TABLE OF CONTENTS—Continued

FORD MOTOR COMPANY—TAB 2

TABLE OF CONTENTS–Continued

GENERAL MOTORS CORPORATION —TAB 3

INFORMATION IS OUR MIDDLE NAME.

www.MOTOR.com

LIGHT TRUCK & VAN REPAIR MANUAL

MECHANICAL REPAIR

20th Edition, Volume 1

First Printing

FOR INFORMATION ON MOTOR PRODUCTS CALL
1-800-4A-MOTOR
(1-800-426-6867)

MOTOR IS A TRADEMARK OF HEARST BUSINESS PUBLISHING, INC.

PUBLISHED BY MOTOR INFORMATION SYSTEMS, A DIVISION OF HEARST BUSINESS PUBLISHING, INC. A UNIT OF THE HEARST CORPORATION
5600 CROOKS ROAD,
TROY, MI 48098

PRINTED IN THE U.S.A.

ISBN 1-58251-262-0

COLLISION DATABASE PRODUCTS
Virginia Hudson, ASE, Team Manager
Robert J. Toles, ASE, SAE, Labor Development Coordinator
SENIOR ANALYST
Jeni Witte
ASSOCIATE ANALYSTS
Norman Lentine
Garry A. Mackew, SAE
Harry Narsesian
Gary Ratiu
Brian Robertson, ASE
Doug Sajor, ASE
ANALYSTS
Steven A. Bielecki, SAE
Deborah Person
Andrew Rundell
James Santo
Helmut H. Schneid, ASE
Jacqueline M. Scruggs
Randy Smith
Richard J. Tracy, ASE
CONTENT PRODUCTION
Joel Van Deven, Senior Analyst

CUSTOMER SUPPORT SERVICES
Holly Wright, National Account Services Manager
ASSOCIATE ANALYSTS
Pieter Dijkstra
Brian Martin
Jeffrey Short
ANALYST
Staranne Maxson

MANUFACTURING & DISTRIBUTION
Donna Kijek

INFORMATION PROCUREMENT
Sheri Aquisto

OFFICE MANAGER
Vita Green

SERVICE & REPAIR PRODUCTS
Kelly L. McKinstry, Team Manager
SENIOR ANALYST
Richard G. Glover, SAE
ASSOCIATE ANALYST
Ron Lathrop
ANALYSTS
Jason Baker
Joe Damron
Anthony W. Dutton
Alan McGregor
Uche-Uwa Ogu
Ken Pakkala, ASE
Daniel G. Paalanen, ASE
CONTENT PRODUCTION
Julie Andrews
Susan J. Porzondek

NATIONAL ACCOUNT PRODUCTS
SENIOR ANALYSTS
Richard C. Grunz, SAE
Jim Jackovatz, ASE
Warren Schildknecht, SAE
Michael A. Zimmerman, ASE

Keith Naszradi, Electronic Data Lead
ANALYSTS
Melissa Campbell
Marquel Cherry
Sherry Ciechorski
Jeff Finamore
Scott Gordon
Ken Hinton
Denise Masterson
Richard Sparkes, ASE

CONTENT PRODUCTION
Amy E. Bouchard
Dawn Finamore
Elaine Finamore
Luisa Harrington
Catherine Starzyk
Jill Zimmerman

CHEK-CHART PRODUCTS
James Pirkola, ASE, Team Manager
ANALYSTS
Joseph DeStefanis
Eric Rogowski, ASE
Marcus Teague

MECHANICAL DATABASE PRODUCTS
Paul M. Schmidt, SAE, Team Manager
SENIOR ANALYSTS
Dennis Green, SAE
Scott Hansen, Content Standards
Daniel W. Owen, ASE, SAE
David Williams, ASE, SAE
ASSOCIATE ANALYST
Robert Basler

GRAPHIC SERVICES
Randy Harwood, Art Director
Michele Hawley
Frank Jannaro
Hilarie McMullen

COMPOSITION
Rose Ahee
Christopher Mallory

MEDIA PRODUCTION
Robert Jaramillo, Chief Information Officer
Steven J. Hollowell, MCP, IT Manager
Tina Wrubel, Manager, Product Development/Technical Support

Victor F. Ganzi
President & Chief Executive Officer, The Hearst Corporation
Frank A. Bennack, Jr.
Vice Chairman, The Hearst Corporation
William M. Wright
Executive Vice President & Deputy Group Head, Hearst Business Media
Kevin F. Carr
President, Motor Information Systems
Philip C. Cunningham
Director of Database Development
John Lypen
Director, Data Content Services

George R. Hearst, Jr.
Chairman, The Hearst Corporation
Richard P. Malloch
President & Group Head, Hearst Business Media
Robert D. Wilbanks
Vice President & Group Controller, Hearst Business Media
Richard B. Laimbeer
Publisher, Motor Manuals
Marian A. Maasshoff
Director of Product Development

VEHICLE IDENTIFICATION

INDEX

DIGIT 1	Country Of Origin
1	= USA
2	= Canada

DIGIT 2	Make
A	= Chrysler
C	= Chrysler

DIGIT *3	Vehicle Type
4	= Multipurpose Passenger Vehicle
8	= Multipurpose Passenger Vehicle w/Side Airbags

DIGIT 4	GVWR
F	= 4001-5000 Lbs
G	= 5001-6000 Lbs

DIGIT 5	Line
F	= Pacifica AWD
H	= Town & Country FWD
J	= Voyager FWD
J	= Grand Voyager FWD
K	= Town & Country AWD
M	= Pacifica FWD
P	= Town & Country FWD
T	= Town & Country AWD
Y	= Town & Country

DIGIT 6	Series
1	= eC
2	= Base
2	= LX - Fleet
3	= eL
4	= LX
4	= SE
4	= LX LWB
4	= Base
4	= Base SWB
5	= Touring
5	= Touring LWB
5	= SX
5	= LXi
5	= LX
5	= Base
6	= Limited
6	= Limited LWB
6	= LXi
6	= Touring
6	= FWD/AWD
7	= Limited
7	= EX

DIGIT 7	Body Type
4	= Extended Wagon
5	= Wagon
8	= Sport Utility 4D

DIGIT 8	Engine
3	= 3.3L V6 SFI
3	= 3.0L V6 MPI
3	= 3.0L V6 EFI
4	= 3.5L V6 MPI SOHC
B	= 2.4L I-4 EFI DOHC
G	= 3.3L V6 SFI Flex
G	= 3.3L V6 MPI Flex
L	= 3.8L V6 SFI
L	= 3.8L V6 OHV SMPI
R	= 3.3L V6 SFI
R	= 3.3L V6 SFI SOHC

DIGIT 10	Model Year
1	= 2001
2	= 2002
3	= 2003
4	= 2004
5	= 2005
6	= 2006
L	= 1990
M	= 1991
N	= 1992
P	= 1993
R	= 1994
S	= 1995
T	= 1996
V	= 1997
W	= 1998
Y	= 2000

DIGIT 11	Assembly Plant
B	= St. Louis Assembly South, Fenton, MO, USA
R	= Windsor, ON, Canada
X	= St. Louis, MO, USA

LTV0500000000567

Fig. 1 DaimlerChrysler. Chrysler

DIGIT 1	Country Of Origin
1	= USA
2	= Canada
3	= Mexico
J	= Japan

DIGIT 1-3	World Manufacturer Identifier
WD1	= Sprinter Cab Chassis
WD2	= Freightliner Cargo Van
WD5	= Freightliner Multipurpose Passenger Vehicle
WDI	= Sprinter Cab Chassis
WDX	= Sprinter Cab Chassis

DIGIT 2	Make
B	= Dodge
D	= Dodge

DIGIT 3	Vehicle Type
3	= Truck
3	= Truck w/Side Airbags
4	= Multi-Purpose Passenger Vehicle
5	= Bus
5	= Truck w/Side Airbags
6	= Incomplete Vehicle
7	= Truck w/o Side Airbags
7	= Truck
8	= Multi-Purpose Passenger Vehicle w/Side Airbags

DIGIT 4	GVWR/Brake System
B	= Manual Seat Belt
D	= 1-3000 Lbs, Hydraulic
E	= 3001-4000 Lbs, Hydraulic
F	= 4001-5000 Lbs, Hydraulic
G	= 5001-6000 Lbs, Hydraulic
H	= 6001-7000 Lbs, Hydraulic
J	= 7001-8000 Lbs, Hydraulic
K	= 8001-9000 Lbs, Hydraulic
L	= 9001-10000 Lbs, Hydraulic
L	= 4001-5000 Lbs, Hydraulic
M	= 10001-14000 Lbs, Hydraulic
M	= 5001-6000 Lbs, Hydraulic
W	= Hydraulic Brakes
W	= Bus's & Incomplete Vehicles w/Hydraulic Brakes
W	= Bus Or Incomplete Vehicle
W	= Bus

DIGIT 4*	Body Type
P	= 4X2
W	= Wagon
Y	= Cargo Van

DIGIT 5	Line
A	= Ram Pickup 4X2
B	= Wagon/Van
B	= Durango 4X4
B	= Ram Van 3500
C	= Ram Pickup 4X2
D	= Caravan AWD
D	= Dodge Ramcharger 4X2
D	= Durango 4X2
D	= Grand Caravan AWD
D	= Ram Pickup 4X2
E	= Dodge Ramcharger 4X2
E	= Ram Pickup 4X2
E	= Dakota 4X2
F	= Ram Pickup 4X4
G	= Dakota 4X4
H	= Grand Caravan FWD
H	= Caravan FWD
K	= Ram 50 4X4
K	= Mini Ram Van
K	= Grand Caravan FWD
K	= Grand Caravan AWD
K	= Caravan FWD
K	= Caravan AWD
L	= Dakota 4X2
M	= Dodge Ramcharger 4X4
M	= Ram Pickup 4X4
N	= Dakota 4X2
P	= Grand Caravan FWD
P	= Ram 50
P	= Caravan FWD
R	= Ram Pickup 4X2
R	= Durango 4X2
R	= Dakota 4X4
S	= Durango 4X4
S	= Ram 50
S	= Ram Pickup 4X4
T	= Power Ram 50
T	= Grand Caravan AWD
U	= Ram Pickup 4X4
W	= Dakota 4X4
W	= Dodge Ramcharger 4X4
W	= Ram Pickup 4X4
Z	= Rampage

DIGIT 5-6	Line/Series
D1	= 118-Inch, 8550 Lbs
D1	= 118-Inch, 8550 Lbs
D2	= 140-Inch, 8550 Lbs
D2	= 140-Inch, 8550 Lbs
D3	= 158-Inch, 8550 Lbs
D3	= 158-Inch, 8550 Lbs
D4	= 140-Inch, 9990 Lbs
D4	= 140-Inch, 9990 Lbs
D5	= 158-Inch, 9990 Lbs
D5	= 158-Inch, 9990 Lbs
D6	= 140-Inch, 8550 Lbs
D6	= 140-Inch, 8550 Lbs
D7	= 158-Inch, 8550 Lbs
D7	= 158-Inch, 8550 Lbs
D8	= 140-Inch, 10,200 Lbs
D8	= 140-Inch, 10,200 Lbs
D9	= 158-Inch, 10,200 Lbs
D9	= 158-Inch, 10,200 Lbs
J4	= Raider
J4	= Raider
L2	= Ram 50
L2	= Ram 50
L4	= Ram 50 Custom
L4	= Ram 50 SE
L4	= Ram 50 Custom
L4	= Ram 50 SE
L5	= Ram 50 LE
L5	= Ram 50 LE
L5	= Ram 50 Sport
L5	= Ram 50 Sport
M2	= Ram 50 4X4
M2	= Ram 50 4X4
M4	= Ram 50 SE 4X4
M4	= Ram 50 Custom 4X4
M4	= Ram 50 Custom 4X4
M4	= Ram 50 SE 4X4
M5	= Ram 50 Sport 4X4
M5	= Ram 50 Sport 4X4
M5	= Ram 50 LE 4X4
M5	= Ram 50 LE 4X4

DIGIT 6	Series
0	= 150S Job Rated
0	= Ramcharger
0	= 100 Job Rated
1	= Ramcharger
1	= 100 Job Rated
1	= 150 Job Rated
1	= Cargo

LTV0500000000568

Fig. 2 DaimlerChrysler (Part 1 of 3). Dodge

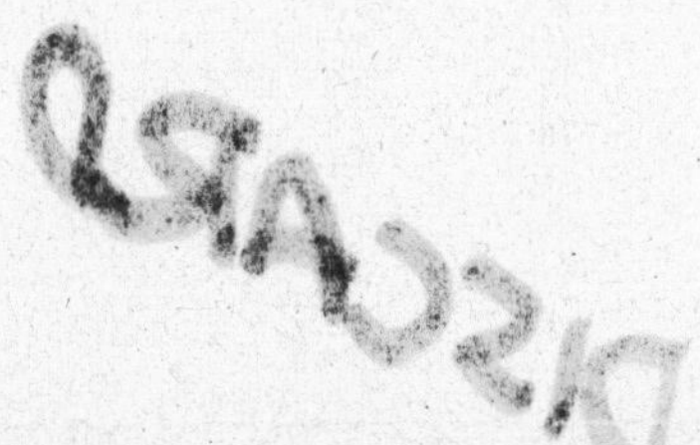

DIGIT 6	Series
1	= Dakota
1	= Dakota Base
1	= Dakota "S"
1	= eC
1	= Dodge Ram "150 Job Rated"
1	= Dodge Ram 1500
2	= Low
2	= SE
2	= Durango
2	= Dodge Ram 2500
2	= Dakota ST
2	= Dakota R/T Sport
2	= Dakota
2	= 250 Job Rated
2	= Base
3	= 350 Job Rated
3	= Dakota Sport
3	= Dodge Ram 3500
3	= Dodge Ram 3500 w/SRW
3	= Durango Sport
3	= eL
3	= Durango ST
3	= SE
3	= Durango SXT
4	= Dodge Ram 3500 w/DRW
4	= SXT
4	= Sport
4	= SE
4	= Rampage
4	= Durango SLT
4	= Dodge 3500 Quad Cab 4WD DRW
4	= Dakota SLT
4	= Base
4	= 450 Job Rated
4	= High
5	= Durango SLT+
5	= ES
5	= LE
5	= Dakota Laramie
5	= 550 Job Rated
5	= Premium
5	= Durango Limited
6	= Dakota Sport
6	= Rampage 2.2
6	= Royal
7	= ES
7	= EX
7	= Durango R/T
7	= Dakota R/T Sport
9	= Shelby Dakota

DIGIT 7	Body Type
0	= Extended Van
0	= Extended Wagon
1	= Conventional Cab - Short
1	= Extended Wagon
1	= Van
1	= Wagon
2	= Club Cab 2D
2	= Club Cab
2	= Conventional Cab - Long
2	= Sport Utility
3	= Club Cab
3	= Club Cab 4D
3	= Extended Cargo Van
3	= Quad Cab - Half Rear Doors
3	= Quad Cab 4D
3	= Van
3	= 3D Metal Top
4	= Conventional Cab
4	= Van
4	= Extended Wagon/Van
4	= Extended Wagon
4	= Conventional Cab - Short
4	= Extended Van
5	= Club Cab
5	= Extended Cab
5	= Wagon
6	= Reg Cab
6	= Conventional Cab
6	= Conventional Cab/Chassis Cab
7	= Sport Utility 2D
8	= Quad Cab - Full Rear Doors
8	= Quad Cab 4D
8	= Sport Utility 4D
9	= Conventional Cab - Long
9	= Convertible
A	= Quad Cab 4D

DIGIT 7-8	Engine
41	= 2.7L I-5 DI Dsl
43	= 2.7L I-5 DI Dsl
44	= 2.7L I-5 DI Dsl

DIGIT 8	Engine
1	= 5.9L V8 4BBL
3	= 3.0L V6 EFI
3	= 3.0L V6 MPI
3	= 3.3L V6 SFI
3	= 3.3L V6 SFI Flex
5	= 5.9L V8 MPI
5	= 2.0L I-4 2BBL
5	= 5.9L V8 MPI HD
5	= 5.9L V8 MPI HDC
6	= 5.9L I-6 FI TDsl
7	= 2.6L I-4 2BBL
7	= 5.9L I-6 FI TDsl HO
8	= 5.9L I-6 Dsl
8	= 5.9L I-6 FI Dsl
B	= 2.2L I-4 2BBL
B	= 2.4L I-4 MPI
B	= 2.4L I-4 MPI DOHC
C	= 5.9L I-6 FI TDsl HO
C	= 5.9L I-6 FI TDSL
C	= 2.2L I-4 2BBL
D	= 2.0L I-4 2BBL
D	= 5.7L V8 HEMI SMPI
D	= 5.7L V8 MPI
D	= 5.7L V8 SMPI Hemi Magnum
D	= 5.9L V6 MPI TDsl
E	= 2.6L I-4 2BBL
E	= 3.3L V6 SFI Flex
E	= 3.7L I-6 1BBL SD
G	= 3.3L V6 MPI Flex
G	= 2.6L I-4 2BBL
G	= 2.5L I-4 TBI
G	= 2.4L I-4 MPI
H	= 8.3L V10 SFI
H	= 3.7L I-6 1BBL SD
J	= 2.5L I-4 FI Tbo
J	= 3.3L V6 MPI CNG
J	= 2.3L I-4 TDsl
J	= 4.7L V8 MPI HO
K	= 3.7L V6 MPI
K	= 3.7L V6 SFI
K	= 2.5L I-4 TBI
K	= 2.5L I-4 EFI
L	= 3.8L V6 MPI
M	= 3.9L V6 2BBL
N	= 4.7L V8 MPI
N	= 3.7L I-6 1BBL
P	= 2.5L I-4 MPI
P	= 5.2L V8 2BBL SD
P	= 4.7L V8 FFV

LTV0500000000569

Fig. 2 DaimlerChrysler (Part 2 of 3). Dodge

DIGIT 8	Engine
P	= 2.5L I-4 EFI
R	= 3.3L V6 MPI
R	= 3.3L V6 SFI
R	= 3.3L V6 SMPI
R	= 5.2L V8 4BBL HD
S	= 3.0L V6 EFI
S	= 3.0L V6 MPI
S	= 5.9L V8 2BBL SD
T	= 5.2L V8 MPI CNG
T	= 5.9L V8 4BBL SD
T	= 5.2L V8 EFI CNG
T	= 5.2L V8 2BBL SD
T	= 5.2L V8 2BBL
U	= 5.9L V8 4BBL
U	= 5.9L V8 4BBL HD Sngl Exh
U	= 5.2L V8 4BBL SD
V	= 5.9L V8 4BBL
V	= 5.9L V8 4BBL HD Dual Exh
W	= 2.4L I-4 EFI
W	= 3.7L I-6 2BBL SD
W	= 5.9L V8 4BBL
W	= 8.0L V10 MPI
X	= 3.9L V6 SFI
X	= 2.4L I-4 EFI DOHC
X	= 3.9L V6 MPI
X	= 3.9L V6 TBI
X	= 3.9L V6 EFI
Y	= 5.2L V8 EFI
Y	= 5.2L V8 MPI
Y	= 5.2L V8 SFI
Y	= 5.2L V8 SMPI
Y	= 5.2L V8 TBI
Z	= 5.9L V8 EFI LD
Z	= 5.9L V8 MPI
Z	= 5.9L V8 MPI LD
Z	= 5.9L V8 MPI LDC
Z	= 5.9L V8 SFI

DIGIT 10	Model Year
1	= 2001
2	= 2002
3	= 2003
4	= 2004
5	= 2005
6	= 2006
B	= 1981
C	= 1982
D	= 1983
E	= 1984
F	= 1985
G	= 1986
H	= 1987
J	= 1988
K	= 1989
L	= 1990
M	= 1991
N	= 1992
P	= 1993
R	= 1994
S	= 1995
T	= 1996
V	= 1997
W	= 1998
X	= 1999
Y	= 2000

DIGIT 11	Assembly Plant
5	= Dusseldorf
A	= Outer Drive, USA
A	= Lynch Road, USA
B	= St. Louis South, MO, USA
D	= Belvidere, IL, USA
F	= Newark, DE, USA
G	= Saltillo, Mexico
G	= Saltillo Assembly - Saltillo, Mexico
J	= Nagoya #3, Japan
J	= St. Louis Assembly North - Fenton, MO, USA
K	= Windsor, ON, Canada
K	= Pillette, Canada
L	= Toledo #1, OH, USA
M	= Lago Alberto Assembly - Mexico City, Mexico
P	= Toledo #2, OH, USA
P	= Nagoya #2, Japan
R	= Windsor, ON, Canada
S	= Dodge City Assembly - Warren, MI, USA
T	= Toluca, Mexico
T	= Warren #2, MI, USA
U	= Mizushima, Japan
U	= Mizushima #1, Japan
V	= Warren #3, MI, USA
W	= Toledo #3, OH, USA
X	= St. Louis #2, MO, USA
Y	= Nagoya #1, Japan
Y	= Nagoya, Japan
Z	= Okazaki, Japan

LTV0500000000570

Fig. 2 DaimlerChrysler (Part 3 of 3). Dodge

DIGIT 1	Country Of Origin
1	= USA
2	= Canada

DIGIT 2	Manufacturer
B	= American Motors Canada
J	= Jeep

DIGIT 3	Vehicle Type
4	= MPV
7	= Truck
8	= MPV w/Side Airbags
C	= Multi-Purpose Vehicle
C	= Multi-purpose Vehicle {MPV}
T	= Truck

DIGIT 4	Engine
B	= 2.5L I-4 2BBL
B	= 2.5L I-4 2BBL
B	= 2.1L I-4 FI TDsl
B	= 2.1L I-4 FI TDsl
C	= 4.2L I-6 2BBL
C	= 4.2L I-6 2BBL
E	= 3001-4000 Lbs, Hydraulic
E	= 3001-4000 Lbs, Hydraulic
F	= 4001-5000 Lbs, Hydraulic
F	= 4001-5000 Lbs, Hydraulic
G	= 5001-6000 Lbs, Hydraulic
G	= 5001-6000 Lbs, Hydraulic
H	= 2.5L I-4 TBI
H	= 6001-7000 Lbs, Hydraulic
H	= 5.0L V8 2BBL
H	= 2.5L I-4 TBI
H	= 6001-7000 Lbs, Hydraulic
H	= 5.0L V8 2BBL
M	= 4.0L I-6 MPI
M	= 4.2L I-6 2BBL
M	= 4.2L I-6 MPI
M	= 4.2L I-6 MPI
M	= 4.0L I-6 MPI
M	= 4.2L I-6 2BBL
N	= 5.9L V8 2BBL
N	= 5.9L V8 2BBL
U	= 2.5L I-4 1BBL
U	= 2.5L I-4 1BBL
W	= 2.8L V6 2BBL
W	= 2.8L V6 2BBL

DIGIT 5	Line
2	= Grand Cherokee 2WD
2	= Grand Cherokee 2WD
4	= Wrangler 4WD
4	= Wrangler 4WD
A	= 3 Spd At Column/Quadra Trac 4WD
A	= 3 Spd At Column/Quadra-Trac 4WD
A	= 3 Spd At Column
A	= Wrangler 4WD
A	= 3 Spd At Column/Quadra-Trac 4WD
A	= 3 Spd At Column/Quadra Trac 4WD
A	= 3 Spd At Column
A	= Wrangler 4WD
B	= 3-Spd At Floor/PT Time 4WD
B	= 3 Spd At Floor/PT Time 4WD
B	= 3-sp At Floor, PT Time 4WD
B	= 3-sp At Floor, PT Time 4WD
B	= 3 Spd At Floor/PT Time 4WD
B	= 3-Spd At Floor/PT Time 4WD
B	= Cherokee 2WD RHD
B	= Cherokee 2WD RHD
C	= 3-sp At Floor, Sel-trac 4WD
C	= 3 Spd At Floor/Selec-Trac 4WD
C	= 3-sp At Floor, Sel-trac 4WD
C	= 3 Spd At Floor/Selec-Trac 4WD
D	= 3 Spd At Floor
D	= 3 Spd At Floor
E	= 3 Spd At Column/PT Time 4WD
E	= 3 Spd At Column/PT Time 4WD
F	= 5 Spd Mt Floor/PT Time 4WD
F	= Cherokee 4WD LHD
F	= 5 Spd Floor/PT Time 4WD
F	= Cherokee 4WD LHD
F	= 5 Spd Mt Floor/PT Time 4WD
F	= 5 Spd Floor/PT Time 4WD
G	= 4 Spd At Column
G	= 4 Spd At Column
H	= Wrangler 4WD
H	= Wrangler 4WD
J	= 3 Spd At Column/Selec-Trac 4WD
J	= 3 Spd At Column/Selec-Trac 4WD
J	= Cherokee 4WD LHD
J	= Cherokee 4WD LHD
K	= Liberty 2WD LHD
K	= Liberty 2WD LHD
L	= 5 Spd Mt Floor/PT Time 4WD
L	= 5-sp Floor, PT Time 4WD
L	= Liberty 4WD LHD
L	= 5-sp Floor, PT Time 4WD
L	= Liberty 4WD LHD
L	= 5 Spd Mt Floor/PT Time 4WD
M	= 4 Spd Manual Floor/PT Time 4WD
M	= 4 Spd Mt Floor/PT Time 4WD
M	= 4 Spd Manual Floor/PT Time 4WD
M	= 4 Spd Mt Floor/PT Time 4WD
N	= Cherokee 4WD RHD
N	= 5 Spd Mt Floor/PT Time 4WD
N	= 5 Spd Mt Floor/PT Time 4WD
N	= 5 Spd Mt Floor/Selec-Trac 4WD
N	= Cherokee 4WD RHD
N	= 5 Spd Mt Floor/Selec-Trac 4WD
P	= 4 Spd At Column/PT Time 4WD
P	= 4 Spd At Column/PT Time 4WD
R	= 4 Spd At Floor/PT Time 4WD
R	= Grand Cherokee 4WD
R	= 4 Spd At Floor/PT Time 4WD
R	= Grand Cherokee 4WD
S	= 4 Spd Mt Floor
S	= Grand Cherokee 2WD
S	= 4 Spd Mt Floor
S	= Grand Cherokee 2WD
T	= Cherokee 2WD LHD
T	= Cherokee 2WD LHD
T	= 4 Spd At Floor/Selec-Trac 4WD
T	= 4 Spd At Floor/Selec-Trac 4WD
U	= 4 Spd At Floor
U	= 4 Spd At Floor
V	= 5 Spd Mt Floor/PT Time 4WD
V	= 5 Spd Mt Floor/PT Time 4WD
W	= Grand Cherokee 4WD
W	= 5 Spd Mt Floor
W	= 5 Spd Mt Floor
W	= Grand Cherokee 4WD
X	= Grand Cherokee 2WD
X	= 4 Spd Mt Floor/PT Time 4WD
X	= Grand Cherokee 2WD
X	= 4 Spd AT Floor/PT Time 4WD
X	= 4 Spd AT Floor/PT Time 4WD
X	= 4 Spd Mt Floor/PT Time 4WD
Y	= Wrangler 4WD
Y	= Wrangler 4WD
Z	= Grand Cherokee 4WD
Z	= 3 Spd At Column/PT Time 4WD
Z	= Grand Cherokee 4WD
Z	= 3 Spd At Column/PT Time 4WD

DIGIT 5-6	Line/Series
J2	= Cherokee 4WD

LTV0500000000577

Fig. 3 DaimlerChrysler (Part 1 of 4). Jeep

DIGIT 5-6	Line/Series
J2	= Comanche 4WD
J2	= Comanche Eliminator 4WD
J2	= Comanche Pioneer 4WD
J3	= Comanche Pioneer 4WD
J3	= Comanche Eliminator 4WD
J3	= Comanche 4WD
J3	= Cherokee Pioneer 4WD
J5	= Cherokee Laredo 4WD
J6	= Comanche Eliminator 4WD
J7	= Cherokee Limited 4WD
J8	= Cherokee 4WD
J8	= Cherokee Sport 4WD
N7	= Cherokee Wagoneer Limited 4WD
N7	= Cherokee Briarwood 4WD
S5	= Grand Wagoneer 4WD
T2	= Comanche 2WD
T2	= Comanche Eliminator 2WD
T2	= Comanche Pioneer 2WD
T2	= Cherokee 2WD
T3	= Cherokee Pioneer 2WD
T3	= Comanche 2WD
T3	= Comanche Eliminator 2WD
T3	= Comanche Pioneer 2WD
T5	= Cherokee Laredo 2WD
T6	= Comanche Eliminator 2WD
T8	= Cherokee 2WD
T8	= Cherokee Sport 2WD
Y1	= Wrangler 4WD
Y1	= Wrangler S 4WD
Y2	= Wrangler 4WD
Y2	= Wrangler S 4WD
Y3	= Wrangler Islander 4WD
Y4	= Wrangler Sahara 4WD
Y5	= Wrangler Laredo 4WD
Y5	= Wrangler Renegade 4WD
Y6	= Wrangler Renegade 4WD

DIGIT 6	Series
1	= Wrangler S
1	= Wrangler Sport
1	= Wrangler Rio Grande
2	= Cherokee SE
2	= Wrangler
2	= Wrangler SE
2	= Wrangler Sport
2	= Wrangler Unlimited LWB
2	= Cherokee
3	= Renegade
3	= Wrangler X
3	= Wrangler Rocky Mountain
3	= Rocky Mountain
3	= Sport
4	= Cherokee Sport
4	= Wrangler Unlimited
4	= Laredo
4	= Rocky Mountain
4	= Special Edition
4	= Sport
4	= Wrangler Sahara
4	= Wrangler Sport
5	= Cherokee Classic
5	= Classic
5	= Laredo
5	= Limited
5	= TSi
5	= Wrangler Sahara
6	= SE
6	= Wrangler Renegade
6	= Overland
6	= Limited
6	= Cherokee Limited
6	= Cherokee Classic
6	= Base
6	= Wrangler Rubicon
6	= Cherokee Sport
7	= Orvis
7	= Cherokee Country
7	= Cherokee Limited
7	= Limited
8	= 5.9 Limited
8	= Grand Wagoneer

DIGIT 6-7	Body Type
15	= Grand Wagoneer 4D Wagon 109 W.B.
16	= Cherokee 2D Wagon 109 W.B.
17	= Cherokee 2D Wagon 109 W.B.
18	= Cherokee 4D Wagon 109 W.B.
25	= Jeep Truck J10 w/Box 119 W.B.
25	= Jeep Truck J20 w/Box 119 W.B.
26	= Jeep Truck J10 w/Box 131 W.B.
27	= Jeep Truck J20 w/Box 131 W.B.
63	= Comanche 4WD 113 W.B.
64	= Comanche 2WD 113 W.B.
65	= Comanche 4WD 120 W.B.
66	= Comanche 2WD 120 W.B.
73	= Cherokee 2D Wagon 2WD 101 W.B.
74	= Cherokee 4D Wagon 2WD 101 W.B.
75	= Cherokee Wagoneer 4D Wagon 4WD 101 W.B.
75	= Wagoneer 4D Wagon 4WD 101 W.B.
77	= Cherokee 2D Wagon 4WD 101 W.B.
78	= Cherokee 4D Wagon 4WD 101 W.B.
81	= 2D Open Body 93.5 W.B.
85	= CJ-5 Open Body 83.5 W.B.
87	= CJ-7 Open Body 93.5 W.B.
88	= CJ-8 Scrambler Open Body 103.5 W.B.
88	= Scrambler Open Body 103.5 W.B.

DIGIT 7	Body Type
4	= 2D Open Body LWB
6	= Conventional Cab
7	= Sport Utility 2D
8	= Sport Utility 4D
9	= 2D Open Body

DIGIT 8	Engine
1	= Comanche 4001-5000#
1	= Cherokee Base, 4001-5000 Lbs
1	= 2.4L I-4 MPI
1	= Wrangler Base, 5001-5000 Lbs
1	= Cherokee Base, 4001-5000 Lbs
1	= Wrangler Base, 5001-5000 Lbs
1	= 2.4L I-4 MPI
1	= Comanche 4001-5000#
2	= Cherokee Pioneer, 4001-5000 Lbs
2	= Wrangler Sahara, 4001-5000 Lbs
2	= 5.7L V8 SFI Hemi
2	= Wrangler Sahara, 4001-5000 Lbs
2	= Cherokee Pioneer, 4001-5000 Lbs
2	= 5.7L V8 SFI Hemi
3	= Cherokee Chief, 4001-5000 Lbs
3	= Wrangler Sport, 4001-5000 Lbs
3	= Wrangler Sport, 4001-5000 Lbs
3	= Cherokee Chief, 4001-5000 Lbs
4	= Wrangler Laredo, 4001-5000 Lbs
4	= Wrangler Laredo, 4001-5000 Lbs
4	= Cherokee Laredo, 4001-5000 Lbs
4	= Cherokee Laredo, 4001-5000 Lbs
5	= Wagoneer, 4001-5000 Lbs
5	= 2.8L I-4 Turbo Diesel
5	= Comanche Eliminator 4001-5000#
5	= Wagoneer, 4001-5000 Lbs
5	= 2.8L I-4 Turbo Diesel
5	= Comanche Eliminator 4001-5000#
6	= Wagoneer Limited, 4001-5000 Lbs

LTV0500000000578

Fig. 3 DaimlerChrysler (Part 2 of 4). Jeep

DIGIT 8	Engine
6	= Wagoneer Limited, 4001-5000 Lbs
7	= 5.9L V8 2BBL
7	= Comanche X 4001-5000#
7	= 5.9L V8 2BBL
7	= Comanche X 4001-5000#
9	= Cherokee Limited, 4001-5000 Lbs
9	= Comanche XLS 4001-5000#
9	= Cherokee Limited, 4001-5000 Lbs
9	= Comanche XLS 4001-5000#
A	= CJ-7, 3001-4000 Lbs
A	= CJ-5, 3001-4000 Lbs
A	= CJ-7, 3001-4000 Lbs
A	= CJ-5, 3001-4000 Lbs
A	= CJ-8 Scrambler, 4001-5000 Lbs
A	= CJ-8 Scrambler, 4001-5000 Lbs
C	= Cherokee Chief, 5001-6000 Lbs
C	= Cherokee Chief, 5001-6000 Lbs
D	= Cherokee Laredo, 5001-6000 Lbs
D	= Cherokee Laredo, 5001-6000 Lbs
E	= 2.5L I-4 TBI
E	= CJ-7, 4001-5000 Lbs
E	= CJ-5, 4001-5000 Lbs
E	= CJ-8 Scrambler, 4001-5000 Lbs
E	= CJ-8 Scrambler, 4001-5000 Lbs
E	= CJ-7, 4001-5000 Lbs
E	= CJ-5, 4001-5000 Lbs
E	= 2.5L I-4 TBI
F	= Comanche Custom 5001-6000#
F	= Comanche 5001-6000#
F	= Comanche Custom 5001-6000#
F	= Comanche 5001-6000#
G	= Comanche X 5001-6000#
G	= Comanche X 5001-6000#
J	= 4.7L V8 MPI HO
J	= Wrangler Base, 3001-4000 Lbs
J	= Comanche XLS 5001-6000#
J	= Comanche XLS 5001-6000#
J	= Cherokee Base, 3001-4000 Lbs
J	= 4.7L V8 MPI HO
J	= Wrangler Base, 3001-4000 Lbs
J	= Cherokee Base, 3001-4000 Lbs
K	= Cherokee Base, 3001-4000 Lbs
K	= Wrangler Sport, 3001-4000 Lbs
K	= 3.7L V6 MPI
K	= 3.7L V6 SFI
K	= Cherokee Pioneer, 3001-4000 Lbs
K	= 3.7L V6 SFI
K	= 3.7L V6 MPI
K	= Cherokee Base, 3001-4000 Lbs
K	= Cherokee Pioneer, 3001-4000 Lbs
K	= Wrangler Sport, 3001-4000 Lbs
L	= Cherokee Pioneer, 3001-4000 Lbs
L	= Cherokee Laredo, 3001-4000 Lbs
L	= 4.0L I-6 MPI
L	= Wrangler Laredo, 3001-4000 Lbs
L	= Cherokee Laredo, 3001-4000 Lbs
L	= 4.0L I-6 MPI
L	= Cherokee Pioneer, 3001-4000 Lbs
L	= Wrangler Laredo, 3001-4000 Lbs
M	= Cherokee Laredo, 3001-4000 Lbs
M	= Wrangler Sahara, 3001-4000 Lbs
M	= 4.2L I-6 2BBL
M	= Cherokee Laredo, 3001-4000 Lbs
M	= Wrangler Sahara, 3001-4000 Lbs
M	= 4.2L I-6 2BBL
N	= 4.7L V8 SFI SOHC
N	= Cherokee, 5001-6000 Lbs
N	= Grand Wagoneer 5001-6000 Lbs
N	= Truck J10, 5001-6000 Lbs
N	= Truck J10, 6001-7000 Lbs
N	= Truck J20, 6001-7000 Lbs

DIGIT 8	Engine
N	= Truck J10, 6001-7000 Lbs
N	= Truck J20, 5001-6000 Lbs
N	= Truck J20, 5001-6000 Lbs
N	= 4.7L V8 MPI
N	= Truck J10, 5001-6000 Lbs
N	= Grand Wagoneer 5001-6000 Lbs
N	= Cherokee, 5001-6000 Lbs
N	= 4.7L V8 SFI SOHC
N	= 4.7L V8 MPI
N	= Truck J20, 6001-7000 Lbs
P	= 2.5L I-4 MPI
P	= Comanche Pioneer 4001-5000#
P	= Truck J20, 6001-7000 Lbs
P	= Comanche Pioneer 4001-5000#
P	= 2.5L I-4 SFI
P	= 2.5L I-4 SFI
P	= 2.5L I-4 MPI
P	= Truck J20, 6001-7000 Lbs
R	= Comanche Pioneer 5001-6000#
R	= Cherokee Chief, 6001-7000 Lbs
R	= Comanche Pioneer 5001-6000#
R	= Cherokee Chief, 6001-7000 Lbs
S	= Truck J20, 7001-8000 Lbs
S	= 4.0L I-6 MPI
S	= 4.0L I-6 SFI
S	= Wrangler S, 3001-4000 Lbs
S	= Comanche Chief 4001-5000#
S	= Wrangler S, 3001-4000 Lbs
S	= 4.0L I-6 MPI
S	= 4.0L I-6 SFI
S	= Comanche Chief 4001-5000#
S	= Truck J20, 7001-8000 Lbs
T	= 4.2L I-6 2BBL
T	= Cherokee Laredo, 6001-7000 Lbs
T	= 4.2L I-6 2BBL
T	= Comanche Laredo 4001-5000#
T	= Cherokee Laredo, 6001-7000 Lbs
T	= Comanche Laredo 4001-5000#
U	= Truck J10, 6001-7000 Lbs
U	= Truck J20, 6001-7000 Lbs
U	= Grand Wagoneer 6001-7000 Lbs
U	= Grand Wagoneer 6001-7000 Lbs
U	= Truck J20, 6001-7000 Lbs
U	= Truck J10, 6001-7000 Lbs
Y	= Truck J20, 8001-9000 Lbs
Y	= Truck J20, 8001-9000 Lbs
Y	= 5.2L V8 MPI
Y	= 5.2L V8 MPI
Z	= 5.9L V8 MPI
Z	= 5.9L V8 MPI

DIGIT 10	Model Year
1	= 2001
2	= 2002
3	= 2003
4	= 2004
5	= 2005
6	= 2006
B	= 1981
C	= 1982
D	= 1983
E	= 1984
F	= 1985
G	= 1986
H	= 1987
J	= 1988
K	= 1989
L	= 1990
M	= 1991
N	= 1992
P	= 1993
R	= 1994

LTV0500000000579

Fig. 3 DaimlerChrysler (Part 3 of 4). Jeep

DIGIT 10	Model Year
S	= 1995
T	= 1996
V	= 1997
W	= 1998
X	= 1999
Y	= 2000

DIGIT 11	Assembly Plant
B	= Brampton, ON, Canada
C	= Detroit, MI, USA
J	= Brampton, ON, Canada
L	= Toledo #1, OH, USA
P	= Toledo #2, OH, USA
T	= Toledo, OH, USA
W	= Toledo North Assembly, Ohio, USA
W	= Toledo North Assembly, OH, USA
W	= Toledo #3, OH, USA
W	= Toledo-North, OH, USA

LTV0500000000580

Fig. 3 DaimlerChrysler (Part 4 of 4). Jeep

DIGIT 1-3	World Manufacturer Identifier
1F1	= Ford Motor Co., USA, MPV-Limousine
1FB	= Ford Motor Co., USA, Bus
1FC	= Ford Motor Co., USA, Truck Stripped Chassis
1FD	= Ford Motor Co., USA, Incomplete Vehicle
1FD	= Ford Motor Co., USA, Truck (Incomplete Vehicle)
1FM	= Ford Motor Co., USA, Multipurpose Vehicle
1FT	= Ford Motor Co., USA, Truck (Complete Vehicle)
2FD	= Ford Motor Co., Canada, Truck (Incomplete Vehicle)
2FD	= Ford Motor Co., Canada, Truck (Incomplete Vehicle)
2FM	= Ford Motor Co., Canada, Multipurpose Vehicle
2FT	= Ford Motor Co., Canada, Truck (Complete Vehicle)
3FD	= Ford Motor Co., Mexico, Incomplete Vehicle
3FT	= Ford Motor Co., Mexico, Truck (Complete Vehicle)
JC2	= Toyo Kogyo Of Japan, Truck (Complete Vehicle)
JC4	= Toyo Kogyo Of Japan, Truck (Incomplete Vehicle)

DIGIT 4	Brake Type/GVWR Class
B	= Hydraulic, 3001-4000 Lbs
C	= Hydraulic, 4001-5000 Lbs
D	= Hydraulic, 5001-6000 Lbs
E	= Hydraulic, 6001-7000 Lbs
F	= Hydraulic, 7001-8000 Lbs
G	= Hydraulic, 8001-8500 Lbs
H	= Hydraulic, 8501-9000 Lbs
J	= Hydraulic, 9001-10000 Lbs
K	= Hydraulic, 10001-14000 Lbs
L	= Hydraulic, 14001-16000 Lbs

DIGIT 4*	Brake Type/GVWR Class/Restraint
B	= Hydraulic, 3001-4000 Lbs, Dual Front & Front Side Airbags
C	= Hydraulic, 4001-5000 Lbs, Dual Front & Front Side Airbags
D	= Hydraulic, 5001-6000 Lbs, Dual Front & Front Side Airbags
E	= Hydraulic, 6001-7000 Lbs, Dual Front & Front Side Airbags
F	= Hydraulic, 7001-8000 Lbs, Dual Front & Front Side Airbags
G	= Hydraulic, 8001-8500 Lbs, No Airbags
H	= Hydraulic, 8501-9000 Lbs, No Airbags
J	= Hydraulic, 9001-10000 Lbs, Without Airbags
J	= Hydraulic, 9001-10000 Lbs, No Airbags
K	= Hydraulic, 10001-14000 Lbs, Without Airbags
N	= Hydraulic, 8501-9000 Lbs, Dual Front Airbags
P	= Hydraulic, 7001-8000 Lbs, Dual Front Airbags
R	= Hydraulic, 6001-7000 Lbs, Dual Front Airbags
S	= Hydraulic, 9001-10000 Lbs, Dual Front Airbags
U	= Hydraulic, 3001-4000 Lbs, Dual Front Airbags
V	= Hydraulic, 8001-8500 Lbs, Dual Front Airbags
W	= Hydraulic, 10001-14000 Lbs, Dual Front Airbags
W	= Hydraulic, 10001-14000 Lbs, Without Airbags
X	= Hydraulic, 14001-16000 Lbs, Dual Front Airbags
Y	= Hydraulic, 4001-5000 Lbs, Dual Front Airbags
Z	= Hydraulic, 5001-6000 Lbs, Dual Front Airbags

DIGIT 4-6	Line, Series, Chassis, Cab Or Body
UA1	= Courier Pickup 2WD, 106.9 WB
UA2	= Courier Pickup 2WD, 112.8 WB

DIGIT 5-7	Line, Series, Chassis, Cab Or Body
A11	= Aerostar Wagon
A14	= Aerostar Cargo Van
A15	= Aerostar Window Van
A21	= Aerostar Wagon 4WD
A24	= Aerostar Cargo Van 4WD
A25	= Aerostar Window Van 4WD
A31	= Aerostar Extended Wagon
A34	= Aerostar Extended Cargo Van
A35	= Aerostar Extended Window Van
A41	= Aerostar Extended Wagon 4WD
A44	= Aerostar Extended Cargo Van 4WD
A45	= Aerostar Extended Window Van 4WD
A50	= Windstar LX Wagon
A50	= Windstar LX 3D Wagon
A50	= Windstar Base Wagon
A50	= Freestar S 4D Wagon
A51	= Freestar SE 4D Wagon

DIGIT 5-7	Line, Series, Chassis, Cab Or Body
A51	= Windstar LX 4D Wagon
A51	= Windstar LX Wagon
A51	= Windstar Wagon
A52	= Windstar SE 4D Wagon
A52	= Freestar SEL 4D Wagon
A53	= Windstar Limited 4D Wagon
A53	= Windstar SEL 4D Wagon
A54	= Windstar Cargo Van
A54	= Freestar Cargo Van
A56	= Windstar SEL 4D Wagon
A57	= Windstar SE Sport 4D Wagon
A57	= Freestar SES 4D Wagon
A58	= Windstar Limited 4D Wagon
A58	= Freestar Limited 4D Wagon
E01	= E100 Club Wagon
E04	= E100 Cargo Van
E05	= E100 Window Van
E06	= E100 Display Van
E11	= E150 Wagon
E14	= E150 Cargo Van
E15	= E150 Window Van
E16	= E150 Display Van
E21	= E250 Club Wagon
E24	= E250 Cargo Van
E25	= E250 Window Van
E25	= E250 HD Cargo Van
E26	= E250 Display Van
E31	= E350 Club Wagon
E34	= E350 Cargo Van
E35	= E350 Window Van
E35	= E350SD Base Cutaway
E36	= E350 Display Van
E37	= E350 Super Duty Commercial Cutaway
E37	= E350 Parcel Delivery Van
E39	= E350SD Commercial Stripped Chassis
F02	= F150 Pickup Regular Cab Flareside 2WD
F04	= F150 Pickup Regular Cab Flareside 4WD
F07	= F150 Pickup Regular Cab Flareside 2WD
F08	= F150 Pickup Regular Cab Flareside 4WD
F10	= F100 Pickup Regular Cab 2WD
F12	= F150 Pickup Regular Cab Styleside 2WD
F14	= F150 Pickup Regular Cab Styleside 4WD
F15	= F150 Pickup Regular Cab Styleside 2WD
F17	= F150 Pickup Regular Cab Styleside 2WD
F18	= F150 Pickup Regular Cab Styleside 4WD
F20	= F250 Super Duty Pickup Regular Cab Styleside 2WD
F21	= F250 Super Duty Pickup Regular Cab Styleside 4WD
F25	= F250HD Pickup Regular Cab Styleside 2WD
F25	= F250 Pickup Regular Cab Styleside 2WD
F26	= F250HD Pickup Regular Cab Styleside 4WD
F26	= F250 Pickup Regular Cab Styleside 4WD
F27	= F250 Pickup Regular Cab Styleside 2WD
F28	= F250 Pickup Regular Cab Styleside 4WD
F30	= F350 Super Duty Pickup Regular Cab 2WD
F31	= F350 Super Duty Pickup Regular Cab 4WD
F32	= F350 Super Duty Pickup Regular Cab 2WD DRW
F33	= F350 Super Duty Pickup Regular Cab 4WD DRW
F35	= F350 Pickup Regular Cab Styleside 2WD
F36	= F350 Pickup Regular Cab Styleside 4WD
F46	= F450 Super Duty Chassis Cab Regular Cab 2WD DRW
F47	= F450 Super Duty Chassis Cab Regular Cab 4WD DRW
F47	= F-Super Duty Chassis Cab Regular Cab 2WD
K01	= Freestyle SE 4D Utility FWD
K02	= Freestyle SEL 4D Utility FWD
K03	= Freestyle Limited 4D Utility FWD
K04	= Freestyle SE 4D Utility AWD
K05	= Freestyle SEL 4D Utility AWD
K06	= Freestyle Limited 4D Utility AWD
R10	= Ranger Regular Cab 2WD
R11	= Ranger Regular Cab 4WD
R14	= Ranger Supercab 2WD

LTV0500000000571

Fig. 4 Ford Motor Company (Part 1 of 3). Ford

DIGIT 5-7	Line, Series, Chassis, Cab Or Body
R15	= Ranger Supercab 4WD
R44	= Ranger 4D Supercab 2WD
R45	= Ranger 4D Supercab 4WD
S11	= E150 Super Club Wagon
S14	= E150 Super Cargo Van
S15	= E150 Super Window Van
S16	= E150 Super Display Van
S21	= E250 Super Club Wagon
S24	= Extended Cargo Van
S24	= E250 Extended Cargo Van
S24	= E250 Super Cargo Van
S25	= E250 Super Window Van
S26	= E250 Super Display Van
S31	= E350 Super Club Wagon
S31	= E350 Super Duty Extended Club Wagon
S34	= E350 Super Cargo Van
S34	= E350 Super Duty Extended Cargo Van
S35	= E350 Super Window Van
S36	= E350 Super Display Van
U01	= Escape XLS 4D Utility 2WD
U02	= Escape XLS 4D Utility 2WD
U02	= Escape XLS 4D Utility 4WD
U03	= Escape XLT 4D Utility 2WD
U04	= Escape XLT 4D Utility 4WD
U04	= Escape Limited 4D Utility 2WD
U04	= Escape Limited 4D Utility 4WD
U12	= Bronco II 2WD
U13	= Expedition XLS 4D Utility 2WD
U14	= Bronco II 4WD
U14	= Expedition XLS 4D Utility 4WD
U15	= Bronco 4WD
U15	= Expedition XLT 4D Utility 2WD
U16	= Expedition XLT 4D Utility 4WD
U17	= Expedition King Ranch 4D Utility 2WD
U17	= Expedition 4D Utility 2WD
U17	= Expedition Eddie Bauer 4D Utility 2WD
U18	= Expedition 4D Utility 4WD
U18	= Expedition Eddie Bauer 4D Utility 4WD
U18	= Expedition King Ranch 4D Utility 4WD
U19	= Expedition Limited 4D Utility 2WD
U20	= Expedition Limited 4D Utility 4WD
U22	= Explorer 2D Utility 2WD
U24	= Explorer 2D Utility 4WD
U32	= Explorer 4D Utility 2WD
U34	= Explorer 4D Utility 4WD
U35	= Explorer 4D Utility AWD
U40	= Excursion XLT 4D Utility 2WD
U40	= Excursion XLS 4D Utility 2WD
U41	= Excursion XLS 4D Utility 4WD
U41	= Excursion XLT 4D Utility 4WD
U42	= Excursion Limited 4D Utility 2WD
U43	= Excursion Limited 4D Utility 4WD
U44	= Excursion Eddie Bauer 4D Utility 2WD
U45	= Excursion Eddie Bauer 4D Utility 4WD
U60	= Explorer Sport 2D Utility 2WD
U61	= Explorer XL 4D Utility 2WD
U62	= Explorer XLS 4D Utility 2WD
U63	= Explorer XLT 4D Utility 2WD
U64	= Explorer Eddie Bauer 4D Utility 2WD
U65	= Explorer Limited 4D Utility 2WD
U67	= Explorer Sport Trac 4D Utility 2WD
U70	= Explorer Sport 2D Utility 4WD
U71	= Explorer XL 4D Utility 4WD
U72	= Explorer XLS 4D Utility 4WD
U73	= Explorer XLT 4D Utility 4WD
U74	= Explorer Eddie Bauer 4D Utility 4WD
U75	= Explorer Limited 4D Utility 4WD
U77	= Explorer Sport Trac 4D Utility 4WD
U82	= Explorer XLS 4D Utility AWD
U83	= Explorer XLT 4D Utility AWD
U84	= Explorer Eddie Bauer 4D Utility AWD

DIGIT 5-7	Line, Series, Chassis, Cab Or Body
U85	= Explorer Limited 4D Utility AWD
U92	= Escape XLS 4D Utility 4WD
U93	= Escape XLT 4D Utility 4WD
U94	= Escape Limited 4D Utility 4WD
U95	= Escape Hybrid 4D Utility 2WD
U96	= Escape Hybrid 4D Utility 4WD
W07	= F150 Pickup SuperCrew 2WD
W08	= F150 Pickup SuperCrew 4WD
W12	= F150 Pickup SuperCrew 2WD
W14	= F150 Pickup SuperCrew 4WD
W20	= F250 Super Duty Pickup Crew Cab 2WD
W21	= F250 Super Duty Pickup Crew Cab 4WD
W25	= F250HD Pickup Crew Cab 2WD
W25	= F250 Pickup Crew Cab 2WD
W26	= F250HD Pickup Crew Cab 4WD
W26	= F250 Pickup Crew Cab 4WD
W30	= F350 Super Duty Pickup Crew Cab 2WD
W31	= F350 Super Duty Pickup Crew Cab 4WD
W32	= F350 Super Duty Pickup Crew Cab 2WD DRW
W33	= F350 Super Duty Pickup Crew Cab 4WD DRW
W35	= F350 Pickup Crew Cab 2WD
W36	= F350 Pickup Crew Cab 4WD
W46	= F450 Super Duty Chassis Cab Crew Cab 2WD DRW
W47	= F450 Super Duty Chassis Cab Crew Cab 4WD DRW
X02	= F150 Pickup Supercab Flareside 2WD
X04	= F150 Pickup Supercab Flareside 4WD
X07	= F150 Pickup Supercab Flareside 2WD
X08	= F150 Pickup Supercab Flareside 4WD
X12	= F150 Pickup Supercab Styleside 2WD
X14	= F150 Pickup Supercab Styleside 4WD
X15	= F150 Pickup Supercab Styleside 2WD
X17	= F150 Pickup Supercab Styleside 2WD
X18	= F150 Pickup Supercab Styleside 4WD
X20	= F250 Super Duty Pickup Supercab Styleside 2WD
X21	= F250 Super Duty Pickup Supercab Styleside 4WD
X25	= F250 Pickup Supercab Styleside 2WD
X25	= F250HD Pickup Supercab Styleside 2WD
X26	= F250 Pickup Supercab Styleside 4WD
X26	= F250HD Pickup Supercab Styleside 4WD
X27	= F250 Pickup Supercab Styleside 2WD
X28	= F250 Pickup Supercab Styleside 4WD
X30	= F350 Super Duty Pickup Supercab 2WD
X31	= F350 Super Duty Pickup Supercab 4WD
X32	= F350 Super Duty Pickup Supercab 2WD DRW
X33	= F350 Super Duty Pickup Supercab 4WD DRW
X35	= F350 Pickup Supercab Styleside 2WD
X46	= F450 Super Duty Chassis Cab Supercab 2WD DRW
X47	= F450 Super Duty Chassis Cab Supercab 4WD DRW

DIGIT 7	GVWR
1	= Class B: 3001-4000 Lbs
2	= Class C: 4001-5000

DIGIT 8	Engine
1	= 2.0L I-4 2BBL
1	= 3.0L V6 DOHC
1	= 3.0L V6 SFI DOHC
1	= 6.9L V8 Dsl
1	= 3.0L Duratec 4V V6
2	= 4.2L V6 EFI OHV
2	= 4.2L V6 SPI
2	= 2.3L I-4 2BBL
3	= 5.4L V8 EFI SOHC S/C
3	= 3.8L V6 2BBL
4	= 3.8L V6 EFI OHV
5	= 5.4L V8 EFI SOHC
5	= 5.4L V8 3V SOHC
6	= 4.6L V8 EFI SOHC
6	= 3.9L V6 SPI
9	= 4.9L I-6 EFI LPG
A	= 2.3L I-4 EFI
A	= 2.3L I-4 1BBL

LTV0500000000572

Fig. 4 Ford Motor Company (Part 2 of 3). Ford

DIGIT 8 Engine
B = 2.0L I-4 SFI DOHC
C = 7.3L V8 IDI TDsl
C = 2.0L I-4 NFC
C = 2.0L I-4 2BBL IFM
C = 2.5L I-4 EFI SOHC
C = 2.0L I-4 1BBL
C = 7.3L V8 DI TDsl
D = 2.3L I-4 EFI
D = 4.2L V8 2BBL
E = 4.0L V6 EFI SOHC
E = 4.9L I-6 1BBL
E = 2.3L I-4 TDsl
F = 5.0L V8 2BBL
F = 7.3L V8 DI TDsl
G = 7.5L V8 EFI
G = 5.8L V8 2BBL
H = 5.8L V8 EFI HO
H = 5.8L V8 EFI
H = 2.3L I-4 w/AC Synchronous Motor
H = 5.8L V8 4BBL HO
K = 4.0L V6 EFI SOHC FFV
K = 4.0L V6 EFI SOHC
K = 7.3L V8 IDI TDsl
L = 7.5L V8 4BBL
L = 5.4L V8 EFI SOHC
M = 7.3L V8 Dsl
M = 5.4L V8 EFI SOHC CNG
N = 5.0L V8 EFI
P = 2.2L I-4 Dsl
P = 5.0L V8 EFI
P = 6.0L V8 DI TDsl
P = 6.0L V8 FI Dsl
R = 5.8L V8 EFI HP
S = 6.8L V10 EFI SOHC
S = 2.8L V6 2BBL
T = 2.9L V6 EFI
U = 3.0L V6 EFI
V = 3.0L V6 EFI Flex Fuel Ethanol
W = 4.6L V8 EFI SOHC
X = 4.0L V6 EFI
Y = 6.8L V10 EFI SOHC
Y = 4.9L I-6 EFI
Y = 4.9L I-6 1BBL
Z = 5.4L V8 EFI SOHC GFP
Z = 6.6L V8 2BBL
Z = 4.9L I-6 EFI GFP
Z = 2.3L I-4 DOHC

DIGIT 10 Model Year
1 = 2001
2 = 2002
3 = 2003
4 = 2004
5 = 2005
6 = 2006
B = 1981
C = 1982
D = 1983
E = 1984
F = 1985
G = 1986
H = 1987
J = 1988
K = 1989
L = 1990
M = 1991
N = 1992
P = 1993
R = 1994
S = 1995
T = 1996
V = 1997

DIGIT 10 Model Year
W = 1998
X = 1999
Y = 2000

DIGIT 11 Assembly Plant
0 = Hiroshima, Japan
0 = Detroit, MI, USA
B = Oakville, ON, Canada
C = Ontario Truck: Oakville, ON, Canada
D = Avon Lake, OH, USA
E = Kentucky Truck: Jefferson County, KY, USA
F = Dearborn: Dearborn, MI, USA
G = Chicago, Illinois
H = Lorain, OH, USA
K = Michigan Truck: Wayne, MI, USA
K = Kansas City: Claycomo, MO, USA
K = Kansas City: Claycomo, MO, USA
L = Michigan Truck: Wayne, MI, USA
M = Cuautitlan, Mexico
N = Norfolk, VA, USA
P = Twin Cities: St. Paul, MN, USA
R = San Jose, CA, USA
T = Edison, NJ, USA
U = Louisville, KY, USA
V = Kentucky Truck: Jefferson County, KY, USA
W = Wayne, MI, USA
Z = St. Louis: Hazelwood, MO, USA

LTV0500000000573

Fig. 4 Ford Motor Company (Part 3 of 3). Ford

DIGIT 1-3 World Manufacturer Identifier
5L1 = Ford Motor Co., USA, Limo
5LM = Ford Motor Co., USA, MPV
5LT = Ford Motor Co., USA, Truck (Complete Vehicle)

DIGIT 4 GVWR/Brake System
E = 6001-7000 Lbs, Hydraulic
F = 7001-8000 Lbs, Hydraulic
P = 7001-8000 Lbs, Hydraulic
P = 7000-8001 Lbs, Hydraulic
R = 6001-7000 Lbs, Hydraulic

DIGIT 5-7 Line/Series/Body Type
U27 = Navigator 4D Utility 2WD
U28 = Navigator 4D Utility 4WD
U68 = Aviator 4D Utility 2WD
U78 = Aviator 4D Utility AWD
U88 = Aviator 4D Utility AWD
W05 = Blackwood 4D 2WD
W16 = Mark LT Supercrew 2WD
W18 = Mark LT Supercrew 4WD

DIGIT 8 Engine
5 = 5.4L V8 3V SOHC
5 = 5.4L V8 EFI DOHC
A = 5.4L V8 EFI DOHC
H = 4.6L V8 EFI DOHC
L = 5.4L V8 EFI
R = 5.4L V8 EFI DOHC

DIGIT 10 Model Year
1 = 2001
2 = 2002
3 = 2003
4 = 2004
5 = 2005
6 = 2006
W = 1998
X = 1999
Y = 2000

DIGIT 11 Assembly Plant
F = Dearborn, MI, USA
K = Kansas City: Claycomo, MO, USA
L = Wayne, MI, USA
Z = St. Louis: Hazelwood, MO, USA

LTV0500000000581

Fig. 5 Ford Motor Company. Lincoln

DIGIT 1-3 World Manufacturer Identifier
2MR = Ford Motor Company of Canada - Mercury, MPV
4M2 = Ford Motor Co., USA, MPV
4M3 = Ford Motor Co., USA, Incomplete Vehicle
4M4 = Ford Motor Co., USA, Truck {Completed Vehicle}

DIGIT 4 GVWR/Brake System
C = 4001-5000 Lbs, Hydraulic
C = 4001-5000 Lbs, Hydraulic, Dual Front Airbags w/Manual Bel
D = 5001-6000 Lbs, Hydraulic
X = 5001-6000 Lbs, Hydraulic
Y = 4001-5000 Lbs, Hydraulic, Dual Front & Side Airbags w/Man
Y = 4001-5000 Lbs, Hydraulic
Z = 5001-6000 Lbs, Hydraulic

DIGIT 4* Brake Type/GVWR Class/Restraint
D = Hydraulic, 5001-6000 Lbs, Dual Front & Front Side Airbags
Z = Hydraulic, 5001-6000 Lbs, Dual Front Airbags

DIGIT 5-7 Line/Series/Body Type
A20 = Monterey 4D Wagon
A21 = Monterey 4D Wagon
A22 = Monterey 4D Wagon
A23 = Monterey 4D Wagon
U36 = Mountaineer 4D Utility - Convenience 2WD
U37 = Mountaineer 4D Utility - Luxury 2WD
U38 = Mountaineer 4D Utility - Premier 2WD
U46 = Mountaineer 4D Utility - Convenience AWD
U47 = Mountaineer 4D Utility - Luxury AWD
U48 = Mountaineer 4D Utility - Premier AWD
U52 = Mountaineer 4D Utility 2WD
U54 = Mountaineer 4D Utility 4WD
U55 = Mountaineer 4D Utility AWD
U56 = Mariner 4D Utility 2WD
U57 = Mariner 4D Utility AWD
U66 = Mountaineer 4D Utility 2WD
U66 = Mariner 4D Utility AWD
U76 = Mountaineer 4D Utility 4WD
U86 = Mountaineer 4D Utility AWD
V11 = Villager Wagon
V12 = Villager Sport Wagon
V14 = Villager Estate Wagon
V14 = Villager Cargo Van

DIGIT 8 Engine
1 = 3.0L V6 MPI
1 = 3.0L Duratec V6
2 = 4.2L V6 SPI
E = 4.0L V6 EFI SOHC
K = 4.0L V6 EFI SOHC FFV
P = 5.0L V8 EFI
T = 3.3L V6 MPI SOHC
W = 3.0L V6 MPI SOHC
W = 4.6L V8 EFI SOHC
Z = 2.3L I4

DIGIT 10 Model Year
1 = 2001
2 = 2002
3 = 2003
4 = 2004
5 = 2005
6 = 2006
P = 1993
R = 1994
S = 1995
T = 1996
V = 1997
W = 1998
X = 1999
Y = 2000

DIGIT 11 Assembly Plant
B = Oakville, Ontario, Canada

DIGIT 11 Assembly Plant
D = Avon Lake, OH, USA
D = Ohio Assembly Plant, Avon Lake, Ohio
U = Louisville, KY, USA
Z = St Louis: Hazelwood, MO

LTV0500000000582

Fig. 6 Ford Motor Company. Mercury

DIGIT 1 Country Of Origin
3 = Mexico
5 = USA

DIGIT 2 Manufacturer
G = General Motors Corporation

DIGIT 3 Vehicle Type
5 = Buick MPV
A = Buick MPV

DIGIT 4 GVWR/Brake System
D = 5001-6000 Lbs, Hydraulic
E = 6001-7000 Lbs, Hydraulic

DIGIT 5-6 Line Chassis/Series
A0 = Utility 4X2
B0 = Utility 4X4
S1 = Utility 4X2
T1 = Utility 4X4
V1 = Incomplete Mobility 4X2
V2 = Terraza CX 4X2
V3 = Terraza CXL 4X2
X2 = Terraza CX 4X4
X3 = Terraza CXL 4X4

DIGIT 7 Body Type
3 = 4D Utility

DIGIT 8 Engine
1 = 3.9L V6 SFI
7 = 3.6L V6 SFI DOHC
E = 3.4L V6 MPI HO
L = 3.5L V6 SFI
M = 5.3L V8 SFI
P = 5.3L V8 SFI
S = 4.2L I6 MPI DOHC

DIGIT 10 Model Year
2 = 2002
3 = 2003
4 = 2004
5 = 2005
6 = 2006

DIGIT 11 Assembly Plant
2 = Moraine, OH, USA
D = Doraville, GA, USA
S = Ramos Arizpe, Mexico

LTV0500000000562

Fig. 7 General Motors Corporation. Buick

DIGIT 1 Country Of Origin
- 1 = USA
- 3 = Mexico

DIGIT 2 Manufacturer
- G = General Motors Corporation

DIGIT 3 Vehicle Type
- Y = Cadillac MPV

DIGIT 4 GVWR/Brake System
- D = 5001-6000 Lbs, Hydraulic
- E = 6001-7000 Lbs, Hydraulic
- F = 7001-8000 Lbs, Hydraulic

DIGIT 5 Line & Chassis
- C = Conventional Cab 4X2
- K = Conventional Cab 4X4

DIGIT 5-6 Line Chassis/Series
- E6 = SRX

DIGIT 6 Series
- 1 = 1/2 Ton
- 4 = 1/2 Ton Platinum
- 6 = 1/2 Ton Luxury

DIGIT 7 Body Type
- 2 = Sport Utility Truck
- 3 = 4D Utility
- 6 = Escalade ESV

DIGIT 8 Engine
- 7 = 3.6L V6 SFI
- A = 4.6L V8 SFI
- N = 6.0L V8 SFI
- R = 5.7L V8 CPI
- T = 5.3L V8 SFI

DIGIT 10 Model Year
- 2 = 2002
- 3 = 2003
- 4 = 2004
- 5 = 2005
- 6 = 2006
- X = 1999
- Y = 2000

DIGIT 11 Assembly Plant
- 0 = Grand River, MI, USA
- 0 = Lansing, MI, USA
- B = Lansing, MI, USA
- G = Silao, Mexico
- L = Lansing, MI, USA
- R = Arlington, TX, USA

LTV0500000000563

Fig. 8 General Motors Corporation. Cadillac

DIGIT 1 Country Of Origin
- 1 = USA
- 2 = Canada
- 3 = Mexico
- J = Japan

DIGIT 2 Manufacturer
- 8 = Isusu
- C = Cami/GM Of Canada/Suzuki J.V.
- G = General Motors Corp.

DIGIT 3 Vehicle Type/Make
- 8 = Chevrolet MPV
- A = Chevrolet Bus {Van W/4th Seat}
- B = Chevrolet Truck {Incomplete Vehicle}
- C = Chevrolet Truck {Complete Vehicle}
- N = Chevrolet MPV
- Y = Chevrolet Luv {Incomplete Vehicle}
- Z = Chevrolet Luv {Complete Vehicle}

DIGIT 4 GVWR/Brake System
- B = 10001-14000 Lbs, Hydraulic
- B = 3001-4000 Lbs, Hydraulic
- C = 4001-5000 Lbs, Hydraulic
- D = 5001-6000 Lbs, Hydraulic
- E = 6001-7000 Lbs, Hydraulic
- F = 7001-8000 Lbs, Hydraulic
- F = 7000-8000 Lbs, Hydraulic
- G = 8001-9000 Lbs, Hydraulic
- H = 9001-10000 Lbs, Hydraulic
- J = 10001-14000 Lbs, Hydraulic
- K = 14001-16000 Lbs, Hydraulic
- L = 16001-19500 Lbs, Hydraulic
- M = 19501-26000 Lbs, Air/Hydraulic

DIGIT 5 Series
- 4 = 4500 Series
- 4 = 4500 Series
- C = Conventional Cab 4X2
- C = Conventional Cab 4X2
- E = Compact Cab 4x2
- E = Compact Cab 4x2
- G = Van
- G = Van, Sport Van
- G = Van
- G = Van, Sport Van
- J = Compact Cab 4X4
- J = Compact Cab 4X4
- K = Conventional Cab 4X4
- K = Conventional Cab 4X4
- L = Small Van 4X4
- L = Luv 4X2
- L = Small Van 4X4
- L = Luv 4X2
- M = Small Van 4X2
- M = Small Van 4X2
- P = Forward Control 4X2
- P = Forward Control 4X2
- R = Conventional Cab 4X2
- R = Luv 4X4
- R = Conventional Cab 4X2
- R = Luv 4X4
- S = Small Cab 4X2
- S = Small Cab 4X2
- T = Small Cab 4X4
- T = Small Cab 4X4
- U = All Purpose Vehicle
- U = All Purpose Vehicle
- V = Conventional Cab 4X4
- V = Conventional Cab 4X4
- W = EL Camino
- W = EL Camino
- X = All Purpose Vehicle - Extended Wheelbase
- X = All Purpose Vehicle - Extended Wheelbase

DIGIT 5-6 Line Chassis/Series
- C1 = Astro 4X2
- C1 = Full Size Truck 4X2, 1500
- C2 = Full Size Truck 4X2, 2500
- C3 = Full Size Truck 4X2, 3500
- C6 = Full Size Truck 4X2, 1500 Luxury
- C7 = Full Size Truck 4X2, 2500 Luxury
- C8 = Full Size Truck 4X2, 3500 Luxury
- C8 = Full Size Truck 4X2, Luxury 3500
- E1 = Tracker 4X2
- E6 = Tracker 4X2 LT
- G1 = Express 4X2 1500
- G2 = Express 4X2 2500
- G3 = Express 4X2 3500
- G6 = Express 4X2 1500, Luxury
- G7 = Express 4X2 2500, Luxury
- G8 = Express 4X2 3500, Luxury
- H1 = Express 4X4 1500
- H2 = Express 4X4 2500
- J1 = Tracker 4X4
- J6 = Tracker 4X4 LT
- J7 = Tracker 4X4 ZR2 Sport
- K1 = Astro 4X4
- K1 = Full Size Truck 4X4, 1500
- K2 = Full Size Truck 4X4, 2500
- K3 = Full Size Truck 4X4, 3500
- K6 = Full Size Truck 4X4, 1500 Luxury
- K7 = Full Size Truck 4X4, 2500 Luxury
- K8 = Full Size Truck 4X4, Luxury 3500
- K8 = Full Size Truck 4X4, 3500 Luxury
- L1 = Astro 4X4
- L1 = Equinox 4X2 LS
- L1 = Equinox 4X2
- L2 = Equinox 4X4
- L2 = Equinox 4X4 LS
- L6 = Astro 4X4 Luxury
- L6 = Equinox 4X2 LT
- L7 = Equinox 4X4 LT
- M1 = Astro 4X2
- M6 = Astro 4X2 Luxury
- P3 = P30 Aluminum Body, Step Van
- S0 = Blazer 4X2, Base
- S0 = Full Size Truck 4X2 - 1SA Trim
- S0 = Trailblazer 4X2, Base
- S1 = Full Size Truck 4X2 - 1SB Trim
- S1 = Trailblazer 4X2, LS
- S1 = S10 4X2
- S1 = Colorado 4X2
- S1 = Blazer 4X2, LS
- S1 = Blazer 4X2
- S1 = Full Size Truck 4X2
- S1 = Trailblazer 4X2
- S2 = Trailblazer 4X2, LT
- S6 = S10 4X2 Luxury
- T0 = Blazer 4X4, Base
- T0 = Full Size Truck 4X2 - 1SA Trim
- T0 = Trailblazer 4X4, Base
- T1 = Blazer 4X4
- T1 = Trailblazer 4X4, LS
- T1 = Trailblazer 4X4
- T1 = S10 4X4
- T1 = Full Size Truck 4X2 - 1SB Trim
- T1 = Blazer 4X4, LS
- T1 = Colorado 4X4
- T2 = Trailblazer 4X4, LT
- T6 = S10 4X4 Luxury
- U0 = Venture APV 4X2
- U0 = Uplander APV 4X2, Base
- U1 = Uplander APV 4X2, Cargo
- U1 = Venture APV 4X2 Luxury
- U2 = Venture APV 4X2 Economy
- U2 = Uplander APV 4X2, LS

LTV0500000000564

Fig. 9 General Motors Corporation (Part 1 of 3). Chevrolet

DIGIT 5-6 Line Chassis/Series
- U3 = Uplander APV 4X2, LT
- V0 = Uplander APV 4X2, Base Ext
- V0 = Venture APV 4X2 Extended
- V0 = Venture APV 4X4
- V1 = Venture APV 4X4 Luxury
- V1 = Uplander APV 4X2, Cargo Ext
- V1 = Venture APV 4X2 Extended Cargo
- V2 = Venture APV 4X4 Economy
- V2 = Uplander APV 4X2, LS Ext
- V2 = Venture APV 4X2 Extended Economy
- V3 = Uplander APV 4X2, LT Ext
- V3 = Venture APV 4X2 Extended Luxury
- X0 = Uplander APV AWD, Base
- X0 = Venture APV 4X2 Extended
- X1 = Uplander, APV AWD, Cargo
- X1 = Venture APV 4X2 Luxury Extended
- X2 = Venture APV 4X2 Economy Extended
- X2 = Uplander, APV AWD, LS
- X3 = Uplander, APV AWD, LT

DIGIT 6 Truck Line & Cab Type
- 0 = All Purpose Vehicle
- 0 = All Purpose Vehicle
- 1 = 1/2 Ton
- 1 = 1/2 Ton
- 2 = 3/4 Ton
- 2 = 3/4 Ton
- 3 = 1 Ton
- 3 = 1 Ton
- 8 = 1/2 Ton
- 8 = 1/2 Ton
- B = Forward/Tiltmaster Medium, Tilt, 67.9 BBC
- B = Forward/Tiltmaster Medium, Tilt, 67.9 BBC

DIGIT 7 Body Type
- 0 = Chassis Cab
- 0 = Sedan Pickup
- 1 = Hi-cube/Cutaway
- 2 = Forward Control
- 2 = Sport Utility Truck
- 3 = 4D All Purpose Vehicle
- 3 = 4D Cab/Utility
- 3 = 4D Utility
- 3 = Crew Cab
- 3 = 4D Cab
- 4 = 2D Cab
- 4 = Ext Cab
- 4 = Extended Cab
- 5 = Van
- 6 = Suburban
- 6 = All Purpose Vehicle
- 6 = 4D Extended Utility
- 8 = 2D Utility
- 9 = Extended Cab
- 9 = Extended Van

DIGIT 7* Chassis Type
- 1 = 4X2 (2 Axles - 1 Driving)

DIGIT 8 Engine
- 1 = 6.6L V8 FI DSL
- 2 = 6.6L V8 OHV Tbo Dsl
- 2 = 6.6L V8 FI DSL
- 4 = 2.2L I-4 MPI
- 4 = 2.5L V6 MPI
- 5 = 2.2L I-4 SFI Flex Fuel
- 6 = 3.5L I5 DOHC MPI
- 6 = 1.6L I-4 MPI
- 8 = 2.8L I4 DOHC MPI
- 9 = 3.4L V6 SFI OHV
- A = 3.8L V6 2BBL
- A = 2.5L I-4 TBI
- A = 1.9L I-4 2BBL

DIGIT 8 Engine
- B = 5.3L V8 SFI
- B = 2.8L V6 2BBL
- B = 4.3L V6 EFI HO
- C = 6.2L V8 Dsl
- C = 6.2L V8 FI DSL
- C = 2.0L I-4 MPI
- D = 4.1L I-6 2BBL
- D = 3.1L V6 TBI
- E = 8.1L V8 MFI
- E = 5.0L V8 TBI
- E = 3.4L V6 SFI HO
- E = 3.4L V6 MPI
- E = 2.5L I-4 TBI
- F = 6.5L V8 FI TDsl HO
- F = 3.4L V6 SFI
- F = 5.0L V8 4BBL
- F = 6.5L V8 FI TDSL
- G = 8.1L V8 MFI
- G = 8.1L V8 SFI OHV
- G = 5.0L V8 2BBL
- H = 2.2L I-4 MPI
- H = 5.0L V8 4BBL
- H = 5.0L V8 TBI
- H = 6.0L OHV SFI V8
- J = 6.2L V8 FI DSL
- J = 6.2L V8 DSL
- J = 7.4L V8 MPI HO
- J = 4.4L V8 2BBL
- K = 3.8L V6 2BBL
- K = 5.7L V8 TBI
- K = 5.7L V8 TBI CNG Capable
- L = 5.7L V8 4BBL
- L = 3.5L V6 SFI
- L = 3.8L V6 MPI
- M = 5.3L V8 SFI OHV
- M = 5.7L V8 4BBL
- M = 5.0L V8 SFI
- M = 5.0L V8 CPI
- M = 5.7L V8 4BBL
- N = 1.8L I-4 2BBL
- N = 4.3L V6 4BBL
- N = 5.7L V8 FI DSL
- N = 6.0L V8 MFI HO
- N = 6.0L V8 SFI
- N = 7.4L V8 TBI
- P = 5.3L V8 SFI Alum
- P = 6.5L V8 FI DSL
- P = 5.3L V8 SFI
- R = 5.7L V8 CPI
- R = 5.7L V8 MPI
- R = 5.7L V8 SFI
- R = 5.7L V8 SFI CNG Capable
- R = 2.8L V6 TBI
- S = 6.5L V8 FI TDsl
- S = 2.2L I-4 DSL
- S = 2.2L I-4 FI DSL
- S = 4.2L I-6 MPI DOHC
- S = 6.5L V8 FI TDsl HO
- T = 5.3L V8 MFI
- T = 4.8L I-6 1BBL
- T = 5.3L V8 SFI
- T = 5.3L V8 MPI
- U = 6.0L V8 MFI
- U = 6.0L V8 SFI
- V = 4.8L V8 SFI
- W = 4.3L V6 CPI
- W = 7.4L V8 4BBL
- X = 4.3L V6 MFI
- X = 4.3L V6 MPI
- X = 4.3L V6 CPI
- X = 4.3L V6 SFI

LTV0500000000565

Fig. 9 General Motors Corporation (Part 2 of 3). Chevrolet

DIGIT 8 Engine
- Y = 2.0L I-4 2BBL
- Y = 6.5L V8 Dsl HO
- Y = 6.5L V8 FI Dsl HO
- Z = 4.3L V6 CPI
- Z = 4.3L V6 TBI
- Z = 5.3L V8 SFI Flex Fuel
- Z = 5.7L V8 FI DSL

DIGIT 10 Model Year
- 1 = 2001
- 2 = 2002
- 3 = 2003
- 4 = 2004
- 5 = 2005
- 6 = 2006
- B = 1981
- C = 1982
- D = 1983
- E = 1984
- F = 1985
- G = 1986
- H = 1987
- J = 1988
- K = 1989
- L = 1990
- M = 1991
- N = 1992
- P = 1993
- R = 1994
- S = 1995
- T = 1996
- V = 1997
- W = 1998
- X = 1999
- Y = 2000

DIGIT 11 Assembly Plant
- 0 = Pontiac West, MI, USA
- 0 = Lansing, MI, USA
- 1 = Wentzville, MO, USA
- 1 = Oshawa, ON, Canada
- 1 = Oshawa #2, ON, Canada
- 2 = Moraine, OH, USA
- 3 = Detroit, MI, USA
- 3 = St. Eustache, PQ, Canada
- 4 = Orion, MI, USA
- 4 = Scarborough, ON, Canada
- 5 = Bowling Green, KY, USA
- 5 = London, ON, Canada
- 6 = Ingersoll, ON, Canada
- 6 = Oklahoma City, OK, USA
- 7 = Lordstown, OH, USA
- 8 = Fujusawa, Japan
- 8 = Shreveport, LA, USA
- 9 = Oshawa #1, ON, Canada
- A = Lakewood, GA, USA
- B = Baltimore, MD, USA
- B = Lansing, MI, USA
- C = Charlotte, Nc, USA
- C = Southgate, CA, USA
- C = Lansing, MI, USA
- D = Doraville, GA, USA
- E = Linden, NJ, USA
- E = Pontiac East, MI, USA
- F = Flint, MI, USA
- G = Silao, Mexico
- H = Flint, MI, USA
- J = Janesville, WI, USA
- K = Linden, NJ, USA
- L = Lansing, MI, USA
- L = Van Nuys, CA, USA
- M = Toluca, Mexico

DIGIT 11 Assembly Plant
- P = Pontiac, MI, USA
- R = Arlington, TX, USA
- S = St. Louis, MO, USA
- S = Ramos Arizpe, Mexico
- T = Tarrytown, NY, USA
- U = Hamtramck, MI, USA
- V = Pontiac, MI, USA
- W = Willow Run, MI, USA
- Z = Ft. Wayne, IN, USA

LTV0500000000566

Fig. 9 General Motors Corporation (Part 3 of 3). Chevrolet

DIGIT 1	Country Of Origin
1	= USA
2	= Canada
3	= Mexico

DIGIT 2	Manufacturer
G	= General Motors Corp.

DIGIT 3	Vehicle Type
0	= GMC Van w/4th Seat
5	= GMC MPV
D	= GMC Truck {Incomplete Vehicle}
J	= GMC Bus {Van W/4th Seat}
K	= GMC MPV
T	= GMC Truck {Complete Vehicle}

DIGIT 4	GVWR/Brake System
B	= 3001-4000 Lbs, Hydraulic
B	= 10001-14000 Lbs, Hydraulic
C	= 4001-5000 Lbs, Hydraulic
D	= 5001-6000 Lbs, Hydraulic
E	= 6001-7000 Lbs, Hydraulic
F	= 7001-8000 Lbs, Hydraulic
G	= 8001-9000 Lbs, Hydraulic
H	= 9001-10000 Lbs, Hydraulic
J	= 10001-14000 Lbs, Hydraulic
K	= 14001-16000 Lbs, Hydraulic

DIGIT 5	Series
4	= 4500 Series
4	= 4500 Series
C	= Conventional Cab 4X2
C	= Conventional Cab 4X2
G	= Van
G	= Van
K	= Conventional Cab 4X4
K	= Conventional Cab 4X4
L	= Small Van 4X4
L	= Small Van 4X4
M	= Small Van 4X2
M	= Small Van 4X2
P	= Forward Control
P	= Forward Control
R	= Conventional Cab 4X2
R	= Conventional Cab 4X2
S	= Small Cab 4X2
S	= Small Cab 4X2
T	= Small Cab 4X4
T	= Small Cab 4X4
V	= Conventional Cab 4X4
V	= Conventional Cab 4X4
W	= Caballero 4X2
W	= Caballero 4X2

DIGIT 5-6	Line Chassis/Series
C1	= Full Size Truck 4X2, 1500
C2	= Full Size Truck 4X2, 2500
C3	= Full Size Truck 4X2, 3500
C6	= Full Size Truck 4X2, 1500 Luxury
C7	= Full Size Truck 4X2, 2500 Luxury
C7	= Full Size Truck 4X2, Luxury 2500
C8	= Full Size Truck 4X2, Luxury 3500
C8	= Full Size Truck 4X2, 3500 Luxury
G1	= Savana 4X2, 1500
G2	= Savana 4X2, 2500
G3	= Savana 4X2, 3500
G3	= G3500
G6	= Savana 4X2, 1500 Luxury
G7	= Savana 4X2, 2500 Luxury
G8	= Savana 4X2, 3500 Luxury
H1	= Savana 4X4, 1500
H2	= Savana 4X4, 2500
H6	= Savana 4X4, 1500 Luxury
H7	= Savana 4X4, 2500 Luxury

DIGIT 5-6	Line Chassis/Series
K1	= Full Size Truck 4X4, 1500
K2	= Full Size Truck 4X4, 2500
K3	= Full Size Truck 4X4, 3500
K6	= Full Size Truck 4X4, 1500 Luxury
K7	= Full Size Truck 4X4, Luxury 2500
K7	= Full Size Truck 4X4, 2500 Luxury
K8	= Full Size Truck 4X4, 3500 Luxury
K8	= Full Size Truck 4X4, Luxury 3500
L1	= Safari 4X4
L6	= Safari 4X4 Luxury
M1	= Safari 4X2
M6	= Safari 4X2 Luxury
P3	= P3500 Aluminum Body Step Van
S0	= Canyon Z85 SL 4X2
S0	= Envoy 4X2 SLE
S1	= Envoy XUV 4X2
S1	= Canyon 4X2
S1	= Canyon Z85 SLE 4X2
S1	= Envoy 4X2
S1	= Envoy XL 4X2
S1	= Jimmy 4X2
S1	= Sonoma 4X2
S1	= Envoy 4X2 SLE
S2	= Canyon Z71 SL 4X2
S2	= Envoy 4X2 SLT
S3	= Canyon Z71 SLE 4X2
S3	= Envoy 4X2 SLT
S6	= Envoy 4X2 Luxury
S6	= Canyon 4X2 Luxury
S6	= Sonoma 4X2 Luxury
S6	= Jimmy 4X2 Luxury
S6	= Envoy 4X2 Denali
S6	= Envoy XL 4X2 Luxury
S6	= Envoy XUV 4X2 Luxury
T0	= Canyon Z85 SL 4X4
T0	= Envoy 4X4 SLE
T1	= Envoy 4X4
T1	= Sonoma 4X4
T1	= Jimmy 4X4
T1	= Envoy XUV 4X4
T1	= Envoy 4X4 SLE
T1	= Canyon Z85 SLE 4X4
T1	= Canyon 4X4
T1	= Envoy XL 4X4
T2	= Canyon Z71 SL 4X4
T2	= Envoy 4X4 SLT
T3	= Envoy 4X4 SLT
T3	= Canyon Z71 SLE 4X4
T6	= Canyon 4X4 Luxury
T6	= Envoy 4X4 Luxury
T6	= Envoy XL 4X4 Luxury
T6	= Envoy XUV 4X4 Luxury
T6	= Jimmy 4X4 Luxury
T6	= Sonoma 4X4 Luxury
T6	= Envoy 4X4 Denali

DIGIT 6	Series
1	= 1/2 Ton
1	= 1/2 Ton
2	= 3/4 Ton
2	= 3/4 Ton
3	= 1 Ton
3	= 1 Ton
8	= 1/2 Ton
8	= 1/2 Ton
B	= Forward/Tiltmaster Medium, Tilt 67.9 BBC
B	= Forward/Tiltmaster Medium, Tilt 67.9 BBC

DIGIT 7	Body Type
0	= Sedan Pickup
1	= Commercial Special & RV Cutaway
2	= Envoy XUV

LTV0500000000574

Fig. 10 General Motors Corporation (Part 1 of 3). GMC

DIGIT 7	Body Type
2	= Forward Control
3	= 4D Utility
3	= Crew Cab
3	= 4D Crew Cab
3	= 4D Cab/Utility
3	= 4D Cab
4	= 2D Cab
5	= Van
6	= Envoy XL
6	= Suburban
6	= Yukon XL
8	= 2D Utility
9	= Extended Cab
9	= Extended Van

DIGIT 7*	Chassis Type
1	= 4X2 (2 Axles - 1 Driving)

DIGIT 8	Engine
1	= 6.6L V8 FI DSL
2	= 6.6L V8 FI DSL
4	= 2.2L I-4 MPI
5	= 2.2L I-4 SFI Flex Fuel
6	= 3.5L I5 DOHC MPI
8	= 2.8L I4 DOHC MPI
A	= 2.5L I-4 FI
A	= 3.8L V6 2BBL
A	= 1.9L I-4 2BBL
B	= 4.3L V6 EFI HO
B	= 5.3L V8 SFI H/O
B	= 2.8L V6 2BBL
C	= 6.2L V8 DSL
C	= 6.2L V8 FI DSL
D	= 4.1L I-6 2BBL
E	= 8.1L V8 MFI
E	= 2.5L I-4 FI
E	= 2.5L I-4 TBI
E	= 5.0L V8 TBI
F	= 5.0L V8 4BBL
F	= 6.5L V8 FI TDSL
F	= 6.5L V8 FI TDsl HO
F	= 6.5L V8 FI TSDL HO
G	= 5.0L V8 4BBL
G	= 8.1L V8 MPI
G	= 5.0L V8 2BBL
G	= 8.1L V8 SFI
H	= 2.2L I-4 MPI
H	= 5.0L V8 4BBL
H	= 5.0L V8 TBI
J	= 6.2L V8 FI DSL
J	= 4.4L V8 2BBL
J	= 6.2L V8 Dsl
J	= 7.4L V8 MPI HO
K	= 5.7L V8 Tbl/LPG
K	= 3.8L V6 2BBL
K	= 5.7L V8 TBI CNG Capable
L	= 5.7L V8 4BBL
L	= 5.7L V8 EFI
M	= 5.7L V8 4BBL
M	= 5.0L V8 CPI
M	= 5.0L V8 MPI
M	= 5.0L V8 SFI
M	= 5.3L V8 SFI
N	= 5.7L V8 DSL
N	= 6.0L V8 SFI
N	= 7.4L V8 Fi
N	= 7.4L V8 TBI
N	= 4.3L V6 4BBL
P	= 4.8L V8 SFI
P	= 5.3L V8 SFI
P	= 5.7L V8 MPI
P	= 6.5L V8 FI DSL

DIGIT 8	Engine
P	= 5.7L V8 MFI
R	= 5.7L V8 SFI CNG Capable
R	= 5.7L V8 SFI
R	= 5.7L V8 MPI
R	= 5.7L V8 CPI
R	= 2.8L V6 TBI
R	= 2.8L V6 FI
S	= 6.5L V8 FI TDsl HO
S	= 6.5L V8 FI TDsl
S	= 2.2L I-4 FI DSL
S	= 4.2L I-6 MPI DOHC
T	= 4.8L I-6 1BBL
T	= 5.3L V8 SFI
T	= 5.3L V8 MFI
T	= 5.3L V8 MPI
U	= 6.0L V8 SFI
U	= 6.0L V8 MPI
V	= 4.8L V8 MPI
V	= 4.8L V8 SFI
W	= 4.3L V6 CPI
W	= 4.3L V6 MPI
W	= 7.4L V8 4BBL
X	= 4.3l V6 CPI
X	= 4.3L V6 MPI
Y	= 6.5L V8 FI DSL
Y	= 6.5L V8 FI Dsl HO
Y	= 2.0L I-4 2BBL
Z	= 5.7L V8 DSL
Z	= 4.3L V6 CPI
Z	= 4.3L V6 Fi
Z	= 4.3L V6 TBI
Z	= 5.3L V8 SFI Flex Fuel

DIGIT 10	Model Year
1	= 2001
2	= 2002
3	= 2003
4	= 2004
5	= 2005
6	= 2006
B	= 1981
C	= 1982
D	= 1983
E	= 1984
F	= 1985
G	= 1986
H	= 1987
J	= 1988
K	= 1989
L	= 1990
M	= 1991
N	= 1992
P	= 1993
R	= 1994
S	= 1995
T	= 1996
V	= 1997
W	= 1998
X	= 1999
Y	= 2000

DIGIT 11	Assembly Plant
0	= Pontiac West, MI, USA
1	= Oshawa #2, ON, Canada
1	= Oshawa (T&B), ON, Canada
1	= Oshawa, ON, Canada
1	= Wentzville, MO, USA
2	= Moraine, OH, USA
3	= Detroit, MI, USA
3	= St. Eustache, PQ, Canada
4	= Scarborough, ON, Canada
6	= Oklahoma City, OK, USA

LTV0500000000575

Fig. 10 General Motors Corporation (Part 2 of 3). GMC

DIGIT 11	Assembly Plant
7	= Lordstown, OH, USA
8	= Shreveport, LA, USA
9	= Oshawa #1, ON, Canada
B	= Baltimore, MD, USA
E	= Pontiac East, MI, USA
E	= Pontiac East, USA
E	= Pontiac, MI, USA
F	= Flint, MI, USA
G	= Silao, Mexico
H	= Flint, MI, USA
J	= Janesville, WI, USA
K	= Linden, NJ, USA
L	= Van Nuys, CA, USA
R	= Arlington, TX, USA
S	= Ramos Arizpe, Mexico
S	= St. Louis, MO, USA
V	= Pontiac, MI, USA
Z	= Ft. Wayne, IN, USA

LTV0500000000576

Fig. 10 General Motors Corporation (Part 3 of 3). GMC

DIGIT 1 Country Of Origin
- 1 = USA

DIGIT 2 Manufacturer
- G = General Motors Corporation

DIGIT 3 Vehicle Type
- H = Oldsmobile APV/MPV

DIGIT 4 GVWR/Brake System
- C = 4001-5000 Lbs, Hydraulic
- D = 5001-6000 Lbs, Hydraulic

DIGIT 5 Line & Chassis
- T = Small Conventional Cab 4X4
- U = All Purpose Vehicle 4X2
- X = All Purpose Vehicle Ext 4X2

DIGIT 5-6 Line Chassis/Series
- S1 = Bravada 4X2
- S6 = Bravada 4X2 Luxury
- T1 = Bravada 4X4
- T6 = Bravada 4X4 Luxury
- V0 = Silhouette 4X4
- V1 = Silhouette 4X4 Luxury
- V2 = Silhouette 4X4 Economy
- X0 = Silhouette 4X2 Ext
- X1 = Silhouette 4X2 Luxury Ext
- X2 = Silhouette 4X2 Economy Ext

DIGIT 6 Series
- 0 = APV
- 1 = 1/2 Ton

DIGIT 7 Body Type
- 3 = 4D Utility
- 6 = All Purpose Vehicle

DIGIT 8 Engine
- D = 3.1L V6 TBI
- E = 3.4L V6 SFI
- L = 3.8L V6 MFI
- S = 4.2L I-6 MFI, DOHC
- S = 4.2L I-6 SFI
- W = 4.3L V6 CPI
- Z = 4.3L V6 TBI

DIGIT 10 Model Year
- 1 = 2001
- 2 = 2002
- 3 = 2003
- 4 = 2004
- L = 1990
- M = 1991
- N = 1992
- P = 1993
- R = 1994
- S = 1995
- T = 1996
- V = 1997
- W = 1998
- X = 1999
- Y = 2000

DIGIT 11 Assembly Plant
- 2 = Moraine, OH, USA
- D = Doraville, GA, USA
- J = Janesville, WI, USA
- T = Tarrytown, NY, USA

LTV0500000000583

Fig. 11 General Motors Corporation. Oldsmobile

DIGIT 1 Country Of Origin
- 1 = USA
- 3 = Mexico

DIGIT 2 Manufacturer
- G = General Motors Corporation

DIGIT 3 Vehicle Type
- 7 = APV
- M = APV

DIGIT 4 GVWR/Brake System
- C = 4001-5000 Lbs, Hydraulic
- D = 5001-6000 Lbs, Hydraulic

DIGIT 5 Line & Chassis
- U = All Purpose Vehicle 2WD
- X = All Purpose Vehicle Ext 2WD

DIGIT 5-6 Line Chassis/Series
- A0 = Aztek SRV 4X2
- B0 = Aztek SRV 4X4
- U0 = Montana 4X2
- U1 = Montana 4X2 Luxury
- U2 = Montana 4X2 Economy
- V0 = Montana 4X2 Ext Economy
- V0 = Montana 4X4
- V1 = Montana 4X4 Luxury
- V1 = Montana 4X2 Ext Cargo
- V2 = Montana 4X4 Economy
- V2 = Montana 4X2 Ext Luxury
- V3 = Montana 4X2 Ext
- X0 = Montana 4X2 Ext
- X1 = Montana 4X2 Ext Luxury
- X2 = Montana 4X4 Ext Economy
- X2 = Montana 4X2 Ext Economy
- X3 = Montana 4X4 Ext Luxury

DIGIT 6 Series
- 0 = All Purpose Vehicle

DIGIT 7 Body Type
- 3 = 4D APV
- 6 = All Purpose Vehicle
- 6 = APV

DIGIT 8 Engine
- D = 3.1L V6 TBI
- E = 3.4L V6 SFI
- L = 3.5L V6 SFI
- L = 3.8L V6 MFI

DIGIT 10 Model Year
- 1 = 2001
- 2 = 2002
- 3 = 2003
- 4 = 2004
- 5 = 2005
- L = 1990
- M = 1991
- N = 1992
- P = 1993
- R = 1994
- S = 1995
- T = 1996
- V = 1997
- W = 1998
- X = 1999
- Y = 2000

DIGIT 11 Assembly Plant
- D = Doraville, GA, USA
- S = Ramos Arizpe, Mexico
- T = Tarrytown, NY, USA

LTV0500000000584

Fig. 12 General Motors Corporation. Pontiac

DIGIT 1-3 World Manufacturer Identifier
- 1G8 = Saturn MPV
- 5GZ = Saturn MPV

DIGIT 4 GVWR/Brake System
- C = 4001-5000 Lbs, Hydraulic
- D = 5001-6000 Lbs, Hydraulic
- Z = Saturn SL

DIGIT 5-6 Line & Chassis
- S5 = FWS 6 Cylinder SL
- U0 = Level 2 Wagon
- U1 = Level 2 Wagon
- U2 = Level 2 Wagon
- U3 = Level 2 Wagon
- V0 = Level 3 Wagon
- V1 = Level 3 Wagon
- V2 = Level 3 Wagon
- V3 = Level 3 Wagon
- X0 = Level 3 AWD Wagon
- X1 = Level 3 AWD Wagon
- X2 = Level 3 AWD Wagon
- X3 = Level 3 AWD Wagon
- Z2 = FWD Manual
- Z3 = FWD Auto
- Z4 = AWD 4 Cylinder
- Z5 = FWD 6 Cylinder
- Z6 = AWD 6 Cylinder

DIGIT 7 Body Type
- 2 = FWD
- 3 = 4D All-Purpose Vehicle

DIGIT 8 Engine
- 4 = 3.5L V6 MPI SOHC
- 8 = 3.0L MFI DOHC HO V6 - Flt
- B = 3.0L V6 MPI DOHC
- D = 2.2L I-4 MPI DOHC
- L = 3.5L V6 SFI OHV

DIGIT 10 Model Year
- 2 = 2002
- 3 = 2003
- 4 = 2004
- 5 = 2005
- 6 = 2006

DIGIT 11 Assembly Plant
- D = Doraville, GA, USA
- S = Spring Hill, TN, USA
- Y = Wilmington, DE, USA
- Z = Spring Hill, TN, USA

LTV0500000000585

Fig. 13 Saturn

AIR BAG SYSTEM PRECAUTIONS

TABLE OF CONTENTS

DaimlerChrysler

INDEX

DISARMING

1. Place ignition switch in Lock position.
2. Disconnect and isolate battery ground cable.
3. **Wait at least 2 minutes after disconnecting battery ground cable before performing any further repairs on vehicle. The system is designed to retain enough voltage to deploy air bags for a short time even after battery has been disconnected.**

ARMING

1. **Ensure no one is inside vehicle.**
2. Connect battery ground cable.
3. Turn ignition switch to On position, **from a safe position below or at the sides of air bag modules.**
4. SRS warning lamp should light for 6–8 seconds, then remain off for at least 45 seconds to indicate SRS is functioning properly.
5. If air bag warning lamp fails to light, or goes on and stays on, there is a system fault. Refer to **MOTOR's "Air Bag Manual" or "Air Bag Diagnostics CD."**

Ford Motor Co.

INDEX

DISARMING

Aviator

To avoid accidental deployment and possible personal injury, the back-up power supply must be depleted before repairing or replacing any air bag supplemental restraint system component.

1. Ensure all vehicle accessories are in Off position.
2. Ensure ignition switch is in Off position.
3. Remove restraints control module (RCM) fuse F2.12 (15A) from central junction box (CJB).
4. Turn ignition switch to On position and visually monitor air bag indicator for 30 seconds. Air bag indicator will remain lit continuously if correct RCM fuse has been removed. Remove correct RCM fuse as required.
5. Turn ignition switch to Off position.
6. Disconnect battery ground cable and wait at least 1 minute prior to any service or repair.

Blackwood

1. Move and tilt front seats to highest and rearmost position.
2. Disconnect battery ground cable and isolate.
3. **On models equipped with auxiliary batteries and power supplies,** disconnect ground cables and isolate.
4. **On all models,** wait at least one minute for back-up power supply to deplete stored energy.

5. Remove driver air bag module as outlined under "Component Service."
6. Connect restraint system diagnostic tool No. 105-R0012, or equivalent, to clockspring side of driver side air bag module electrical connector.
7. Remove instrument panel relay cover from top of instrument panel.
8. Remove passenger air bag module as outlined under "Component Service."
9. Connect restraint system diagnostic tool No. 105-R0012, or equivalent, in place of passenger air bag module.
10. **On models less side impact air bag modules, do not disconnect side impact air bag bridge resistors.**
11. **On models equipped with side impact air bags modules,** proceed as follows:
    a. Disconnect driver and passenger side impact air bag module electrical connectors located under seats.
    b. Connect restraint system diagnostic tools Nos. 40-009, or equivalent, to side impact air bag modules' electrical connectors.
12. **On all models,** disconnect seat belt retractor and pretensioner electrical connectors behind B-pillar.
13. Connect restraint system diagnostic tools No. 40-009, or equivalent, to seat belt retractor and pretensioner electrical connectors.
14. Connect battery ground cable.

Econoline

To avoid accidental deployment and possible personal injury, the back-up power supply must be depleted before repairing or replacing any air bag supplemental restraint system component.

1. Ensure all vehicle accessories are in Off position.
2. Ensure ignition switch is in Off position.
3. **On 2002–03 models,** remove electronic crash sensor (ECS) module fuse F2.19 (10A) and F2.38 (10A) from central junction box (CJB).
4. **On 2004–06 models,** remove restraints control module (RCM) fuse F2.20 (10A) from central junction box (CJB).
5. **On all models,** turn ignition switch to On position and visually monitor air bag indicator for 30 seconds. Air bag indicator will remain lit continuously if correct RCM fuse has been removed. Remove correct RCM fuse as required.
6. Turn ignition switch to Off position.
7. Disconnect battery ground cable and wait at least 1 minute prior to any service or repair.

Escape & Mariner .

To avoid accidental deployment and possible personal injury, the back-up power supply must be depleted before repairing or replacing any air bag supplemental restraint system component.

For Hybrid models, refer to "High-Voltage Traction Battery Systems De-Powering" in "2.3L Engine" section of chassis chapter for required safety precautions

1. Ensure all vehicle accessories are in Off position.
2. Ensure ignition switch is in Off position.
3. **On 2002–04 models,** remove restraints control module (RCM) fuses F2.5 (5A) and F2.7 (10A) from central junction box (CJB).
4. **On 2005–06 models,** remove restraints control module (RCM) fuse F33 (15A) from central junction box (CJB).
5. **On all models,** turn ignition switch to On position and visually monitor air bag indicator for 30 seconds. Air bag indicator will remain lit continuously if correct RCM fuse has been removed. Remove correct RCM fuse as required.
6. Turn ignition switch to Off position.
7. Disconnect battery ground cable and wait at least 1 minute prior to any service or repair.

Excursion & F-Super Duty 250-350

To avoid accidental deployment and possible personal injury, the back-up power supply must be depleted before repairing or replacing any air bag supplemental restraint system component.

1. Ensure all vehicle accessories are in Off position.
2. Ensure ignition switch is in Off position.
3. Remove restraints control module (RCM) fuse F2.26 (10A) from central junction box (CJB).
4. Turn ignition switch to On position and visually monitor air bag indicator for 30 seconds. Air bag indicator will remain lit continuously if correct RCM fuse has been removed. Remove correct RCM fuse as required.
5. Turn ignition switch to Off position.
6. Disconnect battery ground cable and wait at least 1 minute prior to any service or repair.

Expedition & Navigator

To avoid accidental deployment and possible personal injury, the back-up power supply must be depleted before repairing or replacing any air bag supplemental restraint system component.

1. Ensure all vehicle accessories are in Off position.
2. Ensure ignition switch is in Off position.
3. **On 2002 models,** remove restraints control module (RCM) fuse F22 (10A) from central junction box (CJB).
4. **On 2003–06 models,** remove restraints control module (RCM) fuse F1.19 (10A) from central junction box (CJB).
5. **On all models,** turn ignition switch to On position and visually monitor air bag indicator for 30 seconds. Air bag indicator will remain lit continuously if correct RCM fuse has been removed. Remove correct RCM fuse as required.
6. Turn ignition switch to Off position.
7. Disconnect battery ground cable and wait at least 1 minute prior to any service or repair.

Explorer & Mountaineer

To avoid accidental deployment and possible personal injury, the back-up power supply must be depleted before repairing or replacing any air bag supplemental restraint system component.

1. Ensure all vehicle accessories are in Off position.
2. Ensure ignition switch is in Off position.
3. **On models built up to March 2002,** remove restraints control module (RCM) fuse F2.28 (10A) from central junction box (CJB).
4. **On models built from March 2002–05,** remove restraints control module (RCM) fuse F2.19 (10A) from central junction box (CJB).
5. **On 2006 models,** remove restraints control module (RCM) fuse F17 (10A) from central junction box (CJB).
6. **On all models,** turn ignition switch to On position and visually monitor air bag indicator for 30 seconds. Air bag indicator will remain lit continuously if correct RCM fuse has been removed. Remove correct RCM fuse as required.
7. Turn ignition switch to Off position.
8. Disconnect battery ground cable and wait at least 1 minute prior to any service or repair.

Explorer Sport & Explorer Sport-Trac

To avoid accidental deployment and possible personal injury, the back-up power supply must be depleted before repairing or replacing any air bag supplemental restraint system component.

1. Ensure all vehicle accessories are in Off position.
2. Ensure ignition switch is in Off position.
3. **On models built up to February 17, 2002,** remove restraints control module (RCM) fuse F2.6 (7.5A less rear blower, 15A w/rear blower) from central junction box (CJB).
4. **On models built from February 17, 2002** remove restraints control module (RCM) fuse F2.12 (15A) from central junction box (CJB).
5. **On 2003 models,** remove restraints control module (RCM) fuse F2.14 (10A) from central junction box (CJB).
6. **On 2004–05 models,** remove restraints control module (RCM) fuse F2.10 (10A) from central junction box (CJB).
7. **On all models,** turn ignition switch to On position and visually monitor air bag indicator for 30 seconds. Air bag indicator will remain lit continuously if correct RCM fuse has been removed.

Remove correct RCM fuse as required.
8. Turn ignition switch to Off position.
9. Disconnect battery ground cable and wait at least 1 minute prior to any service or repair.

F150

To avoid accidental deployment and possible personal injury, the back-up power supply must be depleted before repairing or replacing any air bag supplemental restraint system component.

1. Ensure all vehicle accessories are in Off position.
2. Ensure ignition switch is in Off position.
3. **On 2002–03 models,** remove restraints control module (RCM) fuse F2.22 (10A) from central junction box (CJB).
4. **On 2004–06 models,** remove restraints control module (RCM) fuse F2.19 (10A) from central junction box (CJB).
5. **On all models,** turn ignition switch to On position and visually monitor air bag indicator for 30 seconds. Air bag indicator will remain lit continuously if correct RCM fuse has been removed. Remove correct RCM fuse as required.
6. Turn ignition switch to Off position.
7. Disconnect battery ground cable and wait at least 1 minute prior to any service or repair.

Freestar & Monterey

To avoid accidental deployment and possible personal injury, the back-up power supply must be depleted before repairing or replacing any air bag supplemental restraint system component.

1. Ensure all vehicle accessories are in Off position.
2. Ensure ignition switch is in Off position.
3. Remove restraints control module (RCM) fuse F2.17 (10A) from central junction box (CJB).
4. Turn ignition switch to On position and visually monitor air bag indicator for 30 seconds. Air bag indicator will remain lit continuously if correct RCM fuse has been removed. Remove correct RCM fuse as required.
5. Turn ignition switch to Off position.
6. Disconnect battery ground cable and wait at least 1 minute prior to any service or repair.

Mark LT

To avoid accidental deployment and possible personal injury, the back-up power supply must be depleted before repairing or replacing any air bag supplemental restraint system component.

1. Ensure all vehicle accessories are in Off position.
2. Ensure ignition switch is in Off position.
3. Remove restraints control module (RCM) fuse F2.19 (10A) from central junction box (CJB).
4. Turn ignition switch to On position and visually monitor air bag indicator for 30 seconds. Air bag indicator will remain lit continuously if correct RCM fuse has been removed. Remove correct RCM fuse as required.
5. Turn ignition switch to Off position.
6. Disconnect battery ground cable and wait at least 1 minute prior to any service or repair.

Ranger

To avoid accidental deployment and possible personal injury, the back-up power supply must be depleted before repairing or replacing any air bag supplemental restraint system component.

1. Ensure all vehicle accessories are in Off position.
2. Ensure ignition switch is in Off position.
3. **On 2002–03 models,** remove restraints control module (RCM) fuses F2.2 (10A) and F2.26 (10A) from central junction box (CJB).
4. **On 2004–06 models,** remove restraints control module (RCM) fuse F2.8 (10A) from central junction box (CJB).
5. **On all models,** turn ignition switch to On position and visually monitor air bag indicator for 30 seconds. Air bag indicator will remain lit continuously if correct RCM fuse has been removed. Remove correct RCM fuse as required.
6. Turn ignition switch to Off position.
7. Disconnect battery ground cable and wait at least 1 minute prior to any service or repair.

Villager

1. Disconnect and isolate battery ground cable.
2. Wait at least three minutes for air bag diagnostic monitor back-up power supply to deplete.
3. Remove cover panel at lower portion of steering wheel to access driver side air bag electrical connector.
4. Disconnect driver air bag electrical connector.
5. Connect air bag simulator tool No. T94P-50-A, or equivalent, to driver air bag module vehicle harness connector.
6. Disconnect passenger air bag module electrical connector, then install Rotunda air bag simulator tool No. T96P-50-A, or equivalent, in place of passenger air bag module.
7. Connect battery ground cable.

Windstar

To avoid accidental deployment and possible personal injury, the back-up power supply must be depleted before repairing or replacing any air bag supplemental restraint system component.

1. Ensure all vehicle accessories are in Off position.
2. Ensure ignition switch is in Off position.
3. Remove restraints control module (RCM) fuse F2.26 (10A) from central junction box (CJB).
4. Turn ignition switch to On position and visually monitor air bag indicator for 30 seconds. Air bag indicator will remain lit continuously if correct RCM fuse has been removed. Remove correct RCM fuse as required.
5. Turn ignition switch to Off position.
6. Disconnect battery ground cable and wait at least 1 minute prior to any service or repair.

ARMING

Aviator

The restraint system diagnostic tool is for restraint system service only. Remove tool from vehicle prior to road use. Failure to remove could result in injury and possible violation of vehicle safety standards.

1. Turn ignition switch from Off to On position.
2. Install RCM fuse F2.12 (15A) to CJB.
3. **Ensure that nobody is in vehicle and that there is nothing blocking or set in front of any air bag module when battery ground cable is connected.** Connect battery ground cable.
4. Prove out SRS system as follows:
   a. Turn ignition from On to Off position.
   b. Wait 10 seconds, then turn key back to On position and monitor air bag indicator with air bag modules installed.
   c. Air bag indicator will light continuously for 6 seconds and then turn Off.
   d. If air bag SRS fault is present, air bag indicator will fail to light, remain lit continuously or flash.
   e. Flashing might not occur until 30 seconds after ignition switch has been turned from Off to On position.
   f. This is time required for RCM to complete testing of SRS.
   g. If air bag indicator is inoperative and a SRS fault exists, a chime will sound in a pattern of 5 sets of 5 beeps.
   h. If this occurs, air bag indicator and any SRS fault discovered must be diagnosed and repaired.
   i. Clear all continuous DTC's from RCM using a suitable scan tool. Refer to **MOTOR's "Air Bag Manual" or "Air Bag Diagnostics CD."**

Blackwood

1. Disconnect battery ground cable and isolate.
2. **On models equipped with auxiliary batteries and power supplies,** disconnect ground cables and isolate.
3. **On all models,** wait at least one minute for back-up power supply to deplete stored energy.
4. Remove restraint system diagnostic tools from seat belt retractor and pretensioner electrical connectors.

5. Connect seat belt retractor and pretensioner electrical connectors.
6. **On models equipped with side impact air bag modules,** proceed as follows:
   a. Remove restraint system diagnostic tools from side impact air bag module electrical connectors.
   b. Connect side impact air bag module electrical connectors.
7. **On all models,** remove restraint system diagnostic tool from passenger air bag module.
8. Install passenger air bag module as outlined under "Component Service."
9. Remove restraint system diagnostic tool from driver side air bag module.
10. Install driver air bag module as outlined under "Component Service."
11. Connect battery ground cable.
12. Prove out SRS system as follows:
    a. Turn ignition from On to Off position.
    b. Wait 10 seconds, then turn key back to On position and monitor air bag indicator with air bag modules installed.
    c. Air bag indicator will light continuously for 6 seconds and then turn Off.
    d. If air bag SRS fault is present, air bag indicator will fail to light, remain lit continuously or flash.
    e. Flashing might not occur until 30 seconds after ignition switch has been turned from Off to On position.
    f. This is time required for RCM to complete testing of SRS.
    g. If air bag indicator is inoperative and a SRS fault exists, a chime will sound in a pattern of 5 sets of 5 beeps.
    h. If this occurs, air bag indicator and any SRS fault discovered must be diagnosed and repaired.
    i. Clear all continuous DTC's from RCM using a suitable scan tool. Refer to **MOTOR's "Air Bag Manual" or "Air Bag Diagnostics CD."**

Econoline

The restraint system diagnostic tool is for restraint system service only. Remove tool from vehicle prior to road use. Failure to remove could result in injury and possible violation of vehicle safety standards.

1. Turn ignition switch from Off to On position.
2. **On 2002–03 models,** install ECS fuses F2.19 (10A) and F2.38 (10A) to CJB and install cover.
3. **On 2004–06 models,** install RCM fuse F2.20 (10A) to CJB and install cover.
4. **On all models, ensure that nobody is in vehicle and that there is nothing blocking or set in front of any air bag module when battery ground cable is connected.** Connect battery ground cable.
5. Prove out SRS system as follows:
   a. Turn ignition from On to Off position.
   b. Wait 10 seconds, then turn key back to On position and monitor air bag indicator with air bag modules installed.
   c. Air bag indicator will light continuously for 6 seconds and then turn Off.
   d. If air bag SRS fault is present, air bag indicator will fail to light, remain lit continuously or flash.
   e. Flashing might not occur until 30 seconds after ignition switch has been turned from Off to On position.
   f. This is time required for ECS or RCM to complete testing of SRS.
   g. If air bag indicator is inoperative and a SRS fault exists, a chime will sound in a pattern of 5 sets of 5 beeps.
   h. If this occurs, air bag indicator and any SRS fault discovered must be diagnosed and repaired.
   i. Clear all continuous DTC's from RCM using a suitable scan tool. Refer to **MOTOR's "Air Bag Manual" or "Air Bag Diagnostics CD."**

Escape & Mariner

The restraint system diagnostic tool is for restraint system service only. Remove tool from vehicle prior to road use. Failure to remove could result in injury and possible violation of vehicle safety standards.

1. Turn ignition switch from Off to On position.
2. **On 2002–04 models,** install RCM fuses F2.5 (5A) and F2.7 (10A) to CJB and install cover.
3. **On 2005–06 models,** install RCM fuse F33 (15A) to CJB and install cover.
4. **On all models, ensure that nobody is in vehicle and that there is nothing blocking or set in front of any air bag module when battery ground cable is connected.** Connect battery ground cable.
5. Prove out SRS system as follows:
   a. Turn ignition from On to Off position.
   b. Wait 10 seconds, then turn key back to On position and monitor air bag indicator with air bag modules installed.
   c. Air bag indicator will light continuously for 6 seconds and then turn Off.
   d. If air bag SRS fault is present, air bag indicator will fail to light, remain lit continuously or flash.
   e. Flashing might not occur until 30 seconds after ignition switch has been turned from Off to On position.
   f. This is time required for RCM to complete testing of SRS.
   g. If air bag indicator is inoperative and a SRS fault exists, a chime will sound in a pattern of 5 sets of 5 beeps.
   h. If this occurs, air bag indicator and any SRS fault discovered must be diagnosed and repaired.
   i. Clear all continuous DTC's from RCM using a suitable scan tool. Refer to **MOTOR's "Air Bag Manual" or "Air Bag Diagnostics CD."**

Excursion & F-Super Duty 250-350

The restraint system diagnostic tool is for restraint system service only. Remove tool from vehicle prior to road use. Failure to remove could result in injury and possible violation of vehicle safety standards.

1. Turn ignition switch from Off to On position.
2. Install RCM fuse F2.26 (10A) to CJB and install cover.
3. **Ensure that nobody is in vehicle and that there is nothing blocking or set in front of any air bag module when battery ground cable is connected.** Connect battery ground cable.
4. Prove out SRS system as follows:
   a. Turn ignition from On to Off position.
   b. Wait 10 seconds, then turn key back to On position and monitor air bag indicator with air bag modules installed.
   c. Air bag indicator will light continuously for 6 seconds and then turn Off.
   d. If air bag SRS fault is present, air bag indicator will fail to light, remain lit continuously or flash.
   e. Flashing might not occur until 30 seconds after ignition switch has been turned from Off to On position.
   f. This is time required for RCM to complete testing of SRS.
   g. If air bag indicator is inoperative and a SRS fault exists, a chime will sound in a pattern of 5 sets of 5 beeps.
   h. If this occurs, air bag indicator and any SRS fault discovered must be diagnosed and repaired.
   i. Clear all continuous DTC's from RCM using a suitable scan tool. Refer to **MOTOR's "Air Bag Manual" or "Air Bag Diagnostics CD."**

Expedition & Navigator

The restraint system diagnostic tool is for restraint system service only. Remove tool from vehicle prior to road use. Failure to remove could result in injury and possible violation of vehicle safety standards.

1. Turn ignition switch from Off to On position.
2. **On 2002 models,** install RCM fuse F22 (10A) to CJB and install cover.
3. **On 2003–06 models,** install RCM fuse F1.19 (10A) to CJB and install cover.
4. **On all models, ensure that nobody is in vehicle and that there is nothing blocking or set in front of any air bag module when battery ground cable is connected.** Connect battery ground cable.
5. Prove out SRS system as follows:
   a. Turn ignition from On to Off position.

b. Wait 10 seconds, then turn key back to On position and monitor air bag indicator with air bag modules installed.
c. Air bag indicator will light continuously for 6 seconds and then turn Off.
d. If air bag SRS fault is present, air bag indicator will fail to light, remain lit continuously or flash.
e. Flashing might not occur until 30 seconds after ignition switch has been turned from Off to On position.
f. This is time required for RCM to complete testing of SRS.
g. If air bag indicator is inoperative and a SRS fault exists, a chime will sound in a pattern of 5 sets of 5 beeps.
h. If this occurs, air bag indicator and any SRS fault discovered must be diagnosed and repaired.
i. Clear all continuous DTC's from RCM using a suitable scan tool. Refer to **MOTOR's "Air Bag Manual" or "Air Bag Diagnostics CD."**

Explorer & Mountaineer

The restraint system diagnostic tool is for restraint system service only. Remove tool from vehicle prior to road use. Failure to remove could result in injury and possible violation of vehicle safety standards.

1. Turn ignition switch from Off to On position.
2. **On models built up to March 2002,** install RCM fuse F2.28 (10A) to CJB and install cover.
3. **On models built from March 2002–05,** install RCM fuse F2.19 (10A) to CJB and install cover.
4. **On 2006 models,** install RCM fuse F17 (10A) to CJB and install cover.
5. **On all models, ensure that nobody is in vehicle and that there is nothing blocking or set in front of any air bag module when battery ground cable is connected.** Connect battery ground cable.
6. Prove out SRS system as follows:
   a. Turn ignition from On to Off position.
   b. Wait 10 seconds, then turn key back to On position and monitor air bag indicator with air bag modules installed.
   c. Air bag indicator will light continuously for 6 seconds and then turn Off.
   d. If air bag SRS fault is present, air bag indicator will fail to light, remain lit continuously or flash.
   e. Flashing might not occur until 30 seconds after ignition switch has been turned from Off to On position.
   f. This is time required for RCM to complete testing of SRS.
   g. If air bag indicator is inoperative and a SRS fault exists, a chime will sound in a pattern of 5 sets of 5 beeps.
   h. If this occurs, air bag indicator and any SRS fault discovered must be diagnosed and repaired.
   i. Clear all continuous DTC's from RCM using a suitable scan tool. Refer to **MOTOR's "Air Bag Manual" or "Air Bag Diagnostics CD."**

Explorer Sport & Explorer Sport-Trac

The restraint system diagnostic tool is for restraint system service only. Remove tool from vehicle prior to road use. Failure to remove could result in injury and possible violation of vehicle safety standards.

1. Turn ignition switch from Off to On position.
2. **On models built up to February 17, 2002,** install RCM fuse F2.6 (7.5A less rear blower, 15A w/rear blower) from central junction box (CJB).
3. **On models built from February 17, 2002–03** install RCM fuse F2.12 (15A) from central junction box (CJB).
4. **On 2003 models,** install RCM fuse F2.14 (10A) from central junction box (CJB).
5. **On 2004–05 models,** install RCM fuse F2.10 (10A) from central junction box (CJB).
6. **On all models, ensure that nobody is in vehicle and that there is nothing blocking or set in front of any air bag module when battery ground cable is connected.** Connect battery ground cable.
7. Prove out SRS system as follows:
   a. Turn ignition from On to Off position.
   b. Wait 10 seconds, then turn key back to On position and monitor air bag indicator with air bag modules installed.
   c. Air bag indicator will light continuously for 6 seconds and then turn Off.
   d. If air bag SRS fault is present, air bag indicator will fail to light, remain lit continuously or flash.
   e. Flashing might not occur until 30 seconds after ignition switch has been turned from Off to On position.
   f. This is time required for RCM to complete testing of SRS.
   g. If air bag indicator is inoperative and a SRS fault exists, a chime will sound in a pattern of 5 sets of 5 beeps.
   h. If this occurs, air bag indicator and any SRS fault discovered must be diagnosed and repaired.
   i. Clear all continuous DTC's from RCM using a suitable scan tool. Refer to **MOTOR's "Air Bag Manual" or "Air Bag Diagnostics CD."**

F150

The restraint system diagnostic tool is for restraint system service only. Remove tool from vehicle prior to road use. Failure to remove could result in injury and possible violation of vehicle safety standards.

1. Turn ignition switch from Off to On position.
2. **On 2002–03 models,** install RCM fuse F2.22 (10A) from central junction box (CJB).
3. **On 2004–06 models,** install RCM fuse F2.19 (10A) from central junction box (CJB).
4. **On all models, ensure that nobody is in vehicle and that there is nothing blocking or set in front of any air bag module when battery ground cable is connected.** Connect battery ground cable.
5. Prove out SRS system as follows:
   a. Turn ignition from On to Off position.
   b. Wait 10 seconds, then turn key back to On position and monitor air bag indicator with air bag modules installed.
   c. Air bag indicator will light continuously for 6 seconds and then turn Off.
   d. If air bag SRS fault is present, air bag indicator will fail to light, remain lit continuously or flash.
   e. Flashing might not occur until 30 seconds after ignition switch has been turned from Off to On position.
   f. This is time required for RCM to complete testing of SRS.
   g. If air bag indicator is inoperative and a SRS fault exists, a chime will sound in a pattern of 5 sets of 5 beeps.
   h. If this occurs, air bag indicator and any SRS fault discovered must be diagnosed and repaired.
   i. Clear all continuous DTC's from RCM using a suitable scan tool. Refer to **MOTOR's "Air Bag Manual" or "Air Bag Diagnostics CD."**

Freestar & Monterey

The restraint system diagnostic tool is for restraint system service only. Remove tool from vehicle prior to road use. Failure to remove could result in injury and possible violation of vehicle safety standards.

1. Turn ignition switch from Off to On position.
2. Install RCM fuse F2.17 (10A) from central junction box (CJB).
3. **Ensure that nobody is in vehicle and that there is nothing blocking or set in front of any air bag module when battery ground cable is connected.** Connect battery ground cable.
4. Prove out SRS system as follows:
   a. Turn ignition from On to Off position.
   b. Wait 10 seconds, then turn key back to On position and monitor air bag indicator with air bag modules installed.
   c. Air bag indicator will light continuously for 6 seconds and then turn Off.
   d. If air bag SRS fault is present, air bag indicator will fail to light, remain lit continuously or flash.
   e. Flashing might not occur until 30

seconds after ignition switch has been turned from Off to On position.
f. This is time required for RCM to complete testing of SRS.
g. If air bag indicator is inoperative and a SRS fault exists, a chime will sound in a pattern of 5 sets of 5 beeps.
h. If this occurs, air bag indicator and any SRS fault discovered must be diagnosed and repaired.
i. Clear all continuous DTC's from RCM using a suitable scan tool. Refer to **MOTOR's "Air Bag Manual" or "Air Bag Diagnostics CD."**

Mark LT

The restraint system diagnostic tool is for restraint system service only. Remove tool from vehicle prior to road use. Failure to remove could result in injury and possible violation of vehicle safety standards.

1. Turn ignition switch from Off to On position.
2. Install RCM fuse F2.19 (10A) from central junction box (CJB).
3. **Ensure that nobody is in vehicle and that there is nothing blocking or set in front of any air bag module when battery ground cable is connected.** Connect battery ground cable.
4. Prove out SRS system as follows:
   a. Turn ignition from On to Off position.
   b. Wait 10 seconds, then turn key back to On position and monitor air bag indicator with air bag modules installed.
   c. Air bag indicator will light continuously for 6 seconds and then turn Off.
   d. If air bag SRS fault is present, air bag indicator will fail to light, remain lit continuously or flash.
   e. Flashing might not occur until 30 seconds after ignition switch has been turned from Off to On position.
   f. This is time required for RCM to complete testing of SRS.
   g. If air bag indicator is inoperative and a SRS fault exists, a chime will sound in a pattern of 5 sets of 5 beeps.
   h. If this occurs, air bag indicator and any SRS fault discovered must be diagnosed and repaired.
   i. Clear all continuous DTC's from RCM using a suitable scan tool. Refer to **MOTOR's "Air Bag Manual" or "Air Bag Diagnostics CD."**

Ranger

The restraint system diagnostic tool is for restraint system service only. Remove tool from vehicle prior to road use. Failure to remove could result in injury and possible violation of vehicle safety standards.

1. Turn ignition switch from Off to On position.
2. **On 2002–03 models,** install RCM fuses F2.2 (10A) and F2.26 (10A) from central junction box (CJB).
3. **On 2004–06 models,** install RCM fuse F2.8 (10A) from central junction box (CJB).
4. **On all models, ensure that nobody is in vehicle and that there is nothing blocking or set in front of any air bag module when battery ground cable is connected.** Connect battery ground cable.
5. Prove out SRS system as follows:
   a. Turn ignition from On to Off position.
   b. Wait 10 seconds, then turn key back to On position and monitor air bag indicator with air bag modules installed.
   c. Air bag indicator will light continuously for 6 seconds and then turn Off.
   d. If air bag SRS fault is present, air bag indicator will fail to light, remain lit continuously or flash.
   e. Flashing might not occur until 30 seconds after ignition switch has been turned from Off to On position.
   f. This is time required for RCM to complete testing of SRS.
   g. If air bag indicator is inoperative and a SRS fault exists, a chime will sound in a pattern of 5 sets of 5 beeps.
   h. If this occurs, air bag indicator and any SRS fault discovered must be diagnosed and repaired.
   i. Clear all continuous DTC's from RCM using a suitable scan tool. Refer to **MOTOR's "Air Bag Manual" or "Air Bag Diagnostics CD."**

Villager

1. Disconnect and isolate battery ground cable.
2. Wait at least three minutes for air bag diagnostic monitor back-up power supply to deplete.
3. Remove air bag simulator from driver air bag connector.
4. Connect driver air bag connector to driver air bag module, then install cover on steering wheel.
5. Remove air bag simulator from passenger air bag module connector.
6. Connect passenger air bag module electrical connector and install passenger air bag module.
7. Connect battery ground cable and prove out system as follows:
   a. Cycle ignition switch from Off to Run **from a safe location at side of or below air bag modules** and visually monitor air bag indicator.
   b. Air bag indicator lamp should light continuously for approximately seven seconds, then go out. Refer to **MOTOR's "Air Bag Manual" or "Air Bag Diagnostics CD."**

Windstar

The restraint system diagnostic tool is for restraint system service only. Remove tool from vehicle prior to road use. Failure to remove could result in injury and possible violation of vehicle safety standards.

1. Turn ignition switch from Off to On position.
2. Install RCM fuse F2.26 (10A) from central junction box (CJB).
3. **Ensure that nobody is in vehicle and that there is nothing blocking or set in front of any air bag module when battery ground cable is connected.** Connect battery ground cable.
4. Prove out SRS system as follows:
   a. Turn ignition from On to Off position.
   b. Wait 10 seconds, then turn key back to On position and monitor air bag indicator with air bag modules installed.
   c. Air bag indicator will light continuously for 6 seconds and then turn Off.
   d. If air bag SRS fault is present, air bag indicator will fail to light, remain lit continuously or flash.
   e. Flashing might not occur until 30 seconds after ignition switch has been turned from Off to On position.
   f. This is time required for RCM to complete testing of SRS.
   g. If air bag indicator is inoperative and a SRS fault exists, a chime will sound in a pattern of 5 sets of 5 beeps.
   h. If this occurs, air bag indicator and any SRS fault discovered must be diagnosed and repaired.
   i. Clear all continuous DTC's from RCM using a suitable scan tool. Refer to **MOTOR's "Air Bag Manual" or "Air Bag Diagnostics CD."**

General Motors Corp.

INDEX

DISARMING

The inflatable restraint sensing and diagnostic module (SDM) maintains a reserved energy supply. The reserved energy supply provides deployment power for the air bags. Deployment power is available for as much as 1 minute after disconnecting the vehicle power. Disabling the SIR system prevents deployment of the air bags from the reserved energy supply.

Astro & Safari

2002

1. Ensure front wheels are in straight ahead position.
2. Turn ignition switch to Off position.
3. Remove key from ignition.
4. Remove AIR BAG fuse from fuse block. **With AIR BAG fuse removed and ignition On, AIR BAG indicator illuminates. This is normal operation and does not indicate an SIR system fault.**
5. Remove driver side insulator panel.
6. Remove connector position assurance (CPA) from driver air bag module yellow 2-way connector located at base of steering column.
7. Disconnect driver air bag module yellow 2-way connector.
8. Remove passenger side insulator panel.
9. Remove CPA from passenger air bag module yellow 2-way connector located under instrument panel insulator panel.
10. Disconnect passenger air bag module yellow 2-way connector.

2003-05

ZONE 1

1. Ensure front wheels are in straight ahead position.
2. Turn ignition switch to Off position.
3. Remove key from ignition.
4. Remove AIR BAG fuse from fuse block. **With AIR BAG fuse removed and ignition On, AIR BAG indicator illuminates. This is normal operation and does not indicate an SIR system fault.**
5. Raise and support vehicle using suitable lift or jack.
6. Remove connector position assurance (CPA) from front end discriminating sensor connector located on frame crossmember.
7. Disconnect front end discriminating sensor connector.

ZONE 3

1. Ensure front wheels are in straight ahead position.
2. Turn ignition switch to Off position.
3. Remove key from ignition.
4. Remove driver side knee bolster.
5. Remove AIR BAG fuse from fuse block. **With AIR BAG fuse removed and ignition On, AIR BAG indicator illuminates. This is normal operation and does not indicate an SIR system fault.**
6. Remove connector position assurance (CPA) from driver air bag module yellow 2-way connector located left of steering column near knee bolster.
7. Disconnect driver air bag module yellow 2-way connector.

ZONE 5

1. Ensure front wheels are in straight ahead position.
2. Turn ignition switch to Off position.
3. Remove key from ignition.
4. Remove passenger side knee bolster.
5. Remove AIR BAG fuse from fuse block. **With AIR BAG fuse removed and ignition On, AIR BAG indicator illuminates. This is normal operation and does not indicate an SIR system fault.**
6. Remove connector position assurance (CPA) from passenger air bag module connector located behind instrument panel support.
7. Disconnect passenger air bag module yellow 2-way connector.

ZONE 7

1. Ensure front wheels are in straight ahead position.
2. Turn ignition switch to Off position.
3. Remove key from ignition.
4. Remove passenger and driver side knee bolster.
5. Remove AIR BAG fuse from fuse block. **With AIR BAG fuse removed and ignition On, AIR BAG indicator illuminates. This is normal operation and does not indicate an SIR system fault.**
6. Remove connector position assurance (CPA) from driver air bag module yellow 2-way connector located left of steering column near knee bolster.
7. Disconnect driver air bag module yellow 2-way connector.
8. Remove CPA from passenger air bag module yellow 2-way connector located behind instrument panel support.
9. Disconnect passenger air bag module yellow 2-way connector.

Avalanche, Escalade ESV, Escalade EXT, Sierra, Silverado, Suburban, SSR, Tahoe & Yukon

2002

1. Ensure front wheels are in straight ahead position.
2. Turn ignition switch to Off position.
3. Remove key from ignition.
4. Remove AIR BAG fuse from fuse block. **With AIR BAG fuse removed and ignition On, AIR BAG indicator illuminates. This is normal operation and does not indicate an SIR system fault.**
5. Remove connector position assurance (CPA) from driver air bag module yellow 2-way connector at base of steering column.
6. Disconnect driver air bag module yellow 2-way connector at base of steering column.
7. Open glove compartment door beyond support stops to access passenger air bag module yellow 2-way connector located behind main instrument panel support.
8. Remove CPA from passenger air bag module yellow 2-way connector.
9. Disconnect passenger air bag module yellow 2-way connector.
10. **On Avalanche, Suburban, Tahoe and Yukon models,** remove and disconnect CPA from driver side impact air bag module yellow 2-way connector from under driver seat.
11. **On Avalanche, Suburban, Tahoe and Yukon models,** remove and disconnect CPA from passenger side impact air bag module yellow 2-way connector from under passenger seat.

2003-06

ZONE 1

1. Ensure steering wheel is in straight ahead position.
2. Turn ignition switch to Off position.
3. Remove key from ignition.
4. Remove SIR fuse from fuse block. **With SIR fuse removed and ignition On, AIR BAG indicator illuminates. This is normal operation and does not indicate an SIR system fault.**
5. Remove connector position assurance (CPA) from both front end sensor connectors from frame crossmember. **This vehicle is equipped with two inflatable restraint front end sensors. Remove both front end sensors.**
6. Disconnect both front end sensor connectors.

ZONE 2

1. Ensure steering wheel is in straight ahead position.
2. Turn ignition switch to Off position.
3. Remove key from ignition.
4. Remove SIR fuse from fuse block. **With SIR fuse removed and ignition On, AIR BAG indicator illuminates. This is normal operation and does not indicate an SIR system fault.**
5. Remove driver side door trim panel using a suitable flat-bladed tool.
6. Remove connector position assurance (CPA) from side impact sensor yellow 2-way connector located at bottom lefthand side of door.
7. Disconnect side impact sensor yellow 2-way connector.
8. **On SSR models,** proceed as follows:
   a. Remove lock pillar trim panel using suitable flat-bladed tool.
   b. Disconnect electrical connector.
   c. Remove CPA from seat belt pretensioner lefthand connector.
   d. Disconnect seat belt pretensioner lefthand connector from vehicle harness connector.

ZONE 3

1. Ensure steering wheel is in straight ahead position.
2. Turn ignition switch to Off position.
3. Remove key from ignition.
4. **On SSR models,** remove knee bolster trim panel.
5. **On all models,** remove SIR fuse from fuse block. **With SIR fuse removed and ignition On, AIR BAG indicator illuminates. This is normal operation and does not indicate an SIR system fault.**
6. Remove connector position assurance (CPA) from driver air bag module yellow 4-way connector located left of steering column near knee bolster.
7. Disconnect driver air bag module yellow 4-way connector.

ZONE 5

1. Ensure steering wheel is in straight ahead position.
2. Turn ignition switch to Off position.
3. Remove key from ignition.
4. Remove SIR fuse from fuse block. **With SIR fuse removed and ignition On, AIR BAG indicator illuminates. This is normal operation and does not indicate an SIR system fault.**
5. Remove connector position assurance (CPA) from passenger air bag module yellow 4-way connector located behind instrument panel support.
6. Disconnect passenger air bag module yellow 4-way connector.

ZONE 6

1. Ensure steering wheel is in straight ahead position.
2. Turn ignition switch to Off position.
3. Remove key from ignition.
4. Remove SIR fuse from fuse block. **With SIR fuse removed and ignition On, AIR BAG indicator illuminates. This is normal operation and does not indicate an SIR system fault.**
5. Remove passenger side door trim panel using a suitable flat-bladed tool.
6. Remove connector position assurance (CPA) from side impact sensor yellow 2-way connector located at bottom of righthand door.
7. Disconnect side impact sensor yellow 2-way connector.
8. **On SSR models,** proceed as follows:
   a. Remove lock pillar trim panel using suitable flat-bladed tool.
   b. Disconnect electrical connector.
   c. Remove CPA from seat belt pretensioner righthand connector.
   d. Disconnect seat belt pretensioner righthand connector from vehicle harness connector.

ZONE 7

Except SSR

1. Ensure steering wheel is in straight ahead position.
2. Turn ignition switch to Off position.
3. Remove key from ignition.
4. Remove SIR fuse from fuse block. **With SIR fuse removed and ignition On, AIR BAG indicator illuminates. This is normal operation and does not indicate an SIR system fault.**
5. Remove connector position assurance (CPA) from driver air bag module yellow 4-way connector located left of steering column near knee bolster.
6. Disconnect driver air bag module yellow 4-way connector.
7. Remove CPA from passenger air bag module yellow 4-way connector located behind instrument panel support.
8. Disconnect passenger air bag module yellow 4-way connector.
9. **On Avalanche and 2003–04 Escalade, Suburban, Tahoe and Yukon models,** proceed as follows:
   a. Remove CPA from passenger side impact air bag module yellow 2-way connector located under passenger seat.
   b. Disconnect passenger side impact air bag module yellow 2-way connector.
   c. Remove CPA from driver side impact air bag module yellow 2-way connector located under driver seat.
   d. Disconnect driver side impact air bag module yellow 2-way connector.

SSR

1. Ensure steering wheel is in straight ahead position.
2. Turn ignition switch to Off position.
3. Remove key from ignition.
4. Remove SIR fuse from fuse block. **With SIR fuse removed and ignition On, AIR BAG indicator illuminates. This is normal operation and does not indicate an SIR system fault.**
5. Remove connector position assurance (CPA) from driver side impact air bag module yellow 2-way connector located under driver seat.
6. Disconnect driver side impact air bag module yellow 2-way connector.

ZONE 8

1. Ensure steering wheel is in straight ahead position.
2. Turn ignition switch to Off position.
3. Remove key from ignition.
4. Remove SIR fuse from fuse block. **With SIR fuse removed and ignition On, AIR BAG indicator illuminates. This is normal operation and does not indicate an SIR system fault.**
5. Remove connector position assurance (CPA) from driver air bag module yellow 4-way connector located left of steering column near knee bolster.
6. Disconnect driver air bag module yellow 4-way connector located left of steering column near knee bolster.
7. Remove CPA from passenger air bag module yellow 4-way connector located behind instrument panel support.
8. Disconnect passenger air bag module yellow 4-way connector.
9. Remove CPA from passenger side impact air bag module yellow 2-way connector located under passenger seat.
10. Disconnect passenger side impact air bag module yellow 2-way connector.
11. Remove lock pillar trim panel using suitable flat-bladed tool.
12. Remove CPA from seat belt pretensioner righthand side connector.
13. Disconnect seat belt pretensioner righthand side connector from vehicle harness connector.
14. Remove CPA from driver side impact air bag module yellow 2-way connector located under driver seat.
15. Disconnect driver side impact air bag module yellow 2-way connector.
16. Remove lock pillar trim panel using suitable flat-bladed tool.
17. Remove CPA from seat belt pretensioner lefthand side connector.
18. Disconnect seat belt pretensioner lefthand side connector from vehicle harness connector.

ZONE 9

1. Ensure steering wheel is in straight ahead position.
2. Turn ignition switch to Off position.
3. Remove key from ignition.
4. Remove SIR fuse from fuse block. **With SIR fuse removed and ignition On, AIR BAG indicator illuminates. This is normal operation and does not indicate an SIR system fault.**
5. Remove connector position assurance (CPA) from passenger side impact air bag module yellow 2-way connector located under passenger seat.
6. Disconnect passenger side impact air bag module yellow 2-way connector.

Aztek & Rendezvous

2002

1. Ensure front wheels are in straight ahead position.
2. Turn ignition switch to Off position.
3. Remove key from ignition.
4. Remove SIR fuse from fuse block. **With SIR fuse removed and ignition On, AIR BAG indicator illuminates. This is normal operation and does not indicate an SIR system fault.**
5. Remove driver side insulator panel.
6. Remove connector position assurance (CPA) from driver air bag module coil connector located at base of steering column.
7. Disconnect driver air bag module coil connector.
8. Remove passenger side insulator panel.
9. Remove CPA from passenger air bag module connector located behind insulator panel.
10. Disconnect passenger air bag module connector.
11. Remove CPA from driver side impact air bag module connector located under driver seat.
12. Disconnect driver side impact air bag module connector.
13. Remove CPA from passenger side impact air bag module connector located under passenger seat.
14. Disconnect passenger side impact air bag module connector.

2003-06

ZONE 1

1. Ensure front wheels are in straight ahead position.
2. Turn ignition switch to Off position.
3. Remove key from ignition.
4. Remove SIR fuse from fuse block. **With SIR fuse removed and ignition On, AIR BAG indicator illuminates. This is normal operation and does not indicate an SIR system fault.**
5. Remove connector position assurance (CPA) from front end sensor harness connector.
6. Disconnect harness connector from front end sensor.

ZONE 2

1. Ensure front wheels are in straight ahead position.
2. Turn ignition switch to Off position.
3. Remove key from ignition.
4. Remove SIR fuse from fuse block. **With SIR fuse removed and ignition On, AIR BAG indicator illuminates. This is normal operation and does not indicate an SIR system fault.**
5. Remove connector position assurance (CPA) from driver side impact sensor and pretensioner yellow 2-way harness connectors.
6. Disconnect driver side impact sensor and pretensioner wiring harness connectors.

ZONE 3

1. Ensure front wheels are in straight ahead position.
2. Turn ignition switch to Off position.
3. Remove key from ignition.
4. Remove SIR fuse from fuse block. **With SIR fuse removed and ignition On, AIR BAG indicator illuminates. This is normal operation and does not indicate an SIR system fault.**
5. Remove driver side insulator panel.
6. Remove connector position assurance (CPA) from driver air bag module coil connector located at base of steering column.
7. Disconnect driver air bag module coil connector.

ZONE 5

1. Ensure front wheels are in straight ahead position.
2. Turn ignition switch to Off position.
3. Remove key from ignition.
4. Remove SIR fuse from fuse block. **With SIR fuse removed and ignition On, AIR BAG indicator illuminates. This is normal operation and does not indicate an SIR system fault.**
5. Remove passenger side insulator panel.
6. Remove connector position assurance (CPA) from passenger air bag module connector located behind insulator panel.
7. Disconnect passenger air bag module connector.

ZONE 6

1. Ensure front wheels are in straight ahead position.
2. Turn ignition switch to Off position.
3. Remove key from ignition.
4. Remove SIR fuse from fuse block. **With SIR fuse removed and ignition On, AIR BAG indicator illuminates. This is normal operation and does not indicate an SIR system fault.**
5. Remove connector position assurance (CPA) from passenger side impact sensor and pretensioner yellow 2-way harness connector.
6. Disconnect passenger side impact sensor and pretensioner wiring harness connectors.

ZONE 7

1. Ensure front wheels are in straight ahead position.
2. Turn ignition switch to Off position.
3. Remove key from ignition.
4. Remove SIR fuse from fuse block. **With SIR fuse removed and ignition On, AIR BAG indicator illuminates. This is normal operation and does not indicate an SIR system fault.**
5. **On 2003 models,** remove connector position assurance (CPA) from driver side impact air bag module connector located under driver seat.
6. **On 2003 models,** disconnect driver side impact air bag module connector.
7. **On 2004–06 models,** remove both CPA's from driver side impact air bag module yellow connector located under driver seat.
8. **On 2004–06 models,** disconnect vehicle harness yellow connector from driver side impact air bag module yellow connector.

ZONE 9

2003

1. Ensure front wheels are in straight ahead position.
2. Turn ignition switch to Off position.
3. Remove key from ignition.
4. Remove SIR fuse from fuse block. **With SIR fuse removed and ignition On, AIR BAG indicator illuminates. This is normal operation and does not indicate an SIR system fault.**
5. **To disable entire SIR system,** proceed as follows:
   a. Remove driver side insulator panel.
   b. Remove connector position assurance (CPA) from driver air bag module coil connector located at base of steering column.
   c. Disconnect driver air bag module coil connector.
   d. Remove passenger side insulator panel.
   e. Remove CPA from passenger air bag module connector located behind insulator panel.
   f. Disconnect passenger air bag module connector.
   g. Remove CPA from driver side impact air bag module connector located under driver seat.
   h. Disconnect driver side impact air bag module connector.
   i. Remove CPA from passenger side impact air bag module connector located under passenger seat.
   j. Disconnect passenger side impact air bag module connector.
6. **To disable passenger side impact air bag module,** proceed as follows:
   a. Remove CPA from passenger side impact air bag module connector located under passenger seat.
   b. Disconnect passenger side impact air bag module connector.

2004

1. Ensure front wheels are in straight ahead position.
2. Turn ignition switch to Off position.
3. Remove key from ignition.
4. Remove SIR fuse from fuse block. **With SIR fuse removed and ignition On, AIR BAG indicator illuminates. This is normal operation and does not indicate an SIR system fault.**
5. Remove both connector position assurance (CPA) from passenger side impact air bag module yellow connector located under passenger seat.
6. Disconnect vehicle harness yellow connector from passenger side impact air bag module yellow connector.

2005-06

1. Ensure front wheels are in straight ahead position.
2. Turn ignition switch to Off position.
3. Remove key from ignition.
4. Remove SIR fuse from fuse block. **With SIR fuse removed and ignition On, AIR BAG indicator illuminates. This is normal operation and does not indicate an SIR system fault.**
5. **To disable entire SIR system,** proceed as follows:
   a. Remove connector position assurance (CPA) from driver side impact sensor and pretensioner harness connectors.
   b. Disconnect driver side impact sensor and pretensioner wiring harness connectors.
   c. Remove CPA from driver side impact air bag module connector located under driver seat.
   d. Disconnect vehicle harness connector from driver side impact air bag module connector.
   e. Remove driver side insulator panel.
   f. Remove CPA from driver air bag module coil connector located at base of steering column.
   g. Disconnect driver air bag module coil connector.
   h. Remove passenger side insulator panel.
   i. Remove CPA from passenger air bag module connector.
   j. Disconnect passenger air bag module connector.
   k. Remove CPA from passenger side impact sensor and pretensioner harness connectors.
   l. Disconnect passenger side impact sensor and pretensioner wiring harness connectors.
   m. Remove CPA from passenger side impact air bag module connector located under passenger seat.

n. Disconnect vehicle harness connector from passenger side impact air bag module connector.

6. **To disable passenger side impact air bag module,**
   a. Remove CPA from passenger side impact air bag module connector located under passenger seat.
   b. Disconnect vehicle harness connector from passenger side impact air bag module connector.

Blazer, Sonoma & S10

2002

1. Ensure front wheels are in straight ahead position.
2. Turn ignition switch to Off position.
3. Remove key from ignition.
4. Remove SIR fuse from fuse block. **With SIR fuse removed and ignition On, AIR BAG indicator illuminates. This is normal operation and does not indicate an SIR system fault.**
5. Remove driver side knee bolster and sound insulator panels.
6. Remove connector position assurance (CPA) from driver air bag module yellow 2-way connector located at base of steering column.
7. Disconnect driver air bag module yellow 2-way connector.
8. Open glove compartment door, lift stop and allow door to fully open.
9. Remove CPA from passenger air bag module yellow 2-way connector located behind glove compartment.
10. Disconnect passenger air bag module yellow 2-way connector.

2003-05

ZONE 1

1. Ensure front wheels are in straight ahead position.
2. Turn ignition switch to Off position.
3. Remove key from ignition.
4. Remove SIR fuse from fuse block. **With SIR fuse removed and ignition On, AIR BAG indicator illuminates. This is normal operation and does not indicate an SIR system fault.**
5. Raise and support vehicle using a suitable jack or lift.
6. Remove connector position assurance (CPA) from both inflatable restraints front end discriminating sensor connectors located on frame crossmember.
7. Disconnect inflatable restraints front end discriminating sensor connectors.

ZONE 3

1. Ensure front wheels are in straight ahead position.
2. Turn ignition switch to Off position.
3. Remove key from ignition.
4. Remove knee bolster.
5. Remove SIR fuse from fuse block. **With SIR fuse removed and ignition On, AIR BAG indicator illuminates. This is normal operation and does not indicate an SIR system fault.**
6. Remove connector position assurance (CPA) from driver air bag module yellow 2-way connector located left of steering column near knee bolster.
7. Disconnect driver air bag module yellow 2-way connector.

ZONE 5

1. Ensure front wheels are in straight ahead position.
2. Turn ignition switch to Off position.
3. Remove key from ignition.
4. Remove SIR fuse from fuse block. **With SIR fuse removed and ignition On, AIR BAG indicator illuminates. This is normal operation and does not indicate an SIR system fault.**
5. Remove connector position assurance (CPA) from passenger air bag module yellow 2-way connector located behind instrument panel support.
6. Disconnect passenger air bag module yellow 2-way connector.

ZONE 8

1. Ensure front wheels are in straight ahead position.
2. Turn ignition switch to Off position.
3. Remove key from ignition.
4. Remove driver panel knee bolster
5. Remove SIR fuse from fuse block. **With SIR fuse removed and ignition On, AIR BAG indicator illuminates. This is normal operation and does not indicate an SIR system fault.**
6. Remove connector position assurance (CPA) from driver air bag module yellow 2-way connector located left of steering column near knee bolster.
7. Disconnect driver air bag module yellow 2-way connector.
8. Remove CPA from passenger air bag module yellow 2-way connector located behind instrument panel support.
9. Disconnect passenger air bag module yellow 2-way connector.

Bravada, Envoy, Rainier & Trailblazer

2002

1. Ensure front wheels are in straight ahead position.
2. Turn ignition switch to Off position.
3. Remove key from ignition.
4. Remove AIR BAG fuse from fuse block. **With AIR BAG fuse removed and ignition On, AIR BAG indicator illuminates. This is normal operation and does not indicate an SIR system fault.**
5. Remove connector position assurance (CPA) from driver air bag module yellow 2-way connector located at base of steering column.
6. Disconnect driver air bag module yellow 2-way connector.
7. Access passenger air bag module yellow 2-way connector located behind instrument panel support by opening glove compartment door and allow to open fully.
8. Remove CPA from passenger air bag module yellow 2-way connector located behind instrument panel support.
9. Disconnect passenger air bag module yellow 2-way connector.
10. Remove CPA from driver side impact air bag module yellow 2-way connector located under driver seat.
11. Disconnect driver side impact air bag module yellow 2-way connector.
12. Remove CPA from passenger side impact air bag module yellow 2-way connector located under passenger seat.
13. Disconnect passenger side impact air bag module yellow 2-way connector.

2003-06

ZONE 1

1. Ensure front wheels are in straight ahead position.
2. Turn ignition switch to Off position.
3. Remove key from ignition.
4. Remove SIR fuse from fuse block. **With SIR fuse removed and ignition On, AIR BAG indicator illuminates. This is normal operation and does not indicate an SIR system fault.**
5. Remove front grille assembly.
6. Remove sensor bracket from bumper.
7. Remove connector position assurance (CPA) from both electronic frontal sensor connectors. **This vehicle is equipped with two inflatable restraint electronic frontal sensors (EFS). Remove both front end sensors.**
8. Disconnect both EFS connectors.

ZONE 2

1. Ensure front wheels are in straight ahead position.
2. Turn ignition switch to Off position.
3. Remove key from ignition.
4. Remove SIR fuse from fuse block. **With SIR fuse removed and ignition On, AIR BAG indicator illuminates. This is normal operation and does not indicate an SIR system fault.**
5. Remove driver door trim panel using suitable flat-bladed tool.
6. Remove connector position assurance (CPA) from driver side impact sensor yellow 2-way connector located near bottom lefthand corner of door.
7. Disconnect driver side impact sensor yellow 2-way connector.

ZONE 3

1. Ensure front wheels are in straight ahead position.
2. Turn ignition switch to Off position.
3. Remove key from ignition.
4. Remove driver side lower instrument panel trim panel.
5. Remove SIR fuse from fuse block. **With SIR fuse removed and ignition On, AIR BAG indicator illuminates. This is normal operation and does not indicate an SIR system fault.**
6. Remove connector position assurance (CPA) from driver air bag module yellow 4-way connector located left of steering column near knee bolster.
7. Disconnect driver air bag module yellow 4-way connector.

ZONE 5

1. Ensure front wheels are in straight ahead position.
2. Turn ignition switch to Off position.
3. Remove key from ignition.
4. Remove SIR fuse from fuse block. **With SIR fuse removed and ignition On, AIR BAG indicator illuminates. This is normal operation and does not indicate an SIR system fault.**
5. Remove connector position assurance (CPA) from passenger air bag module yellow 4-way connector located behind instrument panel support.
6. Disconnect passenger air bag module yellow 4-way connector.

ZONE 6

1. Ensure front wheels are in straight ahead position.
2. Turn ignition switch to Off position.
3. Remove key from ignition.
4. Remove SIR fuse from fuse block. **With SIR fuse removed and ignition On, AIR BAG indicator illuminates. This is normal operation and does not indicate an SIR system fault.**
5. Remove passenger door trim panel using suitable flat-bladed tool.
6. Remove connector position assurance (CPA) from passenger side impact sensor yellow 2-way connector located near bottom of righthand corner of door.
7. Disconnect passenger side impact sensor yellow 2-way connector.

ZONE 7

2003-04

1. Ensure front wheels are in straight ahead position.
2. Turn ignition switch to Off position.
3. Remove key from ignition.
4. Remove SIR fuse from fuse block. **With SIR fuse removed and ignition On, AIR BAG indicator illuminates. This is normal operation and does not indicate an SIR system fault.**
5. Remove connector position assurance (CPA) from driver side impact air bag module yellow 2-way connector located under driver seat.
6. Disconnect driver side impact air bag module yellow 2-way connector.

2005-06

1. Ensure front wheels are in straight ahead position.
2. Turn ignition switch to Off position.
3. Remove key from ignition.
4. Remove SIR fuse from fuse block. **With SIR fuse removed and ignition On, AIR BAG indicator illuminates. This is normal operation and does not indicate an SIR system fault.**
5. Remove connector position assurance (CPA) from driver seat belt pretensioner yellow 2-way connector located under driver seat.
6. Disconnect driver seat belt pretensioner yellow 2-way connector.

ZONE 8

2003-04

1. Ensure front wheels are in straight ahead position.
2. Turn ignition switch to Off position.
3. Remove key from ignition.
4. Remove driver side lower instrument panel trim panel.
5. Remove SIR fuse from fuse block. **With SIR fuse removed and ignition On, AIR BAG indicator illuminates. This is normal operation and does not indicate an SIR system fault.**
6. Remove connector position assurance (CPA) from driver air bag module yellow 4-way connector located left of steering column near knee bolster.
7. Disconnect driver air bag module yellow 4-way connector.
8. Remove CPA from passenger air bag module yellow 4-way connector located behind instrument panel support.
9. Disconnect passenger air bag module yellow 4-way connector.
10. Remove CPA from passenger side impact air bag module yellow 2-way connector located under passenger seat.
11. Disconnect passenger side impact air bag module yellow 2-way connector.
12. Remove CPA from driver side impact air bag module yellow 2-way connector located under driver seat.
13. Disconnect driver side impact air bag module yellow 2-way connector.

2005-06

1. Ensure front wheels are in straight ahead position.
2. Turn ignition switch to Off position.
3. Remove key from ignition.
4. Remove driver side lower instrument panel trim panel.
5. Remove SIR fuse from fuse block. **With SIR fuse removed and ignition On, AIR BAG indicator illuminates. This is normal operation and does not indicate an SIR system fault.**
6. Remove connector position assurance (CPA) from driver air bag module yellow 4-way connector located left of steering column near knee bolster.
7. Disconnect driver air bag module yellow 4-way connector.
8. Remove CPA from passenger air bag module yellow 4-way connector located behind instrument panel support.
9. Disconnect passenger air bag module yellow 4-way connector.
10. Remove CPA from passenger seat belt pretensioner yellow 2-way connector located under passenger seat.
11. Disconnect passenger seat belt pretensioner yellow 2-way connector.
12. Remove passenger side center pillar trim panel.
13. Remove CPA from passenger roof panel air bag module yellow 2-way connector.
14. Disconnect passenger roof panel air bag module yellow 2-way connector from vehicle harness connector.
15. Remove CPA from driver seat belt pretensioner yellow 2-way connector located under driver seat.
16. Disconnect driver seat belt pretensioner yellow 2-way connector.
17. Remove driver side center pillar trim panel.
18. Remove CPA from driver roof panel air bag module yellow 2-way connector.
19. Disconnect driver roof panel air bag module yellow 2-way connector from vehicle harness connector.

ZONE 9

2003-04

1. Ensure front wheels are in straight ahead position.
2. Turn ignition switch to Off position.
3. Remove key from ignition.
4. Remove SIR fuse from fuse block. **With SIR fuse removed and ignition On, AIR BAG indicator illuminates. This is normal operation and does not indicate an SIR system fault.**
5. Remove connector position assurance (CPA) from passenger side impact air bag module yellow 2-way connector located under passenger seat.
6. Disconnect passenger side impact air bag module yellow 2-way connector.

2005-06

1. Ensure front wheels are in straight ahead position.
2. Turn ignition switch to Off position.
3. Remove key from ignition.
4. Remove SIR fuse from fuse block. **With SIR fuse removed and ignition On, AIR BAG indicator illuminates. This is normal operation and does not indicate an SIR system fault.**
5. Remove connector position assurance (CPA) from passenger seat belt pretensioner yellow 2-way connector located under passenger seat.
6. Disconnect passenger seat belt pretensioner yellow 2-way connector.

Canyon & Colorado

ZONE 1

1. Ensure front wheels are in straight ahead position.
2. Turn ignition switch to Off position.
3. Remove key from ignition.
4. Remove SIR fuse from fuse block. **With SIR fuse removed and ignition On, AIR BAG indicator illuminates. This is normal operation and does not indicate an SIR system fault.**
5. Remove connector position assurance (CPA) from both front end sensor connectors from frame crossmember. **This vehicle is equipped with two inflatable restraint front end sensors. Remove both front end sensors.**
6. Disconnect both front end sensor connectors.

ZONE 2

1. Ensure front wheels are in straight ahead position.
2. Turn ignition switch to Off position.
3. Remove key from ignition.
4. Remove SIR fuse from fuse block. **With SIR fuse removed and ignition On, AIR BAG indicator illuminates.**

This is normal operation and does not indicate an SIR system fault.

5. Remove driver front door trim panel using suitable flat-bladed tool.
6. Remove connector position assurance (CPA) from driver side impact sensor yellow 2-way connector located near middle of door.
7. Disconnect driver side impact sensor yellow 2-way connector.
8. **On models equipped with crew cab,** remove lower center pillar trim panel.
9. **On models equipped with extended cab,** remove rear access door wiring harness grommet to access connector.
10. **On models equipped with regular cab,** remove lower body rear corner trim panel.
11. **On all models,** remove CPA from driver seat belt pretensioner connector.
12. Disconnect driver seat belt pretensioner connector from vehicle harness connector.
13. Remove driver windshield garnish molding trim panel.
14. Disconnect driver roof panel air bag module from vehicle harness.

ZONE 3

1. Ensure front wheels are in straight ahead position.
2. Turn ignition switch to Off position.
3. Remove key from ignition.
4. Remove driver knee bolster panel.
5. Remove SIR fuse from fuse block. **With SIR fuse removed and ignition On, AIR BAG indicator illuminates. This is normal operation and does not indicate an SIR system fault.**
6. Remove connector position assurance (CPA) from driver air bag module yellow 4-way connector located left of steering column above lefthand hinge pillar trim panel.
7. Disconnect driver air bag module yellow 4-way connector.

ZONE 5

1. Ensure front wheels are in straight ahead position.
2. Turn ignition switch to Off position.
3. Remove key from ignition.
4. Remove SIR fuse from fuse block. **With SIR fuse removed and ignition On, AIR BAG indicator illuminates. This is normal operation and does not indicate an SIR system fault.**
5. Remove connector position assurance (CPA) from passenger air bag module yellow 4-way connector C208 located above driver kick panel.
6. Disconnect passenger air bag module yellow 4-way connector C208.

ZONE 6

1. Ensure front wheels are in straight ahead position.
2. Turn ignition switch to Off position.
3. Remove key from ignition.
4. Remove SIR fuse from fuse block. **With SIR fuse removed and ignition On, AIR BAG indicator illuminates. This is normal operation and does not indicate an SIR system fault.**
5. Remove passenger front door trim panel using suitable flat-bladed tool.
6. Remove connector position assurance (CPA) from passenger side impact sensor yellow 2-way connector located near middle of door.
7. Disconnect passenger side impact sensor yellow 2-way connector.
8. **On models equipped with crew cab,** remove lower center pillar trim panel.
9. **On models equipped with extended cab,** remove rear access door wiring harness grommet to access connector.
10. **On models equipped with regular cab,** remove lower body rear corner trim panel.
11. **On all models,** remove CPA from passenger seat belt pretensioner connector.
12. Disconnect passenger seat belt pretensioner connector from vehicle harness connector.
13. Remove passenger windshield garnish molding trim panel.
14. Disconnect passenger roof panel air bag module from vehicle harness.

ZONE 8

1. Ensure front wheels are in straight ahead position.
2. Turn ignition switch to Off position.
3. Remove key from ignition.
4. Remove knee bolster trim panel.
5. Remove SIR fuse from fuse block. **With SIR fuse removed and ignition On, AIR BAG indicator illuminates. This is normal operation and does not indicate an SIR system fault.**
6. Remove connector position assurance (CPA) from driver air bag module yellow 4-way connector located left of steering column above lefthand hinge pillar trim panel.
7. Disconnect driver air bag module yellow 4-way connector.
8. Remove driver door trim panel.
9. Remove CPA from driver side impact sensor yellow 2-way connector located near middle of door.
10. Disconnect driver side impact sensor yellow 2-way connector.
11. **On models equipped with crew cab,** remove driver side lower center pillar trim panel.
12. **On models equipped with extended cab,** remove driver side rear access door wiring harness grommet to access connector.
13. **On models equipped with regular cab,** remove driver side lower body rear corner trim panel.
14. **On all models,** remove CPA from driver seat belt pretensioner connector.
15. Disconnect driver seat belt pretensioner connector from vehicle harness connector.
16. Remove driver side windshield pillar garnish molding.
17. Disconnect driver roof panel air bag module connector from vehicle harness.
18. Remove CPA passenger air bag module yellow 4-way connector C208 located above driver side kick panel.
19. Disconnect passenger air bag module yellow 4-way connector C208.
20. Remove passenger door trim panel.
21. Remove CPA from passenger side impact sensor yellow 2-way connector located near middle of door.
22. Disconnect passenger side impact sensor yellow 2-way connector.
23. **On models equipped with crew cab,** remove passenger side lower center pillar trim panel.
24. **On models equipped with extended cab,** remove passenger side rear access door wiring harness grommet to access connector.
25. **On models equipped with regular cab,** remove passenger side lower body rear corner trim panel.
26. **On all models,** remove CPA from passenger seat belt pretensioner connector.
27. Disconnect passenger seat belt pretensioner connector from vehicle harness connector.
28. Remove passenger side windshield pillar garnish molding.
29. Disconnect passenger roof panel air bag module connector from vehicle harness.

Equinox & Torrent

ZONE 1

1. Ensure front wheels are in straight ahead position.
2. Turn ignition switch to Off position.
3. Remove key from ignition.
4. Remove AIR BAG fuse from fuse block. **With AIR BAG fuse removed and ignition On, AIR BAG indicator illuminates. This is normal operation and does not indicate an SIR system fault.**
5. Open hood and locate front end sensor.
6. Remove connector position assurance (CPA) from electronic frontal sensor (EFS).
7. Remove EFS connector from EFS.

ZONE 2

1. Ensure front wheels are in straight ahead position.
2. Turn ignition switch to Off position.
3. Remove key from ignition.
4. Remove AIR BAG fuse from fuse block. **With AIR BAG fuse removed and ignition On, AIR BAG indicator illuminates. This is normal operation and does not indicate an SIR system fault.**
5. **To disable driver roof panel air bag module,** proceed as follows:
   a. Remove upper rear window molding.
   b. Remove lefthand and righthand rear corner trim panels.
   c. Remove rear headliner push-in retainers.
   d. Remove rear coat hooks.
   e. Pull down lefthand rear corner of headliner to access driver roof panel air bag module.
   f. Remove connector position assurance (CPA) from driver roof panel air bag module connector.
   g. Disconnect driver roof panel air bag

module connector from vehicle harness connector.

6. **To disable driver side impact sensor and driver seat belt pretensioner,** proceed as follows:
   a. Remove driver side lower center pillar trim panel.
   b. Remove CPA from driver seat belt pretensioner connector.
   c. Disconnect driver seat belt pretensioner connector from vehicle harness connector.
   d. Remove CPA from driver side impact sensor connector.
   e. Disconnect driver side impact sensor from vehicle harness connector.

ZONE 3

1. Ensure front wheels are in straight ahead position.
2. Turn ignition switch to Off position.
3. Remove key from ignition.
4. Remove AIR BAG fuse from fuse block. **With AIR BAG fuse removed and ignition On, AIR BAG indicator illuminates. This is normal operation and does not indicate an SIR system fault.**
5. Remove connector position assurance (CPA) from driver air bag module coil connector.
6. Disconnect driver air bag module coil connector from vehicle harness connector.

ZONE 5

1. Ensure front wheels are in straight ahead position.
2. Turn ignition switch to Off position.
3. Remove key from ignition.
4. Remove AIR BAG fuse from fuse block. **With AIR BAG fuse removed and ignition On, AIR BAG indicator illuminates. This is normal operation and does not indicate an SIR system fault.**
5. Remove connector position assurance (CPA) from passenger air bag module connector.
6. Disconnect passenger air bag module connector from vehicle harness connector.

ZONE 6

1. Ensure front wheels are in straight ahead position.
2. Turn ignition switch to Off position.
3. Remove key from ignition.
4. Remove AIR BAG fuse from fuse block. **With AIR BAG fuse removed and ignition On, AIR BAG indicator illuminates. This is normal operation and does not indicate an SIR system fault.**
5. **To disable passenger roof panel air bag module,** proceed as follows:
   a. Remove upper rear window molding.
   b. Remove lefthand and righthand rear corner trim panels.
   c. Remove rear headliner push-in retainers.
   d. Remove rear coat hooks.
   e. Pull down righthand rear corner of headliner to access passenger roof panel air bag module.
   f. Remove connector position assurance (CPA) from passenger roof panel air bag module connector.
   g. Disconnect passenger roof panel air bag module connector from vehicle harness connector.
6. **To disable passenger side impact sensor and passenger seat belt pretensioner,** proceed as follows:
   a. Remove passenger side lower center pillar trim panel.
   b. Remove CPA from passenger seat belt pretensioner connector.
   c. Disconnect passenger seat belt pretensioner connector from vehicle harness connector.
   d. Remove CPA from passenger side impact sensor connector.
   e. Disconnect passenger side impact sensor from vehicle harness connector.

ZONE 8

1. Ensure front wheels are in straight ahead position.
2. Turn ignition switch to Off position.
3. Remove key from ignition.
4. Remove AIR BAG fuse from fuse block. **With AIR BAG fuse removed and ignition On, AIR BAG indicator illuminates. This is normal operation and does not indicate an SIR system fault.**
5. Remove upper rear window molding.
6. Remove lefthand and righthand rear corner trim panels.
7. Remove rear headliner push-in retainers.
8. Remove rear coat hooks.
9. Pull down righthand rear corner to access passenger roof panel air bag module connector.
10. Remove connector position assurance (CPA) from passenger roof panel air bag module connector.
11. Disconnect passenger roof panel air bag module connector from vehicle harness connector.
12. Remove passenger side lower center trim panel.
13. Remove CPA from passenger seat belt pretensioner connector.
14. Disconnect passenger seat belt pretensioner connector from vehicle harness connector.
15. Remove CPA from passenger air bag module connector.
16. Disconnect passenger air bag module connector from vehicle harness connector.
17. Remove CPA from driver air bag module coil connector.
18. Disconnect driver air bag module coil connector from vehicle harness connector.
19. Remove driver side lower center trim panel.
20. Remove CPA from driver seat belt pretensioner connector.
21. Disconnect driver seat belt pretensioner connector from vehicle harness connector.
22. Pull down lefthand rear corner to access driver roof panel air bag module connector.
23. Remove CPA from driver roof panel air bag module connector.
24. Disconnect driver roof panel air bag module connector from vehicle harness connector.

Express & Savana

2002

1. Ensure front wheels are in straight ahead position.
2. Turn ignition switch to Off position.
3. Remove key from ignition.
4. Remove AIR BAG fuse from fuse block. **With AIR BAG fuse removed and ignition On, AIR BAG indicator illuminates. This is normal operation and does not indicate an SIR system fault.**
5. Remove driver side knee bolster.
6. Remove connector position assurance (CPA) from driver air bag module yellow 2-way connector located at base of steering column.
7. Disconnect driver air bag module yellow 2-way connector.
8. Remove passenger side knee bolster.
9. Remove CPA from passenger air bag module yellow 2-way connector located under instrument panel extension.
10. Disconnect passenger air bag module yellow 2-way connector.

2003-06

ZONE 1

1. Ensure front wheels are in straight ahead position.
2. Turn ignition switch to Off position.
3. Remove key from ignition.
4. Remove SIR fuse from fuse block. **With SIR fuse removed and ignition On, AIR BAG indicator illuminates. This is normal operation and does not indicate an SIR system fault.**
5. Raise and support vehicle using suitable jack or lift.
6. Remove connector position assurance (CPA) from front end sensor connector located on frame crossmember.
7. Disconnect front end sensor connector.

ZONE 3

1. Ensure front wheels are in straight ahead position.
2. Turn ignition switch to Off position.
3. Remove key from ignition.
4. Remove SIR fuse from fuse block. **With SIR fuse removed and ignition On, AIR BAG indicator illuminates. This is normal operation and does not indicate an SIR system fault.**
5. Remove connector position assurance (CPA) from driver air bag module yellow 4-way connector located left of steering column near knee bolster.
6. Disconnect driver air bag module yellow 4-way connector.

ZONE 5

1. Ensure front wheels are in straight ahead position.
2. Turn ignition switch to Off position.
3. Remove key from ignition.
4. Remove SIR fuse from fuse block. **With SIR fuse removed and ignition On, AIR BAG indicator illuminates. This is normal operation and does not indicate an SIR system fault.**
5. Remove righthand side panel knee bolster bracket.
6. Remove connector position assurance (CPA) from passenger air bag module yellow 4-way connector located behind instrument panel support.
7. Disconnect passenger air bag module yellow 4-way connector.

ZONE 7

2003

1. Ensure front wheels are in straight ahead position.
2. Turn ignition switch to Off position.
3. Remove key from ignition.
4. Remove SIR fuse from fuse block. **With SIR fuse removed and ignition On, AIR BAG indicator illuminates. This is normal operation and does not indicate an SIR system fault.**
5. Remove connector position assurance (CPA) from driver air bag module yellow 4-way connector located left of steering column near knee bolster.
6. Disconnect driver air bag module yellow 4-way connector.
7. Remove righthand side panel knee bolster bracket.
8. Remove CPA from passenger air bag module yellow 4-way connector located behind instrument panel support.
9. Disconnect passenger air bag module yellow 4-way connector.
10. Remove CPA from passenger seat belt pretensioner yellow 2-way connector located under passenger seat.
11. Disconnect passenger seat belt pretensioner yellow 2-way connector.
12. Remove CPA from driver seat belt pretensioner yellow 2-way connector located under driver seat.
13. Disconnect driver seat belt pretensioner yellow 2-way connector.

2004-05

1. Ensure front wheels are in straight ahead position.
2. Turn ignition switch to Off position.
3. Remove key from ignition.
4. Remove SIR fuse from fuse block. **With SIR fuse removed and ignition On, AIR BAG indicator illuminates. This is normal operation and does not indicate an SIR system fault.**
5. Remove connector position assurance (CPA) from driver air bag module yellow 4-way connector located left of steering column near knee bolster.
6. Disconnect driver air bag module yellow 4-way connector.
7. Remove righthand side knee bolster bracket.
8. Remove CPA from passenger air bag module yellow 4-way connector located behind instrument panel support.
9. Disconnect passenger air bag module yellow 4-way connector.

2006

1. Ensure front wheels are in straight ahead position.
2. Turn ignition switch to Off position.
3. Remove key from ignition.
4. Remove SIR fuse from fuse block. **With SIR fuse removed and ignition On, AIR BAG indicator illuminates. This is normal operation and does not indicate an SIR system fault.**
5. Remove connector position assurance (CPA) from driver air bag module yellow 4-way connector located left of steering column near knee bolster.
6. Disconnect driver air bag module yellow 4-way connector.
7. Remove CPA from driver seat belt pretensioner yellow 2-way connector located under driver seat.
8. Disconnect driver seat belt pretensioner yellow 2-way connector.
9. Remove righthand side knee bolster bracket.
10. Remove CPA from passenger air bag module yellow 4-way connector located behind instrument panel support.
11. Disconnect passenger air bag module yellow 4-way connector.
12. Remove CPA from passenger seat belt pretensioner yellow 2-way connector located under passenger seat.
13. Disconnect passenger seat belt pretensioner yellow 2-way connector.

ZONE 9

1. Ensure front wheels are in straight ahead position.
2. Turn ignition switch to Off position.
3. Remove key from ignition.
4. Remove SIR fuse from fuse block. **With SIR fuse removed and ignition On, AIR BAG indicator illuminates. This is normal operation and does not indicate an SIR system fault.**
5. Remove connector position assurance (CPA) from passenger seat belt pretensioner yellow 2-way connector located under passenger seat.
6. Disconnect passenger seat belt pretensioner yellow 2-way connector.

HHR

ZONE 1

1. Ensure front wheels are in straight ahead position.
2. Turn ignition switch to Off position.
3. Remove key from ignition.
4. Remove AIR BAG and SDM fuses from fuse block. **With AIR BAG and SDM fuses removed and ignition On, AIR BAG indicator illuminates. This is normal operation and does not indicate an SIR system fault.**
5. Open hood and locate front end sensor.
6. Remove connector position assurance (CPA) from front end sensor connector.
7. Remove front end sensor connector from front end sensor.

ZONE 2

1. Ensure front wheels are in straight ahead position.
2. Turn ignition switch to Off position.
3. Remove key from ignition.
4. Remove AIR BAG and SDM fuses from fuse block. **With AIR BAG and SDM fuses removed and ignition On, AIR BAG indicator illuminates. This is normal operation and does not indicate an SIR system fault.**
5. Remove driver door trim panel.
6. Remove water deflector shield to access driver side impact sensor.
7. Remove connector position assurance (CPA) from driver side impact sensor connector.
8. Disconnect driver side impact sensor connector from sensor.
9. Remove driver side lower center pillar trim.
10. Remove CPA from driver seat belt pretensioner connector.
11. Disconnect driver seat belt pretensioner connector from vehicle harness connector.
12. Remove driver rear quarter upper trim panel.
13. Remove CPA from driver roof panel air bag module connector.
14. Disconnect driver roof panel air bag module connector from vehicle harness connector.

ZONE 3

1. Ensure front wheels are in straight ahead position.
2. Turn ignition switch to Off position.
3. Remove key from ignition.
4. Remove AIR BAG and SDM fuses from fuse block. **With AIR BAG and SDM fuses removed and ignition On, AIR BAG indicator illuminates. This is normal operation and does not indicate an SIR system fault.**
5. Remove driver outer trim panel from instrument panel.
6. Remove connector position assurance (CPA) from driver air bag module coil connector.
7. Disconnect driver air bag module coil connector from vehicle harness connector.

ZONE 5

1. Ensure front wheels are in straight ahead position.
2. Turn ignition switch to Off position.
3. Remove key from ignition.
4. Remove AIR BAG and SDM fuses from fuse block. **With AIR BAG and SDM fuses removed and ignition On, AIR BAG indicator illuminates. This is normal operation and does not indicate an SIR system fault.**
5. Slide connector position assurance (CPA) of passenger air bag module connector to release position located above righthand side hinge pillar trim panel.
6. Disconnect passenger air bag module connector from vehicle harness connector.

ZONE 6

1. Ensure front wheels are in straight ahead position.
2. Turn ignition switch to Off position.
3. Remove key from ignition.
4. Remove AIR BAG and SDM fuses from fuse block. **With AIR BAG and SDM fuses removed and ignition On, AIR BAG indicator illuminates. This is normal operation and does not indicate an SIR system fault.**
5. Remove passenger door trim panel.
6. Remove water deflector shield to access passenger side impact sensor.
7. Remove connector position assurance (CPA) from passenger side impact sensor connector.
8. Disconnect passenger side impact sensor connector from sensor.
9. Remove passenger lower center pillar trim.
10. Remove CPA from passenger seat belt pretensioner connector.
11. Disconnect passenger seat belt pretensioner connector from vehicle harness connector.
12. Remove passenger rear quarter upper trim panel.
13. Remove CPA from passenger roof panel air bag module connector.
14. Disconnect passenger roof panel air bag module connector from vehicle harness connector.

ZONE 8

1. Ensure front wheels are in straight ahead position.
2. Turn ignition switch to Off position.
3. Remove key from ignition.
4. Remove AIR BAG and SDM fuses from fuse block. **With AIR BAG and SDM fuses removed and ignition On, AIR BAG indicator illuminates. This is normal operation and does not indicate an SIR system fault.**
5. Remove passenger door trim panel.
6. Remove water deflector shield to access passenger side impact sensor.
7. Remove connector position assurance (CPA) from passenger side impact sensor connector.
8. Disconnect passenger side impact sensor connector from sensor.
9. Slide CPA of passenger air bag module connector to release position located above righthand hinge pillar trim.
10. Disconnect passenger air bag module connector from vehicle harness connector.
11. Remove passenger lower center pillar trim panel.
12. Remove CPA from passenger seat belt pretensioner connector.
13. Disconnect passenger seat belt pretensioner connector from vehicle harness connector.
14. Remove passenger rear quarter upper trim molding from upper lock pillar.
15. Remove CPA from passenger roof panel air bag module connector.
16. Disconnect passenger roof panel air bag module connector from vehicle harness connector.
17. Remove driver door trim panel.
18. Remove water deflector shield to access driver side impact sensor.
19. Remove CPA from driver side impact sensor connector.
20. Disconnect driver side impact sensor connector from sensor.
21. Remove driver outer trim panel from instrument panel.
22. Remove CPA from driver air bag module coil connector.
23. Disconnect driver air bag module coil connector from vehicle harness connector.
24. Remove driver lower center pillar trim.
25. Remove CPA from driver seat belt pretensioner connector.
26. Disconnect driver seat belt pretensioner connector from vehicle harness connector.
27. Remove driver rear quarter upper trim panel.
28. Remove CPA from driver roof panel air bag module connector.
29. Disconnect driver roof panel air bag module connector from vehicle harness connector.

Hummer H2

ZONE 1

1. Ensure front wheels are in straight ahead position.
2. Turn ignition switch to Off position.
3. Remove key from ignition.
4. Remove engine protection shield.
5. Remove SIR fuse from fuse block. **With SIR fuse removed and ignition On, AIR BAG indicator illuminates. This is normal operation and does not indicate an SIR system fault.**
6. Raise and support vehicle using suitable lift or jack.
7. Remove connector position assurance (CPA) from both front end sensor connectors located on frame crossmember.
8. Disconnect both front end sensor connectors.

ZONE 3

1. Ensure front wheels are in straight ahead position.
2. Turn ignition switch to Off position.
3. Remove key from ignition.
4. Remove engine protection shield.
5. Remove SIR fuse from fuse block. **With SIR fuse removed and ignition On, AIR BAG indicator illuminates. This is normal operation and does not indicate an SIR system fault.**
6. Remove connector position assurance (CPA) from driver air bag module yellow 2-way connector located left of steering column near knee bolster.
7. Disconnect driver air bag module yellow 2-way connector.

ZONE 5

1. Ensure front wheels are in straight ahead position.
2. Turn ignition switch to Off position.
3. Remove key from ignition.
4. Remove engine protection shield.
5. Remove SIR fuse from fuse block. **With SIR fuse removed and ignition On, AIR BAG indicator illuminates. This is normal operation and does not indicate an SIR system fault.**
6. Remove connector position assurance (CPA) from passenger air bag module yellow 2-way connector located behind air bag module.
7. Disconnect passenger air bag module yellow 2-way connector.

ZONE 7

1. Ensure front wheels are in straight ahead position.
2. Turn ignition switch to Off position.
3. Remove key from ignition.
4. Remove engine protection shield.
5. Remove SIR fuse from fuse block. **With SIR fuse removed and ignition On, AIR BAG indicator illuminates. This is normal operation and does not indicate an SIR system fault.**
6. Remove connector position assurance (CPA) from driver air bag module yellow 2-way connector located left of steering column near knee bolster.
7. Disconnect driver air bag module yellow 2-way connector.
8. Remove connector position assurance (CPA) from passenger air bag module yellow 2-way connector located behind air bag module.
9. Disconnect passenger air bag module yellow 2-way connector.

Hummer H3

ZONE 1

1. Ensure front wheels are in straight ahead position.
2. Turn ignition switch to Off position.
3. Remove key from ignition.
4. Remove engine protection shield.
5. Remove AIR BAG fuse from fuse block. **With AIR BAG fuse removed and ignition On, AIR BAG indicator illuminates. This is normal operation and does not indicate an SIR system fault.**
6. Remove connector position assurance (CPA) from both front end sensor connectors.
7. Disconnect both front end sensor connectors.

ZONE 2

1. Ensure front wheels are in straight ahead position.
2. Turn ignition switch to Off position.
3. Remove key from ignition.
4. Remove engine protection shield.
5. Remove AIR BAG fuse from fuse block. **With AIR BAG fuse removed and ignition On, AIR BAG indicator illuminates. This is normal operation and does not indicate an SIR system fault.**
6. Remove driver door trim panel.
7. Remove connector position assurance (CPA) from driver side impact sensor yellow 2-way connector located near middle of door.
8. Disconnect driver side impact sensor yellow 2-way connector.
9. Remove driver lower center pillar trim panel.

10. Remove CPA from driver seat belt pretensioner connector.
11. Disconnect driver seat belt pretensioner connector from vehicle harness connector.
12. Remove driver windshield pillar trim panel.
13. Disconnect driver roof panel air bag module connector from vehicle harness connector.

ZONE 3

1. Ensure front wheels are in straight ahead position.
2. Turn ignition switch to Off position.
3. Remove key from ignition.
4. Remove engine protection shield.
5. Remove AIR BAG fuse from fuse block. **With AIR BAG fuse removed and ignition On, AIR BAG indicator illuminates. This is normal operation and does not indicate an SIR system fault.**
6. Remove driver knee bolster trim panel.
7. Remove connector position assurance (CPA) from driver air bag module yellow 4-way connector located left of steering column and above left hinge pillar trim panel.
8. Disconnect driver air bag module yellow 4-way connector.

ZONE 5

1. Ensure front wheels are in straight ahead position.
2. Turn ignition switch to Off position.
3. Remove key from ignition.
4. Remove engine protection shield.
5. Remove AIR BAG fuse from fuse block. **With AIR BAG fuse removed and ignition On, AIR BAG indicator illuminates. This is normal operation and does not indicate an SIR system fault.**
6. Access passenger air bag module inline connector C208 above driver kick panel.
7. Remove connector position assurance (CPA) from passenger air bag module yellow 4-way inline connector located above driver kick panel.
8. Disconnect passenger air bag module yellow 4-way inline connector.

ZONE 6

1. Ensure front wheels are in straight ahead position.
2. Turn ignition switch to Off position.
3. Remove key from ignition.
4. Remove engine protection shield.
5. Remove AIR BAG fuse from fuse block. **With AIR BAG fuse removed and ignition On, AIR BAG indicator illuminates. This is normal operation and does not indicate an SIR system fault.**
6. Remove passenger door trim panel.
7. Remove connector position assurance (CPA) from passenger side impact sensor yellow 2-way connector located near middle of door.
8. Disconnect passenger side impact sensor yellow 2-way connector.
9. Remove passenger lower center pillar trim panel.
10. Remove CPA from passenger seat belt pretensioner connector.
11. Disconnect passenger seat belt pretensioner connector from vehicle harness connector.
12. Remove passenger windshield pillar trim panel.
13. Disconnect passenger roof panel air bag module connector from vehicle harness connector.

ZONE 8

1. Ensure front wheels are in straight ahead position.
2. Turn ignition switch to Off position.
3. Remove key from ignition.
4. Remove engine protection shield.
5. Access passenger air bag module inline connector C208 above driver kick panel.
6. Remove AIR BAG fuse from fuse block. **With AIR BAG fuse removed and ignition On, AIR BAG indicator illuminates. This is normal operation and does not indicate an SIR system fault.**
7. Remove connector position assurance (CPA) from driver air bag module yellow 4-way connector located left of steering column above left hinge pillar trim panel.
8. Disconnect driver air bag module yellow 4-way connector.
9. Remove driver door trim panel.
10. Remove CPA from driver side impact sensor yellow 2-way connector located near middle of door.
11. Disconnect driver side impact sensor yellow 2-way connector.
12. Remove driver lower center pillar trim panel.
13. Remove CPA from driver seat belt pretensioner connector.
14. Disconnect driver seat belt pretensioner connector from vehicle harness connector.
15. Remove driver windshield pillar trim panel.
16. Disconnect driver roof panel air bag module connector from vehicle harness connector.
17. Remove CPA from passenger air bag module yellow 4-way inline connector located above driver kick panel.
18. Disconnect passenger air bag module yellow 4-way inline connector C208.
19. Remove passenger door trim panel.
20. Remove CPA from passenger side impact sensor yellow 2-way connector located near middle of door.
21. Disconnect passenger side impact sensor yellow 2-way connector.
22. Remove passenger lower center pillar trim panel.
23. Remove CPA from passenger seat belt pretensioner connector.
24. Disconnect passenger seat belt pretensioner connector from vehicle harness connector.
25. Remove passenger windshield pillar trim panel.
26. Disconnect passenger roof panel air bag module connector from vehicle harness connector.

Montana, Silhouette & Venture

2002

1. Ensure front wheels are in straight ahead position.
2. Turn ignition switch to Off position.
3. Remove key from ignition.
4. Remove SDM fuse from fuse block. **With SDM fuse removed and ignition On, AIR BAG indicator illuminates. This is normal operation and does not indicate an SIR system fault.**
5. Remove driver insulator panel.
6. Remove connector position assurance (CPA) from driver air bag module coil connector located at base of steering column.
7. Disconnect driver air bag module coil connector.
8. Remove passenger insulator panel.
9. Remove CPA from passenger air bag module connector located behind insulator panel.
10. Disconnect passenger air bag module connector.
11. Remove CPA from driver side impact air bag module connector located under driver seat.
12. Disconnect driver side impact air bag module connector.
13. Remove CPA from driver seat belt pretensioner connector located under driver seat.
14. Disconnect driver seat belt pretensioner connector.
15. Remove CPA from passenger side impact air bag module connector located under passenger seat.
16. Disconnect passenger side impact air bag module connector.
17. Remove CPA from passenger seat belt pretensioner connector located under passenger seat.
18. Disconnect passenger seat belt pretensioner connector.

2003-05

ZONE 1

1. Ensure front wheels are in straight ahead position.
2. Turn ignition switch to Off position.
3. Remove key from ignition.
4. Remove SIR fuse from fuse block. **With SIR fuse removed and ignition On, AIR BAG indicator illuminates. This is normal operation and does not indicate an SIR system fault.**
5. Remove connector position assurance (CPA) from both front end sensor connectors from frame crossmember. **This vehicle is equipped with two inflatable restraint front end sensors. Remove both front end sensors.**
6. Disconnect both front end sensor connectors.

ZONE 2

1. Ensure front wheels are in straight ahead position.
2. Turn ignition switch to Off position.
3. Remove key from ignition.

4. Remove SIR fuse from fuse block. **With SIR fuse removed and ignition On, AIR BAG indicator illuminates. This is normal operation and does not indicate an SIR system fault.**
5. Remove driver seat belt retractor trim cover.
6. Remove connector position assurance (CPA) from driver side impact sensor yellow 2-way connector located near bottom of B-pillar.
7. Disconnect driver side impact sensor yellow 2-way connector from sensor.

ZONE 3

1. Ensure front wheels are in straight ahead position.
2. Turn ignition switch to Off position.
3. Remove key from ignition.
4. Remove SIR fuse from fuse block. **With SIR fuse removed and ignition On, AIR BAG indicator illuminates. This is normal operation and does not indicate an SIR system fault.**
5. Remove driver insulator panel.
6. Remove connector position assurance (CPA) from driver air bag module coil yellow 4-way connector located at base of steering column.
7. Disconnect driver air bag module coil yellow 4-way connector.

ZONE 5

1. Ensure front wheels are in straight ahead position.
2. Turn ignition switch to Off position.
3. Remove key from ignition.
4. Remove SIR fuse from fuse block. **With SIR fuse removed and ignition On, AIR BAG indicator illuminates. This is normal operation and does not indicate an SIR system fault.**
5. Remove glove compartment assembly and disconnect electrical connectors.
6. Remove connector position assurance (CPA) from passenger air bag module yellow 4-way connector located behind passenger insulator panel.
7. Disconnect passenger air bag module yellow 4-way connector.

ZONE 6

1. Ensure front wheels are in straight ahead position.
2. Turn ignition switch to Off position.
3. Remove key from ignition.
4. Remove SIR fuse from fuse block. **With SIR fuse removed and ignition On, AIR BAG indicator illuminates. This is normal operation and does not indicate an SIR system fault.**
5. Remove passenger seat belt retractor trim cover.
6. Remove connector position assurance (CPA) from passenger side impact sensor yellow 2-way connector located near bottom of B-pillar.
7. Disconnect passenger side impact sensor yellow 2-way connector from sensor.

ZONE 7

1. Ensure front wheels are in straight ahead position.
2. Turn ignition switch to Off position.
3. Remove key from ignition.
4. Remove SIR fuse from fuse block. **With SIR fuse removed and ignition On, AIR BAG indicator illuminates. This is normal operation and does not indicate an SIR system fault.**
5. Remove connector position assurance (CPA) from driver side impact air bag module yellow 2-way connector located under driver seat.
6. Disconnect driver side impact air bag module yellow 2-way connector.
7. Remove CPA from driver seat belt pretensioner yellow 2-way connector located under driver seat.
8. Disconnect driver seat belt pretensioner yellow 2-way connector.

ZONE 9

1. Ensure front wheels are in straight ahead position.
2. Turn ignition switch to Off position.
3. Remove key from ignition.
4. Remove SIR fuse from fuse block. **With SIR fuse removed and ignition On, AIR BAG indicator illuminates. This is normal operation and does not indicate an SIR system fault.**
5. Remove driver insulator panel.
6. Remove connector position assurance (CPA) from driver air bag module coil yellow 4-way connector located at base of steering column.
7. Disconnect driver air bag module coil yellow 4-way connector.
8. Remove glove compartment assembly and disconnect electrical connectors.
9. Remove CPA from passenger air bag module 4-way connector located behind passenger insulator panel.
10. Disconnect passenger air bag module yellow 4-way connector.
11. Remove CPA from driver side impact air bag module yellow 2-way connector located under driver seat.
12. Disconnect driver side impact air bag module yellow 2-way connector.
13. Remove CPA from driver seat belt pretensioner yellow 2-way connector located under driver seat.
14. Disconnect driver seat belt pretensioner yellow 2-way connector.
15. Remove CPA from passenger side impact air bag module yellow 2-way connector located under passenger seat.
16. Disconnect passenger side impact air bag module yellow 2-way connector.
17. Remove CPA from passenger seat belt pretensioner yellow 2-way connector located under passenger seat.
18. Disconnect passenger seat belt pretensioner yellow 2-way connector.

Relay, SV6, Terraza & Uplander

ZONE 1

1. Ensure front wheels are in straight ahead position.
2. Turn ignition switch to Off position.
3. Remove key from ignition.
4. Remove AIR BAG fuse from fuse block. **With AIR BAG fuse removed and ignition On, AIR BAG indicator illuminates. This is normal operation and does not indicate an SIR system fault.**
5. Open hood and locate both electronic front end sensors.
6. Remove connector position assurance (CPA) from both front end sensors.
7. Disconnect both front end sensor harness connectors from sensors.

ZONE 2

1. Ensure front wheels are in straight ahead position.
2. Turn ignition switch to Off position.
3. Remove key from ignition.
4. Remove AIR BAG fuse from fuse block. **With AIR BAG fuse removed and ignition On, AIR BAG indicator illuminates. This is normal operation and does not indicate an SIR system fault.**
5. Remove driver lower center pillar trim cover.
6. Remove driver side impact sensor from center pillar.
7. Remove connector position assurance (CPA) from driver side impact sensor connector.
8. Disconnect driver side impact sensor harness connector from sensor.
9. Remove CPA from driver seat belt pretensioner connector.
10. Remove vehicle harness connector from driver seat belt pretensioner.

ZONE 3

1. Ensure front wheels are in straight ahead position.
2. Turn ignition switch to Off position.
3. Remove key from ignition.
4. Remove AIR BAG fuse from fuse block. **With AIR BAG fuse removed and ignition On, AIR BAG indicator illuminates. This is normal operation and does not indicate an SIR system fault.**
5. Remove driver knee bolster insulator panel.
6. Remove connector position assurance (CPA) from driver air bag module coil yellow connector located at base of steering column.
7. Disconnect driver air bag module coil connector.

ZONE 5

1. Ensure front wheels are in straight ahead position.
2. Turn ignition switch to Off position.
3. Remove key from ignition.
4. Remove AIR BAG fuse from fuse block. **With AIR BAG fuse removed and ignition On, AIR BAG indicator illuminates. This is normal operation and does not indicate an SIR system fault.**
5. Remove passenger knee bolster insulator panel.
6. Remove connector position assurance (CPA) from passenger air bag module yellow connector.
7. Disconnect passenger air bag module connector.

ZONE 6

1. Ensure front wheels are in straight ahead position.
2. Turn ignition switch to Off position.
3. Remove key from ignition.
4. Remove AIR BAG fuse from fuse block. **With AIR BAG fuse removed and ignition On, AIR BAG indicator illuminates. This is normal operation and does not indicate an SIR system fault.**
5. Remove passenger lower center pillar trim cover.
6. Remove passenger side impact sensor from center pillar.
7. Remove connector position assurance (CPA) from passenger side impact sensor connector.
8. Disconnect passenger side impact sensor harness connector from sensor.
9. Remove CPA from passenger seat belt pretensioner connector.
10. Remove vehicle harness connector from passenger seat belt pretensioner.

ZONE 7

1. Ensure front wheels are in straight ahead position.
2. Turn ignition switch to Off position.
3. Remove key from ignition.
4. Remove AIR BAG fuse from fuse block. **With AIR BAG fuse removed and ignition On, AIR BAG indicator illuminates. This is normal operation and does not indicate an SIR system fault.**
5. Remove connector position assurance (CPA) from driver front side impact air bag module yellow connector located under driver seat.
6. Disconnect vehicle harness connector from driver front side impact air bag module connector.

ZONE 9

1. Ensure front wheels are in straight ahead position.
2. Turn ignition switch to Off position.
3. Remove key from ignition.
4. Remove AIR BAG fuse from fuse block. **With AIR BAG fuse removed and ignition On, AIR BAG indicator illuminates. This is normal operation and does not indicate an SIR system fault.**
5. **To disable entire SIR system,** proceed as follows:
   a. Remove driver lower center pillar trim cover.
   b. Remove connector position assurance (CPA) from driver seat belt pretensioner connector.
   c. Remove vehicle harness connector from driver seat belt pretensioner.
   d. Remove driver knee bolster insulator panel.
   e. Remove CPA from driver air bag module coil yellow connector located at base of steering column.
   f. Disconnect driver air bag module coil connector.
   g. Remove CPA from driver front side impact air bag module yellow connector located under driver seat.
   h. Disconnect vehicle harness connector from driver front side impact air bag module connector.
   i. Remove CPA from driver rear side impact air bag module yellow connector located under driver rear seat.
   j. Disconnect vehicle harness connector from driver rear side impact air bag module connector.
   k. Remove passenger knee bolster insulator panel.
   l. Remove CPA from passenger air bag module yellow connector.
   m. Disconnect passenger air bag module connector.
   n. Remove passenger lower center pillar trim cover.
   o. Remove CPA from passenger seat belt pretensioner connector.
   p. Remove vehicle harness connector from passenger seat belt pretensioner.
   q. Remove CPA from passenger rear side impact air bag module yellow connector located under passenger rear seat.
   r. Disconnect vehicle harness connector from passenger rear side impact air bag module connector.
   s. Remove CPA from passenger front side impact air bag module yellow connector located under passenger seat.
   t. Disconnect vehicle harness connector from passenger front side impact air bag module connector.
6. **To disable passenger front side impact air bag module,** proceed as follows:
   a. Remove CPA from passenger front side impact air bag module yellow connector located under passenger seat.
   b. Disconnect vehicle harness connector from passenger front side impact air bag module connector.

ZONE 10

1. Ensure front wheels are in straight ahead position.
2. Turn ignition switch to Off position.
3. Remove key from ignition.
4. Remove AIR BAG fuse from fuse block. **With AIR BAG fuse removed and ignition On, AIR BAG indicator illuminates. This is normal operation and does not indicate an SIR system fault.**
5. Remove connector position assurance (CPA) from driver rear side impact air bag module yellow connector located under driver rear seat.
6. Disconnect vehicle harness connector from driver rear side impact air bag module connector.

ZONE 12

1. Ensure front wheels are in straight ahead position.
2. Turn ignition switch to Off position.
3. Remove key from ignition.
4. Remove AIR BAG fuse from fuse block. **With AIR BAG fuse removed and ignition On, AIR BAG indicator illuminates. This is normal operation and does not indicate an SIR system fault.**
5. Remove connector position assurance (CPA) from passenger rear side impact air bag module yellow connector located under passenger rear seat.
6. Disconnect vehicle harness connector from passenger rear side impact air bag module connector.

SRX

ZONE 1

1. Ensure front wheels are in straight ahead position.
2. Turn ignition switch to Off position.
3. Remove key from ignition.
4. Place passenger rear seat in farthest back position.
5. Pull carpet away from rear seat to access fuse block.
6. Remove SIR fuse from fuse block. **With SIR fuse removed and ignition On, AIR BAG indicator illuminates. This is normal operation and does not indicate an SIR system fault.**
7. Open hood and remove both connector position assurance (CPA) from front end sensor connectors.
8. Remove both connectors from front end sensors.

ZONE 2

1. Ensure front wheels are in straight ahead position.
2. Turn ignition switch to Off position.
3. Remove key from ignition.
4. Place passenger rear seat in farthest back position.
5. Pull carpet away from rear seat to access fuse block.
6. Remove SIR fuse from fuse block. **With SIR fuse removed and ignition On, AIR BAG indicator illuminates. This is normal operation and does not indicate an SIR system fault.**
7. **To disable driver roof panel air bag module,** proceed as follows:
   a. Remove driver carpet retainer trim, lift carpet to access driver roof panel air bag module connector.
   b. Remove connector position assurance (CPA) from driver roof panel air bag module yellow connector.
   c. Disconnect driver roof panel air bag module connector from air bag module.
8. **To disable driver side impact sensor,** proceed as follows:
   a. Remove driver center pillar trim panel.
   b. Remove driver side impact sensor CPA from sensor connector.
   c. Remove driver side impact sensor connector from sensor.

ZONE 3

1. Ensure front wheels are in straight ahead position.
2. Turn ignition switch to Off position.
3. Remove key from ignition.
4. Place passenger rear seat in farthest back position.
5. Pull carpet away from rear seat to access fuse block.

6. Remove SIR fuse from fuse block. **With SIR fuse removed and ignition On, AIR BAG indicator illuminates. This is normal operation and does not indicate an SIR system fault.**
7. Remove driver insulator panel from side of instrument panel.
8. Remove connector position assurance (CPA) from driver air bag module coil yellow connector.
9. Disconnect driver air bag module coil yellow connector from vehicle harness yellow connector.

ZONE 5

1. Ensure front wheels are in straight ahead position.
2. Turn ignition switch to Off position.
3. Remove key from ignition.
4. Place passenger rear seat in farthest back position.
5. Pull carpet away from rear seat to access fuse block.
6. Remove SIR fuse from fuse block. **With SIR fuse removed and ignition On, AIR BAG indicator illuminates. This is normal operation and does not indicate an SIR system fault.**
7. Remove passenger insulator panel from side of instrument panel.
8. Remove connector position assurance (CPA) from passenger air bag module yellow connector.
9. Disconnect passenger air bag module yellow connector from vehicle harness yellow connector.

ZONE 6

1. Ensure front wheels are in straight ahead position.
2. Turn ignition switch to Off position.
3. Remove key from ignition.
4. Place passenger rear seat in farthest back position.
5. Pull carpet away from rear seat to access fuse block.
6. Remove SIR fuse from fuse block. **With SIR fuse removed and ignition On, AIR BAG indicator illuminates. This is normal operation and does not indicate an SIR system fault.**
7. **To disable passenger roof panel air bag module,** proceed as follows:
   a. Remove passenger carpet retainer trim, lift carpet to access passenger roof panel air bag module connector.
   b. Remove connector position assurance (CPA) from passenger roof panel air bag module yellow connector.
   c. Disconnect passenger roof panel air bag module connector from air bag module.
8. **To disable passenger side impact sensor,** proceed as follows:
   a. Remove passenger center pillar trim panel.
   b. Remove passenger side impact sensor CPA from sensor connector.
   c. Remove passenger side impact sensor connector from sensor.

ZONE 7

1. Ensure front wheels are in straight ahead position.
2. Turn ignition switch to Off position.
3. Remove key from ignition.
4. Place passenger rear seat in farthest back position.
5. Pull carpet away from rear seat to access fuse block.
6. Remove SIR fuse from fuse block. **With SIR fuse removed and ignition On, AIR BAG indicator illuminates. This is normal operation and does not indicate an SIR system fault.**
7. Remove both connector position assurance (CPA) from driver side impact air bag module and seat belt pretensioner yellow connectors located under driver seat.
8. Disconnect driver side impact air bag module and pretensioner yellow connectors from vehicle harness yellow connector.

ZONE 8

1. Ensure front wheels are in straight ahead position.
2. Turn ignition switch to Off position.
3. Remove key from ignition.
4. Place passenger rear seat in farthest back position.
5. Pull carpet away from rear seat to access fuse block.
6. Remove SIR fuse from fuse block. **With SIR fuse removed and ignition On, AIR BAG indicator illuminates. This is normal operation and does not indicate an SIR system fault.**
7. Remove passenger carpet retainer trim.
8. Remove connector position assurance (CPA) from passenger roof panel air bag module yellow connector.
9. Disconnect passenger roof panel air bag module connector from air bag module.
10. Remove passenger insulator panel from side of instrument panel.
11. Remove CPA from passenger air bag module yellow connector.
12. Disconnect passenger air bag module yellow connector from vehicle harness yellow connector.
13. Remove both CPA locks from passenger side impact air bag module and seat belt pretensioner yellow connector located under passenger seat.
14. Disconnect passenger side impact air bag module and pretensioner yellow connector from vehicle harness yellow connector.
15. Remove driver insulator panel from side of instrument panel.
16. Remove CPA from driver air bag module coil yellow connector.
17. Disconnect driver air bag module coil yellow connector from vehicle harness yellow connector.
18. Remove both CPA locks from driver side impact air bag module and seat belt pretensioner yellow connector located under driver seat.
19. Disconnect driver side impact air bag module and pretensioner yellow connector from vehicle harness yellow connector.
20. Remove driver carpet retainer trim.
21. Remove CPA from driver roof panel air bag module yellow connector.
22. Disconnect driver roof panel air bag module connector from air bag module.

ZONE 9

1. Ensure front wheels are in straight ahead position.
2. Turn ignition switch to Off position.
3. Remove key from ignition.
4. Place passenger rear seat in farthest back position.
5. Pull carpet away from rear seat to access fuse block.
6. Remove SIR fuse from fuse block. **With SIR fuse removed and ignition On, AIR BAG indicator illuminates. This is normal operation and does not indicate an SIR system fault.**
7. Remove both connector position assurance (CPA) from passenger side impact air bag module and seat belt pretensioner yellow connector located under passenger seat.
8. Disconnect passenger side impact air bag module and pretensioner yellow connector from vehicle harness yellow connector.

Tracker

2002

1. Ensure front wheels are in straight ahead position.
2. Turn ignition switch to Off position.
3. Remove key from ignition.
4. Remove AIR BAG fuse from fuse block. **With AIR BAG fuse removed and ignition On, AIR BAG indicator illuminates. This is normal operation and does not indicate an SIR system fault.**
5. Remove driver knee bolster trim plate.
6. Remove driver air bag module connector position assurance (CPA).
7. Remove driver air bag module yellow 2-way connector and unlock connector.
8. Remove glove compartment door.
9. Remove CPA and yellow 2-way connector from passenger air bag module and unlock connector.

2003-04

ZONE 3

1. Ensure front wheels are in straight ahead position.
2. Turn ignition switch to Off position.
3. Remove key from ignition.
4. Remove AIR BAG fuse from fuse block. **With AIR BAG fuse removed and ignition On, AIR BAG indicator illuminates. This is normal operation and does not indicate an SIR system fault.**
5. Remove driver knee bolster trim panel.
6. Remove driver air bag module connector position assurance (CPA).
7. Remove driver air bag module yellow 2-way connector and unlock connector.

ZONE 5

1. Ensure front wheels are in straight ahead position.
2. Turn ignition switch to Off position.
3. Remove key from ignition.
4. Remove AIR BAG fuse from fuse block. **With AIR BAG fuse removed and ignition On, AIR BAG indicator illuminates. This is normal operation and does not indicate an SIR system fault.**
5. Remove glove compartment door.
6. Remove CPA and yellow 2-way connector from passenger air bag module and unlock connector.

ZONE 8

1. Ensure front wheels are in straight ahead position.
2. Turn ignition switch to Off position.
3. Remove key from ignition.
4. Remove AIR BAG fuse from fuse block. **With AIR BAG fuse removed and ignition On, AIR BAG indicator illuminates. This is normal operation and does not indicate an SIR system fault.**
5. Remove driver knee bolster trim panel.
6. Remove driver air bag module connector position assurance (CPA).
7. Remove driver air bag module yellow 2-way connector and unlock connector.
8. Remove glove compartment door.
9. Remove CPA and yellow 2-way connector from passenger air bag module and unlock connector.

Vue

ZONE 2

2002-03

1. Ensure front wheels are in straight ahead position.
2. Turn ignition switch to Off position.
3. Remove key from ignition.
4. Remove AIR BAG fuse from fuse block. **With AIR BAG fuse removed and ignition On, AIR BAG indicator illuminates. This is normal operation and does not indicate an SIR system fault.**
5. Remove rear window upper trim panel.
6. Remove both lefthand and righthand rear corner trim panels.
7. Remove rear headliner push-in retainers.
8. Remove rear coat hooks.
9. Pull down corner of headliner to access driver roof panel air bag module connector.
10. Remove connector position assurance (CPA) from driver roof panel air bag module connector.
11. Disconnect driver roof panel air bag module connector from vehicle harness connector.

2004-06

1. Ensure front wheels are in straight ahead position.
2. Turn ignition switch to Off position.
3. Remove key from ignition.
4. Remove AIR BAG fuse from fuse block. **With AIR BAG fuse removed and ignition On, AIR BAG indicator illuminates. This is normal operation and does not indicate an SIR system fault.**
5. **To disable driver roof panel air bag module and driver seat belt pretensioner,** proceed as follows:
   a. Remove upper rear window trim panel.
   b. Remove both lefthand and righthand rear corner trim panels.
   c. Remove rear headliner push-in retainers.
   d. Remove rear coat hooks.
   e. Pull down lefthand rear corner of headliner to access driver roof panel air bag module connector.
   f. Remove connector position assurance (CPA) from driver roof panel air bag module connector.
   g. Disconnect driver roof panel air bag module connector from vehicle harness connector.
   h. Remove driver lower center pillar trim panel.
   i. Remove CPA from driver seat belt pretensioner connector.
   j. Disconnect driver seat belt pretensioner connector.
6. **To disable driver roof panel air bag module,** proceed as follows:
   a. Remove upper rear window trim panel.
   b. Remove both lefthand and righthand rear corner trim panels.
   c. Remove rear headliner push-in retainers.
   d. Remove rear coat hooks.
   e. Pull down lefthand rear corner of headliner to access driver roof panel air bag module connector.
   f. Remove connector position assurance (CPA) from driver roof panel air bag module connector.
   g. Disconnect driver roof panel air bag module connector from vehicle harness connector.

ZONE 3

1. Ensure front wheels are in straight ahead position.
2. Turn ignition switch to Off position.
3. Remove key from ignition.
4. Remove AIR BAG fuse from fuse block. **With AIR BAG fuse removed and ignition On, AIR BAG indicator illuminates. This is normal operation and does not indicate an SIR system fault.**
5. Remove connector position assurance (CPA) from driver air bag module coil connector.
6. Disconnect driver air bag module coil connector from vehicle harness connector.

ZONE 5

1. Ensure front wheels are in straight ahead position.
2. Turn ignition switch to Off position.
3. Remove key from ignition.
4. Remove AIR BAG fuse from fuse block. **With AIR BAG fuse removed and ignition On, AIR BAG indicator illuminates. This is normal operation and does not indicate an SIR system fault.**
5. Remove connector position assurance (CPA) from passenger air bag module connector.
6. Disconnect passenger air bag module connector from vehicle harness connector.

ZONE 6

2002-03

1. Ensure front wheels are in straight ahead position.
2. Turn ignition switch to Off position.
3. Remove key from ignition.
4. Remove AIR BAG fuse from fuse block. **With AIR BAG fuse removed and ignition On, AIR BAG indicator illuminates. This is normal operation and does not indicate an SIR system fault.**
5. Remove upper rear window trim panel.
6. Remove both lefthand and righthand corner trim panels.
7. Remove rear headliner push-in retainers.
8. Remove rear coat hooks.
9. Pull down righthand corner of headliner to access passenger roof panel air bag module connector.
10. Remove connector position assurance (CPA) from passenger roof panel air bag module connector.
11. Disconnect passenger roof panel air bag module connector from vehicle harness connector.

2004-06

1. Ensure front wheels are in straight ahead position.
2. Turn ignition switch to Off position.
3. Remove key from ignition.
4. Remove AIR BAG fuse from fuse block. **With AIR BAG fuse removed and ignition On, AIR BAG indicator illuminates. This is normal operation and does not indicate an SIR system fault.**
5. **To disable passenger roof panel air bag module and passenger seat belt pretensioner,** proceed as follows:
   a. Remove upper rear window trim panel.
   b. Remove both lefthand and righthand rear corner trim panels.
   c. Remove rear headliner push-in retainers.
   d. Remove rear coat hooks.
   e. Pull down righthand rear corner of headliner to access passenger roof panel air bag module connector.
   f. Remove connector position assurance (CPA) from passenger roof panel air bag module connector.
   g. Disconnect passenger roof panel air bag module connector from vehicle harness connector.
   h. Remove passenger lower center pillar trim panel.
   i. Remove CPA from passenger seat belt pretensioner connector.
   j. Disconnect passenger seat belt pretensioner connector.
6. **To disable passenger roof panel air**

bag module, proceed as follows:

a. Remove upper rear window trim panel.
b. Remove both lefthand and righthand rear corner trim panels.
c. Remove rear headliner push-in retainers.
d. Remove rear coat hooks.
e. Pull down right rear corner of headliner to access passenger roof panel air bag module connector.
f. Remove connector position assurance (CPA) from passenger roof panel air bag module connector.
g. Disconnect passenger roof panel air bag module connector from vehicle harness connector.

ZONE 8

2002-03

1. Ensure front wheels are in straight ahead position.
2. Turn ignition switch to Off position.
3. Remove key from ignition.
4. Remove AIR BAG fuse from fuse block. **With AIR BAG fuse removed and ignition On, AIR BAG indicator illuminates. This is normal operation and does not indicate an SIR system fault.**
5. Remove upper rear window trim panel.
6. Remove both lefthand and righthand rear corner trim panels.
7. Remove rear headliner push-in retainers.
8. Remove rear coat hooks.
9. Pull down corner of headliner to access passenger roof panel air bag module connector.
10. Remove connector position assurance (CPA) from passenger roof panel air bag module.
11. Disconnect passenger roof panel air bag module connector from vehicle harness connector.
12. Remove CPA from passenger air bag module connector.
13. Disconnect passenger air bag module connector from vehicle harness connector.
14. Remove CPA from driver air bag module coil connector.
15. Disconnect driver air bag module coil connector from vehicle harness connector.
16. Remove CPA from driver roof panel air bag module connector.
17. Disconnect driver roof panel air bag module connector from vehicle harness connector.

2004-06

1. Ensure front wheels are in straight ahead position.
2. Turn ignition switch to Off position.
3. Remove key from ignition.
4. Remove AIR BAG fuse from fuse block. **With AIR BAG fuse removed and ignition On, AIR BAG indicator illuminates. This is normal operation and does not indicate an SIR system fault.**
5. Remove rear upper window trim panel.
6. Remove both lefthand and righthand side rear corner trim panels.
7. Remove rear headliner push-in retainers.
8. Remove rear coat hooks.
9. Pull down righthand rear corner to access passenger roof panel air bag module connector.
10. Remove connector position assurance (CPA) from passenger roof panel air bag module connector.
11. Disconnect passenger roof panel air bag module connector from vehicle harness connector.
12. Remove passenger lower center pillar trim panel.
13. Remove CPA from passenger seat belt pretensioner connector.
14. Disconnect passenger seat belt pretensioner connector.
15. Remove CPA from passenger air bag module connector.
16. Disconnect passenger air bag module connector from vehicle harness connector.
17. Remove CPA from driver air bag module coil connector.
18. Disconnect driver air bag module coil connector from vehicle harness connector.
19. Remove driver lower center pillar trim panel.
20. Remove CPA from driver seat belt pretensioner connector.
21. Disconnect driver seat belt pretensioner connector.
22. Pull down lefthand rear corner of headliner to access driver roof panel air bag module connector.
23. Remove CPA from driver roof panel air bag module connector.
24. Disconnect driver roof panel air bag module connector from vehicle harness connector.

ARMING

Astro & Safari

2002

1. Remove key from ignition.
2. Connect passenger air bag module yellow 2-way connector located under instrument panel insulator panel.
3. Install CPA to passenger air bag module yellow 2-way connector.
4. Install instrument panel insulator panel.
5. Connect driver air bag module yellow 2-way connector located at base of steering column.
6. Install CPA to driver air bag module yellow 2-way connector.
7. Install driver side insulator panel.
8. Install AIR BAG fuse into fuse block.
9. From a position away from air bag modules, turn On ignition with engine Off.
10. AIR BAG indicator will flash seven times, then AIR BAG indicator will then turn Off.
11. If AIR BAG indicator does not operate as outlined, refer to **MOTOR's "Air Bag Manual" or "Air Bag Diagnostics CD."**

2003-05

ZONE 1

1. Remove key from ignition.
2. Connect front end discriminating sensor connector to front end discriminating sensor located on frame crossmember.
3. Install CPA to front end discriminating sensor connector.
4. Install AIR BAG fuse into fuse block.
5. From a position away from air bag modules, turn On ignition with engine Off.
6. AIR BAG indicator will flash seven times, then AIR BAG indicator will then turn Off.
7. If AIR BAG indicator does not operate as outlined, refer to **MOTOR's "Air Bag Manual" or "Air Bag Diagnostics CD."**

ZONE 3

1. Remove key from ignition.
2. Connect driver air bag module yellow 2-way connector located left of steering column near knee bolster.
3. Install CPA to driver air bag module yellow 2-way connector.
4. Install AIR BAG fuse into fuse block.
5. Install driver side knee bolster.
6. From a position away from air bag modules, turn On ignition with engine Off.
7. AIR BAG indicator will flash seven times, then AIR BAG indicator will then turn Off.
8. If AIR BAG indicator does not operate as outlined, refer to **MOTOR's "Air Bag Manual" or "Air Bag Diagnostics CD."**

ZONE 5

1. Remove key from ignition.
2. Connect passenger air bag module yellow 2-way connector located behind instrument panel support.
3. Install CPA to passenger air bag module yellow 2-way connector.
4. Install passenger side knee bolster.
5. Install AIR BAG fuse into fuse block.
6. From a position away from air bag modules, turn On ignition with engine Off.
7. AIR BAG indicator will flash seven times, then AIR BAG indicator will then turn Off.
8. If AIR BAG indicator does not operate as outlined, refer to **MOTOR's "Air Bag Manual" or "Air Bag Diagnostics CD."**

ZONE 7

1. Remove key from ignition.
2. Connect passenger air bag module yellow 2-way connector located behind instrument panel support.
3. Install CPA to passenger air bag module yellow 2-way connector.
4. Connect driver air bag module yellow 2-way connector located left of steering column near knee bolster.
5. Install CPA to driver air bag module yellow 2-way connector.
6. Install AIR BAG fuse into fuse block.

7. Install passenger and driver side knee bolster.
8. From a position away from air bag modules, turn On ignition with engine Off.
9. AIR BAG indicator will flash seven times, then AIR BAG indicator will then turn Off.
10. If AIR BAG indicator does not operate as outlined, refer to **MOTOR's "Air Bag Manual" or "Air Bag Diagnostics CD."**

Avalanche, Escalade ESV, Escalade EXT, Sierra, Silverado, Suburban, SSR, Tahoe & Yukon

2002

1. Remove key from ignition.
2. **On Avalanche, Suburban, Tahoe and Yukon models,** proceed as follows:
   a. Connect passenger side impact air bag module yellow 2-way connector located under passenger seat.
   b. Install CPA to passenger side impact air bag module yellow 2-way connector located under passenger seat.
   c. Connect driver side impact air bag module yellow 2-way connector located under driver seat.
   d. Install CPA to driver side impact air bag module yellow 2-way connector located under driver seat.
3. **On all models,** connect passenger air bag module yellow 2-way connector located behind main instrument panel support.
4. Install CPA to passenger air bag module yellow 2-way connector located behind instrument panel support.
5. Connect driver air bag module yellow 2-way connector at base of steering column.
6. Install CPA to driver air bag module yellow 2–way connector at base of steering column.
7. Install AIR BAG fuse into fuse block.
8. From a position away from air bag modules, turn On ignition with engine Off.
9. AIR BAG indicator will flash 7 times, then AIR BAG indicator will then turn Off.
10. If AIR BAG indicator does not operate as outlined, refer to **MOTOR's "Air Bag Manual" or "Air Bag Diagnostics CD."**

2003–06

ZONE 1

1. Remove key from ignition.
2. Connect front end sensor connectors to both front end sensors.
3. Install CPA's to both front end sensor connectors.
4. Install SIR fuse into fuse block.
5. From a position away from air bag modules, turn On ignition with engine Off.
6. AIR BAG indicator will flash 7 times, then AIR BAG indicator will then turn Off.
7. If AIR BAG indicator does not operate as outlined, refer to **MOTOR's "Air Bag Manual" or "Air Bag Diagnostics CD."**

ZONE 2

1. Remove key from ignition.
2. **On SSR models,** connect seat belt pretensioner lefthand connector to vehicle harness connector.
3. **On SSR models,** install lock pillar trim panel.
4. **On all models,** connect side impact sensor yellow 2-way connector located at middle of door.
5. Install CPA to side impact sensor yellow 2-way connector.
6. Install driver side door trim panel.
7. Install SIR fuse into fuse block.
8. From a position away from air bag modules, turn On ignition with engine Off.
9. AIR BAG indicator will flash 7 times, then AIR BAG indicator will then turn Off.
10. If AIR BAG indicator does not operate as outlined, refer to **MOTOR's "Air Bag Manual" or "Air Bag Diagnostics CD."**

ZONE 3

1. Remove key from ignition.
2. Connect driver air bag module yellow 4-way connector located left of steering column near knee bolster.
3. Install CPA to driver air bag module yellow 4-way connector.
4. Install SIR fuse into fuse block.
5. From a position away from air bag modules, turn On ignition with engine Off.
6. AIR BAG indicator will flash 7 times, then AIR BAG indicator will then turn Off.
7. If AIR BAG indicator does not operate as outlined, refer to **MOTOR's "Air Bag Manual" or "Air Bag Diagnostics CD."**

ZONE 5

1. Remove key from ignition.
2. Connect passenger air bag module yellow 4-way connector located behind instrument panel support.
3. Install CPA to passenger air bag module yellow 4-way connector.
4. Install SIR fuse into fuse block.
5. From a position away from air bag modules, turn On ignition with engine Off.
6. AIR BAG indicator will flash 7 times, then AIR BAG indicator will then turn Off.
7. If AIR BAG indicator does not operate as outlined, refer to **MOTOR's "Air Bag Manual" or "Air Bag Diagnostics CD."**

ZONE 6

1. Remove key from ignition.
2. **On SSR models,** connect seat belt pretensioner righthand connector to vehicle harness connector.
3. **On SSR models,** install lock pillar trim panel.
4. **On all models,** connect side impact sensor yellow 2-way connector located in middle of righthand side door.
5. Install CPA to side impact sensor yellow 2-way connector.
6. Install passenger side door trim panel.
7. Install SIR fuse into fuse block.
8. From a position away from air bag modules, turn On ignition with engine Off.
9. AIR BAG indicator will flash 7 times, then AIR BAG indicator will then turn Off.
10. If AIR BAG indicator does not operate as outlined, refer to **MOTOR's "Air Bag Manual" or "Air Bag Diagnostics CD."**

ZONE 7

Except SSR

1. Remove key from ignition.
2. Connect driver air bag module yellow 4-way connector located left of steering column at knee bolster.
3. Install CPA to driver air bag module yellow 4-way connector.
4. Connect passenger air bag module yellow 4-way connector located behind instrument panel support.
5. Install CPA to passenger air bag module yellow 4-way connector.
6. **On Avalanche and 2003–04 Escalade, Suburban, Tahoe and Yukon models,** proceed as follows:
   a. Connect passenger side impact air bag module yellow 2-way connector located under passenger seat.
   b. Install CPA to passenger side impact air bag module yellow 2-way connector.
   c. Connect driver side impact air bag module yellow 2-way connector located under driver seat.
   d. Install CPA to driver side impact air bag module yellow 2-way connector.
7. **On all models,** install SIR fuse into fuse block.
8. From a position away from air bag modules, turn On ignition with engine Off.
9. AIR BAG indicator will flash 7 times, then AIR BAG indicator will then turn Off.
10. If AIR BAG indicator does not operate as outlined, refer to **MOTOR's "Air Bag Manual" or "Air Bag Diagnostics CD."**

SSR

1. Remove key from ignition.
2. Connect driver side impact air bag module yellow 2-way connector located under driver seat.
3. Install CPA to driver side impact air bag module yellow 2-way connector.
4. Install SIR fuse into fuse block.

5. From a position away from air bag modules, turn On ignition with engine Off.
6. AIR BAG indicator will flash 7 times, then AIR BAG indicator will then turn Off.
7. If AIR BAG indicator does not operate as outlined, refer to **MOTOR's "Air Bag Manual" or "Air Bag Diagnostics CD."**

ZONE 8

1. Remove key from ignition.
2. Connect driver air bag module yellow 4-way connector located left of steering column and near knee bolster.
3. Install CPA to driver air bag module yellow 4-way connector.
4. Connect passenger air bag module yellow 4-way connector located behind instrument panel support.
5. Install CPA to passenger air bag module yellow 4-way connector.
6. Connect passenger side impact air bag module yellow 2-way connector located under passenger seat.
7. Install CPA to passenger side impact air bag module yellow 2-way connector.
8. Connect righthand side seat belt pretensioner and install CPA.
9. Install lock pillar trim panel.
10. Connect driver side impact module yellow 2-way connector located under driver seat.
11. Install CPA to driver side impact air bag module yellow 2-way connector.
12. Connect lefthand side seat belt pretensioner and install CPA.
13. Install lock pillar trim panel.
14. Install SIR fuse into fuse block.
15. From a position away from air bag modules, turn On ignition with engine Off.
16. AIR BAG indicator will flash 7 times, then AIR BAG indicator will then turn Off.
17. If AIR BAG indicator does not operate as outlined, refer to **MOTOR's "Air Bag Manual" or "Air Bag Diagnostics CD."**

ZONE 9

1. Remove key from ignition.
2. Connect passenger side impact air bag module yellow 2-way connector located under passenger seat.
3. Install CPA to passenger side impact air bag module yellow 2-way connector.
4. Install SIR fuse into fuse block.
5. From a position away from air bag modules, turn On ignition with engine Off.
6. AIR BAG indicator will flash 7 times, then AIR BAG indicator will then turn Off.
7. If AIR BAG indicator does not operate as outlined, refer to **MOTOR's "Air Bag Manual" or "Air Bag Diagnostics CD."**

Aztek & Rendezvous

2002

1. Connect passenger side impact air bag module connector locate under passenger seat.
2. Install CPA to passenger side air bag module connector.
3. Connect driver side impact air bag module connector located under driver seat.
4. Install CPA to driver side impact air bag module connector.
5. Connect passenger air bag module connector located behind passenger side insulator panel.
6. Install CPA to passenger air bag module connector.
7. Install passenger side insulator panel.
8. Connect driver air bag module coil connector located at base of steering column.
9. Install CPA to driver air bag module coil connector.
10. Install driver side insulator panel.
11. Install SIR fuse into fuse block.
12. From a position away from air bag modules, turn On ignition with engine Off.
13. AIR BAG indicator will flash seven times, then AIR BAG indicator will then turn Off.
14. If AIR BAG indicator does not operate as outlined, refer to **MOTOR's "Air Bag Manual" or "Air Bag Diagnostics CD."**

2003-06

ZONE 1

1. Remove key from ignition.
2. Connect harness connector to front end sensor.
3. Install CPA to front end sensor harness connector.
4. Install SIR fuse into fuse block.
5. From a position away from air bag modules, turn On ignition with engine Off.
6. AIR BAG indicator will flash, then AIR BAG indicator will then turn Off.
7. If AIR BAG indicator does not operate as outlined, refer to **MOTOR's "Air Bag Manual" or "Air Bag Diagnostics CD."**

ZONE 2

1. Remove key from ignition.
2. Connect CPA to driver side impact sensor and pretensioner yellow 2-way harness connectors.
3. Install CPA to yellow sensor and pretensioner harness connectors.
4. Install SIR fuse into fuse block.
5. From a position away from air bag modules, turn On ignition with engine Off.
6. AIR BAG indicator will flash seven times, then AIR BAG indicator will then turn Off.
7. If AIR BAG indicator does not operate as outlined, refer to **MOTOR's "Air Bag Manual" or "Air Bag Diagnostics CD."**

ZONE 3

1. Remove key from ignition.
2. Connect driver air bag module coil connector.
3. Install CPA to driver air bag module coil connector located at base of steering column.
4. Install driver side insulator panel.
5. Install SIR fuse into fuse block.
6. From a position away from air bag modules, turn On ignition with engine Off.
7. AIR BAG indicator will flash seven times, then AIR BAG indicator will then turn Off.
8. If AIR BAG indicator does not operate as outlined, refer to **MOTOR's "Air Bag Manual" or "Air Bag Diagnostics CD."**

ZONE 5

1. Remove key from ignition.
2. Connect passenger air bag module connector.
3. Install CPA to passenger air bag module connector located behind passenger side insulator panel.
4. Install passenger side insulator panel.
5. Install SIR fuse into fuse block.
6. From a position away from air bag modules, turn On ignition with engine Off.
7. AIR BAG indicator will flash seven times, then AIR BAG indicator will then turn Off.
8. If AIR BAG indicator does not operate as outlined, refer to **MOTOR's "Air Bag Manual" or "Air Bag Diagnostics CD."**

ZONE 6

1. Remove key from ignition.
2. Connect CPA to passenger side impact sensor and pretensioner yellow 2-way harness connectors.
3. Install CPA to passenger side impact sensor and pretensioner.
4. Install SIR fuse into fuse block.
5. From a position away from air bag modules, turn On ignition with engine Off.
6. AIR BAG indicator will flash seven times, then AIR BAG indicator will then turn Off.
7. If AIR BAG indicator does not operate as outlined, refer to **MOTOR's "Air Bag Manual" or "Air Bag Diagnostics CD."**

ZONE 7

1. Remove key from ignition.
2. **On 2003 models,** connect driver side impact air bag module connector.
3. **On 2003 models,** install connector position assurance (CPA) from driver side impact air bag module connector located under driver seat.
4. **On 2004–06 models,** connect vehicle harness yellow connector from driver side impact air bag module yellow connector.
5. **On 2004–06 models,** install both CPA's from driver side impact air bag module yellow connector located under driver seat.

6. **On all models,** install SIR fuse into fuse block.
7. From a position away from air bag modules, turn On ignition with engine Off.
8. AIR BAG indicator will flash seven times, then AIR BAG indicator will then turn Off.
9. If AIR BAG indicator does not operate as outlined, refer to **MOTOR's "Air Bag Manual" or "Air Bag Diagnostics CD."**

ZONE 9

2003

1. Remove key from ignition.
2. **To enable entire SIR system,** proceed as follows:
   a. Connect passenger air bag module connector located behind passenger side insulator panel.
   b. Install CPA to passenger air bag module connector.
   c. Install passenger side insulator panel.
   d. Connect driver air bag module coil connector located at base of steering column.
   e. Install CPA to driver air bag module coil connector.
   f. Install driver side insulator panel.
   g. Connect driver side impact air bag module connector located under driver seat.
   h. Install CPA to driver side impact air bag module connector.
   i. Connect passenger side impact air bag module connector located under passenger seat.
   j. Install CPA to passenger side impact air bag module connector.
3. **To enable passenger side impact air bag module,** proceed as follows:
   a. Connect passenger side impact air bag module connector located under passenger seat.
   b. Install CPA to passenger side impact air bag module connector.
4. **On all models,** install SIR fuse into fuse block.
5. From a position away from air bag modules, turn On ignition with engine Off.
6. AIR BAG indicator will flash seven times, then AIR BAG indicator will then turn Off.
7. If AIR BAG indicator does not operate as outlined, refer to **MOTOR's "Air Bag Manual" or "Air Bag Diagnostics CD."**

2004

1. Remove key from ignition.
2. Connect vehicle harness yellow connector to passenger side impact sensor yellow connector.
3. Install both CPA's to passenger side impact module yellow connector.
4. Install SIR fuse into fuse block.
5. From a position away from air bag modules, turn On ignition with engine Off.
6. AIR BAG indicator will flash seven times, then AIR BAG indicator will then turn Off.
7. If AIR BAG indicator does not operate as outlined, refer to **MOTOR's "Air Bag Manual" or "Air Bag Diagnostics CD."**

2005-06

1. Remove key from ignition.
2. **To enable entire SIR system,** proceed as follows:
   a. Connect CPA to driver side impact sensor and pretensioner harness connectors.
   b. Install CPA to driver side impact sensor and pretensioner harness connectors.
   c. Connect driver air bag module coil connector.
   d. Install CPA to driver air bag module coil connector located at base of steering column.
   e. Install driver side insulator panel.
   f. Connect passenger air bag module connector.
   g. Install CPA to passenger air bag module connector.
   h. Install passenger side insulator panel.
   i. Connect passenger side impact sensor and pretensioner harness connectors.
   j. Install CPA to passenger side impact sensor and pretensioner harness connectors.
   k. Connect vehicle harness connector to passenger side impact air bag module connector.
   l. Install CPA to passenger side impact air bag module yellow connector.
3. **To enable passenger side impact air bag module,** proceed as follows:
   a. Connect vehicle harness connector to passenger side impact air bag module connector.
   b. Install CPA to passenger side impact air bag module yellow connector.
4. **On all models,** install SIR fuse into fuse block.
5. From a position away from air bag modules, turn On ignition with engine Off.
6. AIR BAG indicator will flash, then AIR BAG indicator will then turn Off.
7. If AIR BAG indicator does not operate as outlined, refer to **MOTOR's "Air Bag Manual" or "Air Bag Diagnostics CD."**

Blazer, Sonoma & S10

2002

1. Remove key from ignition.
2. Connect passenger air bag module yellow 2-way connector located behind glove compartment.
3. Install CPA to passenger air bag module yellow 2-way connector.
4. Close glove compartment door.
5. Connect driver air bag module yellow 2-way connector located at base of steering column.
6. Install CPA to driver air bag module yellow 2-way connector.
7. Install knee bolster and sound insulator panel.
8. Install SIR fuse into fuse block.
9. From a position away from air bag modules, turn On ignition with engine Off.
10. AIR BAG indicator will flash 7 times, then AIR BAG indicator will then turn Off.
11. If AIR BAG indicator does not operate as outlined, refer to **MOTOR's "Air Bag Manual" or "Air Bag Diagnostics CD."**

2003-04

ZONE 1

1. Remove key from ignition.
2. Connect inflatable restraint front end discriminating sensor connectors to inflatable restraints front end discriminating sensor.
3. Install CPA to inflatable restraints front end discriminating sensor connectors.
4. Install SIR fuse into fuse block.
5. From a position away from air bag modules, turn On ignition with engine Off.
6. AIR BAG indicator will flash 7 times, then AIR BAG indicator will then turn Off.
7. If AIR BAG indicator does not operate as outlined, refer to **MOTOR's "Air Bag Manual" or "Air Bag Diagnostics CD."**

ZONE 3

1. Remove key from ignition.
2. Connect driver air bag module yellow 2-way connector located left of steering column near knee bolster.
3. Install CPA to driver air bag module yellow 2-way connector.
4. Install SIR fuse into fuse block.
5. Install knee bolster.
6. From a position away from air bag modules, turn On ignition with engine Off.
7. AIR BAG indicator will flash 7 times, then AIR BAG indicator will then turn Off.
8. If AIR BAG indicator does not operate as outlined, refer to **MOTOR's "Air Bag Manual" or "Air Bag Diagnostics CD."**

ZONE 5

1. Remove key from ignition.
2. Connect passenger air bag module yellow 2-way connector located behind main instrument panel support.
3. Install CPA to passenger air bag module yellow 2-way connector.
4. Install SIR fuse into fuse block.
5. From a position away from air bag modules, turn On ignition with engine Off.
6. AIR BAG indicator will flash 7 times, then AIR BAG indicator will then turn Off.
7. If AIR BAG indicator does not operate as outlined, refer to **MOTOR's "Air Bag Manual" or "Air Bag Diagnostics CD."**

ZONE 8

1. Remove key from ignition.
2. Connect passenger air bag module yellow 2-way connector located behind main instrument panel support.
3. Install CPA to passenger air bag module yellow 2-way connector.
4. Connect driver air bag module yellow 2-way connector located left of steering column near knee bolster.
5. Install CPA to driver air bag module yellow 2-way connector.
6. Install SIR fuse into fuse block.
7. Install knee bolster.
8. From a position away from air bag modules, turn On ignition with engine Off.
9. AIR BAG indicator will flash 7 times, then AIR BAG indicator will then turn Off.
10. If AIR BAG indicator does not operate as outlined, refer to **MOTOR's "Air Bag Manual" or "Air Bag Diagnostics CD."**

Bravada, Envoy, Rainier & Trailblazer

2002

1. Remove key from ignition.
2. Connect passenger side impact air bag module yellow 2-way connector located under passenger seat.
3. Install CPA to passenger side impact air bag module yellow 2-way connector.
4. Connect driver side impact air bag module yellow 2-way connector located under driver seat.
5. Install CPA to driver side impact air bag module yellow 2-way connector.
6. Connect passenger air bag module yellow 2-way connector located behind instrument panel support.
7. Install CPA to passenger air bag module yellow 2-way connector.
8. Connect driver air bag module yellow 2-way connector located at base of steering column.
9. Install CPA to driver air bag module yellow 2-way connector.
10. Install AIR BAG fuse into fuse block.
11. From a position away from air bag modules, turn On ignition with engine Off.
12. AIR BAG indicator will flash 7 times, then AIR BAG indicator will then turn Off.
13. If AIR BAG indicator does not operate as outlined, refer to **MOTOR's "Air Bag Manual" or "Air Bag Diagnostics CD."**

2003-06

ZONE 1

1. Remove key from ignition.
2. Connect EFS connectors to both EFS's.
3. Install CPA's to EFS connectors.
4. Install sensor bracket to bumper.
5. Install grille.
6. Install SIR fuse into fuse block.
7. From a position away from air bag modules, turn On ignition with engine Off.
8. AIR BAG indicator will flash 7 times, then AIR BAG indicator will then turn Off.
9. If AIR BAG indicator does not operate as outlined, refer to **MOTOR's "Air Bag Manual" or "Air Bag Diagnostics CD."**

ZONE 2

1. Remove key from ignition.
2. Connect driver side impact sensor yellow 2-way connector located near bottom lefthand corner of door.
3. Install CPA to driver side impact sensor yellow 2-way connector.
4. Install driver side door trim panel.
5. Install SIR fuse into fuse block.
6. From a position away from air bag modules, turn On ignition with engine Off.
7. AIR BAG indicator will flash 7 times, then AIR BAG indicator will then turn Off.
8. If AIR BAG indicator does not operate as outlined, refer to **MOTOR's "Air Bag Manual" or "Air Bag Diagnostics CD."**

ZONE 3

1. Remove key from ignition.
2. Connect driver air bag module yellow 4-way connector located left of steering column near knee bolster.
3. Install CPA to driver air bag module yellow 4-way connector.
4. Install SIR fuse into fuse block.
5. From a position away from air bag modules, turn On ignition with engine Off.
6. AIR BAG indicator will flash 7 times, then AIR BAG indicator will then turn Off.
7. If AIR BAG indicator does not operate as outlined, refer to **MOTOR's "Air Bag Manual" or "Air Bag Diagnostics CD."**

ZONE 5

1. Remove key from ignition.
2. Connect passenger air bag module yellow 4-way connector located behind main instrument panel support.
3. Install CPA to passenger air bag module yellow 4-way connector.
4. Install SIR fuse into fuse block.
5. From a position away from air bag modules, turn On ignition with engine Off.
6. AIR BAG indicator will flash 7 times, then AIR BAG indicator will then turn Off.
7. If AIR BAG indicator does not operate as outlined, refer to **MOTOR's "Air Bag Manual" or "Air Bag Diagnostics CD."**

ZONE 6

1. Remove key from ignition.
2. Connect passenger side impact sensor yellow 2-way connector located near bottom of righthand corner of door.
3. Install CPA to passenger side impact sensor yellow 2-way connector.
4. Install SIR fuse into fuse block.
5. From a position away from air bag modules, turn On ignition with engine Off.
6. AIR BAG indicator will flash 7 times, then AIR BAG indicator will then turn Off.
7. If AIR BAG indicator does not operate as outlined, refer to **MOTOR's "Air Bag Manual" or "Air Bag Diagnostics CD."**

ZONE 7

2003-04

1. Remove key from ignition.
2. Connect driver side impact air bag module yellow 2-way connector located under driver seat.
3. Install CPA to driver side impact air bag module yellow 2-way connector.
4. Install SIR fuse into fuse block.
5. From a position away from air bag modules, turn On ignition with engine Off.
6. AIR BAG indicator will flash 7 times, then AIR BAG indicator will then turn Off.
7. If AIR BAG indicator does not operate as outlined, refer to **MOTOR's "Air Bag Manual" or "Air Bag Diagnostics CD."**

2005-06

1. Remove key from ignition.
2. Connect driver seat belt pretensioner yellow 2-way connector located under driver seat.
3. Install CPA to driver seat belt pretensioner yellow 2-way connector.
4. Install SIR fuse into fuse block.
5. From a position away from air bag modules, turn On ignition with engine Off.
6. AIR BAG indicator will flash 7 times, then AIR BAG indicator will then turn Off.
7. If AIR BAG indicator does not operate as outlined, refer to **MOTOR's "Air Bag Manual" or "Air Bag Diagnostics CD."**

ZONE 8

2003-04

1. Remove key from ignition.
2. Connect driver air bag module yellow 4-way connector located left of steering column near knee bolster.
3. Install CPA to driver air bag module yellow 4-way connector.
4. Connect passenger air bag module yellow 4-way connector located behind instrument panel support.
5. Install CPA to passenger air bag module yellow 4-way connector.
6. Connect passenger side impact air bag module yellow 2-way connector located under passenger seat.
7. Install CPA to passenger side impact air bag module yellow 2-way connector.
8. Connect driver side impact air bag module yellow 2-way connector located under driver seat.
9. Install CPA to driver side impact air bag

module yellow 2-way connector.
10. Install SIR fuse into fuse block.
11. From a position away from air bag modules, turn On ignition with engine Off.
12. AIR BAG indicator will flash 7 times, then AIR BAG indicator will then turn Off.
13. If AIR BAG indicator does not operate as outlined, refer to **MOTOR's "Air Bag Manual" or "Air Bag Diagnostics CD."**

2005-06

1. Remove key from ignition.
2. Connect driver air bag module yellow 4-way connector located left of steering column near knee bolster.
3. Install CPA to driver air bag module yellow 4-way connector.
4. Connect passenger air bag module yellow 4-way connector located behind instrument panel support.
5. Install CPA to passenger air bag module yellow 4-way connector.
6. Connect passenger seat belt pretensioner yellow 2-way connector located under passenger seat.
7. Install CPA to passenger seat belt pretensioner yellow 2-way connector.
8. Connect passenger roof panel air bag module yellow 2-way connector and install CPA.
9. Install passenger side center pillar trim panel.
10. Connect driver seat belt pretensioner yellow 2-way connector located under driver seat.
11. Install CPA to driver seat belt pretensioner yellow 2-way connector.
12. Connect driver roof panel air bag module yellow 2-way connector and install CPA.
13. Install driver side center pillar trim panel.
14. Install SIR fuse into fuse block.
15. From a position away from air bag modules, turn On ignition with engine Off.
16. AIR BAG indicator will flash 7 times, then AIR BAG indicator will then turn Off.
17. If AIR BAG indicator does not operate as outlined, refer to **MOTOR's "Air Bag Manual" or "Air Bag Diagnostics CD."**

ZONE 9

2003-04

1. Remove key from ignition.
2. Connect passenger side impact air bag module yellow 2-way connector located under passenger seat.
3. Install CPA to passenger side impact air bag module yellow 2-way connector.
4. Install SIR fuse into fuse block.
5. From a position away from air bag modules, turn On ignition with engine Off.
6. AIR BAG indicator will flash 7 times, then AIR BAG indicator will then turn Off.
7. If AIR BAG indicator does not operate as outlined, refer to **MOTOR's "Air Bag Manual" or "Air Bag Diagnostics CD."**

2005-06

1. Remove key from ignition.
2. Connect passenger seat belt pretensioner yellow 2-way connector located under passenger seat.
3. Install CPA to passenger seat belt pretensioner yellow 2-way connector.
4. Install SIR fuse into fuse block.
5. From a position away from air bag modules, turn On ignition with engine Off.
6. AIR BAG indicator will flash 7 times, then AIR BAG indicator will then turn Off.
7. If AIR BAG indicator does not operate as outlined, refer to **MOTOR's "Air Bag Manual" or "Air Bag Diagnostics CD."**

Canyon & Colorado

ZONE 1

1. Remove key from ignition.
2. Connect both front end sensor connectors.
3. Install SIR fuse into fuse block.
4. From a position away from air bag modules, turn On ignition with engine Off.
5. AIR BAG indicator will flash 7 times, then AIR BAG indicator will then turn Off.
6. If AIR BAG indicator does not operate as outlined, refer to **MOTOR's "Air Bag Manual" or "Air Bag Diagnostics CD."**

ZONE 2

1. Remove key from ignition.
2. Connect driver roof panel air bag module and install trim panel.
3. Connect driver seat belt pretensioner and install CPA.
4. **On models equipped with crew cab,** install lower center pillar trim panel.
5. **On models equipped with extended cab,** install rear access door wiring harness grommet to access connector.
6. **On models equipped with regular cab,** install lower body rear corner trim panel.
7. **On all models,** connect driver side impact sensor yellow 2-way connector located near middle of door.
8. Install CPA to driver side impact sensor yellow 2-way connector.
9. Install driver front door trim panel.
10. Install SIR fuse into fuse block.
11. From a position away from air bag modules, turn On ignition with engine Off.
12. AIR BAG indicator will flash 7 times, then AIR BAG indicator will then turn Off.
13. If AIR BAG indicator does not operate as outlined, refer to **MOTOR's "Air Bag Manual" or "Air Bag Diagnostics CD."**

ZONE 3

1. Remove key from ignition.
2. Connect driver air bag module yellow 4-way connector located left of steering column above left hinge pillar trim panel.
3. Install CPA to driver air bag module yellow 4-way connector.
4. Install SIR fuse into fuse block.
5. From a position away from air bag modules, turn On ignition with engine Off.
6. AIR BAG indicator will flash 7 times, then AIR BAG indicator will then turn Off.
7. If AIR BAG indicator does not operate as outlined, refer to **MOTOR's "Air Bag Manual" or "Air Bag Diagnostics CD."**

ZONE 5

1. Remove key from ignition.
2. Connect passenger air bag module 4-way connector C208 located above driver kick panel.
3. Install CPA to passenger air bag module yellow 4-way connector C208.
4. Install SIR fuse into fuse block.
5. From a position away from air bag modules, turn On ignition with engine Off.
6. AIR BAG indicator will flash 7 times, then AIR BAG indicator will then turn Off.
7. If AIR BAG indicator does not operate as outlined, refer to **MOTOR's "Air Bag Manual" or "Air Bag Diagnostics CD."**

ZONE 6

1. Remove key from ignition.
2. Connect passenger roof panel air bag module connector and install trim panel.
3. Connect passenger seat belt pretensioner connector and install CPA.
4. **On models equipped with crew cab,** install lower center pillar trim panel.
5. **On models equipped with extended cab,** install rear access door wiring harness grommet to access connector.
6. **On models equipped with regular cab,** install lower body rear corner trim panel.
7. **On all models,** connect passenger side impact sensor yellow 2-way connector located near middle of door.
8. Install CPA to passenger side impact sensor yellow 2-way connector.
9. Install passenger front door trim panel.
10. Install SIR fuse into fuse block.
11. From a position away from air bag modules, turn On ignition with engine Off.
12. AIR BAG indicator will flash 7 times, then AIR BAG indicator will then turn Off.
13. If AIR BAG indicator does not operate as outlined, refer to **MOTOR's "Air Bag Manual" or "Air Bag Diagnostics CD."**

ZONE 8

1. Remove key from ignition.
2. Connect driver air bag module yellow 4-way connector located left of steering column above left hinge pillar trim panel.
3. Install CPA to driver air bag module yellow 4-way connector.
4. Connect driver roof panel air bag module connector and install trim panel.
5. Connect driver seat belt pretensioner and install CPA.
6. **On models equipped with crew cab,** install driver side lower center pillar trim panel.
7. **On models equipped with extended cab,** install driver side rear access door wiring harness grommet to access connector.
8. **On models equipped with regular cab,** install driver side lower body rear corner trim panel.
9. **On all models,** connect driver side impact sensor yellow 2-way connector located near middle of door.
10. Install CPA to driver side impact sensor yellow 2-way connector.
11. Install driver door trim panel.
12. Connect passenger air bag module yellow 4-way connector C208 located above driver kick panel.
13. Install CPA to passenger air bag module yellow 4-way connector C208.
14. Connect passenger roof panel air bag module connector and install trim panel.
15. Connect passenger seat belt pretensioner and install CPA.
16. **On models equipped with crew cab,** install passenger side lower center pillar trim panel.
17. **On models equipped with extended cab,** install passenger side rear access door wiring harness grommet to access connector.
18. **On models equipped with regular cab,** install passenger side lower body rear corner trim panel.
19. **On all models,** connect passenger side impact sensor yellow 2-way connector located near middle of door.
20. Install passenger door trim panel.
21. Install SIR fuse into fuse block.
22. From a position away from air bag modules, turn On ignition with engine Off.
23. AIR BAG indicator will flash 7 times, then AIR BAG indicator will then turn Off.
24. If AIR BAG indicator does not operate as outlined, refer to **MOTOR's "Air Bag Manual" or "Air Bag Diagnostics CD."**

Equinox & Torrent

ZONE 1

1. Remove key from ignition.
2. Connect EFS connector to EFS.
3. Install CPA to EFS connector.
4. Install AIR BAG fuse into fuse block.
5. From a position away from air bag modules, turn On ignition with engine Off.
6. AIR BAG indicator will flash, then AIR BAG indicator will then turn Off.
7. If AIR BAG indicator does not operate as outlined, refer to **MOTOR's "Air Bag Manual" or "Air Bag Diagnostics CD."**

ZONE 2

1. Remove key from ignition.
2. **To enable driver roof panel air bag module,** proceed as follows:
   a. Connect driver roof panel air bag module connector to vehicle harness connector.
   b. Install CPA to driver roof panel air bag module connector.
   c. Install rear coat hooks.
   d. Install rear headliner push-in retainers.
   e. Install lefthand and righthand rear corner trim panels.
   f. Install upper rear window molding.
3. **To enable driver side impact sensor and driver seat belt pretensioner,** proceed as follows:
   a. Connect driver seat belt pretensioner connector to vehicle harness connector and install CPA.
   b. Connect driver side impact sensor to vehicle harness connector and install CPA.
   c. Install driver side lower center pillar trim.
4. Install AIR BAG fuse into fuse block.
5. From a position away from air bag modules, turn On ignition with engine Off.
6. AIR BAG indicator will flash, then AIR BAG indicator will then turn Off.
7. If AIR BAG indicator does not operate as outlined, refer to **MOTOR's "Air Bag Manual" or "Air Bag Diagnostics CD."**

ZONE 3

1. Remove key from ignition.
2. Connect driver air bag module coil connector to vehicle harness connector.
3. Install CPA to driver air bag module coil connector.
4. Install AIR BAG fuse into fuse block.
5. From a position away from air bag modules, turn On ignition with engine Off.
6. AIR BAG indicator will flash, then AIR BAG indicator will then turn Off.
7. If AIR BAG indicator does not operate as outlined, refer to **MOTOR's "Air Bag Manual" or "Air Bag Diagnostics CD."**

ZONE 5

1. Remove key from ignition.
2. Connect passenger air bag module connector to vehicle harness connector.
3. Install CPA to passenger air bag module connector.
4. Install AIR BAG fuse into fuse block.
5. From a position away from air bag modules, turn On ignition with engine Off.
6. AIR BAG indicator will flash, then AIR BAG indicator will then turn Off.
7. If AIR BAG indicator does not operate as outlined, refer to **MOTOR's "Air Bag Manual" or "Air Bag Diagnostics CD."**

ZONE 6

1. Remove key from ignition.
2. **To enable passenger roof panel air bag module,** proceed as follows:
   a. Connect passenger roof panel air bag module connector to vehicle harness connector.
   b. Install CPA to passenger roof panel air bag module connector.
   c. Install rear coat hooks.
   d. Install rear headliner push-in retainers.
   e. Install lefthand and righthand rear corner trim panels.
   f. Install upper rear window molding.
3. **To enable passenger side impact sensor and passenger seat belt pretensioner,** proceed as follows:
   a. Connect passenger seat belt pretensioner connector to vehicle harness connector and install CPA.
   b. Connect passenger side impact sensor to vehicle harness connector and install CPA.
   c. Install passenger side lower center pillar trim.
4. Install AIR BAG fuse into fuse block.
5. From a position away from air bag modules, turn On ignition with engine Off.
6. AIR BAG indicator will flash, then AIR BAG indicator will then turn Off.
7. If AIR BAG indicator does not operate as outlined, refer to **MOTOR's "Air Bag Manual" or "Air Bag Diagnostics CD."**

ZONE 8

1. Remove key from ignition.
2. Connect driver air bag module coil connector to vehicle harness connector.
3. Install CPA to driver air bag module coil connector.
4. Connect driver seat belt pretensioner connector to vehicle harness connector and install CPA.
5. Install driver side lower center pillar trim.
6. Connect driver roof panel air bag module connector to vehicle harness connector.
7. Install CPA to driver roof panel air bag module connector.
8. Connect passenger air bag module connector to vehicle harness connector.
9. Install CPA to passenger air bag module connector.
10. Connect passenger seat belt pretensioner connector to vehicle harness connector and install CPA.
11. Install passenger side lower center pillar trim.
12. Connect passenger roof panel air bag module connector to vehicle harness connector.
13. Install CPA to passenger roof panel air bag module connector.
14. Install rear coat hooks.
15. Install rear headliner push-in retainers.

16. Install lefthand and righthand rear corner moldings.
17. Install upper rear window molding.
18. Install AIR BAG fuse into fuse block.
19. From a position away from air bag modules, turn On ignition with engine Off.
20. AIR BAG indicator will flash, then AIR BAG indicator will then turn Off.
21. If AIR BAG indicator does not operate as outlined, refer to **MOTOR's "Air Bag Manual" or "Air Bag Diagnostics CD."**

Express & Savana

2002

1. Remove key from ignition.
2. Connect passenger air bag module yellow 2-way connector located under instrument panel extension.
3. Install CPA to passenger air bag module yellow 2-way connector.
4. Install passenger side knee bolster.
5. Connect driver air bag module yellow 2-way connector located at base of steering column.
6. Install CPA to driver air bag module yellow 2-way connector.
7. Install driver side knee bolster.
8. Install AIR BAG fuse into fuse block.
9. From a position away from air bag modules, turn On ignition with engine Off.
10. AIR BAG indicator will flash 7 times, then AIR BAG indicator will then turn Off.
11. If AIR BAG indicator does not operate as outlined, refer to **MOTOR's "Air Bag Manual" or "Air Bag Diagnostics CD."**

2003-06

ZONE 1

1. Remove key from ignition.
2. Connect front end sensor connector to front end sensor.
3. Install CPA to front end sensor connector.
4. Install SIR fuse into fuse block.
5. From a position away from air bag modules, turn On ignition with engine Off.
6. AIR BAG indicator will flash 7 times, then AIR BAG indicator will then turn Off.
7. If AIR BAG indicator does not operate as outlined, refer to **MOTOR's "Air Bag Manual" or "Air Bag Diagnostics CD."**

ZONE 3

1. Remove key from ignition.
2. Connect driver air bag module yellow 4-way connector located left of steering column near knee bolster.
3. Install CPA to driver air bag module yellow 4-way connector.
4. Install SIR fuse into fuse block.
5. From a position away from air bag modules, turn On ignition with engine Off.
6. AIR BAG indicator will flash 7 times, then AIR BAG indicator will then turn Off.
7. If AIR BAG indicator does not operate as outlined, refer to **MOTOR's "Air Bag Manual" or "Air Bag Diagnostics CD."**

ZONE 5

1. Remove key from ignition.
2. Connect passenger air bag module yellow 4-way connector located behind main instrument panel support.
3. Install CPA to passenger air bag module yellow 4-way connector.
4. Install righthand side knee bolster bracket.
5. Install SIR fuse into fuse block.
6. From a position away from air bag modules, turn On ignition with engine Off.
7. AIR BAG indicator will flash 7 times, then AIR BAG indicator will then turn Off.
8. If AIR BAG indicator does not operate as outlined, refer to **MOTOR's "Air Bag Manual" or "Air Bag Diagnostics CD."**

ZONE 7

2003

1. Remove key from ignition.
2. Connect driver air bag module yellow 4-way connector located left of steering column near knee bolster.
3. Install CPA to driver air bag module yellow 4-way connector.
4. Connect passenger air bag module yellow 4-way connector located behind instrument panel support.
5. Install CPA to passenger air bag module yellow 4-way connector.
6. Install righthand side knee bolster bracket.
7. Connect passenger seat belt pretensioner yellow 2-way connector located under passenger seat.
8. Install CPA to passenger seat belt pretensioner yellow 2-way connector.
9. Connect driver seat belt pretensioner yellow 2-way connector located under driver seat.
10. Install CPA to driver seat belt pretensioner yellow 2-way connector.
11. Install SIR fuse into fuse block.
12. From a position away from air bag modules, turn On ignition with engine Off.
13. AIR BAG indicator will flash 7 times, then AIR BAG indicator will then turn Off.
14. If AIR BAG indicator does not operate as outlined, refer to **MOTOR's "Air Bag Manual" or "Air Bag Diagnostics CD."**

2004-05

1. Remove key from ignition.
2. Connect driver air bag module yellow 4-way connector located left of steering column near knee bolster.
3. Install CPA to driver air bag module yellow 4-way connector.
4. Connect passenger air bag module yellow 4-way connector located behind instrument panel support.
5. Install CPA to passenger air bag module yellow 4-way connector.
6. Install righthand side knee bolster bracket.
7. Install SIR fuse into fuse block.
8. From a position away from air bag modules, turn On ignition with engine Off.
9. AIR BAG indicator will flash 7 times, then AIR BAG indicator will then turn Off.
10. If AIR BAG indicator does not operate as outlined, refer to **MOTOR's "Air Bag Manual" or "Air Bag Diagnostics CD."**

2006

1. Remove key from ignition.
2. Connect driver air bag module yellow 4-way connector located left of steering column near knee bolster.
3. Install CPA to driver air bag module yellow 4-way connector.
4. Connect driver seat belt pretensioner yellow 2-way connector located under driver seat.
5. Install CPA to driver seat belt pretensioner yellow 2-way connector.
6. Connect passenger air bag module yellow 4-way connector located behind instrument panel support.
7. Install CPA to passenger air bag module yellow 4-way connector.
8. Install righthand side knee bolster bracket.
9. Connect passenger seat belt pretensioner yellow 2-way connector located under passenger seat.
10. Install CPA to passenger seat belt pretensioner yellow 2-way connector.
11. Install SIR fuse into fuse block.
12. From a position away from air bag modules, turn On ignition with engine Off.
13. AIR BAG indicator will flash 7 times, then AIR BAG indicator will then turn Off.
14. If AIR BAG indicator does not operate as outlined, refer to **MOTOR's "Air Bag Manual" or "Air Bag Diagnostics CD."**

ZONE 9

1. Remove key from ignition.
2. Connect passenger seat belt pretensioner yellow 2-way connector located under passenger seat.
3. Install CPA to passenger seat belt pretensioner yellow 2-way connector.
4. Install SIR fuse into fuse block.
5. From a position away from air bag modules, turn On ignition with engine Off.
6. AIR BAG indicator will flash 7 times, then AIR BAG indicator will then turn Off.
7. If AIR BAG indicator does not operate as outlined, refer to **MOTOR's "Air Bag Manual" or "Air Bag Diagnostics CD."**

HHR

ZONE 1

1. Remove key from ignition.
2. Connect front end sensor connector to front end sensor.
3. Connect CPA to front end sensor connector.
4. Install AIR BAG and SDM fuses into fuse block.
5. From a position away from air bag modules, turn On ignition with engine Off.
6. AIR BAG indicator will flash, then AIR BAG indicator will then turn Off.
7. If AIR BAG indicator does not operate as outlined, refer to **MOTOR's "Air Bag Manual" or "Air Bag Diagnostics CD."**

ZONE 2

1. Remove key from ignition.
2. Connect driver roof panel air bag module connector to vehicle harness connector.
3. Install CPA to driver roof panel air bag module connector.
4. Install driver rear quarter upper trim panel.
5. Connect driver seat belt pretensioner connector.
6. Install CPA to seat belt pretensioner connector.
7. Install driver lower center pillar trim panel.
8. Install driver side impact sensor connector to sensor.
9. Install CPA to driver side impact sensor connector.
10. Install driver door water deflector.
11. Install driver door trim panel.
12. Install AIR BAG and SDM fuses into fuse block.
13. From a position away from air bag modules, turn On ignition with engine Off.
14. AIR BAG indicator will flash, then AIR BAG indicator will then turn Off.
15. If AIR BAG indicator does not operate as outlined, refer to **MOTOR's "Air Bag Manual" or "Air Bag Diagnostics CD."**

ZONE 3

1. Remove key from ignition.
2. Connect driver air bag module coil connector to vehicle harness connector.
3. Install CPA to driver air bag module coil connector.
4. Install driver outer trim panel to instrument panel.
5. Install AIR BAG and SDM fuses into fuse block.
6. From a position away from air bag modules, turn On ignition with engine Off.
7. AIR BAG indicator will flash, then AIR BAG indicator will then turn Off.
8. If AIR BAG indicator does not operate as outlined, refer to **MOTOR's "Air Bag Manual" or "Air Bag Diagnostics CD."**

ZONE 5

1. Remove key from ignition.
2. Connect passenger air bag module connector to vehicle harness connector.
3. Engage CPA of passenger air bag module connector.
4. Install AIR BAG and SDM fuses into fuse block.
5. From a position away from air bag modules, turn On ignition with engine Off.
6. AIR BAG indicator will flash, then AIR BAG indicator will then turn Off.
7. If AIR BAG indicator does not operate as outlined, refer to **MOTOR's "Air Bag Manual" or "Air Bag Diagnostics CD."**

ZONE 6

1. Remove key from ignition.
2. Connect passenger roof panel air bag module connector to vehicle harness connector.
3. Install CPA to passenger roof panel air bag module connector.
4. Install passenger rear quarter upper trim panel.
5. Connect passenger seat belt pretensioner connector.
6. Install CPA to passenger seat belt pretensioner connector.
7. Install passenger lower center pillar trim panel.
8. Install passenger side impact sensor connector to sensor.
9. Install CPA to passenger side impact sensor connector.
10. Install passenger door water deflector.
11. Install passenger door trim panel.
12. Install AIR BAG and SDM fuses into fuse block.
13. From a position away from air bag modules, turn On ignition with engine Off.
14. AIR BAG indicator will flash, then AIR BAG indicator will then turn Off.
15. If AIR BAG indicator does not operate as outlined, refer to **MOTOR's "Air Bag Manual" or "Air Bag Diagnostics CD."**

ZONE 8

1. Remove key from ignition.
2. Connect driver roof panel air bag module connector to vehicle harness connector.
3. Install CPA to driver roof panel air bag module connector.
4. Install driver rear quarter upper trim molding to lock pillar.
5. Connect driver seat belt pretensioner connector.
6. Install CPA to driver seat belt pretensioner connector.
7. Install driver lower center pillar trim panel.
8. Connect driver air bag module coil connector to vehicle harness connector.
9. Install CPA to driver air bag module coil connector.
10. Install driver outer trim cover to instrument panel.
11. Install driver side impact sensor connector to sensor.
12. Install CPA to driver side impact sensor connector.
13. Install driver door water deflector shield.
14. Install driver door trim panel.
15. Connect passenger air bag module connector to vehicle harness connector.
16. Engage CPA to passenger air bag module connector.
17. Connect passenger seat belt pretensioner connector.
18. Install CPA to passenger seat belt pretensioner connector.
19. Install passenger lower center pillar trim panel.
20. Connect passenger roof panel air bag module connector to vehicle harness connector.
21. Install CPA to passenger air bag module connector.
22. Install passenger rear quarter upper trim molding to lock pillar.
23. Install passenger side impact sensor connector to sensor.
24. Install CPA to passenger side impact sensor connector.
25. Install passenger door water deflector shield.
26. Install passenger door trim panel.
27. Install AIR BAG and SDM fuses into fuse block.
28. From a position away from air bag modules, turn On ignition with engine Off.
29. AIR BAG indicator will flash, then AIR BAG indicator will then turn Off.
30. If AIR BAG indicator does not operate as outlined, refer to **MOTOR's "Air Bag Manual" or "Air Bag Diagnostics CD."**

Hummer H2

ZONE 1

1. Remove key from ignition.
2. Connect both front end sensor connectors to sensors.
3. Install CPA to both front end sensor connectors.
4. Install SIR fuse into fuse block.
5. Install engine protection shield.
6. From a position away from air bag modules, turn On ignition with engine Off.
7. AIR BAG indicator will flash seven times, then AIR BAG indicator will then turn Off.
8. If AIR BAG indicator does not operate as outlined, refer to **MOTOR's "Air Bag Manual" or "Air Bag Diagnostics CD."**

ZONE 3

1. Remove key from ignition.
2. Connect driver air bag module yellow 2-way connector located left of steering column near knee bolster.
3. Install CPA to driver air bag module yellow 2-way connector.
4. Install SIR fuse into fuse block.
5. Install engine protection shield.
6. From a position away from air bag modules, turn On ignition with engine Off.
7. AIR BAG indicator will flash seven times, then AIR BAG indicator will then turn Off.
8. If AIR BAG indicator does not operate as outlined, refer to **MOTOR's "Air Bag Manual" or "Air Bag Diagnostics CD."**

ZONE 5

1. Remove key from ignition.
2. Connect passenger air bag module yellow 2-way connector located behind air bag module.
3. Install CPA to passenger air bag module yellow 2-way connector.
4. Install SIR fuse into fuse block.
5. Install engine protection shield.
6. From a position away from air bag modules, turn On ignition with engine Off.
7. AIR BAG indicator will flash seven times, then AIR BAG indicator will then turn Off.
8. If AIR BAG indicator does not operate as outlined, refer to **MOTOR's "Air Bag Manual" or "Air Bag Diagnostics CD."**

ZONE 7

1. Remove key from ignition.
2. Connect driver air bag module yellow 2-way connector located left of steering column near knee bolster.
3. Install CPA to driver air bag module yellow 2-way connector.
4. Connect passenger air bag module yellow 2-way connector located behind air bag module.
5. Install CPA to passenger air bag module yellow 2-way connector.
6. Install SIR fuse into fuse block.
7. Install engine protection shield.
8. From a position away from air bag modules, turn On ignition with engine Off.
9. AIR BAG indicator will flash seven times, then AIR BAG indicator will then turn Off.
10. If AIR BAG indicator does not operate as outlined, refer to **MOTOR's "Air Bag Manual" or "Air Bag Diagnostics CD."**

Hummer H3

ZONE 1

1. Remove key from ignition.
2. Connect sensor connectors to both front end sensors.
3. Install CPA's to both sensor connectors.
4. Install SIR fuse into fuse block.
5. Install engine protection shield.
6. From a position away from air bag modules, turn On ignition with engine Off.
7. AIR BAG indicator will flash seven times, then AIR BAG indicator will then turn Off.
8. If AIR BAG indicator does not operate as outlined, refer to **MOTOR's "Air Bag Manual" or "Air Bag Diagnostics CD."**

ZONE 2

1. Remove key from ignition.
2. Connect driver roof panel air bag module connector and install windshield pillar trim panel.
3. Connect driver seat belt pretensioner and install CPA.
4. Install driver lower center pillar trim panel.
5. Connect driver side impact sensor yellow 2-way connector located near middle of door.
6. Install CPA to driver side impact sensor yellow 2-way connector.
7. Install driver door trim panel.
8. Install SIR fuse into fuse block.
9. Install engine protection shield.
10. From a position away from air bag modules, turn On ignition with engine Off.
11. AIR BAG indicator will flash seven times, then AIR BAG indicator will then turn Off.
12. If AIR BAG indicator does not operate as outlined, refer to **MOTOR's "Air Bag Manual" or "Air Bag Diagnostics CD."**

ZONE 3

1. Remove key from ignition.
2. Connect driver air bag module yellow 4-way connector located left of steering column above left hinge pillar trim panel.
3. Install CPA to driver air bag module yellow 4-way connector.
4. Install SIR fuse into fuse block.
5. Install engine protection shield.
6. From a position away from air bag modules, turn On ignition with engine Off.
7. AIR BAG indicator will flash seven times, then AIR BAG indicator will then turn Off.
8. If AIR BAG indicator does not operate as outlined, refer to **MOTOR's "Air Bag Manual" or "Air Bag Diagnostics CD."**

ZONE 5

1. Remove key from ignition.
2. Connect passenger air bag module yellow 4-way inline connector C208 located above driver kick panel.
3. Install CPA to passenger air bag module yellow 4-way inline connector.
4. Install SIR fuse into fuse block.
5. Install engine protection shield.
6. From a position away from air bag modules, turn On ignition with engine Off.
7. AIR BAG indicator will flash seven times, then AIR BAG indicator will then turn Off.
8. If AIR BAG indicator does not operate as outlined, refer to **MOTOR's "Air Bag Manual" or "Air Bag Diagnostics CD."**

ZONE 6

1. Remove key from ignition.
2. Connect passenger roof panel air bag module connector and install windshield pillar trim panel.
3. Connect passenger seat belt pretensioner and install CPA.
4. Install passenger lower center pillar trim panel.
5. Connect passenger side impact sensor yellow 2-way connector located near middle of door.
6. Install CPA to passenger side impact sensor yellow 2-way connector.
7. Install passenger door trim panel.
8. Install SIR fuse into fuse block.
9. Install engine protection shield.
10. From a position away from air bag modules, turn On ignition with engine Off.
11. AIR BAG indicator will flash seven times, then AIR BAG indicator will then turn Off.
12. If AIR BAG indicator does not operate as outlined, refer to **MOTOR's "Air Bag Manual" or "Air Bag Diagnostics CD."**

ZONE 8

1. Remove key from ignition.
2. Connect driver air bag module yellow 4-way connector located left of steering column above left hinge pillar trim panel.
3. Install CPA to driver air bag module yellow 4-way connector.
4. Connect driver roof panel air bag module connector and install windshield pillar trim panel.
5. Connect driver seat belt pretensioner and install CPA.
6. Install driver lower center pillar trim panel.
7. Connect driver side impact sensor yellow 2-way connector located near middle of door.
8. Install CPA to driver side impact sensor yellow 2-way connector.
9. Install driver door trim panel.
10. Connect passenger air bag module yellow 4-way inline connector C208 located above driver kick panel.
11. Install CPA to passenger air bag module yellow 4-way inline connector.
12. Connect passenger roof panel air bag module connector and install windshield pillar trim panel.
13. Connect passenger seat belt pretensioner and install CPA.
14. Install passenger lower center pillar trim panel.
15. Connect passenger side impact sensor yellow 2-way connector located near middle of door.
16. Install CPA to passenger side impact sensor yellow 2-way connector.
17. Install passenger door trim panel.
18. Install SIR fuse into fuse block.
19. Install engine protection shield.
20. From a position away from air bag

modules, turn On ignition with engine Off.

21. AIR BAG indicator will flash seven times, then AIR BAG indicator will then turn Off.
22. If AIR BAG indicator does not operate as outlined, refer to **MOTOR's "Air Bag Manual" or "Air Bag Diagnostics CD."**

Montana, Silhouette & Venture

2002

1. Connect passenger seat belt pretensioner connector located under passenger seat.
2. Install CPA to passenger seat belt pretensioner connector.
3. Connect passenger side impact air bag module connector located under passenger seat.
4. Install CPA to passenger side impact air bag module connector.
5. Connect driver seat belt pretensioner connector located under driver seat.
6. Install CPA to driver seat belt pretensioner connector.
7. Connect driver side impact air bag module connector located under driver seat.
8. Install CPA to driver side impact air bag module connector.
9. Connect passenger air bag module connector located behind insulator panel.
10. Install CPA to passenger air bag module connector.
11. Install passenger insulator panel.
12. Connect driver air bag module coil connector located at base of steering column.
13. Install CPA to driver air bag module coil connector.
14. Install driver insulator panel.
15. Install SDM fuse into fuse block.
16. From a position away from air bag modules, turn On ignition with engine Off.
17. AIR BAG indicator will flash seven times, then AIR BAG indicator will then turn Off.
18. If AIR BAG indicator does not operate as outlined, refer to **MOTOR's "Air Bag Manual" or "Air Bag Diagnostics CD."**

2003-06

ZONE 1

1. Remove key from ignition.
2. Connect both front end sensor connectors to front end sensors.
3. Install CPA to both front end sensor connectors.
4. Install SIR fuse into fuse block.
5. From a position away from air bag modules, turn On ignition with engine Off.
6. AIR BAG indicator will flash seven times, then AIR BAG indicator will then turn Off.
7. If AIR BAG indicator does not operate as outlined, refer to **MOTOR's "Air Bag Manual" or "Air Bag Diagnostics CD."**

ZONE 2

1. Remove key from ignition.
2. Connect driver side impact sensor yellow 2-way connector to sensor located near bottom of B-pillar.
3. Install CPA to driver side impact sensor yellow 2-way connector.
4. Install driver seat belt retractor trim cover.
5. Install SIR fuse into fuse block.
6. From a position away from air bag modules, turn On ignition with engine Off.
7. AIR BAG indicator will flash seven times, then AIR BAG indicator will then turn Off.
8. If AIR BAG indicator does not operate as outlined, refer to **MOTOR's "Air Bag Manual" or "Air Bag Diagnostics CD."**

ZONE 3

1. Remove key from ignition.
2. Connect driver air bag module coil yellow 4-way connector located at base of steering column.
3. Install CPA to driver air bag module coil yellow 4-way connector.
4. Install driver insulator panel.
5. Install SIR fuse into fuse block.
6. From a position away from air bag modules, turn On ignition with engine Off.
7. AIR BAG indicator will flash seven times, then AIR BAG indicator will then turn Off.
8. If AIR BAG indicator does not operate as outlined, refer to **MOTOR's "Air Bag Manual" or "Air Bag Diagnostics CD."**

ZONE 5

1. Remove key from ignition.
2. Connect passenger air bag module yellow 4-way connector located behind passenger insulator panel.
3. Install CPA to passenger air bag module yellow 4-way connector.
4. Connect electrical connectors and install glove compartment.
5. Install SIR fuse into fuse block.
6. From a position away from air bag modules, turn On ignition with engine Off.
7. AIR BAG indicator will flash seven times, then AIR BAG indicator will then turn Off.
8. If AIR BAG indicator does not operate as outlined, refer to **MOTOR's "Air Bag Manual" or "Air Bag Diagnostics CD."**

ZONE 6

1. Remove key from ignition.
2. Connect passenger side impact sensor yellow 2-way connector to sensor located near bottom of B-pillar.
3. Install CPA to passenger side impact sensor yellow 2-way connector.
4. Install passenger seat belt retractor trim cover.
5. Install SIR fuse into fuse block.
6. From a position away from air bag modules, turn On ignition with engine Off.
7. AIR BAG indicator will flash seven times, then AIR BAG indicator will then turn Off.
8. If AIR BAG indicator does not operate as outlined, refer to **MOTOR's "Air Bag Manual" or "Air Bag Diagnostics CD."**

ZONE 7

1. Remove key from ignition.
2. Connect driver seat belt pretensioner yellow 2-way connector located under driver seat.
3. Install CPA to driver seat belt pretensioner yellow 2-way connector.
4. Connect driver side impact air bag module yellow 2-way connector located under driver seat.
5. Install CPA to driver side impact air bag module yellow 2-way connector.
6. Install SIR fuse into fuse block.
7. From a position away from air bag modules, turn On ignition with engine Off.
8. AIR BAG indicator will flash seven times, then AIR BAG indicator will then turn Off.
9. If AIR BAG indicator does not operate as outlined, refer to **MOTOR's "Air Bag Manual" or "Air Bag Diagnostics CD."**

ZONE 9

1. Remove key from ignition.
2. Connect passenger air bag module yellow 4-way connector located behind passenger insulator panel.
3. Install CPA to passenger air bag module yellow 4-way connector.
4. Connect electrical connectors and install glove compartment.
5. Connect driver air bag module coil yellow 4-way connector located at base of steering column.
6. Install CPA to driver air bag module coil yellow 4-way connector.
7. Install driver insulator panel.
8. Connect driver seat belt pretensioner yellow 2-way connector located under driver seat.
9. Install CPA to driver seat belt pretensioner yellow 2-way connector.
10. Connect driver side impact air bag module yellow 2-way connector located under driver seat.
11. Install CPA to driver side impact air bag module yellow 2-way connector.
12. Connect passenger seat belt pretensioner yellow 2-way connector located under passenger seat.
13. Install CPA to passenger seat belt pretensioner yellow 2-way connector.
14. Connect passenger side impact air bag module yellow 2-way connector located under passenger seat.
15. Install CPA to passenger side impact air bag module yellow 2-way connector.
16. Install SIR fuse into fuse block.
17. From a position away from air bag modules, turn On ignition with engine Off.
18. AIR BAG indicator will flash seven

times, then AIR BAG indicator will then turn Off.

19. If AIR BAG indicator does not operate as outlined, refer to **MOTOR's "Air Bag Manual" or "Air Bag Diagnostics CD."**

Relay, SV6, Terraza & Uplander

ZONE 1

1. Remove key from ignition.
2. Connect both front end sensor harness connectors to front end sensors.
3. Install CPA's to both front end sensor connectors.
4. Install AIR BAG fuse into fuse block.
5. From a position away from air bag modules, turn On ignition with engine Off.
6. AIR BAG indicator will flash, then AIR BAG indicator will then turn Off.
7. If AIR BAG indicator does not operate as outlined, refer to **MOTOR's "Air Bag Manual" or "Air Bag Diagnostics CD."**

ZONE 2

1. Remove key from ignition.
2. Connect vehicle harness connector to driver seat belt pretensioner.
3. Install CPA to driver seat belt pretensioner connector.
4. Connect driver side impact sensor harness connector to sensor.
5. Install CPA to driver side impact sensor connector.
6. Install driver side impact sensor to center pillar and tighten sensor fasteners.
7. Install driver lower center pillar trim cover.
8. Install AIR BAG fuse into fuse block.
9. From a position away from air bag modules, turn On ignition with engine Off.
10. AIR BAG indicator will flash, then AIR BAG indicator will then turn Off.
11. If AIR BAG indicator does not operate as outlined, refer to **MOTOR's "Air Bag Manual" or "Air Bag Diagnostics CD."**

ZONE 3

1. Remove key from ignition.
2. Connect driver air bag module coil yellow connector.
3. Install CPA to driver air bag module coil connector located at base of steering column.
4. Install driver knee bolster insulator panel.
5. Install AIR BAG fuse into fuse block.
6. From a position away from air bag modules, turn On ignition with engine Off.
7. AIR BAG indicator will flash, then AIR BAG indicator will then turn Off.
8. If AIR BAG indicator does not operate as outlined, refer to **MOTOR's "Air Bag Manual" or "Air Bag Diagnostics CD."**

ZONE 5

1. Remove key from ignition.
2. Connect passenger air bag module yellow connector.
3. Install CPA to passenger air bag module connector.
4. Install passenger knee bolster insulator panel.
5. Install AIR BAG fuse into fuse block.
6. From a position away from air bag modules, turn On ignition with engine Off.
7. AIR BAG indicator will flash, then AIR BAG indicator will then turn Off.
8. If AIR BAG indicator does not operate as outlined, refer to **MOTOR's "Air Bag Manual" or "Air Bag Diagnostics CD."**

ZONE 6

1. Remove key from ignition.
2. Connect vehicle harness connector to passenger seat belt pretensioner.
3. Install CPA to passenger seat belt pretensioner connector.
4. Connect passenger side impact sensor harness connector to sensor.
5. Install CPA to passenger side impact sensor connector.
6. Install passenger side impact sensor to center pillar and tighten sensor fasteners.
7. Install passenger lower center pillar trim cover.
8. Install AIR BAG fuse into fuse block.
9. From a position away from air bag modules, turn On ignition with engine Off.
10. AIR BAG indicator will flash, then AIR BAG indicator will then turn Off.
11. If AIR BAG indicator does not operate as outlined, refer to **MOTOR's "Air Bag Manual" or "Air Bag Diagnostics CD."**

ZONE 7

1. Remove key from ignition.
2. Connect vehicle harness connector to driver front side impact air bag module yellow connector.
3. Install CPA to driver front side impact air bag module connector.
4. Install AIR BAG fuse into fuse block.
5. From a position away from air bag modules, turn On ignition with engine Off.
6. AIR BAG indicator will flash, then AIR BAG indicator will then turn Off.
7. If AIR BAG indicator does not operate as outlined, refer to **MOTOR's "Air Bag Manual" or "Air Bag Diagnostics CD."**

ZONE 9

1. Remove key from ignition.
2. **To enable entire SIR system,** proceed as follows:
   a. Connect vehicle harness connector to driver seat belt pretensioner.
   b. Install CPA to driver seat belt pretensioner connector.
   c. Install driver lower center pillar trim cover.
   d. Connect driver air bag module coil yellow connector.
   e. Install CPA to driver air bag module coil connector located at base of steering column.
   f. Install driver knee bolster insulator panel.
   g. Connect vehicle harness connector to driver front side impact air bag module yellow connector.
   h. Install CPA to driver front side impact air bag module connector.
   i. Connect vehicle harness connector to driver rear side impact air bag module yellow connector.
   j. Install CPA to driver rear side impact air bag module connector.
   k. Connect passenger air bag module yellow connector.
   l. Install CPA to passenger air bag module connector.
   m. Install passenger knee bolster insulator panel.
   n. Connect vehicle harness connector to passenger seat belt pretensioner.
   o. Install CPA to passenger seat belt pretensioner connector.
   p. Install passenger lower center pillar trim cover.
   q. Connect vehicle harness connector to passenger rear side impact air bag module yellow connector.
   r. Install CPA to passenger rear side impact air bag module connector.
   s. Connect vehicle harness connector to passenger front side impact air bag module yellow connector.
   t. Install CPA to passenger front side impact air bag module connector.
3. **To enable passenger front side impact air bag module,** proceed as follows:
   a. Connect vehicle harness connector to passenger front side impact air bag module yellow connector.
   b. Install CPA to passenger front side impact air bag module connector.
4. Install AIR BAG fuse into fuse block.
5. From a position away from air bag modules, turn On ignition with engine Off.
6. AIR BAG indicator will flash, then AIR BAG indicator will then turn Off.
7. If AIR BAG indicator does not operate as outlined, refer to **MOTOR's "Air Bag Manual" or "Air Bag Diagnostics CD."**

ZONE 10

1. Remove key from ignition.
2. Connect vehicle harness connector to driver rear side impact air bag module yellow connector.
3. Install CPA to driver rear side impact air bag module connector.
4. Install AIR BAG fuse into fuse block.
5. From a position away from air bag modules, turn On ignition with engine Off.
6. AIR BAG indicator will flash, then AIR BAG indicator will then turn Off.
7. If AIR BAG indicator does not operate as outlined, refer to **MOTOR's "Air Bag Manual" or "Air Bag Diagnostics CD."**

ZONE 12

1. Remove key from ignition.
2. Connect vehicle harness connector to passenger rear side impact air bag module yellow connector.
3. Install CPA to passenger rear side impact air bag module connector.
4. Install AIR BAG fuse into fuse block.
5. From a position away from air bag modules, turn On ignition with engine Off.
6. AIR BAG indicator will flash, then AIR BAG indicator will then turn Off.
7. If AIR BAG indicator does not operate as outlined, refer to **MOTOR's "Air Bag Manual" or "Air Bag Diagnostics CD."**

SRX

ZONE 1

1. Remove key from ignition.
2. Connect both connectors to front end sensors.
3. Install both CPA's to front end sensor connectors.
4. Close hood.
5. Install SIR fuse into fuse block.
6. Install fuse cover and place carpet back under seat.
7. From a position away from air bag modules, turn On ignition with engine Off.
8. AIR BAG indicator will flash, then AIR BAG indicator will then turn Off.
9. If AIR BAG indicator does not operate as outlined, refer to **MOTOR's "Air Bag Manual" or "Air Bag Diagnostics CD."**

ZONE 2

1. Remove key from ignition.
2. **To enable driver side impact sensor,** proceed as follows:
   a. Connect driver side impact sensor connector to sensor.
   b. Connect CPA to driver side impact sensor connector.
   c. Install driver center pillar trim panel.
3. **To enable driver roof panel air bag module,** proceed as follows:
   a. Connect driver roof panel air bag module yellow connector to air bag module.
   b. Install CPA to driver roof panel air bag module connector.
   c. Install driver carpet retainer trim.
4. Install SIR fuse into fuse block.
5. Install fuse cover and place carpet back under seat.
6. From a position away from air bag modules, turn On ignition with engine Off.
7. AIR BAG indicator will flash, then AIR BAG indicator will then turn Off.
8. If AIR BAG indicator does not operate as outlined, refer to **MOTOR's "Air Bag Manual" or "Air Bag Diagnostics CD."**

ZONE 3

1. Remove key from ignition.
2. Connect driver air bag module coil yellow connector to vehicle harness yellow connector.
3. Install CPA to driver air bag module coil yellow connector.
4. Install driver insulator panel to side of instrument panel.
5. Install SIR fuse into fuse block.
6. Install fuse cover and place carpet back under seat.
7. From a position away from air bag modules, turn On ignition with engine Off.
8. AIR BAG indicator will flash, then AIR BAG indicator will then turn Off.
9. If AIR BAG indicator does not operate as outlined, refer to **MOTOR's "Air Bag Manual" or "Air Bag Diagnostics CD."**

ZONE 5

1. Remove key from ignition.
2. Connect passenger air bag module yellow connector to vehicle harness yellow connector.
3. Install CPA to passenger air bag module yellow connector.
4. Install passenger insulator panel to side of instrument panel.
5. Install SIR fuse into fuse block.
6. Install fuse cover and place carpet back under seat.
7. From a position away from air bag modules, turn On ignition with engine Off.
8. AIR BAG indicator will flash, then AIR BAG indicator will then turn Off.
9. If AIR BAG indicator does not operate as outlined, refer to **MOTOR's "Air Bag Manual" or "Air Bag Diagnostics CD."**

ZONE 6

1. Remove key from ignition.
2. **To enable passenger side impact sensor,** proceed as follows:
   a. Connect passenger side impact sensor connector to sensor.
   b. Connect CPA to passenger side impact sensor connector.
   c. Install passenger center pillar trim panel.
3. **To enable passenger roof panel air bag module,** proceed as follows:
   a. Connect passenger roof panel air bag module yellow connector to air bag module.
   b. Install CPA to passenger roof panel air bag module connector.
   c. Install passenger carpet retainer trim.
4. Install SIR fuse into fuse block.
5. Install fuse cover and place carpet back under seat.
6. From a position away from air bag modules, turn On ignition with engine Off.
7. AIR BAG indicator will flash, then AIR BAG indicator will then turn Off.
8. If AIR BAG indicator does not operate as outlined, refer to **MOTOR's "Air Bag Manual" or "Air Bag Diagnostics CD."**

ZONE 7

1. Remove key from ignition.
2. Connect driver side impact air bag module and pretensioner yellow connector to vehicle harness yellow connector.
3. Install both CPA locks to driver side impact air bag module and pretensioner yellow connector.
4. Install SIR fuse into fuse block.
5. Install fuse cover and place carpet back under seat.
6. From a position away from air bag modules, turn On ignition with engine Off.
7. AIR BAG indicator will flash, then AIR BAG indicator will then turn Off.
8. If AIR BAG indicator does not operate as outlined, refer to **MOTOR's "Air Bag Manual" or "Air Bag Diagnostics CD."**

ZONE 8

1. Remove key from ignition.
2. Connect driver roof panel air bag module yellow connector to air bag module.
3. Install CPA to driver roof panel air bag module connector.
4. Install driver carpet retainer trim.
5. Connect driver side impact air bag module and seat belt pretensioner yellow connector to vehicle harness yellow connector located under driver seat.
6. Install both CPA locks to driver side impact air bag module and pretensioner yellow connector.
7. Connect driver air bag module coil yellow connector to vehicle harness yellow connector.
8. Install CPA to driver air bag module coil yellow connector.
9. Install driver insulator panel to side of instrument panel.
10. Connect passenger air bag module yellow connector to vehicle harness yellow connector.
11. Install CPA to passenger air bag module yellow connector.
12. Install passenger insulator panel to side of instrument panel.
13. Connect passenger side impact air bag module and seat belt pretensioner yellow connector to vehicle harness yellow connector located under passenger seat.
14. Install both CPA locks to passenger side impact air bag module and pretensioner yellow connector.
15. Connect passenger roof panel air bag module yellow connector to air bag module.
16. Install CPA to passenger roof panel air bag module connector.
17. Install passenger carpet retainer trim.
18. Install SIR fuse into fuse block.
19. Install fuse cover and place carpet back under seat.
20. From a position away from air bag modules, turn On ignition with engine Off.
21. AIR BAG indicator will flash, then AIR BAG indicator will then turn Off.
22. If AIR BAG indicator does not operate as outlined, refer to **MOTOR's "Air Bag Manual" or "Air Bag Diagnostics CD."**

ZONE 9

1. Remove key from ignition.
2. Connect passenger side impact air bag module and pretensioner yellow connector to vehicle harness yellow connector.
3. Install both CPA locks to passenger side impact air bag module and pretensioner yellow connector.
4. Install SIR fuse into fuse block.
5. Install fuse cover and place carpet back under seat.
6. From a position away from air bag modules, turn On ignition with engine Off.
7. AIR BAG indicator will flash, then AIR BAG indicator will then turn Off.
8. If AIR BAG indicator does not operate as outlined, refer to **MOTOR's "Air Bag Manual" or "Air Bag Diagnostics CD."**

Tracker

2002

1. Remove key from ignition.
2. Install yellow 2-way connector and CPA to passenger air bag module connector.
3. Install glove compartment door.
4. Install yellow 2-way connector and CPA to driver air bag module connector.
5. Install driver knee bolster trim plate.
6. Install AIR BAG fuse into fuse block.
7. From a position away from air bag modules, turn On ignition with engine Off.
8. AIR BAG indicator will flash seven times, then AIR BAG indicator will then turn Off.
9. If AIR BAG indicator does not operate as outlined, refer to **MOTOR's "Air Bag Manual" or "Air Bag Diagnostics CD."**

2003-04

ZONE 3

1. Remove key from ignition.
2. Install yellow 2-way connector and CPA to driver air bag module connector.
3. Install driver knee bolster trim panel.
4. Install AIR BAG fuse into fuse block.
5. From a position away from air bag modules, turn On ignition with engine Off.
6. AIR BAG indicator will flash seven times, then AIR BAG indicator will then turn Off.
7. If AIR BAG indicator does not operate as outlined, refer to **MOTOR's "Air Bag Manual" or "Air Bag Diagnostics CD."**

ZONE 5

1. Remove key from ignition.
2. Install yellow 2-way connector and CPA to passenger air bag module connector.
3. Install glove compartment door.
4. Install AIR BAG fuse into fuse block.
5. From a position away from air bag modules, turn On ignition with engine Off.
6. AIR BAG indicator will flash seven times, then AIR BAG indicator will then turn Off.
7. If AIR BAG indicator does not operate as outlined, refer to **MOTOR's "Air Bag Manual" or "Air Bag Diagnostics CD."**

ZONE 8

1. Remove key from ignition.
2. Install yellow 2-way connector and CPA to passenger air bag module connector.
3. Install glove compartment door.
4. Install yellow 2-way connector and CPA to driver air bag module connector.
5. Install driver knee bolster trim panel.
6. Install AIR BAG fuse into fuse block.
7. From a position away from air bag modules, turn On ignition with engine Off.
8. AIR BAG indicator will flash seven times, then AIR BAG indicator will then turn Off.
9. If AIR BAG indicator does not operate as outlined, refer to **MOTOR's "Air Bag Manual" or "Air Bag Diagnostics CD."**

Vue

ZONE 2

2002-03

1. Remove key from ignition.
2. Connect driver roof panel air bag module connector to vehicle harness connector.
3. Install CPA to driver air bag module connector.
4. Install rear coat hooks.
5. Install rear headliner push-in retainers.
6. Install both lefthand and righthand rear corner trim panels.
7. Install upper rear window trim panels.
8. Install AIR BAG fuse into fuse block.
9. From a position away from air bag modules, turn On ignition with engine Off.
10. AIR BAG indicator will flash, then AIR BAG indicator will then turn Off.
11. If AIR BAG indicator does not operate as outlined, refer to **MOTOR's "Air Bag Manual" or "Air Bag Diagnostics CD."**

2004-06

1. Remove key from ignition.
2. **To enable driver roof panel air bag module,** proceed as follows:
   a. Connect driver roof panel air bag module connector to vehicle harness connector.
   b. Install CPA to driver roof panel air bag module connector.
   c. Install rear coat hooks.
   d. Install rear headliner push-in retainers.
   e. Install both lefthand and righthand rear corner trim panels.
   f. Install upper rear window trim panel.
3. **To enable driver roof panel air bag module and driver seat belt pretensioner,** proceed as follows:
   a. Connect driver roof panel air bag module connector to vehicle harness connector.
   b. Install CPA to driver roof panel air bag module connector.
   c. Install rear coat hooks.
   d. Install rear headliner push-in retainers.
   e. Install both lefthand and righthand rear corner trim panels.
   f. Install upper rear window trim panel.
   g. Connect driver seat belt pretensioner connector and install CPA.
   h. Install driver lower center pillar trim panel.
4. Install AIR BAG fuse into fuse block.
5. From a position away from air bag modules, turn On ignition with engine Off.
6. AIR BAG indicator will flash, then AIR BAG indicator will then turn Off.
7. If AIR BAG indicator does not operate as outlined, refer to **MOTOR's "Air Bag Manual" or "Air Bag Diagnostics CD."**

ZONE 3

1. Remove key from ignition.
2. Connect driver air bag module coil connector to vehicle harness connector.
3. Install CPA to driver air bag module coil connector.
4. Install AIR BAG fuse into fuse block.
5. From a position away from air bag modules, turn On ignition with engine Off.
6. AIR BAG indicator will flash, then AIR BAG indicator will then turn Off.
7. If AIR BAG indicator does not operate as outlined, refer to **MOTOR's "Air Bag Manual" or "Air Bag Diagnostics CD."**

ZONE 5

1. Remove key from ignition.
2. Connect passenger air bag module connector to vehicle harness connector.
3. Install CPA to passenger air bag module connector.
4. Install AIR BAG fuse into fuse block.
5. From a position away from air bag modules, turn On ignition with engine Off.
6. AIR BAG indicator will flash, then AIR BAG indicator will then turn Off.
7. If AIR BAG indicator does not operate as outlined, refer to **MOTOR's "Air Bag Manual" or "Air Bag Diagnostics CD."**

ZONE 6

2002-03

1. Remove key from ignition.
2. Connect passenger roof panel air bag module connector to vehicle harness connector.
3. Install CPA to passenger air bag module connector.
4. Install rear coat hooks.
5. Install rear headliner push-in retainers.

6. Install both lefthand and righthand rear corner trim panels.
7. Install upper rear window trim panel.
8. Install AIR BAG fuse into fuse block.
9. From a position away from air bag modules, turn On ignition with engine Off.
10. AIR BAG indicator will flash, then AIR BAG indicator will then turn Off.
11. If AIR BAG indicator does not operate as outlined, refer to **MOTOR's "Air Bag Manual" or "Air Bag Diagnostics CD."**

2004-06

1. Remove key from ignition.
2. **To enable passenger roof panel air bag module and passenger seat belt pretensioner,** proceed as follows:
   a. Connect passenger roof panel air bag module connector to vehicle harness connector.
   b. Install CPA to passenger roof panel air bag module connector.
   c. Install rear coat hooks.
   d. Install rear headliner push-in retainers.
   e. Install both lefthand and righthand rear corner trim panels.
   f. Install upper rear window trim panel.
   g. Connect passenger seat belt pretensioner connector and install CPA.
   h. Install passenger lower center pillar trim panel.
3. **To enable passenger roof panel air bag module,** proceed as follows:
   a. Connect passenger roof panel air bag module connector to vehicle harness connector.
   b. Install CPA to passenger roof panel air bag module connector.
   c. Install rear coat hooks.
   d. Install rear headliner push-in retainers.
   e. Install both lefthand and righthand rear corner trim panels.
   f. Install upper rear window trim panel.
4. Install AIR BAG fuse into fuse block.
5. From a position away from air bag modules, turn On ignition with engine Off.
6. AIR BAG indicator will flash, then AIR BAG indicator will then turn Off.
7. If AIR BAG indicator does not operate as outlined, refer to **MOTOR's "Air Bag Manual" or "Air Bag Diagnostics CD."**

ZONE 8

2002-03

1. Remove key from ignition.
2. Connect driver air bag module coil connector to vehicle harness connector.
3. Install CPA to driver air bag module coil connector.
4. Connect driver roof panel air bag module connector to vehicle harness connector.
5. Install CPA to driver roof panel air bag module connector.
6. Connect passenger air bag module connector to vehicle harness connector.
7. Install CPA to passenger air bag module connector.
8. Connect passenger roof panel air bag module connector to vehicle harness connector.
9. Install CPA to passenger roof panel air bag module connector.
10. Install rear coat hooks.
11. Install rear headliner push-in retainers.
12. Install both lefthand and righthand rear corner trim panels.
13. Install upper rear window trim panel.
14. Install AIR BAG fuse into fuse block.
15. From a position away from air bag modules, turn On ignition with engine Off.
16. AIR BAG indicator will flash, then AIR BAG indicator will then turn Off.
17. If AIR BAG indicator does not operate as outlined, refer to **MOTOR's "Air Bag Manual" or "Air Bag Diagnostics CD."**

2004-06

1. Remove key from ignition.
2. Connect driver air bag module coil connector to vehicle harness connector.
3. Install CPA to driver air bag module coil connector.
4. Connect driver seat belt pretensioner connector and install CPA.
5. Install driver lower center pillar trim panel.
6. Connect driver roof panel air bag module connector to vehicle harness connector.
7. Install CPA to driver roof panel air bag module connector.
8. Connect passenger air bag module connector to vehicle harness connector.
9. Install CPA to passenger air bag module connector.
10. Connect passenger seat belt pretensioner connector and install CPA.
11. Install passenger lower center pillar trim panel.
12. Connect passenger roof panel air bag module connector to vehicle harness connector.
13. Install CPA to passenger roof panel air bag module connector.
14. Install rear coat hooks.
15. Install rear headliner push-in retainers.
16. Install both lefthand and righthand rear corner trim panels.
17. Install upper rear window trim panel.
18. Install AIR BAG fuse into fuse block.
19. From a position away from air bag modules, turn On ignition with engine Off.
20. AIR BAG indicator will flash, then AIR BAG indicator will then turn Off.
21. If AIR BAG indicator does not operate as outlined, refer to **MOTOR's "Air Bag Manual" or "Air Bag Diagnostics CD."**

COMPUTER RELEARN PROCEDURE

INDEX

DESCRIPTION

A computer relearn procedure may be required on any vehicle equipped with body, engine or transmission control computers whenever battery power to the computer is interrupted. These computers gather and store information on vehicle operation. They use this information to provide maximum driveability and vehicle performance.

DAIMLERCHRYSLER CORP.

Engine Performance

The PCM receives input signals from various switches and sensors. Based on these inputs, the PCM adjusts fuel injector pulse width, idle speed, ignition timing and canister purge operation. If the battery is disconnected, the PCM will need to relearn values sent by the sensors and switches. During the PCM relearning period, a change may be noted in vehicle performance. To allow the PCM to relearn its values, ensure engine is at operating temperature. Drive the vehicle at part throttle, with moderate acceleration and idle conditions until normal performance returns.

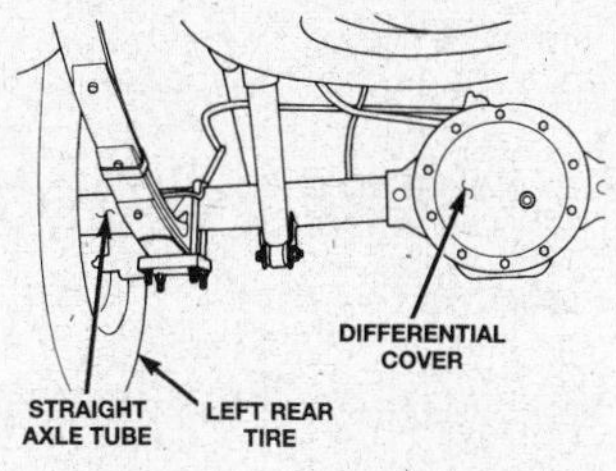

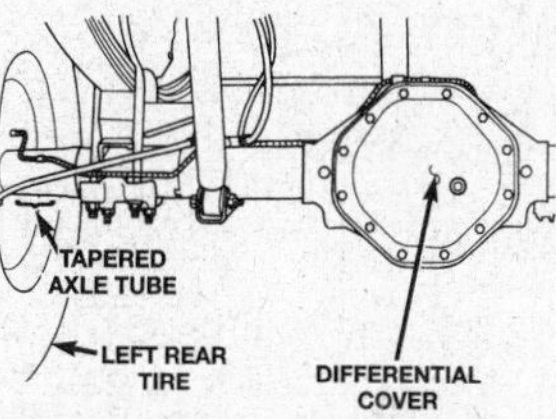

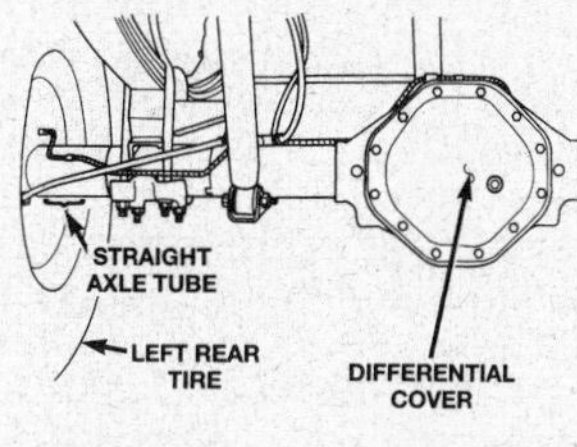

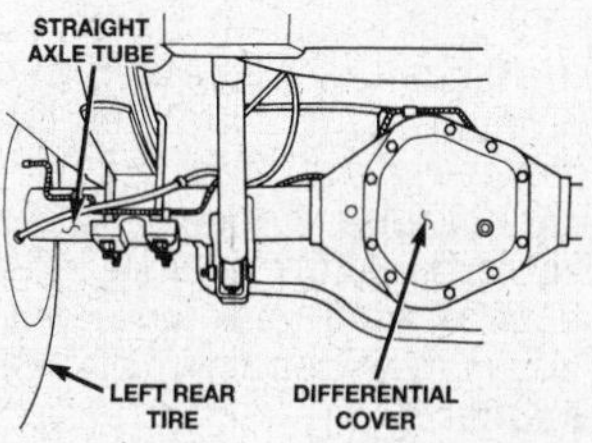

Fig. 1 Rear axle identification. Dakota, Durango, Ram Pick-Up & Ram Van

Transaxle Quick Learn Procedure

The transaxle quick learn procedure requires the use of a DRB III scan tool, or equivalent. This program allows the electronic transaxle system to calibrate itself. Use the following procedure whenever the transaxle assembly, transaxle control module, solenoid pack, clutch plate, clutch plate seal or valve body are replaced.

1. To perform the quick learn procedure, the following conditions must be met:
   a. Brakes must be applied.
   b. Engine speed must be above 500 RPM.
   c. Throttle angle (TPS) must be less than 3°F.
   d. Shift lever position must remain same except when prompted to change position by scan tool.
   e. Calculated oil temperature must be below 200°F and above 60°F.
2. Connect scan tool to Data Link Connector (DLC).
3. Go to transmission screen.
4. Go to miscellaneous screen.
5. Select quick learn procedure.
6. Follow scan tool instructions to perform procedure.

Powertrain Control Module (PCM)

When the PCM is replaced, the new PCM must be programmed using the DRB, or equivalent, scan tool with the original vehicles identification number and the vehicles original miles.

Controller Anti-Lock Brakes (CAB)

DAKOTA, DURANGO, RAM PICK-UP & RAM VAN

If the CAB unit is replaced, the rear axle type and tire revolutions per mile must be programmed into the new CAB unit. Failure to properly program a new CAB unit will result in a blinking ABS light.

1. Place ignition in Off position.
2. Replace CAB unit.
3. Inspect connectors and clean and repair if required.
4. Connect DRB, or equivalent, scan tool to Data Link Connector (DLC).
5. If tire size and rear axle are known,

Fig. 1, select MISC, then MODULE REPLACEMENT.

6. If tire size and rear axle are not known, proceed as follows:
   a. Select MISC, then SET PINION FACTOR on DRB.
   b. If vehicle does not have standardized tires listed on DRB menu, install production size tires.
   c. If size of tires is not known, inspect rear tires for size printed on side wall.
   d. Place ignition in On position with engine Off.
   e. Program tire size into DRB.
   f. Program correct rear axle into DRB.
   g. Road test vehicle above 30 mph for two minutes, then inspect for DTC's. If DTC's are present, refer to "Anti-Lock Brakes" chapter in this manual.

Pinion Factor Procedure

The pinion factor must be set any time the transaxle control module is replaced. This will ensure speedometer readings are correct. The DRB III scan tool, or equivalent, is required to perform this procedure. Failure to perform this procedure could result in an inoperative speedometer. Perform the pinion factor procedure as follows:

1. Connect scan tool to Data Link Connector (DLC).
2. Select transmission menu.
3. Select miscellaneous menu.
4. Select Pinion Factor.
5. Follow scan tool instructions to perform procedure.

Shift Quality

This procedure must be performed whenever battery voltage is interrupted to the Transmission Control Module (TCM) or any transmission internal components are replaced. A Chrysler Diagnostic Readout Box (DRB), or equivalent, scan tool with the specified transmission cartridge must be used to perform this procedure.

1. To perform shift quality reset procedure, following conditions must exist:
   a. Transmission oil temperature must be between 60–200°F (16–94°C).
   b. Engine speed greater than 500 RPM.
   c. Throttle angle less than 3°F.
2. Connect DRB, or equivalent, scan tool to DLC. DLC is located under lefthand side of instrument panel, near top of brake pedal.
3. With correct cartridge installed, select "ADJUSTMENTS" function.
4. Apply brakes and select "QUICK LEARN" function.
5. Place gearshift in NEUTRAL, then "OD" when indicated.
6. Wait until "TEST COMPLETE" is indicated by DRB.
7. Place gearshift in PARK, release brakes and disconnect DRB.

Theft Alarm

This procedure must be done any time the battery is disconnected or the battery is boosted. If the theft alarm is not reset, the alarm system will power up and the vehicle will not start.

1. Before reconnecting battery or connecting booster cables to battery, insert door key into driver side door lock.
2. Connect battery or booster cables and cycle driver door lock once.
3. Vehicle can now be started.

FORD MOTOR CO.

Disconnect battery ground for a minimum of five minutes. After clearing memory, it is required to drive vehicle a minimum of 10 miles to allow processor time to relearn values.

GENERAL MOTORS CORP.

Engine Performance

The PCM/VCM has a learning ability which allows it to make corrections for minor variations in the fuel system to improve driveability. If the battery is disconnected, the learning process resets and begins again. A change may be noted in the vehicle performance. To enact PCM/VCM relearn procedures, ensure engine is at operating temperature. Drive the vehicle at part throttle, with moderate acceleration and idle conditions until normal performance returns. To relearn idle, the engine should be idled in Drive with all accessories off until the vehicle reaches operating temperature and the cooling fan cycles twice.

PCM/VCM

PCM

C & K TRUCKS w/DIESEL ENGINE

1. Perform set up.
   a. Battery is charged.
   b. Ignition is on.
   c. Battery/cigar lighter connection secure.
   d. Data Link Connector attached.
2. Perform programming. Refer to up to date Techline terminal/equipment, or equivalent, for user instructions.
3. After vehicle has been programmed, operate vehicle until coolant temperature is greater than 170°F. This will allow TDC Offset to be programmed.
4. Inspect data list for a TDC Offset.
5. If PCM fails to reprogram, proceed as follows:
   a. Inspect all PCM connections.
   b. Inspect Techline terminal/equipment, or equivalent, for latest software version.
   c. Try again to reprogram PCM. If it fails again, replace PCM.

BODY CONTROL MODULE (BCM)

The BCM must be programmed with proper RPO configurations. The BCM stores information regarding vehicle options and if not programmed properly, the BCM will not control features properly.

1. Ensure following conditions:
   a. Battery is fully charged.
   b. Ignition switch is in Run position.
   c. Data Link Connector (DLC) is accessible.
2. Follow instructions on Techline Terminal and scan tool to program BCM.
3. If BCM fails to accept program, proceed as follows:
   a. Inspect all BCM connections.
   b. Ensure Techline Terminal and scan tool have latest software version.

VCM

EEPROM

1. Perform set up.
   a. Battery is charged.
   b. Ignition is on.
   c. Battery/cigar lighter connection secure.
   d. Data Link Connector attached.
2. Perform programming. Refer to up to date Techline terminal/equipment, or equivalent, for user instructions.
3. If VCM fails to reprogram, proceed as follows:
   a. Inspect all VCM connections.
   b. Inspect Techline terminal/equipment, or equivalent, for latest software version.
   c. Try again to reprogram VCM. If it fails again, replace VCM.

TDC Offset Adjustment

C & K SERIES w/DIESEL ENGINE

The PCM will automatically activate the TDC offset program when the engine coolant is greater than 170°F. If the PCM is not programmed with a TDC offset, a DTC P1214 will set.

Crankshaft Position System Variation Learn

While the learn procedure is in progress, release throttle immediately when the engine starts to decelerate. The engine control is returned to the operator and the engine will respond to throttle position after the learn procedure is complete.

If the CKP system variation learn procedure cannot be completed successfully, refer to the **MOTOR's "Domestic Engine Performance & Driveability Manual"** for DTC P1336 for more information.

1. Install scan tool, then apply parking brake.
2. Block drive wheels and close hood.
3. Place vehicle in Park or Neutral.

4. Idle engine until coolant temperature reaches 150°F.
5. Turn Off all accessories, then enable "Crankshaft Position System Variation Learn Procedure" with scan tool.
6. Apply brakes for duration of procedure, then slowly raise engine speed to 4000 RPM.
7. Immediately release throttle when engine speed decreases, then turn Off ignition for 15 seconds after learn procedure is completed successfully.

Passlock Learn Procedure

WITH TECHLINE TERMINAL & SCAN TOOL

Follow instructions displayed on Techline Terminal in Service Programming System (SPS) and the scan tool for programming procedure.

AUTO LEARN PASSLOCK PROCEDURE

1. Place ignition to RUN position.
2. Turn ignition to CRANK position, then release to RUN position. **Do not start vehicle.**
3. After ignition has been in RUN position for 10 minutes, security indicator lamp will cycle from On to Off.
4. Repeat steps 2 and 3 two more times.
5. After three consecutive cycles of ignition switch are completed, vehicle will learn new component on next ignition lock cylinder cycle from Off position to CRANK position, then to RUN position. Vehicle will then start.
6. Erase Diagnostic Trouble Codes (DTC).

SERVICE REMINDER & WARNING LAMP RESET PROCEDURES

TABLE OF CONTENTS

DaimlerChrysler

INDEX

AIR BAG INDICATOR LAMP

The air bag indicator lamp lights for 6–8 seconds each time the ignition switch is turned on. The light indicates a system self-test is being performed by the air bag control module. If the lamp remains on after the self-test or comes on while driving, an air bag system fault has been detected and the air bag may be inoperative.

ANTI-LOCK BRAKE SYSTEM WARNING INDICATORS

Light Trucks & Vans

The amber lamp monitors anti-lock brake system condition. The lamp will be on during engine starting, but should go off when the self-diagnostic system determines proper system operation. If the lamp remains On, a fault in the anti-lock brake system is indicated. After diagnosis and repair of the system, the lamp may be turned off by disconnecting and reconnecting the anti-lock brake system control module electrical connector or the battery ground cable. The anti-lock brake system control module is located in the passenger compartment and can be accessed after removing the righthand cowl cover.

Jeep

Red and yellow indicator lamps are used to warn of system faults. The red lamp warns of such faults as low brake fluid level, parking brake On, system pressure differential and other system faults. The red indicator lamp will be illuminated for approximately two seconds during engine starting and should go off, unless parking brake is applied or a problem in the brake system exist. The red indicator lamp will reset after repairs to system have been completed and system has returned to normal operation.

The yellow lamp monitors anti-lock brake system condition. The yellow lamp will be On during engine starting, but should go off when the self-diagnostic system determines proper system operation. If yellow lamp remains On, a fault in the anti-lock brake system is indicated. After diagnosis and repair of the system, the yellow lamp may be turn off by cycling the ignition switch off then on. If yellow lamp remains on, it may be required to disconnect and reconnect the battery ground cable.

CHECK CARB LAMP

1980 4-151 CJ

CALIFORNIA MODELS

When the C4 self-diagnostic system detects a problem, the Check Carb lamp on the instrument will be illuminated. After diagnosing and servicing the vehicle, the Check Carb lamp can be reset by disconnecting and reconnecting the battery ground cable.

CHECK ENGINE LAMP

Fuel Injected Engine

The Check Engine lamp will be illuminated for approximately three seconds after

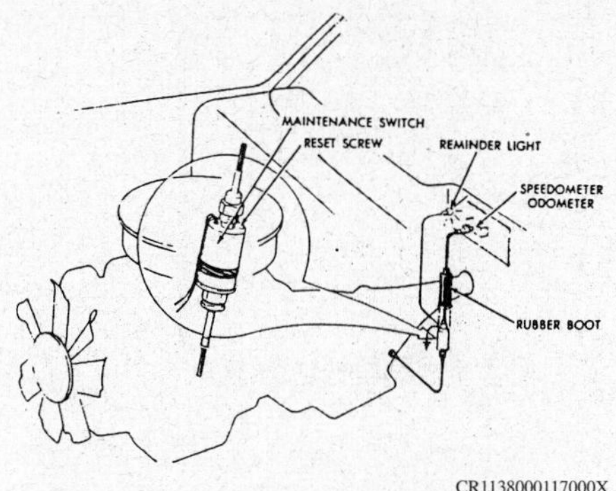

CR1138000117000X

Fig. 1 Emission maintenance reminder system (mechanical type). 1980 Dodge & Plymouth

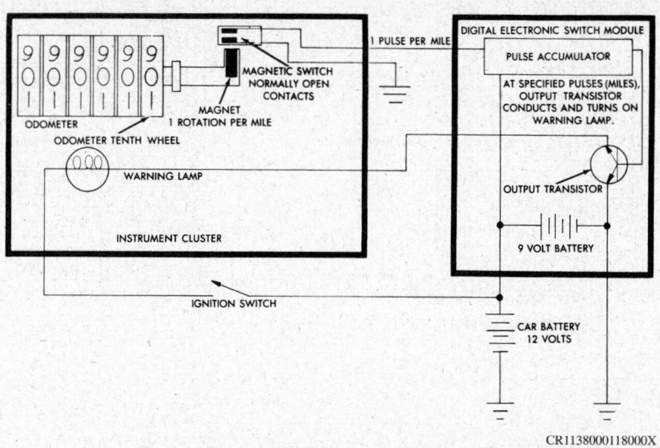

CR1138000118000X

Fig. 2 Emission maintenance reminder system (electronic type). 1980–87 Dodge & Plymouth

the ignition switch has been placed in the On position as a bulb inspection. If incorrect or no signals are received by the Single Module Engine Controller (SMEC) from various sensors, the engine controller will illuminate the Check Engine lamp. After diagnosing and servicing the fuel injection system or emission related systems, the memory will be cleared after approximately 20–100 ignition key on-off cycles or by using the Diagnosis Readout Box II (DRB II) and selecting the fault code erasure mode.

Less Fuel Injected Engine

Refer to "Malfunction Indicator Light" for procedure.

EMISSION MAINTENANCE REMINDER INDICATOR

Chrysler Town & Country, Dodge B Series Vans, Caravan, Dakota, D & W 100-400 & 3500 Series, Mini Ram Van, Ramcharger, Plymouth Trailduster & Voyager

1980

At 30,000 mile intervals, an instrument panel warning lamp will light to indicate need for oxygen sensor replacement. The reminder can either be mechanical, **Fig. 1**, or electronic, **Fig. 2.** After performing the required service, the reminder lamp must be reset.

On the mechanical system, rotate the reset screw located on the switch counterclockwise until it stops, **Fig. 3.**

On the electronic system, remove nine volt battery from module, which is located under the lefthand side of the instrument panel. Insert a suitable rod into hole on module case to reset switch. After resetting switch, install a replacement nine volt battery.

1981-87

This reminder **Fig. 4,** uses mileage impulse counting contacts to calculate maintenance intervals. On front wheel drive van models, the module is located in the upper center of the instrument cluster behind the fuel gauge. On Dakota models, the module is located to the right of the glove compartment. On rear wheel drive van models, the module is located on or near the brake pedal support, **Fig. 5.** On 1981–86 D and W Series pickup trucks and Ramcharger and Trailduster models, the module is located to the right of the steering column. On 1987 D and W Series pickup trucks and Ramcharger models, the module is located to the right of the glove compartment, **Fig. 6.**

After required emission maintenance has been performed, reset module as follows:

1. Slide module from bracket.
2. Insert a small screwdriver into small hole on module case and close switch.
3. Remove module battery cover and install a replacement nine volt battery.
4. Position module on mounting bracket.

1988

This reminder system uses ignition "On" time to calculate maintenance intervals. On front wheel drive van models less tachometer, the module is located in the upper center of the instrument cluster behind the fuel gauge, **Fig. 7.** On front wheel drive van models equipped with tachometer, the module is located behind the tachometer. On Dakota models, the module is located behind the instrument panel on a bracket below the headlamp switch. On rear wheel drive van models, the module is located on or near the brake pedal support, **Fig. 5.** On D and W Series pickup trucks and Ramcharger models, the module is located to the right of the glove compartment, **Fig. 6.**

After required emission maintenance has been performed, reset module by inserting a small screwdriver blade into the hole on module case to depress the reset button.

1989

This reminder system uses ignition "On" time to calculate maintenance intervals. After required emission maintenance has been performed, connect Diagnosis Read-Out Box II (DRB II) to the on-board diagnostic connector, **Figs. 8 through 12.** Follow instructions indicated by DRB II tool.

1990-99

This Emission Maintenance Reminder System (Maintenance Required Lamp) is incorporated into the engine controller. The controller stores vehicle mileage into its memory every eight miles, then at 60,000, 82,500 or 120,000 miles it will light the EMR (Maintenance Required) lamp. When the indicated mileage is reached or the EMR lamp is on at all times the following components must be replaced and the EMR lamp reset.

1. At 60,00 miles, proceed as follows:
   a. Replace EGR valve.
   b. Clean EGR passage.
   c. Replace PCV valve.
2. At 82,500 miles, replace oxygen sensor.
3. At 120,000 miles, proceed as follows:
   a. Replace EGR valve.
   b. Clean EGR passage.
   c. Replace PCV valve.
4. **On 1990–95 models,** after required emission maintenance has been performed, connect Diagnosis Read-Out Box II (DRB II) to the on board diagnosis connector, **Figs. 8 through 13.**
5. **On 1996–99 models,** after required emission maintenance has been performed, connect Diagnosis Read-Out Box II (DRB II) to the on board DLC located under lefthand side of instrument panel.
6. **On all models,** follow instructions indicated by DRB II tool.

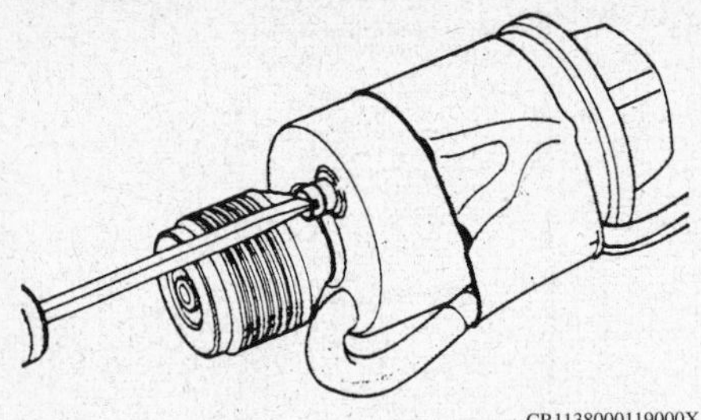

Fig. 3 Resetting maintenance reminder switch (mechanical type). 1980 Dodge & Plymouth

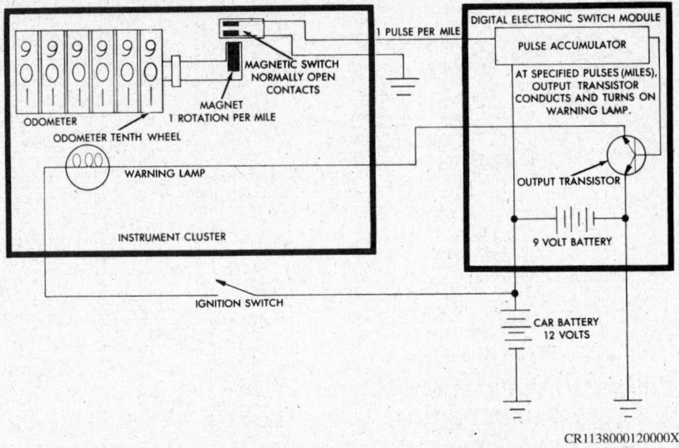

Fig. 4 Emission maintenance reminder system. 1984–87 Dodge Caravan, Dakota, Mini Ram Van & Plymouth Voyager

Jeep

1981-83 CJ 2.5L & SCRAMBLER CALIFORNIA MODELS

At 30,000 mile intervals, an instrument panel warning lamp will light to indicate oxygen sensor service. After performing the required service, the reminder lamp may be reset by rotating the reset screw located on the switch counterclockwise 1/4 turn, **Fig. 3.**

1988-90 COMANCHE, CHEROKEE, WAGONEER & WRANGLER

The emission maintenance timer will light an instrument cluster indicator lamp when vehicle mileage has reached 82,500 miles. At this time, the oxygen sensor and PCV valve should be replaced, in addition to the other required emission maintenance scheduled for this mileage.

If the timer should fail before vehicle has accumulated 82,500 miles, the timer and oxygen sensor should both be replaced to maintain a proper sensor replacement interval.

After performing the required service, replace the emission maintenance timer as follows:

1. **On Comanche, Cherokee and Wagoneer models,** emission maintenance timer is located under instrument panel to right of steering column. On Wrangler models, timer is located under instrument panel to the right of accelerator pedal.
2. **On Comanche, Cherokee and Wagoneer models,** remove cruise control module attaching screws, then remove module, if equipped.
3. **On all models,** remove emission maintenance timer to instrument panel bracket attaching screws.
4. Remove timer, then disconnect electrical connector, **Figs. 14 and 15.**
5. Connect electrical connector to replacement timer, then position timer to dash panel and install and tighten attaching screws.

1991-92 COMANCHE, CHEROKEE & WRANGLER

The emission maintenance timer will light an indicator lamp on the instrument cluster when vehicle mileage has reached 82,500 miles. At this time, the oxygen sensor and other scheduled emission maintenance is required.

If the timer should fail before vehicle has accumulated 82,500 miles, the timer and oxygen sensor should both be replaced to maintain a proper sensor replacement interval. After required emission maintenance has been performed, connect Diagnosis Read-Out Box II (DRB II) to the on board diagnosis connector, **Figs. 16 and 17.** Follow instructions indicated by DRB II tool.

MALFUNCTION INDICATOR LIGHT

1993-94 w/California Emissions & 1995-99

The Powertrain Control Module (PCM) performs an On-Board Diagnostic (OBD) inspection of the EGR system on all California Vehicles. The diagnostic system uses the electronic EGR Transducer (EET) for the system tests.

The OBD inspection activates only during selected engine/driving conditions. When the conditions are met, the PCM energizes the EET solenoid to disable the EGR. The PCM inspects for a change in the oxygen sensor signal. If the air/fuel mixture goes lean, the PCM will attempt to enrich the mixture. The PCM registers a Diagnostic Trouble Code (DTC) if the EGR system has failed or degraded. After registering a DTC, the PCM turns the MALFUNCTION INDICATOR LAMP (MIL) on. (The malfunction indicator lamp was formerly referred to as the Check Engine Lamp). The MIL indicates the need for immediate service.

If a fault is indicated by the MIL and a DTC for the EGR system was set, inspect for proper operation of the EGR system. If the EGR system tests properly, inspect the system using the DRB II scan tool.

Ram Raider & Ram 50

The malfunction indicator light will come on when an irregularity is found in one or more of the following components: engine control unit, injector, fuel pump, or in the oxygen, air flow, intake air temperature, throttle position, engine coolant temperature, crank angle, top dead center or barometric pressure sensors.

When an irregular signal returns to normal or is repaired and the engine control unit judges that it has returned to normal, the malfunction indicator light will turn Off. When the ignition switch is turned Off then malfunction indicator light will turn off until such time as the irregular signal is detected again.

MAINTENANCE REMINDER LAMP/ INDICATOR

1985-87 Ram 50 & 1987 Ram Raider

An EGR warning light on the dash will become illuminated at 50,000 miles to alert the driver to have EGR system inspected and/or serviced.

Following inspection and performance of any needed maintenance, reset mileage sensor. Reset switch is located on the back of instrument panel either to the left of or below speedometer cable junction, **Figs. 18 through 20.** Slide switch to the opposite position to reset sensor lamp.

VEHICLE INFORMATION CENTER (VIC)

Grand Cherokee

1998

The Vehicle Information Center (VIC) is optional on these models and mounts in the instrument panel lower center stack area, above the ashtray and below the HVAC controls. Among its features are reminders for service and distances to the next service interval.

The VIC receives inputs from hard-wired sensors and over the Chrysler Collision Detection (CCD) data bus network.

The "Perform Service" message will display if "Miles/Kms To Service" is zero to indicate that regular service and maintenance are due. The "xxx Miles to Service" message will light each time the vehicle is started.

To reset the counter, turn the ignition On, momentarily press the SELECT button (only if "Miles/Kms To Service" is not currently displayed), then press and hold the SET button for at least two seconds.

This device cannot be repaired. If it has been damaged or proven faulty, the entire module will need replacement.

1999–2006

1. Place ignition in On position.
2. Depress and release menu push button to display first programmable feature.
3. Momentarily depress and release menu push button to step through programmable features list.
4. Momentarily depress and release step push button to step through available options for the following programmable features:
   a. Language.
   b. Display U.S. or metric.
   c. Auto door locks.
   d. Remote unlock.
   e. Remote linked to memory.
   f. Sound horn on lock?
   g. Flash lights with lock?
   h. Headlamp delay and headlamps on with wipers.
   i. Service Intervals.
   j. Reset service distance?
   k. Low fuel chime?
   l. Easy exit seat.
5. Option that lasts appears in display with programmable feature before exiting programming mode becomes newly selected programmable feature option.
6. Electronic Vehicle Information Center (EVIC) exits programming mode and returns to normal operating mode when C/T button is depressed or when end of programmable features menu list is reached.

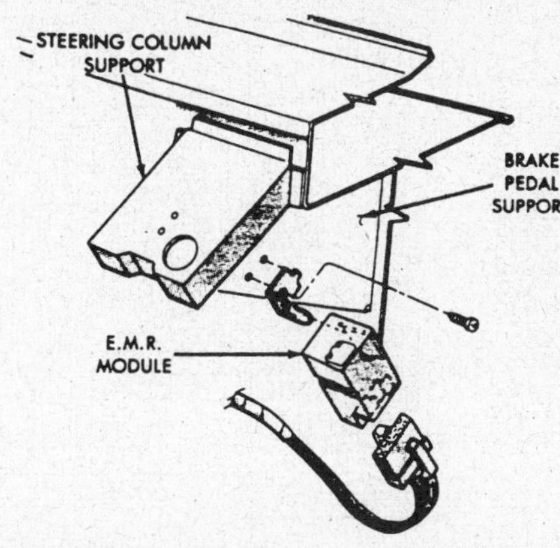

Fig. 5 Emission maintenance reminder module location. Dodge & Plymouth B Series rear wheel drive vans

VEHICLE MAINTENANCE MONITOR

1993–95 Grand Cherokee & Grand Wagoneer

The vehicle maintenance monitor will display a "Perform Service" message at intervals ranging from 2000–7500 miles, depending on the initial operator system setup. To reset the "Perform Service" message after repairs have been performed, depress the SELECT button, then press the SET button.

MAINTENANCE REQUIRED LAMP

Ram Raider

1988

At mileage intervals of 50,000 and 100,000 the Maintenance Required lamp will be illuminated. At 100,000 miles, the bulb should be removed from the Maintenance Required lamp. After performing the required service, reset switch located at rear of instrument cluster to turn lamp off, **Fig. 19.**

1989

At mileage intervals of 50,000, 80,000 and 100,000 the Maintenance Required lamp will be illuminated. At mileage above 120,000 miles, the bulb should be removed from the Maintenance Required lamp. After performing the required service, reset switch located at rear of instrument cluster to turn lamp off, **Fig. 19.**

Ram 50

1988

At mileage intervals of 50,000 and 100,000 the Maintenance Required lamp will be illuminated. At 100,000 miles, the bulb should be removed from the Maintenance Required lamp. After performing the required service, reset switch located at front of instrument cluster to turn lamp off, **Fig. 20.**

1989–93

At mileage intervals of 50,000, 80,000 and 100,000 the Maintenance Required lamp will be illuminated. At mileage above 120,000 miles, the bulb should be removed from the Maintenance Required lamp. After performing the required service, reset switch located at front of instrument cluster to turn lamp off, **Fig. 20.**

TRANSMISSION TEMPERATURE INDICATOR LAMP

Dodge

This indicator lamp is used on some models equipped with snow plow package. When this lamp is illuminated while operating the vehicle, operate engine at idle speed or fast idle with transmission in Neutral until lamp goes off. If lamp is frequently or continually illuminated, transmission service may be required.

WAIT-TO-START LAMP

The wait-to-start lamp is used on diesel engine models. The lamp is lit by the PCM after the ignition switch is turned to the On position. It gives the driver an indication to wait until the intake manifold air heater grid has had sufficient time to warm the intake air for a good quality start. The intake manifold air preheat cycle is controlled by an electronic air heater control module. The lamp will be turned off when the heating cycle is complete or if the ignition is turned to the Start position prior to the end of the heating cycle.

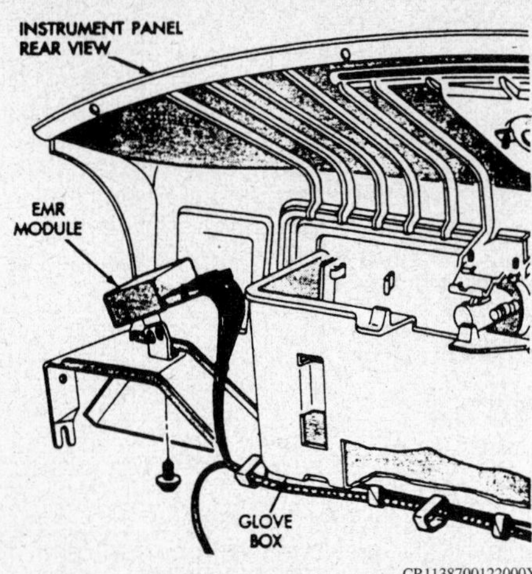

Fig. 6 Emission maintenance reminder module location. 1987–88 Dodge D & W Series

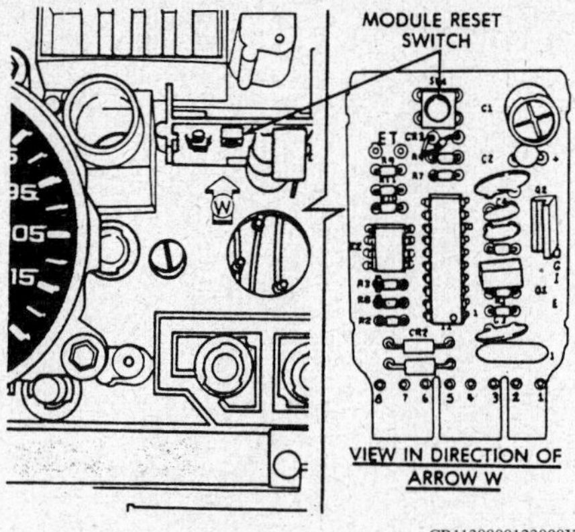

Fig. 7 Emission maintenance reminder module reset switch location. 1988 Dodge Caravan & Plymouth Voyager

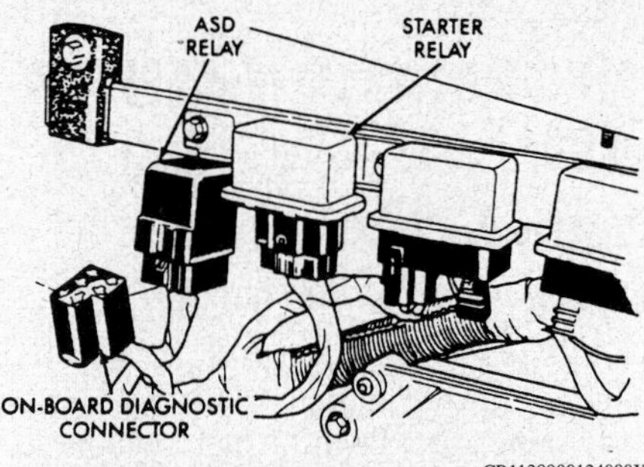

Fig. 8 On board diagnosis connector location. 1989–90 Dodge Caravan & Plymouth Voyager

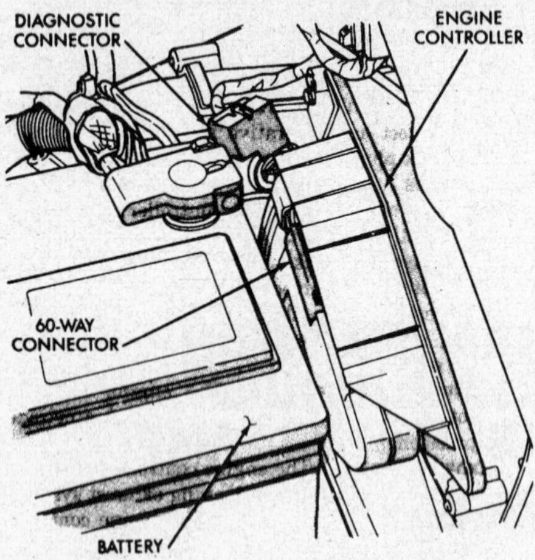

Fig. 9 On board diagnosis connector location. 1991–92 Chrysler Town & Country, Dodge Caravan & Plymouth Voyager

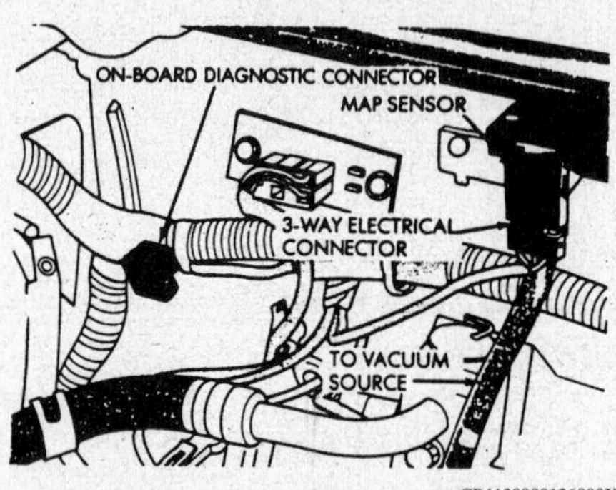

Fig. 10 On board diagnosis connector location. 1989–92 Dodge Dakota

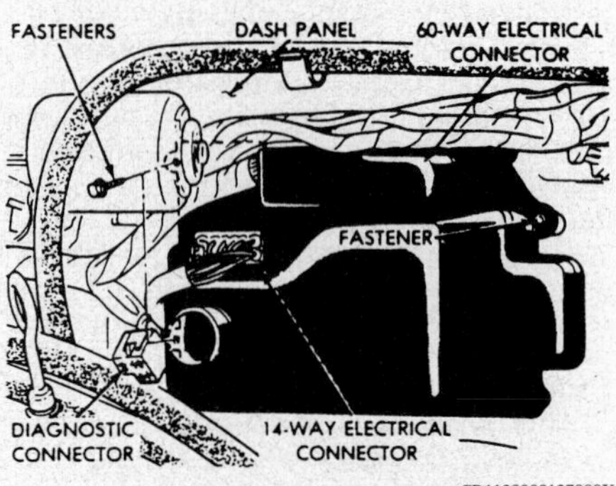

Fig. 11 On board diagnosis connector location. 1989–93 Dodge B Series Vans

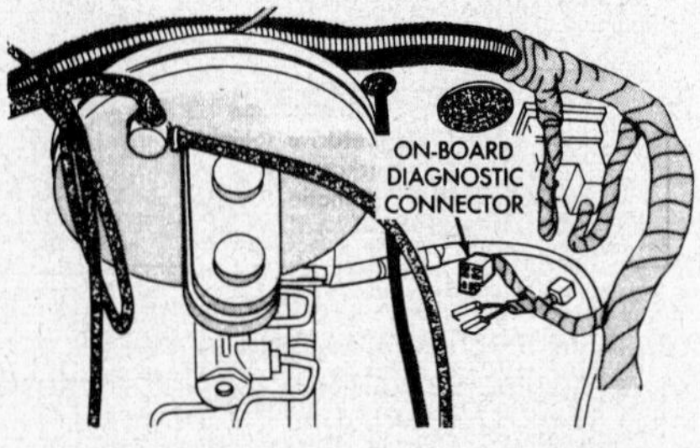

Fig. 12 On board diagnosis connector location. 1989–93 D & W Series & Ramcharger

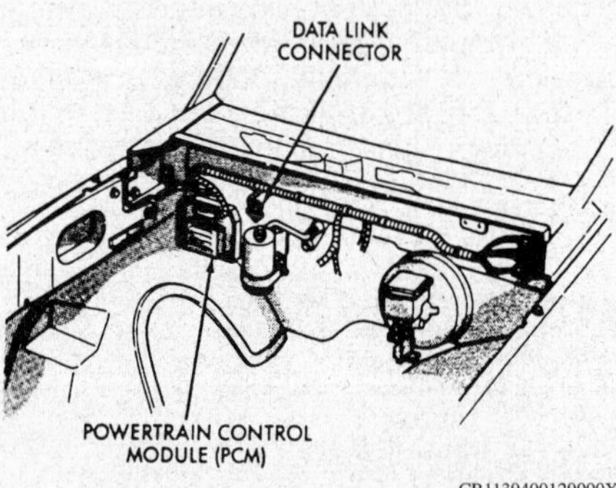

Fig. 13 Data link connector location. 1994–95 Ram Truck 1500–3500

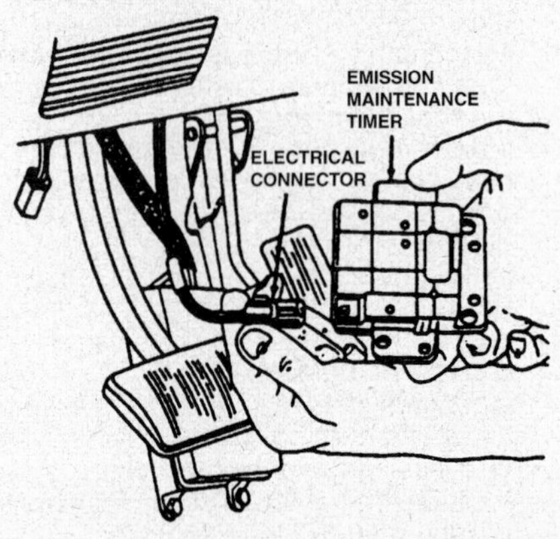

Fig. 14 Emission maintenance timer location. 1988–90 Jeep Cherokee, Comanche & Wagoneer

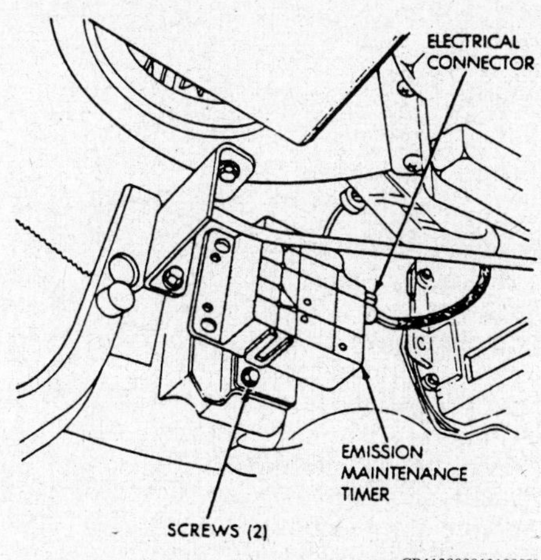

Fig. 15 Emission maintenance timer location. 1988–90 Jeep Wrangler

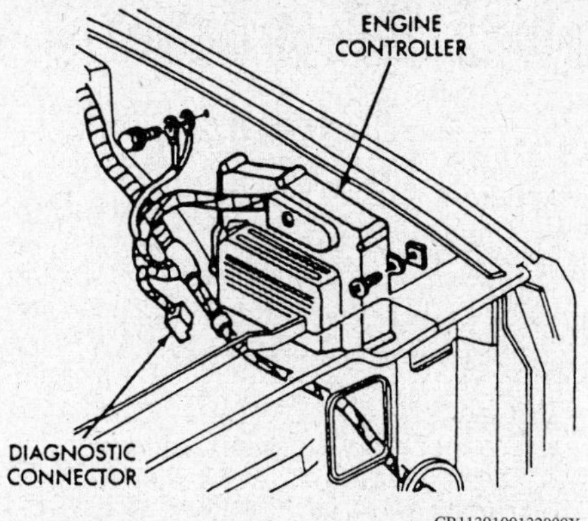

Fig. 16 Diagnostic connector location. 1991–92 Jeep Cherokee & Comanche

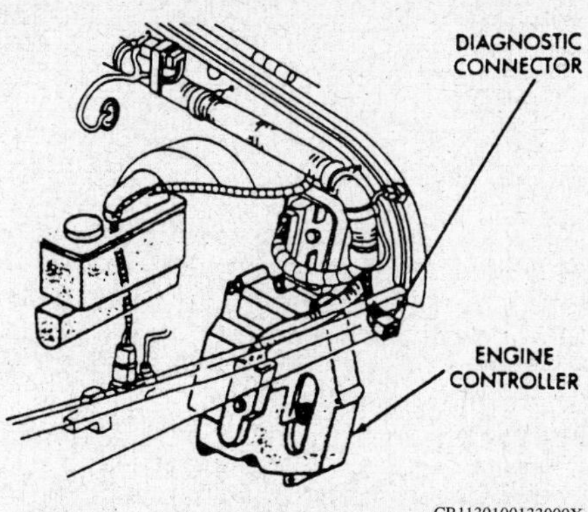

Fig. 17 Diagnostic connector location. 1991–92 Jeep Wrangler

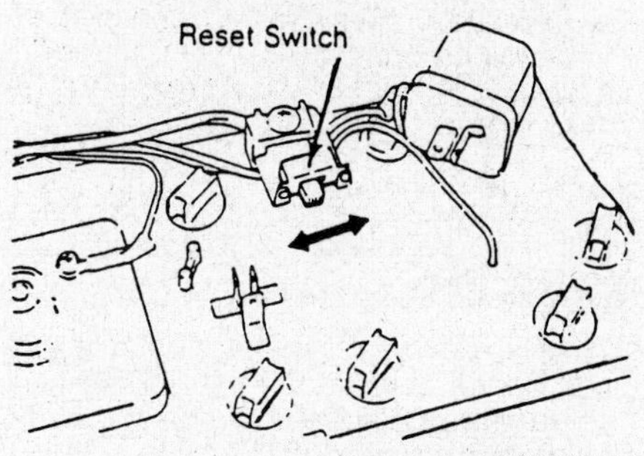

Fig. 18 EGR maintenance reminder lamp reset. 1985–86 Ram 50

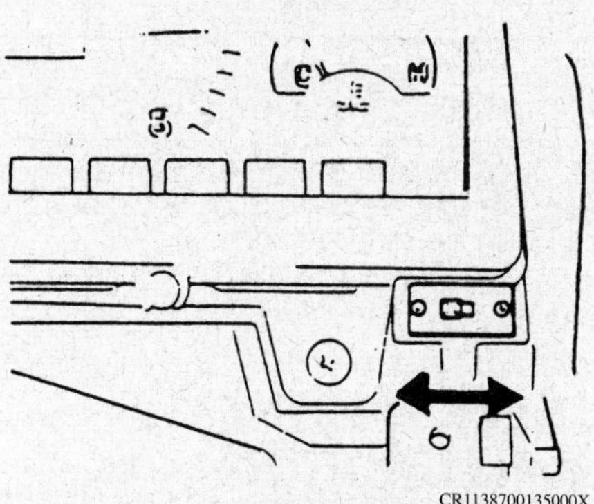

Fig. 19 Resetting EGR/ Maintenance Required reminder lamp. 1987–89 Ram Raider

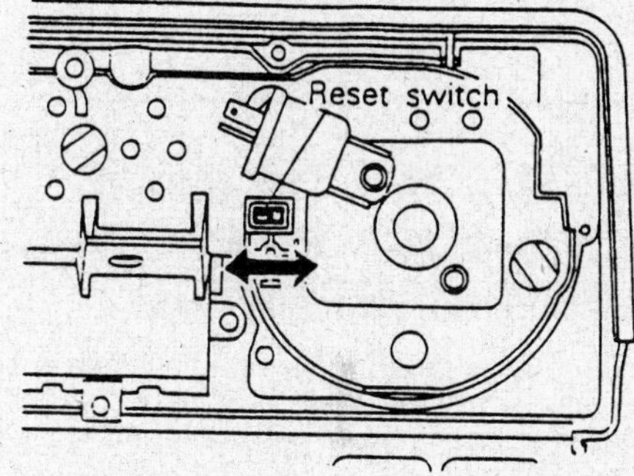

Fig. 20 Resetting EGR/ Maintenance Required reminder lamp. 1987–93 Ram 50

Ford Motor Co.

INDEX

ANTI-LOCK OR REAR ANTI-LOCK BRAKE SYSTEM WARNING

Red and yellow indicator lamps are used to warn of system faults. The red lamp warns of such faults as low brake fluid level, parking brake On, system pressure differential and other system faults. The red indicator lamp will be illuminated for approximately two seconds during engine starting and should go off, unless parking brake is applied or a problem in the brake system exist. The red indicator lamp will reset after repairs to system have been completed and system has returned to normal operation.

The yellow lamp monitors anti-lock brake system condition. The yellow lamp will be on during engine starting, but should go off when the self-diagnostic system determines proper system operation. If yellow lamp remains On, a fault in the anti-lock brake system is indicated. After diagnosis and repair of the system, the yellow may be turn off by cycling the ignition switch Off then On.

CHARGE SYSTEM WARNING INDICATOR

The charge system warning indicator lamps are used to warn of no alternator output. When ignition switch contacts are closed, current flows through charge indicator and parallel resistor to voltage indicator and the indicator lights. When alternator builds enough voltage to energize a circuit in voltage regulator, the indicator will go out.

CHANGE OIL SOON LAMP

Windstar

1. Press RESET and SETUP buttons at same time to activate service mode.
2. Press SETUP to access system inspection, then press RESET to start system inspection.
3. Press and hold RESET button.
4. Press RESET and SETUP buttons for personalized setting.
5. After successfully reset, message center will display oil life reset to 100%.

CHECK ENGINE OR MALFUNCTION INDICATOR LAMP (MIL)

DI Turbo Diesel

STAR II TESTER

Unlatching STAR tester during "fast" code transmission will clear all codes in the PCM. They will be stored in the STAR tester for viewing.

NEW GENERATION STAR (NGS) SCAN TOOL

Select RETRIEVE/CLEAR option from NGS menu for the appropriate test, then press CLEAR ALL button. Diagnostic trouble codes will be cleared from memory.

EEC

EXCEPT MALFUNCTION INDICATOR LIGHT (MIL)

When using NGS tool No. 007-00500, or equivalent, select Diagnostic Test Mode Results, then press CLEAR. Or, disconnect battery ground cable. Codes will be erased from back-up memory after 24 hours.

MALFUNCTION INDICATOR LIGHT

1. Activate diagnostic test mode.
2. Disconnect diagnostic connector.
3. Jump BL/W and GY/BL wires using suitable jumper wires.
4. Wait about two seconds.
5. Remove jumper wire and reconnect diagnostic connector.
6. MIL will stay on, and codes will be erased.

EEC-IV

1988–91

This lamp will be illuminated when the ignition switch is placed in the On position. After engine is started the lamp should go off, unless a problem has been detected by the EEC-IV system. After diagnosis and repair, the Check Engine/MIL lamp will automatically reset when stored codes are cleared from the EEC-IV system memory. After diagnosis and repair, EEC-IV memory may be cleared of stored codes as follows:

1. With ignition switch in Off position, connect a jumper wire between Self Test and Self Test Input (STI) connectors, **Fig. 1.** On Aerostar, Self Test and STI connectors are gray in color and are located on lefthand fender apron, near Electronic Engine Control (EEC) relay. On Bronco and F-Series, Self Test and STI connectors and are located in area of EEC system charcoal canister. On Bronco II, Explorer and Ranger, Self Test connector and STI connector are red in color and they are both located on righthand fender apron near Electronic Engine Control (EEC) relay. On E-Series, Self Test and STI connectors are located on righthand fender apron in area of MAP sensor and starter motor relay.
2. Position ignition switch in On position, then disconnect jumper wire from test connector terminals. Disconnect jumper as soon as Check Engine lamp starts flashing.

1992–97

CONTINUOUS MEMORY

This lamp will be illuminated when the ignition switch is placed in the On position. After the engine is started the lamp should go off, unless a problem has been detected by the EEC-IV system. After diagnosis and repair, the Check Engine/MIL lamp will automatically reset when stored diagnostic trouble codes (DTC's) are cleared from the EEC-IV system memory as follows:

1. Perform Key On Engine Off (KOEO) Self-Test using Super Star II Tester, or equivalent scan tool.
2. When DTC's begin to be displayed, deactivate self-test as follows:
   a. Unlatch center button using **Super Star II Tester.**
   b. Push stop button using **scan tool.**
   c. Remove jumper wire from between self-test input (STI) connector and signal return pin of DLC on all others.

KEEP ALIVE MEMORY (KAM)

Disconnecting the battery ground cable for at least five minutes will also clear PCM memory but will also clear Keep Alive Memory (KAM) which stores certain emission related DTC's. Whenever KAM is cleared, the vehicle must be driven 10 miles or more to allow the PCM to relearn values for optimum driveability.

EEC-V

Codes must be cleared either by performing the PCM reset function of an OBD II scan tool or by disconnecting the battery ground cable for a minimum of five minutes. **Disconnecting the battery ground cable will also clear Keep Alive Memory (KAM) which stores certain emission related DTC's.** Whenever KAM is cleared, the vehicle must be driven 10 miles or more to allow the PCM to relearn values for optimum driveability.

PCM

The PCM Reset allows the scan tool to command the PCM to clear all emission-related diagnostic information. When resetting the PCM, a DTC P1000 will be stored in the PCM until all the OBD II system monitors or components have been tested to satisfy a Trip without any other faults occurring.

1. Following results occur when resetting PCM:
   a. Clears number of DTC's.
   b. Clears DTC's.
   c. Clears freeze frame data.
   d. Clears oxygen sensor test data.
   e. Resets status of OBD II system monitors.
   f. Sets DTC P1000.
2. To reset PCM, perform following:
   a. Connect scan tool to DLC.
   b. Select Vehicle and Engine Selection menu (OPTIONAL).
   c. Select year, model with appropriate qualifier, if needed (transmission, 499 state, California, OPTIONAL).
   d. Follow operating instructions from menu (turn key On).
   e. Select GENERIC OBD II FUNCTIONS. Press CONT button if all OBD II monitors are not complete.
   f. Turn key On.
   g. Select CLEAR DIAGNOSTIC CODES.

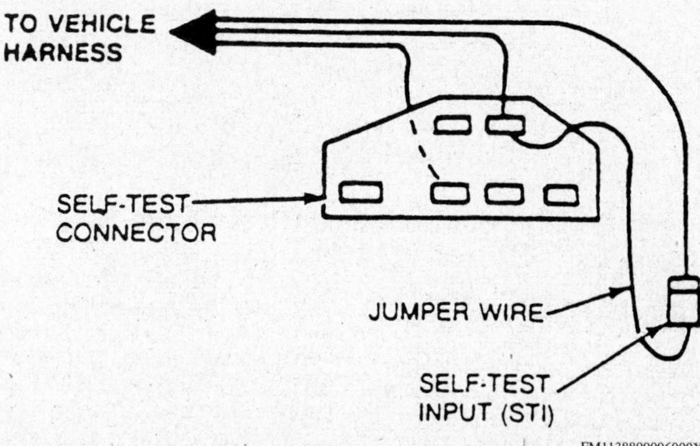

Fig. 1 Jumper wire connections for resetting check engine lamp. EEC-IV

KAM

Disconnect the battery ground cable for a minimum of five minutes (this will also result in PCM reset). Resetting KAM will also clear learned values the PCM has stored for adaptive systems such as idle and Fuel systems. Once the vehicle is driven, the PCM will relearn new adaptive values. It will take a few miles and may run rough until the values are relearned.

EGR INDICATOR LAMP

Courier

After performing the required EGR system maintenance, reset the lamp as follows:

1. Locate switch, which is installed behind speedometer.
2. Remove switch cover, then slide switch knob to opposite position.

EMISSION MAINTENANCE REMINDER LAMP

This lamp will be illuminated after approximately 60,000 miles of operation, **Fig. 2.** The amber lens lamp is located on the instrument panel and has the word Emissions, Emiss or EGR printed on it. On 1988 Ranger models with 2.0L engine, the lamp lens will indicate Check Engine. After performing the required emission control maintenance, the module must be replaced or reset, depending on type of module used. On module equipped with reset feature, reset the module as follows:

1. Place ignition switch in Off position.
2. Insert a suitable Phillips head screwdriver through .2 inch diameter hole located on module near reset sticker and lightly press down and hold.
3. While still lightly pressing down on screwdriver, turn ignition switch to Run position. Emissions maintenance lamp should remain illuminated for as long as screwdriver is pressing down. Hold screwdriver in position for approximately five seconds.
4. Remove screwdriver, lamp should go out after approximately two to five seconds, indicating module has been reset. If lamp fails to go out, repeat reset procedure. Place ignition switch in Off position.
5. Turn ignition switch to Run position and inspect to ensure emission maintenance lamp is illuminated for two to five seconds. After approximately two to five seconds lamp should turn off.

FUEL FILTER WARNING LAMP

Diesel Engine

The fuel filter indicator will be illuminated when fuel filter replacement is required. A vacuum switch located on the fuel filter head, activates the instrument panel lamp. If the lamp is illuminated, replace fuel filter. After replacing fuel filter, the lamp will automatically reset.

FUEL RESET

The FUEL RESET indicator is grounded through the inertia switch whenever vehicle is in a high force situation. The Inertia Fuel Shutoff (IFS) switch cuts off the fuel pump motor. The FUEL RESET indicator illuminates when IFS switch has been tripped.

LOW COOLANT LAMP

This lamp will be illuminated when engine coolant level in the radiator drops below a pre-determined level. To turn lamp off, inspect cooling system, then add coolant to bring system to proper level.

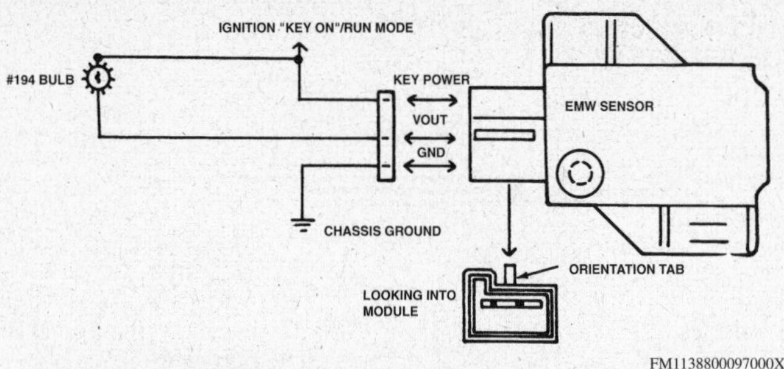

Fig. 2 Emission maintenance reminder lamp system

LOW FUEL INDICATOR

When fuel level drops below a predetermined level, the CHECK GAUGE indicator will light. The CHECK GAUGE indicator will light if engine oil pressure drops below 6 psi, fuel level drops below 1–2 gallons or engine temperature exceeds 250° F.

LOW OIL LEVEL WARNING INDICATOR

This system is used to indicate a low engine oil level condition. The lamp will be illuminated during engine starting. If oil level is sufficient, the lamp will go off when engine is operating. If oil level is low the lamp will remain on until engine oil is added and the ignition switch is placed in the Off position. The module may take a few minutes to reset. If the engine is started during this period, the last recorded reading will be displayed.

REAR LOAD LEVELING (CHECK SUSP)

The CHECK SUSP indicator lights when there is a fault of the rear load leveling system or if the air suspension switch is in the Off position.

SERVICE ENGINE SOON

After the engine is started, the SERVICE ENGINE SOON indicator will cycle for three seconds. If the instrument cluster does not receive a message from the Powertrain Control Module (PCM) within five seconds, the instrument cluster will send two messages to the PCM and attempt to establish communication. If instrument cluster is unable to establish communication it will light the SERVICE ENGINE SOON indicator and record a Diagnostic Trouble Code (DTC).

WATER IN FUEL WARNING LAMP

Diesel Engine

The water in fuel indicator will be illuminated when excessive water has entered the fuel system. As water collects in the fuel filter, a probe located at the water separator section of the filter, will activate the instrument panel lamp. If the lamp is illuminated, drain fuel filter. After fuel filter has been drained, the lamp will automatically reset. If lamp illuminates after drain fuel filter, replacement of fuel filter and or purging of fuel tank may be required.

General Motors Corp.

INDEX

CHECK ENGINE OR SERVICE ENGINE SOON INDICATOR LAMP

Diesel Electronic Control System

The Check Engine Lamp will be illuminated when the ignition switch is placed in the On position. When the engine is started, the lamp should go off. If the lamp remains on after the engine is started, the self diagnosis system has detected a problem and has stored a code in the system Electronic Control Module (ECM). After diagnosis and repair, the ECM memory can be cleared of codes by disconnecting the battery ground cable for approximately 30 seconds with ignition switch in Off position. It should be noted, when battery ground cable is disconnected to clear codes, components such as clocks, electronically tuned radios etc., will have to be reset.

Electronic Engine Controls Or Electronic Fuel Injection

EXCEPT LUV & TRACKER

The Check Engine Lamp will be illuminated when the ignition switch is placed in the On position. When the engine is started, the lamp should go off. If the lamp remains on for 10 seconds or constantly after the engine is started, the self diagnosis system has detected a problem and has stored a code in the system Electronic Control Module (ECM) or Powertrain Control Module (PCM). After diagnosis and repair, the ECM/PCM memory can be cleared of codes either by using a scan tool (OBD II systems) or by disconnecting the battery ground cable for approximately 30 seconds with the ignition switch in the Off position. It should be noted that if the battery ground cable is disconnected to clear codes, components such as clocks, electronically tuned radios etc., will have to be reset.

LUV

The check engine lamp will be illuminated when the ignition switch is in the On position with engine not operating. When engine is started, the Check Engine lamp should go off. If lamp remains on, a code has been stored by the Electronic Control Module (ECM). After diagnosis and repair, place ignition switch in Off position, then clear codes stored in the ECM memory by removing the Emission or ECM fuse, located on the fuse box in engine compartment, for approximately ten seconds.

TRACKER

FEDERAL MODELS

The Check Engine lamp will be illuminated when the ignition switch is in the On position with engine not operating. When engine is started, the Check Engine lamp should go off. If lamp remains on, either a service interval is indicated or a code has been stored by the Electronic Control Module (ECM) memory.

At mileage intervals of 50,000, 80,000 and 100,000 miles, the Check Engine lamp will be illuminated indicating required service and maintenance is to be performed. After performing the required service, the lamp may be turned off by resetting the cancel switch located on the instrument panel.

If a service code has been stored in the ECM memory, perform diagnosis and repair, then place ignition switch in Off position and clear codes stored in the ECM memory by disconnecting the battery ground cable for approximately 20 seconds.

CALIFORNIA MODELS

The Check Engine lamp will be illuminated when the ignition switch is in the On position with engine not operating. When engine is started, the Check Engine lamp should go off. If lamp remains on, a code has been stored by the Electronic Control Module (ECM) memory. After diagnosis and repair, place ignition switch in Off position, then clear codes stored in the ECM memory by disconnecting the battery ground cable, for approximately 20 seconds.

BRAKE WARNING LAMP

Tracker

The electronic brake control module (EBCM) contains the rear wheel anti-lock (RWAL) self-diagnosis programming. Should a failure be detected, the EBCM sets a trouble code and will cause the "BRAKE" warning lamp to illuminate and the RWAL brake system operation will cease its operation.

After the RWAL system is repaired, erase codes by enabling flash code diagnostics as follows:

1. Release parking brake and block drive wheels.
2. Ensure brake fluid level in reservoir is adequate.
3. Turn ignition switch to On position.
4. Connector together for more than two seconds using a jumper wire, short terminals 3 and 5 of diagnostic.
5. After flash code diagnostic mode has been entered, turn ignition switch to Off position.

CHOKE OR OIL/CHOKE WARNING LAMP

Carbureted Engine

On models less gauges, the oil/choke warning indicator lamp should be illuminated when the ignition switch is in the Run or Start position. When the engine is started, the choke warning indicator lamp should go off. If the lamp fails to illuminate with ignition switch in Run or Start position, with engine not operating, a burnt out bulb or fuse or defect in choke electrical system is indicated. If lamp remains on after engine has been started, a problem in the engine oil pressure system or electrical choke system exist.

On models equipped with gauges, the choke warning indicator lamp should be illuminated when the ignition switch is in the Run or Start position. When the engine is started, the choke warning indicator lamp should go off. If the lamp fails to illuminate with ignition switch in Run or Start position, with engine not operating, a burnt out bulb or fuse or defect in choke electrical system is indicated. If lamp remains on after engine has been started, a problem in the alternator circuit is indicated.

After service has been completed, the lamp operation should return to normal.

EMISSION OR SENSOR MAINTENANCE REMINDER FLAG

1980 Caballero & El Camino

At 30,000 mile intervals, an Emission or Sensor reminder flag, if equipped, will appear across the odometer to indicate the need for oxygen sensor replacement. After performing the required service, the flag must be reset for the next 30,000 mile interval. This is accomplished by gaining access to the speedometer head and removing the speedometer lens. Using a suitable pointed tool, rotate edge of flag wheel detents downward, until flag wheel can no longer be rotated. Flag wheel alignment mark should center in odometer.

LOW COOLANT LAMP

This lamp will be illuminated when engine coolant level in the radiator drops below a pre-determined level. To turn lamp off, inspect cooling system, then add coolant to bring system to proper level.

MALFUNCTION INDICATOR LAMP (MIL)

Tracker w/Federal Emissions

The MIL lamp will flash or illuminate at 50,000, 80,000 and 100,000 miles to indicate emission maintenance is required.

1989-91

After performing the required maintenance the MIL lamp may be reset by moving cancel switch to opposite position. The MIL cancel switch is located behind the access panel below the steering column.

1992-95

After performing the required maintenance, reset the MIL cancel switch. The MIL cancel switch is located behind the instrument panel (attached to instrument panel next to left speaker).

WATER IN FUEL OR DRAIN FUEL FILTER WARNING LAMP

Diesel Engine

The water in fuel indicator will be illuminated when excessive water has entered the fuel system. As the fuel filter becomes plugged, a low pressure sensor activates the lamp. The lamp will be illuminated during engine starting as a bulb inspect. Once the engine has started, the lamp should go off. If the lamp is illuminated intermittently, drain fuel filter. If lamp remains illuminated, drain fuel filter. If the lamp still remains on after fuel filter has been drained, replace fuel filter. If lamp is illuminated during high speed operation or during heavy acceleration, replace fuel filter. If after starting, the engine stalls and will not restart and lamp remains illuminated, inspect for plugged fuel filter or fuel lines. If this condition occurs immediately after refueling, inspect fuel tank for large concentration of water in fuel, and if required purge fuel tank and replace fuel filter. After performing the required service, the increased fuel pressure through the fuel filter will reset the water in fuel lamp.

ENGINE OIL LIFE MONITOR

The engine oil life monitor will indicate when to change engine oil usually between 3000–10,000 miles since last oil change. Under severe conditions, the CHANGE OIL SOON light may be displayed before 3000 miles. Vehicle must not be driven more than 10,000 miles or 12 months without an oil change. After oil has been changed, reset oil life monitor as follows:

1. Turn ignition to Run position.
2. Fully push and release accelerator pedal three times within five seconds.
3. If CHANGE OIL SOON light flashes two times, system is reset.
4. If CHANGE OIL SOON light comes on and stays on for five seconds, system did not reset. Repeat procedure until system resets.

MODULE CONFIGURATION PROCEDURE

TABLE OF CONTENTS

Page No.

Ford Motor Co.

Some modules will require configuration after being installed on the vehicle. All configurable modules will be packaged in a kit which contains a warning label and multi-language sheet which lists requirements to configure the modules.

There are two types of configuration data. The first type is used by the module so that it can interact with the vehicle correctly. The second type is customer preference driven. These are items that the customer may or may not want to have enabled. To program customer driven preferences, a Ford service function card (FSF) and the New Generation Star Tester (NGS), tool No. 007-00500, or equivalents, must be used to toggle preferences On or Off.

The New Generation Star Tester (NGS), tool No. 007-00500, or equivalent, must be used to retrieve configuration data from the old module before it is removed from the vehicle. This information will be transferred into the new module so that the new module will contain the same settings as the old module.

On some vehicles the following modules require configuration when being replaced; ABS control module, ABS control module with traction control, interactive vehicle dynamic (IVD) module, instrument cluster, instrument cluster with message center, rear electronic module (REM), front electronic module (FEM), driver door module (DDM), dual automatic temperature control (DATC) module, remote emergency satellite cellular unit (RESCU) module, and the steering column lock module (SCLM) when PCM is replaced on manual transmission equipped models. If configuring PCM, the NGS tester flash cable tool No. 007-00531, or equivalent, must be used.

To perform the configuration process, proceed as follows:

1. Connect New Generation Star Tester tool No. 007-00500 or equivalent, with Ford service function (FSF) card to vehicle DLC.
2. Follow scan tool instructions to upload configuration data.
3. Install new module. **NGS will not retain configuration data for more than 24 hours.**
4. Download stored configuration information to new module using FSF card and NGS tester.
5. If unable to carry out configuration process, proceed as follows:
   a. Inspect for signs of electrical damage.
   b. If NGS does not communicate with vehicle, ensure program card is correctly installed, vehicle connections are secure and that ignition switch is in run position.
   c. If NGS still does not communicate with vehicle, diagnose module communications network concern.

VEHICLE LIFT POINTS

TABLE OF CONTENTS

DaimlerChrysler

INDEX

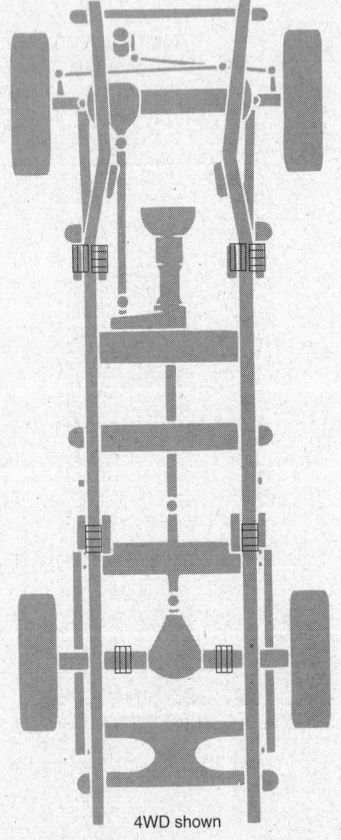

Fig. 1 Dodge Ram Pickups 1500, 2500 & 3500

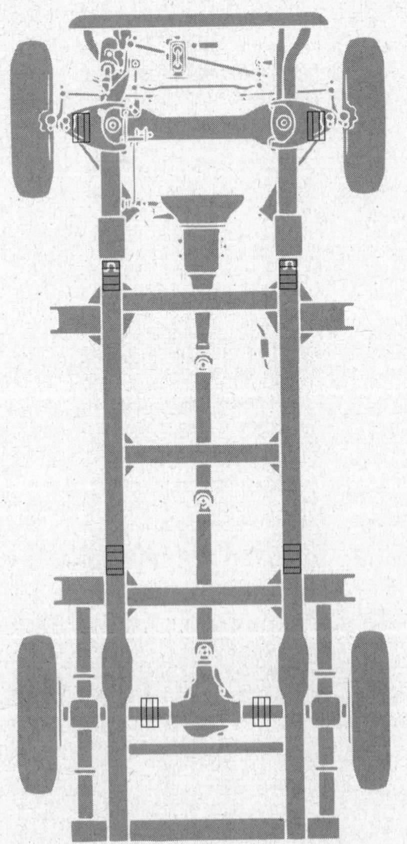

Fig. 2 Dodge Ram Vans

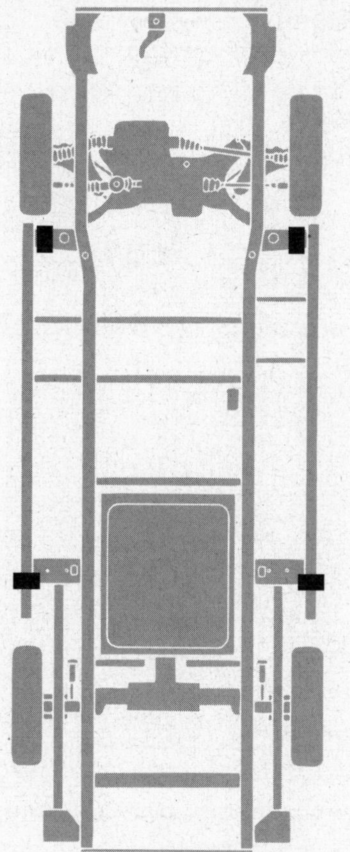

Fig. 3 Caravan, Grand Caravan, Town & Country & Voyager

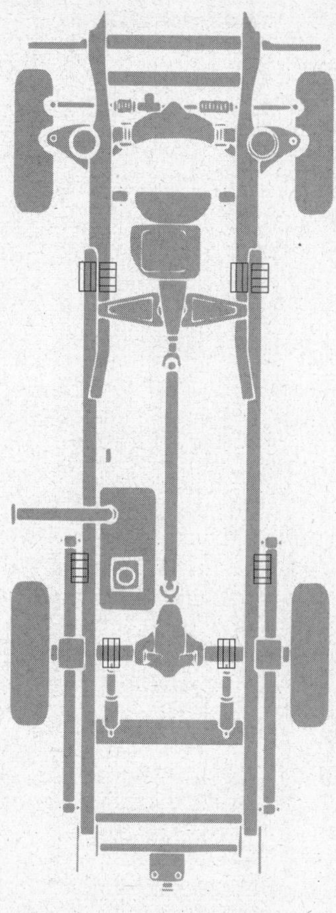

Fig. 4 Dakota & Durango

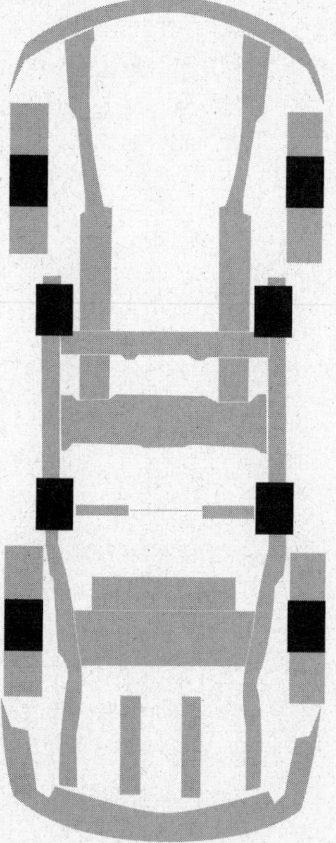

Fig. 5 Pacifica

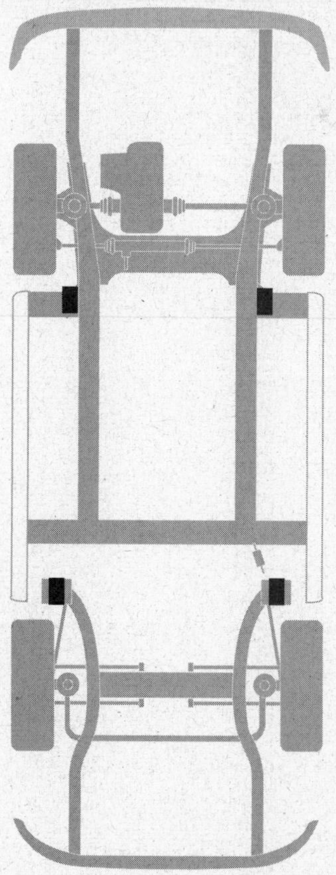

Fig. 6 PT Cruiser

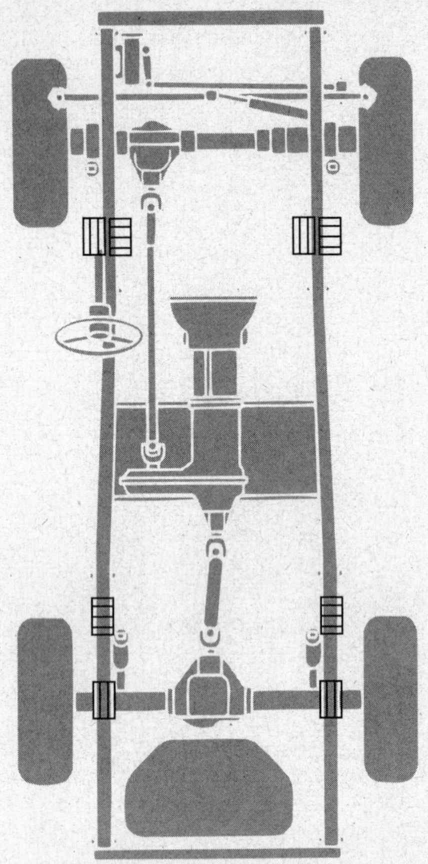

Fig. 7 Wrangler & 2002–04 Grand Cherokee

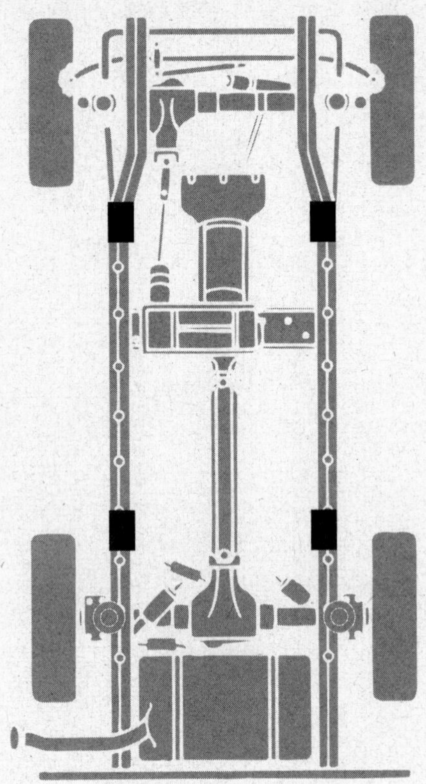

Fig. 8 Commander & 2005–06 Grand Cherokee

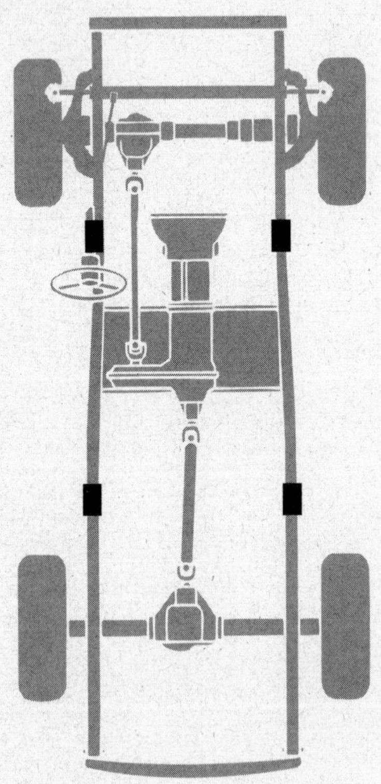

Fig. 9 Liberty

Ford Motor Co.

INDEX

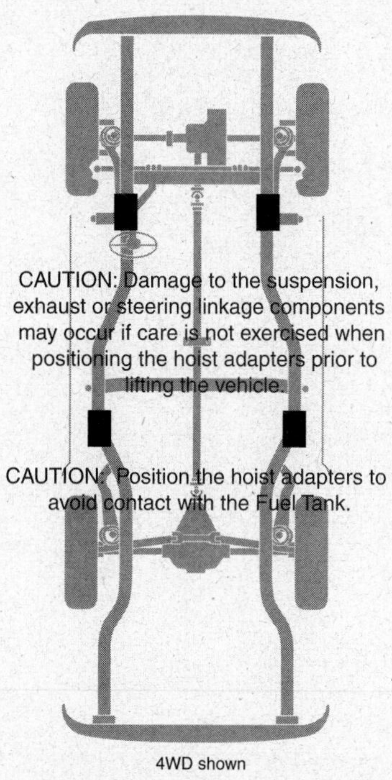
CAUTION: Damage to the suspension, exhaust or steering linkage components may occur if care is not exercised when positioning the hoist adapters prior to lifting the vehicle.
CAUTION: Position the hoist adapters to avoid contact with the Fuel Tank.
4WD shown
ALTF00010

Fig. 1 Escape & Mariner

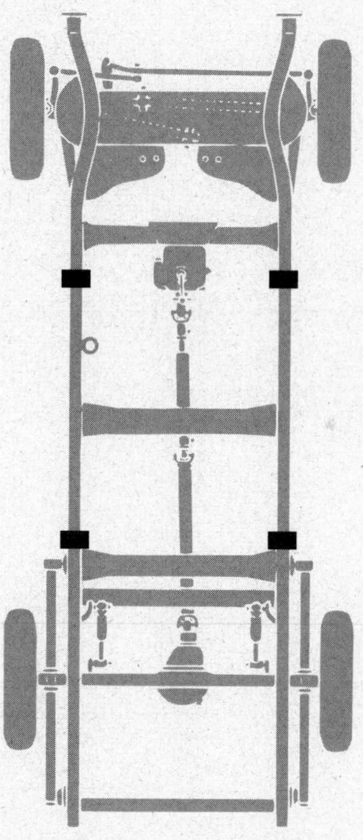
ALTF00002

Fig. 2 E-Series Vans

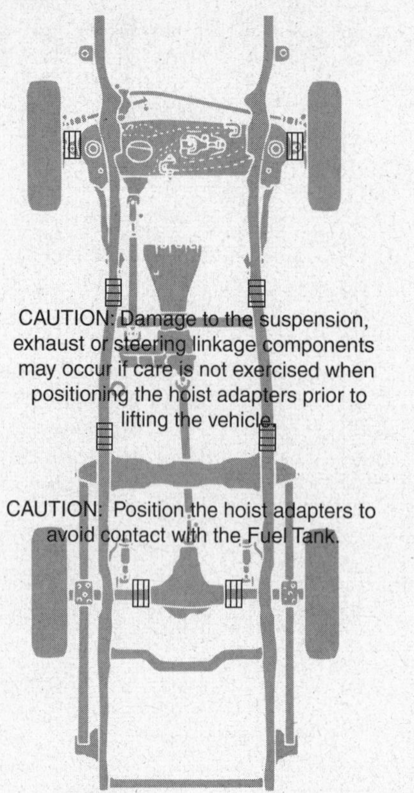
CAUTION: Damage to the suspension, exhaust or steering linkage components may occur if care is not exercised when positioning the hoist adapters prior to lifting the vehicle.
CAUTION: Position the hoist adapters to avoid contact with the Fuel Tank.
ALTF00004

Fig. 3 Excursion, F250HD & F350

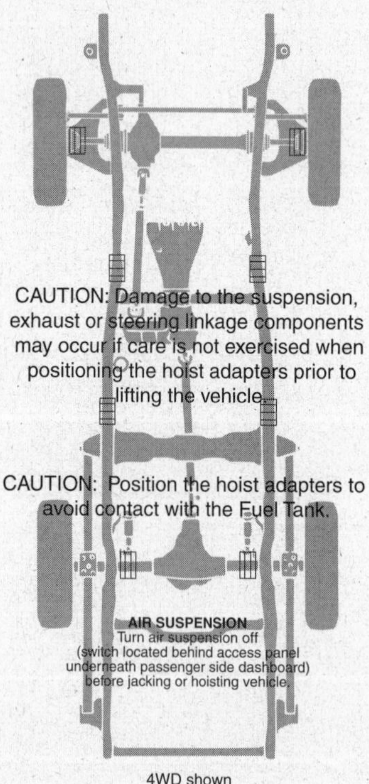
CAUTION: Damage to the suspension, exhaust or steering linkage components may occur if care is not exercised when positioning the hoist adapters prior to lifting the vehicle.
CAUTION: Position the hoist adapters to avoid contact with the Fuel Tank.
AIR SUSPENSION
Turn air suspension off (switch located behind access panel underneath passenger side dashboard) before jacking or hoisting vehicle.
4WD shown
ALTF00008

Fig. 4 Blackwood, Expedition, F150 Pickups & Navigator

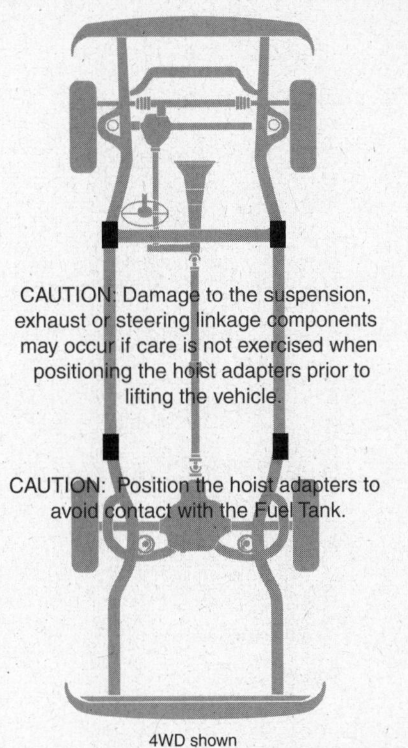
CAUTION: Damage to the suspension, exhaust or steering linkage components may occur if care is not exercised when positioning the hoist adapters prior to lifting the vehicle.
CAUTION: Position the hoist adapters to avoid contact with the Fuel Tank.
4WD shown
ALTF00011

Fig. 5 Aviator, Explorer & Mountaineer

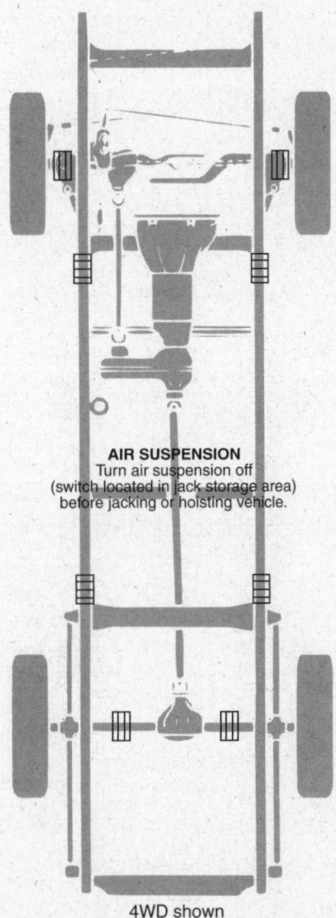
AIR SUSPENSION
Turn air suspension off (switch located in jack storage area) before jacking or hoisting vehicle.
4WD shown
ALTF0001

Fig. 6 Explorer Sport, Explorer Sport-Trac & Ranger

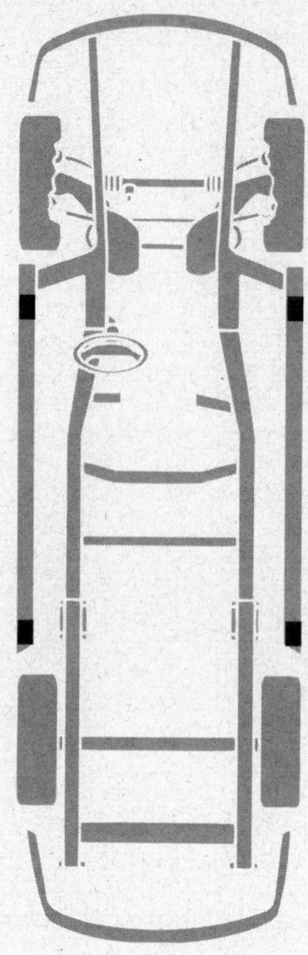
ALND00012

Fig. 7 Villager

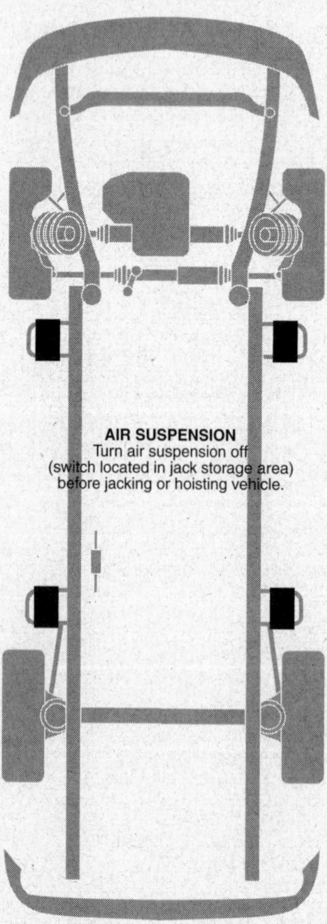
AIR SUSPENSION
Turn air suspension off
(switch located in jack storage area)
before jacking or hoisting vehicle.
ALFD00011

Fig. 8 Windstar

AIR SUSPENSION
Turn air suspension off
(switch located in trunk on right side or
jack storage area)
before jacking or hoisting vehicle.
On 1996-99 Sable/Taurus models
use a cushioned pad on rear
contact pad to prevent paint damage.
ALFD00007

Fig. 9 Freestar & Monterey

General Motors Corp.

INDEX

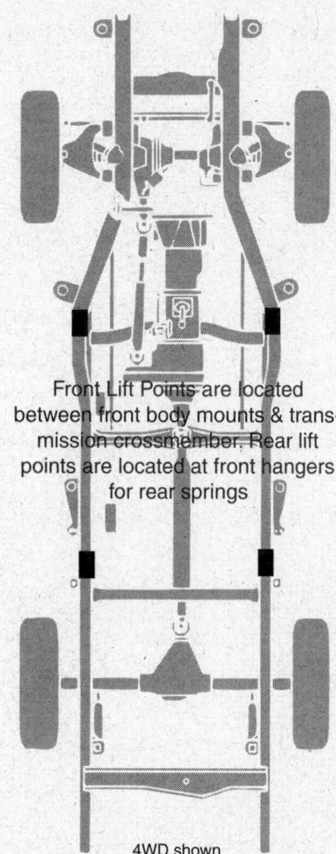

Front Lift Points are located between front body mounts & transmission crossmember. Rear lift points are located at front hangers for rear springs
4WD shown
ALCT00001

Fig. 1 Astro, Bravada, Canyon, Colorado, Envoy, Rainer, Safari, Sonoma, S-Blazer, SSR, S-10 & Trailblazer

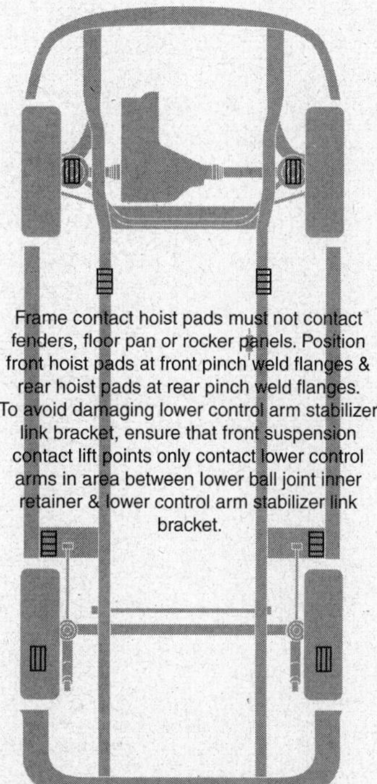

Fig. 2 Aztek, Montana, Rendezvous, Silhouette, Terraza, Uplander & Venture

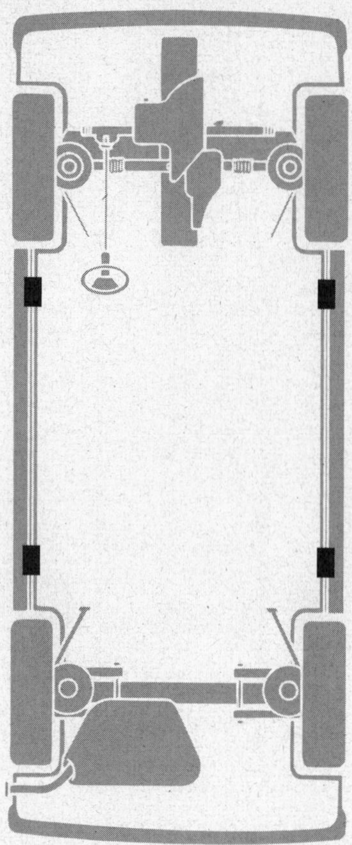

ALTA00007

Fig. 3 Vue

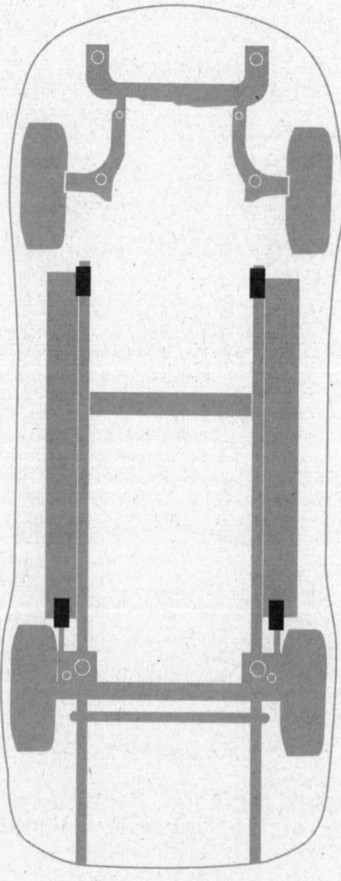

ALSN04003

Fig. 4 Relay

Frame contact hoist pads must not contact rocker panels, fenders or floor. When using tip-up hoist pad, position front frame contact hoist pads under front frame between lower control arm & frame pad or front frame pad. On models with rear leaf springs, position rear frame contact tip-up hoist pad under rear spring just behind hanger.
4WD Shown
ALCT00008

Fig. 5 Avalanche, Denali, Escalade, Escalade ESV, Escalade EXT, Hummer H2, Hummer H3, Sierra, Silverado, Suburban, Tahoe, Yukon & Yukon XL

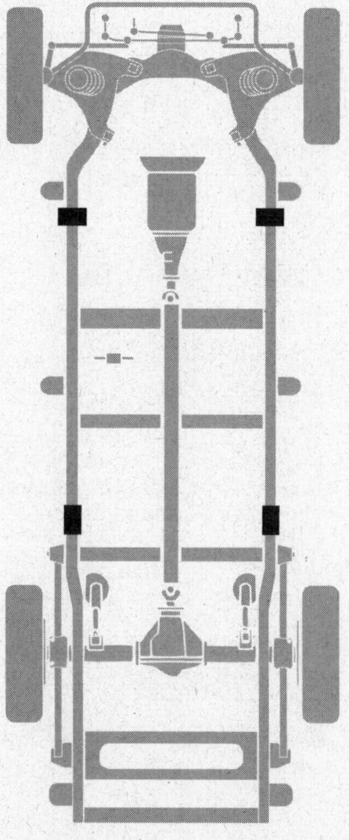

Fig. 6 Express & Savana

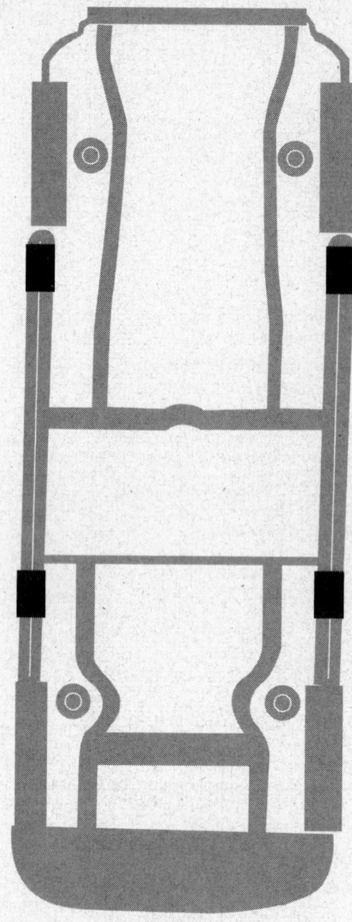

ALGM04040

Fig. 7 Equinox & Torrent

Position the frame contact front hoist pads as follows:
Under the Front frame rail reinforcement.
The long sides of the pads, if applicable parallel to the frame rails.
Under the rear Frame rail at the rear axle cradle mount flange.
The long sides of the pads, if applicable perpendicular to the frame rails.

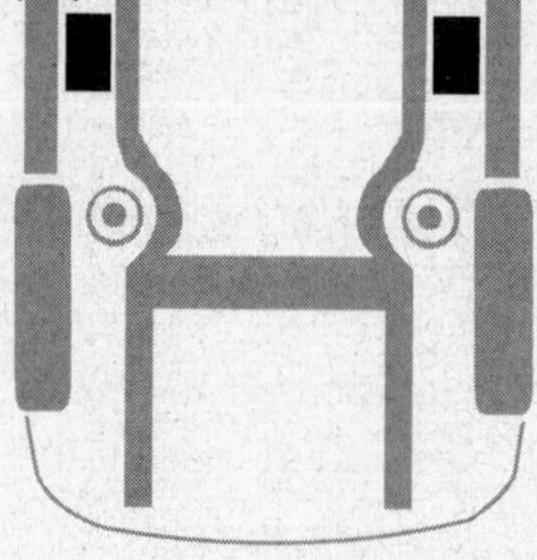

ALGM00035

Fig. 8 SRX

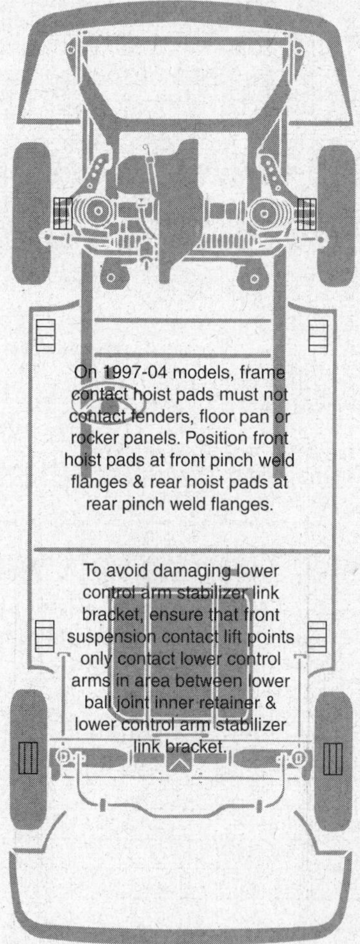
On 1997-04 models, frame contact hoist pads must not contact fenders, floor pan or rocker panels. Position front hoist pads at front pinch weld flanges & rear hoist pads at rear pinch weld flanges.
To avoid damaging lower control arm stabilizer link bracket, ensure that front suspension contact lift points only contact lower control arms in area between lower ball joint inner retainer & lower control arm stabilizer link bracket.
ALGM00018

Fig. 9 HHR

NON-STANDARD TIRE & WHEEL SIZE ADJUSTMENT TO RIDE HEIGHT SPECIFICATIONS & TIRE SIZE ADJUSTMENT CHARTS

INDEX

SECTION WIDTH ADJUSTMENT FOR METRIC RADIAL & BIAS PLY TIRES

These specifications are approximate and are only intended for use in making approximate ride height inspections and adjustments on models with non-standard tires. These specifications should not be used in place of those recommended by the vehicle manufacturer.

Standard Tire	Optional Tire, Tire Section Width Change Adjustment To Ride Height Specification, Inch													
	P145	P155	P165	P175	P185	P195	P205	P215	P225	P235	P245	P255	P265	P275
P145	0	+.25	+.50	—	—	—	—	—	—	—	—	—	—	—
P155	–.25	0	+.25	+.50	—	—	—	—	—	—	—	—	—	—
P165	–.50	–.25	0	+.25	+.50	—	—	—	—	—	—	—	—	—
P175	—	–.50	–.25	0	+.25	+.50	—	—	—	—	—	—	—	—
P185	—	—	–.50	–.25	0	+.25	+.50	—	—	—	—	—	—	—
P195	—	—	—	–.50	–.25	0	+.25	+.50	—	—	—	—	—	—
P205	—	—	—	—	–.50	–.25	0	+.25	+.50	—	—	—	—	—
P215	—	—	—	—	—	–.50	–.25	0	+.25	+.50	—	—	—	—
P225	—	—	—	—	—	—	–.50	–.25	0	+.25	+.50	—	—	—
P235	—	—	—	—	—	—	—	–.50	–.25	0	+.25	+.50	—	—
P245	—	—	—	—	—	—	—	—	–.50	–.25	0	+.25	+.50	—
P255	—	—	—	—	—	—	—	—	—	–.50	–.25	0	+.25	+.50
P265	—	—	—	—	—	—	—	—	—	—	–.50	–.25	0	+.25
P275	—	—	—	—	—	—	—	—	—	—	—	–.50	–.25	0

ASPECT RATIO ADJUSTMENT FOR P145-215 METRIC RADIAL & BIAS PLY TIRES

These specifications are approximate and are only intended for use in making approximate ride height inspections and adjustments on models with non-standard tires. These specifications should not be used in place of those recommended by the vehicle manufacturer.

Standard Tire	Optional Tire, Tire Aspect Ratio Change to Ride Height Specification, Inch				
	60	65	70	75	80
60	0	+.38	+.75	—	—
65	–.38	0	+.38	+.75	—
70	–.75	–.38	0	+.38	+.75
75	—	–.75	–.38	0	+.38
80	—	—	–.75	–.38	0

ASPECT RATIO ADJUSTMENT FOR P225-275 METRIC RADIAL & BIAS PLY TIRES

These specifications are approximate and are only intended for use in making approximate ride height inspections and adjustments on models with non-standard tires. These specifications should not be used in place of those recommended by the vehicle manufacturer.

Standard Tire	Optional Tire, Tire Aspect Ratio Change to Ride Height Specification, Inch				
	60	65	70	75	80
60	0	+.50	+1.00	—	—
65	−.50	0	+.50	+1.00	—
70	−1.00	−.50	0	+.50	+1.00
75	—	−.75	−.50	0	+.50
80	—	—	−1.00	−.50	0

SECTION WIDTH ADJUSTMENT FOR ALPHA-NUMERIC RADIAL PLY TIRES

These specifications are approximate and are only intended for use in making approximate ride height inspections and adjustments on models with non-standard tires. These specifications should not be used in place of those recommended by the vehicle manufacturer.

Standard Tire	Optional Tire, Tire Section Width Change Adjustment To Ride Height Specification, Inch						
	DR	ER	FR	GR	HR	JR	LR
DR	0	+.19	+.44	—	—	—	—
ER	−.19	0	+.25	+.50	—	—	—
FR	−.44	−.25	0	+.25	+.63	—	—
GR	—	−.50	−.25	0	+.31	+.50	—
HR	—	—	−.63	−.31	0	+.19	+.44
JR	—	—	—	−.50	−.19	0	+.25
LR	—	—	—	—	−.44	−.25	0

ASPECT RATIO ADJUSTMENT FOR ALPHA-NUMERIC RADIAL PLY TIRES

These specifications are approximate and are only intended for use in making approximate ride height inspections and adjustments on models with non-standard tires. These specifications should not be used in place of those recommended by the vehicle manufacturer.

Standard Tire	Optional Tire, Change Adjustment to Ride Height Specification, Inch		
	60	70	78
60	0	+.50	+.62
70	−.50	0	+.13
78	−.62	−.13	0

SECTION WIDTH ADJUSTMENT FOR ALPHA-NUMERIC BIAS PLY TIRES

These specifications are approximate and are only intended for use in making approximate ride height inspections and adjustments on models with non-standard tires. These specifications should not be used in place of those recommended by the vehicle manufacturer.

Standard Tire	Optional Tire, Change Adjustment To Ride Height Specifications, Inch							
	A	B	C	D	E	F	G	H
A	0	+.25	+.50	—	—	—	—	—
B	−.25	0	+.25	+.38	—	—	—	—
C	−.50	−.25	0	+.13	+.37	—	—	—
D	—	−.37	−.13	0	+.25	+.50	—	—
E	—	—	−.38	−.25	0	+.25	+.50	—
F	—	—	—	−.50	−.25	0	+.25	+.56
G	—	—	—	—	−.50	−.25	0	+.31
H	—	—	—	—	—	−.56	−.31	0

ELECTRICAL SYMBOL & WIRE COLOR CODE IDENTIFICATION

TABLE OF CONTENTS

Electrical Symbol Identification

INDEX

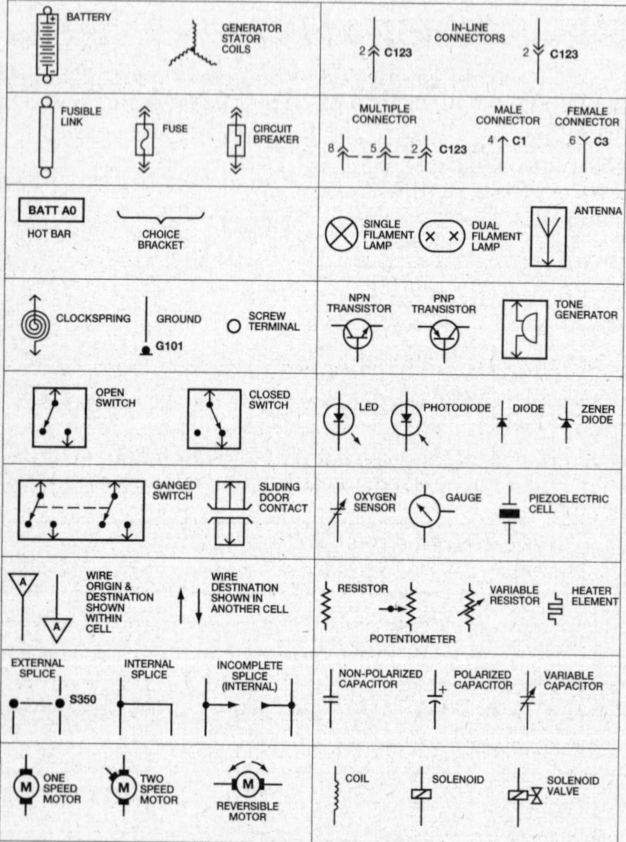

Fig. 1 DaimlerChrysler

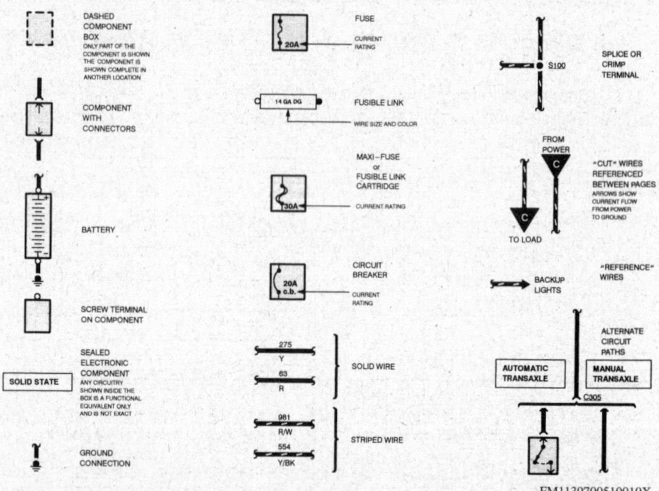

Fig. 2 Ford Motor Co. (Part 1 of 2). Except Escape, Explorer Sport, Explorer Sport-Trac & Villager

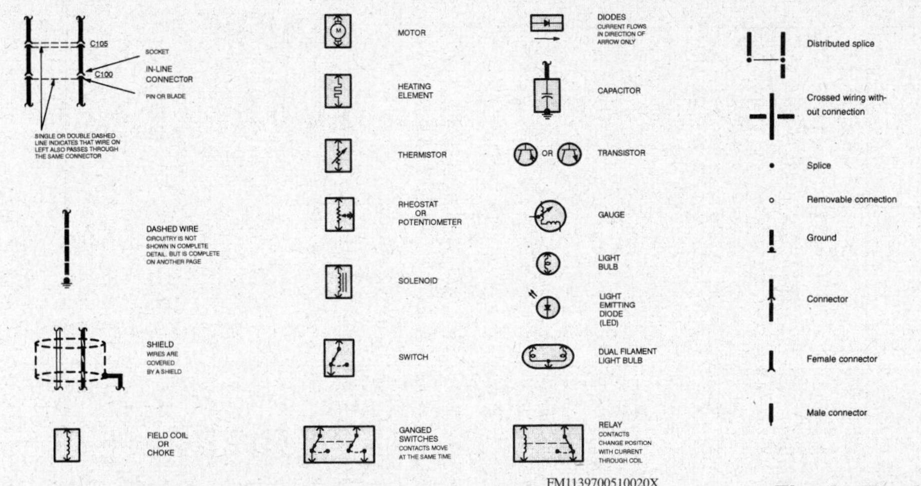

Fig. 2 Ford Motor Co. (Part 2 of 2). Except Escape, Explorer Sport, Explorer Sport-Trac & Villager

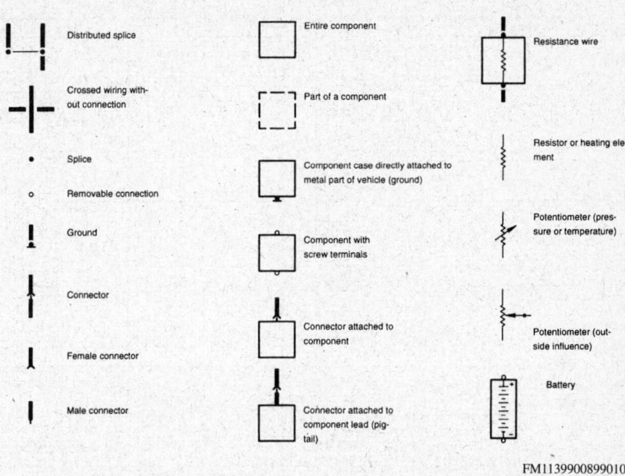

Fig. 3 Ford Motor Co. (Part 1 of 4). Escape, Explorer Sport, Explorer Sport-Trac & Villager

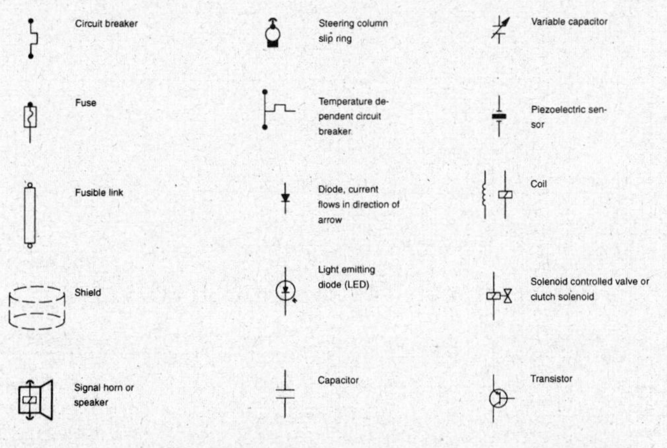

Fig. 3 Ford Motor Co. (Part 2 of 4). Escape, Explorer Sport, Explorer Sport-Trac & Villager

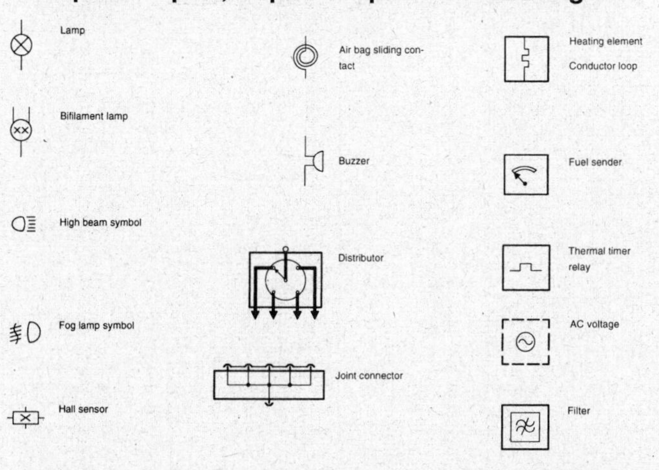

Fig. 3 Ford Motor Co. (Part 3 of 4). Escape, Explorer Sport, Explorer Sport-Trac & Villager

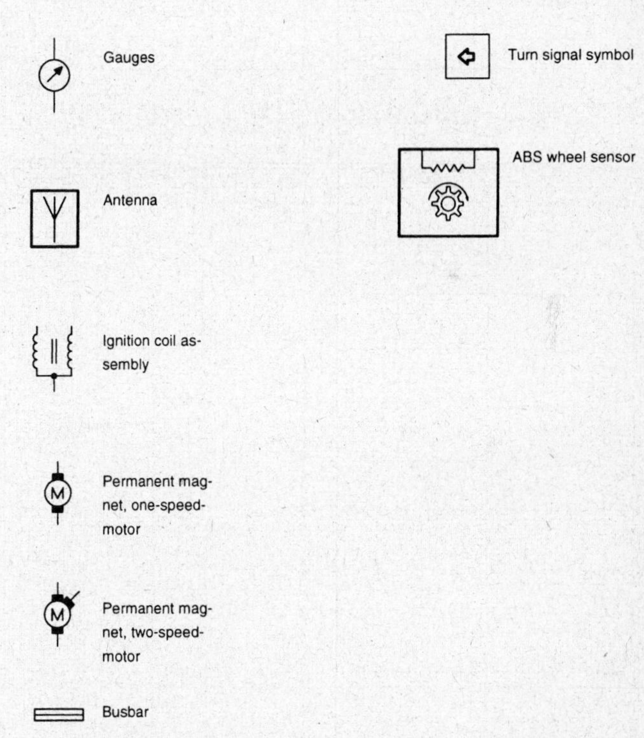

Fig. 3 Ford Motor Co. (Part 4 of 4). Escape, Explorer Sport, Explorer Sport-Trac & Villager

Symbol	Description
	Supplemental Inflatable Restraint (SIR) or Supplemental Restraint System (SRS) Icon This icon is used to alert the technician that the system contains SIR/SRS components that require certain precautions before servicing. Refer to *SIR Handling Caution* in Cautions and Notices.
OBD II	On-Board Diagnostic (OBD II) Icon This icon is used to alert the technician that the circuit is essential for proper OBD II emission controls circuit operation. Any circuit which, if it fails, causes the malfunction indicator lamp (MIL) to turn on, is identified as an OBD II circuit.
	Important Icon This icon is used to alert the technician that there is additional information that will aid in servicing a system.
Hot At All Times Hot In Run Hot In Start Hot In Acc And Run Hot In Run And Start Hot In Run, Bulb Test And Start Hot With Headlamp Switch In Park Or Head Hot In Retained Accessory Power (RAP)	Voltage Indicator Boxes These boxes are used on schematics to indicate when voltage is present at a fuse.
	Partial Component When a component is represented in a dashed box, the component or its wiring is not shown in its entirety.

Symbol	Description
	Entire Component When a component is represented in a solid box the component or its wiring is shown in its entirety.
	Fuse
	Circuit Breaker
	Fusible Link
12	Connector Attached to Component

GM1139901001010X

Fig. 4 General Motors Corp. (Part 1 of 4)

Symbol	Description
12	Pigtail Connector
	Bolt On or Screw On Eyelet Terminal
12 C100	Inline Harness Connector
S100	Splice
P100	Pass Through the Grommet

Symbol	Description
G100	Chassis Ground
	Case Ground
	Single Filament Light Bulbs
	Double Filament Light Bulb
	Light Emitting Diodes

GM1139901001020X

Fig. 4 General Motors Corp. (Part 2 of 4)

Symbol	Description
	Capacitor
	Battery
	Variable Battery
	Resistor
	Variable Resistor

Symbol	Description
	Position Sensor
	I/O Resistors
	I/O Switches
	Diode
	Crystal

GM1139901001030X

Fig. 4 General Motors Corp. (Part 3 of 4)

Symbol	Description
	Heating Elements
M	Motor
	Solenoid
	Coil
	Antenna

Symbol	Description
	Shield
	Switches
	Single Pole Single Throw Relay
	Single Pole Double Throw Relay

GM1139901001040X

Fig. 4 General Motors Corp. (Part 4 of 4)

Wire Color Code Identification

DAIMLERCHRYSLER

Color	Code
Black	BK
Blue	BL
Brown	BR
Dark Blue	DB
Dark Green	DG
Gray	GY
Light Blue	LB
Light Green	LG
Orange	OR
Pink	PK
Red	RD
Silver	SR
Tan	TN
Violet	VT
White	WH
White	WT
Yellow	YE
Yellow	YL

FORD MOTOR CO.

Color	Code
Black	BK
Blue	BU
Brown	BN
Dark Blue	DB
Dark Green	DG
Gray	GY
Green	GN
Light Blue	LB
Light Green	LG
Natural	NA
Orange	OG
Pink	PK
Red	RD
Silver	SR
Tan	TN
Violet	VT
White	WH
Yellow	YE

GENERAL MOTORS CORP.

Color	Code
Black	BLK
Blue	BLU
Brown	BRN
Dark Blue	DKBLU
Dark Green	DKGRN
Gray	GR
Green	GRN
Light Blue	LGTBLU
Light Green	LGTGRN
Orange	ORN
Pink	PNK
Purple	PPL
Red	RED
Tan	TAN
White	WHT
Yellow	YEL

VEHICLE MAINTENANCE SCHEDULES

TABLE OF CONTENTS

DaimlerChrysler

INDEX

CARAVAN, PACIFICA, TOWN & COUNTRY & VOYAGER

Recommended Service & Intervals (Months)	Service Interval In Miles①																																						
	3000	6000	7500	9000	12000	15000	18000	21000	22500	24000	27000	30000	33000	36000	37500	39000	42000	45000	48000	51000	52500	54000	57000	60000	63000	66000	67500	69000	72000	75000	78000	81000	82500	84000	87000	90000	93000	96000	97500	99000
BODY																																								
Replace Cabin Air Filter	Every 12 Months Or 12,000 Miles																																							
BRAKES																																								
Inspect Brake Connections, Hoses & Lines, 2002	Normal Service Every 12 Months Or 7500 Miles; Severe Service 3000 Miles																																							
Inspect Brake Connections, Hoses & Lines, 2003–06	At Every Oil Change Interval																																							
Inspect Brake Drums, Linings & Rotors, 2002				S			S		N		S			S				X				S			S		N		S			S				X				
Inspect Brake Drums, Linings & Rotors, 2003–05	Normal Service Every 18,000 Miles; Severe Service Every 9000 Miles																																							
Inspect Brake Drums, Linings & Rotors, 2006	Normal Service Every 18,000 Miles; Severe Service Every 12,000 Miles																																							
CLUTCH & TRANSMISSION																																								
Adjust Bands 3 Speed Transaxle	Every 15,000 Miles																																							
Change Automatic Transaxle Fluid & Filter, 2002–03②	No Normal Service; Severe Service Every 48,000 Miles																																							
Change Automatic Transaxle Fluid & Filter, 2004–06②	No Normal Service; Severe Service Every 60,000 Miles																																							
Change AWD Overrunning Clutch & Driveline Module/Rear Carrier Lubricants								S									S								S									S						
Change AWD Power Transfer Unit Lubricant②						S						S						S						S						S						S				
DRIVESHAFT & CV JOINTS																																								
Inspect CV & Driveshaft Joint Boots			X			X			X			X			X			X			X			X			X			X			X			X			X	

CARAVAN, PACIFICA, TOWN & COUNTRY & VOYAGER—Continued

Recommended Service & Intervals (Months)	Service Interval In Miles①																																							
	3000	6000	7500	9000	12000	15000	18000	21000	22500	24000	27000	30000	33000	36000	37500	39000	42000	45000	48000	51000	52500	54000	57000	60000	63000	66000	67500	69000	72000	75000	78000	81000	82500	84000	87000	90000	93000	96000	97500	99000
ENGINE																																								
Change Engine Coolant, 2002–05	Every 60 Months Or 100,000 Miles																																							
Change Engine Coolant, 2006	Normal Service Every 60 Months Or 102,000 Miles; Severe Service Every 60 Months Or 100,000 Miles																																							
Change Engine Oil & Filter, 2002	Normal Service Every 6 Months Or 7500 Miles; Severe Service Every 3000 Miles																																							
Change Engine Oil & Filter, 2003–06	Normal Service Every 6 Months Or 6000 Miles; Severe Service Every 3 Months Or 3000 Miles																																							
Inspect Coolant Level	At Every Engine Oil Change																																							
Inspect Cooling System & Protection Level			X			X			X			X			X			X			X			X			X			X			X			X			X	
Inspect Alternator Drive Belt, 2002 2.4L	Inspect Every 30,000 Miles																																							
Inspect Alternator Drive Belt, 2003–06 2.4L	Normal Service Inspect Every 42,000 Miles; Severe Service Inspect Every 15,000 Miles																																							
Inspect Drive Belts, 2002																								X						S										
Inspect PCV Valve③												S												X												X				
Inspect Power Steering Pump Drive Belt, 2003–06 2.4L	Normal Service Every 30,000 Miles; Severe Service Every 15,000 Miles																																							
Inspect Serpentine Belt																								X																
Replace Engine Air & PCV Filters						S						X						S						X						S						X				
Replace Ignition Cables Except, 2.4L & 2002 3.3L & 3.8L	Every 60,000 Miles																																							
Replace Ignition Cables, 2002–03 3.3L & 3.8L	Every 100,000 Miles																																							
Replace Ignition Cables, 2004–06 3.3L & 3.8L	Normal Service Every 100,000 Miles; Severe Service Every 75,000 Miles																																							
Replace PCV Valve, 2002	At 60,000 Miles & 120,000 Miles, Or When Emissions Maintenance Lamp Remains Lit w/Ignition On																																							
Replace PCV Valve, 2003–06	Normal Service Inspect At 60,000 Miles & Replace If Necessary; Severe Service Inspect Every 30,000 Miles & Replace If Necessary Or When Emissions Maintenance Lamp Remains Lit w/Ignition On																																							
Replace Spark Plugs, 2003–06 2.4L	Every 30,000 Miles																																							
Replace Spark Plugs, 2002 2.4L & 3.0L												X												X												X				
Replace Spark Plugs, 2003 3.3L & 3.8L & 2004–06 3.5L	Normal Service Every 100,000 Miles; Severe Service Every 75,000 Miles																																							

CARAVAN, PACIFICA, TOWN & COUNTRY & VOYAGER—Continued

Recommended Service & Intervals (Months)	Service Interval In Miles①																																							
	3000	6000	7500	9000	12000	15000	18000	21000	22500	24000	27000	30000	33000	36000	37500	39000	42000	45000	48000	51000	52500	54000	57000	60000	63000	66000	67500	69000	72000	75000	78000	81000	82500	84000	87000	90000	93000	96000	97500	99000
ENGINE																																								
Replace Timing Belt, 2.4L	Normal Service Every 120,000 Miles; Severe Service Every 90,000 Miles																																							
Replace Timing Belt, 2.5L																																				X				
Replace Timing Belt, 3.0L																								X																
STEERING, SUSPENSION & TIRES																																								
Inspect Ball Joints (Every 24 Mos.)										X														X												X				
Inspect Bushings, Arms, Seals, Springs & Jounce Bumpers	S	X		S	X	S	X	S		X	S	X	S	X		S	X	S	X	S		X	S	X	S	X		S	X	S	X	S		X	S	X	S	X		S
Inspect Power Steering Belt & Tensioner, 2.4L	Every 30,000 Miles																																							
Lubricate Front Suspension Ball Joints, Steering Linkage & Wheel Stops (Every 24 Mos.)										X														X												X				
Rotate Tires & Adjust Pressure, 2002		S	N		S	N	S		N	S		X		S	N		S	N	S		N	S		X		S	N		S	N	S		N	S		X		S		
Rotate Tires & Adjust Pressure, 2003–06	Every 6000 Miles																																							

AWD — All Wheel Drive
N — Normal Service
S — Severe Service
X — Normal Or Severe Service
① — After vehicle passes 99,000 mile mark return to beginning of mileage table & start cycle over again.
② — Operating vehicle more than 50% heavy traffic during hot weather, above 90°F, using vehicle for police, taxi, limousine type operation, or trailer towing require more frequent transaxle & AWD service. Perform these services if vehicle is usually operated under these conditions.
③ — This maintenance is recommended by DaimlerChrysler to owner but is not required to maintain warranty on PCV valve.

DAKOTA & DURANGO

Recommended Service & Intervals (Months)	Service Interval In Miles①																																						
	3000	6000	7500	9000	12000	15000	18000	21000	22500	24000	27000	30000	33000	36000	37500	39000	42000	45000	48000	51000	52500	54000	57000	60000	63000	66000	67500	69000	72000	75000	78000	81000	82500	84000	87000	90000	93000	96000	97500	99000
BRAKES																																								
Inspect Brake Connections, Hoses & Lines	Normal Service Every 6 Months Or 7500 Miles; Severe Service Every 3 Months Or 3000 Miles																																						
Inspect Brake Drums & Rotors					S		S		N		S			S				X				S			S		N		S			S				X				
Inspect Brake Pads & Shoes					S		S		N		S			S				X				S			S		N		S			S				X				
CLUTCH & TRANSMISSION																																								
Change Automatic Transmission Fluid & Filter, 2002–04 Dakota & 4.7L & 5.7L Durango	Normal Service Every 100,000 Miles; Severe Service Every 30,000 Miles																																						
Change Automatic Transmission Fluid & Filter, 2004 Durango 3.7L	Normal Service Every 100,000 Miles; Severe Service At 60,000 Miles Then Every 30,000 Miles Thereafter																																						
Change Automatic Transmission Fluid & Filter, 2005–06 3.7L, 4.7L & 5.7L	Severe Service Every 60,000 Miles																																						
Change Transfer Case Lubricant, 2002–03	Normal Service Inspect Every 60,000 Miles; Drain And Refill Every 120,000 Miles; Severe Service Every 60,000 Miles																																						
Change Transfer Case Lubricant, 2004–06	Normal Service Inspect Every 60,000 Miles; Drain And Refill Every 120,000 Miles; Severe Service Inspect Every 30,000 Miles; Drain & Refill Every 120,000 Miles																																						
Lubricate Clutch Bellcrank									X									X									X									X				
DRIVE AXLE & DRIVESHAFT																																								
Change Differential Lubricants, Except 2004 Dakota & 2005–06 All					S					S				S					S					S					S					S				S		
Change Differential Lubricants, 2004 Dakota & 2005–06 All						S						S						S						S						S						S				
Inspect CV & Driveshaft Joint Boots			X			X			X			X			X			X			X			X			X			X			X			X			X	
Lubricate Driveshaft U-Joints, Slip Splines & Yokes②	S	X		S	X	S	X	S		X	S	X	S	X		S	X	S	X	S		X	S	X	S	X		S	X	S	X	S		X	S	X	S	X		S
ENGINE																																								
Change Engine Coolant, 2002–04 Except 2004 Durango	Every 60 Months Or 100,000 Miles																																						
Change Engine Coolant, 2004 Durango & 2005–06 All	Every 60 Months Or 102,000 Miles																																						
Change Engine Oil & Filter, 2002	Normal Service Every 6 Months Or 7500 Miles; Severe Service Every 3000 Miles																																						

DAKOTA & DURANGO—Continued

Recommended Service & Intervals (Months)	Service Interval In Miles①																																						
	3000	6000	7500	9000	12000	15000	18000	21000	22500	24000	27000	30000	33000	36000	37500	39000	42000	45000	48000	51000	52500	54000	57000	60000	63000	66000	67500	69000	72000	75000	78000	81000	82500	84000	87000	90000	93000	96000	97500	99000
ENGINE																																								
Change Engine Oil & Filter, 2003–06	Normal Service Every 6 Months Or 6000 Miles; Severe Service Every 3000 Miles																																							
Inspect Air Filter, 2003–06	Normal Service Every 30,000 Miles; Severe Service Every 15,000 Miles																																							
Inspect Cooling System & Protection Level			X			X			X			X			X			X			X			X			X			X			X			X			X	
Inspect Drive Belts												X												X												X				
Inspect Ignition Cables, 5.7L	Every 60,000 Miles																																							
Inspect PCV Valve③												S												X												S				
Replace Air Filter, 2002	Every 30,000 Miles																																							
Replace Ignition Cables, 2.5L, 3.9L, 5.2L & 5.9L	Every 60,000 Miles																																							
Replace Spark Plugs												X												X												X				
Replace Timing Belt, 2.5L																																				X				
STEERING, SUSPENSION & TIRES																																								
Inspect Bushings, Arms, Seals, Springs & Jounce Bumpers	S	X		S	X	S	X	S		X	S	X	S	X		S	X	S	X	S		X	S	X	S	X		S	X	S	X	S		X	S	X	S	X		S
Inspect Front Wheel Bearings (Clean & Repack If Required)	Every 18 Months Or 22,500 Miles																																							
Lubricate Ball Joints (Every 18 Mos.)									X									X									X									X				
Lubricate Steering Linkage (Every 12 Mos.)						X						X						X						X						X						X				
Rotate Tires & Adjust Pressure, 2002		S	N		S	N	S		N	S		X		S	N		S	N	S		N	S		X		S	N		S	N	S		N	S		X		S	N	
Rotate Tires & Adjust Pressure, 2003–06	Every 6000 Miles																																							

AWD — All Wheel Drive
N — Normal Service
S — Severe Service
X — Normal Or Severe Service
① — After vehicle passes 99,000 mile mark return to beginning of mileage table & start cycle over again.
② — Lubricate slip splines daily if travelling through water.
③ — Inspect and replace as necessary. This maintenance is recommended by DaimlerChrysler Corporation to the owner, but not required to maintain the warranty of the PCV Valve.

FULL SIZE PICKUPS

	Service Interval In Miles①																																							
Recommended Service & Intervals (Months)	3000	6000	7500	9000	12000	15000	18000	21000	22500	24000	27000	30000	33000	36000	37500	39000	42000	45000	48000	51000	52500	54000	57000	60000	63000	66000	67500	69000	72000	75000	78000	81000	82500	84000	87000	90000	93000	96000	97500	99000
BRAKES																																								
Inspect Brake Connections, Hoses & Lines	Normal Service Every 6 Months Or 7500 Miles; Severe Service Every 3000 Miles																																							
Inspect Brake Linings, 2002 HD	Normal Service Every 18,000 Miles; Severe Service Every 12,000 Miles																																							
Inspect Brake Linings, 2002 MD					S		N			S				X					S			N		S					X					S		N		S		
Inspect Brake Linings, 2002 1500, 2500 & 3500 LD					S				N	S				S				N	S					S			N		S					S		N		S		
Inspect Brake Linings 2003–05 1500, 2500 & 3500	Normal Service Every 18,000 Miles; Severe Service Every 12,000 Miles																																							
Inspect Brake Linings 2006 1500, 2500 & 3500	Normal Service Every 24,000 Miles; Severe Service Every 18,000 Miles																																							
Inspect Brake Linings, Diesel	Normal Service Every 22,500 Miles; Severe Service Every 15,000 Miles																																							
Lubricate Parking Brake Ratio Lever Pivot									X									X									X									X				
CLUTCH & TRANSMISSION																																								
Change Automatic Transmission Filter, Fluid & Adjust Bands, Diesel, 2002–03	Normal Service Every 100,000 Miles; Severe Service Every 30,000 Miles																																							
Change Automatic Transmission Filter, Fluid & Adjust Bands, Diesel, 2004–06 (48RE)	Normal Service Every 100,000 Miles; Severe Service Every 30,000 Miles																																							
Change Automatic Transmission Filter, Fluid & Adjust Bands, Diesel, 2004–06 (54RFE)	Severe Service Every 60,000 Miles																																							
Change Automatic Transmission Filter, Fluid & Adjust Bands, 2002 1500, 2500 & 3500 LD	Normal Service Every 100,000 Miles; Severe Service Every 30,000 Miles																																							
Change Automatic Transmission Filter, Fluid & Adjust Bands, 2003–04 1500, 2500 & 3500	Normal Service Every 100,000 Miles; Severe Service Every 30,000 Miles																																							
Change Automatic Transmission Filter, Fluid & Adjust Bands, 2005 Gasoline Except SRT 10	Normal Service Every 120,000 Miles; Severe Service Every 60,000 Miles																																							

FULL SIZE PICKUPS—Continued

Recommended Service & Intervals (Months)	Service Interval In Miles①																																							
	3000	6000	7500	9000	12000	15000	18000	21000	22500	24000	27000	30000	33000	36000	37500	39000	42000	45000	48000	51000	52500	54000	57000	60000	63000	66000	67500	69000	72000	75000	78000	81000	82500	84000	87000	90000	93000	96000	97500	99000
CLUTCH & TRANSMISSION																																								
Change Automatic Transmission Filter, Fluid & Adjust Bands, 2002 MD, Gasoline④	Normal Service Every 100,000 Miles; Severe Service Every 24,000 Miles																																							
Change Automatic Transmission Filter, Fluid & Adjust Bands, 2002 HD, Gasoline④	Normal Service Every 100,000 Miles; Severe Service Every 30,000 Miles																																							
Change Automatic Transmission Filter, Fluid & Adjust Bands, 2005 Gasoline SRT 10②	Normal Service Every 100,000 Miles; Severe Service Every 30,000 Miles																																							
Change Automatic Transmission Filter, Fluid & Adjust Bands, 2006 Gasoline Except SRT 10	Severe Service Every 60,000 Miles																																							
Change Transfer Case Lubricant, 2002 1500 LD	Normal Service Inspect Every 30,000 Miles, Drain And Refill At 90,000 Miles; Severe Service Drain And Refill Every 60,000 Miles																																							
Change Transfer Case Lubricant, 2002 2500 & 3500 HD	Normal Service At 36,000 Miles, Then Every 18,000 Miles Thereafter; Severe Service Every 18,000 Miles																																							
Change Transfer Case Lubricant, 2002 2500 & 3500 LD & MD	Normal Service Inspect Every 30,000 Miles, Drain And Refill Every 120,000 Miles; Severe Service Drain And Refill Every 60,000 Miles																																							
Change Transfer Case Lubricant, 2003–04	Normal Service, Inspect Every 30,000 Miles & Drain And Refill Every 90,000 Miles; Severe Service Inspect Every 30,000 Miles And Drain And Refill Every 60,000 Miles																																							
Change Transfer Case Lubricant, 2005–06	Normal Service, Inspect Every 30,000 Miles & Drain And Refill Every 120,000 Miles; Severe Service Inspect Every 30,000 Miles And Drain And Refill Every 60,000 Miles																																							
Change 6 Speed Manual Transmission Fluid, 2005–06 Diesel	Severe Service Every 75,000 Miles																																							
Change 6 Speed Manual Transmission Fluid, 2005–06 Gasoline	Severe Service Every 60,000 Miles																																							
Lubricate Clutch Bellcrank									X									X									X									X				
Lubricate O/D 4 Gearshift Mechanism									X									X									X									X				
DRIVE AXLE & DRIVESHAFT																																								
Change Differential Lubricant, 2002					S					S				S					S					S					S					S				S		

FULL SIZE PICKUPS—Continued

Recommended Service & Intervals (Months)	Service Interval In Miles①																																						
	3000	6000	7500	9000	12000	15000	18000	21000	22500	24000	27000	30000	33000	36000	37500	39000	42000	45000	48000	51000	52500	54000	57000	60000	63000	66000	67500	69000	72000	75000	78000	81000	82500	84000	87000	90000	93000	96000	97500	99000
DRIVE AXLE & DRIVESHAFT																																								
Change Differential Lubricant, 2003–06	Severe Service Every 15,000 Miles																																							
Change Front (4X4) & Rear Axle Fluid, 2002 1500	Severe Service Every 12,000 Miles																																							
Change Front (4X4) & Rear Axle Fluid, 2004–06 1500	Severe Service Every 15,000 Miles																																							
Inspect CV & Driveshaft Joint Boots			X			X			X			X			X			X			X			X			X			X			X			X			X	
Inspect Differential Lubricant Level	At Every Engine Oil Change																																							
Lubricate Driveshaft U-Joints, Slip Splines & Yokes③	S	X		S	X	S	X	S		X	S	X	S	X		S	X	S	X	S		X	S	X	S	X		S	X	S	X	S		X	S	X	S	X		S
ENGINE																																								
Adjust Engine Valve Clearance, 2004–06 Diesel	Every 135,000 Miles																																							
Change Engine Coolant, 2002 1500 LD	Normal Service At 60 Months Or 75,000 Miles Then Every 25,000 Miles Thereafter; Severe Service Every 100,000 Miles																																							
Change Engine Coolant, 2002 2500 & 3500 LD	Normal Service At 36 Months Or 45,000 Miles Then Every 24 Months Or 30,000 Miles; Severe Service Every 51,000 Miles																																							
Change Engine Coolant, 2006 Diesel	Every 60 Months Or 100,000 Miles																																							
Change Engine Coolant, 2003–04 1500, 2500 & 3500	Every 60 Months Or 100,000 Miles																																							
Change Engine Coolant, 2005–06 1500, 2500 & 3500	Every 60 Months Or 102,000 Miles																																							
Change Engine Coolant, 2002 MD Gasoline	Green IAT Coolant Every 36 Months Or 48,000 Miles																																							
Change Engine Coolant, 2002 MD Gasoline	Green Coolant Every 48,000 Miles																																							
Change Engine Coolant, 2002 Diesel	Every 36 Months Or 52,500 Miles																																							
Change Engine Oil, LD (Normal Service Every 6 Mos.), 2002	S	S	N	S	S	N	S	S	N	S	S	N	S	S	N	S	S	N	S	S	N	S	S	N	S	S	N	S	S	N	S	S	N	S	S	N	S	S	N	S
Change Engine Oil, MD & HD Gasoline (Normal Service Every 6 Mos.), 2002	S	X		S	X	S	X	S		X	S	X	S	X		S	X	S	X	S		X	S	X	S	X		S	X	S	X	S		X	S	X	S	X		S
Change Engine Oil, 2002 Diesel	Normal Service Every 6 Months Or 7500 Miles; Severe Service Every 3 Months Or 3750 Miles																																							

FULL SIZE PICKUPS—Continued

Recommended Service & Intervals (Months)	Service Interval In Miles①																																							
	3000	6000	7500	9000	12000	15000	18000	21000	22500	24000	27000	30000	33000	36000	37500	39000	42000	45000	48000	51000	52500	54000	57000	60000	63000	66000	67500	69000	72000	75000	78000	81000	82500	84000	87000	90000	93000	96000	97500	99000
ENGINE																																								
Change Engine Oil, 2003–06 Gasoline	Normal Service Every 6 Months Or 6000 Miles; Severe Service Every 3 Months Or 3000 Miles																																							
Change Engine Oil, 2003–04 Diesel Tier 1 EPA (250HO Or 305HP)	Normal Service Every 12 Months Or 15,000 Miles; Severe Service Every 7500 Miles																																							
Change Engine Oil, 2003–04 Diesel, California LEV (235HP)	Normal Service Every 6 Months Or 7500 Miles; Severe Service Every 3750 Miles																																							
Change Engine Oil, 2005–06 Diesel	Normal Service Every 12 Months Or 15,000 Miles; Severe Service Every 7500 Miles																																							
Change Engine Oil Filter, 2002 1500, 2500 & 3500 LD	Normal Service Every 6 Months Or 7500 Miles; Severe Service Every 3000 Miles																																							
Change Engine Oil Filter, 2003–06 Gasoline	Normal Service Every 6000 Miles; Severe Service Every 3000 Miles																																							
Change Engine Oil Filter, 2002 Diesel	Normal Service Every 6 Months Or 7500 Miles; Severe Service Every 3750 Miles																																							
Change Engine Oil Filter, 2002 MD & HD	Normal Service Every 6 Months Or 6000 Miles; Severe Service Every 3000 Miles																																							
Change Engine Oil Filter, 2003–04 Diesel Tier 1 EPA (250HP Or 305HP)	Normal Service Every 12 Months Or 15,000 Miles; Severe Service Every 7500 Miles																																							
Change Engine Oil Filter, 2003–04 Diesel , California LEV (235HP)	Normal Service Every 6 Months Or 7500 Miles; Severe Service Every 3750 Miles																																							
Change Engine Oil Filter, 2005–06 Diesel	Normal Service Every 12 Months Or 15,000 Miles; Severe Service Every 7500 Miles																																							
Clean & Lubricate Crankcase Inlet Air Filter, 2002 HD 5.9L Gasoline					S					X				S					X					S					X					S				X		
Drain Crankcase Breather Bottle, 2002 Diesel	Normal Service Every 15,000 Miles; Severe Service Every 3750 Miles																																							
Inspect Coolant Pump Weep Hole For Blockage, Diesel	Every 15,000 Miles																																							
Inspect Cooling System & Protection Level, Gasoline			X			X			X			X			X			X			X			X			X			X			X			X			X	
Inspect Drive Belts, Replace As Necessary, Diesel	Every 22,500 Miles																																							
Inspect Drive Belts, Replace As Necessary, 2002–03 Gasoline	Every 60,000 Miles																																							

FULL SIZE PICKUPS—Continued

Recommended Service & Intervals (Months)	Service Interval In Miles①																																						
	3000	6000	7500	9000	12000	15000	18000	21000	22500	24000	27000	30000	33000	36000	37500	39000	42000	45000	48000	51000	52500	54000	57000	60000	63000	66000	67500	69000	72000	75000	78000	81000	82500	84000	87000	90000	93000	96000	97500	99000
ENGINE																																								
Inspect Drive Belts, Replace As Necessary, 2004–06 Gasoline	Normal Service Every 90,000 Miles; Severe Service Every 75,000 Miles																																							
Inspect Engine Air Filter, 2003–06	Normal Service Every 30,000 Miles; Severe Service Every 15,000 Miles & Replace As Necessary																																							
Inspect Exhaust System		X			X		X			X		X		X			X		X			X		X		X			X		X			X		X		X		
Inspect Fan Hub & Dampener, Diesel	Every 30,000 Miles																																							
Inspect PCV Valve, 2002 1500 & 2003 1500, 2500 & 3500	Every 60,000 Miles																																							
Inspect PCV Valve, 2004 1500, 2500 & 3500	Normal Service Every 60,000 Miles; Severe Service Every 30,000 Miles																																							
Inspect PCV Valve, 2005–06 1500, 2500 & 3500	Every 60,000 Miles																																							
Lubricate Manifold Heat Riser Valve, 3.9L & 5.2L																					X																			
Replace Distributor Cap & Rotor, 2002 HD 5.9L Gasoline																								X																
Replace Engine Air Filter, 2002 LD & MD Gasoline						S						X						S						X						S						X				
Replace Fuel Filter & Clean Strainer, Diesel, 2002–03	Normal Service At 15,000 Miles & Every 15,000 Thereafter; Severe Service Every 7500 Miles																																							
Replace Fuel Filter & Clean Strainer, Diesel, 2004–06	Every 15,000 Miles																																							
Replace Ignition Cables, 2002 5.9L 1500	Every 60,000 Miles																																							
Replace Ignition Cables, 2003–06 5.7L, 5.9L & 8.0L	Every 60,000 Miles																																							
Replace O2 Sensor, 2002 HD 5.9L Gasoline																																	X							
Replace PCV Valve, 2003–06	Normal Service Inspect Every 60,000 Miles And Replace If Necessary; Severe Service Inspect Every 30,000 Miles																																							
Replace Spark Plugs												X												X												X				
STEERING, SUSPENSION & TIRES																																								
Change Power Steering Fluid, 2003–06	Drain And Replace At 100,000 Miles																																							
Inspect Bushings, Arms, Seals, Springs & Jounce Bumpers③	S	X		S	X	S	X	S		X	S	X	S	X		S	X	S	X	S		X	S	X	S	X		S	X	S	X	S		X	S	X	S	X		S
Inspect & Repack Front Wheel Bearings, 2002 2WD Diesel					S					X				S					X					S					X					S				X		

FULL SIZE PICKUPS—Continued

Recommended Service & Intervals (Months)	Service Interval In Miles①																																						
	3000	6000	7500	9000	12000	15000	18000	21000	22500	24000	27000	30000	33000	36000	37500	39000	42000	45000	48000	51000	52500	54000	57000	60000	63000	66000	67500	69000	72000	75000	78000	81000	82500	84000	87000	90000	93000	96000	97500	99000
STEERING, SUSPENSION & TIRES																																								
Inspect & Repack Front Wheel Bearings, 2002 2WD LD								S	N								S	N							S		N							S		N				
Inspect & Repack Front Wheel Bearing, 2002 2WD MD & HD										X									X										X									X		
Lubricate Center Link	Every 24 Months Or 22,500 Miles																																							
Lubricate Steering Linkage, 2002	Normal Service Every 6 Months Or 7500 Miles; Severe Service Every 3000 Miles																																							
Rotate Tires & Adjust Pressure, 2002 LD & Diesel	Inspect For Wear & Rotate Every 7500 Miles																																							
Rotate Tires & Adjust Pressure, 2002 MD & HD	Inspect For Wear & Rotate Every 6000 Miles																																							
Rotate Tires & Adjust Pressure, 2003–06 Diesel	Inspect For Wear & Rotate Every 7500 Miles																																							
Rotate Tires & Adjust Pressure, 2003–06 Gasoline	Inspect For Wear & Rotate Every 6000 Miles																																							

GVWR — Gross Vehicle Weight Rating
LD — Light Duty 2002 2500 models except 8.0L engine.
MD — Medium Duty 2002 2500 & 3500 models w/CA emissions & 8.0L engine.
HD — Heavy Duty 2002 2500 models w/FED emissions & 8.0L HD engine & 3500 models w/FED emissions & 5.9L & 8.0L engines.
Mos. — Months
N — Normal Service
S — Severe Service
X — Normal Or Severe Service
2WD — Two Wheel Drive
4WD — Four Wheel Drive
① — After vehicle passes 99,000 mile mark return to beginning of mileage table & start cycle over again.
② — If used for frequent wide open throttle upshifts (Drag Racing etc.) every 15,000 miles.
③ — Lubricate slip splines daily if travelling through water.
④ — Off-the-highway operation, trailer towing, snow plowing or prolonged operation w/heavy loading, especially in hot weather require more frequent transmission service. Perform these services if vehicle is usually operated under these conditions.

FULL SIZE VANS

Recommended Service & Intervals (Months)	Service Interval In Miles①																																							
	3000	6000	7500	9000	12000	15000	18000	21000	22500	24000	27000	30000	33000	36000	37500	39000	42000	45000	48000	51000	52500	54000	57000	60000	63000	66000	67500	69000	72000	75000	78000	81000	82500	84000	87000	90000	93000	96000	97500	99000
BRAKES																																								
Inspect Brake Connections, Hoses & Lines, 2002	Normal Service Every 6 Months Or 7500 Miles; Severe Service Every 3000 Miles																																							
Inspect Brake Connections, Hoses & Lines, 2003	Normal Service Every 18,000 Miles; Severe Service Every 12,000 Miles																																							
Lubricate Brake Booster Bellcrank Pivot						X						X						X						X						X						X				
Lubricate Parking Brake Ratio Lever Pivot									X									X									X									X				
CLUTCH & TRANSMISSION																																								
Change Automatic Transmission Fluid, Filter & Adjust Bands	Normal Service Every 100,000 Miles; Severe Service Every 30,000 Miles																																							
DRIVE AXLE & DRIVESHAFT																																								
Change Differential Lubricants					S					S				S					S					S					S					S				S		
Lubricate Driveshaft U-Joints, Slip Splines & Yokes	S	X		S	X	S	X	S		X	S	X	S	X		S	X	S	X	S		X	S	X	S	X		S	X	S	X	S		X	S	X	S	X		S
ENGINE																																								
Change Engine Coolant, 2002 Gasoline	Normal Service Every 45,000 Miles Then Every 30,000 Miles Thereafter; Severe Service At 51,000 Miles Then Every 30,000 Miles Thereafter																																							
Change Engine Coolant, 2003 Gasoline	Normal Service At 36 Months Or 60,000 Miles Then Every 24 Months Or 30,000 Miles Thereafter; Severe Service At 51,000 Miles Then Every 30,000 Miles Thereafter																																							
Change Engine Oil Filter, 2002	Normal Service Every 6 Months Or 7500 Miles; Severe Service Every 3000 Miles																																							
Change Engine Oil Filter, 2003	Normal Service Every 6 Months Or 6000 Miles; Severe Service Every 3000 Miles																																							
Inspect Cooling System & Protection Level			X			X			X			X			X			X			X			X			X			X			X			X			X	
Inspect Exhaust System		X			X		X			X		X		X			X		X			X		X		X			X		X			X		X		X		
Inspect PCV Valve②												S												X												S				
Lubricate Manifold Heat Riser Valve, 3.9L & 5.2L																					X																			
Replace Drive Belts	Inspect And/Or Replace At 60,000 Miles & Then Inspect Every 15,000 Miles Thereafter																																							
Replace Engine Air Filter	Normal Service Every 30,000 Miles; Severe Service Inspect Every 15,000 Miles & Replace As Necessary																																							
Replace Fuel Filter, Van w/FED Emissions																								S																
Replace PCV Valve②												S												X												S				
Replace Spark Plugs												X												X												X				

FULL SIZE VANS—Continued

Recommended Service & Intervals (Months)	Service Interval In Miles①																																						
	3000	6000	7500	9000	12000	15000	18000	21000	22500	24000	27000	30000	33000	36000	37500	39000	42000	45000	48000	51000	52500	54000	57000	60000	63000	66000	67500	69000	72000	75000	78000	81000	82500	84000	87000	90000	93000	96000	97500	99000
STEERING, SUSPENSION & TIRES																																								
Inspect Bushings, Arms, Seals, Springs & Jounce Bumpers	S	X		S	X	S	X	S		X	S	X	S	X		S	X	S	X	S		X	S	X	S	X		S	X	S	X	S		X	S	X	S	X		S
Inspect & Repack Front Wheel Bearings, 2002								S	N								S	N							S		N							S		N				
Lubricate Front Suspension Ball Joints, 2002	Every 18 Months Or 22,500 Miles																																						
Lubricate Front Suspension Ball Joints, 2003	Every 21,000 Miles																																						
Lubricate Steering Linkage, 2002	Every 12 Months Or 15,000 Miles																																						
Lubricate Steering Linkage, 2003	Normal Service Every 12,000 Miles; Severe Service Every 3000 Miles																																						
Rotate Tires, 2002	Normal Service Every 7500 Miles; Severe Service Every 6000 Miles																																						
Rotate Tires, 2003	Normal Service Every 6000 Miles																																						

Mos. — Months
N — Normal Service
S — Severe Service
X — Normal Or Severe Service
① — After vehicle passes 99,000 mile mark return to beginning of mileage table & start cycle over again.
② — This maintenance is recommended by DaimlerChrysler Corporation to the customer but it is not required to maintain warranty on PCV valve.

JEEP

Service Interval In Miles①

Recommended Service	3000	6000	7500	9000	12000	15000	18000	21000	22500	24000	27000	30000	33000	36000	37500	39000	42000	45000	48000	51000	52500	54000	57000	60000	63000	66000	67500	69000	72000	75000	78000	81000	82500	84000	87000	90000	93000	96000	97500	99000
BODY																																								
Lubricate Body Components												X												X												X				
BRAKES																																								
Drain & Replace Brake Fluid, Grand Cherokee	Every 60,000 Miles																																							
Inspect Brake Connections, Hoses & Lines, 2002	Normal Service Every 6 Months Or 7500 Miles; Severe Service Every 3000 Miles																																							
Inspect Brake Connections, Hoses & Lines, 2003–06	Normal Service Every 18,000 Miles; Severe Service Every 12,000 Miles																																							
Inspect Brake Drums & Rotors					S				N	S				S				N	S					S			N		S					S		N		S		
Inspect Brake Pads & Shoes Except Liberty Diesel					S				N	S				S				N	S					S			N		S					S		N		S		
Inspect Brake Pads & Shoes, Liberty Diesel	Normal Service Every 25,000 Miles; Severe Service Every 12,500 Miles																																							
Inspect Brake System												X												X												X				
CLUTCH, TRANSMISSION & TRANSFER CASE																																								
Change Automatic Transmission Fluid & Filter, 2002 Grand Cherokee, Liberty & Wrangler	Normal Service Every 100,000 Miles; Severe Service Every 30,000 Miles																																							
Change Automatic Transmission Fluid & Filter, 2003–04 Grand Cherokee, Liberty & Wrangler	Normal Service Every 102,000 Miles; Severe Service Every 30,000 Miles																																							
Change Automatic Transmission Fluid & Filter, 2005–06 Grand Cherokee, Liberty & Wrangler & 2006 Commander	Gasoline Engine Models Severe Service Every 60,000 Miles; Diesel Engine Models Severe Service Every 62,500 Miles																																							
Change Transfer Case Lubricant, Grand Cherokee	②																																							
Change Transfer Case Lubricant, Liberty Diesel	Normal Service Inspect Every 12,500 Miles; Severe Service Every 62,500 Miles																																							
Change Transfer Case Lubricant, 2002 Liberty	No Normal Service; Severe Service Every 60,000 Miles																																							
Change Transfer Case Lubricant, 2002–03 Wrangler & 2003–06 Liberty Except Diesel	Normal Service At 120,000 Miles; Severe Service Every 60,000 Miles																																							
Change Transfer Case Lubricant, 2006 Commander	Every 60,000 Miles																																							

JEEP—Continued

Recommended Service	Service Interval In Miles①																																							
	3000	6000	7500	9000	12000	15000	18000	21000	22500	24000	27000	30000	33000	36000	37500	39000	42000	45000	48000	51000	52500	54000	57000	60000	63000	66000	67500	69000	72000	75000	78000	81000	82500	84000	87000	90000	93000	96000	97500	99000
CLUTCH, TRANSMISSION & TRANSFER CASE																																								
Inspect Manual Transmission Lubricant, 2006 Liberty Diesel	At 12,500 Miles Then Every 62,500 Miles																																							
DRIVE AXLE & DRIVESHAFT																																								
Change Differential Lubricants, Wrangler④	Severe Service Every 12,000 Miles																																							
Change Differential Lubricants, 2006 Commander. Grand Cherokee, Liberty Except Diesel④	Severe Service Every 12,500 Miles																																							
Change Differential Lubricants, 2006 Liberty Diesel④	Severe Service Every 15,000 Miles																																							
Inspect & Lubricate Driveshaft U-Joints & Slip Splines	S	S	N	S	S	X	S	S	N	S	S	X	S	S	N	S	S	X	S	S	N	S	S	X	S	S	N	S	S	X	S	S	N	S	S	X	S	S	N	S
ENGINE																																								
Change Engine Coolant, 2002–04	Every 60 Months Or 100,000 Miles																																							
Change Engine Coolant, 2005–06	Every 60 Months Or 102,000 Miles																																							
Change Engine Oil & Filter, Liberty Diesel	Normal Service Every 12,500 Miles; Severe Service Every 6250 Miles																																							
Change Engine Oil & Filter, 2002	Normal Service Every 7500 Miles; Severe Service Every 3000 Miles																																							
Change Engine Oil & Filter, 2003–06 Gasoline Engine	Normal Service Every 6000 Miles; Severe Service Every 3000 Miles																																							
Inspect & Adjust Manually Tensioned Drive Belts, 2002 Grand Cherokee	4.0L At 60,000 Miles & Every 15,000 Miles Thereafter; 4.7L At 90,000 Miles & Every 15,000 Miles Thereafter																																							
Inspect & Adjust Manually Tensioned Drive Belts, 2002 Wrangler												X												X												X				
Inspect Coolant Level	At Every Engine Oil Change																																							
Inspect Cooling System & Protection Level			X			X			X			X			X			X			X			X			X			X			X			X			X	
Inspect Drive Belts, 2002–04 Liberty & 2003–04 Grand Cherokee	Normal Service At 60,000 Miles & Every 15,000 Miles Thereafter; Severe Service At 45,000 Miles & Every 15,000 Miles Thereafter																																							
Inspect Drive Belts, 2003 Wrangler	Normal Service At 75,000 Miles & Every 15,000 Miles Thereafter; Severe Service At 60,000 Miles & Every 15,000 Miles Thereafter																																							

JEEP—Continued

Recommended Service	Service Interval In Miles①																																							
	3000	6000	7500	9000	12000	15000	18000	21000	22500	24000	27000	30000	33000	36000	37500	39000	42000	45000	48000	51000	52500	54000	57000	60000	63000	66000	67500	69000	72000	75000	78000	81000	82500	84000	87000	90000	93000	96000	97500	99000
ENGINE																																								
Inspect Drive Belts, 2005	Normal Service At 60,000 Miles & Every 12,000 Miles Thereafter; Severe Service At 45,000 Miles & Every 15,000 Miles Thereafter																																							
Inspect Drive Belts, 2006	Normal Service At 60,000 Miles & Every 30,000 Miles Thereafter; Severe Service At 60,000 Miles & Every 15,000 Miles Thereafter																																							
Inspect Exhaust System	At Every Engine Oil Change																																							
Inspect PCV Valve	Normal Service At 60,000 Miles & Every 30,000 Miles Thereafter; Severe Service Every 30,000 Miles																																							
Inspect PCV Valve, Grand Cherokee, 2002 4.7L & 2003–06 Grand Cherokee, Liberty, Wrangler & 2006 Commander③	Normal Service Inspect Every 60,000 Miles; Severe Service Every 30,000 Miles																																							
Replace Boost Pressure Solenoid Filter, 2006 Liberty Diesel	Every 50,000 Miles																																							
Replace Drive Belts, Liberty Diesel	Normal Service Every 62,500 Miles; Severe Service Every 37,500 Miles																																							
Replace Engine Air Filter, Liberty Diesel	Normal Service Every 25,000 Miles; Severe Service Every 12,500 Miles																																							
Replace Engine Air Filter, 2002 Cherokee, Grand Cherokee, Wrangler & Liberty						S						X						S						X						S						X				
Replace Engine Air Filter, 2003 Grand Cherokee, Liberty & Wrangler	Inspect Every 30,000 Miles & Replace As Necessary																																							
Replace Engine Air Filter, 2004–06 Grand Cherokee, Liberty Except Diesel, Wrangler & 2006 Commander	Normal Service Inspect Every 30,000 Miles & Replace As Necessary; Severe Service Inspect Every 15,000 Miles & Replace As Necessary																																							
Replace Fuel Filter/Water Separator Unit, Liberty Diesel	Every 25,000 Miles																																							
Replace Ignition Cables 2002–05 Wrangler, 2.5L & 2003–06 2.4L Liberty & Wrangler	Every 60,000 Miles																																							
Replace Spark Plugs												X												X												X				
Replace Timing Belt & Idler Pulleys, 2006 Liberty Diesel③	Every 100,000 Miles																																							
Replace Timing Belt, 2.4L③	Normal Service Every 120,000 Miles; Severe Service Every 90,000 Miles																																							
STEERING, SUSPENSION & TIRES																																								
Inspect Chassis Components												X												X												X				

JEEP—Continued

Recommended Service	3000	6000	7500	9000	12000	15000	18000	21000	22500	24000	27000	30000	33000	36000	37500	39000	42000	45000	48000	51000	52500	54000	57000	60000	63000	66000	67500	69000	72000	75000	78000	81000	82500	84000	87000	90000	93000	96000	97500	99000
	Service Interval In Miles①																																							
STEERING, SUSPENSION & TIRES																																								
Inspect Power Steering Fluid Level	At Every Engine Oil Change																																							
Inspect & Lubricate Steering Gear & Linkage, & Suspension Ball Joints	S	S	N	S	S	X	S	S	N	S	S	X	S	S	N	S	S	X	S	S	N	S	S	X	S	S	N	S	S	X	S	S	N	S	S	X	S	S	N	S
Rotate Tires & Adjust Pressure		S	N		S	N	S		N	S		X		S	N		S	N		S	N		S	X		S	N		S	N		S	N		S	X		S	N	

Mos. — Months
N — Normal Service
S — Severe Service
X — Normal Or Severe Service
① — After vehicles passes 99,000 mile mark return to beginning of mileage table & start cycle over again.
② — Quadra Trac drain and refill every 30,000 miles. Select Trac inspect every 30,000 miles, Severe Service drain & refill every 60,000 miles.
③ — This maintenance is recommended to customer but is not required to maintain emissions warranty.
④ — Off highway operation, trailer towing, snow plowing or prolonged operation w/heavy loading, especially in hot weather require more frequent transmission service. Perform services if vehicle is usually operated under these conditions.

PT CRUISER

Recommended Service & Intervals (Months)	Service Interval In Miles①																																						
	3000	6000	7500	9000	12000	15000	18000	21000	22500	24000	27000	30000	33000	36000	37500	39000	42000	45000	48000	51000	52500	54000	57000	60000	63000	66000	67500	69000	72000	75000	78000	81000	82500	84000	87000	90000	93000	96000	97500	99000
BRAKES																																								
Inspect Brake Connections, Hoses & Lines	Normal Service Every 6 Months Or 7500 Miles; Severe Service Every 3 Months Or 3000 Miles																																							
Inspect Brake Drums & Rotors, 2002					S		S		N		S			S				X				S			S		N		S			S				X				
Inspect Brake Drums & Rotors, 2003–06	Normal Service Every 18,000 Miles; Severe Service Every 12,000 Miles																																							
Inspect Brake Pads & Linings, 2002					S		S		N		S			S				X				S			S		N		S			S				X				
Inspect Brake Pads & Linings, 2003–06	Normal Service Every 18,000 Miles; Severe Service Every 12,000 Miles																																							
Replace Brake Fluid ③																			S																			S		
CLUTCH & TRANSMISSION																																								
Change Automatic Transmission Fluid & Filter, 2002–04	Severe Service Replace Every 48,000 Miles																																							
Change Automatic Transmission Fluid & Filter, 2005–06	Severe Service Replace Every 60,000 Miles																																							
Change Manual Transmission Lubricant	Severe Service Replace Every 48,000 Miles																																							
Check Transmission Lubricant & Level Condition	Severe Service At Every Oil Change																																							
DRIVE AXLE & DRIVESHAFT																																								
Inspect CV & Driveshaft Joint Boots			X			X			X			X			X			X			X			X			X			X			X			X			X	
ENGINE																																								
Adjust Alternator Drive Belt Tension	Every 24 Months Or 30,000 Miles																																							
Change Engine Coolant, 2002–04	Every 60 Months Or 100,000 Miles																																							
Change Engine Coolant, 2005–06	Every 60 Months Or 102,000 Miles																																							
Change Engine Oil & Filter, 2002	S	S	N	S	S	N	S	S	N	S	S	N	S	S	N	S	S	N	S	S	N	S	S	N	S	S	N	S	S	N	S	S	N	S	S	N	S	S	N	S
Change Engine Oil & Filter, 2003–06 Non-Turbo	Normal Service Every 6 Months Or 6000 Miles; Severe Service Every 3000 Miles																																							
Change Engine Oil, Turbo	Normal Service Every 6 Months Or 5000 Miles; Severe Service Every 3000 Miles																																							

PT CRUISER—Continued

Recommended Service & Intervals (Months)	Service Interval In Miles①																																						
	3000	6000	7500	9000	12000	15000	18000	21000	22500	24000	27000	30000	33000	36000	37500	39000	42000	45000	48000	51000	52500	54000	57000	60000	63000	66000	67500	69000	72000	75000	78000	81000	82500	84000	87000	90000	93000	96000	97500	99000
ENGINE																																								
Inspect Coolant Level, Hoses & Clamps	At Every Oil Change																																							
Inspect Drive Belts						S						X						S						X						S						X				
Inspect Engine Air Filter & PCV Filter	Normal Service Every 30,000 Miles; Severe Service Every 15,000 Miles																																							
Inspect Exhaust System	At Every Oil Change																																							
Inspect PCV Valve②												S												X												S				
Replace Ignition Cables	Every 60,000 Miles																																							
Replace PCV Filter	Normal Service Inspect at 60,000 Miles, Severe Service Inspect At 30,000 & Every 30,000 Thereafter. Replace If Necessary																																							
Replace Spark Plugs												X												X												X				
Replace Timing Belt, 2002–04	Every 102,000 Miles																																							
Replace Timing Belt, 2005–06	Normal Service Every 105,000 Miles; Severe Service Every 90,000 Miles																																							
STEERING, SUSPENSION & TIRES																																								
Inspect Bushings, Arms, CV Joints, Seals, Springs & Jounce Bumpers	S	X		S	X	S	X	S		X	S	X	S	X		S	X	S	X	S		X	S	X	S	X		S	X	S	X	S		X	S	X	S	X		S
Inspect Tie Rod Ends & Boot Seals	Every 30,000 Miles																																							
Lubricate Ball Joints (Every 18 Mos.)									X									X									X									X				
Lubricate Steering Linkage (Every 12 Mos.)						X						X						X						X						X						X				
Rotate Tires & Adjust Pressure, 2002		S	N		S	N	S		N	S		X		S	N		S	N	S		N	S		X		S	N		S	N	S		N	S		X		S	N	
Rotate Tires & Adjust Pressure, 2003–06 Non-Turbo	Every 6000 Miles																																							
Rotate Tires & Adjust Pressure, 2003–06 Turbo	Every 5000 Miles																																							

N — Normal Service
S — Severe Service
X — Normal Or Severe Service
① — After vehicle passes 99,000 mile mark return to beginning of mileage table & start cycle over again.
② — This maintenance is recommended by DaimlerChrysler Corporation to the owner, but not required to maintain the warranty of the PCV Valve.
③ — If vehicle is used for trailer towing.

SPRINTER

<table>
<tr><th rowspan="2">Recommended Service & Intervals (Months)</th><th colspan="40">Service Interval In Miles①</th></tr>
<tr><th>3000</th><th>6000</th><th>7500</th><th>9000</th><th>12000</th><th>15000</th><th>18000</th><th>21000</th><th>22500</th><th>24000</th><th>27000</th><th>30000</th><th>33000</th><th>36000</th><th>37500</th><th>39000</th><th>42000</th><th>45000</th><th>48000</th><th>51000</th><th>52500</th><th>54000</th><th>57000</th><th>60000</th><th>63000</th><th>66000</th><th>67500</th><th>69000</th><th>72000</th><th>75000</th><th>78000</th><th>81000</th><th>82500</th><th>84000</th><th>87000</th><th>90000</th><th>93000</th><th>96000</th><th>97500</th><th>99000</th></tr>
<tr><td colspan="41">BODY</td></tr>
<tr><td>Inspect Body And Paint For Damage And Corrision</td><td colspan="40">Every 24 Months</td></tr>
<tr><td>Inspect Headlamp Aiming②</td><td colspan="40">Schedule B</td></tr>
<tr><td>Inspect Seat Belts②</td><td colspan="40">Schedule B</td></tr>
<tr><td>Lubricate Hood Hinges And Latches ②</td><td colspan="40">Schedules A And B</td></tr>
<tr><td colspan="41">BRAKES</td></tr>
<tr><td>Inspect Brake Connections, Hoses & Lines②</td><td colspan="40">Schedule B</td></tr>
<tr><td>Inspect Brake Drums & Rotors</td><td colspan="40">Schedule B</td></tr>
<tr><td>Inspect Brake Pads & Linings②</td><td colspan="40">Schedules A And B</td></tr>
<tr><td>Inspect Parking Brake②</td><td colspan="40">Schedule B</td></tr>
<tr><td colspan="41">CLUTCH & TRANSMISSION</td></tr>
<tr><td>Change Automatic Transmission Fluid & Filter</td><td colspan="40">Replace At 80,000 Miles, After This Change, Automatic Transmission Fluid Is Changed For Life</td></tr>
<tr><td>Check Transmission Lubricant & Level Condition②</td><td colspan="40">Schedules A And B</td></tr>
<tr><td colspan="41">DRIVE AXLE & DRIVESHAFT</td></tr>
<tr><td>Inspect Driveshaft Flex Discs</td><td colspan="40">Every 48 Months Or 50,000 Miles</td></tr>
<tr><td>Rear Axle Fluid②</td><td colspan="40">At Fourth Maintenance Service</td></tr>
<tr><td colspan="41">ENGINE</td></tr>
<tr><td>Change Engine Coolant</td><td colspan="40">Every 60 Months Or 100,000 Miles</td></tr>
<tr><td>Change Engine Oil & Filter②</td><td colspan="40">Schedules A And B; Normal Service Every 12 Months Or 10,000 Miles</td></tr>
<tr><td>Inspect Coolant Level, Hoses & Clamps②</td><td colspan="40">Schedules A And B</td></tr>
<tr><td>Inspect Drive Belts②</td><td colspan="40">Schedule B</td></tr>
<tr><td>Inspect Exhaust System②</td><td colspan="40">Schedule B</td></tr>
<tr><td>Replace Air Filter</td><td colspan="40">Every 36 Months Or 30,000 Miles</td></tr>
<tr><td>Replace Fuel Filter</td><td colspan="40">At Oil Change Intervals</td></tr>
<tr><td>Replace Spark Plugs</td><td colspan="40">Every 60 Months Or 100,000 Miles</td></tr>
<tr><td colspan="41">STEERING, SUSPENSION & TIRES</td></tr>
<tr><td>Inspect Chassis Components For Damage And Corrision</td><td colspan="40">Every 48 Months</td></tr>
<tr><td>Inspect Front Ball Joints And Boots②</td><td colspan="40">Schedule B</td></tr>
</table>

SPRINTER—Continued

<table>
<tr><th rowspan="2">Recommended Service & Intervals (Months)</th><th colspan="40">Service Interval In Miles①</th></tr>
<tr><th>3000</th><th>6000</th><th>7500</th><th>9000</th><th>12000</th><th>15000</th><th>18000</th><th>21000</th><th>22500</th><th>24000</th><th>27000</th><th>30000</th><th>33000</th><th>36000</th><th>37500</th><th>39000</th><th>42000</th><th>45000</th><th>48000</th><th>51000</th><th>52500</th><th>54000</th><th>57000</th><th>60000</th><th>63000</th><th>66000</th><th>67500</th><th>69000</th><th>72000</th><th>75000</th><th>78000</th><th>81000</th><th>82500</th><th>84000</th><th>87000</th><th>90000</th><th>93000</th><th>96000</th><th>97500</th><th>99000</th></tr>
<tr><td colspan="41">STEERING, SUSPENSION & TIRES</td></tr>
<tr><td>Inspect Steering Components And Boots②</td><td colspan="40">Schedule B</td></tr>
<tr><td>Inspect Tires②</td><td colspan="40">Schedules A And B</td></tr>
<tr><td>Rotate Tires②</td><td colspan="40">Schedule B</td></tr>
</table>

N — Normal Service
S — Severe Service
X — Normal Or Severe Service
① — After vehicle passes 99,000 mile mark return to beginning of mileage table & start cycle over again.
② — There are two FSS symbols that will appear in the main odometer display next to suggested service. Service Schedule A is represented by one wrench symbol which indicates oil service is necessary.. Service Schedule B is represented by two wrench symbols which indicates maintenace service is necessary. Follow Schedule Schedule A for first service interval, Schedule B for second service interval and so on. If the display shows the number of days a clock sysmbol will appear and the maintenance should be performed in the stated period/distance. The service indicator will be reset after an oil service and or maintenance service has been performed.

Ford Motor Co.

INDEX

AVIATOR, BLACKWOOD, E-SERIES, EXCURSION, EXPEDITION, F-SERIES & F-SUPER DUTY, MARK LT & NAVIGATOR

Recommended Service	Service Interval In Miles①																														
	3000	5000	6000	7500	9000	10000	12000	15000	18000	20000	21000	22500	24000	25000	27000	30000	33000	35000	36000	37500	39000	40000	42000	45000	48000	50000	51000	52500	54000	55000	57000	60000
BODY																																
Inspect Instrument Panel Warning Lamps & Gauges	At Every Engine Oil Change																															
Inspect & Replace Damaged Or Missing Vehicle Noise Shields, Diesel																X																X
Lubricate Body Hardware & Hinges								X								X								X								X
Replace Cabin Air Filter	Every 15,000 Miles, If Equipped																															
Replace Climate Control Seat Filter, Blackwood, Navigator & Aviator																X																X
BRAKES																																
Inspect Brake Systems	Normal Service Every 15,000 Miles; Severe Service Every 5000 Miles																															
Inspect Parking Brake System Operation																X																X
CLUTCH & TRANSMISSION																																
Change Automatic Transmission Fluid & Filter, 2004–06	Normal Service Inspect Every 15,000 Miles Change At 150,000 Miles; Severe ServiceReplace Every 30,000 Miles																															
Change Automatic Transmission Fluid & Filter, 4RTOW & 4R100	Inspect Every 15,000 Miles; Replace Every 30,000 Miles																															
Change Automatic Transmission Fluid & Remote Filter Element, 2005–06 Torqushift	Inspect Fluid Level Every 15,000 Miles; Replace Every 30,000 Miles																															
Change Manual Transmission	Normal Service Every 60,000 Miles; Severe Service 60,000 Miles Or Less If Required																															
Change Transfer Case Lubricant	Normal Service Every 150,000 Miles; Severe Service Every 60,000 Miles																															
Inspect & Lubricate Automatic Transmission Shift Linkage	At Every Engine Oil Change																															
Lubricate Throttle Kickdown Or TV Lever Ball Studs													S			X									S							X
Lubricate Transfer Case Shift Lever Pivot Bolt & Control Rod Connecting Pins								X								X								X								X
DRIVE AXLE & DRIVESHAFT																																
Change Differential Lubricant	③																															
Driveshaft U-Joints & Slip Yoke Grease Fittings	At Every Engine Oil Change																															
Lubricate RH Front Drive Axle Slip Yoke, 4WD																X																X

AVIATOR, BLACKWOOD, E-SERIES, EXCURSION, EXPEDITION, F-SERIES & F-SUPER DUTY, MARK LT & NAVIGATOR—Continued

Recommended Service	Service Interval In Miles①																														
	3000	5000	6000	7500	9000	10000	12000	15000	18000	20000	21000	22500	24000	25000	27000	30000	33000	35000	36000	37500	39000	40000	42000	45000	48000	50000	51000	52500	54000	55000	57000	60000
ENGINE																																
Change Engine Coolant, 2002–03	Green Coolant, Every 45,000 Miles, Then Every 30,000 Miles Thereafter. Replace Orange Coolant, Every 150,000 Miles, Replace Yellow Coolant, Every 5 Years Or 100,000 Miles																														
Change Engine Coolant, 2004–06	Replace Premium Gold Coolant, Every 5 Years Or 100,000 Miles Thereafter Replace Every 36 Months Or 50,000 Miles																														
Change Engine Oil & Filter	S	N	S		S	N	S	X	S	N	S		S	N	S	X	S	N	S		S	N	S	X	S	N	S		S	N	S	X
Drain Coalescent Filter Bowl, 2002–04, NGV	Every 120,000 Miles And Inspect NGV Tanks																														
Drain Coalescent Filter Bowl, 2005–06, NGV	Every 125,000 Miles And Inspect NGV Tanks																														
Drain Water From Diesel Fuel Filter Bowl & Water Separator		X				X		X		X				X		X		X				X		X		X				X		X
Inspect Drive Belts, Ambulance		X				X		X		X				X		X		X				X		X		X				X		X
Inspect Drive Belts, Except Ambulance								X								X								X								X
Inspect Engine Air Induction System, Fan & Shrouds, E-350 & F-350 w/10,000 Lb. GVWR & Over																X																X
Inspect Exhaust System & Instrument Panel Warning Lamps & Gauges	At Every Engine Oil Change																														
Inspect Thermactor Or Secondary Air Injection Hoses, Clamps & System Operation																X																X
Replace Engine Air & Crankcase Filter Elements, Except Diesel																X																X
Replace Engine Air Filter Element, Diesel	Every 30,000 Miles Or When Restriction Gauge Enters Red Zone																														
Replace Fuel Filter, 2002–03②	Every 30,000 Miles																														
Replace Fuel Filter, 2004–06②	Normal Service Every 30,000 Miles; Severe Service Every 15,000 Miles																														
Replace Fuel Filter, 2002–03 Diesel	Every 15,000 Miles Or When Filter Restriction Lamp Lights																														
Replace PCV Valve																																X
Replace Spark Plugs, Expedition, Navigator & F-150 & E-Series Except NGV	Normal Service Every 100,000 Miles; Severe Service Every 60,000 Miles																														
Replace Spark Plugs, E-Series NGV																																X
Replace Spark Plug Wires																																X

AVIATOR, BLACKWOOD, E-SERIES, EXCURSION, EXPEDITION, F-SERIES & F-SUPER DUTY, MARK LT & NAVIGATOR—Continued

Recommended Service	Service Interval In Miles①																														
	3000	5000	6000	7500	9000	10000	12000	15000	18000	20000	21000	22500	24000	25000	27000	30000	33000	35000	36000	37500	39000	40000	42000	45000	48000	50000	51000	52500	54000	55000	57000	60000
STEERING, SUSPENSION & TIRES																																
Inspect Hub Lock & Spindle Needle Bearing Lubrication, 4WD																X																X
Lubricate Front Axle Spindle Pins & Steering Linkage	Normal Service Every 15,000 Miles; Severe Service As Required																															
Tighten Wheel Lugnuts	500 Miles After Rotation Or Wheel Removal, Then At Every Engine Oil Change																															
Rotate Tires	Normal Service Inspect For Wear & Rotate Every 5000 Miles																															

GVWR — Gross Vehicle Weight Rating
HD — Heavy Duty, GVWR of 8501 lbs. or more
LD — Light Duty, GVWR of 8500 lbs. or less
N — Normal Service
NGV — Natural Gas Vehicle
S — Severe Service
X — Normal Or Severe Service
① — After vehicle has passed 60,000 mile mark return to beginning of mileage table & start cycle over again.
② — On models equipped w/California emission service is recommended but not required.
③ — **Normal Vehicle Axle Maintenance:** Front axle, rear axle and power take off (PTO) units containing synthetic lubricant and light duty trucks equipped with Ford-design axles are lubricated for life. These lubricants are not to be checked or changed unless a leak is suspected, service is required or the axle assembly has been submerged in water. The axle lubricant and PTO lubricant should be changed anytime the axle and PTO has been submerged in water. Non-synthetic rear axle lubricants should be replaced every 100,000 miles under normal operating conditions. Non-synthetic rear axle lubricants should be replaced every 3000 miles or 3 months, whichever occurs first, during extended trailer tow operation above (70°F) ambient and wide open throttle for extended periods above 45 mph. The 3000 mile lube change interval may be waived if the axle was filled with 75W140 synthetic gear lubricant meeting Ford specification WSL-M2C192–A, part number F1TZ-19580–B or equivalent. Add four ounces of additive friction modifier C8AZ-19B546–A (EST-M2C118–A) or equivalent for complete refill of Traction-Lok rear axles. The rear axle lubricant should be changed anytime the axle has been submerged in water.

Police and Taxi Vehicle Axle Maintenance: Replace rear axle lubricant every 160,000km (100,000 miles). Rear axle lubricant change may be waived if the axle was filled with 75W140 synthetic gear lubricant meeting Ford specification WSL-M2C192–A. Add four ounces of additive friction modifier C8AZ-19B546–A(EST-M2C118–A) or equivalent for complete refill of Traction-Lok rear axles. The rear axle lubricant should be changed anytime the axle has been submerged in water.

ESCAPE, EXPLORER, MARNIER, MOUNTAINEER & RANGER

Recommended Service	Service Interval In Miles①																											
	3000	5000	6000	9000	10000	12000	15000	18000	20000	21000	24000	25000	27000	30000	33000	35000	36000	39000	40000	42000	45000	48000	50000	51000	54000	55000	57000	60000
BRAKES																												
Inspect Brake Hoses & Lines							X							X							X							X
Inspect Disc & Drum Brake System, Lubricate Caliper Slide Rails	Normal Service Every 15,000 Miles; Severe Service Every 5000 Miles																											
Inspect Parking Brake Operation														X														X
Replace Cabin Air Filter, If Equipped	Every 15,000 Miles																											
CLUTCH & TRANSMISSION																												
Change Automatic Transmission Fluid & Filter, Explorer, Mountaineer & Ranger⑤	Normal Service Inspect Every 15,000 Miles, Change Every 150,000 Miles; Severe Service Change Every 30,000 Miles																											
Change Automatic Transmission Fluid, 2002–03 Explorer & Mountaineer ②	Inspect Every 15,000 Miles; Every 30,000 Miles																											
Change Manual Transmission Lubricant																												X
Change Transfer Case Fluid	Normal Service Every 150,000 Miles; Severe Service Every 60,000 Miles																											
Inspect & Lubricate Automatic Transmission Cable Linkage		N	S			S	N	S			S	N		S		N	S			S	N	S			S	N		S
Lubricate Transfer Case Shift Lever Pivot Bolt & Control Rod Connecting Pins							X							X							X							X
DRIVE AXLE & DRIVESHAFT																												
Change Differential Lubricant	⑥																											
Lubricate Driveshaft Grease Fittings, Double Cardan Joint Centering Ball & Slip Yoke		N	S			S	N	S			S	N		S		N	S			S	N	S			S	N		S
Lubricate RH Front Drive Axle Shaft Slip Yoke, 4WD Models														X														X
ENGINE																												
Change Engine Coolant, 2002–03	Green Coolant, Every 45,000 Miles, Then Every 30,000 Miles Thereafter. Replace Orange Coolant, Every 150,000 Miles, ReplaceYellow Coolant, Every 5 Years Or 100,000 Miles																											
Change Engine Coolant, 2004–06	Replace Premium Gold Coolant, Every 5 Years Or 100,000 Miles Thereafter Replace Every 36 Months Or 50,000 Miles																											
Change Engine Oil & Filter	S	N	S	S	N	S	X	S	N	S	S	N	S	X	S	N	S	S	N	S	X	S	N	S	S	N	S	X
Inspect Cooling System & Protection Level							X							X							X							X
Inspect Drive Belts	Every 100,000 Miles																											
Inspect Exhaust System		N	S			S	N	S			S	N		S		N	S			S	N	S			S	N		S
Inspect NGV Tanks, 2002–03④	Every 30,00 Miles																											
Inspect NGV Tanks, 2004–06④	Every 3 Years From Date Of Tank Manufacture																											
Inspect Spark Plug Wires														X														X
Replace Engine Air Filter & Crankcase Emission Filter Elements														X														X
Replace Fuel Filter ③	Normal Service Every 30,000 Miles; Severe Service Every 15,000 Miles																											
Replace NGV Tanks, 2004–06④	Every 15 Years From Date Of Tank Manufacture																											
Replace PCV Valve	4 Cylinder Every 60,000 Miles; Except 4 Cylinder Every 100,000 Miles																											
Replace Spark Plugs	Normal Service Every 100,000 Miles; Severe Service Every 60,000 Miles																											

ESCAPE, EXPLORER, MARNIER, MOUNTAINEER & RANGER—Continued

Recommended Service	Service Interval In Miles①																											
	3000	5000	6000	9000	10000	12000	15000	18000	20000	21000	24000	25000	27000	30000	33000	35000	36000	39000	40000	42000	45000	48000	50000	51000	54000	55000	57000	60000
STEERING, SUSPENSION & TIRES																												
Inspect Power Steering Fluid Level	At Every Engine Oil Change																											
Inspect Spindle Needle Bearing Thrust Bearing & Hub Lock Lubrication														X														X
Lubricate Steering Linkage			S			S	N	S			S	N		S		N	S			S	N	S			S	N		S
Repack Front Wheel Bearings														X														X
Rotate Tires & Inspect Wheel Lug Nut Security	Normal Service Inspect For Wear And Rotate Every 5000 Miles																											

N — Normal Service
S — Severe Service
X — Normal Or Severe Service
① — After vehicle has passed 60,000 mile mark return to beginning of mileage table & start cycle over again.
② — On models equipped w/4R70W or 4R100 automatic transmissions.
③ — On models equipped with California emissions.
④ — On natural gas equipped models.
⑤ — Except models equipped w/4R70W or 4R100 automatic transmission.
⑥ — **Normal Vehicle Axle Maintenance:** Rear axle and power take off (PTO) units containing synthetic lubricant and light duty trucks equipped with Ford-design axles are lubricated for life. These lubricants are not to be checked or changed unless a leak is suspected, service is required or the axle assembly has been submerged in water. The axle lubricant and PTO lubricant should be changed anytime the axle and PTO has been submerged in water. Non-synthetic rear axle lubricants should be replaced every 3000 miles or 3 months, whichever occurs first, during extended trailer tow operation above (70°F) ambient and wide open throttle for extended periods above 45 mph. The 3000 mile lube change interval may be waived if the axle was filled with 75W140 synthetic gear lubricant meeting Ford specification WSL-M2C192–A, part number F1TZ-19580–B or equivalent. Add four ounces of additive friction modifier C8AZ-19B546–A (EST-M2C118–A) or equivalent for complete refill of Traction-Lok rear axles. The rear axle lubricant should be changed anytime the axle has been submerged in water.

Police and Taxi Vehicle Axle Maintenance: Replace rear axle lubricant every 160,000km (100,000 miles). Rear axle lubricant change may be waived if the axle was filled with 75W140 synthetic gear lubricant meeting Ford specification WSL-M2C192–A. Add four ounces of additive friction modifier C8AZ-19B546–A(EST-M2C118–A) or equivalent for complete refill of Traction-Lok rear axles. The rear axle lubricant should be changed anytime the axle has been submerged in water.

FREESTAR, MONTEREY & WINDSTAR

Recommended Service	Service Interval In Miles①																											
	3000	5000	6000	9000	10000	12000	15000	18000	20000	21000	24000	25000	27000	30000	33000	35000	36000	39000	40000	42000	45000	48000	50000	51000	54000	55000	57000	60000
BRAKES																												
Inspect Brake Drums, Linings, Pads & Rotors	Normal Service Every 15,000 Miles; Servere Service Every 5000 Miles																											
Inspect Brake Lines & Hoses														X														X
Replace Cabin Air Filter	Every 15,000 Miles																											
CLUTCH & TRANSMISSION																												
Change Automatic Transaxle Fluid & Filter, 2002–04	Inspect Every 15,000 Miles; Replace Every 30,000 Miles																											
Change Automatic Transaxle Fluid & Filter, 2005–06	Inspect Every 15,000 Miles; Replace Every 30,000 Miles																											
ENGINE																												
Change Engine Coolant, 2002–03	Replace Green Coolant Every 45,000 Miles, Then Every 30,000 Miles Thereafter. Replace Orange Coolant Every 150,000 Miles, Replace Yellow Coolant, Every 5 Years Or 100,000 Miles																											
Change Engine Coolant, 2004–06	Replace Premium Gold Coolant, Every 5 Years Or 100,000 Miles Thereafter Replace Every 36 Months Or 50,000 Miles																											
Change Engine Oil & Filter	S	N	S	S	N	S	X	S	N	S	S	N	S	X	S	N	S	S	N	S	X	S	N	S	S	N	S	X
Inspect Cooling System & Protection Level							X							X							X							X
Inspect Drive Belts	Every 100,000 Miles																											
Inspect Exhaust System														X														X
Replace Engine Air Filter Element														X														X
Replace Fuel Filter②	Normal Service Every 30,000 Miles; Severe Service Every 15,000 Miles																											
Replace PCV Valve	Every 100,000 Miles																											
Replace Spark Plugs	Normal Service Every 100,000 Miles; Severe Service Every 60,000 Miles																											
STEERING, SUSPENSION & TIRES																												
Rotate Tires	Normal Service Inspect For Wear & Rotate Every 5000 Miles																											
Tighten Wheel Lugnuts	500 Miles After Rotation Or Wheel Removal																											

N — Normal Service
S — Severe Service
X — Normal Or Severe Service
① — After vehicle has passed 60,000 mile mark return to beginning of mileage table & start cycle over again.
② — On models equipped with California emissions. Service is recommended but not required.

VILLAGER

Recommended Service	Service Interval In Miles①																															
	3000	5000	6000	7500	9000	10000	12000	15000	18000	20000	21000	22500	24000	25000	27000	30000	33000	35000	36000	37500	39000	40000	42000	45000	48000	50000	51000	52500	54000	55000	57000	60000
BODY																																
Replace Cabin Air Filter	Every 15,000 Miles																															
BRAKES																																
Inspect Brake Drums, Linings, Pads & Rotors	Normal Service Every 15,000 Miles; Severe Service Every 5000 Miles																															
Inspect Brake Lines & Hoses								X								X								X								X
CLUTCH & TRANSMISSION																																
Change Automatic Transaxle Fluid & Filter	Normal Service Inspect Every 15,000 Miles, Change Every 150,000 Miles; Severe Service Change Every 30,000 Miles																															
ENGINE																																
Change Engine Coolant	Replace Green Coolant, Every 45,000 Miles, Then Every 30,000 Miles Thereafter, Replace Orange Coolant Every 150,000 Miles, Replace Yellow Coolant Every 5 Years Or 100,000 Miles																															
Change Engine Oil & Filter	S	N	S		S	N	S	X	S	N	S		S	N	S	X	S	N	S		S	N	S	X	S	N	S		S	N		X
Inspect Cooling System & Protection Level								X								X								X								X
Inspect Drive Belts																X																X
Replace Accessory Drive Belts	Every 60,000 Miles																															
Replace Drive Belts	At 120,000 Miles																															
Replace Engine Air Filter Element																X																X
Inspect Exhaust System																X																X
Replace Fuel Filter ②	Every 30,000 Miles																															
Replace Spark Plugs	Every 100,000 Miles																															
Replace Timing Belt	Every 105,000 Miles																															
STEERING, SUSPENSION & TIRES																																
Rotate Tires	Normal Service Inspect For Wear And Rotate Every 5000 Miles																															

N — Normal Service
S — Severe Service
X — Normal Or Severe Service
① — After vehicle has passed 60,000 mile mark return to beginning of mileage table & start cycle over again.
② — On models equipped w/California emissions.

General Motors Corp.

INDEX

ASTRO & SAFARI

Recommended Service	Service Interval In Miles①																																						
	3000	6000	7500	9000	12000	15000	18000	21000	22500	24000	27000	30000	33000	36000	37500	39000	42000	45000	48000	51000	52500	54000	57000	60000	63000	66000	67500	69000	72000	75000	78000	81000	82500	84000	87000	90000	93000	96000	97500	99000
BODY																																								
Clean Power Antenna Mast, Inspect Neutral Safety & BTSI Operation	At Least Once Every 3 Months																																							
Flush Vehicle Underside, Inspect Drain Holes	At Least Once Every 12 Months, Especially In Winter & Springtime																																							
Inspect Lamps, Seat Belts & Warning Devices	At Least Once Every 6 Months																																							
Inspect Noise Shields & Underhood Insulation						X						X						X						X						X						X				
Lubricate Hinges, Latches, Lock Cylinders & Strikers	At Engine Oil Changes Or At Least Every 12 Months																																							
BRAKES																																								
Inspect Brake System	At Tire Rotation Or At Least Every 6 Months																																							
Lubricate Brake Cable Guides	S	S	N	S	S	X	S	S	N	S	S	X	S	S	N	S	S	X	S	S	N	S	S	X	S	S	N	S	S	X	S	S	N	S	S	X	S	S	N	S
CLUTCH & TRANSMISSION																																								
Adjust Clutch Pedal Freeplay	At Least Once Every 6 Months																																							
Change Automatic Transmission Fluid & Filter	Normal Service Every 50,000 Miles; Severe Service Every 15,000 Miles																																							
Change Transfer Case Fluid	Every 50,000 Miles																																							
Lubricate Transfer Case & Transmission Linkage, Pedal Pivots & Springs	S	S	N	S	S	X	S	S	N	S	S	X	S	S	N	S	S	X	S	S	N	S	S	X	S	S	N	S	S	X	S	S	N	S	S	X	S	S	N	S
DRIVE AXLE																																								
Lubricate Driveshaft	S	S	N	S	S	X	S	S	N	S	S	X	S	S	N	S	S	X	S	S	N	S	S	X	S	S	N	S	S	X	S	S	N	S	S	X	S	S	N	S
ENGINE																																								
Change Engine Coolant	Every 60 Months Or 150,000 Miles																																							
Change Engine Oil & Filter	S	S	N	S	S	X	S	S	N	S	S	X	S	S	N	S	S	X	S	S	N	S	S	X	S	S	N	S	S	X	S	S	N	S	S	X	S	S	N	S
Inspect Drive Belts, Emission & Fuel System Connections, Hoses, Lines, Filler Cap & Tank																								X																
Inspect Engine Air Filter Element	S	S		S	S	X	S	S		S	S	X	S	S		S	S	X	S	S		S	S	X	S	S		S	S	X	S	S		S	S	X	S	S		S
Inspect Exhaust System	At Engine Oil Changes																																							
Inspect PCV System & Valve	Every 100,000 Miles																																							
Inspect Spark Plug Wires, Distributor Cap & Rotor	Every 30,000 Miles & At Spark Plug Replacements																																							

ASTRO & SAFARI—Continued

Recommended Service	Service Interval In Miles①																																							
	3000	6000	7500	9000	12000	15000	18000	21000	22500	24000	27000	30000	33000	36000	37500	39000	42000	45000	48000	51000	52500	54000	57000	60000	63000	66000	67500	69000	72000	75000	78000	81000	82500	84000	87000	90000	93000	96000	97500	99000
ENGINE																																								
Inspect Thermostatically Controlled Air Cleaner Operation						X						X						X						X						X						X				
Inspect Throttle Linkage Operation	At Engine Oil Or Air Filter Element Changes																																							
Replace Engine Air & PCV Inlet Filter Elements, 2002–04												X												X												X				
Replace Engine Air & PCV Inlet Filter Elements, 2005																		X																		X				
Replace Fuel Filter												X												X												X				
Replace Spark Plugs	Every 100,000 Miles																																							
STEERING, SUSPENSION & TIRES																																								
Lubricate Steering & Suspension Grease Fittings	S	S	N	S	S	X	S	S	N	S	S	X	S	S	N	S	S	X	S	S	N	S	S	X	S	S	N	S	S	X	S	S	N	S	S	X	S	S	N	S
Lubricate Steering Kingpins & Bushings	Normal Service Every 3000 Miles; Severe Service Every 1500 Miles																																							
Repack Front Wheel Bearings, 2WD Only						S						X						S						X						S						X				
Rotate Tires	Normal Service Every 7500 Miles; Severe Service Every 6000 Miles																																							

BTSI — Brake Transmission Shift Interlock
CDRV — Crankcase Depression Regulator Valve
EPR — Exhaust Pressure Regulator
EVR — Electronic Vacuum Regulator N — Normal Service
S — Severe Service
X — Normal Or Severe Service
① — After vehicle passes 99,000 mile mark return to beginning of mileage table & start cycle over again.

AVALANCHE

Recommended Service	Service Interval In Miles①																																							
	3000	6000	7500	9000	12000	15000	18000	21000	22500	24000	27000	30000	33000	36000	37500	39000	42000	45000	48000	51000	52500	54000	57000	60000	63000	66000	67500	69000	72000	75000	78000	81000	82500	84000	87000	90000	93000	96000	97500	99000
BODY																																								
Inspect Lamps, Seat Belts & Warning Devices	At Least Once Every 6 Months																																							
Lubricate Hinges, Latches, Lock Cylinders & Strikers	At Engine Oil Changes Or At Least Every 12 Months																																							
Replace Passenger Compartment Air Filter	Normal Service Every 15,000 Miles; Severe Service Every 10,000 Miles																																							
BRAKES																																								
Inspect Brake System	At Tire Rotation Or At Least Every 6 Months																																							
CLUTCH & TRANSMISSION																																								
Adjust Clutch Pedal Freeplay (Models w/Mechanical Linkage)	At Least Once Every 6 Months																																							
Change Automatic Transmission Fluid & Filter, 2002–03	Every 100,000 Miles																																							
Change Automatic Transmission Fluid & Filter, 2004–06	Normal Service Every 100,000 Miles; Severe Service, Every 50,000 Miles																																							
Change Transfer Case Fluid	Every 50,000 Miles																																							
Manual Transmission Fluid	Does Not Require Change																																							
DRIVE AXLE																																								
Change Rear Axle Lubricant, Trailor Towing	After The First 500 Miles (Break In Period) Of Trailer Towing																																							
Inspect Axle Seals & CV Joints	Normal Service Every 7500 Miles; Severe Service, Every 3000 Miles Or Every 3 Months																																							
Inspect Front & Rear Axle Lubricant Level	Normal Service Every 7500 Miles; Severe Service, Every 3000 Miles Or Every 3 Months																																							
Lubricate Driveshaft Fittings	Normal Service Every 7500 Miles; Severe Service Every 3 Months Or 3000 Miles																																							
ENGINE																																								
Change Engine Coolant	Every 150,000 Miles Or 60 Months																																							
Change Engine Oil & Filter, 2002	S	S	N	S	S	X	S	S	N	S	S	X	S	S	N	S	S	X	S	S	N	S	S	X	S	S	N	S	S	X	S	S	N	S	S	X	S	S	N	S
Change Engine Oil & Filter, 2003–06	Engine Oil Life Monitor Will Indicate When To Change Oil Filter, Vehicle Must Not Be Driven More Than 12 Months Or 10,000 Miles Without An Oil & Filter Change																																							
Inspect Air Intake System & Filter						X						X						X						X						X						X				
Inspect Drive Belts, 2002–03												S												X												S				
Inspect Drive Belts, 2004–06	Every 150,000 Miles																																							

AVALANCHE—Continued

Recommended Service	Service Interval In Miles①																																						
	3000	6000	7500	9000	12000	15000	18000	21000	22500	24000	27000	30000	33000	36000	37500	39000	42000	45000	48000	51000	52500	54000	57000	60000	63000	66000	67500	69000	72000	75000	78000	81000	82500	84000	87000	90000	93000	96000	97500	99000
ENGINE																																								
Inspect Emission & Fuel System Connections, Hoses, Lines, Filler Cap & Tank, 2002–03												S												X												S				
Inspect Evaporative Control System, 2004–06	Every 50,000 Miles																																							
Inspect Exhaust System, 2002–03	At Engine Oil Changes																																							
Inspect Exhaust System, 2004–06	Every 25,000 Miles																																							
Inspect Fuel System For Damage & Leaks, 2004–06	Every 25,000 Miles																																							
Inspect PVC, 2003–04 Except 8.1L V8	At 100,000 Miles																																							
Inspect Thermostatically Controlled Cooling Fan System						X						X						X						X						X						X				
Inspect Throttle Linkage Operation	At Air Filter Element Changes																																							
Replace Engine Air Filter, 2002–03	Every 30,000 Miles																																							
Replace Engine Air Filter, 2004②	Every 25,000 Miles																																							
Replace Engine Air Filter, 2005–06②	Every 50,000 Miles																																							
Replace Fuel Filler Cap, 2002	Severe Service Every 25,000 Miles																																							
Replace Fuel Filter, 2002–03												X												X												X				
Replace Spark Plugs	At 100,000 Miles																																							
STEERING, SUSPENSION & TIRES																																								
Lubricate Steering & Suspension Grease Fittings	S	S	N	S	S	X	S	S	N	S	S	X	S	S	N	S	S	X	S	S	N	S	S	X	S	S	N	S	S	X	S	S	N	S	S	X	S	S	N	S
Rotate Tires	At Engine Oil Change Intervals																																							

N — Normal Service
S — Severe Service
X — Normal Or Severe Service
① — After vehicle passes 150,000 mile mark return to beginning of mileage table & start cycle over again.
② — Models less filter restriction indicator.

AZTEK & RENDEZVOUS

Recommended Service	Service Interval In Miles①																																							
	3000	6000	7500	9000	12000	15000	18000	21000	22500	24000	27000	30000	33000	36000	37500	39000	42000	45000	48000	51000	52500	54000	57000	60000	63000	66000	67500	69000	72000	75000	78000	81000	82500	84000	87000	90000	93000	96000	97500	99000
BODY																																								
Inspect Lamps, Seat Belts & Warning Devices	At Least Once Every 6 Months																																							
Lubricate Hinges, Latches, Lock Cylinders & Strikers	At Engine Oil Changes Or At Least Every 12 Months																																							
Replace Passenger Comparment Air Filter						X						X						X						X						X						X				
BRAKES																																								
Inspect Brake System, 2002–03	Every 7500 Miles																																							
Inspect Brake System, 2004–06	At Engine Oil Changes Or At Least Every 12 Months																																							
CLUTCH & TRANSMISSION																																								
Change Automatic Transmission Fluid & Filter	Normal Service Every 100,000 Miles; Severe Service Every 50,000 Miles																																							
DRIVE AXLE																																								
Change Differential Lubricant, 2002 AWD	Trailer Tow At 7500 Miles Only																																							
ENGINE																																								
Change Engine Coolant	Every 60 Months Or 150,000 Miles																																							
Change Engine Oil & Filter	The Engine Oil Life Monitor Will Indicate When To Change Engine Oil. The Engine Oil & Filter Must Be Changed At Least Once a Year																																							
Inspect Accessory Drive Belt, 2002	Every 60,000 Miles																																							
Inspect Accessory Drive Belt, 2003–06	Every 150,000 Miles																																							
Inspect Emission & Fuel System Connections, Hoses, Lines, Filler Cap & Tank																								X																
Inspect Engine Air Filter	Severe Service Every 15,000 Miles																																							
Inspect Exhaust System, 2002–03	At Engine Oil Changes																																							
Inspect Exhaust System, 2004–06	Every 25,000 Miles																																							
Inspect Fuel System, 2004–06	Every 25,000 Miles																																							
Inspect Spark Plug Wires	Every 100,000 Miles																																							
Replace Engine Air Filter, 2002–03												X												X												X				
Replace Engine Air Filter, 2004	Every 25,000 Miles																																							

AZTEK & RENDEZVOUS—Continued

Recommended Service	Service Interval In Miles①																																							
	3000	6000	7500	9000	12000	15000	18000	21000	22500	24000	27000	30000	33000	36000	37500	39000	42000	45000	48000	51000	52500	54000	57000	60000	63000	66000	67500	69000	72000	75000	78000	81000	82500	84000	87000	90000	93000	96000	97500	99000
ENGINE																																								
Replace Engine Air Filter, 2005–06	Every 50,000 Miles																																							
Replace Spark Plugs	Every 100,000 Miles																																							
STEERING, SUSPENSION & TIRES																																								
Rotate Tires, 2002–03	Every 7500 Miles																																							
Rotate Tires, 2004–06	At Engine Oil Changes Or At Least Every 12 Months																																							

N — Normal Service
S — Severe Service
X — Normal Or Severe Service
① — If equipped, the engine oil life monitor will indicate when to change engine oil, ususally 3000–10,000 miles. Under severe driving conditions, engine oil may need to be changed before 3000 miles. If vehicle is driven in a dusty area, change engine oil every 3000 miles.

BLAZER/JIMMY S-SERIES, SONOMA, SSR, S-10 & S-15—Continued

Recommended Service	Service Interval In Miles①																																							
	3000	6000	7500	9000	12000	15000	18000	21000	22500	24000	27000	30000	33000	36000	37500	39000	42000	45000	48000	51000	52500	54000	57000	60000	63000	66000	67500	69000	72000	75000	78000	81000	82500	84000	87000	90000	93000	96000	97500	99000
STEERING, SUSPENSION & TIRES																																								
Clean & Repack Front Wheel Bearings, 2002–03 2WD S-10 & Sonoma	Every 30,000 Miles																																							
Inspect Steering & Suspension System Components	At Engine Oil Change Intervals																																							
Lubricate Steering & Suspension Grease Fittings, Sonoma GT, Syclone & Typhoon	Initial Service At 2500 Miles, Then Every 3 Months Or 3000 Miles Thereafter																																							
Lubricate Steering & Suspension Grease Fittings, S & T Except Sonoma GT, Syclone & Typhoon	S	S	N	S	S	X	S	S	N	S	S	X	S	S	N	S	S	X	S	S	N	S	S	X	S	S	N	S	S	X	S	S	N	S	S	X	S	S	N	S
Rotate Tires	At Engine Oil Change Intervals																																							

BTSI — Brake Transmission Shift Interlock
EPR — Exhaust Pressure Regulator
N — Normal Service
S — Severe Service
X — Normal Or Severe Service
① — After vehicle passes 99,000 mile mark return to beginning of mileage table & start cycle over again.

BRAVADA, ENVOY, RAINER & TRAILBLAZER

Recommended Service	Service Interval In Miles①																																							
	3000	6000	7500	9000	12000	15000	18000	21000	22500	24000	27000	30000	33000	36000	37500	39000	42000	45000	48000	51000	52500	54000	57000	60000	63000	66000	67500	69000	72000	75000	78000	81000	82500	84000	87000	90000	93000	96000	97500	99000
BODY																																								
Inspect Lamps, Seat Belts & Warning Devices	At Least Once Every 6 Months																																							
Inspect Restraint System	At Oil Change Intervals																																							
Lubricate Body Components	At Oil Change Intervals																																							
BRAKES																																								
Inspect Brake System	At Tire Rotation Or At Least Every 6 Months																																							
CLUTCH & TRANSMISSION																																								
Change Automatic Transfer Case Fluid	Every 50,000 Miles																																							
Change Automatic Transmission Fluid & Filter	Normal Service Every 100,000 Miles; Severe Service Every 50,000 Miles																																							
DRIVE AXLE & DRIVESHAFT																																								
Check Front & Rear Axle Fluid Level, 2002–03	Every 7500 Miles																																							
Check Front & Rear Axle Fluid Level, 2004–06	At Oil Change Intervals																																							
ENGINE																																								
Change Engine Coolant	Every 60 Months Or 150,000 Miles																																							
Change Engine Oil & Filter	Engine Oil Life Monitor Will Indicate When To Change Oil Filter, Vehicle Must Not Be Driven More Than 12 Months Or 10,000 Miles Without An Oil & Filter Change																																							
Inspect Cooling System	At Oil Change Intervals																																							
Inspect Drive Belts	Every 150,000 Miles																																							
Inspect Engine Air Filter	At Oil Change Intervals																																							
Inspect Exhaust System	Every 25,000 Miles																																							
Inspect Fuel System	Every 25,000 Miles																																							
Inspect PCV Valve, 5.3L	Every 100,000 Miles																																							
Inspect Spark Plug Wire, 5.3L	Every 100,000 Miles																																							
Replace Engine Air Filter, 2002–03	Every 30,000 Miles																																							
Replace Engine Air Filter, 2004	Every 25,000 Miles																																							
Replace Engine Air Filter, 2005–06	Every 50,000 Miles																																							
Replace Fuel Filter, 2002–03	Every 30,000 Miles																																							
Replace Fuel Filter, 2004–05	Every 25,000 Miles																																							

BRAVADA, ENVOY, RAINER & TRAILBLAZER—Continued

Recommended Service	Service Interval In Miles①																																						
	3000	6000	7500	9000	12000	15000	18000	21000	22500	24000	27000	30000	33000	36000	37500	39000	42000	45000	48000	51000	52500	54000	57000	60000	63000	66000	67500	69000	72000	75000	78000	81000	82500	84000	87000	90000	93000	96000	97500	99000
ENGINE																																								
Replace Spark Plugs	Every 100,000 Miles																																							
STEERING, SUSPENSION & TIRES																																								
Inspect Suspension And Steering Components	At Oil Change Intervals																																							
Lubricate Steering & Suspension Grease Fittings	At Oil Change Intervals																																							
Rotate Tires, 2002–03	Every 7500 Miles																																							
Rotate Tires, 2004–06	At Oil Change Intervals																																							

BTSI — Brake Transmission Shift Interlock
EPR — Exhaust Pressure Regulator
N — Normal Service
S — Severe Service
X — Normal Or Severe Service
① — After vehicle passes 99,000 mile mark return to beginning of mileage table & start cycle over again.

CANYON & COLORADO

<table>
<tr><th rowspan="2">Recommended Service</th><th colspan="40">Service Interval In Miles①</th></tr>
<tr><th>3000</th><th>6000</th><th>7500</th><th>9000</th><th>12000</th><th>15000</th><th>18000</th><th>21000</th><th>22500</th><th>24000</th><th>27000</th><th>30000</th><th>33000</th><th>36000</th><th>37500</th><th>39000</th><th>42000</th><th>45000</th><th>48000</th><th>51000</th><th>52500</th><th>54000</th><th>57000</th><th>60000</th><th>63000</th><th>66000</th><th>67500</th><th>69000</th><th>72000</th><th>75000</th><th>78000</th><th>81000</th><th>82500</th><th>84000</th><th>87000</th><th>90000</th><th>93000</th><th>96000</th><th>97500</th><th>99000</th></tr>
<tr><td colspan="41">BODY</td></tr>
<tr><td>Inspect Lamps, Seat Belts & Warning Devices</td><td colspan="40">At Least Once Every 6 Months</td></tr>
<tr><td>Inspect Restraint System</td><td colspan="40">At Oil Change Intervals</td></tr>
<tr><td>Lubricate Body Components</td><td colspan="40">At Oil Change Intervals</td></tr>
<tr><td colspan="41">BRAKES</td></tr>
<tr><td>Inspect Brake System</td><td colspan="40">At Tire Rotation Or At Least Every 6 Months</td></tr>
<tr><td colspan="41">CLUTCH & TRANSMISSION</td></tr>
<tr><td>Change Automatic Transmission Fluid & Filter</td><td colspan="40">Normal Service Every 100,000 Miles; Severe Service Every 50,000 Miles</td></tr>
<tr><td colspan="41">ENGINE</td></tr>
<tr><td>Change Engine Coolant</td><td colspan="40">Every 60 Months Or 150,000 Miles</td></tr>
<tr><td>Change Engine Oil & Filter</td><td colspan="40">Engine Oil Life Monitor Will Indicate When To Change Oil Filter, Vehicle Must Not Be Driven More Than 12 Months Or 10,000 Miles Without An Oil & Filter Change</td></tr>
<tr><td>Inspect Cooling System</td><td colspan="40">At Oil Change Intervals</td></tr>
<tr><td>Inspect Drive Belts</td><td colspan="40">Every 150,000 Miles</td></tr>
<tr><td>Inspect Engine Air Filter</td><td colspan="40">At Oil Change Intervals</td></tr>
<tr><td>Inspect Exhaust System</td><td colspan="40">Every 25,000 Miles</td></tr>
<tr><td>Inspect Fuel System For Damage And Leaks</td><td colspan="40">Every 25,000 Miles</td></tr>
<tr><td>Replace Engine Air Filter</td><td colspan="40">Every 50,000 Miles</td></tr>
<tr><td>Replace Fuel Filter, 2005–06</td><td colspan="40">Every 25,000 Miles</td></tr>
<tr><td>Replace Spark Plugs</td><td colspan="40">Every 100,000 Miles</td></tr>
<tr><td colspan="41">STEERING, SUSPENSION & TIRES</td></tr>
<tr><td>Inspect Suspension And Steering Components</td><td colspan="40">At Oil Change Intervals</td></tr>
<tr><td>Rotate Tires</td><td colspan="40">At Oil Change Intervals</td></tr>
</table>

BTSI — Brake Transmission Shift Interlock
EPR — Exhaust Pressure Regulator
N — Normal Service
S — Severe Service
X — Normal Or Severe Service
① — After vehicle passes 99,000 mile mark return to beginning of mileage table & start cycle over again.

DENALI, ESCALADE, ESCALADE ESV & EXT, SIERRA, SILVERADO, SUBURBAN, TAHOE, YUKON & YUKON XL

<table>
<tr><th rowspan="2">Recommended Service</th><th colspan="40">Service Interval In Miles①</th></tr>
<tr><th>3000</th><th>6000</th><th>7500</th><th>9000</th><th>12000</th><th>15000</th><th>18000</th><th>21000</th><th>22500</th><th>24000</th><th>27000</th><th>30000</th><th>33000</th><th>36000</th><th>37500</th><th>39000</th><th>42000</th><th>45000</th><th>48000</th><th>51000</th><th>52500</th><th>54000</th><th>57000</th><th>60000</th><th>63000</th><th>66000</th><th>67500</th><th>69000</th><th>72000</th><th>75000</th><th>78000</th><th>81000</th><th>82500</th><th>84000</th><th>87000</th><th>90000</th><th>93000</th><th>96000</th><th>97500</th><th>99000</th></tr>
<tr><td colspan="41">BODY</td></tr>
<tr><td>Inspect Lamps, Seat Belts & Warning Devices</td><td colspan="40">At Least Once Every 6 Months</td></tr>
<tr><td>Inspect Noise Shields & Underhood Insulation, w/Diesel</td><td colspan="40">Every 10,000 Miles</td></tr>
<tr><td>Lubricate Hinges, Latches, Lock Cylinders & Strikers</td><td colspan="40">At Engine Oil Changes Or At Least Every 12 Months</td></tr>
<tr><td>Replace Passenger Compartment Air Filter, w/Diesel</td><td colspan="40">Every 10,000 Miles</td></tr>
<tr><td>Replace Passenger Compartment Air Filter, w/Gasoline Engine</td><td colspan="40">Every 15,000 Miles</td></tr>
<tr><td colspan="41">BRAKES</td></tr>
<tr><td>Inspect Brake System</td><td colspan="40">At Tire Rotation Or At Least Every 6 Months</td></tr>
<tr><td colspan="41">CLUTCH & TRANSMISSION</td></tr>
<tr><td>Adjust Clutch Pedal Freeplay (Models w/Mechanical Linkage)</td><td colspan="40">At Least Once Every 6 Months</td></tr>
<tr><td>Change Automatic Transfer Case Fluid, w/Gasoline Engine</td><td colspan="40">Every 50,000 Miles</td></tr>
<tr><td>Change Automatic Transmission External Main Control Filter, w/ Allison Transmission</td><td colspan="40">At First Maintenance Service Performed On Vehicle</td></tr>
<tr><td>Change Automatic Transmission Fluid & Filter, w/Allison Transmission</td><td colspan="40">Normal Service Every 50,000 Miles; Severe Service Every 25,000 Miles</td></tr>
<tr><td>Change Automatic Transmission Fluid & Filter, GVW Under 8600 Lbs.</td><td colspan="40">Normal Service Every 100,000 Miles; Severe Service Every 50,000 Miles</td></tr>
<tr><td>Change Automatic Transmission Fluid & Filter, GVW Over 8600 Lbs., Less Allison Transmission</td><td colspan="40">Every 50,000 Miles</td></tr>
<tr><td>Change Clutch Fluid, 2004–05 6 Speed Manual Transmission</td><td colspan="40">Every 24 Months Or 25,000 Miles</td></tr>
</table>

DENALI, ESCALADE, ESCALADE ESV & EXT, SIERRA, SILVERADO, SUBURBAN, TAHOE, YUKON & YUKON XL—Continued

Recommended Service	Service Interval In Miles①																																							
	3000	6000	7500	9000	12000	15000	18000	21000	22500	24000	27000	30000	33000	36000	37500	39000	42000	45000	48000	51000	52500	54000	57000	60000	63000	66000	67500	69000	72000	75000	78000	81000	82500	84000	87000	90000	93000	96000	97500	99000
CLUTCH & TRANSMISSION																																								
Change 5 Speed Manual Transmission 4300 V6, 4800 V8, 2003 Silerado 4WD	At 100,000 Miles																																							
Change 5 Speed Manual Transmission 6000 V8, 2003 Silverado 4WD	At 200,000 Miles																																							
Change 5 Speed Manual Transmission, 2004–06	At 150,000 Miles																																							
DRIVE AXLE																																								
Change Rear Axle Lubricant, Trailor Towing, 2002	After The First 500 Miles (Break In Period) Of Trailer Towing																																							
Inspect Axle Seals & CV Joints, w/Diesel	Every 5000 Miles																																							
Inspect Axle Seals & CV Joints, w/Gasoline Engine	Normal Service Every 7500 Miles; Severe Service, Every 8000 Miles Or Every 3 Months																																							
Inspect Front & Rear Axle Lubricant Level, w/Diesel	Every 5000 Miles																																							
Inspect Front & Rear Axle Lubricant Level, w/Gasoline Engine	Normal Service Every 7500 Miles; Severe Service Every 8000 Miles Or Every 3 Months																																							
Lubricate Driveshaft Fittings, w/Gasoline Engine	Normal Service Every 7500 Miles; Severe Service Every 3 Months Or 8000 Miles																																							
Lubricate Driveshaft Fitting, w/Diesel	Every 5000 Miles																																							
ENGINE																																								
Change Engine Coolant	Every 150,000 Miles Or 60 Months																																							
Change Engine Oil & Filter, 2002 w/Gasoline Engine & All 2003–06②	Every 12 Months Or As Indicated By Oil Life Monitor																																							
Change Engine Oil & Filter, 2002 w/Diesel	Every 3 Months Or 5000 Miles																																							
Inspect Air Intake System & Filter, w/Gasoline Engine						X						X						X						X						X						X				
Inspect Air Intake System & Filter Housing, w/Diesel	Every 10,000 Miles																																							
Inspect CDRV System, w/Diesel																								X																

DENALI, ESCALADE, ESCALADE ESV & EXT, SIERRA, SILVERADO, SUBURBAN, TAHOE, YUKON & YUKON XL—Continued

Recommended Service	Service Interval In Miles①																																							
	3000	6000	7500	9000	12000	15000	18000	21000	22500	24000	27000	30000	33000	36000	37500	39000	42000	45000	48000	51000	52500	54000	57000	60000	63000	66000	67500	69000	72000	75000	78000	81000	82500	84000	87000	90000	93000	96000	97500	99000
ENGINE																																								
Inspect Drive Belts, w/Diesel 2002–03												S												X												S				
Inspect Drive Belts, 2004–06	Every 150,000 Miles																																							
Inspect EGR System																								X																
Inspect Emission & Fuel System Connections, Hoses, Lines, Filler Cap & Tank												S												X												S				
Inspect Engine Idle Speed, w/Diesel	Initially At 5000 & 30,000 Miles, Then Every 30,000 Miles Thereafter																																							
Inspect Evaporative System, 2005–06	Every 50,000 Miles																																							
Inspect Exhaust System, 2002–03	At Engine Oil Changes																																							
Inspect Exhaust System, 2004–06	Every 25,000 Miles																																							
Inspect Fuel System, 2004–06	Every 25,000 Miles																																							
Inspect PCV System & Valve	Every 100,000 Miles																																							
Inspect Spark Plug Wires, Distributor Cap & Rotor	Every 30,000 Miles																																							
Inspect Thermostatically Controlled Cooling Fan System						X						X						X						X						X						X				
Inspect Thermostatically Controlled Cooling Fan System, w/Diesel	Every 12 Months Or 10,000 Miles																																							
Inspect Throttle Linkage Operation	At Air Filter Element Changes																																							
Replace Engine Air Filter, 2003	Every 30,000 Miles																																							
Replace Engine Air Filter, 2004	Every 25,000 Miles																																							
Replace Engine Air Filter, 2005–06③	Every 50,000 Miles																																							
Replace External Main Control Filter, 2003 Silverado w/Allison Transmission	At 7500 Miles																																							
Replace Fuel Filler Cap, 2002	Severe Service Every 25,000 Miles																																							
Replace Fuel Filter												X												X												X				
Replace PCV Inlet Filter Elements	Replace Every 100,000 Miles																																							

DENALI, ESCALADE, ESCALADE ESV & EXT, SIERRA, SILVERADO, SUBURBAN, TAHOE, YUKON & YUKON XL—Continued

Recommended Service	Service Interval In Miles①																																							
	3000	6000	7500	9000	12000	15000	18000	21000	22500	24000	27000	30000	33000	36000	37500	39000	42000	45000	48000	51000	52500	54000	57000	60000	63000	66000	67500	69000	72000	75000	78000	81000	82500	84000	87000	90000	93000	96000	97500	99000
ENGINE																																								
Replace Spark Plugs, 2002 4.3L												X												X												X				
Replace Spark Plugs, Except 2002 4.3L	Every 100,000 Miles																																							
STEERING, SUSPENSION & TIRES																																								
Lubricate Steering & Suspension Grease Fittings, w/Diesel	Every 3 Months Or 5000 Miles																																							
Lubricate Steering & Suspension Grease Fittings, w/Gasoline Engine	At Engine Oil Changes																																							
On 2WD, Clean & Repack Wheel Bearings, 2002–04	Normal Service Every 30,000 Miles; Severe Service Every 15,000 Miles																																							
Rotate Tires	At Engine Oil Changes																																							

BTSI — Brake Transmission Shift Interlock
CDRV — Crankcase Depression Regulator Valve
EPR — Exhaust Pressure Regulator
EVR — Electronic Vacuum Regulator
GVWR — Gross Vehicle Weight Rating
N — Normal Service
S — Severe Service
X — Normal Or Severe Service
① — After vehicle passes 99,000 mile mark return to beginning of mileage table & start cycle over again.
② — The engine Oil Life Monitor will indicate when to change the engine oil. Reset the indicator after the oil has been changed.
③ — Vehicles without filter restriction indicator.

EQUINOX & TORRENT

Recommended Service	Service Interval In Miles①																																							
	3000	6000	7500	9000	12000	15000	18000	21000	22500	24000	27000	30000	33000	36000	37500	39000	42000	45000	48000	51000	52500	54000	57000	60000	63000	66000	67500	69000	72000	75000	78000	81000	82500	84000	87000	90000	93000	96000	97500	99000
BODY																																								
Inspect Seat Belts & Restraint Systems	At Least Once Every 6 Months																																							
Inspect Wiper Blades & Inserts	At Least Once Every 6 Months																																							
Lubricate Door Check Straps & Hinges	At Engine Oil Change Intervals																																							
Lubricate Headlamp Doors	At Engine Oil Change Intervals																																							
Lubricate Hood Latch	At Engine Oil Change Intervals																																							
Replace Cabin Air Filter	Every 12 Months Or 12,000 Miles. In Dusty Areas Change More Often																																							
BRAKES																																								
Inspect Brake Drums & Shoes		X				X				X				X				X				X				X				X				X				X		
Inspect Brake Hoses, Lines & Connections		X				X				X				X				X				X				X				X				X				X		
Inspect Disc Brake Calipers For Freedom Of Movement (Lubricate If Required)		X				X				X				X				X				X				X				X				X				X		
Inspect Disc Brake Pads & Rotors		X				X				X				X				X				X				X				X				X				X		
CLUTCH & TRANSAXLE																																								
Change Automatic Transaxle Fluid & Filter	Normal Service Every 100,000 Miles; Severe Service Every 50,000 Miles																																							
DRIVESHAFT																																								
Inspect CV Joint Boots		X		X		X		X		X		X		X		X		X		X		X		X		X		X		X		X		X		X		X		X
ENGINE																																								
Change Engine Coolant	Every 60 Months Or 150,000 Miles																																							
Change Engine Oil & Filter②	The Engine Oil Life Monitor Will Indicate When To Change Engine Oil. The Engine Oil & Filter Must Be Changed At Least Once a Year																																							
Inspect Air Filter	Severe Service Every 15,000 Miles																																							
Inspect Cooling System & Protection Level						X						X						X						X						X						X				
Inspect Drive Belts	Every 150,000 Miles																																							
Inspect Exhaust System	Every 25,000 Miles																																							
Inspect Fuel System	Every 25,000 Miles																																							
Inspect Fuel Tank Filler Cap										X										X										X										X
Inspect Throttle System	At Engine Oil Change Intervals																																							
Replace Air Filter	Every 50,000 Miles																																							
Replace Spark Plugs	Every 100,000 Miles																																							

EQUINOX & TORRENT—Continued

Recommended Service	Service Interval In Miles① 3000	6000	7500	9000	12000	15000	18000	21000	22500	24000	27000	30000	33000	36000	37500	39000	42000	45000	48000	51000	52500	54000	57000	60000	63000	66000	67500	69000	72000	75000	78000	81000	82500	84000	87000	90000	93000	96000	97500	99000
STEERING, SUSPENSION & TIRES																																								
Inspect Ball Joint Seals	At Engine Oil Change Intervals																																							
Inspect Suspension	At Engine Oil Change Intervals																																							
Rotate Tires	Every 6000 Miles																																							

BTSI — Brake Transaxle Shift Interlock
N — Normal Service
S — Severe Service
X — Normal Or Severe Service
① — After vehicle passes 100,000 mile mark return to beginning of mileage table & start cycle over again.
② — On models equipped with Engine Oil Life Moniter, change engine oil when message appears in message display center. Never drive vehicle more then 6000 miles or 6 months without changing oil and filter.

G SERIES

Recommended Service	Service Interval In Miles① 3000	6000	7500	9000	12000	15000	18000	21000	22500	24000	27000	30000	33000	36000	37500	39000	42000	45000	48000	51000	52500	54000	57000	60000	63000	66000	67500	69000	72000	75000	78000	81000	82500	84000	87000	90000	93000	96000	97500	99000
BODY																																								
Inspect Lamps, Seat Belts & Warning Devices	At Least Once Every 6 Months																																							
Inspect Noise Shields & Underhood Insulation, w/Diesel	Every 10,000 Miles																																							
Lubricate Hinges, Latches, Lock Cylinders & Strikers	At Engine Oil Changes Or At Least Every 12 Months																																							
Replace Cabin Air Filter	Every 15,000 Miles																																							
BRAKES																																								
Inspect Brake System	Every 6 Months																																							
Lubricate Brake Cable Guides, w/Diesel	Normal Service Every 12 Months Or 5000 Miles; Severe Service Every 3 Months Or 2500 Miles																																							
Lubricate Brake Cable Guides, w/Gasoline Engine	S	S	N	S	S	X	S	S	N	S	S	X	S	S	N	S	S	X	S	S	N	S	S	X	S	S	N	S	S	X	S	S	N	S	S	X	S	S	N	S

G SERIES—Continued

Recommended Service	Service Interval In Miles①																																						
	3000	6000	7500	9000	12000	15000	18000	21000	22500	24000	27000	30000	33000	36000	37500	39000	42000	45000	48000	51000	52500	54000	57000	60000	63000	66000	67500	69000	72000	75000	78000	81000	82500	84000	87000	90000	93000	96000	97500	99000
CLUTCH & TRANSMISSION																																								
Adjust Clutch Pedal Freeplay (Models w/Mechanical Linkage)	At Least Once Every 6 Months																																							
Change Automatic Transmission Fluid & Filter	Normal Service Every 100,000 Miles; Severe Service Every 50,000 Miles																																							
Lubricate Transfer Case & Transmission Linkage, Pedal Pivots & Springs, w/Diesel	Normal Service Every 12 Months Or 5000 Miles; Severe Service Every 3 Months Or 2500 Miles																																							
Lubricate Transfer Case & Transmission Linkage, Pedal Pivots & Springs, w/Gasoline Engine	S	S	N	S	S	X	S	S	N	S	S	X	S	S	N	S	S	X	S	S	N	S	S	X	S	S	N	S	S	X	S	S	N	S	S	X	S	S	N	S
DRIVE AXLE																																								
Change Differential Lubricant	Normal Service Once Only At Initial Engine Oil Change; Severe Service Every 15,000 Miles																																							
Change Differential Lubricant, Except 3500HD						S						S						S						S						S						S				
Change Differential Lubricant, Locking Type, Models Less Dana 70/80 Axle	S		N			S						S						S						S						S						S				
Change Differential Lubricant, 3500HD												S												S												S				
Lubricate Driveshaft, w/Diesel	Normal Service Every 12 Months Or 5000 Miles; Severe Service Every 3 Months Or 2500 Miles																																							
Lubricate Driveshaft, w/Gasoline Engine	S	S	N	S	S	X	S	S	N	S	S	X	S	S	N	S	S	X	S	S	N	S	S	X	S	S	N	S	S	X	S	S	N	S	S	X	S	S	N	S
ENGINE																																								
Change Engine Oil & Filter, w/Diesel	Normal Service Every 12 Months Or 5000 Miles; Severe Service Every 3 Months Or 2500 Miles																																							
Change Engine Oil & Filter, w/Gasoline Engine②	S	S	N	S	S	X	S	S	N	S	S	X	S	S	N	S	S	X	S	S	N	S	S	X	S	S	N	S	S	X	S	S	N	S	S	X	S	S	N	S
Inspect Air Intake System & Filter, Gasoline w/HD Emissions						X						X						X						X						X						X				
Inspect Air Intake System & Filter Housing, w/Diesel	Every 10,000 Miles																																							
Inspect CDRV System, w/Diesel																								X																
Inspect Drive Belts, 2002	Every 60,000 Miles																																							
Inspect Drive Belts, 2003–06	Every 150,000 Miles																																							

G SERIES—Continued

Recommended Service	Service Interval In Miles①																																							
	3000	6000	7500	9000	12000	15000	18000	21000	22500	24000	27000	30000	33000	36000	37500	39000	42000	45000	48000	51000	52500	54000	57000	60000	63000	66000	67500	69000	72000	75000	78000	81000	82500	84000	87000	90000	93000	96000	97500	99000
ENGINE																																								
Inspect EGR System, w/Gasoline Engines & VIN S Diesel																								X																
Inspect Emission & Fuel System Connections, Hoses, Lines, Filler Cap & Tank												S												X												S				
Inspect Engine Idle Speed, w/Diesel	Initially At 5000 & 30,000 Miles, Then Every 30,000 Miles Thereafter																																							
Inspect Evaporative Emission Control System, 2005–06	Every 50,000 Miles																																							
Inspect Exhaust System, 2002–04	At Engine Oil Changes																																							
Inspect Exhaust System, 2005–06	Every 25,000 Miles																																							
Inspect Fuel System, 2005–06	Every 25,000 Miles																																							
Inspect PCV System & Valve	Every 100,000 Miles																																							
Inspect Spark Plug Wires, Distributor Cap & Rotor	Every 30,000 Miles																																							
Inspect Thermostatically Controlled Air Cleaner Operation, Gasoline Engines w/LD Emissions						X						X						X						X						X						X				
Inspect Thermostatically Controlled Air Cleaner Operation, Gasoline Engines w/HD Emissions					X					X				X					X					X					X					X				X		
Inspect Thermostatically Controlled Air Cleaner Operation, w/Diesel	Every 10,000 Miles																																							
Inspect Thermostatically Controlled Cooling Fan System, w/Diesel	Every 12 Months Or 10,000 Miles																																							
Inspect Thermostatically Controlled Cooling Fan System, w/Gasoline Engine						X						X						X						X						X						X				
Inspect Throttle Linkage Operation	At Air Filter Element Changes																																							
Replace Engine Air Filter, 2002–04	Every 30,000 Miles																																							

G SERIES—Continued

Recommended Service	Service Interval In Miles①																																							
	3000	6000	7500	9000	12000	15000	18000	21000	22500	24000	27000	30000	33000	36000	37500	39000	42000	45000	48000	51000	52500	54000	57000	60000	63000	66000	67500	69000	72000	75000	78000	81000	82500	84000	87000	90000	93000	96000	97500	99000
ENGINE																																								
Replace Engine Air Filter, 2005–06 Less Filter Restriction Indicator	Every 50,000 Miles																																							
Replace Fuel Filter, w/Diesel												X												X												X				
Replace Fuel Filter, w/Gasoline												X												X												X				
Replace PCV Inlet Filter Elements	Replace Every 100,000 Miles																																							
Replace Spark Plugs, Standard Tip												X												X												X				
Replace Spark Plugs, Platinum Tip	Every 100,000 Miles																																							
STEERING, SUSPENSION & TIRES																																								
Lubricate Steering Kingpins & Bushings	Normal Service Every 3000 Miles; Severe Service Every 1500 Miles																																							
Lubricate Steering & Suspension Grease Fittings, w/Diesel	Normal Service Every 12 Months Or 5000 Miles; Severe Service Every 3 Months Or 2500 Miles																																							
Lubricate Steering & Suspension Grease Fittings, w/Gasoline Engine	S	S	N	S	S	X	S	S	N	S	S	X	S	S	N	S	S	X	S	S	N	S	S	X	S	S	N	S	S	X	S	S	N	S	S	X	S	S	N	S
Repack Front Wheel Bearings						S						X						S						X						S						X				
Rotate Tires, Except Diesel	At Oil Change Intervals																																							
Rotate Tires, w/Diesel	Normal Service Every 7500 Miles; Severe Service Every 5000 Miles																																							

BTSI — Brake Transmission Shift Interlock
CDRV — Crankcase Depression Regulator Valve
EPR — Exhaust Pressure Regulator
EVR — Electronic Vacuum Regulator
GVWR — Gross Vehicle Weight Rating
HD — Heavy Duty, GVWR of 8501 lbs. or more
LD — Light Duty, GVWR of 8500 lbs. or less
N — Normal Service
S — Severe Service
X — Normal Or Severe Service
① — After vehicle passes 99,000 mile mark return to beginning of mileage table & start cycle over again.
② — On models equipped with engine Oil Life Monitor, change oil when message appears in display center. Reset oil monitor when oil has been changed. Vehicle must not be driven more than 10,000 miles or 12 months without an oil and filter change.

HHR

<table>
<tr><th rowspan="2">Recommended Service</th><th colspan="40">Service Interval In Miles①</th></tr>
<tr><th>3000</th><th>6000</th><th>7500</th><th>9000</th><th>12000</th><th>15000</th><th>18000</th><th>21000</th><th>22500</th><th>24000</th><th>27000</th><th>30000</th><th>33000</th><th>36000</th><th>37500</th><th>39000</th><th>42000</th><th>45000</th><th>48000</th><th>51000</th><th>52500</th><th>54000</th><th>57000</th><th>60000</th><th>63000</th><th>66000</th><th>67500</th><th>69000</th><th>72000</th><th>75000</th><th>78000</th><th>81000</th><th>82500</th><th>84000</th><th>87000</th><th>90000</th><th>93000</th><th>96000</th><th>97500</th><th>99000</th></tr>
<tr><td colspan="41">BODY</td></tr>
<tr><td>Inspect Lamps, Seat Belts & Warning Devices</td><td colspan="40">At Least Once Every 6 Months</td></tr>
<tr><td>Inspect Restraint System</td><td colspan="40">At Oil Change Intervals</td></tr>
<tr><td>Lubricate Body Components</td><td colspan="40">At Oil Change Intervals</td></tr>
<tr><td colspan="41">BRAKES</td></tr>
<tr><td>Inspect Brake System</td><td colspan="40">At Tire Rotation Or At Least Every 6 Months</td></tr>
<tr><td colspan="41">CLUTCH & TRANSMISSION</td></tr>
<tr><td>Change Automatic Transmission Fluid & Filter</td><td colspan="40">Severe Service Every 50,000 Miles</td></tr>
<tr><td colspan="41">ENGINE</td></tr>
<tr><td>Change Engine Coolant</td><td colspan="40">Every 60 Months Or 150,000 Miles</td></tr>
<tr><td>Change Engine Oil & Filter</td><td colspan="40">Engine Oil Life Monitor Will Indicate When To Change Oil Filter, Vehicle Must Not Be Driven More Than 12 Months Or 10,000 Miles Without An Oil & Filter Change</td></tr>
<tr><td>Inspect Cooling System</td><td colspan="40">At Oil Change Intervals</td></tr>
<tr><td>Inspect Drive Belts</td><td colspan="40">Every 150,000 Miles</td></tr>
<tr><td>Inspect Engine Air Filter</td><td colspan="40">At Oil Change Intervals</td></tr>
<tr><td>Inspect Exhaust System</td><td colspan="40">Every 25,000 Miles</td></tr>
<tr><td>Inspect Fuel System For Damage And Leaks</td><td colspan="40">Every 25,000 Miles</td></tr>
<tr><td>Replace Engine Air Filter</td><td colspan="40">Every 50,000 Miles</td></tr>
<tr><td>Replace Fuel Filter</td><td colspan="40">Every 25,000 Miles</td></tr>
<tr><td>Replace Spark Plugs</td><td colspan="40">Every 100,000 Miles</td></tr>
<tr><td colspan="41">STEERING, SUSPENSION & TIRES</td></tr>
<tr><td>Inspect Suspension And Steering Components</td><td colspan="40">At Oil Change Intervals</td></tr>
<tr><td>Rotate Tires</td><td colspan="40">At Oil Change Intervals</td></tr>
</table>

N — Normal Service
S — Severe Service
X — Normal Or Severe Service
BTSI — Brake Transmission Shift Interlock
EPR — Exhaust Pressure Regulator
① — After vehicle passes 99,000 mile mark return to beginning of mileage table & start cycle over again.

HUMMER H2 & H3

Recommended Service	Service Interval In Miles①																																							
	3000	6000	7500	9000	12000	15000	18000	21000	22500	24000	27000	30000	33000	36000	37500	39000	42000	45000	48000	51000	52500	54000	57000	60000	63000	66000	67500	69000	72000	75000	78000	81000	82500	84000	87000	90000	93000	96000	97500	99000
BODY																																								
Inspect Lamps, Seat Belts & Warning Devices	At Least Once Every 6 Months																																							
Lubricate Hinges, Latches, Lock Cylinders & Strikers	At Engine Oil Changes Or At Least Every 12 Months																																							
Replace Passenger Compartment Air Filter	Normal Service Every 15,000 Miles; Severe Service Every 10,000 Miles																																							
BRAKES																																								
Inspect Brake System	At Tire Rotation Or At Least Every 6 Months																																							
CLUTCH & TRANSMISSION																																								
Change Automatic Transmission Fluid & Filter	Normal Service Every 100,000 Miles; Severe Service, Every 50,000 Miles																																							
Change Transfer Case Fluid	Every 50,000 Miles																																							
DRIVE AXLE																																								
Inspect Axle Seals & CV Joints	Normal Service Every 7500 Miles; Severe Service, Every 3000 Miles Or Every 3 Months																																							
Inspect Front & Rear Axle Lubricant Level	Normal Service Every 7500 Miles; Severe Service, Every 3000 Miles Or Every 3 Months																																							
Lubricate Driveshaft Fittings	Normal Service Every 7500 Miles; Severe Service Every 3 Months Or 3000 Miles																																							
ENGINE																																								
Change Engine Coolant	Every 150,000 Miles Or 60 Months																																							
Change Engine Oil & Filter③	Engine Oil Life Monitor Will Indicate When To Change Oil Filter, Vehicle Must Not Be Driven More Than 12 Months Or 10,000 Miles Without An Oil & Filter Change, Reset Oil Life System																																							
Inspect Air Intake System & Filter						X						X						X						X						X						X				
Inspect Drive Belts	Every 150,000 Miles																																							
Inspect Emission & Fuel System Connections, Hoses, Lines, Filler Cap & Tank	Every 25,000 Miles																																							
Inspect Exhaust System	Every 25,000 Miles																																							
Inspect Fuel System For Damage & Leaks	Every 25,000 Miles																																							
Inspect PVC, 2003	At 100,000 Miles																																							
Inspect Thermostatically Controlled Cooling Fan System						X						X						X						X						X						X				
Inspect Throttle Linkage Operation	At Air Filter Element Changes																																							
Replace Engine Air Filter, 2003	Every 30,000 Miles																																							

HUMMER H2 & H3—Continued

Recommended Service	Service Interval In Miles①																																							
	3000	6000	7500	9000	12000	15000	18000	21000	22500	24000	27000	30000	33000	36000	37500	39000	42000	45000	48000	51000	52500	54000	57000	60000	63000	66000	67500	69000	72000	75000	78000	81000	82500	84000	87000	90000	93000	96000	97500	99000
ENGINE																																								
Replace Engine Air Filter, 2004–05②	At 100,000 Miles																																							
Replace Engine Air Filter, 2006②	Every 50,000 Miles																																							
Replace Fuel Filter, 2003 H2	Every 30,000 Miles																																							
Replace Spark Plugs	At 100,000 Miles																																							
STEERING, SUSPENSION & TIRES																																								
Lubricate Steering & Suspension Grease Fittings	S	S	N	S	S	X	S	S	N	S	S	X	S	S	N	S	S	X	S	S	N	S	S	X	S	S	N	S	S	X	S	S	N	S	S	X	S	S	N	S
Rotate Tires	Every 7500 Miles																																							

N — Normal Service
S — Severe Service
X — Normal Or Severe Service
① — After vehicle passes 150,000 mile mark return to beginning of mileage table & start cycle over again.
② — Models less filter restriction indicator.
③ — If equipped, the engine oil life monitor will indicate when to change engine oil, usually 3000–10,000 miles. Under severe driving conditions, engine oil may need to be changed before 3000 miles. If vehicle is driven in a dusty area, change engine oil every 3000 miles.

MONTANA, RELAY, SILHOUETTE, TERRAZA, UPLANDER & VENTURE

Service Interval In Miles①

Recommended Service	3000	6000	7500	9000	12000	15000	18000	21000	22500	24000	27000	30000	33000	36000	37500	39000	42000	45000	48000	51000	52500	54000	57000	60000	63000	66000	67500	69000	72000	75000	78000	81000	82500	84000	87000	90000	93000	96000	97500	99000
BODY																																								
Change Passenger Compartment Air Filter	Every 15,000 Miles																																							
Clean Power Antenna Mast, Inspect Neutral Safety & BTSI Operation	At Least Once Every 3 Months																																							
Flush Vehicle Underside, Inspect Drain Holes	At Least Once Every 12 Months, Especially In Winter & Springtime																																							
Inspect Lamps, Seat Belts & Warning Devices	At Least Once Every 6 Months																																							
Lubricate Hinges, Latches, Lock Cylinders & Strikers	At Engine Oil Changes Or At Least Every 12 Months																																							
BRAKES																																								
Inspect Brake System	At Tire Roatations																																							
Lubricate Brake Cable Guides	S	S	N	S	S	X	S	S	N	S	S	X	S	S	N	S	S	X	S	S	N	S	S	X	S	S	N	S	S	X	S	S	N	S	S	X	S	S	N	S
CLUTCH & TRANSMISSION																																								
Change Automatic Transmission Fluid & Filter, 2002	No Normal Service Required; Severe Service Change Every 50,000 Miles																																							
Change Automatic Transmission Fluid & Filter, 2003–06	Normal Service Every 100,000 Miles; Severe Service Change Every 50,000 Miles																																							
DRIVE AXLE & DRIVESHAFT																																								
Change Rear Axle Fluid, AWD Models, 2002④	Severe Service At 7500 Miles																																							
Lubricate Driveshaft	S	S	N	S	S	X	S	S	N	S	S	X	S	S	N	S	S	X	S	S	N	S	S	X	S	S	N	S	S	X	S	S	N	S	S	X	S	S	N	S
ENGINE																																								
Change Engine Coolant	150,000 Miles																																							
Change Engine Oil & Filter③	Every 12 Months Or As Indicated By Oil Life Monitor																																							
Inspect Accessory Drive Belts, 2003–06	Every 150,000 Miles																																							
Inspect Drive Belts, 2002	Every 60,000 Miles																																							
Inspect Emission & Fuel System Connections, Hoses, Lines, Filler Cap & Tank, 2002–03												S												X												S				
Inspect Exhaust System, 2002–03	At Engine Oil Changes																																							

MONTANA, RELAY, SILHOUETTE, TERRAZA, UPLANDER & VENTURE—Continued

Recommended Service	Service Interval In Miles①																																							
	3000	6000	7500	9000	12000	15000	18000	21000	22500	24000	27000	30000	33000	36000	37500	39000	42000	45000	48000	51000	52500	54000	57000	60000	63000	66000	67500	69000	72000	75000	78000	81000	82500	84000	87000	90000	93000	96000	97500	99000
ENGINE																																								
Inspect Exhaust System, 2004–06	Every 25,000 Miles																																							
Inspect EVR Valve & Ignition Timing																								X																
Inspect Fuel System, 2004–06	Every 25,000 Miles																																							
Replace Engine Air Filter, 2004	Every 25,000 Miles																																							
Replace Engine Air Filter, 2005–06	Every 50,000 Miles																																							
Replace Engine Air & PCV Inlet Filter Elements, 2002–03②						S						X						S						X						S						X				
Replace Spark Plugs	Every 100,000 Miles																																							
STEERING, SUSPENSION & TIRES																																								
Lubricate Steering & Suspension Grease Fittings	At Engine Oil Changes																																							
Rotate Tires		S	N		S	N	S		N	S		X		S	N		S	N	S		N	S		X		S	N		S	N	S		N	S		X		S	N	

BTSI — Brake Transmission Shift Interlock
EPR — Exhaust Pressure Regulator
N — Normal Service
S — Severe Service
X — Normal Or Severe Service
① — After vehicle passes 99,000 mile mark return to beginning of mileage table & start cycle over again.
② — Inspect & replace even more frequently in severe dusty conditions, possibly as often as every 3000 miles.
③ — This vehicle is equipped with a GM Oil Life System and will show when to change the engine oil and oil filter. This occurs usually between 3000 miles and 10,000 miles since last oil change. Do not exceed 12 months between oil changes. Severe conditions change every 3000 miles or sooner if the CHANGE OIL SOON light comes on. Reset Oil Life System when the oil and filter have been changed.
④ — If vehicle is used to pull a trailer, change at 7500 miles.

SRX

Recommended Service	Service Interval In Miles①																																						
	3000	6000	7500	9000	12000	15000	18000	21000	22500	24000	27000	30000	33000	36000	37500	39000	42000	45000	48000	51000	52500	54000	57000	60000	63000	66000	67500	69000	72000	75000	78000	81000	82500	84000	87000	90000	93000	96000	97500	99000
BODY																																								
Flush Vehicle Underside, Inspect Drain Holes	At Least Every 12 Months, Especially In Winter & Springtime																																							
Inspect Lamps, Seat Belts & Warning Devices	At Least Once Every 6 Months																																							
Lubricate Hinges, Latches, Lock Cylinders & Strikers	At Engine Oil Changes Or At Least Every 12 Months																																							
Replace Passenger Compartment Air Filter						X						X						X						X						X						X				
BRAKES																																								
Inspect Brake System	At Engine Oil Changes Or At Least Every 12 Months																																							
Inspect Parking Brake Operation	At Least Once Every 12 Months																																							
Lubricate Parking Brake Cable Guides		S	N		S	N	S		N	S		X		S	N		S	N	S		N	S		X		S	N		S	N	S		N	S		X		S	N	
CLUTCH & TRANSAXLE/TRANSMISSION																																								
Change Automatic Transmission Fluid & Filter	Normal Service Every 100,000 Miles; Severe Service Every 50,000 Miles																																							
Change Transfer Case Fluid	Trailer Tow Operation Only Every 50,000 Miles																																							
Inspect Neutral Safety & BTSI Operation		S	N		S	N	S		N	S		X		S	N		S	N	S		N	S		X		S	N		S	N	S		N	S		X		S	N	
Lubricate Transmission Shift Linkage		S	N		S	N	S		N	S		X		S	N		S	N	S		N	S		X		S	N		S	N	S		N	S		X		S	N	
ENGINE																																								
Change Engine Coolant	Every 60 Months Or 150,000 Miles																																							
Change Engine Oil & Filter②	As Indicated By Oil Life System. Do Not Exceed 12 Months Between Oil And Filter Change Intervals																																							
Inspect Air Cleaner Element						X												X												X						X				
Inspect Drive Belts	At 150,000 Miles																																							
Inspect EGR System												X												X												X				
Inspect Exhaust System	Every 25,000 Miles																																							
Inspect Fuel Filler Cap												X												X												X				
Inspect Fuel System Hoses, Lines & Connections	Every 25,000 Miles																																							
Inspect Spark Plug Wires	At Spark Plug Changes																																							
Replace Air Filter	Every 50,000 Miles																																							
Replace Spark Plugs	Every 100,000 Miles																																							

SRX—Continued

Recommended Service	Service Interval In Miles①																																						
	3000	6000	7500	9000	12000	15000	18000	21000	22500	24000	27000	30000	33000	36000	37500	39000	42000	45000	48000	51000	52500	54000	57000	60000	63000	66000	67500	69000	72000	75000	78000	81000	82500	84000	87000	90000	93000	96000	97500	99000
STEERING, SUSPENSION & TIRES																																								
Inspect Steering & Suspension System	At Tire Rotations																																							
Lubricate Chassis & Suspension		S	N		S	N	S		N	S		X		S	N		S	N	S		N	S		X		S	N		S	N	S		N	S		X		S	N	
Rotate Tires	Initial Service At 5000 Miles, Then Every 10,000 Miles Thereafter																																							

BTSI — Brake Transmission Shift Interlock
IAC — Idle Air Control
ISC — Idle Speed Control System
N — Normal Service
S — Severe Service
X — Normal Or Severe Service
① — After vehicle passes 99,000 mile mark return to beginning of mileage table & start cycle over again.
② — If equipped, the engine oil life monitor will indicate when to change engine oil, usually 3000–10,000 miles. Under severe driving conditions, engine oil may need to be changed before 3000 miles. If vehicle is driven in a dusty area, change engine oil every 3000 miles.

TRACKER

Recommended Service	Service Interval In Miles①																																						
	3000	6000	7500	9000	12000	15000	18000	21000	22500	24000	27000	30000	33000	36000	37500	39000	42000	45000	48000	51000	52500	54000	57000	60000	63000	66000	67500	69000	72000	75000	78000	81000	82500	84000	87000	90000	93000	96000	97500	99000
BODY																																								
Inspect Seat Belt Pretensioners & Supplemental Restraint System	10 Years From Vehicle Build Date																																							
Inspect Warning Lamps & Devices	S	S	N	S	S	X	S	S	N	S	S	X	S	S	N	S	S	X	S	S	N	S	S	X	S	S	N	S	S	X	S	S	N	S	S	X	S	S	N	S
Lubricate Door Hinges	At Every Engine Oil Change																																							
Lubricate Lock Cylinders	At Least Once Every 12 Months																																							
Replace AC Evaporator Filter	Every 30,000 Miles																																							
Tighten Body Fasteners		S	N		S	N	S			S		X		S			S	N	S			S		X		S			S	N	S			S		X		S		
BRAKES																																								
Change Brake Fluid																								X																
Inspect Brake Connections, Drums, Hoses, Lines, Pads, Rotors & Shoes	At Tire Rotation																																							
CLUTCH & TRANSMISSION																																								
Change Automatic Transmission Fluid & Filter	Normal Service Every 100,000 Miles; Severe Service Every 15,000 Miles																																							
Change Transfer Case & Manual Transmission Lubricants						S						X						S						X						S						X				
Inspect Clutch						X						X						X						X						X						X				
Inspect Clutch Pedal Freeplay		S	N		S	N	S		N	S		X		S	N		S	N	S		N	S		X		S	N		S	N	S		N	S		X		S	N	
Inspect Neutral Safety & Shift Interlock Switch Operation	At Least Once Every 12 Months																																							
Lubricate Transmission Shift Control Lever & Shaft & Inspect Operation	At Every Engine Oil Change																																							
Replace Automatic Transmission Fluid Cooler Hoses																		X																		X				

TRACKER—Continued

Recommended Service	Service Interval In Miles①																																							
	3000	6000	7500	9000	12000	15000	18000	21000	22500	24000	27000	30000	33000	36000	37500	39000	42000	45000	48000	51000	52500	54000	57000	60000	63000	66000	67500	69000	72000	75000	78000	81000	82500	84000	87000	90000	93000	96000	97500	99000
DRIVE AXLE																																								
Change Differential Lubricant			X			S						X						S						X						S						X				
Inspect CV Joint Boots & Wheel Bearings		S	N		S	N	S		N	S		X		S	N		S	N	S		N	S		X		S	N		S	N	S		N	S		X		S	N	
Inspect & Lubricate Driveshafts			S			X			S			X			S			X			S			X			S			X			S			X			S	
ENGINE																																								
Change Engine Coolant												X												X												X				
Change Engine Oil & Filter	Normal Service Every 7.5 Months Or 7500 Miles; Severe Service Every 3 Months Or 3000 Miles																																							
Inspect Carburetor Or Fuel Injector & Catalytic Converter	Every 100,000 Miles																																							
Inspect Carburetor Or TBI Unit Fastener Security		S	N																																					
Inspect Cooling System & Protection Level						X						X						X						X						X						X				
Inspect Distributor Cap & Rotor						S						S						S						X						S						S				
Inspect Drive Belts						S						X						S						X						S						X				
Inspect ECM & Related Sensors	Every 100,000 Miles																																							
Inspect EGR System	Every 100,000 Miles																																							
Inspect Emission System Hoses & Tubes																								X																
Inspect Engine Air Filter Element	S	S		S	S	S	S	S		S	S	S	S	S		S	S	S	S	S		S	S	S	S	S		S	S	S	S	S		S	S	S	S	S		S
Inspect Fuel & Vapor System & Idle Speed						X						X						X						X						X						X				
Inspect Ignition Coils												X												X												X				
Inspect Ignition Timing																								X																
Inspect PCV Valve						S						X						S						X						S						X				
Inspect Spark Plug Wires						S						S						S						S						S						S				
Inspect Thermostatic Air Cleaner System Operation												X												X												X				
Inspect Underhood Wiring Harness & Connections																								X																
Replace Drive Belts												S												X												S				
Replace Engine Air Filter Element						S						X						S						X						S						X				

TRACKER—Continued

Recommended Service	Service Interval In Miles①																																							
	3000	6000	7500	9000	12000	15000	18000	21000	22500	24000	27000	30000	33000	36000	37500	39000	42000	45000	48000	51000	52500	54000	57000	60000	63000	66000	67500	69000	72000	75000	78000	81000	82500	84000	87000	90000	93000	96000	97500	99000
ENGINE																																								
Replace EVAP Canister, 2002	Every 100,000 Miles																																							
Replace EVAP Canister, 2003–04	Every 120,000 Miles																																							
Replace Exhaust System Hangers																								X																
Replace Fuel Filter	Every 30 Months Or 30,000 Miles																																							
Replace Fuel Hoses, Connections & Filler Cap & Spark Plug Wires																								X																
Replace Spark Plugs												X												X												X				
Replace O2 Sensor	Every 80,000 Miles																																							
Replace PCV Valve	Every 50,000 Miles																																							
Replace Timing Belt	②																																							
STEERING, SUSPENSION & TIRES																																								
Clean & Repack Front Wheel Bearings, 2WD	At 30,000 Miles Or At Brake Relinings																																							
Inspect Leaf Springs						S						X						S						X						S						X				
Inspect Power Steering & Steering & Suspension System		S	N		S	N	S		N	S		X		S	N		S	N	S		N	S		X		S	N		S	N	S		N	S		X		S	N	
Inspect Shock Absorbers			X			X						X						X						X						X						X				
Inspect Steering Wheel Freeplay, Gearbox Lubricant & Linkage	S	S		S	S	S	S	S		S	S	S	S	S		S	S	S	S	S		S	S	S	S	S		S	S	S	S	S		S	S	S	S	S		S
Inspect Wheel Discs & Free-Wheeling Hubs			X			X			X			X			X			X			X			X			X			X			X			X			X	
Rotate Tires		S	N		S	N	S		N	S		X		S	N		S	N	S		N	S		X		S	N		S	N	S		N	S		X		S	N	
Tighten Chassis & Suspension Fasteners		S	N		S	N	S			S		X		S			S	N	S			S		X		S			S	N	S			S		X		S		

N — Normal Service
S — Severe Service
X — Normal Or Severe Service
① — After vehicle passes 99,000 mile mark return to beginning of mileage table & start cycle over again.
② — Inspect every 60,000 miles, then replace at 100,000 miles.

VUE

Recommended Service	Service Interval In Miles①																																							
	3000	6000	7500	9000	12000	15000	18000	21000	22500	24000	27000	30000	33000	36000	37500	39000	42000	45000	48000	51000	52500	54000	57000	60000	63000	66000	67500	69000	72000	75000	78000	81000	82500	84000	87000	90000	93000	96000	97500	99000
BODY																																								
Inspect Seat Belts & Restraint Systems	At Least Once Every 6 Months																																							
Inspect Wiper Blades & Inserts	At Least Once Every 6 Months																																							
Lubricate Door Check Straps & Hinges		X		X		X		X		X		X		X		X		X		X		X		X		X		X		X		X		X		X		X		X
Lubricate Headlamp Doors		X		X		X		X		X		X		X		X		X		X		X		X		X		X		X		X		X		X		X		X
Lubricate Hood Latch		X		X		X		X		X		X		X		X		X		X		X		X		X		X		X		X		X		X		X		X
Lubricate Sunroof		X		X		X		X		X		X		X		X		X		X		X		X		X		X		X		X		X		X		X		X
Replace Cabin Air Filter	Every 12 Months Or 12,000 Miles; In Dusty Areas Change More Often																																							
BRAKES																																								
Inspect Brake Drums & Shoes	At Oil Change Intervals																																							
Inspect Brake Hoses, Lines & Connections	At Oil Change Intervals																																							
Inspect Disc Brake Calipers For Freedom Of Movement (Lubricate If Required)	At Oil Change Intervals																																							
Inspect Disc Brake Pads & Rotors	At Oil Change Intervals																																							
CLUTCH & TRANSAXLE																																								
Add DEX-CVT Additive To VTi Variable Transmission	Every 50,000 Miles																																							
Change Automatic Or VTi Transaxle Fluid & Filter, 2002–03	No Normal Service; Severe Service Every 50,000 Miles																																							
Change Automatic Transmission Fluid, 2004–06	Normal Service Every 100,000 Miles; Severe Service Every 25,000 Miles																																							
Change VTi VariableTransaxle Fluid & Filter	Normal Service Every 100,000 Miles; Severe Service Every 50,000 Miles																																							
DRIVESHAFT																																								
Change Engine Coolant & Inspect Pressure Cap, 2002–03	Every 60 Months Or 100,000 Miles																																							
Change Engine Coolant & Inspect Pressure Cap, 2004–06	Every 60 Months Or 150,000 Miles																																							
Change Engine Oil & Filter②	S	X	S	X	S	X	S	X	S	X	S	X	S	X	S	X	S	X	S	X	S	X	S	X	S	X	S	X	S	X	S	X	S	X	S	X	S	X	S	X
Change Rear Drive Module Fluid, 3.5L	Normal Service Every 100,000 Miles; Severe Service Every 50,000 Miles																																							

VUE—Continued

Recommended Service	Service Interval In Miles①																																							
	3000	6000	7500	9000	12000	15000	18000	21000	22500	24000	27000	30000	33000	36000	37500	39000	42000	45000	48000	51000	52500	54000	57000	60000	63000	66000	67500	69000	72000	75000	78000	81000	82500	84000	87000	90000	93000	96000	97500	99000
DRIVESHAFT																																								
Change Rear Drive Module & Power Take Off Unit Fluid, 2.2L	Normal Service Every 100,000 Miles; Severe Service Every 50,000 Miles																																							
Change Transfer Assembly Fluid, 3.5L	Normal Service At 100,000 Miles Then Every 50,000 Miles Thereafter; Severe Service Every 25,000 Miles																																							
ENGINE																																								
Inspect Air Filter	Severe Service Every 15,000 Miles																																							
Inspect Cooling System & Protection Level						X						X						X						X						X						X				
Inspect CV Joint Boots		X		X		X		X		X		X		X		X		X		X		X		X		X		X		X		X		X		X		X		X
Inspect Drive Belts & Coolant Hoses, 2002–03	Every 18,000 Miles																																							
Inspect Drive Belts & Coolant Hoses, 2004–06	Every 25,000 Miles																																							
Inspect Emission Hoses, Lines & Connections, 2002–03	Every 30,000 Miles																																							
Inspect Exhaust System, 2002–03		X		X		X		X		X		X		X		X		X		X		X		X		X		X		X		X		X		X		X		X
Inspect Exhaust System, 2004–06	Every 25,000 Miles																																							
Inspect Fuel System	Every 25,000 Miles																																							
Inspect Fuel Hoses, Lines & Connections										X										X										X										X
Inspect Fuel Tank Filler Cap										X										X										X										X
Inspect Valve Clearance, 3.5L	Every 100,000 Miles																																							
Replace Air Filter, 2002–03	Normal Service Every 30,000 Miles; More Frequently In Severe Service Or Dusty Conditions																																							
Replace Air Filter, 2004	Every 25,000 Miles																																							
Replace Air Filter, 2005–06	Every 50,000 Miles																																							
Replace Fuel Filter	Every 100,000 Miles																																							
Replace Spark Plugs	Every 100,000 Miles																																							
Replace Timing Belt, 3.0L, 2002–03	Every 100,000 Miles																																							
Replace Timing Belt, 3.5L, 2004–06	Normal Service Every 100,000 Miles; Severe Service Every 50,000 Miles																																							
STEERING, SUSPENSION & TIRES																																								
Inspect Ball Joint Seals		X		X		X		X		X		X		X		X		X		X		X		X		X		X		X		X		X		X		X		X
Inspect Suspension		X		X		X		X		X		X		X		X		X		X		X		X		X		X		X		X		X		X		X		X
Rotate Tires	Every 6000 Miles																																							

BTSI — Brake Transaxle Shift Interlock
N — Normal Service
S — Severe Service
X — Normal Or Severe Service
① — After vehicle passes 100,000 mile mark return to beginning of mileage table & start cycle over again.
② — On models equipped with Engine Oil Life Moniter, change engine oil when message appears in message display center. Do not exceed 12 months between oil and filter change intervals.

DAIMLERCHRYSLER CORP./JEEP

DAIMLERCHRYSLER CORP./JEEP

Page No.

CHRYSLER

DODGE

JEEP

GENERAL SERVICE

FULL SIZE TRUCKS & VAN

NOTE: Refer To The Rear Of This Manual For Vehicle Manufacturer's Special Service Tool Suppliers.

NOTE: Includes Coverage Of Compressed Natural Gas (CNG) Engines.

INDEX OF SERVICE OPERATIONS

Specifications

GENERAL ENGINE SPECIFICATIONS

Year	Engine Liter	Fuel System	Bore & Stroke	Comp. Ratio	Horsepower @ RPM	Torque Ft. Lbs. @ RPM	Normal Oil Pressure, psi
2002	3.7L	EFI	3.66 x 3.40	9.1	215 @ 5200	235 @ 4000	25–110③
	3.9L	EFI	3.91 x 3.31	9.1	175 @ 4800	—	30–80③
	4.7L	EFI	3.66 x 3.40	9.0	235 @ 4800	295 @ 3200	25–110③
	5.2L	EFI	3.91 x 3.31	9.1	230 @ 4400	300 @ 3200	30–80③
	5.2L	CNG	3.91 x 3.31	9.1	200 @ 4400	250 @ 3600	30–80③
	5.9L	EFI	4.00 x 3.58	9.1	245 @ 4000	335 @ 3200	30–80③
	5.9L	Turbo Diesel	4.02 x 4.72	①	⑦	⑧	30②
	8.0L	EFI	4.00 x 3.88	8.6	⑥	⑧	50–60③
2003	3.7L	EFI	3.66 x 3.40	9.1	210 @ 5200	225 @ 4200	25–110③
	3.9L	EFI	3.91 x 3.31	9.1	175 @ 4800	—	30–80③
	4.7L	EFI	3.66 x 3.40	9.0	235 @ 4800	295 @ 3200	25–110③
	5.2L	EFI	3.91 x 3.31	9.1	230 @ 4400	300 @ 3200	30–80③
	5.2L	CNG	3.91 x 3.31	9.1	200 @ 4400	250 @ 3600	30–80③
	5.7L	EFI	3.91 x 3.58	9.6	345 @ 5400	375 @ 4200	25–110③
	5.9L	EFI	4.00 x 3.58	9.1	245 @ 4000	335 @ 3200	30–80③
	5.9L	Turbo Diesel	4.02 x 4.72	17.2	⑤	④	30②
	8.0L	EFI	4.00 x 3.88	8.6	305 @ 4000	440 @ 2800	50–60③
2004–06	3.7L	EFI	3.66 x 3.40	9.1	210 @ 5200	225 @ 4200	25–110③
	4.7L	EFI	3.66 x 3.40	9.0	235 @ 4800	295 @ 3200	25–110③
	5.7L	EFI	3.91 x 3.58	9.6	345 @ 5400	375 @ 4200	25–110③
	5.9L	EFI	4.00 x 3.58	9.1	245 @ 4000	335 @ 3200	30–80③
	5.9L	Turbo Diesel	4.02 x 4.72	17.2	⑤	④	30②
	8.3L	EFI	4.03 x 3.96	9.6	501 @ 5600	525 @ 4100	45–75③

① — On models equipped with 235 HP engine, 16.3:1; On models equipped with 245 HP engine, 17:1.
② — At 2500 RPM.
③ — At 3000 RPM.
④ — Automatic and 5 speed manual transmissions, 460 @ 1400; 6 speed manual transmission, 555 @ 1400.
⑤ — Automatic and 5 speed manual transmissions, 235 @ 2700 CARB, 250 @ 2900 49 State; 6 speed manual transmission, 305 @ 2900.
⑥ — 2002: 310 @ 4000 RPM w/Federal Emissions & 305 @ 4000 RPM w/California Emissions.
⑦ — 2002: Automatic and 5 speed manual transmissions, 235 @ 2700 RPM, 6 speed manual transmission: 245 @ 2700 RPM.
⑧ — 2002: Automatic and 5 speed manual transmissions, 460 @ 1600 RPM, 6 speed manual transmission, 505 @ 1600 RPM.

TUNE UP SPECIFICATIONS

Year & Engine (VIN Code)④	Spark Plug Gap	Ignition Timing, BTDC				Curb Idle Speed②		Fast Idle Speed		Fuel Pump Pressure, psi	Valve Lash
		Firing Order ③	Man. Trans.	Auto. Trans.	Mark Location	Man. Trans.	Auto. Trans.	Man. Trans.	Auto. Trans.		
2002											
3.7L (K)	.042	D	①	①	Damper	⑤	⑤	⑤	⑤	44–54	⑥
3.9L (X)	.040	B	①	①	Damper	⑤	⑤	⑤	⑤	44–54	⑥
4.7L (N)	.040	E	①	①	Damper	⑤	⑤	⑤	⑤	44–54	⑥
5.2L(Y)	.040	A	①	①	Damper	⑤	⑤	⑤	⑤	44–54	⑥
5.2L (T)	.035	A	①	①	Damper	⑤	⑤	⑤	⑤	110–125	⑥
5.9L (Z,5)	.040	A	①	①	Damper	⑤	⑤	⑤	⑤	44–54	⑥
8.0L (W)	.045	C	①	①	Damper	⑤	⑤	⑤	⑤	44–54	⑥
2003											
3.7L (K)	.042	D	①	①	Damper	⑤	⑤	⑤	⑤	47.2–51.2	⑥
3.9L (X)	.040	B	①	①	Damper	⑤	⑤	⑤	⑤	44–54	⑥
4.7L (N)	.040	E	①	①	Damper	⑤	⑤	⑤	⑤	47.2–51.2	⑥

Continued

TUNE UP SPECIFICATIONS—Continued

Year & Engine (VIN Code)④	Spark Plug Gap	Ignition Timing, BTDC				Curb Idle Speed②		Fast Idle Speed		Fuel Pump Pressure, psi	Valve Lash
		Firing Order ③	Man. Trans.	Auto. Trans.	Mark Location	Man. Trans.	Auto. Trans.	Man. Trans.	Auto. Trans.		
2003											
5.2L(Y)	.040	A	①	①	Damper	⑤	⑤	⑤	⑤	44–54	⑥
5.2L (T)	.035	A	①	①	Damper	⑤	⑤	⑤	⑤	110–125	⑥
5.7L (D)	.045	F	①	①	Damper	⑤	⑤	⑤	⑤	47.2–51.2	⑥
5.9L (Z,5)	.040	A	①	①	Damper	⑤	⑤	⑤	⑤	47.2–51.2	⑥
8.0L (W)	.045	C	①	①	Damper	⑤	⑤	⑤	⑤	47.2–51.2	⑥
2004–06											
3.7L (K)	.042	D	①	①	Damper	⑤	⑤	⑤	⑤	47.2–51.2	⑥
4.7L (N)	.040	E	①	①	Damper	⑤	⑤	⑤	⑤	47.2–51.2	⑥
5.7L (D)	.045	F	①	①	Damper	⑤	⑤	⑤	⑤	47.2–51.2	⑥
5.9L (Z,5)	.040	A	①	①	Damper	⑤	⑤	⑤	⑤	47.2–51.2	⑥
8.3L (H)	.033–.038	G	①	①	Damper	⑤	⑤	⑤	⑤	56–60	⑥

BTDC — Before Top Dead Center

① — Non-adjustable.

② — Idle speed is adjusted w/transmission in Neutral (N). When inspecting idle speed, set parking brake & block drive wheels.

③ — Before removing wires from distributor cap, determine location of No. 1 wire in cap, as distributor position may have been altered from that outlined at the end of this chart.

④ — The eighth digit of the VIN denotes engine code.

⑤ — Controlled by an idle speed control motor.

⑥ — Equipped w/hydraulic valve lash adjusters.

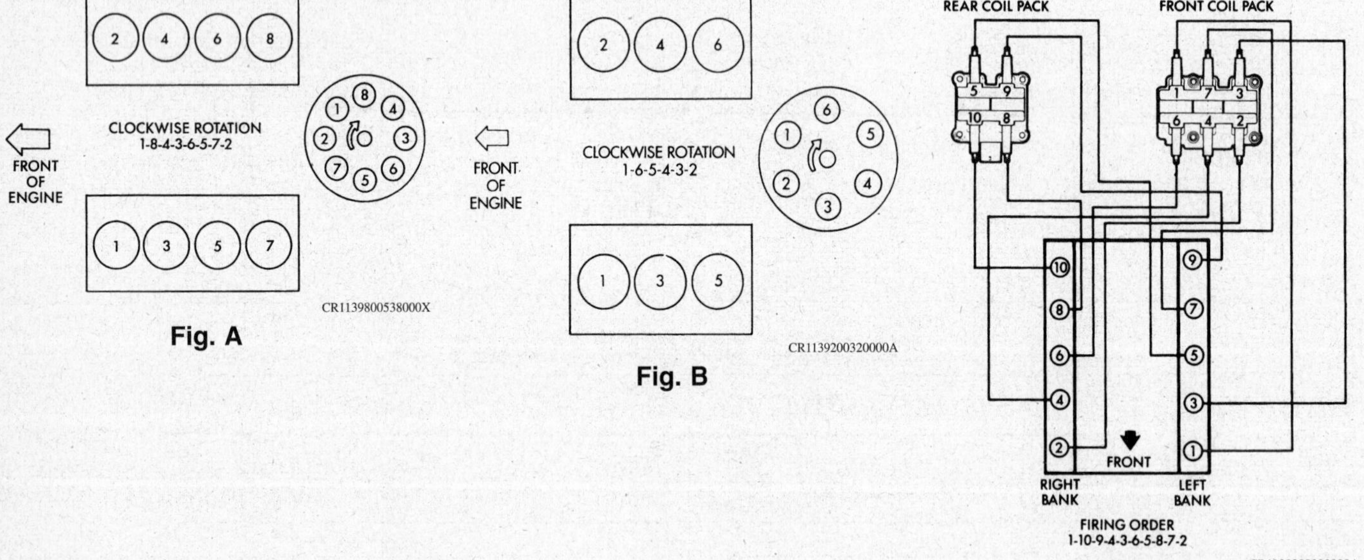

Fig. A

Fig. B

Fig. C

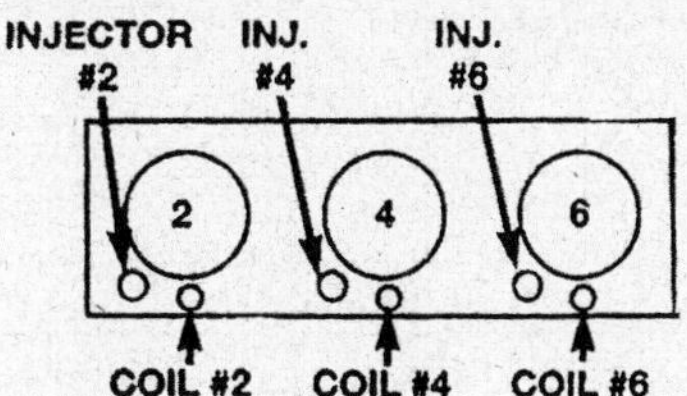

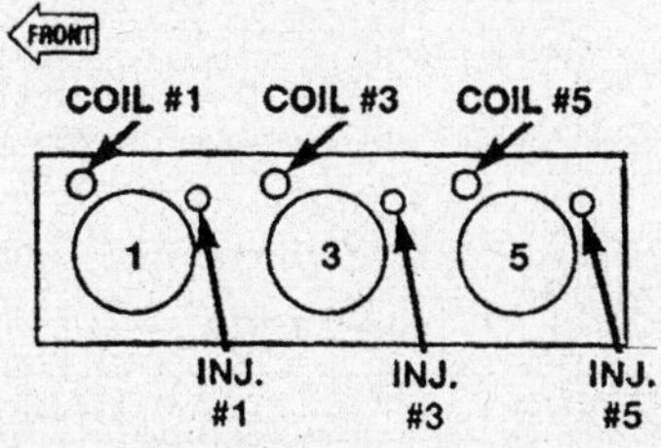

FIRING ORDER: 1 - 6 - 5 - 4 - 3 - 2

CR1130200953000X

Fig. D

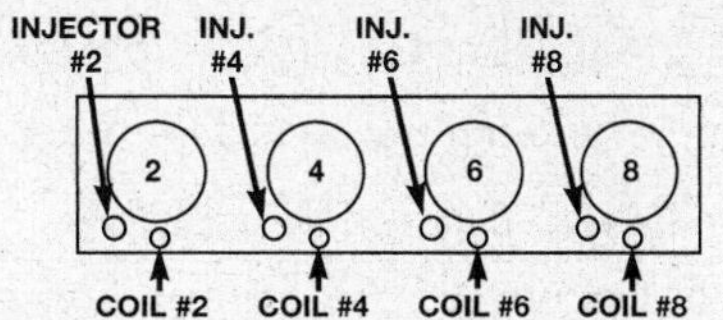

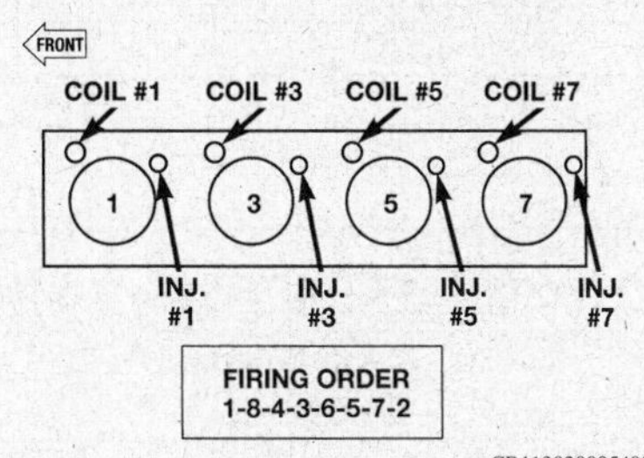

CR1130200954000X

Fig. E

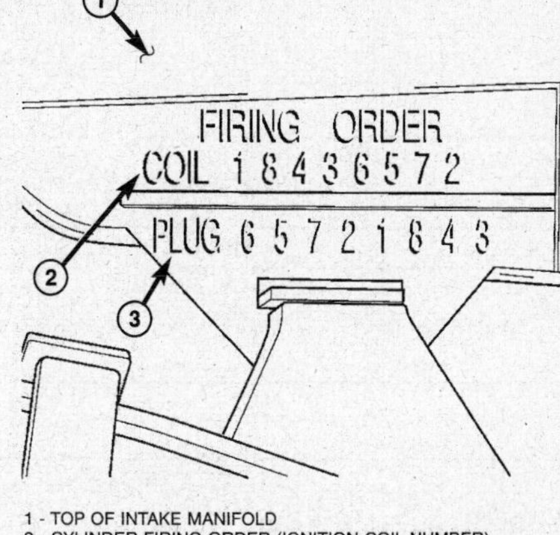

LTV1900000000328

Fig. F

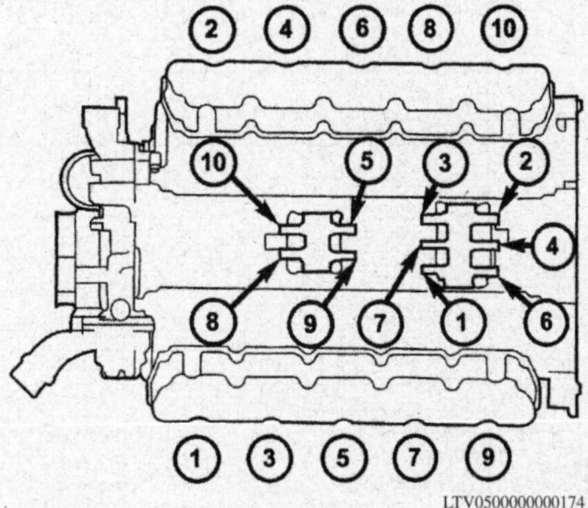

LTV0500000000174

Fig. G

DIESEL ENGINE PERFORMANCE SPECIFICATIONS

Year	Engine Liter	Compres-sion Ratio	Firing Order	Injection Timing	Injection Nozzle Opening Pressure, psi	Low Idle Stop Speed (Min.), RPM	Full Throttle Stop Speed, RPM
2002–06	5.9L	②	1-5-3-6-2-4	①	4250–4750	①	①

① — Timing & fuel adjustments are controlled by the ECM, there are no adjustments available.

② — 2002: 235 HP 16.3, 245 HP 17.0, 2003–04: 305 HP 17.2., 2005–06: 325 HP 17.2

FRONT WHEEL ALIGNMENT SPECIFICATIONS

The specifications listed below are for unloaded vehicles

RAM VAN/WAGON

Year	Model	Caster Angle, Degrees		Camber Angle, Degrees		Toe, Degrees①	
		Limits	Desired	Limits	Desired	Limits	Desired
2002–03	All	+2.50 to +4.50	+3.50	-.3 to +.3	0	0 to +.50	+.25

① — Toe-in (+). Toe-out (-).

2002 RAM 2500-3500

Year	Model	Wheel Base, Inches	GVW, Lbs.	Caster Angle, Degrees		Camber Angle, Degrees		Toe In, Degrees①	
				Limits	Desired	Limits	Desired	Limits	Desired
2002	2WD	118.7	6400	+2.66 to +4.66②	+3.66②	0 to +1③	+.5③	0 to +.2	+.1
		134.7	6400	+2.89 to +4.89②	+3.89②	0 to +1③	0+.5③	0 to +.2	+.1
			8800	+2.53 to +4.53②	+3.53②	0 to +1③	+.5③	0 to +.2	+.1
			10,500	+2.33 to +4.33②	+3.33②	0 to +1③	+.5③	0 to +.2	+.1
		138.7	6400	+2.99 to +4.99②	+3.99②	0 to +1③	+.5③	0 to +.2	+.1
			8800	+2.59 to +4.59②	+3.59②	0 to +1③	+.5③	0 to +.2	+.1
		154.7	6400	+3.17 to +5.17②	+4.17②	0 to +1③	+.5③	0 to +.2	+.1
			8800	+2.78 to +4.78②	+3.78②	0 to +1③	+.5③	0 to +.2	+.1
			10,500	+2.58 to +4.58②	+3.58②	0 to +1③	+.5③	0 to +.2	+.1
	4WD	118.7	6400	+1.86 to +3.86②	+2.86②	—	+.5	0 to +.2	+.1
		134.7	6400	+2.04 to +4.04②	+3.04②	—	+.5	0 to +.2	+.1
			8800	+1.68 to 3.68②	+2.68②	—	+.5	0 to +.2	+.1
			10,500	+1.48 to +3.48②	+2.48②	—	+.5	0 to +.2	+.1
		138.7	6600	+2.19 to +4.19②	+3.19②	—	+.5	0 to +.2	+.1
			8800	+1.74 to +3.74②	+2.74②	—	+.5	0 to +.2	+.1
		154.7	6600	+2.37 to +4.37②	+3.37②	—	+.5	0 to +.2	+.1
			8800	+1.88 to +3.88②	+2.88②	—	+.5	0 to +.2	+.1
			10,500	+1.63 to +3.63②	+2.63②	—	+.5	0 to +.2	+.1

① — Toe-in (+). Toe-out (-). ② — Preferred cross caster 0° (+/–.5°). ③ — Preferred cross camber 0° (+/–.5°).

FRONT WHEEL ALIGNMENT SPECIFICATIONS—Continued

The specifications listed below are for unloaded vehicles

2002-06 RAM 1500

Year	Model	Wheel Base, Inches	Caster Angle, Degrees		Camber Angle, Degrees		Toe In, Degrees①	
			Limits	Desired	Limits	Desired	Limits	Desired
2002–06	2WD	120.5	+3.25 to +4.75②	+4②	-.5 to +.5③	0③	0 to +.2⑤	+.1⑤
		140.5	+3.45 to +4.95②	+4.2②	-.5 to +.5③	0③	0 to +.2⑤	+.1⑤
		160.5	+3.65 to +5.15②	+4.4②	-.5 to +.5③	0③	0 to +.2⑤	+.1⑤
2002–06	4WD	120.5	+3.45 to +4.95②	+4.2②	-.5 to +.5④	0④	0 to +.2⑤	+.1⑤
		140.5	+3.65 to +5.15②	+4.4②	-.5 to +.5④	0④	0 to +.2⑤	+.1⑤
		160.5	+3.85 to +5.35②	+4.6②	-.5 to +.5④	0④	0 to +.2⑤	+.1⑤

2WD — Two Wheel Drive
4WD — Four Wheel Drive
① — Toe-in (+). Toe-out (–).

② — Maximum left/right difference .04°.
③ — Maximum left/right difference .5°.
④ — Maximum left/right difference .6°.
⑤ — Maximum left/right difference .06°.

2003-06 RAM 2500-3500

Year	Model	Wheel Base, Inches	Caster Angle, Degrees		Camber Angle, Degrees		Toe In, Degrees①	
			Limits	Desired	Limits	Desired	Limits	Desired
2003–06	2WD	140	+3.25 to +4.75②	+4.0②	-.50 to +.50③	0③	+.05 to +.15⑤	+.1⑤
		160	+3.55 to +5.05②	+4.3②	-.50 to +.50③	0③	+.05 to +.15⑤	+.1⑤
	4WD	140	+3.75 to +5.25②	+4.5②	-.25 to +.75④	+.25④	+.05 to +.15⑤	+.1⑤
		160	+3.95 to +5.45④	+4.7④	-.25 to +.75④	+.25④	+.05 to +.15④	+.1⑤

2WD — Two Wheel Drive
4WD — Four Wheel Drive
① — Toe-in (+). Toe-out (–).

② — Maximum left/right difference .4°.
③ — Maximum left/right difference .6°.
④ — Maximum left/right difference .5°.
⑤ — Maximum left/right difference .1°.

FRONT WHEEL ALIGNMENT SPECIFICATIONS—Continued

The specifications listed below are for unloaded vehicles

RAM CAB-CHASSIS 2500-3500

Year	Model	Wheel Base, Inches	Caster Angle①		Toe In, Degrees②	
			Hanger Bolt Gauge Hole Measurement, Inch	Caster Correction, Degree Desired	Limits	Desired
2002	2WD 8800 Lb. GVW	134.7	–5.0	+4.27	0 to +.2	+.1
			–4.75	+4.39	0 to +.2	+.1
			–4.5	+4.51	0 to +.2	+.1
			–4.25	+4.64	0 to +.2	+.1
			–4.0	+4.76	0 to +.2	+.1
			–3.75	+4.88	0 to +.2	+.1
			–3.5	+5	0 to +.2	+.1
			–3.25	+5.12	0 to +.2	+.1
			–3.0	+5.25	0 to +.2	+.1
			–2.75	+5.37	0 to +.2	+.1
			–2.5	+5.49	0 to +.2	+.1
			–2.25	+5.61	0 to +.2	+.1
			–2.0	+5.74	0 to +.2	+.1
			–1.75	+5.86	0 to +.2	+.1
			–1.5	+5.98	0 to +.2	+.1
			–1.25	+6.1	0 to +.2	+.1
			–1.0	+6.23	0 to +.2	+.1
			–.75	+6.33	0 to +.2	+.1
			–.5	+6.47	0 to +.2	+.1
			–.25	+6.59	0 to +.2	+.1
			0	+6.71	0 to +.2	+.1
	4WD 8800 Lb. GVW & 2WD & 4WD 11,000 Lb. GVW	134.7 & 138.7	–5.0	+3.77	0 to +.2	+.1
			–4.75	+3.89	0 to +.2	+.1
			–4.5	+4.01	0 to +.2	+.1
			–4.25	+4.14	0 to +.2	+.1
			–4.0	+4.26	0 to +.2	+.1
			–3.75	+4.38	0 to +.2	+.1
			–3.5	+4.5	0 to +.2	+.1
			–3.25	+4.62	0 to +.2	+.1
			–3.0	+4.75	0 to +.2	+.1
			–2.75	+4.87	0 to +.2	+.1
			–2.5	+4.99	0 to +.2	+.1
			–2.25	+5.11	0 to +.2	+.1
			–2.0	+5.24	0 to +.2	+.1
			–1.75	+5.36	0 to +.2	+.1
			–1.5	+5.48	0 to +.2	+.1
			–1.25	+5.6	0 to +.2	+.1
			–1.0	+5.73	0 to +.2	+.1
			–.75	+5.83	0 to +.2	+.1
			–.5	+5.97	0 to +.2	+.1
			–.25	+6.09	0 to +.2	+.1
			0	+6.21	0 to +.2	+.1

Continued

FRONT WHEEL ALIGNMENT SPECIFICATIONS—Continued

The specifications listed below are for unloaded vehicles

RAM CAB-CHASSIS 2500-3500—Continued

Year	Model	Wheel Base, Inches	Caster Angle①		Toe In, Degrees②	
			Hanger Bolt Gauge Hole Measurement, Inch	Caster Correction, Degree Desired	Limits	Desired
2002	2WD & 4WD 11,000 Lb. GVW	162.7	−5.0	+3.81	0 to +.2	+.1
			−4.75	+3.91	0 to +.2	+.1
			−4.5	+4.01	0 to +.2	+.1
			−4.25	+4.11	0 to +.2	+.1
			−4.0	+4.21	0 to +.2	+.1
			−3.75	+4.31	0 to +.2	+.1
			−3.5	+4.41	0 to +.2	+.1
			−3.25	+4.51	0 to +.2	+.1
			−3.0	+4.61	0 to +.2	+.1
			−2.75	+4.71	0 to +.2	+.1
			−2.5	+4.81	0 to +.2	+.1
			−2.25	+4.91	0 to +.2	+.1
			−2.0	+5.01	0 to +.2	+.1
			−1.75	+5.11	0 to +.2	+.1
			−1.5	+5.21	0 to +.2	+.1
			−1.25	+5.31	0 to +.2	+.1
			−1.0	+5.41	0 to +.2	+.1
			−.75	+5.51	0 to +.2	+.1
			−.5	+5.61	0 to +.2	+.1
			−.25	+5.71	0 to +.2	+.1
			0	+5.81	0 to +.2	+.1

① — Take height measurement from ground to center of front gauge hole in frame. Take height measurement from ground to center of rear spring hanger bolt. Refer to **Fig. 1** for measurement locations. Take measurements at both sides of vehicle. Subtract front measurement from rear measurement & use average between left & right side. Use this average (hanger bolt gauge hole) w/caster correction to obtain correct angle.

② — Toe-in (+). Toe-out (-).

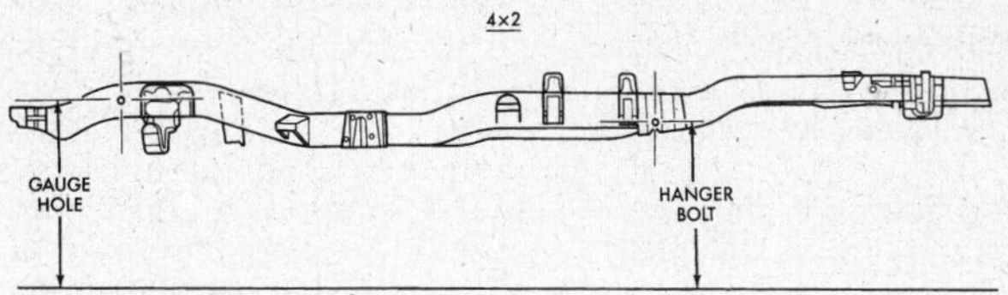

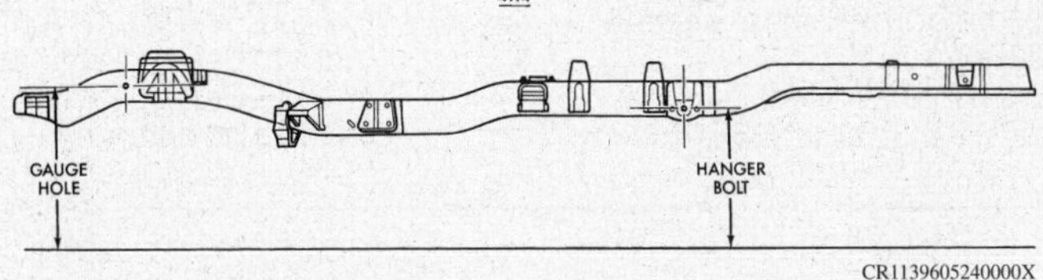

Fig. 1 Ram cab-chassis measurement locations

FLUID CAPACITIES & COOLING SYSTEM DATA

Year	Engine Liter	Cooling Capacit, Qts.	Recommended Coolant Type	Radiator Cap Relief Pressure, Lbs.	Thermo. Opening Temp. °F	Fuel Tank Gals.	Engine Oil Refill Qts.	Transmission Oil		Transfer Case Pts.	Drive Axle Oil Pts.	
								Manual Trans, Pts.	Auto. Trans. Qts.⑦		Front	Rear
CONVENTIONAL CAB												
2003–06	3.7L	16.2	Ethylene Glycol	16	195	④	5.0①	4.8	⑧	3.4	3.50	4.9⑩
	4.7L	16.2	Ethylene Glycol	16	195	④	6.0①	4.8	⑧	3.4	3.50	4.9⑩
	5.9L⑪	16.3	Ethylene Glycol	16	195	④	5.0①	4.8	⑧	3.4	3.50	4.9⑩
	5.9L⑮	29.5	Ethylene Glycol	14	180	⑱	11.0①	⑥	㉚	4.0	4.75	⑬⑨
	8.0L	26.0	Ethylene Glycol	14	195	⑫	7.0①	⑥	⑯	⑰	8.50	⑨
	8.3L	18.0	Ethylene Glycol	18	193	⑭	9.0①	4.8	⑧	3.4	—	—
VANS, WAGONS & FRONT SECTIONS												
2002–03	3.9L	14.5	Ethylene Glycol	16	195	②	4.0①	—	③	—	—	⑤
	5.2L	16.5	Ethylene Glycol	16	195	②	5①	—	③	—	—	⑤
	5.9L	15.0	Ethylene Glycol	16	195	②	5.0①	—	③	—	—	⑤

CNG — Compressed Natural Gas
MPI — Multi-Point Fuel Injection
① — Includes filter.
② — 109 inch wheel base; 31 gal. tank, 127 inch wheel base; 35 gal. tank.
③ — 32H transmission 6.7–6.9 qts., 46RE transmission 8 qts. qts.
④ — Short bed, 26 gals.; long bed, 35 gals.
⑤ — 8¼ inch ring gear, 4.4 pts.; 9¼ inch ring gear, 4.5 pts.; 248 RBI, 6.25 pts.
⑥ — NV4500 transmission, 8 pts.; NV5600 transmission, 9.5 pts.
⑦ — Approximate, make final inspect w/dipstick.
⑧ — 46RE, service fill, 4 qts.; after overhaul, 9.5–10 qts. 45RFE/545RFE, service fill, 2WD, 5.5 qts., 4WD, 6.5 qts., after overhaul, 14.5–16.5 qts.
⑨ — 10 ½ inch, 4.75 pts.; 11 ½ inch, 7.65 pts.
⑩ — For limited slip differentials, include 5 oz. of friction modifier.
⑪ — 1500 Series.
⑫ — 2500 short wheelbase Club Cabs & Quad Cabs, 34 gals.; other models, 35 gals.
⑬ — Except limited slip differential, Model 248–RBI 2WD, 6.1 pts.; Model 248–RBI 4WD, 7.2 pts.; Model 267–RBI 2WD, 7 pts.; Models 267 RBI 4WD, 7.6 pts.; Model 286–RBI 2WD, 6.8 pts.; Model 286–RBI 4WD, 10.1 pts. Limited slip differential, Model 248–RBI 2WD, 5.9 pts.; Model 248–RBI 4WD, 6.8 pts.; Model 267 RBI 2WD, 6.5 pts.; Model 267–RBI 4WD, 7.2 pts.; Model 268–RBI 2WD, 6.3 pts.; Model 268–RBI 4WD, 9.5 pts.
⑭ — 1500 series w/6.5' short box; 26 gal tank, 2500 series Club Cab and Quad Cab w/6.5' short box; 34 gal tank, all 8' long box and Cab/Chassis models; 35 gal tank.
⑮ — Diesel Engine.
⑯ — Refill capacity, 4 qts. Total capacity, 46RE, 9.5–10 qts.; 47RE, 14.5–16.5.
⑰ — NV241, 4.61 pts.; NV241HD, 6.51 pts.

LUBRICANT DATA

Year	Model	Lubricant Type					
		Transmission		Transfer Case	Drive Axle	Power Steering	Brake System
		Manual	Automatic				
PICKUP							
2002	1500	⑥	ATF+4	ATF+4	75W-90 GL-5⑦	ATF+4	DOT 3
	2500 & 3500	⑥	ATF+4	ATF+4	⑧	ATF+4	DOT 3
2003–06	1500	⑥	ATF+4	ATF+4	③	ATF+4	DOT 3
	2500 & 3500	④	ATF+4	ATF+4	①	ATF+4	DOT 3
RAM VAN/WAGON							
2002–03	All	—	ATP+4	—	②	⑤	DOT 3

① — Front axle, Mopar Synthetic Gear Lubricant 75W-90; rear axle, Mopar Synthetic Gear Lubricant 75W-90.

② — 8 ¼ and 9 ¼ inch rear axles, 75W-90 GL-5 lubricant, trailer towing, 75W-140 GL-5 lubricant; 248–RBI rear axle 90W lubricant.

③ — Front axle, Mopar Gear Lubricant 75W-90; rear axle, Mopar Synthetic Gear Lubricant 75W-140.

④ — NV4500, Mopar Synthetic 75W-85 manual transmission lubricant; NV5600 Mopar manual transmission lubricant.

⑤ — Use Mopar power steering fluid or equivalent.

⑥ — Use Mopar Manual Transmission Lubricant Part No. 4874464.

⑦ — Limited slip differentials require 6.5% of friction modifier added whenever fluid is changed.

⑧ — Front axle, 80–90W GL-5; rear axle, thermally stable 90W. Limited slip differentials require 6.5% of friction modifier added whenever fluid is changed.

Electrical

NOTE: On Air Bag Equipped Models, Refer To "Air Bag System Precautions" Located In The Front Of This Manual For System Disarming & Arming Procedures.

NOTE: Refer To "Computer Relearn Procedures" Located In The Front Of This Manual When Battery Power To The Computer Has Been Interrupted.

INDEX

PRECAUTIONS

Air Bag Systems

Refer to "Air Bag System Precautions" in the front of this manual for system disarming and arming procedures.

Battery Ground Cable

Prior to service, disconnect battery ground cable and isolate as required.

FUSE PANEL LOCATION

Pickup

2002 2500 & 3500

An electrical junction block is located behind the left outboard end of the instrument panel cover. The left end of the instrument panel cover has a snap fit fuse panel cover that can be removed for service of the junction block fuses. A fuse puller and spare fuse holders are located at the back of the fuse access cover along with a fuse layout label to ensure proper fuse identification.

1500 & 2003-06 2500 & 3500

The fuse and relay center is located on the left front corner of the engine compartment near the battery.

Van

The junction block is located behind the left outboard end of the instrument panel cover. The hazard flasher and turn signal flasher plug into designated slots next to the fuse panel.

FUEL PUMP RELAY LOCATION

Pickup

2002 2500 & 3500

The fuel pump relay is located on the rear lefthand side of the engine compartment, in the power distribution center.

1500 & 2003-06 2500 & 3500

The fuel pump relay is located in the left front corner of the engine compartment, in the fuse and relay center. **NOTE: 8.3L Engine does not have a fuel pump relay.**

Van

The fuel pump relay is located in the main relay center in the fuse block at the left end of the instrument panel.

RELAY CENTER LOCATION

The main relay center is located at the fuse block.

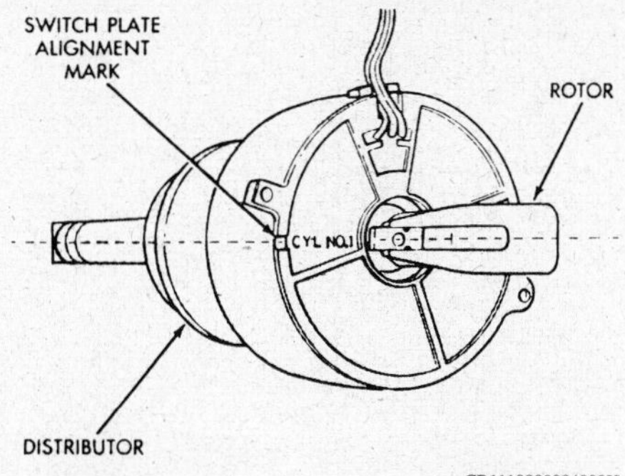

Fig. 1 Rotor alignment mark. 3.9L, 5.2L & 5.9L engines

STARTER

REPLACE

Pickup

2002 2500 & 3500

DIESEL ENGINE

Removal

1. Raise and support vehicle.
2. Pull back protective rubber boot from solenoid battery terminal far enough to access and remove nut from positive cable harness connector eyelet.
3. Remove nut that secures positive cable to solenoid terminal, then remove positive cable.
4. Remove solenoid wire connecting nut from starter solenoid connector.
5. While supporting starter motor with one hand, remove three screws that secure starter motor to transmission housing.
6. Remove starter motor from engine compartment.

Installation

1. Position starter motor in engine compartment.
2. While supporting starter motor with one hand, loosely install three screws that secure starter motor to transmission housing.
3. **Torque** three starter mounting bolts to 32 ft. lbs.
4. Install battery positive cable wire harness connector eyelets over solenoid terminal studs.
5. **Torque** nut that secures battery positive cable wire harness connector eyelet to solenoid terminal stud to 55 inch lbs.
6. Install and **Torque** nut that secures battery positive cable wire harness connector eyelet to solenoid battery terminal stud to 10 ft. lbs.
7. Install protective rubber boot on positive cable.
8. Lower vehicle.

GASOLINE ENGINE

Removal

1. Raise and support vehicle.
2. Remove nut and lockwasher securing starter motor to mounting stud on manual transmission clutch housing or automatic transmission torque converter housing.
3. While supporting starter with one hand, remove upper mounting screw from starter.
4. **On models equipped with automatic transmission,** slide transmission cooler tube bracket forward on tubes far enough for starter motor flange to be removed from lower mounting stud.
5. **On all models,** move starter motor towards front of vehicle far enough for nose of starter pinion housing to clear transmission housing.
6. Do not let starter motor hang from wiring.
7. Tilt motor downwards and lower starter motor far enough to access and remove nut that secures battery positive cable to solenoid.
8. Remove starter positive cable wire harness connector from solenoid terminal connector receptacle.
9. Remove starter motor from engine compartment.

Installation

1. Position starter motor in engine compartment.
2. Reconnect battery positive cable wire harness connector to solenoid terminal connector receptacle.
3. Do not let starter hang from wire harness.
4. Install battery positive cable wire harness connector eyelet over solenoid battery terminal stud.
5. Install nut that secures battery cable wire harness connector eyelet to solenoid battery terminal stud.
6. **Torque** nut to 10 ft. lbs. Support starter during this process, do not let starter hang from harness.
7. Position stater motor to front of transmission housing.
8. **On models equipped with automatic transmission,** slide ATF cooler tube bracket rearward on tubes and into position over upper mounting hole in starter motor mounting flange.
9. **On all models,** loosely install screw that secures upper starter motor mounting flange to transmission housing.
10. **Torque** upper and lower starter mounting bolts to 50 ft. lbs.
11. Lower vehicle.

1500 & 2003-06 2500 & 3500

DIESEL ENGINE

1. Raise and support vehicle.
2. Remove three starter motor mounting bolts.
3. Move starter motor toward front of vehicle far enough for nose of starter pinion housing to clear housing. Do not let starter motor hang from wire harness.
4. Tilt nose downward, then lower far enough to access and remove nuts securing wiring harness.
5. Remove starter motor noting position of aluminum spacer, if equipped.
6. Reverse procedure to install.

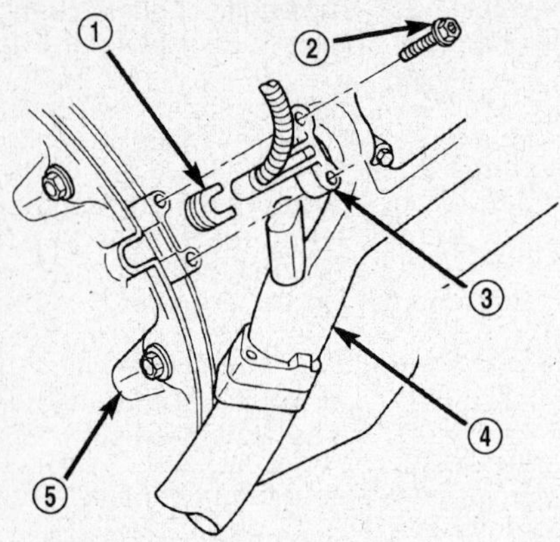

1 – GROMMET
2 – MOUNTING BOLTS (2)
3 – CRANKSHAFT POSITION SENSOR
4 – RIGHT EXHAUST MANIFOLD
5 – TRANSMISSION BELL HOUSING

CR1119900274000X

Fig. 2 Crankshaft position sensor. 3.9L, 5.2L & 5.9L engines

GASOLINE ENGINE

1. Raise and support vehicle.
2. **On models equipped with 4WD,** remove support bracket bolts, then pry support bracket to gain access to lower starter mounting bolt.
3. **On all models,** remove starter motor bolts.
4. Move starter motor toward front of vehicle far enough for nose of starter pinion to clear housing, Do not let starter motor hang from wire harness.
5. Tilt nose downward, then lower far enough to access and remove nut securing battery positive cable connector eyelet to terminal stud.
6. Remove battery positive cable from terminal stud, then disconnect battery positive cable wire harness electrical connector.
7. Remove starter motor.
8. Reverse procedure to install.

Van

1. Raise and support vehicle.
2. Remove nut and lockwasher securing starter motor to mounting stud on manual transmission clutch housing or automatic transmission torque converter housing.
3. While supporting starter with one hand, remove upper mounting screw from starter.
4. Slide transmission cooler tube bracket forward on tubes far enough for starter motor flange to be removed from lower mounting stud.
5. Move starter motor towards front of vehicle far enough for nose of starter pinion housing to clear transmission housing.
6. Do not let starter motor hang from wiring.
7. Tilt motor downwards and lower starter motor far enough to access and remove nut that secures battery positive cable to solenoid.
8. Remove starter positive cable wire harness connector from solenoid terminal connector receptacle.
9. Remove starter motor from engine compartment.
10. Reverse procedure to install, noting the following:
    a. **Torque** nut to 10 ft. lbs. Support starter during this process, do not let starter hang from harness.
    b. **Torque** upper and lower starter mounting bolts to 50 ft. lbs.

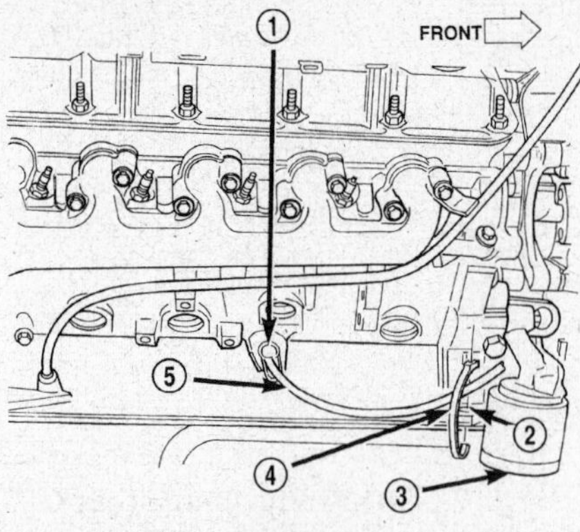

1 – CRANKSHAFT POSITION SENSOR
2 – HOLE
3 – OIL FILTER
4 – PLASTIC TIE STRAP
5 – PIGTAIL HARNESS

CR1119900275000X

Fig. 3 Crankshaft position sensor. 8.0L engine

ALTERNATOR

REPLACE

1. Remove alternator drive belt.
2. **On 2002 models equipped with gasoline engine,** remove alternator pivot bolt and mounting bolts and nuts.
3. **On models equipped with 8.3L engine,** remove air cleaner assembly.
4. **On 2002 models equipped with diesel engine,** loosen, but do not remove alternator mounting bracket to engine bolt.
5. **On all models,** remove battery positive terminal retaining nuts.
6. Remove ground terminal and two field terminal retaining nuts.
7. Remove upper alternator mounting bolt, lower mounting bolt and nut.
8. Disconnect wire connectors, then remove alternator.
9. Reverse procedure to install, noting the following:
    a. **On models equipped with 3.7L and 4.7L engine, torque** mounting bolts to 40 ft. lbs.
    b. **On models equipped with 5.7L and 5.9L engine, torque** mounting bolts to 30 ft. lbs.
    c. **On models equipped with 8.3L engine, torque** mounting bolts to 401 ft. lbs.
    d. **On models equipped with diesel engine, torque** alternator mounting bolts to 30 ft. lbs.
    e. **On all models, torque** battery terminal nut to 105 inch lbs.

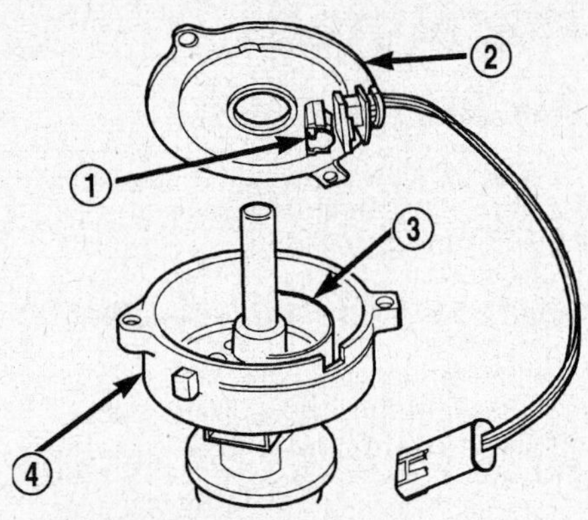

1 – SYNC SIGNAL GENERATOR
2 – CAMSHAFT POSITION SENSOR
3 – PULSE RING
4 – DISTRIBUTOR ASSEMBLY

CR1119900276000X

Fig. 4 Camshaft position sensor. 3.9L, 5.2L & 5.9L engines

DISTRIBUTOR

REPLACE

3.9L, 5.2L & 5.9L Engines

REMOVAL

1. Remove air cleaner assembly.
2. **On Vans,** remove engine cover.
3. **On all models,** remove distributor cap and mark position of distributor housing in relationship to engine or dash panel for installation reference.
4. Bring No. 1 cylinder to TDC position as follows:
    a. Attach a suitable socket to crankshaft vibration damper mounting bolt.
    b. Rotate engine clockwise, as viewed from front, until crankshaft vibration damper is aligned with 0° (TDC) mark on timing chain cover.
    c. Distributor rotor should be aligned to CYL. NO. 1 alignment mark stamped on camshaft position sensor, **Fig. 1.** If rotor is not as specified, then rotate crankshaft through another complete 360° turn.
5. Disconnect camshaft position sensor wiring harness, then remove distributor rotor from shaft.
6. Remove distributor mounting bolt, then the distributor.

INSTALLATION

If engine has been cranked with distributor removed, it will be required to establish the proper relationship between distributor shaft and No. 1 piston position by rotating crankshaft until No. 1 piston is at top of compression stroke. Mark on crankshaft vibration damper should be inline with "0°" TDC mark on timing chain cover.

1. Clean top of cylinder block to ensure a satisfactory seal between distributor base and cylinder block, then apply a thin film of oil to rubber O-ring seal.
2. Position distributor in engine, ensure

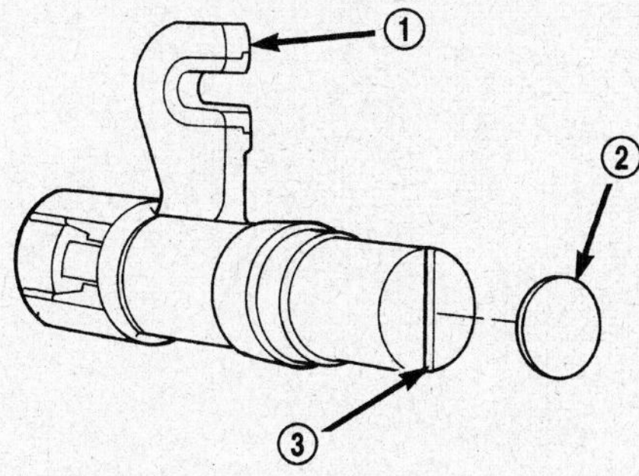

1 – CAMSHAFT POSITION SENSOR
2 – PAPER SPACER
3 – RIB MATERIAL (FOR SENSOR DEPTH POSITIONING)

CR1119900278000X

Fig. 5 Camshaft position sensor depth positioning rib. 8.0L engine

rubber O-ring seal is in groove of distributor housing.

3. Install rotor on distributor shaft.
4. Place distributor into engine. Refer to alignment marks made during removal, and ensure distributor shaft tongue engages in oil pump drive gear slot.
5. Install hold-down clamp and bolt, but do not tighten.
6. Rotate distributor until rotor is aligned to cylinder No. 1 alignment mark on switch plate, **Fig. 1.**
7. **Torque** hold-down bolt to 17 ft. lbs., then connect switch plate or camshaft position sensor wiring and install distributor cap.
8. **On Vans,** install engine cover.
9. **On all models,** install air cleaner assembly.

COIL PACK

REPLACE

3.7L & 4.7L Engines

An individual ignition coil is used for each spark plug. The coil fits into machined holes in the cylinder head. A mounting stud secures each coil to the top of the intake manifold.

1. Depending on which coil is being removed, throttle body, air intake tube or intake box may need to be removed to gain access to coil.
2. Disconnect electrical connector from coil by pushing downward on release lock.
3. Clean area at base of coil with compressed air.
4. Remove coil mounting nut from mounting stud.
5. Pull up coil from cylinder head opening with a slight twisting action.
6. Remove coil from vehicle.
7. Reverse procedure to install. Replace O-ring if required.

3.9L, 5.2L & 5.9L Engines

The ignition coil is an epoxy filled type. If it is replaced, it must be replaced with the same type. On 3.9L, 5.2L or 5.9L LDC gasoline engines, the coil is located on the front of the right cylinder head. On 5.9L HDC gasoline engines, the ignition coil is located on a bracket that is mounted to the AIR injection pump mounting bracket.

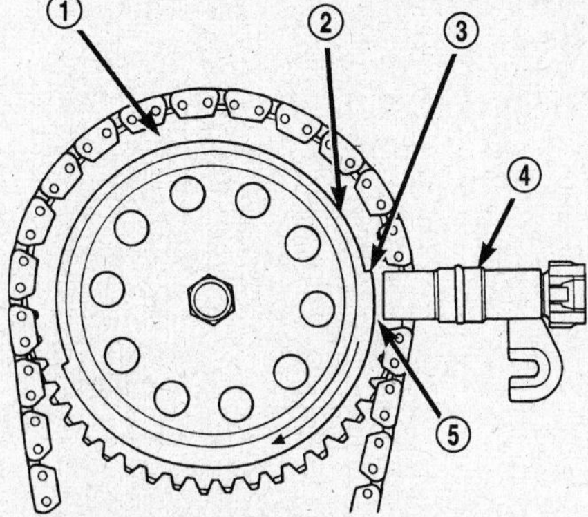

1 – CAM DRIVE GEAR
2 – LOW MACHINED AREA
3 – HIGH MACHINED AREA
4 – CAMSHAFT POSITION SENSOR
5 – AIR GAP

CR1119900279000X

Fig. 6 Camshaft position sensor air gap. 8.0L engine

1. Disconnect primary wiring from ignition coil.
2. Disconnect secondary spark plug cable from ignition coil.
3. **On models equipped with 3.9L, 5.2L and 5.9L LDC gasoline engines, do not remove coil mounting bracket to cylinder head mounting bolts. Bolts are under accessory drive belt tension. If bracket is to be removed for any reason, all belt tension must be relieved first.**
4. **On all models,** remove ignition coil from coil mounting bracket.
5. Reverse procedure to install, **torque** mounting bolts to 50 inch lbs.

5.7L Engine

Before removing or disconnecting any spark plug cables, note their original position to prevent ignition crossfire.

An individual ignition coil is used for each spark plug. The coil mounts to the top of the valve cover with two bolts.

1. Depending on which coil is being removed, throttle body, air intake tube or intake box may need to be removed to gain access to coil.
2. Unlock electrical connector by moving slide lock first, then press on release lock while pulling electrical connector from coil.
3. Disconnect secondary high-voltage cable from coil using a twisting action.
4. Clean area at base of coil using compressed air.
5. Remove two mounting bolts. Bolts are retained to coil.
6. Pull up coil from cylinder head opening with a slight twisting action.
7. Remove coil from vehicle.
8. Reverse procedure to install. Apply dielectric grease to inside of boots

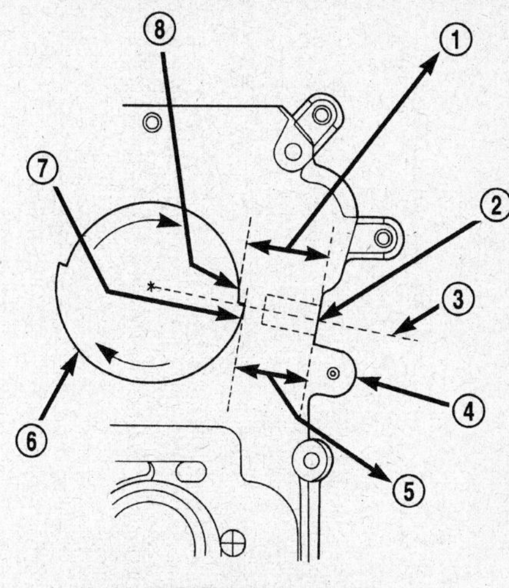

1 – 2.018" DO NOT INSTALL SENSOR
2 – SENSOR MOUNTING HOLE OPENING
3 – SENSOR CENTER LINE
4 – TIMING CHAIN COVER
5 – 1.818" OK TO INSTALL SENSOR
6 – CAM DRIVE GEAR
7 – HIGH MACHINED AREA
8 – LOW MACHINED AREA

CR1119900280000X

Fig. 7 Camshaft position sensor depth dimensions. 8.0L engine

8.0L Engine

Two coil packs containing five independent coils are attached to a common mounting bracket located above the right engine valve cover. Front and rear coil packs may be serviced separately.

1. Remove secondary spark plug cables from coil packs. Tag cables for installation reference.
2. Disconnect primary wiring harness connectors at coil packs.
3. Remove four coil pack mounting bracket bolts for coil pack being serviced.
4. Remove coil from mounting bracket.
5. Reverse procedure to install. **Torque** coil pack mounting bolts to 90 inch lbs.

8.3L Engine

1. Relieve fuel pressure as outlined under "Fuel System Pressure Relief" in "Precautions."
2. Remove air cleaner assembly.
3. Remove intake manifold as outlined under "Intake Manifold, Replace."
4. Disconnect ignition coil electrical connector.
5. Twist and remove ignition cables from ignition coil.
6. Remove four mounting bolts, then coil.
7. Reverse procedure to install.

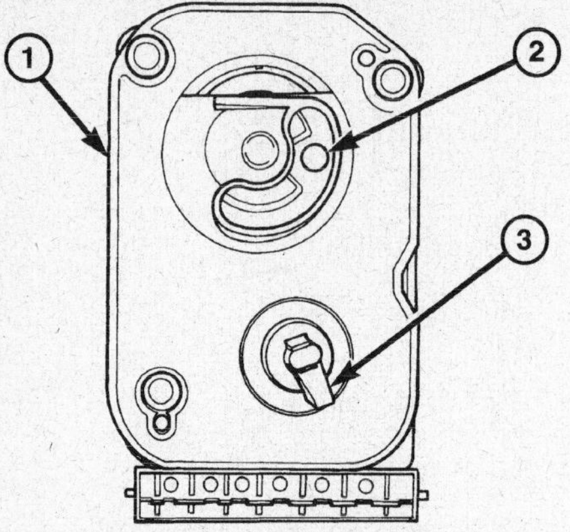

1 - REAR OF IGNITION SWITCH
2 - PARK LOCK DOWEL PIN (RUN POSITION)
3 - FLAG (RUN POSITION)

LTV1900000000329

Fig. 8 Flag in RUN position. 2002 2500 & 3500 Pickup

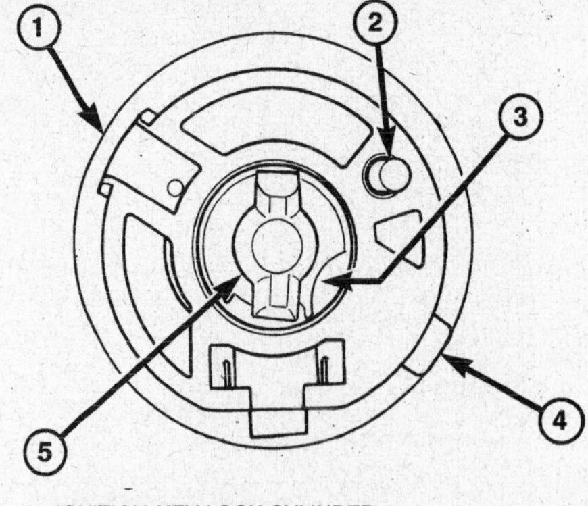

1 - IGNITION KEY LOCK CYLINDER
2 - PUSH PIN
3 - RETAINING PIN SLOT
4 - RETAINING PIN
5 - DRIVER

LTV1900000000330

Fig. 9 Rear view of key cylinder. 2002 2500 & 3500 Pickup

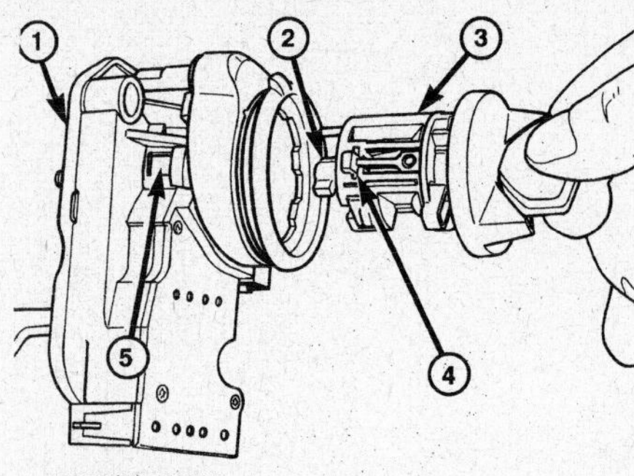

1 - IGNITION SWITCH
2 - DRIVER
3 - IGNITION KEY LOCK CYLINDER
4 - RETAINING PIN
5 - RETAINING PIN SLOT

LTV1900000000331

Fig. 10 Key cylinder installation. 2002 2500 & 3500 Pickup

CRANKSHAFT POSITION SENSOR

3.9L, 5.2L & 5.9L Engines

The sensor is bolted to the top of the cylinder block near the rear of the right cylinder head.

1. Remove air cleaner intake tube.
2. Disconnect crankshaft position sensor pigtail harness form main wiring harness, **Fig. 2.**
3. Remove two sensor mounting bolts, then the sensor.
4. Reverse procedure to install, **torque** mounting bolts to 70 inch lbs.

8.0L Engine

REMOVAL

1. Raise and support vehicle.
2. Disconnect pigtail connector from main engine wiring harness.
3. Remove sensor mounting bolt, **Fig. 3.**
4. Cut plastic tie strap securing sensor pigtail harness to side of engine block.
5. Carefully pry sensor from cylinder block in a rocking action with two small screwdrivers, then remove sensor.

INSTALLATION

1. Apply a small amount of engine oil to sensor O-ring.
2. Install sensor into cylinder block with a slight rocking motion. Do not twist sensor into position or damage to O-ring may occur.
3. Install mounting bolt and **torque** to 70 inch lbs.

CAMSHAFT POSITION SENSOR

3.7L, 4.7L & 5.7L Engines

1. Disconnect electrical connector from camshaft position sensor.
2. Remove sensor mounting bolt.
3. Carefully twist sensor from cylinder head.
4. Reverse procedure to install.

3.9L, 5.2L & 5.9L Engines

Camshaft position sensor is located in the distributor. Distributor removal is not required to remove camshaft position sensor.

1. Remove air cleaner assembly.
2. Remove distributor cap from distributor.
3. Disconnect camshaft position sensor wiring from main engine wiring harness.
4. Remove distributor rotor from distributor shaft.
5. Lift camshaft position sensor assembly from distributor housing, **Fig. 4.**
6. Reverse procedure to install.

5.9L Diesel

The camshaft position sensor is located below the fuel injection pump and bolted to the back of the timing gear cover.

1. Disconnect camshaft position sensor electrical connector.
2. Remove sensor mounting bolt.
3. Carefully twist sensor from timing gear cover.
4. Reverse procedure to install.

8.0L Engine

The camshaft position sensor is located on the timing chain cover on the left front side of the engine. A thin plastic rib is molded into the face of the sensor, **Fig. 5,** to position the depth of the sensor to the upper cam gear sprocket. This rib can be found on both the new replacement sensors and sensors that were originally installed on the engine. The first time the engine has been operated, part of the rib may be sheared (ground) off. Depending on components tolerances, some of the rib material may still be observed after removal.

REPLACING OLD SENSOR WITH ORIGINAL SENSOR

1. Disconnect sensor electrical connector.
2. Remove sensor mounting bolt.
3. Carefully pry sensor from timing chain case/cover using two small screwdrivers and a rocking motion.
4. Remove sensor and inspect O-ring for visible signs of damage.
5. Observe face of sensor. If any of the original rib material remains, it must be cut down flush to the face of the sensor with a razor knife.
6. Remove only enough of the material to make the sensor face flat. Do not remove more material than required or damage to sensor will occur.
7. Do not use an electric grinder to remove material from sensor.
8. Clean face of sensor and apply paper spacer, **Fig. 5.** Paper spacers are of a certain thickness and are used as a tool to set sensor depth.
9. Apply a small amount of engine oil to sensor O-ring.
10. Sensor is positioned in timing gear cover so that a small air gap exists between face of sensor and high machined area of cam gear, **Fig. 6.**
11. Before installation, ensure cam gear

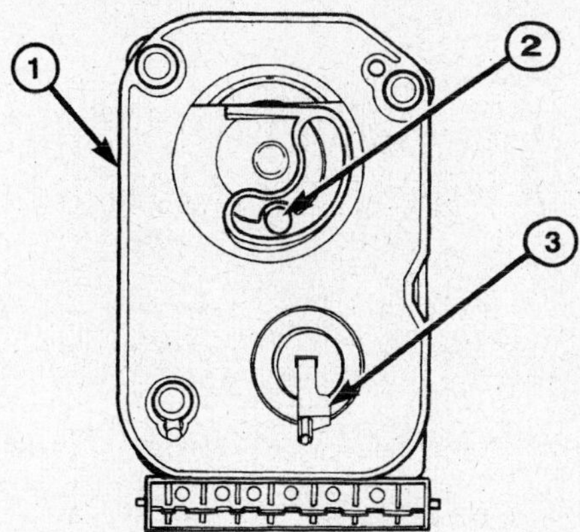

1 - REAR OF IGNITION SWITCH
2 - PARK LOCK DOWEL PIN (LOCK POSITION)
3 - FLAG (LOCK POSITION)

LTV1900000000332

Fig. 11 Ignition switch. 2002 2500 & 3500 Pickup

high area is directly in front of sensor mounting hole on timing cover. Do not install sensor with gear positioned at low area or sensor will be broken on engine startup.

12. Measure distance from cam gear to face of sensor mounting hole opening on timing gear cover using a ½ wide metal ruler, **Fig. 7.**
13. If dimension is approximately 1.818 inches, sensor can be installed. If dimension is approximately 2.108 inches, cam gear will have to be rotated before sensor can be installed.
14. Install sensor into timing case/cover with a slight rocking motion until paper spacer contacts camshaft gear. Do not install sensor mounting bolt. Do not twist sensor into position or damage to O-ring and spacer paper may occur.
15. Scratch a scribe line into timing chain cover to indicate depth of sensor, then remove sensor from cover.
16. Remove paper spacer from sensor, apply a small amount of engine oil to sensor O-ring.
17. Install sensor into timing cover with slight rocking motion until sensor is aligned with scribe line.
18. Install sensor mounting bolt and **torque** to 50 inch lbs.
19. Connect electrical connector to sensor.

REPLACING OLD SENSOR WITH NEW SENSOR

1. Disconnect sensor wiring harness from sensor.
2. Remove sensor mounting bolt, then the sensor with two small screwdrivers and a slight rocking motion.
3. Apply slight amount of clean engine oil to new sensor O-ring.
4. Measure distance from cam gear face to face of sensor mounting hole on timing gear cover using a ½ inch wide metal ruler.
5. If dimension is approximately 1.818 inches, sensor can be installed. If dimension is approximately 2.018 inches, cam gear will have to be rotated to achieve the 1.818 inch measurement.
6. When measurement is approximately 1.818 inches, install sensor into timing case/cover with a slight rocking motion. Do not twist into position or damage to O-ring may occur.
7. Push sensor all the way into case/cover until rib material on sensor contacts camshaft gear.
8. Install mounting bolt and **torque** to 50 inch lbs.
9. Connect sensor wiring harness.
10. When engine is started, rib material will be sheared off of face of sensor, this will automatically set sensor air gap.

8.3L Engine

1. Disconnect sensor wiring electrical connector.
2. Remove sensor mounting bolt. **Note: if original sensor is to be installed, scribe sensor for depth location.**
3. Carefully pry sensor from timing chain cover using two small screw drivers and rocking motion.
4. Remove sensor.
5. Reverse procedure to install.

IGNITION SWITCH

REPLACE

Pickup

1500 & 2003-06 2500 & 3500

1. Remove driver air bag module as outlined in "Passive Restraint Systems."
2. Remove lower and upper shrouds from steering column.
3. Place shifter in PARK position, then rotate key to RUN position.
4. Press in on retaining pin located at side of key cylinder, then pull cylinder from ignition switch.
5. Remove tilt lever mounting screws to gain access to ignition switch mounting screws.
6. Disconnect electrical connector at rear of ignition switch.
7. Remove ignition switch mounting screw.
8. Push on locking tab and remove switch from steering column using a small screwdriver.
9. Reverse procedure to install, noting the following:
   a. Key must be in cylinder for installation.
   b. Rotate slot in ignition switch to ON position.

2002

2500 & 3500

Removal

1. **On models equipped with tilt steering,** remove tilt lever.
2. **On all models,** remove upper and lower shrouds from steering column.

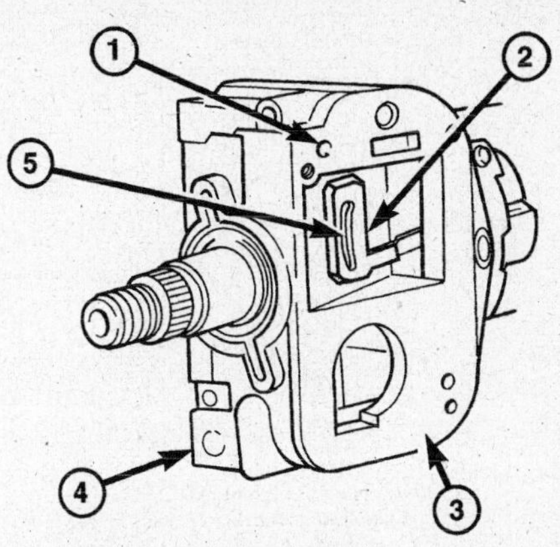

1 - DOWEL LOCATING HOLES (2)
2 - PARK LOCK SLIDER LINKAGE
3 - IGNITION SWITCH MOUNTING PAD
4 - STEERING COLUMN
5 - SLOT

LTV1900000000333

Fig. 12 Park lock linkage. 2002 2500 & 3500 Pickup

3. **On models equipped with automatic transmission,** place shifter in PARK position.
4. **On all models,** rotate key to RUN position.
5. Press in on retaining pin located at side of key cylinder, then pull key cylinder from ignition switch.
6. Remove three ignition switch mounting screws.
7. Pull switch away from column, then disconnect electrical connector.
8. Disconnect halo lamp electrical connector.

Installation

1. Rotate flag on rear of ignition switch to RUN position, **Fig. 8,** to allow tang on key cylinder to fit into slots within ignition switch.
2. With key in lock cylinder, rotate clockwise until retaining pin can be depressed, **Fig. 9.**
3. Install key cylinder into ignition switch by aligning retaining pin slot, **Fig. 10.** Push key cylinder into switch until retaining pin engages, then rotate key to OFF or LOCK position.
4. **On models equipped with automatic transmission,** before attaching ignition switch to steering column, shifter must be in PARK position. Park lock dowel pin on rear of ignition switch, **Fig. 11,** must also be properly indexed into park lock linkage, **Fig. 12,** before installing switch.
5. **On all models,** flag at rear of ignition switch must be properly indexed into steering column before installing switch. This flag is used to operate steering wheel lock lever in steering column, **Fig. 13,** allowing steering wheel position to be locked when key is in LOCK position.
6. Place ignition switch in LOCK position. Switch is in lock position when column lock flag is parallel to ignition switch terminals.

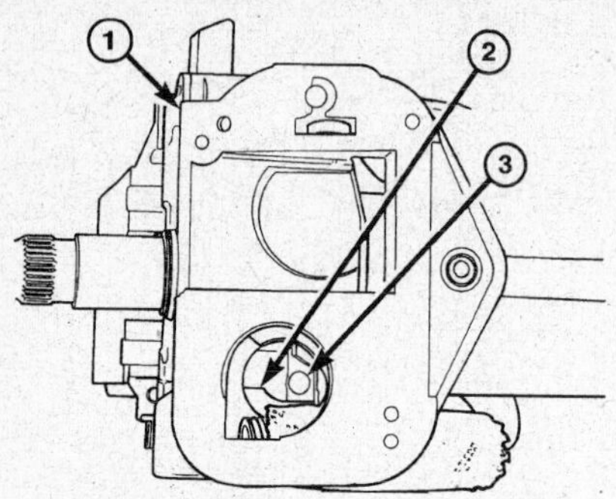

Fig. 13 Steering wheel lock lever. 2002 2500 & 3500 Pickup

7. **On models equipped with automatic transmission,** apply a light coating of grease to park lock dowel pin and park lock slider linkage. Before installing switch, push park lock slider linkage forward until it bottoms. Do a final positioning by pulling it rearward about ¼ inch.
8. **On all models,** apply light coating of grease to both column lock flag and shaft at end of flag.
9. Place ignition switch into openings on steering column.
10. **On models equipped with automatic transmission,** ensure park lock dowel pin on rear of ignition switch enters slot in park lock slider linkage.
11. **On all models,** ensure flag on rear of switch is positioned above steering wheel lock lever.
12. Align dowel pins on rear of switch into holes on side of steering column.
13. Install three ignition switch mounting screws.
14. After installing ignition switch rotate ignition key from LOCK to ON position. Verify that park lock slider moves in slider slot, allowing gear shift lever to be moved out of PARK. If slider does not move and gear shift lever is locked in PARK, remove ignition switch and reinstall.
15. Connect electrical connectors.
16. Install steering column shrouds.
17. **On models equipped with tilt,** install tilt column lever.
18. **On models equipped with automatic transmission,** ensure shifter locks in PARK position with key in LOCK position and unlocks when key is rotated to ON position.
19. **On all models,** inspect proper operation of ignition switch.

Van

REMOVAL

1. Remove upper and lower steering column shrouds.
2. Place transmission shifter in Park position.
3. Rotate key to RUN position.
4. Press in on retaining pin, **Fig. 14,** then pull key cylinder from ignition switch.
5. Disconnect lower clockspring connectors.
6. Remove wire retainer from tilt lever bracket.
7. **On models equipped with tilt steering,** remove tilt lever mounting screws to gain access to ignition switch mounting screws.
8. **On models less tilt steering,** remove bracket to gain access to mounting screws.
9. **On all models,** disconnect electrical connector at rear of ignition switch.
10. Remove ignition switch mounting screw, then push on locking tab and remove switch from steering column.

INSTALLATION

1. Rotate slot in ignition switch to ON position, then connect electrical connector.
2. Position switch on column, then install mounting screw. **Torque** screw to 26 inch lbs.
3. **On models equipped with tilt steering,** install tilt lever bracket mounting screws, **torque** screws to 40 inch lbs.
4. **On models less tilt steering,** install bracket, **torque** screws to 40 inch lbs.
5. **On all models,** Insert wire retainer to tilt lever bracket, then reconnect lower clockspring connector.
6. Install key cylinder into housing using care to align end of cylinder with ignition switch.
7. Push key cylinder in until it clicks.
8. Install upper and lower steering column shrouds.

CLUTCH START SWITCH

REPLACE

The clutch start switch is an integral part of the clutch master cylinder pushrod and cannot be serviced separately.

NEUTRAL SAFETY SWITCH

REPLACE

1. Raise and support vehicle, then place a suitable drain pan beneath switch.
2. **On 2002 models,** remove switch from case.
3. **On 2003–06 models,** move manual lever to Low position.
4. **On all models,** disconnect switch electrical connections.
5. Remove two switch to mounting bracket attaching screws.
6. Remove switch by pulling it straight out from bracket.
7. Reverse procedure to install.

HEADLAMP SWITCH

REPLACE

Pickup

1500 & 2003-06 2500 & 3500

1. Remove left instrument panel bezel using a suitable trim stick.

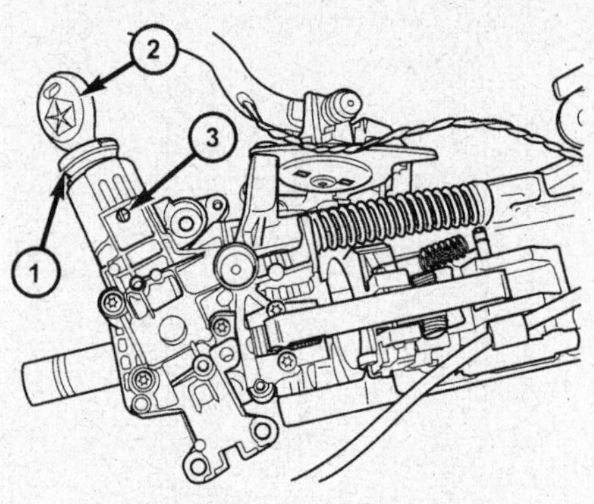

Fig. 14 Key cylinder removal. Van

2. Disconnect headlamp switch electrical connector.
3. Remove screws securing switch to bezel, then remove switch.
4. Reverse procedure to install.

Van

1. Remove cluster bezel from instrument panel.
2. Remove three headlight switch bezel to instrument panel attaching screws.
3. Pull headlamp switch and bezel away from instrument panel far enough to access instrument panel wire harness connectors.
4. Disconnect two instrument panel wire harness connectors from headlamp switch.
5. Pull headlamp switch control knob out to On position.
6. Depress headlamp switch control knob and shaft release button on top of headlamp switch body.
7. While holding down release button, pull headlamp switch control knob and shaft out of headlamp switch.
8. Remove switch bezel and mounting bracket to headlamp switch attaching nut.
9. Remove switch bezel and mounting bracket from headlamp switch.
10. Reverse procedure to install.

STOP LIGHT SWITCH

REPLACE

Pickup

REMOVAL

1. Disconnect switch electrical connector.
2. Press and hold brake pedal in applied position.
3. **On 2002–04 models,** rotate switch counterclockwise about 30° to align locking tab with notch in bracket.
4. **On 2005–06 models,** rotate switch clockwise about 30° to align locking tab with notch in bracket.
5. **On all models,** pull switch rearward out of mounting bracket, then release brake pedal.

INSTALLATION

1. Press and hold brake pedal down.
2. **On 2002–04 models,** align tab on new switch with notch in switch bracket, then insert switch and rotate clockwise 30° to lock in place.
3. **On 2005–06 models,** align tab on new switch with notch in switch bracket, then insert switch and rotate counterclockwise 30° to lock in place.
4. **On all models,** connect electrical connector, then release brake pedal.
5. Move release lever on switch parallel with connector to engage switch plunger. Switch is now adjusted and can not be adjusted again.

Van

REMOVAL

1. Remove lower column cover.
2. Remove DLC, hood release lever and park release lever from knee blocker.
3. Remove knee blocker for access to switch.
4. Press and hold brake pedal in applied position.
5. Rotate brake lamp switch counterclockwise about 30° to unlock switch, then pull straight out of mounting bracket.
6. Disconnect electrical connector, then remove switch.

INSTALLATION

1. Plug electrical connector into new switch.
2. Press and hold brake pedal in applied position.
3. Align switch locking collar index in switch bracket, then insert switch straight into bracket.
4. Turn switch clockwise 30° to lock into place.
5. Release brake pedal, then move release lever on top of switch to engage switch plunger. **Switch can only be adjusted during initial installation. If switch is not adjusted properly, a new switch must be installed.**
6. Install knee blocker.
7. Install DLC, hood release lever and park release lever to knee blocker.
8. Install lower column cover.

MULTI-FUNCTION SWITCH

REPLACE

2002 2500 & 3500

1. **On models equipped with tilt steering wheel,** remove tilt steering column lever.
2. **On all models,** remove upper and lower shrouds from steering column.
3. Remove lower and upper fixed column shroud.
4. Remove multi-function switch tamper proof Torx screws with suitable Torx bit tool.
5. Carefully pull switch away from steering column, remove wire harness connector screw, then connector from multi-function switch.
6. Remove switch.
7. Reverse procedure to install, noting the following:
   a. **Torque** wire harness connector screw to 17 inch lbs.
   b. **Torque** multi-function switch retaining screws to 17 inch lbs.

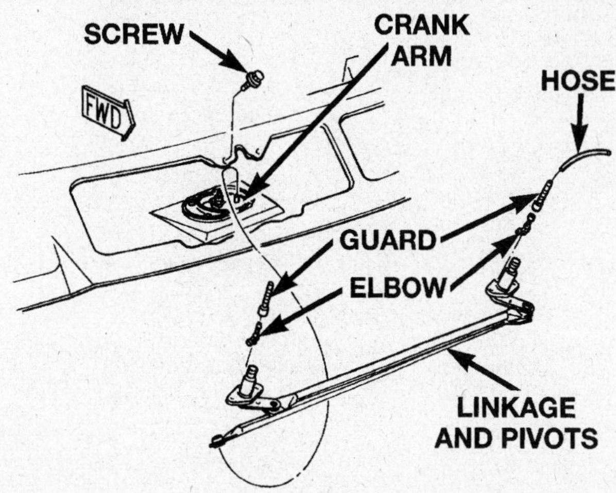

Fig. 15 Windshield wiper transmission assembly. Van

1500 & 2003-06 2500 & 3500

1. Remove steering wheel as outlined in "Steering Wheel, Replace."
2. Remove upper and lower steering column shrouds.
3. Disconnect electrical connector from back of multi-function switch.
4. Remove screws retaining multi-function switch to steering column adapter collar, then remove switch.
5. Remove screws retaining clockspring to multi-function switch.
6. Reverse procedure to install.

STEERING WHEEL

REPLACE

Pickup

2002 2500 & 3500

1. Remove two screws securing driver air bag module to steering wheel.
2. Pull driver air bag module away from steering wheel, then disconnect electrical connectors from air bag module.
3. Remove driver air bag module from steering wheel.
4. Disconnect electrical connectors from steering wheel to clockspring.
5. Remove nut securing steering wheel to steering column shaft.
6. Remove steering wheel using steering wheel puller tool No. C-3428-B or equivalent.
7. Reverse procedure to install. **Torque** steering wheel nut to 45 ft. lbs.

1500 & 2003-06 2500 & 3500

1. From underside of steering wheel, remove two screws securing trim covers or speed control switches to each side of driver air bag module trim cover.
2. Remove two trim covers or speed control switches from driver air bag module trim cover.
3. Remove two screws securing driver air bag module to steering wheel.
4. Pull driver air bag module away from steering wheel and disconnect electrical connectors.
5. Remove driver air bag module from steering wheel.
6. Partially remove steering wheel bolt.
7. Install steering wheel puller tool No. CJ98-1, or equivalent, using top of steering wheel bolt to push on.
8. Remove steering wheel discarding bolt.
9. Reverse procedure to install, noting the following:
   a. Install new steering wheel bolt.
   b. **Torque,** steering wheel bolt to 45 ft. lbs.

Van

1. Ensure front wheels are facing straight ahead.
2. Remove driver air bag module, then disconnect air bag, horn and speed control wiring connectors.
3. Remove steering wheel nut.
4. Remove steering wheel using puller tool No. C-3428-B, or equivalent. **Do not bump or hammer on steering shaft to remove wheel, as damage to shaft may result.**
5. Reverse procedure to install. **Torque** steering wheel retaining nut to 45 ft. lbs.

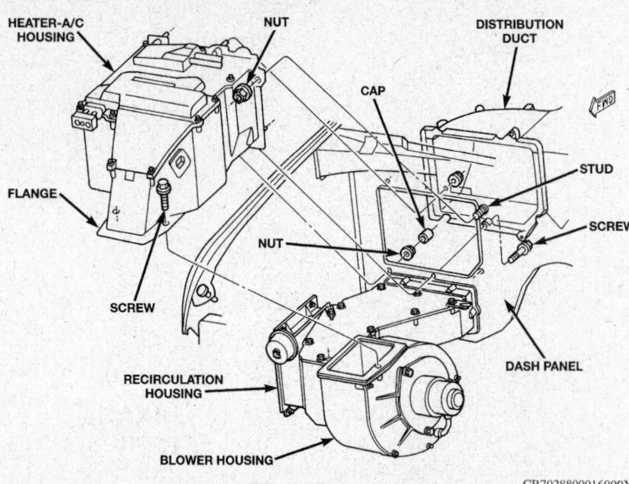

Fig. 16 Heater assembly. Van with A/C

INSTRUMENT CLUSTER

REPLACE

Pickup

2002 2500 & 3500

1. **On models equipped with automatic transmission,** turn ignition switch to the Unlock position, set parking brake and place gear selector lever in Low position.
2. **On models equipped with tilt steering,** tilt steering wheel to its lowest position.
3. **On all models,** using a trim stick or suitable wide blade tool, gently pry around outer perimeter of cluster bezel and separate bezel from instrument panel.
4. Remove four screws securing instrument cluster to instrument panel.
5. Pull cluster bezel far enough away from instrument panel to disconnect wire harness connector from back of power outlet, then remove bezel.
6. Reverse procedure to install.

1500 & 2003-06 2500 & 3500

1. Release top clips on steering column opening cover and lower drivers side bezel using suitable trim stick.
2. Pry headlamp switch bezel from instrument panel using suitable trim stick.
3. Disconnect headlamp switch electrical connector, then remove switch.
4. Open ashtray and cup holder, then remove one center bezel retaining screw.
5. Pry center bezel from instrument panel.
6. Remove four screws securing instrument cluster to instrument panel structural support.
7. Pull instrument cluster far enough away from instrument panel to disconnect wire harness connector from back of power outlet, then remove instrument cluster.
8. Reverse procedure to install.

Van

1. Turn ignition switch to Unlock position and set parking brake.
2. **On models equipped with automatic transmission,** place gear selector lever in Low position.
3. **On models equipped with tilt steering wheel,** tilt steering wheel to its lowest position.
4. **On all models,** using a trim stick or other suitable wide flat bladed tool, gently pry around outer perimeter of cluster bezel to disengage bezel retaining clips from instrument panel.
5. Pull outboard side of cluster bezel away from instrument panel far enough to clear odometer reset button, then remove cluster bezel.
6. Remove four instrument cluster to instrument panel attaching screws.
7. **On models equipped with automatic transmission,** place gear selector into Park position.
8. **On all models,** pull instrument cluster rearward enough to disconnect two self docking instrument panel wire harness connectors and to access gear selector indicator.
9. Remove gear selector indicator from back of cluster housing.
10. Remove instrument cluster.
11. Reverse procedure to install.

RADIO

REPLACE

Pickup

1. Remove cluster bezel and cluster.
2. Remove mounting screws from front of radio, then pull radio out of instrument panel,
3. Disconnect radio wiring and antenna, then remove screw from ground strap.
4. Reverse procedure to install

Van

Do not operate radio with speaker leads detached, as damage to transistors may result.

1. Remove cluster bezel as outlined previously.
2. Remove radio attaching screws and ground strap screw.
3. Pull radio from panel, then disconnect antenna lead, speaker leads and electrical connectors.
4. Remove radio.
5. Reverse procedure to install.

WIPER MOTOR

REPLACE

Pickup

2002 2500 & 3500

1. Remove wiper arms from wiper pivots.
2. Remove weatherstrip along front edge of cowl plenum cover and cowl plenum panel.
3. Remove plastic screws that secure cowl plenum cover panel to studs on top cowl panel near base of windshield.
4. Lift cowl plenum cover panel from cowl far enough to access windshield washer nozzle plumbing near left end of cowl plenum.
5. Disconnect windshield washer supply hose at fitting.
6. Remove cowl plenum cover and set aside.
7. Remove four screws that secure wiper module to cowl plenum panel.
8. Move wiper module as required to access wiper motor wire harness connectors.
9. Unplug wiper motor harness connectors, remove wiper module.
10. Reverse procedure to install.

1500 & 2003-06 2500 & 3500

1. Remove both wiper arms from wiper pivots.
2. Unlatch and open hood.
3. Disconnect washer hose.
4. Remove hood seal, then the six push pin fasteners from front of cowl grille.
5. Remove two rear corner screws, then remove cowl grille.
6. Disconnect wiper motor electrical connector.
7. Remove two screws securing wiper module to top of cowl plenum panel at pivot brackets.
8. Remove two screws securing wiper module to bottom of cowl plenum panel.
9. Remove wiper module.
10. Reverse procedure to install.

Van

1. Disconnect wiper motor electrical connectors, then remove motor attaching screws.
2. Lower motor down enough to gain access to crank arm to drive link retainer bushing.
3. Remove crank arm from drive link by prying retainer bushing from crank arm pin using a two suitable screwdrivers.

4. Place one screwdriver on each side of ball stud and pry between crank arm and metal portion of drive link.
5. Remove motor from vehicle.
6. Reverse procedure to install, noting the following:
   a. Use channel lock pliers to reinstall drive link bushing onto crank arm ball stud. Do not apply pressure directly to plastic bushing.
   b. **Torque** pivot mounting screws to 96 inch lbs.

WIPER SWITCH

REPLACE

Refer to "Multi-Function Switch Replace" for wiper switch replacement procedure.

WIPER TRANSMISSION

REPLACE

Pickup

CRANK ARM

1. Remove wiper motor as outlined in "Windshield Wiper Motor, Replace."
2. Remove crank arm to motor driveshaft attaching nut, then crank arm.
3. Reverse procedure to install.

DRIVE LINK & LEFT PIVOT ASSEMBLY

These components are not independently serviceable. Replace wiper linkage assembly if a pivot is damaged.

RIGHT PIVOT ASSEMBLY

This component is not independently serviceable. Replace wiper linkage assembly if a pivot is damaged.

Van

DRIVE LINK

1. Remove wiper arms and washer hoses, then the cowl cover grille.
2. Remove drive link from crank arm and connecting link pins by prying retainer bushing apart using a suitable screwdriver, **Fig. 15.**
3. Remove drive link through access hole.
4. Reverse procedure to install.

PIVOT LINK

1. Remove cowl cover grille.
2. Remove connecting link from drive link and pivot pins by prying retainer bushings apart using a suitable screwdriver, **Fig. 15.**
3. Remove pivot link through access hole.
4. Reverse procedure to install.

CRANK ARM

1. Remove wiper arms and washer hoses.
2. Remove cowl cover grille.
3. Remove drive link from crank arm pin

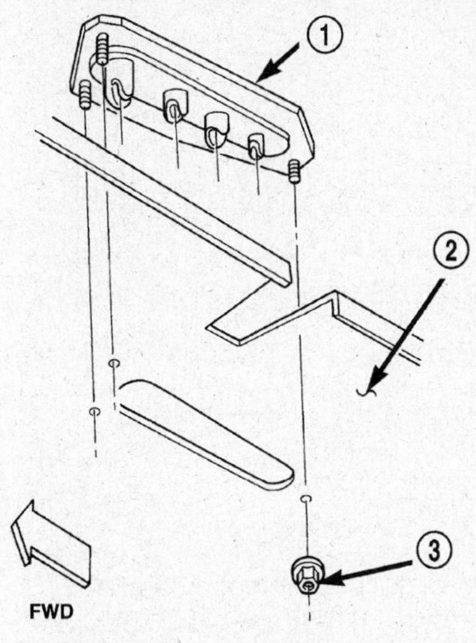

Fig. 17 Rear heater-A/C plumbing plate. Van

by prying retainer bushing apart using a suitable screwdriver, **Fig. 15.**
4. Remove crank arm to motor attaching nut, then the crank arm through access hole.
5. Reverse procedure to install.

PIVOTS

1. Remove wiper arms and washer hoses.
2. Remove cowl cover grille.
3. Remove connecting link from pivot pins by prying retainer bushing apart using a suitable screwdriver, **Fig. 15.**
4. Remove pivot attaching bolts, then lower pivot and remove through access hole.
5. Reverse procedure to install.

BLOWER MOTOR

REPLACE

Pickup

2002

1. Disconnect blower motor cooling tube, then remove blower motor electrical connector from retainer.
2. Disconnect electrical connector, then remove blower motor and wheel assembly mounting screws.
3. Remove blower motor and wheel assembly, then remove wheel and retaining clip from motor shaft.
4. Reverse procedure to install, noting the following:
   a. Wheel retainer clip ears must be over flat surface on motor shaft.
   b. Ensure seal is installed on blower motor housing.

2003–06

1. Disconnect blower motor electrical connection.
2. Remove blower motor to HVAC housing mounting screws.
3. Remove blower motor by rotating and tilting as needed.
4. Reverse procedure to install.

Van

FRONT

1. Remove top half of fan shroud.
2. Disconnect blower motor electrical connector and remove blower motor cooling tube.
3. Remove three retaining nuts from studs holding blower motor.
4. **On models equipped with A/C,** pull suction and discharge lines inboard and upward while pulling blower motor assembly from housing.
5. **On all models,** remove blower motor.
6. Reverse procedure to install.

REAR

The rear blower motor is used only on models with optional rear heater-A/C units.
1. Remove cover from rear heater-A/C unit.
2. Remove vertical and horizontal ducts from heater-A/C unit.
3. Remove upper housing from heater-A/C unit.
4. Remove three screws that secure blower motor mounting plate to rear heater-A/C unit upper housing.
5. Remove blower motor assembly from heater-A/C unit.
6. Remove retainer clip from hub of blower wheel, then the wheel from blower motor shaft.
7. Reverse procedure to install.

HEATER CORE

REPLACE

Pickup

2002 2500 & 3500

1. Remove instrument panel from vehicle as outlined in "Dash Panel Service" chapter.
2. **On models equipped with A/C,** proceed as follows:
   a. Recover refrigerant as outlined in "Air Conditioning" chapter.
   b. Disconnect liquid line refrigerant line fitting from evaporator inlet tube. Install plugs in or tape over all open refrigerant lines and fittings.
   c. Remove accumulator, plug all fittings and hose connections.
3. **On all models,** drain engine coolant into suitable container.
4. Disconnect heater hoses from heater core tubes, plug all open heater core fittings.
5. Remove powertrain control module from dash panel and set aside, but do not unplug PCM wire harness connectors.

6. Remove nuts from heater-A/C housing mounting studs on engine compartment side of dash panel.
7. Remove nuts that secure heater-A/C housing to mounting studs on passengers compartment side of dash panel.
8. Pull heater-A/C housing rearward far enough for mounting studs and evaporator drain tube to clear dash panel holes.
9. Remove heater-A/C housing from vehicle.
10. Place heater-A/C housing upside down on suitable workbench.
11. Remove screw that secures floor duct to bottom of heater-A/C housing and slide floor duct off center heat duct adapter.
12. Unsnap center heat duct adapter from bottom of heater-A/C housing and remove screw that was hidden by adapter.
13. Remove remaining screws on bottom of heater-A/C housing that secure two housing halves together.
14. Place heater-A/C housing right side up on work bench.
15. Separate top half of heater-A/C housing from bottom half and set aside.
16. Remove heater core/evaporator core from housing unit.
17. Reverse procedure to install.

1500 & 2003–06 2500 & 3500

1. Remove instrument panel from vehicle as outlined in "Dash Panel Service" chapter.
2. **On models equipped with A/C,** proceed as follows:
   a. Recover refrigerant as outlined in "Air Conditioning" chapter.
   b. Disconnect liquid line refrigerant line fitting from evaporator inlet tube. Install plugs in or tape over all open refrigerant lines and fittings.
   c. Remove accumulator, plug all fittings and hose connections.
3. **On all models,** drain engine coolant into suitable container.
4. Disconnect heater hoses from heater core tubes, plug all open heater core fittings.
5. Disconnect all electrical connectors from actuators and blower motor.
6. Remove nuts from HVAC housing mounting studs.
7. Remove HVAC housing from inside vehicle.
8. **On models equipped with Dual Zone system,** remove linkage rod from actuator levers for heater core access.
9. **On all models,** remove screws securing heater core to HVAC housing.
10. Lift heater core from HVAC housing.
11. Reverse procedure to install.

Van

FRONT

1. **On models equipped with A/C,** proceed as follows:
   a. Recover refrigerant as outlined in "Air Conditioning" chapter.

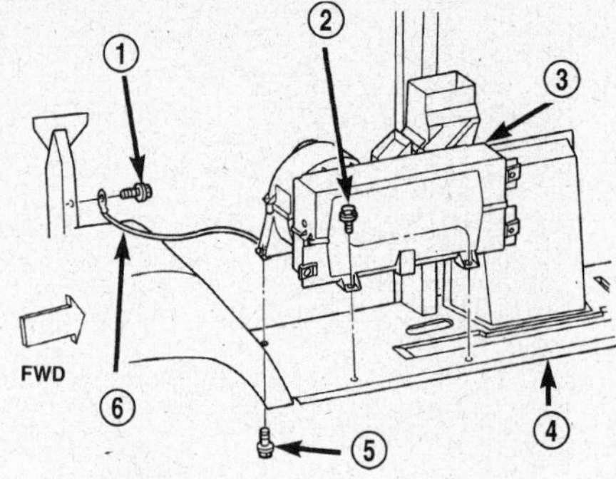

Fig. 18 Rear heater-A/C installation. Van

   b. Disconnect suction line jumper at expansion valve.
   c. Remove screws that secure filter/drier and it's mounting bracket to heater-A/C housing and cowl side panel.
   d. Swing filter drier, mounting bracket and refrigerant plumbing, as an assembly, out of way toward center of vehicle.
   e. Unplug wire harness connector from fin sensing cycling switch.
2. **On all models,** unplug wire harness connectors from blower motor resistor and high speed blower motor relay.
3. Place a waterproof cover over alternator to prevent coolant from spilling over it, drain coolant into suitable container, then disconnect and plug heater core hoses.
4. Remove right headlamp assembly, grille panel, right cowl support panel and right radiator core support assembly.
5. Remove two screws that secure lower heater-A/C housing flange to blower housing.
6. Disconnect link from blend-air door motor on top of distribution duct in passenger compartment.
7. Through glove box opening and under instrument panel, remove screws and nuts retaining evaporator housing to dash panel.
8. From engine compartment, remove one stamped nut that secures heater-A/C housing to stud on dash panel.
9. Remove two screws from flange connection to blower housing. Separate evaporator housing from blower housing and carefully remove evaporator housing from vehicle, **Fig. 16.**
10. Remove cover from housing, then remove heater core strap retaining screw and remove heater core.
11. Reverse procedure to install.

REAR

The heater core for the optional rear heater-A/C unit is integral with the A/C evaporator coil. The unit is referred to as the combination coil.

1. Recover refrigerant as outlined in "Air Conditioning" chapter.
2. Raise and support vehicle.
3. Drain cooling system.
4. Disconnect underbody plumbing at rear heater-A/C unit plumbing connections.
5. Plug all open fittings and lines.
6. Remove three nuts that secure rear heater-A/C unit plumbing plate studs to underbody panel, **Fig. 17.**
7. Remove one screw attaching rear heater-A/C unit to underbody panel from underneath vehicle, **Fig. 18.**
8. Lower vehicle and remove cover from heater-A/C unit.
9. Remove vertical and horizontal duct from heater-A/C unit.
10. Remove screw securing rear heater-A/C unit ground wire outlet to left side panel behind unit, **Fig. 18.**
11. Remove two screws that secure bottom of rear heater-A/C unit to underbody panel.
12. Lift rear heater-A/C unit upward far enough to allow plumbing to clear hole in underbody panel, then pull unit away from side panel far enough to access and unplug wire harness connector from body wire harness near front of unit.
13. Remove rear heater-A/C unit from vehicle.
14. Lift two relay wire harness wire connectors upward to disengage from mounting tabs on rear of heater-A/C housing unit.
15. Unplug wire connectors from rear heater-A/C unit blower motor and rear mode control motor.
16. Disengage blower motor cooling tube from nipple on lower housing of rear heater-A/C unit.
17. Remove control cable from rear heater-A/C unit water valve.
18. Remove clip on rear inboard corner of rear heater-A/C unit, **Fig. 19,** that secures upper housing to lower housing.
19. Remove screws that secure upper housing of rear heater-A/C unit to lower housing.
20. Remove upper housing from rear heater-A/C unit.
21. Reverse procedure to install.

EVAPORATOR CORE

REPLACE

Pickup

Refer to "Heater Core, Replace," for evaporator core replacement procedure.

Van

FRONT

Refer to "Heater Core, Replace," for evaporator core replacement procedure.

REAR

Refer to "Heater Core, Replace," for evaporator core replacement procedure.

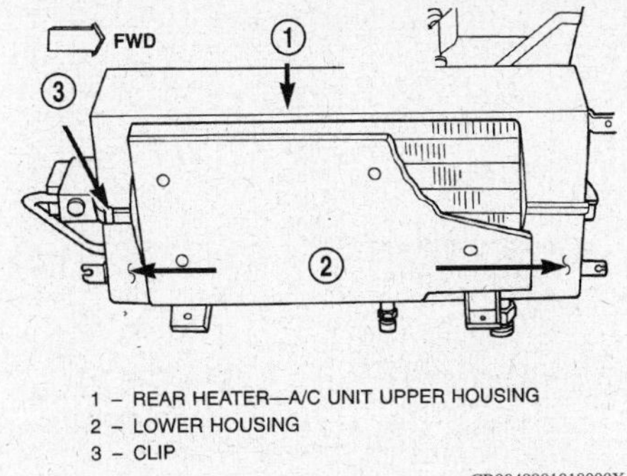

Fig. 19 Rear heater-A/C unit housing clip. Van

3.7L Engine

NOTE: Air Bag Equipped Models, Refer To "Air Bag System Precautions" Located In The Front Of This Manual For System Disarming & Arming Procedures.

NOTE: Refer To "Computer Relearn Procedures" Located In The Front Of This Manual When Battery Power To The Computer Has Been Interrupted.

NOTE: Refer To "3.7L Engine" In The "Liberty" Chapter For Procedures Not Covered In This Section.

INDEX

PRECAUTIONS

Air Bag Systems

Refer to "Air Bag System Precautions" in the front of this manual for system disarming and arming procedures.

Battery Ground Cable

Prior to service, disconnect battery ground cable and isolate as required.

Fuel System Pressure Relief

1. Remove fuel cap, then fuel pump relay from PDC.
2. Start and run engine until it stalls.
3. Attempt to restart engine until it will no longer run.
4. Turn ignition key to Off position.
5. Unplug connector from any injector.
6. Attach one end of a suitable 18 gauge or smaller jumper wire to either injector terminal.
7. Connect other end of jumper wire to positive battery terminal.
8. Connect one end of a second jumper wire to remaining injector terminal.
9. Momentarily touch other end of second jumper wire to negative battery terminal for no more than a few seconds. **Powering an injector for more than a few seconds will damage injector.**
10. Place a suitable rag below fuel line quick connect fitting on fuel rail, then disconnect quick connect fitting.
11. Install fuel pump relay to PDC, then clear any stored DTCs.

COMPRESSION PRESSURE

1. Ensure battery is completely charged and engine starter motor is in good operating condition.
2. Clean spark plug recesses with compressed air, then remove spark plugs.

3. Secure throttle in wide open position.
4. Remove auto shut down (ASD) relay from power distribution center.
5. Install a suitable compression pressure gauge, then rotate engine using starter motor for three revolutions.
6. Record compression pressure on third revolution.

ENGINE MOUNT

REPLACE

Front

1. Remove viscous fan assembly.
2. Raise and support vehicle.
3. Remove skid plate, then the front crossmember.
4. Remove engine oil filter.
5. Remove engine oil drain trough.
6. Support engine using a suitable jack and block of wood across full width of engine oil pan.
7. Support front axle using a suitable jack.
8. Remove four bolts attaching engine mounts to front axle.
9. Remove three bolts attaching front axle to left engine bracket.
10. Lower front axle, then remove six through bolts.
11. Raise engine far enough to be able to remove left and right engine mounts.
12. Remove engine mounts.
13. Reverse procedure to install. Apply Mopar Lock and Seal Adhesive, or equivalent, to mount to engine block and left engine bracket to front axle bolts.

Rear

1. Raise and support vehicle, then support transmission using a suitable jack.
2. Remove nuts from transmission mount.
3. Remove two bolts attaching transmission mount to engine bracket.
4. Raise transmission enough to remove mount from crossmember.
5. Remove rear mount.
6. Reverse procedure to install. Apply suitable threadlock to bolts.

ENGINE

REPLACE

1. Remove hood ensuring to mark hinge locations for reference during installation.
2. Remove air cleaner assembly.
3. Remove radiator core support bracket.
4. Remove fan shroud with electric fan assembly.
5. Remove serpentine drive belt.
6. Remove A/C compressor and position aside with lines attached.
7. Remove alternator and position aside.
8. Remove power steering pump and position aside with lines attached. **Do not remove phenolic pulley from power steering pump.**
9. Drain cooling system into suitable container, then remove coolant bottle.

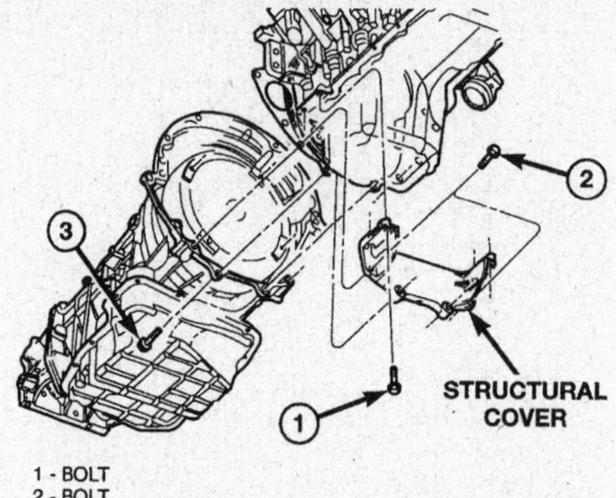

Fig. 1 Structural collar tightening sequence

10. Disconnect heater hoses from engine.
11. Disconnect heater hoses from heater core, then remove hose assembly.
12. Disconnect throttle and speed control cables.
13. Remove upper and lower radiator hoses from engine.
14. Remove radiator.
15. Disconnect engine to body ground straps at lefthand side of cowl.
16. Disconnect electrical connectors from the following:
    a. IAT sensor.
    b. Fuel injectors.
    c. TPS switch.
    d. IAC motor.
    e. Engine oil pressure switch.
    f. ECT sensor.
    g. MAP Sensor.
    h. CMP sensor.
    i. Coil over plugs.
    j. CKP sensor.
17. Remove coil over plugs.
18. Release fuel pressure as outlined in "Precautions."
19. Remove fuel rail and position aside.
20. Remove PCV hose.
21. Remove breather hoses.
22. Remove vacuum hose for power brake booster.
23. Disconnect knock sensors.
24. Remove engine oil dipstick tube.
25. Remove intake manifold as outlined in "Intake Manifold, Replace."
26. Install suitable engine lifting fixture.
27. Secure lefthand and righthand engine wiring harnesses away from engine.
28. Raise and support vehicle.
29. Disconnect oxygen sensor electrical connector.
30. Disconnect CKP sensor electrical connector.
31. Disconnect front propshaft at front differential and secure aside.
32. Remove starter motor.
33. Remove ground straps from lefthand and righthand side of block.
34. Disconnect lefthand and righthand exhaust pipes at manifolds from crossover, then remove from vehicle.
35. Remove structural collar.
36. Remove torque convertor bolts. Mark bolt locations for reference during installation.
37. Remove transmission bellhousing to engine bolts.
38. Remove lefthand and righthand engine mount through bolts.
39. Lower vehicle.
40. Support transmission using a suitable jack.
41. Remove engine using a suitable engine hoist.
42. Reverse procedure to install, noting the following:
    a. Tighten structural collar bolts in sequence, **Fig. 1,** to specifications. **Structural collar must be held tightly against both engine and transmission bell housing during tightening sequence.**
    b. Install new clamps on exhaust manifold flanges.

VALVE COVER

REPLACE

1. Remove resonator assembly, then the air inlet hose.
2. Disconnect fuel injector electrical connectors, then un-clip injector harness.
3. Disconnect and remove lefthand breather tube.
4. Remove bolts, then the valve cover and gasket.
5. Reverse procedure to install. Gasket can be reused.

VALVE ARRANGEMENT

This engine uses two valve per cylinder. Exhaust valves are located on the exhaust manifold side of the cylinder head, intake valves are located on the intake manifold side of the cylinder head.

CAMSHAFT LOBE LIFT SPECIFICATIONS

Exhaust .... **.429 inch**
Intake .... **.472 inch**

VALVE ADJUSTMENT

These engines are equipped with hydraulic lash adjusters. There is no provision for adjustment.

VALVE GUIDES

The valve guides are an integral part of the cylinder head. If valve stem to guide clearance is excessive, the cylinder head must be replaced.

OIL PAN

REPLACE

2002

1. Remove engine as outlined in "Engine, Replace."
2. Mount engine on suitable engine stand.
3. Unbolt and remove oil pump pickup tube.
4. Remove oil pan gasket/windage tray assembly from engine. **Do not pry on oil pan or oil pan gasket.**

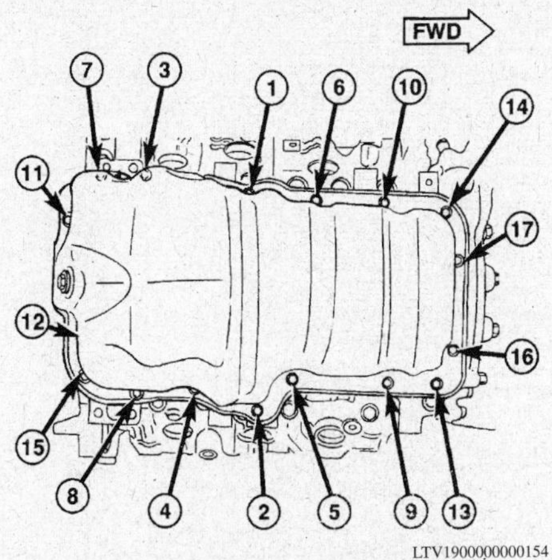

Fig. 2 Oil pan tightening sequence. 2002

5. Reverse procedure to install, noting the following:
   a. Inspect integrated oil pan gasket and replace as required.
   b. Tighten oil pan bolts in sequence, **Fig. 2,** to specifications.

2003–06

1. Install engine support fixture tool No. 8534, or equivalent.
2. Raise and support vehicle.
3. Loosen lefthand and righthand engine mount through bolts. Do not remove bolts.
4. **On models equipped with a structural dust cover,** remove cover.
5. **On all models,** remove skid plate, then drain engine oil into suitable container.
6. Remove front crossmember, then lower vehicle.
7. Raise engine using support fixture to provide clearance for oil pan removal.
8. Raise and support vehicle.
9. Remove oil pan bolts.
10. Remove two nuts and one bolt holding oil pump pickup tube and windage tray in place.
11. Drop oil pump pickup tube into oil pan, then remove oil pan, pickup tube and windage tray as an assembly from front of vehicle.
12. Reverse procedure to install, noting the following:
    a. Clean oil pan and block gasket mating surfaces.
    b. Tighten oil pan bolts in sequence, **Fig. 3,** to specifications.

COOLING SYSTEM BLEED

1. Install cylinder block drain plug and close radiator draincock.
2. Fill cooling system until level reaches COLD FILL RANGE in overflow bottle.
3. Start and run engine until thermostat opens.
4. If required, add coolant to overflow bottle.

RADIATOR

REPLACE

1. Drain cooling system into suitable container.
2. Disconnect upper and lower radiator hoses.
3. Remove coolant overflow tank hose from radiator filler neck.
4. Remove coolant overflow tank by pulling straight up.
5. Unclip power steering hoses from fan shroud.
6. Disconnect electrical connectors from windshield washer reservoir tank, then remove tank.
7. Remove fan shroud mounting bolts, then pull up and out of radiator tank clips.
8. Position shroud rearward over fan blades toward engine.
9. Disconnect transmission cooler lines from transmission cooler, then plug lines to prevent leakage.
10. Disconnect power steering lines from power steering cooler, then plug lines to prevent leakage.
11. Remove two upper radiator mounting bolts.
12. Lift radiator straight up and out of engine compartment.
13. Reverse procedure to install.

FUEL PUMP

REPLACE

1. Loosen clamp, then disconnect rubber fuel vent hose at tank fitting.
2. Support tank using suitable jack.

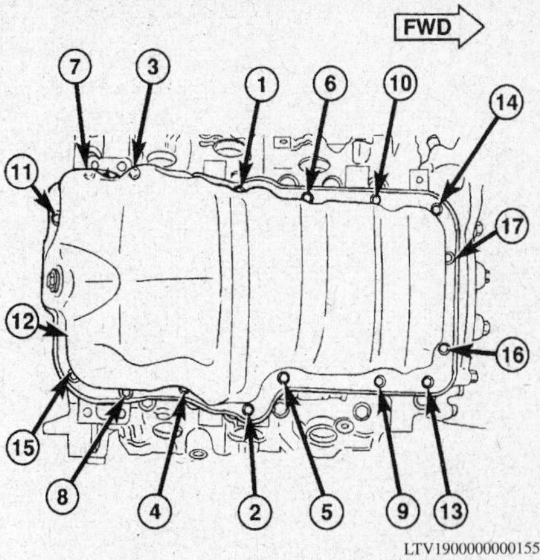

Fig. 3 Oil pan tightening sequence. 2003–06

3. Remove tank strap bolts, then the tank straps.
4. Carefully lower tank a few inches, then disconnect fuel pump electrical connector.
5. Disconnect fuel line at fuel filter by pressing on tabs at side of quick-connect fitting.
6. Disconnect EVAP line at top of tank.
7. Lower and remove tank.
8. Remove fuel pump module lock nut using spanner wrench tool No. 9340, or equivalent.
9. Remove fuel pump module from tank.
10. Reverse procedure to install, noting the following:
    a. Install new fuel pump module gasket.
    b. Install fuel pump module, then rotate until index marks on module are aligned with index marks on fuel tank.
    c. Ensure fitting on fuel filter is pointed toward drivers side of vehicle.

FUEL FILTER

REPLACE

A combination fuel filter and fuel pressure regulator is used. It is located on the top of fuel pump module. The filter is designed for extended service and do not require normal scheduled maintenance.

Refer to "Fuel Pump, Replace" for fuel filter replacement procedure.

TIGHTENING SPECIFICATIONS

Year	Component	Torque Ft. Lbs.
2002–06	Camshaft Bearing Cap	100①
	Camshaft Sprocket	90
	Connecting Rod Cap	20②
	Crankshaft Damper	130
	Engine Mount Bracket To Block	45
	Exhaust Manifold	18
	Flexplate	70
	Hydraulic Tensioner	21
	Intake Manifold	105①
	Oil Fill Tube	105①
	Oil Pan	11
	Oil Pan Drain Plug	25
	Oil Pickup Tube	21
	Oil Pump	21
	Oil Pump Cover	105①
	Rear Mount To Transmission	34
	Structural Collar	40
	Timing Chain Cover	43
	Timing Chain Guide	21
	Timing Chain Primary Tensioner	21
	Timing Chain Tensioner Arm	21
	Timing Drive Idler Sprocket	25
	Thermostat Housing	105①
	Water Pump	43

① — Inch lbs.
② — Plus an additional 90°.

3.9L, 5.2L, 5.9L & 8.0L Gasoline Engines

NOTE: On Air Bag Equipped Models, Refer To "Air Bag System Precautions" Located In The Front Of This Manual For System Disarming & Arming Procedures.

NOTE: Refer To "Computer Relearn Procedure" Located In The Front Of This Manual When Battery Power To The Computer Has Been Interrupted.

INDEX

PRECAUTIONS

Air Bag Systems

Refer to "Air Bag System Precautions" in the front of this manual for system disarming and arming procedures.

Battery Ground Cable

Prior to service, disconnect battery ground cable and isolate as required.

Compressed Natural Gas (CNG) System Service

Although natural gas vapors will disperse in open areas, the vapors may accumulate in an enclosed setting. To prevent explosion and fire, adequate ventilation and/or a natural gas detection system must be provided in areas which are routinely used for storage of CNG vehicles. If a system leak exists, do not bring the vehicle into an unventilated area. If long term storage is required, the manual shut off valve and each fuel control valve should be closed.

Fuel system pressure must be released prior to servicing any fuel related component. However welding of fuel cylinders or any fuel system components should never be attempted. If fuel cylinder outer composite covering exhibits signs of damage such as cuts, fraying or unraveling, do not refill cylinder until outer covering has been replaced.

If a CNG vehicle has been involved in an accident, the fuel system should be fully inspected and pressure tested.

Fuel System Pressure Relief

GASOLINE ENGINE

The fuel system is under constant fuel pressure. This pressure must be released before servicing any fuel related component.

1. Remove fuel tank filler cap to release tank pressure.
2. Remove fuel pump relay from Power Distribution Center (PDC).
3. Start and run engine until it stalls, then attempt to restart engine until it will no longer run.

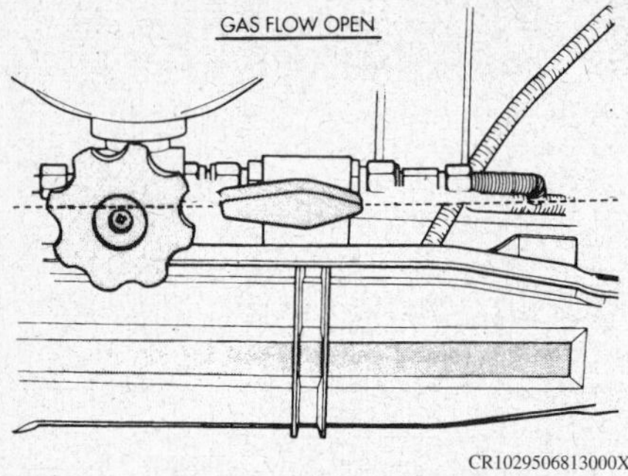

Fig. 1 CNG manual shutoff valve open position. CNG engine

4. Turn ignition key to Off position. **Steps 1, 2 and 3 must be performed to relieve high pressure fuel from within fuel rail. Do not attempt to use following steps to relieve this pressure as excessive fuel will be forced into cylinder chamber.**
5. Unplug electrical connector from any injector.
6. Attach one end of a jumper wire with alligator clips to either injector terminal.
7. Connect other end of jumper wire to positive side of battery.
8. Connect one end of a second jumper wire to remaining injector terminal.
9. Momentarily touch other end of jumper wire to negative terminal of battery for no more than a few seconds. **Powering injector for more than a few seconds will permanently damage injector.**
10. Place a rag below fuel line quick-connect fitting at fuel rail, then disconnect quick-connect fitting.
11. Install fuel pump relay to PDC.
12. One or more DTCs may have been stored in PCM memory due to fuel pump relay removal. Clear DTCs using suitable scan tool.

CNG ENGINE

The fuel system must be purged of natural gas prior to removing or repairing any fuel system component. The fuel tube purge procedure should be used if fuel cylinders or control valves are not to be serviced; however, if these are to be serviced, then fuel cylinder purge procedure should be used. **To prevent accumulation of fumes, perform purge procedures outdoors.**

FUEL TUBE PURGE

1. On all cylinders, close fuel control valves by turning clockwise, then open manual shutoff valve, **Fig. 1.**
2. If engine will run, start and run until residual fuel is consumed and engine stalls, then attempt three more engine starts.
3. When servicing manual shut off valve or fuel gauge pressure transducer, proceed as follows:
   a. Slowly loosen fuel tube fitting at inlet side of fuel pressure regulator until pressure begins to release.
   b. Allow pressure to decrease gradually by loosening fitting in increments until all pressure is released.

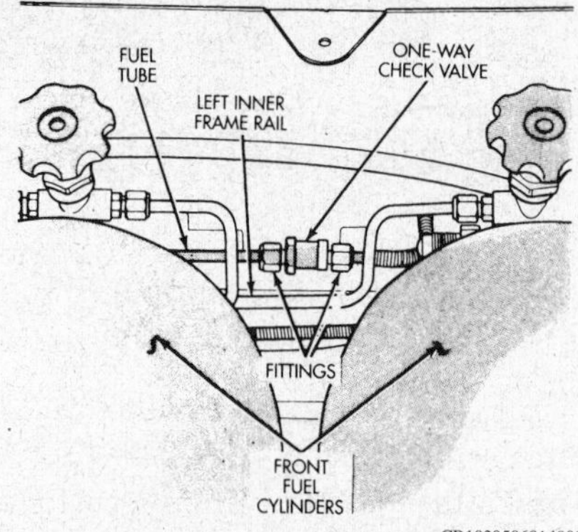

Fig. 2 CNG one-way check valve & fuel tube fittings. CNG engine

4. When servicing fuel filter, fuel pressure regulator or high pressure solenoid, proceed as follows:
   a. Slowly loosen fuel tube fittings at inlet and outlet sides of fuel pressure regulator until pressure begins to release.
   b. Allow pressure to decrease gradually by loosening fitting in increments until all pressure is released.
5. When servicing fuel fill receptacle or one-way check valve, proceed as follows:
   a. Slowly loosen fuel tube fitting at outlet side of check valve, **Fig. 2,** until pressure begins to release.
   b. Allow pressure to decrease gradually by loosening fitting in increments until all pressure is released.
6. When servicing low pressure fuel shutoff solenoid, fuel rail, fuel hose between fuel rail and solenoid, fuel pressure sensor or fuel temperature sensor, proceed as follows:
   a. Slowly loosen fuel tube fitting at inlet side of low pressure fuel shutoff solenoid very slowly.
   b. When pressure release begins, allow pressure to decrease gradually by loosening fitting in increments until all pressure is released.
7. Perform repairs to system as required, noting the following:
   a. **Although fuel tubes have been purged of natural gas, fuel cylinders remain under high pressure. Do not open cylinder valves until all high pressure components have be reconnected and sealed.**
   b. After repairs have been completed and all fuel system components are in place, use a suitable Go-No-Go inspection tool to inspect fuel system high pressure fittings.

FUEL CYLINDER PURGE

1. Open manual shutoff valve, **Fig. 1,** then open fuel control valves on cylinders being serviced by turning clockwise. **Ensure valves on cylinders not being serviced are fully closed.**
2. If engine will run, start and run until all residual fuel is consumed, then attempt three more engine starts.

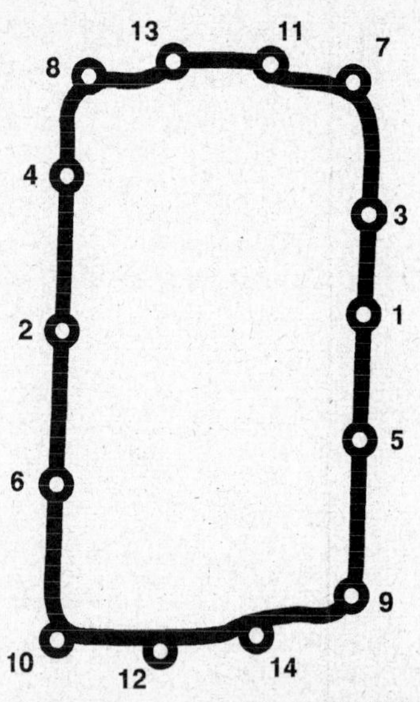

Fig. 3 Intake plenum tightening sequence. 3.9L engine

3. Slowly loosen fuel tube fitting at fuel control valve of cylinder being serviced; allow pressure to decrease gradually by loosening fitting in increments until all pressure is released.
4. Perform repairs to system as required, noting the following:
   a. **Although fuel tubes and opened fuel cylinders have been purged of natural gas, fuel cylinders not being serviced remain under high pressure. Do not open cylinder valves until all high pressure components have be reconnected and sealed.**
   b. After repairs have been completed and all fuel system components are in place, use a suitable Go-No-Go inspection tool to inspect fuel system high pressure fittings.

COMPRESSION PRESSURE

Compression pressure on 3.9L, 5.2L and 5.9L engines minimum pressure should be 100 psi. Maximum variation between cylinders should not exceed 25 percent.

Compression pressure on 8.0L engines should be 170–190 psi.

ENGINE MOUNT

REPLACE

Front

1. Raise hood, then position fan and related components aside as required to obtain required clearance.
2. Raise and support vehicle, then attach a suitable lifting device to engine.
3. Raise engine slightly, then remove through bolts and nuts from brackets and insulators.
4. Remove brackets and insulators as required.
5. Reverse procedure to install.

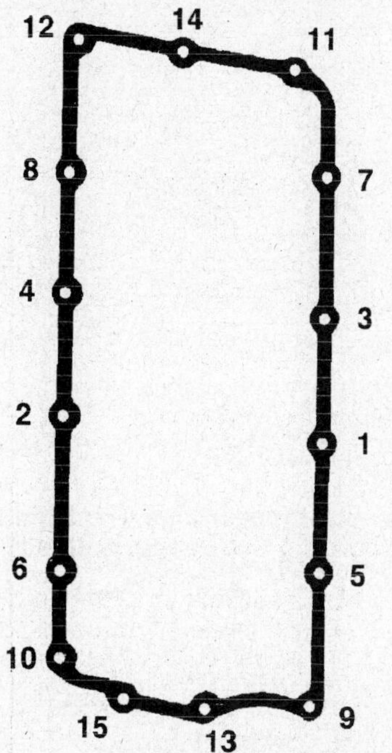

Fig. 4 Intake plenum tightening sequence. 5.2L & 5.9L engines

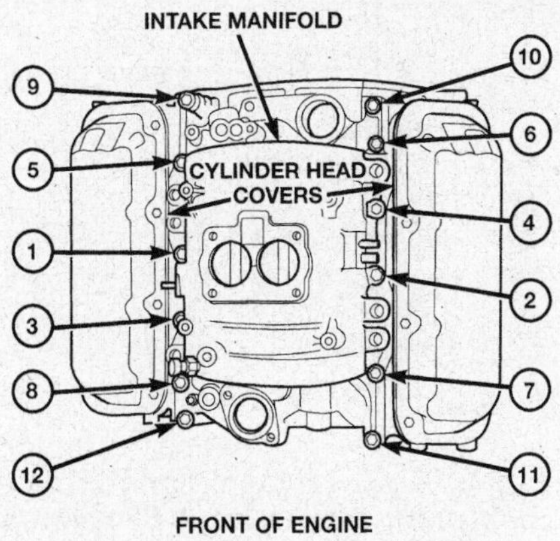

Fig. 5 Intake manifold bolt tightening sequence. 3.9L engine

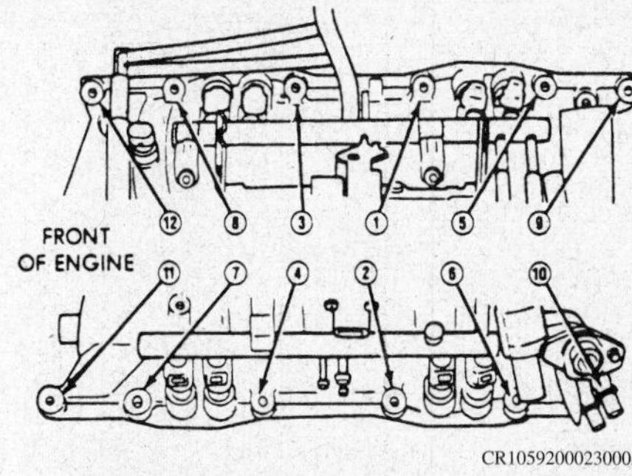

Fig. 6 Intake manifold bolt tightening sequence. 5.2L & 5.9L engines

Rear

PICKUP

1. Raise and support vehicle, then position transmission jack beneath transmission and remove rear support cushion stud nuts.
2. Raise rear of engine/transmission assembly slightly, then remove bolts securing support cushion to transmission support bracket. Remove cushion from vehicle.
3. Remove bolts securing transmission support bracket to transmission.
4. Reverse procedure to install.

VAN

1. Raise and support vehicle, then position transmission jack beneath transmission and raise rear of engine/transmission assembly slightly.
2. Remove rear mount through bolt and nut,
3. Remove U-shaped bracket, then separate insulator from bracket.
4. Remove rear engine support from transmission extension housing.
5. Reverse procedure to install.

ENGINE

REPLACE

Pickup

1. Remove battery and drain cooling system, then remove upper crossmember and top core support.
2. Remove transmission oil cooler and recover A/C system, then remove serpentine belt as outlined in "Serpentine Drive Belt."
3. Remove A/C compressor with lines attached and position aside, then remove condenser, washer bottle and overflow bottle.
4. Disconnect upper radiator hose, then remove fan and shroud.
5. Disconnect lower radiator hose and transmission cooler lines, then remove radiator.
6. Remove alternator with wire connections, then the air cleaner box.
7. Release fuel pressure as outlined in "Fuel System Pressure Relief" in "Precautions."
8. Disconnect throttle linkage and remove throttle body, then remove intake manifold as outlined in "Intake Manifold, Replace."
9. **On models equipped with 3.9L, 5.2L and 5.9L engines,** remove distributor cap and wiring.
10. **On models equipped with 8.0L engine,** remove coil assemblies with ignition cables.
11. **On all models,** disconnect heater hoses, power steering hoses, transmission cooler lines and fuel lines.
12. **On models equipped with manual transmission,** remove shift lever.
13. **On all models,** raise and support vehicle, then drain engine oil and remove front engine mount through bolt nuts.
14. Remove transmission cooler line brackets from oil pan, then disconnect exhaust pipe at manifold.
15. Disconnect starter wires, then remove starter, dust shield and transmission cover.
16. **On models equipped with automatic transmission,** support transmission, then remove torque converter and transmission bolts.
17. **On models equipped with manual transmission,** remove propeller shaft, then support transmission and remove rear transmission support.
18. **On all models,** remove crossmember and clutch slave cylinder, then disconnect all wiring and connectors.
19. Support engine, then remove transmission bolts and transmission, bellhousing, clutch assembly and flywheel and ring gear assembly.
20. Lower vehicle.
21. **On models equipped with automatic transmission,** support transmission with a suitable jack stand.
22. **On all models,** install a suitable engine lifting fixture. **Do not lift engine by intake manifold.**
23. Remove engine from vehicle.
24. Reverse procedure to install.

Van

1. Remove engine cover.
2. Discharge A/C system using suitable A/C recovery equipment.
3. Raise and support vehicle.
4. Drain cooling system and engine oil into suitable containers.
5. Disconnect catalytic converter assembly from exhaust manifolds.
6. Disconnect starter motor wires and remove starter.
7. Remove engine to transmission struts.
8. Remove inspection cover.
9. Remove flexplate to converter bolts.
10. Remove left and right engine mount insulator to mounting bracket nuts.
11. Disconnect transmission cooler lines from radiator using quick connect tool No. 6935, or equivalent.
12. Remove transmission oil cooler lines from oil pan fastening clips.
13. Remove lower transmission to engine mounting bolts.
14. Lower vehicle.
15. Remove grille and mounting bracket.
16. Remove A/C condenser and cap off open ports/hoses to prevent moisture and particle contamination.
17. Remove transmission auxiliary oil cooler (if equipped).
18. Remove upper and lower radiator hoses.
19. Remove cooling fan shroud from radiator and allow it to rest on viscous fan.
20. Remove cowl plenum to upper radiator support rods.
21. Remove coolant recovery and windshield washer bottles from upper radiator support.
22. Remove PDC from upper radiator support and secure out of way.
23. Remove upper radiator support.
24. Remove radiator from engine compartment.
25. Remove fan shroud.

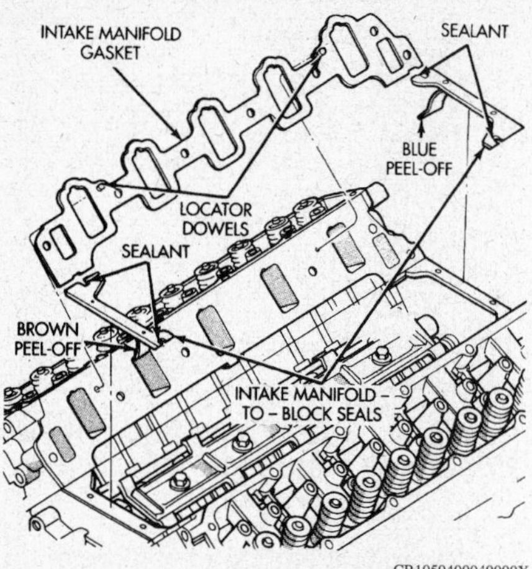

CR1059400049000X

Fig. 7 Lower intake manifold gaskets. 8.0L engine

26. Remove accessory drive belt.
27. Remove A/C suction/discharge hose assembly from compressor (if A/C equipped).
28. Remove A/C compressor, power steering pump, and alternator assembly.
29. Disconnect all engine electrical and vacuum connections, secure all harnesses out of way.
30. Release fuel pressure as outlined in "Fuel System Pressure Relief" in "Precautions."
31. Remove intake manifold.
32. Attach suitable engine lifting device, raise engine and slowly guide out of vehicle. Vehicle may need to be raised slightly.
33. Drain remaining oil into suitable container.
34. Reverse procedure to install. Road test after installation and inspect for fluid and exhaust leaks.

INTAKE MANIFOLD

REPLACE

3.9L, 5.2L & 5.9L Engines

1. Drain cooling system into suitable container.
2. Remove A/C compressor.
3. Remove alternator, accessory drive bracket and air cleaner.
4. Perform fuel system pressure relief procedure as outlined in "Fuel System Pressure Relief."
5. Disconnect accelerator linkage, speed control and transmission kickdown cables.
6. Remove return spring, distributor cap and wires and coil wires.
7. Disconnect heat indicator sending unit wire.
8. Disconnect heater hoses and bypass hose.
9. Remove closed crankcase ventilation and evaporation control systems.

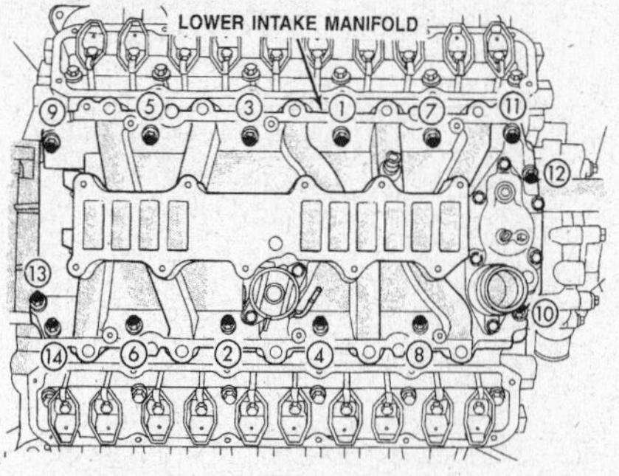

CR1059400050000X

Fig. 8 Lower intake manifold bolt tightening sequence. 8.0L engine

10. Remove intake manifold bolts.
11. Lift intake manifold and throttle body out of engine compartment as an assembly.
12. Remove and discard flange side gaskets and front and rear crossover gaskets.
13. Remove throttle body.
14. Remove plenum pan and gasket, if required.
15. Reverse procedure to install, noting the following:
    a. If plenum pan was removed, position a new gasket and install plenum pan. Tighten bolts in sequence, **Figs. 3 and 4,** in three steps.
    b. Step 1: **On models equipped with 3.9L engine, torque** bolts to 48 inch lbs.
    c. Step 1: **On models equipped with 5.2L and 5.9L engines, torque** bolts to 24 inch lbs.
    d. Step 2: **On all models, torque** bolts to 84 inch lbs.
    e. Step 3: **Torque** bolts to 84 inch lbs.
16. Install new gasket, then the throttle body.
17. Apply Mopar Gen II silicone rubber adhesive sealant to four corner joints of intake manifold.
18. Install front and rear crossover gaskets and flange gaskets. Ensure vertical port alignment tab is resting on deck face of block.
19. Horizontal tabs must be in position with mating cylinder head gasket tabs. The "Manifold Side" should be visible on center of each flange gasket.
20. Install intake manifold and tighten in sequence **Figs. 5 and 6,** as follows:
    a. **On models equipped with 3.9L engine, torque** bolts 1 and 2 to 72 inch lbs., in alternating steps 12 inch lbs., at a time.
    b. **On models equipped with 5.2L and 5.9L engines, torque** bolts 1–4 to 72 inch lbs., in alternating steps 12 inch lbs., at a time.
    c. **On models equipped with 3.9L engine, torque** bolts 3–12 to 72 inch lbs., ensure that all bolts are torqued to 72 inch lbs.
    d. **On models equipped with 5.2L and 5.9L engines, torque** bolts 5–12 to 72 inch lbs., ensure that all bolts are torqued to 72 inch lbs.
    e. **On all models, torque** all bolts to 12 ft. lbs., ensure that all bolts are torqued to 12 ft. lbs.

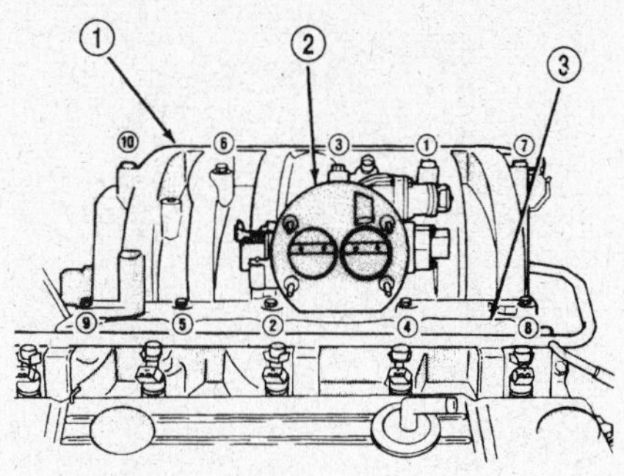

1 - UPPER INTAKE MANIFOLD
2 - THROTTLE BODY (MPI)
3 - LOWER INTAKE MANIFOLD

CR1059400051000X

Fig. 9 Upper intake manifold bolt tightening sequence. 8.0L engine

8.0L Engine

REMOVAL

1. Drain cooling system, then remove accessory drive belt, alternator brace and alternator.
2. Remove A/C compressor brace and compressor and position aside, then remove air cleaner cover, filter and housing. Discard gasket.
3. Release fuel pressure as outlined in "Fuel System Pressure Relief" in "Precautions."
4. Disconnect fuel lines, accelerator linkage and cables for speed control and transmission kickdown.
5. Remove coil assemblies with ignition cables, then disconnect vacuum lines, heater hoses and bypass hose.
6. Remove closed crankcase ventilation and evaporation control systems, then the throttle body bolts.
7. Lift throttle body off upper intake manifold, then remove upper intake manifold bolts and lift manifold out of engine compartment. Discard gaskets.
8. Remove lower intake manifold bolts and manifold, then discard gasket.

INSTALLATION

1. Install intake manifold side gaskets. Ensure locator dowels are positioned in head.
2. Insert dowels in locator holes, then peel protective paper from new intake manifold to block seals and align upon dowels.
3. Install seals on block, pressing firmly to ensure adhesion. **Front seal is brown and rear seal is blue.**
4. Apply suitable silicone rubber adhesive sealant to four corner pockets, **Fig. 7,** then install lower intake manifold within three minutes of sealant aplication.
5. **Torque** lower intake manifold bolts in sequence, **Fig. 8,** to 40 ft. lbs.

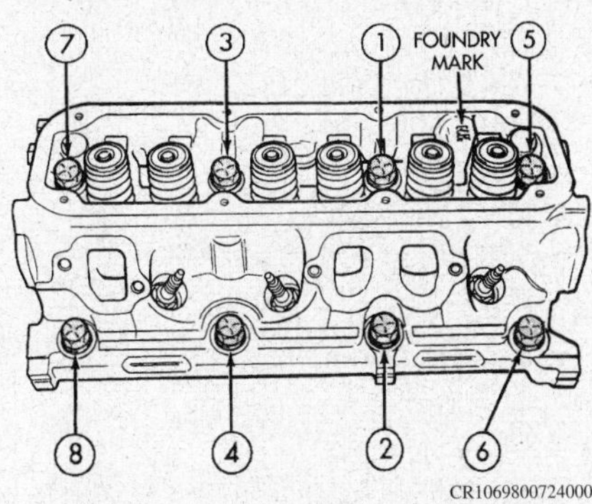

Fig. 10 Cylinder head bolt tightening sequence. 3.9L engine

6. Install upper intake manifold on lower manifold and **torque** bolts in sequence using a new gasket, **Fig. 9,** to 16 ft. lbs.
7. Install throttle body and tighten bolts to specifications using a new gasket, then install closed crankcase ventilation and evaporation control systems.
8. Connect heater hoses, bypass hose and vacuum lines, then install coil assemblies and ignition cables.
9. Connect accelerator linkage and cables for speed control and transmission kickdown, then install fuel lines.
10. Install air cleaner housing using a new gasket, filter and cover. Tighten housing nuts to specifications.
11. Install A/C compressor, alternator and braces. Tighten all bolts to specifications, then install accessory drive belt.
12. Fill cooling system.

EXHAUST MANIFOLD

REPLACE

1. Raise and support vehicle.
2. Remove bolts and nuts attaching exhaust pipe to manifold, then lower vehicle and remove exhaust heat shields.
3. **On models equipped with 8.0L engine,** remove EGR tube, gasket and dipstick bracket from right exhaust manifold.
4. **On all models,** remove bolts, nuts and washers attaching manifold to cylinder head.
5. Remove manifold from cylinder head.
6. Reverse procedure to install, noting the following:
   a. **On models equipped with 3.9L, 5.2L and 5.9L engines,** if exhaust manifold studs came out with nuts, install new studs, applying suitable sealer on coarse thread ends. **If sealer is not applied to stud threads, water leaks may develop at studs.**
   b. **On models equipped with 3.9L, 5.2L and 5.9L engines,** install two bolts and conical washers at inner ends of outboard arms of manifold, then two bolts without washers on center arm of manifold.
   c. **On models equipped with 3.9L, 5.2L and 5.9L engines,** starting at center arm and working outward, tighten manifold bolts to specifications.
   d. **On models equipped with 8.0L engine,** use a new manifold gasket, and tighten all bolts and nuts to specifications.

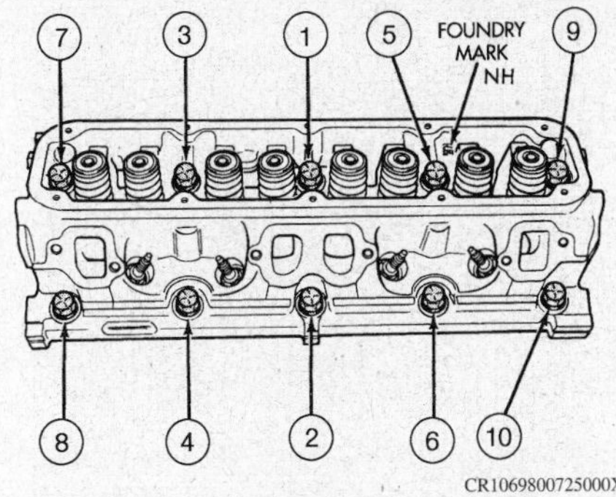

Fig. 11 Cylinder head bolt tightening sequence. 5.2L & 5.9L engines

CYLINDER HEAD

REPLACE

3.9L, 5.2L & 5.9L Engines

1. Drain cooling system into suitable container.
2. Remove heat shields.
3. Remove intake manifold to alternator bracket support rod, remove alternator.
4. Remove closed crankcase ventilation system.
5. Disconnect evaporative control system.
6. Remove air cleaner.
7. Release fuel system pressure as outlined in "Fuel System Pressure Relief" in "Precautions."
8. Disconnect fuel supply line.
9. Disconnect accelerator linkage, speed control linkage and kick down cables.
10. Remove distributor cap and wires.
11. Disconnect coil wire, then the coolant temperature sending unit electrical connector.
12. Disconnect heater hoses, then the bypass hose.
13. Disconnect all electrical and vacuum harnesses.
14. Remove intake manifold and throttle body as an assembly as outlined in "Intake Manifold, Replace."
15. Remove exhaust manifolds as outlined in "Exhaust Manifold, Replace."
16. Remove rocker arm assemblies and pushrods. Identify components for installation reference.
17. Remove head bolts from each cylinder heads, discard head gaskets.
18. Remove spark plugs.
19. Reverse procedure to install, noting the following:
   a. **Torque** bolts in sequence, **Figs. 10 and 11,** in two steps, first to 50 ft. lbs., then to 105 ft. lbs.
   b. Tighten intake manifold bolts as outlined in "Intake Manifold, Replace" in this section.

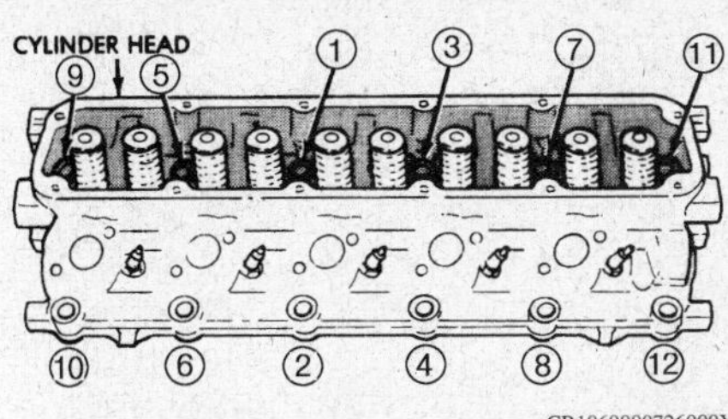

Fig. 12 Cylinder head bolt tightening sequence. 8.0L engine

8.0L Engine

1. Drain cooling system into suitable container.
2. Remove heat shields.
3. Remove intake manifold to alternator bracket support rod, then the alternator.
4. Remove closed crankcase ventilation system.
5. Disconnect evaporation control system.
6. Remove air cleaner.
7. Release fuel system pressure as outlined in "Fuel System Pressure Relief" in "Precautions."
8. Disconnect coil wires.
9. Disconnect heat indicator sending unit wire.
10. Disconnect heater hoses and bypass hose.
11. Remove upper intake manifold and throttle body as an assembly as outlined in "Intake Manifold, Replace."
12. Remove cylinder head covers and gaskets.
13. Remove EGR tube, discard gaskets for right side only.
14. Remove lower intake manifold as outlined in "Intake Manifold, Replace." Discard flange side gaskets and front and rear crossover gaskets.
15. Remove exhaust manifolds as outlined in "Exhaust Manifold, Replace."
16. Remove rocker arm assemblies and pushrods, identify components for installation reference.
17. Remove head bolts from each cylinder head, then the cylinder heads.
18. Remove spark plugs.
19. Reverse procedure to install, noting the following:
   a. **Torque** bolts in sequence, **Fig. 12,** in two steps, first to 43 ft. lbs., then to 105 ft. lbs.
   b. When installing rocker arm bolts, ensure piston is not at TDC or damage to pistons or valves may occur.
   c. Install pushrods and rocker arm assemblies in their original positions and **torque** bolts to 21 ft. lbs.
   d. When installing cross over gaskets, ensure block assembly is oil free.

VALVE LIFTERS

Refer to **Fig. 13** for illustration of the type of hydraulic valve lifters used. Before disassembling any part of the engine to inspect

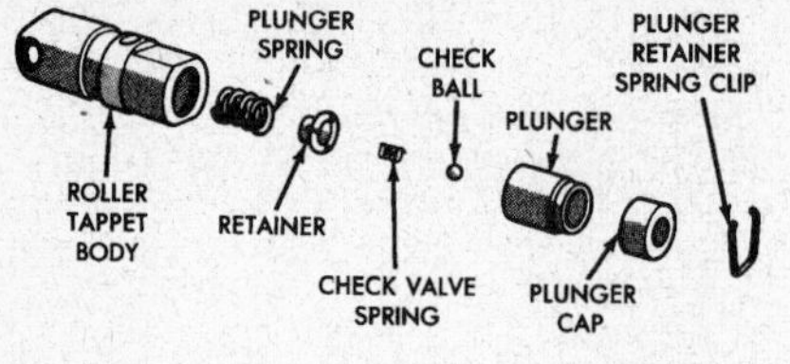

Fig. 13 Hydraulic valve lifter. 3.9L, 5.2L & 5.9L engines

for noise, inspect the oil pressure at the gauge and the oil level in the oil pan. The oil level in the pan should never be above the "full" mark on the dipstick, nor below the "add oil" mark. Either of the two conditions could be responsible for noisy lifters.

VALVE ADJUSTMENT

These engines are equipped with hydraulic lifters with no provision for adjustment.

ROCKER ARMS

When disassembling rocker arms, place all components on the workbench in their proper sequence to ensure correct assembly.

Clean all sludge and gum formation from the inside and outside of the shafts. Clean oil holes and passages in the rocker arms and shafts. Inspect the shafts for wear.

1. Disconnect spark plug wires from plugs and position aside.
2. Remove rocker arm cover and gasket.
3. **On models equipped with 3.9L, 5.2L and 5.9L engines,** remove rocker arm bolts, pivots and pushrods, **Fig. 14.** Mark for installation reference.
4. **On models equipped with 8.0L engine,** remove rocker arm bolts and assemblies, **Fig. 15,** then the pushrods. Mark rocker arm assemblies and pushrods for installation reference.
5. **On all models,** reverse procedure to install, noting the following:
   a. Rotate engine until "V8" mark lines up with TDC mark on front cover.
   b. Tighten rocker arm bolts to specifications.
   c. **Do not crank engine during or immediately after rocker arm installation. Allow up to 20 minutes for hydraulic roller tappets to bleed down.**

VALVE GUIDES

These engines do not have removable valve guides. The valves operate in guide holes bored in the cylinder head. Valves with oversize stems are available for service replacement when it is required to ream the valve guide holes.

Standard production stem diameter should be as follows:

1. **On models equipped with 5.9L engine,** valve stem diameter should be .372–.373 inch for intake valves and .371–.372 inch for exhaust valves.
2. **On models equipped with 3.9L, 5.2L and 8.0L engines,** valve stem diameter should be .311–.312 inch.

On all models, if stem wear exceeds .002 inch, replace valve. When reaming guides for oversize valve stems, do so in two steps from standard size to .015 inch. This must be done in order to maintain a true relationship of the guide to the valve seat. Reamer size to valve guide application is as follows: a reamer oversize of .003 inch has a valve guide size of .316–.317 inch, and a reamer oversize of .015 inch has a valve guide size of .328–.329 inch.

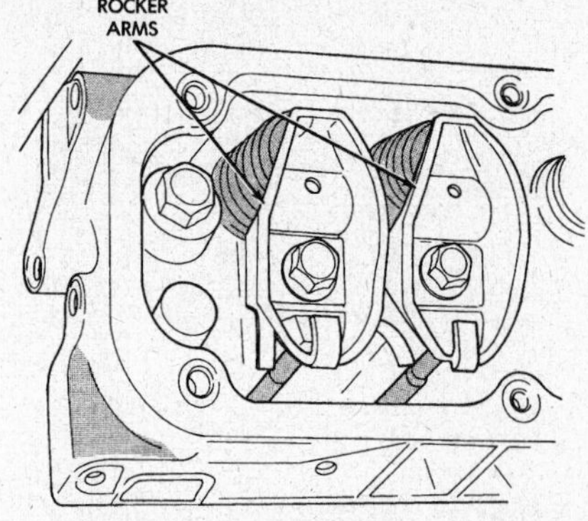

Fig. 14 Rocker arms. 3.9L, 5.2L & 5.9L engines

HYDRAULIC LIFTERS

REPLACE

Worn valve guides or cocked springs are sometimes mistaken for noisy lifters. Determine which lifter is noisy. If the application of side thrust on the valve spring fails to noticeably reduce the noise, the lifter is probably faulty and should be removed for inspection. When installing hydraulic lifters in the engine, fill them with light engine oil to avoid excessive time required to quiet them during initial operation of engine.

1. Remove air cleaner, valve cover, rocker assembly and pushrods. **Mark pushrods for installation reference.**
2. Remove intake manifold as outlined in "Intake Manifold, Replace."
3. **On models equipped with 8.0L engine,** cut cylinder head gasket for accessibility if end lifters are to be replaced.
4. **On all models,** remove yoke retainer and aligning yokes, then pull lifter from bore with a twisting motion. If required, use hydraulic tappet remover/installer tool No. C-4129-A, or equivalent.
5. Mark lifters for installation reference, then inspect. If lifters or bores are scored or show signs of sticking, ream bore to next oversize and obtain corresponding oversize lifters.
6. **On models equipped with 8.0L engine,** inspect camshaft lobes for abnormal wear.
7. **On all models,** reverse procedure to install, noting the following:
   a. **On models equipped with 3.9L, 5.2L and 5.9L engines,** ensure oil feed hole in side of lifter faces away from crankshaft.
   b. **On models equipped with 8.0L engine,** ensure oil bleed hole in lifter faces forward.
   c. **On all models,** do not run engine above fast idle until all hydraulic lifters have filled with oil and are quiet.

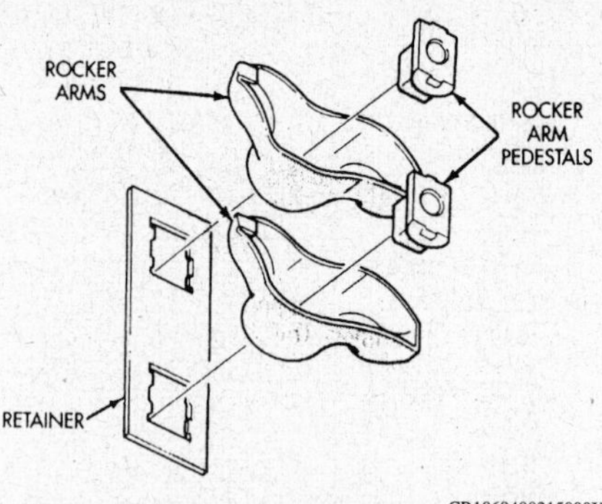

Fig. 15 Rocker arm assembly. 8.0L engine

CRANKSHAFT DAMPER

REPLACE

1. Remove fan shroud retainer bolts and position shroud back over engine.
2. Remove fan, then the serpentine belt as outlined in "Serpentine Drive Belt."
3. **On models equipped with 3.9L, 5.2L and 5.9L engines,** remove vibration damper pulley from damper.
4. **On all models,** remove damper bolt and washer from crankshaft end, then install suitable pulley/damper remover.
5. Remove damper from crankshaft.
6. Reverse procedure to install, noting the following:
   a. **On models equipped with 3.9L, 5.2L and 5.9L engines,** use a suitable tool to draw damper onto crankshaft end.
   b. **On all models,** tighten damper bolt to specifications.

FRONT COVER

REPLACE

3.9L, 5.2L & 5.9L Engines

REMOVAL

1. Drain cooling system into suitable container.
2. Remove serpentine belt.
3. Remove water pump.
4. Remove power steering pump.
5. Remove vibration damper.
6. Loosen oil pan bolts and remove front bolt at each side.
7. Remove cover bolts, then the cover and gasket.
8. From inside of front cover, tap front crankshaft seal outward.

INSTALLATION

1. Ensure mating surfaces of cover and cylinder block are clean and free of burrs.

2. Use a new cover gasket and carefully install cover to avoid damaging oil pan gasket.
3. Use a small amount of Mopar silicone rubber adhesive sealant, or equivalent, at joint between timing chain cover gasket and oil pan gasket.
4. Finger tighten timing chain cover bolts at this time.
5. Place small diameter of oil seal over front oil seal installation seal tool No. 6635, or equivalent, seat oil seal in groove of tool.
6. Position seal and tool onto crankshaft.
7. Tighten four lower cover bolts to 10 ft. lbs., to prevent cover from tipping during seal installation.
8. Draw seal into position on crankshaft using the vibration damper bolt and seal installation tool No. 6635, or equivalent.
9. Loosen four bolts tightened previously to allow for alignment of front cover.
10. Tighten cover bolts and oil pan bolts to specifications.
11. Remove vibration damper bolt and seal installation tool.
12. Install vibration damper, water pump and housing assembly using new gaskets. Tighten bolts to specifications.
13. Install power steering pump.
14. Install serpentine belt.
15. Install cooling fan, tightening bolts to specifications.
16. Install fan shroud.
17. Fill cooling system.

8.0L Engine

REMOVAL

1. Drain cooling system into suitable container.
2. Remove serpentine belt, fan and fan shroud.
3. Unbolt A/C compressor and set on top of engine.
4. Remove alternator, air pump and bracket assembly.
5. Remove water pump.
6. Remove damper bolt and washer.
7. Remove pulley/damper from crankshaft. Attach puller jaws to inside of pulley diameter.
8. Loosen oil pan bolts and remove front oil pan bolts that mount pan to timing chain cover.
9. Remove cover bolts.
10. Remove timing chain cover and gasket using care to avoid damaging oil pan gasket.

INSTALLATION

1. Ensure mating surfaces of engine block and timing chain cover are clean and free of burrs.
2. Lubricate pump rotors using suitable petroleum jelly or lubriplate.
3. Install timing chain cover using care to avoid damaging oil pan gasket using a new cover gasket.
4. Use a small amount of Mopar silicone rubber adhesive sealant, or equivalent, at joint between timing chain cover gasket and oil pan gasket.
5. Finger tighten cover bolts at this time.

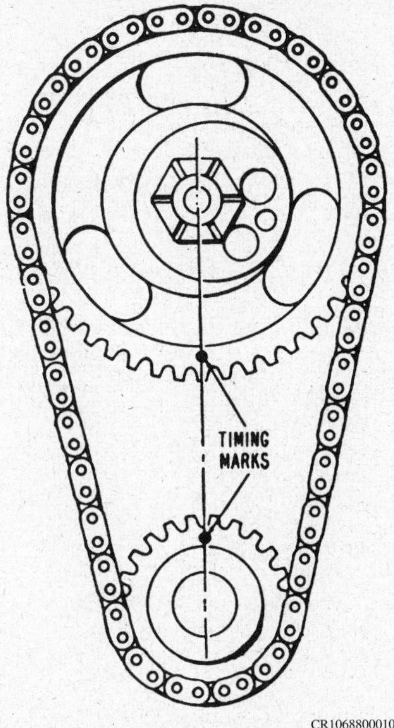

Fig. 16 Timing mark alignment

6. Tighten cover bolts and oil pan bolts to specifications.
7. Install crankshaft pulley/damper using installer tool No. C-3688, or equivalent.
8. Prime oil pump by squirting oil into oil filter mounting hole and filling J-trap of front timing cover.
9. When oil is running out, install filter that has been filled with oil.
10. Install water pump and housing assembly tightening bolts to specifications.
11. Install alternator, air pump and bracket assembly.
12. Install A/C compressor.
13. Install cooling fan, shroud and serpentine belt.
14. Fill cooling system

TIMING CHAIN

REPLACE

Removal

1. Remove crankshaft damper as outlined in "Crankshaft Damper, Replace" and front cover as outlined in "Front Cover, Replace."
2. Remove camshaft sprocket bolt, then the timing chain with crankshaft and camshaft sprockets.

Installation

1. Position camshaft and crankshaft sprockets on bench with timing marks aligned, **Fig. 16,** then place chain around both sprockets.
2. Rotate crankshaft and camshaft as required to align them with keyways in sprockets.
3. Lift sprockets and chain into position over camshaft and crankshaft, keeping sprockets tight against chain, then inspect timing mark alignment with a straightedge.
4. Install camshaft bolt and tighten to specifications, then install front cover as outlined in "Front Cover, Replace" and crankshaft damper as outlined in "Crankshaft Damper, Replace."

CAMSHAFT

REPLACE

Removal

1. Remove radiator as outlined in "Radiator, Replace."
2. Remove A/C condenser, then the engine cover.
3. Remove intake manifold as outlined in "Intake Manifold, Replace."
4. Remove valve covers as outlined in "Valve Cover, Replace."
5. Remove front cover as outlined in "Front Cover, Replace."
6. Remove rocker arms.
7. Remove push rods and tappets marking locations for reference during installation.
8. Remove distributor, then lift out oil pump and distributor drive shaft.
9. Remove camshaft thrust plate, noting location of oil tab, **Fig. 17.**
10. Install a long bolt into front of camshaft to aid in removal, then remove camshaft ensuring not to damage cambearings.

Installation

1. Lubricate camshaft lobes and bearing journals, then insert camshaft to within two inches of its final position in cylinder block.
2. Install camshaft holder tool No. C-3509, or equivalent, with tongue back of distributor drive gear.
3. Hold tool in position with distributor lock plate bolt. This will restrict camshaft from being pushed in too far and knocking out welch plug in rear of cylinder block. Tool should remain installed until camshaft and crankshaft sprockets and timing chain have been installed.
4. Install camshaft thrust plate and chain oil tab ensuring tang enters lower right hole in thrust plate. Top edge of tab should be flat against thrust plate in order to catch oil for chain lubrication.
5. Install timing chain and gears.
6. Measure camshaft endplay. If endplay is not .002–.010 inch, replace thrust plate.
7. Install tapets in original locations. Replace all tappets if installing new camshaft.
8. Install distributor and distributor drive.
9. Install push rods, then the rocker arms.
10. Install front cover as outlined in "Front Cover, Replace."
11. Install valve covers as outlined in "Valve Cover, Replace."
12. Install intake manifold as outlined in "Intake Manifold, Replace."

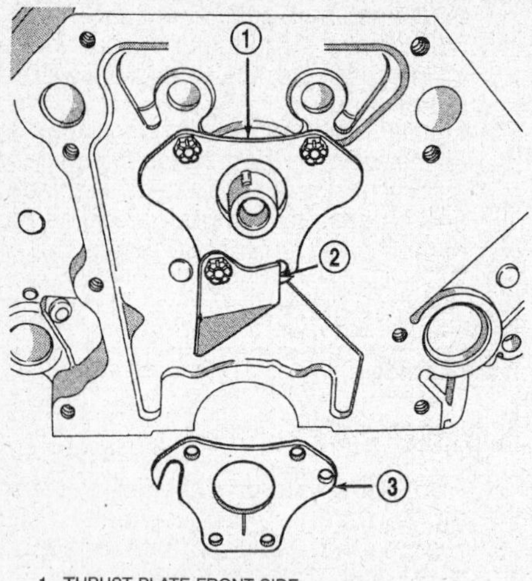

Fig. 17 Thrust plate

13. Install engine cover.
14. Install A/C condenser.
15. Install radiator as outlined in "Radiator, Replace."

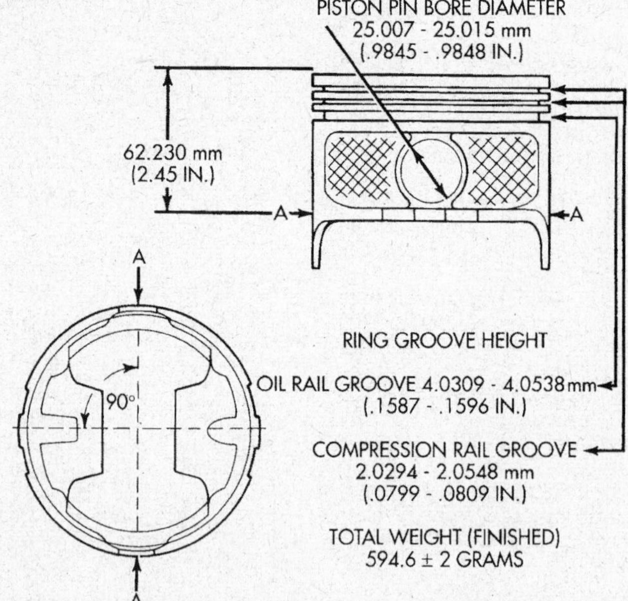

PISTON SIZE	A DIA = PISTON DIAMETER		BORE DIAMETER	
	MIN. mm (IN.)	MAX. mm (IN.)	MIN. mm (IN.)	MAX. mm (IN.)
A	99.280 (3.9087)	99.294 (3.9092)	99.306 (3.9097)	99.319 (3.9102)
B	99.294 (3.9092)	99.306 (3.9097)	99.319 (3.9102)	99.332 (3.9107)
C	99.306 (3.9097)	99.319 (3.9102)	99.332 (3.9107)	99.344 (3.9112)
D	99.319 (3.9102)	99.332 (3.9107)	99.344 (3.9112)	99.357 (3.9117)
E	99.332 (3.9107)	99.344 (3.9112)	99.357 (3.9117)	99.370 (3.9122)

CR1068800017000X

Fig. 18 Piston measurements. 3.9L & 5.2L engines

PISTON & ROD ASSEMBLY

Refer to **Figs. 18 and 19** for piston specifications.

Removal

1. Remove engine from vehicle as outlined in "Engine, Replace," then remove cylinder head and oil pan from engine as outlined in "Cylinder Head, Replace" and "Oil Pan, Replace."
2. **On models equipped with 8.0L engine,** remove oil pump pickup tube.
3. **On all models,** cover piston, then ream ridge at top of cylinder bore with suitable reaming tool.
4. Mark connecting rod and cap for installation reference, then remove cap and install rod bolt guide set on rod bolts.
5. Rotate crankshaft until connecting rod is centered in cylinder bore at BDC, then slide piston and rod out from top of block. **Do not nick crankshaft journals.**
6. After assembly is removed, install cap on mating connecting rod.

Installation

1. Stagger compression ring gaps so that neither aligns with oil ring gap, then ensure oil ring expander ends are butted and rail gaps are positioned properly, **Figs. 20 and 21.**
2. Immerse piston head and rings in clean engine oil, then compress rings with suitable piston ring compressor. **Ensure ring positions do not change.**
3. Install connecting rod bolt protectors on rod bolts with long protector on numbered side of rod, then rotate crankshaft until journal is centered under cylinder bore.
4. Insert rod and piston into cylinder bore, guiding rod end over crankshaft journal, then tap piston down in cylinder bore using a hammer handle or suitable equivalent. **Ensure notch on top of piston points toward front of engine and larger connecting rod bore chamfer faces crankshaft journal fillet.**
5. Install rod caps and tighten nuts to specifications.
6. **On models equipped with 8.0L engine,** install oil pump pickup tube.
7. **On all models,** install oil pump as outlined in "Oil Pump, Replace" and cylinder head as outlined in "Cylinder Head, Replace."
8. Install engine as outlined in "Engine, Replace."

MAIN & ROD BEARINGS

Main and rod bearings are furnished in standard sizes and the following undersizes: .001, .002, .003, .010 and .012 inch.

CRANKSHAFT SEAL

REPLACE

3.9L, 5.2L & 5.9L Engines

The service oil seal is split into lower and upper halves. The upper seal half can be installed with the crankshaft removed or installed, but the lower seal half can only be installed with the rear main bearing cap removed. When a new upper seal is installed, install a new lower seal.

UPPER SEAL

1. With crankshaft installed, proceed as follows:
   a. Remove oil pan as outlined in "Oil Pan, Replace," then remove oil pump from rear main bearing cap.
   b. Remove rear main bearing cap, then carefully remove and discard old lower and upper oil seals.
   c. Loosen two main bearing caps forward of rear cap to facilitate new seal installation.
2. Clean cylinder block mating surfaces and ensure seal groove is free of debris, then apply a thin film of oil to new upper seal lips.
3. Install new upper seal with yellow paint facing rear of engine. If crankshaft was removed, position in cylinder block.
4. Install new lower seal as outlined in this section.
5. Apply a ⅕ inch drop of Loctite 515, or equivalent to each side of rear main bearing cap. **Do not allow sealant to contact rubber seal. Install bearing cap on block immediately after sealant application.**
6. Align bearing cap using cap slot, alignment dowel and cap bolts. **Do not remove excess material after assembly or strike rear cap more**

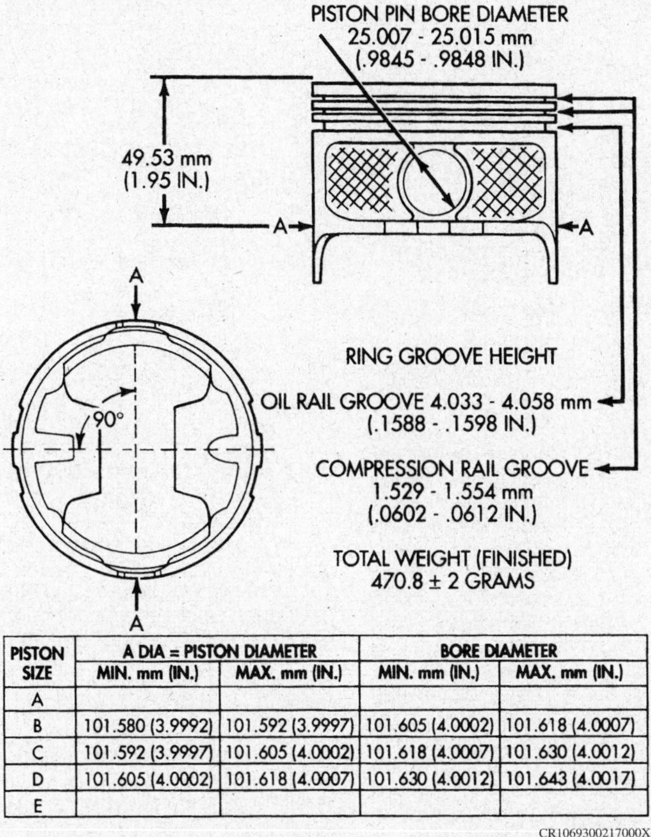

PISTON SIZE	A DIA = PISTON DIAMETER		BORE DIAMETER	
	MIN. mm (IN.)	MAX. mm (IN.)	MIN. mm (IN.)	MAX. mm (IN.)
A				
B	101.580 (3.9992)	101.592 (3.9997)	101.605 (4.0002)	101.618 (4.0007)
C	101.592 (3.9997)	101.605 (4.0002)	101.618 (4.0007)	101.630 (4.0012)
D	101.605 (4.0002)	101.618 (4.0007)	101.630 (4.0012)	101.643 (4.0017)
E				

Fig. 19 Piston measurements. 5.9L & 8.0L engines

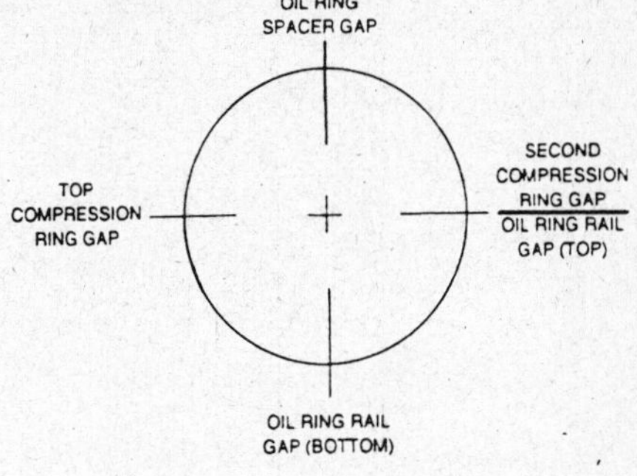

Fig. 20 Ring gap locations. 3.9L, 5.2L & 5.9L engines

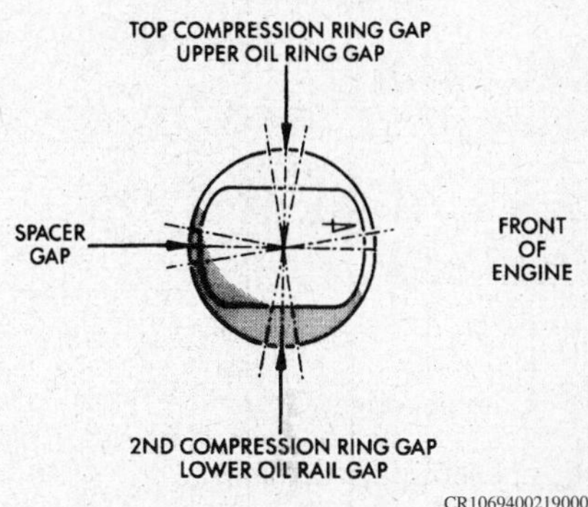

Fig. 21 Ring gap locations. 8.0L engine

than twice when aligning.

7. Install rear main bearing cap and alternately tighten bolts, including bolts loosened to facilitate seal installation, to specifications.
8. Install oil pump, then apply suitable silicone rubber adhesive sealant to joint between bearing cap and block to provide cap to block and oil pan sealing.
9. Install oil pan immediately after sealant application. Refer to "Oil Pan, Replace" for procedure.

LOWER SEAL

1. Remove oil pan as outlined in "Oil Pan, Replace," then the oil pump and rear main bearing cap. Discard old lower seal.
2. Clean rear main cap mating surfaces and oil pan seal grooves, then install new upper seal as outlined in this section.
3. Apply a thin film of oil to new lower seal lips, then install seal in bearing cap with yellow paint facing rear of engine.
4. Apply a ⅕ inch drop of Loctite 515, or equivalent to each side of rear main bearing cap. **Do not allow sealant to contact rubber seal. Install bearing cap on block immediately after sealant application.**
5. Align bearing cap using cap slot, alignment dowel and cap bolts. **Do not remove excess material after assembly or strike rear cap more than twice when aligning.**
6. Install rear main bearing cap and alternately tighten bolts to specifications.
7. Install oil pump, then apply suitable silicone rubber adhesive sealant to joint between bearing cap and block to provide cap to block and oil pan sealing.
8. Install oil pan immediately after sealant application. Refer to "Oil Pan, Replace" for procedure.

8.0L Engine

1. Remove transmission as outlined in **MOTOR's "Domestic Transmission, In-Vehicle Service" or "Transmission Service DVD"** then the flywheel and clutch or torque converter and driveplate assemblies.
2. Remove oil pan as outlined in "Oil Pan, Replace," then the rear seal retainer, **Fig. 22.**
3. Remove and discard old seal and gasket.
4. Reverse procedure to install, noting the following:
   a. Tighten seal retainer bolts to specifications.
   b. Apply a small amount of suitable silicone rubber adhesive sealant at seal split line.

OIL PAN

REPLACE

1. **On models equipped with 3.9L, 5.2L and 5.9L engines,** remove engine oil dipstick.
2. **On all models,** raise and support vehicle.
3. Drain engine oil, then remove exhaust crossover pipe and left engine to transmission strut.
4. Remove oil pan attaching screws, oil pan and gasket(s). **It may be required to loosen right engine support bracket cushion through bolt and raise engine slightly for clearance.**
5. **On models equipped with 8.0L engine,** remove oil pickup tube assembly and discard gasket.
6. **On all models,** reverse procedure to install, noting the following:
   a. Clean oil pan in solvent and inspect condition of oil screen.
   b. **On models equipped with 3.9L, 5.2L and 5.9L engines,** apply a small amount of suitable sealant to corner of cap and block and install new one-piece gasket.
   c. **On models equipped with 8.0L engines,** apply a small amount of suitable sealant at split lines between cylinder block, front cover and crankshaft rear seal assembly.
   d. **On all models,** oil pan and must be installed within three minutes of sealant application.
   e. Install new one-piece gasket.
   f. Tighten oil pan bolts to specifications.

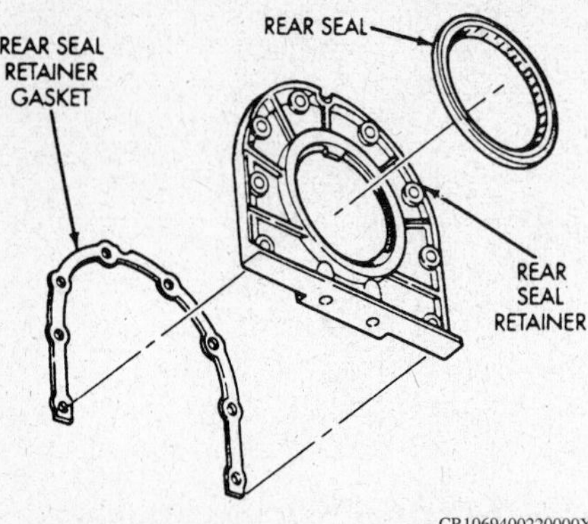

Fig. 22 Crankshaft rear seal & retainer. 8.0L engine

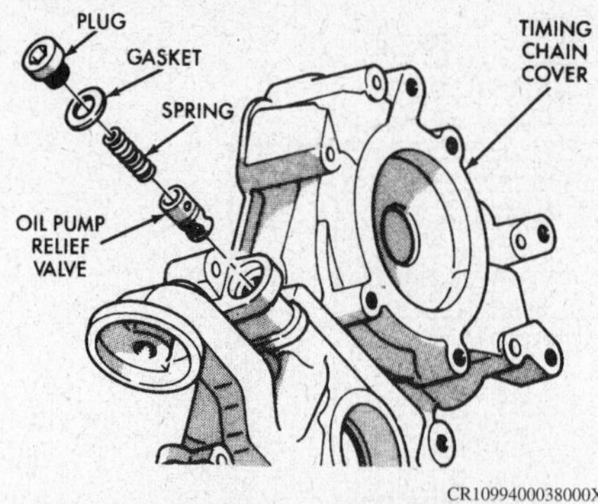

Fig. 23 Oil pressure relief valve assembly. 8.0L engine

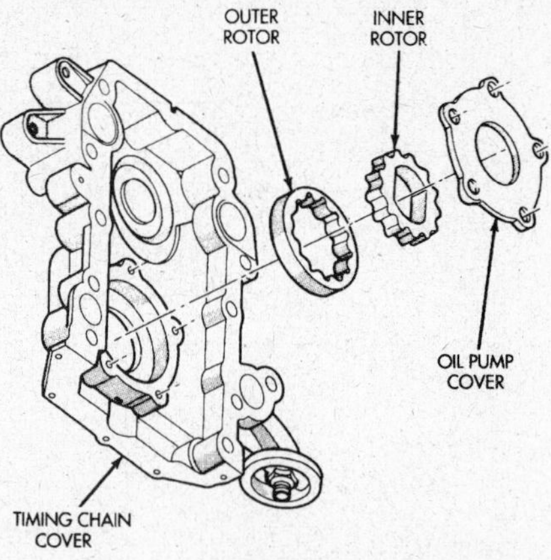

Fig. 24 Oil pump assembly. 8.0L engine

OIL PUMP

REPLACE

3.9L, 5.2L & 5.9L Engines

1. Remove oil pan as outlined in "Oil Pan, Replace," then the oil pump from rear main bearing cap.
2. Reverse procedure to install. Tighten bolts to specifications.

8.0L Engine

1. Remove front cover as outlined in "Front Cover, Replace," then the oil pressure relief valve plug, gasket, spring and valve, **Fig. 23.** Discard gasket.
2. Remove oil pump cover and rotors, **Fig. 24.**
3. Reverse procedure to install, noting the following:
   a. Lubricate pump rotors in clean engine oil. Replace if worn or damaged.
   b. Tighten oil pump cover bolts and relief valve plug to specifications.

OIL PUMP SERVICE

3.9L, 5.2L & 5.9L Engines

Service of oil pump requires pump to be removed. With pump removed, disassemble pressure relief valve by pulling out cotter pins and drilling a 1/8 inch hole into center of relief valve retainer cap, **Fig. 25.** Insert a self-threading sheet metal screw into cap and secure head in vise. While supporting pump body, remove cap by tapping body with soft hammer. Discard retainer cap and remove spring and relief valve. Relief valve spring has a free length of 1.95 inches and should test between 19.5–20.5 lbs. when compressed to 1 11/32 inches. Replace spring that fails to meet specifications. Unbolt oil pump cover and discard oil seal ring. Inner rotor and shaft can now be removed as well as outer rotor. Clean all components thoroughly and inspect for damage or wear. If mating surface of oil pump cover is scratched or grooved, replace pump assembly. Lay a straightedge across pump cover surface. If a .0015 inch feeler gauge can be inserted between cover and straightedge, replace pump assembly, **Fig. 26.** If outer rotor thickness measures .825 inch or less, or the diameter is 2.469 inches or less, replace the outer rotor, **Fig. 27.** If inner rotor measures .825 inch or less, replace inner rotor and shaft assembly, **Fig. 28.** With outer rotor inserted into pump body, press rotor to one side with fingers. If clearance between rotor and pump body is .014 inch or more, replace oil pump assembly, **Fig. 29.** With inner rotor inserted into pump body, place a straightedge across face between bolt holes. If a feeler gauge of .004 inch can be inserted between rotors and straightedge, replace oil pump assembly, **Fig. 30.** Shaft and both rotors should be replaced if tip clearance between inner and outer rotor exceeds .008 inch on 3.9L engine and .010 inch on 5.2L and 5.9L engines, **Fig. 31.** Using new components as required, assemble pump. Prime pump before installation by filling rotor cavity with engine oil. Rotate engine until No. 1 cylinder is at TDC and timing mark on damper is at zero. Coat distributor drive gear and shaft with oil, install shaft so that after gear spirals into place is will index with oil pump shaft. The slot on top of the drive gear should be aligned towards left front intake manifold attaching bolt hole, **Fig. 32.**

8.0L Engine

Refer to **Fig. 24** throughout the following procedure.

1. Lay a straightedge across oil pump cover surface. If a .003 inch feeler gauge blade can be inserted between straightedge and cover, or if surface is scratched or grooved, replace cover.
2. Measure thickness and diameter of both rotors. If thickness of either rotor is .5876 inch or less, or if diameter is 3.246 inches or less, replace rotor set.
3. Slide outer rotor into timing chain cover pump body, then press rotor to one side and measure clearance between rotor and body. If clearance is .007 inch or more, replace timing chain cover.
4. Install inner rotor in timing chain cover pump body with chamfer up. If distance between rotors is .006 inch or more, replace rotor set.
5. Place a straightedge across face of timing chain cover pump body, between bolt holes. If a .003 inch feeler gauge blade can be inserted between rotors and straightedge, and rotors are within specifications, replace timing chain cover.
6. Inspect oil pressure relief valve plunger for scoring. Remove small marks with 400 grit wet/dry sandpaper, then ensure plunger operates freely in bore.
7. Ensure relief valve spring free length is approximately 1.95 inches, then compress to 1 11/32 inches. Spring should exert between 22.5–24.5 lbs. force. Replace spring if not within specifications.

BELT TENSION DATA

A new belt run for 15 minutes is considered a used belt. These engines are equipped with automatic belt tensioners, no adjustment is required.

SERPENTINE DRIVE BELT

Belt Routing

Refer to **Figs. 33 through 35** for serpentine drive belt routing.

Belt Tensioner Replacement

3.9L, 5.2L & 5.9L LD ENGINES

The automatic tensioner is equipped with an indexing arrow on the back of the tensioner housing. If a new belt is being installed, the arrow must be within approximately 1/8 inch of the point B indexing mark. If an old belt is being used, it must not pass the point marked A, **Fig. 36.**

1. Attach a suitable wrench to mounting bolt of automatic tensioner pulley bolt, **Fig. 37.**
2. Remove drive belt as outlined in "Belt Replacement."

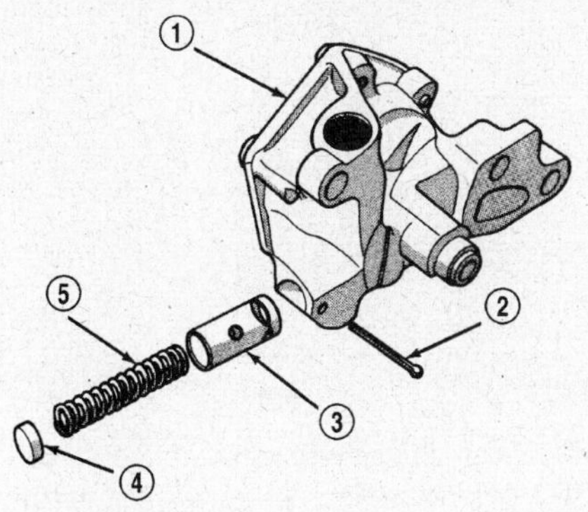

Fig. 25 Oil pressure relief valve. 3.9L, 5.2L & 5.9L engines

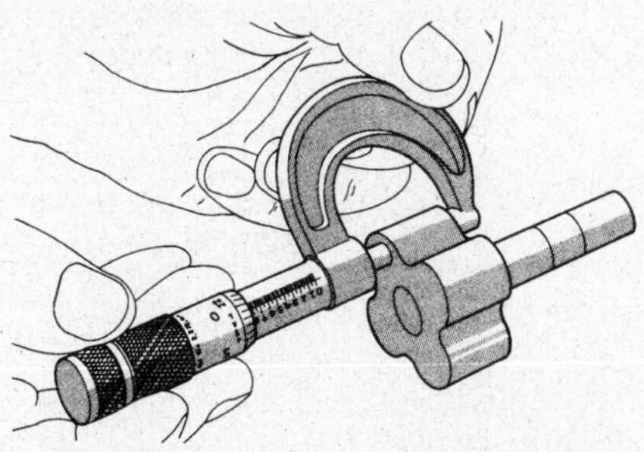

Fig. 28 Inner rotor thickness measurement. 3.9L, 5.2L & 5.9L engines

3. Disconnect wiring and secondary cable from ignition coil.
4. Remove ignition coil from mounting bracket.
5. Remove tensioner assembly from mounting bracket.
6. Remove pulley bolt and remove pulley from tensioner.
7. Reverse procedure to install, aligning indexing tab located on back of tensioner to slot in mounting bracket, **Fig. 36.**

5.9L HD & 8.0L ENGINES

1. Remove drive belt as outlined in "Belt Replacement."
2. Remove tensioner mounting bolt, **Fig. 38,** then tensioner. **Because of high spring tension to not attempt to disassemble automatic tensioner, unit is serviced as an assembly.**
3. Reverse procedure to install, aligning dowel pin on back of tensioner to hole in tensioner in bracket, **Figs. 39 and 40.**

Belt Replacement

3.9L, 5.2L & 5.9L LD ENGINES

1. Attach a suitable wrench to pulley mounting bolt of automatic tensioner, **Fig. 37.**
2. Rotate tensioner assembly clockwise until tension has been relieved.
3. Remove belt from vehicle.
4. Position new drive belt over all pulleys except idler pulley.
5. Attach a suitable wrench to pulley mounting bolt of automatic tensioner.
6. Rotate wrench clockwise, place belt over idler pulley then allow tensioner to rotate back into place. **Ensure belt is properly seated on all pulleys.**
7. Inspect belt indexing marks as outlined in "Belt Tensioner Replacement."

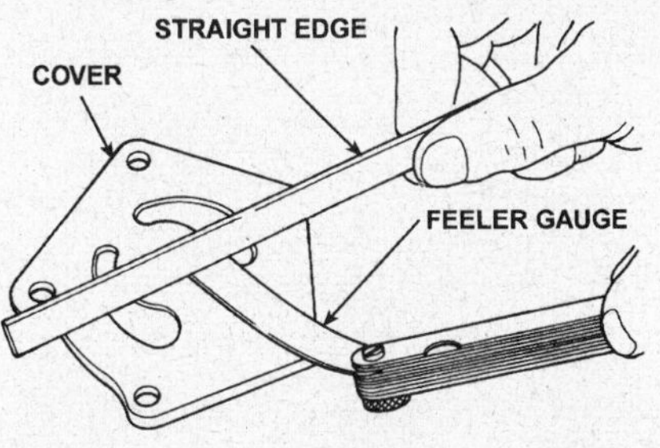

Fig. 26 Oil pump cover flatness inspection. 3.9L, 5.2L & 5.9L engines

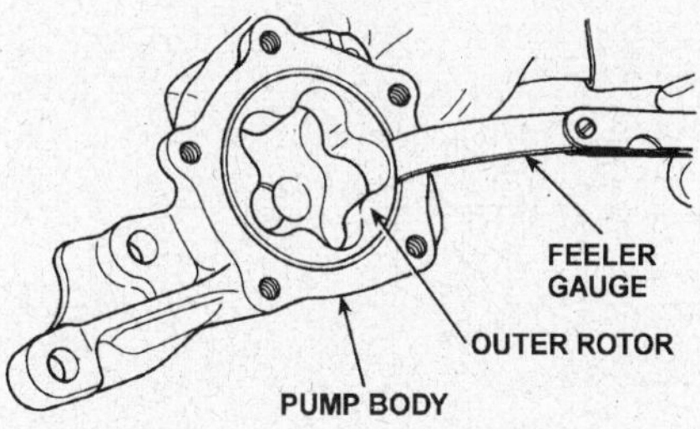

Fig. 29 Outer rotor clearance in pump body measurement. 3.9L, 5.2L & 5.9L engines

5.9L HD & 8.0L ENGINES

1. Attach a wrench to pulley mounting bolt of automatic tensioner. Threads on this bolt are lefthand.
2. Release tension from belt by rotating tensioner counterclockwise. When all belt tension has been released remove belt from tensioner first, then other pulleys.
3. Position new drive belt on all pulleys except tensioner pulley.
4. Attach a wrench to pulley bolt of tensioner, then rotate wrench counterclockwise.
5. Place belt over tensioner pulley, let tension rotate back into place, then ensure belt is properly seated on all pulleys.

COOLING SYSTEM BLEED

These engines do not require a specified bleed procedure. After filling cooling system, run engine to operating temperature with radiator/pressure cap off. Air will then be automatically bled through cap opening.

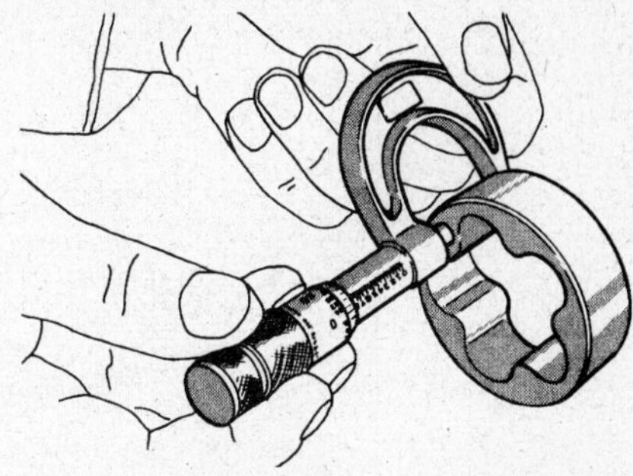

Fig. 27 Outer rotor thickness measurement. 3.9L, 5.2L & 5.9L engines

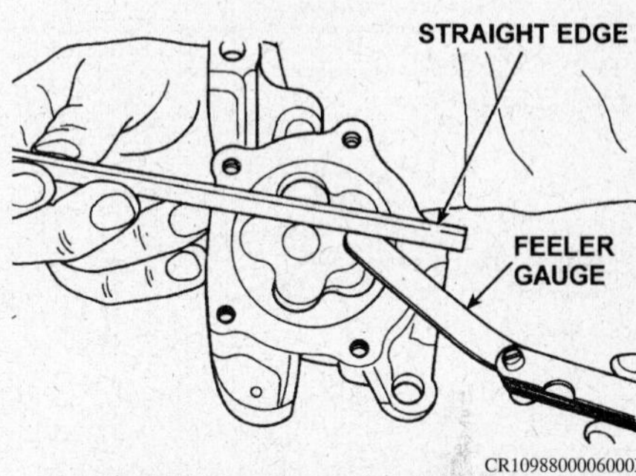

Fig. 30 Clearance over rotor measurement. 3.9L, 5.2L & 5.9L engines

THERMOSTAT

REPLACE

3.9L, 5.2L & 5.9L Engines

1. Drain cooling system into suitable container until coolant level is below thermostat level.
2. **On models equipped with A/C,** proceed as follows:
   a. Remove support bracket rod located at rear of alternator.
   b. Remove drive belt.
   c. Remove two alternator mounting bolts. Do not remove any wiring at alternator.
   d. Unplug 4WD indicator lamp wiring located near rear of alternator.
   e. Remove alternator and position to gain access to thermostat.
3. **On all models,** remove upper radiator hose clamp, then the hose at thermostat housing.
4. A number letter is stamped into tongue of constant tension clamps. If replacement is required, replace only with original equipment clamp of same number or letter.
5. Remove thermostat housing mounting bolts, then the thermostat and gasket.
6. Reverse procedure to install, noting the following:
   a. Install thermostat spring side down

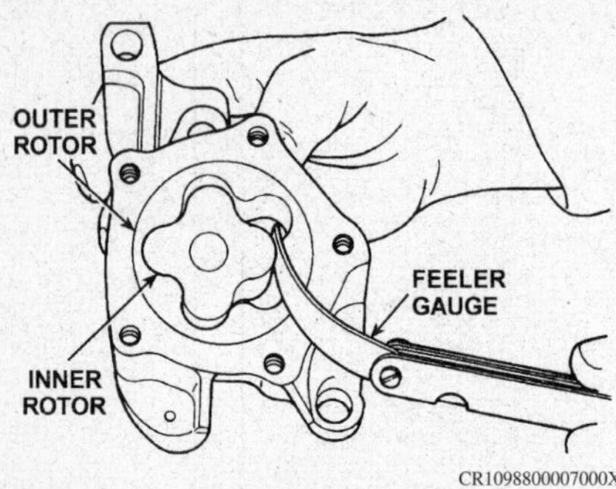

Fig. 31 Clearance measurement between rotors. 3.9L, 5.2L & 5.9L engines

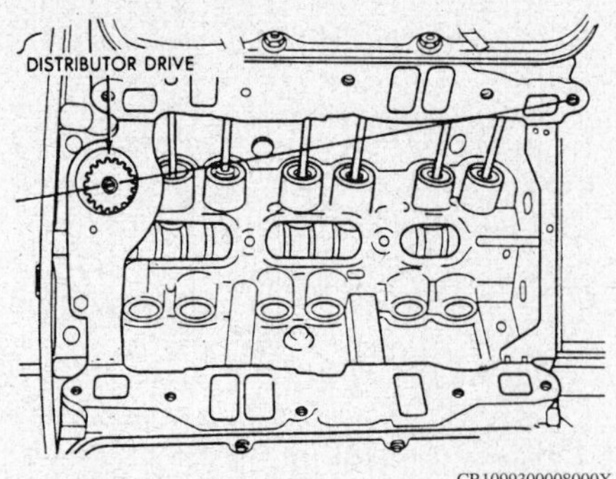

Fig. 32 Distributor drive gear position. 3.9L, 5.2L & 5.9L engines

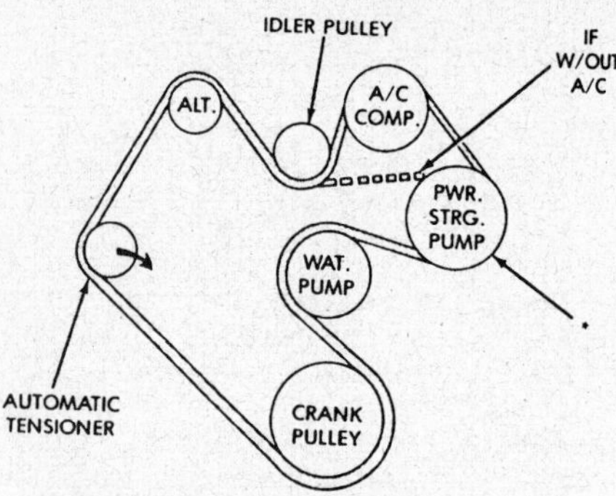

Fig. 33 Serpentine drive belt routing. 3.9L, 5.2L & 5.9L LD engines

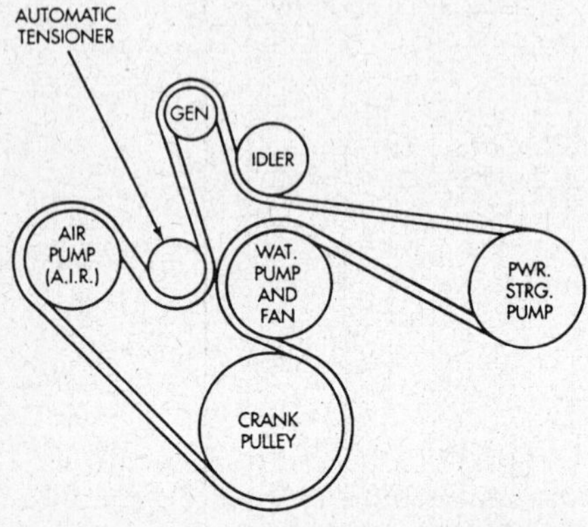

Fig. 34 Serpentine drive belt routing. 5.9L HD & 8.0L engines less A/C

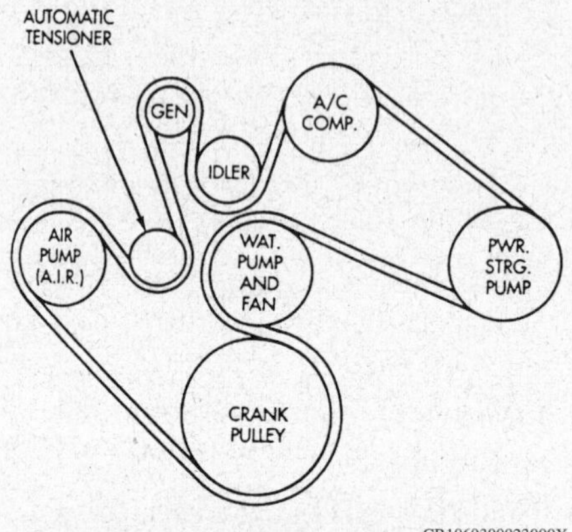

Fig. 35 Serpentine drive belt routing. 5.9L HD & 8.0L engines with A/C

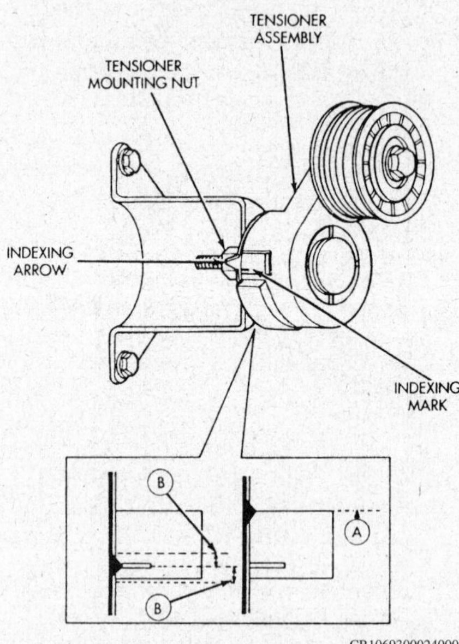

Fig. 36 Automatic belt tensioner assembly. 3.9L, 5.2L & 5.9L LD engines

into recessed machined groove on intake manifold.

b. Install gasket, then position thermostat housing so word "Front" stamped on housing is facing front of vehicle.
c. Install thermostat housing bolts tightening to specifications.
d. Tighten alternator mounting bolts to specifications.

8.0L Engine

1. Drain cooling system until coolant level is below thermostat.
2. Remove intake manifold to alternator support rod, upper radiator hose clamp and upper radiator hose.
3. Disconnect electrical connectors on thermostat housing, then remove six bolts, housing and gasket. Discard gasket.
4. Reverse procedure to install, noting the following:
   a. If rubber thermostat seal requires replacement, coat metal portion of new seal with suitable gasket maker.
   b. Tighten thermostat housing bolts to specifications.

WATER PUMP

REPLACE

When it becomes required to remove a fan clutch of the silicone type, the assembly must be supported in the vertical position to prevent leaks of silicone fluid from the clutch mechanism. This loss of fluid will render the fan clutch inoperative.

1. Drain cooling system and remove windshield washer reservoir from fan shroud.
2. **On models equipped with 3.9L, 5.2L and 5.9L engines,** disconnect coolant reserve/overflow tank to radiator hose at tank.
3. **On all models,** remove fan shroud mounting bolts and upper radiator hose from radiator, then the fan/fan drive assembly from water pump by rotating mounting nut counterclockwise (as viewed from front).
4. **If water pump is being replaced, do not unbolt fan blade assembly from thermal control fan drive.**
5. Remove fan/fan drive and shroud as an assembly, then the serpentine drive belt as outlined in "Belt Replacement" in "Serpentine Drive Belt."
6. Remove water pump pulley and all hoses from pump.
7. **On models equipped with 3.9L, 5.2L and 5.9L engines,** remove heater hose coolant return tube from water pump and discard O-ring.
8. **On all models,** remove water pump bolts, then loosen clamp at pump end of bypass hose and slip hose off water pump while removing pump from vehicle. **Do not remove bypass hose clamp.**
9. Discard water pump gasket.
10. **On models equipped with 8.0L engine,** if water pump is being replaced, remove heater hose fitting from pump body. **Note position for installation reference.**
11. **On all models,** reverse procedure to install. Tighten all bolts to specifications.

RADIATOR

REPLACE

Pickup

1. Drain cooling system into suitable container.
2. Remove hose clamps and hoses from radiator.
3. Remove coolant reserve/overflow tank hose from radiator filler neck nipple.
4. Remove coolant reserve/overflow tank from fan shroud by pulling straight up.

5. Disconnect electrical connectors at windshield washer reservoir tank and remove tank.
6. Remove fan shroud mounting bolts, position shroud rearward over fan blades.
7. Remove plastic clips retaining rubber shields to sides of radiator, position rubber shields to side.
8. Remove two upper radiator mounting bolts, then lift radiator straight up and out of vehicle.
9. Reverse procedure to install.

Van

1. Raise and support vehicle.
2. Drain cooling system into suitable container.
3. Remove radiator lower hose from radiator outlet.
4. Disconnect transmission cooler lines from radiator fittings using quick disconnect tool No. 6935, or equivalent.
5. Cap all lines and fittings to prevent system contamination.
6. Lower vehicle.
7. Remove engine oil filler tube.
8. Remove radiator upper support to cowl brackets.
9. Remove coolant reserve/overflow tank hose from radiator filler neck fitting.
10. Remove windshield washer bottle and coolant recovery bottle.
11. Disconnect upper radiator hose from radiator outlet.
12. Remove fan shroud mounting bolts and position shroud rearward on engine.
13. Remove radiator mounting bolts, then lift radiator up and out of engine compartment.
14. Reverse procedure to install.

FUEL PUMP

REPLACE

The fuel pump is contained within the fuel pump module and is not independently serviceable. If pump requires service, replace module.

1. Relieve fuel system pressure as outlined in "Fuel System Pressure Relief" in "Precautions."
2. Drain fuel tank into suitable container.
3. Remove fuel tank assembly.
4. Clean area around pump module to prevent fuel tank contamination.
5. Install spanner wrench No. 6856, or equivalent, onto fuel pump module locknut.
6. Remove locknut, then the fuel pump module.

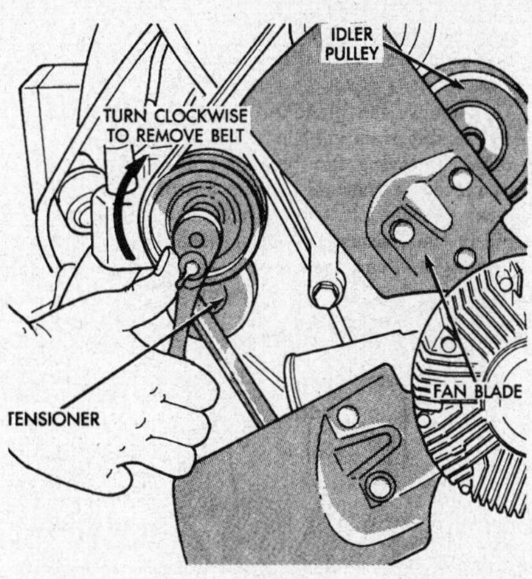

Fig. 37 Automatic belt tensioner replacement. 3.9L, 5.2L & 5.9L LD engines

7. Reverse procedure to install, noting the following:
   a. Replace fuel pump module gasket.
   b. Apply a small amount of oil to module locknut threads.
   c. Install module assembly and rotate until index arrow on module aligns with index marks on fuel tank.
   d. Tighten module locknut to specifications using spanner wrench.
   e. Carefully rotate fuel filter/fuel pressure regulator until pointed toward drivers side of vehicle.

FUEL FILTER

REPLACE

Gasoline Engine

FUEL FILTER/FUEL PRESSURE REGULATOR

1. Relieve fuel system pressure as outlined in "Fuel System Pressure Relief" in "Precautions."
2. Drain fuel tank into suitable container.
3. Remove fuel tank assembly.
4. Clean area around filter/regulator.
5. Fuel filter/regulator is pressed into a rubber grommet. Remove by twisting and pulling straight up.
6. Do not pull filter/regulator more than three inches from fuel pump module or damage to coiled fuel tube line may result.
7. Gently cut old fuel line clamp taking care not to damage plastic fuel tube. Remove and discard old fuel clamp.
8. Remove plastic fuel tube from filter regulator by gently pulling downward.
9. Remove filter/regulator from fuel pump module.
10. Reverse procedure to install, noting the following:
    a. Install new clamp over plastic fuel tube.
    b. Install filter/regulator to fuel tube, rotate in fuel tube until regulator is pointed toward left side of vehicle.
    c. Tighten clamp to fuel line using clamp tool No. C-4124, or equivalent. Do not use conventional side cutters to tighten clamp.
    d. Install regulator, rotate until pointed toward drivers side of vehicle.

FUEL PUMP INLET FILTER

The Fuel pump inlet filter is located on the bottom of the fuel pump module.

1. Remove fuel pump module as outlined in "Fuel Pump, Replace."
2. Remove filter (strainer) by carefully prying 2 lock tabs at bottom of module with 2 screwdrivers. Filter is snapped to module.
3. Clean bottom of fuel pump module.
4. Reverse procedure to install.

CNG Engine

1. Purge fuel system as outlined in "Precautions."
2. Raise and support vehicle, then remove rubber shield from around pressure regulator.
3. Clean area around fittings and fuel tubes at fuel pressure regulator and manual shutoff valve.
4. Remove manual shutoff valve mounting bracket, then disconnect fuel tube from manual shutoff valve.
5. Disconnect fuel tube at fuel pressure regulator, **Fig. 41. Fitting will be under a small spring pressure.**
6. Remove filter retention spring, filter and O-ring.
7. Reverse procedure to install, noting the following:
   a. Apply suitable sealant to pipe threads of tube fitting. **Apply sealant to pipe threads only, do not allow sealant to enter any fuel system opening.**
   b. After repairs have been completed and all fuel system components are in place, use a suitable Go-No-Go inspection tool to inspect fuel system high pressure fittings.
   c. **Torque** manual shutoff valve mounting bracket bolts to 96 inch lbs.

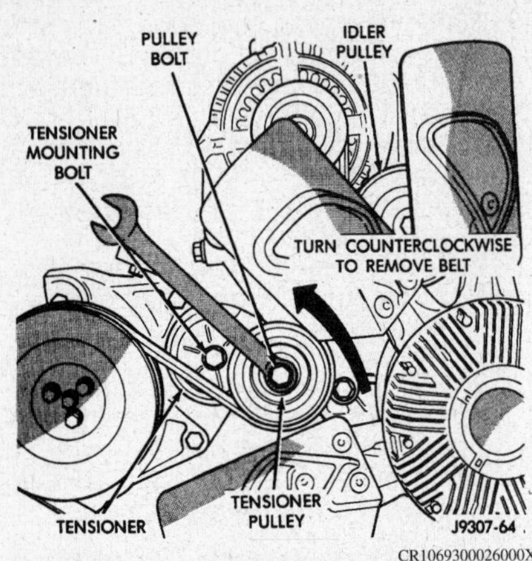

Fig. 38 Automatic belt tensioner replacement. 5.9L HD & 8.0L engines

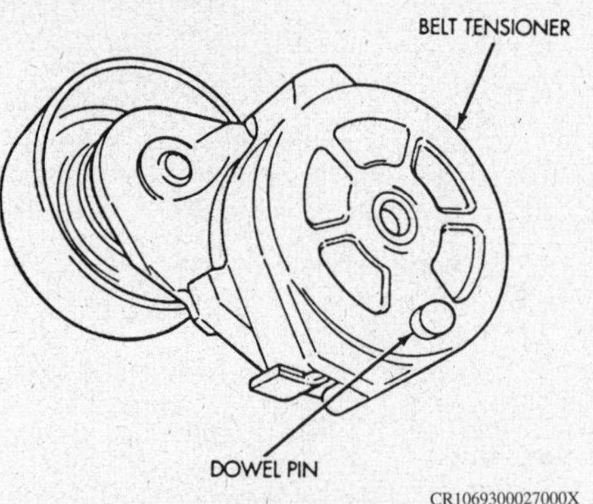

Fig. 39 Automatic belt tensioner dowel pin. 5.9L HD & 8.0L engines

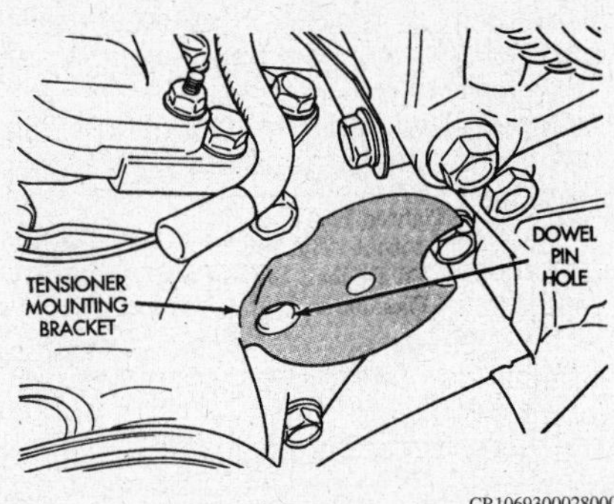

Fig. 40 Automatic belt tensioner mounting bracket dowel hole. 5.9L HD & 8.0L engines

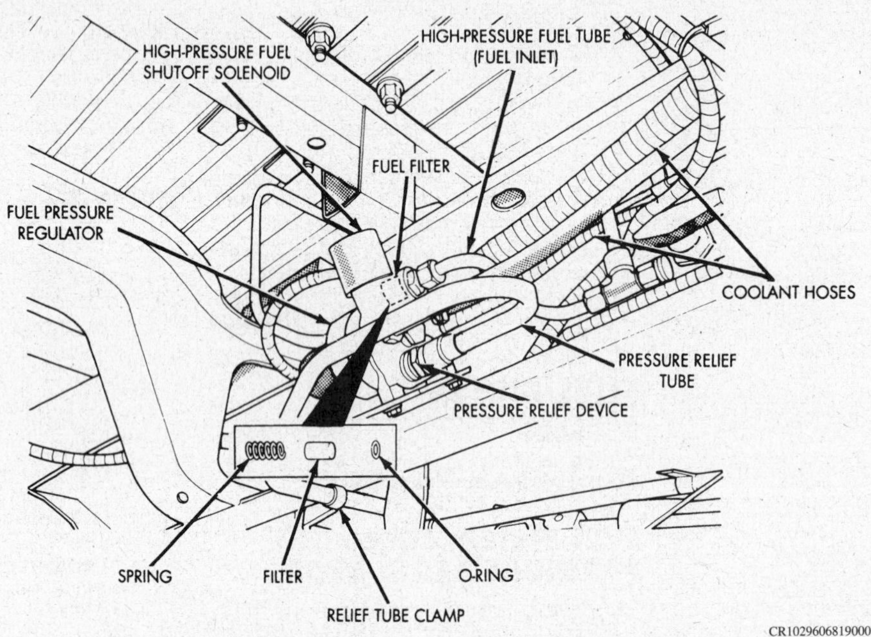

Fig. 41 Fuel filter removal. CNG engine

TIGHTENING SPECIFICATIONS

Year	Component	Torque Ft. Lbs.
3.9L ENGINE		
2002–03	A/C Compressor Bracket To Water Pump Bolt	20
	A/C Compressor Support Bolts	30
	A/C Compressor To Bracket Bolt	20
	Alternator Adjusting Strap Bolt	17
	Alternator Adjusting Strap Mounting Bolt	30
	Alternator Bracket Bolt	30
	Alternator Mounting Pivot Nut	30
	Bracket/Cushion To Block Bolts	60
	Bracket/Cushion To Block Through Bolts	75
	Camshaft Lockbolt	50
	Camshaft Thrust Plate Bolts	17.5
	Catalytic Converter To Manifold Bolts/Nuts	25
	Clutch Housing Bolts	①
	Connecting Rod Nuts	45
	Crankshaft Vibration Damper Bolt	135
	Cylinder Head Bolts	②
	Cylinder Head Cover Bolts	96③
	Distributor Clamp Bolt	17
	Engine Mount Nuts	75
	Exhaust Manifold	25
	Exhaust Pipe Flange Nuts	19
	Fan Blade Attaching Bolts	17
	Fan Shroud	⑤
	Flexplate To Converter Bolts	22.5
	Flexplate To Crankshaft Bolts	55
	Flywheel To Crankshaft Bolts	55
	Front Cover Bolts	30
	Fuel Pump Module Locknut	40
	Intake Manifold Bolts	④
	Main Bearing Cap Bolts	85
	Oil Drain Plug	25
	Oil Filter Attaching Stud	50
	Oil Pan Bolts	17
	Oil Pressure Gauge Sending Unit	17
	Oil Pump Attaching Bolts	30
	Oil Pump Cover Bolts	96③
	Radiator Hose Clamps	⑦
	Radiator Mounting Bolts	96③
	Rear Support Bracket Front Bolts	50
	Rear Support Bracket Rear Bolt	17
	Rear Support Bracket Through Bolt	30
	Rocker Arm Bolts	21
	Rocker Shaft Bracket Bolt	17
	Spark Plugs	30
	Starter Mounting Bolts	50
	Temperature Gauge Sending Unit	60③
	Thermostat Housing Mounting Bolts	19
	Throttle Body Bolts	17
	Water Pump Pulley Bolts	16
	Water Pump To Housing Bolts	30

TIGHTENING SPECIFICATIONS—Continued

Year	Component	Torque Ft. Lbs.
5.2L & 5.9L ENGINES		
2002–03	A/C Compressor Bracket To Water Pump Bolt	20
	A/C Compressor Support Bolts	30
	A/C Compressor To Bracket Bolt	20
	Alternator Adjusting Strap Bolt	17
	Alternator Adjusting Strap Mounting Bolt	30
	Alternator Bracket Bolt	30
	Alternator Mounting Pivot Nut	30
	Bracket/Cushion To Block Bolts	60
	Bracket/Cushion To Block Through Bolts	50
	Camshaft Lockbolt	50
	Camshaft Thrust Plate Bolts	17.5
	Catalytic Converter To Manifold Bolts/Nuts	25
	Clutch Housing Bolts	①
	Connecting Rod Nuts	45
	Crankshaft Vibration Damper Bolt	135
	Cylinder Head Bolts	②
	Cylinder Head Cover Bolts	18
	Distributor Clamp Bolt	17
	Engine Mount Nuts	75
	Exhaust Manifold Bolts	25
	Exhaust Pipe Flange Nuts	19
	Fan Blade Attaching Bolts	17
	Fan Shroud	⑤
	Flexplate To Converter Bolts	22.5
	Flexplate To Crankshaft Bolts	55
	Flywheel To Crankshaft Bolts	55
	Front Cover Bolts	30
	Fuel Pump Module Locknut	40
	Main Bearing Cap Bolts	85
	Oil Drain Plug	25
	Oil Filter Attaching Stud	50
	Oil Pan Bolts	17
	Oil Pressure Gauge Sending Unit	17
	Oil Pump Attaching Bolts	30
	Oil Pump Cover Bolts	96③
	Radiator Hose Clamps	⑦
	Radiator Mounting Bolts	96③
	Rear Mount Bracket Through Bolt	50
	Rear Mount Bracket U-Shaped Bolts	30
	Rocker Arm Bolts	21
	Rocker Shaft Bracket Bolt	17
	Spark Plugs	30
	Starter Mounting Bolts	50
	Temperature Gauge Sending Unit	60③
	Thermostat Housing Mounting Bolts	17
	Throttle Body Bolts	17
	Water Pump To Housing Bolts	30

Continued

TIGHTENING SPECIFICATIONS—Continued

Year	Component	Torque Ft. Lbs.
8.0L ENGINE		
2002–03	A/C Compressor Brace Bolts	20
	Air Cleaner Housing	96③
	Alternator Brace Bolts	30
	Alternator Mounting Bolt	30
	Bracket/Cushion To Block Bolts	60
	Bracket/Cushion To Block Through Bolts	50
	Camshaft Sprocket Bolt	55
	Camshaft Thrust Plate Bolts	16
	Catalytic Converter To Manifold Bolts/Nuts	25
	Coil Pack Bracket Bolts	16
	Crankshaft Pulley/Damper Bolt	135
	Crankshaft Rear Seal Retainer Bolts	16
	Cylinder Head Bolts	②
	Cylinder Head Cover Bolts & Studs	12
	Driveplate To Crankshaft Bolts	55
	Driveplate To Torque Converter Bolts	55
	EGR Nuts	14.5
	EGR Tube Nut	25
	Engine Mount Nuts	75
	Exhaust Manifold Bolts	16
	Fan Shroud	⑤
	Flywheel To Crankshaft Bolts	55
	Front Cover Bolts	35
	Fuel Pump Module Locknut	40
	Hydraulic Valve Lifter Yoke Retainer Bolts	16
	Intake Manifold Bolts	④

TIGHTENING SPECIFICATIONS—Continued

Year	Component	Torque Ft. Lbs.
8.0L ENGINE		
2002–03	Main Bearing Caps	⑥
	Oil Drain Plug	25
	Oil Filter	78③⑧
	Oil Filter Connector	34
	Oil Pan Bolts (1/4 inch)	96③
	Oil Pan Bolts (5/16 inch) & Studs	12
	Oil Pan Pick-Up Tube Bolts	12
	Oil Pump Attaching Bolts	30
	Oil Pump Cover Bolts	11
	Oil Pump Pressure Relief Plug	15
	Radiator Hose Clamps	⑦
	Radiator Mounting Bolts	96③
	Rocker Arm Bolts	27
	Spark Plugs	30
	Starter Mounting Bolts	50
	Thermostat Housing Bolts	18.5
	Throttle Body Bolts	16.5
	Torque Converter Driveplate Bolts	23
	Water Pump Bolts	30
	Water Pump Pulley Bolts	16

①— 3/8 inch bolt, 30 ft. lbs.; 7/16 inch bolt, 50 ft. lbs.
②— Refer to "Cylinder Head, Replace" procedure.
③— Inch lbs.
④— Refer to "Intake Manifold, Replace" procedure.
⑤— Pickup models, 50 inch lbs.; Van models, 96 inch lbs.
⑥— Step 1, 20 ft. lbs.; step 2, 85 ft. lbs.
⑦— Pickup models, 35 inch lbs.; Van models, 15 inch lbs.
⑧— Plus an additional 1/8 turn.

4.7L Engine

NOTE: Air Bag Equipped Models, Refer To "Air Bag System Precautions" Located In The Front Of This Manual For System Disarming & Arming Procedures.

NOTE: Refer To "Computer Relearn Procedures" Located In The Front Of This Manual When Battery Power To The Computer Has Been Interrupted.

NOTE: Refer To "4.7L Engine" In The "Grand Cherokee" Chapter For Procedures Not Covered In This Section.

INDEX

PRECAUTIONS

Air Bag Systems

Refer to "Air Bag System Precautions" in the front of this manual for system disarming and arming procedures.

Battery Ground Cable

Prior to service, disconnect battery ground cable and isolate as required.

Fuel System Pressure Relief

1. Remove fuel cap, then fuel pump relay from PDC.
2. Start and run engine until it stalls.
3. Attempt to restart engine until it will no longer run.
4. Turn ignition key to Off position.
5. Unplug connector from any injector.
6. Attach one end of a suitable 18 gauge or smaller jumper wire to either injector terminal.
7. Connect other end of jumper wire to positive battery terminal.
8. Connect one end of a second jumper wire to remaining injector terminal.
9. Momentarily touch other end of second jumper wire to negative battery terminal for no more than a few seconds. **Powering an injector for more than a few seconds will damage injector.**
10. Place a suitable rag below fuel line quick connect fitting on fuel rail, then disconnect quick connect fitting.

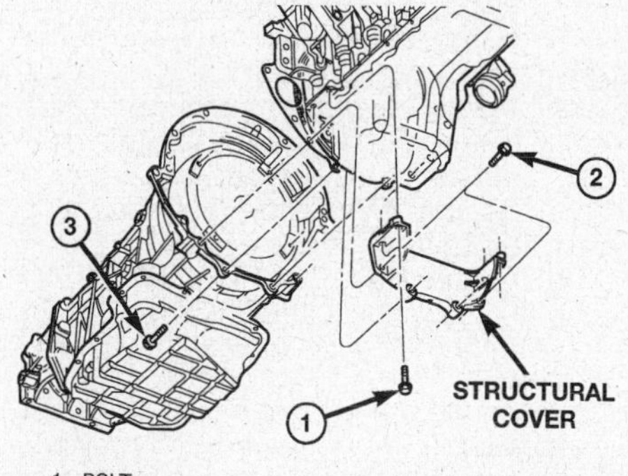

Fig. 1 Structural cover tightening sequence

11. Install fuel pump relay to PDC, then clear any stored DTCs.

COMPRESSION PRESSURES

Correct compression pressure for this engine is 120–150 psi; maximum variation between cylinders is 25%.

ENGINE MOUNT

REPLACE

Refer to "3.7L Engine" section for engine mount replacement procedure.

ENGINE

REPLACE

1. Remove battery, then battery tray.
2. Raise and support vehicle.
3. Remove exhaust crossover pipe from exhaust manifolds.
4. **On models equipped with 4WD,** disconnect axle vent tube from left side of engine mount.
5. **On all models,** remove through bolt retaining nut and bolt from both left and right side engine mounts.
6. **On models equipped with 4WD,** remove locknut from left and right side engine mount brackets.
7. **On all models,** disconnect two ground straps from lower lefthand side and one ground strap from lower righthand side of engine.
8. Disconnect CKP sensor electrical connector.
9. **On models equipped with 4WD and automatic transmission,** remove axle isolator bracket from engine, transmission and axle.
10. **On all models,** remove structural cover.
11. Remove starter motor as outlined under "Starter, Replace" in "Electrical" section.
12. Drain engine cooling system into suitable container.
13. **On models equipped with automatic transmission,** remove torque converter bolts.
14. **On all models,** remove transmission to engine mounting bolts.
15. Disconnect engine block heater power cable from block heater.

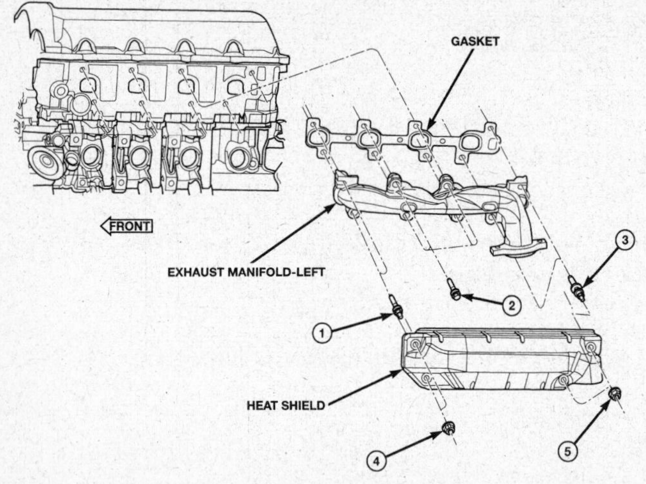

ITEM	DESCRIPTION	TORQUE	ITEM	DESCRIPTION	TORQUE
1	Stud (Qty 2)		4	Nut (Qty 2)	8 N·m (72 in. lbs.), then loosen 45 degrees
2	Bolt (Qty 4)	25 N·m (18 ft. lbs.)	5	Nut (Qty 2)	
3	Stud (Qty 2)				

JP1069900123000X

Fig. 2 Lefthand exhaust manifold tightening sequence

ITEM	DESCRIPTION	TORQUE	ITEM	DESCRIPTION	TORQUE
1	Stud (Qty 2)		4	Nut (Qty 2)	8 N·m (72 in. lbs.), then loosen 45 degrees
2	Bolt (Qty 4)	25 N·m (18 ft. lbs.)	5	Nut (Qty 2)	
3	Stud (Qty 2)				

JP1069900122000X

Fig. 3 Righthand exhaust manifold tightening sequence

16. Lower vehicle.
17. Remove throttle body resonator assembly and air inlet hose.
18. Disconnect throttle and speed control cables.
19. Disconnect tube from both and lefthand and righthand side crankcase breathers.
20. Discharge A/C system as outlined in "Air Conditioning" chapter.
21. Remove A/C compressor.
22. Remove fan shroud, then fan assembly.
23. Remove serpentine drive belt.
24. Disconnect transmission oil cooler lines at radiator.
25. Disconnect upper and lower radiator hoses.
26. Remove radiator, A/C condenser and transmission oil cooler.
27. Remove alternator.
28. Disconnect two heater hoses from timing chain cover and heater core.
29. Unclip, then remove heater hoses and tubes from intake manifold.
30. Disconnect electrical connectors from the following:
    a. IAT sensor.
    b. Fuel injectors.
    c. TPS switch.
    d. IAC motor.
    e. Engine oil pressure switch.
    f. ECT sensor.
    g. MAP sensor.
    h. CMP sensor.
    i. Coil over plugs.
31. Disconnect vacuum lines at throttle body and intake manifold.
32. Relieve fuel pressure as outlined in "Precautions."
33. Disconnect fuel supply quick connect fitting at fuel rail.
34. Remove power steering pump and position aside.
35. Install lifting studs tool No. 8400, or equivalent, into cylinder heads.
36. Install engine lifting fixture tool No. 8347, or equivalent, as follows:
    a. Holding lifting fixture at a slight angle, slide large bore in front plate over hex portion of lifting stud.
    b. Position two remaining fixture arms onto lifting studs.
    c. Pull forward and upward on lifting fixture so that lifting stud rest in slotted area below large bore.
    d. Secure lifting fixture to three studs using 7⁄16 locknuts.
    e. Ensure lifting loop in fixture is in last hole closest to throttle body to minimize angle of engine during removal.
37. Disconnect body ground strap at left side cowl.
38. Support transmission using suitable jack.
39. Remove engine from vehicle.
40. Reverse procedure to install. Tighten structural cover in sequence, **Fig. 1,** to specifications.

EXHAUST MANIFOLD

REPLACE

Lefthand

1. Raise and support vehicle.
2. Disconnect exhaust pipe at manifold.
3. Lower vehicle.
4. Remove front two heat shield retaining nuts, then raise and support vehicle.
5. Remove heat shield retaining nuts at rear of shield, then heat shield.
6. Lower vehicle, then remove upper manifold retaining bolts.
7. Raise and support vehicle.
8. Remove lower manifold retaining bolts, then manifold.
9. Reverse procedure to install. Tighten bolts to specifications, **Fig. 2.**

Righthand

1. Remove air cleaner assembly, resonator assembly and air inlet hose.
2. Remove serpentine drive belt.
3. Remove A/C compressor mounting bolts and position aside.
4. Remove A/C accumulator support bracket.
5. Drain cooling system to below heater hose level into suitable container.
6. Remove heater hoses at engine.
7. Remove heat shield bolts, then heat shield.
8. Remove upper exhaust manifold bolts.
9. Raise and support vehicle.
10. Disconnect exhaust pipe from exhaust manifold.
11. Remove starter motor bolts, then position starter motor aside.
12. Remove lower exhaust manifold bolts.
13. Remove exhaust manifold and gasket.
14. Reverse procedure to install, noting the following:
    a. Install exhaust manifold bolts but do not tighten until all bolts are in place.
    b. Tighten exhaust manifold bolts in sequence, **Fig. 3** to specifications.

CYLINDER HEAD

REPLACE

1. Relieve fuel system pressure as outlined in "Precautions."
2. Raise and support vehicle, then disconnect exhaust pipe from exhaust manifold.
3. Drain coolant into suitable container.
4. Lower vehicle.
5. Remove intake manifold as outlined in "Intake Manifold, Replace."

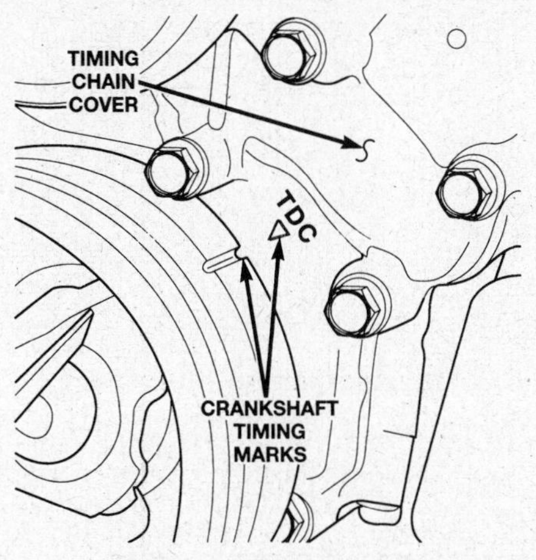

Fig. 4 TDC indicator

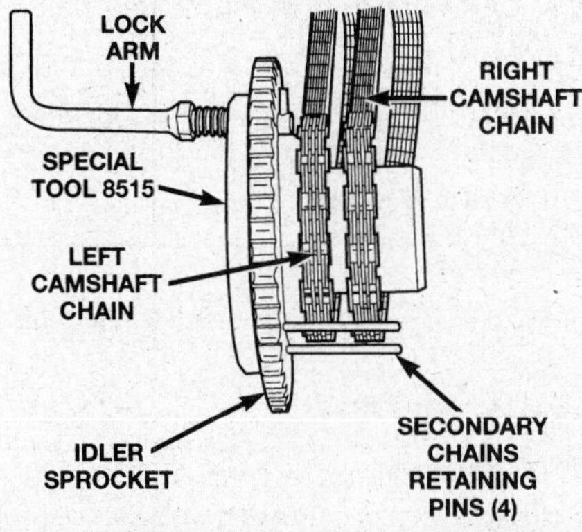

Fig. 6 Secondary timing chain lock down

6. Remove master cylinder and booster assembly.
7. Remove valve cover as outlined in "Valve Cover, Replace."
8. Remove fan shroud and power steering pump.
9. Rotate crankshaft until damper timing mark is aligned with TDC indicator, **Fig. 4.**
10. Verify V8 mark is in position, **Fig. 5.** Rotate crankshaft one turn if required.
11. Remove crankshaft damper.
12. Remove timing chain cover as outlined in "Timing Chain, Replace" in this section.
13. Lock secondary timing chains to idler sprocket, **Fig. 6,** using Special Tool No. 8515, or equivalent.
14. Mark secondary timing chain, **Fig. 5,** one link on each side of V8 mark on cam drive gear.
15. Remove secondary chain tensioner.
16. Remove cylinder head access plug, **Fig. 7.**
17. Remove secondary chain guide.
18. Remove retaining bolt and cam drive gear.
19. Remove cylinder head retaining bolts, then cylinder head and gasket.
20. Reverse procedure to install, noting the following:
    a. Lubricate M11 bolts with oil and install finger tight.

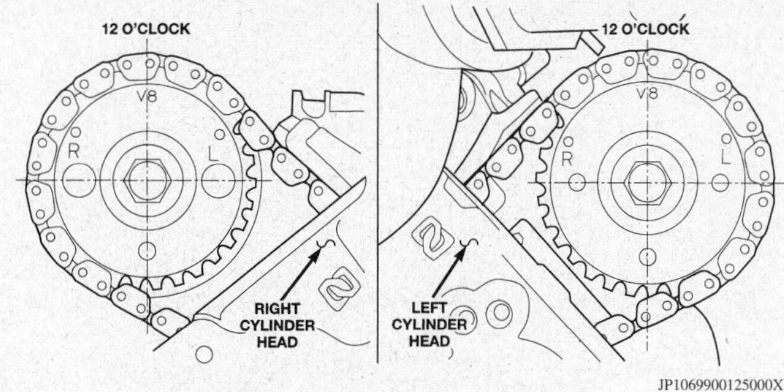

Fig. 5 Camshaft alignment

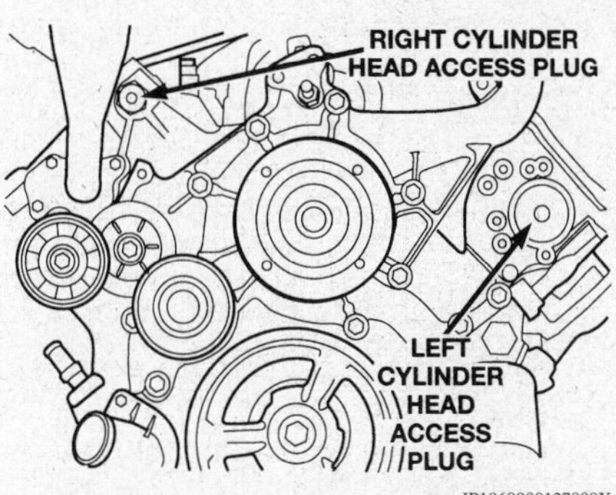

Fig. 7 Cylinder head access plug

    b. Coat four M8 bolts with suitable lock and seal adhesive, then install finger tight.
    c. **Torque** bolt Nos. 1–10 to 15 ft. lbs., refer to **Fig. 8,** for tightening sequence.
    d. **Torque** bolt Nos. 1–10 to 35 ft. lbs.
    e. **Torque** bolt Nos. 11–14 to 18 ft. lbs.
    f. Tighten bolt Nos. 1–10 an additional 90°, then **torque** bolt Nos. 11–14 to 22 ft. lbs.

VALVE COVER

REPLACE

Lefthand

1. Remove air cleaner housing and throttle body resonator.
2. Disconnect injector connectors and unclip injector harness.
3. Route injector harness in front of valve cover.
4. Remove valve cover mounting bolts, then cover and gasket.
5. Reverse procedure to install, noting the following:
    a. Gasket may be used again, provided there are no tears, cuts or deformation.
    b. Tighten bolts to specifications.

Righthand

1. Remove air cleaner housing and throttle body resonator.
2. Drain cooling system into suitable container.
3. Remove serpentine drive belt.
4. Remove A/C compressor retaining bolts and position compressor aside.

Fig. 8 Cylinder head bolt tightening sequence

5. Remove heater hoses from front of engine.
6. Disconnect ignition coil and injector connectors.
7. Remove PCV hose and oil fill tube.
8. Unclip harness from valve cover.
9. Remove rear breather tube and filter assembly.
10. Remove valve cover retaining bolts, then valve cover and gasket.
11. Reverse procedure to install, noting the following:
    a. Gasket may be used again, provided there are no tears, cuts or deformation.
    b. Tighten bolts to specifications.

VALVE ARRANGEMENT

This engine uses four valves per cylinder. Exhaust valves are on the exhaust manifold side of the cylinder head, intake valves are on the intake manifold side of the cylinder head.

CAMSHAFT LOBE LIFT SPECIFICATIONS

Intake .... **.443 inch**
Exhaust .... **.429 inch**

VALVE ADJUSTMENT

These engines are equipped with hydraulic lash adjusters. There is no provision for adjustment.

VALVE GUIDES

The valve guides are an integral part of the cylinder head. If valve stem to guide clearance is excessive, the cylinder head must be replaced.

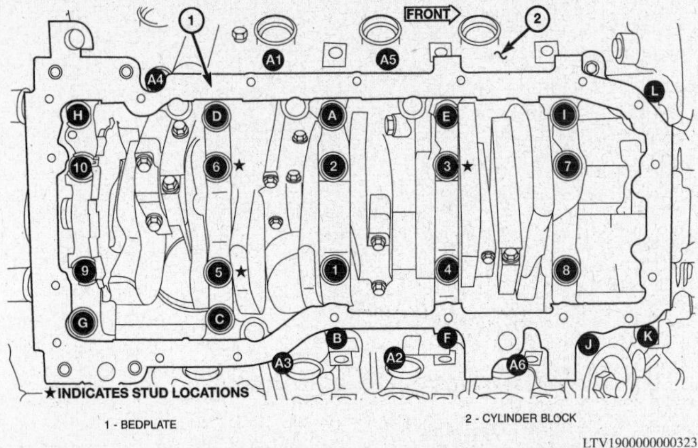

Fig. 9 Main bearing cap & bedplate tightening sequence

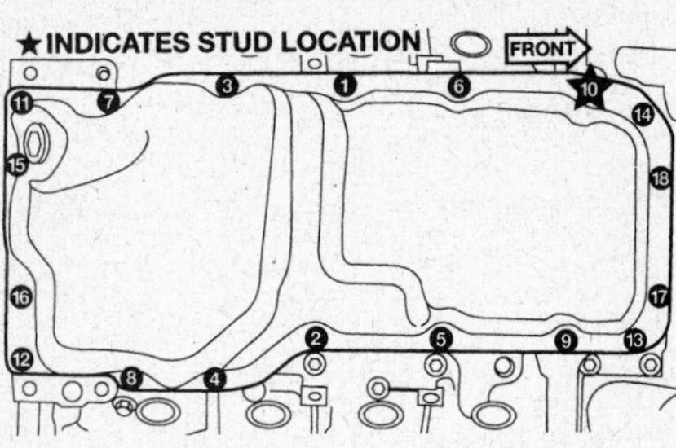

Fig. 10 Oil pan tightening sequence

CRANKSHAFT MAIN BEARING CAP & BEDPLATE

Use the following procedure to tighten the main bearing cap and bedplate bolts.

1. **Torque** bolts 1–10 to 25 inch lbs., in sequence, **Fig. 9.**
2. Tighten bolts 1–10 an additional 90° in sequence.
3. **Torque** bolts A–L to 40 ft. lbs.
4. **Torque** bolts A1–A6 to 20 ft. lbs.

OIL PAN

REPLACE

1. Install engine support fixture tool No. 8534, or equivalent.
2. Loosen but do not remove both left-hand and righthand side engine mount through bolts.
3. Remove structural dust cover.
4. Drain engine oil into suitable container.
5. Remove front crossmember.
6. Raise engine using support fixture enough to provide clearance to remove oil pan.
7. Remove oil pan mounting bolts, then oil pan.
8. Unbolt oil pump pickup tube, then remove tube.
9. Reverse procedure to install, noting the following:
   a. Inspect integral windage tray and gasket and replace as needed.
   b. Install pickup tube with new O-ring.
   c. Tighten oil pan bolts in sequence, **Fig. 10,** to specifications.

OIL PUMP

REPLACE

1. Remove oil pan and pickup tube as outlined in "Oil Pan, Replace."
2. Remove front cover as outlined in "Front Cover, Replace."
3. Remove timing chains and tensioners as outlined in "Timing Chain, Replace."
4. Remove four bolts, primary timing chain tensioner and oil pump.
5. Reverse procedure to install.

COOLING SYSTEM BLEED

Refer to "3.7L Engine" section for cooling system bleed procedure.

RADIATOR

REPLACE

Refer to "3.7L Engine" section for radiator replacement procedure.

FUEL PUMP

REPLACE

Refer to "3.7L Engine" section for fuel pump replacement procedure.

FUEL FILTER

REPLACE

Refer to "3.7L Engine" section for fuel filter replacement procedure.

TIGHTENING SPECIFICATIONS

Year	Component	Torque Ft. Lbs.
2002–06	Automatic Belt Tensioner To Block	30
	Automatic Belt Tensioner To Mounting Bracket	50
	Block Heater Bolt	17①
	Camshaft Bearing Cap	100①
	Camshaft Sprocket	90
	Connecting Rod Cap Bolt	20④
	Cylinder Head Access Plug	60
	Cylinder Head Bolts	②
	Crankshaft Damper	130
	Crankshaft Main Bearing Cap & Bedplate	③
	Exhaust Manifold	18
	Flexplate To Crankshaft	45
	Front Engine Mount Bolt	45
	Idler Sprocket Bolt	25
	Intake Manifold	105①
	Oil Dipstick Tube	21
	Oil Pan Bolts	11
	Oil Pan Drain Plug	25
	Oil Pump Bolt	21
	Oil Pump Tube Bolts	21
	Primary Timing Chain Tensioner Bolts	21
	Rear Engine Mount	34
	Rear Engine Mount Through Bolt Lock Nut	50
	Spark Plugs	27
	Starter Mounting Bolts	33
	Thermostat Housing	115①
	Timing Chain Guide	21
	Timing Chain Primary Tensioner	21
	Timing Chain Secondary Hydraulic Tensioner	21
	Timing Chain Tensioner Arm	12
	Timing Drive Idler Sprocket	25
	Torque Converter To Flexplate	28
	Valve Cover Bolts	105①
	Vibration Damper Or Pulley	130
	Water Pump	30–40

① — Inch lbs.
② — Refer to “Cylinder Head, Replace” for tightening procedure.
③ — Refer to “Crankshaft Main Bearing Cap & Bedplate” for tightening procedure.
④ — Plus an additional 90°.

5.7L Engine

NOTE: Air Bag Equipped Models, Refer To "Air Bag System Precautions" Located In The Front Of This Manual For System Disarming & Arming Procedures.

NOTE: Refer To "Computer Relearn Procedures" Located In The Front Of This Manual When Battery Power To The Computer Has Been Interrupted.

INDEX

PRECAUTIONS

Air Bag Systems

Refer to "Air Bag System Precautions" in the front of this manual for system disarming and arming procedures.

Battery Ground Cable

Prior to service, disconnect battery ground cable and isolate as required.

Fuel System Pressure Relief

1. Remove fuel cap, then fuel pump relay from PDC.
2. Start and run engine until it stalls.
3. Attempt to restart engine until it will no longer run.
4. Turn ignition key to Off position.
5. Unplug connector from any injector.
6. Attach one end of a suitable 18 gauge or smaller jumper wire to either injector terminal.
7. Connect other end of jumper wire to positive battery terminal.
8. Connect one end of a second jumper wire to remaining injector terminal.
9. Momentarily touch other end of second jumper wire to negative battery terminal for no more than a few seconds. **Powering an injector for more than a few seconds will damage injector.**
10. Place a suitable rag below fuel line quick connect fitting on fuel rail, then disconnect quick connect fitting.
11. Install fuel pump relay to PDC, then clear any stored DTCs.

COMPRESSION PRESSURES

All gauge pressure indications should be equal, with no more than 25% leakage.

ENGINE MOUNT

REPLACE

Front

2WD

1. Raise and support vehicle.
2. Remove engine mount through bolts.
3. Install engine support fixture tool No. 8534, or equivalent, then raise engine.
4. Remove engine mount to insulator bolts, then remove insulator.
5. Reverse procedure to install. Apply Mopar Lock and Seal Adhesive Medium Strength Threadlocker, or equivalent, to mount to engine block and left engine bracket to front axle bolts.

4WD

1. Raise and support vehicle, then remove skid plate.
2. Remove front crossmember, then engine oil filter.
3. Support engine using engine support fixture tool No. 8534, or equivalent.
4. Support front axle using suitable jack.
5. Remove four bolts attaching engine mounts to front axle.
6. Remove three bolts attaching front axle to lefthand engine bracket.
7. Lower front axle.
8. Remove six through bolts, then raise engine enough to remove mounts.
9. Remove lefthand and righthand engine mounts.
10. Reverse procedure to install. Apply Mopar Lock and Seal Adhesive Medium Strength Threadlocker, or equivalent, to mount to engine block and lefthand engine bracket to front axle bolts.

Rear

1. Raise and support vehicle.
2. Support transmission using suitable jack.
3. Remove nuts from transmission mount.
4. Remove two bolts attaching transmission mount to engine bracket.
5. Raise transmission enough to remove mount from crossmember.
6. Remove rear mount.
7. Reverse procedure to install. Apply suitable threadlock to bolts.

ENGINE

REPLACE

1. Remove air cleaner resonator and duct work as an assembly.
2. Drain cooling system into suitable container.
3. Remove serpentine drive belt.
4. Remove coolant overflow bottle and position aside.
5. Remove fan blade/viscous fan drive assembly from water pump by turning mounting nut counterclockwise as viewed from front.

Fig. 1 Lefthand exhaust manifold removal & tightening sequence

6. Remove fan shroud mounting bolts, then pull lower shroud mounts out of radiator tank clips.
7. Remove fan shroud and fan blade/ viscous fan drive assembly from vehicle as an assembly. **Do not** store viscous fan drive in a horizontal position.
8. Remove radiator as outlined in "Radiator, Replace."
9. Remove upper crossmember and top core support.
10. Remove A/C compressor with lines attached and position aside.
11. Remove alternator assembly.
12. Relieve fuel pressure as outlined in "Precautions."
13. Remove intake manifold as outlined in "Intake Manifold, Replace."
14. Remove power steering pump and position aside.
15. Disconnect fuel supply line.
16. Raise and support vehicle, then drain engine oil into suitable container.
17. Remove engine front mount through bolts.
18. Disconnect transmission oil cooler lines from their retainers at oil pan bolts.
19. Disconnect exhaust pipe at manifolds.
20. Disconnect electrical connectors from starter motor, then remove starter motor.
21. Remove structural dust cover, then transmission inspection cover.
22. **On models equipped with automatic transmission,** remove drive plate to converter bolts.
23. **On all models,** remove transmission bell housing to engine block bolts.
24. Lower vehicle.
25. Install engine lifting fixture tool No. 8984, or equivalent.
26. Remove engine from vehicle.
27. Reverse procedure to install.

INTAKE MANIFOLD

REPLACE

1. Remove resonator assembly and air inlet hose.
2. Disconnect electrical connectors from the following:
   a. MAP sensor.
   b. IAT sensor.
   c. TPS.
   d. Coolant temperature sensor.
3. Disconnect brake booster and PCV hoses.
4. Remove alternator and position aside.
5. Remove A/C compressor with lines attached and position aside.
6. Relieve fuel system pressure as outlined in "Precautions."
7. Remove intake manifold bolts in a criss-cross pattern starting from outside bolts and ending at middle bolts.

Fig. 2 Righthand exhaust manifold removal & tightening sequence

8. Remove intake manifold.
9. Reverse procedure to install. Tighten bolts in a criss-cross pattern starting with middle bolts and working outward to specifications.

EXHAUST MANIFOLD

REPLACE

1. Raise and support vehicle.
2. Remove exhaust pipe to manifold bolts.
3. Lower vehicle.
4. Install engine support fixture tool No. 8534, or equivalent.
5. Raise engine far enough to remove exhaust manifolds ensuring not to damage engine wiring harness while raising engine.
6. Remove heat shield.
7. Remove exhaust manifold bolts, then exhaust manifold, **Figs. 1 and 2.**
8. Reverse procedure to install.

CYLINDER HEAD

REPLACE

1. Drain cooling system into suitable container.
2. Remove air cleaner resonator and duct work.
3. Remove closed crankcase ventilation system.
4. Disconnect exhaust at exhaust manifolds.
5. Relieve fuel system pressure as outlined in "Precautions."
6. Disconnect heater hoses.
7. Remove valve covers as outlined in "Valve Cover, Replace."
8. Remove intake manifold as outlined in "Intake Manifold, Replace."
9. Remove rocker arm assemblies and push rods. Mark their locations for reference during installation.
10. Remove cylinder head bolts, then cylinder head.
11. Reverse procedure to install, noting the following:
    a. Install new cylinder heads onto engine block. Cylinder head gaskets are not interchangeable, they are marked "L" and "R" to indicate left and right sides.
    b. **Torque** M12 cylinder head bolts in sequence, **Fig. 3,** to 25 ft. lbs and M8 bolts to 15 ft. lbs.
    c. **Torque** M12 cylinder head bolts in sequence to 40 ft. lbs, then verify M8 bolts are at 15 ft. lbs.
    d. Tighten M12 cylinder head bolts in sequence and additional 90°.
    e. **Torque** M8 bolts in sequence to 25 ft. lbs.

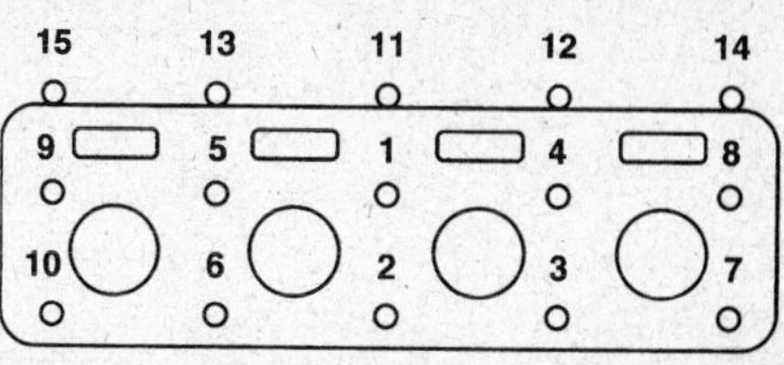

Fig. 3 Cylinder head tightening sequence

VALVE COVER

REPLACE

1. Disconnect coil on plug electrical connectors.
2. Remove valve cover bolts, then ground straps. **Ground straps must be installed in same location as removed.**
3. Remove valve cover.
4. Reverse procedure to install, noting the following:
   a. Valve cover can be reused provided no cuts, tears or deformation has occurred.
   b. Righthand ground strap is located on front inboard stud and lefthand ground strap is located on rear inboard stud.
   c. Tighten valve cover bolts to specifications beginning with middle bolt and moving outward in a criss-cross pattern from top to bottom.

CAMSHAFT LOBE LIFT SPECIFICATIONS

Intake .... .472 inch
Exhaust .... .460 inch

ROCKER ARMS

REPLACE

1. Remove valve cover as outlined in "Valve Cover, Replace."
2. Install pushrod retaining plate tool No. 9070 or equivalent.
3. Loosen rocker shafts using sequence outlined, **Fig. 4.**
4. Remove rocker shafts noting locations for reference during installation.
5. Remove push rods noting locations for reference during installation.
6. Reverse procedure to install, noting the following:
   a. Install push rods in same order as removed. Longer push rods are for exhaust side and shorter push rods are for intake side.
   b. Install rocker shaft assemblies in same order as removed. Intake rocker arm is marked with letter "I."
   c. Tighten rocker shaft bolts using following sequence, **Fig. 4,** to specifications.
   d. Do not rotate or crank engine during or immediately after rocker arm installation, allow hydraulic tappets five minutes to bleed down.

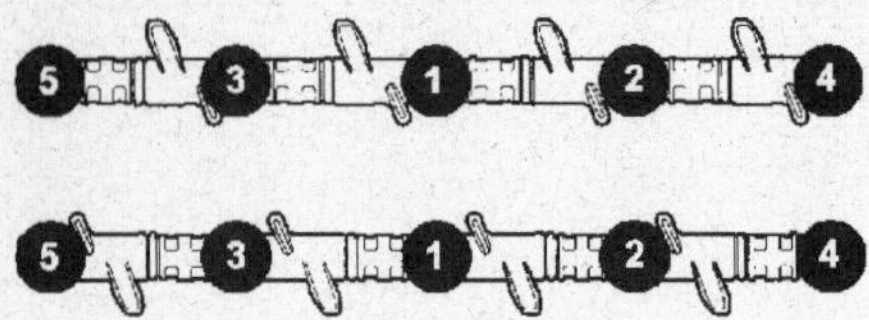

Fig. 4 Rocker arm replace

VALVE GUIDES

The valve guides are not replaceable or serviceable and valve guide reaming is not recommended. If guides are worn beyond acceptable limits, replace cylinder heads.

FRONT COVER

REPLACE

1. Remove air cleaner assembly.
2. Drain cooling system into suitable container.
3. Remove serpentine drive belt.
4. Remove fan blade/viscous fan drive assembly from water pump by turning mounting nut counterclockwise as viewed from front.
5. Remove fan shroud mounting bolts, then pull lower shroud mounts out of radiator tank clips.
6. Remove fan shroud and fan blade/ viscous fan drive assembly from vehicle as an assembly. **Do not** store viscous fan drive in a horizontal position.
7. Remove coolant overflow bottle, then washer fluid bottle.
8. Remove A/C compressor with lines attached and position aside.
9. Remove alternator.
10. Remove upper radiator hose.
11. Disconnect both heater hoses at front cover.
12. Disconnect lower radiator hose at engine.
13. Remove serpentine drive belt tensioner, then both idler pulleys.
14. Remove vibration damper using three jaw puller tool No. 8454 and insert tool No. 8513A, or equivalents.
15. Remove power steering pump with lines attached and position aside.
16. Remove engine oil dipstick support bolt.
17. Drain engine oil into suitable container.
18. Remove oil pan and pickup tube as outlined in "Oil Pan, Replace."
19. Remove front cover bolts, then front cover.
20. Reverse procedure to install using new front cover gasket.

TIMING CHAIN

REPLACE

Removal

1. Drain cooling system into suitable container.
2. Remove front cover as outlined in "Front Cover, Replace."
3. Install vibration damper bolt finger tight.
4. Rotate crankshaft to align timing chain sprockets and key ways using suitable socket and breaker bar, **Fig. 5.**
5. Remove oil pump.
6. Retract tensioner shoe until hole in shoe lines up with hole in bracket, then slide a suitable pin into holes.
7. Remove camshaft sprocket attaching bolt, then remove timing chain with crankshaft and camshaft sprockets.

Installation

1. Align camshaft pin and slot in cam sprocket at 12 o'clock position.
2. Align crankshaft keyway at 2 o'clock position.
3. Install crankshaft sprocket so that dots and or paint mark is at 6 o'clock position.
4. Place both camshaft sprocket and crankshaft sprocket on bench with timing marks on exact imaginary center line through both camshaft and crankshaft bores.
5. Place timing chain around both sprockets. Timing chain must be installed with single plated link aligned with dot or painted marking on camshaft sprocket. Crankshaft sprocket is aligned with dot or painted mark on sprocket between two plated timing chain links.
6. Lift sprockets and chain and slide them evenly over respective shafts. Inspect alignment of timing marks.
7. Install camshaft bolt.
8. Remove tensioner pin, then inspect alignment of timing marks.
9. Install front cover.
10. Fill cooling system.

CAMSHAFT

REPLACE

1. Remove air cleaner assembly.
2. Drain coolant into suitable container.
3. Remove serpentine drive belt, then alternator.
4. Remove A/C compressor with lines attached and position aside.
5. Remove radiator as outlined in "Radiator, Replace."
6. Remove intake manifold as outlined in "Intake Manifold, Replace."
7. Remove valve covers as outlined in "Valve Cover, Replace."
8. Remove cylinder heads as outlined in "Cylinder Head, Replace."
9. Remove oil pan as outlined in "Oil Pan, Replace."
10. Remove front cover as outlined in "Front Cover, Replace."
11. Remove oil pick up tube.
12. Remove oil pump as outlined in "Oil Pump, Replace."
13. Remove timing chain as outlined in "Timing Chain, Replace."
14. Remove camshaft tensioner/thrust plate assembly.
15. Remove lifters and retainer assembly.

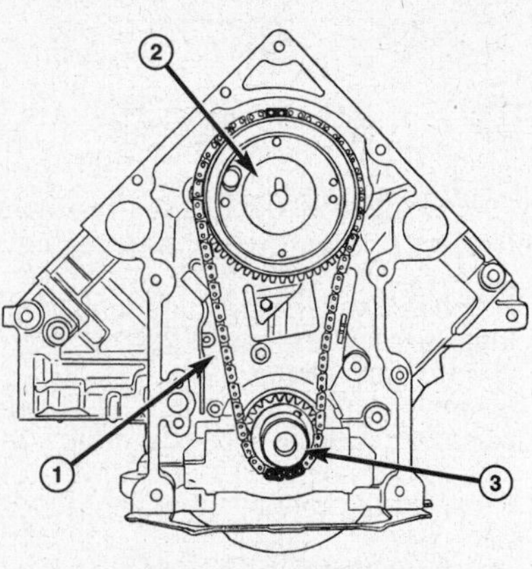

Fig. 5 Timing chain alignment marks

Mark lifter locations for reference during installation.

16. Install a long bolt into front of camshaft to aid in removal.
17. Remove camshaft ensuring not to damage cam bearings with cam lobes.
18. Reverse procedure to install, noting the following:
    a. Lubricate camshaft lobes and camshaft bearing journals with clean engine oil.
    b. Measure camshaft end play. If end play is not .0031–.0114 inch, replace thrust plate.
    c. Ensure lifters are installed in original positions.
    d. If replacing camshaft, all lifters must also be replaced.

PISTON & ROD ASSEMBLY

Install pistons with raised "F" mark or arrow facing toward front of engine.

Install connecting rod with oil slinger slot facing toward front of engine.

Connecting rod bolts are torque to yield and must not be reused. Always replace bolts when they are loosened or removed.

MAIN & ROD BEARINGS

Main bearings are available in three different grades. Refer to **Fig. 6** for main bearing selection chart.

CRANKSHAFT MAIN BEARING CAP

Tighten main bearing caps in sequence, **Fig. 7,** to specifications.

Tighten cross bolts in sequence, **Fig. 7,** to specifications starting with cross bolt A.

GRADE MARKING	SIZE mm (in.)	FOR USE WITH JOURNAL SIZE
A	0.008 mm U/S (0.0004 in.) U/S	64.988–64.995 mm (2.5585– 2.5588in.)
B	NOMINAL	64.996–65.004 mm (2.5588–2.5592 in.)
C	0.008 mm O/S (0.0004 in.) O/S	65.005–65.012 mm (2.5592–2.5595 in.)

LTV1900000000326

Fig. 6 Main bearing selection chart

CRANKSHAFT REAR OIL SEAL

REPLACE

Removal

1. Remove transmission as outlined in **MOTOR's "Domestic Transmission, In-Vehicle Service" or "Transmission Service DVD."**
2. Remove flex plate bolts, then flex plate.
3. Installed deeply into seal using removal tool No. 8506, or equivalent, remove crankshaft oil seal.

Installation

1. Do not lubricate seal lip or outer edge.
2. Position plastic seal guide onto crankshaft rear face, then position seal onto guide.
3. Tap seal into place until seal installer seats against cylinder block crankshaft bore using crankshaft rear oil seal installer tool No. 8349 and driver handle tool No. C-4171, or equivalents.
4. Install flexplate, then transmission.

OIL PAN

REPLACE

1. Install engine support fixture tool No. 8534, or equivalent.
2. **On models equipped with 2WD,** remove lefthand and righthand engine mount through bolts.
3. **On models equipped with 4WD,**

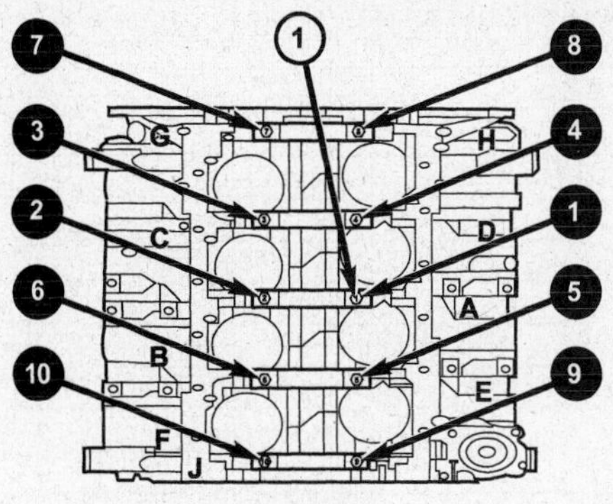

FRONT

1 - Stud Location

LTV1900000000325

Fig. 7 Main bearing tightening sequence

loosen but do not remove both lefthand and righthand side engine mount through bolts.
4. **On all models,** remove structural dust cover.
5. Drain engine oil into suitable container.
6. Remove front crossmember.
7. Raise engine to provide clearance for oil pan removal.
8. Remove oil pan bolts in sequence outlined, **Fig. 8,** then oil pan. **Do not pry on oil pan or gasket.**
9. Unbolt and remove pickup tube.
10. Reverse procedure to install. Install oil pan studs in same location as they were removed from.

OIL PUMP

REPLACE

1. Remove oil pan and pickup tube as outlined in "Oil Pan, Replace."
2. Remove front cover as outlined in "Front Cover, Replace."
3. Remove four bolts, then oil pump.
4. Reverse procedure to install.

COOLING SYSTEM BLEED

Refer to "3.7L Engine" section for cooling system bleed procedure.

WATER PUMP

REPLACE

1. Drain coolant into suitable container.
2. Remove serpentine drive belt.

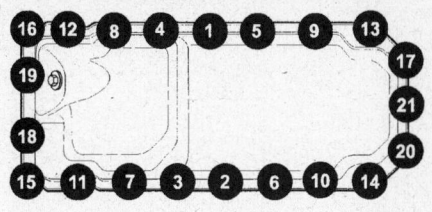

LTV0500000000178

Fig. 8 Oil pan bolt loosen & tightening sequence

3. Remove fan blade/viscous fan drive assembly from water pump by turning mounting nut counterclockwise as viewed from front.
4. Remove fan shroud mounting bolts, then pull lower shroud mounts out of radiator tank clips.
5. Remove fan shroud and fan blade/viscous fan drive assembly from vehicle as an assembly. **Do not** store viscous fan drive in a horizontal position.
6. Remove coolant overflow bottle.
7. Disconnect washer bottle electrical connector and hose.
8. Remove A/C compressor, then alternator brace.
9. Remove idler pulleys.
10. Remove serpentine drive belt tensioner assembly.
11. Remove upper and lower radiator hoses.
12. Remove heater hoses.
13. Remove water pump bolts, then water pump.
14. Reverse procedure to install.

RADIATOR

REPLACE

Refer to "3.7L Engine" section for radiator replacement procedure.

FUEL PUMP

REPLACE

Refer to "3.7L Engine" section for fuel pump replacement procedure.

FUEL FILTER

REPLACE

Refer to "3.7L Engine" section for fuel filter replacement procedure.

TIGHTENING SPECIFICATIONS

Year	Component	Torque Ft. Lbs.
2003–06	Alternator	40
	Camshaft Sprocket	90
	Camshaft Tensioner Plate	21
	Connecting Rod Cap	15③
	Crankshaft Rear Seal Retainer	11
	Cylinder Head	②
	Exhaust Manifold	18
	Flywheel	70
	Front Cover	21
	Front Cover Lifting Stud	40
	Front Insulator To Block (2WD)	70
	Front Insulator To Support Bracket Stud Nut (4WD)	30
	Front Insulator To Support Bracket Through Bolt (4WD)	75
	Front Insulator Through Bolt	70
	Intake Manifold	105①
	Main Bearing Cap	20③
	Main Bearing Cross Bolts	20
	Oil Dipstick Tube	105①
	Oil Pan	105①
	Oil Pan Drain Plug	25
	Oil Pump	21
	Oil Pump Pickup Tube	21
	Rear Insulator Bracket (4WD w/ Automatc Transmission)	50
	Rear Insulator To Bracket Through Bolt (2WD)	50
	Rear Insulator To Crossmember Support Bracket (2WD)	30
	Rear Insulator To Crossmember (4WD)	50
	Rear Insulator To Transmission (4WD)	50
	Rear Support Bracket To Crossmember	30
	Rear Support Plate To Transfer Case	30
	Rocker Arm	16
	Thermostat Housing	21
	Throttle Body	105①
	Transmission Support Bracket (2WD)	50
	Transfer Case To Insulator Mounting Plate	105
	Valve Cover	70①
	Vibration Damper	129
	Water Pump	21

① — Inch lbs.
② — Refer to "Cylinder Head, Replace" for tightening procedure.
③ — Plus an additional 90°.

5.9L Diesel Engine

NOTE: On Air Bag Equipped Models, Refer To "Air Bag System Precautions" Located In The Front Of This Manual For System Disarming & Arming Procedures.

NOTE: Refer To "Computer Relearn Procedure" Located In The Front Of This Manual When Battery Power To The Computer Has Been Interrupted.

INDEX

PRECAUTIONS

Air Bag Systems

Refer to "Air Bag System Precautions" in the front of this manual for system disarming and arming procedures.

Battery Ground Cable

Prior to service, disconnect battery ground cable and isolate as required.

Fuel System Pressure Relief

Fuel supply lines on EFI engines will remain pressurized for sometime after the engine is turned off. This residual pressure must be relieved before servicing the fuel system.

Fuel system pressure may be relieved by one of two methods. The first method is to disconnect the inertia switch and crank the engine for 15–20 seconds. The inertia switch is located in the engine compartment.

The second method is to install fuel pressure relief tool No. T80L-9974-B, , or equivalent, to measuring port on engine fuel rail. Position drain hose in suitable container, then press relief button.

COMPRESSION PRESSURE

The minimum cylinder pressure is 350 psi. Cylinder pressure should be within 20% from cylinder to cylinder.

DESCRIPTION

Air Intake System

The Cummins built engine is an inline six cylinder turbocharged diesel. On turbocharged engines, the flow is from the filter to the turbocharger and then through the air crossover to the manifold. From the intake manifold, air is forced into the cylinder. The exhaust gases flow through the turbocharger to rotate the turbine and impeller, using exhaust energy to force more air into the cylinders. The additional air provided by the turbocharger allows more fuel to be injected to increase power output from the engine, **Fig. 1.**

Fuel System

The function of the fuel system is to inject clean, atomized fuel into the engine cylinders at a precise time near the end of the compression stroke of each piston. The components of the system contribute to the delivery of fuel to the cylinders, **Fig. 2.**

The engine is equipped with a cam actuated lift pump. Fuel flow begins as the lift pump pulls fuel from the supply tank. This pump supplies low pressure fuel (3–5 psi) to the fuel filter head, through the filter and then to the distributor injection pump.

The Bosch distributor type fuel pump builds the high injection pressures required for combustion, and routes the fuel through individual high-pressure fuel lines to each injector. When the high pressure fuel reaches the injector, the pressure lifts the needle valve against the spring tension to let the fuel enter the combustion chamber. Any leakage past the needle valve enters the fuel drain manifold. The fuel drain manifold routes controlled venting from the distributor injection pump and leakage from the injectors back into the fuel tank.

Electrical System

The electrical system consists of the starting circuit, charging circuit, heaters and control devices. The injection pump uses an electrical fuel shutoff valve. The engine has water temperature and oil pressure sensors connected to gauges on the instrument panel. In addition to the ammeter, water and oil gauges, a message center and run circuit is also used, **Fig. 3.** The heater circuits consist of an intake manifold heater, fuel heater and coolant heater, **Figs. 4 through 6.**

Lubrication System

The lubricating gerotor type pump draws oil from the pan and forces it through the lubrication system. The pressure regulation valve controls the oil pressure in the system. This valve is designed to keep the oil pressure from exceeding 60 psi. When the oil pressure is greater than 60 psi, the valve opens uncovering the dump port so part of the oil is routed to the oil pan. The filter bypass valve ensures a supply of oil in the event the filter becomes plugged. The bypass valve, located on oil cooler cover, will let the oil flow bypass a plugged filter. The valve is designed to open when the pressure drop across the filter is more than 20 psi, as with a plugged filter. The piston pins are lubricated by the splash from the piston cooling nozzles. The oil pump idler gear bushing is pressure lubricated. The remainder of the front gear train is lubricated by oil carry over and splash, **Fig. 7.**

The oil coolers are full flow, plate type cooler. The oil flows through a cast passage in the cooler cover and through the element where it is cooled by engine coolant flowing past the plates of the element. After the oil is cooled, it flows through the filter. From the filter oil flows to the turbocharger and engine.

The turbocharger receives cooled and pressurized oil through a supply line from the filter head. A drain line connected to the bottom of the turbocharger housing returns the oil to the oil pan.

TROUBLESHOOTING

The troubleshooting charts cover a partial list of symptoms of various engine systems. Refer to **Figs. 8 through 26** to diagnose and correct a system fault.

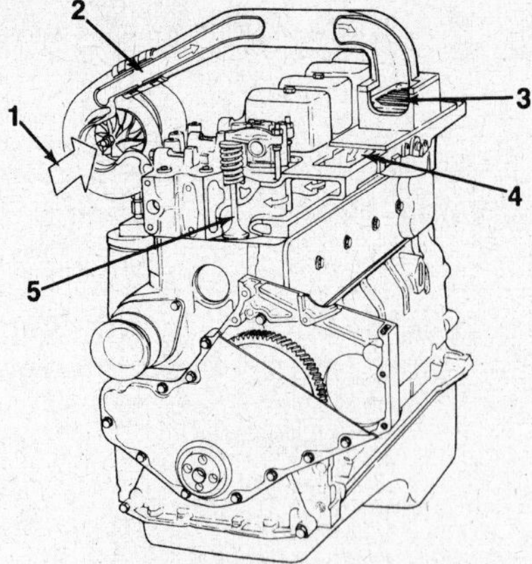

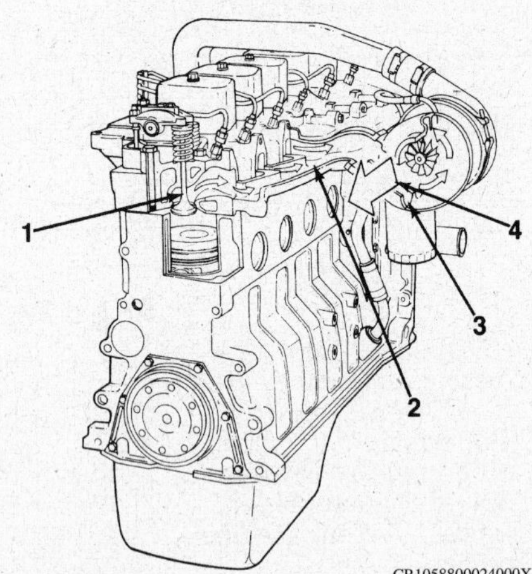

Fig. 1 Air flow system

ENGINE MOUNT

REPLACE

Front

1. Position fan as required to gain clearance, then install suitable engine support fixture.
2. Raise and support vehicle, then lift engine slightly and remove through bolt and nut.
3. Remove engine support bracket/cushion bolts, then the support bracket/cushion.
4. Reverse procedure to install. Tighten bolts and nuts to specifications.

Rear

1. Raise and support vehicle, then position suitable transmission jack beneath transmission and remove support cushion stud nuts.
2. Raise rear of engine/transmission assembly slightly, then remove bolts securing support cushion to transmission support bracket.
3. Remove support cushion and, if required, transmission support bracket.
4. Reverse procedure to install. Tighten bolts and nuts to specifications.

ENGINE

REPLACE

2002

1. Recover refrigerant as outlined in "Air Conditioning" chapter.
2. Relieve fuel pressure as outlined in- "Fuel System Pressure Relief" in "Precautions."
3. Raise and support vehicle.
4. Drain engine coolant and oil into suitable containers.
5. Lower vehicle.
6. Remove radiator upper hose.
7. Remove cooling fan shroud to radiator mounting bolts.
8. Remove viscous fan drive assembly using a suitable 36mm wrench. Fan hub and nut have left hand threads.
9. Remove cooling fan and shroud together.
10. Disconnect coolant recovery bottle hose from radiator filler neck and remove bottle from fan shroud.
11. Disconnect heater core supply and return hoses from cylinder head fitting and coolant pipe.
12. Raise and support vehicle.
13. Remove transmission and transfer case (if equipped).
14. Disconnect exhaust pipe from turbocharger extension pipe.
15. Remove starter motor.
16. Disconnect A/C suction/discharge hose form rear of A/C compressor.
17. Lower vehicle.
18. Disconnect lower radiator hose from radiator outlet.
19. **On models equipped with automatic transmission,** disconnect transmission oil cooler lines from radiator
20. **On all models,** remove radiator mounting screws and lift radiator out of engine, remove upper radiator support panel.
21. Remove front bumper assay.
22. Disconnect A/C condenser refrigerant lines.
23. Disconnect charge air cooler piping.
24. Remove two charge air cooler mounting bolts, then the charge air cooler.
25. Disconnect engine block heater connector and A/C compressor electrical connector.
26. Remove passenger battery ground cable from engine block.
27. Disconnect power steering pump pressure and return lines.
28. Remove accelerator linkage cover.
29. Leaving all cables attached, remove

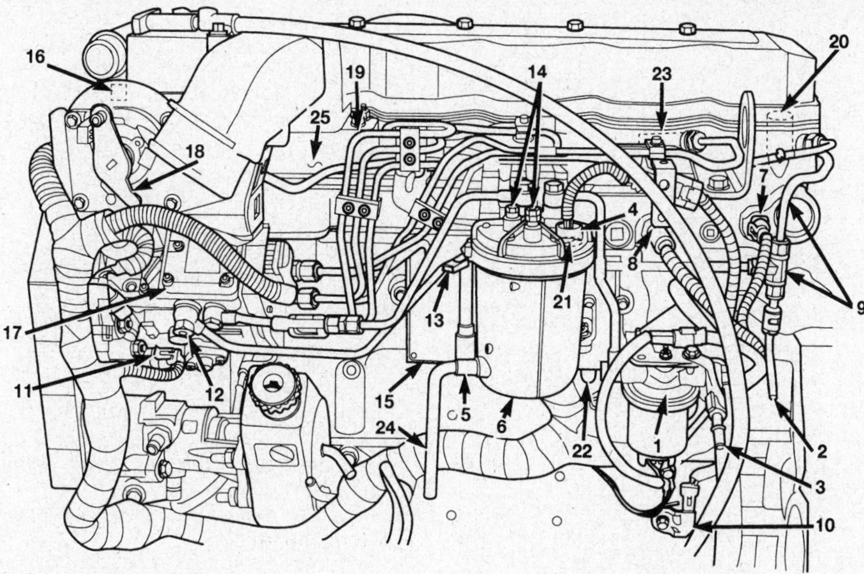

1. FUEL TRANSFER (LIFT) PUMP
2. FUEL RETURN LINE (TO FUEL TANK)
3. FUEL SUPPLY LINE (LOW-PRESSURE, TO ENGINE)
4. FUEL HEATER
5. WATER-IN-FUEL (WIF) SENSOR
6. FUEL FILTER/WATER SEPARATOR
7. IAT SENSOR
8. MAP (BOOST) SENSOR
9. FUEL DRAIN MANIFOLD
10. CKP SENSOR
11. CMP SENSOR
12. OVERFLOW VALVE
13. DRAIN VALVE
14. FUEL PRESSURE TEST PORTS
15. ECM
16. ECT SENSOR
17. FUEL INJECTION PUMP
18. THROTTLE LEVER BELLCRANK AND APPS
19. HIGH-PRESSURE FUEL LINES
20. FUEL INJECTORS
21. FUEL HEATER TEMPERATURE SENSOR (THERMOSTAT)
22. OIL PRESSURE SENSOR
23. FUEL INJECTOR CONNECTOR
24. DRAIN TUBE
25. INTAKE MANIFOLD AIR HEATER/ELEMENTS

CR10288013190000X

Fig. 2 Fuel system components & flow

accelerator pedal position sensor assembly (APPS) from cylinder head bracket and secure out of way.

30. Disconnect APPS sensor electrical connector.
31. Disconnect vacuum pump supply hose.
32. Disconnect engine harness and ground cable from power distribution center.
33. Disconnect fuel supply and return hoses.
34. Remove cylinder head cover.
35. Remove No. 5 and No. 6 cylinder intake and exhaust rocker arms and pedestals, note original location for assembly reference.
36. Loosen but do not remove engine mount through bolts and nuts.
37. Attach suitable chain across engine lift brackets.
38. Lift engine up and out of engine compartment.
39. Reverse procedure to install.

2003-06

1. Disconnect engine grid heater harness at grid heater relays.
2. Disconnect electrical connections from rear of alternator.
3. Recover refrigerant as outlined in "Air Conditioning" chapter.
4. Raise and support vehicle, then drain coolant into suitable container.
5. Drain engine oil into suitable container.
6. Remove fan assembly.
7. Remove upper radiator hose.
8. Remove upper fan shroud mounting bolts.
9. Disconnect coolant recovery bottle hose from radiator fill neck, then remove recovery bottle.
10. Remove cooling fan and shroud together.
11. Disconnect heater core supply and return hoses from cylinder head fitting and coolant pipe.
12. Raise and support vehicle.
13. Remove transmission and transfer case as outlined in **MOTOR's "Domestic Transmission, In-Vehicle Service" or "Transmission Service DVD."**
14. Disconnect exhaust pipe from turbocharger extension pipe.
15. Disconnect engine electrical harness to vehicle electrical harness.
16. Remove starter motor as outlined in "Electrical" section.
17. Remove flywheel/flexplate.
18. Remove transmission adapter.
19. Disconnect A/C suction/discharge hose from rear of A/C compressor.
20. Lower vehicle, then disconnect lower radiator hose from radiator outlet.
21. **On models equipped with automatic transmissions,** using removal tool No. 6931, or equivalent, disconnect transmission oil cooler lines from front of radiator.
22. **On all models,** remove radiator as outlined in "Radiator, Replace."
23. Disconnect A/C condenser refrigerant lines.
24. Disconnect charge air cooler piping.
25. Remove charge air cooler mounting bolts, then the charge air cooler.
26. Remove damper and speed indicator ring from front of engine.
27. Disconnect engine block heater electrical connector.
28. Disconnect A/C compressor and pressure sensor electrical connectors.
29. Remove battery ground cables from engine block.
30. Remove bolts, then the power steering pump.
31. Remove accelerator linkage cover.
32. **On early build models,** disconnect cables from accelerator pedal position sensor.
33. **On late build models,** disconnect ECM power and ground wires.
34. **On all models,** disconnect fuel supply and return hoses.
35. Remove intake manifold cover as outlined in "Intake Manifold Cover, Replace."
36. Disconnect three injector harness connectors at rocker housing.
37. Disconnect electrical connectors from injectors.
38. Remove rear engine lift bracket.
39. Remove cylinder Nos. 4, 5 and 6 intake and exhaust rocker arms, pedestals and push rods, noting location for reference during installation.
40. Loosen No. 6 fuel line shield bolts, then rotate shield aside.
41. Remove cylinder Nos. 5 and 6 high pressure fuel lines.
42. Remove fuel connector tube nut, then the fuel connector tube.
43. Remove cylinder Nos. 5 and 6 fuel injectors.
44. Remove rocker housing.
45. Remove Nos. 4 and 12 cylinder head bolts, then install engine lift bracket tool No. 9009, or equivalent, **Fig. 27.**
46. Loosen but do not remove engine mount through bolts and nuts.
47. Disconnect hod support struts, then position hood out of the way.
48. Attach a suitable chain with two hooks to engine lift brackets.
49. While keeping engine level, lift straight up out of mounts.
50. Rotate nose of engine upward and remove from vehicle.
51. Reverse procedure to install.

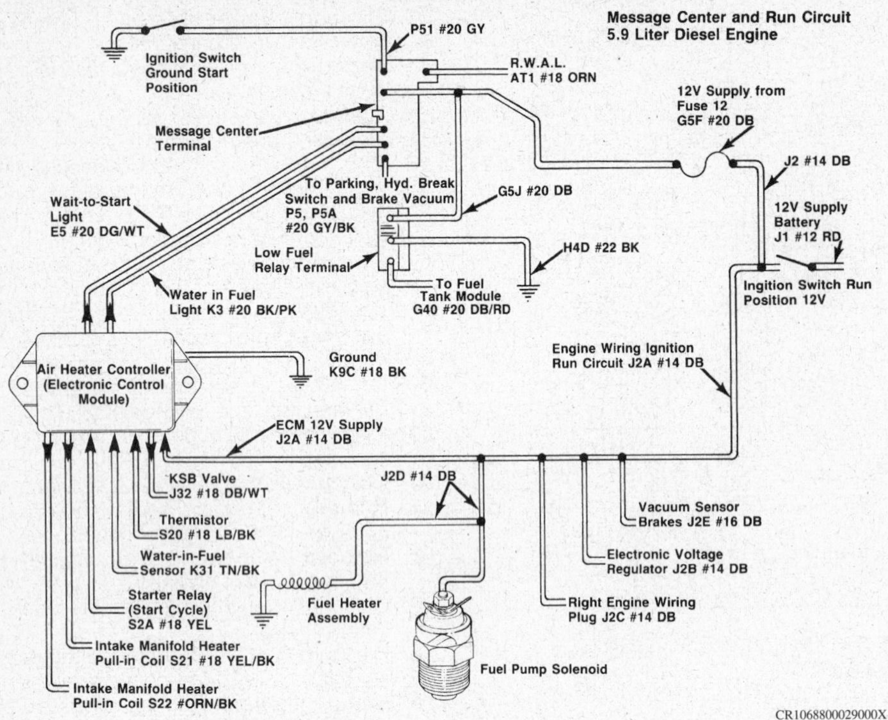

Fig. 3 Message center & run circuit

EXHAUST MANIFOLD

REPLACE

1. Loosen air crossover hose clamps.
2. Disconnect air intake and exhaust piping from turbocharger.
3. Disconnect oil supply line and oil drain tube.
4. Disconnect intercooler inlet duct from turbocharger.
5. Remove turbocharger attaching nuts and turbocharger and gasket.
6. Remove cab heater supply and return lines.
7. Remove manifold attaching bolts, then manifold and gaskets.
8. Reverse procedure to install, noting the following:
   a. Torque exhaust manifold bolts to 25 ft. lbs. in sequence, **Fig. 28.**
   b. Tighten all bolts and nuts to specifications.

INTAKE MANIFOLD COVER

REPLACE

1. Remove charge air cooler outlet duct from air inlet tube, then remove high pressure fuel lines.
2. Remove engine oil dipstick tube mounting bolt, position dipstick to side.
3. Remove air intake heater ground wire, then disconnect air intake heater power supply lines.
4. Disconnect air grid heater power cables at cable mounting studs.
5. Remove four air inlet housing mounting bolts, then housing from top of heater elements.
6. Remove intake air grid heater from manifold.
7. Remove high pressure fuel lines.
8. Remove remaining intake manifold cover to cylinder head bolts, then cover and gasket
9. Reverse procedure to install.

CYLINDER HEAD

REPLACE

2002

1. Raise and support vehicle, then drain coolant into suitable container.
2. Disconnect exhaust pipe from turbocharger elbow.
3. Lower vehicle.
4. Remove air cleaner housing and snorkel from vehicle. Cap off turbocharger air inlet.
5. Disconnect cab heater core supply and return hoses from cylinder head and heater pipe.
6. Disconnect turbocharger oil drain tube at rubber hose connection. Cap open ports.
7. Disconnect turbocharger oil supply line at turbocharger end. Cap open ports.
8. Remove exhaust manifold to cylinder head bolts and spacers, then remove exhaust manifold and turbocharger as an assembly.
9. Remove serpentine drive belt.
10. Remove alternator upper bracket.
11. Disconnect radiator upper hose from thermostat housing.
12. Disconnect coolant temperature sensor electrical connector.
13. Remove engine harness to cylinder head bolt at front of cylinder head.
14. Remove engine harness ground bolt at front of head below thermostat housing.

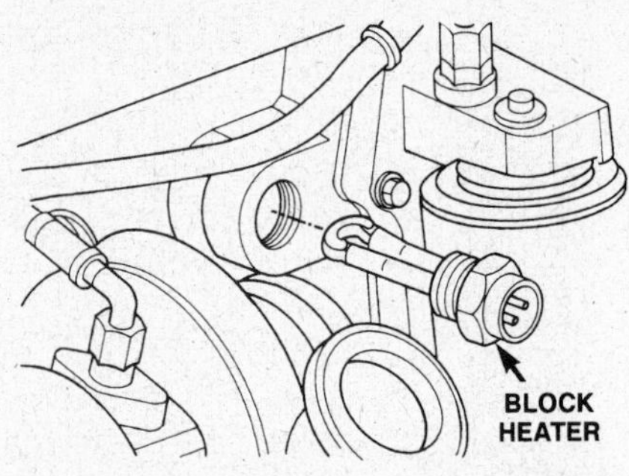

Fig. 4 Block heater

15. Remove six accelerator pedal position sensor assembly to cylinder head bracket bolts, **Fig. 29,** then secure aside.
16. Remove intake air grid heater wire from grid heater.
17. Remove engine oil dipstick tube bolt from air inlet housing.
18. Remove charge air cooler to air inlet housing pipe.
19. Remove air inlet housing and intake grid heater from intake manifold.
20. Remove engine lift bracket from rear of cylinder head.
21. Remove high pressure fuel lines, **Figs. 30 and 31,** from engine as follows:
    a. Remove all injection line to intake manifold cover support bracket bolts.
    b. Loosen No. 1, 2 and 4 cylinder high pressure lines at injection pump and cylinder head.
    c. Remove No. 1, 2 and 4 cylinder high pressure line bundle from engine.
    d. Loosen No. 3, 5 and 6 cylinder high pressure lines at injection pump and cylinder head.
    e. Remove No. 3, 5 and 6 cylinder high pressure line bundle from engine.
22. Remove lift pump to fuel filter low pressure line.
23. Remove fuel filter to injection pump low pressure line.
24. Disconnect water-in-fuel and fuel heater electrical connectors.
25. Remove fuel filter assembly to manifold cover bolts, then filter assembly.
26. Disconnect IAT and MAP sensor electrical connectors.
27. Remove cylinder head cover.
28. Remove rocker arms, cross heads and push rods. Mark locations for reference during installation.
29. Remove fuel return line banjo bolt at rear of cylinder head ensuring not to drop two sealing washers.
30. Reinstall engine lift bracket at rear of cylinder head.
31. Remove 26 cylinder head bolts.
32. Attach suitable engine lift to brackets, the lift cylinder head off engine.
33. Reverse procedure to install noting the following:
    a. Install new gasket with part number side facing upward over dowel sleeves. **Outside edge of head gasket is very sharp.**

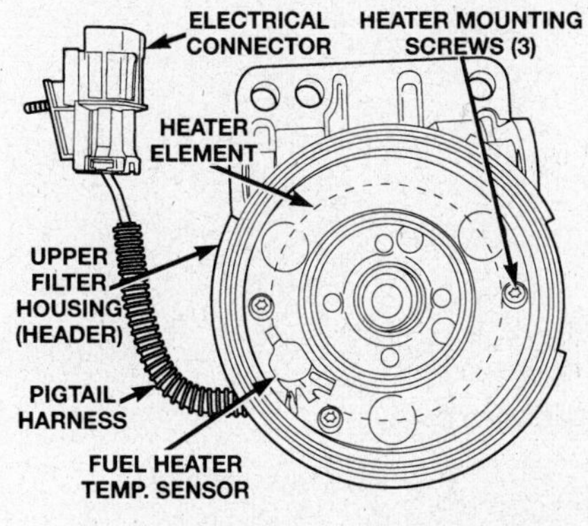

Fig. 5 Fuel heater (Part 1 of 2)

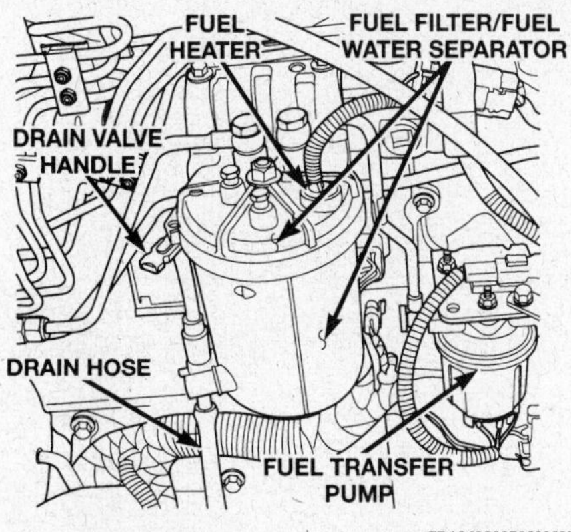

Fig. 5 Fuel heater (Part 2 of 2)

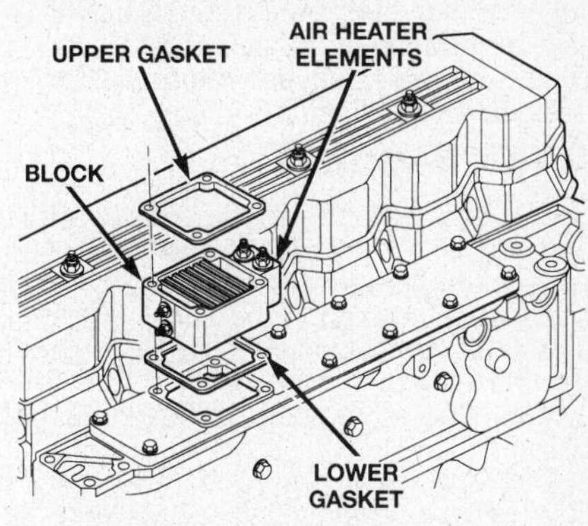

Fig. 6 Intake air heater

b. Lightly lubricate head bolts with clean engine oil.
c. **Torque** cylinder head bolts in sequence, **Fig. 32,** to 59 ft. lbs.
d. **Torque** cylinder head bolts in sequence to 77 ft. lbs.
e. Inspect to ensure all bolts are at 77 ft. lbs.
f. Tighten all bolts in sequence an additional ¼ turn.

2003–06

1. Raise and support vehicle, then drain coolant into suitable container.
2. Disconnect exhaust pipe from turbocharger elbow.
3. Lower vehicle.
4. Disconnect air inlet temperature pressure sensor.
5. Remove air cleaner housing and snorkel from vehicle. Cap turbocharger inlet.
6. Disconnect cab heater core supply and return hoses from cylinder head and heater pipe.
7. Disconnect turbocharger oil drain tube at rubber hose connection. Cap openings.
8. Disconnect turbocharger oil supply line at turbocharger end. Cap openings.
9. Remove exhaust manifold to cylinder head bolts, spacers, heat shield, retention straps and cab heater plumbing.
10. Remove exhaust manifold and turbocharger as an assembly.
11. Remove cooling fan assembly.
12. Remove serpentine drive belt.
13. Remove cooling fan support from cylinder block.
14. Remove upper alternator bolt, then loosen lower bolt and rotate alternator away from cylinder head.
15. Disconnect radiator upper hose from thermostat housing.
16. Disconnect IAT, MAP and coolant temperature sensor electrical connectors.
17. Remove engine harness to cylinder head bolts and P-clips at front of cylinder head.
18. Remove throttle linkage cover.
19. Remove six accelerator pedal position sensor assembly to cylinder head bracket bolts, **Fig. 29,** then secure aside.
20. Remove intake air grid heater wires from grid heater.
21. Remove engine oil dipstick tube bolt at fuel filter housing bracket and inlet connection.
22. Remove charge air cooler to air inlet housing pipe.
23. Remove engine wire harness bolt and push-in fastener from air inlet housing.
24. Remove air inlet housing and intake grid heater from intake manifold cover.
25. Remove two grid heater harness to cylinder head bolts at front of cylinder head.
26. Remove engine lift bracket from rear of cylinder head.
27. Loosen fuel line nuts at fuel pump and fuel rail. Use a back-up wrench on fitting at fuel pump to keep it from loosening.
28. Loosen No. 6 high pressure fuel line shield and position aside.
29. Loosen fuel line nuts at fuel rail and cylinder head.
30. Remove fuel line bracket bolts at intake manifold cover.
31. Remove fuel rail as follows:
    a. Remove fuel rail pressure sensor connector.
    b. Remove banjo fitting at pressure limiting valve.
    c. Remove fuel rail bolts and fuel rail.
    d. Remove fuel rail bolts, then fuel rail.
32. Remove low pressure lines as follows:
    a. Remove fuel drain banjo fitting on front side of fuel filter housing.
    b. Remove fuel drain line support bracket on rear side of filter housing.
    c. Remove fuel drain hose.
    d. Remove banjo fitting at bottom of fuel filter housing.
    e. Disconnect fuel supply hose at lift pump.
33. Disconnect fuel heater, water in fuel sensor and fuel lift pump electrical connectors.
34. Remove fuel filter assembly to cylinder head bolts, then filter assembly.
35. Remove wire harness P-clip from cylinder head.
36. Remove cylinder head cover.
37. Disconnect rocker housing injector harness electrical connectors.
38. Remove injector harness nuts from injectors.
39. Remove rocker arms, cross heads and push rods. Mark locations for reference during installation.
40. Remove fuel return line banjo bolt at rear of cylinder head ensuring not to drop two sealing washers.
41. Remove fuel injectors.
42. Remove rocker housing bolts, then rocker housing and gasket.
43. Reinstall engine lift bracket at rear of cylinder head.
44. Remove 26 cylinder head bolts.
45. Attach suitable engine lift to brackets, the lift cylinder head off engine.
46. Reverse procedure to install, noting the following:
    a. Install new gasket with part number side facing upward over dowel sleeves. **Outside edge of head gasket is very sharp.**
    b. Lightly lubricate head bolts with clean engine oil.
    c. **Torque** cylinder head bolts in sequence, **Fig. 32,** to 52 ft. lbs.
    d. Back off bolts in sequence 360°.
    e. **Torque** bolts to 77 ft. lbs.
    f. Inspect to ensure all bolts are at 77 ft. lbs.
    g. Tighten all bolts in sequence an additional ¼ turn.

CYLINDER HEAD SERVICE

Cylinder Head Refacing

The cylinder head may be resurfaced in whatever increments are required to clean up the head surface. The combined total of stock removed cannot exceed .03937 inch. After resurface is complete, steel stamp the amount removed on the lower right rear face of the head, **Fig. 33.**

Inspect for valve protrusion after head resurface.

CYLINDER BLOCK SERVICE

Cylinder Bore Repair

Cylinder bores can be repaired two

ways. Either over boring and using oversize pistons and rings or by boring and installing a repair sleeve to return the bore to its standard dimension.

OVER BORING

Oversize pistons and rings are available in two sizes of .0197 inch and .0393 inch. Any combination of standard or overbore sizes may be used in the same engine. If more than .0393 inch over bore is required, a repair sleeve must be installed. A sleeved cylinder can not be bored, sleeve must be bored out and a new sleeve installed.

Cylinder bores may be bored twice before use of a repair sleeve is required. The first bore is .0197 inch oversize. the second bore is .0393 inch oversize, **Fig. 34.** After boring to size use a honing stone to chamfer the edge of the bore.

A correctly honed surface will have a crosshatch appearance with the line at 15° to 20° angles to the top of the cylinder head, **Fig. 35.** For the rough hone, use 80 grit honing stones. To finish the hone, use 280 grit honing stones. A maximum of 48 micro inch surface finish must be obtained.

After finish honing is complete, immediately clean cylinder bores with a strong solution of laundry detergent and hot water. After rinsing blow block dry. Inspect bore cleanliness by wiping with a lightly oiled white cloth. There should be grit or residue present. If block is not to be used right away, then lightly coat with a rust prevention compound.

REPAIR SLEEVE

If more than .0393 inch diameter oversize bore is required, the cylinder head must be bored and a repair sleeve installed. A sleeved cylinder can not be bored, sleeve must be bored out and a new sleeve installed.

1. Bore cylinder to 4.1142–4.1148 inch, **Fig. 36.** Repair sleeves may be replaced by using a boring bar to bore out old sleeve. **Do not cut cylinder bore beyond oversize limit.**
2. Thoroughly clean bore of metal chips, debris and oil residue before installing sleeve.
3. Cool repair sleeves to 10° F or below for a minimum of one hour. Be ready to install sleeve immediately after removing it from freezer.
4. Apply a coat of Loctite 620, or equivalent to bore that is to be sleeved, then with protective gloves push cold sleeve into bore as far as possible.
5. Drive sleeve downward until it contacts bottom of bore. A sleeve driver may be constructed as outlined in **Fig. 37.**
6. With a boring bar, or equivalent, machine sleeve to 4.014 inches, **Fig. 38,** then use a honing stone to chamfer edge of bore. A correctly honed surface will have a crosshatch appearance with lines at 15° to 20° angles to top of cylinder head, **Fig. 35.** For rough hone, use 80 grit honing stones. To finish hone, use 280 grit honing stones. A maximum of 48 micro inch surface finish must be obtained.
7. After finish honing is complete, immediately clean cylinder bores with a strong solution of laundry detergent and hot water, then allow blow block dry.
8. Inspect bore cleanliness by wiping with a lightly oiled white cloth. There should be no grit or residue present.
9. If block is not to be used right away lightly coat with a rust prevention compound.
10. A standard diameter piston and piston ring set must be used with a sleeved cylinder bore.

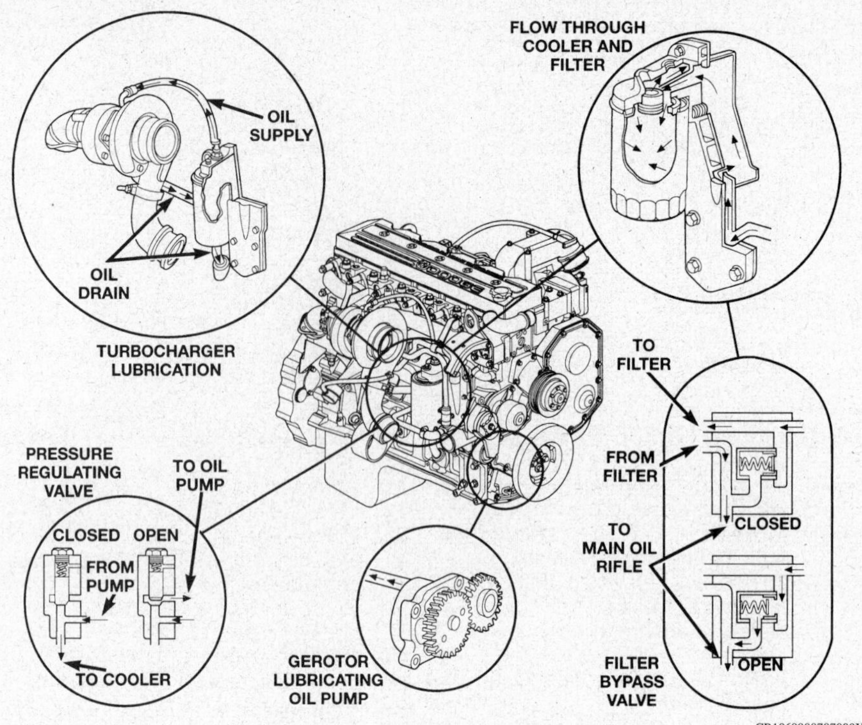

Fig. 7 Lubrication system

ROCKER ARM & PUSHRODS

1. Remove cylinder head cover, then the rocker arms and pedestals. Mark arms and pedestals for installation reference.
2. Remove pushrods and crossheads. Mark pushrods and crossheads for installation reference.
3. Remove rocker shafts, **Fig. 39.** Inspect shafts for cracks and excessive wear, replace as required.
4. Remove socket. Inspect socket and ball insert for wear, replace as required.
5. Measure rocker arm bore with a suitable gauge, **Fig. 40,** replace rocker arm if bore is over .867 inch in diameter.
6. Measure rocker shaft with suitable micrometer, **Fig. 41,** replace rocker arm shafts if measurement is less than .865 inch.
7. Reverse procedure to install, noting the following:
   a. Ensure pushrods are seated in tappets.
   b. Lubricate valve tips, crossheads and push rod sockets before assembly.
   c. Verify valve lash adjustment.

VALVE ARRANGEMENT

Front to rear ....I-E-I-E-I-E-I-E-I-E-I-E

VALVE CLEARANCE SPECIFICATIONS

Clearance specifications for intake valves: .010 inch, exhaust valves: .026 inch.

VALVE ADJUSTMENT

This system is a low maintenance design. Routine adjustments are not required. However, measurements should still be taken place when troubleshooting performance problems, or when completing a repair that included the removal and installation of the valve train components.

1. Remove cylinder head cover.
2. Remove fuel pump gear access cover.
3. Rotate engine and align pump gear mark with top dead center (TDC) mark on gear housing cover using crankshaft barring tool No. 7471B, or equivalent, **Fig. 42.**
4. With engine in this position, (pump gear mark at 12 o'clock position), valve lash can be measured at indicated intake and exhaust valves, **Fig. 42.**
5. Valve lash is measured between rocker arm socket and crosshead. Intake valve lash specification is .006–.015 inch, and exhaust valve specification is .015–.030 inch.
6. Rotate crankshaft one revolution, (pump gear mark is aligned at 6 o'clock

CONDITION	POSSIBLE CAUSES	CORRECTION
ENGINE WILL NOT CRANK OR CRANKS SLOWLY	1. Starting motor operating, but not cranking the engine.	1. Remove the starter motor. Check for broken flywheel teeth or a broken starting motor spring.
	2. Crankshaft rotation restricted.	2. Rotate the engine to check for rotational resistance.
	3. Starting circuit connections loose or corroded.	3. Clean and tighten connections.
	4. Neutral safety switch or starter relay inoperative.	4. Check starter relay supply voltage and proper operation of neutral safety switch if equipped. Replace defective parts.
	5. Battery charge low.	5. Check battery voltage. Replace battery if a charge cannot be held.
	6. No voltage to starter solenoid.	6. Check voltage to solenoid. If necessary, replace the solenoid.
	7. Solenoid or starter motor inoperative.	7. Replace starter motor.

CR1069700684000X

Fig. 8 Engine will not crank or cranks slowly

CONDITION	POSSIBLE CAUSES	CORRECTION
ENGINE HARD TO START, OR WILL NOT START—SMOKE FROM EXHAUST	1. Incorrect starting procedure.	1. The fuel shutoff solenoid control must be in the run position. Ensure proper procedure is being used.
	2. Cranking speed too slow.	2. A. Verify that the transmission is not engaged. B. Check the battery, starting motor and look for loose or corroded wiring connections. C. Rotate the engine with barring tool (Snap-on Tool SP371, MTE No. 3377462, or equivalent) to check for external rotational resistance.
	3. Intake heater system not working.	3. Verify system is working. Repair/replace inoperative parts.
	4. Insufficient intake air.	4. Inspect or replace filter and check for obstructions to the air supply tube.
	5. Air in fuel system or the fuel supply is inadequate.	5. Check the flow through the filter and bleed the system. Locate and eliminate the air source.
	6. Fuel transfer (lift) pump.	6. Measure transfer pump outlet pressure. If needed, repair or replace pump.
	7. Injection pump throttle linkage loose or damaged.	7. Visually check the linkage. Adjust/replace linkage.
	8. Contaminated fuel.	8. Verify by operating the engine with clean fuel from a temporary tank. Check for presence of gasoline. Drain and flush fuel supply tank. Replace fuel/water separator filter.
	9. Fuel screen plugged.	9. Check fuel screen.
	10. One or more injectors worn or not operating properly.	10. Check/replace improperly operating injectors.
	11. Worn or inoperative injection pump.	11. Visually check fuel delivery with an externally connected injector to one of the pump outlets. Repair or replace the pump if fuel is not being delivered.
	12. Injection pump out of time.	12. Check/Time the pump
	13. Valves incorrectly adjusted.	13. Adjust valves.
	14. Engine compression low.	14. Check compression to identify the problem.

CR1069700686000X

Fig. 10 Engine hard to start or will not start-smoke from exhaust

ENGINE CRANKS, BUT WILL NOT START—NO SMOKE FROM EXHAUST	1. No fuel in supply tank.	1. Fill fuel supply.
	2. Electrical fuel shutdown solenoid not operating.	2. Check for loose wires and verify that the fuel shutdown solenoid and fuel shutdown solenoid relay are functioning.
	3. Air intake or exhaust plugged.	3. Remove the obstruction.
	4. Fuel filter plugged.	4. Drain fuel/water separator and replace fuel filter.
	5. Excessive fuel inlet restriction.	5. Check fuel inlet restriction. Correct cause.
	6. Injection pump not getting fuel or fuel is aerated.	6. Check fuel flow/bleed fuel system.
	7. Inoperative fuel transfer (Lift) pump.	7. Check fuel line for restrictions and fuel pressure.
	8. One or more injectors worn or not operating properly.	8. Check/replace bad or improperly operating injectors.
	9. Worn or inoperative injection pump.	9. Visually check delivery with externally connected injector to one of the pump outlets. Repair or replace the pump if fuel is not being delivered.
	10. Internal pump timing incorrect.	10. Time the pump
	11. Camshaft out of time.	11. Check/correct gear train timing alignment.

CR1069700685000X

Fig. 9 Engine cranks, will not start-no smoke from exhaust

CONDITION	POSSIBLE CAUSES	CORRECTION
ENGINE STARTS, BUT WILL NOT KEEP RUNNING	1. Idle speed too low for the accessories.	1 Adjust the idle speed.
	2. Intake air or exhaust system restricted.	2. Visually check for exhaust restriction and inspect the air intake. Repair/replace restricting parts.
	3. Air in the fuel system or the fuel supply is inadequate.	3. Check flow through the filter and bleed the system. Locate and eliminate the air source.
	4. Fuel waxing due to extremely cold weather.	4. Verify by inspecting the fuel filter. Clean the system and use climatized fuel. Replace fuel/water separator filter. Check fuel heater for proper operation.
	5. Contaminated fuel.	5. Verify by operating the engine with clean fuel from a temporary supply tank. Check for presence of gasoline. Replace fuel/water separator filter.

CR1069700687000X

Fig. 11 Engine starts, does not stay running

SURGING (SPEED CHANGE)	1. If the condition occurs at idle, the idle speed is set too low for the accessories.	1. Adjust the idle speed.
	2. Improperly operating injection pump.	2. Replace the injector pump.

CR1069700688000X

Fig. 12 Surging (Speed change)

position), and set valve lash for intake and exhaust valves indicated, **Fig. 42.**
7. Install cylinder head cover and fuel pump access cover.

VALVE LIFTERS

Removal

1. Install lifter removal service tool, **Fig. 43,** insert through to full length of cam bore.
2. Position trough so it will catch lifter when dowel is removed. **Remove only one lifter at a time.** Remove rubber band from two companion lifters, securing lifter not to be removed with rubber band. Pull up dowel from lifter bore, allowing lifter to fall into trough.
3. Carefully pull trough and lifter from cam bore and remove lifter.
4. Identify location of each lifter as it removed for installation reference.

Installation

1. Insert trough full length of cam bore.
2. Lower tappet installation tool through pushrod hole into trough, **Fig. 44.**
3. Retrieve tappet installation tool using hooked rod provided with tool kit, **Fig. 45.**
4. Lubricate lifter on stem and face with Lubriplate 105, or equivalent.
5. Insert installation tool into lifter, then place lifter and tool in trough, **Fig. 46.**
6. Pull tool and lifter through cam bore and up into lifter bore. After lifter has been pulled up into position, slide trough back into cam bore and rotate it ½ turn. This will position round side of trough up, which will hold lifter in place.
7. Remove installation tool, then install dowel into lifter and secure with rubber band.
8. Install camshaft and gear as outlined in "Camshaft, Replace."

FRONT COVER SEAL

REPLACE

Removal

1. Raise and support vehicle.
2. Partially drain engine coolant into suitable container.
3. Lower vehicle.
4. Remove radiator upper hose.
5. Disconnect coolant recovery bottle hose from radiator filler neck and lift bottle off of fan shroud.
6. Disconnect windshield washer pump supply hose and electrical connections and lift washer bottle off of fan shroud.
7. Remove fan shroud to radiator mounting bolts.
8. Remove viscous fan/drive assembly. Fan drive nut has lefthand threads.
9. Remove cooling fan shroud and fan assembly from vehicle.
10. Remove accessory drive belt.
11. Remove cooling fan support/hub from front of engine.
12. Raise and support vehicle. Remove crankshaft damper.
13. Lower vehicle.
14. Remove gear cover to housing bolts and gently pry cover away from housing, use care to prevent marring surfaces.

ROUGH IDLE (IRREGULARLY FIRING OR ENGINE SHAKING)	1. If engine is cold, intake heater system defective. 2. Idle speed too low for the accessories. 3. Engine mounts damaged or lose. 4. High pressure fuel leaks. 5. Air in the fuel system. 6. Sticking needle valve in an injector.	1. Refer to intake heater system 2. Adjust idle speed. 3. Repair or replace mounts. 4. Correct leaks in the high pressure lines, fittings or delivery valves. 5. Bleed the fuel system and eliminate the source of the air. 6. Check and replace the injector with the sticking needle valve.

CR1069700689000X

Fig. 13 Rough idle (misfire or engine shaking)

CONDITION	POSSIBLE CAUSES	CORRECTION
ENGINE RUNS ROUGH CONT.	4. Incorrect valve operation. 5. Injection pump timing incorrect. 6. Improperly operating injectors. 7. Defective injection pump (delivery valve). 8. Camshaft out of time. 9. Damaged camshaft or tappets.	4. Check for a bent push rod and adjust valves. Replace push rod, if necessary. 5. Check/time pump 6. Replace inoperative injectors. 7. Repair or replace injection pump. 8. Check/correct gear train timing alignment. 9. Inspect camshaft valve lift. Replace camshaft and tappets.

CR1069700690020X

Fig. 14 Engine runs rough (Part 2 of 2)

ENGINE RUNS ROUGH	1. Fuel injection lines leaking. 2. Air in the fuel or the fuel supply is inadequate. 3. Contaminated fuel.	1. Correct leaks in the high pressure lines, fittings, injectors sealing washers or delivery valves. 2. Check the flow through the filter and bleed the system. Locate and eliminate the air source. 3. Verify by operating the engine with clean fuel from a temporary supply tank. Check for presence of gasoline. Replace fuel/water separator filter.

CR1069700690010X

Fig. 14 Engine runs rough (Part 1 of 2)

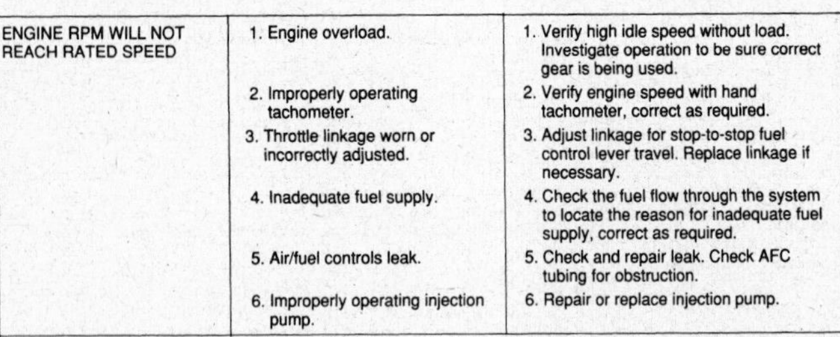

ENGINE RPM WILL NOT REACH RATED SPEED	1. Engine overload. 2. Improperly operating tachometer. 3. Throttle linkage worn or incorrectly adjusted. 4. Inadequate fuel supply. 5. Air/fuel controls leak. 6. Improperly operating injection pump.	1. Verify high idle speed without load. Investigate operation to be sure correct gear is being used. 2. Verify engine speed with hand tachometer, correct as required. 3. Adjust linkage for stop-to-stop fuel control lever travel. Replace linkage if necessary. 4. Check the fuel flow through the system to locate the reason for inadequate fuel supply, correct as required. 5. Check and repair leak. Check AFC tubing for obstruction. 6. Repair or replace injection pump.

CR1069700691000X

Fig. 15 Engine will not reach rated speed

15. Support cover on flat work surface with wooden blocks.
16. Drive old seal out of cover from outside of cover.

Installation

1. Apply a bead of Mopar Stud and Bearing Mount, or equivalent, to outside diameter of seal. Do not lubricate inner diameter of new seal.
2. With cover supported by wood blocks, install seal into rear of cover using crankshaft seal installer tool No. 8281 and handle No. C-4171, or equivalents.
3. Strike driver handle until installation tool bottoms out on inside of cover.
4. Install plastic seal pilot (provided with seal kit) into crankshaft seal.
5. Apply a bead of Mopar Silicone Rubber Adhesive Sealant, or equivalent, to gear housing cover sealing surface.
6. Install cover to gear housing, aligning seal pilot with nose of crankshaft.
7. Install cover bolts tightening to specifications.
8. Install crankshaft damper tightening bolts to specifications. Use engine barring tool to keep engine from rotating during tightening operation. Install fan support/hub assembly tightening bolts to specifications.
9. Install accessory drive belt.
10. Start engine and inspect for leaks.

FRONT COVER

REPLACE

Refer to "Front Cover Seal, Replace" for replacement procedure.

CAMSHAFT

REPLACE

Removal

1. Recover A/C refrigerant as outlined in "Air Conditioning" chapter.
2. Raise and support vehicle.
3. Drain coolant into suitable container, lower vehicle.
4. Remove upper and lower radiator hoses and viscous fan drive assembly.
5. Disconnect coolant recovery bottle hose from radiator filler neck.
6. Remove cooling fan shroud.
7. Disconnect ATC cooler lines, if equipped, using disconnect tool No. 6931, or equivalent.
8. Remove radiator and upper radiator support panel.
9. Remove front bumper.
10. Disconnect A/C condenser refrigerant lines, if equipped, and charge air cooler piping from cooler inlet and outlet.
11. Remove charge air cooler and A/C condenser, if equipped, from vehicle.
12. Remove serpentine drive belt, fan support/hub assembly and crankshaft damper.
13. Remove pump gear access cover by rotating counterclockwise.
14. Rotate crankshaft to bring engine to TDC No.1 using engine barring tool No 7471B, or equivalent.
15. Remove gear cover to housing bolts and gently pry cover away from housing. Take care not to mar gasket surfaces.
16. Remove cylinder head cover, rocker arms, cross heads and pushrods. Mark components for installation reference.
17. Remove tappets using wooden dowels provided with Miller Tool Kit No. 8502 or Cummins tappet replacement tool kit No. 3822513, or equivalent, as follow:
    a. Insert slotted end of dowel rod into tappet. Dowel rods for rear two cylinders will have to be cut for cowl panel clearance.
    b. Press firmly to ensure dowels are seated firmly in tappet.
    c. Raise dowel rod to bring tappet to top of its travel, then wrap a rubber band around dowel rods to prevent tappets from dropping into crankcase.
18. Repeat procedure for remaining cylinders.
19. Verify that camshaft timing marks are aligned with crankshaft and injection pump marks.
20. Remove bolts from thrust late.
21. When removing camshaft and thrust plate, hold on to thrust plate to prevent it from falling into crankcase.
22. Remove camshaft and thrust plate.

Installation

1. Lubricate camshaft bushings and bores with fresh engine oil.
2. Liberally coat camshaft lobes, journals, and thrust washer with fresh engine oil or suitable lubricant.
3. When installing camshaft do not push in farther than it will go with thrust washer in place. Pushing in too far can dislodge plug in the rear of camshaft bore and cause oil leaks.
4. Install camshaft and thrust plate. Align timing marks, **Figs. 47 and 48.**
5. Install thrust plate bolts to and tighten to specifications.
6. Measure camshaft backlash and end clearance.
7. Remove wooden dowel rods and rubber bands from tappets.
8. Lubricate pushrods with engine oil and install in original locations. Ensure they are properly seated in tappets.
9. Lubricate valve tips with engine oil and install cross heads in original locations.
10. Install crossheads and pushrod sockets with engine oil, then install rocker arms and pedestals in their original locations and tighten to specifications.
11. Verify valve lash adjustment.
12. Install cylinder head cover and reusable gasket and tighten bolts to specifications.
13. Apply a bead of suitable silicone adhesive sealant to gear housing cover. Install and tighten bolts to specifications.
14. Install remaining components in reverse order of removal and tighten bolts to specifications.

LOW POWER	1. Fuel control lever not moving to full throttle.	1. Check/correct for stop-to-stop travel.
	2. High oil level.	2. Check/correct oil level.
	3. Engine overloaded.	3. Check for added loading from accessories or driven units, brakes dragging and other changes in vehicle loading. Repair/replace as needed.
	4. Slow throttle response caused by leaking or obstructed air control tube or improperly operating control in the pump.	4. Check for leaks and obstructions. Tighten the fittings. Repair or replace the pump if the controls are not functioning.
	5. Inadequate intake air flow.	5. Inspect/replace air cleaner element. Look for other restrictions.
	6. Inadequate fuel supply. Air in the fuel.	6. Inspect/correct leaks in the high pressure lines, fittings injectors sealing washers or delivery valve seals.
	7. Excessive exhaust restriction.	7. Check/correct the restriction in the exhaust system.

CR1069700692010X

Fig. 16 Low power (Part 1 of 2)

CONDITION	POSSIBLE CAUSES	CORRECTION
LOW POWER CONT.	8. High fuel temperature.	8. Verify that fuel heater is off when engine is warm. Check for restricted fuel drain tube. Repair/replace as needed.
	9. Poor quality fuel or fuel contaminated with gasoline.	9. Verify by operating from a temporary tank with good fuel. Check for presence of gasoline. Replace fuel/water separator filter.
	10. Air leak between the turbocharger and the intake manifold.	10. Check/correct leaks in hoses, gaskets, charge air cooler and around mounting capscrews or through holes in the manifold cover.
	11. Exhaust leak at the manifold or turbocharger.	11. Check/correct leaks in the manifold or turbocharger gaskets. If manifold is cracked, replace manifold.
	12. Improperly operating turbocharger.	12. Inspect/replace turbocharger.
	13. Wastegate operation.	13. Check waste gate operation.
	14. Valve not operating.	14. Check for bent push rod, replace if necessary.
	15. Worn or improperly operating injectors.	15. Check/replace injectors.
	16. Incorrect injection pump timing.	16. Verify injection pump timing
	17. Improperly operating injection pump.	17. Repair or replace injection pump.

CR1069700692020X

Fig. 16 Low power (Part 2 of 2)

EXCESSIVE EXHAUST SMOKE	1. Engine running too cold (white smoke).	1. Refer to troubleshooting for coolant temperature below normal Inspect intake manifold heater system for proper operation.
	2. Improper starting procedure (white smoke).	2. Use proper starting procedures.
	3. Fuel supply inadequate.	3. Check fuel supply pressure and inlet restriction.
	4. Injection pump timing.	4. Check and time pump
	5. Inadequate intake air.	5. Inspect/change air filter. Look for other restriction. Check charge air cooler for obstructions.
	6. Air leak between turbocharger and intake manifold.	6. Check/correct leaks in the air crossover tube, hoses, gaskets, mounting capscrews or through holes in the manifold cover.
	7. Exhaust leak at the manifold or turbocharger.	7. Check/correct leaks in the manifold or turbocharger gaskets. If cracked, replace manifold.
	8. Improperly operating turbocharger.	8. Inspect/replace turbocharger.
	9. Improperly operating injectors.	9. Check and replace inoperative injectors.

CR1069700693010X

Fig. 17 Excessive exhaust smoke (Part 1 of 2)

CONDITION	POSSIBLE CAUSES	CORRECTION
EXCESSIVE EXHAUST SMOKE CONT.	10. Improperly operating or overfueled injector pump.	10. Repair or replace injection pump.
	11. Piston rings not sealing (blue smoke).	11. Perform blow-by check. Correct as required.

CR1069700693020X

Fig. 17 Excessive exhaust smoke (Part 2 of 2)

PISTON & ROD ASSEMBLY

Assemble piston to rod, ensure the "Front" marking on piston and the numbers on rod and cap are oriented as outlined in **Fig. 49.** Pistons do not require heating to install pin. Position piston and rod into cylinder bore with the word "Front" on piston towards front of cylinder block.

The top surfaces of all rings are identified with the word "Top" or suppliers "Mark." Position rings on piston as outlined in **Fig. 50.**

PISTONS, PINS & RINGS

Piston Grading

1. Install any original piston and rod assemblies into cylinder No. 1. **Do not install piston rings**
2. Install upper bearing shell in connecting rod. **Tang on bearing must index with slot on connecting rod and connecting rod bearing shell must be installed in original connecting rod and cap. Four digit number stamped on connecting rod and cap at parting line must match and be installed on oil cooler side of engine.**
3. Install connecting rod and cap screws, then tighten cap screws to specifications.
4. With a suitable fine grit stone remove any burrs or nicks from cylinder block head deck, install and zero a suitable dial indicator to cylinder block head deck.
5. Place dial indicator directly over piston pin to eliminate side to side movement, then bring crankshaft to top dead center (TDC) position.
6. Rotate crankshaft clockwise and counterclockwise, then note highest reading on dial indicator.
7. Remove piston and rod assembly from cylinder.
8. Determine piston grade by referring to four digit grading number located on top of piston head, **Fig. 51,** then to piston protrusion chart, **Fig. 52.** If piston grading number can not be seen, then measure from piston pin to top of piston, **Fig. 53.** Refer to applicable chart, **Fig. 54,** to determine what grade piston is used.
9. Repeat procedure for each cylinder using same piston and rod assembly.

Piston Ring End Gap

1. Determine piston diameter and obtain appropriate ring set.
2. Position each ring set in cylinder and use a piston to square it with bore at a depth of 3.5 inches.
3. Use a feeler gauge to measure ring end gap.
4. Top ring end gap specification is .010–.014 inch, intermediate ring end gap specification is .0334–.0452 inch and oil control ring end gap specification is .0100–.0215 inch.

MAIN & ROD BEARINGS

Crankshaft main bearings are available in standard and undersize. Main bearing sizes are .0197 and .0394. Rod bearings are available in standard and oversizes. Rod bearing sizes are .0098, .0197, .0295 and .0394.

On 2002 models, **torque** connecting rod cap bolts first to 26 ft. lbs., then to 51 ft. lbs., and finally to 73 ft. lbs. **Torque** main bearing cap bolts first to 45 ft. lbs., then to 88 ft. lbs., and finally to 129 ft. lbs.

On 2003–06 models, **torque** connecting rod cap bolts first to 22 ft. lbs., then to 44 ft. lbs., and finally rotate an additional 60°. **Torque** main bearing cap bolts first to 37 ft. lbs., then to 59 ft. lbs., and finally rotate an additional 90°.

CRANKSHAFT REAR OIL SEAL

REPLACE

1. Raise and support vehicle, then remove transmission.
2. **On models equipped with manual transmission,** remove clutch cover and clutch plate.
3. **On all models,** remove flywheel or converter drive plate.
4. Drill holes 180° apart into seal, then use a slide hammer and number ten screw and pull, alternating from side to side, until seal is free.
5. Install seal using seal pilot provided in seal kit. Push seal on pilot and onto crankshaft.
6. Remove pilot and drive seal on using alignment tool and hammer.
7. Reverse remaining procedure to install.

ENGINE WILL NOT SHUT OFF	1. Fuel shutoff solenoid or solenoid relay inoperative. 2. Engine running on fumes drawn into the air intake. 3. Fuel injection pump malfunction.	1. Check/replace fuel shutoff solenoid or relay. 2. Check the air intake ducts for the source of fumes. **WARNING: In case of engine runaway due to flammable fumes from gasoline spills or turbocharger oil leaks being sucked into the engine. Shut off engine ignition switch first then use a CO2 fire extinguisher and direct the spray under the front bumper to remove oxygen supply. The engine air intake is on the passenger side behind the bumper. The fire extinguisher must be directed at this location for emergency shutdown conditions.** 3. Repair or replace fuel injection pump.

CR1069700694000X

Fig. 18 Engine will not shut off

CONDITION	POSSIBLE CAUSES	CORRECTION
COOLANT TEMPERATURE ABOVE NORMAL CONT.	10. Inoperative water pump. 11. Incorrect injection pump timing. 12. Overfueled injection pump. 13. Plugged cooling passages in radiator, head, head gasket or block. 14. Engine overloaded.	10. Check and replace the water pump. 11. Check/time the injector pump 12. Repair or replace the injection pump. 13. Flush the system and fill with clean coolant. 14. Verify that the engine load rating is not being exceeded.

CR1069700695020X

Fig. 19 Coolant temperature above normal (Part 2 of 2)

COOLANT TEMPERATURE ABOVE NORMAL	1. Low coolant level. 2. Incorrect/improperly operating pressure cap. 3. Loose drive belt on water pump/fan. 4. Inadequate air flow to the radiator. 5. Radiator fins plugged. 6. Collapsed radiator hose. 7. Improperly operating temperature sensor/gauge. 8. Improperly operating, incorrect or no thermostat. 9. Air in the cooling system.	1. Check coolant level. Add coolant, if necessary. Locate and correct the source of the coolant loss. 2. Replace cap with the correct rating for the system. 3. Check/replace belt or belt tensioner. 4. Check/repair radiator core, fan shroud and viscous fan drive as required. 5. Blow debris from fins. 6. Replace the hose. Check cap operation, 7. Verify that the gauge and temperature sensor are accurate. Replace gauge/sensor, if bad. 8. Check and replace the thermostat. 9. A. Make sure the fill rate is not being exceeded and the correct vented thermostat is installed. B. Check for loose hose clamps. Tighten if loose. C. If aeration continued, check for a compression leak through the head gasket.

CR1069700695010X

Fig. 19 Coolant temperature above normal (Part 1 of 2)

COOLANT TEMPERATURE BELOW NORMAL	1. Too much air flow across the radiator. 2. Incorrect thermostat or contamination in thermostat. 3. Temperature sensor or gauge inoperative. 4. Coolant not flowing by temperature sensor.	1. Check/repair viscous fan drive as required. 2. Check and replace thermostat. 3. Verify that the gauge and sensor are accurate. If not, replace gauge/sensor. 4. Check and clean coolant passages.

CR1069700696000X

Fig. 20 Coolant temperature below normal

OIL PAN

REPLACE

1. Install engine support fixture tool No. 8534, or equivalent.
2. Raise and support vehicle.
3. Remove transmission and transfer case.
4. Remove flywheel, then disconnect starter cables from starter motor.
5. Remove starter motor, then the transmission adapter plate assembly.
6. Drain engine oil into suitable container, then remove oil pan bolts.
7. Lower pan slightly, then remove oil suction tube fasteners.
8. Remove oil pan, then the suction tube.
9. Reverse procedure to install, tighten bolts to specifications.

OIL PUMP

REPLACE

Removal

1. Remove fan assembly, then the drive belt.
2. Remove radiator, fan clutch assembly, then the fan hub.
3. Remove oil filler tube, crankshaft vibration damper and front cover.
4. Remove pump attaching bolts, then the pump from bore in cylinder block.

Installation

1. Lubricate pump with clean engine oil. Filling pump with clean engine oil during installation will help to prime pump at engine start up.
2. Ensure idler gear pin is installed in locating bore in cylinder block.
3. Install pump, **torque** bolts in numbered sequence, **Fig. 55,** in two steps to specified values.
4. Step 1: **Torque** bolts to 44 inch lbs on 2002 models and to 71 inch lbs., on 2003–06 models.
5. Step 2: **Torque** bolts to 18 ft. lbs.
6. Back plate on pump seats against bottom of bore in cylinder block. When pump is correctly installed, flange on pump will not touch cylinder block.
7. Measure idler gear to pump drive gear backlash and idler gear to crankshaft gear backlash, **Fig. 56.**
8. **On 2002 models,** maximum allowable backlash is .0296–.0335 inch.
9. **On 2003–06 models,** maximum allowable backlash is .006–.010 inch.
10. **On all models,** if oil pump gear backlash measures outside of specified range, replace pump.
11. Apply a bead of suitable rubber adhesive silicone sealant to gear housing cover sealing surface.
12. Install gear housing cover, tighten mounting bolts to specifications.
13. Install vibration damper, tighten to specifications. Use engine barring device to keep engine from rotating during tightening.
14. Install fan support/hub assembly, tighten to specifications.
15. Install remaining components in reverse order of removal.

OIL PUMP SERVICE

1. Visually inspect pump gears for chips, cracks or excessive wear or damage.
2. Remove back plate.
3. Mark "Top" on georotor planetary using a felt tip marker.
4. Remove georotor planetary. Inspect planetary and housing for excessive wear or damage.
5. Install georotor planetary in original position. Chamfer must be on O.D. and down.
6. Measure tip clearance, **Fig. 57.**
7. Maximum allowable clearance is .007 inch. If pump measure outside of specified range, replace pump.
8. Measure clearance of georotor drive/georotor planetary to port plate, **Fig. 58.**
9. Maximum allowable clearance is .005 inch. If pump measure outside of specified range, replace pump.
10. Measure clearance of georotor planetary to body bore, **Fig. 59.**
11. Maximum allowable clearance is .015 inch. If pump measures outside of specified range, replace pump.
12. Measure gear backlash, **Fig. 60.**
13. **On 2002 models,** maximum allowable backlash is .0296–.0335 inch. If pump backlash measures outside of specified range, replace pump.
14. **On 2003–06 models,** maximum allowable backlash is 006–.1010 inch. If pump backlash measures outside of specified range, replace pump.
15. **On all models,** install back plate.

BELT TENSION DATA

This engine is equipped with a spring loaded automatic belt tensioner. **Do not attempt to inspect belt tension with a belt tension gauge.** If tension is not maintained properly, inspect for improper drive belt routing, excessive belt wear or automatic tensioner damage.

SERPENTINE DRIVE BELT

Belt Routing

Refer to **Figs. 61 through 63** for drive belt routing.

CONDITION	POSSIBLE CAUSES	CORRECTION
LUBRICATING OIL PRESSURE LOW	1. Low oil level.	1. A. Check and fill with clean engine oil. B. Check for a severe external oil leak that could reduce the pressure.
	2. Oil viscosity thin, diluted or wrong specification.	2. Verify the correct oil is being used. Check for oil dilution.
	3. Improperly operating pressure switch/gauge.	3. Verify the pressure switch is functioning correctly. If not, replace switch/gauge.
	4. Relief valve stuck open.	4. Check/replace valve.
	5. Plugged oil filter.	5. Change oil filter. Oil filter change interval may need to be revised.
	6. If cooler was replaced, shipping plugs left in cooler.	6. Check/remove shipping plugs.
	7. Worn oil pump.	7. Check and replace oil pump.
	8. Suction tube loose or seal leaking.	8. Check and replace seal.
	9. Loose main bearing cap.	9. Check and install new bearing and tighten cap to proper torque.
	10. Worn bearings or wrong bearings installed.	10. Inspect and replace connecting rod or main bearings. Check and replace piston cooling nozzles.
	11. Oil jet under piston bad fit into main carrier.	11. Check oil jet position.

CR1069700697000X

Fig. 21 Lubricating oil pressure low

LUBRICATING OIL LOSS	1. External leaks.	1. Visually inspect for oil leaks. Repair as required.
	2. Crankcase being overfilled.	2. Verify that the correct dipstick is being used.
	3. Incorrect oil specification or viscosity.	3. A. Make sure the correct oil is being used. B. Look for reduced viscosity from dilution with fuel. C. Review/reduce the oil change intervals.
	4. Oil cooler leak.	4. Check and replace the oil cooler.
	5. High blow-by forcing oil out the breather.	5. Check the breather tube area for signs of oil loss. Perform the required repairs.
	6. Turbocharger leaking oil to the air intake.	6. Inspect the air ducts for evidence of oil transfer. Repair as required.
	7. Piston rings not sealing (oil being consumed by the engine).	7. Perform blow-by check. Repair as required.

CR1069700699000X

Fig. 23 Lubricating oil loss

LUBRICATING OIL PRESSURE TOO HIGH	1. Pressure switch/gauge not operating properly.	1. Verify the pressure switch is functioning correctly. If not, replace switch/gauge.
	2. Engine running to cold.	2. Refer to Coolant Temperature Below Normal
	3. Oil viscosity too thick.	3. Make sure the correct oil being used,
	4. Oil pressure relief valve stuck closed or binding.	4. Check and replace valve.

CR1069700698000X

Fig. 22 Lubricating oil pressure too high

CONDITION	POSSIBLE CAUSES	CORRECTION
COMPRESSION KNOCKS	1. Air in the fuel system.	1. Bleed the fuel system
	2. Poor quality fuel or water/gasoline contaminated fuel.	2. Verify by operating from a temporary tank with good fuel. Clean and flush the fuel supply tanks. Replace fuel/water separator filter.
	3. Engine overloaded.	3. Verify the engine load rating is not being exceeded.
	4. Incorrect injection pump timing.	4. Check and time injection pump
	5. Improperly operating injectors.	5. Check and replace inoperative injectors.

CR1069700700000X

Fig. 24 Compression knocks

Belt Replacement

2002

1. Attach a 3/8 inch long-handle ratchet to square hole in automatic belt tensioner, then rotate tensioner assembly counterclockwise (as viewed from front) until belt tension is relieved.
2. Remove belt from water pump pulley first, then from all other pulleys.
3. Reverse procedure to install.

2003-06

1. Attach a suitable socket wrench to pulley mounting bolt of automatic tensioner, then rotate tensioner clockwise (as viewed from front) until belt tension is relieved.
2. Remove belt from idler pulley first, then from all other pulleys.
3. Reverse procedure to install.

VACUUM PUMP

REPLACE

Removal

1. Place suitable drain pan under power steering pump.
2. Disconnect vacuum and power steering pump hoses.
3. Disconnect lubricating oil feed line from fitting at underside of vacuum pump.
4. Remove lower bolt that attaches pump assembly to engine block.
5. Remove bottom inboard nut attaching adapter to steering pump.
6. Remove upper pump attaching bolt, then the pump.
7. Remove nuts attaching vacuum pump to adapter.
8. Remove vacuum pump from adapter. Turn pump gear back and forth to disengage pump shaft from coupling.
9. Remove coupling from adapter.
10. Remove adapter attaching nuts and remove adapter from steering pump. If steering pump will be serviced, remove spacer from each inboard mounting stud on pump.

Installation

1. Clean and lubricate pump shaft with engine oil.
2. Install spacers on steering pump studs.
3. Install O-ring on adapter, then position adapter on pump studs.
4. Install attaching nuts on outboard studs and on two upper pump studs. Do not install nut on lower, inboard stud at this time.
5. Install coupling on pump shaft. Ensure coupling is securely engaged in shaft drive tangs.
6. Install vacuum pump on adapter. Rotate drive gear until tangs on pump shaft engage in coupling. Ensure pump is seated before installing attaching nuts.
7. Install and tighten vacuum pump attaching nuts to specification.
8. Lubricate adapter O-ring with engine oil.
9. Note position of drive slots in coupling, then rotate drive gear to align tangs on vacuum pump shaft with coupling.
10. Verify that pump is seated in adapter and coupling.
11. Install and tighten pump attaching nuts and washers to specification.
12. Position new gasket on vacuum pump mounting flange. Use suitable silicone adhesive sealer to hold gasket in place.
13. Insert pump assembly upper attaching bolt in mounting flange and gasket. Use sealer or grease to hold bolt in place if required.
14. Position pump assembly on engine and install upper bolt. Tighten upper bolt only enough to hold assembly in place.
15. From under vehicle, install pump assembly lower attaching bolt. Tighten bolts to specifications.
16. Position bracket on steering pump inboard stud. Then install remaining adapter attaching nut on stud and tighten to specifications.
17. Connect oil feed line to vacuum pump connector and tighten.
18. Connect steering pump pressure and return lines to pump and tighten to specifications.
19. Connect vacuum hose to pump.
20. Fill power steering pump reservoir, purge air from lines by starting engine and turning wheel left to right.
21. Stop engine and top up fluid.

COOLING SYSTEM BLEED

These engines do not require a specified bleed procedure. After filling cooling system, run engine to operating temperature with radiator/pressure cap off. Air will then be automatically bled through cap opening.

THERMOSTAT

REPLACE

1. Drain cooling system until level is below thermostat.
2. Remove radiator hose clamp and hose from thermostat housing.
3. Remove three thermostat housing bolts, then the thermostat housing.
4. Reverse procedure to install.

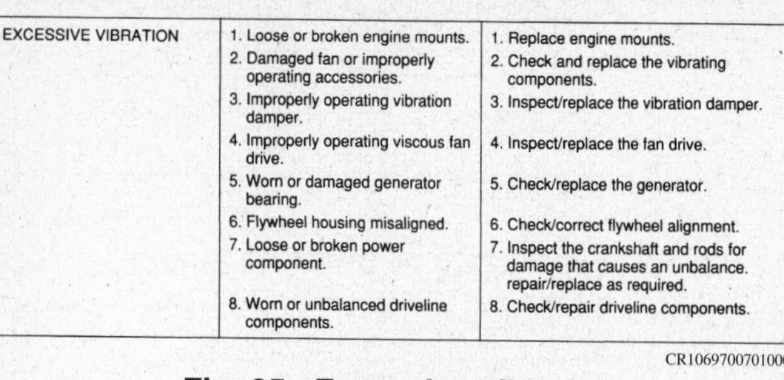

EXCESSIVE VIBRATION	1. Loose or broken engine mounts.	1. Replace engine mounts.
	2. Damaged fan or improperly operating accessories.	2. Check and replace the vibrating components.
	3. Improperly operating vibration damper.	3. Inspect/replace the vibration damper.
	4. Improperly operating viscous fan drive.	4. Inspect/replace the fan drive.
	5. Worn or damaged generator bearing.	5. Check/replace the generator.
	6. Flywheel housing misaligned.	6. Check/correct flywheel alignment.
	7. Loose or broken power component.	7. Inspect the crankshaft and rods for damage that causes an unbalance. repair/replace as required.
	8. Worn or unbalanced driveline components.	8. Check/repair driveline components.

CR1069700701000X

Fig. 25 Excessive vibration

EXCESSIVE ENGINE NOISES	1. Drive belt squeal, insufficient tension or abnormally high loading.	1. Check the automatic tensioner and inspect the drive belt. Make sure water pump, tensioner pulley, fan hub and generator turn freely.
	2. Intake air or exhaust leaks.	2. Refer to Excessive Exhaust smoke (Engine Diagnosis Performance).
	3. Excessive valve lash.	3. Adjust valves. Make sure the push rods are not bent and rocker levers or adjusting screws are not severely worn. Replace bent or severely worn pads.
	4. Turbocharger noise.	4. Check turbocharger impeller and turbine wheel for housing contact. Repair/replace as required.
	5. Gear train noise.	5. Visually inspect and measure gear backlash. Replace gears as required.
	6. Power function knock.	6. Check/replace rod and main bearings.

CR1069700702000X

Fig. 26 Excessive engine noises

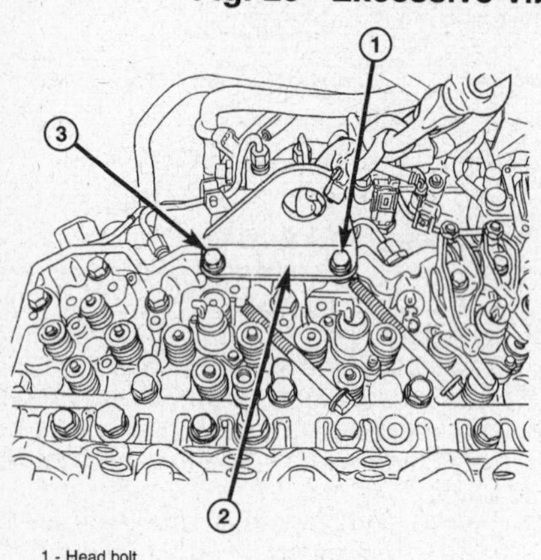

1 - Head bolt
2 - Engine Lift Bracket
3 - Head Bolt

LTV1900000000337

Fig. 27 Engine lift bracket installation

WATER PUMP

REPLACE

1. Drain coolant from system.
2. Remove drive belt as outlined in "Belt Replacement" in "Serpentine Drive Belt."
3. Remove any wiring harness clips from water pump.
4. Remove water pump bolts and pump from cylinder block, **Fig. 64.**
5. Reverse procedure to install. Tighten pump bolts to specifications.

RADIATOR

REPLACE

2002

1. Remove positive cable retaining nuts from radiator top and position cable to rear.
2. Drain cooling system, then disconnect throttle cable.
3. Remove hose clamps and hoses, then the overflow tank hose from filler neck nipple and tank from fan shroud T-slots.
4. Disconnect windshield washer reservoir tank electrical connectors and remove tank, then remove two upper fan shroud metal retaining clips.
5. Remove four fan shroud mounting bolts, then move shroud to rear.
6. Remove two upper mounting bolts and lift radiator from vehicle.
7. Reverse procedure to install.

CR1078800001000X

Fig. 28 Exhaust manifold bolt tightening sequence

2003-06

1. Drain cooling system into suitable container.
2. Remove air box, then turbocharger inlet tube.
3. Remove coolant tank hose, washer bottle hose and positive battery cable from fastening clips located on top of radiator.
4. Remove hose clamps, then hoses from radiator.
5. Remove power steering cooler bolts, then position cooler aside.
6. Disconnect transmission cooler lines at transmission.
7. Remove lower shroud assembly, then electronic viscous fan wiring from upper shroud assembly.
8. Remove two radiator upper mounting bolts.
9. Lift radiator straight up and out of engine compartment.
10. Reverse procedure to install.

TURBOCHARGER

REPLACE

Removal

1. Raise and support vehicle.
2. Disconnect exhaust pipe from turbocharger elbow.
3. Lower vehicle.
4. Disconnect turbocharger air inlet hose.
5. Disconnect turbocharger oil supply line and oil drain tube from turbocharger.
6. Disconnect charge air cooler inlet pipe from turbocharger.
7. Remove turbocharger and gasket from exhaust manifold.

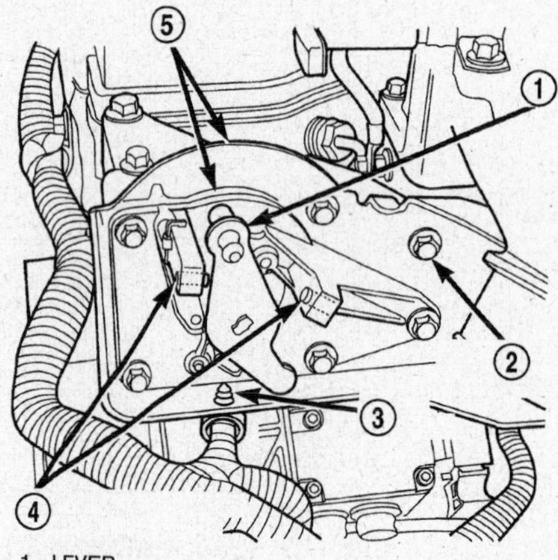

1 - LEVER
2 - MOUNTING BOLTS (6)
3 - WIRE HARNESS CLIP
4 - CALIBRATION SCREWS (NO ADJUSTMENT)
5 - APPS ASSEMBLY

LTV1900000000338

Fig. 29 Accelerator pedal position sensor assembly

8. If turbocharger is not to be installed immediately, cover opening to prevent material from entering manifold.
9. If replacing turbocharger, transfer discharge elbow and clamp to new assembly.
10. Clean and inspect sealing surface.

Installation

1. Apply anti-seize to studs, then tighten turbocharger mounting bolts to specifications.
2. Install oil drain tube to turbocharger and tighten mounting bolts to specifications.
3. Pre-lubricate turbocharger by pouring 2–3 ozs. of clean engine oil into oil supply line fitting. Carefully rotate turbocharger impeller by hand to distribute oil thoroughly.
4. Install oil supply line fitting tightening to specifications.
5. Position charge air cooler inlet pipe to turbocharger. With clamp in position, tighten clamp nut specifications.
6. Position air inlet hose to turbocharger, tighten clamp to specifications.
7. Raise and support vehicle.
8. Connect exhaust pipe to turbocharger, tighten bolts to specifications.
9. Lower vehicle.
10. Start engine and inspect for leaks.

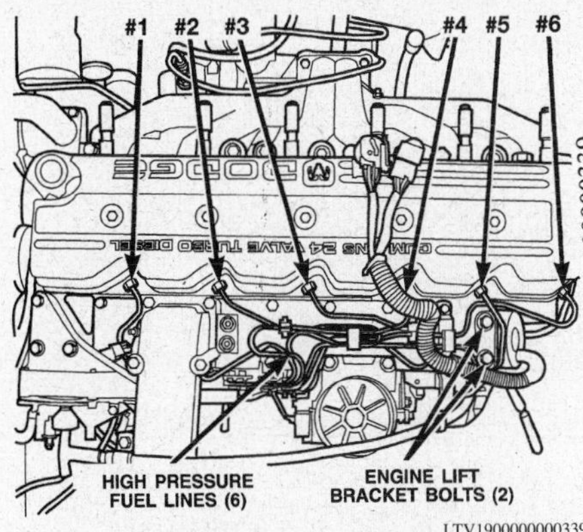

Fig. 30 High pressure lines at cylinder head. 2002

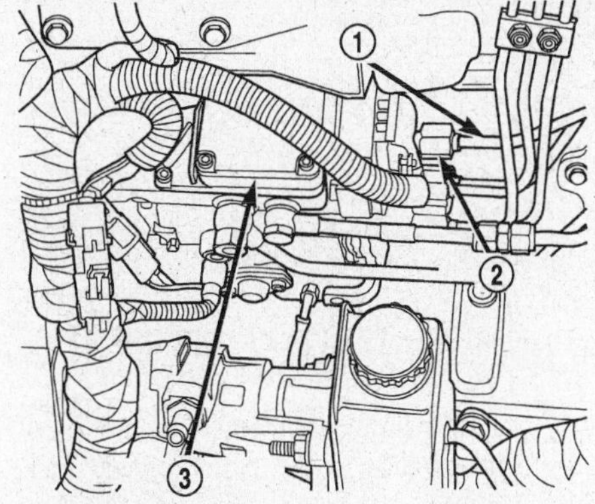

Fig. 31 High pressure lines at fuel injection pump. 2002

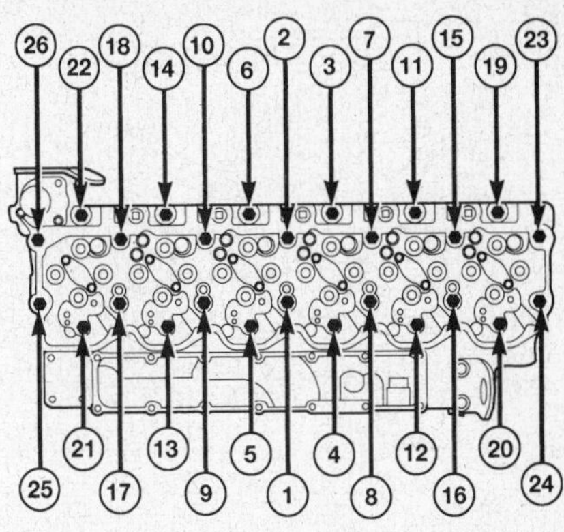

Fig. 32 Cylinder head bolt tightening sequence

FUEL PUMP

REPLACE

2002

REMOVAL

1. Thoroughly clean area around transfer pump and fuel lines.
2. Remove starter motor.
3. Place a suitable drain pan below pump.
4. Disconnect fuel line quick connect fitting at fuel supply line.
5. Remove support bracket bolt at top of pump.
6. Remove front and rear banjo bolts at pump.
7. Disconnect electrical connector at side of pump.
8. Remove three pump bracket nuts and remove pump from vehicle.

INSTALLATION

1. Install new gaskets to fuel supply line support bracket and banjo bolt at rear of pump.
2. Install line at banjo bolt to pump, do not tighten banjo bolt at this time.
3. Install new gaskets to fuel line and banjo bolt at front of pump.
4. Position three pump studs into pump mounting bracket and install three nuts, do not tighten nuts at this time.
5. Install support bracket bolt, do not tighten bolt at this time.
6. **Torque** three pump nuts to 108 inch lbs.
7. **Torque** banjo bolts to 18 ft. lbs.
8. **Torque** support bracket bolt to 108 inch lbs.
9. Connect electrical connector to pump and fuel line quick connect fitting to fuel supply line at rear of pump.
10. Install starter motor.
11. Bleed air at fuel supply line at side of fuel injection pump.
12. Start engine and inspect for leaks.

2003-06

1. Drain fuel into suitable container, then remove fuel tank.
2. Locate arrow on top of module showing rotation direction for removal.

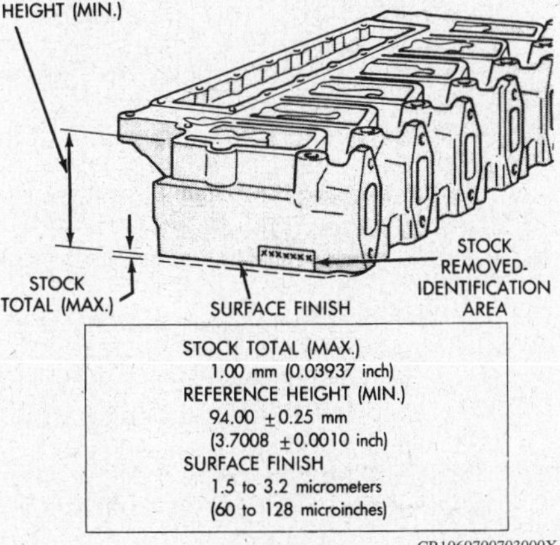

Fig. 33 Cylinder head stock removal

3. Rotate locking ring counterclockwise using tool No. 9340 or equivalent.
4. Remove module from tank ensuring not to bend float during removal.
5. Reverse procedure to install.

INJECTION PUMP

REPLACE

2002

REMOVAL

1. Thoroughly clean fuel lines at cylinder head and injection pump ends.
2. Clean fuel injection pump and supply/return lines at side of pump.
3. Disconnect fuel pump control module electrical connector.
4. Remove fuel return and supply lines, all high pressure fuel lines, intake air tube, accelerator pedal position sensor and air intake housing.
5. Remove engine oil dipstick tube, wiring clips, electrical cables at intake heaters and engine lifting bracket.
6. Remove hose clamp at crankcase vent hose and remove hose from canister, then remove canister (unscrew) from gear cover and nut and washer retaining injection pump gear to injection pump shaft.
7. Insert barring tool, No. SP371, or equivalent, into flywheel housing opening, **Fig. 65.**
8. Rotate engine until keyway is at 12 o'clock position.
9. Use T-bar type puller to separate injection pump gear from injection pump shaft, **Fig. 66.**
10. Pull injection pump gear forward until it loosens from injection pump shaft. **Pull gear only enough to loosen it from injection pump shaft. Pulling gear too far may cause damage or breakage to gear cover.**
11. Remove three lower pump bracket bolts, then the lower pump bracket.
12. Loosen two engine bracket bolts.
13. Remove injection pump to gear housing mounting nuts.
14. Remove injection pump from gear housing. **Use care to not to nick injection pump shaft on aluminum gear housing when removing pump. Do not drop pump keyway into gear housing. Whenever fuel injection pump is removed from engine, pump drive gear is laying loose on camshaft drive gear. Do not attempt to crank or rotate engine with pump removed from engine or serious damage will occur.**

INSTALLATION

1. Clean and inspect injection pump mounting surfaces.
2. Install new rubber O-ring at pump mounting surface.
3. Apply clean engine oil to injection pump O-ring only.
4. Machined tapers on both injection pump shaft and injection pump gear must be absolutely dry, clean and free of any dirt or oil film to ensure proper gear to shaft tightening.
5. Clean pump gear and pump shaft at machined tapers with an evaporative type cleaner such as brake cleaner.
6. Pump/gear keyway has an arrow and a three digit number stamped at top edge, **Fig. 67.**
7. Position keyway into pump shaft with arrow pointed toward rear of pump.

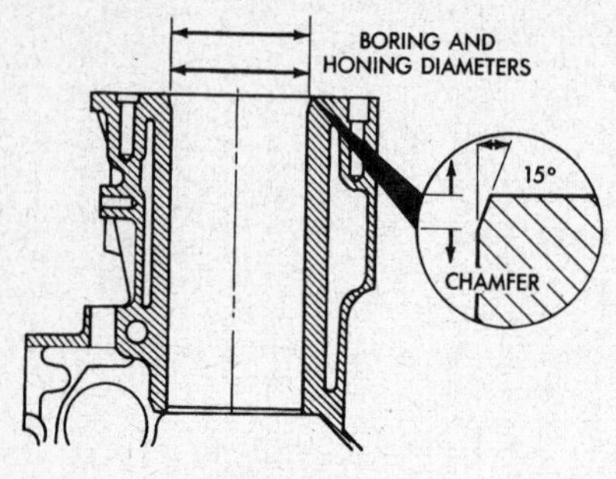

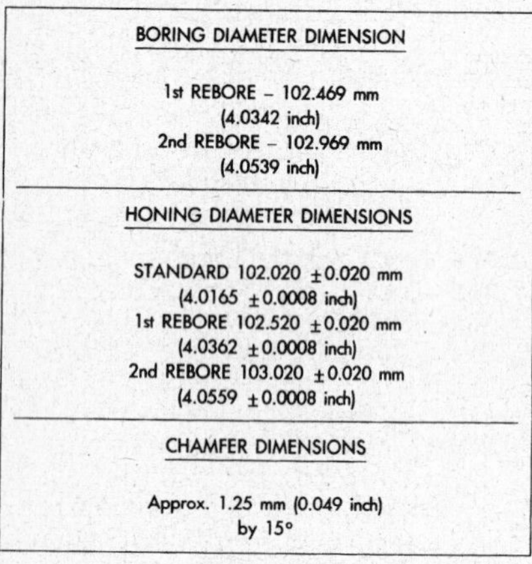

BORING DIAMETER DIMENSION

1st REBORE – 102.469 mm
(4.0342 inch)
2nd REBORE – 102.969 mm
(4.0539 inch)

HONING DIAMETER DIMENSIONS

STANDARD 102.020 ±0.020 mm
(4.0165 ±0.0008 inch)
1st REBORE 102.520 ±0.020 mm
(4.0362 ±0.0008 inch)
2nd REBORE 103.020 ±0.020 mm
(4.0559 ±0.0008 inch)

CHAMFER DIMENSIONS

Approx. 1.25 mm (0.049 inch)
by 15°

CR1069600667000X

Fig. 34 Cylinder bore dimensions. Less repair sleeve

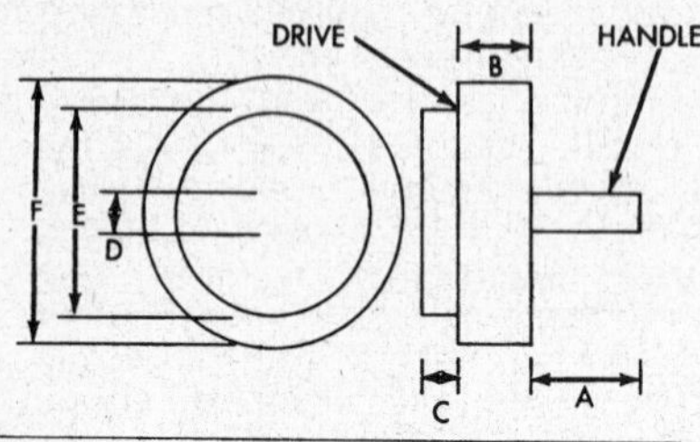

DRIVE – ALUMINUM
HANDLE – STEEL

A = 127 mm (5 inch)
B = 38 mm (1.5 inch)
C = 6.35 mm (0.25 inch)
D = 25.4 mm (1 inch)
E = 101 mm (3.976 inch)
F = 107.343 mm (4.226 inch)

CR1069600670000X

Fig. 37 Sleeve driver construction

8. Ensure three digit number stamped on top of keyway is same as three digit number stamped on injection pump data plate, **Fig. 68.**
9. Position pump assembly to mounting flange on gear cover while aligning injection pump shaft through back of injection pump gear.
10. When installing pump, dowel on mounting flange must align with hole in front of pump.
11. After pump is positioned flat to mounting flange, install four mounting nuts and tighten finger tight only. **Do not attempt to tighten (pull) pump to gear cover using mounting nuts. Damage to pump or gear cover may occur.**
12. To prevent damage or cracking of components, tighten nuts/bolts in the following sequence:
    a. **Torque** injection pump shaft nut to 15–22 ft. lbs.
    b. **Torque** pump mounting nuts to 32 ft. lbs.
    c. **Torque** lower pump bracket to pump bolts to 18 ft. lbs.
    d. **Torque** engine bracket to engine bolts to 18 ft. lbs.
    e. **Torque** injection pump shaft nut to a final torque of 125 ft. lbs. Use barring tool to prevent engine from rotating when tightening.
13. Install plastic access cap on front gear cover.
14. Install fuel return and supply lines using new gaskets.
15. Install engine oil dipstick tube, wiring clips, then the electrical cables at intake heaters and engine lifting bracket.
16. Install intake air tube, accelerator pedal position sensor and air intake housing.
17. Connect fuel pump control module electrical connector.
18. Bleed air from system and inspect fuel system for leaks.

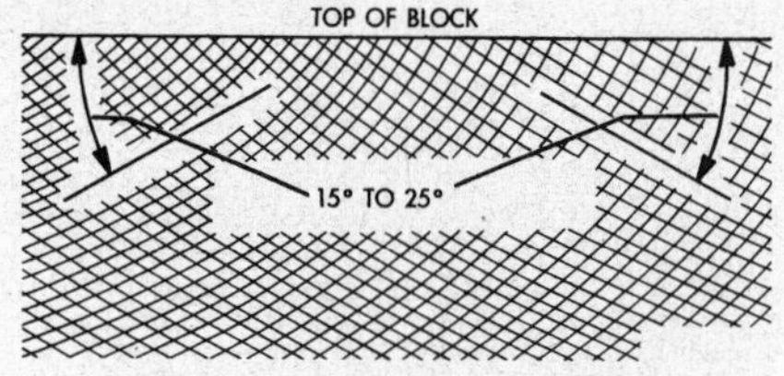

CR1069600668000X

Fig. 35 Honing crosshatch pattern

2003

REMOVAL

1. Remove intake manifold air intake tube and rubber connector hose.
2. Remove five ECM mounting bolts, then position ECM aside. Do not disconnect ECM electrical connector.
3. remove cooling fan shroud, then cooling fan assembly.
4. Remove serpentine drive belt.
5. Thoroughly clean rear of injection pump and attachment points of fuel lines.
6. Disconnect fuel control actuator electrical connector at rear of injection pump.
7. Remove injection pump to overflow valve fuel line.
8. Remove injection pump to fuel rail fuel line.
9. Remove injection pump to fuel filter housing fuel line.
10. Remove fuel pump drive gear access cover.
11. Remove fuel pump drive gear mounting nut and washer, **Fig. 69.**
12. Attach gear puller tool No. C3428B, or equivalent, to pump drive gear using two bolts, then separate gear from pump. Leave gear hanging loose within timing gear cover.
13. Remove three injection pump nuts, then the injection pump.

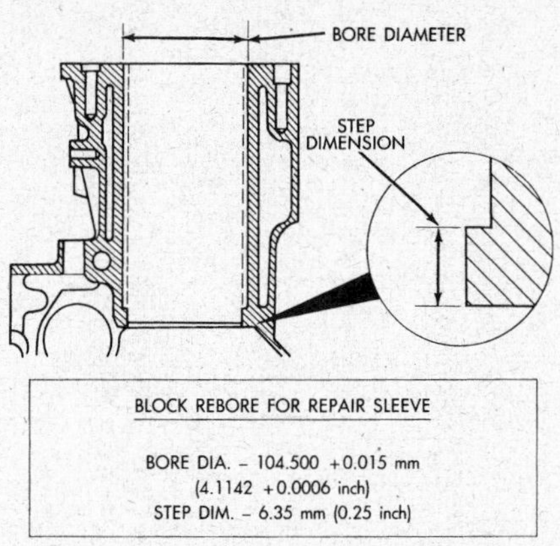

BLOCK REBORE FOR REPAIR SLEEVE

BORE DIA. – 104.500 +0.015 mm
(4.1142 +0.0006 inch)
STEP DIM. – 6.35 mm (0.25 inch)

CR1069600669000X

Fig. 36 Cylinder bore dimensions for repair sleeve

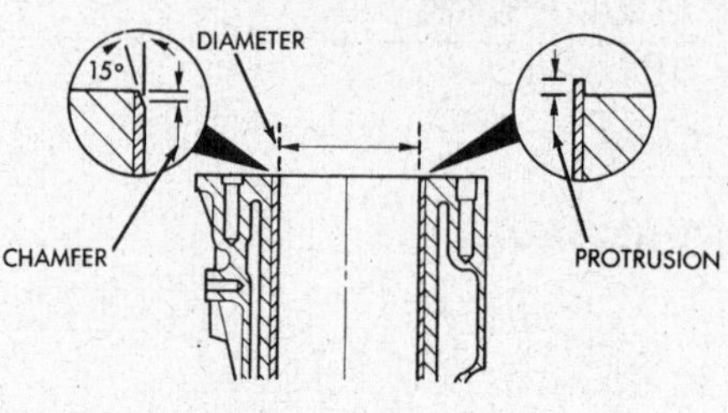

SLEEVE DIAMETER – 101.956 mm
(4.014 inch)
SLEEVE PROTRUSION
MIN. – FLUSH WITH BLOCK
MAX. – 0.050 mm (0.0019 inch)
SLEEVE CHAMFER
APPROX. 1.25 mm (0.049 inch)
BY 15°

CR1069600671000X

Fig. 38 Sleeve boring dimensions

INSTALLATION

1. Inspect pump mounting surfaces at pump and mounting flange for nicks, cuts or damage.
2. Inspect O-ring surfaces for nicks, cuts or damage.
3. Install new O-ring into machined groove of pump mounting surface.
4. Apply clean engine oil to injection pump O-ring only.
5. Clean pump gear and pump shaft at machined tapers with an evaporative type cleaner. **Machined tapers on both injection pump shaft and injection pump gear must be absolutely dry, clean and free of any dirt or oil film.**
6. Position injection pump to mounting flange on gear cover while aligning injection pump shaft through back of injection pump gear.
7. After pump is positioned flat to mounting flange , install three pump mounting nuts and tighten finger tight only. **Do not attempt to pull pump to gear**

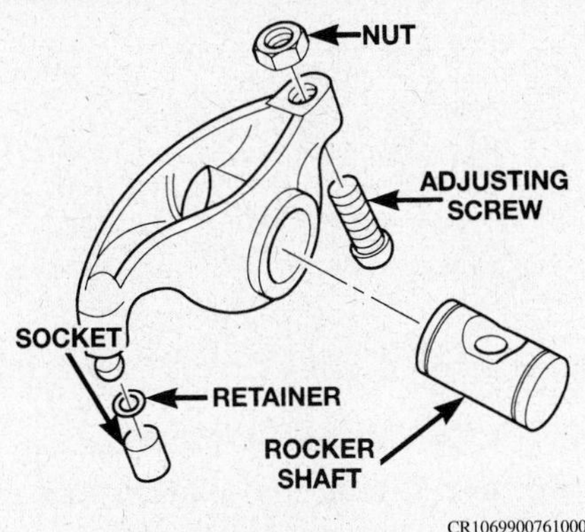

Fig. 39 Rocker arm assembly

cover using mounting nuts, damage to pump or cover may occur.

8. To prevent damage or cracking of components, tighten nuts as follows:
   a. Install injection pump shaft washer and nut to pump shaft. Tighten nut finger tight only.
   b. Do preliminary light tightening of injection pump shaft nut.
   c. **Torque** three injection pump mountings nuts to 17 ft. lbs.
   d. **Torque** pump shaft nut to 77 ft. lbs.
9. Install drive gear access cover.
10. Install ECM to left side of engine.
11. Install injection to pump overflow valve fuel line.
12. Install injection pump to fuel rail fuel line.
13. Install injection pump to fuel filter housing fuel line.
14. Connect fuel control actuator electrical connector to rear of injection pump.
15. Install intake manifold air intake tube.
16. Install serpentine drive belt.
17. Install cooling fan shroud.
18. Install cooling fan assembly.
19. Inspect system for fuel or engine oil leaks.

2004–06

1. Remove intake manifold air intake tube.
2. Remove serpentine drive belt as outlined under "Serpentine Belt, Replace."
3. Thoroughly clean fuel line to injection pump connections.
4. Disconnect fuel control actuator (FCA) electrical connection at back of injection pump.
5. Disconnect the following fuel lines:
   a. Injection pump to fuel pressure limiting valve.
   b. Injection pump to fuel rail using back up wrench on fitting at fuel pump.
   c. injection pump to fuel filter housing.
6. Remove fuel pump drive gear access cover.
7. Attach gear puller tool No. C3428B, or equivalent, to pump drive gear using two bolts, then separate gear from

Fig. 40 Rocker arm bore measurement

pump. Leave gear hanging loose within timing gear cover.
8. Remove three injection pump mounting nuts, then pump.
9. Reverse procedure to install noting the following:
   a. **Torque** three injection pump mounting nuts to 18 ft. lbs.
   b. **Torque** pump shaft nut to 77 ft. lbs.

FUEL FILTER

REPLACE

1. Place suitable drain pan under drain hose.
2. With engine Off, rotate drain handle forward to Open position.
3. After filter is drained, close valve handle.
4. Unscrew and remove fuel filter cap at top of fuel filter housing.
5. Remove and discard O-ring from filter cap.
6. Remove filter from filter cap.
7. Reverse procedure to install noting the following:
   a. Install new O-ring on filter cap, then lubricate O-ring with clean diesel oil.
   b. **On 2002 models,** fill fuel filter housing with clean diesel fuel.
   c. **On 2003–06 models,** turn key to CRANK position and quickly release to ON position before engine starts to operate fuel transfer pump for approximately 25 seconds.

INJECTION PUMP TIMING

2002

With the Bosch VP44 injection pump, there are no mechanical adjustments for

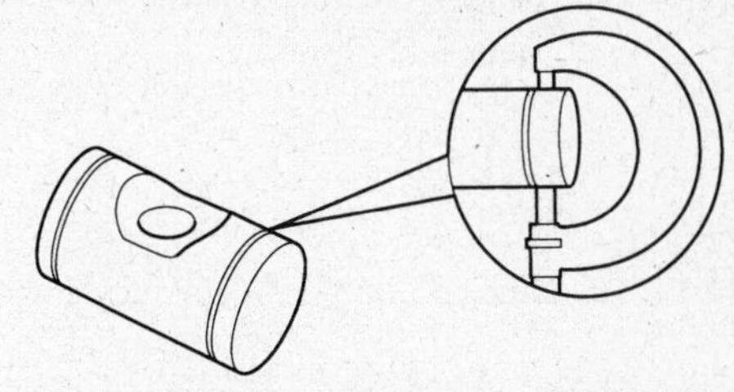

Fig. 41 Rocker arm shaft measurement

fuel injection timing. All timing and fuel adjustments are made by the Engine Control Module (ECM).

If a DTC appears after installation of a new or rebuilt injection pump, the pump keyway has probably been installed backwards. If a DTC has been stored indicating an engine sync error or a static timing error, perform the following procedure.

1. Remove plastic access cover and injection pump nut and washer. Locate keyway behind washer.
2. Ensure keyway aligning fuel injection pump shaft to injection pump gear is in proper position and pump gear has not slipped on pump shaft.
3. Remove timing gear cover to gain access to timing gears.
4. Use a t-type puller to separate injection pump gear from pump shaft.
5. Ensure keyway has been installed with arrow pointed to rear of pump.
6. Pump timing has been calibrated to pump keyway. Ensure three digit number on pump keyway matches three digit number on fuel injection pump data plate.
7. Verify timing marks on cam, crank and pump are aligned.
8. Perform any required gear alignment/ repairs, then erase DTCs using DRB scan tool, or equivalent.

2003–06

With the Bosch injection pump, there are no mechanical adjustments for fuel injection timing. All timing and fuel adjustments are made by the Engine Control Module (ECM).

IDLE SPEED

ADJUST

All timing and fuel adjustments are controlled by the ECU and are not adjustable.

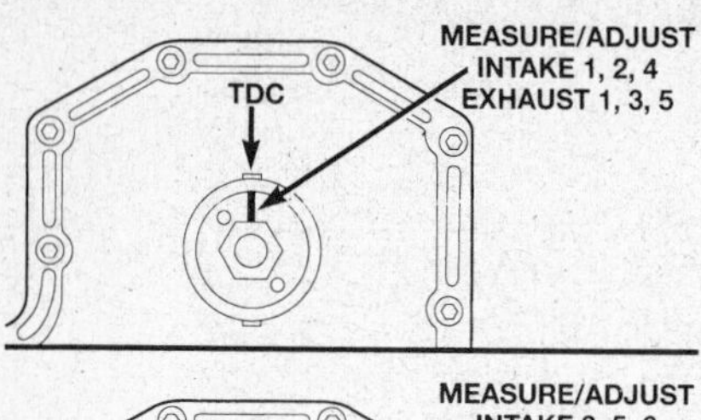

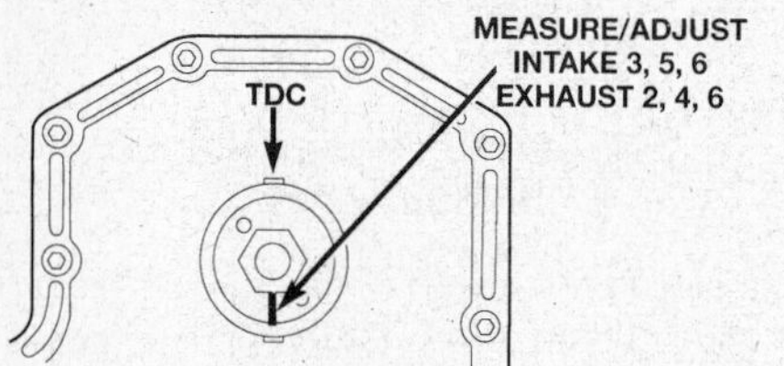

Fig. 42 Valve lash measurement

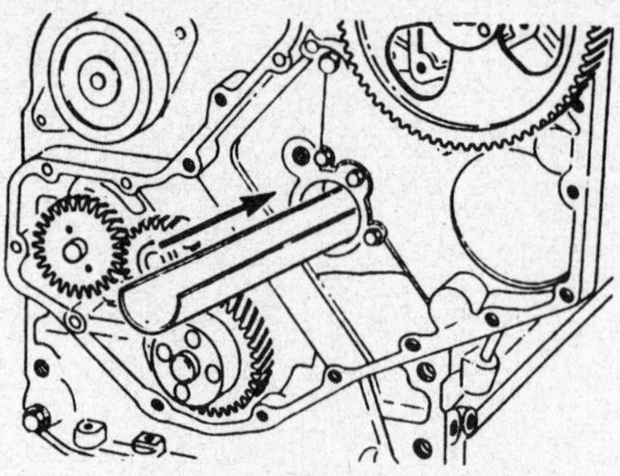

Fig. 43 Lifter removal tool

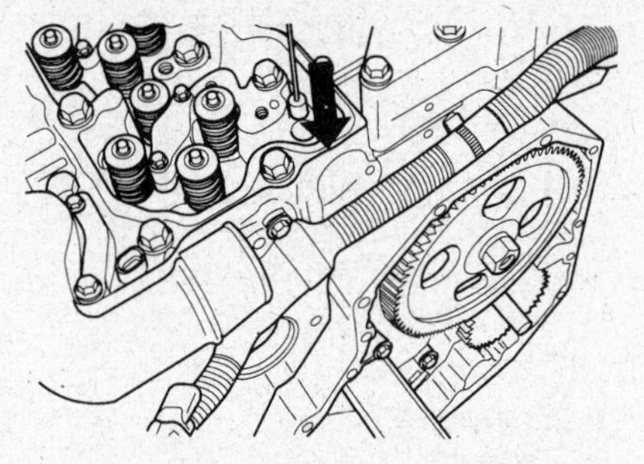

Fig. 44 Tappet installation tool

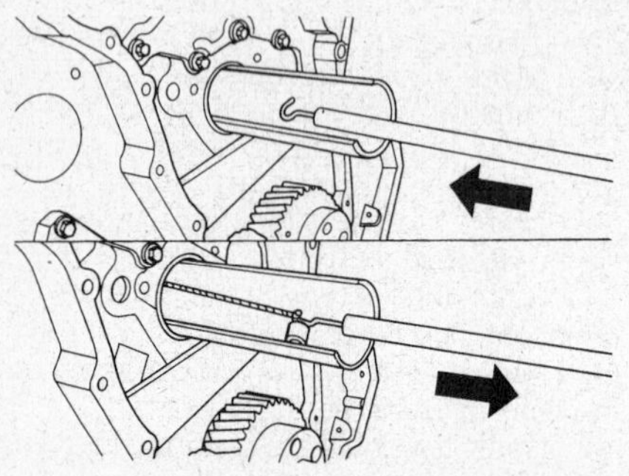

Fig. 45 Tappet installation tool retrieval

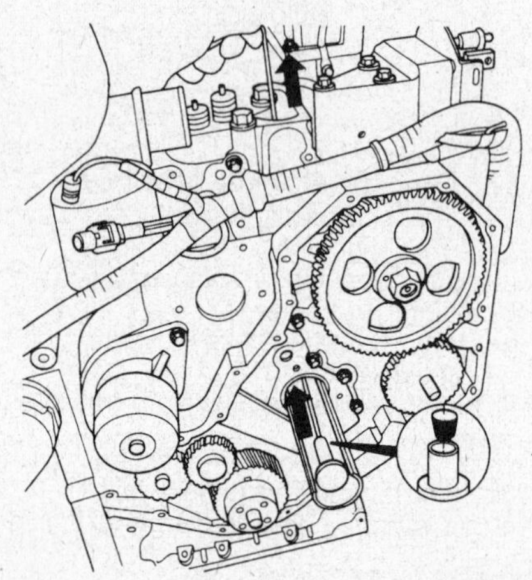

Fig. 46 Tappet tool installation & use

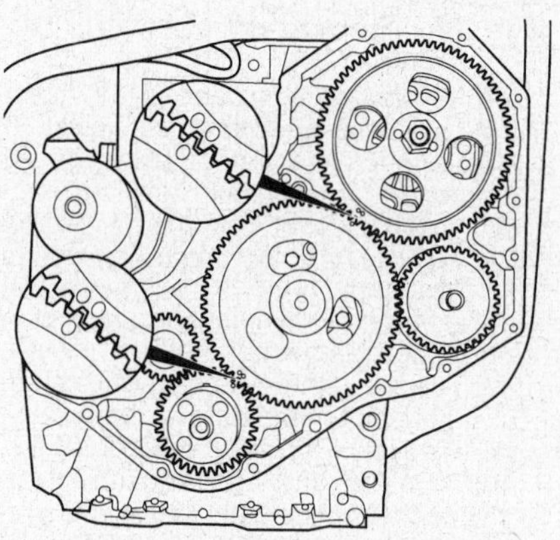

Fig. 47 Camshaft timing mark alignment

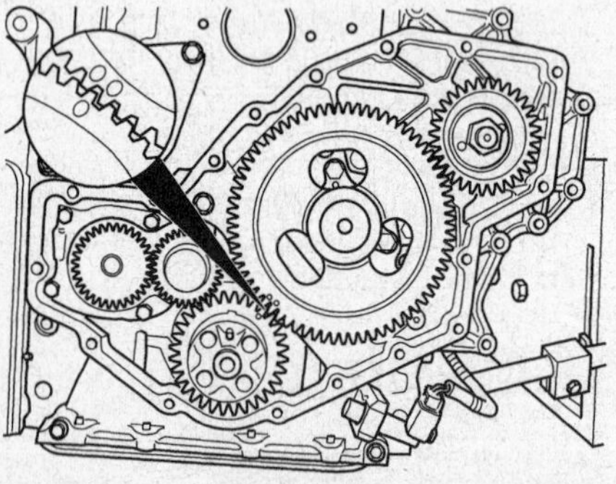

Fig. 48 Camshaft timing mark alignment

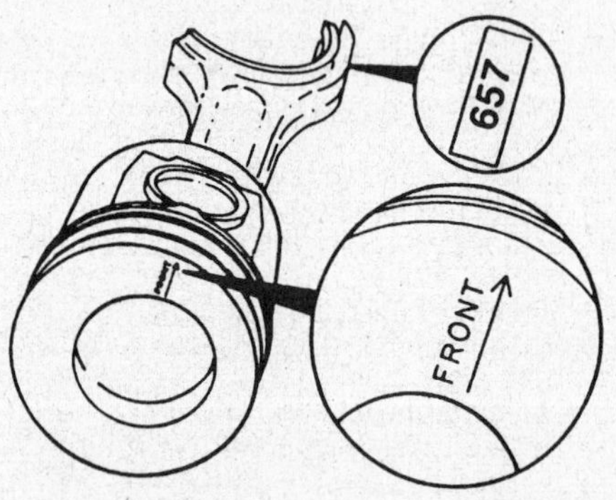

Fig. 49 Piston & rod assembly

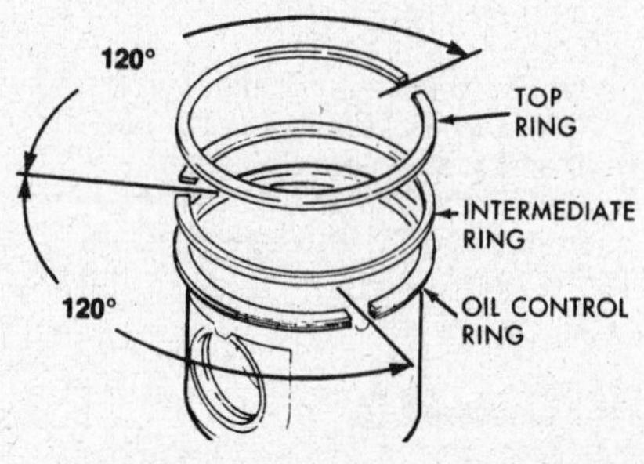

Fig. 50 Ring position on piston

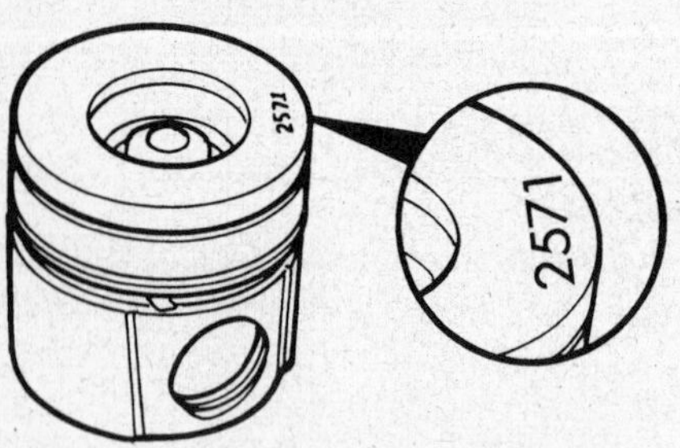

Fig. 51 Piston grading number location

IF MEASURING PISTON IS	AND	USE	
GRADING #:		PROTRUSION IS	GRADE:
245 HP	235 HP		
6050	6153	0.609-0.711 mm (0.024-0.028 in.)	A
6050	6153	0.508-0.609mm (0.020-0.024 in.)	B
6050	6153	0.406-0.508 mm (0.016-0.020 in.)	C
6051	6154	0.711-0.813 mm (0.028-0.032 in.)	A
6051	6154	0.609-0.711 mm (0.024-0.028 in.)	B
6051	6154	0.508-0.609 mm (0.020-0.024 in.)	C
6052	6155	0.813-0.914 mm (0.032-0.036 in.)	A
6052	6155	0.711-0.813 mm (0.028-0.032 in.)	B
6052	6155	0.609-0.711 mm (0.024-0.028 in.)	C

CR1060100935000X

Fig. 52 Piston protrusion chart

Dimension A	Ref. Number	Grade
51.554 to 51.607mm (2.029 to 2.031in)	2571	A
51.654 to 51.707mm (2.033 to 2.035in)	2572	B
51.754 to 51.807mm (2.037 to 2.039in)	2573	C

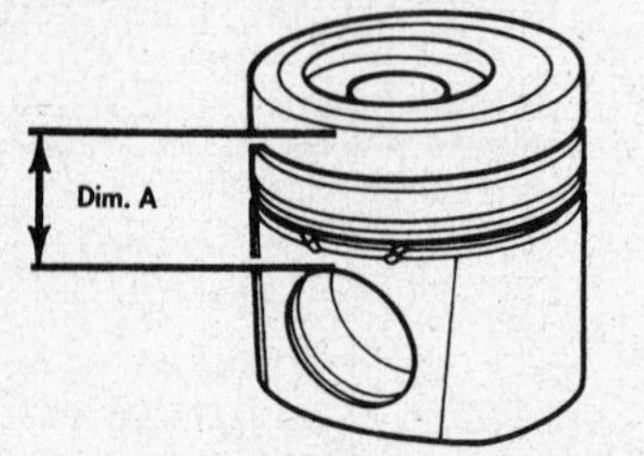

Fig. 53 Piston grading measurement

DIMENSION "A"	REF. NUMBER		GRADE
	235 HP	245 HP	
51.554-51.607 mm (2.029-2.031 in.)	6153	6050	A
51.654-51.707 mm (2.033-2.035 in.)	6154	6051	B
51.754-51.807 mm (2.037-2.039 in.)	6155	6052	C

CR1060100936000X

Fig. 54 Piston grading measurement chart

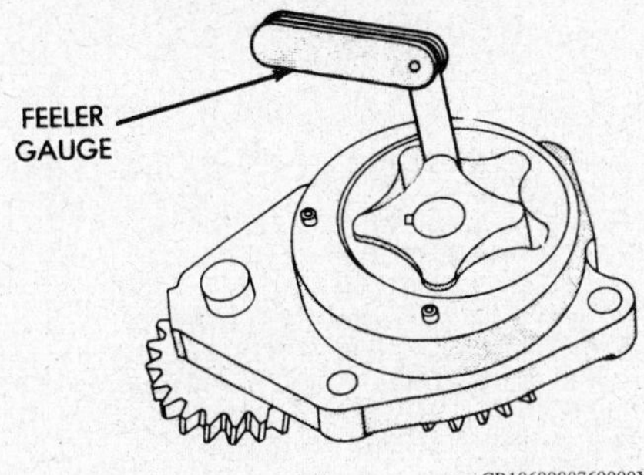

Fig. 57 Oil pump tip clearance

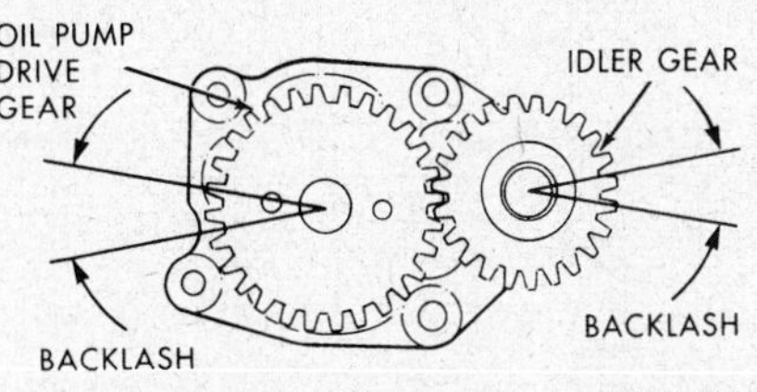

Fig. 60 Oil pump gear backlash

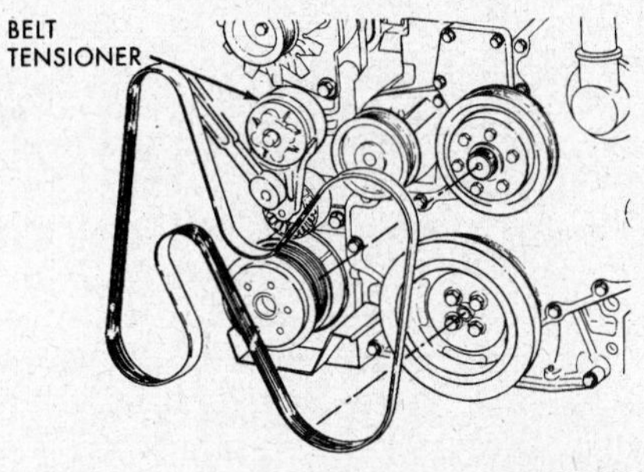

Fig. 61 Serpentine drive belt routing. 2002 With A/C

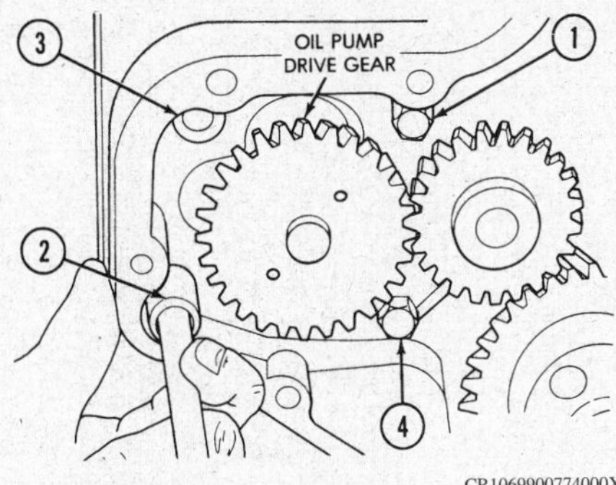

Fig. 55 Oil pump bolt tighten sequence

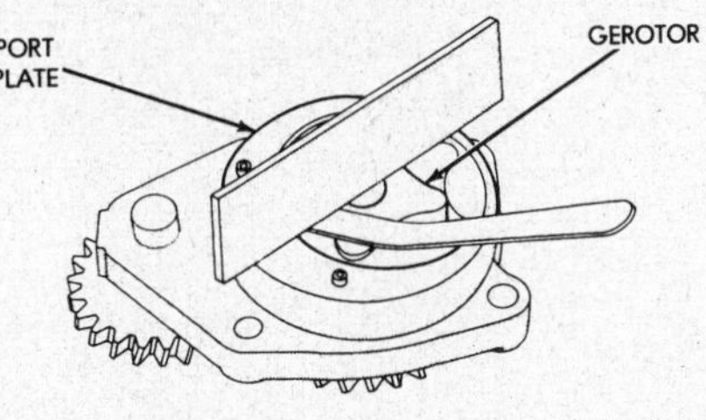

Fig. 58 Oil pump georotor to port plate clearance

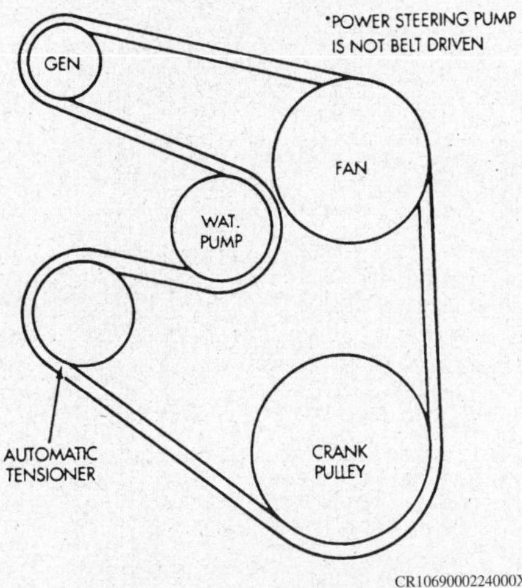

Fig. 62 Serpentine drive belt routing. 2002 Less A/C

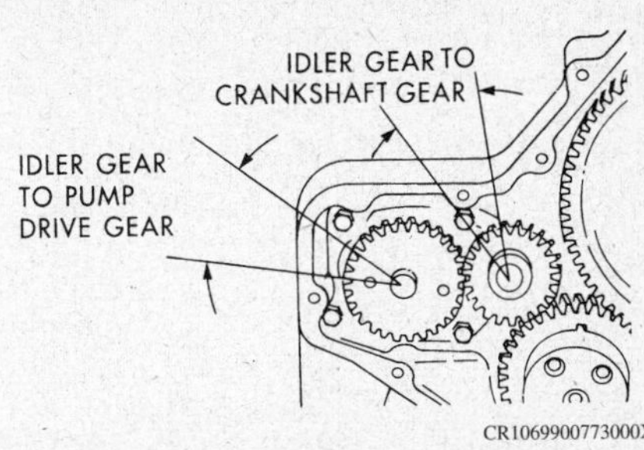

Fig. 56 Idler gear to pump gear & crankshaft gear backlash

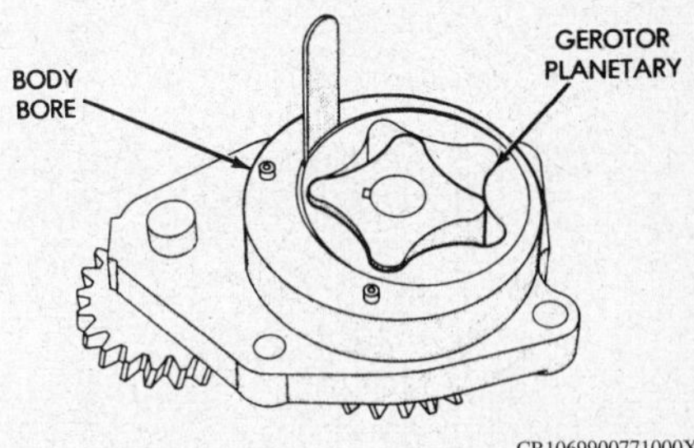

Fig. 59 Oil pump georotor planetary to body bore clearance

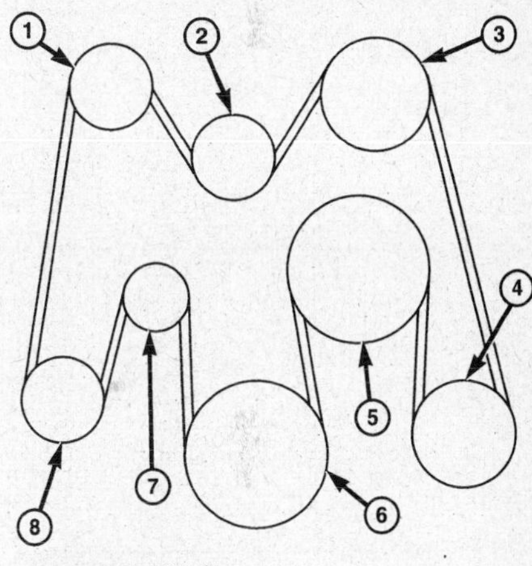

Fig. 63 Serpentine drive belt routing. 2003–06

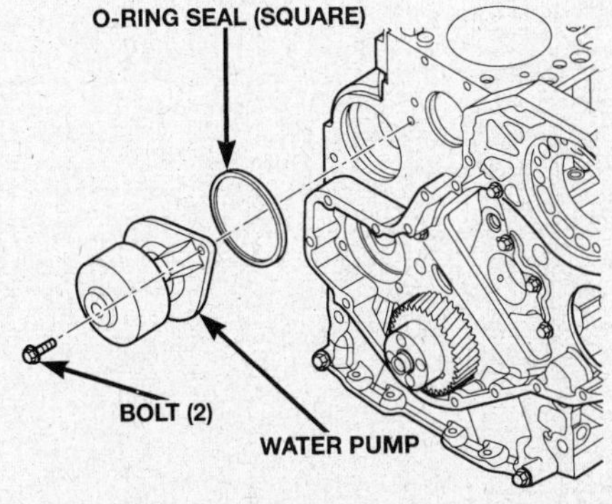

Fig. 64 Water pump

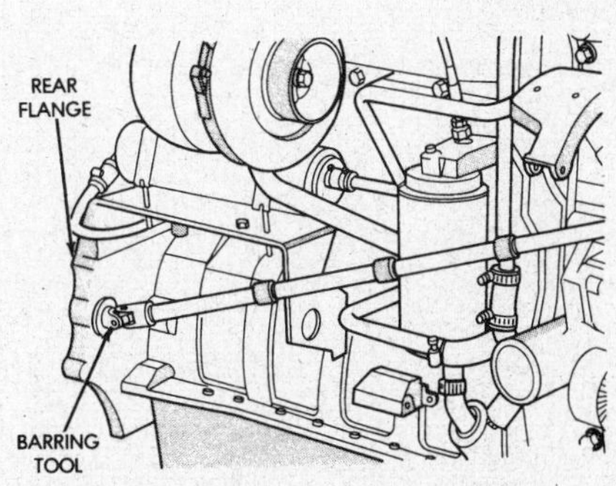

Fig. 65 Engine barring tool installation. 2002

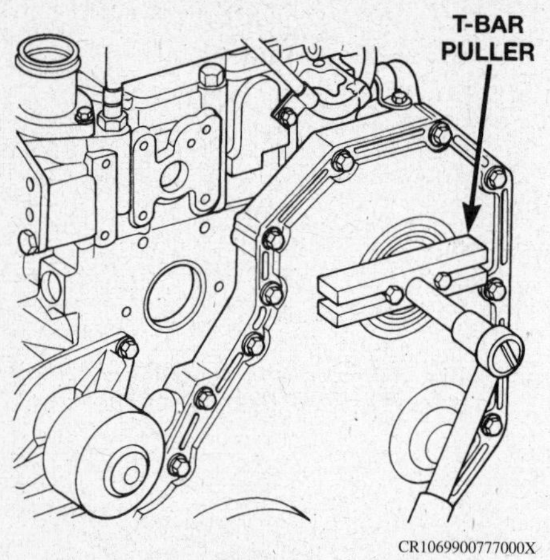

Fig. 66 Injection pump gear removal. 2002

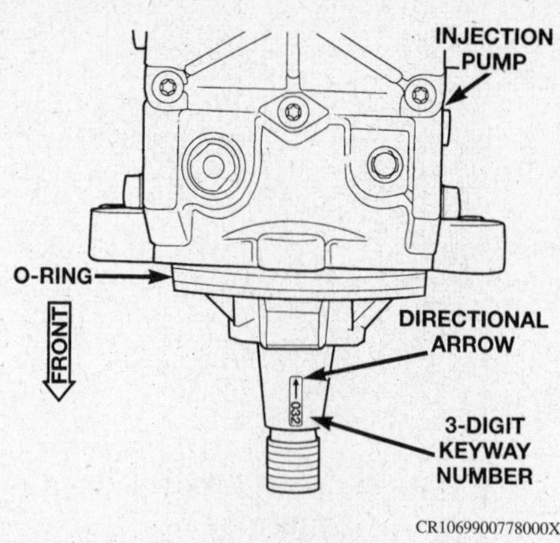

Fig. 67 Keyway arrow & number. 2002

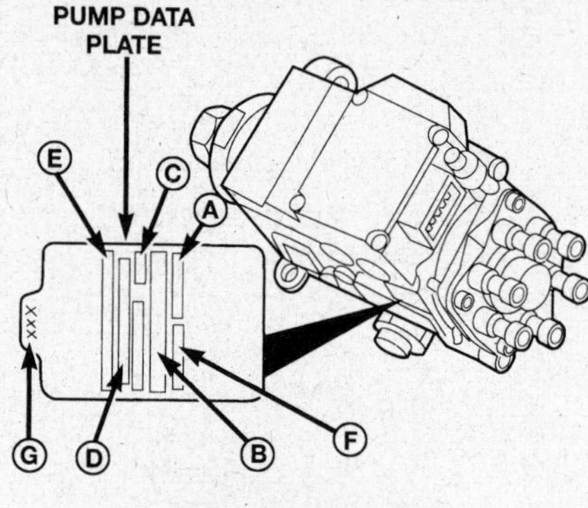

A. ORDER NUMBER
B. BOSCH PART NUMBER
C. FACTORY CODE
D. CUMMINS PART NUMBER
E. MANUFACTURE DATE
F. PUMP SERIAL NUMBER
G. LAST THREE DIGITS OF KEY PART NUMBER

CR1069900779000X

Fig. 68 Injection pump data plate. 2002

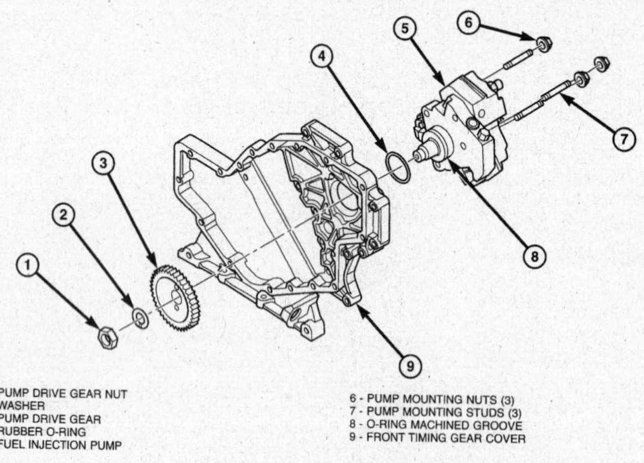

DEPD03CR00005864

Fig. 69 Injection pump. 2003

TIGHTENING SPECIFICATIONS

Year	Component	Torque Ft. Lbs.
2002	A/C Compressor Bolts	35
	A/C Compressor Line Fittings	15
	Air Fuel Control Banjo Screw	108①
	Air Fuel Control Fitting	72①
	Air Intake Tube Clamp	72①
	Alternator Lower Mounting Bolts	32
	Alternator Upper Mounting Bolts	18
	Alternator Pulley Bolt	60
	Battery Ground Cable To Block Bolt	57
	Belt Tensioner Mounting Bolt	32
	Block Heater Mounting Bolt	108①
	Cab Heater Hose Clamp	35①
	Cab Heater Tubing Clamp Mounting	84①
	Cam Thrust Plate Bolts	18
	Charge Air Cooler Outlet Duct Clamps	72①
	Clutch Cover To Flywheel Bolts	17
	Connecting Rod Bolts	②
	Connecting Rod Cap Screws	26
	Cooling Fan To Fan Clutch Bolts	15
	Crankshaft Damper Bolt	92
	Crossover Clamp	44①
	Cylinder Head	④
	Cylinder Head Cover	18
	Engine Front Mount Bracket To Block Bolts	60
	Engine Front Mount Bracket To Insulator Nut	80
	Engine Front Mount Insulator To Mount Nuts	80
	Engine Front Mount Through Bolt Nuts	110
	Engine Lifting Eyes	57
	Engine Rear Mount Nuts & Bolts	30
	Exhaust Manifold Bolts	⑤
	Exhaust Outlet Pipe Bolts	72①
	Exhaust Pipe Clamp Mounting	20
	Exhaust Pipe Steady Rest To Transmission Bolts	50
	Exhaust Pipe To Turbocharger	25
	Fan Clutch To Fan Hub Bolts (LH Threads)	42
	Fan Hub Bearing Retaining Capscrew	57
	Fan Hub Bracket Bolts	18
	Fan Pulley To Fan Hub Bolts	84①
	Fan Shroud Nuts	8
	Flywheel Bolts	101
	Flywheel Housing Bolts	44
	Front Cover Bolts	18
	Fuel Banjo Screw To Fuel Pump	24
	Fuel Banjo Screw To Head	18
	Fuel Banjo Screw To Injector	72①
	Fuel Heater Assembly Bolts	24
	Fuel Heater Ground To Intake Manifold Bolts	9
	Fuel Line Fitting	18
	Fuel High Pressure Supply Fitting	22
	Fuel Low Pressure Supply Fitting	18

TIGHTENING SPECIFICATIONS—Continued

Year	Component	Torque Ft. Lbs.
2002	Fuel Pump Drive Gear	48
	Fuel Pump Lock	22
	Fuel Pump Mounting Bolts	18
	Fuel Pump Solenoid	32
	Fuel Pump Support Bracket	18
	Fuel Pump Unlock	10
	Fuel Vent Screw	72①
	Gear Housing To Block Bolts	18
	Injection Pump Access Plug	11
	Injection Pump Driveshaft To Gear Nut	②
	Injection Pump Mounting Bracket Bolts	18
	Injection Pump Mounting Stud Nuts	18
	Injection Pump Oil Fill Plug	21
	Injection Pump Rear Plug (w/Copper Washer)	84①
	Injection Pump Shaft Nut	15-22
	Injector Retaining Nut	44
	Intake Manifold Cover	18
	Main Bearing Cap Bolts	②
	Oil Cooler Assembly	18
	Oil Drain Plug	37
	Oil Fill Tube Bracket Bolt	32
	Oil Pan Bolts	18
	Oil Pressure Regulator Plug	60
	Oil Pressure Sender/Switch	12
	Oil Pump Mounting	18
	Oil Suction Tube	18
	Oil Suction Tube Brace Bolt	18
	Power Steering Pump To Vacuum Pump	18
	Power Steering Pressure Line Fitting	22
	Radiator Mounting Bolts	96①
	Radiator Hose Clamps	34①
	Rear Seal Mounting	84①
	Rocker Arm Bolts	27
	Starter Mounting	50
	Starter Positive Battery Cable Nut	16
	Starter Solenoid Nut	44①
	Tappet Cover Bolts	18
	Thermostat Bolts	18
	Thermostat Housing Bolts	18
	Throttle Bracket Bolts	18
	Throttle Rod To Throttle Lever Nut	90①
	Thrust Plate Bolts	18
	Timing Pin Flange Bolts	44①
	Torque Converter Access Cover Plate Bolts	35①
	Torque Converter Driveplate To Converter Bolts	23
	Transfer Case To Transmission Bolts	35
	Transmission Cooler Tube To Oil Pan	18
	Transmission Kickdown Cable Bracket Bolts	50

Continued

TIGHTENING SPECIFICATIONS—Continued

Year	Component	Torque Ft. Lbs.
2002	Transmission Oil Cooler Line Connection	40
	Transmission Oil Cooler Line Fittings	50①
	Transmission Oil To Air Cooler Hose Clamps	18①
	Transmission To Clutch Housing Bolts	35
	Transmission To Engine Bolts	30
	Transmission Torque Converter Bolts	35
	Turbine Housing Bolts	96①
	Turbocharger Air Cooler Inlet Pipe Clamp	95①
	Turbocharger Compressor Housing Clamp	72①
	Turbocharger Mounting Nuts	24
	Turbocharger Oil Drain Tube Bolts	18
	Turbocharger Oil Supply Line Fitting	11
	Vacuum Pump	84①
	Vacuum Pump Nuts	18
	Vacuum Pump To Gear Housing	57
	Valve Cover	18
	Valve Adjusting Nuts	18
	Water Hose Clamps	35①
	Water Inlet Connection	32
	Water Pump Mounting	18
	Water In Fuel (WIF) Sensor	15–20①
	Water Temperature Sensor	37

TIGHTENING SPECIFICATIONS—Continued

Year	Component	Torque Ft. Lbs.
2003–06	Breather Cover	18
	Connecting Rod Bolts	②
	Crankshaft Damper	30⑥
	Cylinder Head	④
	Exhaust Manifold	32
	Fan Blade Assembly	17
	Flywheel	101
	Fuel Delivery Lines Banjo Bolt	18
	Fuel Drain Line Banjo Bolt	18
	Fuel Filter Cap	25
	Fuel Pump To Fuel Rail	22
	Fuel Rail To Cylinder Head	22
	Fuel Transfer Pump	61①
	Gear Housing	18
	Injection Pump	⑦
	Injector Fuel Line Brace	18
	Intake Manifold	18
	Main Bearing Cap Bolts	②
	Oil Pan	21
	Oil Pan Drain Plug	37
	Oil Pressure Regulator Plug	60
	Oil Pressure Switch	13
	Oil Pump	③
	Oil Suction Tube Brace	21
	Oil Suction Tube Flange	18
	Rocker Arm	27
	Serpentine Drive Belt Tensioner	43
	Support Cushion	35
	Thermostat Housing	88①
	Transmission Support Bracket	35
	Turbocharger	32
	Water Pump	18

①— Inch lbs.
②— Refer to "Main & Rod Bearings" procedure.
③— Torque in two steps: 1st. step, 72 inch lbs.; 2nd. step, 18 ft. lbs.
④— Refer to "Cylinder Head, Replace" procedure.
⑤— Refer to "Exhaust Manifold, Replace" procedure.
⑥— Plus an additional 60°.
⑦— Refer to "Injection Pump, Replace" procedure.

8.3L Engine

NOTE: Air Bag Equipped Models, Refer To "Air Bag System Precautions" Located In The Front Of This Manual For System Disarming & Arming Procedures.

NOTE: Refer To "Computer Relearn Procedures" Located In The Front Of This Manual When Battery Power To The Computer Has Been Interrupted.

INDEX

PRECAUTIONS

Air Bag Systems

Refer to "Air Bag System Precautions" in the front of this manual for system disarming and arming procedures.

Battery Ground Cable

Prior to service, disconnect battery ground cable and isolate as required.

Fuel System Pressure Relief

1. Remove fuel cap.
2. Disconnect one of two fuel pump module electrical connections located midway along righthand frame rail.
3. Start and run engine until it stalls.
4. Attempt to restart engine until it will no longer run.
5. With ignition off, disconnect quick-connect fitting at fuel rail.
6. Reconnect fuel pump module electrical connector.

COMPRESSION PRESSURE

Compression should not be less than 100 psi and not vary more than 25 percent from cylinder to cylinder.

ENGINE MOUNT

REPLACE

1. Raise and support vehicle.
2. Support oil pan with suitable jack.
3. Loosen engine mount to block bolts for desired mount.
4. Loosen engine mount to frame nut.
5. Raise with jack.
6. Remove engine mount to block bolts, then mount.
7. Reverse procedure to install.

ENGINE

REPLACE

1. Disconnect throttle body air inlet duct, then remove air cleaner cover.
2. Raise and support vehicle, then remove lower engine shield.
3. Drain cooling system into suitable container.
4. Mark driveshaft with suitable felt tip marker for installation reference, then remove driveshaft.
5. Remove transmission as outlined in **MOTOR's "Domestic Transmission, In-Vehicle Service" or "Transmission Service DVD."**
6. Remove starter as outlined under "Starter, Replace" in "Electrical" section.
7. Disconnect righthand front exhaust pipe flange to exhaust manifold.
8. Disconnect hydraulic cooling fan lines at fan motor.
9. Drain engine oil into suitable container and remove oil filter.
10. Separate air conditioning hose from fan shroud.
11. Disconnect lower radiator hose.
12. Disconnect power steering line support bracket at lower left of radiator.
13. Loosen both engine mount through bolts.
14. Disconnect ground strap from floor board, above righthand exhaust flange.
15. Lower vehicle.
16. Recover refrigerant as outlined in "Air Conditioning" chapter.
17. Remove upper radiator hose.
18. Disconnect washer hose at splice.
19. Remove radiator core support.
20. Disconnect cooling fan harness electrical connector.
21. Remove radiator and radiator fan assembly as outlined under "Radiator, Replace."
22. Remove A/C condenser, cap and position hoses aside.
23. Disconnect upper front cover and lower coolant housing heater hoses and position aside.
24. Disconnect oil cooler hoses from engine and position aside.
25. Remove serpentine drive belt as outlined under "Serpentine Belt, Replace."
26. Remove alternator as outlined under "Alternator, Replace" in "Electrical" section.
27. Disconnect power steering pump bracket bolts and position pump aside.
28. Disconnect A/C compressor electrical connector, then A/C lines.
29. Disconnect brake booster vacuum hose and fuel line to fuel rail.
30. Disconnect cruise control, accelerator cable and fuel vapor purge harness AND POSITION ASIDE.
31. Disconnect engine harness electrical connectors on top of intake manifold.
32. Disconnect spark plug wires from spark plugs and place wires on top of engine.
33. Disconnect ground strap at thermostat housing and pull electrical harness underneath intake manifold and set aside.
34. Install engine lifting bracket tool No. 9363 or equivalent, to exhaust manifold heat shield studs.
35. Insert engine lifting bar through access holes in engine lifting brackets.
36. Remove engine with suitable engine hoist.
37. Reverse procedure to install.

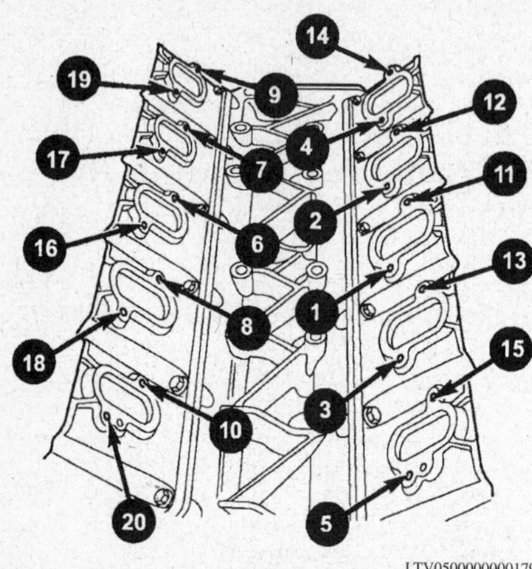

Fig. 1 Intake manifold tightening sequence

INTAKE MANIFOLD

REPLACE

1. Relieve fuel system pressure as outlined in "Precautions."
2. Disconnect throttle body air inlet duct, IAT sensor, CCV hose and remove air cleaner cover.
3. Disconnect throttle cable from throttle cam. Remove throttle cable from bracket and set aside.
4. Disconnect speed control cable from throttle cam and set aside.
5. Disconnect brake booster vacuum hose from intake manifold and set aside.
6. Disconnect fuel line quick connect fitting from fuel rail.
7. Disconnect electrical connectors from the following:
   a. Lefthand cylinder head fuel injectors.
   b. MAP sensor.
   c. Engine Coolant Temperature (ECT) Sensor.
   d. Idle Speed Control Sensor (ISC).
   e. Throttle Position Sensor (TPS).
   f. Righthand cylinder head fuel injectors.
8. Separate fuel injector harness push pins from intake manifold.
9. Disconnect purge solenoid hose from beneath throttle body.
10. Disconnect CCV hoses from lefthand and righthand cylinder head covers.
11. Remove intake manifold bolts and intake manifold.
12. Reverse procedure to install noting the following:
    a. Tighten in sequence to specifications starting from center and working out, **Fig. 1.**

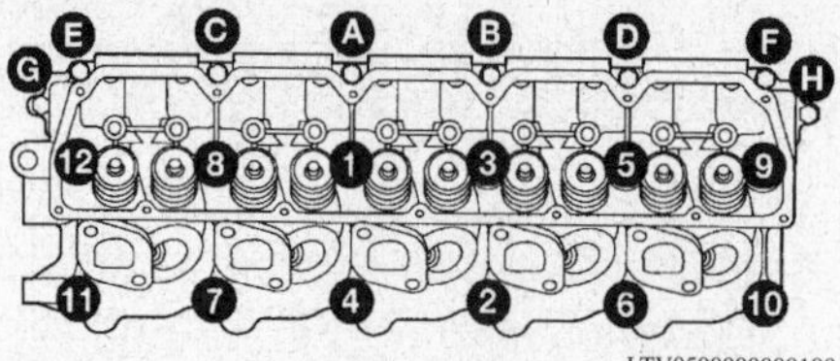

Fig. 2 Cylinder head tightening sequence

EXHAUST MANIFOLD

REPLACE

1. Raise and support vehicle.
2. Disconnect exhaust pipe from exhaust manifold.
3. Lower vehicle, then disconnect spark wires.
4. Remove exhaust manifold heat shield.
5. Remove exhaust manifold to cylinder head bolts, then manifold.
6. Reverse procedure to install.

CYLINDER HEAD

REPLACE

1. Relieve fuel system pressure as outlined in "Precautions."
2. Disconnect throttle body air inlet duct, IAT sensor, CCV hose and remove air cleaner cover.
3. Drain cooling system into suitable container.
4. Raise and support vehicle.
5. Disconnect front exhaust pipe from exhaust manifold.
6. lower vehicle.
7. Remove intake manifold as outlined under "Intake Manifold, Replace."
8. Disconnect spark plug wires and position aside.
9. Remove oil dipstick tube.
10. Disconnect CCV hoses from valve covers.
11. Remove valve covers as outlined under "Valve Cover, Replace."
12. Remove exhaust manifold as outlined under "Exhaust Manifold, Replace."
13. Remove rocker arm and pedestal assemblies. **NOTE: Rocker arm and pedestal assemblies must be installed in original location if not being replace.**
14. Remove push rods.
15. Remove 12 head bolts and 8 cylinder head tappet gallery bolts from cylinder head.
16. Remove cylinder head.
17. Reverse procedure to install, noting the following:
    a. **Torque** cylinder head bolts in sequence in two passes, **Fig. 2.**
    b. **Torque** bolts on first pass to 35 ft. lbs.
    c. **Torque** bolts on second pass to 90 ft. lbs.
    d. **Torque** A-H bolts to 95 inch lbs.

VALVE COVER

REPLACE

1. Disconnect CCV hose from cylinder head cover.

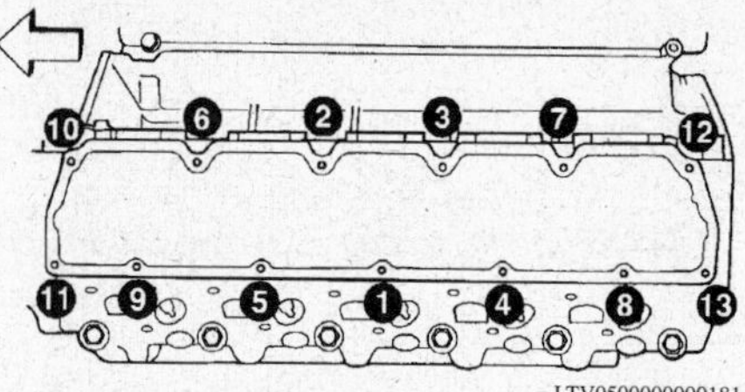

Fig. 3 Valve cover tightening sequence

2. Disconnect spark plug wires from spark plugs and position aside.
3. If removing lefthand valve cover, disconnect power brake booster vacuum hose at intake manifold and set aside.
4. If removing righthand valve cover, remove oil dipstick tube.
5. Remove valve cover mounting bolts.
6. Remove valve cover.
7. Reverse procedure to install, tightening mounting bolts in sequence, **Fig. 3.**

ROCKER ARMS

REPLACE

Refer to "Cylinder Head, Replace" for rocker arm replacement procedure.

VALVE GUIDES

These engines do not have removable valve guides. The valves operate in guide holes bored in the cylinder head. Valves with oversize stems are available for service replacement when it is required to ream the valve guide holes.

Standard production stem diameter should be as follows:

1. Valve stem diameter should be .331–.312 inch for intake and exhaust valves.

If stem wear exceeds .002 inch for intake valve or .027 inch for exhaust valve, replace valve. When reaming guides for oversize valve stems, do so in two steps from standard size to .015 inch. This must be done in order to maintain a true relationship of the guide to the valve seat. Reamer size to valve guide application is as follows: a reamer oversize of .005 inch has a valve guide size of .318–.319 inch, and a reamer oversize of .015 inch has a valve guide size of .328–.329 inch.

FRONT COVER

REPLACE

1. Disconnect throttle body air inlet duct, CCV hose, IAT sensor.
2. Remove air cleaner housing cover.
3. Remove oil dipstick tube.
4. Raise and support vehicle, then remove lower engine shield.
5. Drain engine oil and cooling system into suitable containers.
6. Drain power steering fluid into suitable container.
7. Disconnect cooling fan return hose at radiator fan.
8. Disconnect radiator fan pressure hose to power steering rack.

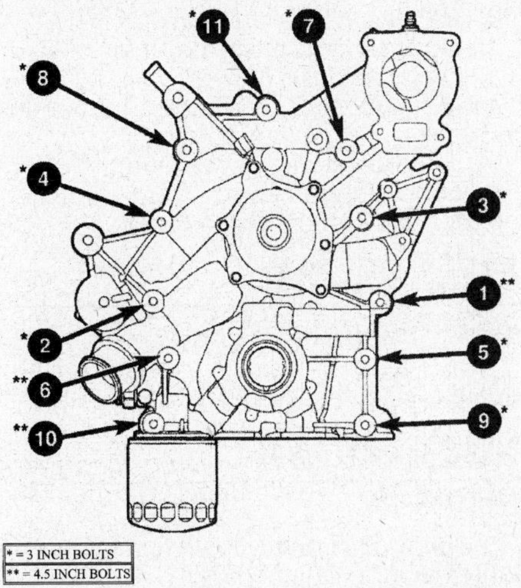

Fig. 4 Front cover bolt tightening sequence

9. Disconnect power steering hose at pump.
10. Separate A/C hose from radiator fan module.
11. Remove lower radiator hoses.
12. Remove front crossmember.
13. Remove flywheel inspection cover.
14. Disconnect oil cooler line at timing cover using tool No. 9005 or equivalent.
15. Loosen lefthand and righthand engine mounts, but do not remove.
16. Remove oil pan and pick up tube as outlined under "Oil Pan, Replace."
17. Remove serpentine drive belt as outlined under "Serpentine Belt, Replace."
18. Remove A/C compressor mounting bolts and position compressor aside.
19. Disconnect power steering line support from radiator.
20. Remove upper radiator hose and coolant recovery bottle.
21. Remove radiator fan motor and shroud.
22. Remove upper idler pulley.
23. Remove power steering pump mounting bolts and position pump aside.
24. Remove alternator as outlined under "Alternator, Replace" in "Electrical" section.
25. Disconnect heater hose at timing cover.
26. Disconnect ground wire at thermostat housing.
27. Disconnect camshaft sensor and engine coolant temperature sensor electrical connections.
28. Remove crankshaft pulley and damper.
29. Remove front cover.
30. Reverse procedure to install noting the following:
    a. **Torque** front cover bolts to 17 ft. lbs., in sequence, **Fig. 4.**

TIMING CHAIN

REPLACE

1. Remove front cover as outlined under "Front Cover, Replace."
2. Rotate crankshaft until timing marks are aligned, **Fig. 5.**
3. Remove camshaft sprocket attaching bolts.
4. Remove timing chain with camshaft sprocket.
5. Reverse procedure to install, noting the following:
    a. Align crankshaft timing mark to 12 O'clock position and camshaft timing mark at six O'clock position with timing chain attached.
    b. Place timing chain around crankshaft sprocket and install camshaft sprocket into position.
    c. **Torque** camshaft mounting bolt to 17 ft. lbs.

CAMSHAFT

REPLACE

1. Relieve fuel system pressure as outlined in "Precautions."
2. Raise and support vehicle.
3. Remove front engine shield.
4. Drain cooling system into suitable container.
5. Drain power steering system into suitable container.
6. Remove oil pan as outlined under "Oil Pan, Replace."
7. Lower vehicle, then remove radiator as outlined under "Radiator, Replace."
8. Remove intake manifold as outlined under "Intake Manifold, Replace."
9. Remove valve covers as outlined under "Valve Cover, Replace."
10. Remove front cover as outlined under "Front Cover, Replace."
11. Remove cylinder heads as outlined under "Cylinder Head, Replace."
12. Remove timing chain as outlined under "Timing Chain, Replace."
13. Remove camshaft thrust plate, then camshaft.
14. Reverse procedure to install.

PISTON & ROD ASSEMBLY

Left bank pistons are labeled "ODD." Right bank pistons are labeled "EVEN". Install pistons with arrow facing toward front of engine.

Connecting rods and pistons are serviced as an assembly.

Connecting rod bolts are torque to yield and must not be reused. Always replace bolts when they are loosened or removed.

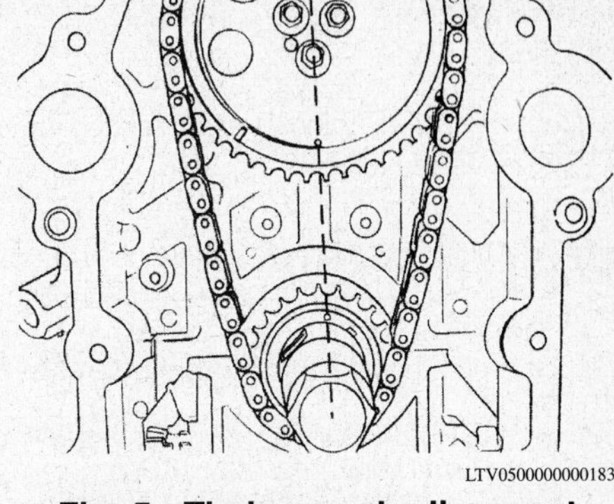

Fig. 5 Timing mark alignment

MAIN & ROD BEARINGS

Bearing shells are available in standard of 3.0008–3.0013 and 3.0013–3.0018 inch and the following undersizes: .001–.003 inch, .010, .012 and .020 inch.

CRANKSHAFT REAR OIL SEAL

REPLACE

1. Remove transmission as outlined in **MOTOR's "Domestic Transmission, In-Vehicle Service" or "Transmission Service DVD."**
2. Remove seal retainer bolts from cylinder block and oil pan.
3. Remove oil seal and retainer.
4. Reverse procedure to install.

OIL PAN

REPLACE

1. Disconnect oil dipstick tube from right valve cover.
2. Install engine lifting tool No. 9363 or equivalent.
3. Raise and support vehicle.
4. Remove lower engine shield.
5. Drain engine oil into suitable container.
6. Remove front crossmember.
7. Remove flywheel inspection cover.
8. Loosen engine mount through bolts.
9. Remove oil dipstick tube.
10. Raise front of engine using suitable engine lifting tool.
11. Remove oil pan mounting bolts, then oil pan.
12. Reverse procedure to install.

OIL PUMP

REPLACE

The oil pump is serviced with the timing chain cover. Refer to "Front Cover, Replace" for removal procedure

COOLING SYSTEM BLEED

Refer to "3.7L Engine" section for cooling system bleed procedure.

WATER PUMP

REPLACE

1. Drain cooling system into suitable container.
2. Remove windshield washer reservoir tank from radiator fan shroud.
3. Remove radiator fan shroud mounting bolts. Do not remove fan shroud at this time.
4. Disconnect upper radiator hose at radiator.
5. Remove serpentine drive belt as outlined under "Serpentine Belt, Replace."
6. Disconnect lower radiator hose at water pump.
7. Disconnect heater hose at water pump fitting.
8. Remove water pump mounting bolts.
9. Loosen bypass hose clamp at water pump, then slip bypass hose from water pump while removing pump from vehicle.
10. Reverse procedure to install.

RADIATOR

REPLACE

1. Drain cooling system into suitable container.
2. Remove radiator fan.
3. Remove power steering cooler mounting bolts and pushpins, then position cooler aside.
4. Remove two upper radiator mounting bolts.
5. Lift radiator straight up and out of engine compartment.
6. Reverse procedure to install.

FUEL PUMP

REPLACE

Refer to "3.7L Engine" section for fuel pump replacement procedure.

FUEL FILTER

REPLACE

Refer to "3.7L Engine" section for fuel filter replacement procedure.

TIGHTENING SPECIFICATIONS

Year	Component	Torque Ft. Lbs.
2004–06	Alternator	30
	Camshaft Sprocket	17
	Camshaft Tensioner Plate	18
	Connecting Rod Cap	50
	Crankshaft Rear Seal Retainer	95①
	Cylinder Head	②
	Engine Mount Bracket To Block	30
	Exhaust Manifold	17
	Flywheel	55
	Front Cover	17
	Intake Manifold	95①
	Oil Pan	③
	Oil Pan Drain Plug	25
	Oil Pump	17
	Oil Pump Pickup Tube	③
	Power Steering Pump	17
	Rocker Arm	26
	Starter Motor	30
	Throttle Body	95①
	Valve Cover	95①
	Water Pump	95①

① — Inch lbs.
② — Refer to "Cylinder Head, Replace" for tightening procedure.
③ — 1/4 inch bolts: 95 inch lbs., 5/16 inch bolts: 17 ft. lbs.

Rear Axle & Suspension

NOTE: Refer To "Computer Relearn Procedure" Located In The Front Of This Manual When Battery Power To The Computer Has Been Interrupted.

INDEX

PRECAUTIONS

Battery Ground Cable

Prior to service, disconnect battery ground cable and isolate as required.

DESCRIPTION

These axle assemblies, **Figs. 1 and 2,** are of the integral carrier housing hypoid gear type with the center line of the drive pinion mounted below the centerline of the ring gear. The drive pinion is supported by two preloaded taper roller bearings and the front and rear pinion bearing cones are pressed on the pinion stem. The front and rear pinion bearing cups are pressed against a shoulder that is recessed within the carrier casting. Drive pinion depth of mesh adjustment is controlled by installing metal shims between the rear pinion bearing cup and carrier casting.

REAR AXLE

REPLACE

1. Raise and support vehicle.
2. Support axle using a suitable jack, then secure axle to jack.
3. Remove rear wheel and tire assemblies.
4. Disconnect hydraulic brake lines at wheel cylinder. Cap fittings to prevent loss of brake fluid.
5. Disconnect parking brake cables, if required.
6. Scribe alignment marks on propeller shaft universal joint and pinion flange to ensure correct position during installation. Disconnect propeller shaft at differential pinion flange and secure to one side.
7. Remove shock absorbers from spring plate studs, then the rear spring U-bolts.
8. Remove axle assembly from vehicle.
9. Reverse procedure to install.

REAR AXLE SHAFT

REPLACE

8¼, 9¼ & 9¾ Inch Differential

1. Raise and support vehicle and remove brake drum.
2. Clean area around housing cover, then loosen housing cover and allow lubricant to drain. Remove cover.
3. Turn differential case until pinion shaft lock screw is accessible and remove lock screw and pinion shaft, **Fig. 3.**
4. Push axle shaft inward and remove C-washer locks from axle shaft, **Fig. 4,** then pull axle shaft from housing being careful not to damage axle shaft bearing. **Inspect axle shaft bearing surfaces for signs of damage or wear. If any of these conditions exist, both shaft and bearing should be replaced. Normal bearing contact on shaft should be a dull gray and may appear lightly dented.**
5. Remove axle shaft bearing and seal from axle housing using suitable removal tools, **Fig. 5.** If bearing shows no sign of excessive wear or damage, it can be reused along with a new seal. Never reuse an axle shaft seal. **Remove any burrs that may be present in housing bearing shoulder, as bearing could become cocked during installation.**
6. Install bearing, making sure it does not become cocked. Drive bearing until it bottoms against shoulder. **Do not use seal to position or bottom bearing as this will damage seal.**
7. With seal installer, **Fig. 6,** install axle shaft bearing seal until outer flange of tool bottoms against housing flange face. This will position seal to proper depth.
8. Reverse disassembly procedure to reassemble axle.

10 ½ & 11 ½ Inch Differential

1. Remove axle shaft flange bolts.
2. Slide axle shaft out of axle tube.
3. Remove axle shaft gasket.
4. Reverse procedure to install, noting the following:
   a. Install new axle shaft gasket.
   b. Use new axle flange bolts or apply Loctite 242 on cleaned existing bolts.

Dana/Spicer Type

1. Remove axle shaft flange nuts and lock washers.
2. Slide axle shaft from axle tube.
3. Reverse procedure to install.

HUB & BEARING

REPLACE

10 ½ & 11 ½ Inch Differential

REMOVAL

1. Remove axle shaft flange bolts, then the axle shaft.
2. Remove retainer ring from axle shaft tube, **Fig. 7.**
3. Remove hub bearing nut locking key, **Fig. 8.**
4. Remove hub bearing nut using socket tool No. 8954, or equivalent.
5. Remove hub and bearing from axle.
6. Pry out hub bearing seal from back of hub. Inner part of seal may stay on axle tube, this part must also be removed, **Fig. 9.**
7. Remove rear bearing.
8. Remove hub bearing cups using a suitable hammer and drift.

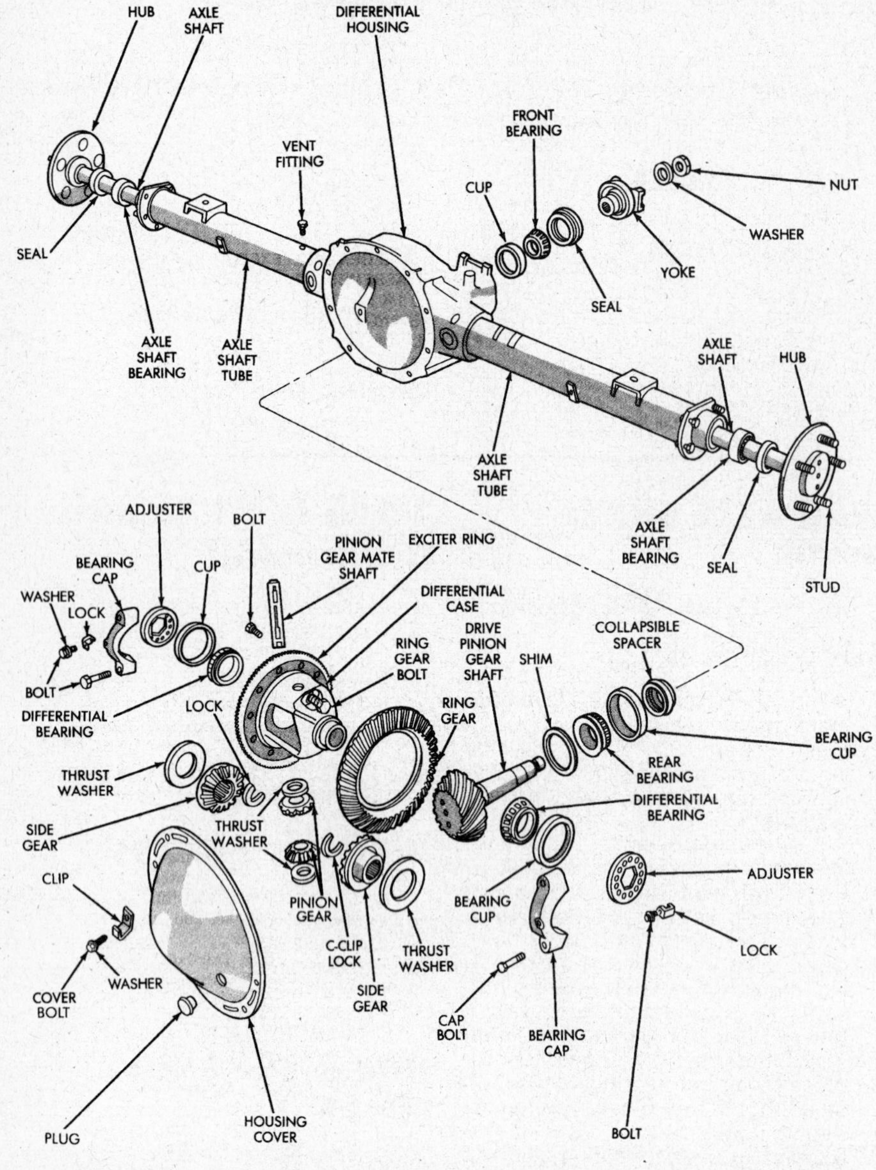

Fig. 1 Exploded view of 8¼ & 9¼ inch integral carrier rear axle assembly

INSTALLATION

1. Install outer hub bearing cup using installer tool No. 8961 and handle tool No. C-4171, or equivalents.
2. Install inner hub bearing cup using installer tool No. 8962 and handle tool No. C-4171, or equivalents.
3. Pack bearings with suitable grease.
4. Install rear bearing with new grease seal using installer tool No. 8963 and handle tool No. C-4171, or equivalents.
5. Slide hub on axle tube, then install front bearing into hub.
6. Install hub bearing nut, then **torque** to 22 ft. lbs., using socket tool No. 8954, or equivalent, while rotating hub.
7. Back off nut 30° and align next hub nut key slot with axle tube key slot, then install locking key. End play should be .001–.010 inch.
8. Install retainer ring with ring end in key slot.
9. Install new axle shaft gasket, then the axle shaft.

Dana/Spicer Type

1. Remove axle shaft as outlined in "Axle Shaft, Replace."
2. Remove locknut and adjustment nut, then slide off rear drum from axle housing.
3. Remove bearings from hub.
4. Reverse procedure to install. **Torque** adjusting nut to 120–140 ft. lbs., then loosen adjusting nut ⅓ turn and tap locknut into spindle keyway and adjusting nut.

SHOCK ABSORBER

REPLACE

Pickup

1. Raise and support vehicle.
2. Support rear axle using suitable jack.
3. Remove upper and lower shock bolt and nut.
4. Remove shock from vehicle.
5. Reverse procedure to install.

Van

1. Raise and support vehicle.
2. Remove lower shock mounting bolt and nut from axle bracket.
3. Remove upper mounting nut, retainers and bolt.
4. Remove shock from vehicle. If required, remove spacer tube from upper shock eye.
5. Reverse procedure to install.

LEAF SPRING

REPLACE

Pickup

1. Raise and support vehicle.
2. Support axle using suitable jack.
3. Remove nuts, lock washers and U-bolts attaching spring to axle.
4. Remove spring shackle attaching bolts, shackle and spring front bolt, then remove spring.
5. Reverse procedure to install.

Van

1. Raise and support vehicle.
2. Remove U-bolt attaching nuts, U-bolts and plate.
3. Remove front pivot attaching bolt, then the rear shackle attaching nuts.
4. Remove outer shackle and bolt from hanger, then the spring. Some vehicles are equipped with one piece shackles.
5. Reverse procedure to install.

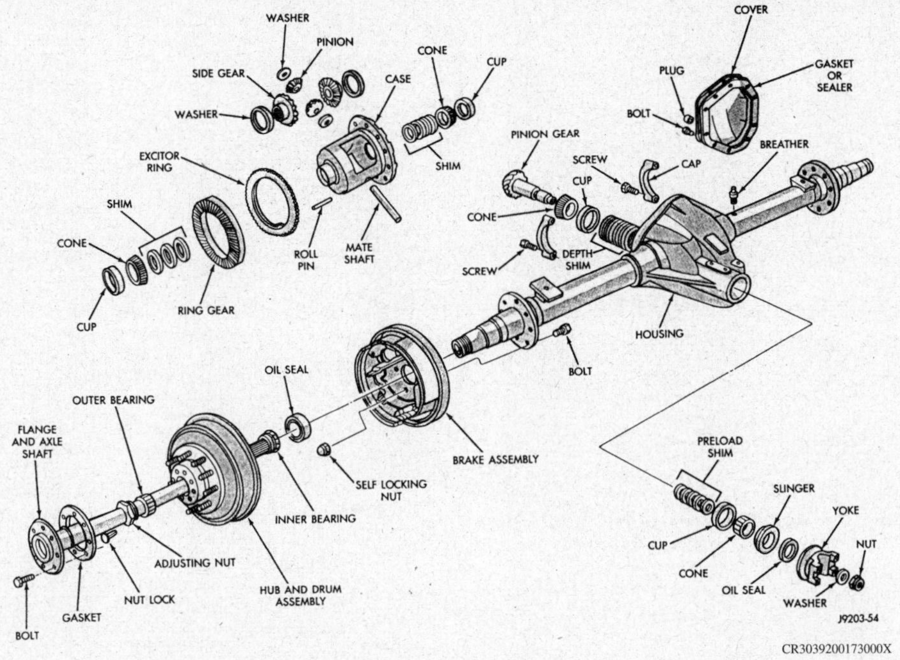

CR3039200173000X

Fig. 2 Exploded view of Spicer Models 60, 70 & 80 rear axle assembly

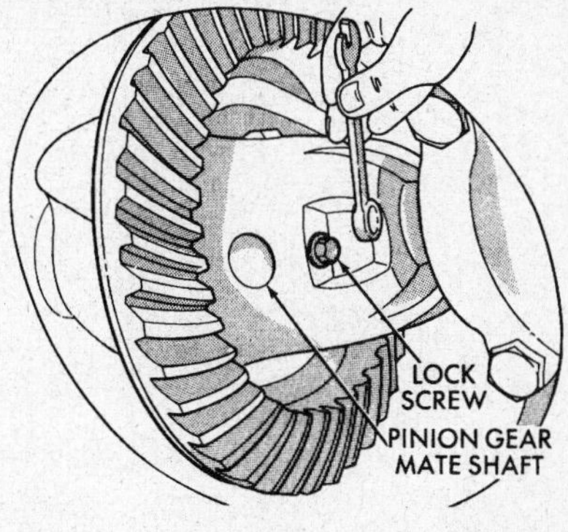

CR3038800137000X

Fig. 3 Differential pinion shaft lockpin removal. 8¼, 9¼ & 9¾ Inch

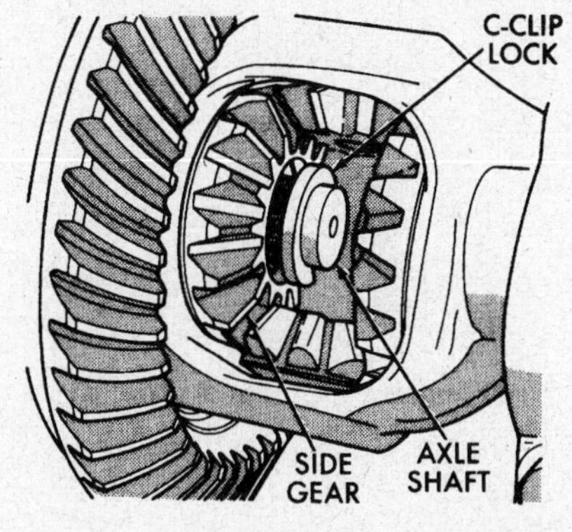

CR3038800138000X

Fig. 4 C-lock washers removal. 8¼, 9¼ & 9¾ Inch

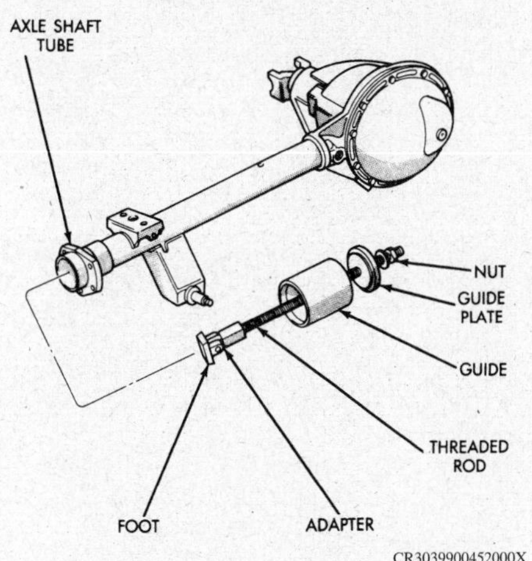

CR3039900452000X

Fig. 5 Axle shaft bearing removal tool. 8¼, 9¼ & 9¾ Inch

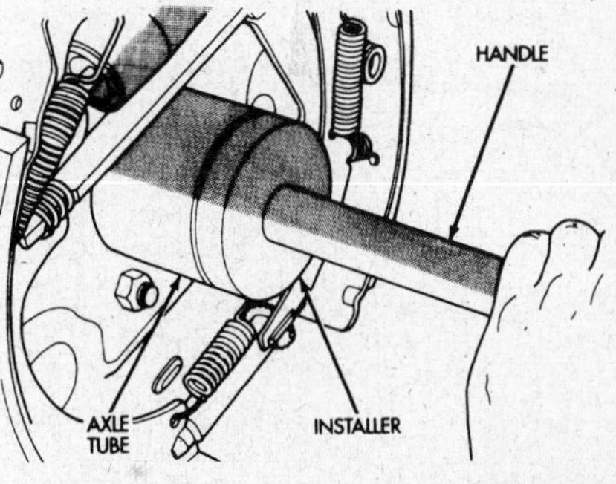

CR3039900453000X

Fig. 6 Axle shaft seal & bearing installer. 8¼, 9¼ & 9¾ Inch

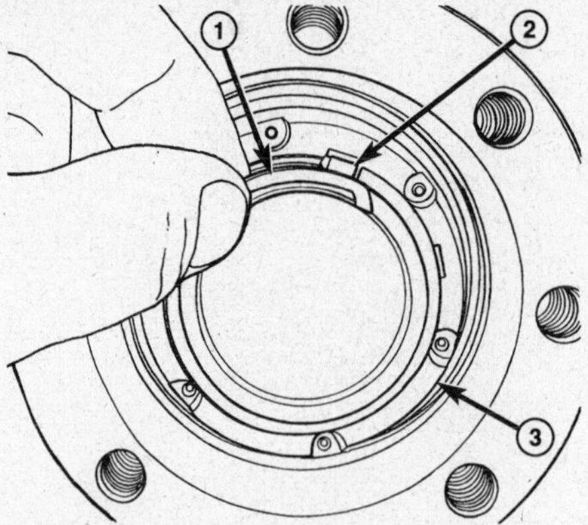

1 - RETAINER RING
2 - LOCKING KEY
3 - BEARING NUT

LTV1900000000342

Fig. 7 Retainer ring. 10 ½ & 11 ½ Inch Differential

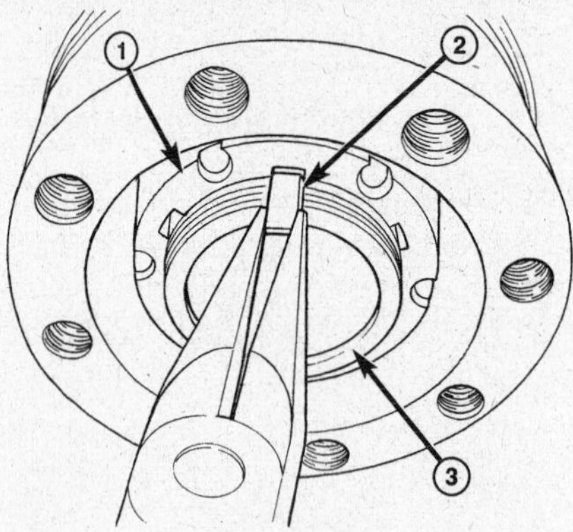

1 - BEARING NUT
2 - LOCKING KEY
3 - AXLE TUBE

LTV1900000000343

Fig. 8 Locking key. 10 ½ & 11 ½ Inch Differential

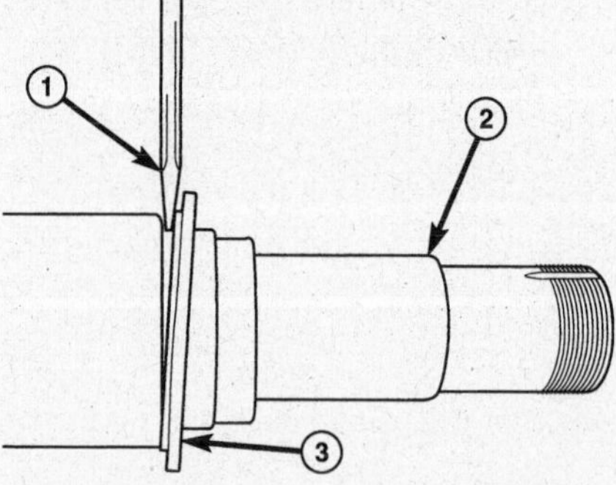

1 - PRY BAR
2 - AXLE TUBE
3 - REMAINING SEAL

LTV1900000000344

Fig. 9 Inner part of seal. 10 ½ & 11 ½ Inch Differential

TIGHTENING SPECIFICATIONS

Year	Component	Torque Ft. Lbs.
PICKUP		
2002–06	Auxiliary Spring Bumper	25
	Axle Flange	95
	Differential Cover	30
	Jounce Bumper LD & SRT-10	30
	Jounce Bumper HD	45
	Power Hop Damper	75
	Shock Absorber Nut	100
	Spring Bolt & Nut	120
	Spring Clamp U-Bolt Nut	110
	Spring Rear Shackle Nuts LD & SRT-10	120
	Spring Rear Shackle Nuts HD	170
	Stabilizer Bar Retainer To Axle SRT-10	55
	Wheel Lug Nuts	①
VAN		
2002–03	Axle Shaft Bolts	90–100
	Shock Absorber	70
	Spring Eye Front Nut	90
	Spring Eye Rear Nut	110
	Spring Shackle Bracket	35
	Spring Shackle Eye Nut	110
	Spring U-Bolt	110
	Wheel Lug Nuts	②

① — 1500, 135 ft. lbs.; 2500–3500, 145 ft. lbs.
② — 15 inch 5 stud wheel, 80–110 ft. lbs.; 16 inch 8 stud wheel, 120–150 ft. lbs.

Front Suspension & Steering

NOTE: Refer To "Computer Relearn Procedure" Located In The Front Of This Manual When Battery Power To The Computer Has Been Interrupted.

NOTE: Prior To Performing Any Service Operations Listed In This Section, Consult The "Technical Service Bulletins" Section For Related Information.

INDEX

PRECAUTIONS

Battery Ground Cable

Prior to service, disconnect battery ground cable and isolate as required.

DESCRIPTION

Independent Front Suspension

These vehicles are equipped with a coil spring front suspension system, **Figs. 1 and 2.** On Van, the upper control arms are mounted on longitudinal rails and the lower control arms are mounted on a removable crossmember. Both control arms have replaceable bushings on the inner ends and ball joints on the outer ends. The upper control arms also control caster and camber adjustments through eccentric pivot bolts at the inner ends or through slots in the upper control arm mounting bracket.

The Pickup are equipped with either a link/coil front suspension, **Fig. 3,** or an independent front suspension, **Fig. 4.** On models equipped with link/coil system, wheels are mounted to knuckles with a non-serviceable hub and bearing assembly. Steering knuckles pivot on replaceable ball studs attached to axle tube yokes and caster and pinion angle adjustments are made with cam bolts located at the axle. On models with the independent front suspension, replaceable suspension arm ball studs are pressed into the arms and the upper arm has a pivot bar mounted to a frame bracket. This bracket is where caster and camber adjustments are made.

WHEEL BEARING

REPLACE

Van

1. Raise and support vehicle.
2. Remove tire and wheel assembly.
3. Remove disc brake caliper.
4. Remove dust cap, cotter pin, nut lock, nut and washer from spindle.
5. Slide hub/rotor from spindle.
6. Remove seal and inner wheel bearing from hub/rotor.
7. Remove inner/outer bearing cups from hub/rotor with a suitable pin punch.
8. Reverse procedure to install, noting the following:
   a. **Torque** nut to 35 ft. lbs., to preload bearing while rotating hub/rotor.
   b. Stop hub/rotor and loosen nut to completely release bearing preload torque.
   c. **Torque** nut to 25 inch lbs., and install nut lock and a new cotter pin.

HUB & BEARING

REPLACE

Pickup

2WD

1. Raise and support vehicle, then remove tire and wheel assembly.
2. Remove brake caliper and rotor.
3. **On models equipped with ABS,** remove ABS wheel speed sensor.
4. **On all models,** remove three hub/bearing mounting bolts.
5. Remove hub/bearing from steering knuckle.
6. Reverse procedure to install.

4WD

INDEPENDENT SUSPENSION

1. Raise and support vehicle, then remove wheel and tire assembly.
2. Remove brake caliper and rotor.
3. **On models equipped with ABS,** remove ABS wheel speed sensor.
4. **On all models,** remove halfshaft nut.
5. Remove tie rod end nut, then separate tie rod from knuckle using tool No. 9360 or equivalent.
6. Separate upper ball joint from knuckle using tool No. 9360 or equivalent.
7. Pull down on steering knuckle to separate halfshaft from hub assembly.
8. Remove three hub assembly mounting

bolts, then slide hub from steering knuckle.
9. Reverse procedure to install.

LINK/COIL SUSPENSION

1. Raise and support vehicle, then remove tire and wheel assembly.
2. **On models equipped with hub extension,** remove extension from rotor.
3. **On all models,** remove brake caliper.
4. Remove cotter pin and hub nut from axle shaft.
5. **On models equipped with ABS,** disconnect ABS wheel sensor electrical connection from under hood, then remove from frame and steering knuckle.
6. **On all models,** loosen hub assembly mounting bolts ¼ inch, then tap bolts with suitable hammer to loosen hub assembly from steering knuckle.
7. Remove hub assembly mounting bolts, then hub assembly.
8. **On models equipped with ABS,** remove ABS wheel speed sensor from hub.
9. **On all models,** separate wheel studs from hub assembly.
10. Reverse procedure to install.

BALL JOINT INSPECTION

Lower

1. Raise and support vehicle, then install dial indicator and clamp assembly to lower suspension arm.
2. Position indicator plunger against knuckle arm and zero indicator.
3. Raise and lower wheel with a pry bar under center of tire.
4. Measure axial movement of knuckle with respect to suspension arm.
5. **On Van, 1500 Pickup and 2003–06 2500–3500 Pickup models,** if travel of suspension arm is .020 inch or more, replace ball joint.
6. **On 2002 2500–3500 Pickup models,** if travel of suspension arm is .030 inch or more, replace ball joint.

Upper

1. Position a suitable floor jack under lower suspension arm, then raise wheel and allow tire to lightly contact floor.
2. Mount a dial indicator on upper suspension arm, then position indicator plunger against upper ball joint boss of steering knuckle.
3. Grasp top of tire and apply force in and out. Inspect for movement at ball joint between upper suspension arm and knuckle.
4. If lateral movement is .020 inch or more, replace the ball joint.

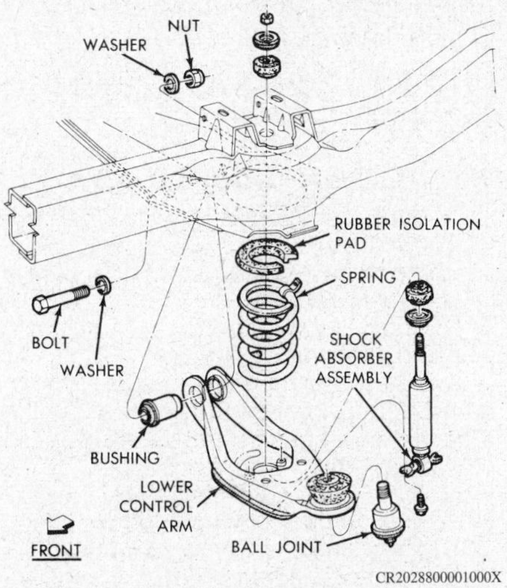

Fig. 1 Lower control arm & coil spring. Van

BALL JOINT

REPLACE

Pickup

2002 2500 & 3500

LOWER

1. Remove snap ring from lower ball joint.
2. Install ball joint removal tool Nos. C4212-F, 8445-3 and 8445-1 or equivalents, **Fig. 5.**
3. Remove ball joint.
4. Reverse procedure to install.

UPPER

1. Install ball joint removal tool Nos. C4212-F, 6761 and 8445-3, or equivalents, **Fig. 6.**
2. Remove ball joint.
3. Reverse procedure to install.

1500 & 2003-06 2500 & 3500

LOWER

Independent Suspension

1. Raise and support vehicle, then remove tire and wheel assembly.
2. Remove brake caliper and rotor.
3. Remove tie rod end using puller tool No. C-4150A, or equivalent.
4. **On models equipped with 4WD,** remove front halfshaft nut.
5. **On all models,** remove upper ball joint nut.
6. Separate ball joint from knuckle using remover tool No. 8677, or equivalent.
7. Remove lower ball joint nut.
8. Separate ball joint from knuckle using remover tool No. 8677, or equivalent.
9. Remove hub and bearing from steering knuckle.
10. **On models equipped with 4WD,** position and support halfshaft aside.
11. **On heavy duty models equipped with 2WD,** remove snap ring from lower control arm.
12. **On all models,** using press tool No. C-4212-F, receiver tool No. 8698-2 and driver tool No. 8698-3, or equivalents, press ball joint from lower control arm, **Fig. 7.**
13. Reverse procedure to install, noting the following
    a. **On light duty models,** stake ball joint flange in four evenly spaced places around ball joint.
    b. **On heavy duty models equipped with 2WD,** install new snap ring.

Link/Coil Suspension

1. Raise and support vehicle, then remove wheel and tire assembly.
2. Remove steering knuckle.
3. Remove axle shaft from axle.
4. Remove lower snap ring from lower ball joint.
5. Remove ball joint using tool No. C-4212-F, receiver tool No. 8698-2 and driver tool No. 8698-3, or equivalents.
6. Reverse procedure to install.

Van

UPPER

1. Place a suitable jack under outer end of lower suspension arm, then raise and support vehicle.
2. Remove tire and wheel assembly.
3. Remove disc brake caliper, then the wheel speed sensor.
4. Support lower control arm.
5. Remove cotter pins and nuts from ball joints.
6. Position ball joint remover tool No. C-3564-A, or equivalent, between ball joints, then rotate threaded portion of tool to apply force to upper ball joint.
7. Unthread ball joint from suspension arm using socket tool No. C-3561, or equivalent. It may be required to strike knuckle with a hammer to separate ball joints from knuckle.
8. Reverse procedure to install, noting the following:
    a. Gap between ball joint hex and suspension arm bore is .01–.05 inch.
    b. Install new seal over ball joint.

LOWER

2002-03

1. Raise and support vehicle, then remove tire and wheel assembly.
2. Separate outer tie rod end from knuckle.
3. Remove disc brake caliper, then the rotor.
4. Support lower control arm.
5. Remove cotter pins and nuts from ball joints.
6. Install ball joint remover tool No. C-3564-A, or equivalent, then rotate threaded portion of tool to apply force to lower ball joint. It may be required to strike knuckle with a hammer to separate ball joints from knuckle.
7. Remove ball joint seal.

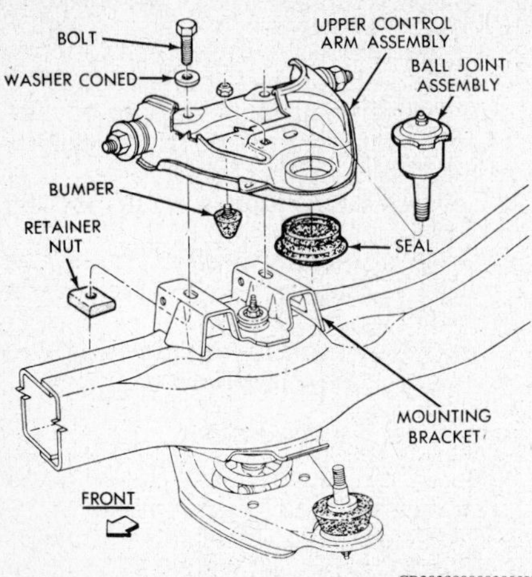

Fig. 2 Upper control arm. Van

8. Press ball joint from lower suspension arm bore.
9. Reverse procedure to install.

COIL SPRING

REPLACE

Pickup

2002 2500 & 3500

2WD

1. Raise and support vehicle.
2. Remove tire and wheel assembly, brake caliper assembly and rotor.
3. Remove cotter pin and nut from tie rod, then the tie rod end from steering knuckle with puller tool No. C-3894, or equivalent.
4. Remove stabilizer link from lower suspension arm.
5. Support lower suspension arm outboard end with suitable jack.
6. Remove cotter pin and nut from lower ball joint, then separate ball joint with remover tool No. C-4150A, or equivalent.
7. Remove lower shock bolt from suspension arm.
8. Lower jack and suspension arm until spring tension is relieved.
9. Remove spring and rubber isolator.
10. Reverse procedure to install.

4WD

1. Raise and support vehicle, then support axle with a suitable hydraulic jack.
2. Scribe alignment marks on lower suspension arm cam adjusters and axle bracket for installation reference, then remove upper suspension arm and loosen lower suspension arm bolts.
3. Disconnect front propeller shaft from axle. Mark orientation for installation reference.
4. Disconnect track bar from frame rail bracket, drag link from pitman arm and stabilizer bar link and shock absorber from axle.
5. Lower axle until spring is free from upper mount, then remove spring.
6. Reverse procedure to install. Use a new cotter pin when connecting drag link to pitman arm.

1500 & 2003-06 2500 & 3500

INDEPENDENT SUSPENSION

1. Raise and support vehicle, then remove tire and wheel assembly.
2. Support lower control arm at outboard side of lower arm.
3. Remove shock absorber as outlined in "Shock Absorber, Replace."
4. Install spring compressor tool No. DD-1278 up through lower suspension arm, coil spring and shock hole in frame. Bell shaped adapter goes against lower suspension arm.
5. Install nut on top of tool at shock hole.
6. Tighten spring compressor nut against bell shaped adapter finger tight, then loosen ½ turn.
7. Remove stabilizer link.
8. Remove lower ball joint nut at steering knuckle.
9. Separate ball joint from knuckle using ball joint remover tool No. 8677, or equivalent. Support upper control arm aside.
10. Remove lower control arm support.
11. Tighten spring compressor tool to allow clearance for lower ball joint to be removed out of knuckle. It may be required to loosen control arm pivot bolt to allow downward swing.
12. Loosen tension on spring compressor slowly allowing lower suspension arm to pivot downward.
13. Remove spring compressor tool.
14. Remove coil spring and isolator pad from vehicle.
15. Reverse procedure to install.

LINK/COIL SUSPENSION

1. Raise and support vehicle.
2. Support axle using a suitable jack.
3. Scribe alignment marks on lower suspension arm cam adjusters and axle bracket for reference during installation.
4. Remove upper suspension arm, then loosen lower suspension arm bolts.
5. Remove front propeller shaft from axle. Mark location for reference during installation.
6. Disconnect track bar from frame rail bracket.
7. Disconnect drag link from pitman arm.
8. Disconnect stabilizer bar link, then the shock absorber from axle.
9. Lower axle until spring is free from upper mount.
10. Remove coil spring.
11. Reverse procedure to install.

Van

1. Block brake pedal in up position.
2. Raise and support vehicle.
3. Remove front wheels, then the caliper retainer and anti-rattle spring assemblies.
4. Remove caliper from disc and position caliper aside, then remove inboard shoe. **Do not allow caliper to hang or be supported by hydraulic brake hose.**
5. Remove shock absorber, upper bushing and sleeve, then the strut.
6. Install spring compressor tool No. DD-1278, or equivalent, finger tight, then back off one half turn.
7. Remove cotter keys and ball joint nuts.
8. Install ball joint breaker tool No. C-3564-A, or equivalent, over lower ball joint stud, then set tool securely against upper ball joint stud.
9. Tighten tool to apply pressure against upper ball joint stud, then strike knuckle with hammer to loosen stud.
10. Remove tool, then slowly loosen coil spring compressor until all tension is relieved from spring.
11. Remove spring compressor and spring.
12. Reverse procedure to install.

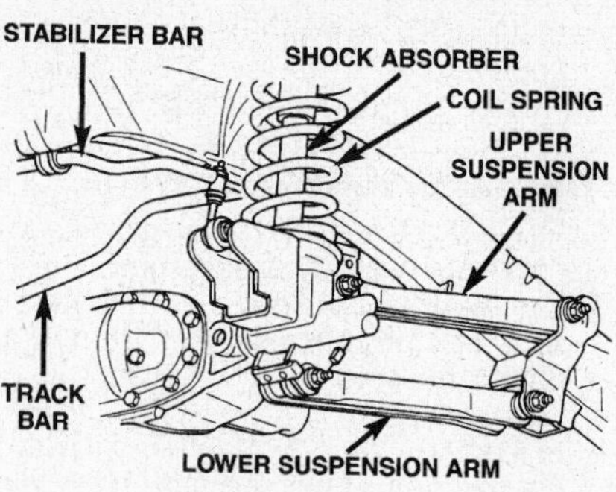

Fig. 3 Link/coil front suspension. Pickup

SHOCK ABSORBER

REPLACE

1. Raise and support vehicle.
2. Turn wheel as needed to gain access to upper shock absorber mount, then remove upper nut and retainer.
3. **On models equipped with link/coil suspension,** remove three nuts from upper shock bracket, then the bracket.
4. **On all models,** remove lower attaching bolts, then the shock.
5. Reverse procedure to install.

CONTROL ARM

REPLACE

Upper Control Arm

PICKUP

INDEPENDENT SUSPENSION

1. Raise and support vehicle, then remove tire and wheel assembly.
2. Remove disc brake caliper adapter with caliper, then remove rotor.
3. **On models equipped with ABS,** remove wheel speed sensor from upper control arm.
4. **On all models,** remove nut from upper ball joint.
5. Separate upper ball joint from steering knuckle using tool No. 9360 or equivalent.

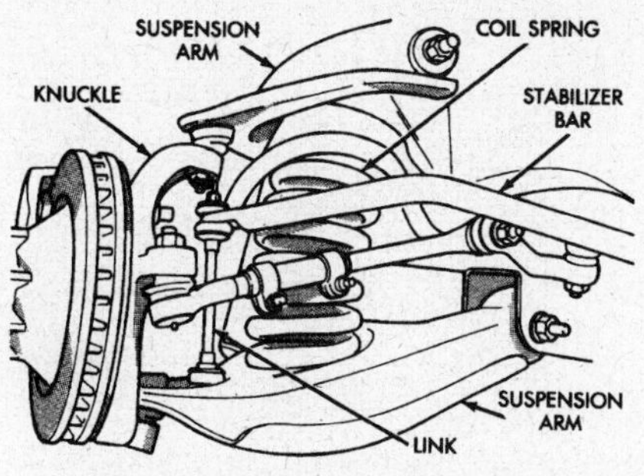

Fig. 4 Independent front suspension. Pickup

6. Remove control arm pivot bolts and flag nuts, then remove control arm.
7. Reverse procedure to install.

LINK/COIL SUSPENSION

1. Raise and support vehicle, then remove tire and wheel assembly.
2. Access righthand control arm by performing the following:
   a. Disconnect exhaust system at manifolds.
   b. Disconnect rubber exhaust mounts at muffler.
   c. Support transmission with suitable jack.
   d. Remove transmission crossmember.
   e. Lower exhaust system for access to upper control arm bolt.
3. Remove mounting bolt at frame rail.
4. Remove mounting bolt at axle bracket.
5. Remove control arm.
6. Reverse procedure to install.

VAN

1. Raise and support vehicle.
2. Remove front tire and wheel assembly.
3. Remove disk brake caliper and rotor.
4. Support lower suspension arm.
5. Remove cotter pin and nut from upper ball joint.
6. Position ball joint remover tool No. C-3564–A, or equivalent, and rotate threaded portion of tool to apply force to lower ball joint.
7. Strike steering knuckle sharply with hammer to loosen ball joint. Do not force ball joint out from knuckle with tool.
8. Separate upper ball joint from steering knuckle.
9. Remove suspension arm pivot bar nuts, then the suspension arm.
10. Reverse procedure to install, noting the following:
    a. Tighten bolts to specifications.
    b. Perform front end alignment.

Lower Control Arm

PICKUP

2002 2500 & 3500

1. Raise and support vehicle.
2. Remove tire and wheel assembly.
3. Remove brake caliper assembly and rotor.
4. Remove tie rod end from steering knuckle with puller tool No. C-3894–A, or equivalent.
5. Remove stabilizer bar link from lower suspension arm.
6. Support lower suspension arm outboard end with suitable jack. Place jack under arm in front of shock mount.
7. Remove cotter pin and nut from lower ball joint.
8. Separate ball joint with removal tool No. C-4150A, or equivalent.
9. Remove lower shock bolt from suspension arm.
10. Lower jack and suspension arm until spring tension is relieved, remove spring and rubber isolator.
11. Remove bolts mounting suspension arm to crossmember, then the arm.
12. Reverse procedure to install tightening bolts to specifications.

1500 & 2003-06 2500 & 3500

2WD Models w/Independent Suspension

1. Raise and support vehicle, then remove tire and wheel assembly.
2. Support lower control arm at outboard side to support vehicle weight.
3. Remove shock absorber as outlined in "Shock Absorber, Replace."
4. Install spring compressor tool No. DD-1278, or equivalent, up through lower suspension arm, coil spring and shock hole in frame. Bell shaped adapter goes against lower suspension arm.
5. Install nut on top of tool at shock hole.
6. Tighten spring compressor nut against bell shaped adapter finger tight then loosen ½ turn.
7. Remove stabilizer link.
8. Remove lower ball joint nut at steering knuckle.
9. Install ball joint remover tool No. 8677, or equivalent, then separate lower ball joint from knuckle.
10. Support upper control arm and steering knuckle out of the way.
11. Remove lower control arm support.
12. Tighten spring compressor tool to allow clearance for lower ball joint to be removed out of knuckle.
13. Loosen tension on spring compressor tool slowly allowing lower suspension arm to pivot downward.
14. Remove spring compressor tool.
15. Remove coil spring and isolator pad from vehicle.
16. Remove front and rear pivot bolts, then the lower control arm.
17. Reverse procedure to install.

4WD Models w/Independent Suspension

1. Raise and support vehicle, then remove tire and wheel assembly.
2. Remove upper ball joint nut.
3. Separate ball joint from steering knuckle using ball joint removal tool No. 8677, or equivalent.
4. Remove front half shaft, then the torsion bar.
5. Remove shock absorber lower bolt.
6. Remove stabilizer bar link.
7. Remove lower ball joint nut.

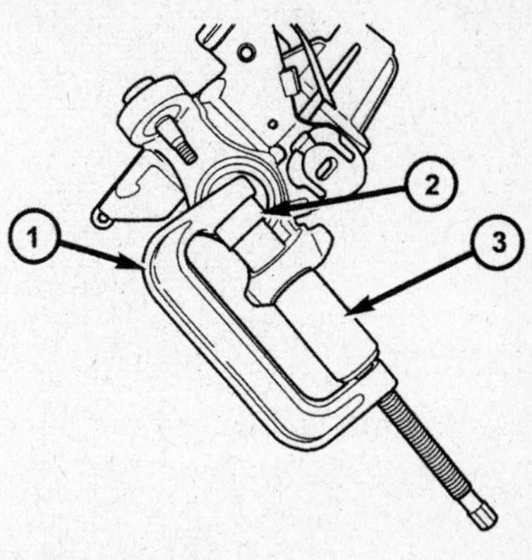

1 - SPECIAL TOOL C4212-F
2 - SPECIAL TOOL 8445-3
3 - SPECIAL TOOL 8445-1

CR2020100176000X

Fig. 5 Lower ball joint removal. 2002 2500 & 3500

8. Separate ball joint from steering knuckle using ball joint removal tool No. 8677, or equivalent.
9. Remove control arm pivot bolts, then the lower control arm.
10. Reverse procedure to install.

4WD Models w/Link/Coil Suspension

1. Raise and support vehicle, then remove front tire and wheel assembly.
2. Scribe alignment marks on cam adjusters and control arm for installation reference.
3. Remove lower control arm nut, cam and cam bolt from axle.
4. Remove nut and bolt from frame rail bracket, then remove lower control arm.

VAN

1. Raise and support vehicle, then remove front tire and wheel assembly.
2. Remove disc brake caliper from steering knuckle.
3. Disconnect stabilizer bar and strut bar from lower suspension arm.
4. Remove shock absorber.
5. Install spring compressor tool No. DD-1278, or equivalent up through the lower suspension arm, coil spring and shock hole in frame. Bell shaped adapter goes against lower suspension arm.
6. Tighten spring compressor nut against adapter finger tight, then loosen ½ turn.
7. Remove cotter pin and lower ball joint nut at steering knuckle.
8. Install ball joint removal tool No. C-3564–A, or equivalent, on lower ball joint.
9. Expand tool enough to place force on ball joint, then strike joint sharply with hammer to loosen joint. Do not attempt to force joint out of steering knuckle with loosening tool.
10. Remove spring compressor tool.
11. Remove lower suspension arm pivot

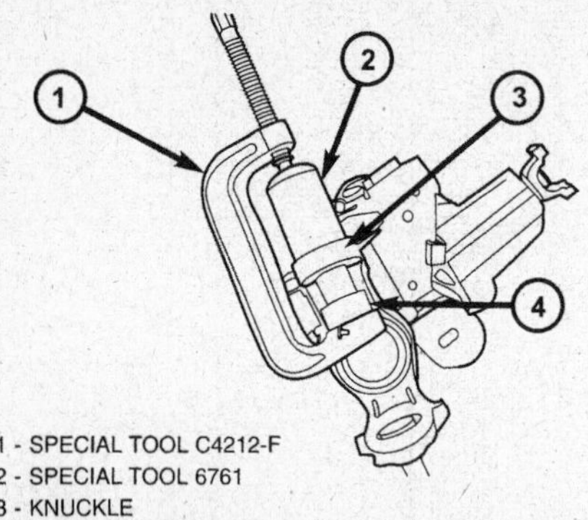

Fig. 6 Upper ball joint removal. 2002 2500 & 3500

bolt from crossmember, then the suspension arm.
12. Reverse procedure to install tightening bolts to specifications.

STEERING KNUCKLE

REPLACE

Independent Suspension

1. Raise and support vehicle, then remove tire and wheel assembly.
2. Remove brake caliper and rotor.
3. Remove brake shield, then the ABS wheel speed sensor.
4. Remove tie rod end nut.
5. Separate tie rod from knuckle.
6. Remove upper ball joint nut.
7. Separate ball joint from steering knuckle.
8. Remove lower ball joint nut.
9. Separate ball joint from steering knuckle using removal tool No. 8677, or equivalent.
10. Remove knuckle.
11. Reverse procedure to install.

4WD

LINK & COIL SUSPENSION

1. Remove hub assembly as outlined under "Hub & Bearing, Replace."
2. Remove tie-rod or drag link end from steering knuckle arm.
3. Remove ABS sensor wire and bracket from knuckle.
4. Remove upper and lower ball stud nuts.
5. Strike steering knuckle with a brass hammer to loosen.
6. Remove knuckle from axle tube yokes.
7. Reverse procedure to install.

STABILIZER BAR

REPLACE

Pickup

INDEPENDENT SUSPENSION

1. Raise and support vehicle, then disconnect link from lower suspension arm and stabilizer bar.
2. Disconnect stabilizer bar clamps from frame rails and remove bar.
3. Reverse procedure to install. Ensure bar is centered in frame.

LINK/COIL SUSPENSION

1. Raise and support vehicle.
2. Hold stabilizer link shafts with wrench and remove nuts at stabilizer bar.
3. Remove retainers and grommets from stabilizer bar links.
4. Remove stabilizer bar link nuts from axle brackets.
5. Remove links from axle brackets using puller tool No. C-3894–A, or equivalent.
6. Remove stabilizer bar clamps, then the stabilizer bar.
7. Reverse procedure to install.

Van

1. Raise and support vehicle, then remove nut and washer from stabilizer bar link bolt at lower suspension arm on both sides of vehicle.
2. Remove link bolt, retainers, insulators and spacers from each lower suspension arm, then remove bolts from U-shaped retainer.
3. Remove retainer and stabilizer bar from vehicle.
4. Reverse procedure to install. Align stabilizer bar bushings before installing bar on bracket.

POWER STEERING GEAR

REPLACE

Pickup

INDEPENDENT SUSPENSION

1. Lock steering wheel.
2. Drain and siphon power steering fluid from reservoir into suitable container.
3. Raise and support vehicle.
4. Remove and discard steering coupler pinch bolt.
5. Disconnect power steering hoses from steering gear.
6. Remove tire and wheel assembly.

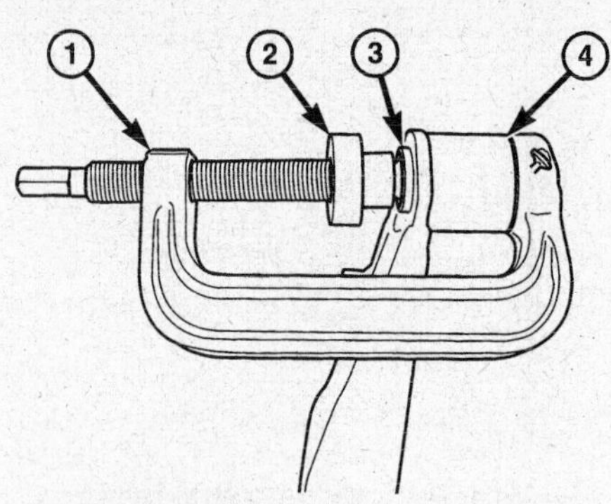

Fig. 7 Lower ball joint removal. 2002–03 1500 & 2003 2500 & 3500

7. Remove tie rod end nuts.
8. Separate tie rod ends from knuckles using remover tool No. 8677, or equivalent.
9. Remove skid plate.
10. Remove steering gear mounting bolts, then the steering gear from vehicle.
11. Reverse procedure to install.

LINK/COIL SUSPENSION

1. Place front wheels in a straight ahead position.
2. Disconnect and cap fluid hoses from steering gear.
3. Remove coupler pinch bolt at steering gear and slide shaft off of gear.
4. Mark pitman shaft and pitman arm for installation reference, then remove pitman arm with puller tool No. C-4150A, or equivalent.
5. Remove steering gear retaining bolts and nuts, then the steering gear.
6. Reverse procedure to install, noting the following:
   a. Align steering coupler on gear shaft.
   b. Align and install pitman arm.
   c. Add fluid.

Van

1. Position front wheels straight ahead.
2. Raise and support vehicle.
3. Remove and cap fluid hoses from steering gear.
4. Remove coupler retaining bolt and slide coupler off of steering gear stub shaft.
5. Mark pitman shaft and pitman arm for installation reference, then remove pitman arm with puller No. C-4150A, or equivalent.
6. Remove steering gear and bracket from vehicle.
7. Reverse procedure to install, noting the following:

a. Align coupler shaft index marks to steering gear and shaft.
b. Install steering coupler with new bolts.
c. Align pitman arm.

POWER STEERING PUMP

REPLACE

Pickup

2002 2500 & 3500

CNG & GASOLINE ENGINES

1. Remove serpentine drive belt.
2. Remove hoses from power steering pump and cap fittings.
3. Unthread battery ground cable stud from cylinder head, do not remove from bracket.
4. Loosen upper bracket bolt and remove lower bracket to engine block bolts.
5. Pivot pump assembly past coolant tube.
6. Remove upper stud and bolt from cylinder head.
7. Remove steering pump and mounting bracket from engine as an assembly.
8. Remove pump pulley with puller tool No. C-4333, or equivalent.
9. Remove front pump bracket.
10. **On models equipped with 8.0L engine,** remove rear pump bracket.
11. **On all models,** reverse procedure to install, tighten bolts to specifications.

DIESEL ENGINE

1. Remove and cap power steering pump hoses and vacuum pump vacuum line.
2. Remove sender unit from engine block and plug hole in block.
3. Remove and cap oil feed line from bottom of vacuum pump.
4. Remove lower bolt that attaches vacuum/steering pump assembly to engine block.
5. Remove nut from steering pump attaching bracket.
6. Remove upper bolt from pump assembly, then the assembly.
7. Remove mounting gasket.
8. Remove steering pump to vacuum pump bracket attaching nuts.
9. Slide steering pump from bracket, use care not to damage internal oil seal in vacuum pump.
10. Remove two pump body spacers.
11. Reverse procedure to install, noting the following:
    a. Install vacuum pump bracket to steering pump nuts, then tighten to specifications.
    b. Position new gasket on vacuum pump assembly. Use sealer to hold gasket in place if required.
    c. Align and install pump assembly on engine, ensure power steering pump stud is inserted into block bracket.
    d. Tighten pump to engine block attaching bolts to specifications.
    e. Tighten steering pump to attaching bracket nut to specifications.
    f. Tighten oil feed line to vacuum pump connection to specifications.
    g. Tighten fluid hoses to power steering pump fittings to specifications.

1500 & 2003-06 2500 & 3500

GASOLINE ENGINE

1. Drain and siphon power steering fluid from reservoir into suitable container.
2. Remove serpentine drive belt.
3. Remove three bolts securing pump to cylinder head. Access can be gained through holes in pulley.
4. Remove power steering pump.
5. Reverse procedure to install.

DIESEL ENGINE

1. Drain and siphon power steering fluid from reservoir into suitable container.
2. Remove serpentine drive belt.
3. Disconnect return hose, then the pressure hose.
4. Loosen pump bracket to block.
5. Remove six intake plenum bolts.
6. Loosen inner cooler tube clamp at intake plenum, then remove plenum.
7. Loosen inner cooler tube clamp at radiator support side, then remove tube from vehicle.
8. Remove power steering pump from top of engine compartment.
9. Reverse procedure to install.

Van

1. Remove drive belt by rotating tensioner clockwise and sliding belt off of tensioner.
2. Disconnect power steering hoses from power steering pump and cap fittings.
3. Remove bracket bolts and remove pump assembly.
4. Remove pump pulley and bracket.
5. Reverse procedure to install, tighten bolts to specifications.

TIGHTENING SPECIFICATIONS

Year	Component	Torque Ft. lbs
2002 2500 & 3500 PICKUP		
2002	Anti-Rattle Spring Fasteners	15
	Ball Joint Nuts	60
	Ball Stud To Steering Knuckle Nuts	55
	Lower Ball Joint Nut (Light Duty, 11⁄16 Inch)	95
	Lower Ball Joint Nut (Heavy Duty, 3⁄4 Inch)	110
	Lower Shock Bolt	105
	Lower Suspension Arm Frame Nuts	145
	Pitman Arm Retaining Nut	185
	Pivot Bar Bolts	125
	Power Steering Gear Fluid Couplings	23
	Power Steering Gear To Frame Rail	130
	Power Steering Pump Oil Feed Line	60①
	Power Steering Pump Bracket	35
	Power Steering Pump To Engine (Diesel)	57
	Stabilizer Bar Bolts	40
	Stabilizer Link Nuts	27
	Steering Arm To Knuckle (Light Duty)	217
	Steering Arm To Knuckle (Heavy Duty)	225
	Steering Coupler To Gear Shaft Pinch Bolt	36
	Suspension Arm Crossover Nut	125
	Tie Rod End Attaching Nut	①
	Upper Ball Stud To Knuckle Nut	60
	Upper Suspension Arm Pivot Bar Bolts	155
	Vacuum Pump Bracket	18
	Wheel Lug Nuts (5-Stud Wheel)	95
	Wheel Lug Nuts (8-Stud Wheel)	145
1500 & 2003–06 2500 & 3500 PICKUP		
2002–06	Hub/Bearing (Light Duty)	120
	Hub/Bearing (Heavy Duty)	130
	Lower Shock Absorber Bolt (2WD)	25
	Lower Shock Absorber Bolt (4WD)	155
	Lower Suspension Arm Ball Joint Nut (Light Duty)	38②
	Lower Suspension Arm Bolt Joint Nut (Heavy Duty)	100
	Lower Suspension Arm Frame Nut (Light Duty)	150
	Lower Suspension Arm Frame Nut (Heavy Duty)	175
	Power Steering Pressure Line	23
	Power Steering Pump	17
	Power Steering Return Line	38
	Stabilizer Bar	45
	Stabilizer Link Lower Control Arm Nut	75
	Stabilizer Link Stabilizer Bar Nut	20
	Steering Gear (Independent Suspension)	235
	Steering Gear (Link/Coil Suspension)	145
	Steering Gear Coupler (Independent Suspension)	36

TIGHTENING SPECIFICATIONS—Continued

Year	Component	Torque Ft. lbs
1500 & 2003–06 2500 & 3500 PICKUP		
2002–06	Steering Gear Pitman Shaft Nut (Link/Coil Suspension)	225
	Tie Rod End Jam Nut	55
	Tie Rod End Nut	45②
	Upper Shock Absorber Nut	40
	Upper Suspension Arm Ball Joint Nut (Light Duty)	40②
	Upper Suspension Arm Frame Nuts (Light Duty)	130
	Upper Suspension Arm Frame Nuts Heavy Duty)	125
VAN		
2002–03	Brake Pad Anti-Rattle Spring Retaining Clips	15
	Lower Ball Joint To Steering Knuckle Nuts (Light Duty, 5⁄8 Inch)	135
	Lower Ball Joint To Steering Knuckle Nuts (Heavy Duty, 3⁄4 Inch)	175
	Pitman Arm Nut	185
	Pivot Arm Bolts	200
	Power Steering Gear Fluid Hoses	21
	Power Steering Pump Assembly	30
	Power Steering Pump Bracket To Pump (3.9L & 5.2L Engines)	40
	Power Steering Pump Bracket To Pump (5.9L Engine)	21
	Steering Arm To Knuckle (Light Duty)	217
	Steering Arm To Knuckle (Heavy Duty)	225
	Steering Gear Bracket On Frame	100
	Steering Knuckle Arm To Steering Knuckle (5⁄8 Inch Bolts)	215
	Steering Knuckle Arm To Steering Knuckle (3⁄4 Inch Bolts)	225
	Suspension Arm Pivot Bolt	175
	Tie Rod End Attaching Nut	①
	Upper Ball Joint To Control Arm Bolt	125
	Upper Ball Joint To Steering Knuckle	135
	Wheel Lug Nuts (15 Inch Wheel)	80–110
	Wheel Lug Nuts (16 Inch Wheel)	120–150

① — 1⁄2–20 nuts, 45 ft. lbs.; 9⁄16–18 nuts, 55 ft. lbs.; 5⁄8–18 nuts, 75 ft. lbs.

② — Plus an additional 90°.

Front Wheel Drive

NOTE: Refer To "Computer Relearn Procedure" Located In The Front Of This Manual When Battery Power To The Computer Has Been Interrupted.

INDEX

PRECAUTIONS

Battery Ground Cable

Prior to service, disconnect battery ground cable and isolate as required.

AXLE

REPLACE

C205F Axle

1. Place transmission in neutral.
2. Raise and support vehicle, then remove tire and wheel assembly.
3. Remove axle half shafts.
4. Remove exhaust crossover pipe.
5. Remove propeller shaft. Mark location for reference during installation.
6. Remove suspension crossmember mounting bolts, then the crossmember, **Fig. 1**.
7. Support axle using suitable jack.
8. Remove axle housing pinion mounting bolts, **Fig. 2.**
9. Remove axle shaft tube mounting bolts, **Fig. 3.**
10. Remove differential housing mounting bolts, **Fig. 4.**
11. Lower axle from vehicle.
12. Reverse procedure to install.

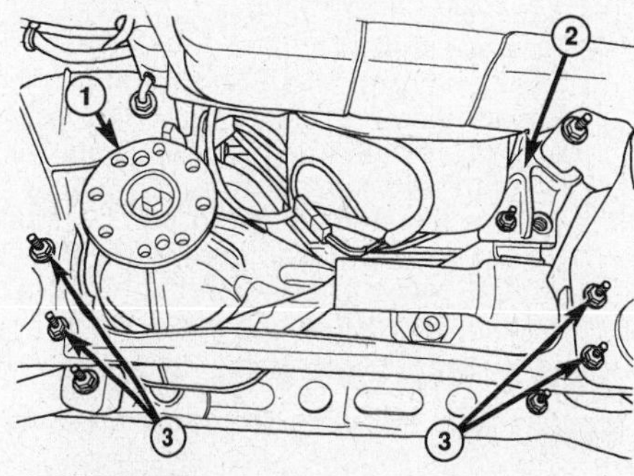

Fig. 1 Suspension crossmember. C205F axle

248 Axle

1. Raise vehicle and support with suitable stands under frame rails behind lower suspension arm brackets, then remove front wheels.
2. Remove brake components and ABS brake sensor, if equipped, then disconnect axle vent hose.
3. Disconnect vacuum hose and electrical connector at disconnect housing, then mark driveshaft yoke, axle pinion yoke and transfer case flange for installation alignment reference.
4. Disconnect driveshaft from axle and transfer case, then disconnect stabilizer bar link at axle bracket.
5. Disconnect shock absorbers and track bar from axle brackets, then disconnect tie rod and drag link from steering knuckle.
6. Support axle under differential with suitable jack, then disconnect upper and lower suspension arms from axle bracket. **Mark cams for installation reference.**
7. Lower jack enough to remove axle, then remove coil springs from axle brackets.
8. Reverse procedure to install, noting the following:
   a. Align suspension arm cams to reference marks, but do not tighten lower/upper suspension arm or track bar bolts and nuts until all other assembly is completed and vehicle is lowered.
   b. Inspect front wheel alignment.

9 ¼ Inch Axle

1. Raise and support vehicle, then remove wheel and tire assembly.
2. Remove brake calipers and rotors.
3. Disconnect ABS wheel speed sensors electrical connectors.
4. Disconnect axle vent hose.
5. Remove front propeller shaft. Mark location for reference during installation.
6. Disconnect stabilizer bar links at axle brackets.
7. Disconnect shock absorbers from axle brackets.
8. Disconnect track bar from axle bracket.
9. Disconnect tie rod and drag link from steering knuckles.
10. Support axle using suitable jack.
11. Mark suspension alignment cams for reference during installation.
12. Disconnect upper and lower suspension arms from axle bracket.
13. Lower axle, coil springs will drop with axle.
14. Remove coil springs from axle bracket.
15. Reverse procedure to install. Tighten suspension components with rubber bushings with weight of vehicle on suspension.

AXLE SHAFT

REPLACE

C205F Axle

1. Remove half shaft from vehicle.
2. Remove skid plate.
3. Clean axle seal area.
4. Remove snap ring from axle shaft.
5. Remove axle shaft using removal tool No. 8420A, collar tool No. 8420-3 and slide hammer tool No. C-3752, or equivalents.
6. Reverse procedure to install, noting the following:
   a. Lubricate bearing bore and seal lip with gear lubricant.
   b. Install axle shaft, pushing firmly to engage snap ring.

248 Axle

1. Raise and support vehicle, then remove wheel and brake components from axle.

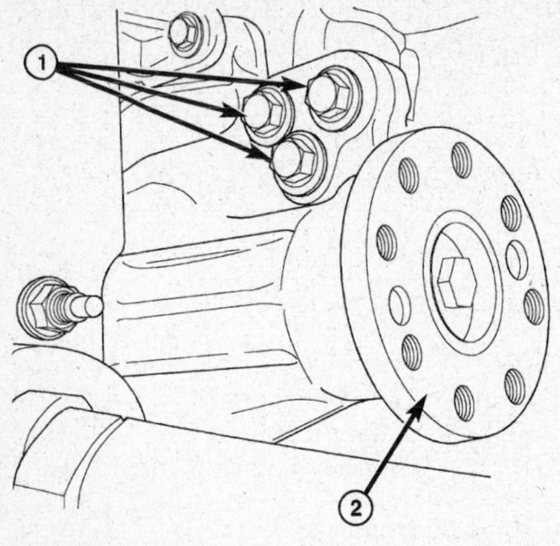

Fig. 2 Housing pinion mounting bolts. C205F axle

2. Remove cotter pin and axle hub nut, then the hub to knuckle bolts.
3. Remove hub bearing from steering knuckle and axle shaft, then remove brake dust shield and slide axle out of housing. **Avoid damaging shaft oil seal.**
4. Reverse procedure to install.

9 ¼ Inch Axle

1. Remove tire and wheel assembly.
2. Remove brake caliper, rotor and ABS wheel speed sensor.
3. Remove axle shaft cotter pin, hub nut and washer.
4. Remove four hub bearing bolts from back of steering knuckle.
5. Remove hub bearing from steering knuckle.
6. Remove axle shaft from steering knuckle and axle housing.
7. Reverse procedure to install.

INTERMEDIATE SHAFT & INNER SEAL

Removal

1. Remove axle shift motor as outlined in "Axle Shift Motor, Replace."
2. Remove outer axle shaft as outlined in "Axle Shaft, Replace."
3. Remove inner axle shaft seal from shift motor housing using a suitable drift or punch.
4. Remove intermediate axle shaft and shift collar.
5. Remove intermediate axle shaft bearing using bearing removal and installation tool Nos. 5041–2, 5041–3 and D–354–2 or equivalents, **Fig. 5.**
6. Remove intermediate shaft.

Installation

1. Install bearing into housing using bearing removal and installation tool Nos. 5041–2, 5041–3 and D-354–3 or equivalents, **Fig. 6.**
2. Clean inside perimeter of axle shaft tube using suitable crocus cloth.
3. Apply a light coating of clean oil to inside lip of new axle shaft seal.
4. Install inner axle seal using seal installer tool Nos. 5041–2, 5041–3 and 5041–60F or equivalents, **Fig. 7.**.
5. Install shift collar to axle housing.
6. Lubricate splined end of intermediate shaft using suitable multi-purpose lubricant.
7. Insert intermediate axle shaft into differential side gear.
8. Lubricate axle shaft splines, then insert axle shaft into axle tube. Engage splined end of shaft with shift collar.
9. Install vacuum shift motor housing.

AXLE SHIFT MOTOR

REPLACE

1. Disconnect vacuum and wiring connector from shift housing, **Fig. 8.**
2. Remove indicator switch.
3. Remove shift motor housing cover, then the gasket and shield from the housing.
4. Remove shift motor.
5. Reverse procedure to install noting the following:
   a. Ensure shift fork is correctly guided onto shift collar groove.
   b. Add 5 ounces of API grade GL 5 or equivalent hypoid gear lubricant to shift motor housing through indicator switch mounting hole.

AXLE SHAFT OIL SEAL

REPLACE

C205F Axle

1. Remove axle shaft as outlined in "Axle Shaft, Replace."
2. Remove axle shaft seal using a suitable small pry bar.
3. Reverse procedure to install, noting the following:
   a. Install new axle seal using installer tool No. 8694 and handle tool No. C-4171, or equivalent.
   b. Lubricate seal lip with suitable gear lubricant.

248 Axle

1. Remove axle shaft as outlined in "Axle Shaft, Replace."
2. Remove axle seal from differential housing.
3. Clean inside perimeter of differential using suitable crocus cloth.
4. Apply a light film of oil to inside lip of new seal.
5. Install inner axle seal, **Fig. 9,** using seal installer tool Nos. 5041–2, C–3972–A and 5041–7 or equivalents. It may be required to substitute installer C–3716–A for C–3972–A or equivalent on 216 axles.

9 ¼ Inch Axle

REMOVAL

1. Remove axle shaft as outlined in "Axle Shaft, Replace."

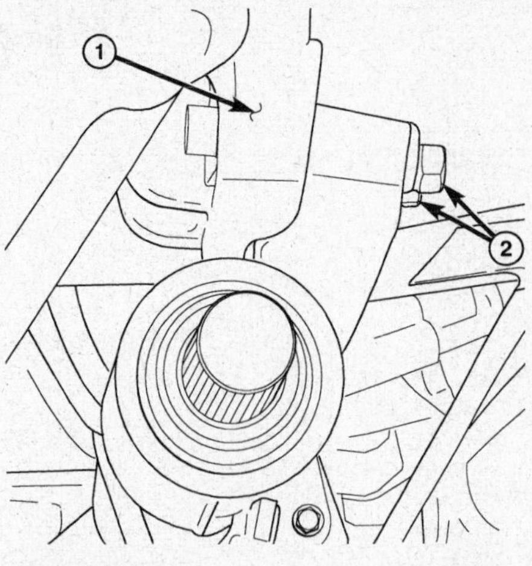

Fig. 3 Axle shaft tube mount. C205F axle

2. Remove differential from differential housing.
3. Remove differential bearing adjusters, **Fig. 10.**
4. Remove axle seals located behind adjusters using receiver tool No. 8498 and extractor tool No. 6310, or equivalent, **Fig. 11.**
5. Install receiver tool No. 8498, or equivalent, into adjuster bore.
6. Install extractor rod tool No. 6310 with extractor foot tool No. 6310-9, or equivalents, through receiver and axle seal, **Fig. 12.**
7. Install extractor plate tool No. 6310-2 and nut tool No. 6310-7, or equivalents, on extractor rod.
8. Tighten nut on extractor rod, **Fig. 13,** pulling seal out and into receiver.

INSTALLATION

1. Install axle seal on installer cups tool No. 8885-2, or equivalent, then position cups with seals into housing. Seals are installed with axle guide facing outward.
2. Install turnbuckle tool No. 8885-1, or equivalent, into installer cups, then expand turnbuckle until seal bottoms in housing, **Fig. 14.**
3. Install differential into axle housing.
4. Install axle shaft and hub bearings.

STEERING KNUCKLE & BALL JOINT

REPLACE

Knuckle Removal

1. Remove hub bearing and axle shaft as outlined in "Axle Shaft, Replace," then remove tie rod or drag link end from steering knuckle arm.
2. Remove ABS sensor wire and bracket from knuckle, then remove cotter pin from upper ball stud nut and nuts from upper and lower ball studs.

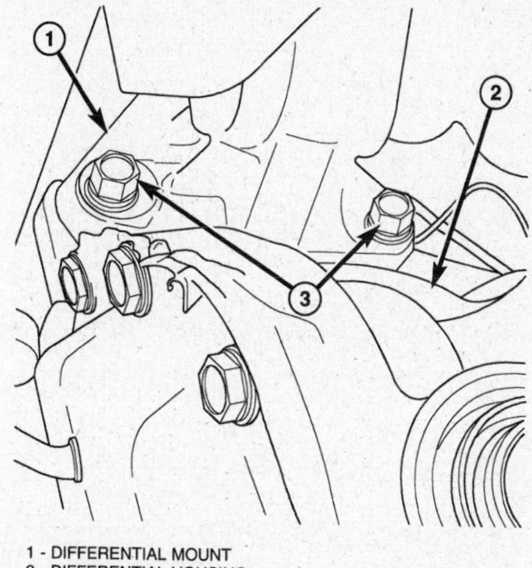

Fig. 4 Differential housing mount. C205F axle

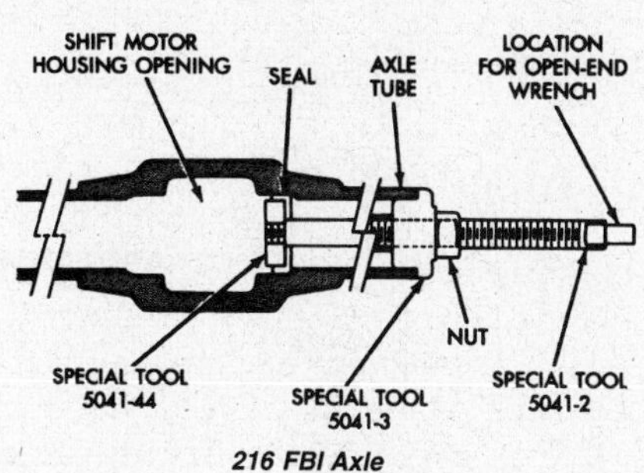

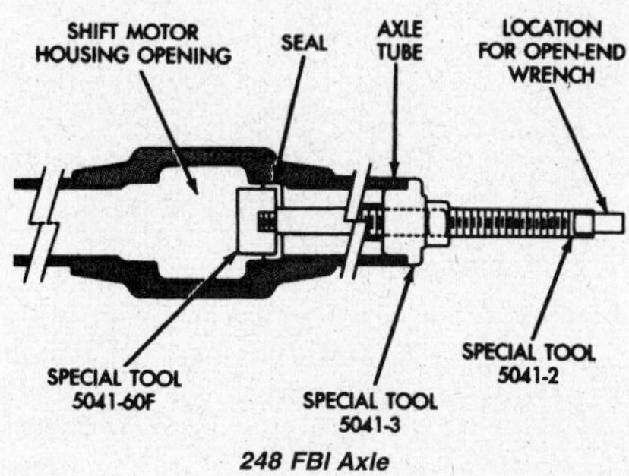

Fig. 7 Inner axle seal installation. 248 Axle

3. Loosen steering knuckle with a brass hammer, then remove from axle tube yokes.

UPPER BALL STUD REPLACEMENT

248 AXLE

Position tools as outlined in **Fig. 15,** to remove upper ball stud and as outlined in **Fig. 16,** to install.

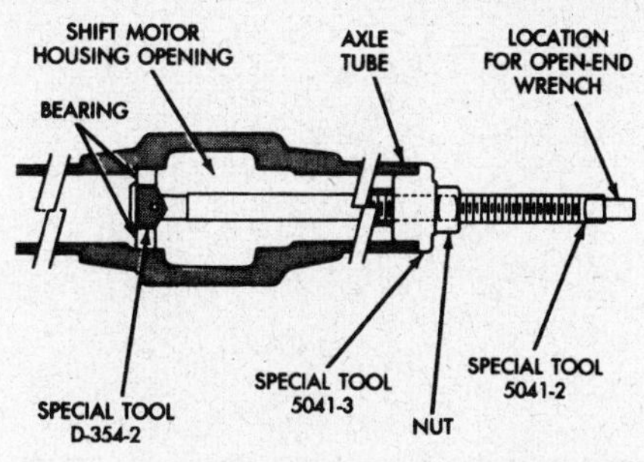

Fig. 5 Intermediate shaft bearing removal. 248 Axle

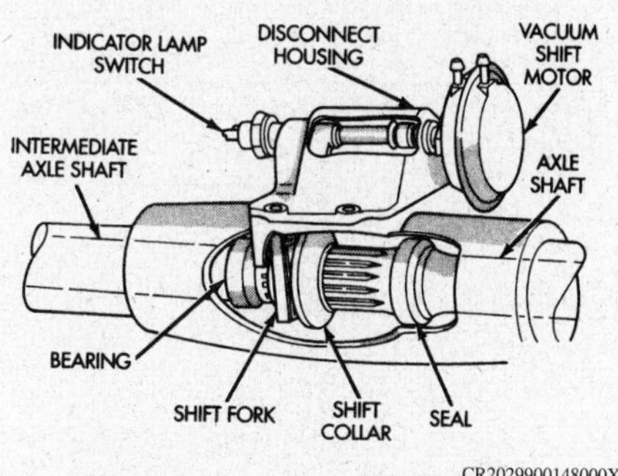

Fig. 8 Axle shift motor

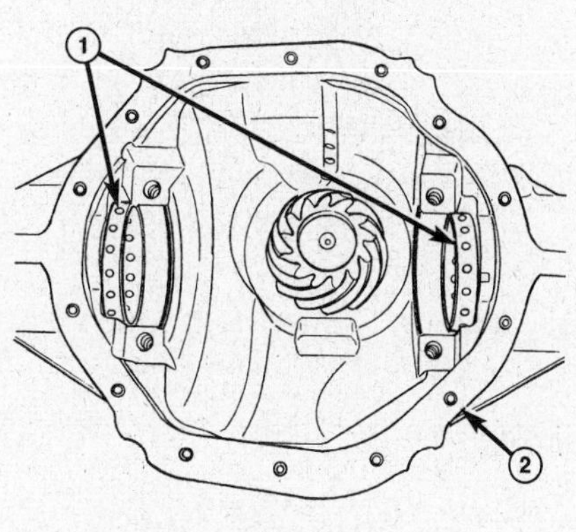

Fig. 10 Differential bearing adjusters. 9 ¼ Inch Axle

LOWER BALL STUD REPLACEMENT

248 AXLE

Position tools as outlined in **Fig. 17,** to remove lower ball stud and as outlined in **Fig. 18,** to install.

KNUCKLE INSTALLATION

248 AXLE

1. Position steering knuckle on ball studs, then install lower ball stud nut and initially **torque** to 35 ft. lbs. **Do not install cotter pin.**
2. Install upper ball stud nut and tighten to specifications, then install new cotter pin.
3. **Torque** lower ball stud nut to 140–160 ft. lbs., and install new cotter pin, then install hub bearing and axle shaft as outlined in "Axle Shaft, Replace."
4. Connect drag link or tie rod to steering knuckle arm, then install ABS sensor wire and bracket.

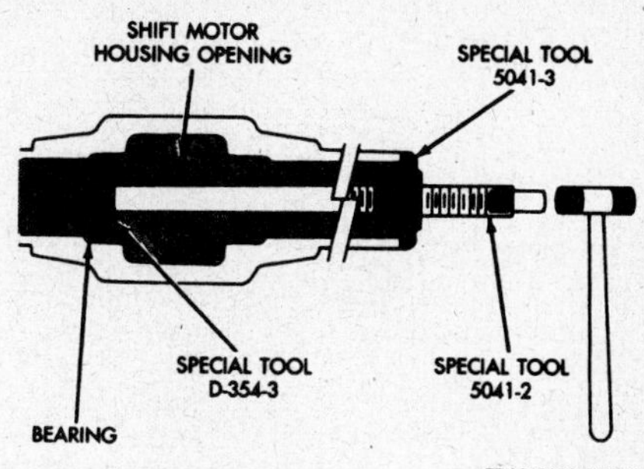

Fig. 6 Intermediate shaft bearing installation. 248 Axle

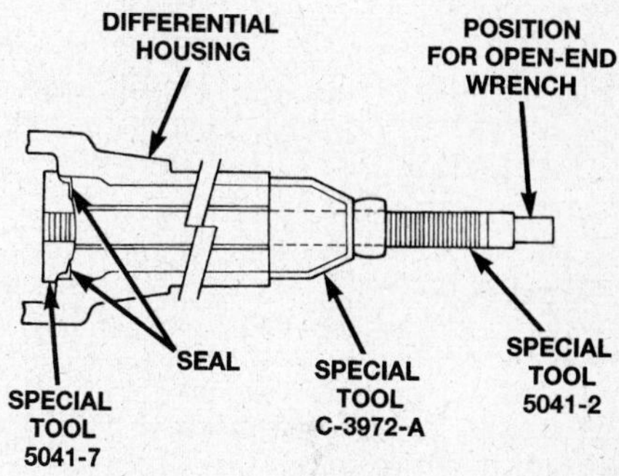

Fig. 9 Axle seal installation. 248 Axle

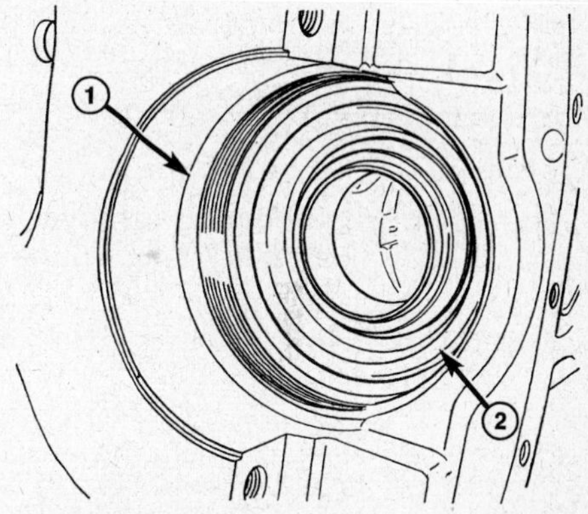

Fig. 11 Axle shaft seal. 9 ¼ Inch Axle

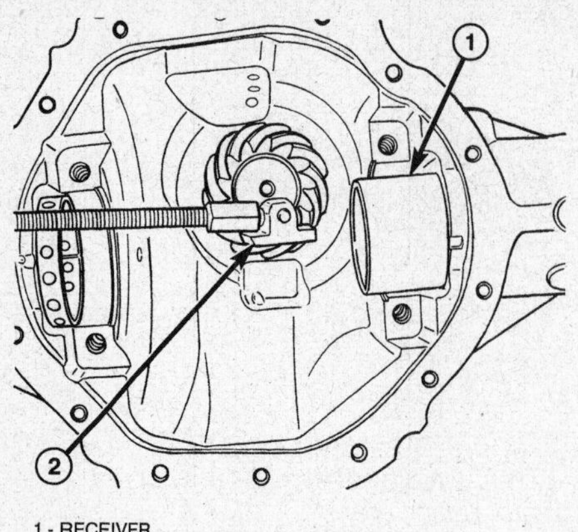

Fig. 12 Seal receiver installation. 9 ¼ Inch Axle

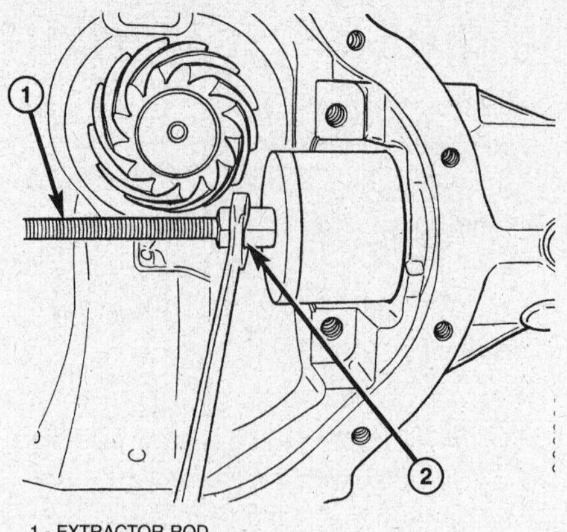

Fig. 13 Seal extractor. 9 ¼ Inch Axle

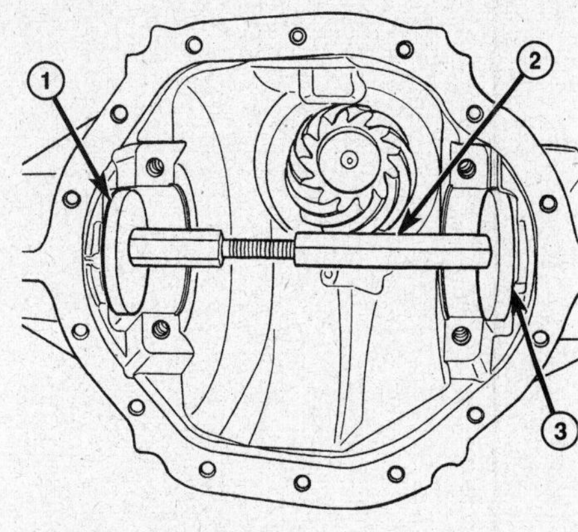

Fig. 14 Axle seal installation. 9 ¼ Inch Axle

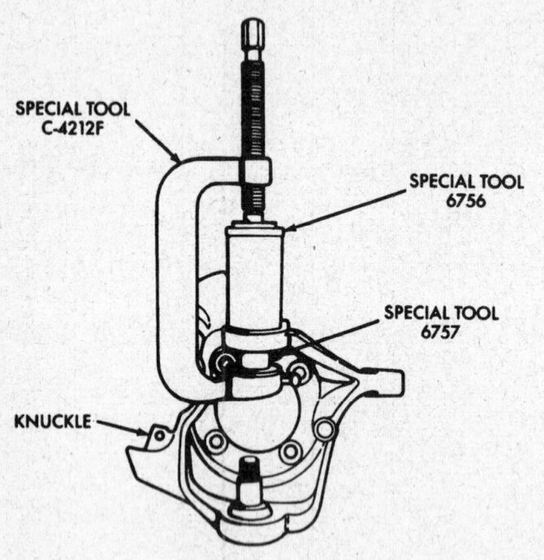

Fig. 15 Upper ball stud removal. 248 axle

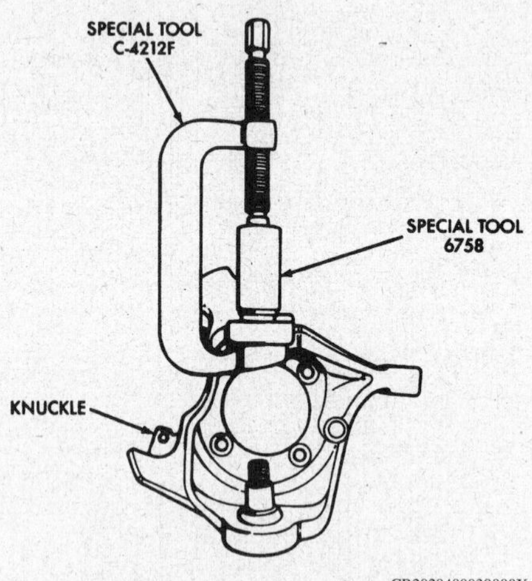

Fig. 16 Upper ball stud installation. 248 axle

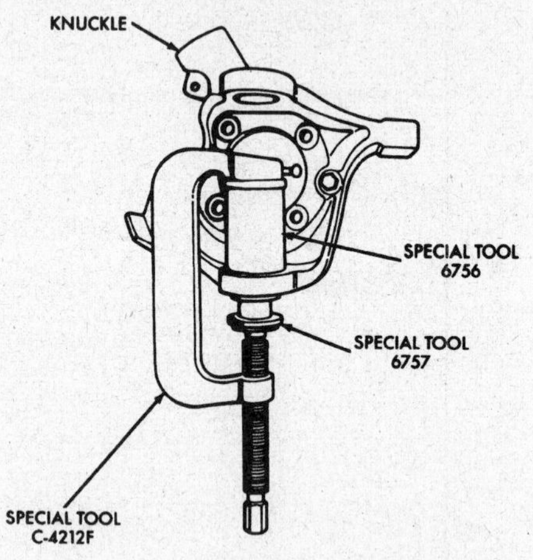

Fig. 17 Lower ball stud removal. 248 axle

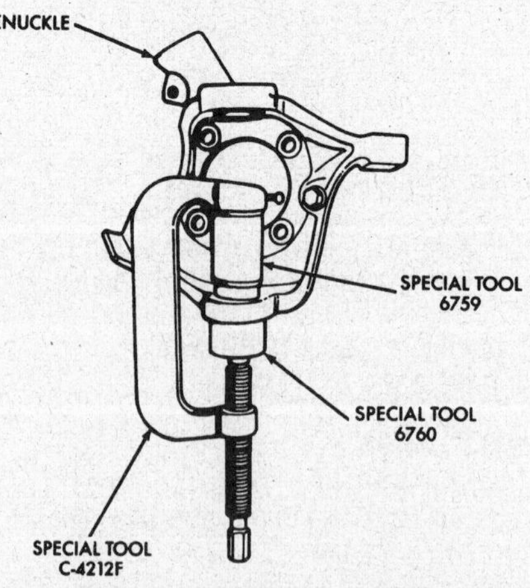

Fig. 18 Lower ball stud installation. 248 axle

TIGHTENING SPECIFICATIONS

Year	Component	Torque Ft. Lbs.
C205F AXLE		
2002–06	Differential Cover	17
	Fill Plug	25
	Mounting Nuts	70
	Pinion Nut	200–350
248 AXLE		
2002–06	Bearing Cap	80
	Differential Cover	35
	Pinion Mate Shaft	20
	Pinion Nut	215–330
	Ring Gear Bolt	130
	Wheel Lug Nuts	①
9 1/4 INCH AXLE		
2002–06	Adjuster Lock Bolt	18
	Axle Nut	263
	Bearing Caps	63
	Differential Cover	30
	Fill Plug	24
	Pinion Shaft Lock Bolt	38
	Ring Gear Bolts	103

① — Coned nuts w/thread size of 1/2 X 20, 95–105 ft. lbs.;
flanged nut w/thread size of 5/8 X 18, 325 ft. lbs.;
flanged nut w/thread size of 1 1/8 X 16, 475 ft. lbs.

Wheel Alignment

INDEX

PRELIMINARY INSPECTION

1. Ensure tires are of correct size and are inflated to recommended pressure.
2. Inspect front wheel bearings for wear and/or to verify proper adjustment.
3. Inspect ball studs, steering linkage pivot points and steering gear for excessive freeplay, roughness, binding or wear.
4. Inspect front wheels for excessive lateral or radial runout or imbalance.
5. Inspect suspension components for wear and improper tightening.

FRONT WHEEL ALIGNMENT

Caster

VAN

Front suspension height must be inspected and corrected as required prior to inspecting wheel alignment.

1. Remove all foreign material from exposed threads of pivot bar adjusting bolt nuts.
2. Record initial camber and caster readings before loosening pivot bar bolt nuts, **Fig. 1.**
3. When performing adjustments, tool No. C-4581, or equivalent, is required to adjust caster and camber. The camber settings should be held as close as possible to "desired" setting, and caster setting should be held as nearly equal as possible on both wheels.

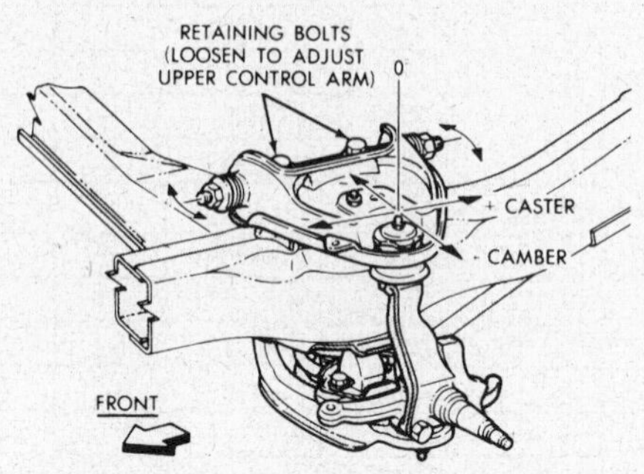

Fig. 1 Alignment adjustment locations & directions

PICKUP

LINK/COIL FRONT SUSPENSION

Refer to "Front Wheel Alignment Specifications" in this chapter when inspecting caster. If caster is not in the acceptable range, record measurement. Caster can be adjusted by rotating cams on lower suspension arm.

INDEPENDENT FRONT SUSPENSION

Move rear end of pivot bar in or out to change caster angle significantly while altering camber angle only slightly. Refer to "Front Wheel Alignment Specifications" for correct settings.

Camber

VAN

Refer to "Pickup With Link Coil Front Suspension" for procedure.

PICKUP

LINK/COIL FRONT SUSPENSION

Caster is preset by the manufacturer with no provision for adjustment. Refer to "Front Wheel Alignment Specifications" in this chapter when inspecting camber due to suspension damage or suspected misalignment.

INDEPENDENT FRONT SUSPENSION

Move forward end of pivot bar in or out to change camber angle significantly while altering caster angle only slightly. Refer to "Front Wheel Alignment Specifications" for correct settings.

Toe-In

With the front wheels in straight ahead position, loosen the clamps at each end of both adjusting tubes. Adjust toe-in by turning the tie rod sleeve which will "center" the steering wheel spokes. If the steering wheel was centered, make the toe-in adjustment by turning both sleeves an equal amount. Position sleeve clamps so ends do not align in the sleeve slot. Refer to "Front Wheel Alignment Specifications" for correct settings.

CARAVAN, TOWN & COUNTRY & VOYAGER

NOTE: Refer To Rear Of This Manual For Vehicle Manufacturer's Special Service Tool Suppliers.

INDEX OF SERVICE OPERATIONS

Specifications

GENERAL ENGINE SPECIFICATIONS

Year	Engine	Fuel System	Bore & Stroke, Inch	Compres-sion Ratio	Horsepower @ RPM	Torque Ft. Lbs. @ RPM	Normal Oil Pressure Pounds @ 3000 RPM, psi
2002–06	2.4L	FI	3.45 x 3.97	9.40	150 @ 5200	167 @ 4000	25–80
	3.3L	FI	3.66 x 3.19	9.35	180 @ 5200	210 @ 4000	30–80
	3.8L	FI	3.78 x 3.43	9.60	215 @ 5000	245 @ 4000	30–80

TUNE UP SPECIFICATIONS

Engine (VIN Code)	Spark Plug Gap	Ignition Timing, °BTDC				Curb Idle Speed②		Fast Idle Speed		Fuel Pump Pres-sure, psi.	Valve Lash
		Firing Order ③	Man. Trans.	Auto. Trans.	Mark Loca-tion	Man. Trans.	Auto. Trans.	Man. Trans.	Auto. Trans.		
2002–06											
2.4L	.048–.053	A	⑤	⑤	①	—	⑥	—	⑥	53–63	④
3.3L	.048–.053	B	⑤	⑤	①	—	⑥	—	⑥	53–63	④
3.8L	.048–.053	B	⑤	⑤	①	—	⑥	—	⑥	53–63	④

BTDC — Before Top Dead Center

① — Equipped w/crankshaft position sensor.

② — Idle speed is adjusted w/transmission in Neutral (N). When inspecting idle speed, set parking brake & block drive wheels.

③ — Before removing wires from distributor cap, determine location of No. 1 wire in cap, as distributor position may have been altered from that outlined at the end of this chart.

④ — Equipped w/hydraulic lash adjusters.

⑤ — Ignition timing cannot be changed or reset.

⑥ — Controlled by an idle speed control motor.

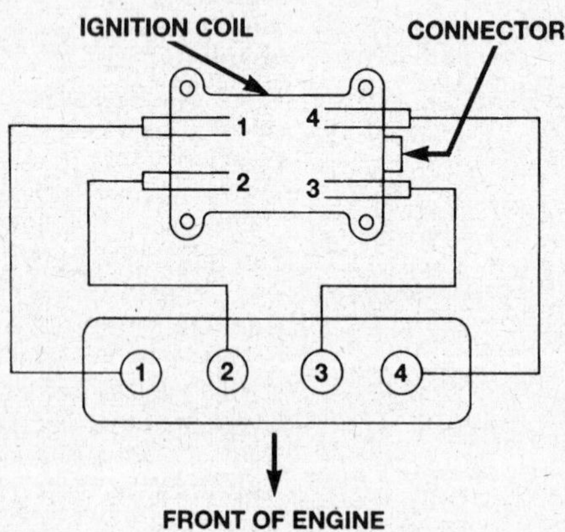

Fig. A

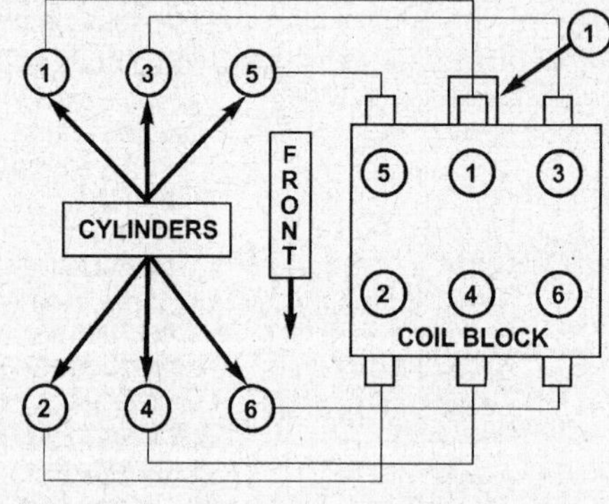

Fig. B

FRONT WHEEL ALIGNMENT SPECIFICATIONS

Year	Tire Size	Caster, Degrees	Camber, Degrees	Toe-In, Inch		Ball Joint Wear
				Individual	Total	
2002–06	P215/65R16 Or P215/70R15	+1.31 to +3.31	–.30 to +.50	—	–.10 to +.30	①

① — Refer to "Ball Joint Inspection" in "Front Suspension & Steering" section.

REAR WHEEL ALIGNMENT SPECIFICATIONS

Year	Caster, Degrees	Camber, Degrees	Toe-In, Inch	Ball Joint Wear
2002–06	—	0②	0	①

① — Refer to "Ball Joint Inspection" in "Rear Axle & Suspension" section.

② — Reference angle only, not adjustable.

FLUID CAPACITIES & COOLING SYSTEM DATA

Year	Engine	Coolant Capacity, Qts.		Engine Coolant Type	Radiator Cap Relief Pressure, Lbs.	Thermo. Opening Temp., °F	Fuel Tank, Gals.	Engine Oil Refill, Qts.	Transaxle Oil	
		Less A/C	With A/C						5 Speed, Pts.	Auto. Trans., Qts.
2002–06	2.4L	11.40	11.40	Ethylene Glycol	15	196	20	5.0①	—	③
	3.3L	13.40②	13.40②	Ethylene Glycol	15	196	20	4.5①	—	③
	3.8L	13.40②	13.40②	Ethylene Glycol	15	196	20	4.5①	—	③

MPI — Multi-Point Fuel Injection

① — Includes filter change.

② — On models w/rear heater add 2.9 qts.

③ — Drain & refill, 4 qts.; After overhaul, 31TH, 9.1 qts., 41TE, 9.7 qts.

LUBRICANT DATA

Year	Model	Lubricant Type					
		Transmission		Transfer Case	Drive Axle	Power Steering	Brake System
		Manual	Automatic				
2002–06	All	—	ATF + 4 Type 9602	80W-90 MS-9020	80W-90 MS-9020	MS-9602	DOT 3

Electrical

NOTE: On Air Bag Equipped Models, Refer To "Air Bag System Precautions" Located In The Front Of This Manual For System Disarming & Arming Procedures.

NOTE: Refer To "Computer Relearn Procedures" Located In The Front Of This Manual When Battery Power To The Computer Has Been Interrupted.

INDEX

PRECAUTIONS

Air Bag Systems

Refer to "Air Bag System Precautions" in the front of this manual for system disarming and arming procedures.

Battery Ground Cable

Prior to service, disconnect battery ground cable and isolate as required.

FUSE PANEL LOCATION

Fuse panel is located below lefthand side of instrument panel.

Turn signal/hazard flasher is a single unit located on fuse panel.

RELAY CENTER LOCATION

The relay bank is located in the fuse box and in the power distribution center on the lefthand side of the engine compartment. Refer to **Figs. 1 and 2** for relay identification.

FUEL PUMP RELAY LOCATION

The fuel pump relay is located in the lefthand side of the engine compartment in the power distribution center.

STARTER

REPLACE

1. Raise and support vehicle.
2. Remove starter motor attaching bolts and nuts.
3. Remove solenoid.
4. Disconnect all electrical connectors from starter motor and remove starter.
5. Reverse procedure to install.

ALTERNATOR

REPLACE

2.4L Engine

1. Disconnect Inlet Air Temperature (IAT) sensor.
2. Remove air box, then EVAP purge solenoid from its bracket and position aside.
3. Disconnect push-in field wire connector from back of alternator.
4. Remove nut holding B+ wire terminal to back of alternator, then B+ terminal.
5. Remove drive belt, then alternator.
6. Reverse procedure to install.

3.3L & 3.8L Engines

1. Disconnect push-in field wire connector from back of alternator.
2. Remove nut holding B+ wire terminal to back of alternator, then the B+ wire.
3. Raise and support vehicle, then remove righthand front lower splash shield.
4. Remove drive belt, then lower oil dip stick tube bolt.
5. Remove wiring harness from oil dip stick tube.
6. Remove three mounting bolts, then lower vehicle.
7. Remove oil dip stick tube, then alternator.
8. Reverse procedure to install.

IGNITION COIL

REPLACE

1. **On models equipped with 3.3L and 3.8L engines,** remove throttle and speed control cables from clip.
2. **On models equipped with 3.3L and 3.8L engines,** remove power steering reservoir bolts and position reservoir aside.
3. **On all models,** remove ignition cables.
4. Disconnect electrical connector from ignition coil.
5. Remove ignition coil.
6. Reverse procedure to install.

IGNITION SWITCH

REPLACE

1. Remove steering column cover screws.
2. Remove parking brake release cable from handle, then the steering column shroud screws and lower shroud.
3. Place ignition key lock cylinder in On position, then depress lock cylinder retaining tab and remove lock cylinder.
4. Remove ignition switch mounting screw with a suitable Torx driver.
5. Depress retaining tab and remove ignition switch from steering column.

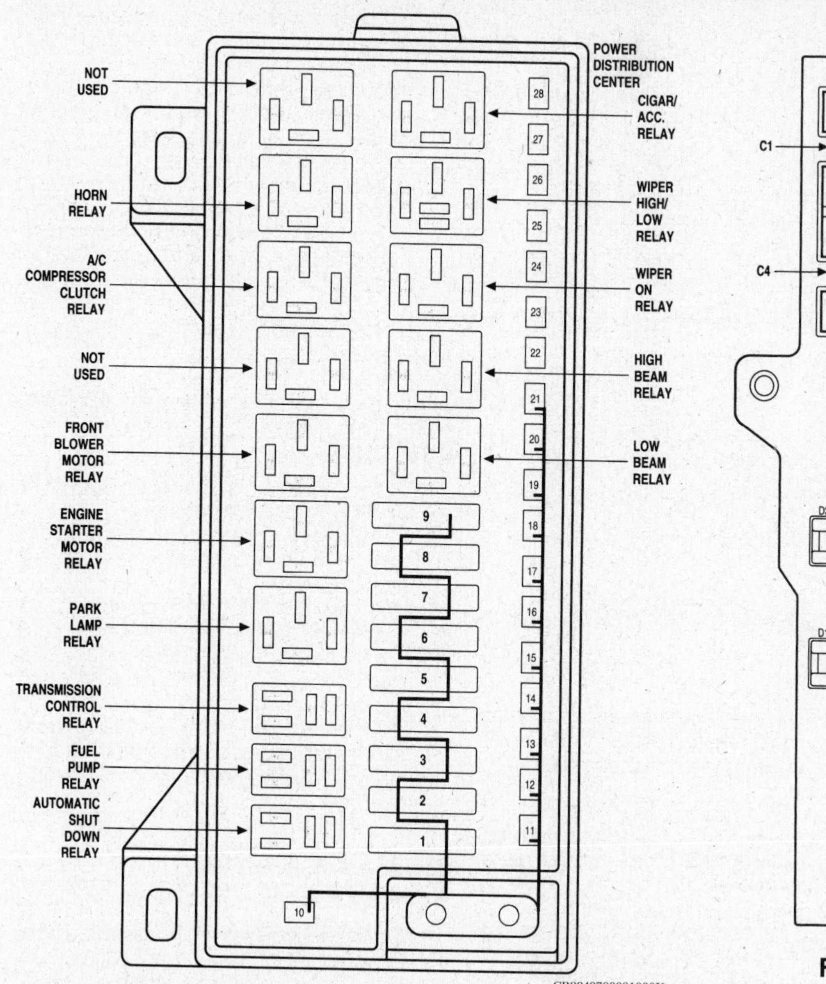

Fig. 1 Power distribution center relay identification

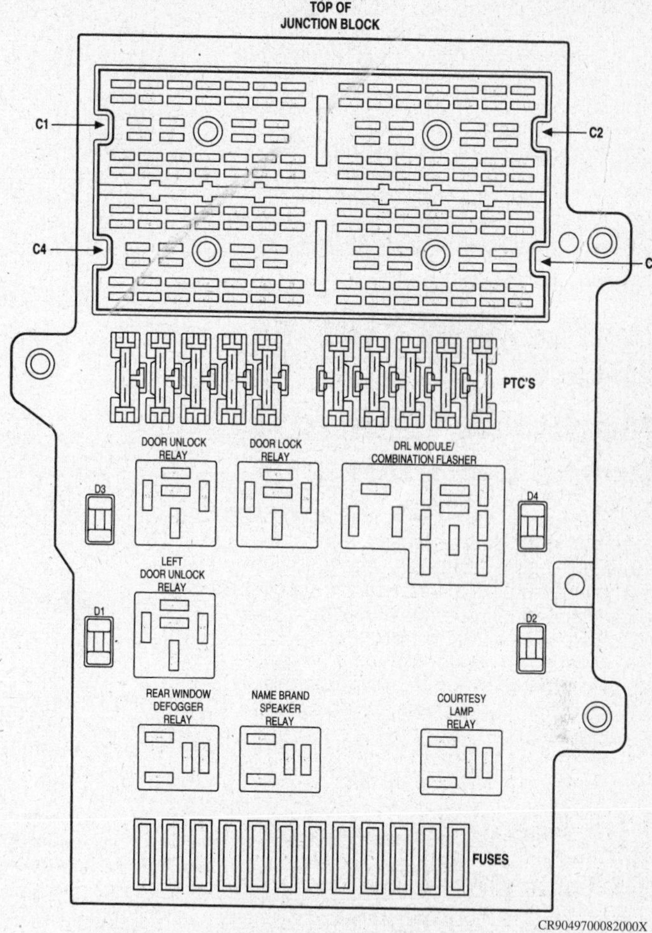

Fig. 2 Fuse panel relay identification

6. Disconnect ignition switch electrical connector, then remove switch.
7. Reverse procedure to install. **Torque** ignition switch mounting screw to 17 inch lbs.

NEUTRAL SAFETY SWITCH

REPLACE

The following procedure applies to automatic transaxle equipped models only. On manual transaxle equipped models, a back-up switch is mounted on the transaxle case.

1. Disconnect switch electrical connector.
2. Remove switch from transaxle case and allow fluid to drain into suitable container.
3. Ensure switch operating lever fingers center in opening when shift selector is in Park and Neutral positions.
4. Reverse procedure to install switch with new seal. **Torque** switch to 24 ft. lbs.

HEADLAMP SWITCH

REPLACE

1. Remove instrument panel lower steering column cover.
2. Reach up behind lefthand side of instrument panel, then depress spring clip on top or bottom of headlamp switch.
3. Firmly push out headlamp switch assembly, then disconnect electrical connector.
4. Remove headlamp switch from vehicle.
5. Reverse procedure to install.

STOP LIGHT SWITCH

REPLACE

Removal

1. Remove trim cover from below steering column and lower steering column cover.
2. Remove brake lamp switch from it's bracket by depressing and holding brake pedal while rotating brake lamp switch in a counterclockwise direction approximately 30°.
3. Disconnect wiring connector from switch.

Installation

Do not reuse original stop light switch, the switch can only be adjusted once.

1. Install switch in bracket by aligning index tab on switch with slot in mounting bracket.
2. With switch fully seated in bracket, rotate switch clockwise 30° to lock into place.
3. With brake pedal in full released position, move lever on back of switch from angled non-adjusted position to vertical position to adjust switch to vehicle.
4. Install steering column cover.
5. Inspect brake lamps to verify proper operation.

MULTI-FUNCTION SWITCH

REPLACE

1. Remove upper and lower steering column shrouds.
2. Disconnect wire connector from back of turn signal multifunction switch.
3. Remove screws holding turn signal switch to steering column adapter collar.
4. Remove turn signal switch.
5. Reverse procedure to install.

STEERING WHEEL

REPLACE

1. Ensure front wheels are straight and steering column is locked.

2. Remove four air bag module attaching nuts from back of steering wheel, then lift module and disconnect rear module connector.
3. Remove vehicle speed control switch and connector.
4. Remove steering wheel retaining nut and pull steering wheel with puller tool No. C-3428B, or equivalent.
5. Reverse procedure to install. **Torque** steering wheel attaching nut to 45 ft. lbs.

INSTRUMENT CLUSTER

REPLACE

Mechanical Transaxle Range Indicator

1. Remove lower steering column cover, then metal knee blocker panel.
2. Disconnect transaxle range indicator cable from shift lever, steering column and steering column receiver.
3. Remove instrument cluster bezel, then instrument cluster mounting screws.
4. Rotate top of cluster outward, then disconnect wire connector from back of cluster.
5. Remove instrument cluster.
6. Reverse procedure to install.

Electronic Transaxle Range Indicator

1. Remove instrument cluster bezel, then remove instrument cluster mounting screws.
2. Rotate top of cluster outward, then disconnect electrical connect from back of cluster.
3. Remove instrument cluster.
4. Reverse procedure to install.

RADIO

REPLACE

1. Remove cup holder, then trim panel above cup holder by pulling straight out.
2. Remove center instrument panel trim panel.
3. Remove screws securing radio, then pull rearward to gain access to back of radio.
4. Disconnect antenna cable from back of radio, then remove bolt securing ground strap to radio.
5. Disconnect electrical connectors from back of radio, then remove radio.
6. Reverse procedure to install.

WIPER MOTOR

REPLACE

Front

1. Remove wiper arms, then cowl cover.
2. Open hood, disconnect wiper unit electrical connector and washer hoses.

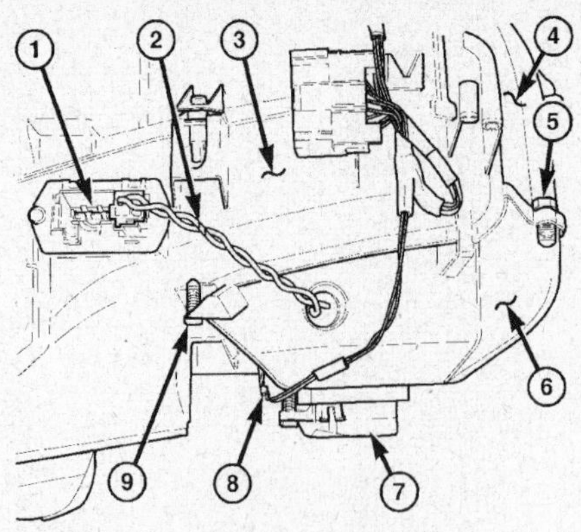

1 - BLOWER MOTOR RESISTOR/POWER MODULE
2 - BLOWER MOTOR WIRE LEAD
3 - LOWER HVAC HOUSING
4 - UPPER AIR INLET HOUSING
5 - UPPER SCREW (1)
6 - LOWER AIR INLET HOUSING
7 - RECIRCULATION DOOR ACTUATOR
8 - ACTUATOR WIRE LEAD
9 - LOWER SCREW (4)

LTV0500000000163

Fig. 3 Blower motor replacement

3. Disconnect drain tubes from bottom of wiper unit.
4. Remove nuts holding wiper unit to lower windshield fence, then bolts holding wiper unit to dash panel.
5. Lift wiper unit from weld studs on lower windshield fence.
6. Remove wiper unit from vehicle, then wiper linkage and motor mount plate from wiper unit.
7. Disconnect wiper motor electrical connectors from wiper motor, then remove wiper linkage from motor crank.
8. Remove wiper motor mounting bolts and remove motor from mount plate.
9. Reverse procedure to install

Rear

1. Remove wiper arm, open liftgate and remove trim panel.
2. Remove wiper motor mounting screws and disconnect electrical connector.
3. Remove motor from liftgate.
4. Reverse procedure to install. **Torque** mounting screws to 25–45 inch lbs.

BLOWER MOTOR

REPLACE

1. Remove righthand cowl trim panel.
2. Position carpet aside for access to front upper air inlet housing mounting screw, **Fig. 3.**
3. Remove recirculation door actuator.
4. Disconnect blower motor electrical connector from either blower motor resistor or power module.
5. Remove one top retaining screw that secures lower air inlet housing to upper inlet housing.
6. Remove four bottom retaining screws that secure lower inlet housing to upper inlet housing and lower HVAC housing.
7. Push rubber grommet on blower motor wires through hole in lower intake air housing.
8. Remove lower intake air housing from evaporator housing and upper intake air housing.
9. Feed blower motor wires and harness connector through grommet hole in lower intake air housing.
10. Relocate recirculation air door as required to access and remove three screws securing blower motor to blower housing in lower half of evaporator housing.
11. Gently flex recirculation air door far enough to remove blower motor from blower housing.
12. Reverse procedure to install.

CABIN AIR FILTER

REPLACE

1. Locate cabin air filter door on bottom of lower evaporator housing.
2. Slide cabin air filter door latch toward rear of vehicle until it engages opened stop on door.
3. Pull cabin air filter door straight down to disengage from air filter opening of lower evaporator housing.
4. Pull cabin air filter straight down and out of evaporator housing.
5. Reverse procedure to install ensuring airflow directional arrow imprinted on filter is pointed toward center of vehicle.

HEATER CORE

REPLACE

1. Drain cooling system into suitable container.
2. Remove silencer boot fasteners located around base of lower steering shaft from instrument panel so it may be positioned aside.
3. Remove stop lamp switch from its mounting bracket as outlined under "Stop Lamp Switch, Replace."
4. Disconnect power brake booster input rod from pin on brake pedal arm.
5. Remove three screws securing heater core shield to lefthand end of HVAC distribution housing.
6. Pull heater core shield rearward far enough to disengage two locating tabs that position front of shield to receptacles in two lower formations of evaporator housing near instrument panel.
7. Remove heater core shield from distribution housing.
8. Take proper precautions to protect carpet below heater core from possible spilled engine coolant.
9. Remove screw securing heater core tube sealing plate to heater core supply and return ports.
10. Push both heater core tubes simultaneously toward instrument panel far enough to disengage fittings from heater core supply and return ports.
11. Plug open heater core ports and tube fittings.
12. Remove two screws securing heater core mounting plate to distribution housing.
13. Pull accelerator pedal upward and push brake pedal downward far

enough for clearance to pull hater core out of distribution housing.
14. Reverse procedure to install.

EVAPORATOR CORE

REPLACE

1. Recover A/C refrigerant as outlined under in "Air Conditioning" chapter.
2. Drain coolant into suitable container.
3. Disconnect liquid line and suction line from expansion valve.
4. Disconnect heater hoses from heater core tubes.
5. Remove four nuts securing heater-A/C unit housing studs to engine compartment side of instrument panel.
6. Remove instrument panel as outlined in "Dash Panel Service" chapter.
7. Remove floor distribution duct from passenger compartment.
8. Remove one screw securing heater-A/C unit housing bracket to passenger side of instrument panel.
9. Pull heater-A/C unit housing rearward far enough for mounting studs to clear dash panel, then remove.
10. Remove heater core tubes from heater core.
11. Remove and discard foam seal from HVAC housing seal flange around fresh air inlet opening and expansion valve/evaporator tube opening on instrument panel side of unit.
12. Remove expansion valve from evaporator inlet and outlet tube fittings.
13. Disconnect blower motor electrical connector, then disengage HVAC wire harness from routing clips molded into outside of HVAC housing components.
14. Remove three screws from instrument panel side of unit securing top of distribution housing to inboard end of evaporator housing.
15. Pull top of distribution housing away from evaporator housing far enough to disengage two hooks on bottom of distribution housing.
16. Remove two screws securing upper intake air housing to lower intake air housing.
17. Remove three screws securing upper intake air housing to top of outboard end of evaporator housing ensuring not to miss screw located inside inboard side of fresh air intake opening.
18. Remove upper intake air housing from top of evaporator housing to expose recirculation air door and blower wheel housing.
19. Remove two screws securing upper half of recirculation air door to lower half of door.
20. Remove upper half of recirculation air door from lower half of door.
21. Remove twelve screws around perimeter of evaporator housing securing upper housing half to lower half.
22. Carefully separate and remove upper half of evaporator housing from lower half.
23. Carefully lift evaporator and its foam wrap out of lower half of evaporator housing as a unit ensuring not to loose clam shell type rubber seal that is fitted to evaporator inlet and outlet tubes where they exit evaporator housing.
24. Reverse procedure to install. If replacing evaporator core add 2 ounces of ND8 PAG, or equivalent.

2.4L Engine

NOTE: On Air Bag Equipped Models, Refer To "Air Bag System Precautions" Located In The Front Of This Manual For System Disarming & Arming Procedures.

NOTE: Refer To "Computer Relearn Procedures" Located In The Front Of This Manual When Battery Power To The Computer Has Been Interrupted.

INDEX

PRECAUTIONS

Air Bag Systems

Refer to "Air Bag System Precautions" in the front of this manual for system disarming and arming procedures.

Battery Ground Cable

Prior to service, disconnect battery ground cable and isolate as required.

Fuel System Pressure Relief

1. Remove fuel pump relay from Power Distribution Center (PDC).
2. Start and run engine until it stalls.
3. Attempt to restart engine until it will no longer run.
4. Turn ignition key to Off position, then place a rag below fuel line quick-connect fitting at fuel rail.
5. Install fuel pump relay in PDC.
6. One or more DTCs may have been stored in PCM due to fuel pump relay removal. Erase any DTCs using suitable scan tool.

COMPRESSION PRESSURE

Compression pressure should be a minimum of 100 psi., with no more than a 25% variation in pressure between cylinders.

ENGINE MOUNT

REPLACE

Front

1. Raise and support vehicle.
2. Remove front engine mount through bolt from insulator, **Fig. 1.**
3. Remove front engine mount bolts, then insulator assembly.
4. Remove front mounting bracket from engine.
5. Reverse procedure to install. Tighten bolts to specifications.

Lefthand

1. Raise and support vehicle, then remove lefthand front wheel.
2. Remove lefthand mount through bolt access cover.
3. Support transaxle with suitable jack.
4. Remove engine front mount through bolt to allow lefthand mount removal clearance.
5. Remove lefthand mount through frame rail bolt, **Fig. 2.**
6. Lower transaxle for access to horizontal bolts, then remove bolts from mount to transaxle.
7. Remove lefthand engine mount.
8. Reverse procedure to install. Tighten bolts to specifications.

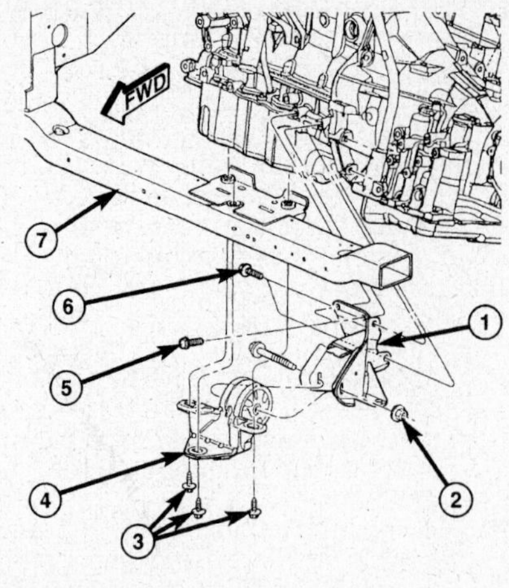

1 - BRACKET - FRONT MOUNT
2 - NUT
3 - BOLT
4 - MOUNT - FRONT INSULATOR
5 - BOLT
6 - BOLT
7 - FRONT CROSSMEMBER

CR1060100937000X

Fig. 1 Front engine mount replacement

Righthand

1. Remove air cleaner housing lid and clean air hose from throttle body.
2. Remove air cleaner element and housing.
3. Disconnect make-up air hose from valve cover.
4. Remove load on righthand engine mount by supporting engine assembly with a floor jack.
5. Disconnect electrical harness support clips from engine mount bracket.
6. Remove vertical bolts attaching engine mount to frame rail, **Fig. 3.**
7. Loosen horizontal bolt attaching engine mount to frame rail.
8. Remove bolts attaching engine mount to engine bracket.
9. Remove righthand engine mount.
10. Reverse procedure to install. Tighten bolts to specifications.

Rear

1. Raise and support vehicle, then remove rear mount heat shield.
2. Remove through bolt from mount and rear mount bracket, **Fig. 4.**
3. Remove mount bolts, then rear mount.
4. Remove rear bracket bolts, then rear bracket.
5. Reverse procedure to install. Tighten bolts to specifications.

ENGINE

REPLACE

1. Relieve fuel system pressure as outlined under "Precautions."
2. Remove air cleaner housing and inlet tube.
3. Disconnect fuel line from fuel rail.
4. Disconnect all vacuum hoses, then drain cooling system into suitable container.
5. Remove radiator fans, then radiator upper and lower hoses.
6. Disconnect automatic transaxle cooler lines.
7. Disconnect transmission shift linkage and electrical connectors.
8. Disconnect throttle body linkage, then engine wiring harness.
9. Disconnect heater hoses from heater.
10. Recover A/C refrigerant as outlined in "Air Conditioning" chapter.
11. Raise and support vehicle, then remove both front wheels.
12. Remove accessory drive belt splash shield, then drive belt.
13. Remove axle shafts.
14. Drain engine oil into suitable container, then remove oil filter.
15. Remove crossmember cradle plate, then disconnect exhaust pipe from manifold.
16. Remove front engine mount and bracket as outlined under "Engine Mount, Replace."
17. Remove structural collar, then rear engine mount bracket.
18. Mark flex plate to torque converter for reference during installation, then remove torque converter bolts.
19. Pinch off power steering supply hose at pump, then remove hose from pump.
20. Remove power steering pump and bracket, then position aside. **Do not disconnect pressure line.**
21. Lower vehicle, then remove A/C lines at compressor capping all open lines.
22. Remove engine ground straps at righthand mount and at starter.
23. Raise vehicle enough to install engine dolly tool No. 6135, cradle tool No. 6710 and posts tool No. 6848, or equivalents.
24. Loosen cradle posts to allow movement for proper positioning, then locate two rear posts into holes on engine bedplate.
25. Locate two front posts on oil pan rails.
26. Lower vehicle and position cradle mounts until engine is resting on mounts, then tighten mounts to cradle frame.
27. Install safety straps around engine to cradle, then tighten and lock.
28. Lower vehicle so weight of only engine and transmission are on cradle.
29. Remove engine and transmission mount bolts.
30. Raise vehicle slowly to remove engine.
31. Reverse procedure to install.

INTAKE MANIFOLD

REPLACE

Upper

1. Disconnect electrical connector from inlet air temperature sensor.
2. Disconnect air intake tube at throttle body, then remove upper air cleaner housing.

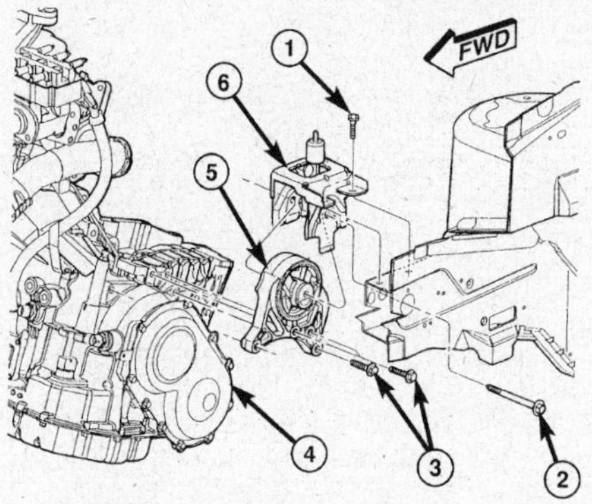

1 - BOLT - BRACKET TO FRAME RAIL
2 - BOLT - MOUNT TO RAIL THRU
3 - BOLT - LEFT MOUNT TO TRANSAXLE
4 - TRANSAXLE
5 - MOUNT - LEFT
6 - BRACKET - LEFT MOUNT

CR1060100938000X

Fig. 2 Lefthand engine mount replacement

3. Disconnect electrical connectors from TPS, IAC and MAP sensors.
4. Remove vacuum lines for purge solenoid and PCV valve at intake manifold.
5. Remove vacuum lines for power brake booster, LDP, EGR transducer and speed control vacuum reservoir at upper intake manifold fittings.
6. Disconnect throttle, speed control and transaxle control cables from throttle lever and bracket.
7. Remove EGR tube, then the upper manifold support bracket bolt.
8. Remove engine oil dipstick from tube.
9. Remove upper intake manifold bolts, then upper intake manifold.
10. Reverse procedure to install. Tighten intake manifold bolts in sequence, **Fig. 5** to specifications.

Lower

1. Relieve fuel pressure as outlined under "Precautions."
2. Remove upper intake manifold as outlined previously.
3. Disconnect fuel line, then drain cooling system into suitable container.
4. Remove heater supply and radiator upper hoses at intake manifold.
5. Disconnect coolant temperature sensor/fuel injector wire harness electrical connector.
6. Remove lower intake manifold support bracket bolts, then disconnect fuel injector harness.
7. Remove bolts attaching power steering reservoir to manifold, then position aside.
8. Remove lower intake manifold bolts, then bolts.
9. Reverse procedure to install. Tighten manifold bolts in sequence, **Fig. 6,** to specifications.

EXHAUST MANIFOLD

REPLACE

1. Raise and support vehicle, then disconnect exhaust pipe from manifold.

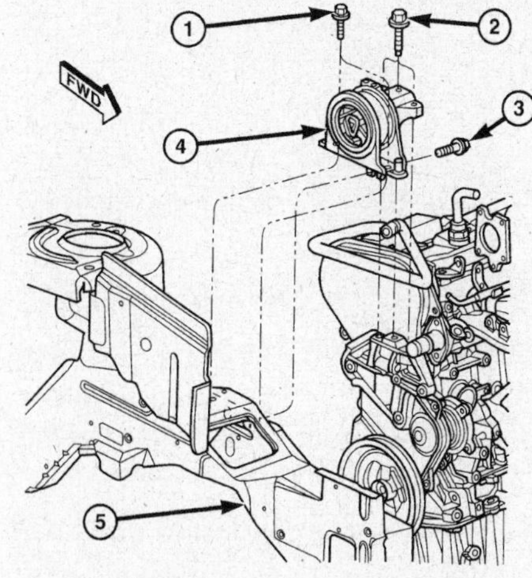

1 - BOLT - MOUNT TO RAIL
2 - BOLT - MOUNT TO ENGINE
3 - BOLT - MOUNT TO RAIL (HORIZONTAL)
4 - RIGHT ENGINE MOUNT
5 - RIGHT FRAME RAIL

CR1060100939000X

Fig. 3 Righthand engine mount replacement

2. Disconnect upstream oxygen sensor electrical connector at rear of exhaust manifold.
3. Remove exhaust manifold bolts, then manifold.
4. Reverse procedure to install. Tighten bolts in sequence, **Fig. 7.**

CYLINDER HEAD

REPLACE

1. Relieve fuel pressure as outlined under "Precautions."
2. Drain cooling system into suitable container, then remove air filter housing and inlet tube.
3. Remove upper intake manifold as outlined under "Intake Manifold, Replace."
4. Remove heater tube support bracket from cylinder head.
5. Disconnect radiator upper and heater supply hoses from intake manifold water outlet connections.
6. Remove accessory drive belts.
7. Raise and support vehicle, then remove exhaust pipe from manifold.
8. Remove power steering pump reservoir and support bracket, then position aside.
9. Remove ignition coil and wires, then disconnect cam sensor and fuel injector electrical connectors.
10. Remove timing belt and camshaft sprockets as outlined under "Timing Belt, Replace."
11. Remove timing belt idler pulley, then the rear timing belt cover.
12. Remove cylinder head cover.
13. Remove camshafts as outlined under "Camshaft, Replace."
14. Identify rocker arm positions for reference during installation, then remove rocker arms.

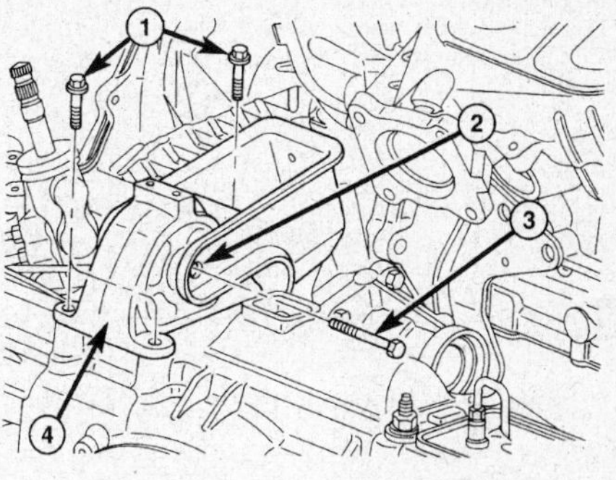

1 - BOLT
2 - REAR MOUNT BRACKET
3 - THRU-BOLT
4 - REAR MOUNT

CR1060100940000X

Fig. 4 Rear engine mount replacement

15. Remove cylinder head bolts in reverse order of tightening sequence, **Fig. 8.**
16. Remove cylinder head from engine.
17. Reverse procedure to install. **Torque** cylinder head bolts in sequence, **Fig. 8,** using four steps, first to 25 ft. lbs., second to 60 ft. lbs., third to 60 ft. lbs., and fourth an additional 1/4 turn.

VALVE COVER

REPLACE

1. Remove upper intake manifold as outlined under "Intake Manifold, Replace."
2. Remove upper manifold support bracket.
3. Remove ignition coil, then spark plug wires.
4. Disconnect PCV and make-up air hoses from valve cover.
5. Remove valve cover bolts, then valve cover.
6. Reverse procedure to install, noting the following:
   a. Apply Mopar Engine RTV GEN II, or equivalent to camshaft cap corners and top edges of 1/2 round seal.
   b. Install valve cover bolts ensuring two bolts with sealing washer are located in center of cover.
   c. Tighten bolts in sequence, **Fig. 9,** first to 40 inch lbs., then to 80 inch lbs., and finally to 105 inch lbs.

VALVE ARRANGEMENT

Intake valves are located on intake manifold side of engine and exhaust valves are located on exhaust manifold side of engine.

CAMSHAFT LOBE LIFT SPECIFICATIONS

Intake lobe lift should be .324 inch and exhaust lobe lift should be .259 inch.

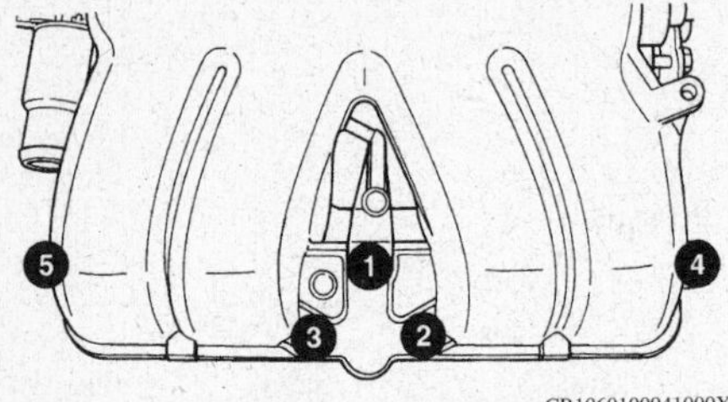

Fig. 5 Upper intake manifold tightening sequence

VALVE CLEARANCE SPECIFICATIONS

Equipped with hydraulic valve lash adjusters.

VALVE ADJUSTMENT

On these engines, the intake and exhaust valves are equipped with hydraulic lash adjusters; there is no provision for adjustment.

FRONT COVER

REPLACE

Upper

1. Remove upper cover mounting bolts, **Fig. 10.**
2. Remove cover.
3. Reverse procedure to install.

Lower

1. Remove crankshaft damper bolt using puller tool No. 1026 and insert tool No. 6827, or equivalents.
2. Remove alternator drive belt tensioner.
3. Remove front cover mounting bolts, **Fig. 10,** then cover.
4. Reverse procedure to install.

TIMING BELT

REPLACE

REMOVAL

With the timing belt removed, avoid turning camshaft or crankshaft. If movement is required, exercise extreme caution to avoid valve damage caused by piston contact.

1. Remove air cleaner assembly.
2. Raise and support vehicle, then remove righthand front wheel.
3. Remove righthand inner splash shield.
4. Remove accessory drive belts, then crankshaft damper.
5. Remove A/C belt tensioner and pulley.
6. Remove timing belt cover as outlined under "Front Cover, Replace."
7. Remove righthand engine mount and bracket as outlined under "Engine Mount, Replace."
8. Align crankshaft and camshaft sprocket marks, **Fig. 11.**

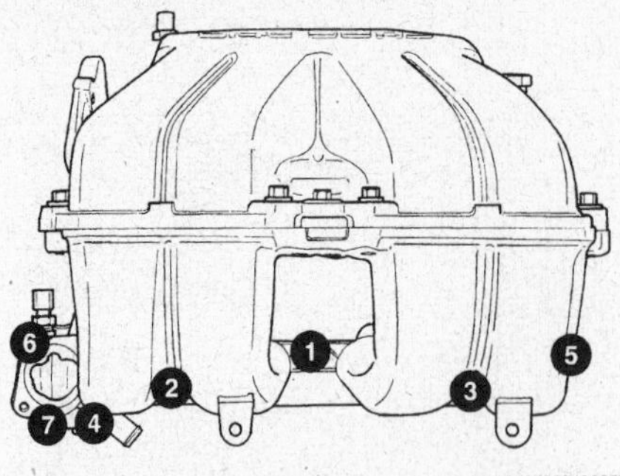

Fig. 6 Lower intake manifold tightening sequence

9. Loosen timing belt tensioner lock bolt, **Fig. 12.**
10. Insert a 6mm allen wrench into the hexagon opening located on top plate of belt tensioner pulley, the rotate top plate clockwise until there is enough slack in timing belt for removal.
11. Remove timing belt.

INSTALLATION

1. Set crankshaft sprocket to TDC by aligning sprocket with arrow on oil pump housing.
2. Set camshafts timing marks so that exhaust camshaft sprocket is a 1/2 notch below intake camshaft sprocket, **Fig. 11.**
3. Install timing belt. Starting at crankshaft, go around water pump sprocket, idler pulley, camshaft sprockets and then around tensioner.
4. Move exhaust camshaft sprocket counterclockwise to align marks and take up belt slack, **Fig. 13.**
5. Insert a 6 mm Allen wrench into hexagon opening located on top plate of belt tensioner pulley. Rotate top plate counterclockwise. The tensioner pulley will move against belt and tensioner setting notch will eventually start to move clockwise. Watching movement of setting notch, continue rotating top plate counterclockwise until setting notch is aligned with spring tang.
6. Rotate crankshaft clockwise two complete revolutions manually for seating of belt, until crankshaft is repositioned at TDC position.
7. Ensure spring tang is within tolerance window, **Fig. 14.**

CAMSHAFT

REPLACE

1. Remove valve cover as outlined under "Valve Cover, Replace."
2. Remove timing belt, sprockets and covers.
3. Bearing caps are identified for location. Remove outside bearing caps L1, R1, L6 and R6 first, **Fig. 15.**
4. Loosen camshaft bearing cap attaching bolts in sequence, **Fig. 16,** one camshaft at a time.
5. Identify camshafts before removing from head. Camshafts are not interchangeable.

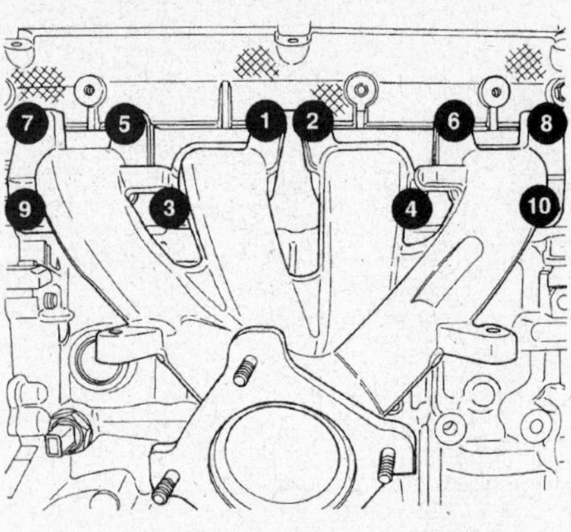

Fig. 7 Exhaust manifold tightening sequence

6. Reverse procedure to install. Using sequence, **Fig. 17,** tighten camshaft bearing caps as follows:
   a. **Ensure none of the cylinders are at TDC when installing camshafts.**
   b. Install righthand and lefthand camshaft bearing caps No. 2 through No. 5 and righthand No. 6, then **torque** bearing cap bolts to 108 inch lbs.
   c. Install camshaft bearing caps No. 1 and No. 6 and **torque** bolts to 21 ft. lbs.

BALANCE SHAFT

REPLACE

1. Raise and support vehicle.
2. Remove oil pan as outlined under "Oil Pan, Replace."
3. Remove oil pick up tube.
4. Remove chain cover, guide and tensioner. Discard pivot and adjuster screws, **Fig. 18.**
5. Remove balance shaft drive sprocket retaining screw, then chain and sprocket, **Fig. 19.**
6. Work crankshaft sprocket back and forth to remove from crankshaft.
7. Remove gear cover double ended retaining stud, then cover and balance shaft gears, **Fig. 20.**
8. Remove rear cover and balance shafts.
9. Remove four carrier to crankcase attaching bolts to separate carrier.
10. Reverse procedure to install, noting the following:
    a. Place matching marks on balance shaft gears must be aligned and balance shaft keys must face upward, **Fig. 21.**
    b. Balance shaft timing chain and gear timing mark must be aligned as outlined in, **Fig. 22.**
    c. When adjusting balance shaft timing chain tension, position a shim .039 inch thick by 2.75 inches long between tensioner and chain. Push tensioner and shim against timing chain with a force of 2.2–6.6 lbs., **Fig. 23.** With force applied to timing chain, **torque** top tensioner bolt, then bottom tensioner bolt to 105 inch lbs.

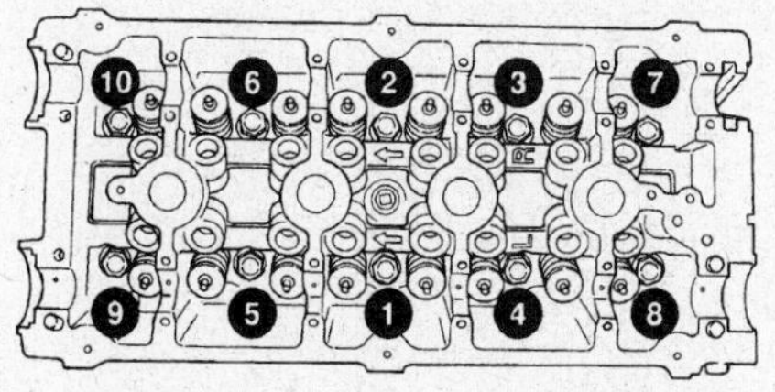

Fig. 8 Cylinder head bolt tightening sequence

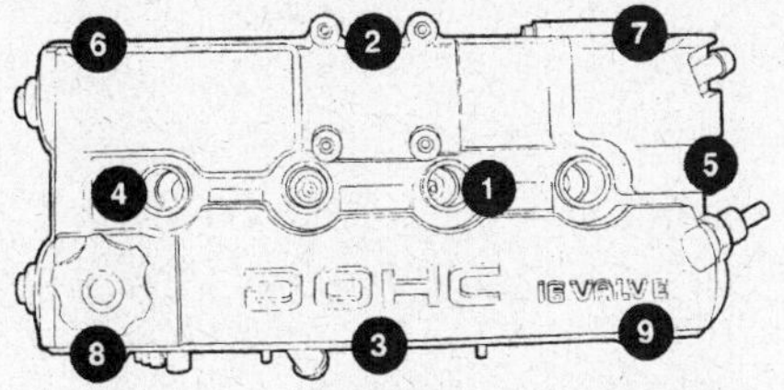

Fig. 9 Valve cover tightening sequence

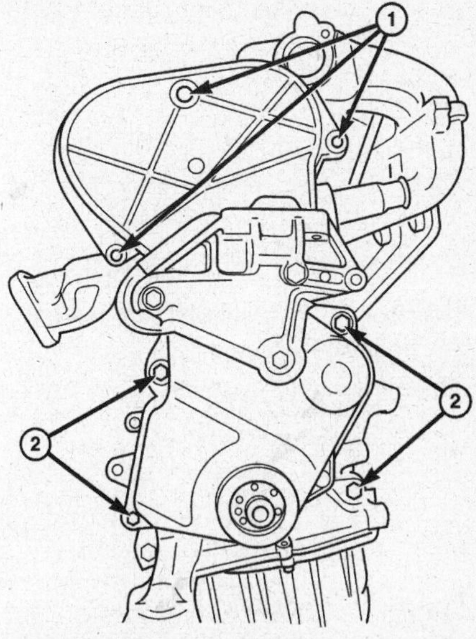

Fig. 10 Front upper & lower cover replacement

PISTON & ROD ASSEMBLY

The stamping on the front portion of the piston must face toward the front of the engine.

1. Install rings as outlined in **Fig. 24.**
2. Tighten main bearing cap bolts in sequence, **Fig. 25,** to specifications.

CRANKSHAFT SEAL

REPLACE

1. Refer to "Timing Belt, Replace" procedure until crankshaft sprocket is accessible.
2. Remove crankshaft sprocket using sprocket remover tool No. 6793 and insert tool No. C-4685-C2, or equivalents, **Fig. 26.**
3. Remove seal using oil seal remover tool No. 6771, or equivalent, **Fig. 27.**
4. Reverse procedure to install, noting the following:
   a. Install new seal using seal installation tool No. 6780-1, or equivalent.
   b. Install crankshaft sprocket using tool No. 6792, or equivalent.

CRANKSHAFT REAR OIL SEAL

REPLACE

1. Remove transaxle as outlined in **MOTOR's "Domestic Transmission, In-Vehicle Service."**
2. Pry out rear seal with screwdriver being careful not to nick or damage crankshaft flange seal surface or retainer bore.
3. Inspect shaft seal surface for nicks or dirt. Polish with 400 grit sandpaper if required.
4. Reverse procedure to install, after tapping new seal into place using suitable seal installer.

OIL PAN

REPLACE

1. Raise and support vehicle, then drain oil into suitable container.
2. Remove structural collar, then A/C compressor bracket to oil pan bolt.
3. Remove oil pan bolts, then oil pan.
4. Reverse procedure to install, noting the following:
   a. Apply Mopar Engine RTV GEN II, or equivalent at oil pump to engine block parting line.
   b. Tighten oil pan bolts to specifications.

OIL PUMP

REPLACE

1. Remove timing belt as outlined in "Timing Belt, Replace."
2. Remove oil pan as outlined in "Oil Pan, Replace."
3. Remove crankshaft sprocket using removal tool No. 6793 and insert C-4685-C2, or equivalents.
4. Remove oil pick up tube.
5. Remove oil pump and front crankshaft seal.
6. Reverse procedure to install, noting the following:
   a. Prime oil pump before installation.
   b. Align oil pump rotor flats with flats on crankshaft.
   c. Tighten attaching bolts to specifications.

OIL PUMP SERVICE

Disassemble

1. Remove relief valve plug and gasket, then spring and relief valve.
2. Remove oil pump attaching bolts and cover.
3. Remove pump rotors.

Inspection

1. Clean all components thoroughly in a suitable solvent. Mating surface of oil pump should be smooth. Replace pump cover if scratched or grooved.
2. Measure thickness and diameter of outer rotor. If outer rotor thickness measures .370 inch or less, or if diameter is 3.148 inches or less, replace outer rotor.
3. If inner rotor measures .370 inch or less, replace inner rotor.
4. Place outer rotor into pump housing and press to one side. Measure clearance between rotor and housing. If measurement is .015 inch or more, replace housing.
5. Install inner rotor into pump housing. If clearance between inner and outer rotors is .008 or more, replace rotors.
6. Place a straightedge across face of pump housing, between bolt holes. If a feeler gauge of .001 inch or more can be inserted between rotors and straightedge, replace pump assembly, only if rotors are in specification.
7. Inspect oil pressure relief valve plunger for scoring and free operation in its bore. Small marks may be removed with 400 grit wet or dry sand paper.
8. Oil pump relief valve spring free length is approximately 2.39 inches in length and should test between 18-19 pounds when compressed to 1.6 inches. Replace spring if not to specification.

Assemble

1. Assemble pump using new components as required. Install inner rotor with chamfer facing cast iron oil pump cover.
2. Prime oil pump before installation by filling rotor cavity with clean engine oil.
3. Apply Mopar gasket maker lightly to cover mounting surface on pump body. Attach cover and tighten to specifications.
4. Install relief valve, spring, gasket and cap and tighten to specifications. **Relief valve must be installed as outlined in Fig. 28.**

BELT TENSION DATA

The A/C compressor and alternator belt tension should be 150 lbs. for a new belt or 80 lbs. for a used belt.

The power steering pump belt tension should be 130 lbs. for a new belt or 80 lbs. for a used belt.

A belt is considered used after 15 minutes of use.

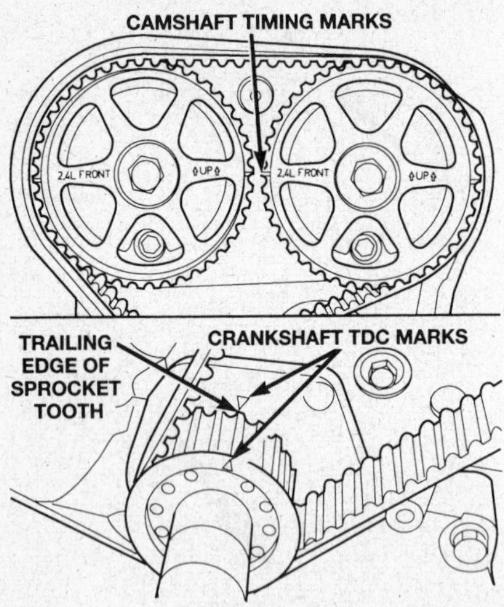

Fig. 11 Crankshaft & camshaft sprocket timing mark alignment

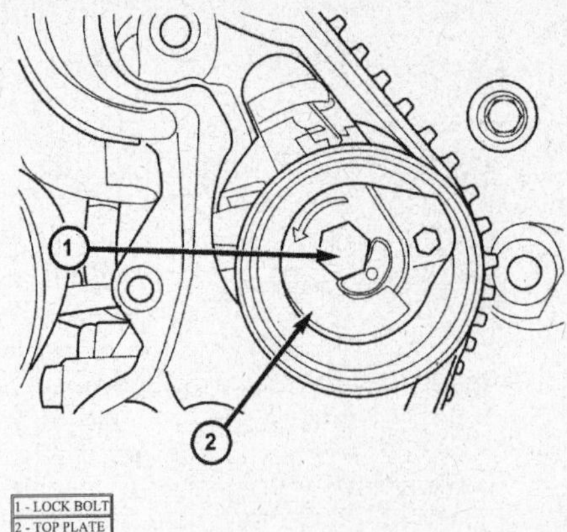

Fig. 12 Timing belt tensioner lock bolt

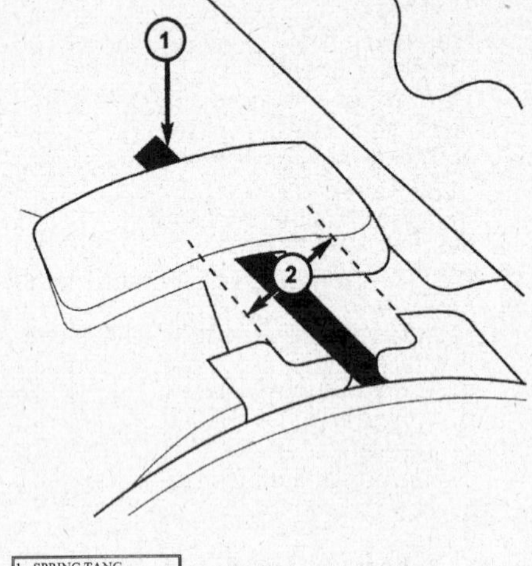

Fig. 14 Timing belt tension verification

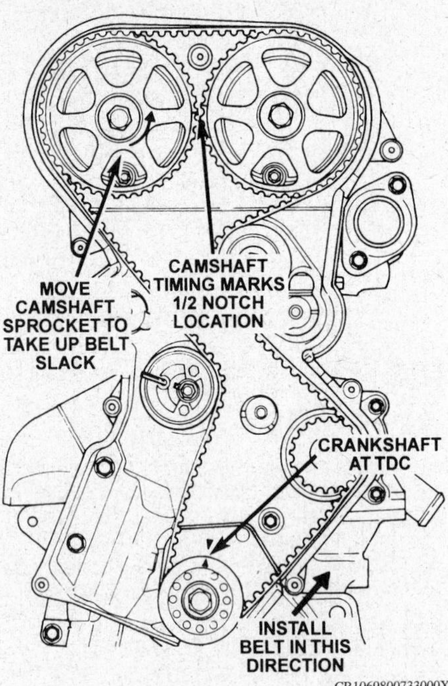

Fig. 13 Camshaft sprocket alignment

COOLING SYSTEM BLEED

The coolant system may be vented during refill by removing engine coolant temperature (ECT) sensor on top of the water outlet connector. Fill system until coolant level reaches this level, then install ECT sensor and tighten to specification. Continue filling system until full, then fill reserve system to MAX level. It may be required to add coolant to reserve tank after three of four warm up and cool down cycles to maintain coolant level.

THERMOSTAT

REPLACE

1. Drain cooling system to thermostat level or below.
2. Remove thermostat assembly, and clean sealing surfaces.
3. Reverse procedure to install. Tighten to specification.

WATER PUMP

REPLACE

1. Raise and support vehicle and remove righthand inner splash shield.
2. Remove accessory drive belts and power steering pump.
3. Drain cooling system.
4. Support engine from bottom and remove righthand engine mount.
5. Remove power steering pump bracket attaching bolts and set pump and bracket assembly aside. Power steering lines do not need to be disconnected.
6. Remove righthand engine mount bracket.
7. Remove timing belt as outlined under "Timing Belt, Replace."
8. Remove inner timing belt cover.
9. Remove water pump attaching bolts and the water pump.
10. Reverse procedure to install, noting the following:
    a. Install new O-ring gasket in water pump body O-ring groove.
    b. Tighten bolts to specification.
    c. Fill cooling system.

RADIATOR

REPLACE

1. Remove radiator upper crossmember support.
2. Drain cooling system into suitable container, then remove radiator fans.
3. Remove A/C condenser side brackets to radiator attaching screws.
4. Separate condenser from radiator by lifting upward to disengage from lower mounts, then allow condenser to rest in front of radiator.
5. Remove radiator from vehicle by lifting upward.
6. Reverse procedure to install.

FUEL PUMP

REPLACE

The electric fuel pump is not serviceable. If the fuel pump needs replacement, the complete fuel pump module must be replaced. The fuel reservoir of the fuel pump does not empty out when fuel tank is drained. The fuel in the reservoir will spill out when pump is removed.

1. Relive fuel system pressure as outlined under "Precautions."
2. With a siphon hose drain fuel tank into a suitable container.
3. Raise and support vehicle, then support fuel tank with a suitable jack and remove fuel tank straps.
4. Clean top of tank to remove dirt and debris.
5. Lower fuel tank slightly, then disconnect fuel filter lines and electrical connector from fuel pump module.
6. Remove locknut securing fuel pump module.
7. Remove fuel pump module and O-ring from tank, then discard O-ring.
8. Reverse procedure to install.

FUEL FILTER

REPLACE

The fuel filter mounts to the top of the fuel tank. The inlet and outlet tubes are permanently attached to the filter.

1. Release fuel system pressure as outlined under "Precautions."
2. Disconnect fuel lines from fuel pump module and chassis fuel supply tube.
3. Remove fuel filter retaining screw, then filter.
4. Reverse procedure to install.

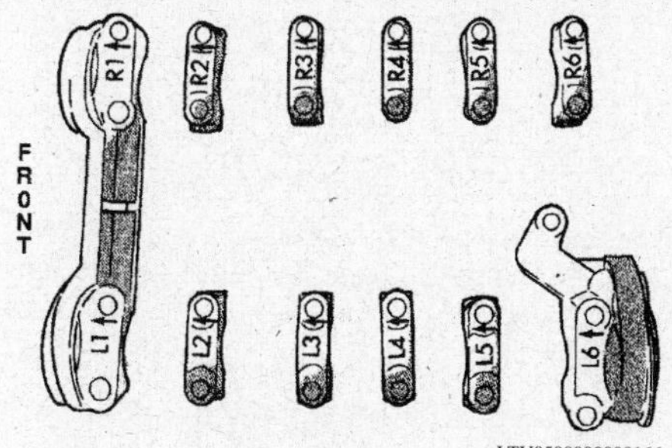

Fig. 15 Camshaft bearing cap identification

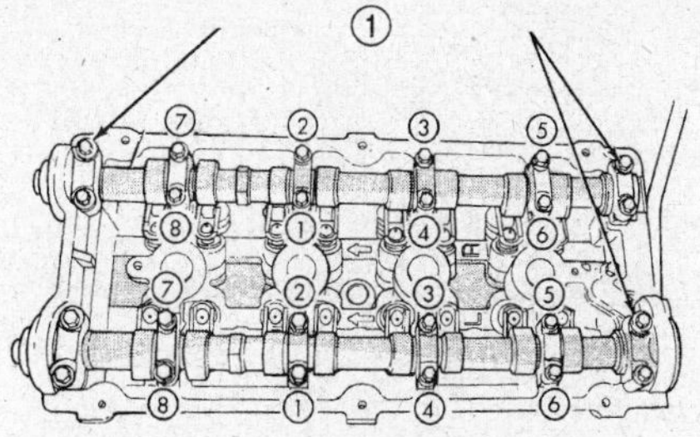

Fig. 16 Camshaft bearing cap removal

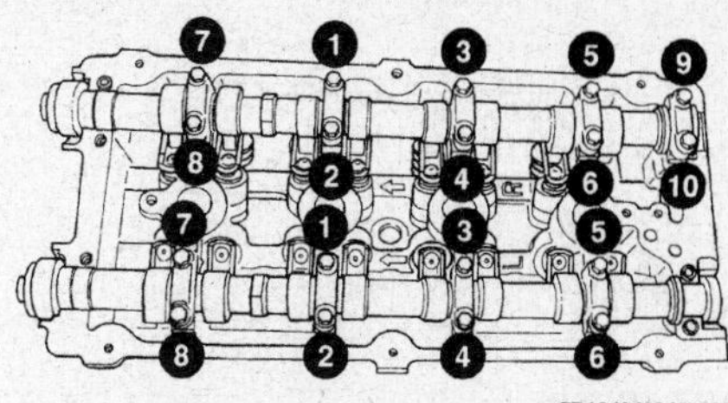

Fig. 17 Camshaft bearing cap tightening sequence

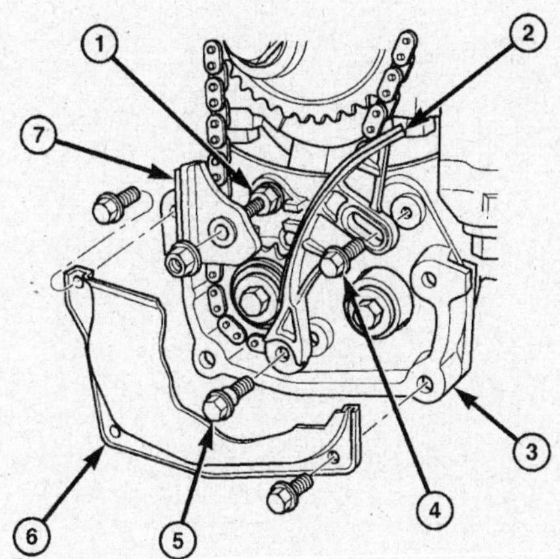

Fig. 18 Chain cover, guide & tensioner

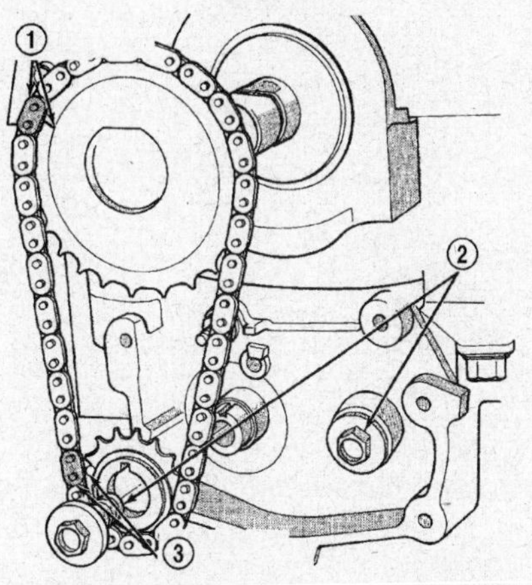

Fig. 19 Balance shaft chain & sprocket

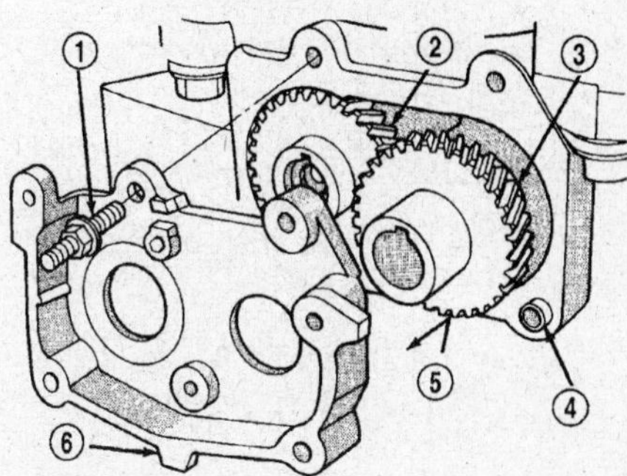

Fig. 20 Gear cover & gears

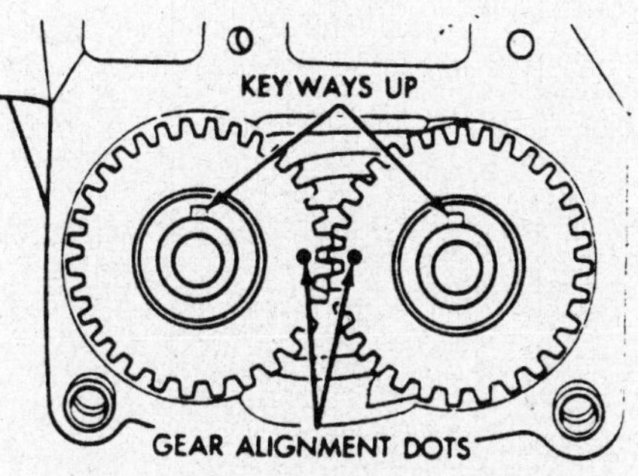

Fig. 21 Balance shaft gear alignment

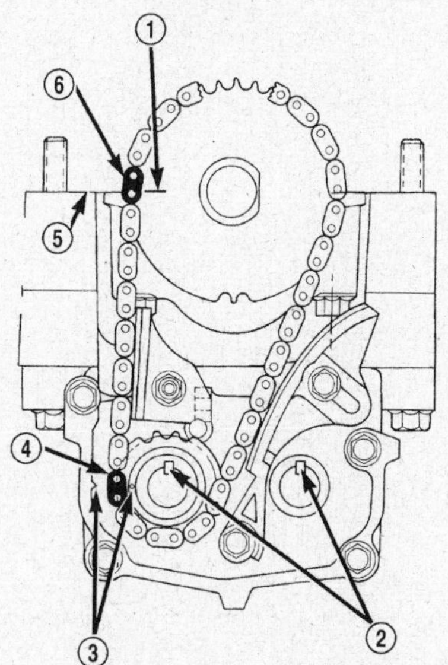

Fig. 22 Balance shaft timing chain & gears

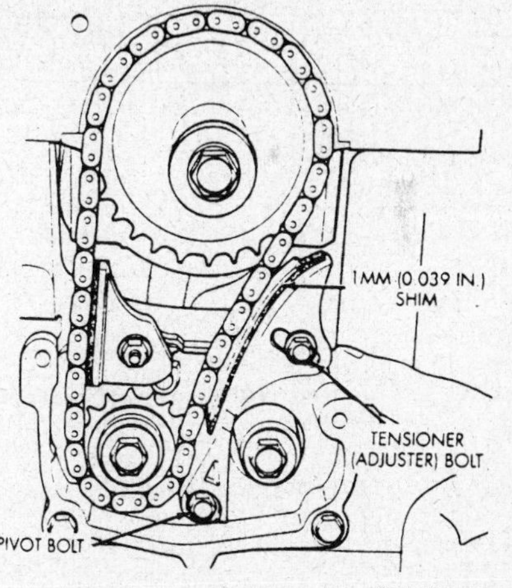

Fig. 23 Balance shaft timing chain tensioner adjustment

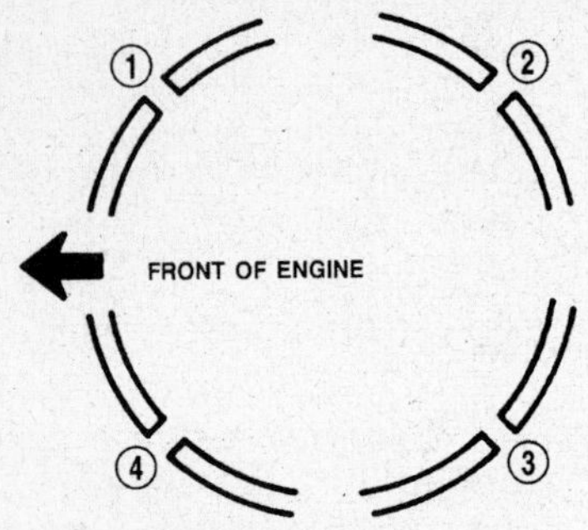

FRONT OF ENGINE
Fig. 68 Piston Ring End Gap Position
1 - GAP OF LOWER SIDE RAIL
2 - NO. 1 RING GAP
3 - GAP OF UPPER SIDE RAIL
4 - NO. 2 RING GAP AND SPACER EXPANDER GAP
CR1060100945000X

Fig. 24 Piston ring end gap position

CR1060100946000X

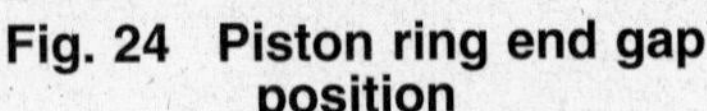

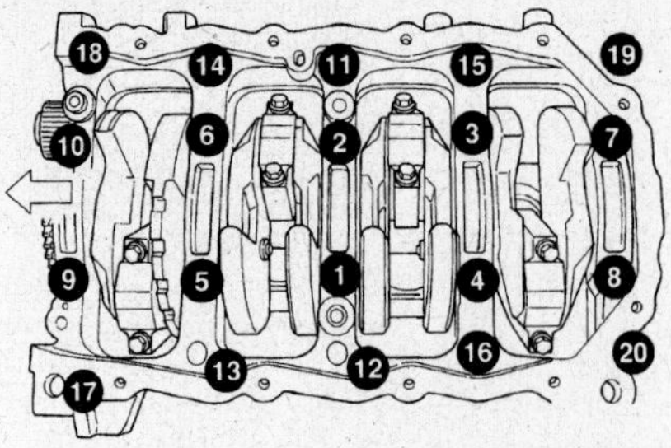

Fig. 25 Main bearing cap tightening sequence

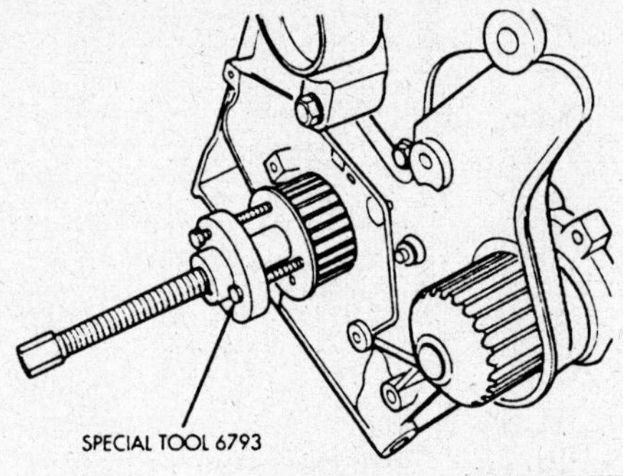

SPECIAL TOOL 6793
CR1069500591000X

Fig. 26 Crankshaft sprocket removal

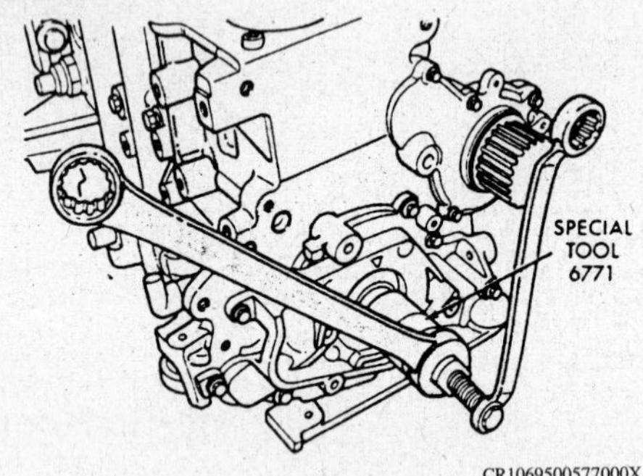

SPECIAL TOOL 6771
CR1069500577000X

Fig. 27 Front crankshaft oil seal removal

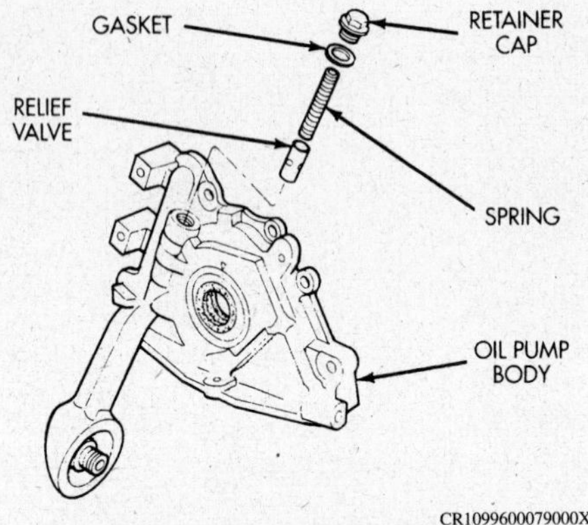

GASKET
RETAINER CAP
RELIEF VALVE
SPRING
OIL PUMP BODY
CR1099600079000X

Fig. 28 Oil pump relief valve installation

TIGHTENING SPECIFICATIONS

Year	Component	Torque Ft. Lbs.
2002–06	Alternator Mounting Bolts	40
	Balance Shaft Sprocket Bolts	21
	Camshaft Sprocket Bolt	75
	Connecting Rod Cap Bolt	③
	Crankshaft Pulley Bolt	100
	Cylinder Head	②
	Engine Coolant Temperature Sensor	60④
	Exhaust Manifold Heat Shield	105④
	Exhaust Manifold To Cylinder Head	15
	Front Cover Bolts	50④
	Front Engine Mount Bolts	50
	Lefthand Engine Mount Bracket To Frame Rail	50
	Lefthand Engine Mount Through Bolt	55
	Lefthand Engine Mount Transaxle Bolt	40
	Lower Intake Manifold Bolts	21
	Main Bearing Caps (M-8 Bolts)	21
	Main Bearing Caps (M-11 Bolts)	①
	Oil Pan Drain Plug	20
	Oil Pan To Engine Block	105④
	Oil Pump	21
	Oil Pump Cover	105④
	Oil Pump Pickup Tube	21
	Oil Pump Relief Valve Retaining Cap	30
	Radiator	45④
	Rear Engine Mount Bolts	40
	Righthand Engine Mount Bolts	50
	Spark Plugs	21
	Thermostat Housing	21
	Timing Belt Tensioner	45
	Timing Belt Tensioner Pulley	45
	Upper Intake Manifold Bolts	21
	Valve Cover Bolts	⑤

① — 30 ft. lbs., plus 1/4 turn.
② — Refer to "Cylinder Head, Replace."
③ — 20 ft. lbs. plus 1/4 turn.
④ — Inch lbs.
⑤ — Refer to "Valve Cover, Replace."

3.3L & 3.8L Engines

NOTE: On Air Bag Equipped Models, Refer To "Air Bag System Precautions" Located In The Front Of This Manual For System Disarming & Arming Procedures.

NOTE: Refer To "Computer Relearn Procedures" Located In The Front Of This Manual When Battery Power To The Computer Has Been Interrupted.

INDEX

PRECAUTIONS

Air Bag Systems

Refer to "Air Bag System Precautions" in the front of this manual for system disarming and arming procedures.

Battery Ground Cable

Prior to service, disconnect battery ground cable and isolate as required.

Fuel System Pressure Relief

1. Remove fuel pump relay from Power Distribution Center (PDC).
2. Start and run engine until it stalls.
3. Attempt to restart engine until it will no longer run.
4. Turn ignition key to Off position, then place a rag below fuel line quick-connect fitting at fuel rail.
5. Install fuel pump relay in PDC.
6. One or more DTCs may have been stored in PCM due to fuel pump relay removal. Erase any DTCs using suitable scan tool.

COMPRESSION PRESSURE

Compression pressure should be 100 psi with no more than a 25 percent variation in compression pressure between cylinders.

ENGINE MOUNT

REPLACE

Refer to "Engine Mount, Replace" as outlined in "2.4L Engine" section.

ENGINE

REPLACE

1. Relieve fuel pressure as outlined under "Precautions."
2. Remove air cleaner and hoses, then disconnect fuel line from fuel rail.
3. Remove wiper module.
4. Block off heater hoses to rear heater system using suitable pinch-off pliers.
5. Drain cooling system into suitable container, then disconnect heater hoses.
6. Remove radiator upper support crossmember, then the radiator fans.
7. Disconnect throttle cables from throttle body.
8. Disconnect MAP, IAC, TPS and EGR transducer electrical connectors.
9. Disconnect vacuum hoses from brake booster, speed control and throttle body.
10. Disengage wire harness clip from righthand engine mount.
11. Remove power steering reservoir and position aside.
12. Disconnect ground strap from rear of cylinder head.
13. Disconnect ECT and ignition coil electrical connectors.
14. Disconnect fuel injector electrical harness connector, then disengage clip from support bracket.
15. Disconnect camshaft and crankshaft sensor electrical connectors.
16. Recover A/C refrigerant as outlined in "Air Conditioning" chapter.
17. Disconnect A/C compressor electrical connector.
18. Disconnect A/C lines from compressor, then plug all openings of compressor and lines.
19. Remove radiator upper hose, then disconnect electrical harness clip at transaxle dipstick tube.
20. Disconnect cooler lines from transaxle, then shift linkage and electrical connectors.
21. Raise and support vehicle, then drain oil into suitable container.
22. Remove axle shafts as outlined under "Front Suspension & Steering."
23. Remove crossmember cradle plate.
24. **On models equipped with AWD,** remove power transfer unit.
25. **On all models,** disconnect exhaust pipe from manifold.
26. Remove front engine mount and bracket as an assembly.
27. Remove rear mount bracket, then engine to transaxle struts.
28. Remove transaxle case cover, then flex plate to torque converter bolts.
29. Remove power steering pressure hose support clip bolt.
30. Remove accessory drive belt splash shield, then drive belt.
31. Disconnect lower radiator hose, then remove A/C compressor.
32. Remove alternator, then water pump pulley bolts.
33. Disconnect oil pressure switch electrical connector, then wiring harness

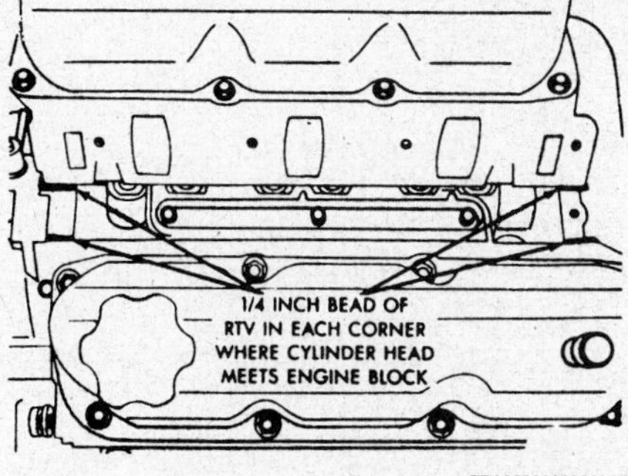

Fig. 1 Intake manifold gasket sealant application

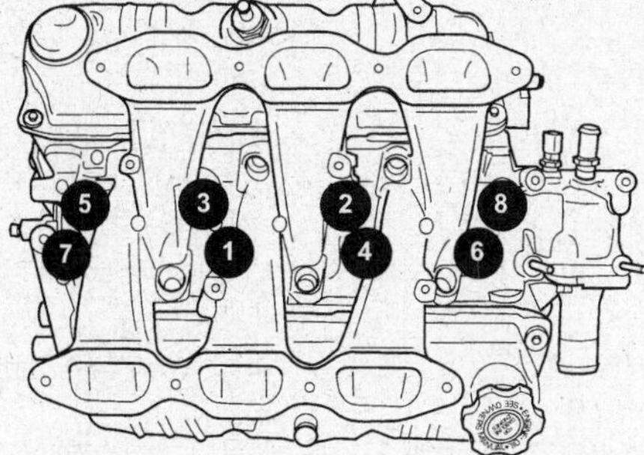

Fig. 2 Lower intake manifold tightening sequence

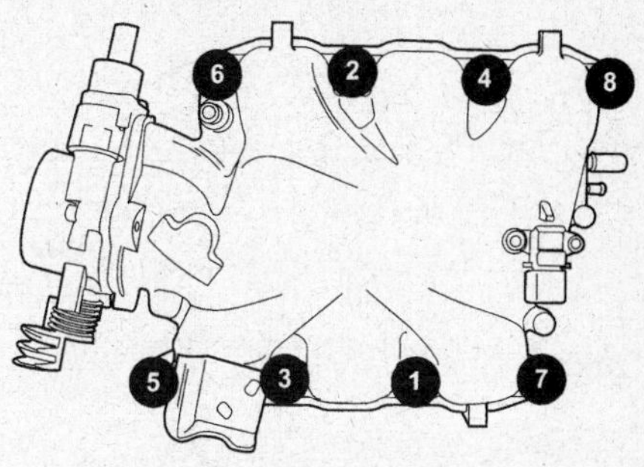

Fig. 3 Upper intake manifold tightening sequence

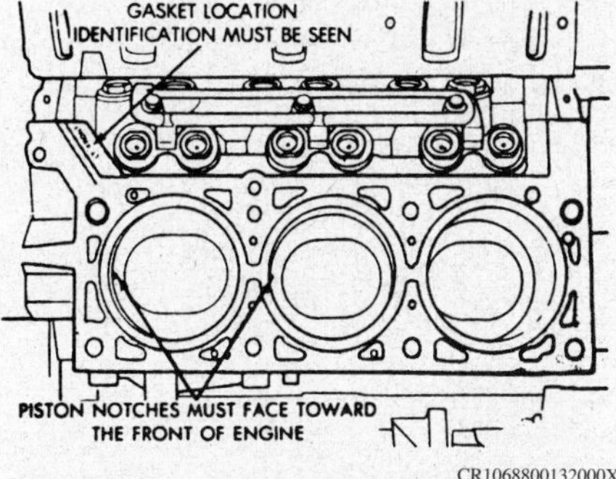

Fig. 4 Head gasket installation

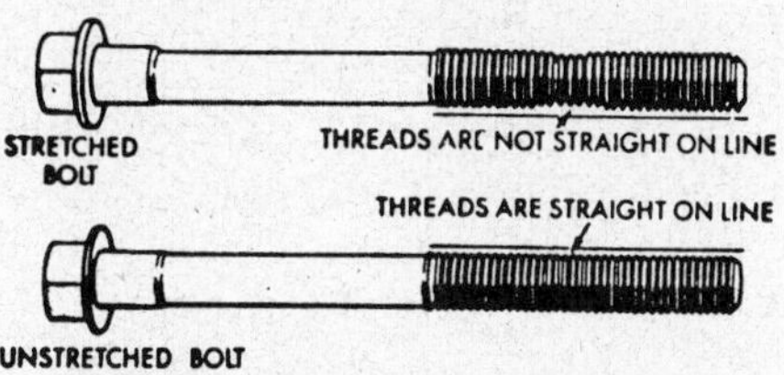

Fig. 5 Cylinder head bolt inspection

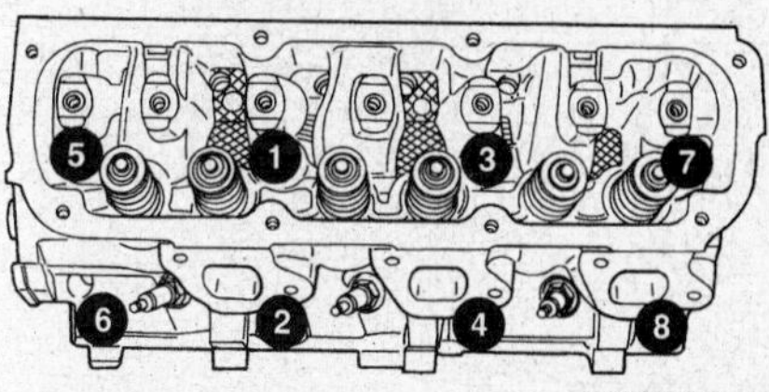

Fig. 6 Cylinder head bolt tightening sequence

support clip from dipstick tube.

34. Install adapter tool Nos. 6912 and 8444, or equivalent to righthand side of engine block.
35. Lower vehicle, then remove power steering pump and position aside.
36. Raise vehicle enough to allow engine dolly tool No. 6135 and cradle tool No. 6710, or equivalents with post tool No. 6848 and adapter tool No. 6909, or equivalents to be installed under vehicle.
37. Lower vehicle positioning cradle mounts until engine is resting on mounts, then tighten mounts to cradle frame.
38. Lower engine so only weight of engine and transaxle is resting on cradle.
39. Install safety straps to cradle around engine.
40. Remove engine righthand side mount bolts, then lefthand mount through bolt.
41. Raise vehicle slowly to remove engine.
42. Reverse procedure to install. Tighten bolts to specifications.

INTAKE MANIFOLD

REPLACE

1. Disconnect air inlet sensor electrical connector, then remove air inlet resonator to throttle body hose assembly.
2. Disconnect throttle and speed control cables.
3. Disconnect make-up air hose support clip from throttle cable bracket.
4. Disconnect AIS, TPS and MAP electrical connectors.
5. Disconnect EGR transducer vacuum hose from bottom of upper intake manifold.
6. Remove EGR tube, then disconnect vapor purge vacuum hose from throttle body.
7. Disconnect PCV hose, then remove power steering reservoir and position aside.
8. Disconnect brake booster and leak detection pump hoses from intake manifold.
9. Remove upper intake manifold bolts, then upper intake manifold.
10. Drain cooling system into suitable container, then remove fuel line.
11. Remove ignition coil and bracket.
12. Disconnect heater supply hose, then ECT sensor electrical connector.
13. Disconnect fuel injector wire harness, then remove fuel injectors and rail assembly.
14. Remove upper radiator hose.
15. Remove lower intake manifold bolts, then lower intake manifold.
16. Reverse procedure to install, noting the following:
    a. Apply a bead of Mopar Engine RTV GEN II, or equivalent to each corner of lower intake manifold to cylinder head corners, **Fig. 1.**
    b. **Torque** lower intake manifold bolts in sequence, **Fig. 2** first to 10 inch lbs., then to 17 ft. lbs., and finally again to 17 ft. lbs.
    c. Tighten upper intake manifold bolts in sequence, **Fig. 3,** to specifications.

EXHAUST MANIFOLD

REPLACE

RIGHT

1. Remove wiper module, then disconnect spark plug wires.
2. Remove bolts securing crossover pipe to exhaust manifold.
3. Remove upstream oxygen sensor.
4. Remove heat shield screws, then upper heat shield.
5. Raise and support vehicle, then remove drive belt shield.
6. Loosen power steering pump support strut lower bolt.
7. Disconnect downstream oxygen sensor electrical connector.
8. Disconnect catalytic converter pipe from exhaust manifold.
9. Lower vehicle, then remove power steering pump support strut upper bolt.
10. Remove exhaust manifold bolts, then exhaust manifold.
11. Reverse procedure to install. Tighten bolts to specifications.

LEFT

1. Remove bolts attaching crossover pipe to exhaust manifold.
2. Disconnect lefthand cylinder bank spark plug wires.
3. Remove heat shield bolts.
4. Remove exhaust manifold bolts, then exhaust manifold.
5. Reverse procedure to install. Tighten bolts to specifications.

CYLINDER HEAD

REPLACE

Removal

1. Drain cooling system.
2. Remove intake manifold and throttle body as outlined under "Intake Manifold, Replace."
3. Disconnect coil wires, sending unit wire, heater hoses and bypass hose.
4. Remove closed ventilation system, evaporation control system and cylinder head covers.
5. Remove exhaust manifolds.

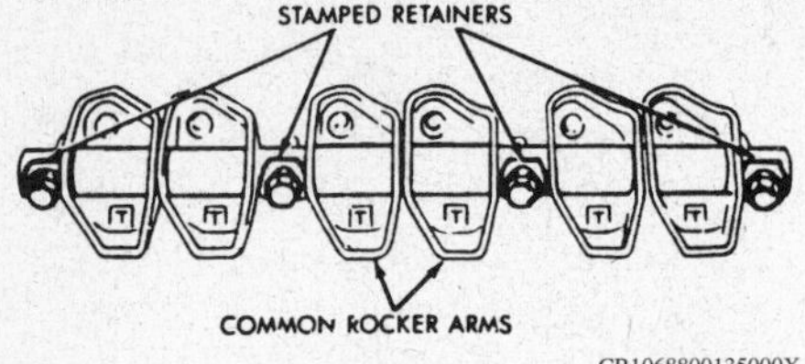

CR1068800135000X

Fig. 7 Rocker arm shaft retainers

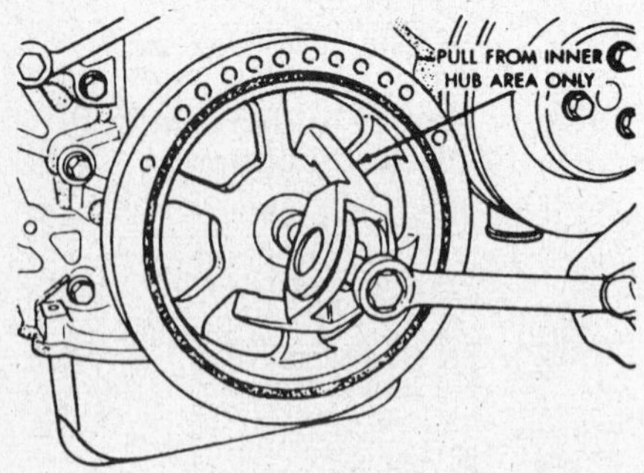

CR1068800123000X

Fig. 9 Crankshaft pulley removal

6. Remove rocker arm and shaft assemblies. Remove pushrods noting position for installation in their original locations.
7. Remove bolts attaching each cylinder head, then cylinder heads.

Installation

1. Clean all surfaces of cylinder heads and cylinder block.
2. Install new head gaskets on cylinder block, **Fig. 4.**
3. Install cylinder heads on cylinder block.
4. Examine cylinder head bolts for stretching as outlined in, **Fig. 5.** Replace any stretched bolts.
5. Tighten cylinder head bolts 1 through 8 in four steps using sequence outlined in **Fig. 6.**
   a. **Torque** all bolts in sequence to 45 ft. lbs.
   b. **Torque** all bolts in sequence to 65 ft. lbs.
   c. **Torque** all bolts in sequence again to 65 ft. lbs.
   d. Turn each bolt an additional ¼ turn, noting bolt torque. **If bolt torque is not over 90 ft. lbs., after tightening an additional ¼ turn, bolt should be replaced and entire tightening procedure repeated.**
6. Install pushrods, rocker arm and shaft assemblies with stamped steel retainers positioned as outlined, **Fig. 7.** Tighten to specifications.
7. Install new cylinder head cover gaskets, then install cylinder head covers. Tighten to specifications.
8. Reverse remaining removal procedure to complete installation.

VALVE ADJUSTMENT

This engine uses hydraulic lash adjusters, no adjustment is required.

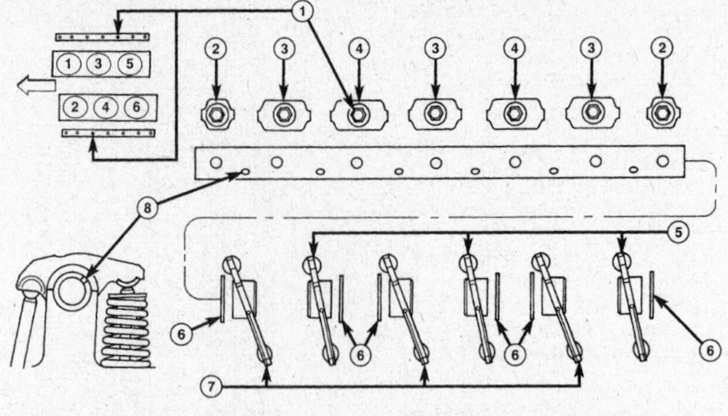

1 - BOLT (ROCKER SHAFT OIL FEED - LONGER LENGTH)
2 - SHAFT RETAINER/SPACER - 21.5 mm (0.84 in.)
3 -SHAFT RETAINER/SPACER - 37.5 mm (1.47 in.)
4 - SHAFT RETAINER/SPACER - 40.9 mm (1.61 in.)
5 - ROCKER ARM - EXHAUST
6 - WASHER
7 - ROCKER ARM - INTAKE (LARGER OFFSET)
8 - ROCKER ARMS LUBRICATION FEED HOLE (POSITION UPWARD & TOWARD VALVE SPRING

CR1060100949000X

Fig. 8 Rocker arms and shaft

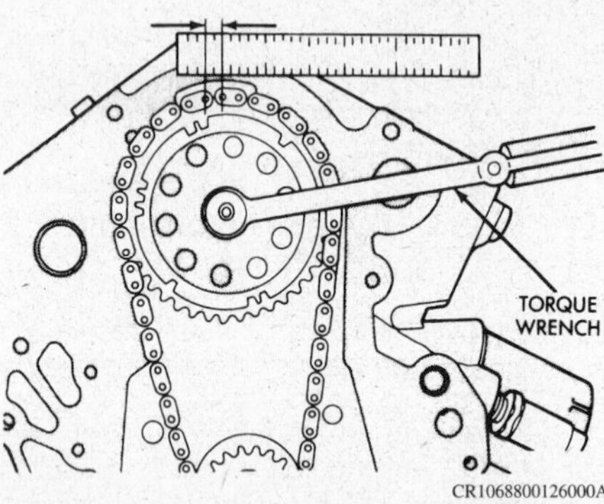

CR1068800126000A

Fig. 10 Timing chain movement inspection

ROCKER ARMS

Rocker Arms & Shaft Assembly, Replace

1. Remove cylinder head covers.
2. Loosen rocker shaft bolts one turn each until all valve spring pressure is relieved.
3. Remove rocker arm and shaft assembly.
4. Reverse procedure to install, noting the following:
   a. Ensure longer shaft retaining bolt is installed in proper location, **Fig. 8.**
   b. Tighten rocker arm bolts to specifications. **Rocker arm shaft should be tightened slowly, starting with center bolts. Allow 20 minutes tappet bleed down time after installation of rocker shafts before engine operation.**

TIMING CHAIN

REPLACE

Cover Removal

1. Drain engine coolant into suitable container.
2. Raise and support vehicle, then drain engine oil into suitable container.
3. Remove righthand wheel, then inner splash shield.

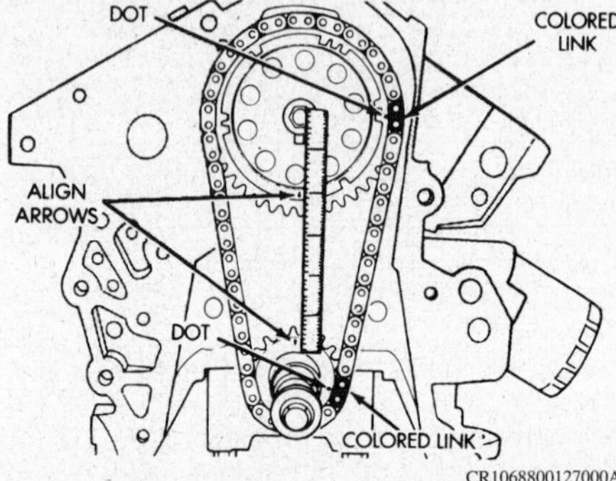

CR1068800127000A

Fig. 11 Timing mark alignment

4. Remove oil pan, then oil pick-up tube.
5. Remove drive belt, then A/C compressor positioning aside.
6. Remove crankshaft pulley, **Fig. 9.**
7. Remove lower radiator hose, then heater hose from timing chain cover.
8. Remove righthand engine mount as outlined under "Engine Mount, Replace."
9. Remove idler pulley from engine bracket, then engine mount bracket.
10. Remove cam sensor from timing chain cover.
11. Remove water pump as outlined under "Water Pump, Replace" for timing cover removal clearance.
12. Remove bolt attaching power steering pump support strut to front cover.
13. Remove front cover bolts, then front cover.

Chain Inspection

1. Place a scale next to timing chain so chain movement can be measured.
2. Install a torque wrench and socket over camshaft sprocket, then apply torque in direction of crankshaft rotation to take up chain slack. Apply 30 ft. lbs., of torque with cylinder heads installed or 15 ft. lbs., of torque with cylinder heads removed. **With torque applied to camshaft sprocket bolt, crankshaft should not move. It may be required to block crankshaft to prevent rotation.**

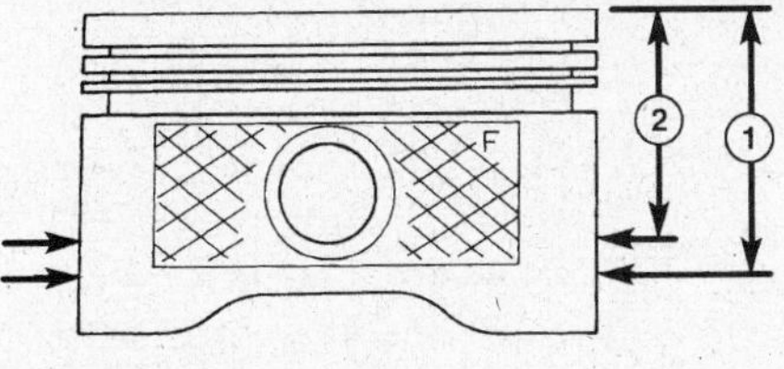

Fig. 12 Piston measurement

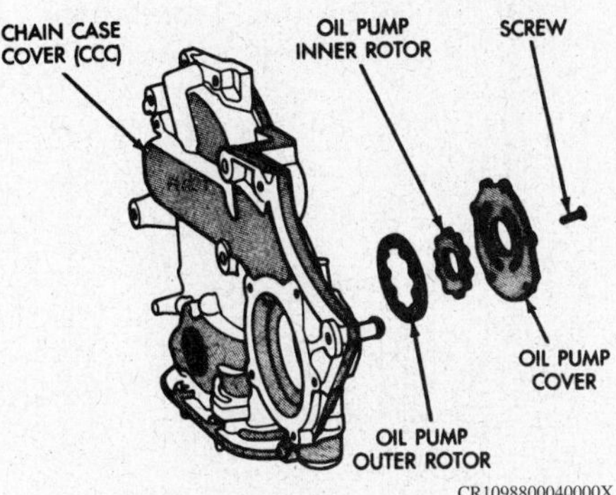

Fig. 15 Oil pump components

3. Holding a scale with dimension reading even with edge of a chain link, apply specified torque in reverse direction and note amount of chain movement, **Fig. 10.**
4. If timing chain movement exceeds ⅛ inch, replace chain.

Chain Replacement

1. Remove camshaft sprocket attaching cup washer, then remove timing chain with crankshaft and camshaft sprockets.
2. Install new timing chain around both sprockets.
3. Turn crankshaft and camshaft to align keyway locations in both sprockets.
4. Lift sprocket and chain, keeping sprockets tight against chain in position.
5. Slide both sprockets with chain evenly over their respective shafts, then use a straightedge to inspect alignment of timing marks, **Fig. 11.**
6. Install cup washer and camshaft sprocket bolt. Tighten bolt to specifications.
7. Inspect camshaft endplay. Endplay should measure .005–.012 inch with a new thrust plate or up to .012 inch with a used thrust plate. If camshaft endplay is not as specified, replace thrust plate.
8. Install timing chain cover.

Cover Installation & Oil Seal Replacement

1. Ensure mating surfaces of chain case cover are clean and free of burrs. **Crankshaft oil seal must be removed to ensure correct oil pump engagement.**
2. Remove crankshaft oil seal using removal tool No. 6314A, or equivalent.
3. Position new gasket on timing cover ensuring lower edge of gasket is flush to .020 inch passed lower edge of cover. **Do not use sealer on cover gasket.**
4. Rotate crankshaft so that oil pump drive flats are in vertical position.
5. Position oil pump inner rotor so mating flats are in same position as crankshaft drive flats.
6. Install timing cover. Tighten bolts to specifications.
7. Install crankshaft oil seal using installer tool No. C-4992-1, or equivalent until seal is flush with cover.
8. Reverse remaining removal procedure to complete installation.

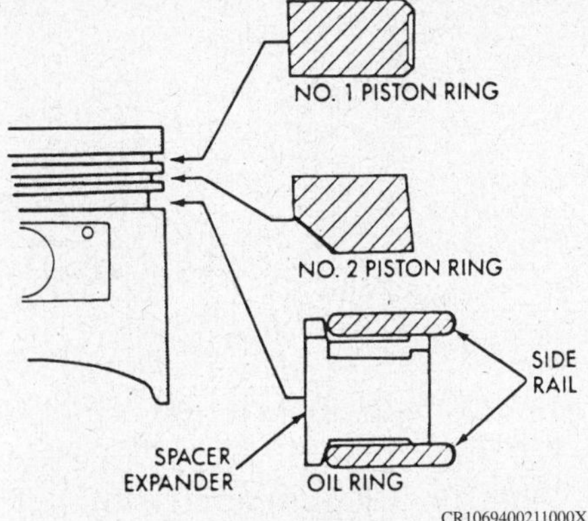

Fig. 13 Piston ring installation

CAMSHAFT

REPLACE

1. Remove engine as outlined under "Engine, Replace."
2. Remove intake manifold as outlined under "Intake Manifold, Replace."
3. Remove timing case cover and chain as outlined under "Timing Chain, Replace."
4. Remove rocker arm and shaft assemblies and cylinder heads as outlined under "Cylinder Head, Replace."
5. Remove camshaft thrust plate.
6. Install a long bolt into camshaft to facilitate removal of camshaft, then remove camshaft.
7. Reverse procedure to install, noting following:
   a. Tighten to specifications.
   b. If new camshaft is installed, new tappets must be used.

PISTON & ROD ASSEMBLY

When installing piston and rod assemblies notch in piston top or F mark near piston pin must point toward front of engine

Refer to **Figs. 12 through 14** for piston measurements and ring installation.

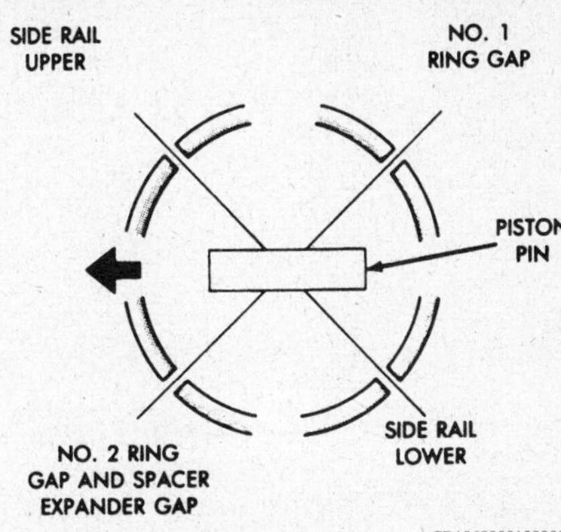

Fig. 14 Ring end gap orientation

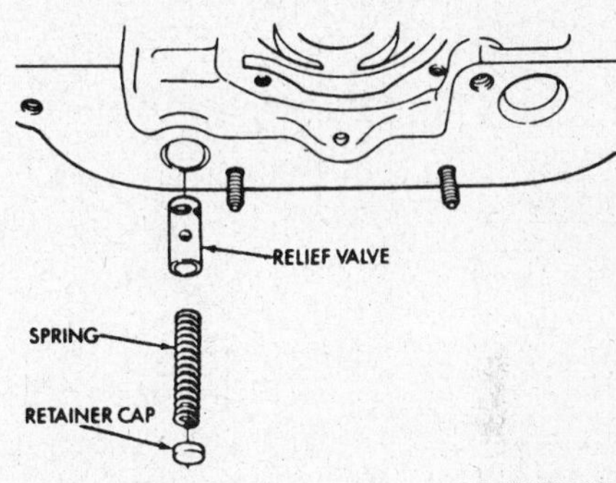

Fig. 16 Oil pressure relief valve components

OIL PAN

REPLACE

1. Raise and support vehicle, then drain engine oil into suitable container.
2. Remove drive belt splash shield.
3. Remove strut to transaxle bolt, then loosen strut to engine block bolt.
4. Remove transaxle case cover, then oil pan bolts.
5. Remove oil pan.
6. Reverse procedure to install noting the following:
   a. Apply a ⅛ inch bead of Mopar Engine RTV GEN II, or equivalent to parting line of chain case cover and rear seal retainer.

OIL PUMP SERVICE

It is required to remove oil pan, oil pickup and chain case cover to service oil pump rotors, **Fig. 15.** Oil pump relief valve can be serviced by removing oil pan and oil pickup tube.

Disassemble

1. Remove relief valve as follows:
   a. Drill a ⅛ inch hole into relief valve retainer cap, **Fig. 16,** then insert a self-threading sheet metal screw into cap.
   b. Clamp screw in a vise, then while supporting chain case cover (CCC), remove cap by tapping CCC with a soft hammer.

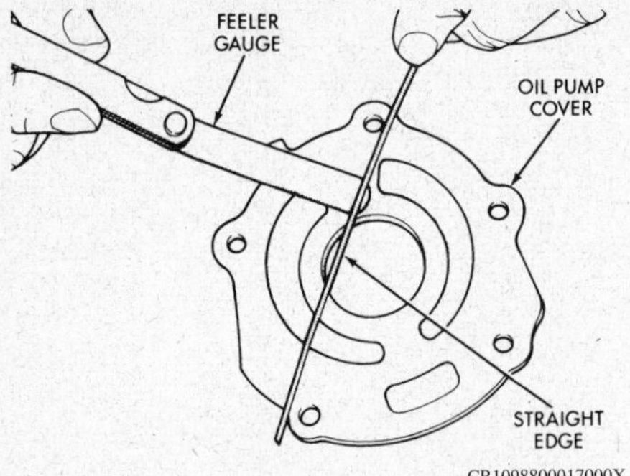

Fig. 17 Oil pump cover flatness inspection

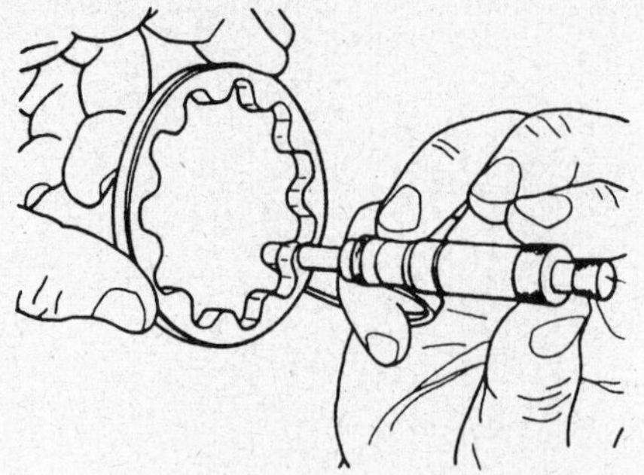

Fig. 18 Oil pump outer rotor thickness inspection

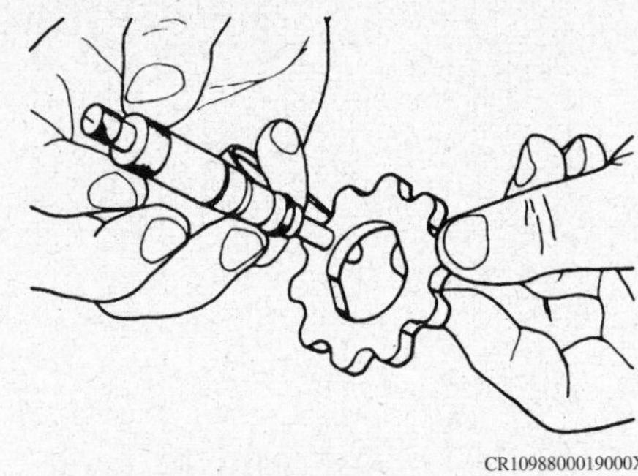

Fig. 19 Oil pump inner rotor thickness inspection

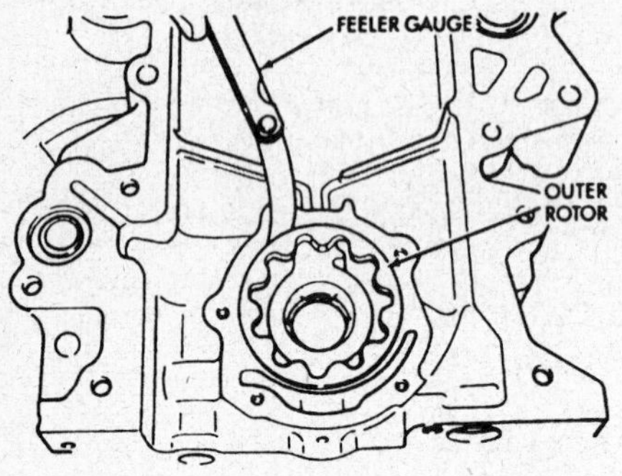

Fig. 20 Oil pump outer rotor clearance in case inspection

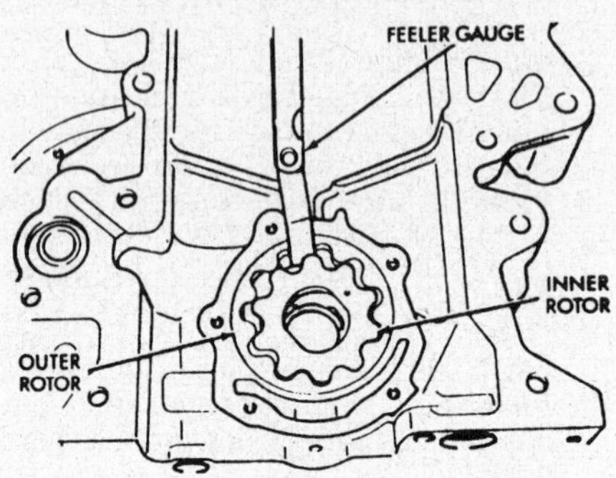

Fig. 21 Oil pump rotor clearance inspection

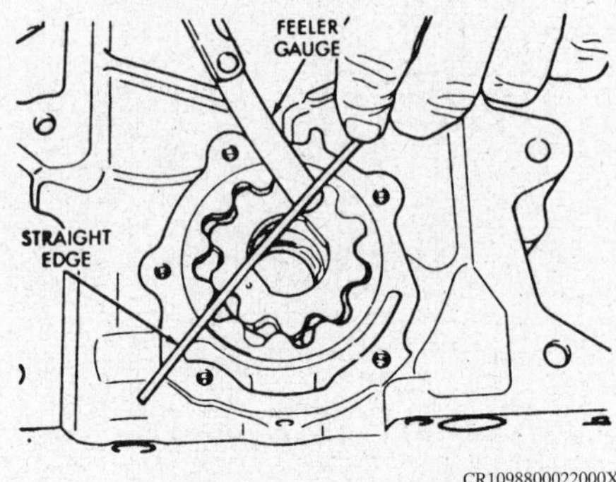

Fig. 22 Oil pump rotor to case clearance inspection

  c. Discard retainer cap, then remove relief spring and relief valve, **Fig. 16.**
2. Remove oil pump cover screws, then lift off cover, **Fig. 15.**
3. Remove pump rotors, **Fig. 15.**
4. Wash all components in a suitable solvent and inspect for damage or wear.

Inspection & Repair

1. Clean all components thoroughly. Mating surfaces of cover should be smooth. Replace pump cover if scratched or grooved.
2. Lay a straightedge across pump cover surface, **Fig. 17.**
3. If a .001 inch feeler gauge can be inserted between cover and straightedge, replace cover.
4. Measure thickness and diameter of outer rotor, **Fig. 18.** If outer rotor thickness measures .301 inch or less, or if diameter is 3.148 inches on or less, replace outer rotor.
5. If inner rotor thickness, **Fig. 19,** measures .301 inch or less, replace inner rotor and shaft assembly.
6. Install outer rotor into cover, press one side with fingers and measure clearance between outer rotor and cover, **Fig. 20.** If measurement is .015 inch or more, and if outer rotor is within specifications, replace cover only.
7. Install inner rotor into cover, then measure clearance between inner and outer rotors, **Fig. 21.** If clearance measured between rotors is .008 inch or more, replace both rotors.
8. Place a straightedge across face of CCC between bolt holes, **Fig. 22.** If a feeler gauge of .004 inch or more can be inserted between rotors and straightedge, replace pump assembly.
9. Inspect oil pressure relief valve plunger for scoring and free operation in it's bore. Small marks can be removed with 400 grit wet or dry sandpaper.
10. Relief valve spring has a free length of approximately 1.95 inches and should test between 19.5–20.5 pounds when compressed to 1 11/32 inches. Replace spring that does not meet specifications.

Assemble & Installation

1. Assemble oil pump as outlined, **Figs. 15 and 16,** using new components as required.
2. Tighten oil pump cover screws to specifications.
3. Prime oil pump prior to installation by filling rotor cavity with engine oil.
4. Refer to "Timing Chain, Replace" to install timing chain case cover.

BELT TENSION DATA

Belt tension is controlled automatically by the dynamic tensioner.

SERPENTINE DRIVE BELT

Routing

Refer to **Fig. 23** for serpentine belt routing.

Replacement

Refer to **Fig. 23** for serpentine belt replacement, noting the following:

1. Raise vehicle and support vehicle.
2. Remove drive belt shield.
3. Rotate dynamic tensioner counterclockwise to release tension.

COOLING SYSTEM BLEED

These engines do require a specific bleed procedure. Fill radiator with water/coolant mixture, then fill coolant recovery container to the MAX mark. To remove air trapped in the cooling system, operate engine through three or four warm up and cool down cycles, then inspect container level. If required fill container to MAX level.

THERMOSTAT

REPLACE

1. Drain cooling system below thermostat level.

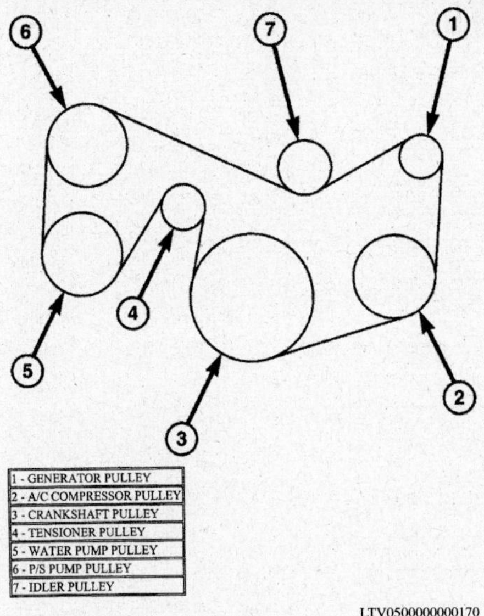

Fig. 23 Serpentine drive belt routing

2. Remove upper radiator hose from coolant outlet housing.
3. Remove coolant outlet housing attaching bolts, then housing.
4. Remove thermostat from coolant outlet housing, discard gasket and clean both gasket sealing surfaces.
5. Reverse procedure to install.

WATER PUMP

REPLACE

1. Drain cooling system into suitable container.
2. Remove accessory drive belt shield.
3. Release belt tension by rotating tensioner counterclockwise, then remove accessory drive belt.
4. Remove water pump pulley bolts.
5. Rotate pulley until openings in pulley align with water pump hub spokes, then move pulley inward between pump housing and hub, **Fig. 24.**
6. Position pulley to allow access to water pump mounting bolts, then remove bolts.
7. Remove water pump and pulley together.
8. Remove and discard O-ring, then clean O-ring groove and seal surfaces.
9. Reverse procedure to install.

RADIATOR

REPLACE

1. Remove radiator upper crossmember support.
2. Drain engine coolant into suitable container, then remove radiator fans.
3. Disconnect coolant reserve/recovery hose.
4. Remove vapor purge solenoid from mounting bracket, then disconnect upper and lower radiator hoses.
5. Remove A/C condenser side brackets to radiator screws, then separate condenser from radiator by lifting upward to disengage from lower mounts.
6. Lift radiator from vehicle.
7. Reverse procedure to install.

FUEL PUMP

REPLACE

1. Relieve fuel pressure as outlined under "Precautions."
2. Drain fuel from fuel tank into suitable container.
3. Remove fuel tank using suitable jack.
4. Remove fuel pump module lock ring using tool No. 9340, or equivalent.
5. Remove fuel pump. Do not reuse O-ring.
6. Reverse procedure to install.

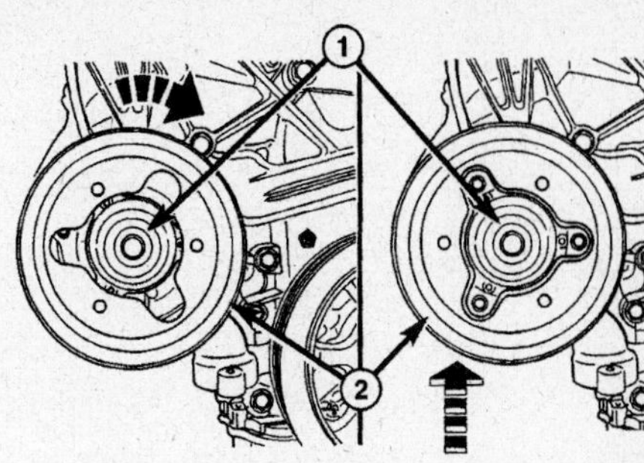

1 - HUB - WATER PUMP
2 - PULLEY - WATER PUMP

LTV0500000000171

Fig. 24 Water pump pulley positioning

FUEL FILTER

REPLACE

1. Remove fuel pump module as outlined under "Fuel Pump, Replace."
2. Pry back locking tabs on fuel pump reservoir.
3. Remove strainer and O-ring from reservoir body.
4. Revers procedure to install.

TIGHTENING SPECIFICATIONS

Year	Component	Torque Ft. Lbs.
2002–06	Alternator Mounting Bolts	40
	Camshaft Sprocket Lockbolt	40
	Camshaft Thrust Plate	105①
	Connecting Rod Nut	②
	Cylinder Head Bolt	③
	Cylinder Head Cover Bolts	105②
	Engine Bracket	40
	Exhaust Crossover Pipe Flange Nut/Bolt	40
	Exhaust Manifold Bolts	17
	Fuel Rail Bolts	95①
	Fuel Tube Retaining Bracket Screw	35①
	Intake Manifold Bolt, Lower	17
	Intake Manifold Bolt, Upper	21
	Main Bearing Cap Bolt	④
	Oil Pan Bolts	105①
	Oil Pan Drain Plug	20
	Oil Pump Cover Screws	105①
	Starter Mounting Bolts	40
	Tappet Yoke Retainer	105①
	Thermostat Housing Bolts	105①
	Timing Chain Case Cover Bolts	⑤
	Water Pump Pulley Bolts	21
	Water Pump To Chain Case Cover Bolt	105①

①— Inch lbs.
②— 40 ft. lbs., plus ¼ turn.
③— Refer to "Cylinder Head, Replace."
④— 30 ft. lbs., plus ¼ turn.
⑤— M-8 bolts, 20 ft. lbs., M-10 bolts, 40 ft. lbs.

Rear Axle & Suspension

INDEX

PRECAUTIONS

Battery Ground Cable

Prior to service, disconnect battery ground cable and isolate as required.

REAR AXLE

REPLACE

FWD Models

1. Raise and support vehicle, then remove rear wheel and tire assemblies.
2. Remove brake assemblies and ABS sensors.
3. Support axle with suitable jack, then remove shock absorber lower bolts, **Fig. 1. If bolts deflect upward during removal, raise axle by adjusting jack. If bolts deflect downward during removal, lower axle by adjusting jack.**
4. Remove track bar bolt and nut, then remove leaf spring mounting pad bolts.
5. Lower axle assembly from vehicle.
6. Reverse procedure to install, noting the following:
   a. Install track bar nut and bolt finger tight. **Do not tighten fully until vehicle is lowered and full vehicle weight is applied to rear axle.**
   b. Tighten to specifications.

WHEEL BEARING

REPLACE

AWD Models

1. Set parking brake, then raise and support vehicle.
2. Remove wheel and tire assembly.
3. Remove cotter pin and nut retainer from stub shaft of outer C/V joint.
4. Remove hub nut and washer.
5. Remove six bolts mounting drive shaft inner joint to output shaft of rear drive line module.
6. Remove rear wheel speed sensor, then release parking brake.
7. Remove disc brake caliper to adapter guide pin bolts.
8. Remove rear caliper from adapter by rotating rear of caliper up from adapter, then pulling front of caliper and outboard brake shoe anti-rattle clip out from under front abutment on adapter.
9. Remove brake rotor from hub/bearing.
10. Remove driveshaft from rear drive line module and hub/bearing.
11. Remove hub/bearing to axle mounting bolts, then hub/bearing.
12. Reverse procedure to install. Tighten hub/bearing bolts in a criss-cross pattern to specifications.

FWD Models

1. Raise and support vehicle, then remove wheel and tire.
2. Remove brake caliper, then the rotor.
3. **On models equipped with anti-lock brakes,** proceed as follows:
   a. Remove secondary yellow retaining clip at rear of wheel speed sensor head.
   b. Push up on metal clip up, then pull back on wheel speed sensor head removing it from hub and bearing.
4. **On all models,** remove four bolts attaching hub and bearing to rear axle.
5. If hub and bearing cannot be removed from axle by hand proceed, press hub and bearing out of axle using tool No. 8458, or equivalent as follows:
   a. Thread guide pins into hub and bearing mounting bolt holes, then remove two outboard spring plate bolts.
   b. Install screw mount tool No. 8458-2, or equivalent using spring plate bolts, **Fig. 2.**
   c. Place push plate tool No. 8458-1, or equivalent on ends of threaded guide pins.
   d. Apply a small amount of grease in dimple of push plate.
   e. Tighten forcing screw tool No. 8458-3, or equivalent against dimple in push plate pressing hub and bearing out of axle.
6. Remove hub and bearing from rear axle.
7. Reverse procedure to install. Tighten hub and bearing bolts in a criss-cross pattern to specifications.

SHOCK ABSORBER

REPLACE

1. Raise and support vehicle.
2. Support axle with suitable jack, then remove shock absorber lower bolts. **If bolts deflect upward during removal, raise axle by adjusting jack. If bolts deflect downward during removal, lower axle by adjusting jack.**
3. While holding shock, remove upper shock bolt.
4. Reverse procedure to install, noting the following:
   a. Install shock absorber bolts finger tight.
   b. Tighten bolts to specifications with vehicle lowered and full vehicle weight on axle.

LEAF SPRING

REPLACE

Removal

1. Raise and support vehicle.
2. Support axle with suitable jack, then remove shock absorber lower bolts. **If bolts deflect upward during removal, raise axle by adjusting jack. If bolts deflect downward during removal, lower axle by adjusting jack.**
3. Raise and support axle assembly to remove axle weight from springs.
4. Remove axle plate bolts from springs.
5. Lower rear axle assembly, allowing rear springs to hang free.
6. Remove four attaching bolts from front spring hanger.
7. Remove rear spring shackle attaching nuts and plate, then shackle from spring.
8. Remove springs from vehicle.
9. Remove front pivot bolt from front spring hanger.

Installation

1. Assemble front spring mount to front of spring and install pivot bolt. **Do not tighten.**
2. Raise front of spring and install four hanger bolts, then tighten hanger bolts to specifications.
3. Install rear of spring onto rear spring shackle, then install shackle plate. **Do not tighten.**
4. Ensure lower spring isolator is in position, then raise axle assembly into correct position with axle centered under spring locator post, **Fig. 3.**
5. Install axle plate bolts, then tighten axle plate bolts to specifications.
6. Install lower shock absorber bolts. **Do not tighten.**
7. Lower vehicle, then with full vehicle weight applied to axle, tighten front pivot bolt, shackle nuts and shock absorber bolts to specifications.

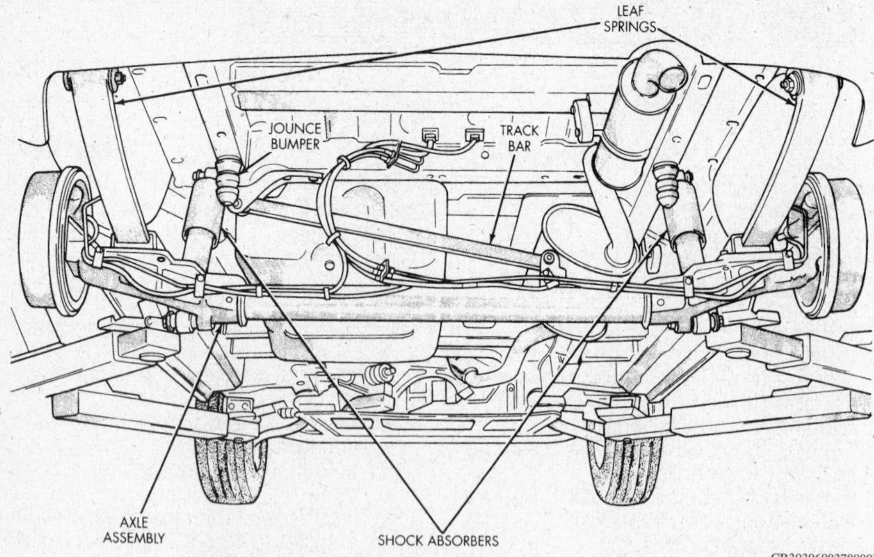

CR3039600378000X

Fig. 1 Rear axle & suspension assembly. FWD models

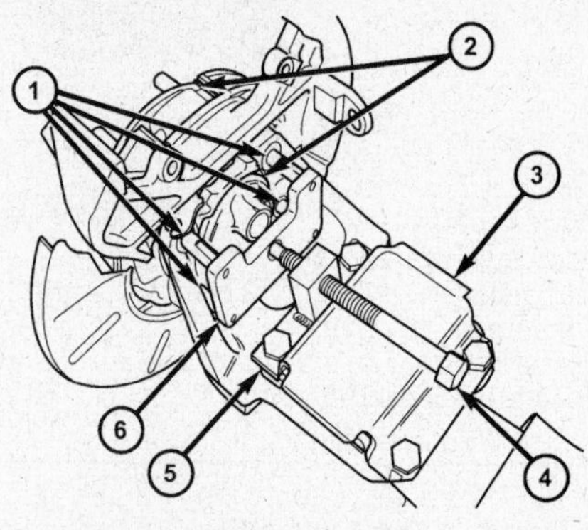

1 - THREADED GUIDE PINS 8458-4
2 - HUB AND BEARING
3 - LEAF SPRING PLATE
4 - FORCING SCREW 8458-3
5 - SCREW MOUNT 8458-2
6 - PUSH PLATE 8458-1

CR2030100106000X

Fig. 2 Hub & bearing removal. FWD models

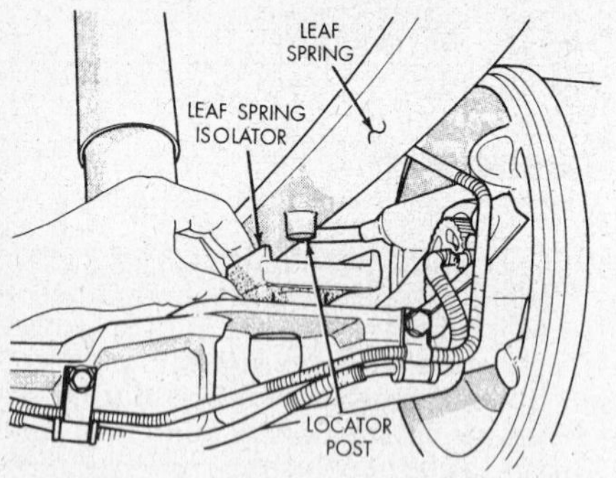

CR3039600380000X

Fig. 3 Leaf spring locator post

STABILIZER BAR

REPLACE

1. Raise and support vehicle.
2. Remove stabilizer bar to link attaching bolts on each side of bar.
3. While holding stabilizer bar in place, remove bolts that attach stabilizer bar bushing retainers to rear axle.
4. Remove stabilizer bar, **Fig. 4.**
5. Reverse procedure to install.

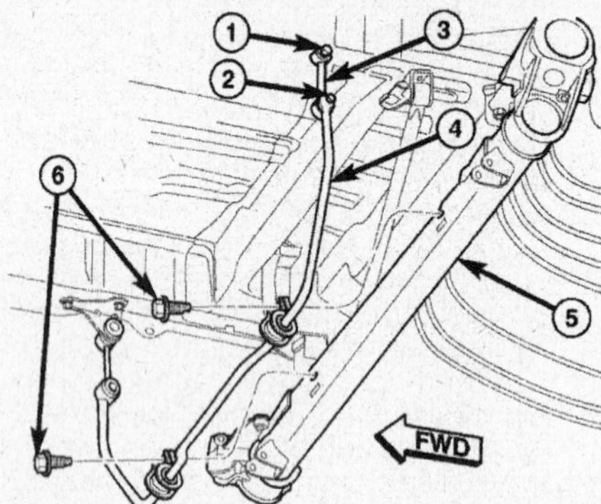

1 - LINK NUT
2 - LINK BOLT AND NUT
3 - STABILIZER LINK
4 - STABILIZER BAR
5 - REAR AXLE
6 - BOLTS

LTV0500000000172

Fig. 4 Stabilizer bar. w/ Fold-In-Floor seating

TRACK BAR, REPLACE

1. Remove lower track bar nut and bolt at axle, **Fig. 5.**
2. Remove upper track bar bolt and nut.

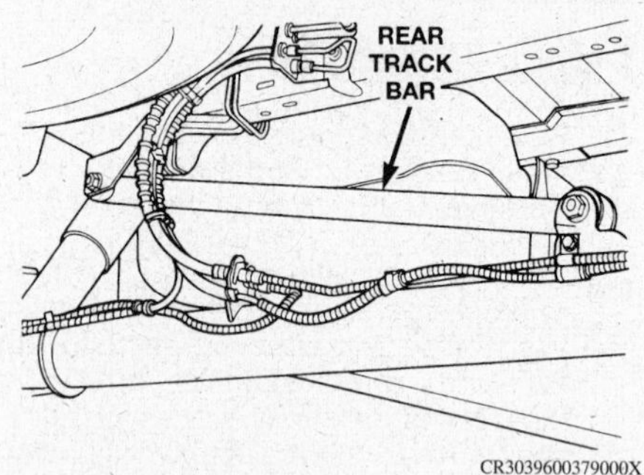

CR3039600379000X

Fig. 5 Rear track bar assembly

3. Remove track bar.
4. Remove three track bar mount retaining bolts.
5. Remove track bar mount.
6. Reverse procedure to install, noting the following:
   a. Install track bar mount retaining bolts and tighten to specifications.
   b. Install track bar bolts with bolt heads facing rear of vehicle.
   c. Tighten bolts to specifications with vehicle lowered and full vehicle weight on axle.

TIGHTENING SPECIFICATIONS

Year	Component	Torque Ft. Lbs.
2002–06	Axle Nut	150
	Brake Assembly Mounting Bolts	95
	Driveshaft Nut	150
	Hub Bearing Mounting Bolts	95
	Hub Nut	150
	Leaf Spring To Hanger Mounting Nut	115
	Shackle Plate Nuts	45
	Shock Absorber Bolts	75
	Spring Front Mount To Body	45
	Spring Plate To Axle	80
	Spring Rear Mount To Body	45
	Track Bar Bolts	70
	Track Bar Bracket To Body	45
	Wheel Lug Nuts	95

Front Suspension & Steering

NOTE: On Air Bag Equipped Models, Refer To "Air Bag System Precautions" Located In The Front Of This Manual For System Disarming & Arming Procedures.

NOTE: Refer To "Computer Relearn Procedures" Located In The Front Of This Manual When Battery Power To The Computer Has Been Interrupted.

INDEX

PRECAUTIONS

Air Bag Systems

Refer to "Air Bag System Precautions" in the front of this manual for system disarming and arming procedures.

Battery Ground Cable

Prior to service, disconnect battery ground cable and isolate as required.

DESCRIPTION

These vehicles use a McPherson type front suspension with vertical shock absorber struts attached to upper fender reinforcement and steering knuckle. The lower control arms are attached inboard to a crossmember and outboard to steering knuckle through a ball joint to provide lower steering knuckle position. During steering maneuvers, strut and steering knuckle rotate as an assembly.

The driveshafts are attached inboard to transaxle output drive flanges and outboard to driven wheel hub.

HUB & BEARING

REPLACE

1. Raise and support vehicle, then remove front wheel and tire assembly.
2. Remove cotter pin, nut lock and spring washer from stub axle.
3. With brakes applied loosen but do not remove hub nut. **Hub and driveshaft are splined together through knuckle and retained by hub nut.**
4. Remove front disc brake caliper to steering knuckle mounting bolts, then remove caliper and support with suitable wire hook. **Do not allow caliper to hang by hydraulic hose.**
5. Remove braking disc from hub and bearing assembly, then remove hub nut and washer from stub axle.
6. Remove four hub and bearing assembly mounting nuts from rear of steering knuckle, then remove hub and bearing assembly.
7. Reverse procedure to install, noting the following:
   a. Tighten to specifications.
   b. Inspect wheel alignment after installation.

DRIVESHAFT

REPLACE

1. Remove cotter pin, nut lock and spring washer from stub axle.
2. With brakes applied loosen but do not remove hub nut. **Hub and driveshaft are splined together through knuckle and retained by hub nut.**
3. Raise and support vehicle, then remove front wheel and tire assembly.
4. Remove front disc brake caliper to steering knuckle mounting bolts.
5. Remove caliper and support with suitable wire hook. **Do not allow caliper to hang by hydraulic hose.**

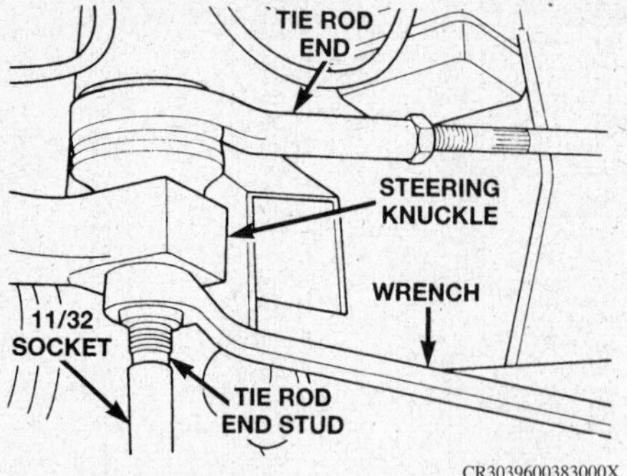

Fig. 1 Tie rod end nut removal

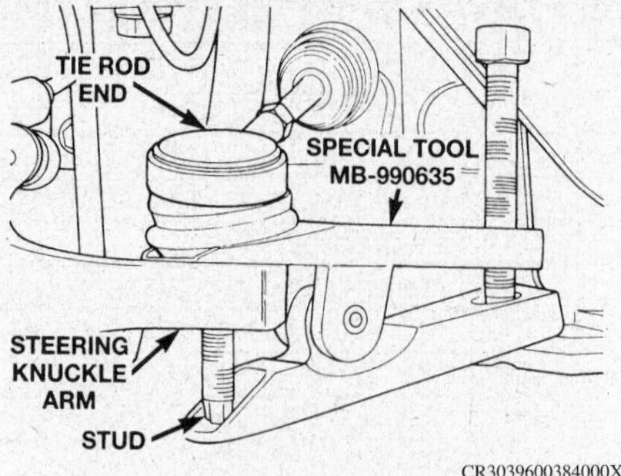

Fig. 2 Tie rod end removal

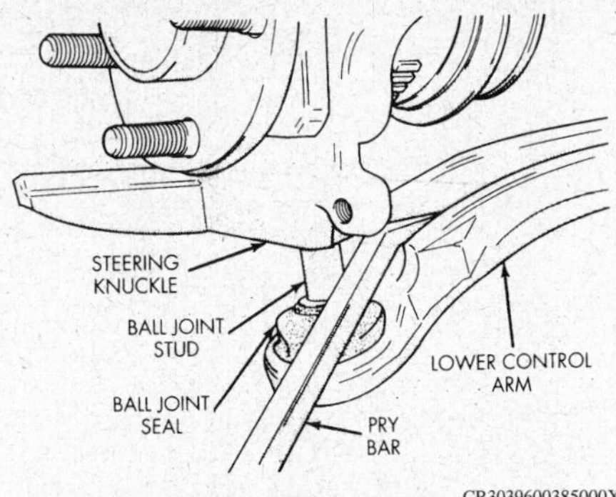

Fig. 3 Steering knuckle & ball joint separation

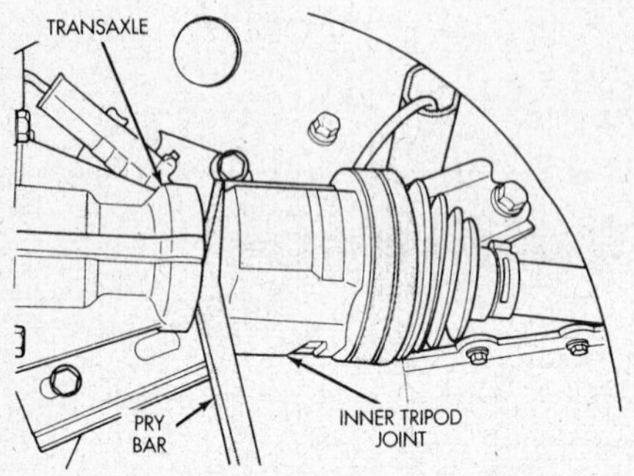

Fig. 4 Righthand side inner tripod joint removal

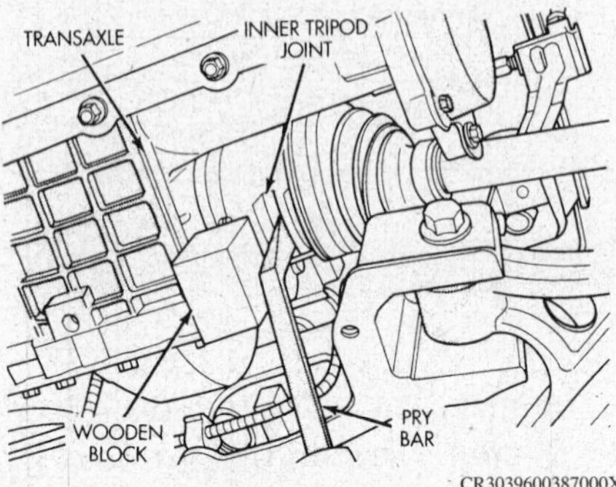

Fig. 5 Lefthand side inner tripod joint removal

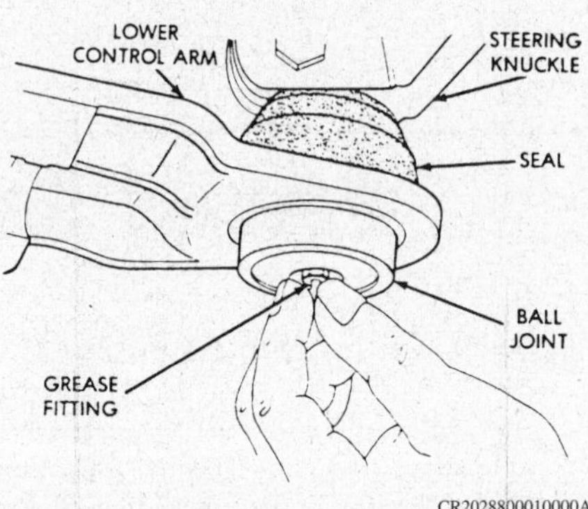

Fig. 6 Ball joint wear inspection

6. Remove brake disc, then hub nut and washer from stub axle.
7. Hold tie rod end with 11/32 socket, then remove outer tie rod end to steering knuckle nut with a suitable wrench, **Fig. 1.**
8. Remove tie rod end from steering knuckle with removal tool No. MB-990635, or equivalent, **Fig. 2.**
9. Remove wheel speed sensor from steering knuckle, then wheel stop.
10. Remove nut and bolt clamping steering knuckle to ball joint stud.
11. With a suitable pry bar separate steering knuckle from ball joint, **Fig. 3. Do not damage ball joint grease seal.**
12. Pull knuckle assembly out and away from outer CV joint of driveshaft.
13. Insert a suitable pry bar between inner tripod joint and transaxle case, then pry against inner tripod joint until snap ring disengages from transaxle side gear, **Figs. 4 and 5.**
14. While holding inner tripod joint and interconnecting shaft, remove driveshaft assembly by pulling straight out from transaxle side gear. **Do not drag spline or snap ring across sealing lip of transaxle to tripod joint oil seal.**
15. Reverse procedure to install, noting the following:
    a. Thoroughly clean and lubricate spline and oil seal sealing surface on tripod joint with suitable transaxle lubricant.
    b. Insert tripod joint into transaxle side gear and push tripod joint in until snap ring engages with side gear.
    c. Install a new steering knuckle to ball joint clamping bolt and nut.
    d. Tighten hub nut with full vehicle load on axle.

BALL JOINT INSPECTION

Ball joint is not serviced separately. If worn, replace lower control arm. With weight of vehicle resting on wheel and tire assembly, attempt to move grease fitting with fingers, **Fig. 6.** Do not use tool or added force to attempt to move grease fitting. If grease fitting moves freely, replace lower control arm.

COIL SPRING

REPLACE

1. Remove strut damper assembly as outlined under "Strut Damper, Replace."
2. Compress coil spring using suitable tool.
3. Remove strut rod nut while holding strut rod to prevent rotation.
4. Remove mount assembly, **Fig. 7.**
5. Remove coil spring from strut dampener.
6. Inspect mount assembly for deterioration of rubber isolator, retainers for cracks and distortion, and bearings for blinding.
7. Install dust shield, jounce bumper, spacer and seat to top of spring. Mount assembly to rod, then install retainer and rod nut.
8. Position spring retainer alignment notch parallel to dampener lower attaching bracket.
9. Tighten strut rod nut to specifications, using suitable tool, then release spring compressor.
10. With weight of vehicle off front wheels, turn both strut rod and strut rod nut in same direction until upper spring seat is properly positioned, then inspect torque of strut rod nut.

CONTROL ARM

REPLACE

Removal

1. Raise and support vehicle, then remove tire and wheel.
2. Remove steering knuckle as outlined under "Steering Knuckle, Replace."
3. Remove power steering cooler to front suspension cradle crossmember reinforcement bolts.
4. Remove lower control arm rear bushing retainer bolts located on each side of each lower control arm rear bushing.
5. Remove cradle crossmember reinforcement to front suspension cradle crossmember bolts.
6. Remove two bolts securing reinforcement and rear cradle crossmember to body of vehicle, then the reinforcement.
7. Remove pivot bolts attaching front bushing of lower control arm to front suspension cradle crossmember.
8. Remove lower control arm.

Installation

1. Position lower control arm assembly

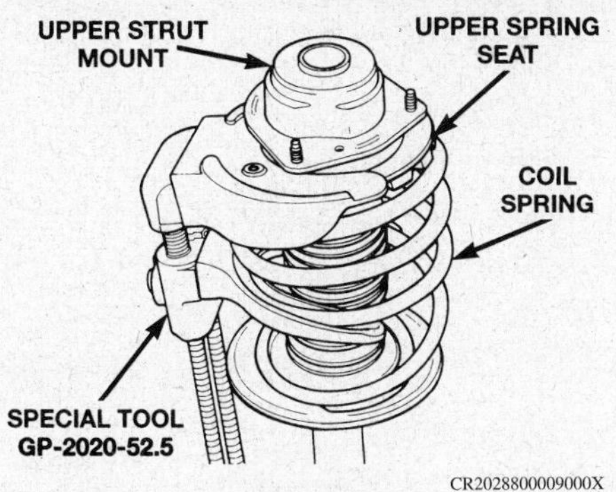

Fig. 7 Strut dampener mount assembly

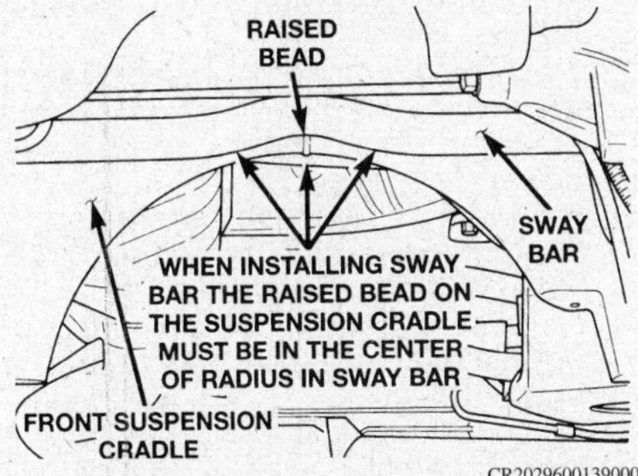

Fig. 10 Stabilizer bar installation

into front suspension cradle crossmember guiding bushings into mounting position.

2. Install new pivot bolt attaching front bushing of lower control arm to front suspension cradie crossmember. Do not tighten bolt at this time.
3. Install reinforcement on front suspension cradle crossmember, then the bolts attaching reinforcement to cradle crossmember. Tighten bolts to specifications.
4. Install lower control arm rear bushing retainer bolts through reinforcement on each side of each lower control arm rear bushing. Tighten bolts to specifications.
5. Install power steering cooler, then steering knuckle.
6. Position jack stands under lower control arms as close to ball joints as possible, then lower vehicle until jack stands are supporting total weight of vehicle.
7. Tighten front lower control arm pivot bolt to specifications.
8. Install tire and wheel, then raise vehicle and remove jack stands.

STEERING KNUCKLE

REPLACE

1. Raise and support vehicle, then remove wheel and tire.
2. Remove cotter pin, nut lock and spring washer from end of stub axle.
3. With brakes applied, remove hub nut.
4. Remove caliper and support with suitable wire hook. **Do not allow caliper to hang by hydraulic hose.**

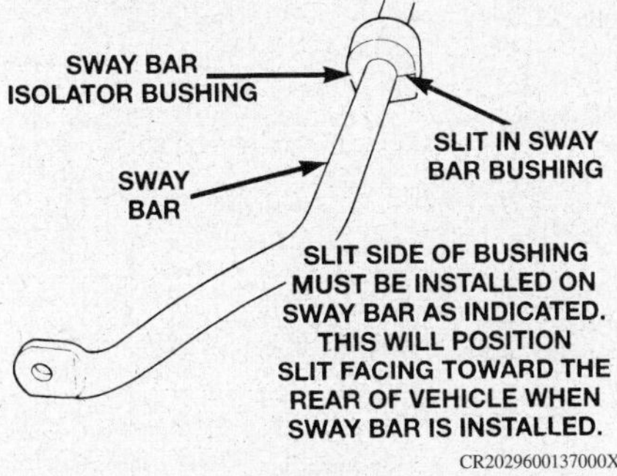

Fig. 8 Stabilizer bar bushing installation

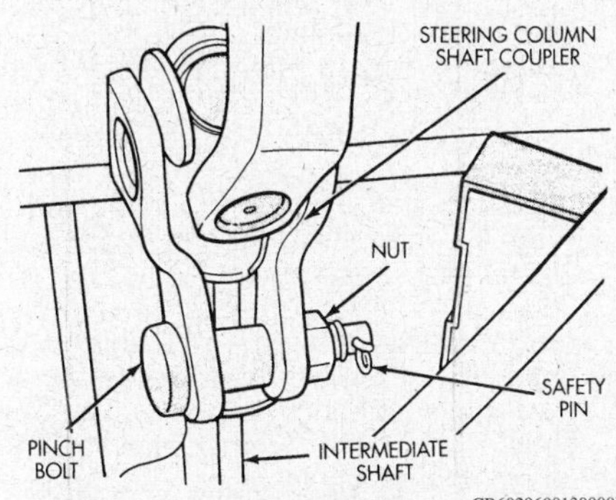

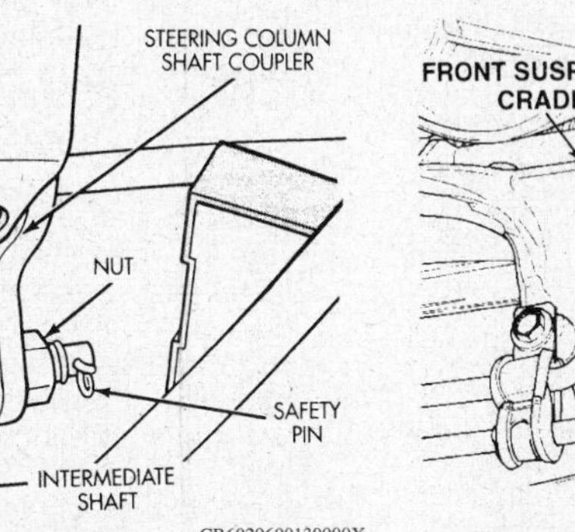

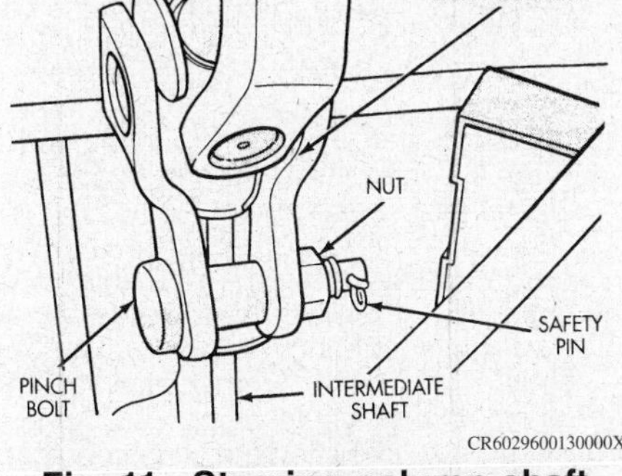

Fig. 11 Steering column shaft coupler to intermediate shaft bolt removal

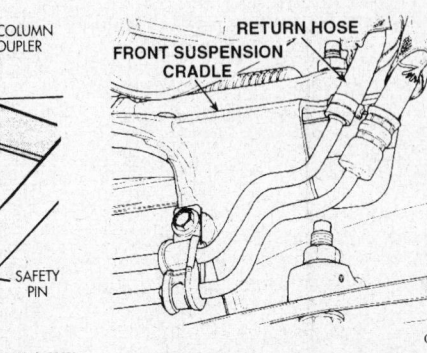

5. Remove nut attaching outer tie rod end to steering knuckle.
6. Remove tie rod end using tool No. C-3894-A, or equivalent.
7. Remove front wheel speed sensor from steering knuckle, then the two steering knuckle to strut clevis bracket bolts.
8. Tip knuckle outward, then remove driveshaft stub axle from hub and bearing. Suspend driveshaft using suitable cord or wire.
9. Remove ball joint nut, then release ball joint stud from steering knuckle using tool No. C-4150-A, or equivalent.
10. Remove steering knuckle from vehicle.
11. Reverse procedure to install. Tighten bolts to specifications.

STABILIZER BAR

REPLACE

1. Raise and support vehicle, then remove power steering cooler to front suspension cradle crossmember bolts.
2. Remove lower control arm rear bushing retainer bolts located on each side of lower control arm rear busing.
3. Remove bolts attaching cradle crossmember reinforcement to front suspension cradle crossmember.
4. Remove two bolts attaching reinforcement and rear cradle crossmember to body of vehicle, then the reinforcement.

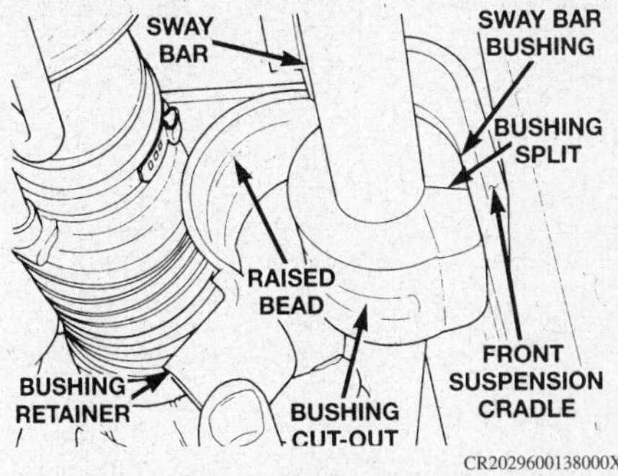

Fig. 9 Stabilizer bar bushing retainer installation

Fig. 12 Power steering fluid return hose connection

5. Remove stabilizer bar links from each end of stabilizer. **When removing nut from stud of stabilizer bar link, do not allow stud to rotate in its socket.**
6. Remove stabilizer bar bushing retainers from front suspension cradle crossmember.
7. Remove stabilizer bar and bushings as an assembly from front suspension cradle crossmember.
8. Reverse procedure to install noting the following:
   a. Install bushings on stabilizer bar so that slit in bushing faces rear of vehicle and flat side faces ground when stabilizer bar is installed, **Fig. 8.**
   b. Position stabilizer bar so bushings are aligned with depression in cradle.
   c. Install bushing retainers so that raised bead is aligned with cutout on bushing, **Fig. 9.**
   d. Center of stabilizer bar curved section must be aligned with raised line in center of front suspension cradle, **Fig. 10.**

STRUT DAMPNER

REPLACE

1. Raise and support vehicle, then remove front wheel and tire assembly.
2. Remove brake hose bracket, then speed sensor cable bracket.

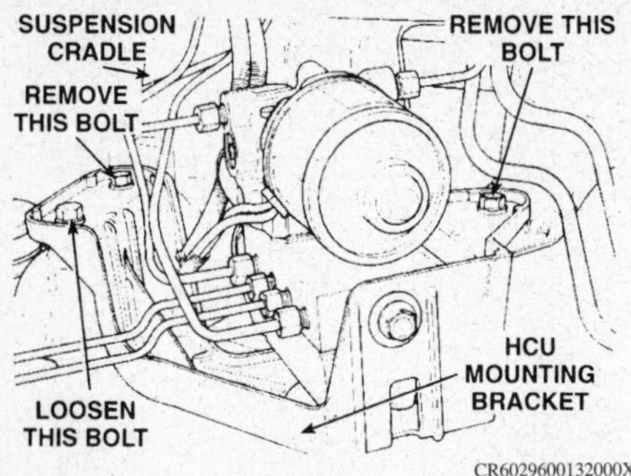

Fig. 13 Hydraulic control unit removal

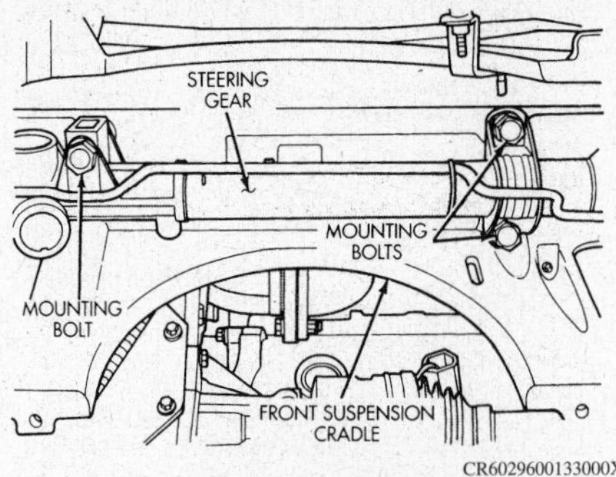

Fig. 14 Steering gear mounting bolt removal

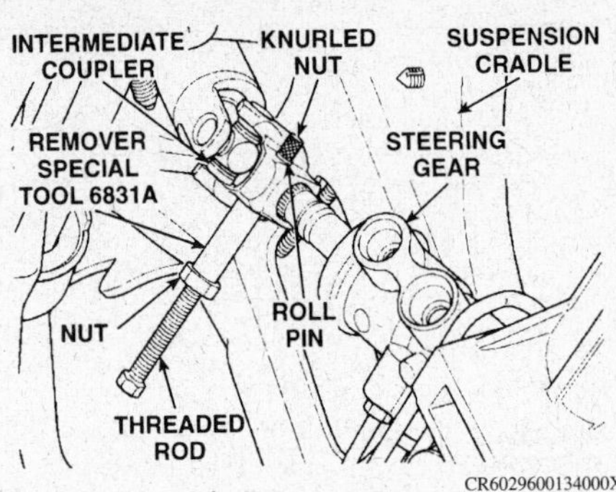

Fig. 15 Intermediate coupler roll pin removal

3. Remove stabilizer bar link from bracket on strut assembly.
4. Remove two strut assembly clevis bracket to steering knuckle mounting bolts.
5. Remove three nuts mounting strut assembly upper mount to strut tower, then strut.
6. Reverse procedure to install, noting the following:
   a. Steering knuckle to strut assembly mounting bolts are serrated and must not be turned during installation. Install nuts while holding bolts stationary in steering knuckles.
   b. If strut assembly is attached to steering knuckle using a cam bolt, then bolt must be installed in lower slotted hole on strut clevis bracket. Bolts should be installed with nuts facing front of vehicle.

POWER STEERING GEAR

REPLACE

1. Place ignition in Off position, then turn steering wheel lefthand until in locked position.
2. Disconnect steering column shaft coupler from intermediate shaft, **Fig. 11,** then raise and support vehicle.
3. Remove front wheel and tire assembly, then disconnect power steering fluid return hose at steel tube connections, **Fig. 12,** and drain into suitable container.
4. Remove tie rod end to steering knuckle mounting nut, then tie rod end from knuckle with puller tool No. MB-990635, or equivalent.
5. Remove anti-lock brake hydraulic control unit (HCU) bolts as outlined in **Fig. 13,** then rotate HCU rearward.
6. Remove ten front suspension cradle plate mounting bolts, then front suspension cradle plate.
7. Remove power steering fluid tube bracket, then the power steering fluid pressure and return hoses at power steering gear.
8. Remove steering gear mounting bolts, **Fig. 14,** then lower steering gear and install replacement tool No. 6831A, or equivalent, through center of intermediate coupler roll pin and secure with knurled nut. Hold threaded rod stationary while rotating knurled nut to remove roll pin from intermediate coupler, **Fig. 15.**
9. Separate intermediate coupler from steering gear, then remove steering gear assembly.
10. Reverse procedure to install.

POWER STEERING PUMP

REPLACE

2.4L Engine

1. Remove cap from power steering fluid reservoir, then siphon as much power steering fluid as possible from reservoir.
2. Raise and support vehicle, then disconnect oxygen sensor wiring harness from vehicle wiring harness at rear engine mount bracket.
3. Remove four bolts securing catalytic converter to exhaust manifold.
4. Disconnect all exhaust system hangers from brackets on exhaust system.
5. Remove exhaust system by moving it rearward as far as possible, then lowering front below crossmember.
6. Remove power steering fluid supply hose from fitting on power steering pump.
7. Move heat sleeve on power steering return hose to expose hose connection at pump, then remove hose from power steering pump.
8. Remove power steering fluid pressure line from power steering pump.
9. Remove drive belt splash shield.
10. Remove adjuster nut attaching rear of power steering pump to cast mounting bracket.
11. Remove front adjuster nut, then the lower pivot bolt.
12. Remove accessory drive belt.
13. Remove power steering pump and front bracket through exhaust tunnel.
14. Reverse procedure to install. Tighten bolts to specifications.

3.3L & 3.8L Engines

1. Remove wiper module, then raise and support vehicle.
2. Remove accessory drive belt splash shield, then loosen pump bracket thru-bolt.
3. Remove pressure hose routing bracket bolt, then lower vehicle.
4. Remove cap from power steering fluid reservoir, then siphon as much fluid as possible from reservoir.
5. Disconnect fluid supply hose from pump, then pressure hose.
6. Remove mounting bolt from rear of pump using care not to lose spacer between pump and bracket.
7. Remove three front mounting bolts through pulley.
8. Remove pump through engine compartment by rocking it over aluminum bracket.
9. Reverse procedure to install. Tighten bolts to specifications.

TIGHTENING SPECIFICATIONS

Year	Component	Torque Ft. Lbs.
2002–06	Axle Nut	180
	Brake Hose Bracket	105①
	Front Brake Caliper Mounting Bolts	16
	Front Lower Control Arm Pivot Bolt	135
	Front Suspension Cradle Plate Mounting Bolts	②
	Hub & Bearing Assembly Mounting Bolts	45
	Hub Nut	180
	Power Steering Fluid Lines	23
	Power Steering Pump Mounting Bolts	40
	Rear Lower Control Arm Bushing Retainer	50
	Speed Sensor	60
	Speed Sensor Cable Bracket	10
	Stabilizer Bar Retainer Mounting Bolts	50
	Stabilizer Link Attaching Nuts	65
	Steering Column Coupler To Intermediate Shaft	21
	Steering Gear To Front Suspension Cradle	135
	Steering Knuckle To Ball Joint	105
	Strut Assembly To Steering Knuckle	65
	Strut Assembly Upper Mount	21
	Strut Damper To Steering Knuckle	65
	Strut Shaft Retaining Nut	75
	Tie Rod End To Steering Knuckle	40
	Wheel Lug Nuts	100

① — Inch lbs.
② — M-12 bolts, 78 ft. lbs., M-14 bolts, 113 ft. lbs.

Wheel Alignment

INDEX

PRELIMINARY INSPECTION

1. Tires are at recommended pressure, are of equal size and have approximately the same wear pattern
2. Inspect front wheel and tire assembly for radial runout and inspect lower ball joints and steering linkage for looseness.
3. Inspect front and rear springs for sagging or damage.
4. Front suspension inspections should be performed on a level floor or alignment rack with fuel tank at capacity, and vehicle free of luggage and passenger compartment load.
5. Prior to each alignment reading, vehicle should be bounced an equal number of times from center of the bumper alternating first from rear, then front, and releasing at bottom of down cycle.

FRONT WHEEL ALIGNMENT

Caster & Camber

If front camber is not within the specified range, it can be adjusted by using an available camber adjustment bolt package. Before installing bolt package, ensure no components are bent or damaged.

1. Raise and support vehicle.
2. Remove front tire and wheel assemblies.

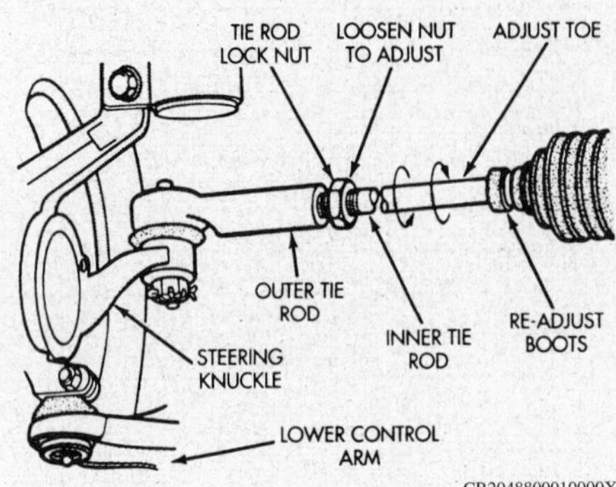

Fig. 1 Toe-in adjustment

3. Remove and discard top and bottom strut clevis bracket to steering knuckle attaching bolts. Attaching bolts are serrated and must not be turned during removal, remove nuts while holding bolts stationary.
4. Separate steering knuckle from strut clevis bracket and position steering knuckle so it is out of way of strut.
5. Use a suitable grinder and grinding wheel, slot bottom hole in both sides of strut clevis bracket.
6. After slotting clevis bracket holes, do not use original attaching bolts and hardware.
7. Position knuckle back into strut clevis bracket.
8. Install flanged bolt from service package into upper hole and a cam bolt into lower hole. Both bolt heads should face forward when installed.
9. Install a dogbone washer on steering knuckle to strut clevis bracket attaching bolts, then install nuts.
10. Tighten bolts just enough to hold steering knuckle in place when adjusting while still allowing steering knuckle to move in clevis bracket.
11. Install front tire and wheel assemblies, lower vehicle, then jounce front and rear an equal amount of times.
12. Adjust front camber to specification by rotating lower eccentric bolt.
13. When camber is set, tighten upper bolt, then the lower bolt. Jounce front and rear of vehicle and verify settings.
14. **Torque** both front strut bolts to 65 ft. lbs., plus an additional ¼ turn.
15. Adjust toe as required.

Toe-In

To adjust toe-in, center steering wheel and hold in position with a suitable tool. Loosen tie rod locknuts and rotate rod, **Fig. 1**, to adjust toe-in to specifications. Use care not to twist steering gear rubber boots. **Torque** tie rod locknuts to 55 ft. lbs. Adjust position of steering gear rubber boots. Remove steering wheel holding tool.

REAR WHEEL ALIGNMENT

Alignment on these vehicles is preset at the factory and cannot be adjusted.

DAKOTA & DURANGO

NOTE: Refer To The Rear Of This Manual For Vehicle Manufacturer's Special Service Tool Suppliers.

INDEX OF SERVICE OPERATIONS

Specifications

GENERAL ENGINE SPECIFICATIONS

Year	Engine Liter	Fuel System	Bore & Stroke, Inch	Comp. Ratio	Horsepower @ RPM	Torque, Ft. Lbs. @ RPM	Normal Oil Pressure, Lbs.
2002–06	2.5L	Fuel Inj.	3.88 x 3.19	9.2:1	120 @ 5200	145 @ 3250	37–75②
	3.7L	Fuel Inj.	3.66 x 3.40	9.6:1	211 @ 5200	263 @ 4000	25–110①
	3.9L	Fuel Inj.	3.91 x 3.31	9.1:1	175 @ 4800	225 @ 3200	30–80①
	4.7L	Fuel Inj.	3.66 x 3.40	9.0:1	235 @ 4800	295 @ 3200	25–110①
	5.7L	Fuel Inj.	3.91 x 3.58	9.6:1	335 @ 5400	375 @ 4200	25–110①
	5.9L	Fuel Inj.	4.00 x 3.58	9.1:1	250 @ 4400	345 @ 3200	30–80①

①— At 3000 RPM.

②— At 1600 RPM or higher.

TUNE UP SPECIFICATIONS

The following specifications are published from latest information available. This data should only be used in absence of decal affixed in engine compartment.

Year & Engine	Spark Plug Gap	Ignition Timing, ° BTDC				Curb Idle Speed②		Fast Idle Speed		Fuel System Pump Pressure, psi	Valve Lash
		Firing Order③	Man. Trans.	Auto. Trans.	Mark Location	Man. Trans.	Auto. Trans.	Man. Trans.	Auto. Trans.		
2002–03											
2.5L	.035	B	⑥	⑥	Damper	—	④	—	④	44–54①	⑤
3.9L	.040	A	—	⑥	Damper	—	④	—	④	44–54①	⑤
4.7L	.040	D	—	⑥	Damper	—	④	—	④	44–54①	⑤
5.9L	.040	C	—	⑥	Damper	—	④	—	④	44–54①	⑤
2004–06											
3.7L	.042	A	—	⑥	Damper	—	④	—	④	56–60①	⑤
4.7L	.040	D	—	⑥	Damper	—	④	—	④	56–60①	⑤
5.7L	.045	D	—	⑥	Damper	—	④	—	④	56–60①	⑤

BTDC — Before Top Dead Center

①— Loosen fuel tank filler cap to release fuel tank pressure. Disconnect injector electrical connector from engine electrical connector. Connect jumper wire between pin No. 1 of injector electrical connector and ground. Connect another jumper wire to pin No. 2 of injector electrical connector and contact battery positive terminal to release system fuel pressure. Do not contact battery positive for more than five seconds. Wrap shop towel around fuel pressure port, then connect suitable fuel pressure gauge to port. Energize fuel pump and note fuel pressure reading.

②— Idle speed is adjusted w/transmission in Neutral (N). When inspecting idle speed, set parking brake & block drive wheels.

③— Before removing wires from distributor cap, determine location of No. 1 wire in cap, as distributor position may have been altered from that outlined at end of this chart.

④— Controlled by idle speed control motor.

⑤— Hydraulic lash adjusters.

⑥— Non-adjustable.

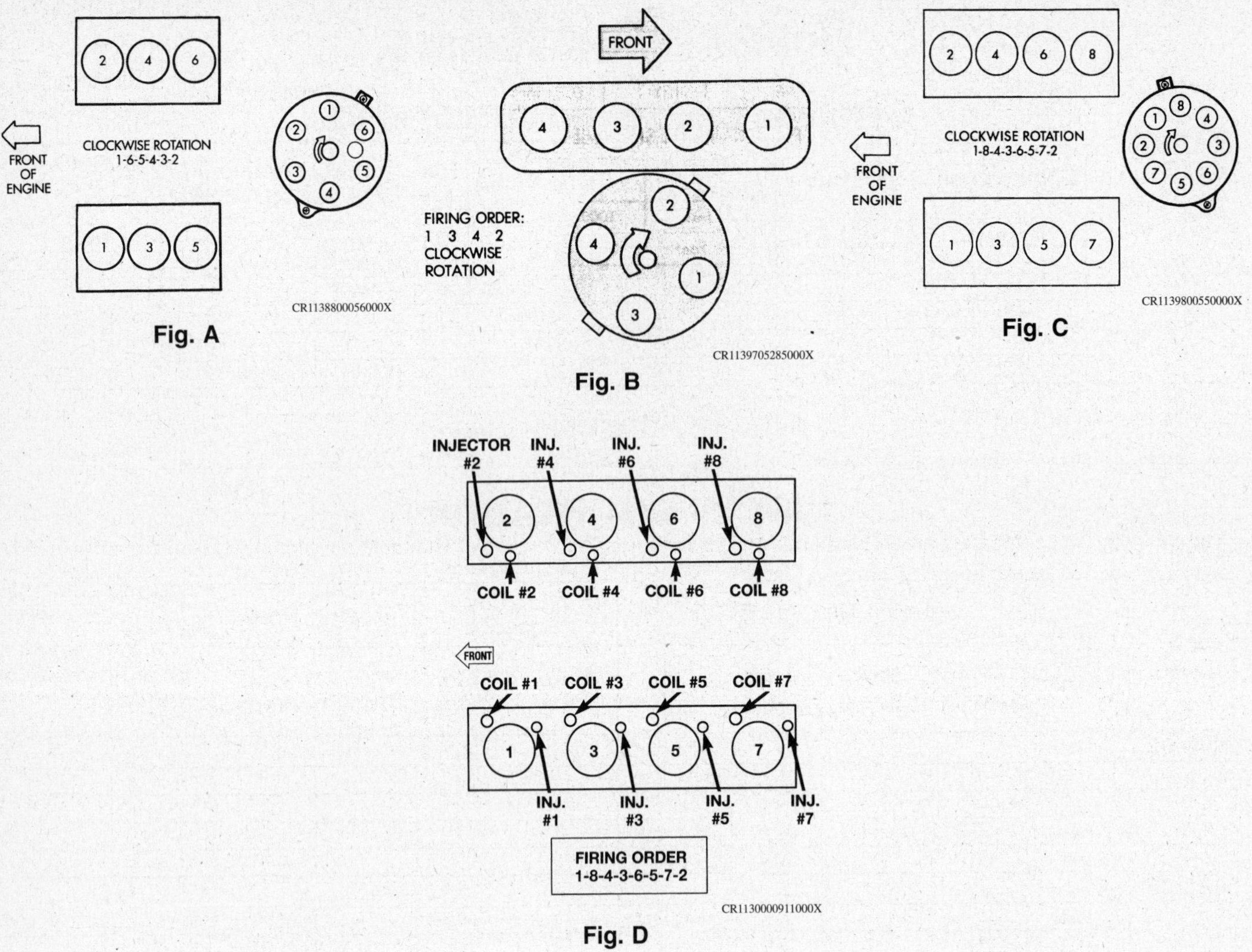

2 4 6
FRONT OF ENGINE
CLOCKWISE ROTATION
1-6-5-4-3-2
1 3 5
CR1138800056000X
FRONT
4 3 2 1
FIRING ORDER:
1 3 4 2
CLOCKWISE
ROTATION
CR1139705285000X
2 4 6 8
FRONT OF ENGINE
CLOCKWISE ROTATION
1-8-4-3-6-5-7-2
1 3 5 7
CR1139800550000X
INJECTOR #2
INJ. #4
INJ. #6
INJ. #8
COIL #2
COIL #4
COIL #6
COIL #8
FRONT
COIL #1
COIL #3
COIL #5
COIL #7
INJ. #1
INJ. #3
INJ. #5
INJ. #7
FIRING ORDER
1-8-4-3-6-5-7-2
CR1130000911000X

Fig. A

Fig. B

Fig. C

Fig. D

FRONT WHEEL ALIGNMENT SPECIFICATIONS

Year	Model	Wheel Base	Caster Angle, Degrees		Camber Angle, Degrees		Toe-In	Ball Joint Wear, Inch
			Limits	Desired	Limits	Desired		
DAKOTA								
2002–04	2WD Except Dakota RT	111.9	+2.49 to +3.49①	+2.99①	-.50 to +.50①	0①	+.04 to +.16	+.1
	2WD Except Dakota RT	130.9	+2.63 to +3.63①	+3.13①	-.50 to +.50①	0①	+.04 to +.16	+.1
	2WD Dakota RT	130.9	+3.17 to +4.17①	+3.67①	-.59 to +.41①	-.09①	+.04 to +.16	+.1
	2WD Dakota RT	111.9	+3.31 to +4.31①	+3.81①	-.59 to +.41①	-.09①	+.04 to +.16	+.1
	4WD	111.9	+2.66 to +3.66①	+3.16①	-.50 to +.50①	0①	+.04 to +.16	+.1
	4WD	130.9	+2.77 to +3.77①	+3.27①	-.50 to +.50①	0①	+.04 to +.16	+.1
2005–06	All	131.0	+3.10–+4.10①	3.60	-.75–.25	-.25	.30 to .10	+.1
DURANGO								
2002–03	2WD	All	+2.60 to +3.60①	+3.1①	-.75 to +.25	-.25①	+.04 to +.16	+.1
	4WD	All	+2.80 to +3.80①	+3.3①	-.75 to +.25①	-.25①	+.04 to +.16	+.1
	Cross Value Except R/T	All	-.50 to +.50	0	-.50 to +.50	0	-.06 to +.06	0
	Cross Value R/T	All	-.30 to +.30	0	-.10 to +.50	+.20	-.06 to +.06	0
2004–06	2WD	119.0	3.00 to 4.00	3.5	-.50 to +.50	0	.05 to .15	+.1
	4WD	119.0	3.00 to 4.00	3.5	-.65 to +.35	0	.05 to .15	+.1

① — Maximum left to right difference is .50°.

FLUID CAPACITIES & COOLING SYSTEM DATA

Year	Engine	Coolant Capacity	Recommended Engine Coolant Type	Radiator Cap Relief Pressure, Lbs.	Thermo. Opening Temp., °F	Fuel Tank, Gals.	Engine Oil Refill, Qts.	Transmission Oil		Transfer Case, Pints	Axle, Pints	
								Manual, Pints	Auto., Qts.		Front	Rear
2002	2.5L	9.8	Ethylene Glycol	16	195	⑪	4.5	⑫	⑬	⑭	3	⑮
	3.9L	14.0	Ethylene Glycol	21	195	⑪	4	⑫	⑬	⑭	3.5	⑮
	4.7L⑨	13.0	Ethylene Glycol	21	195	⑪	6	⑫	⑬	⑭	3.5	⑮
	4.7L⑩	17.0	Ethylene Glycol	21	195	25	6	—	⑬	⑭	3.5	⑧
	5.9L⑨	14.6	Ethylene Glycol	21	195	⑪	5	⑫	⑬	⑭	3.5	⑮
	5.9L⑩	14.3	Ethylene Glycol	21	195	25	5	—	⑬	⑭	3.5	⑧

Continued

FLUID CAPACITIES & COOLING SYSTEM DATA—Continued

Year	Engine	Coolant Capacity	Recommended Engine Coolant Type	Radiator Cap Relief Pressure, Lbs.	Thermo. Opening Temp., °F	Fuel Tank, Gals.	Engine Oil Refill, Qts.	Transmission Oil		Transfer Case, Pints	Axle, Pints	
								Manual, Pints	Auto., Qts.		Front	Rear
2003	3.9L	14.3	Ethylene Glycol	21	195	⑪	4	⑱	①	⑭	3.5	⑮
	4.7L⑨	17.0	Ethylene Glycol	21	195	⑪	6	⑱	①	⑭	3.5	⑮
	4.7L⑩	⑯	Ethylene Glycol	21	195	25	6	—	②	⑭	3.5	⑧
	5.9L⑨	14.3	Ethylene Glycol	21	195	⑪	5	⑱	①	⑭	3.5	⑮
	5.9L⑩	⑰	Ethylene Glycol	21	195	25	5	—	②	⑭	3.5	⑧
2004	3.7L⑨	13.0	Ethylene Glycol	21	195	⑪	5	③	⑬	④	3.5	⑤
	3.7L⑩	16.2	Ethylene Glycol	21	195	27	5	—	⑥	⑦	3.5	⑤
	4.7L⑨	13.0	Ethylene Glycol	21	195	⑪	6	③	⑬	④	3.5	⑤
	4.7L⑩	16.2	Ethylene Glycol	21	195	27	6	—	⑥	⑦	3.5	⑤
	5.7L⑩	16.2	Ethylene Glycol	21	195	27	7	—	⑥	⑦	3.5	⑤
2005–06	3.7L⑨	16.2	Ethylene Glycol	21	195	25	5	4.65	⑥	④	3.5	⑤
	3.7L⑩	16.2	Ethylene Glycol	21	195	27	5	—	⑥	⑦	3.5	⑤
	4.7L⑨	16.2	Ethylene Glycol	21	195	25	6	4.65	⑥	④	3.5	⑤
	4.7L⑩	16.2	Ethylene Glycol	21	195	27	6	—	⑥	⑦	3.5	⑤
	5.7L⑩	16.2	Ethylene Glycol	21	195	27	7	—	⑥	⑦	3.5	⑤

① — 42RE & 46RE, service fill, 4 qts., after overhaul, 19–20 pts.; 545RFE, service fill, 2WD, 11 pts., 4WD, 13 pts., after overhaul, 28 pts.
② — 46RE, service fill, 4 qts, after overhaul, 19–20 pts.; 45RFE, service fill, 2WD, 11 pts., 4WD, 13 pts., after overhaul, 28 pts.
③ — 2WD, 4.8 pts., 4WD, 4.18 pts.
④ — NV233, 2.5 pts.; NV244, 2.85 pts.
⑤ — 8¼ inch, 4.4pts., 9¼ inch, 4.5 pts.
⑥ — 42RLE, service fill, 4 qts., after overhaul, 9.5–10 qts.; 545RFE, service fill, 2WD, 5.5 qts., 4WD, 6.5 qts., after overhaul, 14 qts.
⑦ — NV144, 1.8; NV244 GENII, 3.4.
⑧ — 8¼ inch, 4.4 pts., 9¼ inch, 4.9 pts.
⑨ — Dakota.
⑩ — Durango.
⑪ — 2 door, 22 gals, 4 door 24 gals.
⑫ — NV1500, 4.86 pts.: NV3500, 2WD, 4.8 pts., 4WD, 4.18 pts.
⑬ — 42RE & 46RE, service fill, 4 qts., after overhaul, 9.5–10 qts.; 45RFE, service fill, 2WD, 5.5 qts., 4WD, 6.5 qts., after overhaul, 14 qts.
⑭ — NV133 & NV233, 2.5 pts.; NV244, 2.85 pts.
⑮ — 8¼ inch, 4.7pts., 9¼ inch, 4.9 pts.
⑯ — With rear heat, 14.1 qts.; less rear heat, 13.3 qts.
⑰ — With rear heat, 17.2 qts.; less rear heat, 16.4 qts.
⑱ — 2WD, 4.8 pts.; 4wd, 4.2 pts.

LUBRICANT DATA

Year	Model	Lubricant Data					
		Transmission		Transfer Case	Rear Axle①	Power Steering	Brake System
		Manual	Automatic				
2002–06	All	4874464②	ATF + 4(9062)	ATF + 4(9062)	75W-90 GL-5	ATF + 4(9062)	DOT 3

① — On Trac-Lok differentials, add 4 ounces of friction modifier.
② — DaimlerChrysler Corp. part No.

Electrical

NOTE: On Air Bag Equipped Models, Refer To "Air Bag System Precautions" Located In The Front Of This Manual For System Disarming & Arming Procedures.

NOTE: Refer To "Computer Relearn Procedures" Located In The Front Of This Manual When Battery Power To The Computer Has Been Interrupted.

INDEX

PRECAUTIONS

Air Bag Systems

Refer to "Air Bag System Precautions" in the front of this manual for system disarming and arming procedures.

Battery Ground Cable

Prior to service, disconnect battery ground cable and isolate as required.

FUSE PANEL LOCATION

The fuse panel is located under the left-hand side of the instrument panel.

FLASHER LOCATION

The hazard and turn signal flashers are located on the fuse panel, under the left-hand side of the instrument panel.

FUEL PUMP RELAY LOCATION

The fuel pump relay is located in the relay center.

RELAY CENTER LOCATION

The relay center is located on the left-hand side inner fender of the engine compartment, above the wheel house, **Fig. 1.** Refer to **Fig. 2** for relay identification.

STARTER

REPLACE

2.5L Engine

1. Raise and support vehicle.
2. While supporting starter motor with one hand, remove two screws that secure starter motor to engine block.
3. Lower stater motor enough to access and remove nut that secures battery positive cable connector eyelet to solenoid battery terminal stud.
4. **Always support starter motor, do not let starter motor hang from wire harness.**
5. Remove battery positive cable connector eyelet from solenoid battery terminal stud.
6. Disconnect engine wire harness connector from solenoid terminal connector receptacle.
7. Remove starter motor and any shims from engine compartment.
8. Reverse procedure to install, noting the following:
   a. Install any shims that were removed previously.
   b. **Torque** battery positive cable connector eyelet to solenoid battery terminal stud to 90 inch lbs.
   c. **Torque** both starter motor mounting bolts to 33 ft. lbs.

3.7L, 3.9L, 4.7L & 5.9L Engines

1. Raise and support vehicle.
2. Remove front axle skid plate and skid plate crossmember.
3. Remove nut and lock washer from starter mounting stud.
4. Remove screw from upper starter mounting flange hole, then slide transmission cooler tube bracket forward for clearance.
5. Move starter towards front of vehicle until gear housing nose clears bell housing.
6. Tilt nose downwards, then lower starter far enough to access solenoid wire harness connector.
7. Remove starter from vehicle.
8. Reverse procedures to install, noting the following:
   a. **Torque** upper and lower mounting nuts to 50 ft. lbs.
   b. **Torque** battery cable terminal nut to 10 ft. lbs.

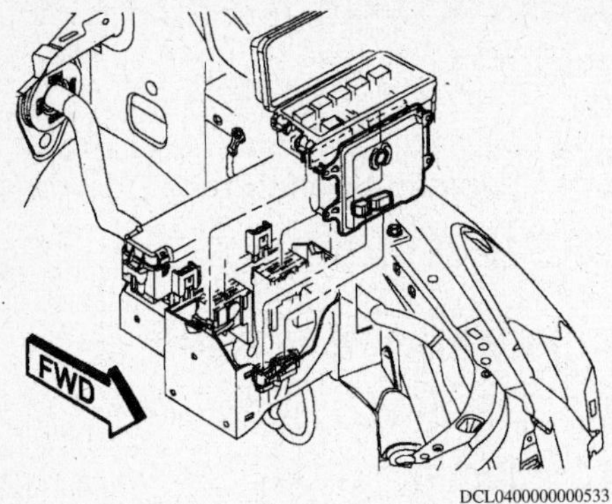

Fig. 1 Relay location

5.7L Engine

1. Raise and support vehicle. **If equipped with 4WD and certain transmissions, a support bracket is used between front axle and side of transmission. Remove 2 support bracket bolts at transmission. Pry support bracket slightly to gain access to lower starter mounting bolts.**
2. Remove two mounting bolts.
3. Move starter motor towards front of vehicle far enough for nose of starter pinion housing to clear housing. Always support starter motor during this process, do not let starter motor hang from wire harness.
4. Tilt nose downwards and lower starter motor far enough to access and remove nut that secures battery positive cable wire harness connector eyelet to solenoid battery terminal stud. Do not let motor hang from wire harness.
5. Remove battery positive cable wire harness connector eyelet from solenoid battery terminal stud.
6. Disconnect battery positive cable wire harness connector from solenoid terminal connector receptacle.
7. Remove starter motor.
8. Reverse procedure to install.

ALTERNATOR

REPLACE

1. Remove alternator belt.
2. Remove pivot and mounting bolts, then position alternator for wire connection access.
3. Remove harness hold-down, battery terminal, ground terminal and two field terminal nuts.
4. Remove wire connectors, then remove alternator.
5. Reverse procedure to install, noting the following:
   a. **On models equipped with 2.5L engine, torque** mounting and pivot bolts to 41 ft. lbs.
   b. **On models equipped with 3.9L, 5.7L and 5.9L engines, torque** mounting and pivot bolts to 30 ft. lbs.
   c. **On models equipped with 4.7L engine, torque** mounting bolts to 40 ft. lbs.

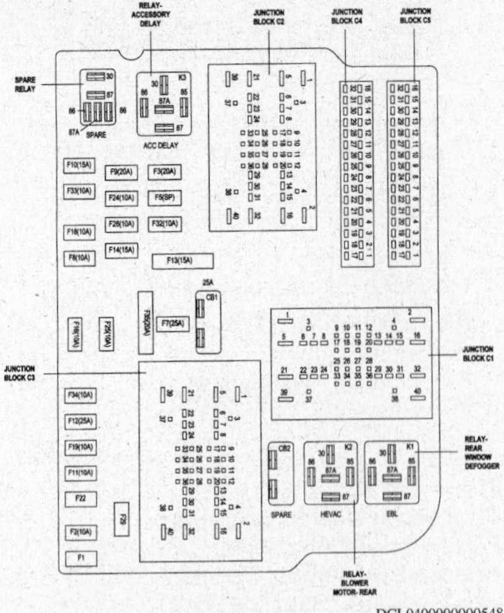

Fig. 2 Relay identification

   d. **On models equipped with serpentine drive belt,** the belt must be routed correctly or water pump will rotate in wrong direction and engine will overheat. See engine compartment belt routing label or "Serpentine Drive Belt" in "3.9L & 5.9L Engines" section.

DISTRIBUTOR

REPLACE

2.5L Engine

REMOVAL

1. Remove air tube between throttle body and air cleaner housing.
2. Disconnect coil secondary cable at coil.
3. Remove distributor cap. **Do not remove cables from distributor cap. Do not remove rotor.**
4. Disconnect distributor wiring harness from main engine wiring harness.
5. Remove cylinder No. 1 spark plug.
6. Hold a finger over open spark plug hole and rotate engine at vibration dampener bolt until compression is felt.
7. Slowly continue to rotate engine until timing index mark on vibration damper pulley aligns with top dead center (TDC) mark (0°) on timing scale. **Do not rotate engine backward to align timing marks.**
8. Remove distributor hold down bolt and clamp.
9. Remove distributor from engine by slowly lifting straight up.
10. Remove and discard old distributor gasket.

INSTALLATION

1. Ensure oil pump gear slot is aligned slightly before 10 o'clock position, **Fig. 3.**
2. Remove camshaft position sensor from distributor housing by lifting straight up.
3. Rotate distributor and install suitable

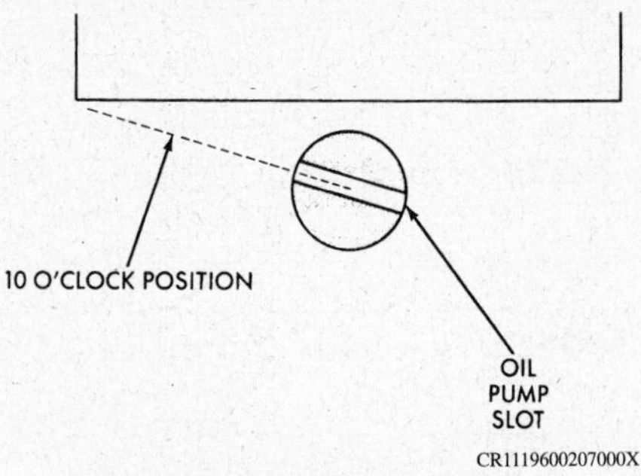

Fig. 3 Oil pump gear slot alignment. 2.5L engine

$^3/_{16}$ inch pin punch through plastic ring and into mating access hole in distributor housing to prevent shaft and rotor from rotating, **Fig. 4.**
4. Clean distributor mounting hole area of engine block and install new gasket.
5. Pre-position distributor into engine block while holding centerline of base slot in the 1 o'clock position, **Fig. 5.**
6. The rotor and distributor will rotate clockwise during installation due to helical gears on distributor and camshaft.
7. When distributor is fully seated to engine block, the centerline of base slot should be aligned to clamp bolt mounting hole on engine, and centerline of base slot should be slightly past 3 o'clock position, **Fig. 6.** It may be required to rotate rotor and distributor shaft very slightly to engage shaft with slot in pump gear. The same may have to be done to engage distributor gear with camshaft gear.
8. The distributor is correctly positioned when:
   a. Rotor is pointed at the 3 o'clock position.
   b. Pin punch is still installed in distributor.
   c. No. 1 cylinder is set at TDC.
   d. Centerline of slot at base of distributor is aligned to centerline of distributor hold-down bolt hole on engine block.
9. Install distributor hold-down clamp bolt and **torque** to 17 ft. lbs.
10. Remove pin punch from distributor.
11. Install camshaft position sensor to distributor, then the rotor.
12. Install distributor cap with all high tension wires connected and **torque** hold-down clamp screws to 26 inch lbs.
13. Connect distributor wiring harness to main engine wiring harness.

3.9L, 5.2L & 5.9L Engines

REMOVAL

Base ignition timing is not adjustable and is controlled by the PCM. Because a conventional timing light can not be used to adjust distributor position after installation, note and mark position of distributor before removal.

1. Remove distributor cap.

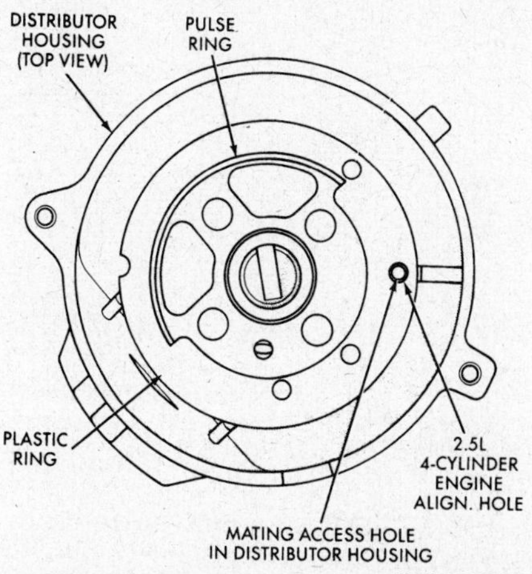

Fig. 4 Mating access hole alignment. 2.5L engine

2. Mark rotation and position of distributor housing to aid in installation.
3. Slowly rotate engine clockwise with a socket on crankshaft vibration damper mounting bolt until indicating mark on damper aligns to 0° mark on timing chain cover. Distributor rotor should align with stamped "CYL. No. 1" alignment mark on distributor plate, **Fig. 7.** If not, rotate engine another 360.°
4. Disconnect camshaft position sensor wiring harness from main engine wiring harness then remove distributor rotor
5. Remove hold-down bolt and distributor. **Do not crank engine with distributor removed.**

INSTALLATION

1. If engine has been cranked while distributor was removed, rotate crankshaft until No. 1 cylinder piston is at top dead center on its compression stroke and indicating mark on damper aligns to 0° mark on timing chain cover.
2. Clean top of cylinder block for a good seal between distributor and block, then lightly oil rubber O-ring on distributor housing.
3. Install rotor on distributor shaft, then position distributor into engine, engage tongue of distributor shaft with slot in oil pump drive gear.
4. Position rotor to No. 1 spark plug cable position, then install distributor hold-down clamp and clamp bolt. **Do not tighten.**
5. Rotate distributor until rotor is aligned to "CYL. NO. 1" alignment mark on camshaft position sensor, **Fig. 7.**
6. **Torque** clamp hold-down bolt to 17 ft. lbs.
7. Connect switch plate wiring harness and install distributor cap.

IGNITION LOCK

REPLACE

Refer to "Ignition Switch, Replace" for ignition lock replacement procedure.

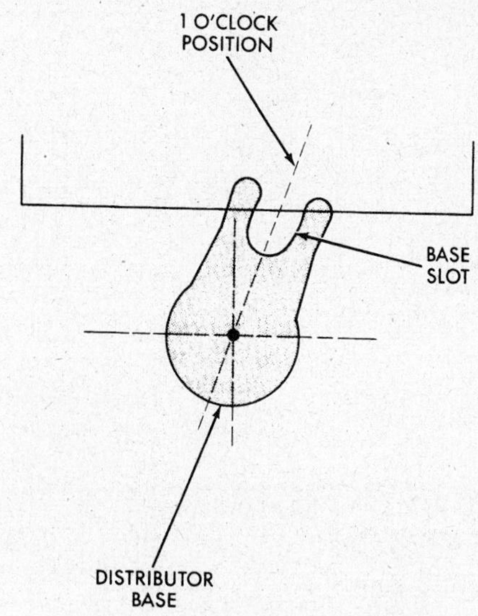

Fig. 5 Distributor base pre-position alignment. 2.5L engine

IGNITION SWITCH

REPLACE

Removal

1. **On models equipped with tilt column,** remove tilt lever.
2. **On models equipped with automatic transmission,** place shifter in Park position.
3. **On all models,** remove upper and lower steering column covers.
4. A retaining pin is located at side of key cylinder assembly. Rotate key to RUN position and press in on retaining pin while pulling key cylinder from ignition switch, **Fig. 8.**
5. Remove ignition switch mounting screws, **Fig. 9,** using Torx tool No. SD-MTR10, or equivalent.
6. Gently pull switch away from column and release connector locks on seven pin terminal wiring connector, then remove connector from ignition switch.
7. Release connector lock on key-in-switch and Halo light four pin terminal connector.

Installation

1. Rotate flag on rear of ignition switch until it is in the Run position, **Fig. 10.**
2. With key in ignition lock cylinder, rotate key clockwise until retaining pin can be depressed, **Fig. 11.**
3. Install key cylinder into ignition switch by aligning retaining pin with retaining pin slot, **Fig. 12.**
4. Push key cylinder into switch until retaining pin engages, after pin engages, rotate key to Off or Lock position.
5. Ensure proper retention of key cylinder by attempting to pull cylinder from switch.

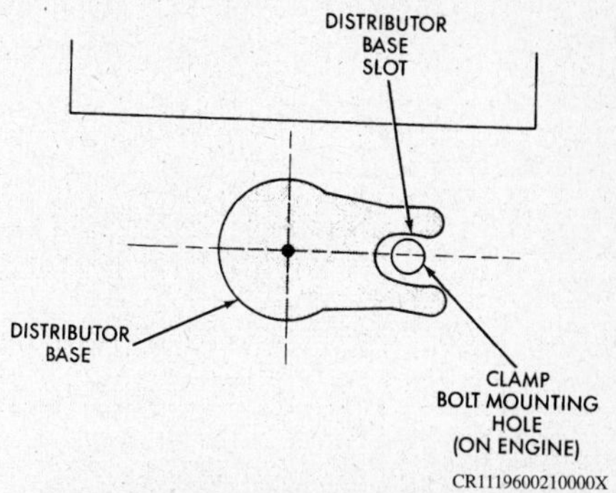

Fig. 6 Distributor base seated position. 2.5L engine

6. **On models equipped with automatic transmission,** before attaching ignition switch to steering column, transmission shifter must be in Park position.
7. **On models equipped with automatic transmission,** park lock dowel pin on rear of ignition switch must be properly indexed into Park/Lock linkage before installing switch.
8. **On all models,** flag at rear of ignition switch must be properly indexed into steering column before installing switch.
9. Place ignition switch in Lock position. Switch is in Lock position when column lock flag is parallel to ignition switch terminals.
10. **On models equipped with automatic transmission,** apply a light coating of suitable grease to park lock dowel pin and park lock slider linkage. Push park lock slider linkage forward until it bottoms out, then pull rearward approximately one-quarter inch.
11. **On all models,** apply a light coating of suitable grease to both column lock flag and shaft at end of flag.
12. Place ignition switch into opening on steering column.
13. **On models equipped with automatic transmission,** proceed as follows:
    a. Ensure park lock dowel pin on rear of ignition switch enters slot in park lock slider linkage.
    b. Ensure flag on rear of switch is positioned above steering wheel lock lever, **Fig. 13.**
    c. Align dowel pins on rear of switch into holes on side of steering column.
    d. Install ignition switch mounting screws and **torque** to 22–30 inch lbs.
14. **On all models,** connect electrical connectors to ignition switch and halo lamp.
15. Install steering column covers, **torque** screws to 17 inch lbs.
16. **On models equipped with tilt steering wheel,** install tilt lever.
17. **On all models,** inspect for proper operation of ignition switch and lock assembly.

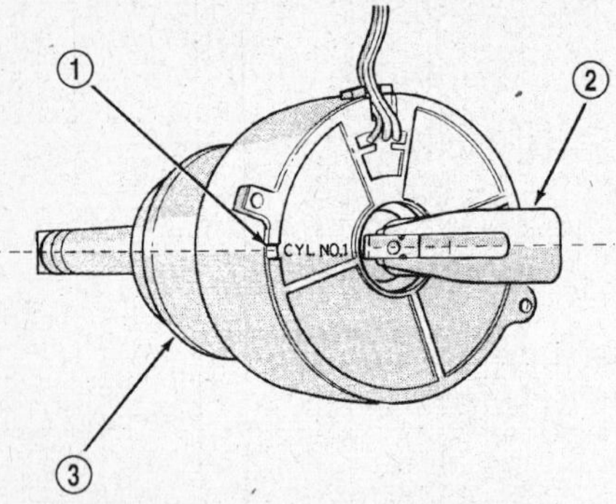

Fig. 7 Rotor alignment mark. 3.9L, 5.2L & 5.9L engines

NEUTRAL SAFETY SWITCH

REPLACE

1. Raise and support vehicle, then position drain pan under switch.
2. Disconnect switch wires and remove switch from case.
3. Ensure switch operating lever fingers center in case opening for switch when shift lever is in Park and Neutral positions.
4. Install switch and new seal. **Torque** switch to 25 ft. lbs.
5. Connect switch wires, lower vehicle and inspect transmission fluid.

HEADLAMP SWITCH

REPLACE

1. Remove the cluster bezel from the instrument panel.
2. Disconnect the wire harness connector from the back of the headlamp switch.
3. Place the cluster bezel face down on a suitable work surface. Be certain to take the proper precautions to protect the face of the bezel from cosmetic damage.
4. Remove the three screws that secure the headlamp switch to the back of the cluster bezel.
5. Remove the headlamp switch from the cluster bezel.
6. Reverse procedure to install. **Torque** three mounting screws to 17 inch lbs.

STOP LIGHT SWITCH

REPLACE

1. Disconnect switch harness.
2. Press and hold brake pedal in applied position.
3. Rotate switch counterclockwise about 30° to align switch lock tab with notch in bracket.
4. Pull switch rearward out of mounting bracket and release brake pedal.
5. Reverse procedure to install.

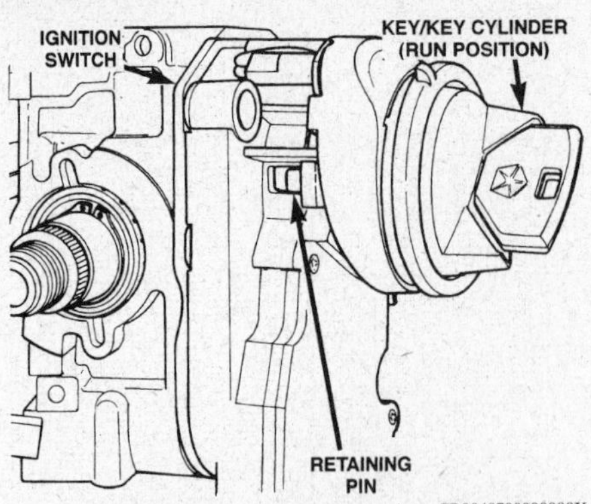

Fig. 8 Key cylinder removal

MULTI-FUNCTION SWITCH

REPLACE

1. Remove driver air bag module from steering wheel as outlined in "Passive Restraint System" chapter.
2. Disconnect steering wheel wire harness connectors from upper clockspring connector receptacles. **Be certain that screws that secure steering wheel puller to steering wheel are fully engaged in steering wheel armature without passing through steering wheel and damaging clockspring.**
3. Remove steering wheel from steering column.
4. Remove screw that secures tilt steering column knob and remove it from tilt actuator on lefthand side of column.
5. From below steering column, remove two outboard screws that secure upper column shroud to lower shroud.
6. Press inward on both sides of upper hand shroud above parting line of lower shroud to release snap feature that secure two shroud halves to each other.
7. Remove upper shroud from lower shroud and steering column.
8. Remove one center screw that secures lower shroud to steering column.
9. Remove lower shroud from steering column.
10. Disconnect wire harness connector from back of multi-function switch housing.
11. Remove two screws that secure switch to multi-function switch mounting housing.
12. Grasp switch control stalk and pull it toward lefthand side of vehicle to remove switch from mounting housing.
13. Reverse procedure to install noting the following:
    a. **Torque** multi-function switch wire harness connector screw to 20 inch lbs.
    b. **Torque** multi-function switch mounting screws to 20 inch lbs.

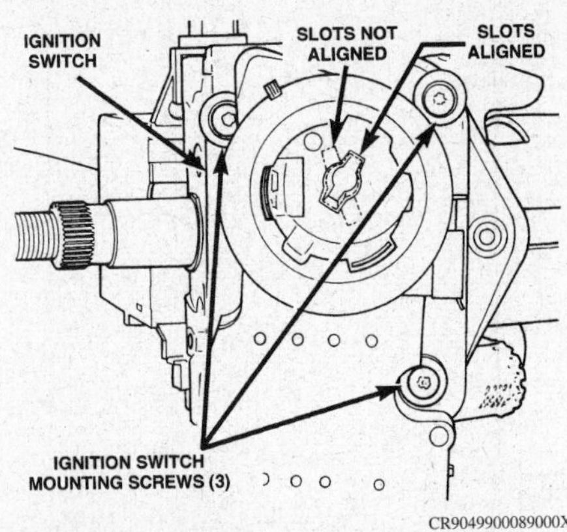

Fig. 9 Ignition switch removal

TURN SIGNAL SWITCH

REPLACE

Refer to "Multi-Function Switch, Replace" for turn signal switch replacement procedure.

DIMMER SWITCH

REPLACE

Refer to "Multi-Function Switch, Replace" for dimmer switch replacement procedure.

STEERING WHEEL

REPLACE

Removal

1. Partially remove steering wheel bolt and leave bolt in column.
2. Install tool No. CJ98-1, or equivalent, using top of bolt to push on.
3. Remove and discard the steering wheel bolt.
4. Remove the steering wheel.

Installation

1. Install steering wheel to column. **Do not reuse old steering wheel bolt, a new bolt must used. Make sure to align spline on steering wheel hub to column shaft. Be certain that steering wheel mounting bolt is tightened to proper torque specification to ensure proper clockspring operation.**
2. Install new steering wheel bolt. **Torque** to 45 inch lbs.

INSTRUMENT CLUSTER

REPLACE

1. Remove cluster bezel from instrument panel.
2. Remove four screws that secure instrument cluster to instrument panel structural support.
3. Pull instrument cluster rearward far enough to access and disconnect instrument panel wire harness connectors from connector receptacles on back of cluster housing.

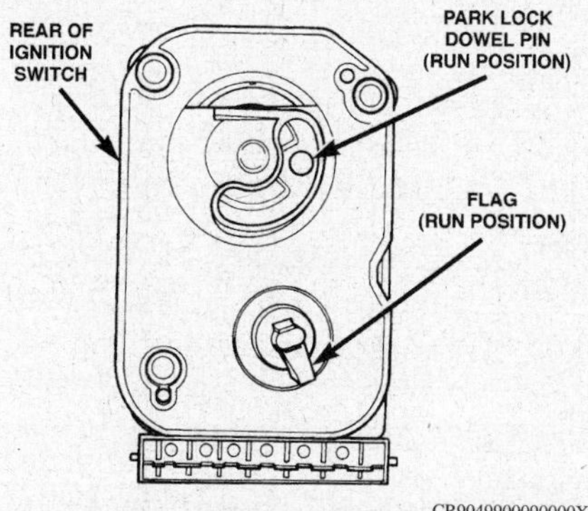

Fig. 10 Ignition switch flag in Run position

4. Remove instrument cluster from instrument panel.
5. Reverse procedure to install. **Torque** instrument cluster support screws to 17 inch lbs.

RADIO

REPLACE

1. Remove steering column cover and instrument cluster bezel.
2. Remove two screws attaching radio to instrument panel, then pull radio through front face of panel and disconnect radio electrical connector, antenna lead and ground strap.
3. Reverse procedure to install.

WIPER MOTOR

REPLACE

1. Remove both front wiper arms from wiper pivots.
2. Remove cowl plenum cover/grill panel from over front wiper module.
3. Disconnect wire harness connector from the front wiper motor connector.
4. Disengage socket bushing of right-hand wiper drive link from ball stud on wiper motor crank arm using two large screwdrivers, one on each side of ball stud. Pry between crank arm and metal portion of drive link until socket unsnaps from ball.
5. Remove sleeve bushing of lefthand wiper drive link from ball stud on wiper motor crank arm.
6. While supporting wiper motor from underside of wiper module bracket, remove three screws that secure motor to bracket.

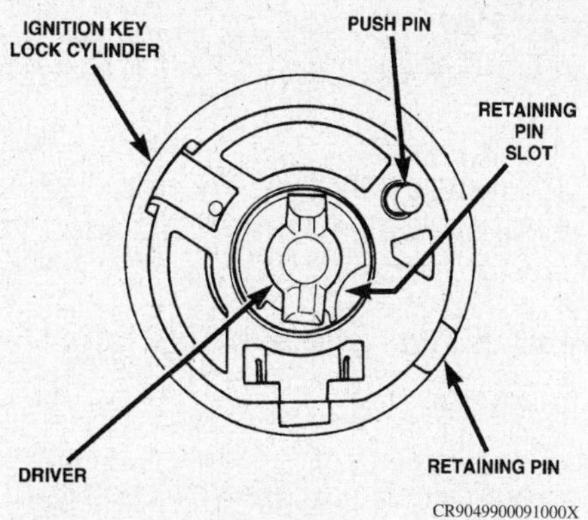

Fig. 11 Lock cylinder retaining pin

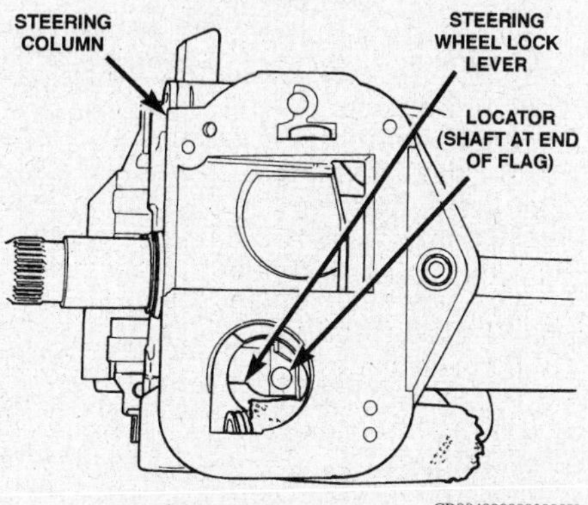

Fig. 13 Steering wheel lock lever

7. Remove wiper motor and crank arm unit from underside of module bracket.
8. Reverse procedure to install, noting the following:
   a. **Torque** motor mounting screws to 62 inch lbs.
   b. **Torque** wiper arm pivot nuts to 18 ft. lbs.

WIPER SWITCH

REPLACE

Refer to "Multi-Function Switch, Replace" for wiper switch replacement procedure.

BLOWER MOTOR

REPLACE

1. Remove instrument panel from vehicle.
2. Remove heater-A/C housing.
3. Remove blower motor housing cover.

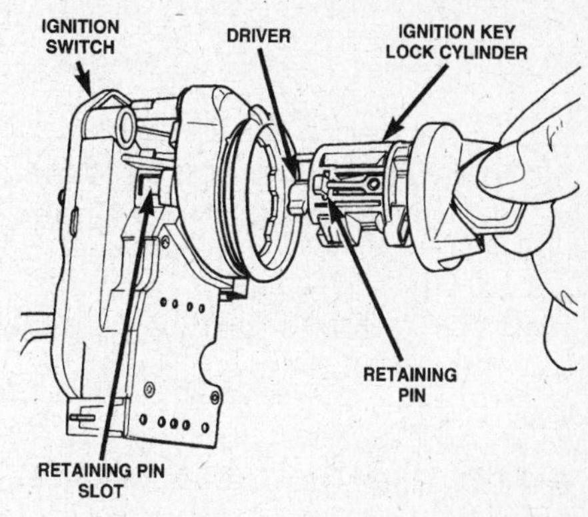

Fig. 12 Lock cylinder installation

4. Remove three screws securing blower motor and blower wheel assembly to heater-A/C housing.
5. Pull blower motor and wheel assembly out of passenger compartment side of heater A/C housing while feeding blower motor wire harness, grommet and connector through hole on dash panel side of housing.
6. Remove blower wheel retainer clip and remove wheel from blower motor shaft.
7. Reverse procedure to install.

HEATER CORE

REPLACE

1. Recover A/C refrigerant as outlined in "Air Conditioning" chapter.
2. Drain engine coolant into suitable container.
3. Remove instrument panel assembly as outlined in "Dash Panel Service" chapter.
4. Remove heater-A/C housing assembly.
5. Lift heater core out of heater-A/C housing.
6. Reverse procedure to install.

EVAPORATOR CORE

REPLACE

1. Recover A/C refrigerant as outlined in "Air Conditioning" chapter.
2. Remove instrument panel assembly as outlined in "Dash Panel Service" chapter.
3. Remove heater-A/C housing assembly.
4. Lift core from housing.
5. Reverse procedure to install.

2.5L Engine

NOTE: On Air Bag Equipped Models, Refer To "Air Bag System Precautions" Located In The Front Of This Manual For System Disarming & Arming Procedures.

NOTE: Refer To "2.5L & 4.0L Engines" In The "Cherokee & Grand Cherokee" Chapter For Service Procedures Not Covered In This Section.

NOTE: Refer To "Computer Relearn Procedures" Located In The Front Of This Manual When Battery Power To The Computer Has Been Interrupted.

INDEX

PRECAUTIONS

Air Bag Systems

Refer to "Air Bag System Precautions" in the front of this manual for system disarming and arming procedures.

Fuel System Pressure Relief

1. Remove fuel fill cap.
2. Fuel filler tube contains a spring loaded flap located below fuel cap. Place a non-metallic object into fuel fill tube and press on flap to relieve any tank pressure.
3. Remove fuel pump relay from Power Distribution Center (PDC).
4. Start and run engine until it stalls.
5. Attempt to restart engine to ensure it will no longer run.
6. Turn key to Off position.

Battery Ground Cable

Prior to service, disconnect battery ground cable and isolate as required.

COMPRESSION PRESSURE

Compression pressure should be 120–150 psi. Maximum variation between cylinders is 30 psi.

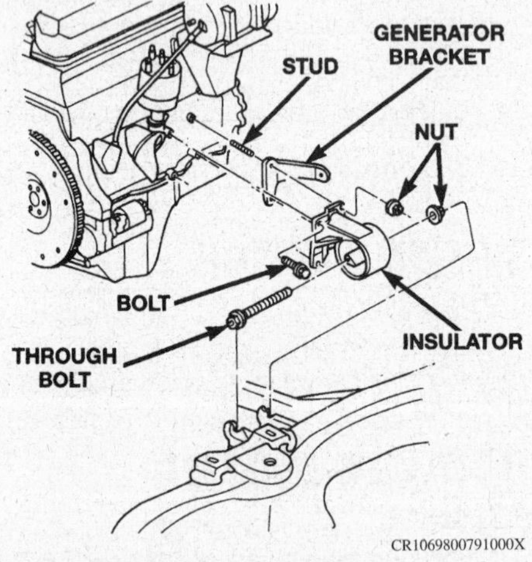

Fig. 1 Right front engine mount

ENGINE MOUNT

REPLACE

Front

REMOVAL

1. Raise and support vehicle.
2. Support engine with a suitable lifting device.
3. Remove through bolt nuts from left and right engine mounts, **Figs. 1 and 2.**
4. Raise engine to allow clearance when removing insulator.
5. Remove engine retaining bolts attaching insulator assembly to engine block.
6. Remove insulator assembly.

INSTALLATION

1. Position insulator assembly on cylinder block and install nuts and bolts.
2. **Torque** bolts to 60 ft. lbs., and nuts to 35 ft. lbs.
3. Install through bolts and retaining nut, **do not tighten at this time.**
4. Lower engine until through bolt and nut are resting in frame bracket and weight of engine is off of supporting device.
5. **Torque** through bolt nut to 60 ft. lbs.
6. Remove engine support, lower vehicle.

Rear

1. Raise and support vehicle.
2. Use a suitable transmission jack to support transmission.
3. **On models equipped with automatic transmission,** remove rear engine support bracket through bolt, **Fig. 3.**
4. **On models equipped with manual transmission,** remove nuts securing insulator to transmission, **Fig. 4.**
5. **On all models,** raise transmission and engine slightly.
6. Remove stud nuts and insulator from transmission mounting crossmember.
7. Remove insulator.
8. Reverse procedure to install. Tighten bolts to specifications.

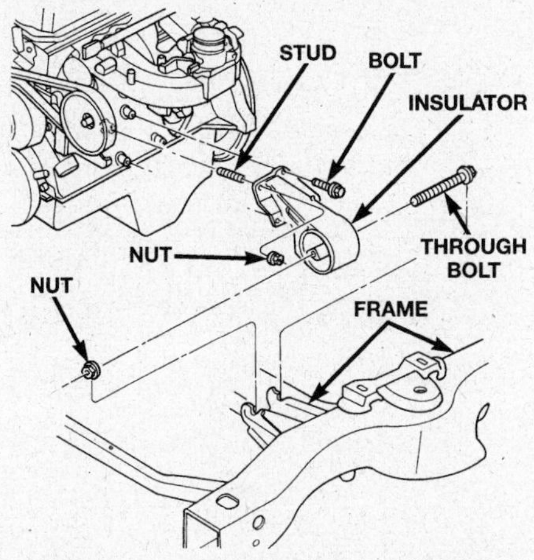

Fig. 2 Left front engine mount

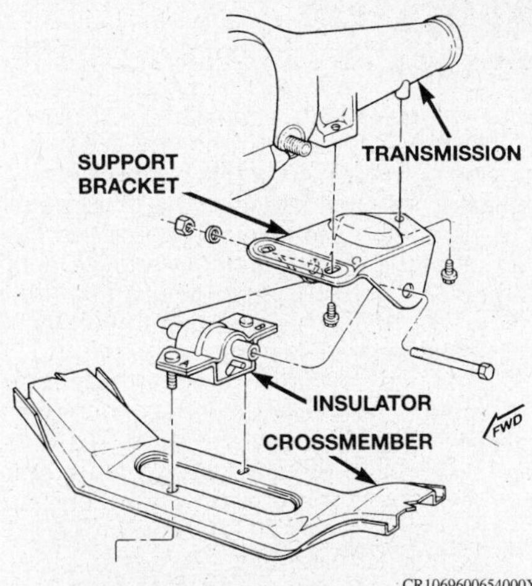

Fig. 3 Rear engine mount. Automatic transmission

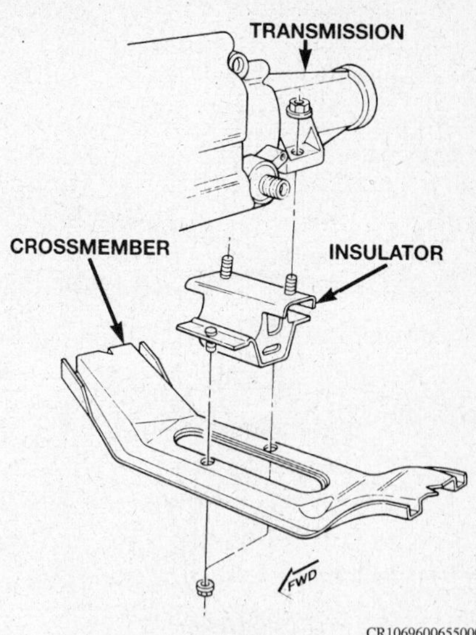

Fig. 4 Rear engine mount. Manual transmission

ENGINE

REPLACE

Refer to "2.5L Engine" In the "Cherokee & Grand Cherokee" chapter.

INTAKE MANIFOLD

REPLACE

Refer To "2.5L & 4.0L Engines" section In the "Cherokee & Grand Cherokee" chapter for Service procedures not covered in this Section.

EXHAUST MANIFOLD

REPLACE

Refer To "2.5L & 4.0L Engines" section In the "Cherokee & Grand Cherokee" chapter for Service procedures not covered in this Section.

CYLINDER HEAD

REPLACE

Refer To "2.5L & 4.0L Engines" section In the "Cherokee & Grand Cherokee" chapter for Service procedures not covered in this Section.

VALVE COVER

REPLACE

Refer To "2.5L & 4.0L Engines" section In the "Cherokee & Grand Cherokee" chapter for Service procedures not covered in this Section.

VALVE ARRANGEMENT

Refer To "2.5L & 4.0L Engines" section In the "Cherokee & Grand Cherokee" chapter for Service procedures not covered in this Section.

CAMSHAFT LOBE LIFT SPECIFICATIONS

Refer To "2.5L & 4.0L Engines" section In the "Cherokee & Grand Cherokee" chapter for Service procedures not covered in this Section.

VALVE ADJUSTMENT

These engines are equipped with hydraulic valve lifters. There is no provision for adjustment.

ROCKER ARMS

REPLACE

Refer To "2.5L & 4.0L Engines" section In the "Cherokee & Grand Cherokee" chapter for Service procedures not covered in this Section.

HYDRAULIC LIFTERS

REPLACE

Refer To "2.5L & 4.0L Engines" section In the "Cherokee & Grand Cherokee" chapter for Service procedures not covered in this Section.

FRONT COVER

REPLACE

Refer To "2.5L & 4.0L Engines" section In the "Cherokee & Grand Cherokee" chapter for Service procedures not covered in this Section.

TIMING CHAIN

REPLACE

Refer To "2.5L & 4.0L Engines" section In the "Cherokee & Grand Cherokee" chapter for Service procedures not covered in this Section.

CAMSHAFT

REPLACE

Refer To "2.5L & 4.0L Engines" section In the "Cherokee & Grand Cherokee" chapter for Service procedures not covered in this Section.

PISTON & ROD ASSEMBLY

Refer To "2.5L & 4.0L Engines" section In the "Cherokee & Grand Cherokee" chapter for Service procedures not covered in this Section.

MAIN & ROD BEARINGS

Refer To "2.5L & 4.0L Engines" section In the "Cherokee & Grand Cherokee" chapter for Service procedures not covered in this Section.

CRANKSHAFT REAR OIL SEAL

REPLACE

Refer To "2.5L & 4.0L Engines" section In the "Cherokee & Grand Cherokee" chapter for Service procedures not covered in this Section.

OIL PAN

REPLACE

Refer To "2.5L & 4.0L Engines" section In the "Cherokee & Grand Cherokee" chapter for Service procedures not covered in this Section.

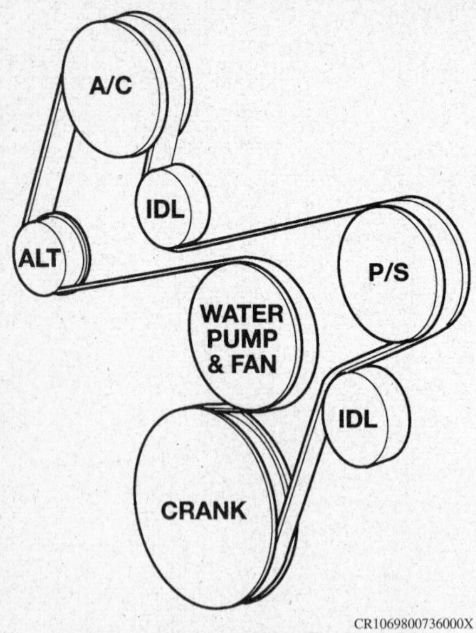

Fig. 5 Serpentine drive belt routing. With A/C

OIL PUMP

REPLACE

Refer To "2.5L & 4.0L Engines" section In the "Cherokee & Grand Cherokee" chapter for Service procedures not covered in this Section.

SERPENTINE DRIVE BELT

BELT ROUTING

Refer to **Figs. 5 and 6** for serpentine drive belt routing.

WATER PUMP

REPLACE

Refer To "2.5L & 4.0L Engines" section In the "Cherokee & Grand Cherokee" chapter for Service procedures not covered in this Section.

RADIATOR

REPLACE

Constant tension hose clamps are used on most cooling system hoses. When removing or installing clamps, use only tools designed for servicing this type of clamp.

A number or letter is stamped into the tongue of the clamp. If clamp replacement is required, use only an original equipment clamp with matching letter or number.

1. Drain cooling system.
2. Remove hose clamps and hoses from radiator, then overflow tank hose from filler neck.
3. Disconnect electric cooling fan motor connector, then remove fan shroud upper clips, and lift fan and shroud assembly from vehicle.
4. **On models equipped with automatic transmission,** disconnect oil cooler lines.
5. **On all models,** remove radiator upper mounting screws and radiator.
6. Reverse procedure to install.

FUEL PUMP

REPLACE

1. Release fuel system pressure as outlined under "Precautions."
2. Drain fuel into a suitable container, then lower fuel tank using suitable jack stand.
3. Note direction of fuel filter/fuel pressure regulator, pressure relief/roll over valve and pump electrical connector.
4. Hold fuel pump module down while loosening locknut. **Pump is under slight spring pressure** and will pop up when locknut is removed.
5. Release fuel pump module and remove from tank.
6. Reverse procedure to install, noting the following:
   a. Do not bend float rod connected to module.
   b. Use new gasket and locknut.
   c. Tighten locknut to specifications.

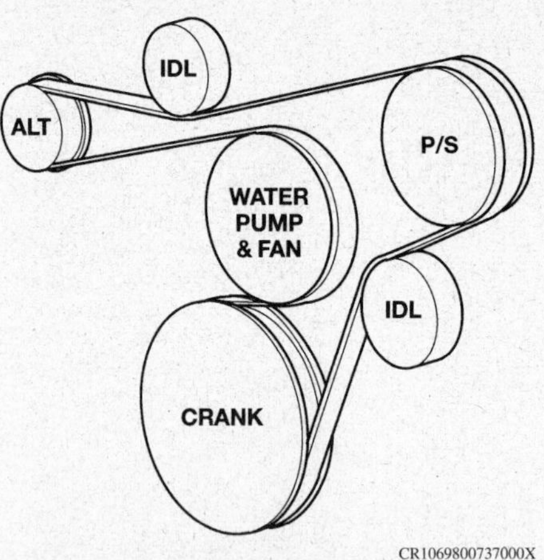

Fig. 6 Serpentine drive belt routing. Less A/C

FUEL FILTER

REPLACE

1. Release fuel system pressure as outlined under "Precautions."
2. Drain and remove fuel tank.
3. Clean area around filter/regulator to prevent contaminants from entering pump module.
4. Remove fuel filter/regulator from rubber grommet by twisting and pulling straight up.
5. Cut old fuel line clamp, using care not to damage plastic fuel line.
6. Remove plastic fuel tube from filter/regulator, then the filter/regulator from fuel pump module.
7. Reverse procedure to install, noting the following:
   a. Install new fuel tube clamp.
   b. Install filter and rotate until fittings are pointed towards driver's side of vehicle.
   c. Tighten line clamp to fuel line using hose clamp pliers No. C-4121, or equivalent. **Do not use conventional side cutters to tighten clamp.**
   d. Inspect for fuel leaks.

TIGHTENING SPECIFICATIONS

Year	Component	Torque, Ft. Lbs.
2002	A/C Compressor Bracket To Engine Bolts	35
	A/C Compressor Mounting Bolts	20
	Camshaft Sprocket Bolt	80
	Cylinder Head Cover	115①
	Exhaust Manifold/Pipe Nuts	20
	Flywheel/Converter Housing Bolts	28
	Flywheel/Crankshaft Bolts	105
	Front Cover To Block Bolts (¼ -20)	60①
	Front Cover To Block Bolts (5⁄16 -18)	16
	Front Engine Mount Insulator Bracket Bolts	60
	Front Engine Mount Insulator Bracket Nuts	35
	Front Engine Mount Thru-Bolt	60
	Oil Pan Bolts (¼-20)	10–11
	Oil Pan Bolts (5⁄16-18)	13
	Rear Engine Mount Support Cushion/ Crossmember Nuts	16
	Rear Engine Mount Support Cushion/Bracket Nuts	34
	Rear Engine Mount Transmission Support Adaptor Bracket	55
	Rear Engine Mount Transmission Support Bracket/Cushion Bolt	55

① — Inch lbs.

3.7L Engine

NOTE: Refer To The "3.7L Engine" In The "Liberty" Chapter For Procedures Not Covered In This Section.

NOTE: On Air Bag Equipped Models, Refer To "Air Bag System Precautions" Located In The Front Of This Manual For System Disarming & Arming Procedures.

NOTE: Refer To "Computer Relearn Procedures" Located In The Front Of This Manual When Battery Power To The Computer Has Been Interrupted.

INDEX

PRECAUTIONS

Air Bag Systems

Refer to "Air Bag System Precautions" in the front of this manual for system disarming and arming procedures.

Fuel System Pressure Relief

1. Remove fuel fill cap.
2. Fuel filler tube contains a spring loaded flap located below fuel cap. Place a non-metallic object into fuel fill tube and press on flap to relieve any tank pressure.
3. Remove fuel pump relay from Power Distribution Center (PDC).
4. Start and run engine until it stalls.
5. Attempt to restart engine to ensure it will no longer run.
6. Turn key to Off position.

Battery Ground Cable

Prior to service, disconnect battery ground cable and isolate as required.

COMPRESSION PRESSURE

Minimum compression pressure should be 100 psi. Maximum variation between cylinders is 25 percent.

ENGINE MOUNT

REPLACE

Dakota

2WD MODELS

FRONT

1. Remove viscous fan. **Remove viscous fan before raising engine. Failure to do so may cause damage to fan blade, fan clutch and fan shroud.**
2. Raise and support vehicle.
3. Remove engine oil filter.
4. Remove oil drain trough.
5. Support engine with a suitable jack and a block of wood across full width of engine oil pan.
6. Support front axle with a suitable jack.
7. Remove bolts that attach engine mounts to front axle.
8. Remove bolts that attach front axle to lefthand engine bracket.
9. Lower front axle.
10. Remove through bolts.
11. Raise engine far enough to be able to remove lefthand and righthand engine mounts.
12. Remove mount to engine attaching bolts.
13. Remove engine mounts.
14. Reverse procedure to install.

REAR

1. Raise vehicle on a hoist.
2. Support transmission using a suitable jack.
3. Remove nuts from transmission mount.
4. Remove two bolts that attach transmission mount to engine bracket.
5. Raise transmission enough to remove mount from crossmember.
6. Remove mount.
7. Reverse procedure to install.

4WD MODELS

FRONT

1. Remove viscous fan. **Remove viscous fan before raising engine. Failure to do so may cause damage to**

fan blade, fan clutch and fan shroud.
2. Raise and support vehicle.
3. Remove skid plate.
4. Remove front crossmember.
5. Remove engine oil filter.
6. Remove oil drain trough.
7. Support engine with a suitable jack and a block of wood across full width of engine oil pan.
8. Support front axle with suitable jack.
9. Remove bolts that attach engine mounts to front axle.
10. Remove bolts that attach front axle to lefthand engine bracket.
11. Lower front axle.
12. Remove trough bolts.
13. Raise engine far enough to be able to remove lefthand and righthand engine mounts.
14. Remove engine mount bolts and mounts.
15. Reverse procedure to install.

REAR

1. Raise vehicle on a hoist.
2. Support transmission using suitable jack.
3. Remove nuts from transmission mount.
4. Remove two bolts that attach transmission mount to engine bracket.
5. Raise transmission enough to remove mount from crossmember.
6. Remove mount.
7. Reverse procedure to install.

Durango

FRONT

2WD

1. Remove viscous fan. **Remove viscous fan before raising engine. Failure to do so may result in damage to fan blade, fan clutch and fan shroud.**
2. Remove engine oil filter.
3. Remove oil drain trough.
4. Install engine support fixture tool No. 8534, or equivalent.
5. Remove thru bolts.
6. Raise engine far enough to be able to remove lefthand and righthand engine mounts.
7. Remove mount to engine attaching bolts.
8. Remove engine mounts.
9. Reverse procedure to install.

4WD

1. Remove viscous fan. **Remove viscous fan before raising engine. Failure to do so may cause damage to fan blade, fan clutch and fan shroud.**
2. Remove skid plate.
3. Remove front crossmember.
4. Remove engine oil filter.
5. Remove oil drain trough.
6. Support front axle with a suitable jack.
7. Install engine support fixture tool No. 8534, or equivalent.
8. Remove bolts that attach engine mounts to front axle.
9. Remove bolts that attach front axle to

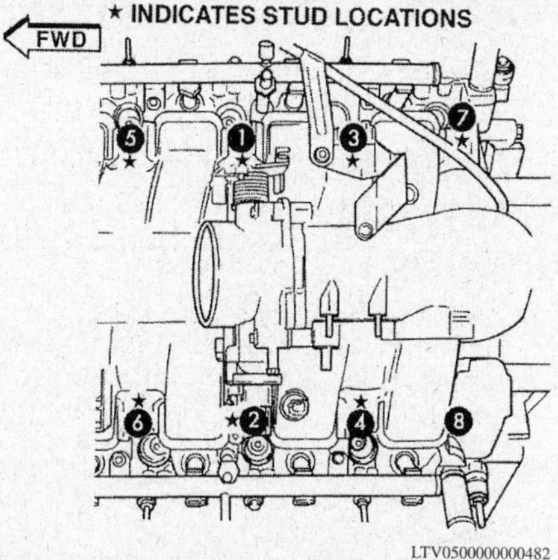

Fig. 1 Intake manifold tightening sequence

lefthand engine bracket.
10. Lower front axle.
11. Remove thru bolts.
12. Raise engine far enough to be able to remove lefthand and righthand engine mounts.
13. Remove engine mount bolts and mounts.
14. Reverse procedure to install.

REAR

2WD

1. Raise vehicle on a hoist.
2. Using a suitable jack, support transmission.
3. Remove nuts from transmission mount.
4. Remove two bolts that attach transmission mount to engine bracket.
5. Raise transmission enough to remove mount from crossmember.
6. Remove mount.
7. Reverse procedure to install.

4WD

1. Raise vehicle on a hoist.
2. Using a suitable jack, support transmission.
3. Remove nuts from transmission mount.
4. Remove two bolts that attach transmission mount to engine bracket.
5. Raise transmission enough to remove mount from crossmember.
6. Remove mount.
7. Reverse procedure to install.

ENGINE

REPLACE

1. Scribe hood hinge outlines on hood, then remove hood.
2. Remove battery, drain cooling system into suitable container and remove air cleaner.
3. Disconnect heater and radiator hoses, then remove radiator. Set fan shroud aside.
4. Remove vacuum lines and all electrical connectors.
5. Disconnect throttle linkage, then remove throttle body.
6. Release fuel system pressure as outlined under "Precautions."
7. Disconnect fuel lines, starter and oil pressure wires.
8. **On models equipped with A/C,** recover refrigerant as outlined in "Air Conditioning" chapter.
9. **On all models,** disconnect power steering hoses, then disconnect A/C hoses.
10. Remove starter motor and alternator, then raise and support vehicle.
11. Disconnect exhaust pipe from exhaust manifold.
12. **On models equipped with automatic transmission,** remove transmission as outlined in **MOTOR's "Domestic Transmission, In-Vehicle Service" or "Transmission Service DVD."**
13. **On models equipped with manual transmission,** remove transmission as outlined in **MOTOR's "Domestic Transmission, In-Vehicle Service" or "Transmission Service DVD."**
14. **On all models,** install suitable engine lifting equipment onto engine lifting eyes.
15. Remove engine mounts as outlined under "Engine Mount, Replace."
16. Lower vehicle and remove engine.
17. Reverse procedure to install. Tighten all nuts and bolts to specifications.

INTAKE MANIFOLD

REPLACE

Removal

1. Remove resonator assembly and air inlet hose.
2. Disconnect throttle and speed control cables.
3. Disconnect electrical connectors for the following components.
   a. Manifold absolute pressure (MAP) sensor.
   b. Intake air temperature (IAT) sensor.
   c. Throttle position (TPS) sensor.
   d. Coolant temperature (CTS) sensor.
   e. Idle air control (IAC) motor.
4. Disconnect vapor purge hose, brake booster hose, speed control servo hose, positive crankcase ventilation (PCV) hose.
5. Disconnect alternator electrical connections.
6. Disconnect air conditioning compressor electrical connections.
7. Disconnect lefthand and righthand radio suppressor straps.
8. Disconnect and remove ignition coil towers.
9. Remove top oil dipstick tube retaining bolt and ground strap.
10. Bleed fuel system.
11. Remove fuel rail.
12. Remove throttle body assembly and mounting bracket.
13. Drain cooling system below coolant temperature level.
14. Remove heater hoses from engine front cover and heater core.
15. Unclip and remove heater hoses and tubes from intake manifold.

16. Remove coolant temperature sensor.
17. Remove intake manifold retaining fasteners in reverse order of tightening sequence.
18. Remove intake manifold.

Installation

1. Install intake manifold gaskets.
2. Install intake manifold.
3. Install intake manifold retaining bolts and tighten in sequence outlined in **Fig. 1,** to 105 inch lbs.
4. Install lefthand and righthand radio suppressor straps.
5. Install throttle body assembly.
6. Connect throttle cable and speed control cable to throttle body.
7. Install fuel rail.
8. Install ignition coil towers.
9. Position and install heater hoses and tubes onto intake manifold.
10. Install heater hoses to heater core and engine front cover.
11. Connect electrical connectors for the following components:
    a. Manifold absolute pressure (MAP) sensor.
    b. Intake air temperature (IAT) sensor.
    c. Throttle position (TPS) sensor.
    d. Coolant temperature (CTS) sensor.
    e. Idle air control (IAC) motor.
    f. Ignition coil towers.
    g. Fuel injectors.
12. Install top oil dipstick tube retaining bolt and ground strap.
13. Connect alternator electrical connections.
14. Connect vapor purge hose, brake booster hose, speed control servo hose, positive crankcase ventilation (PCV) hose.
15. Fill cooling system.
16. Install resonator assembly and air inlet hose.

EXHAUST MANIFOLD

REPLACE

1. Raise and support vehicle.
2. Remove bolts and nuts attaching exhaust pipe to exhaust manifold.
3. Lower vehicle, then remove exhaust manifold bolts, nuts and washers, and exhaust manifold.
4. Reverse procedure to install, noting the following:
    a. Install exhaust manifold on two cylinder head studs using conical washers and nuts.
    b. Install new bolts and washers in remaining holes.
    c. Starting from center, working outward, tighten nuts and bolts to specifications.

CYLINDER HEAD

REPLACE

Refer to "3.7L Engine" in "Liberty" chapter for cylinder head replacement procedure.

VALVE ARRANGEMENT

Refer to "3.7L Engine" in "Liberty" chapter for valve arrangement.

VALVE & VALVE SPRINGS

REPLACE

1. With cylinder head removed, compress valve springs using valve spring compressor tool No. MD-998772-A and adapter No. 6716A, or equivalents.
2. Remove valve retaining locks, valve spring retainers, valve stem cup seals and valve springs.
3. Before removing valves, remove any burrs from valve stem lock grooves to prevent damage to valve guides. Identify valves for installation reference.
4. Reverse procedure to install, noting the following:
    a. Coat valve stems with lubricant before installing.
    b. If valves or seats were ground, inspect valve stem height. If valve is too long, replace cylinder head.
    c. Measure installed height of springs.
    d. Ensure measurement is taken from bottom of spring seat in cylinder head to bottom surface of spring retainer.
    e. If height is greater than 1 11/16 inches, install a 1/16 inch spacer in head counterbore.

VALVE TIMING CHECK

1. Turn crankshaft until No. 6 exhaust valve is closing and No. 6 intake valve is opening.
2. Insert 1/4 inch spacer between rocker arm pad and stem tip of No. 1 intake valve. Allow spring load to bleed valve tappet down, giving effect of solid tappet.
3. Install a suitable dial indicator so plunger contacts valve spring retainer as nearly perpendicular as possible. Zero indicator.
4. Rotate crankshaft clockwise until valve has lifted .010 inch. Do not turn crankshaft any further clockwise as valve spring might bottom and cause serious damage.
5. Crankshaft pulley timing should read between 10° before top dead center to 2° after TDC. Remove spacer.
6. If reading is not as specified, inspect sprocket index marks, timing chain for wear and accuracy of DC mark on timing indicator.

VALVE ADJUSTMENT

These engines are equipped with hydraulic lifters. No provision for adjustment is provided.

ROCKER ARMS

REPLACE

Refer to "3.7L Engine" in "Liberty" chapter for rocker arm replacement procedure.

TIMING CHAIN COVER

REPLACE

1. Drain cooling system.
2. Remove electric cooling fan and fan shroud assembly.
3. Remove radiator fan.
4. Disconnect both heater hoses at timing cover.
5. Disconnect lower radiator hose at engine.
6. Remove accessory drive belt tensioner assembly.
7. Remove crankshaft damper.
8. Remover alternator.
9. Remove A/C compressor. **3.7L engine uses an anerobic sealer instead of a gasket to seal front cover to engine block, from factory. For service, Mopar® Grey Engine RTV sealant, or equivalent, must be substituted. It is not required to remove water pump for timing cover removal.**
10. Remove bolts holding timing cover to engine block.
11. Remove timing cover.
12. Reverse procedure to install.

TIMING CHAIN

REPLACE

Refer to "3.7L Engine" in "Liberty" chapter for timing chain replacement procedure.

CAMSHAFT

REPLACE

Refer to "3.7L Engine" in "Liberty" chapter for camshaft replacement procedure.

PISTON & ROD ASSEMBLY

Refer to "3.7L Engine" in "Liberty" chapter for piston and rod assembly.

MAIN & ROD BEARINGS

Refer to "3.7L Engine" in "Liberty" chapter main and rod bearings.

CRANKSHAFT SEAL

REPLACE

If the timing chain front cover is not misaligned, the front crankshaft oil seal can be replaced without removing the timing chain cover.

1. Remove accessory drive belt.
2. Remove A/C compressor mounting fasteners and set aside.
3. Drain cooling system.
4. Remove upper radiator hose.
5. Disconnect electrical connector for fan mounted inside radiator shroud.
6. Remove radiator cooling fan.
7. Remove crankshaft damper bolt.

8. Remove damper using tool No. 8513, or equivalent, and tool No. 1026, or equivalent.
9. Remove crankshaft front seal using tool No. 8511, or equivalent.
10. Reverse procedure to install.

CRANKSHAFT REAR OIL SEAL

REPLACE

1. If being performed in vehicle, remove transmission.
2. Remove flexplate. **Crankshaft oil seal can not be reused after removal. Crankshaft rear oil seal remover tool No. 8506, or equivalent, must be install deeply into seal. Continue to tighten removal tool into seal until tool can not be turned farther. Failure to install tool correctly the first time will cause tool to pull free of seal without removing seal from engine.**
3. Remove crankshaft rear oil seal using tool No. 8506, or equivalent.
4. Reverse procedure to install.

OIL PAN

REPLACE

Removal

1. Install engine support fixture, tool No. 8534, or equivalent. **Do not raise engine at this time.**
2. Remove both lefthand and righthand side engine mount through bolts.
3. Remove structural dust cover.
4. Drain engine oil into suitable container.
5. Raise engine using tool No. 8534, or equivalent, to provide clearance to remove oil pan. **Only raise engine enough to provide clearance for oil pan removal. Inspect for proper clearance at fan shroud to fan and cowl intake manifold.**
6. **On models equipped with 4WD,** proceed as follows:
   a. Remove pinion bracket. **Front axle must be lowered, to provide clearance for oil pan removal. It is not required to remove front axle from vehicle, or remove axle shafts.**
   b. Disconnect front driveshaft at front axle.
   c. Remove front axle mounting bolts.
   d. Lower axle using suitable jack enough to provide clearance to remove oil pan.
7. **On all models,** remove oil pan mounting bolts and oil pan. **Do not pry on oil pan or oil pan gasket. Gasket is integral to engine windage tray and does not come out with oil pan.**
8. Unbolt oil pump pickup tube and remove tube.
9. Inspect integral windage tray and gasket and replace as required.

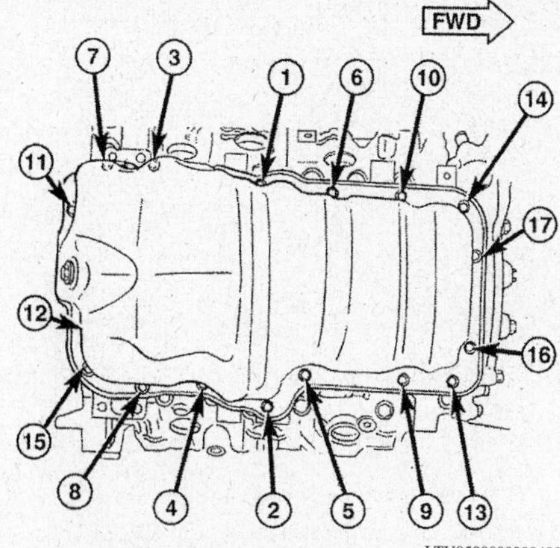

Fig. 2 Oil pan tightening sequence

Installation

1. Clean oil pan gasket mating surface of bedplate and oil pan.
2. Position oil pan gasket and pickup tube with new O-ring. Install mounting bolt and nuts. Tighten bolt and nuts to specification.
3. Position oil pan and install mounting bolts. Tighten mounting bolts to specification in sequence outlined, **Fig. 2.**
4. Lower engine into mounts using tool No. 8534, or equivalent.
5. Install both lefthand and righthand engine mount through bolts. Tighten to specification.
6. Remove tool No. 8534, or equivalent.
7. Install structural dust cover.
8. **On models equipped with 4WD,** proceed as follows:
   a. Raise axle using suitable jack. **Front axle must be lowered, to provide clearance for oil pan removal. It is not required to remove front axle from vehicle, or remove axle shafts.**
   b. Install front axle mounting bolts.
   c. Install pinion bracket.
   d. Install front driveshaft to front axle.
9. **On all models,** fill engine oil.
10. Start engine and inspect for leaks.

OIL PUMP

REPLACE

Refer to "3.7L Engine" in "Liberty" chapter for oil pump replacement procedure.

OIL PUMP SERVICE

Disassemble

1. Remove pressure relief valve as follows:
   a. Remove cotter pin.
   b. Drill a ⅛ inch hole into relief valve retainer cap and insert a self threading sheet metal screw.
   c. Clamp screw into vise and while supporting oil pump remove cap by tapping pump body with soft faced hammer.
   d. Discard retainer cap, then remove spring and relief valve.
2. Remove oil pump cover.
3. Remove pump outer and inner rotor with shaft, then wash all components in solvent.

Inspection

1. Inspect oil pump cover. Replace if scratched or grooved.
2. Position a straightedge across pump cover surface. If a .0015 inch feeler gauge can be inserted between cover and straightedge, replace assembly.
3. Measure thickness and diameter of outer rotor. Replace if thickness is .825 inch or less, or diameter is 2.469 inches or less.
4. Replace inner rotor and shaft assembly if inner rotor is .825 inch or less thick.
5. Slide outer rotor into pump body. Press rotor to side and measure clearance between rotor and pump body. Replace assembly if clearance is .014 inch or more.
6. Install inner rotor and shaft into pump body. Replace shaft and both rotors if clearance between inner and outer rotors is .008 inch or more.
7. Place a straightedge across face of pump between bolt holes. Replace pump assembly if a feeler gauge of .004 inch or more can be inserted between rotors and straightedge.
8. Inspect oil pressure relief valve plunger for scoring and free operation in its bore.
9. Ensure relief valve spring has a free length of approximately 1.95 inches.
10. Relief valve spring should test between 19.5–20.5 lbs. when compressed to 1.34 inches.

Assemble

1. Install pump rotors and shaft.
2. Position oil pump cover onto pump body. Tighten cover bolts to specification.
3. Install relief valve and spring, then insert cotter pin.
4. Tap on new retainer cap.
5. Prime oil pump before installing.

BELT TENSION DATA

Belt tension is automatically adjusted.

SERPENTINE DRIVE BELT

Belt Routing

Refer to **Fig. 3** for belt routing.

Belt Replacement

REMOVAL

Belt tension is not adjustable. Belt adjustment is maintained by automatic (spring load) belt tensioner. **Do not let tensioner arm snap back to freearm position, severe damage may occur to tensioner.**

1. Rotate belt tension until it contacts it's stop. Remove belt, then slowly rotate tensioner into freearm position.

INSTALLATION

Belt tension is not adjustable. Belt adjustment is maintained by an automatic (spring load) belt tensioner.

1. Inspect condition of all pulleys. **When installing serpentine accessory drive belt, belt must be routed correctly. If not, engine may overheat due to water pump rotating in wrong direction.**
2. Install new belt. Route belt around all pulleys except idler pulley. Rotate tensioner arm until it contacts it's stop position. Route belt around idler and slowly let tensioner rotate into belt. Make sure belt is seated onto all pulleys.
3. With drive belt installed, inspect belt wear indicator.

Belt Tensioner Replacement

A used belt should be replaced if tensioner indexing arrow has moved to minimum tension indicator. Tensioner travel stops at this point.

1. Remove accessory drive belt.
2. Remove tensioner assembly from mounting bracket.
3. Remove pulley bolt. Remove pulley from tensioner. **Because of high spring pressure, do not attempt to disassemble automatic tensioner, unit is serviced as an assembly except for pulley on tensioner.**
4. Reverse procedure to install noting the following:
   a. An indexing slot is located on back of tensioner. Align this slot to head of bolt on front cover.
   b. Inspect belt indexing marks.

COOLING SYSTEM BLEED

Refer to "3.7L Engine" in "Liberty" chapter for cooling system bleed procedure.

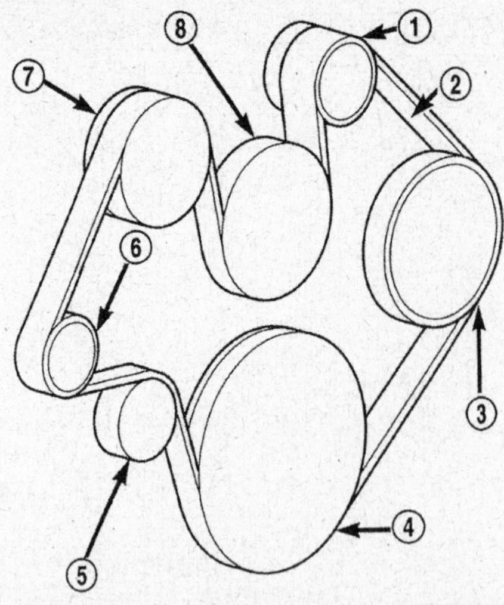

Fig. 3 Serpentine belt routing

THERMOSTAT

REPLACE

1. Drain cooling system into suitable container.
2. Raise vehicle on hoist.
3. Remove splash shield.
4. Remove lower radiator hose clamp and lower radiator hose at thermostat housing.
5. Remove thermostat housing mounting bolts, thermostat housing, then thermostat.
6. Reverse procedure to install.

WATER PUMP

REPLACE

1. Drain cooling system into suitable container.
2. Remove viscous fan drive assembly from water pump.
3. If water pump is being replaced, do not unbolt fan blade assembly from thermal viscous fan drive.
4. Remove two fan shroud-to-radiator screws. Disconnect coolant overflow hose, windshield washer fluid hose and washer pump electrical connector.
5. Remove fan shroud and fan blade/viscous fan drive assembly from vehicle.
6. After removing fan blade/viscous fan drive assembly, do not place thermal viscous fan drive in horizontal position. If stored horizontally, silicone fluid in visous fan drive could drain into its bearing assembly and contaminate lubricant.
7. Remove accessory drive belt from water pump pulley.
8. Remove lower radiator hose clamp and remove lower hose at water pump.
9. Remove seven water pump mounting bolts and one stud bolt.
10. Remove water pump and gasket. Discard gasket. **Do not pry water pump at timing chain case/cover. Machined surfaces may be damaged resulting in leaks.**
11. Reverse procedure to install.

RADIATOR

REPLACE

1. Drain cooling system into suitable container.
2. Remove pushpins and upper condenser radiator seal.
3. Remove upper radiator hose.
4. Disconnect power steering hoses from power steering fluid transmission cooler.
5. Remove overflow tube.
6. Remove radiator fan shroud from radiator and position over radiator fan.
7. Raise and support vehicle.
8. Disconnect power steering cooler lines.
9. Remove lower radiator hose.
10. Lower vehicle.
11. Remove upper radiator mounting bolts.
12. Remove radiator.
13. Remove power steering fluid and transmission oil cooler from radiator, if required.
14. Reverse procedure to install.

FUEL PUMP

REPLACE

Fuel system is under a constant pressure (even with engine off). Before servicing fuel pump module, fuel system pressure must be released.

1. Drain and remove fuel tank.
2. Note rotational position of module before attempting removal. An indexing arrow is located on top of module for this purpose.
3. Position lockring remover installer tool No 9340, or equivalent, into notches on outside edge of lockring.
4. Install ½ inch drive breaker bar to lockring remover installer tool No. 9340, or equivalent.
5. Rotate breaker bar counter-clockwise to remove lockring.
6. Remove lockring. Module will spring up slightly when lockring is removed.
7. Remove module from fuel tank. Be careful not to bend float arm while removing.
8. Reverse procedure to install.

FUEL FILTER

REPLACE

Refer to "3.7L Engine" in "Liberty" chapter for fuel filter replacement procedure.

TIGHTENING SPECIFICATIONS

Year	Component	Torque Ft. Lbs.
2004–2006	Bed Plate	③
	Camshaft Bearing Cap	100①
	Camshaft Sprocket	90
	Connecting Rod Cap	20②
	Crankshaft Damper	130
	Cylinder Head	④
	Engine Mount Bracket To Block	45
	Exhaust Manifold	18
	Flexplate	70
	Hydraulic Tensioner	21
	Intake Manifold	105①
	Oil Fill Tube	105①
	Oil Pan	11
	Oil Pan Drain Plug	25
	Oil Pickup Tube	21
	Oil Pump	21
	Oil Pump Cover	105①
	Rear Mount To Transmission	34
	Structural Collar	40
	Timing Chain Cover	43
	Timing Chain Guide	21
	Timing Chain Primary Tensioner	21
	Timing Chain Tensioner Arm	21
	Timing Drive Idler Sprocket	25
	Thermostat Housing	105①
	Water Pump	43

① — Inch lbs.
② — Plus an additional 90°.
③ — Refer to “Main & Rod Bearings” for specification.
④ — Refer to “Cylinder Head, Replace” for specification.

3.9L & 5.9L Engines

NOTE: On Air Bag Equipped Models, Refer To "Air Bag System Precautions" Located In The Front Of This Manual For System Disarming & Arming Procedures.

NOTE: Refer To "Computer Relearn Procedures" Located In The Front Of This Manual When Battery Power To The Computer Has Been Interrupted.

INDEX

PRECAUTIONS

Air Bag Systems

Refer to "Air Bag System Precautions" in the front of this manual for system disarming and arming procedures.

Fuel System Pressure Relief

1. Remove fuel fill cap.
2. Fuel filler tube contains a spring loaded flap located below fuel cap. Place a non-metallic object into fuel fill tube and press on flap to relieve any tank pressure.
3. Remove fuel pump relay from Power Distribution Center (PDC).
4. Start and run engine until it stalls.
5. Attempt to restart engine to ensure it will no longer run.
6. Turn key to Off position.

Battery Ground Cable

Prior to service, disconnect battery ground cable and isolate as required.

COMPRESSION PRESSURE

Minimum compression pressure should be 100 psi. Maximum variation between cylinders is 25 percent.

ENGINE MOUNT

REPLACE

Dakota

2WD MODELS

FRONT

1. Raise hood and position fan to ensure clearance for radiator top tank and hose.
2. Install suitable engine lifting equipment. **Do not lift engine by intake manifold.**
3. Raise and support vehicle.
4. Remove attaching bolts and washers from front support insulator assembly, **Figs. 1 through 3.**
5. Raise engine with lifting fixture slightly. Remove insulator retaining bolts, then the insulator assembly and heat shield.

REAR

1. Raise and support vehicle.
2. Support transmission with transmission jack.
3. **On models equipped with automatic transmission,** raise engine and transmission slightly.
4. **On models equipped with automatic transmission,** remove stud nuts attaching insulator to crossmember, **Fig. 4.**
5. **On models with manual transmission,** raise engine and transmission slightly.
6. **On models with manual transmission,** remove stud nuts attaching insulator to transmission extension, **Fig. 5.**
7. **On all models,** remove insulator.
8. Reverse procedure to install. Tighten nuts and bolts to specifications.

4WD MODELS

FRONT

1. Raise and support vehicle.
2. Install suitable engine lifting device.
3. Remove front axle.
4. On lefthand front insulator mount only, remove starter wires and starter motor assembly.

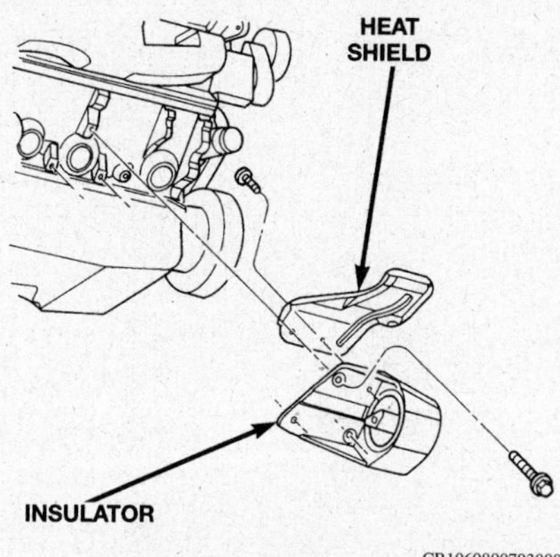

Fig. 1 Righthand front engine mount. Dakota w/2WD

5. On all front insulator mounts, remove insulator to frame through bolts, **Figs. 6 through 8.**
6. Raise engine slightly.
7. Remove upper insulator to support bracket stud nut and insulator to support through bolt.
8. Remove engine mount insulator.
9. If engine support bracket is being replaced, remove support bracket to transmission bell housing bolts and three support bracket to engine block bolts.
10. Remove support bracket.

REAR

1. Raise and support vehicle.
2. Support transmission with suitable transmission jack, then remove stud nuts holding insulator to crossmember, **Figs. 9 and 10.**
3. Raise rear of transmission slightly.
4. **On models equipped with automatic transmission,** remove bolts holding insulator to bracket, then remove insulator.
5. **On models equipped with manual transmission,** remove bolts holding insulator to transmission, then remove insulator.
6. **On all models,** reverse procedure to install. Tighten all nuts and bolts to specifications.

Durango

FRONT

Engine and front axle must be supported during any service procedures involving the front support assemblies.

1. Raise and support vehicle.
2. Install engine support fixture tool No. C-3487-A, or equivalent, then remove the front axle.
3. On lefthand mount insulator, remove starter wires and starter motor as outlined under "Starter, Replace" in "Electrical" section.
4. Remove insulator to frame through bolt, **Fig. 8,** then raise engine slightly.
5. Remove upper insulator to support bracket stud nut, then the insulator to support through bolt.

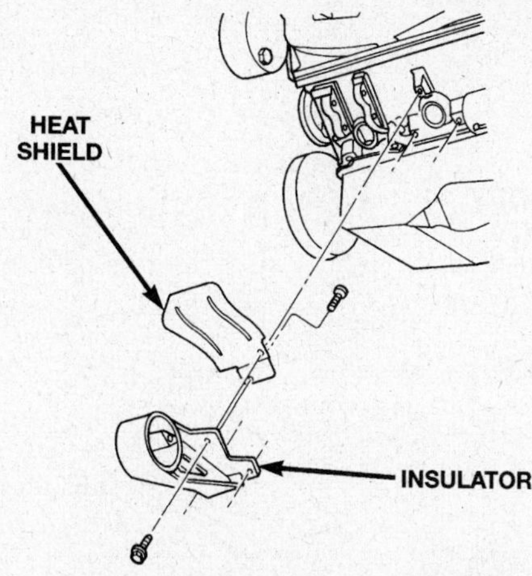

Fig. 2 Lefthand front engine mount. Dakota w/2WD

6. Remove engine mount insulator, **Figs. 6 and 7.**
7. If engine support bracket removal is required, proceed as follows:
   a. Remove support bracket to transmission bell housing retaining bolts.
   b. Remove three support bracket to engine block bolts.
   c. Remove support bracket.
8. Reverse procedures to install. Tighten nuts and bolts to specification.

REAR

1. Raise and support vehicle.
2. Support transmission with a suitable transmission jack.
3. Remove insulator to crossmember retaining nuts.
4. Raise rear of transmission slightly.
5. Remove insulator to insulator bracket retaining nuts, then the insulator.
6. Reverse procedure to install. Tighten nuts and bolts to specification.

ENGINE

REPLACE

1. Scribe hood hinge outlines on hood, then remove hood.
2. Remove battery, drain cooling system into suitable container and remove air cleaner.
3. Disconnect heater and radiator hoses, then remove radiator. Set fan shroud aside.
4. Remove vacuum lines, distributor cap and all electrical connectors.
5. Disconnect throttle linkage, then remove throttle body.
6. Release fuel system pressure as outlined under "Precautions."
7. Disconnect fuel lines, starter and oil pressure wires.
8. **On models equipped with A/C,** recover refrigerant as outlined in "Air Conditioning" chapter.
9. **On all models,** disconnect power steering hoses, then disconnect A/C hoses.

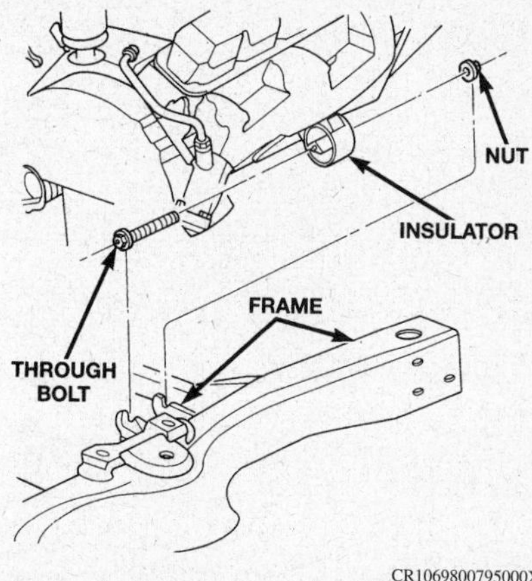

Fig. 3 Engine mount insulator at frame. Dakota w/2WD

10. Remove starter motor and alternator, then raise and support vehicle.
11. Disconnect exhaust pipe from exhaust manifold.
12. **On models equipped with automatic transmission,** remove transmission as outlined in **MOTOR's "Domestic Transmission, In-Vehicle Service" or "Transmission Service DVD."**
13. **On models equipped with manual transmission,** remove transmission as outlined in **MOTOR's "Domestic Transmission, In-Vehicle Service" or "Transmission Service DVD."**
14. **On all models,** install suitable engine lifting equipment onto engine lifting eyes.
15. Remove engine mounts as outlined under "Engine Mount, Replace."
16. Lower vehicle and remove engine.
17. Reverse procedure to install. Tighten all nuts and bolts to specifications.

INTAKE MANIFOLD

REPLACE

Removal

1. Drain cooling system into suitable container.
2. Remove A/C compressor and position aside. It is not required to disconnect A/C hoses or pipes.
3. Remove air cleaner and alternator.
4. Release fuel system pressure as outlined in "Precautions."
5. Remove fuel lines and fuel rail.
6. Disconnect throttle linkage, speed control and transmission kickdown cables, then remove throttle return spring.
7. Remove distributor cap and wires, then disconnect coil wires.
8. Disconnect heat indicator sending unit wire, then remove heater and bypass hoses.
9. Remove closed crankcase ventilation and evaporation control systems.
10. Remove intake manifold bolts, then lift intake manifold and throttle body out of engine compartment.

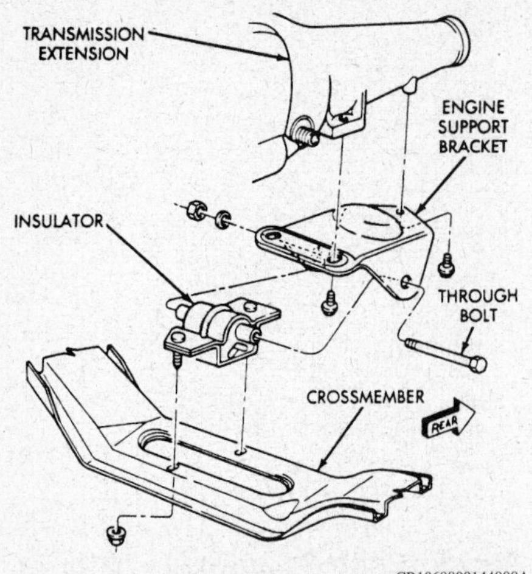

Fig. 4 Rear engine mount. Dakota w/2WD & automatic transmission

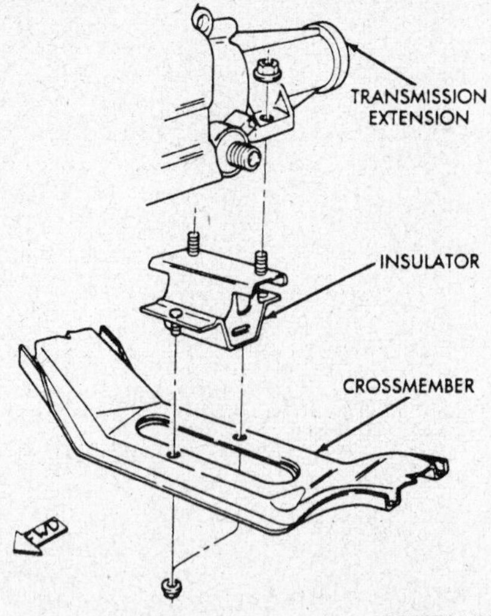

Fig. 5 Rear engine mount. Dakota w/2WD & automatic transmission

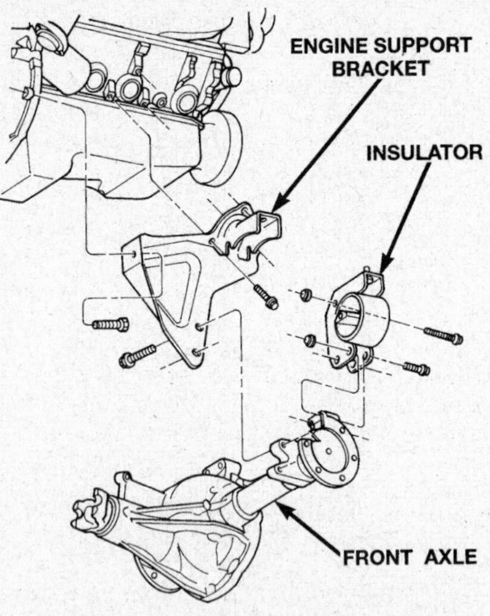

Fig. 6 Righthand front engine mount. 4WD models

11. Remove and discard flange side, front and rear crossover gaskets.
12. Remove throttle body and discard gasket.
13. Support upside down manifold, then remove plenum pan bolts and lift pan off manifold. Discard gaskets.

Installation

1. Install plenum pan using a new gasket, hand tighten bolts.
2. **Torque** bolts first to 24 inch lbs., then to 48 inch lbs., and finally to 84 inch lbs., using sequence outlined in **Fig. 11.**
3. Install throttle body with new gasket.
4. Install four plastic locator dowels into block holes, **Fig. 12.**
5. Apply silicone rubber adhesive sealant slightly higher than crossover gasket (approximately .2 inch) to four corner joints. Excessive sealant may reduce flange gasket effectiveness.
6. Install front and rear crossover gaskets onto dowels, then install flange gasket. Ensure vertical port alignment tab is resting on block deck face and horizontal tabs align with mating cylinder head gasket tabs.
7. Lower manifold into position and ensure seal placement, then remove alignment studs.
8. **On models equipped with 3.9L engine,** tighten intake manifold bolts in sequence, **Fig. 13,** as follows:
   a. Step 1: **Torque** bolts 1 and 2 in alternating steps of 12 inch lbs., to 72 inch lbs.
   b. Step 2: **Torque** bolts 3 through 12 to 72 inch lbs.
   c. Step 3: Inspect all bolts are **torqued** to 72 inch lbs.
   d. Step 4: **Torque** all bolts in sequence to 12 ft. lbs.
   e. Step 5: Inspect all bolts are **torqued** to 12 ft. lbs.
9. **On models equipped with 5.9L engine,** tighten intake manifold bolts in sequence, **Fig. 14,** as follows:
   a. Step 1: **Torque** bolts 1 through 4 in alternating steps of 12 inch lbs., to 72 inch lbs.
   b. Step 2: **Torque** bolts 5 through 12 to 72 inch lbs.
   c. Step 3: Inspect that all bolts are **torqued** to 72 inch lbs.
   d. Step 4: **Torque** all bolts in sequence, to 12 ft. lbs.
   e. Step 5: Inspect that all bolts are **torqued** to 12 ft. lbs.
10. **On all models,** install closed crankcase ventilation and evaporation control systems.
11. Connect coil and heat indicator sending unit wires, then install heater and bypass hoses.
12. Install distributor cap and wires, then connect accelerator linkage, speed control and transmission kickdown cables.
13. Install fuel lines, fuel rail, alternator, serpentine belt and air cleaner.
14. Fill cooling system.

EXHAUST MANIFOLD

REPLACE

1. Raise and support vehicle.
2. Remove bolts and nuts attaching exhaust pipe to exhaust manifold.
3. Lower vehicle, then remove exhaust manifold bolts, nuts and washers, and exhaust manifold.
4. Reverse procedure to install, noting the following:
   a. Install exhaust manifold on two cylinder head studs using conical washers and nuts.
   b. Install new bolts and washers in remaining holes.
   c. Starting from center, working outward, tighten nuts and bolts to specifications.

CYLINDER HEAD

REPLACE

1. Drain cooling system into suitable container.
2. Remove alternator and closed crankcase ventilation system, then disconnect evaporation control system.
3. Remove air cleaner, then release fuel system pressure as outlined under "Precautions."
4. Disconnect fuel lines, accelerator linkage, speed control and transmission kickdown cables, then remove throttle return spring.
5. Remove distributor cap and wires, then disconnect coil and coolant temperature sending unit wires as well as heater and bypass hoses.
6. Disconnect all vacuum supply hoses and fuel injector wiring harnesses from intake manifold.
7. Remove cylinder head cover and gasket, then the intake manifold and throttle body. Discard flange side, front and rear crossover gaskets.
8. Remove exhaust manifolds.
9. Remove rocker arm assemblies and push rods. **Identify pushrods for installation reference.**
10. Remove cylinder head bolts, and cylinder heads. Discard head gasket.
11. Reverse procedure to install, noting the following:
    a. **Torque** cylinder head bolts in two steps; first step to 50 ft. lbs., second step to 105 ft. lbs., using sequence outlined, **Figs. 15 and 16.**
    b. When tightening rocker arm bolts, ensure piston is not at TDC.
    c. Allow hydraulic roller tappets five minutes to bleed down before rotating or cranking engine.

VALVE ARRANGEMENT

3.9L Engine

Front to Rear ....E-I-I-E-E-I

5.9L Engine

Front to Rear ....E-I-I-E-E-I-I-E

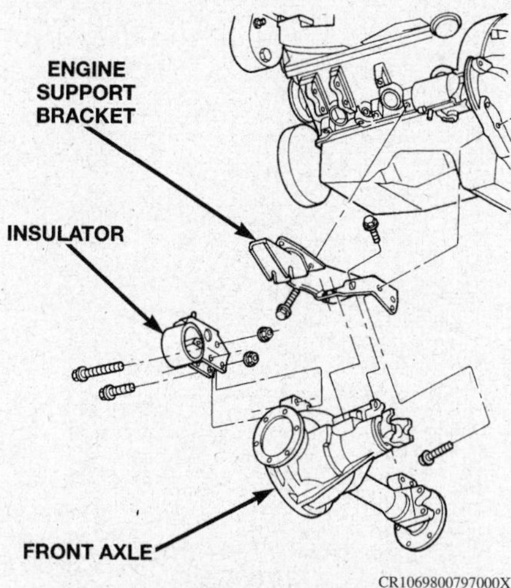

Fig. 7 Lefthand front engine mount. 4WD models

VALVE & VALVE SPRINGS

REPLACE

1. With cylinder head removed, compress valve springs using valve spring compressor tool No. MD-998772-A and adapter No. 6716A, or equivalents.
2. Remove valve retaining locks, valve spring retainers, valve stem cup seals and valve springs.
3. Before removing valves, remove any burrs from valve stem lock grooves to prevent damage to valve guides. Identify valves for installation reference.
4. Reverse procedure to install, noting the following:
   a. Coat valve stems with lubricant before installing.
   b. If valves or seats were ground, inspect valve stem height. If valve is too long, replace cylinder head.
   c. Measure installed height of springs.
   d. Ensure measurement is taken from bottom of spring seat in cylinder head to bottom surface of spring retainer.
   e. If height is greater than $1\frac{11}{16}$ inches, install a $\frac{1}{16}$ inch spacer in head counterbore.

VALVE TIMING CHECK

1. Turn crankshaft until No. 6 exhaust valve is closing and No. 6 intake valve is opening.
2. Insert $\frac{1}{4}$ inch spacer between rocker arm pad and stem tip of No. 1 intake valve. Allow spring load to bleed valve tappet down, giving effect of solid tappet.
3. Install a suitable dial indicator so plunger contacts valve spring retainer as nearly perpendicular as possible. Zero indicator.
4. Rotate crankshaft clockwise until valve has lifted .010 inch. Do not turn crankshaft any further clockwise as valve spring might bottom and cause serious damage.

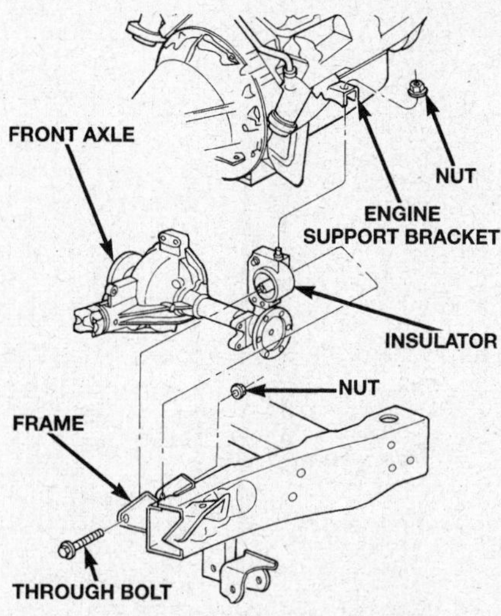

Fig. 8 Engine mount insulator at frame. 4WD models

5. Crankshaft pulley timing should read between 10° before top dead center to 2° after TDC. Remove spacer.
6. If reading is not as specified, inspect sprocket index marks, timing chain for wear and accuracy of DC mark on timing indicator.

VALVE ADJUSTMENT

These engines are equipped with hydraulic lifters. No provision for adjustment is provided.

ROCKER ARMS

REPLACE

1. Disconnect spark plug wires, then remove cylinder head cover and gasket.
2. Remove rocker arm bolt, pivot and rocker arm, keeping them in order for installation.
3. Reverse procedure to install, noting the following:
   a. Rotating crankshaft until "V6" or "V8" mark lines up with TDC mark on timing chase case cover 147° after TDC.
   b. Tighten bolts to specifications.

TIMING CHAIN COVER

REPLACE

1. Drain cooling system into suitable container.
2. Remove serpentine drive belt as outlined under "Serpentine Drive Belt."
3. Remove water pump as outlined under "Water Pump, Replace."
4. Remove power steering pump as outlined under "Power Steering Pump, Replace" in "Front Suspension & Steering" section.
5. Remove vibration damper.
6. Loosen oil pan bolts, then remove front bolt at each side.
7. Remove timing chain cover retaining bolts.

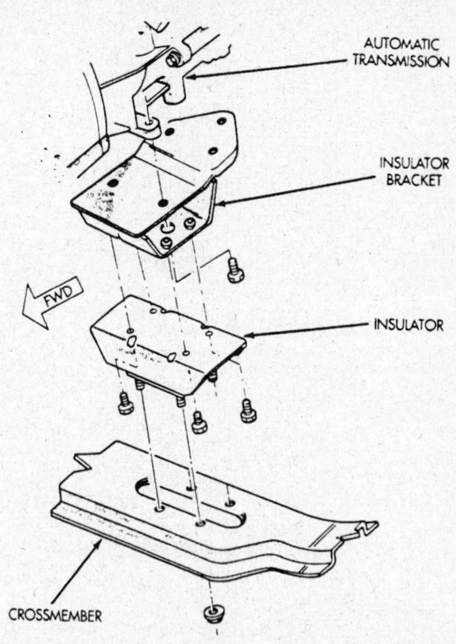

Fig. 9 Rear engine mount. Dakota w/4WD & automatic transmission

8. Remove cover and gasket. **Do not damage oil pan gasket.**
9. Reverse procedures to install.

TIMING CHAIN

REPLACE

Removal

1. Drain cooling system into suitable container.
2. Remove timing chain cover as outlined under "Timing Chain Cover, Replace."
3. Rotate crankshaft to align timing marks to number one TDC, **Fig. 17.**
4. Remove camshaft sprocket retaining bolt, then the timing chain with crankshaft and camshaft sprockets.
5. **On models, equipped with 3.9L engine,** proceed as follows:
   a. Place crankshaft sprocket onto crankshaft, then compress tensioner shoe by placing a large screwdriver between crankshaft sprocket and tensioner shoe, **Fig. 18.**
   b. Compress shoe until hole in shoe aligns with hole in bracket.
   c. Slide a suitable pin into holes, then remove screw driver.

Installation

1. Place both camshaft sprocket and crankshaft sprocket on bench with timing marks on an exact imaginary center line through both camshaft and crankshaft bores.
2. Place timing chain around both sprockets.
3. Slide both sprockets evenly over their respective shafts and verify alignment of timing marks with straight-edge if required.
4. Install camshaft bolt. Tighten bolt to specifications.

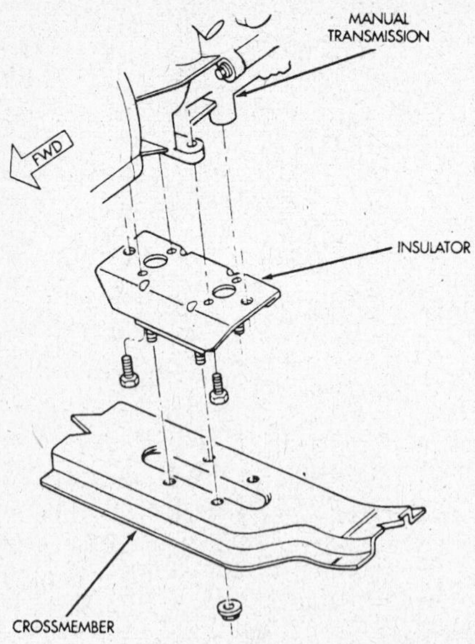

Fig. 10 Rear engine mount. Dakota w/4WD & manual transmission

5. **On models equipped with 3.9L engine,** remove tensioner pin.
6. **On all models,** verify alignment of timing marks.
7. Install timing chain cover.

CAMSHAFT

REPLACE

1. Drain cooling system into suitable container.
2. Remove radiator as outlined under "Radiator, Replace."
3. Remove intake manifold as outlined under "Intake Manifold, Replace."
4. Remove distributor assembly.
5. Remove cylinder head covers, then the timing chain cover as outlined under "Timing Chain Cover, Replace."
6. Remove rocker arms.
7. Remove pushrods and tappets. Identify each part for installation reference.
8. Remove distributor as outlined under "Distributor, Replace" in "Electrical" section, then lift out oil pump and distributor drive shaft.
9. **On models equipped with 3.9L engine,** remove three tensioner to block retaining bolts, then the tensioner.
10. **On all models,** install a long bolt into front of camshaft, then remove camshaft. **Do not to damage cam bearings with cam lobes.**
11. Reverse procedures to install. Tighten all fasteners to specification.

PISTON & ROD ASSEMBLY

Identify connecting rods and caps by cylinder before removing. Remove pistons and connecting rods from top of cylinder only, with crankshaft centered at bottom dead center. **Do not nick crankshaft journals.**

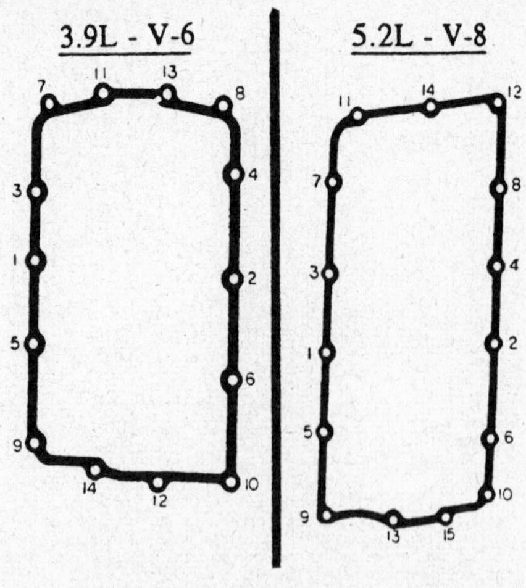

Fig. 11 Plenum pan bolt tightening sequence

It is important that pistons be inspected for taper and elliptical shape, **Fig. 19.**

Before installing pistons and connecting rods, ensure compression ring gaps are staggered so that neither is on-line with oil ring rail gap. Install piston and connecting rod assembly into engine with notch or groove on piston top facing front of engine and larger chamber on connecting rod bore facing crankshaft journal fillet.

Fit rods one bank at a time; do not alternate from side to side. Connecting rods and pistons are not interchangeable between banks.

MAIN & ROD BEARINGS

Install connecting rod bearings in pairs. Do not use a new bearing half with an old bearing half. Do not file rods or bearing caps. Ensure V-groove in lower bearing shell is in line with V-groove in cap parting face. Install shells with tangs in rod and cap machined grooves. Bearings are available in are available in .001, .002, .003, .010 and .012 inch underseas.

On 3.9L engine, lower main bearing halves of Nos. 1 and 3 are interchangeable. Upper and lower No. 2 bearing halves are flanged to carry thrust loads and are not interchangeable with any other bearing halves.

On 5.9L engine, lower main bearing halves of Nos. 2 and 4 are interchangeable. Upper and lower No. 3 bearing halves are flanged to carry thrust loads and are not interchangeable with any other bearing halves.

CRANKSHAFT SEAL

REPLACE

If the timing chain front cover is not misaligned, the front crankshaft oil seal can be replaced without removing the timing chain cover.

1. Remove vibration damper.
2. To inspect front cover alignment, insert front seal installation tool No. 6335, or equivalent.

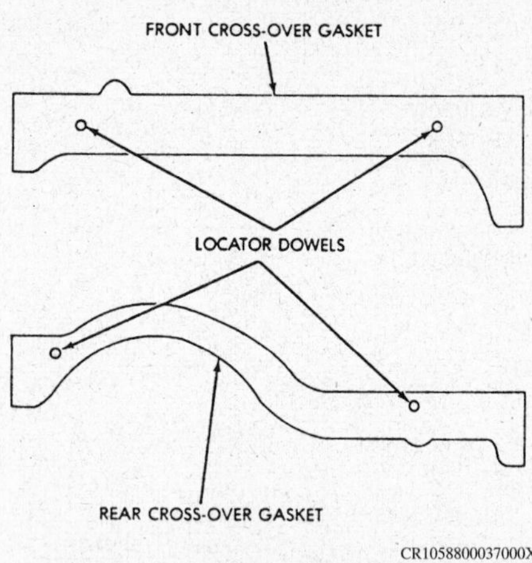

Fig. 12 Intake manifold locator dowels

3. If tool fits with a minimum of interference, proceed to next step. If tool does not fit with a minimum of interference, remove cover as outlined under "Timing Chain Cover, Replace" and install properly, then proceed to next step.
4. Place a suitable tool behind lips of oil seal and pry seal outward. Use care to avoid damaging crankshaft seal bore of cover.
5. Place smaller diameter of new seal over front oil seal installation tool No. 6635, or equivalent.
6. Seat oil seal in groove of tool.
7. Position seal and tool onto crankshaft.
8. Draw seal into position onto crankshaft using vibration damper bolt.
9. Remove vibration damper bolt and seal tool.
10. Install vibration damper.

CRANKSHAFT REAR OIL SEAL

REPLACE

The service seal is a two piece, Viton seal. The upper seal half can be installed with the crankshaft installed. When a new upper seal is installed, a new lower seal must be installed. The lower seal half can only be installed with the rear main bearing cap removed.

Removal

1. Remove oil pan, then the oil pump from rear main bearing cap.
2. Remove rear main bearing cap, then remove lower seal.
3. Carefully remove upper oil seal.

Installation

1. Clean cylinder block mating surfaces.
2. Inspect for burrs at oil hole on cylinder block to rear cap mating surface.
3. Lightly coat new upper seal lips with engine oil.
4. Loosen at least two main bearing caps forward of rear bearing cap to ease seal installation.
5. Rotate new upper seal into cylinder

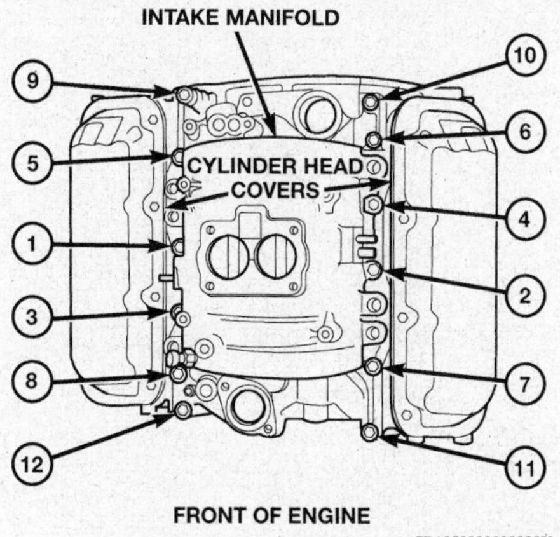

Fig. 13 Intake manifold tightening sequence. 3.9L engine

block using care not to shave or cut outer surface of seal.

6. Install new seal with white paint facing toward rear of engine.
7. Install new lower rear bearing oil seal into bearing cap with white paint facing toward rear of engine.
8. Apply .020 inch drop of Loctite 518, or equivalent, on each side of rear main bearing cap. **Do not over-apply sealant or allow sealant to contact rubber seal.**
9. Assemble bearing cap to cylinder block immediately after sealant application. Ensure white paint faces toward rear of engine.
10. Align bearing cap with cap slot alignment dowel and cap bolts. **Do not remove excess material after assembly.**
11. Install rear main bearing cap with clean and oiled cap bolts.
12. Alternately tighten cap bolts to specification.
13. Install oil pump.
14. Apply suitable silicone adhesive sealant at bearing cap to block joint to provide cap to block and oil pan sealing, **Fig. 20.**
15. Apply sealant until a small amount is squeezed out.
16. Wipe excess sealant off oil pan seal groove, then immediately install oil pan.

OIL PAN

REPLACE

2WD Models

1. Remove oil dipstick.
2. Disconnect distributor cap and set aside away from cowl, then raise and support vehicle.
3. Drain engine oil, then remove exhaust crossover pipe.
4. Loosen side engine mount bolts, then using suitable jack and wood block positioned at oil pan, raise engine slightly and remove side engine mount bolts.
5. When engine is high enough, place bolts similar to engine mount bolts in mount attaching points on frame

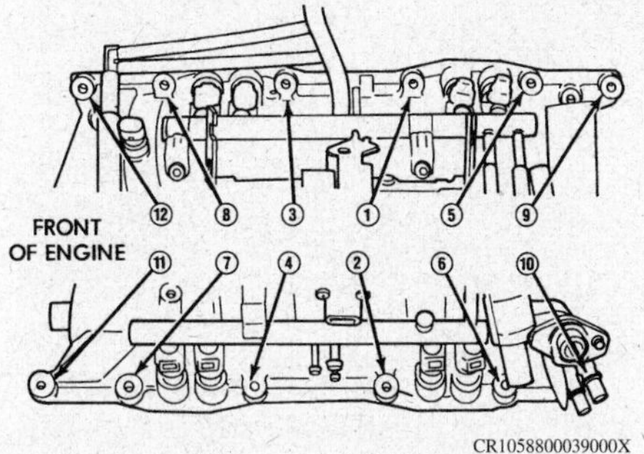

Fig. 14 Intake manifold tightening sequence. 5.9L engine

brackets. Lower engine so mount bottoms rest on installed bolts.

6. Remove oil pan and gasket.
7. Reverse procedure to install. Apply in corner of cap and block. Tighten attaching bolts to specifications.

4WD Models

1. Remove oil dipstick.
2. Raise and support vehicle, then drain engine oil.
3. Remove front drive axle, both engine mount support brackets and transmission inspection cover.
4. Remove oil pan and gasket.
5. Reverse procedure to install. Apply in corner of cap and block. Tighten attaching bolts to specifications

OIL PUMP

REPLACE

1. Remove oil pan.
2. Remove oil pump from rear main bearing cap.
3. Reverse procedure to install, slowly rotating pump body to ensure proper derivations to pump rotor engagement. Hold pump flush against mating surface and finger tighten bolts, then tighten to specifications.

OIL PUMP SERVICE

Disassemble

1. Remove pressure relief valve as follows:
   a. Remove cotter pin.
   b. Drill a 1/8 inch hole into relief valve retainer cap and insert a self threading sheet metal screw.
   c. Clamp screw into vise and while supporting oil pump remove cap by tapping pump body with soft faced hammer.
   d. Discard retainer cap, then remove spring and relief valve.
2. Remove oil pump cover.
3. Remove pump outer and inner rotor with shaft, then wash all components in solvent.

Inspection

1. Inspect oil pump cover. Replace if scratched or grooved.

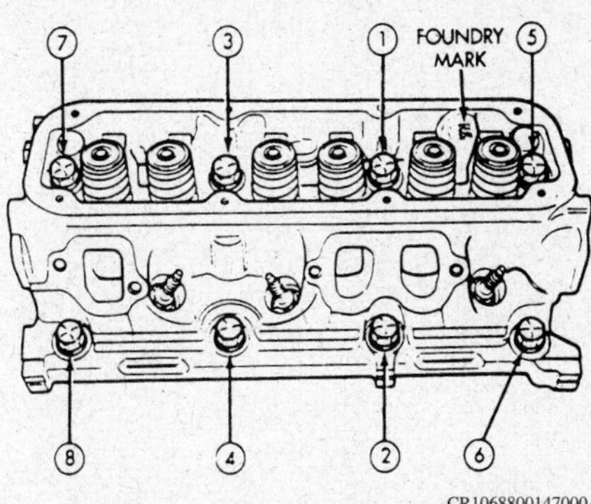

Fig. 15 Cylinder head bolt tightening sequence. 3.9L engine

2. Position a straightedge across pump cover surface. If a .0015 inch feeler gauge can be inserted between cover and straightedge, replace assembly.
3. Measure thickness and diameter of outer rotor. Replace if thickness is .825 inch or less, or diameter is 2.469 inches or less.
4. Replace inner rotor and shaft assembly if inner rotor is .825 inch or less thick.
5. Slide outer rotor into pump body. Press rotor to side and measure clearance between rotor and pump body. Replace assembly if clearance is .014 inch or more.
6. Install inner rotor and shaft into pump body. Replace shaft and both rotors if clearance between inner and outer rotors is .008 inch or more.
7. Place a straightedge across face of pump between bolt holes. Replace pump assembly if a feeler gauge of .004 inch or more can be inserted between rotors and straightedge.
8. Inspect oil pressure relief valve plunger for scoring and free operation in its bore.
9. Ensure relief valve spring has a free length of approximately 1.95 inches.
10. Relief valve spring should test between 19.5–20.5 lbs. when compressed to 1.34 inches.

Assemble

1. Install pump rotors and shaft.
2. Position oil pump cover onto pump body. Tighten cover bolts to specification.
3. Install relief valve and spring, then insert cotter pin.
4. Tap on new retainer cap.
5. Prime oil pump before installing.

BELT TENSION DATA

Belt tension is automatically adjusted.

SERPENTINE DRIVE BELT

Belt Routing

Refer to **Figs. 21 and 22** for serpentine drive belt routing.

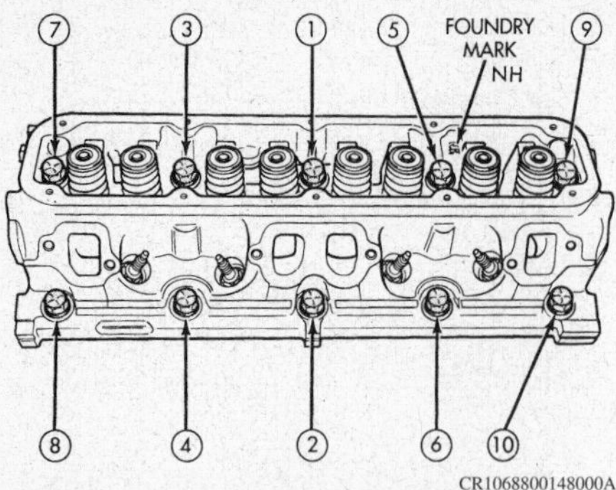

Fig. 16 Cylinder head bolt tightening sequence. 5.9L engine

Belt Replacement

The automatic tensioner is equipped with an indexing arrow on the back of tensioner housing. If a new belt is being installed, arrow must be within approximately 1/8 inch of point B indexing mark. If an old belt is being used, it must not pass indexing point marked A, **Fig. 23.**

REMOVAL

1. Attach a suitable wrench to automatic tensioner pulley mounting bolt, **Fig. 24.**
2. Rotate tensioner assembly clockwise until tension has been relieved.
3. Remove belt from idler puller, then from vehicle.

INSTALLATION

Serpentine belt must be routed correctly. If routed incorrectly water pump will rotate in wrong direction and engine will overheat.

1. Position drive belt over all pulleys except idler pulley.
2. Attach a suitable wrench to automatic tensioner pulley mounting bolt.
3. Rotate wrench clockwise, place belt over idler pulley, then allow tensioner to rotate back into place. **Ensure belt is properly seated on all pulleys.**
4. Inspect belt indexing.

Belt Tensioner Replacement

1. Attach a suitable wrench to automatic tensioner pulley mounting bolt, **Fig. 24.**
2. Remove drive belt as outlined under "Belt Replacement."
3. Disconnect wiring and secondary cable from ignition coil, then remove ignition coil from mounting bracket.
4. Remove tensioner assembly from mounting bracket, then remove pulley bolt and remove pulley from tensioner.
5. Reverse procedure to install, aligning indexing tab located on back of tensioner to slot in mounting bracket, **Fig. 23.**

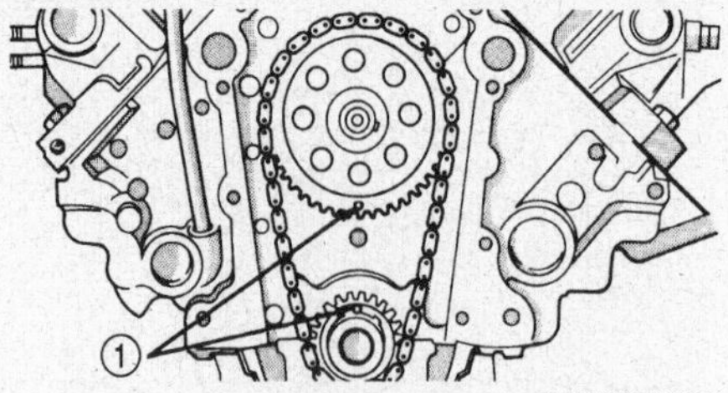

Fig. 17 Aligning valve timing marks

COOLING SYSTEM BLEED

These engines do not require a specified bleed procedure. After filling cooling system, run engine to operating temperature with radiator/pressure cap off. Air will automatically bleed through cap opening.

THERMOSTAT

REPLACE

1. Drain coolant to below thermostat level.
2. **On models equipped with A/C,** remove alternator support bracket, **Fig. 25,** then partially remove alternator for access to thermostat.
3. **On all models,** remove upper radiator hose at thermostat housing.
4. Move wiring harness behind thermostat housing out of the way.
5. Remove thermostat housing bolts, then housing, thermostat and gasket.
6. Reverse procedure to install with housing FRONT stamp pointed toward vehicle front. Tighten all bolts to specifications.

WATER PUMP

REPLACE

1. Drain cooling system.
2. Remove upper radiator hose clamp and hose at radiator.
3. Place bar or screw driver between water pump pulley bolts and attach Snap-On fan wrench tool No. 36 MM, or equivalent, to thermal viscous fan drive mounting nut. As fan drive threads are righthand, turn mounting nut counterclockwise to remove from water pump. Do not remove assembly from vehicle now.
4. Remove fan shroud mounting bolts. then remove shroud and viscous fan assembly. **Do not place viscous fan in a horizontal position, as fan drive fluid could drain into bearing assembly and contaminate lubricant.**
5. Do not remove water pump pulley bolts at this time.
6. Remove accessory drive belt by rotating tensioner clockwise to release all belt tension.
7. Remove four water pump pulley bolts and pulley, then remove lower radiator hose clamp and hose at water pump.

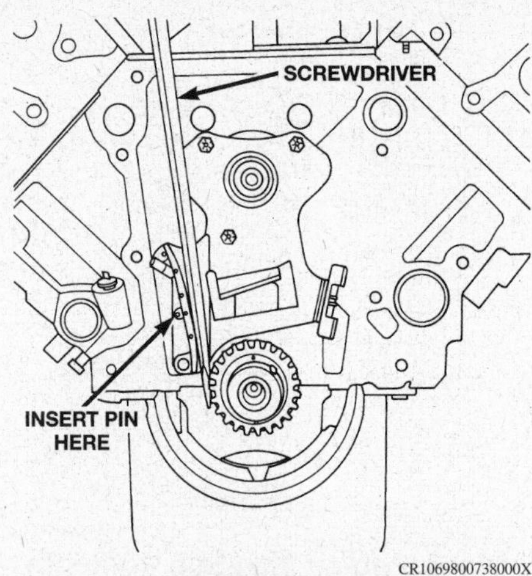

Fig. 18 Timing chain tensioner compression

8. Remove heater hose clamp and hose from coolant return tube, then loosen heater hose coolant return tube mounting bolt and remove from water pump. Discard old tube O-ring.
9. Loosen bypass hose clamp at water pump and slip hose off pump while removing water pump from vehicle.
10. Reverse procedures to install using new gasket and O-ring. Ensure impeller does not rub timing chase cover by spinning water pump. Tighten bolts to specifications.

RADIATOR

REPLACE

1. Drain cooling system into suitable container.
2. Remove throttle cable at fan shroud, then unsnap and remove overflow tank from shroud.
3. Remove two fan shroud retaining clips and move toward engine. Shroud does not have to be removed from vehicle.
4. Disconnect transmission cooler lines, then remove upper and lower radiator hose clamps and hoses.
5. Remove two upper radiator support bolts and lift radiator out of vehicle.
6. Reverse procedure to install. Insert two bottom alignment pins into holes in lower support.

FUEL PUMP

REPLACE

Wrap shop towels around fuel filler hoses to catch any fuel spill.

1. Remove fuel tank cap.
2. Release fuel system pressure as outlined in "Precautions" at beginning of this section.
3. If fuel pump works, drain fuel through supply hose.
4. If fuel pump does not work and fuel level is lower than filler hose, disconnect filler neck and siphon fuel through filler hose.

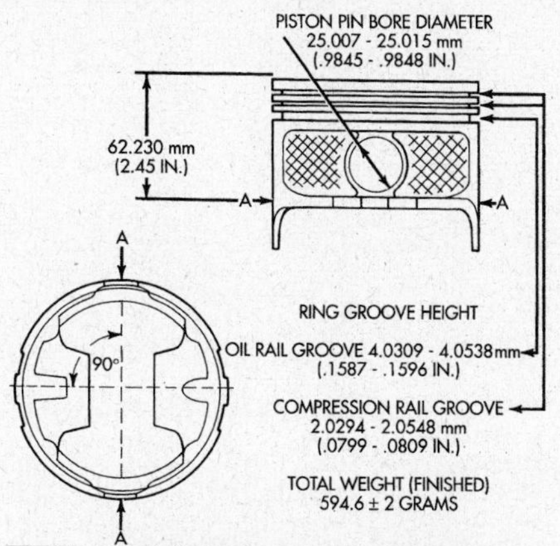

PISTON SIZE	A DIA = PISTON DIAMETER		BORE DIAMETER	
	MIN. mm (IN.)	MAX. mm (IN.)	MIN. mm (IN.)	MAX. mm (IN.)
A	99.280 (3.9087)	99.294 (3.9092)	99.306 (3.9097)	99.319 (3.9102)
B	99.294 (3.9092)	99.306 (3.9097)	99.319 (3.9102)	99.332 (3.9107)
C	99.306 (3.9097)	99.319 (3.9102)	99.332 (3.9107)	99.344 (3.9112)
D	99.319 (3.9102)	99.332 (3.9107)	99.344 (3.9112)	99.357 (3.9117)
E	99.332 (3.9107)	99.344 (3.9112)	99.357 (3.9117)	99.370 (3.9122)

CR1068800152000A

Fig. 19 Piston measurements. 3.9L engine

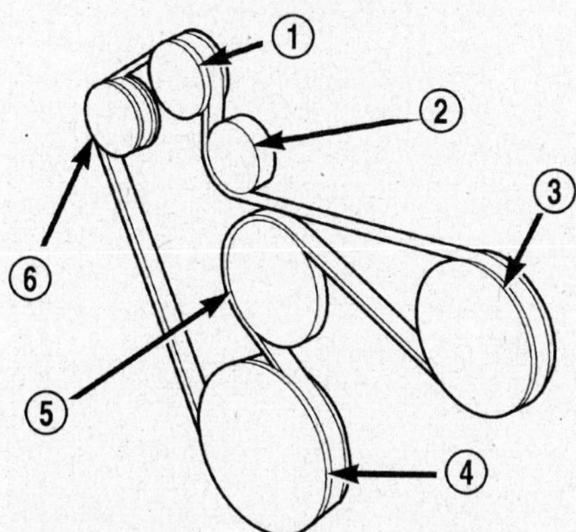

1 - GENERATOR PULLEY
2 - IDLER PULLEY
3 - POWER STEERING PULLEY
4 - CRANKSHAFT PULLEY
5 - WATER PUMP PULLEY
6 - TENSIONER PULLEY

FM1060101332000X

Fig. 22 Serpentine drive belt routing. 3.9L, 5.3L & 5.9L engines less A/C

5. If fuel pump does not work and tank is full, drain fuel from neck as follows:
   a. Support fuel tank with suitable transmission jack, then loosen fuel tank mounting straps (passenger side fuel mounting strap slightly more than driver side).
   b. Lower tank slightly, then loosen filler neck-hose clamp and slide back on hose.
   c. Disconnect hose from neck and drain tank through hose.
6. Raise and support vehicle, then disconnect all vent and filler hoses.
7. Remove vent hoses from hose routing bracket at top of frame rail, then place

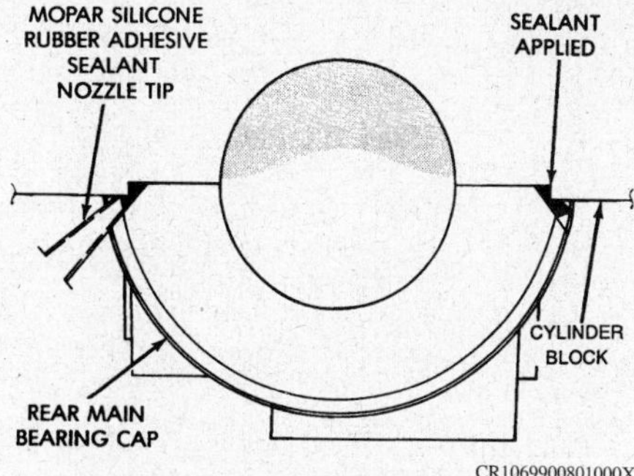

CR1069900801000X

Fig. 20 Main bearing cap sealant application

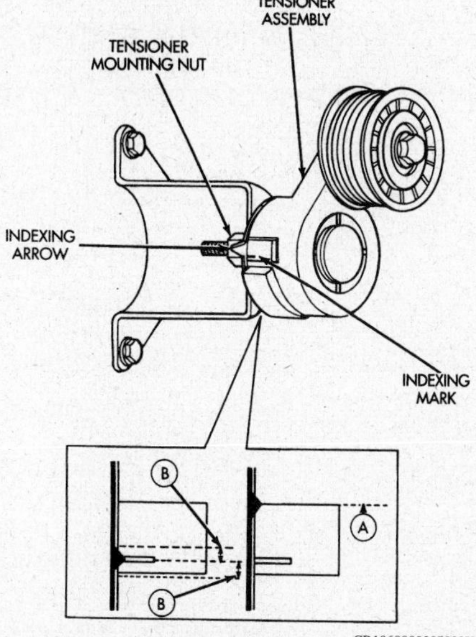

CR1068800207000X

Fig. 23 Automatic belt tensioner assembly

transmission jack under center of fuel tank and apply slight pressure.

8. Remove nuts from two mounting straps inboard ends and lower tank far enough to disconnected fuel pump module electrical connector.
9. Disconnect fuel supply and return lines from fuel pump, then fuel vapor line from pressure relief/roll over valve.
10. Lower tank from vehicle.
11. Note direction of fuel filter/pressure regulator, pressure relief/rollover valve and electrical connector, then remove pump locknut and module will spring up.
12. Remove fuel pump being careful not to bend wire rod connecting float to module.
13. Reverse procedure to install, ensure proper alignment of module with retaining bracket on bottom of tank. Tighten bolts to specifications.

FUEL FILTER

REPLACE

The combination fuel filter and pressure

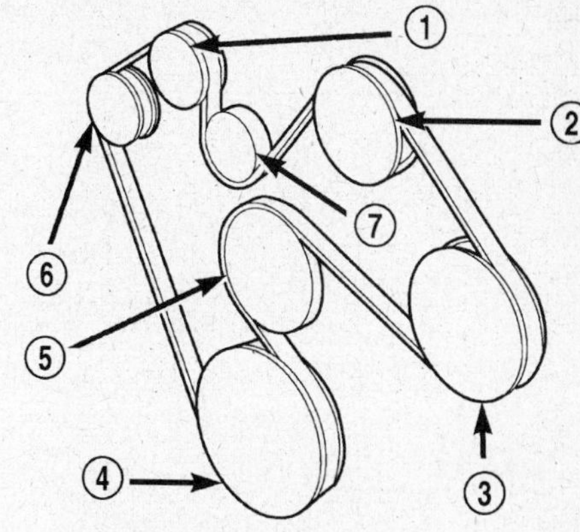

1 - GENERATOR PULLEY
2 - A/C PULLEY
3 - POWER STEERING PULLEY
4 - CRANKSHAFT PULLEY
5 - WATER PUMP PULLEY
6 - TENSIONER PULLEY
7 - IDLER PULLEY

FM1060101331000X

Fig. 21 Serpentine drive belt routing. 3.9L, 5.3L & 5.9L engines with A/C

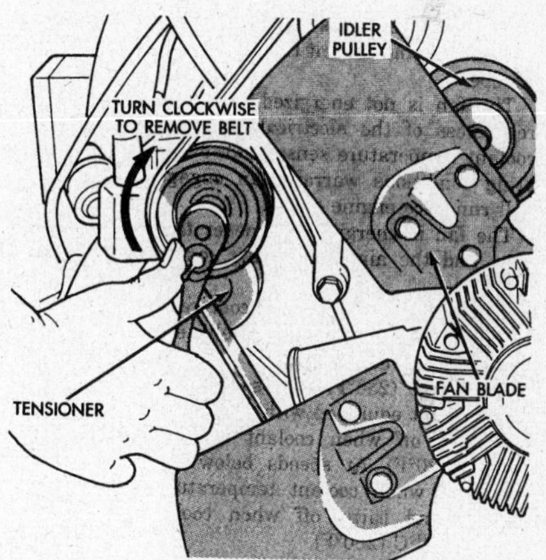

CR1068800208000X

Fig. 24 Serpentine drive belt removal

regulator is pressed into the rubber grommet on top of the fuel pump module.

1. Release fuel system pressure as outlined under "Precautions."
2. Drain and remove fuel tank as outlined in "Fuel Pump, Replace." Fuel pump does not have to be removed from tank.
3. Twist fuel filter/regulator and pull straight up. **Do not lift filter/regulator more than 3 inches.**
4. Cut line clamp, remove and discard.
5. Gently pull fuel down and off filter/regulator, then remove filter/regulator.
6. Reverse procedure to install. Ensure filter/regulator is pointed to vehicle's driver side. Use hose clamp pliers tool No. C-4124, or equivalent, to tighten line clamp to fuel line.

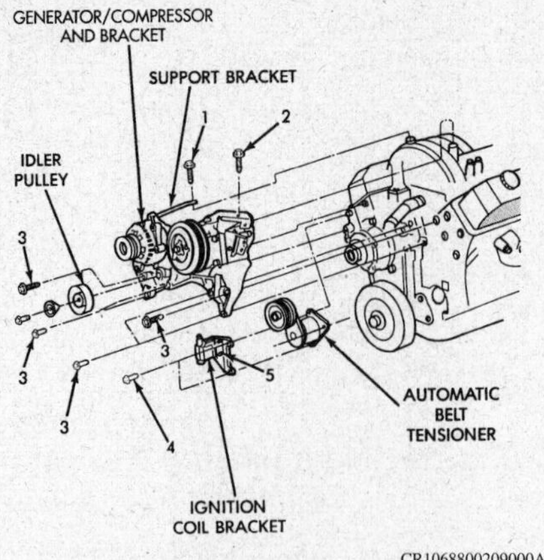

Fig. 25 Alternator support bracket

TIGHTENING SPECIFICATIONS

Year	Component	Torque Ft. Lbs.
2002–03	A/C Compressor Bracket	20
	A/C Compressor To Bracket Bolts	20
	Alternator Bracket Bolt	30
	Alternator Pivot Nut	30
	Automatic Belt Tensioner Pulley Bolt	45
	Automatic Belt Tensioner To Bracket Nut	50
	Camshaft Sprocket Lock Bolt	50
	Camshaft Thrust Plate	17
	Chain Case Cover Bolt	30
	Clutch Housing Bolt	③
	Connecting Rod Nut Or Cap Bolt	45
	Crankshaft Bolt (Vibration Damper)	⑤
	Cylinder Head Bolt	②
	Cylinder Head Cover (Bolts)	96①
	Cylinder Head Cover (Nut)	78①
	Distributor Clamp Bolt	17
	Engine Mount Through Bolt (2WD)	50
	Exhaust Manifold Bolts & Nuts	25
	Exhaust Manifold (Screw)	20
	Exhaust Pipe Flange	20
	Fan Blade Attaching Bolts	17
	Flexplate To Convertor	23
	Flexplate To Crankshaft	55
	Flywheel To Crankshaft	55
	Front Insulator Through Bolt	70
	Front Insulator To Support Bracket Stud Nut (4WD)	30
	Front Insulator To Support Bracket Through Bolt (4WD)	75
	Front Insulator To Block Bolts (2WD)	70
	Fuel Pump Locknut	40①
	Fuel Tank Retaining Strap Nuts	35
	Heat Shield Bolts	30
	Intake Manifold Bolts	④
	Insulator Bracket To Crossmember Bolts (2WD)	50
	Main Bearing Cap Bolts	85

TIGHTENING SPECIFICATIONS—Continued

Year	Component	Torque Ft. Lbs.
2002–03	Oil Filter Attaching Stud	50
	Oil Pan Bolts	18
	Oil Pan Drain Plug	25
	Oil Pressure Gauge Sending Unit	60①
	Oil Pump Attaching Bolts	30
	Oil Pump Cover Bolts	96①
	Rear Insulator To Bracket Through Bolt (2WD)	50
	Rear Insulator To Crossmember Support Bracket Nut (2WD)	30
	Rear Insulator To Crossmember Nuts (4WD)	50
	Rear Insulator To Transmission Bolts (4WD)	50
	Rear Insulator Bracket Bolts (4WD w/Automatic Transmission)	50
	Rear Support Bracket To Crossmember Flange Nuts	30
	Rear Support Plate To Transfer Case Bolts	30
	Rocker Arm Bolt	21
	Spark Plug	30
	Temperature Gauge Sending Unit	60①
	Thermostat Bolts	16
	Throttle Body Bolts	16
	Vibration Damper Bolt To Crankshaft	⑤
	Water Pump To Chain Case Cover Bolt	30
	Water Pump Pulley Bolt	20

① — Inch lbs.

② — Refer to "Cylinder Head, Replace" for procedure.

③ — $5/16$ bolts, 17 ft. lbs.; $3/8$ bolts, 30 ft. lbs.; $7/16$ bolts, 50 ft. lbs.

④ — Refer to "Intake Manifold, Replace" for tightening procedure.

⑤ — 3.9L engine, 135 ft. lbs.; 5.9L engine, 180 ft. lbs.

4.7L Engine

NOTE: Refer To The "4.7L Engine" Section In The "Commander & Grand Cherokee" Chapter For Procedures Not Covered In This Section.

NOTE: On Air Bag Equipped Models, Refer To "Air Bag System Precautions" Located In The Front Of This Manual For System Disarming & Arming Procedures.

NOTE: Refer To "Computer Relearn Procedures" Located In The Front Of This Manual When Battery Power To The Computer Has Been Interrupted.

INDEX

PRECAUTIONS

Air Bag Systems

Refer to "Air Bag System Precautions" in the front of this manual for system disarming and arming procedures.

Fuel System Pressure Relief

1. Remove fuel fill cap.
2. Fuel filler tube contains a spring loaded flap located below fuel cap. Place a non-metallic object into fuel fill tube and press on flap to relieve any tank pressure.
3. Remove fuel pump relay from Power Distribution Center (PDC).
4. Start and run engine until it stalls.
5. Attempt to restart engine to ensure it will no longer run.
6. Turn key to Off position.

Battery Ground Cable

Prior to service, disconnect battery ground cable and isolate as required.

ENGINE MOUNT

REPLACE

Lefthand & Righthand

1. Remove fan blade, fan clutch and fan shroud.
2. Remove engine oil filter.
3. Support engine with suitable jack and a block of wood across full width of engine oil pan.
4. **On models equipped with 2WD,** remove four cylinder block to insulator mount bolts and nut from engine insulator mount through bolt, **Figs. 1 and 2.**
5. **On models equipped with 4WD,** remove three cylinder block to insulator mount bolts and loosen nut from engine insulator mount through bolt, **Figs. 3 and 4.**
6. **On all models,** raise engine high enough to remove engine insulator mount through bolt and insulator mount.
7. Reverse procedure to install, tighten to specification.

Rear

1. Raise and support vehicle.
2. Support transmission with a suitable jack.
3. Remove nut from insulator mount through bolt, **Figs. 5 and 6.**
4. Remove four bolts and washers retaining mount to transmission, **Fig. 7.**
5. Raise transmission enough to remove through bolt.
6. Remove bolts retaining mount to crossmember.
7. Remove two nuts retaining insulator to crossmember.
8. Remove bolts retaining insulator bracket to transmission.
9. Reverse procedure to install.

ENGINE

REPLACE

1. Remove battery and battery tray.
2. Raise and support vehicle.
3. Remove exhaust crossover pipe from exhaust manifolds.
4. **On models equipped with 4WD,** proceed as follows:
   a. Disconnect vent tube from lefthand side engine mount.
   b. Remove bolt retaining nut and bolt from both lefthand and righthand side engine mounts.

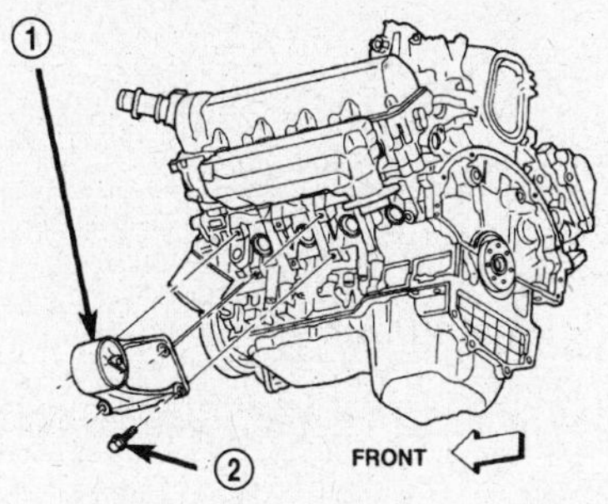

1 – ENGINE INSULATOR MOUNT-LEFT SIDE
2 – MOUNTING BOLT

CR1060000872000X

Fig. 1 Lefthand side engine mount. 2WD

   c. Remove locknut from lefthand and righthand side engine mount brackets.
5. **On all models,** disconnect two ground straps from lower lefthand side of engine and one ground strap from lower righthand side of engine.
6. Disconnect crankshaft position sensor.
7. **On models equipped with 4WD,** remove righthand side axle isolator bracket from engine, transmission and axle.
8. **On all models,** remove lefthand exhaust pipe from exhaust manifold.
9. Loosen righthand exhaust manifold to exhaust pipe retaining bolts.
10. Remove eight bolts retaining structural cover.
11. Pivot exhaust pipe downward and remove structural cover.
12. Remove starter.
13. Drain cooling system into suitable container.
14. Remove torque converter bolts.
15. Remove transmission to engine mounting bolts.
16. Disconnect engine block heater connector.
17. Lower vehicle.
18. Remove throttle body resonator assembly and air inlet hose.
19. Disconnect throttle and speed control cables.
20. Recover refrigerant as outlined in the "Air Conditioning" chapter.
21. Remove A/C compressor.
22. Remove shroud, fan assemblies and accessory drive belt.
23. Disconnect transmission oil cooler lines at radiator.
24. Disconnect upper and lower radiator hoses.
25. Remove radiator, A/C condenser and transmission oil cooler as an assembly.
26. Remove alternator.
27. Disconnect two heater hoses from timing chain cover and heater core.
28. Unclip and remove heater hoses and tubes from intake manifold.
29. Disconnect engine harness connectors at the following:

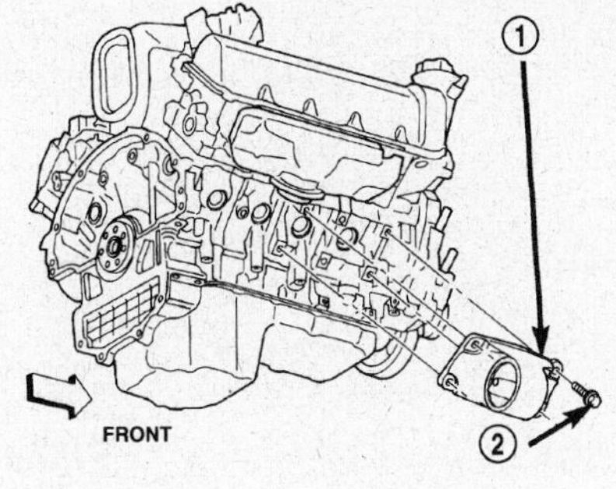

1 – ENGINE INSULATOR MOUNT-RIGHT SIDE
2 – MOUNTING BOLT

CR1060000873000X

Fig. 2 Righthand side engine mount. 2WD

   a. Intake Air Temperature (IAT) sensor.
   b. Fuel injectors.
   c. Throttle Position (TPS) switch.
   d. Idle Air Control (IAC) motor.
   e. Engine oil pressure switch.
   f. Engine Coolant Temperature (ECT) sensor.
   g. Manifold Absolute Pressure (MAP) sensor.
   h. Camshaft Position (CMP) sensor
   i. Coil over plugs.
30. Disconnect vacuum lines at throttle body and intake manifold.
31. Release fuel system pressure as outlined under "Precautions."
32. Remove power steering pump and position out of way.
33. Install suitable lifting studs onto engine.
34. Install engine lifting fixture tool No. 8347, or equivalent, as follows:
   a. Hold lifting fixture at a slight angle, then slide large bore in front plate over hex portion of lifting stud.
   b. Position two remaining fixture arms onto lifting studs in cylinder head.
   c. Pull forward and upward on lifting fixture so that lifting stud rests in slotted area below large bore.
   d. Secure lifting fixture to three studs with suitable locknuts.
   e. Ensure lifting loop in lifting fixture is in last hole, closest to throttle body, to minimize angle of engine during removal.
35. Disconnect body ground strap at righthand side, then lefthand side cowl.
36. Position suitable jack under transmission.
37. Remove engine from vehicle.
38. Reverse procedure to install.

INTAKE MANIFOLD

REPLACE

Refer to "4.7L Engine" section in "Commander & Grand Cherokee" chapter for intake manifold replacement procedure.

EXHAUST MANIFOLD

REPLACE

Refer to "4.7L Engine" section in "Commander & Grand Cherokee" chapter for exhaust manifold replacement procedure.

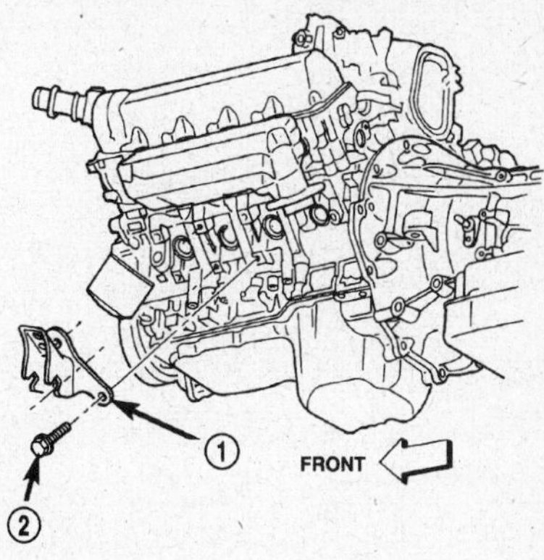

1 – ENGINE INSULATOR MOUNT-LEFT SIDE
2 – MOUNTING BOLT

CR1060000874000X

Fig. 3 Lefthand side engine mount. 4WD

CYLINDER HEAD

REPLACE

Refer to "4.7L Engine" section in "Commander & Grand Cherokee" chapter for cylinder head replacement procedure.

VALVE COVER

REPLACE

Refer to "4.7L Engine" section in "Commander & Grand Cherokee" chapter valve cover replacement procedure.

VALVE ARRANGEMENT

Refer to "4.7L Engine" section in "Commander & Grand Cherokee" chapter valve arrangement.

HYDRAULIC LASH ADJUSTERS

REPLACE

CAMSHAFT LOBE LIFT SPECIFICATIONS

Refer to "4.7L Engine" section in "Commander & Grand Cherokee" chapter camshaft lobe lift specifications.

VALVE ADJUSTMENT

These engines are equipped with hydraulic lash adjusters. There is no provision for adjustment.

ROCKER ARMS

REPLACE

Refer to "4.7L Engine" section in "Commander & Grand Cherokee" chapter for rocker arms replacement procedure.

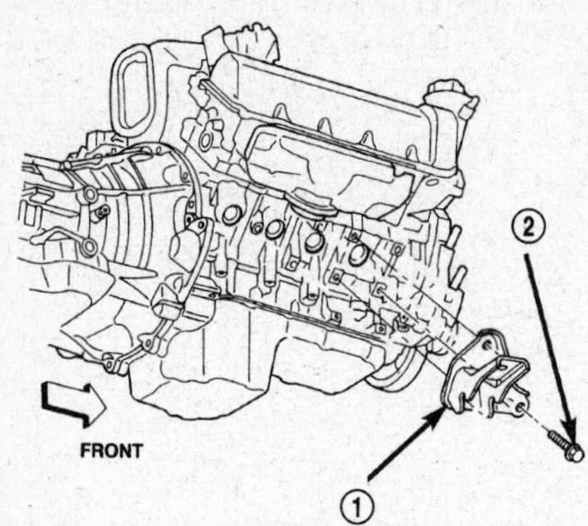

Fig. 4 Righthand side engine mount. 4WD

VALVE GUIDES

The valve guides are an integral part of the cylinder head. If valve stem to guide clearance is excessive, the cylinder head must be replaced.

FRONT COVER

REPLACE

Refer to "4.7L Engine" section in "Commander & Grand Cherokee" chapter for front cover replacement procedure.

TIMING CHAIN

REPLACE

Refer to "4.7L Engine" section in "Commander & Grand Cherokee" chapter for timing chain replacement procedure.

CAMSHAFT

REPLACE

Refer to "4.7L Engine" section in "Commander & Grand Cherokee" chapter for camshaft replacement procedure.

PISTON & ROD ASSEMBLY

Refer to "4.7L Engine" section in "Commander & Grand Cherokee" chapter piston and rod assembly.

MAIN & ROD BEARINGS

Refer to "4.7L Engine" section in "Commander & Grand Cherokee" chapter main and rod bearings.

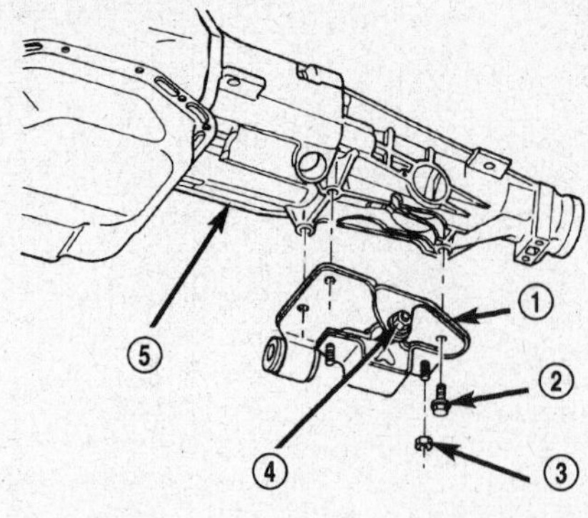

Fig. 5 Rear engine mount. 2WD w/automatic transmission

CRANKSHAFT MAIN BEARING CAP & BEDPLATE

Refer to "4.7L Engine" section in "Commander & Grand Cherokee" chapter crankshaft main bearing cap and bedplate.

CRANKSHAFT REAR OIL SEAL

REPLACE

Refer to "4.7L Engine" section in "Commander & Grand Cherokee" chapter crankshaft rear oil seal replacement procedure.

OIL PAN

REPLACE

2WD

1. Drain cooling system into suitable container.
2. Remove upper fan shroud.
3. Remove throttle body resonator, air inlet hose and intake manifold.
4. Raise and support vehicle.
5. Disconnect exhaust pipe at exhaust manifold.
6. Remove structural cover.
7. Drain engine oil into suitable container and remove oil filter.
8. Position suitable jack under engine.
9. Remove both righthand and lefthand side engine mount through bolts.
10. Raise engine to provide clearance for oil pan removal.
11. Place blocks of wood between engine brackets and lower mounts to provide stability to engine.
12. Remove oil pan mounting bolts, then the oil pan. **Do not pry on oil pan or oil pan gasket. Gasket is mounted to engine and does not come out with oil pan.**

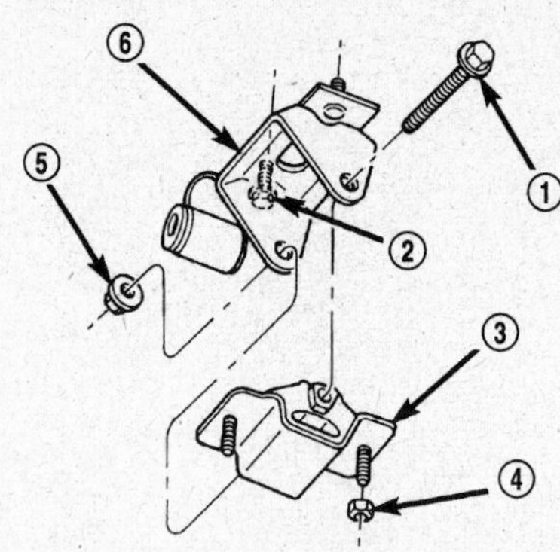

Fig. 6 Rear engine mount. Manual transmission

13. Remove oil pump pickup tube, then the pan gasket from engine.
14. Reverse procedure to install, noting the following:
    a. Clean pan and gasket mating surfaces.
    b. Position oil pan gasket and pickup tube with new O-ring.
    c. Tighten oil pan bolts in sequence, **Fig. 8,** to specification.

4WD

1. Remove front axle as outlined in "Front Wheel Drive" section.
2. Remove structural cover.
3. Drain engine oil into suitable container and remove oil filter.
4. Remove oil pan mounting bolts, then the oil pan. **Do not pry on oil pan or pan gasket. Gasket is mounted to engine and does not come out with oil pan.**
5. Remove oil pump pickup tube and oil pan gasket from engine.
6. Reverse procedure to install, noting the following:
    a. Clean oil pan gasket mating surfaces.
    b. Position oil pan gasket and pickup tube with new O-ring.
    c. Tighten oil pan bolts in sequence, **Fig. 8,** to specification.

OIL PUMP

REPLACE

Refer to "4.7L Engine" section in "Commander & Grand Cherokee" chapter oil pump replacement procedure.

BELT TENSION DATA

Refer to "4.7L Engine" section in "Commander & Grand Cherokee" chapter for belt tension data.

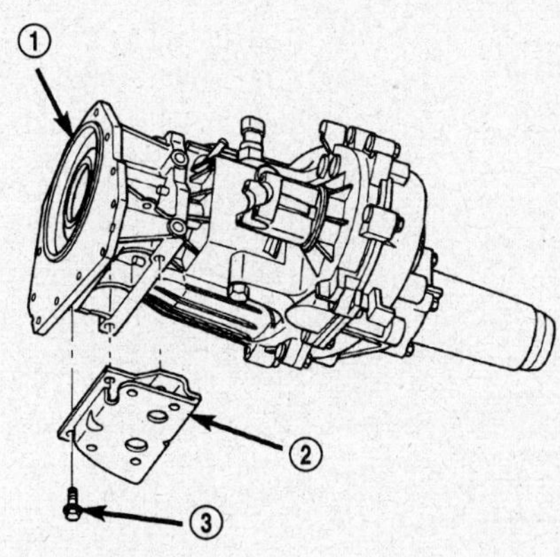

1 - TRANSMISSION
2 - ENGINE REAR MOUNT
3 - BOLT

CR1060000878000X

Fig. 7 Rear engine mount. 4WD w/automatic transmission

SERPENTINE DRIVE BELT

Refer to "4.7L Engine" section in "Commander & Grand Cherokee" chapter for serpentine drive belt removal and installation.

COOLING SYSTEM BLEED

Refer to "4.7L Engine" section in "Commander & Grand Cherokee" chapter for cooling system bleed procedure.

WATER PUMP

REPLACE

Refer to "4.7L Engine" section in "Commander & Grand Cherokee" chapter for water pump replacement procedure.

RADIATOR

REPLACE

A number or letter is stamped into the tongue of constant tension clamps. If replacement is required, use only an original equipment clamp with matching letter or number.

1. Drain cooling system into suitable container.
2. Remove hose clamps and hoses from radiator.
3. Disconnect coolant reserve/overflow hose and washer bottle connector and hose.
4. Remove upper fan shroud.
5. Disconnect electric cooling fan connector.
6. Remove upper radiator mounting screws, then lift radiator up and out of vehicle.

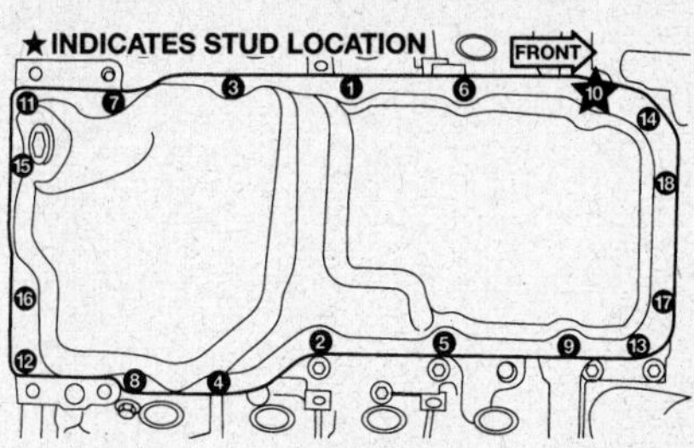

CR1060000879000X

Fig. 8 Oil pan tightening sequence

7. Reverse procedure to install, noting the following:
   a. Position lower radiator isolator pins into alignment holes in radiator lower support.
   b. Install and tighten radiator mounting bolts to specification.

FUEL PUMP

REPLACE

Refer to "4.7L Engine" section in "Commander & Grand Cherokee" chapter fuel pump replacement procedure.

FUEL FILTER

REPLACE

Refer to "4.7L Engine" section in "Commander & Grand Cherokee" chapter for fuel filter replacement procedure.

TIGHTENING SPECIFICATIONS

Year	Component	Torque Ft. Lbs.
2002–06	A/C Compressor Mounting (M-8 Bolts)	17–25
	A/C Compressor Mounting (M-10 Bolts)	30–50
	Front Motor Mount Insulator To Cylinder Block	45
	Front Motor Mount Through Bolt (R & L)	45
	Oil Pan	11
	Oil Pump Pickup Tube	20
	Radiator Mounting	17
	Rear Motor Mount Isolator Bracket To Transmission	30
	Rear Motor Mount Isolator Mount To Crossmember	21
	Rear Motor Mount Bracket To Crossmember	21
	Rear Motor Mount Bracket To Transmission	50
	Rear Motor Mount Through Bolt	75
	Transmission To Engine	30

5.7L Engine

NOTE: Refer To The "3.7L Engine" Section In The "Liberty" Chapter For Procedures Not Covered In This Section.

NOTE: Refer To The "4.7L Engine" Section In The "Commander & Grand Cherokee" Chapter For Procedures Not Covered In This Section.

NOTE: Refer To The "5.7L Engine" Section In The "Full Size Trucks & Van" Chapter For Procedures Not Covered In This Section.

NOTE: On Air Bag Equipped Models, Refer To "Air Bag System Precautions" Located In The Front Of This Manual For System Disarming & Arming Procedures.

NOTE: Refer To "Computer Relearn Procedures" Located In The Front Of This Manual When Battery Power To The Computer Has Been Interrupted.

INDEX

PRECAUTIONS

Air Bag Systems

Refer to "Air Bag System Precautions" in the front of this manual for system disarming and arming procedures.

Fuel System Pressure Relief

1. Remove fuel cap, then fuel pump relay from PDC.
2. Start and run engine until it stalls.
3. Attempt to restart engine until it will no longer run.
4. Turn ignition key to OFF position.
5. Unplug connector from any injector.
6. Attach one end of a suitable 18 gauge or smaller jumper wire to either injector terminal.
7. Connect other end of jumper wire to positive battery terminal.
8. Connect one end of a second jumper wire to remaining injector terminal.
9. Momentarily touch other end of second jumper wire to negative battery terminal for no longer than a few seconds. **Powering an injector for more than a few seconds will damage injector.**
10. Place a suitable rag below fuel line quick connect fitting on fuel rail, then disconnect quick connect fitting.
11. Install fuel pump relay to PDC, then clear any stored DTC's.

Battery Ground Cable

Prior to service, disconnect battery ground cable and isolate as required.

ENGINE MOUNT

REPLACE

Front

2WD

1. Raise and support vehicle.
2. Remove engine mount through bolts.
3. Install engine support fixture tool No. 8534, or equivalent, then raise engine.
4. Remove engine mount to insulator bolts, then remove insulator.
5. Reverse procedure to install. Apply suitable sealant to mount, engine block and lefthand engine bracket to front axle bolts.

4WD

1. Raise and support vehicle.
2. Remove front crossmember, then engine oil filter.
3. Support engine using engine support fixture tool No. 8534, or equivalent.
4. Support front axle using suitable jack.
5. Remove four bolts attaching engine mounts to front axle.
6. Remove three bolts attaching front axle to lefthand engine bracket.
7. Lower front axle.
8. Remove six through bolts, then raise engine enough to remove mounts.

9. Remove lefthand and righthand engine mounts.
10. Reverse procedure to install. Apply suitable sealant to mount, engine block and lefthand engine bracket to front axle bolts.

Rear

1. Raise and support vehicle.
2. Support transmission using suitable jack.
3. Remove nuts from transmission mount.
4. Remove two bolts attaching transmission mount to engine bracket.
5. Raise transmission enough to remove mount from crossmember.
6. Remove rear mount.
7. Reverse procedure to install. Apply suitable threadlock to bolts.

ENGINE

REPLACE

1. Remove air cleaner resonator and duct work as an assembly.
2. Drain cooling system into suitable container.
3. Remove serpentine drive belt.
4. Remove coolant overflow bottle and position aside.
5. Remove fan blade/viscous fan drive assembly from water pump by turning mounting nut counterclockwise as viewed from front.
6. Remove fan shroud mounting bolts, then pull lower shroud mounts out of radiator tank clips.
7. Remove fan shroud and fan blade/ viscous fan drive assembly from vehicle as an assembly. Do not store viscous fan drive in a horizontal position.
8. Remove radiator as outlined in "Radiator, Replace."
9. Remove upper crossmember and top core support.
10. Remove A/C compressor with lines attached and position aside.
11. Remove alternator assembly.
12. Relieve fuel pressure as outlined in "Precautions."
13. Remove intake manifold as outlined in "Intake Manifold, Replace."
14. Remove power steering pump and position aside.
15. Disconnect fuel supply line.
16. Raise and support vehicle, then drain engine oil into a suitable container.
17. Remove engine front mount through bolts.
18. Disconnect transmission oil cooler lines from their retainers at oil pan bolts.
19. Disconnect exhaust pipe at manifolds.
20. Disconnect electrical connectors from starter motor, then remove starter motor.
21. Remove structural dust cover, then transmission inspection cover.
22. **On models equipped with automatic transmission,** remove drive plate to converter bolts.
23. **On all models,** remove transmission bell housing to engine block bolts.
24. Lower vehicle.
25. Install engine lifting fixture tool No. 8984, or equivalent.
26. remove engine from vehicle.
27. Reverse procedure to install.

INTAKE MANIFOLD

REPLACE

Refer to "5.7L Engine" section in "Full Size Trucks & Van" chapter for intake manifold replacement procedure.

EXHAUST MANIFOLD

REPLACE

Refer to "5.7L Engine" section in "Full Size Trucks & Van" chapter for exhaust manifold replacement procedure.

CYLINDER HEAD

REPLACE

Refer to "5.7L Engine" section in "Full Size Trucks & Van" chapter for cylinder head replacement procedure.

VALVE COVER

REPLACE

Refer to "5.7L Engine" section in "Full Size Trucks & Van" chapter for valve cover replacement procedure.

VALVE ARRANGEMENT

Refer to "4.7L Engine" section in "Commander & Grand Cherokee" chapter for valve arrangement.

CAMSHAFT LOBE LIFT SPECIFICATIONS

Refer to "4.7L Engine" section in "Commander & Grand Cherokee" chapter for camshaft lobe lift specifications.

VALVE ADJUSTMENT

These engines are equipped with hydraulic lash adjusters. There is no provision for adjustment.

ROCKER ARMS

REPLACE

Refer to "5.7L Engine" section in "Full Size Trucks & Van" chapter for rocker arms replacement procedure.

VALVE GUIDES

The valve guides are an integral part of the cylinder head. If valve stem to guide clearance is excessive, the cylinder head must be replaced.

FRONT COVER

REPLACE

Refer to "5.7L Engine" section in "Full Size Trucks & Van" chapter for front cover replacement procedure.

TIMING CHAIN

REPLACE

Refer to "5.7L Engine" section in "Full Size Trucks & Van" chapter for timing chain replacement procedure.

CAMSHAFT

REPLACE

Refer to "5.7L Engine" section in "Full Size Trucks & Van" chapter for camshaft replacement procedure.

PISTON & ROD ASSEMBLY

Refer to "5.7L Engine" section in "Full Size Trucks & Van" chapter for piston and rod assembly.

MAIN & ROD BEARINGS

Refer to "5.7L Engine" section in "Full Size Trucks & Van" chapter for main and rod bearings.

CRANKSHAFT REAR OIL SEAL

REPLACE

Refer to "5.7L Engine" section in "Full Size Trucks & Van" chapter for crankshaft rear oil seal replacement procedure.

OIL PAN

REPLACE

1. Install engine support fixture tool No. 8534, or equivalent.
2. Loosen but do not remove both lefthand and righthand side engine mount through bolts.
3. Remove structural dust cover.
4. Drain engine oil into suitable container.
5. Remove front crossmember.
6. Raise engine to provide clearance for oil pan removal.
7. Remove oil pan bolts, then oil pan. **Do not pry on oil pan or gasket.**
8. Unbolt and remove pickup tube.
9. Reverse procedure to install. Install oil pan studs in same location

OIL PUMP

REPLACE

1. Remove oil pan and pickup tube as outlined in "Oil Pan, Replace."
2. Remove front cover as outlined in "Front Cover, Replace."
3. Remove four bolts, then oil pump.
4. Reverse procedure to install.

BELT TENSION DATA

Belt tension is automatically adjusted.

SERPENTINE DRIVE BELT

Belt Routing

Refer to **Fig. 1** for belt routing.

Belt Replacement

REMOVAL

Belt tension is not adjustable. Belt adjustment is maintained by automatic (spring load) belt tensioner. **Do not let tensioner arm snap back to freearm position, severe damage may occur to tensioner.**

1. Rotate belt tension until it contacts it's stop. Remove belt, then slowly rotate tensioner into freearm position.

INSTALLATION

Belt tension is not adjustable. Belt adjustment is maintained by an automatic (spring load) belt tensioner.

1. Inspect condition of all pulleys. **When installing serpentine accessory drive belt, belt must be routed correctly. If not, engine may overheat due to water pump rotating in wrong direction.**
2. Install new belt. Route belt around all pulleys except idler pulley. Rotate tensioner arm until it contacts it's stop position. Route belt around idler and slowly let tensioner rotate into belt. Make sure belt is seated onto all pulleys.
3. With drive belt installed, inspect belt wear indicator.

Belt Tensioner Replacement

A used belt should be replaced if tensioner indexing arrow has moved to minimum tension indicator. Tensioner travel stops at this point.

1. Remove accessory drive belt.
2. Remove tensioner assembly from mounting bracket.
3. Remove pulley bolt. Remove pulley from tensioner. **Because of high spring pressure, do not attempt to disassemble automatic tensioner, unit is serviced as an assembly except for pulley on tensioner.**
4. Reverse procedure to install noting the following:
   a. An indexing slot is located on back of tensioner. Align this slot to head of bolt on front cover.
   b. Inspect belt indexing marks.

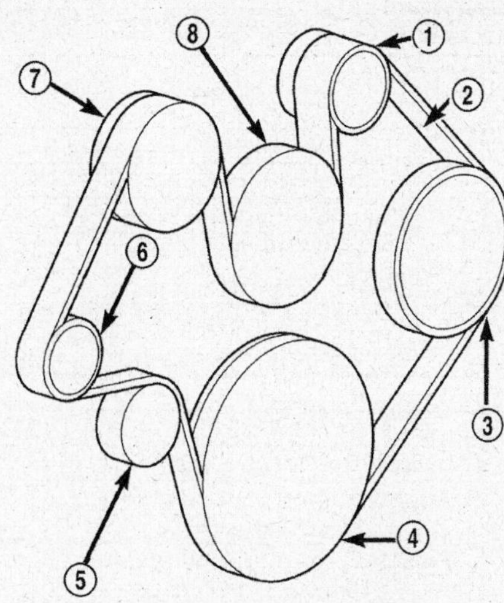

Fig. 1 Serpentine belt routing

COOLING SYSTEM BLEED

Refer to "3.7L Engine" section in "Liberty" chapter for cooling system bleed procedure.

WATER PUMP

REPLACE

1. Drain coolant into suitable container.
2. Remove serpentine drive belt.
3. Remove fan blade/viscous fan drive assembly from water pump by turning mounted nut counterclockwise as viewed from front.
4. Remove fan shroud mounting bolts, then pull lower shroud mounts out of radiator tank clips.
5. Remove fan shroud and fan blade/viscous fan drive assembly from vehicle as an assembly. Do not store viscous fan drive in a horizontal position.
6. Remove coolant overflow bottle.
7. Disconnect washer bottle electrical connector and hose.
8. Remove A/C compressor, then the alternator brace.
9. Remove idler pulleys.
10. Remove serpentine drive belt tensioner assembly.
11. Remove upper and lower radiator hoses.
12. Remove heater hoses.
13. Remove water pump bolts, then water pump.
14. Reverse procedure to install.

RADIATOR

REPLACE

Refer to "3.7L Engine" section in "Liberty" chapter for radiator replacement procedure.

FUEL PUMP

REPLACE

Refer to "3.7L Engine" section in "Liberty" chapter for fuel pump replacement procedure.

FUEL FILTER

REPLACE

Refer to the "3.7L Engine" section in the "Liberty" chapter for fuel filter replacement procedure.

TIGHTENING SPECIFICATIONS

Year	Component	Torque Ft. Lbs.
2002–06	Alternator	40
	Camshaft Sprocket	90
	Camshaft Tensioner Plate	21
	Connecting Rod Cap	15③
	Crankshaft Rear Seal Retainer	11
	Cylinder Head	②
	Exhaust Manifold	18
	Flywheel	70
	Front Cover	21
	Front Insulator To Block (2WD)	70
	Front Insulator To Support Bracket Stud Nut (4WD)	30
	Front Insulator To Support Bracket Through Bolt (4WD)	75
	Front Insulator Through Bolt	70
	Front Cover Lifting Stud	40
	Intake Manifold	105①
	Main Bearing Cap	20③
	Main Bearing Cross Bolts	20
	Oil Dipstick Tube	105①
	Oil Pan	105①
	Oil Pan Drain Plug	25
	Oil Pump	21
	Oil Pump Pickup Tube	21
	Rear Insulator Bracket (4WD W/ Automatic Transmission)	50
	Rear Insulator To Bracket Through Bolt (2WD)	50
	Rear Insulator To Crossmember Support Bracket (2WD)	30
	Rear Insulator To Crossmember (4WD)	50
	Rear Insulator To Transmission (4WD)	50
	Rear Support Bracket To Crossmember	30
	Rear Support Plate To Transfer Case	30
	Rocker Arm	16
	Thermostat Housing	21
	Throttle Body	105①
	Transmission Support Bracket (2WD)	50
	Transfer Case To Insulator Mounting Plate	105
	Valve Cover	70①
	Vibration Damper	129
	Water Pump	21

① — Inch lbs.
② — Refer to "Cylinder Head, Replace" for tightening procedure.
③ — Plus an additional 90°.

Rear Axle & Suspension

INDEX

DESCRIPTION

These axle assemblies, **Fig. 1** are integral carrier housing hypoid gear type with centerline of drive pinion mounted below center line of ring gear. Drive pinion is supported by two preloaded taper roller bearings and front and rear pinion bearing cones are pressed on pinion stem. Front and rear pinion bearing cups are pressed against a shoulder that is recessed within carrier casting. Drive pinion depth of mesh adjustment is controlled by installing metal shims between rear pinion bearing cup and carrier casting.

Gear ratio is identified by small tag on housing cover.

REAR AXLE

REPLACE

1. Raise and support vehicle.
2. Position a suitable lifting device under axle.
3. Secure brake drums to axle shaft.
4. Remove RWAL sensor from differential housing, if applicable.
5. Disconnect brake hose at axle junction block. Do not disconnect brake hydraulic lines at wheel cylinders.
6. Disconnect parking brake cables and cable brackets.
7. Disconnect vent hose from axle shaft tube.
8. Mark propeller shaft and yoke for installation reference.
9. Remove propeller shaft.
10. Disconnect shock absorbers from axle.
11. Remove spring clamps and spring brackets.
12. Remove axle from vehicle.
13. Reverse procedure to install. Tighten all fasteners to specification.

REAR AXLE SHAFT

REPLACE

1. Raise and support vehicle, ensure transmission is in neutral.
2. Remove wheel and tire assembly, then the brake drum.
3. Clean all foreign material from housing cover area.
4. Loosen cover bolts, drain lubricant from housing and axle shaft tubes, then remove cover from differential case.

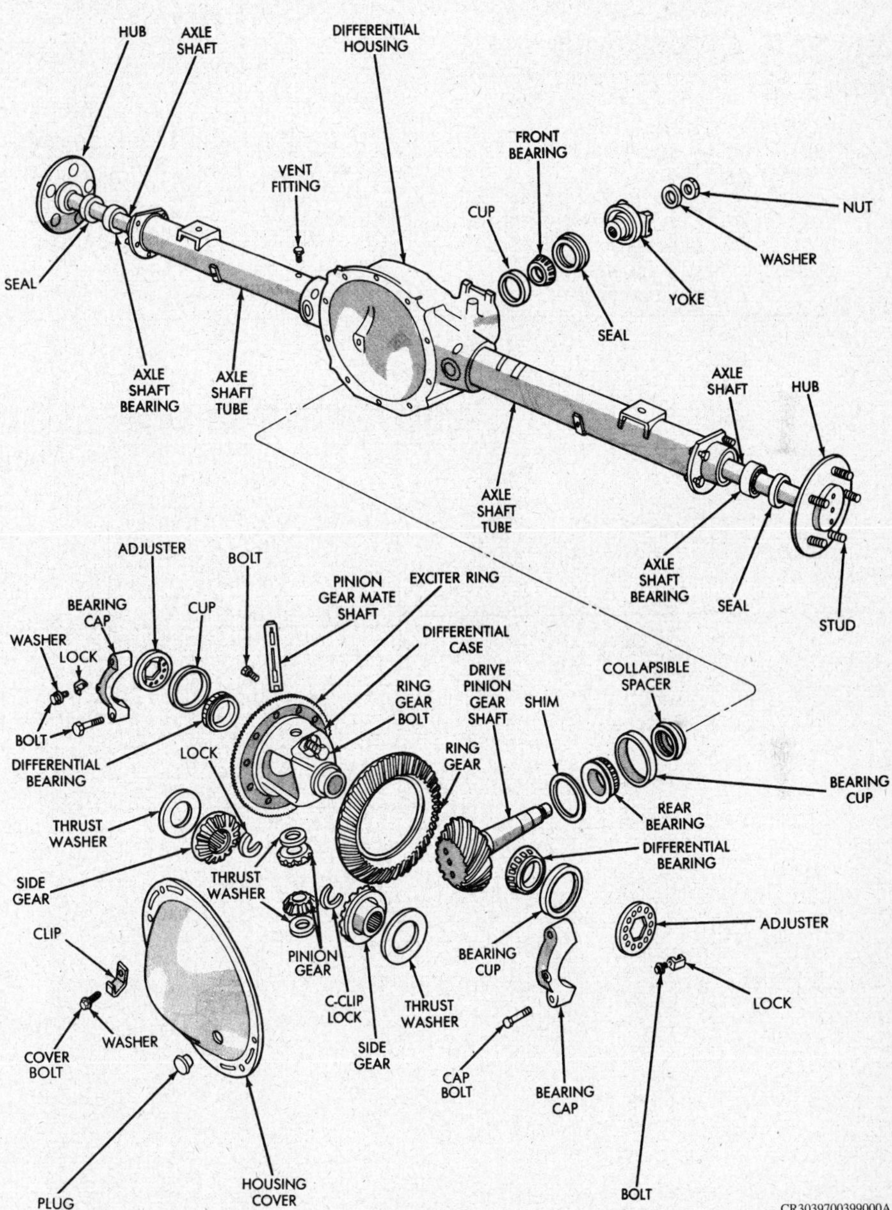

Fig. 1 Exploded view of 8¼ or 9¼ inch integral carrier rear axle assembly

5. Rotate differential case so pinion mate gear shaft lock screw is accessible, **Fig. 2.**
6. Remove lock screw and pinion mate gear shaft from differential case.
7. Push axle shaft inward and remove axle shaft C-clip lock from axle shaft.
8. Remove axle shaft, use care to prevent damage to axle shaft bearing and seal.
9. Inspect seal for signs of leakage or damage.

10. Inspect roller bearing contact surface on axle shaft for signs of brinneling, galling and pitting.
11. Replace axle shaft and/or bearing and seal if damage is as indicated.
12. Reverse procedure to install, noting the following:
    a. Insert C-clip in end of axle shaft, then push axle shaft outward to seat clip in side gear.
    b. Install mate shaft lock screw with Loctite on threads and tighten to specification.

SHOCK ABSORBER

REPLACE

1. Raise and support vehicle.
2. Remove shock absorber lower nut and bolt from axle bracket.
3. Remove shock absorber upper nut and bolt from frame bracket and remove shock absorber.
4. Reverse procedure to install.

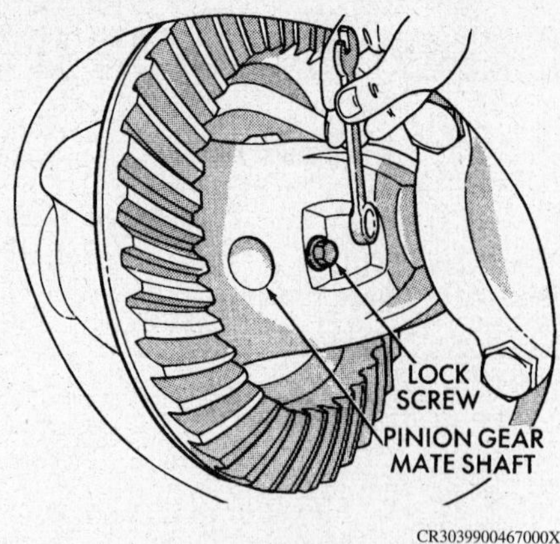

Fig. 2 Mate shaft lock screw

LEAF SPRING

REPLACE

1. Raise and support vehicle at frame.
2. Use a suitable hydraulic jack to relieve axle weight.
3. Remove wheel and tire assemblies.
4. Remove nuts, U-bolts, and spring plate from axle.
5. Remove nut and bolt from spring front eye.
6. Remove nut and bolt that attaches spring shackle to rear frame bracket.
7. Remove spring from vehicle, then the shackle from spring assembly.
8. Reverse procedure to install.

TIGHTENING SPECIFICATIONS

Year	Component	Torque Ft. Lbs.
2002–06	Bell Crank To Differential Bolt	185
	Lower Control Arm	180
	Shock Absorber Lower Nut	75
	Shock Absorber Upper Bolt	75
	Stabilizer Link Stabilizer Bar	75
	Stabilizer Link To Frame	75
	Stabilizer Retainer To Axle	45
	Watts Lateral Link To Frame	125
	Watts Link To Bell Crank	80
	Upper Control Arm	115

Front Suspension & Steering

NOTE: On Air Bag Equipped Models, Refer To "Air Bag System Precautions" Located In The Front Of This Manual For System Disarming & Arming Procedures.

NOTE: Refer To "Computer Relearn Procedures" Located In The Front Of This Manual When Battery Power To The Computer Has Been Interrupted.

INDEX

PRECAUTIONS

Air Bag Systems

Refer to "Air Bag System Precautions" in the front of this manual for system disarming and arming procedures.

Battery Ground Cable

Prior to service, disconnect battery ground cable and isolate as required.

DESCRIPTION

The front suspension system is designed to allow each wheel to adapt to different road surfaces independently. The wheels are mounted to hub bearings on cast iron steering knuckle spindles. The hub bearings are sealed and lubricated for life. The 4WD models use a torsion bar spring suspension whereas the 2WD models use a coil spring suspension.

WHEEL BEARING

ADJUST

Front wheel hub and bearing are preadjusted at factory and are not adjustable.

BALL JOINT INSPECTION

Lower

1. Raise front of vehicle and support both lower suspension arms with safety stands. Place stands as far outboard as possible. Upper arms must not contact rebound bumpers.
2. Clamp dial indicator to lower suspension arm, position plunger against bottom of steering knuckle lower ball joint boss.
3. The dial indicator plunger must be perpendicular to the machined surface of the steering knuckle lower ball joint boss.
4. Position a pry bar over top of upper suspension arm and under pivot bar of upper suspension arm.
5. Pry down on upper suspension arm and then zero dial indicator.
6. Reposition pry bar under upper suspension arm and on top of frame rail. Pry up on upper suspension arm and record dial indicator reading.
7. If travel exceeds .060 inch, replace lower suspension arm.

Upper

1. Position a suitable floor jack under lower suspension arm.
2. Raise wheel and allow tire to lightly contact the floor.
3. Mount a dial indicator solidly on the upper suspension arm, position indicator plunger against upper ball joint boss of steering knuckle.
4. Grasp top of tire and apply force in and out. Inspect for movement at all joint between upper suspension arm and steering knuckle.
5. If lateral movement is greater than .060 inch, replace upper suspension arm.

BALL JOINT

REPLACE

Upper and lower ball joints are integrated into their respective control arms and cannot be serviced separately. If ball joints exceed the specified service limit, replace the upper or lower control arm.

COIL SPRING

REPLACE

1. Raise and support vehicle, then remove wheel and tire.
2. Disconnect stabilizer bar from control arm and remove shock absorber.
3. Install spring compressor tool No. DD-1278, or equivalent, through lower suspension arm and coil spring, then tighten tool nut and compress spring.
4. Remove lower ball joint nut and separate ball joint from knuckle with removal tool No. C-415A, or equivalent.
5. Loosen spring compressor lower nut to remove spring tension.
6. Remove tool and pull down on lower suspension arm to remove spring.
7. Reverse procedure to install, noting the following:
   a. Ramped or open end of coil spring is bottom of spring.
   b. Tape insulator pad to top of coil spring.
   c. Ensure coil spring is seated in pocket.

SHOCK ABSORBER

REPLACE

1. Remove upper shock nut, retainer and grommet from shock absorber stud.
2. Raise and support vehicle.
3. Remove lower mounting bolts, then the shock absorber through the lower suspension arm.
4. Reverse procedure to install.

STEERING KNUCKLE

REPLACE

2WD

1. Raise and support vehicle.
2. Remove wheel and tire assembly, disc brake caliper, rotor, shield and ABS speed sensor and position aside. **Do not allow caliper to hang from hydraulic line.**
3. Remove tie rod from steering knuckle arm.

4. Remove hub/bearing and shock absorber.
5. Install spring compressor tool No. DD-1278, or equivalent, up through lower suspension arm, coil spring and upper shock mounting hole.
6. Tighten tool lower nut to compress coil spring.
7. Remove lower ball joint nut and separate lower ball joint from knuckle with removal tool No. C-4150A, or equivalent.
8. Remove upper ball joint nut and separate upper ball joint from knuckle with removal tool No. MB-991113, or equivalent. **Ensure damage does not occur to ball joint seal.**
9. Remove steering knuckle.
10. Reverse procedure to install.

4WD

1. Raise and support vehicle.
2. Remove wheel and tire assembly, then the brake caliper, rotor, shield and ABS wheel speed sensor.
3. Remove front driveshaft, tie rod end cotter pin and nut.
4. Separate tie rod end from knuckle using removal tool No. MB991113, or equivalent.
5. Support lower suspension arm with suitable hydraulic jack, then raise jack to unload rebound bumper.
6. Remove upper ball joint cotter pin and nut, then separate ball joint from knuckle with removal tool No. MB991113, or equivalent.
7. Use care to ensure damage does not occur to ball joint seals.
8. Remove lower ball joint cotter pin and nut, then separate lower ball joint from knuckle with removal tool No. C-4150A, or equivalent.
9. Remove hub/bearing from steering knuckle.
10. Reverse procedure to install, noting the following:
    a. When installing hub/bearing with ABS brakes, position speed sensor opening towards front of vehicle.
    b. Ball joint stud tapers must be clean and dry before installing the knuckle. Clean stud tapers with mineral spirits to remove dirt and grease.
    c. Tighten all nuts and bolts to specification.

TORSION BAR

REPLACE

The lefthand and righthand side torsion bars are not interchangeable. The bars are identified and stamped R or L for their respective sides. The bars do not have a front or rear end and can be installed with either end facing forward.

1. Raise and support vehicle.
2. Turn adjustment bolt counterclockwise to release spring tension. Count and record number of turns for installation reference.
3. Remove adjustment bolt from swivel.
4. Remove torsion bar and anchor, then separate anchor from torsion bar.
5. Reverse procedure to install, noting the following:
    a. Remove all foreign material from torsion bar mounting in anchor and suspension arm.
    b. Inspect adjustment bolt, bearing and swivel for damage, replace components as required.

STABILIZER BAR

REPLACE

2WD

1. Raise and support vehicle.
2. Remove upper link nut, retainer and grommet from each link.
3. Remove lower link nut from lower suspension arm on each side.
4. Remove stabilizer bar retainer bolts and remove retainers and stabilizer from vehicle.
5. Remove bushings from stabilizer bar.
6. Reverse procedure to install.

4WD

To service the stabilizer bar the vehicle must be on a drive-on hoist. The vehicle suspension must be at curb height for stabilizer bar installation.

1. Remove stabilizer bar retainer bolts from lower suspension arms, then remove retainers.
2. Remove stabilizer bar retainer nuts, bolts and retainers from frame crossmember, then remove the bar.
3. If required, remove bushings from stabilizer bar.
4. Reverse procedure to install.

POWER STEERING GEAR

REPLACE

1. Place wheels in straight ahead position with steering wheel centered.
2. Disconnect and cap fluid lines from steering gear.
3. Remove lower shaft coupler bolt and slide coupler off of gear
4. Raise and support vehicle.
5. Remove cotter pin and nut from pitman arm ball stud.
6. Separate pitman arm from center link with pitman arm puller tool No. C-3894-A, or equivalent.
7. Remove splash shield under cooling module.
8. Remove steering gear mounting bolts, then the steering gear from by lowering it through opening between cooling module and frame crossmember.
9. Remove pitman arm from gear with removal tool No. C-4150A, or equivalent.
10. Reverse procedure to install.

POWER STEERING PUMP

REPLACE

5.7L Engine

1. Drain and siphon power steering fluid from pump.
2. Remove serpentine drive belt.
3. Remove reservoir return hose at reservoir.
4. Remove pressure hose from pump.
5. Remove three pump mounting bolts through pulley access holes.
6. Remove pump from engine.
7. Reverse procedure to install.

TIGHTENING SPECIFICATIONS

Year	Component	Torque Ft. Lbs.
2002–06	Hub/Bearing Bolts	120
	Lower Suspension Arm Ball Joint Nut	70
	Lower Suspension Arm Frame Nuts	180
	Shock Absorber Upper Nut	75
	Shock Absorber Lower Bolt	60
	Stabilizer Bar Frame Bolt	45
	Stabilizer Link To Lower Control Arm	125
	Stabilizer Link Stabilizer Bar Nut	40
	Tie Rod End Jam Nut	96
	Tie Rod End To Knuckle Nut	55
	Upper Suspension Arm Frame Nuts	75
	Upper Suspension Arm Ball Joint Nut	55

Wheel Alignment

INDEX

PRELIMINARY INSPECTION

1. Road test vehicle noting any abnormal steering or handling characteristics.
2. Ensure tires are the proper type, correctly inflated, properly balanced and same size on each axle.
3. Inspect ball joints, suspension arms, bushings and tie rods, and repair or replace any component that is damaged or excessively worn.
4. Ensure wheel runout is not excessive and bearings are properly adjusted.
5. Inspect suspension components for wear and correct tightening.
6. Jounce vehicle several times to settle suspension.
7. Place vehicle on suitable alignment rack following manufacturers instructions. Remove hub cap and cotter pin (2WD) or free wheeling hub (4WD Models), and attach alignment gauges to wheel hub.
8. Inspect and correct alignment angles in the following sequence:
   a. **On models equipped with 4WD,** proceed to "Vehicle Ride Height."
   b. **On all models,** camber, caster and toe-in.

FRONT WHEEL ALIGNMENT

Caster & Camber

On 4WD models, front suspension height must be inspected and corrected as required prior to inspecting wheel alignment. Refer to "Vehicle Ride Height" for procedure.

1. Remove all foreign material from exposed threads of pivot bar adjusting nuts.
2. Record initial camber and caster readings before loosening pivot bar adjusting nuts, **Fig. 1.**
3. Moving only rear pivot of upper control arm in or out will greatly affect caster while changing camber only slightly. Moving front pivot of upper control arm in or out will greatly affect camber while changing caster only slightly.
4. Caster should be held as nearly equal as possible on both wheels.
5. Camber settings should be held as close as possible to desired specifications.
6. After adjusting, **torque** pivot bar attaching nuts to 155 ft. lbs.

Toe-In

1. Start engine, turn wheels both ways before straightening, then secure steering wheel with wheels pointed straight ahead.
2. Loosen tire rod adjustment sleeve camp bolts or nut.
3. Adjust toe-in by turning sleeves. **Each wheel should be adjusted ½ total specification to ensure steering wheel being centered.**
4. **Torque** locknut to 55 ft. lbs., or clamp bolts to 17 ft. lbs.

VEHICLE RIDE HEIGHT

Front Suspension Height

4WD MODELS

The vehicle suspension height must be measured and adjusted if required before performing wheel alignment on 4WD vehicles. Measurement must be taken on both sides of vehicle and should be performed with vehicle supporting it's own weight.

1. Inspect tires for correct size and air pressure.
2. Jounce front of vehicle.
3. Measure and record distance between ground and center of lower suspension arm rear mounting bolt head, **Fig. 2.**
4. Measure and record distance between ground and center of front wheel, **Fig. 2.**
5. Subtract first measurement from second measurement. Difference between two measurements should be 1.725–1.975 inches.
6. To adjust vehicle height, turn torsion bar adjustment bolt clockwise to raise vehicle height and counterclockwise to lower vehicle height.
7. Always raise vehicle height to correct suspension height. If vehicle height is too high, lower vehicle, then raise to proper height specification.

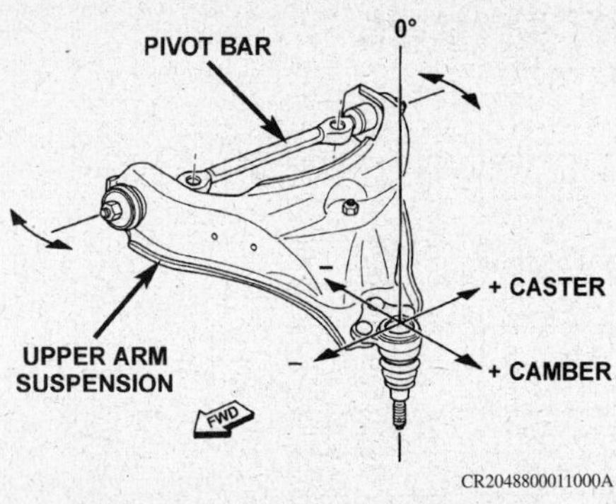

Fig. 1 Loosening pivot bar adjusting nuts

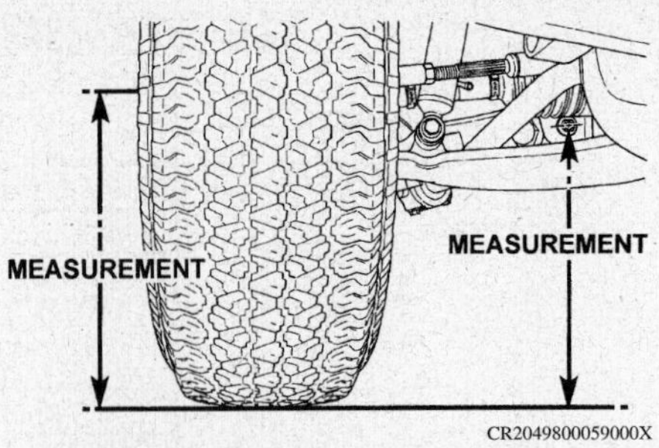

Fig. 2 Vehicle ride height measurement. 4WD models

PACIFICA

NOTE: Refer To The Rear Of This Manual For Vehicle Manufacturer's Special Service Tool Suppliers.

INDEX OF SERVICE OPERATIONS

Specifications

GENERAL ENGINE SPECIFICATIONS

Year	Engine Liter	Fuel System	Bore & Stroke, Inch	Comp. Ratio	Horsepower @ RPM	Torque, Ft. Lbs. @ RPM	Normal Oil Pressure, Lbs. @ 300 RPM
2004–06	3.5L	SMPI	3.780 x 3.189	10	250 @ 6400	250 @ 3950	45–105

TUNE UP SPECIFICATIONS

The following specifications are published from latest information available. This data should only be used in absence of decal affixed in engine compartment.

Year & Engine	Spark Plug Gap	Ignition Timing, ° BTDC				Curb Idle Speed		Fast Idle Speed		Fuel System Pump Pressure, psi⑥	Valve Lash
		Firing Order, Fig. ①	Man. Trans.	Auto. Trans.	Mark Location	Man. Trans.	Auto. Trans.	Man. Trans.	Auto. Trans.		
2004–06	.048–.053	A	—	②	③	—	④	—	④	58	⑤

BTDC — Before Top Dead Center

① — Before disconnecting wires from coil unit, determine location of No. 1 wire, as position may have been altered from that in **Fig. A.**

② — Direct (Distributorless) Ignition System (DIS). Not adjustable.

③ — Equipped w/crankshaft position sensor.

④ — Controlled by PCM/TCM.

⑤ — Equipped w/hydraulic lash adjusters. No adjustment is required.

⑥ — Remove cover from service valve on fuel rail. Connect suitable fuel pressure test gauge to service valve. With ignition switch in Run position, use Diagnostic Read-Out Box to activate fuel pump & pressurize system.

Fig. A

FRONT WHEEL ALIGNMENT SPECIFICATIONS

Year	Caster Angle, Degrees		Camber Angle, Degrees		Toe-In	Ball Joint Wear, Inch
	Limits	Desired	Limits	Desired		
2004–06	+4.00 to +5.00	+4.50	–.60 to +.20	–.20	+.10	①

① — Refer to "Ball Joint Inspection" in "Front Suspension & Steering."

REAR WHEEL ALIGNMENT SPECIFICATIONS

Year	Caster Angle, Degrees		Camber Angle, Degrees		Toe-In	Ball Joint Wear, Inch
	Limits	Desired	Limits	Desired		
2004–06	0	0	–.90 to +.10	–.40	0	①

① — Refer to "Ball Joint Inspection" in "Front Suspension & Steering."

FLUID CAPACITIES & COOLING SYSTEM DATA

Year	Engine	Coolant Capacity	Recommended Engine Coolant Type	Radiator Cap Relief Pressure, Lbs.	Thermo. Opening Temp., °F	Fuel Tank, Gals.	Engine Oil Refill, Qts.①	Transmission Oil		Transfer Case, Pints	Axle, Pints	
								Manual, Pints	Auto., Qts.		Front	Rear
2004–06	3.5	10.5	Ethylene Glycol	16	—	23	5.5	—	9.7	2.1	—	1.48

① — Includes filter.

LUBRICANT DATA

Year	Model	Lubricant Data					
		Transmission		Transfer Case	Rear Axle	Power Steering	Brake System
		Manual	Automatic				
2004–06	All	—	Mopar ATF Plus 4	75W-90 GL-5	75W-90 GL-5	MS-9602	DOT 3

Electrical

NOTE: On Air Bag Equipped Models, Refer To "Air Bag System Precautions" Located In The Front Of This Manual For System Disarming & Arming Procedures.

NOTE: Refer To "Computer Relearn Procedures" Located In The Front Of This Manual When Battery Power To The Computer Has Been Interrupted.

INDEX

PRECAUTIONS

Air Bag Systems

Refer to "Air Bag System Precautions" in the front of this manual for system disarming and arming procedures.

Battery Ground Cable

Prior to service, disconnect battery ground cable and isolate as required.

FUSE PANEL LOCATION

Fuse panel is located below lefthand side of instrument panel.

Turn signal/hazard flasher is a single unit located on fuse panel.

RELAY CENTER LOCATION

The relay bank is located in the fuse box and in the power distribution center on the lefthand side of the engine compartment. Refer to **Fig. 1** for relay identification.

FUEL PUMP RELAY LOCATION

The fuel pump relay is located in the lefthand side of the engine compartment in the power distribution center.

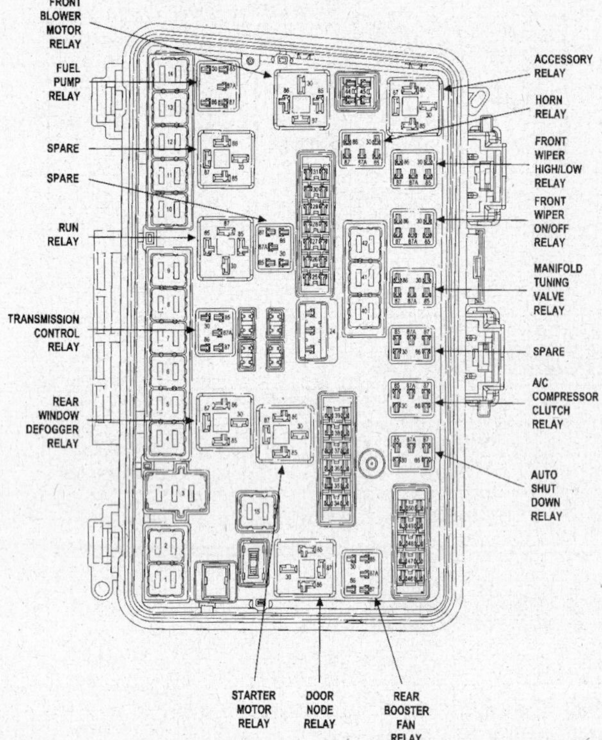

Fig. 1 Power distribution center relay identification

STARTER

REPLACE

1. Remove screws attaching radiator closure to upper grille, then the panel from vehicle.
2. Remove push pin fasteners attaching cooling upper seal to radiator crossmember.
3. Remove screws attaching hood latch to radiator crossmember, then disconnect remote hood latch release cable clip.
4. Remove radiator top attaching bolts to radiator crossmember.
5. Remove bolts sides of radiator crossmember, then crossmember from vehicle.
6. Remove radiator fan module, then the wiring harness clip from front mount.
7. Remove coolant line clamp bolt, then the upper nut from front mount.
8. Remove upper starter mounting bolt, then the middle starter bolt.
9. Raise and support vehicle, then remove lower front mount nut.
10. Raise and support engine, then remove lower bracket bolts to transmission and engine.
11. Reposition front mount and bracket, then disconnect positive battery cable from starter.
12. Remove lower starter bolt, then starter from vehicle.
13. Reverse procedure to install.

ALTERNATOR

REPLACE

1. Remove engine cover, then the alternator drive belt.
2. Remove nut holding B+ wire terminal to back of alternator, then the B+ terminal.
3. Disconnect push-in field wire connector from back of alternator.
4. Remove upper and lower mounting bolts, then the alternator from vehicle.
5. Reverse procedure to install.

IGNITION COIL

REPLACE

1. Remove electrical connector from ignition coil.
2. Remove upper intake manifold as outlined under "Intake Manifold" in "3.5L Engine" section to access front coils.
3. Prior to removing ignition coils, spray compressed air around coil area and spark plug.
4. It is required to loosen screws by alternating back and forth. Do not lose spacers under coil when loosening screws.
5. Remove ignition coils from engine.
6. Reverse procedure to install.

IGNITION LOCK

REPLACE

1. Remove bezel ignition switch ring.
2. Pull center console bezel loose from instrument panel.
3. Insert ignition key and turn to ON position.
4. Depress locking tab on ignition switch housing.
5. Pull key cylinder from the ignition switch housing.
6. Reverse procedure to install noting the following:
   a. Shaft at end of lock cylinder aligns with socket in end of housing. To align socket with lock cylinder, ensure socket is in ON position.
   b. Align lock cylinder with grooves in housing. Slide lock cylinder into housing until tab sticks through opening in housing.

IGNITION SWITCH

REPLACE

1. Remove knee blocker air bag module as outlined in "Passive Restraint Systems" chapter.
2. Remove instrument panel center bezel panel.
3. Remove switch mounting nuts.
4. Loosen rear mounting nut.
5. Slide assembly rearward.
6. Disconnect electrical connector from ignition switch and SKREEM Module.
7. Remove interlock and interlocking cables.
8. Remove ignition switch mounting screw, then the ignition switch from lockhousing.
9. Reverse procedure to install.

NEUTRAL SAFETY SWITCH

REPLACE

1. Disconnect switch electrical connector.
2. Remove switch from transaxle case and allow fluid to drain into suitable container.
3. Ensure switch operating lever fingers center in opening when shift selector is in Park and Neutral positions.
4. Reverse procedure to install switch with new seal. **Torque** switch to 24 ft. lbs.

HEADLAMP SWITCH

REPLACE

1. Remove instrument panel lower steering column cover.
2. Reach up behind lefthand side of instrument panel, then depress spring clip on top or bottom of headlamp switch.
3. Firmly push out headlamp switch assembly, then disconnect electrical connector.
4. Remove headlamp switch from vehicle.
5. Reverse procedure to install.

STOP LIGHT SWITCH

REPLACE

Removal

1. Rotate switch in a clockwise direction approximately 30° and pull out of mount.
2. Release locking tab, then disconnect wiring connector from switch.
3. Discard brake lamp switch.

Installation

Do not reuse the original brake lamp switch. The switch can only be adjusted once. That is during initial installation of the switch. If the switch is not adjusted properly or has been removed for some service, a new switch must be installed and adjusted.

1. Connect electrical connector to switch and latch locking tab.
2. Install switch in its bracket by aligning index tab on switch with slot in mounting bracket.
3. When switch is fully seated in its mount, rotate switch counterclockwise approximately 30° to lock switch into place.
4. With brake pedal in fully released position, move lever on back of brake lamp switch from angled non-adjusted position to the vertical position.
5. Ensure stop lamps operate properly and not staying on when pedal is in released position.
6. Road test vehicle to ensure proper operation of brakes including ABS and speed control.

MULTI-FUNCTION SWITCH

REPLACE

1. Remove lower and upper steering column shrouds.
2. Disconnect electrical connector from switch.
3. Remove two screws that secure multi-function switch to housing.
4. Remove lefthand multi-function switch from column and vehicle.
5. Reverse procedure to install. **Torque** multi-function switch to column screws to 22 inch lbs.

TURN SIGNAL SWITCH

REPLACE

Refer to "Multi-Function Switch, Replace" for turn signal switch replacement procedure.

DIMMER SWITCH

REPLACE

Refer to "Multi-Function Switch, Replace" for dimmer switch replacement procedure.

STEERING WHEEL

REPLACE

1. Remove driver air bag module as outlined in "Passive Restraint Systems" chapter.
2. Remove steering wheel retaining nut, then the damper.
3. Remove steering wheel using standard wheel puller.
4. Remove speed control switches from steering wheel.
5. Remove remote audio switches from steering wheel.
6. Reverse procedure to install.

INSTRUMENT CLUSTER

REPLACE

1. Remove cluster bezel.
2. **On models equipped with navigation system,** remove nuts to column and lower on to seat.
3. **On all models,** disconnect electrical connectors from bottom of cluster, accessed from underneath instrument panel.
4. **On models less navigation system,** remove retaining screws to both multi-function switches.
5. **On all models** remove cluster retaining screws, then pull cluster straight out of instrument panel opening. **Use care not to scratch cluster face.**
6. Reverse procedure to install.

RADIO

REPLACE

1. Remove instrument panel center bezel, then the radio mounting screws.
2. Pull radio rearward to gain access to back of radio. **Pulling antenna cable straight out of radio without pulling on locking antenna connector could damage cable or radio.**
3. Disconnect antenna cable by pulling locking antenna connector away from radio.
4. Disconnect electrical connectors from back of radio.
5. Reverse procedure to install.

WIPER MOTOR

REPLACE

Front

1. Gently pry arm retaining nut cap off using trim stick tool No. C-4755 or equivalent.
2. Remove nut holding wiper arm to wiper pivot.
3. Separate wiper arm from wiper pivot using a suitable two jaw puller.
4. Open hood as required, then push pin fasteners from cowl plenum panel.
5. Disengage locking tabs and remove grille from body and vehicle using trim stick tool No. C-4755 or equivalent.
6. Disconnect wiper motor electrical connector, then remove retaining bolts to wiper module.
7. Remove wiper module from vehicle.
8. With wiper module on bench, pry apart socket and ball joint at end of bell crank.
9. Remove front wiper motor mounting bolts, then the motor from module/linkage.
10. Reverse procedure to install.

Rear

1. Lift up wiper arm nut cover by pivoting out of way, then remove rear wiper arm retaining nut.
2. Lift rear wiper arm off rear window and gently rock arm back and forth until it comes off or use an appropriate battery terminal puller to pull arm off rear motor shaft.
3. Open liftgate, then remove liftgate trim panel and disconnect rear wiper motor electrical connector.
4. Remove rear wiper motor mounting screws, then the rear wiper motor from vehicle.
5. Reverse procedure to install.

WIPER SWITCH

REPLACE

Refer to "Multi-Function Switch, Replace" for wiper switch replacement procedure.

BLOWER MOTOR

REPLACE

1. Disarm air bag system as outlined in "Precautions."
2. Remove glove box from instrument panel.
3. Disconnect electrical connectors from front blower motor power module.
4. Remove screws that secure front blower motor power module to front HVAC housing then the blower power module.
5. Reverse procedure to install.

HEATER CORE

REPLACE

1. Drain cooling system into suitable container.
2. Remove silencer boot fasteners located around base of lower steering shaft from instrument panel so it may be positioned aside.
3. Remove stop lamp switch from its mounting bracket as outlined under "Stop Lamp Switch, Replace."
4. Disconnect power brake booster input rod from pin on brake pedal arm.
5. Remove three screws securing heater core shield to lefthand end of HVAC distribution housing.
6. Pull heater core shield rearward far enough to disengage two locating tabs that position front of shield to receptacles in two lower formations of evaporator housing near instrument panel.
7. Remove heater core shield from distribution housing.
8. Take proper precautions to protect carpet below heater core from possible spilled engine coolant.

9. Remove screw securing heater core tube sealing plate to heater core supply and return ports.
10. Push both heater core tubes simultaneously toward instrument panel far enough to disengage fittings from heater core supply and return ports.
11. Plug open heater core ports and tube fittings.
12. Remove two screws securing heater core mounting plate to distribution housing.
13. Pull accelerator pedal upward and push brake pedal downward far enough for clearance to pull heater core out of distribution housing.
14. Reverse procedure to install.

EVAPORATOR CORE

REPLACE

1. Recover A/C refrigerant as outlined under in "Air Conditioning" chapter.
2. Drain coolant into a suitable container.
3. Disconnect liquid line and suction line from expansion valve.
4. Disconnect heater hoses from heater core tubes.
5. Remove nuts securing heater-A/C unit housing studs to engine compartment side of instrument panel.
6. Remove instrument panel as outlined in "Dash Panel Service" chapter.
7. Remove floor distribution duct from passenger compartment.
8. Remove screw securing heater-A/C unit housing bracket to passenger side of instrument panel.
9. Pull heater-A/C unit housing rearward far enough for mounting studs to clear dash panel, then remove.
10. Remove heater core tubes from heater core.
11. Remove and discard foam seal from HVAC housing seal flange around fresh air inlet opening and expansion valve/evaporator tube opening on instrument panel side of unit.
12. Remove expansion valve from evaporator inlet and outlet tube fittings.
13. Disconnect blower motor electrical connector, then disengage HVAC wire harness from routing clips molded into outside of HVAC housing components.
14. Remove screws from instrument panel side of unit securing top of distribution housing to inboard end of evaporator housing.
15. Pull top of distribution housing away from evaporator housing far enough to disengage hooks on bottom of distribution housing.
16. Remove screws securing upper intake air housing to lower intake air housing.
17. Remove screws securing upper intake air housing to top of outboard end of evaporator housing ensuring not to miss screw located inside inboard side of fresh air intake opening.
18. Remove upper intake air housing from top of evaporator housing to expose recirculation air door and blower wheel housing.
19. Remove screws securing upper half of recirculation air door to lower half of door.
20. Remove upper half of recirculation air door from lower half of door.
21. Remove screws around perimeter of evaporator housing securing upper housing half to lower half.
22. Carefully separate and remove upper half of evaporator housing from lower half.
23. Carefully lift evaporator and its foam wrap out of lower half of evaporator housing as a unit ensuring not to loose clam shell type rubber seal that is fitted to evaporator inlet and outlet tubes where they exit evaporator housing.
24. Reverse procedure to install. If replacing evaporator core add 2 ounces of ND8 PAG, or equivalent.

3.5L Engine

NOTE: On Air Bag Equipped Models, Refer To "Air Bag System Precautions" Located In The Front Of This Manual For System Disarming & Arming Procedures.

NOTE: Refer To "Computer Relearn Procedures" Located In The Front Of This Manual When Battery Power To The Computer Has Been Interrupted.

INDEX

PRECAUTIONS

Air Bag Systems

Refer to "Air Bag System Precautions" in the front of this manual for system disarming and arming procedures.

Fuel System Pressure Relief

1. Remove fuel pump relay for power distribution center.
2. Start and run engine until it stalls.
3. Attempt to start engine until it no longer runs.
4. Turn ignition switch to Off position.
5. Place rag or towel under fuel line quick-connector fitting at fuel rail.
6. Install fuel pump relay.
7. One or more Diagnostic Trouble Codes (DTCs) may have been stored because of removing fuel pump relay. Clear these DTCs with suitably programmed scan tool.

Battery Ground Cable

Prior to service, disconnect battery ground cable and isolate as required.

COMPRESSION PRESSURE

The minimum compression pressure should be no less than 100 psi and the maximum variation between cylinders should be no more than 25%.

ENGINE MOUNT

REPLACE

Upper

1. Support engine assembly with a suitable floor jack, ensure it does not rotate.
2. Disconnect intake air temperature sensor connector, then remove air inlet hose at throttle body.
3. Disconnect air circulation hose element housing, then remove housing retaining bolt.
4. Pull housing off locating pin and remove air cleaner housing from vehicle.

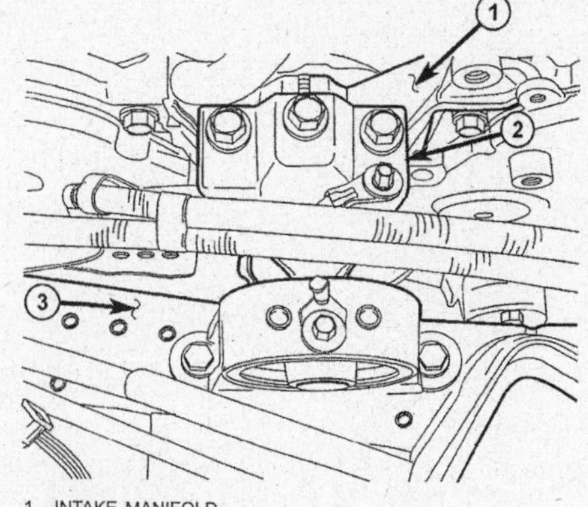

Fig. 1 Upper engine mount replacement

5. Remove upper engine mount bolts from inner frame rail and engine.
6. Remove mount from engine, **Fig. 1.**
7. Reverse procedure to install.

Lefthand

1. Open hood, then remove headlamp retaining screws.
2. Pull headlamps forward unsnaping it from retaining clips.
3. Disconnect electrical connector and remove headlamps.
4. Raise and support vehicle, then remove fascia air dam to radiator closure panel.
5. Remove front fascia to splash shield screws, then the fascia to front fenders retaining screws.
6. Disconnect fog lamps electrical connectors, then lower vehicle.
7. Remove push pins attaching upper appearance panel to upper crossmember.
8. Remove push pins attaching upper grille support to headlamp mounting panel at each side of grille.
9. Remove bumper fascia from vehicle.
10. Disconnect radiator fan electrical connector, then remove screw and radiator fan.
11. Raise and support vehicle, then remove both engine mount to cradle nuts.
12. Lower the vehicle, then connect engine support fixture and support engine weight.
13. Remove engine mount bolts and mount, **Fig. 2.**
14. Reverse procedure to install.

Righthand

1. Raise and support vehicle, then remove both engine mount to cradle nuts.
2. Lower vehicle, then connect engine fixture and support engine weight.
3. Raise and support vehicle, then remove mount bracket bolts.
4. Remove engine mount top nut, then the engine mount plate and engine mount, **Fig. 3.**
5. Reverse procedure to install.

ENGINE

REPLACE

1. Recover A/C refrigerant as outlined under in "Air Conditioning" chapter.
2. Drain coolant into a suitable container.
3. Remove fuel pump relay for power distribution center.
4. Start and run engine until it stalls.
5. Attempt to start engine until it no longer runs.
6. Turn ignition switch to Off position.
7. Place rag or towel under fuel line quick-connector fitting at fuel rail.
8. Install fuel pump relay.
9. Remove engine cover, then the cruise control servo and upper radiator hose.
10. Remove headlamp retaining screws.
11. Pull headlamps forward unsnaping it from retaining clips.
12. Disconnect electrical connector and remove headlamps.
13. Raise and support vehicle, then remove fascia air dam to radiator closure panel screws.
14. Remove front fascia to splash shield screws, then the fascia to front fenders retaining screws.
15. Disconnect fog lamps electrical connectors, then lower vehicle.
16. Remove push pins attaching upper appearance panel to upper crossmember.
17. Remove push pins attaching upper grille support to headlamp mounting panel at each side of grille.
18. Remove bumper fascia from vehicle.
19. Disconnect radiator fan electrical connector, then remove screw and radiator fan.
20. Disconnect intake air temperature

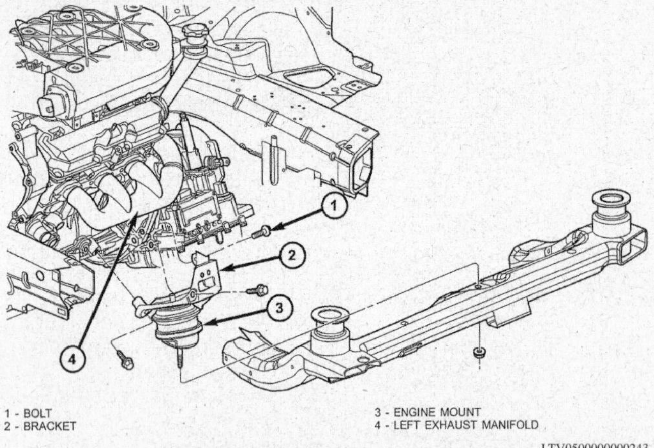

Fig. 2 Lefthand engine mount replacement

sensor connector, then remove air inlet hose at throttle body.

21. Disconnect air circulation hose element housing, then remove housing retaining bolt.
22. Pull housing off locating pin and remove air cleaner housing from vehicle.
23. Disconnect throttle and cruise control cables from throttle body.
24. Disconnect cruise control and power brake booster vacuum hoses at engine.
25. Disconnect transmission electrical connector from solenoid pack, input and output sensors and range sensor connectors.
26. Disconnect engine grounds at lefthand inner frame rail, then the transmission shift cable and cooler lines.
27. Disconnect engine block heater connector and set aside.
28. Disconnect coolant reservoir hoses at thermostat housing, then the heater hoses at heater core and upper radiator hose at thermostat housing.
29. Disconnect both front brake lines from Hydraulic Control Unit, then the air condition suction discharge hoses at compressor and plug openings to prevent contamination.
30. Disconnect lower radiator hose at engine outlet and remove.
31. Disconnect A/C clutch, oil pressure sending unit and alternator electrical connectors.
32. Disconnect fuel supply line at fuel rail, then the ignition connector at intake manifold.
33. Raise and support vehicle, then remove front wheels.
34. Remove lefthand and righthand inner fender wells.
35. Disconnect connector from powertrain control module, then wheel speed sensors and retainers.
36. Remove sway bar links at front struts, then the drive axle nuts.
37. Remove steering knuckle pinch bolts, then separate steering knuckles from struts and suitably support steering knuckles.
38. Disconnect battery ground cable from transmission, then the starter connectors, harness retainers and exhaust manifold oxygen sensor electrical connector.
39. Disconnect catalytic converter oxygen sensor electrical connector, then remove exhaust system from manifold and set aside.
40. Match mark rear driveshaft front and rear positions, then remove drive shaft.
41. Remove engine to transmission support plate, then transmission inspection shield.
42. Remove flex plate to torque converter bolts. **Secure steering wheel to prevent rotation and possible damage to steering column clock spring when coupling is separated.**
43. Remove lower steering column coupling pin with tool No. 6831–A or equivalent and separate union.
44. Remove both lower engine mount nuts, then match mark front cradle to body location and position engine cradle support under vehicle.
45. Lower vehicle until just above cradle support fixture, then align cradle support dowels with cradle access holes.
46. Adjust engine support fixture to fit flush with oil pan and adjust cradle support fixture arms to fit flush with cradle.
47. Lower vehicle onto cradle support fixture, then remove upper engine mount.
48. Carefully remove front and rear cradle mounting bolts and raise vehicle to separate engine, transmission and cradle assembly from vehicle.
49. Connect engine lifting brackets to engine, then separate power transfer unit, engine and transmission from engine cradle using lifting brackets.
50. Separate transmission from engine.
51. Reverse procedure to install.

INTAKE MANIFOLD

REPLACE

Upper

1. Remove air cleaner housing and inlet hose.
2. Remove throttle and speed control cables from throttle arm and bracket.
3. Disconnect Secondary Runner Valve (SRV), Manifold Tuning Valve (MTV), Throttle Position Sensor (TPS), Idle Air Control (IAC) and Intake Air Temperature/Manifold Absolute Pressure (TMAP) electrical connectors.
4. Disconnect SRV reservoir, speed control reservoir and Positive Crankcase Ventilation (PCV) vacuum hoses.
5. Remove lefthand and righthand side intake manifold supports, then support brackets at intake manifold front corners and MTV.
6. Remove EGR tubes mounting clips.
7. Remove mounting bolts and upper manifold.
8. Reverse procedure to install, noting the following:
   a. Hand start all intake manifold mounting bolts.
   b. Tighten bolts gradually starting in center working outward until to 105 inch lbs.

Lower

1. Remove fuel pump relay for power distribution center.
2. Start and run engine until it stalls.
3. Attempt to start engine until it no longer runs.
4. Turn ignition switch to Off position.
5. Place rag or towel under fuel line quick-connector fitting at fuel rail.
6. Install fuel pump relay.
7. Drain cooling system into suitable container.
8. Remove air cleaner housing and inlet hose.
9. Remove throttle and speed control cables from throttle arm and bracket.
10. Disconnect Secondary Runner Valve (SRV), Manifold Tuning Valve (MTV), Throttle Position Sensor (TPS), Idle Air Control (IAC) and Intake Air Temperature/Manifold Absolute Pressure (TMAP) electrical connectors.
11. Disconnect SRV reservoir, speed control reservoir and Positive Crankcase Ventilation (PCV) vacuum hoses.
12. Remove lefthand and righthand side intake manifold supports, then support brackets at intake manifold front corners and MTV.
13. Remove EGR tubes mounting clips.
14. Remove mounting bolts and upper manifold.
15. Disconnect fuel injectors and coolant temperature sensor electrical connectors, then heater hose quick connect tee from heater tube.
16. Disconnect fuel rail fuel supply hose from fuel rail, then remove fuel rail support bracket to throttle body support bracket mounting screw.
17. Remove fuel rail and injector assembly mounting bolts, then fuel rail and injectors.
18. Remove lower intake manifold mounting bolts and manifold.
19. Reverse procedure to install. Gradually **torque** mounting bolts in sequence to 21 ft. lbs., **Fig. 4.**

EXHAUST MANIFOLD

REPLACE

Righthand

1. Disconnect upstream oxygen sensor electrical connector.
2. Remove exhaust manifold crossover pipe retaining bolts, then raise and support vehicle.
3. Disconnect downstream oxygen sensor electrical connector.
4. Remove exhaust manifold flange retaining bolts, then disconnect exhaust system hangers from pipe assembly.
5. Remove exhaust system from vehicle, then the EGR tube support bracket bolt.
6. Remove lower exhaust manifold retaining bolts and manifold, then the oxygen sensor from exhaust manifold.
7. Reverse procedure to install.

Lefthand

1. Open hood, then remove headlamp retaining screws.
2. Pull headlamps forward unsnaping it from retaining clips.
3. Disconnect electrical connector and remove headlamps.
4. Raise and support vehicle, then remove fascia air dam to radiator closure panel.
5. Remove front fascia to splash shield screws, then the fascia to front fenders retaining screws.
6. Disconnect fog lamps electrical connectors, then lower vehicle.
7. Remove push pins attaching upper appearance panel to upper crossmember.
8. Remove push pins attaching upper grille support to headlamp mounting panel at each side of grille.
9. Remove bumper fascia from vehicle.
10. Disconnect radiator fan electrical connector, then remove screw and radiator fan.
11. Loosen oil dipstick tube retaining bolt and position dipstick out of way.
12. Remove exhaust manifold crossover pipe retaining bolts.
13. Remove exhaust manifold retaining bolts, exhaust manifold, and discard gasket.
14. Reverse procedure to install.

CYLINDER HEAD

REPLACE

Righthand

1. Relieve fuel pressure as outlined under "Precautions."
2. Drain cooling system into a suitable container, then remove engine cover.
3. Disconnect intake air temperature sensor connector, then remove air inlet hose at throttle body.
4. Disconnect air circulation hose element housing, then remove housing retaining bolt.

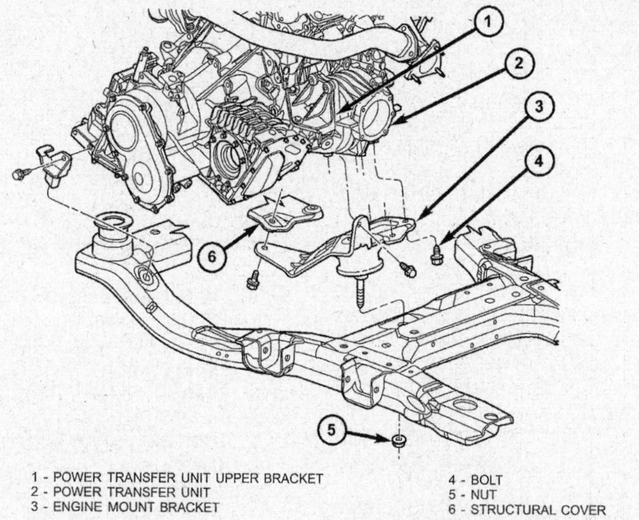

Fig. 3 Righthand engine mount replacement

5. Pull housing off locating pin and remove air cleaner housing from vehicle.
6. Disconnect fuel line at fuel rail.
7. Remove upper and lower intake manifolds as outlined under "Intake Manifold, Replace."
8. Raise and support vehicle, then remove righthand front tire, righthand inner splash shield, and accessory drive belt.
9. Remove vibration damper bolt, then damper using puller tool No. 1023 and insert No. 9020–R or equivalents.
10. Remove lower accessory drive belt idler pulley, the power steering mounting bolts and set the pump aside.
11. Remove lower outer timing belt cover bolts, then catalytic converter mounting nuts.
12. Disconnect both oxygen sensor connectors, then separate muffler to tail pipe union and remove catalytic converter.
13. Remove exhaust cross over pipe lower bolts.
14. Remove righthand exhaust manifold as outlined under "Exhaust Manifold, Replace."
15. Lower vehicle and remove upper accessory drive belt idler pulley.
16. Remove belt tensioner, then support engine with a block of wood and floor jack.
17. Remove upper engine mount as outlined under"Engine Mount, Replace."
18. Remove power steering reservoir bolts and set reservoir aside, then the remaining outer timing belt cover bolts and cover.
19. Rotate engine to TDC and align timing belt marks, then remove timing belt tensioner and reset tensioner.
20. Remove timing belt as outlined under "Timing Belt, Replace."
21. Remove righthand valve cover to cylinder head ground strap, then the EGR valve and tube assembly.
22. Remove righthand cylinder head cover, then the righthand rocker arm assembly.
23. Remove righthand rear camshaft thrust plate, then counterhold cam gear and righthand cam gear retaining bolt.
24. Push camshaft out of back of cylinder head approximately 3.5 inches and remove cam gear.
25. Remove inner timing cover to cylinder head retaining bolts, then the cylinder head bolts in REVERSE of tightening sequence.
26. **Because of clearance restrictions when removing righthand cylinder head, front four cylinder head bolts must be loosened, raised and supported with a rubber band before cylinder head can be removed.**
27. Remove cylinder head from vehicle.
28. Reverse procedure to install, noting the following:
    a. Cylinder head bolts are tightened using a torque plus angle procedure, bolts with stretched threads must be replaced.
    b. Lubricate bolt threads with suitable, clean engine oil.
    c. **Torque** cylinder head bolts to 45 ft. lbs.
    d. Then **torque** head bolt bolts to 65 ft. lbs.
    e. **Torque** cylinder head bolt again to 65 ft. lbs.
    f. Tighten bolts an additional 90°. **Do not use a torque wrench for this step.** Bolt torque after 90° turn should be over 90 ft. lbs., in tightening direction, if not replace bolt.

Lefthand

1. Relieve fuel pressure as outlined under "Precautions."
2. Drain cooling system into a suitable container, then remove engine cover.
3. Disconnect intake air temperature sensor connector, then remove air inlet hose at throttle body.

4. Disconnect air circulation hose element housing, then remove housing retaining bolt.
5. Pull housing off locating pin and remove air cleaner housing from vehicle.
6. Remove headlamp retaining screws.
7. Pull headlamps forward unsnaping it from retaining clips.
8. Disconnect electrical connector and remove headlamps.
9. Raise and support vehicle, then remove fascia air dam to radiator closure panel.
10. Remove front fascia to splash shield screws, then the fascia to front fenders retaining screws.
11. Disconnect fog lamps electrical connectors, then lower vehicle.
12. Remove push pins attaching upper appearance panel to upper crossmember.
13. Remove push pins attaching upper grille support to headlamp mounting panel at each side of grille.
14. Remove bumper fascia from vehicle.
15. Disconnect radiator fan electrical connector, then remove screw and radiator fan.
16. Disconnect fuel line at fuel rail.
17. Remove upper and lower intake manifolds as outlined under "Intake Manifold, Replace."
18. Remove lefthand exhaust manifold as outlined under "Exhaust Manifold, Replace."
19. Raise and support vehicle, then remove righthand front tire, righthand inner splash shield, and accessory drive belt.
20. Remove vibration damper bolt, then damper using puller tool No. 1023 and insert No. 9020–R or equivalents.
21. Remove lower accessory drive belt idler pulley, the power steering mounting bolts and set pump aside.
22. Remove lower outer timing belt cover bolts, then catalytic converter mounting nuts.
23. Remove power steering reservoir bolts and set reservoir aside, then the remaining outer timing belt cover bolts and cover.
24. Rotate engine to TDC and align timing belt marks, then remove timing belt tensioner and reset tensioner.
25. Remove timing belt as outlined under "Timing Belt, Replace."
26. Remove lefthand valve cover to cylinder head ground strap.
27. Remove lefthand cylinder head cover, then the lefthand rocker arm assembly.
28. Remove lefthand rear camshaft thrust plate, then counterhold cam gear and righthand cam gear retaining bolt.
29. Push camshaft out of back of cylinder head approximately 3.5 inches and remove cam gear.
30. Remove front timing belt housing to cylinder head retaining bolts, then the cylinder head bolts in REVERSE of tightening sequence.
31. Remove cylinder head from vehicle.
32. Reverse procedure to install, noting the following:
    a. Cylinder head bolts are tightened using a torque plus angle procedure, bolts with stretched threads must be replaced.
    b. Lubricate bolt threads with suitable, clean engine oil.
    c. **Torque** cylinder head bolts to 45 ft. lbs.
    d. Then **torque** head bolt bolts to 65 ft. lbs.
    e. **Torque** cylinder head bolt again to 65 ft. lbs.
    f. Tighten bolts an additional 90°. **Do not use a torque wrench for this step.** Bolt torque after 90° turn should be over 90 ft. lbs., in tightening direction, if not replace bolt.

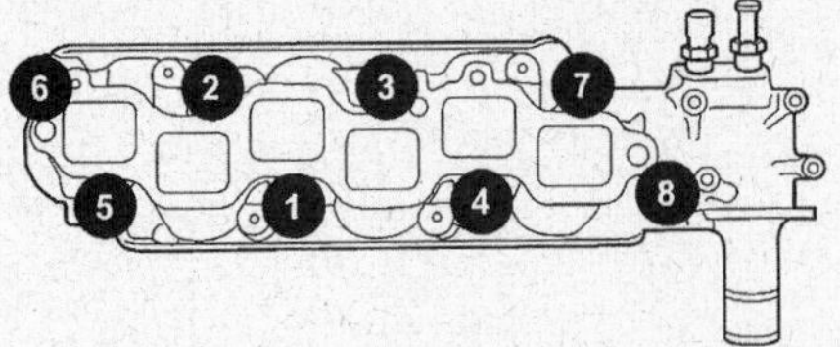

Fig. 4 Lower intake manifold bolt tightening sequence

VALVE COVER

REPLACE

1. Remove upper intake manifold from engine as outlined under "Intake Manifold Replace."
2. Cover lower intake manifold with a suitable cover during service.
3. Disconnect and remove ignition coils.
4. Remove upper intake manifold support brackets from front and rear of engine.
5. Lift up on wire harness track retaining tabs, then remove ground strap/resistor retaining bolt from cylinder head cover.
6. Completely loosen cylinder head cover retaining bolts and remove covers.
7. Remove PCV valve from valve cover assembly.
8. Reverse procedure to install.

SPARK PLUG TUBES

REPLACE

1. Remove cylinder head cover as outlined under "Valve Cover, Replace."
2. Remove tube from cylinder head using suitable locking pliers.
3. Apply suitable lubricant to new tube approximately .039 inch from tube end, in a .118 inch wide area.
4. Install seater end of tube into cylinder head, then carefully install tube using suitable hardwood block and mallet until seated into bore bottom.
5. Install cylinder head cover.

VALVE ADJUSTMENT

Rocker arms are equipped with hydraulic lash adjusters. No adjustment is required.

ROCKER ARMS

REPLACE

Removal

1. Remove cylinder head covers as outlined under "Valve Cover, Replace."
2. Identify rocker arm assembly and rocker arm for installation alignment.
3. Remove mounting bolts and rocker arm assembly. **To prevent air ingestion into lash adjusters, avoid turning rocker arm assembly upside down. Do not rest rocker arm assembly on lash adjusters.**
4. Install screw, nut, spacer and washer into pin, then tighten screw into pin, loosen nut and pull out shaft support dowel, **Fig. 5.**
5. Remove rocker arms and pedestals in order.

Installation

1. Install rocker arms and pedestals into shaft. Rocker shaft notches face up. Righthand cylinder bank notches face toward rear and lefthand notches face toward front.
2. Press new dowel pins until they bottom against shaft in pedestal. Pins pass through pedestal into exhaust rocker shafts.
3. Rotate camshafts until lobes are in neutral position, **Fig. 6.**
4. Install rocker arm and shaft assembly. Ensure identification marks face front of engine on lefthand head and toward rear of engine on righthand head.
5. Tighten mounting bolts in sequence, **Fig. 7.**

VALVE SPRINGS

REPLACE

1. Remove upper intake manifold as outlined under "Intake Manifold, Replace."
2. Remove cylinder head cover as outlined under "Valve Cover, Replace."
3. Remove rocker arm and shaft assembly as outlined under "Rocker Arm, Replace."
4. Remove spark plugs, then rotate crankshaft clockwise until number 1 piston is at TDC on compression stroke.
5. Install suitable spark plug adapter into cylinder being serviced, then apply 90–100 psi air pressure to hold valves in place.
6. Compress valve spring using valve spring compressor tool No. MD-998772-A with adapter tool No. 6527, or equivalent, then remove valve locks, retainer and spring.
7. Remove valve stem seals using suitable valve seal tool.
8. Repeat procedure in firing sequence 1-2-3-4-5-6. **Ensure piston is at TDC on cylinder from which valve spring(s) is being removed.**
9. Reverse procedure to install, noting the following:

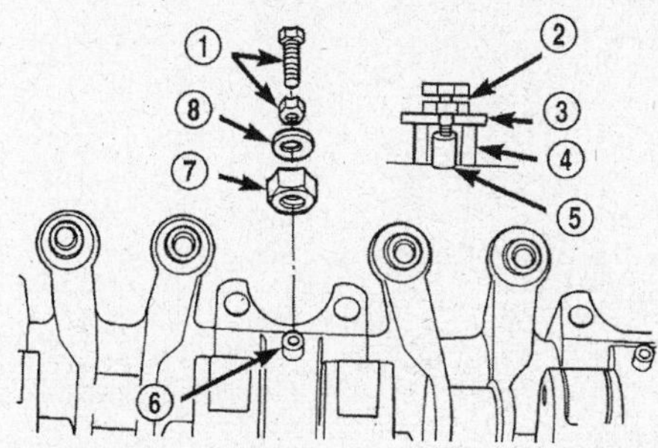

Fig. 5 Rocker arm dowel removal

a. Push valve steam seal/seat firmly and squarely over valve guide with stem as guide.
b. Do not force seal against guide top.
c. When installer retainer locks, compress spring only enough to install locks.

CRANKSHAFT DAMPER

REPLACE

1. Raise and support vehicle, then remove righthand front wheel and accessory drive belt splash shield.
2. Remove accessory drive belts.
3. Remove damper using three-jaw puller tool No. 1023 and crankshaft damper remover insert tool No. 9020–R or equivalents.
4. Reverse procedure to install.

FRONT COVER

REPLACE

1. Raise and support vehicle, then remove righthand front wheel and accessory drive belt splash shield.
2. Remove accessory drive belts.
3. Remove accessory drive belt tensioner.
4. Remove bolts, then reposition power steering pump aside.
5. Remove damper using three-jaw puller tool No. 1023 and crankshaft damper remover insert tool No. 9020–R or equivalents.
6. Remove lower front timing belt cover fasteners, then lower vehicle.
7. Support engine with a floor jack.
8. Disconnect intake air temperature sensor connector, then remove air inlet hose at throttle body.
9. Disconnect air circulation hose element housing, then remove housing retaining bolt.
10. Pull housing off locating pin and remove air cleaner housing from vehicle.
11. Remove lefthand engine mount as outlined under "Engine Mount, Replace."
12. Disconnect fuel supply line at fuel rail.
13. Remove upper timing belt cover bolts and front timing belt cover.
14. Reverse procedure to install.

TIMING BELT

REPLACE

Removal

The 3.5L engine is NOT a freewheeling engine. Therefore, loosen the valve train rocker assemblies before servicing the timing drive.

1. Relieve fuel pressure as outlined under "Precautions."
2. Remove both cylinder head covers as outlined under "Valve Cover, Replace" then loosen rocker arm assemblies.
3. Remove front timing belt cover as outlined under "Front Cover, Replace."
4. Mark belt running direction, if timing belt is to be reused. **When aligning timing marks, always rotate engine by turning crankshaft. Failure to do so will result in valve and/or piston damage.**
5. Rotate engine clockwise until crankshaft mark aligns with TDC mark on oil pump housing and camshaft sprocket timing marks are aligned with marks on rear cover, **Fig. 8.**
6. Remove timing belt tensioner and timing belt.
7. Inspect tensioner for fluid leakage then the pivot and bolt for free movement, bearing grease leakage, and smooth rotation. If not rotating freely replace the arm and pulley assembly.
8. When tensioner is removed from engine it is required to compress plunger into tensioner body.
9. **Index tensioner in vise same way it is installed on engine. This ensures proper pin orientation when tensioner is installed on engine.**
10. Place tensioner into a vise and slowly compress plunger. Total bleed down of tensioner should take about five minutes.
11. When plunger is compressed into tensioner body install a pin through body and plunger to retain plunger in place until tensioner is installed.

Installation

1. Align crankshaft sprocket with TDC mark on oil pump cover, **Fig. 8.**
2. Align camshaft sprockets timing reference marks with marks on rear cover.
3. Install timing belt in a counterclockwise direction starting at crankshaft sprocket.
4. Ensure camshaft sprocket marks are still between rear cover marks.
5. Hold tensioner pulley against belt, then install tensioner.
6. Pull retaining pin and allow tensioner to extend to pulley bracket.
7. Ensure camshaft sprocket marks are still aligned.
8. Rotate crankshaft sprocket two revolutions and ensure timing marks align.
9. Install front timing belt cover, then tighten rocker arm assemblies.
10. Install cylinder head covers as outlined under "Valve Cover, Replace."

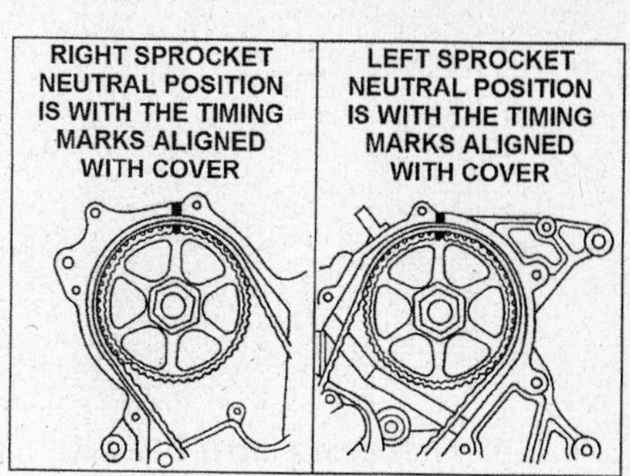

Fig. 6 Camshaft sprockets neutral position

CAMSHAFT

REPLACE

Camshafts are removed from the rear of each cylinder head.

1. Remove cylinder head as outlined under "Cylinder Head, Replace."
2. Carefully remove camshaft from rear of cylinder head, **Fig. 9. Care must be taken not to nick or scratch journals when removing the camshaft.**
3. Reverse procedure to install. Lubricate camshaft journals and cam with suitable, clean engine oil before installation.

CAMSHAFT OIL SEAL

REPLACE

Righthand

1. Relieve fuel pressure as outlined under "Precautions."
2. Drain cooling system into a suitable container, then remove engine cover.
3. Disconnect intake air temperature sensor connector, then remove air inlet hose at throttle body.
4. Disconnect air circulation hose element housing, then remove housing retaining bolt.
5. Pull housing off locating pin and remove air cleaner housing from vehicle.
6. Disconnect fuel line at fuel rail.
7. Remove upper and lower intake manifolds as outlined under "Intake Manifold, Replace."
8. Raise and support vehicle, then remove righthand front tire, righthand inner splash shield, and accessory drive belt.
9. Remove vibration damper bolt, then damper using puller tool No. 1023 and insert No. 9020–R or equivalent.
10. Remove lower accessory drive belt idler pulley, the power steering mounting bolts and set the pump aside.
11. Remove lower outer timing belt cover bolts, then catalytic converter mounting nuts.
12. Disconnect both oxygen sensor connectors, then separate muffler to tail pipe union and remove catalytic converter.
13. Remove exhaust cross over pipe lower bolts.

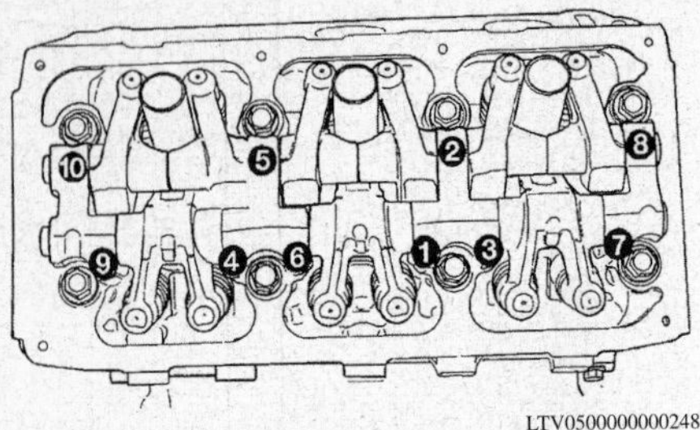

LTV0500000000248

Fig. 7 Rocker arm & shaft assembly bolt tightening sequence

14. Remove righthand exhaust manifold as outlined under "Exhaust Manifold, Replace."
15. Lower vehicle and remove upper accessory drive belt idler pulley.
16. Remove belt tensioner, then support engine with a block of wood and floor jack.
17. Remove upper engine mount as outlined under "Engine Mount, Replace."
18. Remove power steering reservoir bolts and set reservoir aside, then the remaining outer timing belt cover bolts and cover.
19. Rotate engine to TDC and align timing belt marks, then remove timing belt tensioner and reset tensioner.
20. Remove timing belt as outlined under "Timing Belt, Replace."
21. Remove righthand valve cover to cylinder head ground strap, then the EGR valve and tube assembly.
22. Remove righthand cylinder head cover, then the righthand rocker arm assembly.
23. Remove righthand rear camshaft thrust plate, then counterhold cam gear and righthand cam gear retaining bolt.
24. Push camshaft out of back of cylinder head approximately 3.5 inches.
25. Remove camshaft oil seal.

Lefthand

1. Relieve fuel pressure as outlined under "Precautions."
2. Drain cooling system into a suitable container, then remove engine cover.
3. Disconnect intake air temperature sensor connector, then remove air inlet hose at throttle body.
4. Disconnect air circulation hose element housing, then remove housing retaining bolt.
5. Pull housing off locating pin and remove air cleaner housing from vehicle.
6. Remove headlamp retaining screws.
7. Pull headlamps forward unsnaping it from retaining clips.
8. Disconnect electrical connector and remove headlamps.
9. Raise and support vehicle, then remove fascia air dam to radiator closure panel.
10. Remove front fascia to splash shield screws, then the fascia to front fenders retaining screws.
11. Disconnect fog lamps electrical connectors, then lower vehicle.
12. Remove push pins attaching upper appearance panel to upper crossmember.
13. Remove push pins attaching upper grille support to headlamp mounting panel at each side of grille.
14. Remove bumper fascia from vehicle.
15. Disconnect radiator fan electrical connector, then remove screw and radiator fan.
16. Disconnect fuel line at fuel rail.
17. Remove upper and lower intake manifolds as outlined under "Intake Manifold, Replace."
18. Remove lefthand exhaust manifold as outlined under "Exhaust Manifold, Replace."
19. Raise and support vehicle, then remove righthand front tire, righthand inner splash shield, and accessory drive belt.
20. Remove vibration damper bolt, then damper using puller tool No. 1023 and insert No. 9020–R or equivalent.
21. Remove lower accessory drive belt idler pulley, then power steering mounting bolts and set pump aside.
22. Remove lower outer timing belt cover bolts, then catalytic converter mounting nuts.
23. Remove power steering reservoir bolts and set reservoir aside, then the remaining outer timing belt cover bolts and cover.
24. Rotate engine to TDC and align timing belt marks, then remove timing belt tensioner and reset tensioner.
25. Remove timing belt as outlined under "Timing Belt, Replace."
26. Remove lefthand valve cover to cylinder head ground strap.
27. Remove lefthand cylinder head cover, then the lefthand rocker arm assembly.
28. Remove lefthand rear camshaft thrust plate, then counterhold cam gear and righthand cam gear retaining bolt.
29. Push camshaft out of back of cylinder head approximately 3.5 inches.
30. Remove camshaft oil seal.

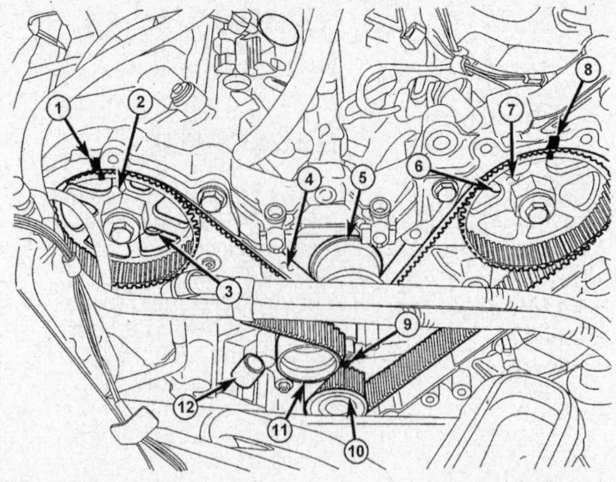

1 - RIGHT CAMSHAFT GEAR ALIGNMENT MARK
2 - RIGHT CAMSHAFT GEAR
3 - CYLINDER HEAD TO INNER TIMING BELT COVER BOLTS - RIGHT
4 - TIMING BELT
5 - WATER PUMP PULLEY
6 - CYLINDER HEAD TO INNER TIMING BELT COVER BOLTS - LEFT
7 - LEFT CAMSHAFT GEAR
8 - LEFT CAMSHAFT GEAR ALIGNMENT MARK
9 - CRANKSHAFT GEAR ALIGNMENT MARK
10 - CRANKSHAFT GEAR
11 - TIMING BELT TENSIONER PULLEY
12 - TIMING BELT TENSIONER

LTV0500000000249

Fig. 8 Timing gear marks

CAMSHAFT TIMING

ADJUST

With the timing belt removed, avoid turning the camshaft or crankshaft. If movement is required, exercise caution to avoid valve damage caused by piston contact.

1. Align crankshaft sprocket timing mark with oil pump housing TDC mark, **Fig. 8.**
2. Install dial indicator into cylinder No. 1, then rotate crankshaft until piston is exactly at TDC.
3. Install camshaft alignment tools No. 6642, or equivalent, on rear of each cylinder head.
4. Slowly preload tensioner with suitable vise and install locking pin. Store pin with plunger facing up until ready to install.
5. Install camshaft sprockets, align timing marks between rear cover timing marks.
6. Install new mounting bolts. Lefthand mounting bolt is 10 inches long, righthand 8⅜ inches. Do not tighten at this time.
7. Install timing belt starting at crankshaft sprocket and going in counterclockwise direction. Maintain tension on belt when installing belt around tensioner pulley.
8. Ensure camshaft sprocket timing marks are still fall between rear cover marks.
9. Hold tensioner pulley against belt, install tensioner.
10. Pull retaining pin and allow tensioner to extend to pulley bracket.
11. Ensure No. 1 piston is at TDC, then hold camshaft sprocket hex with suitable wrench and tighten camshaft bolts.
12. Remove dial indicator and install spark plug.

PISTON & ROD ASSEMBLY

Removal

1. Remove cylinder bores top ridge with suitable ridge reamer before removing pistons.
2. Rotate crankshaft so connecting rod is centered in cylinder bore.
3. Mark connecting rod and bearing caps with permanent ink marker or suitable scribe tool for assembly. Do not use stamp or punch to mark connecting rods.
4. Remove connecting rod cap.
5. Remove piston and rod assembly from top of cylinder block. using connecting rod guide tools No. 8189, or equivalent.
6. Install bearing cap on mating rod.

Installation

1. Install oil ring expander.
2. Place one end of upper side rail between piston ring groove and expander, then hold end firmly and press down portion to be installed until side rail is in position. **Do not use piston ring expander.**
3. Place one end of lower side rail between piston ring groove and expander, then hold end firmly and press down portion to be installed until side rail is in position. **Do not use piston ring expander.**
4. Install No. 2 intermediate piston ring. Ensure manufacturers I.D. dot mark faces up, towards top of piston, **Fig. 10.**
5. Install piston ring No. 1.
6. Position piston ring end gaps, **Fig. 11.**
7. Ensure compression ring gaps are staggered so neither is in line with oil ring rail gap.
8. Ensure oil ring expander ends are butted and rail gaps properly located before installing ring compressor.
9. Immerse piston head and rings in clean engine oil, slide ring compressor over piston and tighten. Ensure ring position does not change.
10. Position bearing onto connecting rod. Ensure bearing half hole aligns with connecting rod hole.
11. Lubricate bearing surface with engine oil.
12. Install connecting rod guide tool No. 8189, or equivalent.
13. Pistons are marked on top with arrow and F above pin boss. These marks must point toward front of engine in both cylinder banks.
14. Connecting rod oil squirt hole faces major thrust (righthand) side of block.
15. Rotate crankshaft so connecting rod journal is centered in cylinder bore, then insert rod and piston into bore and guide rod over crankshaft journal.

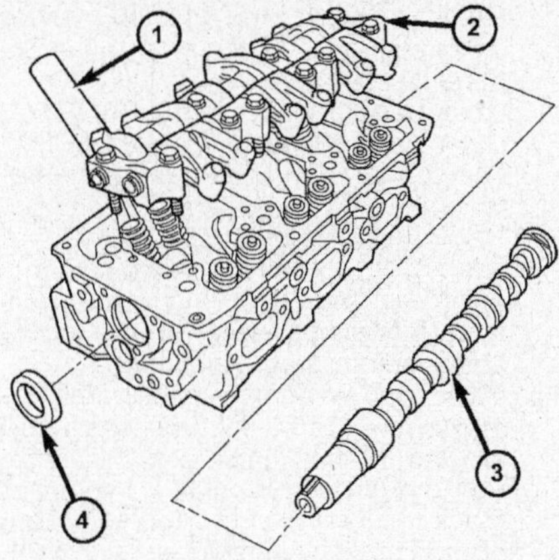

1 - SPARK PLUG TUBE
2 - ROCKER ARM ASSEMBLY
3 - CAMSHAFT
4 - SEAL

LTV0500000000250

Fig. 9 Camshaft replacement

16. Tap piston down cylinder bore and guide connecting rod onto connecting rod journal using suitable hammer handle.
17. Lubricate rod bolts and bearing surfaces with engine oil.
18. Install connecting rod cap and bearing.

CRANKSHAFT

REPLACE

Removal

1. Remove engine as outlined under "Engine, Replace."
2. Drain engine oil into suitable container.
3. Remove mounting bolts, then structural collar from oil pan and transmission housing.
4. Remove engine oil cooler line, then transmission oil cooler line clips.
5. Remove mounting bolts, oil pan and gasket.
6. Remove oil pickup tube and windage tray, then the front timing belt cover.
7. Remove timing belt and tensioner, then the crankshaft sprocket using remover tool No. L-4407A or equivalent.
8. Tap dowel pin out of crankshaft, then remove oil pump assembly.
9. Remove crankshaft rear oil seal retainer.
10. Mark connecting rod bearing caps for assembly, then remove.
11. Mark main bearing caps for assembly, then remove.
12. Remove crankshaft.

Installation

Upper and lower bearing halves are not interchangeable.

1. Lubricate upper main bearing halves with engine oil.
2. Push crankshaft forward.
3. Roll lubricate front thrust washer onto machined shelf between No. 2 upper main bulk head and crankshaft thrust surface.
4. Move crankshaft rearward.
5. Roll lubricate rear thrust washer onto machined shelf between No. 2 upper main bulk head and crankshaft thrust surface.
6. Lubricate lower main bearings with engine oil, then install main bearings and caps.
7. **Torque** inside main bearing cap bolts to 15 ft. lbs., then tighten an additional ¼ turn.
8. Measure crankshaft end play.
9. Install connecting rods and measure side clearance.
10. Install windage tray.
11. Lubricate windage tray mounting bolts with engine oil, **torque** to 20 ft. lbs., then tighten an additional ¼ turn.
12. Install main cap tie bolts.
13. Install rear crankshaft oil seal retainer and oil seal.
14. Install oil pump, crankshaft dowel pin, crankshaft sprocket, timing belt, covers and crankshaft damper.
15. Install accessory drive idler pulley, then oil pickup tube and pan.
16. Install engine and fill crankcase with suitable oil.

MAIN & ROD BEARINGS

Refer to "Crankshaft, Replace" for main and rod bearings service.

CRANKSHAFT SEAL

REPLACE

Removal

1. Remove timing belt as outlined under "Timing Belt, Replace."
2. Remove crankshaft sprocket using crankshaft sprocket puller tool No. L-4407-A, or equivalent.
3. Tape dowel pin out of crankshaft.
4. Remove seal using crankshaft seal remover tool No. 6341A, or equivalent.

Installation

1. Install crankshaft seal using crankshaft seal installer tool No. 6342, or equivalent.
2. Install crankshaft dowel pin to .047 inch protrusion.
3. Install crankshaft sprocket using crankshaft sprocket installer tool No. 6641, or equivalent.
4. Install timing belt.

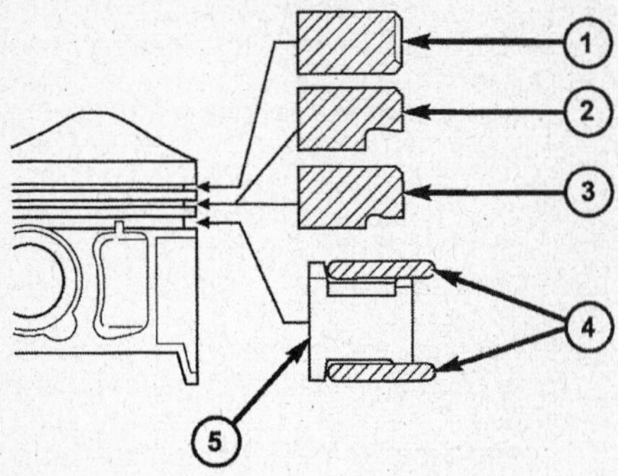

Fig. 10 Piston ring installation

CRANKSHAFT REAR OIL SEAL

REPLACE

Removal

1. Remove transmission and drive plate.
2. Insert suitable 3⁄16 inch wide flat bladed screwdriver between lip and seal metal case.
3. Angle screwdriver through dust lip against metal case and pry out seal. **Do not allow screwdriver blade to contact seal surface.**

Installation

1. Place magnetic base of crankshaft rear seal pilot guide tool No. 6926-1, or equivalent, on crankshaft.
2. Place seal over pilot tool, ensure seal lip faces towards crankshaft.
3. Drive seal into retainer housing until seal is flush with surface using crankshaft rear seal installer tool No. 6926-2 and handle tool No. C-4171, or equivalents.
4. Install drive plate and transmission.

OIL PAN

REPLACE

1. Open hood, then remove headlamp retaining screws.
2. Pull headlamps forward unsnaping it from retaining clips.
3. Disconnect electrical connector and remove headlamps.
4. Raise and support vehicle, then remove fascia air dam to radiator closure panel.
5. Remove front fascia to splash shield screws, then the fascia to front fenders retaining screws.
6. Disconnect fog lamps electrical connectors, then lower vehicle.
7. Remove push pins attaching upper appearance panel to upper crossmember.
8. Remove push pins attaching upper grille support to headlamp mounting panel at each side of grille.
9. Remove bumper fascia from vehicle.
10. Disconnect radiator fan electrical connector, then remove screw and radiator fan.
11. Remove engine oil indicator,
12. **It is not required to recover refrigerant from refrigerant system to perform this procedure.** Remove top air conditioning compressor bolts.
13. Raise and support vehicle, then remove lower bolts and reposition compressor with a suitable retaining strap.
14. Remove air conditioning compressor bracket, then the structural collar from oil pan and transmission housing.
15. Remove inspection shield between transmission and oil pan.
16. Drain engine oil, then remove fasteners, oil pan and gasket.
17. Reverse procedure to install.

OIL PUMP

REPLACE

1. Drain cooling system into a suitable container.
2. Remove timing belt, as outlined under "Timing Belt, Replace".
3. Remove crankshaft sprocket using crankshaft sprocket puller tool No. L-4407-A, or equivalent.
4. Remove oil pan as oulined in "Oil Pan, Replace."
5. Remove oil pickup tube, then the oil pump fasteners, pump and gasket from engine.
6. Reverse procedure to install, noting the following:
   a. Prime oil pump before installing.
   b. Install new O-ring with oil pickup tube.

OIL PUMP SERVICE

1. Remove cotter pin and drill 1⁄8 inch hole into relief valve retainer cap, then insert self-threading sheet metal screw into cap.
2. Clamp screw into suitable vise, support oil pump body and remove cap by tapping on body with suitable soft hammer.
3. Discard cap, then remove spring and pressure relief valve.
4. Remove mounting screws and lift cover plate off.
5. Remove pump rotors.
6. Wash components in suitable solvent, then inspect for damage or wear.
7. Lay straight-edge across pump cover surface. If .001 inch feeler gauge can be inserted between cover and straight-edge, replace cover.
8. Measure thickness and diameter of rotors.
9. If outer rotor thickness is less than .563 inch, or rotor diameter is less than 3.141 inches, replace rotor.
10. If inner rotor thickness is less than .563 inch, replace rotor.

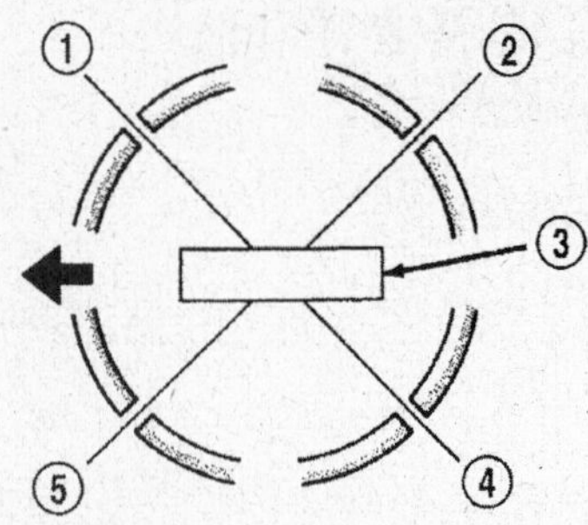

Fig. 11 Piston ring end gap positions

11. Slide outer rotor into body, press to one side with fingers and measure clearance between rotor and body. If clearance is more than .015 inch, replace body.
12. Install inner rotor and measure clearance between rotors. If clearance is more than .008 inch, replace pump assembly.
13. Place straight-edge across body face between bolt holes. If clearance between rotors and straight-edge is more than .003 inch replace pump assembly.
14. Inspect oil pressure relief valve plunger for scoring and free operation in bore. Small marks may be removed with 400-grit wet or dry sandpaper.
15. Relief valve spring free length should be approximately 1.95 inches. Compress spring with 23–25 lbs. If length is not 1.34 inches, replace spring.
16. Reverse procedure to assemble.

BELT TENSION DATA

Belt tension is controlled automatically by the tensioner.

SERPENTINE DRIVE BELT

Routing

Refer to **Fig. 12** serpentine belt routing.

Replacement

Refer to **Fig. 12,** serpentine belt replacement, noting the following:

1. Raise and support vehicle, then remove drive belt shield.
2. Position a wrench on belt tensioner lug, then release belt tension by rotating tensioner counterclockwise.
3. Remove drive belt, Carefully return tensioner to its relaxed position.

COOLING SYSTEM BLEED

It may be required to add coolant to the coolant pressure container after three or four warm up/cool down cycles to maintain coolant level between the MAX and MIN mark. This will allow trapped air to be removed from the system.

THERMOSTAT

REPLACE

1. Drain cooling system into a suitable container.
2. Disconnect electrical connectors from engine oil and power steering pressure switches.
3. Disconnect radiator and heater hoses from thermostat housing.
4. Remove thermostat housing bolts, then the housing, thermostat, and gasket.
5. Reverse procedure to install.

WATER PUMP

REPLACE

1. Drain cooling system into suitable container.
2. Remove accessory drive belts.
3. Remove timing belt components required to access water pump as outlined under "Timing Belt, Replace."
4. Remove mount bolt and water pump.
5. Reverse procedure to install. Apply suitable dielectric grease to O-ring.

RADIATOR

REPLACE

1. Recover A/C refrigerant as outlined under in "Air Conditioning" chapter.
2. Open hood, then remove headlamp retaining screws.
3. Pull headlamps forward unsnaping it from retaining clips.
4. Disconnect electrical connector and remove headlamps.
5. Raise and support vehicle, then remove fascia air dam to radiator closure panel.
6. Remove front fascia to splash shield screws, then the fascia to front fenders retaining screws.
7. Disconnect fog lamps electrical connectors, then lower vehicle.

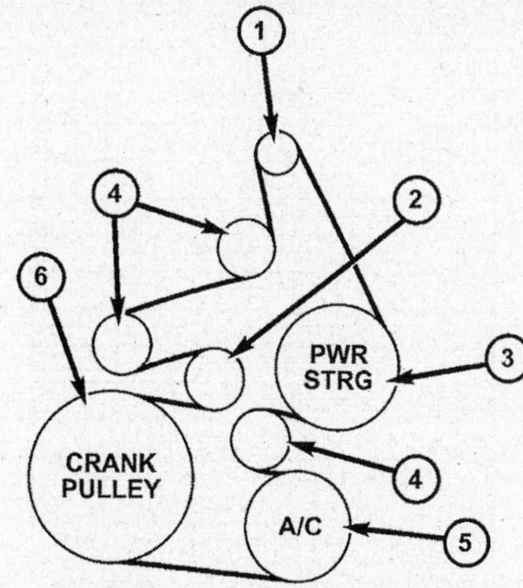

Fig. 12 Accessory drive belt routing

8. Remove push pins attaching upper appearance panel to upper crossmember.
9. Remove push pins attaching upper grille support to headlamp mounting panel at each side of grille.
10. Remove bumper fascia from vehicle.
11. Disconnect radiator fan electrical connector.
12. Disconnect coolant reverse/recovery hose, then drain cooling system into suitable container.
13. Remove A/C lines, then the auxiliary transmission cooler hoses.
14. Remove pushpins, then upper radiator seal and lefthand and righthand radiator seals.
15. Remove A/C condenser side brackets to radiator attaching screws, then separate condenser from radiator by lifting upward to disengage from lower mount stand allow condenser to rest in front of radiator.
16. Remove upper and lower radiator hoses.
17. Lift radiator from engine, then remove the auxiliary transmission from radiator module.
18. Remove cooling fan assembly from radiator module.
19. Reverse procedure to install.

FUEL PUMP

REPLACE

1. Relieve fuel pressure as outlined under "Precautions."
2. Drain fuel tank dry into holding tank or a properly labeled GASOLINE safety container.
3. Raise vehicle support vehicle, then disconnect exhaust system between catalytic converter and muffler.
4. Support exhaust system with jack stands, then remove muffler hanger rubber grommets.
5. Remove center exhaust hanger rubber grommets, then the rear portion of exhaust system and set on floor.
6. Disconnect fuel tank electrical connector, then the fuel line, EVAP line and vapor recirculation tube.
7. Mark driveshaft rear connection, then disconnect driveshaft rear connection.
8. Remove driveshaft support/bearing, then support driveshaft on jack.
9. Remove lefthand rear tire and splash shield, then the fuel filler tube from rubber hose at fuel tank.
10. Support fuel tank with a transmission jack, then remove two fuel tank straps.
11. Lower fuel tank and remove from vehicle.
12. Vacuum area before removing fuel pump module lock ring.
13. Disconnect vapor line and electrical connector.
14. Remove fuel pump module lock ring, then fuel pump module top.
15. Disconnect electrical connector from passenger side level sensor.
16. Tab location in fuel pump module for return line and fuel supply line.
17. Remove return line from pump module. **Ensure not crack or break locking tabs or supply line fitting.**
18. Remove fuel line from top of pump module, then tip fuel pump module on its side to remove fuel from reservoir.
19. Remove fuel pump module.
20. Reverse procedure to install.

FUEL FILTER

REPLACE

1. Release fuel system pressure as outlined under "Precautions."
2. Disconnect fuel lines from fuel pump module and chassis fuel supply tube.
3. Remove fuel filter retaining screw, then filter.
4. Reverse procedure to install.

TIGHTENING SPECIFICATIONS

Year	Component	Torque Ft. Lbs.
2004–06	Accessory Drive Belt Tensioner	21
	A/C Compressor	25
	A/C Compressor Bracket	85
	A/C Condenser Mounting	45①
	Alternator	40
	Camshaft Sprocket	②
	Camshaft Thrust Plate	21
	Connecting Rod Cap	20
	Crankshaft Damper	70
	Crankshaft Main Bearing Cap (Horizontal, Tie Bolts)	21
	Crankshaft Main Bearing Cap (Inner)	15③
	Crankshaft Main Bearing Cap (Out)	20③
	Cylinder Head	④
	Cylinder Head Cover	105①
	Engine Mount Righthand & Lefthand	55
	Engine Mount Upper To Frame	50
	Engine Mount Upper To Timing Cover	40
	Exhaust Manifold	17
	Exhaust Manifold Heat Shield	105
	Flex Plate To Crankshaft	70
	Flex Plate To Torque Converter	55
	Fuel Tank Strap	40
	Intake Manifold (Lower)	21
	Intake Manifold (Upper)	105①
	Oil Filter	12
	Oil Filter Adaptor	30
	Oil Pan (M6 Bolts)	105①
	Oil Pan (M8 Bolts)	21
	Oil Pan Drain Plug	20
	Oil Pump To Block (M6 Bolts)	105①
	Oil Pump To Block (M8 Bolts)	21
	Oil Pump Pick Up Tube	21
	Radiator Mounting	105①
	Rear Crankshaft Seal	105①
	Rocker Shaft Pedestal Retaining	23
	Structural Collar	⑤
	Timing Belt Cover	⑥
	Timing Belt Tensioner	21
	Timing Belt Tensioner Pulley	45
	Water Pump	105①
	Water Pump Pulley	21
	Windage Tray	20

①— Inch lbs.
②— Righthand, 75 ft. lbs., plus 1/4 turn; lefthand, 85 ft. lbs., plus 1/4 turn.
③— Plus 1/4 turn.
④— Refer to "Cylinder Head, Replace" for tightening specifications and sequence.
⑤— Initial torque to 20 ft. lbs., final torque to 40 ft. lbs.
⑥— M6 bolts to 105 inch lbs.; M8 bolts to 21 ft. lbs.; M10 bolts to 40 ft. lbs.

Rear Axle & Suspension

NOTE: On Air Bag Equipped Models, Refer To "Air Bag System Precautions" Located In The Front Of This Manual For System Disarming & Arming Procedures.

NOTE: Refer To "Computer Relearn Procedures" Located In The Front Of This Manual When Battery Power To The Computer Has Been Interrupted.

INDEX

PRECAUTIONS

Air Bag Systems

Refer to "Air Bag System Precautions" in the front of this manual for system disarming and arming procedures.

Battery Ground Cable

Prior to service, disconnect battery ground cable and isolate as required.

HUB & BEARING

REPLACE

1. Raise and support vehicle, then remove tire and wheel assembly.
2. **On models equipped with FWD,** while a helper applies brakes, remove cotter pin, nut lock, spring washer and hub nut.
3. **On all models** remove brake caliper and rotor from hub and bearing assembly.
4. Disconnect vehicle wheel speed sensor connector
5. Unclip wheel speed sensor connector from spare tire mounting support.
6. Disconnect two sensor cable routing clips on rear suspension crossmember, then two sensor cable routing clips along toe link.
7. Disconnect sensor cable from bracket on brake support.
8. Completely loosen but do not remove four hub and bearing bolts, then push bolts up against rear of hub and bearing to keep brake support plate in place when hub and bearing is removed.
9. **On models equipped with AWD,** thread wheel speed sensor cable through hole in brake support plate as it is removed with hub and bearing.
10. **On all models,** pull hub and bearing off knuckle and half shaft.
11. Reverse procedure to install.

SHOCK ABSORBER

REPLACE

1. Raise and support vehicle, then remove wheel and tire assembly.
2. Position an extra pair of jack stands under and support forward end of engine cradle to help stabilize vehicle.
3. Position transmission jack under center of rear suspension crossmember or rear driveline module.
4. Raise jack head to contact driveline module/suspension crossmember and secure in place.
5. Remove shock absorber upper mounting bolts, then the lower mounting bolt and nut.
6. Remove both front and rear crossmember mounting bolts on repair-side of vehicle. **Do not lower crossmember any further than required to remove shock absorber or coil spring.**
7. Slowly lower jack just enough to allow top of shock absorber to clear body flange.
8. Remove shock absorber by tipping top outward and lifting lower end out of pocket in spring link **Fig. 1.**
9. Reverse procedure to install.

COIL SPRING

REPLACE

Refer to "Shock Absorber, Replace" for coil spring replacement procedure.

KNUCKLE

REPLACE

1. Lock out automatic adjuster in parking brake lever.
2. Raise and support vehicle, then remove parking brake cable bolt at knuckle.
3. Remove hub and bearing as outlined under "Hub And Bearing Replace."
4. Remove parking brake shoe return spring, then shoe actuator from between parking brake shoes and end of cable.
5. Remove support and parking brake shoes from knuckle, then brake caliper adapter mounting bolts and adapter.
6. Position jack stand under spring link, then raise jack head to contact spring link at shock mount and secure in place.
7. Remove spring link-to-knuckle nut and bolt, then place guide tool No. 9050A-2 or equivalent against sleeve in knuckle.
8. Insert tap tool No. 9050A-1 or equivalent, on an appropriate handle, through guide and into sleeve.
9. Cut threads approximately halfway through bushing or about six complete threads. **It is important to back tap out often and clean out burrs that can build up inside guide. Keep tap well lubricated to avoid damaging it.**
10. Assemble remover tool No. 9050A or equivalent as outlined **Fig. 2.**
11. Remove sleeve retaining spring link ball joint in knuckle, discard knuckle sleeve.
12. Remove bolt and nut attaching compression link to knuckle, then bolt attaching toe link to knuckle.
13. Remove nuts and bolts attaching stabilizer link to knuckle, then tension link to knuckle and camber link to knuckle.
14. Remove knuckle, then hub mounting bolts from knuckle.
15. Reverse procedure to install.

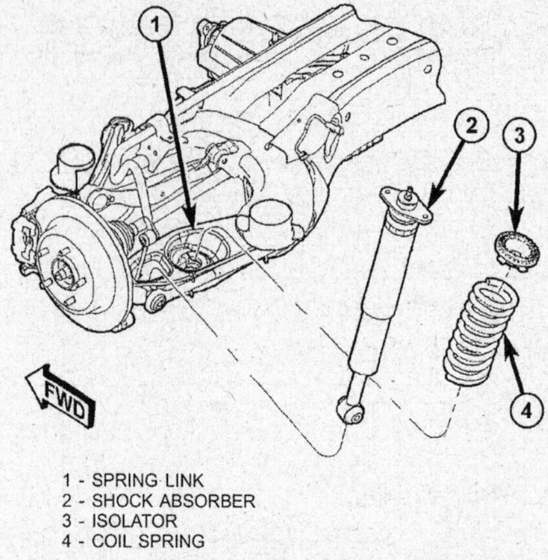

Fig. 1 Shock absorber & coil spring removal

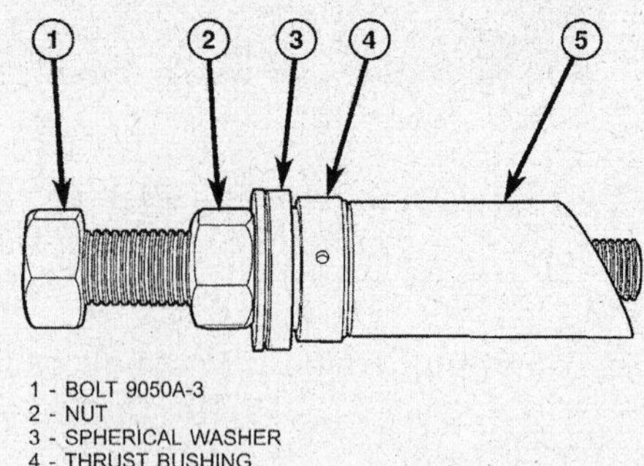

Fig. 2 Sleeve remover tool assembled

TIGHTENING SPECIFICATIONS

Year	Component	Torque Ft. Lbs.
2004–06	Brake Caliper Knuckle Bolts	85
	Camber Link Crossmember Bolt	50
	Camber Link Knuckle Bolt	70
	Compression Link Crossmember Bolt	50
	Compression Link Knuckle Bolt 60	60
	Crossmember Mounting Bolt	120
	Hub And Bearing Mounting	60
	Hub Nut	180
	Shock Absorber Mounting (Upper)	45
	Shock Absorber Mounting (Lower)	75
	Spring Link Crossmember Bolt	80
	Spring Link Knuckle Nut	95
	Stabilizer Bar Cushion	95
	Stabilizer Bar Cushion Retainer Bolt	45
	Stabilizer Bar Nut	45
	Tension Link Knuckle Bolt	88
	Toe Link Crossmember Nut	127
	Toe Link Knuckle Bolt	80

Front Suspension & Steering

NOTE: On Air Bag Equipped Models, Refer To "Air Bag System Precautions" Located In The Front Of This Manual For System Disarming & Arming Procedures.

NOTE: Refer To "Computer Relearn Procedures" Located In The Front Of This Manual When Battery Power To The Computer Has Been Interrupted.

INDEX

PRECAUTIONS

Air Bag Systems

Refer to "Air Bag System Precautions" in the front of this manual for system disarming and arming procedures.

Battery Ground Cable

Prior to service, disconnect battery ground cable and isolate as required.

HUB & BEARING

REPLACE

Replacement of front hub and bearing assembly can normally be done without having to remove steering knuckle from vehicle. In event that hub/bearing is frozen in steering knuckle and cannot be removed by hand, it will have to be pressed out of steering knuckle. Steering knuckle will then require removal before hub and bearing can be pressed out.

1. Raise and support vehicle, then remove tire and wheel assembly.
2. Remove cotter pin, then nut lock and spring washer from halfshaft stub shaft.
3. With aid of a helper applying brakes to keep front hub from turning, remove hub nut.
4. Access and remove front brake rotor, then disconnect wheel speed sensor connector.
5. Unclip wheel speed sensor connector and routing clip from frame rail outer reinforcement.
6. Remove screw attaching wheel speed sensor routing bracket to strut assembly.
7. Open routing clip at knuckle and remove wheel speed sensor cable.
8. Push in on end of halfshaft stub shaft, pushing its splines out of hub splines.
9. Remove four hub and bearing mounting bolts from rear of steering knuckle, **Fig. 1.**
10. Remove hub and bearing with wheel speed sensor from steering knuckle.
11. Reverse procedure to install.

BALL JOINT INSPECTION

Lower

With the weight of the vehicle resting on the wheels, grasp the special fitting cap on the bottom of the ball joint and with no mechanical assistance or added force, attempt to rotate the grease fitting. If the ball joint is worn, the grease fitting will rotate easily. If movement is noted, replacement of the control arm is recommended.

STRUT

REPLACE

Do not remove nut from strut rod while strut assembly is installed in vehicle or before strut assembly spring is compressed.

1. Raise and support vehicle, then remove tire and wheel assembly.
2. If both strut assemblies are to be removed, mark strut assemblies righthand or lefthand according to which side of vehicle they originated.
3. Remove screw attaching wheel speed sensor routing bracket to strut assembly.
4. Remove stabilizer bar link from bracket on strut assembly.
5. Remove bolts and nuts attaching strut clevis to steering knuckle.
6. If servicing lefthand strut assembly, remove nuts fastening coolant recovery bottle in place and reposition bottle with hoses attached out of way.
7. Remove nuts attaching strut assembly upper mount to strut tower, then remove strut assembly from vehicle, **Fig. 2.**
8. Diassemble strut assembly as outlined under "Coil Spring & Strut Service."
9. Reverse procedure to install.

COIL SPRING & STRUT SERVICE

1. Position strut assembly in strut coil spring compressor following manufacturers instructions, then position lower hooks on coil spring first, then uppers.
2. Compress coil spring until all coil spring tension is removed from upper mount, **Fig. 3.**
3. Install strut nut wrench tool No. 6864 or equivalent, on strut shaft retaining nut, then a 10 mm socket onto hex located on end of strut shaft.
4. While holding strut shaft from turning, remove nut from strut shaft.
5. Remove upper mount from strut shaft, then pivot bearing.
6. Remove upper spring seat or isolator from top coil spring.
7. Remove clamp from bottom of coil spring and remove strut out through bottom of coil spring.
8. Release tension from coil spring by backing off compressor drive fully. Push back compressor upper hooks and remove coil spring from spring compressor.
9. Remove dust shield and jounce bumper as an assembly from strut shaft.
10. Remove spring isolator from lower spring seat on strut.
11. Reverse procedure to assemble.

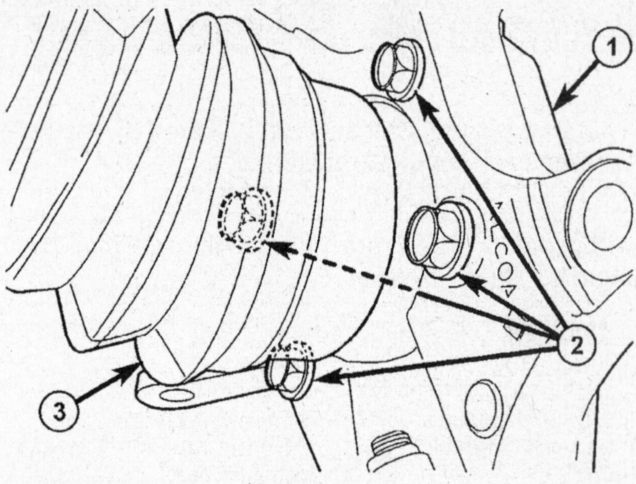

1 - KNUCKLE
2 - HUB AND BEARING MOUNTING BOLTS
3 - HALFSHAFT

LTV0500000000256

Fig. 1 Hub & bearing mounting bolts removal

CONTROL ARM

REPLACE

Lower

1. Raise and support vehicle, then remove wheel and tire assembly.
2. Remove steering knuckle as outlined under "Steering Knuckle, Replace."
3. Remove bolts and nuts attaching lower control arm to engine cradle.
4. Remove lower control arm.
5. Reverse procedure to install.

STEERING KNUCKLE

REPLACE

1. Raise and support vehicle, then remove wheel and tire assembly.
2. Remove cotter pin, then nut lock and spring washer from halfshaft stub shaft.
3. With aid of a helper applying brakes to keep front hub from turning, remove hub nut.
4. Access and remove front brake rotor, then disconnect wheel speed sensor connector.
5. Unclip wheel speed sensor connector and routing clip from frame rail outer reinforcement.
6. Remove screw attaching wheel speed sensor routing bracket to strut assembly.
7. Open routing clip at knuckle and remove wheel speed sensor cable.
8. Push in on end of halfshaft stub shaft, pushing its splines out of hub splines.
9. Remove nut attaching outer tie rod to steering knuckle by holding outer tie rod stud stationary while loosening nut with a wrench.
10. Remove tie rod from steering knuckle using remover tool No. C-3894-A or equivalent.
11. Remove bolts attaching strut clevis to steering knuckle.
12. Tip knuckle outward at top and remove halfshaft stub shaft from hub and bearing.
13. Suspend driveshaft straight outward using a bungee cord or wire. Do not allow driveshaft to hang by inner joint.
14. Remove ball joint nut using a power impact wrench. **Because tapered stud is held sufficiently in knuckle at this time, it is not required to hold stud stationary to remove nut.**
15. Reinstall ball joint nut until top of nut is even with top of ball joint stud. **This will keep stud from distorting while stud is released from knuckle.**
16. **Do not remove ball joint stud from steering knuckle using a hammer. Damage to Aluminum knuckle, ball joint or control arm will result.**
17. Release ball joint stud from steering knuckle using remover tool No. C-4150A or equivalent. **To ease remover installation and use, rotate knuckle around so inside of knuckle faces outward.**
18. Remove tool and nut from top of ball joint stud.
19. Remove steering knuckle from vehicle.
20. If hub and bearing needs to be transferred, remove bolts attaching hub and bearing to knuckle, then the hub and bearing.
21. Reverse procedure to install.

STABILIZER BAR

REPLACE

1. Raise and support vehicle, then remove wheel and tire assembly.
2. Remove nut attaching outer tie rod to steering knuckle by holding rod end stud stationary while loosening a nut with a wrench.
3. Remove tie rod end from steering knuckle using remover, tool No. C-3894-A or equivalent.
4. Remove stabilizer bar links from each end of stabilizer bar.
5. Remove stabilizer bar cushion retainers.
6. Remove stabilizer bar out through righthand wheel opening by carefully rotating bar up-and-down, and back-and-forth as needed.
7. Reverse procedure to install.

TIE ROD END

REPLACE

1. Place front wheels of vehicle in straight-ahead position.
2. Raise and support vehicle, then remove front tire and wheel assembly.
3. Loosen tie rod jam nut.
4. Remove nut attaching outer tie rod to steering knuckle by holding tie rod end stud stationary while loosening nut with a wrench.
5. Remove outer tie rod end from steering knuckle using remover tool No. C-3894-A or equivalent.
6. Remove outer tie rod from inner tie rod threads. Count how many rotations it takes to remove outer tie rod for installation reference.
7. Reverse procedure to install. Perform wheel alignment setting toe to specifications as outlined under "Wheel Alignment" chapter.

POWER STEERING GEAR

REPLACE

1. Place front wheels of vehicle in straight-ahead position.
2. Install steering wheel holder locking steering wheel in straight-ahead position.
3. Remove as much power steering fluid as possible from power steering fluid reservoir.
4. Raise and support vehicle, then remove both front tire and wheel assemblies.
5. If outer tie rods need to be transferred to new gear, loosen tie rod jam nuts on both sides of vehicle.
6. Remove nut attaching outer tie rods to steering knuckle by holding rod end studs stationary while loosening nut with a wrench.
7. Remove each outer tie rod end from steering knuckle using remover tool No. C-3894-A or equivalent.
8. Insert remover tool No. 6831A or equivalent, through roll pin attaching intermediate shaft extension to power steering gear.
9. Thread knurled nut all way onto end of tool, then while holding tool head stationary, turn hex nut pulling roll pin from shafts, **Fig. 4.**
10. Remove roll pin from tool, then slide intermediate shaft extension off steering gear shaft.
11. Remove tube nut attaching return hose to power steering gear, then the return hose from gear port.

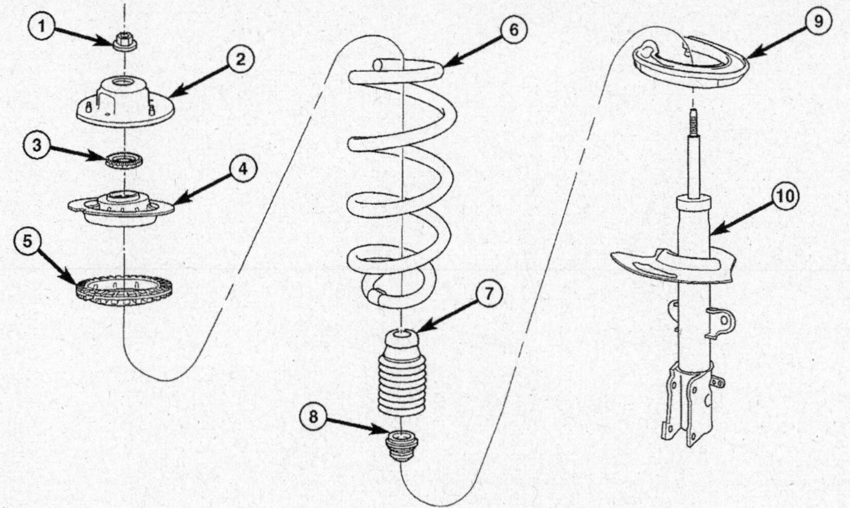

1 - NUT
2 - UPPER MOUNT
3 - PIVOT BEARING
4 - UPPER SPRING SEAT
5 - UPPER SPRING ISOLATOR
6 - COIL SPRING
7 - DUST SHIELD
8 - JOUNCE BUMPER
9 - LOWER SPRING ISOLATOR
10 - STRUT (DAMPER)

LTV0500000000257

Fig. 2 Exploded view of strut assembly

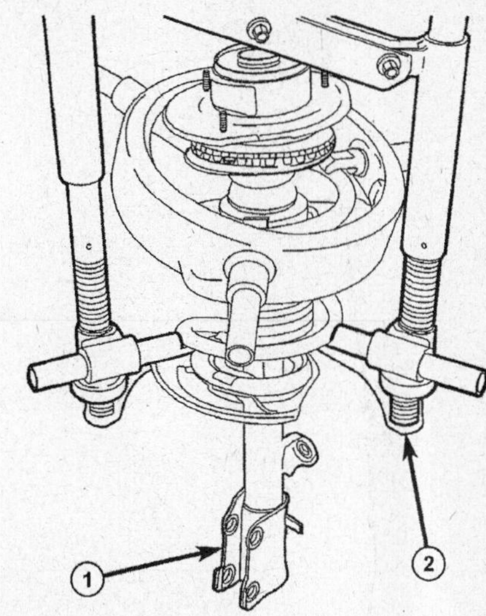

1 - STRUT ASSEMBLY
2 - STRUT SPRING COMPRESSOR

LTV0500000000258

Fig. 3 Strut assembly compressor tool

12. Remove tube nut attaching pressure hose to power steering gear, then the pressure hose from gear port.
13. Remove power steering gear mounting bolts, then tip gear forward at top and slide out lefthand wheel opening. **Do not cut tie rod boots on shields as gear is removed.**
14. Reverse procedure to install.

POWER STEERING PUMP

REPLACE

1. Remove as much power steering fluid as possible from power steering fluid reservoir.
2. Remove engine appearance cover, then upper and lower radiator closure panels.
3. Remove power steering return and supply hoses, then the upper reservoir retaining bolt from reservoir.
4. Loosen but do not remove power steering reservoir lower retaining bolt, then slide reservoir upward and out.
5. Remove clamp, then the fluid supply hose from pump.
6. Remove nuts attaching lefthand and righthand motor mounts to engine cradle.
7. Remove accessory drive belt, then lower vehicle.
8. Disconnect intake air temperature sensor connector, then remove air inlet hose at throttle body.
9. Disconnect air circulation hose element housing, then remove housing retaining bolt.
10. Pull housing off locating pin and remove air cleaner housing from vehicle.
11. Remove bolts attaching righthand motor mount to frame rail, then move pressure and return hoses away from pump toward cooling module.
12. Place floor jack with block of wood on it below engine oil pan.
13. Carefully raise accessory drive end of engine with floor jack approximately two inches to access pump mounting bolts.
14. Remove pump with pulley from engine, **Fig. 5.**
15. Reverse procedure to install.

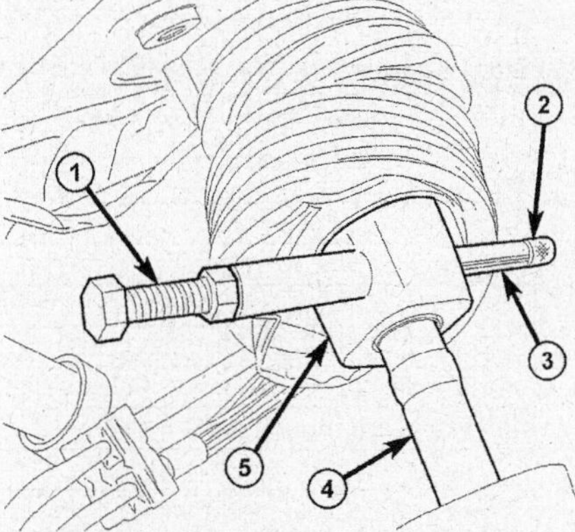

1 - INSTALLER 6831A
2 - KNURLED NUT
3 - ROLL PIN
4 - STEERING GEAR SHAFT
5 - INTERMEDIATE SHAFT EXTENSION

LTV0500000000259

Fig. 4 Roll pin removal

POWER STEERING SYSTEM BLEED

1. Fill fluid reservoir to proper level and let fluid settle for at least two minutes.
2. Start engine and let run for a few seconds, then turn engine off add fluid if required until fluid level remains constant after running engine.
3. Raise front wheels off ground, then start engine.
4. Slowly turn steering wheel righthand and lefthand lightly contacting wheel stops. Add fluid if required.
5. Lower vehicle, then turn steering wheel slowly from lock-to-lock.
6. Stop engine, then inspect fluid level and refill as required.
7. If fluid is extremely foamy allow vehicle to stabilize a few minutes, then repeat procedure.

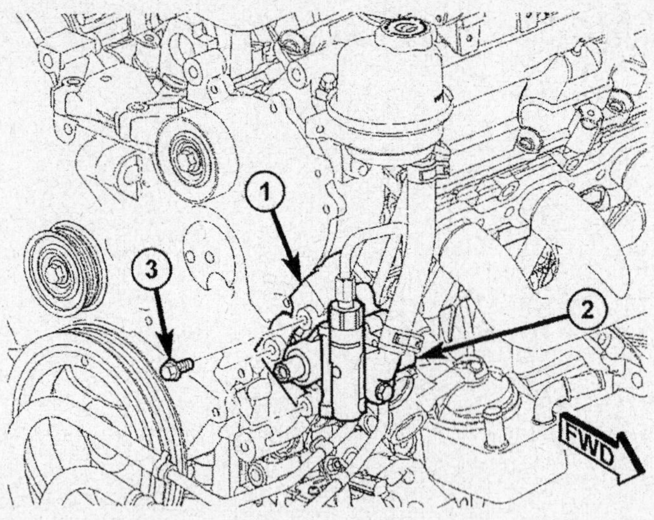

1 - PUMP MOUNTING BRACKET ON ENGINE
2 - POWER STEERING PUMP
3 - MOUNTING BOLTS

LTV0500000000260

Fig. 5 Power steering pump removal

TIGHTENING SPECIFICATIONS

Year	Component	Torque Ft. Lbs.
2004–06	Axle Nut	180
	Ball Joint Nut	60①
	Brake Hose Bracket Bolt	13
	Disc Brake Caliper Mounting Bolt	125
	Engine Cradle Mounting Bolts	120
	Hub & Bearing Mounting Bolts	45
	Lower Control Arm Frame Bolt	120
	Power Steering Gear Mounting Bolts	120
	Power Steering Pump Mounting Bolts	23
	Power Steering Reservoir Mounting Bolts	105③
	Power Steering Fluid Lines	23
	Power Steering Pump Pressure Fitting	65
	Stabilizer Bar Cushion Retainer Bolt	40
	Stabilizer Bar Link Nuts	65
	Strut Body/Tower Nuts	20
	Strut Clevis To Knuckle Nuts	65①
	Strut Shaft Nut	75
	Tie Rod Jam Nut	55
	Tie Rod Steering Arm Nut	35②
	Wheel Lug Nut	100

① — Plus 90° turn.
② — Plus 180° turn.
③ — Inch lbs.

Wheel Alignment

INDEX

PRELIMINARY INSPECTION

1. Verify that fuel tank is full of fuel. If tank is not full, reduction in weight will affect curb height of vehicle and alignment angles.
2. Passenger and luggage compartments of vehicle should be free of any load that is not factory equipment.
3. Inspect tires on vehicle. All tires must be same size and in good condition with approximately same amount of tread wear. Inflate all tires to recommended air pressure.
4. Inspect front wheel and tire assemblies for excessive radial runout.
5. Inspect lower ball joints and all steering linkage for looseness, binding, wear or damage. Repair as required.
6. Inspect suspension retainers for proper torque and retighten as required.
7. Inspect all suspension component rubber bushings for signs of wear or deterioration. Replace any faulty bushings or components before aligning vehicle.
8. Inspect vehicle's curb height to verify it is within specifications.

FRONT WHEEL ALIGNMENT

Caster & Camber

If front camber is not within the specified range, it can be adjusted by using an available camber adjustment bolt package. Before installing bolt package, ensure no components are bent or damaged.

1. Raise and support vehicle.
2. Remove front tire and wheel assemblies.
3. Remove and discard top and bottom strut clevis bracket to steering knuckle attaching bolts. Attaching bolts are serrated and must not be turned during removal, remove nuts while holding bolts stationary.
4. Separate steering knuckle from strut clevis bracket and position steering knuckle so it is out of way of strut.
5. Use a suitable grinder and grinding wheel, slot bottom hole in both sides of strut clevis bracket.
6. After slotting clevis bracket holes, do not use original attaching bolts and hardware.
7. Position knuckle back into strut clevis bracket.
8. Install flanged bolt from service package into upper hole and a cam bolt into lower hole. Both bolt heads should face forward when installed.
9. Install a dogbone washer on steering knuckle to strut clevis bracket attaching bolts, then install nuts.
10. Tighten bolts just enough to hold steering knuckle in place when adjusting while still allowing steering knuckle to move in clevis bracket.
11. Install front tire and wheel assemblies, lower vehicle, then jounce front and rear an equal amount of times.
12. Adjust front camber to specification by rotating lower eccentric bolt.
13. When camber is set, tighten upper bolt, then the lower bolt. Jounce front and rear of vehicle and verify settings.
14. **Torque** both front strut bolts to 65 ft. lbs., plus an additional ¼ turn.
15. Adjust toe as required.

Toe-In

To adjust toe-in, center steering wheel and hold in position with a suitable tool. Loosen tie rod locknuts and rotate rod, **Fig. 1,** to adjust toe-in to specifications. Use care not to twist steering gear rubber boots. **Torque** tie rod locknuts to 55 ft. lbs. Adjust position of steering gear rubber boots. Remove steering wheel holding tool.

REAR WHEEL ALIGNMENT

Toe

1. Loosen cam bolt nut securing toe link to rear crossmember just enough to rotate cam bolt.
2. Rotate adjustment link as required to set rear wheel toe.
3. While holding cam bolt from turning, tighten cam bolt nut to specifications.
4. Adjust rear toe on opposite side of vehicle using above procedure as required.
5. Once rear toe is set, proceed to front toe to set vehicle's front toe.

VEHICLE RIDE HEIGHT

Vehicle height should be inspected with vehicle on a flat surface, preferably an alignment rack. Ensure tires are inflated to proper pressure and are all of the same size. Inspect vehicle height with full fuel tank and no passenger or luggage load.

Vehicle height is not adjustable. If measurement is not within specification, inspect vehicle for bent or weak suspension components.

1. Measure from inboard edge of wheel opening fender lip directly above wheel center (spindle), to floor or alignment rack surface.
2. Maximum righthand to lefthand differential should not exceed .5 inch.
3. Vehicle height specifications are front height specification is 31.03–31.81 inches and rear specification is 31.61–32.39 inches.

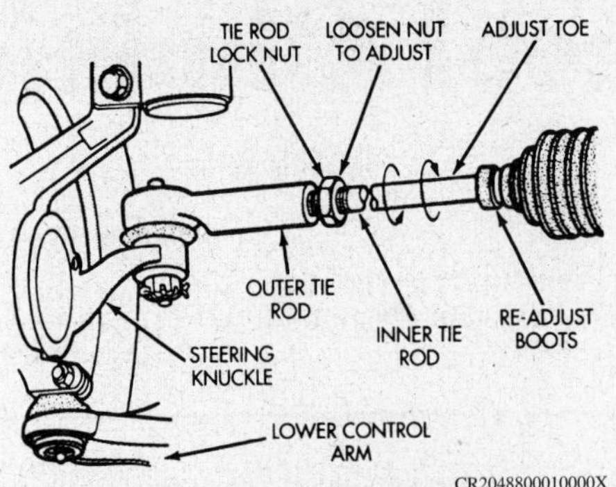

Fig. 1 Toe-in adjustment

PT CRUISER

NOTE: Refer To Back Of This Manual For Vehicle Manufacturer's Special Service Tool Suppliers.

INDEX OF SERVICE OPERATIONS

Specifications

GENERAL ENGINE SPECIFICATIONS

Year	Engine	Bore x Stroke, Inch	Comp. Ratio	Horsepower @ RPM	Torque Ft. Lbs. @ RPM	Normal Oil Pressure, psi
2002	2.4L	3.44 x 3.98	9.4	150 @ 5500	162 @ 4000	25–80 @ 3000 RPM
2003–06	2.4L	3.44 x 3.98	9.5	150 @ 5500	162 @ 4000	25–80 @ 3000 RPM
	2.4L Turbo	3.44 x 3.98	8.1	215 @ 5000	245 @ 3600	25–80 @ 3000 RPM

TUNE UP SPECIFICATIONS

The following specifications are published from the latest information available. This data should only be used in the absence of a decal affixed in the engine compartment.

Year & Engine Liters	Spark Plug Gap	Ignition Timing, °BTDC				Curb Idle Speed, RPM②		Fast Idle Speed, RPM②		Fuel Pump Pressure, psi	Valve Lash Specifications
		Firing Order, Fig.①	Man. Trans.	Auto. Trans.	Mark Location	Man. Trans.	Auto. Trans.	Man. Trans.	Auto. Trans.		
2002											
2.4L	.048–.053	A	③	③	Damper	④	④	④	④	53–63	⑤
2003–06											
2.4L	.048–.053	1-3-4-2	③	③	Damper	④	④	④	④	53–63	⑤
2.4L Turbo	.048–.053	1-3-4-2	③	③	Damper	④	④	④	④	53–63	⑤

① — Before removing wires from distributor cap, determine location of No. 1 wire in cap, as distributor position may have been altered from that outlined.

② — Neutral when inspecting idle speed, set parking brake and block drive wheels.

③ — Non-adjustable.

④ — Controlled by idle speed control motor.

⑤ — Equipped w/hydraulic valve tappets.

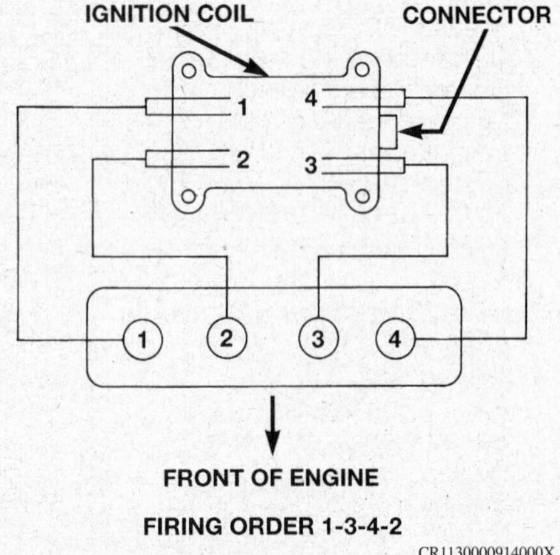

Fig. A

FRONT WHEEL ALIGNMENT SPECIFICATIONS

Year	Caster Angle, Degrees①		Camber Angle, Degrees②		Toe, Degrees③	
2002–06	Limits	Desired	Limits	Desired	Limits	Desired
	+1.45 to +3.45	+2.45	-.4 to +.4	0	0 to +.4	+.2

① — Cross caster maximum side to side difference, 0 to 1°.

② — Cross camber maximum side to side difference, 0 to .5°.

③ — Toe in (+). Toe out (–).

REAR WHEEL ALIGNMENT SPECIFICATIONS

Year	Model	Camber Angle, Degree		Total Toe, Degree①		Thrust Angle, Degree
		Limits	Desired	Limits	Desired	
2002–06	All	-.25 to +.25	0	0 to +.4	+.2	-.3 to +3

① — Toe in (+). Toe out (–).

FLUID CAPACITIES & COOLING SYSTEM DATA

Year	Engine Liter	Coolant Capacity, Qts.	Recom-mended Coolant Type	Radiator Cap Relief Pres-sure, Lbs.	Thermo. Opening Temp., Deg. °F.	Fuel Tank, Gals.	Engine Oil Refill, Qts.	Transmission Oil	
								Manual Trans., Pts.	Auto. Trans., Qts.②
2002	2.4L	7.4	Ethylene Glycol	14–18	195	15	5①	5–5.6	③
2003	2.4L	6.5	Ethylene Glycol	14–18	192–199	15	5①	5–5.6	③
2004–06	2.4L	6.5	Ethylene Glycol	14–18	192–199	15	5 ①	5–5.6	③
	2.4L Turbo	6.5	Ethylene Glycol	14–18	192–199	15	5 ①	3.8	③

① — Includes filter.

② — Approximate. Make final inspection w/dipstick.

③ — Drain & refill, 4 qts.; total capacity, 8.6 qts.

LUBRICANT DATA

Year	Model	Lubricant Type				
		Transmission		Hydraulic Clutch Fluid	Power Steering	Brake System
		Manual	Automatic			
2002	All	Type MS-9417	ATF+ 4 9602	DOT 3	①	DOT 3
2003–06	All	ATF+ 4	ATF+ 4 9602	DOT 3	①	DOT 3

① — Mopar power steering fluid or equivalent.

Electrical

NOTE: On Air Bag Equipped Models, Refer To "Air Bag System Precautions" Located In The Front Of This Manual For System Disarming & Arming Procedures.

NOTE: Refer To "Computer Relearn Procedures" Located In The Front Of This Manual When Battery Power To The Computer Has Been Interrupted.

INDEX

PRECAUTIONS

Air Bag Systems

Refer to "Air Bag System Precautions" in the front of this manual for system disarming and arming procedures.

Battery Ground Cable

Prior to service, disconnect battery ground cable and isolate as required.

FUSE PANEL & FLASHER LOCATION

The fuse panel is located in the lefthand front lower instrument panel and is accessed through a cover located on the lower dash panel. The flasher is located on the back side of the multi-function switch and requires removal of the steering column shrouds for access.

FUEL PUMP RELAY LOCATION

The fuel pump relay is located in the Power Distribution Center (PDC) in the lefthand front corner of the engine compartment, just behind the air cleaner housing and the battery.

STARTER

REPLACE

Non-Turbocharged Engine

1. Remove air cleaner box cover.
2. Raise and support vehicle.
3. Remove engine structural collar.
4. Disconnect starter motor wiring.
5. Remove starter motor mounting bolts, then the starter motor.
6. Reverse procedure to install, noting the following:
   a. **Torque** starter mounting bolts to 40 ft. lbs.
   b. **Torque** solenoid battery cable nut to 90 inch lbs.

Turbocharged Engine

1. Remove air cleaner box.
2. Remove upper starter motor bolt and ground wire.
3. Raise and support vehicle.
4. Remove lower inner cooler hose.
5. Remove nuts securing inner cooler tube.
6. Remove studs securing power steering lines.
7. Loosen and position power steering lines aside.
8. Remove engine structural collar.
9. Disconnect starter motor wiring.
10. Remove lower starter motor bolt, then the starter motor.
11. Reverse procedure to install, noting the following:
    a. **Torque** starter mounting bolts to 40 ft. lbs.
    b. **Torque** solenoid battery cable nut to 90 inch lbs.

IGNITION COIL

REPLACE

Non-Turbocharged Engine

1. Disconnect electrical connector from ignition coil.
2. Remove ignition coil bolts, then the ignition coil.
3. Reverse procedure to install.

Turbocharged Engine

1. Remove throttle control shield.
2. Disconnect throttle cables from throttle body lever.
3. Remove throttle body cable bracket and position aside.
4. Disconnect spark plug cables from ignition coil.
5. Disconnect electrical connector from ignition coil.
6. Remove bolt from ignition coil. Twist coil to remove two of the bolts.
7. Pull coil up and out throttle body side of intake manifold.
8. Reverse procedure to install.

IGNITION LOCK

REPLACE

1. Place ignition in Run position.
2. Through hole in lower steering column shroud, depress lock cylinder retaining tab and remove key and cylinder assembly.
3. Reverse procedure to install. When installing key cylinder, cylinder retaining tab will only depress in Run position.

IGNITION SWITCH

REPLACE

Removal

1. Remove lock cylinder as outlined in "Ignition Lock, Replace."
2. Remove upper and lower shrouds from steering column.
3. Disconnect electrical connectors from ignition switch.
4. Remove two screws at top of multi-function switch and relocate switch.
5. Remove igniting switch mounting screw with No. 10 Torx bit.
6. Remove ignition switch from steering column.

Installation

1. Ensure ignition switch is in Run position and actuator shaft in lock housing is in Run position.
2. Install ignition switch. Switch will snap over retaining tabs.
3. Install mounting screw.
4. Install electrical connectors to ignition switch.
5. Install multi-function switch and upper and lower steering column shrouds.
6. Install key cylinder. Cylinder retaining tab will depress only in Run position.

CLUTCH START SWITCH

REPLACE

A clutch Interlock/Upstart switch is utilized. The switch is an assembly consisting of two switches, and engine starter inhibitor switch and a clutch pedal upstop switch.

Removal

1. Remove lefthand lower instrument panel bezel.
2. Disconnect upstop switch and brake lamp switch connectors.
3. Disconnect clutch master cylinder rod from clutch pedal pin.
4. Remove brake booster push rod retaining clip from brake pedal, then disengage rod from pedal.
5. Remove four brake booster/pedal bracket to cowl panel nuts.
6. From under hood, pull brake master cylinder/booster far enough forward to obtain pedal to bracket stud clearance.
7. Remove brake pedal bracket assembly.
8. Remove pedal pivot shaft, then the clutch and brake pedals.
9. Remove interlock/upstop switch assembly from brake/clutch pedal bracket assembly by depressing four plastic wing tabs on each switch.

Installation

Proper switch harness routing is critical to switch durability. Note harness routing and location of fasteners intended to keep wires from contacting pedals.

1. Install switches into pedal bracket assembly.
2. Route harness as required.
3. Install clutch and brake pedals to pedal bracket.
4. Install pivot shaft and nut. **Torque** nut to 25 ft. lbs.
5. Install brake/clutch pedal bracket assembly into position.
6. Install brake booster mounting nuts and **torque** to 25 ft. lbs.
7. Install pedal bracket to instrument panel nuts and **torque** to 25 ft. lbs.
8. Install new stop lamp switch.
9. Connect brake booster rod to brake pedal and install retainer clip.
10. Connect clutch master cylinder push rod.
11. Loosen adjustment screw and gently lift clutch pedal upwards. **Torque** adjustment screw to 70 inch lbs.
12. Connect interlock/upstop and stop lamp switch connectors.
13. Verify proper switch operation.

HEADLAMP SWITCH

REPLACE

The headlamp switch is incorporated into the multi-function switch. Refer to "Multi-Function Switch, Replace" for replacement procedures.

STOP LIGHT SWITCH

REPLACE

Removal

1. Remove silencer pad below knee blocker.
2. Fold down and remove knee blocker.
3. Remove brake lamp switch by rotating switch in counterclockwise direction approximately 30°.
4. Pull switch rearward and remove from mounting bracket.

Installation

Do not reuse original brake lamp switch. The switch can only be adjusted once during the initial installation of the switch. If switch is not adjusted properly or has been removed, a new switch must be installed and adjusted.

1. Install switch in it's bracket by aligning index tab on switch with slot in mounting bracket.
2. When switch is fully seated in it's bracket, rotate switch clockwise approximately 30° to lock switch into position.
3. With brake pedal in fully released position, move lever on back of brake lamp switch from angled non-adjusted position to full vertical position.
4. Install knee blocker and silencer pad below knee blocker.
5. Inspect stop lamp operation to ensure proper operation.

MULTI-FUNCTION SWITCH

REPLACE

1. Remove upper and lower steering column shrouds.
2. Disconnect both posi-lock harness connectors at rear of multi-function switch.
3. Remove multi-function switch mounting screws, then the switch.
4. Reverse procedure to install.

TURN SIGNAL SWITCH

REPLACE

The turn signal switch is incorporated into the multi-function switch . Refer to "Multi-Function Switch, Replace" for replacement procedures.

STEERING WHEEL

REPLACE

1. **On 2002 models,** adjust steering wheel so that tires are pointed straight ahead, then rotate steering wheel one half turn 180° in clockwise direction.
2. **On 2003–06 models,** adjust steering wheel so that tires are pointed straight ahead.
3. **On all models,** lock column with ignition cylinder lock.
4. Disarm, then remove driver air bag module as outlined under "Passive Restraint Systems" chapter.
5. Remove one retaining bolt to steering wheel.
6. Remove steering wheel with suitable steering wheel puller. Feed wires through holes in steering wheel.
7. Reverse procedure to install, noting the following:
   a. **On 2002 models,** ensure steering wheel is a half turn to 180° clockwise direction and that column is locked with ignition switch.
   b. **On 2003–06 models,** ensure front wheels are pointed straight ahead.
   c. **On all models,** ensure turn signal stalk is in Neutral position.
   d. Install steering wheel ensuring flats on hub align with clockspring.
   e. Pull horn lead, air bag and speed control leads through larger slot. Ensure leads do not get pinched under steering wheel.
   f. Install steering wheel retaining bolt and **torque** to 40 ft. lbs.

INSTRUMENT CLUSTER

REPLACE

Turning cluster upside down causes dampening fluid within the gauge pointer assembly to leak causing permanent damage to instrument cluster. Do not turn cluster upside down for more than 30 minutes (preferably Never).

Do not expose instrument cluster to direct sunlight for extended periods of time. Overexposure to direct sunlight permanently warps the internal mask of the instrument cluster causing the pointers to stick.

Do not do an electrical hot swap when replacing or testing clusters. Ensure ignition is Off with the M1 fuse removed or battery ground battery terminal is disconnected.

Do not swap clusters between vehicles. The instrument cluster has learned information stored in it's microprocessor for Air Bags, Anti-Lock Brakes, Cruise Control and Smart Key Immobilizer. Swapping clusters between vehicles may result in improper illumination of cluster indicators associated with these systems.

1. Remove instrument cluster bezel as follows:
   a. Remove instrument panel top cover.
   b. Remove lefthand lower instrument panel bezel.
   c. Remove lefthand instrument panel end cap.
   d. Grab sides of instrument cluster bezel and pull to unsnap cluster bezel.
   e. Disconnect turn signal lamps from instrument cluster bezel, then remove bezel.
2. Remove four screws to instrument cluster and pull straight back to release off of self docking connectors.
3. Reverse procedure to install.

RADIO

REPLACE

1. Remove instrument panel center bezel as follows:
   a. Pry out front power window switch from instrument panel switch bezel using a thin trim stick or equivalent.
   b. Disconnect switch electrical connector.
   c. Remove HVAC control knobs from control head.
   d. Remove one retaining screw to center bezel inside window switch opening.
   e. Pry center bezel out of instrument panel and remove using a trim stick, or equivalent.
2. Remove four screws on radio and pull out from instrument panel.
3. Disconnect wiring, antenna cable and ground wire, then the radio.
4. Reverse procedure to install.

WIPER MOTOR

REPLACE

Front

1. Gently pry up on wiper arm nut cap and remove using a trim stick, or equivalent.
2. Remove wiper arm retaining nut.
3. Remove arm from pivot using a rocking motion while the arm is in over/centered position.
4. Remove lefthand and righthand cowl covers.
5. Disconnect front windshield wiper motor posi-lock harness connector.
6. Remove three front windshield wiper module mounting bolts, then the module.
7. Remove bell crank retaining nut, then the bell crank.
8. Remove three bolts to front windshield wiper motor and separate from module.
9. Reverse procedure to install.

Rear

1. Remove rear wiper arm nut cap and nut.
2. Use a battery terminal puller to remove wiper arm from wiper pivot.
3. Remove liftgate trim panel.
4. Disconnect harness connector.
5. Remove three bolts to rear wiper motor, then the wiper motor.
6. Ensure when removing motor to prevent damage to grommet or window.
7. Reverse procedure to install.

WIPER SWITCH

REPLACE

1. Remove multi-function switch as outlined in this section.
2. Remove two Torx retaining screws, then the wiper switch.
3. Reverse procedure to install.

WIPER TRANSMISSION

REPLACE

Refer to "Wiper Motor, Replace" for wiper transmission replacement procedure.

BLOWER MOTOR

REPLACE

1. Remove two push pin fasteners that secure righthand silencer pad to lower edge of instrument panel.
2. Pull righthand silencer pad rearward to remove it from under instrument panel.
3. Disconnect instrument panel wire harness connector from blower motor pigtail wiring connector.
4. **On models less A/C,** proceed as follows:
   a. Pull down on blower motor locking tab located on edge of blower motor mounting flange nearest dash panel.
   b. While holding locking tab down, grasp blower motor firmly and rotate it approximately ⅛ turn counterclockwise.
5. **On models equipped with A/C,** remove four screws that secure blower motor to heater and A/C unit housing.
6. **On all models,** lower blower motor and wheel straight down from heater unit housing.
7. Reverse procedure to install.

HEATER CORE

REPLACE

1. Drain cooling system into suitable container.
2. Recover refrigerant as outlined under "Air Conditioning" chapter.
3. Remove instrument panel as outlined under "Dash Panel Service" chapter.
4. Remove refrigerant lines from evaporator connections.
5. Remove heater core coolant supply hoses from heater core.
6. Working from inside engine compartment, remove A/C-heater housing retaining fasteners from bulk head.
7. Remove A/C-heater housing drain tube.
8. Remove A/C-heater housing bolts, then disconnect electrical connectors.
9. Remove A/C-heater housing from vehicle and place on a suitable bench.
10. Separate air distribution outlet foam seals at case parting line.
11. Remove evaporator lines foam seal and heater core tubes foam seal from unit.
12. Remove retaining clips and screws, then separate two halves of housing.
13. Lift out heater core.
14. Reverse procedure to install.

EVAPORATOR CORE

REPLACE

Refer to "Heater Core, Replace" for evaporator core replacement procedures.

2.4L Engine

NOTE: On Air Bag Equipped Models, Refer To "Air Bag System Precautions" Located In The Front Of This Manual For System Disarming & Arming Procedures.

NOTE: Refer To "Computer Relearn Procedures" Located In The Front Of This Manual When Battery Power To The Computer Has Been Interrupted.

INDEX

PRECAUTIONS

Air Bag Systems

Refer to "Air Bag System Precautions" in the front of this manual for system disarming and arming procedures.

Battery Ground Cable

Prior to service, disconnect battery ground cable and isolate as required.

Fuel System Pressure Relief

1. Remove fuel pump relay from Power Distribution Center (PDC).
2. Start and run engine until it stalls.
3. Attempt restarting engine until it will no longer run.
4. Turn ignition key to Off position.
5. Place a rag or shop towel below fuel line quick connect fitting at fuel rail.
6. Return fuel pump relay to PDC.
7. One or more diagnostic trouble codes may have been stored in PCM memory due to fuel pump relay removal. Use suitable scan tool to erase codes.

COMPRESSION PRESSURE

Recommended compression pressures are 170–225 psi. Recommended pressures are used only as a guide to diagnosing engine problem. An engine should not be disassembled to determine the cause of low compression unless a fault is present.

1. Ensure battery is fully charged and starter is in good operating condition.
2. Inspect engine oil level and top up if required.
3. Drive vehicle until engine is at normal operating temperature.
4. Remove spark plugs from engine and inspect for abnormal firing indicators.
5. Disconnect coil wire from distributor and secure to good ground. For direct ignition system,. disconnect coil connector.
6. Ensure throttle blade is fully open during compression test.
7. Insert compression gauge adapter tool No. 8116, or equivalent, into No. 1 cylinder spark plug hole.
8. Connect 0–500 psi (Blue) transducer with cable adapters to DRBIII.
9. Crank engine until maximum pressure is reached on gauge, repeat for all cylinders.
10. Compression should not be less than 100 psi or vary by more than 25 percent from cylinder to cylinder.

ENGINE MOUNT

REPLACE

Lefthand

1. Remove air cleaner assembly.
2. Remove bolts attaching PDC bracket to lefthand mount and battery tray.
3. Support transaxle with suitable jack.
4. Remove mount to transaxle bolts, **Fig. 1.**
5. Remove lefthand mount bracket to body frame rail fasteners, then the motor mount.
6. Reverse procedure to install, noting the following:
    a. Install engine mount bracket to body frame rail and tighten to specification.
    b. Position engine/transaxle for installation of mount to transaxle bolts.
    c. Install bolts and tighten to specification.

Righthand

Engine removal is required for required clearance to access the righthand motor

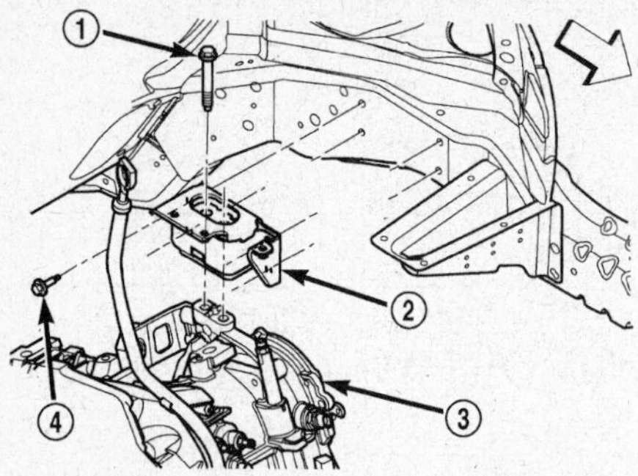

Fig. 1 Lefthand engine mount

mount. The righthand engine mount attaching holes are slightly oversize to compensate for manufacturing tolerances. The mount has been set at the factory for proper powertrain alignment. If mount is to be removed, it will be required to mark the position of the mount before removing the attaching bolts.

1. Mark position of engine mount to body frame rail using a permanent marker or equivalent.
2. Remove bolts attaching mount to body, **Fig. 2**, then the mount.
3. Reverse procedure to install, tighten to specification.

Torque Struts

UPPER

1. Remove bolts attaching strut to shock tower bracket and engine mount bracket, **Fig. 3.**
2. **On models equipped with A/C,** remove timing belt front upper cover.
3. **On all models,** remove upper torque strut.
4. Reverse procedure to install, adjust torque strut according to adjustment procedure.

LOWER

1. Raise and support vehicle.
2. Remove accessory belt splash shield.
3. Remove pencil strut, **Fig. 4.**
4. Remove bolts attaching lower strut to crossmember and strut bracket, then the lower torque strut.
5. Reverse procedure to install, adjust torque strut according to adjustment procedure.

ADJUSTMENT PROCEDURE

The upper and lower torque struts need to be adjusted together to assure proper engine mount load balance and engine positioning. Whenever a torque strut bolt is loosened, the following adjustment procedure must be performed.

1. Remove pencil strut.
2. Loosen upper and lower torque strut attaching bolt at suspension crossmember and shock tower bracket.
3. Position a suitable floor jack on forward edge of transmission bell housing, **Fig. 5.**
4. Floor jack must be positioned to prevent minimal upward lifting of engine.
5. Apply upward force, allowing upper engine to rotate rearward until distance between center or rearmost attaching bolt on engine mount bracket (point "A") and center of hole on shock tower bracket (point "B") is 4.70 inches, **Fig. 6.**
6. With engine held at proper position, **torque** upper and lower torque strut bolts to 87 ft. lbs.
7. Remove floor jack.
8. Install pencil strut and **torque** nuts to 43 ft. lbs.

STRUCTURAL COLLAR

REPLACE

Automatic Transaxle

REMOVAL

1. Raise and support vehicle.
2. Remove bolts attaching bending strut to engine and transaxle, **Fig. 7.**
3. Remove bolts attaching collar and strut to engine, oil pan and transaxle.
4. Remove strut and collar.

INSTALLATION

Torque procedure for structural collar and bending strut must be followed or damage could occur to oil pan, collar and/or bending strut. Refer to **Fig. 7** for bolt locations while performing this procedure.

1. Place collar into position between transaxle and oil pan.
2. Install collar to transaxle bolt (1), hand start bolt only.
3. Position power steering hose support bracket and install collar to oil pan bolt (4), hand tight only.
4. Position bending strut in place and hand start only, bolt (3) into upper transaxle hole.
5. Install bolt (2), through strut and collar, hand start only.
6. Install bolt (6), strut to cylinder block, hand tight only.
7. Position power steering hose support bracket and install remaining collar to oil pan bolt (5), hand tight only.
8. **Torque** collar to transaxle bolts 1–3 to 75 ft. lbs.
9. Install bolts (7) and (8) through strut and into cylinder block.
10. **Torque** bolts 4–8 to 45 ft. lbs.

Manual Transaxle

REMOVAL

1. Raise and support vehicle.
2. Remove bolts attaching bending strut to engine and transaxle, **Fig. 8,** then the strut.
3. Remove bolts attaching collar and clutch slave cylinder to oil pan and transaxle, then the collar.

INSTALLATION

Torque procedure for structural collar and bending strut must be followed or damage could occur to oil pan, collar and/or bending strut. Refer to **Fig. 8** for bolt position when performing this procedure.

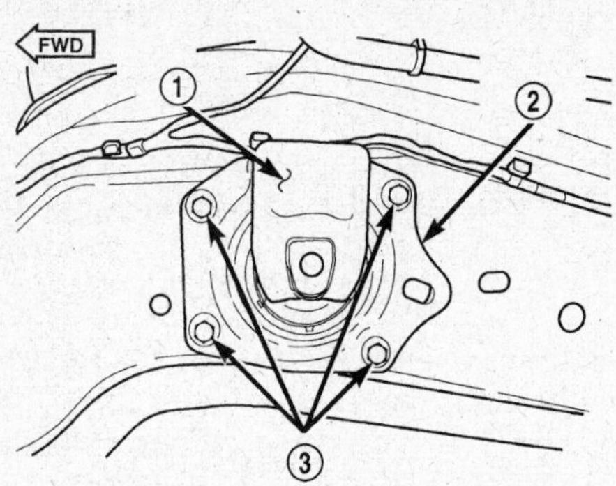

Fig. 2 Righthand engine mount

1. Place collar into position between transaxle and oil pan. Install collar to transaxle bolt (1), hand start only.
2. Position power steering hose support bracket and install collar to oil pan bolt (2), hand tight only.
3. Position clutch slave cylinder into mounting position and install bolts (3) and (4), hand tight only.
4. Position bending strut in place and install bolt (5), hand tight only, into upper transaxle hole.
5. Position power steering hose support bracket and install remaining collar to oil pan bolt (6), hand tight only.
6. Tighten all bolts in sequence as follows:
   a. **Torque** bolts 1 and 5 to 75 ft. lbs.
   b. **Torque** bolts 2 and 6 to 45 ft. lbs.
   c. **Torque** bolts 3 and 4 to 20 ft. lbs.

ENGINE

REPLACE

1. Perform fuel system pressure release procedure as outlined under "Precautions."
2. Remove air cleaner housing assembly and clean air hose.
3. Disconnect positive and battery grounds.
4. Remove battery and battery tray.
5. Drain cooling system into suitable container.
6. **On models equipped with A/C,** recover refrigerant as outlined under "Air Conditioning" chapter.
7. **On all models,** disconnect throttle and speed control cables.
8. Disconnect engine wiring harness at PCM connector.
9. Disconnect positive cable from PDC and ground wire from vehicle body.
10. Remove power distribution center attaching bolts and set PDC aside.
11. Disconnect wiring connectors at lower battery tray support.
12. Disconnect ground wire from vehicle body to engine at righthand side strut tower.
13. Disconnect brake booster vacuum hose from intake manifold.

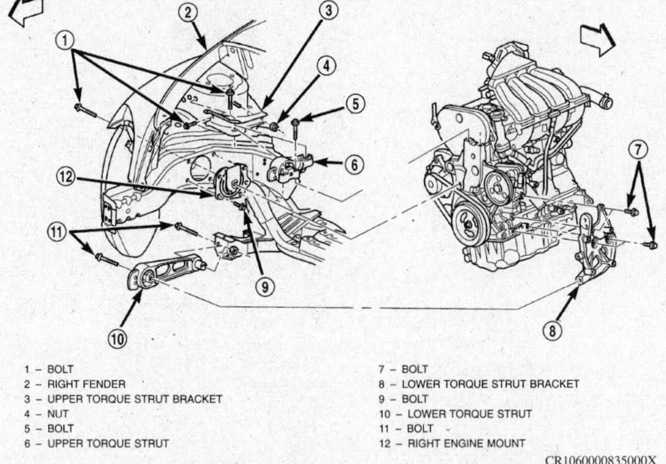

Fig. 3 Upper & lower strut mounts

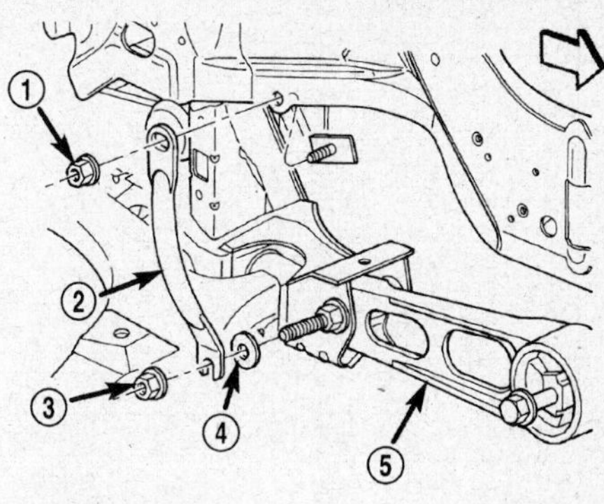

Fig. 4 Pencil strut

14. Disconnect proportional purge hoses from intake manifold.
15. Disconnect coolant reserve/recovery hose from coolant outlet connector.
16. Disconnect heater hoses.
17. Remove upper radiator support crossmember.
18. Remove upper and lower radiator hoses.
19. Disconnect upper A/C line from condenser.
20. Disconnect A/C lines at junction near upper torque strut.
21. Disconnect automatic transmission cooler lines and plug lines to prevent leakage.
22. Disconnect electrical fan connector and remove cooling module assembly fan.
23. Disconnect shift linkage and transaxle electrical connectors.
24. Disconnect clutch hydraulic line at quick disconnect fitting using removal tool No. 6638, or equivalent.
25. Raise and support vehicle.
26. Remove front wheels, righthand inner splash shield and axle shafts.
27. Remove accessory drive belts, alternator and support brackets.
28. **On models equipped with turbochargers,** remove charge air cooler hoses.
29. **On all models,** drain engine oil into suitable container.
30. Disconnect downstream oxygen sensor connector.
31. Disconnect exhaust system from manifold.
32. Disconnect power steering pressure hose from steering gear.
33. **On models equipped with turbochargers,** remove upper and lower heat shields, elbow support bracket, turbocharger support bracket and elbow.
34. **On all models,** remove lower engine torque strut and structural collar.
35. Remove torque converter bolts.
36. Lower vehicle and remove A/C compressor.
37. Disconnect power steering fluid return line from reservoir.
38. Remove power steering pump.
39. Raise and support vehicle and position engine dolly and cradle tool No. 6135 and tool No. 6710, or equivalents, **Fig. 9,** below engine and transaxle assembly.
40. Loosen engine support posts to allow movement for positioning onto engine locating holes and flange on engine bedplate.
41. Lower vehicle and position cradle until engine is resting on support posts.
42. Tighten mounts to cradle frame.
43. Install suitable safety straps around engine to cradle. Tighten straps and lock into position.
44. Raise vehicle enough to determine if straps are secure enough to hold cradle assembly to engine.
45. Lower vehicle so weight of engine and transmission only is on cradle assembly.
46. Remove upper engine torque strut.
47. Remove righthand mount through bolt and lefthand mount attaching bolt.
48. Raise vehicle slowly until engine/transaxle assembly clears engine compartment. It may be required to move engine/transmission assembly with cradle to allow for removal around body flanges.
49. Reverse procedure to install.

INTAKE MANIFOLD

REPLACE

Upper

NON-TURBOCHARGED ENGINE

REMOVAL

1. Disconnect inlet air temperature sensor and make up air hose from clean air hose.
2. Remove engine cover by pulling upward to release from ball stud retainers.
3. Remove throttle and speed control cables from throttle lever and bracket.
4. Disconnect Manifold Absolute Pressure (MAP) sensor, Idle Air Control (IAC) motor and Throttle Position Sensor (TPS) wiring connectors, **Figs. 10 and 11.**
5. Disconnect proportional purge hose, **Fig. 12,** brake booster hose and PCV hose from intake manifold.
6. Remove EGR tube bolts at upper intake manifold.
7. Remove upper intake manifold fasteners, then the upper intake manifold.
8. If further service is required, cover lower intake manifold to prevent foreign material from entering engine.

INSTALLATION

1. Clean all surfaces, replace seals as required.
2. Position upper intake manifold onto EGR tube, then position upper intake manifold on lower manifold.
3. Tighten upper intake manifold fasteners in sequence, **Fig. 13,** to specification.
4. Install throttle body support bracket bolt at throttle body.
5. Position EGR tube retainer plate. Tighten smaller bolts to specification.
6. Connect PCV hose to intake manifold.
7. Connect electrical connectors and vacuum hoses.
8. Install throttle and speed control cables to bracket, then to throttle lever.
9. Install air cleaner housing and clean air hose.
10. Tighten clean air hose clamp to 15 inch lbs.
11. Connect make up air hose and inlet air temperature sensor.
12. Install engine cover.

TURBOCHARGED ENGINE

1. Disconnect IAT sensor electrical connector.
2. Disconnect throttle inlet pressure hose.
3. Disconnect charge air cooler hose at throttle body.
4. Disconnect IAC motor and TP sensor electrical connectors.
5. Remove throttle control shield, then the throttle cable from throttle body lever.
6. Remove speed control cable from throttle lever by sliding clasp out of

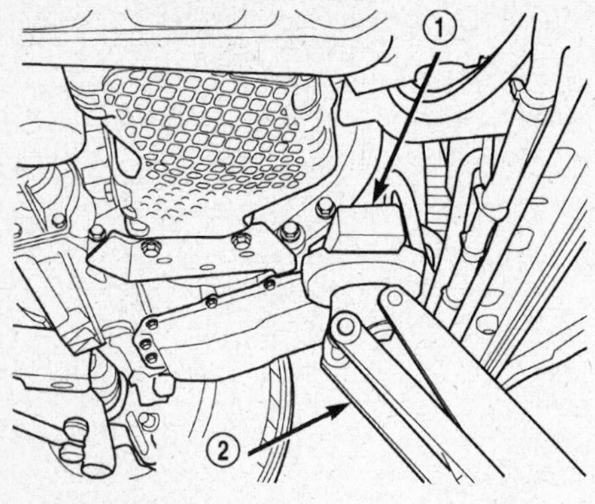

1 – WOOD BLOCK
2 – FLOOR JACK

CR1060000837000X

Fig. 5 Floor jack positioning

hole used for throttle cable.

7. Remove two screws for throttle cable bracket, then position bracket aside.
8. Disconnect brake booster hose and PCV hose from intake manifold.
9. Disconnect purge solenoid hose from throttle body.
10. Remove upper intake manifold support bracket.
11. Remove bolts, then the intake manifold.
12. Reverse procedure to install. Tighten intake manifold in sequence, **Fig. 13.**

Lower

REMOVAL

1. Relieve fuel system pressure as outlined under "Precautions."
2. Disconnect inlet air temperature sensor and make up air hose.
3. Remove air cleaner housing and clean air hose.
4. Remove upper intake manifold as outlined previously.
5. Drain cooling system into suitable container to level below thermostat.
6. Remove upper radiator hose.
7. Remove coolant outlet connector.
8. Disconnect fuel supply line quick connect at fuel rail assembly. Wrap shop towels around hose to catch any fuel spillage.
9. Disconnect fuel injector wiring harness.
10. Remove screw attaching oil dipstick tube to lower intake manifold.
11. Remove lower intake manifold fasteners, then the lower intake manifold.

INSTALLATION

1. Clean all gasket surfaces, replace gaskets as required.
2. Position new seals on lower intake manifold.
3. Install lower intake manifold.
4. Tighten intake manifold bolts in sequence, **Fig. 14,** to specification.
5. If removed, install fuel rail assembly to intake manifold. Tighten screws to specification.
6. Connect fuel injector wiring harness.
7. Inspect quick connect fittings for damage and replace as required.

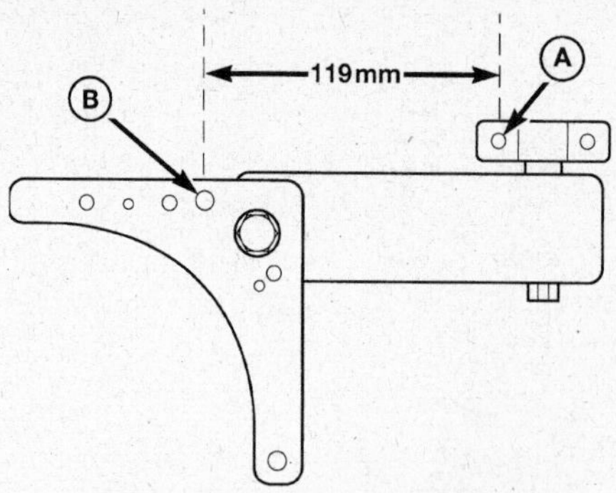

CR1060000839000X

Fig. 6 Engine position measurement

8. Lubricate tube with clean engine oil and connect fuel supply hose to fuel rail assembly.
9. Inspect connection by pulling on connector to ensure it locked into position.
10. Install oil dipstick attaching screw, upper radiator hose and upper intake manifold.
11. Install air cleaner housing and clean air hose.
12. Connect inlet air temperature sensor and make up air hose.
13. Fill cooling system.
14. Activate "ASD Fuel System Test" to inspect for leaks using suitable scan tool.
15. "ASD Fuel System" Test activates auto shutdown relay for seven minutes or until ignition switch is turned to the Off position, or "Stop All Test" is selected.

EXHAUST MANIFOLD

REPLACE

Removal

1. Remove clean air hose and air cleaner housing.
2. Disconnect throttle and speed control cables from throttle lever and bracket.
3. Disconnect MAP sensor electrical connector.
4. Remove power steering fluid reservoir from mounting bracket.
5. Remove coolant recovery bottle.
6. Remove upper heat shield.
7. Raise and support vehicle.
8. Disconnect exhaust pipe from manifold.
9. Remove engine wiring heat shield.
10. Remove manifold support bracket.
11. Remove lower exhaust manifold heat shield.
12. Disconnect oxygen sensor electrical connector.
13. Remove exhaust manifold lower fasteners.
14. Lower vehicle and remove upper exhaust manifold fastening retainers.
15. Remove exhaust manifold from above, between engine and cowl panel.
16. Remove and discard manifold gasket.

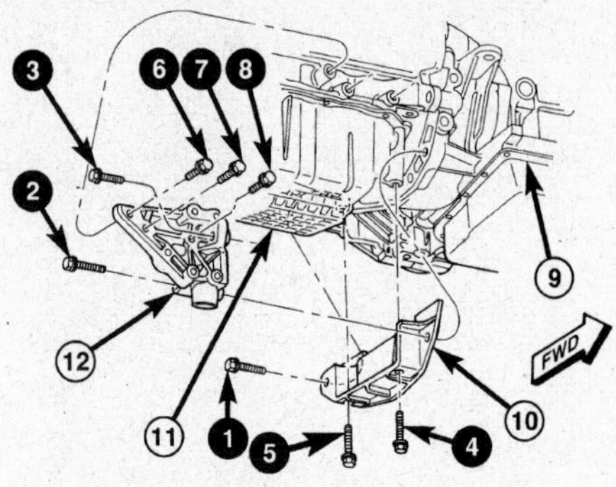

1–8 – BOLT TIGHTENING SEQUENCE
9 – TRANSAXLE
10 – COLLAR
11 – OIL PAN
12 – STRUT

CR1060000838000X

Fig. 7 Structural collar & bending strut w/automatic transaxle

Installation

1. Install new manifold gasket. Do not apply sealer.
2. Position exhaust manifold in place, tighten fasteners starting at center and working outward, **Fig. 15,** to specification.
3. Install exhaust manifold heat shields, tighten bolts to specification.
4. Install exhaust manifold support bracket.
5. Install engine wiring heat shield.
6. Connect oxygen sensor wiring connector.
7. Install exhaust pipe to manifold, tighten mounting bolts to specification.
8. Install coolant recovery bottle.
9. Install power steering fluid reservoir to mounting bracket.
10. Connect MAP sensor electrical connector.
11. Connect throttle and speed control cables.
12. Install clean air hose and air cleaner housing.

CYLINDER HEAD

REPLACE

1. Perform fuel system pressure relief procedure as outlined under "Precautions."
2. Disconnect inlet air temperature sensor and make up air hose.
3. Remove clean air hose and air cleaner housing.
4. Drain cooling system into suitable container.
5. Remove upper intake manifold as outlined under "Intake Manifold, Replace."
6. Disconnect fuel supply line quick connect at fuel rail assembly.
7. Remove heater tube support bracket from cylinder head.
8. Disconnect upper radiator and heater supply hoses from coolant outlet connections.
9. Remove accessory drive belts.
10. Raise and support vehicle.

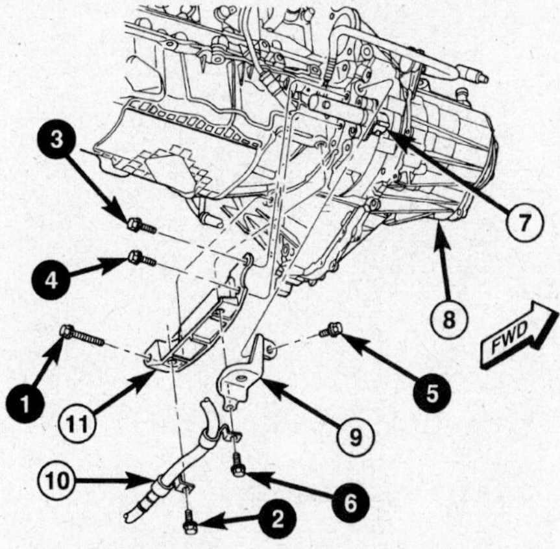

1–6 – BOLT TIGHTENING SEQUENCE
7 – HYDRAULIC CLUTCH SLAVE CYLINDER
8 – TRANSAXLE
9 – STRUT
10 – POWER STEERING HOSE
11 – COLLAR

CR1060000840000X

Fig. 8 Structural collar & bending strut w/manual transaxle

11. Disconnect exhaust pipe from manifold.
12. **On models equipped with turbochargers,** proceed as follows:
    a. Remove turbocharger heat shields.
    b. Remove elbow and turbocharger support brackets.
    c. Remove oil supply and return lines.
    d. Remove coolant supply and return lines.
13. **On all models,** lower vehicle.
14. Disconnect ignition coil wiring connector.
15. Remove ignition coil and plug wires.
16. Disconnect cam sensor wiring connector.
17. Remove timing belt as outlined under "Timing Belt, Replace."
18. Remove camshaft as outlined under "Camshaft, Replace."
19. Remove timing belt idler pulley and rear timing belt cover.
20. Remove power steering pump fluid reservoir and support bracket.
21. Remove cylinder head cover, camshafts, and camshaft followers.
22. Remove cylinder head bolts in reverse order of tightening sequence, **Fig. 16.**
23. Remove cylinder head from engine block.
24. Reverse procedure to install, noting the following:
    a. Ensure cylinder head bolts hole in block are clean, dry and that threads are not damaged. Inspect cylinder head bolts for necking (stretching).
    b. Hold a steel scale or straight edge against threads and note whether all threads are touching scale. If all threads do not contact straight edge, bolt should be replaced.
    c. Position new cylinder head gasket on cylinder block with part number facing up.
    d. Ensure gasket is seated over locating dowels in block.
    e. Before installing bolts, lightly coat threads with engine oil.
    f. **Torque** cylinder head bolts in four steps, in sequence, **Fig. 16,** to the following specifications:
    g. First step: **Torque** all bolts to 25 ft. lbs.
    h. Second step: **Torque** all bolts to 50 ft. lbs.
    i. Third step: **Torque** all bolts to 50 ft. lbs.
    j. Fourth step: Turn all bolts an additional 1/4 turn.

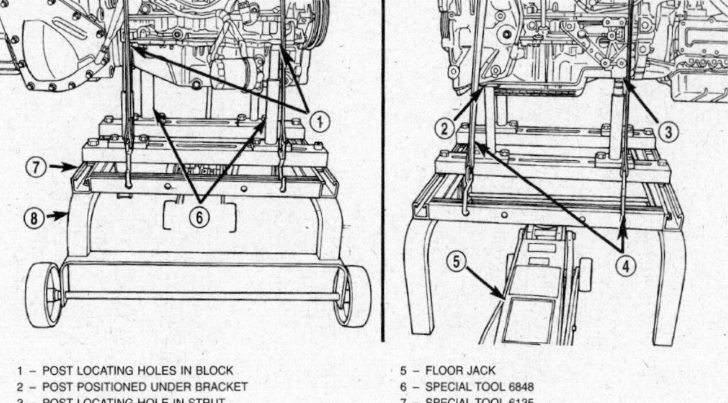

1 – POST LOCATING HOLES IN BLOCK
2 – POST POSITIONED UNDER BRACKET
3 – POST LOCATING HOLE IN STRUT
4 – SAFETY STRAPS
5 – FLOOR JACK
6 – SPECIAL TOOL 6848
7 – SPECIAL TOOL 6135
8 – SPECIAL TOOL 6710

CR1060000841000X

Fig. 9 Engine cradle support

VALVE LIFTERS

This procedure is for in-vehicle service with camshafts installed.

1. Remove cylinder head cover, cam followers and lash adjusters.
2. If components are to be reused, mark for installation reference.
3. Reverse procedure to install.

CAMSHAFT LOBE LIFT SPECIFICATIONS

Exhaust ....259 inch
Intake .... .324 inch

VALVE ADJUSTMENT

These engines use hydraulic lifters. No adjustment is required.

CAMSHAFT FOLLOWERS

This procedure is for in-vehicle service with camshafts installed.

1. Remove cylinder head cover, fuel rail and spark plugs.
2. Rotate engine until camshaft lobe, on follower being removed, is positioned on it's base circle (heel). Piston should be a minimum of .025 inch below TDC position.
3. If cam follower assemblies are to be reused, mark followers for installation reference.
4. Slowly depress valve assembly until cam follower can be removed using valve spring compressor tool No. 8215 and adapter tool No. 8436, or equivalent, **Fig. 17.**
5. It may be required to remove additional brackets to allow clearance for tool handle movement.
6. Reverse procedure to install.

FRONT COVER

REPLACE

Upper

1. Remove upper torque strut attaching bolts and set strut aside.
2. **On models equipped with turbochargers,** recover refrigerant as outlined under "Air Conditioning" chapter, then disconnect air conditioning lines at junction block near upper timing belt cover.
3. **On all models** remove timing belt cover bolts, **Fig. 18,** then the cover.
4. Reverse procedure to install.

Lower

1. Raise and support vehicle.
2. Remove righthand front wheel.
3. Remove righthand splash shield.
4. Remove accessory drive belts.
5. Remove crankshaft damper.
6. Remove lower torque strut.
7. Disconnect exhaust system from manifold.
8. Disconnect A/C pressure switch at rear of compressor housing.
9. Recover refrigerant as outlined under "Air Conditioning" chapter.
10. Remove upper torque strut and bracket.
11. Remove upper radiator support crossmember.
12. Remove power steering pump and bracket. Set pump aside. Do not disconnect lines from pump.
13. With engine properly supported, remove righthand engine mount through bolt.
14. Raise engine with suitable jack until engine support bracket bolts are accessible, **Fig. 19.**

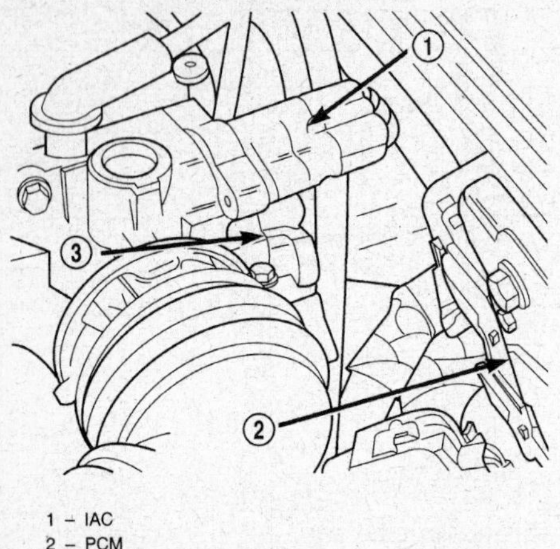

Fig. 10 IAC motor & TPS wiring connectors. Non-turbocharged engine

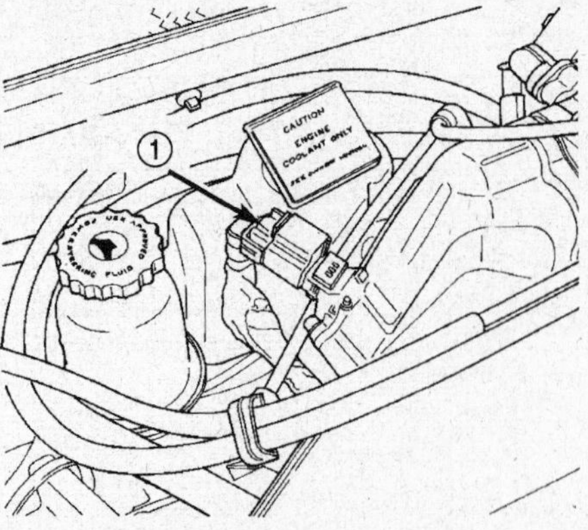

Fig. 11 MAP sensor. Non-turbocharged engine

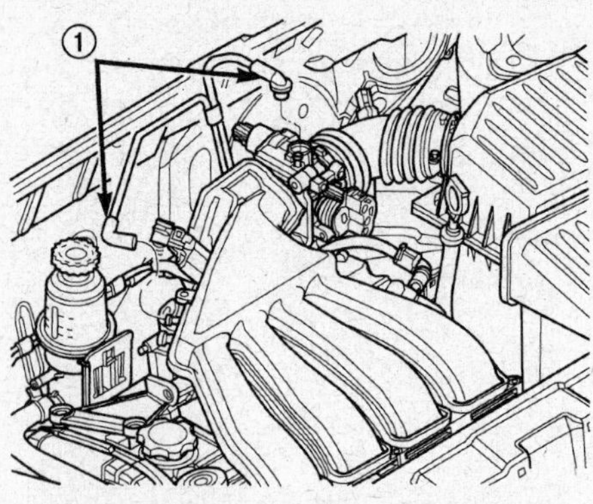

Fig. 12 Proportional purge hose. Non-turbocharged engine

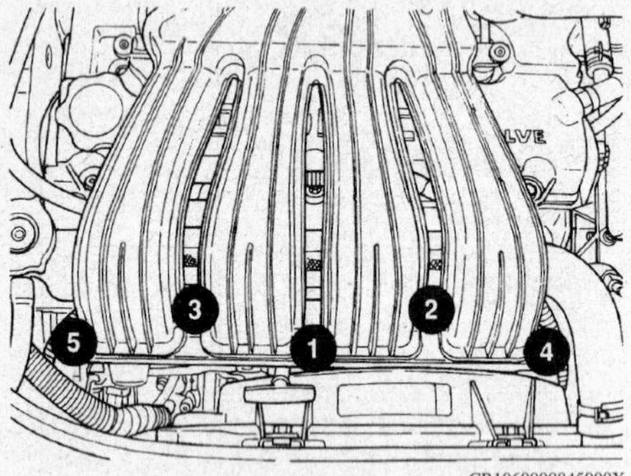

Fig. 13 Upper intake manifold tightening sequence

15. Remove engine support bracket, then the lower timing belt cover.
16. Reverse procedure to install.

TIMING BELT

REPLACE

Removal

1. Raise and support vehicle.
2. Remove timing belt cover bolts, **Fig. 18,** then the cover.
3. Before removal of timing belt, rotate crankshaft until TDC mark on oil pump housing aligns with TDC mark on crankshaft sprocket, **Fig. 20.**
4. When aligning crankshaft and camshaft timing marks, always rotate engine from crankshaft. Do not rotate camshaft after timing belt has been removed.
5. Install a 6mm Allen wrench into belt tensioner. Before rotating tensioner, insert long end of ⅛ inch or 3mm Allen wrench into pin hole on front tensioner, **Fig. 21.**
6. While rotating tensioner counterclockwise, push in slightly on ⅛ inch or 3mm Allen wrench until it slides into locking hole.
7. Remove timing belt.

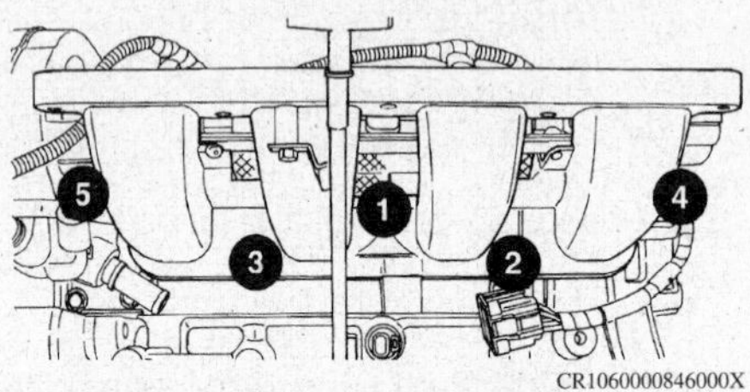

Fig. 14 Lower intake manifold tightening sequence

Installation

1. Set crankshaft sprocket to TDC by aligning sprocket with arrow on oil pump housing, **Fig. 20.**
2. Set camshafts timing marks so that exhaust camshaft timing mark is ½ notch below intake camshaft sprocket, **Fig. 22.**
3. Ensure arrows on both camshaft sprockets are facing up.
4. Install timing belt. Starting at crankshaft, go around water pump sprocket, idler pulleys, camshaft sprockets and tensioner.
5. Move exhaust camshaft sprocket counterclockwise to take up belt slack and align marks.
6. New tensioners are held in place by a pull pin. Remove pull pin or Allen wrench from belt tensioner.
7. Once timing belt has been installed and tensioner released, rotate crankshaft two complete revolutions and verify that TDC marks on camshafts are aligned, **Fig. 20.**
8. Install lower and upper timing belt covers and bolts.
9. Install righthand engine support bracket, ensure power steering pump is properly located in mounting location on bracket.
10. **Torque** mount bracket bolts to 45 ft. lbs.
11. Lower engine into mounting position and install righthand engine mount through bolt. **Torque** bolt to 87 ft. lbs.
12. Install power steering pump and brackets, upper radiator support crossmember and torque strut bracket to strut tower.
13. Install ground strap to bracket.
14. Install upper torque strut.
15. Connect A/C lines and recharge A/C system as outlined under "Air Conditioning" chapter.
16. Raise and support vehicle.
17. Connect exhaust system to exhaust manifold.
18. Connect A/C pressure switch connector and install crankshaft damper.
19. Install accessory drive belts and lower torque strut.
20. Perform torque strut adjustment procedure as outlined in torque struts under "Engine Mounts, Replace."
21. Install righthand splash shield and righthand front wheel.
22. Perform camshaft/crankshaft synchronization procedure as follows:
    a. Connect DRBIII scan tool, or equivalent, to data link connector.
    b. Turn ignition switch On and access "Miscellaneous" screen.
    c. Select "Re-Set Values" option.
    d. Perform Cam/Crank synchronization procedure following on screen prompts from scan tool.

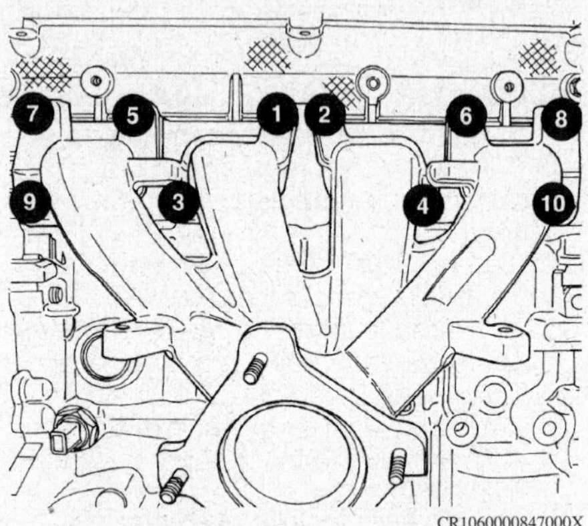

Fig. 15 Exhaust manifold tightening sequence

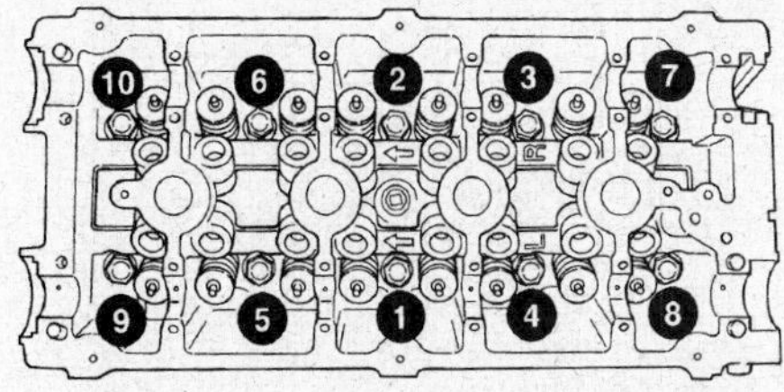

Fig. 16 Cylinder head tightening sequence

CAMSHAFT

REPLACE

Removal

Camshafts are not interchangeable. The lefthand (intake) camshaft thrust bearing face (No. 6) spacing is wider.

1. Remove cylinder head cover.
2. Remove camshaft position sensor and camshaft target magnet.
3. Remove timing belt as outlined under "Timing Belt, Replace" then the camshaft sprockets and rear timing belt cover.
4. Bearing caps are identified for location, remove outside bearing caps first, **Fig. 23.**
5. Loosen camshaft bearing cap attaching fasteners in sequence, **Fig. 24.**
6. Identify camshafts, then remove from cylinder head.

Inspection

1. Oil camshaft journals and install camshaft without cam follower assemblies.
2. Install rear cam caps and tighten to specification.
3. Move camshaft as far rearward as it will go.
4. Mount and zero a suitable dial indicator on cylinder head and camshaft, **Fig. 25.**
5. Move camshaft as far forward as it will go and note dial indicator reading.
6. End play travel specification is .002–.010 inch.
7. If end play is excessive, inspect cylinder head and camshafts for excessive wear and replace as required.

Installation

Ensure no piston is at TDC when installing camshafts.

1. Lubricate all camshaft bearing journals, cam followers and camshafts.
2. Install cam followers and camshafts.
3. Install righthand and lefthand camshaft bearing caps No. 2–5 and righthand No. 6. Tighten M6 fasteners to specification, in sequence, **Fig. 26.**
4. Apply Mopar Gasket Maker, or equivalent, to No. 1 and lefthand No. 6 bearing caps. Install caps and tighten M8 fasteners to specification.
5. Camshaft end caps must be installed before camshaft seals are installed.
6. Install camshaft seals, rear timing belt cover, camshaft sprockets and timing belt.
7. Install camshaft target magnet and camshaft position sensor.
8. Install cylinder head cover.
9. Perform camshaft/crankshaft synchronization procedure as follows:
   a. Connect DRBIII scan tool, or equivalent, to data link connector.
   b. Turn ignition switch On and access "Miscellaneous" screen.
   c. Select "Re-Set Values" option.
   d. Perform Cam/Crank synchronization procedure following on screen prompts from scan tool.

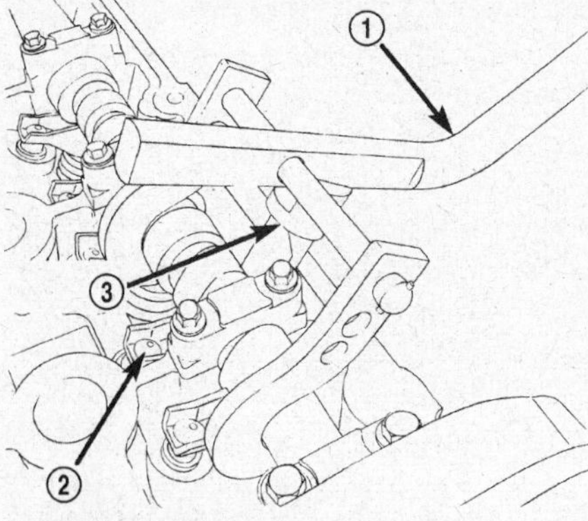

Fig. 17 Camshaft follower replacement

BALANCE SHAFT

REPLACE

Balance Shafts & Balance Shaft Carrier

The following components will remain intact during carrier removal, **Fig. 27:** Gear covers, gears, balance shafts and rear cover.

1. Drain engine oil into suitable container.
2. Remove oil pan and oil pickup tube.
3. Remove chain cover, guide and tensioner, **Fig. 28.**
4. Remove gear sprocket retaining screws.
5. Remove chain and sprocket assembly. Using two wide pry bars, work sprocket back and forth until it is off of shaft.
6. Remove gear cover retaining stud (double ended to also retain chain guide), gear cover and balance shaft gears.
7. Remove gear cover and balance shafts.
8. Remove four carrier to crankcase attaching bolts to separate carrier from engine bedplate.
9. Remove chain cover and driven balance shaft chain sprocket screw.
10. Loosen tensioner pivot and adjusting screws, move driven balance shaft inboard through driven chain sprocket. Sprocket will hang in lower chain loop.
11. Remove carrier to crankcase attaching bolts, then the carrier.
12. Reverse procedure to install.

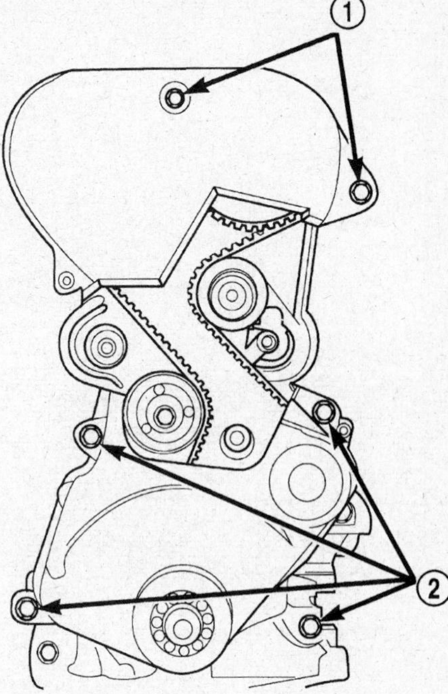

Fig. 18 Upper & lower timing belt covers

BALANCE SHAFT TIMING

1. With balance shafts installed in carrier, **Fig. 27,** position carrier on crankcase and install four attaching bolts. Tighten bolts to specification.
2. Turn balance shafts until both shaft keyways are up, parallel to vertical centerline of engine.
3. Install short hub drive gear on sprocket driven shaft and long hub gear on gear driven shaft.
4. Gear and balance shaft keyways must be up with gear timing marks meshed, **Fig. 29.**
5. Install gear cover and tighten double ended stud/washer to specification.
6. Align flat on balance shaft sprocket to flat on crankshaft, **Fig. 30.**
7. Install balance shaft drive sprocket on crankshaft using sprocket installer tool No. 6052, or equivalent.
8. Turn crankshaft until No. 1 cylinder is at TDC. Timing marks on chain sprocket should line up with parting line on lefthand side of No. 1 main bearing cap, **Fig. 31.**
9. Place chain over crankshaft sprocket so that plated link of chain is over No. 1 cylinder timing mark on balance shaft crankshaft sprocket, **Fig. 31.**
10. Place balance shaft sprocket into timing chain and align timing mark on sprocket with lower plated link on chain, **Fig. 31.**
11. Lower plated link is eight links from upper link.
12. With balance shaft keyways pointing

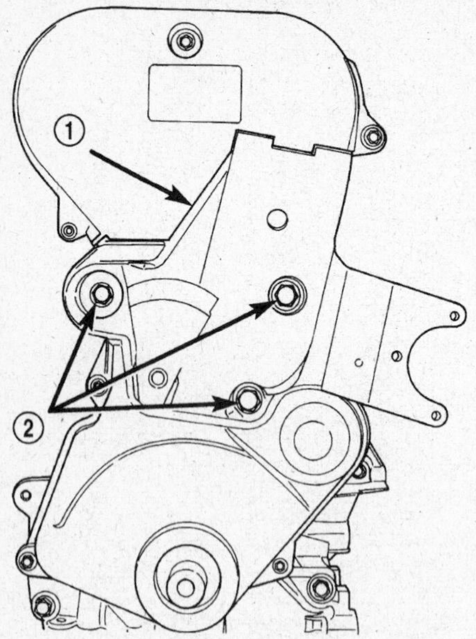

Fig. 19 Engine support bracket

up, slide balance shaft sprocket onto nose of balance shaft. Balance shaft may have to be pushed in slightly to allow for clearance.

13. Timing mark on sprocket, lower nickel plated link and arrow on side of gear cover should line up when balance shafts are timed correctly.
14. Install balance shaft bolts, tighten to specification. A wood block placed between crankcase and crankshaft counterbalance will prevent crankshaft and gear rotation.
15. Install chain tensioner loosely.
16. Position guide on double ended stud. Ensure tab on guide fits into slot on gear cover, then install and **torque** nut/washer to 105 inch lbs.
17. Place a shim .039 inch thick and 2.75 inches long between tensioner and chain.
18. Push tensioner and shim up against chain. Apply firm pressure of 5.5–6.6 lbs., directly behind adjustment slot to take up all slack.
19. Chain must have shoe radius contact, **Fig. 32.**
20. With load applied, tighten top bolt first, then bottom pivot bolt. Tighten bolts to specification, then remove shim.
21. Install carrier covers and tighten bolts to specification.
22. Install pickup tube and oil pan.
23. Fill crankcase with proper oil to correct level.

PISTON & ROD ASSEMBLY

The directional stamp on the piston should face toward the front of the engine.

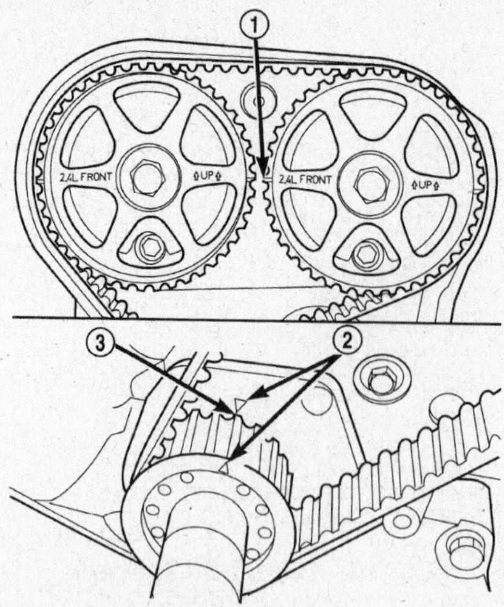

Fig. 20 Crankshaft & camshaft timing marks

CRANKSHAFT REAR OIL SEAL

REPLACE

Removal

1. Remove transaxle and flexplate as outlined in **MOTOR'S "Domestic Transmission, In-Vehicle Service."**
2. Insert a 3⁄16 inch flat bladed screwdriver between dust lip and metal case of crankshaft seal.
3. Pry out seal.
4. Do not allow screwdriver blade to contact crankshaft seal surface.
5. If burrs or scratches are present on crankshaft edge, polish with 400 grit sand paper to prevent seal damage during installation of new seal.

Installation

When installing new seal, no lube on seal is needed.

1. Place seal guide tool No. 6926–1, or equivalent, on crankshaft.
2. Position seal over guide tool, guide tool should remain on crankshaft during installation of seal.
3. Ensure lip of seal is facing toward crankcase during installation.
4. Drive seal into block using seal driver tool No. 6926–2 and handle tool No. C-4171, or equivalents, until tool bottoms out against block.
5. Install flexplate.
6. Apply Mopar Lock and Seal adhesive to bolt threads and tighten to specification.
7. Install transaxle as outlined in **MOTOR'S "Domestic Transmission, In-Vehicle Service."**

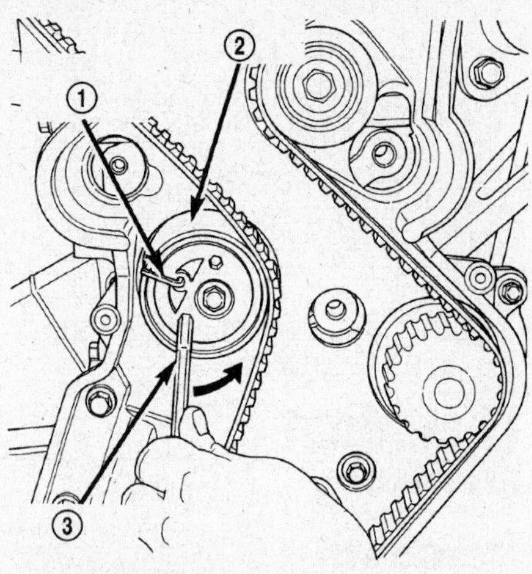

Fig. 21 Locking timing belt tensioner

OIL PAN

REPLACE

1. Raise and support vehicle.
2. Drain engine oil into suitable container.
3. Remove oil filter.
4. Remove righthand inner splash shield.
5. **On models equipped with turbochargers,** remove turbocharger to charge air cooler hose assembly.
6. **On models equipped with turbochargers,** remove oil cooler connector bolt. **Do not disconnect coolant lines from oil cooler.**
7. **On all models,** remove structural collar as outlined under "Structural Collar, Replace."
8. Remove lower torque strut.
9. Remove oil filter adapter and gasket.
10. Remove oil pan and gasket.
11. Clean oil pan and all gasket surfaces.
12. Reverse procedure to install, noting the following:
    a. Apply Mopar Engine RTV GEN II, or equivalent, at oil pump to engine block parting lines.
    b. Install oil pan and gasket and tighten to specification.
    c. Install oil filter adapter and gasket, tighten to specification.

OIL PUMP

REPLACE

1. Remove timing belt as outlined under "Timing Belt, Replace" then the timing belt rear cover.
2. Remove oil pan as outlined under "Oil Pan, Replace."
3. Remove crankshaft sprocket using tools No. 6793 and C-4685–C2, or equivalents.
4. Remove crankshaft key.
5. Remove oil pickup tube.
6. Remove oil pump and front crankshaft seal, **Fig. 33.**
7. Reverse procedure to install, noting the following:

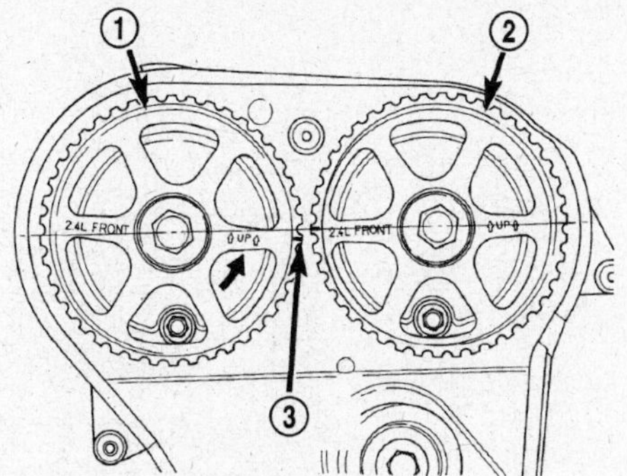

1 – CAMSHAFT SPROCKET-EXHAUST
2 – CAMSHAFT SPROCKET-INTAKE
3 – 1/2 NOTCH LOCATION

CR1060000854000X

Fig. 22 Camshaft sprocket alignment

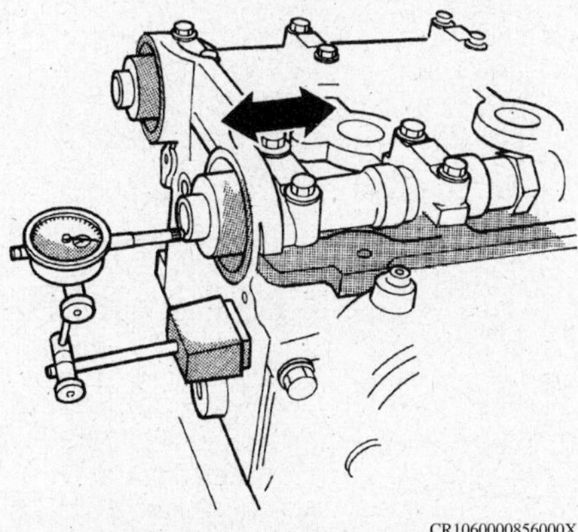

CR1060000856000X

Fig. 25 Camshaft end play

a. Ensure all surfaces are clean and free of oil and dirt.
b. Apply Mopar Gasket Maker, or equivalent, to oil pump, **Fig. 34.**
c. Install O-ring into oil pump body discharge passage.
d. Prime oil pump with engine oil before installation.

ACCESSORY DRIVE BELTS

The accessory drive consist of two Poly-V type drive belts. One belt drives the alternator, the other drives the power steering pump and air conditioning. The power steering and air conditioning belt is tensioned by an automatically controlled belt tensioner. The alternator belt is manually tensioned by an adjusting bolt and locknut.

COOLING SYSTEM BLEED

1. Open cooling system bleed valve, **Fig. 35.**
2. Attach a 48 inch length of clear hose to bleed valve, route hose away from accessory drive and radiator fan.
3. Place other end of hose into suitable container.
4. Fill cooling system with proper amount of recommended coolant.

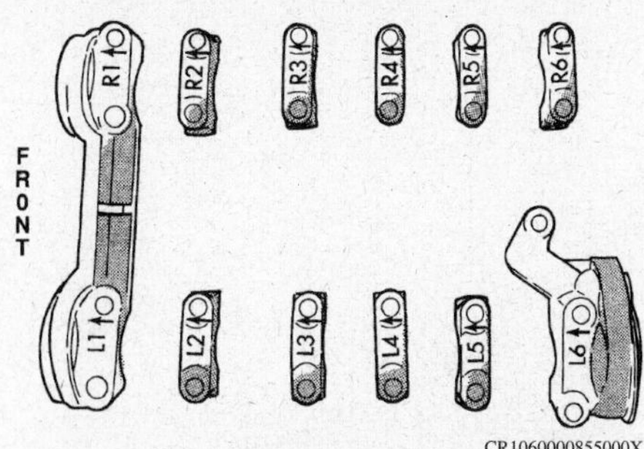

CR1060000855000X

Fig. 23 Camshaft bearing cap identification

5. Slowly continue filling system until a steady stream of coolant flows from attached hose on bleed valve.
6. Close bleed valve and remove hose.
7. Fill coolant level to top of pressure cap neck, then install pressure cap.
8. Fill coolant recovery bottle to at least Full Hot mark.
9. Perform 3–4 warm up and cool down cycles, top up coolant as required.

THERMOSTAT

REPLACE

1. Remove upper intake manifold as outlined under “Intake Manifold, Replace.”
2. Drain cooling system into suitable container to level below thermostat.
3. Remove upper radiator hose from outlet connector.
4. Remove coolant recovery system hose from outlet connector.
5. Remove thermostat/outlet connector.
6. Remove thermostat assembly.
7. Reverse procedure to install, noting the following:
   a. Clean sealing surfaces.
   b. Place new thermostat into coolant outlet connector aligning air bleed with location notch on outlet connector, **Fig. 36.**
   c. Install outlet connector, tighten to specification.

WATER PUMP

REPLACE

1. Drain cooling system into suitable container.
2. Remove timing belt as outlined under “Timing Belt, Replace.”
3. Remove camshaft sprockets and rear timing belt cover.
4. Reverse procedure to install, noting the following:
   a. Apply Mopar Dielectric Grease, or equivalent, to new O-ring before installation.
   b. Install O-ring gasket in water pump body groove. Ensure O-ring seal is properly seated in water pump groove.
   c. Assemble pump to block, install bolts and tighten to specification.

RADIATOR

REPLACE

1. Remove battery and battery tray.

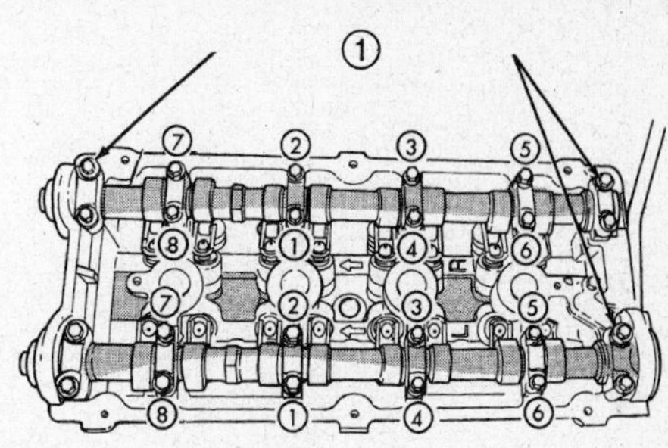

1 – REMOVE OUTSIDE BEARING CAPS FIRST

CR1060000857000X

Fig. 24 Camshaft bearing cap removal sequence

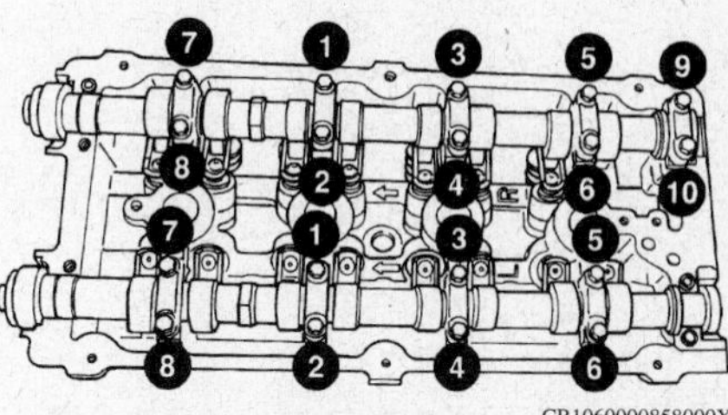

CR1060000858000X

Fig. 26 Camshaft bearing cap tightening sequence

2. Drain cooling system into suitable container.
3. Recover refrigerant as outlined under “Air Conditioning” chapter.
4. Remove grille and upper radiator support crossmember.
5. Remove upper radiator hose from radiator.
6. Raise and support vehicle.
7. Disconnect and cap automatic transmission cooler hoses.
8. Disconnect radiator fan motor electrical connector.
9. Remove lower radiator hose.
10. Lower vehicle.
11. Remove A/C lines from condenser.
12. Remove cooling module assembly (radiator, fan and A/C condenser), by lifting it up from engine compartment.
13. Use care to avoid damaging cooling fins and tubes.
14. Place cooling module on workbench and remove bolts attaching radiator fan to radiator.
15. Remove bolts attaching A/C condenser and transmission oil cooler to radiator.
16. Remove lower air shield from radiator.
17. Reverse procedure to install.

FUEL PUMP

REPLACE

The fuel pump is part of the fuel pump module assembly which includes the fuel pump, fuel pump reservoir, inlet strainer, fuel pressure regulator, fuel gauge sending unit, fuel supply line connection and the fuel filter. The fuel pump module is located on the top of the fuel tank. The fuel level sensor is the only serviceable component on

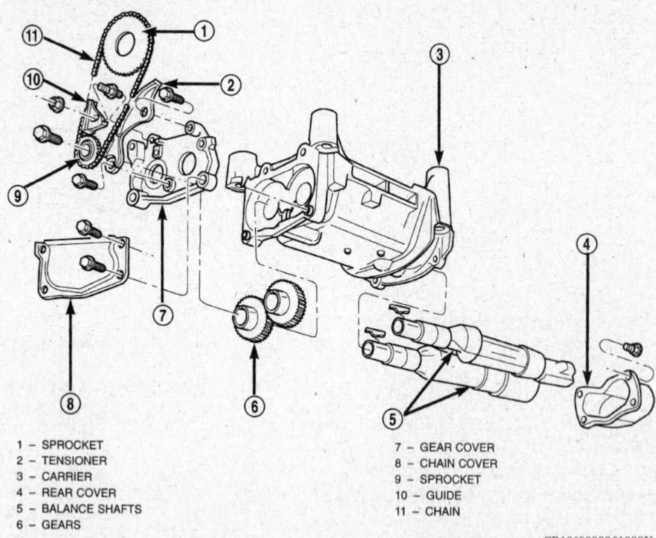

1 – SPROCKET
2 – TENSIONER
3 – CARRIER
4 – REAR COVER
5 – BALANCE SHAFTS
6 – GEARS
7 – GEAR COVER
8 – CHAIN COVER
9 – SPROCKET
10 – GUIDE
11 – CHAIN

CR1060000861000X

Fig. 27 Exploded view of balance shafts and carrier

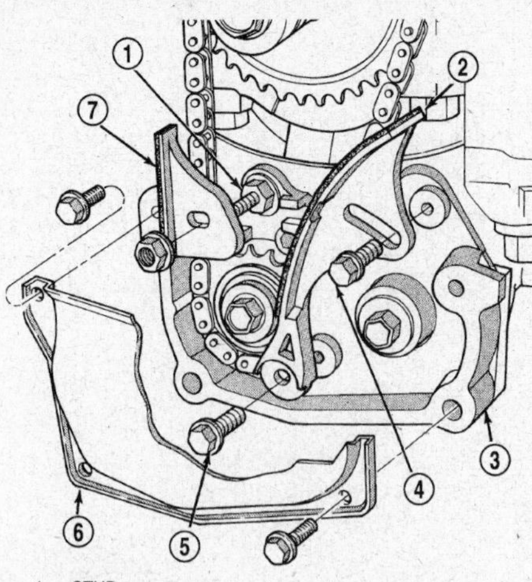

1 – STUD
2 – TENSIONER (ADJUSTER)
3 – GEAR COVER
4 – ADJUST SCREW
5 – PIVOT SCREW
6 – CHAIN COVER (CUTAWAY)
7 – GUIDE

CR1060000859000X

Fig. 28 Chain cover, guide & tensioner

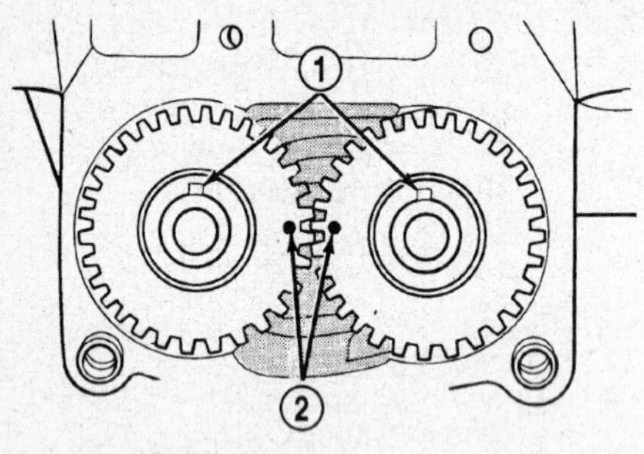

1 – KEY WAYS UP
2 – GEAR ALIGNMENT DOTS

CR1060000862000X

Fig. 29 Balance shaft gear timing marks

the fuel pump module. If any other components are faulty, the entire fuel pump module must be replaced.

1. Remove fuel filler cap and relieve fuel system pressure as outlined under "Precautions."
2. Remove air cleaner lid.
3. Disconnect inlet air temperature sensor and makeup air hose.
4. Raise and support vehicle.
5. Remove fuel tank as follows:
   a. Drain fuel into suitable container.
   b. Support fuel tank with a suitable support device such as a transmission jack.
   c. Disconnect fuel tank rubber fill hose.
   d. Remove bolts from fuel tank straps.
   e. Lower fuel tank and remove EVAP line and recirculation line.
   f. Remove vacuum line from LDP.
   g. Disconnect quick connect fuel line fitting in front of fuel tank.
   h. Unlock electrical connector, then disconnect connector.
   i. Remove hoses from EVAP canister.
   j. Remove fuel tank from vehicle.
6. Clean top of fuel tank to remove loose dirt and debris.
7. Disconnect fuel lines from fuel pump module.
8. Remove locknut to release fuel pump module using spanner wrench tool No. 6856, or equivalent.
9. Fuel reservoir of fuel pump module does not empty out when fuel tank is drained. Ensure residual fuel does not spill onto vehicle surfaces.
10. Remove fuel pump module and seal from tank.
11. Reverse procedure to install, tighten to specification.

TURBOCHARGER

REPLACE

If turbocharger is being replaced due to a bearing failure, replacement of oil pressure feed line is required. Oil return tube should be cleaned also.

1. Drain engine cooling system into suitable container.
2. Remove air cleaner housing and lid.
3. Disconnect clean air hose from turbocharger.
4. Disconnect throttle and speed control cables at throttle body.
5. Disconnect IAT, MAP, IAC motor, TP, ignition coil capacitor and upstream HO2 sensor electrical connectors.
6. Disconnect air inlet hose at throttle body.
7. Disconnect vacuum hoses from throttle body and upper intake manifold.
8. Remove upper intake manifold support bracket.
9. Remove upper intake manifold as outlined under "Intake Manifold, Replace." Cover lower intake manifold to prevent foreign objects from entering engine.
10. Remove turbocharger upper heat shield.
11. Disconnect oil supply line at turbocharger.
12. Disconnect coolant return line.
13. Disconnect vacuum hoses from turbocharger.
14. Raise and support vehicle.
15. Disconnect muffler ground strap, then

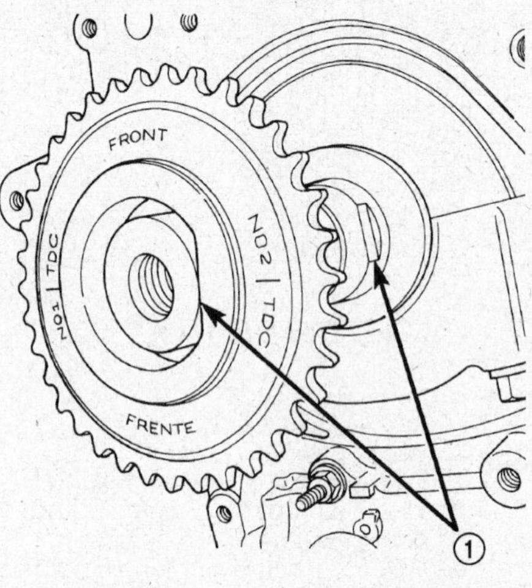

1 - ALIGN FLATS

CR1060000863000X

Fig. 30 Balance shaft sprocket alignment to crankshaft

the downstream oxygen sensor.

16. Remove bolts securing catalytic converter to exhaust manifold.
17. Remove catalytic converter and intermediate pipe as an assembly.
18. Remove turbocharger to charge air cooler hose assembly.
19. Remove turbocharger and elbow support brackets.
20. Remove oil return tube, then the turbocharger coolant supply line.
21. Remove turbocharger lower heat shield, then the elbow.
22. Remove lower exhaust manifold bolts, then lower vehicle.
23. Remove upper exhaust manifold bolts.
24. Remove turbocharger/exhaust manifold assembly from engine and cowl panel.
25. Reverse procedure to install. Use new exhaust manifold gasket positioning steel layer against cylinder head.

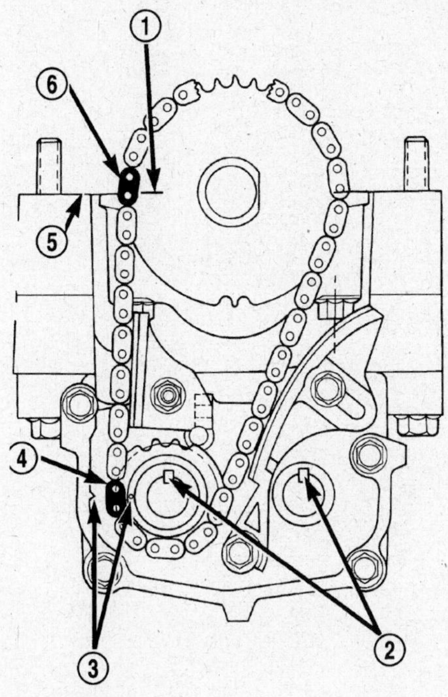

1 – MARK ON SPROCKET
2 – KEYWAYS UP
3 – ALIGN MARKS
4 – PLATED LINK
5 – PARTING LINE (BEDPLATE TO BLOCK)
6 – PLATED LINK

CR1060000864000X

Fig. 31 Balance shaft timing

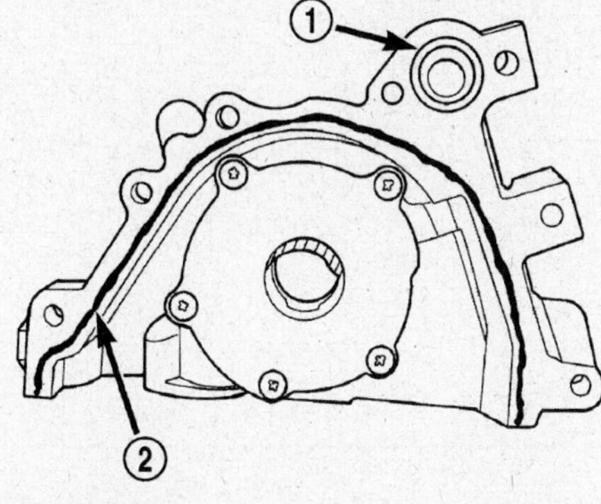

1 – O-RING
2 – SEALER LOCATION

CR1060000867000X

Fig. 34 Oil pump sealing

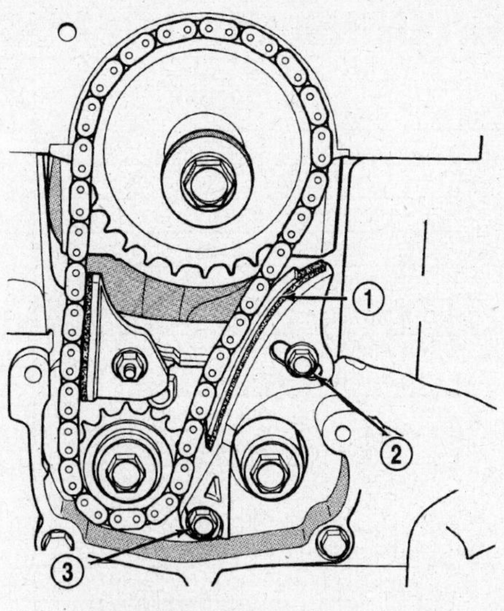

1 – 1MM (0.039 IN.) SHIM
2 – TENSIONER (ADJUSTER) BOLT
3 – PIVOT BOLT

CR1060000865000X

Fig. 32 Chain tensioner adjustment

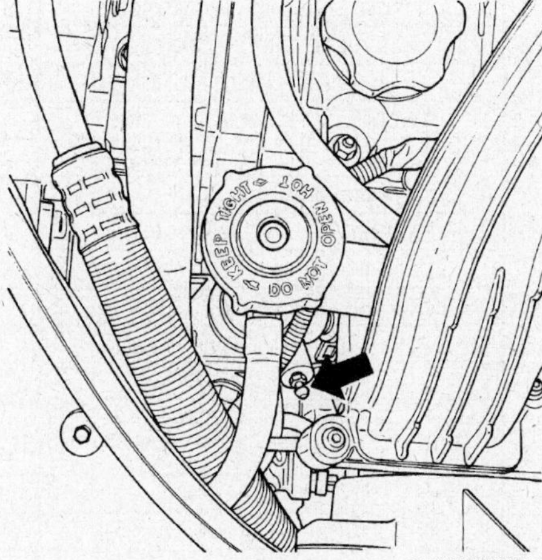

CR1080000288000X

Fig. 35 Cooling system bleed valve

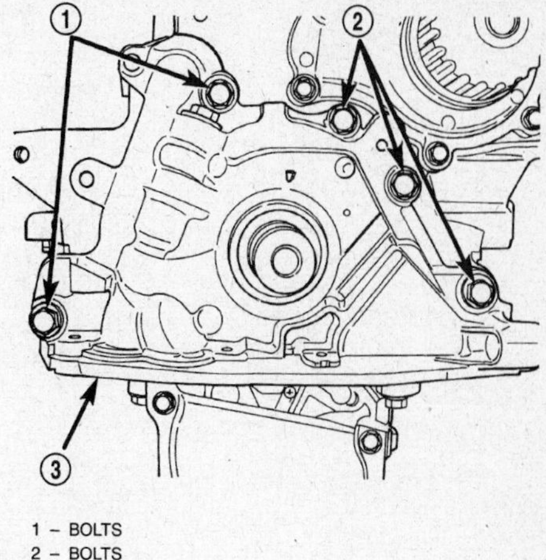

1 – BOLTS
2 – BOLTS
3 – OIL PUMP

CR1060000866000X

Fig. 33 Oil pump

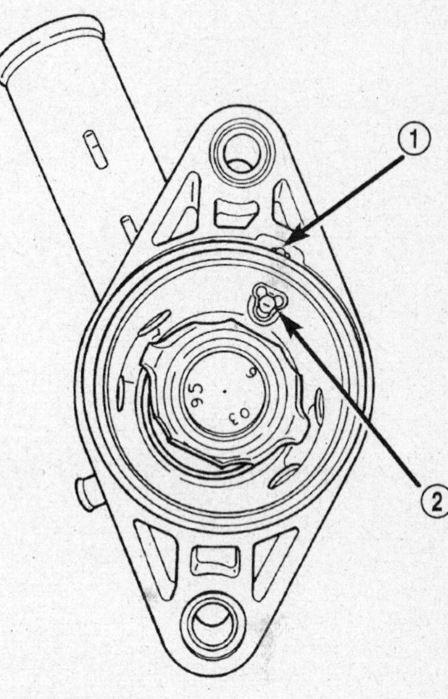

1 – LOCATOR NOTCH
2 – AIR BLEED

CR1080000289000X

Fig. 36 Thermostat installation

TIGHTENING SPECIFICATIONS

Year	Component	Torque Ft. Lbs.
2002–06	Balance Shaft Carrier	40
	Balance Shaft Chain Tensioner	105①
	Balance Shaft Gear Cover	105①
	Balance Shaft Sprockets	21
	Camshaft Bearing Caps (M-6)	105①
	Camshaft Bearing Caps (M-8)	18
	Catalytic Converter To Exhaust Manifold	21
	Coolant Line Banjo Bolt	22
	Coolant/Oil Line Brass Bolt	30
	Coolant/Oil Line Flared Fitting	23
	Connecting Rod Cap	20②
	Crankshaft Damper	100
	Crankshaft Main Bearing Cap (M-8)	21
	Crankshaft Main Bearing Cap (M-11)	55
	EGR Retainer Plate (Small Bolt)	95①
	EGR Retainer Plate (Large Bolt)	20
	Exhaust Manifold	17
	Exhaust Manifold/Turbocharger Assembly	21
	Exhaust Manifold Heat Shields	105①
	Exhaust Pipe To Manifold	21
	Flex Plate	70
	Fuel Pump Module Locknut	55
	Fuel Rail Assembly To Intake Manifold	18
	Intake Manifold (Lower)	105①
	Intake Manifold, Except Turbo (Upper)	105①
	Intake Manifold, Turbo (Upper)	21
	Motor Mount (L) Bracket To Body Rail	21
	Motor Mount (L) To Transaxle	87
	Motor Mount (R)	21
	Oil Filter Adapter	105①
	Oil Pan	105①
	Thermostat Outlet	110①
	Turbocharger Support Bracket	40
	Water Pump	105①

① — Inch lbs.
② — Plus ¼ turn.

Rear Axle & Suspension

NOTE: Refer To "Computer Relearn Procedures" Located In The Front Of This Manual When Battery Power To The Computer Has Been Interrupted.

INDEX

PRECAUTIONS

Battery Ground Cable

Prior to service, disconnect battery ground cable and isolate as required.

REAR AXLE

REPLACE

The automatic adjusting feature of this parking brake lever contains a clockspring loaded to approximately 19 lbs. Do not release the automatic adjuster lockout device unless the rear parking brake cables and equalizer are connected to the lever output cable. Keep hands out of automatic adjuster sector and pawl area.

Removal

1. Unclip air cleaner and move aside.
2. Block tires and wheels so vehicle does not move once parking brake lever is released.
3. Remove transmission shift knob.
4. Remove center console.
5. Grasp parking brake lever output cable, **Fig. 1,** and pull upward.
6. Continue pulling on cable until an appropriate sized pin punch (drill bit or locking pin) can be inserted sufficiently through hole in lefthand side of lever mounting bracket.
7. Slowly release output cable, there should be slack in cable.
8. Remove rear parking brake cables from parking brake equalizer.
9. Raise and support vehicle.
10. Remove both rear tires and wheel assemblies.
11. **On models equipped with drum brakes,** proceed as follows:
    a. Remove bolts securing drum brake flex hoses to axle trailing arms.
    b. Remove brake drum retaining clips, then the drums.
12. **On models equipped with rear disc brakes,** proceed as follows:
    a. Remove bolts securing disc brake flex hoses to trailing arms.
    b. Remove disc brake caliper guide pin bolts, then the calipers from disc brake adapters.
    c. Hang calipers out of way using suitable wire hanger or bungee cord.
    d. Remove brake rotor from rear hub and bearing.
13. **On all models,** remove dust cap from rear hub and bearing, **Fig. 2.**
14. Remove hub and bearing retaining nut from spindle, then the hub and bearing.
15. **On models equipped with rear disc brakes,** proceed as follows:
    a. Remove upper return spring and both shoe hold down clips.
    b. Spread rear parking brake shoes apart at top enough to clear shoe anchor.
    c. Remove parking brake shoes as an assembly from disc brake adapter.
16. **On models equipped with rear drum brakes,** proceed as follows:
    a. Remove parking brake cable from actuator lever.
    b. Remove actuator spring between brake shoe adjustment lever.
    c. Remove brake shoe and parking brake cable from rear brake support plate.
17. **On models equipped with rear disc brakes,** proceed as follows:
    a. Remove parking brake actuating lever from parking brake cable.
    b. Remove parking brake cable from rear disc brake adapter using ½ offset box wrench, **Fig. 3,** to compress fingers on cable retainer.
18. **On all models,** remove two bolts on each axle trailing arm securing cable and routing brackets to arm.
19. Pull cable through hole in trailing arm.
20. **On models equipped with anti-lock brakes,** remove bolts securing wheel speed sensors to disc brake adapters, then remove sensors.
21. **On all models,** remove four bolts securing each brake shoe support plate or disc brake adapter, and spindle to axle.
22. On each side of vehicle, remove support plate or disc brake adapter and spindle from axle. Hang support plate out of way using suitable wire hanger or bungee cord.
23. Remove bolt securing watts link bell crank to center of axle, **Fig. 4.**
24. Remove bolts securing stabilizer bar cushion retainers to rear axle, then the stabilizer bar.
25. Position a suitable transmission jack, or equivalent, under center of axle raising it enough to support axle.
26. Remove shock absorber lower mounting nuts and bolts at axles.
27. Lower transmission jack until coil springs can be removed from axle.
28. Remove coil springs and rubber isolators.
29. Scribe a line marking location of axle trailing arm bracket using an awl, side to side and front to rear, on body of vehicle.
30. Remove bolts securing trailing arm forward brackets to body of vehicle.
31. Remove axle from vehicle.

Installation

1. If removed, install trailing arm forward brackets on each side of trailing arm as follows:
    a. From above axle, place bracket down over axle trailing arm bushing aligning hole in bracket with center hole in bushing, **Fig. 4.**
    b. From outboard side of axle and bracket, push bolt through bracket and bushing. Trailing arm bracket through bolts must be installed from outside, in toward center of axle assembly.
    c. Install nut on inboard end of nut. Tighten nut until bracket has resistance when turned, but still moves independent of axle bushing. Fully tighten after vehicle is at curb height.
2. Center axle beam on transmission jack standing at axle removal height.
3. Swing trailing arms up aligning brackets with previously scribed marks, then install eight mounting bolts. Thread bolts in but do not tighten fully.
4. Tap trailing brackets as required to align with scribed marks, then **torque** bolts to 40 ft. lbs.

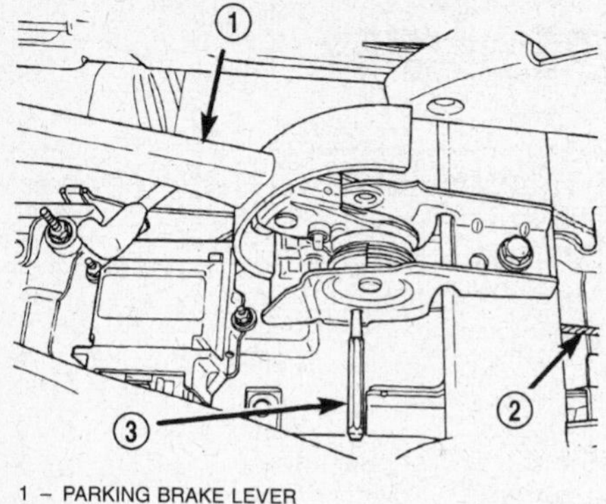

Fig. 1 Parking brake lever & output cable

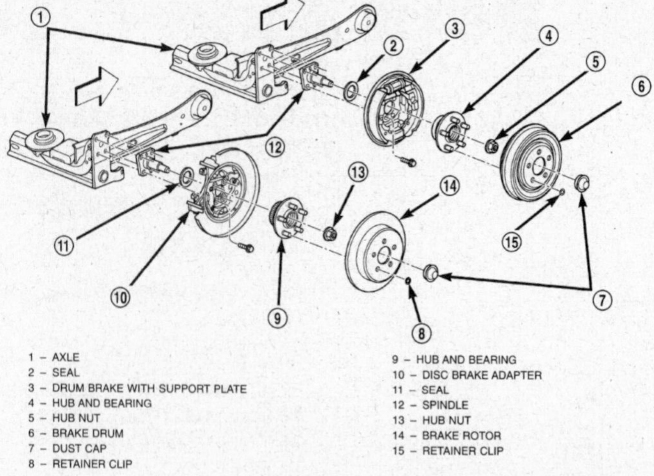

Fig. 2 Exploded view of rear axle assembly

5. Install a rubber isolator on each end of coil springs, wrapping rubber fingers around coil. Turn isolators until rubber abutment butts up against flat end of coil spring.
6. Both ends of coil spring are identical, either end of spring can be top or bottom.
7. Place coil springs on top of axle spring perches.
8. Coil springs require proper orientation to body when installed. To do this, turn coil springs and isolators until flat end of each upper spring coil lines up with an imaginary line running parallel with axle beam, **Fig. 5.**
9. Ensure upper coil springs end near outboard sides of vehicle and not 180° of that location.
10. Raise transmission jack guiding coil springs into spring mounting brackets on body of vehicle.
11. Raise jack until shock absorber lower mounting bolts can be installed through axle brackets and shock absorber lower mounting eyes.
12. Install washer and nut on each end of shock absorber lower mounting bolt. **Torque** mounting bolts to 50 ft. lbs.
13. Remove jack.
14. Hook lower ends of stabilizer bar cushion retainers into slots in back of axle, then rotate opposite end of retainers upward so mounting bolts can be installed.
15. Install mounting bolt through each cushion retainer into threads in rear axle.
16. **Torque** rear stabilizer bar cushion retainer bolts to 40 ft. lbs.
17. When installing watts links and bell crank to axle, ensure crank is correct side up. When mounted properly, the words "Back Up" should be able to be read from rear over top of axle, **Fig. 6.**
18. Install bolt from front securing watts link bell crank to center of axle. Place washer and nut on end of mounting bolt, **torque** to 90 ft. lbs.
19. On each side of vehicle, install spindle and support plate (drum brakes) or disc brake adapter on end of axle.
20. Clean threads of bolts used to mount brake shoe support plates or disc brake adapters and apply Mopar Thread Locker and Seal, or equivalent, to threads.
21. Install four bolts securing each brake shoe support plate or disc brake adapter, and spindle to axle, **torque** mounting bolts to 70 ft. lbs.
22. **On models equipped with anti-lock brakes,** install wheel speed sensors, **torque** bolts to 105 inch lbs.
23. **On all models,** guide end of each parking brake cable through hole in trailing arm toward brake.
24. Align cable routing brackets with their mounts on trailing arm. Install and **torque** mounting bolts to 100 inch lbs.
25. On each side of vehicle, install parking brake cable into brake support plate or rear disc brake adapter. Ensure locking fingers on cable retainer are expanded once cable is pushed all the way into support plate or brake adapter hole.
26. **On models equipped with drum brakes,** on each side of vehicle, install parking brake cable actuating lever and actuating spring to brake shoe and brake adjustment lever.
27. **On models equipped with rear disc brakes,** install parking brake shoe actuator lever on parking brake cable and parking brake shoe assemblies on disc brake adapter.
28. **On all models,** install hub and bearing on each rear spindle. Install new nut and **torque** to 160 ft. lbs.
29. Install hub and bearing dust cap.
30. Install brake drums or calipers and rotors.
31. Install rear wheel and tire assemblies.
32. Lower vehicle and install parking brake cables into equalizer.
33. Keeping your hands clear of automatic adjuster sector and pawl area, firmly grasp parking brake lever pin punch and quickly remove from parking brake lever mechanism.
34. Parking brake lever mechanism will automatically adjust parking brake cables.
35. Cycle parking brake lever once to position parking brake cables, then return lever to it's released position.
36. Ensure rear wheels rotate freely without excessive dragging with lever in it's released position.
37. Install center console and shift knob.
38. Apply parking brake and remove blocks from wheels and tires, then reinstall air cleaner.
39. Place vehicle on drive-on hoist or an alignment rack.
40. With vehicle at curb height, **torque** both trailing arm to mounting bracket pivot through bolts to 80 ft. lbs.
41. Inspect rear wheel alignment.

REAR AXLE PIVOT BUSHING

REPLACE

Removal

1. Raise and support vehicle.
2. Remove both rear tire and wheel assemblies.
3. Remove bolts securing rear brake flex hoses and wheel speed sensors, to vehicle body immediately behind axle trailing arm forward brackets.
4. Remove two bolts on each axle trailing arm securing parking brake cables and routing brackets to arm.
5. Move parking brake cables from their mounting positions away from bottom of trailing arm pivot bushing and forward brackets.
6. Remove bolt securing watts link bell crank to center of axle.
7. Position a suitable transmission jack, or equivalent, under center of axle raising it just enough to support axle.
8. Scribe a line marking location of axle trailing arm bracket using an awl, side to side and front to rear, on body of vehicle.
9. Remove bolts securing trailing arm froward brackets to body of vehicle.
10. Pry down on froward end of trailing arm and place a block of wood between top of arm and body of vehicle just rear of forward mounting bracket using lower

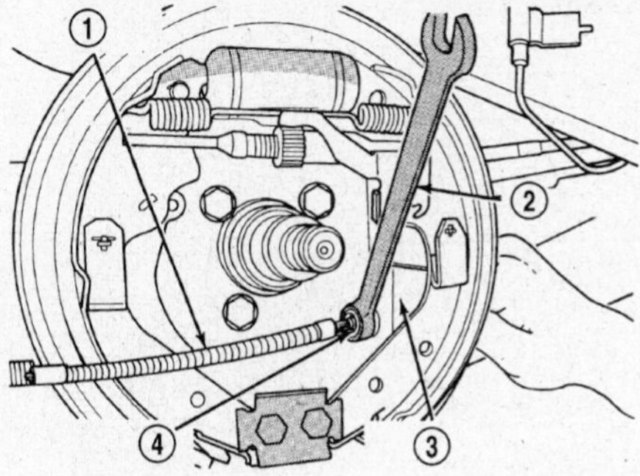

Fig. 3 Parking brake cable removal

shock mounts as a pivot point. Use care to avoid pinching hoses or cables.

11. Remove pivot through bolt securing forward bracket to trailing arm.
12. Place receiver tool No. 8405–1, or equivalent, on press tool No. C-4212F, or equivalent, and tighten set screw, **Fig. 7.**
13. When properly installed, screw drive on tool will be toward center of vehicle.
14. Curve on trailing arm prevents tool from being properly installed in opposite direction.
15. Tighten screw drive, pressing bushing from trailing arm.
16. Remove tool and bushing from trailing arm, discard bushing.

Installation

1. Apply Mopar Rubber Bushing Installation Lube to outside edges of new bushing and to inside surface of installation tool.
2. Place stepped end of installer on end of trailing arm bushing sleeve that has curved flange at arm, **Fig. 8.**
3. Place lubricated bushing inside large opening in installation tool.
4. Place bushing and tool as indicated, **Fig. 8.** When properly installed, screw drive on tool will be positioned toward center of vehicle.
5. Tighten screw drive, pressing bushing into trailing arm sleeve. Do not overly install bushing.
6. Push bushing in until freed from installer and centered in trailing arm sleeve. Outer lips of bushing must hang out past end of sleeve on each side of trailing arm.
7. Remove tools from arm.
8. Install trailing arm forward brackets on axle as follows:
    a. From above axle, place bracket down over axle trailing arm bushing aligning hole in bracket with center hole in bushing.
    b. From outboard side of axle and bracket, push bolt through bracket and bushing. Trailing arm bracket bolts must be installed from outside, in toward center of axle assembly or bolt threaded ends will contact body.
    c. Install nut on inboard end of bolt and tighten until bracket has resistance when turned but still moves independent of axle bushing.
9. Remove wood block between arm and body of vehicle.
10. Swing trailing arms up aligning brackets with scribed marks made previously.
11. Install all eight mounting bolts, thread bolts in but do not tighten fully.
12. Tap axle trailing arm brackets as required to align with scribed marks, then tighten to specification.
13. When installing watts link and bell crank, ensure crank is correct side up. When mounted properly, the words "Back Up" are readable from rear over top of axle.
14. Install bolt from front securing watts link bell crank to center of axle. Place washer and nut on mounting bolt and tighten to specification.
15. Move parking brake cable to their original location, align cable mounting brackets, then install mounting bolt and tighten to specification.
16. Ensure parking brake cable and grommet is still in proper position at body access hole.
17. Install brake flex hoses and speed sensors.
18. Install tires and wheels, then lower vehicle.
19. Place vehicle on an alignment rack or drive on hoist.
20. With vehicle at curb height, tighten both trailing arm to mounting bracket pivot through bolts to specification.

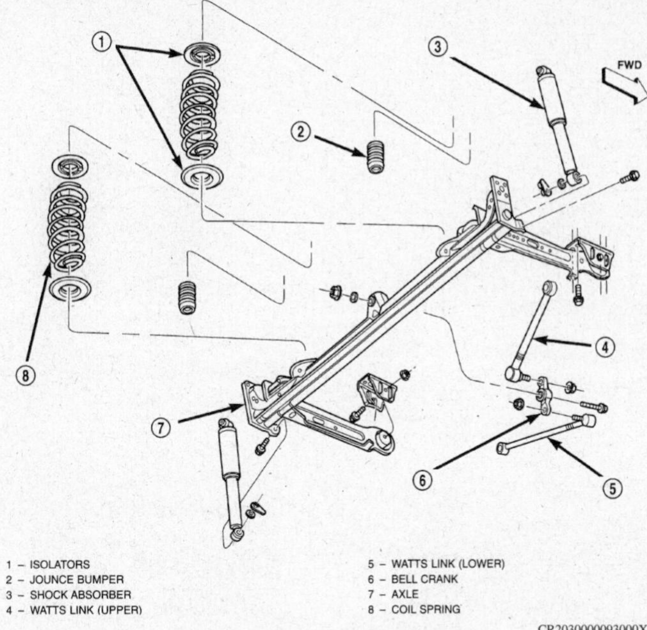

Fig. 4 Rear suspension

REAR HUB & BEARING

REPLACE

1. Raise and support vehicle.
2. Remove rear wheel and tire assembly.
3. **On models equipped with drum brakes,** remove brake drum retaining clips, then the brake drum.
4. **On models equipped with rear disc brakes,** proceed as follows:
    a. Remove brake caliper guide pin bolts, then the caliper.
    b. Hang caliper out of way using suitable wire hanger or bungee cord.
    c. Remove brake rotor retaining clips, then the brake rotor.
5. **On all models,** remove dust cap from hub and bearing.
6. Remove hub and bearing retaining nut from spindle, then the hub and bearing.
    a. Reverse procedure to install, noting the following:
    b. Install new hub and bearing nut, **torque** to 160 ft. lbs.
    c. Install caliper guide pin bolts, **torque** to 16 ft. lbs.
    d. Install wheels and tires, **torque** lug nuts to 100 ft. lbs.

SHOCK ABSORBER

REPLACE

1. Raise and support vehicle.
2. Remove tire and wheel assembly.
3. Position a suitable transmission jack, or equivalent, under center of axle raising it enough to support axle.
4. Remove shock absorber lower mounting bolt and nut at axle.
5. Remove upper mounting bolt, then the shock absorber from vehicle.
6. Reverse procedure to install, tighten bolts and nuts to specification.

COIL SPRING

REPLACE

1. Raise and support vehicle.
2. Remove both rear tire and wheel assemblies.

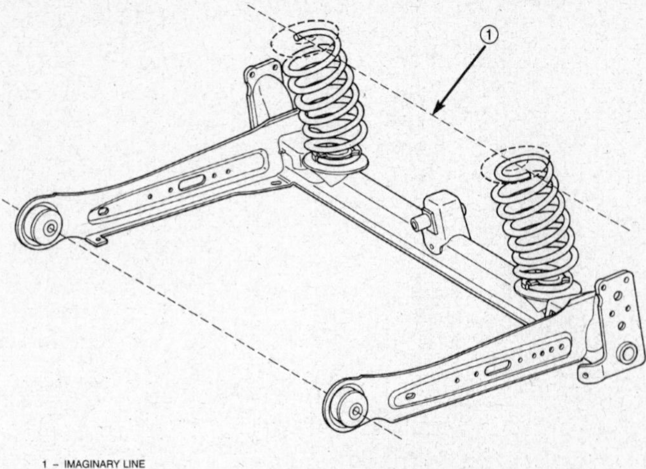

Fig. 5 Coil spring orientation

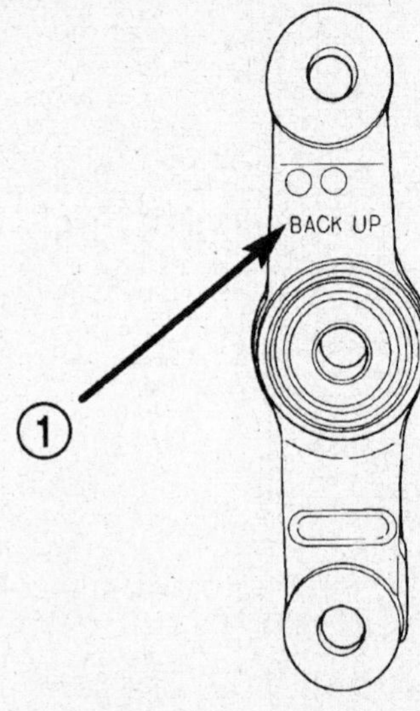

Fig. 6 Bellcrank

3. Remove bolt securing watts link bell crank, **Fig. 4,** to center of axle.
4. Remove stabilizer bar from axle.
5. Position a suitable transmission jack, or equivalent, under center of axle, raising it enough to support axle.
6. Remove shock absorber lower mounting bolts and nuts at axle.
7. Lower transmission jack until coil springs can be removed from axle.
8. Remove coil springs and rubber isolators.
9. Reverse procedure to install, tighten all nuts and bolts to specification.

STABILIZER BAR

REPLACE

1. Raise and support vehicle.
2. Remove both rear wheel and tire assemblies.
3. Remove nut from end of each rear stabilizer link bolt fastening bar to link, **Fig. 9.**
4. Pull bolt out far enough to free stabilizer. While holding rear stabilizer bar, remove bolts that secure cushion retainers to rear axle.
5. Remove cushion retainers, cushions and stabilizer bar from vehicle.
6. Remove cushions from stabilizer bar.
7. Reverse procedure to install, tighten to specification.

JOUNCE BUMPER

REPLACE

1. Raise and support vehicle.
2. Grasp jounce bumper and with a twisting motion, remove jounce bumper from bracket mounted to body.
3. Reverse procedure to install, do not use any type of lubricant or premature jounce bumper failure may occur.

SPINDLE

REPLACE

Removal

1. Raise and support vehicle.
2. Remove rear tire and wheel assembly.
3. **On models equipped with drum brakes,** remove bolts securing drum brake flex hose to trailing arm, then the brake drum retaining clips and drum.
4. **On models equipped with rear disc brakes,** remove bolts securing flex hose to trailing arm, rear brake caliper and rear rotor. Hang caliper out of way using suitable wire hanger or bungee cord.
5. **On all models,** remove dust cap from rear hub and bearing.
6. Remove hub and bearing retaining nut, then the hub and bearing.
7. Remove two bolts on each axle trailing arm securing parking brake cable and routing bracket to axle trailing arm.
8. **On models equipped with anti-lock brakes,** remove wheel speed sensor from adapter.
9. **On all models,** remove four bolts securing brake shoe support plate or disc brake adapter and spindle to axle.
10. Move support plate or disc brake adapter away from axle, loosen spindle from axle and remove from back of support plate or disc brake adapter.
11. Reverse procedure to install, tighten all nuts and bolts to specification.

WATTS LINK

REPLACE

Removal

1. Raise and support vehicle.
2. If lower watts link is being removed, proceed as follows:
   a. Remove nut securing bell crank pivot bolt in center of axle.
   b. With bolt still installed, slide bell crank away from axle just far enough to remove nut securing lower link to bell crank.
3. Remove nut securing ball joint to bell crank.
4. Install joint removal tool No. MB991113, or equivalent, on link ball joint at bell crank and release ball joint from bell crank.
5. Remove bolt securing link to bracket on body of vehicle, remove link.

Installation

When installing the link, do not attempt to turn the ball joint end of the link independently.

1. Ensure ball joint end is properly positioned for mounting to bell crank, then install link into bracket on body of vehicle.
2. Install bolt (and flag nut for upper link) securing link to bracket, do not fully tighten at this time.
3. Upper link extends from righthand side of vehicle to upper end of bell crank, lower link extends from lefthand side of vehicle to lower end of bell crank.
4. Install upper or lower link to bell crank.
5. Install nut on ball joint stud and tighten to specification.
6. If lower link is being installed, slide bell crank pivot bolt all the way through axle, place washer and nut on pivot bolt and tighten to specification.
7. When installing watts links or bell crank, ensure crank is properly positioned. When mounted properly, words "Back Up" should be readable from rear over top of axle.
8. Lower vehicle.
9. Place on alignment rack or drive on hoist.
10. With suspension at curb height, tighten link mounting bolt at body bracket to specification.

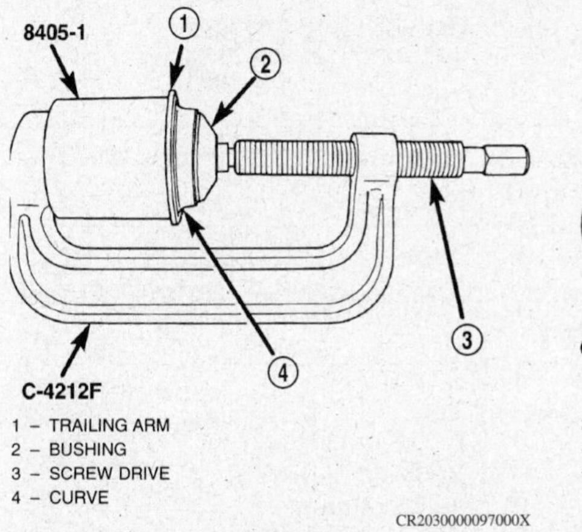

Fig. 7 Rear axle pivot bushing removal

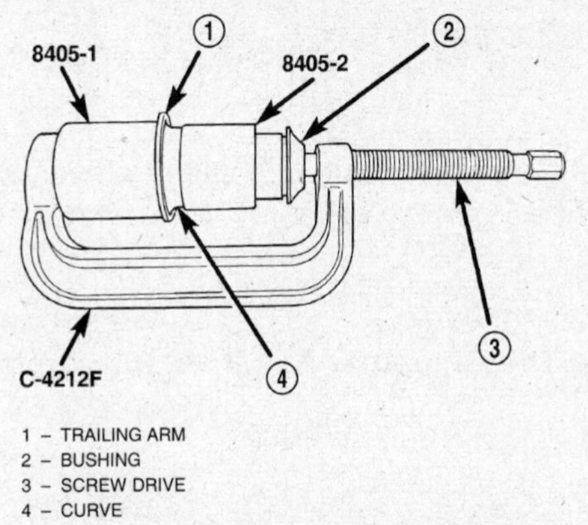

Fig. 8 Rear axle pivot bushing installation

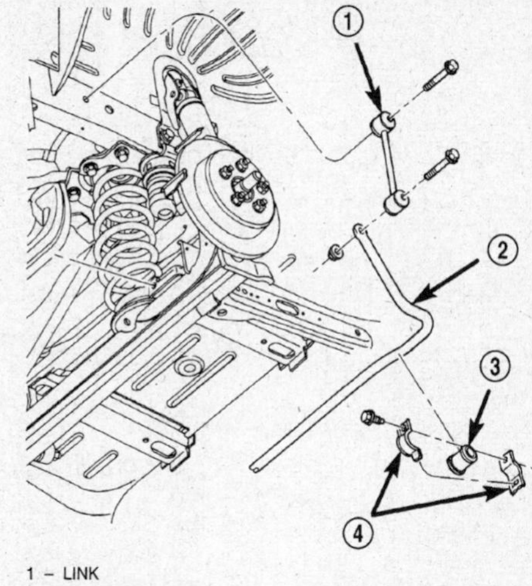

Fig. 9 Rear stabilizer bar & link

TIGHTENING SPECIFICATIONS

Year	Component	Torque Ft. Lbs.
2002–06	Caliper Guide Pin	16
	Hub & Bearing Retaining Nut	160
	Lug Nuts	100
	Parking Brake Cable Routing Brackets & Mounts	100①
	Shock Absorber Lower Mounting	65
	Shock Absorber Upper Mounting	73
	Stabilizer Bar Cushion Retainer	45
	Trailing Arm Mounting	40
	Trailing Arm To Mounting Bracket Pivot	90
	Watts Link Ball Joint Stud	10②
	Watts Link Bell Crank To Axle	90
	Watts Link Mounting Bolt At Body	60
	Watts Link Pivot Bolt	110
	Wheel Speed Sensor	105①

① — Inch lbs.
② — Plus 180°.

Front Suspension & Steering

NOTE: On Air Bag Equipped Models, Refer To "Air Bag System Precautions" Located In The Front Of This Manual For System Disarming & Arming Procedures.

NOTE: Refer To "Computer Relearn Procedures" Located In The Front Of This Manual When Battery Power To The Computer Has Been Interrupted.

INDEX

PRECAUTIONS

Air Bag Systems

Refer to "Air Bag System Precautions" in the front of this manual for system disarming and arming procedures.

WHEEL BEARING

REPLACE

Removal and installation of wheel bearing and hub from the steering knuckle can only be done with the steering knuckle removed from the vehicle.

1. Remove steering knuckle as outlined under "Steering Knuckle, Replace."
2. Three wheel studs across from one another must be removed from flange hub.
3. Rotate hub to align each wheel mounting stud with notch in bearing retainer plate.
4. Press three wheel mounting studs out of hub flange using stud removal tool No. C-4150A, or equivalent, **Fig. 1.**
5. Remove studs from hub through open notch in hub, **Fig. 2.**
6. Rotate hub so stud mounting holes in hub are facing, **Fig. 3.**
7. Install bearing splitter tool No. 1130, or equivalent, between hub and bearing retainer plate, **Fig. 3.**
8. Hand tighten nuts to hold bearing splitter in place on steering knuckle.
9. Place steering knuckle face down in a suitable arbor press supported by bearing splitter, **Fig. 4.**
10. Remove hub from wheel bearing using press tool No. 6644–2, or equivalent. Bearing race will normally come out with hub.
11. Remove bearing splitter from steering knuckle.
12. Remove bearing retainer plate from steering knuckle.
13. Place steering knuckle back in arbor press face down and press wheel bearing out of steering knuckle.
14. Use bearing splitter to remove race that is still pressed onto hub.
15. Reverse procedure to install, tighten all nuts and bolts to specification.

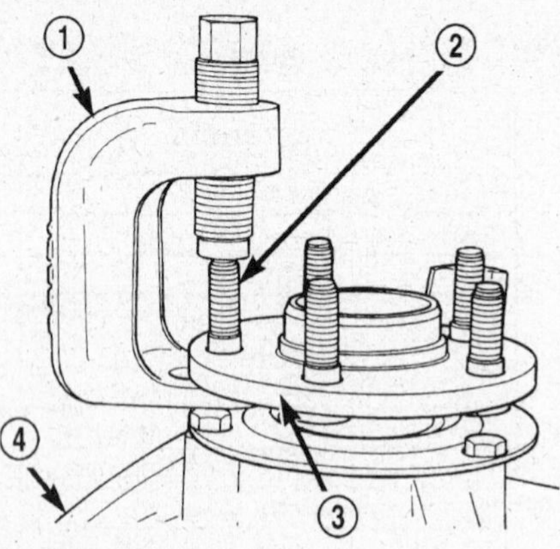

1 – SPECIAL TOOL 4150A
2 – WHEEL MOUNTING STUD
3 – HUB FLANGE
4 – STEERING KNUCKLE

CR2020000159000X

Fig. 1 Wheel stud removal

BALL JOINT

REPLACE

1. Remove lower control arm as outlined under "Control Arm, Replace."
2. Pry seal off of boot of ball joint using a screwdriver or other suitable pry tool.
3. Position receiver tool No. 6908–2, or equivalent, on a hydraulic press to support lower control arm.
4. Place control arm on top of support tool so that bottom of ball joint sets into receiver cup.
5. Place larger end of adapter tool No. 6804, or equivalent, on top of ball joint.
6. Press ball joint completely out of lower control arm using a suitable hydraulic press, into receiver.
7. Remove tools, ball joint and arm from hydraulic press.
8. Reverse procedure to install, noting the following:
   a. When installing ball joint, position ball joint so that notch in joint is facing lower control arm front isolator bushing.
   b. When installing sealing boot on ball joint, position upward lip on outside perimeter of seal boot outward away from control arm.
   c. If ball joint is equipped with a grease fitting, joint will need to be lubricated once control arm has been installed.

COIL SPRING & STRUT SERVICE

Removal

1. Raise and support vehicle.
2. Remove tire and wheel assembly.
3. If both strut assemblies are to be removed, mark righthand and lefthand assemblies for installation reference.
4. Remove screw attaching ground strap to rear of strut.
5. **On models equipped with ABS system,** remove screws attaching ABS wheel speed sensor to rear of strut.
6. **On all models,** remove two bolts attaching strut to steering knuckle.
7. Strut assembly to steering knuckle attaching bolts are serrated and must not be turned during removal. Hold bolts stationary in steering knuckle while removing nuts, then tap bolts out with a suitable punch.
8. Lower vehicle just enough to open hood without letting tires touch floor.
9. Remove three nuts attaching upper mount to vehicles strut tower, then the strut assembly from vehicle.
10. If both struts are being serviced at the

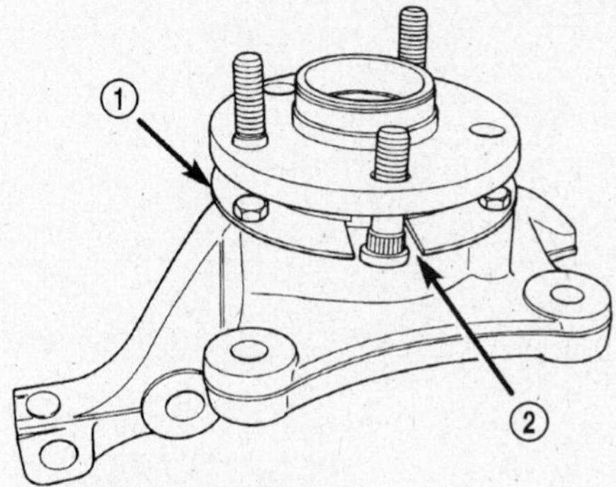

Fig. 2 Wheel bearing retainer notch

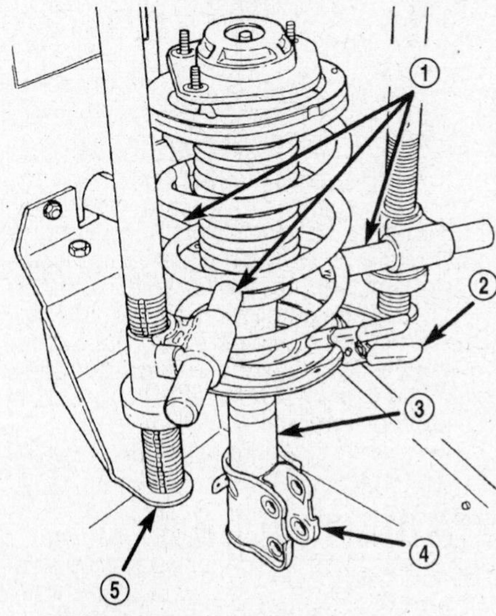

Fig. 5 Strut assembly in compressor tool (lower)

same time, mark springs and struts for assembly reference.

11. Position strut assembly in suitable coil spring compressor following manufacturers instructions.
12. Set lower hooks, then upper hooks, **Fig. 5.**
13. Position strut clevis bracket straight outward away from spring compressor.
14. Place a clamp on lower end of coil spring, so that strut is held in place once strut shaft nut is removed.
15. **Do not remove strut shaft nut before compressing spring.**
16. Compress coil spring until all coil spring tension is relieved from upper mount.
17. **Do not use impact or high speed tools to remove strut shaft nut. Damage to strut internal bearings may occur.**
18. When spring is sufficiently compressed, install strut nut tool No. 6864, or equivalent, on strut shaft retaining nut, **Fig. 6.**

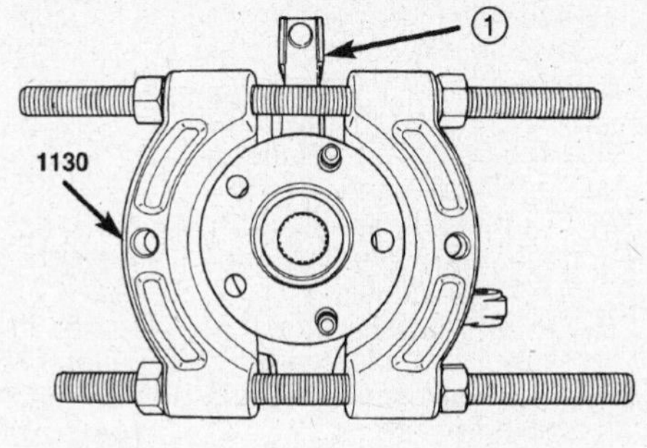

Fig. 3 Bearing splitter installation

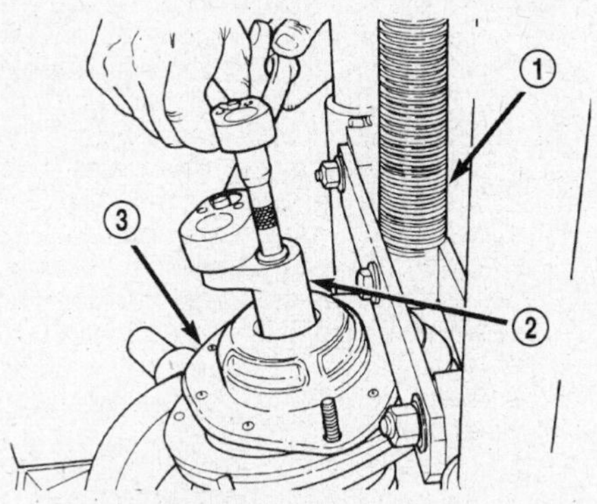

Fig. 6 Shaft nut replacement

19. Install socket on hex on end of strut shaft.
20. Hold strut shaft from turning and remove nut from shaft.
21. Remove upper mount from strut, **Fig. 7.**
22. Remove upper spring seat and bearing along with upper spring isolator as an assembly.
23. Remove dust shield, then the jounce bumper from strut shaft by pulling each straight up.
24. Remove clamp on bottom of coil spring, then the strut out through bottom of coil spring.
25. Remove lower spring isolator from lower spring seat on strut.
26. Release tension from coil spring and remove from compressor tool.

Installation

1. Inspect strut assembly components for the following:
   a. Inspect strut for signs of shaft binding over the full stroke of the shaft.
   b. Inspect jounce bumper for cracks and sign of deterioration.
   c. Inspect upper mount for cracks and distortion and it's studs for signs of damage.
   d. Inspect upper spring seat and bearing for cracks or distortion.

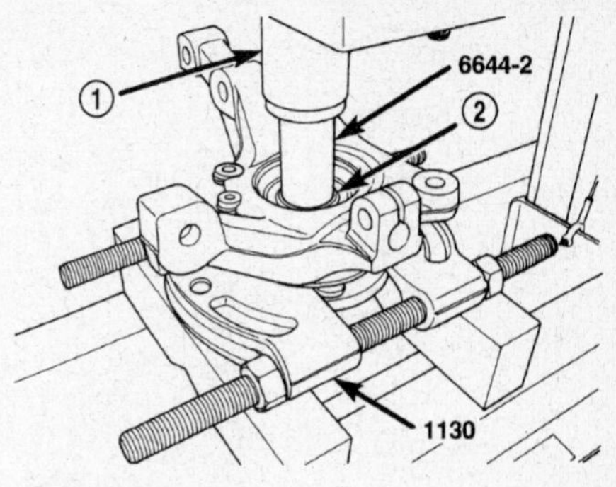

Fig. 4 Steering knuckle positioning in press

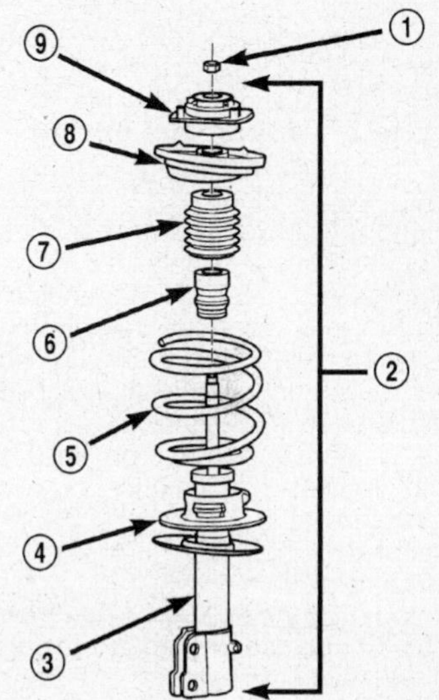

Fig. 7 Exploded view of strut assembly

   e. Inspect for binding of upper spring seat and bearing pivot bearing.
   f. Inspect dust shield for rips and deterioration.
   g. Inspect upper and lower spring isolators for material deterioration and distortion.
   h. Inspect coil spring for signs of damage to coating.
2. Place coil spring in compressor following manufacturers instructions.
3. Before compressing spring, rotate spring so end of top coil is directly in front, **Fig. 8.**
4. Slowly compress coil spring until enough room is available for strut assembly.
5. Install lower spring isolator on lower spring seat of strut.
6. Install strut through bottom of coil

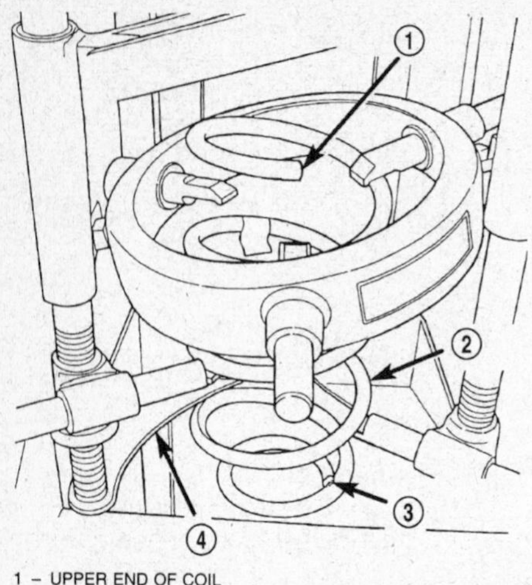

Fig. 8 Upper coil spring positioning

spring until lower spring seat contacts lower end of coil spring.

7. Rotate strut as required until clevis bracket is positioned straight outward away from compressor, **Fig. 5,** then install clamp on lower end of coil spring and strut so strut is held in place.
8. Install jounce bumper on strut shaft with smaller end pointing downward toward lower seat.
9. Install dust shield on strut shaft. Bottom of dust shield will snap to retainer on top of strut housing.
10. Install upper spring isolator on upper spring seat and bearing.
11. Install upper spring seat and bearing on top of coil spring.
12. Position notch formed into upper edge of upper seat straight out away from compressor, **Fig. 9,** so it lines up with very end of coil spring coil.
13. Install strut upper mount over strut shaft and onto top of upper spring seat and bearing.
14. Position mount so that third mounting stud on mounting top is inward toward compressor, opposite of clevis bracket.
15. Loosely install retaining nut on strut shaft.
16. Install strut nut socket on strut shaft retaining nut.
17. Install socket on hex end of strut shaft.
18. While holding strut shaft from turning, tighten strut shaft retaining nut to specification.
19. Slowly release tension from coil spring, ensure upper mount and seat and bearing are properly aligned.
20. Verify that upper mount does not bind.
21. Remove clamp from lower end of coil spring and strut.
22. Remove strut assembly from compressor tool.
23. Install strut assembly into strut tower, then the three nuts on mounting studs and tighten to specification.
24. Close hood of vehicle.
25. Position lower end of strut assembly in line with upper end of steering knuckle and align mounting holes.
26. Install two attaching bolts with nuts facing toward front of vehicle.
27. Holding bolts in place, tighten nuts to specification.
28. **On models equipped with ABS,** attach wheel sensor to rear of strut, tighten to specification.
29. **On all models,** attach ground strap to rear of strut, tighten to specification.
30. Install tire and wheel assembly and lower vehicle.

CONTROL ARM

REPLACE

1. Raise and support vehicle.
2. Remove front tire and wheel assembly.
3. Remove both stabilizer links.
4. Rotate forward ends of stabilizer bar downward. It may be required to loosen stabilizer bar cushion retainer bolts to ease any turning resistance.
5. Remove nut and pinch bolt clamping ball joint stud to steering knuckle, then separate ball joint from steering knuckle.
6. If lower righthand arm is being serviced, proceed as follows:
   a. Remove screws fastening front fascia to reinforcement as required to access drive belt splash shield forward fastener screw.
   b. Remove drive belt splash shield fasteners, then the splash shield.
   c. Remove pencil strut from righthand front corner of crossmember and body.
   d. Remove engine torque strut.
7. Remove front pivot bolt attaching lower control arm to front suspension crossmember.
8. Remove rear pivot bolt attaching lower control arm to front suspension crossmember and frame rail.
9. Remove lower control arm from crossmember.
10. Reverse procedure to install, tighten all nuts and bolts to specification.

STEERING KNUCKLE

REPLACE

1. Raise and support vehicle.
2. Remove front tire and wheel assembly.
3. Remove cotter pin, locknut and spring washer from hub nut.
4. Remove front disc brake caliper and adapter as an assembly.
5. Remove brake rotor from steering knuckle.
6. Remove tie rod end from steering knuckle with suitable ball joint/tie rod removal tool.
7. Remove tie rod heat shield.
8. Remove nut and pinch bolt clamping ball joint stud to steering knuckle.
9. Strut to steering knuckle attaching bolts are serrated and must not be turned during removal. Hold bolts stationary in knuckle while removing nuts, then tap out bolts with suitable punch.
10. Remove two bolts attaching strut to steering knuckle.

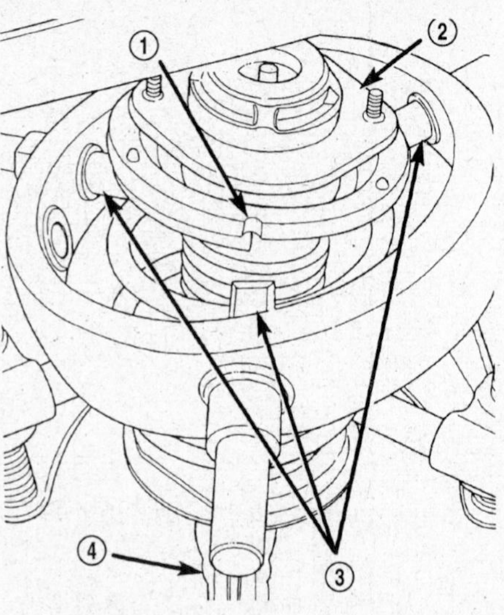

Fig. 9 Strut assembly in compressor (upper)

11. Separate ball joint stud from steering knuckle by prying down on lower control arm and up against ball joint boss on steering knuckle.
12. Do not allow driveshaft to hang from inner CV joint. Axle must be supported to keep joint from separating during knuckle removal.
13. Reverse procedure to install.

STABILIZER BAR

REPLACE

1. Raise and support vehicle.
2. Remove both stabilizer bar links from vehicle by holding upper nut with wrench and turning link bolt.
3. Remove stabilizer bar cushion retainer bolts and retainers.
4. Remove stabilizer bar with cushions attached.
5. Reverse procedure to install, noting the following:
   a. Inspect cushions and links for excessive cracks, wear or damage. Replace as required.
   b. Clean threads of stabilizer bar link bolts and apply Mopar Lock and Seal, or equivalent.
   c. It may be required to put vehicle on platform hoist or alignment rack to gain access to stabilizer bar mounting bolts with vehicle at curb height.

POWER STEERING GEAR

REPLACE

Removal

1. Place steering wheel in straight ahead position.
2. Lock in position with suitable steering wheel holder.

3. Remove silencer pad below knee blocker panel below steering column.
4. Fold down and remove knee blocker.
5. Remove steering column coupling retainer pin, back off pinch bolt nut and remove steering column coupling pinch bolt (nut is not removable).
6. Separate upper and lower steering column couplings.
7. Raise and support vehicle.
8. Remove both front tire and wheel assemblies.
9. Remove nuts attaching both outer tie rods to steering knuckles.
10. Remove both outer tie rods from steering knuckles using suitable joint removal tool.
11. Remove tie rod heat shields.
12. Remove wiring harness connector from power steering fluid pressure switch.
13. Back out tube nut securing power steering fluid pressure hose to gear.
14. Disconnect cooler hose from power steering gear fitting.
15. Remove cooler tube from righthand routing clip.
16. Remove screws securing cooler to front suspension crossmember. Allow cooler to hang out of way.
17. Remove pencil strut from righthand corner of crossmember and body of vehicle.
18. Remove washer behind strut from torque strut bolt.
19. Remove screws fastening front fascia to reinforcement as required in order to access drive belt splash shield forward fastener screw.
20. Remove drive belt splash shield.
21. Remove bolt mounting engine torque strut to righthand forward corner of front suspension crossmember.
22. Scribe a line marking location of front suspension crossmember to body of vehicle.
23. If front suspension crossmember location is not marked before removal, alignment settings will be lost.
24. Position a suitable transmission jack under center of front suspension crossmember and raise it to support bottom of crossmember.
25. Loosen all six bolts attaching front suspension crossmember to frame rails of vehicle.
    a. **Do not completely remove two mounting bolts going through lower control arm rear isolator bushings.**
    b. Back two bolts out just enough to disengage the threaded tapping plates in body of vehicle.
    c. Completely remove other four bolts.
26. Lower front suspension crossmember enough to allow power steering gear to be removed from rear of crossmember. Do not let crossmember hang from lower control arms.
27. Remove roll pin securing steering column lower coupling to power steering gear pinion shaft.
28. Push steering column lower coupling up and off of power steering gear pinion shaft.

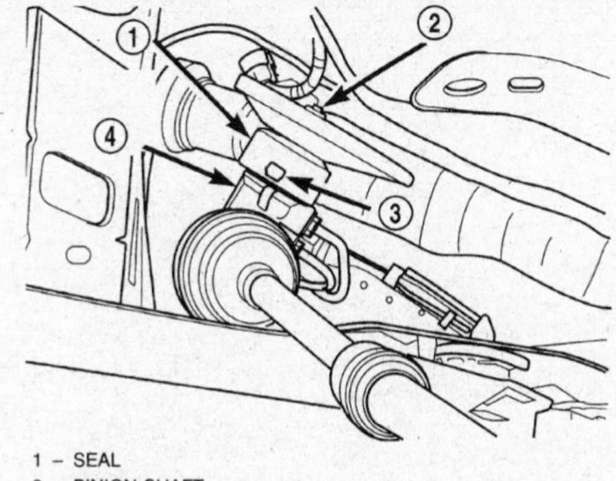

1 – SEAL
2 – PINION SHAFT
3 – TAB
4 – POWER STEERING GEAR

CR6020000212000X

Fig. 10 Pinion shaft dash cover seal

29. Release pinion shaft dash cover seal from tabs cast into power steering gear housing and remove seal from power steering gear.
30. Remove four bolts attaching power steering gear to front suspension crossmember.
31. Remove power steering gear from suspension crossmember.

Installation

1. Install steering gear on front suspension crossmember, tighten mounting bolts to specification.
2. Install pinion shaft dash cover seal over power steering pinion shaft and onto power steering gear housing.
3. Align holes on each side of seal with tabs cast into power steering gear housing, **Fig. 10.**
4. With steering column lower coupling pushed partway up through it's hole in dash panel, match flat on inside of steering column lower coupling to flat on power steering gear pinion shaft and slide coupling onto top of pinion shaft.
5. Align roll pin hole in coupling with groove in pinion shaft and install roll pin.
6. Center power steering rack in it's travel.
7. Raise front suspension crossmember and power steering gear until crossmember contacts it's mounting spot against body and frame rails.
8. Guide steering column lower coupling up through it's hole in dash panel.
9. Start two crossmember bolts through lower control arm rear isolator bushings into tapping plates mounted in body.
10. Install two front and two rear mounting bolts.
11. Lightly tighten all six mounting bolts to approximately 20 inch lbs., to hold front crossmember in position.
12. Tap front suspension into position previously scribed onto body using a soft tipped hammer.
13. Tighten two bolts through lower control arm rear isolator bushings to specification, then the remaining four bolts to specification.
14. Fasten engine torque strut to righthand forward corner of front suspension crossmember.
15. Install pencil strut and tighten to specification.
16. Install drive belt splash shield and attach front fascia screws.
17. Wipe the open power steering hose ends and power steering gear ports using a lint free towel.
18. Replace pressure hose O-ring, lubricate with power steering fluid.
19. Install power steering cooler.
20. Connect power steering fluid cooler hose onto steel gear fitting, **Fig. 11.**
21. Secure clamp on hose past bead on steel fitting.
22. Attach power steering fluid pressure hose to it's port on power steering gear, **Fig. 11,** tighten to specification.
23. Forward of steering gear, power steering fluid pressure hose routes between front suspension crossmember and driveshaft. When tightening pressure hose tube nut to steering gear, pressure hose must be positioned so that it's final routing offers .157–.393 inch clearance measured at pressure hose steel to rubber coupling.
24. Connect wiring harness connector from power steering fluid pressure switch.
25. Install tie rods and heat shields to steering knuckle, tighten to specification.
26. Install tire and wheel assemblies, lower vehicle.
27. Verify that grease is present on lip of dash to coupling seal where it contacts coupling's plastic collar.
28. Inside passenger compartment, connect steering column lower coupling to steering column upper coupling.
29. Install coupling pinch bolt, tighten to specification.
30. Remove steering wheel holder.
31. Install knee blocker and silencer pad.
32. Add suitable power steering fluid and bleed system as follows:
    a. Fluid level should read between MIN. COLD and MAX. COLD when fluid temperature is approximately 70–80°F.
    b. Fill fluid to proper level and let set for at least two minutes.
    c. Start engine, run for a few seconds, then shut off.
    d. Add fluid as required and repeat.
    e. Raise and support vehicle until front wheels are off of ground.
    f. Start engine and slowly turn steering wheel righthand and lefthand lightly contacting wheel stops.
    g. Add power steering fluid as required, lower vehicle.
    h. Turn steering wheel from lock to lock, stop engine.
    i. Inspect fluid level and refill as required.
    j. If fluid is extremely foamy, allow vehicle to stand a few minutes and repeat procedure.

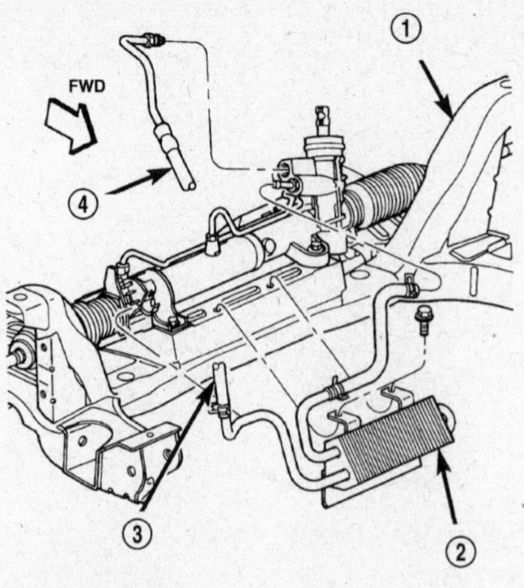

Fig. 11 Cooler & fluid hose mounting

TIGHTENING SPECIFICATIONS

Year	Component	Torque Ft. Lbs.
2002–06	Ball Joint Stud Pinch Bolt	70
	Crossmember Mounting Bolts	113
	Crossmember Through Bolts (To Lower Control Arm)	185
	Ground Strap To Strut	120①
	Lower Control Arm Front Pivot	120
	Lower Control Arm Rear Pivot	185
	Lug Nuts	100
	Pencil Strut Nuts	43
	Power Steering Cooler To Crossmember	90①
	Power Steering Coupling Pinch Bolt	21
	Power Steering Gear Mounting	45
	Power Steering Pressure Hose To Steering Gear	35
	Stabilizer Bar Cushion Nuts	21
	Stabilizer Bar Link Nuts	21
	Strut Lower Mounting Bolts	40②
	Strut Shaft Retaining Nut	55
	Strut Upper Mounting Nut	25
	Tie Rod End To Steering Knuckle	40
	Wheel Bearing Retainer	21
	Wheel Speed Sensor	120①

① — Inch lbs.
② — Plus an additional 90°.

Wheel Alignment

INDEX

PRELIMINARY INSPECTION

Before any attempt is made to change or correct the wheel alignment, the following inspection and required corrections must be performed.

1. Ensure fuel tank is filled with fuel.
2. Passenger and luggage compartments of vehicle should be free of any load that is not factory equipment.
3. Inspect all tires. All tires must be same size, in good condition and inflated to proper pressure with approximately same tread wear.
4. Inspect front tires and wheels for excessive radial runout.
5. Inspect all suspension components and fasteners for looseness and proper torque.
6. Inspect lower front ball joint and all steering linkages for looseness and signs of wear or damage.
7. Inspect all rubber suspension bushings for wear or deterioration.
8. Inspect vehicle curb height as outlined under "Vehicle Ride Height."

FRONT WHEEL ALIGNMENT

Refer to "Specifications" for alignment measurements.

Camber & Caster

There is no required adjustment of camber and caster when servicing suspension components. Camber and caster should be inspected to ensure they meet vehicle specifications.

If front camber is found to be out of the specified range, it can be adjusted using an available camber adjustment bolt package. Before installing camber bolt package, inspect all suspension components for damage and excessive wear. The camber adjustment bolt package contains new nuts and bolts for attaching the strut clevis bracket to the steering knuckle. The bolts are slightly undersized to allow for approximately two degrees of camber adjustment per side of the vehicle. To install and adjust camber adjustment bolt package, proceed as follows:

1. Raise and support vehicle until wheels are and tires are not supporting weight of vehicle.
2. The knuckle to strut assembly attaching bolts are serrated and must not be turned during removal. Remove nuts while holding bolts stationary.
3. Remove original upper bolt attaching strut clevis bracket to knuckle, **Fig. 1.**
4. Install a bolt from adjustment package into hole where original bolt was removed. Install bolt from rear.
5. Install a nut provided in adjustment package on bolt and tighten until snug but still allowing knuckle to slide in clevis bracket.
6. Remove original lower bolt and install a bolt from the package into bottom hole, install bolt from rear.
7. Install nut provided in adjustment package and tighten until snug.
8. Perform procedure to any remaining strut as required.
9. Install tire and wheel assemblies.
10. Lower vehicle and jounce front and rear of vehicle.
11. Adjust front camber to preferred setting by pushing or pulling on top of tire.
12. When camber is set to specified value, tighten upper and lower strut clevis bolts.
13. Jounce front and rear of vehicle and verify settings.
14. **Torque** front strut clevis bracket to steering knuckle attaching bolts to 40 ft. lbs., plus an additional 1/4 turn after torque is met.
15. Once camber is within specification, adjust toe.

Toe-In

1. Center steering wheel and lock in place.
2. Loosen tie rod adjusting jam nuts, grasp each inner tie rod at it's splines and rotate it one way or another to set toe to specification.
3. Do not twist inner tie rod to steering gear rubber boots while turning inner tie rod during adjustment.
4. **Torque** tie rod adjusting jam nuts to 55 ft. lbs.
5. Road test vehicle to verify that steering wheel is straight and vehicle does not pull or wander.

REAR WHEEL ALIGNMENT

Rear camber and toe adjustments are not required when servicing suspension components. Rear camber and toe can be changed when required through the use of specially designed shims. To install shims, proceed as follows:

1. Raise and support vehicle until wheels and tires are off of floor or alignment rack.
2. Remove tire and wheel assembly.
3. Loosen four spindle mounting bolts just enough to slide adjustment shim in between spindle and axle mounting flange.
4. Each shim is .010 inch thick. Do not place more than two shims at any one spindle.
5. Hook shim on mounting bolts utilizing slots cut into shim.
6. Shim placement should be as follows:
   a. To achieve more positive camber, place shim across two upper mounting bolts.
   b. To achieve more negative camber, place shim across two lower mounting bolts.
   c. To achieve more positive toe, place shim across two rearward mounting bolts.
   d. To achieve more negative toe, place shim across two froward mounting bolts.
7. **Torque** four mounting bolts to 70 ft. lbs.
8. Assemble remaining components in reverse order of removal.
9. Lower vehicle.

VEHICLE RIDE HEIGHT

Vehicle height is inspected with vehicle on a flat, level surface, preferably a vehicle alignment rack. Vehicle ride height is not adjustable. If measurement is not within specification, inspect for bent or weak suspension components. Prior to reading curb height measurements, front and rear of vehicle should be jounced by grasping center of rear, then front bumper and jouncing vehicle an equal number of times.

1. Measure from edge of wheel opening fender lip directly above wheel center (spindle) down to floor or alignment rack surface.
2. When measuring, maximum lefthand to righthand differential should not exceed .39 inch.
3. Front curb height specification is 27.37–27.69 inches, rear curb height is 27.95–28.59 inches.

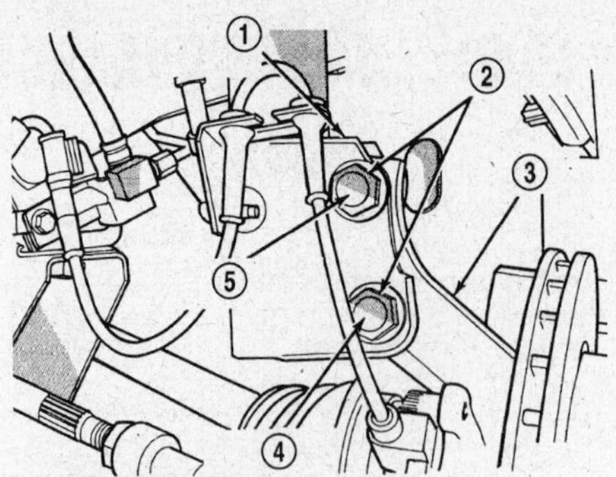

1 – STRUT CLEVIS BRACKET
2 – STRUT CLEVIS BRACKET TO STEERING KNUCKLE ATTACHING BOLTS
3 – STEERING KNUCKLE
4 – LOOSEN THIS BOLT
5 – REMOVE AND REPLACE THIS BOLT

CR2020000172000X

Fig. 1 Front strut clevis bracket attaching bolts

SPRINTER

NOTE: Refer To The Rear Of This Manual For Vehicle Manufacturer's Special Service Tool Suppliers.

INDEX OF SERVICE OPERATIONS

Specifications

GENERAL ENGINE SPECIFICATIONS

Engine Liter	Year	Fuel System	Bore & Stroke	Comp. Ratio	Horsepower @ RPM	Torque/Ft. Lbs. @ RPM	Normal Oil Pressure, psi
2.7L	2003–06	CDI	3.46 X 3.48	18:1	154 @ 3800 RPM	243 @ 1600–2400	—

CDI — Common Rail Diesel Injection.

DIESEL ENGINE PERFORMANCE SPECIFICATIONS

Engine Liter	Year	Compress-ion Ratio	Firing Order	Injection Timing	Fuel Pressure	Low Idle Stop Speed (Min.), RPM	Full Throttle Stop Speed, RPM
2.7L	2003–06	18:1	1-2-4-5-3	①	②	①	①

① — Timing & fuel adjustments are controlled by the ECM, there are no adjustments available.

② — Starter Speed, 6–22 psi; Idle Speed, 29–36 psi; Max. 44–58 psi.

FRONT WHEEL ALIGNMENT SPECIFICATIONS

The specifications listed below are for unloaded vehicles

Year	Caster Angle, Degrees		Camber Angle, Degrees		Toe, Degrees①		Steering Knuckle Inclination	
	Limits	Desired	Limits	Desired	Limits	Desired	Limits	Desired
2003–06	.5 to +.5	0	-.75 to +.75②	0	-.16 to +.16	0	.5 to +.5③	0

① — Toe-in (+). Toe-out (-).

② — Max. difference left to right, 1.33°.

③ — Max. difference left to right, 1°

REAR WHEEL ALIGNMENT SPECIFICATIONS

The specifications listed below are for unloaded vehicles

Year	Camber Angle, Degrees		Toe, Degrees①	
	Limits	Desired	Limits	Desired
2003–06	-.66 to +.33	0	-.25 to + 2.5	0

① — Toe-in (+). Toe-out (-).

FLUID CAPACITIES & COOLING SYSTEM DATA

Year	Engine Liter	Cooling Capacity, Qts.	Recom-mended Coolant Type	Radiator Cap Relief Pres-sure, Lbs.	Thermo. Opening Temp. °F	Fuel Tank, Gals.	Engine Oil Refill, Qts. w/Filter	Transmission Oil		Drive Axle Oil, Pts.
								Service Fill, Qts.	Overhaul Fill, Qts.	
2003–06	2.7L	10.5	Ethylene-Glycol①	18–21	192	②	9.5	10.6	16.3	4.0③

① — Glycol-based coolant w/corrosion inhibitors (Hybrid Organic Additive Technology (HOAT).

② — Primary, 26.4 gals.; Reserve, 2.8 gals.

③ — Plus or minus 1 ounce.

LUBRICANT DATA

Year	Model	Transmission	Drive Axle	Power Steering	Brake System
2003–06	All	①	②	③	DOT 4

①— Shell 3403 ATF. Mopar ATF +4 ATF, or other fluids meeting MS-9602 may be used if Shell 3403 ATF is not available.

②— Synthetic Gear & Axle Lubricant SAE 75W-140.

③— Mopar ATF +4 ATF, or equivalent.

Electrical

NOTE: On Air Bag Equipped Models, Refer To "Air Bag System Precautions" Located In The Front Of This Manual For System Disarming & Arming Procedures.

NOTE: Refer To "Computer Relearn Procedures" Located In The Front Of This Manual When Battery Power To The Computer Has Been Interrupted.

INDEX

PRECAUTIONS

Air Bag Systems

Refer to "Air Bag System Precautions" in the front of this manual for system disarming and arming procedures.

Battery Ground Cable

Prior to service, disconnect battery ground cable and isolate as required.

FUSE PANEL LOCATION

Fuse block No. 1 is under the steering column, **Fig. 1.** Fuse block No, 2 is under the driver's seat, **Fig. 2.**

The power distribution center is in the lefthand front corner of the engine compartment on the battery positive cable.

RELAY CENTER LOCATION

The relay block is under the driver's seat, **Fig. 2.**

STARTER

REPLACE

1. Remove wiring to transmission bellhousing bolt.
2. Cut tie-wraps and position wiring harness aside.
3. Remove two mounting nuts and solenoid wire connector and battery cable.
4. Raise and support vehicle.
5. Remove two mounting bolts and starter, **Fig. 3.**
6. Reverse procedure to install, noting the following:
   a. **Torque** starter mounting bolts to 30 ft. lbs.
   b. **Torque** battery cable nut to 124 inch lbs.
   c. **Torque** start solenoid nut to 52 inch lbs.

ALTERNATOR

REPLACE

1. Relieve belt tension by rotating ratchet and tensioner counterclockwise using suitable long handle drive ratchet.
2. Remove drive belt starting at water pump pulley.
3. Raise and support vehicle.
4. Remove plastic cover and battery output cable mounting nut
5. Disconnect alternator field terminal connector.
6. Remove four mounting bolts and alternator, **Fig. 4.**
7. Reverse procedure to install, noting the following:
   a. **Torque** alternator mounting bolts to 40 ft. lbs.
   b. **Torque** terminal nut to 115 inch lbs.
   c. Place belt over all pulleys except water pump.
   d. Rotating ratchet and tensioner counterclockwise using suitable long handle drive ratchet.
   e. Place belt over water pump pulley and remove ratchet.

IGNITION SWITCH

REPLACE

1. Remove central electronics cover and steering column shroud.
2. Remove ignition lock transponder coil.
3. Insert key and turn ignition lock to first detent.
4. Turn cap 1/4 trim to left, **Fig. 5.**

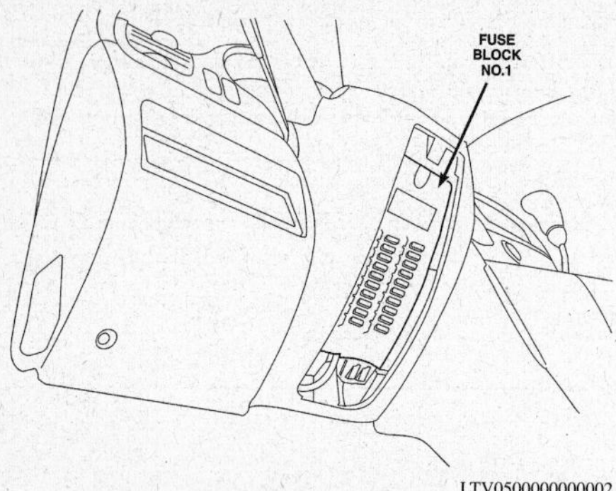

Fig. 1 Fuse block No. 1

5. Remove cap with lock cylinder.
6. Reverse procedure to install.

NEUTRAL SAFETY SWITCH

REPLACE

The Transmission Control Module (TCM) monitors the transmission temperature sensor and shift position signals to deter park and neutral position.

HEADLAMP SWITCH

REPLACE

Refer to "Multi-Function Switch, Replace" for headlamp switch replacement procedure.

STOP LIGHT SWITCH

REPLACE

1. Depress locking tab and rotate switch approximately 30° counterclockwise, **Fig. 6.**
2. Disconnect switch plunger form pedal bracket mounting hole by pull switch toward vehicle front.
3. Disconnect wire harness and remove switch.
4. Reverse procedure to install.

MULTI-FUNCTION SWITCH

REPLACE

1. Remove fuse block cover by rotating locking screw 90°.
2. Remove steering column cover.
3. Disconnect fuse block and electrical connectors.
4. Remove fuse block, **Fig. 2.**
5. Ensure front wheels are in straight-ahead position.
6. Disarm air bag system as outlined in "Precautions."
7. Remove mounting screws and driver air bag module from steering wheel, **Fig. 7.**
8. Disconnect clockspring upper pigtail with connectors from horn switch terminals.
9. Ensure steering wheel is locked.
10. Remove mounting bolt and steering wheel.

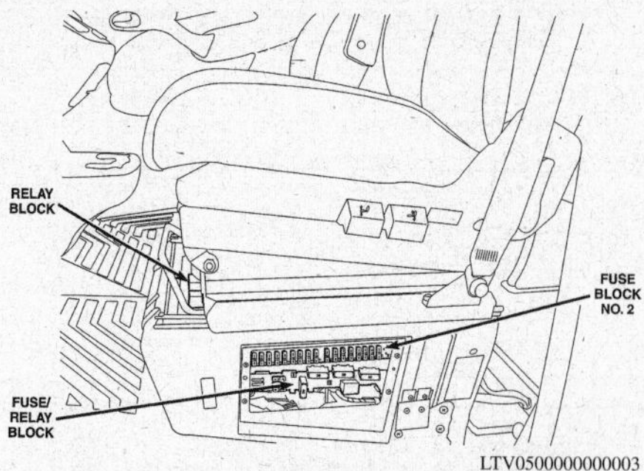

Fig. 2 Fuse block No. 2 & relay block

11. Remove steering column opening cover from instrument panel.
12. Disconnect two clockspring lower pigtail connectors from vehicle wire harness connectors.
13. Loosen two mounting screws and remove clockspring, **Fig. 8.**
14. Remove two mounting screws and upper shroud, **Fig. 9.**
15. Remove two mounting screws and multi-function switch.
16. Reverse procedure to install, noting the following:
    a. **Torque** clockspring mounting screws to 18 inch lbs.
    b. **Torque** driver air bag module mounting screws to 53 inch lbs.
    c. **Torque** steering wheel mounting bolt to 59 ft. lbs.

DIMMER SWITCH

REPLACE

Refer to "Multi-Function Switch, Replace" for dimmer switch replacement procedure.

STEERING WHEEL

REPLACE

1. Ensure front wheels are in straight-ahead position.
2. Disarm air bag system as outlined in "Precautions."
3. Remove mounting screws and driver air bag module from steering wheel, **Fig. 7.**
4. Disconnect clockspring upper pigtail with connectors from horn switch terminals.
5. Ensure steering wheel is locked.
6. Remove mounting bolt and steering wheel.
7. Remove steering column opening cover from instrument panel.
8. Reverse procedure to install, noting the following:
    a. **Torque** driver air bag module mounting screws to 53 inch lbs.
    b. **Torque** steering wheel mounting bolt to 59 ft. lbs.

INSTRUMENT CLUSTER

REPLACE

1. Remove mounting screws and disconnect instrument cluster cover using trim stick tool C-4755, or equivalent.

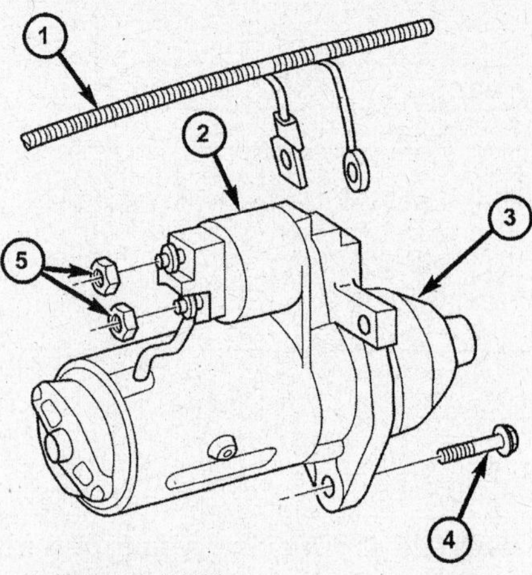

Fig. 3 Starter replacement

2. Disconnect electrical connectors and remove instrument cluster bezel.
3. Remove two instrument cluster ear mounting screws, **Fig. 10.**
4. Roll cluster rearward and disconnect RKE/immobilizer module, **Fig. 11.**
5. Depress release and left lever arm, then disconnect two frame wire harness connectors from cluster housing.
6. Lift cluster and disconnect two molded plastic pivot loops from hooks.
7. Remove instrument cluster.
8. Reverse procedure to install. **Torque** mounting screws to 20 inch lbs.

RADIO

REPLACE

1. Insert lock tools No. 9241, or equivalent, into each radio face slot.
2. Remove radio, then disconnect wire harness connectors and antenna, **Fig. 12.**
3. Reverse procedure to install.

WIPER MOTOR

REPLACE

1. Disconnect wiper motor pigtail from vehicle wire harness, **Fig. 13.**
2. Remove motor crank arm to shaft nut.
3. Mark output shaft and crank arm for installation alignment.
4. Remove three mounting screws and wiper motor from linkage module bracket.
5. Reverse procedure to install. **Torque** mounting screws and shaft nut to 105 inch lbs.

WIPER SWITCH

REPLACE

Refer to "Multi-Function Switch, Replace" when replacing the wiper switch.

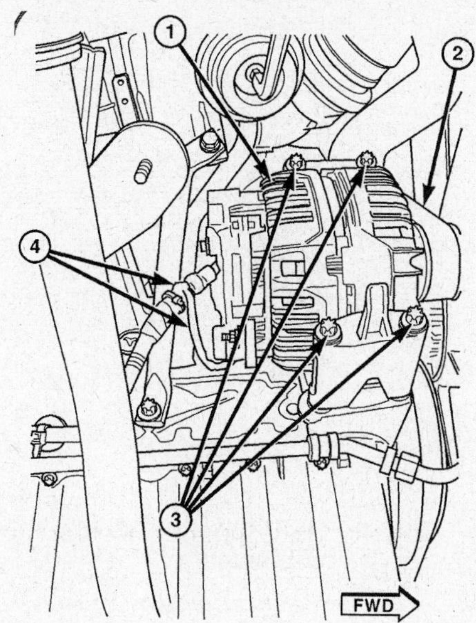

Fig. 4 Alternator replacement

WIPER MODULE

REPLACE

1. Disconnect washer nozzle hose from wiper arm pivot end.
2. Disconnect and remove cover away from wiper arm hinge pin.
3. Remove mounting nut and wiper arm using suitable battery terminal puller tool.
4. Remove five mounting nuts, then disconnect and lower ventilation housing from cowl panel to rest on engine, **Fig. 14.**
5. Disconnect wiper motor pigtail connector for vehicle wiring harness.
6. Remove wiper pivot housings' mounting nuts and washers, **Fig. 15.**
7. Remove two mounting screws, then the wiper linkage module and motor.
8. Remove mounting screws and wiper motor.
9. Reverse procedure to install, noting the following:
   a. **Torque** wiper linkage module mounting screws to 50 inch lbs.
   b. **Torque** wiper arm mounting nit to 18 ft. lbs.
   c. Position wiper arm pivot ends onto pivots so lower edge of wiper arm top aligns with black alignment line near lower edge of windshield glass.

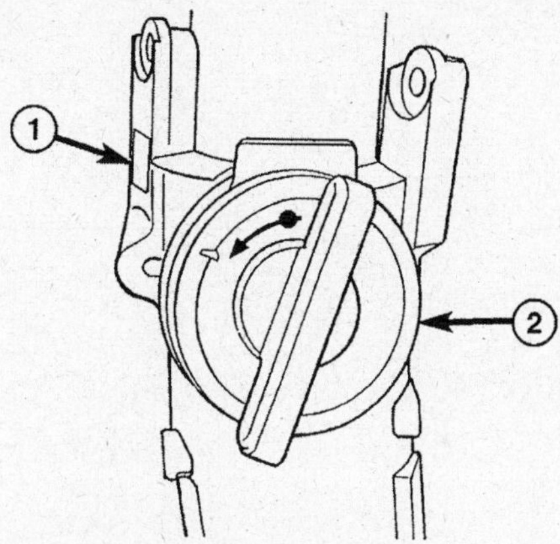

Fig. 5 Ignition switch replacement

BLOWER MOTOR

REPLACE

Front

1. Remove upper turbocharge heat shield.
2. Disconnect Manifold Air Flow (MAF) sensor air hose and electrical connector.
3. Remove mounting screws and MAF sensor.
4. Disconnect and remove air cleaner housing top, then remove air cleaner element, **Fig. 16.**
5. Disconnect air cleaning housing bottom.
6. Remove air intake hose from inner fender and air cleaner.
7. Remove air cleaner housing bottom.
8. Position ventilation housing insulation blanket aside.
9. Disconnect blower motor electrical connector, **Fig. 17.**
10. Remove three mounting screws and blower motor.
11. Reverse procedure to install. **Torque** blower motor mounting screws to 17 inch lbs.

Rear

1. Remove rear dome lamp and disconnect connector.
2. Remove six push-pin fasteners and roof duct panel, **Fig. 18.**
3. Remove five evaporator panel front mounting screws, then disconnect and remove interior motion sensor, **Fig. 19.**
4. Remove three push-pin rear evaporator panel fasteners.
5. Remove rear evaporator panel.
6. Disconnect electrical connector, then remove flour mounting screws and blower motor, **Fig. 20.**

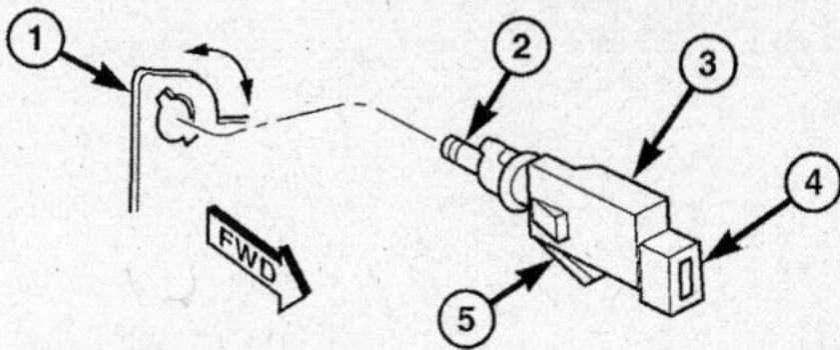

Fig. 6 Stop lamp switch replacement

7. Reverse procedure to install, noting the following:
   a. **Torque** blower motor mounting screws to 45 inch lbs.
   b. **Torque** evaporator panel mounting screws to 17 inch lbs.

CABIN AIR FILTER

REPLACE

Front

1. Remove ventilation housing insulation blanket.
2. Open locking clips and slide ventilation housing cover to right, **Fig. 21.**
3. Remove cabin air filter.

Rear

1. Unlock four fasteners by turning them counterclockwise.
2. Remove inlet grate, cover and air filter, **Fig. 22.**
3. Disconnect straps and remove filter from grate.
4. Reverse procedure to install.

HEATER CORE

REPLACE

1. Remove heater housing as outlined under "Evaporator Case, Replace."
2. Remove five mounting bolts and heater housing.
3. Remove evaporator and heater core tubes' gasket, **Fig. 23.**
4. Lift heater core out of lower housing.
5. Remove wiring harness.
6. Remove three mounting bolts and heater core tube. Discard seals.
7. Reverse procedure to install, noting the following:
   a. **Torque** heater core tube mounting bolts to 45 inch lbs.
   b. **Torque** heater cover mounting screws to 17 inch lbs.

EVAPORATOR CASE

REPLACE

1. Recover refrigerant as outlined in "Air Conditioning" chapter.
2. Partially drain cooling system into suitable container.

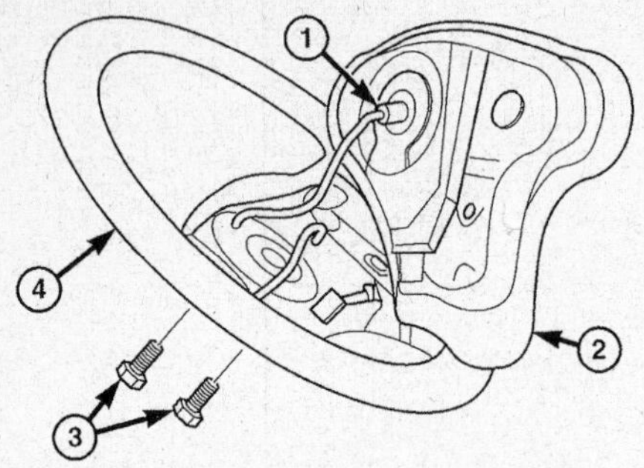

1 - AIRBAG CONNECTOR
2 - DRIVER AIRBAG
3 - SCREW (2)
4 - STEERING WHEEL

LTV0500000000010

Fig. 7 Driver air bag module replacement

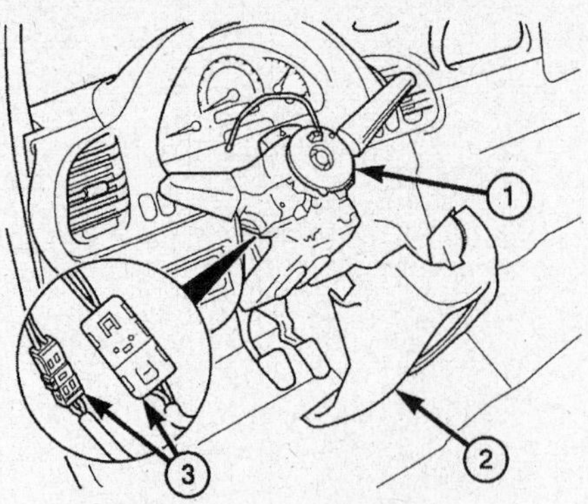

1 - CLOCKSPRING
2 - SHROUD
3 - LOWER PIGTAIL CONNECTOR (2)

LTV0500000000009

Fig. 8 Clockspring replacement

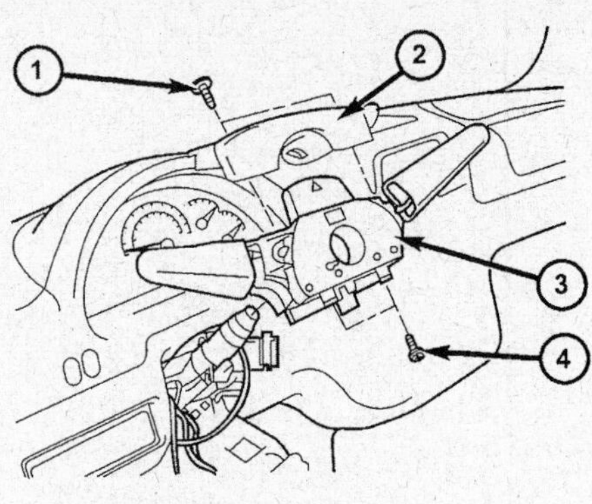

1 - SCREW (2)
2 - UPPER SHROUD
3 - SWITCH
4 - SCREW (2)

LTV0500000000008

Fig. 9 Multi-function switch replacement

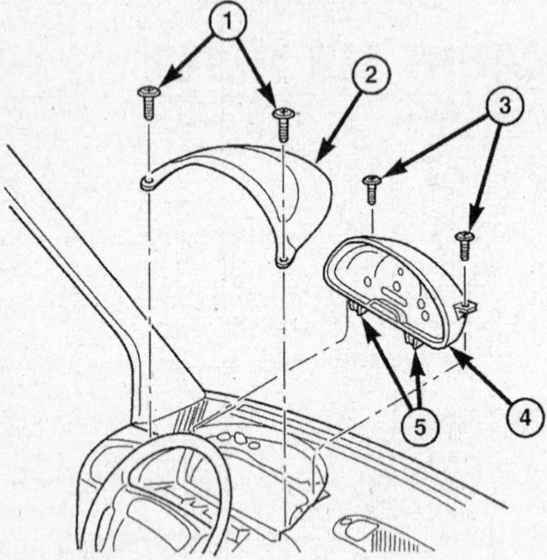

1 - SCREW (2)
2 - COVER
3 - SCREW (2)
4 - INSTRUMENT CLUSTER
5 - LOOP (2)

LTV0500000000011

Fig. 10 Instrument cluster replacement

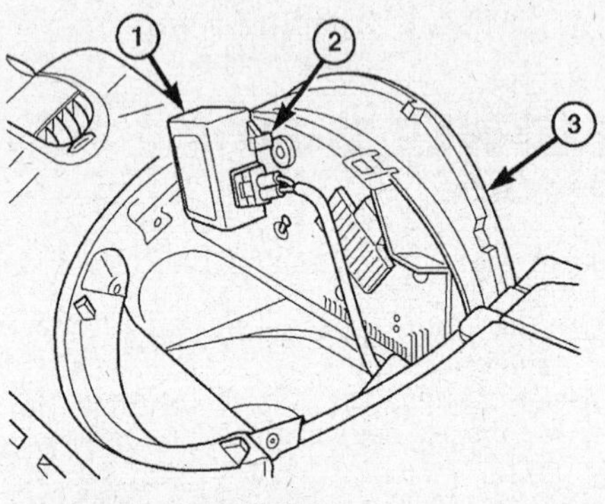

1 - RKE/IMMOBILIZER MODULE
2 - LATCH
3 - INSTRUMENT CLUSTER

LTV0500000000012

Fig. 11 RKE/immobilizer module replacement

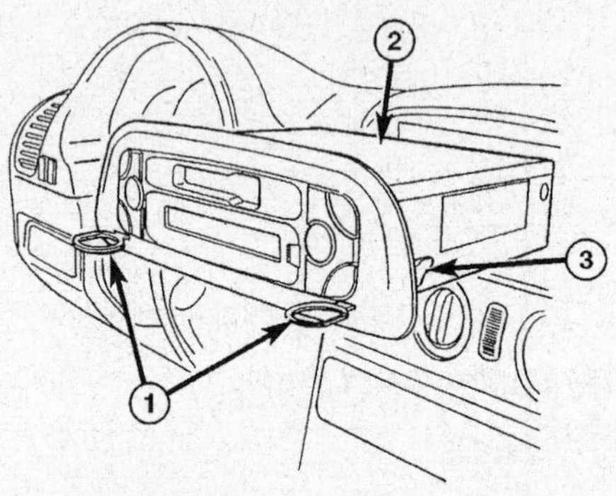

1 - SPECIAL TOOL 9241
2 - RADIO
3 - RETAINING TAB

LTV0500000000013

Fig. 12 Radio replacement

3. Remove upper turbocharge heat shield, **Fig. 16.**
4. Disconnect Manifold Air Flow (MAF) sensor air hose and electrical connector.
5. Remove mounting screws and MAF sensor.
6. Disconnect and remove air cleaner housing top, then remove air cleaner element.
7. Disconnect air cleaning housing bottom.
8. Remove air intake hose from inner fender and air cleaner.
9. Remove air cleaner housing bottom.
10. Disconnect washer pump/motor electrical connector and washer reservoir harness routing clip, **Fig. 24.**
11. Remove washer supply hose from pump/motor outlet and reservoir trough.
12. Remove mounting nut and washer, then the washer reservoir.
13. Remove ventilation housing insulation blanket.
14. Open locking clips, slide ventilation housing cover to right and remove cabin air filter, **Fig. 21.**
15. Disconnect recirculation door actuator electrical and vacuum connectors, **Fig. 25.**
16. Disconnect blower resistor block and blower motor electrical connectors.
17. Remove mounting nuts and washers, then the ventilation housing, **Fig. 14.**
18. Disconnect hoses from heater core and tubes. Plug or tape hoses and openings.
19. Remove two mounting bolts, then disconnect refrigerant lines and evaporator tubes. Plug or tape openings.
20. Remove instrument panel as outlined in “Dash Panel Service” chapter.
21. Remove mounting screws, then the lefthand and righthand defroster ducts.
22. Remove mounting screws, then the lefthand and righthand floor distribution ducts.
23. Remove mounting screws, then the lefthand and righthand instrument panel distribution ducts.
24. Disconnect instrument cluster area bulkhead ground connections.
25. Remove four mounting bolts and passenger air bag module bracket, **Fig. 26.**
26. Disconnect evaporator and air outlet temperature sensors' connectors, **Fig. 27.**
27. Remove righthand HVAC housing wire harness from bracket.
28. Disconnect heater-air conditioning control cables from mode door levers.
29. Disconnect evaporator drain tube from housing.
    a. **Torque** line and tube block mounting bolt to 45 inch lbs.
    b. **Torque** heater housing mounting bolts to 40 inch lbs.
    c. **Torque** passenger air bag module mounting bolts to 89 inch lbs.
    d. **Torque** duct mounting screws to 17 inch lbs.
    e. **Torque** washer reservoir mounting nut to 50 inch lbs.

EVAPORATOR CORE

REPLACE

1. Remove heater housing as outlined under “Evaporator Case, Replace.”
2. Remove five mounting bolts and heater housing.
3. Remove evaporator and heater core tubes' gasket, **Fig. 23.**
4. Lift evaporator core out of lower housing.
5. Reverse procedure to install, noting the following:
    a. **Torque** heater core tube mounting bolts to 45 inch lbs.
    b. **Torque** heater cover mounting screws to 17 inch lbs.

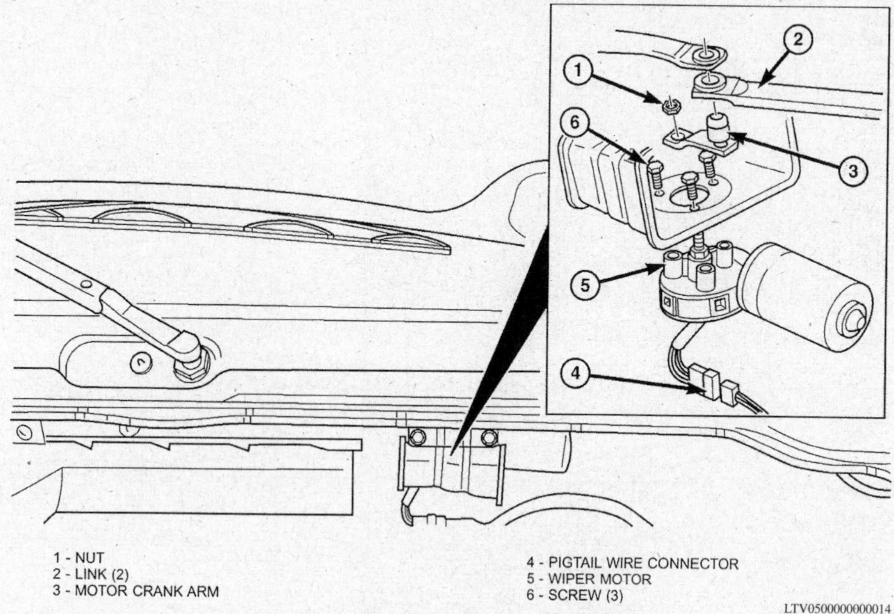

1 - NUT
2 - LINK (2)
3 - MOTOR CRANK ARM
4 - PIGTAIL WIRE CONNECTOR
5 - WIPER MOTOR
6 - SCREW (3)

LTV0500000000014

Fig. 13 Wiper motor replacement

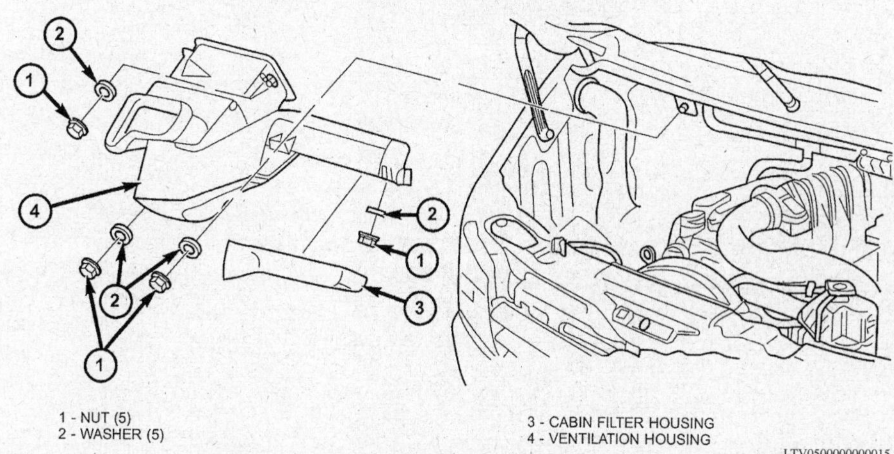

1 - NUT (5)
2 - WASHER (5)
3 - CABIN FILTER HOUSING
4 - VENTILATION HOUSING

LTV0500000000015

Fig. 14 Ventilation housing replacement

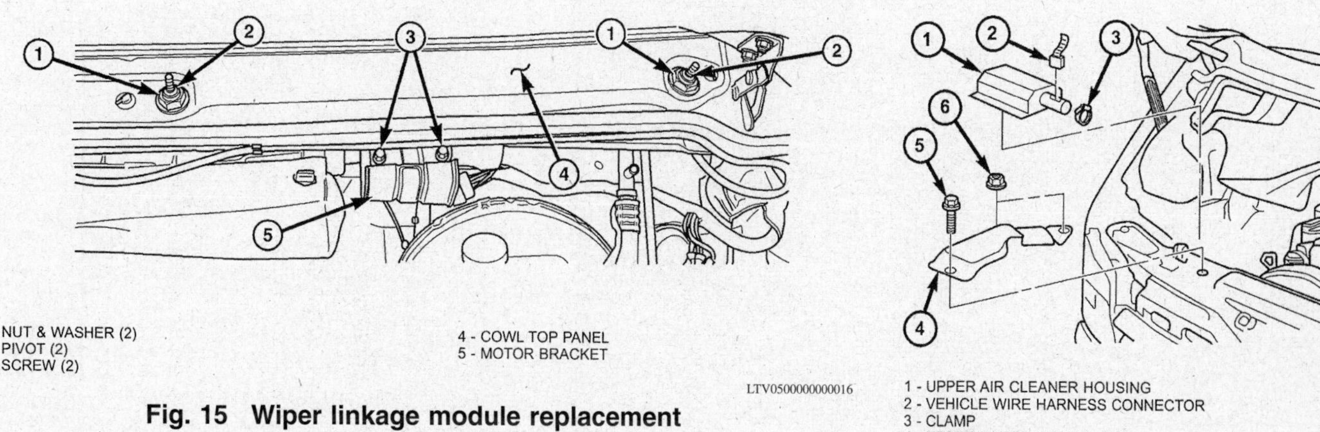

1 - NUT & WASHER (2)
2 - PIVOT (2)
3 - SCREW (2)
4 - COWL TOP PANEL
5 - MOTOR BRACKET

LTV0500000000016

Fig. 15 Wiper linkage module replacement

1 - UPPER AIR CLEANER HOUSING
2 - VEHICLE WIRE HARNESS CONNECTOR
3 - CLAMP
4 - UPPER TURBO HEAT SHIELD
5 - SCREW
6 - NUT (2)

LTV0500000000023

Fig. 16 Air cleaner housing replacement

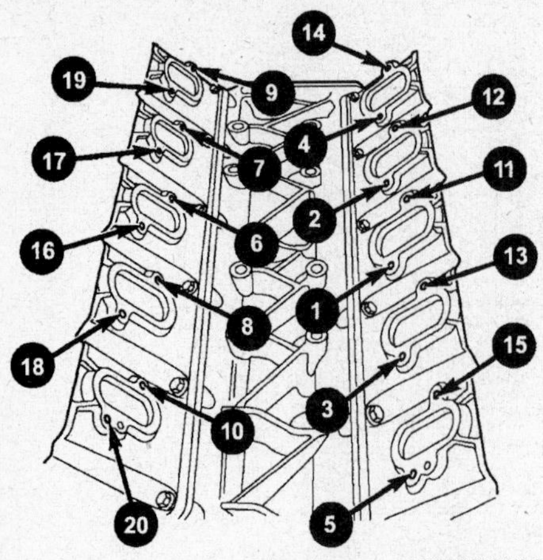

Fig. 17 Front blower motor replacement

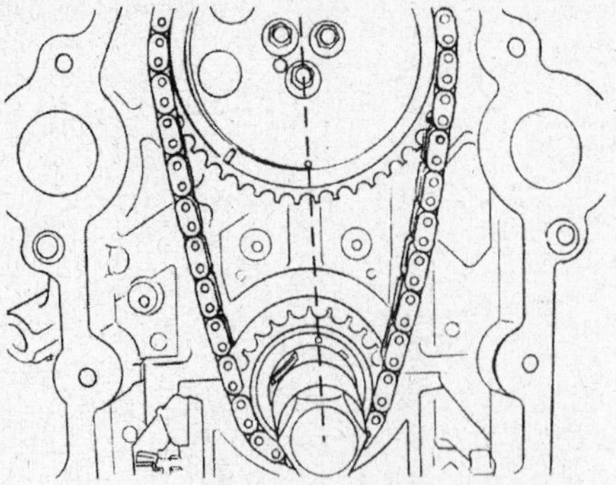

LTV0500000000018

Fig. 18 Rear roof duct panel replacement

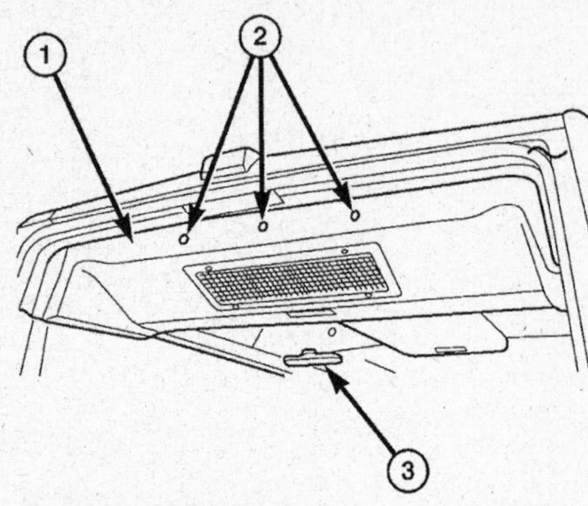

1 - REAR EVAPORATOR PANEL
2 - PUSH-PIN FASTENER (3)
3 - INTERIOR MOTION SENSOR

LTV0500000000020

Fig. 19 Rear evaporator panel replacement

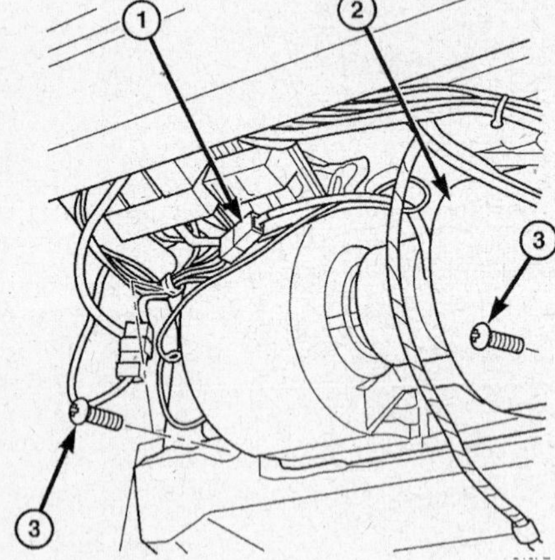

1 - WIRE HARNESS CONNECTOR
2 - REAR A/C BLOWER MOTOR
3 - SCREW (4)

LTV0500000000021

Fig. 20 Rear blower motor replacement

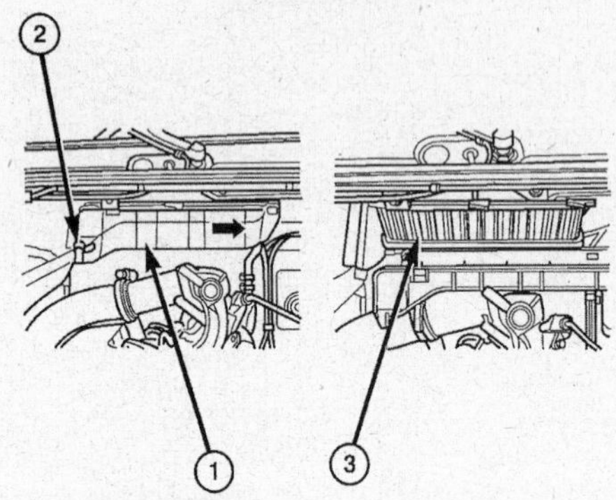

1 - VENTILATION HOUSING INSULATION BLANKET
2 - LOCKING CLIP (2)
3 - AIR FILTER

LTV0500000000022

Fig. 21 Front cabin air filter replacement

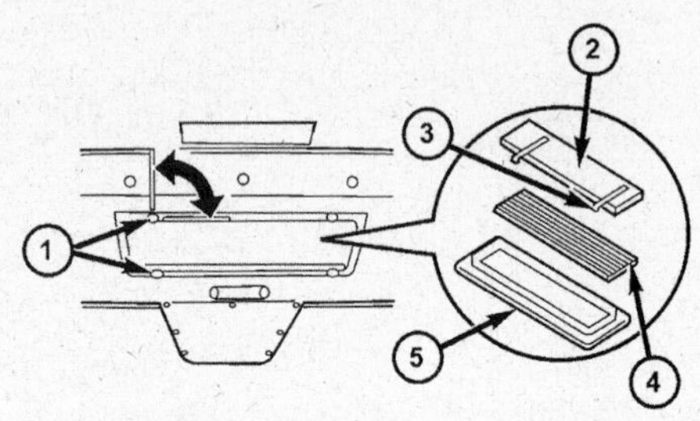

1 - QUICK-DISCONNECT FASTENER (4)
2 - AIR FILTER
3 - RETAINING STRAP (2)
4 - AIR INLET GRATE
5 - COVER

LTV0500000000019

Fig. 22 Rear cabin air filter replacement

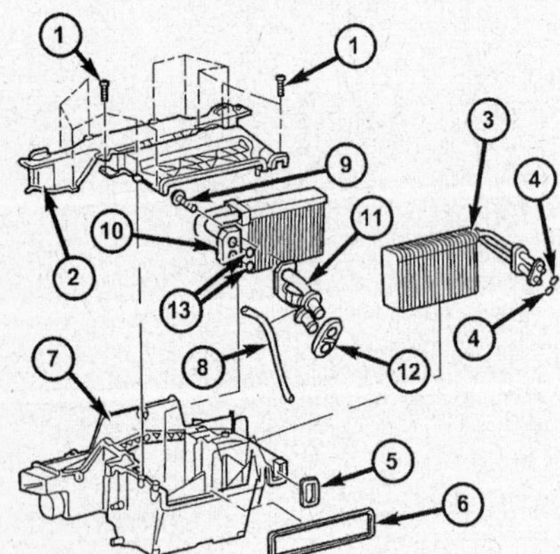

1 - SCREW (12)
2 - HEATER HOUSING COVER
3 - EVAPORATOR
4 - EVAPORATOR O-RING SEAL (2)
4 - EVAPORATOR GASKET
6 - VENTILATION HOUSING GASKET
7 - HEATER HOUSING
8 - WIRING HARNESS
9 - BOLT (3)
10 - HEATER CORE
11 - HEATER CORE TUBE ASSEMBLY
12 - HEATER CORE TUBE GASKET
13 - HEATER CORE TUBE O-RING SEAL (2)

LTV0500000000028

Fig. 23 Heater core replacement

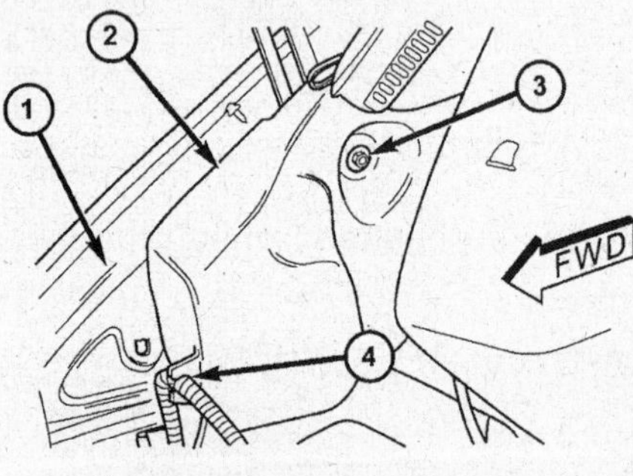

1 - RIGHT INNER FENDER
2 - WASHER RESERVOIR
3 - NUT & WASHER
4 - ROUTING CLIP

LTV0500000000024

Fig. 24 Washer reservoir replacement

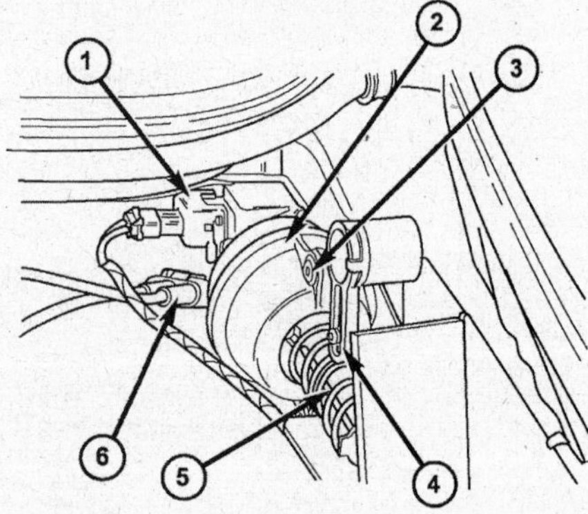

1 - WIRE HARNESS CONNECTOR
2 - RECIRCULATION DOOR ACTUATOR
3 - SCREW (2)
4 - PIVOT LEVER
5 - ACTUATOR SHAFT
6 - VACUUM LINE

LTV0500000000025

Fig. 25 Recirculation door actuator connectors

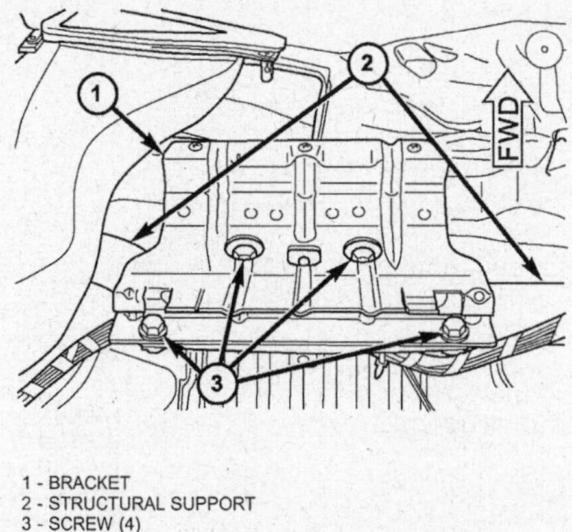

Fig. 26 Passenger air bag module bracket replacement

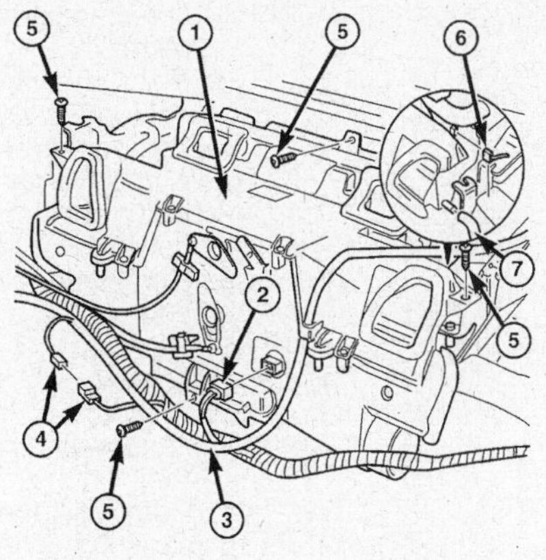

Fig. 27 Heater housing wiring replacement

2.7L Diesel Engine

NOTE: On Air Bag Equipped Models, Refer To "Air Bag System Precautions" Located In The Front Of This Manual For System Disarming & Arming Procedures.

NOTE: Refer To "Computer Relearn Procedure" Located In The Front Of This Manual When Battery Power To The Computer Has Been Interrupted.

INDEX

PRECAUTIONS

Air Bag Systems

Refer to "Air Bag System Precautions" in the front of this manual for system disarming and arming procedures.

Battery Ground Cable

Prior to service, disconnect battery ground cable and isolate as required.

DESCRIPTION

This 2.7 liter five-cylinder Common Rail Diesel Injection (CDI) engine is an in-line overhead valve diesel engine. This engine utilizes a cast iron cylinder block and an aluminum cylinder head. The engine is turbocharged and intercooled. This engine also has four valve per cylinder and dual overhead camshafts.

ENGINE MOUNT

REPLACE

1. Support and slightly raise engine using engine fixture tool No. 8534, or equivalent.

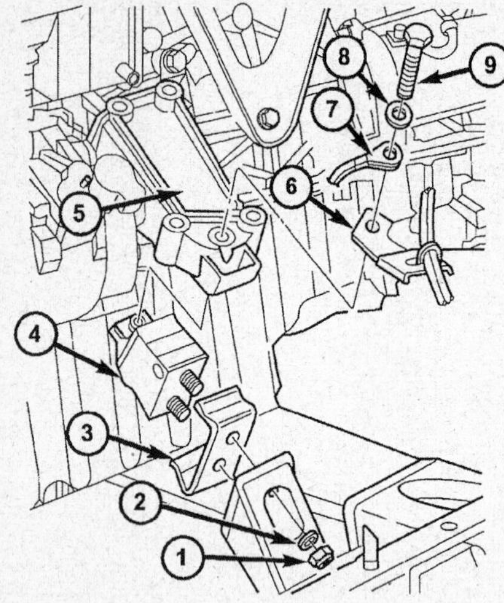

Fig. 1 Lefthand engine mount replacement

2. Raise and support vehicle.
3. Remove engine mount bolts, **Figs. 1 and 2.**
4. Lower vehicle.
5. Remove weight from mounts by raising engine using support fixture tool.
6. Remove mounting nuts and mount.
7. Reverse procedure to install.

COMPRESSION PRESSURE

1. Warm engine to operating temperature (176°F).
2. Turn engine off.
3. Remove mounting bolts and engine cover.
4. Remove glow plug connectors using flow plug pliers tool No. 9286, or equivalent.
5. Remove glow plugs.
6. Eliminate combustion residue by cranking engine several times using starter motor.
7. Install suitable compression tester.
8. Crank engine at least eight revolutions using starter motor.
9. Maximum compression per cylinder is 420–507 psi. Minimum compression is 261 psi.
10. Maximum permissible difference between cylinders is 44 psi.

ENGINE

REPLACE

1. Raise and support hood.
2. Remove clip, then disconnect prop rod and spring from hood.
3. Mark hood hinges for installation alignment.
4. Remove mounting nuts and hood.
5. Drain engine coolant into suitable container.
6. Recover air conditioning refrigerant as outlined in "Air Conditioning" chapter.
7. Disconnect vehicle-side engine side wiring harness and guide it through into engine compartment through cowl.
8. Remove mounting bolts and engine cover.
9. Remove upper turbocharge heat shield.
10. Disconnect Manifold Air Flow (MAF) sensor air hose and electrical connector.
11. Remove mounting screws and MAF sensor.
12. Disconnect and remove air cleaner housing top, then remove air cleaner element.
13. Disconnect air cleaning housing bottom.
14. Remove air intake hose from inner fender and air cleaner.
15. Remove air cleaner housing bottom.
16. Disconnect charge air hose at mixing chamber, **Fig. 3.**
17. Remove radiator as outlined under "Radiator, Replace."
18. Disconnect power steering pump high pressure and return hoses.
19. Disconnect fuel filter lines.
20. Disconnect air conditioning compressor refrigerant line.
21. Disconnect brake booster vacuum pump line.
22. Disconnect water pump heating return hose.
23. Disconnect cylinder head heater supply hose.
24. Disconnect turbocharger vacuum and air inlet hoses.
25. Raise and support vehicle.
26. Remove mounting bolts and disconnect front exhaust at turbocharger.
27. Disconnect transmission electrical connector, **Fig. 4.**
28. Disconnect locking clamp, shifter cable and catch.
29. Remove steering gear mounting bolts.
30. Disconnect transmission cooler lines.
31. Remove access plate and torque converter mounting bolts.
32. Disconnect connector, then remove mounting bolts and Crankshaft Position (CKP) sensor.
33. Remove transmission to engine mounting bolts.
34. Remove starter motor mounting bolts.
35. Support transmission with suitable jack.
36. Place suitable wood block between transmission housing and front frame crossover.
37. Remove righthand exhaust bracket.
38. Remove lefthand ground strap.
39. Lower vehicle.
40. Remove filter and lower heater housing.
41. Support engine with suitable lifting fixture, **Fig. 5.**
42. Remove engine mount bolts.
43. Remove transmission oil dipstick tube mounting bolt.
44. Remove front crossplate by cutting edges using suitable tin snips, **Fig. 6.**

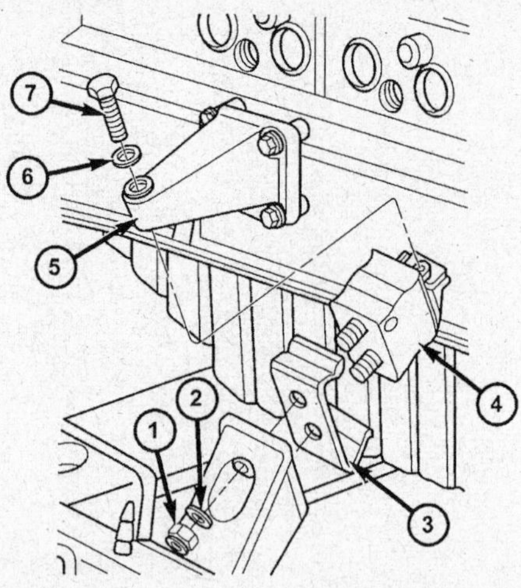

Fig. 2 Righthand engine mount replacement

45. Remove engine.
46. Reverse procedure to install.

INTAKE MANIFOLD

REPLACE

1. Drain radiator coolant into suitable container.
2. Remove mounting bolts and engine cover.
3. Disconnect vehicle-side engine side wiring harness and guide it through into engine compartment through cowl.
4. Disconnect intake manifold charge air hose, **Fig. 7.**
5. Disconnect EGR connector.
6. Remove wiring harness to intake manifold mounting bolt.
7. Disconnect coolant hose at connection junction through intake manifold support bracket.
8. Disconnect fuel filter lines.
9. Remove mounting bolts, then the lower and righthand intake manifold support brackets.
10. Disconnect fuel pressure sensor connector.
11. Raise and support vehicle.
12. Remove intake manifold rear coolant hose.
13. Remove intake manifold rear mounting bolts.
14. Lower vehicle.
15. Remove mounting bolts and intake manifold, guiding wiring harness and fuel lines through manifold openings. Discard gasket.
16. Reverse procedure to install.

EXHAUST MANIFOLD

REPLACE

1. Remove tubrocharger as outlined under "Turbocharger, Replace."

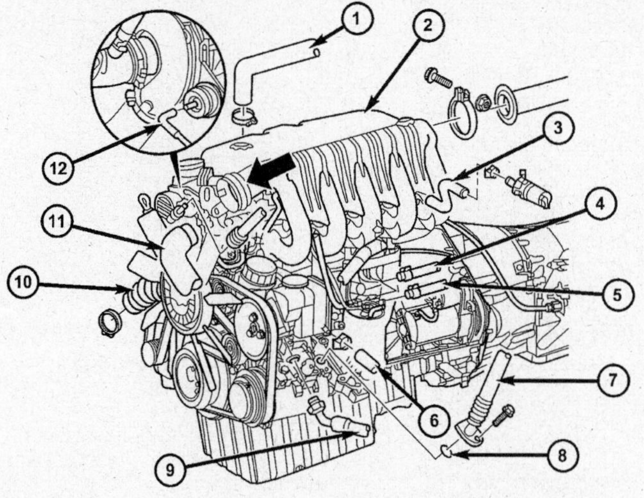

Fig. 3 Engine hose replacements

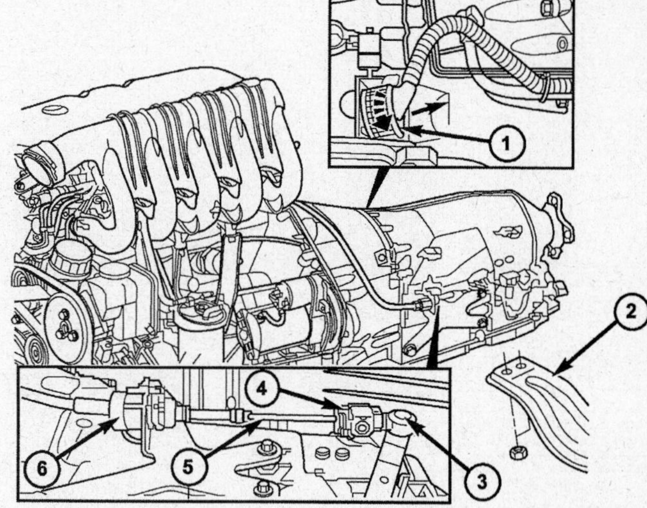

Fig. 4 Transmission connections

2. Remove mounting nuts and exhaust manifold.
3. Reverse procedure to install using new gasket.

CYLINDER HEAD

REPLACE

1. Position cylinder No. 1 at ignition TDC. **Do not rotate engine counterclockwise.**
2. Raise and support vehicle.
3. Lock crankshaft/starter ring gear using retaining lock tool No. 8932, or equivalent.
4. Drain cooling system into suitable container.
5. Lower vehicle.
6. Remove camshafts as outline under "Camshaft, Replace."
7. Remove tappets, **Fig. 8.**
8. Remove camshaft housing.
9. Remove mounting bolt, bushing and injection pump intermediate gear.
10. Disconnect and set engine side harness aside.
11. Disconnect charge air pipe from cylinder head and set it aside with engine harness attached.
12. Disconnect turbocharger oil supply line from cylinder head and turbocharger.
13. Remove mounting bolts and disconnect turbocharger from exhaust manifold.
14. Remove transmission dipstick tube mounting bolt.
15. Disconnect upper radiator and pass hoses from thermostat.
16. Disconnect fuel rail rear line.
17. Remove upper timing case to cylinder head mounting bolts, **Fig. 9.**
18. Loosen and remove cylinder head bolts in reverse of tightening sequence, **Fig. 10.**
19. Remove cylinder head.
20. Reverse procedure to install, noting the following:
    a. Replace cylinder head bolts more than 4.09 inches long, **Fig. 11.**
    b. Apply small amount of clean, suitable engine oil to cylinder head bolts.
    c. Install M12 cylinder head bolts hand tight.
    d. **Torque** M12 cylinder head bolts to 133 inch lbs., in sequence, **Fig. 10.**
    e. **Torque** cylinder head bolts to 44 ft. lbs., in sequence.
    f. Install and **torque** M8 timing chain cover to cylinder head bolts to 15 ft. lbs.
    g. Tighten M12 cylinder head bolts an additional 90° in sequence.
    h. Final tighten M12 cylinder head bolts an additional 90° in sequence.

VALVE COVER

REPLACE

1. Disconnect and position air inlet aside.
2. Disconnect oil separator hose.
3. Disconnect Camshaft Position (CMP) sensor connector, **Fig. 12.**
4. Disconnect and position fuel injector and glow plug harness aside.
5. Remove mounting bolts and engine cover.
6. Raise and support vehicle.
7. Remove lower radiator deflector plate.
8. Drain cooling system into suitable container.
9. Remove turbocharger down pipe.
10. Remove mounting bolt and oil dipstick tube.
11. Lower vehicle.
12. Remove upper turbocharge heat shield.
13. Disconnect Manifold Air Flow (MAF) sensor air hose and electrical connector.
14. Remove mounting screws and MAF sensor.
15. Disconnect and remove air cleaner housing top, then remove air cleaner element.
16. Disconnect air cleaning housing bottom.
17. Remove air intake hose from inner fender and air cleaner.
18. Remove air cleaner housing bottom.
19. Disconnect charge air hose, **Fig. 3.**
20. Remove turbocharger righthand mount.
21. Remove hold-downs and battery.
22. Disconnect clip and position Power Distribution Center (PDC) aside.
23. Remove mounting bolts and battery tray.
24. Siphon as much fluid as possible, then remove power steering reservoir.
25. Remove charger air cooler outlet hose.
26. Remove intake manifold to lefthand engine mount bracket.
27. Recover air conditioning refrigerant as outlined in "Air Conditioning" chapter.
28. Disconnect air conditioning compressor suction/discharge lines.
29. Disconnect pedal position sensor connector.
30. Disconnect fuel injector electrical connectors.
31. Remove fuel/water separator mounting bolts.
32. Support engine with suitable hoist.
33. Support engine with suitable lifting fixture, **Fig. 5.**
34. Remove engine mount through bolts and righthand mount sill plate.
35. Disconnect fuel injector high pressure line counterholding lines with suitable wrench socket, **Fig. 13.**
36. Remove fuel injector mounting bolt and tension claw.
37. Lower engine and remove fuel injectors.
38. Disconnect outlet line.

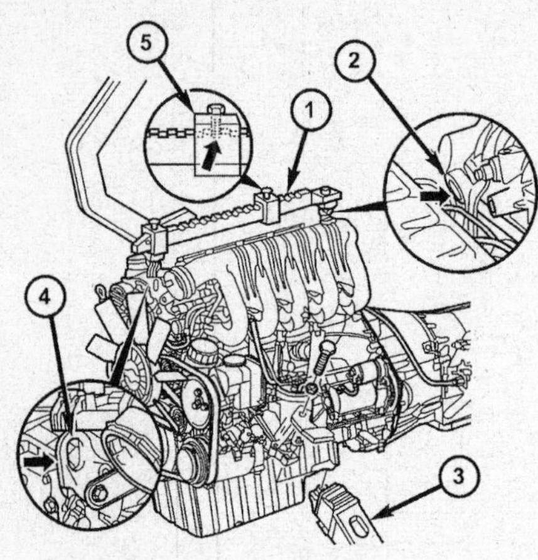

Fig. 5 Engine lifting fixture

39. Remove mounting bolts and valve cover.
40. Reverse procedure to install, noting the following:
    a. Install valve cover with new gasket.
    b. **Do not tighten valve cover mounting bolts before installing, aligning and tightening fuel injectors.**
    c. Coat fuel injector body with suitable anti-seize lubricant.
    d. Install new fuel injector seals.
    e. **Torque** fuel injectors to 62 inch lbs., No. 3, No. 4, No. 5, No. 2 and No. 1 in sequence.
    f. Final tighten fuel injectors an additional 90° in sequence.
    g. Loosen fuel rail line to install high pressure lines free of stress.

VALVE ARRANGEMENT

Exhaust valves are on the righthand side of the engine, with the intake valves on the lefthand side.

VALVE CLEARANCE SPECIFICATIONS

These engines are equipped with tappets. There is no provision for adjustment.

VALVE ADJUSTMENT

These engines are equipped with tappets. There is no provision for adjustment.

CRANKSHAFT DAMPER

REPLACE

1. Relieve belt tension by rotating ratchet and tensioner counterclockwise using suitable long handle drive ratchet.
2. Remove drive belt starting at water pump pulley.
3. Lock crankshaft/starter ring gear using retaining lock tool No. 8932, or equivalent, **Fig. 14.**
4. Remove mounting bolt and washer, then the pulley/vibration damper using vibration damper puller tool No. 8940, or equivalent. **Do not tilt puller.**
5. Reverse procedure to install, noting the following:
    a. Front crankshaft seal must be replaced as outlined under "Crankshaft Seal, Replace."
    b. Align parallel key and hold in place using suitable grease.
    c. **Torque** M8.8 damper mounting bolt to 148 ft. lbs, then tighten an additional 90°.
    d. **Torque** M10.9 damper mounting bolt to 240 ft. lbs, then tighten an additional 90°.

FRONT COVER

REPLACE

1. Remove valve cover as outlined under "Valve Cover, Replace."
2. Position cylinder No. 1 at ignition TDC. **Do not rotate engine counterclockwise.**
3. Lock camshaft using locking pin tool No. 8929 through first camshaft bearing cap into lefthand inlet camshaft sprocket hole, **Fig. 15.**
4. Ensure two intake camshaft sprockets are positioned opposite and bearing cap markings align.
5. **Do not rotate engine with locking pin in place.**
6. Drain coolant into suitable container.
7. Lock crankshaft/starter ring gear using retaining lock tool No. 8932, or equivalent.
8. Drain engine oil into suitable container. Remove oil filter.
9. Remove radiator as outlined under "Radiator, Replace."
10. Remove mounting bolts and engine cover.
11. Remove mounting bolts and engine cover.
12. Remove intake air scoop.
13. Relieve belt tension by rotating ratchet and tensioner counterclockwise using suitable long handle drive ratchet.
14. Remove drive belt starting at water pump pulley.
15. Remove timing chain tensioner, **Fig. 16.**
16. Remove cylinder head front cover mounting bolts.
17. Raise top guide rail locking pawl and remove cylinder head front cover.
18. Remove injection pump as outlined under "Injection Pump, Replace."
19. Remove water pump as outlined under "Water Pump, Replace."
20. Remove mounting bolt and washer, then the pulley/vibration damper using suitable puller. **Do not tilt puller.**
21. Siphon as much fluid as possible from power steering pump reservoir.
22. Remove high pressure and return hoses from power steering pump.
23. Remove mounting bolts and power steering pump.
24. Disconnect air conditioning compressor electrical connector.
25. Remove mounting bolt and position air conditioning compressor aside. **Do not open refrigerant system.**

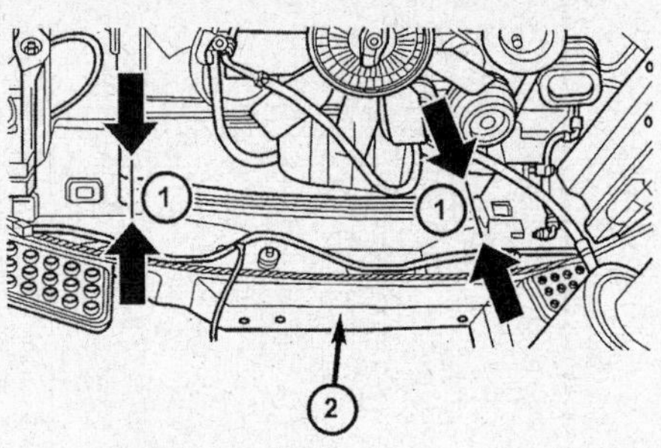

Fig. 6 Front crossplate replacement

26. Remove four mounting bolts and position alternator aside with electrical wiring attached.
27. Support engine with suitable lifting fixture, **Fig. 5.**
28. Remove mounting bolts and position sway bar aside.
29. Remove wiring harness duct from oil pan mounting bolts and position it aside.
30. Lower vehicle and remove turbocharger upper heat shield.
31. Support and slightly raise engine with suitable lifting fixture, **Fig. 5.**
32. Remove engine mount bolts, **Figs. 1 and 2.**
33. Disconnect oil level sensor.
34. Remove transmission cooler lines from oil pan mounting bolts and position them aside.
35. Remove mounting bolts, oil pan and gasket.
36. Disconnect oil-water heat exchange coolant hose, **Fig. 17.**
37. Remove cylinder head to front cover mounting bolts.
38. Remove mounting bolts and front cover.
39. Reverse procedure to install, noting the following:
    a. Front crankshaft seal must be replaced as outlined under "Crankshaft Seal, Replace."
    b. Apply .039–.079 inch suitable sealant to front cover, **Fig. 18. Cylinder head front cover must be installed with 10 minutes of sealant application.**
    c. Align parallel key and hold in place using suitable grease.
    d. **Torque** M8.8 damper mounting bolt to 148 ft. lbs, then tighten an additional 90°.
    e. **Torque** M10.9 damper mounting bolt to 240 ft. lbs, then tighten an additional 90°.

TIMING CHAIN

REPLACE

1. Remove mounting bolts and engine cover.
2. Remove valve cover as outlined under "Valve Cover, Replace."
3. Remove vacuum line, **Fig. 19.**
4. Remove mounting bolts and vacuum pump. Discard seals.

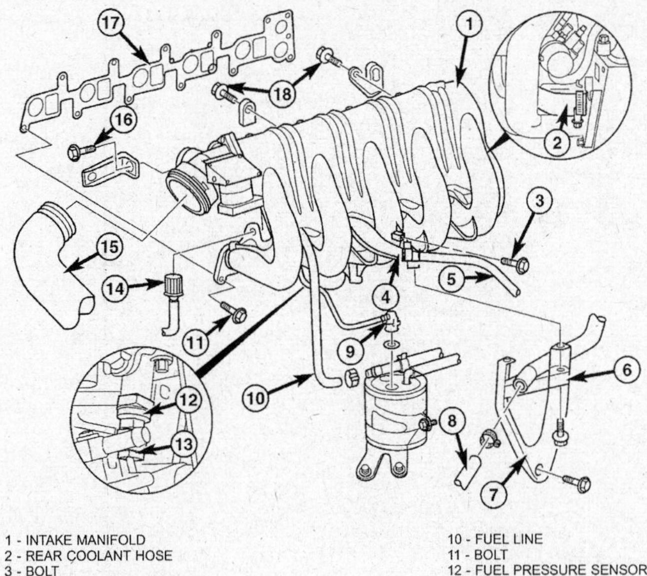

1 - INTAKE MANIFOLD
2 - REAR COOLANT HOSE
3 - BOLT
4 - ENGINE HARNESS DUCTING
5 - ENGINE HARNESS
6 - CONNECTING JUNCTION
7 - SUPPORT BRACKET
8 - COOLANT HOSE FROM HEATER
9 - FUEL LINE
10 - FUEL LINE
11 - BOLT
12 - FUEL PRESSURE SENSOR
13 - HARNESS CONNECTOR
14 - HARNESS CONNECTOR
15 - CHARGE AIR HOSE
16 - BRACKET
17 - GASKET
18 - SUPPORT BRACKETS

LTV0500000000039

Fig. 7 Intake manifold replacement

1 - CAMSHAFT HOUSING
2 - DOWEL
3 - FUEL PIPE
4 - O-RING
5 - COOLANT HOSE
6 - COOLANT HOSE
7 - BOLT
8 - BUSHING
9 - HIGH PRESSURE PUMP INTERMEDIATE GEAR
10 - EXHAUST MANIFOLD
11 - COOLANT PIPE
12 - TURBOCHARGER
13 - O-RING
14 - TURBOCHARGER OIL SUPPLY LINE
15 - BANJO BOLT
16 - TAPPET

LTV0500000000052

Fig. 8 Camshaft housing replacement

5. Disconnect fuel lines.
6. Remove mounting bolts and fuel pump, **Fig. 20.**
7. Position cylinder No. 1 at ignition TDC. **Do not rotate engine counterclockwise.**
8. Lock camshaft using locking pin tool No. 8929 through first camshaft bearing cap into lefthand inlet camshaft sprocket hole, **Fig. 15.**
9. Ensure two intake camshaft sprockets are positioned opposite and bearing cap markings align.
10. **Do not rotate engine with locking pin in place.**
11. Remove intake air scoop.
12. Relieve belt tension by rotating ratchet and tensioner counterclockwise using suitable long handle drive ratchet.
13. Remove drive belt starting at water pump pulley.
14. Remove timing chain tensioner, **Fig. 16.**
15. Secure timing chain to camshaft sprocket using suitable tie straps.
16. Remove mounting bolt and sprocket with chain attached.
17. Separate timing chain using suitable timing chain separator tool.
18. Remove tool and install sprocket with chain on camshaft. **Do not remove chain from sprocket.**
19. Remove chain press-out pin.
20. Secure chain in place using timing chain retainer tool No. 8931, or equivalent.
21. Remove tie straps.
22. Attach new timing chain to old using assembly link, plate and locking element.
23. Draw new timing chain in by rotating crankshaft in normal rotational direction slowly keeping new chain meshed with camshaft sprocket.
24. Draw out old chain as new chain is drawn in.
25. Remove assembly locking element, outer plate and link.
26. Attach and retain new timing chain to sprocket.
27. Install new riveted link and middle plate.
28. Remove retaining tool.
29. Remove camshaft sprocket from camshaft with chain attached.
30. Press new riveted link using riveting tool.
31. Rivet link and install sprocket and chain on camshaft.
32. Reverse procedure to install, noting the following:
    a. Prime fuel pump before installation.
    b. Install new timing chain tensioner gasket.
    c. Place belt over all pulleys except water pump.
    d. Rotating ratchet and tensioner counterclockwise using suitable long handle drive ratchet.
    e. Place belt over water pump pulley and remove ratchet.

TIMING CHAIN TENSIONER

REPLACE

1. Remove mounting bolts and engine cover.
2. Remove valve cover as outlined under "Valve Cover, Replace."
3. Position cylinder No. 1 at ignition TDC. **Do not rotate engine counterclockwise.**
4. Lock camshaft using locking pin tool No. 8929 through first camshaft bearing cap into lefthand inlet camshaft sprocket hole, **Fig. 15.**
5. Ensure two intake camshaft sprockets are positioned opposite and bearing cap markings align.
6. **Do not rotate engine with locking pin in place.**
7. Remove intake air scoop.
8. Relieve belt tension by rotating ratchet and tensioner counterclockwise using suitable long handle drive ratchet.
9. Remove drive belt starting at water pump pulley.
10. Remove timing chain tensioner, **Fig. 16.**
11. Reverse procedure to install, noting the following:
    a. Install new timing chain tensioner gasket.
    b. Place belt over all pulleys except water pump.
    c. Rotating ratchet and tensioner counterclockwise using suitable long handle drive ratchet.
    d. Place belt over water pump pulley and remove ratchet.

CAMSHAFT

REPLACE

Removal

1. Remove timing chain tensioner as outlined under "Timing Chain Tensioner, Replace."
2. Remove vacuum line, **Fig. 21.**
3. Remove mounting bolts and vacuum pump. Discard seals.
4. Disconnect fuel lines.
5. Remove mounting bolts and fuel pump.
6. Remove cylinder head front cover mounting bolts.
7. Raise top guide rail locking pawl and remove cylinder head front cover.
8. Remove top guide rail.
9. Mark camshaft sprocket to timing chain for installation alignment.
10. Remove exhaust camshaft sprocket

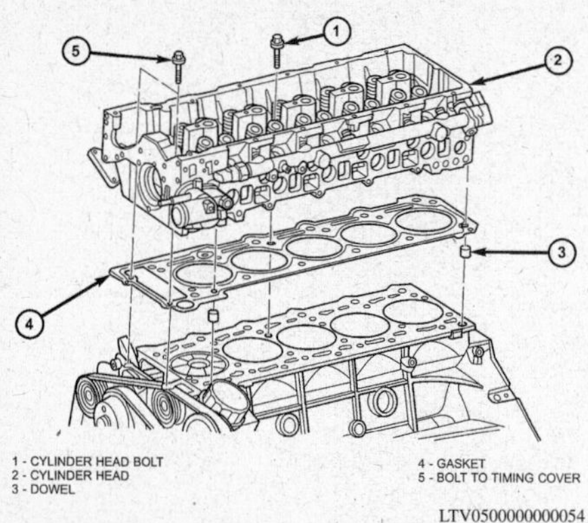

Fig. 9 Cylinder head replacement

mounting bolt. Record dowel pin position for installation alignment.

11. Mark camshaft bearing caps for install in original position.
12. Remove camshaft bearing caps.
13. Remove camshafts, **Fig. 22.**

Installation

1. Lubricate tappets and bearing points with suitable oil.
2. Install camshafts with sprockets' holes opposite, and camshaft and bearing caps aligned.
3. Align camshafts at axial bearing, **Fig. 15.**
4. Position cylinder No. 1 at ignition TDC. **Do not rotate engine counterclockwise.**
5. Install exhaust camshaft bearing caps No. 2 and 5, then intake camshaft bearing caps No. 2 and 5.
6. **Torque** camshaft bearing caps No. 2 and 5 evenly to 80 inch lbs., in one turn revolutions, **Fig. 23.**
7. Install remaining bearing caps, then **torque** evenly to 80 inch lbs., in one turn revolutions, **Fig. 24.**
8. Ensure cylinder No. 1 is at ignition TDC. **Do not rotate engine counterclockwise.**
9. Lock camshaft using locking pin tool No. 8929 through first camshaft bearing cap into lefthand inlet camshaft sprocket hole, **Fig. 15.**
10. Install camshaft sprocket with timing chain onto exhaust camshaft. Ensure dowel pin is properly positioned.
11. Install and tighten new camshaft sprocket mounting bolt.
12. Ensure camshafts are properly aligned, **Fig. 15.**
13. Apply .039–.079 inch suitable sealant to cylinder head front cover, **Fig. 25. Cylinder head front cover must be installed with 10 minutes of sealant application.**
14. Raise top guide locking pawl and install front cover onto guide pins. Install and tighten mounting bolts.
15. Prime fuel pump before installation.
16. Install fuel pump and tighten mounting bolts.
17. Install fuel lines.
18. Install vacuum pump using new gaskets and tighten mounting bolts.
19. Install vacuum pump line.

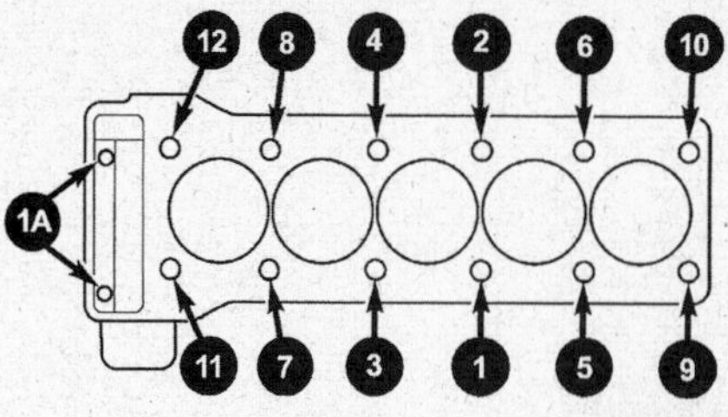

Fig. 10 Cylinder head tightening sequence

20. Install timing chain tensioner as outlined under "Timing Chain Tensioner, Replace."

PISTON & ROD ASSEMBLY

1. Mark connecting rod and bearing cap to each other on intake side.
2. Mark bearing shell and bearing cap to each other.
3. **Do not mix top and bottom connecting rod bearing shells.**
4. Install piston with arrow pointing in direction travel (opposite power flow), **Fig. 26.**
5. Connecting rod marking should point toward intake side.

PISTONS, PINS & RINGS

Align ring gaps as follows:

1. Oil spacer gap on piston skirt centerline, **Fig. 27.**
2. Oil rails gap 180° apart on piston pin bore centerline.
3. Compression ring No. 2 gap 120° from top oil rail gap.
4. Compression ring No. 1 gap 120° from compression ring No. 2 gap.

MAIN & ROD BEARINGS

The crankshaft bearing caps are numbered consecutively, beginning with the first crankshaft bearing cap at the front of the engine, **Fig. 28.**

1. Oil bearing shells before inserting in crankshaft.
2. Thrust washer oil grooves must point toward thrust collars.
3. Thrust washers have two retaining lugs as anti-twist locks.
4. Ensure anti-twist locks are located in connecting rod bearing cap slots.
5. Oil bolt thread and head contact surfaces.
6. Tighten bolts from inside to out, beginning at fit bearing.
7. **Torque** crankshaft bearing caps to 40 ft. lbs.
8. Final tighten bearing caps at additional 90°.
9. **Torque** connecting rod bearing caps to 44 inch lbs.
10. **Torque** connecting rod bearing caps to 18 ft. lbs.
11. Final tighten caps an additional 90°.

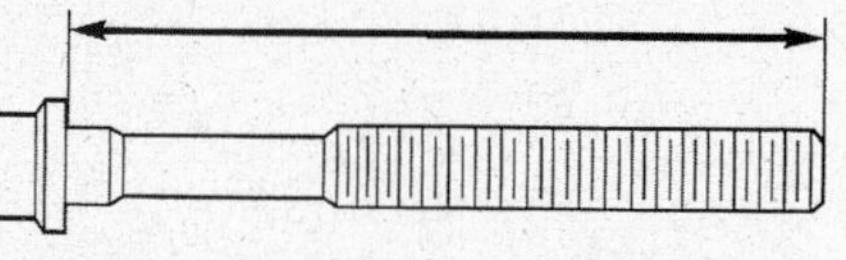

Fig. 11 Cylinder head bolt measurement

CRANKSHAFT SEAL

REPLACE

1. Relieve belt tension by rotating ratchet and tensioner counterclockwise using suitable long handle drive ratchet.
2. Remove drive belt starting at water pump pulley.
3. Lock crankshaft/starter ring gear using retaining lock tool No. 8932, or equivalent, **Fig. 14.**
4. Remove mounting bolt and washer, then the pulley/vibration damper using suitable puller. **Do not tilt puller.**
5. Remove front crankshaft seal using suitable prying tool. **Do not damage crankshaft and mounting hole.**
6. Reverse procedure to install, noting the following:
   a. Install seal using front crankshaft seal installer tool No. 8936, or equivalent.
   b. Align parallel key and hold in place using suitable grease.
   c. **Torque** M8.8 damper mounting bolt to 148 ft. lbs., then tighten an additional 90°.
   d. **Torque** M10.9 damper mounting bolt to 240 ft. lbs., then tighten an additional 90°.

CRANKSHAFT REAR OIL SEAL

REPLACE

1. Raise and support vehicle.
2. Drain engine oil into suitable container.
3. Loose oil pan mounting bolts.
4. Remove transmission as outlined in **MOTOR's "Domestic Transmission, In-Vehicle Service" or "Transmission Service DVD."**
5. Lock crankshaft/starter ring gear using retaining lock tool No. 8932, or equivalent, **Fig. 14.**
6. Remove mounting bolts, inner and outer washers, and flywheel.
7. Remove mounting bolts and rear seal adapter, **Fig. 29. Do not damage oil pan gasket.**
8. Reverse procedure to install, noting the following:
   a. Position rear main oil seal/adaptor with rear main seal installer tool No. 8944, or equivalent, so dowel sleeves fit into guide holes.
   b. **Rear mail oil seal lip must not roll over tool edge.**
   c. **Do not damage oil pan gasket.**
   d. **Torque** flywheel mounting bolts to 33 ft. lbs., then tighten an additional 90°.

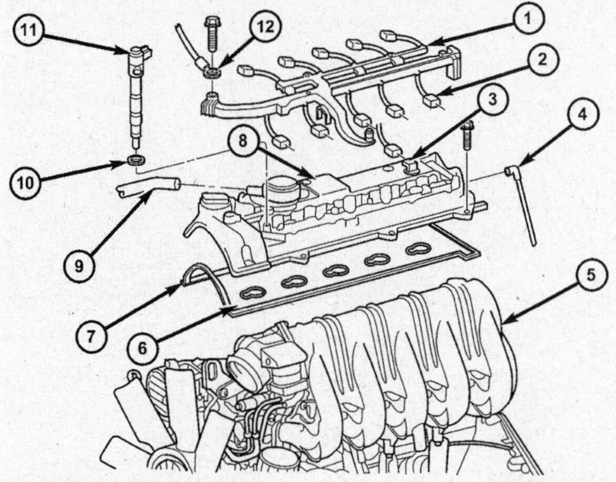

1 - ENGINE WIRING HARNESS
2 - GLOW PLUG CONNECTOR
3 - CAMSHAFT POSITION SENSOR
4 - OUTLET LINE
5 - INTAKE MANIFOLD
6 - GASKET
7 - GASKET
8 - CYLINDER HEAD COVER
9 - CRANKCASE VENT LINE
10 - GASKET
11 - FUEL INJECTOR
12 - GROUND

LTV0500000000041

Fig. 12 Valve cover replacement

1 - FUEL INJECTOR RETURN LINE
2 - RETAINING CLIP
3 - INJECTOR HIGH PRESSURE LINE
4 - INJECTOR SEAL
5 - FUEL INJECTOR
6 - TENSIONING CLAW
7 - SPECIAL TOOLS #8938 AND # 8937

LTV0500000000040

Fig. 13 Fuel injector replacement

OIL PAN

REPLACE

1. Raise and support vehicle.
2. Drain engine oil into suitable container.
3. Remove mounting bolts and position sway bar aside.
4. Remove wiring harness duct from oil pan mounting bolts and position it aside, **Fig. 30.**
5. Lower vehicle and remove turbocharger upper heat shield.
6. Support and slightly raise engine with suitable lifting fixture, **Fig. 5.**
7. Remove engine mount bolts, **Figs. 1 and 2.**
8. Disconnect oil level sensor.
9. Remove transmission cooler lines from oil pan mounting bolts and position them aside.
10. Remove mounting bolts, oil pan and gasket.
11. Reverse procedure to install, noting the following:
    a. Coat oil pan gasket with suitable sealant, **Fig. 31.**
    b. **Torque** M6 oil pan mounting bolts to 80 inch lbs., **Fig. 32.**
    c. **Torque** M8 mounting bolts to 15 ft. lbs.
    d. **Torque** oil pan to bell housing mounting bolts to 30 ft. lbs.

OIL PUMP

REPLACE

1. Remove oil pan as outlined under "Oil Pan, Replace."
2. Remove oil pump mounting bolts, **Fig. 30.**
3. Press tensioner off chain and remove pump from chain.
4. Remove oil pump, pick-up tube and O-ring.
5. Reverse procedure to install.

BELT TENSION DATA

This engine is equipped with a spring loaded automatic belt tensioner. **Do not attempt to inspect belt tension with a belt tension gauge.** If tension is not maintained properly, inspect for improper drive belt routing, excessive belt wear or automatic tensioner damage.

SERPENTINE DRIVE BELT

Replace

1. Relieve belt tension by rotating ratchet and tensioner counterclockwise using suitable long handle drive ratchet.
2. Remove drive belt starting at water pump pulley.
3. Reverse procedure to install, noting the following:
    a. Place belt over all pulleys except water pump.
    b. Rotating ratchet and tensioner counterclockwise using suitable long handle drive ratchet.
    c. Place belt over water pump pulley and remove ratchet.

Routing

Refer to **Fig. 33** for drive belt routing.

VACUUM PUMP

REPLACE

1. Remove vacuum line, **Fig. 19.**
2. Remove mounting bolts and vacuum pump. Discard seals.
3. Reverse procedure to install.

COOLING SYSTEM BLEED

These engines do not require a specified bleed procedure. After filling cooling system, run engine to operating temperature with radiator/pressure cap off. Air will then be automatically bled through cap opening.

THERMOSTAT

REPLACE

1. Drain engine coolant into suitable container.
2. Disconnect connector, then remove locking element and coolant temperature sensor, **Fig. 34.**
3. Disconnect air intake hose at charge air distribution pipe.
4. Remove fuel line bracket.
5. Remove oil filter housing cap.
6. Remove mounting bolts and thermostat.
7. Reverse procedure to install using new gasket.

WATER PUMP

REPLACE

1. Drain coolant into suitable container.
2. Remove mounting screws and cover, then the push pin fasteners and fascia mounting screws.
3. Pull bumper off support brackets and disconnect electrical connectors.
4. Remove rivets, mounting screws and grille.
5. Remove mounting bolts and headlamps.
6. Remove heat shield, **Fig. 35.**
7. Remove clamps and rubber mounts, then the mounting bolts and radiator crossmember.
8. Push radiator forward.
9. Disconnect coolant line from lower radiator shroud.
10. Hold fan pulley using suitable 36 mm fan wrench.
11. Counterhold water pump drive belt pulley using suitable wrench.
12. Remove fan blade/viscous clutch mounting bolt counterclockwise. Mounting nut has righthand threads.
13. Remove fan and shroud.
14. Disconnect fuel lines from water pump brackets.
15. Disconnect water pump coolant hoses, **Fig. 36.**

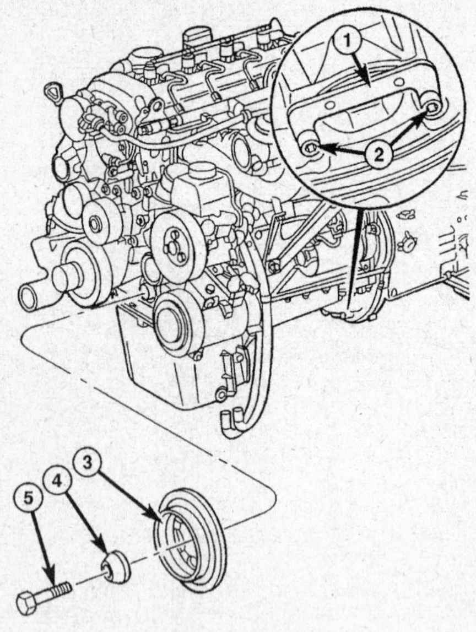

1 - SPECIAL TOOL #8932
2 - RETAINING BOLTS
3 - VIBRATION DAMPER/CRANKSHAFT PULLEY
4 - WASHER
5 - CRANKSHAFT BOLT

LTV0500000000057

Fig. 14 Pulley/vibration damper replacement

16. Remove caps, mounting bolts and belt guide pulley.
17. Remove mounting bolts and water pump.
18. Reverse procedure to install using new gasket.

RADIATOR

REPLACE

1. Drain radiator coolant into suitable container.
2. Remove mounting screws and cover, then the push pin fasteners and fascia mounting screws.
3. Pull bumper off support brackets and disconnect electrical connectors.
4. Remove rivets, mounting screws and grille.
5. Remove mounting bolts and headlamps.
6. Remove heat shield, **Fig. 35.**
7. Remove clamps and rubber mounts, then the mounting bolts and radiator crossmember.
8. Remove mounting bolts and front bumpers.
9. Recover air conditioning refrigerant as outlined in "Air Conditioning" chapter.
10. Disconnect condenser outlet port liquid line fitting, **Fig. 37.** Discard seal, then plug or tape opening.
11. Disconnect condenser inlet port liquid line fitting. Discard seal, then plug or tape opening.
12. Disconnect electrical connector, then remove mounting bolts, auxiliary fan and upper bracket.
13. Remove fasteners and lower bracket.
14. Remove four mounting screws and condenser.
15. Disconnect charge air hose from tubrocharger and air intake pipe, **Fig. 38.**

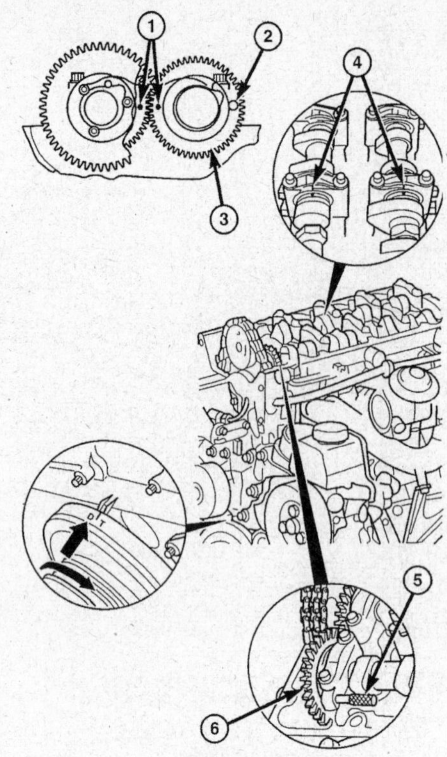

1 - CAMSHAFT SPROCKET ALIGNMENT DOTS
2 - CAMSHAFT LOCK POSITION
3 - INTAKE CAMSHAFT SPROCKET
4 - CAMSHAFT AND BEARING CAP ALIGNMENT MARKS
5 - CAMSHAFT LOCKING PIN (SPECIAL TOOL #8929)
6 - INTAKE CAMSHAFT SPROCKET

LTV0500000000042

Fig. 15 Camshaft alignment

16. Disconnect air intake pipe from body.
17. Disconnect coolant reservoir hoses and coolant level sensor connector.
18. Drain power steering pump reservoir steering gear oil into suitable container.
19. Disconnect power steering pump reservoir hydraulic oil hose, then the hose from line.
20. Disconnect righthand lower radiator hose.
21. Disconnect transmission cooler lines.
22. Remove mounting bolts, then the lefthand and righthand radiator trim.
23. Remove radiator from rubber grommets.
24. Remove radiator top trim.
25. Remove charge air cooler with steering cooling loop, **Fig. 39.**
26. Remove radiator bottom trim and disconnect coolant hose.
27. Disconnect coolant pipe with hose and remove fan shroud.
28. Reverse procedure to install.

TURBOCHARGER

REPLACE

1. Remove heat shield, **Fig. 40.**
2. Remove clamp and disconnect front exhaust pipe from turbocharger.
3. Remove clamps, then disconnect charge and intake air hoses from turbocharger.

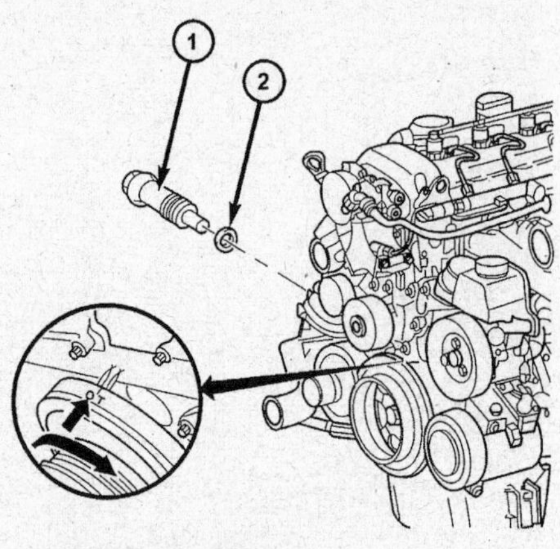

1 - TIMING CHAIN TENSIONER
2 - TIMING CHAIN TENSIONER SEAL

LTV0500000000044

Fig. 16 Timing chain tensioner replacement

4. Remove vacuum unit line.
5. Disconnect oil supply line at cylinder head and turbocharger.
6. Disconnect oil return line from turbocharger.
7. Remove mounting bolts and support bracket.
8. Remove mounting bolts and turbocharger.
9. Reverse procedure to install using new gaskets.

FUEL PUMP

REPLACE

1. Remove vacuum line, **Fig. 19.**
2. Remove mounting bolts and vacuum pump. Discard seals.
3. Disconnect fuel lines.
4. Remove mounting bolts and fuel pump, **Fig. 20.**
5. Reverse procedure to install. Prime fuel pump before installation.

INJECTION PUMP

REPLACE

1. Remove mounting screws and cover, then the push pin fasteners and fascia mounting screws.
2. Pull bumper off support brackets and disconnect electrical connectors.
3. Remove rivets, mounting screws and grille.
4. Remove mounting bolts and headlamps.
5. Remove heat shield, **Fig. 35.**
6. Remove clamps and rubber mounts, then the mounting bolts and radiator crossmember.
7. Push radiator forward.
8. Disconnect coolant line from lower radiator shroud.
9. Hold fan pulley using suitable 36 mm fan wrench.
10. Counterhold water pump drive belt pulley using suitable wrench.
11. Remove fan blade/viscous clutch mounting bolt counterclockwise. Mounting nut has righthand threads.
12. Remove fan and shroud.

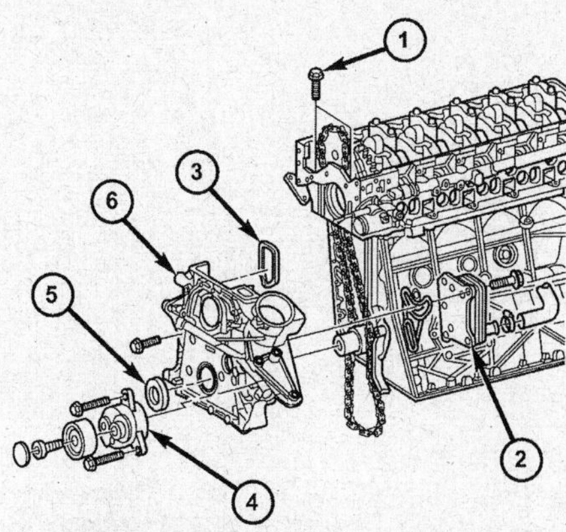

Fig. 17 Front cover replacement

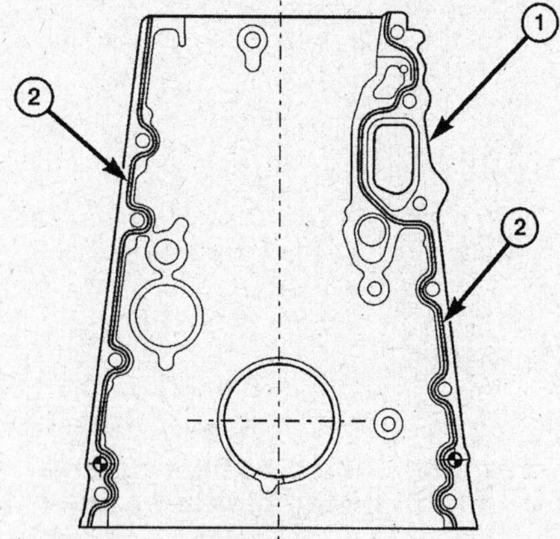

Fig. 18 Front cover sealant application

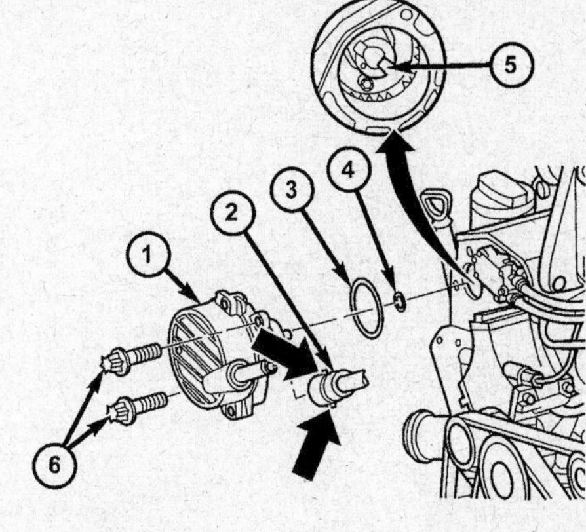

Fig. 19 Vacuum pump replacement

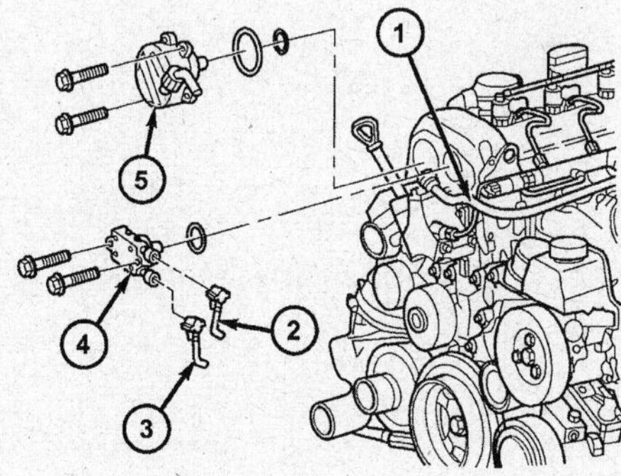

Fig. 20 Fuel pump replacement

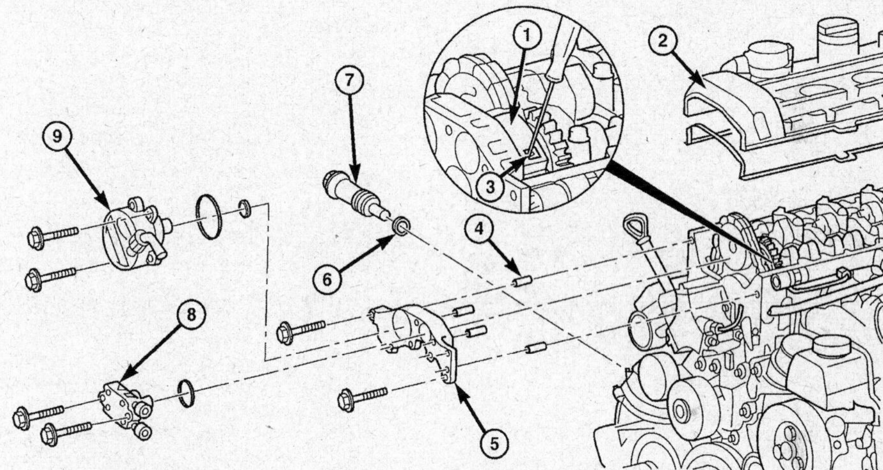

Fig. 21 Cylinder head front cover replacement

13. Disconnect injection pump electrical connector.
14. Mark outside fuel return line for installation alignment.
15. **Do not crimp or bend fuel lines. Counterhold thread connections with suitable wrench.**
16. Remove mounting bolt and bracket, then the fuel supply and return lines, **Fig. 41.**
17. Remove mounting bolts and injection pump.
18. Reverse procedure to install.

FUEL FILTER

REPLACE

1. Disconnect fuel outlet line connector, **Fig. 42.**
2. Loosen clamp and disconnect fuel inlet line.
3. Remove mounting bolt and preheating valve.
4. Remove bracket mounting bolt and fuel filter.
5. Reverse procedure to install. Fill filter with approximately 13 ounces new diesel fuel.

INJECTION PUMP TIMING

All timing and fuel adjustments are controlled by the ECM and are not adjustable.

IDLE SPEED

ADJUST

All timing and fuel adjustments are controlled by the ECM and are not adjustable.

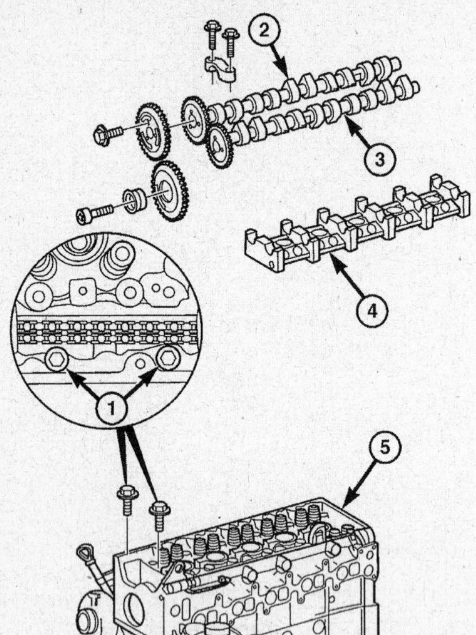

1 - CYLINDER HEAD BOLTS
2 - EXHAUST CAMSHAFT
3 - INTAKE CAMSHAFT
4 - CAMSHAFT HOUSING
5 - CYLINDER HEAD

LTV0500000000043

Fig. 22 Camshaft replacement

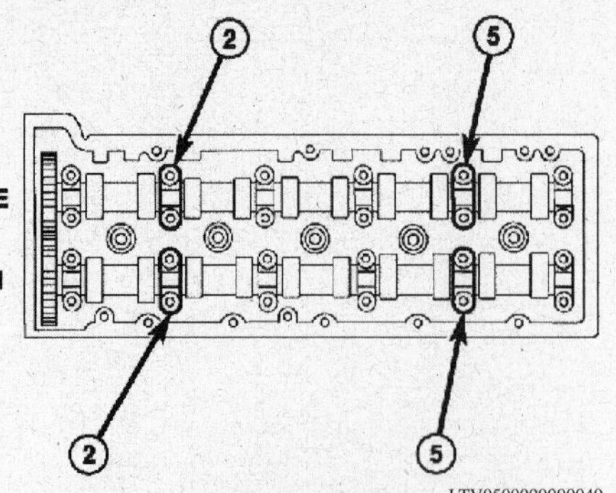

LTV0500000000049

Fig. 23 Camshaft bearing cap first tightening sequence

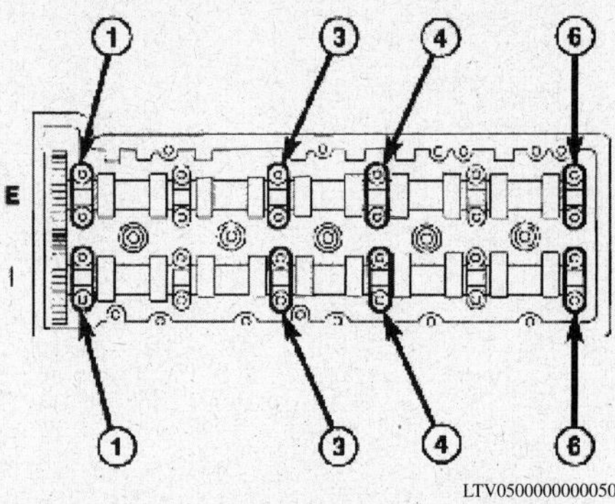

LTV0500000000050

Fig. 24 Camshaft bearing cap second tightening sequence

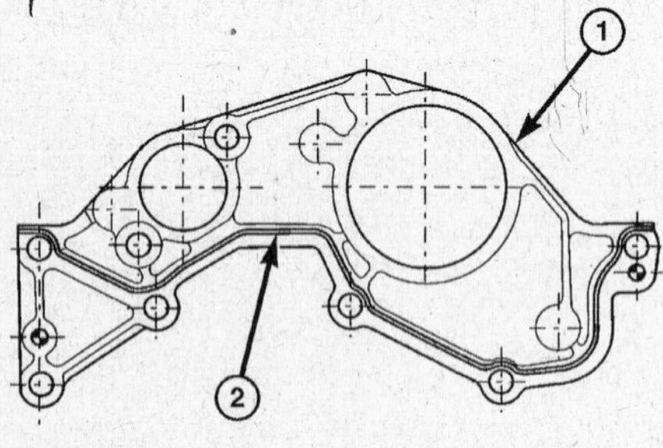

1 - CYLINDER HEAD FRONT COVER
2 - SEALANT BEAD

LTV0500000000051

Fig. 25 Cylinder head front cover replacement

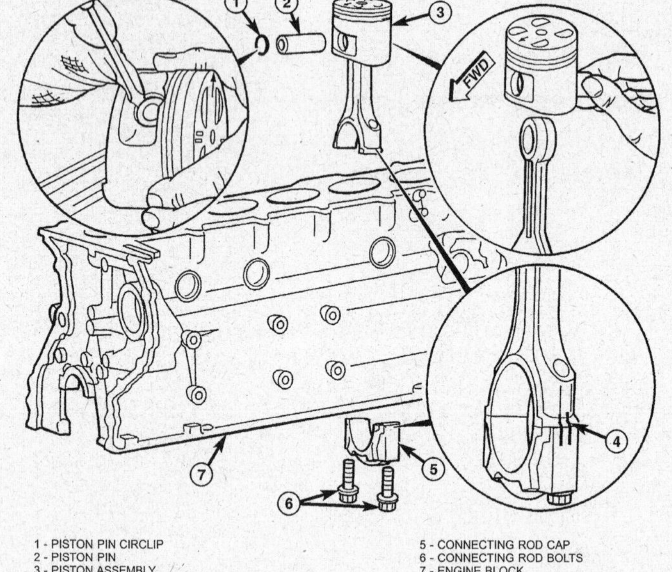

1 - PISTON PIN CIRCLIP
2 - PISTON PIN
3 - PISTON ASSEMBLY
4 - CONNECTING ROD AND CAP ALIGNMENT MARKS
5 - CONNECTING ROD CAP
6 - CONNECTING ROD BOLTS
7 - ENGINE BLOCK

LTV0500000000063

Fig. 26 Piston & connecting rod assembly

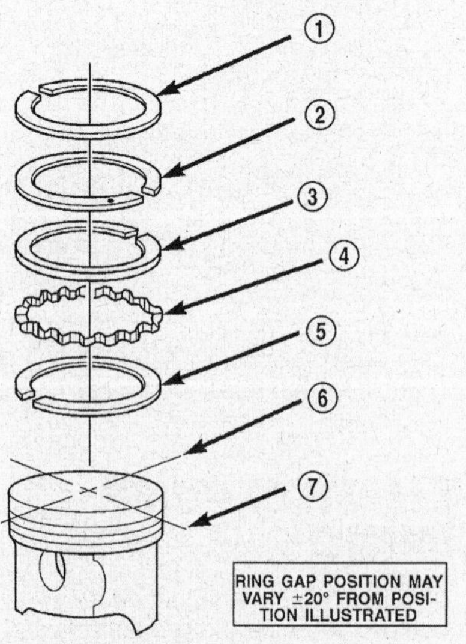

RING GAP POSITION MAY VARY ±20° FROM POSITION ILLUSTRATED

1 - TOP COMPRESSION RING
2 - BOTTOM COMPRESSION RING
3 - TOP OIL CONTROL RAIL
4 - OIL RAIL SPACER
5 - BOTTOM OIL CONTROL RAIL
6 - IMAGINARY LINE PARALLEL TO PISTON PIN
7 - IMAGINARY LINE THROUGH CENTER OF PISTON SKIRT

LTV0500000000064

Fig. 27 Ring gap orientation

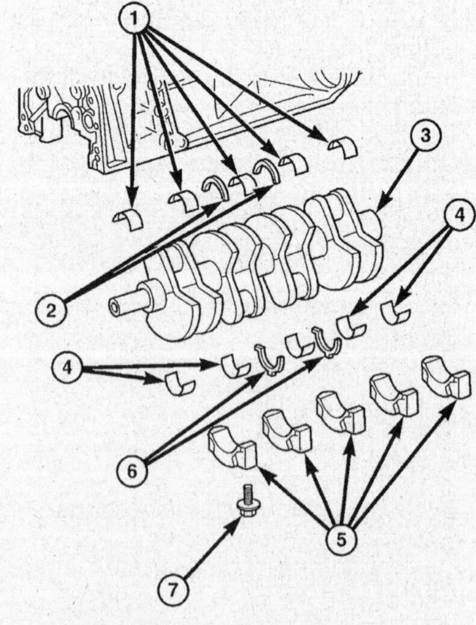

1 - BEARING HALVES IN ENGINE BLOCK
2 - THRUST WASHERS IN ENGINE BLOCK
3 - CRANKSHAFT
4 - BEARING HALVES IN MAIN BEARING CAPS
5 - MAIN BEARING CAPS
6 - THRUST WASHERS IN MAIN BEARING CAPS
7 - MAIN BEARING BOLTS

LTV0500000000065

Fig. 28 Crankshaft assembly

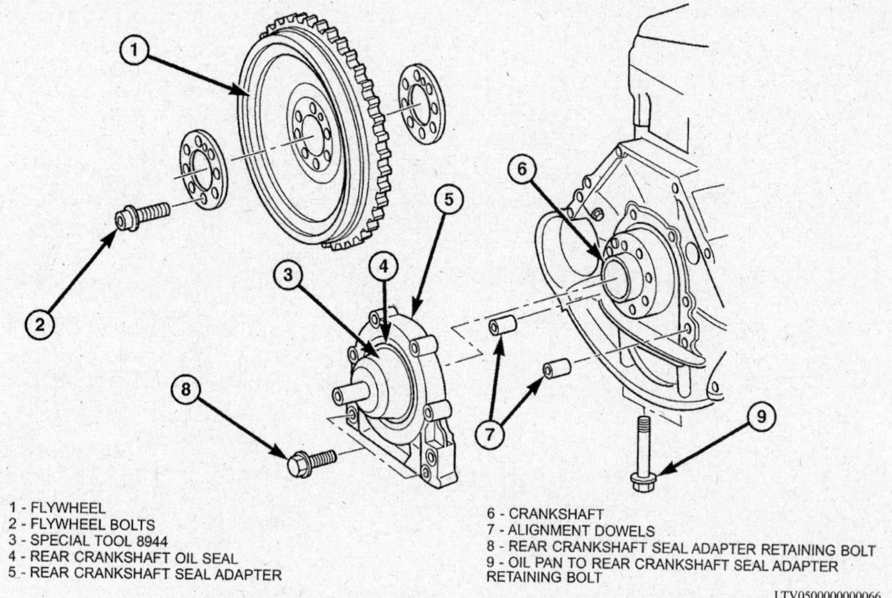

Fig. 29 Crankshaft rear oil seal replacement

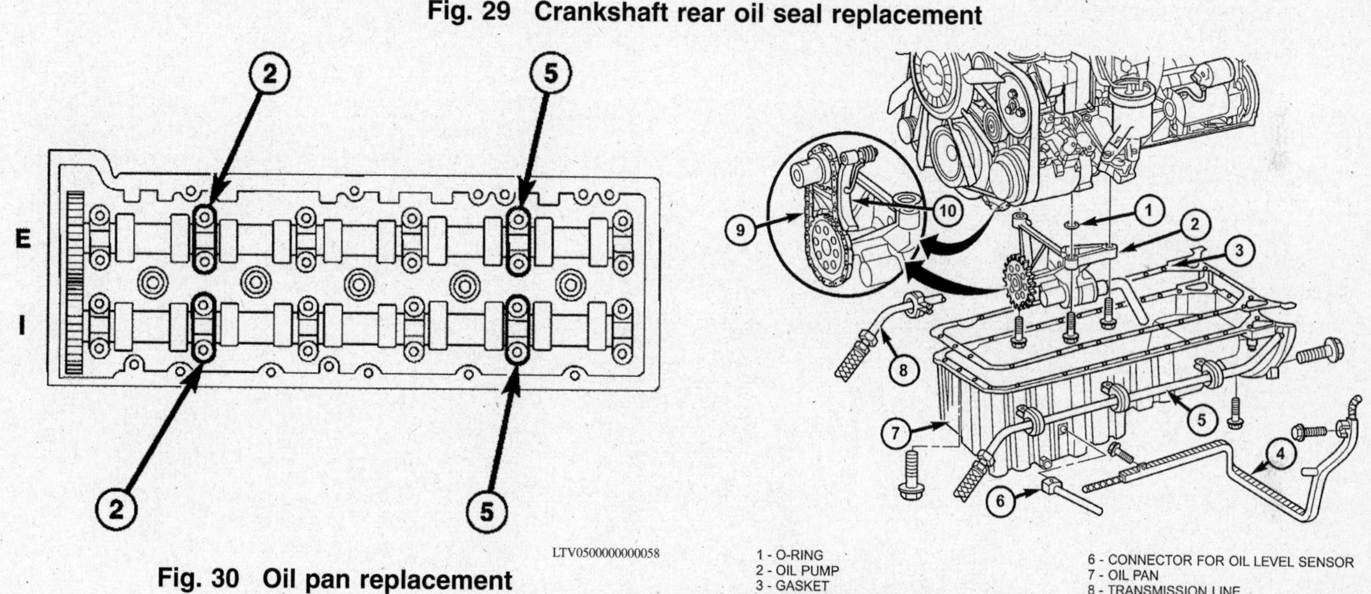

Fig. 30 Oil pan replacement

Fig. 31 Oil pan gasket sealant application points

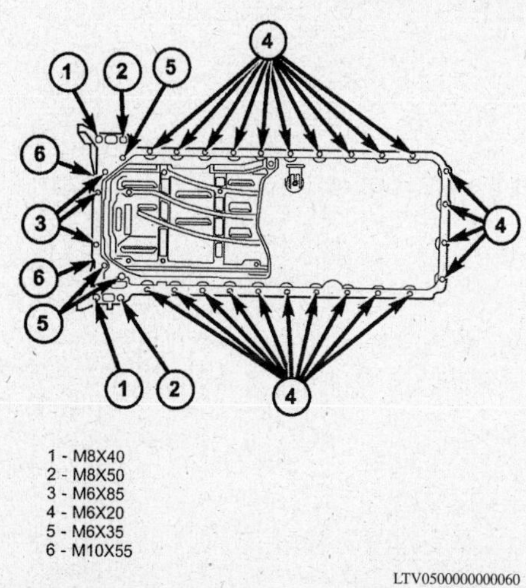

Fig. 32 Oil pan mounting bolts

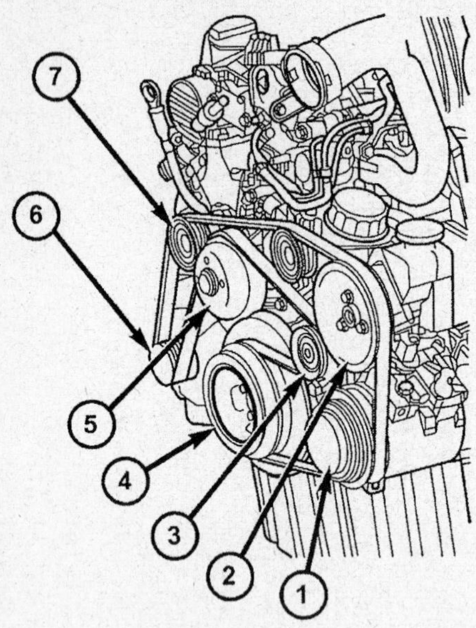

1 - A/C COMPRESSOR
2 - POWER STEERING
3 - DRIVE BELT TENSIONER
4 - CRANKSHAFT PULLEY
5 - WATER PUMP PULLEY
6 - GENERATOR
7 - IDLER PULLEY

LTV0500000000067

Fig. 33 Drive belt routing

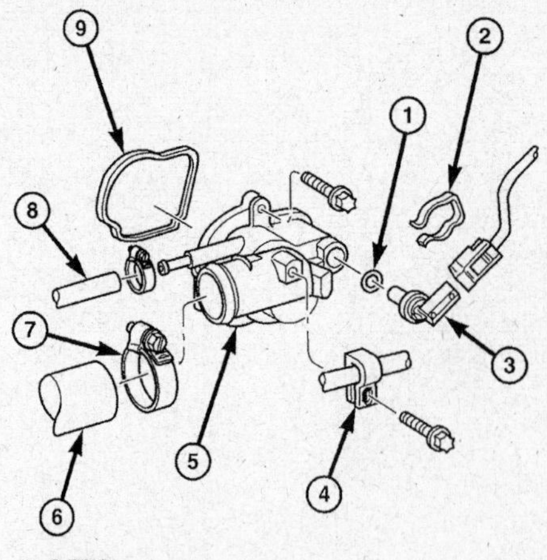

1 - O-RING
2 - CLAMP
3 - COOLANT TEMPERATURE SENSOR
4 - FUEL LINE W/BRACKET
5 - THERMOSTAT HOUSING ASSEMBLY
6 - COOLANT HOSE
7 - CLAMP
8 - COOLANT HOSE
9 - GASKET

LTV0500000000068

Fig. 34 Thermostat replacement

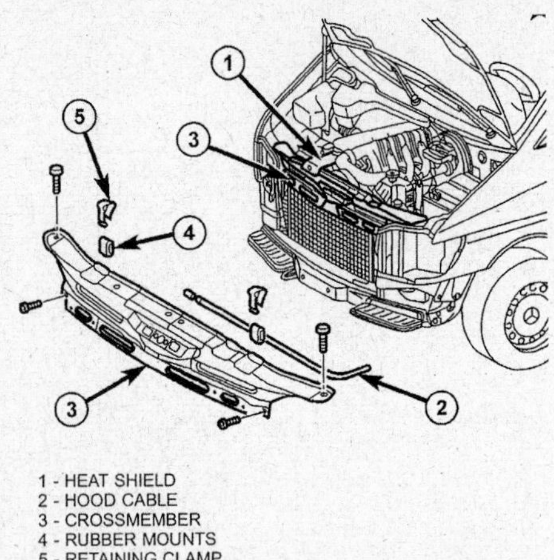

1 - HEAT SHIELD
2 - HOOD CABLE
3 - CROSSMEMBER
4 - RUBBER MOUNTS
5 - RETAINING CLAMP

LTV0500000000032

Fig. 35 Radiator crossmember replacement

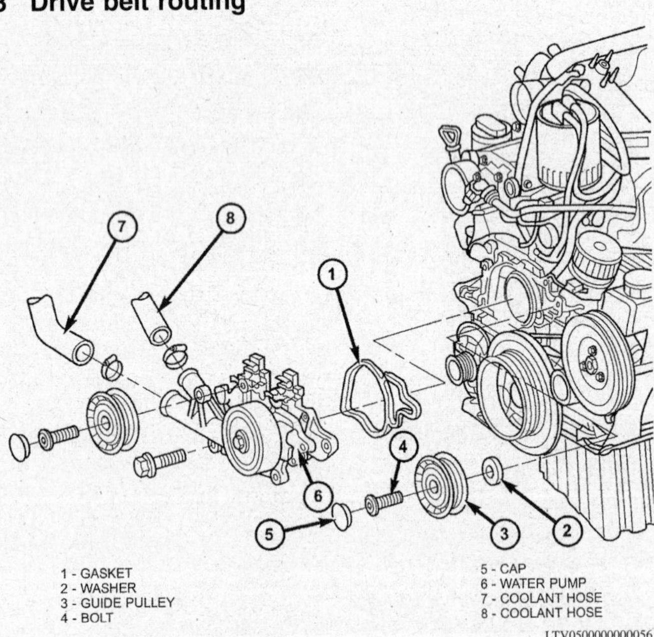

1 - GASKET
2 - WASHER
3 - GUIDE PULLEY
4 - BOLT
5 - CAP
6 - WATER PUMP
7 - COOLANT HOSE
8 - COOLANT HOSE

LTV0500000000056

Fig. 36 Water pump replacement

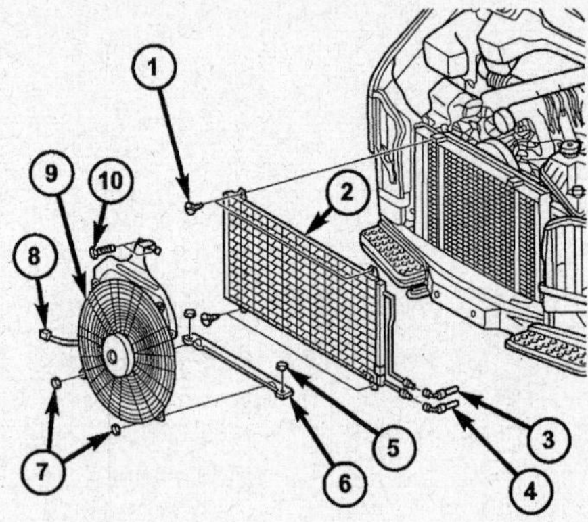

1 - SCREW (4)
2 - CONDENSER
3 - LIQUID REFRIGERANT LINE
4 - COMPRESSOR DISCHARGE LINE
5 - NUT (2)
6 - LOWER AUXILIARY FAN BRACKET
7 - NUT (2)
8 - WIRE HARNESS CONNECTOR
9 - AUXILIARY COOLING FAN
10 - SCREW (2)

LTV0500000000034

Fig. 37 Air conditioning condenser replacement

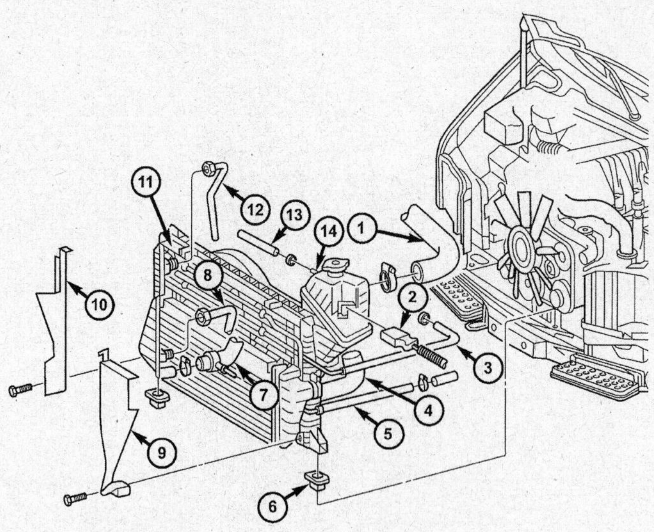

1 - COOLANT HOSE
2 - SENSOR HARNESS CONNECTOR
3 - HYDRAULIC HOSE
4 - CHARGE AIR HOSE
5 - HYDRAULIC HOSE
6 - RUBBER GROMMET
7 - COOLANT HOSE
8 - ATF LINE
9 - LEFT RADIATOR TRIM PANEL
10 - RIGHT RADIATOR TRIM PANEL
11 - RADIATOR
12 - ATF LINE
13 - COOLANT HOSE
14 - COOLANT RESERVOIR

LTV0500000000033

Fig. 38 Radiator replacement

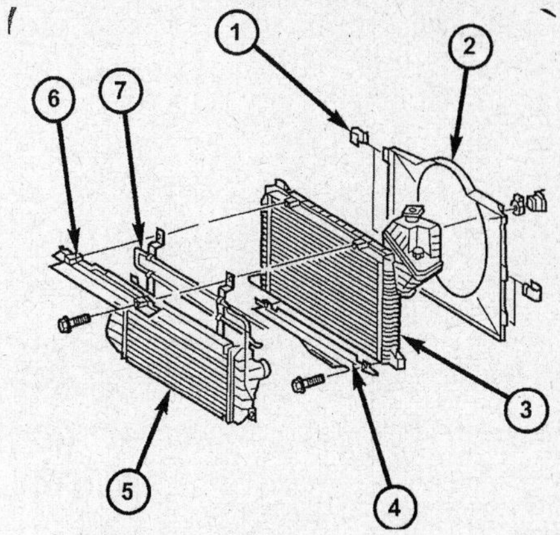

1 - CLIP
2 - SHROUD
3 - RADIATOR
4 - BOTTOM RADIATOR TRIM PANEL
5 - CHARGE AIR COOLER
6 - TOP RADIATOR TRIM PANEL
7 - POWER STEERING COOLER LOOP

LTV0500000000035

Fig. 39 Radiator & fan shroud replacement

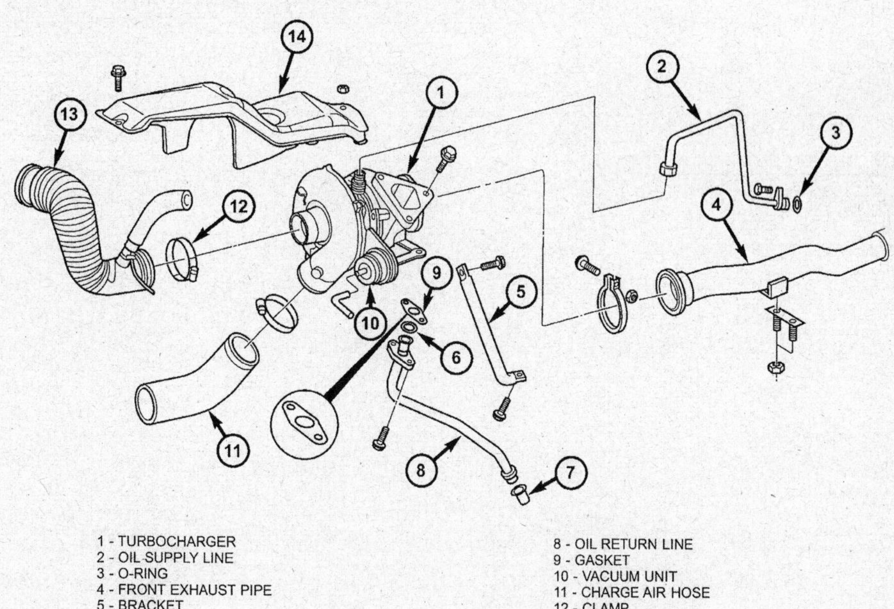

1 - TURBOCHARGER
2 - OIL SUPPLY LINE
3 - O-RING
4 - FRONT EXHAUST PIPE
5 - BRACKET
6 - O-RING
7 - GASKET
8 - OIL RETURN LINE
9 - GASKET
10 - VACUUM UNIT
11 - CHARGE AIR HOSE
12 - CLAMP
13 - AIR INTAKE HOSE
14 - HEAT SHIELD

LTV0500000000069

Fig. 40 Turbocharger replacement

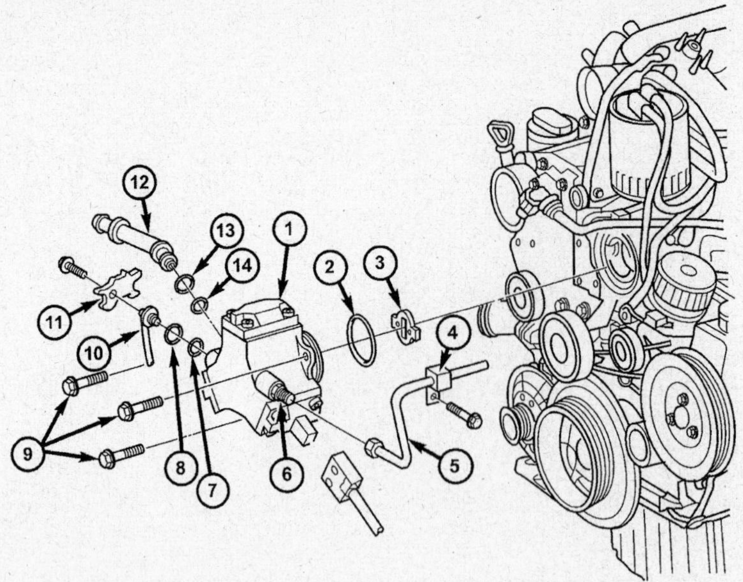

1 - HIGH PRESSURE INJECTION PUMP
2 - SEALING RING
3 - INJECTION PUMP DRIVER
4 - BRACKET
5 - HIGH PRESSURE LINE
6 - THREADED UNION
7 - SEALING RING
8 - SEALING RING
9 - BOLTS
10 - FUEL RETURN LINE
11 - BRACKET
12 - FUEL SUPPLY LINE FROM LOW PRESSURE PUMP
13 - SEALING RING
14 - SEALING RING

LTV0500000000045

Fig. 41 Fuel injection pump replacement

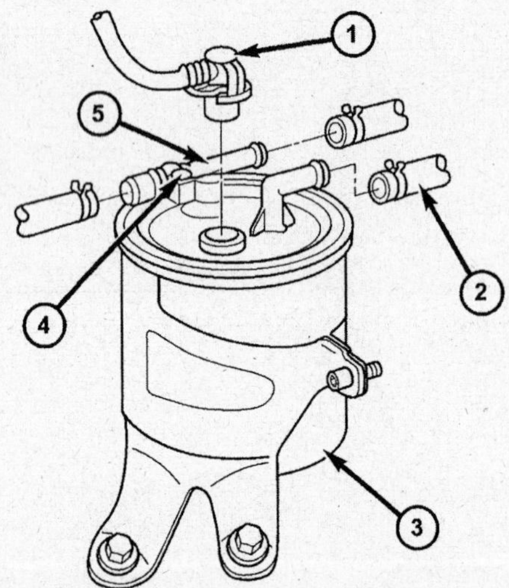

1 - FUEL LINE PLUG CONNECTION
2 - FUEL LINE INLET
3 - FUEL FILTER
4 - BOLT OF PREHEATING VALVE
5 - PREHEATING VALVE

LTV0500000000070

Fig. 42 Fuel filter replacement

TIGHTENING SPECIFICATIONS

Year	Component	Torque Ft. Lbs.
2003–06	Air Condition Compressor	15
	Air Conditioning Condenser	17①
	Air Conditioning Condenser Inlet Port Fitting	24
	Air Conditioning Condenser Outlet Port Fitting	12
	Alternator	40
	Auxiliary Fan Bracket	45①
	Battery Holdown	70①
	Battery Tray	105①
	Belt Guide Pulley	26
	Bumper	15
	Camshaft Bearing Caps	⑤
	Camshaft Position (CMP) Sensor	97①
	Camshaft Sprocket, Exhaust	13
	Camshaft Sprocket, Intake	37
	Crankshaft Damper	⑦
	Crankshaft Position (CKP) Sensor	70①
	Crankshaft Pulley	⑦
	Cylinder Head Front Cover	10
	Engine Cover	97①
	Engine Mount Bracket	⑩
	Engine Mount, Rear Crossmember To Body	30
	Engine Mount, Rear Mount to Rear Crossmember	26
	Engine Mount, Rear Mount To Transmission	26
	Engine Mount, Through Bolt	30
	Engine Mount To Bracket, Bolt	40
	Engine Mount To Bracket, Nut	48
	Engine Mount To Front Axle Carrier	26
	Engine Mount To Vehicle Frame	26
	Exhaust Manifold	22
	Fan	80①
	Fascia	127
	Front Cover	15
	Front Exhaust Pipe To Turbocharger	22
	Fuel Injector	④
	Fuel Line Bracket	80①
	Fuel Line, High Pressure	16

TIGHTENING SPECIFICATIONS—Continued

Year	Component	Torque Ft. Lbs.
2003–06	Fuel Pump	80①
	Fuel Rail	10
	Glow Plug	115①
	Hood	17
	Injection Pump	10
	Intake Manifold	12③
	Main Bearing	⑨
	Oil Pan	⑧
	Oil Pan Drain Plug	18
	Oil Pump	13
	Power Steering Pump	15
	Power Steering Pump Hose, High Pressure	28
	Radiator Crossmember	10
	Rear Main Seal/Adaptor	80①
	Steering Gear	②
	Thermostat	80①
	Timing Chain Tensioner	59
	Torque Converter	33
	Transmission To Engine	28
	Transmission Oil Cooler Line	25
	Turbocharger Bracket To Engine	15
	Turbocharger Bracket To Turbocharge	22
	Turbocharger To Exhaust Manifold	22
	Turbocharger Oil Supply Line To Cylinder Head	80①
	Turbocharger To Oil Supply Line	13
	Vacuum Pump	10
	Valve Cover	80①
	Vibration Damper	⑦
	Viscous Clutch	33
	Water Pump	10⑥

① — Inch lbs.
② — **Torque** to 18 ft. lbs., then to 33 ft. lbs.
③ — Tighten in cross directional pattern. Begin with middle bolts and work outward.
④ — Refer to "Valve Cover, Replace" for tightening specifications and sequence.
⑤ — Refer to "Camshaft, Replace" for tightening specifications and sequence.
⑥ — **Torque** M8 bolts 15 ft. lbs.
⑦ — Refer to "Crankshaft Damper, Replace" for tightening specifications and sequence.
⑧ — Refer to "Oil Pan, Replace" for tightening specifications and sequence.
⑨ — Refer to "Main & Rod Bearings" for tightening specifications and sequence.
⑩ — **Torque** to 15 ft. lbs., then tighten an additional 90°.

Rear Axle & Suspension

NOTE: Refer To "Computer Relearn Procedure" Located In The Front Of This Manual When Battery Power To The Computer Has Been Interrupted.

INDEX

PRECAUTIONS

Battery Ground Cable

Prior to service, disconnect battery ground cable and isolate as required.

DESCRIPTION

The rear axle consist of a cast iron center section with axle tubes extending from either side. The tubes are pressed into and welded to the differential housing from a one-piece axle housing.

Models equipped with Single Rear Wheels (SRW) have semi-flooting axle shafts, **Fig. 1**.

Models equipped with Dual Rear Wheels (DRW) have full floating axle shafts, **Fig. 2.**

Axle seals, axle bearings, pinion seals and differential cover are the only service components.

The rear suspension consists of: shock absorbers, jounce bumpers, stabilizer bar and leaf springs.

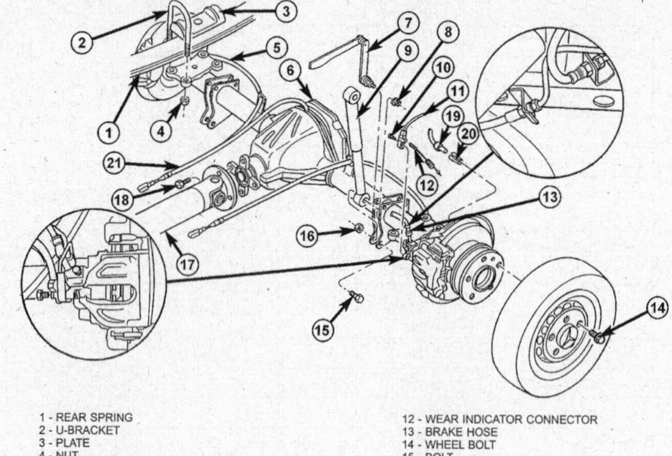

Fig. 1 SRW rear axle & suspension

REAR AXLE

REPLACE

1. Raise and support vehicle.
2. Support axle with suitable lifting device.
3. Remove tire and wheel assemblies.
4. Disconnect wear indicator cable, **Figs. 1 and 2.**
5. Disconnect brake pad wear indicator cable connector.
6. Remove ABS sensor and clamp bushing from mounting bore.
7. Remove park brake cables ties.
8. Disconnect brake pad wear indicator and ABS sensor cable up to parking brake relay.
9. Remove brake cables from adjust.
10. Remove guide bolt and brake caliper, **Figs. 3 and 4.** Support caliper aside with adapters and lines attached.
11. Remove mounting nuts and disconnect stabilizer bar from axle brackets.
12. Remove shock absorber mounting bolts.
13. Remove mounting nuts and disconnect ALB lever from bracket.
14. Disconnect clips and brakes hoses.
15. Remove rear axle vent line from frame.
16. Mark propeller shaft for installation alignment, **Figs. 5 and 6.**
17. Remove propeller shaft to transmission and rear axle flanges' mounting bolts, **Figs. 7 and 8.**
18. Remove intermediate bearing bracket mounting nuts.
19. **On models with 140-inch wheelbase,** remove mounting bolts and brake cable bracket.
20. **On all models,** remove propeller shaft.
21. Remove mounting nuts, U-brackets and plates.
22. Remove rear axle.
23. Reverse procedure to install.

REAR AXLE SHAFT

REPLACE

DRW

1. Raise and support vehicle, then remove tire and wheel assembly.
2. Remove hub nuts and axle shaft, **Fig. 9.**
3. Reverse procedure to install. Coat axle shaft flange with Hylomar SQ 32 M, or equivalent sealant.

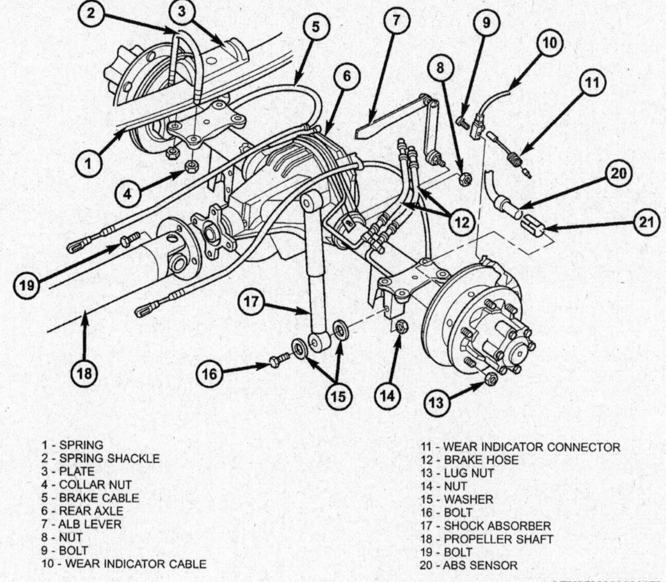

Fig. 2 DRW rear axle & suspension

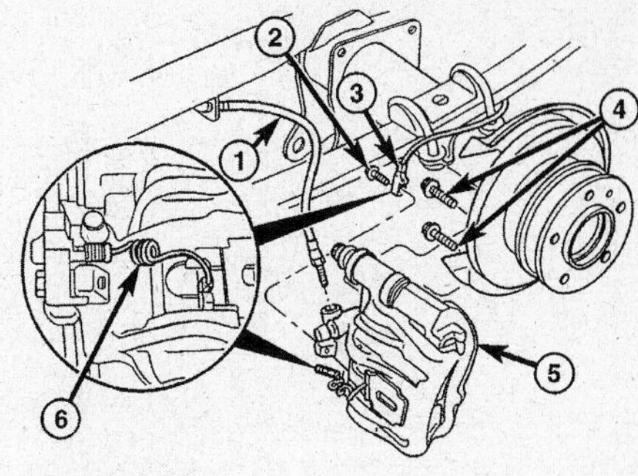

Fig. 3 Brake caliper replacement. SRW

SRW

1. Raise and support vehicle, then remove tire and wheel assembly.
2. Disconnect front brake cable, **Fig. 10. Do not remove cables.**
3. Remove ABS sensor with clamp bushing from bearing cap.
4. Remove brake fluid reservoir cap.
5. Remove cable and brake pad wear indictor.
6. Remove brake caliper guide pin.
7. **On models equipped with 15-inch wheel,** fold brake caliper top section up, **Fig. 11.**
8. **On models equipped with 16-inch wheel,** proceed as follows:
   a. Remove brake caliper from adapter, **Fig. 12.**
   b. Remove retaining spring.
9. **On all models,** remove disc brake pads.
10. Remove caliper adapter.
11. Apply parking brake.
12. Secure disc brake rotor using two lug studs.
13. Remove locking bolt and two lugs nuts.
14. Release parking brake.
15. Loosen park brake adjuster and remove rear brake rotor, **Fig. 13.**
16. Remove retracting springs using return spring pulling hook tool No. 9280, or equivalent, **Fig. 14.**
17. Remove adjuster.
18. Remove pressure springs using retaining spring tool No. 9281, or equivalent.
19. Pull parking brake shoes apart at bottom and remove with adjuster.
20. Remove brake control lock.
21. Remove bearing cap bolts and axle shaft.
22. Remove seal and gasket.
23. Reverse procedure to instal using new U-bolt nuts.

PROPELLER SHAFT

REPLACE

1. Secure vehicle from rolling.
2. Mark propeller shaft for installation alignment, **Figs. 5 and 6.**
3. Remove propeller shaft to transmission and rear axle flanges' mounting bolts, **Figs. 7 and 8.**
4. Remove intermediate bearing bracket mounting nuts.
5. **On models with 140-inch wheelbase,** remove mounting bolts and brake cable bracket.
6. **On all models,** remove propeller shaft.
7. Reverse procedure to install.

HUB & BEARING

REPLACE

SRW

REMOVAL

1. Remove rear axle shaft as outlined under "Rear Axle Shaft, Replace."
2. Straighten locking pin using suitable punch and hammers.
3. Loosen bearing nut using bearing nut wrench tool No. 9279, or equivalent, noting the following:
   a. Lefthand rear axle nut with groove has lefthand threads.
   b. Righthand rear axle nut less groove has righthand threads.
4. Remove bearing nut and locking ring.
5. Push axle bearing plate tool No. 9277, or equivalent, between bearing cover and rear axle shaft.
6. Place axle shaft with plate into suitable press.
7. Press axle shaft through bearing cover and tapered roller bearing.
8. Remove tapered roller bearing, sealing ring, dust shield and bearing cap, **Fig. 15.**
9. Drive shaft seal out of bearing cover using suitable drift and hammer.

INSTALLATION

1. Drive axle shaft flush within .12 inch deep into bearing cover using installer tool No. 9278, or equivalent.
2. Grease roller bearings.
3. Install bearing cover with axle shaft seal, new gasket and dust shield.
4. Install tapered roller bearing and race.
5. Install new locking ring with flat side toward nut.
6. Position axle shaft through axle bearing plate tool No. 9277, or equivalent, in suitable press.
7. Press tapered roller bearing onto shaft as far as stop. **Turn outer race while pressing bearing.**
8. Tighten bearing nut, noting the following:
   a. Lefthand rear axle nut with groove has lefthand threads.
   b. Righthand rear axle nut less groove has righthand threads.
9. Bend locking ring at both grooves using suitable punch and hammer.
10. Install sealing ring.

DRW

REMOVAL

1. Remove brake fluid reservoir cap.
2. Raise and support vehicle, then remove tire and wheel assembly.
3. Disconnect wear indicator cable, **Fig. 2.**
4. Remove guide bolt and brake caliper, **Fig. 4.** Support caliper aside with adapters and lines attached.
5. Back off parking brake.
6. Remove locking plate, inner hub nut and thrust washer.
7. Pry hub off axle tube.
8. Pry out ABS sensor and remove hub seal.
9. Remove hub bearings.
10. Remove inner and outer bearing cups using suitable drift and hammer.

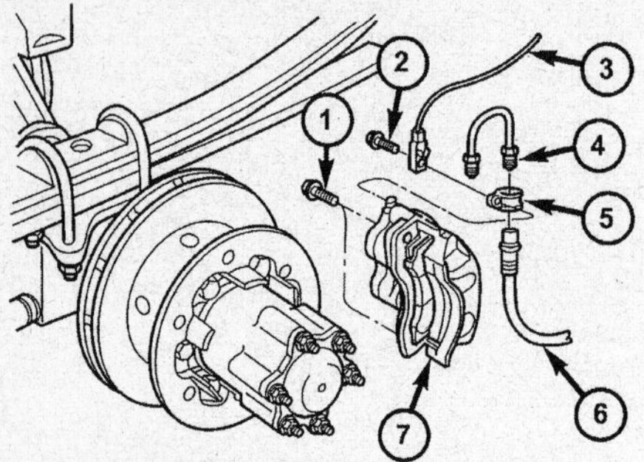

Fig. 4 Brake caliper replacement. DRW

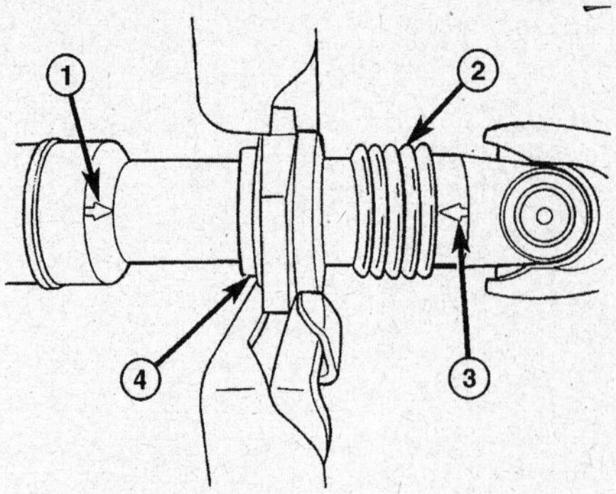

1 - ALIGNMENT MARK
2 - BOOT
3 - ALIGNMENT MARK
4 - CENTER BEARING
LTV0500000000076

Fig. 5 Propeller shaft alignment. Two-piece

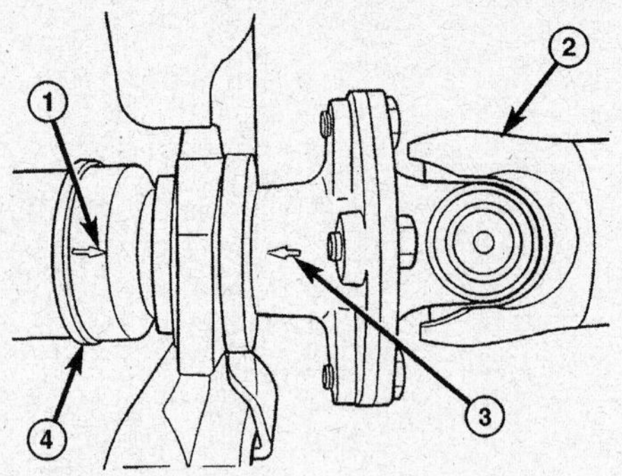

1 - REFERNCE MARK
2 - CENTER SHAFT
3 - REFERENCE MARK
4 - REAR SHAFT
LTV0500000000077

Fig. 6 Propeller shaft alignment. Three-piece

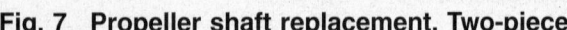

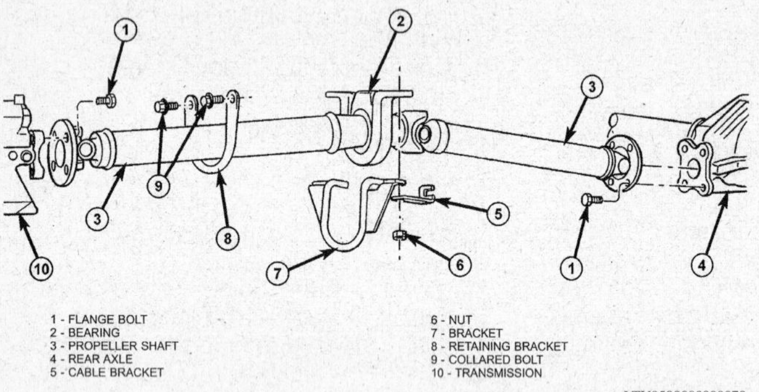

Fig. 7 Propeller shaft replacement. Two-piece

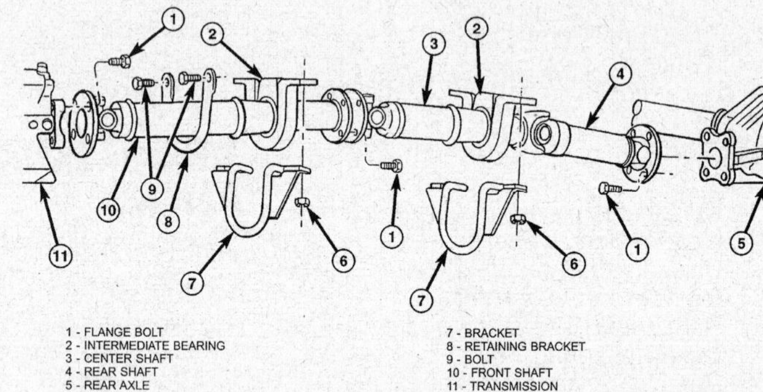

Fig. 8 Propeller shaft replacement. Three-piece

INSTALLATION

1. Install bearing cups using drift tool No. 9291, or equivalent, and suitable hammer.
2. Thoroughly grease bearings.
3. Install inner wheel bearing.
4. Coat new seal outer circumference using Hylomar SQ 32 M, or equivalent sealant. **Do not coat rubberized sealing surface.**
5. Install seal flush within .12 inch deep into hub using suitable installer tool.
6. Coast ABS sensor ring contact surface using Hylomar SQ 32 M, or equivalent sealant.
7. Drive ABS sensor ring in as far as stop using suitable plastic hammer.
8. Install hub on axle tube.
9. Install outer hub bearing.
10. Install thrust washer and inner hub nut.
11. **Torque** inner hub nut to 221 ft. lbs., using wrench tool No. 9290, or equivalent, while constantly spinning wheel hub.
12. Turn back inner nut and tighten until it touches thrust washer without play.
13. Tighten an additional 45°.
14. Install locking plate.
15. Install outer hub nut and tighten.

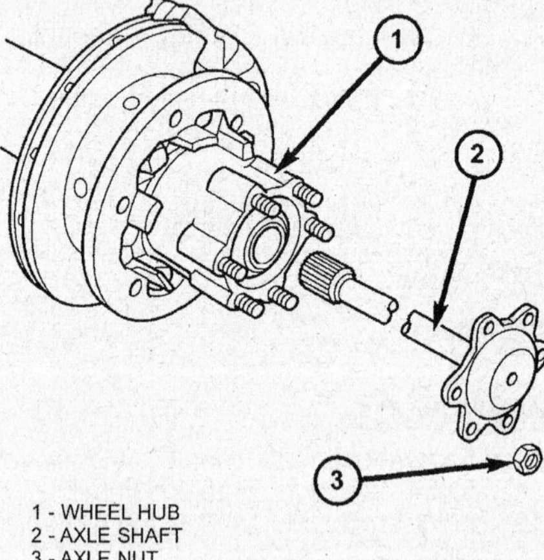

Fig. 9 Axle shaft replacement. DRW

SHOCK ABSORBER

REPLACE

1. Raise and support vehicle.
2. Remove shock absorber rear axle mounting bolt, **Fig. 16.**
3. Disconnect ALB lever clip.
4. Remove upper shock absorber ALB lever.
5. Remove upper shock absorber frame mounting bolt.
6. Remove shock absorber.
7. Reverse procedure to install.

LEAF SPRING

REPLACE

1. Raise and support vehicle, then the rear axle.
2. Remove mounting nuts, U-bolt and plate, **Figs. 17 and 18.**
3. Remove spring from front bracket.
4. Remove spring with shackle from bracket.
5. Lower axle and remove spring.
6. Reverse procedure to install.

STABILIZER BAR

REPLACE

1. Raise and support vehicle.
2. Remove mounting bolt, nut and stabilizer links at bar, **Figs. 19 and 20.**
3. Remove clamp, bracket and stabilizer bar.
4. Reverse procedure to install.

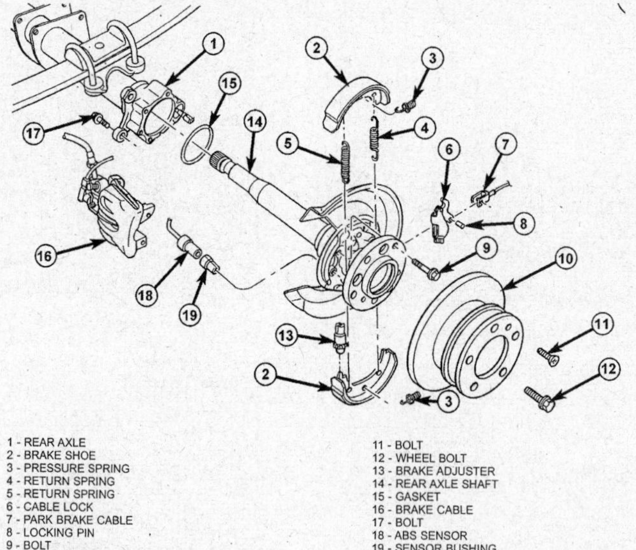

1 - REAR AXLE
2 - BRAKE SHOE
3 - PRESSURE SPRING
4 - RETURN SPRING
5 - RETURN SPRING
6 - CABLE LOCK
7 - PARK BRAKE CABLE
8 - LOCKING PIN
9 - BOLT
10 - BRAKE DISC
11 - BOLT
12 - WHEEL BOLT
13 - BRAKE ADJUSTER
14 - REAR AXLE SHAFT
15 - GASKET
16 - BRAKE CABLE
17 - BOLT
18 - ABS SENSOR
19 - SENSOR BUSHING

LTV0500000000080

Fig. 10 Rear axle shaft replacement. SRW

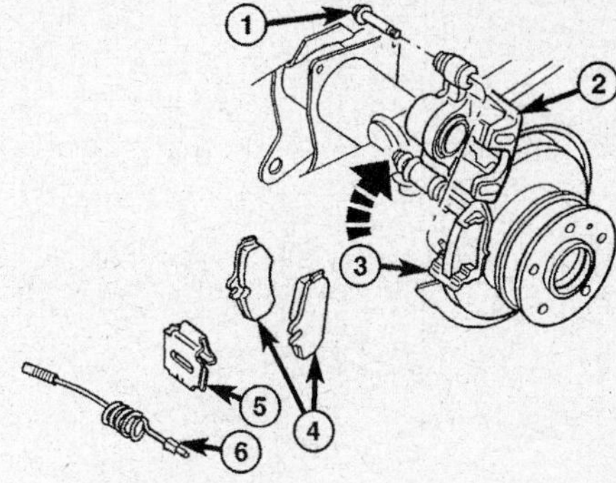

1 - CALIPER GUIDE PIN
2 - DISC BRAKE CALIPER
3 - CALIPER ADAPTER
4 - DISC BRAKE PADS
5 - RETAINING SPRING
6 - WEAR INDICATOR

LTV0500000000082

Fig. 11 Brake pad replacement. SRW w/15-inch wheel

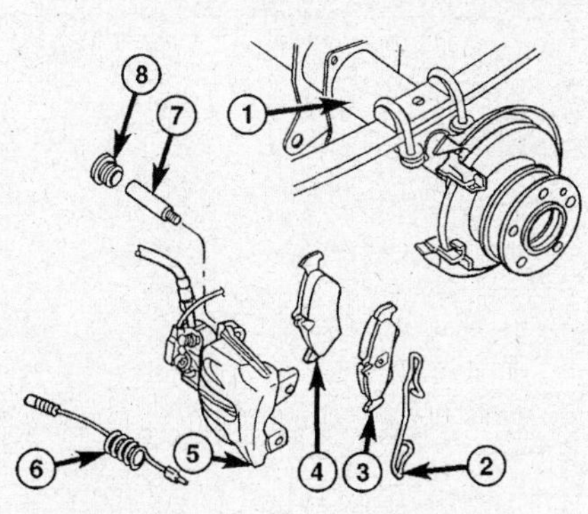

1 - AXLE
2 - RETAINING SPRING
3 - OUTBOARD PADS
4 - INBOARD PAD
5 - DISC BRAKE CALIPER
6 - WEAR INDICATOR
7 - GUIDE PIN
8 - DUST CAP

LTV0500000000081

Fig. 12 Brake pad replacement. SRW w/16-inch wheel

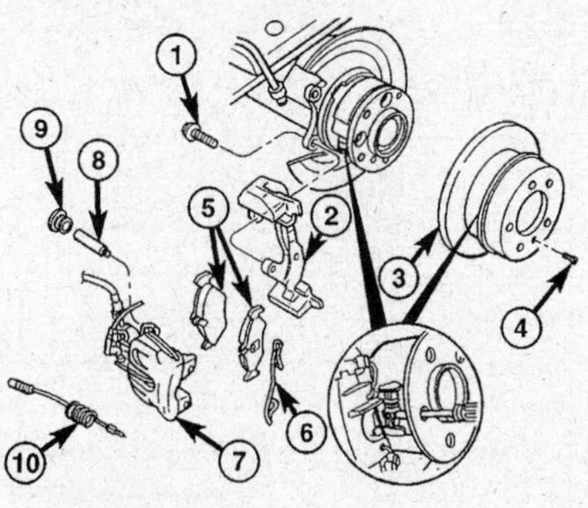

1 - M8 BOLT
2 - CALIPER ADAPTER
3 - DISC BRAKE ROTOR
4 - LOCKING BOLT
5 - DISC BRAKE PADS
6 - RATTLE SPRING
7 - DISC BRAKE CALIPER
8 - GUIDE BOLT
9 - COVER
10 - WEAR INDICATOR

LTV0500000000083

Fig. 13 Rear disc rotor replacement. SRW

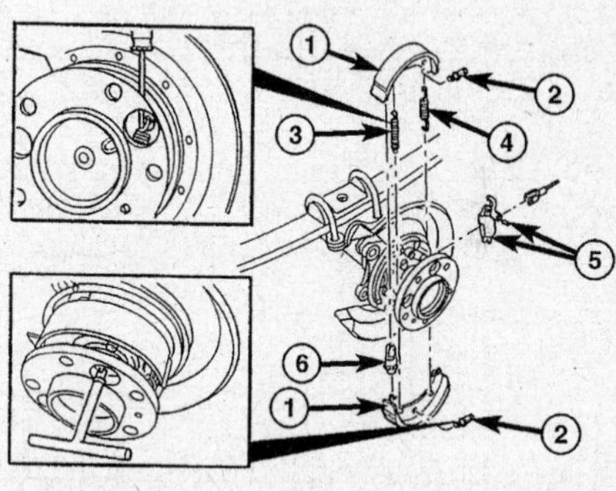

1 - PARK BRAKE SHOES
2 - PRESSURE SPRING
3 - RETRACTING SPRING (SHORT HOOK EYE)
4 - RETRACTING SPRING (LONG HOOK EYE)
5 - CABLE LOCK
6 - ADJUSTER

LTV0500000000084

Fig. 14 Parking brake shoe replacement. SRW

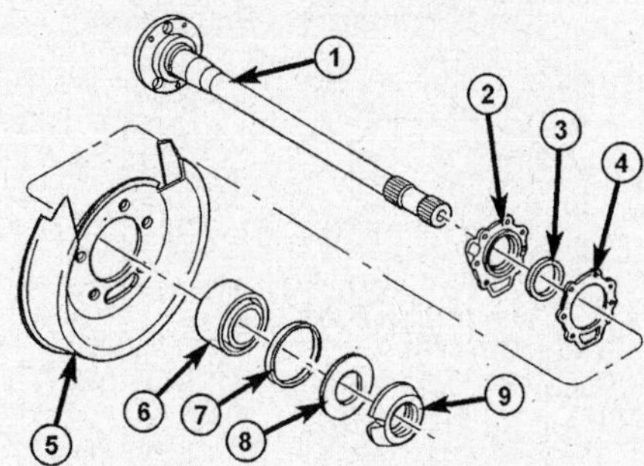

1 - AXLE SHAFT
2 - BEARING COVER
3 - RADIAL SHAFT SEAL
4 - GASKET
5 - DUST SHIELD
6 - BEARING
7 - SEALING RING
8 - LOCKING RING
9 - BEARING NUT

LTV0500000000086

Fig. 15 Axle bearing replacement. SRW

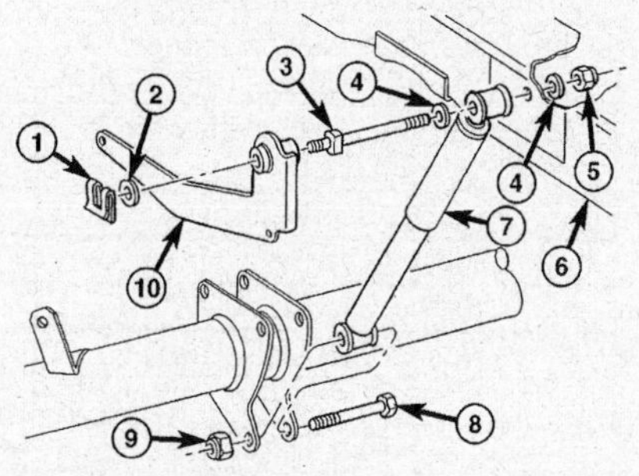

1 - CLIP
2 - WASHER
3 - MOUNTING STUD/BOLT
4 - WASHER
5 - NUT
6 - FRAME
7 - SHOCK ABSORBER
8 - BOLT
9 - NUT
10 - ALB LEVER

LTV0500000000071

Fig. 16 Shock absorber replacement

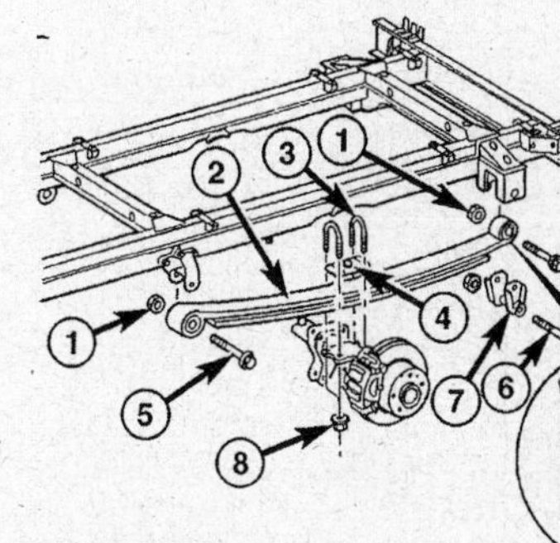

1 - NUT
2 - LEAF SPRING
3 - U-BOLTS
4 - PLATE
5 - SPRING BOLT
6 - SHACKLE BOLT
7 - SPRING SHACKLE
8 - U-BOLT NUTS

LTV0500000000087

Fig. 17 Leaf spring replacement. SRW

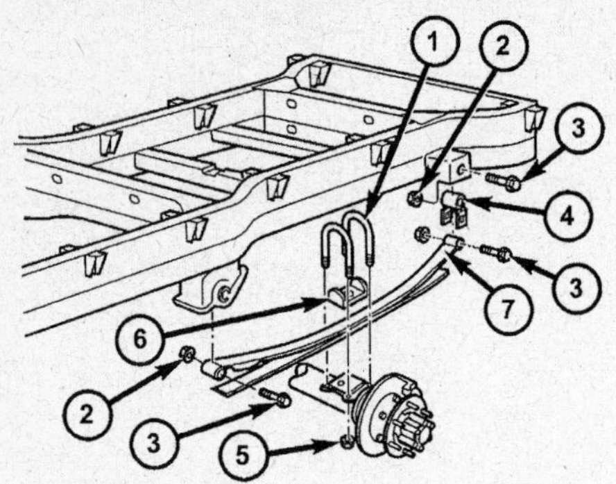

1 - U-BOLTS
2 - NUT
3 - BOLT
4 - SPRING SHACKLE
5 - U-BOLT MOUNTING NUT
6 - U-BOLT BRACKET ALIGNING PLATE
7 - LEAF SPRING

LTV0500000000088

Fig. 18 Leaf spring replacement. DRW

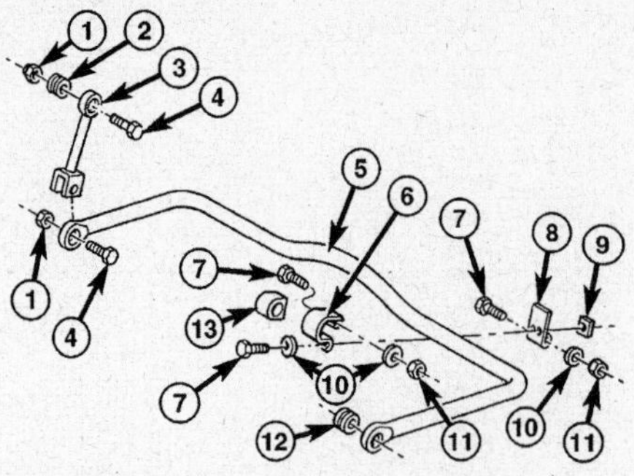

1 - M12 NUT
2 - BUSHING
3 - SWAY BAR LINK
4 - M12 BOLT
5 - SWAY BAR
6 - CLAMP
7 - M8 BOLT
8 - BRACKET
9 - FOUR POINT NUT M8
10 - WASHER
11 - M8 NUT
12 - BUSHING
13 - MOUNT

LTV0500000000089

Fig. 19 Stabilizer bar replacement. SRW

1 - STABILIZER LINK
2 - SWAY BRA BOLT
3 - SWAY BAR NUT
4 - SWAY BAR
5 - RUBBER MOUNT
6 - SWAY BAR CLAMP
7 - CLAMP MOUNTING BOLTS

LTV0500000000090

Fig. 20 Stabilizer bar replacement. DRW

TIGHTENING SPECIFICATIONS

Year	Component	Torque Ft. Lbs.
2003–06	ALB Lever	46
	Axle Bearing Cap	53
	Axle, Grooved Nut	369
	Axle Shaft Hub	48
	Brake Caliper	②
	Brake Hose	10
	Brake Wear Indicator	89①
	Differential Cover	48
	Drain & Fill Plugs	74
	Hub, Inner Nut	⑤
	Hub, Outer Nut	184
	Leaf Spring To Bracket, DRW	136
	Leaf Spring To Front Bracket, SRW	70
	Leaf Spring To Rear Bracket, SRW	63
	Propeller Shaft	52
	Propeller Shaft Bracket	74
	Propeller Shaft Center Bearing To Frame	70
	Propeller Shaft Center Bearing To Support	77
	Shock Absorber, Lower	③
	Shock Absorber, Upper	⑥
	Spring Shackle, DRW	136
	Spring Shackle, SRW	66
	Stabilizer Bar	④
	Stabilizer Bar Link	60
	U-Bolt	125

① — Inch lbs.
② — M8 bolt, 18 ft. lbs.; M10, 22 ft. lbs.
③ — M12 bolt, 52 ft. lbs.; M14 bolt, 81 ft. lbs.
④ — DRW, 52 ft. lbs.; SRW, 18 ft. lbs.
⑤ — Refer to "Hub & Bearing, Replace" for tightening specifications and sequence.
⑥ — SRW, 59 ft. lbs; DRW, 103 ft. lbs.

Front Suspension & Steering

NOTE: Refer To "Computer Relearn Procedure" Located In The Front Of This Manual When Battery Power To The Computer Has Been Interrupted.

INDEX

PRECAUTIONS

Battery Ground Cable

Prior to service, disconnect battery ground cable and isolate as required.

WHEEL BEARING

ADJUST

1. Raise and support vehicle, then remove grease cap.
2. Position suitable dial indicator against wheel hub face.
3. Tighten clamping nut locking screw.
4. Pull wheel hub back and forth firmly.
5. If wheel bearing play is not .000787–.00158 inch, loosen locking screw and adjust clamping nut.

HUB & BEARING

REPLACE

1. Raise and support vehicle, then remove front tire and wheel assembly.
2. Remove cable and wear indicator, **Figs. 1 and 2.**
3. Remove brake caliper hose. Seal hose and caliper connection.
4. Remove guide bolt and brake caliper, then the brake pads.
5. Remove brake caliper adapter.
6. Loosen bolt and remove clamping nut, **Figs. 3 and 4.**
7. Remove thrust washer, hub and tapered roller bearing.
8. Reverse procedure to install, noting the following:
   a. Grease outer tapered roller bearing thoroughly.
   b. Inspect wheel bearing as outlined under "Wheel Bearing Adjust."
   c. Pack grease cap half with grease and coat edge with suitable sealant.

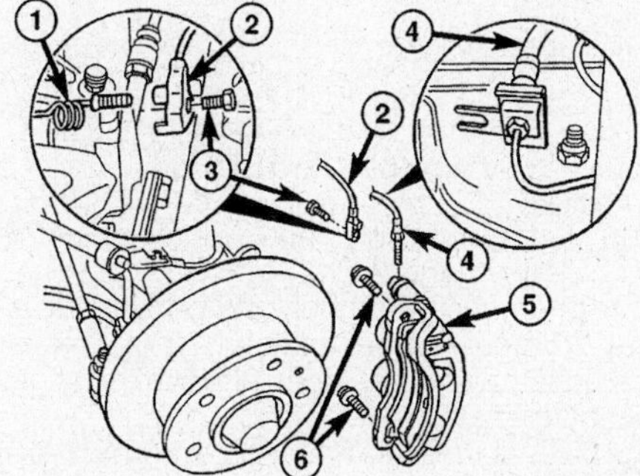

Fig. 1 Front brake caliper replacement. SRW

BALL JOINT

REPLACE

Lower

1. Remove strut as outlined under "Strut, Replace."
2. Remove steering knuckle as outlined under "Steering Knuckle, Replace."
3. Remove lower ball joint using driver tool No. 9294-1 with receiver tool No. 9294-2 and puller tool No. C-4212-F, or equivalents.
4. Reverse procedure to install using install ring tool No. 9294-3, or equivalent.

STRUT

REPLACE

1. **If removing lefthand strut,** remove lefthand side floor covering.
2. **If removing righthand strut,** remove tool cover.
3. **On all models,** remove cover and strut upper, **Fig. 5.**

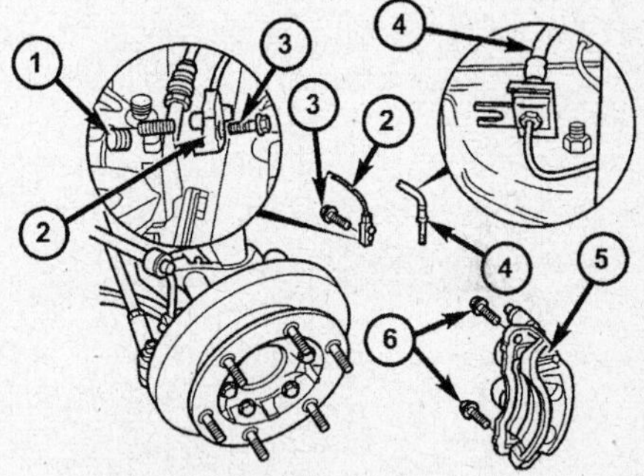

Fig. 2 Front brake caliper replacement. DRW

4. Raise and support vehicle, then remove tire and wheel assembly.
5. Eliminate strut tensile force by raising lower control arm approximately .39 inches using suitable jack.
6. Remove mounting bolts and strut.
7. Reverse procedure to install. **Hand tighten upper mounting nut until vehicle weight in on ground.**

LEAF SPRING

REPLACE

1. Remove lefthand and righthand spring clamp plates' front and rear mounting bolts, **Fig. 6.**
2. Remove lower control arm as outlined under "Control Arm, Replace."
3. Support transverse leaf spring using suitable jack with cushioning pad.
4. Remove mounting bolts, then the lefthand and righthand spring clamp plates.
5. Mark spring blocks for installation in original position. **Do not mix upper spring blocks between engine cradle and spring.**

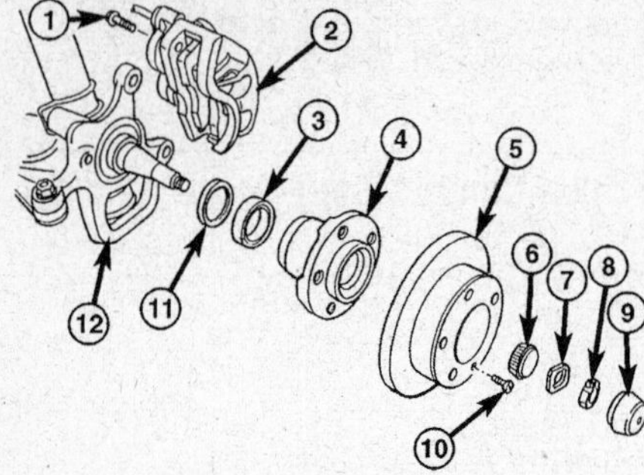

1 - CALIPER ADAPTER BOLT
2 - DISC BRAKE CALIPER
3 - INNER BEARING
4 - WHEEL HUB
5 - DISC BRAKE ROTOR
6 - OUTER BEARING
7 - THRUST WASHER
8 - CLAMPING NUT
9 - GREASE CAP
10 - LOCKING BOLT
11 - GREASE SEAL
12 - STEERING KNUCKLE

LTV0500000000093

Fig. 3 Hub & bearing replacement. SRW

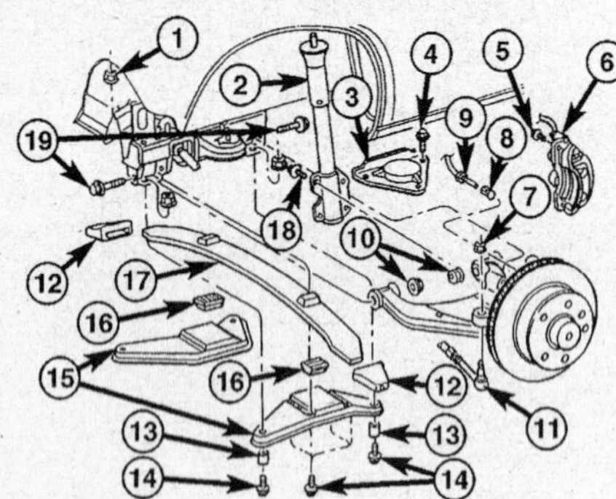

1 - NUT
2 - STRUT
3 - STOP PLATE
4 - STOP PLATE BOLT
5 - CALIPER ADAPTER BOLT
6 - DISC BRAKE CALIPER
7 - OUTER TIE ROD END NUT
8 - ABS SENSOR
9 - SPEED SENSOR
10 - LOWER CONTROL ARM RETAINING NUTS
11 - OUTER TIE ROD END
12 - RUBBER SPRING MOUNT
13 - SHEAR BUSHING
14 - SPRING CLAMP PLATE BOLT
15 - SPRING CLAMP PLATE
16 - LOWER RUBBER SPRING MOUNT
17 - SPRING
18 - STRUT BOLTS

LTV0500000000098

Fig. 6 Spring replacement

6. Lower jack and remove transverse leaf spring.
7. Reverse procedure to install.

CONTROL ARM

REPLACE

Lower

1. Install spring block tool No. 9288, or equivalent.
2. Raise and support vehicle, then remove tire and wheel assembly.

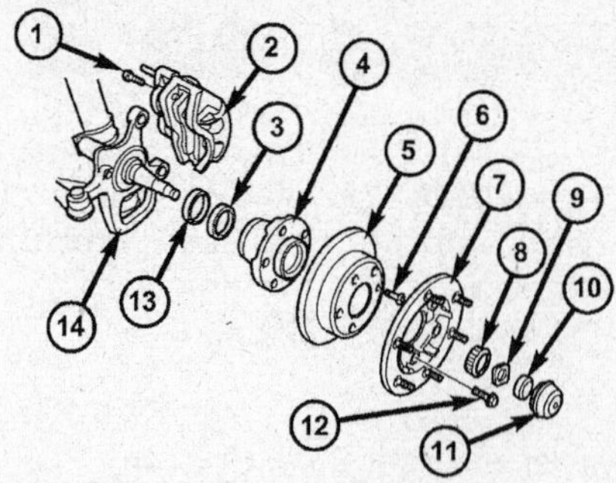

1 - ADAPTER BOLT
2 - DISC BRAKE CALIPER
3 - INNER BEARING RACE
4 - WHEEL HUB
5 - DISC BRAKE ROTOR
6 - LOCKING BOLT
7 - WHEEL FLANGE RING
8 - OUTER BEARING
9 - THRUST WASHER
10 - CLAMPING NUT
11 - GREASE CAP
12 - WHEEL FLANGE RING MOUNTING BOLT
13 - GREASE SEAL
14 - STEERING KNUCKLE

LTV0500000000094

Fig. 4 Hub & bearing replacement. DRW

3. Remove cable and wear indicator, **Figs. 1 and 2.**
4. Remove guide bolt and brake caliper. Support caliper aside.
5. Remove brake pads and brake caliper adapter.
6. Remove tie rod to steering knuckle nut, **Fig. 7.**
7. Separate outer tie rod from steering knuckle using tie rod puller tool No. C-3894-A, or equivalent.
8. Eliminate strut tensile force by raising lower control arm approximately .39 inches using suitable jack.
9. Remove strut to steering knuckle mounting bolts.
10. Remove mounting bolts and rotate stop plate upward with stabilizer link attached.
11. Lower control arm and remove ball joint nut from steering knuckle.
12. Separate lower ball joint from steering knuckle using ball joint separator tool No. 9282, or equivalent.
13. Remove mounting bolt, nuts and lower control arm.
14. Reverse procedure to install.

STEERING KNUCKLE

REPLACE

1. Raise and support vehicle, then remove tire and wheel assembly.
2. Remove cable and wear indicator, **Figs. 1 and 2.**
3. Remove brake caliper hose. Seal hose and caliper connection.
4. Remove guide bolt and brake caliper, then the brake pads.
5. Remove brake caliper adapter.
6. Loosen bolt and remove clamping nut, **Figs. 3 and 4.**

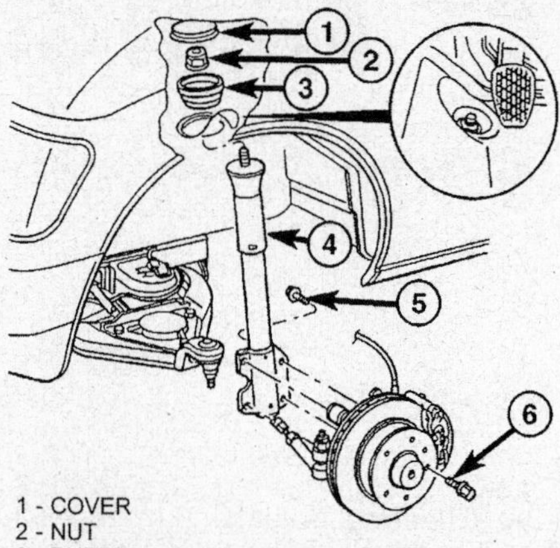

1 - COVER
2 - NUT
3 - RUBBER MOUNT
4 - STRUT
5 - STRUT BOLT
6 - LOCKING BOLT

LTV0500000000096

Fig. 5 Strut replacement

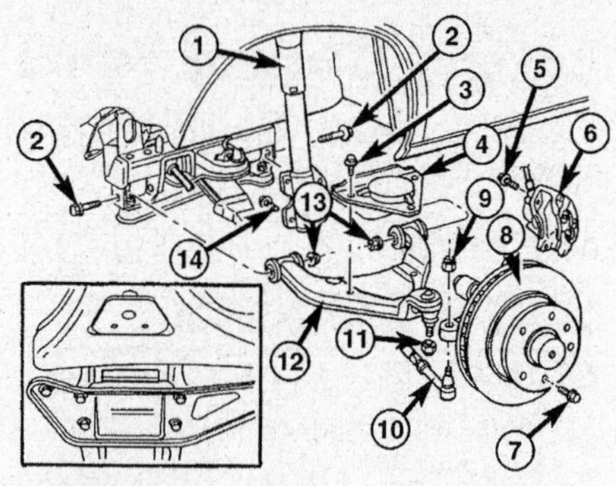

1 - STRUT
2 - LOWER CONTROL ARM BOLT
3 - STOP PLATE BOLT
4 - STOP PLATE
5 - CALIPER ADPTER BOLT
6 - DISC BRAKE CALIPER
7 - LOCKING BOLT
8 - DISC BRAKE ROTOR
9 - OUTER TIE ROD END RETAINING NUT
10 - OUTER TIE ROD END
11 - LOWER BALL JOINT NUT
12 - LOWER BALL JOINT
13 - LOWER CONTROL ARM NUTS
14 - STRUT BOLT

LTV0500000000097

Fig. 7 Lower control arm replacement

7. Remove thrust washer, hub and tapered roller bearing.
8. Separate outer tie rod from steering knuckle using tie rod puller tool No. C-3894-A, or equivalent.
9. Eliminate strut tensile force by raising lower control arm approximately .39 inches using suitable jack.
10. Remove ABS sensor from knuckle.
11. Remove mounting bolts and disconnect strut from knuckle, **Fig. 8.**
12. Separate lower ball joint from steering knuckle using ball joint separator tool No. 9282, or equivalent.
13. Remove steering knuckle.
14. Reverse procedure to install, noting the following:
    a. Grease outer tapered roller bearing thoroughly.
    b. Inspect wheel bearing as outlined under "Wheel Bearing Adjust."

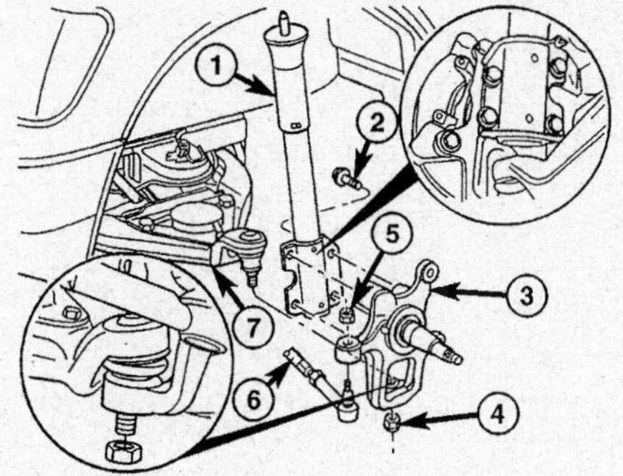

1 - STRUT
2 - STRUT BOLT
3 - STEERING KNUCKLE
4 - LOWER BALL JOINT NUT
5 - OUTER TIE ROD END RETAINING NUT
6 - INNER TIE ROD END
7 - LOWER CONTROL ARM

LTV0500000000095

Fig. 8 Steering knuckle replacement

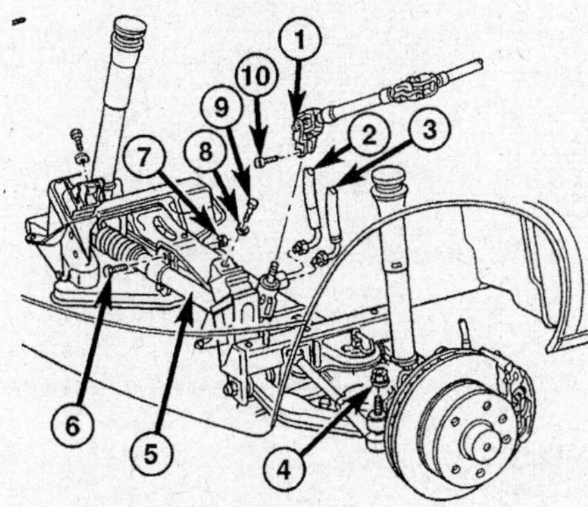

1 - U-JOINT
2 - HIGH PRESSURE POWER STEERING HOSE
3 - RETURN HOSE
4 - OUTER TIE ROD END RETAINING NUT
5 - STEERING GEAR
6 - STEERING GEAR RETAINING BOLT
7 - STEERING GEAR NUT
8 - WASHER
9 - ENGINE MOUNT BOLT
10 - U-JOINT CLAMPING BOLT

LTV0500000000100

Fig. 11 Steering gear replacement

c. Pack grease cap half with grease and coat edge with suitable sealant.

STABILIZER BAR

REPLACE

1. Raise and support vehicle.
2. Remove stabilizer bar clamp bolts, **Fig. 9.**
3. Press rubber mounts out of brackets.
4. Remove stabilizer links.
5. Reverse procedure to install.

TIE ROD END

REPLACE

1. Raise and support vehicle, then remove tire and wheel assembly.

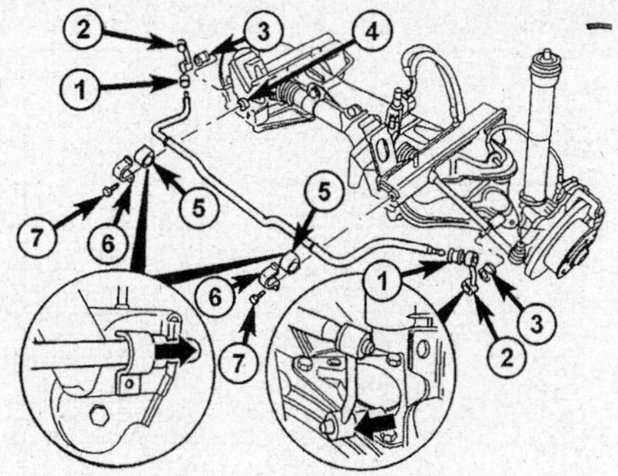

1 - RUBBER MOUNT
2 - STABILIZER LINK
3 - RUBBER MOUNT
4 - NUT
5 - RUBBER MOUNT
6 - CLAMP BRACKET
7 - BOLT

LTV0500000000099

Fig. 9 Stabilizer bar replacement

2. Loose luck nut, **Fig. 10.**
3. Remove tie rod end nut.
4. Separate outer tie rod from steering knuckle using tie rod puller tool No. C-3894-A, or equivalent.
5. Remove outer from inner tie rod end.
6. Reverse procedure to install.

POWER STEERING GEAR

REPLACE

1. Siphon as much fluid as possible from power steering pump reservoir.
2. Raise and support vehicle, then remove front tire and wheel assemblies.
3. Remove mounting bolts and stabilizer bar from upper link.
4. Remove outer tie rod end nuts.
5. Separate outer tie rod from steering knuckle using tie rod puller tool No. C-3894-A, or equivalent, **Fig. 11.**
6. Remove outer tie rod end from steering gear.
7. Remove mounting bolts and spring clamp plates.
8. Remove high pressure and return hoses from steering gear.
9. Remove steering shaft clamping bolt and separate universal joint from steering gear.
10. Slight steering gear toward righthand side of vehicle, then tilt it downward on lefthand side and remove.
11. Reverse procedure to install, noting the following:
    a. **Torque** steering gear mounting bolts to 18 ft. lbs.
    b. **Torque** gear mounting bolts to 33 ft. lbs.
    c. Final tighten mounting bolts an additional 90°.

POWER STEERING PUMP

REPLACE

1. Remove power steering pump belt.

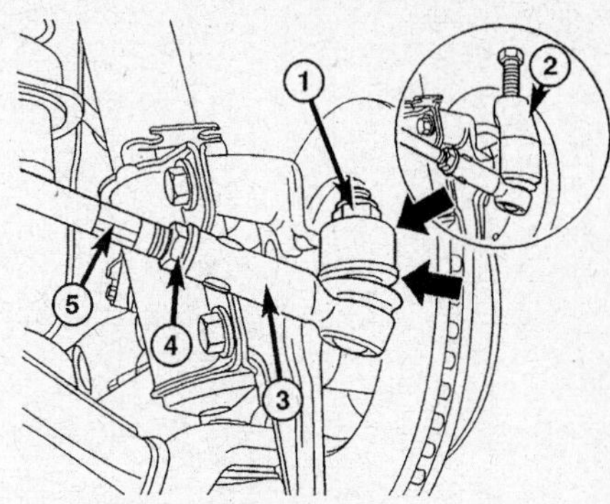

1 - OUTER TIE ROD END RETAINING NUT
2 - TIE ROD SEPERATOR TOOL
3 - OUTER TIE ROD END
4 - LOCKING NUT
5 - INNER TIE ROD END

LTV0500000000101

Fig. 10 Tie rod end replacement

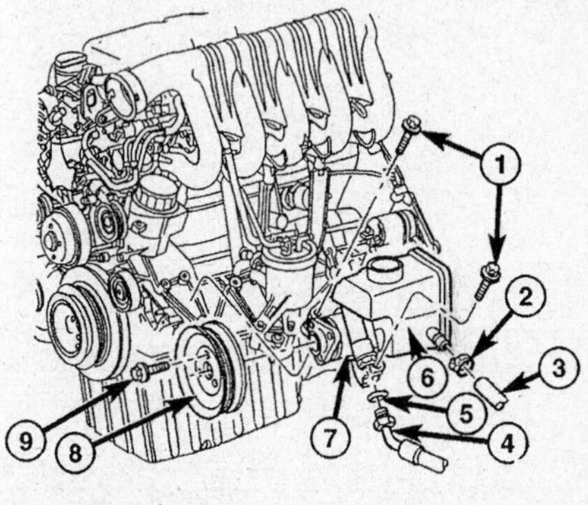

1 - PUMP MOUNTING BOLT
2 - CLAMP
3 - RETURN HOSE
4 - HIGH PRESSURE HOSE
5 - O-RING
6 - PUMP RESERVOIR
7 - PUMP
8 - PULLEY
9 - PULLEY BOLT

LTV0500000000102

Fig. 12 Power steering pump replacement

2. Siphon as much fluid as possible from power steering pump reservoir.
3. Remove power steering pump high pressure and return hoses, **Fig. 12.**
4. Remove mounting bolts and power steering pump.
5. Reverse procedure to install.

POWER STEERING SYSTEM BLEED

1. Remove fluid reservoir cap.
2. Fill pump with suitable fluid. **Do fill above MAX mark.**
3. Raise and support front of vehicle.
4. Start engine and idle engine.
5. Turn steering wheel with engine idling.
6. Turn engine off and adjust oil level.
7. Ensure there are no bubbles in system.

TIGHTENING SPECIFICATIONS

Year	Component	Torque/Ft. lbs
2003–06	Brake Caliper	③
	Brake Hose	10
	Lower Ball Joint	206
	Lower Control Arm	110
	Lower Control Arm Stop Plate	44
	Outer Tie Rod End	96
	Outer Tie Rod End Jam Nut	37
	Power Steering Pump	15
	Power Steering Pump High Pressure Flexible Hose	28
	Power Steering Pump Pulley	22
	Spring Clamp Plate, Bottom To Front Axle	②
	Steering Gear	④
	Steering Gear Boot Clamp	62①
	Steering Gear High Pressure Hose	27
	Steering Gear Return Line	27
	Steering Gear U-Joint	18
	Strut to Body	74
	Strut To Steering Knuckle	136
	Sway Bar Clamp	22
	Wheel Bearing Play Adjust Clamp	106①

① — Inch lbs.
② — M10, 48 ft. lbs.; M12, 96 ft. lbs.
③ — SRW, 18 ft. lbs.; DRW, M8, 18 ft. lbs.; M10.9, 22 ft. lbs.
④ — Refer to "Power Steering Gear, Replace" for tightening specifications and sequence.

Wheel Alignment

INDEX

PRELIMINARY INSPECTION

1. Ensure tire size and air pressure are correct.
2. Inspect tread wear.
3. Inspect front wheel bearings.
4. Inspect front wheels for excessive radial or lateral runout.
5. Inspect front wheel balance.
6. Inspect ball studs, linkage pivot points and steering gear for looseness, roughness or binding.
7. Inspect suspension components for wear and noise.
8. Road test vehicle.

FRONT WHEEL ALIGNMENT

Caster

Caster is not adjustable on this vehicle.

Camber

Camber is not adjustable on this vehicle.

Toe-In

1. Start engine and turn wheels in both directions before straightening.
2. Secure steering wheel with front wheels straight ahead.
3. Loose tie rod jam nuts.
4. Adjust toe by turning inner tie rod. **Each wheel should be adjusted for one-half total toe.**
5. **Torque** tie rod jam nut to 37 ft. lbs.
6. Ensure toe measurement.

WRANGLER

NOTE: Refer To Back Of This Manual For Vehicle Manufacturer's Special Service Tool Suppliers.

INDEX OF SERVICE OPERATIONS

Specifications

GENERAL ENGINE SPECIFICATIONS

Year	Engine Liters	VIN Code	Fuel Type	Bore x Stroke	Comp. Ratio	Horsepower @ RPM	Torque Ft. Lbs. @ RPM	Normal Oil Pressure, psi
2002	2.5L	P	MPI	3.88 x 3.19	9.1	120 @ 5400	140 @ 3500	①
	4.0L	S	MPI	3.88 x 3.41	8.8	190 @ 4600	235 @ 3200	①
2003	2.4L	P	MPI	3.45 x 3.98	9.4	150 @ 5200	165 @ 4000	②
	4.0L	S	MPI	3.88 x 3.41	8.8	190 @ 4600	235 @ 3200	①
2004–06	2.4L	1	MPI	3.45 x 3.98	9.4	150 @ 5200	165 @ 4000	②
	4.0L	S	MPI	3.88 x 3.41	8.8	190 @ 4600	235 @ 3200	①

① — At 600 RPM, 13 psi; at idle, 25–35 psi; above 1600 RPM, 37–75 psi.

② — At idle 4 psi; at 3000 RPM, 25–80 psi.

TUNE UP SPECIFICATIONS

The following specifications are published from the latest information available. This data should only be used in the absence of a decal affixed in the engine compartment.

Year & Engine Liters	Spark Plug Gap	Ignition Timing, °BTDC				Curb Idle Speed, RPM②		Fast Idle Speed, RPM		Fuel Pump Pressure, psi	Valve Lash Specifications
		Firing Order, Fig.③	Man. Trans.	Auto. Trans.	Mark Location	Man. Trans.	Auto. Trans.	Man. Trans.	Auto. Trans.		
2002											
2.5L	.035	A	④	④	Damper	①	①	①	①	44–54	④
4.0L	.035	1-5-3-6-2-4-	④	④	Damper	①	①	①	①	44–54	④
2003–04											
2.4L	.048–.053	B	④	④	Damper	①	①	①	①	47–51	④
4.0L	.040	1-5-3-6-2-4-	④	④	Damper	①	①	①	①	47–51	④
2005–06											
2.4L	.037–.042	B	④	④	Damper	①	①	①	①	56–60	④
4.0L	.030–.035	1-5-3-6-2-4-	④	④	Damper	①	①	①	①	56–60	④

BTDC — Before Top Dead Center

① — Controlled by idle speed control motor.

② — Idle speed for man. trans. models is adjusted in Neutral. On auto. trans. models, idle speed is adjusted in Drive. When inspecting idle speed, set parking brake & block drive wheels.

③ — Before removing wires from distributor cap, determine location of No. 1 wire in cap, as distributor position may have been altered from that outlined.

④ — Non-adjustable.

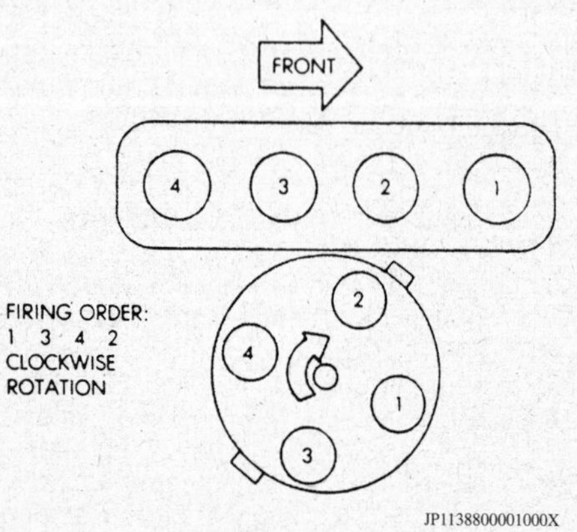

Fig. A

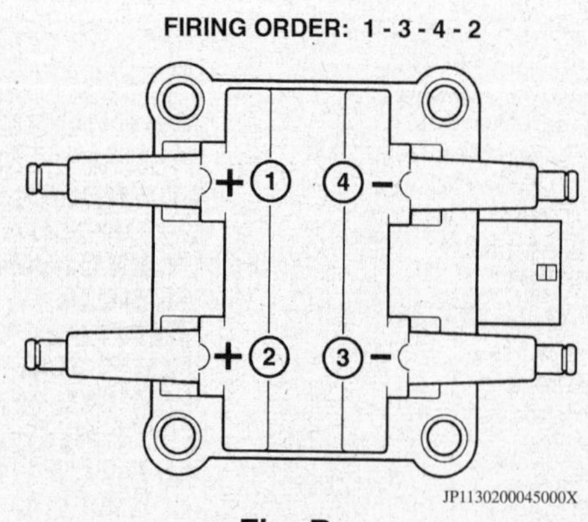

Fig. B

FRONT WHEEL ALIGNMENT SPECIFICATIONS

Year	Caster, Degree	Camber, Degree	Toe-In, Degree
2002–06	+6 to +8	-.88 to +.38	+.08 to +.22

REAR WHEEL ALIGNMENT SPECIFICATIONS

Year	Camber, Degree		Thrust Angle, Degree		Total Toe, Degree	
	Limits	Desired	Limits	Desired	Limits	Desired
2002–06	0–.50	.25	-.25 to +.25	0	-.50 to +.50	.25

FLUID CAPACITIES & COOLING SYSTEM DATA

Year	Engine Liter	Coolant Capacity, Qts.	Recommended Coolant Type	Radiator Cap Relief Pressure, Lbs.	Thermo. Opening Temp., Deg. °F.	Fuel Tank, Gals.	Engine Oil Refill, Qts.①	Transmission Oil		Transfer Case, Pts.	Drive Axle	
								5 Speed, Pts.	Auto. Trans., Qts.②		Front, Pts.	Rear, Pts.
2002	2.5L	9.0	Ethylene Glycol	16	195	19	4	⑦	4.9	2.2	2.50	④⑨
	4.0L	10.5	Ethylene Glycol	16	195	19	6	⑦	6.7	2.2	2.50	④⑧
2003	2.4L	9.0	Ethylene Glycol	16	195	19	4	⑥	4.0	⑤	③	④⑧
	4.0L	10.5	Ethylene Glycol	16	195	19	6	⑥	4.0	⑤	③	④⑧
2004–06	2.4L	9.0	Ethylene Glycol	18–21	195	19	4	⑥	⑩	⑤	③	④⑧
	4.0L	10.5	Ethylene Glycol	18–21	195	19	6	⑥	⑩	⑤	③	④⑧

① — With or without filter change.
② — Approximate. Make final inspect w/dipstick.
③ — Model 181 FBI, 2.5 pts.; model 216 RBI, 4 pts.
④ — Models w/Trac-Loc include 4 ozs., friction modifier additive.
⑤ — NV231, 2.2 pts.; NV241, 4.2 pts.
⑥ — NV1500, 4.8 pts.; NV3550, 4.2 pts.
⑦ — AX5 transmission, 7 pts.; NV3550 transmission, 4.8 pts.
⑧ — Model 216, 4.0 pts., model 194, 3.5pts.
⑨ — Models 194 & 198 RBI axles, 3.8 pts. Models 216 & 226 RBA axles, 4.8 pts.
⑩ — 42RLE Automatic transmission, service fill, 8.0 pts, overhaul fill 17.6 pts.

LUBRICANT DATA

Year	Model	Lubricant Type					
		Transmission		Transfer Case	Front/Rear Axle	Power Steering	Brake System
		Manual	Automatic				
2002	2.5L	②	ATF+4	ATF+4	③	④	DOT 3
	4.0L	②	ATF+4	ATF+4	③	④	DOT 3
2003–06	2.4L	①	ATF+4	ATF+4	③	ATF+4	DOT 3
	4.0L	①	ATF+4	ATF+4	③	ATF+4	DOT 3

① — Mopar manual transmission lubricant.
② — AX5 Mopar 75W-90 API grade GL-3; NV3550, Mopar manual transmission lubricant.
③ — Mopar Hypoid Gear Lubricant, or equivalent thermally stable 80W–90 GL5 for normal driving. Use 75W-140 synthetic gear lubricant in heavy duty trailer towing situations. On Trac-Loc differentials add 4 ounces of friction modifier.
④ — Mopar power steering fluid.

Electrical

NOTE: On Air Bag Equipped Models, Refer To "Air Bag System Precautions" Located In The Front Of This Manual For System Disarming & Arming Procedures.

NOTE: Refer To "Computer Relearn Procedures" Located In The Front Of This Manual When Battery Power To The Computer Has Been Interrupted.

INDEX

PRECAUTIONS

Air Bag Systems

Refer to "Air Bag System Precautions" in the front of this manual for system disarming and arming procedures.

Battery Ground Cable

Prior to service, disconnect battery ground cable and isolate as required.

FUSE PANEL & FLASHER LOCATION

The fuse panel is located behind the glove compartment, above the heater and A/C unit. The fuse panel can be accessed by removing the glove compartment.

Turn signal/flasher is located to the back of the lefthand multi-function switch on top of the steering column.

FUEL PUMP RELAY LOCATION

The fuel pump relay is located on the righthand side of the engine compartment in the relay/power distribution center.

RELAY CENTER LOCATION

The relay/power distribution center is located on the righthand side of the engine compartment, forward of the battery.

Refer to **Figs. 1 through 3** for relay identification.

STARTER

REPLACE

2.4L & 2.5L Engines

1. Raise and support vehicle.
2. Remove two bolts that secure starter motor to engine block.
3. Lower starter motor to gain access to solenoid harness connector eyelet to solenoid terminal retaining nut, then remove nut and wiring from starter.
4. Remove battery cable harness connector eyelet to solenoid battery terminal retaining nut. **Support starter using suitable wire.**
5. Remove battery cable wiring from starter, then starter from vehicle.
6. Retain any starter motor shims for installation.
7. Reverse procedure to install.

4.0L Engine

1. Raise and suitably support vehicle.
2. Remove starter motor lower mounting bolt.
3. While supporting starter motor, remove starter motor upper mounting bolt.
4. Lower starter motor from front of transmission housing far enough to access wiring connector retaining nut.
5. Remove battery cable eyelet to solenoid battery terminal retaining nut.
6. Disconnect solenoid terminal wire harness connector from starter solenoid.
7. Remove starter motor from vehicle.
8. Reverse procedure to install.

DISTRIBUTOR

REPLACE

Removal

1. Rotate crankshaft, and position cylinder number one at Top Dead Center (TDC) of its compression stroke, align crankshaft pulley timing mark. **Rotate engine in normal direction of rotation only.**
2. Disconnect coil secondary wire at coil only, then disconnect distributor primary wiring connector.

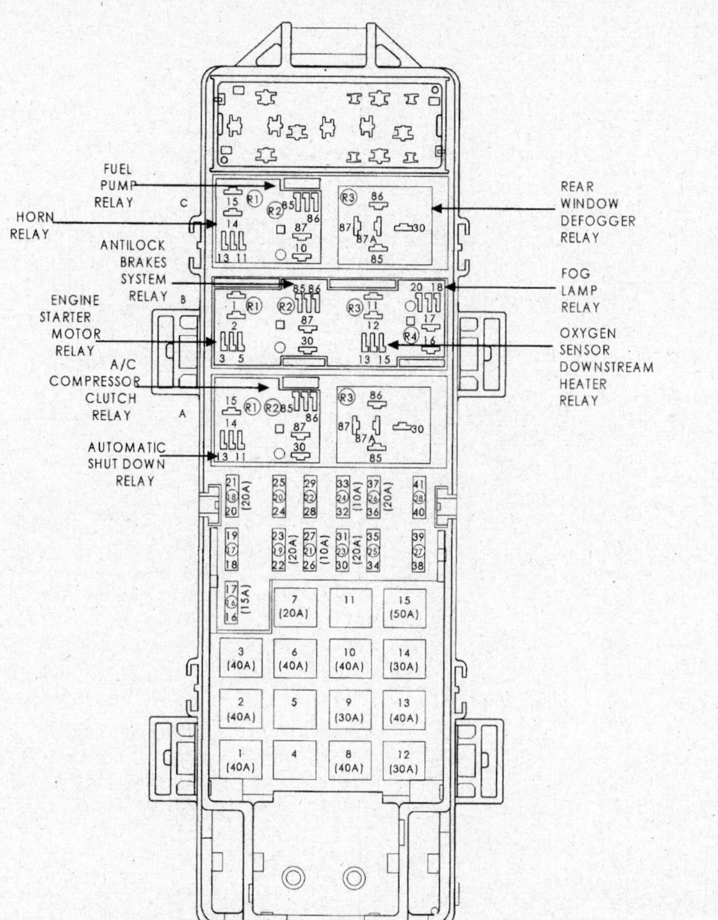

Fig. 1 Relay location & identification. 2002

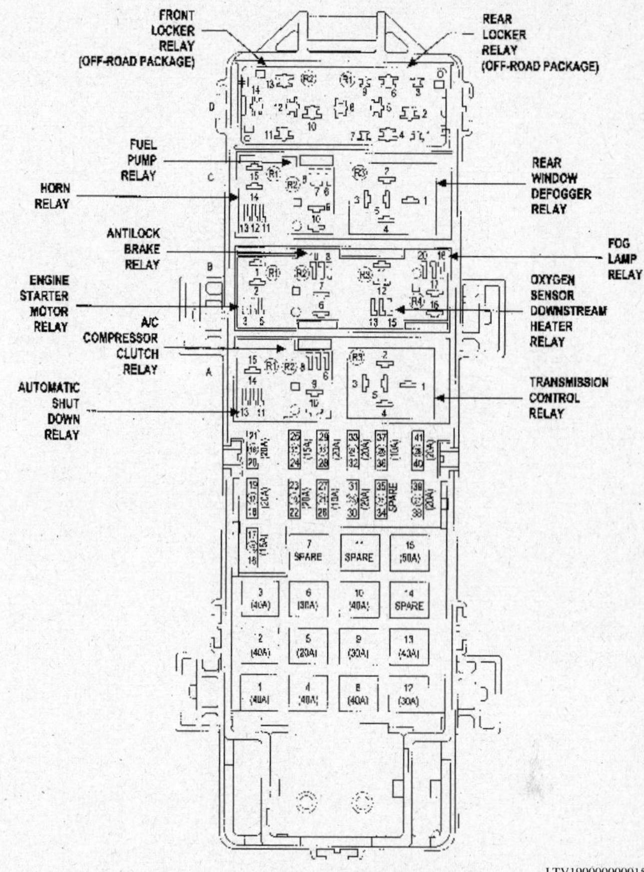

Fig. 2 Relay location & identification. 2003–04

3. Remove distributor cap and position aside. **Do not remove rotor.**
4. **On models equipped with air conditioning,** remove electrical cooling fan and shroud assembly from radiator.
5. **On all models,** remove distributor hold-down bolt, then pull distributor straight out of engine.
6. Mark position of rotor onto body of distributor for installation reference.

Installation

1. Ensure cylinder No. 1 is at TDC of its compression stroke and oil pump drive slot is positioned as outlined, **Fig. 4.**
2. Install new distributor base gasket.
3. **If installing old distributor,** align rotor to match marks on distributor body, then align mount tab to mounting hole and insert distributor.
4. **If installing new distributor,** proceed as follows:
   a. Ensure plastic shipping/installation pin is engaged into correct hole in plate, **Fig. 5.**
   b. Insert distributor partially, just short of distributor drive gear engagement, then align distributor mount tab bolt slot to one o'clock position, **Fig. 6.**
   c. Push distributor straight into block, allowing distributor to turn as drive gears engage. Rotor and distributor will rotate clockwise during installation due to helical cut gears on distributor and camshaft.
   d. Remove shipping/installation pin.
5. **On all distributors,** ensure distributor is fully seated into block. If required, wiggle distributor and/or shaft slightly to allow engagement of distributor drive gears and/or oil pump drive.
6. Install distributor hold-down bolt and **torque** to 17 ft. lbs.
7. Install remaining components and **torque** distributor cap screws to 26 inch lbs.
8. Connect high tension lead to coil, then primary lead to distributor.

IGNITION COIL

REPLACE

2.4L Engine

1. Disconnect electrical connector at rear of coil.
2. Remove all secondary cables from coil.
3. Remove four bolts, then coil.
4. Reverse procedure to install.

2.5L Engine

1. Disconnect ignition coil secondary cable from ignition coil, **Fig. 7.**
2. Disconnect engine harness connector from ignition coil.
3. Remove ignition coil mounting bolts.
4. Remove ignition coil from vehicle.
5. Reverse procedure to install, **torque** mounting bolts to 50 inch lbs.

4.0L Engine

A one piece coil rail assembly containing three individual coils is used on the 4.0L engine, **Fig. 8.** The coil rail must be replaced as an assembly. The bottom of the coil is equipped with 6 individual rubber boots to seal the 6 spark plugs to the coil.

1. Remove four coil mounting bolts.
2. Carefully pry up coil assembly from spark plugs, alternately prying up at each end of coil until rubber boots have disengaged from all spark plugs.
3. Disconnect coil electrical connector by pushing slide tab outward to righthand side of vehicle, then push in on secondary release lock on side of connector and pull connector from coil.
4. Remove coil from vehicle.
5. Reverse procedure to install.

IGNITION LOCK

REPLACE

1. **On models equipped with a automatic transmission,** place shifter in PARK position.
2. **On all models,** rotate key to ON position.

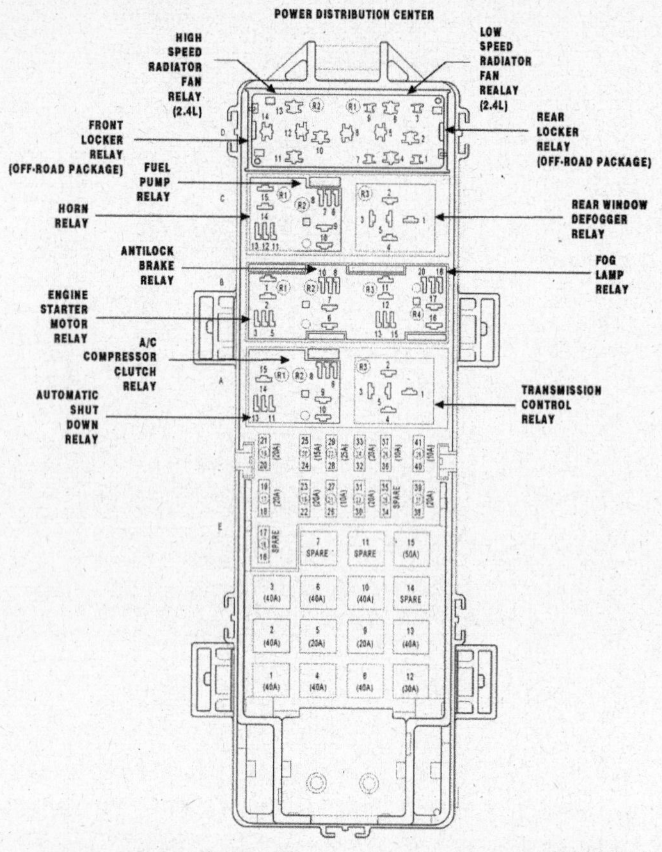

LTV0500000000322

Fig. 3 Relay location & identification. 2005–06

3. A release tang is located on bottom of key cylinder. Position a small screwdriver or pin punch into tang access hole on bottom of steering column lower cover.
4. Push pin punch up while pulling key cylinder from steering column.
5. Reverse procedure to install.

IGNITION SWITCH

REPLACE

Removal

1. Remove ignition lock as outlined under "Ignition Lock, Replace."
2. Remove lower steering column cover screws and remove cover.
3. Remove multi-function switch.
4. Disconnect electrical connector at rear of ignition switch.
5. Remove ignition switch mounting screw using a suitable tamper proof torx bit.
6. Pull ignition switch straight out to remove from locking tabs.

Installation

1. Before installing ignition switch, rotate slot in switch to ON position, **Fig. 9.**
2. Connect electrical connector to rear of ignition switch. Make sure that locking tab is fully seated into wiring connector.
3. Position switch to column and install tamper proof screw to specification.
4. Test operation of lock cylinder for smooth rotating.
5. Instal multi-function switch.
6. Install steering column lower cover.

CLUTCH START SWITCH

REPLACE

The clutch interlock switch is an integral part of the clutch master cylinder push rod and cannot be serviced separately.

NEUTRAL SAFETY SWITCH

REPLACE

2002

1. Raise and support vehicle.
2. Disconnect electrical connector from switch and remove switch from transmission. Allow transmission fluid to drain into a suitable container.
3. Move selector lever to Park and Neutral positions. Inspect switch operating fingers for proper operation.
4. Reverse procedure to install, noting the following:
   a. Install new seal on switch.
   b. Tighten switch to specification.
   c. Add transmission fluid as required.

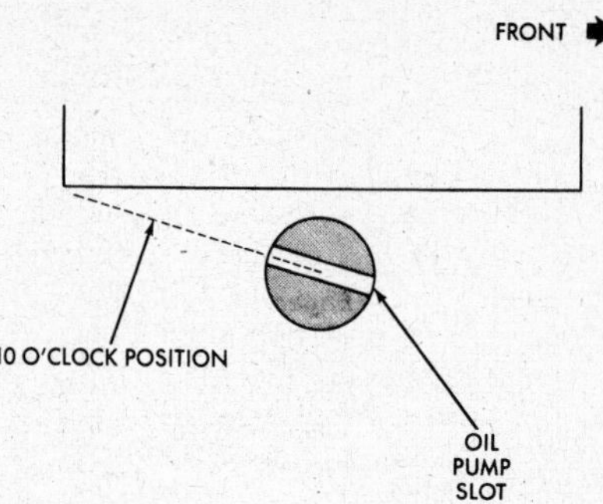

Slot At 10 O'clock Position—2.5L Engine

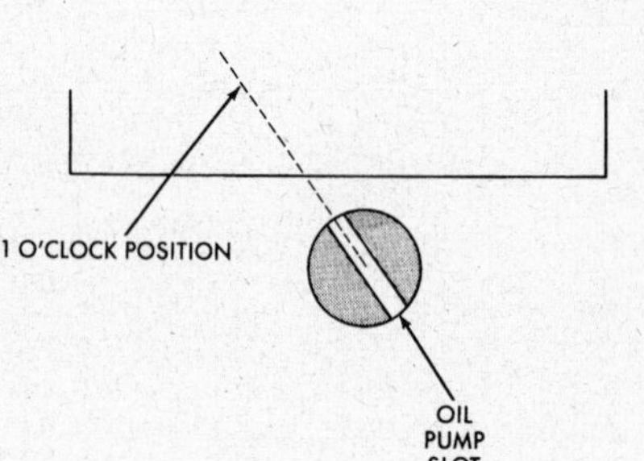

Slot At 11 O'clock Position—4.0L Engine

CR1119500211000X

Fig. 4 Oil pump drive slot position

2003–06

Refer to **MOTOR's "Domestic Transmission, In-Vehicle Service" or "Transmission Service DVD."**

HEADLAMP SWITCH

REPLACE

Refer to "Multi-Function Switch, Replace" for headlamp switch replacement procedure.

STOP LIGHT SWITCH

REPLACE

1. Remove lower steering column cover mounting screws, then pull top edge of cover back and down to disengage hooks on lower edge.
2. Remove lower trim panels as required to access switch.
3. While holding brake pedal down, rotate switch 30° counter clockwise to disengage switch from mounting bracket.
4. Disconnect switch electrical connector.
5. Reverse procedure to install, noting the following.
   a. Ensure switch plunger is fully extended before installation.
   b. Hold pedal down while installing switch.
   c. After switch is installed, pull pedal fully rearward to allow self adjustment. Switch will make ratcheting noise as it self adjusts.
   d. Ensure pedal returns fully to pedal stop.

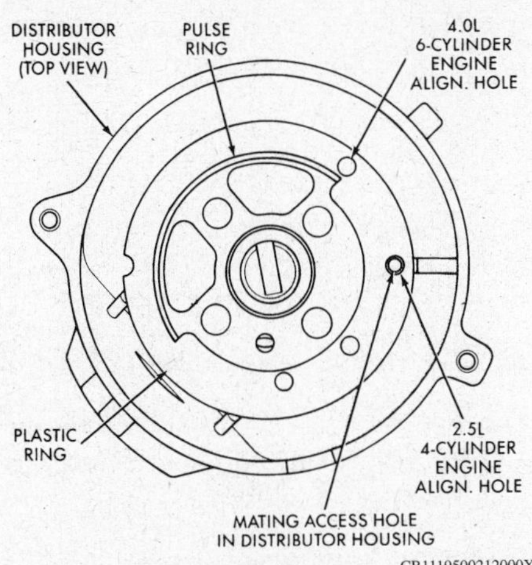

Fig. 5 Distributor alignment pin holes

MULTI-FUNCTION SWITCH

REPLACE

1. Remove steering column opening cover from instrument panel.
2. Remove two screws securing lower steering column shroud to upper shroud.
3. **On models equipped with tilt steering,** tilt steering column to fully lowered position.
4. **On all models,** remove upper and lower steering column shrouds.
5. Disconnect cross body wire harness electrical connector from back of left-hand multi-function switch.
6. Remove two screws securing multi-function switch to upper steering column housing.
7. Remove multi-function switch assembly from upper steering column housing.
8. Reverse procedure to install.

TURN SIGNAL SWITCH

REPLACE

Refer to "Multi-Function Switch, Replace" for turn signal switch replacement procedure.

STEERING WHEEL

REPLACE

1. Remove driver air bag module as outlined in "Passive Restraint Systems" chapter.
2. Loosen steering wheel retaining nut, then place match marks on column and steering wheel.
3. Remove wheel from column using a suitable steering wheel puller pushing on top of nut.
4. Reverse procedure to install. **Torque** steering wheel nut to 40 ft. lbs.

INSTRUMENT CLUSTER

REPLACE

1. Remove cluster bezel from instrument panel.

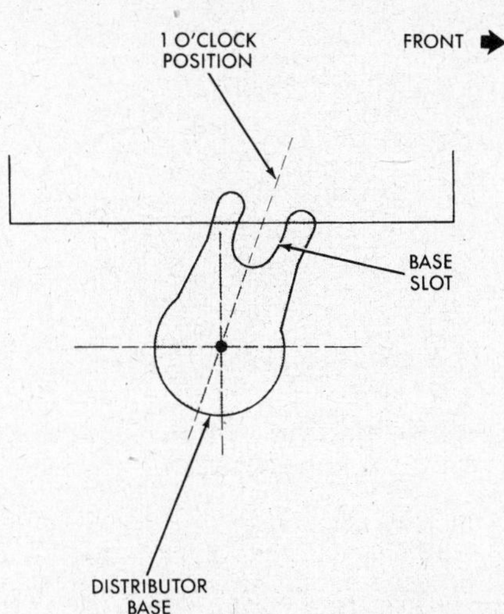

Fig. 6 Distributor mount tab alignment

2. Remove four instrument cluster retaining screws.
3. Pull cluster rearward to disconnect self-connecting electrical connectors, then remove cluster from vehicle.
4. Reverse procedure to install. Ensure self-connecting electrical connectors are properly aligned when installing instrument cluster into place.

RADIO

REPLACE

2002

1. Pry top cover away from instrument panel and remove cover from vehicle.
2. Remove top of center unit to instrument panel attaching screws.
3. Remove ashtray, then screw from ashtray opening.
4. Pry lower edge of center unit away from instrument panel. Lift center unit upwards to disengage hooks.
5. **On models equipped with CD radio,** remove glove box, then reach through opening to remove radio bracket and ground strap from back of radio.
6. **On all models,** remove radio to instrument panel retaining screws.
7. Slide radio out from instrument panel and disconnect electrical connectors and antenna lead.
8. Reverse procedure to install.

2003-06

1. Remove instrument panel top cover from instrument panel.
2. Remove center bezel.
3. Remove screws that secure radio to instrument panel.
4. **On model equipped with a CD radio,** remove glove compartment from instrument panel.
5. **On model equipped with a CD radio,** reach through instrument panel glove box opening to access and remove

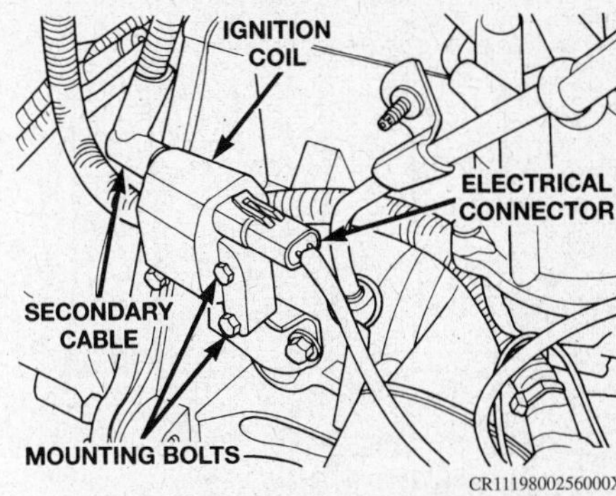

Fig. 7 Ignition coil. 2.5L engine

screw that secures CD radio bracket and ground strap to back of radio.
6. **On all models,** pull radio out from instrument panel far enough to access wire harness connectors and antenna coaxial cable connector.
7. Unplug wire harness connectors from rear of radio.
8. Disconnect antenna cable by pulling locking antenna connector away from radio.
9. Remove radio from instrument panel.
10. Reverse procedure to install. **Torque** screws to 20 inch lbs.

WIPER MOTOR

REPLACE

Front

2002

1. Lift wiper arm fully away from windshield to release tension on base latch.
2. Pull out latch at base of arm, then, while rocking arm, pull from pivot shaft, **Fig. 10.**
3. Open hood, pull up each end of hood seal in cowl area to expose screws, then remove cowl retaining screws.
4. Close hood, remove one screw from top center of cowl grille and four cowl to windshield base screws.
5. Remove cowl grille and screen.
6. Disconnect motor electrical connector from inside cowl opening.
7. Remove wiper assembly mounting screws, then lift assembly out through cowl opening.
8. Dismount wiring connector from linkage frame.
9. Remove nut from wiper motor shaft and remove arm.
10. Remove motor retaining screws and motor.
11. Reverse procedure to install.

2003-06

1. Lift front wiper arm far enough to raise wiper blade off of glass and permit wiper arm latch plate to be pulled out to its holding position, then release arm. Wiper arm and blade will remain off glass with latch in this position.
2. Remove front wiper arm pivot end from wiper pivot driver.
3. Unlatch, open and support hood.

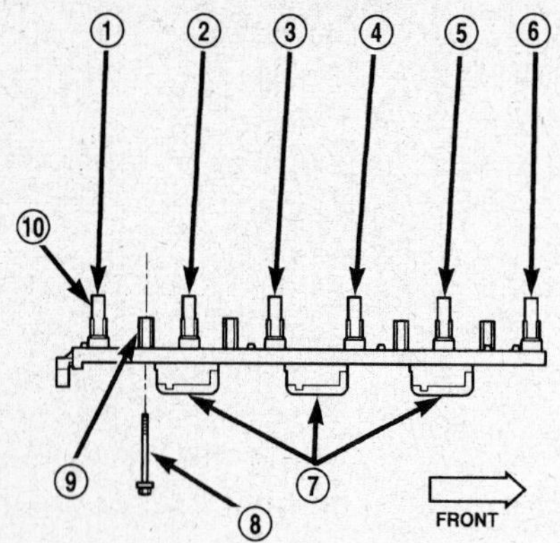

Fig. 8 Ignition coil. 4.0L engine

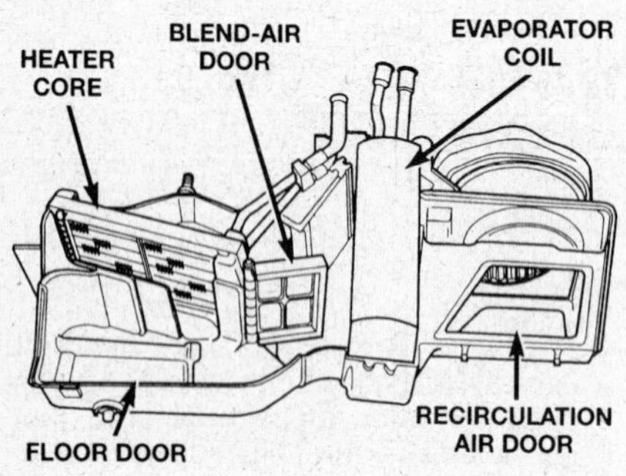

Fig. 11 Lower half of heating & A/C housing. 2002–04

4. Remove four screws at rear of cowl grille.
5. Open hood and remove screws that attach cowl grille and screen to cowl.
6. Remove grille and screen from cowl.
7. Disconnect body wire harness connector for front wiper motor from motor pigtail wire connector.
8. Remove three screws that secure front wiper module mounting bracket to cowl plenum panel.
9. Remove front wiper module from cowl plenum panel as a unit.
10. Reverse procedure to install. **Torque** screws to 105 inch lbs.

Rear

2002

1. Lift wiper arm fully away from rear window to release tension on base latch.
2. Pull out latch at base of arm, then while rocking arm pull from pivot shaft.
3. Remove wiper shaft nut, bezel and gasket.
4. Remove motor cover attaching

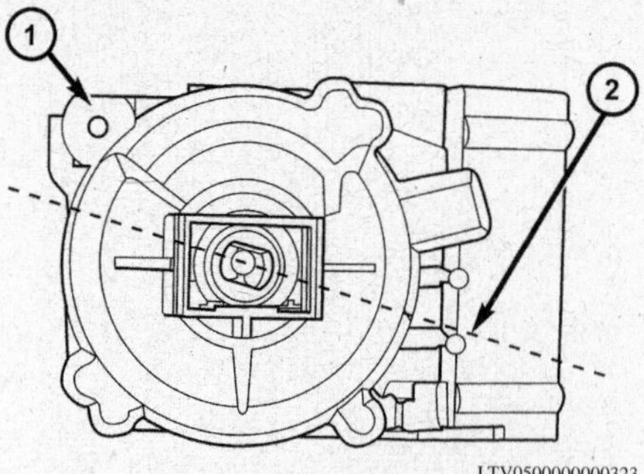

Fig. 9 Ignition switch alignment on position

screws, then cover.
5. Disconnect electrical connectors.
6. Loosen but do not remove righthand side lift glass hinge retaining nut.
7. Pull motor rearward until wiper shaft clears glass, then move motor sideways until mounting tab is free of hinge.
8. Reverse procedure to install.

2003-06

1. Lift up wiper arm pivot cover.
2. Remove nut securing wiper arm to wiper motor output shaft.
3. Lift wiper arm to its over-center position to hold wiper blade off glass and relieve spring tension on wiper arm.
4. Remove wiper arm from output shaft.
5. Remove nut securing threaded sleeve of wiper motor output shaft to outside of liftglass.
6. Remove washer from wiper motor output shaft sleeve.
7. Remove trim cover from wiper motor.
8. Disconnect wiper motor electrical connector.
9. Remove nut and washer securing wiper motor bracket insulator to stud on liftglass.
10. Remove washer from stud securing wiper motor bracket insulator to liftglass.
11. From inside liftglass, gently pull wiper motor away from liftglass until output shaft clears rubber grommet in liftglass output shaft hole.
12. Remove wiper motor and mounting bracket from liftglass as a unit.
13. Reverse procedure to install.

WIPER SWITCH

REPLACE

Front

Refer to "Multi-Function Switch, Replace" for wiper switch replacement procedure.

Rear

1. Remove accessory switch bezel from instrument panel center bezel from instrument panel.
2. Gently pry latch tabs at top and bottom of rear wiper and washer switch receptacle on back of accessory switch

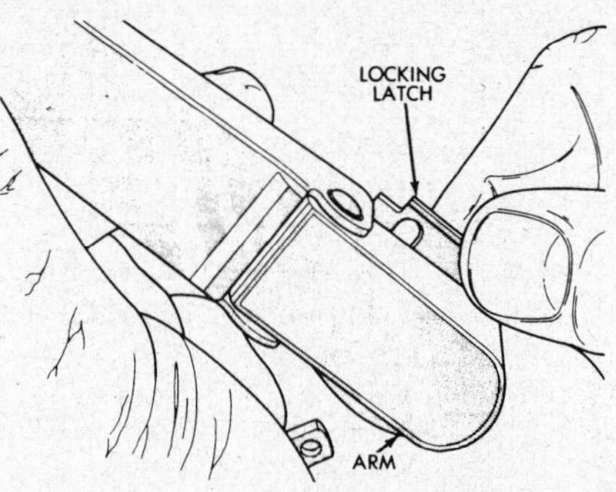

Fig. 10 Front wiper arm latch. 2002

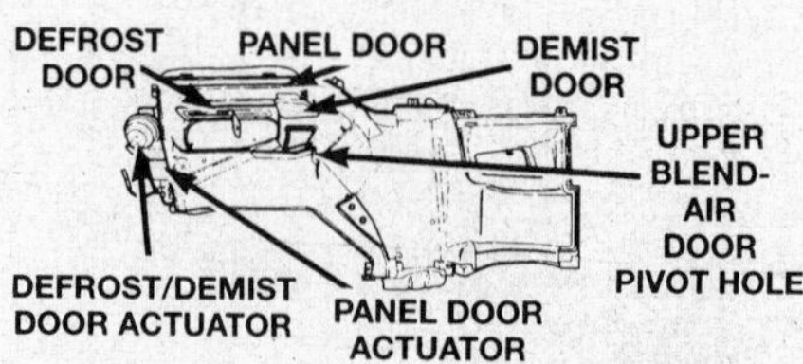

Fig. 12 Upper half of heating & A/C housing. 2002–04

bezel far enough to disengage snap features on top and bottom of switch housing, then pull switch out of receptacle.

WIPER TRANSMISSION

REPLACE

The wiper transmission is part of the wiper motor. Refer to "Wiper Motor, Replace" for wiper transmission replacement procedure.

BLOWER MOTOR

REPLACE

1. Disconnect blower motor electrical connector.
2. Release blower motor retaining tab, then rotate blower motor assembly counterclockwise.
3. Remove blower motor assembly from HVAC housing.
4. Reverse procedure to install.

HEATER CORE

REPLACE

2002-04

1. Remove instrument panel. as outlined in "Dash Panel Service" chapter.
2. **On models equipped with A/C,** recover refrigerant from A/C system as outlined in "Air Conditioning" chapter, then disconnect and seal refrigerant lines and fittings from evaporator coil.
3. **On all models,** drain cooling system, then disconnect hoses from heater core.
4. Disconnect vacuum supply hose to heating and A/C housing.
5. From engine compartment, remove five nuts from heating and A/C housing

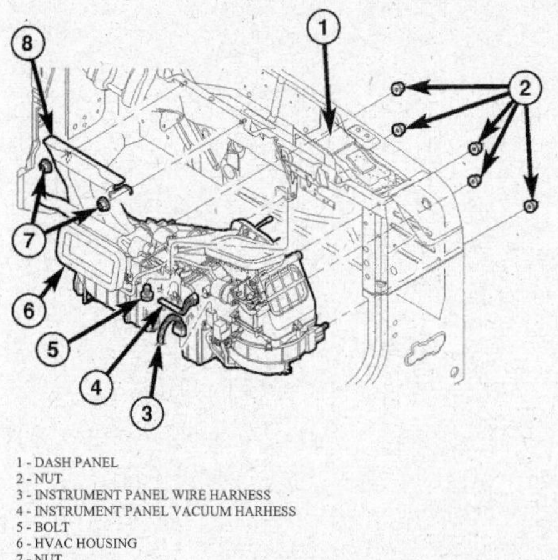

Fig. 13 HVAC housing removal. 2005–06

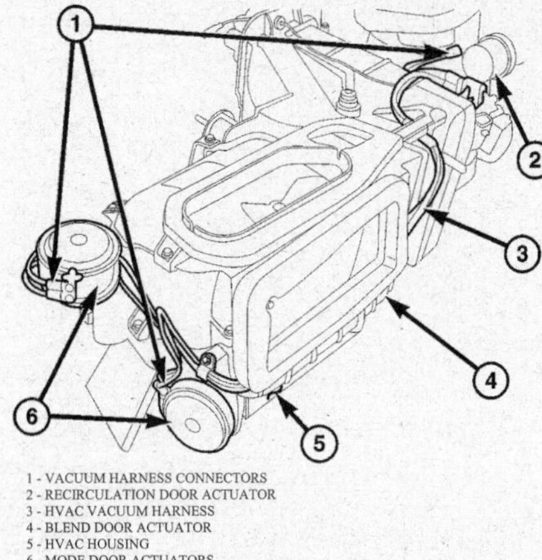

Fig. 14 Vacuum harness & actuators. 2005–06

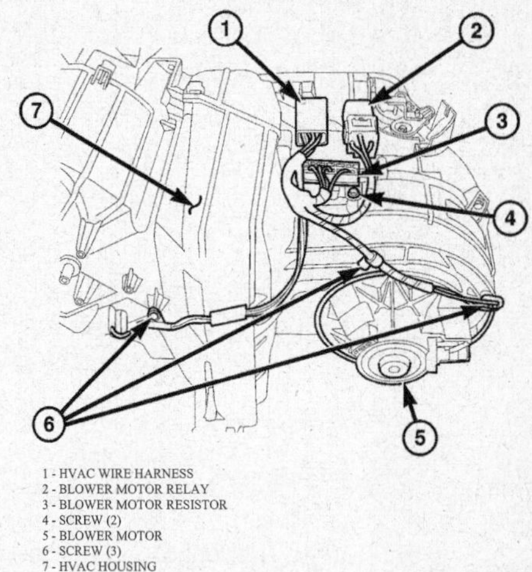

Fig. 15 HVAC wire harness. 2005–06

mounting studs, reposition or remove battery if required.
6. Remove cowl plenum drain tube from stud behind engine.
7. From inside vehicle, remove heating and A/C housing to firewall attaching screw.
8. Pull heating and A/C housing downward to clear ducts while pulling rearward to clear studs from firewall, then remove unit from vehicle.
9. Disengage wiring harness and connector retaining clips from heating and A/C housing.
10. Disconnect vacuum harness connectors at recirculation air door actuator and floor air door actuator.
11. Disconnect blower motor electrical connector.
12. Remove blower motor mounting screws, then blower assembly.
13. Remove snap clips and screws holding upper and lower halves of heater and A/C unit together, then separate unit, **Figs. 11 and 12.**
14. Lift heater core from lower half of assembly.
15. Reverse procedure to install. Ensure foam insulators are installed.

2005–06

1. Remove instrument panel as outlined under "Dash Panel Service" chapter.
2. **On models equipped with A/C,**
   a. Recover refrigerant as outlined in "Air Conditioning" chapter.
   b. Disconnect A/C liquid and suction lines from A/C evaporator and remove and discard O-ring seals.
   c. Install plugs in, or tape over opened suction and liquid line fittings and both evaporator tubes.
3. **On all models,** drain engine cooling system into suitable container.
4. Disconnect heater hoses from heater core tubes. Install plugs in, or tape over opened heater core tubes.
5. Disconnect HVAC system vacuum supply line connector from tee fitting near heater core tubes.
6. Remove five nuts that secure the HVAC housing to dash panel in engine compartment, **Fig. 13.**
7. Remove two push-nuts that secure defroster duct to dash panel in passenger compartment and remove duct.
8. Remove bolt that secures HVAC housing to bracket located on dash panel in passenger compartment.
9. Remove HVAC housing from inside vehicle taking care not to allow any remaining coolant to drain on vehicles interior.
10. Remove HVAC housing assembly.
11. Disconnect HVAC vacuum harness connectors from mode door actuators and recirculation door actuator, **Fig. 14.**
12. Disengage vacuum harness from any retaining clips located on HVAC housing and carefully pull vacuum supply line through foam seal located at front of housing and remove vacuum harness.
13. Remove mode door actuators and blend door actuator from HVAC housing.
14. Disconnect wire harness connectors from blower motor resistor and blower motor, **Fig. 15.**
15. Disengage push-in retainers for HVAC wire harness connector and blower motor relay from HVAC housing.
16. Remove three screws that secure HVAC wire harness to HVAC housing and remove wire harness.
17. Remove two screws that secure blower motor resistor to HVAC housing and remove resistor.
18. Disengage blower motor retaining tab and turn blower motor counterclockwise and remove blower motor from HVAC housing.
19. Remove five screws that secure air inlet housing to top of HVAC housing and remove inlet housing, **Fig. 16.**
20. Remove three screws that secure floor distribution duct to bottom of HVAC housing and remove duct, **Fig. 17.**
21. Remove one screw that secures upper and lower HVAC housing halves together at bottom of HVAC housing.
22. Cut foam seal for defrost/demister outlet cover along two parting lines of outlet cover.
23. Cut foam seal for panel outlet along parting line of two HVAC housing halves.
24. Remove five screws that secure defrost/demister outlet cover to top of HVAC housing and remove cover.
25. Cut foam seal for evaporator and heater core tubes along parting line of two HVAC housing halves.
26. Remove foam seal from evaporator condensate drain tube.
27. Remove fourteen screws and two clips that secure upper and lower HVAC housing halves together.
28. Separate two HVAC housing halves.
29. Release retaining tab that secures panel door lever to panel-air door and remove lever.
30. Remove panel-air door from lower half of HVAC housing.
31. Remove floor/defrost-air door and blend-air door from lower half of HVAC housing.
32. Lift heater core and foam insulator out of lower half of HVAC housing.
33. **On models equipped with A/C,** disengage rubber seal from around tubes of A/C evaporator and carefully lift A/C evaporator and foam insulator out of lower half of HVAC housing.
34. **On all models,** remove rubber seal for evaporator tubes from lower half of HVAC housing, if required.
35. Remove screw that secures evaporator tube clamp to evaporator tubes and remove clamp.
36. Lift heater core out of lower half of HVAC housing.
37. Reverse procedure to install. Ensure foam insulators are undamaged, and installed.

EVAPORATOR CORE

REPLACE

Refer to "Heater Core, Replace" for evaporator core replacement procedure.

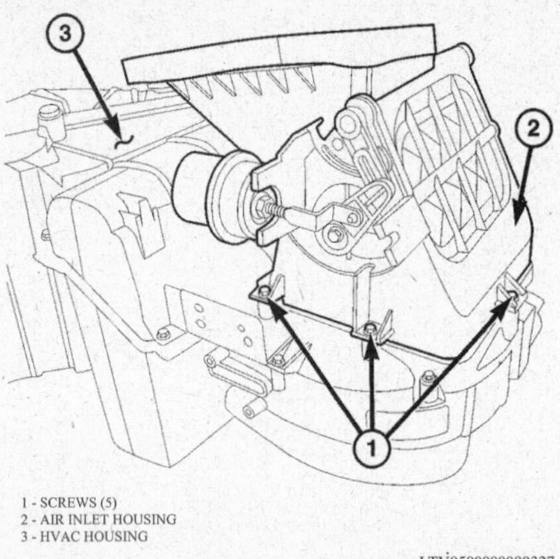

Fig. 16 HVAC air inlet housing. 2005–06

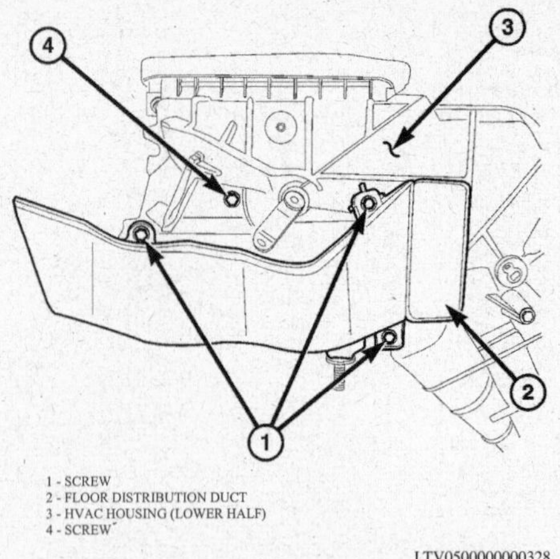

Fig. 17 Floor distribution duct and screw. 2005–06

2.4L Engine

NOTE: Refer To "2.4L Engine" Section Of "Liberty" Chapter In This Manual For Service Procedures & Tightening Specifications Not Found In This Section.

NOTE: Air Bag Equipped Models, Refer To "Air Bag System Precautions" Located In The Front Of This Manual For System Disarming & Arming Procedures.

NOTE: Refer To "Computer Relearn Procedures" Located In The Front Of This Manual When Battery Power To The Computer Has Been Interrupted.

INDEX

PRECAUTIONS

Air Bag Systems

Refer to "Air Bag System Precautions" in the front of this manual for system disarming and arming procedures.

Battery Ground Cable

Prior to service, disconnect battery ground cable and isolate as required.

Fuel System Pressure Relief

1. Remove fuel cap, then fuel pump relay from PDC.
2. Start and run engine until it stalls.
3. Attempt to restart engine until it will no longer run.
4. Turn ignition key to Off position.
5. Unplug connector from any injector.
6. Attach one end of a suitable 18 gauge or smaller jumper wire to either injector terminal.
7. Connect other end of jumper wire to positive battery terminal.
8. Connect one end of a second jumper wire to remaining injector terminal.
9. Momentarily touch other end of second jumper wire to negative battery terminal for no more than a few seconds. **Powering an injector for more than a few seconds will damage injector.**
10. Place a suitable rag below fuel line quick connect fitting on fuel rail, then disconnect quick connect fitting.
11. Install fuel pump relay to PDC, then clear any stored DTC's.

INTAKE MANIFOLD

REPLACE

1. Disconnect IAT sensor electrical connector.
2. Disconnect air intake tube at throttle body, then remove upper air cleaner housing.
3. Disconnect electrical connector from TPS, IAC and MAP sensor.
4. Disconnect vacuum lines for purge solenoid and PCV valve at intake manifold.
5. Disconnect vacuum lines for power brake booster, leak detection pump, EGR transducer and speed control vacuum reservoir at intake manifold.
6. Disconnect throttle, speed control and

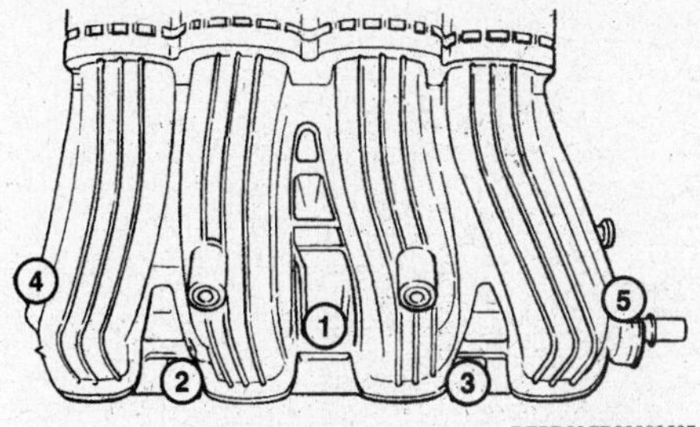

Fig. 1 Intake manifold tightening sequence

transmission control cables from throttle lever and bracket.

7. Release fuel system pressure as outlined in "Precautions."
8. Disconnect fuel line.
9. Disconnect ECT and fuel injector wire harness electrical connectors.
10. Remove intake manifold bolts, then intake manifold.
11. Reverse procedure to install, noting the following:
    a. Install new intake manifold gasket.
    b. Tighten intake manifold bolts in sequence, **Fig. 1,** to specifications.

CAMSHAFT LOBE LIFT SPECIFICATIONS

Exhaust .... .259 inch
Intake .... .324 inch

VALVE ADJUSTMENT

These engines use hydraulic lifters. No adjustment is required.

SERPENTINE DRIVE BELT

Routing

Refer to **Figs. 2 through 5** for drive belt routing.

Replacement

Refer to "2.4L Engine" in the "Liberty" chapter for serpentine drive belt replacement procedure.

WATER PUMP

REPLACE

1. Drain cooling system into suitable container.
2. Remove timing belt as outlined in "Timing Belt, Replace."
3. Remove both cam sprockets using holding tool No. 6793 and adaptor tool No. C-4685-C2, or equivalents.
4. Remove timing belt rear cover.
5. Remove bolts, then water pump.
6. Reverse procedure to install, noting the following:
    a. Install new O-ring in water pump body groove.
    b. Install water pump, then pressurize cooling system to 15 psi., and inspect for leaks at shaft seal and O-ring.

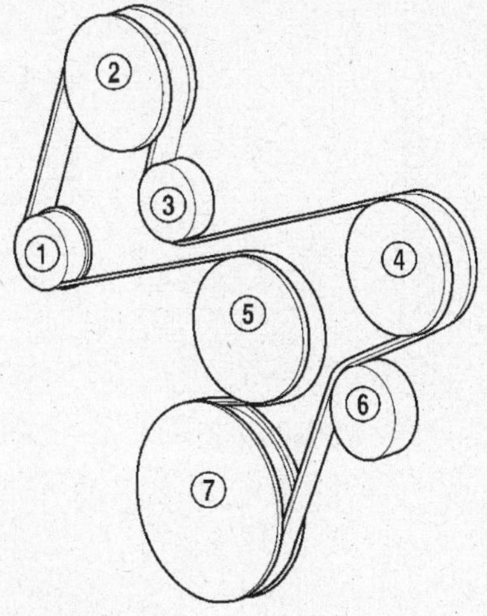

1 - ALT
2 - A/C
3 - IDL
4 - P/S
5 - WATER PUMP AND FAN
6 - IDL
7 – CRANK

LTV0500000000331

Fig. 2 Drive belt routing. 2002 2.4L engine w/air conditioning

RADIATOR

REPLACE

1. Remove radiator cap.
2. Remove condenser lower seal from lower core support.
3. Drain cooling system into a suitable container.
4. Remove radiator upper and lower hose clamps, and hoses.
5. Disconnect coolant reserve/overflow tank hose from radiator.
6. **On 2002 models equipped with a 2.4L engine and power steering,** remove four fan shroud mounting bolts, tie reservoir back to prevent spillage, and position fan shroud back over fan blades.
7. **On models equipped with a automatic transmission,** disconnect and plug transmission fluid cooler lines.
8. **On all models,** remove six radiator mounting bolts and position front axle vent hose to side.
9. Lift radiator straight up and out of vehicle.
10. Reverse procedure to install. Tighten bolts to specification.

FUEL PUMP

REPLACE

1. Drain fuel tank into a suitable container.
2. Remove fuel filler cap.
3. Remove plastic fuel filler bezel to body screws and remove plastic fuel filler bezel.

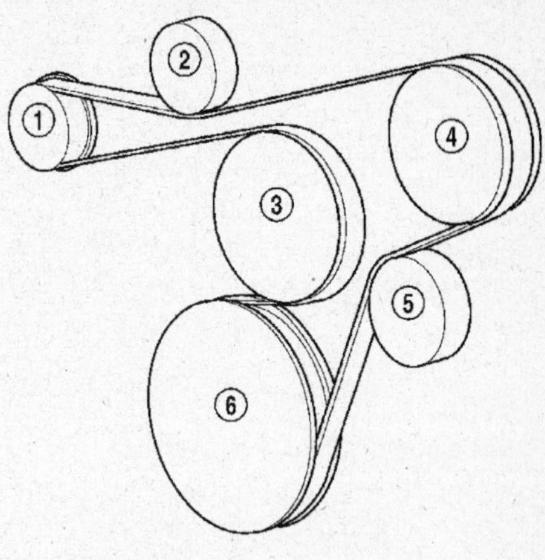

1 - ALT
2 - IDL
3 - WATER PUMP AND FAN
4 - P/S
5 - IDL
6 - CRANK

LTV0500000000332

Fig. 3 Drive belt routing. 2002 2.4L engine less air conditioning

4. To prevent contaminants from entering tank, temporarily install fuel cap to fill hoses.
5. Remove right/rear tire/wheel.
6. Remove wheelhouse liner at right/rear wheel.
7. Remove vertical support bracket to gain access to ORVR vapor line.
8. Disconnect vapor line (ORVR VAPOR LINE).
9. Cut plastic tie wrap securing rear axle vent hose to fuel fill hose.
10. Disconnect fuel tank electrical connector at left/front of fuel tank.
11. Disconnect 2 vapor lines at left/front of fuel tank.
12. Disconnect quick-connect fitting from fuel supply line at front of fuel tank.
13. Centrally position a transmission jack or equivalent, under skid plate/fuel tank assembly.
14. Remove three skid plate-to-body nuts at front of tank.
15. Remove four skid plate-to-body nuts at rear of tank.
16. Lower tank assembly.
17. Disconnect fuel filler hose at tank.
18. Note rotational position of module before attempting removal. An indexing arrow is located on top of module for this purpose.
19. Position Lockring Remover/Installer tool No. 9340 or equivalent into notches on outside edge of lockring.
20. Remove lockring.
21. Remove module from fuel tank.
22. Reverse procedure to install.

FUEL FILTER

REPLACE

1. Remove fuel pump as outlined under "Fuel Pump, Replace."
2. Remove fuel filter using suitable screwdrivers.
3. Clean bottom of pump module.
4. Reverse procedure to install.

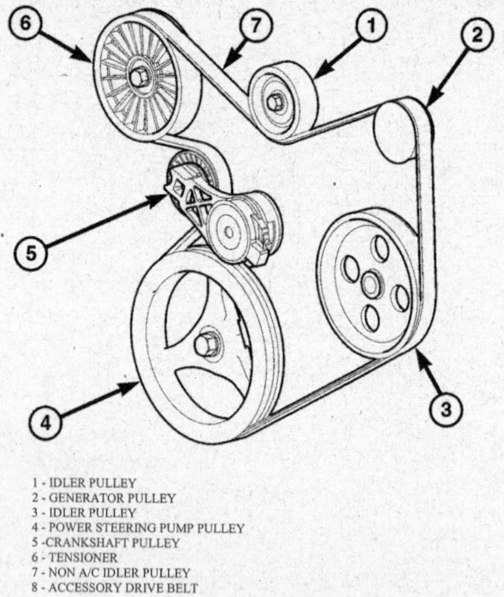

Fig. 4 Drive belt routing. 2003–06 2.4L engine w/air conditioning

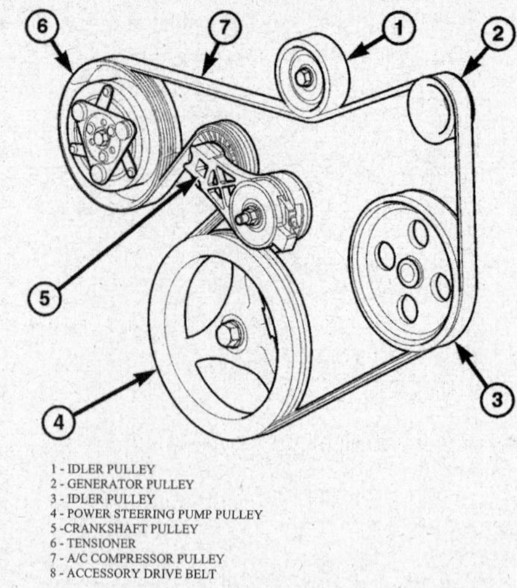

Fig. 5 Drive belt routing. 2003–06 2.4L engine less air conditioning

TIGHTENING SPECIFICATIONS

Year	Component	Torque Ft. Lbs.
2002–06	Balance Shaft Carrier Cover	105
	Balance Shaft Carrier To Block	40
	Balance Shaft Chain Tensioner	105①
	Balance Shaft Gear Cover	105①
	Balance Shaft Sprocket	21
	Camshaft Sprocket	75
	Connecting Rod Cap	40②
	Crankshaft Damper	100
	Exhaust Manifold	17
	Exhaust Manifold Heat Shield	105①
	Flex Plate To Crankshaft	70
	Flywheel	60
	Front Cover	105①
	Lower Intake Manifold	21
	Oil Pan	105①
	Oil Pan Drain Plug	20
	Oil Pump Cover	105①
	Oil Pump Pick Up Tube	20
	Oil Pump Relief Valve Cap	30
	Oil Pump To Block	21
	Righthand Engine Mount Bracket	45
	Timing Belt Rear Cover	105①
	Timing Belt Tensioner	45
	Timing Belt Tensioner Lock Nut	22
	Valve Cover	105①

① — Inch lbs.
② — Plus 1/4 turn.

2.5L Engine

NOTE: On Air Bag Equipped Models, Refer To "Air Bag System Precautions" Located In The Front Of This Manual For System Disarming & Arming Procedures.

NOTE: Refer To "Computer Relearn Procedures" Located In The Front Of This Manual When Battery Power To The Computer Has Been Interrupted.

INDEX

PRECAUTIONS

Air Bag Systems

Refer to "Air Bag System Precautions" in the front of this manual for system disarming and arming procedures.

Battery Ground Cable

Prior to service, disconnect battery ground cable and isolate as required.

Fuel System Pressure Relief

1. Remove fuel pump relay from power distribution center.
2. Start and run engine until it stalls.
3. Crank engine until it will no longer run.
4. Turn ignition key to off position.

COMPRESSION PRESSURE

Pressure is 120–150 psi. Maximum allowable variation between cylinders is 30 psi.

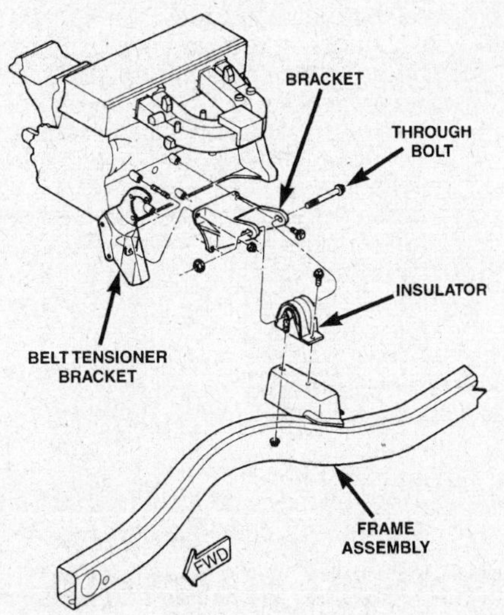

Fig. 1 Lefthand front engine mount

ENGINE MOUNT

REPLACE

Front

1. Raise and support vehicle.
2. Support engine with appropriate engine support stand.
3. Remove through bolt nut, **Figs. 1 and 2. Do not remove through bolt at this time.**
4. Remove retaining bolts/nuts from support cushion, then through bolt.
5. Remove cushion.
6. Reverse procedure to install. Tighten nuts and bolts to specifications.

Rear

1. Raise and support vehicle, then support transmission.
2. Remove support cushion to crossmember retaining nuts, then crossmember.
3. **On models equipped with manual transmission,** proceed as follows:
   a. Remove support cushion retaining nuts, then cushion.
   b. If required, remove transmission support bracket to transmission retaining bolts, then bracket.
4. **On models equipped with automatic transmission,** remove support cushion retaining bolts, then cushion and transmission support bracket.
5. **On all models,** reverse procedure to install. Tighten nuts and bolts to specifications.

ENGINE

REPLACE

1. Remove battery and drain cooling system.

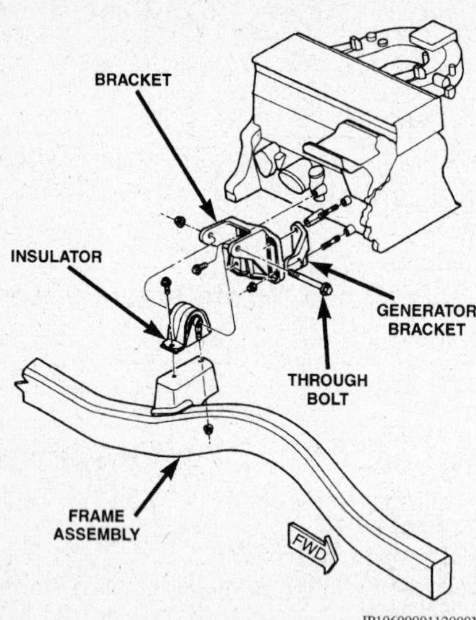

Fig. 2 Righthand front engine mount

2. Cover windshield frame with a protector.
3. Raise hood and rest it against windshield frame.
4. Disconnect electrical connectors from alternator, ignition coil, distributor, oil pressure switch and starter motor, then separate CEC system engine harness connector. **Mark connectors for installation reference.**
5. Disconnect quick disconnect fuel lines at fuel rail and return line.
6. Remove fuel line bracket from intake manifold.
7. Remove air cleaner, then disconnect engine ground strap.
8. Disconnect vacuum purge from canister, idle speed actuator connector, throttle cable and if equipped, speed control cable.
9. Remove throttle cable from bracket.
10. Disconnect throttle rod at bellcrank, then disconnect oxygen sensor connector.
11. Remove vacuum check valve from brake booster.
12. Disconnect coolant hoses from radiator, rear of intake manifold and thermostat housing and heater core.
13. Remove fan shroud and radiator retaining bolts, then fan shroud and radiator assembly.
14. Remove fan and spacer or thermostatic clutch, as equipped.
15. Install 5/16 x 1/2 inch SAE bolt through fan pulley and thread it into water pump in order to maintain pulley alignment as crankshaft is rotated.
16. **On models equipped with power steering,** proceed as follows:
    a. Disconnect hoses from steering gear.
    b. Drain power steering fluid into suitable container.
    c. Plug hoses and open fittings.
17. **On all models,** raise and support vehicle.
18. Remove oil filter, starter motor, flywheel housing cover and front motor mount through bolts.
19. Disconnect exhaust pipe from manifold.
20. Remove upper flywheel housing bolts and loosen lower bolts.
21. Remove engine shock damper bracket from sill, if equipped.
22. Lower vehicle and attach suitable lifting device to engine.
23. Raise engine off mounts, then place suitable support under flywheel housing.
24. Remove lower flywheel housing to engine retaining bolts.
25. Separate engine from flywheel housing.
26. Remove engine from vehicle.
27. Reverse procedure to install. Tighten nuts and bolts to specification.

INTAKE MANIFOLD

REPLACE

Mark installation position of all components, hoses and wiring prior to removal to aid reassembly.

1. Drain cooling system.
2. Remove air inlet hose from throttle body and air cleaner.
3. Loosen accessory drive belt tension, then remove belt from power steering pump.
4. Remove power steering pump and brackets. Position assembly aside.
5. Remove fuel tank filler cap to relieve tank pressure, then reinstall cap.
6. Disconnect fuel line from fuel rail, then accelerator cable from throttle body and hold-down bracket.
7. Disconnect all required electrical connectors, then pull harnesses away from manifold.
8. Remove crankcase ventilation hose.
9. Disconnect MAP sensor vacuum hose at manifold.
10. Disconnect vacuum hose from port on manifold, then remove molded vacuum harness.
11. Disconnect vacuum brake booster hose at manifold.
12. Remove manifold to cylinder head retaining bolts, then manifold.
13. Reverse procedure to install noting following:
    a. Install new gaskets.
    b. Tighten manifold bolts to specification in sequence outlined, **Fig. 3.**

EXHAUST MANIFOLD

REPLACE

1. Remove intake manifold as outlined in "Intake Manifold, Replace."
2. Remove manifold retaining nuts, then manifold.
3. Reverse procedure to install. Tighten bolts to specification in sequence outlined in **Fig. 3.**

CYLINDER HEAD

REPLACE

Removal

1. Drain coolant, then disconnect hoses from thermostat housing.

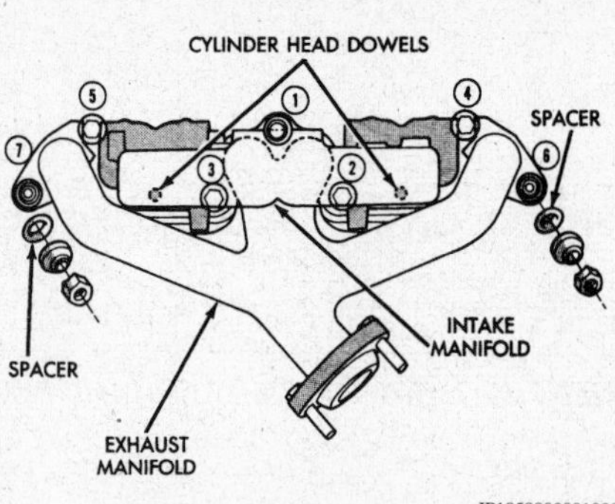

Fig. 3 Intake & exhaust manifold tightening sequence

2. Remove air cleaner.
3. Remove cylinder head cover retaining bolts, then cover.
4. Remove capscrews, bridges, pivots and rocker arms.
5. Remove pushrods. **Retain push rods, bridges, pivots and rocker arms in same order as removed.**
6. **On models equipped with power steering,** loosen drive belt at pump bracket.
7. **On models equipped with manual steering,** loose drive belt at idler pulley.
8. **On models equipped with A/C,** proceed as follows:
    a. Remove compressor mounting bracket retaining bolts and position compressor aside.
    b. Remove compressor bracket bolts from engine cylinder head.
    c. Loosen through bolt at bottom of bracket.
9. **On models equipped with power steering,** remove pump bracket and position aside.
10. **On all models,** relieve fuel system pressure as outlined in "Fuel System Pressure Relief."
11. Remove latch clip, then disconnect fuel supply hose.
12. Remove intake manifold as outlined in "Intake Manifold, Replace."
13. Remove exhaust manifold as outlined in "Exhaust Manifold, Replace."
14. Disconnect ignition wires, then remove spark plugs.
15. Disconnect coolant temperature sending unit connector.
16. Remove cylinder head retaining bolts, then cylinder head and gasket.
17. If this was the first time bolts were removed, put a dab of paint on top of bolt head. If bolts have a paint mark or it isn't known if they were used before, discard bolts.

Installation

1. Thoroughly clean gasket mating surfaces.
2. Fabricate two alignment dowels from a pair of longest used head bolts as follows:
    a. Cut bolt head off just below hex head.
    b. Cut a slot in top of bolt to allow removal with a screwdriver.

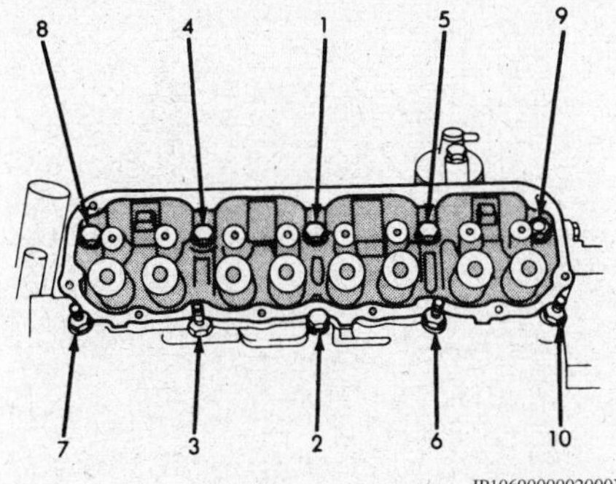

Fig. 4 Cylinder head tightening sequence

3. Install fabricated dowels in cylinder block bolt holes No. 8 and No. 10.
4. Position cylinder head gasket, with numbers facing upward, on cylinder block.
5. Install cylinder head.
6. Apply a suitable sealant to threads of No. 7 head bolt.
7. Install all except No. 8 and No. 10 head bolts.
8. Remove fabricated dowels and install No. 8 and No. 10 head bolts.
9. Tighten cylinder head bolts using sequence outlined in **Fig. 4.**
   a. **Torque** bolts to 22 ft. lbs.
   b. **Torque** bolts to 45 ft. lbs.
   c. **Torque** bolts 1–6 and 8–10 to 110 ft. lbs.
   d. **Torque** bolt 7 to 100 ft. lbs.
10. Install exhaust manifold as outlined in "Exhaust Manifold, Replace."
11. Install intake manifold as outlined in "Intake Manifold, Replace."
12. Install latch clip, then connect fuel supply hose.
13. **On models equipped with power steering,** install pump bracket.
14. **On models equipped with A/C,** install A/C compressor bracket bolts.
15. **On all models,** install capscrews, bridges, pivots and rocker arms.
16. Install crankcase ventilation vacuum hoses onto cylinder head cover.
17. Connect fresh air inlet hose into cover.
18. Install cylinder head cover, then retaining bolts.
19. Install air cleaner.
20. Connect coolant hoses to thermostat housing.
21. Install ignition wires and spark plugs.
22. Connect coolant temperature sending unit connector.

VALVE ARRANGEMENT

Front To Rear

2.5L Engine........................E-I-I-E-E-I-I-E

VALVE LIFTERS

Valve lifters can be removed after removing rocker arm assemblies and pushrods, using tool No. J-21884, or equivalent, **Fig. 5.** Failure of hydraulic lifters used in these engines is generally caused by dirt or insufficient lubrication due to low oil levels, oil contamination or foaming.

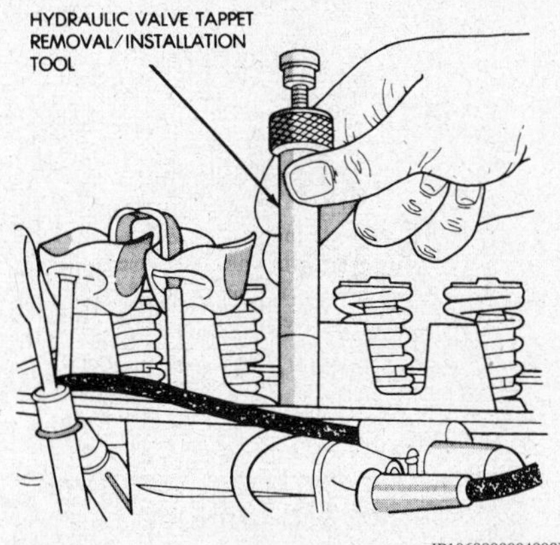

Fig. 5 Hydraulic lifter removal

CAMSHAFT LOBE LIFT SPECIFICATIONS

Exhaust.................................... .259 inch
Intake .... .255 inch

VALVE ADJUSTMENT

These engines use hydraulic lifters. No provision for adjustment is provided.

ROCKER ARMS

1. Remove rocker arm cover retaining screws, then rocker arm cover. Silicone sealant is used between rocker arm cover and cylinder head mating surfaces. To avoid damaging rocker arm cover, do not pry cover upward until seal has been completely broken.
2. Inspect for rocker arm bridges that are causing misalignment of rocker arm to valve tip area.
3. Remove rocker arm cap screws by alternately loosening one turn at a time to prevent damage to bridge, **Fig. 6.**
4. Remove rocker arm bridge, pivots and rocker arms. Tag all components so they can be reinstalled in same position as removed.
5. Reverse procedure to install. When installing rocker arm cap screws, tighten each screw alternately and evenly approximately one turn at a time to prevent damage to bridge.

VALVE GUIDES

The valve guides are an integral part of the cylinder head. If valve system to guide clearance is excessive, the guide should be reamed to the next oversize and the approximate oversize valve installed. Valves are available in standard size and oversizes of .003 inch and .015 inch.

FRONT COVER

REPLACE

Refer to "Timing Chain, Replace" for front cover replacement procedure.

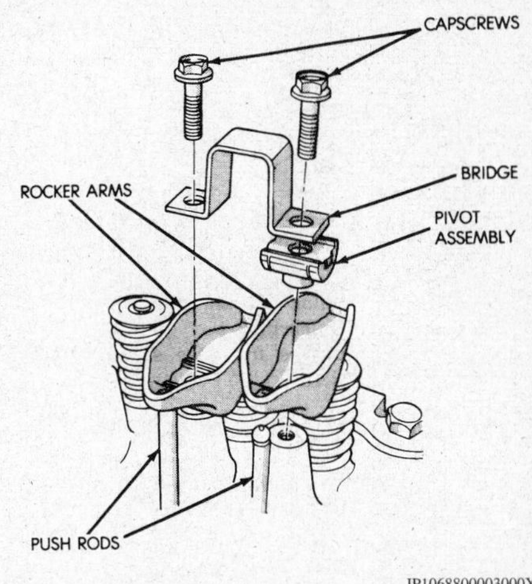

Fig. 6 Rocker arm, bridge & pivot assembly

TIMING CHAIN

REPLACE

Removal

1. Remove accessory drive belts/ serpentine drive belt.
2. Remove engine cooling fan, hub and shroud.
3. Remove crankshaft damper hub bolt, then damper, using suitable puller.
4. Remove alternator bracket assembly and position alternator aside.
5. Remove oil pan to timing cover and timing cover to block retaining bolts, then timing cover and crankshaft oil slinger.
6. Rotate crankshaft until zero degree mark on crankshaft sprocket is aligned with timing mark on camshaft sprocket (A), **Fig. 7.**
7. Remove camshaft sprocket retaining bolt, then timing chain and sprockets as an assembly.
8. Cut off oil pan side gaskets flush with engine block and remove ends of gaskets.
9. Pry oil seal from timing cover using suitable lever.
10. Clean all old gasket material from block, timing cover and front of oil pan.

Installation

1. Rotate lever on timing chain tensioner to unlocked position, **Fig. 8.**
2. Pull tensioner block toward tensioner to compress spring, then rotate lever up to locked position.
3. Apply suitable silicone adhesive sealant to keyway in crankshaft and insert key.
4. Position cam and crankshaft sprockets in timing chain with timing marks aligned, then mount assembly on engine.
5. Install camshaft sprocket retaining bolt and tighten to specification.
6. Turn chain tensioner to unlocked (down) position.
7. Install oil slinger.

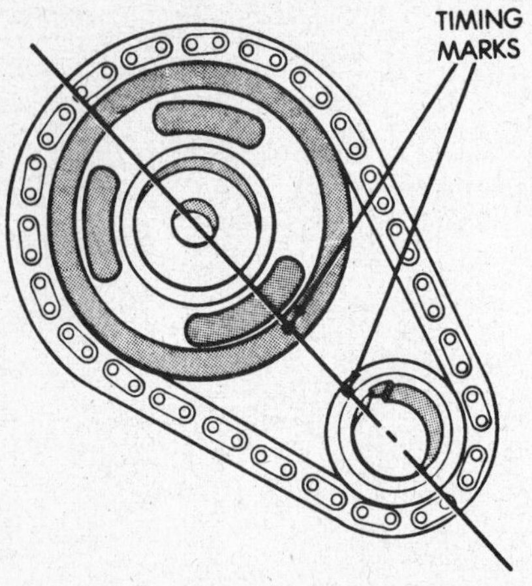

Fig. 7 Valve timing mark alignment

8. Replace oil seal in timing case cover.
9. Install timing case cover and gasket.
10. With key inserted in keyway in crankshaft, install vibration damper, washer and bolt.
11. Lubricate and tighten bolt to specification.
12. Install fan and shroud.

CAMSHAFT

REPLACE

1. Drain cooling system into a suitable container.
2. Remove radiator as outlined in "Radiator, Replace."
3. **On models equipped with A/C,** remove condenser.
4. **On all models,** mark position of distributor housing and rotor, then remove distributor and ignition wires.
5. Remove cylinder head cover and rocker arms as outlined in "Rocker Arms, Replace."
6. Remove pushrods.
7. Remove valve lifters as outlined in "Valve Lifters."
8. Remove timing case cover, timing chain and gears as outlined in "Timing Chain, Replace."
9. Remove camshaft.
10. Reverse procedure to install, noting the following:
    a. Tighten timing case cover to block bolts to specifications.
    b. Tighten oil pan to timing case cover bolts to specifications.
    c. Tighten camshaft sprocket bolts to specifications.

PISTON & ROD ASSEMBLY

Pistons are marked with an arrow on the top perimeter, **Fig. 9.** When installing piston in engine, the arrow must face toward front of engine. Always assemble rods and caps with oil spurt holes facing camshaft. Inspect side clearance between connecting rod and crankshaft journal. Clearance should be .010–.019 inch.

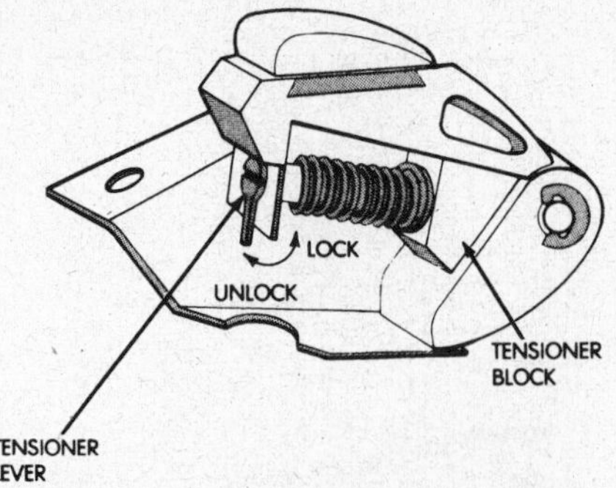

Fig. 8 Timing chain tensioner unlocked position

1. Remove cylinder head as outlined in "Cylinder Head, Replace."
2. Position piston one at a time near bottom of stroke. Using a suitable ridge reamer, to remove ridge from top end of cylinder walls. Use a protective shop towel to collect shavings.
3. Raise and support vehicle, then drain engine oil.
4. Remove oil pan as outlined in "Oil Pan, Replace."
5. Remove connecting rod bearing caps and inserts. Mark rods and caps with cylinder bore location. Connecting rods and caps are stamped with a two letter combination, **Fig. 10.**
6. Lower vehicle to approximately 2 ft. from floor.
7. With assistance, push piston/ connecting rod up and through top of cylinder bore. **Ensure connecting rod bolts do not scratch crankshaft journals or cylinder bores. Short pieces of rubber hose, slipped over rod bolts will provide protection during removal.**
8. Reverse procedure to install.

MAIN & ROD BEARINGS

The main bearing journal size (diameter) is identified by a color coded paint mark on adjacent cheek toward flanged (rear) end of crankshaft, except for rear main journal which is on crankshaft rear flange. Color codes used to indicate journal and corresponding bearing sizes, **Figs. 11 and 12.**

The connecting rod journal is identified by a color coded paint mark on adjacent cheek or counterweight toward flanged (rear) end of crankshaft. Color codes used to indicate journal sizes and corresponding bearing sizes, **Fig. 13.**

OIL PAN

REPLACE

Removal

1. Raise and support vehicle.
2. Remove oil pan drain plug and drain engine oil.
3. Remove starter motor.
4. Remove flywheel torque converter housing access cover.

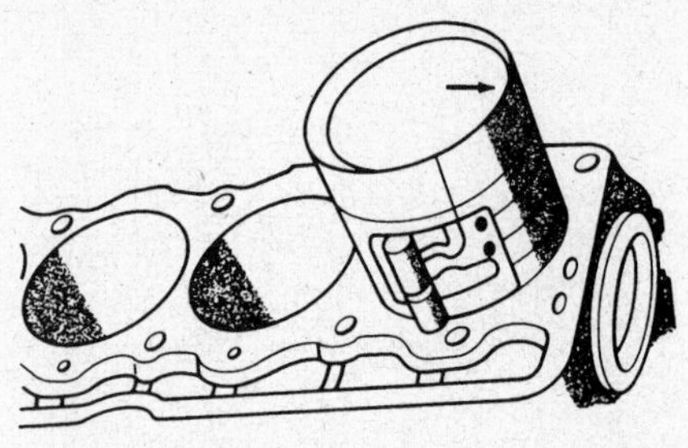

Fig. 9 Piston & rod assembly

5. Position a suitable jack stand directly under engine vibration damper.
6. Place a piece of wood between jack stand and engine vibration damper.
7. Remove engine mount through bolts.
8. Raise engine until adequate clearance is obtained to remove oil pan.
9. Remove oil pan retaining bolts, then oil pan.

Installation

1. Clean block and oil pan gasket surfaces.
2. Fabricate four alignment dowels from ¼ x 1½ inch bolts.
3. Cut head off bolts, then cut a slot into top of dowel to allow removal and installation with a screwdriver.
4. Install two dowels in timing case cover and two in cylinder block.
5. Slide one-piece gasket over dowels and onto block and timing case cover.
6. Position oil pan over dowels and onto gasket.
7. Install retaining bolts and tighten to specification.
8. Remove dowels.
9. Install remaining retaining bolts and tighten to specification.

OIL PUMP

REPLACE

1. Drain crankcase, then remove oil pan as outlined in "Oil Pan, Replace."
2. Remove oil pump to cylinder block retaining bolts, then oil pump and gasket. Do not disturb positioning of oil pump strainer and tube. If tube is moved, a replacement tube and screen assembly must be installed.
3. Reverse procedure to install. Tighten to specifications.

BELT TENSION DATA

Belt	New, Lbs.	Used, Lbs.
Serpentine	180–200	140–160

SERPENTINE DRIVE BELT

Routing

Refer to **Figs. 14 through 16** for correct routing.

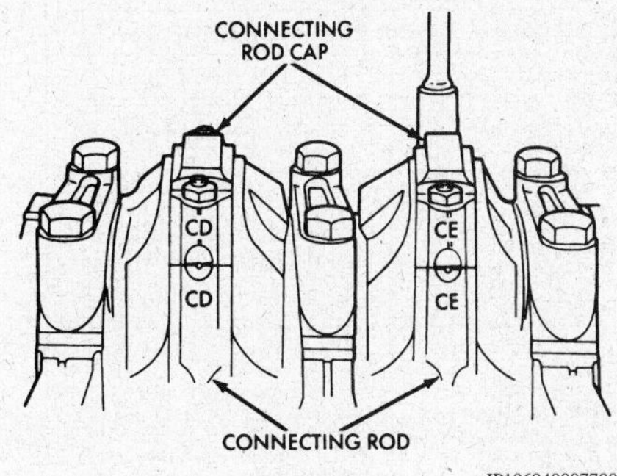

Fig. 10 Stamped connecting rods & caps

If belt routing differs from routing outlined in these diagrams, refer to the belt routing label located in the engine compartment.

Replacement

Belt tension is adjusted at the power steering pump or idler pulley if not equipped with power steering.

1. Loosen power steering or idler pulley rear mounting bolts.
2. Loosen power steering pump pivot bolt and locknut.
3. Loosen adjusting bolt to remove belt.
4. Tighten to adjust belt tension. Refer to "Belt Tension Data."

COOLING SYSTEM BLEED

This engine does not require a specified bleed procedure. After filling cooling system, run engine to operating temperature with radiator/pressure cap off. Air will then be automatically bled through cap opening.

THERMOSTAT

REPLACE

Constant tension hose clamps are used on most cooling system hoses. When removing or installing this style clamp, use only tools designed for constant tension clamps. A number or letter is stamped into the clamp. If replacing a clamp, use only an original equipment clamp with matching number or letter.

1. Drain coolant from radiator until level is below thermostat housing.
2. Disconnect coolant temperature sensor wiring, if applicable.
3. Remove thermostat housing and gasket, then thermostat.
4. Install new thermostat, ensuring pellet which is encircled by a coil spring faces engine.
5. Ensure thermostat is in recess groove with arrow and air bleed hole on outer flange.
6. Install new gasket, then thermostat housing.
7. Tighten to specifications. Fill coolant to proper level.

CRANKSHAFT JOURNALS #1 - 4		CORRESPONDING CRANKSHAFT BEARING INSERT	
Color Code	Diameter	Upper Insert Size	Lower Insert Size
Yellow	63.5025 - 63.4898 mm (2.5001 - 2.4996 in.)	Yellow - Standard	Yellow - Standard
Orange	63.4898 - 63.4771mm (2.4996 - 2.4991 in.) 0.0127 mm (0.0005 in.) Undersize	Yellow - Standard	Blue- Undersize 0.025 mm (0.001 in.)
Blue	63.4771 - 63.4644 mm (2.4991 - 2.4986 in.) 0.0254 mm (0.001 in.) Undersize	Blue- Undersize 0.025 mm (0.001 in.)	Blue- Undersize 0.025 mm (0.001 in.)
Green	63.4644 - 63.4517 mm (2.4986 - 2.4981 in.) 0.0381 mm (0.0015 in.) Undersize	Blue - Undersize 0.025 mm (0.001 in.)	Green - Undersize 0.051 mm (0.002 in.)
Red	63.2485 - 63.2358 mm (2.4901 - 2.4896 in.) 0.254 mm (0.010 in.) Undersize	Red - Undersize 0.254 mm (0.010 in.)	Red - Undersize 0.254 mm (0.010 in.)

JP1068800009000X

Fig. 11 Main bearing selection chart. Main bearing Nos. 1, 2, 3, 4

WATER PUMP

REPLACE

All engines have a reverse rotating (counterclockwise) water pump. The letter "R" is stamped into the back of the water pump impeller to identify this style of pump. Engines from previous model years, depending upon application, may be equipped with a forward rotating water pump. Installation of the wrong water pump will cause engine overheating.

1. Drain coolant into suitable container.
2. Loosen four hub to water pump pulley mounting bolts. Do not remove bolts at this time.
3. Remove accessory drive belt, then power steering pump.
4. Remove lower radiator hose and heater hose from water pump.
5. Remove four hub to water pump pulley bolts, then fan blade assembly and pulley.
6. Do not store viscous fan drive in horizontal position.
7. Remove four pump mounting bolts, then pump.
8. Reverse procedure to install.

RADIATOR

REPLACE

Do not service radiator while system is hot. Allow system to cool before attempting removal procedure.

1. Remove radiator cap, then drain radiator into suitable container.
2. Disconnect coolant reserve tank hose from radiator.
3. Remove upper and lower radiator hoses.
4. Remove four shroud mounting bolts, then move shroud back over fan blades.
5. **On models equipped with power steering,** if reservoir tank is attached to side of fan shroud, tie reservoir back to prevent spillage.
6. **On models equipped with automatic transmission,** disconnect and plug automatic transmission cooler lines.
7. **On all models,** remove radiator mounting bolts, then position front axle vent hose to one side.
8. Lift radiator straight up and out of vehicle.
9. Reverse procedure to install. Tighten to specifications.

FUEL PUMP

REPLACE

1. Drain fuel tank, then remove tank as follows:
   a. Remove fuel filler cap.
   b. Relieve fuel system pressure as outlined in "Fuel System Pressure Relief."
   c. Remove fuel filler bezel to body retaining bolts, then filler bezel.
   d. Cut plastic tie wrap securing rear axle vent hose to filler hoses.
   e. Disconnect electrical connector at front of fuel tank.
   f. Disconnect evaporator hose from evaporator line at front of tank.
   g. Position a suitable jack under fuel tank assembly, then secure tank to jack.
   h. Remove skid plate to body retaining nuts at front of tank.
   i. Remove skid plate to body retaining nuts at rear of tank. **Do not loosen tank strap nuts.**
   j. Lower tank assembly from vehicle.
2. Thoroughly clean area around pump module to prevent contaminants from entering tank.
3. Remove fuel pump module locknut using spanner wrench tool No. 6856, or equivalent. Fuel pump module will spring up when locknut is removed.
4. Remove module from fuel tank.
5. Reverse procedures to install.

FUEL FILTER

REPLACE

Removal

These models use a combination fuel filter/fuel pressure regulator which has no replacement service interval. Fuel filters should be replaced only in the event of failure.

1. Remove fuel tank as outlined in "Fuel Pump, Replace."
2. Clean area of fuel pump module to prevent fuel system contamination during replacement procedures.
3. Release fuel filter/pressure regulator retainer clamp, **Fig. 17.** Note position of fuel line outlet for installation reference.
4. Pry fuel filter/pressure regulator from fuel pump module using two suitable screwdrivers. Discard gasket below fuel filter/pressure regulator.
5. Inspect removed unit for old O-ring seals, **Fig. 18.** It may be required to remove old lower O-ring from fuel pump module. **Discard O-rings.**

Installation

1. Lightly lubricate new O-rings with clean motor oil, then install O-rings onto fuel filter/pressure regulator unit.
2. Install new gasket to fuel pump module.
3. Install fuel filter/pressure regulator unit into module and press down firmly until unit snaps into place.
4. With arrow on fuel pump module considered as 12 o'clock, rotate fuel filter/ pressure regulator until fuel outlet is positioned at 10 o'clock.
5. Install retainer clamp.
6. Install fuel tank as outlined in "Fuel Pump, Replace."

CRANKSHAFT JOURNAL #5 ONLY		CORRESPONDING CRANKSHAFT BEARING INSERT	
Color Code	Diameter	Upper Insert Size	Lower Insert Size
Yellow	63.4873 - 63.4746 mm (2.4995 - 2.4990 in.)	Yellow - Standard	Yellow - Standard
Orange	63.4746 - 63.4619 mm (2.4990 - 2.4985 in.) 0.0127 mm (0.0005 in. Undersize	Yellow - Standard	Blue - Undersize 0.025 mm (0.001 in.)
Blue	63.4619 - 63.4492 mm (2.4985 - 2.4980 in.) 0.0254 mm (0.001 in.) Undersize	Blue- Undersize 0.025 mm (0.001 in.)	Blue- Undersize 0.025 mm (0.001 in.)
Green	63.4492 - 63.4365 mm (2.4980- 2.4975 in.) 0.0381 mm (0.0015 in.) Undersize	Blue - Undersize 0.025 mm (0.001 in.)	Green - Undersize 0.051 mm (0.002 in.)
Red	63.2333 - 63.2206 mm (2.4895 - 2.4890 in.) 0.254 mm (0.010 in.) Undersize	Red - Undersize 0.254 mm (0.010 in.)	Red - Undersize 0.254 mm (0.010 in.)

JP1068800010000X

Fig. 12 Main bearing selection chart. Main bearing No. 5

CRANKSHAFT JOURNAL		CORRESPONDING CONNECTING ROD BEARING INSERT	
Color Code	Diameter	Upper Insert Size	Lower Insert Size
Yellow	53.2257-53.2079 mm (2.0955-2.0948 in.)	Yellow - Standard	Yellow - Standard
Orange	53.2079 - 53.1901 mm (2.0948 - 2.0941 in.) 0.0178 mm (0.0014 in.) Undersize	Yellow - Standard	Blue - Undersize 0.025 mm (0.001 in.)
Blue	53.1901 - 53.1724 mm (2.0941 - 2.0934 in.) 0.0356 mm (0.0014 in.) Undersize	Blue - Undersize 0.025 mm (0.001 in.)	Blue - Undersize 0.025 mm (0.001 in.)
Red	52.9717 - 52.9539 mm (2.0855 - 2.0848 in.) 0.254 mm (0.010 in.) Undersize	Red - Undersize 0.254 mm (0.010 in.)	Red - Undersize 0.254 mm (0.010 in.)

JP1068800011000X

Fig. 13 Connecting rod bearing chart

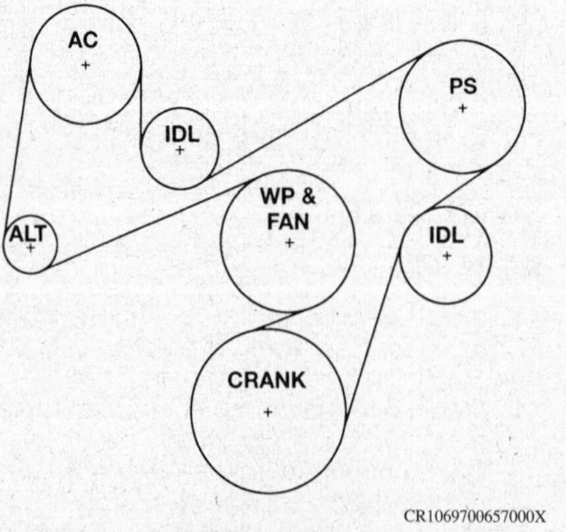

Fig. 14 Serpentine drive belt routing. With A/C

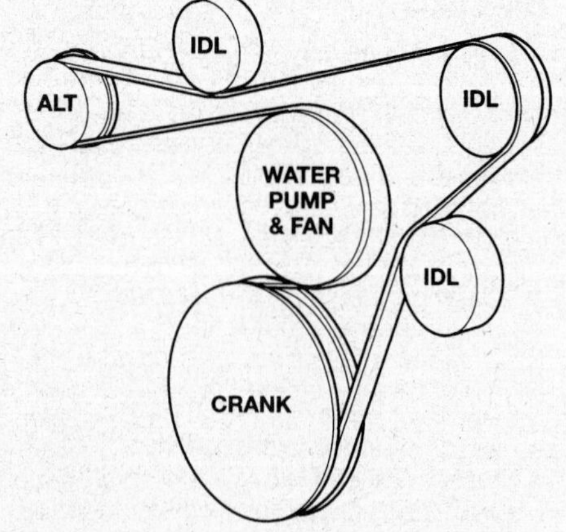

Fig. 15 Serpentine drive belt routing. Less A/C & P/S

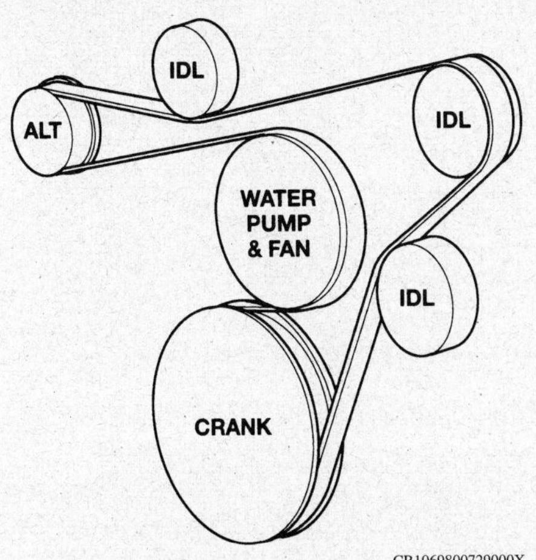

Fig. 16 Serpentine drive belt routing. Less A/C

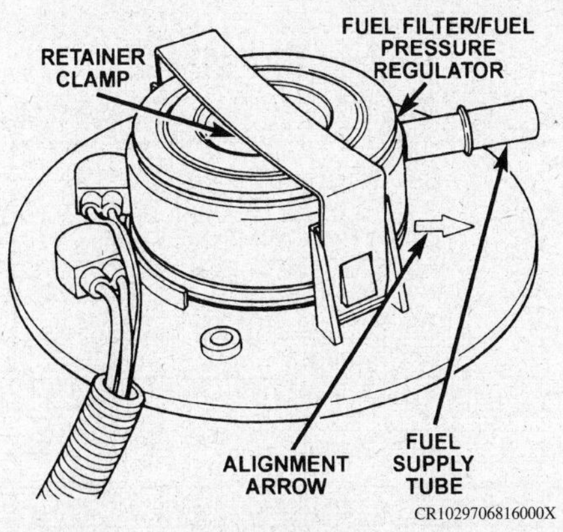

Fig. 17 Fuel filter/fuel pressure regulator

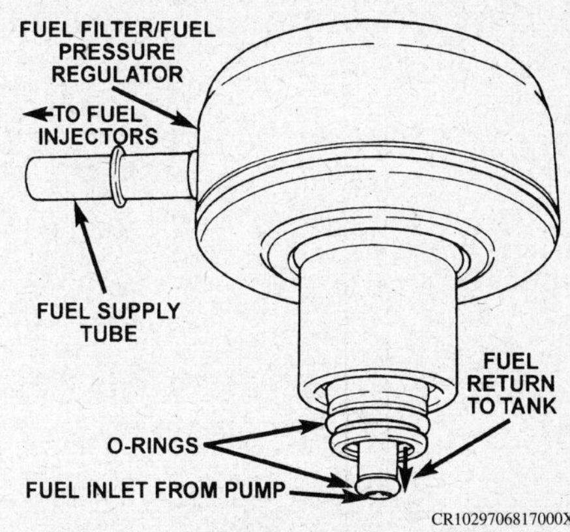

Fig. 18 Fuel filter/fuel pressure regulator O-ring location

TIGHTENING SPECIFICATIONS

Year	Component	Torque Ft. Lbs.
2002	Accelerator Pedal Bracket Mounting Bolts	72–84①
	A/C Compressor Bracket To Engine Bolts	35
	A/C Compressor Mounting Bolts	20
	A/C Condenser Mounting Bolt	55①
	Alternator Adjusting Bolt	20
	Alternator Mounting Bolt To Head	33
	Alternator Mounting Bracket To Engine	28
	Alternator Pivot Bolt Or Nut	28
	Block Heater Nut	16①
	Camshaft Sprocket Bolt	80
	Carburetor Hold-Down Nuts	14
	Clutch Cover To Flywheel Bolts	23
	Clutch Housing To Block Screws	55
	Coil Bracket To Chassis	85①
	Connecting Rod Bolt Nuts	33
	Crankshaft Damper Bolt	80
	Cylinder Head Bolts	③
	Cylinder Head Capscrews	85
	Cylinder Head Cover Nuts	55①
	Dimmer/Ignition Switch Mounting Screws	35①
	Dipstick Tube Bracket Bolt To Cylinder Block	14
	Distributor Cap Hold-Down Screws	26①
	Distributor Clamp Bracket Screw	22
	Distributor Hold-Down Bolt	17
	Driver Air Bag Module Screws	84–96①
	EGR Valve	13
	EGR Valve Tube Nuts	30
	Engine Mount Bolts	45
	Engine Mount Stud Nuts	34
	Exhaust Manifold Bolts	23

Continued

TIGHTENING SPECIFICATIONS—Continued

Year	Component	Torque Ft. Lbs.
2002	Exhaust Pipe To Manifold Bolts	23
	Fan & Hub Assembly Bolts	18
	Flywheel To Crankshaft Bolts	105
	Front Crossmember To Sill	65
	Front Support Bracket To Cylinder Block	45
	Front Support Cushion To Engine Mount (Through Bolt)	48
	Front Support Cushion To Sill Bracket	30
	Fuel Hose Clamps	25①
	Fuel Pump Module Locknut	45
	Fuel Rail Mounting Bolts Or Nuts	96①
	Fuel Supply Tube To Throttle Body	13
	Fuel Tank Skid Plate Bolts	11–12
	Intake Manifold Coolant Fittings	20
	Intake Manifold Screws	23
	Lock Cylinder Retaining Screws	40①
	Main Bearing Capscrews	80
	Neutral Safety Switch	25
	Oil Filter Adapter	48
	Oil Level Sensor In Oil Pan	25
	Oil Pan Drain Plug	25
	Oil Pan Screws (1/4-20)	84①
	Oil Pan Screws (5/16-18)	11
	Oil Pump Attaching Screws (Long)	17
	Oil Pump Attaching Screws (Short)	10
	Oil Pump Cover Screws	70①
	Oxygen Sensor	35
	Power Steering Pump Adapter Screw	23
	Power Steering Pump Bracket Screw	28
	Power Steering Pump Mounting Screw	28
	Power Steering Pump Pressure Hose Nut	38
	Power Steering Pump Pulley Nut	58
	Radiator Mounting Bolts	55①
	Rear Crossmember to Side Sill Nut	30
	Rear Support Bracket To Transmission Bolts	33
	Rocker Arm Assembly To Cylinder Head Bolts	21
	Spark Plugs	27
	Starter Motor To Cylinder Block Bolts	33
	Steering Wheel Retaining Nut	25
	Tensioner Bracket To Cylinder Block Bolt	14
	Thermostat Housing Bolt	13
	Throttle Body To Intake Manifold Attaching Nuts	16
	Timing Case Cover To Block Screws	60①
	Timing Case Cover To Block Studs	16
	Torque Converter Driveplate To Crankshaft Bolts	40②
	Vibration Damper Bolt (Lubricated)	80
	Water Pump Bolt	23
	Wiper Motor Mounting Bolt	96①

①— Inch lbs.
②— Tighten an additional 60.°
③— Refer to "Cylinder Head, Replace."

4.0L Engine

NOTE: Refer To "2.5L & 4.0L Engines" Section Of "Commander & Grand Cherokee" Chapter In This Manual For Service Procedures & Tightening Specifications Not Found In This Section.

NOTE: On Air Bag Equipped Models, Refer To "Air Bag System Precautions" Located In The Front Of This Manual For System Disarming & Arming Procedures.

NOTE: Refer To "Computer Relearn Procedures" Located In The Front Of This Manual When Battery Power To The Computer Has Been Interrupted.

INDEX

PRECAUTIONS

Air Bag Systems

Refer to "Air Bag System Precautions" in the front of this manual for system disarming and arming procedures.

Battery Ground Cable

Prior to service, disconnect battery ground cable and isolate as required.

Fuel System Pressure Relief

1. Remove fuel pump relay from power distribution center.
2. Start and run engine until it stalls.
3. Attempt restarting engine until it will no longer run.
4. Turn ignition key to off position.

COMPRESSION PRESSURE

Pressure is 120–150 psi. Maximum allowable variation between cylinders is 30 psi.

ENGINE MOUNT

REPLACE

Front Mount

1. Raise and support vehicle using a suitable lift of jack.
2. Support engine with suitable jack, then remove through bolt retaining nut, **Figs. 1 and 2.** Do not remove through bolt at this time.

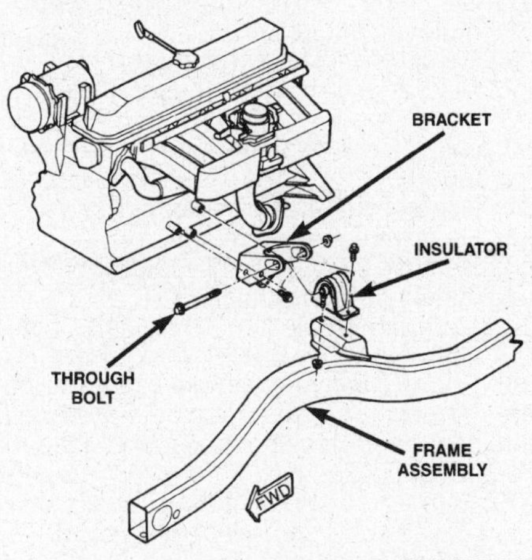

Fig. 1 Lefthand front engine mount

3. Remove retaining bolts and nuts from engine support cushions.
4. Remove through bolt and engine support cushions.
5. Reverse procedure to install, noting the following:
   a. **Torque** engine support bracket bolts to 37 ft. lbs.
   b. **Torque** retaining bolts and nuts to 38 ft. lbs.
   c. **Torque** through bolt and retaining nut to 35 ft. lbs.

Rear Mount

1. Raise and support vehicle and transmission.
2. Remove attaching nuts securing transmission support cushion and insulator stud nut, **Figs. 3 and 4.**
3. **On models equipped with manual transmission,** proceed as follows:
   a. Remove nuts holding transmission support bracket.
   b. Remove support cushion, then bolts holding transmission support bracket to transmission.
   c. Remove transmission support bracket.
4. **On models equipped with automatic transmission,** proceed as follows:
   a. Remove nuts holding support cushion to transmission support bracket.
   b. Remove support cushion.
   c. Remove bolts holding transmission bracket to transmission, then transmission support bracket.
5. **On all models,** remove transmission support cushions and support bracket to transmission, **Figs. 3 and 4.**
6. Separate transmission support cushion from transmission support bracket.
7. Reverse procedure to install, noting the following:
   a. **Torque** transmission mount bracket bolts to 40 ft. lbs.
   b. **Torque** support cushion nuts to 30 ft. lbs.
   c. **Torque** bracket to skid plate nuts (automatic transmission) to 21 ft. lbs.
   d. **Torque** skid plate bolts to sill to 55 ft. lbs.

ENGINE

REPLACE

1. Remove engine compartment lamp.
2. Mark hinge locations on hood panel for alignment reference and remove hood.
3. Drain engine coolant into a suitable container.
4. Remove upper and lower radiator hose and coolant recovery hose.

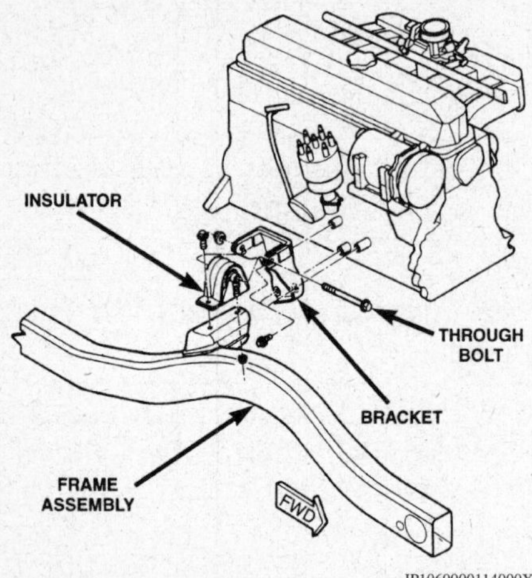

Fig. 2 Righthand front engine mount

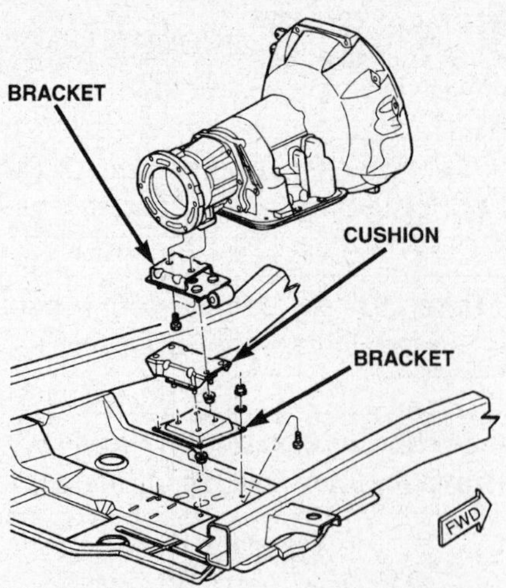

Fig. 3 Rear engine mount replacement. Automatic transmission

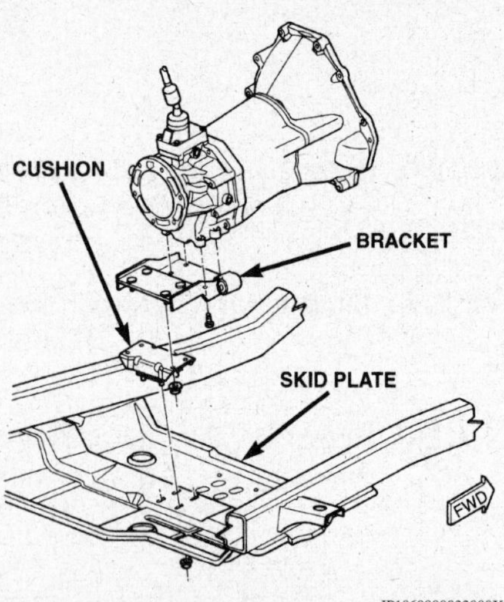

Fig. 4 Rear engine mount replacement. Manual transmission

5. Remove upper radiator support retaining bolts and remove radiator support.
6. Remove fan assembly from water pump.
7. Remove fan shroud.
8. Disconnect transmission fluid cooler lines.
9. **On models equipped with A/C,** discharge A/C system as outlined under "Air Conditioning" chapter.
10. **On models equipped with A/C,** remove service valves and cap compressor ports.
11. **On all models,** remove radiator.
12. **On models equipped with A/C,** remove condenser.
13. **On all models,** disconnect heater hoses at engine thermostat housing and water pump.
14. Disconnect accelerator cable, transmission line pressure cable and speed control cable from throttle body.
15. Remove cables from bracket and secure out of way.
16. Disconnect body ground at engine.
17. Disconnect the following:
    a. Power steering pressure switch.
    b. Coolant temperature sensor.
    c. Six (6) fuel injector connectors.
    d. Intake air temperature sensor.
    e. Throttle position sensor.
    f. Map sensor.
    g. Crankshaft position sensor.
    h. Oxygen sensor.
    i. Camshaft position sensor.
    j. Alternator connector and B+ terminal wire.
18. Disconnect coil rail electrical connections and oil pressure switch connector.
19. Perform fuel pressure release procedure.
20. Disconnect fuel supply line at injector rail.
21. Remove fuel line bracket from intake manifold.
22. Remove air cleaner assembly.
23. Disconnect hoses from fittings at steering gear.
24. Drain pump reservoir.
25. Cap fittings on hoses and steering gear to prevent foreign objects from entering system.
26. Raise and suitably support vehicle.
27. Disconnect wires from engine starter motor solenoid.
28. Remove engine starter motor.
29. Disconnect oxygen sensor from exhaust pipe.
30. Disconnect exhaust pipe from manifold.
31. Remove exhaust pipe support.
32. Remove bending brace.
33. Remove engine flywheel/converter housing access cover.
34. Mark converter and drive plate location.
35. Remove converter-to-drive plate bolts.
36. Remove upper engine flywheel/converter housing bolts and loosen bottom bolts.
37. Remove engine mount cushion-to-engine compartment bracket bolts.
38. Lower vehicle.
39. Attach a suitable lifting device to engine.
40. Raise engine off front supports.
41. Place a suitable support or floor jack under converter housing.
42. Remove remaining converter housing bolts.
43. Lift engine out of engine compartment using suitable lift.
44. Reverse procedure to install.

SERPENTINE DRIVE BELT

Routing

Refer to **Figs. 5 and 6** for serpentine drive belt routing and service.

Replacement

1. Rotate belt tensioner until it contacts its stop. Remove belt, then slowly rotate tensioner into freearm position.
2. Reverse procedure to install.

RADIATOR

REPLACE

Do not remove the cylinder block drain plugs or loosen the radiator draincock with the system hot and pressurized. serious burns from the coolant can occur.

1. Remove radiator cap.
2. Remove condenser lower seal from lower core support.
3. Drain cooling system into a suitable container.
4. Remove radiator upper and lower hose clamps. Remove radiator hoses.
5. Disconnect coolant reserve/overflow tank hose from radiator.
6. Remove reservoir tank and power steering reservoir and position out of way.
7. Remove four fan shroud mounting bolts and position fan shroud back over fan blades.
8. **On models equipped with a automatic transmission,** disconnect and plug transmission fluid cooler lines.
9. **On all models,** remove six radiator mounting bolts and position front axle vent hose to side.
10. Lift radiator straight up and out of vehicle taking care not to damage radiator fins.
11. Note position of rubber seals located on top and bottom of radiator. These seals must be installed to their original positions.
12. Reverse procedure to install. Tighten bolts to specification.

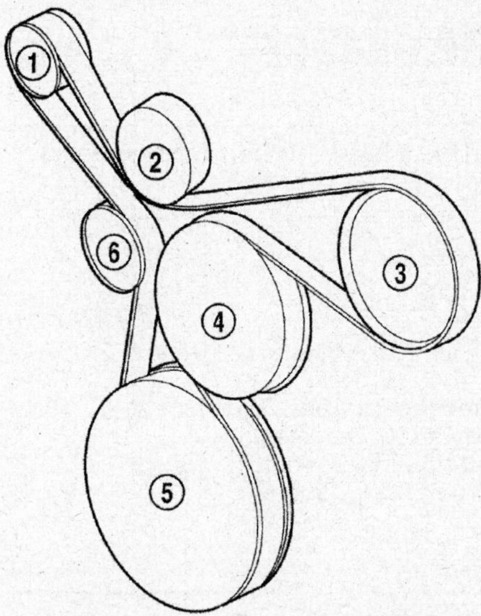

Fig. 5 Drive belt routing. 4.0L engine less air conditioning

FUEL PUMP

REPLACE

Refer to "Fuel Pump, Replace" in "2.4L Engine" section for fuel pump replacement procedure.

FUEL FILTER

REPLACE

Refer to "Fuel Filter, Replace" in "2.5L Engine" section for fuel filer replacement procedure.

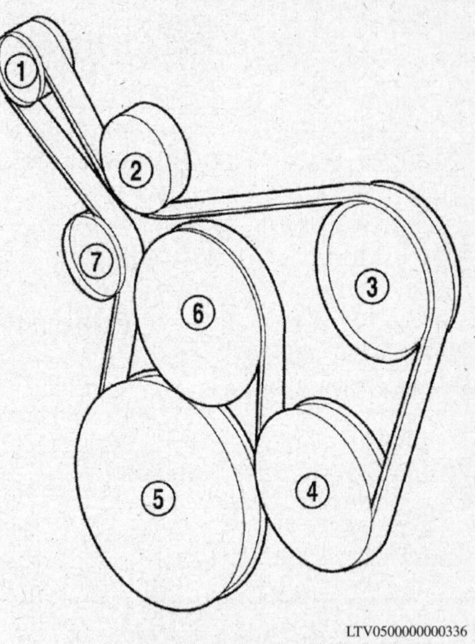

Fig. 6 Drive belt routing. 4.0L engine w/air conditioning

TIGHTENING SPECIFICATIONS

Year	Component	Torque Ft. Lbs.
2002–06	Camshaft Sprocket	50
	Connecting Rod Cap	33
	Crankshaft Damper	80
	Crankshaft Main Bearing Cap	80
	Electric Fan To Fan Shroud Bolts	53①
	Flex Plate To Crankshaft	105
	Flex Plate To Converter Housing	28
	Front Cover	②
	Oil Pan	③
	Oil Pan Drain Plug	25
	Oil Pump Cover	70①
	Oil Pump To Block	17
	Radiator Crossmember Bolts	70①
	Radiator Upper Isolator To Crossmember Bolts	80
	Righthand Engine Mount Bracket	④
	Valve Cover	85①
	Water Pump Bolts	17

① — Inch lbs.
② — Torque 1/4 bolts to 60 inch lbs. and 5/16 bolts to 192 inch lbs.
③ — Torque ¼ bolts to 84 inch lbs., and 5⁄16 bolts to 132 inch lbs.
④ — Refer to "Engine Mount, Replace" procedure to tightening specifications.

Rear Axle & Suspension

NOTE: Refer To "Computer Relearn Procedures" Located In The Front Of This Manual When Battery Power To The Computer Has Been Interrupted.

INDEX

PRECAUTIONS

Battery Ground Cable

Prior to service, disconnect battery ground cable and isolate as required.

REAR AXLE

REPLACE

1. Raise and support vehicle.
2. Support axle with a suitable lifting device. **Secure axle to lifting device to prevent axle movement.**
3. Remove wheel and tire assemblies.
4. Disconnect brake fluid flex line between chassis and axle, then plug lines and fittings.
5. Disconnect electrical connectors for speed sensors.
6. Remove brake system components as required.
7. Disconnect axle vent hose.
8. **On models equipped with a locker differential,** disconnect pressure hose from differential housing and locker indicator connector.
9. **On all models,** scribe match marks on propeller shaft for installation reference, then remove shaft.
10. Disconnect stabilizer bar links from axle.
11. Disconnect shock absorbers from axle.
12. Disconnect track bar, then upper and lower control arms from axle.
13. Lower axle from vehicle. **Secure springs while lowering.**
14. Reverse procedure to install, noting the following:
    a. Do not tighten track arm or control arm bolts completely until vehicle is resting with weight on wheels and suspension is at normal ride height.
    b. Ensure springs are properly aligned in their seats.
    c. Bleed brake system as outlined in "Hydraulic Brake Systems" chapter.

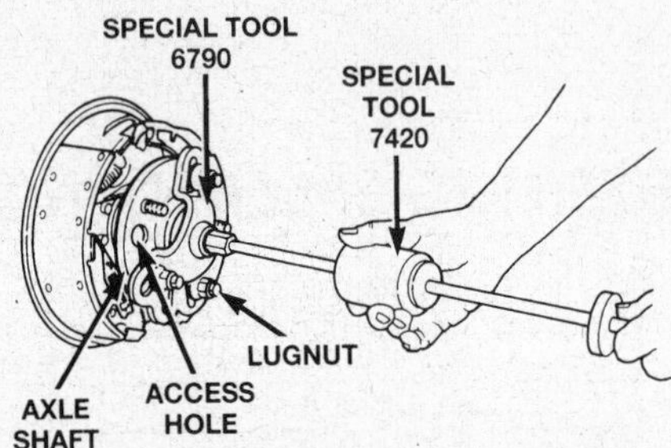

Fig. 1 Rear axle shaft pulling. 216 RBI axle

REAR AXLE SHAFT

REPLACE

194 RBI Axle

1. Place transmission in neutral.
2. Raise and support vehicle, then remove tires and wheels.
3. Remove brake drum.
4. Remove differential housing cover, then drain fluid.
5. Rotate differential case to access pinion mate gear shaft lock screw.
6. Remove lock screw and shaft from differential case.
7. Push axle shaft inward, then remove axle C-clip lock.
8. Remove axle shaft.
9. Reverse procedure to install.

216 RBI Axle

1. Raise and support vehicle.
2. Remove rear wheel and tire assemblies.
3. **On models equipped with drum brakes,** remove brake drums as outlined in "Drum Brakes" chapter.
4. **On models equipped with disc brakes,** remove brake caliper and rotor as outlined in "Disc Brakes" chapter.
5. Remove axle retainer plate nuts through access hole in axle flange.
6. Pull axle shaft with bearing and seal from housing using slide hammer tool, or equivalent, **Fig. 1.**
7. Reverse procedure to install, noting the following:
    a. Ensure flat edge of axle retainer plate is facing up.
    b. Tighten nuts and bolts to specifications.
    c. Fill axle fluid as required.

REAR WHEEL BEARING & SEAL

REPLACE

194 RBI Axle

1. Remove axle shaft as outlined in "Rear Axle Shaft, Replace" in this section.
2. Pry axle seal from housing using a suitable pry bar.
3. Pull bearing from axle housing using axle bearing puller tool set No. 6310, or equivalent, **Fig. 2.**
4. Inspect bearing seat in housing for damage, scratches or burrs, repair or replace as required.
5. Ensure part number of new bearing is facing outward, then using installer plate tool No. 6436 with handle tool No. C-4171, or equivalents, drive new bearing into housing.
6. Drive new seal into housing using installer C-6437 with handle tool No. C-4171, or equivalents.
7. Install axle shaft as outlined in "Rear Axle Shaft, Replace" in this section.

216 RBI Axle

1. Remove axle shaft as outlined in "Rear Axle Shaft, Replace" in this section.
2. Drill a 3/8 inch hole partially through soft metal retaining ring, **Fig. 3. Do not drill through ring into axle.**
3. Cut through soft metal retaining ring at drilled hole, then remove ring from axle.
4. Remove wheel bearing from axle using a suitable separator plate and

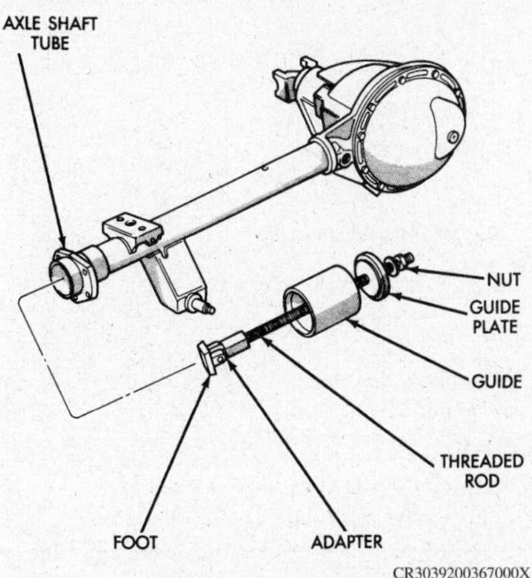

Fig. 2 Rear axle shaft bearing removal. 194 RBI axle

press, **Fig. 4,** then remove retainer plate and seal.
5. Thoroughly clean and inspect axle components.
6. Place retainer plate, seal and bearing onto axle, then using suitable support plates and press, push bearing into position.
7. Place soft metal retaining ring onto axle and press into position.
8. Install axle shaft as outlined in "Rear Axle Shaft, Replace" in this section.

PINION FLANGE SEAL

REPLACE

Removal

1. With vehicle in neutral, raise vehicle and suitably support.
2. **On models equipped with drum brakes,** remove brake drums as outlined under "Drum Brakes" chapter.
3. **On models equipped with disc brakes,** remove disc brakes as outlined under "Disc Brakes" chapter.
4. **On all models,** remove propeller shaft from yoke.
5. Rotate pinion gear three or four times.
6. Record torque required to rotate pinion gear with a suitable inch pound dial-type torque wrench.
7. Hold yoke with a suitable wrench and remove pinion nut and washer.
8. Remove pinion yoke with pinion yoke remover tool No. C-452 or equivalent and a suitable wrench.
9. Remove pinion seal with a suitable pry tool or slide hammer mounted screw.

Installation

1. Apply a light coating of gear lubricant on lip of pinion seal and install seal with a suitable installer.
2. Install pinion yoke screw tool No. 8112, Cup tool No. 8109 and spanner wrench tool No. 6958 or equivalent.
3. Install yoke washer and new nut on pinion gear and tighten nut until there is zero bearing end-play.
4. **Torque** pinion nut to 200 ft. lbs. **Never loosen pinion gear nut to decrease pinion gear bearing rotating torque and never exceed specified preload torque. This may result in damage.**
5. Rotate pinion shaft using a suitable inch pound torque wrench. Rotating torque should be equal to reading recorded during removal plus an additional 5 inch lbs.
6. If rotating torque is low, use a suitable wrench to hold pinion yoke, and **torque** pinion nut in 60 inch lbs. increments until proper rotating torque is achieved. **If maximum tightening torque 350 ft. lbs. is reached prior to reaching required rotating torque, the collapsible spacer may have been damaged. This may result in damage.**
7. Install propeller shaft.
8. **On models equipped with drum brakes,** install brake drums as outlined under "Drum Brakes" chapter.
9. **On models equipped with disc brakes,** install disc brakes as outlined under "Disc Brakes" chapter.

SHOCK ABSORBER

REPLACE

1. Raise and support vehicle.
2. Position a suitable jack under axle assembly, then raise axle slightly.
3. Remove bolt and nut from lower mounting and bolts from upper mounting.
4. Remove shock absorber from shock mounting.
5. Reverse procedure to install. Tighten to specifications.

COIL SPRING

REPLACE

1. Raise and suitably support vehicle, and position a suitable hydraulic jack under axle to support it.
2. Disconnect stabilizer bar links as outlined under "Stabilizer Bar, Replace."
3. Disconnect shock absorbers from axle brackets "Shock Absorber, Replace."
4. Disconnect track bar from frame rail bracket "Track Rod, Replace."
5. Lower axle until spring is free from upper mount seat and remove spring.
6. Reverse procedure to install. Tighten fasteners to specifications.

CONTROL ARM

REPLACE

Lower

1. Raise vehicle and suitably support.
2. Remove lower suspension arm nut and bolt at axle bracket.

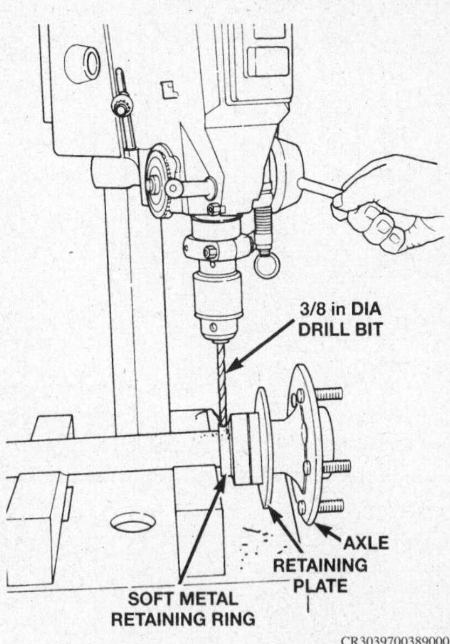

Fig. 3 Rear axle bearing retaining ring removal. 216 RBI axle

3. Remove nut and bolt at frame rail mount and remove lower suspension arm.
4. Reverse procedure to install. Tighten fasteners to specifications.

Upper

1. Raise vehicle and suitably support.
2. Remove parking brake cable/bracket and ABS wiring bracket from arm.
3. Remove upper suspension arm nut and bolt from axle bracket.
4. Remove nut and bolt from frame rail bracket and remove upper suspension arm.
5. Reverse procedure to install. Tighten fasteners to specifications.

STABILIZER BAR

REPLACE

1. Raise and support vehicle.
2. Disconnect stabilizer bar links from frame mounts and stabilizer bar.
3. Remove axle mount bolts and mount bracket, then remove bar from vehicle.
4. Reverse procedure to install, noting the following:
   a. Ensure stabilizer bar is centered on axle with equal spacing between bar ends and axle mounts.
   b. Tighten to specification.

TRACK ROD

REPLACE

1. Raise and support vehicle.
2. Remove nut and bolt attaching track bar to frame rail bracket.
3. Remove bolt and nut attaching track bar to axle bracket.
4. Remove track bar from vehicle.
5. Reverse procedure to install.

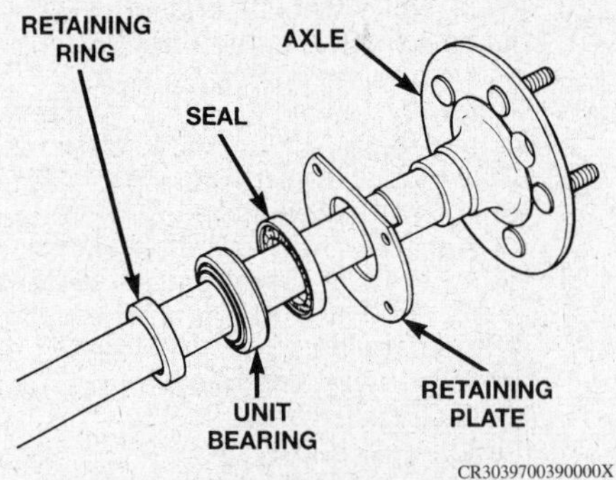

Fig. 4 Wheel bearing removal. 216 RBI axle

TIGHTENING SPECIFICATIONS

Year	Component	Torque Ft. Lbs.
2002–06	Anti-Lock Sensor Bolt	②
	Backing Plate Bolt	32–45
	Bearing Cap Bolt	57
	Brake Line To Axle Hose	11–13
	Brake Line To Wheel Cylinder	11–13
	Control Arm Lower	130
	Control Arm Upper	55
	Differential Cover Bolt	30
	Fill Plug	25
	Front Propeller Shaft Front Yoke Bolts	30
	Front Propeller Shaft Rear Yoke Bolts	20
	Pinion Nut	③
	Rear Propeller Shaft Rear Yoke Bolts	14
	Shock Absorber Lower Nut	74
	Shock Absorber Upper Bolt	23
	Stabilizer Bar	40
	Stabilizer Link	40
	Track Bar Axle Bracket Nut	74
	Track Bar Frame Bracket Nut	74
	Wheel Cylinder Bolts	84①
	Wheel Lug Nuts	85–115
	Wheel Speed Sensor Bolt	②

① — Inch lbs.
② — 2002–03 models, torque to 9–10 ft. lbs.; 2004–06 models, torque to 18 ft. lbs.
③ — On models equipped w/194 RBI, torque to 200–350 ft. lbs.; on models equipped w/216 RBI, torque to 160–200 ft. lbs.

Front Suspension & Steering

NOTE: On Air Bag Equipped Models, Refer To "Air Bag System Precautions" Located In The Front Of This Manual For System Disarming & Arming Procedures.

NOTE: Refer To "Computer Relearn Procedures" Located In The Front Of This Manual When Battery Power To The Computer Has Been Interrupted.

INDEX

PRECAUTIONS

Air Bag Systems

Refer to "Air Bag System Precautions" in the front of this manual for system disarming and arming procedures.

WHEEL BEARING

REPLACE

1. Raise vehicle and support vehicle using a suitable lift or jack.
2. Remove wheel and tire assembly.
3. Remove brake caliper, rotor and ABS wheel speed sensor as outlined under "Disc Brakes" chapter.
4. Remove cotter pin, nut retainer and axle hub nut.
5. Remove hub bearing mounting bolts from back of steering knuckle.
6. Remove hub bearing from steering knuckle and off axle shaft.
7. Reverse procedure to install. Tighten fasteners to specifications.

BALL STUD

REPLACE

1. Remove hub bearing and axle shaft as outlined under "Axle Shaft, Replace" and "Hub & Bearing, Service."
2. Removing upper and lower ball studs require using a ball stud remover/installer tool No. 6289 or equivalent, **Fig. 1.**
3. Reverse procedure to install.

COIL SPRING

REPLACE

1. Raise vehicle and support vehicle using a suitable lift or jack.
2. Remove wheel and tire assemblies.
3. Position a suitable hydraulic jack under axle to support it.

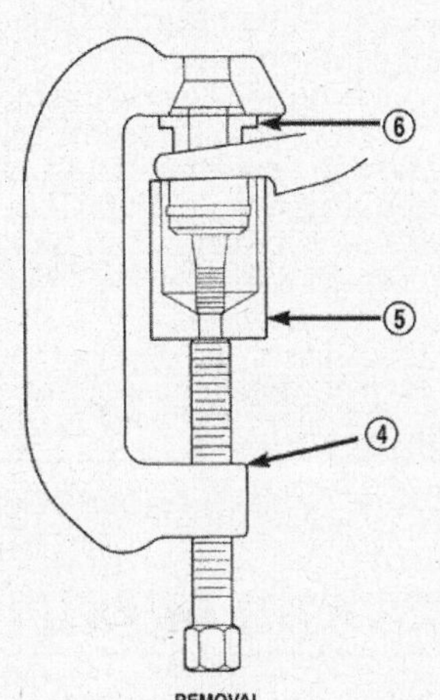

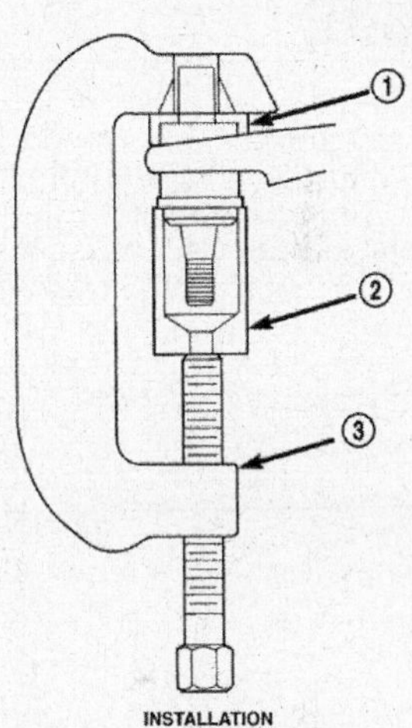

Fig. 1 Ball stud removal & installation

4. Remove front shocks at lower mountings as outlined under "Shock Absorber, Replace."
5. **On models equipped with ABS,** remove ABS wire mounting brackets at axle.
6. **On all models,** remove lower suspension arms mounting nuts and bolts from frame.
7. Remove track bar from axle bracket.
8. Remove righthand side of drag link from righthand side knuckle.
9. Lower axle until spring is free from upper mount.
10. Remove upper spring isolator and jounce bumper out of mount if needed.
11. Reverse procedure to install. Tighten lower suspension arm nuts to specification with vehicle at normal ride height.

SHOCK ABSORBER

REPLACE

1. Remove nut, retainer and grommet from upper stud through engine compartment access hole.
2. Remove lower nuts and bolts from axle bracket and remove shock absorber.
3. Reverse procedure to install. Tighten to specification.

CONTROL ARM

REPLACE

Lower

1. Raise vehicle and suitably support.
2. **On models equipped with ABS,** remove sensor wire from inboard side of arm.
3. **On all models,** paint or scribe alignment marks on cam adjusters and suspension arm for installation reference.
4. Remove lower suspension arm nut and bolt from axle.
5. Remove nut and bolt/cam bolt from frame rail bracket and remove lower suspension arm.
6. Reverse procedure to install. Tighten to specification.

Upper

1. Raise vehicle and suitably support.
2. Remove upper suspension arm nut and bolt at axle bracket.
3. Remove nut and bolt at frame rail and remove upper suspension arm.
4. Reverse procedure to install. Tighten to specification.

STEERING KNUCKLE

REPLACE

1. Remove hub bearing and axle shaft. as outlined under "Axle Shaft, Replace" and "Hub & Bearing, Service."
2. Disconnect tie-rod or drag link from steering knuckle arm.
3. Remove cotter pins from upper and lower ball studs and ball stud nuts.
4. Separate ball joints from steering knuckle using a ball joint separator tool No. C-4150A or equivalent.
5. Reverse procedure to install. Tighten to specifications.

TRACK BAR

REPLACE

1. Raise vehicle and suitably support.
2. Remove cotter pin and nut from ball stud end at frame rail bracket.
3. Use a suitable puller tool to separate track bar ball stud from frame rail bracket.
4. Remove bolt and flag nut from axle bracket and remove track bar.
5. Reverse procedure to install. Tighten to specification.

STABILIZER BAR

REPLACE

1. Remove upper link nuts and separate links from stabilizer bar using a remover tool No. MB-991113 or equivalent.
2. Remove front bumper valence.
3. Remove stabilizer retainer bolts and remove retainers.
4. Remove stabilizer bar.
5. Remove lower link nuts and bolts and remove links.
6. Reverse procedure to install. Tighten to specification.

POWER STEERING GEAR

REPLACE

2002

The steering column on vehicles with an automatic transmission may not be equipped with an internal locking shaft that allows the ignition key cylinder to be locked with the key. Alternative methods of locking the steering wheel for service will have to be used.

1. Place front wheels in straight ahead position with steering wheel centered and locked.
2. Disconnect and cap fluid hoses/tubes from power steering pump.
3. Remove column coupler shaft from gear.
4. Remove pitman arm from gear.
5. Remove steering gear retaining bolts and remove gear.
6. Remove power steering hoses/tubes from steering gear.
7. Reverse procedure to install. Tighten to specification

2003–06

The steering column on vehicles with an automatic transmission may not be equipped with an internal locking shaft that allows the ignition key cylinder to be locked with the key. Alternative methods of locking the steering wheel for service will have to be used.

1. Place front wheels in straight ahead position with steering wheel centered and locked.
2. Siphon out as much power steering fluid as possible.
3. Remove bumper shield.
4. Remove power steering hoses/tubes from steering gear.
5. Remove column coupler shaft from gear.
6. Remove pitman arm from gear.
7. Remove steering gear retaining bolts and remove gear.
8. Reverse procedure to install. Tighten to specification.

TIGHTENING SPECIFICATIONS

Year	Component	Torque Ft. Lbs.
2002–06	Control Arm Lower (Axle Bracket)	130
	Control Arm Lower (Frame Bracket)	130
	Control Arm Upper	60
	Drag Link To Pitman Arm	60
	Driveshaft U-Joint Strap Bolt	14
	Pitman Arm To Pitman Shaft	185
	Power Steering Gear To Frame	70
	Shock Absorber Lower Nut	21
	Shock Upper Nut	17
	Stabilizer Bar Frame Bracket Bolt	45
	Stabilizer Bar To Upper Link Nut	45
	Stabilizer Bar Link To Axle Bracket Bolt	75
	Track Bar Ball Stud Nut	60
	Track Bar Axle Bracket Bolt	40
	Wheel Lug Nut	85–115

Front Wheel Drive

INDEX

AXLE

REPLACE

1. Raise vehicle and suitably support.
2. Position a suitable lift under axle and secure to axle.
3. Remove wheels and tires.
4. **On models equipped with ABS,** remove wheel speed sensors.
5. **On all models,** remove brake calipers, rotors and as outlined under "Disc Brakes" chapter.
6. Disconnect vent hose from axle shaft tube.
7. Mark propeller shaft and yoke for installation alignment reference.
8. Remove propeller shaft.
9. Remove stabilizer bar links at axle.
10. Remove shock absorbers from axle brackets.
11. Remove track bar.
12. Remove tie rod and drag link from steering knuckle.
13. Remove steering damper from axle bracket.
14. Remove upper and lower suspension arms from axle brackets.
15. Lower lifting device enough to remove axle. Coil springs will drop with axle.
16. Remove coil springs from axle.
17. Reverse procedure to install, noting the following:
    a. To prevent bushing bind or damage, do not tighten suspension component bolts completely until vehicle is resting with weight on wheels and suspension is at normal ride height.
    b. Ensure springs are properly aligned in their seats.
    c. Tighten nuts and bolts to specification.
    d. Inspect and align vehicle as required as outlined in "Wheel Alignment."

AXLE SHAFT

REPLACE

1. Raise and support front of vehicle.
2. Remove wheel and tire assembly.
3. Remove brake caliper and rotor. Support caliper aside without disconnecting lines.
4. Remove ABS wheel sensor, if applicable.
5. Disconnect tie rod end from knuckle using a suitable tie rod end removal tool.
6. Remove axle cotter pin, nut lock and axle hub nut.
7. Remove steering knuckle to hub and bearing assembly attaching bolts, then hub and bearing assembly and rotor splash shield from knuckle.
8. Remove axle shaft from vehicle.
9. Reverse procedure to install, noting the following:
    a. Ensure axle shaft is properly engaged with intermediate shaft and shift collar is properly positioned.
    b. When installing shift motor, ensure shift fork engages shift collar.
    c. Tighten nuts and bolts to specifications.

PINION FLANGE SEAL

REPLACE

Refer to "Rear Axle & Suspension" section for pinion flange seal replacement procedures.

AXLE BEARING SEAL

REPLACE

1. Raise and support vehicle.
2. Remove axle shafts as outlined under "Axle Shaft, Replace."
3. Remove differential assembly.
4. Remove inner axle shaft seals with a suitable pry bar.
5. Reverse procedure to install, noting the following:
    a. Remove any sealer remaining from original seals.
    b. Remove sealer from axle tube to housing junction, if required.
    c. Install new axle shaft seals with disc tool No. 8110 and turnbuckle tool No. 6797, or equivalents.

HUB & BEARING SERVICE

The hub and bearing on this vehicle are serviced as an assembly.

Remove hub and bearing as outlined in "Axle Shaft, Replace" in this section.

TIGHTENING SPECIFICATIONS

Year	Component	Torque Ft. Lbs.
2002–06	Axle Hub Nut	175
	Ball Stud To Knuckle Nuts (Upper)	80
	Ball Stud To Knuckle Nuts (Lower)	75
	Differential Bearing Cap Bolt	①
	Differential Housing Cover Bolt	30
	Driveshaft U-Joint Strap Bolt	14
	Fill Plug	25
	Hub & Bearing To Knuckle Bolts	75
	Hub Nut	175
	Pinion Bearing Nut (2002 181FBI)	260
	Pinion Bearing Nut (2003–06 181 RBI)	160–500
	Pinion Bearing Nut (2003–06 216 RBI)	160–200
	Ring Gear Bolts (181FBI)	80
	Ring Gear Bolts (216FBI)	100

Continued

TIGHTENING SPECIFICATIONS—Continued

Year	Component	Torque Ft. Lbs.
2002–06	Shock Absorber Lower Nut	20
	Shock Upper Nut	23
	Track Bar Ball Stud To Frame Bracket	60
	Track Bar To Axle Bracket Nut	40
	Wheel Bearing And Hub Assembly To Knuckle Bolt	75
	Wheel Lug Nut	85–115

① — On models equipped w/181FBI axle, torque to 45 ft. lbs.; on models equipped w/216RBI axle, torque to 80 ft. lbs.

Wheel Alignment

INDEX

PRELIMINARY INSPECTION

Inspect the following components. Adjust, repair or replace as required prior to performing front wheel alignment.

1. Inflate tires to cold specifications.
2. Ensure front tires are of same size, ply rating and load rating.
3. Inspect for excessive wheel bearing endplay.
4. Inspect for worn or damaged spindle ball joints.
5. Inspect steering gear mounting bolts for proper torque.
6. Inspect radius arm or bent or damaged condition.
7. Inspect radius arm to frame bushings for looseness or wear.
8. Inspect suspension components for wear or damage.

FRONT WHEEL ALIGNMENT

Refer to "Specifications" for alignment measurements.

Camber

Camber is set at time of manufacture and cannot be adjusted.

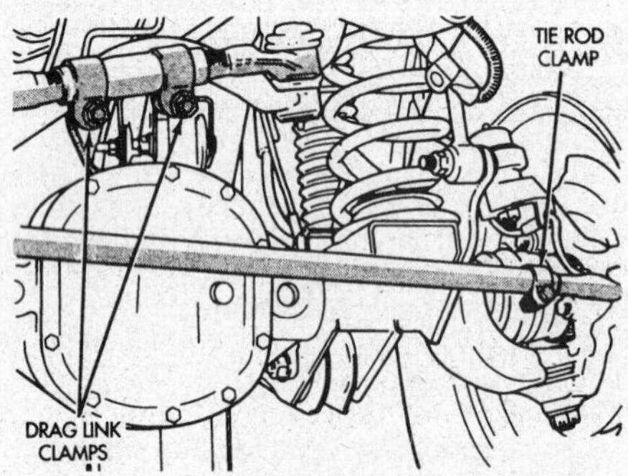

Fig. 1 Toe-in adjustment clamp bolts location

Caster

Caster may be adjusted by turning adjustment cams on the axle end of the lower control arms.

Toe-In

If vehicle is equipped with power steering, this adjustment must be performed with the engine running

1. Start engine and turn steering wheel both ways before straightening steering wheel.
2. Center and secure steering wheel.
3. Loosen adjustment sleeve clamp bolts.
4. Adjust righthand wheel toe position with drag link.
5. Turn sleeve until righthand wheel is at correct positive toe-in position. Refer to "Front Wheel Alignment Specifications" in "Specifications" section.
6. Position clamp bolts as outlined, **Fig. 1.**
7. Adjust lefthand wheel toe position with tie rod.
8. Turn sleeve until lefthand wheel is at same toe-in position as righthand wheel.
9. Position clamp bolts as outlined, **Fig. 1.**
10. Verify righthand toe specifications and turn off engine.
11. **Torque** righthand drag link and tie rod end clamp bolt to 36 ft lbs.
12. **Torque** lefthand drag link and tie rod end clamp bolt to 20 ft lbs.

COMMANDER & GRAND CHEROKEE

NOTE: Refer To Rear Of This Manual For Vehicle Manufacturer's Special Service Tool Suppliers.

INDEX OF SERVICE OPERATIONS

Specifications

GENERAL ENGINE SPECIFICATIONS

Year	Engine Liters (VIN)	Fuel System	Bore & Stroke, Inch	Compression Ratio	Net H.P. @ RPM	Maximum Torque Ft. Lbs. @ RPM	Normal Oil Pressure, psi①
2002–04	4.0L (S)	MPI	3.88 x 3.41	8.8	190 @ 4600	225 @ 3000	13
	4.7L (N)	MPI	3.66 x 3.40	9.0	235 @ 4800	295 @ 3200	7
	4.7L H.O. (J)	MPI	3.66 x 3.40	9.7	270 @ 5100	330 & 3600	4
2005–06	3.7L (K)	MPI	3.66 x 3.40	9.6	211 @ 5200	236 @ 4000	4
	4.7L (N)	MPI	3.66 x 3.40	9.0	235 @ 4800	295 @ 3200	7
	5.7L (2)	EFI	3.91 x 3.58	9.6	330 @ 5000	375 @ 4000	4

VIN — Eight digit of Vehicle Identification Number.

① — At curb idle.

TUNE UP SPECIFICATIONS

The following specifications are published from the latest information available. This data should only be used in the absence of a decal affixed in the engine compartment.

Year & Engine	Spark Plug Gap, Inch	Firing Order, Fig.	Ignition Timing	Mark Location	Ignition Coil Resistance, Ohms⑥ Primary	Ignition Coil Resistance, Ohms⑥ Secondary	Curb Idle Speed	Fast Idle Speed	Fuel Pump Pressure, psi	Valve Lash, Inch
2002–03										
4.0L	.035	B②	④	Damper	.71–.88	—	④	④	44.2–54.2	①
4.7L	.040	C③	④	Damper	.60–.90	6000–9000	④	④	44.2–54.2	①
2004										
4.0L	.040	B②	④	Damper	.71–.88	—	④	④	44.2–54.2	①
4.7L	.040	C③	④	Damper	.60–.90	6000–9000	④	④	44.2–54.2	①

Continued

TUNE UP SPECIFICATIONS—Continued

The following specifications are published from the latest information available. This data should only be used in the absence of a decal affixed in the engine compartment.

Year & Engine	Spark Plug Gap, Inch	Firing Order, Fig.	Ignition Timing	Mark Location	Ignition Coil Resistance, Ohms⑥		Curb Idle Speed	Fast Idle Speed	Fuel Pump Pressure, psi	Valve Lash, Inch
					Primary	Secondary				
2005–06										
3.7L	.042	A⑤	④	Damper	.60–.90	6000–9000	④	④	56–60	①
4.7L	.040	C③	④	Damper	.60–.90	6000–9000	④	④	56–60	①
5.7L (D)	.045	D③	④	Damper	.60–.90	6000–9000	④	④	56–60	①

BTDC — Before Top Dead Center
① — Equipped w/hydraulic valve lash adjusters.
② — Firing order: 1-5-3-6-2-4.
③ — Firing order: 1-8-4-3-6-5-7-2.
④ — Controlled by Powertrain Control Module (PCM).
⑤ — Firing order: 1-6-5-4-3-2.
⑥ — @ 70–80°F.

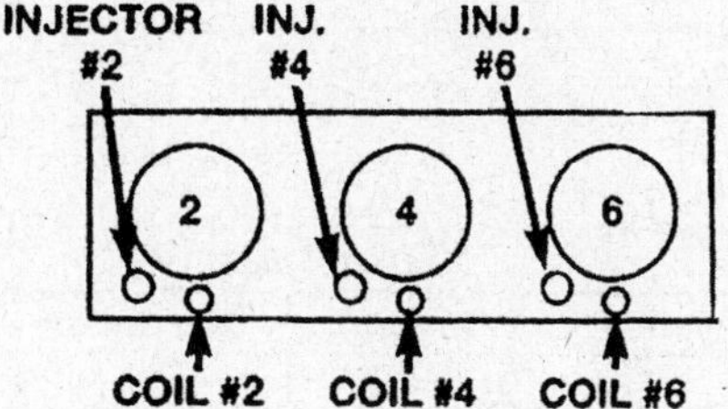

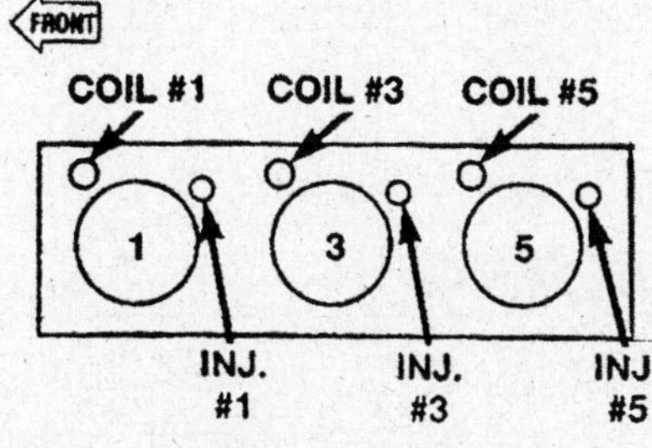

FIRING ORDER: 1 - 6 - 5 - 4 - 3 - 2

JP1130200046000X

Fig. A

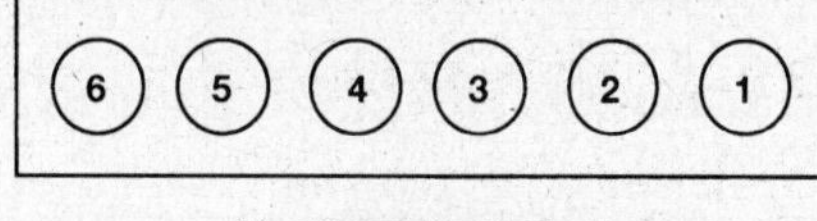

FIRING ORDER
1-5-3-6-2-4

COILS PAIRED:
CYLINDERS 1-6
CYLINDERS 2-5
CYLINDERS 3-4

JP1139900034000X

Fig. B

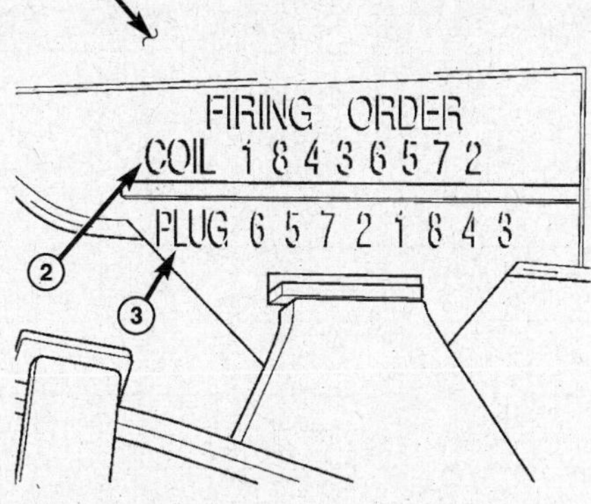

1 - TOP OF INTAKE MANIFOLD
2 - CYLINDER FIRING ORDER (IGNITION COIL NUMBER)
3 - CORRESPONDING SPARK PLUG NUMBER

LTV1900000000328

Fig. D

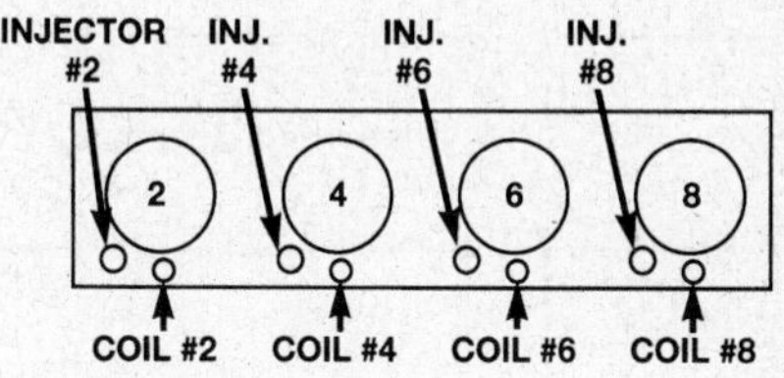

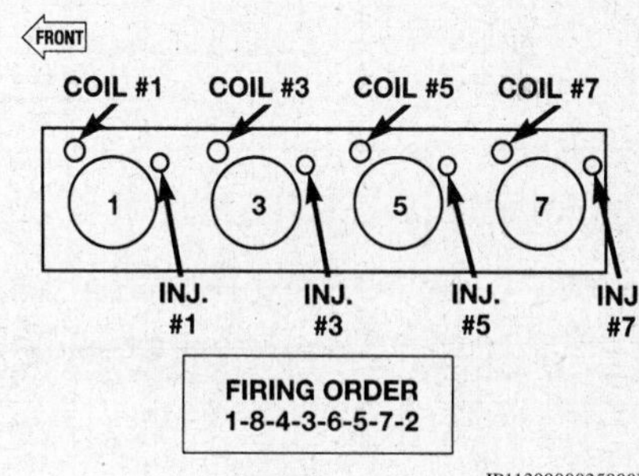

JP1139900035000X

Fig. C

COMMANDER & GRAND CHEROKEE

FRONT WHEEL ALIGNMENT SPECIFICATIONS

The specifications listed below are for unloaded vehicles

Model	Year	Suspension	Caster Angle, Degrees		Camber Angle, Degrees		Toe, Degrees①	
			Limits	Desired	Limits	Desired	Limits	Desired
Commander	2006	All	+3.55 to +4.45	+4.00	-.70 to +.15	-.25	0 to +.50	+.250
Grand Cherokee	2002–04	Standard	+6.00 to +7.50	+6.75	-.75 to +.50	-.37	+.14 to +.26	+.200
		Up-Country	+5.70 to +7.20	+6.50	-.75 to +.50	-.37	0 to +.36	+.200
	2005	All	+3.55 to +4.45	+4.00	-.70 to +.15	-.25	0 to +.50	+.250
	2006	All	+3.55 to +4.45	+4.00	-.70 to +.15	-.25	0 to +.25	+.125

① — Toe-in (+). Toe-out (-).

REAR WHEEL ALIGNMENT SPECIFICATIONS

The specifications listed below are for unloaded vehicles

Model	Year	Camber Angle, Degrees		Toe, Degrees①		Thrust Angle	
		Limits	Desired	Limits	Desired	Limits	Desired
Commander	2006	-.50 to +.50	-.25	0 to +.50	+.250	-.25 to +.25	0
Grand Cherokee	2002–04	-.75 to 0	-.37	0 to +.70	+.370	-.25 to +.25	0
	2005	-.50 to +.50	-.25	0 to +.50	+.250	-.25 to +.25	0
	2006	-.50 to +.50	-.25	0 to +.25	+.125	-.25 to +.25	0

① — Toe-in (+). Toe-out (-).

FLUID CAPACITIES & COOLING SYSTEM DATA

Year	Engine	Coolant Capacity, Qts.②	Recommended Engine Coolant Type	Radiator Cap Relief Pressure, Lbs.	Thermo. Opening Temp., °F	Fuel Tank, Gals.	Engine Oil Refill, Qts.①	Transmission Oil, Qts	Transfer Case, Pts.	Axle Oil, Pts.	
										Front	Rear
2002–04	4.0L	15.0	Ethylene Glycol	15	195	20	6	⑤	④	2.5⑥⑦	③⑥⑦
	4.7L	14.5	Ethylene Glycol	14.5	195	20	6	⑤	④	2.5⑥⑦	③⑥⑦
2005–06	3.7L	10.0	Ethylene Glycol	18–21	195	20	5	⑧	⑨	3.6⑪	⑩⑪
	4.7L	14.5	Ethylene Glycol	14.5	195	20	6	⑧	⑨	3.6⑪	⑩⑪
	5.7L	14.5	Ethylene Glycol	16	195	20	7	⑧	⑨	3.6⑪	⑩⑪

① — Approximate, make final inspect w/dipstick.

② — Includes 1 Qt. for coolant recovery bottle.

③ — 198 RBI (Model 35), 3.5 pts., 226 RBA (Model 44), 4.75 pts.

④ — With NV242, 2.85 pts.; w/NV247, 4.75 pts.

⑤ — 42RE service fill, 4.0 qts.; overhaul, 9.5–10 qts.

⑥ — With Trac-Lock or Vari-Lock, add 2.5 ounces Friction Modifier.

⑦ — Plus or minus 1 ounce.

⑧ — 545RFE service fill 2WD, 5.5 Qts.; 4WD, 6.5 Qts.; overhaul, 14 Qts.

⑨ — NV140, 1.4 Pts.; NV245, 3.8 Pts.

⑩ — C213R, 4.375 Pts.; C213RE, 4.718 Pts.

⑪ — Plus or minus 2 ounces.

LUBRICANT DATA

Model	Year	Lubricant Type					
		Transmission	Transfer Case	Axle		Power Steering	Brake System
				Front	Rear		
Commander	2006	Mopar ATF +4	②	③	③	①	DOT 3
Grand Cherokee	2002–04	Mopar ATF +4	⑥	③	④⑤	①	DOT 3
	2005–06	Mopar ATF +4	②	③	③	①	DOT 3

① — DaimlerChrysler specification MS-10838, or equivalent.

② — NV140: Mopar ATF+4; NV245: Mopar NV245/247 Transfer Case Fluid.

③ — Mopar Synthetic Gear Lubricant 75W-140.

④ — Mopar Gear Lubricant 80W-90. For Heavy Duty or Trailer Towing: Mopar Synthetic Gear Lubricant 75W-140.

⑤ — Trac-lok & Vari-lok® equipped axles require 4 ounces of Limited Slip Additive be added.

⑥ — NV147 & NV242: Mopar Transfer Case Lubricant (part No. 05016796); NV242: Mopar ATF+4.

Electrical

NOTE: **On Air Bag Equipped Models, Refer To "Air Bag System Precautions" Located In The Front Of This Manual For System Disarming & Arming Procedures.**

NOTE: **Refer To "Computer Relearn Procedures" Located In The Front Of This Manual When Battery Power To The Computer Has Been Interrupted.**

NOTE: **Prior To Performing Any Service Operations Listed In This Section, Consult The "Technical Service Bulletins" Section For Related Information.**

INDEX

PRECAUTIONS

Air Bag Systems

Refer to "Air Bag System Precautions" in the front of this manual for system disarming and arming procedures.

Battery Ground Cable

Prior to service, disconnect battery ground cable and isolate as required.

FUSE PANEL & FLASHER LOCATION

The fuse panel is located under the left-hand side of the instrument panel. The combination turn signal and hazard lamp flasher is located in the fuse panel.

On 2005–06 models, the junction block contains six relays that are integral to the housing assembly. The relays cannot be replaced separately. If any of the relays are diagnosed inoperative or damaged, the complete junction block unit must be replaced. The six relays are: Lock, unlock, driver door unlock, rear wiper, ignition RUN and ignition RUN/ACCESSORY DELAY.

FUEL PUMP RELAY LOCATION

The fuel pump relay is located Power Distribution Center (PDC).

RELAY CENTER LOCATION

On 2002–04 models, the Power Distribution Center (PDC) is located in righthand front corner of the engine compartment, between the battery and the righthand front inner fender shield.

On 2005–06 models, the Power Distribution Center (PDC) is located in the left-hand front corner of the engine compartment, between the Integrated Power Module (IPM) and the brake master cylinder.

STARTER

REPLACE

2002–04

1. Raise and support vehicle.
2. Remove lower mounting bolt.
3. Support starter motor with hand and remove upper mounting bolt.
4. Lower starter slightly and disconnect solenoid electrical connector.
5. Remove battery cable and solenoid terminal wire.
6. Remove starter motor.
7. Reverse procedure to install, noting the following:
   a. **Torque** solenoid battery terminal nut to 100 inch lbs.
   b. **Torque** starter upper mounting bolt to 40 ft. lbs.
   c. **On 4.0L engines, torque** starter lower mounting bolt to 30 ft. lbs.
   d. **On 4.7L engines, torque** starter lower mounting bolt to 40 ft. lbs.

2005–06

1. Raise and support vehicle.
2. **On models equipped with 3.7L and 4.7L engines and 4WD,** proceed as follows:
   a. Ensure transmission is in Neutral.
   b. Mark axle pinion flange, propeller shaft, flange yoke and transfer case for install alignment.
   c. Support transmission and cross-member.
   d. Remove mounting bolts, then the propeller shaft from the transfer case and axle pinion flanges.
3. **On models equipped with 4WD,** proceed as follows:
   a. Remove support bracket between front axle and transmission side two mounting bolts.
   b. Position bracket aside to access starter motor lower mounting bolt.
4. **On all models,** remover starter motor mounting bolts.
5. Support starter using hand and move it forward until starter pinion nose clears housing.
6. Tilt starter downward and lower starter, then remove battery cable wire connector.
7. Remove starter motor, noting the following:
   a. **Torque** battery connector nut to 19 ft. lbs.
   b. **Torque** starter motor mounting bolts to 50 ft. lbs.
   c. **Torque** propeller shaft to axle pinion flange mounting bolts to 80 ft. lbs.
   d. **Torque** propeller shaft to transfer case flange mounting bolts to 24 ft. lbs.

ALTERNATOR

REPLACE

1. Rotate belt tensioner until it contacts stop, then remove drive belt and slowly rotate tensioner into freearm position.
2. Disconnect cap, remove mounting nut and disconnect B+ terminal.
3. Disconnect field wire connector.
4. Remove mounting bolts and alternator.
5. Reverse procedure to install. **Torque** M8 mounting bolts to 21 ft. lbs., and M10 mounting bolts to 40 ft. lbs.

IGNITION COIL

REPLACE

4.0L Engine

The coil is a one piece rail assembly containing three individual coils. The bottom of the coil has six rubber boots that attach to the spark plugs. Springs inside the boots contact the spark plug to complete the electrical connection. The boots and springs are permanent components of the coil. The coil is only serviced as an assembly.

1. Remove four coil mounting bolts.
2. Gently pry coil from spark plugs alternating each end using suitable spark plug boot removal tool.
3. Disconnect electrical connector and remove coil rail.
4. Reverse procedure to install. **Torque** mounting bolts to 29 ft. lbs.

3.7L, 4.7L & 5.7L Engines

An individual ignition coil is used for each cylinder. The coil fits into a machined hole in the cylinder head. A mounting stud/nut secures each coil to the top of the intake manifold.

Depending on which coil is being removed, throttle body air intake tube or intake box may need to be removed.

Remove ignition coils as follows:

1. Disconnect electrical connector.
2. Clean area at base of ignition coil using suitable compressed air.
3. Remove mounting nut and coil using slight twisting motion.
4. Reverse procedure to install, noting the following:
   a. **On 3.7L and 4.7L engines, torque** mounting bolt to 70 inch lbs.
   b. **On 5.7L engines, torque** mounting bolt to 62 inch lbs.

IGNITION LOCK

REPLACE

2002–04

1. Place gear shifter in Park.
2. Place ignition in ON position.
3. Press release tab on key lock cylinder housing bottom up while pulling and removing key cylinder.
4. Reverse procedure to install.

2005–06

1. Remove switch bezel using suitable plastic trim removal stick.
2. Turn key lock cylinder to ON position while pressing release tab on side of assembly.
3. Pull and remove cylinder.
4. Reverse procedure to install.

IGNITION SWITCH

REPLACE

2002–04

1. Place gear shifter in Park.
2. Place ignition in ON position.
3. Press release tab on key lock cylinder housing bottom up while pulling and removing key cylinder.
4. Remove mounting screws and lower steering column cover.
5. Remove ignition switch Torx screws.

6. Push locking tab using suitable small screwdriver and remove ignition switch.
7. Disconnect electrical connectors.
8. Reverse procedure to install.

2005–06

1. Remove switch bezel using suitable plastic trim removal stick.
2. Remove two mounting screws and silencer pad.
3. Remove mounting bolts and lefthand hush panel.
4. Separate upper clips using trim stock tool No. C-4755, or equivalent, and rotate cover down.
5. Disconnect lower hinges at bottom and remove steering column opening cover.
6. Remove two key cylinder housing lower mounting screws.
7. Remove instrument panel cluster bezel using suitable plastic trim removal stick.
8. Remove one key cylinder housing mounting screw behind instrument panel cluster.
9. Lower key/cylinder/switch/cable/SKREEM assembly and disconnect ignition switch and SKREEM electrical connectors.
10. Disconnect cable with simultaneously pressing tab.
11. Remove mounting screw and SKREEM.
12. Remove mounting screw and ignition switch by simultaneously pressing two release tabs using two suitable small screwdrivers.
13. Remove key lock cylinder by rotating key to ON position while pressing on release tab.
14. Reverse procedure to install.

NEUTRAL SAFETY SWITCH

REPLACE

2002–04

The neutral start and back-up lamp switches are an integral assembly and cannot be replaced separately.

1. Raise and support vehicle.
2. Disconnect switch electrical connector.
3. Place suitable container under switch.
4. Remove switch and allow fluid to drain into container.
5. Move shift linkage to Park and Neutral positions, observing switch operating fingers for proper positioning.
6. Reverse procedure to install.

2005–06

The Transmission Control Module (TCM) monitors the Solenoid switch valve to deter park and neutral position.

HEADLAMP SWITCH

REPLACE

Refer to "Multi-Function Switch, Replace" for headlamp switch replacement procedure.

STOP LIGHT SWITCH

REPLACE

Removal

1. Remove steering column cover and lower trim panel.
2. Press brake pedal downward to fully applied position and unlock retainer by rotating switch approximately 30° counterclockwise.
3. Pull switch out of bracket and disconnect electrical connector.

Installation

1. Pull switch plunger out all the way to extended position.
2. Connect electrical connector.
3. Press and hold brake pedal fully applied position.
4. Align switch tab with bracket notch, then install switch and lock in position by turning it approximately 30° clockwise.
5. Release and pull brake pedal lightly rearward, Switch will ratchet as it self adjusts.

MULTI-FUNCTION SWITCH

REPLACE

The lefthand and righthand switches are separate and can be replaced individually.

1. Remove mounting screw and lower tilting steering column cover.
2. Disconnect and remove upper steering column cover.
3. Disconnect electrical connector.
4. Remove mounting screws and switch.
5. Reverse procedure to install, noting the following:
   a. **On 2002–04 models, torque** switch mounting screws to 22 inch lbs.
   b. **On 2005–06 models, torque** switch mounting screws to 30 inch lbs.
   c. **On all models, torque** cover mounting screws to 17 inch lbs.

TURN SIGNAL SWITCH

REPLACE

Refer to "Multi-Function Switch, Replace" for turn signal switch replacement procedure.

DIMMER SWITCH

REPLACE

Refer to "Multi-Function Switch, Replace" for dimmer switch replacement procedure.

STEERING WHEEL

REPLACE

1. Ensure front wheels are positioned straight forward.
2. Disarm driver air bag module as outlined under "Air Bag System Disarming & Arming."
3. Remove driver air bag module mounting screws from steering wheel back.
4. Disconnect driver air bag module and horn switch connectors.
5. Remove driver air bag module.
6. Partially remove steering wheel mounting bolt.
7. Remove steering wheel using puller tool No. C-3894-A, or equivalent.
8. Reverse procedure to install, noting the following:
   a. **On 2002–04 models, torque** steering wheel mounting bolt to 40 ft. lbs.
   b. **On 2005–06 models, torque** steering wheel mounting bolt to 45 ft. lbs.
   c. **On all models, torque** driver air bag module nuts to 90 inch lbs.

INSTRUMENT CLUSTER

REPLACE

2002–04

1. Place tilt column fully forward.
2. Disconnect instrument cluster bezel snap clips using trim stick tool No. C-4755, or equivalent.
3. Roll and remove cluster bezel top over steering column.
4. Remove four cluster mounting screws.
5. Pull upper mounting tabs downward and cluster rearward.
6. Disconnect electrical connector and remove cluster.
7. Reverse procedure to install. **Torque** cluster mounting screws to 20 inch lbs.

2005–06

1. Tilt steering column down, then grasp and remove cluster bezel.
2. Remove two mounting screws, pull instrument cluster rearward and disconnect electrical connectors.
3. Disconnect mounting posts at bottom and remove instrument cluster.
4. Reverse procedure to install. **Torque** cluster mounting screws to 17 inch lbs.

RADIO

REPLACE

1. Remove instrument cluster bezel using trim stick tool No. C-4755, or equivalent, to disconnect corners.

2. Remove mounting screws, then disconnect electrical connectors and antenna.
3. Remove radio.
4. Reverse procedure to install. **Torque** mounting screws to 20 inch lbs.

WIPER MOTOR

REPLACE

Front

2002-04

1. Remove wiper arms from pivots.
2. Pull hood to plenum seal off forward cowl grille cover and plenum panel flanges.
3. Remove six cowl grille cover to studs plastic nuts.
4. Lift cowl cover lefthand end and disconnect washer fluid lines.
5. Remove cowl cover through opening between hood and windshield.
6. Remove four wiper module mounting screws.
7. Lift wiper module lefthand end and disconnect motor electrical connector.
8. Remove wiper module.
9. Reverse procedure to install. **Torque** module mounting screws to 72 inch lbs.

2005-06

1. Remove wiper arms and plenum seal.
2. Disconnect and remove lefthand and righthand cowl grille covers.
3. Remove inboard front wiper module bracket to cowl plenum mounting nut.
4. Remove two module bracket mounting screws.
5. Disconnect electrical connector and remove wiper module.
6. Reverse procedure to install. **Torque** module mounting screws and nut to 55 inch lbs.

Rear

2002-04

1. Remove wiper arm.
2. Disconnect liftgate trim panel from wiper motor output shaft bezel and gasket using suitable door trim panel removal tool.
3. Remove wiper motor shaft nut, bezel and gasket.
4. Remove liftgate mounting screws and disconnect rear window defroster connector.
5. Remove liftgate trim panel using trim stick tool No. C-4755, or equivalent.
6. Disconnect electrical connector.
7. Loosen rear wiper module mounting bracket mounting nuts.
8. Disconnect mounting nuts from keyed slots by sliding module and bracket forward.
9. Remove rear wiper module and bracket.
10. Reverse procedure to install, noting the following:
    a. **Torque** motor shaft nut to 43 inch lbs.
    b. **Torque** mounting bracket nuts to 47 inch lbs.

2005-06

1. Remove wiper arm.
2. Remove wiper motor shaft nut, bezel and gasket.
3. Remove mounting screws and liftgate lower trim panel mounting screws using suitable wide flat-bladed tool.
4. Disconnect lower liftgate trim panel lamp electrical connector.
5. Disconnect rear wiper motor electrical connector.
6. Loosen rear wiper module mounting bracket mounting screws.
7. Disconnect mounting screws from keyed slots by sliding module and bracket forward.
8. Remove rear wiper module and bracket.
9. Reverse procedure to install, noting the following:
    a. **Torque** motor shaft nut to 43 inch lbs.
    b. **Torque** mounting bracket nuts to 50 inch lbs.

WIPER SWITCH

REPLACE

Front

Refer to "Multi-Function Switch, Replace" for wiper switch replacement procedure.

Rear

Refer to "Multi-Function Switch, Replace" for wiper switch replacement procedure.

BLOWER MOTOR

REPLACE

2002-04

1. Remove retainers and blower motor electrical connector.
2. Remove three mounting screws, then the blower motor and fan.
3. Remove clip and blower fan.
4. Reverse procedure to install. **Torque** mounting screws to 20 inch lbs.

2005-06

1. Remove instrument panel righthand side silencer.
2. Disconnect damper rod, then open glove compartment and press stops down.
3. Turn down, release door hinges and remove glove compartment.
4. Remove blower motor electrical connector.
5. Remove three mounting screws, then the blower motor and fan.
6. Remove clip and blower fan.
7. Reverse procedure to install. **Torque** mounting screws to 20 inch lbs.

HEATER CORE

REPLACE

2002-04

1. Recover refrigerant as outlined in "Air Conditioning" chapter.
2. Drain engine coolant into suitable container.
3. Remove instrument panel as outlined in "Dash Panel Service" chapter.
4. Disconnect refrigerant lines from evaporator tubes and heater hoses from tubes.
5. Remove coolant reserve/overflow bottle, then the mounting bolts and position Powertrain Control Module (PCM) aside.
6. Remove heater-air conditioning housing mounting nuts from engine compartment studs and disconnect rear floor heat duct from center adapter.
7. Disconnect heater-air conditioning housing wire connectors, then remove passenger compartment side mounting nut and heater-air conditioning housing.
8. Remove mounting screws and heater core.
9. Reverse procedure to install. **Torque** heater-air conditioning housing nuts to 60 inch lbs.

2005-06

1. Recover refrigerant as outlined in "Air Conditioning" chapter.
2. Drain engine coolant into suitable container.
3. Remove instrument panel as outlined in "Dash Panel Service" chapter.
4. Remove five heater mounting screws, then the core and tube cover.
5. **On models equipped with dual zone heating-air conditioning,** remove righthand side blend door actuator.
6. **On all models,** remove heater core tubes and bracket mounting screws.
7. Remove heater tubes mounting bolt.
8. Disconnect and remove heater core tubes. Discard O-ring seals. **Plug or tape openings and ports.**
9. Disconnect refrigerant lines from evaporator tubes and heater hoses from tubes.
10. Remove coolant reserve/overflow bottle, then the mounting bolts and position Powertrain Control Module (PCM) aside.
11. Remove heater core.
12. Reverse procedure to install, noting the following:
    a. **Torque** tube and cover mounting screws to 20 inch lbs.
    b. **Torque** heater-air conditioning housing nuts to 60 inch lbs.

EVAPORATOR CORE

REPLACE

2002-04

1. Recover refrigerant as outlined in "Air Conditioning" chapter.

2. Drain engine coolant into suitable container.
3. Remove instrument panel as outlined in "Dash Panel Service" chapter.
4. Disconnect refrigerant lines from evaporator tubes and heater hoses from tubes.
5. Remove coolant reserve/overflow bottle, then the mounting bolts and position Powertrain Control Module (PCM) aside.
6. Remove heater-air conditioning housing mounting nuts from engine compartment studs and disconnect rear floor heat duct from center adapter.
7. Disconnect heater-air conditioning housing wire connectors, then remove passenger compartment side mounting nut and heater-air conditioning housing.
8. Remove mounting screws and separate housing halves.
9. Remove evaporator core out.
10. Reverse procedure to install. **Torque** heater-air conditioning housing nuts to 60 inch lbs.

2005-06

1. Recover refrigerant as outlined in "Air Conditioning" chapter.
2. Drain engine cooling system into suitable container.
3. Apply parking brake.
4. Turn ignition switch to ON position, apply brakes and place gear selector lever into Neutral position.
5. Turn ignition switch to OFF position and release brakes.
6. Remove mat from floor console front cubby bin.
7. Open lid and remove mat from rear bin.
8. Remove two console shifter bezel mounting screws.
9. Disconnect bezel from console using suitable trim stick.
10. Remove shifter bezel from around gear selector lever.
11. Remove three console rear mounting bolts from rear bin and two screws at front.
12. Remove floor console.
13. Remove instrument panel as outlined in "Dash Panel Service" chapter.
14. Disconnect push-pin, then disconnect and remove front console duct.
15. Remove mounting screws and position gear selector aside.
16. Disconnect lefthand and righthand floor ducts.
17. Disconnect and remove rear flood distribution duct.
18. Disconnect then remove lefthand and righthand floor ducts.
19. Disconnect evaporator liquid and suction lines, then the heater core hoses.
20. Remove two mounting bolts from engine compartment and remove housing.
21. Remove air distribution and air inlet housings.
22. Disconnect evaporator temperature sensor and blower motor resistor or power module electrical connectors.
23. Disconnect retainers and remove wiring harness.
24. Remove mounting bolts, blower motor and resistor or power module.
25. Remove evaporator temperature sensor.
26. Remove two mounting bolts and expansion valve. Discard O-ring seals. **Install plugs or tape fittings and ports.**
27. Cut foam seal and remove halves mounting clips.
28. Remove 10 mounting screws and separate housing halves.
29. Open rubber seal, then remove evaporator core and insulator.
30. Reverse procedure to install, noting the following:
    a. **Torque** halves mounting screws to 20 inch lbs.
    b. **Torque** housing mounting bolts to 62 inch lbs.

TECHNICAL SERVICE BULLETINS

Remote Starter Inoperative

2005 MODELS

On some of these models the remote starter may chirp once by the engine will not remote start. Or it may chirp twice and the engine will not start. Or the remote starter may chirp once, the engine start and then turn off. This condition may be intermittent.

This condition may be caused by hood switch.

To correct this condition, replace the remote hood switch.

3.7L Engine

NOTE: Air Bag Equipped Models, Refer To "Air Bag System Precautions" Located In The Front Of This Manual For System Disarming & Arming Procedures.

NOTE: For Procedures Not Found In This Section, Refer To "3.7L Engine" Section In The "Liberty" Chapter.

INDEX

PRECAUTIONS

Air Bag Systems

Refer to "Air Bag System Precautions" in the front of this manual for system disarming and arming procedures.

Battery Ground Cable

Prior to service, disconnect battery ground cable and isolate as required.

Fuel System Pressure Relief

1. Remove fuel cap and fuel pump relay from PDC.
2. Start and run engine until it stalls.
3. Attempt to start engine until it will no longer run.
4. Turn ignition key to OFF position.
5. Disconnect any fuel injector connector.
6. Attach one end of suitable 18 gauge, or smaller, jumper wire to either injector terminal.
7. Connect other end of jumper wire to positive battery terminal.
8. Connect one end of second jumper wire to remaining injector terminal.
9. Momentarily touch other end of second jumper wire to negative battery terminal for no more than a few seconds. **Do not power injector for more than a few seconds.**
10. Place suitable rag below fuel line quick connect fitting on fuel rail.
11. Disconnect quick connect fitting.
12. Install fuel pump relay and clear stored Diagnostic Trouble Codes (DTCs).

COMPRESSION PRESSURES

Correct compression pressure for these engines is 170–225 psi; maximum variation between cylinders is 30 psi.

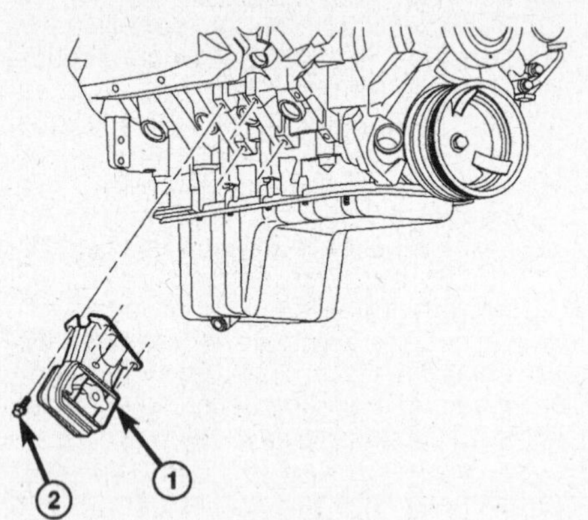

Fig. 1 Front engine mount replacement

ENGINE MOUNT

REPLACE

Front

1. Raise and support vehicle.
2. Remove engine mount through bolt.
3. Support and raise engine using suitable jack.
4. Remove mounting bolts and engine mount, **Fig. 1.**
5. Reverse procedure to install.

Rear

1. Raise and support vehicle.
2. Support transmission using suitable jack.
3. Remove crossmember.
4. Remove mounting bolts and mount, **Figs. 2 and 3.**
5. Reverse procedure to install.

ENGINE

REPLACE

1. Relieve fuel system pressure as outlined under "Precautions."
2. Remove mounting nuts and strut tower support.
3. Remove air cleaner.
4. Rotate belt tensioner until it contacts stop, then remove drive belt and slowly rotate tensioner into freearm position.
5. Remove fan blade/viscous fan drive from water pump using spanner wrench tool No. 6958 and adapter pin tools No. 8346, or equivalents. adapters. Mounting nut turns counterclockwise.
6. Disconnect connector, then remove mounting bolts and fan shroud with viscous fan.
7. Recover refrigerant as outlined in "Air Conditioning" chapter.
8. Remove air cleaner housing resonator.
9. Remove discharge and suction lines' compressor mounting nuts.
10. Disconnect compressor refrigerant lines, then remove and discard dual plane seals. **Plug or tape openings.**
11. Disconnect air conditioning compressor electrical connector.
12. Loosen accessory mounting bracket mounting bolt.
13. Remove mounting bolts and position air conditioning compressor aside.
14. Remove three mounting bolts and position alternator aside.
15. Remove three mounting bolts and position power steering pump aside with lines attached. **Do not remove power steering pump phenolic pulley.**
16. Drain cooling system into suitable container.
17. Disconnect heater core hoses.
18. Disconnect throttle and speed control cables.
19. Remove upper and lower radiator hoses.
20. Remove radiator as outlined under "Radiator, Replace."
21. Disconnect lefthand engine to body ground straps.
22. Disconnect Intake Air Temperature (IAT) sensor and fuel injectors' connectors.
23. Disconnect Throttle Position (TP)

switch and Idle Air Control (IAC) motor connectors.
24. Disconnect engine oil pressure switch and Engine Coolant Temperature (ECT) sensor connectors.
25. Disconnect Manifold Absolute Pressure MAP) and Camshaft Position (CMP) sensors' connectors.
26. Disconnect coil over plugs and Crankshaft Position (CKP) sensor connectors.
27. Remove mounting bolts and coil over plugs.
28. Disconnect clip and fuel rail line.
29. Remove throttle body vacuum lines.
30. Remove mounting bolts and position fuel rail aside.
31. Remove PCV and breather hoses, then the power brake booster vacuum hose.
32. Disconnect knock sensors.
33. Remove intake manifold as outlined in "3.7L Engine" section of the "Liberty" chapter.
34. Install engine lifting fixture tool No. 8427, or equivalent.
35. Remove engine oil dipstick tube.
36. Disconnect oxygen sensor.
37. Disconnect engine block heater power cable.
38. Remove mounting bolts at differential, then disconnect and position front propeller shaft aside.
39. Remove mounting bolts and starter motor.
40. Remove lefthand and righthand engine block ground straps.
41. Remove mounting bolts and structural cover, **Fig. 2.**
42. Disconnect lefthand and righthand exhaust pipes at manifold and crossover, then remove them.
43. Mark torque converter for installation alignment.
44. Remove mounting bolts and torque converter.
45. Remove bellhousing to engine mounting bolts.
46. Remove lefthand and righthand engine mount through bolts.
47. Lower vehicle.
48. Support transmission using suitable jack.
49. Remove engine using suitable engine hoist and engine lift plate.
50. Reverse procedure to install, noting the following:
    a. **Torque** structural collar mounting bolts to 40 ft. lbs., in sequence, **Fig. 2.**
    b. Install new exhaust manifold flange clamps.

OIL PAN

REPLACE

1. Remove radiator as outlined under "Radiator, Replace."

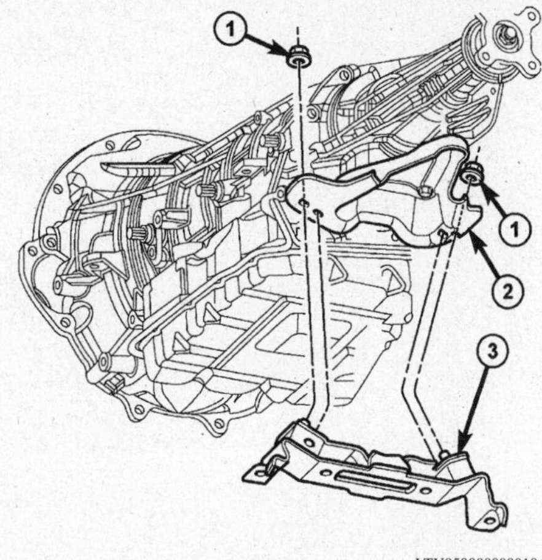

Fig. 2 Rear engine mounting replacement. 2WD

2. Remove intake manifold as outlined in "3.7L Engine" section of "Liberty" chapter.
3. Install engine support fixture tool No. 8534, or equivalent.
4. Raise and support vehicle, then remove front tires and wheels.
5. Remove mounting bolts and structural cover, **Fig. 2.**
6. Raise engine using support fixture.
7. Drain engine oil into suitable container. Remove oil filter.
8. Remove mounting bolts and oil pan. **Do not pry on oil pan or gasket.**
9. Remove mounting bolt, oil pump pickup tube and oil pan gasket.
10. Remove two nuts and one bolt holding oil pump pickup tube and windage tray in place.
11. Drop oil pump pickup tube into oil pan, then remove oil pan, pickup tube and windage tray as an assembly from front of vehicle.
12. Reverse procedure to install. **Torque** oil pan bolts to 11 ft. lbs., in sequence, **Fig. 4.**

WATER PUMP

REPLACE

1. Drain coolant into suitable container.
2. Remove serpentine drive belt.
3. Remove lower radiator hose at water pump.
4. Remove water pump mounting bolts, then the water pump and gasket.
5. Reverse procedure to install. Tighten water pump bolts to specification.

RADIATOR

REPLACE

1. Drain radiator coolant into suitable container.
2. Remove six upper push pins and front grill.
3. Remove two radiator mounting bolts.
4. Disconnect transmission cooler lines.
5. Disconnect fan control solenoid electrical connector.
6. Disconnect power steering cooling line from cooler and filter.
7. Disconnect upper and lower radiator hoses, then the overflow hose.
8. Remove air inlet duct at grille.
9. Disconnect two hydraulic fan drive high pressure fluid lines an low pressure return hose.
10. Remove radiator. **Do not scrape fins against other components.**
11. **Do not disturb air conditioning condenser.**
12. Reverse procedure to install, noting the following:
    a. Guide two radiator alignment dowels through rubber air seals, then through air conditioning support brackets.
    b. Hose clamps' tangs must be positioned straight down.

FUEL PUMP

REPLACE

1. Relieve fuel pressure as outlined under "Precautions."
2. Drain fuel tank into suitable container.
3. Loosen clamp and disconnect tank rubber fill hose.
4. Disconnect fuel pump module electrical jumper connector from body connector at rear of tank.
5. Disconnect EVAP lines at rear of tank.
6. Disconnect fuel and EVAP lines at front of tank.
7. Support fuel tank with suitable jack.
8. Remove mounting bolts and remove fuel tank.
9. Remove lock ring by turning remover/installer tool No. 9340, or equivalent, and suitable ½ inch drive breaker bar counterclockwise.
10. Remove fuel pump module. **Do not bend float arm.**
11. Reverse procedure to install. Tighten lock ring clockwise until all seven notches have engaged.

FUEL FILTER

REPLACE

Two fuel filters are used. One is located at the bottom of the fuel pump module. The other is located inside the module.

A separate frame mounted fuel filter is not used.

Both fuel filters are designed for extended service. They do not require normal scheduled maintenance. Filters should only be replaced if a diagnostic procedure indicates to do so.

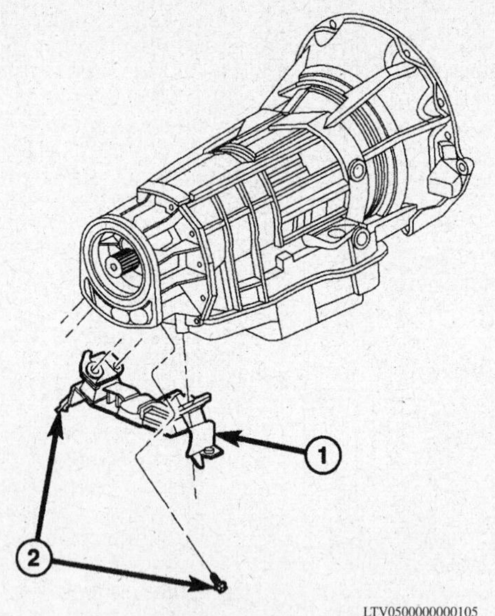

Fig. 3 Rear engine mount replacement. 4WD

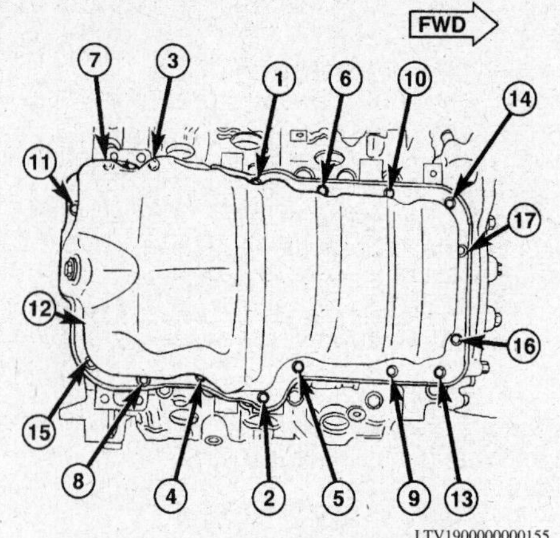

Fig. 4 Oil pan tightening sequence

TIGHTENING SPECIFICATIONS

Year	Component	Torque Ft. Lbs.
2005–06	Alternator	⑤
	Air Conditioning Compressor	41
	Air Conditioning Compressor to Accessory Bracket	30
	Bellhousing	30
	Engine Mount	22
	Fan	20
	Fan Shroud	53①
	Hydraulic Fan Drive Pressure Line Fitting	④
	Oil Pan	③
	Oil Pan Drain Plug	25
	Oil Pump Tube	20
	Refrigerant Lines	15
	Structural Collar	②

① — Inch lbs.

② — Refer to "Engine, Replace" for tightening specifications and sequence.

③ — Refer to "Oil Pan, Replace" for tightening specifications and sequence.

④ — ½ inch, 36 ft. lbs.; ⅜ inch, 21 ft. lbs.

⑤ — M8, 21 ft. lbs.; M10, 40 ft. lbs.

4.0L Engine

NOTE: Air Bag Equipped Models, Refer To "Air Bag System Precautions" Located In The Front Of This Manual For System Disarming & Arming Procedures.

NOTE: Refer To "Computer Relearn Procedures" Located In The Front Of This Manual When Battery Power To The Computer Has Been Interrupted.

NOTE: Prior To Performing Any Service Operations Listed In This Section, Consult The "Technical Service Bulletins" Section For Related Information.

INDEX

PRECAUTIONS

Air Bag Systems

Refer to "Air Bag System Precautions" in the front of this manual for system disarming and arming procedures.

Battery Ground Cable

Prior to service, disconnect battery ground cable and isolate as required.

Fuel System Pressure Relief

1. Remove fuel cap and fuel pump relay from PDC.
2. Start and run engine until it stalls.
3. Attempt to start engine until it will no longer run.
4. Turn ignition key to OFF position.
5. Disconnect any fuel injector connector.
6. Attach one end of suitable 18 gauge, or smaller, jumper wire to either injector terminal.
7. Connect other end of jumper wire to positive battery terminal.
8. Connect one end of second jumper wire to remaining injector terminal.
9. Momentarily touch other end of second jumper wire to negative battery terminal for no more than a few seconds. **Do not power injector for more than a few seconds.**
10. Place suitable rag below fuel line quick connect fitting on fuel rail.
11. Disconnect quick connect fitting.
12. Install fuel pump relay and clear stored Diagnostic Trouble Codes (DTCs).

COMPRESSION PRESSURES

Correct compression pressure for these engines is 120–150 psi; maximum variation between cylinders is 30 psi.

ENGINE MOUNT

REPLACE

Front

1. Raise and support vehicle.
2. Raise engine.
3. Remove lower front sill bolts, **Figs. 1 and 2.**
4. Raise engine slightly.
5. Remove through bolt and insulator.
6. Remove engine bracket.
7. Reverse procedure to install.

Rear

1. Raise and support vehicle, then support transmission using suitable jack.
2. Remove mount to transmission bolts, **Figs. 3 and 4.**
3. Raise transmission slightly, then remove bolt, nut and rear isolator mount.
4. Remove rear mount bracket to crossmember mounting bolts.
5. Reverse procedure to install, noting the following:
   a. Do not tighten through bolt until weight of transmission is applied.
   b. Refer to **Fig. 4** for bolt locations and tightening specifications.

ENGINE

REPLACE

1. Mark hoof hinge locations installation alignment.
2. Remove engine compartment lamp and hood.
3. Drain radiator coolant into suitable container.
4. Remove upper and lower radiator hoses, then the coolant recovery hose.
5. Remove thermal viscous fan mounting

bolt. **Fan drive threads are right-hand. Do not remove fan now.**
6. Remove fan shroud to upper cross-member mounting nuts.
7. Remove fan shroud and viscous fan.
8. Disconnect transmission cooler lines.
9. Recover refrigerant as outlined in "Air Conditioning" chapter.
10. Remove air conditioning compressor service valves and cap ports.
11. Remove mounting bolts and front grille.
12. Disconnect fan motor and harness electrical connectors.
13. Remove air inlet duct from grille.
14. Remove radiator. **Do not damage auxiliary transmission oil cooler line seal. Do not damage radiator fins. Do not damage condenser.**
15. Disconnect air conditioning compressor suction/discharge hose.
16. Cap or tape lines and ports.
17. Disconnect thermostat housing and water pump heater hoses.
18. Disconnect throttle body accelerator, transmission line pressure and speed control cables.
19. Remove cables from bracket and position aside.
20. Disconnect engine body ground.
21. Disconnect power steering pressure switch and Engine Coolant Temperature (ECT) sensor connectors.
22. Disconnect fuel injector and Intake Air Temperature (IAT) sensor connectors.
23. Disconnect Throttle Position (TP) and Manifold Absolute Pressure (MAP) sensors' connectors.
24. Disconnect Crankshaft Position (CKP), Camshaft Position (CMP) and oxygen sensors' connectors.
25. Disconnect alternator connector and battery positive terminal wire.
26. Disconnect coil rail and oil pressure switch connectors.
27. Release fuel system pressure as outlined under "Precautions."
28. Remove latch clip and disconnect fuel line quick connect at fuel rail.
29. Remove intake manifold fuel line bracket.
30. Disconnect clamp and air cleaner duct.
31. Raise and support vehicle.
32. Remove clips and pry back rubber inner fender shield.
33. Remove lower air cleaner housing three lower mounting nuts. **Do not remove upper mounting nuts and bolts.**
34. Remove air cleaner.
35. Disconnect power steering gear hoses and drain pump reservoir into suitable container. Cap fittings on hoses and steering gear.
36. Raise and support vehicle.
37. Disconnect starter motor solenoid wires.
38. Remove mounting bolts and starter motor.
39. Disconnect oxygen sensor from exhaust pipe.
40. Disconnect exhaust pipe from manifold.
41. Remove mounting bolts and engine support bending brace.
42. Remove mounting bolts and converter housing access cover.
43. Mark torque converter and drive plate for installation alignment.
44. Remove torque converter mounting bolts.
45. Remove converter housing upper mounting bolts and loosen lower mounting bolts.
46. Remove engine mount bracket bolts.
47. Lower vehicle.
48. Support engine with suitable lifting device.
49. Raise engine slightly off front supports.
50. Support converter housing using suitable floor jack.
51. Place a support stand under converter or flywheel housing.
52. Remove lower converter housing mounting bolts and engine.
53. Reverse procedure to install.

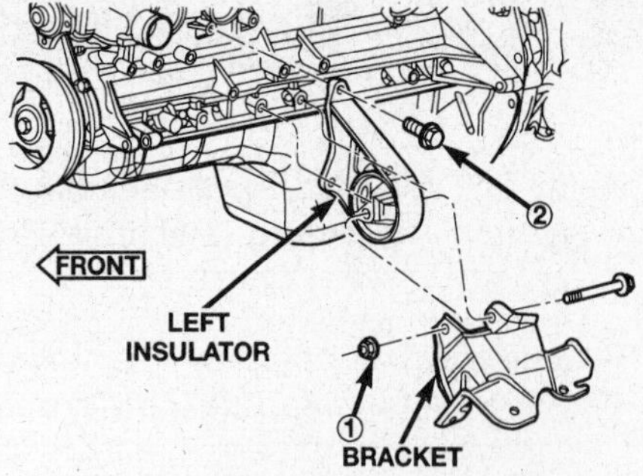

Fig. 1 Lefthand front engine mount replacement

INTAKE MANIFOLD

REPLACE

The intake and exhaust manifolds must be removed together because the two manifolds share a common gasket at the cylinder head.

1. Disconnect clamp and air cleaner duct.
2. Raise and support vehicle.
3. Remove clips and pry back rubber inner fender shield.
4. Remove lower air cleaner housing three lower mounting nuts. **Do not remove upper mounting nuts and bolts.**
5. Remove air cleaner.
6. Disconnect throttle, speed control and transmission line pressure cables.
7. Disconnect Throttle Position (TP) sensor and Idle Air Control (IAC) motor connectors.
8. Disconnect Engine Coolant Temperature (ECT) and Intake Air Temperature (IAT) sensor connectors.
9. Disconnect Oxygen and Crankshaft Position (CKP) sensors' connectors.
10. Disconnect fuel injector and Manifold Absolute Pressure (MAP) sensor connectors.
11. Disconnect HVAC and brake booster vacuum lines from intake manifold.
12. Relieve fuel pressure as outlined under "Precautions."
13. Disconnect and remove fuel rail supply line.
14. Rotate belt tensioner until it contacts stop, then remove drive belt and slowly rotate tensioner into freearm position.
15. Remove mounting bolts and position power steering pump aside.
16. Raise and support vehicle.
17. Disconnect exhaust pipes from manifolds.
18. Lower vehicle.
19. Remove mounting bolts, then the intake and exhaust manifolds.
20. Reverse procedure to install, noting the following:
    a. Install new exhaust/intake manifold gasket over alignment dowels.
    b. Install exhaust manifolds and hand tighten mounting bolt/nut No. 3, **Fig. 5.**
    c. Install intake manifold.
    d. Install washers and mounting bolts/nuts Nos. 1, 2, 4, 5, 8, 9, 10 and 11.
    e. Install washers and mounting bolts/nuts Nos. 6 and 7.
    f. **Torque** mounting bolts/nuts 1–5 to 24 ft. lbs.
    g. **Torque** mounting bolts/nuts 6 and 7 to 23 ft. lbs.
    h. **Torque** mounting bolts/nuts 8–11 to 24 ft. lbs.

EXHAUST MANIFOLD

REPLACE

The intake and exhaust manifolds must be removed together because the two manifolds share a common gasket at the cylinder head.

Refer to "Intake Manifold, Replace" for exhaust manifold replacement procedure.

CYLINDER HEAD

REPLACE

1. Drain cooling system into suitable container.
2. Disconnect clamp and air cleaner duct.
3. Raise and support vehicle.
4. Remove clips and pry back rubber inner fender shield.
5. Remove lower air cleaner housing three lower mounting nuts. **Do not remove upper mounting nuts and bolts.**
6. Remove air cleaner.
7. Disconnect Crankcase Ventilation (CCV) vacuum and fresh air inlet hoses from engine valve cover.
8. Disconnect accelerator, transmission and speed control cables from throttle body.
9. Remove three control cable bracket mounting bolts.
10. Remove control cables from valve cover clip.
11. Position control cables and bracket aside.
12. Remove mounting bolts, valve cover and gasket.
13. Remove rocker arm bridge and pivot capscrews one turn at a time.
14. Remove bridges, pivots and rocker arm pairs. Maintain order for installation in original positions.
15. Remove push rods and maintain order for installation in original positions.
16. Rotate belt tensioner until it contacts

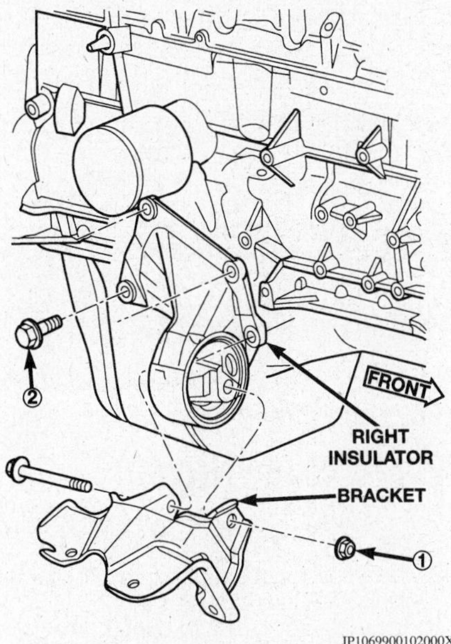

Fig. 2 Righthand front engine mount replacement

stop, then remove drive belt and slowly rotate tensioner into freearm position.

17. Remove mounting bolts and position air condition compressor aside.
18. Remove mounting bolts, power steering pump and bracket. Position pump aside with lines attached.
19. Relieve fuel pressure as outlined under "Precautions."
20. Disconnect fuel rail supply line.
21. Remove intake and exhaust manifolds as outlined under "Intake Manifold, Replace."
22. Remove four mounting bolts and pry coil from spark plugs alternating each end using suitable spark plug boot removal tool.
23. Disconnect electrical connector and remove coil rail.
24. Disconnect ignition wires and remove spark plugs.
25. Disconnect temperature sending unit.
26. Remove cylinder head mounting bolts. Pull bolt No. 14 as far as it will go and suspend in position using suitable tape around bolt. Bolt No. 14 cannot be removed until head is forward. Discard bolts that have been reused more than once.
27. Remove cylinder head and gasket.
28. Reverse procedure to install, noting the following:
    a. Coat stud bolt No. 11 with 11, with Loctite 592, or equivalent sealant.
    b. **Torque** cylinder head bolts to 22 ft. lbs., in sequence, **Fig. 6.**
    c. **Torque** head bolts to 45 ft. lbs., in sequence.
    d. Ensure heads are **torqued** to 45 ft. lbs.
    e. **Torque** bolts 1–10 to 110 ft. lbs.
    f. **Torque** bolt 11 to 100 ft. lbs.
    g. **Torque** bolts 12–14 to 110 ft. lbs.

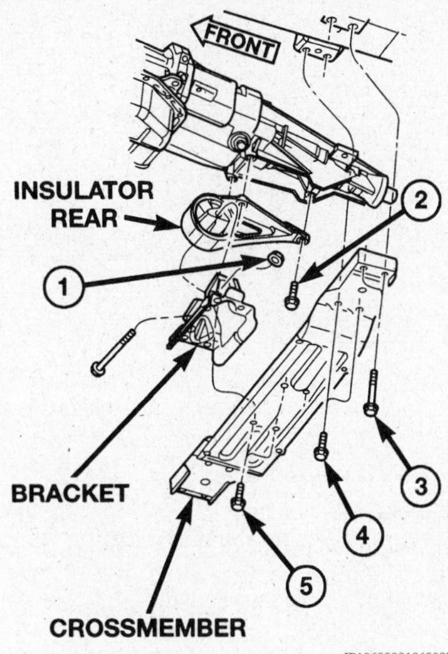

Fig. 3 Rear motor mount replacement. 2WD

ITEM	DESCRIPTON	TORQUE
1	NUT (Qty 1)	45 N·m (33 ft. lbs.)
2	BOLT (Qty 4)	46 N·m (34 ft. lbs.)
3	BOLT (Qty 2 Per Side)	68 N·m (50 ft. lbs.)
4	BOLT (Qty 2 Per Side)	46 N·m (34 ft. lbs.)
5	BOLT (Qty 4)	46 N·m (34 ft. lbs.)

JP1069900108000X

Fig. 4 Rear motor mount replacement (Part 2 of 2). 4WD

VALVE COVER

REPLACE

1. Disconnect Crankcase Ventilation (CCV) vacuum and fresh air inlet hoses from engine valve cover.
2. Disconnect accelerator, transmission and speed control cables from throttle body.
3. Remove three control cable bracket mounting bolts.
4. Remove control cables from valve cover clip.
5. Position control cables and bracket aside.
6. Remove mounting bolts, valve cover and gasket.
7. Reverse procedure to install.

VALVE ARRANGEMENT

Front To Rear

4.0L Engine ....E-I-I-E-I-E-E-I-E-I-I-E

CAMSHAFT LOBE LIFT SPECIFICATIONS

Exhaust ....4145 inch
Intake ....4705 inch

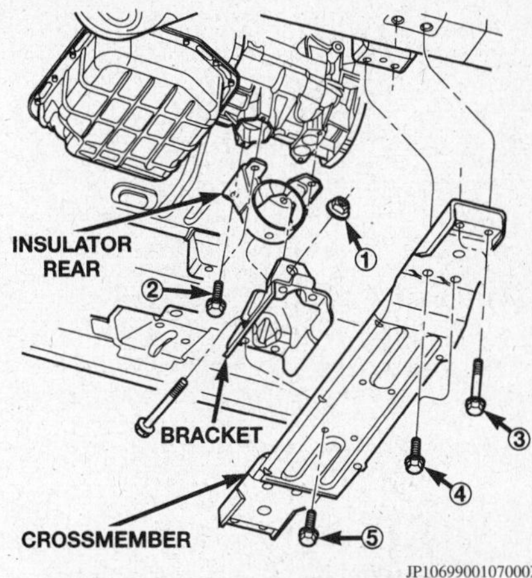

Fig. 4 Rear motor mount replacement (Part 1 of 2). 4WD

VALVE ADJUSTMENT

These engines are equipped with hydraulic valve lifters. There is no provision for adjustment.

ROCKER ARMS

REPLACE

1. Disconnect Crankcase Ventilation (CCV) vacuum and fresh air inlet hoses from engine valve cover.
2. Disconnect accelerator, transmission and speed control cables from throttle body.
3. Remove three control cable bracket mounting bolts.
4. Remove control cables from valve cover clip.
5. Position control cables and bracket aside.
6. Remove mounting bolts, valve cover and gasket.
7. Remove rocker arm bridge and pivot capscrews one turn at a time, **Fig. 7.**
8. Remove bridges, pivots and rocker arm pairs. Maintain order for installation in original positions.

HYDRAULIC LIFTERS

REPLACE

1. Remove cylinder head as outlined under "Cylinder Head, Replace."
2. Remove tappets through push rod openings using suitable hydraulic valve tappet removal/installation tool.
3. Reverse procedure to install, noting the following:
    a. Dip each tappet in Mopar Engine Oil Supplement, or equivalent.
    b. Pour remain engine oil supplement over valve system.

CRANKSHAFT DAMPER

REPLACE

1. Rotate belt tensioner until it contacts stop, then remove drive belt and slowly rotate tensioner into freearm position.
2. Remove mounting bolt, washer and

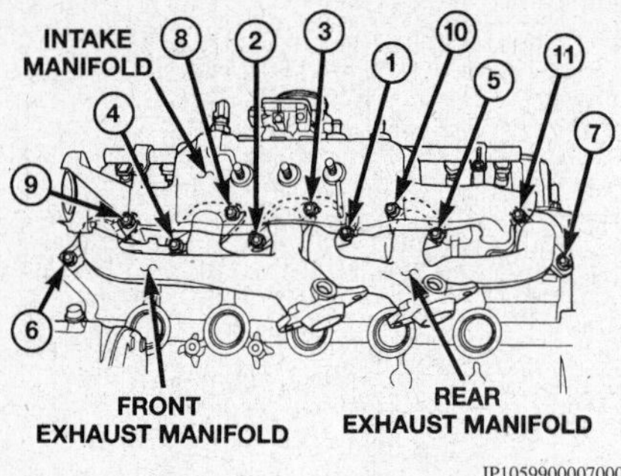

Fig. 5 Intake & exhaust manifold tightening sequence

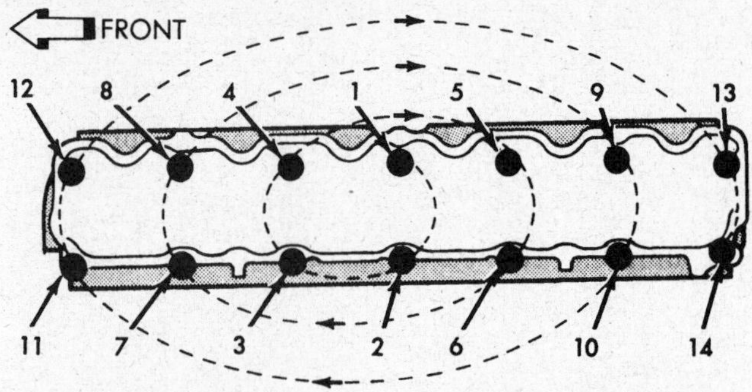

Fig. 6 Cylinder head tightening sequence

damper using vibration damper removal tool No. 7697, or equivalent.
3. Reverse procedure to install. Apply suitable silicone rubber adhesive sealant to keyway.

FRONT COVER

REPLACE

1. Rotate belt tensioner until it contacts stop, then remove drive belt and slowly rotate tensioner into freearm position.
2. Remove mounting bolt, washer and damper using vibration damper removal tool No. 7697, or equivalent.
3. Remove upper and lower radiator hoses, then the coolant recovery hose.
4. Remove thermal viscous fan mounting bolt. **Fan drive threads are righthand . Do not remove fan now.**
5. Remove fan shroud to upper crossmember mounting nuts.
6. Remove fan shroud and viscous fan.
7. Remove mounting bolts and accessory drive brackets.
8. Remove mounting bolts, then position air conditioning compressor and alternator bracket aside.
9. Remove mounting bolts, timing case cover and gasket.
10. Reverse procedure to install, noting the following:
    a. Install new crankshaft oil seal.
    b. Install timing case cover using timing case cover alignment and seal installation tool No. 6139, or equivalent.

TIMING CHAIN

REPLACE

1. Remove timing case cover as outlined under "Front Cover, Replace."
2. Rotate crankshaft until zero timing mark is closest to and on center line with camshaft sprocket timing mark, **Fig. 8.**
3. Remove crankshaft oil slinger.
4. Remove camshaft sprocket mounting bolt and washer.
5. Remove crankshaft sprocket, camshaft sprocket and timing chain as an assembly.
6. Reverse procedure to install. Ensure correct timing by rotating crankshaft two revolutions and inspecting alignment, **Fig. 8.**

CAMSHAFT

REPLACE

1. Remove radiator as outlined under "Radiator, Replace."
2. Remove engine cylinder head as outlined under "Cylinder Head, Replace."
3. Remove tappets through push rod openings using suitable hydraulic valve tappet removal/installation tool.
4. Remove timing chain as outlined under "Timing Chain, Replace."
5. Remove two mounting bolts, thrust plate and camshaft, **Fig. 9.**
6. Reverse procedure to install. Lubricate camshaft with Mopar Engine Oil Supplement, or equivalent.

PISTON & ROD ASSEMBLY

When assembling piston to rod, ensure arrow faces front of engine and oil spurt hole on connecting rod faces toward camshaft, **Fig. 10.**

PISTONS, PINS & RINGS

Align ring gaps as follows:

1. Oil spacer gap on piston skirt centerline, **Fig. 11.**
2. Oil rails gap 180° apart on piston pin bore centerline.
3. Compression ring No. 2 gap 120° from top oil rail gap.
4. Compression ring No. 1 gap 120° from compression ring No. 2 gap.

MAIN & ROD BEARINGS

Connecting Rod

1. Lubricate and install upper bearing insert.
2. Install piston and rod assembly.
3. Install dry lower bearing insert with full-width Plastigage strip.
4. **Torque** bearing cap to 33 ft. lbs. **Do not rotate crankshaft.**
5. Remove bearing cap and ensure clearance is .001–.003 inch.

Main Bearings

1. Lubricate each bearing surface using suitable engine oil.
2. Loose all main bearing caps and install main bearing upper inserts.
3. Install lower bearing inserts into main bearing caps.
4. Apply .125 inch diameter Mopar Gasket Maker sealer, or equivalent, on rear main cap, **Fig. 12.**
5. Install main bear caps and lower inserts, **Fig. 13.**
6. **Torque** cap bolts 1, 2, 4, 5, 6 and 7 to 40 ft. lbs.
7. **Torque** cap bolts 1, 2, 4, 5, 6 and 7 to 70 ft. lbs.
8. **Torque** cap bolts 1, 2, 4, 5, 6 and 7 to 80 ft. lbs.
9. Push crankshaft forward and backward.
10. **Torque** cap bolts 3 to 40 ft. lbs.
11. **Torque** cap bolts 3 to 70 ft. lbs.
12. **Torque** cap bolts 3 to 80 ft. lbs.

CRANKSHAFT SEAL

REPLACE

1. Remove timing case cover as outlined under "Front Cover, Replace."
2. Remove crankshaft oil seal from timing case cover.
3. Reverse procedure to install using seal installation tool No. 6139, or equivalent.

CRANKSHAFT REAR OIL SEAL

REPLACE

Removal

1. Remove transmission inspection cover.
2. Remove oil pan as outlined under "Oil Pan, Replace."
3. Remove main bearing cap brace and No. 7 main bearing cap.
4. Push upper seal out of groove. **Do not damage crankshaft and seal groove.**
5. Remove lower half of seal from bearing cap.

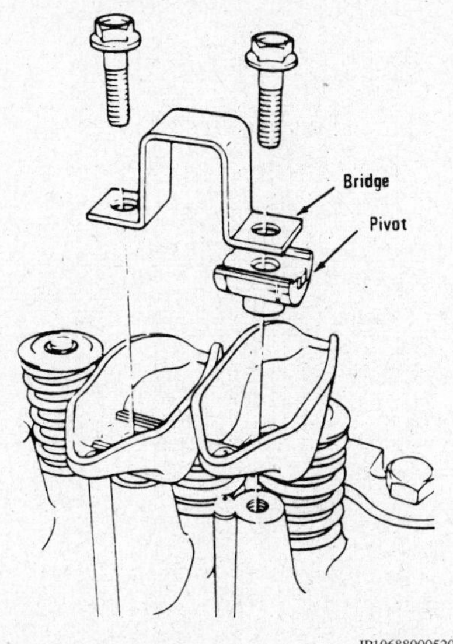

Fig. 7 Rocker arm replacement

Installation

1. Wipe seal surface area clean and apply thin coat of suitable engine oil.
2. Coat seal lip with suitable engine oil.
3. Position upper seal into cylinder block. Lip seal faces toward front of engine.
4. Apply .125 inch diameter Mopar Gasket Maker sealer on both sides of cylinder block, **Fig. 12.**
5. Apply .09 inch diameter Mopar Gasket Maker sealer on rear bearing cap. **Do not apply sealer to seal lip.**
6. Firmly seat lower seal into bearing cap flush with cylinder block pan rail.
7. Coat lower seal curved surface with soap and seal lip with engine oil.
8. Install rear main bearing cap. **Do not strike cap more than twice.**
9. **Torque** main bearing bolts to 80 ft. lbs.
10. Install main bearing cap brace.
11. Install oil pan and gasket as outlined under "Oil Pan, Replace."
12. Apply suitable silicone rubber adhesive sealer to rear main bearing cap corners and cylinder block front joints, **Fig. 14.**
13. Install inspection cover.

OIL PAN

REPLACE

1. Raise and support vehicle, then drain engine oil into suitable container.
2. Disconnect exhaust pipe at exhaust manifold.
3. Disconnect exhaust hanger at catalytic converter and lower pipe.
4. Remove mounting bolts and starter motor.
5. Remove mounting bolts and torque converter housing access cover.
6. Disconnect oil level sensor.
7. Support engine using suitable wood piece and jack stand under vibration damper.
8. Remove engine mount through bolts.
9. Raise engine.
10. Remove transmission oil cooler lines

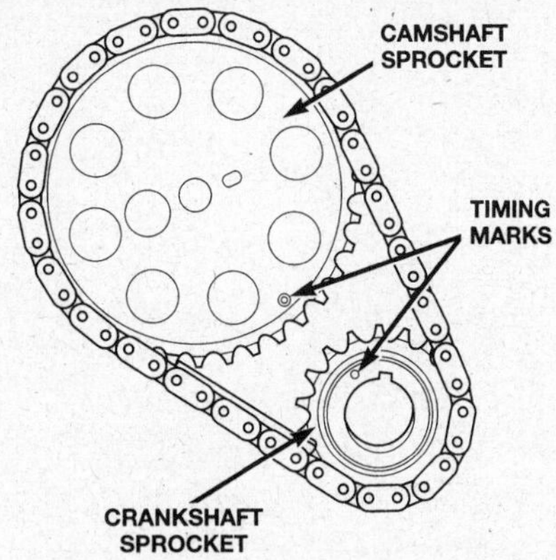

Fig. 8 Valve timing mark alignment.

and oxygen sensor wiring supports from oil pan studs.

11. Remove mounting bolts and studs, then the oil pan and gasket. **Do not damage oil level sensor.**
12. Reverse procedure to install, noting the following:
    a. Fabricated four alignment dowels by cutting head off 1 ½ x ¼ inch bolts and cut slot into top.
    b. Install two dowels in timing case cover and cylinder block.
    c. Apply suitable silicone rubber adhesive sealer to rear main bearing cap corners and cylinder block front joints, **Fig. 14.**
    d. **Torque** ¼ inch oil pan mounting bolts to 84 inch lbs.
    e. **Torque** 5/16 inch oil pan mounting bolts to 11 ft. lbs., **Fig. 15.**

OIL PUMP

REPLACE

1. Remove oil pan as outlined under "Oil Pan, Replace."
2. Remove mounting bolts, oil pump and gasket.
3. Reverse procedure to install, using new gasket

BELT TENSION DATA

This engine is equipped with an automatic belt tensioner.

SERPENTINE DRIVE BELT

Routing

Refer to **Fig. 16** for serpentine drive belt routing.

Replacement

1. Rotate belt tensioner until it contacts stop.
2. Remove drive belt.
3. Slowly rotate tensioner into freearm position.
4. Reverse procedure to install.

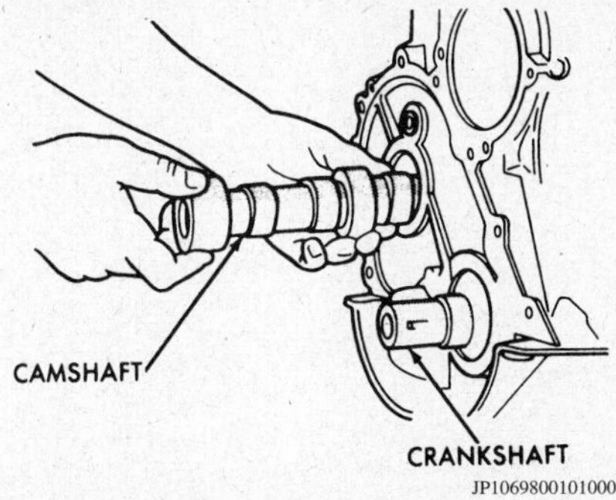

Fig. 9 Camshaft replacement

COOLING SYSTEM BLEED

After filling cooling system, start and run engine until it reaches operating temperature with radiator cap removed. Air in system is automatically bled through radiator cap opening. Adjust coolant level, then install radiator cap and inspect coolant level in recovery reservoir.

THERMOSTAT

REPLACE

1. Drain radiator coolant until level is below thermostat housing into suitable container.
2. Remove thermostat housing upper radiator and heater hoses.
3. Disconnect Engine Coolant Temperature (ECT) sensor connector.
4. Remove mounting bolts, housing, gasket and thermostat. Discard gasket
5. Reverse procedure to install, noting the following:
    a. Ensure pellet, which is encircled by coil spring, faces engine.
    b. Position thermostat in groove with arrow and air bleed hole on outer flange pointing up.

WATER PUMP

REPLACE

1. Drain radiator coolant into suitable container.
2. If replacing water pump. **Do not unbolt fan blade.**
3. Remove upper and lower radiator hoses, then the coolant recovery hose.
4. Remove thermal viscous fan mounting bolt. **Fan drive threads are righthand . Do not remove fan now.**
5. Remove fan shroud to upper crossmember mounting nuts.
6. Remove fan shroud and viscous fan.
7. Rotate belt tensioner until it contacts stop, then remove drive belt and slowly rotate tensioner into freearm position.
8. Loosen mounting bolts and remove water pump pulley. **Do not remove mounting bolts.**
9. Remove idler pulley over water pump.
10. Remove water pump lower radiator and heater hoses.
11. Remove five mounting bolt and water pump. Discard gasket.
12. Reverse procedure to install.

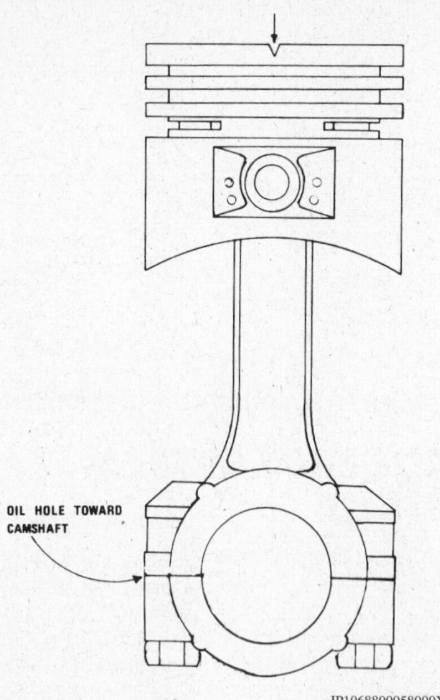

Fig. 10 Piston & rod assembly

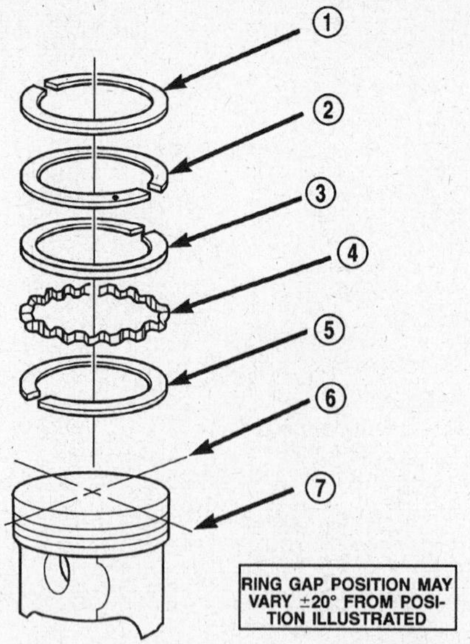

Fig. 11 Ring gap orientation

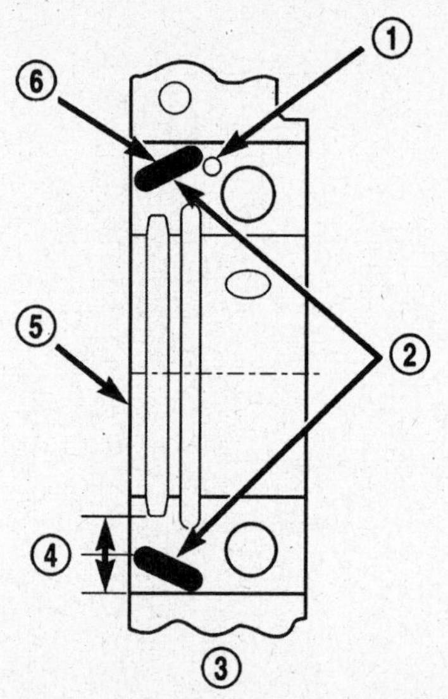

Fig. 12 Rear main cap sealer application

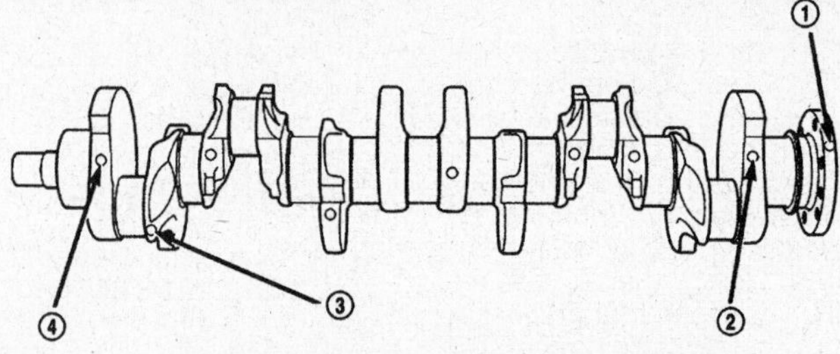

Fig. 13 Crankshaft journal I.D.

RADIATOR

REPLACE

1. Drain radiator coolant into suitable container.
2. Remove viscous fan mounting nut. **Do not remove fan assembly now.**
3. Remove mounting bolts and front grille.
4. Remove two radiator mounting bolts.
5. Disconnect transmission cooler lines.
6. Disconnect fan motor and harness electrical connectors.
7. Remove upper and lower radiator hoses.
8. Remove air inlet duct from grille.
9. Remove radiator. **Do not damage radiator fins or condenser.**
10. Reverse procedure to install.

FUEL PUMP

REPLACE

1. Relieve fuel pressure as outlined under "Precautions."
2. Raise and support vehicle, then remove lefthand rear wheel and tire assembly.
3. Drain fuel tank into suitable container.
4. Drill out plastic rivets and remove stone shield behind lefthand rear wheel.
5. Remove three LDP mounting bolts.
6. Remove support brace bracket mounting bolt.
7. Loosen two support bracket mounting nuts. **Do not remove mounting nuts.**
8. Remove three mounting bolts, then lower support bracket and disconnect LDP wiring clip.
9. Remove clamp and fuel fill tube.
10. Cut and discard tie wrap, then disconnect fuel vent hose.
11. Disconnect EVAP canister ORVR hose elbow.
12. Support fuel tank using suitable hydraulic jack.
13. Remove fuel tank to rear bumper fascia clips.
14. Remove fuel tank heat shield mounting bolts.
15. Disconnect fuel filter/pressure regulator return and pressure lines.
16. Disconnect EVAP canister vent line.
17. Disconnect fuel pump module electrical connector.
18. Remove tank support bracket mounting bolt.
19. **On models equipped with trailer hitch,** remove mounting bolts.
20. **On models equipped less trailer hitch,** remove mounting bolts and support bracket bolt.
21. **On all models,** remove fuel tank.
22. Remove fuel module locknut using rotating tool No. 6856, or equivalent.
23. Remove fuel module.
24. Reverse procedure to install, noting the following:
    a. Install new gasket.
    b. Apply clean water to locknut threads.
    c. Rotate module until indexing arrow points toward vehicle rear, **Fig. 17.**

FUEL FILTER

REPLACE

1. Remove fuel module as outlined under "Fuel Pump, Replace."
2. Remove fuel filter by prying from bottom of module using two suitable screwdrivers.
3. Remove procedure to install.

TECHNICAL SERVICE BULLETINS

Multiple Cylinder Misfire

2002-04

On some of these models there may be a engine misfire between 50–70 mph under light load conditions such as slight uphill grades. Condition may be more noticeable at less than 32°F. Diagnostic Trouble Code (DTC) P0300 may be set. High frequency misfire may place engine in Limp-In mode.

This condition may be caused by one or more exhaust valves closing slow because of no valve rotation and associated carbon build-up on valve stem.

To correct this condition, inspect and decarbonize all exhaust valves as follows:

1. Remove valve cover and all exhaust

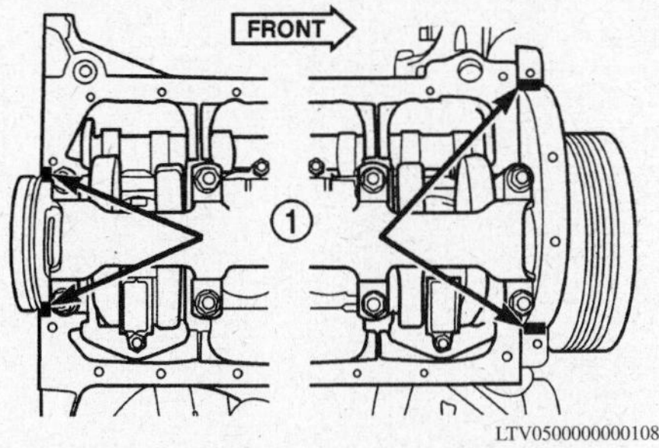

Fig. 14 Oil pan sealer locations

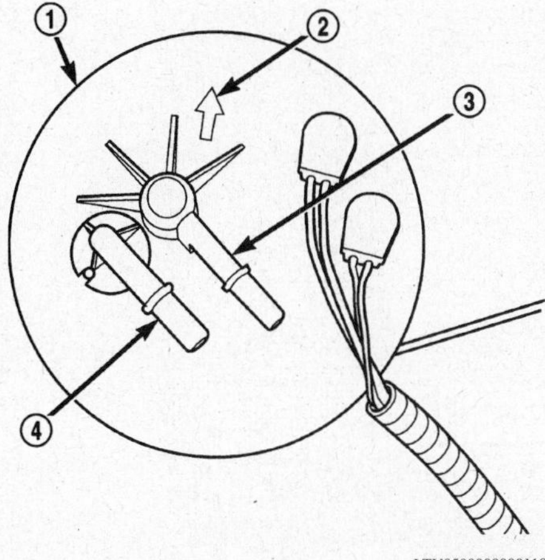

Fig. 17 Fuel module replacement

rocker arms as outlined under "Rocker Arm, Replace."

2. Inspect exhaust valve stem when it contacts rocker arm, noting the following:
   a. If valve has bulls eye or circular wear pattern, it is rotating properly and further diagnosis is required.
   b. If valve has straight mark-like pattern, proceed to next step.
3. Clean and mark all exhaust valve stems with paint marker.
4. Bring cylinder No. 1 to TDC using crankshaft front damper/pulley mark.
5. Install valve spring compressor tool No. MD-998772 A, or equivalent, to cylinder No. 1 exhaust valve spring.
6. Compress spring and rotate exhaust valve 90°.
7. Slowly remove valve spring compression, then ensure valve keeper is properly seated on stem and retainer.
8. Repeat procedure on cylinder No. 6.
9. Rotate crankshaft 120°, then repeat procedure on cylinders Nos. 2 and 5.
10. Rotate crankshaft another 120°, then repeat procedure on cylinders Nos. 3 and 4.
11. Install rocker arms and retaining bridge. Ensure push rods are properly seated.
12. **Torque** bridge/rocker arm caps to 21 ft. lbs., when respective cylinder is at

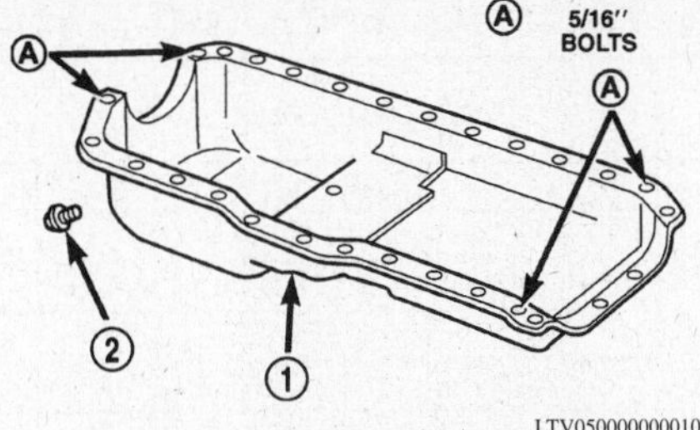

Fig. 15 Oil pan 5/16 inch mounting bolt locations

TDC (valves are closed.

13. Install cylinder head cove and **torque** mounting bolts to 85 inch lbs.
14. Start engine and run to normal operating temperature.
15. Remove throttle body air tube.
16. With engine at idle, spray can of Mopar Combustion Chamber Cleaner, or equivalent, directly into throttle body.Run engine to load-up to stall point and maintain condition until entire cleaner can is ingested.
17. Stop engine and install air tube.
18. Allow engine to heat soak for 2–3 hour with hood closed inside garage.
19. After soak, start and drive vehicle until engine reaches normal operating temperature.
20. Place transmission in L positions and drive vehicle until engine reaches 4500 RPM.
21. Hold engine at 4500 RPM for 15 seconds.
22. Slow down, pull off road and allow engine to idle for five seconds.
23. Repeat driving procedure five more times.

Engine Compartment Ticking

2002-04

On some of these models there may be a ticking sound when the engine is idling. Condition may be more noticeable in colder ambient temperatures.

This condition may be caused by mechanical contact between Duty Cycle Purge (DCP) solenoid and body.

To correct this condition, install narrow slot bushing (part No. 53030987) and new isolation U-bracket (P/N 05114514AA), as follows:

1. Turn ignition switch to OFF position, disconnect DCP solenoid evaporative vapor lines and electrical connector, **Fig. 18.**
2. Remove DCP solenoid from plastic body mounting bracket by lifting it upward.
3. Record rubber bushing orientation.
4. Remove bushing with wide slot and install replacement bushing with narrow slot.

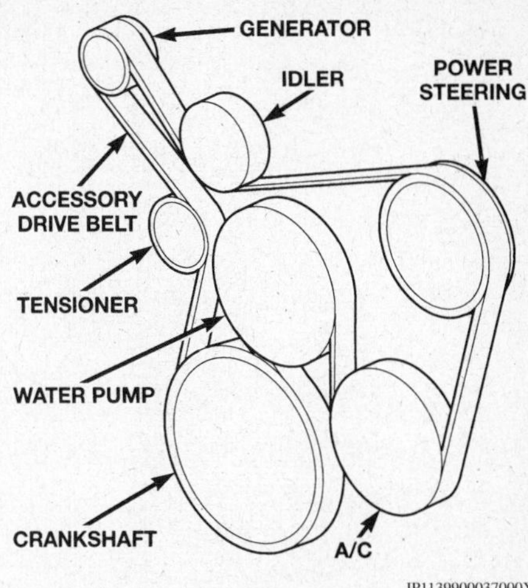

Fig. 16 Serpentine drive belt routing

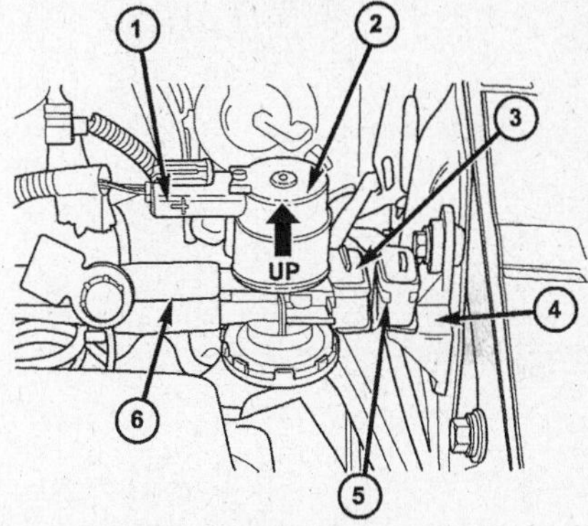

1 - DCP Electrical Connector
2 - DCP Solenoid - Note Proper Orientation
3 - New Bushing w/Narrow Slot
4 - Plastic Body Mounting Bracket
5 - Isolating U-Bracket
6 - Evaporative Vapor Line Connection

LTV0500000000146

Fig. 18 DCP solenoid replacement

5. Install new isolation U-bracket into plastic body mounting bracket.
6. Install DCP solenoid. Ensure it is correctly oriented.
7. Install vapor lines and electrical connector.

Fuel Cap Difficult To Remove

2002

On some of these models the fuel cap may be difficult to remove.

This condition may be caused by the fuel cap.

To correct this condition, install revised fuel cap (P/N 52102464AB).

TIGHTENING SPECIFICATIONS

Year	Component	Torque Ft. Lbs.
2002–04	Air Cleaner	93①
	Air Conditioning Compressor	20
	Air Conditioning Compressor Bracket	30
	Camshaft Sprocket	50
	Camshaft Thrust Plate	18
	Connecting Rod	33
	Cylinder Head	②
	Crankshaft Damper	80
	Engine Mount Through Bolt	48
	Exhaust Manifold	④
	Exhaust Pipe To Manifold	23
	Front Cover	③
	Front Engine Mount	30
	Fuel Hose Clamp	28
	Fuel Pump Module	55
	Fuel Tank	65
	Fuel Tank Bracket, Large	⑥
	Fuel Tank Bracket, Small	45①
	Fuel Tank Heat Shield To Body	25①
	Fuel Tank Heat Shield To Tank	85①
	Fuel Injector Rail	100①
	Idler Pulley	35
	Intake Manifold	④
	Main Bearing	⑤
	Main Bearing Cap Brace	35
	Main Bearing Brace	35
	Power Steering Gear Fitting	38
	Rear Engine Mount	18
	Rocker Arm	21
	Thermostat	16
	Torque Converter	28
	Valve Cover	77①
	Vibration Damper	80
	Water Pump	22
	Water Pump Pulley	21

①— Inch lbs.
②— Refer to "Cylinder Head, Replace" for tightening specifications and sequence.
③— 1/4 inch cover to block bolts, 60 inch lbs.; 5/16 inch cover to block bolts, 16 ft. lbs; 1/4 inch cover to pan bolts, 84 inch lbs.;
④— Refer to "Intake Manifold, Replace" for tightening specifications and sequence.
⑤— Refer to "Main & Rod Bearings" for tightening specifications and sequence.
⑥— Bolts, 25 ft. lbs.; nuts, 45 ft. lbs.

4.7L Engine

NOTE: Air Bag Equipped Models, Refer To "Air Bag System Precautions" Located In The Front Of This Manual For System Disarming & Arming Procedures.

NOTE: Refer To "Computer Relearn Procedures" Located In The Front Of This Manual When Battery Power To The Computer Has Been Interrupted.

NOTE: Prior To Performing Any Service Operations Listed In This Section, Consult The "Technical Service Bulletins" Section For Related Information.

INDEX

PRECAUTIONS

Air Bag Systems

Refer to "Air Bag System Precautions" in the front of this manual for system disarming and arming procedures.

Battery Ground Cable

Prior to service, disconnect battery ground cable and isolate as required.

Fuel System Pressure Relief

1. Remove fuel cap and fuel pump relay from PDC.
2. Start and run engine until it stalls.
3. Attempt to start engine until it will no longer run.
4. Turn ignition key to OFF position.
5. Disconnect any fuel injector connector.
6. Attach one end of suitable 18 gauge, or smaller, jumper wire to either injector terminal.
7. Connect other end of jumper wire to positive battery terminal.
8. Connect one end of second jumper wire to remaining injector terminal.
9. Momentarily touch other end of second jumper wire to negative battery terminal for no more than a few seconds. **Do not power injector for more than a few seconds.**
10. Place suitable rag below fuel line quick connect fitting on fuel rail.
11. Disconnect quick connect fitting.
12. Install fuel pump relay and clear stored Diagnostic Trouble Codes (DTCs).

COMPRESSION PRESSURES

Correct compression pressure for these engines is 120–150 psi; maximum variation between cylinders is 30 psi.

ENGINE MOUNT

REPLACE

2002–04

FRONT

1. Raise and support vehicle, then drain cooling system into suitable container.
2. Disconnect two hydraulic fan drive high pressure lines. Discard O-rings.
3. Disconnect hydraulic fan drive low pressure line.

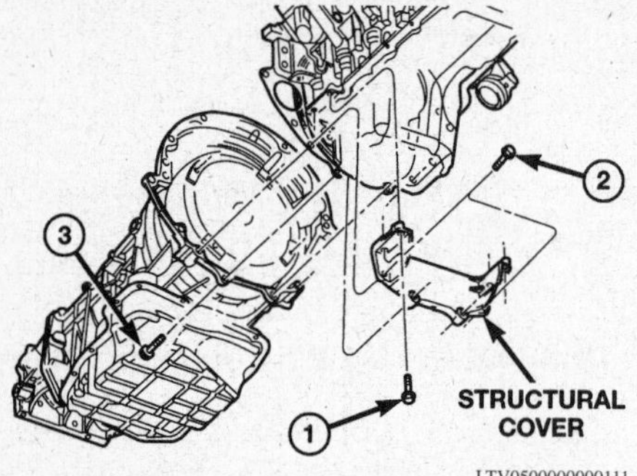

Fig. 1 Structural collar loosening & tightening sequence

4. Remove two fan shroud lower mounting bolts.
5. Lower vehicle and disconnect fan control solenoid electrical connector.
6. Disconnect and position upper radiator hose aside.
7. Disconnect power steering gear cooler outlet and fluid return hoses.
8. Remove two upper mounting bolts and fan shroud with drive.
9. Remove oil filter.
10. Support engine using suitable jack and wood block across full width of oil pan.
11. Remove four engine block to insulator mounting bolts and through bolt nut
12. Raise engine slightly, then remove through bolt and insulator mount.
13. Reverse procedure to install.

REAR

1. Raise and support vehicle.
2. Support transmission using suitable jack.
3. Remove through bolt locknut and insulator to transmission mounting bolts.
4. Raise transmission slightly, then remove through bolt and mount.
5. Reverse procedure to install.

2005–06

Refer to "3.7L Engine" section for engine replacement procedures.

ENGINE

REPLACE

2002–04

1. Remove mounting bolts and front fascia.
2. Raise and support vehicle.
3. Remove exhaust crossover pipe from manifold.
4. Disconnect two lower lefthand and one lower righthand ground straps.
5. Disconnect Crankshaft Position (CKP) sensor.
6. Loosen righthand exhaust pipe to manifold mounting bolts.
7. Remove eight structural collar mounting bolts in sequence, **Fig. 1.**
8. Pivot exhaust pipe downward and remove structural collar.

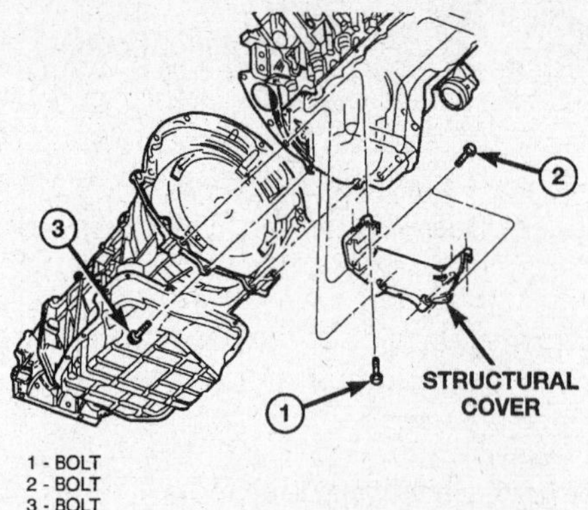

Fig. 2 Structural collar tightening sequence

9. Remove starter motor lower mounting bolt.
10. Support starter motor with hand and remove upper mounting bolt.
11. Lower starter slightly and disconnect solenoid electrical connector.
12. Remove battery cable and solenoid terminal wire.
13. Remove starter motor.
14. Remove rubber splash shield.
15. Drain coolant into suitable container.
16. Remove torque converter mounting bolts.
17. Remove transmission to engine mounting bolts.
18. Disconnect engine block heater power cable.
19. Lower vehicle.
20. Remove throttle body resonator and inlet hose.
21. Disconnect throttle and speed control cables.
22. Disconnect lefthand and righthand crankcase breathers tube.
23. Recover air conditioning refrigerant as outlined in "Air Conditioning" chapter.
24. Disconnect two hydraulic fan drive high pressure lines and one low pressure return hose.
25. Remove two fan shroud lower mounting bolts.
26. Disconnect fan control solenoid electrical connector.
27. Disconnect and position upper radiator hose aside.
28. Disconnect power steering gear cooler outlet and fluid return hoses.
29. Remove two upper mounting bolts, then the shroud and fan drive.
30. Rotate belt tensioner until it contacts stop, then remove drive belt and slowly rotate tensioner into freearm position.
31. Remove mounting bolts and position power steering pump aside with lines connected.
32. Disconnect air conditioning compressor clutch coil connector.
33. Remove mounting bolts, then the suction and discharge lines. Plug or tape fittings.
34. Remove mounting bolts and position air conditioning compressor aside.
35. Disconnect transmission cooler lines at radiator.

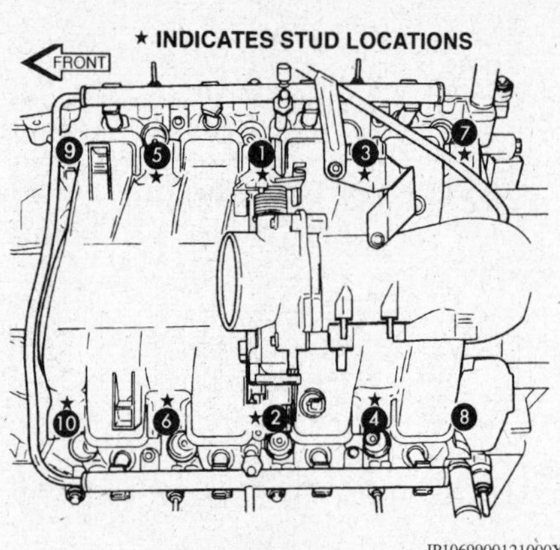

Fig. 3 Intake manifold tightening sequence

36. Disconnect thermostat lower radiator hose.
37. Remove headlamps.
38. Remove hood latch and brace mounting nuts.
39. Mark radiator upper crossmember for installation alignment.
40. Remove mounting bolts and radiator upper crossmember.
41. Remove headlamp mounting module.
42. Remove mounting bolts and condenser.
43. Remove radiator as outlined under "Radiator, Replace."
44. Disconnect cap, remove mounting nut and disconnect B+ terminal.
45. Disconnect field wire connector.
46. Remove mounting bolts and position alternator aside.
47. Disconnect heater hoses from timing chain cover.
48. Disconnect Intake Air Temperature (IAT) sensor and fuel injector connectors.
49. Disconnect Throttle Position (TP) sensor and Idle Air Control (IAC) motor connectors.
50. Disconnect engine oil pressure switch and Engine Coolant Temperature (ECT) sensor connectors.
51. Disconnect Manifold Absolute Pressure (MAP) and Camshaft Position (CMP) sensors' connectors.
52. Disconnect coil over plugs' connectors.
53. Relieve fuel pressure as outlined under "Precautions."
54. Disconnect fuel rail supply line.
55. Support engine using engine lifting fixture tool No. 8347, or equivalent.
56. Disconnect lefthand and righthand cowl body ground strap.
57. Support transmission using suitable jack.
58. Remove engine mounting through bolts.
59. Raise engine slightly, then remove lefthand and righthand engine mounts.
60. Remove engine.
61. Reverse procedure to install. **Torque** rear structural cover mounting bolts to 40 ft. lbs., in sequence, **Fig. 2.**

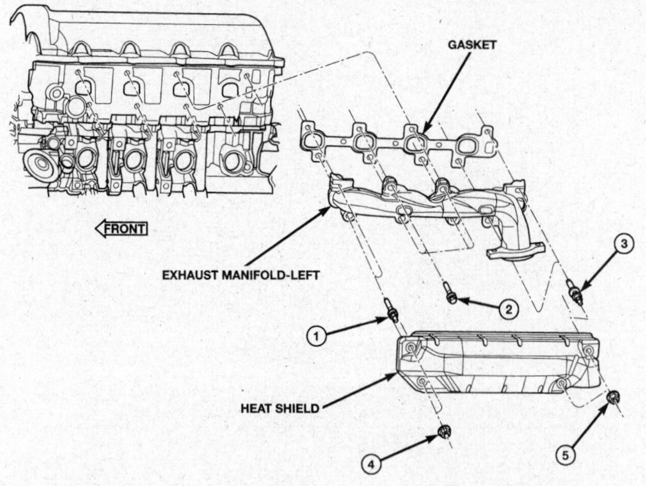

ITEM	DESCRIPTION	TORQUE	ITEM	DESCRIPTION	TORQUE
1	Stud (Qty 2)	25 N·m (18 ft. lbs.)	4	Nut (Qty 2)	8 N·m (72 in. lbs.), then loosen 45 degrees
2	Bolt (Qty 4)		5	Nut (Qty 2)	
3	Stud (Qty 2)				

JP1069900123000X

Fig. 4 Lefthand exhaust manifold replacement

ITEM	DESCRIPTION	TORQUE	ITEM	DESCRIPTION	TORQUE
1	Stud (Qty 2)	25 N·m (18 ft. lbs.)	4	Nut (Qty 2)	8 N·m (72 in. lbs.), then loosen 45 degrees
2	Bolt (Qty 4)		5	Nut (Qty 2)	
3	Stud (Qty 2)				

JP1069900122000X

Fig. 5 Righthand exhaust manifold replacement

2005–06

1. Remove mounting nuts and strut tower support.
2. Relieve fuel pressure as outlined under "Precautions."
3. Disconnect fuel rail supply line.
4. Disconnect two lower lefthand and one lower righthand ground straps.
5. Remove lefthand and righthand engine mounting through bolts.
6. Disconnect Crankshaft Position (CKP) sensor.
7. Raise and support vehicle.
8. Remove exhaust crossover pipe from manifold.
9. Remove lefthand exhaust pipe from exhaust manifold.
10. Loosen righthand exhaust pipe to manifold mounting bolts.
11. Remove eight structural collar mounting bolts in sequence, **Fig. 2.**
12. Pivot exhaust pipe downward and remove structural collar.
13. Remove starter motor lower mounting bolt.
14. Support starter motor with hand and remove upper mounting bolt.
15. Lower starter slightly and disconnect solenoid electrical connector.
16. Remove battery cable and solenoid terminal wire.
17. Remove starter motor.
18. Drain coolant into suitable container.
19. Remove torque converter mounting bolts.
20. Remove transmission to engine mounting bolts.
21. Disconnect engine block heater power cable.
22. Lower vehicle.
23. Remove throttle body resonator and inlet hose.
24. Disconnect throttle and speed control cables.
25. Disconnect lefthand and righthand crankcase breathers tube.
26. Recover air conditioning refrigerant as outlined in "Air Conditioning" chapter.
27. Remove mounting nuts and refrigerant lines.
28. Remove and discard dual plane seals. Plug or tape fittings.
29. Disconnect air conditioning compressor connector.
30. Loosen accessory mounting bracket bolt, then mounting bolts and air conditioning compressor.
31. Disconnect fan electrical connector.
32. Remove two mounting bolts, then the shroud and fan drive.
33. Rotate belt tensioner until it contacts stop, then remove drive belt and slowly rotate tensioner into freearm position.
34. Disconnect transmission cooler lines at radiator.
35. Disconnect upper and lower radiator hoses.
36. Remove radiator as outlined under "Radiator, Replace."
37. Mark radiator upper crossmember for installation alignment.
38. Remove mounting bolts and radiator upper crossmember.
39. Disconnect condenser discharge line.
40. Remove receiver/drier mounting bolt.
41. Disconnect receiver/drier tube from condenser.
42. Remove four mounting bolts and condenser.
43. Remove transmission oil cooler.
44. Disconnect cap, remove mounting nut and disconnect B+ terminal.
45. Disconnect field wire connector.
46. Remove mounting bolts and position alternator aside.
47. Disconnect heater hoses from timing chain cover and intake manifold.
48. Disconnect Intake Air Temperature (IAT) sensor and fuel injector connectors.
49. Disconnect Throttle Position (TP) sensor and Idle Air Control (IAC) motor connectors.
50. Disconnect engine oil pressure switch and Engine Coolant Temperature (ECT) sensor connectors.
51. Disconnect Manifold Absolute Pressure (MAP) and Camshaft Position (CMP) sensors' connectors.
52. Disconnect coil over plugs' connectors.
53. Disconnect throttle body and intake manifold vacuum lines.
54. Remove mounting bolts and position power steering pump aside with lines connected.
55. Support engine using engine lifting fixture tool No. 8347, or equivalent.
56. Disconnect lefthand and righthand cowl body ground strap.
57. Support transmission using suitable jack.
58. Remove engine.
59. Reverse procedure to install. **Torque** rear structural cover mounting bolts to 40 ft. lbs., in sequence, **Fig. 2.**

INTAKE MANIFOLD

REPLACE

1. Remove air cleaner housing and throttle body resonator.
2. Disconnect throttle and speed control cables.
3. Disconnect Manifold Absolute Pressure (MAP) and Intake Air Temperature (IAT) sensors' connectors.
4. Disconnect Throttle Position (TP) and Engine Coolant Temperature (ECT) sensors' connectors.
5. Disconnect Idle Air Control (IAC) motor connector.
6. Disconnect vapor purge, brake booster, speed control servo and Positive Crankcase Ventilation (PCV) hoses.
7. Rotate belt tensioner until it contacts

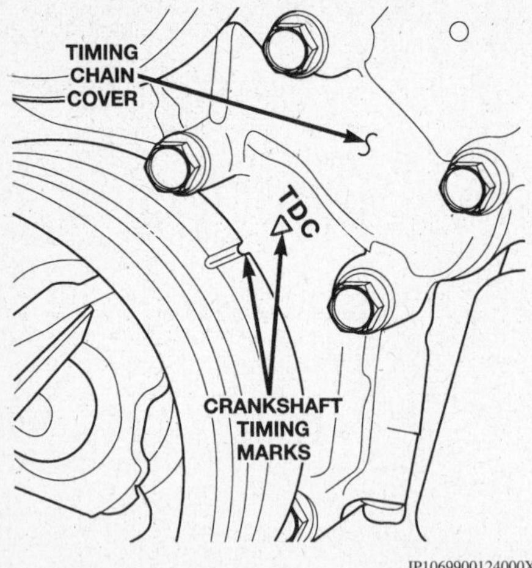

Fig. 6 TDC indicator alignment

stop, then remove drive belt and slowly rotate tensioner into freearm position.

8. Disconnect cap, remove mounting nut and disconnect B+ terminal.
9. Disconnect field wire connector.
10. Remove mounting bolts and position alternator aside.
11. Disconnect electrical connector, then remove mounting bolts and position air conditioning compressor aside.
12. Disconnect lefthand and righthand radio suppressor straps.
13. Disconnect connector, then remove mounting bolts and ignition coil towers.
14. Remove top oil dipstick tube mounting bolt and ground strap.
15. Relieve fuel system pressure as outlined under "Precautions."
16. Disconnect fuel rail line and fuel injector connectors.
17. Remove four fuel rail mounting bolts.
18. Gently rock and pull left, then righthand fuel rail until injectors clear machined holes.
19. Remove fuel rail with injectors.
20. Remove three mounting bolts and throttle body.
21. Drain coolant into suitable container.
22. Disconnect connector and remove ECT sensor.
23. Remove cowl to hood seal.
24. Remove righthand side lifting stud.
25. Remove intake manifold mounting bolts in reverse of tightening sequence, **Fig. 3.**
26. Remove intake manifold.
27. Reverse procedure to install. **Torque** intake manifold mounting bolts to 105 inch lbs, **Fig. 3.**

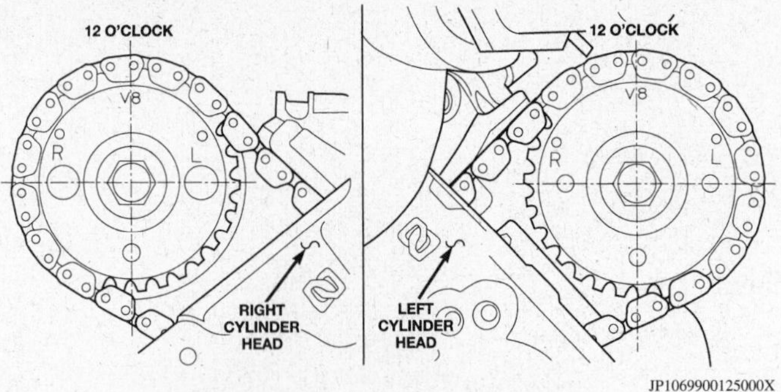

Fig. 7 Camshaft alignment

EXHAUST MANIFOLD

REPLACE

Lefthand

1. Raise and support vehicle, then disconnect exhaust pipe at manifold.
2. Lower vehicle and remove air cleaner housing and tube.
3. Remove two heat shield front mounting nuts, then raise and support vehicle.
4. Remove rear mounting nuts and heat shield, **Fig. 4.**
5. Lower vehicle and remove exhaust manifold upper mounting bolts.
6. Raise and support vehicle.
7. Remove lower mounting bolts and exhaust manifold.
8. Reverse procedure to install.

Righthand

1. Remove battery.
2. Remove mounting bolts and set Power Distribution Center (PDC) aside.
3. Remove battery tray and washer fluid reservoir.
4. Rotate belt tensioner until it contacts stop, then remove drive belt and slowly rotate tensioner into freearm position.
5. Disconnect electrical connector, then remove mounting bolts and position air conditioning compressor aside.
6. Remove air conditioning accumulator support bracket mounting bolts.
7. Drain coolant into suitable container.
8. Remove engine heater hoses.
9. Remove mounting nuts and exhaust heat shield, **Fig. 5.**
10. Remove exhaust manifold upper mounting bolts.
11. Raise and support vehicle.
12. Disconnect exhaust pipe from manifold.
13. Remove mounting bolts and position starter motor aside.
14. Remove lower mounting bolts and exhaust manifold.
15. Reverse procedure to install.

CYLINDER HEAD

REPLACE

2002-04

1. Raise and support vehicle, then disconnect lefthand and/or exhaust pipe from manifold.
2. Drain coolant into suitable container.
3. Lower vehicle.
4. Remove intake manifold as outlined under "Intake Manifold, Replace."
5. Remove valve cover as outlined under "Valve Cover, Replace."
6. **If removing righthand cylinder head,** remove oil fill housing.
7. **On all models,** rotate belt tensioner until it contacts stop, then remove drive belt and slowly rotate tensioner into freearm position.
8. Remove mounting bolts and position power steering pump aside with lines connected.
9. Rotate crankshaft until damper timing mark is aligned with TDC indicator, **Fig. 6.**
10. Ensure camshaft sprocket V8 mark is aligned, **Fig. 7.** Crankshaft may have to be rotate one turn to align V8 marks.
11. Remove mounting bolt, then the vibration damper using three-jaw puller tool No. 1026 and insert tool No. 8513, or equivalents.
12. Remove as outlined under "Front Cover, Replace."
13. Lock secondary timing chains to idler sprocket using secondary chain holder tool No. 8515, or equivalent, **Fig. 8.**
14. Mark secondary timing chain one link on each side of V8 mark on cam drive gear for installation alignment
15. Collapse and pin primary chain tensioner, then cover pan opening.
16. Remove secondary chain tensioner.
17. Remove cylinder head access plug, **Fig. 9.**
18. Remove secondary chain guide.
19. Remove mounting bolt and camshaft drive gear.
20. Remove mounting bolts and cylinder head. Discard gasket.
21. Reverse procedure to install, noting the following:
    a. Replace head bolts if threads are necked down.
    b. Lubricate M11 bolts with suitable oil and install hand tight.
    c. Coat four M8 bolts with suitable

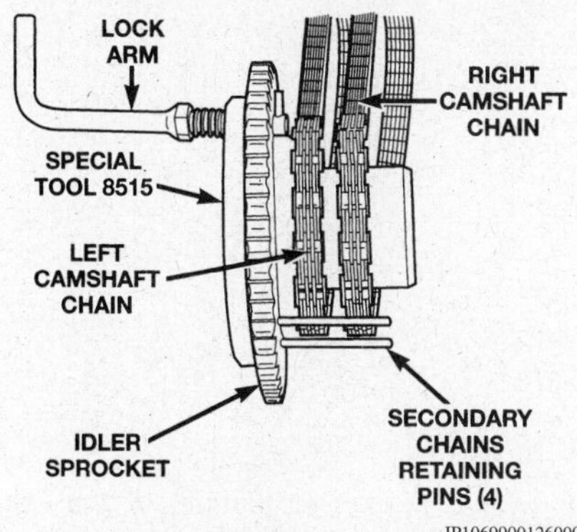

Fig. 8 Secondary timing chain lock

lock and seal adhesive, then install hand tight.
   d. **Torque** bolts Nos. 1–10 to 20 ft. lbs., in sequence, **Fig. 10.**
   e. Ensure bolts at **torqued** to 20 ft. lbs., by repeating sequence without loosening bolts.
   f. **Torque** bolts Nos. 11–14 to 10 ft. lbs.
   g. Tighten bolt Nos. 1–10 an additional 90°.
   h. Final tighten bolt Nos. 1–10 an additional 90°.
   i. **Torque** bolt Nos. 11–14 to 19 ft. lbs.
   j. Press damper onto crankshaft using assembly tool No. 8512-A, or equivalent.

2005-06

1. Raise and support vehicle, then disconnect lefthand and/or exhaust pipe from manifold.
2. Drain coolant into suitable container.
3. Lower vehicle.
4. Remove intake manifold as outlined under "Intake Manifold, Replace."
5. **If removing lefthand cylinder head,** proceed as follows:
   a. Siphon fluid, then remove master cylinder primary and secondary brake lines.
   b. Disconnect brake fluid level switch.
   c. Remove two mounting nuts and master cylinder.
   d. Remove power brake booster as outlined in "Power Brake Unit" chapter.
6. **On all models,** remove valve cover as outlined under "Valve Cover, Replace."
7. Rotate belt tensioner until it contacts stop, then remove drive belt and slowly rotate tensioner into freearm position.
8. Drain cooling system into suitable container.
9. Remove mounting bolts and upper fan shroud.
10. Loosen fan blade/viscous fan drive from water pump using spanner wrench tool No. 6958 and adapter pin tools No. 8346, or equivalents. adapters. Mounting nut turns counterclockwise.
11. Disconnect connector, then remove mounting bolts and fan shroud with viscous fan.

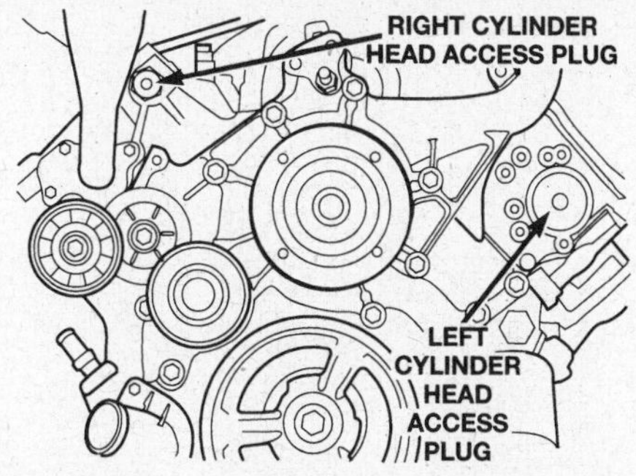

Fig. 9 Cylinder head access plug replacement

12. **If removing lefthand cylinder head,** remove mounting bolts and position power steering pump aside with lines connected.
13. **If removing righthand cylinder head,** remove oil fill housing.
14. **On all models,** rotate crankshaft until damper timing mark is aligned with TDC indicator, **Fig. 6.**
15. Ensure camshaft sprocket V8 mark is aligned, **Fig. 7.** Crankshaft may have to be rotated one turn to align V8 marks.
16. Remove mounting bolt, then the vibration damper using three-jaw puller tool No. 1026 and insert tool No. 8513, or equivalents.
17. Remove as outlined under "Front Cover, Replace."
18. Lock secondary timing chains to idler sprocket using secondary chain holder tool No. 8515, or equivalent, **Fig. 8.**
19. Mark secondary timing chain one link on each side of V8 mark on cam drive gear for installation alignment.
20. Collapse and pin primary chain tensioner, then cover pan opening.
21. Remove secondary chain tensioner.
22. Remove cylinder head access plug, **Fig. 9.**
23. Remove secondary chain guide.
24. Remove mounting bolt and camshaft drive gear.
25. Remove mounting bolts and cylinder head. Discard gasket.
26. Reverse procedure to install, noting the following:
   a. Replace head bolts if threads are necked down.
   b. Lubricate M11 bolts with suitable oil and install hand tight.
   c. Coat four M8 bolts with suitable lock and seal adhesive, then install hand tight.
   d. **Torque** bolts Nos. 1–10 to 15 ft. lbs in sequence, **Fig. 10.**
   e. **Torque** bolts Nos. 1–10 to 35 ft. lbs in sequence.
   f. **Torque** bolts Nos. 11–14 to 18 ft. lbs.
   g. Tighten bolt Nos. 1–10 an additional 90°.
   h. **Torque** bolt Nos. 11–14 to 22 ft. lbs.
   i. Press damper onto crankshaft using assembly tool No. 8512-A, or equivalent.

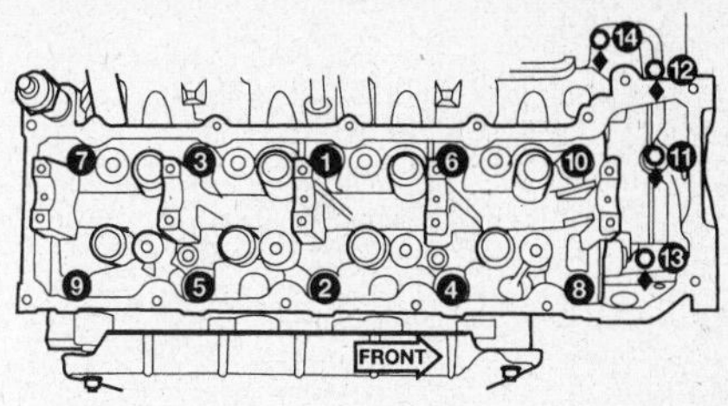

Fig. 10 Cylinder head bolt tightening sequence

VALVE COVER

REPLACE

Left

1. Remove resonator and air inlet hose.
2. Disconnect injector connectors and unclip injector harness.
3. Route injector harness in front of valve cover.
4. Remove mounting bolts, valve cover and gasket.
5. Reverse procedure to install. Gasket may be used, again.

Right

1. Remove battery, air cleaner housing and throttle body resonator.
2. Disconnect battery lugs from PDC.
3. Unclip PDC and move to left of fender well.
4. Drain coolant below heater hose level into suitable container.
5. Remove air conditioning compressor mounting bolts and position compressor aside.
6. Remove battery tray, then disconnect battery temperature sensor.
7. Remove heater hoses from front of engine.
8. Loosen accumulator bracket.
9. Disconnect ignition coil and injector connectors.
10. Remove PCV hose and oil fill tube.
11. Unclip harness from valve cover.
12. Remove rear breather tube and filter assembly.
13. Remove valve cover mounting bolts, then the valve cover and gasket.
14. Reverse procedure to install, noting the following:
   a. Gasket may be used again, provided there are no tears, cuts or deformation.
   b. Tighten bolts to specifications.

VALVE ARRANGEMENT

This engine uses four valves per cylinder. Exhaust valves are on the exhaust manifold side of the cylinder head, intake valves are on the intake manifold side of the cylinder head.

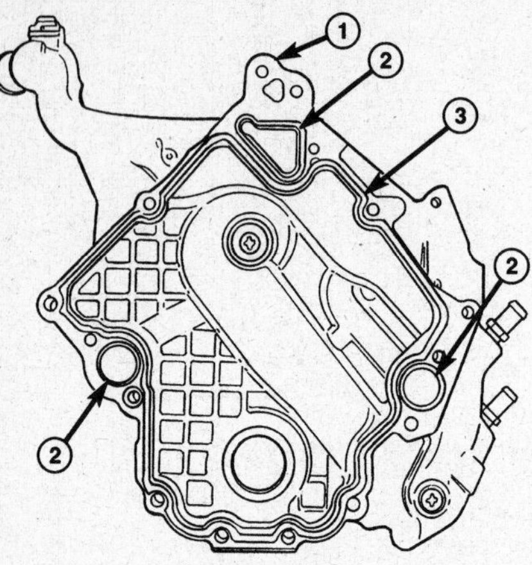

Fig. 11 Front cover sealer application

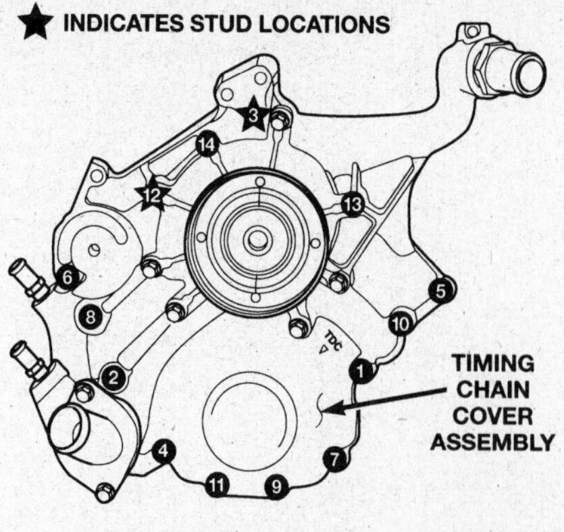

Fig. 12 Front cover tightening sequence

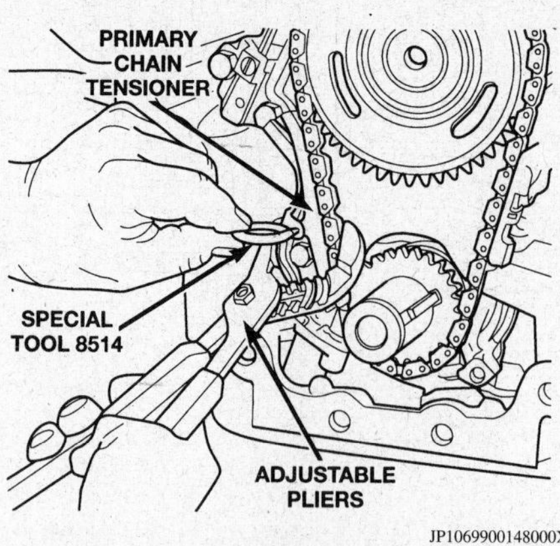

Fig. 13 Collapsing primary tensioner

CAMSHAFT LOBE LIFT SPECIFICATIONS

Intake ....443 inch
Intake (H.O.) ....472 inch
Exhaust ....429 inch

VALVE ADJUSTMENT

These engines are equipped with hydraulic lash adjusters. There is no provision for adjustment.

ROCKER ARMS

REPLACE

1. Remove valve cover as outlined under "Valve Cover, Replace."
2. Rotate crankshaft until cylinder No. 1 is at exhaust TDC, then remove cylinders Nos. 3 and 5 rocker arms.
3. Press downward on valve spring and remove rocker arm using valve spring compressor tool No. 8516, or equivalent.
4. Rotate crankshaft until cylinder No. 1 is at TDC stroke TDC, then remove cylinders Nos. 2 and 8 rocker arms.
5. Rotate crankshaft until cylinder No. 3 is at compression TDC, then remove cylinder Nos. 4 and 6 rocker arm s.
6. Rotate crankshaft until cylinder No. 2 is at TDC compression TDC, then remove cylinders Nos. 1 and 7 rocker arms.
7. Reverse procedure to install, noting the following:
   a. Coat rocker arms with suitable, clean engine oil.
   b. Ensure concave pocket on rocker arm is installed over lash adjuster.

HYDRAULIC LIFTERS

REPLACE

1. Remove Valve cover as outlined under "Valve Cover, Replace."
2. Remove rocker arms as outlined under "Rocker Arm, Replace."
3. Remove lash adjuster.
4. Reverse procedure to install. Ensure lash adjuster is at least partially full of clean engine oil prior to installation.

CRANKSHAFT DAMPER

REPLACE

2002–04

1. Rotate belt tensioner until it contacts stop, then remove drive belt and slowly rotate tensioner into freearm position.
2. Remove mounting bolt, then the vibration damper using three-jaw puller tool No. 1026 and insert tool No. 8513, or equivalents.
3. Reverse procedure to install. Press damper onto crankshaft using assembly tool No. 8512-A, or equivalent.

2005–06

1. Rotate belt tensioner until it contacts stop, then remove drive belt and slowly rotate tensioner into freearm position.
2. Drain cooling system into suitable container.
3. Remove mounting bolts and upper fan shroud.
4. Loosen fan blade/viscous fan drive from water pump using spanner wrench tool No. 6958 and adapter pin tools No. 8346, or equivalents. adapters. Mounting nut turns counterclockwise.
5. Disconnect connector, then remove mounting bolts and fan shroud with viscous fan.
6. Disconnect fan connector inside radiator shroud.
7. Remove mounting bolt, then the vibration damper using three-jaw puller tool No. 1026 and insert tool No. 8513, or equivalents.
8. Reverse procedure to install. Press damper onto crankshaft using assembly tool No. 8512-A, or equivalent.

FRONT COVER

REPLACE

1. Drain coolant into suitable container.
2. Remove viscous fan assembly and radiator shroud.
3. Disconnect heater hoses from front cover.
4. Disconnect lower radiator hose at engine.
5. Rotate belt tensioner until it contacts stop, then remove drive belt and slowly rotate tensioner into freearm position.
6. Remove mounting bolt, then the vibration damper using three-jaw puller tool No. 1026 and insert tool No. 8513, or equivalents.
7. Disconnect cap, remove mounting nut and disconnect B+ terminal.
8. Disconnect field wire connector.
9. Remove mounting bolts and position alternator aside.
10. Recover air conditioning refrigerant as outlined in "Air Conditioning" chapter.
11. Remove mounting bolts and position power steering pump aside with lines connected.
12. Disconnect air conditioning compressor clutch coil connector.
13. Remove mounting bolts, then the suction and discharge lines. Plug or tape fittings.
14. Remove mounting bolts and position air conditioning compressor aside.
15. Remove mounting bolts and cover. **Do not remove water pump.**
16. Reverse procedure to install, noting the following:
    a. Apply .118–.157 inch thick bead of suitable engine RTV sealer to front cover, **Fig. 11.**
    b. **Torque** mounting bolts to 43 ft. lbs., in sequence, **Fig. 12.**
17. Press damper onto crankshaft using assembly tool No. 8512-A, or equivalent.

TIMING CHAIN

REPLACE

Removal

1. Drain coolant into suitable container.
2. Remove lefthand and righthand valve covers as outlined under "Valve Cover, Replace."
3. **On 2002–04 models,** proceed as follows:
   a. Disconnect two hydraulic fan drive

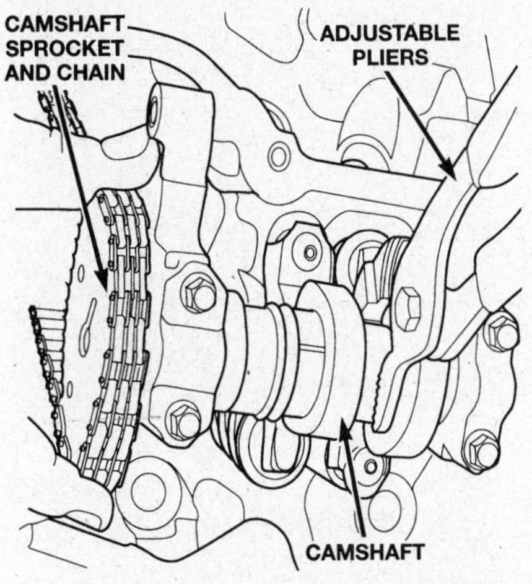

Fig. 14 Lefthand camshaft sprocket removal

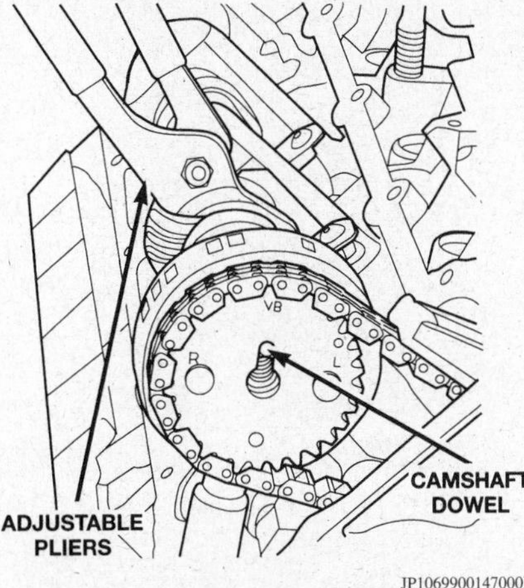

Fig. 15 Righthand camshaft sprocket removal

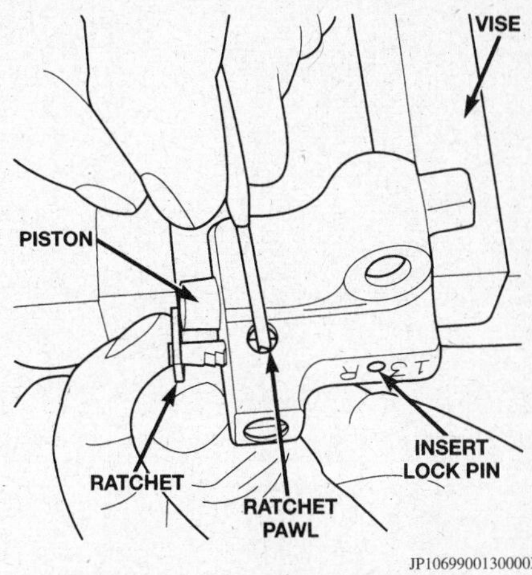

Fig. 16 Tensioner reset

high pressure lines and one low pressure return hose.
   b. Remove two fan shroud lower mounting bolts.
   c. Disconnect fan control solenoid electrical connector.
   d. Disconnect and position upper radiator hose aside.
   e. Disconnect power steering gear cooler outlet and fluid return hoses.
   f. Remove two upper mounting bolts, then the shroud and fan drive.
4. **On 2005–06 models,** proceed as follows:
   a. Remove mounting bolts and upper fan shroud.
   b. Loosen fan blade/viscous fan drive from water pump using spanner wrench tool No. 6958 and adapter pin tools No. 8346, or equivalents. adapters. Mounting nut turns counterclockwise.
   c. Disconnect connector, then remove mounting bolts and fan shroud with viscous fan.
5. **On all models,** rotate crankshaft until damper timing mark is aligned with TDC indicator, **Fig. 6.**
6. Ensure camshaft sprocket V8 mark is aligned, **Fig. 7.** Crankshaft may have to be rotate one turn to align V8 marks.
7. Remove mounting bolts and position power steering pump aside with lines connected.
8. Remove cylinder head access plug, **Fig. 9.**
9. Remove oil fill housing.
10. Rotate belt tensioner until it contacts stop, then remove drive belt and slowly rotate tensioner into freearm position.
11. Remove mounting bolt, then the vibration damper using three-jaw puller tool No. 1026 and insert tool No. 8513, or equivalents.
12. Remove timing chain cover as outlined under "Front Cover, Replace."
13. Collapse and pin primary timing chain tensioner, **Fig. 13.** Cover pan opening.
14. Remove secondary chain tensioners.
15. Remove Camshaft Position (CMP) sensor from righthand cylinder head.
16. Remove lefthand and righthand camshaft sprocket mounting bolts.
17. Remove lefthand camshaft sprocket by slowly rotate camshaft approximately 15° clockwise to neutral position while holding lefthand camshaft using suitable adjustable pliers, **Fig. 14.**
18. Remove righthand camshaft sprocket by slowly rotating camshaft approximately 45° counterclockwise to a neutral position, while holding righthand camshaft using suitable adjustable pliers, **Fig. 15.**
19. Remove idler sprocket mounting bolt.
20. Remove primary and secondary timing chains by sliding idler and crankshaft sprockets forward together.
21. Remove pivoting tensioner arms and chain guides.
22. Remove chain tensioner.

Installation

1. Lightly compress secondary timing chain tensioner piston until piston step is flush with tensioner body using suitable vice.
2. Release ratchet pawl by pulling pawl back through access hole on side of tensioner.
3. Push ratchet device to .079 inch from tensioner body while holding pawl back, then install lock pin tool No. 8514, or equivalent, into hole on front of tensioner, **Fig. 16.**
4. Transfer piston spring force to lock pin by slowly opening vise.
5. Position primary timing chain tensioner over oil pump and tighten mounting bolts into tensioner bracket lower two holes.
6. Install righthand side tensioner arm, apply suitable lock and seal to threads and tighten mounting bolt.
7. Install and tighten lefthand chain guide. **Silver bolts retain guides to cylinder heads and the black bolts retain guides to block.**
8. Install lefthand side tensioner arm, apply suitable lock and seal to threads and tighten mounting bolt.
9. Install and tighten righthand chain guide. **Silver bolts retain guides to cylinder heads and the black bolts retain guides to block.**
10. Install both secondary chains onto idler sprocket. Align two plated links to be visible through idler sprocket openings in, **Fig. 17.**
11. Lock timing chains to idler sprocket using secondary chain holder tool No. 8515, or equivalent, **Fig. 18.**
12. Align primary chain double plated links with timing mark on idler sprocket at 12 o'clock position.
13. Align primary chain single plated link with timing mark on crankshaft sprocket at 6 o'clock position.
14. Lubricate idler shaft and bushings with suitable, clean engine oil.
15. Install chains, crankshaft and idler sprockets as an assembly.
16. Guide both secondary chains through block and cylinder head openings, then maintain chain tension by attaching suitable elastic strap.
17. Align lefthand camshaft sprocket L dot to chain plated link and righthand camshaft sprocket R dot to chain plated link on chain
18. Remove special tool No. 8515 and attach both sprockets to camshafts. **Do not tighten now.**
19. Ensure all plated links and camshaft sprockets' V8 marks are properly aligned.
20. Install and tighten both secondary chain tensioners.
21. Lubricate washer with suitable engine oil, then install and tighten idler sprocket bolt.
22. Remove tensioners' lock pins from all tensioners. **Do not manually extend tensioners' ratchets.**
23. Tighten camshaft sprocket bolts using spanner tool No. 6958 with adaptor pins tools Nos. 8346, or equivalents, using special tools outlined, **Figs. 19 and 20.**
24. Rotate engine two full revolutions and ensure all timing marks align, **Fig. 17.**
25. Lubricate chains with suitable, clean engine oil.
26. Ensure idler gear end play is .004–.010 inch. If end play is more than

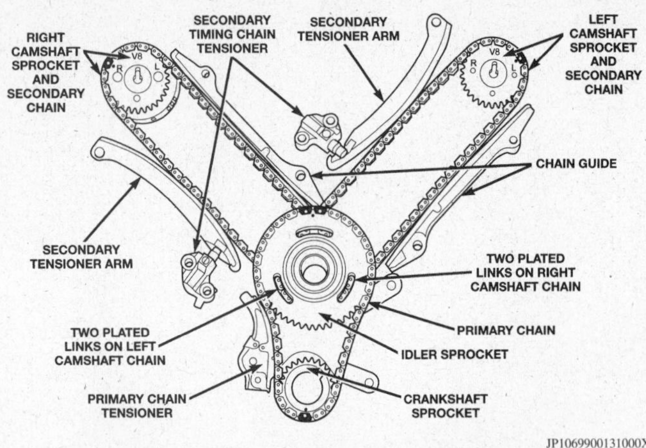

Fig. 17 Timing chain alignment

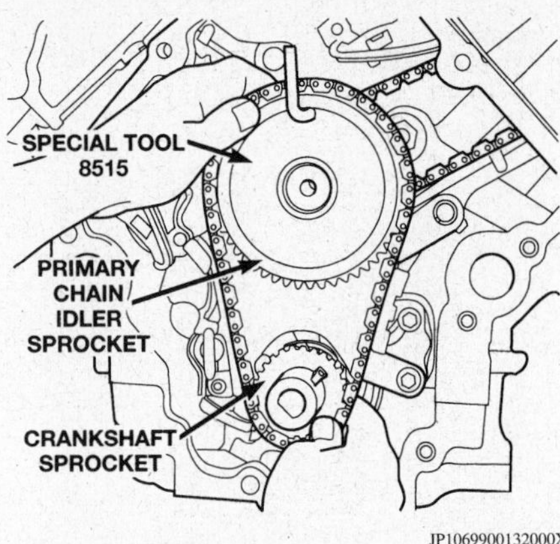

Fig. 18 Timing chain installation

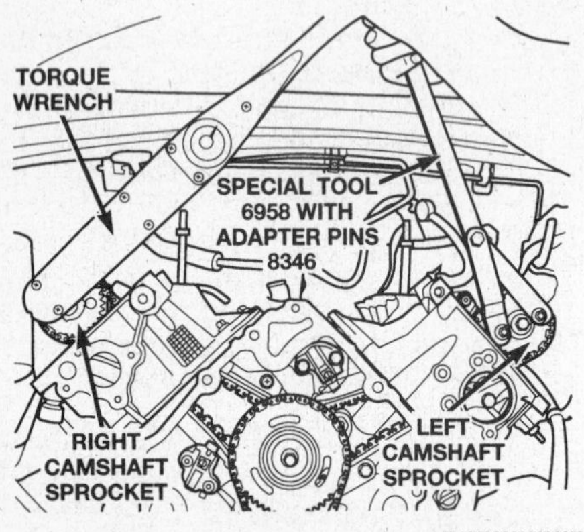

Fig. 19 Righthand camshaft sprocket installation

specified, replace idler sprocket.

27. Install timing chain cover as outlined under "Front Cover, Replace."
28. Press damper onto crankshaft using assembly tool No. 8512-A, or equivalent.
29. Install valve covers as outlined under "Valve Cover, Replace.".
30. Coat access plug with Teflon thread sealant, then install and tighten into righthand cylinder head.
31. Install oil fill housing.
32. Install access plug into lefthand cylinder head.
33. Install power steering pump and radiator fan shroud.

TIMING CHAIN TENSIONER

REPLACE

Refer to "Timing Chain, Replace" for tensioner replacement procedures.

CAMSHAFT

REPLACE

When the timing chain is removed and the cylinder heads are still installed, do not forcefully rotate the camshafts or crankshaft independently of each other.

Removal

1. Remove valve cover as outlined under "Valve Cover, Replace."
2. Rotate crankshaft until damper timing mark is aligned with TDC indicator, **Fig. 6.**
3. Ensure camshaft sprocket V8 mark is aligned, **Fig. 7.** Crankshaft may have to be rotate one turn to align V8 marks.
4. Mark one link on secondary timing chain on both sides V8 mark on camshaft sprocket for installation alignment.
5. Loosen camshaft sprocket mounting bolt. Leave bolt snug against sprocket. **Do not remove mounting bolt.**
6. Lock timing chain by tapping wedge tool No. 8350, or equivalent, between timing chain strands, then against tensioner arm and guide, **Figs. 21 through Fig. 23.**
7. Remove mounting bolt and camshaft sprocket while holding camshaft with suitable adjustable pliers.
8. **When removing lefthand camshaft,** gently rotate camshaft 15° clockwise until camshaft is in neutral, no valve-load position.
9. **When removing righthand camshaft,** gently rotate camshaft 45° counterclockwise until camshaft is in neutral, no valve-load position.
10. **On all models,** starting outside and working in, loosen bearing cap mounting bolts ½ turn at a time until all load is off of bearing caps.
11. Mark rocker arms prior to camshaft removal.
12. Remove bearing caps and camshaft.

Installation

1. Lubricate camshaft journals with suitable, clean engine oil.
2. **On lefthand camshaft,** position camshaft in neutral position with sprocket dowel near 1 o'clock position.
3. **On righthand camshaft,** position camshaft in neutral position with sprocket dowel near 10 o'clock position.

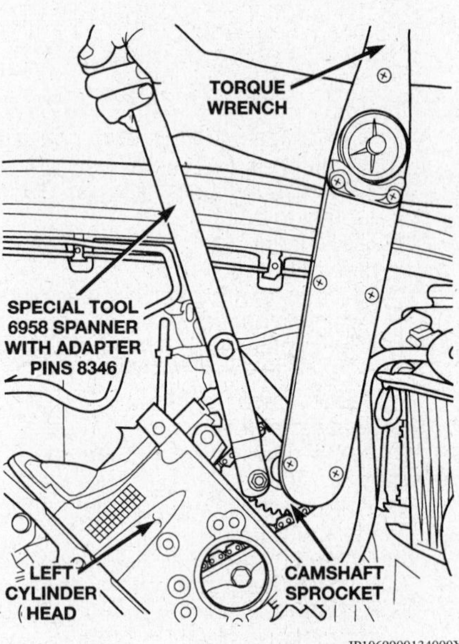

Fig. 20 Lefthand camshaft sprocket installation

4. **On all models,** install bearing caps and hand tighten mounting bolts.
5. Tighten bearing cap mounting bolts in ½ turn increments, starting in middle and working outward,
6. **Torque** bearing cap bolts to 100 inch lbs. in sequence.
7. Position camshaft sprocket into chain aligning V8 mark with links marked during removal.
8. Rotate camshaft until sprocket dowel is aligned with sprocket slot using suitable adjustable pliers.
9. Remove excess oil from camshaft sprocket mounting bolt.
10. Install sprocket and hand tighten mounting bolt.
11. Remove timing chain wedge tool.
12. Tighten camshaft sprocket mounting bolt using spanner wrench tool No. 6958 with adapter pins tools No. 8346, or equivalent, **Fig. 20.**
13. Install valve cover as outlined under "Valve Cover, Replace."

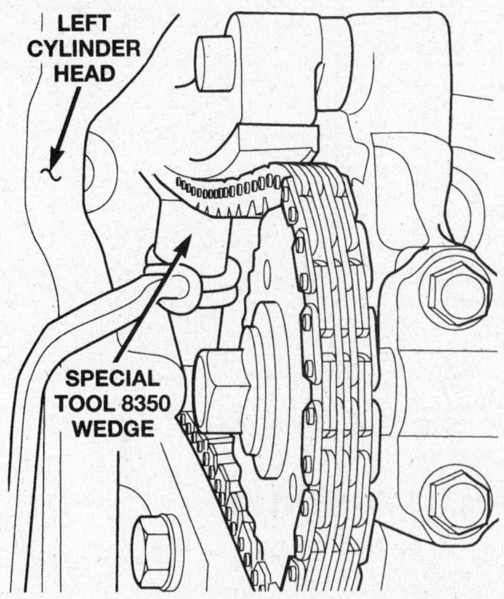

Fig. 21 Timing chain locking. Lefthand

PISTON & ROD ASSEMBLY

Pistons are marked with an F on the piston pin bore surface. When installing piston, ensure F faces front of engine, **Fig. 24.** The connecting rod oil slinger slot faces the front of the engine.

PISTONS, PINS & RINGS

Position piston ring end gaps, **Fig. 25.** It is important that expander ring gap (5) is at least 45° from the side rail gaps, but not on the piston pin center or on the thrust direction.

MAIN & ROD BEARINGS

Connecting Rod

1. Position bearing onto connecting rod. Ensure bearing shell and connecting rod holes align.
2. Lubricate bearing surface with suitable, clean engine oil.
3. Rotate crankshaft until connecting rod journal is on center of cylinder bore.
4. Insert rod and piston into cylinder bore and carefully position connecting rod guides tool No. 8507, or equivalent, over crankshaft journal.
5. Tap piston down in cylinder bore using suitable hammer handle, at the same time, guide connecting rod into position on rod journal.
6. Lubricate new rod bolts and bearing surfaces with suitable engine oil.
7. **Torque** connecting rod cap and bearing to 20 ft. lbs.
8. Final tighten bolts an additional 90°.

Main Bearing

Main bearings are available in three grades, **Fig. 26.**

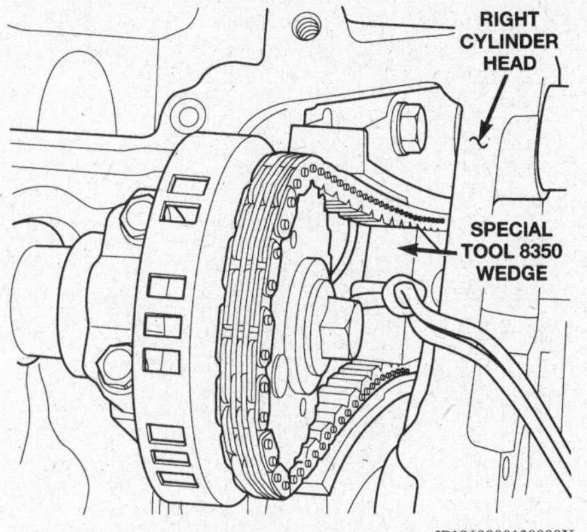

Fig. 22 Timing chain locking. Righthand

REMOVAL

1. Remove bedplate mounting bolts. Mark three stud bolts to installation alignment.
2. Remove bedplate by prying at cast pry points, **Fig. 27. Do not pry on or damage bedplate to cylinder block mating surface. Do not drop or damage lower main bearing halves.**
3. Remove connecting rods from crankshaft.
4. Remove crankshaft and target wheel.

INSTALLATION

1. Lubricate upper main bearing halves with suitable, clean engine oil.
2. Apply sealant to target wheel mounting screws.
3. Install target wheel and tighten mounting screws.
4. Install crankshaft and thrust washers.
5. Apply .100 inch bead of Mopar Gen II Silicone Rubber Adhesive sealant, or equivalent, to cylinder block-to-bedplate mating surface, **Fig. 28.**
6. Coat crankshaft main bearing journals with suitable, clean engine oil and position bedplate onto cylinder block.
7. Lubricate bedplate mounting bolts with suitable, clean engine oil.
8. Ensure stud bolts are in proper positions.
9. **Torque** bolts A–K to 40 ft. lbs., in sequence, **Fig. 29.**
10. **Torque** bolts 1–10 to 25 inch lbs. in sequence.
11. Tighten bolts 1–10 an additional 90° in sequence.
12. **Torque** bolts A1–A6 to 20 ft. lbs.

CRANKSHAFT SEAL

REPLACE

1. Rotate belt tensioner until it contacts stop, then remove drive belt and slowly rotate tensioner into freearm position.
2. Remove mounting bolts and position air conditioning compressor aside.
3. Drain cooling system into suitable container.
4. Remove upper radiator hose.
5. Disconnect fan electrical connector mounted inside radiator shroud.

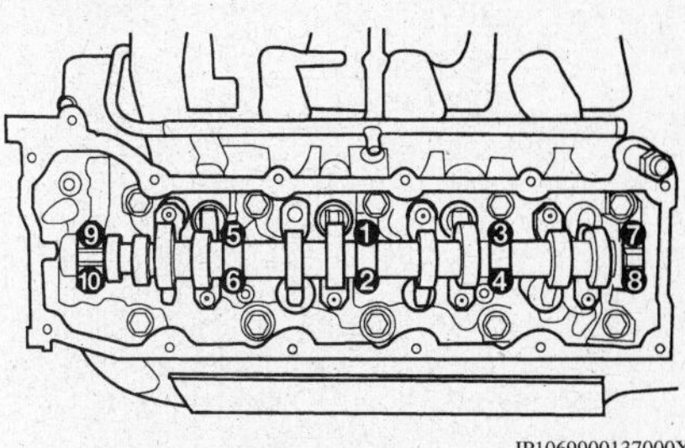

Fig. 23 Camshaft bearing cap tightening sequence

6. Remove mounting bolts, radiator cooling fan and shroud.
7. Remove mounting bolt, then the vibration damper using three-jaw puller tool No. 1026 and insert tool No. 8513, or equivalents.
8. Remove crankshaft front seal using front crankshaft deal remover tool No. 8511, or equivalent.
9. Reverse procedure to install using crankshaft seal installer tool No. 8348 and crankshaft damper tool No. 8512, or equivalent.

CRANKSHAFT REAR OIL SEAL

REPLACE

Removal

1. Remove transmission as outlined in **MOTOR's "Domestic Transmission, In-Vehicle Service" or "Transmission Service DVD."**
2. Remove flexplate.
3. Remove seal using seal remover tool No. 8506, or equivalent.

Installation

1. Lubricate crankshaft flange with suitable engine oil.
2. Position magnetic seal guide tool No. 8349-2, or equivalent.
3. Position crankshaft rear oil seal onto guide.
4. Install seal using seal installer tool No. 8349 and driver tool No. C-4171, or equivalents. Tap seal into place until it is seated against crankshaft bore.
5. Install flexplate and transmission as outlined in **MOTOR's "Domestic Transmission, In-Vehicle Service" or "Transmission Service DVD."**

OIL PAN

REPLACE

2002–04

1. Raise and support vehicle.
2. Loosen righthand exhaust pipe to manifold mounting bolts.
3. Remove eight structural collar mounting bolts in sequence, **Fig. 1.**

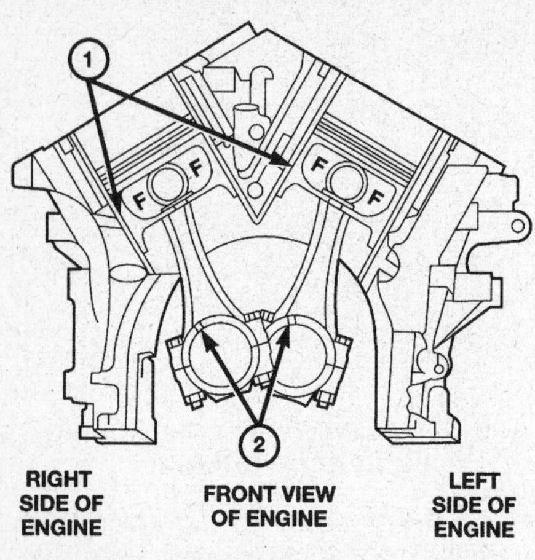

1. MAJOR THRUST SIDE OF PISTON
2. OIL SLINGER SLOT

LTV0500000000114

Fig. 24 Piston orientation

4. Pivot exhaust pipe downward and remove structural collar.
5. Remove exhaust system Y-pipe.
6. Remove mounting bolts and position starter motor aside.
7. Drain engine oil into suitable container.
8. Disconnect transmission cooler lines from oil pan stud and position aside.
9. Remove mounting bolts and oil pan. **Do not pry on oil pan gasket.** Oil pan gasket is mounted to cylinder block in three locations and remains attached to block.
10. Remove oil pump pick up tube and pan gasket.
11. Reverse procedure to install, noting the following:
    a. Install new pick-up tub O-ring.
    b. **Torque** pan mounting bolts to 11 ft. lbs., in sequence, **Fig. 30.**

2005-06

1. Support engine using engine support fixture tool No. 8534, or equivalent. **Do not raise engine now.**
2. Loosen left and righthand engine mount through bolts. **Do not remove bolts.**
3. Remove eight structural collar mounting bolts in sequence, **Fig. 2.**
4. Drain engine oil into suitable container.
5. Raise engine only to provide removal clearance. Ensure there is proper clearance at fan shroud to fan and cowl to intake manifold.
6. Remove mounting bolts and oil pan. **Do not pry on oil pan or oil pan gasket.**
7. Remove mounting bolt and oil pump pick-up tube.
8. Reverse procedure to install, noting the following:
    a. Install new oil pump pick-up tube O-ring.
    b. **Torque** pan mounting bolts to 11 ft. lbs., in sequence, **Fig. 30.**

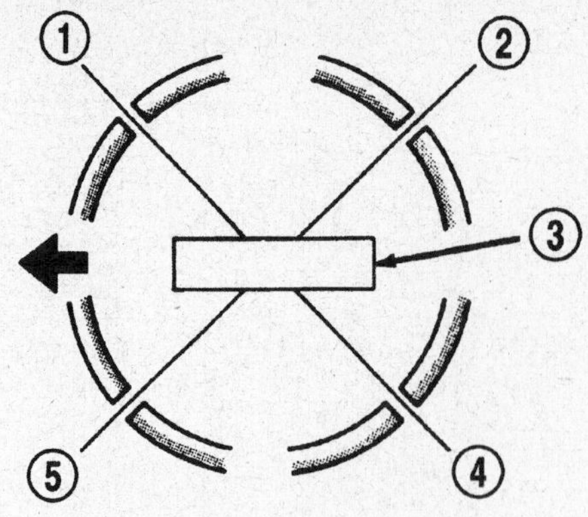

1 SIDE RAIL UPPER
2 NO. 1 RING GAP
3 PISTON PIN
4 SIDE RAIL LOWER
5 NO. 2 RING GAP AND SPACER EXPANDER GAP

LTV0500000000115

Fig. 25 Piston ring end gap position

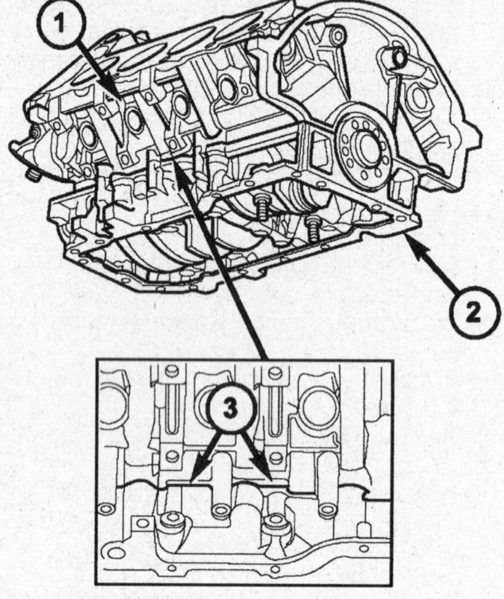

1. CYLINDER BLOCK
2. BEDPLATE
3. PRY POINT

LTV0500000000116

Fig. 27 Bedplate replacement

OIL PUMP

REPLACE

1. Remove oil pan and pick-up tube as outlined under "Oil Pan, Replace."
2. Remove timing chain cover as outlined under "Front Cover, Replace."
3. Remove timing chains and tensioners as outlined under "Timing Chain, Replace."
4. Remove four bolts, primary timing chain tensioner and oil pump.
5. Reverse procedure to install.

OIL PUMP SERVICE

Oil pump is an assembly. There are no part numbers for components. If the oil pump is not functioning or out of specification it must be replaced as an assembly.

GRADE MARKING	SIZE mm (in.)	FOR USE WITH JOURNAL SIZE
A	.008 mm (.0004 in.) U/S	63.488-63.496 mm (2.4996-2.4999 in.)
B	STANDARD	63.496-63.504 mm (2.4999-2.5002 in.)
C	.008 mm (.0004 in.) O/S	63.504-63.512 mm (2.5002-2.5005 in.)

JP1069900140000X

Fig. 26 Main bearing grade

Disassemble

1. Remove mounting screws and cover plate.
2. Remove inner and outer rotors.
3. If required, remove pressure relief valve and drive roll pin from pump housing, then remove cup plug, spring and valve.
4. Once oil pressure relief valve, cup plug, and pin are removed, pump assembly must be replaced.

Inspection

1. If pump cover is scratched or grooved, oil pump should be replaced.
2. Lay suitable straight edge across pump cover surface. If clearance is .001 inch, or more, replace oil pump.
3. Measure outer rotor thickness. If measurement is more than .472 inch, replace oil pump.
4. Measure outer rotor diameter. Of measurement is 3.382 inches, or less, replace oil pump.
5. Measure inner rotor thickness. If measurement is .472 inch, or more, replace oil pump.
6. Slide outer rotor into oil pump body.
7. Press outer rotor to one side, then measure clearance between outer rotor and body. If measurement is .009 inch, or more, replace oil pump.
8. Install inner rotor into oil pump body.
9. Measure clearance between inner and outer rotors. If measurement is .006 inch, or more, replace oil pump.
10. Place suitable straight edge across oil pump body. If clearance between straight edge and rotors is .001 inch, or more, replace oil pump.

Assemble

1. Install inner and outer rotors.
2. Install cover and tighten mounting bolts.
3. Prime oil pump by filling rotor cavity with suitable engine oil.

BELT TENSION DATA

The belt tensioner on this engine is equipped with an indexing tang on the back

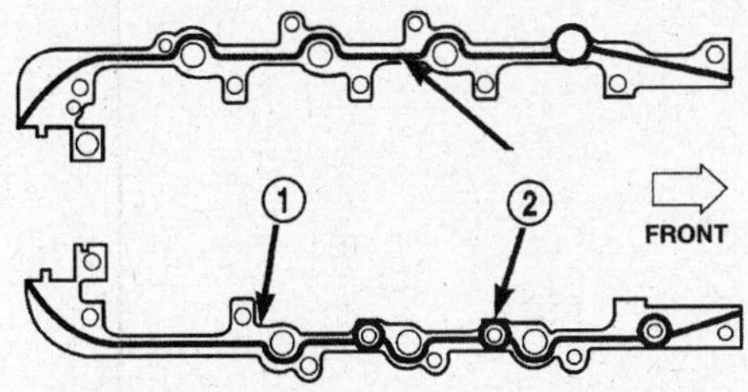

1. CYLINDER BLOCK
2. SEALANT BEAD LOCATION

LTV0500000000117

Fig. 28 Cylinder block-to-bedplate sealant bead location

of the tensioner and an indexing stop on the tensioner housing, **Fig. 31.** If distance between indexing tang and indexing stop is more than .94 inches, replace the belt.

SERPENTINE DRIVE BELT

Replacement

1. Rotate belt tensioner until it contacts stop.
2. Remove drive belt and slowly rotate tensioner into freearm position.
3. Reverse procedure to install. After installation, inspect belt wear indicator, **Fig. 31.** If wear exceeds .94 inches, replace belt.

Routing

Refer to **Fig. 32** for serpentine drive belt routing.

COOLING SYSTEM BLEED

1. Remove cooling system bleed plug from radiator upper hose inlet housing.
2. Fill coolant system until coolant flows out of bleed hole.
3. Install bleed plug, then fill radiator to top and install cap.
4. Adjust reservoir level to FULL mark.
5. Fill reservoir to Full mark.
6. Start and operate engine with heater control in HEAT position.
7. When engine reaches normal operating temperature, shut engine off and allow it to cool.
8. Adjust reservoir level
9. Preform procedure three times to purge system of all air.

THERMOSTAT

REPLACE

1. Drain coolant into suitable container.
2. Raise and support vehicle, then remove splash shield.
3. Remove clamp and thermostat housing lower radiator hose.
4. Remove mounting bolts, housing and thermostat.
5. Reverse procedure to install.

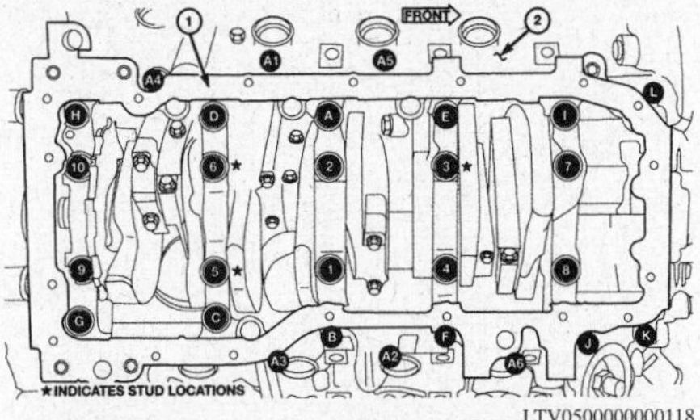

LTV0500000000118

Fig. 29 Main bearing cap & bedplate tightening sequence

WATER PUMP

REPLACE

1. Drain coolant into suitable container.
2. Rotate belt tensioner until it contacts stop, then remove drive belt and slowly rotate tensioner into freearm position.
3. Remove water pump lower radiator hose.
4. Remove pump mounting bolts and one stud bolt, then the water pump. Discard gasket.
5. Reverse procedure to install.

RADIATOR

REPLACE

2002–04

1. Drain radiator coolant into suitable container.
2. Remove viscous fan mounting nut. **Do not remove fan assembly now.**
3. Remove mounting bolts and front grille.
4. Remove two radiator mounting bolts.
5. Disconnect transmission cooler lines.
6. Disconnect fan motor and harness electrical connectors.
7. Disconnect power steering cooler line from cooler and filter.
8. Remove upper and lower radiator hoses, then the overflow hose.
9. Remove air inlet duct from grille.
10. Disconnect two fan drive high hydraulic pressure fluid lines, and one low pressure return hose.
11. Remove radiator. **Do not damage radiator fins or condenser.**
12. Reverse procedure to install.

2005–06

1. Drain radiator coolant into suitable container.
2. Remove six upper push pins and front grill.
3. Remove two radiator mounting bolts.
4. Disconnect transmission cooler lines.
5. Disconnect fan control solenoid electrical connector.
6. Disconnect power steering cooling line from cooler and filter.
7. Disconnect upper and lower radiator hoses, then the overflow hose.
8. Remove air inlet duct at grille.
9. Disconnect two hydraulic fan drive high pressure fluid lines an low pressure return hose.

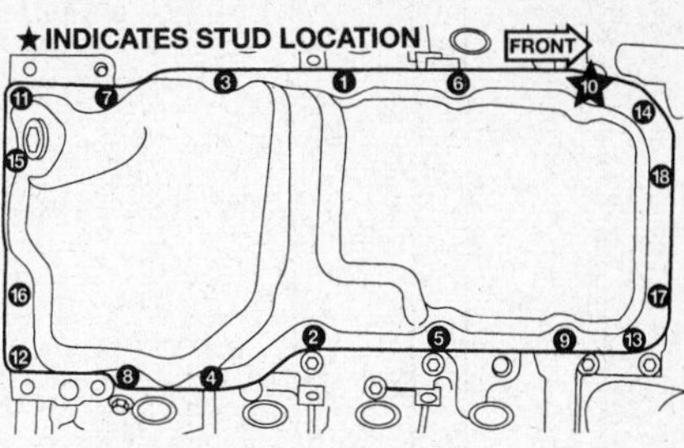

JP1069900142000X

Fig. 30 Oil pan tightening sequence

10. Remove radiator. **Do not scrape fins against other components.**
11. **Do not disturb air conditioning condenser.**
12. Reverse procedure to install, noting the following:
    a. Guide two radiator alignment dowels through rubber air seals, then through air conditioning support brackets.
    b. Hose clamps' tangs must be positioned straight down.

FUEL PUMP

REPLACE

2002–04

Refer to the "4.0L Engine" section for fuel pump replacement procedures.

2005–06

Refer to the "3.7L Engine" section for fuel pump replacement procedures.

FUEL FILTER

REPLACE

2002–04

Refer to the "4.0L Engine" section for fuel filter replacement procedures.

2005–06

Refer to the "3.7L Engine" section for fuel filter replacement procedures.

TECHNICAL SERVICE BULLETINS

Engine Compartment Ticking

2002–04

On some of these models there may be a ticking sound when the engine is idling. Condition may be more noticeable in colder ambient temperatures.

This condition may be caused by mechanical contact between Duty Cycle Purge (DCP) solenoid and body.

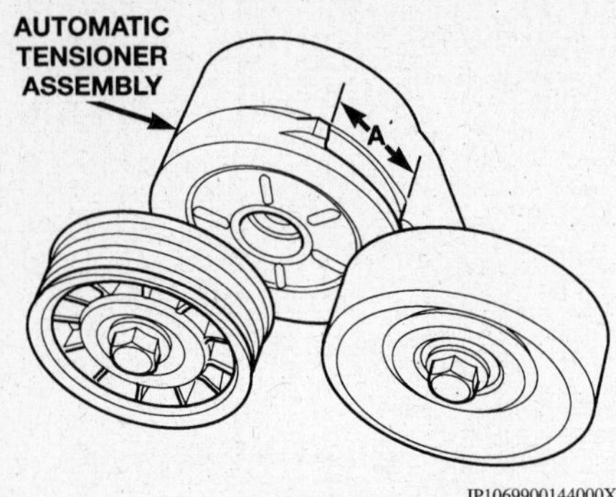

Fig. 31 Belt wear indicator

To correct this condition, install narrow slot bushing (part No. 53030987) and new isolation U-bracket (part No. 05114514AA), as follows:

1. Turn ignition switch to OFF position, disconnect DCP solenoid evaporative vapor lines and electrical connector, **Fig. 33.**
2. Remove DCP solenoid from plastic body mounting bracket by lifting it upward.
3. Record rubber bushing orientation.
4. Remove bushing with wide slot and install replacement bushing (part No. 53030987) with narrow slot.
5. Install new isolation U-bracket (P/N 05114514AA) into plastic body mounting bracket.

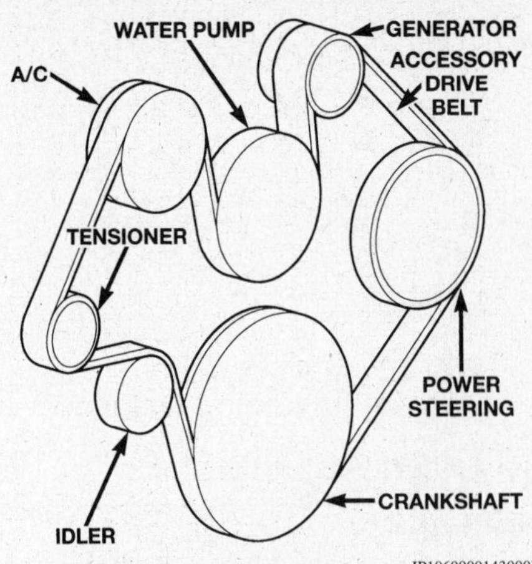

Fig. 32 Serpentine drive belt routing

6. Install DCP solenoid. Ensure it is correctly oriented.
7. Install vapor lines and electrical connector.

Fuel Cap Difficult To Remove

2002

On some of these models the fuel cap may be difficult to remove.

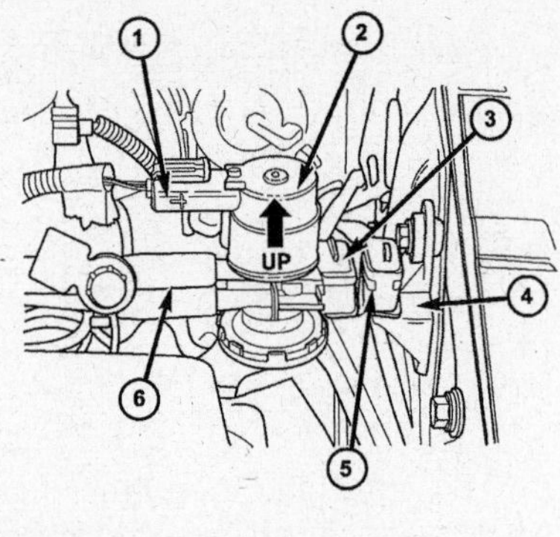

1 - DCP Electrical Connector
2 - DCP Solenoid - Note Proper Orientation
3 - New Bushing w/Narrow Slot
4 - Plastic Body Mounting Bracket
5 - Isolating U-Bracket
6 - Evaporative Vapor Line Connection

LTV0500000000147

Fig. 33 DCP solenoid replacement

This condition may be caused by the fuel cap.

To correct this condition, install revised fuel cap (par No. 52102464AB).

TIGHTENING SPECIFICATIONS

Year	Component	Torque Ft. Lbs.
2002–06	Access Plug	60
	Air Conditioning Compressor, Front (2002–04)	35–50
	Air Conditioning Compressor, Rear (2002–04)	25–35
	Air Conditioning Compressor (2005–06)	41
	Air Conditioning Compressor To Accessory Bracket (2005–06)	30
	Air Conditioning Compressor Line Fitting	18
	Alternator	⑨
	Camshaft Bearing Cap	⑥
	Camshaft Sprocket	90
	Connecting Rod	③
	Condenser	44①
	Crankshaft Damper Or Pulley	130
	Cylinder Head	②
	Engine Mount Through Bolt	70
	Exhaust Manifold	18
	Exhaust Manifold Heat Shield	⑦
	Fan Shroud (2002–04)	50①
	Fan Shroud (2005–06)	95①
	Flexplate	45
	Front Engine Mount (2002–04)	45
	Front Engine Mount (2005–06)	22
	Idler Sprocket	25
	Intake Manifold	④
	Oil Pan	⑤
	Oil Pan Drain Plug	25
	Oil Pump	21
	Oil Pump Cover	105①
	Oil Pump Tube	20
	Primary Timing Chain Tensioner	21
	Rear Engine Mount	34
	Structural Cover	⑧
	Target Wheel	12
	Thermostat	115①
	Throttle Body	105①
	Timing Chain Guide	21
	Timing Chain Tensioner Arm	12
	Transmission To Engine	30
	Valve Cover	105①
	Vibration Damper Or Pulley	130
	Water Pump	43

①— Inch lbs.
②— Refer to "Cylinder Head, Replace" for tightening specifications and sequence.
③— Refer to "Main & Rod Bearings" for tightening specifications and sequence.
④— Refer to "Intake Manifold, Replace" for tightening specifications and sequence.
⑤— Refer to "Oil Pan, Replace" for tightening specifications and sequence.
⑥— Refer to "Camshaft, Replace" for tightening specifications and sequence.
⑦— **Torque** to 72 inch lbs., then loosen 45°.
⑧— Refer to "Engine, Replace" for tightening specifications and sequence.
⑨— M8, 21 ft. lbs.; M10, 40 ft. lbs.

5.7L Engine

NOTE: Air Bag Equipped Models, Refer To "Air Bag System Precautions" Located In The Front Of This Manual For System Disarming & Arming Procedures.

NOTE: Refer To "Computer Relearn Procedures" Located In The Front Of This Manual When Battery Power To The Computer Has Been Interrupted.

NOTE: For Procedures Not Found In This Section, Refer To "5.7L Engine" Section In The "Full Size Trucks & Vans" Chapter.

INDEX

PRECAUTIONS

Air Bag Systems

Refer to "Air Bag System Precautions" in the front of this manual for system disarming and arming procedures.

Battery Ground Cable

Prior to service, disconnect battery ground cable and isolate as required.

Fuel System Pressure Relief

1. Remove fuel cap and fuel pump relay from PDC.
2. Start and run engine until it stalls.
3. Attempt to start engine until it will no longer run.
4. Turn ignition key to OFF position.
5. Disconnect any fuel injector connector.
6. Attach one end of suitable 18 gauge, or smaller, jumper wire to either injector terminal.
7. Connect other end of jumper wire to positive battery terminal.
8. Connect one end of second jumper wire to remaining injector terminal.
9. Momentarily touch other end of second jumper wire to negative battery terminal for no more than a few seconds. **Do not power injector for more than a few seconds.**
10. Place suitable rag below fuel line quick connect fitting on fuel rail.
11. Disconnect quick connect fitting.
12. Install fuel pump relay and clear stored Diagnostic Trouble Codes (DTCs).

COMPRESSION PRESSURES

The maximum variation between cylinders is 25%.

ENGINE MOUNT

REPLACE

Refer to "3.7L Engine" section for engine mount replacement procedures.

ENGINE

REPLACE

1. Remove mounting nuts and strut tower support, then the engine cover.
2. Relieve fuel system pressure as outlined in "Precautions."
3. Remove air cleaner air cleaner resonator and duct work.
4. Raise and support vehicle.
5. Drain cooling system into suitable container.
6. Release belt tension by rotating tensioner counterclockwise.
7. Rotate belt tensioner and remove belt, then gently release tensioner.
8. Position suitable container to catch power steering fluid that may exit hydraulic fan drive driven by power steering pump.
9. Disconnect two hydraulic fan drive high pressure lines. Discard fittings' O-rings.
10. Disconnect hydraulic fan drive low pressure return hose.
11. Remove two fan shroud lower mounting bolts.
12. Lower vehicle.
13. Disconnect fan control solenoid electrical connector.
14. Disconnect radiator upper hose and position side.
15. Disconnect power steering gear outlet and fluid return hoses at cooler.
16. Remove two upper mounting bolts, then the shroud and fan drive.
17. Remove mounting bolts and position air conditioning compressor aside with lines attached.
18. Disconnect cap, remove mounting nut and disconnect B+ terminal.
19. Disconnect field wire connector.

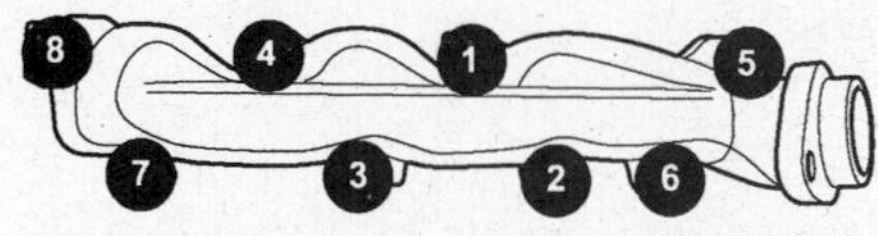

Fig. 1 Exhaust manifold loosening & tightening sequence (Part 1 of 2)

20. Remove mounting bolts and alternator.
21. Remove intake manifold as outlined under "Intake Manifold, Replace."
22. Remove ground wires from rear of each cylinder head.
23. Disconnect the heater hoses.
24. Remove mounting bolts and position power steering pump aside with lines attached.
25. Disconnect fuel supply line.
26. Raise and support vehicle, then drain engine oil into suitable container.
27. Remove front engine mount frame bolts and nuts.
28. Disconnect transmission oil cooler lines from oil pan bolt retainers.
29. Disconnect exhaust pipe at manifolds.
30. Disconnect wires, then remove mounting bolts and starter motor.
31. Remove mounting bolts and structural cover.
32. Remove drive plate to converter mounting bolts.
33. Remove oil pan to transmission and bell housing to engine bolt mounting bolts.
34. Support engine with lift fixture tools Nos. 8984 and 8984-UPD, or equivalent.
35. Separate from transmission and remove engine.
36. Reverse procedure to install.

INTAKE MANIFOLD

REPLACE

1. Remove engine cover.
2. Relieve fuel system pressure as outlined in "Precautions."
3. Remove air inlet hose.
4. Remove ignition wires from intake manifold.
5. Disconnect Manifold Absolute Pressure (MAP) sensor and fuel injectors' electrical connectors.
6. Disconnect Electrical Throttle Control (ETC) electrical connectors.
7. Remove intake manifold wire harness.
8. Disconnect brake booster, purge and Make Up Air (MUA) hoses.
9. Remove EGR tube from intake manifold.
10. Remove intake manifold bolts in crisscross pattern starting from outside and ending at middle.
11. Remove intake manifold.
12. Reverse procedure to install. **Torque** mounting bolts to 105 inch lbs. in crisscross pattern starting with middle bolts and working outward.

EXHAUST MANIFOLD

REPLACE

1. Raise and support vehicle.
2. Remove exhaust pipe to manifold bolts.
3. Remove engine mount to frame bolts.
4. Raise engine using suitable jack. **Do not damage engine harness.**
5. Remove engine mount and heat shield.
6. Remove mounting bolts in sequence, **Fig. 1,** and exhaust manifold.
7. Reverse procedure to install. **Torque** mounting bolts to 18 ft. lbs., in sequence, **Fig. 1.**

CYLINDER HEAD

REPLACE

1. Relieve fuel system pressure as outlined in "Precautions."
2. Disconnect fuel supply line.
3. Drain cooling system into suitable container.
4. Remove air cleaner resonator and duct work.
5. Remove closed crankcase ventilation system.
6. Disconnect exhaust pipe at manifolds.
7. Disconnect evaporative control system.
8. Disconnect heater hoses.
9. Remove mounting bolts and position power steering pump aside with lines attached.
10. Disconnect ignition coil connector.
11. Remove mounting bolts and ignition coil.
12. Remove mounting bolts and valve cover.
13. Remove intake manifold and throttle body as outlined under "Intake Manifold, Replace."
14. Loosen rocker shafts in sequence, **Fig. 2.**
15. Remove rocker shafts. Record locations for installation alignment. Rocker shafts are not interchangeable. Intake rocker arms are marked with an I.
16. **Do not remove rocker shaft retainers.**
17. Remove bolts in sequence **Fig. 3** and cylinder head. Discard gasket.
18. Reverse procedure to install, noting the following:
    a. Cylinder head gaskets are not interchangeable, they are marked L and R to indicate lefthand and righthand sides. Gaskets are also mark TOP to indicate up side.
    b. **Torque** M12 cylinder head bolts to 25 ft. lbs., and M8 bolts to 15 ft. lbs., in sequence, **Fig. 3.**
    c. **Torque** M12 head bolts to 40 ft. lbs., and ensure M8 bolts are at 15 ft. lbs., in sequence.
    d. Tighten M12 bolts an additional 90° in sequence.
    e. **Torque** M8 bolts to 25 ft. lbs., in sequence.
    f. **Torque** rocker shafts to 16 ft. lbs., in sequence, **Fig. 2.**
    g. **Torque** cover bolts to 70 inch lbs. in sequence, **Fig. 4.**

VALVE COVER

REPLACE

1. Disconnect ignition coil connector.

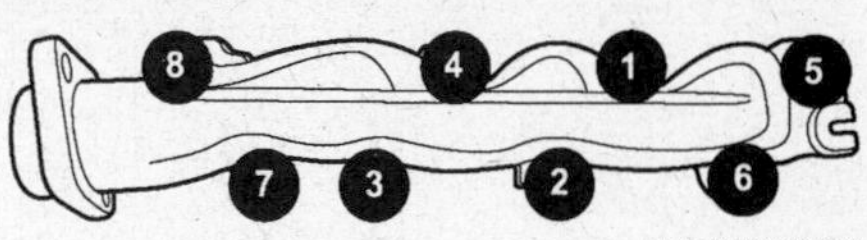

Fig. 1 Exhaust manifold loosening & tightening sequence (Part 2 of 2)

2. Remove mounting bolts and ignition coil.
3. Remove mounting bolts and valve cover.
4. Reverse procedure to install, noting the following:
    a. Ensure all double ended studs are in correct locations.
    b. Apply suitable dielectric grease to inside of spark plug boots.
    c. **Torque** cover bolts to 70 inch lbs., in sequence, **Fig. 4.**

CAMSHAFT LOBE LIFT SPECIFICATIONS

Intake ....472 inch
Exhaust ....460 inch

VALVE CLEARANCE SPECIFICATIONS

These engines are equipped with hydraulic tappets. The dry lash at the valve is .1181 inch.

VALVE ADJUSTMENT

These engines are equipped with hydraulic tappets. There are no provision for adjustment.

ROCKER ARMS

REPLACE

1. Disconnect ignition coil connector.
2. Remove mounting bolts and ignition coil.
3. Remove mounting bolts and valve cover.
4. Hold pushrods in place using pushrod retaining plate tool No. 9070, or equivalent.
5. Loosen rocker shafts in sequence, **Fig. 2.**
6. Remove rocker shafts. Record locations for installation alignment. Rocker shafts are not interchangeable. Intake rocker arms are marked with an I.
7. **Do not remove rocker shaft retainers.**
8. Reverse procedure to install, noting the following:
9. Reverse procedure to install, noting the following:
    a. **Torque** rocker shafts to 16 ft. lbs., in sequence, **Fig. 2.**
    b. **Torque** cover bolts to 70 inch lbs., in sequence, **Fig. 4.**

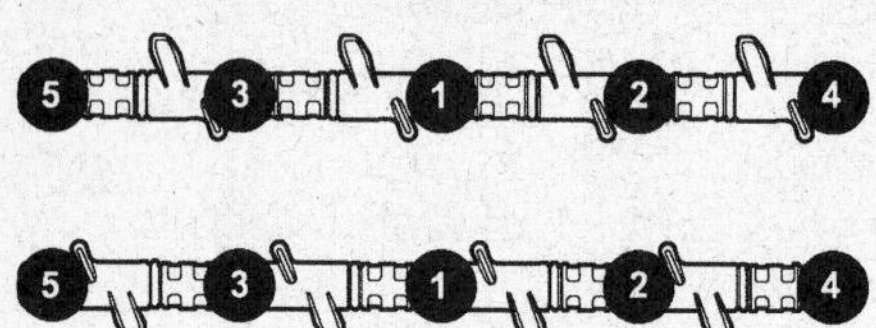

Fig. 2 Rocker shaft loosening & tightening sequence

PUSH RODS

1. Disconnect ignition coil connector.
2. Remove mounting bolts and ignition coil.
3. Remove mounting bolts and valve cover.
4. Hold pushrods in place using pushrod retaining plate tool No. 9070, or equivalent.
5. Loosen rocker shafts in sequence, **Fig. 2.**
6. Remove rocker shafts. Record locations for installation alignment. Rocker shafts are not interchangeable. Intake rocker arms are marked with an I.
7. Remove pushrods. Record pushrod location for installation alignment. Longer push rods are for exhaust side and shorter ones are for intake side.
8. Reverse procedure to install, noting the following:
   a. **Torque** rocker shafts to 16 ft. lbs., in sequence, **Fig. 2.**
   b. **Torque** cover bolts to 70 inch lbs., in sequence, **Fig. 4.**

HYDRAULIC LIFTERS

REPLACE

1. Disconnect cylinder head as outlined under "Cylinder Head, Replace."
2. Remove mounting bolt and tappet guide holder.
3. Remove tappet using twisting motion. Mark tappets for installation in original positions.
4. Reverse procedure to install, noting the following:
   a. Multi Displacement System (MDS) engines use both standard an deactivating roller tappets.
   b. Deactivating roller tappets must be used in cylinders Nos. 1,4,6 and 7.
   c. Deactivating tappets can be identified by two body holes for latching pins.

CRANKSHAFT DAMPER

REPLACE

1. Release belt tension by rotating tensioner counterclockwise.
2. Rotate belt tensioner and remove belt, then gently release tensioner.
3. Raise and support vehicle.
4. Drain cooling system into suitable container.

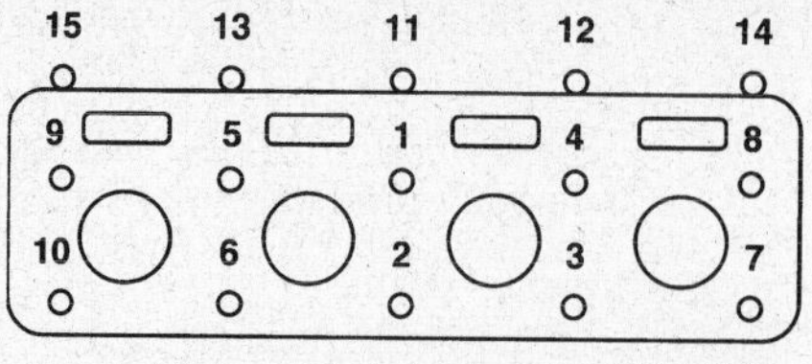

Fig. 3 Cylinder head loosening & tightening sequence

5. Position suitable container to catch power steering fluid that may exit hydraulic fan drive driven by power steering pump.
6. Disconnect two hydraulic fan drive high pressure lines. Discard fittings' O-rings.
7. Disconnect hydraulic fan drive low pressure return hose.
8. Remove two fan shroud lower mounting bolts.
9. Lower vehicle.
10. Disconnect fan control solenoid electrical connector.
11. Disconnect radiator upper hose and position side.
12. Disconnect power steering gear outlet and fluid return hoses at cooler.
13. Remove two upper mounting bolts, then the shroud and fan drive.
14. Remove mounting bolt and crankshaft damper using three-jaw puller tool No. 1023 and insert tool No. 8513A, or equivalents.
15. Reverse procedure to install. Press damper onto crankshaft using damper installation tool No. 8512-A, or equivalent.

FRONT COVER

REPLACE

1. Release belt tension by rotating tensioner counterclockwise.
2. Rotate belt tensioner and remove belt, then gently release tensioner.
3. Raise and support vehicle.
4. Drain cooling system into suitable container.
5. Position suitable container to catch power steering fluid that may exit hydraulic fan drive driven by power steering pump.
6. Disconnect two hydraulic fan drive high pressure lines . Discard fittings' O-rings.
7. Disconnect hydraulic fan drive low pressure return hose.
8. Remove two fan shroud lower mounting bolts.
9. Lower vehicle.
10. Disconnect fan control solenoid electrical connector.
11. Disconnect radiator upper hose and position side.
12. Disconnect power steering gear outlet and fluid return hoses at cooler.
13. Remove two upper mounting bolts, then the shroud and fan drive.
14. Remove coolant and washer fluid bottles.
15. Remove mounting bolts and position

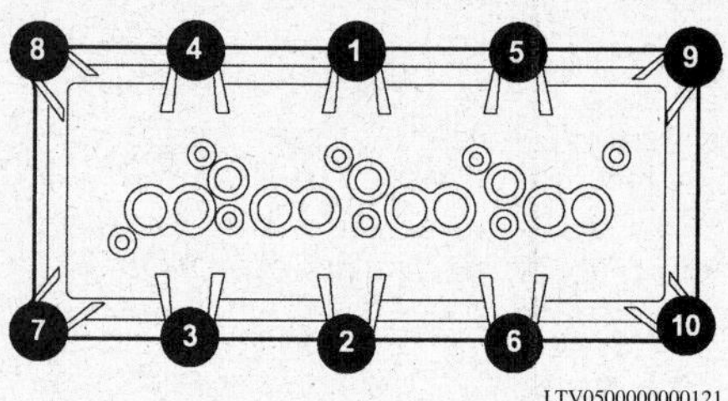

Fig. 4 Valve cover tightening sequence

air conditioning compressor aside with lines attached.

16. Disconnect cap, remove mounting nut and disconnect B+ terminal.
17. Disconnect field wire connector.
18. Remove mounting bolts and alternator.
19. Remove upper radiator hose.
20. Disconnect both heater hoses at front cover.
21. Disconnect lower radiator hose at engine.
22. Remove serpentine drive belt tensioner and both idler pulleys.
23. Remove mounting bolt and crankshaft damper using three-jaw puller tool No. 1023 and insert tool No. 8513A, or equivalents.
24. Remove mounting bolts and position power steering pump aside with lines attached.
25. Remove engine oil dipstick support bolt.
26. Drain engine oil into suitable container.
27. Remove oil pan and pickup tube as outlined in "Oil Pan, Replace."
28. Remove mounting bolts and timing cover. Discard gasket. **Water pump does not have to be removed.**
29. Reverse procedure to install.

TIMING CHAIN

REPLACE

Removal

1. Remove timing chain cover as outlined in "Front Cover, Replace."
2. Install vibration damper bolt hand tight.
3. Rotate crankshaft to align timing chain sprockets and key ways using suitable socket and breaker bar, **Fig. 5. Ensure camshaft pin and sprocket slot are at 12 o'clock position.**
4. Remove oil pan and pickup tube as outlined under "Oil Pan, Replace."
5. Remove four mounting bolts and oil pump.
6. Retract tensioner shoe until shoe and bracket hole align, then slide suitable pin into holes.
7. Remove camshaft sprocket mounting bolt, then remove timing chain with crankshaft and camshaft sprockets.

Installation

1. Align camshaft pin and cam sprocket slot at 12 o'clock position.

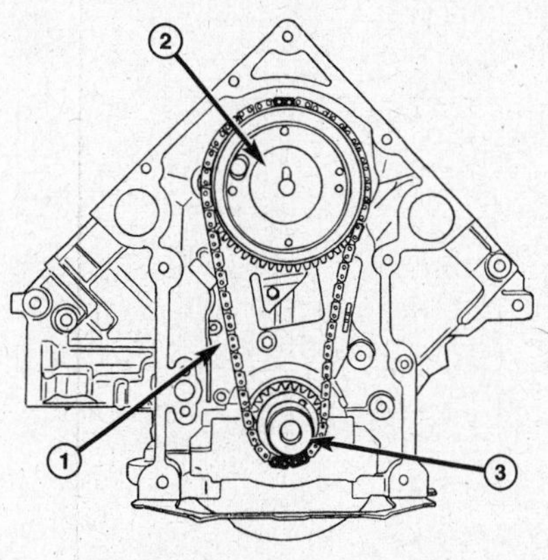

Fig. 5 Timing mark alignment

2. Align crankshaft keyway at 2 o'clock position.
3. Install crankshaft sprocket so that dots and or paint mark is at 6 o'clock position.
4. Place both camshaft sprocket and crankshaft sprocket on bench with timing marks on exact imaginary center line through camshaft and crankshaft bores.
5. Place timing chain around both sprockets with single plated link aligned with dot or painted marking on camshaft sprocket. Crankshaft sprocket aligns with dot or painted mark on sprocket between two plated timing chain links.
6. Lift sprockets and chain, then slide them evenly over respective shafts. Keep sprockets tight against chain.
7. Inspect timing mark alignment.
8. Install and tighten camshaft bolt.
9. Remove tensioner pin and inspect alignment of timing marks.
10. Install and tighten oil pump.
11. Install timing chain cover as outlined under "Front Cover, Replace."

TIMING CHAIN TENSIONER

REPLACE

Refer to "Timing Chain, Replace" for timing chain tensioner replacement procedure.

CAMSHAFT

REPLACE

1. Remove air cleaner air cleaner resonator and duct work.
2. Raise and support vehicle.
3. Drain cooling system into suitable container.
4. Release belt tension by rotating tensioner counterclockwise.
5. Rotate belt tensioner and remove belt, then gently release tensioner.
6. Disconnect cap, remove mounting nut and disconnect B+ terminal.
7. Disconnect field wire connector.
8. Remove mounting bolts and alternator.
9. Remove mounting bolts and position air conditioning compressor aside with lines attached.
10. Remove radiator as outlined in "Radiator, Replace."
11. Remove intake manifold as outlined in "Intake Manifold, Replace."
12. Remove cylinder heads as outlined in "Cylinder Head, Replace."
13. Remove oil pan as outlined in "Oil Pan, Replace."
14. Remove timing chain cover as outlined in "Front Cover, Replace."
15. Remove mounting bolts and oil pump.
16. Remove timing chain as outlined in "Timing Chain, Replace."
17. Remove camshaft tensioner/thrust plate.
18. Remove mounting bolt and tappet guide holder.
19. Remove tappet using twisting motion. Mark tappets for installation in original positions.
20. Install long bolt into camshaft front.
21. Remove camshaft. **Do not damage cam bearings with cam lobes.**
22. Reverse procedure to install, noting the following:
    a. If installing new camshaft, ensure it is compatible with Multi Displacement System (MDS).
    b. Lubricate camshaft lobes and bearing journals with suitable, clean engine oil.
    c. Measure camshaft end play. If end play is not .0031–.0114 inch, replace thrust plate.
    d. Ensure lifters are installed in original positions.
    e. Multi Displacement System (MDS) engines use both standard an deactivating roller tappets.
    f. Deactivating roller tappets must be used in cylinders Nos. 1,4,6 and 7.
    g. Deactivating tappets can be identified by two body holes for latching pins.

PISTON & ROD ASSEMBLY

The pistons are marked on the piston pin bore surface with an raised F or arrow on top of piston indicating installation position. This mark must point toward the front of engine on both cylinder banks, **Fig. 6.**

PISTONS, PINS & RINGS

Position piston ring end gaps, **Fig. 7.** It is important that expander ring gap is at least 45° from the side rail gaps, but not on the piston pin center or on the thrust direction.

MAIN & ROD BEARINGS

Connecting Rod

1. Position bearing onto connecting rod.

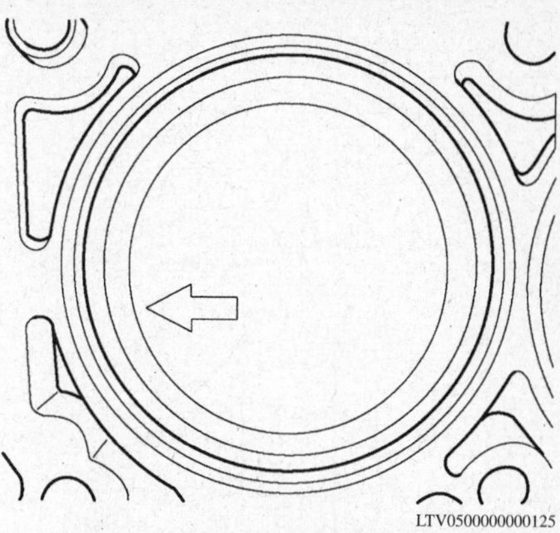

Fig. 6 Piston orientation

Lubricate bearing surface with suitable, clean engine oil.

2. Rotate crankshaft until connecting rod journal is on cylinder bore center.
3. Install rod and piston into cylinder bore and carefully position connecting rod guides tool No. 8507, or equivalent, over crankshaft journal.
4. Tap piston down in cylinder bore using suitable hammer handle while at same time, guiding connecting rod into position on rod journal.
5. Lubricate new rod bolts and bearing surfaces with suitable engine oil.
6. Install connecting rod cap and bearing.
7. **Torque** connecting rod bolts to 15 ft. lbs.
8. Final tighten bolts an additional 90°.

Main Bearings

Main bearings are available in three different grades, **Fig. 8.**

1. Mark rod bearing caps before removal.
2. Remove main bearing caps and bearings one at a time.
3. Install main bearings in block and caps, then lubricate bearings.
4. Position crankshaft into cylinder block and install thrust washers.
5. Clean and oil cap bolts.
6. Install main bearing caps.
7. Install cap bolts and alternately tighten.
8. **Torque** main cap bolts to 20 ft. lbs., in sequence, **Fig. 9.**
9. Final tighten main bearing caps an additional 90°.
10. Install cross bolts with new washer/gasket
11. **Torque** cross bolts to 21 ft. lbs., in sequence, **Fig. 9.**

CRANKSHAFT SEAL

REPLACE

1. Rotate belt tensioner and remove belt, then gently release tensioner.
2. Raise and support vehicle.
3. Drain cooling system into suitable container.
4. Position suitable container to catch power steering fluid that may exit hydraulic fan drive driven by power steering pump.

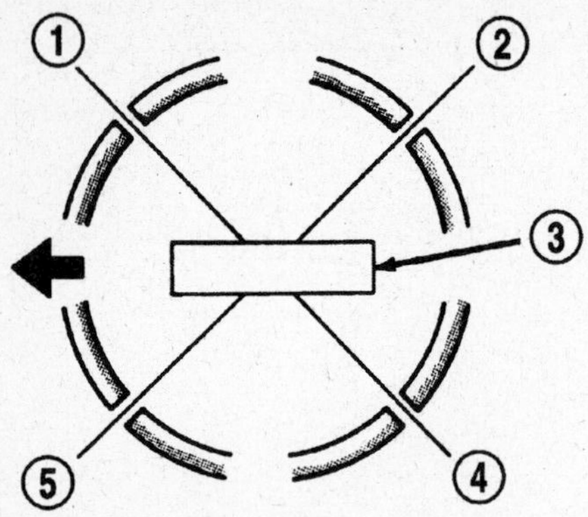

1 SIDE RAIL UPPER
2 NO. 1 RING GAP
3 PISTON PIN
4 SIDE RAIL LOWER
5 NO. 2 RING GAP AND SPACER EXPANDER GAP

LTV0500000000126

Fig. 7 Piston ring end gap position

5. Disconnect two hydraulic fan drive high pressure lines . Discard fittings' O-rings.
6. Disconnect hydraulic fan drive low pressure return hose.
7. Remove two fan shroud lower mounting bolts.
8. Lower vehicle.
9. Disconnect fan control solenoid electrical connector.
10. Disconnect radiator upper hose and position side.
11. Disconnect power steering gear outlet and fluid return hoses at cooler.
12. Remove two upper mounting bolts, then the shroud and fan drive.
13. Remove mounting bolt and crankshaft damper using three-jaw puller tool No. 1023 and insert tool No. 8513A, or equivalents.
14. Remove crankshaft front seal using front seal removal tool No. 9071, or equivalent.
15. Reverse procedure to install, noting the following:
    a. Install front crankshaft seal dry. **Do not apply lubricant to sealing lip or to outer edge.**
    b. Install using crankshaft front seal installer tools Nos. 8512A and 9072, or equivalents.

CRANKSHAFT REAR OIL SEAL

REPLACE

Removal

1. Remove transmission as outlined in **MOTOR's "Domestic Transmission, In-Vehicle Service" or "Transmission Service DVD."**
2. Remove flexplate.
3. Remove seal using seal remover tool No. 8506, or equivalent.

GRADE MARKING	SIZE mm (in.)	FOR USE WITH JOURNAL SIZE
A	0.008 mm U/S (0.0004 in.) U/S	64.988–64.995 mm (2.5585– 2.5588in.)
B	NOMINAL	64.996–65.004 mm (2.5588–2.5592 in.)
C	0.008 mm O/S (0.0004 in.) O/S	65.005–65.012 mm (2.5592–2.5595 in.)

LTV1900000000326

Fig. 8 Main bearing selection chart

Installation

The rear seal must be installed dry. **Do not lubricate the seal lip or outer edge.**

1. Position suitable plastic seal guide tool onto crankshaft rear face.
2. Position crankshaft rear oil seal onto guide.
3. Install seal using crankshaft rear oil seal installer tool No. 8349 and driver handle tool No. C-4171, or equivalents. Tap seal into place until it is seated against crankshaft bore.
4. Install flexplate and transmission as outlined in **MOTOR's "Domestic Transmission, In-Vehicle Service" or "Transmission Service DVD."**

OIL PAN

REPLACE

1. Remove engine cover.
2. Remove intake manifold as outlined under "Intake Manifold, Replace."
3. Raise and support vehicle.
4. Remove lefthand and righthand engine mount to frame bolts.
5. Drain engine oil into suitable container.
6. Remove engine oil dipstick and tube from oil pan.
7. Lower vehicle.
8. Support engine using fixture tool No. 8534, or equivalent.
9. Raise engine to provide oil pan removal clearance.
10. Remove front axle as outlined under "Front, Replace" in "Front Wheel Drive" section.
11. Remove mounting bolts and structural cover.
12. Remove vertical and horizontal M10 mounting bolts. **Horizontal M10 bolts are .197 inch longer and must be installed in original locations.**
13. Remove oil pan bolts in sequence, **Fig. 10,** and oil pan. **Do not pry on oil pan or gasket.**
14. Discard gasket and windage tray.
15. Remove oil pump pick-up tube.
16. Reverse procedure to install, noting the following:
    a. Apply .177 X .984 inch suitable engine RTV to four T-joints, **Fig. 11.** RTV should cover gasket bottom.

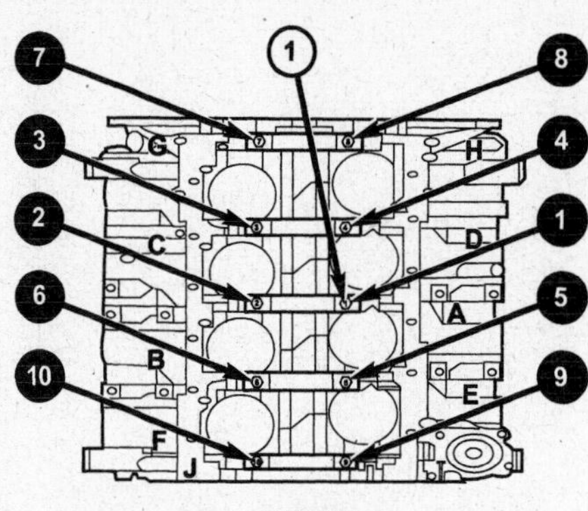

1 - Stud Location

LTV1900000000325

Fig. 9 Main bearing tightening sequence

    b. Install new oil pump pick-up tube O-ring.
    c. Align oil pan and engine block rears, then install M10 and new M6 mounting bolts hand tight.
    d. **Torque** new M6 mounting bolts to 44 inch lbs. in sequence , **Fig. 10.**
    e. **Torque** M10 bolts to 39 ft. lbs.
    f. **Torque** M6 bolts to 106 inch lbs.
    g. **Torque** lefthand and righthand oil pan to transmission bolts to 39 ft. lbs.

OIL PUMP

REPLACE

1. Remove oil pan and pickup tube as outlined under "Oil Pan, Replace."
2. Remove front cover as outlined under "Front Cover, Replace."
3. Remove four mounting bolts and oil pump.
4. Reverse procedure to install.

OIL PUMP SERVICE

Oil pump is an assembly. There are no part numbers for components. If the oil pump is not functioning or out of specification it must be replaced as an assembly.

Disassemble

1. Remove mounting screws and cover plate.
2. Remove inner and outer rotors.
3. If required, remove pressure relief valve and drive roll pin from pump housing, then remove cup plug, spring and valve.
4. Once oil pressure relief valve, cup plug, and pin are removed, pump assembly must be replaced.

Inspection

1. If pump cover is scratched or grooved, oil pump should be replaced.
2. Slide outer rotor into oil pump body.
3. Press outer rotor to one side, then measure clearance between outer

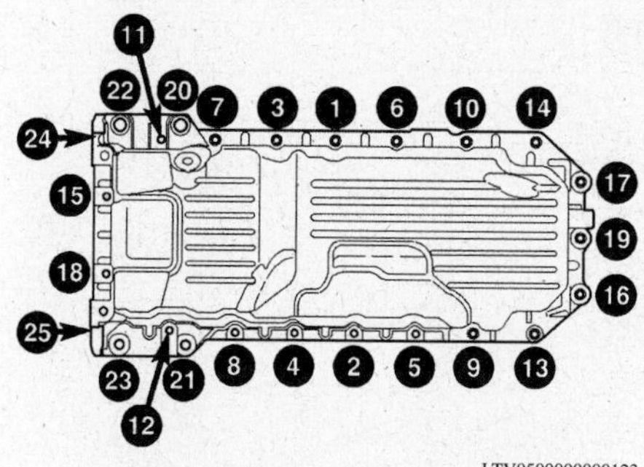

Fig. 10 Oil pan loosening & tightening sequence

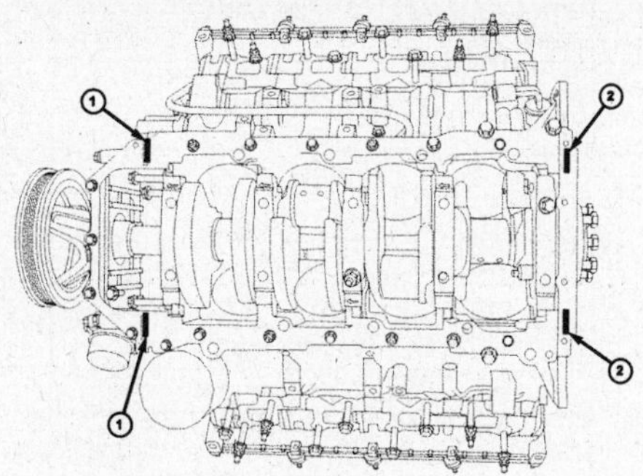

Fig. 11 Oil pan RTV application

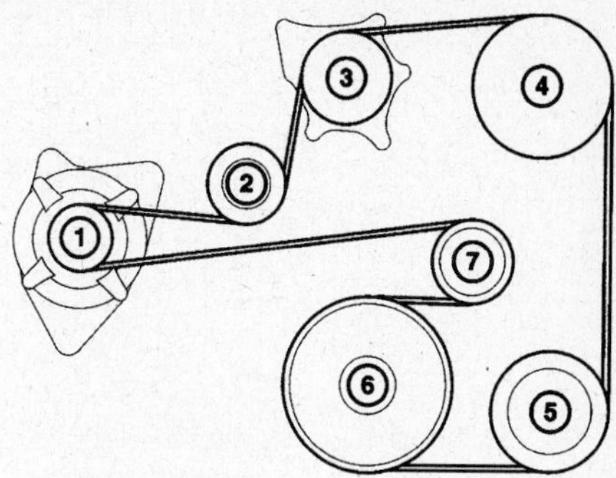

Fig. 12 Serpentine belt routing

rotor and body. If measurement is .009 inch, or more, replace oil pump.

4. Install inner rotor into oil pump body.
5. Measure clearance between inner and outer rotors. If measurement is .006 inch, or more, replace oil pump.
6. Place suitable straight edge across oil pump body. If clearance between straight edge and rotors is .0038 inch, or more, replace oil pump.

Assemble

1. Install inner and outer rotors.
2. Install cover and tighten mounting bolts.
3. Prime oil pump by filling rotor cavity with suitable engine oil.

SERPENTINE DRIVE BELT

Replace

1. Remove air intake tube between intake manifold and air filter.
2. Release belt tension by rotating tensioner counterclockwise with suitable wrench on tensioner pulley bolt.
3. Rotate belt tensioner until belt can be removed from pulleys.
4. Gently release tensioner.
5. Ensure belt is properly routed and all V-grooves make proper contact with pulleys.
6. Position drive belt over all pulleys except water pump pulley.
7. Rotate tensioner counterclockwise and slip belt over water pump pulley.
8. Gently release tensioner.

Routing

Refer to **Fig. 12** for serpentine belt routing.

COOLING SYSTEM BLEED

Refer to "Cooling System Bleed" in the "3.7L Engine" section for cooling system bleed procedure.

THERMOSTAT

REPLACE

1. Drain cooling system into suitable container.
2. Remove clamp and thermostat housing radiator hose.
3. Remove mounting bolts, housing and thermostat.
4. Reverse procedure to install.

WATER PUMP

REPLACE

1. Raise and support vehicle.
2. Drain cooling system into suitable container.
3. Position suitable container to catch power steering fluid that may exit hydraulic fan drive driven by power steering pump.
4. Disconnect two hydraulic fan drive high pressure lines . Discard fittings' O-rings.
5. Disconnect hydraulic fan drive low pressure return hose.
6. Remove two fan shroud lower mounting bolts.
7. Lower vehicle.
8. Disconnect fan control solenoid electrical connector.
9. Disconnect radiator upper hose and position side.
10. Disconnect power steering gear outlet and fluid return hoses at cooler.
11. Remove two upper mounting bolts, then the shroud and fan drive.
12. Rotate belt tensioner and remove belt, then gently release tensioner.
13. Remove clamp and thermostat housing radiator hose.
14. Remove mounting bolts, housing and thermostat.
15. Remove mounting bolts and water pump. Mark mounting bolts for replacement in original positions.
16. Reverse procedure to install.

RADIATOR

REPLACE

Refer to "Radiator, Replace" in the "3.7L Engine" section for radiator replacement procedure.

FUEL PUMP

REPLACE

Refer to "Fuel Pump, Replace" in the "3.7L Engine" section for fuel pump replacement procedure.

FUEL FILTER

REPLACE

Refer to "Fuel Filter, Replace" in the "3.7L Engine" section for fuel filter replacement procedure.

TIGHTENING SPECIFICATIONS

Year	Component	Torque Ft. Lbs.
2005–06	Alternator	⑦
	Camshaft Sprocket	90
	Camshaft Tensioner Plate	21
	Coil	62①
	Connecting Rod	③
	Crankshaft Damper	129
	Cylinder Head	②
	Exhaust Manifold	⑤
	Front Cover	21⑧
	Heat Shield	70①
	Intake Manifold	④
	Main Bearing	③
	Main Bearing Cross Bolts	③
	Oil Pan	⑨
	Oil Pan Drain Plug	25
	Oil Pump	21
	Oil Pump Cover	11
	Oil Pump Pickup Tube	21
	Rocker Arm	②
	Tappet Guide	106①
	Thermostat	112①
	Timing Chain Tensioner	21
	Timing Cover	21⑧
	Valve Cover	⑥
	Vibration Damper	129
	Water Pump	20

①— Inch lbs.
②— Refer to "Cylinder Head, Replace" for tightening procedure.
③— Refer to "Main & Rod Bearings" for tightening specifications and sequence.
④— Refer to "Intake Manifold, Replace" for tightening specifications and sequence.
⑤— Refer to "Exhaust Manifold, Replace" for tightening specifications and sequence.
⑥— Refer to "Valve Cover, Replace" for tightening specifications and sequence.
⑦— M8, 21 ft. lbs.; M10, 40 ft. lbs.
⑧— **Torque** large lifting studs to 40 ft. lbs.
⑨— Refer to "Oil Pan, Replace" for tightening specifications and sequence.

Rear Axle & Suspension

NOTE: Prior To Performing Any Service Operations Listed In This Section, Consult The "Technical Service Bulletins" Section For Related Information.

INDEX

DESCRIPTION

The rear suspension is comprised of: drive axle, shock absorbers, coil springs, lower suspension arms, upper suspension arm and stabilizer bar, **Figs. 1 and 2.**

The rear axle has a differential housing with axle shaft tubes extending from either side. The tubes are pressed into differential housing The axles are semi-floating supported by the axle shaft and bearings.

REAR AXLE

REPLACE

2002–04

1. Raise and support vehicle, then support axle with suitable hydraulic jack.
2. Remove wheels and tires, then the brake calipers and rotors as outlined in "Disc Brakes" chapter.
3. Disconnect parking brake cables from brackets and levers.
4. Remove wheel speed sensors.
5. Disconnect brake hose at axle junction block. **Do not disconnect hydraulic lines at calipers.**
6. Disconnect axle shaft tube vent hose.
7. Mark propeller shaft and yokes for installation alignment.
8. Remove propeller shaft.
9. Disconnect stabilizer bar links from axle.
10. Remove upper suspension arm rear axle ball joint nut.
11. Separate rear axle ball joint from upper suspension arm using remover tool No. 8278, or equivalent.
12. Disconnect shock absorbers from axle.
13. Disconnect track bar.
14. Remove lower suspension arms from axle brackets.
15. Remove axle.
16. Reverse procedure to install. **Weight of vehicle must be supported by springs when upper and lower suspension arms and track bar mounting bolts and nuts are being tightened.**

2005–06

1. Place gear selector in Neutral, then raise and support vehicle.
2. Remove differential cove and drain fluid into suitable container.
3. Remove brake calipers and rotors as outlined in "Disc Brakes" chapter.
4. Remove speed sensors from axle tube flange.
5. Remove axle flange nuts, then pull axle shaft and backing plate out of axle tube until bearing is exposed.
6. Remove axle bearing O-ring, then remove axle shaft from axle tube and backing plate.
7. Remove axle vent hose from vent and cover bracket.
8. Remove mounting bolts and propeller shaft.
9. Remove stabilizer bar clamp from axle.
10. Support axle using suitable jack.
11. Remove track bar from axle.
12. Remove shock absorbers, then the upper and lower control arms from axle bracket.
13. Lower axle, then remove coil springs and insulators.
14. Remove rear axle.
15. Reverse procedure to install.

REAR AXLE SHAFT

REPLACE

2002–04

1. Place transmission in neutral, then raise and support vehicle.
2. Remove wheel and tire assembly, then the brake caliper and rotor as outlined in "Disc Brakes" chapter.
3. Remove retainer plate mounting nuts.
4. Remove axle shaft from housing using puller tool No. 6790, or equivalent, and suitable slide hammer.
5. Reverse procedure to install.

2005–06

1. Place transmission in neutral, then raise and support vehicle.
2. Remove brake caliper and rotor as outlined in "Disc Brakes" chapter.
3. **On models equipped with C215R and C215RE axles,** proceed as follows:
   a. Tap axle end plug loose from flange using suitable hammer and punch.
   b. Pull plug out of axle flange.
4. **On all models,** remove speed sensors from axle tube flange.
5. Remove axle flange nuts.
6. Pull axle shaft and backing plate out exposing axle bearing.
7. Remove axle bearing O-ring.
8. Remove axle shaft from tube and backing plate.
9. Tap axle shaft out of bearing and axle flange through plug hole using suitable hammer and brass drift.
10. Reverse procedure to install. **On models equipped with C215R and C215RE axles,** coat new axle flange plug with Mopar Stud N' Bearing Mount Adhesive, or equivalent, and it with suitable freeze plug installer.
11.

PROPELLER SHAFT

REPLACE

1. Shift transmission (and transfer case) to neutral position.
2. Raise and support vehicle.
3. Make pinion and propeller shaft yokes (and transfer case yoke) for installation alignment.
4. Remove universal joint clamp bolts from pinion yokes (and CV joint bolts from transfer case).
5. Remove propeller shaft.
6. Reverse procedure to install.

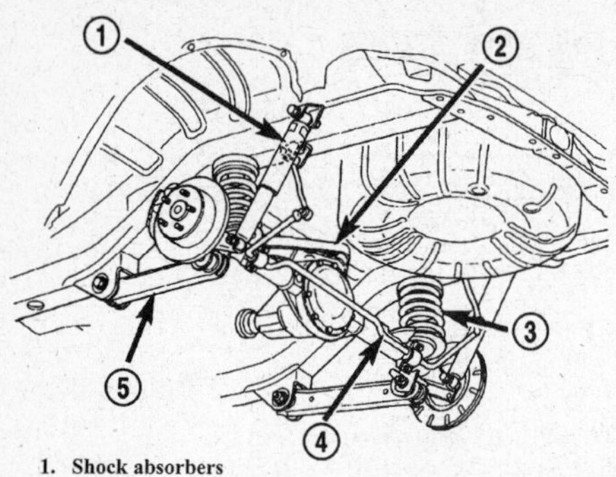

Fig. 1 Exploded view of rear suspension. 2002–04

SHOCK ABSORBER

REPLACE

1. Raise and support vehicle, then support axle with suitable hydraulic jack.
2. Remove upper mounting nut and bolt from frame bracket, **Figs. 3 and 4.**
3. Remove lower mounting nut and bolt from axle bracket.
4. Remove shock absorber.
5. Reverse procedure to install.

COIL SPRING

REPLACE

1. Raise and support vehicle, then support axle with suitable hydraulic jack.
2. Remove tire and wheel assembly.
3. Disconnect stabilizer link from bar.
4. Remove shock absorber lower mounting bolt from axle bracket, **Figs. 4 and 5.**
5. Lower and tilt axle, then remove coil spring.
6. Remove upper and lower spring isolators.
7. Reverse procedure to install.

BALL JOINT

REPLACE

1. Raise and support vehicle, then support axle with suitable hydraulic jack.
2. Remove nut and disconnect ball joint using remover tool No. 8278, or equivalent.
3. Remove mounting bolts and ball joint from differential housing.
4. Reverse procedure to install using new mounting nut.

CONTROL ARM

REPLACE

2002–04

LOWER

1. Raise and support vehicle, then support axle with suitable hydraulic jack.

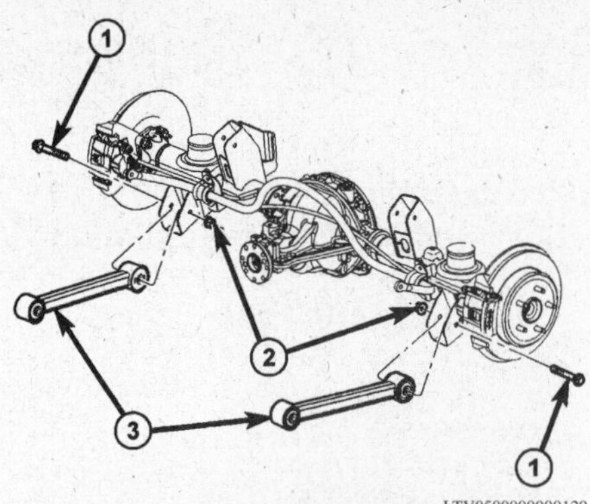

Fig. 2 Exploded view of rear suspension. 2005–06

2. Disconnect parking brake cables and hose from control arm.
3. Remove axle bracket mounting nut and bolt, **Fig. 6.**
4. Remove frame rail mounting nut and bolt, then the lower control arm.
5. Reverse procedure to install.

UPPER

1. Raise and support vehicle, then support axle with suitable hydraulic jack.
2. Disconnect parking brake cables and hose from control arm.
3. Remove wheel speed sensors.
4. Remove upper suspension arm rear axle ball joint nut.
5. Separate rear axle ball joint from upper suspension arm using remover tool No. 8278, or equivalent.
6. Remove mounting bolts and upper control arm, **Fig. 7.**
7. Reverse procedure to install.

2005–06

LOWER

1. Raise and support vehicle, then support rear axle with suitable jack.
2. **If removing lefthand,** proceed as follows:
   a. Relieve fuel pressure as outlined under "Precautions."
   b. Drain fuel tank into suitable container.
   c. Loosen clamp and disconnect tank rubber fill hose.
   d. Disconnect fuel pump module electrical jumper connector from body connector at rear of tank.
   e. Disconnect EVAP lines at rear of tank.
   f. Disconnect fuel and EVAP lines at front of tank.
   g. Support fuel tank with suitable jack.
   h. Remove mounting bolts and remove fuel tank.
3. **On all models,** remove axle bracket lower suspension arm mounting nut and bolt, **Fig. 8.**
4. Remove frame rail mounting nut and bolt, then the lower suspension arm.
5. Reverse procedure to install.

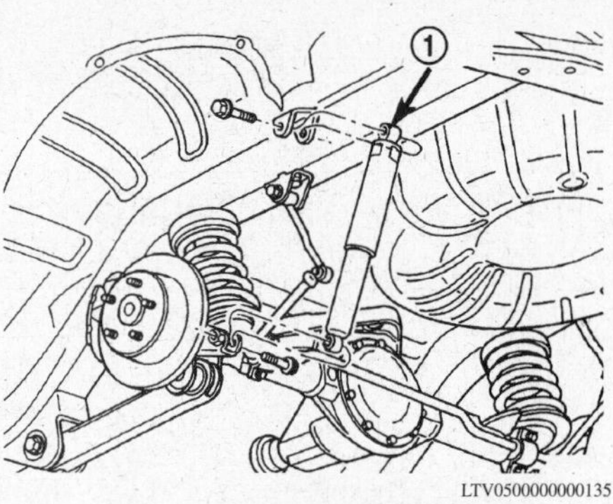

Fig. 3 Shock absorber replacement. 2002–04

UPPER

1. Raise and support vehicle, then support rear axle with suitable hydraulic jack.
2. **If removing lefthand,** proceed as follows:
   a. Relieve fuel pressure as outlined under "Precautions."
   b. Drain fuel tank into suitable container.
   c. Loosen clamp and disconnect tank rubber fill hose.
   d. Disconnect fuel pump module electrical jumper connector from body connector at rear of tank.
   e. Disconnect EVAP lines at rear of tank.
   f. Disconnect fuel and EVAP lines at front of tank.
   g. Support fuel tank with suitable jack.
   h. Remove mounting bolts and lower fuel tank.
3. **On all models,** remove axle bracket upper suspension arm mounting nut and bolt, , **Fig. 8.**
4. Remove frame rail mounting and bolt, then the upper suspension arm.
5. Reverse procedure to install.

STABILIZER BAR

REPLACE

1. Raise and support vehicle.
2. Remove stabilizer bar links from stabilizer bar and frame mount, **Fig. 9.**
3. Remove mounting bolts and stabilizer bar.
4. Reverse procedure to install.

TRACK ROD

REPLACE

1. Raise and support vehicle, then support rear axle with suitable jack.
2. Remove track bar mounting bolt and nut from frame bracket, **Fig. 10.**
3. Remove lefthand lower shock bolt at axle.
4. Pry between coil springs, then remove track bar mounting bolt and nut from axle bracket, **Fig. 11.**
5. Remove track bar.
6. Reverse procedure to install.

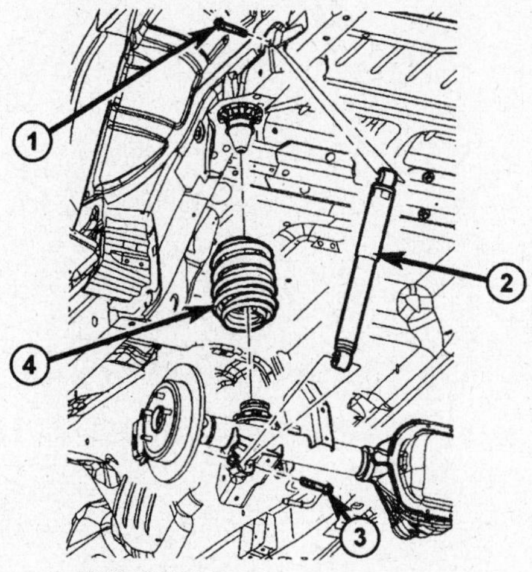

1. UPPER SHOCK BOLT
2. SHOCK
3. LOWER SHOCK BOLT
4. SPRING

LTV0500000000130

Fig. 4 Shock absorber replacement. 2005–06

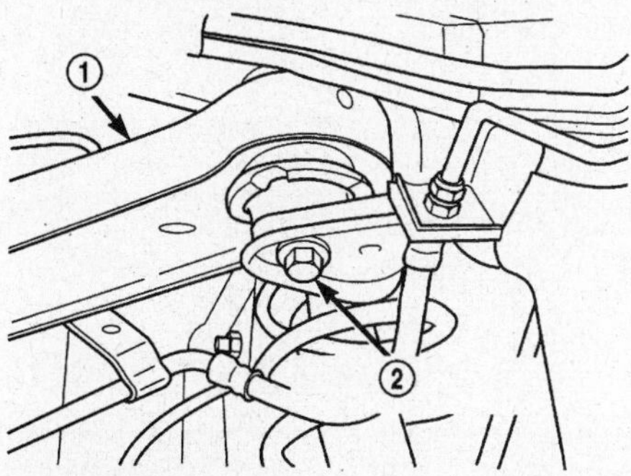

1. Upper Control Arm
2. Mounting Bolt

LTV0500000000138

Fig. 7 Upper control arm replacement. 2002–04

TECHNICAL SERVICE BULLETINS

Rear Axle Vent Line Jiggle Cap Fluid Weepage

2002-04 WITH DANA 44 REAR AXLE

On some of these models axle fluid may weep past the rear axle vent line jiggle cap and track down the outside of the vent tube. There may be a small deposit of axle fluid on the ground from the accumulated fluid tracking. This condition will normally occur following a vehicle cold soak period and a drive cycle where the engine is started and

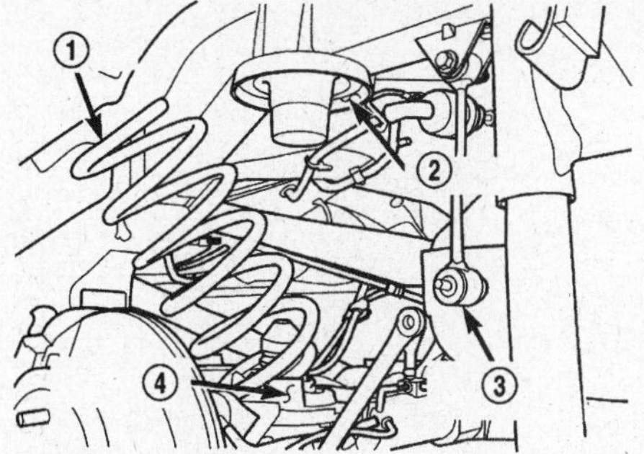

1. Coil Spring
2. Upper spring isolators
3. Stabilizer Bar
4. Lower spring isolators

LTV0500000000136

Fig. 5 Coil spring replacement. 2002–04

the vehicle driven at highway speeds almost immediately.

This condition may be caused by residual fluid in the vent line being forced past the jiggle cap because of rapid pressure build up in the axle housing.

To correct this condition, install fluid accumulator canister (P/N 52070409AA) in the rear axle vent line as follows:

1. Raise and support vehicle.
2. Remove four plastic push pins and two rear bumper fascia mounting screws in liftgate opening, then remaining four plastic push pins at fascia bottom.
3. Remove three plastic rivets and fascia to quarter panel mounting nut in each rear wheel well opening.
4. Disconnect large fascia to quarter panel retainer, then the tabs using a suitable long, narrow trim stick between fascia and quarter panel.
5. Remove rear bumper fascia.
6. Remove lefthand rear wheel splash/stone shield.
7. **On models equipped with ORVR,** proceed as follows:
   a. Loosen two evaporative canister support bracket mounting nuts and a mounting bolt. **Do not remove mounting nuts and bolt.**
   b. Remove support bracket brace mounting nut.
   c. Remove evaporative canister support bracket.
   d. Disconnect evaporative vapor ORVR hose elbow from canister top.
   e. Position canister aside.
8. **On all models,** remove rear axle vent line to support bracket plastic tie wrap.
9. Cut rubber rear axle vent line 1.5 inches from end. **Do not include jiggle valve in measurement.**
10. Install jiggle cap with 1.5 inches length vent line to quick connector fitting on fluid accumulator canister end, **Fig. 12.** Canister FLOW arrow points toward jiggle cap.

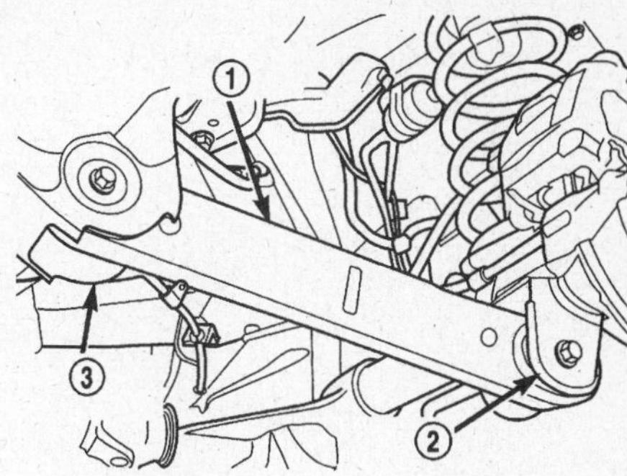

1. Lower Control Arm
2. Axle Bracket
3. Frame Bracket

LTV0500000000137

Fig. 6 Lower control arm replacement. 2002–04

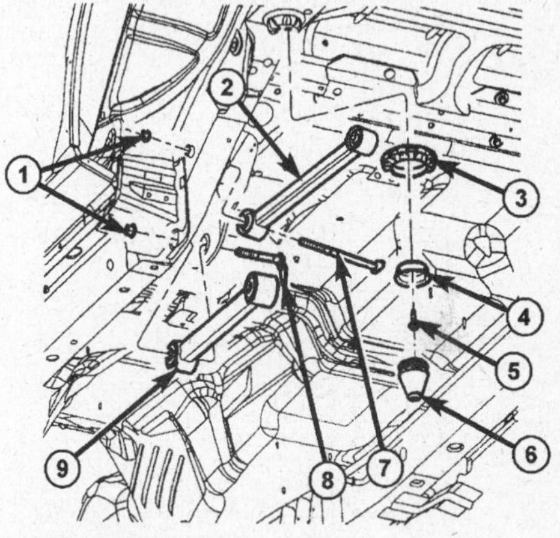

1. NUT
2. UPPER SUSPENSION ARM
3. UPPER SPRING ISOLATOR
4. JOUNCE BUMPER RETAINER
5. BOLT
6. JOUNCE BUMPER
7. UPPER FLAG BOLT
8. LOWER FLAG BOLT
9. LOWER SUSPENSION ARM

LTV0500000000131

Fig. 8 Control arm replacement. 2005–06

11. Install vent line from rear axle in other end of canister.
12. Secure fluid accumulator canister to metal fuel line tube and fuel vent hose using suitable plastic tie wraps. FLOW arrow must point upward. **Ensure canister does not rattle.**
13. **On models equipped with ORVR,** proceed as follows:
    a. Install ORVR elbow hose.
    b. Install evaporative canister support bracket and brace.
    c. **Torque** support bracket and brace mounting nuts and bolts to 21 ft. lbs.
14. **On all models,** install splash/stone shield and rear bumper fascia.

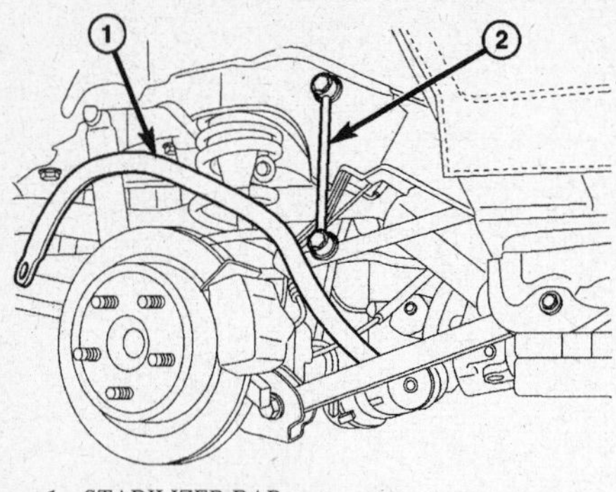

1. STABILIZER BAR
2. STABILIZER LINK

LTV0500000000132

Fig. 9 Stabilizer bar replacement. 2005–06

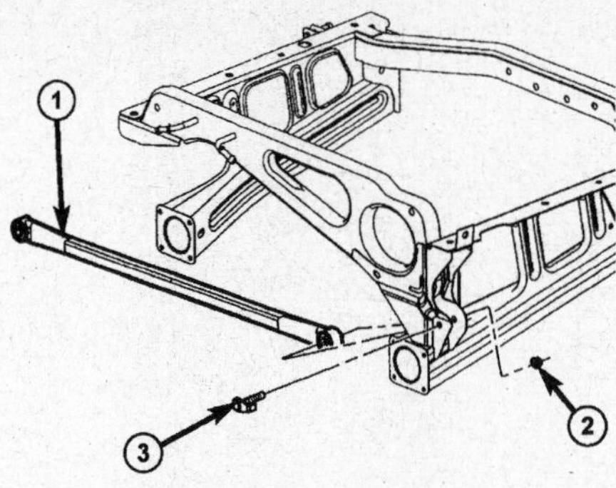

1. TRACK BAR
2. NUT
3. BOLT

LTV0500000000133

Fig. 10 Track bar replacement to frame bracket. 2005–06

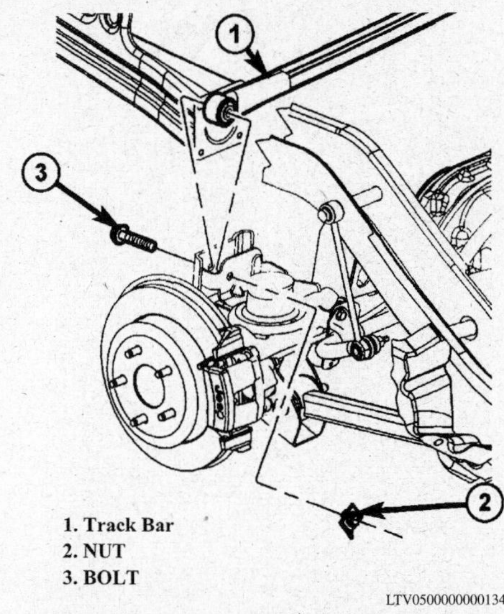

1. Track Bar
2. NUT
3. BOLT

LTV0500000000134

Fig. 11 Track bar replacement to axle bracket. 2005–06

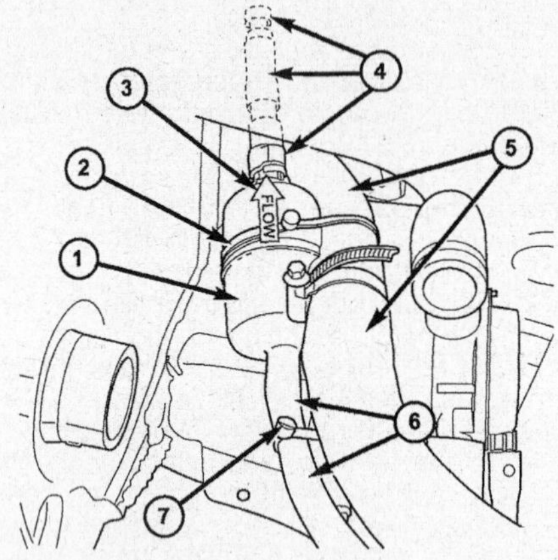

1 - Fluid Accumulator Canister

2 - Plastic Tie Wrap - Canister Body To Fuel Fill Tube

3 - "FLOW" Arrow Pointing Up And Toward Jiggle Valve

4 - Jiggle Valve, Vent Line Hose, and Quick Connect Fitting

5 - Fuel Fill Tube And Fill Hose

6 - Rear Axle Vent Line Between Fluid Canister And Axle

7 - Plastic Tie Wrap - Axle Vent Hose To Fuel Vent Hose

LTV0500000000148

Fig. 12 Fluid accumulator

TIGHTENING SPECIFICATIONS

Year	Component	Torque Ft. Lbs.
2002–04	Axle Bearing Retainer Plate	45
	Axle Flange	88
	Ball Joint Bolt	100
	Ball Joint Nut	105
	Bearing Cap (198RBI)	57
	Bearing Cap (226RBA)	63
	Control Arm, Lower To Axle Bracket	120
	Control Arm, Lower To Frame	115
	Control Arm, Upper	74
	Different Cover	30
	Pinion Mate Shaft (198RBI)	12
	Pinion Mate Shaft (226RBA)	13
	Pinion Nut (198RBI)	200–250
	Pinion Nut (226RBA)	220–280
	Propeller Shaft, CV Joint	24
	Propeller Shaft, Universal Joint Clamp	14
	Ring Gear (198RBI)	95–105
	Ring Gear (226RBA)	100
	Shock Absorber, Lower	85
	Shock Absorber, Upper	80
	Stabilizer Bar	40
	Stabilizer Bar Bracket	68
	Stabilizer Bar Link	27
	Suspension Arm, Lower	130
	Track Bar	74
	U-Bolt Strap	14
2005–06	Adjuster Lock Screw (213R & C213RE)	97①
	Axle Flange (C213R)	88
	Bearing Cap (C213R & C213RE)	100
	Bearing Cap (226RBI)	80
	Control Arm, Lower To Axle Bracket	155
	Control Arm, Lower To Frame	130
	Control Arm, Upper To Axle Bracket	100
	Control Arm, Upper To Frame	95
	Differential Cover	30
	Pinion Nut (C213R & C213RE)	210
	Pinion Nut (226RBI)	220–500
	Pinion Shaft Lock Screw (C213R & C213RE)	97①
	Propeller Shaft	80
	Ring Gear (C213R & C213RE)	75
	Ring Gear (226RBI)	125
	Shock Absorber, Lower	85
	Shock Absorber, Upper	70
	Stabilizer Bar	90
	Stabilizer Bar Bracket	31
	Stabilizer Link To Body	75
	Track Bar	140

① — Inch lbs.

Front Suspension & Steering

NOTE: On Air Bag Equipped Models, Refer To "Air Bag System Precautions" Located In The Front Of This Manual For System Disarming & Arming Procedures.

NOTE: Refer To The "Front Wheel Drive" Section For 4WD Front Axle Service Procedures Not Covered In This Section.

NOTE: Prior To Performing Any Service Operations Listed In This Section, Consult The "Technical Service Bulletins" Section For Related Information.

INDEX

PRECAUTIONS

Air Bag Systems

Refer to "Air Bag System Precautions" in the front of this manual for system disarming and arming procedures.

DESCRIPTION

2002–04

The front suspension is a link/coil design comprised of: drive axle, shock absorbers, coil springs, upper and lower suspension arms, stabilizer bar, track bar, and jounce bumpers, **Fig. 1.**

2005–06

The front suspension wheels are mounted to hub bearings on the steering knuckle spindles, **Fig. 2.** The double-row hub bearings are sealed and lubricated for life. The steering knuckles turn (pivot) on ball joints integral to the outboard portion of the upper control arms and pressed into the lower steering knuckle. The ball joints are lubricated for life.

HUB & BEARING

REPLACE

2002–04

1. Raise and support vehicle, then remove wheel and tire assembly.
2. Remove brake caliper, anchor and rotor as outlined in "Disc Brakes" chapter.
3. Remove ABS wheel speed sensor.
4. Remove cotter pin, retainer and axle hub nut.
5. Remove mounting bolts and hub bearing from steering knuckle and axle shaft.
6. Reverse procedure to install.

2005–06

1. Raise and support vehicle, then remove wheel and tire assembly.
2. Remove brake caliper, anchor and rotor as outlined in "Disc Brakes" chapter.
3. Remove mounting nut and ABS wheel speed sensor.
4. Remove three mounting bolts and bearing from steering knuckle.
5. Reverse procedure to install.

BALL JOINT INSPECTION

1. Raise and support vehicle.
2. Grasp bottom of wheel and tire assembly and shake from side to side, inspect ball joint for any movement.
3. Push tire and wheel assembly up and down, inspect ball joint for any movement.
4. If any ball joint movement is observed, replace ball joint.

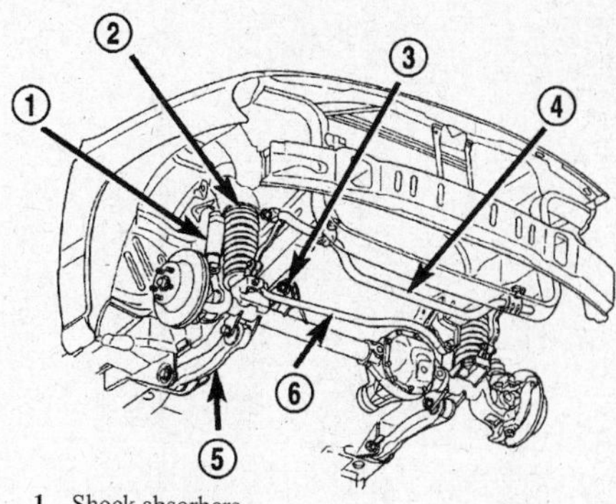

1. Shock absorbers
2. Coil springs
3. Upper suspension arms
4. Stabilizer bar
5. Lower suspension arms
6. Track bar

LTV0500000000140

Fig. 1 Exploded view of front suspension. 2002–04

BALL JOINT

REPLACE

2002-04

1. Raise and support vehicle, then remove wheel and tire assembly.
2. Remove brake caliber and rotor as outlined in "Disc Brakes" chapter.
3. Remove ABS wheel speed sensor,
4. Remove cotter pin, retainer and axle nut.
5. Remove mounting bolts, hub bearing and axle shaft.
6. Remove brake rotor shield.
7. Remove ball joint using removal tool kit No. 6289, or equivalent.
8. Reverse procedure to install. Apply thin film of Mopar Wheel Bearing Grease, or equivalent, to shaft splines, seal contact surface and hub bore.

2005-06

LOWER

1. Raise and support vehicle, then remove tire and wheel assembly.
2. Remove brake caliper, adapter and rotor as outlined in "Disc Brakes" chapter.
3. Remove wheel speed sensor mounting bolt and disconnect wire from knuckle retaining clips.
4. **On models equipped with 4WD,** remove axle shaft nut.
5. **On all models,** remove three mounting bolts and bearing from steering knuckle.
6. Remove retaining nut and separate outer tie rod end from steering knuckle using special removal tool No. 8677, or equivalent.
7. Remove nut and separate lower ball joint from knuckle using removal tool No. C-4150A, or equivalent.
8. Remove nut and separate upper ball joint from knuckle using removal tool No. 8677, or equivalent.
9. Remove knuckle.
10. **On models equipped with 4WD,** remove clevis bracket and support halfshaft aside.
11. **On all models,** press ball joint from lower control arm using special tools removal tool No. C-4212-F, or equivalent.
12. Reverse procedure to install.

UPPER

1. Raise and support vehicle, then support axle using suitable jack.
2. Remove tire and wheel assembly.
3. Remove mounting nut and separate upper ball joint from knuckle using removal tool No. 8677, or equivalent.
4. Position knuckle aside.
5. Press ball joint from upper control arm using special tools removal tool No. C-4212-F, or equivalent.
6. Reverse procedure to install.

COIL SPRING

REPLACE

2002-04

1. Raise and support vehicle, then remove wheel and tire assemblies.
2. Support axle using suitable jack.
3. Remove shock absorber lower mounting nuts from axle brackets.
4. Remove track bar mounting bolt from axle bracket.
5. Ensure shock absorber does not hold brake line tension at axle tube housing.
6. Lower axle, then remove spring from upper mount and isolator.
7. Remove upper and lower spring isolators.
8. Reverse procedure to install.

2005-06

1. Remove shock absorber as outlined under "Shock Absorber, Replace."
2. Install shock with coil-over spring in suitable spring removal/installation tool.
3. Compress spring and remove upper shock nut.
4. Remove shock and upper mount, then the upper and lower spring isolators.
5. Reverse procedure to install.

SHOCK ABSORBER

REPLACE

2002-04

1. Remove shock absorber upper mounting nut, retainer and grommet.
2. Raise and support vehicle.
3. Remove lower mounting nuts and bolts, then the shock absorber.
4. Reverse procedure to install.

2005-06

LEFTHAND

1. Remove air box cover and intake hose.
2. Remove three bracket nuts and position Power Distribution Center (PDC) aside.
3. Remove four shock absorber upper mounting nuts.

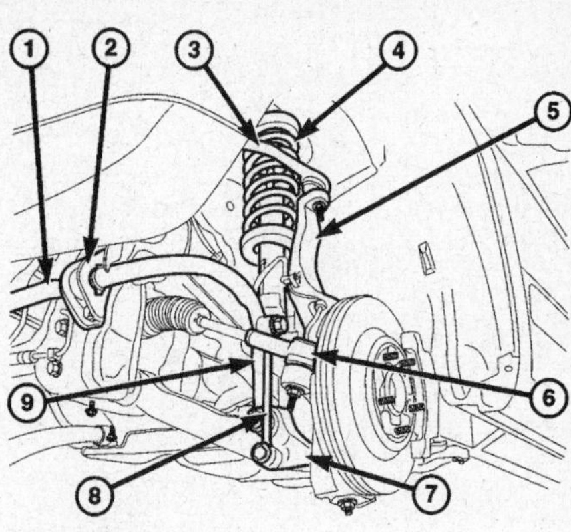

1. Stabilizer Bar
2. Bracket
3. Upper Control Arm
4. Coil Spring
5. Steering Knuckle
6. Tie Rod
7. Lower Control Arm
8. Stabilizer Link
9. Stabilizer Bar

LTV0500000000145

Fig. 2 Exploded view of front suspension. 2005–06

4. Raise and support vehicle, then remove tire and wheel assembly.
5. Remove adapter, brake caliper and rotor as outlined in "Disc Brakes" chapter.
6. Remove nut and separate upper ball joint from knuckle using removal tool No. 8677, or equivalent.
7. Remove lower clevis and stabilizer bolts from lower control arm.
8. Remove shock with coil-over spring.
9. Reverse procedure to install.

RIGHTHAND

1. Remove air box cover and intake hose.
2. Disconnect cruise control servo electrical connector.
3. Remove mounting bolt and position coolant reservoir aside.
4. Remove four shock absorber upper mounting nuts.
5. Raise and support vehicle, then remove tire and wheel assembly.
6. Remove adapter, brake caliper and rotor as outlined in "Disc Brakes" chapter.
7. Remove nut and separate upper ball joint from knuckle using removal tool No. 8677, or equivalent.
8. Remove lower clevis and stabilizer bolts from lower control arm.
9. Remove shock with coil-over spring.
10. Reverse procedure to install.

CONTROL ARM

REPLACE

2002-04

UPPER

1. Raise and support vehicle, then support axle using suitable jack.

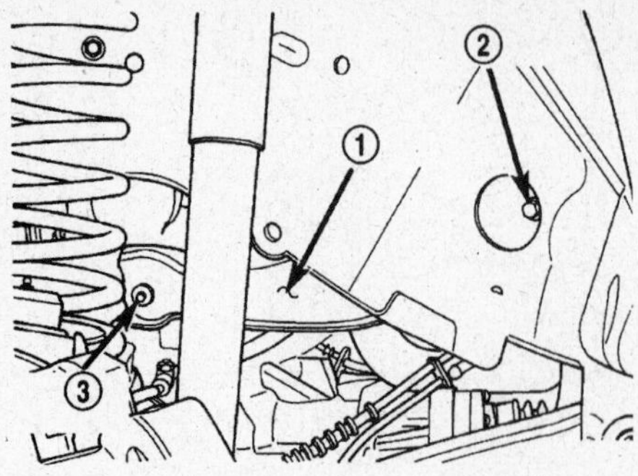

Fig. 3 Upper control arm replacement. 2002–04

2. Remove upper suspension arm mounting nut and bolt from axle bracket, then the frame rail bracket, **Fig. 3.**
3. Remove lower suspension arm.
4. Reverse procedure to install.

LOWER

1. Raise and support vehicle, then support axle using suitable jack.
2. Remove lower suspension arm mounting nut and bolt from axle bracket, then the frame rail bracket, **Fig. 4.**
3. Remove lower suspension arm.
4. Reverse procedure to install.

2005–06

LOWER

1. Raise and support vehicle, then remove tire and wheel assembly.
2. Remove brake caliper, adapter and rotor as outlined in "Disc Brakes" chapter.
3. Remove wheel speed sensor mounting bolt and disconnect wire from knuckle retaining clips.
4. **On models equipped with 4WD,** remove axle shaft nut.
5. **On all models,** remove three mounting bolts and bearing from steering knuckle.
6. Remove retaining nut and separate outer tie rod end from steering knuckle using special removal tool No. 8677, or equivalent.
7. Remove nut and separate lower ball joint from knuckle using removal tool No. C-4150A, or equivalent.
8. Remove nut and separate upper ball joint from knuckle using removal tool No. 8677, or equivalent.
9. Remove knuckle.
10. Remove shock clevis bracket and stabilizer link from lower control arm.
11. Remove mounting nuts and bolts, then the lower control arm.
12. Reverse procedure to install.

UPPER

1. Raise and support vehicle, then support axle using suitable jack.
2. Remove tire and wheel assembly, then the inner fender well.
3. Remove nut and separate upper ball joint from knuckle using removal tool No. 8677, or equivalent.
4. Remove mounting nut and bolt, then the upper control arm.
5. Reverse procedure to install.

STEERING KNUCKLE

REPLACE

2002–04

1. Raise and support vehicle, then remove wheel and tire assembly.
2. Remove brake caliper, anchor and rotor as outlined in "Disc Brakes" chapter.
3. Remove ABS wheel speed sensor.
4. Remove cotter pin, retainer and axle hub nut.
5. Remove mounting bolts and hub bearing from steering knuckle and axle shaft, **Fig. 5.**
6. Remove tie rod clamp nut and damper.
7. Remove cotter pins and tie rod ends nuts from steering knuckle.
8. Remove tie rod ends from steering knuckles using puller tool No. C-3894-A, or equivalent.
9. Loosen adjustment sleeve clamp bolts and unscrew tie rod ends from sleeve.
10. Remove cotter pins, then the upper and lower ball stud nuts.
11. Remove axle shaft as outlined under "Front Wheel Drive" section.
12. Remove ABS sensor wire and bracket from knuckle.
13. Remove drag link and tie rod ends,
14. Remove cotter pins and mounting nuts from upper and lower ball joints.
15. Loosen steering knuckle from ball studs by strike it using suitable brass hammer.
16. Remove steering knuckle.
17. Reverse procedure to install.

2005–06

1. Raise and support vehicle, then remove tire and wheel assembly.
2. Remove brake caliper, adapter and rotor as outlined in "Disc Brakes" chapter.
3. Remove wheel speed sensor mounting bolt and disconnect wire from knuckle retaining clips.
4. **On models equipped with 4WD,** remove axle shaft nut.
5. **On all models,** remove three mounting bolts and bearing from steering knuckle.
6. Remove retaining nut and separate outer tie rod end from steering knuckle using special removal tool No. 8677, or equivalent.
7. Remove nut and separate lower ball joint from knuckle using removal tool No. C-4150A, or equivalent.
8. Remove nut and separate upper ball joint from knuckle using removal tool No. 8677, or equivalent.
9. Remove knuckle.
10. Reverse procedure to install.

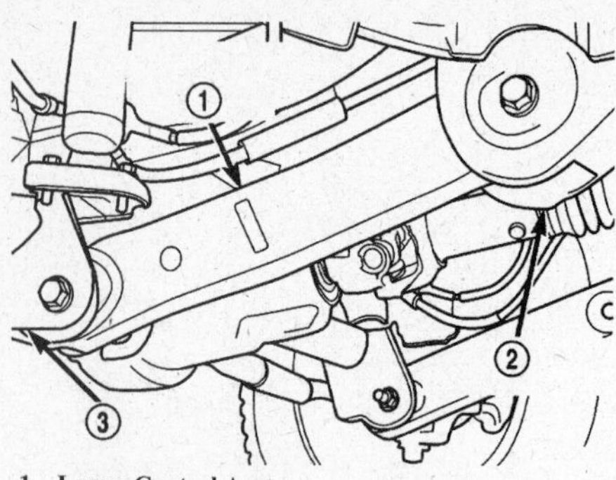

Fig. 4 Lower control arm replacement. 2002–04

STABILIZER BAR

REPLACE

2002–04

1. Raise and support vehicle.
2. Remove mounting nuts and bolts, then the stabilizer links, **Fig. 6.**
3. Remove mounting bolts and stabilizer bar.
4. Reverse procedure to install.

2005–06

1. Raise and support vehicle, then remove front splash shield.
2. Remove stabilizer bar link upper mounting nut and bolt.
3. Remove two bushing clamp bolts and stabilizer bar.
4. Reverse procedure to install.

TRACK BAR

REPLACE

1. Raise and support vehicle.
2. Remove track bar to frame rail bracket mounting nut and bolt.
3. Remove axle bracket mounting bolt and track bar.

TIE ROD END

REPLACE

2002–04

1. Raise and support vehicle, then remove wheel and tire assemblies.
2. Remove tie rod clamp nut and damper.
3. Remove cotter pins and nuts from tie rod ends at steering knuckles.
4. Remove tie rod ends from steering knuckles using puller tool No. C-3894-A, or equivalent.
5. Loosen adjustment sleeve clamp bolts and remove tie rod ends from sleeve.
6. Reverse procedure to install.

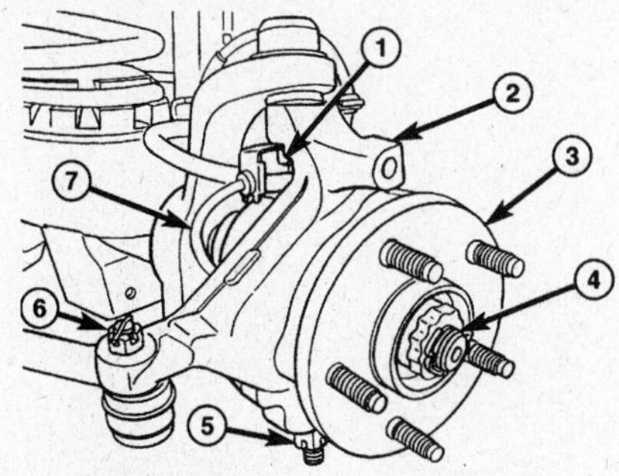

1. Upper Ball Joint
2. Steering Knuckle
3. Brake Rotor
4. Axle nut
5. Lower Ball Joint
6. Tie Rod

LTV0500000000141

Fig. 5 Steering knuckle replacement. 2002–04

2005–06

1. Remove jam and tie rod end nut.
2. Remove tie rod end from steering knuckle using puller tool No. 8677, or equivalent.
3. Remove outer tie rod end form inner tie rod. Count number of turns when removing tie rod end to determined starting point when installing and toe adjustment.
4. Reverse procedure to install.

POWER STEERING GEAR

REPLACE

2002–04

1. Place front wheels straight with steering wheel centered and locked.
2. Remove air cleaner housing.
3. Drain or siphon power steering system fluid into suitable container.
4. Disconnect steering gear pressure and return hoses.
5. Remove steering column coupler shaft bolt.
6. Raise and support vehicle, then remove lefthand front wheel and tire assembly.
7. Remove pitman arm from steering gear using puller tool No. C-4150A, or equivalent.
8. Remove windshield washer fluid reservoir.
9. Remove mounting bolts and steering gear.
10. Reverse procedure to install.

2005–06

1. Place front wheels straight with steering wheel centered and locked.
2. Drain or siphon power steering system fluid into suitable container.
3. Remove bolt and disconnect steering column coupler shaft from steering gear.
4. Remove oil drip tray.
5. Disconnect steering gear pressure and return hoses.
6. Raise and support vehicle, then remove front wheel and tire assemblies
7. Loosen tie rod end jam nuts, the remove end nut and separate tie rod from steering knuckle using puller tool No. 8677, or equivalent.
8. Remove front splash shield.
9. **On models equipped with 4WD,** remove front axle as outlined under "Axle, Replace" in "Front Wheel Drive" section.
10. **On all models,** remove two mounting bolts and move steering gear to full righthand position.
11. Lower and remove gear past control arm.
12. Reverse procedure to install.

POWER STEERING PUMP

REPLACE

3.7L & 4.7L Engines

1. Rotate belt tensioner until it contacts stop, then remove drive belt and slowly rotate tensioner into freearm position.
2. Remove power steering pump pressure and return hoses, then drain fluid into suitable container.
3. Remove three mounting bolts through pulley access holes, then remove pump downward
4. Reverse procedure to install.

4.0L Engine

1. Rotate belt tensioner until it contacts stop, then remove drive belt and slowly rotate tensioner into freearm position.
2. Remove power steering pump pressure and return hoses, then drain fluid into suitable container.
3. Loosen pump bracket mounting bolt.
4. Remove three mounting bolts through pulley access holes, then downward and remove pump.
5. Reverse procedure to install.

5.7L Engine

1. Siphon power steering reservoir fluid into suitable container.
2. Remove air intake tube.
3. Release belt tension by rotating tensioner counterclockwise.
4. Rotate belt tensioner and remove belt, then gently release tensioner.
5. Disconnect pump supply hose and pressure line.
6. Remove three mounting bolts and power steering pump.
7. Reverse procedure to install.

STEERING DAMPER

REPLACE

1. Remove tie rod ball stud nut.
2. Remove steering damper from tie rod.
3. Remove mounting nut and bolts, then the steering damper axle bracket.
4. Reverse procedure to install.

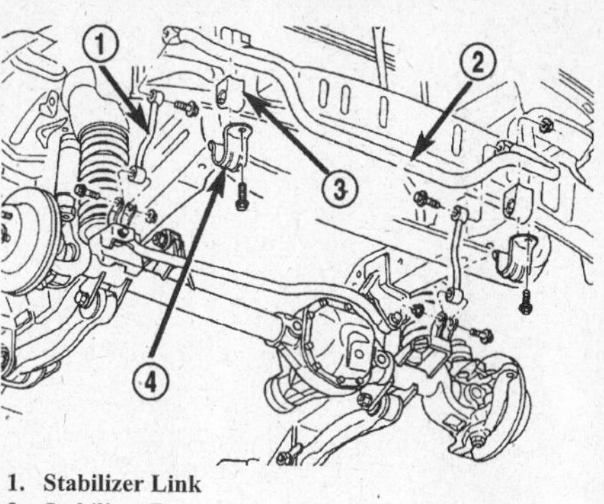

1. Stabilizer Link
2. Stabilizer Bar
3. Bushing
4. Bracket

LTV0500000000144

Fig. 6 Stabilizer bar replacement. 2002–04

POWER STEERING SYSTEM BLEED

2002–04

LESS HYDRAULIC COOLING FAN

The dipstick should indicate COLD when the fluid is at normal ambient temperature.

1. Fill pump fluid reservoir to proper level and let for at least two minutes.
2. Start and run engine for a few seconds, then turn engine off.
3. Adjust fluid level.
4. Repeat procedure until the level remains constant after running engine.
5. Raise front wheels and support vehicle.
6. Slowly turn steering wheel right and left, lightly contacting wheel stops at least 20 times.
7. Adjust fluid level.
8. Lower vehicle, start engine and turn steering wheel slowly from lock to lock.
9. Stop engine and adjust fluid level.
10. If fluid is extremely foamy or milky looking, allow vehicle to stand a few minutes and repeat procedure.

WITH HYDRAULIC COOLING FAN

The dipstick should indicate COLD when the fluid is at normal ambient temperature.

1. Fill pump fluid reservoir to proper level and let for at least two minutes.
2. Start and run engine for a few seconds, then turn engine off.
3. Adjust fluid level.
4. Repeat procedure until the level remains constant after running engine.
5. Raise front wheels and support vehicle.
6. Slowly turn steering wheel right and left, lightly contacting wheel stops at least 20 times.
7. Adjust fluid level.
8. Lower vehicle, start engine and use suitably programmed scan tool to activate hydraulic fan on full fan operation.
9. Turn steering wheel slowly from lock to lock.
10. Stop engine and adjust fluid level.

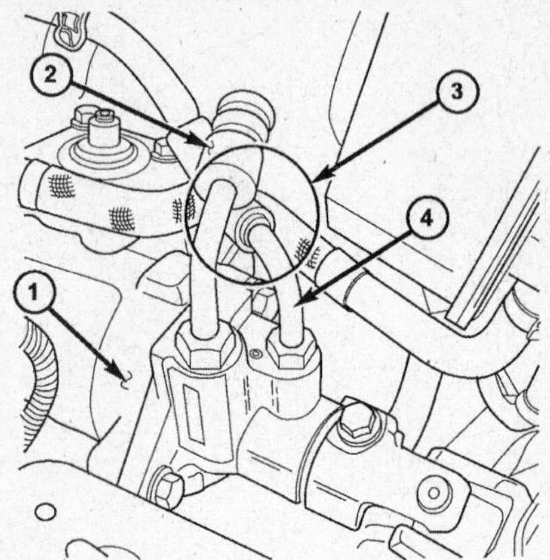

1 - Power Steering Gear Assembly

2 - High Pressure Inlet Power Steering Hose

3 - Location of Possible Hose Contact

4 - Low Pressure Outlet/Return Power Steering Hose

LTV0500000000149

Fig. 7 Power steering gear hose contact

11. If fluid is extremely foamy or milky looking, allow vehicle to stand a few minutes and repeat procedure.
12. With vehicle in park, use suitably programmed scan tool to activate hydraulic fan on full fan operation and briefly rev engine up to 3000 RPM to fully engage hydraulic fan.
13. Adjust fluid level.

2005-06

The procedure has been revised by a Technical Service Bulletin.

The dipstick should indicate COLD when the fluid is at normal ambient temperature.

1. Install Miller power steering cap adapter tool No. 9688, or equivalent, onto power steering pump reservoir.
2. Apply 20–25 in Hg. vacuum to power steering system for at least three minutes using suitable hand pump.
3. Slowly release vacuum, remove tools and adjust fluid level.
4. Repeat procedure until the level remains constant.
5. Start engine and turn steering wheel slowly from lock to lock three times. **Do not hold steering wheel on stops.**
6. Adjust fluid level.

TECHNICAL SERVICE BULLETINS

Cold Temperature Power Steering Whine

MODELS BUILT BEFORE OCT. 29, 2005 w/5.7L ENGINE

On some of these models there may be a short duration power steering whine during initial cold engine start-up at ambient temperatures of 32°F, or less.

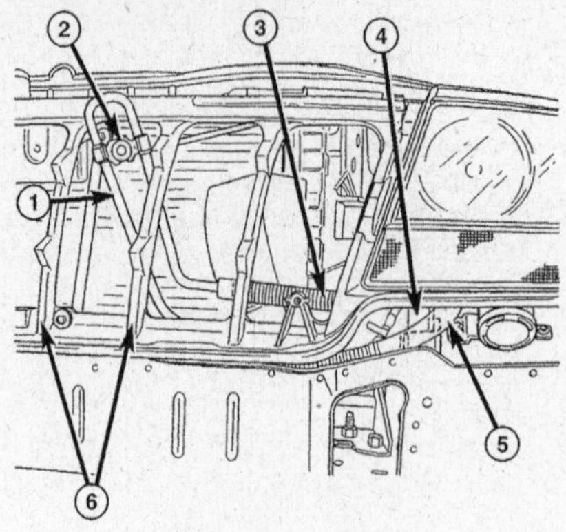

1 - New Power Steering Pressure Hose

2 - Bracket For Attaching Hose To Lower Radiator Support Panel

3 - Pump End Of Hose - Route Hose Next To Radiator

4 - Radiator Support Post

5 - Gear End Of Hose - Route Hose Under Left Headlamp

6 - Opening In Radiator Grill Support Panel

LTV0500000000150

Fig. 8 Power steering pressure hose grill routing

This condition may be caused by the remote mounted power steering reservoir.

To correct this condition, install revised reservoir (part No. 52124317AA). Revisions are internal. Exterior of reservoir is unchanged.

Power Steering Whine

MODELS BUILT BEFORE NOV. 9, 2004, w/5.7L ENGINE

On some of these models there may be a power steering whine during parking lot maneuvers.

This condition may be caused by power steering pressure hose grounding.

To correct this condition, adjust hose as follows:

1. Inspect power steering pressure hose between pump and Hydraulic Engine Cooling (HEC) module.
2. Ensure hose is at least one inch from the lefthand frame rail and Electronic Limited Slip Differential (ELSD) harness/connector.
3. If hose is not as specified, loose hose flare nut on lefthand side of power steering pump to allow hose rotation inside flare not.
4. Rotate hose to at least one inch from the lefthand frame rail and ELSDI harness/connector.
5. **Torque** flare nut to 35 ft. lbs.

Suspension Squeak/ Squawk

2002-04

On some of these models there may be a suspension squeak or squawk. Sound may occur most often when ambient temperature is approximately 32°F.

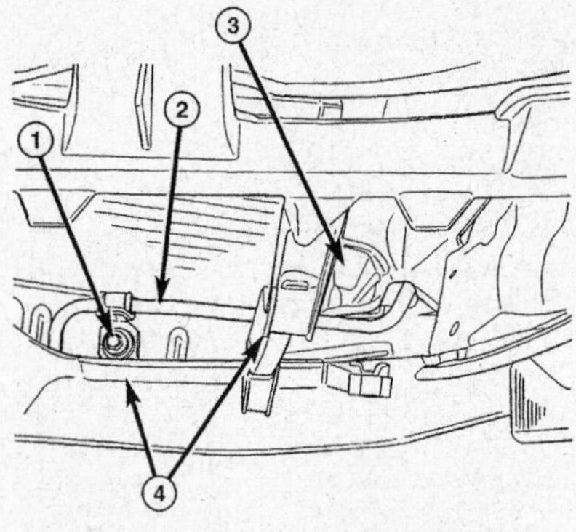

1 - Screw Securing Pressure Hose To Lower Radiator Panel

2 - New Power Steering Pressure Hose

3 - Black Air Deflector

4 - Radiator Grill Support Panel

LTV0500000000151

Fig. 9 Power steering pressure hose body attachment

This condition may be caused by the front stabilizer bar bushings.

To correct this condition, lubricate the front stabilizer bar and bushings, as follows:

1. Raise and support vehicle.
2. Remove mounting bolts and front stabilizer bar bracket, then the bushings.
3. Thoroughly clean stabilizer bar bushing contact area. Ensure there is no foreign material or rubber build-up on bar.
4. Apply liberal coating of Mopar lubricant No. 0501961AA, or equivalent, to stabilizer bar bushing position.
5. **On 2004 models,** replace bushings (part No. 52088284AE).
6. **On all models,** thoroughly lubricate entire inside bushings' surface.
7. Install bushings and **torque** mounting bolts to 68 ft. lbs.

Power Steering Moan Or Whine While Turning

2002-03

On some of these models there may be a moan or whine when turning.

This condition may be caused by contact between high and low pressure power steering hoses.

To correct this condition, separate high and low pressure power steering hoses at the steering gear as follows:

1. Clean power steering gear hose connections area.
2. Slightly loosen low and high pressure power steering gear hoses' connections.
3. Position hoses so there is no contact, **Fig. 7.**
4. Maintain at least .125 inch between hoses. **Do not separate hoses too far or hoses will contact other vehicle components such as air box snorkel.**
5. **Torque** hose connections to 17 ft. lbs.

Power Steering Honk

2002

On some of these models, equipped less hydraulic cooling, there may be a power steering honk. The is sound most often occurs during low-speed, righthand turns.

This condition may be caused by the power steering pressure and return hoses and tubes.

To correct this condition, replace the power steering pressure and return hoses and tubes as follows:

4.0L ENGINE

1. Remove front fascia panel and air cleaner housing, then the lefthand headlamp housing module.
2. Clean power steering gear and pump pressure hose connections.
3. Siphon fluid from power steering reservoir into suitable container.
4. Remove power steering pressure hose from power steering pump and gear.
5. Install new pressure hose (part No. 52088452AE) through grill support panel opening, **Fig. 8.**
6. Route power steering pump pressure hose end through radiator and under black air deflector at same time.
7. Route power steering gear pressure hose end through opening under lefthand headlamp. **Do not damage leak detection pump hose, nipple or electrical harness and connector.**
8. Secure pressure hose in front of radiator to lower radiator panel using mounting screw (part No. 061921411AA), **Fig. 9.**
9. Set black air deflector in place, around pressure hose.
10. Remove reservoir power steering return hose.
11. Remove power steering gear return hose and tube.
12. Loosely install new return hose (part No. 52088775AB) to power steering gear.
13. Slide two new hose clamps (part No. 06504502) over new return hose (part No. 52088774AC).

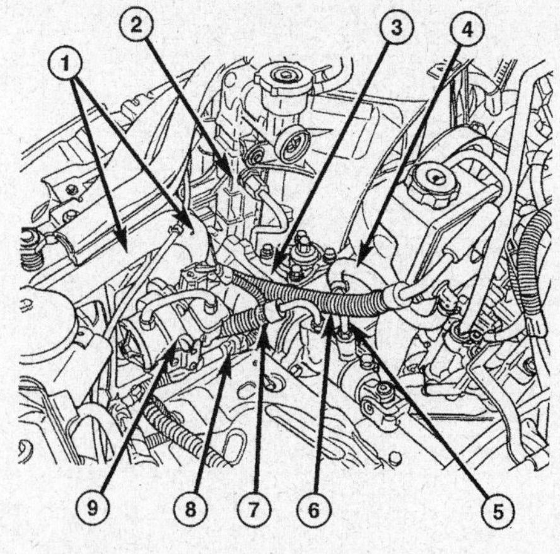

1 - Radiator Support
2 - Radiator
3 - Power Steering Gear
4 - New Power Steering Return Hose
5 - New Power Steering Return Tube
6 - Steering Pump End Of The New Pressure Hose
7 - Steering Gear End Of the New Pressure Hose
8 - Harness To The Leak Detection Pump
9 - Leak Detection Pump

LTV0500000000152

Fig. 10 Power steering engine compartment hose routing

14. Loosely install hose to return tube and reservoir. Ensure there are no kinks or interference between pressure and return hoses, **Fig. 10.**
15. Hand tighten pressure hose fittings, then **torque** fittings to 21 ft. lbs.
16. Tighten return hose clamps.
17. Install lefthand headlamp housing module, air cleaner housing and front fascia panel.
18. Fill and bleed power steering system as outlined under "Power Steering System Bleed"

4.7L ENGINE

1. Remove air cleaner housing.
2. Clean power steering gear and pump pressure hose connections.
3. Siphon fluid from power steering reservoir into suitable container.
4. Remove power steering pressure hose from power steering pump and gear.
5. Install new power steering pressure hose quick connect fitting (part No. 52088116AB) to power steering pump.
6. Install new power steering pressure hose (part No. 05080950AA) to pump and gear. **Torque** fittings to 21 ft. lbs.
7. Remove power steering gear metal return tube.
8. Remove short rubber hose between metal return tube and oil cooler.
9. Slide hose clamp (part No. 06504502) onto new return hose (part No. 05080951AA).
10. Loosely install return hose onto oil cooler. **Do not lubricate hose. Connection must be dry fit.**
11. Loosely install return hose onto power steering gear. Ensure hose is not kinked.
12. Tighten return hose oil cooler end clamp.
13. **Torque** return hose steering gear fitting to 21 ft. lbs.
14. Install air cleaner housing.
15. Fill and bleed power steering system as outlined under "Power Steering System Bleed"

Slight Lead Or Drift

2002-04

On some of these models there may be a slight lead or drift to either side with no driver steering system input. This condition may also occur when driver is maintaining a constant steering system input in order to maintain a straight ahead direction.

This condition may be caused by front end caster and/or camber angles.

To correct this condition, install offset ball joints as outlined in "Wheel Alignment" section.

TIGHTENING SPECIFICATIONS

Year	Component	Torque Ft. Lbs.
2002–04	Axle Nut	175
	Axle Shaft	96
	Ball Joint, Lower	80
	Ball Joint, Upper	75
	Control Arm, Lower To Axle Bracket	120
	Control Arm, Lower To Frame Bracket	115
	Control Arm, Upper	45
	Hub Bearing	75
	Lower Ball Joint	70
	Pitman Arm	185
	Power Steering Pump (4.0L Engine)	20
	Power Steering Pump (4.7L Engine)	21
	Steering Power Pump Hose	21
	Power Steering Pump Bracket	42
	Shock Absorber, Lower	21
	Shock Absorber Upper	26
	Stabilizer Bar	68
	Stabilizer Bar Link	78
	Steering Damper	65
	Steering Gear	80
	Steering Power Steering Hose	14–18
	Tie Rod Ball Joint	30
	Tie Rod End	35
	Tie Rod End Clamp	30
	Track Bar	74
	Upper Ball Joint	70
	Wheel Lug Nuts	85–115
2005–06	Control Arm, Lower Front	125
	Control Arm, Lower Rear	65
	Control Arm, Upper	80
	Power Steering Hose	21
	Power Steering Pump	21
	Shock Absorber, Lower Clevis	125
	Shock Absorber, Upper	70
	Shock Absorber Upper Shaft	25
	Stabilizer Bar	95
	Stabilizer Link	85
	Steering Gear	180
	Steering Gear Couple Shaft	36
	Tie Rod End	70
	Tie Rod Jam Nut	55
	Upper Ball Joint	70

Front Wheel Drive

INDEX

AXLE

REPLACE

2002–04

1. Raise and support vehicle, then support axle with suitable hydraulic jack.
2. Remove tire and wheel assemblies, then the brake calipers and rotors as outlined in "Disc Brakes" chapter.
3. Disconnect wheel sensor wiring from vehicle harness.
4. Remove stabilizer bar links.
5. Remove shock absorbers from axle brackets.
6. Remove track bar.
7. Remove tie rod and drag link from steering knuckle.
8. Remove steering damper from axle bracket.
9. Remove upper and lower suspension arms from axle bracket.
10. Lower and remove axle. Coil springs will drop from axle.

2005–06

1. With transmission in neutral, raise and support vehicle, then remove skid plate.
2. Drain differential fluid into suitable container.
3. Mark front propeller shaft and pinion flange for installation alignment.
4. Remove mounting bolts and propeller shaft from pinion flange.
5. Remove half shaft hub/bearing mounting nuts.
6. Remove wheel speed sensors.
7. Remove mounting bolts and brakes calipers from caliper adapters.
8. Remove stabilizer links mounting bolts from lower control arms.
9. Remove end nuts and separate outer tie rods from knuckles using remover tool No. 8677, or equivalent.
10. Remove nuts and separate upper ball joints from knuckles using remover tool No. 8677, or equivalent.
11. Remove lower shock clevis mounting bolts from lower control arm.
12. Lean knuckles out and push half shafts out of hub/bearings.
13. Pry half shafts off axles.
14. Remove ELSD connector and remove differential vent hose.
15. Remove axle tube bushing and pinion nose bushing mounting bolts.
16. Support axle with suitable lift or jack.
17. Remove differential cover bracket bushing mounting bolts and remove axle.
18. Reverse procedure to install.

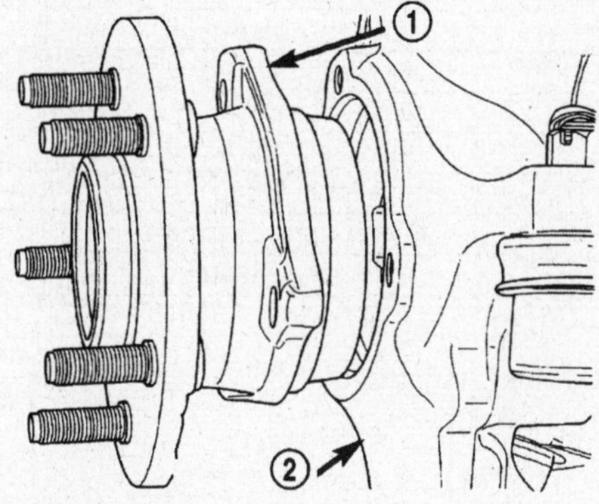

Fig. 1 Hub & bearing replacement

AXLE SHAFT

REPLACE

2002–04

If the axle shaft and hub bearing are being removed to service another component, the axle shaft and hub bearing can be removed as an assembly.

1. Raise and support vehicle, then remove wheel and tire assembly.
2. Remove brake caliber and rotor as outlined in "Disc Brakes" chapter.
3. Remove ABS wheel speed sensor,
4. Remove cotter pin, retainer and axle nut.
5. Remove mounting bolts, hub bearing and axle shaft.
6. Remove brake rotor shield.
7. Reverse procedure to install. Apply thin film of Mopar Wheel Bearing Grease, or equivalent, to shaft splines, seal contact surface and hub bore.

2005–06

1. Remove half shaft.
2. Remove snap ring and O-ring.
3. Remove axle using remove tool No. 8420A, or equivalent, and suitable slide hammer.
4. Reverse procedure to install. Lubricate bearing bore and seal lip with suitable gear lubricant.

HUB & BEARING SERVICE

2002–04

1. Raise and support vehicle, then remove wheel and tire assembly.
2. Remove brake caliper, anchor and rotor as outlined in "Disc Brakes" chapter.
3. Remove ABS wheel speed sensor.
4. Remove cotter pin, retainer and axle nut.
5. Remove mounting bolts and hub bearing, **Fig. 1.**
6. Reverse procedure to install.

2005–06

1. Remove axle shaft.
2. Remove axle shaft tube seal using seal remover tool No. 7794-A, or equivalent, and suitable slide hammer.
3. Remove bearing using axle bearing remover tool No. C-4660-A, or equivalent.
4. Reverse procedure to install using installer tool No. 5063 and handle tool No. C-4171, or equvialents.

TIGHTENING SPECIFICATIONS

Year	Component	Torque Ft. Lbs.
2002–04	Axle Nut	175
	Coil Spring	17
	Control Arm, Lower	35
	Control Arm, Upper	55
	Hub Bearing	75
	Shock Absorber	17
	Stabilizer Bar Link	70
	Steering Damper	55
	Track Bar	74
	Wheel Lug Nut	80–110
2005–06	Axle Tube Bushing	70
	Axle Tube Bushing	35
	Axle Tube Bushing	100
	Drain Plug	44
	Pinion Nose Bushing	70
	Propeller Shaft	80

Wheel Alignment

INDEX

PRELIMINARY INSPECTION

Inspect following components, adjust, repair or replace as required prior to performing front wheel alignment.

2002–04

1. Inflate tires to cold specifications.
2. Ensure tires are of same size, ply rating and load rating.
3. Inspect for excessive wheel bearing endplay.
4. Inspect for worn or damaged ball joints.
5. Inspect steering gear mounting bolts for proper torque.
6. Inspect control arm for bent or damaged condition.
7. Inspect control arm to frame bushings for looseness or wear.
8. Inspect suspension components for wear or damage.
9. Inspect vehicle ride height.

2005–06

1. Inspect tires for size, air pressure and tread wear.
2. Inspect front wheel bearings for wear.
3. Inspect front wheels for excessive radial or lateral runout and balance.
4. Inspect ball studs, linkage pivot points and steering gear for looseness, roughness or binding.
5. Inspect suspension components for wear and noise.

FRONT WHEEL ALIGNMENT

Refer to "Specifications" for specifications.

Camber

2002–04

The procedure has been revised by a Technical Service Bulletin.

Camber is preset at the factory and is not adjustable.

If cross-camber is more than 1°, select the wheel furthest from desired camber angle and replace ball joint with appropriate offset as outlined under "Ball Joint, Replace."

The camber angle of the adjusted side should equal the unadjusted side, providing a cross-camber of zero degrees.

Cross-camber of no more than 1° is allowed provided both lefthand and righthand camber angles are within camber angle limits.

2005–06

Camber adjustments involve changing the position of the lower control arm with the slots in the frame brackets to move the lower control arm in or outward for proper adjustment. **Do not use the upper control arm for camber adjustments.**

1. Loosen lower control arm pivot bolts. Lower control arm will move outward.
2. Move lower control arm using suitable long pry bar with curved tip.
3. Insert pry bar into lower control arm frame brackets and prying in or outward.
4. Move both front and rear of lower control arm together in or out.
5. This will change camber angle significantly and caster angle slightly.
6. **Torque** front pivot bolt to 125 ft. lbs., and rear bolt to 65 ft. lbs.

Caster

2002–04

The procedure has been revised by a Technical Service Bulletin.

Caster is preset at the factory and is not adjustable.

If individual caster is more than specified or if cross-caster difference between sides is more than .5°, replace ball joint with appropriate offset as outlined under "Ball Joint, Replace."

Offset ball joints will not effect front propeller shaft angles.

2005–06

Caster angle adjustments involve changing the position of the lower control arm with the slots in the frame brackets to move the lower control arm in or outward for proper adjustment. **Do not use the upper control arm for caster adjustments.**

1. Loosen lower control arm pivot bolts. Lower control arm will move outward.
2. Move lower control arm using suitable long pry bar with curved tip.
3. Insert pry bar into lower control arm frame brackets and prying in or outward.
4. Move rear position of lower control arm at frame in or out, will change caster angle significantly and camber angle only slightly.
5. To maintain camber angle while adjusting caster, move rear of lower control arm in or out.
6. Then move front of lower control arm slightly in opposite direction.
7. **Torque** front pivot bolt to 125 ft. lbs., and rear bolt to 65 ft. lbs.

Toe-In

2002–04

The engine must be running during this procedure.

1. Apply parking brake, then start engine and turn wheel in both directions.
2. Center and lock steering wheel.
3. Loosen tie rod adjustment sleeve clamp bolts.
4. Turn sleeve to obtain desired toe.
5. Each front wheel should be adjusted for one-half of total toe position specification.
6. **Torque** clamp bolts to 50 ft. lbs. Ensue toe setting does change during tightening.

2005–06

The engine must be running during this procedure.

1. Apply parking brake, then start engine and turn wheel in both directions.
2. Center and lock steering wheel.
3. Loosen tie rod jam nuts.
4. Turn inner tie rod to obtain desired toe.
5. Each front wheel should be adjusted for one-half of total toe position specification.
6. **Torque** tie rod jam nut to 55 ft. lbs. Ensue toe setting does change during tightening.

BALL JOINT

REPLACE

The procedure has been revised by a Technical Service Bulletin.

The front end camber and caster angles on 2002–04 models are not adjustable. Offset ball joints are available to adjust fixed front end alignment angles up to 1.5°, **Fig. 1.**

Offset Angle°	Part No.
.5	05014876AC
1.0	05014877AC
1.5	05016972AC

Fig. 1 Off-set ball joint selection table

If cross-camber is more than 1°, select the wheel furthest from desired camber angle and replace ball joint as follows.

The camber angle of the adjusted side should equal the unadjusted side, providing a cross-camber of zero degrees.

Cross-camber of no more than 1° is allowed provided both lefthand and righthand camber angles are within camber angle limits.

If individual caster is more than specified or if cross-caster is difference between sides is more than .5°, replace ball joint with appropriate offset as follows:

Offset ball joints will not effect front propeller shaft angles.

1. Raise and support vehicle, then support front axle with suitable jack.
2. Remove tire and wheel assembly.
3. Remove axle shaft wheel hub/bearing cotter pin, retainer and nut.
4. Mark brake rotor to axle hub/bearing for installation alignment.
5. Remove two slide pins, brake caliper, pads and rotor. Support caliper aside. **Do not use brake line to support caliper.**
6. Remove tie rod from steering knuckle. **Do not damage boot.**
7. Mark wheel hub/bearing to steering knuckle for installation alignment.
8. Remove wheel hub/bearing and brake rotor shield.
9. Carefully remove axle shaft.
10. Remove upper and lower ball joint cotter pins and nuts.
11. Loosen steering knuckle from ball joint by striking knuckle with suitable brass hammer.

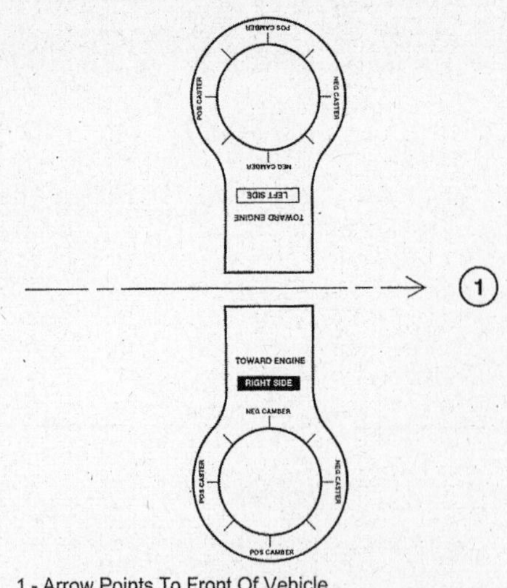

Fig. 2 Ball joint template positioning

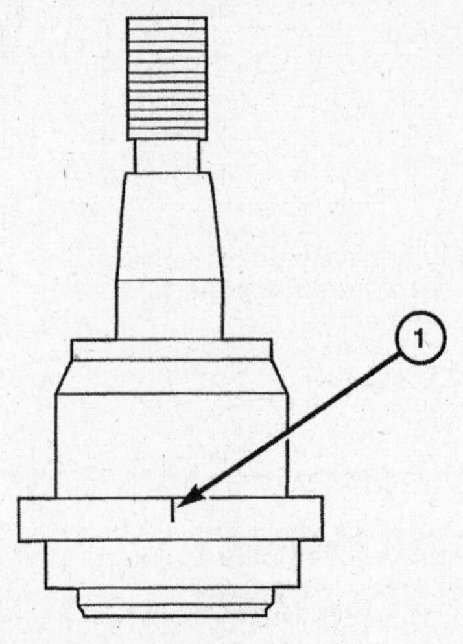

Fig. 3 Ball joint index mark

12. Lower steering knuckle from all joints studs.
13. Remove upper ball joint using ball joint installation and removal kit tool No. 6289, or equivalent.
14. Position template supplied in new offset ball joint package on top of axle yoke. Ensure template is oriented correctly, **Fig. 2.**
15. Temporarily friction fit offset ball joint to axle yoke by hand.
16. Position ball joint index mark to template to obtain desired angle, **Fig. 3.**
17. Remove template.
18. Press ball joint into axle yoke bore.
19. Ensure ball joint is fully seated and is correctly positioned relative to template.
20. Install ball joint dust boot and grease fitting.
21. Install steering knuckle.
22. **Torque** lower ball joint nut to 80 ft. lbs., and install new cotter pin.
23. **Torque** upper ball joint nut to 75 ft. lbs., and install new cotter pin.
24. Install tie rod to steering knuckle.
25. **Torque** tie rod to knuckle mounting nut to 35 ft. lbs., and install new cotter pin.
26. Install axle. **Do not damage axle seal.**
27. Align wheel hub/bearing and steering knuckle marks.
28. Install brake dust shield and wheel hub/bearing.
29. **Torque** wheel hub/bearing mounting bolts to 75 ft. lbs.
30. Install axle shaft washer and nut.
31. **Torque** axle nut to 175 ft. lbs. Install axle nut retainer and new cotter pin.
32. Align brake rotor and wheel hub/bearing marks, then install brake rotor.
33. Install brake caliper and brake pads to steering knuckle.
34. **Torque** caliper slide bolts to 26 ft. lbs.
35. Grease ball joint.
36. Install tire and wheel assembly. **Torque** lug nuts to 100 ft. lbs.
37. Inspect wheel alignment.

LIBERTY

NOTE: Refer To Rear Of This Manual For Vehicle Manufacturer's Special Service Tool Suppliers.

INDEX OF SERVICE OPERATIONS

Specifications

GENERAL ENGINE SPECIFICATIONS

Year	Engine Liters	Fuel System	Bore & Stroke, Inch	Compression Ratio	Net H.P. @ RPM	Maximum Torque, Ft. Lbs. @ RPM	Normal Oil Pressure, psi①
2002–06	2.4L	MPI	3.45 x 3.98	9.4:1	150 @ 5200	165 @ 4000	4
	2.8L Turbo Diesel	DI	3.54 x 3.94	17.5:1	163 @ 3800	295 @ 1800	28 @ 3800 RPM
	3.7L	MPI	3.66 x 3.40	9.1:1	210 @ 5000	225 @ 4000	4

DI— Direct Injection

MPI— Multi Port Injection

① — At curb idle.

TUNE UP SPECIFICATIONS

The following specifications are published from the latest information available. This data should only be used in the absence of a decal affixed in the engine compartment.

Year & Engine	Spark Plug Gap, Inch	Ignition Timing: Firing Order, Fig.	Ignition Timing: Man. Trans.	Ignition Timing: Auto. Trans.	Ignition Timing: Mark Location	Curb Idle Speed: Man. Trans.	Curb Idle Speed: Auto. Trans.	Fast Idle Speed: Man. Trans.	Fast Idle Speed: Auto. Trans.	Fuel Pump Pressure, psi	Valve Lash, Inch
2002–06											
2.4L	.048–.053	A	①	①	—	②	②	②	②	47.2–51.2	③
2.8L Turbo Diesel	—	1-3-4-2	①	①	—	②	②	②	②	—	—
3.7L	.042	B	①	①	Damper	②	②	②	②	47.2–51.2	③

① — Non-adjustable.

② — Controlled by idle speed control motor.

③ — Equipped w/hydraulic valve tappets.

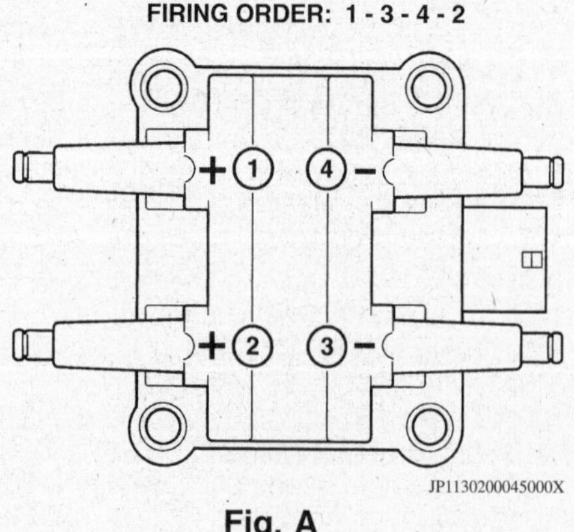

Fig. A

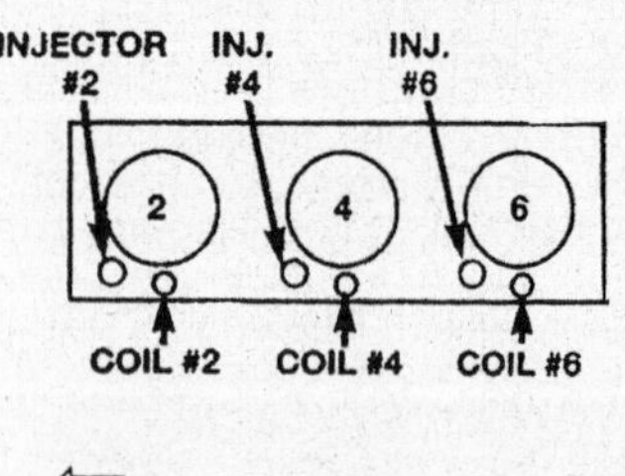

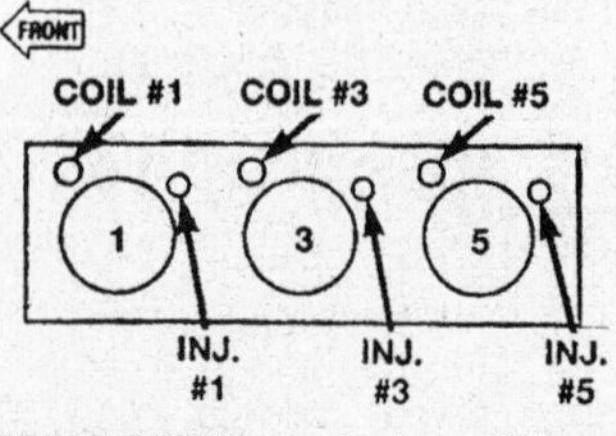

FIRING ORDER: 1 - 6 - 5 - 4 - 3 - 2

JP1130200046000X

Fig. B

FRONT WHEEL ALIGNMENT SPECIFICATIONS

Year	Caster, Degree		Camber, Degree		Toe-In, Inch		Ball Joint Wear Limit
	Limits	Desired	Limits	Desired	Limits	Desired	
2002	+2.9 to +4.1①	+3.5①	-.375 to +.375②	0②	+.070 to +.330③	+.2③	④
2003–06	+3.4 to +4.4①	+3.9①	-.750 to 0②	-.375②	+.075 to +.325③	+.2③	④

① — Maximum lefthand to righthand difference, .5°.
② — Maximum lefthand to righthand difference, .7°.
③ — Maximum lefthand to righthand difference, .13°.
④ — Refer to "Ball Joint Inspection" in "Front Suspension & Steering" section.

REAR WHEEL ALIGNMENT SPECIFICATIONS

Year	Camber		Thrust Angle		Total Toe	
	Limits	Desired	Limits	Desired	Limits	Desired
2002–06	-.625 to +.125	-.25	-.25 to +.25	0	-.16 to +.66	+.25

FLUID CAPACITIES & COOLING SYSTEM DATA

Year	Engine	Coolant Capacity, Qts.	Recommended Engine Coolant Type	Radiator Cap Relief Pressure, Lbs.	Thermo. Opening Temp., °F	Fuel Tank, Gals.	Engine Oil Refill, Qts.①	Transmission Oil			Axle Oil, Pts.
								Man. Trans., Pts.	Auto. Trans., Qts.②	Transfer Case, Pts.	
2002	2.4L	10.1	Ethylene Glycol	18–21	195	18.5	5	4.82	③	④	⑤
	3.7L	13.0	Ethylene Glycol	18–21	195	18.5	5	4.82	③	④	⑤
2003	2.4L	10.0	Ethylene Glycol	18–21	195	18.5	5	⑦	③	⑥	⑤
	3.7L	14.0	Ethylene Glycol	18–21	195	18.5	5	⑦	③	⑥	⑤
2004	2.4L	10.0	Ethylene Glycol	18–21	195	19.5	5	⑦	⑧	⑥	⑤
	3.7L	14.0	Ethylene Glycol	18–21	195	19.5	5	⑦	⑧	⑥	⑤
2005	3.7L	14.0	Ethylene Glycol	18–21	195	19.5	5	3.17	⑧	⑨	⑤
	2.8L Turbo Diesel	11.8	Ethylene Glycol	14–18	195	19.5	6.3	3.17	⑧	⑨	⑤
2006	2.4L	10.0	Ethylene Glycol	18–21	195	19.5	5	3.17	⑧	⑨	⑤
	2.8L Turbo Diesel	11.8	Ethylene Glycol	14–18	195	19.5	6.3	3.17	⑧	⑨	⑤
	3.7L	14.0	Ethylene Glycol	18–21	195	19.5	5	3.17	⑧	⑨	⑤

① — Includes filter.
② — Approximate. Make final inspection w/dipstick.
③ — Service fill, 5 qts.; after overhaul, 14 qts.
④ — Model NV231, 2.2 pts.; model NV242, 2.85 pts.
⑤ — Front axle, 2.6 pts. Rear axles, 8.25 inch, 4.4 pts.; 198-RBI, 3.8 pts. When equipped with Trac-Lok, include 4 oz. of friction modifier.
⑥ — Model NV231, 2.95 pts.; model NV242, 3.4 pts.
⑦ — Model NV1500, 4.8 pts.; Model NV3550, 2WD 4.8 pts., 4WD 4.2 pts.
⑧ — 545RFE Service fill 5 qts.; Overhaul 14 qts; 42RLE Service fill 4 qts.; Overhaul 8.8 qts.
⑨ — Model NV231, 2.95 pts.; model NV242, 3.4 pts.; model NV241 GENII, 4.2 pts.

LUBRICANT DATA

Year	Model	Lubricant Type					
		Transmission		Transfer Case	Front/ Rear Axle	Power Steering	Brake System
		Manual	Automatic				
2002–04	All	①	ATF+4	ATF+4	③	②	DOT 3
2005–06	All	①	ATF+4	ATF+4	④	②	DOT 3

① — Mopar Manual Transmission Lubricant.
② — Use Mopar Power Steering Fluid or equivalent.
③ — Front axle, 75W-140 Synthetic gear lubricant. Rear axle, 198RBI, 75W-140 Synthetic gear lubricant. Rear axle 8.25 inch, models not intended for heavy duty or trailer tow use 75W-90 GL-5 gear lubricant; models intended for heavy duty use or trailer tow use 75W-140 Synthetic gear lubricant. On models with Trac-Lok, include 4 oz. of friction modifier.
④ — Front axle, 80W-90. Rear axle 8.25 inch, models not intended for heavy duty or trailer tow use 75W-90 GL-5 gear lubricant; models intended for heavy duty use or trailer tow use 75W-140 Synthetic gear lubricant. On models with Trac-Lok, include 4 oz. of friction modifier.

Electrical

NOTE: On Air Bag Equipped Models, Refer To "Air Bag System Precautions" Located In The Front Of This Manual For System Disarming & Arming Procedures.

NOTE: Refer To "Computer Relearn Procedures" Located In The Front Of This Manual When Battery Power To The Computer Has Been Interrupted.

INDEX

PRECAUTIONS

Air Bag Systems

Refer to "Air Bag System Precautions" in the front of this manual for system disarming and arming procedures.

Battery Ground Cable

Prior to service, disconnect battery ground cable and isolate as required.

FUSE PANEL & FLASHER LOCATION

The fuse panel is located on the lefthand end of the instrument panel. The combination turn signal and hazard lamp flasher is part of the hard switch module located in the center of the instrument panel.

FUEL PUMP RELAY LOCATION

The fuel pump relay is located on the lefthand side of the engine compartment in the relay/power distribution center.

RELAY CENTER LOCATION

The relay/power distribution center is located on the lefthand side of the engine compartment.

STARTER

REPLACE

2.4L Engine

1. Raise and support vehicle.
2. Remove solenoid wire from solenoid terminal.
3. Remove battery cable from stud on starter solenoid.
4. Remove two starter motor bolts, then the starter motor.
5. Reverse procedure to install.

2.8L Turbo Diesel

1. Raise and support vehicle.
2. Disconnect solenoid wire connector from solenoid terminal.
3. Remove battery cable from stud on starter solenoid.
4. Remove three starer mounting bolts.
5. Remove starter from bellhousing.
6. Reverse procedure to install.

3.7L Engine

1. Raise and support vehicle.
2. Remove two flange bolts securing left-hand exhaust downpipe to crossover pipe, then lower pipe slightly to allow for propeller shaft removal.
3. Remove propeller shaft.
4. Remove two starter motor heat shield bolts, then the heat shield nut.
5. Remove starter motor heat shield.
6. Remove solenoid wire from solenoid terminal.
7. Remove battery cable from stud on starter solenoid.
8. Remove two starter motor mounting bolts.
9. Position front of starter motor to face rear of vehicle, then rotate until solenoid position is located below starter.
10. Remove starter motor from vehicle through opening between exhaust pipe and transmission bellhousing.
11. Reverse procedure to install.

IGNITION COIL

REPLACE

2.4L Engine

1. Disconnect electrical connector at rear of coil.
2. Remove all secondary cables from coil.
3. Remove four coil mounting bolts, then the coil.
4. Reverse procedure to install.

3.7L Engine

An individual ignition coil is used for each cylinder. The coil fits into a machined hole in the cylinder head. A mounting stud/nut secures each coil to the top of the intake manifold. Remove ignition coils as follows:

1. Depending on which coil is being removed, throttle body air intake tube or

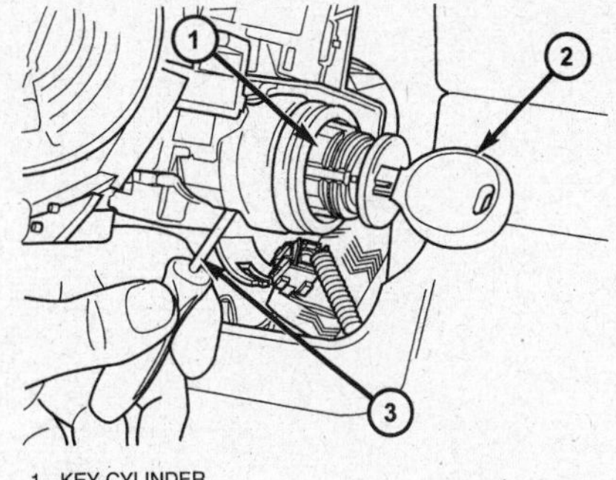

Fig. 1 Key cylinder release

intake box may need to be removed to gain access to ignition coil.
2. Disconnect electrical connector from coil by pushing downward on release lock on top of connector and pulling connector from coil.
3. Clean area at base of ignition coil before removing from cylinder head.
4. Remove mounting nut and carefully pull up on coil using a slight twisting motion.
5. Reverse procedure to install.

IGNITION LOCK

REPLACE

Removal

1. **On models equipped with automatic transmission,** place shifter in PARK position.
2. **On all models,** remove lower shroud cover.
3. Remove remote keyless entry module.
4. Insert a suitable pin punch through access hole on bottom of steering column, **Fig. 1.**
5. Push pin punch while pulling key cylinder from steering column.

Installation

1. Ignition key must be in key cylinder for installation.
2. Install key cylinder into housing aligning end of key cylinder with ignition switch.
3. Push key cylinder in until it clicks.
4. Rotate key to insert position.
5. Install halo ring around key cylinder housing.
6. Install remote keyless entry module.
7. Install lower shroud cover.

IGNITION SWITCH

REPLACE

Removal

1. Remove lower steering column cover.
2. Remove lock cylinder as outlined in "Ignition Lock, Replace."
3. Remove multi-function switch.
4. Disconnect electrical connector from rear of ignition switch.
5. Remove ignition switch screw using suitable torx bit.
6. Pull ignition switch straight out to remove from locking tabs.

Installation

1. Rotate slot in ignition switch to ON position, **Fig. 2.**
2. Connect electrical connector to rear of ignition switch ensuring locking tab is fully seated into wiring connector.
3. Install ignition switch to column, then **torque** screw to 17 inch lbs.
4. Install lock cylinder as outlined in "Ignition Lock, Replace."
5. Ensure lock cylinder operates smoothly.
6. Install multi-function switch, then the steering column lower cover.

HEADLAMP SWITCH

REPLACE

Refer to "Multi-Function Switch, Replace" for headlamp switch replacement procedure.

STOP LIGHT SWITCH

REPLACE

Removal

1. Disconnect stop light switch harness electrical connector.
2. Rotate stop light switch housing counterclockwise 30° to align tabs on locking collar with keyed mounting hole in steering column support bracket.
3. Pull switch straight back from mounting hole to remove it from steering column support bracket.
4. Discard stop light switch.

Installation

Stop light switch is a one time only component and is not intended for reinstallation.

1. Apply and hold brake pedal, then align tabs on stop light switch locking collar with keyed mounting hole in support bracket.
2. Insert tabs on stop light switch housing through keyed mounting hole in support bracket until switch is firmly seated against bracket.
3. Rotate switch clockwise 30° to lock tabs on switch locking collar to keyed mounting hole in support bracket.
4. Release brake pedal.
5. Rotate plunger adjustment release lever clockwise until it locks into place parallel to stop light switch connector. This will set switch plunger length to a final adjustment position and cannot be undone. If not performed properly first time, a new stop light switch must be installed. **Do not pull up on brake pedal before switch plunger adjustment has been completed.**
6. Connect stop light switch electrical connector.

MULTI-FUNCTION SWITCH

REPLACE

1. **On models equipped with tilt steering,** tilt steering column to fully lowered position and leave tilt release lever in released position.
2. **On all models,** remove screws securing lower shroud to upper shroud.
3. Push inward on both sides of upper shroud near parting line between upper and lower shrouds to release snap features securing two halves together.
4. Remove both shrouds from steering column.
5. Disconnect two multi-function switch electrical connectors.
6. Remove multi-function switch from steering column lock housing by carefully rocking switch and pulling switch housing upward far enough to disengage its alignment posts and locator tabs from lock housing.
7. Reverse procedure to install.

TURN SIGNAL SWITCH

REPLACE

Refer to "Multi-Function Switch, Replace" for turn signal switch replacement procedure.

DIMMER SWITCH

REPLACE

Refer to "Multi-Function Switch, Replace" for dimmer switch replacement procedure.

STEERING WHEEL

REPLACE

1. Remove driver air bag module as outlined in "Passive Restraint Systems" chapter.
2. Partially remove steering wheel bolt.
3. Remove steering wheel using steering wheel puller tool No. C-3894-A, or equivalent, using top of bolt to push on.
4. Reverse procedure to install. **Torque** new steering wheel bolt to 40 ft. lbs.

INSTRUMENT CLUSTER

REPLACE

1. Remove drivers side trim bezels, then the instrument panel top cover.
2. Remove seven screws, then the cluster bezel.
3. Remove four screws securing instrument cluster to instrument panel.
4. Pull instrument cluster rearward far enough to access and disconnect electrical connector.
5. Remove instrument cluster.
6. Reverse procedure to install.

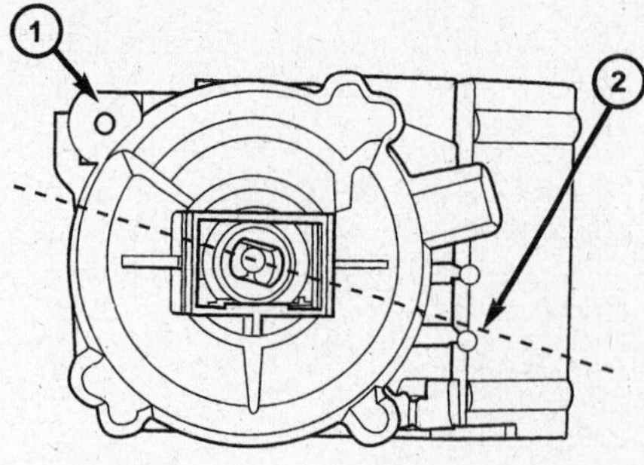

Fig. 2 Ignition switch ON position

RADIO

REPLACE

1. Remove instrument panel center trim panel.
2. Remove radio mounting screws.
3. Disconnect antenna cable by pulling locking antenna connector away from radio.
4. Disconnect radio electrical connector.
5. Remove radio from instrument panel.

WIPER MOTOR

REPLACE

Front

1. Unlatch and open hood.
2. Remove both wiper arms from wiper pivots.
3. Remove cowl plenum cover panel.
4. Disconnect wiper motor electrical connector.
5. Remove two screws securing front wiper module to top of cowl plenum panel at pivot brackets.
6. Remove two nuts that secure front wiper module to two weld studs on bottom of cowl plenum panel.
7. Lift front wiper module up from cowl plenum panel far enough to disengage two lower insulators from weld studs.
8. Remove front wiper module as a unit.
9. Reverse procedure to install.

Rear

1. Remove rear wiper arm from wiper motor output shaft.
2. Gently pry at notch in base of wiper motor output shaft bezel to unsnap nut cover from bezel using a suitable small thin bladed tool.
3. Remove nut securing wiper motor output shaft to outer swing gate panel.
4. Remove bezel and gasket from wiper motor output shaft.
5. Remove inner trim panel from tailgate.
6. Disconnect rear glass ajar switch electrical connector.
7. Disconnect wiper motor electrical connector.
8. Loosen two screws securing wiper motor mounting bracket to top of tailgate inner panel.
9. Slide rear wiper motor and mounting bracket forward far enough to disengage two mounting screws from keyed slots in top of tailgate inner panel.
10. Remove rear wiper motor and mounting bracket from tailgate as a unit.
11. Reverse procedure to install.

WIPER SWITCH

REPLACE

Refer to "Multi-Function Switch, Replace" for wiper switch replacement procedure.

BLOWER MOTOR

REPLACE

1. Unplug blower motor electrical harness connector.
2. Release locking tab to blower motor and wheel assembly to HVAC housing.
3. Rotate and tilt blower motor and wheel from HVAC housing.
4. Reverse procedure to install.

HEATER CORE

REPLACE

1. Remove instrument panel as outlined in "Dash Panel Service" chapter.
2. Recover refrigerant as outlined in "Air Conditioning" chapter.
3. Disconnect liquid refrigerant line fitting from evaporator inlet tube, plug all open lines.
4. Disconnect accumulator inlet tube refrigerant line fitting from evaporator outlet tube, plug all open lines.
5. Drain cooling system, then disconnect heater hoses from heater core tubes plugging all open tubes.
6. Disconnect heater and A/C system vacuum supply line from tee fitting near heater core tubes.
7. Disconnect heater and A/C unit wire harness fastened to housing next to blower motor relay.
8. Remove five nuts from housing mounting studs on engine compartment side of dash panel.
9. Pull housing rearward far enough for studs and evaporator condensate drain tube to clear dash panel holes, then remove housing.
10. Remove two heater core retaining screws.
11. Gently push back on two of heater core retaining tabs and pull up on heater core to remove.
12. Reverse procedure to install.

EVAPORATOR CORE

REPLACE

1. Remove heater and A/C housing as outlined in "Heater Core, Replace."
2. Remove top housing retaining screws, then the top of heater and A/C housing.
3. Remove thermostatic switch and capillary tube.
4. Remove evaporator retaining screws, then the evaporator.
5. Separate evaporator valve from evaporator core.
6. Reverse procedure to install.

2.4L Engine

NOTE: Air Bag Equipped Models, Refer To "Air Bag System Precautions" Located In The Front Of This Manual For System Disarming & Arming Procedures.

NOTE: Refer To "Computer Relearn Procedures" Located In The Front Of This Manual When Battery Power To The Computer Has Been Interrupted.

INDEX

PRECAUTIONS

Air Bag Systems

Refer to "Air Bag System Precautions" in the front of this manual for system disarming and arming procedures.

Battery Ground Cable

Prior to service, disconnect battery ground cable and isolate as required.

Fuel System Pressure Relief

1. Remove fuel cap, then the fuel pump relay from PDC.
2. Start and run engine until it stalls.
3. Attempt to restart engine until it will no longer run.
4. Turn ignition key to Off position.
5. Unplug connector from any injector.
6. Attach one end of a suitable 18 gauge or smaller jumper wire to either injector terminal.
7. Connect other end of jumper wire to positive battery terminal.
8. Connect one end of a second jumper wire to remaining injector terminal.
9. Momentarily touch other end of second jumper wire to negative battery terminal for no more than a few seconds. **Powering an injector for more than a few seconds will damage injector.**
10. Place a suitable rag below fuel line quick connect fitting on fuel rail, then disconnect quick connect fitting.
11. Install fuel pump relay to PDC, then clear any stored DTC's.

COMPRESSION PRESSURE

1. Ensure battery is fully charged and starter is in good operating condition.
2. Inspect engine oil level and top off if required.
3. Drive vehicle until engine is at normal operating temperature.
4. Remove spark plugs from engine and inspect for abnormal firing indicators.
5. Remove Auto Shut Down (ASD) relay from power distribution center.
6. Ensure throttle blade is fully open during compression test.
7. Insert compression gauge adapter tool No. 8116, or equivalent, into No. 1 cylinder spark plug hole.
8. Connect 0–500 psi (Blue) transducer with cable adapters to DRBIII.
9. Crank engine until maximum pressure is reached on gauge, repeat for all cylinders.
10. Compression should not be less than 100 psi or vary by more than 25 percent from cylinder to cylinder.

ENGINE MOUNT

REPLACE

Front

1. Raise and support vehicle.
2. Remove front engine mount through bolt from insulator.
3. Remove front engine mount bolts, then the front engine mounts, **Figs. 1 and 2.**
4. Reverse procedure to install.

Rear

1. Raise and support vehicle.
2. Support transmission using suitable jack.
3. Remove bolts holding mount to crossmember, then remove crossmember.
4. Remove bolts, then the mount, **Fig. 3.**

ENGINE

REPLACE

1. Remove hood ensuring to mark hinge locations for reference during installation.
2. Remove air cleaner assembly.
3. Remove radiator core support bracket.
4. Remove fan shroud with electric fan assembly.
5. Remove serpentine drive belt.
6. Remove A/C compressor and position aside with lines attached.
7. Remove alternator and position aside.

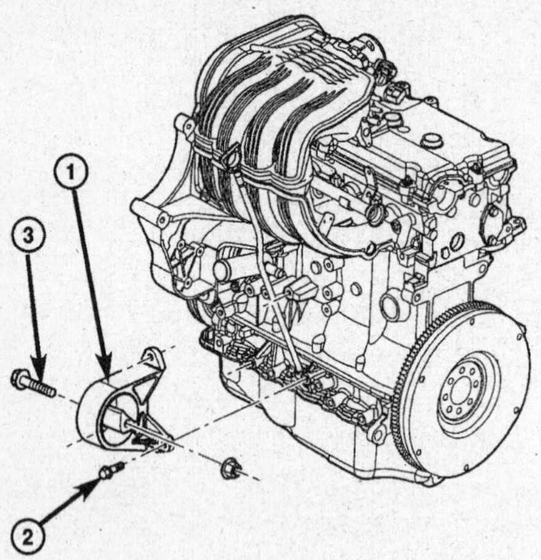

Fig. 1 Lefthand front engine mount

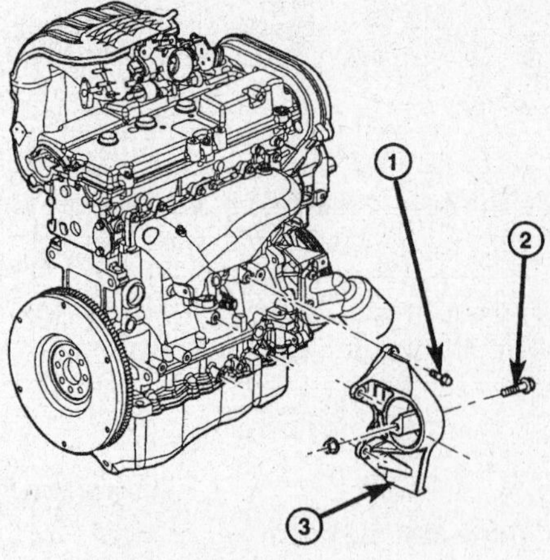

Fig. 2 Righthand front engine mount

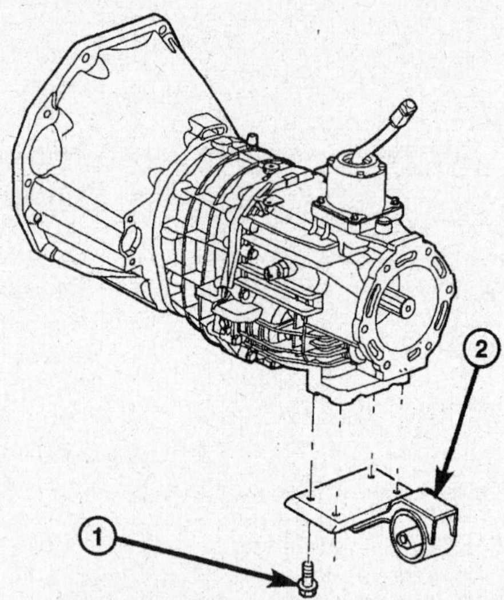

Fig. 3 Rear engine mount

8. Remove power steering pump and position aside with lines attached. **Do not remove phenolic pulley from power steering pump.**
9. Drain cooling system into suitable container, then remove coolant bottle.
10. Disconnect heater hoses from engine.
11. Disconnect heater hoses from heater core, then remove hose assembly.
12. Disconnect throttle and speed control cables.
13. Remove upper and lower radiator hoses from engine.
14. Disconnect engine to body ground straps at lefthand side of cowl.
15. Disconnect electrical connectors from the following:
    a. IAT sensor.
    b. Fuel injectors.
    c. TPS switch.
    d. IAC motor.
    e. Engine oil pressure switch.
    f. ECT sensor.
    g. MAP Sensor.
    h. CMP sensor.
    i. Coil over plugs.
    j. CKP sensor.
16. Remove coil over plugs.
17. Release fuel pressure as outlined in "Precautions."
18. Remove fuel rail and position aside.
19. Remove PCV hose.
20. Remove breather hoses.
21. Remove vacuum hose for power brake booster.
22. Disconnect knock sensors.
23. Secure lefthand and righthand engine wiring harnesses away from engine.
24. Raise and support vehicle.
25. Disconnect oxygen sensor electrical connector.
26. Disconnect CKP sensor.
27. Disconnect engine block heater power cable if equipped.
28. Disconnect front propeller shaft at front differential and position aside.
29. Remove starter motor, then the ground straps from engine.

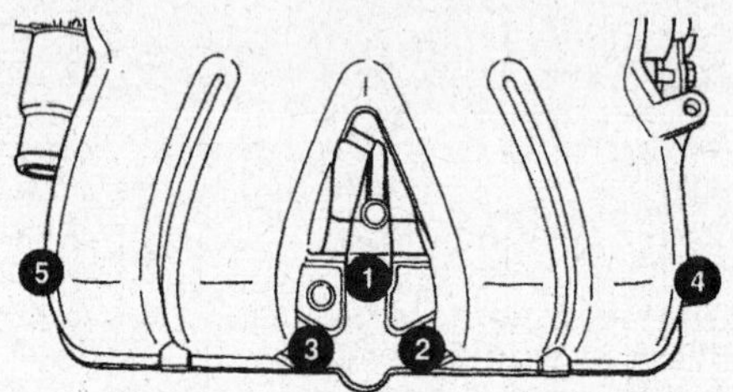

Fig. 4 Upper intake manifold tightening sequence

30. Disconnect exhaust pipes at exhaust manifold.
31. Remove structural collar.
32. Remove torque convertor bolts. Mark bolt locations for reference during installation.
33. Remove transmission bellhousing to engine bolts.
34. Loosen lefthand and righthand engine mount through bolts. **It is not required to completely remove engine mount through bolts for engine removal.**
35. Lower vehicle, then support transmission with suitable jack.
36. Remove engine using suitable engine hoist.
37. Reverse procedure to install.

INTAKE MANIFOLD

REPLACE

Upper

1. Disconnect electrical connector from inlet air temperature sensor.
2. Disconnect air intake tube at throttle body, then remove upper air cleaner housing.
3. Disconnect TPS, IAC motor and MAP sensor electrical connectors.
4. Disconnect vacuum lines for purge solenoid and PCV valve at intake manifold.
5. Disconnect vacuum lines for power brake booster, leak detection pump, EGR transducer and speed control vacuum reservoir at upper intake manifold.
6. Disconnect throttle, speed control and transmission control cables from throttle lever and bracket.
7. Remove EGR tube.
8. Remove upper manifold support bracket bolt to manifold.
9. Remove engine oil dipstick from tube.
10. Remove upper intake manifold bolts, then the upper intake manifold.
11. Reverse procedure to install, noting the following:
    a. Apply a .06 inch bead of Mopar Gasket maker or equivalent to perimeter of lower intake manifold runner openings.
    b. Tighten upper intake manifold bolts in sequence, **Fig. 4,** to specifications.

Lower

1. Disconnect electrical connector from inlet air temperature sensor.
2. Disconnect air intake tube at throttle body, then remove upper air cleaner housing.
3. Disconnect TPS, IAC motor and MAP sensor electrical connectors.
4. Disconnect vacuum lines for purge solenoid and PCV valve at intake manifold.
5. Disconnect vacuum lines for power brake booster, leak detection pump, EGR transducer and speed control vacuum reservoir at upper intake manifold.
6. Disconnect throttle, speed control and transmission control cables from throttle lever and bracket.
7. Release fuel pressure as outlined in "Precautions."
8. Disconnect fuel line.
9. Disconnect coolant temperature sensor electrical connector.
10. Disconnect fuel injector harness.

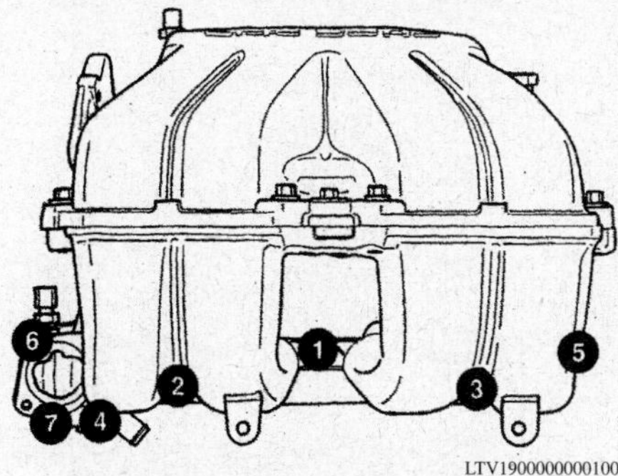

Fig. 5 Lower intake manifold tightening sequence

11. Remove lower intake manifold bolts, then the lower intake manifold.
12. Reverse procedure to install, noting the following:
    a. Install new lower intake manifold gasket.
    b. Tighten lower intake manifold in sequence, **Fig. 5,** to specifications.

EXHAUST MANIFOLD

REPLACE

1. Raise and support vehicle.
2. Disconnect exhaust pipe from exhaust manifold.
3. Lower vehicle.
4. Disconnect upstream oxygen sensor electrical connector at rear of exhaust manifold.
5. Remove air cleaner bracket, then the heat shield.
6. Remove bolts, then the exhaust manifold.
7. Reverse procedure to install.

CYLINDER HEAD

REPLACE

1. Release fuel pressure as outlined in "Precautions."
2. Drain cooling system into suitable container.
3. Remove air filter housing and inlet tube.
4. Remove intake manifold as outlined in "Intake Manifold, Replace."
5. Remove heater tube support bracket from cylinder head.
6. Disconnect radiator upper and heater supply hoses from water outlet connections.
7. Remove serpentine drive belt.
8. Raise and support vehicle.
9. Remove exhaust pipe from exhaust manifold.
10. Remove power steering pump and position aside. Do not disconnect lines.
11. Remove accessory drive bracket.
12. Remove ignition coil and wires.
13. Disconnect cam sensor and fuel injector wiring connectors.
14. Remove timing belt and camshaft sprockets as outlined in "Timing Belt, Replace."
15. Remove timing belt idler pulley and rear cover.
16. Remove valve cover as outlined in "Valve Cover, Replace."

- Fourth Turn an additional 1/4 Turn,

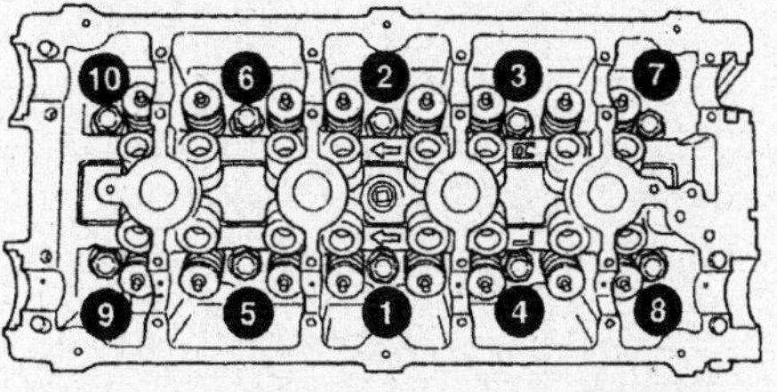

Fig. 6 Cylinder head tightening sequence

17. Remove camshafts as outlined in "Camshaft, Replace."
18. Remove rocker arms as outlined in "Rocker Arms, Replace."
19. Remove cylinder head bolts in reverse order of tightening sequence, **Fig. 6.**
20. Remove cylinder head.
21. Reverse procedure to install, noting the following:
    a. Ensure cylinder head bolts hole in block are clean, dry and that threads are not damaged. Inspect cylinder head bolts for necking (stretching).
    b. Hold a steel scale or straight edge against threads and note whether all threads are touching scale. If all threads do not contact straight edge, bolt should be replaced.
    c. Position new cylinder head gasket on cylinder block with part number facing up.
    d. Ensure gasket is seated over locating dowels in block.
    e. Before installing bolts, lightly coat threads with engine oil.
    f. **Torque** cylinder head bolts in four steps, in sequence, **Fig. 6,** to the following specifications:
    g. First step: **Torque** all bolts to 25 ft. lbs.
    h. Second step: **Torque** all bolts to 50 ft. lbs.
    i. Third step: **Torque** all bolts to 50 ft. lbs.
    j. Fourth step: Turn all bolts an additional ¼ turn.

VALVE COVER

REPLACE

1. Remove intake manifold as outlined in "Intake Manifold, Replace."
2. Remove ignition coil and spark plug wires.
3. Disconnect PCV and make-up hoses from valve cover.
4. Remove valve cover bolts, then the valve cover.
5. Reverse procedure to install, noting the following:
    a. Install new spark plug well seals, bolt assemblies and valve cover gasket.
    b. Apply Mopar Engine RTV GEN II or equivalent to camshaft cap corners and at top edges of half round seal, **Fig. 7.**
    c. Install valve cover bolts with bolts containing sealing washer located in center of cover.

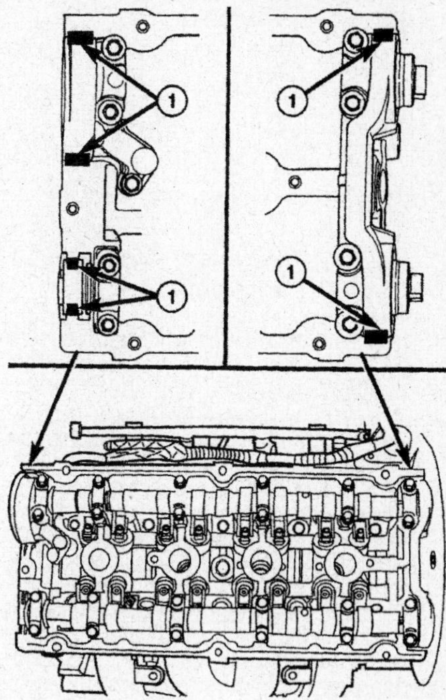

Fig. 7 Sealer location

    d. **Torque** valve cover bolts in sequence, **Fig. 8,** using three steps. First to 40 inch lbs., second to 80 inch lbs., and finally to 105 inch lbs.

VALVE LIFTERS

This procedure is for in-vehicle service with camshafts installed.

1. Remove valve cover as outlined in "Valve Cover, Replace."
2. Remove camshafts as outlined in "Camshaft, Replace."
3. Remove rocker arms as outlined in "Rocker Arms, Replace."
4. Remove hydraulic lifter. If reusing lifter mark location for reference during installation.
5. Reverse procedure to install.

CAMSHAFT LOBE LIFT SPECIFICATIONS

Exhaust ....259 inch
Intake .... .324 inch

VALVE ADJUSTMENT

These engines use hydraulic lifters. No adjustment is required.

ROCKER ARMS

REPLACE

1. Remove valve cover as outlined in "Valve Cover, Replace."
2. Release fuel pressure as outlined in "Precautions" then remove fuel rail.
3. Remove spark plugs.
4. Rotate engine until camshaft lobe, on follower being removed , is positioned

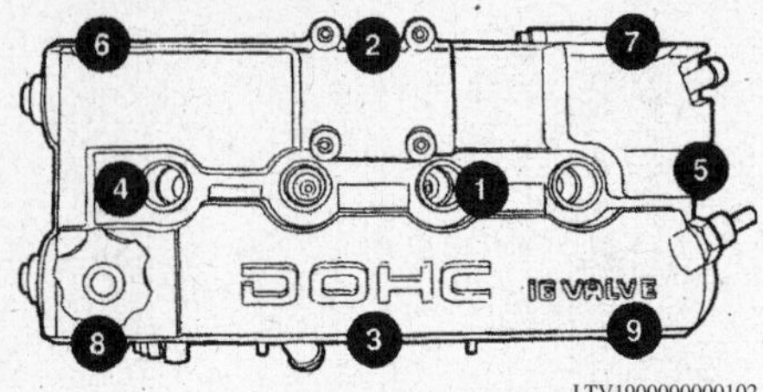

Fig. 8 Valve cover tightening sequence

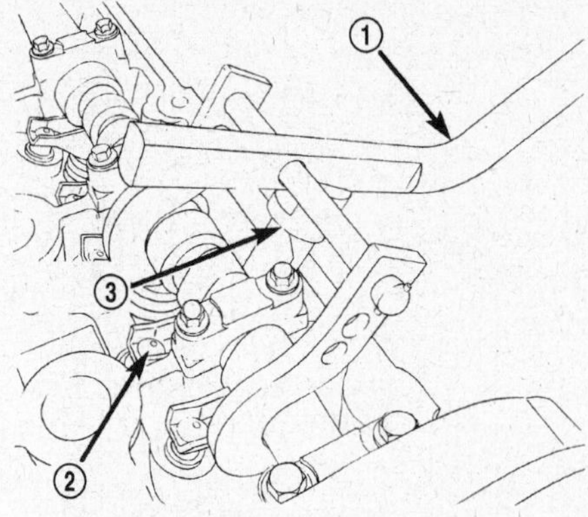

Fig. 9 Camshaft follower replacement

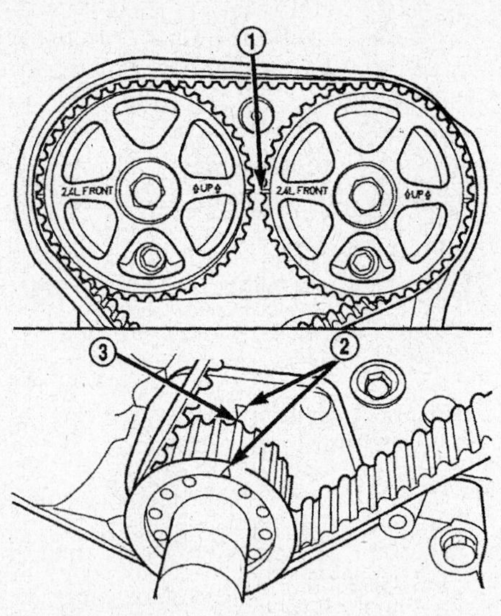

Fig. 10 Crankshaft and camshaft timing marks

on it's base circle (heel). Piston should be a minimum of .025 inch below TDC position.

5. If cam follower assemblies are to be re-used, mark followers for installation reference.
6. Slowly depress valve assembly until cam follower can be removed using valve spring compressor tool No. 8215 and adapter tool No. 8436, or equivalent, **Fig. 9.**
7. It may be required to remove additional brackets to allow clearance for tool handle movement.
8. Reverse procedure to install.

FRONT COVER

REPLACE

1. Remove serpentine drive belt.
2. Remove crankshaft vibration damper bolt.
3. Remove vibration damper using three jaw puller tool No. 1026 and insert tool No. 6827-A, or equivalents.
4. Remove serpentine drive belt tensioner.
5. Remove front cover bolts, then the front cover.
6. Reverse procedure to install.

TIMING BELT

REPLACE

Removal

1. Remove air cleaner upper cover, housing and clean air tube.
2. Raise and support vehicle.
3. Remove serpentine drive belt.
4. Remove crankshaft vibration damper bolt.
5. Remove vibration damper using three jaw puller tool No. 1026 and insert tool No. 6827-A, or equivalents.
6. Remove air conditioner/alternator belt tensioner and pulley assembly.
7. Remove timing belt lower front cover bolts, then the cover.
8. Lower vehicle.
9. Remove upper front cover bolts, then the cover.
10. Rotate crankshaft until TDC mark on oil pump housing aligns with TDC mark on crankshaft sprocket, **Fig. 10. Crankshaft sprocket TDC mark is located on trailing edge of sprocket tooth.**
11. Install a 6 mm wrench into belt tensioner. Before rotating tensioner, insert long end of a 1⁄8 inch or 3 mm wrench into pin hole on front of tensioner, **Fig. 11.**
12. While rotating tensioner counterclockwise, push in lightly on 1⁄8 inch or 3 mm wrench until it slides into locking hole.
13. Remove timing belt.

Installation

1. Set crankshaft sprocket to TDC by aligning sprocket with arrow on oil pump housing.
2. Set camshaft timing marks so that exhaust camshaft sprocket is a 1⁄2 notch below intake camshaft sprocket, **Fig. 12. Ensure that arrows on both camshaft sprockets are facing up.**
3. Install timing belt, starting at crankshaft, go around water pump sprocket, idler pulley, camshaft sprockets and then tensioner.
4. Move exhaust camshaft sprocket counterclockwise to align marks and take up belt slack, **Fig. 13.**
5. Insert a 6 mm wrench into hexagon opening located on top plate of belt tensioner pulley.
6. Rotate top plate counterclockwise. Tensioner pulley will move against belt and tensioner setting notch will eventually start to move clockwise. Watching movement of setting notch, continue rotating top plate counterclockwise until setting notch is aligned with spring tang, **Fig. 14.**
7. Tighten tensioner lock nut to specifications using three jaw puller tool No. 1026 and insert tool No. 6827-A, or equivalents. Setting notch and spring tang should remain aligned after nut is torqued.
8. Remove wrench and torque wrench.
9. **Repositioning crankshaft to TDC position must be done only during clockwise rotation. If TDC is missed, rotate two revolutions until TDC is achieved. Do not rotate crankshaft counterclockwise.**
10. Once timing belt has been installed and tensioner adjusted, rotate crankshaft clockwise two complete revolutions manually for seating belt until crankshaft is repositioned at TDC position.
11. Verify that camshaft and crankshaft timing marks are in proper position, **Fig. 15.**
12. Ensure spring tang is within tolerance window, **Fig. 16.** If spring tang is not within tolerance window, repeat steps 5–11.
13. Install timing belt front covers.
14. Install air conditioner/alternator belt tensioner and pulley.
15. Install crankshaft vibration damper.
16. Install serpentine drive belt, then the splash shield.
17. Install air cleaner housing, upper cover and clean air tube.

CAMSHAFT

REPLACE

Camshafts are not interchangeable. The lefthand (intake) camshaft thrust bearing face (No. 6) spacing is wider.

Removal

1. Remove valve cover as outlined in "Valve Cover, Replace."
2. Remove camshaft position sensor and camshaft target magnet.
3. Remove timing belt as outlined in "Timing Belt, Replace."
4. Bearing caps are identified for location, remove outside bearing caps first, **Fig. 17.**
5. Loosen camshaft bearing cap bolts in sequence, **Fig. 18,** one camshaft at a time.
6. Identify camshafts for reference during installation, then remove camshafts.

Inspection

1. Inspect camshaft bearing journals for

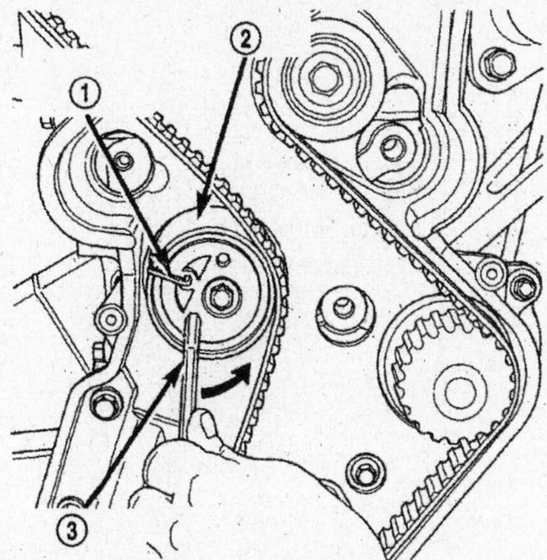

Fig. 11 Locking belt tensioner

damage and binding.

2. Inspect cylinder head oil holes for clogging.
3. Inspect cam lobe and bearing surfaces for abnormal wear or damage.
4. Inspect camshaft lobe wear, **Fig. 19,** wear limit is .010 inch.

Installation

Ensure no piston is at TDC when installing camshafts.

1. Lubricate all camshaft bearing journals, rocker arms and camshafts.
2. Install rocker arms in original positions.
3. Install camshafts on cylinder head bearing journals.
4. Install righthand and lefthand camshaft bearing caps No. 2–5 and righthand No. 6. Tighten M6 fasteners to specification, in sequence, **Fig. 20.**
5. Apply Mopar Gasket Maker, or equivalent, to No. 1 and lefthand No. 6 bearing caps. Install caps and tighten M8 fasteners to specification.
6. Camshaft end caps must be installed before camshaft seals are installed.
7. Install camshaft seals until they are flush with cylinder head using installation tool No. MD-998306, or equivalent.
8. Install camshaft target magnet and position sensor as follows:
9. Install valve cover, then the timing belt rear cover.
10. Install camshaft sprocket, then the timing belt.

BALANCE SHAFT

REPLACE

Balance Shafts

1. Remove oil pan as outlined in "Oil Pan, Replace."
2. Remove chain cover, guide and tensioner, **Fig. 21.**
3. Remove gear cover retaining stud.

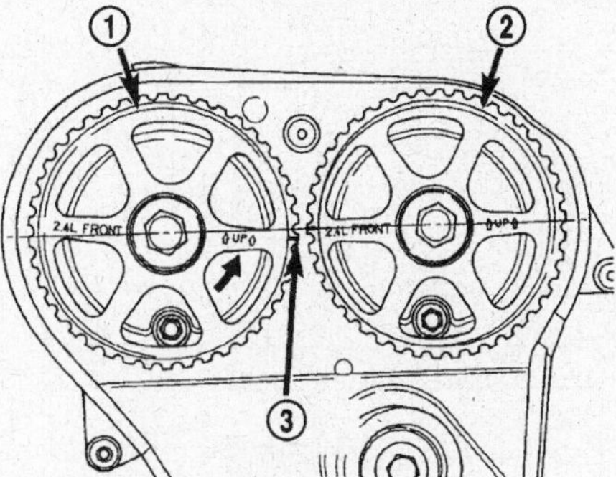

Fig. 12 Camshaft sprocket alignment

4. Remove cover and balance shaft gears.
5. Remove balance shaft gear, chain sprocket retaining screws and crankshaft chain sprocket.
6. Remove chain and sprocket assembly, **Fig. 22,** using two wide pry bars to work sprocket back and forth until its off shaft.
7. Remove carrier gear cover and balance shafts, **Fig. 23.**
8. Remove four carrier to crankshaft attaching bolts to separate carrier from engine bedplate.
9. Reverse procedure to install. Time crankshaft to balance shaft as outlined in "Balance Shaft Timing."

Balance Shaft Carrier

The following components will remain intact during carrier removal, **Fig. 21.** Gear cover, gears, balance shafts and the rear cover.

1. Remove chain cover and driven balance shaft chain sprocket screw.
2. Loosen tensioner pivot and adjusting screws, then move driven balance shaft inboard through driven chain sprocket. Sprocket will hang in lower chain loop.
3. Remove carrier to crankcase attaching bolts, then the carrier.
4. Reverse procedure to install. Time crankshaft to balance shaft as outlined in "Balance Shaft Timing."

Balance Shaft Timing

1. With balance shafts installed in carrier, position carrier on crankcase and install four attaching bolts.
2. Turn balance shafts until both shaft key ways are up parallel to vertical centerline of engine, **Fig. 24.**
3. Install short hub drive gear on sprocket driven shaft and long drive gear on gear driven shaft. Ensure gear and balance shaft keyways are up with gear timing marks aligned, **Fig. 24.**
4. Install gear cover and tighten double ended stud/washer to specifications.
5. Align flat on balance shaft drive sprocket with flat on crankshaft, **Fig. 25.**
6. Install balance shaft drive sprocket on crankshaft using installation tool No. MD-998306, or equivalent.
7. Turn crankshaft until number one cylinder is at TDC. Timing marks on chain sprocket should line up with parting line on lefthand side of number one main bearing cap, **Fig. 26.**
8. Install chain over crankshaft sprocket so that plated link of chain is over number one cylinder timing mark on balance shaft crankshaft sprocket, **Fig. 26.**
9. Install balance shaft sprocket into timing chain and align timing mark on sprocket (dot) with lower plated link on chain, **Fig. 26.** Lower plated link is eight links from upper link.
10. With balance shaft keyways pointing up, slide balance shaft sprocket onto nose of balance shaft. Balance shaft may have to be pushed in slightly to allow for clearance.
11. Timing mark on sprocket, lower nickel plated link and arrow on side of gear cover should line up when balance shafts are timed correctly.
12. Install balance shaft bolts, tighten to specification. A wood block placed between crankcase and crankshaft counterbalance will prevent crankshaft and gear rotation.
13. Install chain tensioner loosely.
14. Position guide on double ended stud. Ensure tab on guide fits into slot on gear cover, then install and **torque** nut/washer to 105 inch lbs.
15. Place a shim .039 inch thick and 2.75

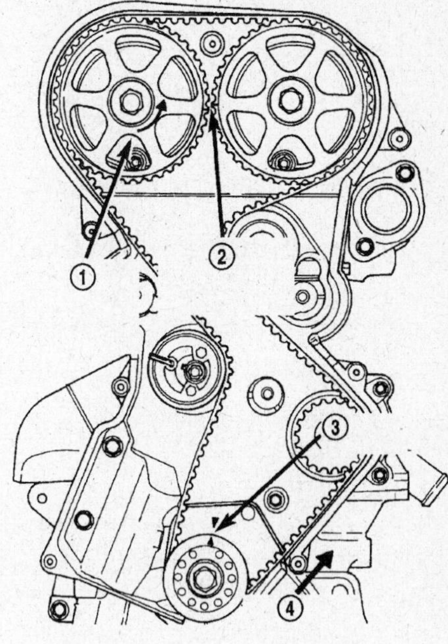

Fig. 13 Timing belt installation

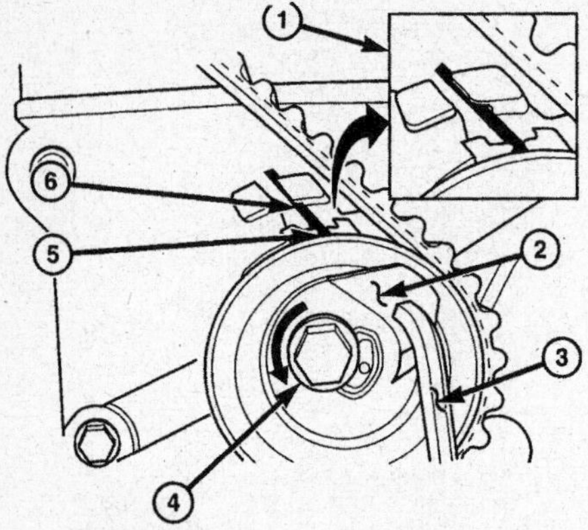

1 - ALIGN SETTING NOTCH WITH SPRING TANG
2 - TOP PLATE
3 - 6mm ALLEN WRENCH
4 - LOCK NUT
5 - SETTING NOTCH
6 - SPRING TANG

LTV1900000000127

Fig. 14 Timing belt tensioner adjustment

inches long between tensioner and chain.

16. Push tensioner and shim up against chain. Apply firm pressure (5.5–6.6 lbs.) directly behind adjustment slot to take up all slack.
17. Chain must have shoe radius contact, **Fig. 27.**
18. With load applied, tighten top bolt first, then bottom pivot bolt. Tighten bolts to specification, then remove shim.
19. Install carrier covers and tighten bolts to specification.
20. Install pickup tube and oil pan.
21. Fill crankcase with proper oil to correct level.

PISTON & ROD ASSEMBLY

The directional stamp on the piston should face toward the front of the engine.

MAIN & ROD BEARINGS

The crankshaft is supported by five main bearings. End play is controlled by a flanged bearing on the number three main bearing journal, **Fig. 28.** The number three bearings halves are not interchangeable with other bearings. Bearings are available in standard and .001 and .010 inch undersizes.

Ensure correct thrust bearing alignment as follows:

1. Rotate crankshaft until number four piston is at TDC.
2. Move crankshaft rearward to limit of travel, then move forward to limit of travel.
3. Wedge a suitable tool between rear of cylinder block **(not bed plate)** and rear crankshaft counterweight to crankshaft in its furthest forward position.
4. Install and **torque** bolts 1–10 in sequence, **Fig. 29,** to 30 ft. lbs.
5. Remove wedge tool used to hold crankshaft.

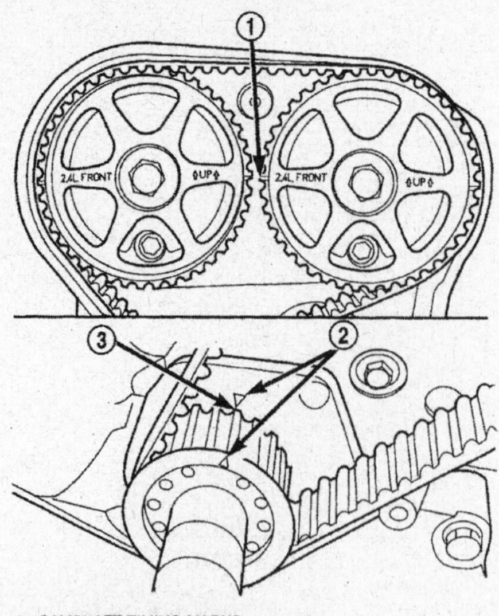

1 - CAMSHAFT TIMING MARKS
2 - CRANKSHAFT TDC MARKS
3 - TRAILING EDGE OF SPROCKET TOOTH

LTV1900000000128

Fig. 15 Crankshaft and camshaft timing

6. **Torque** bolts again in sequence to 30 ft. lbs., plus an additional ¼ turn.
7. Install and **torque** bolts 11–20 in sequence, **Fig. 29,** to 20 ft. lbs.
8. Inspect crankshaft turning torque, it should not exceed 50 inch lbs.

CRANKSHAFT REAR OIL SEAL

REPLACE

Removal

1. Remove transmission as outlined in **MOTOR's "Domestic Transmission, In-Vehicle Service Manual" or "Transmission Service DVD."**
2. Remove flexplate.
3. Insert a 3⁄16 inch flat bladed screwdriver between dust lip and metal case of crankshaft seal.
4. Pry out seal.
5. Do not allow screwdriver blade to contact crankshaft seal surface.
6. If burrs or scratches are present on crankshaft edge, polish with 400 grit sand paper to prevent seal damage during installation of new seal.

Installation

When installing new seal, no lube on seal is needed.

1. Place seal guide tool No. 6926–1, or equivalent, on crankshaft.
2. Position seal over guide tool, guide tool should remain on crankshaft during installation of seal.
3. Ensure lip of seal is facing toward crankcase during installation.
4. Drive seal into block using seal driver tool No. 6926–2 and handle tool No. C-4171, or equivalents, until tool bottoms out against block.
5. Install flexplate.

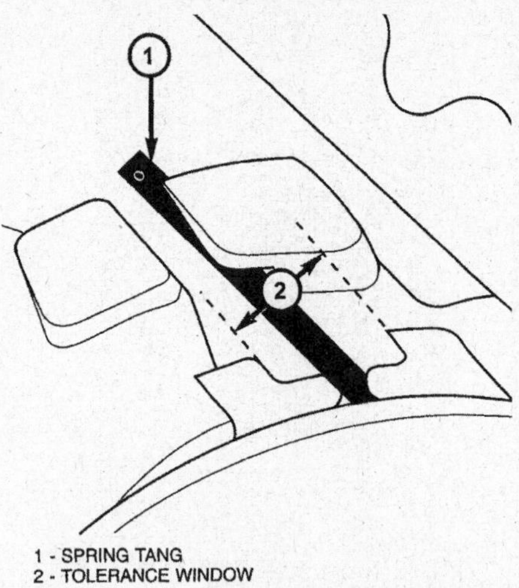

1 - SPRING TANG
2 - TOLERANCE WINDOW

LTV1900000000129

Fig. 16 Timing belt tension verification

6. Apply Mopar Lock and Seal adhesive to bolt threads and tighten to specification.
7. Install transaxle.

OIL PAN

REPLACE

1. Remove air cleaner assembly.
2. Raise and support vehicle, then drain oil into suitable container.
3. Loosen engine mount through bolts.
4. Disconnect exhaust pipe at exhaust manifold.
5. Remove structural collar.
6. **On models equipped with 4WD,** remove front axle mounting bolts and lower axle as far as possible.
7. **On all models,** install support tool No. 8534, or equivalent, on fender lip and align slots in brackets with fender mounting holes.
8. Secure brackets to fender using four M6 x 1.0 x 25 mm flanged cap screws.
9. Tighten thumbscrews to secure sleeves to support tube.
10. Secure support tube in upright position.
11. Assemble flat washer, thrust bearing, hook and T handle.
12. Secure chain to front cover and hook using capscrew supplied with support fixture.
13. Support engine as needed.
14. Remove oil pan bolts, then the oil pan.
15. Reverse procedure to install, noting the following:
    a. Clean oil pan and all gasket surfaces.
    b. Apply Mopar Engine RTV GEN II, or equivalent, at oil pump to engine block parting lines.

OIL PUMP

REPLACE

1. Remove timing belt as outlined in "Timing Belt, Replace" then the timing belt rear cover.
2. Remove oil pan as outlined in "Oil Pan, Replace."

Fig. 17 Camshaft bearing cap identification

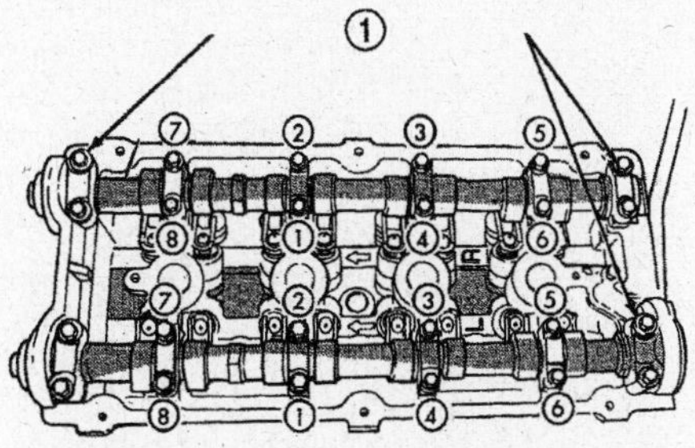

Fig. 18 Camshaft bearing cap removal

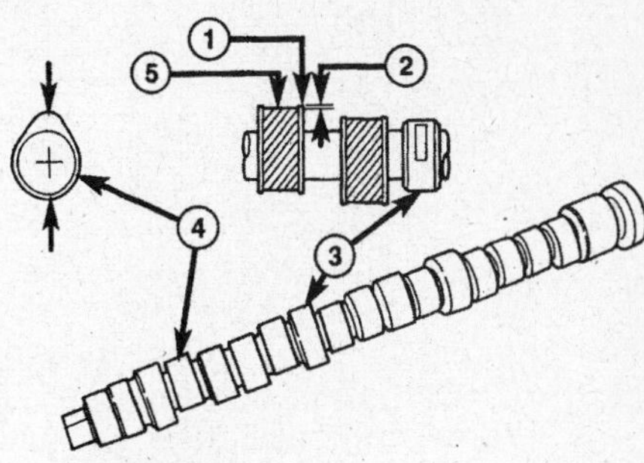

Fig. 19 Inspecting camshaft wear

3. Remove crankshaft sprocket using tools No. 6793 and C-4685–C2, or equivalents.
4. Remove crankshaft key.
5. Remove oil pickup tube.
6. Remove oil pump and front crankshaft seal, **Fig. 30.**
7. Reverse procedure to install, noting the following:
   a. Ensure all surfaces are clean and free of oil and dirt.
   b. Apply Mopar Gasket Maker, or equivalent, to oil pump, **Fig. 31.**
   c. Install O-ring into oil pump body discharge passage.
   d. Prime oil pump with engine oil before installation.

BELT TENSION DATA

Belt tension is maintained by an automatic belt tensioner. Replace belt if measurement between tang and housing stop on belt tensioner, **Fig. 32,** is more than .94 inches.

SERPENTINE DRIVE BELT

Routing

Refer to **Figs. 33 and 34** for drive belt routing.

Replacement

1. Rotate belt tensioner until it contacts its stop.
2. Remove belt, then slowly rotate tensioner into free arm position.
3. Reverse procedure to install ensuring belt is seated onto all pulleys.

COOLING SYSTEM BLEED

1. Ensure cooling system is full and coolant in pressure bottle is at service line.
2. Turn heater control unit to HEAT position, then run engine with pressure bottle cap installed.
3. Add coolant to pressure bottle as required. **Only add coolant to pressure bottle when engine is cold.**

WATER PUMP

REPLACE

1. Raise and support vehicle.
2. Remove serpentine drive belt, then the drive belt tensioner.
3. Drain cooling system into suitable container.
4. Remove alternator, then the power steering pump.
5. Remove A/C compressor, then the accessory drive bracket.
6. Remove timing belt as outlined in "Timing Belt, Replace."
7. Remove timing belt idler pulley.
8. Remove both cam sprockets using holding tool No. C-4687 and adaptor tool No. C-4687-1, or equivalents.
9. Remove timing belt rear cover.
10. Remove bolts, then the water pump.
11. Reverse procedure to install, noting the following:
    a. Install new O-ring in water pump body groove.
    b. Install water pump, then pressurize cooling system to 15 psi and inspect for leaks at shaft seal and O-ring.

RADIATOR

REPLACE

1. Drain engine coolant into suitable container.
2. Remove screws, then the front grille.
3. Remove cooling fan from engine.
4. Remove two radiator mounting bolts.
5. Disconnect both transmission cooler lines from radiator.
6. Disconnect electric fan electrical connector.
7. Disconnect power steering cooler line from cooler.
8. Disconnect radiator upper and lower hoses.
9. Disconnect overflow hose from radiator.
10. Gently lift and remove radiator from vehicle.
11. Reverse procedure to install, noting the following:
    a. Ensure all radiator rubber air seals are in their original locations.
    b. Guide two radiator alignment dowels into rubber grommets located in lower radiator crossmember.

FUEL PUMP

REPLACE

1. Remove two rearward cargo hold down clamps from cargo area by drilling out rivets.
2. Fold carpet forward to gain access to fuel pump module access plate.
3. Remove four fuel pump module access plate nuts.
4. While applying heat from a heat gun, carefully pry up fuel pump module access plate taking care not to bend plate.
5. Clean area around top of fuel pump module.
6. Release fuel pressure as outlined in "Precautions."
7. Disconnect two fuel lines at fuel pump module by pressing on buttons at side of fitting.
8. Disconnect electrical connector at top of fuel pump module by sliding red colored tab first to unlock, then pushing grey colored tab down.
9. Disconnect On-Board Refueling Vapor Recovery (ORVR) hose clamp and hose at fuel pump module fitting, **Fig. 35.**
10. Tap fuel pump module lock ring counterclockwise using suitable brass drift and hammer.
11. Carefully lift upper section of fuel pump module from fuel tank very slowly until rubber gasket can be retained.
12. Disconnect electrical connector at bottom of upper pump module section, **Fig. 36.**
13. Disconnect fuel pressure regulator at bottom of upper fuel pump module section.
14. Disconnect fuel return line at bottom of upper pump module section.
15. Remove upper section of fuel pump module from fuel tank.
16. Drain fuel tank into suitable container through pump module opening.
17. Push on plastic release tab while sliding lock tab upward, **Fig. 37.**
18. Sides of lower fuel pump module are equipped with tension springs. These springs hold module to bottom of fuel tank into two formed guides.
19. Release lower fuel pump module from guides by sliding toward righthand side

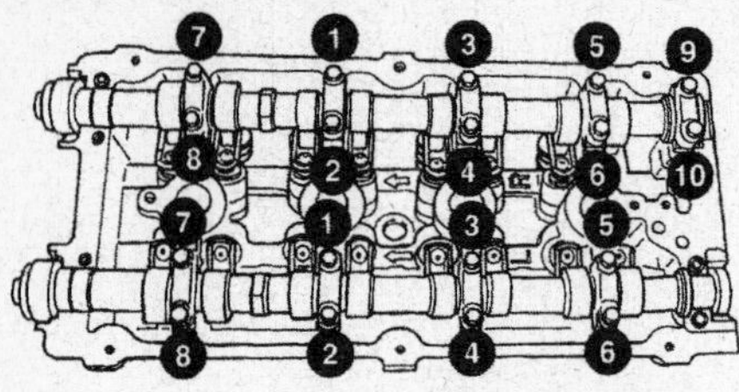

Fig. 20 Camshaft bearing cap tightening sequence

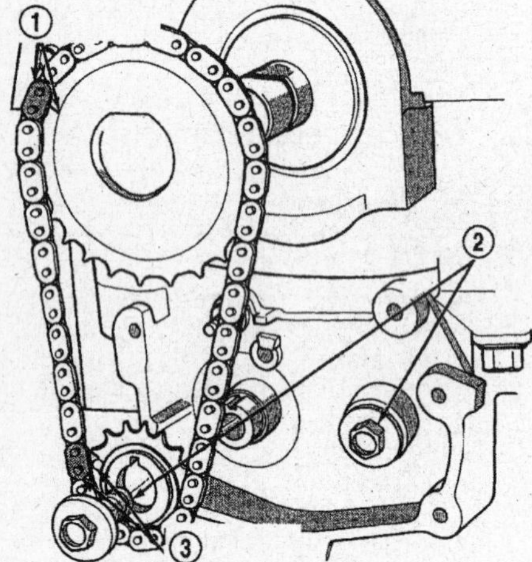

Fig. 22 Drive chain and sprockets

of tank, then lift and remove.

20. Reverse procedure to install, noting the following:
    a. Install new fuel pump module gasket.
    b. Position fuel pump module in tank with notch facing toward rear of tank.
    c. Apply silicone sealant to bottom of fuel pump module access plate.

FUEL FILTER

REPLACE

1. Release fuel pressure as outlined in "Precautions."
2. Remove two rearward cargo hold down clamps from cargo area by drilling out rivets.
3. Fold carpet forward to gain access to fuel pump module access plate.
4. Remove four fuel pump module access plate nuts.
5. While applying heat from a heat gun, carefully pry up fuel pump module access plate taking care not to bend plate.
6. Clean area around top of fuel pump module.

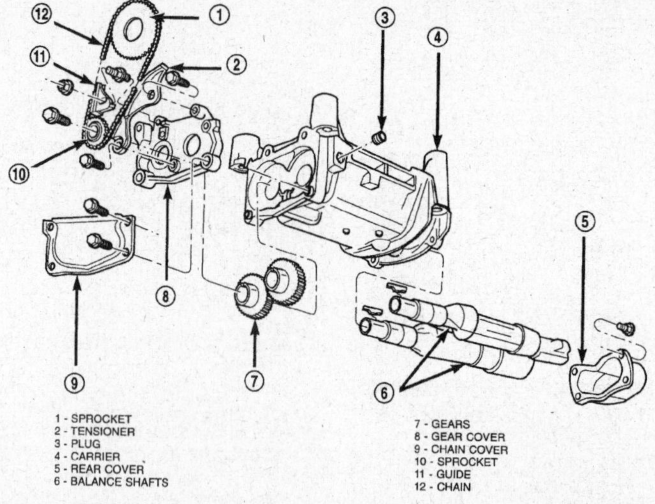

Fig. 21 Exploded view of balance shaft and carrier

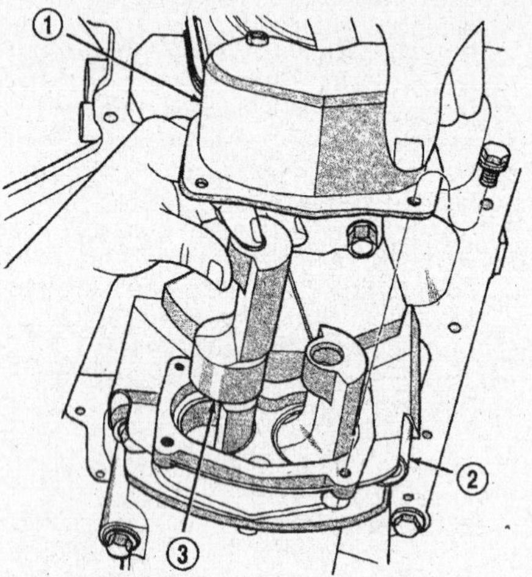

Fig. 23 Balance shaft removal

7. Disconnect two fuel lines at fuel pump module by pressing on buttons at side of fitting.
8. Raise and support vehicle, then place drain pan under fuel filter.
9. Disconnect fuel line from fuel filter.
10. Disconnect fuel line from body retention clip.
11. Remove fuel filter ground strap at fuel tank mounting strap.
12. Remove nut, then the fuel filter.
13. Reverse procedure to install, noting the following:
    a. Position fuel lines on filter toward top of fuel tank.
    b. Apply silicone sealant to fuel pump module access plate.

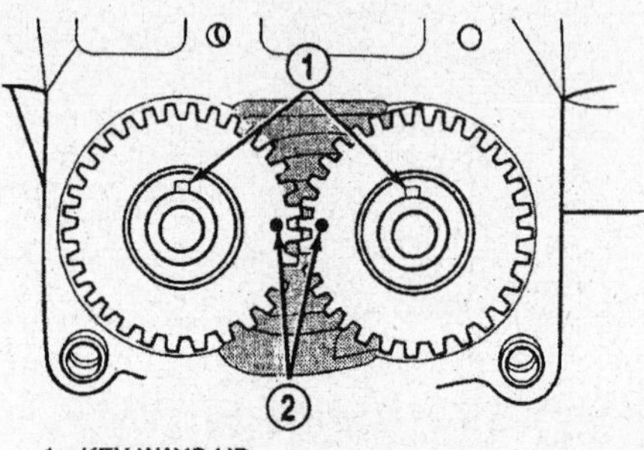

Fig. 24 Gear timing

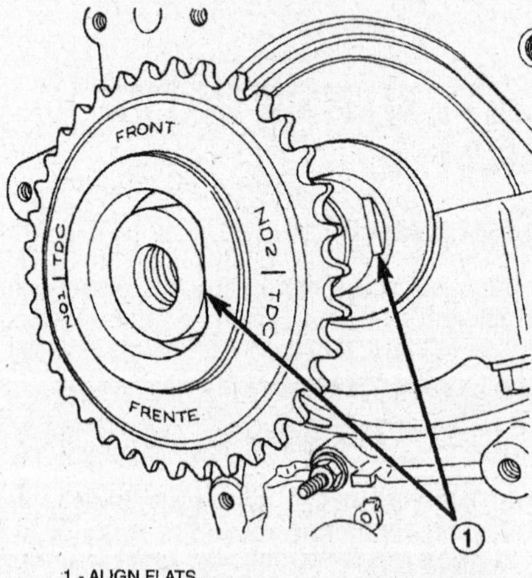

Fig. 25 Balance shaft sprocket alignment to crankshaft

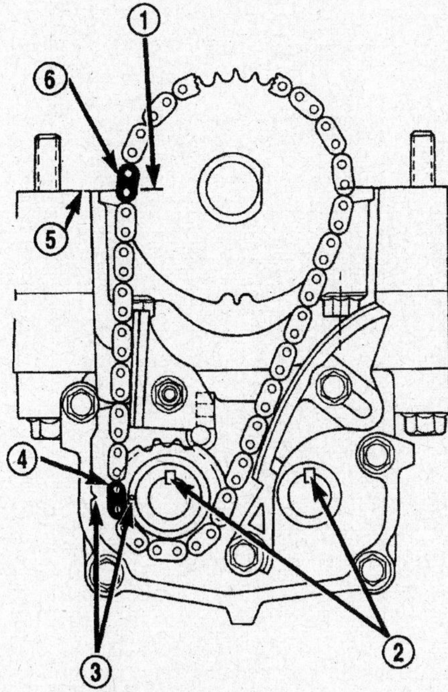

1 - MARK ON SPROCKET
2 - KEYWAYS UP
3 - ALIGN MARKS
4 - PLATED LINK
5 - PARTING LINE (BEDPLATE TO BLOCK)
6 - PLATED LINK

LTV1900000000121

Fig. 26 Balance shaft timing

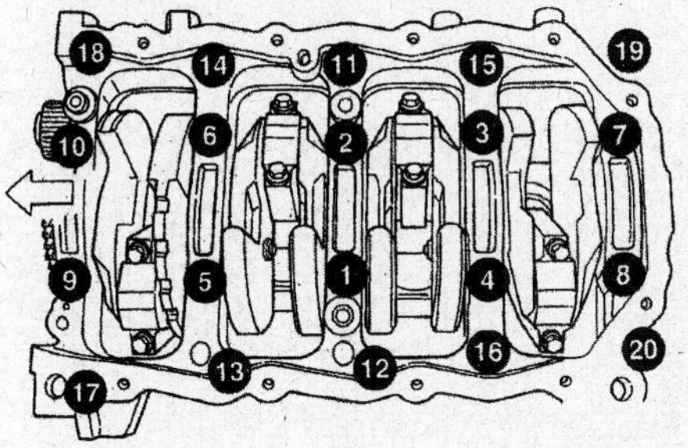

LTV1900000000104

Fig. 29 Main bearing tightening sequence

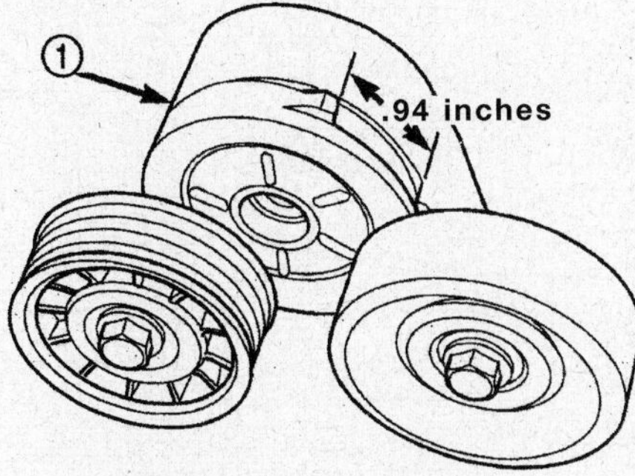

1 - AUTOMATIC TENSIONER ASSEMBLY

LTV1900000000105

Fig. 32 Belt tensioner

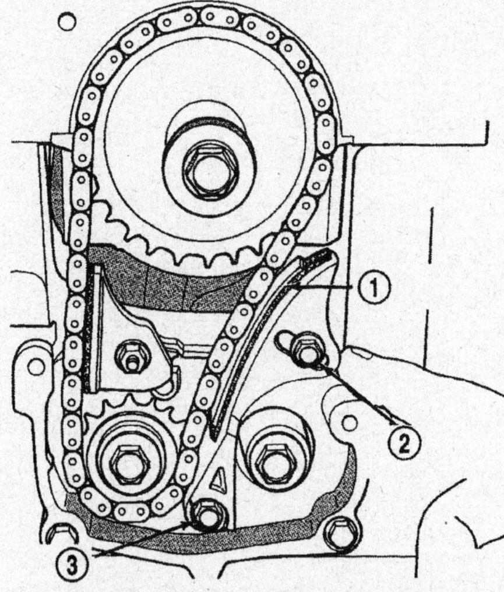

1 - 1MM (0.039 IN.) SHIM
2 - TENSIONER (ADJUSTER) BOLT
3 - PIVOT BOLT

LTV1900000000122

Fig. 27 Chain tension adjustment

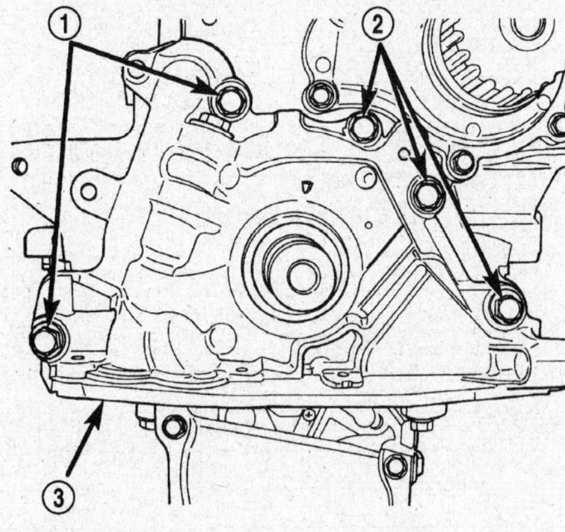

1 – BOLTS
2 – BOLTS
3 – OIL PUMP

CR1060000866000X

Fig. 30 Oil pump

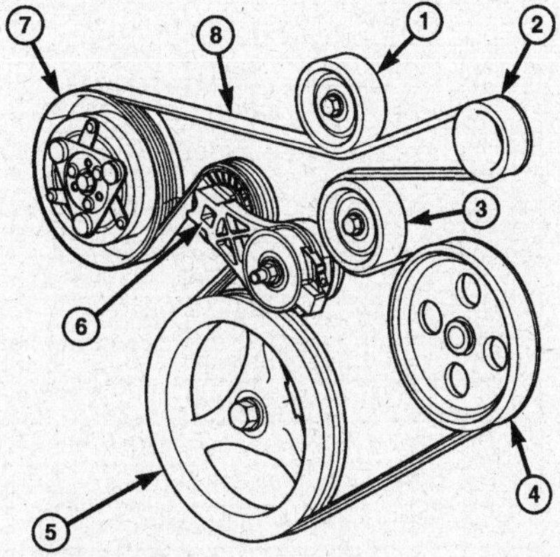

1 - IDLER PULLEY
2 - GENERATOR PULLEY
3 - IDLER PULLEY
4 - POWER STEERING PUMP PULLEY
5 -CRANKSHAFT PULLEY
6 - TENSIONER
7 - A/C COMPRESSOR PULLEY
8 - ACCESSORY DRIVE BELT

LTV1900000000106

Fig. 33 Drive belt routing w/A/C

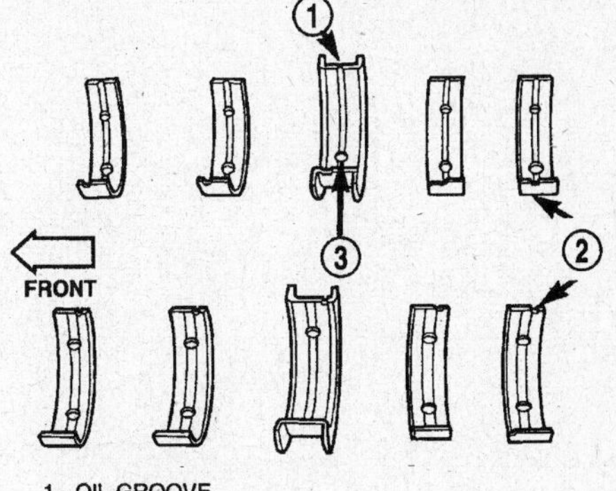

1 - OIL GROOVE
2 - MAIN BEARINGS
3 - OIL HOLE

LTV1900000000103

Fig. 28 Main bearing identification

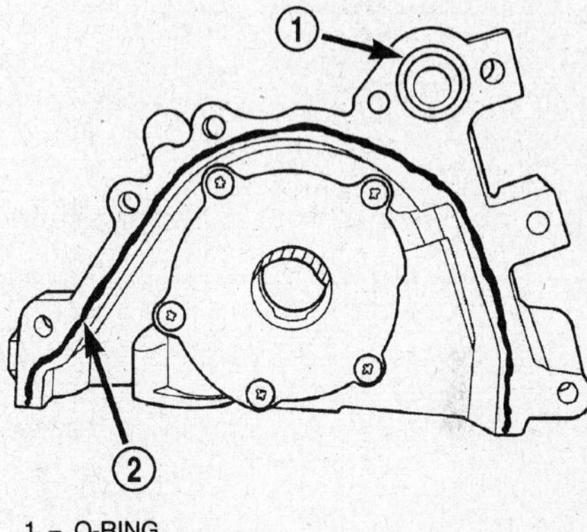

1 – O-RING
2 – SEALER LOCATION

CR1060000867000X

Fig. 31 Oil pump sealing

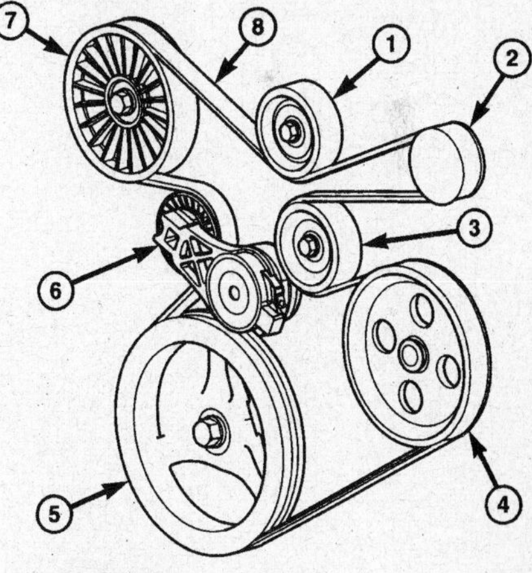

1 - IDLER PULLEY
2 - GENERATOR PULLEY
3 - IDLER PULLEY
4 - POWER STEERING PUMP PULLEY
5 -CRANKSHAFT PULLEY
6 - TENSIONER
7 - NON A/C IDLER PULLEY
8 - ACCESSORY DRIVE BELT

LTV1900000000107

Fig. 34 Drive belt routing less A/C

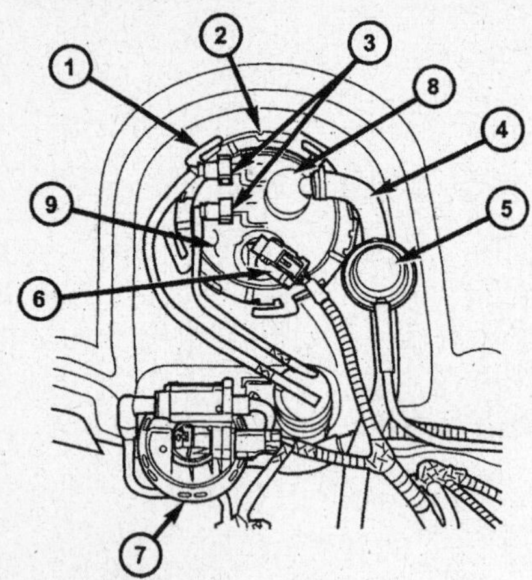

1 - LOCK RING
2 - ALIGNMENT NOTCH
3 - FUEL FILTER FITTINGS (2)
4 - ORVR SYSTEM HOSE AND CLAMP
5 - FLOW MANAGEMENT VALVE
6 - ELECTRICAL CONNECTOR
7 - LEAK DETECTION PUMP
8 - FUEL TANK CHECK (CONTROL) VALVE
9 - FUEL PUMP MODULE (UPPER SECTION)

LTV1900000000108

Fig. 35 Top of fuel pump module

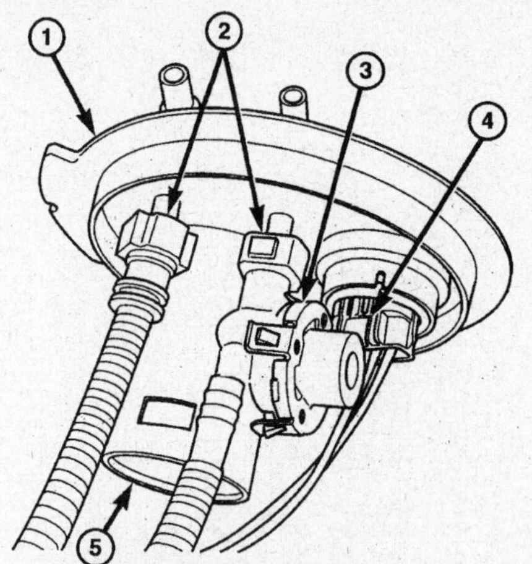

1 - UPPER SECTION OF PUMP MODULE
2 - QUICK-CONNECT FITTINGS
3 - FUEL PRESSURE REGULATOR
4 - 4-WIRE ELECTRICAL CONNECTOR
5 - FUEL TANK CHECK (CONTROL) VALVE

LTV1900000000109

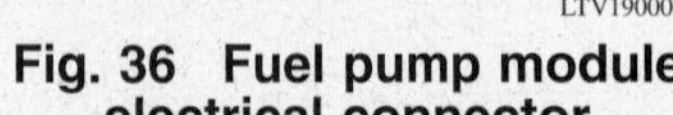

Fig. 36 Fuel pump module electrical connector

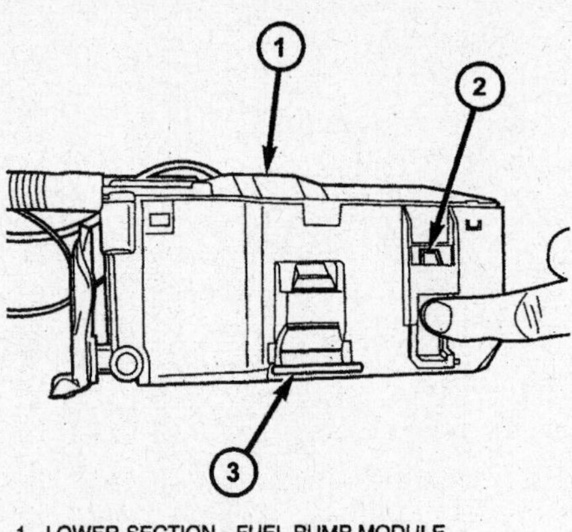

1 - LOWER SECTION - FUEL PUMP MODULE
2 - RELEASE LOCK AND TAB
3 - TENSION SPRINGS

LTV1900000000110

Fig. 37 Lower fuel pump module

TIGHTENING SPECIFICATIONS

Year	Component	Torque Ft. Lbs.
2002–06	Balance Shaft Carrier Cover	105
	Balance Shaft Carrier To Block	40
	Balance Shaft Chain Tensioner	105①
	Balance Shaft Gear Cover	105①
	Balance Shaft Sprocket	21
	Camshaft Sprocket	75
	Connecting Rod Cap	40②
	Crankshaft Damper	100
	Crankshaft Main Bearing Cap	③
	Cylinder Head	④
	Exhaust Manifold	17
	Exhaust Manifold Heat Shield	105①
	Flex Plate To Crankshaft	70
	Flywheel	60
	Front Cover	105①
	Lower Intake Manifold	21
	Oil Pan	105①
	Oil Pan Drain Plug	20
	Oil Pump Cover	105①
	Oil Pump Pick Up Tube	20
	Oil Pump Relief Valve Cap	30
	Oil Pump To Block	21
	Righthand Engine Mount Bracket	45
	Timing Belt Rear Cover	105①
	Timing Belt Tensioner	45
	Timing Belt Tensioner Lock Nut	22
	Valve Cover	105①

① — Inch lbs.
② — Plus ¼ turn.
③ — Refer to "Main & Rod Bearings" procedure for tightening specifications.
④ — Refer to "Cylinder Head, Replace" procedure for tightening specifications.

3.7L Engine

NOTE: Refer To "2.4L Engine" For Service Procedures Not Covered In This Section.

NOTE: Air Bag Equipped Models, Refer To "Air Bag System Precautions" Located In The Front Of This Manual For System Disarming & Arming Procedures.

NOTE: Refer To "Computer Relearn Procedures" Located In The Front Of This Manual When Battery Power To The Computer Has Been Interrupted.

INDEX

PRECAUTIONS

Air Bag Systems

Refer to "Air Bag System Precautions" in the front of this manual for system disarming and arming procedures.

Battery Ground Cable

Prior to service, disconnect battery ground cable and isolate as required.

Fuel System Pressure Relief

1. Remove fuel cap, then the fuel pump relay from PDC.
2. Start and run engine until it stalls.
3. Attempt to restart engine until it will no longer run.
4. Turn ignition key to Off position.
5. Unplug connector from any injector.
6. Attach one end of a suitable 18 gauge or smaller jumper wire to either injector terminal.
7. Connect other end of jumper wire to positive battery terminal.
8. Connect one end of a second jumper wire to remaining injector terminal.
9. Momentarily touch other end of second jumper wire to negative battery terminal for no more than a few seconds. **Powering an injector for more than a few seconds will damage injector.**
10. Place a suitable rag below fuel line quick connect fitting on fuel rail, then disconnect quick connect fitting.
11. Install fuel pump relay to PDC, then clear any stored DTC's.

COMPRESSION PRESSURES

1. Ensure battery is completely charged and engine starter motor is in good operating condition.
2. Clean spark plug recesses with compressed air, then remove spark plugs.
3. Secure throttle in wide open position.
4. Remove auto shut down (ASD) relay from power distribution center.
5. Install a suitable compression pressure gauge, then rotate engine using starter motor for three revolutions.
6. Record compression pressure on third revolution.

ENGINE MOUNT

REPLACE

Front

1. Remove fan blade, fan clutch and shroud.
2. Remove engine oil filter.
3. Support engine using suitable jack and block of wood across full width of engine oil pan.
4. Remove four cylinder block to insulator mount bolts and nut from engine insulator mount through bolt.
5. Raise engine high enough to remove engine insulator mount through bolt, then the insulator mount, **Figs. 1 and 2.**
6. Reverse procedure to install.

Rear

1. Raise and support vehicle.
2. Support transmission using suitable jack.
3. Remove nuts holding support cushion to crossmember, then remove crossmember.
4. Remove support cushion nuts, then the support cushion.
5. Reverse procedure to install.

ENGINE

REPLACE

1. Remove hood ensuring to mark hinge locations for reference during installation.
2. Remove air cleaner assembly.
3. Remove radiator core support bracket.
4. Remove fan shroud with electric fan assembly.
5. Remove serpentine drive belt.

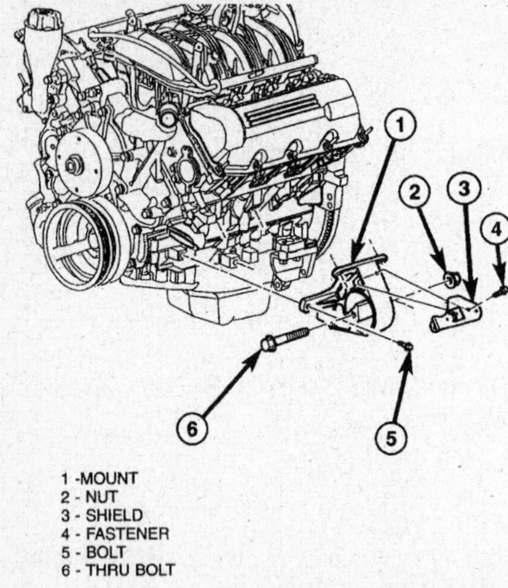

Fig. 1 Lefthand insulator mount

6. Remove A/C compressor and position aside with lines attached.
7. Remove alternator and position aside.
8. Remove power steering pump and position aside with lines attached. **Do not remove phenolic pulley from power steering pump.**
9. Drain cooling system into suitable container, then remove coolant bottle.
10. Disconnect heater hoses from engine.
11. Disconnect heater hoses from heater core, then remove hose assembly.
12. Disconnect throttle and speed control cables.
13. Remove upper and lower radiator hoses from engine.
14. Disconnect engine to body ground straps at lefthand side of cowl.
15. Disconnect electrical connectors from the following:
    a. IAT sensor.
    b. Fuel injectors.
    c. TPS switch.
    d. IAC motor.
    e. Engine oil pressure switch.
    f. ECT sensor.
    g. MAP Sensor.
    h. CMP sensor.
    i. Coil over plugs.
    j. CKP sensor.
16. Remove coil over plugs.
17. Release fuel pressure as outlined in "Precautions."
18. Remove fuel rail and position aside.
19. Remove PCV hose.
20. Remove breather hoses.
21. Remove vacuum hose for power brake booster.
22. Disconnect knock sensors.
23. Remove engine oil dipstick tube.
24. Remove intake manifold as outlined in "Intake Manifold, Replace."
25. Install suitable engine lifting fixture.
26. Secure lefthand and righthand engine wiring harnesses away from engine.
27. Raise and support vehicle.
28. Disconnect oxygen sensor electrical connector.
29. Disconnect CKP sensor electrical connector.
30. Disconnect front propshaft at front differential and secure aside.

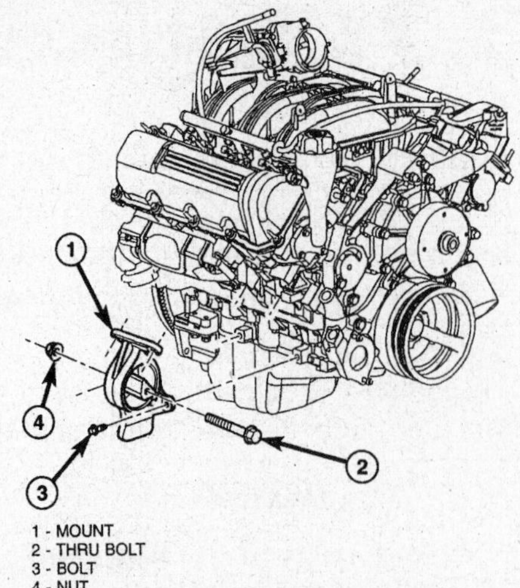

Fig. 2 Righthand insulator mount

31. Remove starter motor.
32. Remove ground straps from lefthand and righthand side of block.
33. Disconnect lefthand and righthand exhaust pipes at manifolds from crossover, then remove from vehicle.
34. **On models equipped with manual transmission,** remove transmission.
35. **On all models,** remove structural collar.
36. **On models equipped with automatic transmission,** remove torque convertor bolts. Mark bolt locations for reference during installation.
37. **On models equipped with automatic transmission,** remove transmission bellhousing to engine bolts.
38. **On all models,** loosen lefthand and righthand engine mount through bolts.
39. Lower vehicle.
40. **On models equipped with automatic transmission,** support transmission using a suitable jack.
41. **On all models,** remove engine using a suitable engine hoist.
42. Reverse procedure to install, noting the following:
    a. Tighten structural collar bolts in sequence, **Fig. 3,** to specifications. **Structural collar must be held tightly against both engine and transmission bell housing during tightening sequence.**
    b. Install new clamps on exhaust manifold flanges.

INTAKE MANIFOLD

REPLACE

1. Remove resonator assembly and air inlet hose.
2. Disconnect throttle and speed control cables.
3. Disconnect electrical connections from the following:
    a. MAP sensor.
    b. IAT sensor.
    c. TP sensor.
    d. Coolant temperature sensor.
    e. IAC motor.

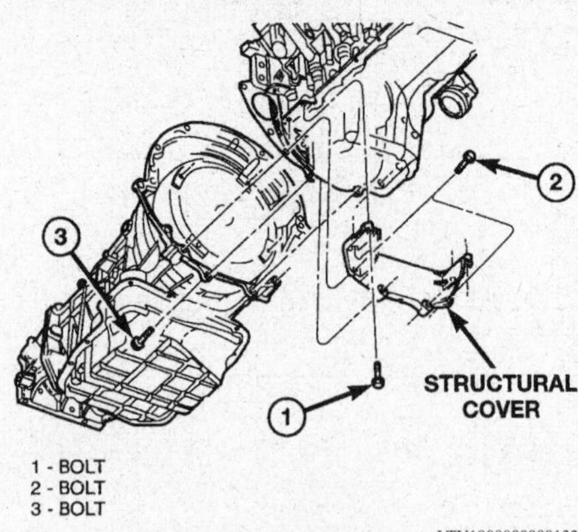

Fig. 3 Structural collar tightening sequence

4. Disconnect vapor purge hose, then the brake booster hose.
5. Disconnect speed control servo hose, then the PCV hose.
6. Disconnect electrical connector from alternator and A/C compressor.
7. Disconnect lefthand and righthand radio suppressor straps.
8. Disconnect and remove ignition coil towers.
9. Remove top oil dipstick tube retaining bolt and ground strap.
10. Release fuel system pressure as outlined in "Precautions."
11. Remove fuel rail.
12. Remove throttle body assembly and mounting bracket.
13. Drain cooling system to below coolant temperature sensor level into suitable container.
14. Remove heater hoses from engine front cover and heater core.
15. Unclip and remove heater hoses and tubes from intake manifold.
16. Remove coolant temperature sensor.
17. Remove intake manifold bolts in reverse order of tightening sequence, **Fig. 4.**
18. Remove intake manifold.
19. Reverse procedure to install. Tighten intake manifold bolts in sequence, **Fig. 4,** to specifications.

EXHAUST MANIFOLD

REPLACE

1. Raise and support vehicle.
2. Remove bolts attaching exhaust pipe to exhaust manifold.
3. Lower vehicle.
4. Remove exhaust heat shield.
5. Remove exhaust manifold nuts, then the exhaust manifold with gasket.
6. Reverse procedure to install, noting the following:
    a. If studs came out with nuts when removing exhaust manifold, install new studs. Apply sealer to coarse thread ends of stud.
    b. Tighten nuts starting with center and working outward to specifications.

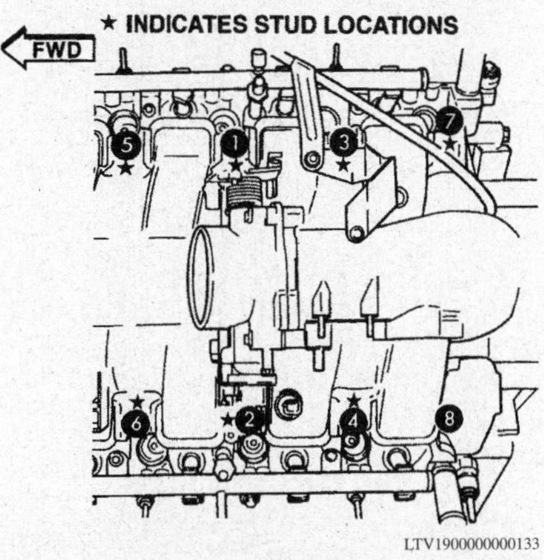

Fig. 4 Intake manifold tightening sequence

CYLINDER HEAD

REPLACE

1. Raise and support vehicle.
2. Disconnect exhaust pipe at exhaust manifold.
3. Drain cooling system into suitable container.
4. Lower vehicle.
5. Remove intake manifold as outlined in "Intake Manifold, Replace."
6. Remove valve cover as outlined in "Valve Cover, Replace."
7. Remove fan shroud and fan blade assembly.
8. Remove serpentine drive belt.
9. Remove power steering pump and position aside.
10. Rotate crankshaft until damper timing mark is aligned with TDC indicator mark, **Fig. 5.**
11. Verify V6 mark on camshaft sprocket is at 12 o'clock position, **Fig. 6.** Rotate crankshaft one turn if required.
12. Remove crankshaft damper bolt.
13. Remove crankshaft damper using puller tool No. 1026 and insert tool No. 8513, or equivalents.
14. Remove timing chain cover as outlined in "Front Cover, Replace."
15. Lock secondary timing chains to idler sprocket using holding tool No. 8429, or equivalent, **Fig. 7.**
16. Mark secondary timing chain one link on each side of V6 mark on camshaft drive gear.
17. Remove secondary timing chain tensioner.
18. Remove cylinder head access plug, **Fig. 8.**
19. Remove secondary timing chain guide.
20. Remove retaining bolt, then the camshaft drive gear.
21. Remove 12 cylinder head bolts. Do not overlook four smaller bolts at front of cylinder head.
22. Remove cylinder head and gasket.
23. Reverse procedure to install noting the following:
    a. Inspect cylinder head bolts for stretching by holding suitable straight edge against threads. If all threads do not contact straight edge, replace bolt.
    b. Install new cylinder head gasket on locating dowels.
    c. Lubricate eight M11 cylinder head bolts with clean engine oil.
    d. Coat four M8 cylinder head bolts with Mopar Lock and Seal or equivalent adhesive.
    e. **Torque** cylinder head bolts 1–8 in sequence, **Fig. 9,** to 20 ft. lbs. Verify bolts reached 20 ft. lbs., by repeating sequence.
    f. **Torque** cylinder head bolts 9–12 in sequence, **Fig. 9,** to 10 ft. lbs.
    g. Tighten cylinder head bolts 1–8 in sequence an additional 90°.
    h. Tighten cylinder head bolts 1–8 in sequence an additional 90° again.
    i. **Torque** cylinder head bolts 9–12 in sequence to 19 ft. lbs.
    j. Install secondary timing chain onto camshaft drive gear with one marked link on either side of V6 mark on gear.
    k. Position gear onto camshaft using camshaft wrench tool No. 8428, or equivalent.

VALVE COVER

REPLACE

1. Remove air cleaner assembly, resonator assembly and air inlet hose.
2. Drain cooling system into suitable container.
3. Remove serpentine drive belt.
4. Remove A/C compressor and position aside.
5. Remove heater hoses.
6. Disconnect fuel injector and ignition coil electrical connectors.
7. Disconnect and remove PCV hose.
8. Remove oil fill tube.
9. Unclip injector and ignition coil harness, then position aside.
10. Remove righthand rear breather tube and filter assembly.
11. Remove valve cover bolts, then the valve cover.
12. Reverse procedure to install, noting the following:
    a. Do not use harsh cleaners to clean valve cover.
    b. Valve cover gaskets may be reused, provided there are no cuts tears or deformation.

VALVE ARRANGEMENT

This engine uses two valve per cylinder. Exhaust valves are located on the exhaust manifold side of the cylinder head, intake valves are located on the intake manifold side of the cylinder head.

CAMSHAFT LOBE LIFT SPECIFICATIONS

Exhaust ....**.429 inch**
Intake ....**.472 inch**

VALVE ADJUSTMENT

These engines are equipped with hydraulic lash adjusters. There is no provision for adjustment.

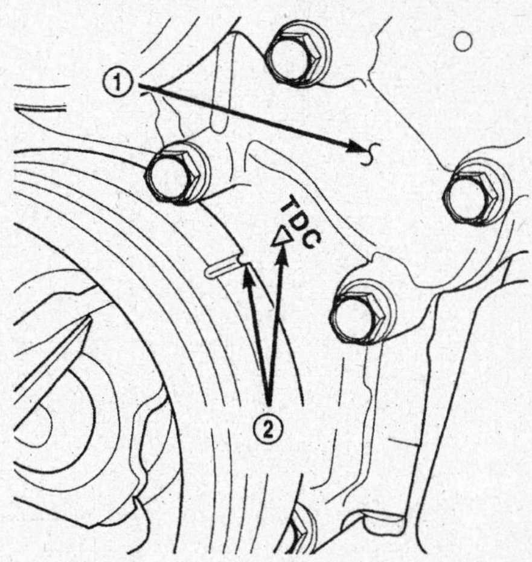

Fig. 5 Engine TDC alignment

ROCKER ARMS

REPLACE

1. Remove valve cover as outlined in "Valve Cover, Replace."
2. For rocker arm removal on cylinder No. 4, rotate crankshaft until cylinder No. 1 is at BDC on intake stroke.
3. For rocker arm removal on cylinder No. 1, rotate crankshaft until cylinder No. 1 is at BDC on combustion stroke.
4. For rocker arm removal on cylinder Nos. 3 and 5, rotate crankshaft until cylinder No. 1 is at TDC on exhaust stroke.
5. For rocker arm removal on cylinder Nos. 2 and 6, rotate crankshaft until cylinder No. 1 is at TDC on ignition stroke.
6. Press downward on valve spring and remove rocker arm using rocker arm removal tool No. 8516, or equivalent.
7. Reverse procedure to install, noting the following:
    a. Ensure rocker arms are installed with concave pocket over lash adjusters.
    b. Coat rocker arms with clean engine oil.

VALVE GUIDES

The valve guides are an integral part of the cylinder head. If valve stem to guide clearance is excessive, the cylinder head must be replaced.

FRONT COVER

REPLACE

1. Drain cooling system into suitable container.
2. Remove electric cooling fan and fan shroud assembly.
3. Disconnect both heater hoses at timing cover.
4. Disconnect lower radiator hose at engine.
5. Remove serpentine drive belt tensioner.

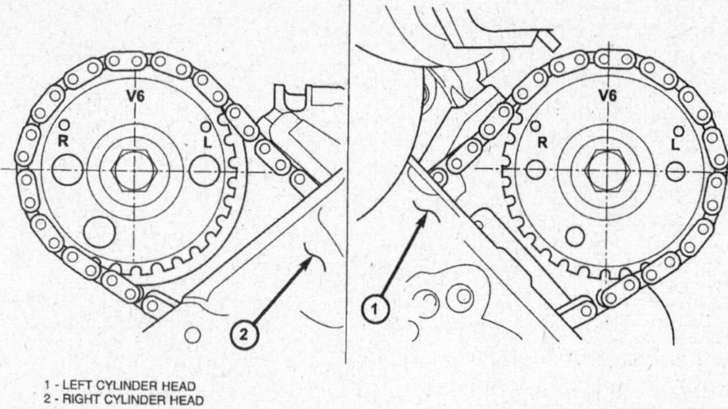

Fig. 6 Camshaft sprocket V6 marks

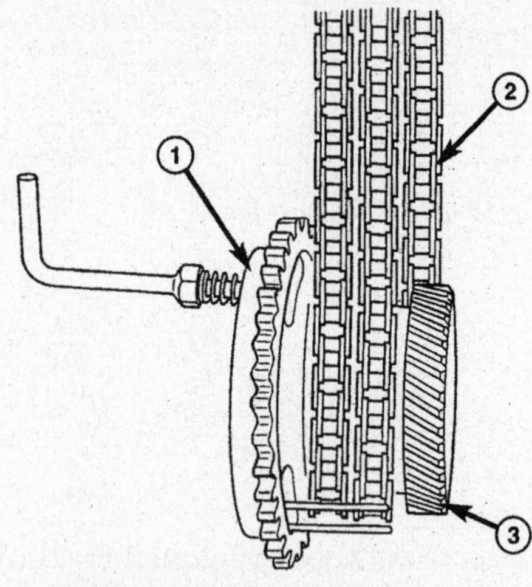

Fig. 7 Locking secondary timing chains

6. Remove crankshaft damper bolt.
7. Remove crankshaft damper using puller tool No. 1026 and insert tool No. 8513, or equivalents.
8. Remove alternator, then the A/C compressor.
9. Remove bolts, then the front cover.
10. Reverse procedure to install, noting the following:
    a. Apply a .12–.15 inch bead of Mopar Engine RTV sealer, or equivalent, to front cover, **Fig. 10.**
    b. Tighten front cover in sequence, **Fig. 11,** to specifications.

TIMING CHAIN

REPLACE

Removal

1. Drain cooling system into suitable container.
2. Remove valve covers as outlined in "Valve Cover, Replace."
3. Remove radiator fan shroud.
4. Rotate engine until timing mark on crankshaft damper aligns with TDC mark on timing chain cover, **Fig. 5,** and camshaft sprocket V6 marks are at 12 o'clock position, **Fig. 6.**
5. Remove power steering pump.
6. Remove access plug from lefthand and righthand cylinder heads for access to chain guide fasteners, **Fig. 8.**
7. Remove oil fill housing to gain access to righthand side tensioner arm fastener.
8. Remove crankshaft damper bolt.
9. Remove crankshaft damper using puller tool No. 1026 and insert tool No. 8513, or equivalents.
10. Remove front cover as outlined in "Front Cover, Replace."
11. Collapse primary chain tensioner, then hold tensioner in collapsed position using a suitable pin.
12. Remove secondary timing chain tensioners. **Cover oil pan opening. Plate behind lefthand secondary chain tensioner could fall into oil pan.**
13. Remove camshaft position sensor. **Use care not to damage CMP sensor. Do not place sensor near any magnetic source.**
14. Remove lefthand and righthand camshaft sprocket bolts.
15. Remove lefthand camshaft sprocket using camshaft wrench tool No. 8428, or equivalent. Slowly rotate camshaft approximately 5° clockwise to neutral position.
16. Remove righthand camshaft sprocket using camshaft wrench tool No. 8428, or equivalent.
17. **Do not forcefully rotate camshafts or crankshaft independently of each other, intake valve to piston contact will occur.**
18. Remove idler sprocket assembly bolt.
19. Slide idler sprocket assembly and crankshaft sprocket forward simultaneously to remove primary and secondary timing chains.
20. Remove primary chain tensioner.

Installation

1. Lightly compress secondary chain tensioner piston until piston is flush with tensioner body.
2. Release ratchet pawl by pulling pawl back against spring force through access hole on side of tensioner.
3. While continuing to hold pawl back, push ratchet device to approximately 2 mm from tensioner body.
4. Install pin tool No. 8514, or equivalent, into hole on front of tensioner, **Fig. 12.** Slowly open vise to transfer piston spring force to lock pin.
5. Position primary chain tensioner over oil pump and insert bolts into lower two holes on tensioner bracket.
6. Install righthand side chain tensioner arm.
7. Install lefthand side chain guide. **Silver bolts retain guides to cylinder heads and black bolts retain guides to engine block.**
8. Install lefthand side chain tensioner arm.
9. Install righthand side chain guide.
10. Install both secondary chains onto idler sprocket.
11. Align two plated links on secondary chains to be visible through two lower openings on idler sprocket (4 o'clock and 8 o'clock position).
12. Once secondary timing chains are installed, position holding tool No. 8429, or equivalent, to hold chains in place for installation.
13. Align primary chain double plated links with timing mark at 12 o'clock position on idler sprocket.
14. Align primary chain single plated link with timing mark at 6 o'clock position on crankshaft sprocket.
15. Lubricate idler shaft and bushings with clean engine oil.
16. Install all chains, crankshaft sprocket and idler sprocket as an assembly, **Fig. 13.**
17. After guiding both secondary chains through block and cylinder head openings, affix chains using suitable elastic strap.
18. Align timing mark on idler sprocket gear to timing mark on counterbalance shaft drive gear, then fully seat idler sprocket, **Fig. 14.**
19. Align lefthand camshaft sprocket L dot to plated link on chain.
20. Align righthand camshaft sprocket R dot to plated link on chain.
21. Remove holding tool, then install both sprockets to camshafts. Remove excess oil from bolts, then install sprocket bolts, but do not tighten at this time.
22. Verify that all plated links are aligned with marks on sprockets and V6 marks on camshaft sprockets are at 12 o'clock position. **Ensure plate between lefthand secondary chain tensioner and block is correctly installed.**
23. Install both secondary chain tensioners. Lefthand and righthand chain tensioners are not common.
24. Remove all three locking pins from tensioners. After pulling locking pins out of each tensioner, do not manually extend tensioner ratchets.
25. Tighten lefthand and righthand camshaft sprocket bolts to specifications using spanner wrench tool No. 6958 with adapter pins tool No. 8346, or equivalents.
26. Rotate engine two full revolutions, then verify timing marks are at the following locations:
    a. Primary timing chain idler sprocket

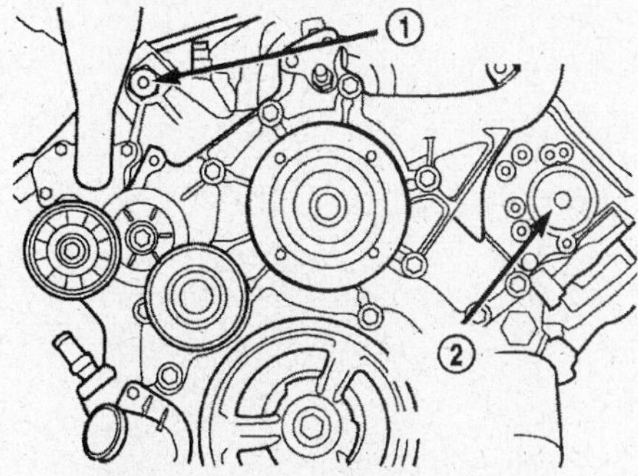

Fig. 8 Cylinder access plug

dot is at 12 o'clock position.

b. Primary timing chain crankshaft sprocket dot is at 6 o'clock position.

c. Secondary timing chain camshaft sprockets V6 marks are at 12 o'clock position.

d. Counterbalance shaft drive gear dot is aligned to idler sprocket gear dot.

27. Lubricate all three timing chains with clean engine oil.
28. After installing timing chains, inspect idler gear end play. End play should be .004–.010 inch. If not within specification, replace idler gear.
29. Install front cover, then the crankshaft damper.
30. Install valve covers.
31. Coat large threaded cylinder access plug with Mopar Thread Sealant with Teflon, or equivalent, then install into righthand cylinder head.
32. Install oil fill housing.
33. Install lefthand cylinder head access plug.
34. Install power steering pump.
35. Fill cooling system.

CAMSHAFT

REPLACE

Removal

When timing chain is removed and cylinder heads are still installed, do not forcefully rotate camshafts or crankshaft independently of each other. Severe valve and/or piston damage can occur.

When removing cam sprocket, timing chains or camshaft, failure to use chain tensioner wedge tool No. 8379, or equivalent, will result in hydraulic tensioner ratchet over extension requiring timing chain cover removal to set tensioner ratchet.

1. Remove valve cover as outlined in "Valve Cover, Replace."
2. Set engine to TDC on cylinder No. 1 and camshaft sprocket V6 marks at 12 o'clock position.
3. Mark one link on secondary timing chain sprocket on both sides of V6 mark on camshaft sprocket to aid in installation.
4. Loosen but do not remove camshaft sprocket retaining bolt. Leave bolt snug against sprocket.
5. Position timing chain wedge tool No. 8379, or equivalent, between timing chain strands. Tap tool to securely wedge timing chain against tensioner arm and guide.
6. Remove camshaft position sensor.
7. Hold camshaft using camshaft wrench tool No. 8428, or equivalent, while removing camshaft sprocket bolt and sprocket.
8. Starting at outside and working inward, loosen camshaft bearing cap retaining bolts ½ turn at a time until load is off bearing caps.
9. When camshaft is removed rocker arms may slide downward, mark rocker arm locations before removing camshaft.
10. Remove camshaft bearing caps, then the camshaft.

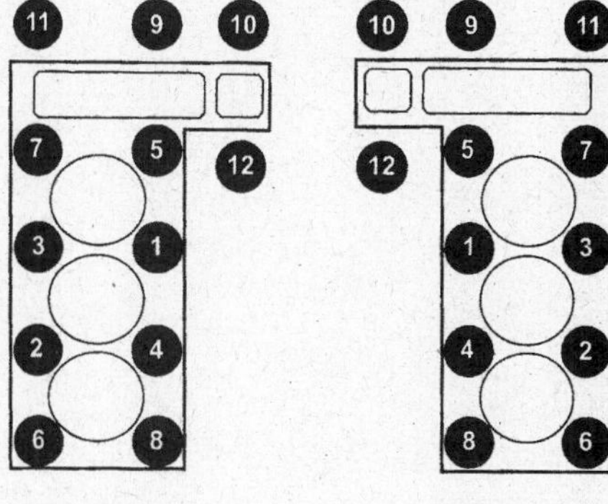

Fig. 9 Cylinder head bolt tightening sequence

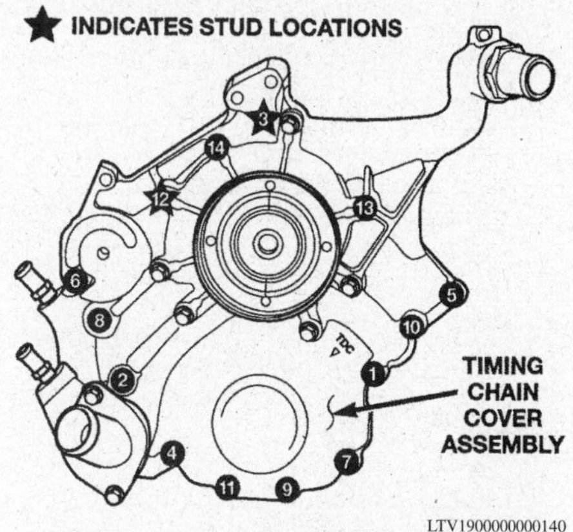

Fig. 11 Front cover tightening sequence

Installation

1. Lubricate camshaft journals with clean engine oil.
2. Install camshaft into cylinder head. Position righthand side camshaft so that camshaft sprocket dowel is near 10 o'clock position, this will ease bearing cap installation.
3. Install camshaft bearing caps hand tightening retaining bolts. Caps should be installed with stamped numbers on caps in numerical order from front to rear and arrows pointing toward front of engine.
4. Working in ½ turn increments, tighten bearing caps in sequence, **Fig. 15**, to specifications.
5. Position camshaft drive gear into timing chain aligning V6 mark between two chain links marked during removal.
6. Rotate camshaft until camshaft sprocket dowel is aligned with slot in camshaft sprocket using camshaft wrench tool No. 8428, or equivalent.
7. Install camshaft sprocket onto camshaft.
8. Remove excess oil from camshaft sprocket bolt, then install camshaft sprocket retaining bolt hand tight.
9. Remove timing chain wedge tool.
10. Tighten camshaft sprocket bolt to specifications using spanner wrench tool No. 6958 with adapter pins tool No. 8346, or equivalents.
11. Install camshaft position sensor.
12. Install valve cover.

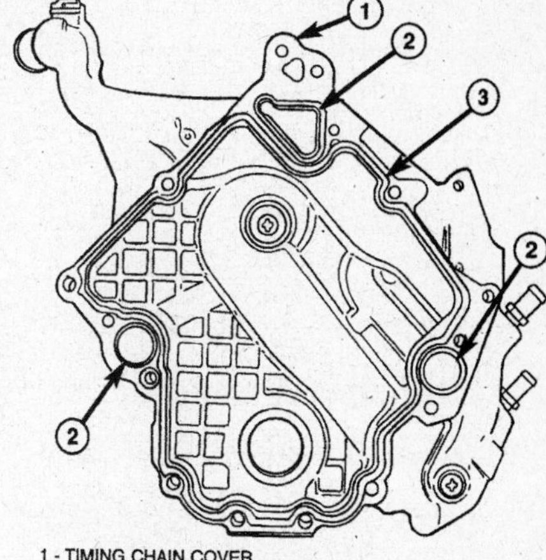

Fig. 10 Front cover sealant

PISTON & ROD ASSEMBLY

Pistons are marked with an "F" near the piston wrist pin bore. When assembling piston to rod, ensure "F" faces toward front of engine. Oil slinger slots in connecting rods also face toward front of engine, **Fig. 16.**

MAIN & ROD BEARINGS

Connecting rod bearings are available in three sizes, **Fig. 17.**

The main bearings are "select fit" to achieve proper oil clearances. The crankshaft position sensor target wheel has grade identification marks stamped into it, **Fig. 18.** These marks are rear from lefthand to righthand and correspond with journal Nos. 1, 2, 3 and 4. Service main bearings are available in four grades,

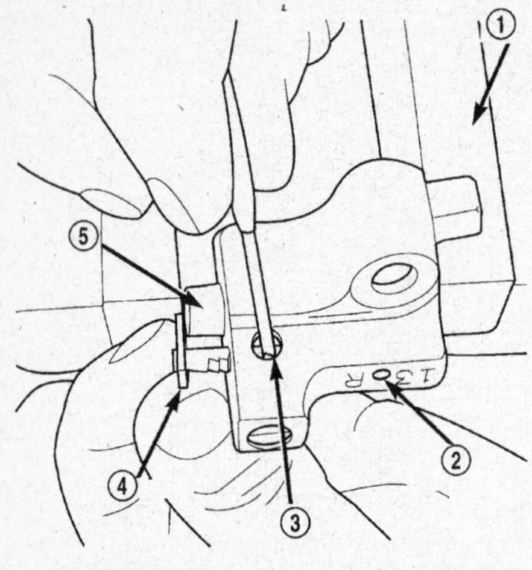

Fig. 12 Resetting secondary chain tensioner

Fig. 19. **Torque** bedplate bolts 1A-1J in sequence, **Fig. 20,** to 40 ft. lbs. **Torque** bolts 1–8 in sequence to 60 inch lbs., plus an additional 90°. **Torque** bolts A–E in sequence to 20 ft. lbs.

CRANKSHAFT REAR OIL SEAL

REPLACE

Removal

1. Remove transmission as outlined in **MOTOR's "Domestic Transmission, In-Vehicle Service Manual" or "Transmission Service DVD."**
2. Remove bolts, then the flex plate.
3. Remove crankshaft rear oil seal using removal tool No. 8506, or equivalent.

Installation

1. Position magnetic seal guide tool No. 8349-2, or equivalent, onto crankshaft rear face.
2. Position crankshaft rear oil seal onto guide.
3. Tap seal into place until seal installer seats against cylinder block bore using oil seal installer tool No. 8349 and driver handle tool No. C-4171, or equivalents.
4. Install flexplate tightening bolts in sequence, **Fig. 21,** to specifications.
5. Install transmission.

OIL PAN

REPLACE

2002

1. Remove engine as outlined in "Engine, Replace."
2. Mount engine on suitable engine stand.

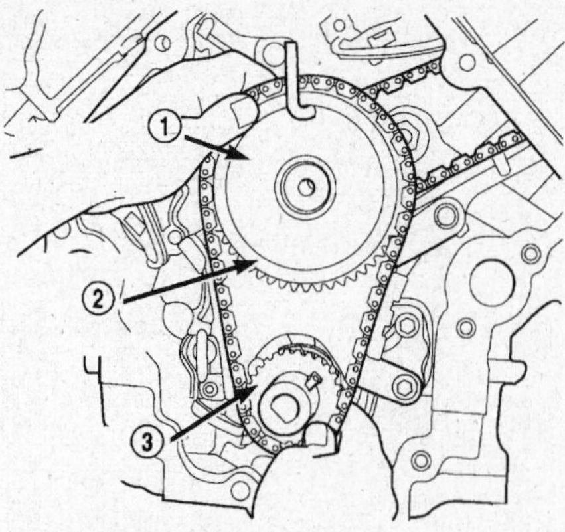

Fig. 13 Timing chain installation

3. Unbolt and remove oil pump pickup tube.
4. Remove oil pan gasket/windage tray assembly from engine. **Do not pry on oil pan or oil pan gasket.**
5. Reverse procedure to install, noting the following:
   a. Inspect integrated oil pan gasket and replace as required.
   b. Tighten oil pan bolts in sequence, **Fig. 22,** to specifications.

2003–06

1. Install engine support fixture tool No. 8534, or equivalent.
2. Raise and support vehicle, then remove front tires and wheels.
3. Remove skid plate, then drain engine oil into suitable container.
4. Remove engine to transmission structural collar.
5. Remove transmission oil cooler line bracket.
6. Remove front axle assembly as outlined in "Axle Housing Assembly, Replace" in "Front Wheel Drive" section.
7. Loosen both engine mount through bolts, then lower vehicle.
8. Raise engine using support fixture until viscous fan almost touches fan shroud.
9. Raise and support vehicle.
10. Remove oil pan bolts.
11. Remove two nuts and one bolt holding oil pump pickup tube and windage tray in place.
12. Drop oil pump pickup tube into oil pan, then remove oil pan, pickup tube and windage tray as an assembly from front of vehicle.
13. Reverse procedure to install, noting the following:
    a. Clean oil pan and block gasket mating surfaces.
    b. Tighten oil pan bolts in sequence, **Fig. 23,** to specifications.

OIL PUMP

REPLACE

1. Remove oil pan as outlined in "Oil Pan, Replace."

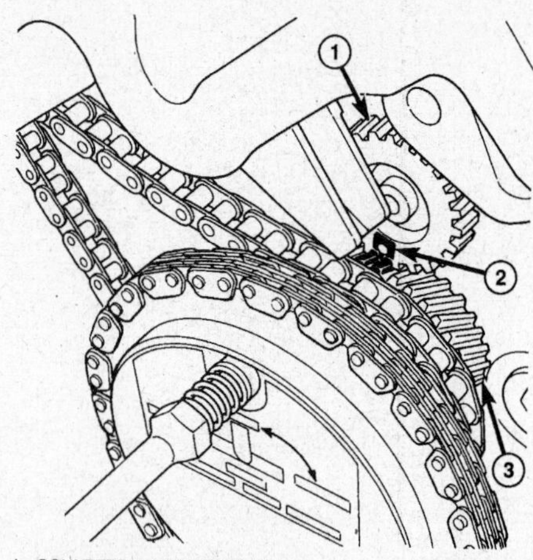

Fig. 14 Counterbalance shaft alignment marks

2. Remove front cover as outlined in "Front Cover, Replace."
3. Remove timing chain and tensioners as outlined in "Timing Chain, Replace."
4. Remove four bolts, primary timing chain, then the oil pump.
5. Reverse procedure to install. Tighten oil pump bolts in sequence, **Fig. 24,** to specifications.

BELT TENSION DATA

Refer to "2.4L Engine" in this section for procedure.

SERPENTINE DRIVE BELT

Routing

Refer to **Fig. 25** for serpentine drive belt routing.

Replacement

1. Rotate belt tensioner until it contacts its stop.
2. Remove belt, then slowly rotate tensioner into freearm position.
3. Reverse procedure to install ensuring belt is seated onto all pulleys.

COOLING SYSTEM BLEED

Refer to "Cooling System Bleed" in the "2.4L Engine" section for procedure.

WATER PUMP

REPLACE

1. Drain cooling system into suitable container.
2. Remove serpentine drive belt.
3. Remove viscous fan drive assembly from water pump using spanner wrench tool No. 6958 and adapters

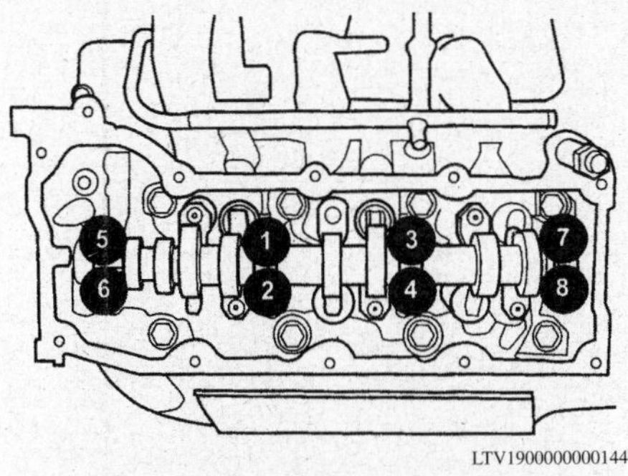

Fig. 15 Camshaft bearing cap tightening sequence

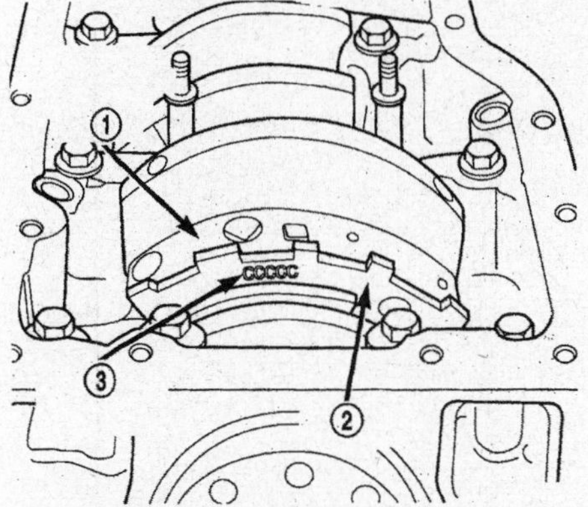

Fig. 18 Main bearing target wheel marks

tool No. 8346, or equivalents, by turning mounting nut counterclockwise as viewed from front. Do not attempt to remove fan drive assembly from vehicle at this time.

4. If water pump is being replaced, do not unbolt fan blade assembly from viscous fan drive.
5. Remove two fan shroud to radiator screws, then disconnect coolant overflow hose.
6. Remove upper fan shroud and viscous fan drive assembly from vehicle. **Do not place viscous fan drive assembly in horizontal position.**
7. Remove lower radiator hose from water pump.
8. Remove seven bolts and one stud, then the water pump.
9. Reverse procedure to install, noting the following:
   a. Install new water pump gasket.
   b. Instal water pump bolts and stud in proper locations, **Fig. 26.**

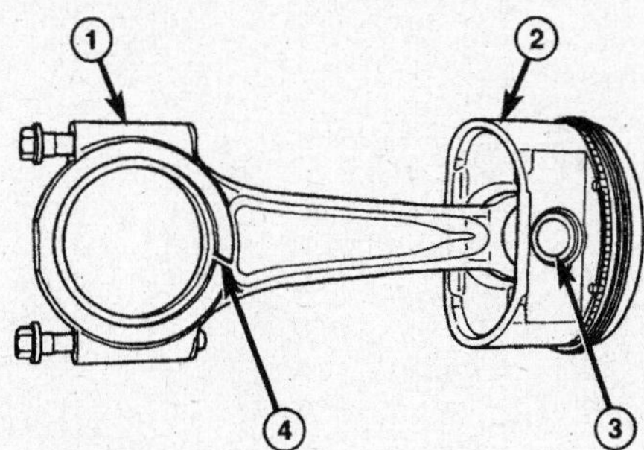

Fig. 16 Piston and rod assembly

Crankshaft MARKING	JOURNAL SIZE SIZE mm (in.)	
"R" Size	63.488 - 63.496 mm (2.4995 - 2.4998 in.)	
"S" Size	63.496 - 63.500 mm (2.4998 - 2.4999 in.)	
"T" Size	63.500 - 63.504 mm (2.4999 - 2.501 in.)	
"U" Size	63.504 - 63.512 mm (2.5001 - 2.5004 in.)	
Bearing size		
Bearing Code	Size	Application
Upper Bearing		
A	2.443 - 2.447 mm (.0961 - .0963 in.)	Use with crankshaft size "R"
B	2.439 - 2.443 mm (0.960 - .0961 in.)	Use with crankshaft "S, T"
C	2.435 - 2.439 mm (.0958 - .0960 in.)	Use with crankshaft "U"
Lower Bearing Main "1" and "4"		
"1"	2.441 - 2.447 mm (.0961 -.0963 in.)	Use with crankshaft "R, S"
"2"	2.435 - 2.441 mm (.0958 - .0962 in.)	Use with crankshaft "T, U"
Lower Main Bearing "2" and "3"		
"3"	2.429 - 2.435 mm (.0956 - .0958 in.)	Use with crankshaft "R, S"
"4"	2.423 - 2.429 mm (.0953 - .0956 in.)	Use with crankshaft "T, U"

LTV1900000000148

Fig. 19 Main bearing selection chart (Part 1 of 2)

Bearing Mark	SIZE	USED WITH JOURNAL SIZE
.025 US	.025 mm (.001 in.)	57.883-57.871 mm (2.2788-2.2783 in.)
Std.	STANDARD	57.908-57.892 mm (2.2798-2.2792 in.)
.250 US	.250 mm (.010 in.)	57.658-57.646 mm (2.27-2.2695 in.)

LTV1900000000146

Fig. 17 Connecting rod bearing size

Crankshaft MARKING	JOURNAL SIZE SIZE mm (in.)
Bearing Clearances	
Main "1, 4"	
Crankshaft "R"	.004 - .034 mm (.00015 - .0013 in.)
Crankshaft "S"	.004 - .030 mm (.00015 - .0011 in.)
Crankshaft "T"	.006 - .032 mm (.0002 - .0012 in.)
Crankshaft "U"	.002 - .032 mm (.00007 -. 0012 in.)
Main "2, 3"	
Crankshaft "R"	.016 - .046 mm (.0006 - .0018 in.)
Crankshaft "S"	.016 - .042 mm (.00062 - .016 in.)
Crankshaft "T"	.018 - .044 mm (.0007 - .0017 in.)
Crankshaft "U"	.014 - .044 mm (.0005 - .0017 in.)

LTV1900000000149

Fig. 19 Main bearing selection chart (Part 2 of 2)

RADIATOR

REPLACE

Refer to “Radiator, Replace” in the “2.4L Engine” section for radiator replacement procedure.

FUEL PUMP

REPLACE

Refer to “Fuel Pump, Replace” in the “2.4L Engine” section for fuel pump replacement procedure.

FUEL FILTER

REPLACE

Refer to “Fuel Filter, Replace” in the “2.4L Engine” section for fuel filter replacement procedure.

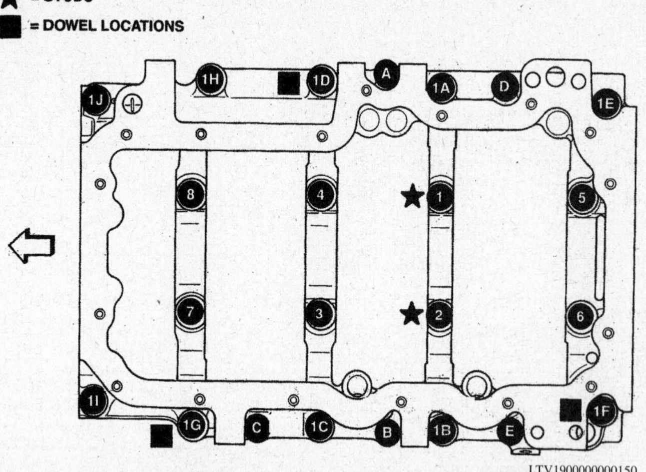

Fig. 20 Bedplate tightening sequence

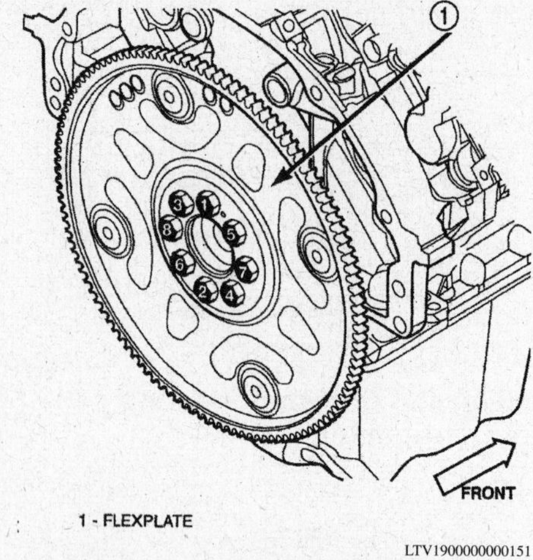

Fig. 21 Flexplate tightening sequence

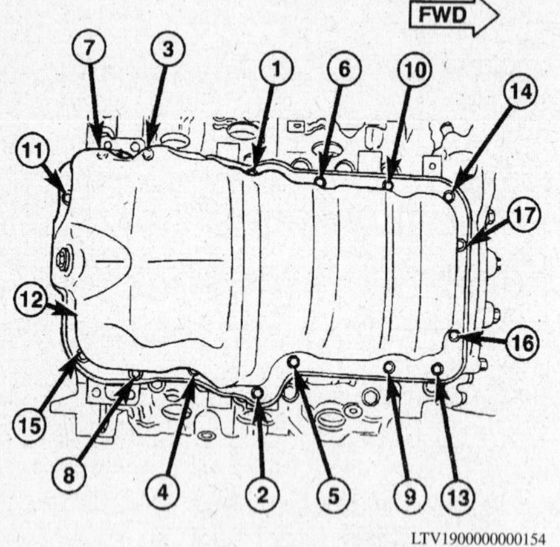

Fig. 22 Oil pan tightening sequence. 2002

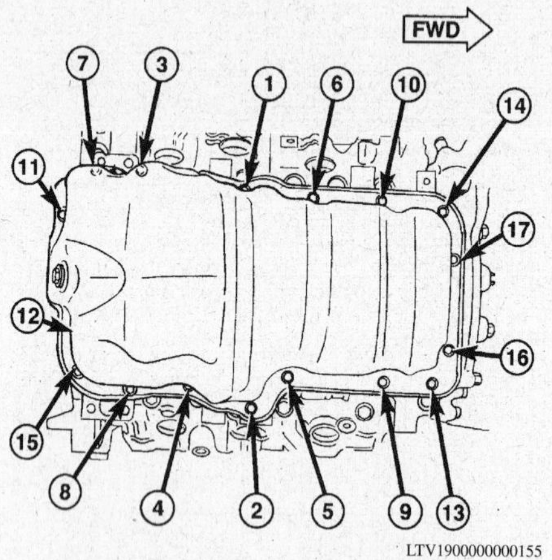

Fig. 23 Oil pan tightening sequence. 2003–06

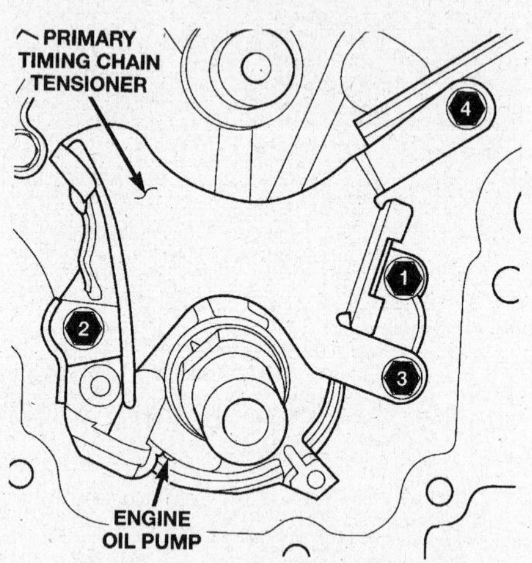

Fig. 24 Oil pump tightening sequence

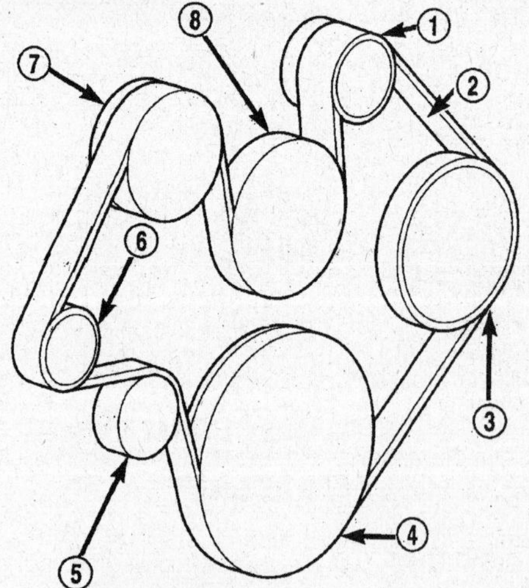

Fig. 25 Serpentine drive belt routing

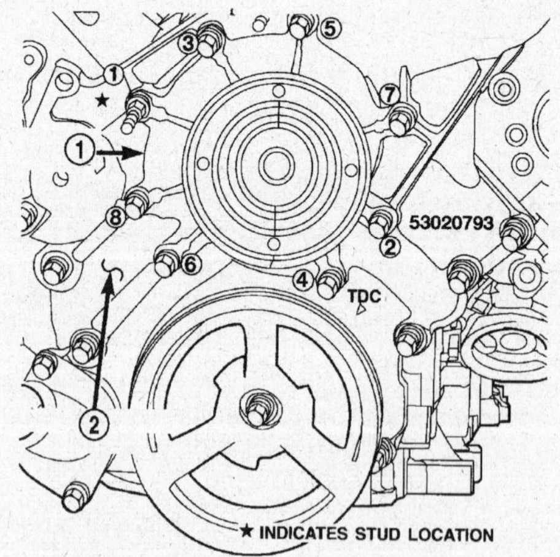

Fig. 26 Water pump installation

TIGHTENING SPECIFICATIONS

Year	Component	Torque Ft. Lbs.
2002–06	Bed Plate	③
	Camshaft Bearing Cap	100①
	Camshaft Sprocket	90
	Connecting Rod Cap	20②
	Crankshaft Damper	130
	Cylinder Head	④
	Engine Mount Bracket To Block	45
	Exhaust Manifold	18
	Flexplate	70
	Hydraulic Tensioner	21
	Intake Manifold	105①
	Oil Fill Tube	105①
	Oil Pan	11
	Oil Pan Drain Plug	25
	Oil Pickup Tube	21
	Oil Pump	21
	Oil Pump Cover	105①
	Rear Mount To Transmission	34
	Structural Collar	40
	Thermostat Housing	105①
	Timing Chain Cover	43
	Timing Chain Guide	21
	Timing Chain Primary Tensioner	21
	Timing Chain Tensioner Arm	21
	Timing Drive Idler Sprocket	25
	Water Pump	43

① — Inch lbs.

② — Plus an additional 90°.

③ — Refer to "Main & Rod Bearings" for specification.

④ — Refer to "Cylinder Head, Replace" for specification.

2.8L Turbo Diesel Engine

NOTE: Air Bag Equipped Models, Refer To "Air Bag System Precautions" Located In The Front Of This Manual For System Disarming & Arming Procedures.

NOTE: Refer To "Computer Relearn Procedures" Located In The Front Of This Manual When Battery Power To The Computer Has Been Interrupted.

INDEX

PRECAUTIONS

Air Bag Systems

Refer to "Air Bag System Precautions" in the front of this manual for system disarming and arming procedures.

Battery Ground Cable

Prior to service, disconnect battery ground cable and isolate as required.

Fuel Injector Harness

Fuel injector harness red-striped wires carry 115 volts. If harness integrity is compromised, severe shock will occur.

COMPRESSION PRESSURE

Compression should not be less than 100 psi and not vary more than 25 percent from cylinder to cylinder.

ENGINE MOUNT

REPLACE

Lefthand

1. Remove cooling fan and fan shroud.
2. Raise and support vehicle.
3. Loosen both engine mount through bolts.
4. Raise and support engine using a suitable jack. **Care must be taken not to damage any wiring above transmission when raising engine.**
5. Remove engine mount retaining bolts and remove mount.
6. Reverse procedure to install.

Righthand

1. Remove cooling fan and shroud.
2. Loosen upper engine mount fastener at engine mount bracket.
3. Raise and support vehicle.
4. Loosen lower engine mount fastener.
5. Raise and support engine using a suitable jack. **Care must be taken not to damage wiring harnesses above transmission when lifting engine.**
6. Remove engine mount bolts and engine mount.
7. Reverse procedure to install.

ENGINE

REPLACE

1. Disconnect under hood lamp from hood assembly.
2. Drain cooling system into suitable container.
3. Remove engine cover.
4. Remove air cleaner assembly from engine bay.
5. Recover A/C refrigerant as outlined in "Air Conditioning" chapter.
6. Disconnect high side refrigerant line from upper radiator support bracket.
7. Remove upper radiator support bracket retaining bolts and remove support bracket.
8. Remove front grille and head lamp panel.
9. Remove from fascia.
10. Remove high side refrigerant line retaining nut and remove line from condenser assembly. Position line out of way.
11. Remove cooling fan and fan drive viscous clutch assembly.
12. Remove fan shroud retaining bolts and remove fan assembly and shroud together.
13. Disconnect charge air cooler hosed from charge air cooler.
14. Disconnect engine coolant hoses from engine assembly.
15. Disconnect coolant reservoir hose from radiator.
16. Remove low side refrigerant line retaining nut and remove line from condenser assembly. Position out of way.
17. Remove condenser assembly retaining nut and remove condenser from vehicle.
18. Remove power steering cooler retaining bolts and unclip air deflectors from both sides of radiator (cooling module) assembly.
19. Remove cooling module assembly.
20. Remove charge air cooler hose from intake manifold.
21. Remove high side refrigerant line from A/C compressor and remove high side line from engine bay.
22. Remove coolant reservoir retaining nuts and clips retaining electrical harness, position reservoir aside to allow access to remaining hoses.
23. Disconnect remaining hoses from

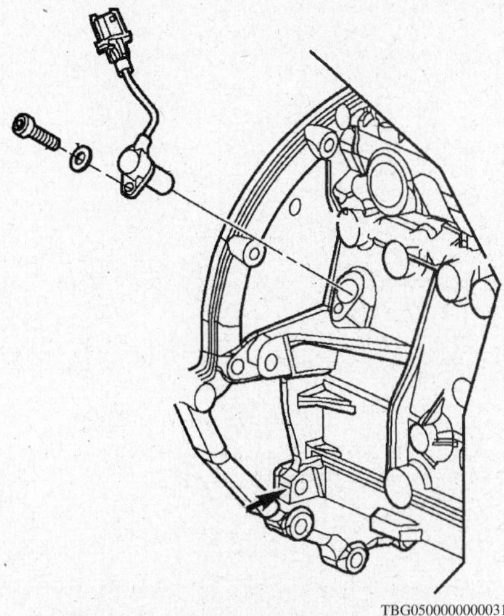

Fig. 1 Flywheel locking tool installation

coolant reservoir and remove reservoir.
24. Remove accessory drive belt from engine.
25. Accessing bolts through pump pulley, remove power steering pump retaining bolts and position pump aside with lines still attached.
26. Remove engine cover mounting bracket retaining bolts and remove bracket from top of engine.
27. Disconnect heater core inlet and outlet hoses from heater core.
28. Remove alternator as outlined under "Alternator, Replace" in "Electrical" section.
29. Remove low side refrigerant line retaining nuts from accumulator and compressor and remove from engine bay.
30. Trace engine wiring and disconnect electrical connectors and ties straps one at a time until all wiring is disconnected from engine assembly. When all engine electrical harness is disconnected position harness aside.
31. Remove coolant elbow retaining bolts from rear of water pump.
32. Disconnect coolant hoses leading from coolant elbow and remove coolant elbow from engine.
33. Remove oil cooler adapter.
34. Raise and support vehicle using a suitable lift or jack.
35. Remove oil filter and adapter assembly.
36. Remove starter as outlined under "Starter, Replace" in "Electrical" section.
37. Remove chassis ground wire above starter mounting location on engine block.
38. Support transmission with a jackstand.
39. Remove flex plate access cover.
40. Remove flex plate fasteners.
41. Remove transmission cross member fasteners.
42. Lower transmission.
43. Remove upper transmission to engine fasteners.
44. Raise transmission.
45. Install transmission cross member fasteners.
46. Remove transmission jack.
47. Remove exhaust inlet pipe retaining bolts and disconnect exhaust pipe from turbocharger.
48. Remove transmission to engine retaining bolts.
49. Separate transmission cooler line from retainer.
50. Connect a suitable lifting device to engine assembly.
51. Remove righthand side engine mount retaining nut.
52. Lower vehicle.
53. Remove lefthand side engine mount retaining mount.
54. Remove exhaust manifold rear heat shield.
55. Disconnect fuel supply and return lines.
56. Remove crankshaft sensor heat shield.
57. Disconnect crankshaft position sensor, located on righthand rear of engine.
58. Remove oil separator from cylinder head cover/intake manifold.
59. Disconnect oil pressure sensor. Make certain everything is disconnected from engine assembly.
60. Place a floor jack under transmission to support transmission.
61. With engine and transmission supported by lifting device separate engine from transmission.
62. Lift engine assembly out of engine bay.
63. Reverse procedure to install.

CYLINDER HEAD

REPLACE

Before removing cylinder head cover/ intake manifold witness mark on crankshaft hub must be rotated to 3 O'clock position or, 90° after TDC to assure proper alignment of camshafts and crankshaft. Failure to do so could result in valve and/or piston damage during reassembly.

1. Remove engine cover and bracket.
2. Remove air cleaner housing.
3. Drain cooling system into suitable container.
4. Recover A/C refrigerant as outlined in "Air Conditioning" chapter.
5. Disconnect coolant recovery hose at radiator.
6. Remove charge air inlet hose at radiator.
7. Remove upper radiator hose at radiator.
8. Separate A/C hoses from cooling fan shroud.
9. Remove cooling fan and fan drive viscous drive assembly, along with fan shroud.
10. Remove accessory drive belt.
11. Remove cooling fan support.
12. Disconnect EGR cooler pipe behind inner timing cover.
13. Remove alternator and alternator rear support bracket.
14. Remove accessory drive belt idler pulleys.

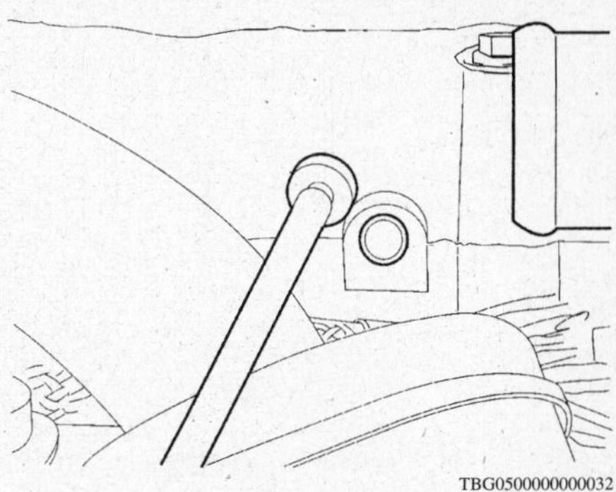

Fig. 2 Exhaust camshaft locking tool installation

15. Remove drive belt tensioner.
16. Remove power steering pump pulley.
17. Remove vibration damper.
18. Rotate crankshaft hub to 90° after TDC.
19. Remove heater hose pipe fasteners.
20. Install intake camshaft locking pin, tool no. 1052, or equivalent, and exhaust camshaft locking pin, tool no. 1053, or equivalent. **It may be required to rotate camshaft gear bolt slightly to gain proper camshaft alignment pin seating against intake manifold. Alignment pins must seat flush against intake manifold.**
21. Remove outer timing belt cover.
22. Remove timing belt.
23. Install tool no. 1085, or equivalent, and remove camshaft gears.
24. Remove timing belt idler pulleys.
25. Remove inner timing belt cover.
26. Disconnect coolant temperature sensor, camshaft position sensor, boost pressure/intake air temperature sensor, fuel injectors, fuel temperature sensor, fuel rail solenoid, and EGR air flow electrical connectors.
27. Disconnect main engine harness connectors at righthand inner fender well and position harness over lefthand side of engine and aside.
28. Disconnect brake booster vacuum pipe from EGR air control valve.
29. Disconnect EGR cooler pipe from EGR air control valve.
30. Separate main engine harness from bracket on EGR air control valve.
31. Remove EGR tube from underside of EGR air control valve.
32. Separate block heater wiring harness from oil dipstick tube.
33. Remove oil dipstick tube from EGR air control valve.
34. Remove fuel injectors.
35. Remove fuel rail.
36. Disconnect oil separator outlet hose at separator.
37. Remove oil separator from intake manifold/cylinder head cover.
38. Disconnect return fuel junction block from intake manifold/cylinder head cover.
39. Remove cylinder head cover/intake manifold retaining bolts.
40. Lift cylinder head cover/intake manifold from cylinder head.

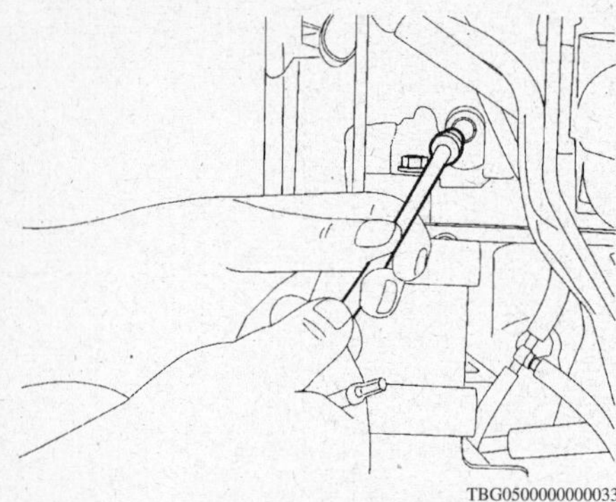

Fig. 3 Intake camshaft locking tool installation

41. Remove rocker arm and lifter assemblies from cylinder head. **When removing rocker arm and lifter assemblies, always keep lifters in an upright position and in order that they were removed from cylinder head.**
42. Remove cylinder head cover/intake manifold gasket from cylinder head.
43. Reverse procedure to install.

VALVE COVER

REPLACE

Refer to "Cylinder Head, Replace" for valve cover replacement procedure.

ROCKER ARM & PUSHRODS

Before removing cylinder head cover/intake manifold the engine must be rotated to 90° after TDC to assure proper alignment of engine timing components. Failure to do so could result in valve and/or piston damage during reassembly.

1. Drain cooling system into a suitable container.
2. Remove cooling fan and fan drive viscous clutch assembly.
3. Remove accessory drive belt.
4. Remove vibration damper.
5. Remove cooling fan support.
6. Remove power steering pump pulley.
7. Rotate crankshaft to 90° ATDC.
8. Remove outer timing belt cover.
9. Remove timing belt.
10. Remove inner timing belt cover.
11. Remove cylinder head cover/intake manifold.
12. Remove rocker arms and lifters. **Lifters must be kept in order of removal and stored in upright position.**
13. Reverse procedure to install.

VALVE ADJUSTMENT

These engine use hydraulic lifters and there is no provision for adjustment.

FRONT COVER

REPLACE

Refer to "Timing Belt, Replace" for front cover removal procedure.

TIMING BELT

REPLACE

Removal

With the timing belt removed, avoid turning the camshaft or crankshaft. If movement is required, exercise extreme caution to avoid valve damage caused by piston contact.

1. Remove engine cover.
2. Remove fan blade/viscous fan drive assembly to water pump mounting nut using spanner wrench tool No. 6958, or equivalent. **Threads on the viscous fan drive assembly mounting nut are righthand thread.**
3. Remove fan shroud to radiator attaching bolts.
4. Remove fan shroud and fan blade/viscous fan drive assembly as a complete unit from vehicle. **Do not place the fan blade/viscous fan drive assembly in a horizontal position. Silicone fluid will leak from the assembly.**
5. Remove accessory drive belts.
6. Remove cooling fan support.
7. Place a paint mark on crankshaft hub and oil pump cover.
8. Remove crankshaft dampner attaching bolts, then the dampner.
9. Rotate engine 90° ATDC, then install flex plate locking tool No. V 1080 through access hole, **Fig. 1.**
10. Remove EGR valve and EGR cooler to exhaust manifold retaining nuts, then position EGR assembly out of way.
11. Remove plug in cylinder head cover/intake manifold, then insert the exhaust camshaft locking tool No. V 1053 into position, **Fig. 2.**
12. Disconnect alternator electrical connectors, then remove the alternator assembly.
13. Remove plug in cylinder head cover/intake manifold, then insert intake camshaft locking tool No. V 1052 into position, **Fig. 3.**
14. Remove timing belt outer cover.
15. Loosen timing belt tensioner, then remove the timing belt.

Installation

1. With camshaft holding tools installed and engine locked at 90° after TDC, ensure camshaft gears are loose.
2. Install timing belt over crankshaft hub and hold in place with timing belt holding tool No. VM 1074, or equivalent, **Fig. 4.**
3. Route timing belt around high pressure injection pump, idler pulley, intake camshaft gear, exhaust camshaft gear, idler pulley and water pump gear, **Fig. 5.**
4. Turn timing belt tensioner in a clockwise direction with tensioner tool No. 9660, or equivalent, until center notch of tensioner aligns with the aluminum cover dowel pin.
5. Install camshaft gear locking tool No. VM 1085, or equivalent, over camshaft gears, **Fig. 6.**

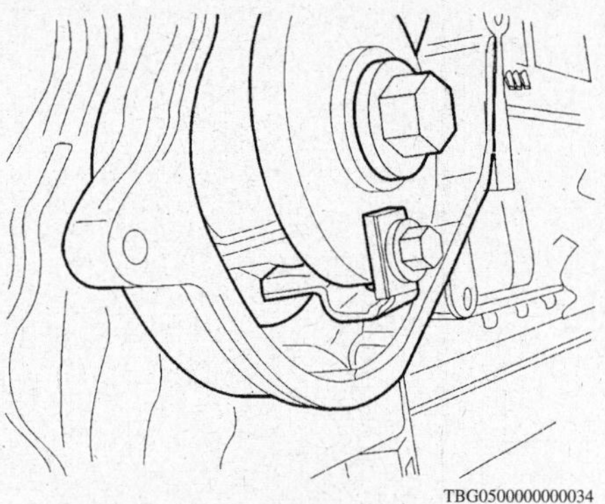

Fig. 4 Timing belt holding tool installation

6. **Torque** camshaft gear retaining bolts to 80 ft. lbs.
7. Remove the camshaft locking tool, the camshaft intake and exhaust locking pins and the timing belt holding tool from the crankshaft hub.
8. Install the timing belt cover and secure with the attaching bolts.
9. Install the crankshaft dampner.
10. Remove flywheel locking tool.
11. Install cooling fan support.
12. Install accessory drive belts.
13. Install fan shroud and fan blade/viscous fan drive assembly.
14. Install engine cover.

CAMSHAFT

REPLACE

1. Remove engine cover and bracket.
2. Drain cooling system into a suitable container.
3. Remove cooling fan and fan drive viscous clutch assembly.
4. Remove accessory drive belt.
5. Remove cooling fan support.
6. Rotate engine to 90° after TDC and install tool no. 1089, or equivalent.
7. Remove vibration damper.
8. Remove alternator as outlined in "Alternator, Replace" in "Electrical" section.
9. Remove timing belt outer cover. **Before removing cylinder head cover/intake manifold or timing belt engine must be rotated to 90° ATDC, or 3 O'clock position and tool no 1089, or equivalent, installed in 90° ATDC alignment hole. Failure to do so could result in valve and/or piston damage during reassembly.**
10. Remove timing belt.
11. Remove timing belt inner cover.
12. Remove cylinder head cover/intake manifold.
13. With cylinder head cover/intake manifold on work bench, remove plugs at rear of cylinder head cover/intake manifold.
14. Remove camshaft oil seals.
15. Remove snap ring and thrust washer from camshaft.
16. Slide camshaft through access hole at rear of cylinder head cover/intake manifold.
17. Reverse procedure to install.

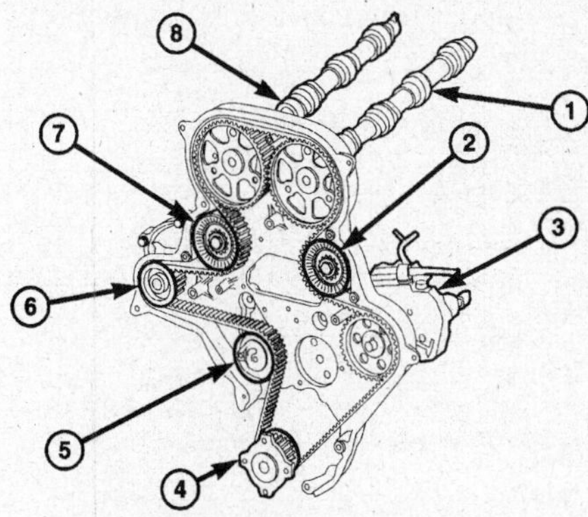

Fig. 5 Timing belt installation

PISTON & ROD ASSEMBLY

Connecting rod bolts must be replaced when disassembled. When assembling connecting rod, be sure that pawl on each connecting rod caps is facing rear (fly wheel) side of the engine.

1. Assemble bearing shells and bearing caps to their respective connecting rods ensuring that serrations on cap and reference marks are aligned.
2. Tighten connecting cap bolts to specification.
3. Without loosening connecting rod bolts, tighten all bolts to specification.
4. Tighten each bolt an additional 40° using a torque angle gauge.
5. Inspect all bolt tightening with a torque wrench set to specification.
6. Inspect and record internal diameter of crank end of connecting rod. **When changing connecting rods, Do Not use a stamp to mark cylinder location. Identify connecting rods and caps location using a paint marker. All four must have same weight and same number. Replacement connecting rods will only be supplied in sets of four. Connecting rods are supplied in sets of four since they all must be of same weight category.**

PISTONS, PINS & RINGS

Removal

1. ID mark on face of top and second piston rings must point toward piston crown.
2. Remove top and second piston rings using a suitable ring expander.
3. Remove upper oil ring side rail, lower oil ring side rail and then oil expander from piston.
4. Carefully clean carbon from piston crowns, skirts and ring grooves ensuring four oil holes in oil control ring grooves are clear.

Installation

1. Install rings on pistons using a suitable ring expander.
2. Top compression ring is tapered and chromium plated. Second ring is of scraper type and must be installed with scraping edge facing bottom of piston. Third is an oil control ring. Ring gaps must be positioned, before inserting piston into liners, as follows in, **Fig. 7.**
3. Top ring gap must be positioned at number 3 position, **Fig. 7.**
4. Second piston ring gap should be positioned at number 1 position, **Fig. 7.**
5. Oil control ring gap should be positioned at number 2 position, **Fig. 7.**
6. When assembling pistons, ensure that components are installed in same position as before disassembly, determined by numbers stamped on crown of individual pistons. Engine cylinders are numbered starting from gear train end of engine. Face arrow on top of piston toward front of engine. Therefore, numbers stamped on connecting rod big end should face toward injection pump side of engine. To insert piston into cylinder use a ring compressor.

MAIN & ROD BEARINGS

Removal

Crankshaft support halves can be identified by aligning witness marks scribed on face, located between halves. These witness marks must face towards front of engine when installing crankshaft and support assembly. Engine must be removed from vehicle and completely disassembled to replace front main bearing.

1. With crankshaft assembly removed from engine, identify crankshaft support witness marks.
2. Remove crankshaft supports from crankshaft and remove bearing halves from supports.
3. Push front main bearing out of front of engine block using tool no. 1073, or equivalent.

Installation

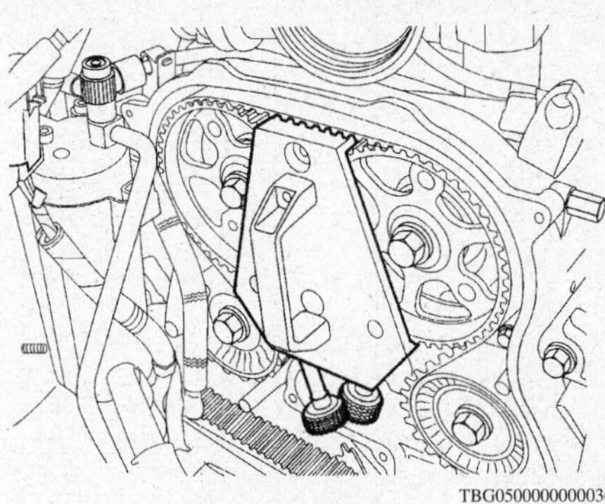

Fig. 6 Camshaft gear locking tool installation

1. Identify crankshaft support witness marks and install bearing halves in crankshaft supports. **Identify correct crankshaft by noting groove on front of crankshaft.**
2. Lubricate crankshaft and main bearings with clean engine oil.
3. Install crankshaft supports on crankshaft. Tighten to specification. **Crankshaft support witness marks must be facing toward front of engine before installing crankshaft. Crankshaft supports have oil passages that must be aligned properly. Crankshaft support bolt heads should be facing balance shaft.**
4. Push front crankshaft main bearing in engine block using tool no. 1073, or equivalent.
5. Ensure oil hole in bearing lines up with oil gally in engine block.
6. Reassemble engine and install in vehicle.

ENGINE OIL COOLER

REPLACE

1. Drain cooling system into suitable container.
2. Remove air cleaner assembly.
3. Remove coolant reservoir and hoses.
4. Remove charge air cooler hose between turbocharger and cooler.
5. Remove lower radiator hose at water pump housing assembly.
6. Remove water pump housing assembly.
7. Remove engine oil cooler.
8. Reverse procedure to install.

CRANKSHAFT SEAL

REPLACE

Front

1. Remove cooling fan and fan drive viscous clutch assembly.
2. Remove accessory drive belt.
3. Remove cooling fan support.
4. Remove vibration damper/crankshaft pulley.
5. Remove outer timing belt cover.

6. Remove timing belt as outlined in "Timing Belt, Replace."
7. Remove timing belt inner cover.
8. Remove crankshaft hub. **Crankshaft hub retaining bolt has lefthand thread.**
9. Remove front engine cover.
10. With cover on work bench, pry out old seal.
11. Reverse procedure to install noting the following: **To prevent potential leaks, do not touch front crankshaft inner seal. Always handle seal from outer diameter.**

Rear

This must be done with either engine or transmission removed from vehicle.

1. Remove flywheel assembly.
2. Paint mark or scribe a witness mark on engine block to be used for alignment purposes during assembly.
3. Pry out old crankshaft oil seal.
4. Reverse procedure to install.

OIL PUMP

REPLACE

Removal

1. Remove cooling fan and fan drive viscous clutch assembly.
2. Remove accessory drive belt.
3. Remove cooling fan support.
4. Remove vibration damper.
5. Remove timing belt outer cover.
6. Remove timing belt as outlined in "Timing Belt, Replace."
7. Remove timing belt inner cover.
8. Remove front engine cover.
9. Remove crankshaft sprocket.
10. Remove oil pump retaining bolts and remove pump from engine block.

Installation

1. Lubricate oil pump rotor with engine oil.
2. Install oil pump in bore in engine block.
3. Install oil pump retaining bolts. Tighten to specification.
4. Install crankshaft sprocket. Tighten to specification.
5. Install front engine cover and seal.
6. Install timing belt inner cover.
7. Install lower timing belt gear and hand tighten fastener.
8. Connect tool no. 6958, or equivalent, to lower timing gear using vibration damper bolts and tighten timing gear fastener to specification.
9. Remove tool no 6958, or equivalent.
10. Install timing belt as outlined in "Timing Belt, Replace."
11. Install timing belt outer cover.
12. Install vibration damper.
13. Install power steering pump.
14. Install cooling fan support.
15. Install accessory drive belt.
16. Install cooling fan and fan drive viscous clutch assembly.
17. Remove crankshaft and camshaft alignment pins.

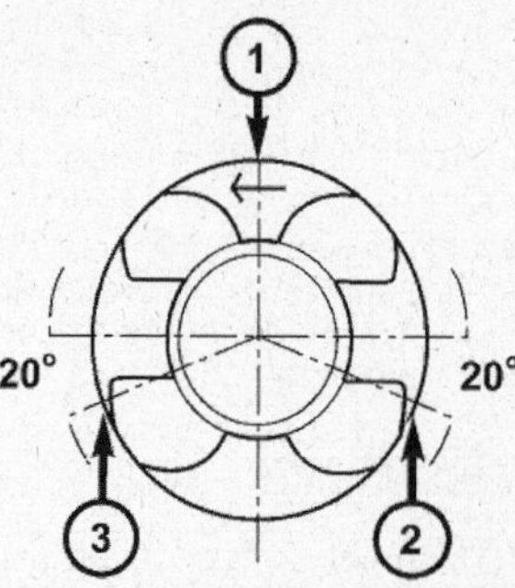

1 - SECOND COMPRESSION RING GAP POSITION
2 - OIL CONTROL RING GAP POSITION
3 - TOP COMPRESSION RING GAP POSITION
LTV0500000000488

Fig. 7 Piston ring gap location

BELT TENSION DATA

Automatic tensioners are calibrated at factory to provide correct amount of tension to belt. Belt wear is measured at tensioner with use of index marks incorporated into tensioner. Tension is correct if belt tensioner is within marks.

SERPENTINE DRIVE BELT

Routing

Refer to **Fig. 8** for drive belt routing.

Belt Replacement

REMOVE

1. Rotate belt tensioner until it contacts its stop.
2. Remove belt, then slowly rotate tensioner into freearm position.

INSTALL

1. Inspect condition of all pulleys.
2. Install new belt. Route belt around all pulleys except idler pulley.
3. Rotate tensioner arm until it contacts its stop position. Route belt around idler and slowly let tensioner rotate into belt.
4. Make sure belt is seated onto all pulleys.

COOLING SYSTEM BLEED

1. Run engine until it reaches normal operating temperature.
2. Turn engine off and allow to cool.
3. Add correct engine coolant mixture to degas bottle until coolant level is between coolant fill level marks.
4. Start engine and allow idle until normal operating temperature is reached. Hot air should discharge from vents with climate control setting to full heat. Coolant temperature gauge should maintain a stabilized reading in middle of normal range and upper radiator hose should feel hot to touch.
5. Repeat procedure until degas bottle level is acceptable.

THERMOSTAT

REPLACE

Thermostat is not serviced separately. Thermostat and housing must be replaced as an assembly.

1. Remove engine cover.
2. Partially drain cooling system.
3. Disconnect upper radiator hose and bypass hoses at thermostat housing.
4. Remove thermostat housing retaining bolts, support bracket and housing from cylinder head, discard gasket.
5. Reverse procedure to install.

WATER PUMP

REPLACE

1. Drain cooling system into a suitable container.
2. Remove timing belt inner and outer covers.
3. Remove water pump retaining bolts and pump.
4. Reverse procedure to install.

TURBOCHARGER

REPLACE

Removal

1. Remove engine cover.
2. Disconnect MAF and inlet air pressure sensors wiring harness connectors, disconnect air outlet duct from turbocharge, and remove air cleaner assembly.
3. Remove charge air cooler inlet hose form turbocharger.
4. Drain cooling system into suitable container.
5. Remove coolant recovery pressure container.
6. Disconnect turbocharger actuator vacuum hose and position aside.
7. Remove turbocharger upper heat shield.
8. Raise and support vehicle.
9. Remove lower splash shield.
10. Disconnect front exhaust pipe from turbocharger.
11. Remove turbocharger support bracket.
12. Disconnect turbocharger oil return line at turbocharger.
13. Lower vehicle.
14. Remove turbocharger oil supply line.
15. Remove turbocharger to exhaust manifold retaining nuts and separate turbocharger from exhaust manifold.

Installation

1. Connect turbocharger to exhaust manifold with new gasket. Tighten to specification. **After tightening exhaust manifold to specification using a diagonal-cross pattern, retrace pattern inspecting correct torque value again.**

2. Install exhaust manifold and turbocharger assembly with new gasket in position on studs in cylinder head. Install retaining nuts and tighten to specification.
3. Install thermostat housing.
4. Install viscous heater.
5. Install accessory drive belt.
6. Raise vehicle on hoist.
7. Connect turbocharger oil return line at turbocharger.
8. Connect exhaust pipe at turbocharger downpipe.
9. Lower vehicle from hoist.
10. Connect oil supply line at turbocharger. Tighten banjo fitting to specification.
11. Install exhaust manifold heat shield.
12. Reposition EGR cooler and or EGR valve assembly on exhaust manifold. Tighten to specification.
13. Connect EGR pipe to EGR valve. Tighten to specification.
14. Connect EGR cooler coolant hoses at cooler.
15. Install coolant recovery pressure container.
16. Refill cooling system.
17. Connect charge air cooler inlet hose at turbocharger.
18. Install air cleaner assembly.
19. Connect air inlet hose to turbocharger.
20. Install engine cover.

RADIATOR

REPLACE

If replacement of constant tension clamp is required, use only an original equipment clamp with matching number or letter.

1. Drain coolant from radiator into suitable container.
2. Remove front grille.
3. Remove cooling fan from engine, if equipped.
4. Remove two radiator mounting bolts.
5. Disconnect connector for electric fan.
6. Disconnect power steering cooler line from cooler.
7. Disconnect radiator upper and lower hoses.
8. Disconnect overflow hose from radiator.

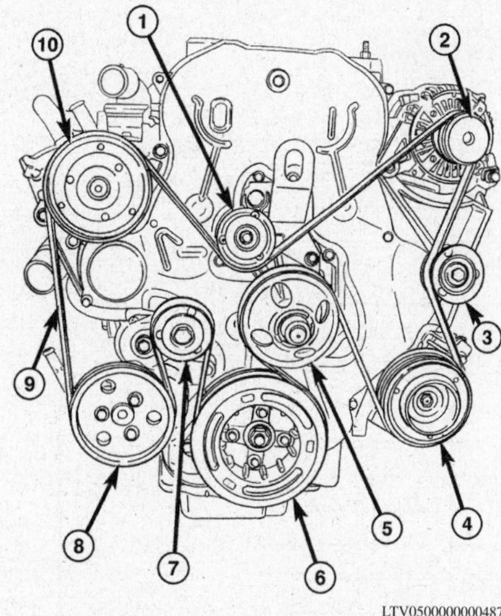

Fig. 8 Drive belt routing

9. Lower part of radiator is equipped with two alignment dowel pins. They are located on bottom of radiator tank and fit into rubber grommets. These rubber grommets are pressed into radiator lower crossmember.
10. Gently lift and remove radiator from vehicle. Be careful not to scrape radiator fins against any other component. Also be careful not to disturb air conditioning condenser (if equipped). **Air conditioning system (if equipped) is under a constant pressure even with engine off. Refer to refrigerant warnings in, heating and air conditioning before handling any air conditioning component. Radiator and radiator cooling fan can be removed as an assembly. It is not required to remove cooling fan before removing or installing radiator.**
11. Reverse procedure to install.

FUEL PUMP

REPLACE

Fuel system may be under a constant pressure (even with engine off). Before servicing fuel pump module, fuel system pressure must be released.

1. Drain and remove fuel tank.
2. Note rotational position of module before attempting removal. An indexing arrow is located on top of module for this purpose.
3. Position lockring remover/installer tool no. 9340, or equivalent, into notches on outside edge of lockring.
4. Install ½ inch drive breaker bar to lockring remover installer tool no. 9340, or equivalent.
5. Rotate breaker bar counterclockwise to remove lockring.
6. Remove lockring. Module will spring up slightly when lockring is removed.
7. Remove module from fuel tank. Be careful not to bend float arm while removing.
8. Reverse procedure to install.

FUEL FILTER

REPLACE

Capture all fuel in approved and appropriately marked containers. Wear safety goggles and adequate protective clothing when servicing fuel system.

1. Disconnect water in fuel (WIF) sensor wiring harness connector.
2. Drain fuel filter/water separator.
3. Unscrew filter assembly from head assembly by rotating housing counterclockwise.
4. Separate WIF sensor and seal from housing by rotating counterclockwise.
5. Reverse procedure to install.

GLOW PLUG SYSTEM

1. Remove alternator.
2. Disconnect glow plug electrical connectors.
3. Remove glow plugs from cylinder head. **Intake manifold inlet tube must be removed to remove cylinder No. 3 glow plug.**
4. Reverse procedure to install.

TIGHTENING SPECIFICATIONS

Year	Component	Torque Ft. Lbs.
2005–06	Accessory Drive Bracket Bolts	33
	Accessory Drive Belt Idler Pulley Bolts	39
	Balance Shaft Bolts	24
	Boost Pressure/Intake Air Temp. Sensor Bolts	48①
	Camshaft Access Plugs	59
	Camshaft Position Sensor Bolt	8
	Camshaft Sprocket Bolts	80
	Camshaft Timing Access Bolt	18
	Camshaft Timing Access Plugs	18
	Coolant Pipe To EGR Valve Bolts	18
	Crankshaft Gear Bolts	
	Crankshaft Hub Bolts	
	Crankshaft Position Sensor Bolts	
	Crankshaft Pulley Bolts	
	Crankshaft Support Bolts	
	Cylinder Head/Intake Manifold Bolts	
	EGR Air Control Valve To Cylinder Head Cover	96①
	EGR Valve Bolts	18
	Engine Block Plug In Front Of Oil Cooler	43
	Engine Lift Hook Bolts	33
	Engine Mount Bracket To Cylinder Head Bolts	33
	Exhaust Manifold Heatshield Bolts	21
	Exhaust Manifold Heat Shield	18
	Exhaust Manifold Nuts	26.5
	Front Engine Cover Bolts	53①
	Fuel Injection Pump Gear Nut	65
	Fuel Injection Pump Retaining Nuts	18
	Fuel Line Fittings At Pump	21
	Fuel Pump Nuts	21
	Fuel Rail Retaining Bolts	18
	Glow Plug	110①
	Intake Inlet Tube Bolts	8

TIGHTENING SPECIFICATIONS—Continued

Year	Component	Torque Ft. Lbs.
2005–06	Oil Cooler Mounting Stud	37
	Oil Cooler To Engine Block Bolt	35
	Oil Dipstick To Cylinder Head Cover	96①
	Oil Dipstick Tube To Pan	96①
	Oil Jet Bolts	8
	Oil Pan Bolts	8
	Oil Pump Bolts	8
	Oil Pump Pick-Up Tube	24
	Oil Separator Bolts	8
	Rear Main Bearing Support Bolts	21
	Reluctor Wheel Bolts	11
	Structural Support To Engine And Transmission Bolts	33
	Thermostat Housing Bolts	18
	Timing Belt Idler Pulley Bolt	35
	Timing Belt Tensioner Bolt	22
	Transmission To Engine Bolts	62
	Turbocharger Downpipe Nuts	24
	Turbocharger Oil Supply Line Fitting	18
	Turbocharger Oil Return Line Bolts	96①
	Turbocharger Support Bracket Bolts	18
	Turbocharger To Exhaust Manifold Nuts	24
	Vacuum Line Fitting Bolt	42
	Vacuum Pump Bolts	8
	Vacuum Pump Pipe To Block	42
	Vibration Damper To Crankshaft Hub Bolts	21
	Water Pump Housing Nuts	18
	8mm Fuel Rail Retaining Bolts	8
	10mm Inner Timing Belt Cover Bolts	33
	3mm Outer Timing Belt Cover Bolts	54①
	8mm Outer Timing Belt Cover Bolts	8

① — Inch lbs.

Rear Axle & Suspension

INDEX

REAR AXLE

REPLACE

1. Raise and support vehicle.
2. Secure axle to suitable jack positioned under vehicle.
3. Remove wheels and tires.
4. Mark propeller shaft and pinion yoke for reference during installation.
5. Remove propeller shaft and suspend under vehicle.
6. Remove disc brake and parking brake components.
7. Disconnect brake hose at body junction block.
8. Remove vent hose from axle shaft tube.
9. Remove stabilizer bar, **Fig. 1.**
10. Remove upper control arm ball joint pinch bolt from bracket, **Fig. 2.**
11. Remove shock absorbers from axle brackets.
12. Loosen all lower control arm mounting bolts.
13. Lower axle enough to remove coil springs and spring insulators.
14. Remove lower control arm bolts from axle brackets.
15. Lower and remove axle from vehicle.
16. Reverse procedure to install. **Weight of vehicle must be supported by springs before lower control arms are tightened to maintain vehicle ride height.**

REAR AXLE SHAFT

REPLACE

198RBI Axle

1. Place transmission in neutral, then raise and support vehicle.
2. Remove wheels and tires, then the brake drum.
3. Remove axle retainer plate nuts from rear of axle flange.
4. Remove axle shaft from axle using slide hammer tool No. 7420 and puller tool No. 6790, or equivalents.
5. Reverse procedure to install, noting the following:
   a. It is normal for axle bearing race to be loose in axle tube.
   b. Install axle into axle tube with flat area of retainer plate upward.

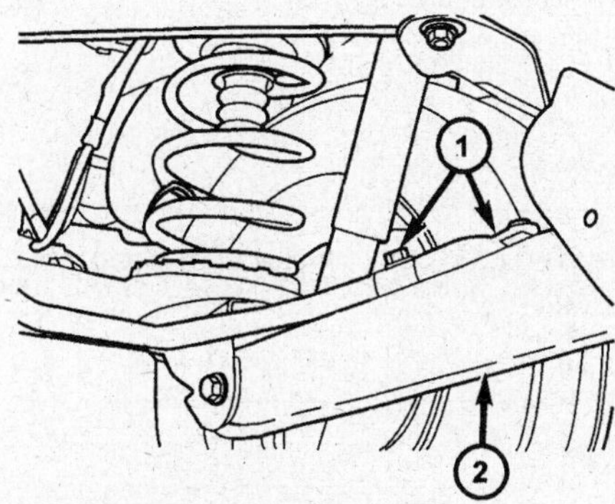

1 - STABILIZER BAR MOUNTING BOLTS
2 - LOWER SUSPENSION ARM

LTV1900000000084

Fig. 1 Stabilizer bar

8 1/4 Inch Axle

1. Place transmission in neutral, then raise and support vehicle.
2. Remove tires and wheels.
3. Remove brake caliper, caliper adapter and rotor.
4. Remove axle housing cover and drain lubricant.
5. Rotate differential case to access pinion shaft lock screw.
6. Remove lock screw and pinion shaft from differential case, **Fig. 3.**
7. Push axle shaft inward, then remove axle shaft C-lock, **Fig. 4.**
8. Remove axle shaft ensuring not to damage shaft bearing and seal.
9. Reverse procedure to install, noting the following:
   a. Lubricate bearing bore and seal lip with gear lubricant.
   b. Insert C-lock in end of axle shaft, then push axle shaft outward to seat C-lock in side gear.
   c. Apply Loctite to threads of pinion shaft lock screw.
   d. Tighten differential cover to specifications in a criss-cross pattern.

SHOCK ABSORBER

REPLACE

1. Raise and support vehicle, then place a suitable jack under rear axle.
2. Remove upper and lower nuts, then the shock absorber.
3. Reverse procedure to install.

COIL SPRING

REPLACE

1. Raise and support vehicle, then place a suitable jack under rear axle.
2. Remove shock absorber lower bolt from axle bracket.
3. Lower jack and tilt axle to remove coil spring.
4. Remove and inspect upper and lower spring insulators.
5. Reverse procedure to install.

CONTROL ARM

REPLACE

Lower

1. Raise and support vehicle, then place a suitable jack under rear axle.
2. Remove stabilizer bar retaining bolts from suspension arm.
3. Remove lower suspension arm nut and bolt from axle bracket.
4. Remove nut and bolt from frame rail, then the lower suspension arm.
5. Reverse procedure to install. End of suspension arm with voided round bushing attaches to axle bracket.

Upper

1. Raise and support vehicle, then place a suitable jack under rear axle.
2. Remove ball joint pinch bolt from top of differential housing bracket, **Fig. 2.**
3. Remove bolts, then lower heat shield down enough to gain proper clearance to remove righthand side bolt from body.
4. Remove bolts, then the upper suspension arm.
5. Reverse procedure to install.

STABILIZER BAR

REPLACE

1. Raise and support vehicle.
2. Remove stabilizer bar bolts from lower suspension arm.
3. Remove stabilizer bar.
4. Reverse procedure to install.

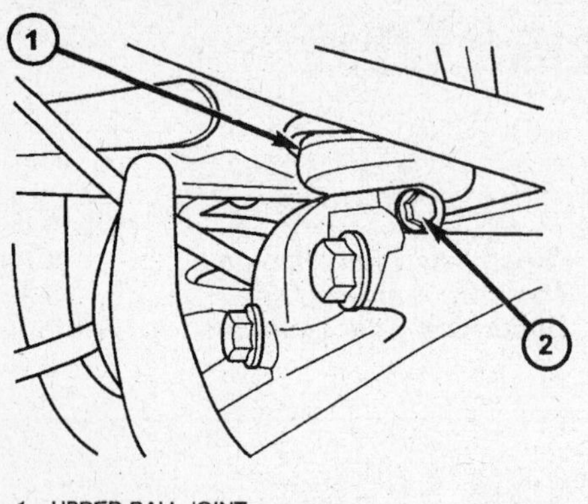

Fig. 2 Ball joint pinch bolt

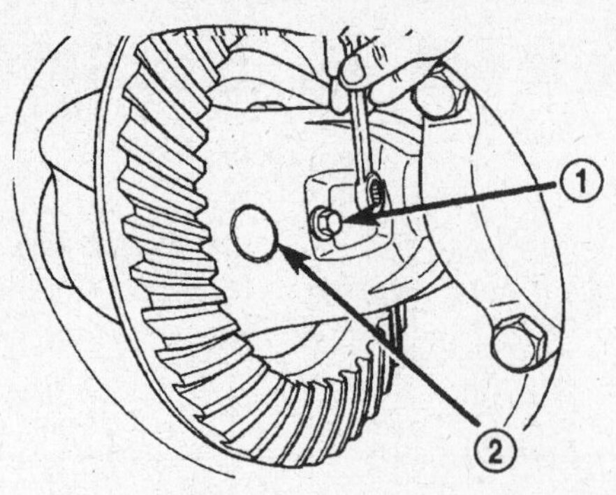

Fig. 3 Pinion shaft lock screw

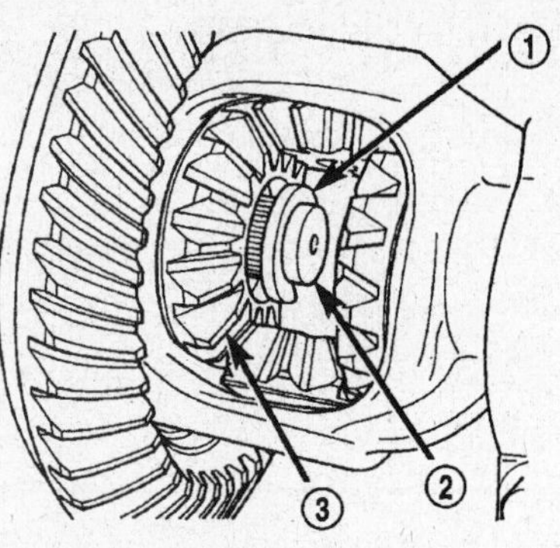

Fig. 4 Axle shaft C-lock

TIGHTENING SPECIFICATIONS

Year	Component	Torque Ft. Lbs.
2002–06	Differential Cover	30
	Pinion Shaft Lock Screw	96①
	Rear Upper Ball Joint Bracket Bolt	100
	Shock Absorber Lower Nut	85
	Shock Absorber Upper Nut	80
	Stabilizer Bar Bolts	73
	Suspension Arm Lower Axle Bracket Nut	120
	Suspension Arm Lower Frame Bracket Nut	120
	Suspension Arm Upper Ball Joint Nut	70
	Suspension Arm Upper Frame Bolt	74

① — Inch lbs.

Front Suspension & Steering

NOTE: **On Air Bag Equipped Models, Refer To "Air Bag System Precautions" Located In The Front Of This Manual For System Disarming & Arming Procedures.**

NOTE: **Refer To The Front Wheel Drive Section For 4WD Front Axle Service Procedures Not Covered In This Section.**

INDEX

PRECAUTIONS

Air Bag Systems

Refer to "Air Bag System Precautions" in the front of this manual for system disarming and arming procedures.

DESCRIPTION

The front suspension is designed to allow each wheel to adapt to different road surfaces independently. The wheels are mounted to hub bearings on the steering knuckle spindles. The steering knuckles pivot on ball joints integral to the outboard portion of the upper and lower control arms. The ball joints are lubricated for life.

HUB & BEARING

REPLACE

1. Raise and support vehicle, then remove tires and wheels.
2. Remove brake caliper, then the rotor.
3. Remove wheel speed sensor, then the bracket securing wire harness.
4. **On models equipped with 4WD,** remove axle shaft nut.
5. **On all models,** remove three hub and bearing mounting nuts.
6. Remove hub and bearing.
7. Reverse procedure to install.

BALL JOINT INSPECTION

1. Raise and support front of vehicle using blocks of wood placed under lower control arms. Lower control arms should support weight of vehicle.
2. Remove tires and wheels.
3. Attach a dial indicator to base of lower control arm and align contact point with the direction of stud axis, touch machined flat on knuckle and zero dial indicator.
4. From front of vehicle, using a suitable pry bar push knuckle up until arm of dial indicator no longer moves.
5. End play should not be more than .06 inch.

BALL JOINT

REPLACE

1. Remove tires and wheels.
2. Remove brake caliper, then the rotor.
3. Remove tie rod end jam nut.
4. Separate tie rod end from knuckle using puller tool No. C3894A, or equivalent.
5. Remove knuckle as outlined in "Steering Knuckle, Replace."
6. **On models equipped with 4WD,** move halfshaft aside and support out of the way.
7. **On all models,** secure steering knuckle in a suitable vise.
8. Press ball joint from steering knuckle using press tool No. C-4212-F, receiver tool No. 8859-2 and driver tool No. 8859-1, or equivalents, **Fig. 1.**

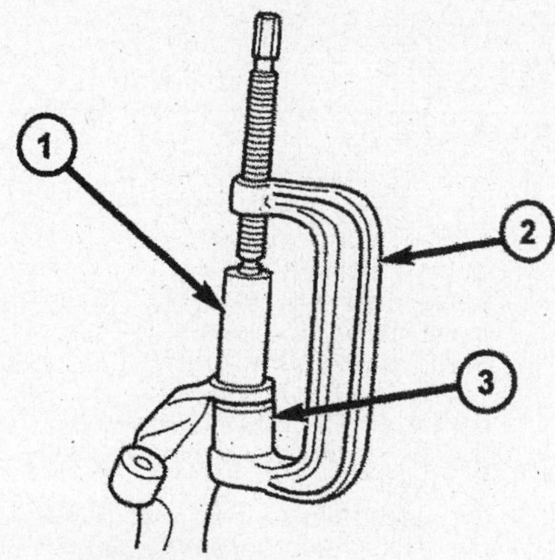

Fig. 1 Lower ball joint removal

9. Reverse procedure to install noting the following:
   a. Install ball joint into steering knuckle using press tool No. C-4212-F, driver tool No. 8859-2 and receiver tool No. 6761, or equivalents, **Fig. 2.**
   b. Inspect ride height and alignment.

COIL SPRING

REPLACE

1. Raise and support vehicle, then remove tires and wheels.
2. Remove shock absorber as outlined in "Shock Absorber, Replace."
3. Secure shock assembly into a Pentastar Service Equipment Spring compressor tool No. W-7200, or equivalent, then compress spring.
4. Remove shock mount nut, then the shock from spring compressor.
5. Reverse procedure to install.

SHOCK ABSORBER

REPLACE

Lefthand

1. Remove battery.
2. Unclip power center and position aside.
3. Remove battery tray, then disconnect battery temperature sensor.
4. Remove four upper shock mounting bolts.
5. Raise and support vehicle, then remove lefthand tire and wheel.
6. Remove lower bolt at lower control arm securing clevis bracket.
7. Remove stabilizer link, then the lower ball joint nut.
8. Separate lower ball joint from lower control arm using puller tool No. C-4150A, or equivalent.
9. Rotate lower control arm downward to allow access.
10. Remove clevis bracket at shock.
11. Remove shock assembly from vehicle.
12. Reverse procedure to install.

Righthand

1. Remove air box assembly.
2. Remove two cruise control servo mounting nuts.
3. Raise and support vehicle, then remove righthand tire and wheel.
4. Remove lower bolt at lower control arm securing clevis bracket.
5. Remove stabilizer link, then the lower ball joint nut.
6. Separate lower ball joint from lower control arm using puller tool No. C-4150A, or equivalent.
7. Rotate lower control arm downward to allow access.
8. Remove clevis bracket at shock.
9. Remove shock assembly from vehicle.
10. Reverse procedure to install.

CONTROL ARM

REPLACE

Lower

1. Raise and support vehicle, then remove tires and wheels.
2. Remove lower clevis bracket bolt at lower control arm.
3. Remove stabilizer link bolt at lower control arm.
4. Remove lower ball joint nut.
5. Separate lower ball joint from lower control arm using puller tool No. C-4150A, or equivalent.
6. Remove front and rear cam/pivot bolts, **Fig. 3,** marking their location for reference during installation.
7. Remove lower control arm from vehicle.
8. Reverse procedure to install.

Upper

1. Raise and support vehicle, then remove tires and wheels.
2. Remove upper ball joint nut.
3. Separate upper ball joint from steering knuckle using puller tool No. C-4150A, or equivalent.
4. Lower vehicle.
5. If removing righthand upper control arm, proceed as follows:
   a. Remove air box assembly.
   b. Remove cruise control servo mounting nuts.
6. If removing lefthand upper control arm, proceed as follows:
   a. Remove battery.
   b. Unclip power center and position aside.
   c. Remove battery tray, then disconnect battery temperature sensor from battery tray.
7. Remove upper control arm front and rear bolts.
8. Remove upper control arm from vehicle.
9. Reverse procedure to install.

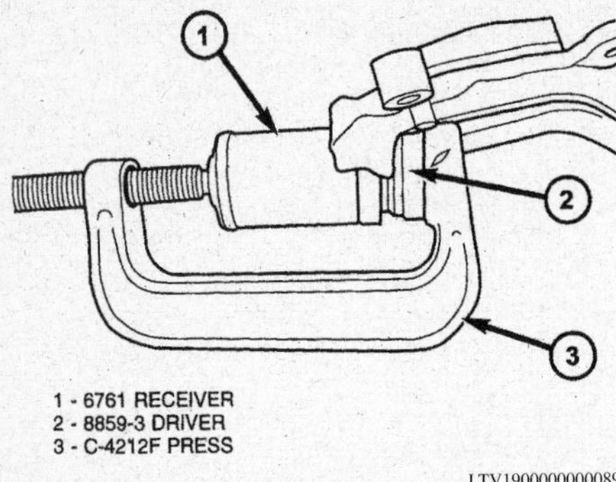

Fig. 2 Lower ball joint installation

STEERING KNUCKLE

REPLACE

1. Raise and support vehicle, then remove tires and wheels.
2. Remove brake caliper, then the brake rotor.
3. Remove wheel speed sensor.
4. **On models equipped with 4WD,** remove axle shaft nut.
5. **On all models,** remove bolts, then the hub and bearing.
6. Separate tie rod end from knuckle using puller tool No. C3894A, or equivalent.
7. Remove lower ball joint nut.
8. Separate upper ball joint from knuckle using puller tool No. C-4150A, or equivalent.
9. Remove knuckle from vehicle.
10. Reverse procedure to install.

STABILIZER BAR

REPLACE

1. Raise and support vehicle, then remove tires and wheels.
2. Remove upper stabilizer link bolts at stabilizer bar.
3. Remove stabilizer bar bushing clamps from frame.
4. Remove stabilizer bar from vehicle.
5. Reverse procedure to install.

POWER STEERING GEAR

REPLACE

1. Siphon power steering fluid from power steering reservoir.
2. Lock steering wheel to prevent spinning of clockspring.
3. Raise and support vehicle, then remove tires and wheels.
4. Remove skid plate from under front of vehicle.
5. **On models equipped with 4WD,** remove lower control arms as outlined in "Control Arm, Replace."
6. **On models equipped with 4WD,** remove front axle assembly as outlined in "Front Wheel Drive" section.
7. **On all models,** remove tie rod end nuts.
8. Separate tie rod ends from knuckles using puller tool No. C-3894-A, or equivalent.
9. Remove intermediate shaft lower coupler bolt and slide coupler off gear.
10. Remove power steering pressure hose bracket.
11. Remove power steering lines from steering gear.
12. Remove mounting bolts from gear to front cradle.
13. Remove steering gear from vehicle.
14. Reverse procedure to install.

POWER STEERING PUMP

REPLACE

2.4L Engine

On models equipped with 2.4L engine, do not reuse power steering pulley if removed. A new pulley must be installed.

1. Siphon out as much power steering fluid as possible.
2. Remove serpentine drive belt.
3. Remove power steering high pressure hose at pump using care not to remove flow control valve.
4. Remove return hose at pump.
5. Remove two nuts securing pump to bracket through holes in pulley.

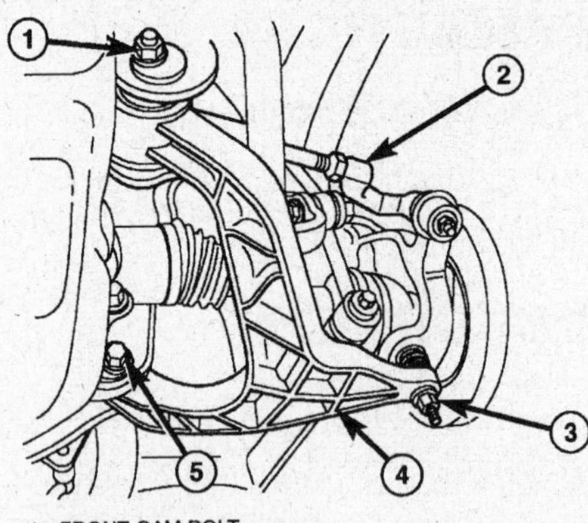

Fig. 3 Lower control arm

6. Remove pump from vehicle.
7. Reverse procedure to install.

2.8L Turbo Diesel

1. Siphon out as much power steering fluid as possible.
2. Remove engine cooling fan.
3. Remove fan shroud.
4. Remove serpentine drive belt.
5. remove three bolts securing pulley to pump.
6. Remove power steering hoses.
7. Remove three bolts securing pump to bracket.
8. Remove pump from vehicle.
9. Reverse procedure to install.

3.7L Engine

1. Siphon out as much power steering fluid as possible.
2. Remove radiator cross member.
3. Remove engine cooling fan, then the fan shroud.
4. Remove serpentine drive belt.
5. Remove power steering high pressure hose at pump.
6. Remove return hose at pump.
7. Remove three bolts securing pump to bracket through holes in pulley.
8. Remove pump from vehicle.
9. Reverse procedure to install.

TIGHTENING SPECIFICATIONS

Year	Component	Torque Ft. Lbs.
2002–06	Ball Joint	60
	Hub & Bearing	96
	Hub & Bearing Halfshaft	100
	Lower Clevis Bracket	110
	Lower Stabilizer Bar Link Nut	85
	Lower Suspension Arm	125
	Power Steering Gear	120
	Power Steering Gear Intermediate Shaft	36
	Power Steering Pump To Bracket	21
	Power Steering Pump To Engine	35
	Power Steering Pump Pressure Line	21
	Shock Absorber Top Mounting Nuts	80
	Shock To Spring & Insulator Nut	30
	Stabilizer Bar Clamp	110
	Upper Clevis Bracket	100
	Upper Stabilizer Bar Link Nut	100
	Upper Suspension Arm	90

Front Wheel Drive

INDEX

AXLE HOUSING ASSEMBLY

REPLACE

1. Raise and support vehicle, then remove tires and wheels.
2. Remove skid plate.
3. Remove differential drain plug and drain fluid into suitable container.
4. Remove half shaft hub nuts.
5. Remove stabilizer bar links from lower control arms.
6. Remove tie rod end nuts.
7. Separate tie rod ends from knuckles using puller tool No. C-3894-A, or equivalent.
8. Remove lower ball joint nuts.
9. Separate lower ball joint from lower control arm using puller tool No. C-4150A, or equivalent.
10. Remove lower shock clevis bolts.
11. Pull out on steering knuckles, then push half shaft out of knuckles.
12. With a pry bar remove half shafts from axle. **Righthand half shaft has a splined axle that may come out with shaft.**
13. Remove differential vent hose from cover.
14. Mark location of propeller shaft and pinion flange for reference during installation, then remove propeller shaft.
15. Support axle using a suitable jack.
16. Remove bolts from lefthand front axle bracket, **Fig. 1.**

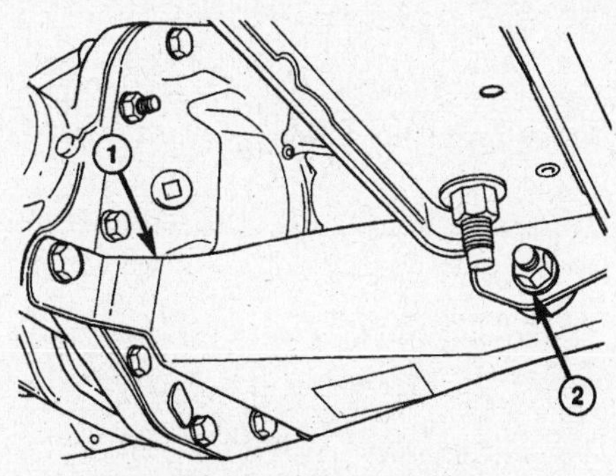

Fig. 1 Lefthand front axle bracket

17. Remove oil filter drip tray.
18. Mark and remove righthand control arm cam bolt.
19. Remove bolts from righthand axle bracket frame mounts, **Fig. 2.**
20. Remove bolt from lefthand rear axle bracket frame mount, **Fig. 3.**
21. Lower axle from vehicle.
22. Reverse procedure to install.

AXLE SHAFT

REPLACE

1. Place transmission in neutral.
2. Raise and support vehicle, then remove righthand tire and wheel.
3. Remove righthand half shaft.
4. Remove snap-ring from axle shaft.
5. Install remover tool No. 8420A, or equivalent, onto axle shaft, **Fig. 4.**
6. Thread slide hammer into remover, then remove axle shaft.
7. Reverse procedure to install, noting the following:
   a. Lubricate bearing bore and seal lip with gear lubricant before installing axle shaft.
   b. Push on axle shaft until axle shaft snap-ring passes through side gear.

HUB & BEARING SERVICE

1. Raise and support vehicle, then remove tires and wheels.
2. Remove brake caliper, then the rotor.
3. Remove wheel speed sensor, then the bracket securing wire harness.
4. Remove axle shaft nut.
5. Remove three hub and bearing mounting nuts.
6. Remove hub and bearing.
7. Reverse procedure to install.

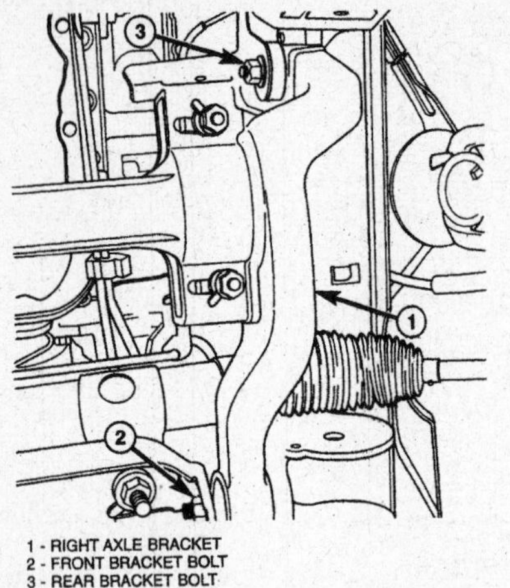

Fig. 2 Righthand axle bracket

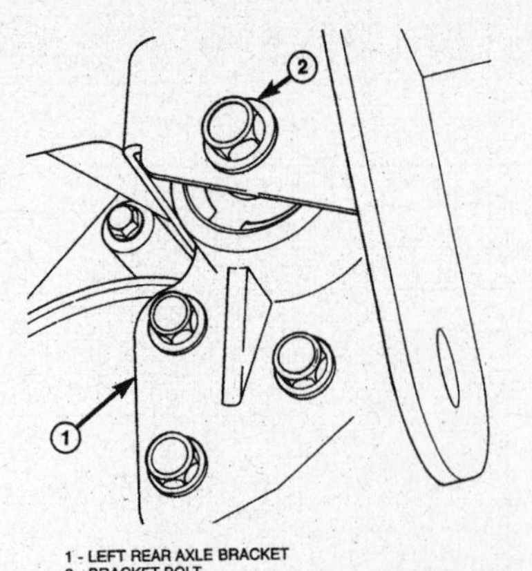

Fig. 3 Lefthand rear axle bracket

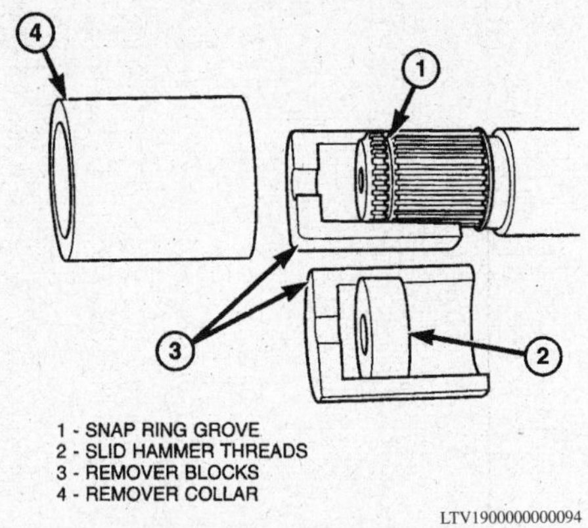

Fig. 4 Axle shaft puller

TIGHTENING SPECIFICATIONS

Year	Component	Torque Ft. Lbs.
2002–06	Axles Brackets To Frame	65
	Differential Cover	14–19
	Front Axle Bracket	45
	Lefthand Axle Bracket	45
	Righthand Axle Bracket	65

Wheel Alignment

INDEX

PRELIMINARY INSPECTION

1. Inflate tires to proper specifications.
2. Ensure tires are same size and rating.
3. Inspect for excessive wheel bearing play.
4. Inspect for worn or damaged ball joints.
5. Inspect suspension components for wear or damage.
6. Inspect vehicle ride height.

FRONT WHEEL ALIGNMENT

Camber

Move both cam bolts together in or out, **Fig. 1.** This will change the camber angle significantly and the caster angle slightly.

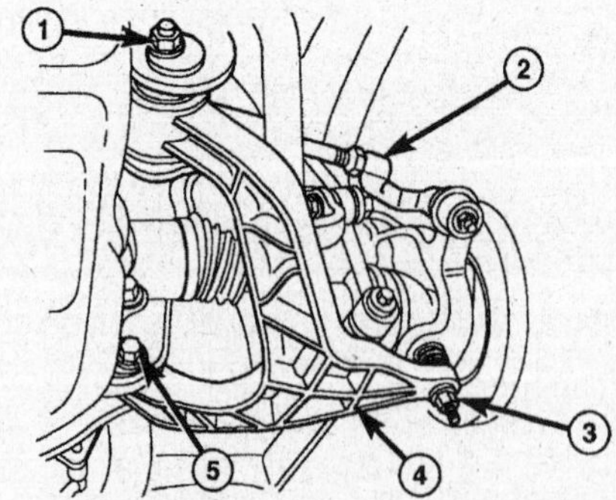

Fig. 1 Lower control arm

Caster

Moving the rear position of the cam bolt in or out will change the caster angle significantly and camber angle only slightly. To maintain the camber angle while adjusting caster, move the rear of the cam bolt in or out, then move the front of the cam bolt slightly in the opposite direction. To increase positive caster angle, move the rear position of the cam bolt outward from engine. Move the front cam bolt inward toward engine slightly until original camber angle is obtained.

Toe

1. Start engine and turn wheel both directions before straightening wheels, then secure steering wheel with wheels in straight ahead position.
2. Loosen tie rod end jam nuts.
3. Adjust wheel toe position by turning tie rod as required. **Each front wheel should be adjusted for one-half of total toe position specification. This will ensure steering wheel will be centered when the wheels are positioned straight ahead.**
4. **Torque** tie rod jam nut to 55 ft. lbs.

AIR CONDITIONING

NOTE: On Air Bag Equipped Models, Refer To "Air Bag System Precautions" Located In The Front Of This Manual For System Disarming & Arming Procedures.

NOTE: Refer To "Computer Relearn Procedures" Located In The Front Of This Manual When Battery Power To The Computer Has Been Interrupted.

TABLE OF CONTENTS

System Testing

INDEX

PRECAUTIONS

Air Bag Systems

Refer to "Air Bag System Precautions" in the front of this manual for system disarming and arming procedures.

Battery Ground Cable

Prior to service, disconnect battery ground cable and isolate as required.

R-134a System

R-134a is a non-toxic, non-flammable liquefied gas that is clear and odorless.

R-134a is not compatible with R-12. Even small amounts of R-12 in an R-134a system can cause lubricant contamination, improper A/C performance and compressor failure. Never add R-12 to an R-134a system.

New service ports have been added to the compressor to prevent charging the system with R-12. **R-134a systems require a special compressor lubricant.** Refer to "Specifications" for correct lubricant.

Avoid breathing A/C R-134a, lubricant vapor or mist. Exposure may irritate eyes, nose and throat. Use only approved service equipment to discharge R-134a systems.

The system must be completely discharged before opening any fitting or connection of the refrigeration system. Open fittings with caution even after the system has been discharged. If any pressure is noticed as fitting is loosened, allow trapped pressure to bleed off very slowly.

Kinks in the refrigerant tubing or sharp bends will greatly reduce the capacity of the entire system. Use a suitable tube bender when bending the refrigerant lines to avoid kinking. **Use the correct line for the installation you are servicing. Keep the radius of flexible hose bends to ten times the diameter of the hose. Sharper bends will reduce the flow of refrigerant. The flexible hose lines should be routed so they are at least three inches from the exhaust manifold.**

O-rings used on tube fittings and unified plumbing plates need to be coated with refrigerant oil prior to installation. Unified plumbing connections with aluminum N-gaskets do not require lubrication before installation.

DESCRIPTION

High Pressure Relief Valve

A high pressure relief valve is located on the compressor cylinder head, which is at the rear of the compressor. This mechanical valve is designed to vent refrigerant from system to protect against damage to the compressor and other system components, caused by condenser air flow restriction or an overcharge of refrigerant.

The high pressure relief valve vents the system when a discharge pressure of 500–

Ambient Temperature	21°C (34-46°F)	26.5°C (80°F)	32°C (90°F)	37.5°C (100°F)	43°C (110°F)
Air Temperature at Left Center Panel Outlet	1-8°C (34-46°F)	3-9°C (37-49°F)	4-10°C (39-50°F)	6-11°C (43-52°F)	7-18°C (45-65°F)
Compressor Discharge Pressure After the Filter Drier	1034-1724 kPa (150-250 PSI)	1517-2275 kPa (220-330 PSI)	1999-2620 kPa (290-380 PSI)	2068-2965 kPa (300-430 PSI)	2275-3421 kPa (300-500 PSI)
Evaporator Suction Pressure	103-207 kPa (15-30 PSI)	117-221 kPa (17-32 PSI)	138-241 kPa (20-35 PSI)	172-269 kPa (25-39 PSI)	207-345 kPa (30-50 PSI)

CR7029600274000X

Fig. 1 Performance temperature chart. Caravan, Town & Country & Voyager

Performance Temperature and Pressure					
Ambient Air Temperature	21°C (70°F)	27°C (80°F)	32°C (90°F)	38°C (100°F)	43°C (110°F)
Maximum Allowable Air Temperature at Center Panel Outlet	7°C (45°F)	7°C (45°F)	13°C (55°F)	13°C (55°F)	18°C (64°F)
Compressor Inlet Pressure at Service Port (Low Side)	138 to 207 kPa (20 to 30 psi)	172 to 241 kPa (25 to 35 psi)	207 to 276 kPa (30 to 40 psi)	241 to 310 kPa (35 to 45 psi)	276 to 345 kPa (40 to 50 psi)
Condensor Out Pressure at Service Port (High Side)	1034 to 1724 kPa (150 to 250 psi)	1379 to 2068 kPa (200 to 300 psi)	1724 to 2413 kPa (250 to 350 psi)	1999 to 2689 kPa (290 to 390 psi)	2413 to 2965 kPa (350 to 430 psi)

CR7020100000635X

Fig. 2 Performance temperature chart. 2002–04 Dakota

600 psi or above is reached. The valve closes when a minimum discharge pressure of 400 psi is reached. The valve is factory calibrated and cannot be adjusted or repaired.

Compressor Clutch

The compressor clutch assembly consists of the stationary electromagnetic coil, hub bearing and pulley assembly and clutch plate. These components provide a means to engage and disengage the compressor from engine serpentine drive belt.

When the clutch coil is energized, it magnetically draws the clutch into contact with the pulley and drives the compressor shaft. When coil is not energized, pulley free wheels on the clutch hub bearing, which is part of the pulley. The clutch and coil are the only serviced components on the compressor.

High Pressure Cutoff Switch

The high pressure cutoff switch is located on the discharge line near the compressor. The switch is screwed onto a fitting that contains a schraeder type valve, which allows switch to be serviced without discharging refrigerant.

The switch contacts open and close causing the PCM to turn the compressor clutch on and off. This prevents compressor operation when discharge line pressure approaches high levels. The high pressure cutoff switch contacts are open when discharge line pressure rises above 450–490 psi. The switch contacts close when the discharge line pressure drops to 270–330 psi. The switch is factory calibrated and cannot be serviced or adjusted.

Low Pressure Cycling Clutch Switch

The low pressure cycling clutch switch is located on the side of the accumulator. The switch is screwed onto a fitting that contains a schraeder type valve, which allows the switch to be serviced without discharging refrigerant.

The switch contacts open and close causing the PCM to turn the compressor clutch on and off. This regulates refrigerant system pressure and controls evaporator temperature. Controlling evaporator temperature prevents condensate water on fins of evaporator from freezing and obstructing air conditioning system air flow.

The low pressure cycling clutch switch contacts are open when suction pressure is about 20.5 psi or lower. The switch contacts will close when suction pressure rises to 34–38 psi or above. Lower ambient temperature, below 30°F, will also cause the switch contacts to open. The switch is factory calibrated and cannot be serviced or adjusted.

PERFORMANCE TEST

Except Jeep

Air temperature in shop should be at least 70°F when performing this test.

1. Connect manifold gauge set and tachometer.
2. Set A/C controls to Max A/C, temperature lever to cool, and blower on High.
3. Start engine and adjust idle speed to 1000 RPM with compressor clutch engaged.
4. Engine should be warmed up with vehicle doors and windows closed.
5. Place thermometer in lefthand center A/C air outlet. Run engine for five minutes to allow temperatures to stabilize. Compressor clutch may cycle.
6. After five minutes, note discharge air temperature. If compressor clutch is cycling, read thermometer before clutch disengages, then compare discharge temperature to performance temperature chart, **Figs. 1 through 13.**

Jeep

1. Connect a tachometer and manifold gauge set.
2. Set heater A/C mode control switch to Recirculation mode, temperature control knob to Full Cool position and blower motor switch in highest speed position.
3. Start engine and hold idle at 1000 RPM with compressor clutch engaged.
4. Engine should be at normal operating temperature.
5. **On Grand Cherokee and Wrangler models,** doors and windows should be open.
6. **On Commander and Liberty models,** doors and windows should be closed.
7. Insert a thermometer in driver side center A/C outlet, operate engine for five minutes.
8. Compressor clutch may cycle depending on ambient air temperature and humidity. If clutch cycles, unplug low pressure cycling clutch switch and place a jumper wire across terminals of connector.
9. With compressor clutch engaged, record discharge air temperature and compressor discharge pressure.
10. Compare discharge air temperature to performance temperature and pressure charts, **Figs. 14 through 18.**

Charge Determination Test

CARAVAN, TOWN & COUNTRY & VOYAGER

This test is used to determine the charge level of R-134a in the system.

1. Attach a suitable manifold gauge set to system.
2. Attach clamp-on thermocouple tool No. 66–324–0014, or equivalent, to liquid line as close to pressure transducer as possible.
3. Start engine and idle at 700 RPM.
4. Set A/C controls to Outside Air, Panel Mode, Full Cool and blower on High.
5. Ensure vehicle windows are open with A/C button On and Recirculation button Off.
6. Operate for five minutes to stabilize system.
7. Set system pressure to about 260 psi, by placing a piece of cardboard over part of front side of condenser. To place cardboard properly, remove upper radiator-condenser cover and insert cardboard between condenser and radiator front. This will maintain a constant pressure.
8. Observe liquid line pressure and temperature.
9. Determine where system is currently operating using Charge determination chart, **Fig. 19.**
10. If reading is in the Undercharged region, add 2 oz. of R-134a to system and inspect readings.
11. If reading is in the Overcharged region, recover 2 oz. of R-134a from system and inspect readings.
12. Continue this process until reading is within proper charge area.

Ambient Air Temperature	21° C (70° F)	27° C (80° F)	32° C (90° F)	38° C (100° F)	43° C (110° F)
Maximum Allowable Air Temperature at Center Panel Outlet	9° C (48° F)	9° C (48° F)	12° C (54° F)	15° C (59° F)	18° C (65° F)
Suction Pressure at Service Port (Low Side)	138 to 310 kPa (20 to 45 psi)	138 to 345 kPa (20 to 50 psi)	207 to 365 kPa (30 to 55 psi)	207 to 414 kPa (30 to 60 psi)	241 to 448 kPa (35 to 65 psi)
Discharge Pressure at Service Port (High Side)	1034 to 1724 kPa (150 to 250 psi)	1379 to 2068 kPa (200 to 300 psi)	1551 to 2241 kPa (225 to 325 psi)	1724 to 2413 kPa (250 to 350 psi)	2068 to 2758 kPa (300 to 400 psi)

LTV0500000000184

Fig. 3 Performance temperature chart. 2005–06 Dakota

Performance Temperature and Pressure					
Ambient Air Temperature	21°C (70°F)	27°C (80°F)	32°C (90°F)	38°C (100°F)	43°C (110°F)
Maximum Allowable Air Temperature at Center Panel Outlet	9°C (48°F)	9°C (48°F)	12°C (54°F)	15°C (59°F)	18°C (65°F)
Maximum Allowable Air Temperature at Driverside 2nd Row Headliner Outlet	10° C (50° F)	10° C (50° F)	13° C (56° F)	15° C (60° F)	18° C (65° F)
Compressor Inlet Pressure at Service Port (Low Side)	138 to 207 kPa (20 to 30 psi)	138 to 207 kPa (20 to 30 psi)	207 to 276 kPa (30 to 40 psi)	207 to 276 kPa (30 to 40 psi)	241 to 310 kPa (35 to 45 psi)
Condensor Out Pressure at Service Port (High Side)	1034 to 1724 kPa (150 to 250 psi)	1379 to 2068 kPa (200 to 300 psi)	1551 to 2241 kPa (225 to 325 psi)	1724 to 2413 kPa (250 to 350 psi)	2068 to 2758 kPa (300 to 400 psi)

LTV1900000000355

Fig. 4 Performance temperature chart. 2002–03 Durango

LEAK TEST

Leak Detectors

FLAME-TYPE (HALIDE) LEAK DETECTORS

Avoid inhaling fumes produced by burning refrigerant when using flame-type detectors. Use caution when using detector near flammable materials such as interior trim components. Do not use flame-type detector where concentrations of combustible or explosive gases, dusts or vapors may exist.

1. Light leak detector and adjust flame as low as possible to obtain maximum sensitivity.
2. Allow detector to warm until copper element is cherry-red. Flame should be almost colorless.
3. Test reaction plate sensitivity by passing end of sensor hose near an opened can of refrigerant. Flame should react violently, turning bright blue.
4. If flame does not change color, replace reaction plate following manufacturer's instructions.
5. Allow flame to clear, then slowly move sensor hose along areas suspected of leakage while observing flame. **Position sensor hose under areas of suspected leakage, as refrigerant is heavier than air.**
6. Move sensor hose under all lines, fittings and components. Insert hose into evaporator case, if possible, and inspect compressor shaft seal.
7. The presence of refrigerant will cause flame to change color as follows: Pale blue, no refrigerant; yellow-yellow/green, slight leak; bright blue-purple/blue, major leak or concentration of refrigerant.
8. If detector indicates a large leak or heavy concentration of refrigerant, ventilate area using a small fan in order to pinpoint leak.
9. Repair leaks as needed, evacuate and recharge system, then inspect system for leaks.

ELECTRONIC LEAK DETECTORS

The procedure for using an electronic leak detector is similar to the procedure for flame-type leak detectors, except that the presence of refrigerant is indicated by an audible tone or flashing light. **An R-12 electronic leak detector is not compatible with R-134a systems.** Refer to operating instructions for unit being used, and observe the following procedures:

1. Move detector probe one inch per second along areas of suspected leakage.
2. Position probe under area to be tested as refrigerant is heavier than air.
3. Inspect gauge manifold, hoses and service ports for leakage.

FLUID LEAK DETECTORS

Apply leak detector solution around joints to be tested. A cluster of bubbles will form immediately if there is a leak. A white foam that forms after a short while will indicate an extremely small leak. In some confined areas, such as sections of the evaporator and condenser, electronic leak detectors will be more useful.

System Leak Tests

SYSTEM EMPTY

Do not pressure test the R-134a system with compressed air. Some mixtures of air and R-134a have been outlined to be combustible at higher pressures. Use leak detector designed for R-134a systems.

1. Evacuate A/C system.
2. Prepare 10 oz. R-134a charge to be injected into system. Refer to "Charging System" for procedure.
3. With engine Off, use an electronic leak detector designed for R-134a systems and inspect for leaks. Fittings, lines or components that appear to be oily may indicate a refrigerant leak.
4. To inspect the evaporator core for leaks, it is possible to insert the leak detector probe into the recirculating air door opening.
5. With the blower at low speed and the selector in FLOOR and RECIRC mode, inspect for leaks at lefthand and righthand heater outlets. If no leak is present, fill system as outlined under "Performance Test."

LOW LEVEL

1. Start engine with A/C On for five minutes to allow system to reach operating temperature and pressure.
2. With engine Off, use an electronic leak detector designed for R-134a systems and inspect for leaks. Fittings, lines or components that appear to be oily may indicate a refrigerant leak.
3. To inspect the evaporator core for leaks, it is possible to insert the leak detector probe into the recirculating air door opening.
4. With the blower at low speed and the selector in FLOOR and RECIRC mode, inspect for leaks at lefthand and righthand heater outlets. If no leak is present, fill system as outlined under "Performance Test."

DISCHARGING SYSTEM

Refrigerant Recovery

The use of refrigerant recovery and recycling stations allows the recovery and reuse of refrigerant after contaminants and moisture have been removed.

When using a recovery or recycling station, follow the manufacturer's operating instructions, noting the following:

1. **Use extreme caution and observe all safety and service precautions related to use of refrigerants.**
2. Connect refrigerant recycling station hose(s) to vehicle A/C service ports and recovery station inlet fitting. **Center manifold hose (yellow or white with black stripe) is used to discharge, recycle, recover, evacuate and charge the refrigerant system. When the low or high pressure valves on the manifold set are opened, the refrigerant will escape through this hose.** Hoses used should have shut off devices or check valves within 12 inches of hose ends to minimize introduction of air into recycling station.
3. Turn recycling station On to start recovery process. Allow recycling station to pump refrigerant from A/C system until station pressure gauge indicates vacuum.
4. After vehicle A/C system has been evacuated, close station inlet valve, if equipped.
5. Turn station Off. On some stations, the pump will automatically be turned Off by a low pressure switch.
6. Allow vehicle A/C system to remain closed for approximately two minutes. Observe vacuum level indicated on gauge. If pressure does not rise, disconnect recycling station hose(s).
7. If system pressure rises, repeat Steps 3 through 6 until vacuum level indicated remains stable for two minutes.

Ambient Air Temperature	21°C (70° F)	27°C (80° F)	32°C (90° F)	38°C (100° F)	43°C (110° F)
Maximum Allowable Air Temperature at Center Panel Outlet	9°C (48°F)	9°C (48°F)	12°C (54° F)	15°C (59°F)	18°C (65°F)
Maximum Allowable Air Temperature at Driver side 2nd Row Headliner Outlet	10° C (50° F)	13° C (55° F)	15° C (59° F)	17° C (63° F)	19° C (67° F)
Suction Pressure at Service Port (Low Side)	138 to 310 kPa (20 to 45 psi)	138 to 345 kPa (20 to 50 psi)	207 to 365 kPa (30 to 55 psi)	207 to 414 kPa (30 to 60 psi)	241 to 448 kPa (35 to 65 psi)
Discharge Pressure at Service Port (High Side)	1034 to 1724 kPa (150 to 250 psi)	1379 to 2068 kPa (200 to 300 psi)	1551 to 2241 kPa (225 to 325 psi)	1724 to 2413 kPa (250 to 350 psi)	2068 to 2758 kPa (300 to 400 psi)

LTV0500000000185

Fig. 5 Performance temperature chart. 2004–05 Durango

Ambient Air Temperature	21° C (70° F)	27° C (80° F)	32° C (90° F)	38° C (100° F)	43° C (110° F)
Maximum Allowable Air Temperature at Center Panel Outlet	9° C (48° F)	9° C (48° F)	12° C (54° F)	15° C (59° F)	24° C (75° F)
Maximum Allowable Air Temperature at Driver Side 2nd Row Headliner Outlet	10° C (50° F)	13° C (55° F)	15° C (59° F)	17° C (63° F)	24° C (75° F)
Suction Pressure at Service Port (Low Side)	138 to 310 kPa (20 to 45 psi)	138 to 345 kPa (20 to 50 psi)	207 to 365 kPa (30 to 55 psi)	207 to 414 kPa (30 to 60 psi)	241 to 448 kPa (35 to 65 psi)
Discharge Pressure at Service Port (High Side)	1034 to 1724 kPa (150 to 250 psi)	1379 to 2068 kPa (175 to 300 psi)	1551 to 2241 kPa (175 to 325 psi)	1724 to 2413 kPa (250 to 350 psi)	2068 to 2758 kPa (300 to 475 psi)

LTV0500000000186

Fig. 6 Performance temperature chart. 2006 Durango

8. Service A/C system as required, then evacuate and recharge A/C system.

System Evacuation

VACUUM PUMP

Keep all R-134a components capped to prevent moisture from entering the system. If the refrigerant system has been opened to the atmosphere, it must be evacuated.

The system must be completely discharged before it can be evacuated. Damage to the vacuum pump may result if pressurized refrigerant is allowed to enter.

1. Connect suitable charging station, refrigerant recovery machine and a manifold gauge set with vacuum pump.
2. Open suction and discharge valves and start vacuum pump. When suction gauge reads 26 inch Hg or greater, close all valves and turn off vacuum pump. If system fails to reach specified vacuum, refrigerant system likely has a leak that must be corrected. If refrigerant system maintains specified vacuum for at least 5 minutes, start vacuum pump and open discharge and suction valves, and allow system to evacuate for an additional ten minutes.
3. Close all valves, turn off and disconnect pump and charge with refrigerant.

CHARGING STATION

A vacuum pump is built into the charging station that is constructed to withstand repeated and prolonged use without damage. Complete moisture removal from the A/C system is possible only with a pump of this type. **System must be completely discharged prior to evacuation. If pressurized refrigerant is allowed to enter vacuum pump, damage will occur to pump.**

1. Connect charging station and discharge system as outlined.
2. Reconnect vacuum hose to vacuum pump and ensure vacuum control valve is closed.
3. Fully open low and high pressure control valves.
4. Connect station to a suitable voltage source and operate vacuum pump.
5. Slowly open vacuum control valve and observe low side compound gauge. If system does not "pump-down" to 28–29½ inches Hg (at sea level) within approximately five minutes, inspect connections and leak test system.
6. Continue to operate vacuum pump for 15–30 minutes, longer if system was open for an extended period of time, then close all control valves and stop pump.
7. Inspect ability of system to hold vacuum. Watch low side compound gauge and ensure reading does not rise at a rate faster than 1 inch Hg every four to five minutes.
8. If system fails to hold vacuum, inspect fittings and connections, and leak test system.
9. If system holds vacuum, charge system with refrigerant.

SYSTEM EVACUATION

Refer to "Discharging System" for evacuation procedures.

CHARGING SYSTEM

Bulk Refrigerant Supply

Refer to "Charging Station J-23500-01 Method."

Multi-Can Refrigerant Supply

1. Connect pressure gauge and manifold assembly tool No. J-23575, or equivalent. Keep both service valves in mid-position.
2. Close both gauge hand valves and disconnect service hose from vacuum pump.
3. Connect service hose to center of refrigerant can supply. Close valves on dispenser.
4. Attach refrigerant cans to adapter.
5. Open one petcock valve and loosen center service hose at gauge to allow refrigerant to purge air from hose. Tighten hose and close petcock valve.
6. Open suction gauge hand valve and one petcock valve. Do not open high pressure gauge hand valve.
7. Start engine and set A/C system controls to maximum cooling position. Compressor will help pull refrigerant gas into suction side of system. **Refrigerant cans can be placed in pan of water no hotter than 125°F to aid charging process.**
8. When first can is empty, open next valve to continue charging until specified amount of refrigerant is in system. Frost line on can may be used as a guide when specifications call for using part of full can. If a scale is available, weigh cans before and during charging procedure to ensure accurate filling.
9. When system is fully charged, close suction gauge hand valve and all petcock valves.
10. Operate system for five to ten minutes to allow it to stabilize and to determine if system cycles properly.
11. After inspecting operation of system, back-seat suction and discharge service valves to normal operating position by turning valves fully counterclockwise.
12. Loosen pressure gauge and manifold assembly service hoses to release refrigerant trapped in hoses. Remove pressure gauge and manifold assembly and install dust caps on fittings.

Charging Station J-23500-01 Method

SYSTEM EMPTY

1. Connect manifold gauge set.
2. Measure refrigerant, refer to "Specifications" and heat to 125°F with charging station. Refer to manufacturer's instructions provided with equipment being used.
3. Open low (suction) and high (discharge) side valves. Open charge valve to allow heated refrigerant to flow into system. When transfer of refrigerant has stopped, close low and high side valves.
4. If all the charge did not transfer from the dispensing device, run engine at a high idle (1500 RPM). Set A/C control to A/C, low blower speed, and open windows. If A/C compressor does not engage, test compressor clutch control circuit and correct any failure.
5. Open low side valve to allow remaining refrigerant to transfer to the system.

Performance Temperature and Pressure						
Ambient Temperature	**21° C (70° F)**	**27° C (80° F)**	**32° C (90° F)**	**38° C (100° F)**	**43° C (110° F)**	**49° C (120° F)**
Center Panel OutletDischarge Air Temperature	5 to 7° C (40 to 45° F)	13 to 16° C (55 to 60° F)	16 to 21° C (60 to 70° F)	21 to 24° C (70 to 75° F)	27 to 29° C (80 to 85° F)	29 to 32° C (85 to 90° F)
*Suction Pressure (Low Side)	241 to 276 kPa (35 to 40 psi)	276 to 345 kPa (40 to 50 psi)	345 to 414 kPa (50 to 60 psi)	414 to 483 kPa (60 to 70 psi)	483 to 552 kPa (70 to 80 psi)	552 to 586 kPa (85 to 90 psi)
*Discharge Pressure (High Side)	931 to 1000 kPa (135 to 145 psi)	1207 to 1482 kPa (175 to 215 psi)	1482 to 1862 kPa (215 to 270 psi)	1862 to 2275 kPa (270 to 330 psi)	2344 to 2551 kPa (340 to 370 psi)	2758 to 2965 kPa (400 to 430 psi)
*Note: If pressures are lower than shown, but center panel outlet discharge air temperatures are OK, then the A/C system is OK.						

CR7029800526000X

Fig. 7 Performance temperature chart. 2002 2500 & 3500 Full Size Pickups

Performance Temperature and Pressure					
Ambient Air Temperature	21° C (70° F)	27° C (80° F)	32° C (90° F)	38° C (100° F)	43° C (110° F)
Air Temperature at Center Panel Outlet	7° C (45° F)	7° C (45° F)	13° C (55° F)	13° C (55° F)	18° C (64° F)
Compressor Inlet Pressure at Service Port (low Side)	138 to 207 kPa (20 to 30 psi)	172 to 241 kPa (25 to 35 psi)	207 to 276 kPa (30 to 40 psi)	241 to 310 kPa (35 to 45 psi)	276 to 345 kPa (40 to 50 psi)
Condensor Out Pressuree at Service Port (High Side)	1034 to 1724 kPa (150 to 250 psi)	1379 to 2068 kPa (200 to 300 psi)	1724 to 2413 kPa (250 to 350 psi)	1999 to 2689 kPa (290 to 390 psi)	2413 to 2965 kPa (350 to 430 psi)

LTV1900000000356

Fig. 8 Performance temperature chart. 1500 & 2003–06 2500 & 3500 Full Size Pickups

Garage Ambient Temperature	21°C (70°F)	26.5°C (80°F)	32°C (90°F)	37.5°C (100°F)	43°C (110°F)
Discharge Air Temperature,	4-13°C (40-56°F)	6-16°C (42-60°F)	4-17°C (40-63°F)	9-19°C (48-67°F)	12-22°C (53-71°F)
Compressor Discharge Pressure	827 1344 kPag	1103 1620 kPag	1379 1861 kPag	1655 2103 kPag	1379 2344 kPag
	120 195 psig	160 235 psig	200 270 psig	240 305 psig	280 340 psig
Evaporator Suction Pressure	124 207 kPag	138 241 kPag	152 269 kPag	172 296 kPag	179 324 kPag
	18 30 psig	20 35 psig	22 39 psig	25 43 psig	26 47 psig

CR7029800527010X

Fig. 9 Performance temperature chart (Front). Full Size Van

Garage Ambient Temperature	21°C (70°F)	26.5°C (80°F)	32°C (90°F)	37.5°C (100°F)	43°C (110°F)
Discharge Air Temperature	3-10°C (38-50°F)	6-12°C (42-54°F)	8-14°C (46-58°F)	10-17°C (50-62°F)	12-19°C (54-66°F)
Compressor Discharge Pressure	827 1344 kPag	1103 1620 kPag	1379 1861 kPag	1655 2103 kPag	1379 2344 kPag
	120 195 psig	160 235 psig	200 270 psig	240 305 psig	280 340 psig
Evaporator Suction Pressure	124 207 kPag	138 241 kPag	152 269 kPag	172 296 kPag	179 324 kPag
	18 30 psig	20 35 psig	22 39 psig	25 43 psig	26 47 psig

CR7029800527020X

Fig. 10 Performance temperature chart (Rear). Full Size Van

Ambient Temperature	21° C (70° F)	27° C (80° F)	32° C (90° F)	38° C (100° F)	43° C (110° F)
Left Center Panel Outlet Discharge Air Temperature	1 to 8° C (34 to 46° F)	3 to 9° C (37 to 49° F)	4 to 10°C (39 to 50° F)	6 to 11°C (43 to 52° F)	7 to 18° C (45 to 65° F)
Discharge Pressure (High Side Service Port)	1034 to 1724 kPa (150 to 250 psi)	1517 to 2275 kPa (220 to 330 psi)	1999 to 2620 kPa (290 to 380 psi)	2068 to 2965 kPa (300 to 430 psi)	2275 to 3421 kPa (330 to 450 psi)
Suction Pressure (Low Side Service Port)	103 to 207 kPa (15 to 30 psi)	117 to 221 kPa (17 to 32 psi)	138 to 241 kPa (20 to 35 psi)	172 to 269 kPa (25 to 39 psi)	207 to 345 kPa (30 to 50 psi)

LTV0500000000187

Fig. 11 Performance temperature chart. Pacifica

Ambient Temperature	21°C (70°F)	27°C (80°F)	32°C (90°F)	38°C (100°F)	43°C (110°F)
Air Temperature at Center Panel Outlet	-2 - 6°C (29-42°F)	2-10°C (37-49°F)	7-15°C (45-58°F)	11-19°C (52-65°F)	15-23°C (59-72°F)
Compressor Discharge Pressure	999-1206 kPa (145-175 PSI)	1033-1378 kPa (150-200 PSI	1240-1757 kPa (180-255 PSI)	1584-2136 kPa (230-310 PSI)	2067-2722 kPa (300-395 PSI)
Accumulator Out Pressure at Service Port	122-221 kPa (18-32 PSI)	137-235 kPa (20-34 PSI)	186-290 kpa (27-42 PSI)	220-324 kpa (32-47 PSI)	275-379 kPa (40-55 PSI)

LTV1900000000357

Fig. 12 Performance temperature chart. PT Cruiser w/Non-turbocharged engine

Do not open high side valve at this time.

6. Close all valves and test A/C system performance. Refer to "Performance Test."
7. Disconnect charging station or manifold gauge set. Install service port caps.

Adding Partial Refrigerant Charge

CARAVAN, TOWN & COUNTRY & VOYAGER

1. Attach manifold gauge set.
2. Open windows of the passenger compartment and set air conditioning controls to A/C, RECIRC and low blower speed.
3. Start engine and allow it to reach normal operating temperature.
4. If compressor clutch does not engage, disconnect low pressure cutoff switch and place a jumper wire across the terminals in the connector boot. If the compressor still does not engage, a problem exists in the clutch feed circuit. Repair circuit as required.
5. Run engine at 1400 RPM.
6. Charge system through suction side of air conditioning system with enough refrigerant to clear sight glass of bubbles.
7. When the sight glass clears, note weight of refrigerant supply drum or level in charging cylinder, then add an additional 12 oz. of refrigerant to system.
8. Remove jumper wire from low pressure cutoff switch boot, then connect boot to switch.
9. Test overall performance of air conditioning system as outlined under "Performance Test."
10. Close all valves on charging equipment, then disconnect hoses from service ports.
11. Install service port protective caps.

Sight Glass Refrigerant Level Inspection

CARAVAN, FULL SIZE PICKUP, FULL SIZE VAN, TOWN & COUNTRY & VOYAGER

The filter-drier is equipped with a sight glass that is used as a refrigerant level indicator only. **This sight glass is not to be used for A/C performance testing. The filter/drier used in an R-134a system is not compatible with the filter/drier in an R-12 system.**

To inspect the refrigerant level, clean the sight glass, start and run engine to operating temperature, then hold idle at 1100 RPM. Set air conditioning control on A/C, RECIRC and high blower. The work area temperature should be at least 70°F. If the compressor clutch does not engage, the refrigerant level is probably too low for the pressure cutoff switch to detect. Refer to "Leak Test" for testing procedures for the low pressure condition indicated. If no leak is found, evacuate and recharge the system as required. If compressor clutch engages, allow approximately one minute for refrigerant to stabilize, then view the refrigerant through the sight glass. The suction line should be cold to the touch and the sight glass should be clear. If foam or bubbles are visible in sight glass, the refrigerant level is probably low. Occasional bubbles are normal when the work area is above 110°F or below 70°F.

If suction line is cold and occasional bubbles are visible in the sight glass, block the condenser air flow to increase the compressor discharge pressure. **Ensure engine does not overheat.** Bubbles should disappear, if not the refrigerant level is low.

Ambient Temperature	21°C (70°F)	27°C (80°F)	32°C (90°F)	38°C (100°F)	43°C (110°F)
Air Temperature at Center Panel Outlet	6 - 16°C (43-60°F)	11-21°C (52-69°F)	16-25°C (60-76°F)	17-28°C (63-83°F)	19-32°C (67-89°F)
Compressor Discharge Pressure	1139-1795 kPa (165-260 PSI)	1828-2070 kPa (265-300 PSI	1932-2070 kPa (280-300 PSI)	1932-2484 kPa (280-360 PSI)	2104-2898 kPa (305-420 PSI)
Accumulator Out Pressure at Service Port	195-319 kPa (28-46 PSI)	257-381 kPa (37-55 PSI)	312-443 kpa (45-64 PSI)	332-512 kpa (48-74 PSI)	360-581 kPa (52-84 PSI)

LTV1900000000358

Fig. 13 Performance temperature chart. PT Cruiser w/Turbocharged engine

Ambient Air Temperature	21° C (70° F)	27° C (80° F)	32° C (90° F)	38° C (100° F)	43° C (110° F)
Maximum Allowable Air Temperature at Center Panel Outlet	9° C (48° F)	9° C (48° F)	12° C (54° F)	15° C (59° F)	18° C (65° F)
Suction Pressure at Service Port (Low Side)	138 to 207 kPa (20 to 30 psi)	138 to 207 kPa (20 to 30 psi)	207 to 276 kPa (30 to 40 psi)	207 to 276 kPa (30 to 40 psi)	241 to 310 kPa (35 to 45 psi)
Discharge Pressure at Service Port (High Side)	1034 to 1724 kPa (150 to 250 psi)	1379 to 2068 kPa (200 to 300 psi)	1551 to 2241 kPa (225 to 325 psi)	1724 to 2413 kPa (250 to 350 psi)	2068 to 2758 kPa (300 to 400 psi)

LTV0500000000188

Fig. 14 Temperature/pressure performance chart. Commander

Performance Temperature and Pressure					
Ambient Air Temperature and Humidity	21° C (70° F @ 80% humidity)	27° C (80° F @ 80% humidity)	32° C (90° F @ 80% humidity)	38° C (100° F @ 50% humidity)	43° C 110° F @ 20% humidity)
Air Temperature at Center Panel Outlet	10 to 13° C (50 to 55° F)	14 to 17° C (58 to 63° F)	15 to 18° C (60 to 65° F)	17 to 20° C (63 to 68° F)	14 to 17° C (58 to 63° F)
Evaporator Inlet Pressure at Charge Port	241 to 276 kPa (35 to 40 psi)	262 to 290 kPa (38 to 42 psi)	269 to 296 kPa (39 to 43 psi)	275 to 303 kPa (40 to 44 psi)	262 to 290 kPa (38 to 42 psi)
Compressor Discharge Pressure	1241 to 1792 kPa (180 to 260 psi)	1380 to 1930 kPa (200 to 280 psi)	1380 to 1930 kPa (200 to 280 psi)	1655 to 2206 kPa (240 to 320 psi)	1567 to 2068 kPa (220 to 300 psi)
Note: The discharge air temperatures will be lower if the humidity is less than the percentages shown.					

LTV1900000000359

Fig. 15 Temperature/pressure performance chart. 2002–04 Grand Cherokee

Ambient Air Temperature	21°C (70°F)	27°C (80°F)	32°C (90°F)	38°C (100°F)	43°C (110°F)
Maximum Allowable Air Temperature at Center Panel Outlet	9°C (48°F)	9°C (48°F)	12°C (54°F)	15°C (59°F)	18°C (65°F)
Suction Pressure at Service Port (Low Side)	138 to 207 kPa (20 to 30 psi)	138 to 207 kPa (20 to 30 psi)	207 to 276 kPa (30 to 40 psi)	207 to 276 kPa (30 to 40 psi)	241 to 310 kPa (35 to 45 psi)
Discharge Pressure at Service Port (High Side)	1034 to 1724 kPa (150 to 250 psi)	1379 to 2068 kPa (200 to 300 psi)	1551 to 2241 kPa (225 to 325 psi)	1724 to 2413 kPa (250 to 350 psi)	2068 to 2758 kPa (300 to 400 psi)

LTV0500000000189

Fig. 16 Temperature/pressure performance chart. 2005–06 Grand Cherokee

Performance Temperature and Pressure					
Ambient Air Temperature	21° C (70° F)	27° C (80° F)	32° C (90° F)	38° C (100° F)	43° C (110° F)
Air Temperature at Center Panel Outlet	7° C (45° F)	7° C (45° F)	13° C (55° F)	13° C (55° F)	18° C (64° F)
Compressor Inlet Pressure at Service Port (Low Side)	138 to 207 kPa (20 to 30 psi)	172 to 241 kPa (25 to 35 psi)	207 to 276 kPa (30 to 40 psi)	241 to 310 kPa (35 to 45 psi)	276 to 345 kPa (40 to 50 psi)
Condensor Outlet Pressuree at Service Port (High Side)	1034 to 1724 kPa (150 to 250 psi)	1379 to 2068 kPa (200 to 300 psi)	1724 to 2413 kPa (250 to 350 psi)	1999 to 2689 kPa (290 to 390 psi)	2413 to 2965 kPa (350 to 430 psi)

LTV1900000000360

Fig. 17 Temperature/pressure performance chart. Liberty

Ambient Temperature	21°C (70°F)	27°C (80°F)	32°C (90°F)	38°C (100°F)	43°C (110°F)
Air Temperature at Center Panel Outlet	-3 to 3°C (27-38°F)	1 to 7°C (33-44°F)	3 to 9°C (37-48°F)	6 to 13°C (43-55°F)	10 to 18°C (50-64°F)
Evaporator Inlet Pressure at Charge Port	179-241 kPa (26-35 psi)	221-283 kPa (32-41 psi)	262-324 kPa (38-47 psi)	303-365 kPa (44-53 psi)	345-414 kPa (50-60 psi)
Compressor Discharge Pressure	1240-1655 kPa (180-240 psi)	1380-1790 kPa (200-260 psi)	1720-2070 kPa (250-300 psi)	1860-2345 kPa (270-340 psi)	2070-2690 kPa (300-390 psi)

CR7019600087000X

Fig. 18 Temperature/pressure performance chart. Wrangler

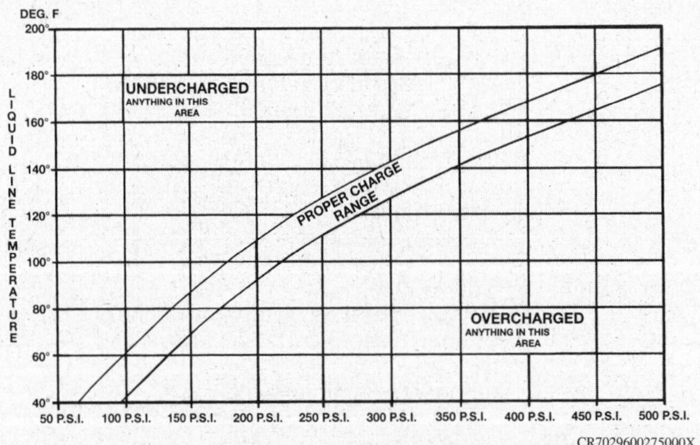

CR7029600275000X

Fig. 19 Charge determination chart. Caravan, Town & Country & Voyager

System Service

INDEX

OIL CHARGE

Except Jeep

If there are no signs of external oil leakage, proceed as follows to add oil to system during component replacement.

1. Discharge system as outlined in "System Testing" and measure amount of oil collected in discharge container. **The amount of oil collected when discharging system must be replaced with new refrigeration oil to maintain proper oil charge.**
2. Remove faulty components. Measure amount of oil remaining in compressor, if removed.
3. Add correct amount of oil to components.
4. Install replacement components, then evacuate and recharge system.

Jeep

A R-134a refrigerant recovery/recycling/charging station that meets SAE standard J2210 must be used to charge refrigerant system with R-134a refrigerant. Refer to operating instructions supplied by equipment manufacture for proper care and use of equipment.

OIL LEVEL CHECK

It will not be required to inspect oil level in compressor or to add oil, unless there has been an oil loss. If a leak occurs, add 1 oz. of oil to refrigerant system after repair has been made.

Refrigerant oil must be added when an accumulator, evaporator coil, or condenser are replaced. Refer to **Fig. 1** for oil quantities. When a compressor is replaced, oil must be drained from old compressor and measured. Drain all oil from new compressor, then fill new compressor with same amount of oil that was drained from old compressor.

Model	Year	Model Compressor	Total Capacity	Component Oil Capacity, Ounces				
				Compressor	Condenser	Evaporator	Filter-Drier	Line
Caravan, Town & Country & Voyager	2002③	10PA17	5.00	5.0	1.00	2.00	1.00	—
	2002④	10PA17	7.40	7.4	1.00	2.00①	1.00	—
	2003③	10S20	5.00	②	.90	1.80	.90	—
	2003④	10S20	6.43	②	.90	1.80	.90	—
	2004–06③	10S17	6.10	②	1.70	1.70	.80	—
	2004–06④	10S20	7.80	②	1.70	1.70	.80	—
Commander	2006	10S17	—	②	—	—	—	—
Dakota	2002–03	SD7H15	7.10	②	1.00	2.00	3.00	—
	2004–06	10S17	7.10	②	1.00	2.00	3.00	—
Durango	2002–03③	SD7H15	⑥	②	1.00	2.00	1.00	—
	2002–03④	SD7H15	10.10	②	1.00	1.00	1.00	—
	2004–06③	10S20	5.10	②	1.00	2.00	1.00	—
	2004–06④	10S20	7.40	②	1.00	2.00	1.00	—
Full Size Pickup	2002⑦	SD-7	6.00	②	1.00	2.00	2.00	—
	2002⑤	SD7H15	6.20	②	1.00	2.00	2.00	—
	2003	SD-7	6.00	②	1.00	2.00	2.00	—
	2004–06	10S17	6.00	②	1.00	2.00	2.00	—
	2004–06	HS-18	6.00	②	1.00	2.00	2.00	—
Full Size Van	2002–03③	TR-105	8.00	②	1.00	2.00	1.00	—
	2002–03④	TR-105	10.00	②	1.00	2.00	1.00	—
Grand Cherokee	2002–04	10PA17	4.40	②	.34	1.69	2.37	—
	2005–06	10S17	4.40	②	1.00	1.40	1.00	—
Liberty	2002–06	SD-7	8.0	②	.75	1.50	3.00	—
Pacifica	2004	10S17	5.00	②	1.00	2.00	1.00	—
	2005–06	10S20	5.00	②	1.00	2.00	1.00	—
PT Cruiser	2002–06⑧	10S15	6.10	②	1.00	2.00	1.00	1.50
	2002–06⑨	10S17	6.10	②	1.00	2.00	1.00	—
Wrangler	2002–06	10PA17	6.10	②	.75	1.50	3.00	—

① — Front & rear.
② — Drain & measure oil from old compressor.
③ — Less rear A/C.
④ — With rear A/C.
⑤ — 2500 & 3500.
⑥ — 7.1 oz. w/4.7L engine & 7.1 oz. w/5.9L engine.
⑦ — 1500.
⑧ — Manual transaxle.
⑨ — Automatic transaxle.

Fig. 1 A/C system component oil capacities chart

Specifications

INDEX

A/C SPECIFICATIONS

Model	Year	Refrigerant Capacity, Lbs.	Refrigerant Type	Refrigerant Oil			Compressor Clutch Air Gap, Inch
				PAG Type	Total System Capacity, Ounces	Compressor, Oil Level	
DAIMLERCHRYSLER							
Caravan, Town & Country & Voyager Less Rear A/C	2002	2.13	R-134a	ND-8	7.40	③	.020–.035
	2003	2.69	R-134a	ND-8	6.43	③	.020–.035
	2004–06	①	R-134a	ND-8	6.1	③	.014–.024
Caravan, Town & Country & Voyager w/Rear A/C	2002	2.88	R-134a	ND-8	5.00	③	.020–.035
	2003	1.94	R-134a	ND-8	5.00	③	.020–.035
	2004	①	R-134a	ND-8	10.14	③	.014–.025
	2005–06	①	R-134a	ND-8	7.80	③	.014–.024
Dakota	2002–03	2.00	R-134a	SP-20	7.10	③	.016–.031
	2004–06	①	R-134a	ND-8	7.10	③	.014–.024
Durango Less Rear A/C	2002–03	1.75	R-134a	SP-20	④	③	.016–.031
Durango Less Rear A/C	2004–06	①	R-134a	ND-8	5.10	③	.014–.024
Durango w/Rear A/C	2002–03	1.90	R-134a	SP-20	10.10	③	.016–.031
Durango w/Rear A/C	2004–06	①	R-134a	ND-8	7.40	③	.014–.024
Full Size Pickup/Truck 1500 3.7L & 4.7L	2002	1.50	R-134a	SP-15	6.00	③	.016–.031
Full Size Pickup/Truck 1500 5.9L	2002	1.63	R-134a	SP-15	6.00	③	.016–.031
Full Size Pickup/Truck 2500 & 3500	2002	2.00	R-134a	SP-20	6.20	③	.016–.031
Full Size Pickup/Truck	2003	1.63	R-134a	SP-15	6.00	③	.016–.031
Full Size Pickup/Truck 3.7L, 4.7L, 5.7L & 8.3L	2004–06	①	R-134a	ND-8	6.00	③	.014–.024
Full Size Pickup/Truck 5.9L	2004–06	①	R-134a	VC-46	6.00	③	.014 - .030
Full Size Vans Less Rear A/C	2002–03	2.12	R-134a	SP-15	8.00	③	.013–.025
Full Size Vans w/Rear A/C	2002–03	2.87	R-134a	SP-15	10.00	③	.013–.025
Pacifica	2004–06	①	R-134a	ND-8	5.00	③	.014–.024
PT Cruiser	2002–04	①	R-134a	ND-8	6.10	③	.014–.026
	2005–06	①	R-134a	ND-8	6.10	③	.014–.024
JEEP							
Commander	2006	①	R-134a	ND-8	—	③	.014 - .024
Grand Cherokee	2002–04	1.69	R-134a	ND-8	4.40	②	.016–.031
	2005–06	①	R-134a	ND-8	4.40	③	.014 - .024
Liberty	2002	1.63	R-134a	SP-10	8.00	③	.016–.031
	2003–05	1.63	R-134a	SP-15	8.00	③	.016–.031
	2006	①	R-134a	VC-46	8.00	③	.014 - .025
Wrangler	2002–03	1.25	R-134a	ND-8	6.10	②	.016–.031
	2004–06	①	R-134a	ND-8	6.10	②	.014 - .026

①— Refer to underhood specification label.
②— See text for inspection procedure.
③— Oil level inches cannot be inspected. Refer to total capacity & see text for inspection procedure.
④— 4.7L engine, 5.5 ounces; 5.9L engine, 6.1 ounces.

BELT TENSION

Engine①	A/C Compressor Belt Tension	
	New, Lbs.	Used, Lbs.
2.4L	190	115
4.0L	180–200	140–160

① — For engines not listed, correct belt tension is maintained automatically.

COOLING FANS

TABLE OF CONTENTS

Electric Cooling Fans, DaimlerChrysler

NOTE: "Electrical Symbol & Wire Color Code Identification" Located In The Front Of This Manual May Be Used As An Aid When Using Wiring Circuits Found In This Section.

NOTE: Refer To "Computer Relearn Procedures" Located In The Front Of This Manual When Battery Power To The Computer Has Been Interrupted.

INDEX

PRECAUTIONS

Battery Ground Cable

Prior to service, disconnect battery ground cable and isolate as required.

DESCRIPTION

The electric cooling fan, **Figs. 1 through 4,** is controlled by the Powertrain Control Module (PCM) with inputs from the temperature of the coolant, which is sensed by the coolant temperature sensor, and vehicle speed which is measured by the vehicle speed sensor. The PCM turns on the fan through either the high or low speed fan relay.

SYSTEM DIAGNOSIS & TESTING

Caravan, Pacifica, Town & Country & Voyager

ACCESSING DIAGNOSTIC TROUBLE CODES

If a problem is sensed by the engine controller, often enough to be considered a fault, a DTC is stored in the module memory. If the problem is repaired, or ceases to occur, the module will cancel the DTC after 50–100 vehicle key On/Off cycles. DTCs that remain in the module memory can be called up and displayed either by using a suitable diagnostic scan tool or by observing flashes of the Malfunction Indicator Lamp (MIL). DTCs can be obtained using the following procedures:

1. Connect scan tool to diagnostic connector located under lefthand side of instrument panel, **Fig. 5.**
2. Follow scan tool manufacturer's instructions to access DTCs.

DIAGNOSTIC TROUBLE CODE INTERPRETATION

Connect a suitable scan tool to the Diagnostic Link Connector (DLC) located under the lefthand side of instrument panel, **Fig. 5,** then follow scan tool manufacturer's instructions to access the DTCs.

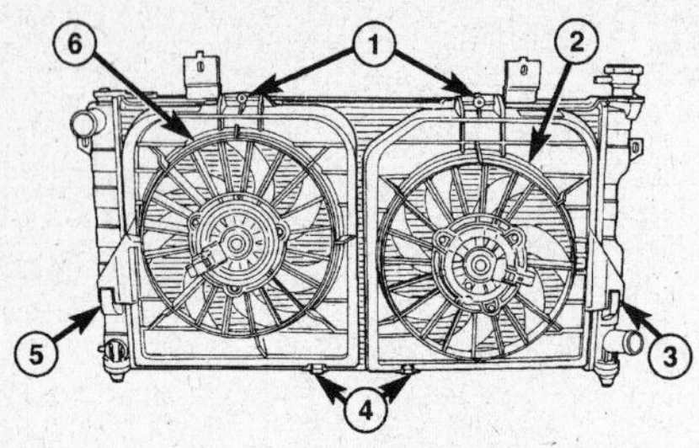

1 - SCREWS - RADIATOR FAN ATTACHING
2 - RADIATOR FAN - RIGHT
3 - MOUNT - RIGHT RADIATOR FAN
4 - CLIPS - RADIATOR FAN LOWER
5 - MOUNT - LEFT RADIATOR FAN
6 - RADIATOR FAN - LEFT

CR1080100306000X

Fig. 1 Electric cooling fan module. Caravan, Voyager, Town & Country

WIRING DIAGRAMS

Refer to **Figs. 6 and 7** when performing diagnostic test procedures.

CLEARING DIAGNOSTIC TROUBLE CODES

Clearing diagnostic trouble codes can be accomplished by following the scan tool manufacturers instructions or by disconnecting the battery ground cable for at least two minutes.

Dakota & Durango

ACCESSING DIAGNOSTIC TROUBLE CODES

These models are equipped with an engine controller which will detect and store a diagnostic trouble code for the cooling fan system. This information may be accessed by using a DRB diagnostic tool, or equivalent.

Obtain DRB diagnostic trouble codes as follows:

1. Connect the DRB to diagnostic connector, located near engine controller, then start engine.
2. **On models equipped with A/C,** turn A/C on and off.
3. **On all models,** shut engine off.
4. Turn ignition switch on, then access DRB Read Fault screen and record all diagnostic trouble codes.
5. If display reads "Radiator Fan Relay," inspect for short or open condition in cooling fan relay control unit; repair as required.

WIRING DIAGRAMS

Refer to wiring diagram, **Figs. 8 through 12** when performing diagnostic test procedures.

CLEARING DIAGNOSTIC TROUBLE CODES

Clearing diagnostic trouble codes can be accomplished by following the scan tool manufacturers instructions or by disconnecting the battery ground cable for at least two minutes.

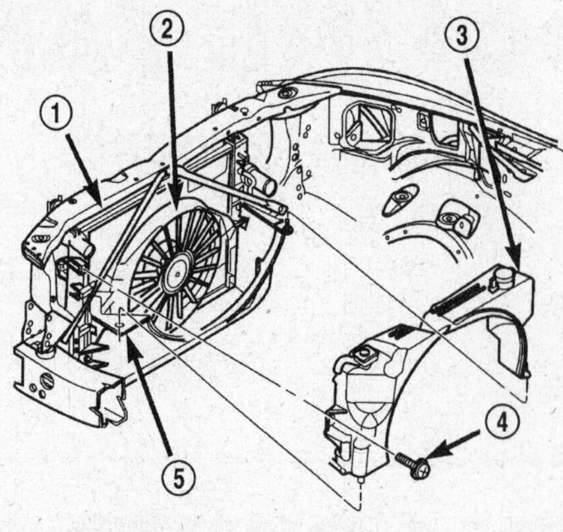

1 – RADIATOR
2 – ELECTRIC COOLING FAN
3 – UPPER SHROUD AND OVERFLOW BOTTLE
4 – SCREW
5 – LOWER SHROUD

CR1080000281000X

Fig. 2 Electric cooling fan module. 2002–03 Durango & 2002–04 Dakota

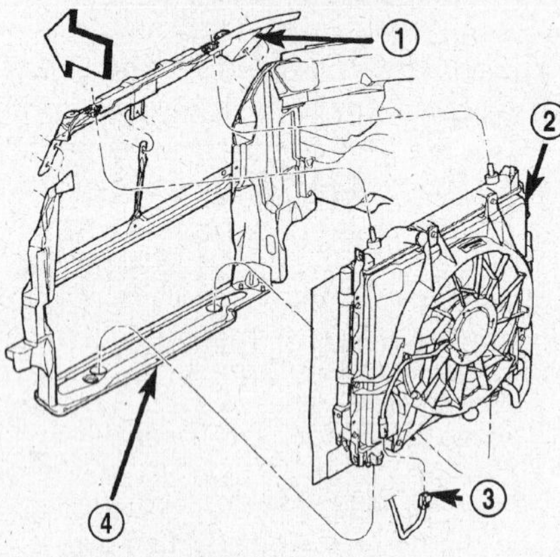

1 – UPPER RADIATOR CROSSMEMBER
2 – COOLING MODULE
3 – RADIATOR FAN CONNECTOR
4 – LOWER RADIATOR CROSSMEMBER

CR1080000284000X

Fig. 4 Electric cooling fan module. PT Cruiser

PT Cruiser

ACCESSING DIAGNOSTIC TROUBLE CODES

These models are equipped with an engine controller which will detect and store a diagnostic trouble code for the cooling fan system. This information may be accessed by using a DRB diagnostic tool, or equivalent.

1. To access DTCs using DRB scan tool proceed as follows:
   a. Connect DRB to data link connector located under dash near steering column.
   b. Turn ignition switch On, then access Read Fault screen.
   c. Record all DTCs and freeze frame information outlined on DRB.

WIRING DIAGRAMS

Refer to wiring diagram, **Figs. 13 through 16** when performing diagnostic test procedures.

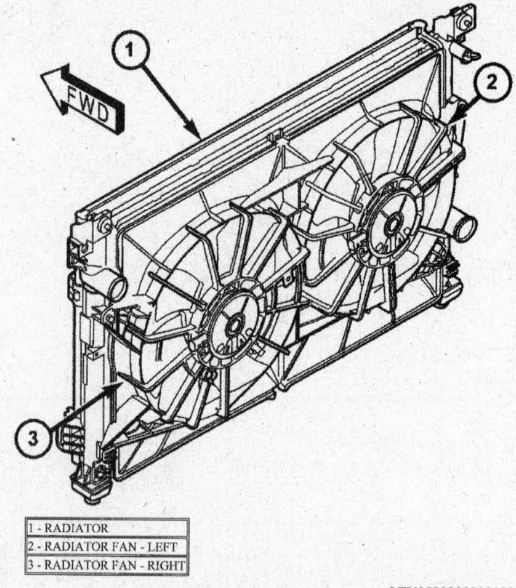

LTV0500000000193

Fig. 3 Electric cooling fan module. Pacifica

CLEARING DIAGNOSTIC TROUBLE CODES

Clearing diagnostic trouble codes can be accomplished by following the scan tool manufacturers instructions.

COMPONENT DIAGNOSIS & TESTING

Electric Fan Motor

1. Disconnect fan motor electrical connector.
2. Connect jumper wire to positive side of fan motor connector.
3. Fan should operate properly; if not, replace fan motor.
4. If fan is noticeably overheated, system voltage may be too high. Inspect charging system as required.

COMPONENT REPLACEMENT

Cooling Fan

CARAVAN, VOYAGER, TOWN & COUNTRY

1. Remove bolts securing hood latch to crossmember, then position latch aside.
2. Remove radiator sight shield, then engine air inlet resonator.
3. Remove hood cable, then prop rod.
4. Remove screw securing coolant recovery bottle to crossmember.
5. Remove bolts securing radiator isolators to crossmember.
6. Remove bolts securing ends of crossmember to radiator closure panel.
7. Remove crossmember from vehicle.
8. Disconnect cooling fans electrical connectors.

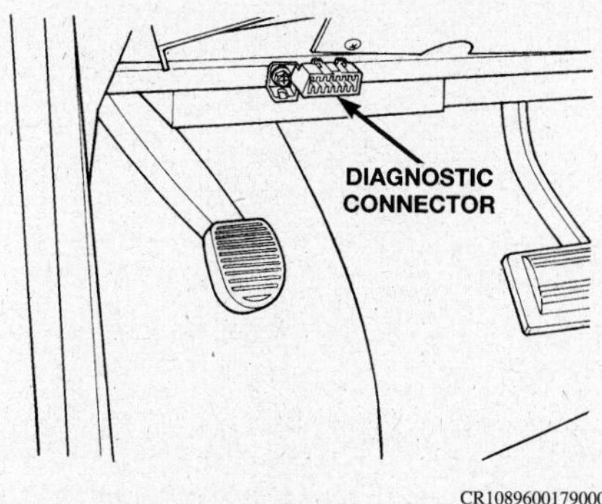

Fig. 5 Diagnostic link connector. Caravan, Voyager, Town & Country

9. Remove cooling fans retaining screws.
10. Remove cooling fans by lifting upward to release from mounts.
11. Reverse procedure to install.

DAKOTA & DURANGO

1. Partially drain cooling system into suitable container.
2. Remove upper radiator hose.
3. Remove fan/viscous fan drive assembly from water pump, using tool Nos. 6958 and adapter pins 8346 or equivalent. Do not remove drive assembly from vehicle at this time.
4. Position fan/fan drive assembly in radiator shroud to remove two shroud mounting screws.
5. Remove radiator shroud and fan drive assembly.
6. Reverse procedure to install.

PT CRUISER

1. Remove battery, then battery tray.
2. Drain cooling system to below upper radiator hose into suitable container.
3. Remove screws securing grille to radiator closure panel.
4. Pull top of grille downward to disengage hooks from fender, then remove grille from vehicle.
5. Mark bolt locations on upper radiator closure panel.
6. Remove radiator closure panel bolts, then closure panel.
7. Disconnect upper radiator hose from radiator.
8. **On models equipped with turbocharger,** remove radiator inlet neck.
9. **On all models,** raise and support vehicle.
10. Disconnect cooling fan electrical connectors.
11. Remove two lower and lefthand side cooling fan screws.
12. Lower vehicle, then remove remaining cooling fan screws.
13. Remove cooling fan from vehicle.
14. Reverse procedure to install.

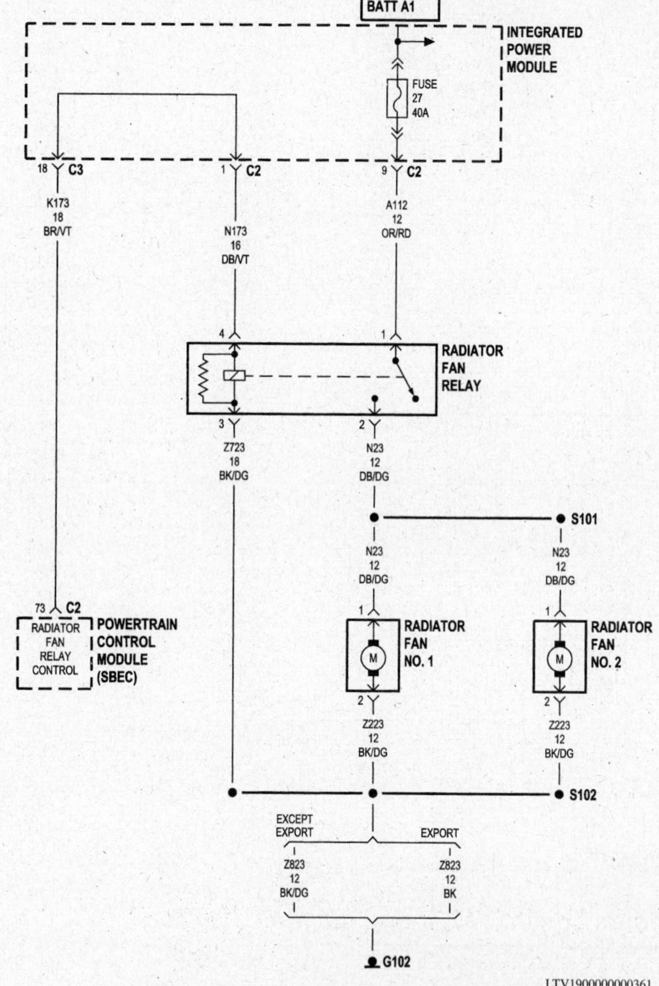

Fig. 6 Electric cooling fan wiring diagram. Caravan, Voyager, Town & Country

SPRINTER

1. Disconnect coolant line from lower radiator shroud.
2. Remove fan blade/viscous fan drive assembly from water pump by turning mounting nut counterclockwise.
3. Remove radiator fan shroud and radiator fan.
4. Reverse procedure to install.

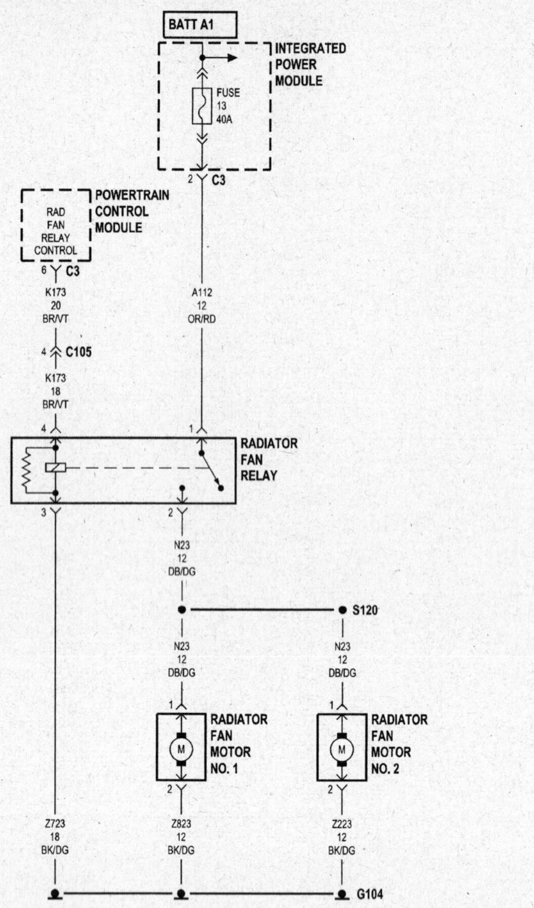

Fig. 7 Electric cooling fan wiring diagram. Pacifica

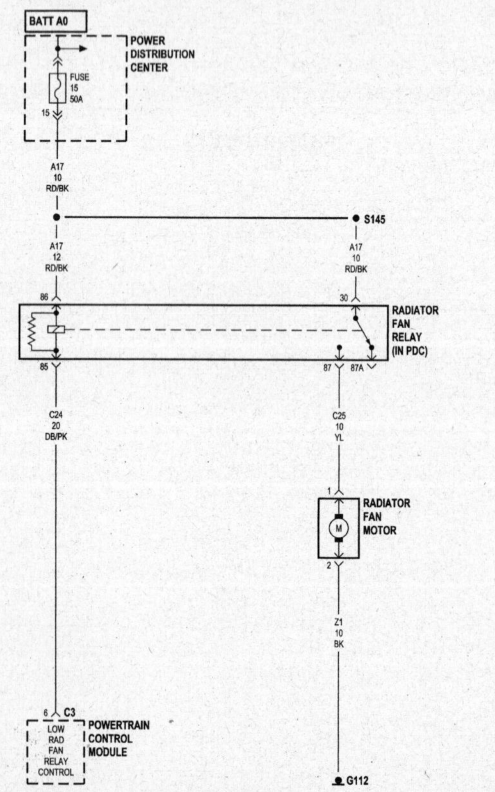

Fig. 9 Electric cooling fan wiring diagram. 2002–04 Dakota w/4.7L engine & 2004 3.7L engine

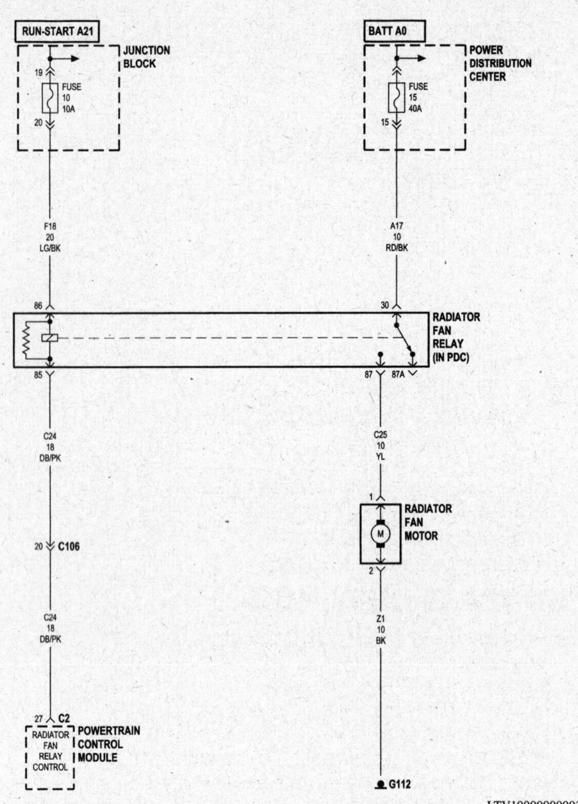

Fig. 8 Electric cooling fan wiring diagram. 2002–03 Dakota w/3.9L & 5.9L engines

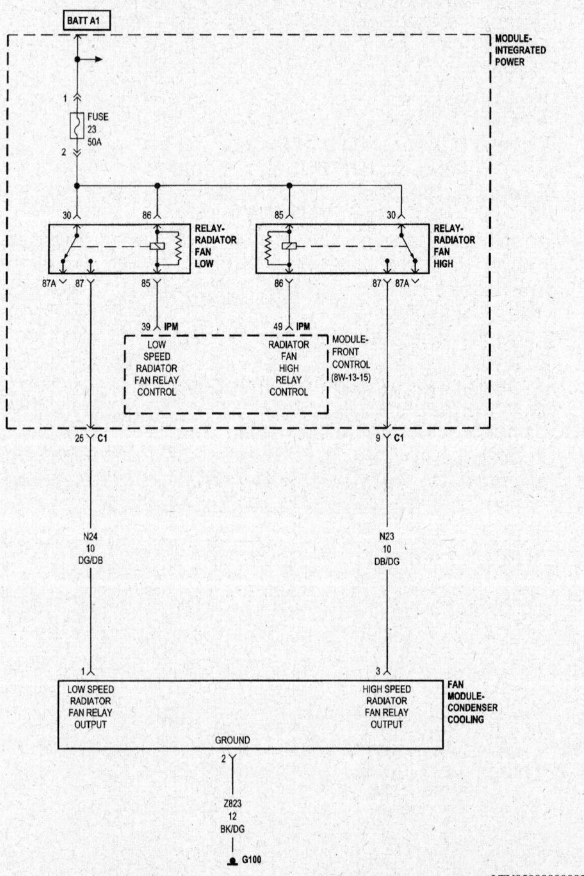

Fig. 10 Electric cooling fan wiring diagram. 2005–06 Dakota w/3.7L & 4.7L engines

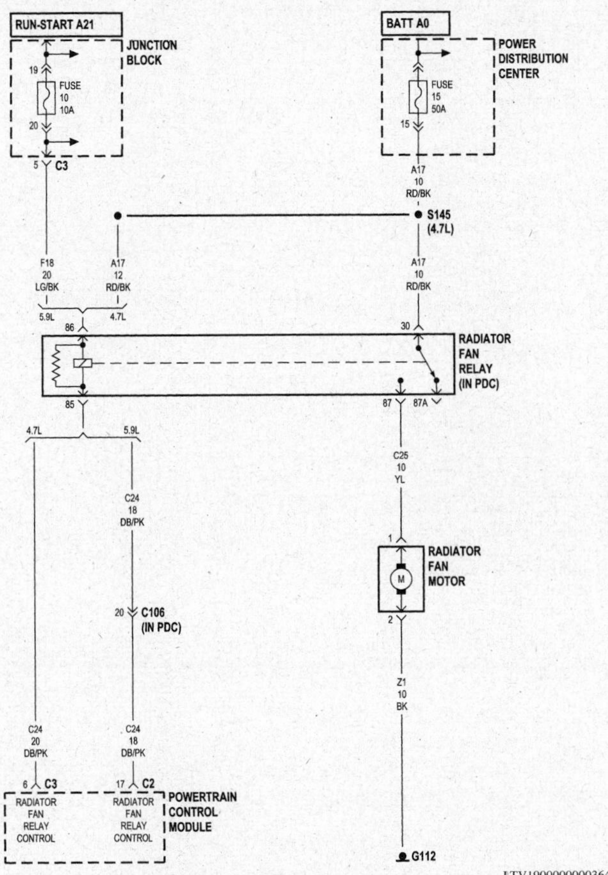

Fig. 11 Electric cooling fan wiring diagram. 2002–04 Durango

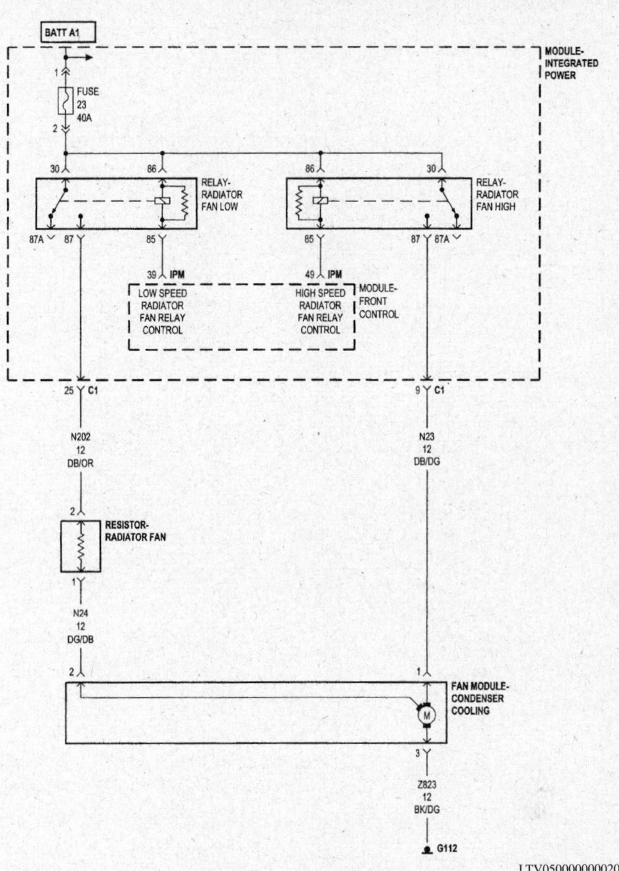

Fig. 12 Cooling fan wiring diagram. 2005–06 Durango

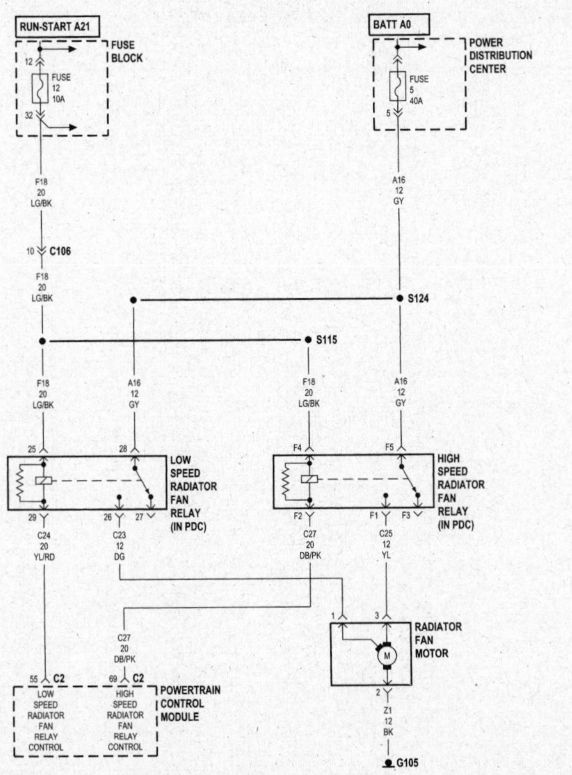

Fig. 13 Electric cooling fan wiring diagram. PT Cruiser less turbocharged engine

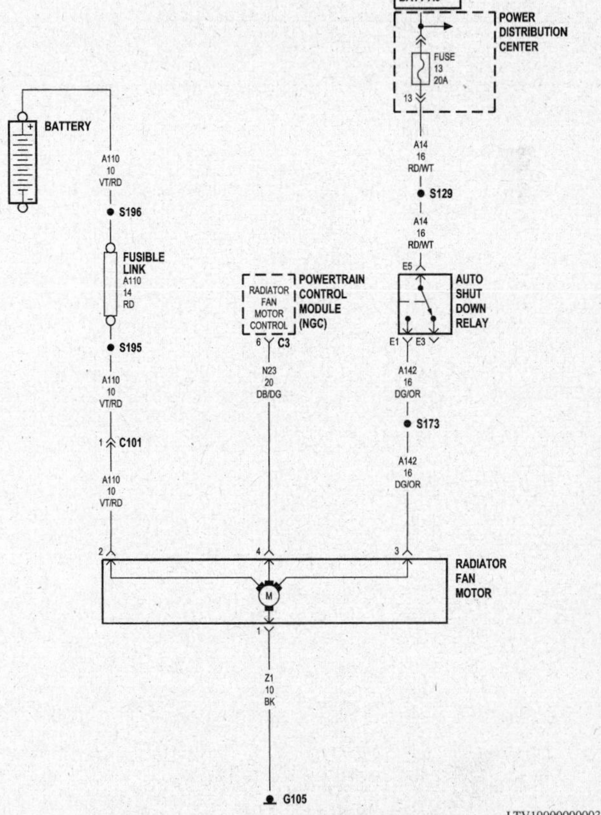

Fig. 14 Electric cooling fan wiring diagram. PT Cruiser w/turbocharged engine

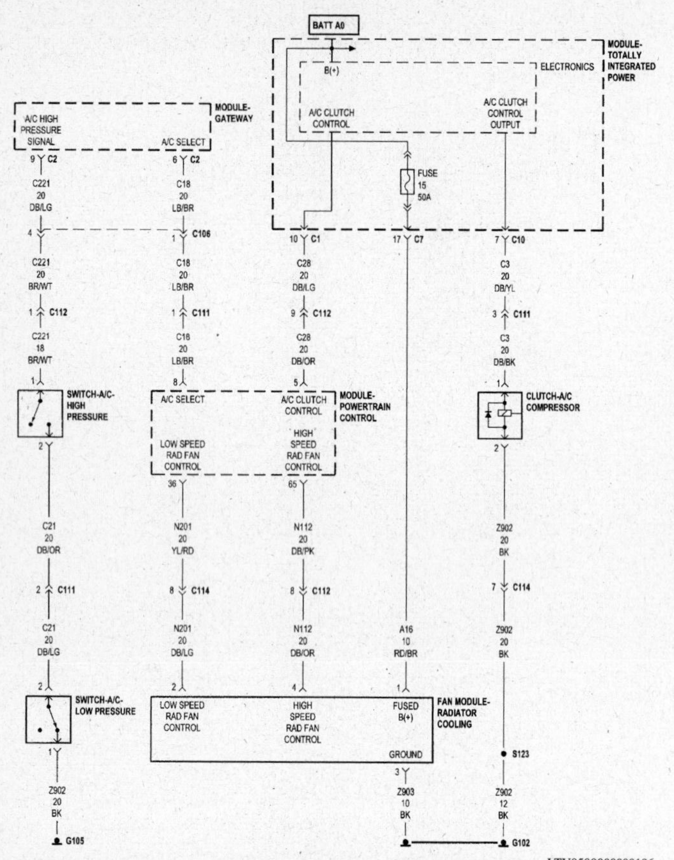

Fig. 15 Electric cooling fan wiring diagram. PT Cruiser 1.6L engine

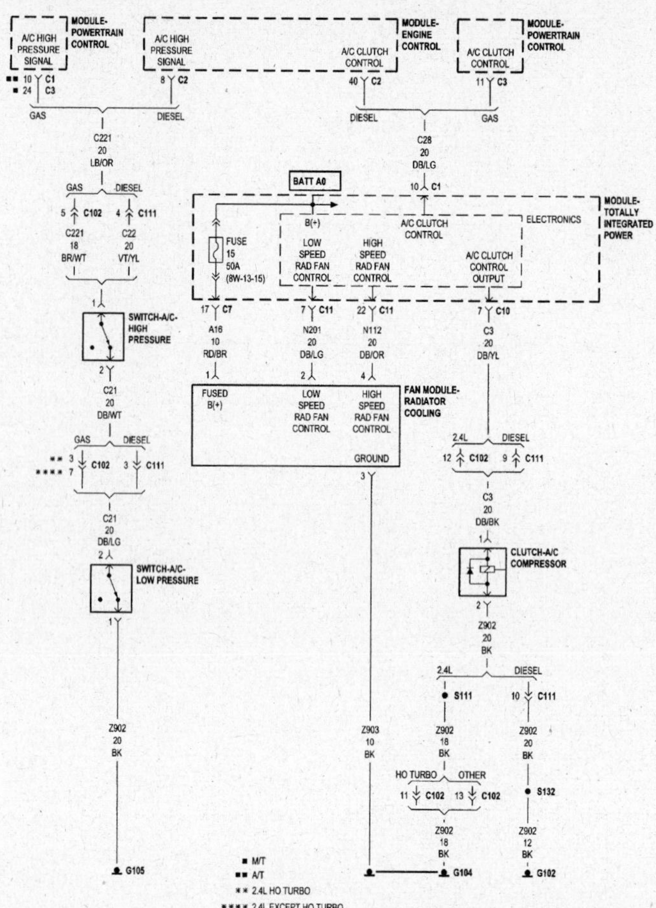

Fig. 16 Electric cooling fan wiring diagram. PT Cruiser except 1.6L engine

Electric Cooling Fans, Jeep

NOTE: "Electrical Symbol & Wire Color Code Identification" Located In The Front Of This Manual May Be Used As An Aid When Using Wiring Circuits Found In This Section.

NOTE: Refer To "Computer Relearn Procedures" Located In The Front Of This Manual When Battery Power To The Computer Has Been Interrupted.

INDEX

PRECAUTIONS

Battery Ground Cable

Prior to service, disconnect battery ground cable and isolate as required.

DESCRIPTION

Commander & Grand Cherokee

On models equipped with 3.7L or 4.0L engine, an electric fan is standard. On models equipped with 4.7L engine, a hybrid designed system is used. The hybrid fan system consists of a low speed viscous driven mechanical fan and a electrical fan. On models equipped with 5.7L engine, a hydraulic cooling fan is used. The power steering pump supplies the hydraulic fluid and pressure to rotate the cooling fan blade, while the electrical part of the fan is controlled by the FCM, **Figs. 1 and 2.**

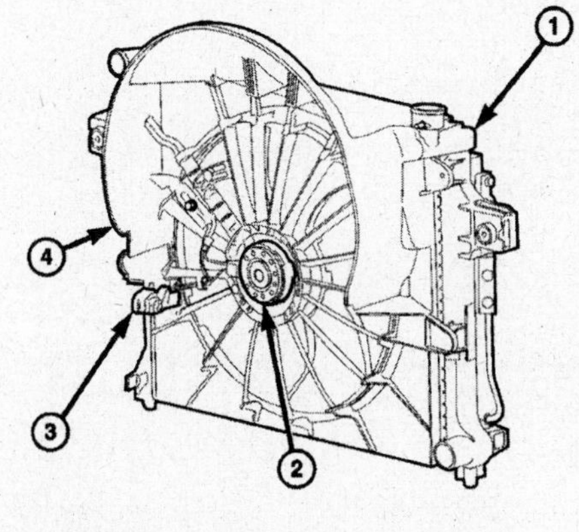

1 - RADIATOR
2 - ELECTRIC COOLING FAN MOTOR
3 - COOLING FAN ELECTRICAL CONNECTOR
4 - FAN SHROUD

LTV0500000000190

Fig. 1 Cooling fan module. Commander & Grand Cherokee w/3.7L engine

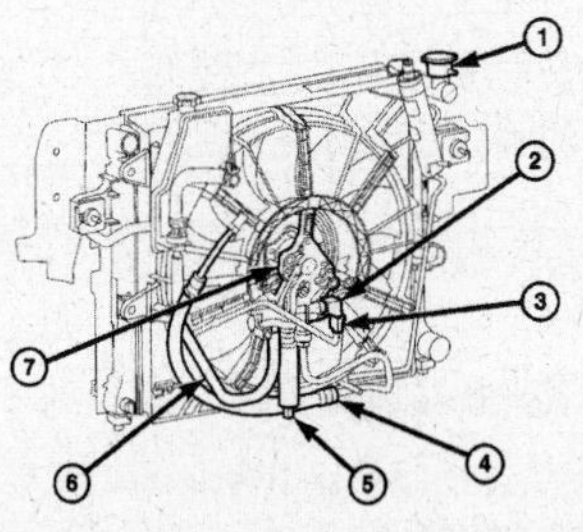

1 - RADIATOR
2 - HYDRAULIC FAN MOTOR SOLENOID
3 - ELECTRICAL CONNECTOR
4 - HIGH PRESSURE LINE FROM HYDRAULIC FAN MOTOR TO STEERING GEAR
5 - HIGH PRESSURE LINE
6 - RETURN LINE
7 - FAN MOTOR

LTV0500000000191

Fig. 2 Cooling fan module. Commander & Grand Cherokee w/5.7L engine

Liberty

The electric cooling fan is controlled by the PCM through the cooling fan relay. The PCM regulates fan operation based on input from the ECT sensor, battery temperature sensor, A/C select switch and vehicle speed.

On models less A/C, the relay is energized when the coolant temperature is above 176°F or battery temperature sensor is above 10°F. The relay will de-energize when coolant temperature drops below 180°F or battery temperature sensor drops below 16°F.

On models with A/C, the cooling fan will be engaged when the A/C system is activated. The relay is also energized when A/C is selected and coolant temperature is above 203°F and battery temperature sensor is above 106°F. The relay will de-energize when A/C is selected and coolant temperature is below 198°F or battery temperature is below 100°F, **Fig. 3.**

Wrangler

On models equipped with 2.4L or 2.5L engine, the electric cooling fan is standard and is integral to the fan shroud. The electric fan is controlled by the electronic control module ECM. The cooling fan is not serviceable. Any failure of the fan blade, electric motor or fan shroud requires replacement of the fan module. Models equipped with 4.0L engine, refer to "Variable Speed Fans" section.

SYSTEM DIAGNOSIS & TESTING

Cooling Fan & Circuit

ACCESSING DIAGNOSTIC TROUBLE CODES

1. Connect a DRB or equivalent scan tool to data link connector (DLC).
2. Start engine, turn air conditioning on and off, then shut engine off.
3. Turn ignition switch to On position and access Read Diagnostic Trouble Code screen.
4. Record all diagnostic trouble code messages.
5. If display reads "Radiator Fan Relay," proceed to "Diagnostic Trouble Code Interpretation."

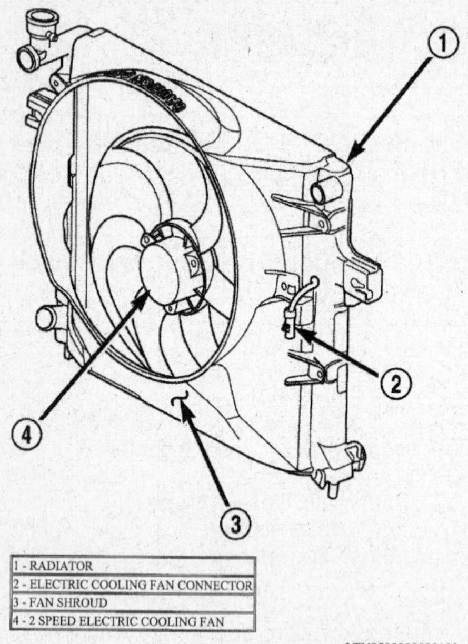

Fig. 3 Electric cooling fan module. Liberty

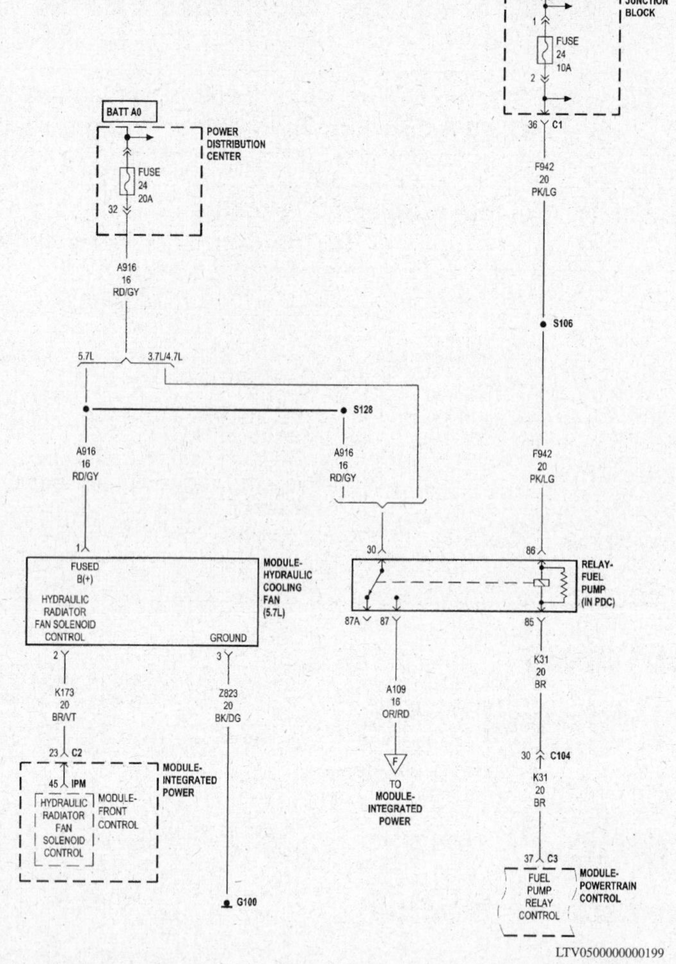

Fig. 4 Cooling fan wiring diagram. Commander

DIAGNOSTIC TROUBLE CODE INTERPRETATION

With scan tool connected to Diagnostic Link Connector (DCL), locate correct test flow chart.

WIRING DIAGRAMS

Refer to **Figs. 4 through 8** when troubleshooting these systems.

CLEARING DIAGNOSTIC TROUBLE CODES

Follow scan tool manufacturers instructions to access code clearing function and menu or disconnect vehicle battery for at least two minutes.

COMPONENT REPLACEMENT

Cooling Fan

COMMANDER

3.7L & 4.7L ENGINES

1. Disconnect cooling electrical connector.
2. Remove shroud mounting bolts
3. Remove fan and shroud from vehicle.
4. Reverse procedure to install.

5.7L & 6.1L ENGINES

1. Raise and support vehicle.
2. Drain cooling system into suitable container.
3. Disconnect two high pressure lines at hydraulic fan drive.
4. Disconnect low pressure line at hydraulic fan drive.
5. Remove two lower fan shroud mounting bolts.
6. Lower vehicle.
7. Disconnect fan control solenoid electrical connector.
8. Disconnect upper radiator hose at radiator and position aside.
9. Disconnect power steering gear outlet hose and return hose at cooler.
10. Remove fan shroud upper mounting bolts.
11. Remove fan drive and shroud from vehicle.
12. Reverse procedure to install.

GRAND CHEROKEE

4.0L ENGINE

1. Remove fan blade/viscous fan drive mounting nut from water pump by turning counterclockwise. Do not remove viscous fan drive at this time.
2. Remove fan shroud to upper crossmember attaching nuts.
3. Remove fan shroud, fan blade/viscous fan drive as an assembly.
4. Remove four fan blade to viscous fan drive mounting bolts.
5. Reverse procedure to install.

4.7L ENGINE

2002-04

Refer to "Commander, 5.7L Engine" for replacement procedures.

2005-06

Refer to "Commander, 3.7 & 4.7L Engines" for replacement procedure.

5.7L & 6.1L ENGINES

Refer to "Commander, 5.7L Engine" for replacement procedures.

LIBERTY

1. Disconnect cooling fan electrical connector.
2. Remove cooling fan electrical connector from fan shroud.
3. Remove two fan shroud bolts, then fan shroud and electric cooling fan assembly.
4. Reverse procedure to install.

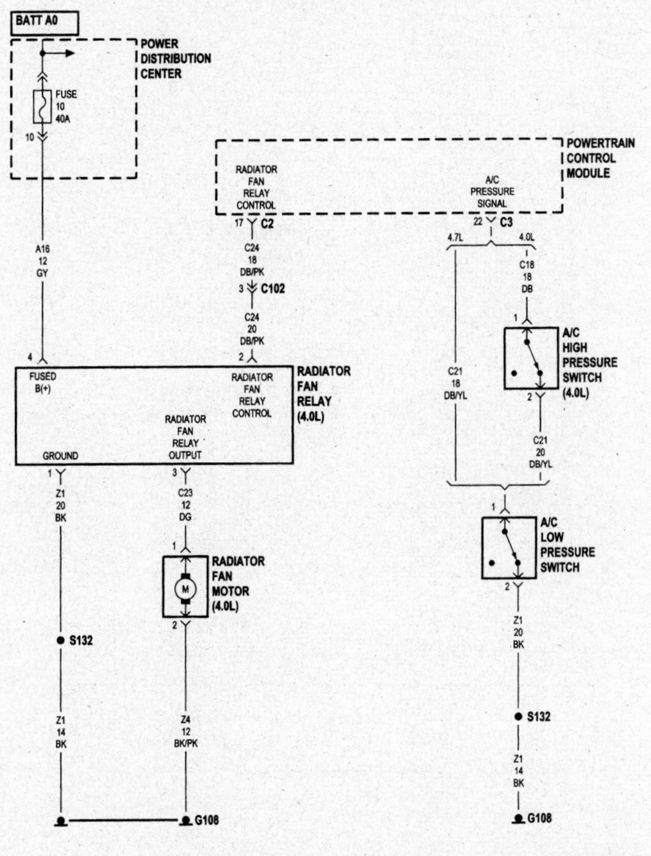

Fig. 5 Electric cooling fan wiring diagram. 2002–04 Grand Cherokee

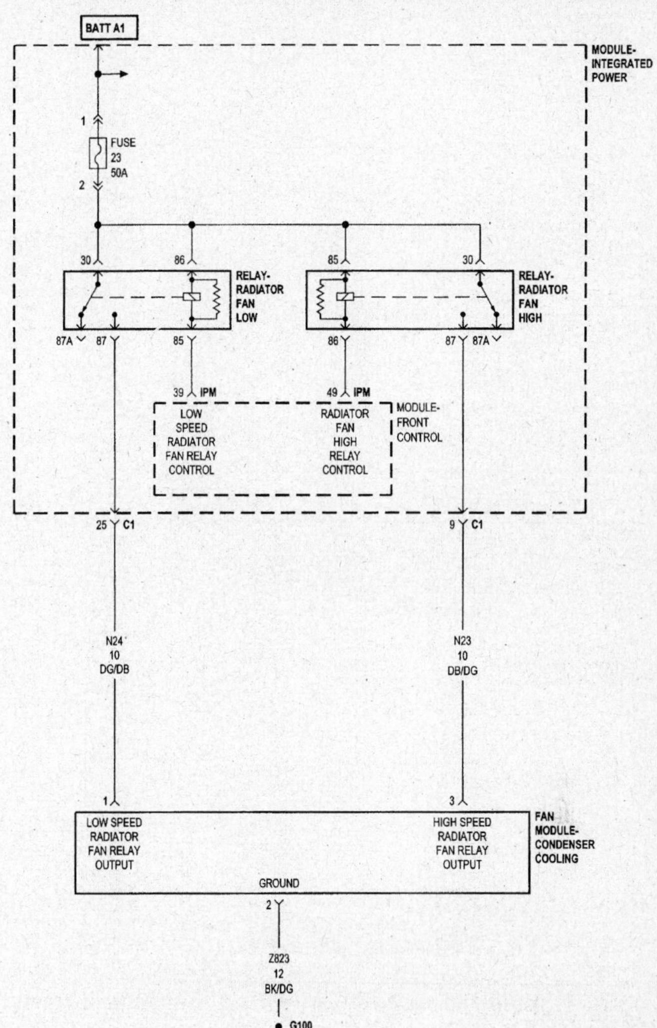

Fig. 6 Cooling fan wiring diagram. 2005–06 Grand Cherokee

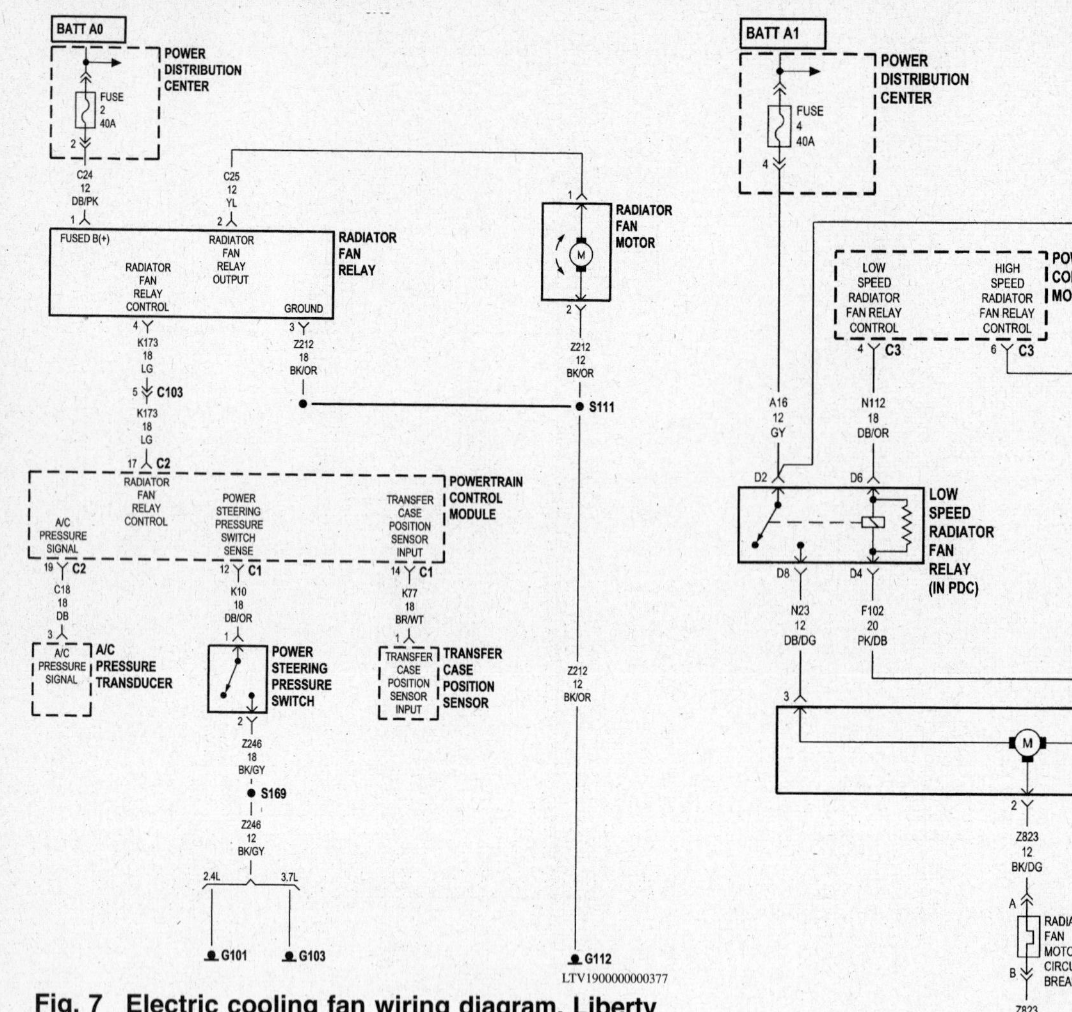

Fig. 7 Electric cooling fan wiring diagram. Liberty

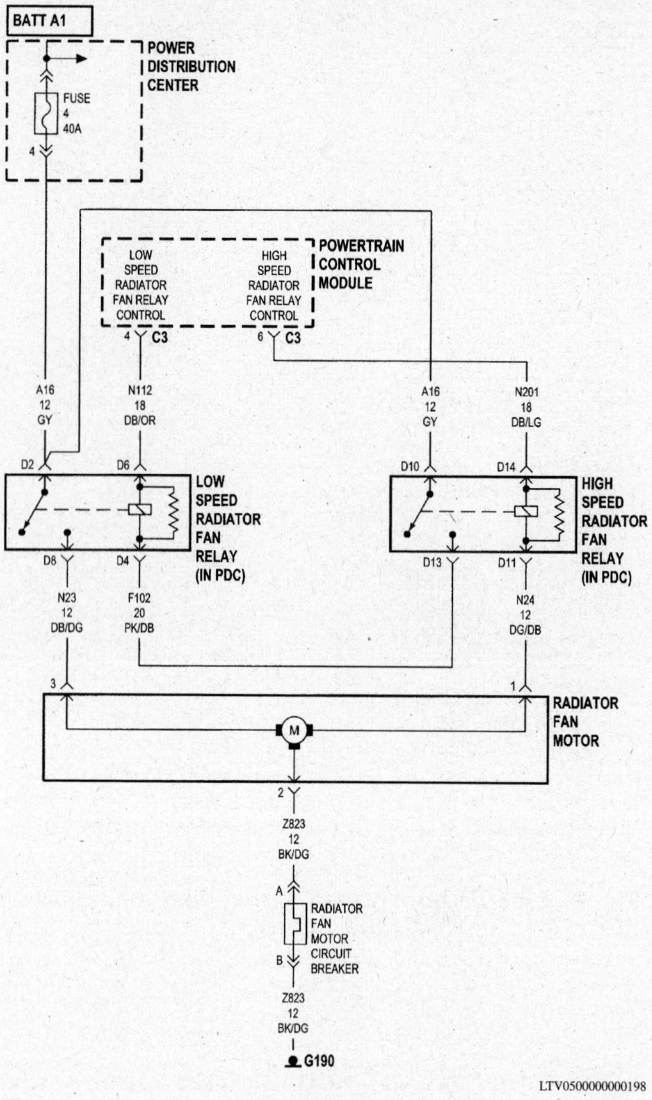

BATT A1
POWER DISTRIBUTION CENTER
FUSE 4 40A
LOW SPEED RADIATOR FAN RELAY CONTROL
HIGH SPEED RADIATOR FAN RELAY CONTROL
POWERTRAIN CONTROL MODULE
4 C3
6 C3
A16 12 GY
N112 18 DB/OR
A16 12 GY
N201 18 DB/LG
D2
D6
D10
D14
LOW SPEED RADIATOR FAN RELAY (IN PDC)
HIGH SPEED RADIATOR FAN RELAY (IN PDC)
D8
D4
D13
D11
N23 12 DB/DG
F102 20 PK/DB
N24 12 DG/DB
RADIATOR FAN MOTOR
Z823 12 BK/DG
RADIATOR FAN MOTOR CIRCUIT BREAKER
Z823 12 BK/DG
G190
LTV0500000000198

Fig. 8 Cooling fan wiring diagram. Wrangler w/2.4L engine

Variable Speed Fans

INDEX

PRECAUTIONS

Do not operate engine until fan has been inspected for cracks and/or separations. If a fan blade is found to be bent or damaged in any way, do not attempt to repair or reuse damaged part. Proper balance is essential in fan assembly operation. Balance cannot be assured once a fan assembly has been found to be bent or damaged and failure may occur during operation, creating an extremely dangerous condition. Always replace a damaged fan assembly.

When removing fan assembly, do not place fan horizontally. Silicone oil may seep out of fluid coupling and damage bearing.

Before replacing fan or fan clutch, ensure replacement is of correct rotation. Some serpentine drive systems require fan and clutch of opposite rotation.

DESCRIPTION

The fan drive clutch, **Figs. 1 through 3**, is a fluid coupling containing silicone oil. Fan speed is regulated by the torque-carrying capacity of the silicone oil. The more silicone oil in the coupling, the greater the fan speed, and the less silicone oil, the slower the fan speed.

The fan drive clutch uses a heat-sensitive, coiled bimetallic spring connected to an opening plate. This unit causes the fan speed to increase with a rise in temperature and to decrease as temperature decreases.

COMPONENT REPLACEMENT

Ram Pick-Up

3.7L, 4.7L & 5.7L ENGINES

1. Remove coolant overflow bottle from fan shroud and position aside. Do Not disconnect hoses or drain coolant from bottle.
2. Remove fan blade/viscous fan drive assembly from water pump by turning mounting nut counterclockwise.
3. Remove fan shroud to radiator mounting bolts. Do Not unbolt fan blade assembly from viscous fan drive at this time.
4. Pull lower shroud mounts out of radiator tank clips.

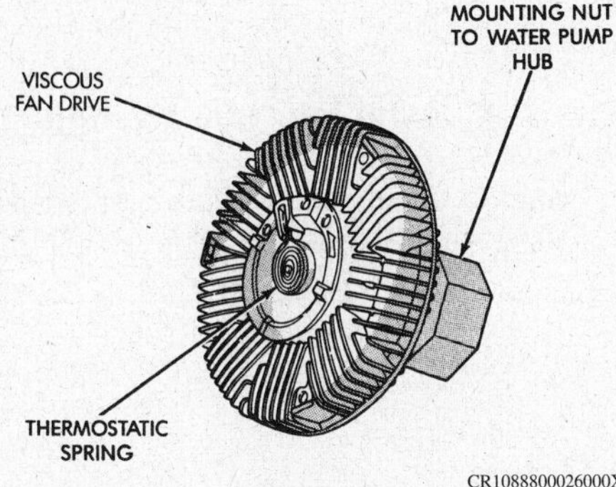

Fig. 1 Fan drive clutch assembly

5. Remove fan shroud and fan blade/viscous fan drive assembly as a complete unit from vehicle.
6. Reverse procedure to install.

8.3L ENGINE

1. Drain cooling system into suitable container.
2. Remove air intake tube between intake manifold and air filter assembly.
3. Unclip A/C lines from radiator fan shroud, and position aside.
4. Remove coolant overflow bottle and container tube.
5. Remove upper radiator hose from radiator and position aside.
6. Raise and support vehicle.
7. Disconnect high and low pressure hydraulic hoses at hydraulic fan motor.
8. Disconnect solenoid electrical connector, then lower vehicle.
9. Remove four fan shroud retaining bolts.
10. Remove fan motor and shroud assembly from vehicle.
11. Reverse procedure to install.

TROUBLESHOOTING

Fan Clutch Noise

Fan clutch noise can sometimes be noticed when clutch is engaged for maximum cooling. Clutch noise is also noticeable within the first few minutes after starting engine while clutch is redistributing the silicone fluid back to its normal, disengaged operating condition after settling for long periods of time (overnight). However, continuous fan noise or an excessive roar indicates the clutch assembly is locked-up due

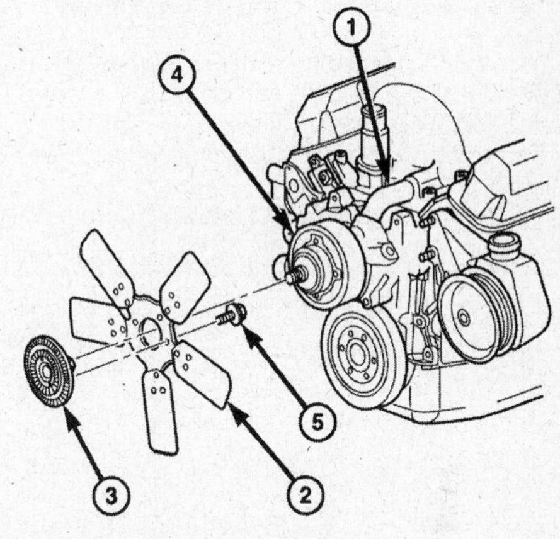

Fig. 2 Cooling fan. Ram Pick-Up, 2005–06 Dakota & 2004–06 Durango

to internal failure. This condition can be inspected by attempting to manually rotate fan. If fan cannot be rotated manually or there is a rough, abrasive feel as fan is rotated, the clutch should be replaced.

Fan Looseness

Lateral movement can be observed at the fan blade tip under various temperature conditions because of the type bearing used. This movement should not exceed ¼ inch (6.5 mm) as measured at the fan tip. If this lateral movement does not exceed specifications, there is no cause for replacement.

Clutch Fluid Leak

Small fluid leaks do not generally affect the operation of the unit. If the leaks appear to be excessive, engine overheating may occur. If the fan is removed, do not place it in a horizontal position as the silicone fluid may drain into the bearing assembly and contaminate the lubricant. Inspect for clutch and fan free wheeling by attempting to rotate fan and clutch assembly by hand five times. If no drag is felt, replace clutch.

Fan Blade Inspection

Place fan on flat surface with leading edge facing down. If there is a clearance between fan blade touching surface and opposite blade of more than .090 inch (2 mm), replace fan.

COMPONENT DIAGNOSIS & TESTING

Fan Drive Clutch Test

Do not operate the engine until the fan has been inspected for possible cracks and separations.

1. Drill a 1/8 inch diameter hole in top center of fan shroud.
2. Insert thermometer through hole in shroud ensuring adequate clearance from fan blades using a dial thermometer with a range of 0–220°F.
3. Connect a tachometer and ignition timing light to be used as a strobe light.
4. Block air flow through radiator using a sheet of plastic, then ensure A/C is turned off.
5. Start engine and run at 2400 RPM for 10 minutes until temperature indicated on dial thermometer is 190°F.
6. Fan drive engagement should occur as follows:
   a. 4.0L engines 165–185°F.
   b. 4.7L engine 185–195°F.
   c. 5.7L and 8.3L engines 199–212°F.
   d. 3.9L and 5.9L gas engines 175°F.
   e. 5.9L diesel engine 160–179°F.
   f. 8.0L engine 190–205°F.
7. When fan drive engagement is verified, remove plastic sheet.
8. Fan drive should start to disengage between 135–175°F, if not replace fan drive unit.

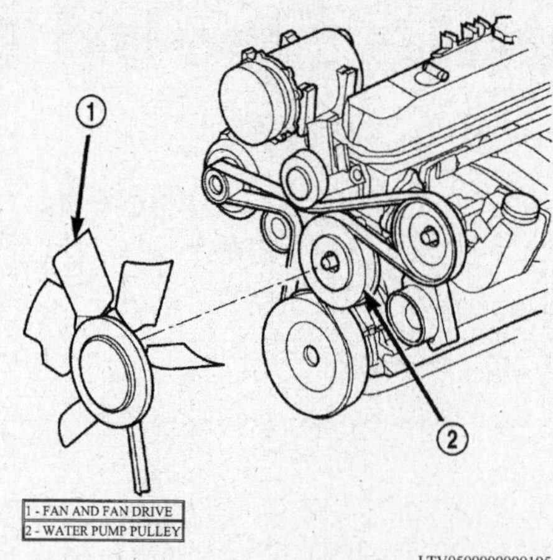

Fig. 3 Cooling fan. 4.0L Wrangler

STARTER MOTORS

TABLE OF CONTENTS

Nippondenso Starters

NOTE: On Air Bag Equipped Models, Refer To "Air Bag System Precautions" Located In The Front Of This Manual For System Disarming & Arming Procedures.

NOTE: Refer To "Computer Relearn Procedures" Located In The Front Of This Manual When Battery Power To The Computer Has Been Interrupted.

INDEX

APPLICATION CHART

Year	Engine Liter	Starter		
		Make	ID. No.	Type
CARAVAN, VOYAGER & TOWN & COUNTRY				
2002–06	2.4L	Nippondenso	—	Gear Reduction
	3.3L	Nippondenso	—	Gear Reduction
	3.8L	Nippondenso	—	Gear Reduction
COMMANDER				
2006	3.7L, 4.7L & 5.7L	Nippondenso	—	Gear Reduction
DAKOTA				
2002–03	3.9L & 5.9L	Nippondenso	56027702	Gear Reduction
2002–06	3.7L & 4.7L	Nippondenso①	①	Gear Reduction
DURANGO				
2002–03	5.9L	Nippondenso	56027702	Gear Reduction
2002–06	3.7L, 4.7L & 5.7L	Nippondenso	56028715	Gear Reduction
1500 FULL SIZE TRUCKS				
2002–06	3.7L, 4.7L, 5.7L & 5.9L	Nippondenso	56028715	Gear Reduction
2002–06	5.9L Diesel	Nippondenso	4741012	Conventional
2002–03	8.0L	Nippondenso	56027703AD	Gear Reduction
2004–06	8.3L	Nippondenso	—	Offset Gear Reduction
2500 & 3500 FULL SIZE TRUCKS				
2002	5.9L	Nippondenso	56027702	Gear Reduction
	5.9L Diesel	Nippondenso	4741012	Gear Reduction
	8.0L	Nippondenso	56027703	Gear Reduction
2003–06	5.7L	Nippondenso	56028715	Gear Reduction
	5.9L Diesel	Nippondenso	4741012	Gear Reduction
	8.0L	Nippondenso	56027703	Gear Reduction

Continued

APPLICATION CHART—Continued

Year	Engine Liter	Starter		
		Make	ID. No.	Type
FULL SIZE VAN				
2002–03	3.9L, 5.2L & 5.9L	Nippondenso	56027702	Gear Reduction
PACIFICA				
2004–06	3.5L & 3.8L	Nippondenso	—	Gear Reduction
PT CRUISER				
2002–06	2.4L	Nippondenso	—	Gear Reduction

① — 56027702 (Manual transmission), 56028715 (Automatic transmission)

PRECAUTIONS

Air Bag Systems

Refer to "Air Bag System Precautions" in the front of this manual for system disarming and arming procedures.

Battery Ground Cable

Prior to service disconnect battery ground cable and isolate as required.

DESCRIPTION

The Nippondenso starters are reduction gear field coil units; Bosch permanent magnet reduction gear starters contain a planetary gear train which transmits power between the starter motor and its pinion shaft.

TROUBLESHOOTING

Refer to **Figs. 1 and 2** for troubleshooting procedure and system components.

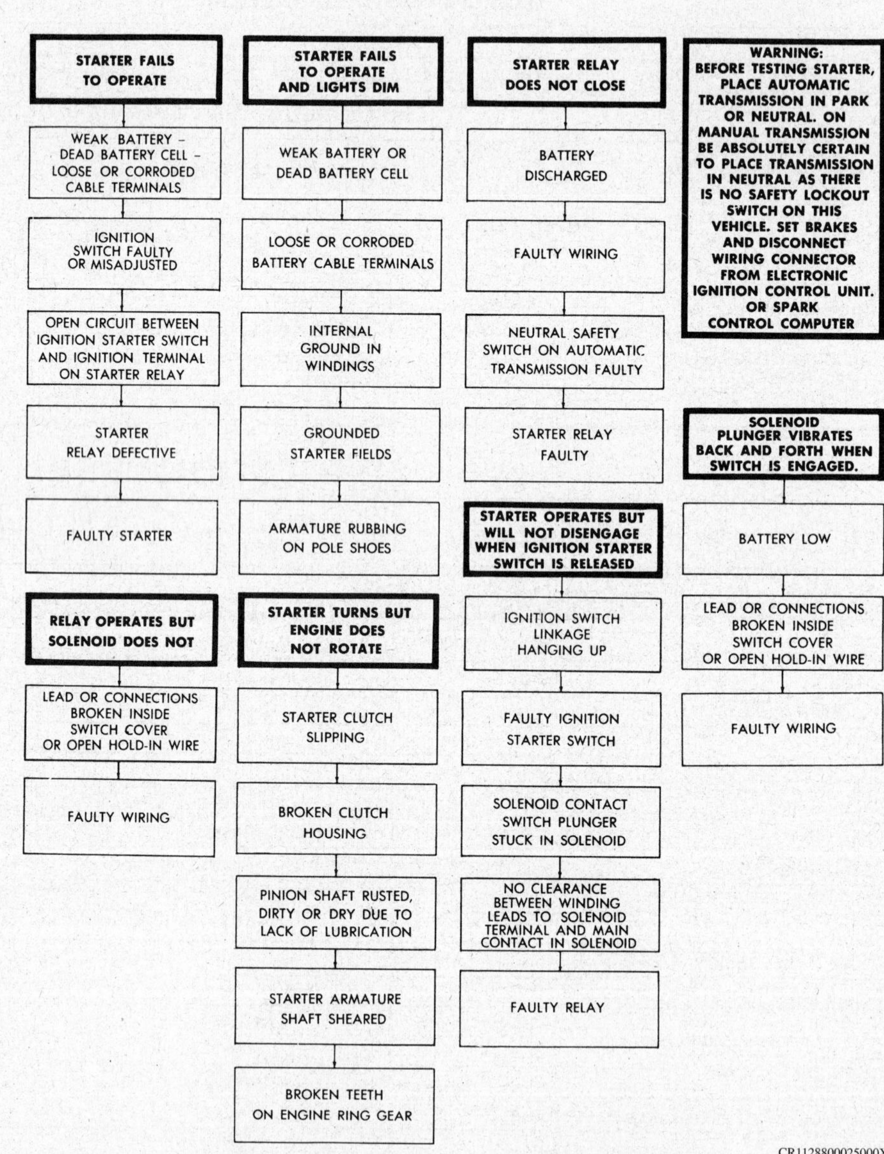

Fig. 1 Starter motor troubleshooting

DIAGNOSIS & TESTING

When performing cranking tests on models with diesel engines, ensure the fuel solenoid has been disabled.

Starter Feed Circuit

LOAD TESTS

1. Disable ignition system on gasoline engines or fuel system on diesel engines.
2. Connect volt/ampere tester to battery terminals. Refer to operating instructions provided with tester being used.
3. Verify that all lights and accessories are Off and transmission shift selector is in Park for automatic transmissions/transaxles or Neutral for manual transmissions/transaxles, then set parking brake.
4. Hold ignition switch in Start position. Observe tester.
   a. If voltage reads above 9.6 volts and amperage draw reads above 250 amps, proceed to starter feed circuit resistance test.
   b. If voltage reads 12.4 volts or greater and amperage reads 0–10 amps, proceed to starter control circuit test.
   c. If starter motor turns engine freely at times, but starting system is still suspected, engage starter several times while observing tester. A starting system that has a problem

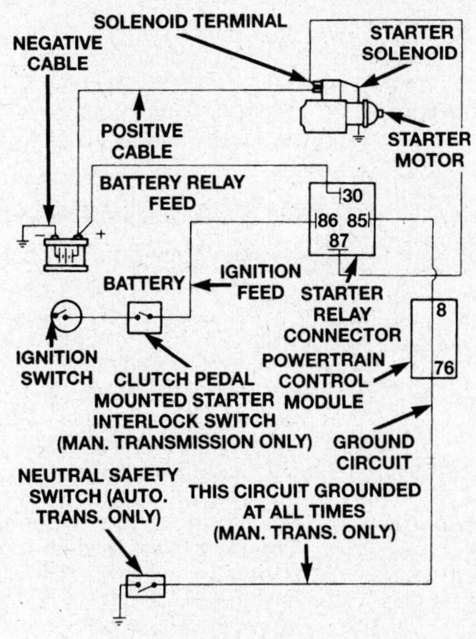

Fig. 2 Starting system components

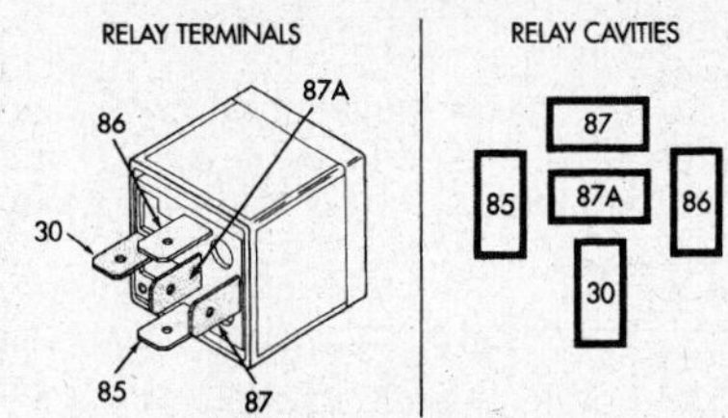

TERMINAL LEGEND	
NUMBER	IDENTIFICATION
30	COMMON FEED
85	COIL GROUND
86	COIL BATTERY
87	NORMALLY OPEN
87A	NORMALLY CLOSED

CR1120000351000X

Fig. 3 Starter relay terminal identification. Full Size Pickup, PT Cruiser, Caravan, Voyager, Town & Country & 2002–03 Dakota & Durango

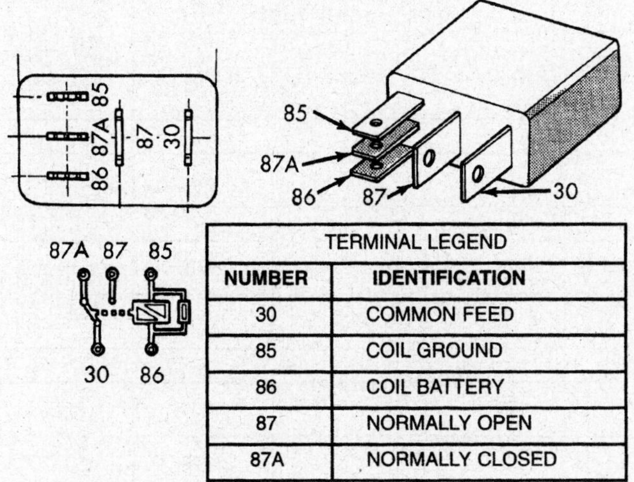

TERMINAL LEGEND	
NUMBER	IDENTIFICATION
30	COMMON FEED
85	COIL GROUND
86	COIL BATTERY
87	NORMALLY OPEN
87A	NORMALLY CLOSED

CR1120000352000X

Fig. 4 Starter relay terminal identification. Full Size Van

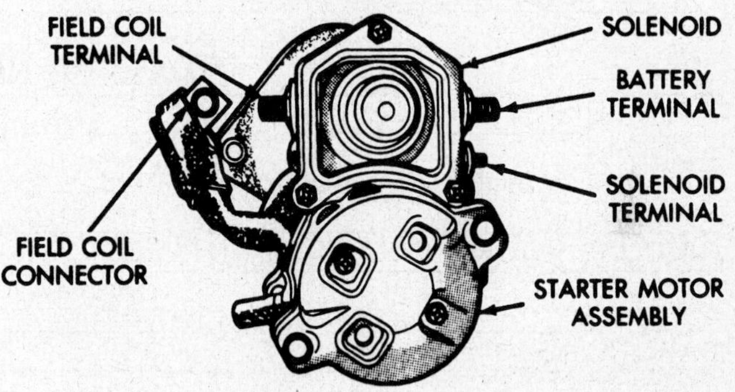

Fig. 5 Nippondenso starter solenoid terminal identification

should fail while performing this procedure.

5. After starting system repairs have been completed, verify battery state of charge, disconnect all testing equipment and connect distributor.

RESISTANCE TESTS

The following test will require a voltmeter accurate to 1⁄10 volt.

1. Disable ignition system on gasoline engines or fuel system on diesel engines.
2. With all wiring harness and components connected properly, perform the following:
   a. Connect positive lead of voltmeter to battery ground post, and negative lead to battery ground cable clamp. Rotate and hold ignition switch in Start position. Observe voltmeter. If voltage is not detected, correct poor contact between cable clamp and post.
   b. Connect positive lead of voltmeter to battery positive post, and negative lead to battery cable positive clamp. Rotate and hold ignition switch in Start position. Observe voltmeter. If voltage is not detected, correct poor contact between cable clamp and post.
   c. Connect positive lead of voltmeter to battery ground terminal, and negative led to engine block near battery cable attaching point.
3. Rotate and hold ignition switch in Start position. If voltage reads above .2 volt, correct poor contact at ground cable attaching point. If reading is still above .2 volt, replace ground cable.
4. Remove starter heat shield (if equipped), then perform the following:
   a. Connect positive voltmeter lead to starter motor housing and negative lead to battery ground terminal. Rotate and hold ignition switch in Start position. If voltage reads above .2 volt, correct poor starter to engine ground.
   b. Connect positive voltmeter lead to positive battery terminal and negative lead to battery cable terminal on starter solenoid. Rotate and hold ignition switch in Start position. If voltage reads above .2 volt, correct poor contact at battery cable to solenoid connection. If reading is still above .2 volt, replace positive battery cable.
5. If resistance tests detect no feed circuit failures, remove starter motor and proceed to "Starter Solenoid Bench Test."

Starter Control Circuit Tests

The starter control circuit consists of a starter solenoid, starter relay, ignition switch and clutch pedal interlock switch (manual transmission) or neutral safety switch (automatic transmission).

Disable ignition system on gasoline engines or fuel system on diesel engines prior to performing test procedures.

SOLENOID TEST

1. Connect heavy jumper wire to starter relay between battery and solenoid terminals. If engine cranks, perform starter relay test.
2. If engine does not crank or solenoid chatters, inspect wiring and connectors from relay to starter for loose connections or corroded terminals.
3. Repeat test, if engine still does not crank properly, repair or replace starter as required.

STARTER RELAY TEST

Refer to **Figs. 3 and 4** when inspecting starter relays.

1. Remove starter relay from relay center.
2. A de-energized relay should have continuity between terminals 87A and 30, and no continuity between terminals 87 and 30. If relay inspection is satisfactory, go to step 3. If not, replace relay.
3. Resistance between terminals 85 and 86 should be 70–80 ohms. If satisfactory go to step 4. If not, replace relay.
4. Apply battery voltage to terminal 86 and ground lead to terminal 85, relay should click. Test for continuity between terminals 30 and 87, and no continuity between terminals 87A and 30. If not, replace relay.

CLUTCH PEDAL SWITCH

The clutch pedal switch is a normally open type switch.

1. Locate and disconnect clutch pedal switch connector.
2. Inspect circuit through switch with pedal released, there should be no continuity.
3. With continuity tester still attached, push clutch pedal to floor, tester should show full continuity.
4. Tester should not show continuity until pedal is fully depressed, replace switch if it fails any test.

Starter Solenoid Bench Test

1. Remove starter assembly from vehicle.
2. Disconnect field coil wire from field coil terminal, **Fig. 5.**
3. Inspect for continuity between solenoid terminal and field coil terminal. Continuity should exist.
4. Inspect for continuity between solenoid terminal and solenoid housing. Continuity should exist.
5. If there is no continuity in either step 3 or 4, solenoid has an open circuit and must be replaced.

STARTER SPECIFICATIONS

Year	Starter				Free Speed Test			Cranking Amp Draw Test③
	Make	ID. No.	Type	Power Rating, Kw	Amps①	Volts	RPM②	
CARAVAN, TOWN & COUNTRY & VOYAGER								
2002–06	Nippondenso	—	Gear Reduction	1.2	73	11	3401	150–200
DAKOTA & DURANGO								
2002–03④	Nippondenso	56027702AC	Gear Reduction	1.4	73	7.5	3601	125–250
2002–06⑤	Nippondenso	56028715	Gear Reduction	1.4	73	7.5	3601	125–250
FULL SIZE TRUCKS & VANS								
2002–06	Nippondenso	56027702/03	Gear Reduction	1.4	73	11	3601	125–250
	Nippondenso	4741012	Gear Reduction	2.7	200	11	3000	450–700
	Nippondenso	56004757	Gear Reduction	1.4	73	11	3601	125–250
	Nippondenso	56028715	Gear Reduction	1.4	73	11	3601	125–250
PT CRUISER								
2002–06	Nippondenso	—	Gear Reduction	1.2	—	12	—	150–280

① — Maximum.
② — Minimum.
③ — With engine @ operating temperature.
④ — 3.9L, 4.7L & 5.9L engines w/manual transmission.
⑤ — 3.7L, 4.7L & 5.7L engines w/automatic transmission.

Mitsubishi Starters

NOTE: On Air Bag Equipped Models, Refer To "Air Bag System Precautions" Located In The Front Of This Manual For System Disarming & Arming Procedures.

NOTE: Refer To "Computer Relearn Procedures" Located In the Front Of This Manual When Battery Power To The Computer Has Been Interrupted.

INDEX

APPLICATION CHART

Year	Engine Liter	Starter Type
COMMANDER		
2006	3.7L, 4.7L & 5.7L	Gear Reduction
DAKOTA		
2002–2003	2.5L	Gear Reduction
GRAND CHEROKEE		
2002–06	2.5L	Gear Reduction
	4.0L, 3.7L, 4.7L, 5.7L & 6.1	Gear Reduction
LIBERTY		
2002–06	2.4L & 3.7	Gear Reduction
2005–06	2.8L Diesel	Gear Reduction
WRANGLER		
2002–06	2.4L, 2.5L & 4.0L	Gear Reduction

PRECAUTIONS

Air Bag Systems

Refer to "Air Bag System Precautions" in the front of this manual for system disarming and arming procedures.

Battery Ground Cable

Prior to service disconnect battery ground cable and isolate as required.

TROUBLESHOOTING

Refer to "Bosch & Nippondenso Starters" for troubleshooting procedures.

DIAGNOSIS & TESTING

Starter Feed Circuit

LOAD TEST

1. Disable ignition system.
2. Connect volt/ampere tester to battery terminals. Refer to tester operating instructions.
3. Verify that all lights and accessories are Off, parking brake is set and transmission shift selector is in Park for automatic transmissions/transaxles or Neutral for manual transmissions/transaxles.
4. While observing tester, hold ignition switch in Start position and inspect as follows:
   a. If voltage reads above 9.6 volts and amperage draw reads above 250 amps, refer to "Starter Feed Circuit Resistance Test."
   b. If voltage reads 12.4 volts or greater and amperage reads 0–10 amps, refer to "Starter Control Circuit Test."
   c. If starter motor turns engine freely at times, but starting system is still suspected, engage starter several times while observing tester. A starting system that has a problem should fail while performing this procedure.
5. After starting system problem have been corrected, ensure battery is fully charged, disconnect all testing equipment and enable ignition system.

RESISTANCE TEST

The following test will require a voltmeter accurate to 1/10 volt.

1. Disable ignition system.
2. Ensure wiring harness and components connected properly, then proceed as follows:
   a. Connect positive lead of voltmeter to battery ground post, and negative lead to battery ground cable clamp. Rotate and hold ignition switch in Start position and observe voltmeter. If voltage is detected, proceed to step b. If voltage is not detected, correct poor contact between cable clamp and battery post.
   b. Connect positive lead of voltmeter to battery positive post, and negative lead to battery cable positive clamp. Rotate and hold ignition switch in Start position and observe

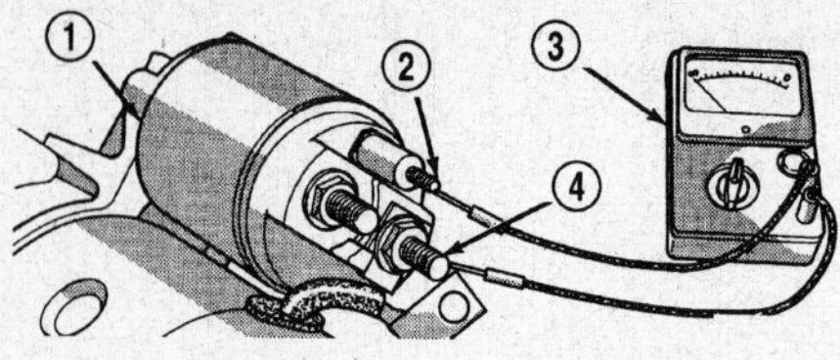

Fig. 1 Starter solenoid continuity test

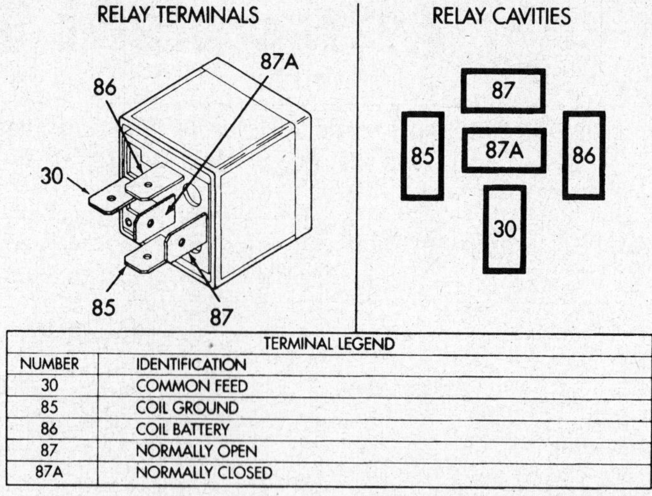

TERMINAL LEGEND	
NUMBER	IDENTIFICATION
30	COMMON FEED
85	COIL GROUND
86	COIL BATTERY
87	NORMALLY OPEN
87A	NORMALLY CLOSED

CR1129200224000X

Fig. 2 Starter relay terminal identification. Cherokee & Dakota

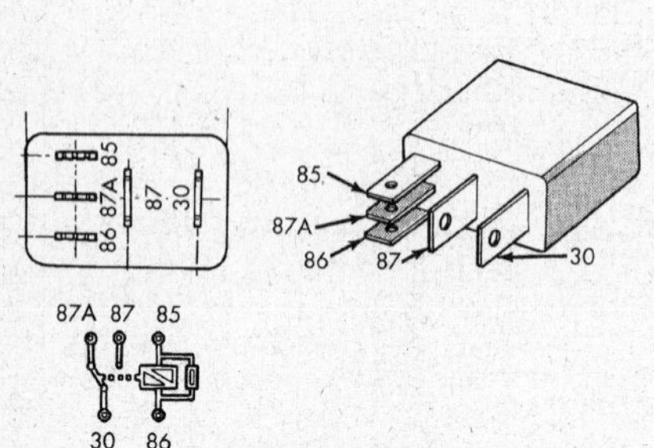

TERMINAL LEGEND	
NUMBER	IDENTIFICATION
30	COMMON FEED
85	COIL GROUND
86	COIL BATTERY
87	NORMALLY OPEN
87A	NORMALLY CLOSED

CR1120000354000X

Fig. 3 Starter relay terminal identification. Grand Cherokee & Wrangler

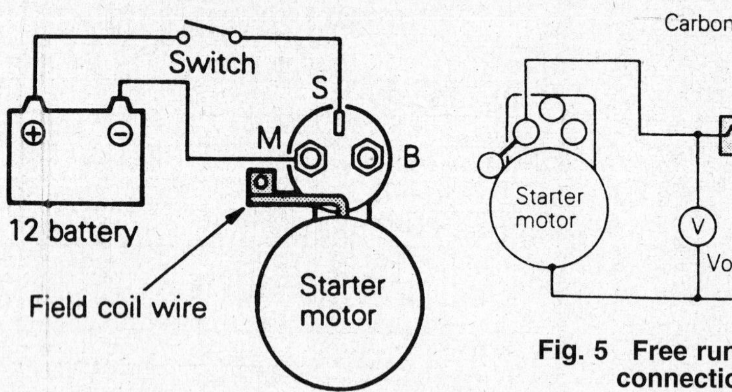

Fig. 4 Magnetic switch terminal identification

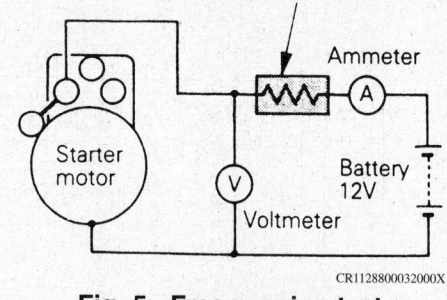

Carbon-pile rheostat
Ammeter
Starter motor
Battery 12V
Voltmeter
CR1128800032000X

Fig. 5 Free running test connections

voltmeter. If voltage is detected, proceed to step c. If voltage is not detected, correct poor contact between cable clamp and battery post.

c. Connect positive lead of voltmeter to battery ground terminal, and negative lead to engine block near battery cable attaching point. Rotate and hold ignition switch in Start position. If voltage reads above .2 volt, correct poor contact at ground cable attaching point. If reading is still above .2 volt, replace ground cable.

3. Remove starter heat shield, then perform the following:
   a. Connect positive voltmeter lead to starter motor housing and negative lead to battery ground terminal. Rotate and hold ignition switch in Start position. If voltage is below .2 volts, proceed to step b. If voltage reads above .2 volt, correct poor contact at starter to engine ground.
   b. Connect positive voltmeter lead to positive battery terminal and negative lead to battery cable terminal on starter solenoid. Rotate and hold ignition switch in Start position. If voltage reads above .2 volt, correct poor contact at battery cable to solenoid connection. If reading is still above .2 volt, replace positive battery cable.
4. If resistance tests detect no feed circuit failures, remove starter motor and proceed to "Starter Solenoid Bench Test."

Starter Control Circuit

The starter control circuit consists of a starter solenoid, starter relay, ignition switch and clutch pedal interlock switch (manual transmission) or safety neutral switch (automatic transmission).

Testing procedures for these components should be followed in order as outlined.

SOLENOID TEST

1. Remove starter motor.
2. Disconnect wire from solenoid field coil terminal.
3. Inspect for continuity between solenoid terminal and solenoid field coil terminal, **Fig. 1.** There should be continuity, if not replace starter motor.
4. Inspect for continuity between solenoid terminal and solenoid case. There should be continuity, if not replace starter motor.

STARTER RELAY TEST

Refer to **Figs. 2 and 3.**

1. Remove starter relay located in relay center.
2. A de-energized relay should have continuity between terminal Nos. 87 A and 30, and no continuity between terminal Nos. 87 and 30.
3. Resistance between terminal Nos. 85 and 86 should be 70–80 ohms.
4. Apply battery voltage to terminal Nos. 85 and 86, inspect for continuity between terminal Nos. 30 and 87 and no continuity between terminal Nos. 87A and 30.

CLUTCH PEDAL SWITCH

The clutch pedal switch is a normally open type switch.

1. Locate and disconnect clutch pedal switch connector.
2. Inspect circuit through switch with pedal released, there should be no continuity.
3. With continuity tester still attached, push clutch pedal to floor, tester should show full continuity.
4. Tester should not show continuity until pedal is fully depressed, replace switch if it fails any test.

Magnetic Switch Pull-In Test

This test must be performed in less than 10 seconds to prevent coil from burning.

1. Disconnect field coil wire from M terminal of magnetic switch, **Fig. 4.**
2. Connect a 12 volt battery between S terminal and M terminal.
3. If pinion moves out, pull-in coil is satisfactory. If pinion does not move, replace magnetic switch.

Magnetic Switch Hold-In Test

This test must be performed in less than 10 seconds to prevent coil from burning.

1. Disconnect field coil wire from M terminal of magnetic switch.
2. Connect a 12 volt battery between S terminal and body.
3. If pinion remains out, system is satisfactory.
4. If pinion moves in, hold-in circuit is open. Replace magnetic switch.

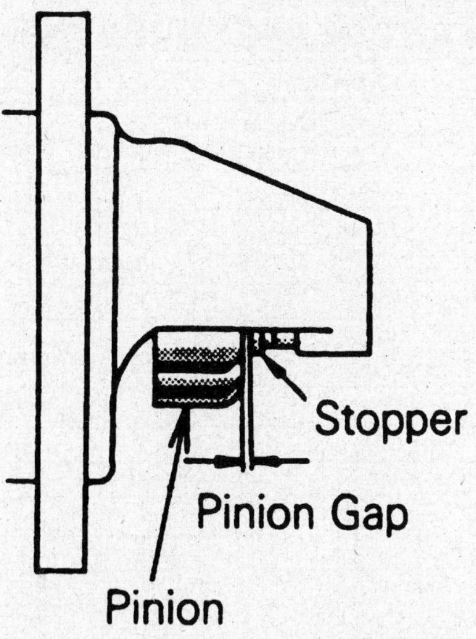

Fig. 6 Pinion gap measurement

Free Running Test

1. Place starter motor in soft jaw vise.
2. Connect a fully charged 12 volt battery to starter motor as follows:
   a. Connect a test ammeter (100 ampere scale) and carbon pile rheostat in series with battery positive post and starter motor terminal, **Fig. 5.**
   b. Connect a voltmeter (15 volt scale) across starter motor.
   c. Rotate carbon pile to full resistance position.
   d. Connect battery cable from battery ground post to starter motor body.
   e. Adjust rheostat until battery voltage outlined on voltmeter.
3. Confirm maximum amperage is within rating of starter and that starter motor turns smoothly and freely.

Magnetic Switch Return Test

This test must be performed in less than 10 seconds to prevent coil from burning.

1. Disconnect field coil wire from M terminal of magnetic switch.
2. Connect a 12 volt battery between M terminal and starter motor body.
3. Pull pinion out and release. If pinion quickly returns to is original position, system is satisfactory. If pinion returns slowly, replace magnetic switch.

Pinion Gap Adjustment Test

This test must be performed in less than 10 seconds to prevent coil from burning.

1. Disconnect field coil wire from M terminal of magnetic switch, **Fig. 4.**
2. Connect a 12 volt battery between S terminal and M terminal.
3. Set ignition switch to On position, pinion should move out.
4. Inspect pinion to stopper clearance (pinion gap) with feeler gauge, **Fig. 6.** Clearance should be .020–.079 inch.
5. If pinion gap is out of specification, adjust by adding or removing gaskets between magnetic switch and front bracket.

STARTER SPECIFICATIONS

Year	Engine Liter	Starter		Free Speed Test			Cranking Amp Draw Test
		Type	Power Rating, Kw	Amps①	Volts	RPM②	
DAKOTA							
2002	2.5L	Gear Reduction	1.2	90	11.2	2600	130
GRAND CHEROKEE							
2002–04	4.0L & 4.7L	Gear Reduction	1.4	90	11.2	2400	160
2005–06	3.7L & 4.7L	Gear Reduction	1.2	73	11	3601	125–250
2005–06	5.7L	Gear Reduction	1.4	73	11	3601	125–250
LIBERTY							
2002–06	2.4L & 3.7L	Gear Reduction	1.4	90	11.2	2400	160
2005–06	2.8L Diesel	Gear Reduction	—	160	11.5	5500	500
WRANGLER							
2002–06	2.4L	Gear Reduction	1.4	90	11.2	2400	160
	2.5L	Gear Reduction	1.2	90	11.2	2600	130
	4.0L	Gear Reduction	1.4	90	11.2	2500	160

① — Maximum. ② — Minimum.

ALTERNATORS

NOTE: "Electrical Symbol & Wire Color Code Identification" Located In The Front Of This Manual May Be Used As An Aid When Using Wiring Diagrams Found In This Section.

NOTE: Refer To "Computer Relearn Procedures" Located In The Front Of This Manual When Battery Power To The Computer Has Been Interrupted.

INDEX

APPLICATION CHART

Year	Rating, Amps	Part No.
CARAVAN, TOWN & COUNTRY & VOYAGER		
2002–06	80 (2.4L Engine)	③
	100 (3.3L & 3.8L)	③
COMMANDER		
2006	160 (3.7L & 4.7L Engine)	—
	160 (5.7L Engine)	—
DAKOTA		
2002–03	117 (2.5L Engine)	56028686AA
	136 (2.5L Engine)	56028687AA
	117 (3.9L & 5.9L Engines)	56029913AA
	136 (3.9L & 5.9L Engines)	56030914AA
	117 (4.7L Engine)	56028692AA
	136 (4.7L Engine)	56041693AB
2002–06	136 (3.7L Engine)	56041693AA
	160 (3.7L Engine)	56029914AA
	117 (4.7L Engine)	56028692AA
	136 (4.7L Engine)	56041693AB
DURANGO		
2002–06	136 (5.2L & 5.9L Engines)	56029701AA
	160 (5.2L & 5.9L Engines)	56029915AA
	136 (3.7L & 4.7L Engines)	56029700AA
	160 (3.7L & 4.7L Engines)	56029914AA
	136 (3.7L & 4.7L Engines)	56041120AC
	136 (5.7L Engine)	56028699AA
	160 (5.7L Engine)	56028697AA
1500 FULL SIZE TRUCKS		
2002–06	136 (3.7L & 4.7L Engines)	56029700AA①
	136 (3.7L & 4.7L Engines)	56041120AC②
	136 (5.7L & 5.9L Gas/5.9L Diesel)	56029701AA①
	136 (5.7L & 5.9L Gas/5.9L Diesel)	56028238AB②
2500 & 3500 FULL SIZE PICKUPS		
2002–06	117 (Gas Engine)	56027912AB
	117 (Gas Engine)	56029913AA
	136 (Gas Engine)	56028920AA
	136 (Gas Engine)	56030914AB
	136 (Diesel Engine)	56027221AB

Continued

APPLICATION CHART—Continued

Year	Rating, Amps	Part No.
2500 & 3500 FULL SIZE PICKUPS		
2003–06	136 (5.7L Gasoline & 5.9L Diesel Engines)	56028696AA ①
	136 (5.7L Gasoline & 5.9L Diesel Engines)	56028699AA ②
	136 (5.9L Gasoline Engine)	56029701AA ①
	136 (5.9L Gasoline Engine)	56028238AB ②
FULL SIZE VAN		
2002–03	117 (Gas Engine)	56027912AB
	117 (Gas Engine)	56029913AA
	136 (Gas Engine)	56028920AA
	136 (Gas Engine)	56030914AB
	136 (Diesel Engine)	56027221AB
GRAND CHEROKEE		
2002–04	136 (4.0L Engine)	56041322
	136 (4.7L Engine)	56041324
2005–06	160 (3.7L & 4.7L Engines)	—
	160 (5.7L Engine)	—
LIBERTY		
2002–06	124 (2.4L Engine)	56044530AB
	136 (2.4L Engine)	56044532AB
	136 (3.7L Engine)	56041693AA
	160 (3.7L Engine)	56029914AA
PACIFICA		
2004–06	—	—
PT CRUISER		
2002–04	120 (2.0L Engine)	4794222AC
2005–06	85 (1.6L Engine)	—
	136 (2.4L Turbo Engine)	—
WRANGLER		
2002	81 (2.5L Engine)	56005684AB
	81 (4.0L Engine)	56041565AA
	117 (2.5L Engine)	56005685AC
	117 (4.0L Engine)	56041685AA
	124 (2.5L & 4.0L Engine)	56041822AA
2003–06	81 (4.0L Engine)	56041565AA
	117 (4.0L Engine)	56041685AA
	124 (2.4L Engine)	56044530AB
	124 (4.0L Engine)	56041822AA
	136 (2.4L Engine)	56044530AB

① — Denso.
② — Bosch.
③ — Located on the side of alternator.

DESCRIPTION

The main components of the alternator are the rotor, stator, rectifier, end shields and drive pulley. Direct current is available at the output "B+" terminal.

Alternator output is controlled by voltage regulator circuitry contained within the power and logic modules of the Engine Controller.

TROUBLESHOOTING

Refer to **Fig. 1** for charging system diagnosis.

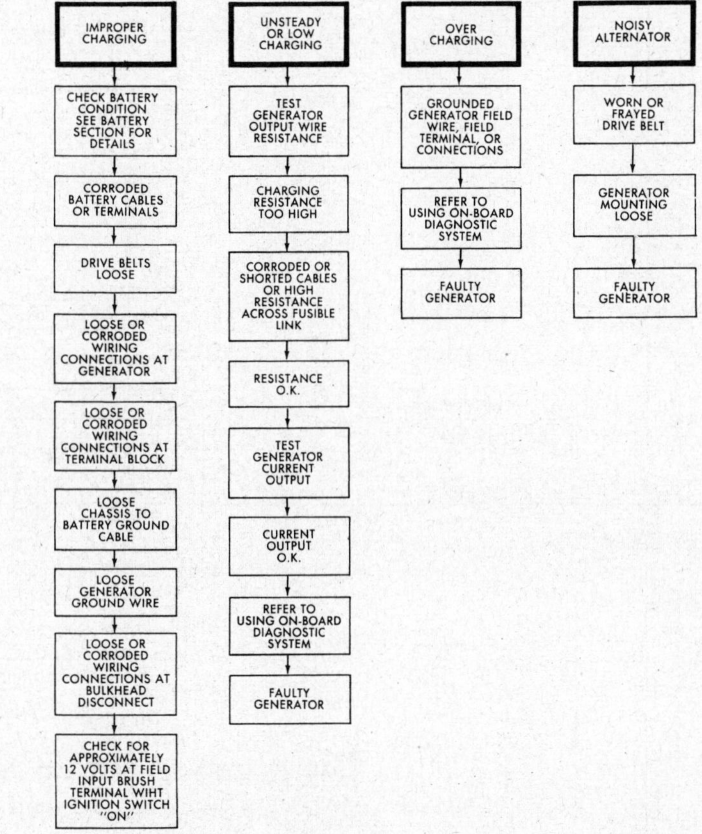

Fig. 1 Charging system troubleshooting chart

DIAGNOSIS & TESTING

Charging System Resistance & Voltage Drop Test

The following test is used to show the amount of voltage drop across the alternator output wire from alternator output (B+) terminal to the battery positive post. The test will also show the amount of voltage drop from the alternator ground (-) terminal or case ground to the battery ground post.

1. Inspect condition of battery and battery cables, replace if required.
2. Start and run engine until it reaches operating temperature.
3. Shut engine off and connect a suitable engine tachometer.
4. Fully engage parking brake, then start engine.
5. Place heater blower in high position, then turn headlamps on to high-beam position.
6. Turn rear window defogger on and bring engine speed up to 2400 RPM and hold.
7. Touch negative lead of a suitable voltmeter with a 0–18 volt DC scale directly to positive battery post.
8. Touch positive lead of voltmeter to alternator (B+) terminal stud (not terminal mounting nut), **Fig. 2.** If voltage is .6 volts or lower, proceed to step 9. If voltage is more than .6 volts, proceed as follows:
   a. Touch positive lead of voltmeter to terminal mounting stud nut and then to wiring connector.
   b. If voltage now reads below .6 volts, inspect for dirty, loose or poor connection at this point, repair as required.
   c. Inspect condition of alternator output wire to battery bullet connector, repair as required.
   d. Inspect voltage drop at circuit ground connections by touching positive lead to every ground connection within the circuit. If voltage reads below .6 volts at any connection, repair as required.
9. Touch positive lead of voltmeter directly to battery ground post, then touch negative lead to alternator case. If voltage is .3 volts or less, alternator ground circuit is satisfactory. If voltage is greater than .3 volts, proceed as follows:
   a. Touch negative lead to alternator case, then to engine block.
   b. If voltage is now lower than .3 volts, inspect for a dirty, loose or poor connection at this point, repair as required.
   c. If voltage is still higher than .3 volts, inspect entire ground circuit between alternator and engine for voltage drop, repair as required.
   d. If voltage is still higher than .3 volts, inspect for corrosion at alternator mounting points or for a loose alternator mounting bracket, repair as required.

Current Output Test

This test will determine if the charging system can produce its minimum test amperage output. Refer to "Alternator Specifications" for minimum test amperage output specifications.

1. Before beginning test, inspect the following:
   a. System Diagnostic Trouble Codes (DTC)s, diagnose and repair as required.
   b. Condition of battery and battery cables, repair or replace as required.
   c. Alternator drive belt for proper tension.
   d. Perform charging system resistance and voltage drop test.
2. Start and run engine until it reaches operating temperature.
3. Shut engine off, then turn off all electrical accessories and lighting.
4. Connect a suitable volt/amp tester with both a battery load control (carbon pile rheostat) and an inductive type pickup clamp (ammeter probe) to battery. **Ensure carbon pile rheostat is in the OPEN or OFF position before connecting leads to battery.**
5. Connect inductive type pickup clamp (ammeter probe) according to tool manufacturer's instructions.
6. Connect a suitable tachometer to engine and fully engage parking brake.
7. Start engine and raise engine speed to 2500 RPM.
8. Maintaining engine speed at 2500 RPM, slowly adjust rheostat control on tester to obtain highest amperage reading. **Do not allow voltage to drop below 12 volts. Perform this load test within 15 seconds to prevent damage to test equipment.**
9. Compare ammeter reading to minimum test amperage specifications, refer to "Alternator Specifications."
10. If minimum test amperage output is less than specified, refer to "Diagnostic Tests."

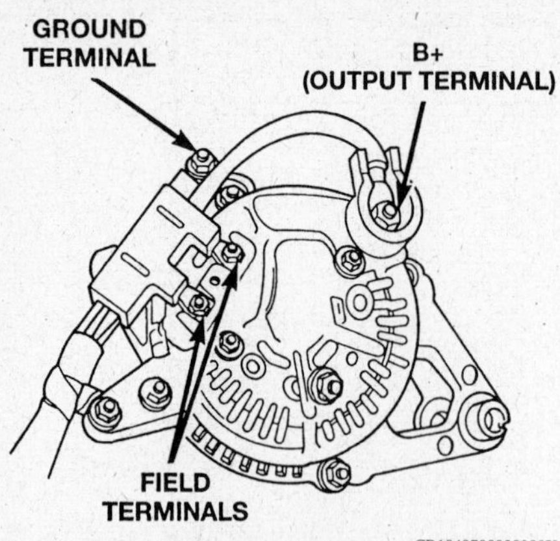

Fig. 2 Alternator terminals

Accessing Diagnostic Trouble Codes

SCAN TOOL

1. Connect DRB test tool, or equivalent scan tool, to DCL located under the instrument panel.
2. Follow scan tool manufactures instructions to access Diagnostic Trouble Codes (DTCs).
3. Refer to "Diagnostic Chart Index" for test identification and location.

Code	Description
P0560	System Voltage Too High
	System Voltage Too Low
P0562	Battery Voltage Low
P0563	Battery Voltage High
P0620	Alternator Field Control Fault
	Battery Voltage Too High/Low
	Open/Short Circuit
	Unstable Circuit
P0622	Alternator Field Fault
P0625	Alternator Field Control Circuit Low
P0626	Alternator Field Control Circuit High
P065A	Alternator System Performance
P1492	Ambient/Battery Temp Sensor Volts Too High
P1493	Ambient/Battery Temp Sensor Volts Too Low
P1594	Charging System Voltage Too High
P1610	Voltage Regulator Signal Voltage Too High
	Voltage Regulator Signal Voltage Too Low
P1682	Charging System Voltage Too Low
P2502	Charging System Error
P2503	Charging System Output Low
P2504	Charging System Output High
U1132	Lost Communication With Alternator

Fig. 3 Diagnostic trouble code interpretation

Diagnostic Trouble Code Interpretation

Refer to **Fig. 3** for diagnostic trouble code interpretation.

CLEARING DIAGNOSTIC TROUBLE CODES

Diagnostic Trouble Codes (DTCs) may only be cleared with the use of a suitable scan tool.

Follow scan tool manufacturers instructions to clear DTCs.

ALTERNATOR SPECIFICATIONS

Year	Alternator Part No.	Rating, Amps	Minimum Test Amps
CARAVAN, TOWN & COUNTRY & VOYAGER			
2002–06	③	—	④
COMMANDER			
2006	—	160	—
DAKOTA			
2002–06	56028686AA	117	88
	56029913AA	117	90
	56028692AA	117	90
	56028687AA	136	95
	56030914AA	136	100
	56041693AB	136	100
DURANGO			
2002–06	56041120AC	136	—
	56029700AA	136	—
	56028699AA	136	—
	56029701AA	136	100
	56029915AA	160	—
	56028697AA	160	—
	56029914AA	160	100
FULL SIZE TRUCKS w/DIESEL ENGINE			
2002–06	56027221①	136	120
	56028238AB②	136	120
	56028696AA	136	—
	56028699AA	136	—
FULL SIZE TRUCKS & VANS w/GASOLINE ENGINE			
2002–06	52067912①	117	90
	52067913①	136	100
	56028238AB②	136	100
	56029700AA	136	—
	56029701AA	136	—
	56041120AC	136	—
	56028238AB	136	—
	56028699AA	136	—
GRAND CHEROKEE			
2002–06	56041322⑤	136	100
	56041324⑥	136	100
	—	160	—
LIBERTY			
2002–06	56044530AB	124	88
	56044532AB	136	96
	56041693AA	136	96
	56029914AA	160	112
PACIFICA			
2004–06	—	—	—

Continued

ALTERNATOR SPECIFICATIONS—Continued

Year	Alternator Part No.	Rating, Amps	Minimum Test Amps
PT CRUISER			
2002–04	4794222AC	120	75
2005–06	—	85	—
	—	136	—
WRANGLER			
2002	56041565AA	81	57
	56005684AB	81	57
	56041685AA	117	88
	56005685AC	117	88
	56041822AA	124	90
2003–06	56041565AA	81	57
	56041685AA	117	88
	56044530AB	124	88
	56041822AA	124	90
	56044530AB	136	96

① — Denso.
② — Bosch.
③ — Located on the side of alternator.
④ — 2.4L engine, 80 amps; 3.3L and 3.8L engines, 100 amps or 115 amps hot.
⑤ — 4.0L engine.
⑥ — 4.7L engine.

DASH PANEL SERVICE

NOTE: On Air Bag Equipped Models, Refer To "Air Bag System Precautions" Located In The Front Of This Manual For System Disarming & Arming Procedures.

NOTE: Refer To "Computer Relearn Procedures" Located In The Front Of This Manual When Battery Power To The Computer Has Been Interrupted.

NOTE: Refer To "Dash Gauges" Section For Related Information.

INDEX

PRECAUTIONS

Air Bag Systems

Refer to "Air Bag System Precautions" in the front of this manual for system disarming and arming procedures.

Battery Ground Cable

Prior to service, disconnect battery ground cable and isolate as required.

DASH PANEL

REPLACE

Caravan, Town & Country & Voyager

1. Remove lower console retaining screws, then lower console.
2. Remove bolts securing lower supports to instrument panel frame.
3. Remove bolts securing lower supports to floor pan.
4. Disconnect electrical connector from passenger air bag module.
5. Remove two screws from righthand and lefthand cowl trim covers.
6. Remove lefthand and righthand side A-pillar trim covers using trim stick tool No. C-4755, or a suitable flat-bladed equivalent.
7. Push in on sides of glove box bin, then lower and remove from instrument panel.
8. Disconnect antenna lead connector from behind glove box.
9. Remove screws from lower steering column cover, then screws from plastic knee blocker reinforcement.
10. Unclip Data Link Connector (DLC) from instrument panel reinforcement.
11. Remove one screw from lefthand side instrument panel silencer, then silencer.
12. Disconnect the following electrical connectors:
    a. Brake switch.
    b. Main bulkhead connector.
    c. Five harness connectors.
    d. Driver air bag module connector.
13. Remove two screws from hood release handle.
14. Remove screws from lefthand under column instrument panel reinforcement brace, then brace.
15. Remove two steering column shroud retaining screws, then separate shrouds and remove.
16. Disconnect seven steering column electrical connectors, then unclip harness from column.
17. Disconnect ORC harness electrical connector.
18. Remove four nuts retaining steering column, then lower to floor.
19. Remove four nuts attaching instrument panel to brake pedal support.
20. Loosen lefthand side roll-down bolt.
21. Remove lefthand side A-pillar retaining bolts.
22. **On models equipped with mechanical transmission range indicator,** proceed as follows:
    a. Remove indicator cable loop.
    b. Remove clip holding gear shift cable end to gear selector adapter.
    c. Pull cable end from gear selector.
    d. Disconnect clip for indicator cable and guide tube from shift cable bracket, then position aside.
23. **On all models,** using trim stick gently pry up on front edge of top cover, then pull rearward and remove.
24. Disconnect electrical connectors from HVAC behind glove box area and two antenna connectors behind glove box hinge.
25. Remove righthand end cover by pulling outward.
26. Remove righthand side A-pillar retaining bolts, then loosen roll-down bolt.
27. Disconnect two front window defroster grid electrical connectors on each side of vehicle.
28. Remove lefthand and righthand power mirrors, then feed power mirror wiring harness through A-pillar.
29. Remove bolts securing instrument panel frame to dash panel below windshield opening.
30. Lift instrument panel up off HVAC and remove from vehicle.
31. Reverse procedure to install. Tighten fasteners to specifications.

Commander

1. Remove bolts then lower instrument panel cover, **Fig. 1.**
2. Remove lower steering column cover, then upper and lower column shrouds.
3. Disconnect steering column electrical connectors.
4. Place front wheels in straight ahead position.
5. Remove pinch bolt, then steering column support bolts.
6. Remove column cross bolt and slide column downward off bracket and remove steering column.
7. Remove instrument panel to pedal support bracket attaching nuts.
8. Remove lefthand instrument panel side cover.
9. Remove lefthand door sill trim, then cowl trim panel.
10. Disconnect electrical connections on

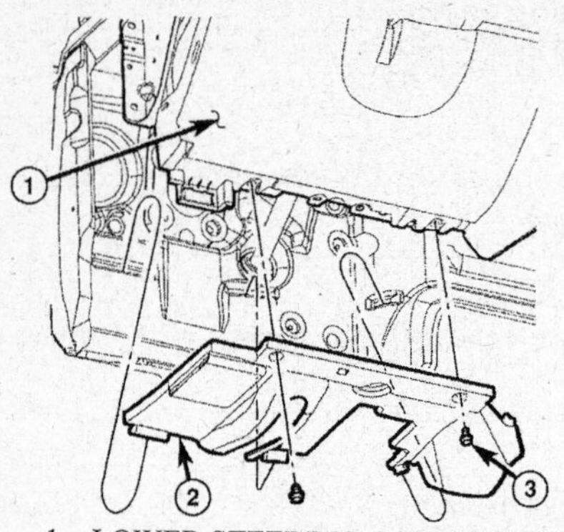

1- LOWER STEERING COLUMN COVER
2- LOWER INSTRUMENT PANEL
3- BOLTS

LTV0500000000205

Fig. 1 Lower instrument panel cover

lefthand side of instrument panel.

11. Remove bolts and disconnect ground wires within steering column opening to lefthand of steering column.
12. Disconnect white adjustable pedal electrical connector.
13. Disconnect HVAC electrical connector.
14. Remove A-pillar trim panels.
15. Remove lefthand a-pillar support bolts and screw.
16. Remove shifter bezel trim ring, then shifter bezel.
17. Remove center console back cover and disconnect electrical connector.
18. Remove console mounting screws and console.
19. Disconnect electrical connectors under console.
20. Separate wire harness push pin hangers and remove screw, then disconnect ground strap.
21. Remove shifter assembly.
22. Remove center HVAC duct.
23. Separate glove box damper rod from glove box by sliding rod towards rear of vehicle to release it from bin.
24. Open glove box and push stop tabs down to drop glove box out of instrument panel.
25. Rotate box down and release door hinges at bottom and remove glove box.
26. Remove righthand lower instrument panel cover.
27. Remove righthand door sill plate, then cowl cover.
28. Remove righthand instrument panel end side cover.
29. Disconnect electrical connectors on righthand side of instrument panel.
30. Disconnect antenna cable.
31. Remove righthand a-pillar support bolts and screw.
32. Remove defroster grill.
33. Remove radio trim bezel.
34. Remove center bezel and disconnect electrical connectors.
35. Remove nut from HVAC support stud behind center bezel.
36. Remove screw to HVAC from under glove box opening.
37. Remove HVAC bracket bolt from glove box opening.
38. Remove lefthand and righthand center support brackets.
39. Remove center floor duct.
40. Remove radio.
41. Remove two HVAC bolts from radio opening.
42. Remove instrument panel assembly.
43. Reverse procedure to install.

Dakota & Durango

2002-04

1. Place wheels in straight ahead position.
2. Remove defroster grille, then the end caps from outboard ends of instrument panel, **Fig. 2.**
3. Remove trim from lefthand and righthand cowl side inner panels.
4. Remove cluster bezel, then the steering column opening cover.
5. Remove lower bezel, then the floor console assembly.
6. Disconnect two halves of radio antenna coaxial cable connector.
7. Remove nut securing instrument panel wiring harness ground to ground stud.
8. Remove two screws securing inside hood release bracket to instrument panel.
9. Disengage 16-way Data Link Connector (DLC) from inner hood release bracket.
10. Disconnect instrument panel wiring harness connector for Air Bag Control Module (ACM).
11. Remove two screws that secure instrument panel wiring harness ground.
12. Disconnect two instrument panel electrical connectors for Central Timer Module (CTM).
13. Disconnect electrical connector for park brake switch and park brake lamp.
14. Disconnect headlamp and instrument panel wiring harness bulkhead electrical connectors.
15. Disconnect two body wiring harness connectors from two instrument panel wiring harness connectors.
16. Disconnect body, headlamp and instrument panel wiring harness connectors from junction block.
17. Remove air bag module, then the steering wheel using a suitable puller tool. **Ensure puller bolts are fully engaged into steering wheel and not into clockspring before attempting to remove steering wheel.**
18. Remove steering column opening cover and knee blocker.
19. **On models equipped with column shift,** proceed as follows:
    a. Pry shift cable from shift lever and remove from cable bracket.

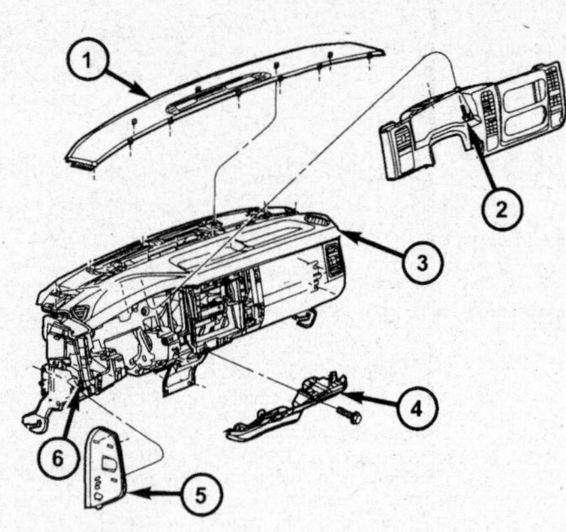

1 - DEFROSTER GRILLE
2 - CLUSTER BEZEL
3 - TOP COVER
4 - LOWER BEZEL
5 - END CAP
6 - INSTRUMENT PANEL

CR9080100088000X

Fig. 2 Instrument panel. 2002–04 Dakota & Durango

    b. Place shift lever in Park position, pull PRNDL cable and twist to remove from PRNDL lever.
    c. Push tab on top of cable retainer, then squeeze sides to remove retainer from column.

20. **On models equipped with tilt steering column,** remove tilt lever.
21. **On all models,** remove upper and lower column shrouds.
22. Remove multi-function switch using suitable 7 MM socket.
23. Remove remaining electrical connectors from column switches.
24. Remove bolt and nut from upper shaft, then slide upper shaft off column shaft.
25. Remove column mounting nuts, then the steering column.
26. Loosen righthand and lefthand instrument panel cowl side roll-down bracket screws ½ inch.
27. Remove two screws securing instrument panel end brackets to each A-pillar.
28. Remove two screws securing center bracket to ACM mounting bracket on floor panel transmission tunnel.
29. Remove five screws that secure top of instrument panel to top of dash panel, removing center screw last.
30. Roll down instrument panel, then install a temporary hook from center hole on instrument panel to center hole on top of dash panel.
31. With instrument panel supported in roll-down position, disconnect electrical connector from HVAC housing.
32. With aid of an assistant, lift instrument panel assembly off roll-down bracket screws and remove from vehicle.
33. Reverse procedure to install.

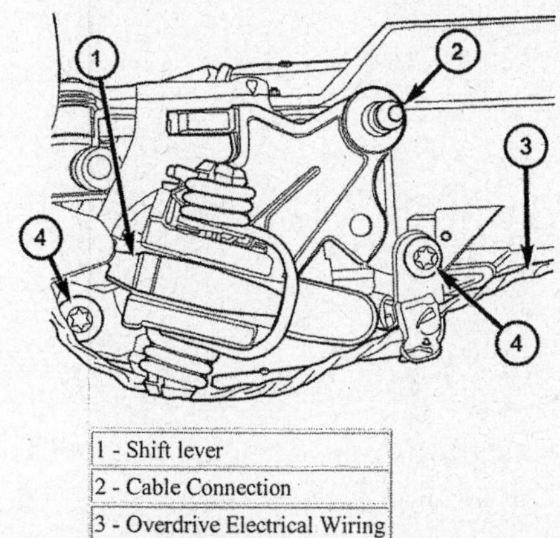

Fig. 3 Shift cable removal. 2005–06 Dakota

2005-06 DAKOTA

1. Remove center console.
2. Remove lefthand door sill trim.
3. Remove steering column cover.
4. Place front wheel in straight ahead position.
5. Remove steering column tilt lever knob, then steering column shrouds.
6. Disconnect brake switch electrical connector.
7. Disconnect steering column wire harness electrical connections.
8. Remove shift cable from column shift lever actuator, **Fig. 3.**
9. Release and shift cable from column bracket.
10. Remove SKIM module, then disconnect electrical connector.
11. Remove upper steering shaft coupler bolt from column, then separate shaft from coupler.
12. Remove steering column mounting nuts, then remove steering column.
13. Remove pedal support mounting bolts.
14. Remove defroster grille.
15. Remove upper instrument panel mounting bolts, **Fig. 4.**
16. Disconnect HVAC electrical connector.
17. Disconnect electrical connections from lefthand side of instrument panel.
18. Disconnect ground strap from lefthand cowel.
19. Separate center wire harness from center support.
20. Remove instrument panel center support bolts, then lefthand support bolts.
21. Remove righthand door sill trim.
22. Remove righthand instrument panel end cap.
23. Disconnect antenna cable.
24. Disconnect ground straps at righthand side of instrument panel.
25. Remove righthand instrument panel support bolts.
26. With aid of an assistant, remove instrument panel assembly from vehicle.
27. Reverse procedure to install.

2005-06 DURANGO

1. Remove lefthand and righthand door sill plates.
2. Remove lefthand cowl trim cover, then instrument panel end cap.
3. Remove steering column cover retaining screws, then cover.
4. Remove hood release handle and position aside.
5. Remove steering column opening reinforcement.
6. Remove steering column tilt lever.
7. Remove upper and lower steering column shrouds.
8. Disconnect wire harness electrical connectors to steering column.
9. Remove shift cable from shift lever actuator.
10. Disconnect shift cable and remove from column bracket.
11. Remove SKIM module, then disconnect electrical connector.
12. Remove upper steering shaft coupler bolt and slide shaft down.
13. Remove brake light switch. **Do not reuse switch.**
14. Remove steering column mounting nuts, then remove steering column.
15. Remove pedal support bracket bolts.
16. Disconnect release rod from arm on pedal assembly.
17. Disconnect electrical connectors from fuse block.
18. Remove A-pillar trim panels.
19. Remove floor console.
20. Disconnect two body wire harness connectors from Occupant Restraint Controller.
21. Remove drivers seat.
22. Remove instrument panel wiring harness from under carpet.
23. Remove center instrument panel support bolts.
24. Remove lefthand floor duct.
25. Remove lefthand instrument panel support bolts.
26. Remove righthand instrument panel end cap, then cowl panel.
27. Remove righthand instrument panel support bolts.
28. Remove amplifier, then disconnect amplifier and antenna electrical connectors.
29. Remove righthand rear floor duct.

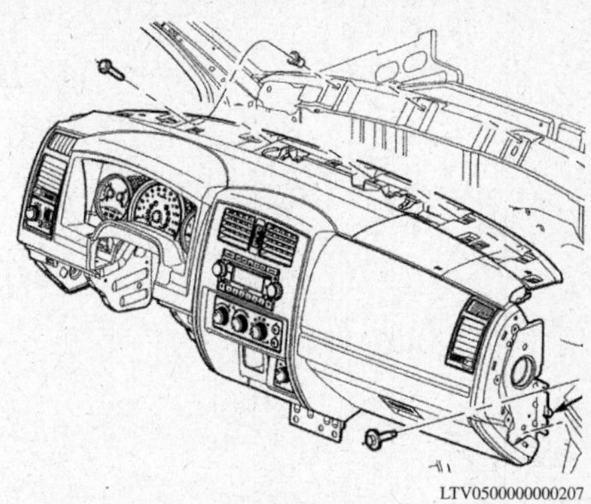

Fig. 4 Instrument panel. 2005–06 Dakota

30. Remove instrument panel defroster grille.
31. Disconnect sensor electrical connector.
32. Remove upper instrument panel mounting bolts.
33. Remove instrument panel assembly through drivers door.
34. Reverse procedure to install.

Full Size Pickup

2002 2500 & 3500

1. Place front wheels in straight ahead position
2. Remove Air Bag Control Module (ACM) and bracket from floor panel transmission tunnel.
3. Remove trim panels from lefthand and righthand cowl side inner panels.
4. Remove steering column opening cover and knee blocker from instrument panel.
5. Remove air bag module, then the steering wheel using a suitable puller tool. **Ensure puller bolts are fully engaged in steering wheel and not into clockspring.**
6. Remove shift link rod from inside engine compartment, if equipped. Pry rod out from grommet in shift lever.
7. Scribe or paint reference mark on steering column shaft to coupler for installation reference, then remove coupler bolt.
8. Remove steering column opening cover/knee bolster.
9. **On models equipped with column shift,** remove PRNDL cable as follows:
   a. Place shift lever in Park position.
   b. Pull cable and twist to remove from

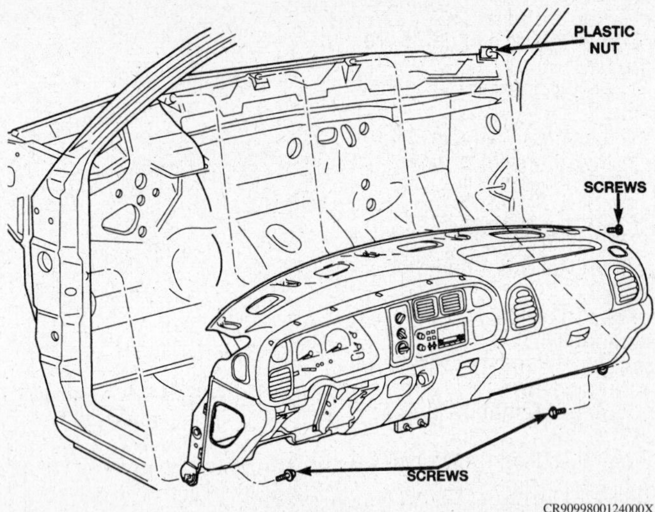

Fig. 5 Instrument panel. 2002 2500 & 3500 Full Size Pickups

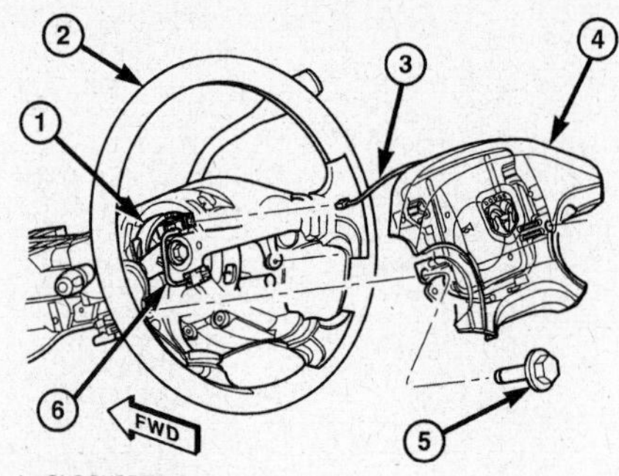

Fig. 6 Driver air bag module replacement. 1500 & 2003–06 2500 & 3500 Full Size Pickups

position arm.

c. Push tab up on bottom of cable retainer, then squeeze sides to remove retainer from column.

10. **On models equipped with tilt steering column,** remove tilt lever.
11. **On all models,** remove upper and lower lock housing shroud and lower fixed shroud.
12. Remove multi-function switch using a suitable 7 MM socket.
13. Loosen upper support bracket nuts to allow some clearance to aid in removal of upper fixed shroud.
14. Disconnect electrical connectors from Key-In lamp, ignition switch, horn and clockspring.
15. Remove wiring harness from column by prying out plastic retainer buttons.
16. Remove toe plate fasteners, then the steering column.
17. Disconnect park release handle linkage rod from park brake mechanism on lefthand cowl side inner panel.
18. Disconnect electrical connector from parking brake switch on parking brake mechanism.
19. Disconnect three junction block wiring harness connectors that are closest to dash panel.
20. Remove screw in center of instrument panel to bulkhead wiring harness connector, then unplug connector.
21. Disconnect instrument panel to door electrical connector located directly below bulkhead wiring harness connector.
22. **On models equipped with Infinity sound system,** disconnect wiring harness connector located on outboard side of bulkhead electrical connector.
23. **On all models,** disconnect electrical connector from stop lamp switch.
24. Disconnect HVAC vacuum harness connector located near inboard end of HVAC housing.
25. Remove two inside hood latch release handle to instrument panel lower reinforcement retaining screws, then lower release handle to floor.
26. Disconnect radio antenna cable connector.
27. Loosen righthand and lefthand instrument panel cowl side roll-down bracket screws approximately ½ inch, **Fig. 5.**
28. Remove five top instrument panel to top of dash panel retaining screws, then the center screw.
29. Roll the instrument panel down and install a temporary hook in center hole on top of instrument panel. Secure other end of hook to center hole in top of dash panel. Hook should support instrument panel in its rolled-down position.
30. With instrument panel in its rolled-down position, reach over to passenger's side and disconnect the following:
    a. Two electrical connectors located on HVAC housing.
    b. Temperature control cable flag retainer from top of HVAC housing, then pull cable core adjuster clip off blend-air door lever.
31. Remove temporary hook and lift instrument panel assembly off of roll-down bracket screws.
32. Remove instrument panel from vehicle.
33. Reverse procedure to install. Tighten fasteners to specifications.

1500 & 2003-06 2500 & 3500

1. Remove A-pillar trim plugs and bolts.
2. Remove trim/grab handle from A-pillar.
3. Pry up on rear of top cover using trim stick No. C-4755, or equivalent, to release attachment clips.
4. Pull top cover backward to release remaining clips and remove cover.
5. Disconnect headliner wire harness electrical connector at A-pillar.
6. Remove lefthand side cover.
7. Place front wheels in a straight ahead position.
8. Remove two switches from steering wheel.
9. Remove two screws that secure trim covers/speed control switches on each side of air bag trim cover.
10. Remove two trim covers/speed control switches from pockets on each side of air bag.
11. Remove two screws that secure air bag to steering wheel, **Fig. 6.**
12. Pull driver air bag module away from steering wheel far enough to disconnect electrical connections.
13. Remove driver air bag module.
14. Remove steering wheel using steering wheel puller CJ98–1, or equivalent.
15. Remove steering column opening cover, tilt lever and clockspring.
16. Disconnect wire harness to column.
17. Remove shift cable from column shift lever actuator.
18. Release and remove shift cable from column bracket
19. Remove SKIM module in order to disconnect electrical connector.
20. Remove upper steering shaft coupler bolt and slide shaft down.
21. Remove brake light switch and discard.
22. Remove steering column mounting nuts.
23. Remove steering column from vehicle.
24. Remove two bolts at steering column support bracket, **Fig. 7.**
25. Remove lefthand cowl trim panel.
26. Remove instrument panel drivers side bezel.
27. Remove lefthand side mounting bolts, **Fig. 8.**
28. Disconnect wire harness electrical connector above brake pedal.
29. Remove hood release handle from bracket.
30. Disconnect park brake release handle actuator rod.
31. Remove Air Bag Control Module trim cover, if equipped.
32. Remove console from floor as outlined under "Floor Console."
33. Remove center bracket bolts.
34. Disconnect air bag control module electrical connector
35. Remove righthand cowl trim cover.
36. Disconnect electrical connectors and radio antenna on righthand side of cowl panel.

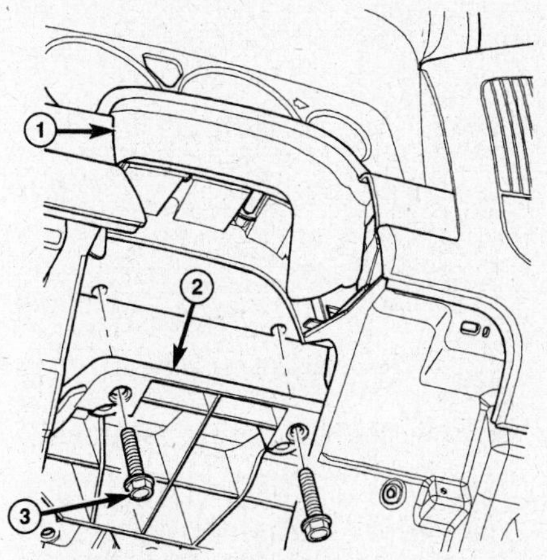

Fig. 7 Steering column support bracket. 1500 & 2003–06 2500 & 3500 Full Size Pickups

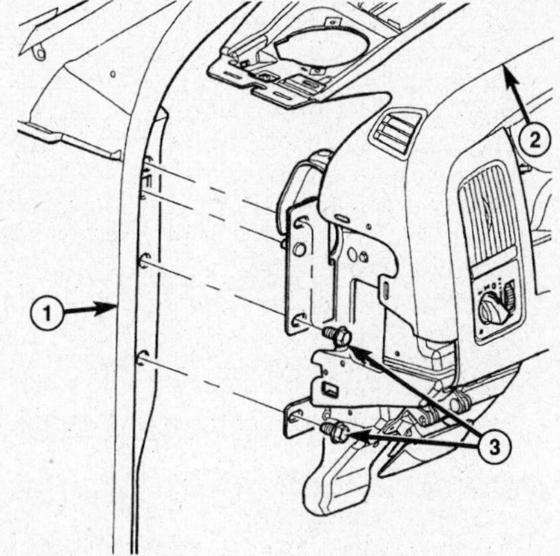

Fig. 8 Lefthand side mounting bolts. 1500 & 2003–06 2500 & 3500 Full Size Pickups

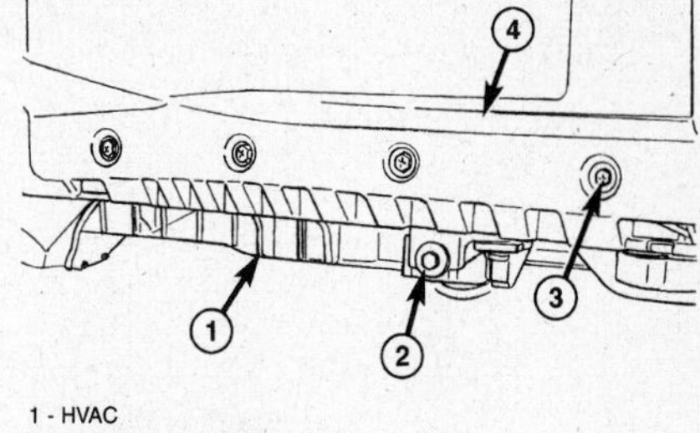

Fig. 9 HVAC/Instrument panel mounting. 1500 & 2003–06 2500 & 3500 Full Size Pickups

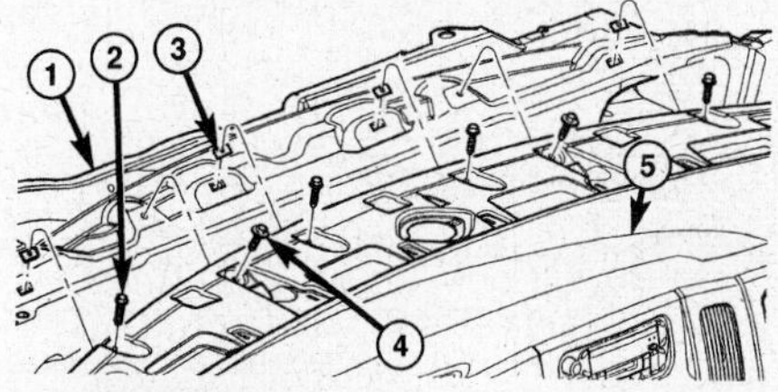

Fig. 10 Upper cowl panel bolts. 1500 & 2500 & 3500 Full Size Pickups

37. Remove HVAC screw, **Fig. 9.**
38. Remove righthand side end cap.
39. Remove righthand side A-pillar trim.
40. Remove righthand side mounting bolts on A-pillar and bolt on cowl side panel.
41. Remove four top instrument panel screws and two bolts, **Fig. 10.**
42. Remove instrument panel.
43. Reverse procedure to install.

Full Size Van

1. Place front wheels in straight ahead position.
2. Remove engine cover, driver side front seat, driver side step sill trim and driver side cowl side trim from passenger compartment.
3. Remove knee blocker, then the instrument panel end caps.
4. Remove interior trim moldings from both A-pillars.
5. Remove two screws that retain outboard ends of top cover to instrument panel, **Fig. 11.**
6. Gently pry rear edge of instrument panel top cover up and away from top of instrument panel using trim stick tool No. C-4755, or a suitable flat-bladed

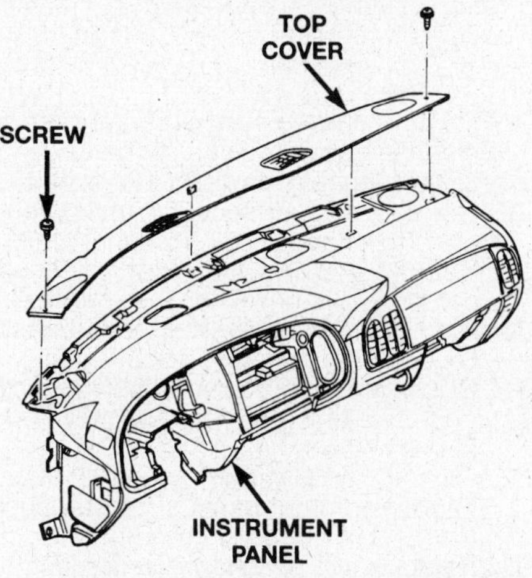

Fig. 11 Instrument panel top cover. Full Size Van

equivalent, then release snap clip retainers.

7. Remove top cover from instrument panel.
8. Open glove box and locate two stop bumpers on sides of instrument panel glove box opening.
9. Depress both sides of glove box inward far enough so that glove box stops can be moved past rubber stop bumpers, **Fig. 12.**
10. Holding sides depressed, roll glove box downward until stops beyond clear rubber bumpers.
11. Remove air bag, then the steering wheel with a suitable puller. **Ensure puller bolts are fully engaged into steering wheel and not into clockspring before attempting to remove steering wheel.**
12. Remove fuse access panel and lower column cover.
13. Remove data link connector, hood release lever and parking brake release

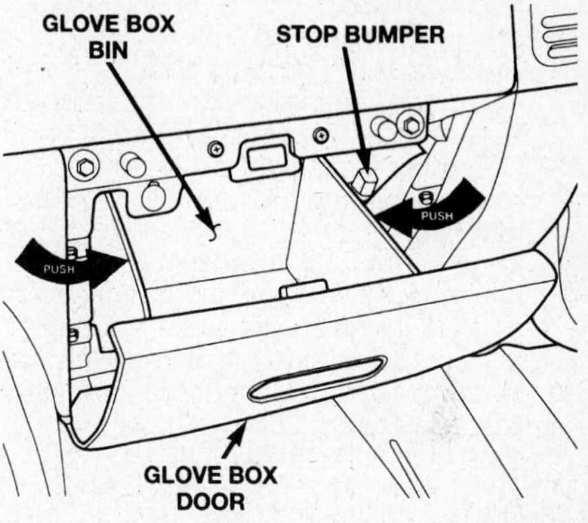

Fig. 12 Glove box roll-down. Full Size Van

lever from knee blocker, then the knee blocker.

14. Disconnect column wiring harness, then the harness block and air bag harness from steering column.
15. Remove shift cable and PRNDL cable, **Fig. 13,** from column shift lever actuator.
16. Release and remove shift cable from column bracket.
17. Remove two PRNDL cable adjuster mounting nuts, **Fig. 14,** then the adjuster.
18. Remove upper steering shaft coupler bolt and slide shaft downward.
19. Remove steering column mounting nuts, then the steering column assembly.
20. Disconnect electrical connectors secured to outboard side of bulkhead wiring harness connector.
21. Remove screw in center of instrument panel to bulkhead wiring harness connector, then disconnect connector.
22. Disconnect electrical connector from air bag control module located on front floor panel under driver side front seat.
23. Lift carpet on driver side front floor far enough to access and disengage air bag control module wiring harness from trough on floor panel.
24. Disconnect heater and air conditioner vacuum harness connector.
25. Reach through glove box opening and disconnect instrument panel to door and instrument panel to body wiring

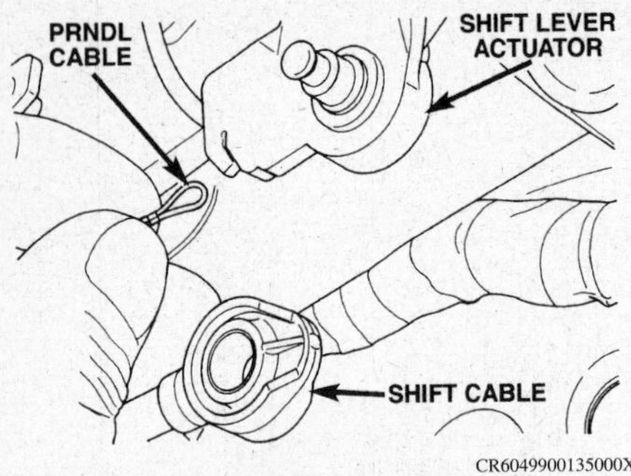

Fig. 13 PRNDL cable & shift cable. Full Size Van

harness connectors.
26. Disconnect radio antenna cable connector on passenger side end bracket of instrument panel.
27. Remove four righthand and lefthand instrument panel end brackets to A-pillar retaining bolts, **Fig. 15.**
28. Remove righthand and lefthand instrument panel end brackets to cowl side inner panels retaining bolts.
29. Loosen two nuts that retain instrument panel righthand and lefthand center support brackets to studs on instrument panel engine housing extension.
30. Remove five top of instrument panel to top of instrument panel retaining bolts, then the center screw.
31. Lift instrument panel assembly off studs on engine cover extension, then remove it from vehicle.
32. Reverse procedure to install. Tighten fasteners to specifications.

Grand Cherokee

2002-04

1. Place front wheels in straight ahead position
2. Remove trim panels from righthand and lefthand A-pillars.
3. Remove top cover from instrument panel, then the four nuts securing instrument panel to studs near windshield fence line.
4. Remove scuff plates from righthand and lefthand door sills.
5. Remove trim panels from righthand and lefthand inner cowl sides.
6. Remove floor console assembly.
7. Remove fuse cover from junction block.
8. Remove instrument cluster bezel.
9. Remove driver air bag module.
10. Remove steering wheel using suitable puller.
11. Remove cluster bezel, then the lower steering column shroud mounting screw.
12. Unsnap two halves of column shrouds by pressing on sides of upper shroud and tilting rear of upper shroud up, then remove shrouds.
13. Remove upper fixed shroud.
14. Disconnect multi-function switch and ignition switch electrical connectors.
15. Remove multi-function switch screw from under switch, then slide switch and clock spring off column as an assembly.
16. Turn ignition On, then release and remove shifter interlock cable from ignition lock cylinder housing.
17. Remove column coupler bolt, then slide coupler off column shaft.
18. Remove column mounting nuts, then lower column off mounting studs and remove from vehicle.
19. Disconnect bulkhead connectors from junction block.
20. Disconnect electrical connectors from floor mounted components.
21. Remove nuts securing ground straps to floor pan.
22. Disengage retainers securing wiring harness to floor pan.
23. Remove instrument panel to center floor tunnel bracket from instrument panel and floor pan.
24. Remove lefthand floor duct attached to HVAC housing.
25. **On models equipped with manual HVAC controls,** disconnect vacuum harness connector.
26. **On all models,** remove screws securing instrument panel steering column support bracket to lefthand end of HVAC housing and intermediate bracket on lefthand side.
27. Remove nut securing instrument panel steering column support bracket to stud on lefthand cowl plenum panel.
28. Remove screws securing instrument panel to lefthand cowl side inner panel.
29. Remove end cap and lower righthand center bezel from instrument panel.
30. Disconnect instrument panel harness connector from righthand cowl panel.
31. Disconnect two antenna cable halves and two electrical connectors from HVAC housing.
32. Remove two screws securing righthand instrument panel structural duct to HVAC housing.
33. Remove two screws securing instrument panel to righthand side cowl side inner panel.
34. Lift instrument panel assembly upward off of studs near windshield fence line and disengage molded hooks from guide holes.
35. Pull instrument panel rearward from dash panel and remove through lefthand front door.
36. Loosen three nuts securing intermediate bracket and accelerator pedal assembly to studs on instrument panel prior to installation.
37. Reverse procedure to install. Tighten fasteners to specifications.

2005-06

Refer to "Commander" for dash panel replacement procedures

Liberty

1. Remove grab handle trim plugs using suitable pry tool.
2. Remove grab handle attaching screws, then the grab handle and a-pillar trim.
3. Remove top cover trim panel using trim stick tool No. C-4755, or equivalent, to release attaching clips, **Fig. 16.**
4. Remove instrument panel speakers.
5. Remove center floor console.
6. Remove instrument panel center trim panel.
7. Remove radio mounting screws, disconnect antenna and electrical harness.
8. Remove radio assembly.
9. Remove center support bracket attaching nuts, then the center support, **Fig. 17.**
10. Ensure front wheels are in straight ahead position.
11. Remove driver air bag module as follows:
    a. Remove driver air bag module to steering wheel armature attaching screws from underside of steering wheel, **Fig. 18.**
    b. Disconnect steering wheel wire harness connector for horn switch from feed pigtail wire connector at back of driver air bag module.
    c. Disconnect clockspring electrical connectors from connector receptacles.
    d. Remove driver air bag module from steering wheel.
12. Remove steering wheel using suitable steering wheel puller tool.
13. Remove lower driver knee bolster panel below steering column.
14. Remove lower column shroud and both upper and lower shrouds.
15. Turn ignition key to On position.
16. **On models equipped with automatic transmission,** disconnect shift interlock cable from column.
17. **On all models,** remove steering coupler bolt and column mounting nuts and bolts, then lower column off mounting studs, **Fig. 19.**
18. Disconnect and remove wiring harness from column.
19. Remove steering column.
20. Remove drivers side cowl trim cover.
21. Disconnect wire harness connector from behind drivers side cowl trim.
22. Disconnect green and light blue wire harness connectors at junction block, **Fig. 20.**
23. Disconnect electrical connector at inner side of pedal support bracket, **Fig. 21.**
24. Remove front pedal support bracket attaching bolts, **Fig. 21.**
25. Remove bottom side of pedal support

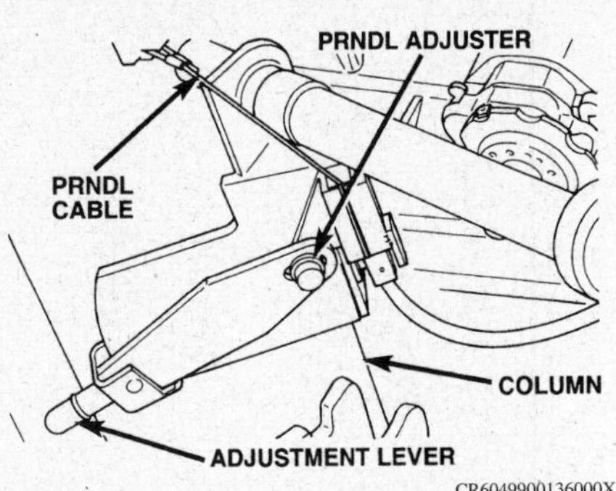

Fig. 14 PRNDL cable adjuster. Full Size Van

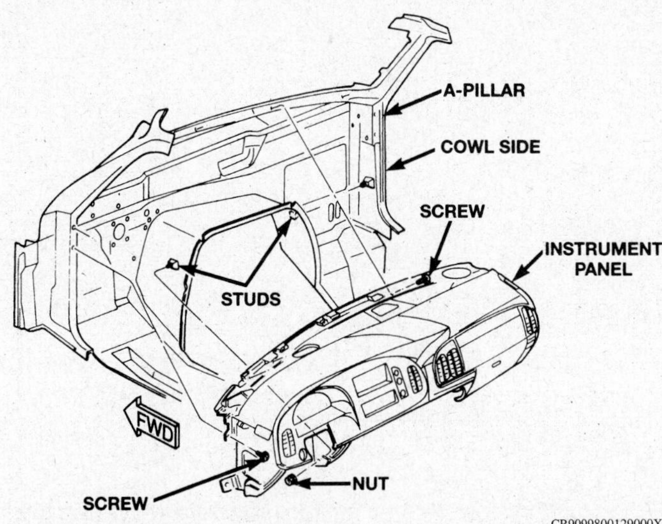

Fig. 15 Instrument panel assembly. Full Size Van

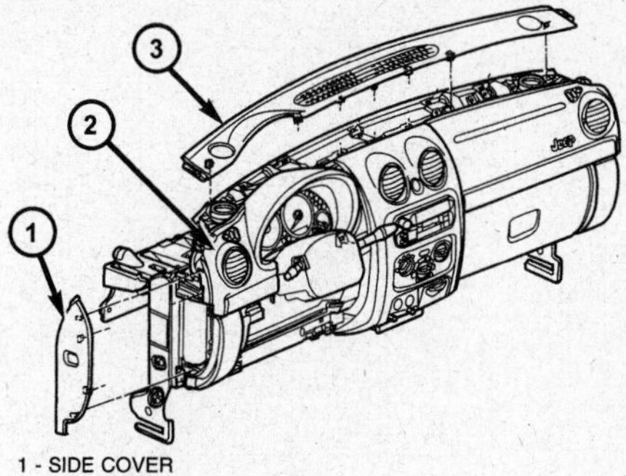

Fig. 16 Instrument panel cover replacement. Liberty

bracket attaching bolts, **Fig. 21.**

26. Remove roll down bracket bolts from lefthand cowl side panel, **Fig. 17.**
27. Remove ground strap attaching bolt, then the restraint module electrical connector, **Fig. 22.**
28. Remove glove compartment.
29. Remove passenger side trim bezel.
30. Remove HVAC mounting bolt above glove compartment striker, **Fig. 23.**
31. Remove HVAC attaching bolt at lower outside corner of glove compartment opening, **Fig. 24.**
32. Remove passenger side cowl trim cover.
33. Disconnect blower resistor electrical connector, **Fig. 24.**
34. Remove roll down bracket attaching bolts from righthand side cowl trim panel.
35. Disconnect vacuum check valve and reservoir, then the blower motor electrical connector.
36. Remove instrument panel top attaching bolts to cowl front panel.
37. Roll instrument panel rearward and remove wire harness from routing channel in rear.
38. Disconnect push pin fastener and position aside radio wire harness. Note location for installation.
39. Remove instrument panel assembly.
40. Reverse procedure to install.

Pacifica

1. Remove front floor console assembly, **Fig. 25.**
2. Remove nuts attaching floor braces to instrument panel.
3. Remove steering column opening cover.
4. Remove inflatable knee blocker and instrument panel trim outlet plate mounting screws, **Fig. 26.**
5. Disengage locking tabs attaching instrument panel trim plate.
6. Disengage parking brake release handle from bracket, leave rod engaged.
7. Remove instrument panel reinforcement, **Fig. 27.**
8. Disconnect bulkhead and body control module wiring connectors.
9. Remove upper and lower steering column shrouds.
10. Disconnect steering column wiring electrical connectors.
11. Remove steering column pinch bolt and retaining nuts, **Fig. 28.**
12. Disconnect brake light electrical connectors.
13. Remove shift interlock cable.
14. Remove A-pillar trim panels.
15. Remove instrument panel end caps.
16. Remove front door sill scuff plates, then cowl side trim panels.
17. Disconnect antenna lead connector.
18. Remove glove box.
19. Disconnect passenger air bag module electrical connector.
20. Remove top cover, then remove righthand instrument panel mounting screws.
21. Disconnect HVAC electrical connectors.
22. Disconnect electrical connectors behind cowl panel.
23. Disconnect righthand electrical connector from A-pillar.
24. Remove screws attaching instrument panel frame to dash panel below windshield opening.
25. With aid of an assistant lift instrument panel up off HVAC, then remove instrument panel.
26. Reverse procedure to install.

PT Cruiser

2002-05

Refer to **Fig. 29** when replacing the instrument panel.

1. Pry off lefthand and righthand A-pillar trim using suitable trim stick.
2. Pry out front power window switch from center bezel using suitable trim stick.
3. Remove one center bezel retaining screw, then pull off HVAC control knobs.
4. Pry off center bezel using suitable trim stick.
5. Remove two top cover retaining screws.
6. Pull rearward on top cover to unlatch it from instrument panel and remove.
7. Remove two screws retaining HVAC control panel, then disconnect electrical connector, vacuum harness connector and control cables.
8. Remove HVAC control panel.
9. Remove upper and lower steering column shrouds.
10. Remove lefthand lower instrument panel bezel.
11. Disconnect ignition switch, multifunction switch and clockspring electrical connectors from steering column.
12. Ensure front wheels are in straight ahead position.
13. Remove key from ignition, then remove silencer pad below steering column.
14. Fold down and remove knee blocker.
15. Remove two screws attaching lower shroud to steering column and upper shroud.
16. Unclip shrouds from each other, then remove them from steering column.
17. Remove driver air bag module.
18. Disconnect speed control switch electrical connector.
19. Holding steering wheel firmly in place, remove retaining bolt from steering column shaft in center of steering wheel.
20. Thread wheel retaining bolt back into end of shaft until .5 inch of thread is showing between wheel and head of bolt.
21. Remove steering wheel using suitable puller.
22. Remove steering coupling retainer pin, then back off pinch bolt nut and remove steering column coupling pinch bolt.
23. Separate upper and lower steering column couplings.
24. **On models equipped with automatic transaxle,** disconnect interlock cable from steering column.
25. **On all models,** remove two lower mounting nuts attaching steering column to instrument panel.
26. Remove two upper mounting nuts attaching steering column to instrument panel.

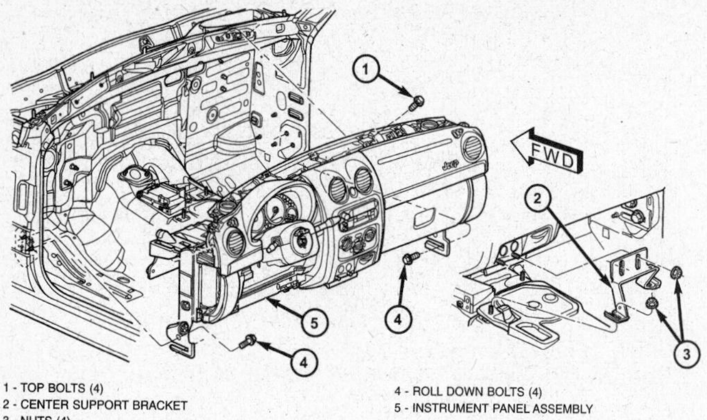

Fig. 17 Instrument panel assembly replacement. Liberty

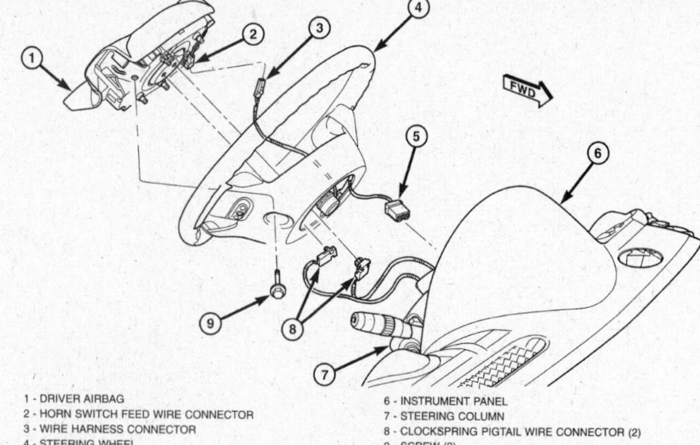

Fig. 18 Driver air bag module replacement. Liberty

27. Lower steering column away from instrument panel.
28. Disconnect electrical connectors from clockspring, multi-function switch, windshield wiper switch and ignition switch.
29. Disconnect electrical connector from Sentry Key Immobilizer Module (SKIM), if equipped.
30. Remove steering column from vehicle.
31. Remove two brake pedal support bracket retaining bolts.
32. Remove two lefthand end cap screws, then pull end cap rearward to unsnap and remove.
33. Disconnect following wiring electrical connectors from lefthand side of instrument panel:
    a. Data Link Connector.
    b. Two main connectors.
    c. Brake switch.
    d. Lefthand side body harness.
    e. Lefthand door harness.
34. Remove three lefthand side A-pillar instrument panel retaining bolts.
35. Remove two retaining bolts at lefthand side of center support bracket.
36. Remove floor console assembly.
37. **On models equipped with automatic transaxle,** remove shifter handle and bezel.
38. **On all models,** disconnect ORC and park brake switch electrical connectors.
39. Remove two retaining bolts at righthand side of center support bracket.
40. Loosen center console heater duct to allow wiring harness to be removed from underneath it.
41. Open glove box and push in on sides to allow retainers to clear instrument panel, then pull glove box downward to remove.
42. Remove two screws to righthand end cap, then pull end cap rearward to remove.
43. Remove two righthand side A-pillar instrument retaining bolts and one nut.
44. Disconnect following righthand side instrument panel electrical connectors:
    a. Antenna.
    b. Overhead systems.
    c. Blower motor.
    d. Lefthand door harness.
    e. Body harness.
45. Remove four fence line instrument panel retaining bolts.
46. Remove instrument panel.
47. Reverse procedure to install. Tighten fasteners to specifications.

2006

1. Remove center instrument panel bezel, then disconnect control cables and electrical connection from back of bezel.
2. Remove floor center console.
3. Remove floor distribution ducts as required to gain access to instrument panel wire harness connections.
4. Disconnect following wiring electrical connectors:
    a. Power outlet.
    b. Gearshift assembly.
    c. Ground wire.
    d. Side air bag controller.
    e. Body wire harness.
    f. Radio amplifier.
5. Disconnect wire harness retainers from floor and console brackets, then position wire harness leads aside.
6. Remove lefthand A-pillar trim panel.
7. Place front wheel in straight ahead position.
8. Remove steering column as noted in "Steering Columns" section.
9. Remove lefthand cowl trim panel.
10. Disconnect wire harness electrical connectors for driver door harness, two main instrument panel connectors and driver side body harness.
11. Remove data link connector from its mounting bracket and disengage two wire harness retainers from side cowl panel.
12. Remove carpeting to floor bracket push pin retainers.
13. Move carpet for access, then remove center instrument panel support to floor bracket bolts.
14. Remove righthand A-pillar trim panel.
15. Remove glove box.
16. Remove righthand instrument panel silencer, then cowl trim panel.
17. Disconnect following wire harness electrical connectors:
    a. Recirculation door actuator.
    b. Blower motor.
    c. Righthand body harness.
    d. Radio coax.
    e. Righthand door harness.
18. Disconnect wire harness retainer from side cowl panel.
19. Remove instrument panel support bracket to driver side of dash panel mounting bolts through steering column opening, **Fig. 30.**
20. Remove instrument panel top cover.
21. Remove top of instrument panel to dash panel mounting bolts.
22. Remove instrument panel end caps.
23. Remove instrument panel support to cowl panel mounting bolts and nut, **Fig. 31.**
24. With aid of an assistant remove instrument panel.
25. Reverse procedure to install.

Sprinter

1. Remove radio using tool No. 9241, or equivalent.
2. Remove glove box mounting screws, then glove box.
3. Remove cup holders.
4. Remove instrument cluster bezel.
5. Remove instrument cluster mounting screws, then cluster.
6. Remove instrument panel top cover tray from over the passenger air bag.
7. Remove two screws that secure passenger air bag door upper clips to instrument panel base.
8. Remove passenger air bag housing to instrument panel support retaining screws.
9. Disconnect passenger air bag electrical connectors.
10. Remove passenger air bag and air bag door from instrument panel as a unit.
11. Remove righthand and lefthand speakers, then center bezel.
12. Remove air conditioning push-button control module.
13. Remove Power Distribution Center (PDC) cover.
14. Remove steering column shrouds.
15. Disconnect PDC electrical connectors,

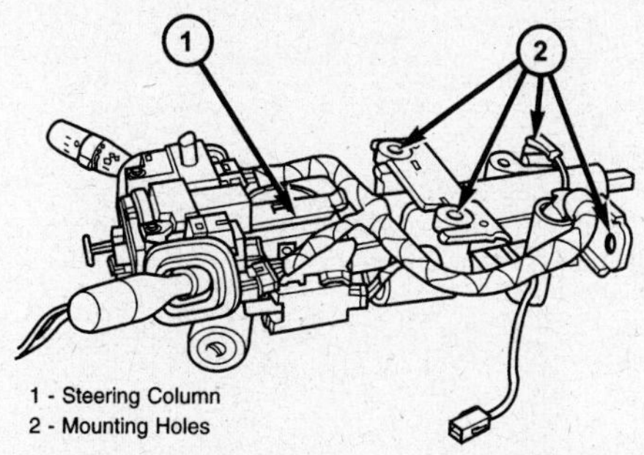

Fig. 19 Steering column mounting locations. Liberty

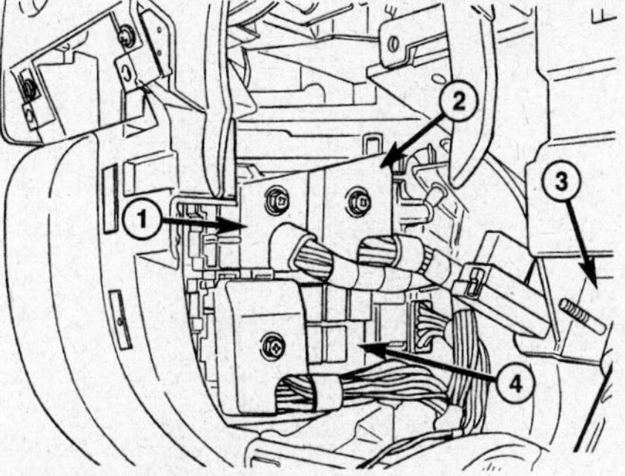

Fig. 20 Junction block connectors. Liberty

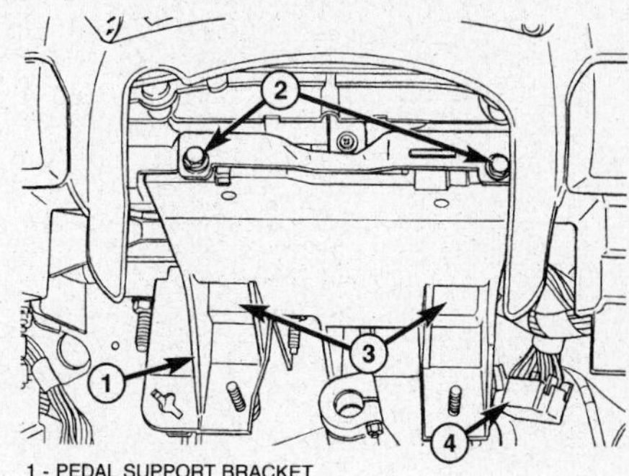

Fig. 21 Pedal support bracket replacement. Liberty

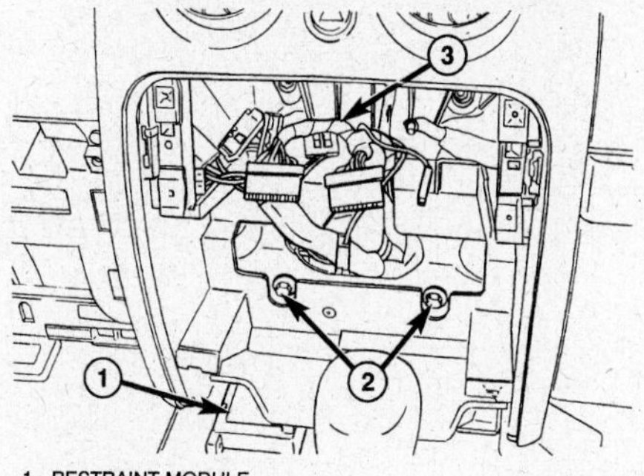

Fig. 22 Restraint module bolt replacement. Liberty

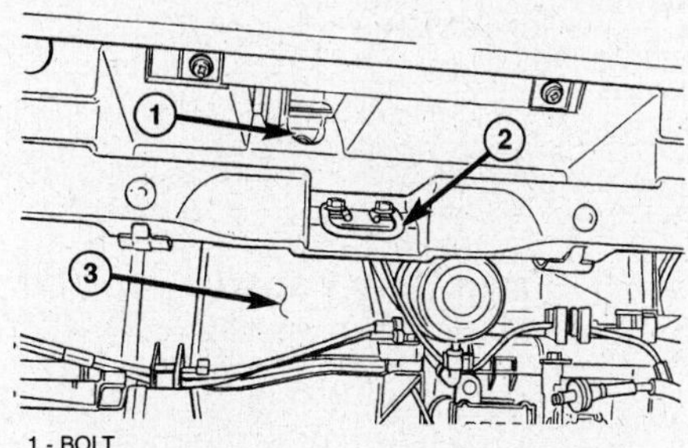

Fig. 23 HVAC upper bolt replacement. Liberty

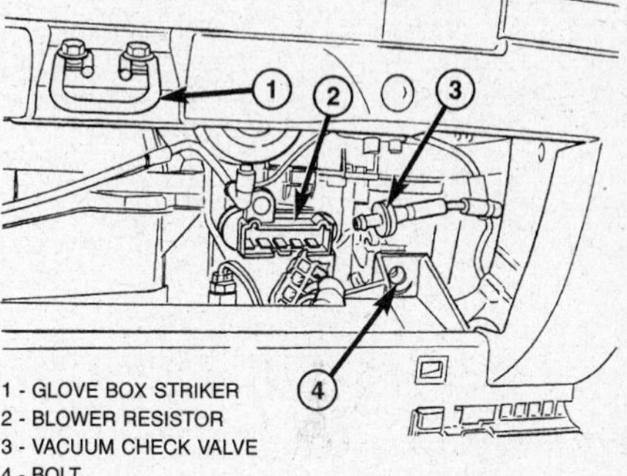

Fig. 24 HVAC connection replacement. Liberty

then remove PDC.

16. Remove all air nozzle covers.
17. Remove protective matting from cluster location.
18. Remove instrument panel top cover screws and cover.
19. Remove brake pedal spring.
20. Remove ignition transponder.
21. Place front wheels in straight ahead position.
22. Remove steering column support bolts.
23. Remove instrument panel screws, then instrument panel.
24. Reverse procedure to install.

Wrangler

1. Place front wheels straight ahead.
2. Remove steering column cover and knee blocker, then insert key and turn to On position. Insert a small screwdriver through access hole and remove ignition lock cylinder.
3. Remove three screws that hold lower shroud to upper, then disconnect all electrical connectors.
4. Remove pinch bolt from upper half of steering shaft coupler, then the four nuts holding steering column mounts to steering column support bracket.
5. Lower steering column mounts off support bracket studs and remove steering column from vehicle.
6. Reach through steering column opening and disconnect instrument panel 100-way electrical connector near cowl side panel, then the side window demister/defroster duct.
7. Remove glove box by depressing retainer tab, then lift off the pivots.
8. Reach through glove compartment opening and disconnect the following:
   a. Temperature control cable.
   b. HVAC housing vacuum harness.
   c. Passenger air bag connector and radio power connector.
   d. Side window demister hose at HVAC housing and radio antenna cable.
9. Remove two nuts securing lower passenger air bag module bracket to studs on instrument panel.
10. Pry off instrument panel top cover using a suitable wide-bladed tool, then remove two screws securing each end of instrument panel to door hinge pillars, **Fig. 32.**
11. Remove four nuts securing top of instrument panel, then lift instrument panel from vehicle.
12. Reverse procedure to install. Tighten fasteners to specifications.

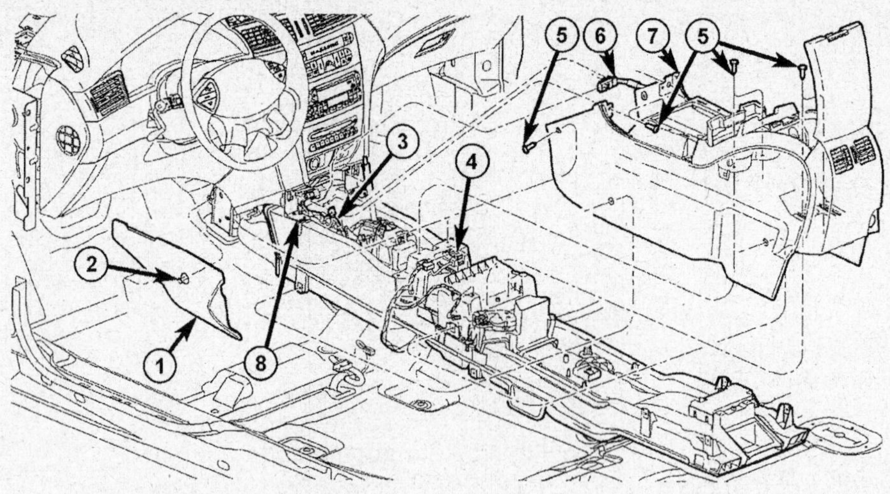

1 - FORWARD CONSOLE CLOSEOUT PANEL
2 - CLOSEOUT PANEL PUSH PIN RETAINER
3 - INSTRUMENT PANEL WIRING
4 - FLOOR CONSOLE BASE
5 - FRONT FLOOR CONSOLE ATTACHING SCREWS TO LOWER INSTRUMENT PANE AND BASE
6 - FRONT FLOOR CONSOLE WIRING CONNECTOR
7 - FRONT FLOOR CONSOLE
8 - ATTACHING L-BRACKETS

LTV0500000000208

Fig. 25 Front floor console replace. Pacifica

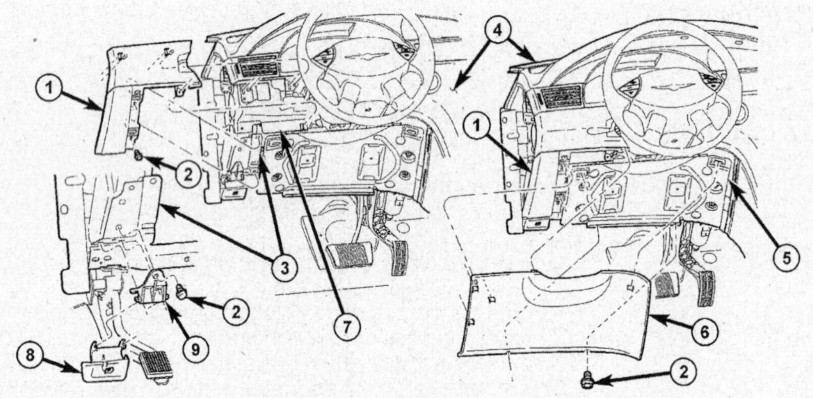

1 - INSTRUMENT PANEL TRIM OUTLET PLATE
2 - ATTACHING SCREWS
3 - INSTRUMENT PANEL PARKING BRAKE RELEASE HANDLE BRACKET
4 - INSTRUMENT PANEL
5 - INFLATABLE KNEE BLOCKER AIRBAG
6 - INSTRUMENT PANEL STEERING COLUMN OPENING COVER
7 - INSTRUMENT PANEL CLUSTER POCKET
8 - BRAKE RELEASE HANDLE
9 - BRAKE HANDLE BRACKET ASSEMBLY

LTV0500000000209

Fig. 26 Park brake handle & lefthand lower instrument panel. Pacifica

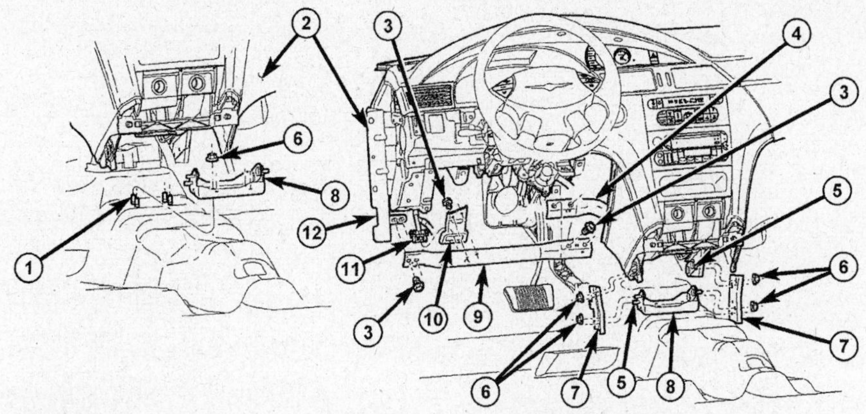

1 - WELD STUDS
2 - INSTRUMENT PANEL
3 - MOUNTING SCREWS
4 - INSTRUMENT PANEL REINFORCEMENT
5 - STUDS
6 - ATTACHING NUTS
7 - INSTRUMENT TO FLOOR BRACKET
8 - INSTRUMENT PANEL BRACE TO FLOOR BRACKET
9 - INSTRUMENT PANEL REINFORCEMENT
10 - DIAGNOSTIC REMOTE CONNECTOR BRACKET
11 - DIAGNOSTIC WIRE CONNECTOR
12 - INSTRUMENT PANEL SIDE COWL BRACKET

LTV0500000000210

Fig. 27 Instrument panel lower reinforcement. Pacifica

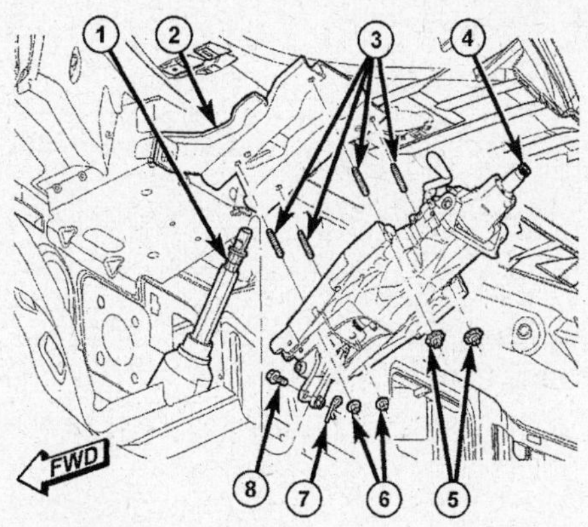

1 - INTERMEDIATE SHAFT
2 - COLUMN MOUNTING BRACKET
3 - COLUMN MOUNING STUDS
4 - STEERING COLUMN
5 - UPPER MOUNTING NUTS
6 - LOWER MOUNTING NUTS
7 - HAIR PIN
8 - COUPLING PINCH BOLT

LTV0500000000211

Fig. 28 Steering column. Pacifica

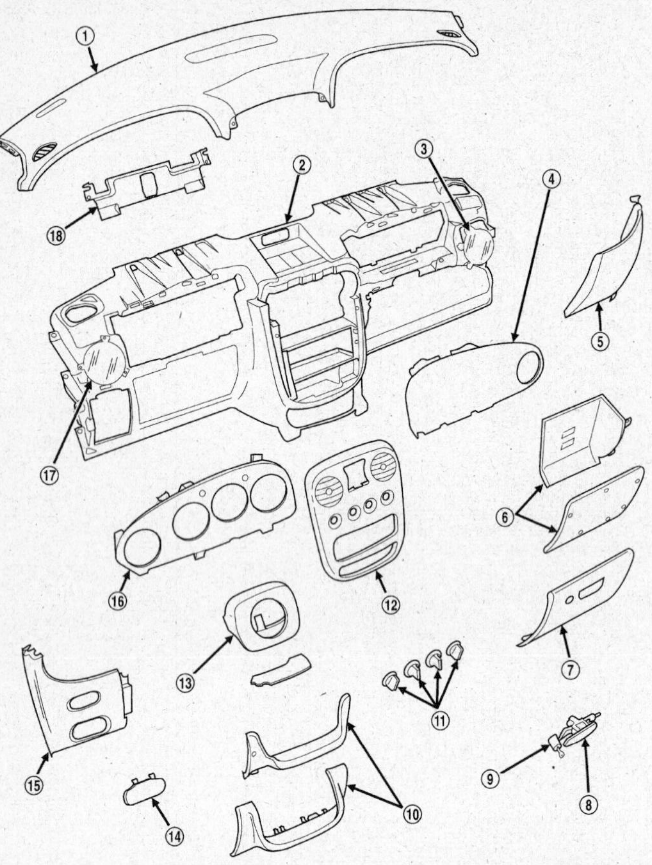

CR9090000194010X

Fig. 29 Exploded view of instrument panel (Part 1 of 2). 2002–05 PT Cruiser

1 – COVER, INSTRUMENT PANEL TOP
2 – ASSEMBLY, INSTRUMENT PANEL
3 – HOUSING, INSTRUMENT PANEL OUTBOARD A/C OUTLET ASSEMBLY
4 – MODULE, PASSENGER AIRBAG COVER, PASSENGER AIRBAG MODULE
5 – ENDCAP, INSTRUMENT PANEL
6 – BOX, INSTRUMENT PANEL GLOVE BOX ASSEMBLY
7 – DOOR, INSTRUMENT PANEL GLOVE BOX
8 – LATCH, INSTRUMENT PANEL GLOVE BOX ASSEMBLY
9 – CYLINDER, LOCK
10 – BEZEL, INSTRUMENT PANEL LOWER
11 – KNOBS, A/C CONTROL ASSEMBLY
12 – BEZEL, INSTRUMENT PANEL CENTER
13 – SHROUD, STEERING COLUMN
14 – COVER, FUSES
15 – ENDCAP, INSTRUMENT PANEL
16 – BEZEL, INSTRUMENT CLUSTER
17 – HOUSING, INSTRUMENT PANEL CLUSTER BEZEL A/C OUTLET ASSEMBLY
18 – PANEL, CLUSTER AREA SUPPORT

CR9090000194020X

Fig. 29 Exploded view of instrument panel (Part 2 of 2). 2002–05 PT Cruiser

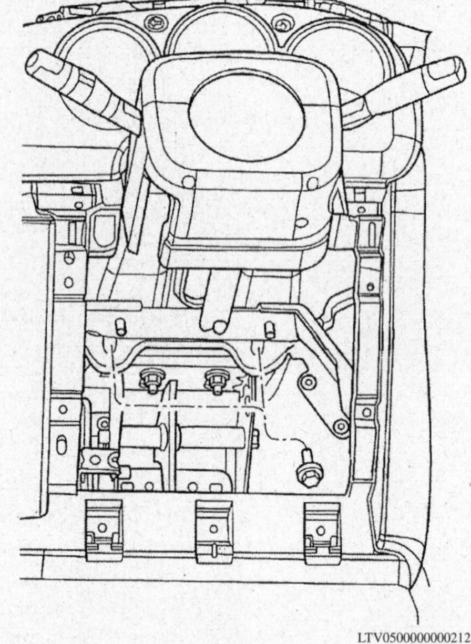

LTV0500000000212

Fig. 30 Instrument panel support bracket

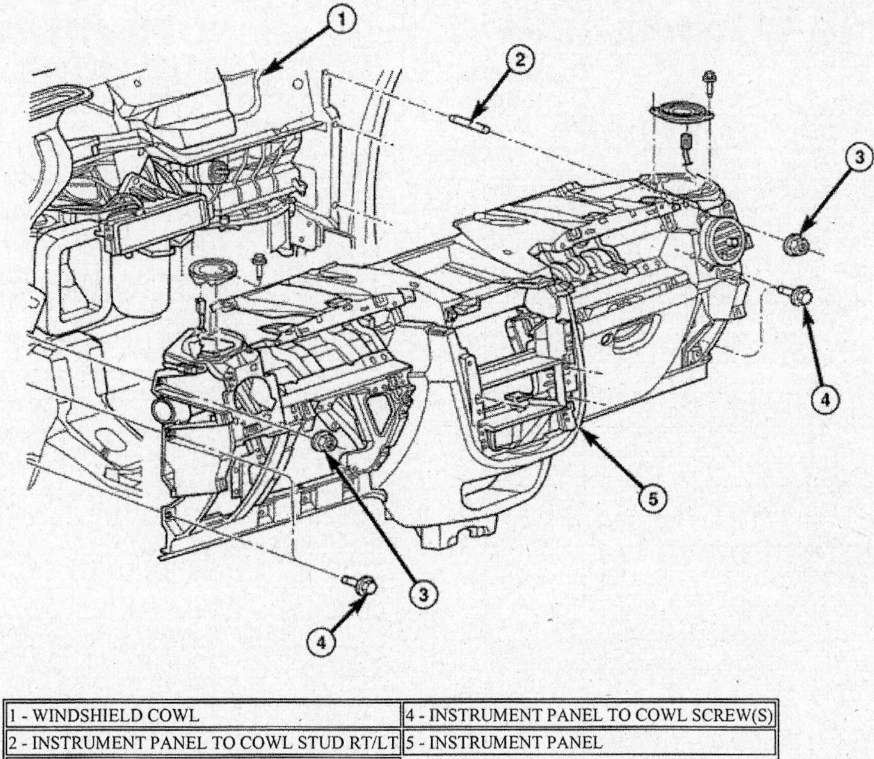

1 - WINDSHIELD COWL	4 - INSTRUMENT PANEL TO COWL SCREW(S)
2 - INSTRUMENT PANEL TO COWL STUD RT/LT	5 - INSTRUMENT PANEL
3 - INSTRUMENT PANEL TO COWL NUT(S)	

LTV0500000000213

Fig. 31 Instrument panel replace. 2006 PT Cruiser

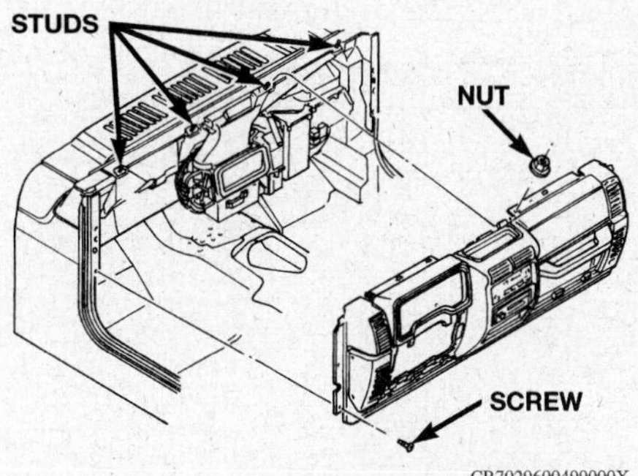

Fig. 32 Instrument panel. Wrangler

TIGHTENING SPECIFICATIONS

Component	Torque Ft. Lbs.
CARAVAN, TOWN & COUNTRY & VOYAGER	
Steering Column Pinch Bolt	21
Steering Column Upper Bracket Washer/Nuts	108①
Steering Wheel Nut	45
COMMANDER	
Center Support Bracket Nuts	105①
Instrument Panel to Cowl Panel Bolts	95①
Steering Column Pinch Bolt	36
Steering Column Support Bolts	105①
2002–04 DAKOTA & DURANGO	
Floor Console	35①
Instrument Panel To Dash Panel	28①
Instrument Panel Roll-Down Screws	108①
Steering Column Nuts	21
Steering Column Pinch Bolt	36
Steering Wheel Nut	45
2005–06 DAKOTA	
Center Support Bolts	105①
Electrical Connector Retaining Bolt	40①
Instrument Panel To Cowl Panel Bolts	105①
Pedal Support Bracket Bolts	10
Steering Column Mounting Bolts	21
Steering Column Pinch Bolt	42
Upper Instrument Panel Bolts	85①
2005–06 DURANGO	
A-Pillar Mounting Bolts	55①
Front Seat Frame Mounting Bolts	20
Instrument Panel To Cowl Support Bolts	20
Instrument Panel Center Support Bolts	95①
Pedal Support Bolts	10
Rear Seat Frame Mounting Bolts	35
Steering Column Mounting Nuts	21
Steering Column Pinch Bolt	28
Upper Instrument Panel Mounting Bolts	70①
2002 2500 & 3500 FULL SIZE PICKUPS	
Instrument Panel Roll-Down Screws	105①
Instrument Panel To Dash Panel	28①
Steering Column Pinch Bolt	36
Steering Column Shroud Screws	20①
Steering Column Upper Bracket Nuts	105①
Steering Wheel Nut	45
Toe Plate Nuts	17
2002–03 1500 & 2003–06 2500 & 3500 FULL SIZE PICKUPS	
Instrument Panel Center Bracket	108①
Instrument Panel Column Support Bolts	10
Instrument Panel Side Mounting Bolts	108①
Instrument Panel Top Bolts	108①
Steering Column Pinch Bolt	42

TIGHTENING SPECIFICATIONS—Continued

Component	Torque Ft. Lbs.
2002–03 1500 & 2003–06 2500 & 3500 FULL SIZE PICKUPS	
Steering Wheel Nut	45
FULL SIZE VAN	
Instrument Panel Center Support Bracket	20
Instrument Panel Screws	96①
Steering Column Nuts	21
Steering Shaft Coupler	36
Steering Wheel Nut	35
2002–04 GRAND CHEROKEE	
Steering Column Coupler Bolt	36
Steering Column Mounting Nuts	105①
Steering Wheel Nut	45
2005–06 GRAND CHEROKEE	
A-Pillar Trim Screws	55①
Instrument Panel Center Support Bracket Nuts	105①
Instrument Panel Pedal Support Nuts	105①
Instrument Panel Side Support Bolts	95①
Steering Column Cross Bolt	108①
Steering Column Pinch Bolt	36
Steering Column Support Bolts	105①
LIBERTY	
Cowl Front Panel To Instrument Panel	21
Driver's Cowl Side Panel	40
HVAC Mounting Bolt At Glove Compartment Opening	55①
Instrument Center Panel Attaching Nuts	17
Roll Down Bracket	40
Steering Column Coupler Bolt	36
Steering Column Mounting Nuts	13
Steering Wheel Nut	45
PACIFICA	
Instrument Panel to Cowl Panel	21
Instrument Panel Column Support Bracket Nuts	17
Instrument Panel Floor Bracket To Floor Nuts	13
Instrument Panel Floor Bracket to Center Stack Brace Nuts	13
PT CRUISER	
Steering Column Mounting Nut	13
Steering Column Pinch Bolt	21
Steering Wheel Nut	40
SPRINTER	
Steering Column Mounting Bolts	18
WRANGLER	
Steering Column Mounting Nuts	17
Steering Column Pinch Bolt	36
Steering Wheel Nut	40

① — Inch lbs.

STEERING COLUMNS

NOTE: On Air Bag Equipped Models, Refer To "Air Bag System Precautions" Located In The Front Of This Manual For System Disarming & Arming Procedures.

NOTE: Refer To "Computer Relearn Procedures" Located In The Front Of This Manual For Computer Relearn Procedures.

NOTE: Prior To Performing Any Service Operations Listed In This Section, Consult The "Technical Service Bulletins" Section For Related Information.

INDEX

PRECAUTIONS

Air Bag Systems

Refer to "Air Bag System Precautions" in the front of this manual for system disarming and arming procedures.

Battery Ground Cable

Prior to service, disconnect battery ground cable and isolate as required.

SERVICE

When the steering column is installed in the vehicle it is not susceptible to damage through ordinary use. However, when it is removed, care must be taken during handling. Such actions as a sharp blow on the end of the steering shaft or shift levers, leaning on the column assembly or dropping of the assembly could loosen or shear the plastic shear joints or rivets used to maintain column rigidity. **Hammering, jolting or bumping on the steering shaft and gearshift tube must be avoided during all service operations. If the shear pins are broken, the controlled length of the telescoping design will be altered making these components unfit for further service. When removing the steering wheel, only a steering wheel puller designed for this purpose must be used.**

It is important that only the specified screws, bolts and nuts be used during the assembly procedure and tightened to specifications to ensure proper breakaway action of the column under impact. Avoid using excessively long bolts or fasteners as they may prevent a portion of the steering column from collapsing. When replacing fasteners, replace with ones of the same part number, or equivalent.

Refer to the appropriate vehicle chapter when removing or installing the steering wheel, ignition switch, lock cylinder, turn signal switch, neutral start switch, back-up lamp switch or adjusting column shift manual transmission linkage.

Do not attempt pivot pin removal to disassemble the tilt mechanism. Do not remove shaft lock plate, plate retainer, park lock link or slider.

DESCRIPTION

The energy absorbing function of the steering column allows the column to collapse at a controlled rate during a severe collision. The collapsing action reduces the possibility of the steering wheel being driven rearward toward the driver. If the driver is thrown forward into the steering wheel, the column can collapse even further at the same controlled rate, thereby reducing the force of impact.

Several designs of steering column jackets are used. There is the slip tube design which is held together with plastic inserts or rivets that shear upon impact and allow the column to collapse. And there is the slotted or corrugated mesh design and bellows type design which shorten in length during impact.

The shift tube is a two piece design which is held together by injections of plastic that form the interconnecting inserts and shear pins. Under impact, there is a gradual paring away of the inserts by the knife-like edge in the adjoining tube section.

The steering shaft is a two piece assembly. The upper piece is solid and has a double flattened lower end. The lower piece is hollow and formed to fit over the double flattened section of the upper piece. The purpose of the double flattened section is to provide continued steering action even though the shaft is completely collapsed. Upon impact, the shear pins break off and the shaft gradually telescopes against resistance provided by the plastic injections.

The steering column mounting bracket prevents the column from being shifted toward the driver during impact. It uses two

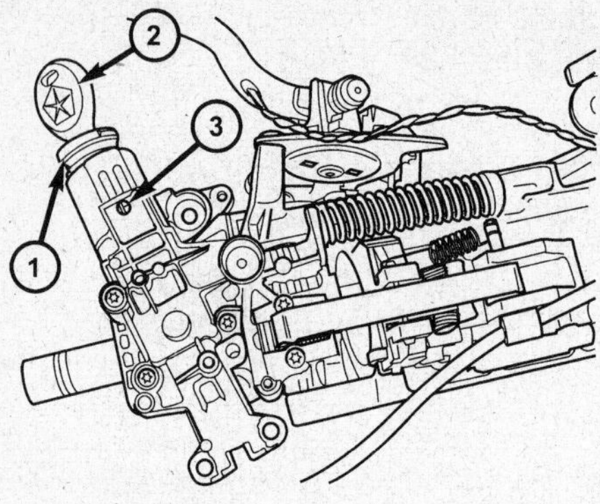

1 - Key Lock Cylinder
2 - Key
3 - Reataining Pin Hole

CR6049800153000X

Fig. 1 Ignition lock cylinder removal. Full Size Van

breakaway capsules that allow the mounting bracket to slip off its attaching points, allowing the steering column to compress or yield in a forward direction under a severe impact from the driver's end.

STEERING COLUMN

REPLACE

Full Size Van

REMOVAL

1. Ensure front wheels are in straight-ahead position.
2. Remove driver air bag module as outlined in "Passive Restraint Systems" chapter.
3. Remove steering wheel retaining nut.
4. Ensure puller tool bolts are fully engaged into steering wheel and not into clockspring before attempting to remove steering wheel.
5. Remove steering wheel.
6. Remove fuse access panel and lower column cover.
7. Remove Data Link Connector (DLC), hood release lever and parking brake release lever from knee blocker.
8. Disconnect column wiring harness, then the harness block and air bag harness from steering column.
9. Remove column shrouds.
10. Remove ignition lock cylinder as follows:
    a. Ensure transmission lever is in Park.
    b. Turn key to Run.
    c. Press in on retaining pin while pulling cylinder out of ignition switch, **Fig. 1.**
11. Remove knee blocker.
12. Remove shift cable and PRNDL cable, **Fig. 2,** from column shift lever actuator.
13. Release and remove shift cable from column bracket.
14. Remove two PRNDL cable adjuster mounting nuts, **Fig. 3,** then the adjuster.

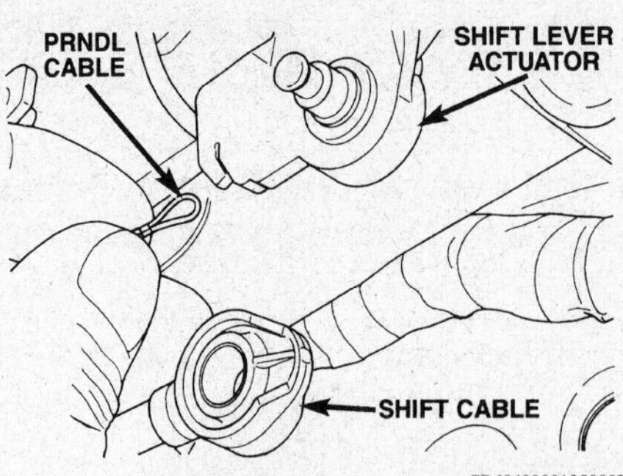

CR6049900135000X

Fig. 2 PRNDL cable & shift cable. Full Size Van

15. Remove upper steering shaft coupler bolt and slide shaft downward. Discard the bolt.
16. Remove steering column mounting nuts, then the steering column assembly.
17. Remove switches and clockspring.

INSTALLATION

New steering columns may be shipped with a locking pin installed. Do not remove lockpin until the column and the steering wheel are installed. When installing a non-tilt column, ensure the column is tilted up against the tilt stop and locked into position.

1. Install switches, clockspring, key cylinder and shrouds. Refer to "Passive Restraint Systems" chapter for procedures.
2. Position steering column on dash panel support and loosely install mounting nuts.
3. Slide steering column firmly upward against studs in dash panel and hand tighten nuts.
4. Install steering shaft coupler on steering shaft with new bolt.
5. Center steering column in dash and **torque** mounting nuts to 21 ft. lbs. Tighten lower lefthand nut first, then the lower righthand nut followed by the upper lefthand and righthand nuts.
6. **Torque** coupler bolt to 36 ft. lbs.
7. Install PRNDL cable and adjust if required by moving adjustment lever.
8. Install shifter cable, column wiring harness block and air bag harness.
9. Connect column wiring harness to block.
10. Connect driver air bag module wiring.
11. Install knee blocker, data link connector, hood release lever and parking brake release lever.
12. Install lower column cover.
13. Align master spline on steering wheel and shaft. Wheel should be at 12 o'clock position.
14. Install retaining nut.
15. **Torque** nut to 45 ft. lbs.
16. Remove shipping lockpin as required.
17. Install driver air bag module as outlined in "Passive Restraint Systems" chapter.

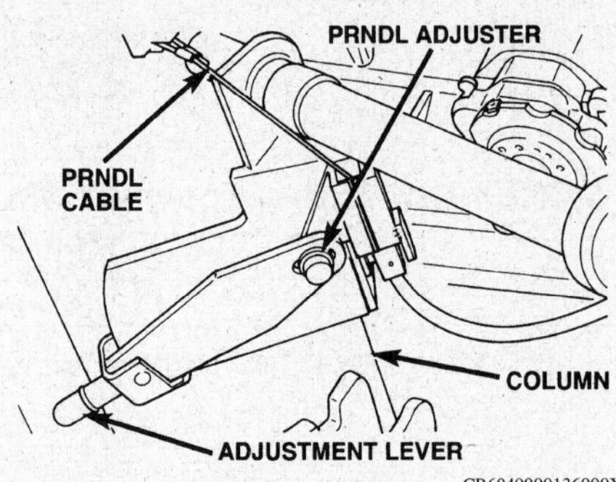

CR6049900136000X

Fig. 3 PRNDL cable adjuster. Full Size Van

Full Size Pickup

2002 2500 & 3500

REMOVAL

1. Ensure front wheels are in straight-ahead position.
2. Remove driver air bag module as outlined in "Passive Restraint Systems" chapter.
3. Remove steering wheel retaining nut.
4. Ensure puller tool bolts are fully engaged in steering wheel and not into clockspring before attempting to remove steering wheel.
5. Remove steering wheel.
6. Remove shift link rod in engine compartment, if equipped. Pry rod out from shift lever grommet. Discard grommet.
7. Scribe or paint reference a mark on steering column shaft to coupler for installation reference, then remove and discard coupler bolt.
8. Remove steering column opening cover and knee blocker.
9. **On models equipped with column shift,** remove PRNDL cable as follows:
    a. Place shift lever in Park position.
    b. Pull cable and twist to remove from position arm.
    c. Push tab up on bottom of cable retainer, then squeeze sides to remove retainer from column.
10. **On models equipped with tilt steering column,** remove tilt lever.
11. **On all models,** remove upper and lower lock housing shroud and lower fixed shroud.
12. Remove multi-function switch electrical connector using a suitable 7 MM socket.
13. Loosen upper support bracket nuts to allow some clearance to aid in removal of upper fixed shroud.
14. Remove electrical connectors from Key-In lamp, ignition switch, horn, overdrive switch and clockspring.
15. Remove wiring harness from column by carefully prying out plastic retainer buttons.
16. Remove toe plate fasteners, then the steering column from vehicle.
17. Remove ignition and multi-function switches.
18. Remove clockspring, then secure it with tape to prevent it from turning.

INSTALLATION

1. Install clockspring and switches. Refer to "Passive Restraint Systems" chapter for procedures.
2. **On models equipped with column shift,** proceed as follows:
   a. A new shift linkage grommet should be used whenever the rod is disconnected.
   b. Install new grommet using suitable lubricant to aid installation.
3. **On all models,** remove shipping lockpin.
4. Install ground clip on lefthand spacer slot, then the column through floor pan.
5. Position column bracket breakaway capsules on mounting studs.
6. Install and loosely assemble two upper bracket nuts.
7. With front wheels in straight-ahead position, align steering column shaft to coupler.
8. Install coupler with new pinch bolt and **torque** to 36 ft. lbs.
9. Install wiring harness to column, then connect multi-function switch electrical connector.
10. Install upper fixed shroud.
11. Ensure both breakaway capsules are fully seated in slots in column support bracket.
12. Pull column rearward and **torque** upper bracket nuts to 105 inch lbs.
13. **Torque** toe plate to floor pan attaching nuts to 17 ft. lbs.
14. Install remaining wiring connections to column, then the lower fixed shroud.
15. **On models equipped with column shift,** install PRNDL driver cable. Adjust if required with thumb screw on cable retainer.
16. **On models equipped with tilt steering column,** install tilt lever.
17. **On all models,** install lock housing shrouds, then **torque** mounting screws to 17 inch lbs.
18. Install knee blocker and steering column opening cover, then **torque** mounting screws to 20 inch lbs.
19. Install steering wheel and retaining nut, then **torque** to 45 ft. lbs.
20. Install driver air bag module as outlined in "Passive Restraint Systems" chapter.
21. **On models equipped with column shift,** connect shift link rod to transmission shift lever using multi-purpose lubricant to aid installation.
22. **On all models,** inspect shift linkage operation and adjust as required.

1500 & 2003-06 2500 & 3500

REMOVAL

1. Ensure front wheels are in straight-ahead position.
2. Remove two switches from steering wheel.
3. Remove driver air bag module as outlined in "Passive Restraint Systems" chapter.
4. Remove steering wheel using puller tool No. CJ98-1, or equivalent. **Ensure puller tool bolts are fully engaged into steering wheel and not into clockspring.**
5. Remove steering column opening cover.
6. Remove tilt lever, then the column shrouds.
7. Remove clockspring, then disconnect wiring harness to column.
8. **On models equipped with automatic transmission,** remove shift cable from column shift lever actuator.
9. **On models equipped with automatic transmission,** release shift cable from column bracket and remove.
10. **On all models,** remove SKIM module in order to disconnect electrical connector.
11. Remove upper steering shaft coupler bolt, then slide shaft down.
12. Remove and discard brake light switch.
13. Remove four steering column mounting nuts.
14. Remove steering column.

INSTALLATION

1. Position steering column on dash panel support, then loosely install mounting nuts.
2. Firmly slide steering column upward against studs in dash panel, then hand tighten nuts.
3. Install steering shaft coupler on steering shaft, then loosely install new bolt.
4. Center steering column in dash opening.
5. **Torque,** mounting nuts to 21 ft. lbs., starting with upper left nut, lower right nut, lower left nut and finally upper right nut.
6. **Torque** coupler bolt to 42 ft. lbs., **using new bolt.**
7. Press and hold brake pedal down, then align new brake light switch with notch in switch bracket.
8. Insert brake light switch into bracket, then rotate clockwise 30° to lock in place.
9. Connect brake light switch electrical connector, then release brake pedal.
10. Move release lever on brake light switch parallel with connector to engage switch plunger. Switch is now adjusted and can not be adjusted again.
11. Install shift cable, then connect wiring harness to column.
12. Install SKIM module.
13. Install clockspring, then the steering column shrouds.
14. Install steering column opening cover.
15. Align spline on wheel hub to shaft.
16. Install steering wheel and new bolt. **Torque** bolt to 45 ft. lbs.
17. Install driver air bag module as outlined in "Passive Restraint Systems" chapter.
18. Install two steering wheel switches, then the tilt lever handle.

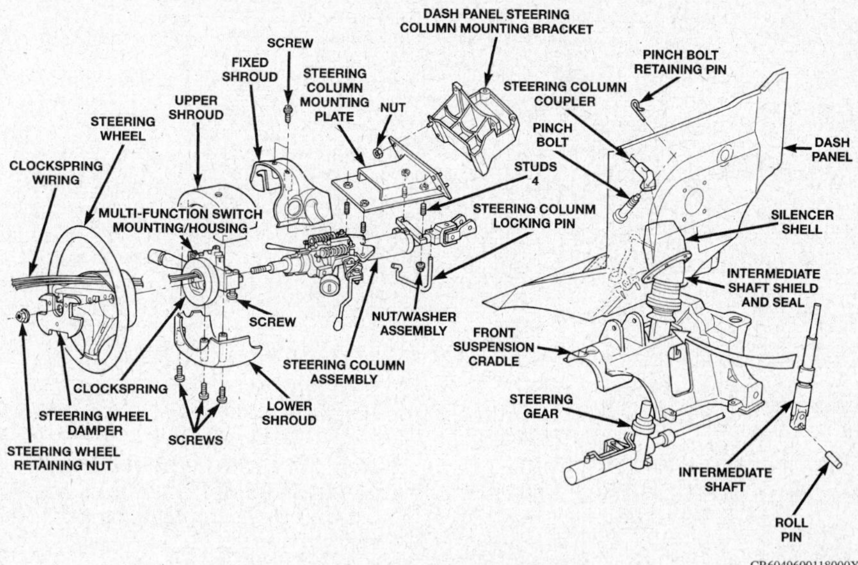

Fig. 4 Exploded view of steering column. 2002–04 Caravan, Town & Country & Voyager

Caravan, Town & Country & Voyager

2002-04

1. Ensure front wheels are in straight-ahead position.
2. Remove two shroud mounting screws, then unsnap upper shroud from lower shroud, **Fig. 4.**
3. Remove traction off switch, then the upper shroud.
4. Remove instrument cluster trim bezel.
5. Remove knee blocker.
6. Remove parking brake handle link.
7. Remove knee blocker reinforcement.
8. Remove driver air bag module as outlined in "Passive Restraint Systems" chapter.
9. Remove steering wheel retaining nut.
10. Remove vibration damper weight.
11. Remove steering wheel using suitable puller.
12. Disconnect electrical connector from the following:
    a. Clockspring.
    b. Multi-function switch.

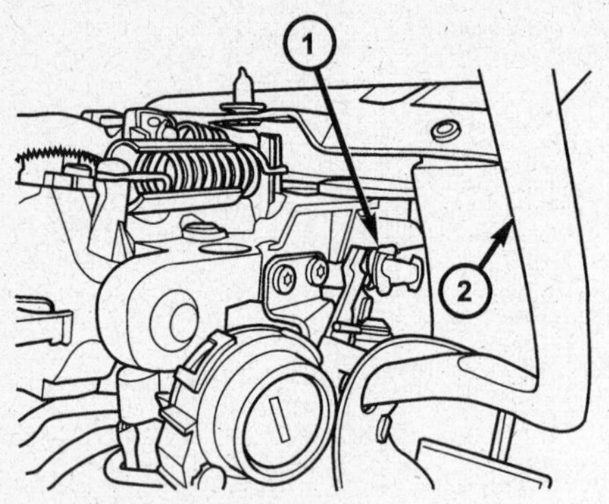

1 - SHIFT CABLE MOUNT
2 - SHIFT LEVER

LTV1900000000382

Fig. 5 Shift cable mounting. 2002–04 Caravan, Town & Country & Voyager

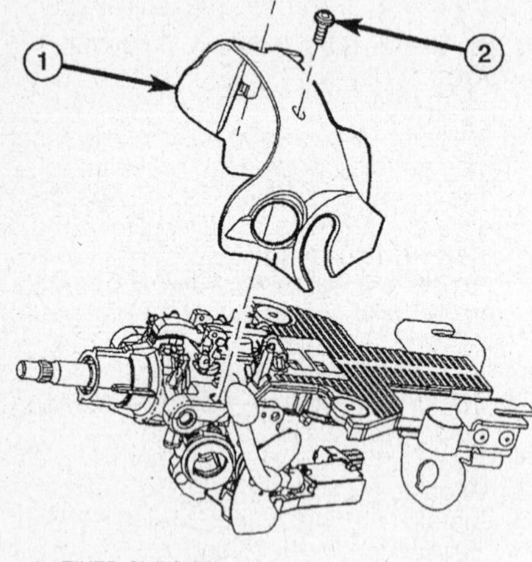

1 - FIXED SHROUD
2 - MOUNTING SCREWS

LTV0500000000588

Fig. 8 Fixed shroud removal. 2005–06 Caravan, Town & Country & Voyager

c. Halo lamp.
d. SKIM module.
e. Ignition switch.
f. Brake transmission shift interlock solenoid.

13. Disconnect shift cable at lever, **Fig. 5.**
14. Remove pinch side clip, then the cable from bracket on column.
15. Remove pinch bolt coupling.
16. Loosen two lower mounting nuts.
17. Remove two upper mounting nuts.
18. Remove steering column.
19. Reverse procedure to install, noting the following:
    a. **Torque** steering column mounting nuts to 105 inch lbs.
    b. **Torque** coupling pinch bolt to 21 ft. lbs.
    c. **Torque** steering wheel nut to 45 ft. lbs.

2005–06

1. Ensure front wheels are in straight-ahead position.
2. Remove driver air bag module as outlined in "Passive Restraint Systems" chapter.

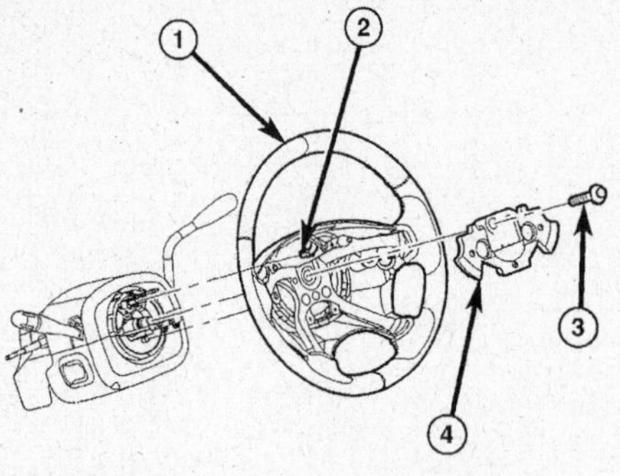

1 - STEERING WHEEL
2 - REMOTE AUDIO CONTROL WIRING CONNECTOR (IF EQUIPPED)
3 - RETAINING BOLT
4 - DAMPER

LTV0500000000586

Fig. 6 Steering wheel damper removal. 2005–06 Caravan, Town & Country & Voyager

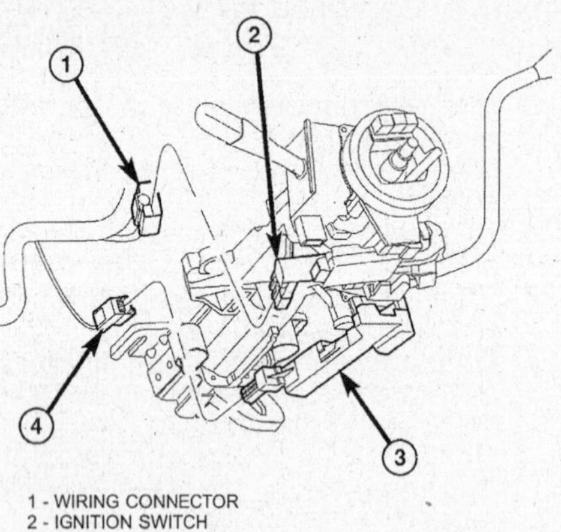

1 - WIRING CONNECTOR
2 - IGNITION SWITCH
3 - BTSI
4 - WIRING CONNECTOR

LTV0500000000589

Fig. 9 Ignition switch & BTSI removal. 2005–06 Caravan, Town & Country & Voyager

3. Remove steering wheel retaining bolt.
4. Remove damper, **Fig. 6.**
5. On models equipped with remote audio system, disconnect control switch wiring from clockspring, **Fig. 6.**
6. Remove steering wheel using suitable puller. **Do not bump or hammer on steering column of steering column shaft when removing steering wheel from steering column shaft.**
7. Remove steering column opening cover knee blocker panel.
8. Remove parking brake release handle link.
9. Remove steering column cover plate knee blocker panel.
10. Remove upper shroud mounting screws using hands on each side of column, gently press inward at seams between shroud points to disconnect inner locking tabs.
11. **On models equipped with traction control,** lower shroud will need to be removed once upper shroud is released to disconnect traction control wiring connector and remove upper shroud with traction control switch intact.

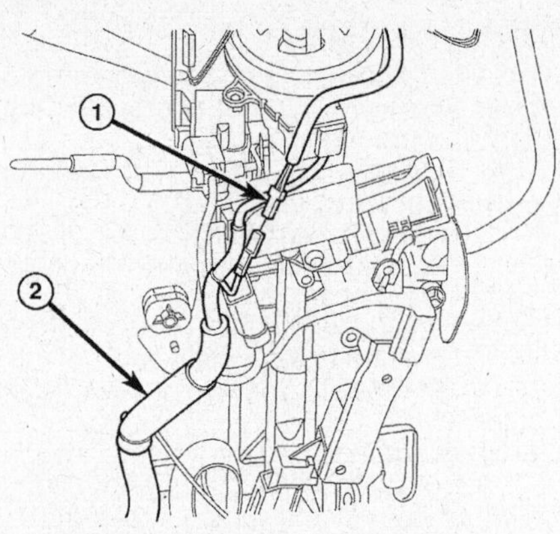

1 - TRACTION CONTROL WIRING CONNECTOR
2 - COLUMN WIRING HARNESS

LTV0500000000587

Fig. 7 Traction control wiring connection. 2005–06 Caravan, Town & Country & Voyager

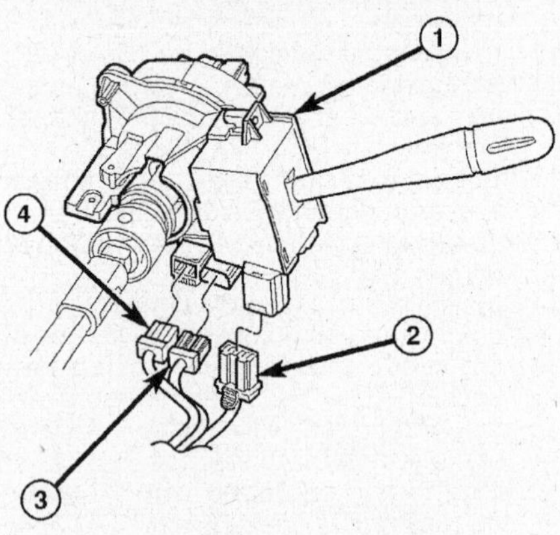

1 - MULTI-FUNCTION SWITCH MOUNTING HOUSING
2 - MULTI-FUNCTION WIRING CONNECTOR
3 - CLOCKSPRING WIRING CONNECTOR
4 - CLOCKSPRING SQUIB WIRING CONNECTOR

LTV0500000000590

Fig. 10 Multi-function & clockspring connections. 2005–06 Caravan, Town & Country & Voyager

12. **On models equipped with adjustable pedals,** disconnect electrical connector for switch.
13. **On all models,** remove lower shroud mounting screw, then the lower shroud.
14. **On models equipped with traction control,** disconnect electrical connector from column wiring harness, **Fig. 7.** Remove upper shroud with traction control switch.
15. **On all models,** remove instrument cluster trim bezel.
16. Remove fixed shroud screws, then the fixed shroud, **Fig. 8.**
17. Disconnect column harness electrical connectors from Brake Transmission

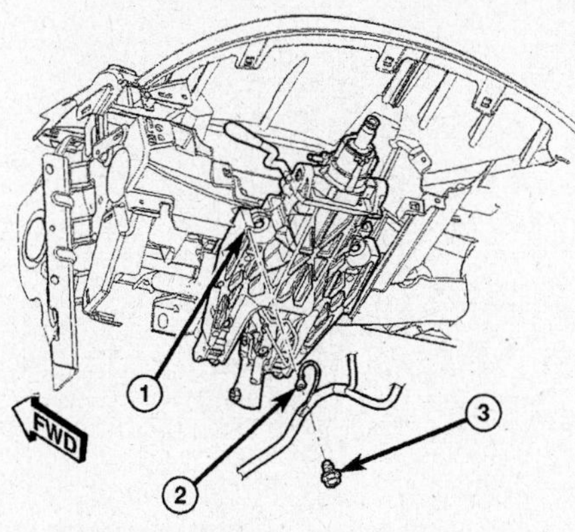

1 - STEERING COLUMN
2 - HORN GROUND WIRE
3 - SCREW

LTV0500000000591

Fig. 11 Horn ground to column. 2005–06 Caravan, Town & Country & Voyager

Shift Interlock (BTSI) and ignition switch, **Fig. 9.**

18. Disconnect column harness electrical connector for multi-function switch.
19. Disconnect column harness electrical connectors for clockspring and SQUIB, **Fig. 10.**
20. **On models equipped with Sentry Key Immobilizer (SKIM),** disconnect wiring connector from SKIM.
21. **On all models,** remove horn ground wire to column screw, **Fig. 11.**
22. Disconnect shift cable at lever pin, **Fig. 12.**
23. Disconnect shift cable at bracket, then feed cable out through bracket, **Fig. 12.**
24. Remove hair pin, then pinch bolt and disconnect column coupling.
25. Loosen column lower mounting nuts.
26. Remove column upper mounting nuts.
27. Remove steering column, **Fig. 13.**
28. If steering column is being replaced, proceed as follows:
    a. Remove set-screw attaching multi-function switch mounting housing to column.
    b. Slide multi-function switch mounting housing off column.
    c. Remove SKIM.
    d. Remove halo from ignition key cylinder housing.
    e. Remove ignition key lock cylinder as outlined in "Caravan, Town & Country & Voyager" chassis chapter.
29. Reverse procedure to install, noting the following:
    a. **Torque** SKIM to ignition key cylinder housing to 30 inch lbs.
    b. **Torque** driver air bag module mounting screws to 90 inch lbs.
    c. **Torque** multi-function switch mounting housing set-screw to 12 ft. lbs.
    d. **Torque** fixed shroud screws to 23 inch lbs.
    e. **Torque** lower and upper shroud screws to 17 inch lbs.
    f. **Torque** steering column coupling pinch bolt to 21 ft. lbs.

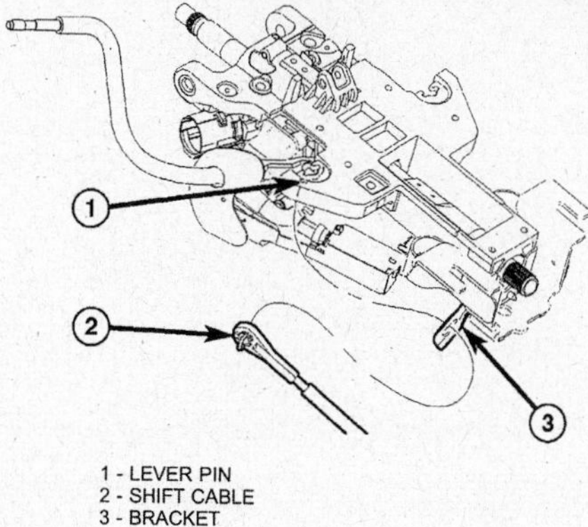

1 - LEVER PIN
2 - SHIFT CABLE
3 - BRACKET

LTV0500000000592

Fig. 12 Shift cable attachment to column removal. 2005–06 Caravan, Town & Country & Voyager

    g. **Torque** steering column mounting nuts to 10 ft. lbs.
    h. **Torque** steering wheel retaining bolt to 45 ft. lbs.

Dakota & Durango

2002-03

1. Ensure front wheels are in straight-ahead position.
2. Remove driver air bag module as outlined in "Passive Restraint Systems" chapter.
3. Remove steering wheel nut.
4. Ensure puller tool bolts are fully engaged into steering wheel and not into clockspring before attempting to remove steering wheel.
5. Remove steering wheel.
6. Remove steering column opening cover and knee blocker.
7. **On models equipped with tilt steering column,** remove tilt lever by pulling it straight rearward and out.
8. **On all models,** remove upper and lower shrouds.
9. **On models equipped with column shift,** proceed as follows:
    a. Pry shift cable from shift lever and remove from cable bracket.
    b. Put shift lever in Park position, pull PRNDL cable and twist to remove from PRNDL lever.
    c. Push tab on top of cable retainer, then squeeze sides to remove retainer from column.
10. **On all models,** remove multi-function switch screws, then the switch.
11. Remove remaining electrical connectors from column switches.
12. Remove bolt and nut from upper shaft, then slide upper shaft off column shaft.
13. Remove column mounting nuts, then the steering column.
14. Remove clockspring, switches and key cylinder.
15. Reverse procedure to install, noting the following:
    a. Remove shipping lockpin.
    b. Position column to panel bracket and attaching studs.
    c. Loosely install mounting nuts.

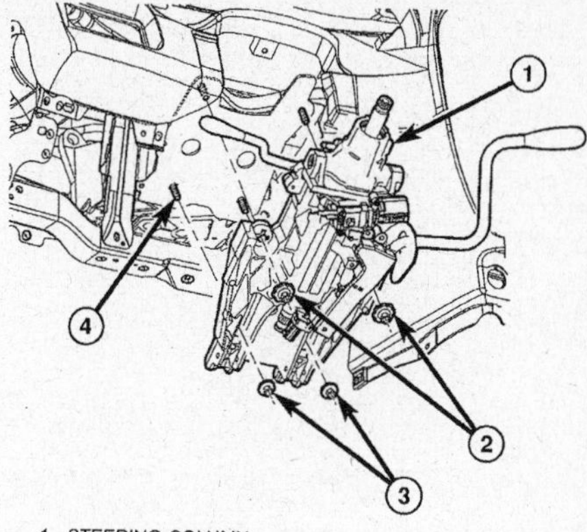

1 - STEERING COLUMN
2 - UPPER MOUNTING NUTS
3 - LOWER MOUNTING NUTS
4 - MOUNTING STUDS

LTV0500000000593

Fig. 13 Steering column removal. 2005–06 Caravan, Town & Country & Voyager

    d. Slide upper shaft onto column shaft, install a new pinch bolt and **torque** to 36 ft. lbs.
    e. **Torque** column mounting nuts to 21 ft. lbs.
    f. Connect multi-function switch electrical connector, **torque** screws to 20 inch lbs.
    g. Install steering wheel and retaining nut and **torque** nut to 45 ft. lbs.
    h. Install driver air bag module as outlined in "Passive Restraint Systems" chapter.

2004-06

1. Ensure front wheels are in straight-ahead position.
2. Remove driver air bag module as outlined in "Passive Restraint Systems" chapter.
3. Remove steering wheel using suitable puller. **Ensure that puller bolts are fully engaged into steering wheel and not into clockspring before removing steering wheel. Failure to do so may damage steering wheel clockspring.**
4. Remove steering column opening cover, **Fig. 14.**
5. Remove steering column opening cover reinforcement panel, **Fig. 15.**
6. Remove tilt lever.
7. Remove both column shroud covers.
8. Remove clockspring as outlined in "Passive Restraint Systems" chapter.
9. Disconnect wiring harness to column, **Fig. 16.**
10. Remove shift cable from column shift lever actuator.
11. Release shift cable from column bracket and remove from bracket.
12. Remove SKIM module and disconnect electrical connector.
13. Remove upper steering column shaft coupling bolt from column, **Fig. 17.**
14. Separate shaft from coupler, in numbered sequence, **Fig. 17.**
15. Remove brake light switch and discard.
16. Remove steering column mounting nuts, **Fig. 18.**

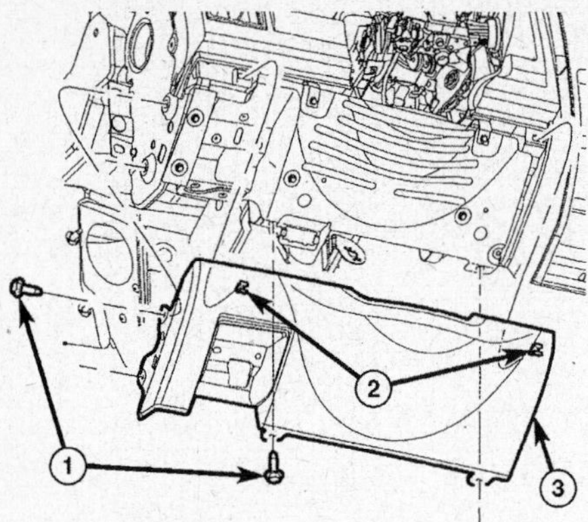

1- STEERING COLUMN COVER BOLTS
2- STEERING COLUMN COVER CLIPS
3- STEERING COLUMN COVER

LTV0500000000594

Fig. 14 Steering column opening cover removal. 2004–06 Dakota & Durango

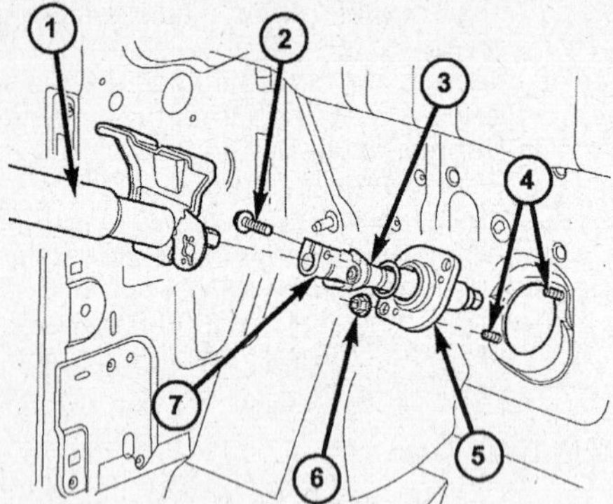

1- UPPER STEERING SHAFT
2- UPPER STEERING SHAFT COUPLER BOLT
3- COLUMN
4- COLUMN BOLT STUDS
5- COLUMN PLATE
6- UPPER STEEERING SHAFT COUPLER NUT
7- COUPLER

LTV0500000000597

Fig. 17 Upper steering shaft coupling bolt removal. 2004–06 Dakota & Durango

17. Remove steering column assembly from vehicle, **Fig. 18.**
18. Reverse procedure to install, noting the following:
    a. **Torque** tilt lever release knob bracket screws to 40 inch lbs.
    b. **Torque** ignition switch screws to 26 inch lbs.
    c. **Torque** gear shift lever assembly screws to 10 ft. lbs.
    d. **Torque** steering column nuts to 21 ft. lbs., as follows: **Tighten upper lefthand nut first, then the lower righthand nut, then tighten lower lefthand nut and upper righthand nut in sequence.**
    e. **Torque** steering wheel bolt to 45 ft. lbs.
    f. **Torque** new steering coupler shaft upper and lower pinch bolts to 28 ft. lbs.
    g. **Torque** toe plate nuts to 10 ft. lbs.

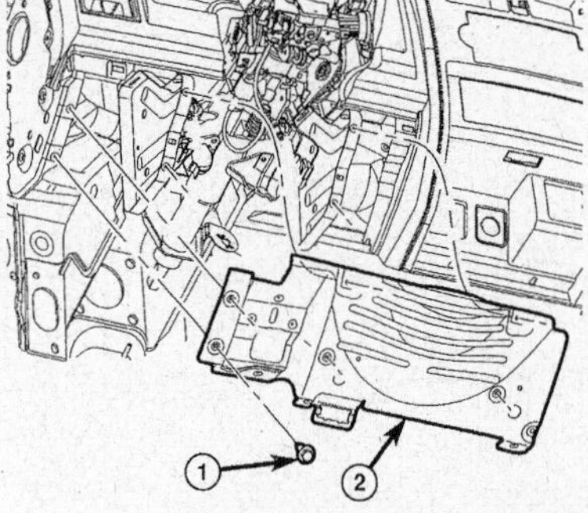

1- STEERING COLUMN COVER REINFORCEMENT BOLT
2- STEEERING COLUMN COVER REINFORCEMENT

LTV0500000000595

Fig. 15 Steering column opening cover reinforcement removal. 2004–06 Dakota & Durango

Commander & Grand Cherokee

2002–04

1. Ensure front wheels are in straight-ahead position.
2. Remove driver air bag module as outlined in "Passive Restraint Systems" chapter.
3. Remove steering wheel bolt/nut.
4. Remove steering wheel using suitable puller. **Ensure puller jaws are securely seated in wheel armature pockets.**
5. Remove cluster bezel.
6. Remove knee blocker.
7. Remove lower steering column shroud mounting screw.
8. Unsnap two halves of column shrouds by pressing on sides of upper shroud and tilting rear of upper shroud up, then remove shrouds.
9. Remove upper fixed shroud.
10. Disconnect multi-function switch and ignition switch electrical connectors.
11. Remove multi-function switch screw from under switch, then slide switch and clockspring off column as an assembly.
12. Turn ignition On, then release and remove shifter interlock cable from ignition lock cylinder housing.
13. Remove column coupler bolt, then slide coupler off column shaft.
14. Remove column mounting nuts, then lower the column off mounting studs and remove from vehicle.
15. Reverse procedure to install, noting the following:
    a. **Torque** column mounting nuts to 105 inch lbs.
    b. **Torque** coupler bolt to 36 ft. lbs.
    c. **Torque** steering wheel nut to 45 ft. lbs.

2005–06

1. Ensure front wheels are in straight-ahead position.
2. Remove driver air bag module as outlined in "Passive Restraint Systems" chapter.

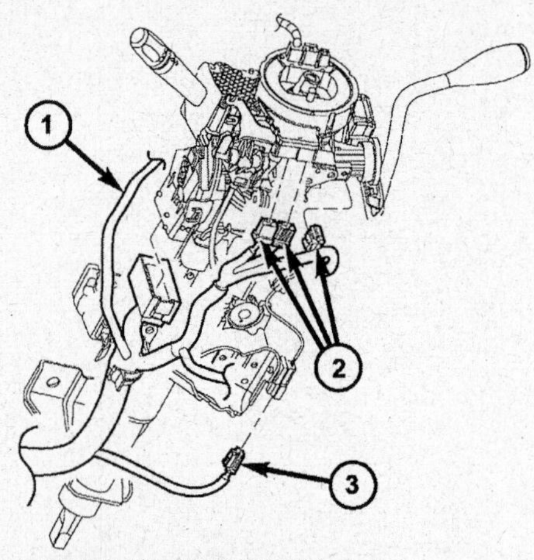

1- UPPER STEERING SHAFT
2- CLOCKSPRING WIRING HARNESS TO STEERING COLUMN
3- WIRING HARNESS TO STEERING COLUMN

LTV0500000000596

Fig. 16 Wiring harness to column connector removal. 2004–06 Dakota & Durango

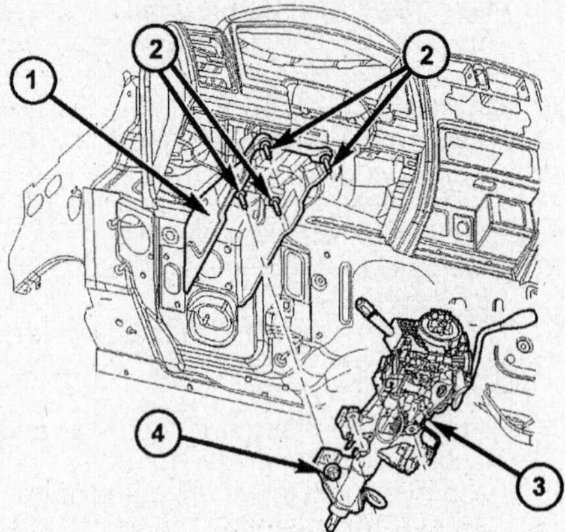

1- STEERING COLUMN ASSEMBLY BRACKET
2- STEERING COLUMN BRACKET BOLTS
3- STEERING COLUMN ASSEMBLY
4- STEERING COLUMN ASSEMBLY NUTS

LTV0500000000598

Fig. 18 Steering column & component removal. 2004–06 Dakota & Durango

3. Remove steering wheel bolt, then the steering wheel using a suitable puller.
4. Remove driver lower instrument panel hush panel, **Fig. 19.**
5. Remove driver instrument panel access cover, **Fig. 20.**
6. Remove steering column shroud covers to access multi-function switch electrical connectors.
7. Disconnect multi-function switch harness.
8. Remove multi-function switch, sliding switch and clockspring off column as an assembly.
9. Remove column cross bolt and slide column downward off from bracket.
10. Remove pinch bolt at lower end of column and upper intermediate shaft coupling.

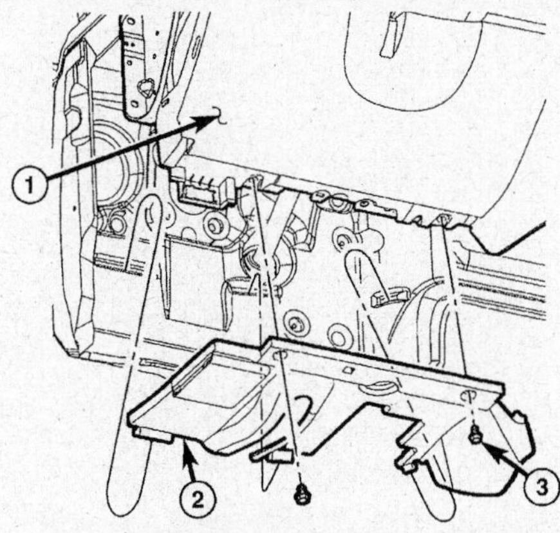

Fig. 19 Driver lower instrument panel hush panel removal. Commander & 2005–06 Grand Cherokee

11. Remove column mounting bolts and lower column downward.
12. Remove column from vehicle.
13. Reverse procedure to install, noting the following:
    a. **Steering column module is centered to vehicle steering system. Failure to keep system and steering column module centered and locked/inhibited from rotating can result in steering column module damage.**
    b. **Torque** steering wheel mounting nut to 45 ft. lbs.
    c. **Torque** steering column bracket nuts to 105 inch lbs.
    d. **Torque** steering column cross bolt to 105 inch lbs.
    e. **Torque** steering column shaft coupler bolts to 36 ft. lbs.

Wrangler

REMOVAL

1. Ensure front wheels are in straight-ahead position.
2. Remove driver air bag module as outlined in "Passive Restraint Systems" chapter.
3. **On models equipped with cruise control,** disconnect clockspring electrical connectors from switch harness on steering wheel.
4. **On all models,** remove steering wheel nut.
5. Remove steering wheel using a suitable puller tool.
6. Turn ignition cylinder to On position, then remove cylinder by pressing release through lower shroud access hole, **Fig. 21.**
7. Remove knee blocker cover and knee blocker.
8. Remove lower column shroud.
9. Remove steering coupler bolt and column mounting nuts, then lower the column, **Fig. 22.**
10. Remove upper column shroud.

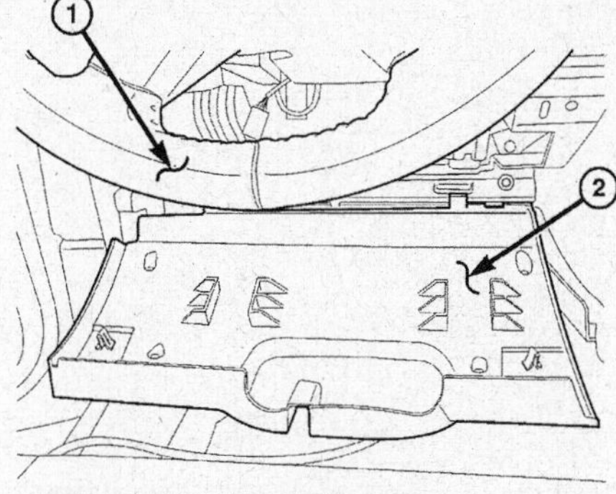

Fig. 20 Driver instrument panel access cover removal. Commander & 2005–06 Grand Cherokee

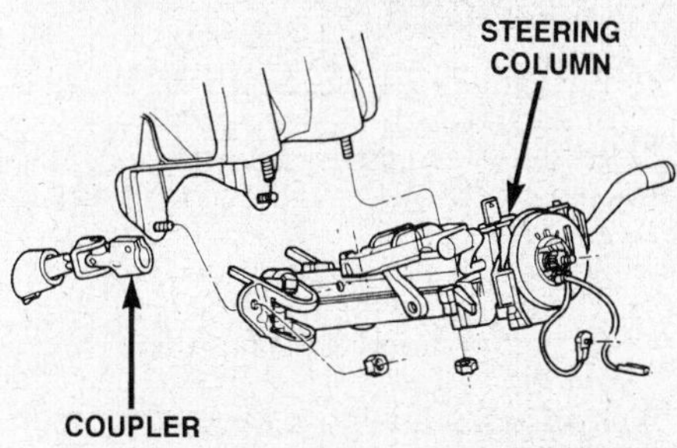

Fig. 22 Steering column mounting. Wrangler

11. Disconnect and remove wiring harness from column.
12. **On models equipped with automatic transmission,** remove shifter interlock cable by disengaging lock tab holding cable end to steering column, then pull cable end from steering column.
13. **On all models,** carefully remove steering column from vehicle.
14. **On models equipped with non-tilt column,** note location and orientation, then remove upper column mounting bracket.

INSTALLATION

1. **On models equipped with non-tilt column,** install upper column mounting bracket onto column, then **torque** bolt to 13 ft. lbs.
2. **On all models,** align and install column into steering coupler.
3. Install column harness and connect harness to switches.
4. **On models equipped with automatic transmission,** install shifter interlock cable.
5. **On all models,** install upper column shrouds.
6. Install column onto mounting studs.
7. Install mounting nuts and **torque** to 17 ft. lbs.
8. Install steering column coupler bolt and **torque** to 36 ft. lbs.
9. Install lower column shrouds, then the ignition cylinder.

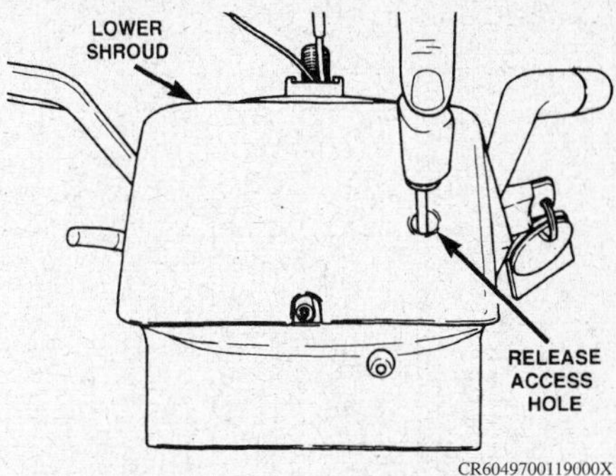

Fig. 21 Key cylinder release access hole. Wrangler

10. Install knee blocker and knee blocker cover.
11. Install steering wheel onto column shaft, then **torque** steering wheel nut to 40 ft. lbs.
12. Install driver air bag module as outlined in "Passive Restraint Systems" chapter.

Liberty

1. Ensure front wheels are in straight-ahead position.
2. Remove driver air bag module as outlined in "Passive Restraint Systems" chapter.
3. Partially remove steering wheel bolt leaving bolt in column.
4. Remove steering wheel using top of bolt to push on using puller tool No. C-3894-A, or equivalent.
5. Remove knee blocker cover, then the knee blocker.
6. Remove screws from lower steering column shroud, then the upper and lower shrouds.
7. Turn ignition switch to ON position.
8. **On models equipped with automatic transmission,** disconnect shift interlock cable from column.
9. **On all models,** remove steering coupler bolt.
10. Remove column mounting nuts and bolts, then lower column off mounting studs.
11. Disconnect and remove wiring harness from column.
12. Slide shifter interlock cable from tie straps.
13. Remove steering column.
14. Reverse procedure to install, noting the following:
    a. Lower steering column nuts must be installed and tightened first, then the upper nuts to prevent damage to capsules.
    b. **Torque** steering wheel bolt to 40 ft. lbs.
    c. **Torque** steering column mounting bolts to 13 ft. lbs.
    d. **Torque** steering column coupling bolt to 36 ft. lbs.
    e. **Torque** intermediate shaft lower support bearing nut to 10 ft. lbs.
    f. **Torque** ignition switch screws to 17 inch lbs.

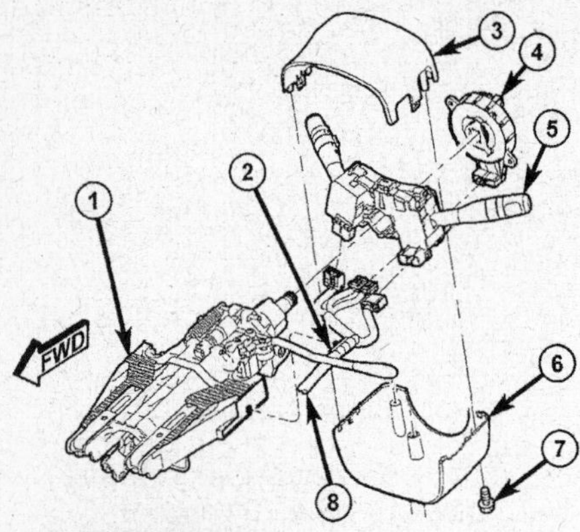

Fig. 23 Steering column lower & upper shroud cover removal. Pacifica

Pacifica

1. Ensure front wheels are in straight-ahead position.
2. Remove driver air bag module as outlined in "Passive Restraint Systems" chapter.
3. Disconnect speed control wiring harness connector at clockspring terminal.
4. Remove steering wheel nut, then the damper.
5. Remove steering wheel using suitable puller.
6. Access and remove driver knee blocker air bag module as outlined in "Passive Restraint Systems" chapter.
7. Remove steering column lower and upper shroud covers, **Fig. 23.**
8. Remove column wiring harness routing clip from lefthand side of column.
9. Remove screw on bottom of column, **Fig. 24,** then slide multi-function switch housing with switches and clockspring off column.
10. Disconnect steering column coupling at intermediate shaft as follows:
    a. Remove hair pin at end of coupling pinch bolt.
    b. Remove pinch bolt.
    c. Remove intermediate shaft from coupling.
11. Remove four nuts attaching column to dash, then the column, **Fig. 25.**
12. Reverse procedure to install, noting the following:
    a. **Torque** driver air bag module bolts to 90 inch lbs.
    b. **Torque** steering column coupling pinch bolt to 21 ft. lbs.
    c. **Torque** steering column mounting nuts to 10 ft. lbs.
    d. **Torque** steering column shroud screws to 18 inch lbs.
    e. **Torque** steering wheel nut to 45 ft. lbs.

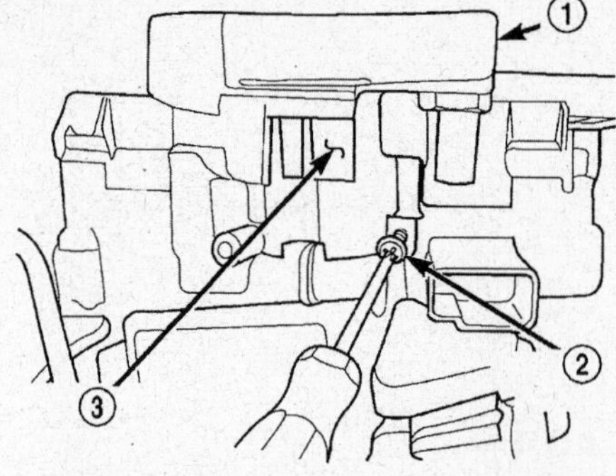

Fig. 24 Multi-function switch housing screw removal. Pacifica

PT Cruiser

1. Ensure front wheels are in straight-ahead position.
2. Remove ignition key from ignition, then remove silencer pad below steering column.
3. Fold down and remove knee blocker.
4. Remove two screws attaching lower shroud to steering column and upper shroud.
5. Unclip shrouds from each other, then remove them from column.
6. Remove driver air bag module as outlined in "Passive Restraint Systems" chapter.
7. Disconnect speed control switch electrical connector.
8. Holding steering wheel firmly in place, remove retaining bolt from steering column shaft in center of steering wheel.
9. Thread wheel retaining bolt back into end of shaft until .5 inch of thread is showing between wheel and head of bolt.
10. Remove steering wheel using suitable puller tool.
11. Remove steering coupling retainer pin, then back off pinch bolt nut and remove steering column coupling pinch bolt.
12. Separate upper and lower steering column couplings.
13. **On models equipped with automatic transaxle,** disconnect interlock cable from steering column.
14. **On all models,** remove two lower mounting nuts attaching steering column to instrument panel.
15. Remove two upper mounting nuts attaching steering column to instrument panel.
16. Lower steering column away from instrument panel.
17. Disconnect electrical connectors from clockspring, multi-function switch, windshield wiper switch and ignition switch.
18. Disconnect electrical connector from Sentry Key Immobilizer Module (SKIM), if equipped.
19. Remove steering column from vehicle.
20. If replacing steering column, proceed as follows:

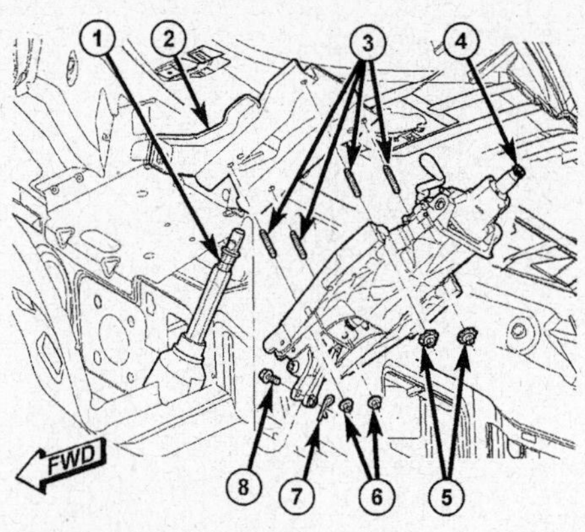

Fig. 25 Steering column removal. Pacifica

    a. Insert key and turn ignition On, then depress retaining tab and remove ignition cylinder by pulling straight out.
    b. Remove clockspring from column by disengaging latch hooks on back of clockspring.
    c. Remove multi-function/windshield wiper switch from steering column.
    d. Remove SKIM, if equipped.
    e. If required, remove ignition switch from steering column.
21. Reverse procedure to install, noting the following:
    a. **Torque** steering column mounting nuts to 13 ft. lbs.
    b. **Torque** pinch bolt nut to 21 ft. lbs.
    c. **Torque** steering wheel nut to 40 ft. lbs.

Sprinter

1. Ensure front wheels are in straight-ahead position. **Position of steering column gear must not be altered again for entire duration of procedure.**
2. Remove driver air bag module as outlined in "Passive Restraint Systems" chapter.
3. Remove electrical center.
4. Remove steering wheel bolt.
5. Remove steering wheel from column.
6. Remove clockspring. **Unscrew retaining bolts enough to be able to remove clockspring. Do not twist or disassemble clockspring.**
7. Remove combination switch as outlined in "Sprinter" chassis chapter.
8. Disconnect electrical connector for ignition lock.
9. Remove spring for brake pedal from steering column.
10. Remove fitted bolt from universal joint.
11. Remove bolts in steering column bracket.
12. Remove steering shaft with universal joint off steering gear driver shaft.
13. Remove steering shaft out of rubber

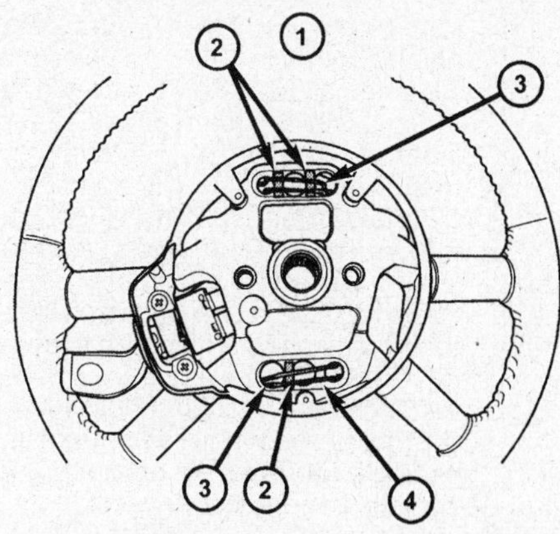

Fig. 26 Foam pad installation. PT Cruiser

grommet in cab floor.

14. Reverse procedure to install, noting the following:
    a. **Torque** steering wheel with air bag to steering shaft to 59 ft. lbs.
    b. **Torque** jacket tube for steering shaft to waist rail to 18 ft. lbs.
    c. **Torque** U-joint to steering gear shaft to 18 ft. lbs.

STEERING COLUMN SERVICE

These steering columns are designed to be serviced as an assembly. Electrical switches may be serviced. Refer to "Electrical" section in appropriate truck section for switch replacement procedures.

TECHNICAL SERVICE BULLETINS

Lower Steering Column Noise And/Or Minor Column Movement

FULL SIZE PICKUP

On some of these models there may be a lower steering column noise and/or minor lower steering column movement.

Apply a vertical up and down force to steering column, note any vertical movement at lower end of column. If there is more than .079 inch of travel, inspect part number of toe plate. If part number of toe plate is 52078177, use the following procedure to install additional toe plate:

1. Remove steering column upper mounting bracket nuts, then lower steering column until it rests on drivers seat.
2. Pull steering column rearward about one inch for additional clearance.
3. Remove lower steering column toe plate retaining nuts.
4. Slide toe plate part No. 05012029AA over existing plate studs. Toe plate cutout portion should face right.
5. Turn plate 90° until it aligns with existing plate, then slide new plate over studs.
6. Install lower steering column toe plate retaining nuts, then **torque** nuts to 15 ft. lbs.
7. Lift steering column back onto upper mounts, then **torque** retaining nuts to 108 inch lbs.
8. Install knee blocker.
9. Inspect for proper PRNDL operation and adjust shift linkage as required.

Popping Sensation & Steering Column Noise During Sharp Turns & Parking Lot Maneuvers

DAKOTA & DURANGO

On these models there may be a popping sensation and steering column noise during sharp turns and parking lot maneuvers.

To correct this condition, proceed as follows:

1. Start engine, then rotate steering wheel until it is in an upside down position.
2. Stop engine and remove key from ignition.
3. Remove three screws securing lower edge of steering column opening to lower instrument panel reinforcement.
4. Gently pry upper edge of steering column opening cover using a suitable trim stick tool. Pry just below cluster bezel on each side of column away from instrument panel far enough to disengage snap clip retainers.
5. Remove steering column opening cover from instrument panel.
6. Loosen steering column attaching nuts.
7. Lightly bounce steering wheel in a vertical motion to normalize alignment.
8. Position steering column opening cover to instrument panel and align

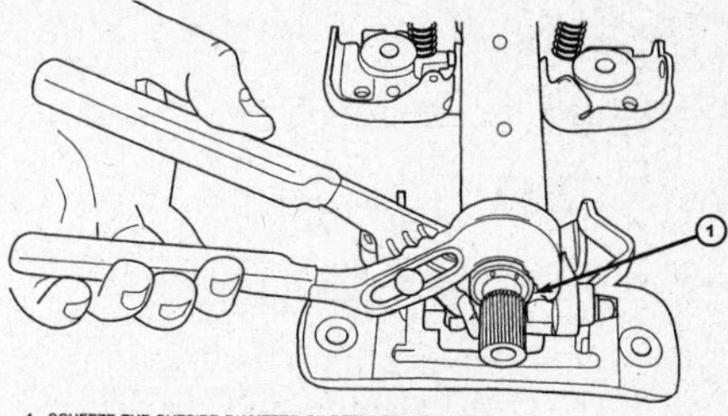

Fig. 27 Spring retainer removal. PT Cruiser

clips with retainers.

9. Press firmly on opening cover until each clip is securely located.
10. Install opening cover screws, then **torque** to 20 inch lbs.

Foam Rubber Pads Beneath The Driver's Side Air Bag Module May Fall Off During Air Bag Module Removal

PT CRUISER

On these models the foam rubber pads beneath the driver air bag module may fall off during air bag module removal, leading to a buzzing or rattling condition.

To correct this condition, install foam pad kit part No. 5072250AA as follows:

1. Remove driver air bag module as outlined in "Passive Restraint Systems" chapter.
2. Disconnect speed control switch electrical connector.
3. Holding steering wheel firmly in place, remove retaining bolt from steering column shaft in center of steering wheel.
4. Thread wheel retaining bolt back into end of shaft until .5 inch of thread is showing between wheel and head of bolt.
5. Remove steering wheel using suitable puller tool.
6. Remove three existing foam pads from between steering wheel base and retaining clips using a suitable small screwdriver, **Fig. 26.**
7. Install three new foam pads. **Ensure pads are positioned as illustrated to prevent horn ground contact interference.**
8. Reverse procedure to install. **Torque** steering wheel nut to 40 ft. lbs.

Click Noise From Lower Steering Column

2002-03 PT CRUISER

On some models, a click noise may be heard from the lower steering column when turning.

1. Turn steering wheel and listen for click noise.
2. If clock noise is heard, remove steering column shrouds.
3. If click noise is eliminated, determine source of interference with steering column shrouds.
4. Ensure wheels are in straight-ahead position.
5. Remove driver air bag module as outlined in "Passive Restraint Systems" chapter.
6. Remove steering wheel bolt, then thread bolt back in until ½ inch of threads are showing.
7. Remove steering wheel using head of bolt to push on.
8. Disconnect intermediate shaft to steering gear lower coupling.
9. Turn steering shaft and listen for click. Turn shaft no more than one revolution in either direction from center keeping track of centered position.
10. If click sound is eliminated, reattach lower coupling and install steering wheel ensuring clockspring is centered. **Torque** coupling pinch bolt to 21 ft. lbs., and steering wheel bolt to 40 ft. lbs.
11. Turn steering wheel to listen if click sound remains.
12. If click sound returns, loosen lower coupling pinch bolt and four steering column mounting bracket nuts.
13. Jiggle steering column, then **torque** coupling pinch bolt to 21 ft. lbs.
14. Tighten two lower steering column mounting nuts to hold column in place. Ensure both break-away capsules are still fully seated in slots of upper steering column mounting bracket and mounting studs are centered fore and aft in plastic capsules.
15. Equally tighten both steering column mounting nuts until upper mounting bracket is seated against support bracket, then **torque** nuts to 13 ft. lbs.
16. Turn steering wheel to listen if click sound still remains.
17. If click sound is eliminated, replace lower coupling pinch bolt with part No. 06506382AA. **Torque** pinch bolt to 21 ft. lbs.
18. If click sound remains, remove clockspring.
19. Disconnect lower coupling.
20. Turn steering wheel to listen if click sound still remains.
21. If sound is eliminated, determine source of interference with clockspring and repair.

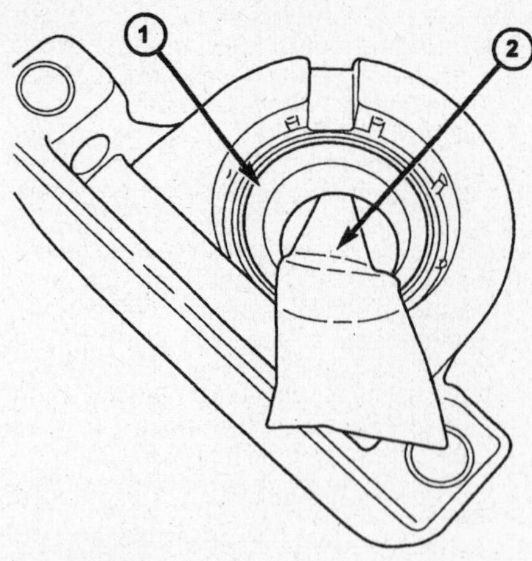

Fig. 28 Inspecting fully seated bearing. PT Cruiser

22. If click sound remains, remove steering column.
23. Remove two screws attaching multi-function switch, then remove switch.
24. Remove upper steering column coupler from steering column shaft.
25. Remove spring retainer by squeezing outside diameter with pliers, then sliding it off end of steering column shaft, **Fig. 27.**
26. Remove spring, wedge and steering column shaft.
27. Stand steering column on end so outer race of upper bearing is supported on a 1 1/16 inch socket. Using a 7/8 inch deep well socket placed against lower bearing outer race, tap bearing downward several times until bearing is fully seated.
28. Use a .005 inch feeler gauge to ensure no clearance exists between lower casting and outer race of bearing, **Fig. 28.**
29. Install steering column shaft, wedge and spring.
30. Thread steering wheel bolt into steering column shaft.
31. Stand column assembly on head of steering wheel bolt ensuring surface is flat.
32. Install new retainer part No. 04664130 onto steering column shaft using 7/8 inch deep well socket and small hammer to tap retainer into place. Distance between lower housing and outside of retainer is .47–.55 inch, **Fig. 29.**
33. If retainer is installed less than .47 inch, remove and install new retainer.
34. If click sound still remains, further diagnosis is required.
35. Install steering column.
36. If air bag retainer clips or foam silencer pads are damaged, they must be replaced as follows:
    a. Use a large flat tipped screwdriver to pry up on middle of driver air bag module retaining clip to remove it from steering wheel armature holes, **Fig. 30.**
    b. Use a small screwdriver to remove three existing foam pads from steering wheel base.
    c. Insert new retaining clips part No. 05086385AA in steering wheel armature holes. Round end goes in small hole and open end goes in larger hole. Put round end in first, then press open end in with screwdriver, **Fig. 31.**
    d. Install three new foam pads. **Positioning of foam pads is critical as ground for horn is affected by position of pads.**

Steering Column Vertical Movement

2002 FULL SIZE PICKUP

Some models may exhibit a slight amount of vertical movement or play in steering column.

Hold the steering wheel in 12 o'clock and 6 o'clock positions, then apply pressure to the top and then the bottom. If movement is more than .010 inch proceed as follows:

1. Remove knee blocker.
2. Pull tilt actuator lever from steering column.
3. Remove steering column shroud.
4. **Torque** steering column mounting nuts to 21 ft. lbs.
5. Inspect tilt mechanism pivot pin and surrounding area for yellow plastic debris used during assembly, **Fig. 32.**
6. Remove any plastic debris which can cause binding in mechanism.
7. Operate tilt mechanism a few time, then inspect for play.
8. If play still remains, using suitable pliers, remove adjuster cable from retaining loop and move cable retaining loop from outside of casting to inside, **Fig. 33.**
9. Install a tie strap around cable. Tighten tie strap until a distance of 1 5/8 inch is measured between two cable sections, **Fig. 34.**
10. Operate tilt mechanism a few time, then inspect for play.
11. If play still remains, measure travel of metal actuator, **Fig. 35,** travel should be 1/4 inch.
12. If cable adjustment is more than 1/4 inch, play can be eliminated by pushing adjuster further into retainer one click at a time until correct travel is obtained, **Fig. 36.**
13. If adjuster is less than 1/4 inch, carefully pry up on white plastic retainer tab and release black cable adjuster.
14. Insert adjuster under retainer and push adjuster in to retainer one click at a time until correct travel is obtained.
15. If play is still present, replace steering column.

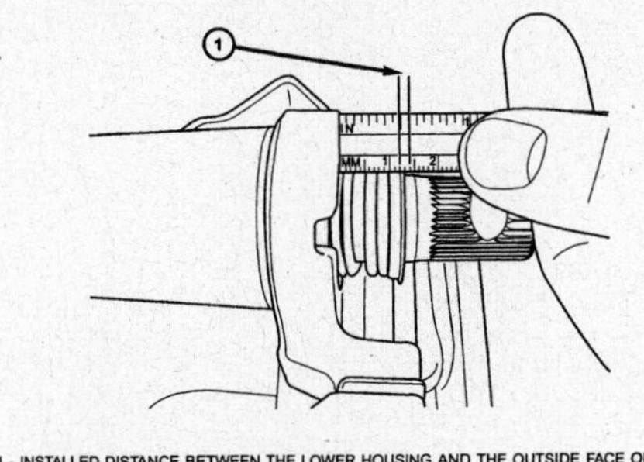

Fig. 29 Retainer installation. PT Cruiser

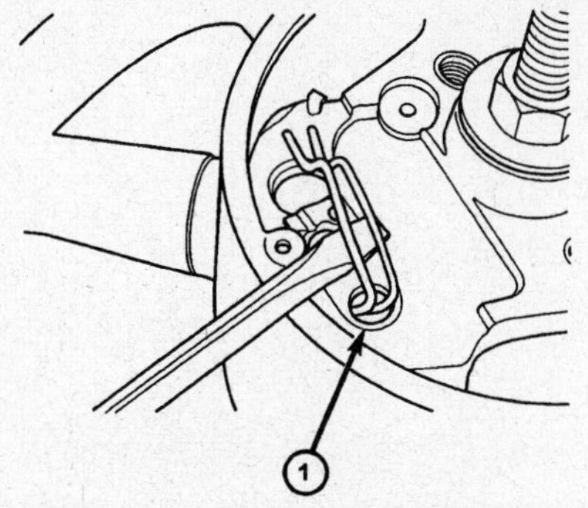

Fig. 30 Air bag retaining clip removal. PT Cruiser

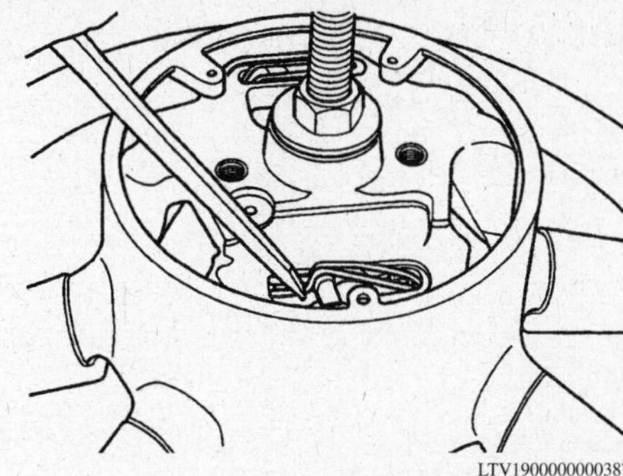

Fig. 31 Air bag retaining clip installation. PT Cruiser

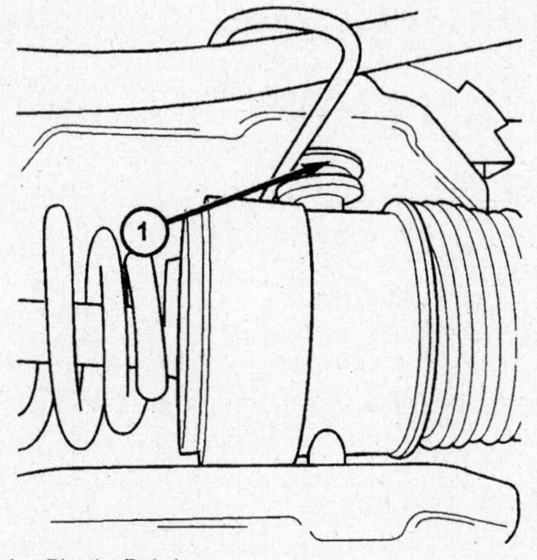

Fig. 32 Tilt pivot inspection. 2002 Full Size Pickup

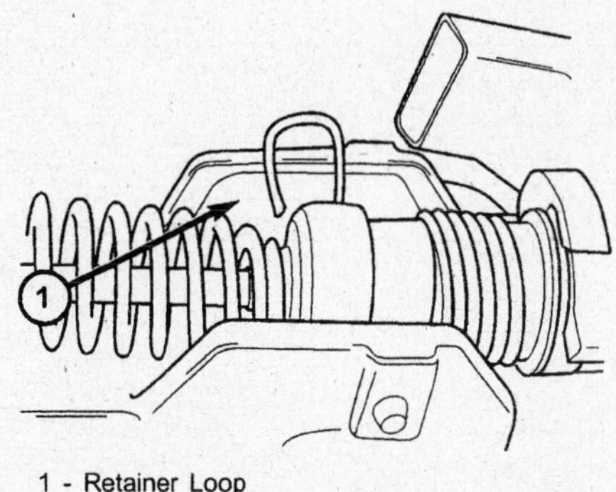

Fig. 33 Cable retainer loop. 2002 Full Size Pickup

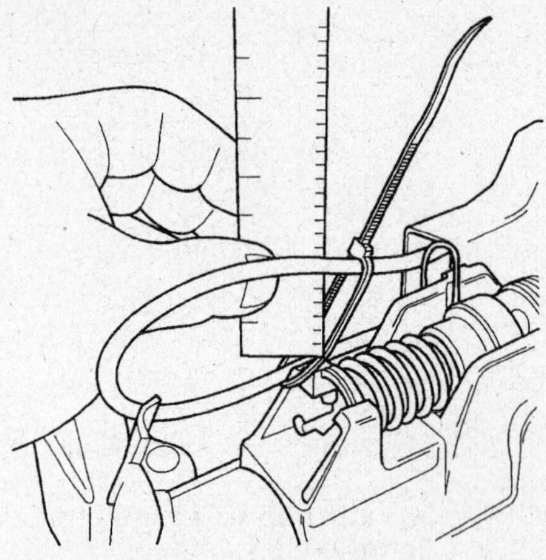

LTV1900000000390

Fig. 34 Cable routing. 2002 Full Size Pickup

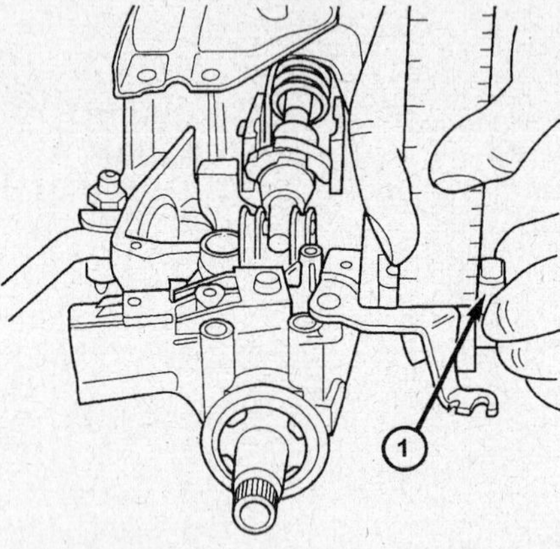

1 - Tilt Actuator Lever

LTV1900000000391

Fig. 35 Tilt mechanism actuator. 2002 Full Size Pickup

1 - Retainer Tab

2 - Adjuster

LTV1900000000392

Fig. 36 Cable adjustment. 2002 Full Size Pickup

POWER STEERING

TABLE OF CONTENTS

Application Chart

Year	Model	Steering Gear
2002–06	Caravan, Town & Country & Voyager	TRW Rack & Pinion
	Dakota	TRW Rack & Pinion
	Durango	DaimlerChrysler Variable Ratio
	Full Size Pickup	DaimlerChrysler Variable Ratio
	Full Size Van	DaimlerChrysler Variable Ratio
	Jeep	DaimlerChrysler Variable Ratio & Rack & Pinion
	Pacifica	DaimlerChrysler Variable Ratio
	PT Cruiser	TRW Rack & Pinion
	Sprinter	Rack & Pinion

Power Steering Pressure Specifications

Model	Year	Initial Pressure, psi	Maximum Pressure, psi	Relief Pressure, psi
Caravan, Voyager, Town & Country	2002–06	100–275	⑤	⑥
Dakota	2002–06	50–80	1500	1450①②⑦
Durango	2002	50–80	1500	1500
	2003	50–80	1450	1500
	2004–06	50–80	1800	1750–1850
Full Size Pickup	2002⑧	50–80	1680	1550–1680
	2002⑨	50–80	1500③	1400–1500④
	2003–04	50–80	1680	1550–1680
	2003⑨	50–80	1800	1800–1850
	2005–06	50–80	1400	1400–1450
Full Size Van	2002–03	50–80	1450	1350–1450
Jeep	2002–06	50–80	1450	1350–1450
Pacifica	2004–06	100–175	1500	1400–1500
PT Cruiser	2002–06	50–80	1450	1350–1450

① — 2.5L engine, 1250 psi.
② — 4.7L engine, 1450 psi.
③ — 2002 1550 psi.
④ — 2002 1450–1550 psi.
⑤ — 2.4L engine, 1350psi; 3.3L & 3.8L engines, 1500 psi.
⑥ — 2.4L engine, 1200–1350 psi; 3.3L & 3.8L engines, 1400–1500 psi.
⑦ — 3.9L & 5.9L engines, 1500 psi.
⑧ — 1500.
⑨ — 2500 & 3500.

Power Steering Flow Rate Specifications

Model	Year	Engine	Flow Rate, psi	Flow Rate, GPM
Caravan, Town & Country & Voyager	2002–06	All	100–275	1.5
Commander & Grand Cherokee	2005–06	All	75–100	2.6–3.0
Dakota	2002–06	All	50–80	2.4–2.8
Durango	2002–03	All	50–80	2.4–2.8
	2004–06	3.7L & 4.7L	50–80	2.7–3.1
	2004–06	5.7L	50–80	3.1–3.5
Full Size Van	2002–03	All	50–80	2.4–2.8
Liberty & Wrangler	2002–06	All	50–80	2.4–2.8
Pacifica	2004–06	All	100–175	1.5
PT Cruiser	2002–06	All	50–80	1.5–1.7
Ram 1500–3500	2002③	All Except 5.9L Diesel	1400–1500	2.7–3.1
		5.9L Diesel	1450–1550	3.1–3.5
		All with Hydraulic Booster	1450–1550	3.1–3.5
	2002–05②	All	1550–1680	3.1–3.5
	2003–05①	All	1750–1850	3.5–4.0
	2006	All	1350–1450	2.4–2.8

GPM — Gallons Per Minute
① — 2500 & 3500.
② — 1500.
③ — Except 2002 1500.

Vane Type Power Steering Pump

NOTE: On Air Bag Equipped Models, Refer To "Air Bag System Precautions" Located In The Front Of This Manual For System Disarming & Arming Procedures.

NOTE: Refer To "Computer Relearn Procedures" Located In The Front Of This Manual When Battery Power To The Computer Has Been Interrupted.

INDEX

PRECAUTIONS

Air Bag Systems

Refer to "Air Bag System Precautions" in the front of this manual for system disarming and arming procedures.

Battery Ground Cable

Prior to service disconnect battery ground cable and isolate as required.

TROUBLESHOOTING

Excessive Steering Play

1. Excessive play in steering gearbox.
2. Loose steering gear.
3. Loose or worn tie rod end stud.

Hard Steering Wheel Operation

1. Air in fluid line.
2. Loose or damaged belt.
3. Low or leaking fluid.
4. Twisted or damaged power steering hoses.
5. Gearbox or pump fault.

Noisy Operation

1. Loose oil pump or gearbox.
2. Loose pulley nut.
3. Interference between pressure hose and other components.
4. Air entering oil pump.
5. Pump seizure.
6. Loose belt.

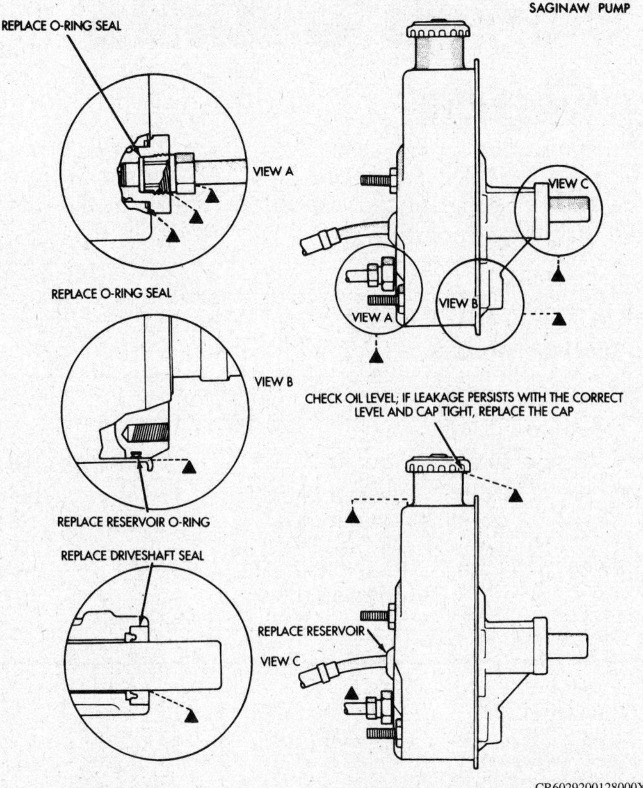

Fig. 1 Pump oil leak inspecting. Saginaw submerged vane pump w/integral reservoir (P type)

1. **BUSHING (BEARING) WORN, SEAL WORN. REPLACE PUMP.**
2. **REPLACE RESERVOIR O-RING SEAL.**
3. **TORQUE HOSE FITTING NUT TO SPECIFICATIONS. IF LEAKAGE PERSISTS, REPLACE O-RING SEAL.**
4. **TORQUE FITTING TO SPECIFICATIONS. IF LEAKAGE PERSISTS, REPLACE O-RING SEAL.**
5. **REPLACE PUMP.**
6. **CHECK OIL LEVEL: IF LEAKAGE PERSISTS WITH THE LEVEL CORRECT AND CAP TIGHT, REPLACE THE CAP.**

CR6029200129000X

Fig. 2 Pump oil leak inspecting. Saginaw vane pump w/external reservoir (TC type)

7. Gearbox port section damage.
8. Return hose fault.
9. Loose oil pump or pump bracket.
10. Excessive oil pump body wear.
11. Fault at steering stopper.
12. Wheel and tire to body interference.
13. Fault in gearbox.

Oil Leaks

Refer to **Figs. 1 and 2** for pump leakage inspect points and repair recommendations.

DIAGNOSIS & TESTING

Flow Rate & Pressure Test

1. Ensure power steering belt is in good condition and adjusted properly.
2. Connect pressure gauge hose from power steering analyzer tool No. 6815, or equivalent, to tube tool No. 6865, or equivalent.
3. Connect adapter tool No. 6826, or equivalent, to power steering analyzer, tool No. 6815, test valve end.
4. Disconnect high pressure hose from power steering pump.
5. Connect tube, tool No. 6865, to pump hose fitting.
6. Connect power steering hose from steering gear to adapter.
7. Open test valve completely.
8. Start engine and let idle long enough to circulate power steering fluid through flow/pressure test gauge.
9. Shut off engine and inspect fluid level. Add fluid as required.
10. Start engine and let idle.
11. Gauge should read below 125 psi. If above, inspect hoses for restrictions and repair as required.
12. Increase engine RPM to 1500 and read flow meter.
13. Reading should be 2.4–2.8 GPM. If below, replace pump.
14. Close valve fully three times for three seconds and record highest pressure indicated each time. Do not leave test valve closed for more than three seconds as pump could be damaged.
15. Readings must be above pump relief pressure specifications and within 50 psi of each other.
16. If pressures are above specification, but are not within 50 psi of each other, replace pump.
17. If pressures are below specification, but are within 50 psi of each other, replace pump.
18. Open test valve, then turn steering wheel from lock to lock. Do not force pump to operate against lock for more than 2–4 seconds.
19. Record highest indicated pressure at each position and compare to relief specifications. If highest output pressures are not within 50 psi against either stop, gear is leaking internally.

POWER STEERING SYSTEM SERVICE

Component Service

Refer to "Vane Type Power Steering Pump, With Integral Reservoir" or "Vane Type Power Steering Pump, Less Integral Reservoir" in the "General Motors" section for service procedures on these types of pumps.

DaimlerChrysler Variable Ratio Steering Gear

NOTE: On Air Bag Equipped Models, Refer To "Air Bag System Precautions" Located In The Front Of This Manual For System Disarming & Arming Procedures.

NOTE: Refer To "Computer Relearn Procedures" Located In The Front Of This Manual When Battery Power To The Computer Has Been Interrupted.

INDEX

PRECAUTIONS

Air Bag Systems

Refer to "Air Bag System Precautions" in the front of this manual for system disarming and arming procedures.

Battery Ground Cable

Prior to service disconnect battery ground cable and isolate as required.

DESCRIPTION

The power steering gear is a recirculating ball type gear, **Fig. 1.** The gear acts as a rolling thread between the worm shaft and the rack piston. The worm shaft is supported by a thrust bearing at the lower end and a bearing assembly at the upper end. When the worm shaft is turned, the rack piston moves. The rack piston teeth mesh with the pitman shaft. Turning the worm shaft turns the pitman shaft, which turns the steering linkage.

TROUBLESHOOTING

Refer to **Figs. 2 through 5** for troubleshooting symptom charts.

DIAGNOSIS & TESTING

Flow Rate & Pressure Test

This test will provide the gallons per minute or flow rate of the power steering pump along with the maximum relief pressure. Perform this test any time a power steering system problem is present.

1. Inspect power steering pump belt to ensure it is in good condition and adjusted properly.
2. Disconnect high pressure hose from power steering pump and install tool No. 6815, or equivalent, **Fig. 6.**
3. Open test valve completely.
4. Start engine and let idle long enough to circulate power steering fluid through flow/pressure test gauge and to release air from system.
5. Shutoff engine, inspect fluid level and top up as required.
6. Start engine and let idle.
7. Initial pressure reading should be approximately 50–80 psi.
8. If gauge reading is above 150 psi, inspect hoses for restrictions and repair or replace as required.
9. Increase engine speed to 1500 RPM and read flow meter.
10. If flow rate (GPM) is below specification, pump should be replaced.
11. Refer to "Power Steering Flow Rate Specifications" chart for specified values.
12. Close valve fully three times and record the highest pressure indicated. **Do not leave valve closed for more than three seconds or damage to pump could occur.**
13. All three readings must be above specified values and within 50 psi of each other.
14. If pump fails to perform as indicated, replace pump.
15. Open test valve and turn steering wheel to extreme left and right positions against the stops. **Do not force the pump to operate against the stops for more than two or three seconds or damage to pump will occur.**
16. Record highest pressure reading at each position.
17. If highest output pressures are not the same against either stop, the gear is leaking internally and must be replaced.

POWER STEERING SYSTEM SERVICE

System Bleed

1. With fluid at room temperature, ensure reservoir is at correct level.
2. Allow fluid to settle for a minimum of two minutes.
3. Start and run engine for a few minutes.
4. Add fluid as required, then repeat above steps until fluid level is constant.
5. Raise front wheels off ground.
6. Start engine, then slowly turn steering wheel left and right. Lightly contacting stops. **Do not force the pump to operate against the stops for more than two or three seconds or damage to pump will occur.**
7. Stop engine and inspect fluid level, fill as required.
8. If fluid is extremely foamy, let stand for a few minutes, then repeat procedure.

Component Service

HOUSING END PLUG

REMOVAL

1. Rotate retaining ring until one end is under hole, **Fig. 7,** in housing.
2. Unseat ring and remove from groove.
3. Rotate stub shaft slowly counterclockwise to remove end plug from housing. **Do not turn stub shaft any further than required. Recirculating balls will drop out of rack piston circuit and fall into rack piston chamber.**
4. Remove O-ring and seal.

INSTALLATION

1. Lubricate O-ring seal with power steering fluid.
2. Install O-ring seal, then the housing end plug. Tap lightly with a plastic mallet to seat plug.
3. Install retaining ring with open end, **Fig. 8,** one inch from access hole.
4. Adjust pitman arm shaft, refer to "Adjustments" in this section.

PITMAN SHAFT/SEALS/ BEARING

REMOVAL

1. Clean exposed end of pitman shaft and housing with a wire brush.
2. Remove preload adjuster nut, **Fig. 9.**
3. Rotate stub shaft with a suitable 12 point socket from stop to stop and count the number of turns.
4. Center stub shaft by rotating it from the stop ½ the total amount of turns.
5. Remove side cover bolts, **Fig. 9,** then the side cover and pitman shaft as an assembly.
6. **Pitman shaft will not clear housing if it is not centered.**
7. Remove pitman shaft from side cover.
8. Remove dust seal from housing, **Fig. 10,** with a seal pick. **Do not score housing bore when prying out seals and washer.**
9. Remove retaining ring with suitable snap ring pliers.
10. Remove washer and oil seal from housing.
11. Remove pitman shaft bearing from housing with a suitable bearing driver and handle, **Fig. 11.**

INSTALLATION

1. Install pitman shaft bearing into housing with a suitable bearing driver and handle.
2. Coat seals and washer with grease.
3. Install back-up washer.
4. Install retainer ring with suitable snap ring pliers.
5. Install dust seal with suitable driver and handle.
6. Install pitman shaft to side cover by screwing shaft in until it fully seats into side cover.
7. Install preload adjuster nut. **Do not tighten nut until over-center rotation torque adjustment has been made.**
8. Install gasket to side cover and bend tabs around edges of side cover, **Fig. 9.**
9. Install side cover bolts and tighten to specification.
10. Adjust over-center rotation torque, refer to "Adjustments" in this section.

SPOOL VALVE

REMOVAL

1. Remove locknut, **Fig. 12.**
2. Remove adjuster nut with spanner wrench tool No. C-4381, or equivalent.
3. Remove thrust support assembly from housing, **Fig. 13.**
4. Pull stub shaft and valve assembly from housing, **Fig. 14.**

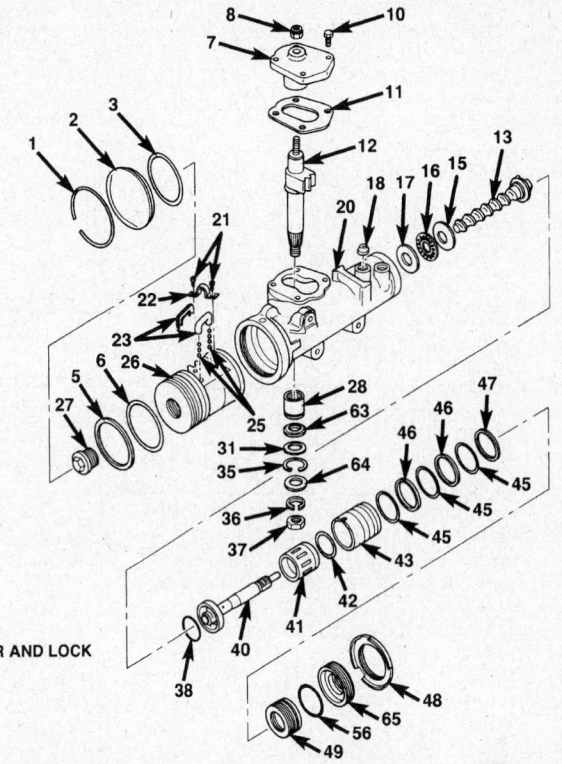

1 - RING, RETAINING
2 - PLUG
3 - SEAL, O-RING
5 - RING, TEFLON
6 - SEAL, O-RING
7 - COVER, SIDE
8 - NUT, ADJUSTER LOCK
10 - BOLT
11 - GASKET
12 - SHAFT, PITMAN
13 - SHAFT, WORM
15 - RACE, FLAT
16 - BEARING, THRUST
17 - RACE, FLAT
18 - VALVE, CHECK
20 - HOUSING
21 - SCREW
22 - CLAMP
23 - GUIDE, BALL
25 - BALLS
26 - PISTON, RACK
27 - PLUG
28 - BEARING, NEEDLE
31 - WASHER, BACKUP
35 - RING, RETAINING
36 - WASHER, LOCK
37 - NUT
38 - SEAL
40 - SHAFT, STUB
41 - SPOOL, VALVE
42 - SEAL
43 - BODY, VALVE
45 - SEAL, O-RING VALVE BODY
46 - RING
48 - NUT, COUPLING SHIELD RETAINER AND LOCK
49 - THRUST SUPPORT ASSEMBLY
56 - SEAL, O-RING
63 - SEAL, PITMAN SHAFT
64 - SEAL, DUST
65 - ADJUSTER NUT ASSEMBLY

CR6028800013000X

Fig. 1 Exploded view of variable ratio type power steering gear

5. Remove stub shaft from valve assembly by lightly tapping shaft on a block of wood to loosen shaft.
6. Remove stub shaft pin from hole in spool valve and separate valve assembly from stub shaft, **Fig. 15.**
7. Remove spool valve from body, **Fig. 16,** by pulling and rotating spool valve.
8. Remove spool valve O-ring and valve body teflon rings, **Fig. 17,** then the O-rings underneath teflon rings.
9. Remove O-ring between worm shaft and stub shaft.

INSTALLATION

1. Clean all components, then lubricate with power steering fluid.
2. Install spool valve O-ring.
3. Install spool valve in valve body by pushing and rotating.
4. Hole in spool valve for stub shaft pins must be accessible from opposite end of valve body.
5. Install stub shaft in valve spool and engage locating pin on stub shaft into spool valve hole, **Fig. 18. Notch in stub shaft cap must fully engage valve body pin and seat against valve body shoulder.**
6. Install O-rings and teflon rings over O-rings on valve body.
7. Install O-ring into back of stub shaft cap, **Fig. 19.**
8. Install stub shaft and valve assembly in housing. Line up worm shaft to slots in valve assembly.
9. Install thrust support assembly. **Thrust support is serviced as an assembly. If any component of thrust support is damaged, assembly must be replaced.**
10. Install adjuster and locknut.
11. Adjust thrust bearing preload and over-center rotating torque as outlined in "Adjustments."

RACK PISTON & WORM SHAFT

REMOVAL

1. Remove housing end plug, rack piston plug, side cover and pitman shaft, **Fig. 20.**
2. Turn stub shaft counterclockwise until rack piston begins to come out of housing.
3. Insert arbor tool No. C-4175, or equivalent, into bore of rack piston, **Fig. 21,** and hold tool tightly against worm shaft.
4. Turn stub shaft counterclockwise with a suitable 12 point socket, to force rack piston onto tool which holds rack piston balls in place.
5. Remove rack piston and tool from housing.
6. Remove tool from rack piston, then the piston balls.
7. Remove clamp bolts, clamp and ball guide, **Fig. 22.**
8. Remove teflon ring and O-ring from rack piston, **Fig. 23.**
9. Remove adjuster locknut and adjuster nut from stub shaft.
10. Pull stub shaft with spool valve and thrust support assembly out of housing.
11. Remove worm shaft, **Fig. 24,** from housing.

INSTALLATION

1. Clean and dry all components, then lubricate with power steering fluid.
2. Inspect rack piston finished surfaces for nicks, scratches and excessive wear. Slight wear is normal on worm gear surfaces.
3. Install O-ring and teflon ring on rack piston.
4. Install worm shaft in rack piston and align worm shaft spiral groove with rack piston ball guide hole, **Fig. 25.**
5. Lubricate and then install rack piston balls through return guide hole while turning worm shaft counterclockwise, **Fig. 25.**
6. Install remaining balls in guide using suitable grease to hold balls in place, **Fig. 26.**
7. Install guide onto rack piston, then the clamp and clamp bolts.
8. Insert arbor tool No. C-4175, or equivalent, into bore of rack piston and hold tool tightly against worm shaft.
9. Turn worm shaft counterclockwise while pushing on arbor tool to force rack piston onto arbor and to hold rack piston balls in place.
10. Install races and thrust bearing on worm shaft, **Fig. 24,** then install the shaft in housing.
11. Install stub shaft with spool valve, thrust support assembly and adjuster nut into housing.
12. Install rack piston and arbor tool into housing.
13. Hold arbor tool tightly against worm shaft and turn stub shaft clockwise until rack piston is seated on worm shaft.
14. Install pitman shaft and side cover.
15. Install rack piston plug and tighten to specification.
16. Install housing end plug.
17. Adjust worm shaft thrust bearing preload and over-center rotating torque, refer to "Adjustments" in this section.

CONDITION	POSSIBLE CAUSES	CORRECTION
OBJECTIONAL HISS OR WHISTLE	1. Steering intermediate shaft to dash panel seal. 2. Noisy valve in power steering gear.	1. Check and repair seal at dash panel. 2. Replace steering gear.
RATTLE OR CLUNK	1. Gear mounting bolts loose. 2. Loose or damaged suspension components. 3. Loose or damaged steering linkage. 4. Internal gear noise. 5. Pressure hose in contact with other components.	1. Tighten bolts to specification. 2. Inspect and repair suspension. 3. Inspect and repair steering linkage. 4. Replace gear. 5. Reposition hose.
CHIRP OR SQUEAL	1. Loose belt.	1. Adjust or replace.
WHINE OR GROWL	1. Low fluid level. 2. Pressure hose in contact with other components. 3. Internal pump noise.	1. Fill to proper level. 2. Reposition hose. 3. Replace pump.
SUCKING AIR SOUND	1. Loose return line clamp. 2. O-ring missing or damaged on hose fitting. 3. Low fluid level. 4. Air leak between pump and reservoir.	1. Replace clamp. 2. Replace o-ring. 3. Fill to proper level. 4. Repair as necessary.
SCRUBBING OR KNOCKING	1. Wrong tire size. 2. Wrong gear.	1. Verify tire size. 2. Verify gear.

CR6029800157000X

Fig. 2 Steering noise

CONDITION	POSSIBLE CAUSE	CORRECTION
DIFFICULT TO TURN WHEEL STICKS OR BINDS	1. Low fluid level. 2. Tire pressure. 3. Steering components (ball joints/tie rod ends). 4. Loose belt. 5. Low pump pressure. 6. Column shaft coupler binding. 7. Steering gear worn or out of adjustment.	1. Fill to proper level. 2. Adjust tire pressure. 3. Lube, inspect and repair as necessary. 4. Adjust or replace. 5. Pressure test and replace if necessary. 6. Replace coupler. 7. Repair or replace gear.

CR6029800158000X

Fig. 3 Binding & sticking

Adjustments

The steering gear must be adjusted in the proper order. If adjustments are not performed in order, gear damage and improper steering response may result.

Adjusting the steering gear in the vehicle is not recommended. Remove steering gear from vehicle and drain the fluid. Then mount gear in a suitable vise and perform adjustments.

WORM BEARING PRELOAD

1. Mount steering gear carefully in a vise. Do not overtighten vise or adjustments may be affected.
2. Remove adjuster plug locknut, **Fig. 27.**
3. Rotate stub shaft back and forth with a suitable 12 point socket to drain remaining fluid.
4. Turn adjuster nut in with spanner wrench tool No. C-4381, or equivalent.
5. Tighten plug and thrust bearing in housing until firmly bottomed in housing.
6. Place an index mark on housing even with one of the holes in adjuster plug, **Fig. 28.**
7. Measure back counterclockwise .020 inch and mark housing, **Fig. 29.**
8. Rotate adjustment cap counterclockwise with spanner wrench until hole is aligned with second mark, **Fig. 30.**
9. Install and tighten locknut to specification. **Ensure cap does not turn while tightening locknut.**

OVER-CENTER

Adjust worm bearing preload before performing this procedure.

1. Rotate stub shaft with a suitable 12 point socket from stop to stop and count number of turns.
2. Starting at either stop, turn stub shaft back ½ the total number of turns to center of gear travel, **Fig. 31.**
3. Place a suitable inch lb., torque wrench in vertical position on stub shaft.
4. Rotate wrench 45° each side of center, **Fig. 32,** and record highest rotational torque in this range. This is the over-center rotating torque.
5. Rotate stub shaft between 90° and 180° to left of center and record left off center preload.
6. Repeat to right of center and record right off center preload.
7. Average of these two readings is preload rotating torque.
8. Over-center rotating torque should be 4–8 inch lbs., higher than preload rotating torque.
9. If an adjustment to over-center rotating torque is required, first loosen adjuster locknut.
10. Turn pitman shaft adjuster screw counterclockwise until fully extended.
11. Turn adjuster screw clockwise one full turn.
12. Measure over-center rotating torque. If required turn adjuster screw and repeat measurement until correct over-center rotating torque is reached.
13. **Turning adjuster screw clockwise increases the over-center rotating torque.**
14. Tighten adjuster locknut to specification. Ensure adjuster screw does not turn while securing locknut.

CONDITION	POSSIBLE CAUSE	CORRECTION
HARD TURNING OR MOMENTARY INCREASE IN TURNING EFFORT	1. Tire pressure. 2. Low fluid level. 3. Loose belt. 4. Lack of lubrication. 5. Low pump pressure. 6. Internal gear leak.	1. Adjust tire pressure. 2. Fill to proper level. 3. Adjust or replace. 4. Inspect and lubricate steering and suspension compnents. 5. Pressure test and repair as necessary. 6. Pressure and flow test, and repair as necessary.
STEERING WHEEL DOES NOT WANT TO RETURN TO CENTER POSITION	1. Tire pressure. 2. Wheel alignment. 3. Lack of lubrication. 4. High friction in steering gear.	1. Adjust tire pressure. 2. Align front end. 3. Inspect and lubricate steering and suspension compnents. 4. Test and adjust as necessary.

CR6029800159000X

Fig. 4 Insufficient assist or poor return to center

CONDITION	POSSIBLE CAUSE	CORRECTION
EXCESSIVE PLAY IN STEERING WHEEL	1. Worn or loose suspension or steering components. 2. Worn or loose wheel bearings. 3. Steering gear mounting. 4. Gear out of adjustment. 5. Worn or loose steering coupler.	1. Inspect and repair as necessary. 2. Inspect and repair or adjust bearings. 3. Tighten gear mounting bolts to specification. 4. Adjust gear to specification. 5. Inspect and replace as necessary.
VEHICLE PULLS OR LEADS TO ONE SIDE.	1. Tire Pressure. 2. Radial tire lead. 3. Brakes dragging. 4. Wheel alignment.	1. Adjust tire pressure. 2. Rotate tires. 3. Repair as necessary. 4. Align front end.

CR6029800160000X

Fig. 5 Loose steering & vehicle lead

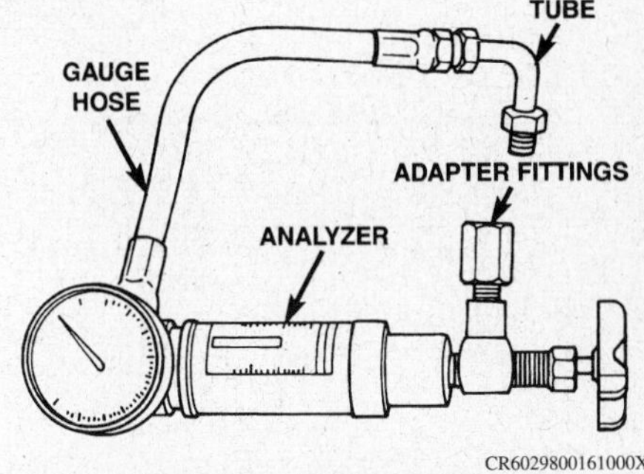

Fig. 6 Power steering pressure test gauge

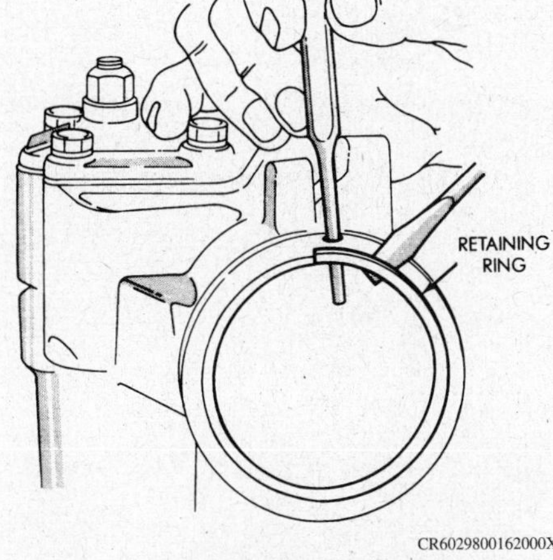

Fig. 7 End plug retaining ring

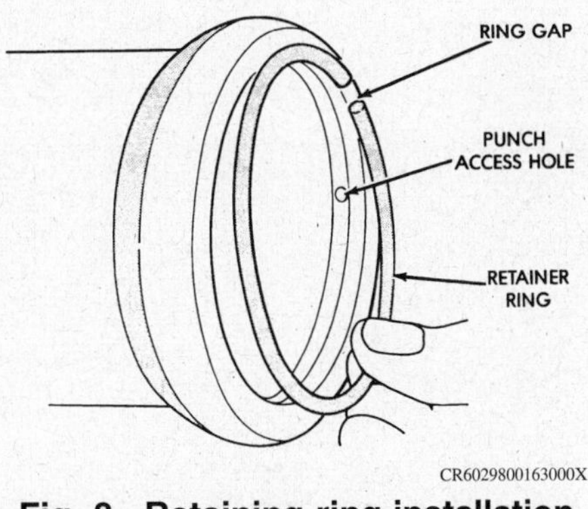

Fig. 8 Retaining ring installation

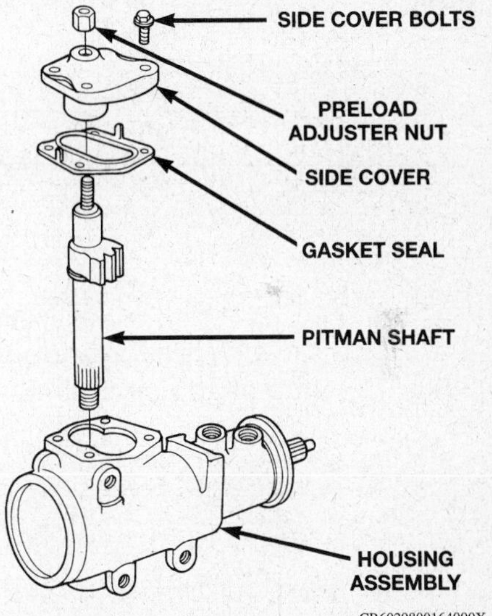

Fig. 9 Side cover & pitman shaft

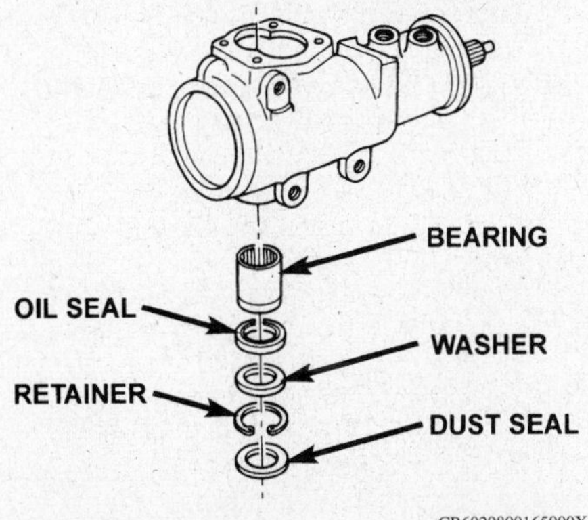

Fig. 10 Pitman shaft seals & bearing

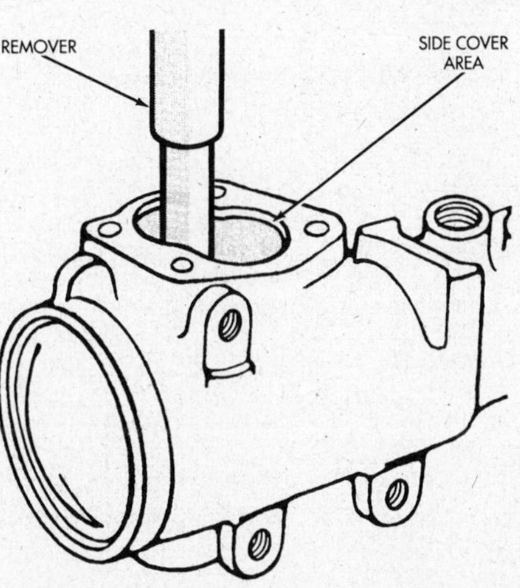

Fig. 11 Needle bearing removal

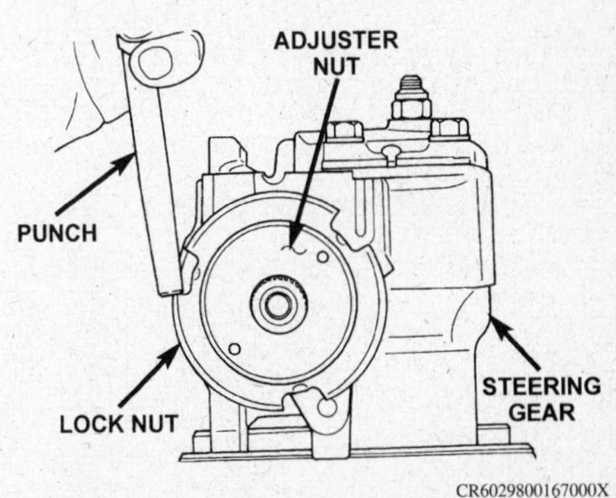

Fig. 12 Lock & adjuster nuts

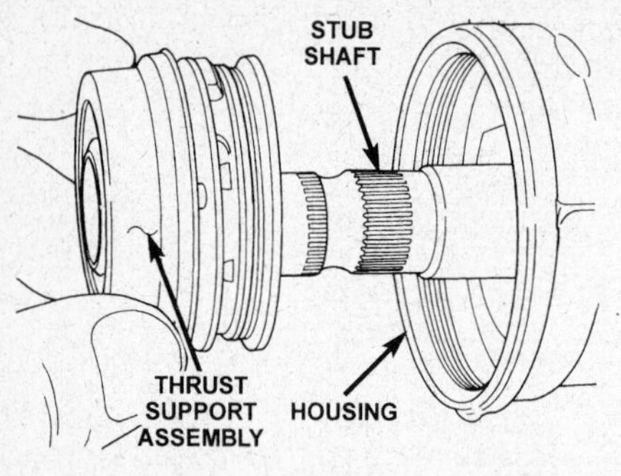

Fig. 13 Thrust support assembly

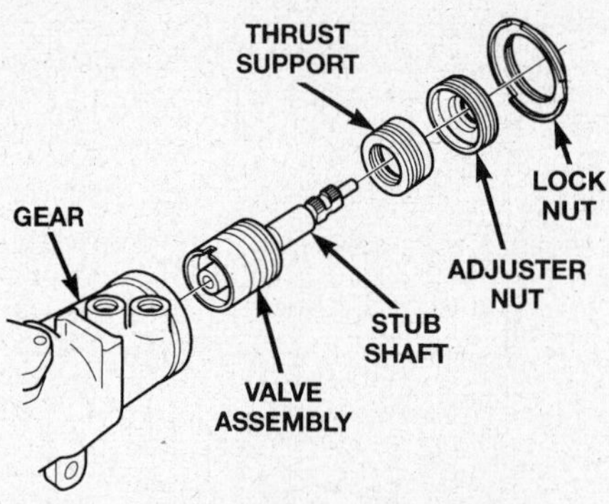

Fig. 14 Exploded view of spool valve

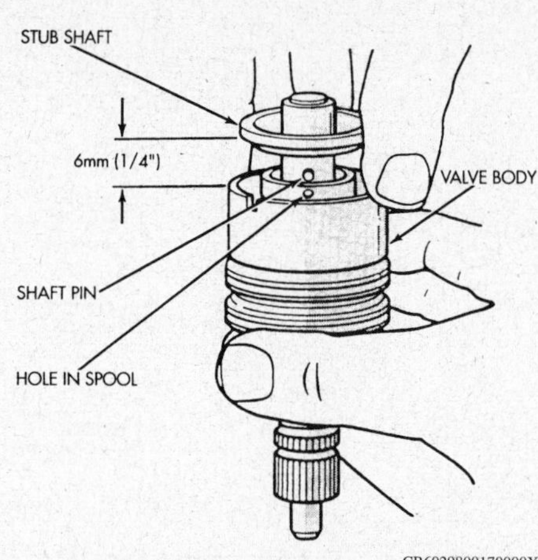

Fig. 15 Stub shaft removal

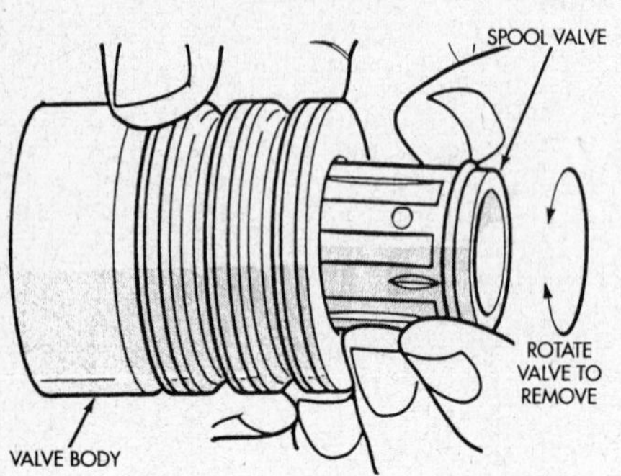

Fig. 16 Spool valve

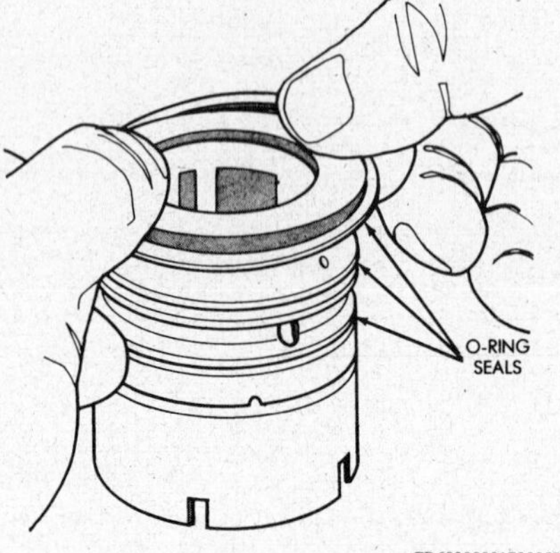

Fig. 17 Valve seals

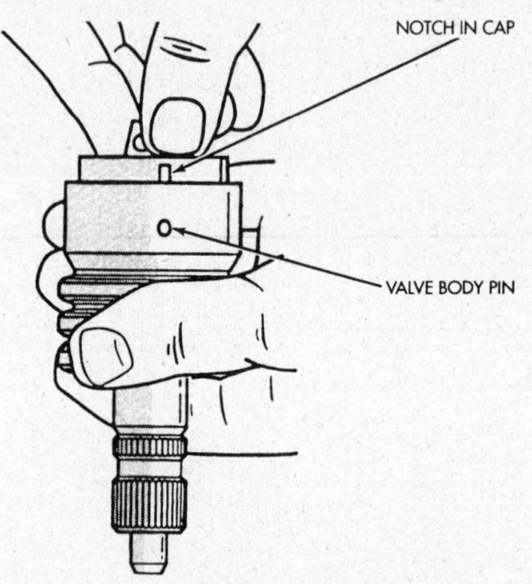

Fig. 18 Stub shaft installation

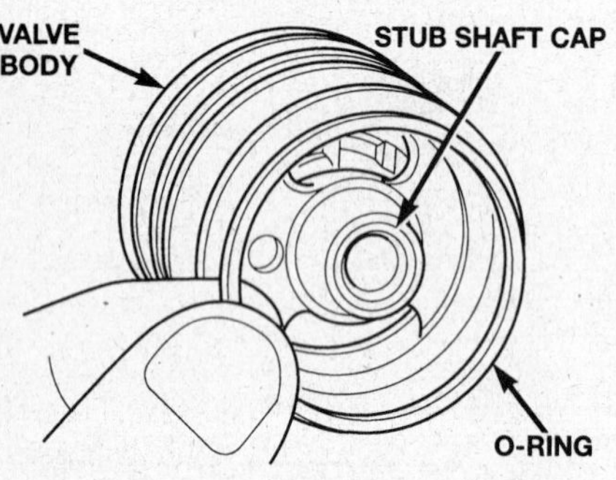

Fig. 19 Stub shaft cap O-ring

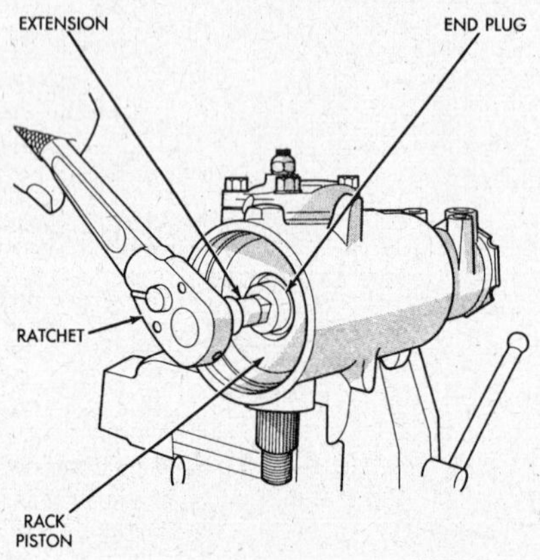

Fig. 20 Rack piston end plug

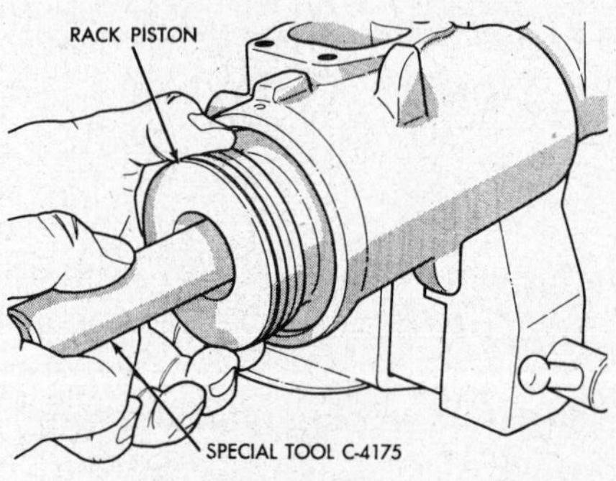

Fig. 21 Rack piston arbor tool installation

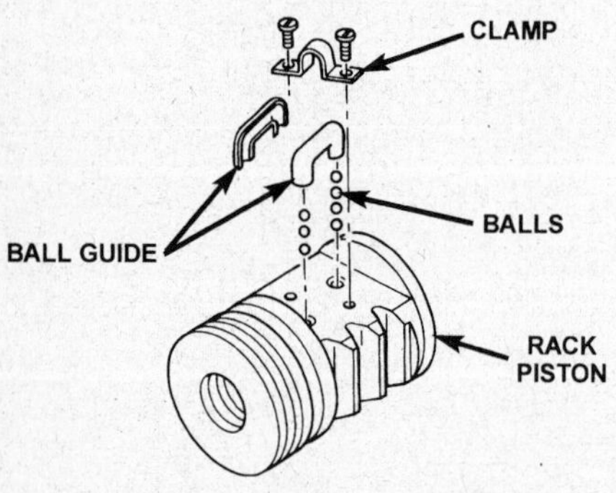

Fig. 22 Rack piston

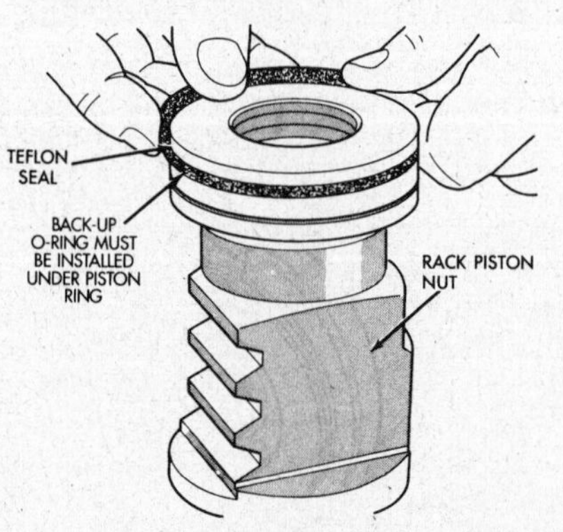

Fig. 23 Rack piston teflon ring & O-ring

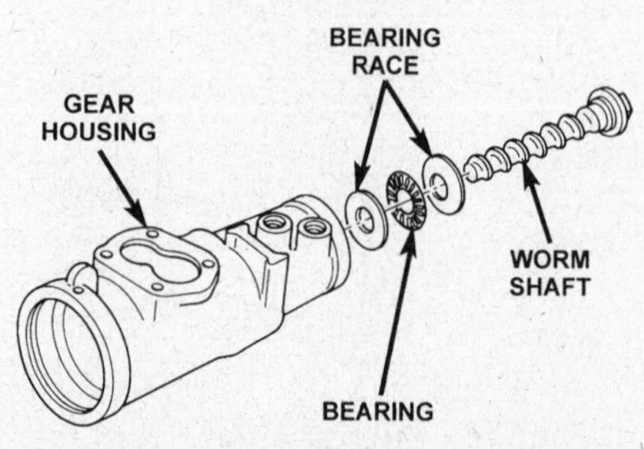

Fig. 24 Worm shaft replacement

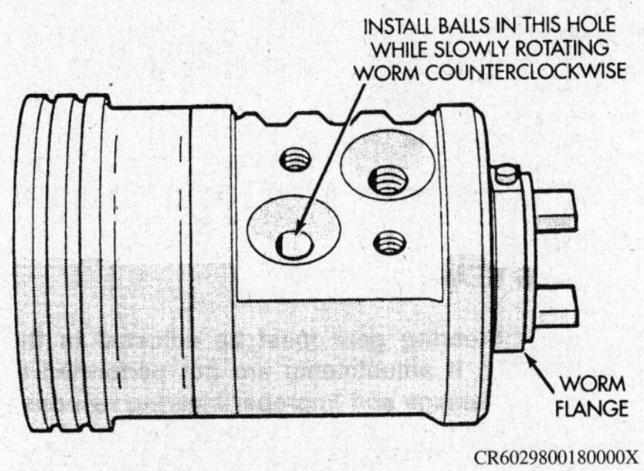

Fig. 25 Rack piston ball installation

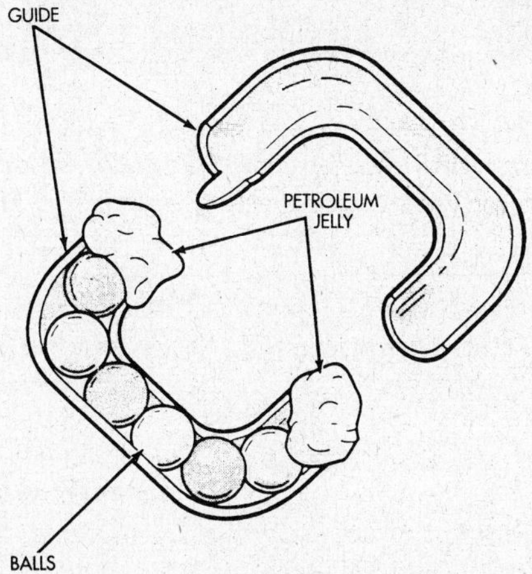

Fig. 26 Rack piston balls in return guide

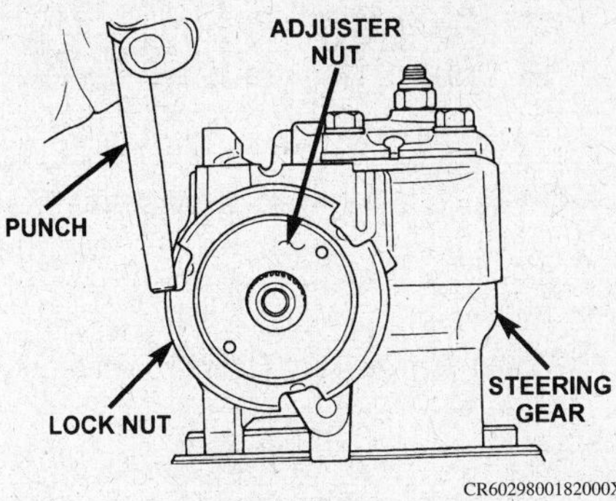

Fig. 27 Bearing preload adjuster locknut

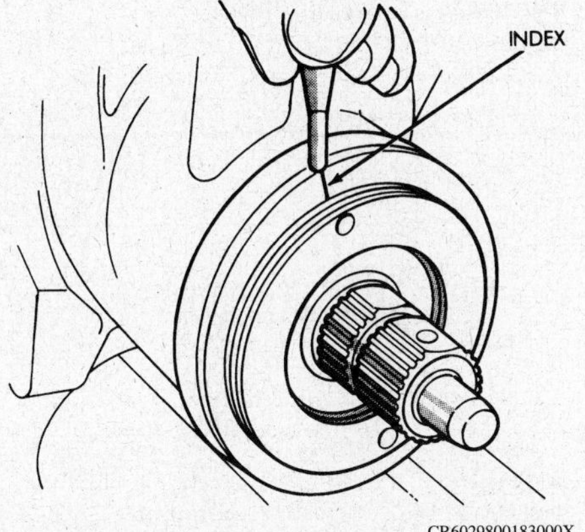

Fig. 28 Housing alignment mark

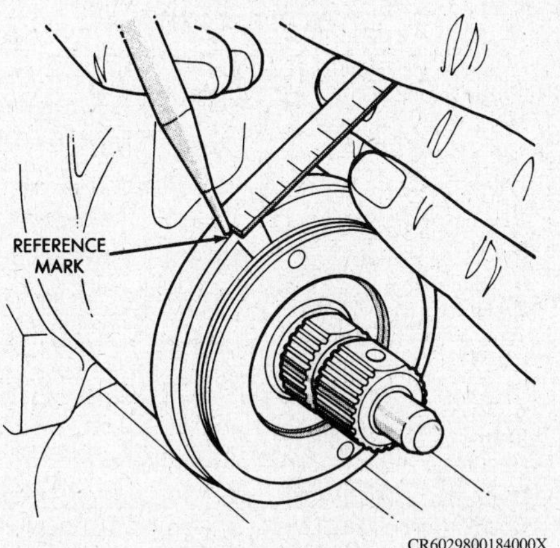

Fig. 29 Housing second mark

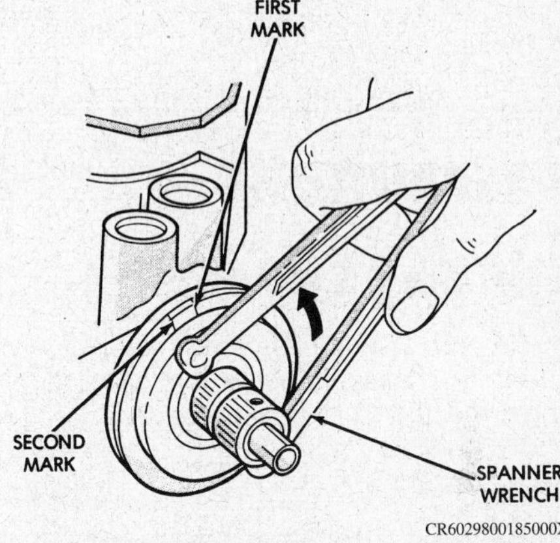

Fig. 30 Second mark alignment

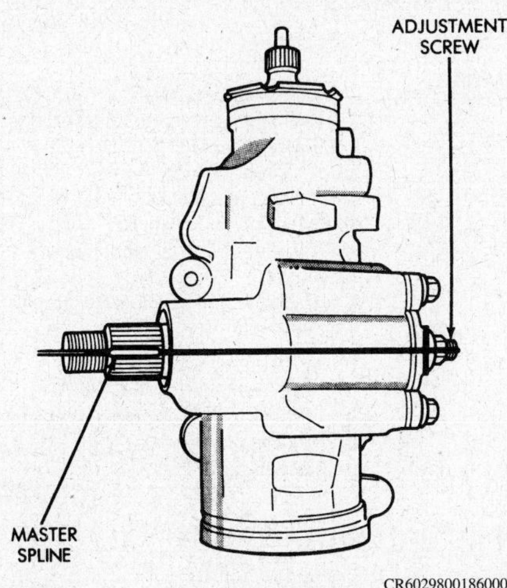

Fig. 31 Steering gear centered position

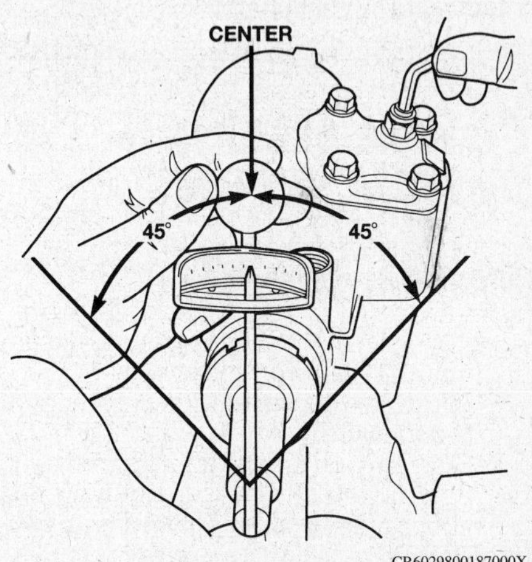

Fig. 32 Over-center rotation torque inspection

TRW Rack & Pinion Steering Gear

NOTE: On Air Bag Equipped Models, Refer To "Air Bag System Precautions" Located In The Front Of This Manual For System Disarming & Arming Procedures.

NOTE: Refer To "Computer Relearn Procedures" Located In The Front Of This Manual When Battery Power To The Computer Has Been Interrupted.

INDEX

PRECAUTIONS

Air Bag Systems

Refer to "Air Bag System Precautions" in the front of this manual for system disarming and arming procedures.

TROUBLESHOOTING

Refer to **Figs. 1 through 3** for troubleshooting symptom charts.

CONDITION	POSSIBLE CAUSE	CORRECTION
DIFFICULT TO TURN WHEEL STICKS OR BINDS	1. Low fluid level. 2. Tire pressure. 3. Steering components 4. Loose belt. 5. Low pump pressure. 6. Column shaft coupler binding. 7. Steering gear worn or out of adjustment.	1. Fill to proper level. 2. Adjust tire pressure. 3. Inspect and lube. 4. Adjust or replace. 5. Pressure test and replace if necessary. 6. Replace coupler. 7. Repair or replace gear.

CR6029800188000X

Fig. 1 Binding or sticking

CONDITION	POSSIBLE CAUSE	CORRECTION
HARD TURNING OR MOMENTARY INCREASE IN TURNING EFFORT	1. Tire pressure. 2. Low fluid level. 3. Loose belt. 4. Lack of lubrication. 5. Low pump pressure. 6. Internal gear leak.	1. Adjust tire pressure. 2. Fill to proper level. 3. Adjust or replace. 4. Inspect and lubricate steering and suspension compnents. 5. Pressure test and repair as necessary. 6. Pressure and flow test, and repair as necessary.
STEERING WHEEL DOES NOT WANT TO RETURN TO CENTER POSITION	1. Tire pressure. 2. Wheel alignment. 3. Lack of lubrication. 4. High friction in steering gear.	1. Adjust tire pressure. 2. Align front end. 3. Inspect and lubricate steering and suspension compnents. 4. Test and adjust as necessary.

CR6029800189000X

Fig. 2 Insufficient assist or poor return to center

CONDITION	POSSIBLE CAUSE	CORRECTION
EXCESSIVE PLAY IN STEERING WHEEL	1. Worn or loose suspension or steering components. 2. Worn or loose wheel bearings. 3. Steering gear mounting. 4. Gear out of adjustment. 5. Worn or loose steering coupler.	1. Inspect and repair as necessary. 2. Inspect and repair or adjust bearings. 3. Tighten gear mounting bolts to specification. 4. Adjust gear to specification. 5. Inspect and replace as necessary.
VEHICLE PULLS OR LEADS TO ONE SIDE.	1. Tire Pressure. 2. Radial tire lead. 3. Brakes dragging. 4. Wheel alignment.	1. Adjust tire pressure. 2. Rotate tires. 3. Repair as necessary. 4. Align front end.

CR6029800190000X

Fig. 3 Loose steering & vehicle lead

POWER STEERING SYSTEM SERVICE

System Bleed

1. With fluid at room temperature, ensure reservoir is at correct level.
2. Allow fluid to settle for a minimum of two minutes.
3. Start and run engine for a few minutes.
4. Add fluid as required, then repeat above steps until fluid level is constant.
5. Raise front wheels off ground.
6. Start engine, then slowly turn steering wheel left and right. Lightly contacting stops.
7. Stop engine and inspect fluid level, fill as required.
8. If fluid is extremely foamy, let stand for a few minutes, then repeat procedure.

Component Service

This steering gear is not serviceable. If a problem is indicated, the unit must be replaced.

TIGHTENING SPECIFICATIONS

Year	Component	Torque Ft. Lbs.
CARAVAN, TOWN & COUNTRY & VOYAGER		
2002–06	High Pressure Hose Tube Nuts	25
	Return Tube Nut	25
	Steering Gear To Crossmember Bolts	135
	Tie Rod End Locknut	55
	Tie Rod End to Steering Knuckle Attaching Nut	55
COMMANDER & GRAND CHEROKEE		
2005–06	Intermediate Shaft Bolt	36
	Power Steering 3/8 Tube Nuts	21
	Power Steering 1/2 Tube Nuts	35
	Rack & Pinion Gear To Frame Bolts	180
	Tie Rod End To Knuckle End Nut	70
	Tie Rod End Jam Nut	55
DAKOTA & 2002–03 DURANGO		
2002–04	Intermediate Shaft Bolt	42
	Power Steering Pressure Line	23
	Power Steering Return Line	23
	Rack & Pinion Gear To Frame Bolts	200
	Tie Rod End Knuckle Nut	60
	Tie Rod End Jam Nut	55
DAKOTA & 2004–06 DURANGO		
2005–06	Intermediate Shaft Bolt	28
	Power Steering Pressure Line	27
	Power Steering Return Line	48
	Rack & Pinion Gear To Frame Bolts	190
	Tie Rod End Knuckle Nut	55
	Tie Rod End Jam Nut	96
FULL SIZE VAN		
2002–03	Adjustment Cap Locknut	80
	Adjustment Screw Locknut	28
	End Plug	25
	Gear Bracket To Frame Crossmember Bolts	30
	Gear To Frame Bolts	150
	High Pressure Fluid Line	22
	Housing Head Spanner Nut	162
	Pitman Adjustment Cap Spanner Nut	155
	Pitman Shaft Nut	185
	Valve Body Screw	96④
	Worm Shaft Adjustment Nut	20
GRAND CHEROKEE		
2002–04	Pitman Arm Shaft Nut	185
	Power Steering Pump Bolts	21
	Power Steering Pump Pressure Line	28①
	Power Steering Pump Pressure Line	35
	Power Steering Pump Return Line	28
	Steering Damper Axle Bolt	65
	Tie Rod Knuckle Nut	35
	Tie Rod Clamp Nuts	30

TIGHTENING SPECIFICATIONS—Continued

Year	Component	Torque Ft. Lbs.
LIBERTY		
2002–06	Intermediate Shaft Bolt	36
	Rack & Pinion Gear To Frame Bolts	120
	Steering Pressure Line	20
	Steering Return Line	20
	Tie Rod End Knuckle Nut	80
	Tie Rod End Jam Nut	55
PACIFICA		
2004–06	Gear Mounting Bolts	120
	Hose Tube Nut At Gear	23
	Hose Tube Nut At Pump (3.5L)	23
	Pump Mounting Bolts	17
	Tie Rod Steering Arm Nut	35⑤
	Tie Rod Jam Nut	55
PT CRUISER		
2002–06	Hose Routing Clamp Bolt	45
	Pump Mounting Bolts	21
	Pump Tube Nut At Gear	23
	Pump Tube Nut At Pump	23
	Steering Gear Mounting Bolts	45
	Tie Rod End-to-Knuckle Nut	40
	Tie Rod Jam Nut	55
SPRINTER		
2004–06	High Pressure Hose To Steering Gear	27
	Power Steering Return Line To Gear	27
	Steering Gear To Frame Bolts	⑧
	U-Joint To Steering Gear	18
WRANGLER		
2002–06	Steering Gear Adjustment Lock Nut	48
	Steering Gear To Frame Bolts	70
	Steering Gear Pitman Shaft Nut	185
	Steering Gear Pressure Line	21
	Steering Gear Return Line	21
2002 2500 & 3500 FULL SIZE PICKUPS		
2002	Adjustment Cap Locknut	80
	Adjustment Screw Locknut	43
	Gear To Frame Bolts	140
	High Pressure Fluid Line	22
	Intermediate Shaft Pinch Bolts	36
	Pitman Shaft Nut	185
	Pump Assembly To Engine Block②	57
	Pump Bracket To Engine③	30
	Pump To Bracket③	35
	Pump To Support Bracket②	18
	Pump To Vacuum Pump②	18
	Rack-Piston Plug	110
	Reservoir To Body	42
	Return Pressure Fluid Line	25
	Side Cover Bolt	45

Continued

TIGHTENING SPECIFICATIONS—Continued

Year	Component	Torque Ft. Lbs.
2002 2500 & 3500 FULL SIZE PICKUPS		
2002–06	Power Steering Pressure Line	23
	Power Steering Pressure Line To Pump	27
	Power Steering Pressure Switch	80④
	Power Steering Pump	27
	Power Steering Pump Bracket	60④
	Power Steering Pump Reservoir	60④
	Power Steering Return Line	37
	Rack & Pinion To Frame Bolts	235⑥
	Tie Rod End To Knuckle Nut	45⑦
	Tie Rod End Jam Nut	94

①— 4.0L engine

②— Diesel engine.

③— Gasoline engine.

④— Inch lbs.

⑤— Plus an additional 180°.

⑥— Light duty.

⑦— Plus an additional 90°.

⑧— 18 ft. lbs., first pass, 33 ft. lbs., second pass, then an additional 90° turn.

DISC BRAKES

NOTE: Prior To Performing Any Service Operations Listed In This Section, Consult The "Technical Service Bulletins" Section For Related Information.

INDEX

PRECAUTIONS

Brake Lines & Linings

Remove one of the front wheels and inspect the brake disc, caliper and linings. The wheel bearings should be inspected at this time and repacked if required.

Do not get any oil or grease on the linings. It is recommended that both front wheel sets be replaced whenever a respective pad is worn or damaged. Inspect and, if required, replace rear brake linings also.

If the caliper is cracked or fluid leakage through the casting is evident, it must be replaced as a unit.

Brake Roughness

The most common cause of brake chatter on disc brakes is a variation in thickness of the disc. If roughness or vibration is encountered during highway operation or if pedal pumping is experienced at low speeds, the disc may have excessive thickness variation. To inspect for this condition, measure the disc at 8 points with a micrometer at a radius approximately one inch from edge of disc. If thickness measurements vary more than specifications allow, the disc should be replaced with a new one.

Excessive lateral runout of braking disc may cause a "knocking back" of the pistons, possibly creating increased pedal travel and vibration when brakes are applied.

Before inspecting the runout, wheel bearings should be adjusted. Ensure to make the adjustment according to the recommendations given in the individual truck chapters.

Brake Disc Service

Servicing of disc brakes is extremely critical due to the close tolerances required in machining the brake disc to ensure proper brake operation.

The maintenance of these close controls on the friction surfaces is required to prevent brake roughness. In addition, the surface finish must be non-directional and maintained at a micro-inch finish. This close control of the rubbing surface finish is required to avoid pulls and erratic performance and promote long lining life and equal lining wear of both lefthand and righthand brakes.

Refinishing of the rubbing surfaces should not be attempted unless precision equipment, capable of measuring in microinches (millionths of an inch) is available.

To inspect runout of a disc, mount a dial indicator on a convenient part (steering knuckle, tie rod, disc brake caliper housing) so that the plunger of the dial indicator contacts the disc at a point one inch from the outer edge. If the total indicated runout exceeds specifications, install a new disc.

General Precautions

1. Grease or any other foreign material must be kept off the caliper, surfaces of the disc and external surfaces of the hub, during service procedures. Handling the brake disc and caliper should be done in a way to avoid deformation of the disc and nicking or scratching brake linings.
2. If inspection reveals rubber piston seals are worn or damaged, they should be replaced immediately.
3. During removal and installation of a wheel assembly, exercise care so as not to interfere with or damage the caliper splash shield, the bleeder screw or the transfer tube (if equipped).
4. Front wheel bearings should be adjusted to specifications.
5. Ensure vehicle is centered on hoist before servicing any of the front end components to avoid bending or damaging the disc splash shield on full righthand or lefthand wheel turns.
6. Before the vehicle is moved after any brake service work, ensure to obtain a firm brake pedal.
7. The assembly bolts of the two caliper housings (if equipped) should not be disturbed unless the caliper requires service.

Caliper Inspection

If it is required to remove the caliper for installation of new components, clean all components in alcohol, wipe dry using lint-free cloths. Using an air hose, blow out drilled passages and bores. Inspect dust boots for punctures or tears. If punctures or tears are evident, new boots should be installed upon reassembly.

Inspect piston bores in both housings for scoring or pitting. Bores that show light scratches or corrosion can usually be cleaned with crocus cloth. However, bores that have deep scratches or scoring may be honed, provided the diameter of the bore is not increased more than .002 inch. If the bore does not clean up within this specification, a new caliper housing should be installed (black stains on the bore walls are caused by piston seals and will do no harm).

When using a hone, ensure to install the hone baffle before honing bore. The baffle is used to protect the hone stones from damage. Use extreme care in cleaning the caliper after honing. Remove all dust and grit by flushing the caliper with alcohol. Wipe dry with clean lint-free cloth and then clean a second time in the same manner.

Brake Bleed

The disc brake hydraulic system can be bled manually or with pressure bleeding equipment.

Never use brake fluid that has been drained from hydraulic system when bleeding the brakes. Ensure the disc brake pistons are returned to their normal positions and that the pad assemblies are properly seated. Before driving the vehicle, inspect brake operation to ensure that a firm pedal has been obtained.

DESCRIPTION

These vehicles are equipped with dual piston calipers, sliding single piston systems, single non-metallic calipers, floating caliper-single piston or single piston caliper mounted disc brake systems.

Upon brake application, fluid pressure exerted against the caliper piston increases equally in all directions, creating the same pressure in the caliper bore and on the piston.

Pressure applied to the piston is transmitted directly to the inboard brake pad, forcing it against the inner surface of the rotor. At the same time, pressure in the bore forces the caliper to slide inward on the mounting bolts to bring the outboard brake pad into contact with the outer surface of the rotor. These actions create a simultaneous, even braking pressure on both sides of the rotor.

TROUBLESHOOTING

Pedal Falls Away

1. System leak at brake line, fitting, hose or caliper/wheel cylinder.
2. Internal leakage in master cylinder caused by worn or damaged piston cups.
3. Internal leak in ABS or RWAL system.

Low Pedal

1. Worn brake linings.
2. Worn drums or rotors.
3. Rear brakes out of adjustment.

Spongy Pedal

1. Air in hydraulic system.
2. Thin brake drums.
3. Substandard brake lines and hoses.

Hard Pedal Or High Pedal Effort

1. Linings that are water soaked, contaminated or glazed.
2. Faulty power booster or check valve.

Pedal Pulsation

1. Disc brake rotors have excessive lateral runout or thickness variation.
2. Out of round brake drums.
3. Loose wheel bearings or calipers.
4. Damaged tires.

Brake Drag

1. Seized or improperly adjusted parking brake cables.
2. Loose or worn wheel bearings.
3. Seized caliper or wheel cylinder piston.
4. Caliper binding on corroded bushings or rusted slide surfaces.
5. Loose caliper mounting.
6. Drum brake shoes binding on worn or damaged support plates.
7. Mis-assembled components.

8. Long booster output rod.
9. If drag occurs at all wheels, inspect for blocked master cylinder return port or faulty power booster.

Brake Fade

1. Overheated brakes caused by excessive brake drag.
2. Customer riding brake pedal.
3. Repeated high speed stops in a short time span.
4. Constant braking on steep mountain roads.

Brake Pull

1. Contaminated lining in one caliper.
2. Seized caliper piston.
3. Binding or loose caliper.
4. Rusty caliper slide surfaces.
5. Improper brake shoes.
6. Damaged rotor.
7. Worn or damaged wheel bearing or suspension component.

Rear Brake Grab Or Pull

1. Improperly adjusted or seized parking brake cables.
2. If both rear wheels are affected, inspect master cylinder or proportioning valve.

Brake Squeal Or Squeak

1. Wet brake linings.
2. Brake linings contaminated with brake fluid, grease or oil.
3. Glazed linings and rotors with hard spots.
4. Dirt or foreign material embedded in brake lining.
5. Severely worn brake linings.

Brake Chatter

1. Loose or worn components.
2. Glazed or burnt linings.
3. Rotors with hard spots.
4. Out of tolerance rotors.
5. Brake lining not securely attached to shoes.
6. Loose wheel bearings.
7. Contaminated brake linings.

BRAKE SYSTEM BLEED

Refer to the "Hydraulic Brake Systems" chapter for brake system bleed procedures.

ROTOR

REPLACE

Caravan, Town & Country & Voyager

1. Raise and support vehicle, then remove wheel and caliper as outlined under "Brake Pad Service." **Support caliper at all times to prevent brake hose damage.**
2. Slide brake rotor off hub.
3. Reverse procedure to install. Clean brake rotor with alcohol or other suitable solvent.

Commander

FRONT

1. Raise and support vehicle using suitable lift or jack.
2. Remove tire and wheel assembly.
3. Remove caliper as outlined in "Caliper Service."
4. Secure caliper anchor assembly using suitable wire.
5. Remove and discard O-ring securing disc brake rotor on hub.
6. Remove rotor from hub and bearing.
7. Reverse procedure to install, noting the following:
   a. Caliper slide pins should be clean and slightly lubricated.
   b. Tighten to specification.

REAR

1. Raise and support vehicle using suitable lift or jack.
2. Remove tire and wheel assembly.
3. Remove caliper as outlined in "Caliper Service."
4. Secure caliper anchor assembly using suitable wire.
5. Remove rotor and discard O-ring securing rotor to axle studs.
6. Reverse procedure to install, noting the following:
   a. Pump brake pedal until caliper pistons and brake pads are seated.
   b. Tighten to specifications.

Dakota & Durango

1. Raise and support vehicle, then remove wheel.
2. Remove caliper and brake pads as outlined under "Brake Pad Service."**It is not required to disconnect brake line from caliper. After caliper has been removed from rotor, support it to prevent brake line damage.**
3. Remove stamped retainer clips, then the rotor.
4. Reverse procedure to install, noting the following:
   a. Inspect ABS tone wheel for damage. Rotor assembly must be replaced if tone wheel is damaged.
   b. Tighten wheel lug nuts to specifications.

Full Size Pickup

2002 2500 & 3500

5-STUD ROTORS

1. Raise and support vehicle.
2. Remove wheel and tire assembly.
3. Remove brake caliper from steering knuckle as outlined under "Brake Pad Service."
4. Remove rotor from hub bearing.
5. Reverse procedure to install.

8-STUD ROTORS

1. Raise and support vehicle.
2. Remove wheel and tire assembly.
3. Remove hub extension mounting nuts, then the hub extension.
4. Remove brake caliper.
5. Remove cotter pin and hub nut from axle shaft.
6. Disconnect ABS wheel sensor wire from under hood, then remove sensor wire from frame and steering knuckle.
7. Remove hub/bearing mounting bolts from inboard side of steering knuckle.
8. Remove rotor hub/bearing assembly, brake shield and spacer from steering knuckle.
9. If rotor hub assembly will not come out of the knuckle, use puller No. C-844 with extra puller leg No. C-884-1, or equivalents, to remove the assembly.
10. Press out wheel studs/hub extension studs and separate rotor from hub.
11. Reverse procedure to install, noting the following:
    a. Apply anti-seize compound to splines of front drive shaft.
    b. If equipped with ABS, position wheel speed sensor wire at top of knuckle.
    c. Tighten to specifications.

1500 & 2003-05 2500 & 3500

FRONT

1. Raise and support vehicle, then remove tire and wheel assembly.
2. Remove caliper from steering knuckle as outlined under "Brake Pad Service."
3. **On 2500 and 3500 models,** remove extension to rotor nuts.
4. **On all models,** remove rotor from hub and bearing wheel studs.
5. Reverse procedure to install. Tighten to specifications.

REAR w/SINGLE WHEEL

1. Raise and support vehicle, then remove tire and wheel assembly.
2. Remove caliper as outlined under "Brake Pad Service."
3. Remove brake caliper adapter bolts, then the caliper adapter.
4. Remove retaining clips, then the rotor.
5. Reverse procedure to install. Tighten to specifications.

REAR w/DUAL WHEELS

1. Raise and support vehicle, then remove tire and wheel assembly.
2. Remove caliper as outlined under "Brake Pad Service."
3. Remove brake caliper adapter bolts, then the caliper adapter.
4. Remove rear axle shaft from housing on dual wheels as outlined under "Full Size Trucks & Vans" chassis chapter.
5. **On 3500C models,** remove hub and rotor assembly.
6. **On all models,** reverse procedure to install. Tighten to specifications.

Full Size Van

FRONT

1. Raise and support vehicle, then remove wheel.
2. Remove caliper as outlined under "Caliper Service." **It is not required to disconnect brake line from caliper, but caliper must be supported at all times to prevent brake line damage.**
3. Remove grease cap, cotter pin, nut lock, hub nut, thrust washer and outer wheel bearing, then lift rotor off spindle.
4. Reverse procedure to install, noting the following:
   a. Pack wheel bearings with suitable high temperature grease; if inner bearing is removed for packing, replace inner grease seal.
   b. To adjust wheel bearing, **torque** hub nut to 20–25 ft. lbs., with rotor rotating. Loosen nut completely and retighten only finger tight. Bearing end play should not exceed .003 inch.
   c. After assembly is complete, apply brakes several times to ensure brake pads are properly seated in caliper.

REAR

1. Raise and support vehicle, then remove wheel.
2. Remove caliper as outlined under "Caliper Service." **It is not required to disconnect brake line from caliper, but caliper must be supported at all times to prevent brake line damage.**
3. Remove caliper adapter bolts, then the caliper adapter.
4. Remove retaining clips and rotor assembly.
5. Reverse procedure to install.

Grand Cherokee

FRONT

1. Raise and support vehicle, then remove tire and wheel assembly.
2. Remove caliper as outlined under "Caliper Service."
3. Remove retainers securing rotor to hub, then slide rotor off hub studs.
4. Reverse procedure to install.

REAR

1. Raise and support vehicle, then remove wheel and caliper as outlined under "Caliper Service."
2. Remove access plug from brake splash shield, then rotate adjuster screw with brake tool to back off parking brake shoes. **Driver side screw must be rotated clockwise and passenger side counterclockwise as viewed from rear of vehicle.**
3. Remove push nuts securing rotor to axle shaft studs, then slide rotor off axle hub and studs. A soft mallet may be required to loosen rotor.
4. Reverse procedure to install, noting the following:
   a. Rotate parking brake adjuster screws until shoes contact friction surface using brake tool, then back off screws ½–1 turn to ensure correct parking brake adjustment.
   b. Pump brake pedal to seat caliper piston and brake pads prior to operating vehicle. **Do not operate vehicle until brake pedal feels firm.**

Liberty

FRONT

1. Raise and support vehicle using suitable lift or jack.
2. Remove tire and wheel assembly.
3. Remove caliper as outlined in "Caliper Service."
4. Remove rotor.
5. Reverse procedure to install, tighten to specifications.

REAR

1. Raise and support vehicle using suitable lift or jack.
2. Remove tire and wheel assembly.
3. Remove caliper and pads as outlined in "Caliper Service."
4. Remove retaining clips, then the rotor.
5. Reverse procedure to install, tighten to specifications.

Pacifica

1. Raise and support vehicle using suitable lift or jack.
2. Remove tire and wheel assembly.
3. Remove caliper as outlined in "Caliper Service."
4. Remove retaining clips, then the rotor.
5. Reverse procedure to install, noting the following:
   a. Ensure a clean surface to rotor.
   b. Ensure any abutment shims are in place as required.
   c. Pump brake pedal several times to ensure caliper and pads are seated.
   d. Inspect and adjust fluid level as required.
   e. Tighten to specifications.

PT Cruiser

1. Raise and support vehicle, then remove tire and wheel assembly.
2. Slide caliper outward to retract caliper piston into its bore.
3. Remove two bolts securing disc brake, then remove caliper. **Support caliper to prevent brake hose damage.**
4. Remove clips retaining brake rotor to wheel studs, then remove rotor.
5. Reverse procedure to install. Tighten to specifications.

Sprinter

DUAL REAR WHEEL

1. Raise and support vehicle.
2. Remove wheels.
3. Remove brake pads.
4. Remove caliper adapter.
5. Remove wheel flange ring.
6. Install two lug studs to secure disc brake rotor when locking bolt is removed.
7. Remove locking bolt for disc brake rotor.
8. Remove two lug nuts.
9. Remove disc brake rotor.
10. Reverse procedure to install. Tighten to specifications.

SINGLE REAR WHEEL

1. Raise and support vehicle.
2. Remove wheels.
3. Remove brake pads.
4. Remove caliper adapter.
5. **When removing rear rotors,** apply parking brake.
6. **On all removal,** install two lug studs to secure disc brake rotor when locking bolt is removed.
7. Remove locking bolt for disc brake rotor.
8. Remove two lug nuts.
9. Remove disc brake rotor.
10. Reverse procedure to install. Tighten to specifications.

Wrangler

1. Raise and support vehicle.
2. Remove wheel and tire assembly.
3. Remove caliper as outlined in "Caliper Service."
4. Remove retainers from hub studs.
5. Remove rotor from hub.
6. Reverse procedure to install. Tighten to specifications.

BRAKE PAD SERVICE

Caravan, Town & Country & Voyager

FRONT

REMOVAL

1. Raise and support vehicle.
2. Remove front wheel and tire assemblies.
3. Remove two caliper-to-knuckle attaching bolts, then remove caliper by sliding away from adapter and lifting off rotor, **Fig. 1.** Support caliper firmly to prevent weight of caliper from damaging flexible hose.
4. Remove outboard pad by prying pad retaining clip over raised area of caliper, then sliding pad down and off of caliper.
5. Pull inboard pad away from caliper piston, until springs release from piston.

INSTALLATION

1. Inspect piston seal for leaks and for ruptures in piston dust boot. Replace all seals, boots or bushings as required.
2. Lubricate adapter ways with a liberal amount of multipurpose lubricant.
3. Install anti-rattle on upper abutment of caliper mounting adapter.
4. Install inboard pad by pressing firmly into caliper piston bore, ensuring pad is flat against piston.

5. Slide outboard pad onto caliper, one side halfway down.
6. Install caliper mounting bolts, then tighten to specifications.
7. Install tire and wheel assemblies.

REAR

REMOVAL

1. Raise and support vehicle, then remove rear wheels.
2. Remove caliper to adapter guide pin bolts.
3. Rotate rear of caliper up from adapter.
4. Pull front of caliper and outboard brake pad anti-rattle clip out from under front abutment on adapter.
5. Support caliper to prevent damage to flexible brake hose.
6. Remove rear rotor from hub by pulling it straight off wheel mounting studs.
7. Remove outboard pad from caliper by prying brake pad retaining clip over raised area on caliper.
8. Remove inboard pad from caliper by pulling it out of caliper piston.

INSTALLATION

1. Completely retract caliper piston back into piston bore of caliper assembly.
2. Lubricate both adapter abutments with liberal amount of Mopar Multipurpose Lubricant, or equivalent.
3. If removed, install rear rotor on hub.
4. Remove protective paper from noise suppression gasket on both inner and outer brake pads (if equipped).
5. Install inboard brake pad into caliper piston by firmly pressing in into piston bore using your thumbs.
6. Install outboard brake pad on caliper.
7. Carefully lower caliper over rotor and onto adapter, reversing removal procedure.
8. Install caliper guide pin bolts and tighten to specification.
9. Install wheels and lug nuts and tighten in proper sequence to specification.

Commander

REMOVAL

1. Raise and support vehicle.
2. Remove wheel and tire assembly.
3. Drain a small amount of fluid from master cylinder brake reservoir with clean suction tool.
4. **On front calipers,** remove caliper mounting bolts.
5. **On rear calipers,** bottom caliper pistons into caliper by prying caliper over.
6. **On rear calipers,** remove caliper slide pins.
7. **On all models,** compress caliper and remove from adapter.
8. Secure caliper using suitable wire.
9. Remove brake pads from caliper.
10. Remove anti-rattle clips from brake caliper adapter.

INSTALLATION

1. Remove and clean all debris from anti-rattle clip mounting surfaces on brake caliper adapter.

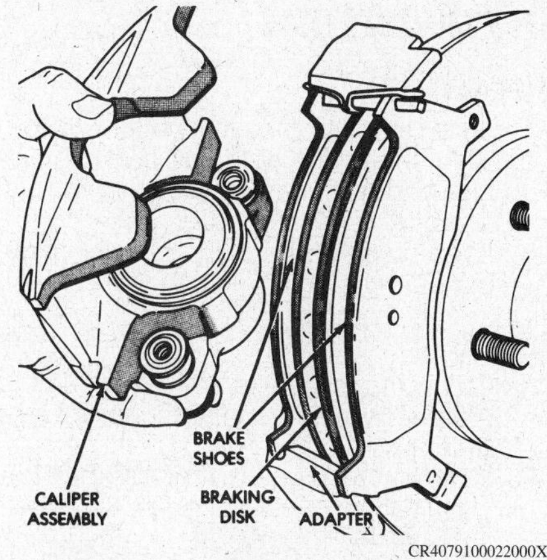

Fig. 1 Double pin caliper. Caravan, Town & Country & Voyager

2. Install new anti-rattle clips into caliper adapter.
3. Install brake pads onto caliper adapter.
4. Install caliper onto caliper adapter.
5. Install caliper slide pin bolts and tighten to specifications.
6. Install wheel and tire assembly.
7. Remove support and lower vehicle.
8. Pump brake pedal until caliper pistons and brake pads are seated and firm brake pedal is obtained.
9. Fill brake fluid.

Dakota & Durango

REMOVAL

1. Clean master cylinder reservoir and filler caps, then remove caps and drain approximately 1/4 of fluid from reservoir using a suitable suction tool.
2. Raise and support vehicle, then remove front wheel.
3. Use a large C-clamp positioned over caliper body and outboard brake pad, bottom caliper piston by threading clamp screw inward upon outboard pad.
4. Remove caliper slide pins, then the caliper with brake pads attached.
5. Remove outboard brake pad by prying one end of retainer spring, away from caliper, then tilt pad upward and rotate out of caliper.
6. Remove inboard pad by tilting pad outward until retainer spring is clear of caliper piston.

INSTALLATION

1. Clean sliding surfaces of adapter ledges with a wire brush, then lubricate with a thin coating of suitable high temperature grease.
2. Install new slide pin bushings if required.
3. Install inboard brake pad and ensure retaining spring is fully seated in caliper piston.
4. Position outboard pad in caliper, ensure outboard pad retaining spring are seated in caliper.
5. Position caliper and brake pads over rotor and into adapter ledges, then install caliper slide pins and tighten to specifications.
6. Install wheel, then lower vehicle and ensure brake fluid reservoir is full.
7. Apply brakes several times to ensure new brake pads are seated properly. **Do not operate vehicle until brake pedal is firm.**

Full Size Pickup

REMOVAL

1. Raise and support vehicle, then remove tire and wheel assemblies.
2. Press caliper piston back into bore using suitable large, flat blade screwdriver, use large C-clamp if additional force is needed.
3. Remove caliper mounting bolts.
4. Rotate caliper rearward off rotor and out of steering knuckle support ledges.
5. Remove inboard and outboard brake pads, then the anti-rattle springs from caliper adjuster.
6. Secure caliper to convenient chassis or suspension component. **Do not allow brake hose to support caliper as this will cause damage to hose and fittings.**

INSPECTION

1. Inspect pad lining for wear. Replace riveted lining if worn to within 1/16 of rivet heads. Replace bonded lining if thickness is 3/16 or less.
2. If pads are to be reused, do not intermix them. Keep pads with the caliper they were removed from.
3. Inspect caliper area for signs of fluid leaks or damage.

INSTALLATION

1. Apply a coat of suitable multi-purpose grease to slide surfaces.
2. Lubricate caliper mounting bolts, collars, bushings and bores with suitable silicone grease.
3. Install anit-rattle springs, then the inboard and outboard brake pads.
4. Install caliper over rotor and into steering knuckle mounting arms. **Ensure caliper is seated flush on mounting arm surfaces,** Tighten to specifications.
5. Install wheel and tire assemblies, then test brakes for proper operation.
6. Lower vehicle and retest brakes for proper operation before moving vehicle.

Full Size Van

REMOVAL

1. Remove caliper assembly as outlined under "Caliper Service."
2. Remove inboard and outboard pads from caliper adapter.
3. Remove anti-rattle springs from caliper adapter.

INSTALLATION

Remove approximately 1/4 of the brake

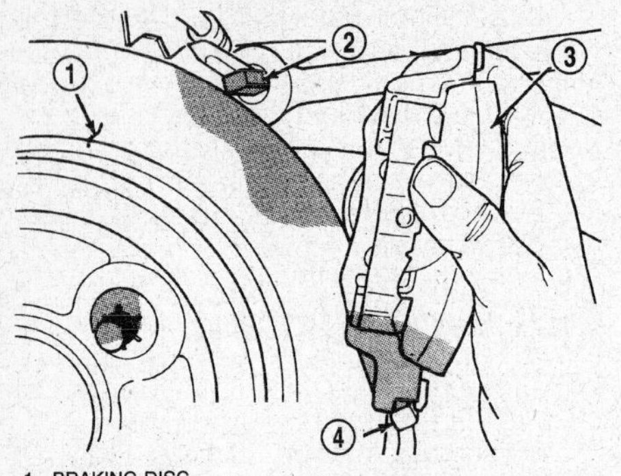

Fig. 2 Rear caliper removal. PT Cruiser

fluid from the reservoir to prevent overflow when pistons are pushed back into their bores.

1. Carefully push pistons back into bores until bottomed.
2. Install anti-rattle springs.
3. Install inboard then outboard pads.
4. Install caliper as outlined under "Caliper Service."

Grand Cherokee, Liberty & Wrangler

REMOVAL

FRONT

1. Unfasten caliper as outlined under "Caliper Service." **It is not required to disconnect brake hose from caliper. Support caliper at all times to prevent brake hose damage.**
2. Remove outboard brake pad from caliper by pressing one end inward to release pad lug.
3. Rotate shoe upward until spring clears caliper.
4. Press other end of pad inward to release other lug, then rotate upwards and out of caliper.
5. Grasp ends of inboard pad and tilt outward to release springs from caliper piston.
6. Clean caliper interior using clean shop cloths. Do not use compressed air, as damage to dust boot may result.

REAR

1. Unfasten caliper as outlined under "Caliper Service." **It is not required to disconnect brake hose from caliper. Support caliper at all times to prevent brake hose damage.**
2. Remove outboard pad by pressing one corner of pad inward and prying upward with a suitable tool.
3. Remove inboard brake pad and anti-rattle clip or retaining spring.
4. Clean caliper interior using clean shop cloths. Do not use compressed air, as damage to dust boot may result.

INSTALLATION

FRONT

1. Install inboard shoe into caliper piston.
2. Start one end of outboard pad into caliper and rotate downward until pad is seated.
3. Install caliper as outlined under "Caliper Service."

REAR

1. Clean brake pad to caliper mounting bracket contact surfaces using wire brush.
2. Position brake pads in caliper, then position caliper over rotor and into mounting bracket.
3. Ensure brake pads are positioned properly, then complete caliper installation as outlined under "Caliper Service."

Pacifica

REMOVAL

1. Remove master cylinder fluid reservoir cap.
2. Raise and support vehicle.
3. Remove tire and wheel assembly.
4. Remove caliper as outlined in "Caliper Service."
5. Remove brake pads from caliper.
6. Install master cylinder fluid reservoir cap.

INSTALLATION

1. Place brake pads in anti-rattle clips on adapter.
2. If required, remove protective paper from noise suppression gasket on rear of both inner and outer brake pads.
3. Completely retract caliper piston back into bore of caliper.
4. Install caliper over brake pads on caliper adapter.
5. Align caliper guide pin bolt holes with guide pins, then install caliper guide pin bolts and tighten to specifications.
6. Install tire and wheel assembly.
7. Lower vehicle.
8. Pump brake pedal several times to set pads to caliper and brake rotor.
9. Inspect and adjust brake fluid as required.
10. Road test vehicle making several stops to wear off any debris and to seat brake pads.

PT Cruiser

REMOVAL

FRONT

1. Raise and support vehicle, then remove tire and wheel assembly.
2. Remove two brake caliper guide pin bolts.
3. Remove disc brake caliper from disc brake adapter. **Support caliper to prevent brake hose damage.**
4. Remove brake pads from disc brake caliper adapter.

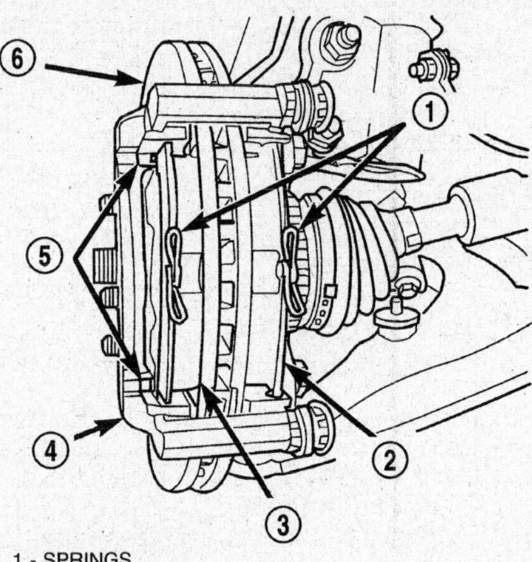

Fig. 3 Front brake pad installation. PT Cruiser

REAR

1. Raise and support vehicle, then remove tire and wheel assembly.
2. Remove two caliper guide pin bolts.
3. Remove caliper assembly from brake adapter by rotating top of caliper away from rotor, then lifting off machined abutment on adapter, **Fig. 2. Support caliper to prevent brake hose damage.**
4. Remove outboard brake shoe from caliper by prying brake pad retaining clip over raised area on caliper, then slide brake pad down and off brake caliper.
5. Pull inboard brake pad away from caliper piston until retaining clip is free from cavity in piston.

INSTALLATION

FRONT

1. Install brake pads in abutment shims clipped into disc brake caliper adapter, **Fig. 3,** ensuring pad with wear indicator is on inboard side.
2. Completely retract caliper piston back into bore of caliper.
3. Install disc brake caliper over brake pads on brake caliper adapter. Ensure springs on pads do not get caught in hole formed into center of caliper housing.
4. Align caliper guide pin bolts holes, then install guide pins.
5. Install tire and wheel assembly, then lower vehicle.
6. Pump brake pedal several times to ensure vehicle has a firm pedal.

REAR

1. Completely retract caliper piston back into piston bore of caliper.
2. Install inboard brake pad into caliper piston by firmly pressing on pad.
3. Slide outboard brake pad onto caliper assembly, ensuring retaining clip is squarely seated in depressed areas on caliper.

4. Lubricate both adapter caliper slide abutments using Mopar Multipurpose Lubricant, or equivalent.
5. Starting with lower end, carefully lower caliper and brake pads over brake rotor catching calipers bottom edge behind slide abutment.
6. Rotate top of caliper into mounting position on adapter.
7. Install caliper guide pin bolts.
8. Install tire and wheel assembly, then lower vehicle.
9. Pump brake pedal several times to ensure vehicle has a firm pedal.

Sprinter

REMOVAL

FRONT

1. Remove brake fluid reservoir cap.
2. Raise and support vehicle.
3. Remove front wheel assembly.
4. Remove caliper as outlined in "Caliper Service."
5. Remove wear indicator cable and wear indicator.
6. Remove brake pads.

REAR

1. Remove brake fluid reservoir cap.
2. Raise and support vehicle.
3. Remove rear wheels.
4. Remove caliper as outlined in "Caliper Service."
5. Remove wear indicator cable and wear indicator.
6. Remove retaining spring, then the pads.

INSTALLATION

FRONT

1. Install brake pads.
2. Install wear indicator cable and wear indicator, tighten to specifications.
3. Install brake caliper as outlined in "Caliper Service."
4. Bleed brake system.
5. Inspect brake system for leaks.
6. Install front wheel assembly.
7. Lower vehicle.

REAR

1. Install brake pads.
2. Install new wear indicator cable and wear indicator. Tighten to specifications.
3. Install caliper as outlined in "Caliper Service."
4. Install retaining spring.
5. Install rear wheels.
6. Lower vehicle.

CALIPER SERVICE

Caravan, Town & Country & Voyager

Refer to "Brake Pad Service" for caliper replacement procedures.

DISASSEMBLE

1. Remove caliper from adapter and rotor as outlined under "Brake Pad Service." **Do not disconnect brake hose from caliper. Support caliper at all times to prevent brake hose damage.**
2. Position caliper away from rotor to prevent brake fluid spillage on machined surface, then place a small block of wood between caliper fingers to prevent piston damage during removal.
3. Gently depress brake pedal to force caliper piston out of bore, then secure brake pedal at any position below one inch of pedal travel to prevent master cylinder brake fluid loss.
4. Disconnect brake hose at caliper, then mount caliper assembly in a soft jawed vise. **Do not apply excessive vise pressure; caliper damage will result.**
5. Use a suitable screwdriver to remove dust boot, then use a plastic trim stick or other suitable non-metallic tool to pry piston seal out of piston bore groove. **Using a metallic tool for this operation may score piston bore.**
6. Discard dust boot and piston seal; then, if required, remove caliper bushing and sleeve assembly as follows:
   a. Push inner sleeve out of bushing far enough to grasp sleeve end, then pull sleeve from bushing, **Fig. 4.**
   b. Gently collapse one side of bushing, then pull on opposite end to remove from caliper assembly.

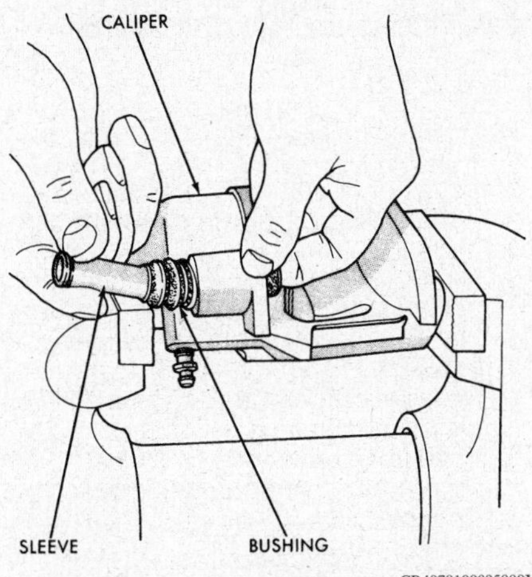

Fig. 4 Inner sleeve removal. Caravan, Town & Country & Voyager

INSPECTION

1. Clean all caliper components in alcohol or other suitable solvent and wipe dry. Ensure bores and drilled passages are cleaned thoroughly.
2. Inspect piston bore for scoring or pitting. Crocus cloth may be used to remove minor scratches or corrosion.
3. If piston bore exhibits deep scratches or severe scoring, use caliper honing tool No. C-4095, or equivalent, to hone caliper bore. **Do not increase bore diameter more than .001 inch.**
4. If caliper piston bore is to be honed, honing tool stones and piston bore should be coated with clean brake fluid, and honing should be followed by cleaning with a stiff, non-metallic rotary brush.
5. If scoring and scratches cannot be removed without increasing piston bore beyond the specified limit, caliper must be replaced.
6. Replace caliper piston if scored or pitted.

ASSEMBLE

1. Clamp caliper in soft jawed vise. **Do not apply excessive vise pressure; caliper damage will result.**
2. Immerse new piston seal in clean brake fluid, then install in piston bore groove.
3. Coat new piston boot with clean brake fluid, then position boot over piston and install piston in caliper bore. **Apply uniform force when pressing piston into bore.**
4. Position dust boot in caliper piston counterbore, then drive boot into counterbore using piston caliper boot installer tool No. C-4689 and handle tool No. C-4171, or equivalents.
5. Install guide pin sleeve bushings as follows:
   a. Fold bushing in half lengthwise at solid middle section, then carefully insert bushing into caliper assembly.
   b. Unfold bushing to seat in caliper assembly using fingers or a suitable soft dowel. Ensure flanges are seated evenly on both sides of bushing hole.
6. Gently press guide pin sleeves through bushings until bushings seat in seal grooves, then ensure bushings and sleeves are installed properly by sliding each back and forth. Sleeves should slide easily and bushings should remain seated in grooves.
7. Install caliper as outlined under "Brake Pad Service."

Commander

REMOVAL

1. Raise and support vehicle.
2. Remove wheel and tire assembly.
3. Drain a small amount of fluid from master cylinder brake reservoir using clean suction tool.
4. Bottom caliper pistons into caliper by prying caliper over.
5. Remove brake hose banjo bolt and gasket washers, then discard gasket washers.
6. Remove caliper slide bolts.
7. Remove caliper from adapter/anchor.

DISASSEMBLE

1. Drain brake fluid from caliper.
2. C-clamp a block of wood over one piston.
3. Place a second block of wood and pad it with one inch thickness shop towels. Place this piece in outboard shoe side of caliper in front of other piston.
4. Remove caliper piston using direct short bursts of low pressure air with a blow gun through caliper brake hose

port. **Do not blow piston out of bore with sustained air pressure, as this could result in a cracker piston.**
5. Remove C-clamp and block of wood from caliper and clamp it over dust boot of first piston removed.
6. Move padded piece of wood in front of other piston.
7. Remove second piston using same procedure.
8. Remove piston dust boots using suitable pry tool.
9. Remove piston seals from caliper.
10. Push caliper mounting bolt bushings out of boot seals and remove boot seals from caliper.
11. Remove caliper bleed screw.

INSPECTION

1. Clean caliper components with clean brake fluid or brake clean only.
2. Wipe caliper and piston dry with lint free towels or low pressure compressed air.
3. Piston should be smooth and clean.
4. Piston must be replaced if cracked or scored.

ASSEMBLE

1. Lubricate caliper pistons, piston seals and piston bores using clean brake fluid.
2. Install new piston seals into caliper bores.
3. Lightly lubricate lip of new boot with silicone grease, then install boot on piston and work boot lip into groove at top of piston.
4. Stretch boot rearward to straighten boot folds, then move boot forward until folds snap into place.
5. Install caliper into caliper bore and press piston down to bottom of caliper bore using a suitable hammer handle.
6. Seat dust boot in caliper using tool No. C-4171 or equivalent, and installer.
7. Install second piston and dust boot.
8. Lubricate caliper mounting bolt bushings, boot seals and bores using suitable grease.
9. Install boot seals into caliper seal bores and center seals in bores.
10. Install mounting bolt bushings into boot seals and insure seal lip is engaged into bushing grooves at either end of bushing.
11. Install caliper bleed screw.

INSTALLATION

1. Install caliper on adapter/anchor.
2. Install brake pads.
3. Caliper slide pins should be clean and lightly lubricated.
4. Install caliper slide pin bolts and tighten to specification.
5. Equalize air pressure by lifting one end of slide pin boot, then release boot and verify boot is fully covering slide pin.
6. Install brake hose to caliper with **new copper washers** and tighten to specifications.
7. Fill and bleed brake system.
8. Install wheel and tire assembly.
9. Remove supports and lower vehicle.
10. Inspect brake fluid level.

Dakota & Durango

REMOVAL

1. Raise vehicle, then remove front wheel.
2. Disconnect brake hose at caliper and discard fitting washers if worn or damaged.
3. Compress caliper, then remove banjo bolt and discard copper washers, caliper slide pins, then lift caliper and brake pads off rotor.
4. Remove caliper slide pins, then lift caliper and brake pads off rotor.
5. If required, remove brake pads from caliper as outlined under "Brake Pad Service."

DISASSEMBLE

1. Clean outside of caliper with suitable solvent.
2. Drain fluid from caliper and place clean shop cloths in caliper opposite piston.
3. Slowly apply compressed air to caliper inlet port until piston moves out of bore. **Do not "blow" piston out of bore; damage and personal injury may result.**
4. Remove and discard dust boot using a suitable screwdriver. Use care to avoid scratching caliper piston bore.
5. Remove and discard piston seal, using a suitable wooden or plastic tool.
6. Remove bleeder screw and protective cap, if equipped.
7. Remove and discard inner and outer bushings and plastic sleeves, if equipped.
8. Clean all components with clean brake fluid and compressed air.

ASSEMBLE

1. Lubricate slide pin boots and bushings with suitable silicone grease.
2. Lubricate piston bore and new piston seal with clean brake fluid.
3. Install seal in bore groove by hand and lubricate piston with clean brake fluid.
4. Apply a light coating of suitable silicone grease to edge and groove of piston and dust seal.
5. Install new dust boot on piston, sliding metal retainer portion of boot over open end of piston and pulling boot rearward until boot lip seats in piston groove.
6. Push metal retainer portion of boot forward until retainer is flush with rim at open end of piston, then snap boot fold into place.
7. Install piston into caliper bore, using care to avoid unseating piston seal.
8. Press piston to bottom of bore.
9. Seat piston dust boot with installer tool No. C-8248 and handle tool No. C-4171, or equivalents.
10. Install bleeder screw, then new inner and outer bushings and plastic sleeves, if equipped, in caliper mounting ears.

INSTALLATION

1. Install brake pads in caliper, then position caliper and pad assembly over rotor and into sliding ledges. Ensure brake pads are seated properly.
2. Align caliper with holes in adapter, then start both slide pins into holes by hand and tighten to specifications.
3. Connect brake hose to caliper and, if required, install new fitting washers.
4. Bleed hydraulic system as outlined under "Brake System Bleed," then install wheel and lower vehicle.
5. Apply brakes several times to ensure brake pads are fully seated. **Ensure brake pedal is firm prior to operating vehicle.**
6. Inspect and add brake fluid as required.

Full Size Pickup

REMOVAL

1. Install suitable prop rod on brake pedal to keep pressure on brake system.
2. Raise and support vehicle, then remove tire and wheel assembly.
3. Drain small amount of fluid from master cylinder brake reservoir.
4. Remove brake hose banjo bolt.
5. Remove caliper mounting slide pin bolts, then the caliper.

DISASSEMBLE

1. Drain brake fluid from caliper.
2. C-clamp a block of wood over one piston.
3. Take another piece of wood and pad it with shop towels, then place it on outboard pad side of caliper in front of other piston.
4. Remove caliper piston by directing short bursts of compressed air through caliper brake hose port.
5. Remove C-clamp and block of wood, then clamp it over dust boot of first removed piston.
6. Move padded piece of wood to in front of remaining piston, then remove piston by directing short bursts if compressed air through caliper brake hose port.
7. Remove piston dust boots using suitable pry tool.
8. Remove piston seals from caliper.
9. Push caliper mounting bolt bushings out of boot seals, then remove boot seals from caliper.
10. Remove caliper bleed screw.

INSPECTION

1. Inspect condition of caliper bore. A fiber brush can be used to clean the bore if needed. The bore should be free of corrosion, pitting, or scoring. Discoloration of the bore is normal. The bore can be lightly polished by hand using crocus cloth only.
2. Inspect condition of piston and replace if corroded, pitted, or scored. **Do not use any kind of abrasive material to restore surface finish of piston.**
3. Inspect condition of threads of inlet and bleed screw ports. Replace caliper if thread damage is evident. **Do not attempt to salvage threads.**
4. Inspect bushings in caliper mounting bolt bores. Replace bushings if required.

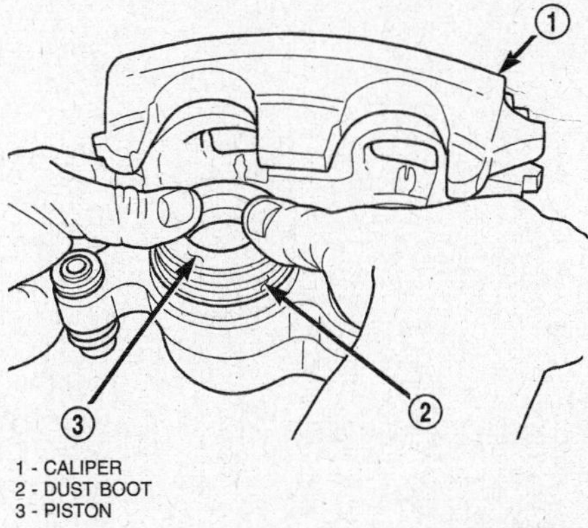

1 - CALIPER
2 - DUST BOOT
3 - PISTON

LTV1900000000400

Fig. 5 Caliper piston installation. Full Size Pickup

ASSEMBLE

1. Lubricate caliper pistons, piston seals and piston bores with clean brake fluid.
2. Install new piston seals into caliper bores.
3. Lightly lubricate lip of new boot with silicone grease.
4. Install boot on piston, then work boot lip into groove at top of piston.
5. Stretch boot rearward to straighten boot folds, then move boot forward until folds snap into place.
6. Install piston into caliper bore, then press piston down to bottom of caliper bore by hand, **Fig. 5.**
7. **On models equipped with LD calipers,** using handle tool No. C-4171 and installer tool No. C-3716-A, or equivalents, seat dust boot in caliper, **Fig. 6.**
8. **On models equipped with HD calipers,** using handle tool No. C-4171 and installer tool No. C-4340, or equivalents, seat dust boot in caliper, **Fig. 6.**
9. Install second piston and dust boot.
10. Lubricate caliper mount bolt bushings, boot seals and bores with Mopar brake grease or equivalent. **Use of alternative grease may cause damage to boot seals.**
11. Install mounting bolt bushings into boot seals, then ensure seal lip is engaged into bushing grooves at either end of bushing.
12. Install caliper bleed screw.

INSTALLATION

1. Install caliper to caliper adapter.
2. Coat caliper mounting slide pin bolts with silicone grease, then install bolts.
3. Install brake hose banjo bolt.
4. Install brake hose to caliper using new seal washers.
5. Remove prop rod from brake pedal, then bleed brakes as outlined in "Hydraulic Brake Systems."
6. Install tire and wheel assembly, then lower vehicle.
7. Verify pedal is firm before moving vehicle.

Full Size Van

REMOVAL

1. Raise and support vehicle, then remove front wheels.
2. Disconnect and cap flexible brake line.
3. Remove caliper retaining bolts.
4. Remove caliper from disc by slowly sliding caliper assembly out and away from disc.

DISASSEMBLE

1. Drain brake fluid from caliper.
2. Clamp a suitable block of wood over one of the pistons.
3. Remove piston with several short bursts of low pressure compressed air directed through fluid inlet port.
4. Block piston bore with block of wood and clamp, then repeat above procedure for other piston.
5. Remove and discard piston dust boots using a suitable pry tool. **Do not scratch piston bores when removing boots.**
6. Remove and discard seals from caliper pistons.
7. Remove mounting bolts from calipers and inspect seals, boots and bushings.
8. Remove caliper bleed screw.

ASSEMBLE

1. Ensure assembly area is clean and dry to avoid any contamination to caliper unit.
2. Lubricate caliper piston seal, piston, and piston bore with liberal amounts of fresh, clean, brake fluid.
3. Lightly lubricate lip of new boot with suitable silicone grease, then work boot lip into boot groove at top of piston.
4. Stretch boot rearward to straighten boot folds, then move boot forward until folds snap into place.
5. Install new seal on piston and seat in groove, ensure square cut seal is not twisted.
6. Install caliper piston into bore, seating it ¾ of way to bottom using hand or suitable hammer handle.
7. **On models equipped with HD calipers,** seat new dust boot in caliper with appropriate installer tool No. C-4340, or equivalent.
8. **On models equipped with LD calipers,** seat new dust boot in caliper with appropriate installer tool No. C-3716–A, or equivalent.
9. **On all calipers,** finish pressing caliper piston to bottom of bore after dust boot is seated.
10. Install but do not fully tighten caliper bleed screw.
11. Install inboard brake pad, ensure spring clip is centered and seated.

INSTALLATION

1. Clean sliding surfaces of caliper mounting adapter with wire brush and lubricate surfaces with suitable high

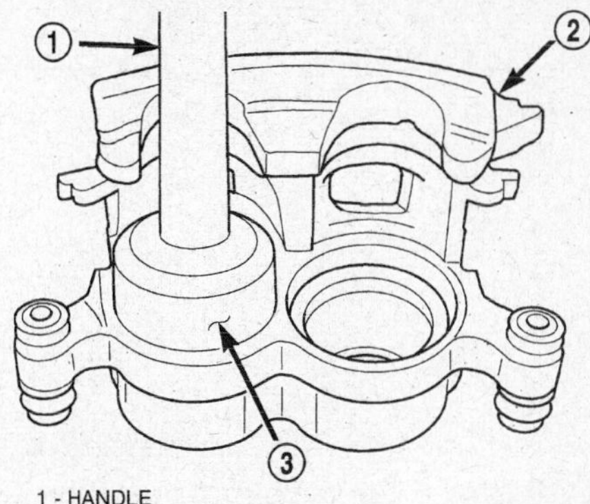

1 - HANDLE
2 - CALIPER
3 - DUST BOOT INSTALLER

LTV1900000000401

Fig. 6 Seating dust boot. Full Size Pickup

temperature grease.

2. Tilt top of caliper over rotor and under adapter.
3. Push bottom of caliper onto adapter.
4. Install caliper mounting bolts and tighten to specification.
5. Connect brake hose to caliper and tighten fitting to specifications. **Use new fitting seal washers. Ensure brake hose is free of kinks and is clear of nearby suspension or body components.**
6. Fill and bleed brake system as outlined under "Brake System Bleed," then install wheels and lower vehicle.
7. Ensure brake pedal feels firm prior to moving vehicle.

Grand Cherokee, Liberty & Wrangler

REMOVAL

FRONT

1. Remove and discard ⅔ of brake fluid from largest master cylinder reservoir.
2. Raise and support vehicle, then remove front wheel.
3. Press caliper piston to bottom of bore using suitable screwdriver or C-clamp.
4. Disconnect brake hose at caliper and cap hose.
5. Remove caliper slide pin bushing caps and slide pins.
6. Lift caliper up and out of anchor plate and off rotor.

REAR

1. Raise and support vehicle, then remove wheel and caliper mounting bolts, **Fig. 7.**
2. Remove caliper slide pin bushing caps, then the slide pins.
3. Rotate caliper rearward, then off mounting bracket ledges.
4. Remove caliper fitting bolt and disconnect brake hose at caliper, then discard metal fitting bolt washers.
5. Remove rear caliper from vehicle.

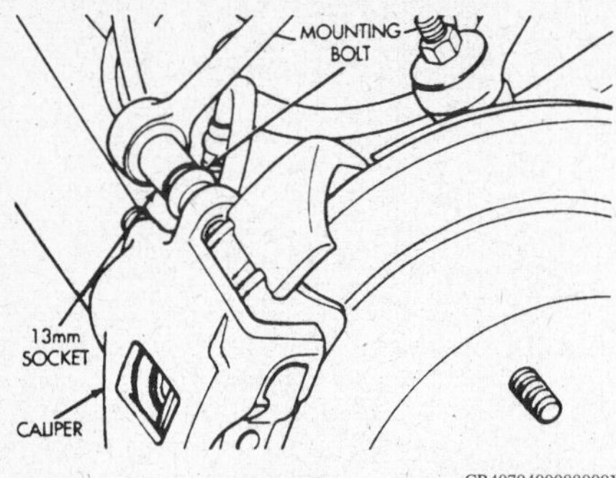

Fig. 7 Rear caliper mounting bolts. Grand Cherokee, Liberty & Wrangler

DISASSEMBLE

FRONT

1. Clean outside of caliper with suitable solvent.
2. Drain fluid from caliper and place clean shop cloths in caliper opposite piston, **Fig. 8.**
3. C-clamp a block of wood over one of the pistons.
4. Slowly apply compressed air to caliper inlet port until piston moves out of bore. **Do not "blow" piston out of bore; damage and personal injury may result.**
5. Remove wood block and C-clamp in position over dust boot of removed piston bore. Remove remaining piston with compressed air.
6. Remove and discard dust boots using a suitable screwdriver. Use care to avoid scratching caliper piston bore.
7. Remove and discard piston seal, using a suitable wooden or plastic tool.
8. Remove bleeder screw and protective cap, if equipped.
9. Remove and discard inner and outer bushings and plastic sleeves, if equipped.
10. Clean all components with clean brake fluid and compressed air.

REAR

1. Remove brake pads from caliper as outlined under "Brake Pad Service" then remove caliper mounting bolt boots and bushings or slide pins.
2. Fill interior portion of caliper with a thick padding of shop rags to prevent piston damage during removal, **Fig. 8.**
3. With compressed air nozzle directed into brake fluid inlet port, gently drive caliper piston out using short bursts of air at low pressure. **Do not "blow" piston out of bore; damage and personal injury may result.**
4. Remove caliper piston dust boot using suitable pry tool, then remove and discard piston seal ring with pencil or other suitable non-metallic tool, **Fig. 9.**
5. Clean caliper and piston with clean brake fluid or suitable brake components cleaning solvent. **Do not use other solvents or thinners, as residual chemicals may cause piston and seal damage.**

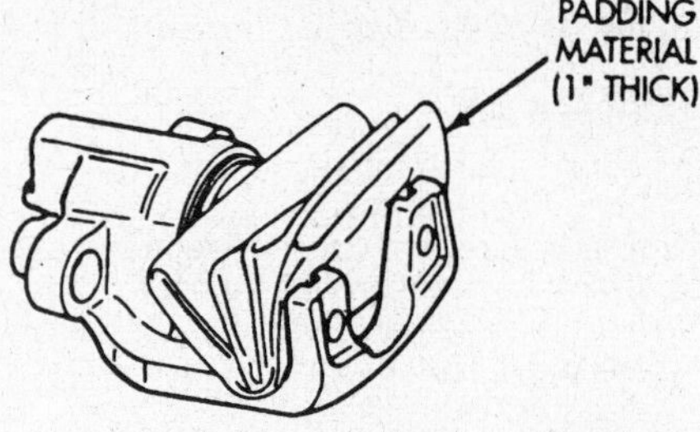

Fig. 8 Caliper piston protective cloth. Grand Cherokee, Liberty & Wrangler

ASSEMBLE

FRONT

1. Lubricate piston bore and new piston seal with clean brake fluid.
2. Install seal in bore groove by hand and lubricate piston with clean brake fluid.
3. Install new dust boot on piston, sliding metal retainer portion of boot over open end of piston and pulling boot rearward until boot lip seats in piston groove.
4. Push metal retainer portion of boot forward until retainer is flush with rim at open end of piston, then snap boot fold into place.
5. Install piston into caliper bore, using care to avoid unseating piston seal.
6. Press piston to bottom of bore.
7. Use handle tool No. C4171 and seal installer tool No. 8280, or equivalents, to seat metal retainer portion of dust boot in counterbore at upper end of bore.
8. Install caliper slide pin bushings into caliper.
9. Install bleeder screw, then new inner and outer bushings and plastic sleeves, if equipped, in caliper mounting ears.

REAR

1. Lubricate caliper piston bore and new piston seal with clean brake fluid, then install seal in piston bore groove. **Ensure seal is fully seated and is not twisted.**
2. Lubricate surface of caliper piston with clean brake fluid, then start piston into bore by hand with a gentle rocking and twisting motion. **Ensure seal is not folded over during piston insertion.**
3. Install dust boot over piston, ensure lip is fully seated in groove at top of piston.
4. Seat dust boot in caliper by hand or with a suitable installer tool as outlined, **Fig. 10,** then press piston to bottom of bore.
5. Install caliper bleed screw and bushing and boot assemblies. Ensure boots are centered in caliper bores.
6. Install mounting bolt bushings in boots with boot lips seated in bushing end grooves.
7. Install brake pads as outlined under "Brake Pad Service."

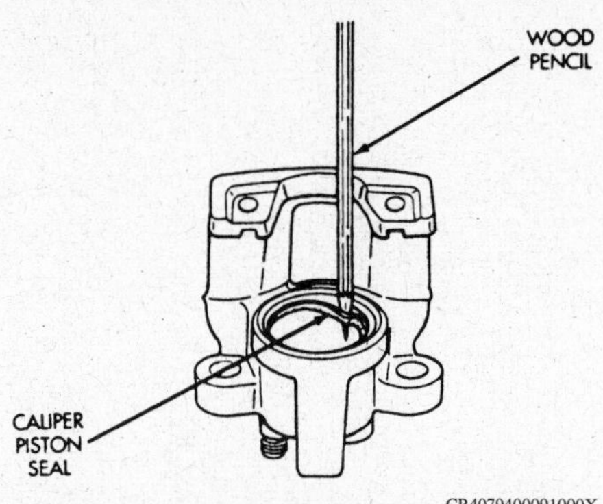

Fig. 9 Rear caliper piston seal removal. Grand Cherokee, Liberty & Wrangler

INSTALLATION

FRONT

1. Lubricate slide pins/bushings with suitable grease.
2. Install caliper over rotor and in anchor plate.
3. Align caliper and anchor plate, then install caliper mounting pins and tighten to specifications.
4. Install new washers on brake line connector or fitting and connect brake line to caliper. Tighten brake line bolt to specifications.
5. Fill master cylinder to within ¼ inch of reservoir rims, then depress brake pedal several times to seat brake pads.
6. Install wheel and tire assemblies, then lower vehicle.
7. Inspect master cylinder fluid level and correct as required, then inspect operation of brake system.

REAR

1. Position caliper over rotor and into bracket, ensure brake pads are positioned properly.
2. Connect rear brake hose to caliper and install new metal fitting washers, then tighten fitting bolt to specifications.
3. Lubricate caliper mounting bolts, then install and tighten to specifications.
4. Ensure brake fluid reservoir is full, then bleed brakes as outlined under "Brake System Bleed."
5. Install wheel and lower vehicle, then turn ignition switch to On position and run HCU pump until it stops.
6. Pump brake pedal several times to seat brake pads. Brake warning indicator lamps should go out.

Pacifica

REMOVAL

1. Install a suitable brake pedal holding tool to depress brake pedal past its first inch of travel and hold it in position.
2. Raise and support vehicle.
3. Remove tire and wheel assembly.
4. Remove banjo bolt connecting brake hose to caliper. Discard washers upon removal.

5. Install suitable C-clamp over brake caliper, placing screw-drive head against outboard shoe and hook against rear of caliper. Slowly tighten screw-drive retracting caliper pistons into bores and breaking outboard brake shoe free from caliper fingers. **Do not overtighten C-clamp.**
6. Slide caliper inboard on guides providing clearance between rotor and inboard brake shoe.
7. Slide suitable pry tool through center opening in top of caliper behind inboard brake shoe between two caliper pistons.
8. Remove brake caliper guide pin bolts, then slide disc brake caliper off pads and remove caliper.

DISASSEMBLE

1. Drain brake fluid from caliper.
2. C-clamp a block of wood over one piston.
3. Place a second block of wood and pad it with one inch thickness shop towels. Place this piece in outboard shoe side of caliper in front of other piston.
4. Remove caliper piston using direct short bursts of low pressure air with a blow gun through caliper brake hose port. **Do not blow piston out of bore with sustained air pressure, as this could result in a cracker piston.**
5. Remove C-clamp and block of wood from caliper and clamp it over dust boot of first piston removed.
6. Move padded piece of wood in front of other piston.
7. Remove second piston using same procedure.
8. Remove piston dust boots using suitable pry tool.
9. Remove piston seals from caliper.
10. Push caliper mounting bolt bushings out of boot seals and remove boot seals from caliper.
11. Remove caliper bleed screw.

INSPECTION

1. Clean caliper components with clean brake fluid or brake clean only.
2. Wipe caliper and piston dry with lint free towels or low pressure compressed air.
3. Piston should be smooth and clean.
4. Piston must be replaced if cracked or scored.

ASSEMBLE

1. Ensure all components are clean and dry.
2. Lubricate caliper pistons, piston seals and piston bores using clean brake fluid.
3. Install **new** piston seals into caliper piston bores.
4. Install new boot on each piston and work boot lip into groove at top of piston. Stretch boot rearward to straighten boot folds.
5. Install first piston into caliper piston bore, pressing piston down to bottom of bore using hand-pressure.
6. Seat dust boot in caliper counterbore

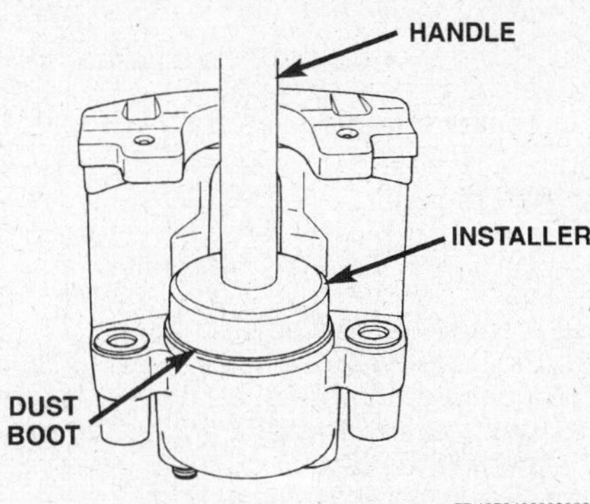

Fig. 10 Rear caliper piston dust boot installation. Grand Cherokee, Liberty & Wrangler

using installer tool No. L-4410 or equivalent, with handle. Install dust boot until it bottoms out.

7. Install second piston and dust boot using previous procedure.
8. Install caliper bleeder screw.
9. Install caliper on vehicle.

INSTALLATION

1. Install brake caliper over brake pads on brake caliper adapter.
2. Align caliper guide pin bolt holes with guide pins, then install caliper guide pin bolts and tighten to specifications.
3. Install banjo bolt attaching brake hose to caliper with **new** washers on each side of hose fitting as banjo bolt is placed through fitting, tighten to specifications.
4. Install tire and wheel assembly.
5. Lower vehicle.
6. Remove brake pedal holding tool.
7. Inspect vehicle braking using several stops to wear off any foreign material and to seat brake pads.

PT Cruiser

REMOVAL

FRONT

1. Depress brake pedal past its first one inch of travel, then hold in this position using suitable holding tool.
2. Raise and support vehicle, then remove tire and wheel assembly.
3. Remove banjo bolt connecting brake hose to caliper. Discard washers.
4. Remove two brake caliper guide pin bolts, then remove caliper from adapter.

REAR

1. Depress brake pedal past its first one inch of travel, then hold in this position using suitable holding tool.
2. Raise and support vehicle, then remove tire and wheel assembly.
3. Remove banjo bolt connecting brake hose to caliper. Discard washers.
4. Remove caliper assembly from brake adapter by rotating top of caliper away from rotor, then lifting off machined abutment on adapter.

DISASSEMBLE

FRONT

1. Remove brake caliper.
2. Mount caliper in a suitable soft jawed vise.
3. Place a wooden block in caliper.
4. Apply short spurts of low pressure compressed air to caliper fluid inlet to remove piston from caliper.
5. Remove piston seal from its groove in caliper piston bore using a suitable plastic trim stick. Discard old seal.
6. Clean piston bore and drilled passage ways with alcohol or suitable solvent, then wipe dry using lint free cloth.
7. Inspect piston and bore for scoring or pitting. Light scratches can be removed using a crocus cloth.

REAR

1. Remove brake caliper from brake rotor. Support caliper to prevent brake hose damage.
2. Remove brake pads, then place a small piece of wood between piston and caliper fingers.
3. Carefully depress brake pedal to hydraulically push piston out of its bore.
4. Hold brake pedal down past its first one inch of travel using suitable holding tool.
5. Disconnect brake fluid flex hose from caliper, then remove caliper.
6. Mount caliper in a suitable soft jawed vise.
7. Remove and discard piston dust boot.
8. Remove piston seal from its groove in caliper piston bore using suitable plastic trim stick. Discard old seal.
9. Clean piston bore and drilled passage ways with alcohol or suitable solvent, then wipe dry using lint free cloth.
10. Inspect piston and bore for scoring or pitting. Light scratches can be removed using a crocus cloth.
11. Bores that have deep scratches should be honed using caliper hone tool No. C-4095, or equivalent. Do not increase diameter of bore more than .001 inch.

ASSEMBLE

FRONT

1. Dip new piston seal in clean brake fluid, then install in groove of caliper bore.
2. Coat new piston with clean brake fluid.
3. Coat new piston boot with clean brake fluid leaving a generous amount inside boot.
4. Position dust boot over lower section of piston, **Fig. 11.**
5. Extend dust boot below bottom of piston, then guide lip seal into groove in caliper piston bore.
6. Install piston into bore carefully pushing it past piston seal using hand pressure.
7. Push piston in until it bottoms in caliper bore and dust boot lip seal falls into groove near top of piston.

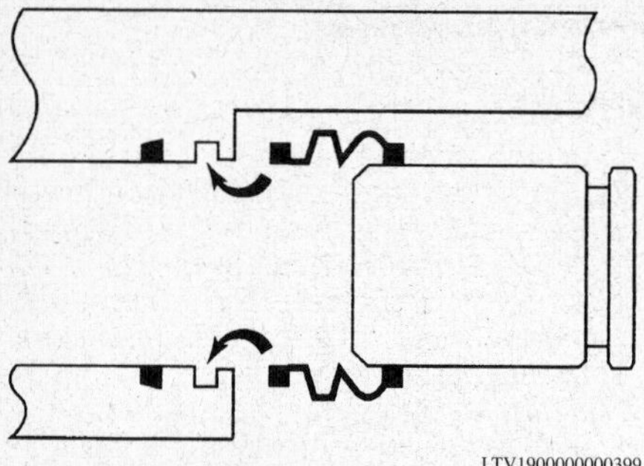

Fig. 11 Front caliper dust boot installation. PT Cruiser

REAR

1. Dip new piston seal in clean brake fluid, then install in groove of caliper bore.
2. Coat new piston boot with clean brake fluid leaving a generous amount inside boot.
3. Position dust boot over piston after coating with brake fluid.
4. Install piston into caliper bore pushing it past piston seal until it bottoms in caliper bore.
5. Position dust boot into counterbore of caliper assembly piston bore.
6. Drive boot into counterbore of caliper using hammer with installer tool No. C-4689 and handle tool No. C-4171, or equivalents.

INSTALLATION

FRONT

1. Place a block of wood over piston, then retract piston completely using suitable C-clamp.
2. Install caliper over brake pads on adapter ensuring springs on shoes do not get caught in hole formed into center of caliper housing.
3. Align caliper guide pin bolt holes, then install guide pins.
4. Install banjo bolt connecting brake hose to caliper using new washers on each side of hose fitting.
5. Install tire and wheel assembly, then lower vehicle.
6. Remove brake pedal holding tool, then bleed brakes as outlined in "Hydraulic Brake Systems."

REAR

1. Place a block of wood over piston, then retract piston completely using suitable C-clamp.
2. Lubricate both adapter caliper slide abutments using Mopar Multipurpose Lubricant, or equivalent.
3. Starting with lower end, carefully lower caliper and brake pads over brake rotor catching calipers bottom edge behind slide abutment.
4. Rotate top of caliper into mounting position on adapter.
5. Align caliper guide pin bolt holes, then install guide pins.
6. Install banjo bolt connecting brake hose to caliper using new washers on each side of hose fitting.
7. Install tire and wheel assembly, then lower vehicle.
8. Remove brake pedal holding tool, then bleed brakes as outlined in "Hydraulic Brake Systems."

Sprinter

1. Unscrew cap from brake fluid reservoir.
2. Remove rear wheels.
3. Remove wear indicator cable and wear indicator. **Seal off line ends and connection threads in brake calipers with plugs.**
4. Remove brake hose at brake caliper.
5. Remove brake caliper guide bolt.
6. Remove brake caliper.
7. Reverse procedure to install.

PARKING BRAKE SERVICE

Caravan, Town & Country & Voyager

PARK BRAKE SHOES

1. Set parking brake. **Parking brake is set to keep hub/bearing and axle shaft from rotating when loosening hub nut.**
2. Raise and support vehicle allowing rear suspension to hang free.
3. Remove rear wheels.
4. Remove cotter pin and nut retainer from stub shaft of outer C/V joint.
5. Remove spring washer, hub nut and washer from stub shaft of outer C/V joint.
6. Release parking brake.
7. Create slack in rear park brake by locking out automatic adjuster as follows:
   a. Grasp exposed section of front park brake and pull downward on it.
   b. Install a pair of suitable locking pliers on front park brake cable just rear of secondary body outrigger bracket, **Fig. 12.**
8. Remove disc brake caliper to adapter guide pin bolts.
9. Remove rear caliper from adapter.
10. Support caliper to prevent damage to flex hose.
11. Remove rotor from hub/bearing.
12. Remove horseshoe clip from retainer on end of park brake cable.
13. Remove end of park brake cable from actuator lever on adapter.
14. Remove end of park brake cable from adapter. Park brake cable is removed from adapter using a suitable wrench slipped over park brake cable retainer to compress locking tabs on park brake cable retainer.
15. Remove attaching bolt from wheel speed sensor, then the wheel speed sensor from hub/bearing and adapter.
16. Remove hub/bearing to axle mounting bolts.
17. Remove hub/bearing from axle.
18. Remove adapter from rear axle.
19. Mount adapter in vice using anchor boss for park brake cable.
20. Remove lower return spring, hold down spring and pin, then the adjuster from leading and trailing park brake shoes.
21. Remove leading park brake shoe from adapter by rotating bottom of brake shoe inward until top of brake shoe can be removed from anchor.
22. Remove upper return springs from leading brake shoe.
23. Remove upper return springs from trailing brake shoe.
24. Remove hold down spring and pin from trailing park brake shoe.
25. Remove trailing park brake shoe from adapter.
26. Remove park brake shoe actuator from adapter and inspect for signs of abnormal wear and binding at pivot point.
27. Reverse procedure to install, noting the following:
   a. Tighten all nuts and bolts to specifications.
   b. When installing hold down pin ensure line on face of pin is positioned strait up and down so pin is correctly engaged with adapter.
   c. Install a new horseshoe clip on park brake cable retainer to prevent cable from rattling in adapter.

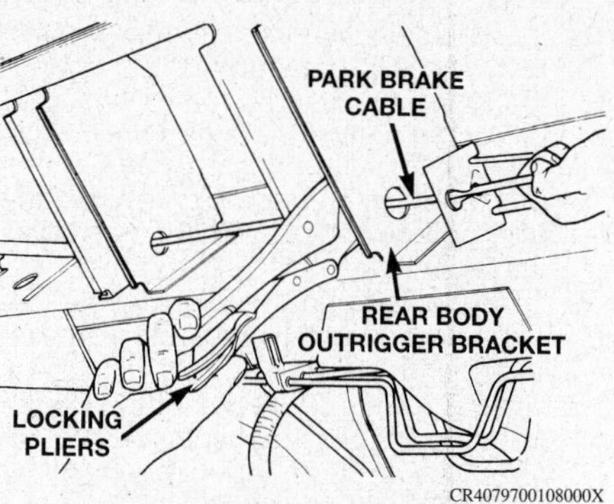

Fig. 12 Locking out automatic adjuster. Caravan, Town & Country & Voyager

Grand Cherokee, Liberty & Wrangler

1. Raise and support vehicle.
2. Remove rear wheel and tire assembly, then the caliper and anchor as an assembly.
3. Remove rubber access plug from back of rear disc brake splash shield.
4. If required, retract parking brake shoes with suitable brake adjuster tool.
5. remove rotor from axle hub flange.
6. Remove lower shoe to shoe spring/ adjuster spring with needle nose pliers.
7. Remove upper shoe to shoe spring/ return spring with brake pliers.
8. Remove shoe hold down clips and pins. Clip is held in place by pin which fits in clip notch.
9. Remove shoes and adjusters.
10. Reverse procedure to install, noting the following:
   a. Lubricate adjuster screw before installation. Ensure notched ends of

adjuster assembly are properly seated on shoes.
b. Adjust parking brake shoes.
c. Tighten all bolts to specification.

TECHNICAL SERVICE BULLETINS

Full Size Pickup

DISC BRAKE SQUEAL

RAM 2500 & 3500

On some 4x4 2500 models with a 8800 GVW rating and 3500 models with 3.38 inch diameter caliper pistons, there may be a front brake squeal on normal stops.

To correct this condition, use the following procedure to grind or file a chamfer or bevel on both ends of the front brake pads.

1. Remove front calipers, then the inner and outer pads. Refer to "Brake Pad Service" for procedure.
2. Replace pads if there is less than ½ inch of lining remaining.
3. Grind or file a chamfer or bevel on inner and outer pads.

Dakota & Durango

SLIGHT BRAKE DRIFT & LEAD

On these models, there may be a slight drift or lead to lefthand or righthand side may on braking.

To correct this condition, proceed as follows:

1. Refer to "Wheel Alignment" for procedure, then set wheel alignment to the following specifications:
   a. Set caster to +1.5°, maximum lefthand to righthand difference =.25.°
   b. Set camber to +.50°, maximum lefthand to righthand difference =.25.°
   c. Set total toe in to +.25°, maximum lefthand to righthand difference =.05.°
2. Resurface front brake rotors and install replacement brake pads (P/N. 4796368).

Grand Cherokee, Liberty & Wrangler

SQUEAK LIKE SOUND FROM PARKING BRAKE CABLE

2002 LIBERTY

On some models a squeak like sound may occur when rear suspension moves while vehicle is driven. The squeak like sound may be the result of one or both parking brake cable housings rubbing against one of the four cable guide loops. The cable guide loops are located on the rear axle spring seats and rear axle upper control arm.

Bounce rear of vehicle to exercise suspension. If squeak like sound is present, raise and support vehicle and slide each parking brake cable against guide loop. If squeak like sound results from contact between cable and guide loop, install low friction sleeve part No. 05093426AA over parking brake cable through each guide loop. Secure each friction sleeve with plastic zip tie.

DISC BRAKE SPECIFICATIONS

Model	Year	Front Disc Brake						Rear Disc Brake					
			Rotor						Rotor				
		Brake Lining Wear Limit, Inch②	Thickness, Inch			Thickness Variation Parallelism Inch	Lateral Run Out (T.I.R.) Inch	Brake Lining Wear Limit, Inch②	Thickness, Inch			Thickness Variation Parallelism Inch	Lateral Run-Out (T.I.R.) Inch
			Nominal	Min. Refinish	Discard Limit ①				Nominal	Min. Refinish	Discard Limit ①		
DAIMLERCHRYSLER													
B150–250	2002–03	.125	1.245	—	1.1810	.0005	.0040	—	—	—	—	—	—
B350	2002–03	.125	1.245	—	1.1810	.0005	.0040	—	—	—	—	—	—
Caravan, Town & Country & Voyager	2002–06	.312④	⑤	—	.9960	⑥	.0014	.281④	.482–.502	—	.443	.0005	.0055
Dakota	2002	.250④	.945	—	.8900	.0005	.0040	—	—	—	—	—	—
	2003–06	—	1.000	—	.9650	.0004	.0010	—	.600	—	.585	.0004	.0010
Durango	2002	.250④	.945	—	.8900	.0005	.0040	—	—	—	—	—	—
	2003	—	1.100	—	1.0470	.0004	.0009	—	.866	—	.811	.0004	.0009
	2004–06	—	1.100	—	1.0390	.0004	.0010	—	.870	—	.803	.0010	.0050
Pacifica	2004–06	—	1.097	1.040	—	.0004	.0014	—	.546	.492	—	.0004	.0055
PT Cruiser	2002–06	.312④	.902–.909	—	.8030	.0004	.0050	.375④	.344–.364	—	.285	.0005	.0050
	2003–06③	.312④	1.099–1.106	—	1.0390	.0004	.0050	.375④	.463–.482	—	.404	.0005	.0050
Ram Truck 1500	2002–06	⑦	1.100	—	1.0390	.0010	.0050	⑦	—	—	1.117	.0010	.0050
Ram Truck 2500–3500	2002	⑦	1.500	—	1.3340	.0010	.0050	⑦	—	—	1.117	.0010	.0050
	2003–06	⑦	1.100	—	1.0390	.0010	.0050	⑦	—	—	1.117	.0010	.0050
Sprinter 901 & 902	2003–06	—	.866	—	.748	—	.0070	—	.470	—	.400	—	.0070
Sprinter, Others	2003–06	—	.866	—	.748	—	.0070	—	.629	—	.550	—	.0070
JEEP													
Commander	2006	—	—	—	1.1220	.0004	.0020	—	—	—	.492	.0004	.0008
Grand Cherokee	2002–06	⑦	1.024	—	.9646	.0005	.0020	⑦	.394	—	.335	.0005	.0030
Liberty	2002	⑦	—	—	.8940	.0005	.0050	—	—	—	—	—	—
	2003–06	—	1.102	—	1.0236	.0006	.0040	—	.472	—	.433	.0007	.0040
Wrangler	2002–06	⑦	.944	—	.8940	.0005	.0050	—	.472	—	.433	.0007	.0040

① — Discard thickness is stamped on rotor.
② — Above rivet head or backing plate. Original equipment type brake lining.
③ — Heavy duty.
④ — Includes backing plate.
⑤ — Teves front disc brake, 1.098–1.106 inch; TRW front disc brake, 1.097–1.107 inch.
⑥ — Teves front disc brake, .0003 inch; TRW front disc brake, .0004 inch.
⑦ — Wear limit, riveted lining, 1⁄16 inch above rivet head; bonded lining, 3⁄16 inch lining thickness.

TIGHTENING SPECIFICATIONS

Year	Component	Torque Ft. Lbs.
CARAVAN, TOWN & COUNTRY & VOYAGER		
2002–06	Booster Mounting	19
	Brake Hose Caliper Banjo Bolt	35
	Brake Hose To Intermediate Bracket	108①
	Brake Line Fittings	12
	Caliper Pin Guide Bolts	16
	Hub/Bearing Mounting Bolts	95
	Hub Nut	180
	Master Cylinder Mounting	19
	Wheel Speed Sensor Mounting Bolt	105①
	Wheel Lug Nuts	85–115
COMMANDER		
2006	Brake Booster Mounting Nuts	29
	Brake Pedal Bracket Adjustable Pedals	21
	Brake Pedal Bracket To Dash	21
	Brake Pedal Pivot Nut	23
	Brake Pedal Support Bolt	17
	Front Caliper Adapter Bolts To Knuckle	125
	Front Caliper Bleed Screw	19
	Front Caliper Brake Hose Banjo Nut	23
	Front Caliper Slide Bolts	32
	Master Cylinder Mounting Nuts	18
	Master Cylinder Primary Brake Line	17
	Master Cylinder Secondary Brake Line	17
	Rear Caliper Bleed Screw	19
	Rear Caliper Brake Hose Banjo Bolt	23
	Rear Caliper Slide Bolts	32
DAKOTA & DURANGO		
2002–06	Brake Booster Mounting Bolts	21
	Brake Hose Front Fitting	12
	Brake Hose Front Bolt	21
	Brake Hose Rear Fitting	14
	Brake Line Fittings At Combination Valve	14
	Brake Line Fittings At Master Cylinder	14
	Brake Line Fittings At Wheel Cylinders	12
	Brake Shield Bolts	18
	Caliper Adapter Bolts	95–125
	Caliper Mounting Pins	22
	Master Cylinder Mounting Bolts	13
	Wheel Lug Nuts	85–117
2002 1500 FULL SIZE PICKUP & 2003–06 ALL		
2002–06	Brake Booster Mounting Nuts	28
	Brake Hose Front Bolts To Frame	96①
	Brake Hose Fitting	14
	Brake Pedal Bracket Nuts	21
	Brake Line Fittings Junction Block	14
	Brake Line Fittings Master Cylinder	14
	Caliper Adapter Mounting Bolts	130
	Caliper Brake Line Banjo Bolt	20
	Caliper Mounting Pins	24
	Hub & Bearing Bolts	120

TIGHTENING SPECIFICATIONS—Continued

Year	Component	Torque Ft. Lbs.
2002 1500 FULL SIZE PICKUP & 2003–06 ALL		
2002–06	Junction Block Bolts To Frame	96①
	Master Cylinder Mounting Nuts	13
	Parking Brake Pedal	14
	Support Plate Mounting Bolts & Nuts	47
2500 & 3500 FULL SIZE PICKUP		
2002	Booster Mounting Nuts To Dashpanel	21
	Caliper Banjo Bolts	30
	Combination Valve Brake Lines	16
	Combination Valve Mounting Bolt	17
	Front Caliper HD Adapter Bolts	210
	Front Caliper Mounting Bolts	24
	Hub & Bearing HD 4x2 Spindle Nut	280
	Hub & Bearing 4x4 Hub Bearing Bolts	125
	Master Cylinder Brake Lines	16
	Master Cylinder Mounting Nuts	17
	Park Brake Pedal Assembly Mounting Bolts & Nuts	21
	Proportioning Valve Brake Hose	23
	Proportioning Valve Brake Lines	16
	Proportioning Valve Mounting Nuts	25
	Rear Caliper Slide Pins	24
	Rotor To Hub Rear Bolt	95
	Support Plate Mounting Bolts	43
FULL SIZE VAN		
2002–03	Booster Mounting Nut	13
	Brake Hose To Caliper Fitting	35
	Brake Line Fittings (3/8 Or 7/16 Inch)	9–14
	Brake Line Fittings, (1/2 Or 9/16 Inch)	14–20
	Brake Line Retaining Clip Screws	40–60①
	Caliper Mounting	24
	Caliper Adapter (B-150 Series)	130
	Caliper Adapter (B-250 & B-350 Series)	210
	Master Cylinder Mounting	17
	Wheel Lug Nuts (1/2 Inch)	80–115
	Wheel Lug Nuts (5/8 Coned)	175–225
	Wheel Lug Nuts (5/8 Flanged)	300–350
GRAND CHEROKEE		
2002–06	Brake Booster Mounting Nuts	29
	Brake Hose Banjo Bolt	23
	Front Caliper Anchor Bolts	66–85
	Front Caliper Bleeder Screw	12
	Front Caliper Slide Pins	21–30
	Master Cylinder Mounting Nuts	18–20
	Master Cylinder Primary Brake Line	12
	Master Cylinder Secondary Brake Line	12
	Power Brake Booster Mounting Nuts	21
	Proportioning Valve Axle Bracket Mounting Bolts	175①
	Proportioning Valve Mounting Bolts	40
	Rear Caliper Slide Pins	21–30
	Rear Caliper Anchor Bolts	66–85

Continued

TIGHTENING SPECIFICATIONS—Continued

Year	Component	Torque Ft. Lbs.
LIBERTY		
2002–06	Booster Mounting	18
	Caliper Banjo Bolt	23
	Front Caliper Bolts	11
	Master Cylinder	18
	Master Cylinder Lines	15
	Rear Caliper Bolts	18
PACIFICA		
2004–06	Brake Hose Bracket Bolt	13
	Brake Hose Caliper Banjo Bolt	35
	Brake Tube Nuts	10
	Caliper Bleed Screw	10
	Front Disc Brake Caliper Adapter Mounting Bolts	125
	Front Disc Brake Caliper Guide Pin Bolts	32
	Master Cylinder Mounting Nuts	19
	Pedal Mounting Nuts	21
	Rear Disc Brake Caliper Adapter Mounting Bolts	85
	Rear Disc Brake Caliper Guide Pin Bolts	17
	Wheel Lug Nuts	100
PT CRUISER		
2002–06	Brake Hose Banjo Bolt	18
	Brake Tube Nuts	12
	Caliper Bleeder Screw	115
	Front Disc Brake Caliper Guide Pin Bolt	26
	Front Disc Brake Caliper To Knuckle	77
	Rear Disc Brake Caliper Guide Pin Bolt	16
	Rear Disc Brake Caliper To Knuckle	70
	Wheel Lug Nuts	100

TIGHTENING SPECIFICATIONS—Continued

Year	Component	Torque Ft. Lbs.
SPRINTER		
2003–06	ALB Operating Linkage Lever To Rear Axle	25
	Booster To Pedal Bracket	18
	Brake Caliper Adapter Front	125
	Brake Caliper Adapter Rear M12 Bolt	66
	Brake Caliper Adapter Rear M14 Bolt	125
	Brake Caliper Guide Pins M8 Bolt	18
	Brake Caliper Guide Pins M10 Bolt	22
	Brake Lines	10
	Disc Brake Rotor Locking Bolt	17
	Master Cylinder To Brake Booster Nut	21
	Pedal Bracket To Firewall	17
	Wear Indicator To Caliper Bolt	89①
	Wheel Flange Ring To Front Rotor	133
	Wheel Flange Ring To Rear Rotor	148
WRANGLER		
2002–06	Booster Mounting	29
	Brake Hose Bolt	23
	Brake Line To Combination Valve	14
	Brake Line To Master Cylinder	14
	Caliper Mounting Bolts	11
	Combination Valve Mounting	13
	Master Cylinder Mounting	13
	Wheel Lugs	85–115

① — Inch lbs.

DRUM BRAKES

TABLE OF CONTENTS

DaimlerChrysler

NOTE: Prior To Performing Any Service Operations Listed In This Section, Consult The "Technical Service Bulletins" Section For Related Information.

INDEX

PRECAUTIONS

When working on or around brake assemblies, care must be taken to prevent breathing asbestos dust, as many manufacturers incorporate asbestos fibers in the production of brake linings. During routine service operations, the amount of asbestos dust from brake lining wear is at a low level due to a chemical breakdown during use, and a few precautions will minimize exposure. **Do not sand or grind brake linings unless suitable local exhaust ventilation equipment is used to prevent excessive asbestos exposure.**

1. Wear a suitable respirator approved for asbestos dust use during all repair procedures.
2. Do not use compressed air or dry brush to clean brake components. Many brake components contain asbestos fibers which, if inhaled, can cause serious injury. To clean brake components, use a water soaked rag or a suitable vacuum cleaner to minimize airborne dust.
3. Keep work area clean, using same equipment as for cleaning brake components.
4. Properly dispose of rags and vacuum cleaner bags by placing them in plastic bags.

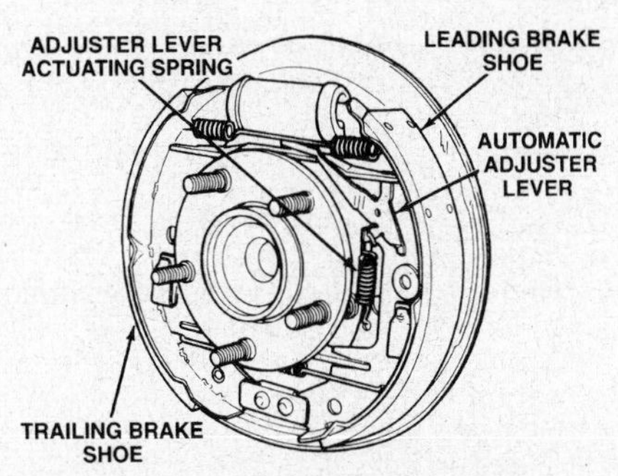

Fig. 1 Rear brake assembly. Caravan, Dakota, Durango, Town & Country & Voyager

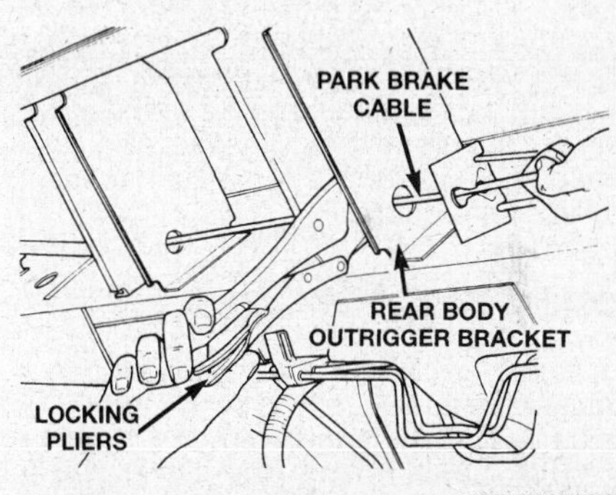

Fig. 2 Park brake cable auto adjuster release. Caravan, Dakota, Durango, Town & Country & Voyager

INSPECTION

Brake Drums

Any time the brake drums are removed for brake service, the braking surface diameter should be inspected with a suitable brake drum micrometer at several points to determine if they are within the safe oversize limit stamped on the brake drum outer surface. If the braking surface diameter exceeds specifications, the drum must be replaced. If the braking surface diameter is within specifications, drums should be cleaned and inspected for cracks, scores, deep grooves, taper, out of round and heat spotting. If drums are cracked or heat spotted, they must be replaced. Minor scores should be removed with sandpaper. Grooves and large scores can only be removed by machining with special equipment, as long as the braking surface is within specifications stamped on brake drum outer surface. Any brake drum sufficiently out of round to cause vehicle vibration or noise while braking, or showing taper should also be machined, removing only enough stock to true up the brake drum.

After a brake drum is machined, wipe the

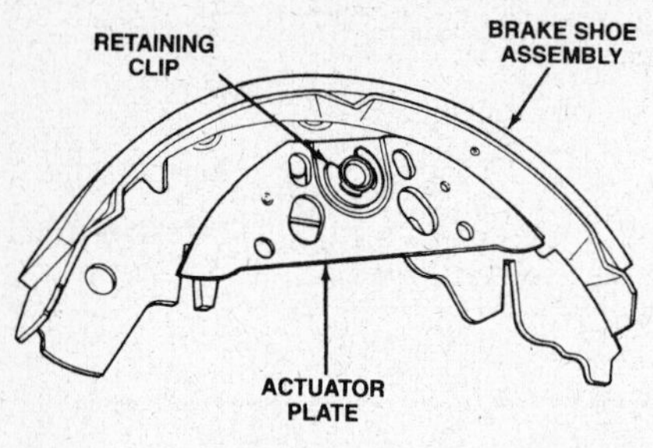

Fig. 3 Park brake actuator plate. Caravan, Dakota, Durango, Town & Country & Voyager

braking surface diameter with a cloth soaked in denatured alcohol. If one brake drum is machined, the other should also be machined to the same diameter to maintain equal braking forces.

Brake Linings & Springs

Inspect brake linings for excessive wear, damage, oil, grease or brake fluid contamination. If any of the above conditions exists, brake linings should be replaced. Do not attempt to replace only one set of brake shoes; they should be replaced as an axle set only to maintain equal braking forces. Examine brake shoe webbing, hold-down retainers and return springs for signs of overheating indicated by a slight blue color. If any component exhibits signs of overheating, replace hold-down and return springs with new ones. Overheated springs lose their pull and could cause brake linings to wear out prematurely. Inspect all springs for sags, bends and external damage, and replace as required.

Backing Plate

Inspect backing plate shoe contact surface for grooves that may restrict shoe movement and cannot be removed by lightly sanding with emery cloth or other suitable abrasive. If backing plate exhibits above condition, it should be replaced. Also inspect for signs of cracks, warping and excessive rust, indicating need for replacement.

Adjuster Mechanism

Inspect all components for rust, corrosion, bends and fatigue. Replace as required. On adjuster mechanism equipped with adjuster cable, inspect cable for kinks, fraying or elongation of eyelet.

Parking Brake Cable

Inspect parking brake cable end for kinks, fraying and elongation, and replace as required.

BRAKE SERVICE

Brake Shoe, Replace

Do not intermix automatic adjuster components from side to side.

9, 10, 11 & 13 INCH DRUMS

CARAVAN, DAKOTA, DURANGO, TOWN & COUNTRY & VOYAGER

Removal

1. Raise and support vehicle, then remove rear wheels.
2. Remove drum retaining nuts if equipped, then the drums. If drum will not separate from brake shoes or axle, proceed as follows:
   a. Ensure parking brake is disengaged.
   b. Remove adjuster hole plug from backing plate.
   c. Insert small screwdriver or equivalent, through adjuster hole, then push and hold self adjuster lever off adjuster screw assembly, **Fig. 1.**
   d. Back off adjuster screw assembly until drum is free of shoes using a suitable brake adjuster tool.
   e. If drum is rusted to axle flange, use a suitable hammer to tap on drum and flange area until drum is free.
3. Pull back front park brake cable, **Fig. 2,** to release tension in self-adjusting parking brake system.
4. Place suitable locking pliers onto cable to maintain slack in system. Place pliers at rear body outrigger bracket only, **Fig. 2.**
5. Remove adjustment lever spring, then the adjustment lever.
6. Remove lower brake shoe to brake shoe spring.
7. Remove tension clip from upper spring and automatic adjuster assembly. **Note position of tension clip for assembly reference.**
8. Remove upper brake shoe to brake shoe spring.
9. Remove trailing brake shoe hold-down spring clip and pin.
10. Lift out trailing brake shoe and disconnect park brake arm, then remove park brake strut.
11. Remove automatic adjuster screw assembly.
12. Remove leading brake shoe hold-down spring clip and pin.
13. Lift out leading brake shoe and disconnect park brake actuator plate from shoe, **Fig. 3.**

Inspection

1. Inspect components for damage and wear. Replace as required.
2. Inspect wheel cylinders, boots which are torn, cut or heat damaged indicate need for wheel cylinder replacement. Peel back lower edge of boot, if fluid

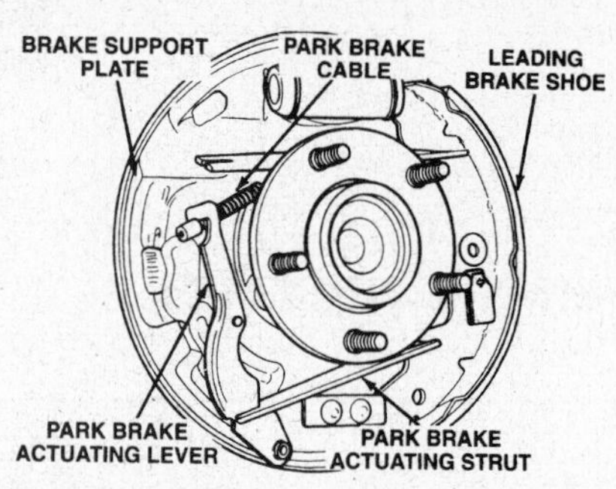

Fig. 4 Park brake actuating strut. Caravan, Dakota, Durango, Town & Country & Voyager

spills out, cup leakage is indicated and wheel cylinder should be replaced. **A small amount of fluid is always present and considered normal.**
3. Inspect backing plate for evidence of seal leakage. If leakage exists, refer to individual truck chassis chapter for axle seal replacement procedure.
4. Inspect backing plate attaching bolts.
5. Inspect adjuster screw operation. If satisfactory, lightly lubricate adjusting screw and washer with suitable brake lube. If adjuster screw does not move easily or does not move at all, replace adjuster.

Installation

1. Clean rust and dirt from shoe contact surfaces on backing plate using fine emery cloth or other suitable abrasive.
2. Lubricate backing plate shoe contact pads with a suitable lubricant.
3. Install park brake actuator plate onto leading brake shoe, **Fig. 3.**
4. Attach leading brake shoe to backing plate with hold-down pin and spring clip.
5. Install park brake actuating strut to leading brake shoe and to park brake actuating lever, **Fig. 4.**
6. Install automatic adjuster assembly onto leading shoe. Ensure automatic adjuster and park brake actuating strut are in proper contact with actuator plate.
7. Install park brake actuating lever onto trailing shoe.
8. Attach trailing shoe to backing plate with hold-down pin and spring clip.
9. Install upper shoe to shoe spring, then the tension clip to spring and automatic adjuster assembly. **Ensure tension clip is installed on threaded portion of adjuster assembly.**
10. Install lower shoe to shoe spring, then the automatic adjuster lever and spring. **Ensure adjuster lever is in contact with star wheel.**
11. Remove locking pliers from front parking brake cable and allow parking brake system to auto adjust.
12. Install drums and retaining nuts if equipped.

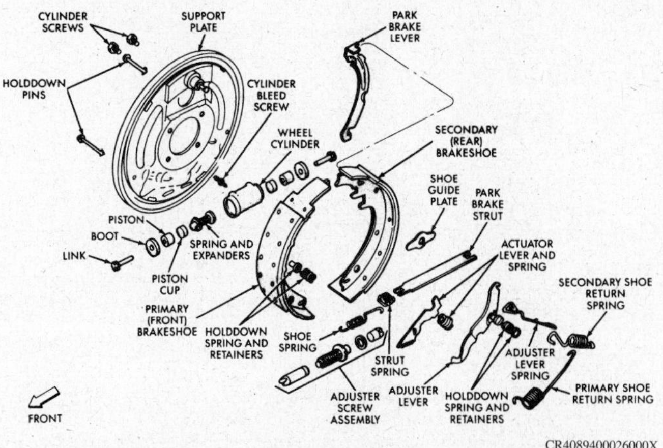

Fig. 5 Exploded view of 11 inch drum brake. Full size pickup

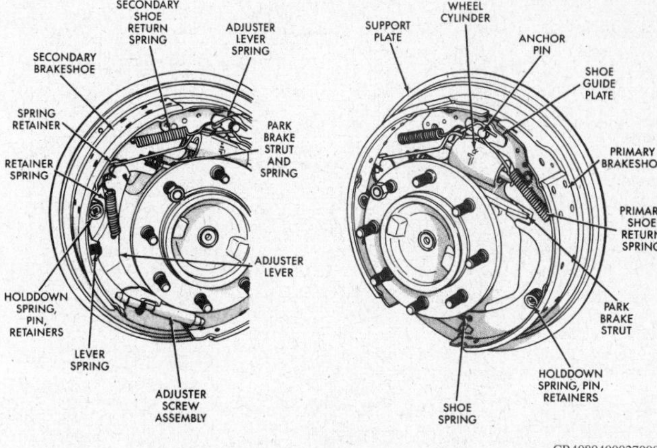

Fig. 6 13 inch drum brake. Full size pickup

13. Install rear wheels and tighten wheel lug nuts to specification.
14. Adjust brakes as outlined under "Adjustments."

FULL SIZE PICKUP

Removal

Do not mix brake self adjuster components. Lefthand adjuster screw assembly has a righthand thread. Righthand adjuster screw assembly has a lefthand thread.

1. Raise and support vehicle, then remove rear wheels.
2. Remove drum retaining nuts, if equipped, then the drums. If drum will not separate from brake shoes or axle, proceed as follows:
   a. Inspect parking brake for engagement and free movement.
   b. Remove adjustment plug from backing plate.
   c. Insert suitable small screwdriver through adjuster hole, then push and hold self adjuster lever off of star wheel of adjuster screw assembly.
   d. Back off star wheel of adjuster screw assembly until drum can be removed using a suitable brake adjustment tool.
   e. If drum is rusted to axle flange, use a suitable hammer to tap on joining area of drum and flange until drum is free.
3. Remove return spring for primary shoe using suitable brake spring tools, **Figs. 5 and 6,** then the primary shoe hold-down retainer, spring and pin.
4. Tilt primary shoe out and disengage from shoe spring.
5. Remove shoe spring, self adjuster screw assembly and parking brake strut with spring.
6. Remove secondary shoe hold-down retainer using a suitable brake spring tool, then the spring and pin.
7. Remove self adjuster levers, spring and retainers from secondary shoe.
8. Tilt secondary shoe up, then remove return spring and self adjuster spring.
9. Disconnect parking brake cable from lever and remove secondary brake shoe.
10. Remove and discard parking brake arm retaining clip, then the arm from the secondary shoe.

Inspection

1. Inspect components for damage and wear. Replace as required.
2. Inspect wheel cylinders. Boots that are torn, cut or heat damaged indicate need for wheel cylinder replacement. Peel back lower edge of boot, if fluid spills out, cup leakage is indicated and wheel cylinder should be replaced. **A small amount of fluid is always present and considered normal.**
3. Inspect backing plate for evidence of seal leakage. If leakage exists, refer to individual truck chassis chapter for axle seal replacement procedure.
4. Inspect backing plate attaching bolts.
5. Inspect adjuster screw operation. If satisfactory, lightly lubricate adjusting screw and washer with suitable brake lube. If adjuster screw does not move easily or does not move at all, replace adjuster.

Installation

Do not mix brake self adjuster components. Lefthand adjuster screw assembly has a righthand thread. Righthand adjuster screw assembly has a lefthand thread.

1. Clean rust and dirt from shoe contact surfaces on backing plate using fine emery cloth or other suitable abrasive.
2. Lubricate backing plate shoe contact pads with a suitable brake lubricant.
3. Attach parking brake lever to secondary brake shoe using a new clip.
4. Attach parking brake cable to arm, then position self adjuster lever onto secondary brake shoe.
5. **On models equipped with 13 inch brake drums,** if self adjuster lever was disassembled, proceed as follows:
   a. Position center portion of adjuster lever into a suitable vise, **Fig. 7.**
   b. Position adjuster spring retainer into lever. A clamp or locking pliers may be used to hold retainer in place during spring installation.
   c. Install retainer spring using a suitable spring tool.
6. **On all models,** attach secondary shoe assembly to backing plate using hold-down pin, spring and retainer.
7. **On models equipped with 13 inch brake drums,** install adjuster lever spring between shoe and lever. Ensure spring is installed over adjuster lever tang.
8. **On all models,** attach long end of shoe spring to secondary brake shoe.
9. Install oval anti-rattle spring onto parking brake strut, then slide non spring end of strut onto secondary brake shoe and spring end onto primary brake shoe.
10. Attach primary shoe assembly to backing plate using hold-down pin, spring and retainer.
11. **On models equipped with 11 inch brake drums,** install actuator lever and spring into adjuster lever on secondary brake shoe. Large diameter of actuator lever spring goes against shoe.
12. **On all models,** install adjuster screw assembly, star wheel end towards secondary shoe.
13. Attach shoe spring to primary shoe using a suitable brake spring tool.
14. Install brake shoe guide plate onto anchor pin of backing plate.
15. Attach self adjuster lever spring to self adjuster lever, install secondary brake shoe return spring to shoe and adjuster lever spring, then using a suitable brake spring tool assemble onto anchor pin.
16. Install primary brake shoe return spring to shoe and anchor pin.
17. Adjust brake shoes using a suitable brake adjustment gauge.
18. Install brake drum and wheels, then tighten wheel lug nuts to specifications.

12 INCH DRUM

REMOVAL

1. Raise and support vehicle.
2. Remove wheel and tire assembly.
3. Remove axle shaft nuts, washers, and cones, then the axle shaft. **If cones do**

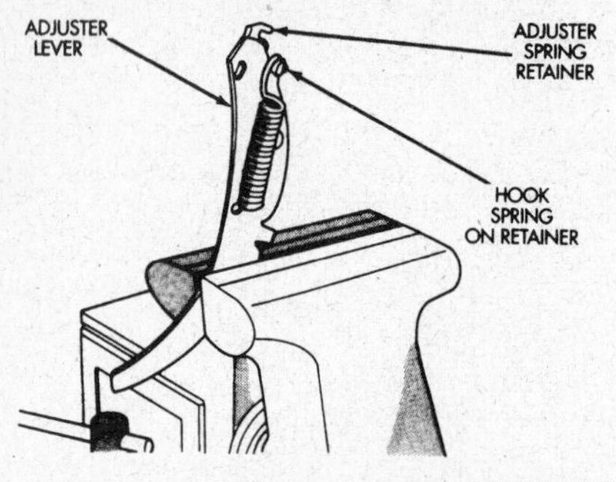

Fig. 7 Self adjuster lever assembly. Full Size Pickup w/13 inch brake drum

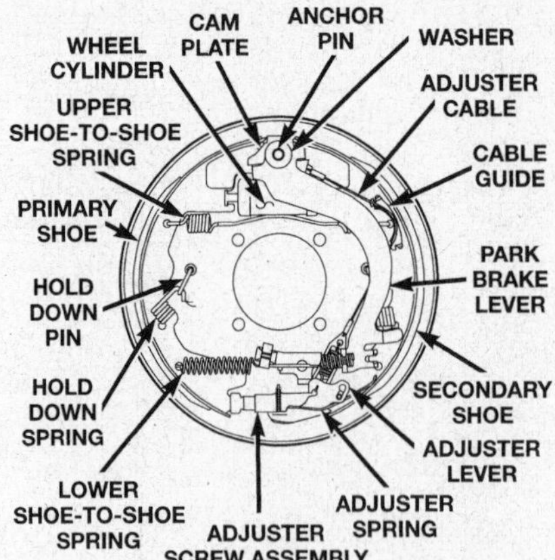

Fig. 8 12 inch drum brake

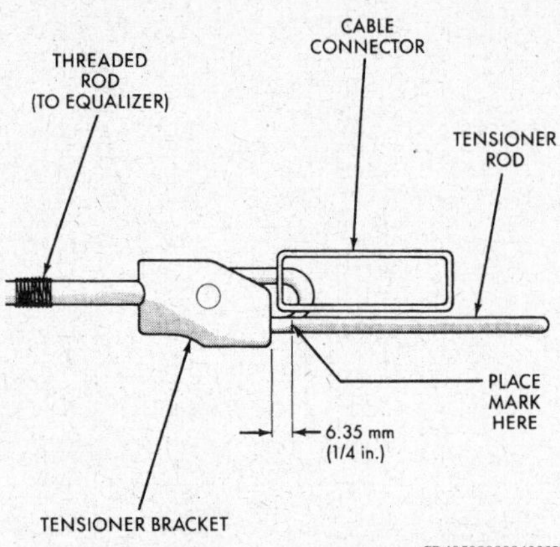

Fig. 9 Tensioner rod adjustment mark. Except FWD models

not release, rap axle shaft sharply at center.

4. Remove outer hub nut, then straighten lock washer and remove washer, inner nut, and bearing.
5. Remove brake drum. If brake lining is dragging on brake drum, back off brake adjustment by rotating adjusting screw.
6. Unhook adjusting lever return spring from lever, remove lever and return spring from lever pivot pin, and unhook adjuster lever from adjuster cable assembly, **Fig. 8.**
7. Unhook upper shoe to shoe spring, then unhook and remove shoe hold-down springs.
8. Disconnect parking brake cable from parking brake lever.
9. Remove shoes, lower shoe to shoe spring and star wheel as an assembly.

INSPECTION

1. Clean support, then inspect for burrs and remove as required.
2. Clean and lubricate threads of adjusting screws, then inspect for pulled or stripped threads.
3. If spring paint shows discoloration, end coils are distorted, or spring strength is questionable, replace spring.

INSTALLATION

Pivot screw and adjusting nut have lefthand threads on lefthand side brakes and righthand threads on righthand side brakes.

1. Lubricate and assemble star wheel assembly, then lubricate guide pads on support plates.
2. Assemble star wheel, lower shoe to shoe spring, and brake shoes and position assembly on support plate.
3. Connect parking brake cable to parking brake lever.
4. Install and hook hold-down springs.
5. Install upper shoe to shoe spring.
6. Position adjuster lever return springs on pivots.
7. Install adjuster lever and route adjuster cable and connector to adjuster.
8. Position drum on axle housing.
9. Install bearing and inner nut.
10. Install lock washer and outer nut, bending washer to lock in place.
11. Place new gasket on hub and install axle shaft, cones, lock washers and nuts.
12. Adjust brakes.
13. Install tire and wheel assembly.
14. If any hydraulic connections have been opened, bleed brake system.
15. Inspect fluid level in master cylinder, filling as required.
16. Inspect brake pedal for proper feel and return.
17. Lower vehicle and road test.

PT CRUISER

REMOVAL

1. Raise and support vehicle, then remove rear wheels.
2. Remove brake drum retaining nuts if equipped, then drum.
3. Remove dust cap from hub and bearing.
4. Remove hub nut, then slide hub and bearing from spindle.
5. Compress cable return spring, then remove parking brake cable from parking brake lever.
6. Remove lower return spring.
7. Compress and remove both shoe hold-down spring clips.
8. Remove both shoes and remaining components as an assembly from anchor and wheel cylinder.
9. Remove adjuster spring from leading shoe and lever pawl.
10. Remove lever pawl from pivot on leading shoe and slide it out from under adjuster.
11. Remove adjuster and upper return spring from shoes.

INSPECTION

1. Inspect components for damage and wear. Replace as required.
2. Inspect wheel cylinders. Boots that are torn, cut or heat damaged indicate need for wheel cylinder replacement. Peel back lower edge of boot, if fluid spills out, cup leakage is indicated and wheel cylinder should be replaced. **A small amount of fluid is always present and considered normal.**
3. Inspect backing plate for evidence of seal leakage. If leakage exists, refer to individual truck chassis chapter for axle seal replacement procedure.
4. Inspect backing plate attaching bolts.
5. Inspect adjuster screw operation. If satisfactory, lightly lubricate adjusting screw and washer with suitable brake lube. If adjuster screw does not move easily or does not move at all, replace adjuster.

INSTALLATION

Do not mix brake self adjuster components. Lefthand adjuster screw assembly has a lefthand thread. Righthand adjuster screw assembly has a righthand thread.

1. Lubricate shoe contact areas on support plate and anchor with suitable lubricant.
2. Place one leading shoe and one trailing shoe on bench, then install adjuster and upper return spring.
3. Slide lever pawl under adjuster and onto pivot on leading shoe.
4. Install adjuster spring between leading shoe and lever pawl.
5. Install pre-assembled brake shoe assembly over wheel cylinder and anchor on brake support plate.
6. Install both shoe hold-down pins from rear, through support plate and shoes.
7. Compress and install shoe hold-down spring clips on pins.
8. Install lower return spring.
9. Compress parking brake cable return spring, then install cable on parking brake lever. Release spring guiding it beneath retaining tab on lever.
10. Slide hub and bearing onto spindle.
11. Adjust brake shoes to drum diameter using a brake shoe gauge.

ADJUSTMENTS

Service Brake

EXCEPT FWD MODELS

SELF-ADJUSTING BRAKES

These brakes have self-adjusting shoe mechanisms that ensure correct lining to drum clearances at all times. The automatic adjusters operate only when the brakes are applied as the vehicle is moving rearward.

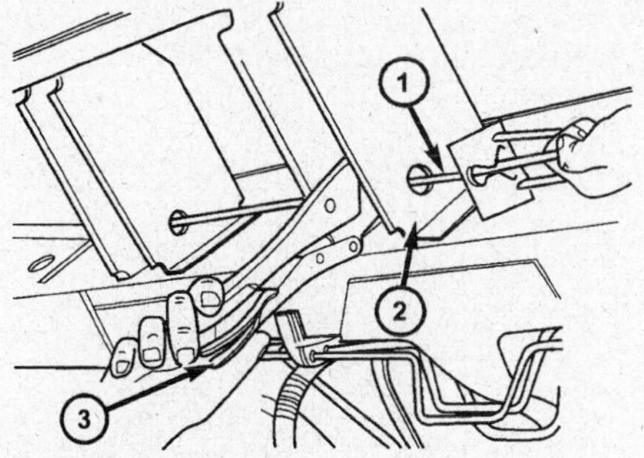

1 - PARK BRAKE CABLE
2 - REAR BODY OUTRIGGER BRACKET
3 - LOCKING PLIERS

LTV1900000001162

Fig. 10 Park brake cable slack. Caravan, Town & Country & Voyager

Although the brakes are self-adjusting, an initial adjustment is required when the brake shoes have been relined, replaced or when the length of the star wheel adjuster has been changed during some other service operation.

Frequent usage of an automatic transmission forward range to halt reverse vehicle motion may prevent the automatic adjusters from functioning, thereby inducing low pedal heights. Should low pedal heights be encountered, it is recommended that numerous forward and reverse stops be made until satisfactory pedal height is obtained. **If a low pedal height condition cannot be corrected by making numerous reverse stops (provided the hydraulic system is free of air), it indicates that the self-adjusting mechanism is not functioning. Therefore, it will be required to remove the drum, clean, free up and lubricate the adjusting mechanism. Then adjust the brakes, ensuring the parking brake is fully released.**

ADJUSTMENT

1. Raise vehicle so wheels are free to turn, then remove rear adjusting hole cover.
2. Back off parking brake cable adjustment so there is slack in the cable. Ensure parking brake lever is fully released.
3. **On models equipped with release type adjuster,** insert adjusting tool into star wheel of adjusting screw. Move tool handle downward until slight drag is felt when wheel is rotated.
4. **On models equipped with application type adjuster,** insert adjusting tool into star wheel of adjusting screw. Move tool handle upward until slight drag is felt when wheel is rotated.
5. **On all models,** insert a suitable screwdriver into brake adjusting hole and push adjusting lever out of engagement with star wheel. **Care should be taken not to bend adjusting lever.**
6. Back off star wheel 10–12 notches until wheel rotates freely with no drag.
7. Install adjusting hole cover.
8. Adjust parking brake cable.

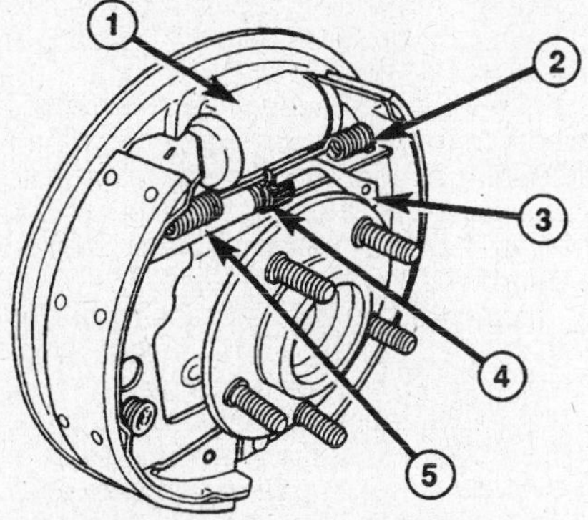

1 - WHEEL CYLINDER
2 - BRAKE SHOE UPPER RETURN SPRING
3 - AUTOMATIC ADJUSTER LEVER
4 - TENSION CLIP
5 - AUTOMATIC ADJUSTER ASSEMBLY

LTV1900000001163

Fig. 11 Tension clip removal. Caravan, Town & Country & Voyager

FWD MODELS

The rear brakes are self-adjusting. An initial adjustment is required after the brake shoes have been relined or replaced, or when the length of the star wheel adjuster has been changed during other service operations. To adjust the rear brakes, proceed as follows:

1. Raise and support vehicle.
2. Remove adjusting hole covers from brake support plates.
3. Insert brake adjusting tool No. C-3784, or equivalent, through adjusting hole and into contact with star wheel of adjusting screw.
4. Move handle of tool upward to turn star wheel until a slight drag is felt while turning wheel.
5. Insert a suitable tool into brake adjusting hole and push adjusting lever out of engagement with star wheel. **Use caution not to bend adjusting lever or distort lever spring.**
6. Back off star wheel until no brake shoe drag is felt while turning wheel using adjusting tool.

Parking Brake

EXCEPT FWD MODELS

1. Raise and support vehicle.
2. Back off tensioner adjusting nut to create slack in cables.
3. Remove rear wheels and drums.
4. Inspect rear brake shoe adjustment with suitable brake gauge.
5. Replace worn brake shoes if required.
6. Verify parking brake cables operate freely, if cables or mechanisms are binding, repair or replace components as required.
7. Install drums, ensure drums rotate freely without drag.
8. Install wheels, then lower vehicle enough for access to parking brake foot pedal.
9. Fully apply parking brakes and leave brakes applied until adjustment is complete.
10. Raise vehicle and mark tensioner rod, **Fig. 9,** ¼ inch from edge of tensioner bracket.
11. Tighten adjusting nut at equalizer until mark on tensioner rod moves into alignment with tensioner bracket. **Do not loosen, or tighten tensioner adjusting nut for any reason after completing adjustment.**
12. Release parking brake and verify rear wheels rotate freely without drag.
13. Lower vehicle.

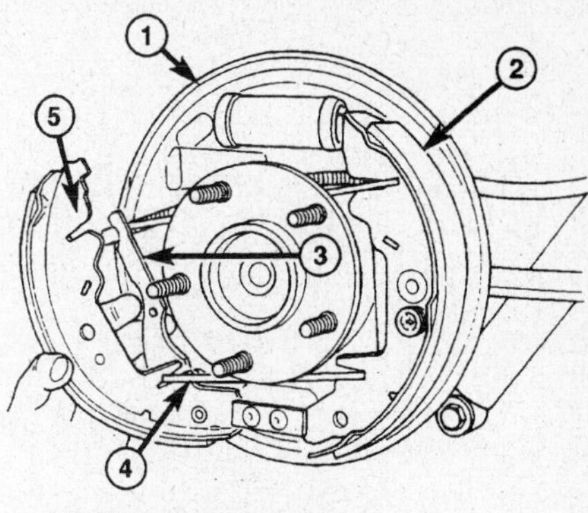

1 - BRAKE SUPPPORT PLATE
2 - LEADING BRAKE SHOE
3 - PARK BRAKE ACTUATING LEVER
4 - PARK BRAKE ACTUATING STRUT
5 - TRAILING BRAKE SHOE

LTV1900000001164

Fig. 12 Trailing brake shoe removal. Caravan, Town & Country & Voyager

FWD MODELS

The parking brake mechanism on these vehicles is self-adjusting.

TECHNICAL SERVICE BULLETINS

Squawk Or Grunt Noise From Rear Brakes

2002-03 CARAVAN, TOWN & COUNTRY & VOYAGER

A cyclic swoosh, squawk or grunt noise from rear of vehicle during medium to light brake applications on vehicles equipped with rear drum brakes. The noise can be related to the speed at which the tire turns (one sound per revolution). This noise could be coming from the wheel cylinders. Use the following procedure to correct this condition.

1. Raise and support vehicle.
2. Remove rear wheels and drums.

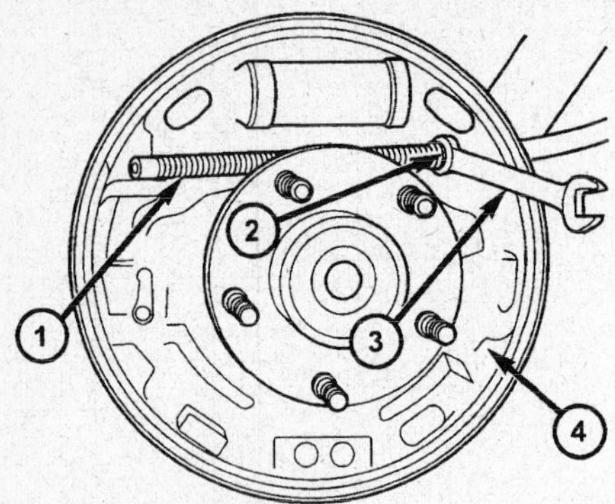

1 - PARK BRAKE CABLE

2 - CABLE RETAINER

3 - 14mm BOX END WRENCH

4 - BRAKE SUPPORT PLATE

LTV1900000001165

Fig. 13 Park brake cable removal. Caravan, Town & Country & Voyager

3. Remove both rear brake shoes from backing plate and clean area around wheel cylinder boots.
4. Peel back edge of both wheel cylinder boots to separate them from groove in casting.
5. Remove boots and attached pistons from wheel cylinder.
6. Apply wheel cylinder lubricant No. 04883068, or equivalent, liberally to surfaces of pistons and inside bore of wheel cylinders without disturbing rubber cup seals.
7. Presence of small amounts of rust visible inside the bore of wheel cylinders can be ignored provided there is no evidence of fluid leakage.
8. Install pistons and boots to wheel cylinders. Ensure boots seat properly onto casting groove around wheel cylinder.
9. With your fingers, move piston back and forth to distribute lubricant.
10. Do not allow boots to become dislodged from wheel cylinder casting groove.
11. Install brake shoes, ensure all three inspection and adjustment plugs are installed in backing plate and that wheel cylinder is sealed to backing plate with suitable RTV sealant.
12. Wipe spilled fluid from outside of wheel cylinder and other brake components.
13. Repeat procedure on other side of vehicle.
14. Install drums and wheels, lower vehicle.

Snow/Water Ingestion Into Rear Brake Drum

CARAVAN, TOWN & COUNTRY & VOYAGER

While driving through deep snow/water, the snow/water may enter the rear brake drums causing rust to develop on rear brake drum and shoe friction surfaces. This condition can lead to temporary freezing of the rear brake linings to the drums. This symptom is experienced after the vehicle has been parked in below freezing temperatures long enough for the snow/water to freeze inside of the rear brake drums. When the parking brake has been applied the symptom is more likely to occur.

If this condition exists, proceed as follows:

1. Raise and support vehicle, then remove tire and wheel assembly.
2. Remove both brake drums.
3. With park brake pedal in released position, pull down and rearward on core of front park brake cable and install a pair of locking pliers on core of front park brake cable just rearward of rear body outrigger bracket, **Fig. 10.**
4. Depress and hold brake pedal past its first one inch of travel to prevent brake fluid from draining out of master cylinder when brake tube is removed from wheel cylinder.
5. Remove adjustment lever spring from adjustment lever and leading brake shoe, **Fig. 1.**
6. Remove adjustment lever from leading brake shoe.
7. Remove brake shoe lower return springs.
8. Remove tension clip attaching upper return spring to automatic adjuster assembly, **Fig. 11.**
9. Remove brake shoe to brake shoe upper return spring.
10. Remove trailing brake shoe assembly hold down spring and pin.
11. Remove trailing brake shoe assembly from brake support plate, park brake actuating lever and park brake actuating strut, **Fig. 12.**
12. Remove automatic adjuster assembly from leading shoe.
13. Remove leading brake shoe assembly hold down spring and pin, then the leading brake shoe.
14. If shoe replacement is required, remove park brake actuator plate from leading brake shoe and install it on replacement shoe.
15. Disconnect park brake cable from park brake actuation lever.
16. Remove rear wheel speed sensor.
17. Compress flared legs on park brake cable retainer using a suitable 14 mm box end wrench, then pull cable out of support plate, **Fig. 13.**
18. Disconnect brake tube from wheel cylinder.
19. Remove two bolts attaching wheel cylinder to brake support plate, then separate wheel cylinder from vehicle.
20. Remove four bolts attaching hub/bearing assembly to flange of rear axle.
21. **On 2002–03 models,** if hub/bearing cannot be removed by hand, proceed as follows:
    a. Thread guide pins tool No. 8458-4, or equivalent, into hub/bearing mounting holes, **Fig. 14.**
    b. Remove two outboard spring plate bolts.
    c. Install screw mount tool No. 8458-2, or equivalent using spring plate bolts.
    d. Place push plate tool No. 8458-1, or equivalent, on ends of threaded guide pins.
    e. Place a dab of grease in dimple of push plate.
    f. Tighten forcing screw tool No. 8458-3, or equivalent, against dimple in push plate and press hub/bearing assembly out of axle.
    g. Remove tool, then install two outboard spring plate bolts and **torque** to 75 ft. lbs.

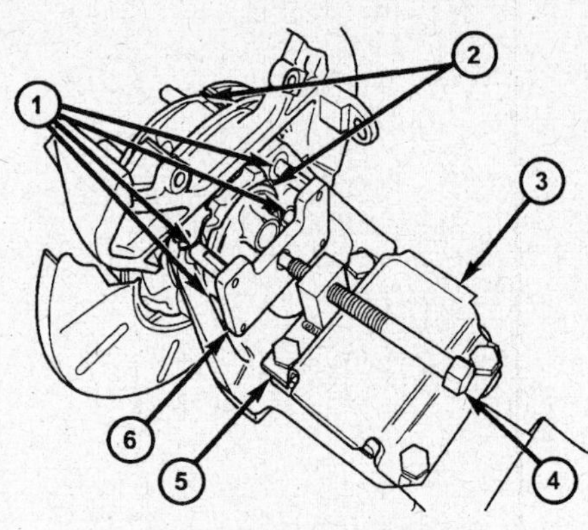

1 - THREADED GUIDE PINS 8458-4

2 - HUB AND BEARING

3 - LEAF SPRING PLATE

4 - FORCING SCREW 8458-3

5 - SCREW MOUNT 8458-2

6 - PUSH PLATE 8458-1**

LTV1900000001167

Fig. 14 Hub/bearing removal. 2002–03 Caravan, Town & Country & Voyager

22. **On all models,** remove brake support plate.
23. Insert four hub/bearing mounting bolts into holes in flange of rear axle.
24. Install revised brake support plate P/N 05016612/3AA on four bolts inserted in flange of rear axle. Ensure park brake cable hole in support plate faces toward front of vehicle.
25. Align hub/bearing with four mounting bolts, then tighten bolts into hub/bearing in a crisscross pattern until hub/bearing is fully seated into flange of rear axle.
26. **Torque** hub/bearing bolts to 95 ft. lbs.
27. Apply Mopar RTV P/N 05010884AA, or equivalent around wheel cylinder opening in brake support plate.
28. Attach wheel cylinder to brake support plate before sealant cures.
29. Install brake tube into wheel cylinder.
30. **On models equipped with ABS,** install rear wheel speed sensor.
31. **On models less ABS,** fill any existing gap between bearing flange and ABS sensor hole in support plate with Mopar RTV sealant, or equivalent.
32. **On all models,** install rear park brake cable into its mounting hole in brake support plate.
33. Install park brake cable to park brake actuator lever.
34. Lubricate eight brake shoe contact

areas on support plate using Mopar Brake Lubricant p/n 04796269, or equivalent.

35. Install leading brake shoe, hold down, pin and spring onto brake support plate.
36. Install park brake actuator strut on leading brake shoe, then install park brake actuator lever on strut.
37. Install automatic adjuster assembly on leading brake shoe, then install trailing brake shoe on park brake actuator lever and park brake actuator strut.
38. Position trailing brake shoe on brake support plate.
39. Install trailing brake shoe hold down, pin and spring onto brake support plate.
40. Install upper brake shoe to brake shoe return spring.
41. Install tension clip attaching upper return spring to automatic adjuster. **When install tension clip on automatic adjuster, clip must be located on threaded area of adjuster assembly.**
42. Install lower brake shoe to brake shoe return springs.
43. Install automatic adjuster lever on leading brake shoe.
44. Install actuating spring on automatic adjuster lever and leading brake shoe.
45. Verify automatic adjuster lever has positive contact with star wheel on automatic adjuster assembly.
46. Remove locking pliers from front park brake cable.
47. Install brake drum, then the tire and wheel assembly.
48. Adjust brakes as outlined under "Adjustments."

DRUM BRAKE SPECIFICATIONS

Model	Year	Brake Lining Wear Limit, Inch②	Brake Drum Inside Diameter, Inches			Drum Runout Limit, Inch	Drum Maximum Out Of Roundness, Inch
			Nominal	Maximum Refinish	Maximum Inside Diameter (Discard Limit)①		
B1500	2002–03	③	11.030	11.090	—	.008	.007
B2500	2002–03	③	12.125	12.185	—	.008	.007
B3500	2002	③	12.125	12.185	—	.006	.007
Caravan, Town & Country & Voyager	2002–06	③	9.842	9.874	9.904	.006	—
Dakota HD Brake	2002	③	11.000	11.060	11.090	.008	—
Dakota Standard Brake	2002	③	9.000	9.060	9.090	.008	—
	2003–06	③	11.000	①	①	.008	—
Durango	2002	①	11.000	11.060	11.090	.008	—
	2003	③	8.110	①	①	.005	—
PT Cruiser	2002–03	③	8.661	8.691	8.705	.006	—
	2004–06	③	—	—	9.079	.005	—

HD — Heavy Duty

① — Maximum brake drum inside diameter (discard limit) is stamped on drum.

② — Above rivet head or shoe. Original equipment type brake linings.

③ — Wear limit, riveted lining, 1/32 inch above rivet head; bonded lining, 1/16 inch lining thickness.

TIGHTENING SPECIFICATIONS

Year	Component	Torque Ft. Lbs.
CARAVAN, TOWN & COUNTRY & VOYAGER		
2002–06	ABS Cab To HCU Mounting Screws	17①
	ABS ICU Mounting Bracket To Cradle Bolts	21
	ABS ICU Mounting Bolts To Bracket	97①
	Anti-Lock Speed Sensor Attaching Bolt	105–108①
	Bleeder Screw	84①
	Booster Mounting	21
	Brake Hose Intermediate Bracket Bolt	105①
	Brake Hose To Caliper Mounting Bolt	35
	Brake Line Fittings	12
	Brake Tube Nuts	145①
	Disc Brake Caliper Bleeder Screw	125①
	Disc Brake Caliper Guide Pin Bolts	26

Continued

TIGHTENING SPECIFICATIONS—Continued

Year	Component	Torque Ft. Lbs.
CARAVAN, TOWN & COUNTRY & VOYAGER		
2002–06	Drum Brake Support Plate Mounting Bolts	95
	Drum Brake Wheel Cylinder Mounting Bleeder Screw	80①
	Drum Brake Wheel Cylinder Mounting Bolts	75①
	Junction Block (Non ABS Brakes) Mounting Bolts	21
	Master Cylinder Mounting	21
	Parking Brake Lever (Pedal) Mounting Bolts and Nuts	21
	Power Brake Booster Mounting Nuts	21
	Proportioning Valve Axle Bracket Mounting Bolt	175①
	Proportioning Valve Mounting Bolts	40
	Support Plate To Rear Axle	95
	Wheel Cylinder To Support Plate	72①
	Wheel Lug Nuts	100
DAKOTA & 2002–03 DURANGO		
2002–06	Booster Mounting Nuts	21
	Brake Line To Control Valves	14
	Brake Line To Flexible Hoses	14
	Brake Line To Master Cylinder	14
	Brake Line To Wheel Cylinders	12
	Master Cylinder Mounting Nuts	90①
	Support Plate Mounting Bolt/Nut	55
	Wheel Cylinder Attaching Screw ¼ -20	11
	Wheel Cylinder Attaching Screw 5/16 -18	16
	Wheel Lug Nuts	85–117
FULL SIZE PICKUP		
2002	Brake Line Fittings	14–17
	Rear Caliper Slide Pins	24
	Support Plate To Axle Bolt	35–50
	Wheel Cylinder Brake Line	115①
	Wheel Cylinder Attaching Screw	15
	Wheel Lug Nut (5 Stud)	80–110
	Wheel Lug Nut (8 Stud w/Dual Wheel)	130–160
	Wheel Lug Nut (8 Stud w/Single Wheel)	120–150
FULL SIZE VAN		
2002–03	Booster Bracket Mounting Nuts	20–40
	Booster Mounting Nuts (In-Line Booster)	18
	Booster Mounting Nuts (Transverse Booster)	30
	Brake Line Nuts, 3/8 Or 7/16 Inch	21
	Brake Line Nuts, ½ Or 9/16 Inch	18
	Drum Support Plate Mounting Nuts	②
	Wheel Cylinder Nuts	15
	Wheel Lug Nuts ½ Inch	80–110
	Wheel Lug Nuts 5/8 Inch (Coned)	175–225
	Wheel Lug Nut 5/8 Inch (Flanged)	300–350

① — Inch lbs.
② — B-150 & B-250 3/8 inch nut, 40 ft. lbs.; B-350 single wheel 7/16 inch nut, 60 ft. lbs.; B-350 dual wheel 1/2 inch nut, 85 ft. lbs.

Jeep

INDEX

PRECAUTIONS

When working on or around brake assemblies, care must be taken to prevent breathing asbestos dust, as many manufacturers incorporate asbestos fibers in the production of brake linings. During routine service operations, the amount of asbestos dust from brake lining wear is at a low level due to a chemical breakdown during use, and a few precautions will minimize exposure. **Do not sand or grind brake linings unless suitable local exhaust ventilation equipment is used to prevent excessive asbestos exposure.**

1. Wear a suitable respirator approved for asbestos dust use during all repair procedures.
2. When cleaning brake dust from brake components, use a vacuum cleaner with a highly efficient filter system. If a suitable vacuum cleaner is not available, use a water soaked rag. **Do not use compressed air or dry brush to clean brake components.**
3. Keep work area clean, using same equipment as for cleaning brake components.
4. Properly dispose of rags and vacuum cleaner bags by placing them in plastic bags.

BRAKE SERVICE

Prior to removing brake shoes it is recommended that a suitable clip or restraining device be applied to the wheel cylinders to prevent the wheel cylinder pistons from being pushed out of their bores.

Brake Shoe Removal

1. Raise and support vehicle.
2. Remove wheel and tire assemblies, then the brake drums.
3. Remove U-clip and washer from parking brake lever pivot pin, **Figs. 1 and 2**, then discard clip.
4. Remove primary and secondary return springs.
5. Remove spring retainers, hold-down springs, and retaining pins.
6. Install suitable clamps over ends of wheel cylinders to hold pistons in place.
7. Remove adjuster lever, adjuster screw, and spring from brake shoes.
8. Remove brake shoes.

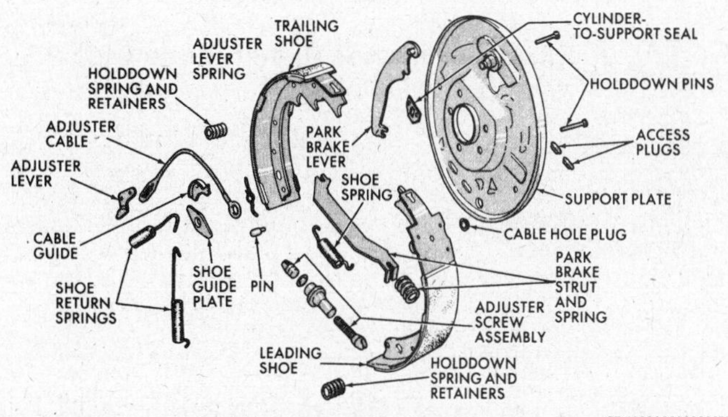

Fig. 1 Exploded view of 9 inch drum brake assembly

Brake Shoe Installation

1. Lubricate support plate ledges, anchor pins, adjuster cable guides, adjuster screw and pivot, and parking brake lever and lever pivot pin.
2. Attach parking brake lever to secondary brake shoe and secure with washer and new U-clip.
3. Remove clamps from wheel cylinders.
4. Install brake shoes and secure with hold-down springs, pins and retainers.
5. Install parking brake lever strut and spring.
6. Install guide plate and adjuster cable on anchor pin.
7. Install primary and secondary return springs with cable guide.
8. Install adjuster screw, spring, and lever, then connect adjuster cable at adjuster lever.
9. Install drums.
10. If any hydraulic lines were opened, bleed brake system and adjust brakes.
11. Install wheel and tire assemblies, and lower vehicle.
12. Inspect master cylinder fluid level, filling as required.
13. Inspect brake pedal for proper feel and return, then road test vehicle.

ADJUSTMENTS

Service Brakes

1. Raise and support vehicle.
2. Remove access slot cover at rear of brake support plate.
3. Rotate adjuster star wheel while turning wheel and tire until brake locks using a suitable brake adjustment tool.
4. Insert a suitable thin tool through adjustment hole and disengage automatic adjuster arm from star wheel, then back off screw approximately one turn.
5. Install access slot cover, then lower vehicle and inspect for proper brake operation.
6. Drive vehicle in Reverse, make 10–15 firm brake applications with one forward stop between each reverse application to equalize adjustment.

Parking Brake

GRAND CHEROKEE

Brakes must be properly adjusted before adjusting parking brake mechanism.

1. Fully apply and release parking brake lever approximately five times.
2. Pull parking brake lever up to 5th click, then raise and support vehicle.
3. Loosen equalizer locknut, then install parking brake adjustment gauge tool No. J-34651, or equivalent, onto an inch pound torque wrench.
4. Position adjustment gauge on one rear cable, then apply and hold **torque** of 45–50 inch lbs., on adjustment gauge. Note position of gauge pointer.
5. If adjustment gauge pointer is not in OK band, turn equalizer locknut in or out until pointer is within OK band.
6. Remove tools and lower vehicle.
7. Apply and release parking brakes four or five times, then inspect adjustment again. Readjust cable if drag is noted.

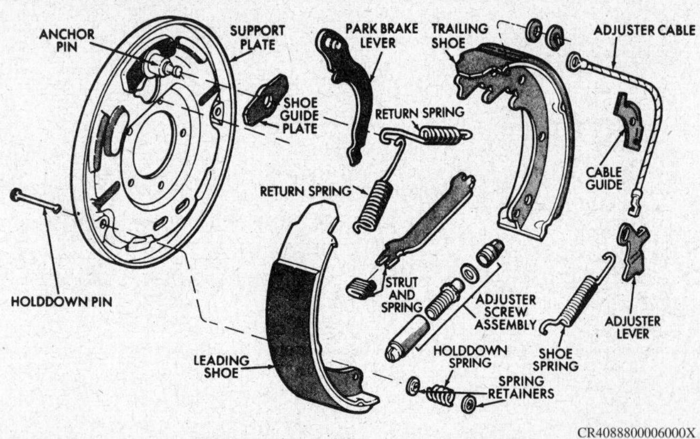

Fig. 2 Exploded view of 10 inch drum brake assembly

WRANGLER

Brakes must be properly adjusted before adjusting parking brake mechanism.

1. Raise and support vehicle.
2. Back off tensioner nuts to create slack in cables.
3. Remove wheels and drums and inspect rear brakes for excessive wear.
4. Ensure parking brake cables operate freely and are not binding or seized.
5. Install wheels and drums and lower vehicle enough to allow access to parking brake lever.

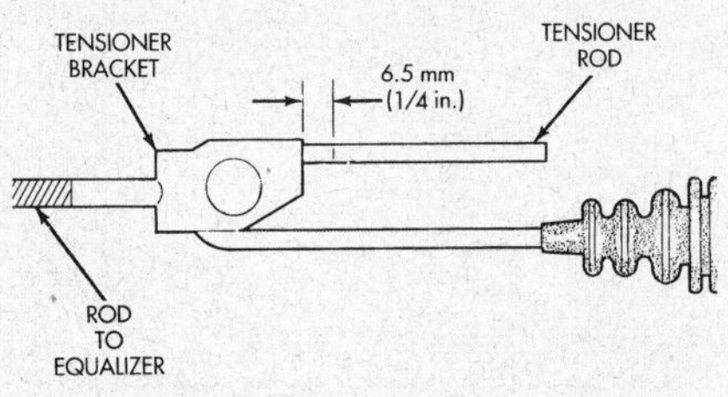

Fig. 3 Tensioner rod measurement. Wrangler

6. Fully apply parking brake, leave brakes applied until adjustment procedure is complete.
7. Raise vehicle and mark tensioner rod 1/4 inch from tensioner bracket, **Fig. 3.**
8. Tighten adjusting nut at equalizer until mark on tensioner rod moves into alignment with tensioner bracket.
9. Lower vehicle until rear wheels are 6–8 inches off floor.
10. Release parking brakes and ensure rear wheels rotate freely without drag.
11. Lower vehicle.

DRUM BRAKE SPECIFICATIONS

Model	Year	Brake Lining Wear Limit, Inch②	Brake Drum Inside Diameter, Inches			Drum Runout Limit, Inch	Drum Maximum Out Of Roundness, Inch
			Nominal	Maximum Refinish	Maximum Inside Diameter (Discard Limit)①		
Liberty 9" Drum Brake	2002–06	③	9.00	9.06	—	.008	.003
Liberty 10" Drum Brake	2002–06	③	10.00	10.06	—	.008	—
Wrangler	2002–06	③	9.00	9.06	—	.008	.007

HD — Heavy Duty
① — Maximum brake drum inside diameter (discard limit) is stamped on drum.
② — Above rivet head or shoe. Original equipment type brake linings.
③ — Wear limit, riveted lining, 1/32 inch above rivet head; bonded lining, 1/16 inch lining thickness.

TIGHTENING SPECIFICATIONS

Year	Component	Torque Ft. Lbs.
2002–06	Booster Mounting	29
	Brake Line To Combination Valve Fitting	15
	Brake Line To Master Cylinder Fitting	11
	Brake Line To Wheel Cylinder Fitting	12
	Master Cylinder Mounting	18
	Support Plate Bolts/Nuts	21
	Wheel Cylinder Mounting	84①
	Wheel Lug Nuts	90

① — Inch lbs.

HYDRAULIC BRAKE SYSTEMS

INDEX

DESCRIPTION

Master Cylinder

EXCEPT CARAVAN, TOWN & COUNTRY & VOYAGER

The cylinder body containing the primary and secondary pistons is made of aluminum. The removable fluid reservoir is made of nylon reinforced with glass fiber. The reservoir is the only serviceable component.

The fluid compartments of the nylon reservoir are interconnected to permit fluid level equalization. The equalization feature does not affect circuit separation in the event of a front or rear brake fault. The reservoir compartments will retain enough fluid to operate the functioning hydraulic circuit.

CARAVAN, TOWN & COUNTRY & VOYAGER

The body of the master cylinder is cast anodized aluminum. It has a machined bore to accept pistons and threaded ports with seats for brake line connections. The brake fluid reservoir is made of a see-through polypropylene type plastic. A low fluid switch is also part of the reservoir assembly.

These models use three different master cylinders. On models not equipped with traction control or four wheel disc brakes, a conventional compensating port master cylinder is used. If the vehicle is equipped with traction control, a dual center port master cylinder is used. On models equipped with four wheel disc brakes, the master cylinder has a different bore diameter and stroke then the master cylinder used for other applications.

The master cylinder primary outlet port supplies hydraulic pressure to the righthand front and lefthand rear brakes. The secondary outlet port supplies hydraulic pressure to the lefthand front and righthand rear brakes.

The master cylinder is not a repairable component and must be replaced if a fault occurs.

Hydraulic Control Valves

COMBINATION VALVE

Some models use a combination valve, which consists of a one-piece housing that contains a rear brake proportioning valve section and a pressure differential valve and switch. The proportioning section of the valve provides balanced front to rear braking action during high pressure pedal stops. When brakes are applied, the valve modulates hydraulic system pressure to the rear brakes to balance operation and prevent excessive rear brake action.

The pressure differential valve section activates the brake warning lamp whenever a pressure loss occurs in front or rear brakes.

METERING VALVE

The metering valve is used to balance braking action between the front and rear brakes. The valve meters full apply pressure to the front disc brakes until the rear brake shoes are in full contact with drums.

FIXED PROPORTIONING VALVE

The fixed proportioning valve is made out of aluminum and has an integral mounting bracket. The fixed proportioning valve is non-serviceable component and must be replaced as an assembly.

The valve operates by allowing full hydraulic pressure to rear brakes up to a set point called the valves "split point." Beyond this "split point" the proportioning valve reduces the amount of hydraulic pressure to the rear brakes according to a certain ratio.

On light brake applications the valve allows approximately equal brake hydraulic brake pressure to be supplied to both front and rear brakes. On heavier brake pedal applications the valve will control hydraulic pressure to the rear brakes so that pressure at rear brakes will be lower than that at the front brakes. This controlled pressure to rear brakes prevents excessive rear wheel ABS cycling during moderate stops.

HEIGHT SENSING PROPORTIONING VALVE

Models not equipped with anti-lock brakes (ABS) use a height sensing proportioning valve. The valve uses an actuator assembly to attach the valve to the lefthand rear spring for sensing vehicle height.

The valve regulates hydraulic pressure to the rear brakes by sensing the load condition of the vehicle through the movement of the valve actuator assembly. The actuator assembly is mounted between the valve and actuator bracket on the lefthand rear leaf spring. As the rear height of the vehicle changes due to the load it is carrying, the height change is transferred through the movement of the lefthand rear leaf spring. As the spring changes position this movement is transferred through the actuator bracket to the actuator assembly and then to the valve. Under a light load condition, hydraulic pressure to the rear brakes is minimized. As the load condition of the vehicle increases, so does the hydraulic pressure to the rear brakes.

DIAGNOSIS & TESTING

Master Cylinder/ Power Booster Test

1. Start engine and inspect booster vacuum hose connections for leaks.
2. Stop engine and shift transmission into neutral.
3. Pump brake pedal until all vacuum reserve in booster is depleted.
4. Press and hold brake pedal under light foot pressure. Pedal should hold firm. If it falls away master cylinder is faulty.
5. Start engine and note pedal action.

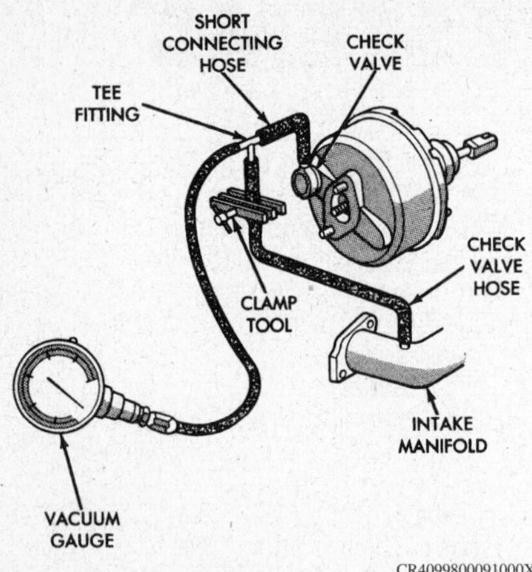

Fig. 1 Vacuum booster test connections

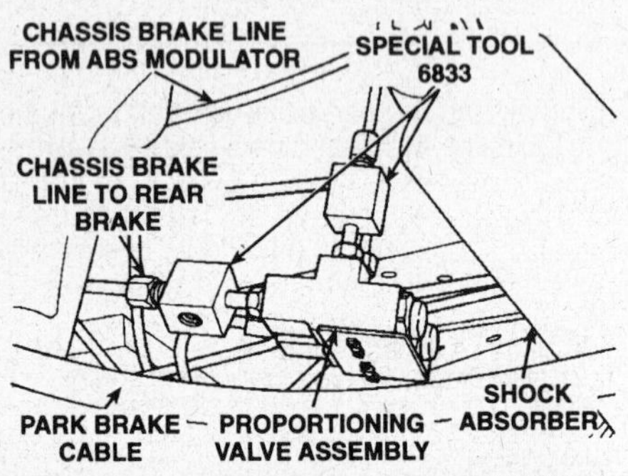

Fig. 4 Fixed proportioning valve test fitting installation. Caravan, Town & Country & Voyager

Pedal should fall away slightly under light foot pressure, then hold firm.

6. If no pedal action is felt, the power booster, vacuum supply or vacuum check valve are faulty. Proceed to "Power Booster Vacuum Test."
7. If pedal operates as specified, restore booster vacuum reserve as follows:
   a. Release brake pedal.
   b. Increase engine speed to 1500 RPM, close throttle and turn off ignition.
   c. Wait a minimum of 90 seconds and try brake action again.
   d. Booster should provide two or more vacuum assisted pedal applications. If vacuum assist is not provided, booster is faulty.

Power Booster Vacuum Test

1. Connect vacuum gauge to booster check valve with short length of hose and a T-fitting, **Fig. 1.**
2. Start and run engine at curb idle speed for one minute.
3. Observe vacuum. If vacuum supply is inadequate, inspect hoses and connections for leaks.
4. If vacuum supply is adequate, clamp hose shut between vacuum source and check valve.

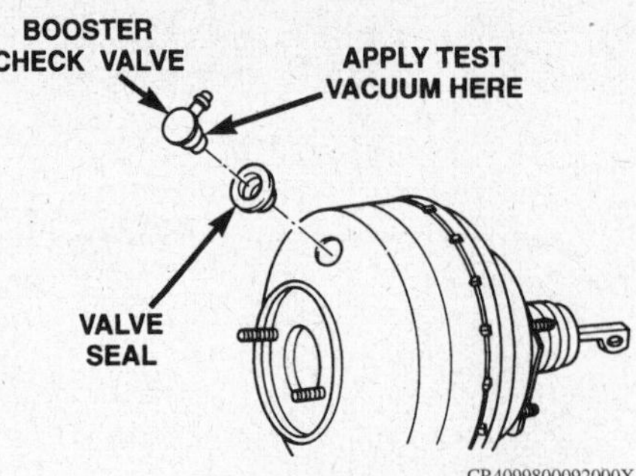

Fig. 2 Vacuum check valve & seal location

5. Stop engine and observe vacuum gauge.
6. If vacuum drops more than one inch within 15 seconds, booster diaphragm or check valve are faulty.

Power Booster Check Valve Test

1. Disconnect vacuum hose from check valve.
2. Remove check valve and valve seal from booster.
3. Apply 15–20 inches vacuum at large end of check valve, **Fig. 2.**
4. If vacuum holds steady. check valve is satisfactory.
5. If vacuum does not hold steady, check valve is faulty and should be replaced.

Combination Valve Test

PRESSURE DIFFERENTIAL SWITCH

1. Apply brake pedal and observe red brake warning light.
2. Raise and support vehicle.
3. Connect bleed hose to a rear wheel cylinder and immerse hose end in container partially filled with brake fluid.
4. Press and hold brake pedal to floor and observe brake warning lamp. If warning lamp lights, switch is operating properly. If lamp does not light, proceed as follows:
   a. Apply parking brake. If lamp does not light, inspect parking brake switch, circuit fuse, bulb and wiring. Repair or replace components as required, then test system again.
   b. If lamp still does not light, switch is faulty. Replace combination valve assembly, then bleed brake system.

Fixed Proportioning Valve Test

CARAVAN, TOWN & COUNTRY & VOYAGER

On models equipped with ABS, premature or excessive rear wheel ABS cycling

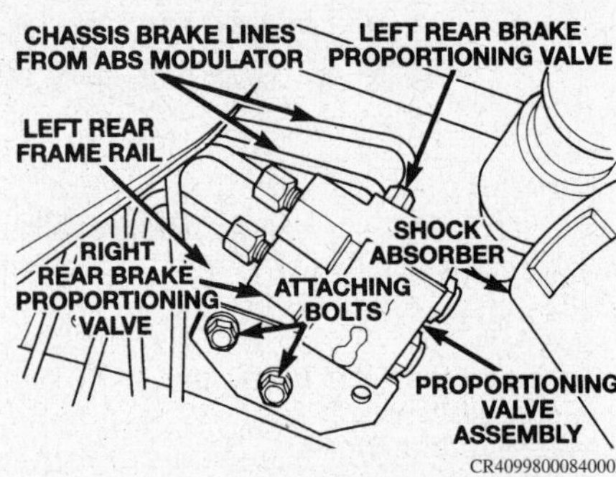

Fig. 3 Fixed proportioning valve & brake line locations. Caravan, Town & Country & Voyager

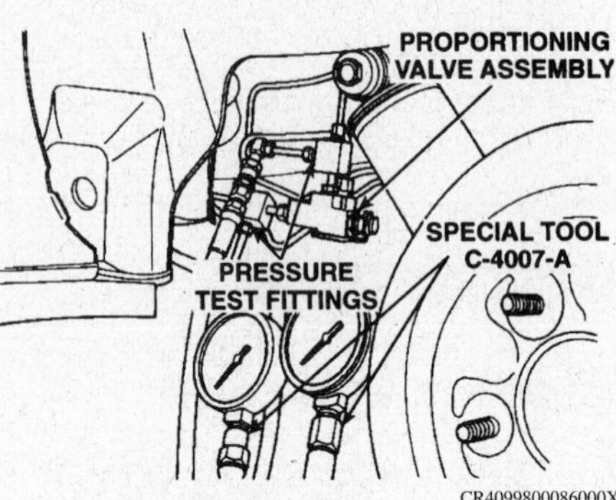

Fig. 5 Pressure gauge installation. Caravan, Town & Country & Voyager

may be an indication that brake fluid pressure to the rear brakes is above desired output.

Prior to testing proportioning valve for function, ensure all tire pressures meet specifications and front and rear brake linings are in satisfactory condition. Since ABS cycles both rear brakes together, both proportioning valves of assembly must be tested.

1. Remove one brake line coming from ABS modulator at proportioning valve assembly, **Fig. 3.**
2. Disconnect brake line for one of the rear wheels from the proportioning valve.
3. Remove valve to frame rail retaining bolts.
4. Lower the valve, then install fitting from pressure test fittings tool No. 6833, or equivalent, into inlet port of valve assembly, **Fig. 4.**
5. Install removed brake line into pressure test fitting.
6. Install fitting from pressure test fittings tool No. 6833, or equivalent, into outlet ports of valve.
7. Install removed brake line into test fitting.
8. Install pressure gauge from gauge set tool No. C-4007-A, or equivalent, into each pressure test fitting, **Fig. 5.**
9. Bleed air out of hose from test fittings to pressure gauges, at pressure gauge.
10. Bleed air out of brake line being tested, at rear wheel cylinder.
11. With aid of an assistant, apply pressure to brake pedal until a pressure of

WHEEL BASE	DRIVE TRAIN	SALES CODE	BRAKE SYSTEM	SPLIT POINT	SLOPE	INLET PRESSURE PSI	OUTLET PRESSURE PSI
SWB	FWD	BRB-BGF	15" DISC/DRUM W/O ANTILOCK	VAR.	.59	1000 PSI	675-875 PSI

CR4090100111000X

Fig. 6 Proportioning valve pressure specifications. Caravan, Town & Country & Voyager

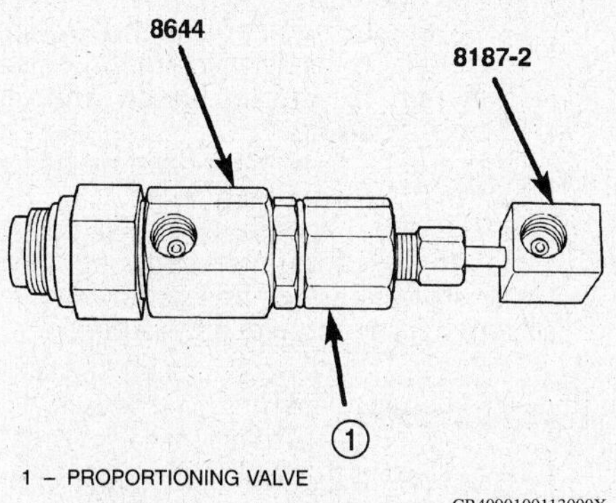

Fig. 8 Pressure adapters installed onto proportioning valve. PT Cruiser

1000 psi is obtained on valve inlet gauge.

12. Compare pressure reading on outlet gauge to specifications listed in **Fig. 6.** If outlet pressure at valve is not within specifications when required inlet pressure is obtained, replace valve.

PT CRUISER

Proportioning valves will only be found on models without anti-lock brakes (ABS). Models equipped with ABS have electronic brake distribution built into the Integrated Control Unit (ICU).

Ensure all tire pressures meet specifications and front and rear brake linings are in satisfactory condition before testing the proportioning valve.

Drive vehicle on a road test through a safe area. Apply the brakes and determine which wheel is skidding first, then proceed as follows:

1. Depress brake pedal past its first inch of travel, then hold in this position using a suitable brake pedal holding tool.
2. Disconnect brake fluid line from proportioning valve, **Fig. 7.**
3. Remove proportioning valve from master cylinder outlet port.
4. Install pressure adapters tool No. 8644 and 8187-2, or equivalent, onto proportioning valve, **Fig. 8.** Ensure pressure test fittings include proper required sizes.
5. Install proportioning valve with adapters into master cylinder outlet port.
6. Connect pressure gauge tool No. C-4007-A, **Fig. 9,** or equivalent, to each adapter.
7. Remove brake pedal holding tool, then bleed any air out of pressure gauge hoses at gauge.
8. Find an assistant to apply pressure on brake pedal until reading on proportioning valve inlet gauge is at target inlet pressure listed in **Fig. 10.**
9. If inlet gauge pressure is over target pressure when brake pedal is depressed, release brake pedal before applying it again. This is required in order to get an accurate reading.
10. After inlet pressure has been reached, measure pressure reading on the proportioning valve outlet gauge.
11. If outlet valve pressure disagrees with specifications in **Fig. 10,** replace that proportioning valve.
12. If outlet pressure is within specifications, that valve is operating properly.
13. Install brake pedal holding tool as before, then remove all test equipment from vehicle.
14. Remove test tools from proportioning valve.
15. Install proportioning valve into master cylinder and hand tighten until its O-ring is fully seated. **Torque** to 30 ft. lbs.
16. Install brake fluid line into proportioning valve. Tighten nut to specifications listed in **Fig. 11.**
17. Bleed affected brake lines as outlined under "Brake System Bleed."

Height Sensing Proportioning Valve Test

Prior to testing proportioning valve for function, ensure all tire pressures meet specifications and front and rear brake linings are in satisfactory condition. If both front and rear brakes are satisfactory, ensure actuator assembly for valve is properly adjusted. If valve is adjusted properly, proceed with test procedure.

1. Remove brake fluid line leading to suspected rear brake from junction block at proportioning valve.
2. Disconnect brake lines from front and rear of valve, **Fig. 12.**
3. Install fitting from pressure test fittings tool No. 6833, or equivalent, into inlet and outlet ports of valve assembly, **Fig. 13.**
4. Install removed brake lines into test fittings.
5. Install pressure gauge from gauge set tool No. C-4007-A, or equivalent, into each pressure test fitting, **Fig. 14.**
6. Bleed air out of hose from test fittings to pressure gauges at pressure gauge.
7. Bleed air out of brake line being tested at rear wheel cylinder.
8. Remove proportioning valve actuator lever bracket to rear axle screw, then raise lever to full upward position.
9. With aid of an assistant, apply pressure to brake pedal until a pressure of

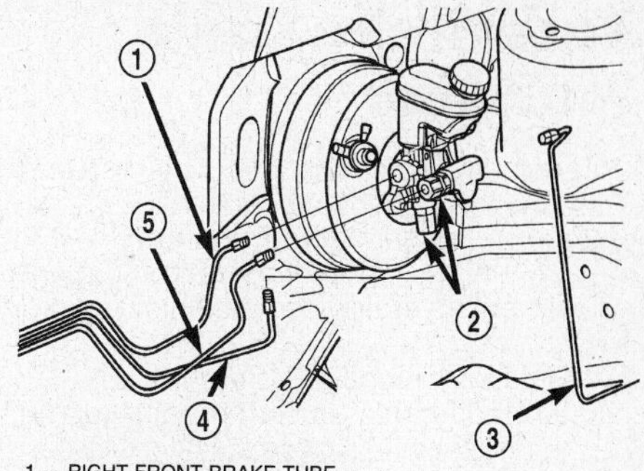

Fig. 7 Proportioning valves. PT Cruiser

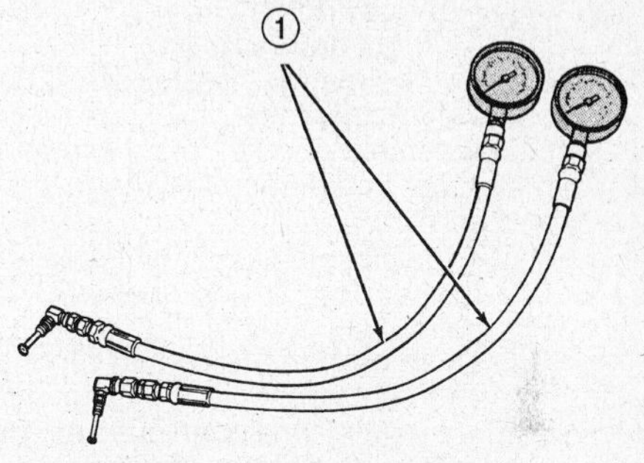

Fig. 9 Pressure gauge tool No. C-4007-A. PT Cruiser

1000 psi is obtained on valve inlet gauge.

10. The proportioning valve is not adjustable. Do not attempt to make adjustments.
11. Bleed both rear hydraulic circuits at rear brakes as outlined under "Brake System Bleed."

ADJUSTMENTS

Height Sensing Proportioning Valve

On these models the proportioning valve is not adjustable. Do not attempt to make adjustments.

Stop Lamp Switch

1. Push and hold brake pedal in applied position.
2. Push switch forward until fully seated against bracket.
3. Release brake pedal.
4. Lightly pull brake pedal rearward until master cylinder pushrod bottoms against master cylinder internal stop. This action will set switch plunger at proper stroke length.

Park Brake Cable Tensioner

Tensioner adjustment is only required when the tensioner, or a cable has been replaced or disconnected for service. To avoid faulty park brake operation, perform adjustment as outlined in the following procedure:

1. Raise and support vehicle.
2. Back off cable tensioner adjusting nut at equalizer to create slack in cables.
3. Remove rear wheel and tire assemblies, then the brake drums.
4. Ensure brakes are in good condition and operating properly.
5. Ensure park brake cables operate freely and are not binding or seized.
6. Inspect rear brake shoe adjustment with a standard brake gauge.
7. Install drums and ensure drums rotate freely without drag.
8. Install wheel and tire assemblies after brake shoe adjustment is complete.
9. Lower vehicle enough to access park brake foot pedal, then fully apply park brakes.
10. Raise vehicle, then mark tensioner rod ¼ inch from edge of tensioner bracket, **Fig. 15.**
11. Tighten adjusting nut at equalizer until mark on tensioner rod moves into alignment with tensioner bracket. **Do not loosen or tighten tensioner adjusting nut for any reason after completing adjustment.**
12. Lower vehicle until rear wheels are six to eight inches off floor.
13. Release park brake foot pedal and ensure rear wheels rotate freely without drag.

COMPONENT REPLACEMENT

Master Cylinder

EXCEPT CARAVAN, TOWN & COUNTRY & VOYAGER

1. With engine off, pump brake pedal five times to deplete vacuum in brake booster.
2. Siphon fluid from brake reservoir.
3. **On Wrangler models,** remove evaporative canister.
4. **On PT Cruiser models,** remove air cleaner housing, then disconnect power distribution center and position aside.
5. **On all models,** disconnect low fluid switch electrical connector.
6. Remove brake lines from master cylinder.
7. Remove master cylinder mounting nuts.
8. **On Durango models with ESP,** remove inner fender well, then remove integrated power module (IPM) fasteners and move IPM to allow clearance to remove master cylinder.
9. **On all models,** remove master cylinder.
10. Reverse procedure to install. **NEW master cylinder should be bled before installing.**

Sales Code	Brake System Type	Split Point	Slope	Identification	Inlet Pressure	Outlet Pressure
BRB	15" Disc/Drum	400 psi	0.34	Black Band	1000 psi	600-700 psi

CR4090100114000X

Fig. 10 Brake proportioning valve applications & pressure specifications. PT Cruiser

CARAVAN, TOWN & COUNTRY & VOYAGER

1. With engine stopped, pump brake pedal four or five times to deplete vacuum in power booster.
2. Remove battery.
3. Thoroughly clean all surfaces of filler neck, brake fluid reservoir and area where master cylinder assembly attaches to booster using Mopar Brake Parts Cleaner, or an equivalent solvent.
4. Remove vehicle wiring harness connector from brake fluid level sensor in master cylinder fluid reservoir.
5. Disconnect primary and secondary brake tubes from master cylinder housing. Install suitable sealing plugs in open outlets on master cylinder assembly.
6. Remove master cylinder from vacuum booster.
7. Remove vacuum seal from master cylinder mounting flange by carefully pulling it off rear of master cylinder. **Do not use any sharp tools.**
8. Reverse procedure to install, noting the following:
   a. Install new vacuum seal when mounting master cylinder.
   b. **Torque** master cylinder mounting nuts to 19 ft. lbs.
   c. **Torque** brake fluid tube nuts to 12 ft. lbs.

BRAKE SYSTEM BLEED

Manual

1. Remove reservoir filler caps and fill reservoir with proper brake fluid.
2. If calipers or wheel cylinders were overhauled, open all caliper and wheel cylinder bleed screws.
3. Close each bleed screw as fluid starts to drip from them.
4. Fill master cylinder reservoir once more before proceeding.
5. Attach one end of bleed hose to bleed screw and insert opposite end in glass container partially filled with brake fluid, **Fig. 16. Ensure bleed hose is immersed in fluid.**
6. Open up bleeder, then have an assistant press down brake pedal.
7. Once brake pedal is down, close bleeder. Repeat bleeding until fluid stream is clear and free of bubbles.
8. Repeat procedure at each wheel.

Pressure

Follow manufacturers instructions carefully when using pressure equipment. Do not exceed the tank manufacturer's pressure recommendations. A tank pressure of 15–20 psi is sufficient for bleeding.

Do not pressure bleed without a proper master cylinder adapter. The improper adapter can lead to leakage or air being draw back into the system.

1. Remove filler neck from master cylinder reservoir.
2. Install appropriate adapter from adapter master cylinder pressure bleed cap tool No. 6921, or equivalent.
3. Attach fluid hose from pressure bleeder to fitting on adapter.
4. Attach a clear plastic hose to bleeder screw at one wheel and feed hose into a clear jar containing fresh brake fluid.
5. Open lefthand rear wheel bleeder screw at least one full turn or more.
6. After four to eight ounces of fluid have been bled through system and an air-free flow is maintained in hose and jar, a good system bleeding has been obtained.
7. Repeat procedures to remaining bleeder screws. Ensure pressure bleeder stays at a proper level so air will not enter system.

Master Cylinder

A new master cylinder should be bled before installation on vehicle.

1. Mount master cylinder in suitable vise.
2. Attach bleed tubes to cylinder outlet ports, then position each tube end into reservoir, **Fig. 17.**
3. Fill reservoir with fresh brake fluid.
4. Press cylinder pistons inward with a wooden dowel, then release pistons and allow them to return.

Model	Mounting Nuts, Ft. Lbs.	Fluid Line Nuts, Ft. Lbs.
Commander	18	17
Dakota & Durango	13	14
Full Size Pickup	17	16
Full Size Van	15	12
Grand Cherokee	18	12
Liberty	18	15
Pacifica	19	10
PT Cruiser	13	12
Sprinter	21	10
Wrangler	14	14

Fig. 11 Master cylinder tightening specifications. Except Caravan, Town & Country & Voyager

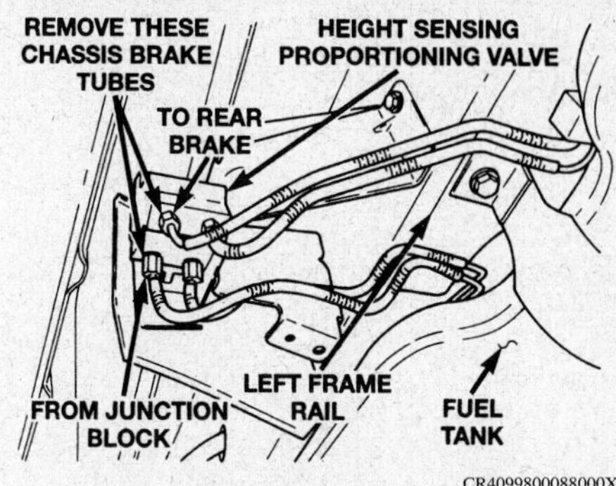

Fig. 12 Brake line connection to proportioning valve. Height sensing proportioning valve

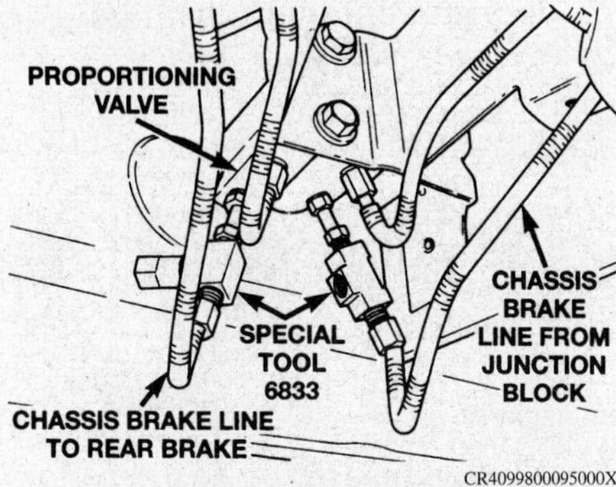

Fig. 13 Test fitting installation. Height sensing proportioning valve

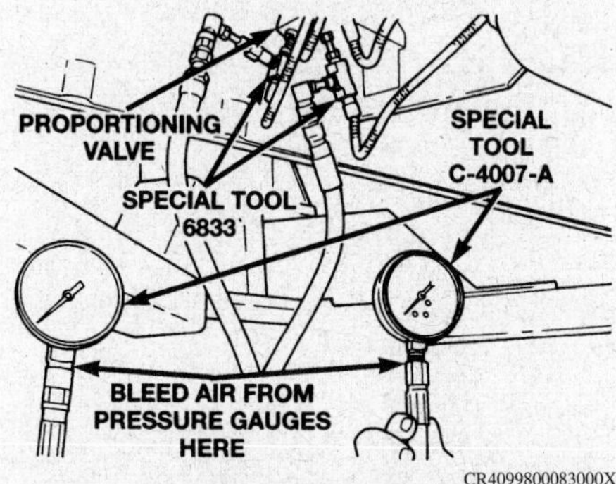

Fig. 14 Pressure gauge installed on test fittings. Height sensing proportioning valve

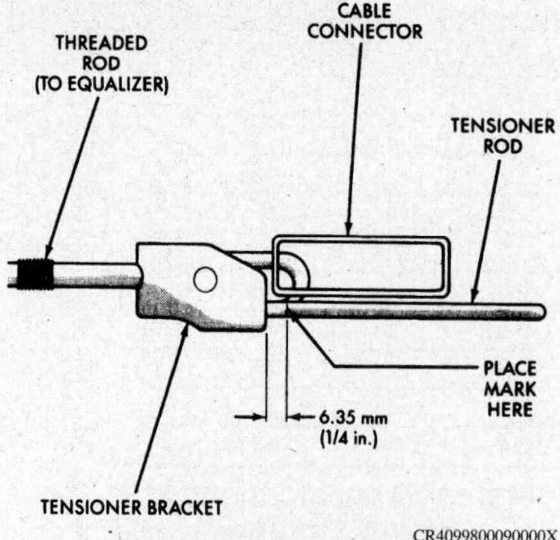

Fig. 15 Cable tensioner adjustment mark location

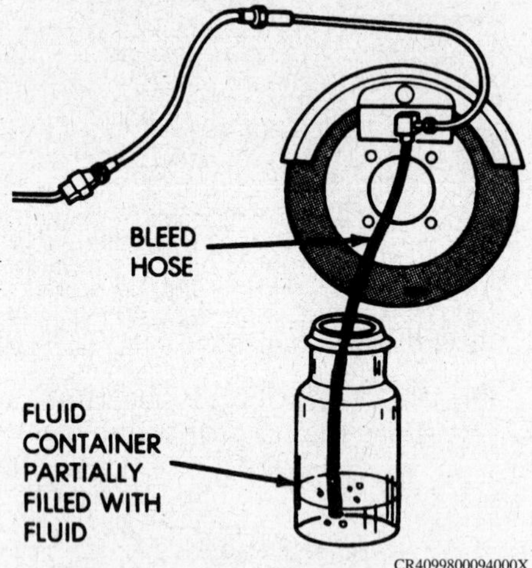

Fig. 16 Bleed hose setup

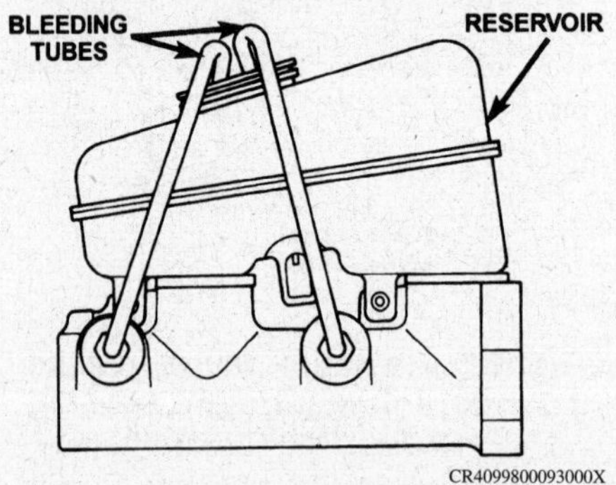

Fig. 17 Master cylinder bleeding

POWER BRAKE UNITS

INDEX

DESCRIPTION

These self contained vacuum hydraulic power braking units are of the vacuum suspended type. They use engine intake manifold vacuum or a vacuum pump along with atmospheric pressure for their power, eliminating the need for a vacuum reservoir. A mechanically operated control valve, with integral vacuum power diaphragms, controls the degree of brake application or release depending on amount of foot pressure applied to the valve operating rod through the brake pedal linkage.

The control valve is a single poppet type valve with an atmospheric and vacuum port. The vacuum port seal is a part of the valve body attached to the diaphragm assembly. The atmospheric port is a part of the valve plunger which moves within the valve housing and vacuum power diaphragm assembly.

These units require no maintenance and must be replaced as a complete assembly.

POWER BRAKE UNIT SERVICE

The only serviceable power brake booster components are the vacuum hose and the check valve. **The power brake booster must be serviced as an assembly. If diagnosis indicates a power brake booster fault condition, the unit must be replaced as an assembly.**

Replacement

CARAVAN, TOWN & COUNTRY & VOYAGER

1. With engine stopped, pump brake pedal four or five times to deplete power booster vacuum.
2. Disconnect both battery cables, then remove battery thermo guard and battery from tray.
3. Remove air inlet resonator and hoses as an assembly from throttle body and air cleaner housing.
4. Remove coolant filler tube to battery tray mounting bolt.
5. **On models equipped with speed control,** disconnect wiring harness connector from speed control servo, then vacuum lines from servo and vacuum reservoir on battery tray.
6. **On all models,** remove bolt securing speed control servo bracket to battery tray, then slide bracket forward to unhook and separate from battery tray.

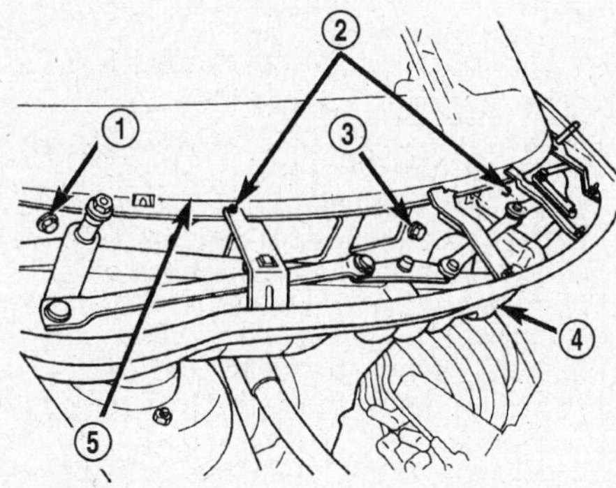

Fig. 1 Front wiper unit removal. Caravan, Town & Country & Voyager

7. Remove battery tray.
8. Remove front wiper unit as follows:
   a. Remove wiper arms.
   b. Remove cowl cover retainers, then the cover.
   c. Disconnect wiper unit electrical connectors.
   d. Disconnect windshield washer hose from connector inside unit.
   e. Disconnect drain tubes from lower side of wiper unit.
   f. Remove wiper unit to lower windshield opening mounting nuts and bolts, **Fig. 1.**
   g. Lift wiper unit off weld studs. **Do not allow wiper unit to sit on master cylinder reservoir.**
9. Remove vehicle wiring harness connector from brake fluid level sensor in master cylinder fluid reservoir.
10. Remove bracket for wiring harness connectors from studs on strut tower.
11. Clean area where master cylinder assembly attaches to booster using Mopar Brake Parts Cleaner, or equivalent solvent.
12. Remove clip attaching drain hose to brake tube at master cylinder, then the drain hose from wiper module.
13. Remove master cylinder from vacuum booster and position aside. **Removing brake tubes from master cylinder when removing master cylinder from vacuum booster is not required.**
14. Discard seal between master cylinder and booster.
15. Disconnect vacuum hose from booster check valve. **Do not remove check valve from booster.**
16. Working under instrument panel inside vehicle, locate vacuum booster input rod to brake pedal attachment and position a small suitable screwdriver between the center tang on booster input rod to brake pedal pin retaining clip.
17. Rotate screwdriver enough to allow retaining clip center tang to pass over end of brake pedal pin, then pull clip off brake pedal pin. **Discard clip and replace with new one during assembly procedure.**
18. Remove Controller Anti-Lock Brakes (CAB) from vacuum booster mounting studs. Position CAB aside without removing wiring connector.
19. Remove vacuum booster from firewall by removing nuts under instrument panel.
20. Remove and discard brake lamp switch by rotating counterclockwise approximately 30°, then pulling rearward out of mounting bracket. Disconnect electrical connector.
21. Reverse procedure to install, noting the following:
   a. **Torque** vacuum booster mounting nuts to 21 ft. lbs.
   b. Always use new retaining clip to connect brake pedal pin to input rod.
   c. Install new brake lamp switch in its bracket by aligning switch index tab with bracket slot.
   d. After brake lamp switch has fully seated in bracket, rotate switch approximately 30° clockwise and ensure it locks securely into place.
   e. Ensure brake pedal is in fully released position, then move lever on rear of brake lamp switch from angled non-adjusted position to full vertical position. This will adjust switch to that particular vehicle.
   f. **Torque** CAB mounting bolts to 21 ft. lbs.
   g. **Torque** EGR mounting bolts to 16–17 ft. lbs.
   h. Install new vacuum seal when mounting master cylinder.
   i. **Torque** master cylinder mounting nuts to 19 ft. lbs.
   j. **Torque** wiring harness bracket mounting nuts to 84–96 inch lbs.

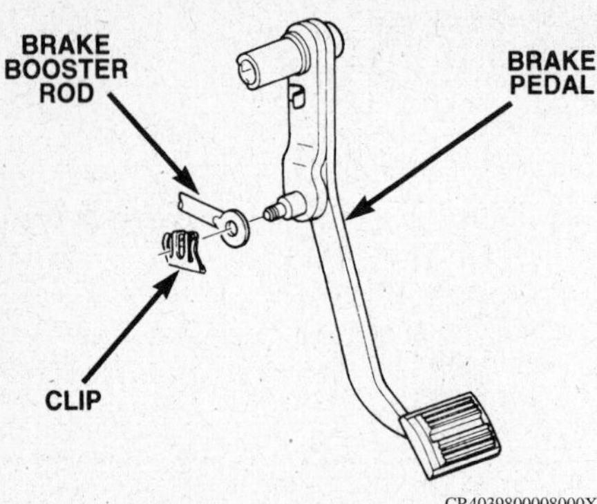

Fig. 2 Booster rod clip removal. Dakota & Durango

k. **Torque** throttle body mounting bolts to 19 ft. lbs.
l. Install front wiper unit, ensuring all hoses and electrical connectors are securely connected.
m. **On all models, torque** battery tray mounting nut and bolts to 10–11 ft. lbs.

COMMANDER

REMOVAL

1. Drain master cylinder using suitable suction tool.
2. Remove primary brake line at master cylinder.
3. Remove primary brake line from Hydraulic Control Unit (HCU).
4. Remove secondary brake line at master cylinder.
5. Remove secondary brake line at HCU.
6. Remove 4 chassis lines at HCU.
7. Disconnect HCU electrical connector.
8. Remove three mounting nuts at HCU bracket.
9. Remove HCU with bracket from vehicle.
10. Disconnect brake fluid level sensor electrical connector from fluid reservoir.
11. Remove two master cylinder mounting nuts.
12. Remove master cylinder.
13. Disconnect vacuum hose at booster check valve.
14. Remove driver knee bolster panel.
15. Remove steering column opening cover and lower instrument panel.
16. Remove retainer clip that holds booster push rod on pedal pin, then slide push rod off pin.
17. Disconnect brake lamp switch wire connector.
18. Remove brake lamp switch.
19. Remove booster to dash attaching nuts.
20. In engine compartment, disconnect wire harness routing clips and move harness to side and downward.
21. Remove booster from vehicle.

INSTALLATION

1. Inspect condition of grommet that secures check valve, replace as required.
2. Install new booster dash seal.
3. Align and position booster in mounting holes of dash panel.
4. Inside vehicle, lubricate pedal pin using Mopar multi-milage grease.
5. Install booster nuts to studs and **torque** to 29 ft. lbs.
6. Slide booster push rod on pedal pin, then secure rod to pin with retainer clip.
7. Install new brake lamp switch and connect electrical connector.
8. Install steering column opening panel.
9. Install driver knee bolster panel.
10. In engine compartment, attach vacuum hose to booster check valve.
11. Install master cylinder to power brake booster using new gasket and nuts.
12. Route wire harness back into position and install routing clip.
13. Connect brake fluid level electrical connector.
14. Install HCU with bracket to vehicle and tighten mounting nuts.
15. Connect HCU electrical connector.
16. Install four chassis lines to HCU.
17. Install secondary brake line to HCU.
18. Install secondary brake line to master cylinder.
19. Install primary brake line to HCU.
20. Install primary brake line to master cylinder.
21. Fill and bleed brake system as required.

DAKOTA & DURANGO

1. Remove master cylinder.
2. Disconnect vacuum lines at booster.
3. Remove clip retaining booster pushrod to brake pedal, **Fig. 2.**
4. Remove retaining nuts from booster mounting studs, **Fig. 3.**
5. Remove booster and gasket from front cowl panel.
6. Reverse procedures to install, noting the following:
   a. **Torque** booster retaining nuts to 21 ft. lbs.
   b. **Torque** master cylinder mounting nuts to 13 ft. lbs.
   c. **Torque** brake line fittings to 14 ft. lbs.

FULL SIZE PICKUP

VACUUM BOOSTER

1. With engine stopped, pump brake pedal four or five times to deplete power booster vacuum.
2. Remove brake lines from master cylinder.
3. Remove nuts attaching master cylinder and valves to power brake booster unit studs, then remove master cylinder and valves as an assembly.
4. Disconnect vacuum hose at booster check valve.
5. Remove knee bolster for access to brake pedal, then the clip and washer securing booster pushrod to brake pedal.
6. Slide booster pushrod off of pedal, then remove nuts attaching booster mounting studs to firewall and pedal mounting bracket.
7. Remove booster from engine compartment.

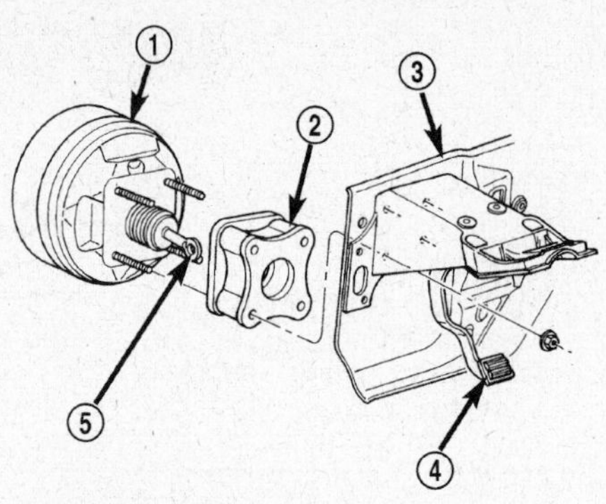

1 - BRAKE BOOSTER
2 - SPACER
3 - FRONT COWL PANEL
4 - BRAKE PEDAL
5 - BRAKE BOOSTER ROD

CR4039700023000X

Fig. 3 Power brake booster removal. Dakota & Durango

8. Reverse procedure to install, noting the following:
   a. **Torque** booster mounting stud nuts and master cylinder mounting nuts to 16–18 ft. lbs.
   b. **Torque** brake line fittings to 12–16 ft. lbs.
   c. Fill and bleed brake system.

HYDRAULIC BOOSTER

The accumulator contains high pressure gas. Do not carry the booster by the accumulator or drop the unit on the accumulator.

1. With engine off depress brake pedal several times to discharge accumulator.
2. Remove brake lines from master cylinder.
3. Remove master cylinder mounting nuts.
4. Remove bracket from hydraulic booster lines and master cylinder mounting studs.
5. Remove master cylinder.
6. Remove return hose and two pressure lines from hydraulic booster.
7. Remove booster pushrod clip, washer and rod from brake pedal.
8. Remove mounting nuts from hydraulic booster, then the booster.
9. Reverse procedure to install, noting the following:
   a. Ensure snap ring holding accumulator in place is properly seated.
   b. **Torque** hydraulic booster mounting nuts to 21 ft. lbs.
   c. **Torque** master cylinder mounting nuts to 21 ft. lbs.
   d. **Torque** hydraulic booster pressure lines to 21 ft. lbs.
   e. Fill and bleed brake system.
   f. Bleed hydraulic booster.

FULL SIZE VAN

TRANSVERSE MOUNT

1. Remove vacuum hoses from power brake booster check valve.
2. Disconnect master cylinder brake lines.
3. Remove shoulder bolt, O-ring and nut

that retains booster pushrod to mounting bracket arm.
4. Remove booster to mounting bracket retaining nuts, **Fig. 4.**
5. Remove booster and master cylinder as an assembly.
6. Remove master cylinder attaching nuts, then the cylinder from booster.
7. Reverse procedures to install, noting following:
   a. **Torque** master cylinder to booster retaining nuts to 15 ft. lbs.
   b. **Torque** booster mounting nuts to 30 ft. lbs.
   c. **Torque** shoulder bolt locknut to 30 ft. lbs.

INLINE MOUNT

1. Remove master cylinder.
2. Remove vacuum hoses from booster check valve.
3. Remove steering column knee bolster for access to brake pedal.
4. Remove clip retaining booster pushrod to brake pedal pin, **Fig. 5.**
5. Remove nuts retaining booster to firewall, then the booster and booster to firewall seal.
6. Reverse procedure to install, noting the following:
   a. **Torque** booster mounting nuts to 18 ft. lbs.
   b. **Torque** master cylinder mounting nuts to 17 ft. lbs.
   c. **Torque** brake fluid line fittings to 12 ft. lbs.

GRAND CHEROKEE

1. Disconnect brake fluid level sensor electrical connector.
2. Disconnect brake fluid lines at master cylinder.
3. Remove master cylinder mounting nuts, then the master cylinder.
4. Disconnect vacuum hose at booster check valve.
5. Remove retainer clip holding pushrod on pedal pin, **Fig. 6,** then slide pushrod off pin.
6. Remove booster to firewall mounting nuts.
7. In engine compartment, slide booster forward, tilt upward, then remove booster assembly. Discard booster to firewall seal.
8. Reverse procedure to install, noting the following:
   a. **Do not substitute aftermarket mounting nuts. Use originals or factory replacements.**
   b. Install new booster to firewall seal.
   c. **Torque** booster mounting nuts to 29 ft. lbs.
   d. **Torque** master cylinder mounting nuts to 18 ft. lbs.

LIBERTY

1. Disconnect electrical connector from fluid level switch at bottom of reservoir.
2. Remove master cylinder.
3. Disconnect vacuum hoses from booster check valve.
4. Remove brake lines from master cylinder and hydraulic control unit or junction block for clearance.

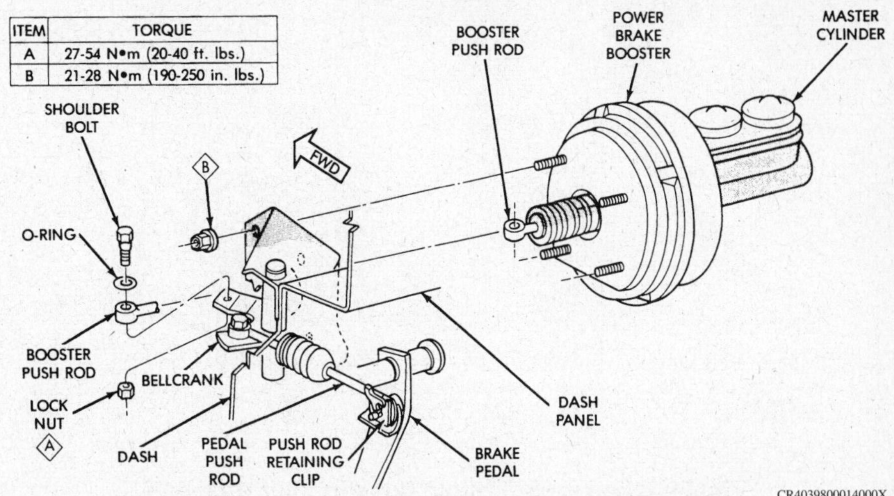

Fig. 4 Transverse mount brake booster. Full Size Van

5. Disconnect hydraulic control unit from mounts, then position aside for clearance.
6. Remove knee blocker under steering column.
7. Remove retaining clip securing booster push rod to brake pedal.
8. Remove nuts attaching booster to dash panel.
9. Slide booster studs out of dash panel, then tilt booster upward and remove booster from engine compartment.
10. Reverse procedure to install, noting the following:
    a. **Torque** booster mounting bolts to 18 ft. lbs.
    b. **Torque** master cylinder bolts to 18 ft. lbs.
    c. **Torque** hydraulic control unit to 10 ft. lbs.

PACIFICA

REMOVAL

Vaccum in power brake booster must be pumped down (removed) before removing master cylinder from brake booster.

1. Place driver seat in full rearward position.
2. Remove battery from vehicle.
3. With engine off, pump brake pedal until firm pedal is achieved using approximately 4–5 compressions.
4. Remove coolant recovery bottle nuts, then place bottle aside with hoses attached.
5. Clean all surfaces of brake fluid reservoir and master cylinder using Mopar Brake Parts Cleaner or suitable equivalent.
6. Disconnect wiring harness connector from brake fluid level switch in master cylinder brake fluid reservoir.
7. Disconnect primary and secondary brake tubes from master cylinder at ABS ICU. Cap off brake tubes and install plugs in open brake tube outlet ports of ICU.
8. Remove two attaching nuts to master cylinder power brake booster.
9. Slide master cylinder straight out of power brake booster.
10. Remove vacuum seal located on mounting flange of master cylinder.
11. Loosen two bolts attaching ABS ICU bracket to frame rail.
12. Lift ICU off frame rail bolts and lower ICU onto top of transaxle.
13. Disconnect vacuum hose from check valve on face of booster. **Do not remove check valve from booster.**
14. Remove knee block air bag module as outlined in "Passive Restraint Systems" chapter.
15. Remove booster push rod from pin on brake pedal as follows:
    a. Place a small screwdriver between center tang on power brake booster brake pedal pin retaining clip.
    b. Rotate screwdriver to allow retaining clip center tang to pass over end of brake pedal pin, then slide retaining clip off brake pedal pin.
    c. Discard retaining clip, it is not to be reused. Install NEW retaining clip during installation procedure.
16. Slide booster push rod off brake pedal pin.
17. Remove and discard brake lamp switch.
18. Remove four power brake booster mounting nuts.
19. Slide power brake booster forward and remove through engine compartment.

INSTALLATION

Before installing booster, ensure there is a NEW booster seal placed over push rod and mounting studs on rear of booster.

1. Install power brake booster through engine compartment, guiding push rod and mounting studs through dash panel.
2. Install four power brake booster nuts and **torque** to 25 ft. lbs.
3. Slide booster push rod onto brake pedal pin and install NEW retaining clip securing push rod to brake pedal.
4. Install and adjust NEW brake lamp switch.

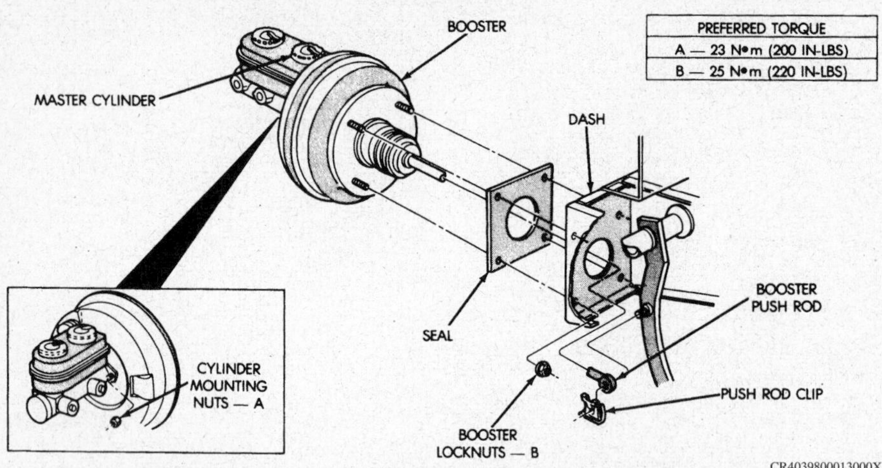

Fig. 5 Inline mount brake booster. Full Size Van

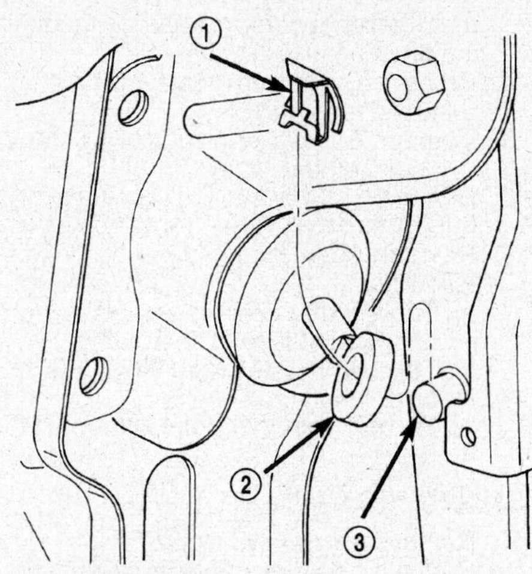

Fig. 6 Booster pushrod clip removal. Grand Cherokee

5. Install knee blocker air bag module as outlined in "Passive Restraint Systems" chapter.
6. Install ABS ICU and **torque** bolts to 18 ft. lbs.
7. Install NEW vacuum seal on rear of master cylinder, ensure seal fits squarely in mounting groove.
8. Install master cylinder on studs of power brake booster, aligning booster push rod with master cylinder piston.
9. Install two master cylinder nuts, **torque** nuts to 19 ft. lbs.
10. Thread primary and secondary brake tubes into ICU ports, **torque** to 10 ft. lbs.
11. Connect wiring harness connector to brake fluid level switch mounted in brake fluid reservoir.
12. Install coolant recovery bottle.
13. Install battery.
14. Fill master cylinder using clean Mopar Brake Fluid or equivalent and bleed system as required.
15. Road test vehicle to ensure proper orientation of brakes.

PT CRUISER

REMOVAL

1. With engine stopped, pump brake pedal four or five times to deplete power booster vacuum.
2. Remove air cleaner cover and hose to TBI unit.
3. Remove air cleaner housing by pulling straight upward.
4. Disconnect and isolate battery ground cable.
5. Unlock the Power Distribution Center, lift upward and position aside.
6. Remove vehicle wiring harness connector from brake fluid level sensor in master cylinder fluid reservoir.
7. Tag their locations, then disconnect brake fluid lines from master cylinder and proportioning valves. Install suitable plugs at all open master cylinder outlets.
8. Clean area around master cylinder to booster mounting surfaces using Mopar Brake Parts Cleaner, or a suitable equivalent. Do not allow any debris to enter booster.
9. Remove master cylinder to booster mounting nuts.
10. Slide master cylinder straight out of booster.
11. **On models equipped with anti-lock brakes,** proceed as follows:
    a. Disconnect brake fluid level switch electrical connector.
    b. Tag their locations, then disconnect brake fluid lines coming from master cylinder at Integrated Control Unit (ICU).
    c. Disconnect brake fluid lines leading to each individual brake at ICU, **Fig. 7.**
    d. Pull outward on connector lock, then disconnect 25-pin electrical connector from Controller Anti-Lock Brake (CAB) unit mounted on ICU.
    e. Remove ICU bracket mounting bolts, then the ICU.
12. **On all models,** disconnect brake booster check valve vacuum hoses. **Do not remove check valve from booster.**
13. Remove instrument panel sound insulator from below knee blocker.
14. Fold down and remove knee blocker.
15. Working under instrument panel inside vehicle, locate vacuum booster input rod to brake pedal attachment and position a suitable small screwdriver between the center tang on booster input rod to brake pedal pin retaining clip.
16. Rotate screwdriver enough to allow retaining clip center tang to pass over end of brake pedal pin, then pull clip off brake pedal pin. **Discard clip and replace with new one during assembly procedure.**
17. Remove four booster to firewall mounting nuts.
18. Slide booster forward until mounting studs have cleared firewall, then remove from vehicle.

INSTALLATION

1. Install booster mounting studs and input rod through firewall. **Torque** mounting nuts to 25 ft. lbs.
2. Coat brake pedal pin to booster input rod contact surface with Mopar Lubriplate, or equivalent.
3. Connect booster input rod to brake pedal pin with a new retaining clip.
4. Install knee blocker and sound insulator.
5. Connect vacuum hoses at booster check valve.
6. **On models equipped with anti-lock brakes,** proceed as follows:
    a. Install ICU onto mounting bracket. **Torque** bolts to 97 inch lbs.
    b. Ensure 25-pin CAB electrical connector seal is properly in place.
    c. After connector has fully seated in CAB socket, push connector lock inward.
    d. Install brake fluid lines into proper ports. **Torque** nuts to 12 ft. lbs.
7. **On all models,** if proportioning valves were removed, install them at this time with new O-rings. They are identical so they can be installed in either port leading to rear brakes.
8. Bleed master cylinder on bench before attempting installation.
9. Ensure master cylinder mounting surface on booster is clean. Do not allow any debris to enter booster.
10. Position master cylinder onto mounting studs, ensuring booster pushrod aligns with master cylinder piston pushrod.
11. Install master cylinder mounting nuts. **Torque** to 21 ft. lbs.
12. Install brake fluid lines into proper ports. **Torque** nuts to 12 ft. lbs., using a suitable crowfoot wrench.
13. Connect brake fluid level switch electrical connector.
14. Install Power Distribution Center (PDC).
15. Connect battery ground cable.
16. Install air cleaner housing.

17. Install hose to TBI unit and air cleaner cover.
18. Bleed base brake system.

SPRINTER

REMOVAL

1. Remove brake fluid from brake reservoir using a suitable suction tool.
2. Disconnect brake level switch electrical connector.
3. Remove brake lines from master cylinder. **Seal off ends and bore holes with plugs.**
4. Remove master cylinder from booster.
5. Remove booster vacuum hose and check valve.
6. Remove pedal push rod clip.
7. Remove booster mounting nuts.
8. Remove booster from the vehicle.

INSTALLATION

1. Install brake booster to vehicle.
2. Install booster mounting nuts and **torque** to 18 ft. lbs.
3. Install push rod pin and clip.
4. Install brake booster vacuum line and check valve.
5. Install master cylinder to brake booster and **torque** to 21 ft. lbs.
6. Install brake lines to master cylinder and **torque** to 10 ft. lbs.
7. Install brake level switch electrical connector.
8. Fill and bleed brake system as required.

WRANGLER

1. Remove EVAP canister as required.
2. Remove combination valve and master cylinder.
3. Disconnect vacuum hose from booster check valve.
4. Remove retaining clip that secures booster pushrod to brake pedal.
5. Remove nuts attaching booster to cowl panel.
6. Slide booster studs out of cowl panel in engine compartment, then remove booster from the compartment.
7. Remove cowl panel seal from booster.
8. Reverse procedure to install, noting the following:
   a. Ensure booster to cowl panel seal is securely in place. Replace if damaged.
   b. **Do not substitute aftermarket mounting nuts. Use originals or factory replacements.**
   c. **Torque** booster mounting nuts to 29 ft. lbs.
   d. **Torque** master cylinder mounting nuts to 14 ft. lbs.
   e. **Torque** combination valve mounting nuts to 14 ft. lbs.

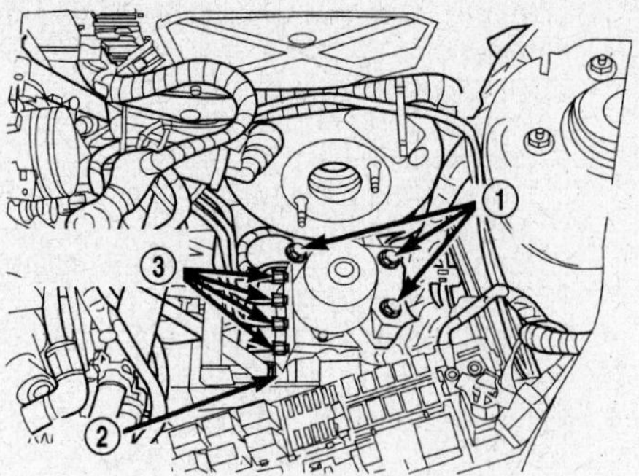

1 – ICU MOUNTING BOLTS
2 – CAB CONNECTOR
3 – BRAKE TUBES TO BRAKES

CR4020002022000X

Fig. 7 ICU connections. PT Cruiser

VACUUM PUMPS

NOTE: On Air Bag Equipped Models, Refer To "Air Bag System Precautions" Located In The Front Of This Manual For System Disarming & Arming Procedures.

INDEX

PRECAUTIONS

Air Bag Systems

Refer to "Air Bag System Precautions" in the front of this manual for system disarming and arming procedures.

Battery Ground Cable

Prior to service disconnect battery ground cable and isolate as required.

DESCRIPTION

The vacuum pump and power steering pump used on the Cummins Turbo Diesel is one assembly and is driven from a common shaft from the front gear train. To service the vacuum pump, the complete assembly must be removed from the front gear housing, **Fig. 1. Do not separate the vacuum pump from the adapter. The vacuum pump is not serviceable and must be replaced as a unit.**

Liberty models use an internal vacuum pump. This vacuum pump is mounted in the front of the engine block under the engine front cover. The vacuum pump is driven by a sprocket on the crankshaft.

PT Cruiser models use a vane type pump. The pump supplies vacuum to the brake booster, EGR system, turbocharger wastegate solenoid, and the swirl valve actuator. The vacuum pump is mounted to the rear of the cylinder head next to the high pressure pump

Sprinter models vacuum pump is operated by a slotted extension attached to the vacuum pump shaft. The vacuum pump shaft slotted extension fits into, and is driven by, the exhaust camshaft gear. The vacuum pump is a constant displacement, vane-type pump. Vacuum is generated by vanes mounted in the pump rotor. The rotor is located in the pump housing and is pressed onto the pump shaft. The vacuum pump rotating components are internally lubricated. The vacuum pump is not serviceable and must be replaced as a unit. Do not disassemble or attempt to repair the pump.

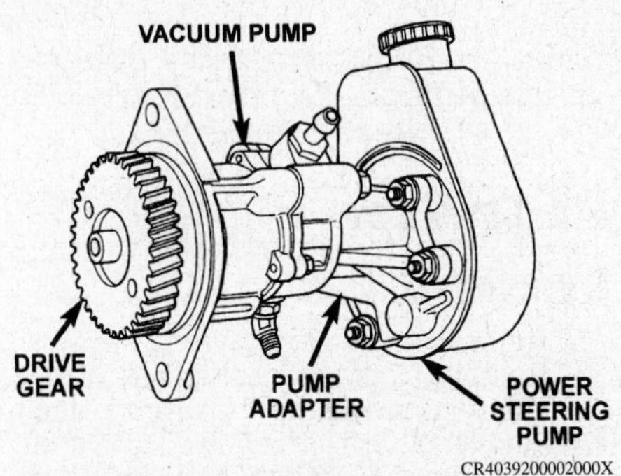

Fig. 1 Power steering & vacuum pump assembly. Except Liberty & PT Cruiser

VACUUM PUMP

REPLACE

Except Liberty, PT Cruiser & Sprinter

REMOVAL

1. Position suitable drain pan under power steering pump.
2. Disconnect vacuum and power steering pump hoses.
3. If required, disconnect engine oil pressure sender unit electrical connector, then remove sender unit.
4. Disconnect lubricating oil feed line from fitting at underside of vacuum pump.
5. Remove pump lower attaching bolt, **Fig. 2.**
6. Remove bottom inboard nut securing adapter to steering pump, nut and bracket must be removed before pump assembly can be removed from block.
7. Remove pump upper mounting bolt, then the pump, **Fig. 3.**
8. Remove power steering pump to adapter nuts, **Fig. 4.**
9. Remove power steering pump from adapter, turning pump gear back and forth to disengage pump shaft from coupling.
10. If steering pump will be serviced, note locations, then remove two spacers from each inboard mounting stud on pump.

INSTALLATION

1. Install spacers on power steering pump studs, **Fig. 5.**
2. Align power steering pump drive dog with vacuum pump drive assembly slot, then slide steering pump into place on adapter. **Avoid damaging adapter body seal.**
3. Position adapter on pump studs.
4. Install attaching nuts on outboard stud and on upper pump studs. Do not install nut on lower inboard stud at this time.
5. **Torque** nuts to 18 ft. lbs.
6. Install new pump mounting flange gasket with Mopar Perfect Seal, or an equivalent silicone adhesive sealer on both sides, **Fig. 6.**
7. Insert pump assembly upper attaching bolts in mounting flange and gasket. Use sealer or grease to hold bolt in place if required.
8. Position pump assembly on engine and install upper bolt. Tighten bolt only enough to hold assembly in place.
9. Working from under vehicle, install pump assembly lower attaching bolt.
10. **Torque** upper and lower bolts to 57 ft. lbs.
11. Position bracket on steering pump inboard stud, then install remaining adapter attaching nut on stud. **Torque** nut to 18 ft. lbs.
12. Connect oil feed line to vacuum pump and tighten fitting.
13. Connect steering pump pressure and return lines to pump. **Torque** pressure line fitting to 22 ft. lbs.
14. Connect vacuum hose to pump.
15. Install engine oil pressure sender unit and connect electrical connector.
16. Fill power steering reservoir with proper power steering fluid.
17. Start vehicle and slowly turn steering wheel from left to right to circulate fluid and purge air from system.
18. Stop engine, then inspect power steering fluid level.
19. Ensure steering system functions properly and that there are no leaks.

1 - PUMP ASSEMBLY LOWER MOUNTING BOLT
2 - ADAPTER BRACKET
3 - BOTTOM—INBOARD ADAPTER BRACKET NUT

CR4039700018000X

Fig. 2 Vacuum pump mounting. Except Liberty, PT Cruiser & Sprinter

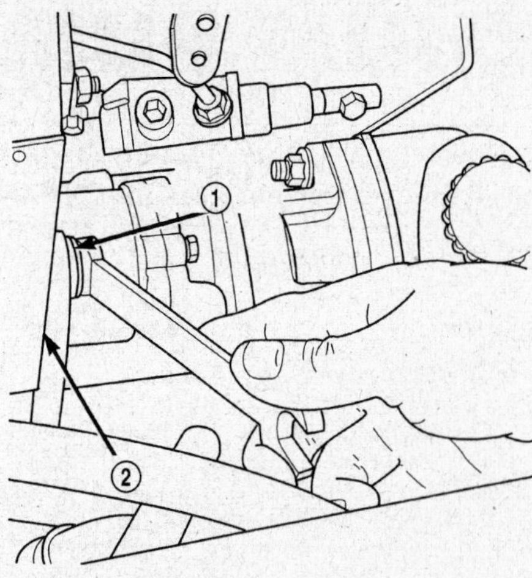

1 - PUMP UPPER BOLT
2 - DRIVE COVER

CR4039700019000X

Fig. 3 Pump assembly upper mounting bolt. Except Liberty, PT Cruiser & Sprinter

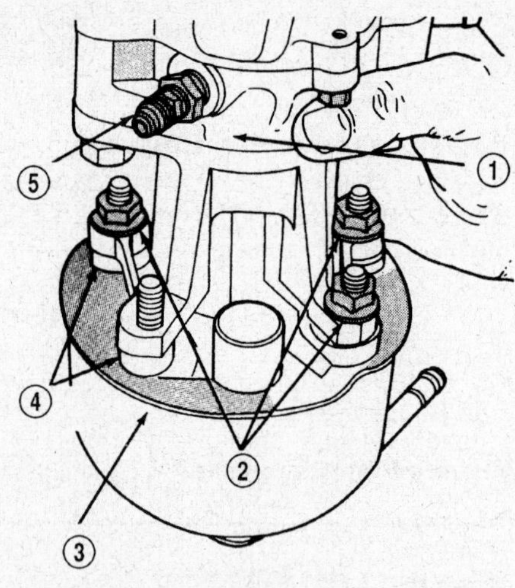

1 - VACUUM PUMP
2 - ATTACHING NUTS
3 - STEERING PUMP
4 - PUMP SPACERS
5 - OIL FEED FITTING

CR4039700020000X

Fig. 4 Adapter to power steering pump nuts. Except Liberty, PT Cruiser & Sprinter

Liberty

1. Remove cooling fan and viscous drive clutch as outlined in "Cooling Fans" chapter.
2. Remove accessory drive belt.
3. Remove cooling fan support.
4. Remove vibration damper/crankshaft pulley.
5. Remove timing belt as outlined under "Timing Belt, Replace" in chassis chapter.
6. Remove crankshaft hub.
7. Remove front engine cover.
8. Remove crankshaft sprocket, **Fig. 7.**
9. Remove vacuum pump.
10. Reverse procedure to install, noting the following:
    a. Refer to **Fig. 8** for pump blade to pump body position.
    b. **Torque** pump mounting bolts to 96 inch lbs.
    c. **Torque** vacuum pump pipe to block nuts to 42 ft. lbs.

PT Cruiser

REMOVAL

1. Remove engine top cover.
2. Remove air cleaner assembly.
3. Disconnect vacuum hose from vacuum pump.
4. Disconnect PDC from bracket and position aside.
5. Remove vacuum pump mounting bolts, then pump from cylinder head.

INSTALLATION

1. With O-ring installed on vacuum pump, align pump with pump drive on camshaft, **Fig. 9.**
2. Slide vacuum pump into cylinder head and **torque** mounting bolts to 12 ft. lbs.
3. Reposition and connect PDC to mounting bracket.
4. Connect vacuum hose to vacuum pump.
5. Install air cleaner housing assembly, then engine top cover.

Sprinter

1. Remove vacuum line at vacuum pump.
2. Remove vacuum pump and seals, **Fig. 10. Note position of driver on rear of pump.**
3. Reverse procedure to install. **Torque** vacuum pump mounting bolts to 12 ft. lbs.

VACUUM PUMP SERVICE

Do not separate the vacuum pump from the adapter. The vacuum pump is not serviceable and must be replaced as a unit.

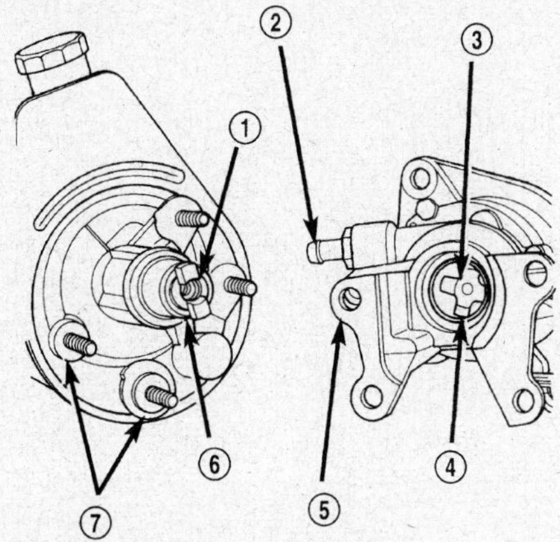

Fig. 5 Power steering pump to adapter installation. Except Liberty, PT Cruiser & Sprinter

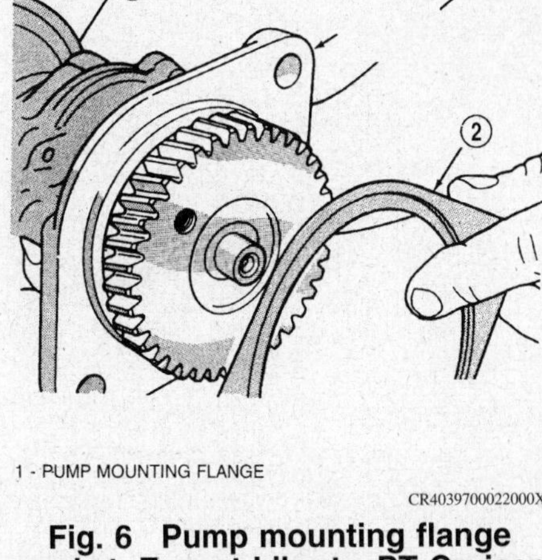

Fig. 6 Pump mounting flange gasket. Except Liberty, PT Cruiser & Sprinter

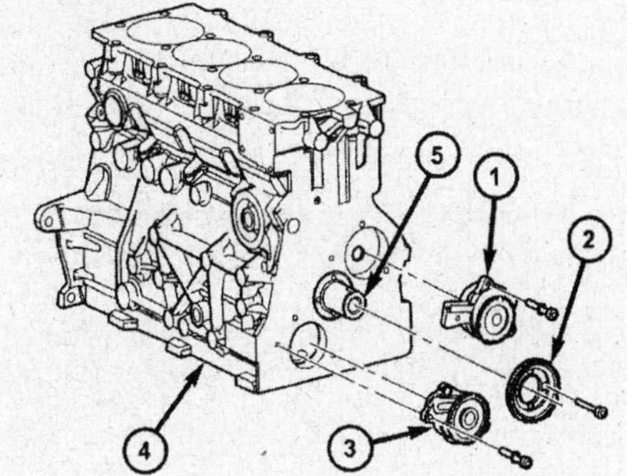

1 - VACUUM PUMP
2 - CRANKSHAFT SPROCKET
3 - OIL PUMP
4 - ENGINE BLOCK
5 - CRANKSHAFT

LTV0500000000214

Fig. 7 Internal vacuum pump removal. Liberty

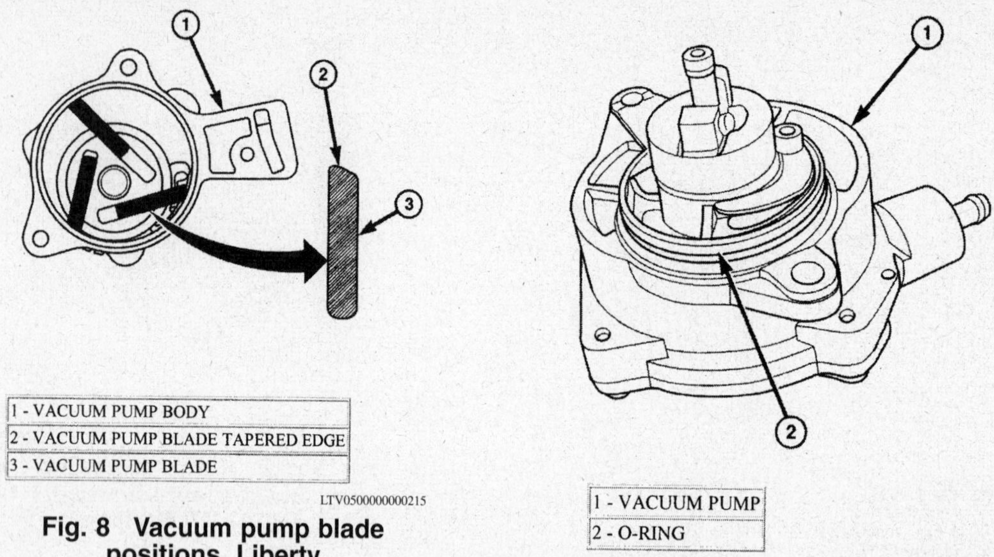

Fig. 8 Vacuum pump blade positions. Liberty

Fig. 9 Vacuum pump. PT Cruiser

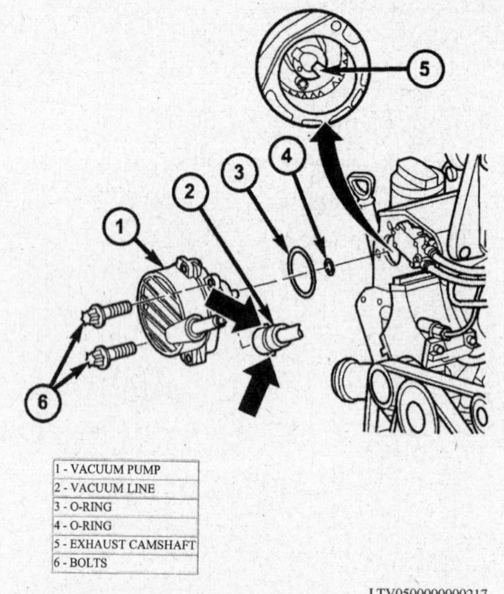

Fig. 10 Vacuum pump. Sprinter

TRANSFER CASES

NOTE: See Individual Truck Chapters For Transfer Case Adjustment & Removal Procedures.

TABLE OF CONTENTS

Application Chart

Year	Model	Transfer Case
2002	Dakota	NV-233 & 244
	Durango	NV-133, 233 & 244
	Full Size Pickup (1500)	NV-241 Gen II & NV-243
	Full Size Pickup (2500 & 3500)	NV-241LD & 241HD
	Grand Cherokee	NV-242 & 247
	Liberty	NV-231 & 242
	Wrangler	NV-231
2003	Dakota	NV-233 & 244
	Durango	NV-133, 233 & 244
	Full Size Pickup (1500)	NV-241 Gen II & NV-243
	Full Size Pickup (2500 & 3500)	NV-271 & 273
	Grand Cherokee	NV-242 & 247
	Liberty	NV-231 & 242
	Wrangler	NV-231 & 241
2004–06	Commander	NV-140 & NV-245
	Dakota	NV-233 & 244
	Durango	NV-144 & NV-244 Gen II
	Full Size Pickup	NV-241 Gen II, NV-243, NV-244 Gen II, NV-246, NV-273, NV-277
	Grand Cherokee	NV-140, NV-146, NV-147, NV-242, NV-245, NV-247
	Liberty	NV-231, NV-241 Gen II & NV-242
	Wrangler	NV-231 & 241

Model NV-231HD & NV-241LD Transfer Cases

INDEX

DIAGNOSIS & TESTING

Before repairing any transfer case, inspect all other driveline components first. The actual cause of a problem may be front hubs, axles, propeller shaft, wheels, tires, transmission or clutch. Ensure hub seals are intact, maintenance of the hubs is critical. Avoid prolonged exposure to dirt and water as damage to internal components will result. If a problem still exists after the inspection and verification, refer to **Fig. 1** for further transfer case diagnosis.

DISASSEMBLE

Rear Extension, Retainer & Rear Case

1. Position transfer case in a suitable shallow drain pan.
2. Remove drain plug and drain.
3. Remove rear extension bolts, then the rear extension.
4. Tap extension with a plastic mallet to break sealer and loosen.
5. Remove output bearing retaining ring with heavy duty snap ring pliers.
6. Remove rear retainer bolts.
7. Loosen rear retainer with suitable pry bar placed under flange, then remove rear retainer and output bearing as an assembly.

Companion Flange & Shift Lever

1. Shift transfer case into neutral.
2. Remove and discard companion flange nut.
3. Remove companion flange from front output shaft. Use a suitable puller if flange cannot be removed by hand.
4. Remove companion flange rubber seal from front output shaft.
5. Remove shift lever from sector shaft, **Fig. 2.**

Front Output Shaft & Drive Chain

1. Remove output bearing retaining ring with suitable snap ring pliers, then the output shaft bearing.
2. Remove rear case to front case bolts. Note position of bolts with flat washers for installation reference.
3. Loosen rear case with pry tool to break sealer bead. Insert tool at each end of case.
4. Remove rear case and oil pump assembly.
5. Remove shift rail cup and spring, **Fig. 3.**
6. Remove front sprocket retaining ring, **Fig. 4.**
7. Pull mainshaft, front sprocket and chain outward approximately 1 inch.
8. Remove chain from mainshaft drive sprocket, then front sprocket and chain as an assembly.

Shift Fork & Mainshaft

1. Remove vacuum indicator switch.
2. Remove poppet plunger screw, spring and O-ring seal, **Fig. 5,** discard O-ring seal.
3. Remove poppet plunger with a magnet.
4. Remove front output shaft from bearing in case.
5. Remove mainshaft assembly.
6. Remove mode fork, mode sleeve and shift rail as an assembly, **Fig. 6.**
7. Note which way sleeve fits in fork, short side of sleeve goes to front.
8. Remove range fork retaining ring, then the range fork and hub as an assembly, **Fig. 7.** Note fork position for installation reference.
9. Remove shift sector, shift sector shaft nylon retainer and O-ring from shaft bore in case.

Mainshaft

1. Remove mode hub retaining ring using suitable snap ring pliers, slide mode hub off mainshaft, **Fig. 8.**
2. Slide drive sprocket off mainshaft, **Fig. 9.**

Input & Planetary Gear

1. Remove front bearing retainer attaching bolts, then front bearing retainer. Pry retainer off with suitable pry tools positioned at slots at each end of retainer.
2. Remove front bearing retainer seal by tapping out with suitable drift and hammer.
3. Remove input gear retaining ring with suitable snap ring pliers.
4. Place front case in horizontal position, then remove input gear and low range gear as an assembly, **Fig. 10.**
5. Tap gear out of bearing with plastic mallet if required.
6. Remove snap ring that retains input gear in low range gear.
7. Remove retainer, front tabbed washer, input gear and rear tabbed washer.

INSPECTION

Transfer Case

Clean transfer case components with a standard components cleaning solvent. Remove all traces of sealer from cases and retainers with a scraper and all purpose cleaner. Use compressed air to remove solvent residue from oil feed passages in the case halves, retainers, gears and shafts.

The oil pickup screen can be cleaned with solvent. Shake excess solvent from the screen after cleaning and allow to air dry. Do not use compressed air on the pickup screen.

Condition	Possible Cause	Correction
TRANSFER CASE DIFFICULT TO SHIFT OR WILL NOT SHIFT INTO DESIRED RANGE	(1) Vehicle speed too great to permit shifting.	(1) Stop vehicle and shift into desired range. Or reduce speed to 3-4 km/h (2-3 mph) before attempting to shift.
	(2) If vehicle was operated for extended period in 4H mode on dry paved surface, driveline torque load may cause difficulty.	(2) Stop vehicle, shift transmission to Neutral, shift transfer case to 2H mode and operate vehicle in 2H on dry paved surfaces.
	(3) Transfer case external shift linkage binding.	(3) Lubricate, repair or replace linkage bushings or tighten loose components as necessary.
	(4) Insufficient or incorrect lubricant.	(4) Drain and refill to edge of fill hole with DEXRON II® or MOPAR-MERCON® Automatic Transmission Fluid.
	(5) Internal components binding, worn or damaged.	(5) Disassemble unit and replace worn or damaged components as necessary.
TRANSFER CASE NOISY IN ALL DRIVE MODES	(1) Insufficient or incorrect lubricant.	(1) Drain and refill to edge of fill hole with DEXRON II® or MOPAR-MERCON® Automatic Transmission Fluid. Check for leaks and repair if necessary. **Note: If unit is still noisy after drain and refill, disassembly and inspection may be required to locate source of noise.**
NOISY IN – OR JUMPS OUT OF – FOUR WHEEL DRIVE LOW RANGE	(1) Transfer case not completely engaged in 4L position.	(1) Stop vehicle, shift transfer case to Neutral, then shift back into 4L position.
	(2) Shift linkage out of adjustment.	(2) Adjust linkage.
	(3) Shift linkage loose or binding.	(3) Tighten, lubricate or repair linkage as necessary.
	(4) Range fork damaged, inserts worn, or fork is binding on shift rail.	(4) Disassemble unit and repair as necessary.
	(5) Low range gear worn or damaged.	(5) Disassemble and repair as necessary.
LUBRICANT LEAKING FROM OUTPUT SHAFT SEALS OR FROM VENT	(1) Transfer case overfilled.	(1) Drain to correct level.
	(2) Vent closed or restricted.	(2) Clear or replace vent if necessary.
	(3) Output shaft seals damaged or installed incorrectly.	(3) Replace seals. Be sure seal lip faces interior of case when installed. Also be sure yoke seal surfaces are not scored or nicked. Remove scores and nicks with fine sandpaper or replace yoke(s) if necessary.
ABNORMAL TIRE WEAR	(1) Extended operation on dry hard surface (paved) roads in 4H range.	(1) Operate in 2H on hard surface (paved) roads.

CR3049500125000X

Fig. 1 Transfer case diagnosis chart

Mainshaft Sprocket & Hub

Inspect the splines on the hub and shaft and the teeth on the sprocket. Minor nicks and scratches can be smoothed with an oilstone. Replace any part that is damaged beyond repair.

Inspect contact surfaces in the sprocket bore and on the mainshaft. Minor nicks and scratches can be smoothed with 320–400 grit emery cloth. If nicks or wear is severe, replace the shaft.

Input Gear & Planetary Carrier

Inspect teeth on gear. Minor nicks can be polished out with an oilstone, but replace the gear if any teeth are broken, cracked, or chipped. The bearing surface on the gear can be smoothed with 300–400 grit emery cloth if required.

Examine the carrier body and pinion gears for wear or damage. The carrier body will have to be replaced as an assembly if the body, pinion pins, or pinion gears are damaged.

Inspect the lock ring and both thrust washers for wear or cracks. Replace as required. Inspect the lock retaining ring and replace if it is bent, distorted or broken.

Shift Forks/Hubs/ Sleeves

Inspect condition of shift forks and mode fork shift rail, **Fig. 11.** Minor nicks on shift rail can be polished with 320–400 grit emery cloth.

Inspect shift fork wear pads, **Fig. 12.** The mode fork pads are serviceable and can be replaced if required. The range fork pads are not serviceable. The fork must be replaced as an assembly if the pads are worn or damaged.

Fig. 2 Shift lever removal

Inspect both of the sleeves for wear or damage, especially on the interior teeth. Replace the sleeves if wear or damage is evident.

Rear Retainer Components

Inspect rear retainer components. Replace the bearing if it's rotation is rough or noisy. Inspect the retainer for cracks or wear in the bearing bore. Clean the retainer sealing surfaces with a scraper and all purpose cleaner to ensure proper adhesion of sealer during assembly.

Inspect retaining rings and washers. Replace any component that is distorted, bent or broken.

Inspect rear extension bushing. Replace if worn or scored.

Drive Chain

Inspect the drive chain and shaft bearings. Replace the chain if it is stretched, distorted, or if any of the links bind. Replace the bearings if their rotation is rough or noisy.

Low Range Annulus Gear

Carefully inspect the condition of the annulus gear. The gear is only serviced as part of the front case. If the gear is damaged, it will be required to replace the gear and the front case as an assembly. Do not attempt to remove the gear, **Fig. 13.**

Front/Rear Cases & Front Retainer

Inspect the cases and retainer for wear and damage. Clean the sealing surfaces with a scraper and all purpose cleaner. This will ensure proper adhesion during assembly. Replace the input retainer seal, do not reuse the seal.

Inspect the case condition. If leaks were a problem, look for gouges and severe scoring of the case sealing surfaces.

Inspect the front case mounting studs and vent tube. The tube can be secured with Loctite 271/680, or equivalent, if loose. The stud threads can be cleaned up with a

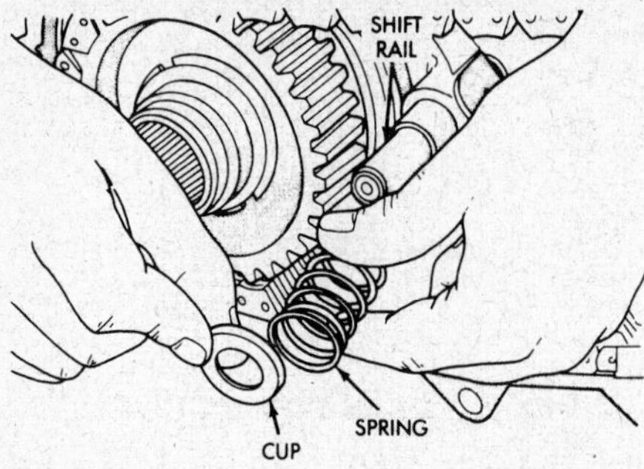

Fig. 3 Shift rail cup & spring

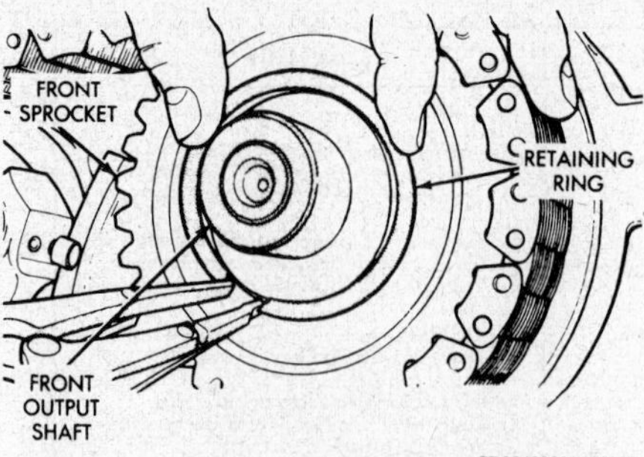

Fig. 4 Front sprocket retaining ring

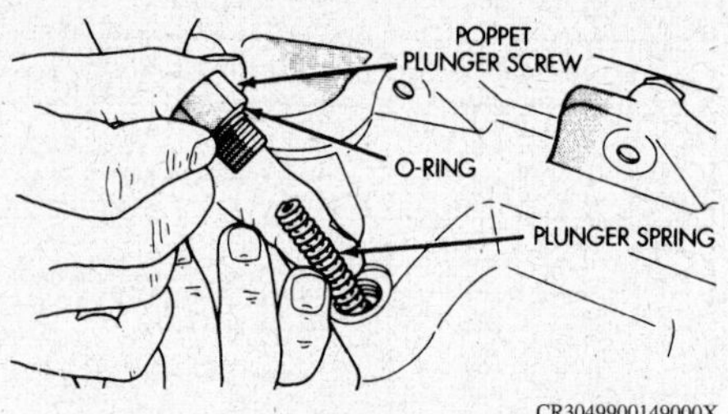

Fig. 5 Poppet plunger screw & spring

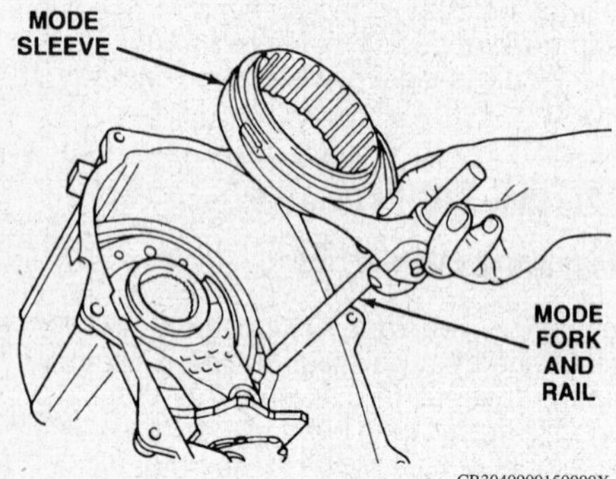

Fig. 6 Mode fork & sleeve

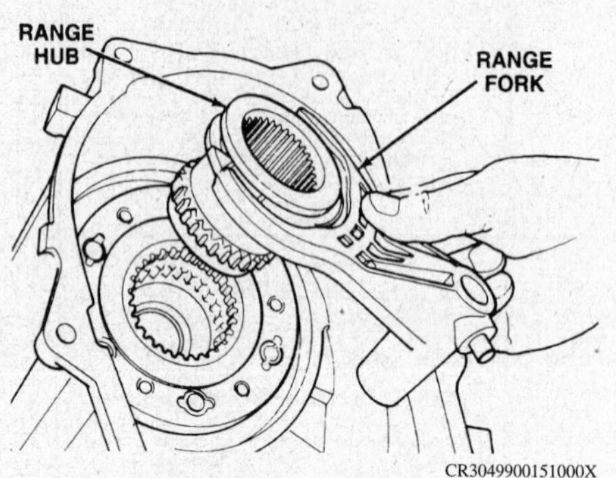

Fig. 7 Range fork & hub removal

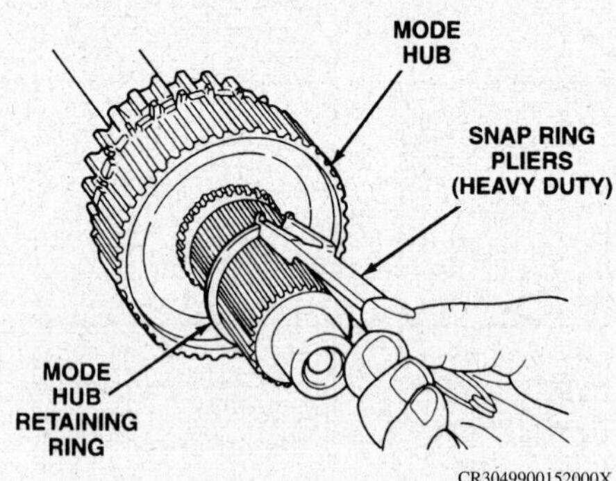

Fig. 8 Mode hub retaining ring

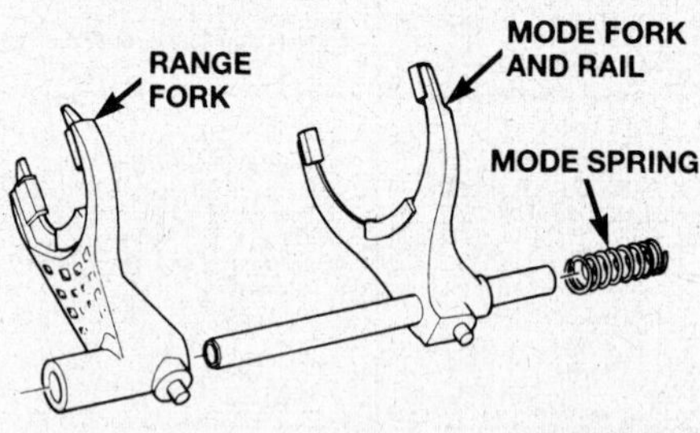

Fig. 11 Shift forks inspection

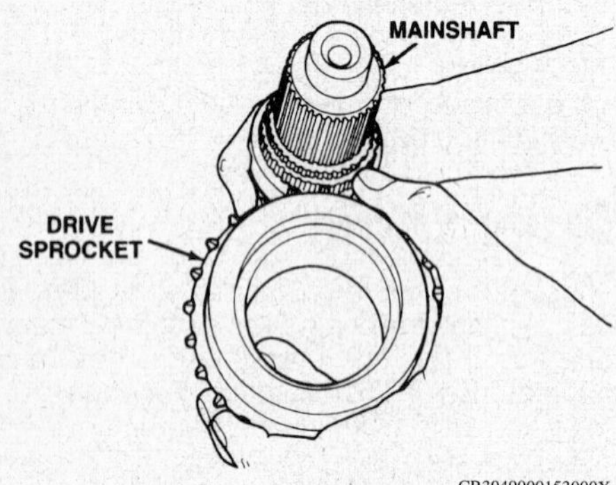

Fig. 9 Drive sprocket

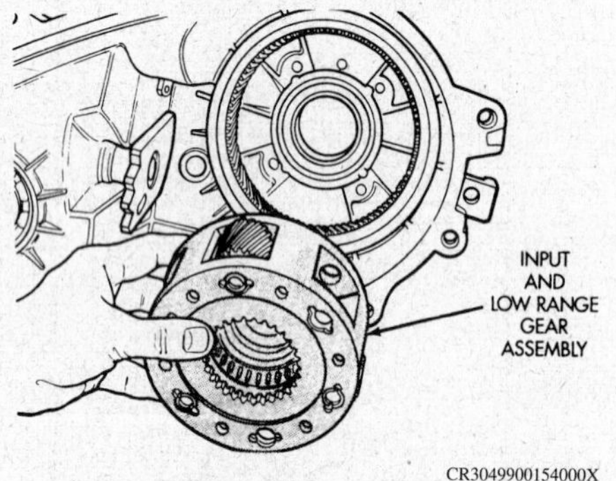

Fig. 10 Input gear & low range gear assembly

suitable die if required. Inspect the condition of the fill/drain plug threads in the rear case. The threads can be repaired with a suitable thread chaser or tap if required. If threads are damaged beyond repair, install a stainless steel threaded insert.

Oil Pump & Oil Pickup

Inspect the oil pump pickup components. Replace the pump if any components appear to be worn or damaged. Do not disassemble the pump, the pump is only available as a complete assembly. The pickup screen, hose and tube are the only serviceable components and are available separately.

ASSEMBLE

Bearing & Seals

1. Drive input shaft bearing from case from inside annulus gear opening using remover tool No. C-4210 and handle tool No. C-4171, or equivalents.
2. Install locating ring on new bearing.
3. Position case so that forward end is facing upward.
4. Drive input shaft bearing into case ensuring locating rings fully seats on case using remover tool No. C-4210 and handle tool No. C-4171, or equivalents.
5. Remove front output shaft bearing using installer tool No. 6953, or equivalent.
6. Start front output shaft bearing in case, then seat bearing with handle tool and installer tool No. 6953, or equivalents.
7. Install front output bearing retaining ring.
8. **On models equipped with 241LD transfer cases,** proceed as follows:
   a. Install new front output seal in case with installer tool No. 6888 and handle tool No. C-4171 or equivalents.
   b. Place new seal on tool with garter spring facing interior of case.
   c. Start seal in bore with light taps from hammer, continue until installer tool bottoms out in case.
   d. Remove installer tool and verify that seal is recessed .080–.100 inch below top edge of seal bore.
   e. Ensure seal is recessed as indicated, seal could loosen or become cocked if not seated properly.
9. **On models equipped with 231HD transfer cases,** proceed as follows:
   a. install new front output seal with installer tool No. 8143, or equivalent.
   b. Place new seal on tool with garter spring facing interior of case.
   c. Start seal in bore with light taps from hammer, continue tapping until seal tool is fully seated against case.
10. **On all transfer cases,** remove seal from front bearing retainer with suitable pry tool.
11. Install new oil seal in front bearing retainer with installer tool No. 7884, or equivalent.
12. Remove seal from oil pump with suitable pry tool.

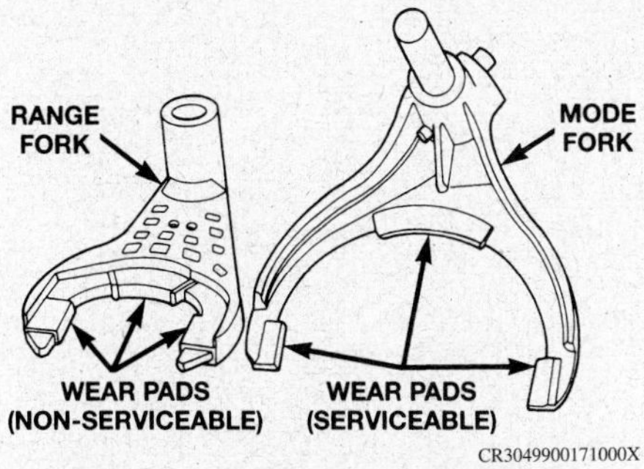

Fig. 12 Shift fork wear pads

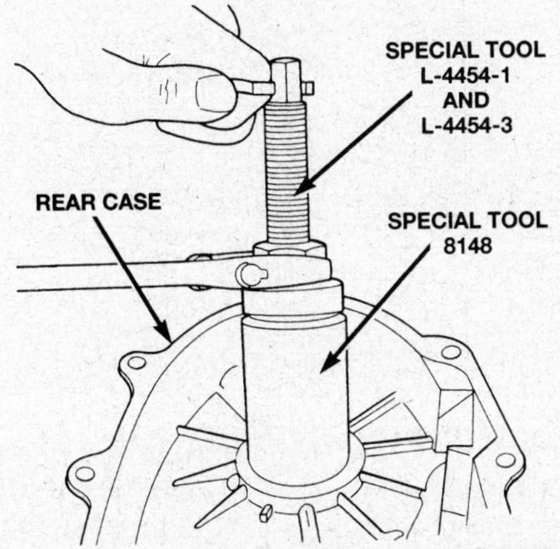

Fig. 15 Output shaft rear bearing removal

13. Install new seal in oil pump with installer tool No. 788, or equivalent.
14. Remove input gear pilot bearing by inserting a suitably sized drift into the splined end of input gear, **Fig. 14.** Driving bearing out with drift and hammer.
15. Install new pilot bearing with Plug No. C-293-3, or equivalent.
16. Remove output shaft rear bearing with screw and jaws from remover tool No. L4454 and cup No. 8148, or equivalents, **Fig. 15.**
17. Install new bearing with tool handle No. C-4171 and installer tool No. 5066, or equivalents.
18. Bearing bore is chamfered at top, install bearing so it is flush with lower edge of this chamfer.

Input & Planetary Gear Assembly

1. Lubricate gears and thrust washers with Dexron II automatic transmission fluid.
2. Install first thrust washer in low range gear, **Fig. 16,** ensure washer tabs are properly aligned in gear notches.
3. Install input gear in low range gear, ensure gear is fully seated.
4. Install remaining thrust washer in low range gear and on top of input gear, ensure washer tabs are properly aligned in gear notches.
5. Install retainer on input gear and install snap ring.

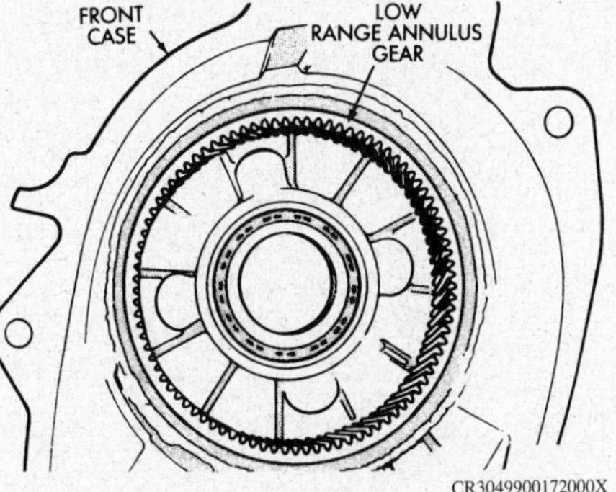

Fig. 13 Low range annulus gear

6. Align and install low range input gear assembly in front case.
7. Ensure low range gear pinions are engaged in annulus gear and that input gear shaft is fully seated in front bearing.
8. Install snap ring to hold input/low range gear into front bearing.
9. Clean gasket sealer residue from retainer and inspect retainer for cracks or other damage.
10. Apply a 1/8 inch bead of suitable silicone adhesive to sealing surface of retainer.
11. Align cavity in seal retainer with fluid return hole in front of case.
12. Do not block fluid return cavity on sealing surface of retainer when applying sealer.
13. Install retainer bolts and tighten to specification.

Mainshaft Assembly

1. Lubricate mainshaft splines with Dexron II automatic transmission fluid.
2. Slide drive sprocket onto main shaft, **Fig. 17,** then the mode hub.
3. Install mode hub retaining ring, ensure retaining ring is fully seated in mainshaft groove.

Shift Forks & Mainshaft

1. Support front case on wood blocks so case interior is facing up. Place blocks between mounting studs on forward surface of case.
2. Ensure blocks will not interfere with input gear installation.
3. Lubricate mainshaft components with Dexron II automatic transmission fluid.
4. Lubricate sector shaft with Dexron II automatic transmission fluid, then install in case.
5. Position slot in sector so it will be aligned with shift fork pin when shift forks are installed.
6. Assemble and install range fork and hub, **Fig. 18,** ensure hub is properly seated in low range gear and engaged in input gear.
7. Align and insert range fork pin in shift sector slot.
8. Install assembled mainshaft, ensure

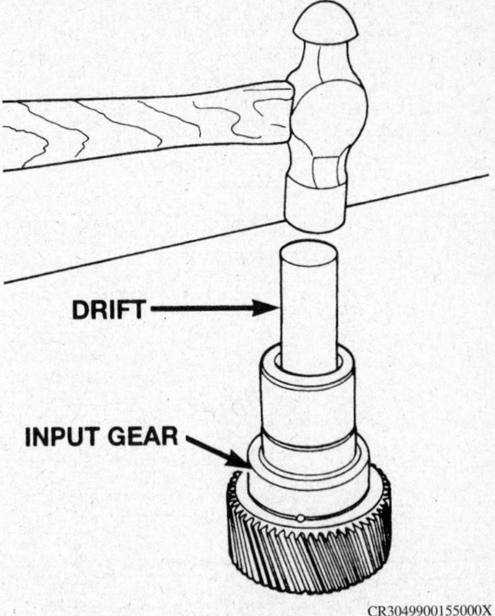

Fig. 14 Input gear pilot bearing removal

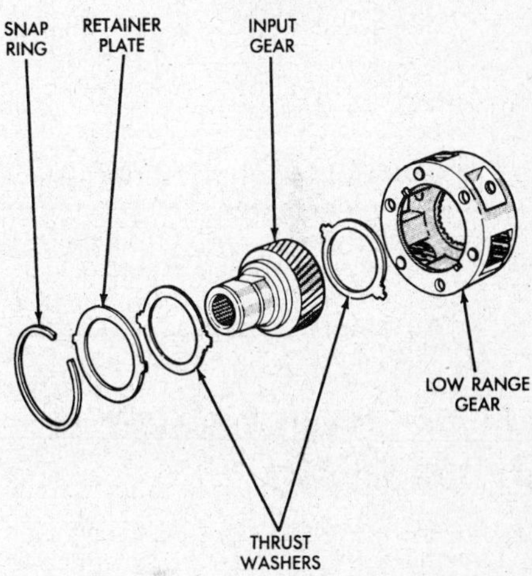

Fig. 16 Exploded view of input/low range gear assembly

shaft is seated in pilot bearing and input gear.

9. Install new pads on mode fork if required.
10. Insert mode sleeve in mode fork, ensure long side of sleeve is toward long end of shift rail.
11. Install assembled mode fork and sleeve, **Fig. 19,** ensure fork rail goes through range fork and into case bore and that sleeve is aligned and seated on mainshaft hub.
12. Replace vacuum indicator switch O-ring if required, then install vacuum indicator switch and tighten to specification.
13. Install new sector shaft O-ring and O-ring retainer, **Fig. 20,** in sector shaft bore.
14. Lubricate O-ring with transmission fluid or petroleum jelly after installation. Install shift lever on sector shaft.
15. Apply one or two drops of Mopar Lock-N-Seal, or equivalent, to threads of sector shaft, then install nut and washer and tighten to specification.

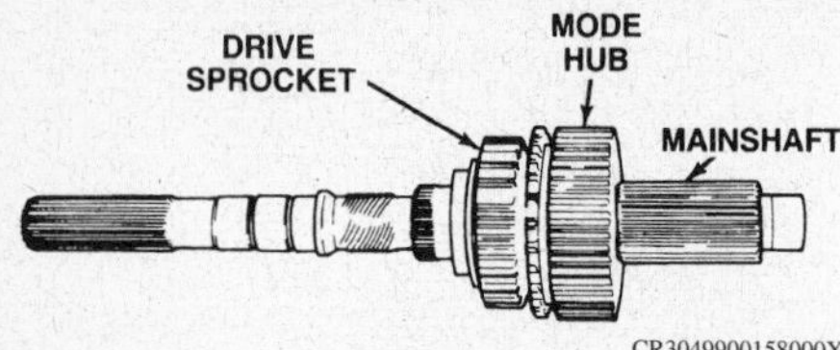

Fig. 17 Drive sprocket, mode hub & mainshaft

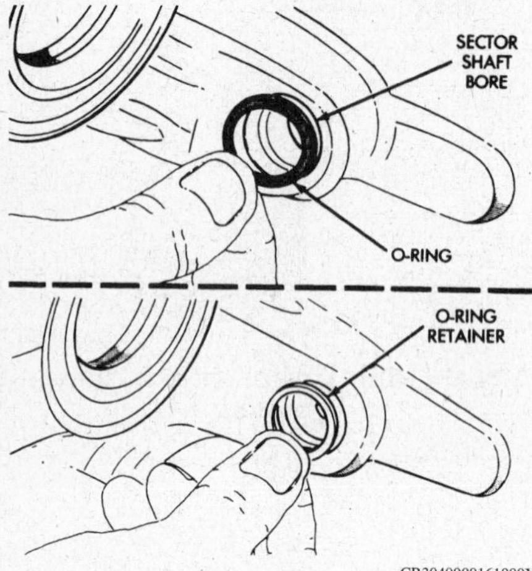

Fig. 20 Sector shaft O-ring & retainer

16. Install poppet plunger and spring.
17. Install new O-ring on poppet screw and install screw in front case. Tighten to specification.

Front Output Shaft & Drive Chain

1. Install front output shaft in bearing.
2. Insert front sprocket in drive chain.
3. Install drive chain around mainshaft sprocket, then position front sprocket over front shaft.
4. Raise mainshaft approximately one inch and seat front sprocket on front output shaft.
5. If mainshaft and mode sleeve were unseated during chain installation, align and reseat mainshaft in input gear and hub.
6. Install front sprocket and retaining ring, **Fig. 21.**
7. Install spring and cup on shift rail, insert magnet in front case pocket.

Oil Pump & Rear Case Assembly

Lubricate oil pump components with Dexron II automatic transmission fluid before installation. Prime oil pump pickup tube by pouring a little oil into the tube before installation.

1. Install new O-ring in pickup tube inlet, **Fig. 22,** of oil pump.
2. Position oil pickup tube and filter in rear case. Ensure pickup filter is seated in case pocket, **Fig. 23,** and that pickup tube is aligned in case notches.

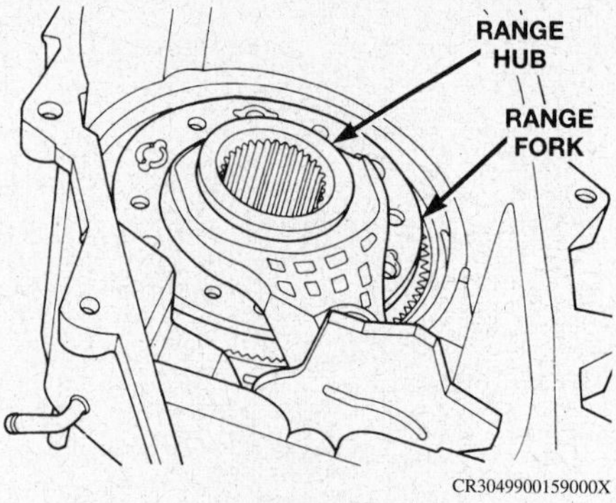

Fig. 18 Range fork & hub assembly

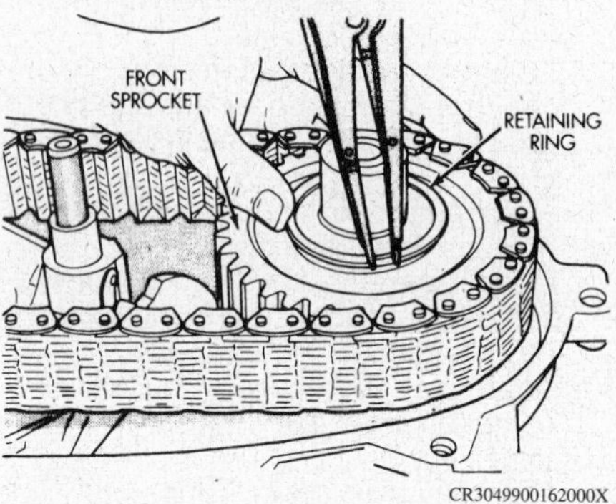

Fig. 21 Front sprocket retaining ring

3. Insert oil pickup tube in oil pump and position pump in rear case, **Fig. 24.**
4. Apply a bead of Mopar Gasket maker or equivalent, to mating surface of front case. Keep sealer bead width to a maximum of 3⁄16 inch.
5. Align oil pump with mainshaft and align shift rail with bore in rear case.
6. Install rear case and oil pump assembly. Ensure oil pump and pickup tube remain in position during case installation.
7. Verify that shift rail and case alignment dowels are seated before installing any bolts. Case could be cracked if shift rail or dowels are misaligned.
8. Install 4–5 case bolts to hold rear case in position. Tighten bolts snug but not to specification at this time.
9. Verify that oil pump is aligned and seated on rear case. Reposition pump if required.
10. Inspect stud at end of case halves. If stud was loosened or came out during disassembly, apply Loctite 242, or equivalent, to stud threads and reseat stud in case.
11. Apply Loctite 242, or equivalent to remainder of case bolt threads and install bolts. Ensure lock washers are used on stud/bolts at case ends.
12. Tighten all bolts and nuts to specification.
13. Install oil pump retaining ring, **Fig. 25,** on mainshaft.
14. Install rear output bearing and snap ring to output shaft.

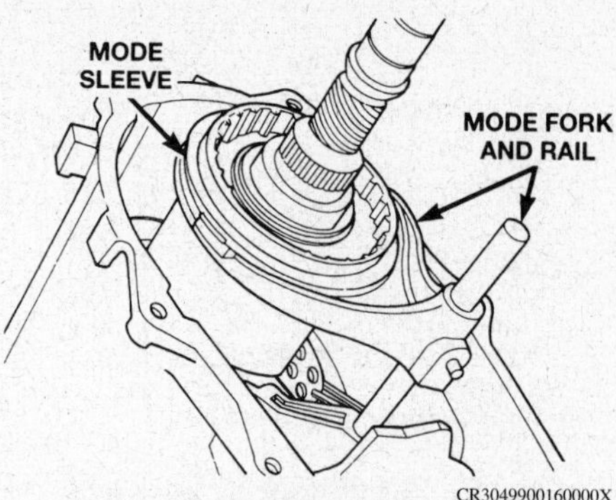

Fig. 19 Mode fork & sleeve

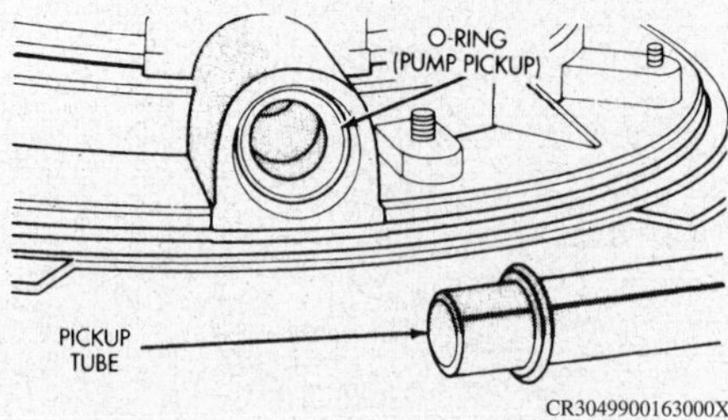

Fig. 22 Pickup tube O-ring

Companion Flange

1. Install companion flange seal, **Fig. 26,** on front shaft.
2. Install companion flange on front shaft, then install and tighten flange nut to specification.

Rear Retainer & Extension

1. Clean mating surfaces of transfer case housing and rear retainer. Remove all old gasket material.
2. Install new retainer gasket onto transfer case housing or rear retainer.
3. Align and install rear retainer on rear case.
4. Apply suitable silicone sealer to threads of rear retainer bolts. Install retainer bolts finger tight.
5. Install output bearing on mainshaft and seat it in rear retainer with suitable size pipe tool, **Fig. 27.**
6. Install output bearing retaining ring, **Fig. 28.**
7. Tighten rear retainer bolts to specification.
8. Install new seal in rear extension with suitable installation tool.
9. Apply bead of Mopar gasket Maker, or equivalent, to mating surfaces of rear extension.
10. Keep sealer bead width to a maximum of 3⁄16 inch.
11. Align and install rear extension on retainer.
12. Apply suitable silicone sealer to threads of rear extension bolts. Install bolts and tighten to specification.

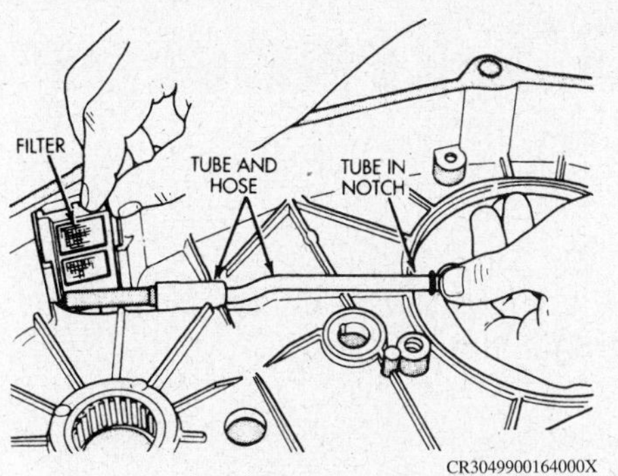

Fig. 23 Oil pickup tube & filter position

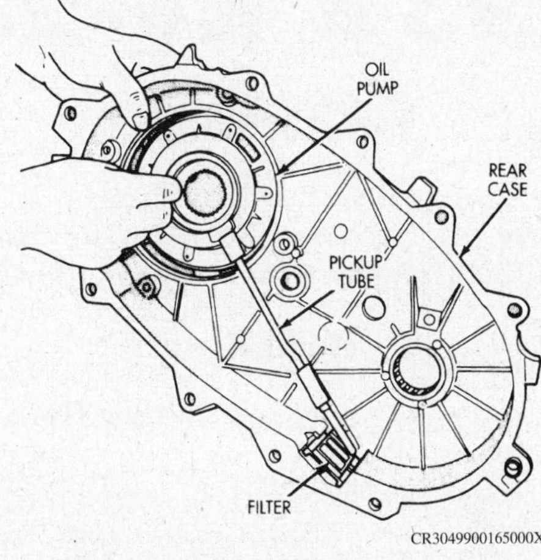

Fig. 24 Oil pump in rear case

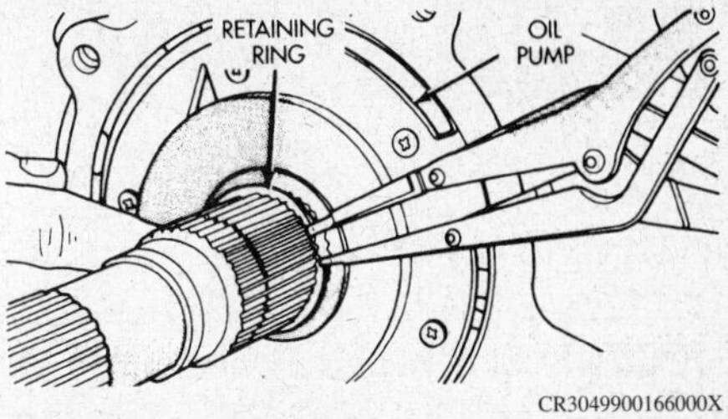

Fig. 25 Oil pump retaining ring

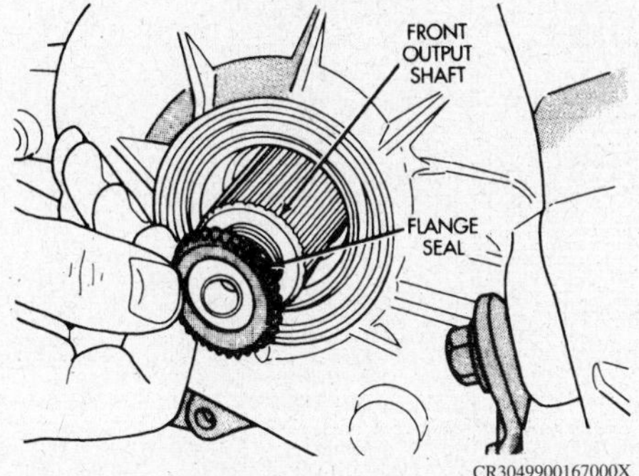

Fig. 26 Flange seal on front shaft

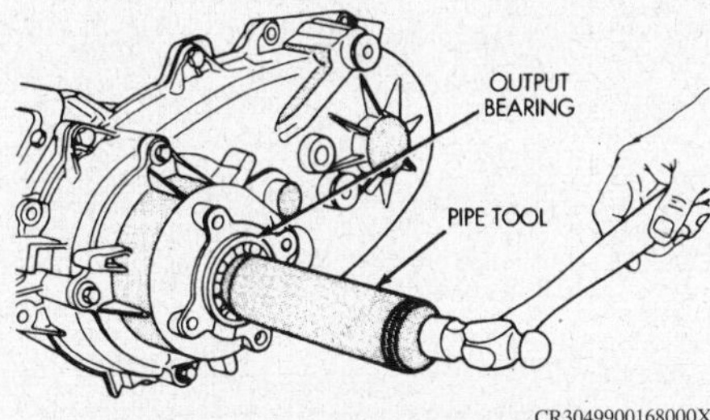

Fig. 27 Output bearing installation

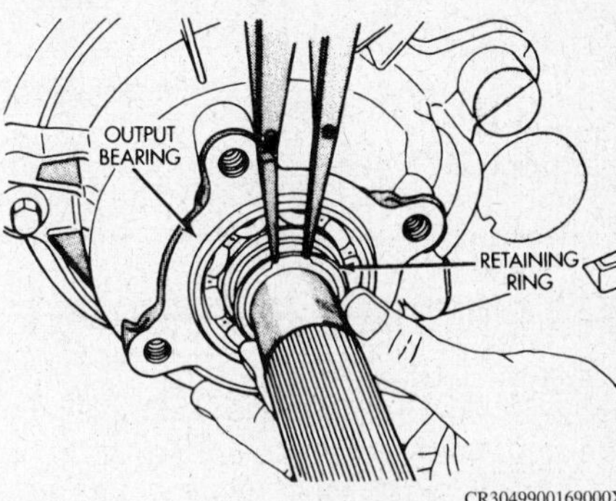

Fig. 28 Output bearing retaining ring installation

TIGHTENING SPECIFICATIONS

Year	Component	Torque Ft. Lbs.
2002–06	Companion Flange Nut	190–230
	Detent Plug	12–18
	Differential Case	15–24
	Drain/Fill Plug	15–25
	Extension Housing	12–18
	Front Bearing Retainer	12–20
	Front Case To Rear Case Nuts/Bolts	20–25
	Front Yoke Nut	90–130
	Range Lever	20–25
	Rear Retainer	26–34
	Shift Lever	15–25
	Transfer Case Mounting	20–30
	U-Joint Clamp	17

Model NV-133 & NV-233 Transfer Cases

NOTE: For Repair Procedures On This Transfer Case, Refer To The "New Venture Gear 233, 236, 241, 243, 246 & 261" Section Of The "Transfer Cases" Chapter In General Motors Corp.

INDEX

DIAGNOSIS & TESTING

Before repairing any transfer case, inspect all other driveline components first. The actual cause of a problem may be front hubs, axles, propeller shaft, wheels, tires, transmission or clutch. Ensure hub seals are intact, maintenance of the hubs is critical. Avoid prolonged exposure to dirt and water as damage to internal components will result. If a problem still exists after the inspection and verification, refer to **Figs. 1 and 2** for further transfer case diagnosis.

DISASSEMBLE

Refer to the "New Venture Gear 233, 236, 241, 243, 246 & 261" section of the "Transfer Cases" chapter in General Motors Corp. for transfer case disassemble procedure.

INSPECTION

Refer to the "New Venture Gear 233, 236, 241, 243, 246 & 261" section of the "Transfer Cases" chapter in General Motors Corp. for transfer case inspection.

ASSEMBLE

Refer to the "New Venture Gear 233, 236, 241, 243, 246 & 261" section of the "Transfer Cases" chapter in General Motors Corp. for transfer case assemble procedure.

Condition	Possible Cause	Correction
Transfer case difficult to shift or will not shift into desired range.	1) Transfer case electronically controlled shift system malfunction.	1) Verify proper operation per the appropriate diagnostic manual.
	2) If vehicle was operated for an extended period in 4HI mode on dry surface, driveline torque load may cause difficulty.	2) Drive the vehicle in a straight line and momentarily release the accelerator. The transfer case can then be shifted to the desired mode.
	3) Insufficient or incorrect lubricant.	3) Drain and refill transfer case with the correct quantity of Mopar® ATF +4, type 9602, Automatic Transmission Fluid.
	4) Internal transfer case components binding, worn, or damaged.	4) Repair or replace components as necessary.
Transfer case noisy in all drive modes.	1) Insufficient or incorrect lubricant.	1) Drain and refill transfer case with the correct quantity of Mopar® ATF +4, type 9602, Automatic Transmission Fluid.
	2) Internal transfer case components binding, worn, or damaged.	2) Repair or replace components as necessary.

CR3040100301010X

Fig. 1 Transfer case diagnosis chart

Condition	Possible Cause	Correction
Transfer case noisy while in, or jumps out of, 4LO mode.	1) Transfer case not completely engaged in 4LO position.	1) While rolling 2-3 MPH and the transmission in NEUTRAL, or clutch depressed on vehicles equipped with a manual transmission, shift transfer case to the 2WD or 4HI position, and then back into the 4LO position.
	2) Range fork damaged, inserts worn, or fork is binding on the shift rail.	2) Repair or replace components as necessary.
	3) Low range gear worn or damaged.	3) Repair or replace components as necessary.
Lubricant leaking from transfer case seals or vent.	1) Transfer case overfilled.	1) Drain lubricant to the correct level.
	2) Transfer case vent closed or restricted.	2) Clean or replace vent as necessary.
	3) Transfer case seals damaged or installed incorrectly.	3) Replace suspect seal.
Abnormal tire wear.	1) Extended operation in 4HI mode on dry surfaces,	1) Operate vehicle in 2WD mode on dry surfaces.

CR3040100301020X

Fig. 2 Transfer case diagnosis chart

Model NV-244 Transfer Case

INDEX

DIAGNOSIS & TESTING

Before repairing any transfer case, inspect all other driveline components first. The actual cause of a problem may be front hubs, axles, propeller shaft, wheels, tires, transmission or clutch. Ensure hub seals are intact, maintenance of the hubs is critical. Avoid prolonged exposure to dirt and water as damage to internal components will result. If a problem still exists after the inspection and verification, refer to **Fig. 1.**

CONDITION	POSSIBLE CAUSE	CORRECTION
Transfer case difficult to shift or will not shift into desired range.	1) Transfer case electronically controlled shift system malfunction.	1) Verify proper operation per the appropriate diagnostic manual.
	2) Insufficient or incorrect lubricant.	2) Drain and refill transfer case with the correct quantity of Mopar® ATF +4, type 9602, Automatic Transmission Fluid.
	3) Internal transfer case components binding, worn, or damaged.	3) Repair or replace components as necessary.
Transfer case noisy in all drive modes.	1) Insufficient or incorrect lubricant.	1) Drain and refill transfer case with the correct quantity of Mopar® ATF +4, type 9602, Automatic Transmission Fluid.
	2) Internal transfer case components binding, worn, or damaged.	2) Repair or replace components as necessary.

CR3040100332000X

Fig. 1 Transfer case diagnosis chart (Part 1 of 2)

CONDITION	POSSIBLE CAUSE	CORRECTION
Transfer case noisy while in, or jumps out of, 4LO.	1) Transfer case not completely engaged in 4LO position.	1) While rolling 2-3 MPH and the transmission in NEUTRAL, or the clutch depressed on vehicles equipped with a manual transmission, shift the transfer case to the AWD or 4HI position, and then back into the 4LO position.
	2) Range fork damaged, inserts worn, or fork is binding on the shift rail.	2) Repair or replace components as necessary.
	3) Low range gear worn or damaged.	3) Repair or replace components as necessary.
Lubricant leaking from transfer case seals or vent.	1) Transfer case overfilled.	1) Drain lubricant to the correct level.
	2) Transfer case vent closed or restricted.	2) Clean or replace vent as necessary.
	3) Transfer case seals damaged or installed incorrectly.	3) Replace suspect seal.
Transfer case will not shift through 4HI (Part-time) range.	1) Incomplete shift due to drivetrain torque load.	1) Drive in a straight line and momentarily release the accelerator pedal to complete the shift.
	2) Incorrect tire pressure.	2) Correct tire pressure as necessary.
	3) Excessive tire wear.	3) Correct tire condition as necessary.
	4) Excessive vehicle loading.	4) Correct as necessary.

CR3040100333000X

Fig. 1 Transfer case diagnosis chart (Part 2 of 2)

DISASSEMBLE

Rear Retainer & Oil Pump

1. Position transfer case in a suitable shallow drain pan.
2. Remove drain plug and drain.
3. Remove extension housing attaching bolts, then separate housing from rear retainer using a suitable plastic hammer to loosen housing, **Fig. 2.**
4. Remove rear bearing snap-ring.
5. Remove rear retainer to rear case half bolts.
6. Separate rear retainer from rear case using a suitable pry tool to brake sealer bead. Pry only against retainer boss.
7. Remove oil pickup tube from oil pump, then the oil pump assembly from transfer case, **Fig. 3.**
8. Remove pickup tube O-ring from oil pump. **Do not disassemble oil pump, it is not serviceable.**
9. Remove rear case to front case attaching bolts, **Fig. 4.** Note position of two black finish bolts at each end of case. These bolts go through case dowels and require a washer under bolt head.
10. Separate rear case from front case by inserting a suitable pry tool into slots cast into each end of case, then pry upward to break sealer bead.

Front Output Shaft & Drive Chain

1. Remove drive sprocket using suitable snap-ring pliers, **Fig. 5.**
2. Remove drive sprocket and chain, **Fig. 6.**
3. Remove front output shaft, **Fig. 7.**

Shift Forks & Mainshaft

1. Remove shift detent plug, spring and pin, **Fig. 8.**
2. Remove shift rail by pulling straight up and out of fork.
3. Remove mode fork and mainshaft as an assembly, **Fig. 9.**
4. Separate mode shift sleeve and mode fork assembly from mainshaft, **Fig. 10.** Note position of mode sleeve in fork and remove sleeve.
5. Remove intermediate clutch shaft using suitable snap ring pliers.
6. Remove clutch shaft thrust ring, **Fig. 11.**
7. Remove intermediate clutch shaft.
8. Remove differential snap ring using suitable snap ring pliers, **Fig. 12.**
9. Remove differential, needle bearings and both needle bearing thrust washers from mainshaft.
10. Slide low range fork pin out of shift sector slot, **Fig. 13.**

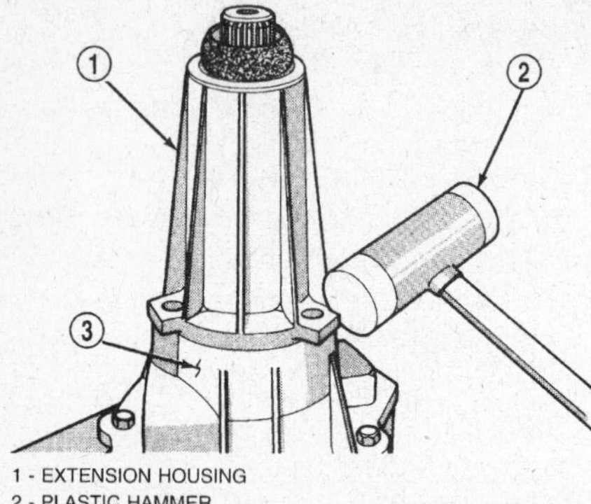

1 - EXTENSION HOUSING
2 - PLASTIC HAMMER
3 - REAR RETAINER

CR3040100334000X

Fig. 2 Extension housing removal

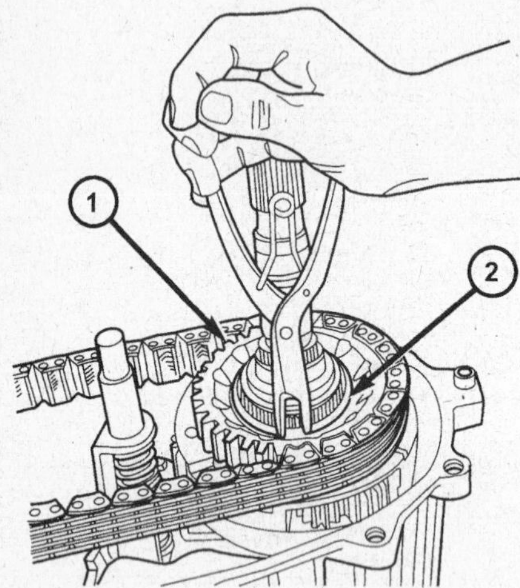

1 - DRIVE SPROCKET
2 - DRIVE SPROCKET SNAP-RING

CR3040100340000X

Fig. 5 Drive sprocket snap-ring removal

11. Remove low range fork and hub.
12. Remove shift sector and shift sector O-ring.

Input Gear/Low Range Assembly

1. Remove front bearing retainer bolts.
2. Carefully pry front bearing retainer loose using a suitable screwdriver, **Fig. 14,** then remove front bearing retainer.
3. Remove input gear snap ring using suitable snap ring pliers.
4. Remove input/low range gear assembly from bearing with tool handle No. C–4171 and gear removal tool No. 7829-A, or equivalents, **Fig. 15.**
5. Remove low range gear snap ring using suitable snap ring pliers, then the low range gear.
6. Remove input gear retainer, thrust washers and input gear from low range gear, **Fig. 16.**
7. Inspect low range annulus gear. **Gear is not a serviceable component. If**

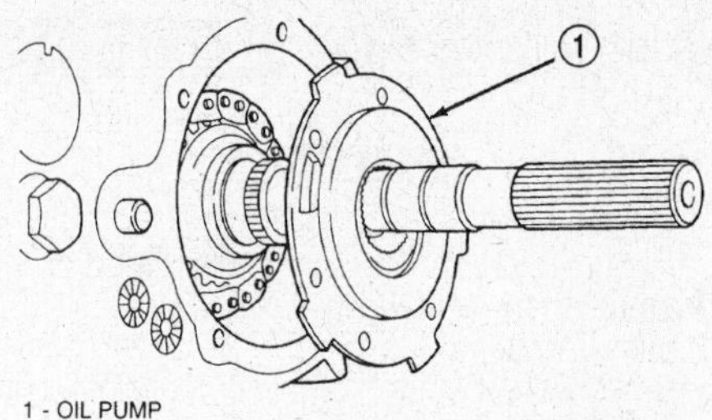

1 - OIL PUMP

CR3040100337000X

Fig. 3 Oil pump removal

damaged, replace gear and front case as an assembly.

8. Remove oil seals from front bearing retainer, rear retainer, oil pump and case halves.

Differential

1. Mark differential case halves for assembly reference.
2. Remove differential case bolts.
3. Invert differential on workbench.
4. Separate top case from bottom case using slots in case halves to pry them apart.
5. Remove thrust washers and planet gears from case pins, **Fig. 17.**
6. Remove mainshaft and sprocket gears from bottom case.

Bearings & Seals

1. Remove front output shaft front bearing retaining snap ring from case with suitable flat-bladed tool, **Fig. 18.**
2. Remove front output shaft front bearing from case.
3. Remove input shaft bearing with tool handle No. C-4171 and bearing remover tool No. C-4210, or equivalents, **Fig. 19.**
4. Remove input gear pilot bearing by inserting a suitably sized drift into splined end of input gear and driving bearing out with drift and hammer, **Fig. 20.**
5. Remove front output shaft rear bearing with screw and jaws from remover tool No. L-4454 and Cup tool No. 8148, or equivalents, **Fig. 21.**
6. Remove rear retainer bearing with bearing remover tool No. 5065 and tool handle No. C-4171, or equivalents.

INSPECTION

Mainshaft/Sprocket/ Hub Inspection

Inspect splines on hub and shafts and teeth on sprocket. Minor nicks and scratches can be smoothed with an oil stone. Replace any part that is damaged beyond repair. Inspect contact surfaces in sprocket bore and on mainshaft. Minor nicks and scratches can be smoothed with 320–400 grit emery cloth. If nicks or wear is severe, replace the shaft.

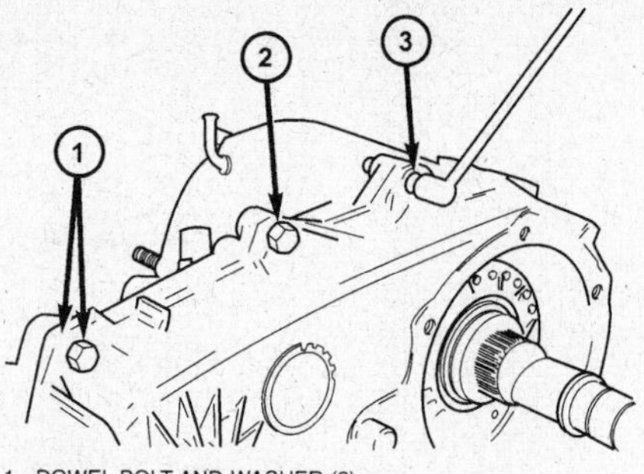

1 - DOWEL BOLT AND WASHER (2)
2 - CASE BOLT (5)
3 - SPLINE HEAD BOLT (1)

CR3040100339000X

Fig. 4 Spline & dowel bolt locations

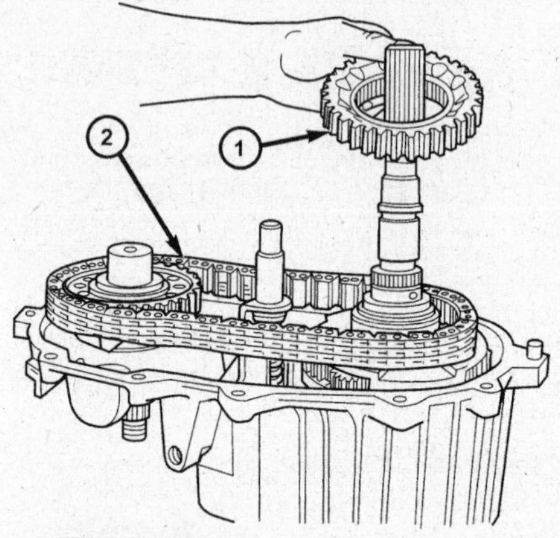

1 - FRONT OUTPUT SHAFT
2 - DRIVE CHAIN
3 - DRIVE SPROCKET

CR3040100341000X

Fig. 6 Drive sprocket & chain removal

Input Gear & Planetary Carrier

Inspect teeth on gear. Minor nicks can be polished out with an oilstone, but replace gear if any teeth are broken, cracked, or chipped. The bearing surface on gear can be smoothed with 300–400 grit emery cloth if required. Examine carrier body and pinion gears for wear or damage. The carrier body will have to be replaced as an assembly if body, pinion pins, or pinion gears are damaged. Inspect lock ring and both thrust washers for wear or cracks. Replace as required. Inspect lock retaining ring and replace if it is bent, distorted or broken.

Shift Forks/Hubs/ Selves

Inspect condition of shift forks and mode fork shift rail. Minor nicks on shift rail can be smoothed with 320–400 grit emery cloth. Inspect shift fork wear pads, **Fig. 22.** Mode and range pads are serviceable and can be replaced if required. Inspect both of sleeves for wear or damage, especially on interior teeth. Replace sleeves if wear or damage is evident.

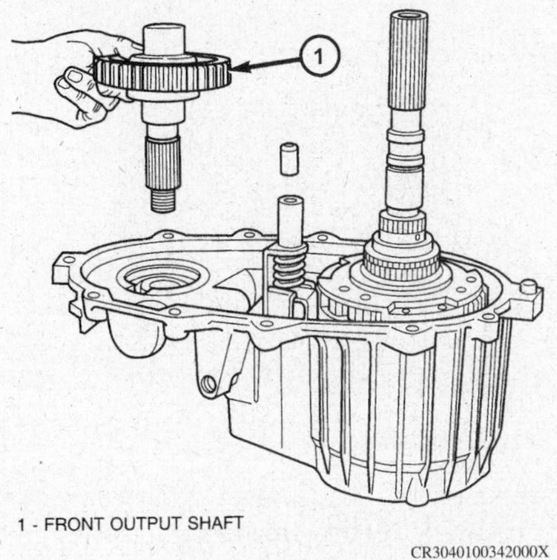

Fig. 7 Front output shaft removal

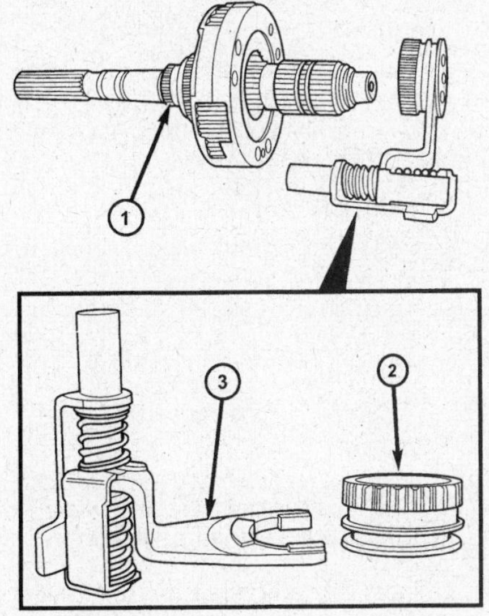

Fig. 10 Mode fork & sleeve

Rear Retainer & Extension Housing

Inspect condition of seal contact surfaces on companion flange slinger. This surface must be clean and smooth to ensure proper seal life. Replace flange nut and seal washer as neither part should be reused. Inspect shaft threads, sprocket teeth, and bearing surfaces. Minor nicks on teeth can be smoothed with oilstone. Use 320–40 grit emery to smooth minor scratches on shaft bearing surfaces. Rough threads on shaft can be chased if required with suitable tool. Replace shaft if threads are damaged, bearing surfaces are scored, or if any sprocket teeth are cracked or broken. Examine the drive chain and shaft bearings. Replace chain and both sprockets if chain is stretched, distorted, or if any of links bind. Replace bearings if rough, or noisy.

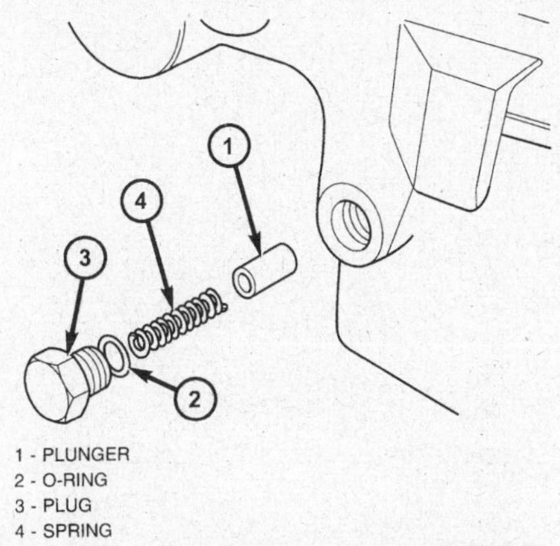

Fig. 8 Detent pin, spring & plug removal

Low Range Annulus Gear

Inspect annulus gear condition carefully. Gear is only serviced as part of front case. If gear is damaged, it will be required to replace gear and front case as an assembly. Do not attempt to remove gear, **Fig. 23.**

Front/Rear Cases & Front Retainer

Inspect cases and retainer for wear and damage. Clean sealing surfaces with a scraper and all purpose cleaner. This will ensure proper adhesion during assembly. Replace input retainer seal, do not reuse seal. Inspect case condition. If leaks were a problem, look for gouges and severe scoring of case sealing surfaces. Inspect front case mounting studs and vent tube. The tube can be secured with Loctite 271/680, or equivalent, if loose. The stud threads can be cleaned up with a suitable die if required. Inspect condition of fill/drain plug threads in rear case. The threads can be repaired with a suitable thread chaser or tap if required. If threads are damaged beyond repair, install a stainless steel threaded insert.

Oil Pump & Oil Pickup

Inspect oil pump pickup components. Replace pump if any components appear to be worn or damaged. Do not disassemble pump, pump is only available as a complete assembly. The pickup screen, hose and tube are the only serviceable components and are available separately.

ASSEMBLE

Bearings & Seals

1. Install new front output shaft front bearing with tapered cone upward using tool handle No. C-4171 and bearing installer tool No. 8033-A, or equivalents.

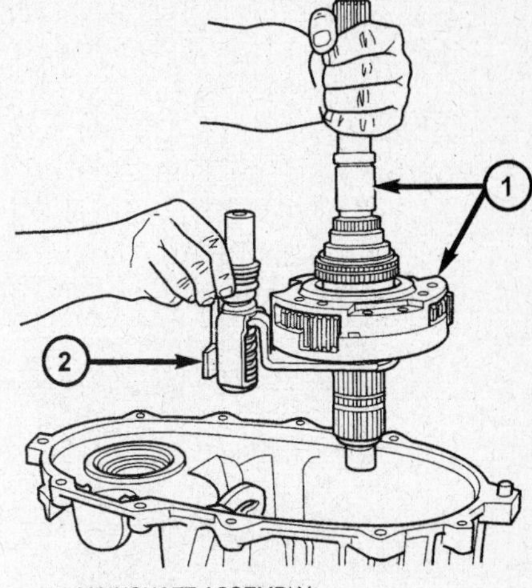

Fig. 9 Mainshaft & mode fork removal

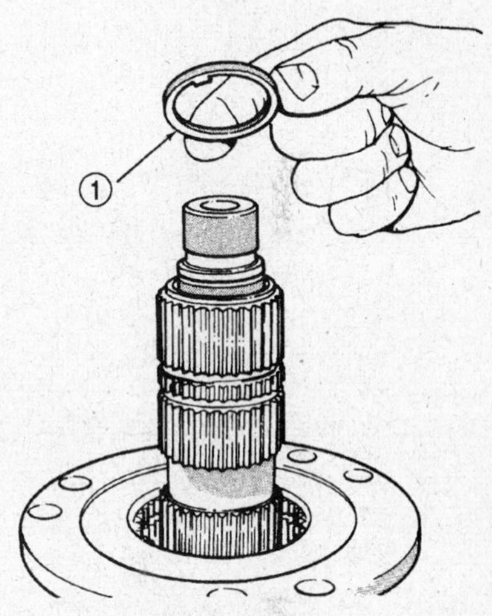

Fig. 11 Intermediate clutch shaft thrust ring removal

2. Install front bearing snap ring.
3. Install new front output shaft oil seal with seal installer tool No. 6952-A, or equivalent.
4. Install snap ring on new input shaft bearing.
5. Install new input shaft bearing with tool handle No. C-4171 and bearing remover tool No. C-4210, or equivalents. Install bearing far enough to seat snap ring against case.
6. Install new pilot bearing with bearing installer tool No. 8128 and handle tool No. C-4171, or equivalents, **Fig. 24.**
7. Install new seal in front bearing retainer with seal installer tool No. 7884, or equivalent.
8. Install new front output shaft bearing with tool handle No. C-4171 and bearing installer tool No. 5066, or equivalents, **Fig. 25.**
9. Install new seal in oil pump feed housing with seal installer tool No. 7888, or equivalent.

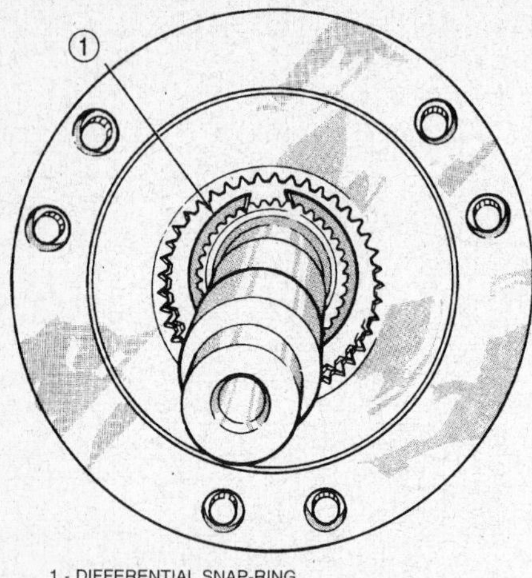

Fig. 12 Differential snap-ring removal

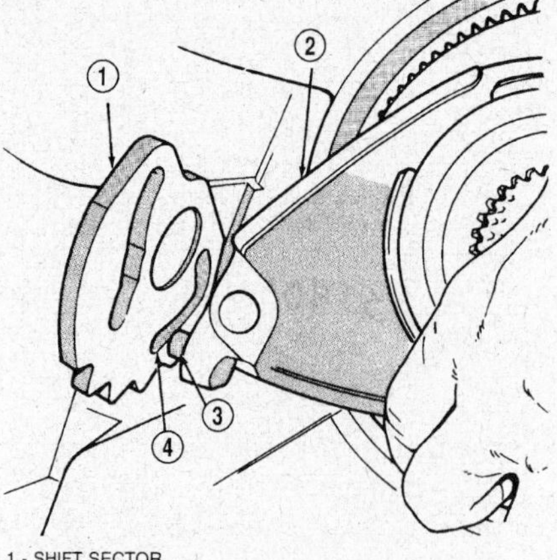

Fig. 13 Low range fork removal

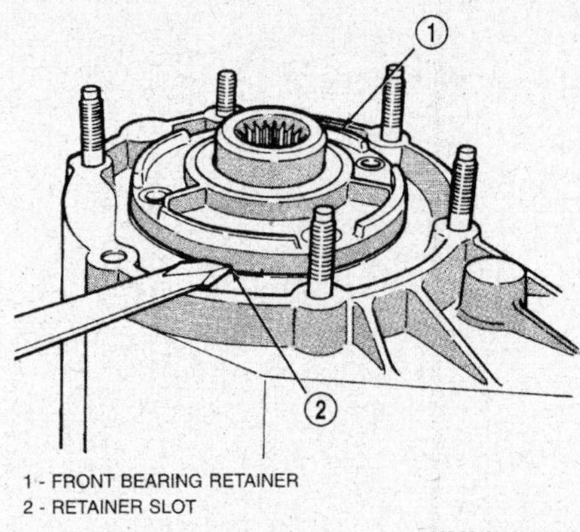

Fig. 14 Front bearing retainer removal

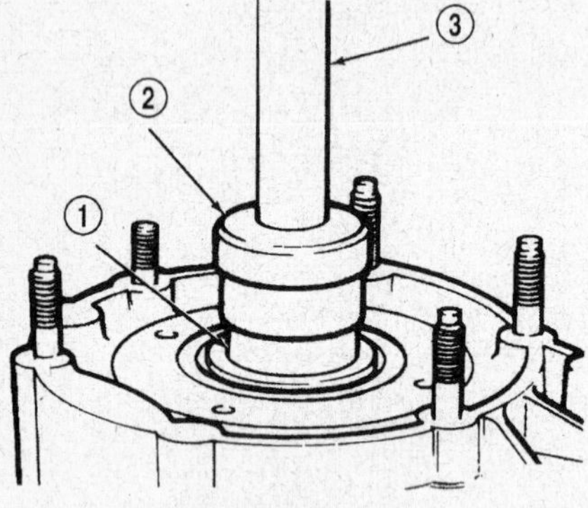

Fig. 15 Input & low range gear assembly removal

10. Install new pickup tube O-ring in oil pump, **Fig. 26.**
11. Install rear bearing in retainer with tool handle No. C-4171 and bearing installer tool No. 5064, or equivalents.

Differential

1. Lubricate differential components with Dexron II automatic transmission fluid.
2. Install sprocket gear in differential bottom case.
3. Install differential planet gears and new thrust washers, **Fig. 27. Ensure thrust washers are installed at top and bottom of each planet gear.**
4. Install differential mainshaft gear.
5. Position differential top case on bottom case by aligning match marks made during disassembly, **Fig. 28.**
6. While holding differential case halves together, invert differential and finger tighten differential case bolts.
7. Tighten differential case bolts to specifications.

Input Gear & Low Range

1. Assemble low range gear, input gear thrust washers, input gear and input gear retainer, **Fig. 29.**
2. Install low range gear snap ring.
3. Lubricate input gear and low range gears with Dexron II automatic transmission fluid.
4. Press input gear shaft into front bearing.
5. Install new input gear snap ring with suitable snap ring pliers.
6. Apply ⅛ inch wide bead of silicone adhesive sealer, Mopar Gasket Maker, or equivalent.
7. Install front bearing retainer and tighten retainer bolts to specifications.

Shift Forks & Mainshaft

1. Install new sector shaft O-ring, then the shift sector.
2. Install new pads on low range fork, if required.
3. Assemble low range fork and hub.
4. Position low range fork and hub in case. Ensure low range fork pin is engaged in shift sector slot **Fig. 13.**
5. Install first mainshaft bearing spacer on mainshaft.
6. Install bearing rollers on mainshaft. **Coat bearings rollers with generous amount of petroleum jelly to hold them in place.**
7. Install remaining bearing spacer on mainshaft. Do not displace bearings while installing spacer.
8. Install differential and snap ring.
9. Install intermediate clutch shaft, thrust ring and snap ring.
10. Install mode sleeve in mode fork, then install assembled sleeve and fork on mainshaft. Ensure mode sleeve

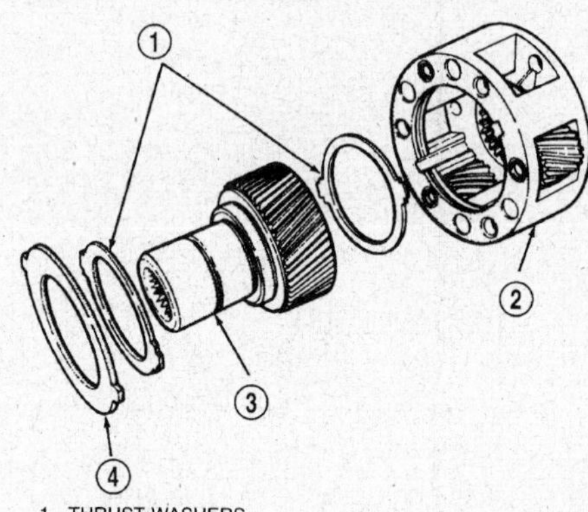

Fig. 16 Exploded view of low range & input gear assembly

splines are engaged in differential splines.

11. Install mode fork and mainshaft assembly in case. Rotate mainshaft slightly to engage shaft with low range gears.
12. Rotate mode fork pin into shift sector slot.
13. Install shift rail, ensure rail is seated in both shift forks.
14. Install detent plunger and spring, then the detent plug in case, **Fig. 8.**

Front Output Shaft & Drive Chain

1. Install front output shaft and drive chain, engage chain with front output shaft sprocket teeth.
2. Install drive sprocket, engage sprocket teeth with chain, then the sprocket splines with mainshaft splines.
3. Install drive sprocket snap ring.

Oil Pump & Rear Case

1. Insert oil pickup tube in oil pump and attach oil screen and connector hose to pickup tube.

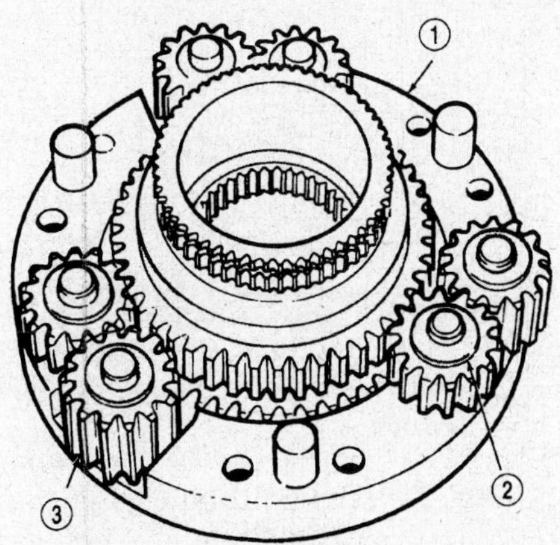

Fig. 17 Planet gears & thrust washer removal

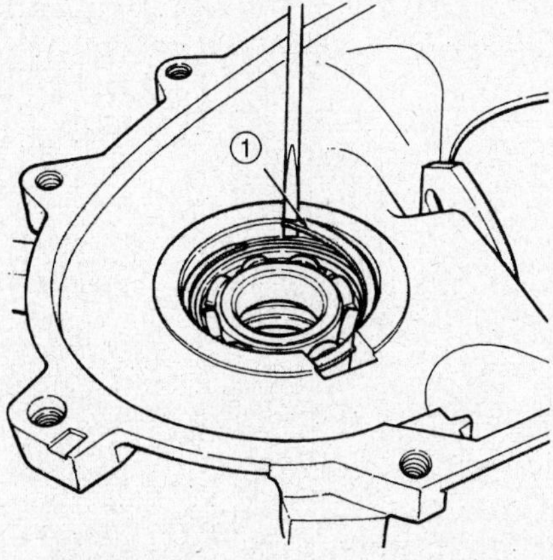

Fig. 18 Front output shaft snap ring removal

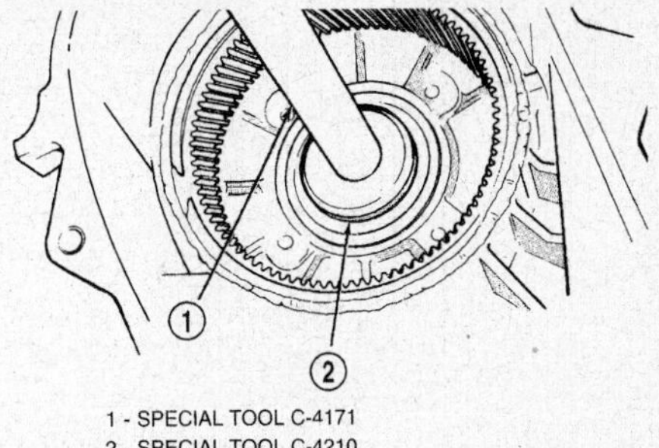

Fig. 19 Input shaft bearing removal

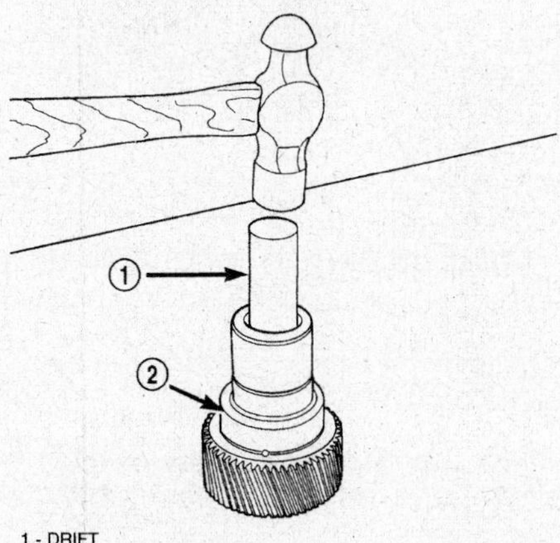

Fig. 20 Input gear pilot bearing removal

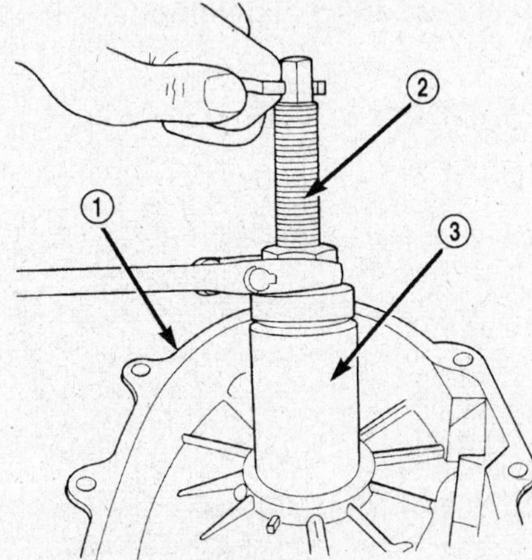

Fig. 21 Front output shaft rear bearing removal

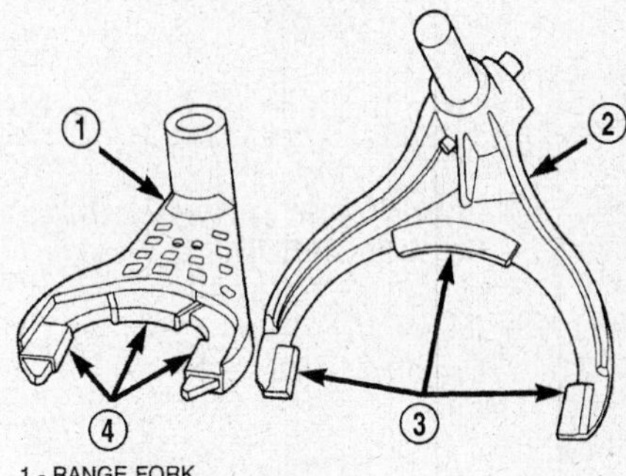

Fig. 22 Shift fork & wear pad locations

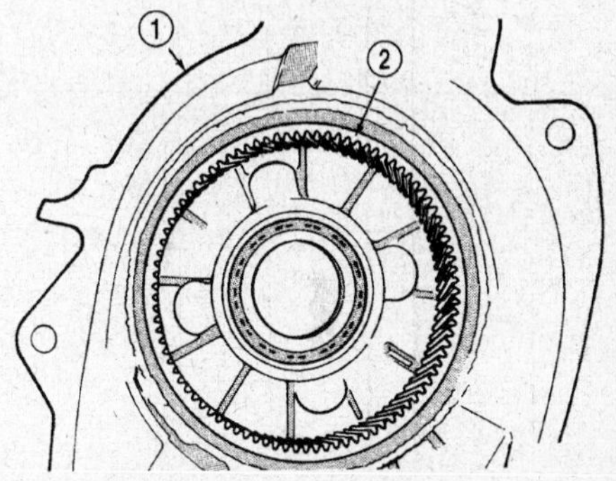

Fig. 23 Low range annulus gear

2. Install assembled pump, tube and screen into rear case. Ensure screen is seated in case slot, **Fig. 30.**
3. Clean transfer case magnet, then install magnet in front case pocket, **Fig. 31.**
4. Apply ⅛ inch wide bead of silicone sealant, Mopar Gasket Maker, or equivalent, to seal surface.
5. Align and install rear case onto front case. Ensure case locating dowels are in place and main shaft splines are engaged in oil pump inner gear.
6. Install and tighten front case to rear case bolts to specifications.

Rear Retainer

1. Apply ⅛ inch wide bead of silicone sealant, Mopar Gasket Maker, or equivalent, to mounting surface of rear retainer.
2. Install rear retainer on rear case and tighten bolts to specification.
3. Install new output shaft bearing snap ring. Lift mainshaft slightly to seat snap ring in shaft groove, if required.
4. Apply ⅛ inch wide bead of silicone sealant, Mopar Gasket Maker, or equivalent, to mounting surface of extension housing.
5. Install extension housing on rear retainer, then tighten housing bolts to specification.

Companion Flange, Shift Motor & Mode Sensor

1. Position shift motor and mode sensor assembly onto transfer case.
2. Apply thread sealer Loctite 242, or equivalent, on shift motor and mode sensor retaining bolts, then install bolts and tighten to specification.
3. Install new seal washer onto front output shaft.
4. Lubricate companion flange hub with Dexron II transmission fluid and install flange onto front output shaft.
5. Install a new companion flange nut onto front output shaft.
6. Tighten companion flange nut to specifications while holding flange with holding tool No. 6958, or equivalent.

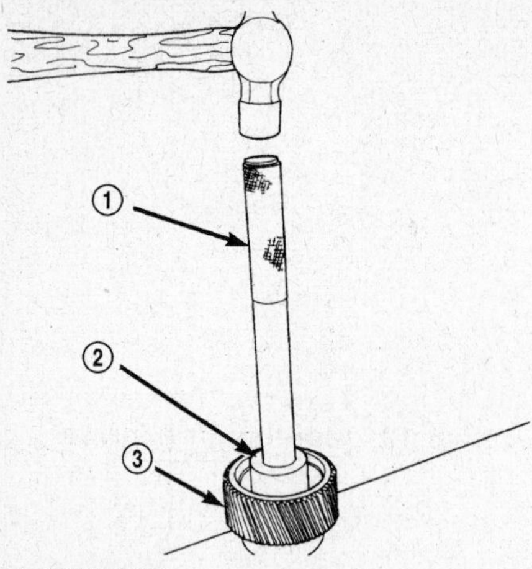

1 - HANDLE C-4171
2 - INSTALLER 8128
3 - INPUT GEAR

CR3040100364000X

Fig. 24 Input gear pilot bearing installation

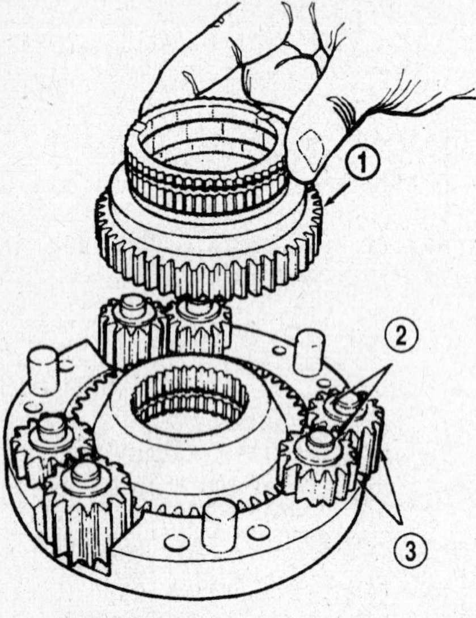

1 - MAINSHAFT GEAR
2 - THRUST WASHERS (12)
3 - PLANET GEARS (6)

CR3040100368000X

Fig. 27 Mainshaft & planet gears installation

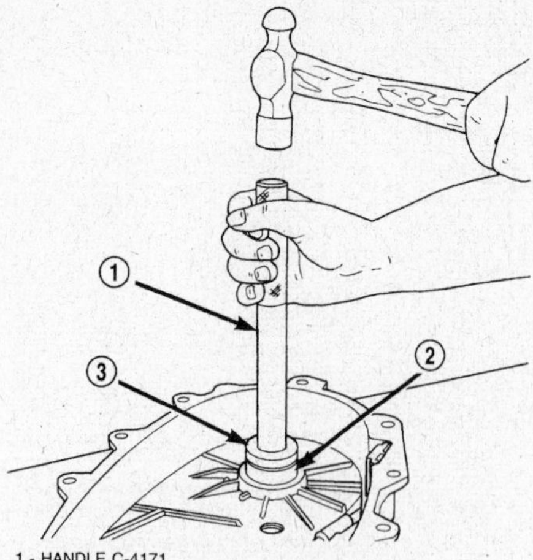

1 - HANDLE C-4171
2 - OUTPUT SHAFT INNER BEARING
3 - INSTALLER 5066

CR3040100366000X

Fig. 25 Front output shaft rear bearing installation

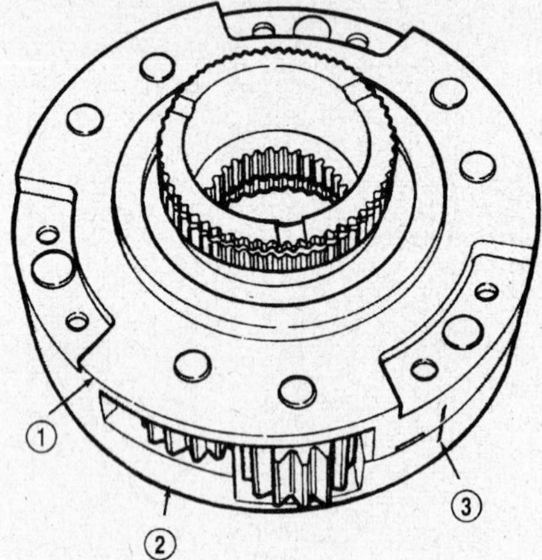

1 - TOP CASE
2 - BOTTOM CASE
3 - CASE ALIGNMENT MARKS

CR3040100369000X

Fig. 28 Differential case alignment marks

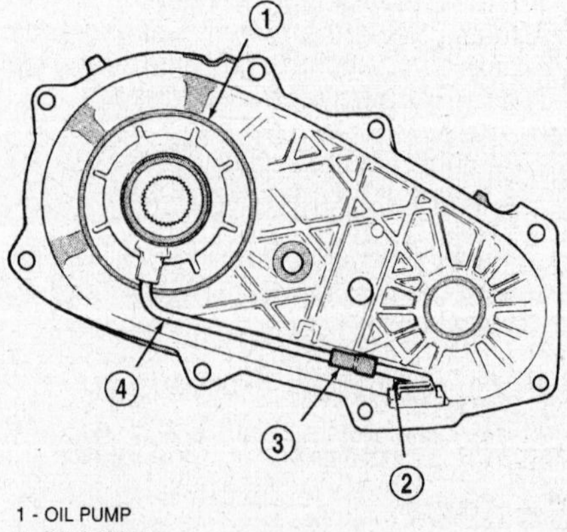

1 - OIL PUMP
2 - OIL SCREEN
3 - CONNECTOR
4 - PICKUP TUBE

CR3040100380000X

Fig. 30 Oil screen & pickup tube installation

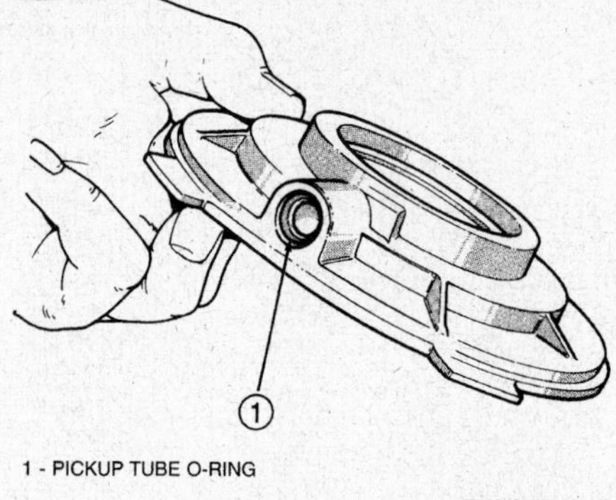

1 - PICKUP TUBE O-RING

CR3040100367000X

Fig. 26 Pickup tube O-ring installation

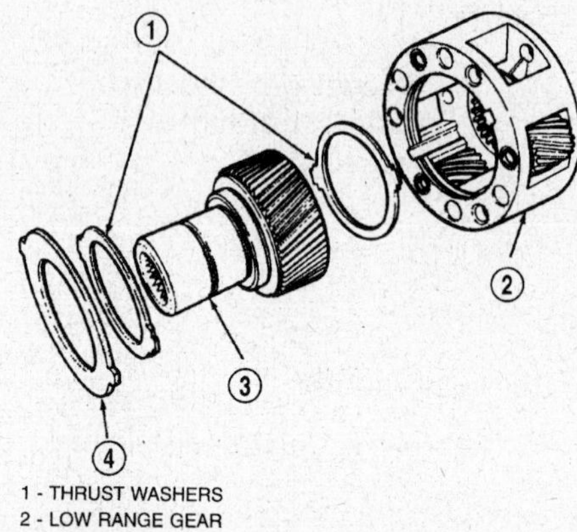

1 - THRUST WASHERS
2 - LOW RANGE GEAR
3 - INPUT GEAR
4 - RETAINER

CR3040100370000X

Fig. 29 Exploded view of low range & input gear assembly

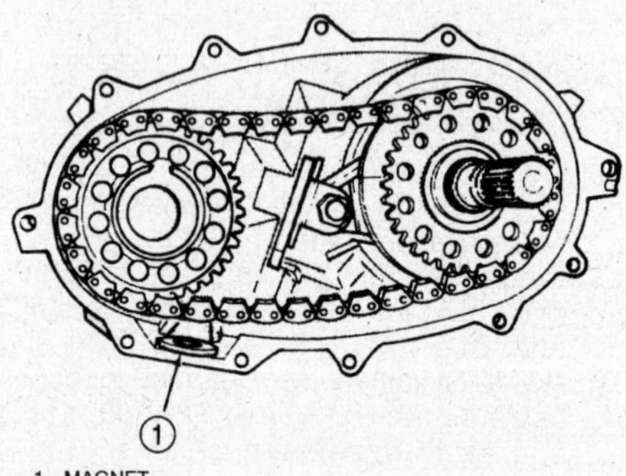

1 - MAGNET

CR3040100381000X

Fig. 31 Case magnet installation

TIGHTENING SPECIFICATIONS

Year	Component	Torque Ft. Lbs.
2002–06	Case Half	20–25
	Companion Flange Nut	90–130
	Detent Plug	12–18
	Differential Case	15–24
	Drain Plug	15–25
	Extension Housing	20–25
	Front Bearing Retainer	12–18
	Mounting Nut	20–25
	Rear Retainer	20–25
	Shift Motor & Mode Sensor Assembly	12–18

Model NV-241HD Transfer Case

INDEX

DIAGNOSIS & TESTING

Before repairing any transfer case, inspect all other driveline components first. The actual cause of a problem may be front hubs, axles, propeller shaft, wheels, tires, transmission or clutch. Ensure hub seals are intact, maintenance of the hubs is critical. Avoid prolonged exposure to dirt and water as damage to internal components will result. If a problem still exists after the inspection and verification, refer to **Fig. 1** for further transfer case diagnosis.

DISASSEMBLE

Extension Housing

1. Remove extension housing snap ring access cover.
2. Remove bolts holding extension housing to rear case half.
3. Tap extension housing with plastic or rawhide hammer to loosen sealant.
4. Remove extension housing snap ring from rear output shaft bearing.
5. Separate extension housing from transfer case.

Companion Flange & Shift Lever

1. Shift transfer case into neutral.
2. Remove and discard companion flange nut, it is not reusable.
3. Remove companion flange from front output shaft. Use a suitable puller if flange cannot be removed by hand.
4. Remove companion flange rubber seal from front output shaft.
5. Remove shift lever from sector shaft.

Front Output Shaft & Drive Chain

1. Remove output bearing retaining ring with suitable snap ring pliers, then the bearing.
2. Note position of bolts that attach rear case half to front case half. Mark position of bolts that require flat washers.
3. Remove case bolts, then loosen rear case with suitable pry tool placed in slot at each end of case.
4. Remove rear case and oil pump assembly.
5. Remove shift rail cup and spring.
6. Remove front sprocket retaining spring, **Fig. 2.**
7. Pull mainshaft, front sprocket and chain outward approximately one inch simultaneously.
8. Remove chain from mainshaft drive sprocket and remove front sprocket and chain assembly.

Shift Fork & Mainshaft

1. Remove vacuum indicator switch.
2. Remove poppet plunger screw and spring.
3. Poppet screw has an O-ring seal, remove and discard O-ring seal, then remove poppet plunger with magnet.
4. Remove front output shaft from bearing in case.
5. Remove mainshaft assembly from input gear, sliding clutch and case, **Fig. 3.**
6. Remove mode fork, **Fig. 4,** then sliding clutch and shift rail as an assembly.
7. Note which way clutch fits in fork, long side of clutch goes to front.
8. Remove range fork retaining ring, **Fig. 5.**
9. Remove range fork, **Fig. 6,** and support sleeve as an assembly.
10. Remove shift selector, then remove shift selector nylon retainer and O-ring from shaft bore in front case, **Fig. 7.**
11. Remove retaining ring that secures synchro hub on mainshaft, **Fig. 8,** using standard snap ring pliers.
12. Remove synchro hub.
13. Inspect synchro hub struts and springs, **Fig. 9.** If struts appear worn, remove struts and springs from hub. Note position of springs for installation reference.
14. Remove brass stop ring. Discard stop ring if worn, cracked or damaged.
15. Remove drive sprocket.

Input & Planetary Gear

1. Remove input bearing retainer bolts.
2. Loosen bearing retainer with suitable pry tool. Insert tool in retainer slot, then remove retainer.
3. Remove input gear retaining ring, **Fig. 10,** using heavy duty parallel jaw pliers.
4. Tap input gear out of bearing with plastic mallet.
5. Remove input gear and planetary/PTO gear as an assembly, **Fig. 11.**
6. Position planetary assembly so PTO gear is on bench.
7. Remove retaining ring that secures input gear and lock ring in planetary assembly, **Fig. 12.**
8. Remove lock ring and front thrust washer from carrier. Note that lock ring and thrust washer are both tabbed.
9. Remove input gear from planetary carrier by lifting straight up.
10. Remove support sleeve from carrier, **Fig. 13.**
11. Remove rear thrust washer.

INSPECTION

Transfer Case

Wash all components thoroughly in clean solvent. Ensure all old lubricant, sealant, metal particles, dirt and foreign material are removed from surfaces of all components.

Apply compressed air to each oil feed port and channel in both case halves to remove any foreign material or cleaning solvent residue.

Inspect two case halves for cracks, porosity, damaged mating surfaces, stripped bolt threads or distortion. Replace or repair case halves as required. Stripped threads

Condition	Possible Cause	Correction
TRANSFER CASE DIFFICULT TO SHIFT OR WILL NOT SHIFT INTO DESIRED RANGE	(1) Vehicle speed too great to permit shifting. (2) If vehicle was operated for extended period in 4H mode on dry paved surface, driveline torque load may cause difficulty. (3) Transfer case external shift linkage binding. (4) Insufficient or incorrect lubricant. (5) Internal components binding, worn or damaged.	(1) Stop vehicle and shift into desired range. Or reduce speed to 3-4 km/h (2-3 mph) before attempting to shift. (2) Stop vehicle, shift transmission to Neutral, shift transfer case to 2H mode and operate vehicle in 2H on dry paved surfaces. (3) Lubricate, repair or replace linkage bushings or tighten loose components as necessary. (4) Drain and refill to edge of fill hole with DEXRON II® or MOPAR-MERCON® Automatic Transmission Fluid. (5) Disassemble unit and replace worn or damaged components as necessary.
TRANSFER CASE NOISY IN ALL DRIVE MODES	(1) Insufficient or incorrect lubricant.	(1) Drain and refill to edge of fill hole with DEXRON II® or MOPAR-MERCON® Automatic Transmission Fluid. Check for leaks and repair if necessary. **Note: If unit is still noisy after drain and refill, disassembly and inspection may be required to locate source of noise.**
NOISY IN – OR JUMPS OUT OF – FOUR WHEEL DRIVE LOW RANGE	(1) Transfer case not completely engaged in 4L position. (2) Shift linkage out of adjustment. (3) Shift linkage loose or binding. (4) Range fork damaged, inserts worn, or fork is binding on shift rail. (5) Low range gear worn or damaged.	(1) Stop vehicle, shift transfer case to Neutral, then shift back into 4L position. (2) Adjust linkage. (3) Tighten, lubricate or repair linkage as necessary. (4) Disassemble unit and repair as necessary. (5) Disassemble and repair as necessary.
LUBRICANT LEAKING FROM OUTPUT SHAFT SEALS OR FROM VENT	(1) Transfer case overfilled. (2) Vent closed or restricted. (3) Output shaft seals damaged or installed incorrectly.	(1) Drain to correct level. (2) Clear or replace vent if necessary. (3) Replace seals. Be sure seal lip faces interior of case when installed. Also be sure yoke seal surfaces are not scored or nicked. Remove scores and nicks with fine sandpaper or replace yoke(s) if necessary.
ABNORMAL TIRE WEAR	(1) Extended operation on dry hard surface (paved) roads in 4H range.	(1) Operate in 2H on hard surface (paved) roads.

CR3049900173000X

Fig. 1 Transfer case diagnosis chart

can be repaired with stainless steel threaded inserts. Rescuer case vent tube with Loctite 680, or equivalent, if required.

Synchronizer Hubs & Rings

Inspect the spline teeth on the synchronizer hub. If evidence of chipping or excessive wear is apparent, replace the hub. The hooked end of each synchro spring should be inserted in one of the struts. In addition, the springs should not interfere with the polished gear cone or inside diameters of the hub.

Inspect the stop rings for cracks and wear. Replace as required. Inspect synchronizer struts for wear or damage.

Gears & Snap Rings

Inspect all gear teeth and splines for burrs, nicks, wear or damage. Remove minor nicks and scratches with an oil stone. Replace any part with damaged splines.

Inspect annulus gear for wear or damage. If damage is apparent, replace front case and annulus gear as an assembly.

It is recommended that all retaining snap rings be replaced during overhaul. Most retaining rings will become distorted during the removal process and cannot be reused.

Shift Forks & Sleeves

Inspect the condition of shift fork pads, **Fig. 14.** The pads should be replaced if cracked, worn or lose.

Inspect the shift forks, clutch and sleeve for cracks, wear or any visible damage. The shift sector shaft and detente should also

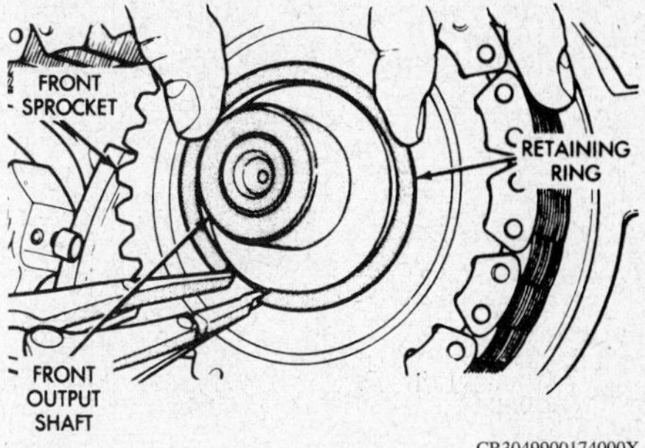

Fig. 2 Front sprocket retaining ring removal

be inspected for wear or damage. The mode fork and shift rail are a one piece unit. If either part is damaged, replace the fork and rail as an assembly. Replace the shift rail cup and spring if they exhibit wear.

Planetary Carrier

Inspect the planetary thrust washers for wear or damage. Replace both washers if required.

The planetary carrier cannot be disassembled. It must be serviced as an assembly if damaged. Inspect the condition of the pinion teeth and the PTO gear teeth. If pinion tooth wear is evident, it will be required to inspect the annulus gear teeth.

ASSEMBLE

Bearing & Seal

1. Drive input shaft seal from case from inside annulus gear opening using removal tool No. C-4210 and handle tool No. C-4171, or equivalents.
2. Install locating ring on new bearing.
3. Position case so that forward end is facing upward.
4. Drive input shaft bearing into case using removal tool No. C-4120 and handle tool No. C-4171, or equivalents.
5. Bearing locating ring must be fully seated on case.
6. Remove front output shaft bearing using installer tool No. 6953, or equivalent. Start new front output shaft bearing into case, then seat bearing with handle tool and installer No. 6953, or equivalent.
7. Install front output bearing retaining ring.
8. Install new front output seal in front case with handle tool and installer tool No. 6888, or equivalent, as follows:
   a. Start seal in bore with light taps from hammer.
   b. Once seal is started, continue tapping seal into bore until installer bottoms out against case.
   c. Remove installer and verify that seal is .080–.100 inch below top edge of seal bore.
9. Remove seal from front bearing retainer with suitable pry tool.

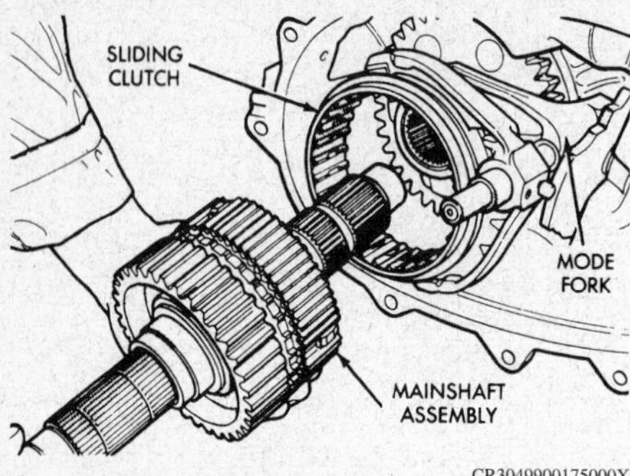

Fig. 3 Mainshaft assembly removal

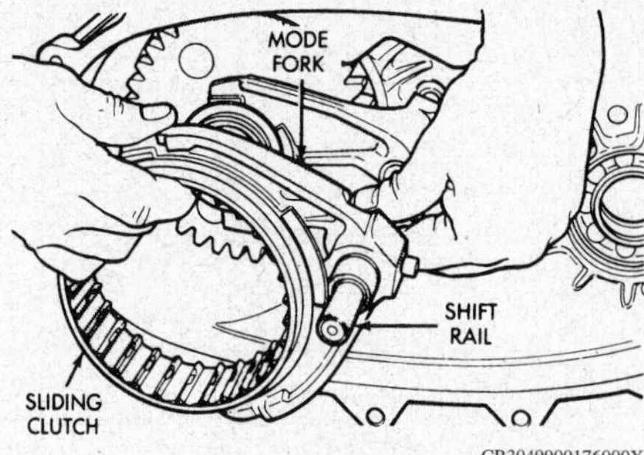

Fig. 4 Mode fork, sliding clutch & shift rail

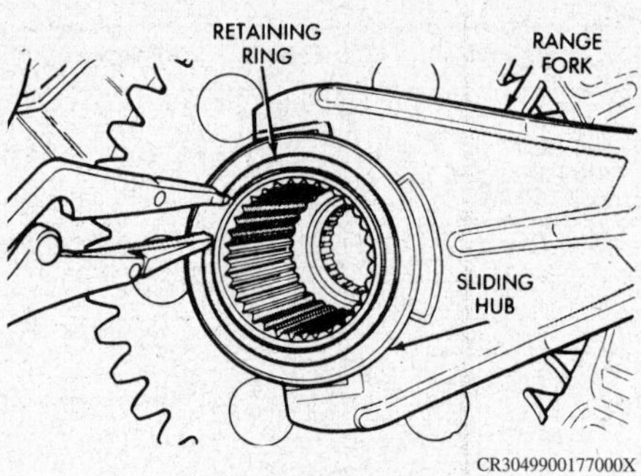

Fig. 5 Range fork retaining ring

Fig. 6 Range fork & support sleeve

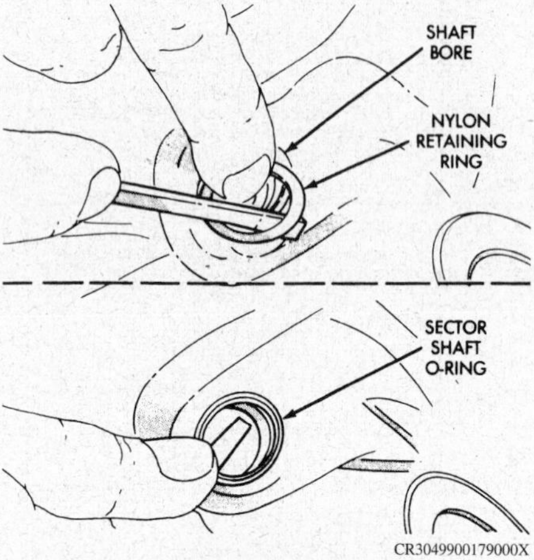

Fig. 7 Sector shaft O-ring & retainer

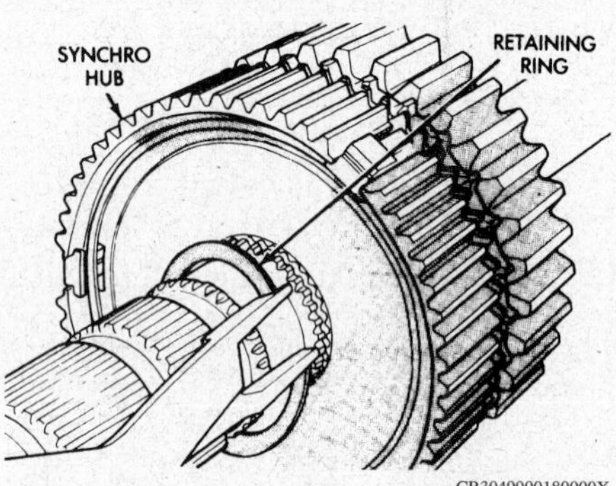

Fig. 8 Synchro hub retaining ring

10. Install new oil seal in front bearing retainer with installer No. 7884, or equivalent.
11. Remove seal from oil pump with suitable pry tool.
12. Install new seal in oil pump with installer No. 7888, or equivalent.
13. Inspect carrier needle bearing, if bearing is worn, rough or damaged, remove it with brass punch and a hammer, **Fig. 15.**
14. Install new needle bearing in planetary carrier using handle tool and installer No. 5062, or equivalents.
15. Remove input gear pilot bearing by inserting a suitable sized drift into splined end of input gear, **Fig. 16.** Drive bearing out with drift and hammer.
16. Install new pilot bearing with Plug tool No. C-293-3, or equivalent.
17. Remove output shaft rear bearing with screw and jaws from remover tool No. L-4454 and cup tool No. 8148, or equivalents **Fig. 17.**
18. Install new bearing with handle tool and installer tool No. 5066, or equivalents.
19. Bearing bore is chamfered at top, install bearing so it is flush with lower edge of chamfer.

Input & Planetary Gear

1. Lubricate planetary components with suitable transmission fluid.
2. Install first thrust washer in carrier, lube washer with petroleum jelly before installation.
3. Support carrier with wood blocks, **Fig. 18,** under PTO gear.
4. Install support sleeve in planetary carrier, ensure sleeve is fully seated.
5. Install input gear in planetary carrier.
6. Install second thrust washer in planetary carrier, ensure washer tabs are seated in carrier slots.
7. Install lock ring and retaining ring.
8. Lubricate planetary pinions and annulus gear with transmission fluid.
9. Install planetary/input gear assembly into case.
10. Start planetary pinions in low range annulus gear, then tap PTO gear with hammer handle to seat planetary pinions in annulus gear.
11. Install retaining ring on input gear, **Fig. 19.**
12. Apply a bead of Mopar Gasket maker, or equivalent, to mating surface of input retainer.
13. Keep sealer bead width to a maximum of 3/16 inch.
14. Align oil channel in retainer with oil feed hole in front case, **Fig. 20.**
15. Install retainer on input gear shaft and front case.
16. Apply suitable silicone sealer to threads of input retainer bolts.
17. Install bolts and tighten to specification.

Mainshaft Assembly

1. Install drive sprocket on mainshaft.
2. Install brass stop ring on drive sprocket, **Fig. 21.**
3. Install three synchro struts and two springs in hub as follows:
   a. Insert first strut in hub, **Fig. 22.** Strut shoulders rest (and slide) on sides of hub slot.
   b. Insert hooked end of first spring in center of strut **Fig. 23,** then work spring into hub.
   c. Press spring inward and install last two struts in hub slots. Ensure spring is positioned under struts to properly secure in place.
   d. Turn hub over and install remaining spring in hub. Position hooked end of second spring 180° away from first spring end.
4. Install assembled synchro hub on mainshaft. Hub has a shoulder on one side which goes toward sprocket or rear of shaft. Flat side of hub faces front of shaft.
5. Install synchro hub retaining ring, **Fig. 24.** Ensure ring is fully seated.
6. Install sliding clutch (sleeve) on synchro hub.
7. Sliding clutch must be correctly positioned to ensure proper shifting. Position clutch hub so that clutch spline is centered over each strut, **Fig. 25.**
8. If clutch is installed so a gap between splines is aligned with one or more struts, gear clash will result.

Shift Forks & Mainshaft

1. Support front case with wood blocks so case interior is facing up.
2. Place blocks between mounting studs on forward surface of case. Ensure blocks will not interfere with input gear installation.
3. Lubricate mainshaft components with Dexron II transmission fluid.

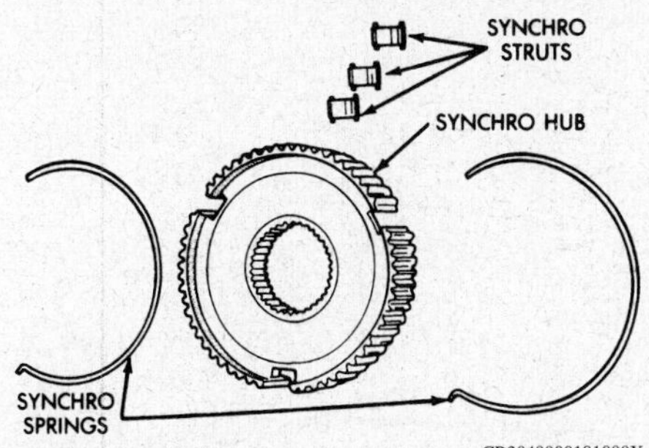

Fig. 9 Synchro strut & spring

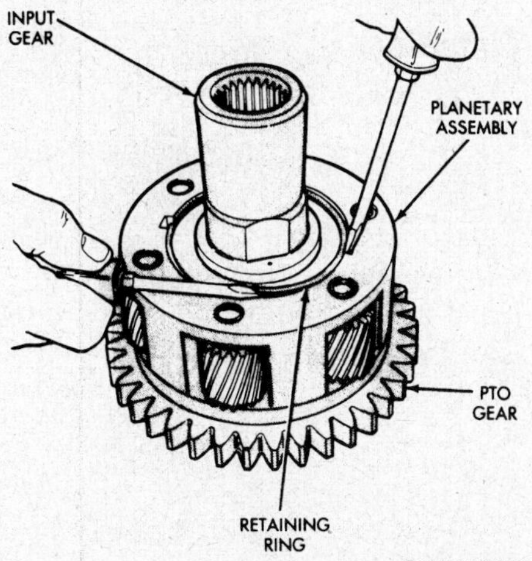

Fig. 12 Lock ring/input gear retaining ring

4. Lubricate sector shaft with ATF and install shift sector in case. Position slot in sector so it will be aligned with shift fork when forks are installed.
5. Assemble range fork and synchro clutch and hub.
6. Install fork and hub in case. seat hub on support sleeve and seat fork pin in shift sector slot, **Fig. 26.**
7. Install sliding hub and retaining ring, **Fig. 27.** Ensure ring is fully seated.
8. Install mode fork and shift rail, **Fig. 28,** in sliding clutch.
9. Install mainshaft/mode fork assembly, **Fig. 29.** Guide mainshaft through hub and into input gear and shift rail through range fork and into case bore.
10. Replace O-ring on vacuum switch if required, then install vacuum switch and tighten to specification.
11. Install new sector shaft O-ring and O-ring retainer, **Fig. 30,** in sector shaft bore.
12. Lubricate O-ring with ATF or petroleum jelly after installation.
13. Install shift lever on sector shaft.
14. Apply one or two drops of Mopar Lock-N-Seal, or equivalent, on nut threads, then install washer and nut and tighten to specification.
15. Install poppet plunger and spring.

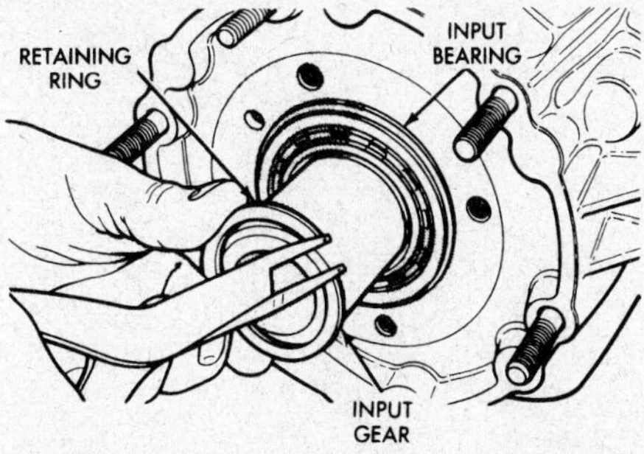

Fig. 10 Input gear retaining ring removal

16. Install new O-ring on poppet screw and tighten to specification.

Front Output Shaft & Chain Drive

1. Install front output shaft in bearing.
2. Install front sprocket in drive chain.
3. Install drive chain around mainshaft sprocket, then position front sprocket over front shaft.
4. Raise mainshaft approximately one inch and seat front sprocket on front output shaft.
5. If mainshaft and sliding clutch were unseated during chain installation, align and reseat mainshaft in input gear and hub.
6. Then reseat synchro hub in sliding clutch. Press synchro struts inward to ease clutch back onto hub. Install front sprocket retaining ring, **Fig. 31.**
7. Realign sliding clutch on synchro hub if required.
8. Press synchro struts inward to ease realignment. Ensure mainshaft is fully seated before proceeding.
9. Install spring and cup on shift rail.
10. Insert magnet in front case pocket.

Oil Pump & Rear Case

Lubricate oil pump components with Dexron II ATF before installation. Prime the oil pickup tube by pouring a little ATF into tube before installation.

1. Install new O-ring in pickup tube inlet of oil pump, **Fig. 32.**
2. Position oil pickup tube and filter in case, **Fig. 33.** Ensure pickup tube is seated in case pocket and aligned in case notches and that hose that connects tube to filter is securely positioned.
3. Insert oil pickup tube in oil pump and position in rear case, **Fig. 34.**
4. Apply a bead of Mopar Gasket Maker, or equivalent, to mating surfaces of front case.
5. Keep sealer bead width to a maximum of 3⁄16 inch.
6. Align oil pump with mainshaft and align shift rail with bore in rear case.
7. Ensure oil pump and pickup tube remain in position during case installation.
8. Verify that shift rail, **Fig. 35,** and case alignment dowels are seated before installing any bolts.
9. Install 4–5 case bolts to hold rear case in position. Tighten bolts snug but do not tighten to specification at this time.
10. Verify that oil pump is aligned and seated on case. Reposition pump if required.
11. Inspect stud at end of case halves. If stud was loosened or came out during disassembly, apply Loctite 242, or equivalent, to stud threads and reseat stud in case.
12. Apply Loctite 242, or equivalent, to remainder of rear case bolt threads and install bolts.
13. Ensure lock washers are used on studs/bolts at case ends.
14. Tighten all bolts or nuts to specification.
15. Install oil pump retaining ring on mainshaft, **Fig. 36.**
16. Install rear output bearing and snap ring onto output shaft.

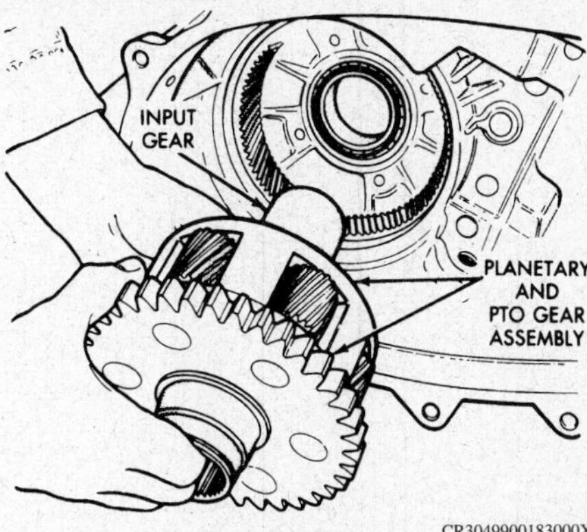

Fig. 11 Input gear & planetary assembly

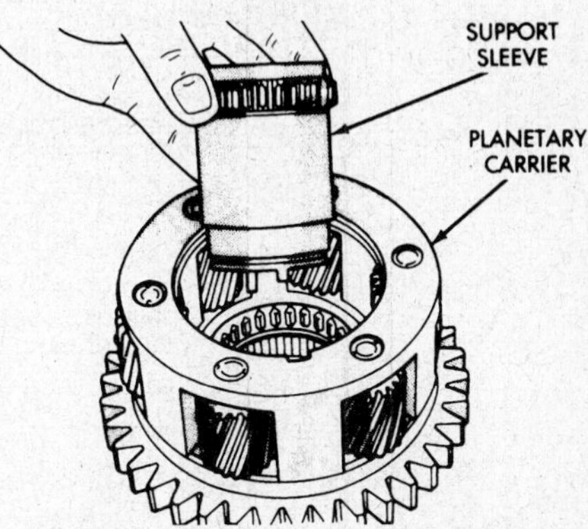

Fig. 13 Support sleeve removal

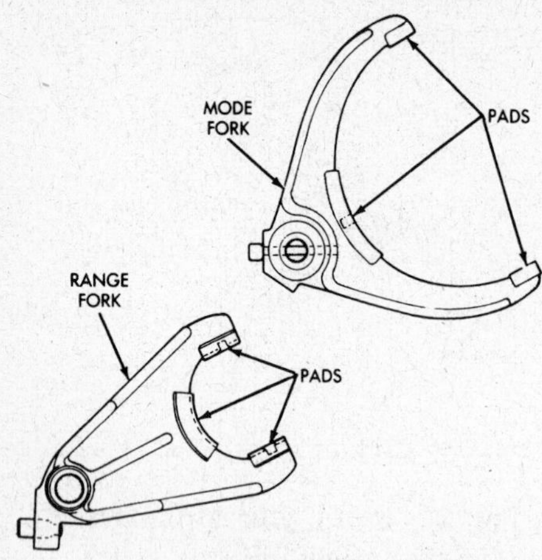

Fig. 14 Shift fork pads

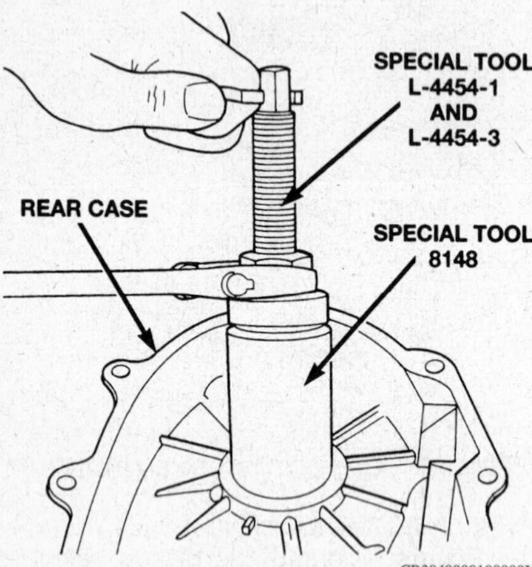

Fig. 17 Output shaft bearing removal

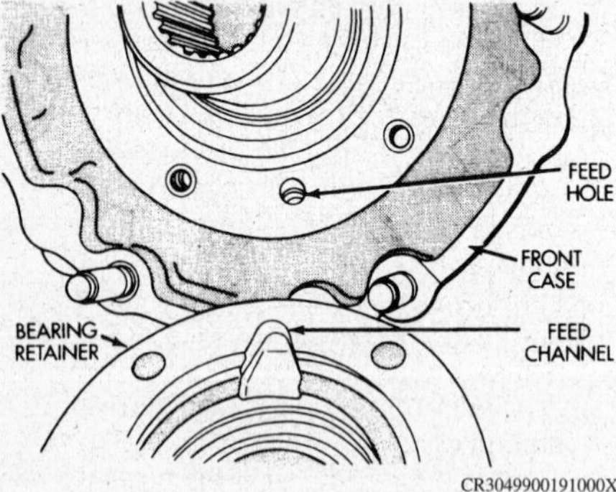

Fig. 20 Retainer oil channel & case feed holes alignment

Companion Flange

1. Install companion flange seal, **Fig. 37**, on front shaft.
2. Install companion flange and flange nut and tighten to specification.

Extension House & PTO Cover

1. Apply bead of Mopar Gasket Maker, or equivalent, to mating surface of extension housing.
2. Keep sealer bead width to a maximum of 3⁄16 inch.
3. Position extension housing over output shaft.
4. Spread extension housing retaining ring and seat extension housing on rear case. Verify that retaining ring is seated in output shaft rear bearing.
5. Install retaining ring access cover.
6. Apply suitable silicone sealer to threads of extension housing bolts and install finger tight.
7. Tighten extension housing bolts to specification.
8. Apply suitable silicone sealer to mating surfaces of PTO cover and to cover bolt shanks and underside of bolt heads.
9. Install cover and bolts and tighten to specification.

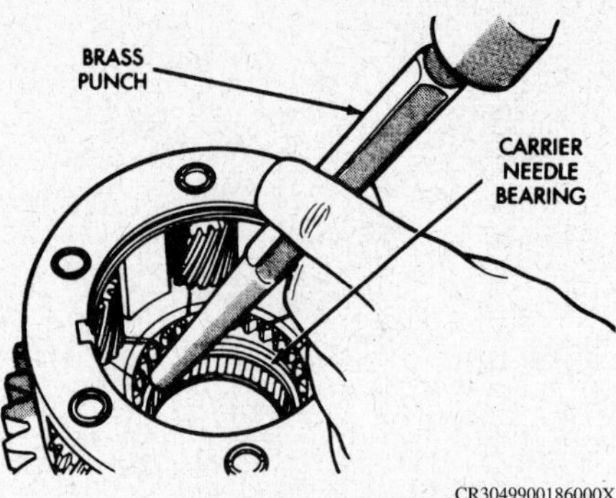

Fig. 15 Carrier needle bearing inspection

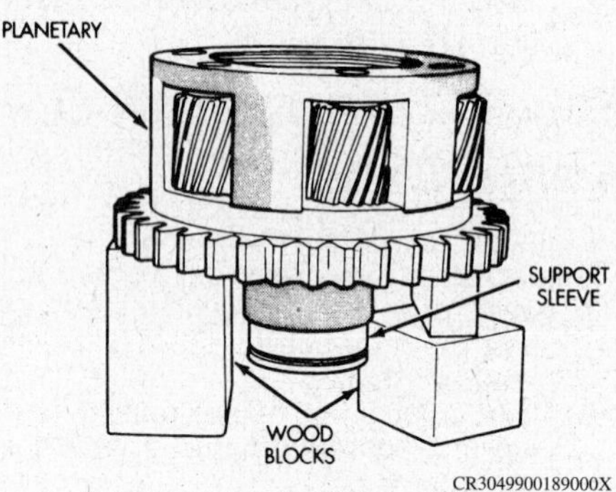

Fig. 18 Supported sleeve installation

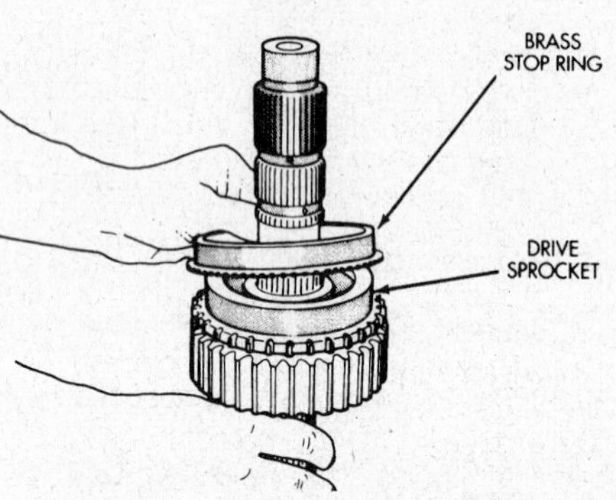

Fig. 21 Synchro stop ring installation

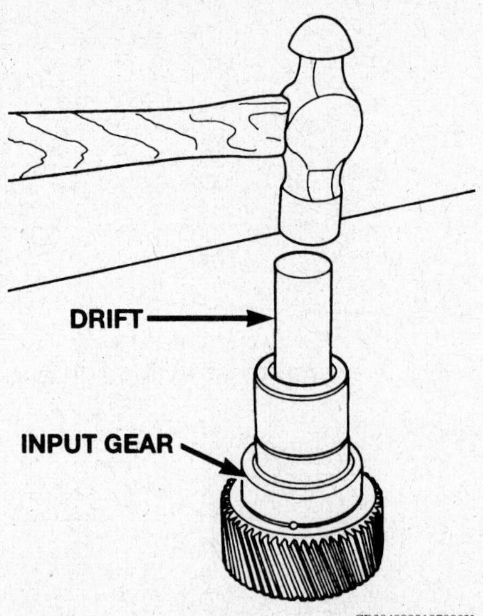

Fig. 16 Input gear pilot bearing removal

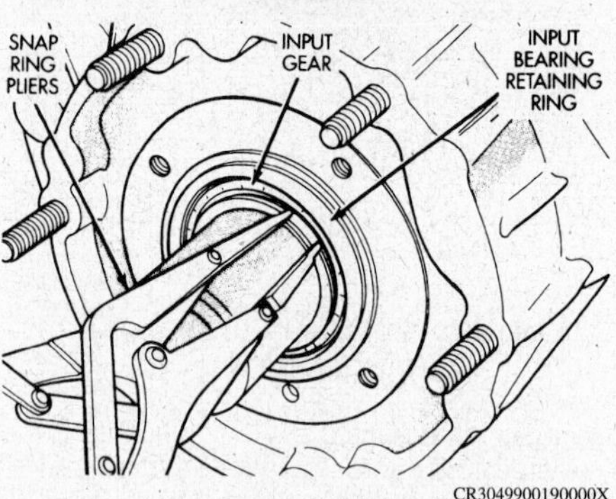

Fig. 19 Input gear retaining ring installation

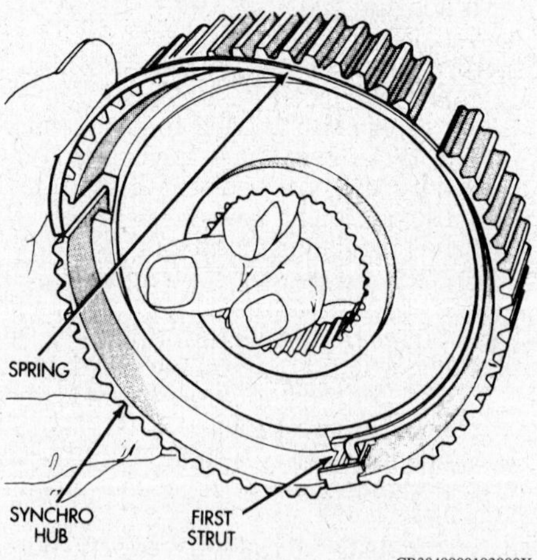

Fig. 22 First synchro strut & spring installation

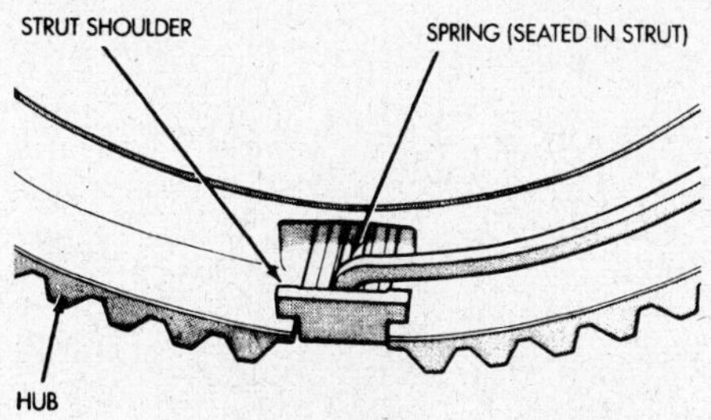

Fig. 23 Synchro spring installation

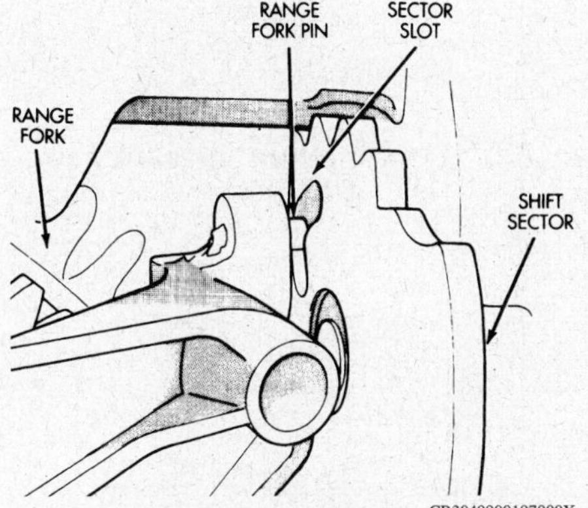

Fig. 26 Range fork & hub installation

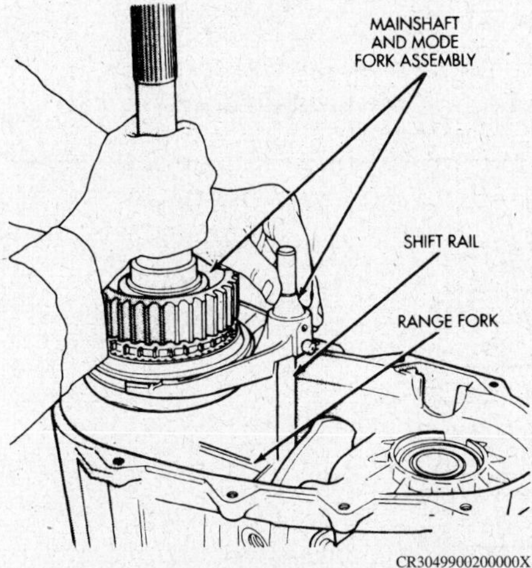

Fig. 29 Mainshaft & mode fork installation

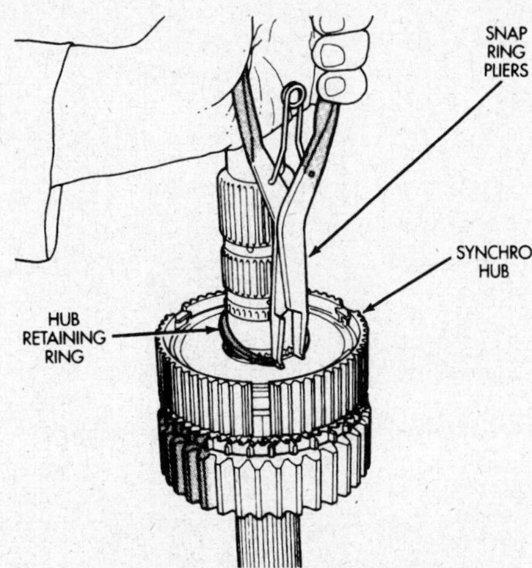

Fig. 24 Synchro hub retaining ring installation

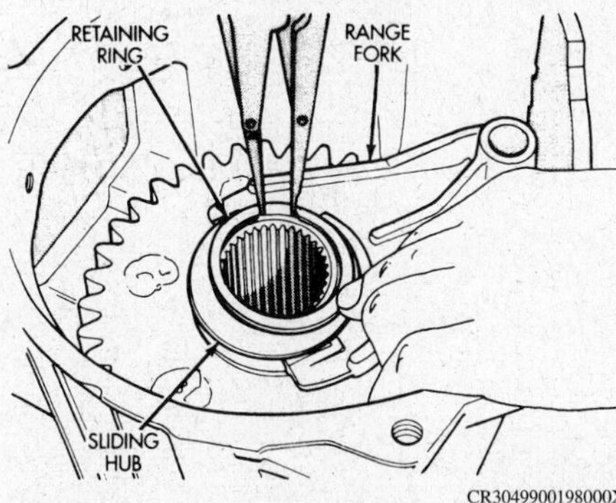

Fig. 27 Sliding hub retaining ring installation

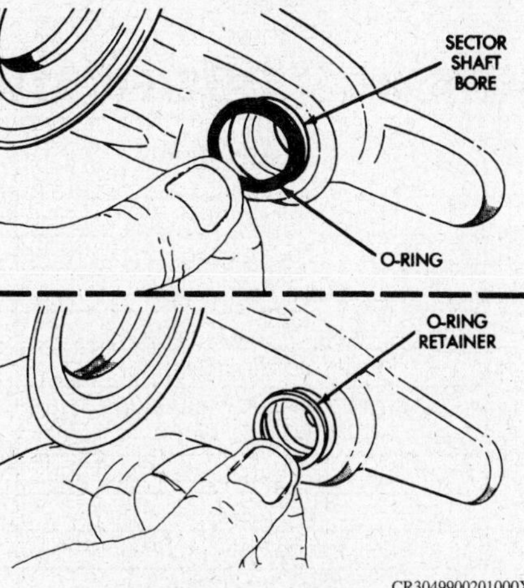

Fig. 30 Sector shaft O-ring & retainer installation

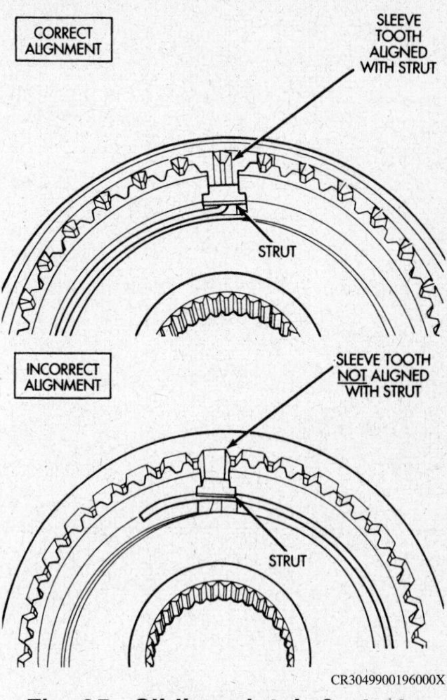

Fig. 25 Sliding clutch & struts alignment

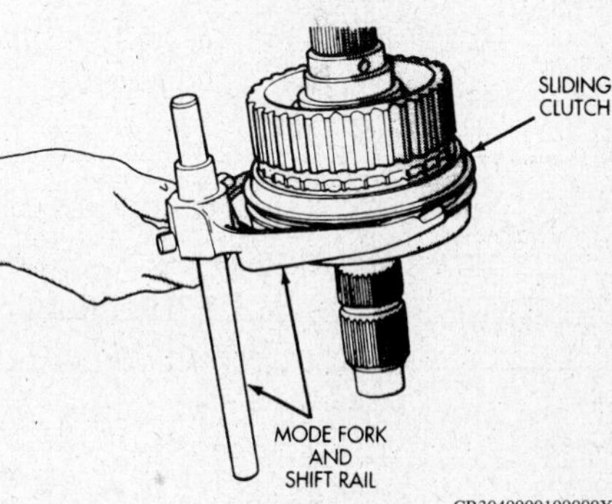

Fig. 28 Mode fork & mainshaft installation

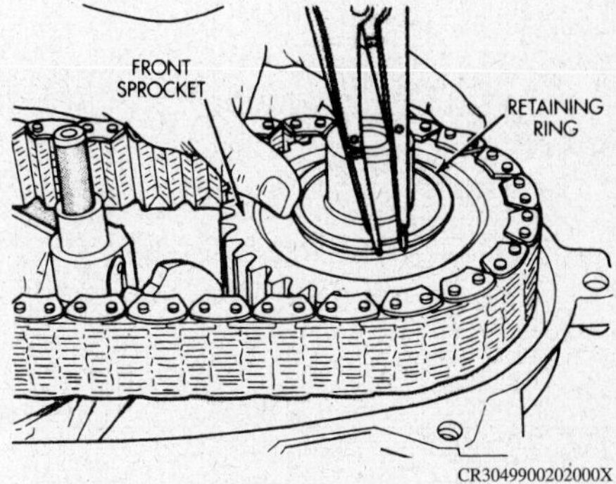

Fig. 31 Front sprocket retaining ring installation

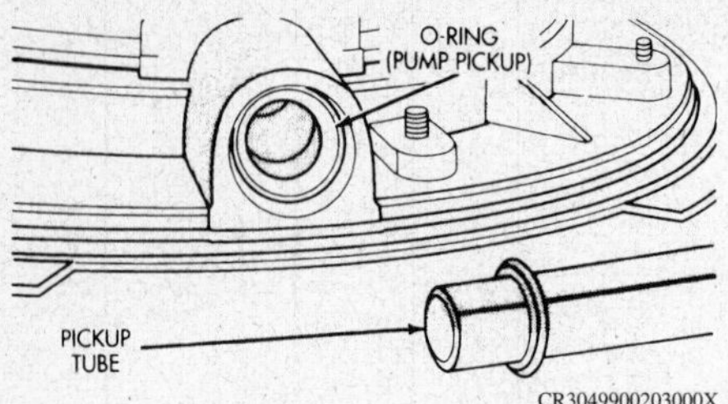

Fig. 32 Oil pump pickup tube O-ring installation

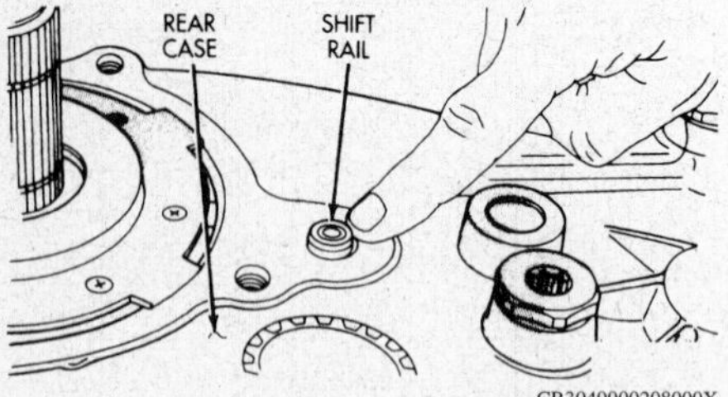

Fig. 35 Shift rail alignment

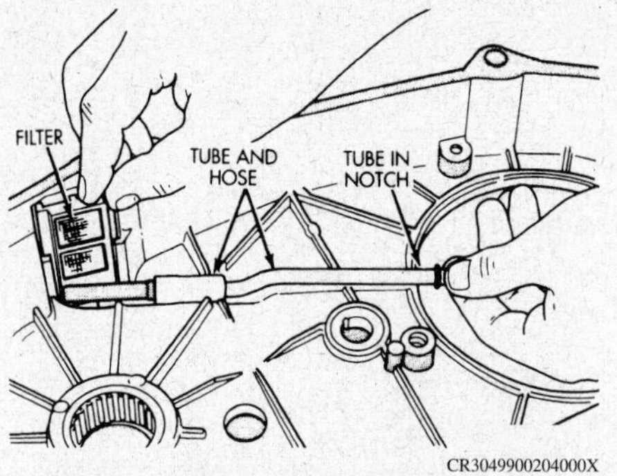

Fig. 33 Oil pickup tube & filter position

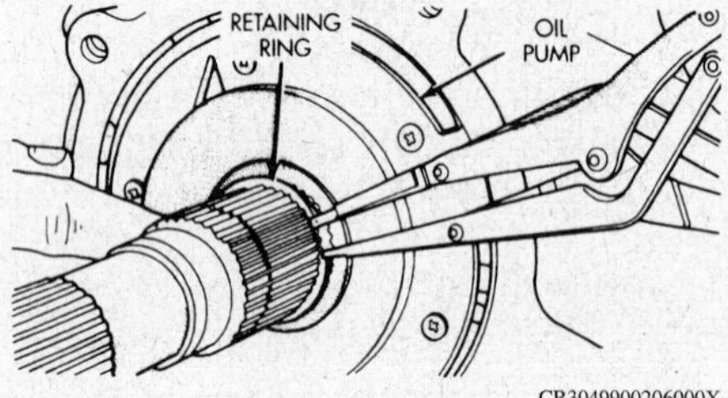

Fig. 36 Oil pump retaining ring installation

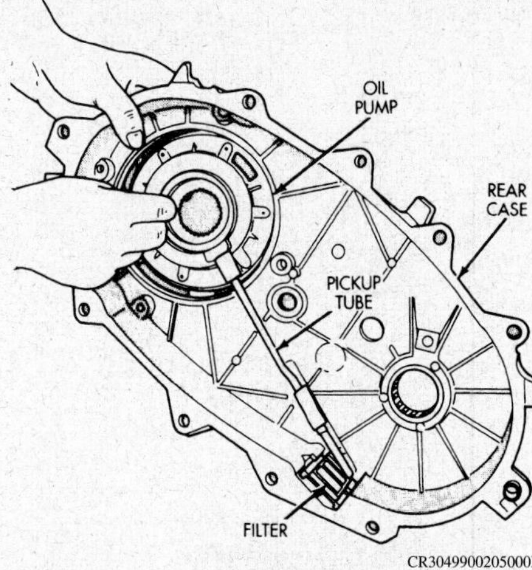

Fig. 34 Oil pump in rear case position

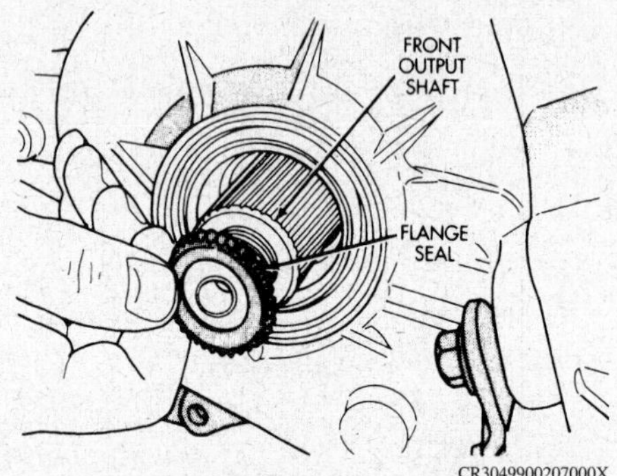

Fig. 37 Front shaft flange seal installation

TIGHTENING SPECIFICATIONS

Year	Component	Torque Ft. Lbs.
2002	Companion Flange Nut	130–200
	Detent Plug	12–18
	Drain/Fill Plug	30–40
	Extension Housing	26–34
	Front Bearing Retainer	12–20
	Front Case To Rear Case (Flange Head)	35–45
	Front Case To Rear Case (Hex Head)	20–25
	Front Yoke Nut	90–130
	Indicator Switch	15–25
	Input Bearing Retainer	20–25
	Oil Pump Screw	12–15①
	Poppet Plunger Screw	12–18
	Power Takeoff Cover (5/16 Inch Head)	20–25
	Power Takeoff Cover (3/8 Inch Head)	30–35
	Propeller Shaft Clamp	14
	Range Lever	20–25
	Shift Lever	20–25
	U-Joint Bolts	17
	Vacuum Switch	15–25

① — Inch lbs.

Model NV-231LD Transfer Case

NOTE: Prior To Performing Any Service Operations Listed In This Section, Consult The "Technical Service Bulletins" Section For Related Information.

INDEX

DIAGNOSIS & TESTING

Before repairing any transfer case, inspect all other driveline components first. The actual cause of a problem may be front hubs, axles, propeller shaft, wheels, tires, transmission or clutch. Ensure hub seals are intact, maintenance of the hubs is critical. Avoid prolonged exposure to dirt and water as damage to internal components will result. If a problem still exists after the inspection and verification, refer to **Fig. 1.**

DISASSEMBLE

Position transfer case on suitable shallow drain pan. Remove drain plug and drain lubricant remaining in case.

Rear Retainer & Oil Pump

1. Remove extension housing bolts.
2. Tap extension housing with plastic or rawhide mallet to loosen sealer.
3. Separate extension housing from rear retainer.
4. Remove rear bearing snap ring, then the bolts holding rear retainer to rear case half.
5. Loosen rear retainer with suitable pry tool to break sealer bead.
6. Pry only against retainer boss, **Fig. 2.**
7. Remove oil pickup tube from oil pump and remove oil pump assembly.
8. Remove pickup tube O-ring from oil pump if required. Do not disassemble oil pump, it is not serviceable.

Yoke & Range Lever

1. Remove transfer case indicator switch.
2. Move range lever to 4L position.
3. Remove yoke nut with impact wrench, then the yoke.
4. If yoke is difficult to remove by hand, remove it with bearing splitter, or with standard two jaw puller, **Fig. 3.**
5. Ensure puller tool is positioned on yoke and not on slinger or slinger will be damaged.
6. Remove and discard seal washer from front output shaft.
7. Remove range lever from sector shaft.

Front Output Shaft & Drive Chain

1. Support transfer case so rear case is facing upward.
2. Remove bolts from front case to rear case.
3. Case alignment bolts require flat washers. Note position of washers for installation reference.
4. Loosen case with suitable pry tool to break sealer bead.
5. Insert suitable pry tool blade only into notches provided at end of case.
6. Remove rear case from front case.
7. Remove oil pickup tube from rear case.

Shift Forks & Mainshaft

1. Remove detent plug, O-ring, detent spring and detent plunger, **Fig. 4.**
2. Remove mainshaft from mode sleeve and input gear pilot bearing.
3. Remove mode fork and sleeve as an assembly, **Fig. 5.**
4. Note position of sleeve for assembly reference. The short side of sleeve faces upward.
5. Remove fork and hub as an assembly, **Fig. 6.**
6. Note fork position for assembly reference.
7. Remove shift sector from front case, then remove sector bushing and O-ring, **Fig. 7,** from sector shaft bore.

Mainshaft

1. Remove mode hub retaining ring using suitable snap ring pliers, **Fig. 8.**
2. Slide mode hub off of mainshaft, then slide sprocket off of mainshaft.

Input & Low Range Gear

1. Remove front bearing retainer attaching bolts.
2. Pry front bearing retainer off using suitable pry tool positioned at slots in each end of retainer.
3. Remove front bearing retainer seal. Tap seal out with suitable drift and hammer.
4. Remove input gear retaining ring using suitable snap ring pliers, **Fig. 9.**
5. Place front case in horizontal position, then remove input gear and low range gear as an assembly.
6. Tap gear out of bearing with plastic mallet if required.
7. Remove snap ring that retains input gear in low range gear. Remove retainer, front tabbed thrust washer, input gear and rear tabbed thrust washer.

INSPECTION

Transfer Case

Clean transfer case components with a standard components cleaning solvent. Remove all traces of sealer from cases and retainers with a scraper and all purpose cleaner. Use compressed air to remove solvent residue from oil feed passages in the case halves, retainers, gears and shafts.

The oil pickup screen can be cleaned with solvent. Shake excess solvent from the screen after cleaning and allow to air dry. Do not use compressed air on the pickup screen.

Condition	Possible Cause	Correction
Transfer case difficult to shift or will not shift into desired range.	1) Vehicle speed to great to permit shifting.	1) Slow vehicle and shift into desired range.
	2) If vehicle was operated for an extended period in 4H mode on dry surface, driveline torque load may cause difficulty.	2) Stop vehicle and shift transfer case to Neutral position. Transfer case can then be shifted to the desired mode.
	3) Transfer case shift linkage binding.	3) Repair or replace linkage as necessary.
	4) Insufficient or incorrect lubricant.	4) Drain and refill transfer case with the correct type and quantity of lubricant.
	5) Internal transfer case components binding, worn, or damaged.	5) Repair or replace components as necessary.
Transfer case noisy in all drive modes.	1) Insufficient or incorrect lubricant.	1) Drain and refill transfer case with the correct type and quantity of lubricant.
Transfer case noisy while in, or jumps out of, 4L mode.	1) Transfer case not completely engaged in 4L position.	1) Slow vehicle, shift transfer case to the Neutral position, and then shift into the 4L mode.
	2) Transfer case shift linkage out of adjustment.	2) Adjust linkage as necessary.
	3) Transfer case shift linkage loose or binding.	3) Repair, replace, or tighten linkage components as necessary.
	4) Range fork damaged, inserts worn, or fork is binding on the shift rail.	4) Repair or replace components as necessary.
	5) Low range gear worn or damaged.	5) Repair or replace components as necessary.
Lubricant leaking from transfer case seals or vent.	1) Transfer case overfilled.	1) Drain lubricant to the correct level.
	2) Transfer case vent closed or restricted.	2) Clean or replace vent as necessary.
	3) Transfer case seals damaged or installed incorrectly.	3) Replace suspect seal.
Abnormal tire wear.	1) Extended operation in 4H mode on dry surfaces,	1) Operate vehicle in 2H mode on dry surfaces.

CR3049900241000X

Fig. 1 Transfer case diagnosis chart

Mainshaft, Sprocket & Hub

Inspect the splines on the hub and shaft and the teeth on the sprocket. Minor nicks and scratches can be smoothed with an oilstone. Replace any part that is damaged beyond repair.

Inspect contact surfaces in the sprocket bore and on the mainshaft. Minor nicks and scratches can be smoothed with 320–400 grit emery cloth. If nicks or wear is severe, replace the shaft.

Input Gear & Planetary Carrier

Inspect teeth on gear. Minor nicks can be polished out with an oilstone, but replace the gear if any teeth are broken, cracked, or chipped. The bearing surface on the gear can be smoothed with 300–400 grit emery cloth if required.

Examine the carrier body and pinion gears for wear or damage. The carrier body will have to be replaced as an assembly if the body, pinion pins, or pinion gears are damaged.

Inspect the lock ring and both thrust washers for wear or cracks. Replace as required. Inspect the lock retaining ring and replace if it is bent, distorted or broken.

Shift Forks, Hubs & Sleeves

Inspect condition of shift forks and mode fork shift rail. Minor nicks on shift rail can be polished with 320–400 grit emery cloth.

Inspect shift fork wear pads, the mode fork pads are serviceable and can be replaced if required. The range fork pads are not serviceable. The fork must be replaced as an assembly if the pads are worn or damaged.

Inspect both of the sleeves for wear or damage, especially on the interior teeth. Replace the sleeves if wear or damage is evident.

Rear Retainer & Extension Housing

Inspect rear retainer components. Replace the bearing if it's rotation is rough or noisy. Inspect the retainer for cracks or wear in the bearing bore. Clean the retainer sealing surfaces with a scraper and all purpose cleaner to ensure proper adhesion of sealer during assembly.

Inspect retaining rings and washers. Replace any component that is distorted, bent or broken.

Inspect rear extension bushing. Replace if worn or scored.

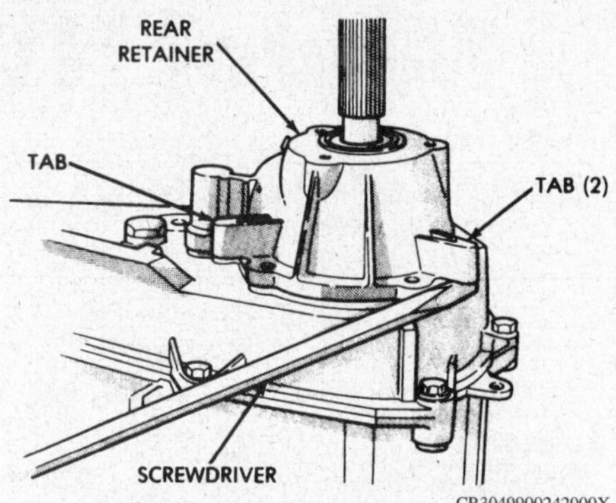

Fig. 2 Rear retainer removal

Front Output Shaft, Yoke & Drive Chain

Inspect condition of seal contact surfaces of yoke slinger. This surface must be clean and smooth to ensure proper seal life. Replace the yoke nut and seal washer, these components should not be reused.

Inspect shaft threads, sprocket teeth and bearing surfaces. Minor nicks can be smoothed with an oilstone. Use 320–400 grit emery cloth to smooth minor scratches on the shaft bearing surfaces. Rough threads on shaft can be chased if required. Replace the shaft if threads are damaged, bearing surfaces are scored, or if any sprocket teeth are cracked or broken.

Examine the drive chain and shaft bearings. Replace the chain and both sprockets if the chain is stretched, distorted, or if any of the links bind. Replace the bearing if rotation is rough or noisy.

Low Range Annulus Gear

Carefully inspect the condition of the annulus gear. The gear is only serviced as part of the front case. If the gear is damaged, it will be required to replace the gear and the front case as an assembly. Do not attempt to remove the gear.

Front-Rear Cases & Front Retainer

Inspect the cases and retainer for wear and damage. Clean the sealing surfaces with a scraper and all purpose cleaner. This will ensure proper adhesion during assembly. replace the input retainer seal, do not reuse the seal.

Inspect the case condition. If leaks were a problem, look for gouges and severe scoring of the case sealing surfaces.

Inspect the front case mounting studs and vent tube. The tube can be secured with Loctite 271/680, or equivalent, if loose. The stud threads can be cleaned up with a suitable die if required. Inspect the condition of the fill/drain plug threads in the rear case. The threads can be repaired with a suitable thread chaser or tap if required. If threads are damaged beyond repair, install a stainless steel threaded insert.

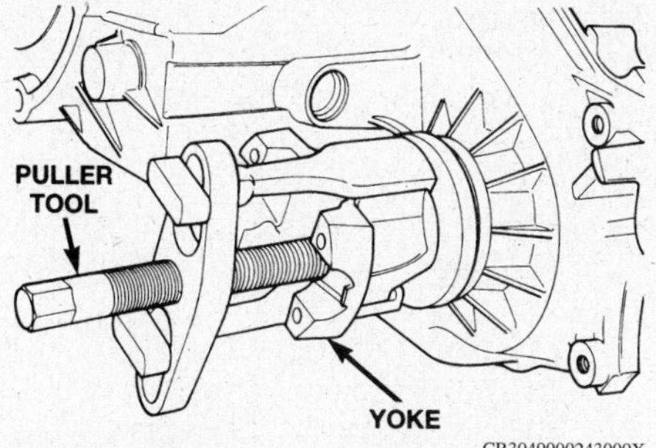

Fig. 3 Yoke removal

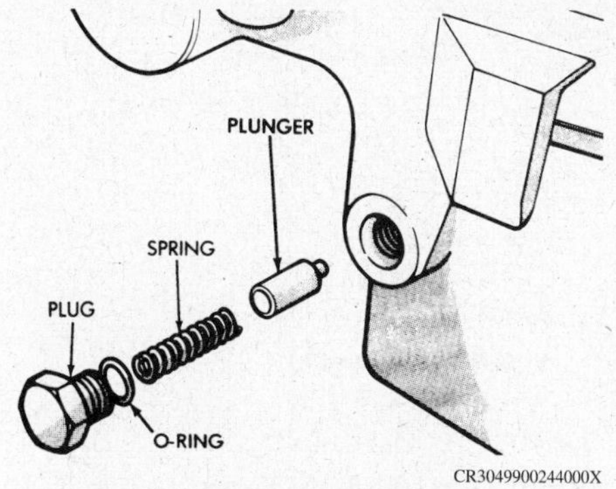

Fig. 4 Detent plug, spring & plunger removal

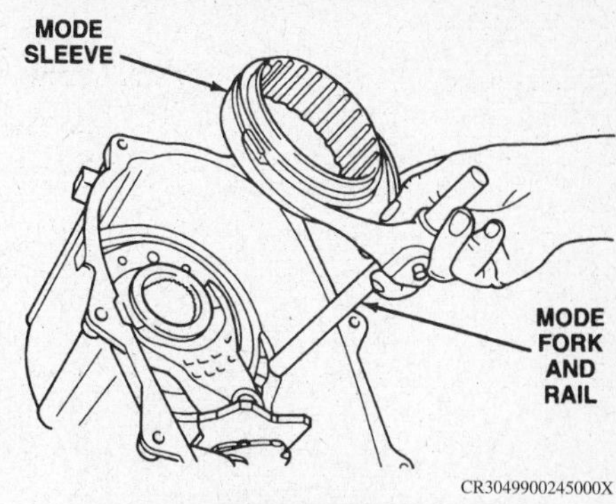

Fig. 5 Mode fork & sleeve assembly

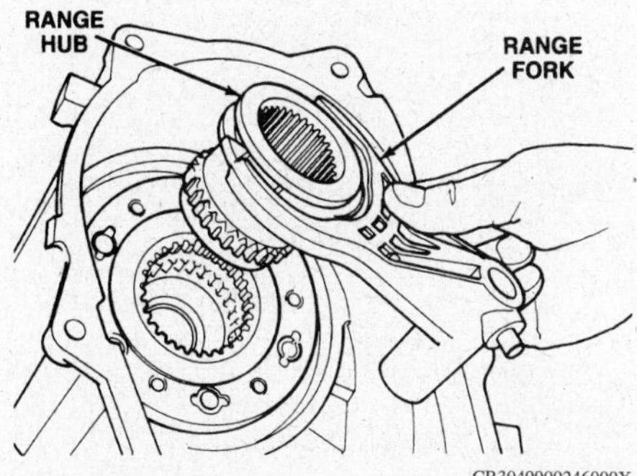

Fig. 6 Range fork & hub removal

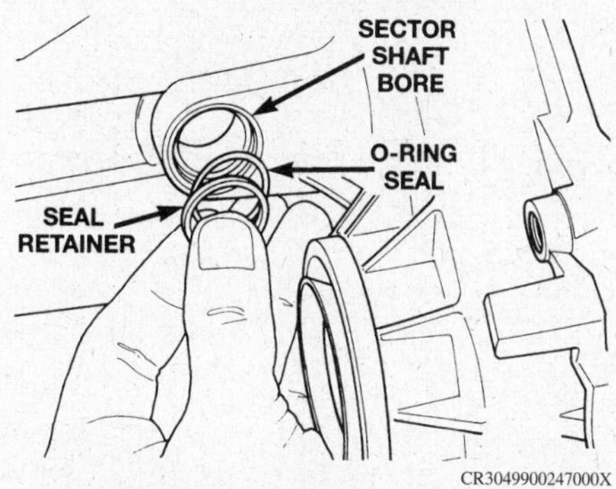

Fig. 7 Sector bushing & O-ring removal

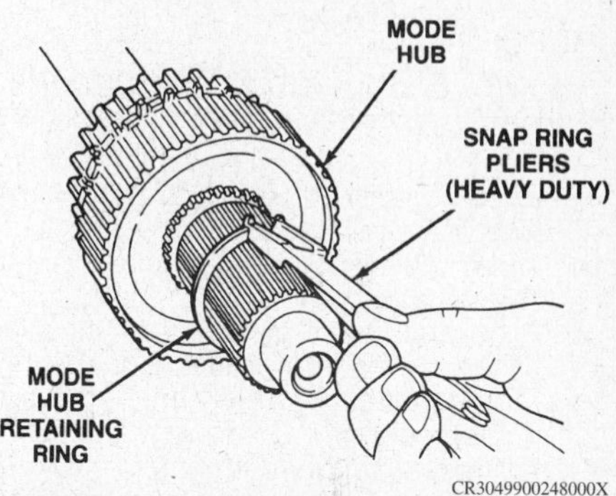

Fig. 8 Mode hub retaining ring removal

Oil Pump & Oil Pickup

Inspect the oil pump pickup components. Replace the pump if any components appear to be worn or damaged. Do not disassemble the pump, the pump is only available as a complete assembly. The pickup screen, hose and tube are the only serviceable components and are available separately.

ASSEMBLE

Bearing & Seal

The bearing bores in various transfer case components contain oil feed holes. Ensure replacement bearings do not block the holes.

1. Remove front output seal from case with suitable pry tool.
2. Remove bearing retaining ring with suitable screwdriver.
3. Remove bearing with tool handle No. C-4171 and removal tool No. 5065, or equivalents.
4. Install front output shaft front bearing in case with tool handle and installer tool No. 5064, or equivalents.
5. Install front output shaft front bearing retaining ring. Start ring into place by hand, then use a suitable small screwdriver to work ring into case groove.
6. Ensure ring is fully seated before proceeding.
7. Install new front output seal in front case using installer tool No. 8143, or equivalent.
   a. Place new seal on tool with garter spring on seal facing toward interior of case.

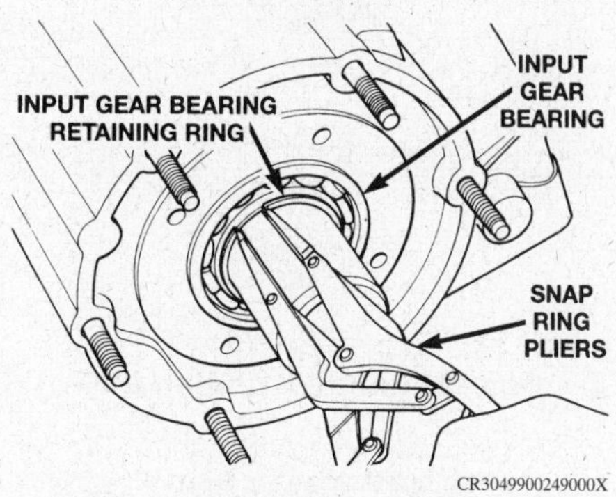

Fig. 9 Input gear retaining ring removal

   b. Start seal in bore with light taps of hammer.
   c. Once seal is started, continue tapping until installer tool bottoms against case.
8. Remove output shaft rear bearing with screw and jaws from remover tool No. L-4454 and cup tool No. 8148, or equivalents, **Fig. 10.**
9. Install new bearing with handle tool and installer No. 5066, or equivalents.
10. Bearing bore is chamfered at top, install bearing so it is flush with lower edge of chamfer.
11. Drive input shaft bearing from inside the annulus gear opening in case using handle tool and remover tool No. C-4171, or equivalents.
12. Install locating ring on new bearing.
13. Position case so forward end is facing upward.
14. Drive input shaft bearing into case using handle tool and remover tool No. C-4120, or equivalent.
15. The bearing locating ring must be fully seated against case surface.
16. Remove input gear pilot bearing by inserting a suitable sized drift into splined end of input gear, **Fig. 11,** and driving bearing out with drift and a hammer.
17. Install new pilot bearing, using handle tool and installer tool No. C-4171, or equivalent, **Fig. 12.**
18. Remove front bearing retainer seal with suitable pry tool.
19. Install new front bearing retainer with installer tool No. 7884, or equivalent.
20. Remove seal from oil pump housing with a suitable pry tool.
21. Install new seal in pump housing with installer tool No. 7888, or equivalent.
22. Remove rear retainer bearing with handle tool and installer tool No. C-4171, or equivalent.
23. Install new rear bearing with handle tool and installer tool No. 5064, or equivalent.

Input Gear & Low Range Gear

1. Lubricate gears and thrust washers with ATF.
2. Install first thrust washer in low range gear, **Fig. 13.** Ensure washer tabs are properly aligned in gear notches.
3. Install input gear in low range gear. Ensure input gear is fully seated.
4. Install remaining thrust washer in low range gear and on top of input gear.

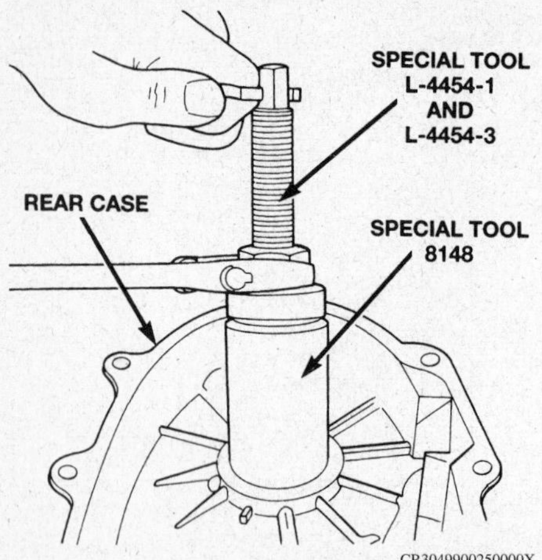

Fig. 10 Output shaft rear bearing removal

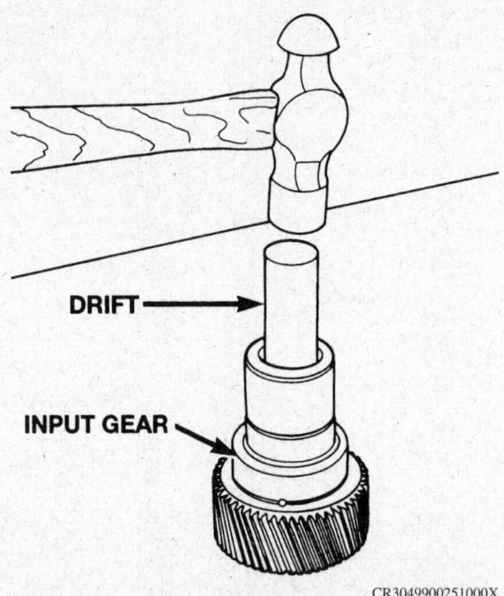

Fig. 11 Input gear pilot bearing removal

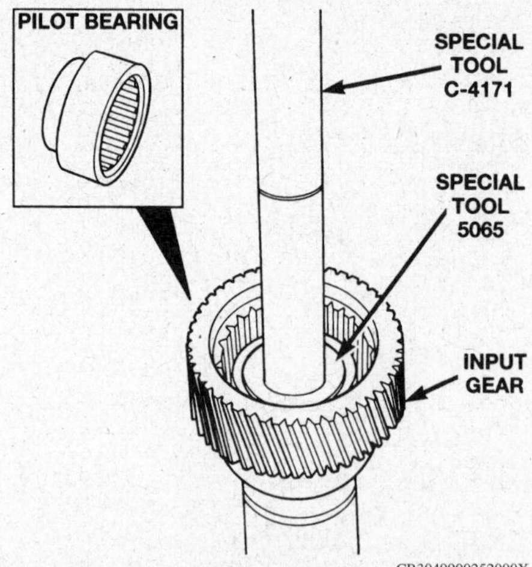

Fig. 12 Input gear pilot bearing installation

Ensure washer tabs are properly aligned in gear notches.

5. Install retainer on input gear and install snap ring.
6. Align and install low range/input gear assembly in front case. Ensure low range gear pinions are engaged in annulus gear and that input gear shaft is fully seated in front bearing.
7. Install snap ring to hold input/low range gear into front bearing.
8. Clean gasket sealer residue from retainer and inspect retainer for cracks and other damage.
9. Apply a 1/8 inch bead of suitable silicone adhesive sealer to sealing surface of retainer.
10. Align cavity in seal retainer with fluid return hole in front of case.
11. Do not block fluid return cavity on sealing surface of retainer when applying silicone sealer.
12. Install bolts that attach retainer to transfer case and tighten to specification.

Mainshaft Assembly

1. Lubricate mainshaft splines with ATF.
2. Slide drive sprocket and mode hub onto mainshaft.
3. Install mode hub retaining ring. Verify that retaining ring is fully seated in mainshaft groove.

Shift Forks & Mainshaft

1. Install new sector shaft O-ring and bushing, **Fig. 7.**
2. Install shift sector in case. lubricate sector shaft with ATF before installation.
3. Install range lever, washer and nut on sector shaft, then tighten range lever nut to specification.
4. Assemble and install range fork and hub, **Fig. 6.** Ensure hub is properly seated in low range gear and engaged to input gear.
5. Align and insert range fork pin in shift sector slot.

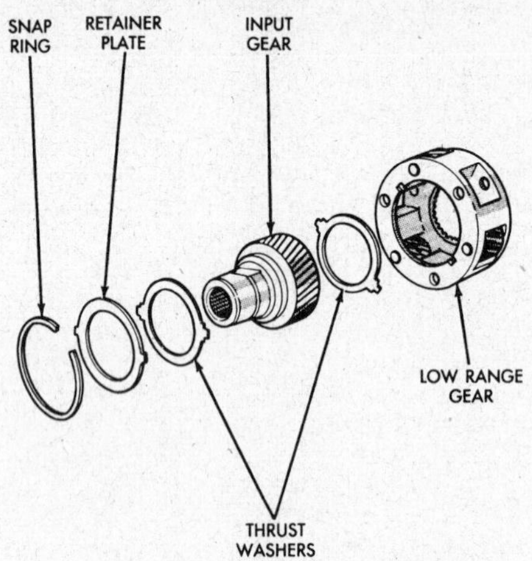

Fig. 13 Exploded view of input/ low range gear installation

6. Install assembled mainshaft, **Fig. 14.** Ensure shaft is seated in pilot bearing and input gear.
7. Install new pads on mode fork as required.
8. Insert mode sleeve into mode fork. Ensure long side of sleeve is toward long end of shift rail.
9. Install assembled mode fork and sleeve into case. Ensure fork rail goes through range fork and into case bore.
10. Ensure sleeve is aligned and seated on mainshaft hub.
11. Rotate sector to Neutral position.
12. Install new O-ring on detent plug, **Fig. 4.**
13. Lubricate detent plunger with ATF or petroleum jelly.
14. Install detent plunger, spring and plug.
15. Verify that plunger is properly engaged in sector.

Front Output Shaft & Drive Chain

1. Lubricate front output shaft/sprocket assembly, drive chain and drive sprocket with ATF.
2. Assemble drive chain and front output shaft.
3. Start chain on mainshaft drive sprocket.
4. Guide front shaft into bearing and drive sprocket onto mainshaft drive gear.
5. Install mode spring on upper end of mode fork shift rail.

Oil Pump & Rear Case

1. Install magnet in front case pocket.
2. Assemble oil pickup screen, connecting hose and tube.
3. Install new pickup tube O-ring in oil pump, **Fig. 15.**
4. Insert oil pickup tube in oil pump inlet.
5. Position assembled oil pump and pickup tube into rear case. Ensure pickup screen is securely seated in case slot.
6. Ensure oil pump locating tabs are outside rear case.
7. Apply a 1/8 inch wide bead of suitable silicone adhesive sealer to mounting flange of front case. Work sealer bead around bolt holes.
8. Lift rear case and oil pump and carefully position assembly on front case. Ensure case dowels are aligned and mode fork rail extends through rear case.
9. Install case attaching bolts.
10. Alignment bolts at each end of case are the only ones requiring washers.
11. Tighten case bolts to specification.

Yoke & Range Lever

1. Install indicator switch in front case, tighten to specification.
2. Install range lever, washer and locknut on sector shaft. Tighten locknut to specification.
3. Install new seal washer on front output shaft, **Fig. 16.**
4. Lubricate yoke hub with ATF and install yoke on front shaft.
5. Install new seal washer on front shaft.
6. Install new yoke nut on front output shaft and tighten to specification. Use

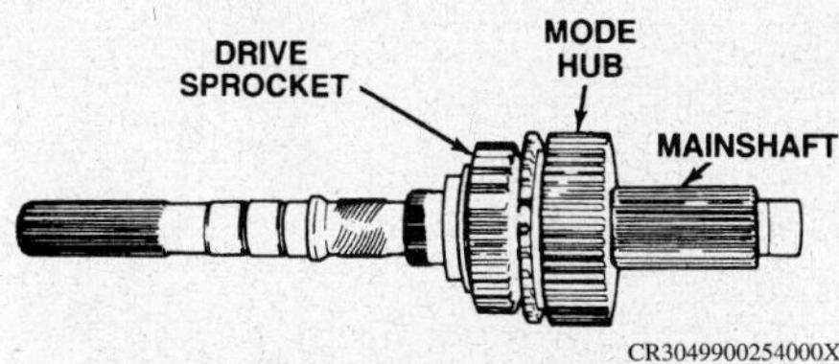

Fig. 14 Mainshaft assembly

yoke holder tool No. C-3281, or equivalent, to hold yoke while tightening nut.

Rear Retainer

1. Apply a ⅛ inch bead of suitable silicone adhesive sealer to mounting surface of rear retainer.
2. Allow sealer to set up before proceeding.
3. Install rear retainer on rear case and tighten bolts to specification.
4. Install new output shaft bearing snap ring. Lift mainshaft slightly to seat snap ring in groove, if required.
5. Apply a ⅛ inch wide bead of suitable silicone adhesive sealer to mounting surface of extension housing.
6. Allow sealer to set up before proceeding.
7. Install extension housing to rear retainer, tighten bolts to specification.

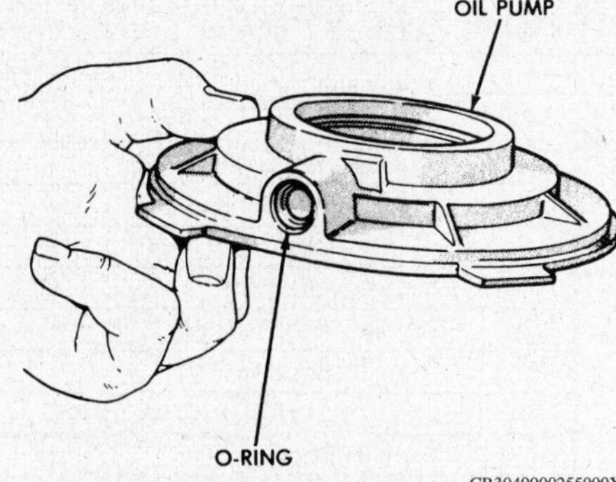

Fig. 15 Oil pump pickup tube O-ring installation

TECHNICAL SERVICE BULLETINS

Transfer Case Shifter Noise

WRANGLER

A thumping or creaking noise may be heard coming from transmission tunnel area on acceleration while driving over bumpy roads. Road test vehicle, if noise is present and there are no worn or damaged components relating to the transfer case mechanism, perform the repair procedure.

This repair involves replacing transfer case shifter components provided in repair kit No. 05014148AA.

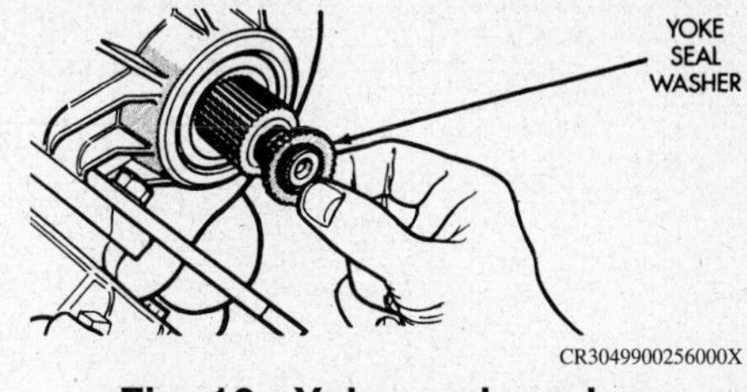

Fig. 16 Yoke seal washer

1. Disconnect shift rods from torque shaft.
2. Remove torque shaft by prying shaft out of green shaft bushing in transmission bracket.
3. Install new bushings on shaft.
4. Remove bronze bushing/retainer and rubber gasket from body bracket.
5. Remove green torque shaft bushing from transmission bracket and install new bushings.
6. Install new gasket into body bracket.
7. Install bronze bushing/retainer and **torque** screws to 45 inch lbs.
8. Use the original torque shaft with new components.
9. Slide boot onto torque shaft and apply multi-purpose grease to area that bronze bushing will contact.
10. Install torque shaft and seat boot on bushing retainer flange.
11. Connect transfer case shift linkage and adjust as required.

TIGHTENING SPECIFICATIONS

Year	Component	Torque Ft. Lbs.
2002–06	Case Half Bolts	20–25
	Case Half Nuts	26–35
	Detent Plug	12–18
	Drain/Fill Plug	15–25
	Front Bearing Retainer	16
	Front Yoke	90–130
	Indicator Switch	15–25
	Range Lever	20–25
	Rear Retainer	26–34
	Shift Lever Bolt	200①

① — Inch lbs.

Model NV-242 Transfer Case

INDEX

DIAGNOSIS & TESTING

Before repairing any transfer case, inspect all other driveline components first. The actual cause of a problem may be front hubs, axles, propeller shaft, wheels, tires, transmission or clutch. Ensure hub seals are intact, maintenance of the hubs is critical. Avoid prolonged exposure to dirt and water as damage to internal components will result. If a problem still exists after the inspection and verification, refer to **Fig. 1** for further diagnosis.

DISASSEMBLE

Rear Retainer

LD

1. Spread band clamp securing output shaft boot on slinger, then slide boot off shaft.
2. Remove rear slinger sing puller tool No. MD-998056-A, or equivalent.
3. Remove rear seal from retainer.
4. Remove rear output bearing retaining ring.
5. Remove rear retainer bolts.
6. Remove rear retainer by tapping with a mallet and prying upward to break sealer bead.

HD

1. Remove extension housing bolts.
2. Tap extension housing with plastic or rawhide hammer to loosen sealer.
3. Separate extension housing from rear retainer.
4. Remove rear bearing snap ring, **Fig. 2.**
5. Remove bolts holding rear retainer to rear case half.
6. Loosen rear retainer with suitable pry tool, **Fig. 3,** to break sealer bead. Pry only against retainer boss.
7. Remove rear bearing O.D. retaining ring with suitable snap ring pliers.
8. Tilt pump and slide it off of output shaft.
9. Remove pickup tube O-ring, **Fig. 4,** from pump, but do not disassemble pump. Pump is not serviceable.
10. Remove seal from oil pump with suitable pry tool.
11. Remove bolts attaching rear case to front case.
12. Note position of two black finish bolts at each end of case, these bolts go through case dowels and require a washer under bolt head.
13. Insert screwdrivers into slots cast into each end of case. Pry upward to break sealer bead, then remove the rear case.
14. Do not pry on sealing surface of either case half, damage to sealing surface will occur.
15. Remove oil pickup tube and screen from rear case.

Yoke & Range Lever

1. Move range lever to 4L position, then using an suitable impact wrench, remove the front yoke nut.
2. Remove yoke, If yoke is difficult to remove by hand, remove it with bearing splitter, or with standard two jaw puller, **Fig. 5.**
3. Ensure puller tool is positioned on yoke and not on slinger as slinger will be damaged.
4. Remove and discard seal washer from front output shaft.
5. Move sector shaft to neutral position, remove nut and washer, then the range lever.

Front Output Shaft & Drive Chain

1. Remove drive sprocket snap ring, **Fig. 6.**
2. Remove drive sprocket and chain, then the front output shaft.

Shift Forks & Mainshaft

1. Remove shift detent plug, spring and pin, **Fig. 7.**
2. Remove seal plug from low range fork lockpin access hole.
3. Move shift selector to align low range fork lockpin with access hole.
4. Remove range fork lockpin with a No. 1 easy-out tool as follows:
    a. Insert easy-out tool through access hole in side of transfer case and into lock pin.
    b. Tap easy-out tool into lockpin with a hammer until tool is securely engaged into lockpin.
    c. Install a T-handle onto easy-out tool.
    d. In one motion, pull upward and turn T-handle counterclockwise to remove lockpin.
5. Remove mode fork, **Fig. 8,** and mainshaft as an assembly.
6. Remove mode shift sleeve and mode fork assembly from mainshaft, **Fig. 9.** Note position of mode sleeve in fork and remove sleeve.
7. Remove intermediate clutch shaft snap ring, **Fig. 10.**
8. Remove clutch shaft thrust ring and intermediate clutch shaft.
9. Remove differential snap ring, **Fig. 11,** then the differential.
10. Remove differential needle bearings and both needle bearing thrust washers from mainshaft.
11. Slide low range fork pin out of shift sector slot, then remove low range fork and hub.
12. Remove shift sector, then the shift sector bushing and O-ring, **Fig. 12.**

Condition	Possible Cause	Correction
Transfer case difficult to shift or will not shift into desired range.	1) Transfer case shift linkage binding.	1) Repair or replace linkage as necessary.
	2) Insufficient or incorrect lubricant.	2) Drain and refill transfer case with the correct type and quantity of lubricant.
	3) Internal transfer case components binding, worn, or damaged.	3) Repair or replace components as necessary.
Transfer case noisy in all drive modes.	1) Insufficient or incorrect lubricant.	1) Drain and refill transfer case with the correct type and quantity of lubricant.
Lubricant leaking from transfer case seals or vent.	1) Transfer case overfilled.	1) Drain lubricant to the correct level.
	2) Transfer case vent closed or restricted.	2) Clean or replace vent as necessary.
	3) Transfer case seals damaged or installed incorrectly.	3) Replace suspect seal.
Transfer case will not shift through 4X4 part time range (light remains on)	1) Incomplete shift due to drivetrain torque load.	1) Momentarily release the accelerator pedal to complete the shift.
	2) Incorrect tire pressure.	2) Correct tire pressure as necessary.
	3) Excessive Tire wear.	3) Correct tire condition as necessary.
	4) Excessive vehicle loading.	4) Correct as necessary.

CR3049900210000X

Fig. 1 Transfer case diagnosis chart

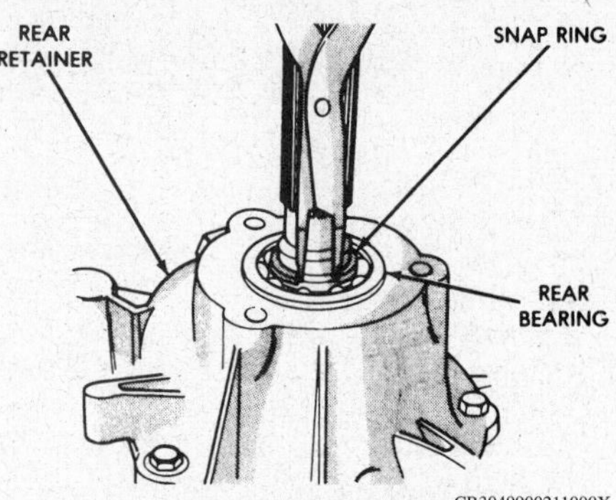

Fig. 2 Rear bearing snap ring removal. HD

Input Gear/Low Range Assembly

1. Remove front bearing retainer bolts, then the retainer.
2. Carefully pry retainer lose with suitable pry tools positioned in slots cast into retainer.
3. Remove input gear snap ring, **Fig. 13.**
4. Remove input/low range gear assembly from bearing with handle tool No. C-4171 and removal tool No. 7829A, or equivalents.
5. Remove low range gear snap ring, **Fig. 14.**
6. Remove input gear retainer, thrust washers and input gear from low range annulus gear, **Fig. 15.**
7. Inspect low range annulus gear. Gear is not serviceable, if damaged, replace gear and front case as an assembly.
8. Remove oil seals from front bearing retainer, rear retainer, oil pump and case halves.

Differential

1. Mark differential case halves for reference.
2. Remove differential case bolts, then invert differential on workbench.
3. Separate top case from bottom case, use slots in case halves, **Fig. 16.**
4. Remove thrust washers and planet gears from case pins, **Fig. 17.**
5. Remove mainshaft and sprocket gears from bottom case. Note gear position for reference before separating components.

INSPECTION

Transfer Case

Clean transfer case components with a standard components cleaning solvent. Remove all traces of sealer from cases and retainers with a scraper and all purpose cleaner. Use compressed air to remove solvent residue from oil feed passages in the case halves, retainers, gears and shafts.

The oil pickup screen can be cleaned with solvent. Shake excess solvent from the screen after cleaning and allow to air dry. Do not use compressed air on the pickup screen.

Mainshaft, Sprocket & Hub

Inspect the splines on the hub and shaft and the teeth on the sprocket. Minor nicks and scratches can be smoothed with an oilstone. Replace any part that is damaged beyond repair.

Inspect contact surfaces in the sprocket bore and on the mainshaft. Minor nicks and scratches can be smoothed with 320–400 grit emery cloth. If nicks or wear is severe, replace the shaft.

Input Gear & Planetary Carrier

Inspect teeth on gear. Minor nicks can be polished out with an oilstone, but replace the gear if any teeth are broken, cracked, or chipped. The bearing surface on the gear can be smoothed with 300–400 grit emery cloth if required.

Examine the carrier body and pinion gears for wear or damage. The carrier body will have to be replaced as an assembly if the body, pinion pins, or pinion gears are damaged.

Inspect the lock ring and both thrust washers for wear or cracks. Replace as required. Inspect the lock retaining ring and replace if it is bent, distorted or broken.

Shift Fork, Hubs & Sleeves

Inspect condition of shift forks and mode fork shift rail, minor nicks on shift rail can be polished with 320–400 grit emery cloth.

Inspect shift fork wear pads. The mode fork pads are serviceable and can be replaced if required. The range fork pads are not serviceable. The fork must be replaced as an assembly if the pads are worn or damaged.

Inspect both of the sleeves for wear or damage, especially on the interior teeth. Replace the sleeves if wear or damage is evident.

Rear Retainer & Extension Housing

Inspect rear retainer components. Replace the bearing if it's rotation is rough or noisy. Inspect the retainer for cracks or wear in the bearing bore. Clean the retainer sealing surfaces with a scraper and all purpose cleaner to ensure proper adhesion of sealer during assembly.

Inspect retaining rings and washers. Replace any component that is distorted, bent or broken.

Inspect rear extension bushing. Replace if worn or scored.

Front Output Shaft, Yoke & Drive Chain

Inspect condition of seal contact surfaces of yoke slinger. This surface must be clean and smooth to ensure proper seal life. Replace the yoke nut and seal washer, these components should not be reused.

Inspect shaft threads, sprocket teeth and bearing surfaces. Minor nicks can be smoothed with an oilstone. Use 320–400 grit emery cloth to smooth minor scratches on the shaft bearing surfaces. Rough threads on shaft can be chased if required. Replace the shaft if threads are damaged, bearing surfaces are scored, or if any sprocket teeth are cracked or broken.

Examine the drive chain and shaft bearings. Replace the chain and both sprockets if the chain is stretched, distorted, or if any

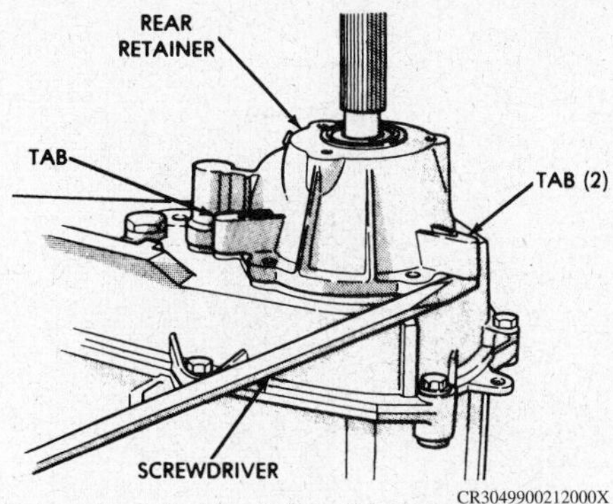

Fig. 3 Loosening rear retainer. HD

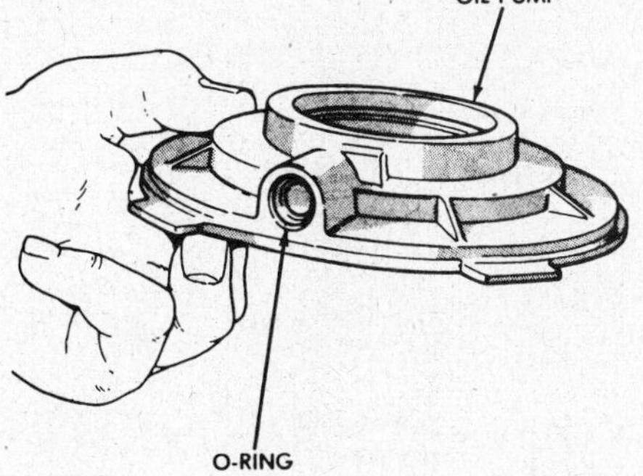

Fig. 4 Pickup tube O-ring. HD

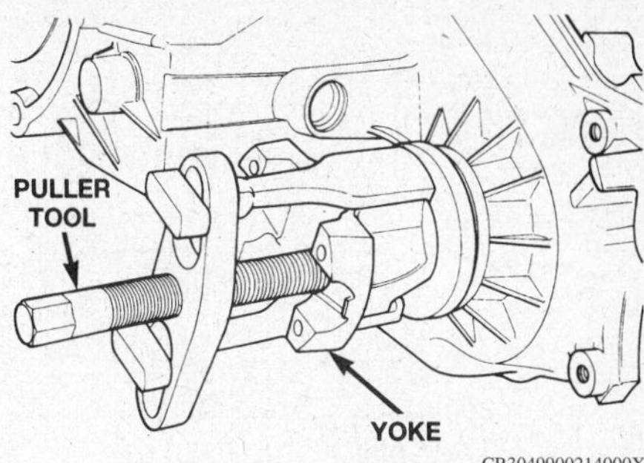

Fig. 5 Yoke removal

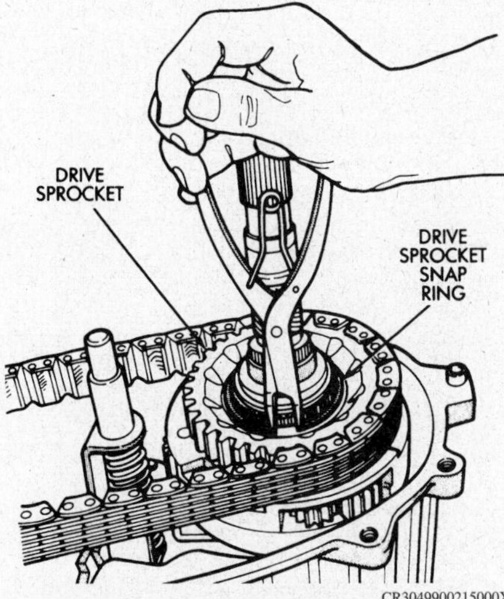

Fig. 6 Drive sprocket snap ring removal

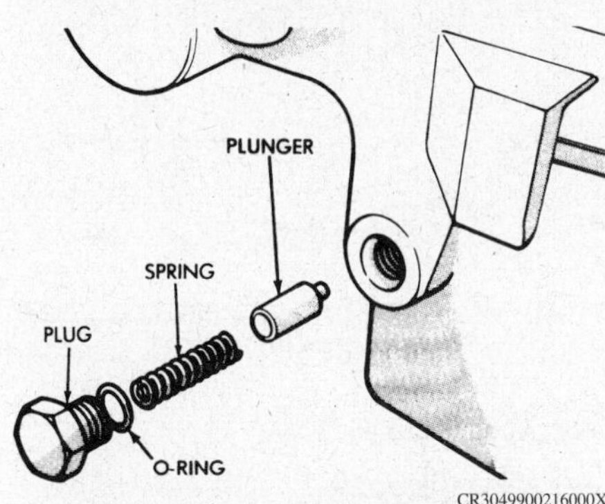

Fig. 7 Detent components

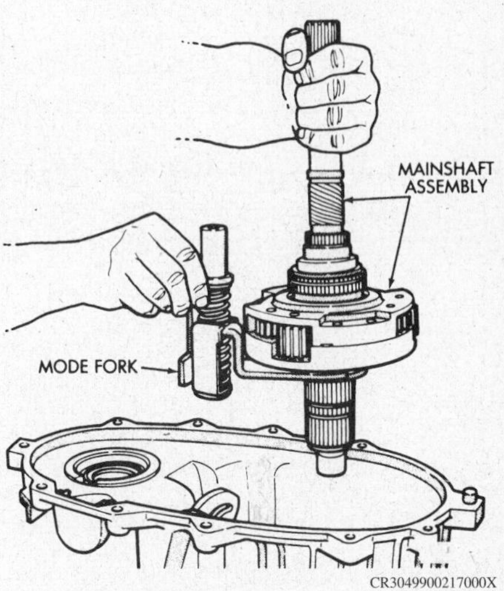

Fig. 8 Mode fork & mainshaft removal

of the links bind. Replace the bearing if rotation is rough or noisy.

Low Range Annulus Gear

Carefully inspect the condition of the annulus gear. The gear is only serviced as part of the front case. If the gear is damaged, it will be required to replace the gear and the front case as an assembly. Do not attempt to remove the gear.

Front-Rear Cases & Front Retainer

Inspect the cases and retainer for wear and damage. Clean the sealing surfaces with a scraper and all purpose cleaner. This will ensure proper adhesion during assembly. Replace input retainer seal, do not reuse the seal.

Inspect the case condition. If leaks were a problem, look for gouges and severe scoring of the case sealing surfaces.

Inspect the front case mounting studs and vent tube. The tube can be secured with Loctite 271/680, or equivalent, if loose. The stud threads can be cleaned up with a suitable die if required. Inspect the condition of the fill/drain plug threads in the rear case. The threads can be repaired with a suitable thread chaser or tap if required. If threads are damaged beyond repair, install a stainless steel threaded insert.

Oil Pump & Oil Pickup

Inspect the oil pump pickup components. Replace the pump if any components appear to be worn or damaged. Do not disassemble the pump, the pump is only available as a complete assembly. The pickup screen, hose and tube are the only serviceable components and are available separately.

ASSEMBLE

Lubricate transfer case components with ATF or petroleum jelly during assembly.

Bearing & Seal

The bearing bores in various transfer case components contain oil feed holes. Ensure replacement bearings do not block the holes.

1. Remove snap ring that retains front output shaft bearing in case, then remove the bearing.
2. Use a hammer handle or brass drift to tap bearing out of case.
3. Install new front output shaft front bearing with tapered cone upward using handle tool No. C-4171 and installer tool No. 8033A, or equivalents.
4. Install front bearing snap ring.
5. Remove front output shaft seal using a suitable pry tool.
6. Install new front output shaft oil seal with installer tool No. 6952-A, or equivalent.
7. Remove input gear bearing with handle tool and remover tool No. C-4120, or equivalent.
8. Install snap ring on new input gear bearing, then install bearing with handle tool and installer tool No. C-4120, or equivalent.
9. Install bearing until snap ring seats against case.
10. Remove input gear pilot bearing using a suitable sized drift and hammer, **Fig. 18.**
11. Install new pilot bearing using handle tool and installer tool No. 8128, or equivalents.
12. Install new front seal in front bearing retainer using installer tool No. 7884, or equivalent.
13. Remove output shaft rear bearing using screw and jaws from remover L-4454 and cup 8148, or equivalents, **Fig. 19.**
14. Install new bearing using handle tool and installer tool No. 5066, or equivalents.
15. Lubricate bearing after installation.
16. Install new seal in oil pump feed housing using tool No. 7888, or equivalent.
17. Install new pickup tube O-ring in oil pump, **Fig. 4.**
18. Remove rear retainer bearing with

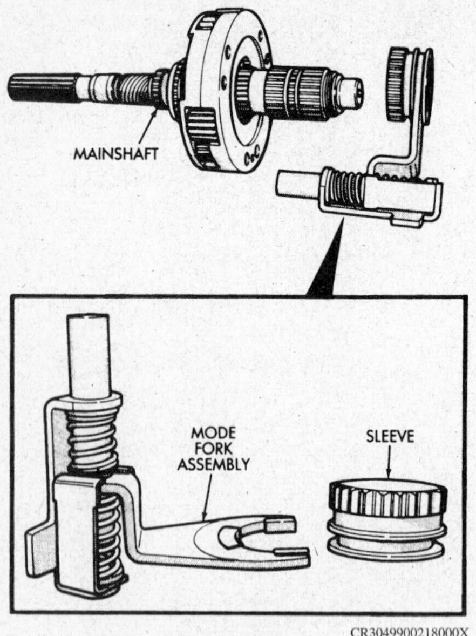

Fig. 9 Mode fork & sleeve removal

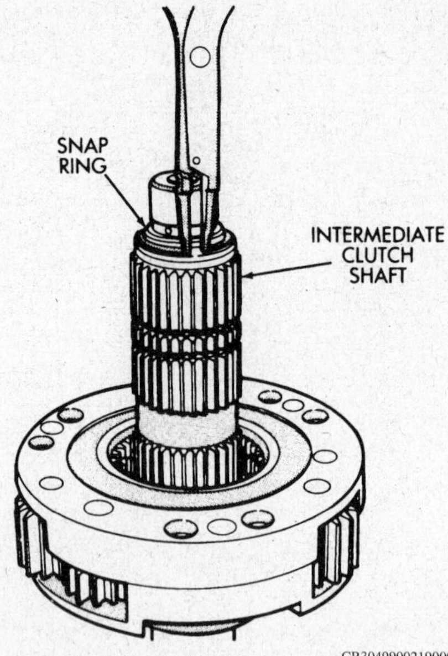

Fig. 10 Intermediate clutch snap ring removal

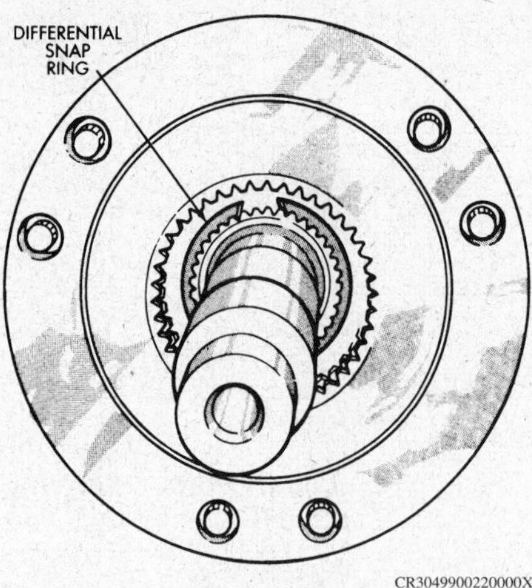

Fig. 11 Differential snap ring removal

handle tool and installer tool No. 5064, or equivalent.

19. Install rear bearing in retainer with handle tool and installer tool No. 5064, or equivalents.

Differential

1. Lubricate differential components with ATF.
2. Install sprocket gear in differential bottom case.
3. Install differential planet gears and new thrust washers, **Fig. 17.** Ensure thrust washers are installed at top and bottom of each planet gear.
4. Install differential mainshaft gear, **Fig. 20.**
5. Align and position differential top case on bottom case. Align using marks made during disassembly.
6. While holding differential case halves together, invert differential and start differential case bolts.
7. Tighten differential case bolts to specification.

Input Gear & Low Range

1. Assemble low range gear, input gear thrust washers, input gear and input gear retainer.
2. Install low range gear snap ring.
3. Lubricate input gear and low range gears with ATF.
4. Start input gear shaft into front case bearing, then press shaft into front bearing.
5. Install new input gear snap ring.
6. Apply a ⅛ inch wide bead of suitable silicone adhesive sealer to seal surface of front bearing retainer.
7. Install front bearing retainer and tighten bolts to specification.

Shift Forks & Mainshaft

1. Install new sector shaft O-ring and bushing, **Fig. 12.**
2. Install shift sector.
3. Inspect pads on low range fork, and replace if required.
4. Assemble low range fork and hub and position in case. Ensure low range fork pin is engaged in shift sector slot, **Fig. 21.**
5. Install first mainshaft bearing spacer on mainshaft.
6. Install bearing rollers on mainshaft, **Fig. 22.**
7. Coat bearing rollers with petroleum jelly to hold in place.
8. Install remaining bearing spacer on mainshaft. Do not displace any bearings while installing spacer.
9. Install differential on mainshaft. Do not displace mainshaft bearings when installing differential.
10. Install differential snap ring, intermediate clutch shaft, clutch shaft thrust washer and clutch shaft snap ring, **Figs. 23 through 26.**
11. Inspect ensure assembly. Replace pads and bushing if required.
12. Replace fork tube if bushings inside tube are worn or damaged. Inspect springs and slider bracket for worn or damaged components.
13. Install mode sleeve in ensure, **Fig. 9,** then install assembled sleeve and fork on mainshaft.
14. Ensure mode sleeve splines are engaged in differential splines.
15. Install mode fork and mainshaft assembly into case. Rotate mainshaft slightly to engage shaft with low range gears.
16. Rotate mode fork pin into shift sector slot.
17. Insert shift rail, ensure rail is seated in both shift forks.
18. Rotate shift sector to align lockpin hole in low range fork with access hole in case.
19. Insert an easy-out tool in range fork lockpin to hold it securely for installation.
20. Lockpin is slightly tapered on one end. Insert tapered end into fork and rail.
21. Insert lockpin through access hole and into shift fork, **Fig. 27.**
22. Then remove easy-out and seat pin with suitable drift.
23. Install plug in lockpin access hole.
24. Install detent plunger, detent spring and detent plug in case, **Fig. 7.**

Front Output Shaft & Drive Chain

1. Install front output shaft and drive chain.
2. Engage chain with front output shaft sprocket teeth.
3. Install drive sprocket, engage drive sprocket teeth with chain.
4. Engage sprocket splines with mainshaft splines.
5. Install drive sprocket snap ring.

Oil Pump & Rear Case

1. Insert oil pickup tube in oil pump and attach oil screen and connector hose to pickup tube.
2. Install assembled pump, tube and screen in rear case, **Fig. 28,** ensure screen is seated in case slot.
3. Install magnet in front case pocket.
4. Apply a ⅛ inch wide bead of suitable silicone adhesive sealer to seal surface of front case.
5. Align and install rear case on front case. Ensure locating dowels are in place and that mainshaft splines are engaged in oil pump inner gear.
6. Install and tighten front case bolts to specification.
7. Install a washer under each bolt used at case dowel locations.

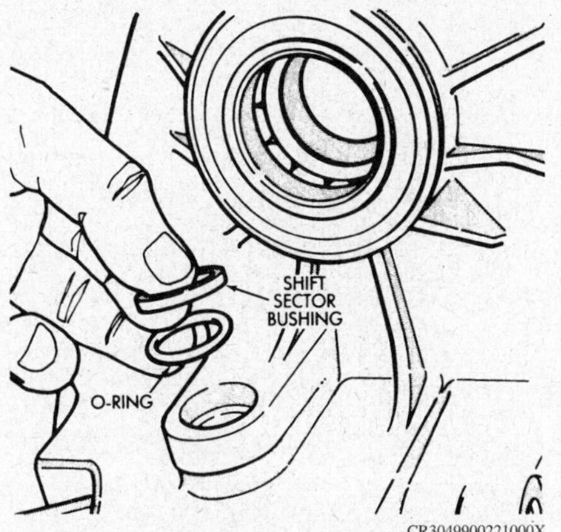

Fig. 12 Shift sector bushing & O-ring removal

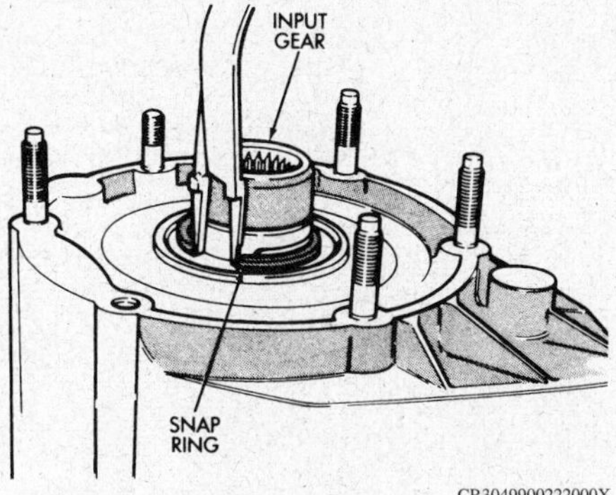

Fig. 13 Input gear snap ring

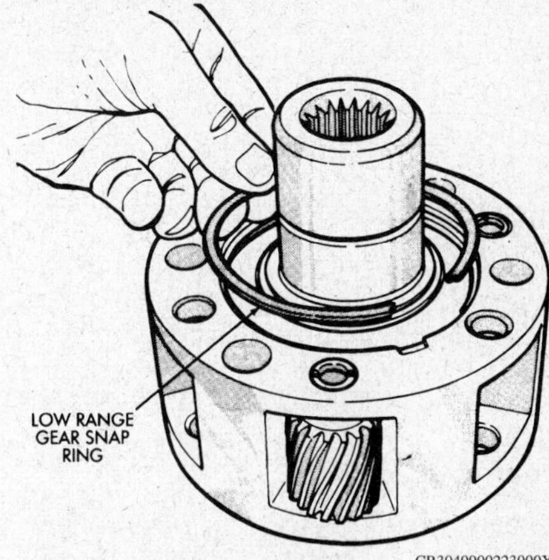

Fig. 14 Low range gear snap ring removal

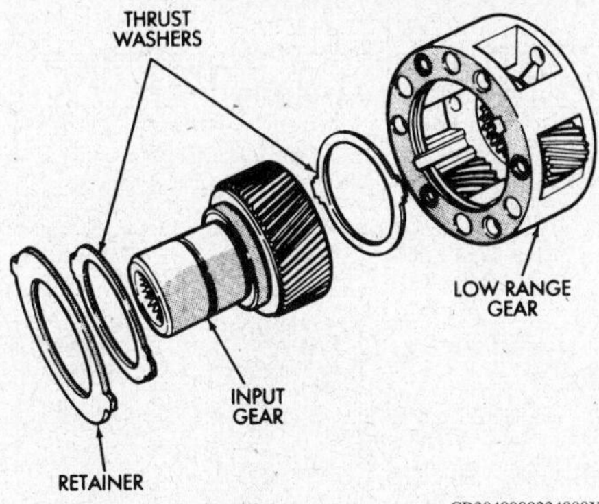

Fig. 15 Exploded view of low range gear

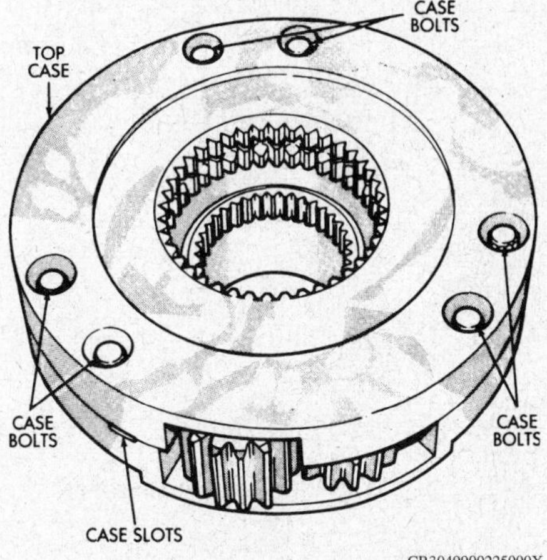

Fig. 16 Differential case halves

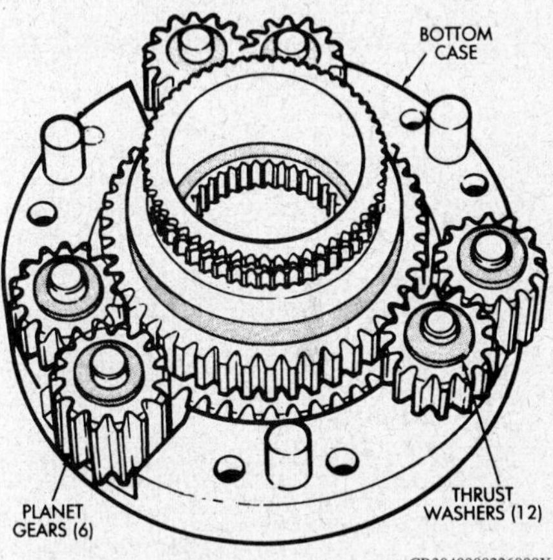

Fig. 17 Planet gears & thrust washers removal

Rear Retainer

LD

1. Apply a bead of Mopar Sealer or Loctite Ultra Gray to mating surfaces of rear retainer. Sealer bead should be a maximum of 3⁄16 inch.
2. Install rear retainer on rear case.
3. Install rear bearing retaining ring and spacer on output shaft.
4. Apply liberal quantity of petroleum jelly to new rear seal and to output shaft to protect seal lips during installation.
5. Slide seal onto protector tool No. 6992, or equivalent, then slide seal protector and seal onto output shaft.
6. Slide installer tool No. C-4076-B, or equivalent onto seal protector with recessed side of tool toward seal.
7. Drive seal into rear bearing retainer using installer tool No. C-4076-B and handle tool No. MD-998323, or equivalents.
8. Install rear slinger using installer tool No. 8408, or equivalent.
9. Install boot on output shaft slinger, then crimp clamp using boot clamp installer tool No. C-4975-A, or equivalent.

HD

1. Install rear bearing O.D. retaining ring, **Fig. 29,** with suitable snap ring pliers.
2. Ensure retaining ring is fully seated in retainer groove.
3. Apply a bead of Mopar sealer No. 82300234, or Loctite Ultra Gray, or equivalents, to mating surfaces of rear retainer.
4. Sealer bead width should be a maximum of 3⁄16 inch.
5. Install rear retainer on case and tighten bolts to specification.
6. Install new output shaft bearing snap ring, **Fig. 30.** Lift mainshaft slightly to seat snap ring in groove.
7. Apply a 1⁄8 inch bead of suitable silicone sealer to mounting surface of extension housing. Allow sealer to set up before proceeding.
8. Install extension housing on rear retainer, install bolts and tighten to specification.

Front Yoke & Switch

1. Install indicator switch in front case and tighten to specification.
2. Lubricate yoke hub with transmission fluid and install yoke on front shaft.
3. Install new seal washer on front shaft, then install yoke and secure with new nut.
4. Tighten yoke nut to specification.

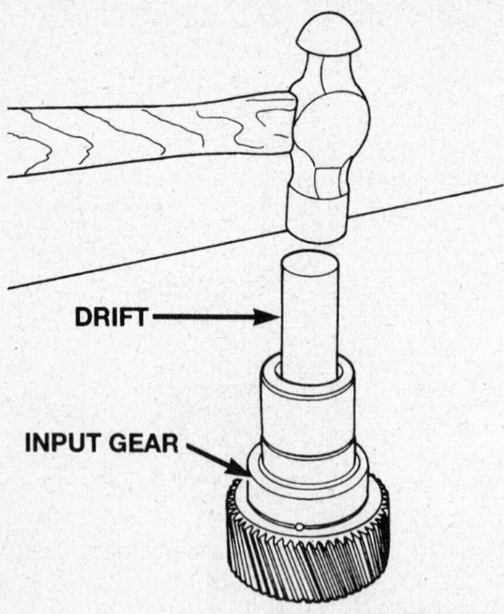

Fig. 18 Input gear pilot bearing removal

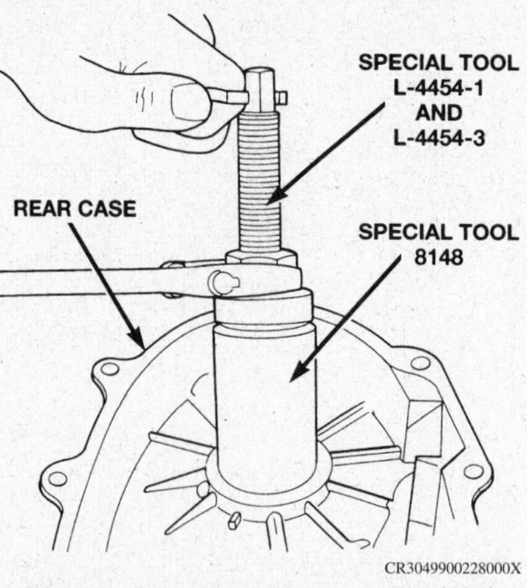

Fig. 19 Front output shaft rear bearing removal

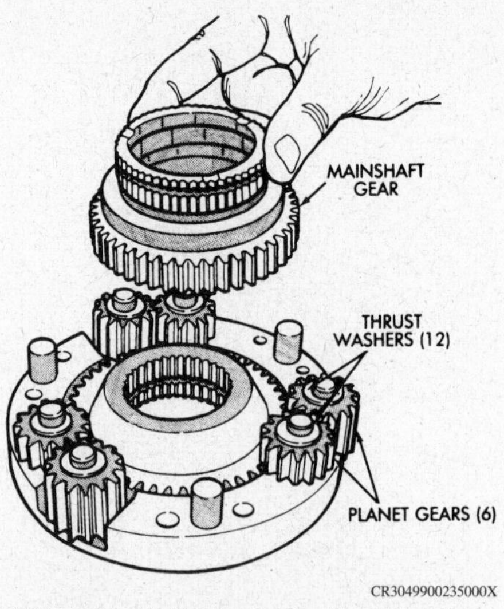

Fig. 20 Mainshaft & planet gears installation

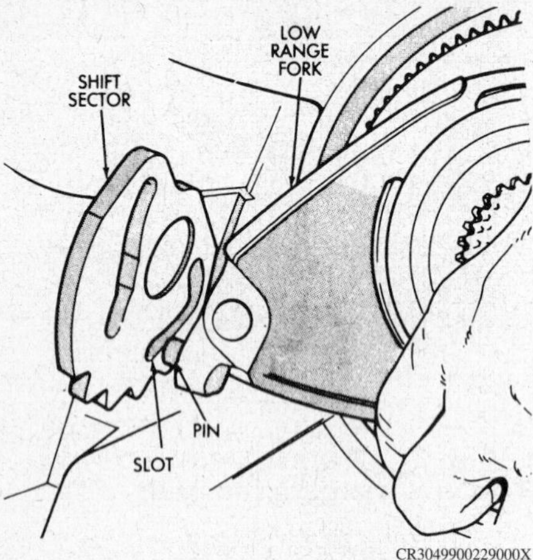

Fig. 21 Low range fork installation

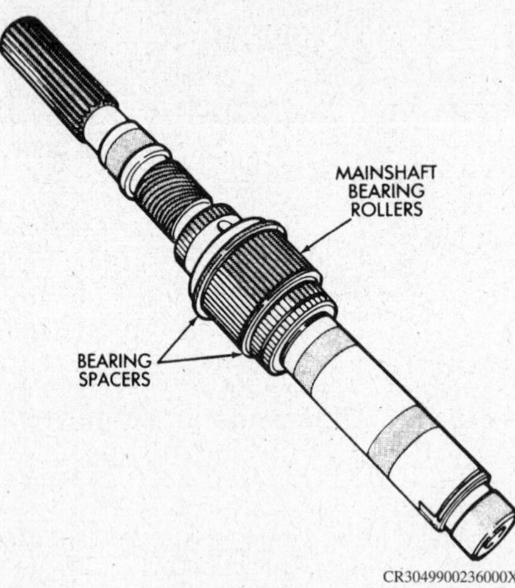

Fig. 22 Mainshaft bearing rollers & spacers

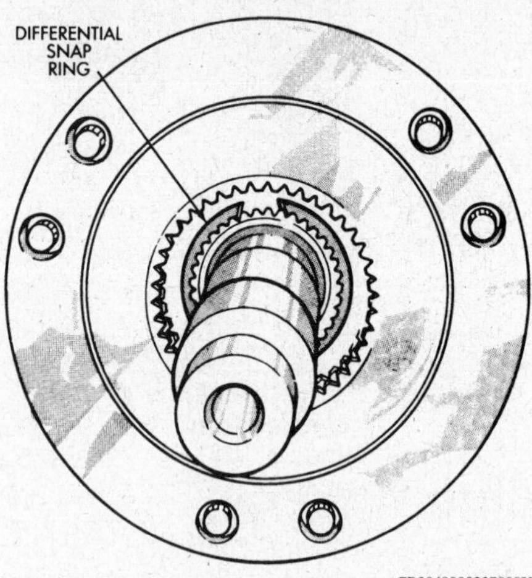

Fig. 23 Differential snap ring installation

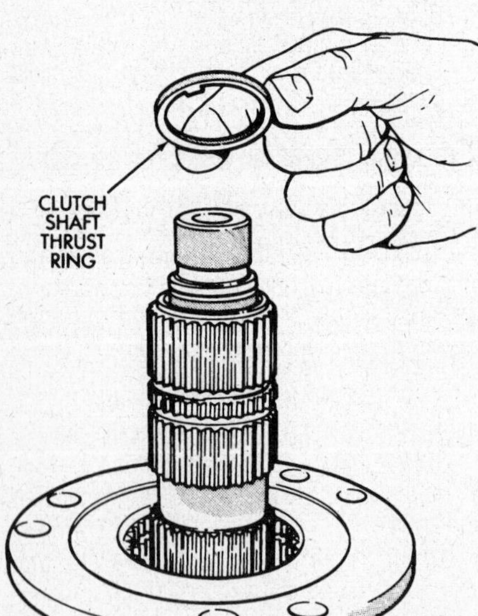

Fig. 24 Intermediate clutch shaft installation

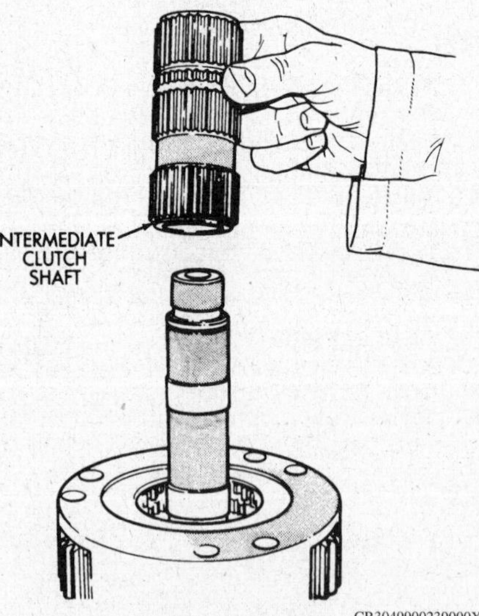

Fig. 25 Clutch shaft thrust washer installation

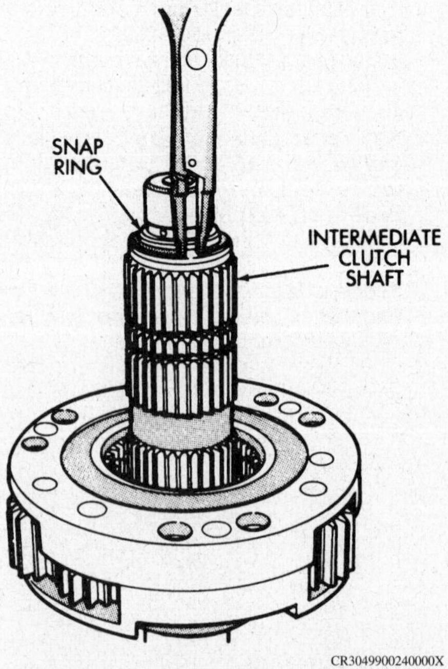

Fig. 26 Clutch shaft snap ring installation

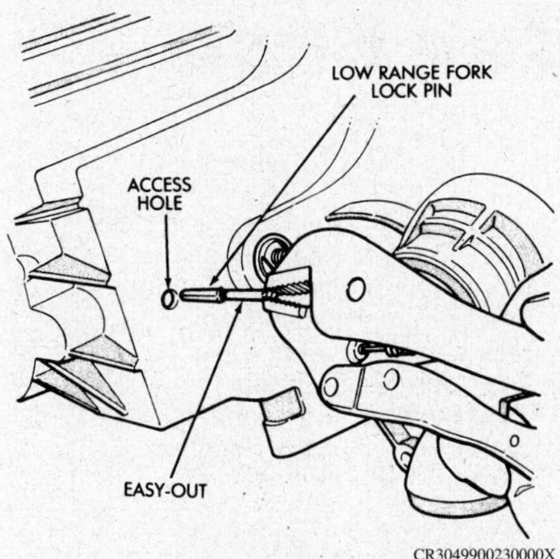

Fig. 27 Low range fork lockpin installation

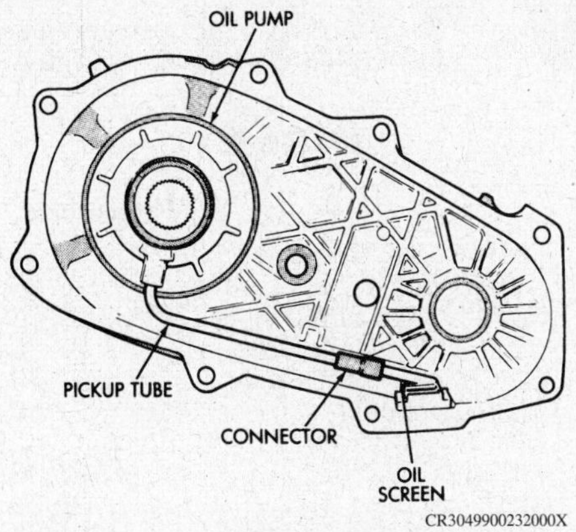

Fig. 28 Oil screen & pickup tube installation

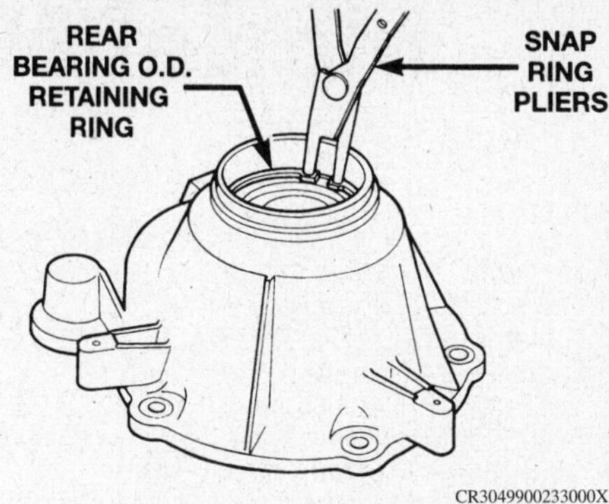

Fig. 29 Rear bearing retaining ring installation. HD

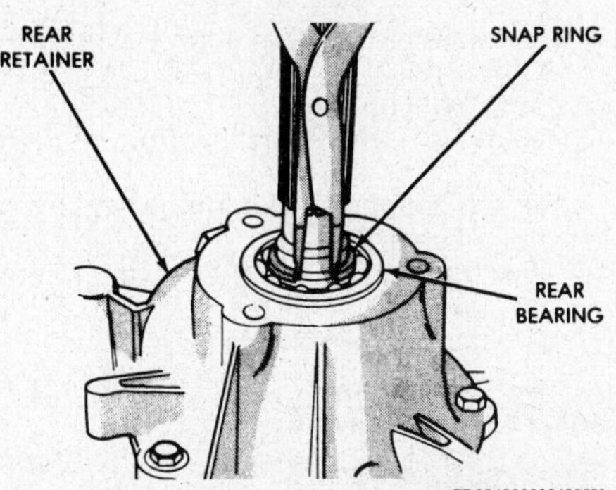

Fig. 30 Output bearing snap ring installation. HD

TIGHTENING SPECIFICATIONS

Year	Component	Torque Ft. Lbs.
2002–06	Detent Plug	12–18
	Differential Case	15–24
	Drain/Fill Plug	15-25
	Extension Housing	26–34
	Front Bearing Retainer	12–20
	Front Case To Rear Case	26–34
	Front Yoke Nut	90–130
	Indicator Switch	15–25
	Oil Pump Screw	12–15①
	Range Lever	20–25
	Rear Retainer	26–34
	Transfer Case Mounting	26
	U-Joint Clamp	17
	Vacuum Switch	15–25

① — Inch lbs.

Model NV-246 Transfer Case

INDEX

DIAGNOSIS & TESTING

Before repairing any transfer case, inspect all other driveline components first. The actual cause of a problem may be front hubs, axles, propeller shaft, wheels, tires, transmission or clutch. Ensure hub seals are intact, maintenance of the hubs is critical. Avoid prolonged exposure to dirt and water as damage to internal components will result. If a problem still exists after the inspection and verification, refer to **Fig. 1** for further diagnosis.

DISASSEMBLE

Shift Motor & Front Output Shaft Seal

1. Remove transfer case isolator from transfer case.
2. Remove front output shaft speed sensor.
3. Remove front propeller shaft boot retaining clamp, then boot.
4. Remove front output shaft seal slinger by bending slinger ears away from transfer case.
5. Remove slinger from output shaft using suitable pry tool.
6. Remove shift motor mounting bolts, then shift motor.
7. Remove shift motor isolator.
8. Remove front output shaft seal using suitable slide hammer.

Oil Pump & Rear Case

1. Remove rear output shaft speed sensor.
2. Remove extension housing seal from extension housing.
3. Remove rear case to front case attaching bolts.
4. Remove access plug in rear extension housing.
5. Release output shaft bearing from rear case with a suitable pair of snap ring pliers through access hole in extension housing.
6. Separate rear case from front case.
7. Remove rear output shaft bearing retaining ring from output shaft, then output shaft bearing.
8. Remove wave washer from output shaft.
9. Remove output shaft tone wheel from output shaft.
10. Disengage oil pump pick-up tube from oil pump.
11. Remove oil pump from output shaft.

Drive Chain, Sprockets & Mainshaft

1. Remove front sprocket retaining ring.
2. Remove mainshaft drive sprocket retaining ring.
3. Remove mainshaft drive sprocket, front drive sprocket and chain as assembly, **Fig. 2.**
4. Remove mainshaft and clutch assembly.

Shift Components

1. Remove clutch fork pivot bolt from transfer case, then clutch fork, **Fig. 3.**
2. Remove shift rail from range fork assembly.
3. Remove range hub and range fork assembly from transfer case, **Fig. 4.**
4. Remove snap-ring that holds shift sector into transfer case.
5. Remove shift sector.

Front Output Shaft

1. Remove front output shaft retaining ring.
2. Remove front output shaft from bearing in front case, **Fig. 5.**

Input & Planetary Gear

1. Remove input gear seal from front case with suitable screw and slide hammer.
2. Remove input gear retaining ring with suitable snap ring pliers.
3. Remove input gear and low range gear as an assembly. Tap gear out of bearing with plastic mallet, if required.

INSPECTION

Mainshaft, Sprocket & Hub

Inspect the splines on the hub and shaft and the teeth on the sprocket. Minor nicks and scratches can be smoothed with an oilstone, however, replace any part that is damaged.

Input Gear & Planetary Carrier

Inspect the teeth on the input gear. Minor nicks can be dressed off with an oilstone but replace the gear if any teeth are broken, cracked, or chipped. The bearing surface on the gear can be smoothed with 300-400 grit emery cloth if required. Examine the planetary carrier body and pinion gears for wear or damage. The carrier will have to be replaced as an assembly if the body, pinion pins, or pinion gears are damaged. Inspect the carrier lock ring and both thrust washers for wear or cracks. Replace them if required. Also replace the carrier lock retaining ring if bent, distorted, or broken

Shift Forks, Hubs & Sleeves

Inspect condition of the shift forks and mode fork shift rail. Minor nicks on the shift rail can be smoothed with 320-400 grit emery cloth. Inspect the shift fork wear pads. The mode fork pads are serviceable and can be replaced if required. The range fork pads are not serviceable. The fork must be replaced as an assembly if the pads are worn or damaged. Inspect both of the sleeves for wear or damage, especially on the interior teeth. Replace the sleeves if wear or damage is evident.

Condition	Possible Cause	Correction
Transfer case difficult to shift or will not shift into desired range.	1) Transfer case electronically controlled shift system malfunction.	1) Verify proper operation per the appropriate diagnostic manual.
	2) If vehicle was operated for an extended period in 4HI mode on dry surface, driveline torque load may cause difficulty.	2) Drive the vehicle in a straight line and momentarily release the accelerator. The transfer case can then be shifted to the desired mode.
	3) Insufficient or incorrect lubricant.	3) Drain and refill transfer case with the correct quantity of fluid.
	4) Internal transfer case components binding, worn, or damaged.	4) Repair or replace components as necessary.
Transfer case noisy in all drive modes.	1) Insufficient or incorrect lubricant.	1) Drain and refill transfer case with the correct quantity of fluid.
	2) Internal transfer case components binding, worn, or damaged.	2) Repair or replace components as necessary.
Transfer case noisy while in, or jumps out of, 4LO mode.	1) Transfer case not completely engaged in 4LO position.	1) While rolling 2-3 MPH and the transmission in NEUTRAL, or clutch depressed on vehicles equipped with a manual transmission, shift transfer case to the 2WD or 4HI position, and then back into the 4LO position.
	2) Range fork damaged, inserts worn, or fork is binding on the shift rail.	2) Repair or replace components as necessary.
	3) Low range gear worn or damaged.	3) Repair or replace components as necessary.
Lubricant leaking from transfer case seals or vent.	1) Transfer case overfilled.	1) Drain lubricant to the correct level.
	2) Transfer case vent closed or restricted.	2) Clean or replace vent as necessary.
	3) Transfer case seals damaged or installed incorrectly.	3) Replace suspect seal.
Abnormal tire wear.	1) Extended operation in 4HI mode on dry surfaces,	1) Operate vehicle in 2WD mode on dry surfaces.

LTV0500000000218

Fig. 1 Transfer case diagnosis chart

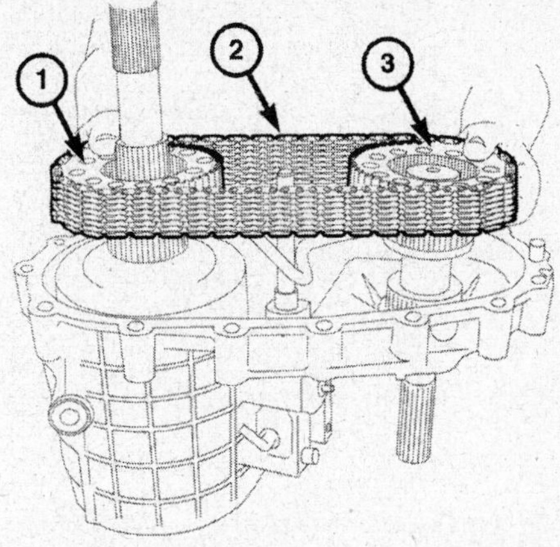

1 - MAINSHAFT DRIVE SPROCKET
2 - DRIVE CHAIN
3 - FRONT DRIVE SPROCKET

LTV0500000000219

Fig. 2 Mainshaft & front drive sprocket assembly

Rear Retainer Components

Inspect the retainer components. Replace the bearing if rough or noisy. Inspect the retainer for cracks or wear in the bearing bore. Inspect the retaining rings and washers. Replace any part if distorted, bent, or broken. Reuse is not recommended. Inspect rear extension bushing. Replace if worn or scored.

Drive Chain

Examine the drive chain and shaft bearings. Replace the chain if stretched, distorted, or if any of the links bind. Replace the bearings if rough, or noisy.

Low Range Annulus Gear

Inspect annulus gear condition carefully. The gear is only serviced as part of the front case. If the gear is damaged, it will be required to replace the gear and front case as an assembly. Do not attempt to remove the gear.

Front Case & Rear Case

Inspect the cases for wear and damage. Inspect case condition. If leaks were a problem, look for gouges and severe scoring of case sealing surfaces. Also make sure the front case mounting studs are in good condition. Inspect the front case mounting studs and vent tube. The tube can be secured with Loctite 271 or 680 if loose. The stud threads can be cleaned up with a die if required. Also inspect condition of the fill/drain plug threads in the rear case. The threads can be repaired with a thread chaser or tap if required. Or the threads can be repaired with Helicoil stainless steel inserts if required.

Oil Pump & Oil Pickup

Examine the oil pump pickup components. Replace the pump if any part appears to be worn or damaged. Do not disassemble the pump as individual components are not available. The pump is only available as a complete assembly. The pickup screen, hose, and tube are the only serviceable components and are available separately.

ASSEMBLE

Front Output Shaft

1. Install front output shaft into bearing in front case.
2. Install retaining ring onto front output shaft.
3. Install new front output shaft seal with suitable seal installer.

Shift Components

1. Install shift sector into transfer case.
2. Install snap-ring that holds shift sector to transfer case.
3. Install range hub and range fork assembly.
4. Install shift rail into range fork assembly.
5. Install clutch fork into transfer case.
6. Install clutch fork pivot bolt into transfer case.

Drive Chain, Sprockets & Mainshaft

1. Install oil pump pick-up tube.
2. Install mainshaft and clutch assembly into transfer case and input gear. **Ensure that tab on clutch apply plate is located toward outside of transfer case and clutch fork pivot bolt.**

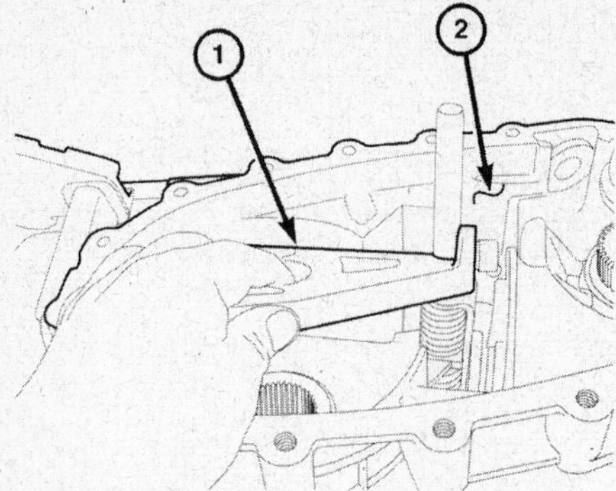

1 - CLUTCH FORK
2 - TRANSFER CASE

LTV0500000000220

Fig. 3 Clutch fork

3. Install mainshaft drive sprocket, front drive sprocket and chain as an assembly, **Fig. 6.**
4. Install mainshaft drive sprocket retaining ring onto mainshaft.
5. Install front sprocket retaining ring.

Oil Pump & Rear Case

1. Install oil pump onto output shaft.
2. Install a new O-ring onto oil pump pick-up tube.
3. Engage oil pump pick-up tube to oil pump.
4. Install output shaft tone wheel onto output shaft.
5. Install wave washer onto output shaft.
6. Install rear output shaft bearing onto output shaft.
7. Install rear output shaft bearing retaining ring.
8. Apply bead of MOPAR® Gasket Maker, or equivalent, to mating surface of front case. Keep sealer bead width to maximum of 3 mm.
9. Assemble case halves together.
10. Through access hole in top of transfer case extension expand output shaft bearing retaining ring in rear extension with a suitable pair of snap ring pliers until snap ring engages groove in bearing.
11. Install access plug.
12. Install case half attaching bolts.
13. Install extension housing seal using suitable seal installer.
14. Install rear output shaft speed sensor.

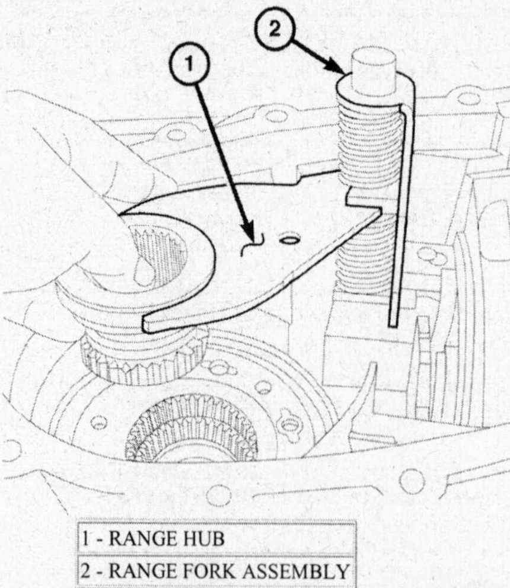

LTV0500000000221

Fig. 4 Range hub & range fork assembly

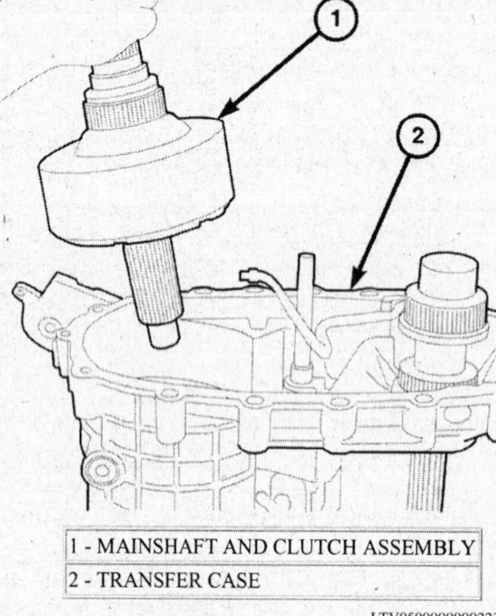

LTV0500000000223

Fig. 6 Mainshaft & clutch assembly

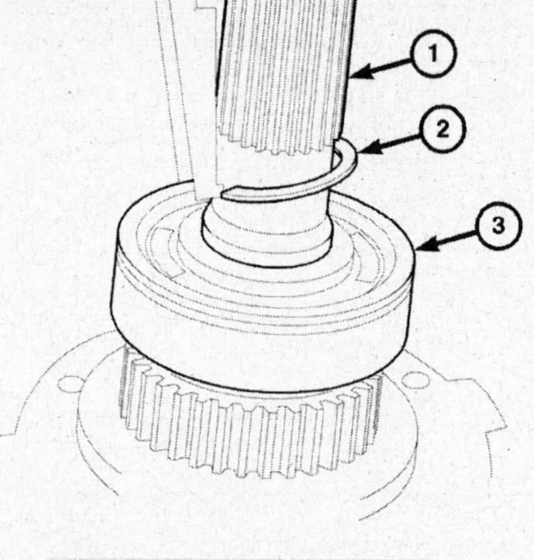

1 - OUTPUT SHAFT
2 - RETAINING RING
3 - REAR OUTPUT SHAFT BEARING

LTV0500000000222

Fig. 5 Rear output shaft bearing & shaft

Shift Motor & Front Output Shaft Boot

1. Install shift motor isolator.
2. Install shift motor and mode sensor assembly, tighten bolts to specifications.
3. Install front output shaft seal slinger with suitable installer until tool contacts rear of output shaft.
4. Install front propeller shaft seal boot and a new retaining clamp.
5. Install front output shaft sensor.
6. Install new transfer case isolator.
7. Install drain plug and fill case.

TIGHTENING SPECIFICATIONS

Year	Component	Torque Ft. Lbs.
2006	Case Half Bolts	27
	Clutch Pivot Bolt	45
	Drain Plug	20
	Front Output Shaft Speed Sensor	13
	Mounting Nuts	25
	Rear Output Shaft Speed Sensor	13
	Shift Motor and Mode Sensor Bolts	17

Model NV-247 Transfer Case

INDEX

DIAGNOSIS & TESTING

Before repairing any transfer case, inspect all other driveline components first. The actual cause of a problem may be front hubs, axles, propeller shaft, wheels, tires, transmission or clutch. Ensure hub seals are intact, maintenance of the hubs is critical. Avoid prolonged exposure to dirt and water as damage to internal components will result. If a problem still exists after the inspection and verification, refer to **Fig. 1** for further diagnosis.

DISASSEMBLE

Rear Retainer & Oil Pump

1. Remove rear retainer bolts.
2. Remove rear bearing locating ring access plug, **Fig. 2.**
3. Loosen rear retainer with suitable pry tool to break sealer bead. Pry only on retainer boss, **Fig. 3.**
4. Spread rear bearing locating ring with suitable snap ring pliers, **Fig. 4.**
5. Slide retainer off of mainshaft and rear bearing.
6. Remove rear bearing snap ring.
7. Remove rear bearing. Note position of rear bearing locating ring groove for installation reference.
8. Remove oil pump pickup tube, **Fig. 5,** from oil pump and remove oil pump assembly.
9. Remove pickup tube O-ring, **Fig. 6,** from oil pump if required. Do not disassemble oil pump, it is not serviceable.

Progressive Coupling

1. Remove oil pump locating snap ring, **Fig. 7,** and progressive coupling snap ring from mainshaft.
2. Remove progressive coupling from mainshaft.

Companion Flange & Range Lever

1. Move range lever to 4L position.
2. Remove nut with socket and impact wrench, then the companion flange.
3. If flange is difficult to remove by hand, remove it with a bearing splitter, or suitable two jaw puller.
4. Ensure puller tool is positioned on flange and not on slinger as slinger will be damaged.
5. Remove and discard seal washer from front output shaft.
6. Remove nut and washer, move the sector to neutral position, then remove range lever from shaft.
7. Note position of range lever for installation reference.

Front Output Shaft & Drive Chain

1. Support transfer case so rear case is facing upward.
2. Remove bolts holding front case to rear case. Case alignment bolts require washers.
3. Loosen rear case with a suitable flat blade screwdriver to break sealer bead.
4. Insert screwdriver blade only into notches provided at each end of case.
5. Remove rear case.
6. Remove oil pickup tube from rear case.
7. Remove drive gear snap ring.
8. Pry gear upward and off of mainshaft.
9. Remove front output shaft, drive chain and drive gear as an assembly, **Fig. 8.**
10. Remove output shaft drive gear snap ring, then the output shaft drive gear.

Shift Forks & Mainshaft

1. Remove detent plug, O-ring, detent spring and detent plunger, **Fig. 9.**
2. Remove shift rail from shift fork and transfer case housing.
3. Rotate range shift fork until it disengages from sector shaft.
4. Remove mainshaft and shift fork from input gear pilot bearing.
5. **Do not lift mainshaft by drive sprocket hub or needle bearings will become dislodged.**
6. Wrap rag around mainshaft underneath drive sprocket and remove drive sprocket hub from mainshaft.
7. Retrieve all drive sprocket hub needle bearings.
8. Remove snap ring holding clutch sleeve onto mainshaft.
9. Remove range clutch sleeve, **Fig. 10,** blockout spring, locking clutch and locking clutch spring from mainshaft.
10. Rotate and tilt sector shaft to remove.
11. Remove shift sector bushing, **Fig. 11,** and O-ring.

Input Gear/Low Range Assembly

1. Turn front case on side so front bearing retainer is accessible.
2. Remove front bearing retainer bolts, then the retainer. Loosen retainer with flat blade screwdriver to break sealer bead.
3. Remove snap ring that retains input gear shaft in front bearing, **Fig. 12.**
4. Remove input and low range gear assembly.
5. Remove oil seals from front bearing retainer, rear retainer and case halves.
6. Remove snap ring, **Fig. 13,** that retains input gear in low range gear.
7. Remove retainer, front tabbed thrust washer, input gear and rear tabbed thrust washer.

INSPECTION

Mainshaft

Inspect the mainshaft components for evidence of wear or damage. Replace thrust washers if worn or damaged. Replace the mainshaft and sprocket gears if the teeth or gear bores are worn or damaged. Replace the mainshaft bearings if worn flat spotted, brinelled or damaged in any way. Replace mainshaft if it is bent, exhibits wear or damage to the bearing surfaces, splines or gear teeth.

CONDITION	POSSIBLE CAUSE	CORRECTION
TRANSFER CASE DIFFICULT TO SHIFT OR WILL NOT SHIFT INTO DESIRED RANGE	1. Vehicle speed too great to permit shifting	1. Reduce speed to 3-4 km/h (2-3 mph) before attempting to shift
	2. Transfer case external shift cable binding	2. Lubricate, repair or replace cable, or tighten loose components as necessary
	3. Insufficient or incorrect lubricant	3. Drain and refill to edge of fill hole with Mopar ATF PLUS (Type 7176) or DEXRON II Automatic Transmission Fluid
	4. Internal components binding, worn, or damaged	4. Disassemble unit and replace worn or damaged components as necessary
TRANSFER CASE NOISY IN ALL MODES	1. Insufficient or incorrect lubricant	1. Drain and refill to edge of fill hole with Mopar ATF PLUS (Type 7176) or DEXRON II Automatic Transmission Fluid. **If unit is still noisy after drain and refill, disassembly and inspection may be required to locate source of noise**
NOISY IN—OR JUMPS OUT OF 4WD LOW RANGE	1. Transfer case not completely engaged in 4WD LOW (possibly from shift to 4L while rolling)	1. Stop vehicle, shift transfer case to neutral, then shift back to 4WD LOW
	2. Shift linkage loose, binding, or is misadjusted	2. Tighten, lubricate, or repair linkage as necessary. Adjust linkage if necessary
	3. Range fork cracked, inserts worn, or fork is binding on shift rail	3. Disassemble unit and repair as necessary
	4. Annulus gear or lockplate worn or damaged	4. Disassemble unit and repair as necessary
LUBRICANT LEAKING FROM OUTPUT SHAFT SEALS OR FROM VENT	1. Transfer case over filled	1. Drain to correct level
	2. Vent closed or restricted	2. Clear or replace vent if necessary
	3. Output shaft seals damaged or installed correctly	3. Replace seals. Be sure seal lip faces interior of case when installed. Also be sure yoke seal surfaces are not scored or nicked. Remove scores and nicks with fine sandpaper or replace yoke(s) if necessary.

CR3049900259000X

Fig. 1 Transfer case diagnosis chart

Input & Low Range Gears

Inspect the low range gear pinions and pinion pins. Replace the low range gear if any of the pins or pinions are worn or damaged. Inspect the thrust washers, retainer, and snap ring. Replace the snap ring if bent or distorted. Replace the thrust washers and retainer if worn, cracked or damaged in any way.

Inspect the input gear carefully, ensure gear teeth and bearing surfaces are in good condition. Replace the gear if wear or damage is evident. Inspect the input gear pilot bearings for rotational roughness or noise. Inspect bearing for position in bore. The bearing should be recessed approximately .100 inch below the top edge of the bore. The bearing should not be seated at the bottom of the bore. Replace the bearing if worn, or roughness is evident. Replace both gear and bearing if bearing is a loose fit in the bore.

Gear Case & Retainers

Inspect both case halves and retainers, replace any retainer or case half that exhibits wear, cracks or other obvious damage. Inspect condition of annulus gear and shift rail bushing in the front case. The low range annulus gear is not serviceable. Replace the case and gear as an assembly if the gear is lose, worn, or damaged. The shift rail bushing is a serviceable part and can be replaced if required. Inspect the bushing in the rear retainer, replace bushing if it is worn or scored.

Examine the sealing surfaces of both case halves and retainers. Small burrs, or scratches on the surfaces can be polished out with emery cloth or a fine tooth file.

Inspect the condition of the shift rail bushing in the front case. If the bushing is worn or damaged, it can be removed with a blind hole type puller. Install replacement bushing with a suitable driver. Recess the bushing slightly below the edge of the bore but do not seat it all the way into the case.

Geartrain

Inspect the mainshaft splines, gear teeth and bearing surfaces for wear or visible damage. Repair shaft if required. The shift rail and range fork are an assembly. Replace both components if either is damaged. The nylon pads in the fork can be replaced if worn or cracked.

Inspect the transfer case snap rings. Replace any snap ring that is bent or distorted. Inspect the low range gear thrust washer retainer and snap ring. The low range gear is serviced as an assembly only. Replace the gear if the case or pinions are damaged. Inspect the seal surface of the input gear. Minor nicks can be polished out with emery cloth. Replace the gear if the seal surface is severely scored or worn.

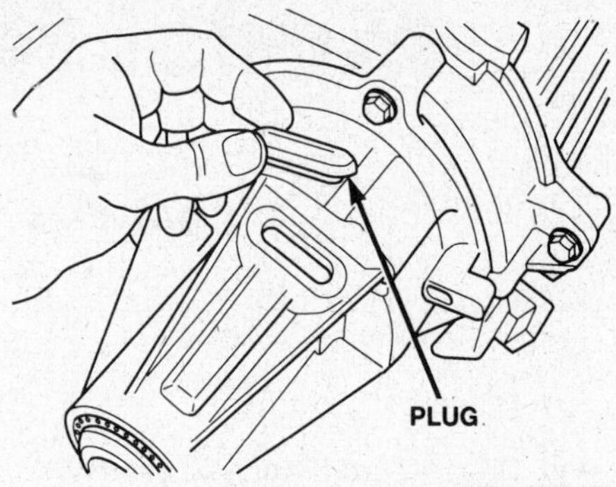

CR3049900260000X

Fig. 2 Rear bearing locating ring access plug

Oil Pump & Progressive Coupling

The oil pump and progressive coupling are not serviceable components. Replace the coupling as an assembly if it is leaking or damaged. Replace the oil pump as an assembly if the gear teeth are worn or if the pump has become damaged.

Bearings & Seals

The transfer case seals should be replaced during overhaul. Use new seals in the input gear bearing retainer, front case and rear retainer. Replace the yoke seal washer and detent plug O-ring.

Inspect the condition of the transfer case bearings. Replace any bearing that exhibits signs of roughness, wear or damage.

ASSEMBLE

Lubricate transfer case components with ATF or petroleum jelly (where indicated) during assembly.

Bearings & Seals

1. Remove front output shaft seal from case with suitable pry tool.
2. Remove snap ring that retains front output shaft bearing in front case.
3. Remove bearing from front case using replacement tool No. 6953, or equivalent.
4. Install new bearing using installer tool No. 6953, or equivalent.
5. Install snap ring to hold bearing into case.
6. Place new front output seal on installer tool No. 6952-A, or equivalent. Garter spring on seal faces toward interior of case.
7. Start seal into bore with light taps from a hammer. Once seal is started, continue tapping until installer tool bottoms against case.
8. Remove output shaft rear bearing with screw and jaws from remover tool No.

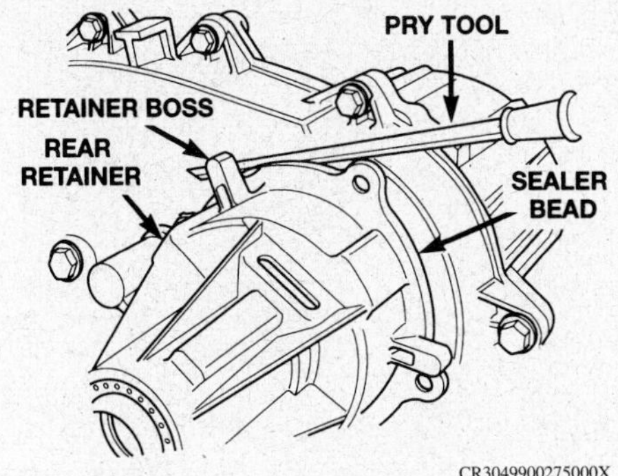

Fig. 3 Rear retainer boss

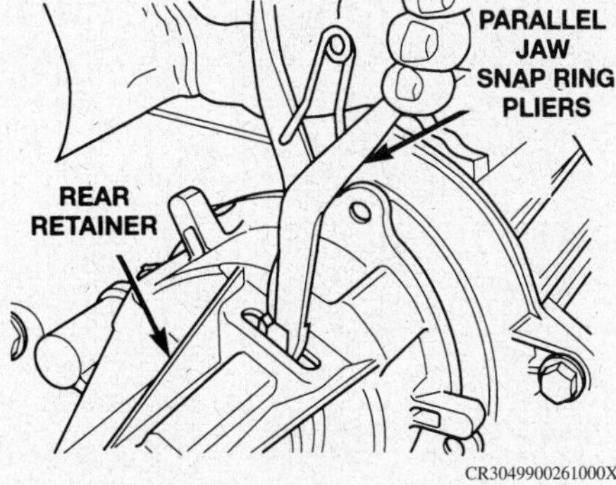

Fig. 4 Rear bearing locating ring

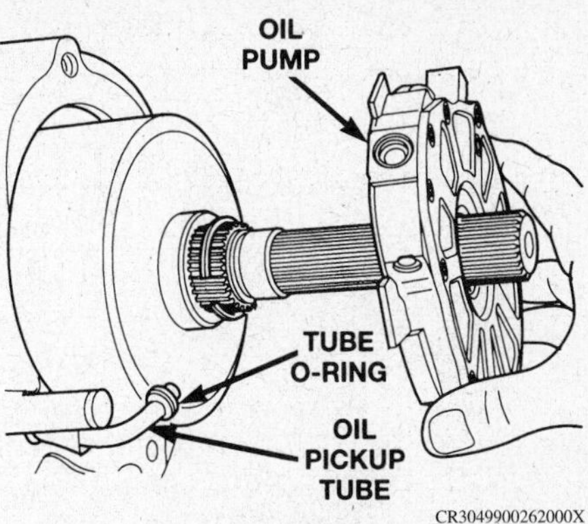

Fig. 5 Rear bearing & oil pump removal

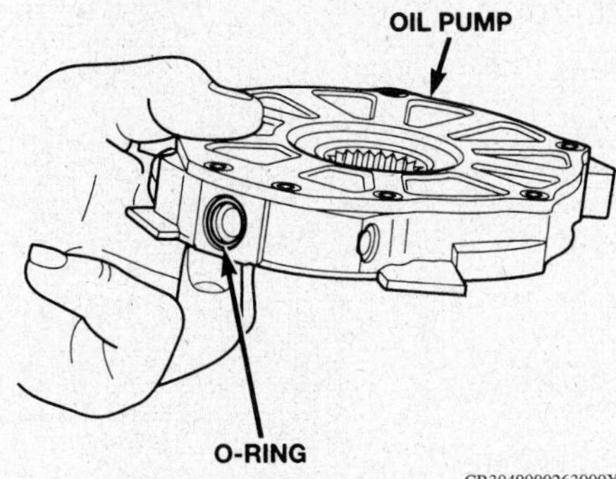

Fig. 6 Pickup tube O-ring removal

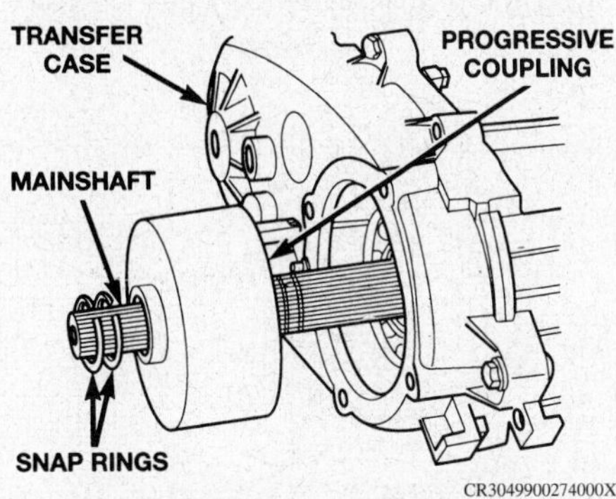

Fig. 7 Progressive coupling

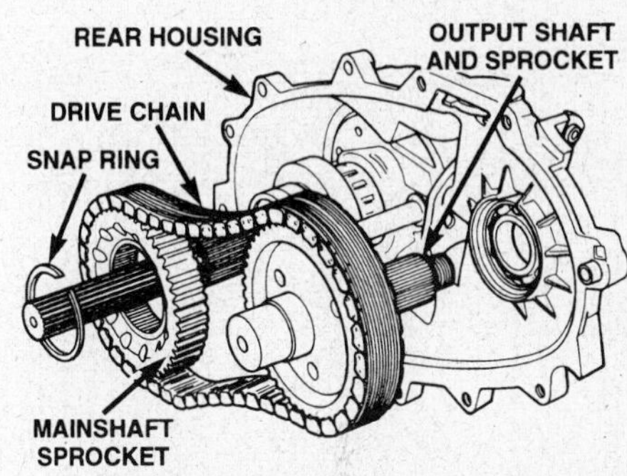

Fig. 8 Front output shaft, drive gear & chain removal

L-4454 and cup tool No. 8148, or equivalents, **Fig. 14.**

9. Install new bearing using handle tool No. C-4171 and installer tool No. 5066, or equivalents.
10. Bearing bore is chamfered at top. Install bearing so it is flush with lower edge of chamfer.
11. Drive input shaft bearing from inside of annulus gear opening in case using handle tool and remover tool No. C-4120, or equivalents.
12. Install locating ring on new bearing.
13. Position case so forward end is facing upward.
14. Drive input shaft bearing into case. bearing locating ring must be fully seated against case using handle tool and remover tool No. C-4120, or equivalents.
15. Remove input gear pilot bearing using a suitable drift, **Fig. 15,** and hammer.
16. Install new pilot bearing using handle tool and installer tool No. C-4171, or equivalents, **Fig. 16.**
17. Remove front bearing retainer seal with suitable pry tool, then install new front bearing retainer with installer tool No. 7884, or equivalent.

Input Gear & Low Range Gear

1. Lubricate gears and thrust washers, **Fig. 17,** with ATF.
2. Install first thrust washer in low range gear, ensure washer tabs are properly aligned in gear notches.
3. Install input gear in low range gear, ensure input gear is fully engaged.
4. Install remaining thrust washer in low range gear and on top of input gear. Ensure washer tabs are properly aligned in gear notches.
5. Install retainer on input gear, then install snap ring.
6. Align and install low range/input gear assembly in front case. Ensure low range gear pinions are engaged in annulus gear and that input gear shaft is fully seated in front bearing.
7. Install snap ring to hold input/low range gear into front bearing.
8. Clean gasket sealer residue from retainer and inspect retainer for cracks or other damage.
9. Apply a ⅛ inch bead of suitable silicone adhesive to sealing surface of retainer.
10. Align cavity in seal retainer with fluid return hole in front of case.
11. Install retainer bolts and tighten to specification.

Shift Forks & Mainshaft

1. Install new sector shaft O-ring, **Fig. 11,** and bushing.
2. Install shift sector.
3. Install locking clutch spring, locking clutch, blockout spring and range clutch sleeve to mainshaft, **Fig. 10.**
4. Install drive sprocket hub to mainshaft and manually load needle bearings.
5. Install new pads on range fork if required.
6. Install range shift fork to range clutch sleeve.
7. Install mainshaft/range shift fork assembly into transfer case and input planetary assembly. Rotate fork until it engages with slot in shift sector.
8. Install shift rail to shift range fork and transfer case housing.
9. Rotate shift sector to Neutral position.
10. Install new O-ring on detent plug, lubricate detent plunger with ATF or a light coat of petroleum jelly.
11. Install detent plunger, spring and plug. Verify that plunger is properly engaged in sector.

Front Output Shaft & Drive Chain

1. Lubricate front output shaft sprocket assembly, drive chain and drive sprocket with transmission fluid.
2. Assemble drive chain, drive sprocket and front output shaft, **Fig. 8.**
3. Start drive sprocket on mainshaft, then guide front shaft into bearing and drive sprocket onto mainshaft drive gear.
4. Install drive sprocket snap ring, roller bearings if removed, and progressive coupling, **Fig. 7.**
5. Install oil pickup tube in rear case, ensure tube is seated in case notch.
6. Install magnet in front case pocket.
7. Clean sealing surfaces of front and rear case with suitable wax and grease remover.
8. Apply a ⅛ wide bead of suitable silicone adhesive sealer to mounting flange of front case. Work sealer bead around bolt holes.
9. Align and install rear case on front case, ensure oil pickup tube is still

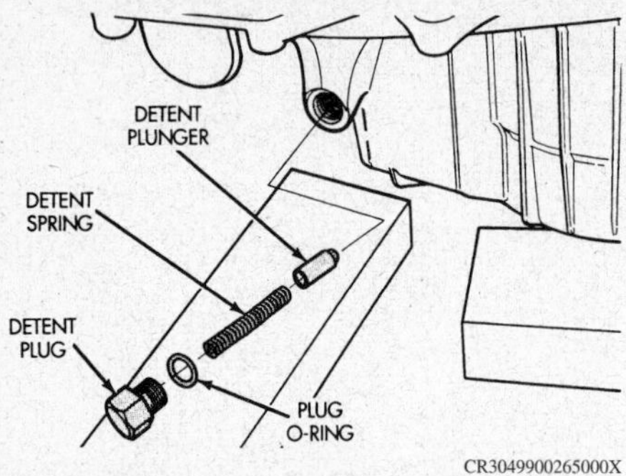

Fig. 9 Detent plug, spring & plunger

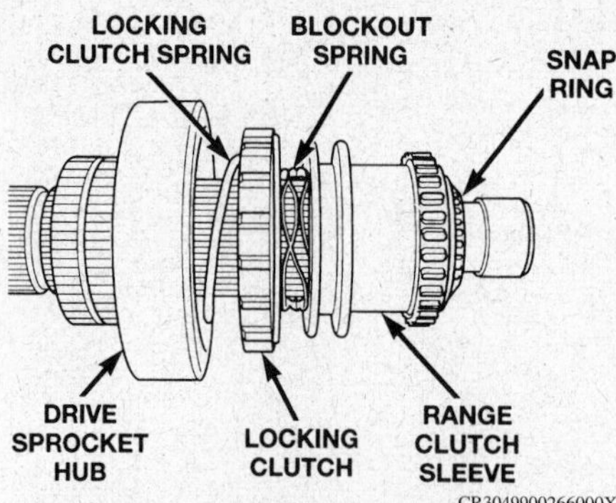

Fig. 10 Range clutch sleeve, blockout spring & locking clutch & spring

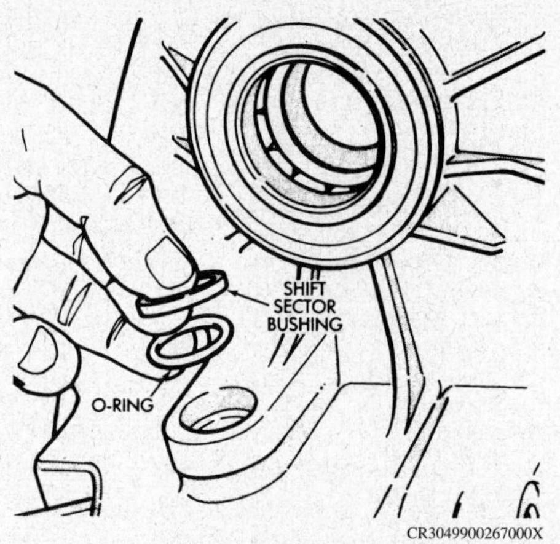

Fig. 11 Sector bushing & O-ring removal

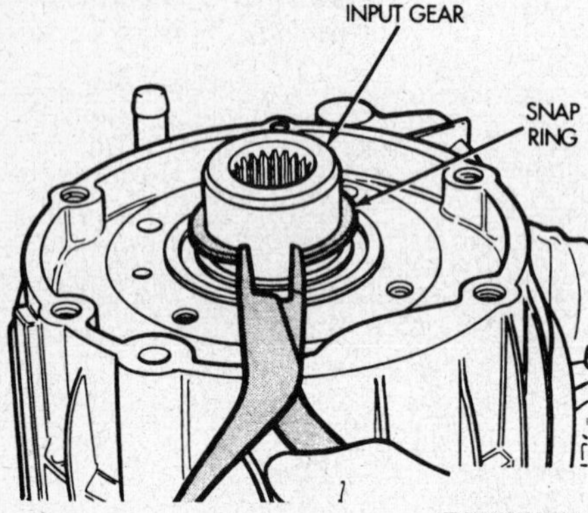

Fig. 12 Input gear snap ring removal

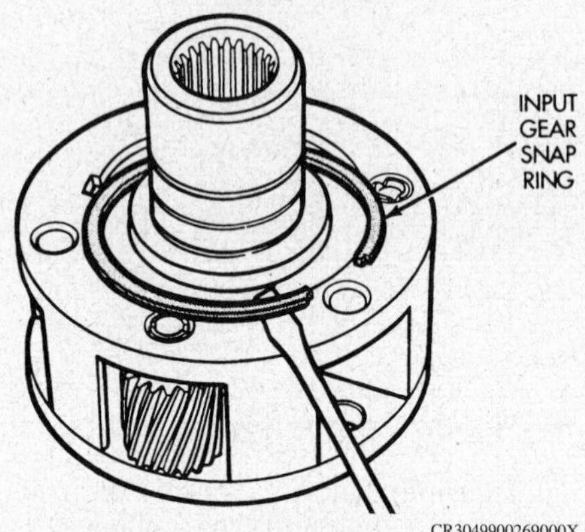

Fig. 13 Input gear snap ring removal

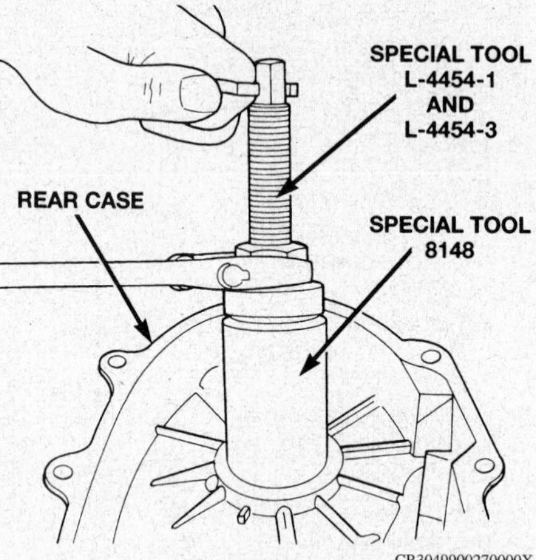

Fig. 14 Output shaft rear bearing removal

seated in case notch and tube end is pointed toward mainshaft.

10. Install case attaching bolts, alignment bolts at each end of case are the only ones requiring flat washers.
11. Tighten all case bolts to specification.

Companion Flange & Range Lever

1. Install range lever, washer and lock nut on sector shaft. Tighten to specification.
2. Install new seal washer on front output shaft.
3. Lubricate flange hub with ATF and install flange on front hub.
4. Install new seal washer on front shaft.
5. Install companion flange and a new nut on front output shaft.
6. Tighten flange nut to specification. Use holding tool No. C-3281, or equivalent to hold flange while tightening yoke nut.

Progressive Coupler

1. Install coupling on mainshaft.
2. Install coupling retaining snap ring first, ensure snap ring is fully seated before proceeding.
3. Install oil pump locating snap ring on mainshaft, **Fig. 18.**

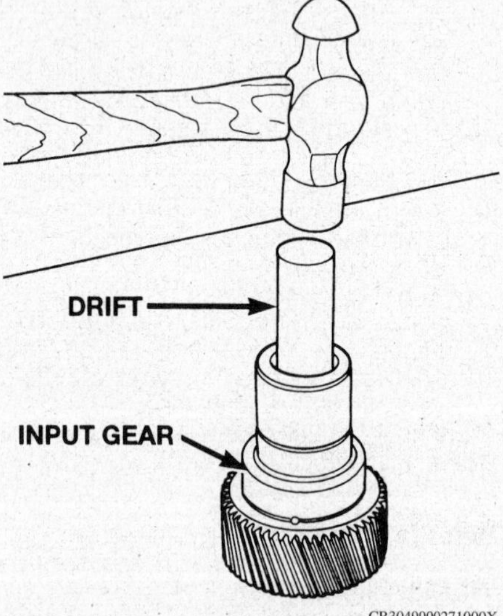

Fig. 15 Input gear pilot bearing removal

Rear Retainer & Oil Pump

1. Install new O-ring on flanged end of oil pickup tube, **Fig. 19,** then install oil pump.
2. Insert oil pickup tube in pump, then install rear bearing on mainshaft, **Fig. 20.**
3. Locating ring groove in bearing goes toward end of mainshaft.
4. Install rear bearing retaining snap ring, **Fig. 21.**
5. Install rear bearing locating ring in rear retainer, if removed.
6. Apply a 1/8 inch wide bead of suitable silicone adhesive sealer to mounting surface or rear retainer. Allow sealer to set up before proceeding.
7. Spread rear bearing locating ring and slide rear retainer into place on rear case.
8. Install and tighten rear bearing retainer bolts to specification.
9. Install rubber access plug.

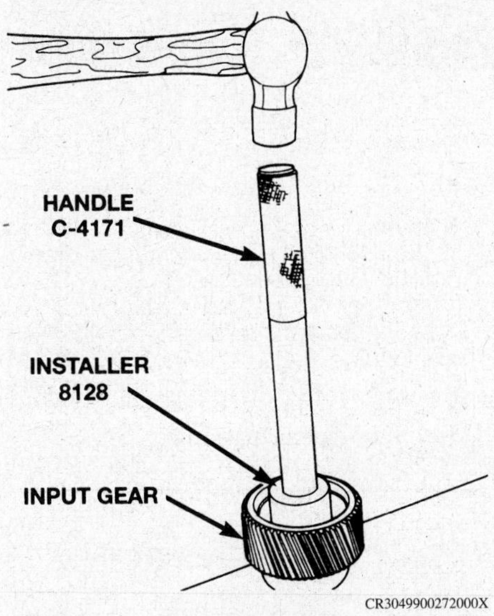

Fig. 16 Input gear pilot bearing installation

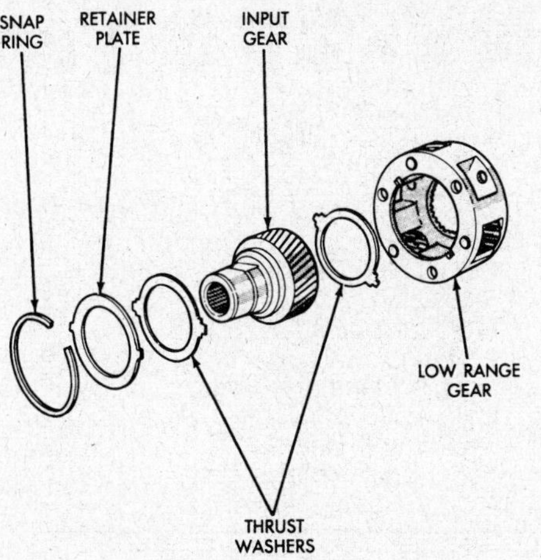

Fig. 17 Exploded view of input/low range gear

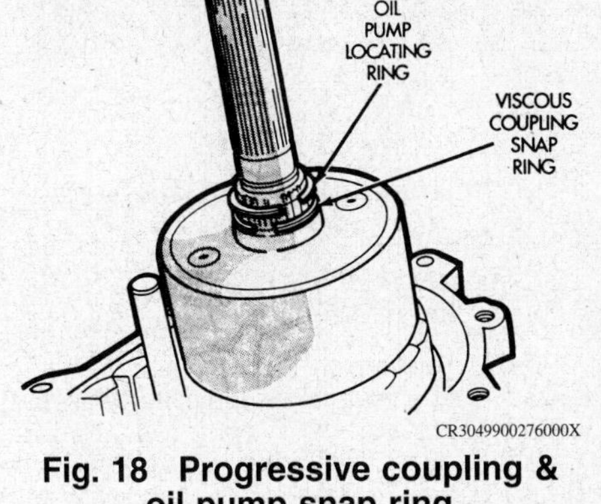

Fig. 18 Progressive coupling & oil pump snap ring

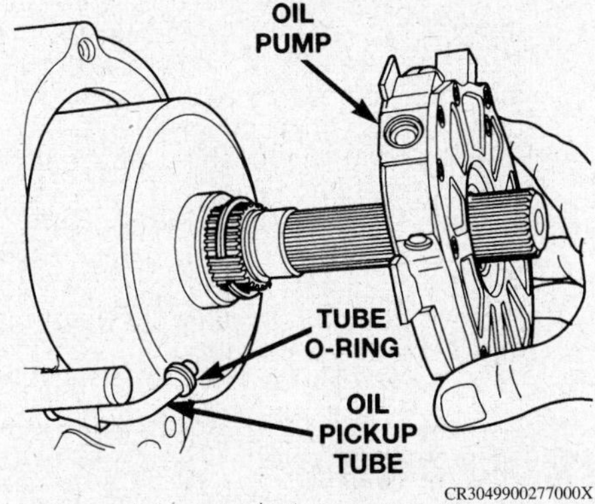

Fig. 19 Oil pump & O-ring installation

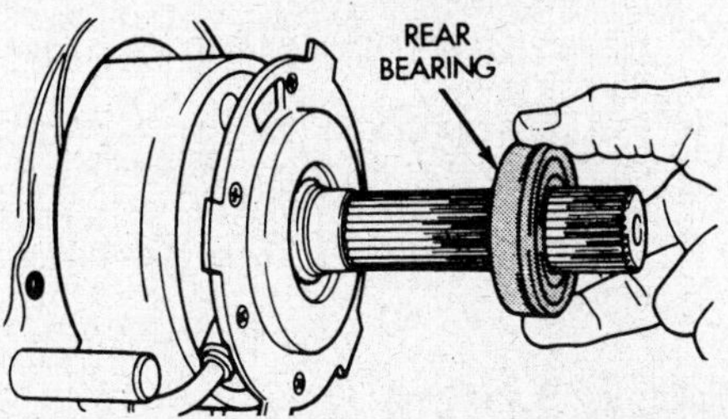

Fig. 20 Rear bearing installation

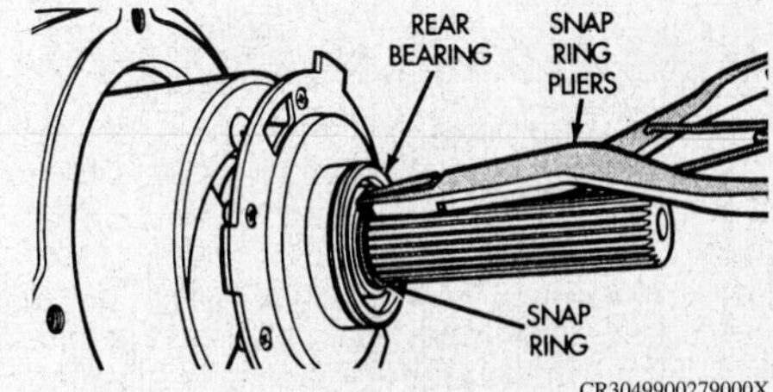

Fig. 21 Rear bearing snap ring installation

TIGHTENING SPECIFICATIONS

Year	Component	Torque Ft. Lbs.
2002–04	Companion Flange Nut	90–130
	Crossmember Bolts	30–35
	Detent Plug	12–18
	Drain/Fill Plugs	30–40
	Front Bearing Retainer	12–18
	Rear Extension	20–25
	Shift Lock Nut	20–25
	Transfer Case Bolts	20–25
	Transfer Case Stud Nuts	24–30

NV-271 & NV-273 Transfer Cases

INDEX

DIAGNOSIS & TESTING

Before repairing any transfer case, inspect all other driveline components first. The actual cause of a problem may be front hubs, axles, propeller shaft, wheels, tires, transmission or clutch. Ensure hub seals are intact, maintenance of the hubs is critical. Avoid prolonged exposure to dirt and water as damage to internal components will result. If a problem still exists after the inspection and verification, refer to **Fig. 1** for further transfer case diagnosis.

DISASSEMBLE

Companion Flange & Extension Housing

1. Install two bolts 180° apart into front output shaft companion flange.
2. Place holder over bolts and against companion flange, **Fig. 2.**
3. Remove and discard front companion flange nut.
4. Remove companion flange from front output shaft using puller tool No. 8992, or equivalent, if required.
5. Remove rear extension housing dust boot.
6. Remove rear extension housing seal.
7. Remove rear extension bolts, then the rear extension housing. Tap with plastic mallet to break loose.

Oil Pump & Rear Case

1. Disengage oil pump pick-up tube from oil pump, **Fig. 3.**
2. Remove oil pump, **Fig. 4.**
3. Remove rear case to front case bolts.
4. Remove rear output shaft bearing inner snap ring, **Fig. 5.**
5. Loosen rear case using suitable pry tool at each end of case.
6. Unseat rear case from alignment dowels, then remove from front case.

Front Output Shaft & Drive Chain

1. Remove oil pick-up tube and screen from front case half.
2. Remove shift rail spring, **Fig. 6.**
3. Remove front output shaft drive sprocket retaining ring.
4. Remove rear output drive sprocket retaining ring.
5. Pull front sprocket, rear sprocket and chain upward until they clear front and rear output shaft sprocket splines.
6. Remove chain and sprockets as an assembly, **Fig. 7.**

Shift Forks & Mainshaft

1. Shift transfer case into neutral.
2. Remove nut securing shift lever to sector shaft, then remove shift lever and spacer from shaft, **Fig. 8.**
3. Remove sector support using socket tool No. 9033, or equivalent.
4. Remove transfer case position sensor, **Fig. 9.**
5. Loosen detent plug.
6. Remove detent plug, spring and plunger, **Fig. 10.** Discard O-ring seal.
7. Remove front output shaft seal using a screw mounted in a slide hammer.
8. Remove front output shaft snap ring, **Fig. 11.**
9. Remove front output shaft from bearing in case, **Fig. 12.**
10. Pull mainshaft assembly out of input gear, mode sleeve and case, **Fig. 13.**
11. Remove mode fork, mode sleeve and shift rail as an assembly, **Fig. 14.** Note which way sleeve fits in fork, long side of sleeve goes to front.
12. Remove range fork and hub as an assembly noting position for reference during installation, **Fig. 15.**
13. Remove shift sector, **Fig. 16.**

Mainshaft

1. Remove clutch gear from output shaft, **Fig. 17.**
2. Remove mode hub retaining ring, then the mode hub from mainshaft, **Fig. 18.**
3. Remove drive sprocket drive hub from mainshaft.

Input & Planetary Gear

1. Remove input gear seal using suitable screw and slide hammer.
2. Remove input gear retaining ring using heavy duty snap ring pliers, **Fig. 19.**
3. Place front case in a horizontal position, then remove input gear and low range gear as an assembly, **Fig. 20.**
4. Remove snap ring retaining input gear in low range gear, **Fig. 21.**
5. Remove retainer and thrust plate, **Figs. 22 and 23.**
6. Remove input gear, **Fig. 24.**
7. Remove bottom tabbed thrust washer from low range planetary.

INSPECTION

Mainshaft, Sprocket & Hub

Inspect the splines on the hub and shaft and on teeth of sprocket. Minor nicks and scratches can be smoothed using an oilstone. Replace any part that is damaged.

Inspect contact surfaces in sprocket bore and on mainshaft. Minor nicks and scratches can be smoothed with 320–400 grit emery cloth. Replace shaft if nicks or wear is severe.

Input Gear & Planetary Carrier

Inspect the teeth on input gear, **Fig. 25.** Minor nicks can be removed using an oilstone. Replace gear if any teeth are broken, cracked or chipped. The bearing surface on gear can be smoothed using 300–400 grit emery cloth.

Examine carrier body and pinion gears for wear or damage. Inspect pinion gear thrust washers on pinion pins for damage. The carrier will have to be replaced as an assembly if the body, pinion pins or pinion gears are damaged.

Inspect lock ring and both thrust washers

Condition	Possible Cause	Correction
Transfer Case difficult to shift or will not shift into desired range.	1) Vehicle speed too great to permit shifting.	1) Stop vehicle and shift into desired range. Or, reduce speed to below 3-4 km/h (2-3 mph) before attempting the shift.
	2) If vehicle was operated for an extended period in 4H on a dry paved surface, the driveline torque load may be causing a bind.	2) Stop vehicle and shift the transmission into neutral. Shift the transfer case to 2H and operate vehicle in 2H on dry paved surfaces.
	3) Transfer case external shift linkage binding.	3) Lubricate, repair, or replace linkage bushings, or tighten loose components as necessary.
	4) Insufficient or incorrect lubricant.	4) Drain and refill to edge of fill hole with Mopar® ATF +4, Automatic Transmission fluid.
	5) Internal components binding, worn, or damaged.	5) Disassemble the transfer case and replace worn or damaged components as necessary.
Transfer Case noisy in all operating ranges.	1) Insufficient or incorrect lubricant.	1) Drain and refill to edge of fill hole with Mopar® ATF +4, Automatic Transmission fluid.

LTV1900000001123

Fig. 1 Transfer case diagnosis chart (Part 1 of 2)

Condition	Possible Cause	Correction
Noisy in, or jumps out of, four wheel drive low range.	1) Transfer case not completely engaged in 4L position.	1) With the transmission in NEUTRAL, or the clutch depressed in the case of a manual transmission and the vehicle moving under 3-4 km/h (2-3 mph), shift the transfer case to NEUTRAL and then shift into the 4L position.
	2) Shift linkage out of adjustment.	2) Adjust linkage.
	3) Shift linkage loose or binding.	3) Tighten, lubricate, or repair linkage as necessary.
	4) Range fork damaged, inserts worn, or fork is binding on the shift rail.	4) Disassemble unit and repair as necessary.
	5) Low range gear worn or damaged.	5) Disassemble unit and repair as necessary.
Lubricant leaking from output shaft seal or vent.	1) Transfer case overfilled.	1) Drain lubricant to the correct level.
	2) Vent closed or restricted.	2) Clear or replace vent as necessary.
	3) Output shaft seals damaged or installed incorrectly.	3) Replace seal as necessary. Check to ensure that another component, the propeller shaft slip yoke for example, is not causing damage to seal.
Abnormal tire wear.	1) Extended operation on hard, dry surfaces in the 4H position.	1) Operate vehicle in the 2H position on hard, dry surfaces.

LTV1900000001124

Fig. 1 Transfer case diagnosis chart (Part 2 of 2)

for wear or cracks. Replace them if required. Replace lock retaining ring if bent, distorted or broken.

Shift Forks, Hubs & Sleeves

Inspect condition of shift forks and mode fork shift rail. Minor nicks on shift rail can be smoothed using 320–400 grit emery cloth.

Inspect shift fork wear pads, **Fig. 26.** Replace if required.

Inspect both of the sleeves for wear or damage, especially on interior teeth. Replace sleeves if wear or damage is evident.

Drive Chain

Examine drive chain and shaft bearings. Replace the chain if stretched, distorted or if any of the links bind. Replace bearings if rough or noisy.

Low Range Annulus Gear

Inspect annulus gear condition carefully. The gear is only serviced as part of the front case. If the gear is damaged, it will be required to replace the gear and front case as an assembly. Do not attempt to remove gear.

Front & Rear Case

Inspect cases for wear and damage. Inspect case condition. If leaks were a problem, look for gouges and severe scoring of case sealing surfaces. Also make sure front case mounting studs are in good condition.

Inspect front case mounting studs and vent tube. The tube can be secured with Loctite 271 or 680 if loose. The stud threads can be cleaned up with a die if required. Also inspect condition of the fill/drain plug threads in the rear case. The threads can be repaired with a thread chaser or tap if required. Threads can also be repaired using a Helicoil stainless insert.

Oil Pump & Pickup

Examine oil pump pickup components. Replace the pump if any part appears to be worn or damaged. Do not disassemble the pump as individual components are not available. The pump is only available as a complete assembly. The pickup screen, hose and tube are the only components available separately.

ASSEMBLE

Bearings & Seals

1. Remove input shaft bearing snap ring from front case half.
2. Remove input shaft bearing from front case half using installer tool No. 6953 and handle tool No. C-4171, or equivalents, **Fig. 27.**
3. Install input shaft bearing into front case half using installer tool No. 8151 inverted on handle tool No. C-4171, or equivalents, **Fig. 28.**
4. Install input shaft bearing snap ring.
5. Remove front output shaft bearing snap ring from front case half.
6. Remove front output shaft bearing using installer tool No. 6953 and handle tool No. C-4171, or equivalents.
7. Start front output shaft bearing in case, then seat using installer tool No. 8891, or equivalent.
8. Install front output shaft bearing retaining ring.
9. Remove input gear pilot bearing by inserting a suitably sized drift into splined end of input gear and driving bearing out with drift and hammer.
10. Install new pilot bearing using installer tool No. 9035, or equivalent.
11. Remove front output shaft rear bearing with screw and jaws from remover tool No. L-4454 and cup tool No. 8148, or equivalents, **Fig. 29.**
12. Install new bearing using handle tool No. C-4171 and installer tool No. 8128, or equivalents. Bearing bore is chamfered at top, install bearing so it is flush with lower edge of chamfer.
13. Remove seal from oil pump using suitable pry tool.
14. Install new seal in oil pump using installer tool No. 7888, or equivalent.
15. Remove rear output shaft bearing snap ring from rear case half.
16. Remove rear output shaft bearing from rear case using installer tool No. 7888, or equivalent.
17. Install rear output shaft bearing using installer tool No. 8152 and handle tool No. C-4171, or equivalent.
18. Install rear output shaft bearing snap ring into rear case half.

Input & Planetary Gear

1. Lubricate gears and thrust washers with transmission fluid.
2. Install bottom thrust washer in low range gear planetary ensuring tabs are properly aligned in gear notches, **Fig. 30.**
3. Install input gear in low range gear ensuring input gear is fully seated, **Fig. 24.**
4. Install remaining thrust washer in low range gear on top of input gear.
5. Install retainer on input gear, **Fig. 22,** then the snap ring.
6. Align and install low range/input gear assembly in front case. Ensure low range gear pinions are engaged in annulus gear and input gear shaft is fully seated in front bearing.
7. Install snap ring to hold input/low range gear into front bearing.
8. Install new input gear seal using installer tool No. 8841 and handle tool No. C-4171, or equivalents.
9. Install new input gear oil seal using installer tool No. 9036 and handle tool No. C-4171, or equivalents.

Shift Forks & Mainshaft

1. Lubricate mainshaft splines with transmission fluid.
2. Coat interior of drive sprocket hub with

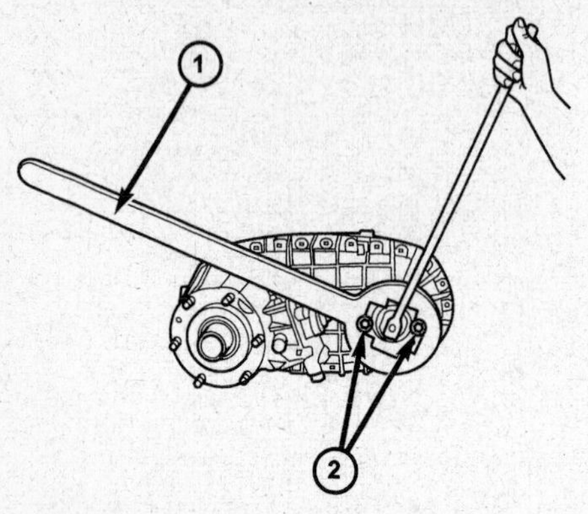

Fig. 2 Companion flange removal

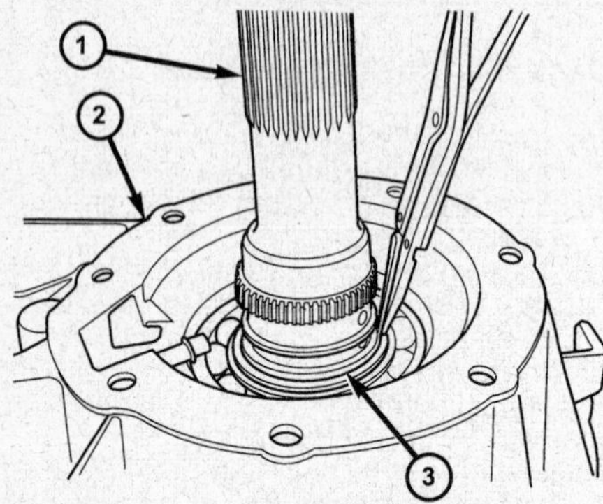

Fig. 5 Rear bearing inner snap ring

transmission fluid, then install hub onto mainshaft.

3. Install mode hub onto mainshaft, then the retaining ring.
4. Install clutch gear onto output shaft ensuring pointed ends of clutch gear teeth are pointing to front of mainshaft, **Fig. 17.**
5. Lubricate sector shaft with transmission fluid and install shift sector in case, **Fig. 16.** Position slot in sector so it will be aligned with shift fork pin when shift forks are installed.
6. Apply Loctite 242, or equivalent, to threads of sector support, then install shift sector support. Use socket tool No. 9033, or equivalent, to tighten.
7. Assemble and install range fork and hub ensuring hub is properly seated in low range gear and engaged to input gear, **Fig. 31.**
8. Align and insert range fork pin in shift sector slot.
9. Install mode fork and shift rail onto mode sleeve.
10. Install mode fork, sleeve and shift rail into transfer case.

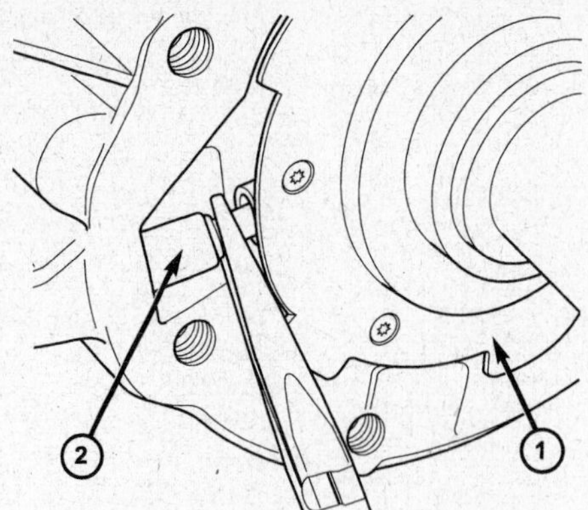

Fig. 3 Oil pump pick-up tube

11. Install mainshaft into transfer case guiding through mode and range sleeves and into input gear.
12. Install transfer case position sensor.
13. Install manual shift lever and spacer onto sector shaft, **Fig. 8.**
14. Install washer and nut on sector shaft. Apply Mopar Lock and Seal, or equivalent, to nut threads before installation.
15. Install new O-ring on detent plug.
16. Install detent plunger, spring and plug, **Fig. 32.**

Front Output Shaft & Drive Chain

1. Install front output shaft into bearing, **Fig. 12.**
2. Install front output shaft bearing inner snap ring onto output shaft, **Fig. 11.**
3. Install new front output shaft seal using installer tool No. MB991168A, or equivalent.
4. Insert front drive sprocket in drive chain.
5. Install drive chain around rear drive sprocket.
6. Position rear drive sprocket over output shaft, then lower sprocket and chain assembly until front sprocket is positioned over front output shaft.
7. Align splines in sprockets to splines on output shafts, then install sprockets onto output shafts.
8. Install front and rear sprocket retaining rings.
9. Install spring onto shift rail, **Fig. 6.**
10. Install magnet in front case pocket, **Fig. 33.**

Rear Case

1. Install oil pick-up tube and screen into rear case half.
2. Apply a 3⁄16 inch bead of Mopar Gasket Maker, or equivalent, to mating surface of front case.
3. Align mainshaft with rear output shaft

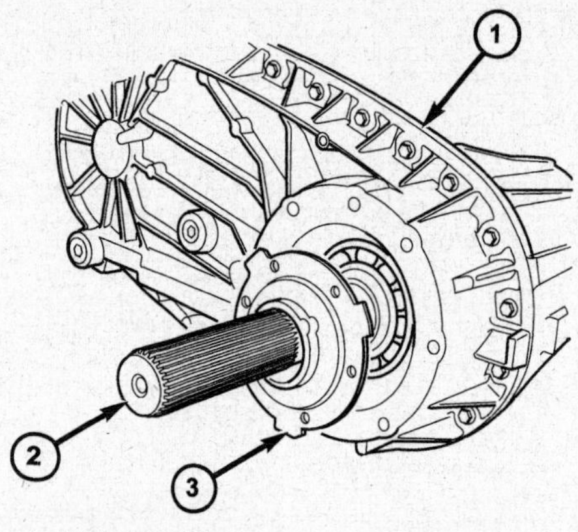

Fig. 4 Oil pump removal

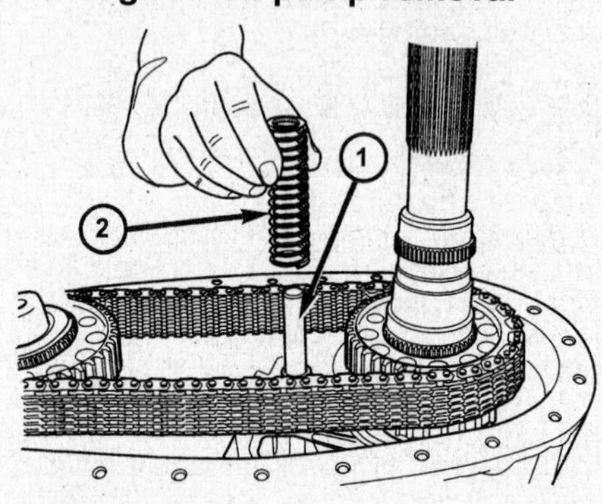

Fig. 6 Shift rail spring

bearing, then align shift rail with bore in rear case.

4. Install rear case ensuring that case alignment dowels correctly seat into their mating recesses.
5. Install rear case to front case bolts.
6. Install rear output bearing inner snap ring to output shaft.

Oil Pump & Rear Extension

1. Install oil pump onto output shaft, **Fig. 4.**
2. Engage oil pump pick-up tube into oil pump, **Fig. 3.**
3. Ensure that pick-up tube O-ring is on tube and correctly installed to oil pump.
4. Apply a 3⁄16 inch bead of Mopar Gasket Maker, or equivalent, to mating surface of rear extension housing.
5. Install extension housing, then the housing bolts onto rear case half.
6. Install extension housing boot using installer tool No. 9037 and handle tool No. C-4171, or equivalents.

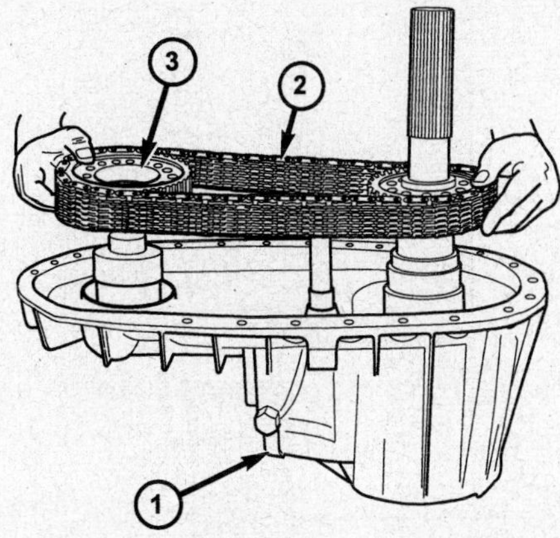

1 - FRONT CASE HALF
2 - CHAIN
3 - DRIVE SPROCKETS

LTV1900000001130

Fig. 7 Drive chain & sprockets

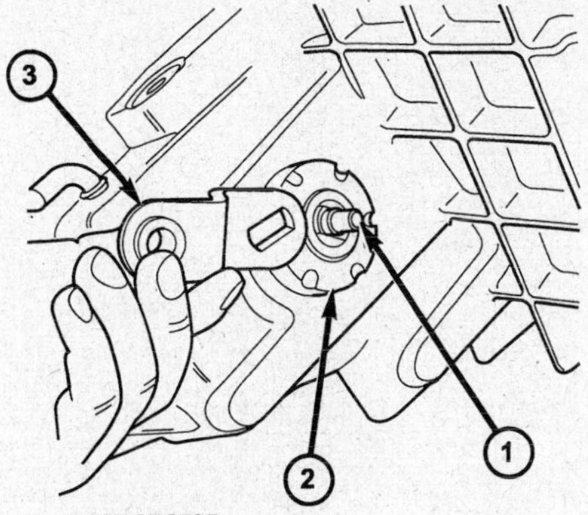

1 - SHIFT SECTOR
2 - SECTOR SUPPORT
3 - MANUAL SHIFT LEVER

LTV1900000001131

Fig. 8 Manual shift lever

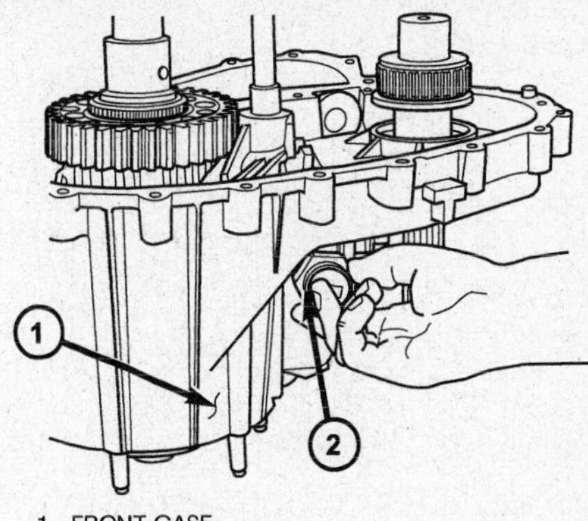

1 - FRONT CASE
2 - POSITION SENSOR

LTV1900000001132

Fig. 9 Position sensor

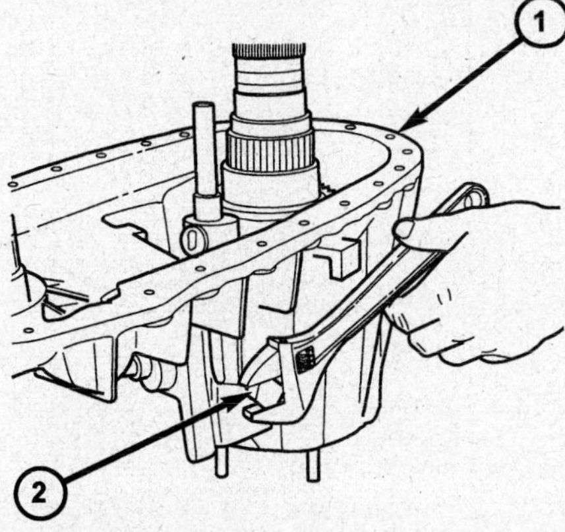

1 - FRONT CASE HALF
2 - DETENT PLUG

LTV1900000001133

Fig. 10 Detent plug, spring and plunger

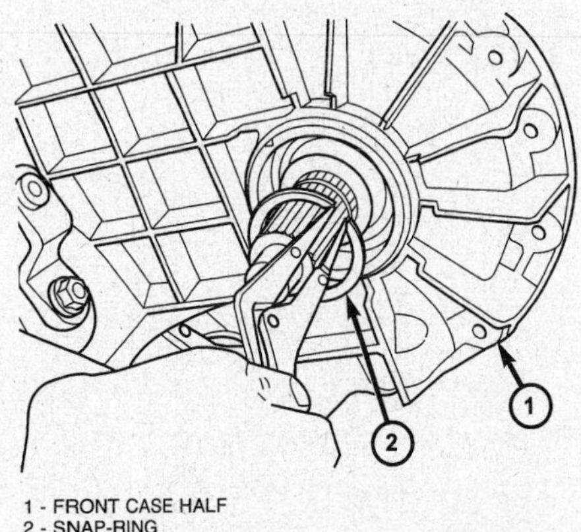

1 - FRONT CASE HALF
2 - SNAP-RING

LTV1900000001134

Fig. 11 Front output shaft bearing inner snap ring

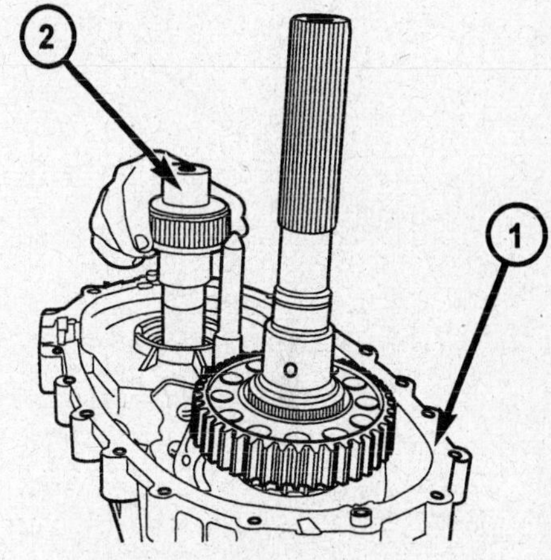

1 - FRONT CASE
2 - FRONT OUTPUT SHAFT

LTV1900000001135

Fig. 12 Front output shaft

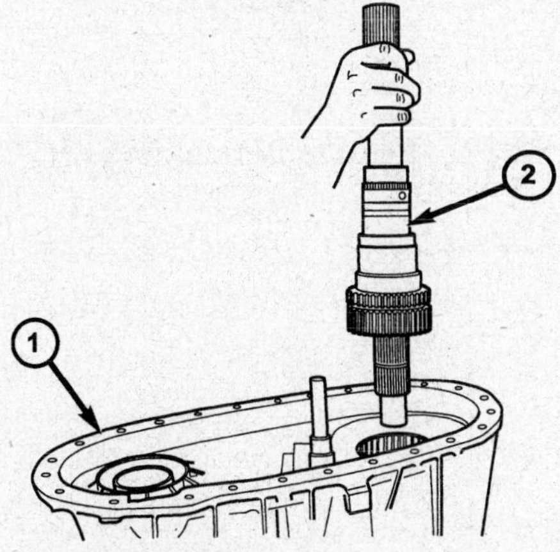

1 - FRONT CASE HALF
2 - MAINSHAFT ASSEMBLY

LTV1900000001136

Fig. 13 Mainshaft assembly

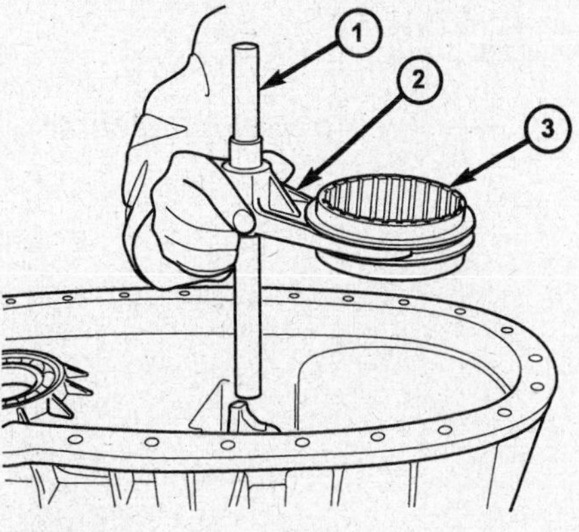

1 - SHIFT RAIL
2 - MODE FORK
3 - MODE SLEEVE

LTV1900000001137

Fig. 14 Mode fork, sleeve and shift rail assembly

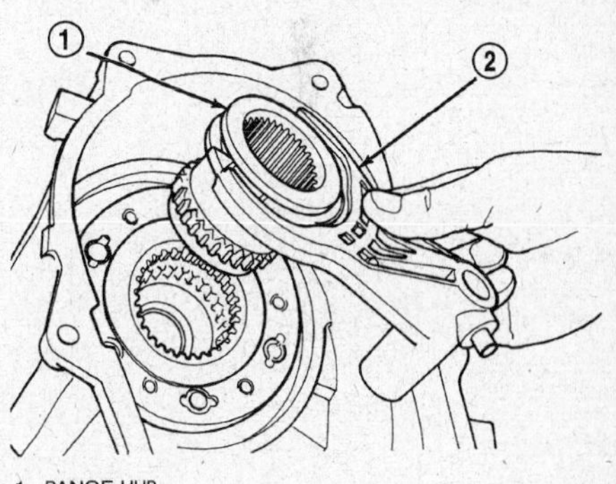

1 - RANGE HUB
2 - RANGE FORK

LTV1900000001138

Fig. 15 Range fork & hub

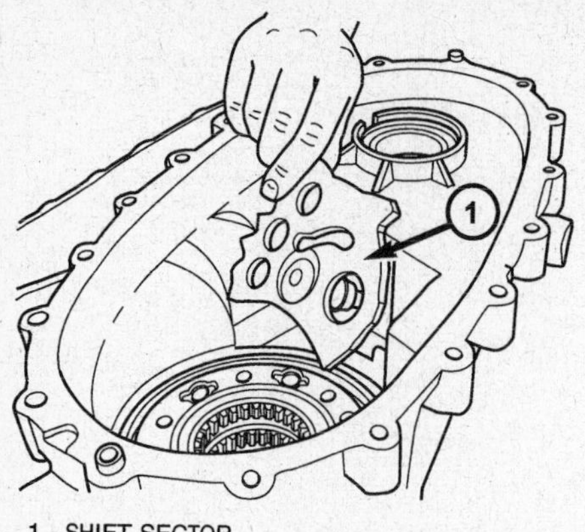

1 - SHIFT SECTOR

LTV1900000001139

Fig. 16 Shift sector

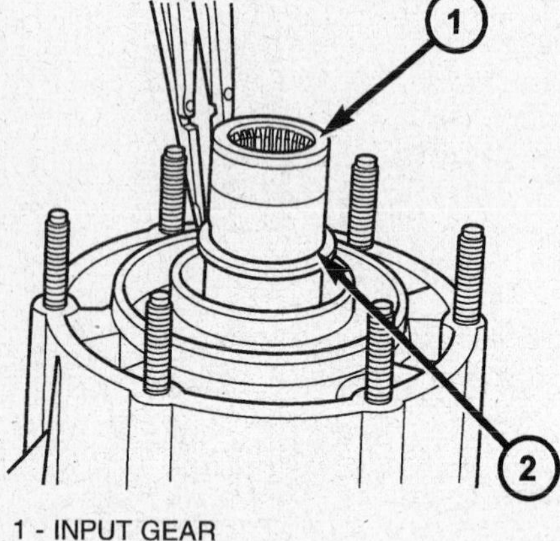

1 - INPUT GEAR
2 - RETAINING RING

LTV1900000001142

Fig. 19 Input gear retaining ring

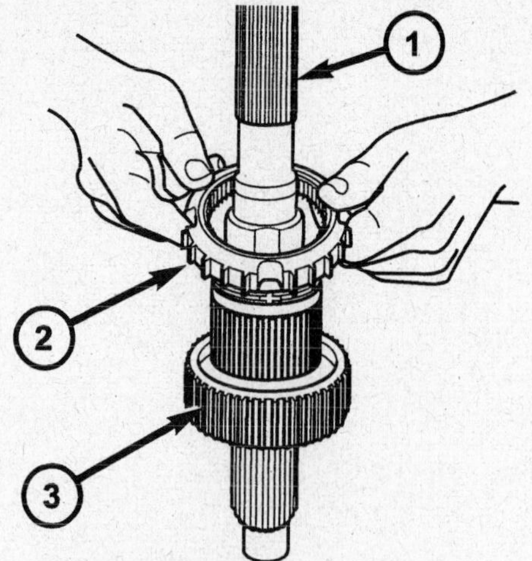

1 - OUTPUT SHAFT
2 - CLUTCH GEAR
3 - MODE HUB

LTV1900000001140

Fig. 17 Clutch gear

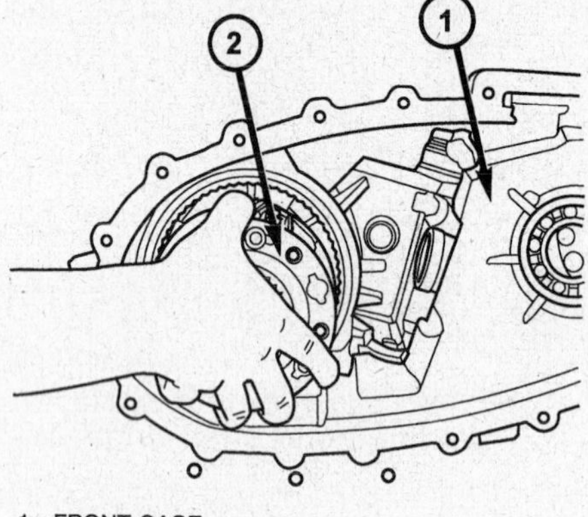

1 - FRONT CASE
2 - INPUT PLANETARY ASSEMBLY

LTV1900000001143

Fig. 20 Input planetary assembly

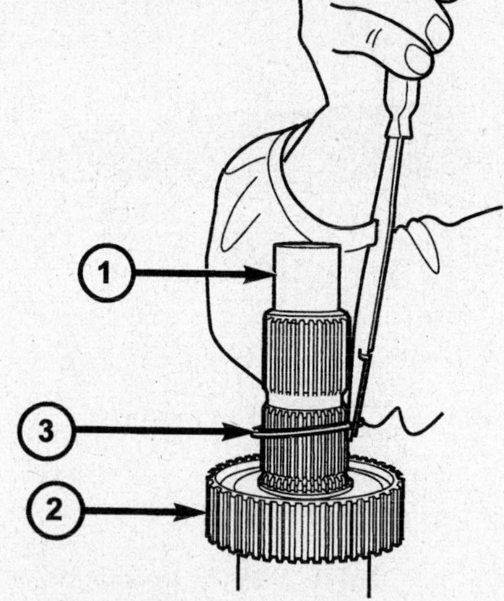

1 - MAINSHAFT
2 - MODE HUB
3 - RETAINING RING

LTV1900000001141

Fig. 18 Mode hub

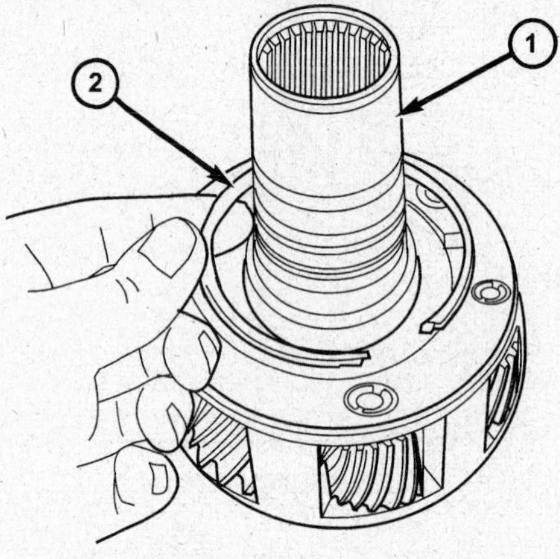

1 - INPUT GEAR
2 - RETAINING RING

LTV1900000001144

Fig. 21 Input gear retaining ring

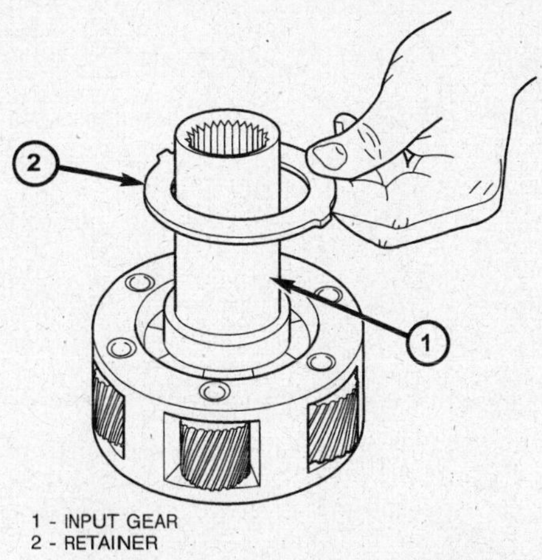

Fig. 22 Input gear retainer

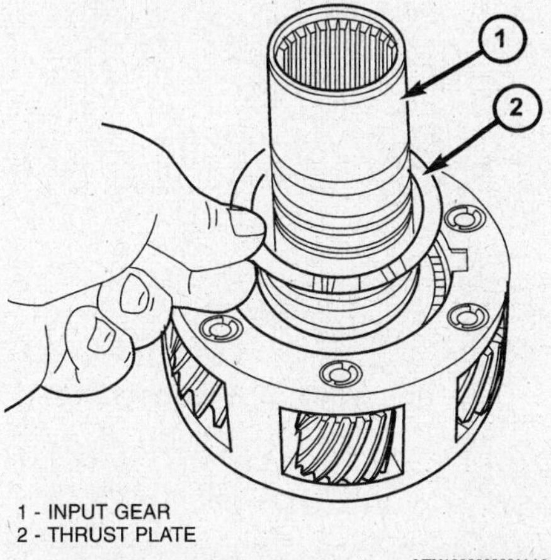

Fig. 23 Input gear thrust plate

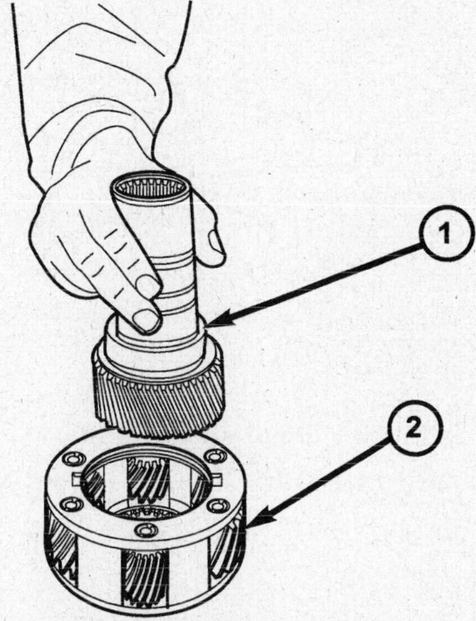

Fig. 24 Input gear

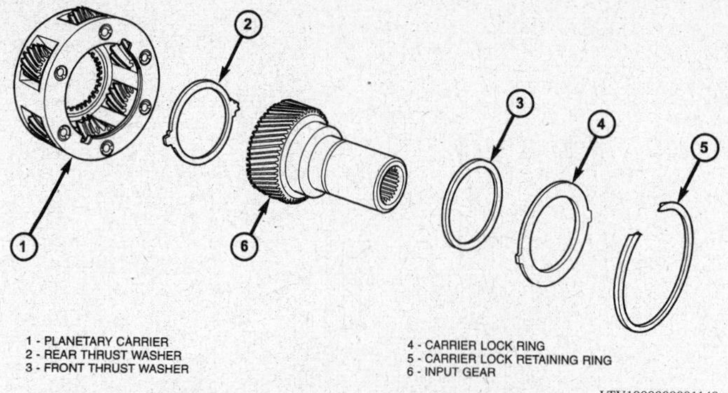

1 - PLANETARY CARRIER
2 - REAR THRUST WASHER
3 - FRONT THRUST WASHER
4 - CARRIER LOCK RING
5 - CARRIER LOCK RETAINING RING
6 - INPUT GEAR

LTV1900000001148

Fig. 25 Exploded view of input gear and carrier

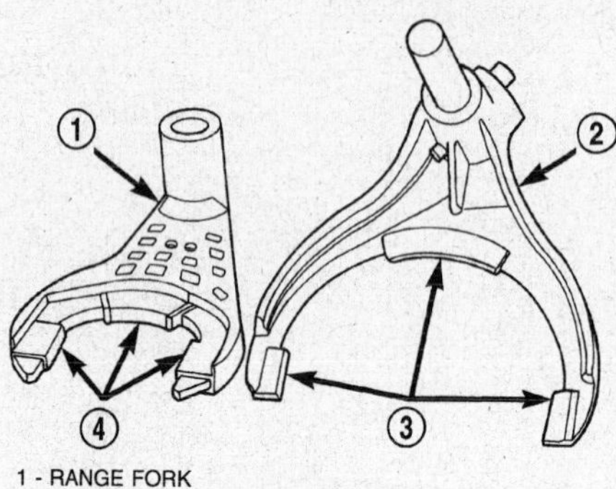

1 - RANGE FORK
2 - MODE FORK
3 - WEAR PADS (SERVICEABLE)
4 - WEAR PADS (SERVICEABLE)

LTV1900000001149

Fig. 26 Shift fork wear pads

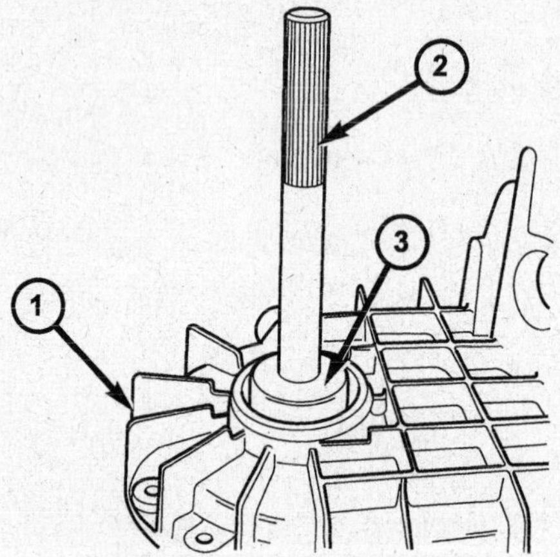

1 - FRONT CASE HALF
2 - HANDLE C-4171
3 - INSTALLER 6953

LTV1900000001151

Fig. 27 Input shaft bearing removal

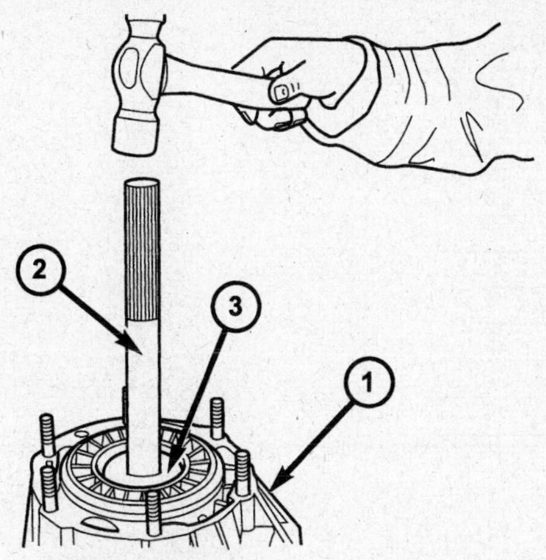

1 - FRONT CASE HALF
2 - HANDLE C-4171
3 - INSTALLER 8151 (INVERTED)

LTV1900000001150

Fig. 28 Input shaft bearing installation

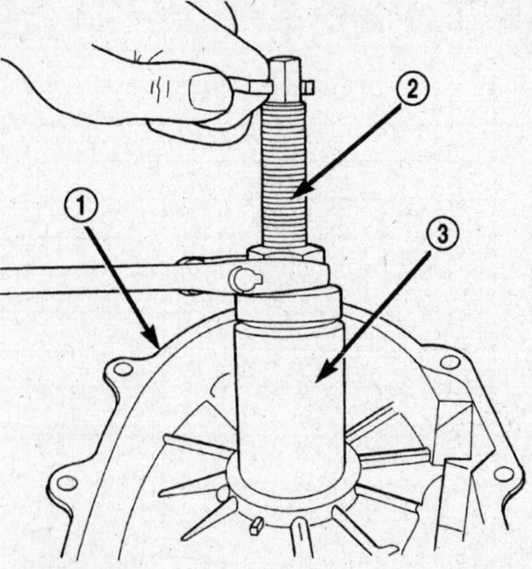

1 - REAR CASE
2 - SPECIAL TOOL L-4454-1 AND L-4454-3
3 - SPECIAL TOOL 8148

LTV1900000001152

Fig. 29 Front output shaft rear bearing removal

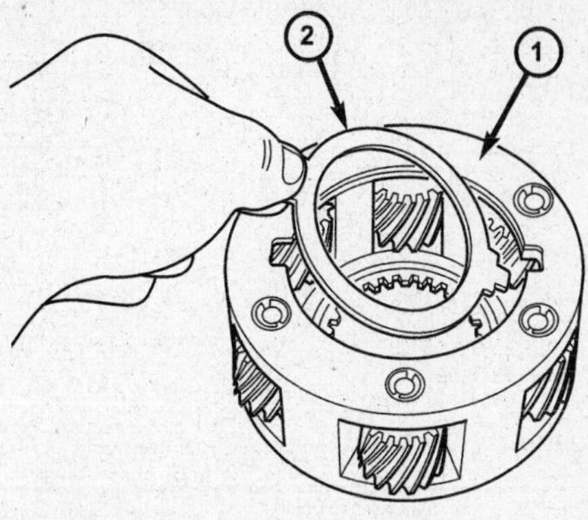

1 - PLANETARY
2 - THRUST PLATE

LTV1900000001153

Fig. 30 Bottom thrust washer installation

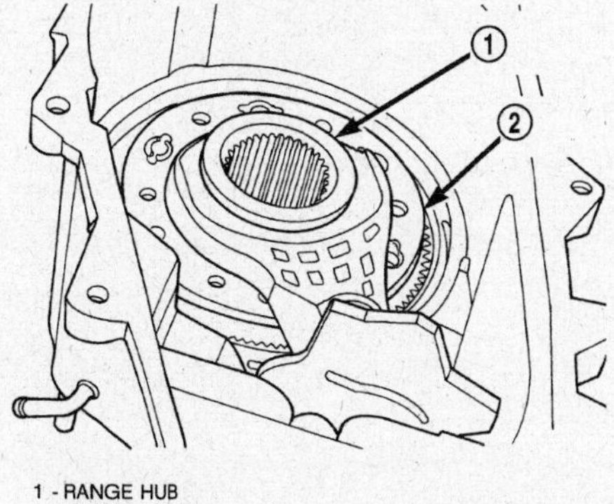

1 - RANGE HUB
2 - RANGE FORK

LTV1900000001154

Fig. 31 Range fork & hub assembly installation

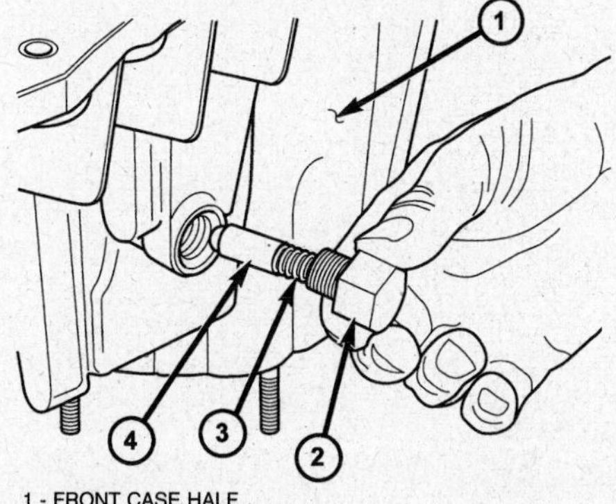

1 - FRONT CASE HALF
2 - DETENT PLUG
3 - SPRING
4 - PLUNGER

LTV1900000001155

Fig. 32 Detent plug, spring & plunger

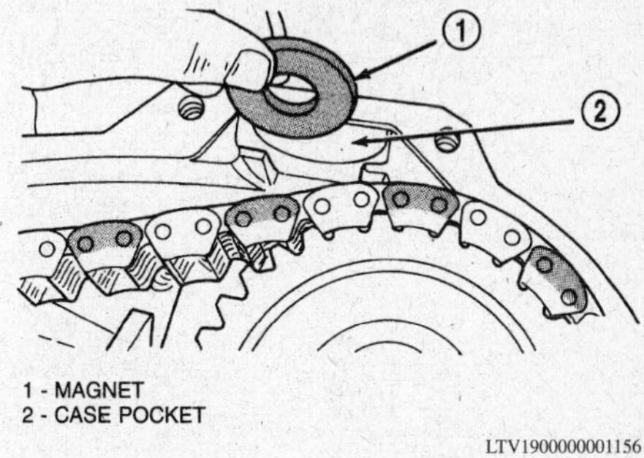

1 - MAGNET
2 - CASE POCKET

LTV1900000001156

Fig. 33 Case magnet

TIGHTENING SPECIFICATIONS

Year	Component	Torque Ft. Lbs.
2003–06	Case Half	20–25
	Companion Flange	130–200
	Detent Plug	12–18
	Drain/Fill Plug	15–25
	Extension Housing	20–25
	Position Sensor	15–25
	Range Lever Nut	20–25
	Sector Support	20–25

FRONT WHEEL DRIVE AXLES

NOTE: For Service Procedures On Rear Wheel & 4WD Vehicles, Refer To "Drive Axles" Section. For Service Procedures On All Wheel Drive Vehicles, Refer To "All-Wheel Drive System" Section.

NOTE: On Air Bag Equipped Models, Refer To "Air Bag System Precautions" Located In The Front Of This Manual For System Disarming & Arming Procedures.

NOTE: Prior To Performing Any Service Operations Listed In This Section, Consult The "Technical Service Bulletins" In This Section For Related Information.

INDEX

PRECAUTIONS

Battery Ground Cable

Prior to service, disconnect battery ground cable and isolate as required.

DESCRIPTION

These models use only the unequal length driveshaft system, **Fig. 1.** This system has a short solid interconnecting shaft on the lefthand side of the vehicle for all engine and transaxle applications. The righthand side of the vehicle interconnecting shafts vary depending on the transaxle used.

The driveshaft assemblies are three piece units, **Figs. 2 and 3.** Each driveshaft has a tripod joint, an interconnecting shaft and a Rzeppa joint. The tripod joint is splined into the transaxle side gear and the Rzeppa joint has a stub shaft that is splined into the wheel hub.

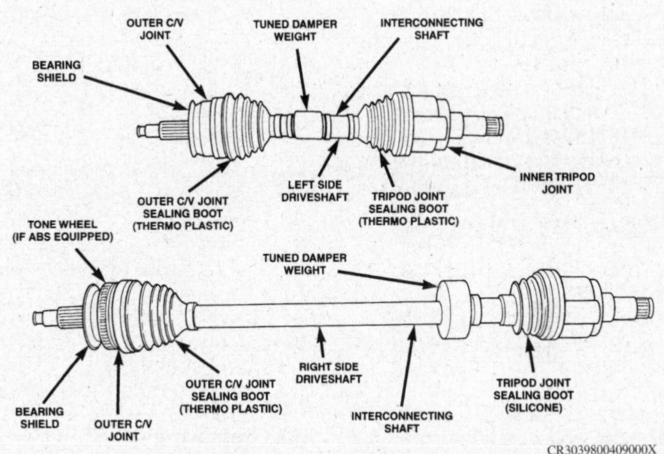

Fig. 1 Driveshaft identification

DRIVESHAFT

REPLACE

Removal

CARAVAN, TOWN & COUNTRY & VOYAGER

1. Remove cotter pin, nut lock and spring washer from end of outer C/V joint stub shaft.
2. With vehicle on the ground and brakes applied, loosen, but do not remove stub axle to hub/bearing retaining nut.
3. Raise and support vehicle, then remove front tire and wheel assembly from hub.
4. Remove front disc brake caliper assembly to steering knuckle guide pin attaching bolts.
5. Lift bottom of caliper away from steering knuckle, then remove top of caliper out from under steering knuckle, **Fig. 4.**
6. Support brake caliper assembly using a wire hook.
7. Remove brake rotor, then the nut retaining outer tie rod end to steering knuckle, **Fig. 5.**
8. Remove tie rod end stud from steering knuckle arm using tie rod end remover tool No. MB-991113, or equivalent, **Fig. 6.**
9. **On models equipped with anti-lock brakes,** remove speed sensor cable routing bracket from steering knuckle.
10. **On all models,** remove cotter pin and castle nut from lower ball joint stud at steering knuckle.
11. Turn steering knuckle so front of steering knuckle is facing as far outboard in wheelwell as possible.
12. Strike steering knuckle boss until steering knuckle separates from stud of lower ball joint using a hammer, **Fig. 7. Do not to strike lower control arm or ball joint grease seal.**
13. Pull steering knuckle assembly out and away from outer C/V joint.
14. Support outer end of driveshaft assembly, then insert a pry bar between inner tripod joint and transaxle case.
15. Pry against inner tripod joint until tripod joint retaining snap ring is disengaged from transaxle side gear.

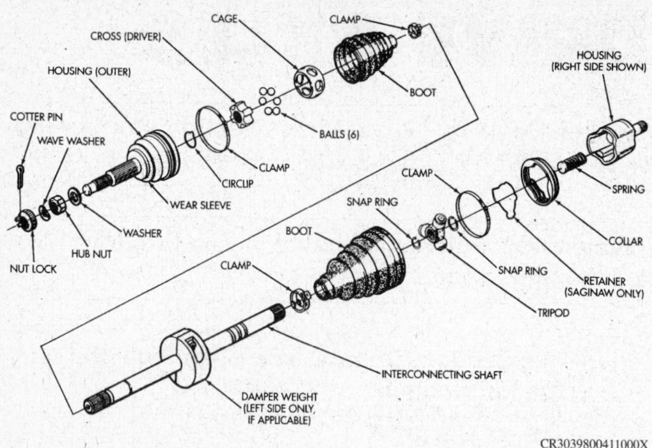

Fig. 2 Exploded view of driveshaft assembly. Caravan, Town & Country & Voyager

16. Hold inner tripod joint and interconnecting shaft of driveshaft assembly, then remove inner tripod joint from transaxle by pulling it straight out of transaxle side gear and oil seal, **Fig. 8.**

LIBERTY

1. Raise and support vehicle, then remove tire and wheel assembly.
2. Remove half shaft hub nut.
3. Remove stabilizer link.
4. Remove lower clevis bolt, **Fig. 9.**
5. Separate lower ball joint from lower control arm, **Fig. 10.**
6. Pull out on steering knuckle, then push half shaft out of knuckle.
7. Remove half shaft from axle using suitable pry bar. Righthand side half shaft has an axle shaft that may come out.

PACIFICA & PT CRUISER

1. Place transaxle in park, then raise and support vehicle.
2. Remove wheel and tire assembly.
3. Remove cotter pin, nut lock and spring washer from end of outer C/V joint stub axle.
4. Remove driveshaft to hub and bearing retaining nut and washer.
5. **On models equipped with anti-lock brakes,** disconnect front wheel speed sensor and position aside.
6. **On all models,** remove nut and bolt retaining ball joint stud into steering knuckle.
7. Separate ball joint stud from steering knuckle by prying down on lower control arm. **Do not allow driveshaft to hang by inner C/V joint.**
8. Remove driveshaft from steering knuckle by pulling outward on knuckle while pressing in on driveshaft, support outer end of driveshaft assembly. If driveshaft is difficult to separate from steering knuckle, proceed as follows:
   a. Install puller tool No. 6790 or equivalent, using wheel lug nuts to secure it in place.
   b. Install a wheel lug nut on wheel stud to protect threads on stud.
   c. Install a suitable flat blade pry tool to keep hub from turning, then using puller, force driveshaft outer stub axle from hub and bearing assembly.
   d. Pull steering knuckle assembly out away from C/V joint of driveshaft assembly.
9. Support outer end of driveshaft assembly.
10. Remove inner tripod joints from side gears of transaxle using a suitable punch to dislodge inner tripod joint retaining ring from transaxle side gear, **Figs. 11 and 12.**
11. Hold inner tripod joint and interconnecting shaft of driveshaft assembly, **Fig. 13,** then remove inner tripod joint from transaxle by pulling it straight out. **Do not let spline or snap ring drag across sealing lip of transaxle to tripod joint oil seal.**

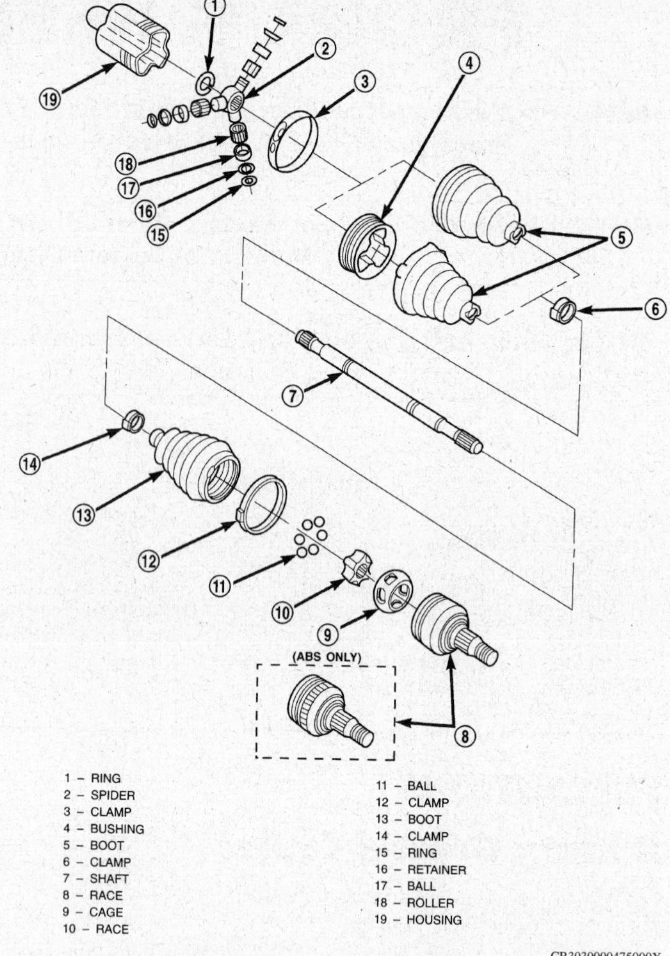

Fig. 3 Exploded view of driveshaft assembly. Pacifica & PT Cruiser

Installation

CARAVAN, TOWN & COUNTRY & VOYAGER

1. Thoroughly clean spline and oil seal sealing surface on tripod joint. Lightly lubricate oil seal sealing surface on tripod joint with fresh clean transmission lubricant.
2. Holding driveshaft assembly by tripod joint and interconnecting shaft, install tripod joint into transaxle side gear as far as possible by hand.
3. Grasp inner tripod joint and interconnecting shaft and forcefully push tripod joint into side gear of transaxle until snap ring is engaged with transaxle side gear.
4. Ensure snap ring is fully engaged with side gear by attempting to remove tripod joint from transaxle by hand. If snap ring is fully engaged with side gear, tripod joint cannot be removed by hand.
5. Clean all debris and moisture out of steering knuckle.
6. Ensure front of outer C/V joint, which fits against face of hub and bearing, is free of debris and moisture before installing outer C/V joint into hub and bearing assembly, **Fig. 14.**
7. Slide driveshaft back into front hub, then install steering knuckle onto lower control arm ball joint stud.
8. Install steering knuckle to ball joint stud castle nut and tighten to specification.
9. **On models equipped with anti-lock brakes,** install speed sensor cable on steering knuckle.
10. **On all models,** install tie rod end into steering knuckle, then start tie rod end to steering knuckle nut onto stud of tie rod end.

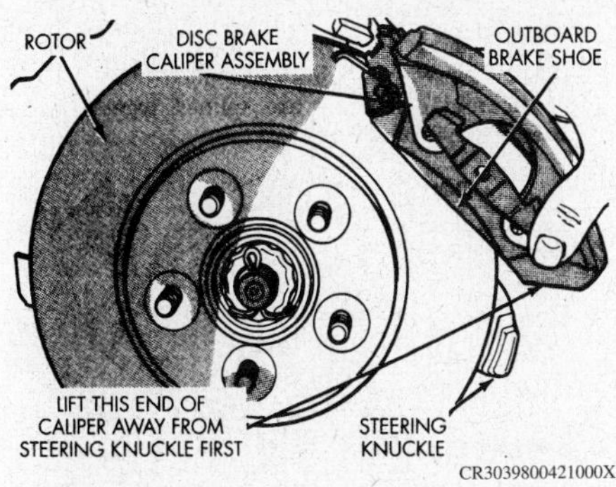

Fig. 4 Brake caliper removal. Caravan, Town & Country & Voyager

11. While holding stud of tie rod end stationary, tighten tie rod end to steering knuckle nut to specification. Use a crowfoot and 11/32 inch socket to tighten nut, **Fig. 15.**
12. Install brake rotor on hub and bearing assembly.
13. Install brake caliper assembly on steering knuckle by first sliding caliper under top abutment on steering knuckle, then installing bottom of caliper against bottom abutment of steering knuckle.
14. Install caliper assembly to steering knuckle guide pin bolts. Tighten bolts to specification.
15. Clean all foreign matter from threads of outer C/V joint stub axle, then install hub nut onto threads of stub axle.
16. With vehicle brakes applied, tighten hub nut to specification.
17. Install spring washer, hub nut lock and new cotter pin on end of stub axle. Wrap cotter pin prongs tightly around hub nut lock.
18. Install front wheel and tire assembly, tighten wheel lug nuts to specification.

LIBERTY

1. Apply a light coat of wheel bearing grease on female splines of inner C/V joint.
2. Install half shaft on axle shaft spline pushing firmly to engage snap ring. Pull on half shaft to verify it has engaged.
3. Clean hub bearing bore, then apply a light coat of wheel bearing grease.
4. Pull out on steering knuckle, then push half shaft through knuckle.
5. Install lower ball joint into lower control arm.
6. Align clevis with knuckle, then install bolt.
7. Install stabilizer link, then the half shaft hub nut.
8. Install tire and wheel assembly.

PACIFICA & PT CRUISER

1. Thoroughly clean spline and oil seal sealing surface on tripod joint. Lightly lubricate oil seal sealing surface on tripod joint with fresh clean transmission lubricant.
2. Holding driveshaft assembly by tripod joint and interconnecting shaft, install tripod joint into transaxle side gear as far as possible by hand.
3. Carefully align tripod joint with transaxle side gears. then grasp driveshaft interconnecting shaft and push tripod into transaxle side gear until fully seated. **Ensure snap ring is fully engaged with side gear by attempting to remove tripod by hand.**
4. Clean all debris and moisture out of steering knuckle, **Fig. 16.**
5. Ensure outer C/V joint which fits into steering knuckle is free of debris and moisture before assembling into steering knuckle.
6. Slide driveshaft back into front hub, then install steering knuckle onto ball joint stud.
7. Install a new steering knuckle to ball joint stud bolt and tighten nut to specifications.
8. Clean all foreign matter from threads of driveshaft outer stub axle, then install washer and hub nut onto threads of stub axle, tighten to specifications.
9. Install spring washer, nut lock and cotter pin.
10. Install front wheel and tire assembly, then lower vehicle.

DRIVESHAFT SERVICE

The inner seal boot may be replaced as required. If joint is damaged, replace driveshaft assembly.

Inner Seal Boot

CARAVAN, PACIFICA, PT CRUISER, TOWN & COUNTRY & VOYAGER

1. Remove driveshaft as outlined under "Driveshaft, Replace."
2. Remove boot clamps and discard, then slide boot down interconnecting shaft.
3. Slide tripod joint housing off of spider assembly, **Fig. 17.**
4. Remove snap ring retainer from spider assembly, **Fig. 18.**
5. Remove spider assembly and boot from interconnecting shaft.
6. Inspect spider assembly, joint housing and interconnecting shaft for excessive wear. Replace driveshaft if excessive wear is present.
7. Reverse procedure to install, noting the following:
   a. Slide new inner boot clamp onto interconnecting shaft first.
   b. Apply half of grease supplied with service kit into tripod housing. Apply other half into boot.
   c. Gently lift large end of boot to vent any excess air in boot after small clamp is secured.

LIBERTY

REMOVAL

1. Clamp half shaft in a soft jawed vise,

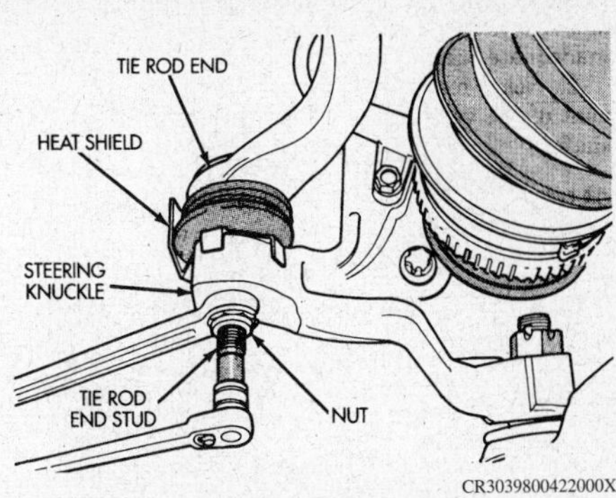

Fig. 5 Tie rod end retaining nut location. Caravan, Town & Country & Voyager

then support C/V joint.

2. Remove clamps using a suitable cut off wheel.
3. Slide boot down shaft.
4. Remove lubricant to expose C/V housing snap ring, then remove snap ring, **Fig. 19.**
5. Remove bearings from cage, **Fig. 20.**
6. Rotate cage 30°, then slide cage off inner race and down shaft.
7. Remove inner race snap ring, then the race from shaft.
8. Remove and discard boot from shaft.

INSTALLATION

1. Apply a coat of grease to C/V joint components before assembling them.
2. Place new clamps on new boot, then slide boot down shaft.
3. Slide cage onto shaft with small diameter end toward boot.
4. Install inner race onto shaft. Pull on race to ensure snap ring engaged.
5. Align cage with inner race, then slide over race.
6. Turn cage 30° to align cage windows with race.
7. Apply grease to inner race and bearings, then install bearings.
8. Apply grease to housing bore, then install bearing assembly into housing.
9. Install housing snap ring ensuring it is seated in groove.
10. Fill housing and boot with grease.
11. Slide boot onto C/V housing ensuring boot is not twisted. Remove any excess air.
12. Secure both boot clamps using clamp installer tool No. C-4975A, or equivalent.

TECHNICAL SERVICE BULLETINS

CV Boot Grease Seepage

The righthand side half shaft inner CV boot may show heavy grease seepage. Although unsightly, seepage will stop eventually and function or durability is not affected.

No replacement of half shaft or boot is needed.

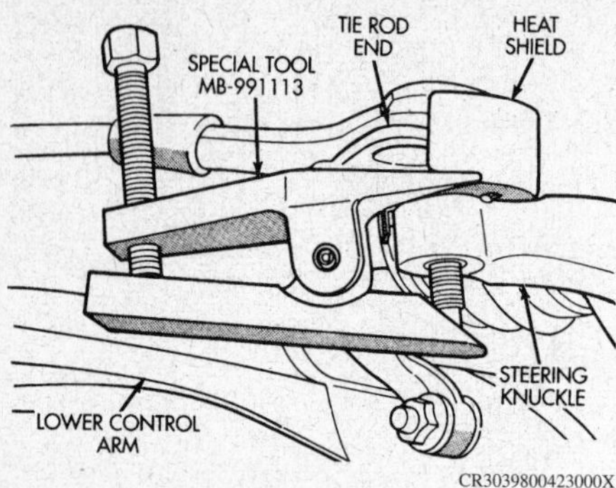

Fig. 6 Tie rod end removal. Caravan, Town & Country & Voyager

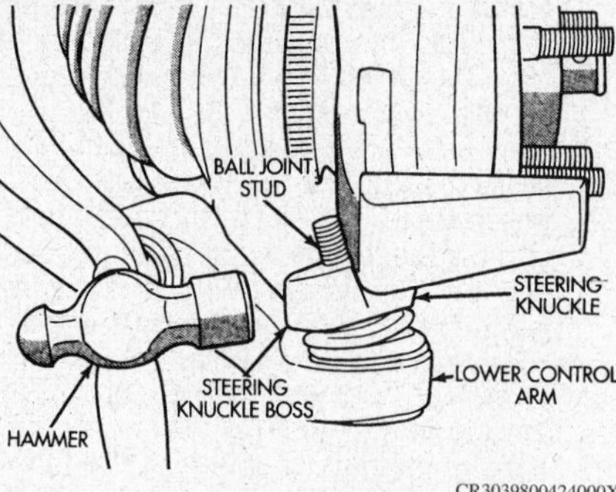

Fig. 7 Ball joint stud separation. Caravan, Town & Country & Voyager

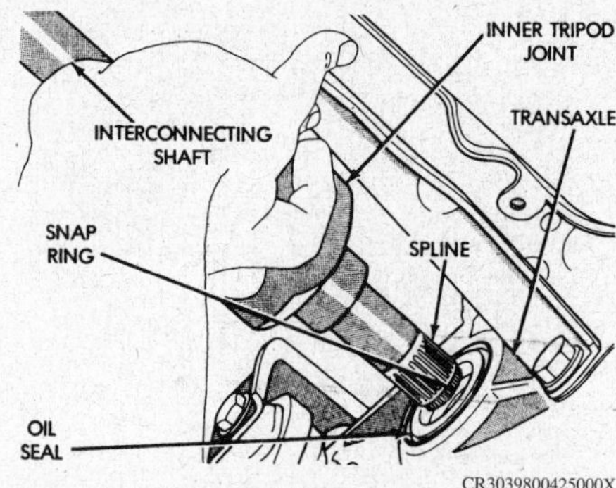

Fig. 8 Tripod joint from transaxle removal. Caravan, Town & Country & Voyager

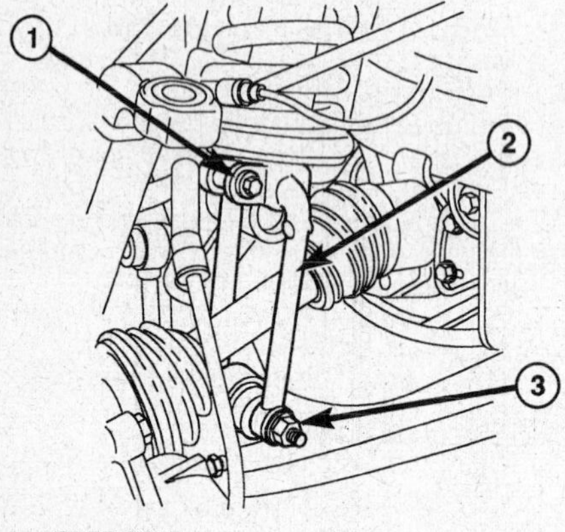

1 - UPPER BOLT
2 - CLEVIS BRACKET
3 - LOWER BOLT

LTV1900000001158

Fig. 9 Clevis bracket. Liberty

1 - FRONT CAM BOLT
2 - OUTER TIE ROD END
3 - LOWER BALL JOINT NUT
4 - LOWER CONTROL ARM
5 - REAR CAM BOLT

LTV1900000001159

Fig. 10 Lower control arm. Liberty

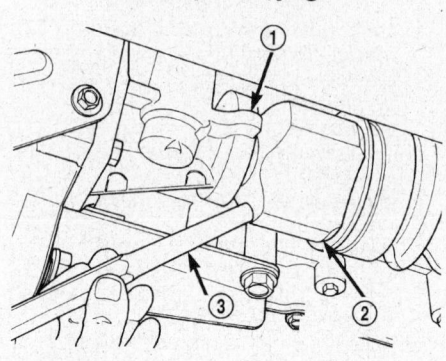

1 – TRANSAXLE
2 – RIGHT INNER TRIPOD JOINT
3 – PUNCH

CR3030000471000X

Fig. 11 Righthand inner tripod joint removal. Pacifica & PT Cruiser

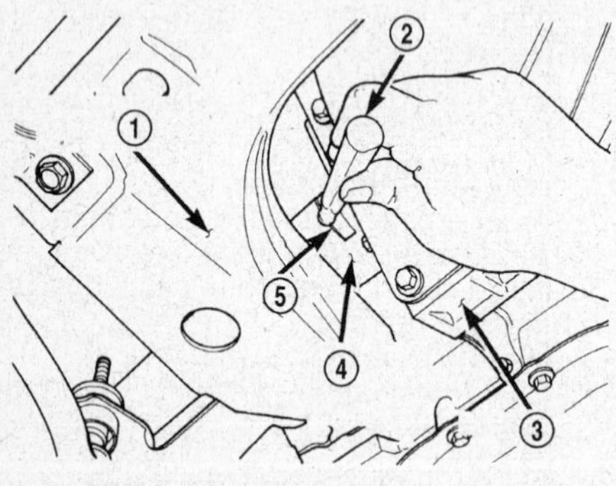

1 – FRONT SUSPENSION CROSSMEMBER
2 – DRIFT
3 – TRANSAXLE
4 – DRIVESHAFT INNER TRIPOD JOINT
5 – NOTCH

CR3030000472000X

Fig. 12 Lefthand inner tripod joint removal. Pacifica & PT Cruiser

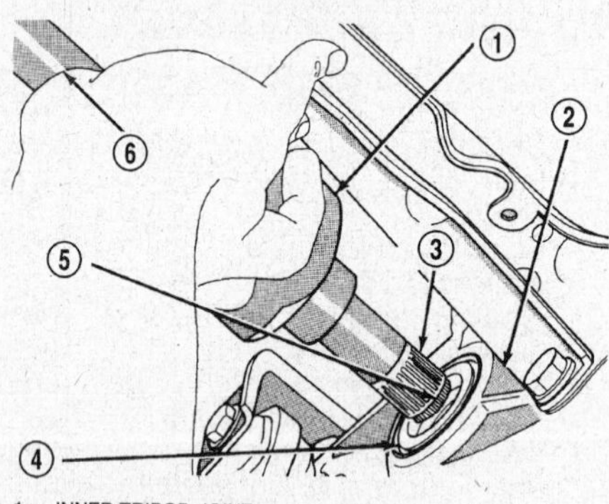

1 – INNER TRIPOD JOINT
2 – TRANSAXLE
3 – SPLINE
4 – OIL SEAL
5 – SNAP RING
6 – INTERCONNECTING SHAFT

CR3030000473000X

Fig. 13 Tripod joint removal from transaxle. Pacifica & PT Cruiser

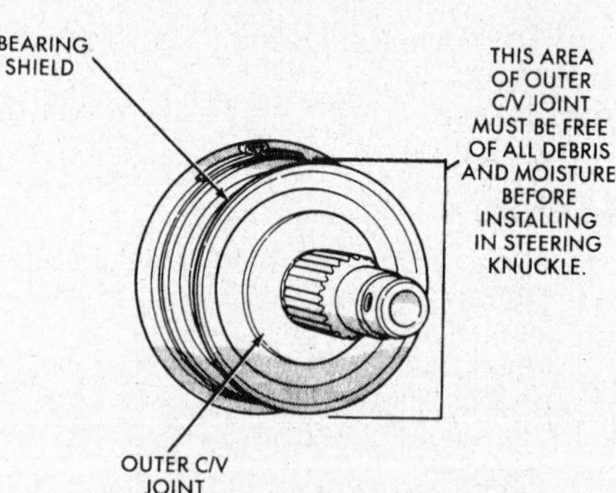

Fig. 14 Outer C/V joint inspection. Caravan, Town & Country & Voyager

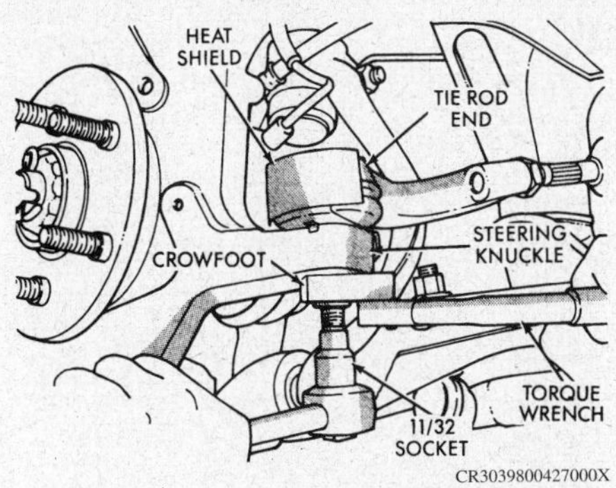

Fig. 15 Tie rod end installation. Caravan, Town & Country & Voyager

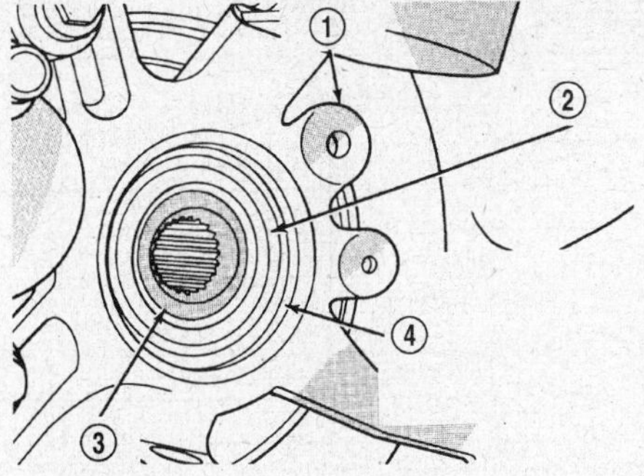

Fig. 16 Steering knuckle to C/V joint sealing area. Pacifica & PT Cruiser

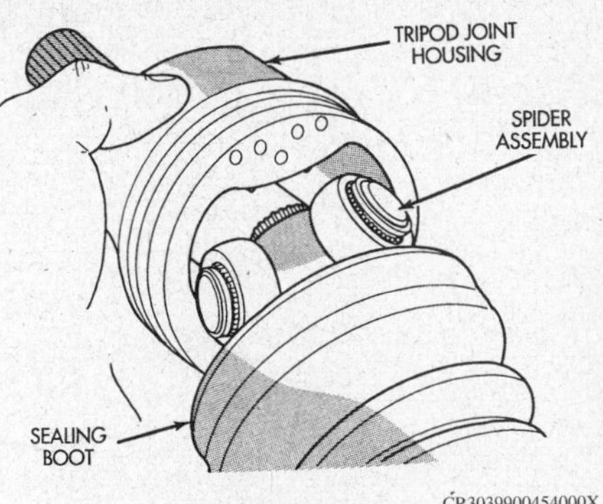

Fig. 17 Housing removal. Caravan, PT Cruiser, Town & Country & Voyager

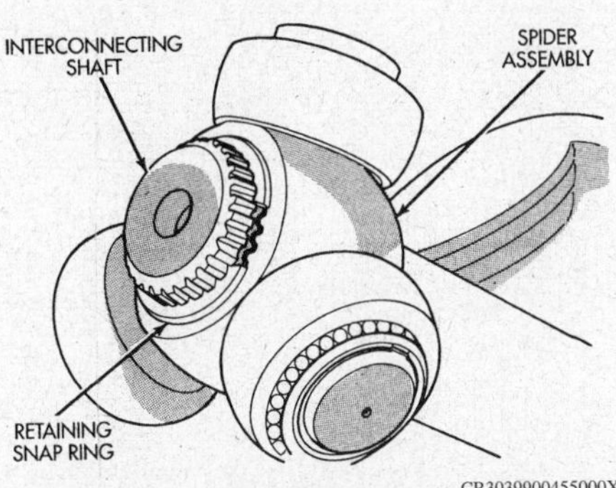

Fig. 18 Snap ring removal. Caravan, PT Cruiser, Town & Country & Voyager

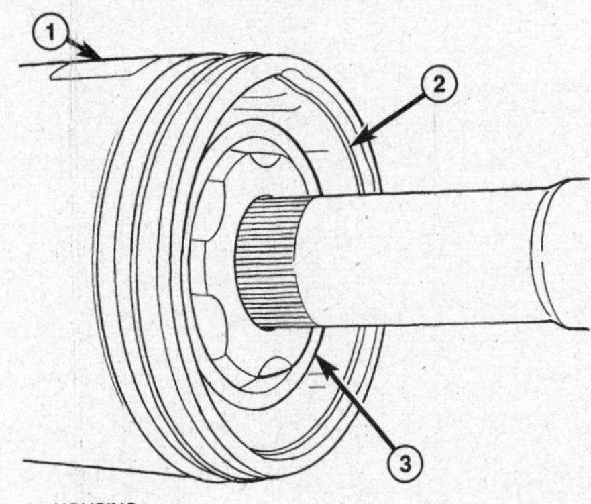

Fig. 19 C/V housing snap ring. Liberty

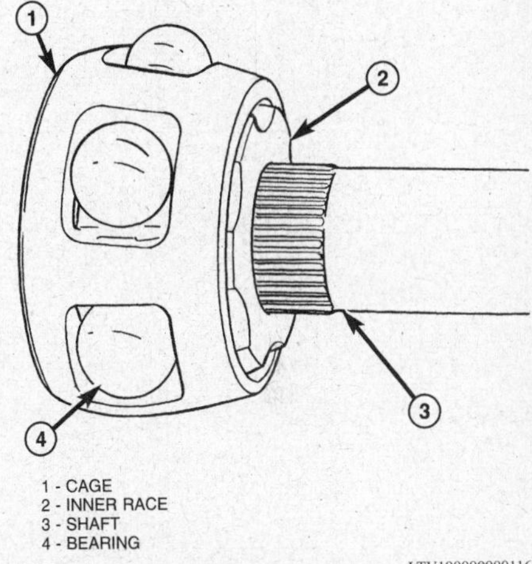

Fig. 20 C/V bearings. Liberty

TIGHTENING SPECIFICATIONS

Year	Component	Torque Ft. Lbs.
2002–06	Caliper Adapter To Knuckle Bolts	125
	Hub Nut	180
	Strut Clevis To Knuckle Nut	60①
	Strut Damper To Steering Knuckle Bolts	65①
	Tie Rod End To Knuckle Nut	55
	Wheel Nuts	100

① — Tighten an additional 90°.

ALL-WHEEL DRIVE SYSTEMS

INDEX

DESCRIPTION

The Power Transfer Unit (PTU) is attached to a modified automatic transaxle case where the right halfshaft extension housing would normally be located. The PTU provides rear wheel power through a hypoid ring gear and pinion seat.

TROUBLESHOOTING

Refer to **Fig. 1** for troubleshooting procedures.

CONDITION	POSSIBLE CAUSES	CORRECTION
Rear wheels not overrunning	1) Bi-directional overrunning clutch failure	1) Replace overrunning clutch components as required
No AWD in forward or reverse directions, propeller shaft turning	1) Bi-directional overrunning clutch failure	1) Replace overrunning clutch components as required
	2) Viscous coupling failure	2) Replace viscous coupling
	3) Rear differential failure	3) Replace the rear differential assembly
No AWD in forward or reverse directions, propeller shaft not turning	1) Power transfer unit failure.	1) Replace power transfer unit components as necessary
Vibration at all speeds, continuous torque transfer	1) Mis-matched tires, worn tires on front axle.	1) Replace worn or incorrect (mis-matched) tires with same make and size

LTV1900000001399

Fig. 1 Driveline module diagnosis chart

HALFSHAFT

REPLACE

Except Pacifica

1. Raise and support vehicle.
2. Remove rear wheel and tire assembly.
3. Remove hub cotter pin, locknut and spring washer, then the hub nut and washer.
4. **The halfshaft outer CV joint, when installed, serves as a bolt and attaches hub/bearing assembly. If vehicle is to be supported or moved on its wheels, install a bolt through hub to ensure hub/bearing assembly will not loosen.**
5. Remove innershaft attaching bolts.
6. Compress inner halfshaft joint slightly, then pull downward to clear differential. Pull halfshaft assembly outward to remove.
7. Reverse procedure to install, noting the following:
   a. Tighten innershaft to carrier attaching bolts to specifications.
   b. Tighten rear brake assembly and spindle attaching bolt to specifications. Tighten wheel lug nuts to specifications.

Pacifica

Rear suspension and drivetrain design require this procedure to be performed on a drive-on hoist as the front and rear suspension needs to be compressed to ride height to facilitate rear halfshaft removal.

1. Place vehicle on drive-on hoist.
2. Remove wheel center cap, cotter pin, nut lock and spring washer.
3. Remove hub nut and washer.
4. Raise vehicle.
5. Remove exhaust system center hanger at propeller shaft bearing support.
6. Disconnect exhaust system at rear most hanger and lower.
7. Lower exhaust system at least 10 inches and support using suitable wire.
8. Place a matchmark on propeller shaft and rear driveline module flanges using suitable paint for installation alignment.
9. Remove three propeller shaft-to-driveline module bolts. **Do not attempt to disconnect shaft from module as it will be disconnected upon lowering driveline module.**
10. Support driveline module using suitable transmission jack.
11. Partially dislodge halfshaft from differential using suitable screwdriver. **Install tool No. 9099 or equivalent to protect seal upon disassembly.**
12. Remove three rear driveline module-to-crossmember bolts.
13. Lower driveline module assembly to remove shaft from differential, ensure tool No. 9099 or equivalent engages seal.
14. Disconnect propeller shaft from driveline module and secure to exhaust system using suitable wire.
15. Remove halfshaft from hub and bearing assembly.
16. Reverse procedure to install, tighten to specifications.

HALFSHAFT & CV JOINT SERVICE

Except Pacifica

1. Clamp shaft in suitable soft jawed vise.
2. Remove shaft boot clamps.
3. Carefully pull back boot assembly.
4. Remove halfshaft joint housing assembly.
5. Remove tripod joint snap ring, then remove tripod joint.
6. Carefully slide boot assembly from axle shaft.
7. Reverse procedure to install.

Pacifica

1. Remove halfshaft boot from vehicle.
2. Remove boot clamp that retains inner tripod joint sealing boot to tripod joint housing and discard.
3. Remove boot clamp which retains inner tripod boot to interconnecting shaft and discard.
4. Remove sealing boot from tripod housing and slide down interconnecting shaft.
5. Slide tripod joint housing off spider assembly and interconnecting shaft.
6. Remove snap ring from spider assembly to interconnecting shaft. **Do not hit outer tripod bearings in an attempt to remove spider assembly from interconnecting shaft.**
7. Remove spider assembly from interconnecting shaft.
8. Remove sealing boot off interconnecting shaft.
9. Clean and inspect spider assembly, tripod joint housing and interconnecting shaft for damage or excessive wear.
10. Reverse procedure to install.

DIFFERENTIAL CARRIER
REPLACE

Except Pacifica

The rear differential assembly can only be serviced as an assembly.

1. Raise and support vehicle.
2. Drain fluid from overrunning clutch housing and differential assembly into suitable container.
3. Remove propeller shaft and lefthand and righthand rear halfshafts from output flanges.
4. Remove torque arm mount to body bolts.
5. Position and secure transmission jack to driveline module assembly.
6. Remove driveline module to body bolts, then lower module from vehicle.
7. Reverse procedure to install.

Pacifica

Rear suspension and drivetrain design require this procedure to be performed on a drive-on hoist.

1. Raise and support vehicle.
2. Drain fluid from overrunning clutch housing and differential assembly into suitable container.
3. Remove exhaust system center hanger at propeller shaft bearing support.
4. Disconnect exhaust system at rear most hanger and lower.
5. Lower exhaust system at least 10 inches and support using suitable wire.
6. Place suitable matchmarks on propeller shaft and rear driveline module flanges using suitable paint mark for installation.
7. Remove three propeller shaft-to-driveline module bolts. Do not attempt to disconnect shaft from module.
8. Support driveline module with transmission jack.

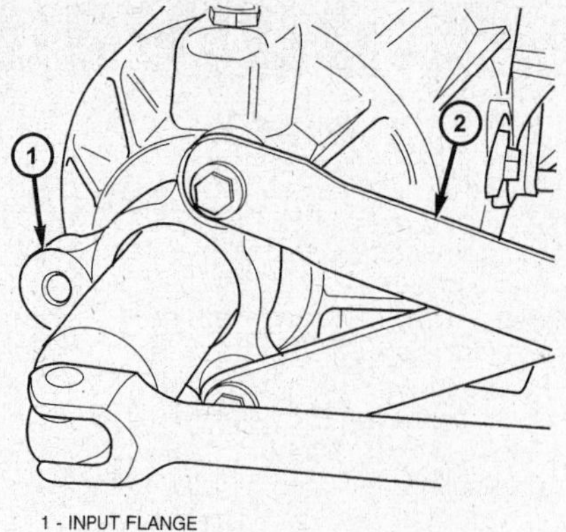

1 - INPUT FLANGE
2 - TOOL 6958

LTV1900000001400

Fig. 2 Input flange nut replacement

9. Partially dislodge halfshafts from differential using suitable screwdriver.
10. Remove three rear driveline module-to-crossmember bolts.
11. Lower driveline module assembly enough to facilitate removal of halfshafts from differential.
12. Disconnect propeller shaft from driveline module and secure to exhaust system using suitable jack.
13. Remove driveline module.
14. Reverse procedure to install, tighten to specifications.

DIFFERENTIAL CARRIER SERVICE

Driveline Module

DISASSEMBLE

1. Remove six torque arm to differential case bolts, then the torque arm assembly.
2. Remove input flange nut and washer using holding tool No. 6958 and a suitable breaker bar, **Fig. 2.**
3. Remove input flange, then pry flange seal from overrunning clutch housing with suitable screwdriver.
4. Remove four overrunning clutch housing to differential assembly bolts, then remove housing.
5. Remove front bearing snap ring, front bearing, **Fig. 3,** O-ring and washer from overrunning clutch assembly.
6. Remove overrunning clutch assembly from viscous coupler.
7. Remove viscous coupler from differential pinion shaft.
8. Remove select fit shim from differential pinion gear, **Fig. 4.**
9. Remove overrunning clutch housing large O-ring from differential assembly, **Fig. 3.**
10. Remove output flanges with suitable screwdriver and blocks of wood, **Fig. 5.**
11. Remove output flange seals.

ASSEMBLE

1. Install output flange seals with installation tools No. C4171 and 8493, or equivalents.
2. Install large overrunning clutch housing O-ring to differential assembly, **Fig. 3.**
3. Install shim to differential pinion shaft.
4. Install viscous coupler to differential pinion shaft.
5. Install overrunning clutch assembly to viscous coupler.
6. Install washer and O-ring to overrunning clutch.
7. Align overrunning clutch ground tab to 12 o'clock position.
8. Install overrunning clutch housing into position with notch, **Fig. 6,** in housing engaging tab on overrunning clutch.
9. Install overrunning clutch housing to differential assembly bolts and tighten to specification.
10. Install input flange seal using tool No. 8802, or equivalent.
11. Install flange/shield assembly.
12. Install input flange washer and nut.
13. Install holding tool, **Fig. 2,** and tighten nut to specification.
14. Install torque arm assembly into position, install torque arm to differential assembly bolts.

Torque Arm

1. Raise and support vehicle.
2. Remove rear driveline module as outlined under "Driveline Module."
3. Remove six torque arm to differential assembly bolts.
4. Remove torque arm.
5. Reverse procedure to install.

Input Flange Seal

1. Raise and support vehicle.
2. Remove propeller shaft.
3. Remove input flange nut and washer, then the input flange.
4. Remove input flange seal from overrunning clutch housing with suitable screwdriver.
5. Reverse procedure to install.

Output Flange Seal

REMOVAL

1. Raise and support vehicle.
2. Remove rear halfshaft inner joint at differential output flange.
3. Pry output flange from differential using two screwdrivers and wood blocks to protect differential housing, **Fig. 5.**
4. Remove output flange seal with suitable screwdriver.

INSTALLATION

1. Install output flange seal to differential housing with installation tools No. C4171A and 8493, or equivalents.
2. Install output flange to differential assembly. Verify that flange is properly seat by attempting to pull out by hand.
3. Install rear halfshaft inner joint to output flange.
4. Install flange bolts and tighten to specification.
5. Inspect fluid levels and top up as required.

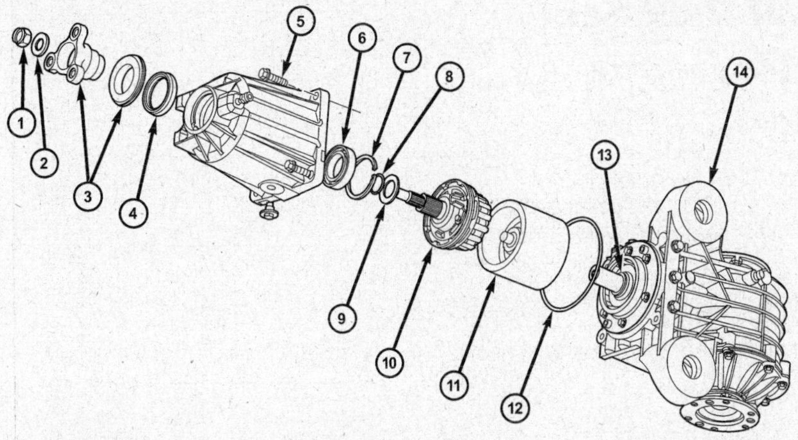

Fig. 3 Driveline module assembly

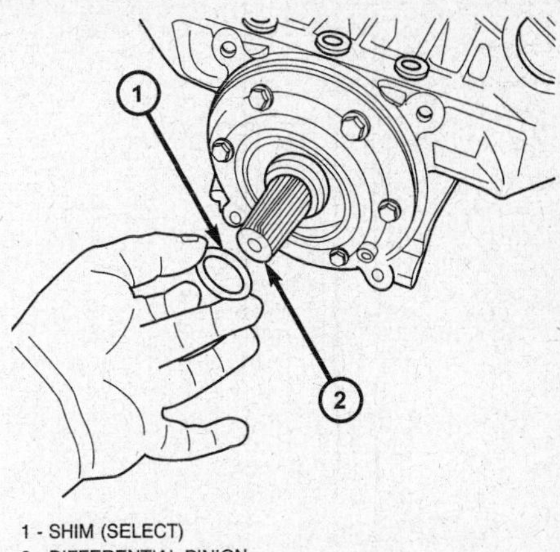

Fig. 4 Differential pinion shim

PROPELLER SHAFT

REPLACE

Except Pacifica

The propeller shaft is serviced as an assembly.

1. Place vehicle in Neutral position, then raise and support.
2. Support propeller shaft assembly. Do not allow shaft to hang unsupported.
3. Remove propeller shaft front and rear retaining bolts, then the shaft.
4. Reverse procedure to install.

Pacifica

Driveshaft removal is a two-person operation. Never allow propeller shaft to hang from the center bearing or while only connected to Power Transfer Unit (PTU) or rear driveline module flanges.

1. Raise vehicle using a suitable lift.
2. Remove hanger from rear muffler.
3. Remove exhaust system center hanger brackets and support exhaust system with screwjack.
4. Ensure transaxle is in neutral position. Place matchmarks on propeller shaft flanges at PTU and rear driveline module for installation.
5. Remove six propeller shaft-to-power transfer unit bolts, do not remove from PTU at this time.
6. Remove three propeller shaft rubber coupler-to-driveline module bolts, do not remove from driveline module at this time.
7. With assistant supporting front segment by hand, remove center segment bearing support-to-body bolts. Support front and center segments by hand.
8. Remove rear segment bearing support while supporting front and center.
9. Lower propeller shaft assembly to ground.
10. Reverse procedure to install, tighten to specifications.

POWER TRANSFER UNIT

REPLACE

Except Pacifica

1. Raise and support vehicle, then remove front wheel and tire assemblies.
2. Remove righthand front driveshaft, then reference mark propeller shaft front flange.
3. Separate propeller shaft from PTU assembly, then suspend securely from vehicle underside.
4. Remove cradle plate, **Fig. 7.**
5. Remove PTU mounting bracket bolts at rear of unit.
6. Remove right outboard support bracket and bolts near right axle shaft.
7. Remove four PTU mounting bolts, then assembly from vehicle.
8. Reverse procedure to install, tighten to specifications.

Pacifica

1. Remove righthand halfshaft assembly as outlined in "Halfshaft, Replace."
2. Remove engine cradle crossmember.
3. Remove propeller shaft assembly as outlined in "Propeller Shaft, Replace."
4. Remove PTU rear mount bracket.
5. Remove oil pan-to-transaxle collar.
6. Remove heat shield.
7. Remove bracket and brace.
8. Remove PTU-to-transaxle upper bolts.
9. Remove PTU-to-bracket lower bolts.
10. Remove PTU from vehicle.
11. Reverse procedure to install, tighten to specifications.

POWER TRANSFER UNIT SERVICE

Seal Location

Refer to **Fig. 8** for seal identification and locations.

Fluid Level Inspection

1. Raise and support vehicle.
2. Remove PTU inspection plug.
3. Fluid level should be within 3⁄16 inch from bottom of inspection hole.
4. Add fluid as required.
5. Install inspection plug and tighten to specification.
6. Lower vehicle.

Fluid Change

1. Raise and support vehicle.
2. Remove PTU inspection plug.
3. Draw fluid from PTU. Ensure hose contacts bottom of case to remove all fluid.
4. Add 1.22 qts., of Mopar Gear and Axle Lubricant 80W-90 with suction gun.
5. Install inspection plug and tighten to specification.
6. Lower vehicle.

Leak Diagnosis

When diagnosing fluid leaks on the power transfer unit, two weep holes are provided to diagnose certain seal leaks. These holes are located on the bottom side of the assembly, **Fig. 9.**

If fluid leak is detected from either weep hole, seal replacement is required. Do not attempt to repair leak by sealing weep holes, they must be kept clear of sealant for proper seal operation.

If fluid is leaking from weep hole "A," **Fig. 9,** the type of fluid leaking will determine which seal needs to be replaced. If the fluid leaking is red in color, this indicates that the transmission differential carrier seal should be replaced. If fluid leaking is light brown in color, this indicates that the PTU input seal should be replaced.

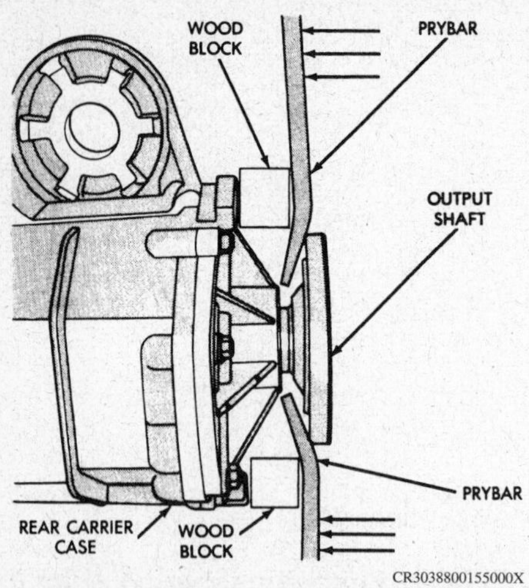

Fig. 5 Output flange removal

If fluid is leaking from weep hole "B," **Fig. 9,** is red in color, the input shaft end seal should be replaced. If the fluid leaking is brown, the halfshaft inner seal and PTU input shaft cover seal should be replaced.

Before replacing any seal or gasket, ensure rocker on engine is not the cause of the leak.

Input Shaft Cover Seal

The power transfer unit input shaft seal is the larger of the two seals located on the inside of the end cover. The differential bearing cup must be removed to service this seal.

REMOVAL

1. Remove PTU as outlined under "Power Transfer Unit, Replace."
2. Remove PTU end cover retaining bolts.
3. Gently tap end cover ears, **Fig. 10,** to separate cover from case.
4. Remove differential bearing race from end cover with removal tool No. 6514, or equivalent, **Fig. 11.**
5. Remove cover seal using seal tool No. 7794-A, or equivalent, **Fig. 12.**

INSTALLATION

1. Clean and inspect seal mating surfaces.
2. Insert seal on installation tool No. MD998803, or equivalent, with spring side of seal facing tool.
3. Use a suitable hammer to drive seal into position.
4. Install original bearing race and shim with installation tool No. 6522, or equivalent, **Fig. 13.**
5. Original shim must be installed behind bearing cup to maintain proper bearing preload.
6. Apply Mopar Gasket Maker, Loctite Gasket Eliminator No. 518, or equivalent, to sealing surfaces of end cover.
7. Install end cover and tighten bolts to specification in sequence outlined, **Fig. 14.**
8. Inspect and fill fluids as required.

Input Shaft Seal

EXCEPT PACIFICA

REMOVAL

1. Remove PTU as outlined in "Power Transfer Unit, Replace."
2. Remove PTU end cover bolts.
3. Gently tap on end cover tabs to release cover from case.
4. Remove ring gear oil trough, **Fig. 15.**
5. Remove input shaft and ring gear from case.
6. Remove seal from case with seal puller tool No. 7794–A, or equivalent, **Fig. 16.**

INSTALLATION

1. Clean and inspect seal area.
2. Lay housing on bench and install new seal with installation tool No. C-4657 and handle tool No. C-4171, or equivalents. Seal spring side must face toward ring gear. Drive seal in until it bottoms against case shoulder.
3. Install input shaft and oil trough.
4. Apply Mopar gasket Maker or equivalent to sealing surfaces of end cover.
5. Install end cover bolts and tighten to specification.
6. Inspect and fill fluids as required.

PACIFICA

REMOVAL

1. Remove power transfer unit as outlined in "Power Transfer Unit, Replace."
2. Drill hole in input shaft seal using suitable drill and bit to facilitate removal with slide hammer.
3. Remove input shaft seal using slide hammer and screw.

INSTALLATION

1. Install input shaft seal using tool Nos. C4171 and 9321 or equivalents.
2. Install power transfer unit as outlined in "Power Transfer Unit, Replace."

Input Shaft End Seal

The input shaft end seal is located on the end of the input shaft.

REMOVAL

1. Remove power transfer unit as outlined under "Power Transfer Unit, Replace."
2. Remove end cover bolts.
3. Tap on end cover ears to release cover from case.
4. Pry out seal with suitable pry bar, **Fig. 17.**

INSTALLATION

1. Clean and inspect seal area.
2. Remove input shaft from housing and stand on soft block of wood.
3. Install input shaft end seal with installation tool No. 5065, handle No. C-4171, or equivalents.

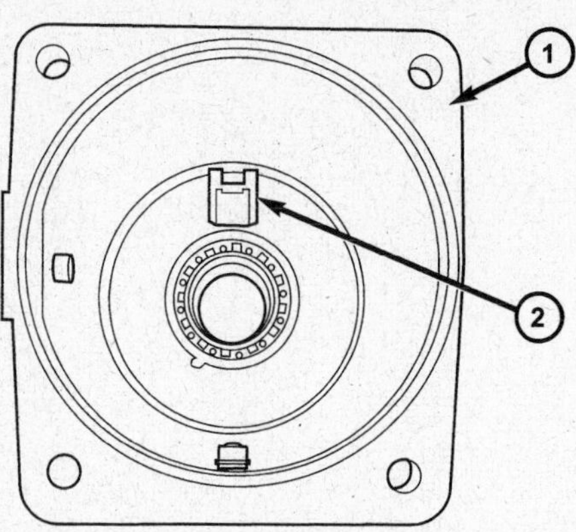

Fig. 6 Overrunning clutch housing notch location

4. Lubricate seal lip after installing seal into input shaft.
5. Clean surfaces of end cover and PTU case.
6. Apply a bead of Mopar Gasket Maker, Loctite Gasket Eliminator No. 518, or equivalent.
7. Place end cover onto PTU case and install bolts.
8. Tighten bolts to specification, in sequence, **Fig. 14.**
9. Retighten first bolt after all others have been tightened.
10. Inspect and fill fluids as required.

Output Seal & Flange

REMOVAL

1. Mark rear cover relationship to case for installation alignment.
2. Remove rear cover retaining bolts, then the cover.
3. Remove output flange retaining nut.
4. Mark pinion relationship to flange for installation alignment.
5. Remove output flange from pinion using suitable hydraulic press.
6. Remove output seal.
7. If output flange is replaced, install a new shim.

INSTALLATION

1. Install seal using seal tool No. 5049, or equivalent.
2. If original flange is used, align marks, then press flange on pinion.
3. If new flange is used, select a new shim that protrudes same distance from new flange as original shim protruded from original flange. Use a feeler gauge to measure protrusion distances.
4. Install flange nut and tighten to specifications.
5. Install rear cover and tighten bolts to specifications. Use care not to damage O-ring.
6. Install propeller shaft and tighten to specifications.
7. Inspect and fill fluids as required.

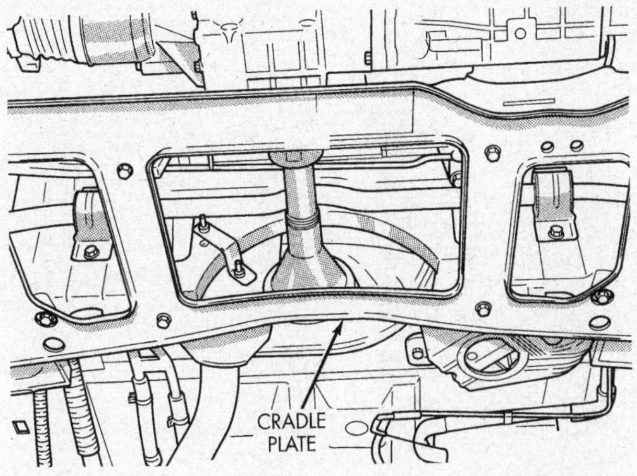

CR3039900457000X

Fig. 7 Cradleplate. Except Pacifica

End Cover Bearing

REMOVAL

1. Remove output seal.
2. Remove bearing snap ring.
3. Remove bearing using bearing puller tool No. MD998346, or equivalent.

INSTALLATION

1. Install bearing using bearing driver tool No. L-4530 and handle tool No. C-4171-2, or equivalents.
2. Install bearing snap ring.
3. Install new seal using seal installation tool No. MD998334, or equivalent.
4. Inspect and fill fluids as required.

End Cover Seal

1. Remove PTU as outlined under "Power Transfer Unit, Replace."
2. Remove PTU end cover retaining bolts.
3. Gently tap on end cover ears with a suitable hammer to separate end cover from case, **Fig. 18.**
4. Clean and inspect sealer surfaces, then apply Mopar gasket maker, Loctite gasket eliminator No. 518, or equivalent, to sealing surfaces.
5. Install cover. Tighten bolts to specification in sequence outlined in **Fig. 14.**
6. Install PTU, then inspect and fill fluids as required.

Halfshaft Inner Seal

REMOVAL

The power transfer unit halfshaft inner seal is the smaller of the two seals located on the inside of the end cover.

1. Remove PTU as outlined under "Power Transfer Unit, Replace."
2. Remove end cover retaining bolts, then tap ears to separate cover from case.
3. Drive seal out with a suitable hammer and chisel, **Fig. 19.**

INSTALLATION

1. Clean and inspect seal area.

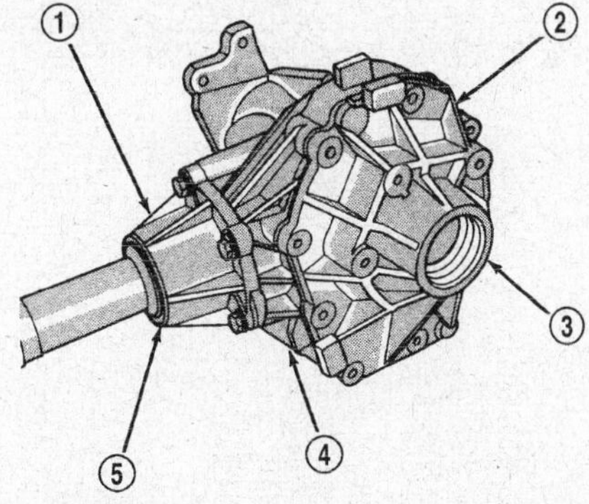

REAR COVER
END COVER
OUTER HALFSHAFT SEAL
P.T.U. CASE
P.T.U. OUTPUT SEAL

LTV1900000001418

Fig. 8 Seal locations (Part 2 of 4)

2. Install seal using a $1\frac{1}{16}$ inch socket, **Fig. 20,** or suitable equivalent. Seal must be installed with spring side of seal facing end cover ball bearing. Seal will bottom against a machined shoulder in cover.
3. Clean sealing surfaces of end cover and PTU case, then apply a bead of Mopar gasket maker, Loctite gasket eliminator No. 518, or equivalent.
4. Place end cover onto PTU case and install bolts. Tighten bolts to specification in sequence outlined in **Fig. 14.** Retighten first bolt after all others are tight.
5. Install PTU into vehicle, then inspect and fill fluids as required.

Halfshaft Outer Seal

REMOVAL

The outer halfshaft seal is located on the outside of the end cover. The PTU does not have to be removed to replace this seal.

1. Raise and support vehicle.
2. Remove righthand front halfshaft from vehicle.
3. Remove seal with a suitable chisel and hammer, **Fig. 21.**

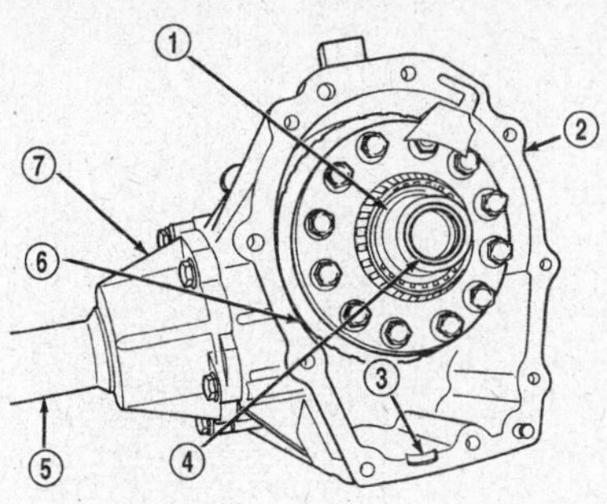

1 - INPUT SHAFT
2 - P.T.U. CASE
3 - MAGNET
4 - INPUT SHAFT END SEAL
5 - OUTPUT SHAFT
6 - RING GEAR
7 - REAR COVER

LTV1900000001417

Fig. 8 Seal locations (Part 1 of 4)

INSTALLATION

1. Clean and inspect seal area.
2. Install new seal with seal tool No. MD998334, or equivalent.
3. Install right front halfshaft.
4. Inspect and fill fluids as required.

Rear Cover O-Ring

1. Raise and support vehicle.
2. Remove rear cover retaining bolts, **Fig. 22.**
3. With paint, place index marks on rear cover to case for installation reference, **Fig. 23.**
4. Pull rear cover out of PTU case.
5. Remove rear cover O-ring, **Fig. 24.**
6. Reverse procedure to install.

ADJUSTMENTS

Output Flange Shim Selection

Perform this procedure whenever the output flange is replaced. The shim must protrude from the new output flange the same distance that the original shim protruded from the original flange.

1. Stand original output flange on end with shim pointing upward.
2. Place original shim into groove in top of flange.
3. Place a straight edge across shim, **Fig. 25.**
4. With a suitable feeler gauge, measure distance between straight edge and top of flange, **Fig. 25.** Record this measurement.
5. Repeat steps with new flange and original shim. Record this measurement.
6. If measurements are not equal, use a new shim that protrudes from new output flange the same amount as old shim and flange.
7. Install output flange and torque flange nut to specification.
8. Inspect running torque of pinion before installing rear cover into PTU. Turning torque should be between 17–22 inch lbs.

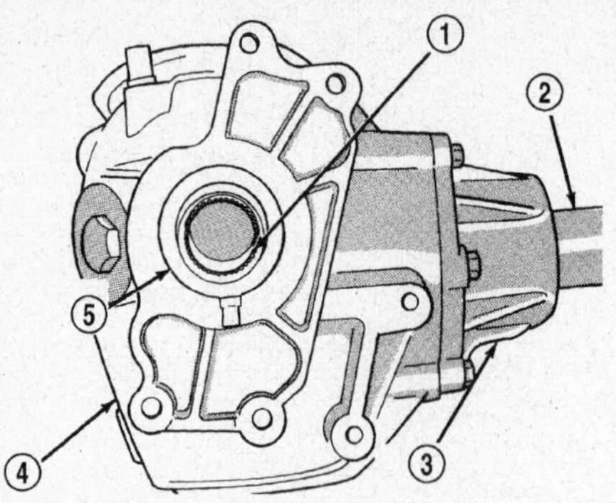

Fig. 8 Seal locations (Part 3 of 4)

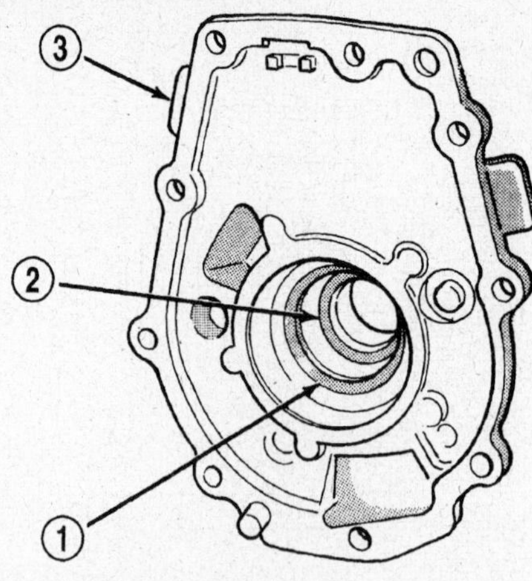

Fig. 8 Seal locations (Part 4 of 4)

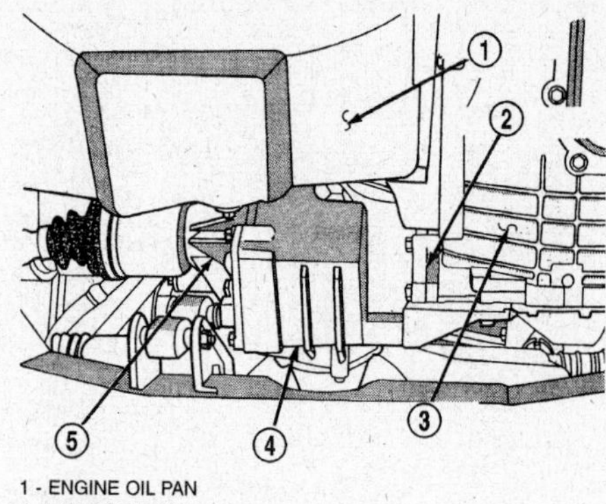

Fig. 9 Weep hole locations

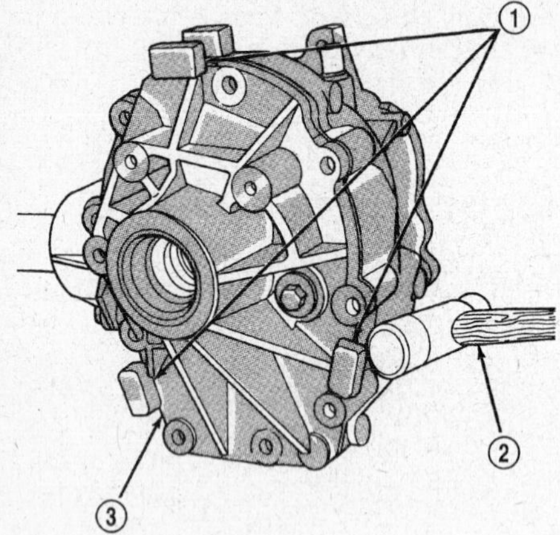

Fig. 10 End cover ears

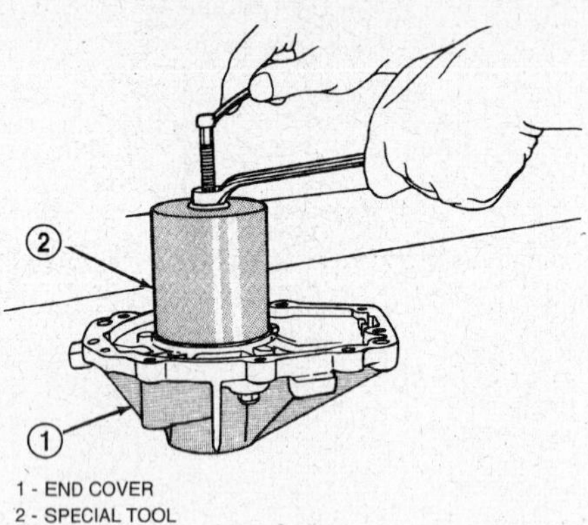

Fig. 11 Differential bearing removal

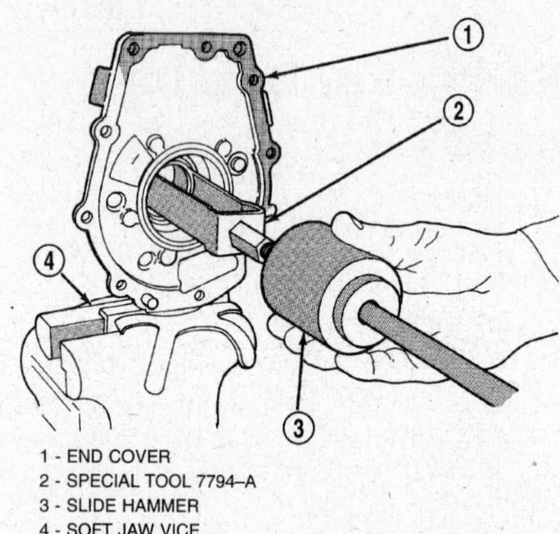

Fig. 12 End cover seal removal

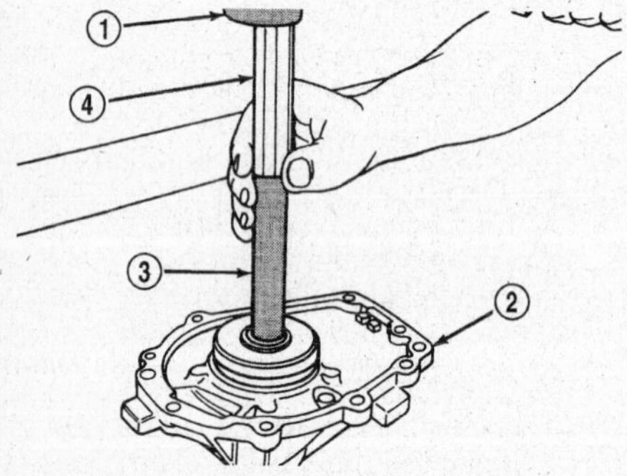

Fig. 13 Bearing race & shim installation

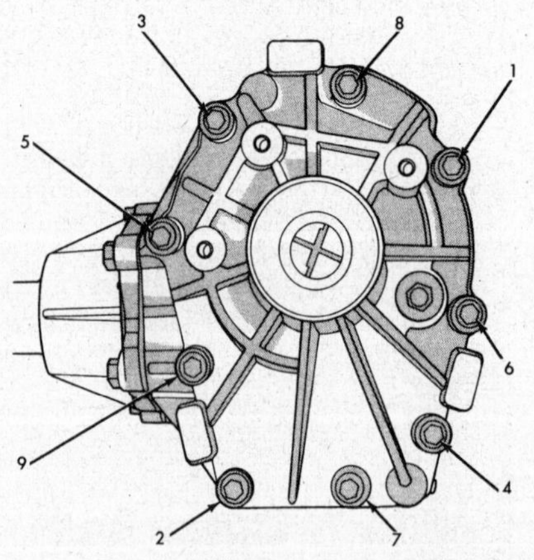

Fig. 14 End cover tightening sequence

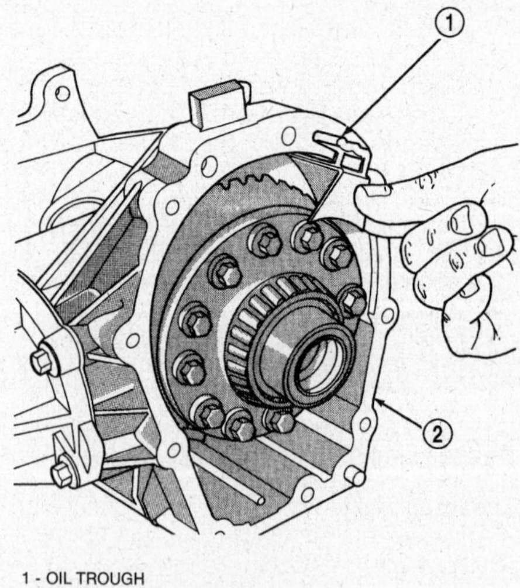

Fig. 15 Ring gear oil trough. Except Pacifica

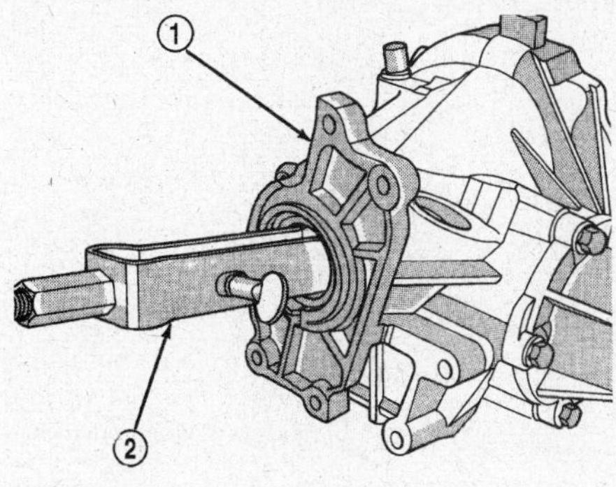

Fig. 16 Seal puller tool. Except Pacifica

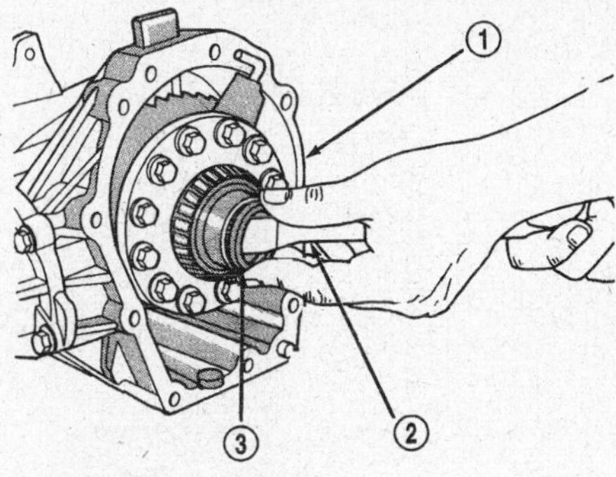

Fig. 17 Input shaft end seal removal

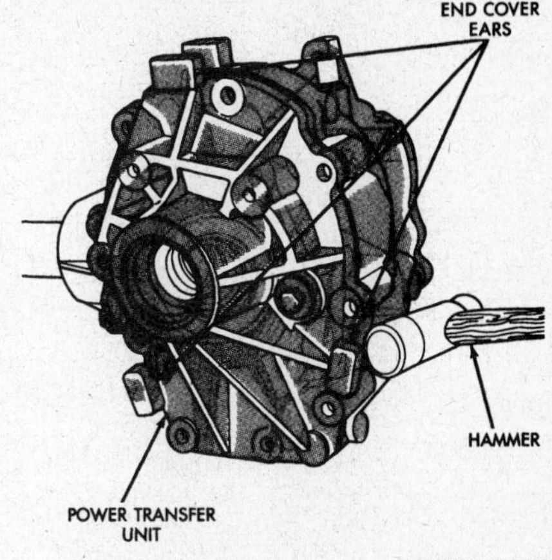

Fig. 18 End cover removal

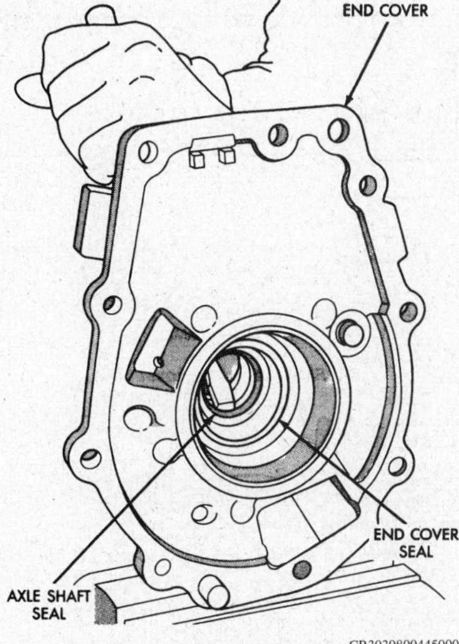

Fig. 19 Inner halfshaft seal removal

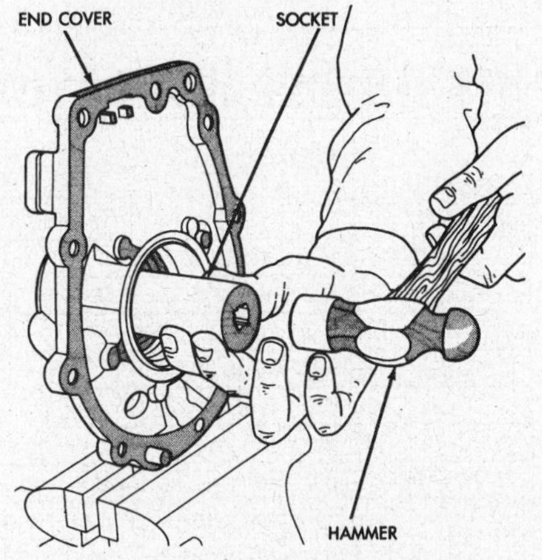

Fig. 20 Inner halfshaft seal installation

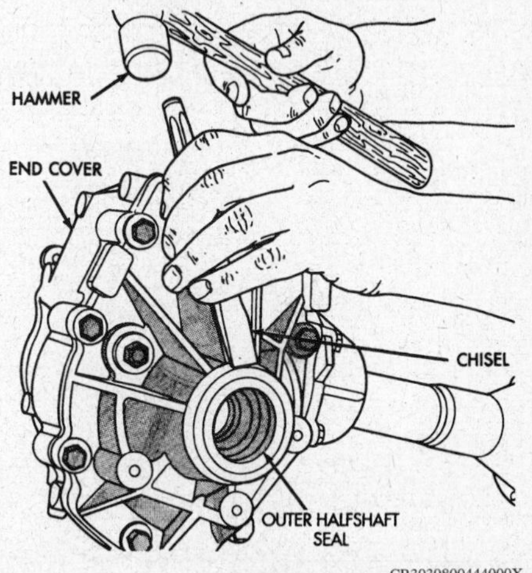

Fig. 21 Outer halfshaft seal removal

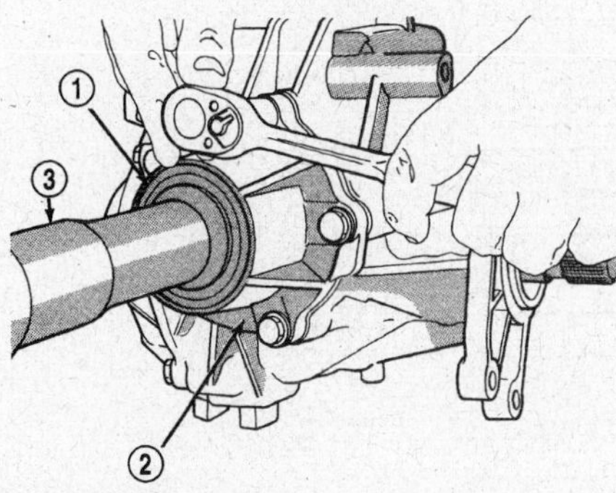

Fig. 22 Rear cover removal

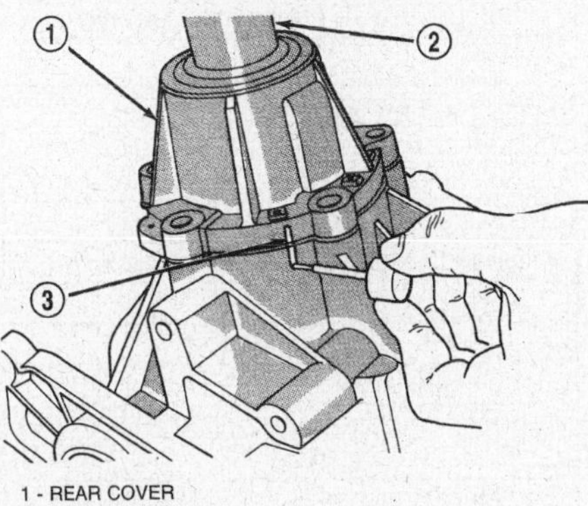

Fig. 23 Rear cover to case index marks

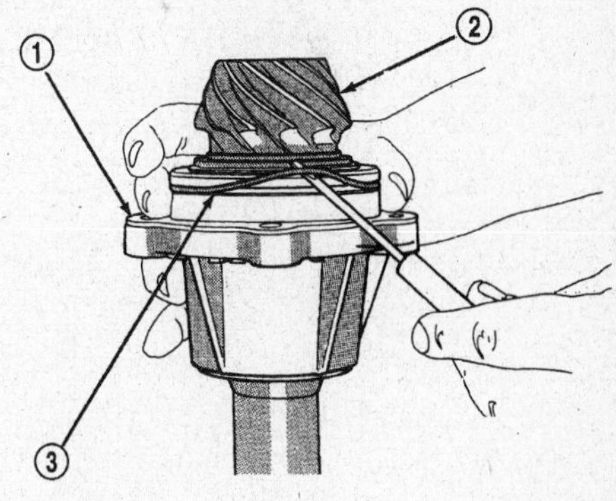

Fig. 24 Rear cover O-ring replacement

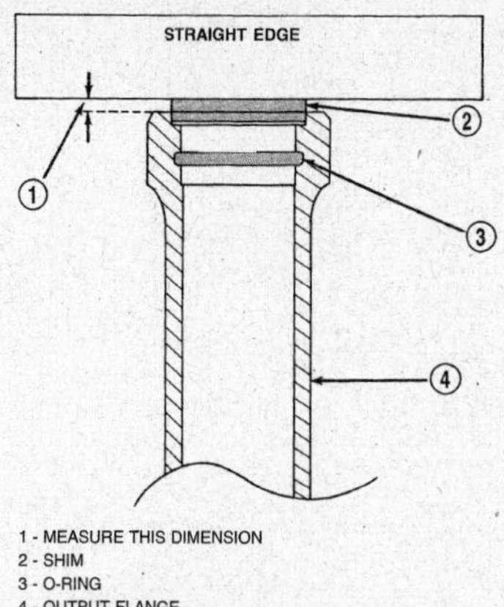

Fig. 25 Output flange shim measurement

TIGHTENING SPECIFICATIONS

Year	Component	Torque Ft. Lbs.
EXCEPT PACIFICA		
2002–04	Differential Drain Fill Plug	26
	Driveline Module To Body Bolt	40
	Halfshaft To Output Flange	45
	Input Flange Nut	100
	Output Flange Nut	180
	Overrunning Clutch Housing Drain/Fill Plug	22
	Overrunning Clutch Housing To Differential	44
	PTU End Cover	250①
	PTU Inspection Plug	180①
	Rear Cover	250①
	Ring Gear	70
	Torque Arm Mount To Body	40
	Torque Arm To Differential Assembly	44
PACIFICA		
2004–06	Differential Drain Fill Plug	26
	Differential Overrunning Clutch Housing Vent	110①
	Driveline Module-To-Body Bolt	40
	Driveline Module-To-Cradle Bolt & Nut	75
	Hub Nut	180
	Input Flange Nut	100
	Mount Bracket-To-PTU Bolt	40
	Overrunning Clutch Housing-To-Differential Bolt	44
	Overrunning Clutch Housing Drain Fill Plug	22
	Propeller Shaft Front Flange-To-PTU Flange Bolt	22
	Propeller Shaft-To-Driveline Module Bolts	40
	Propeller Shaft Rear Flange-To-Driveline Module Flange Bolt	40
	PTU Drain Fill Plug	26
	PTU-To-Transaxle Lower Bolt	21
	PTU-To-Transaxle Upper Bolt	40
	Support Bearing-To-Body Bolt	40
	Wheel Lug Nuts	100

① — Inch lbs.

DRIVE AXLES

NOTE: For Service On Front Wheel Drive Vehicles, Refer To "Front Wheel Drive Axles" Chapter. For Service On All Wheel Drive Vehicles, Refer To "All Wheel Drive" Section.

TABLE OF CONTENTS

Application Chart

Year	Model	Ring Gear Diameter, Inch	Gear Ratios①
COMMANDER			
2006	C213R	8¼	3.21, 3.55 Or 3.73
	C213RE	8¼	3.07, 3.55 Or 3.73
DAKOTA & DURANGO			
2002–06	8¼	8¼	3.21, 3.55 Or 3.92
	9¼	9¼	3.21, 3.55 Or 3.92
FULL SIZE PICKUP			
2002	9¼	9¼	3.21, 3.55 Or 3.92
	248②	9¾	3.55 Or 4.10
	267②	10½	3.55 Or 4.10
	286②	11¼	3.55 Or 4.10
2003–06	9¼	9¼	3.21, 3.55 Or 3.92
	10½	10½	3.73 Or 4.10
	11½	11½	3.73 Or 4.10
FULL SIZE VAN			
2002–03	8¼	8¼	3.21, 3.55 Or 3.92
	9¼	9¼	3.21, 3.55 Or 3.92
	248②	9¾	3.55 Or 4.10
GRAND CHEROKEE			
2002–04	198②	7⅘	3.07, 3.55, 3.73, Or 4.10
	226②	8⁹⁄₁₀	3.55 Or 3.73
2005–06	C213R	8¼	3.21, 3.55 Or 3.73
	C213RE	8¼	3.07, 3.55 Or 3.73
LIBERTY			
2002–06	8¼	8¼	3.55, 3.73 Or 4.10
SPRINTER			
2003–06	8½	8½	3.73 Or 4.11
WRANGLER			
2002	194②	7⅝	3.07, 3.55, 3.73 Or 4.11
	216②	8½	3.07, 3.55 Or 4.10
2003–06	194②	7⅝	3.07, 3.73, 4.11 Or 4.56
	216②	8½	3.07, 3.73 Or 4.11

① — Stamped on differential housing tag.
② — Dana/Spicer.

8¼ & 9¼ Inch DaimlerChrysler Drive Axles

INDEX

DISASSEMBLE

1. Raise and support vehicle.
2. Remove wheels and propeller shaft.
3. Remove cover and gasket, **Fig. 1,** and drain lubricant.
4. Rotate differential to gain access to differential pinion shaft lock screw, then remove lock screw and pinion shaft, **Fig. 2.**
5. Push axle shafts toward center of housing, and remove axle shaft "C" locks and axle shafts, **Fig. 3.**
6. Inspect differential side play by positioning a screwdriver or pinch bar between lefthand side of axle housing and differential case flange, then using a prying motion, determine if side play is present.
7. No side play should exist. Side play resulting from bearing cones becoming loose on differential case hubs requires replacement of case. Otherwise, use threaded adjuster to remove side play.
8. Inspect ring gear runout, **Fig. 4,** with suitable dial indicator to aid assembly. **If original ring gear and pinion are reused, backlash should be adjusted to measured value in order to maintain established gear tooth contact pattern.**
9. **On models equipped with anti-lock brakes,** remove anti-lock brake sensor retaining bracket, then the sensor.
10. **On all models,** mark axle housing and differential side bearing caps to aid assembly, **Fig. 5,** remove side bearing adjuster locks, then loosen but do not remove side bearing cap bolts.
11. Insert tool No. C-4164, or equivalent, through each axle tube, **Fig. 6,** and loosen side bearing adjusters.
12. Support differential assembly and remove side bearing caps, adjusters and differential assembly. On 7¼ inch axles, adjusters will remain in differential housing. **Use caution to avoid damaging RWAL brake exciter ring and ring gear.**
13. Place differential cup and threaded adjuster with respective bearings.
14. Measure pinion rotating torque (bearing preload) using an inch pound torque wrench, **Fig. 7.**
15. Holding companion flange with suitable tool, remove pinion nut and washer.
16. Remove companion flange using tool Nos. C-452 and C-3281, or equivalents, **Fig. 8,** then pry pinion seal from housing.
17. To remove drive pinion or front pinion bearing cone, pinion stem must be driven rearward out of bearing. **Pinion removal will cause excessive impact loading of front pinion bearing assembly. If pinion removal is required, front bearing assembly must be replaced.** Discard collapsible spacer.
18. Remove front and rear bearing cups from housing using remover tool No. C-4306 and handle tool No. C-4171, or equivalents.
19. Remove rear bearing from drive pinion shaft using suitable pullers.
20. Inspect components as outlined in "Cleaning & Inspection" keeping components in order, and replace as required. **Components that are reused must be installed in original position.**

SUBASSEMBLY SERVICE

Differential Overhaul

Standard, Trac-Lok and Sure-Grip limited slip differential assemblies, are used with DaimlerChrysler-built rear axles. Ring gear and side bearing service procedures are identical for both types of differential assemblies. However, due to critical tolerances required for proper operation, the Sure-Grip differential, **Fig. 9,** should not be disassembled for service. If the differential assembly on these models requires service, the complete assembly should be replaced.

STANDARD DIFFERENTIAL

Do not remove ring gear from differential case unless gear or case is to be replaced, or ring gear runout measured during disassembly exceeds .005 inch.

1. Support case assembly, then remove and discard ring gear bolts. Ring gear bolts have lefthand threads.
2. Tap ring gear from case using brass drift and hammer. Do not pry gear from case.
3. Rotate side gears until pinion gears are located at differential case opening, then remove pinion gears.
4. Remove side gears and thrust washers.
5. Inspect components as outlined in "Cleaning & Inspection" and replace as needed.
6. If side bearings are to be replaced, remove bearings using suitable puller, **Fig. 10.** If bearings are loose on case, both case and side bearings must be replaced. **Coat components with specified lubricant prior to assembly. Components that are reused should be installed in original position to ensure proper operation.**
7. Install side gears and thrust washers in respective sides of case.
8. Install thrust washers on differential pinions, using grease to adhere washers.
9. Position pinion assemblies 180° apart in case, in mesh with side gears, then roll pinions into case until they align with pinion shaft bores.
10. Insert pinion shaft and temporarily secure with lock bolt.
11. Relieve sharp edge of chamfer on inside diameter of ring gear with hard Arkansas stone, then ensure ring gear and case mounting surfaces are clean and free from burrs.
12. Fabricate three pilot studs from old ring gear bolts and install studs evenly spaced around ring gear, **Fig. 11.**
13. Heat ring gear evenly using oven, sun lamp or hot fluid. **Do not allow temperature of gear to exceed 300°F. Do not heat gear with torch.**
14. Mount ring gear on case and install new ring gear bolts.
15. Support case, then evenly tighten bolts to specifications in crisscross pattern.
16. Install side bearings on case using suitable driver, **Fig. 12.** Support case on pilot when installing second bearing to prevent damage to bearing already installed.

TRAC-LOK DIFFERENTIAL

Refer to **Fig. 13** during Trac-Lok differential repair or service.

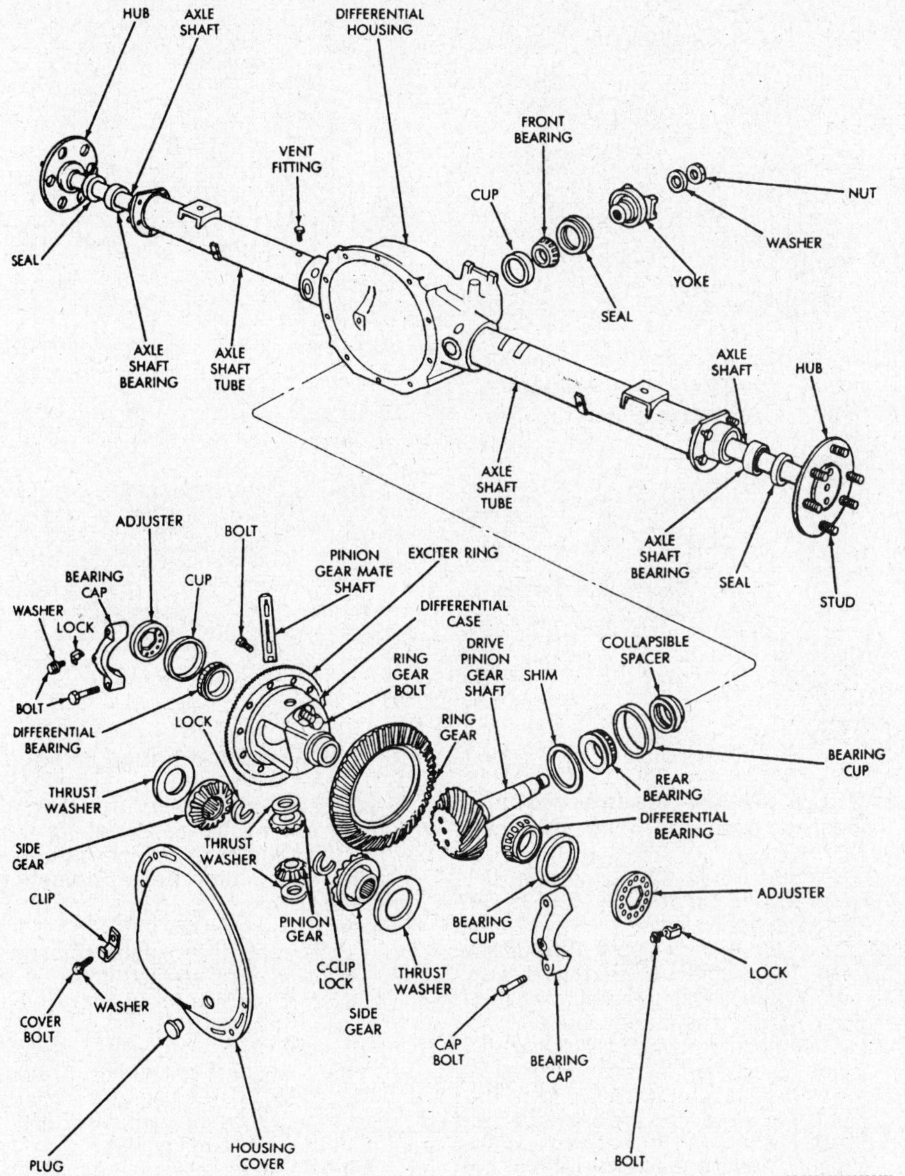

Fig. 1 Exploded view of Chrysler drive axle

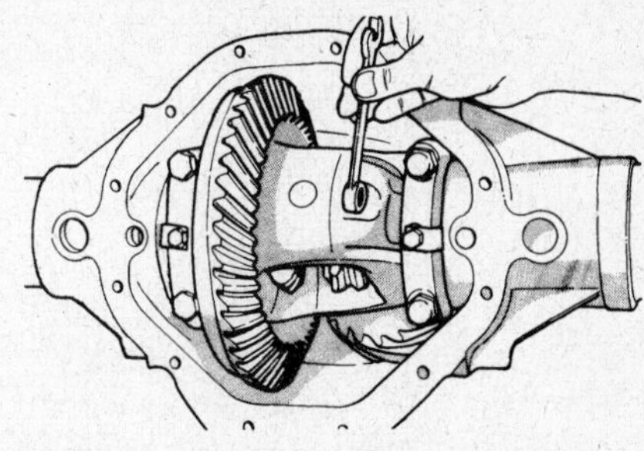

Fig. 2 Differential pinion shaft removal

1. Clamp side gear holding tool No. 8138, or equivalent, in a vise.
2. Position differential case on side gear holding tool.
3. Remove ring gear, if required. Ring gear removal is required only if ring gear is to be replaced. The Trac-Lok differential can be serviced with ring gear installed.
4. Remove pinion gear mate shaft lock screw.
5. Remove pinion gear mate shaft. If required, use a drift and hammer.
6. Install and lubricate step plate tool No. 8140-2, or equivalent, **Fig. 14.**
7. Assemble threaded adapter tool No. 8140-1, or equivalent, into top side gear.
8. Thread forcing screw No. 6960–4, or equivalent, into adapter until it becomes centered in adapter plate.
9. Position a small screw driver in slot of threaded adapter to prevent adapter from turning, **Fig. 15.**
10. **Torque** forcing screw tool to 90 ft. lbs., maximum to compress belleville springs in clutch packs.
11. Remove thrust washers from behind pinion gears using an appropriate size feeler gauge.
12. Insert turning bar tool No. 6960-2, or equivalent, into case, **Fig. 16.**
13. Loosen forcing screw tool in small increments until clutch pack tension is relieved and differential case can be turned using turning bar tool.
14. Rotate differential case until pinion gears can be removed.
15. Remove pinion gears from differential case.
16. Remove forcing screw, step plate and threaded adapter tools from differential.
17. Remove top side gear, clutch pack retainer and clutch pack. Keep plates in correct order during removal, **Fig. 17.**
18. Remove differential case from side gear holding tool, then the side gear, clutch pack retainer, and clutch pack. Keep plates in correct order during removal.

CLEANING & INSPECTION

1. Clean components in suitable solvent and blow dry with compressed air, noting the following:
   a. Do not use brush when cleaning bearings.
   b. Do not "spin dry" bearings as they will be damaged.
   c. Lightly lubricate components after cleaning to retard corrosion.
   d. Keep all components in order to ensure proper assembly.
2. **On models equipped with Trac-Lok differential,** inspect clutch pack plates for wear, scoring or damage. Replace both clutch packs if any one component in either pack is damaged.
3. **On models equipped with Trac-Lok differential,** plates and discs with fiber coating (no grooves or lines) must be presoaked in friction modifier before assembly. Soak plates and discs for a minimum of 20 minutes.
4. **On all models,** inspect gears for cracks, chipped or broken teeth, wear and scoring. Replace gears that are damaged or excessively worn. **Ring gear and pinion must be replaced as an assembly.**
5. Inspect differential case for cracks, damage, distortion, and worn or scored bearing and thrust surfaces. Replace case if damaged or scored.
6. Mount differential case along with side bearings in housing, adjust bearing preload to zero and inspect runout of case flange with suitable dial indicator, **Fig. 18.** If runout exceeds .003 inch, case must be replaced.
7. Inspect axle housing for damaged or scored bearing bores, cracks, distortion, and damaged bearing adjuster threads. Ensure housing is clean and free from burrs and foreign material.
8. Inspect bearing rollers and races for pitting, scoring, overheating and damage.
9. Mate each bearing with race and inspect operation.
10. Replace any bearing that is damaged, excessively worn, or that fails to operate smoothly.

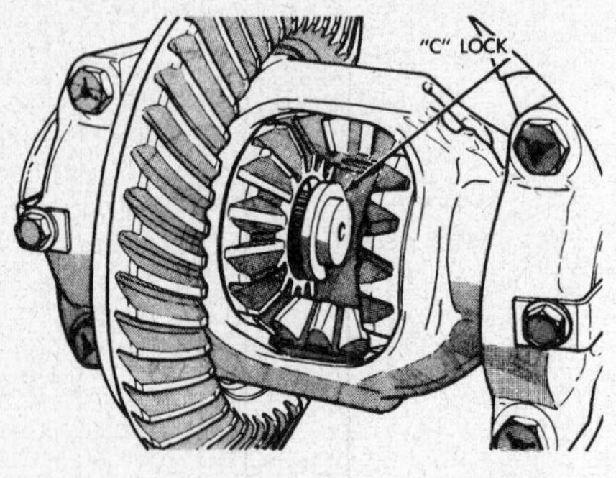

Fig. 3 Axle shaft "C" lock removal

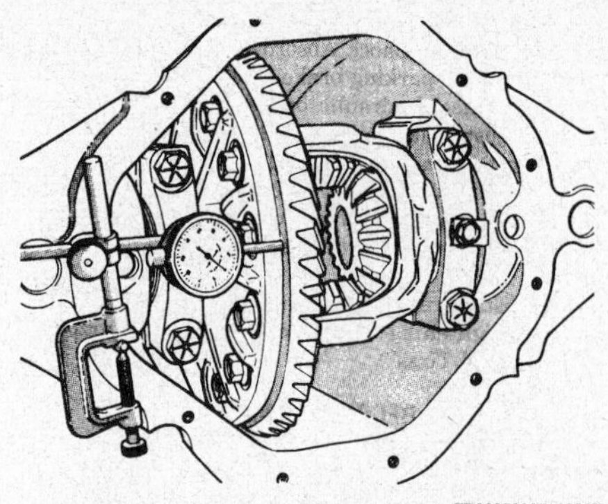

Fig. 4 Ring gear runout inspection

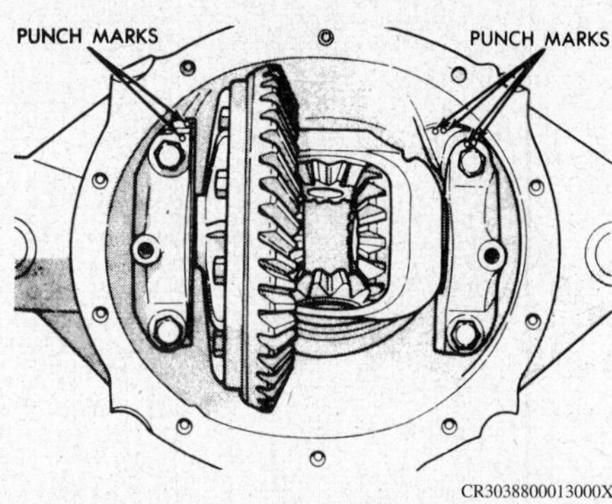

Fig. 5 Side bearing cap marks

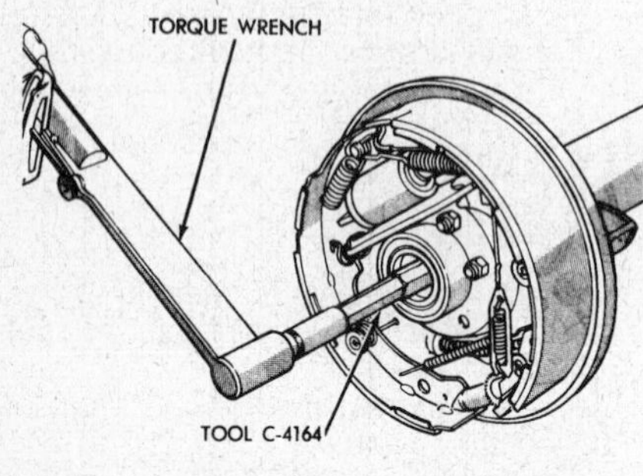

Fig. 6 Side bearing adjustment

Fig. 7 Pinion rotating torque (bearing preload) measurement

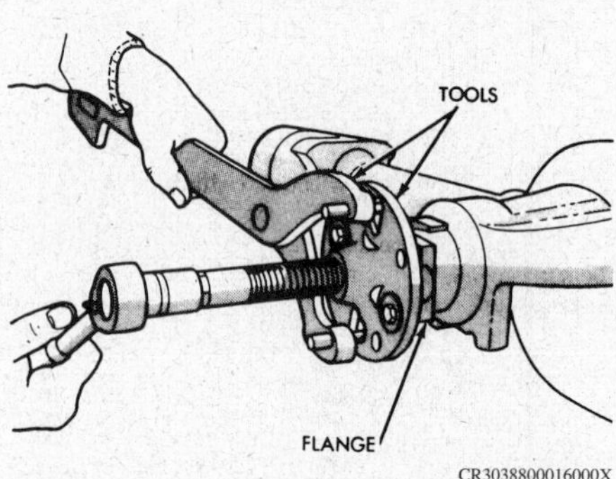

Fig. 8 Companion flange removal

ASSEMBLE

Pinion Depth Adjustment

Correct pinion depth must be established to ensure proper ring gear and pinion tooth contact. Pinion depth is adjusted by varying thickness of shims installed either between rear pinion bearing and gear, or between rear pinion bearing race and housing. If original ring gear and pinion, rear pinion bearing and housing are to be reused, original shims removed during disassembly can be used to adjust pinion depth. However, if gear set, rear pinion bearing assembly or housing are replaced, proper pinion depth must be adjusted using following procedures.

8¼ INCH RING GEAR

Pinion setting gauge assembly and adapter set, **Fig. 19,** or suitable equivalents must be used to select pinion depth adjusting shim and install pinion bearing races. Depth adjusting shims are installed between rear pinion bearing race and gear.

1. Start both pinion bearing races in respective housing bores, ensuring races are not cocked, then lubricate pinion bearings and races.
2. Assemble spacer part No. SP-6030 on shaft part No. SP-5385 followed by rear bearing cone, then insert assembly into housing from case side.
3. Hold assembly in case, then install shaft locating sleeve part No. SP-5382, front bearing cone, washer part No. SP-6022, compression sleeve part No. SP-3194-B, washer part No. SP-534 and nut part Nos. SP-5385 or SP-3193, or equivalents.
4. Hold compression sleeve with suitable tool, then tighten nut to draw bearing races into housing, rotating shaft to prevent damage to bearings.
5. When bearing races are fully seated, loosen nut, then retighten in small increments to obtain 15–25 inch lbs., preload, inspecting preload with suitable torque wrench after each adjustment. **Ensure bearing rollers are lubricated to ensure accurate reading.**
6. Rotate tool to ensure bearings are properly seated, inspect preload and adjust as needed.
7. Mount gauge block part No. SP-5383 onto shaft part No. SP-5385 and wrench part No. SP-531, then securely tighten screw part No. SP-5.
8. Mount arbor part No. SP-6029 in housing side bearing bores, ensuring arbor is centered.
9. Install side bearing caps in proper position, then insert .002 inch shim stock between each bearing cap and arbor. Tighten bearing cap bolts to specifications.
10. Insert progressively thicker shims between arbor and gauge block until fit of shim is snug but not excessively tight, then record thickness of shim.
11. Inspect head of pinion for pinion depth modification code and select shim as follows: **To ensure proper tooth contact, pinion may be marked with a plus (+) or minus (–) code number, indicating in thousandths of an inch required modifications to "nominal" depth setting. It is essential that this modification code be factored when selecting pinion depth adjusting shim.**
   a. If pinion is marked with a minus (–) code, add that number of thousandths to dimension obtained in step 10, and select shim thickness equal to sum.
   b. If pinion is marked with a plus (+) code, subtract that number of thousandths from dimension obtained in step 10 and select shim thickness equal to remainder.
12. Remove gauge tool and adapter assemblies from housing and pinion bearings from shaft.
13. Retain selected shim for pinion installation.

9¼ INCH RING GEAR

Pinion setting gauge assembly outlined in **Fig. 19,** or suitable equivalent, may be used to install pinion bearing races and to select proper shim thickness for pinion depth adjustment. Pinion depth shims are installed between rear pinion bearing and gear.

1. Start both pinion bearing races into housing, ensuring races are not cocked, then lubricate pinion bearings and races.
2. Assemble spacer part No. SP-6017 and rear pinion bearing on shaft part No. SP-526, then insert shaft assembly into housing from case side.
3. Install front pinion bearing, washer part No. SP-6022, compression sleeve part No. SP-535-A, centering washer part No. SP-534 and nut part No. SP-533 on shaft.

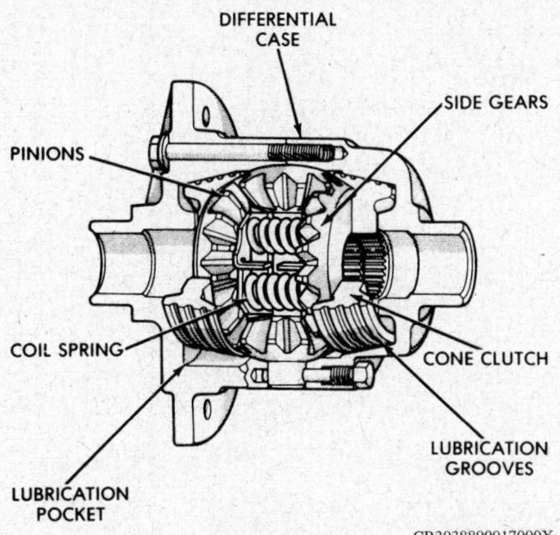

Fig. 9 Sure-Grip differential assembly

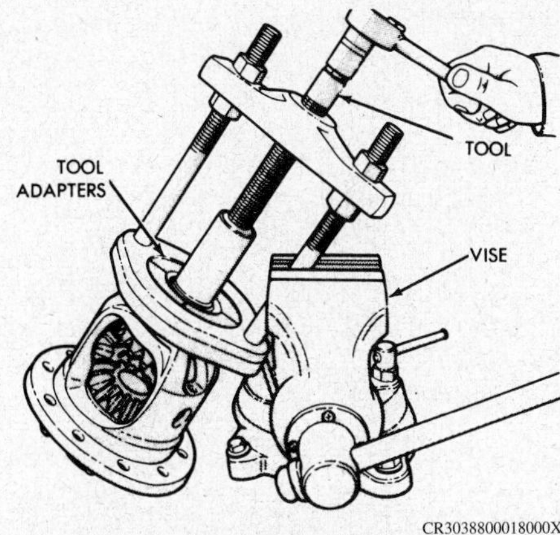

Fig. 10 Differential case side bearing removal

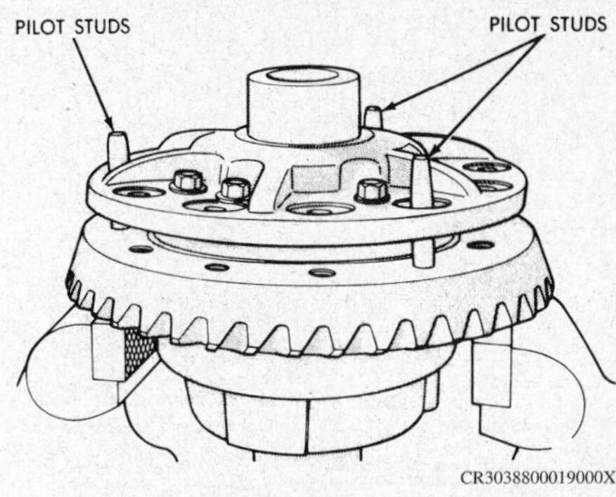

Fig. 11 Ring gear installation

4. Hold compression sleeve with suitable tool, then tighten nut to draw bearing races into housing, rotating tool to prevent damage to bearings.
5. When bearing races are seated, loosen nut on tool until endplay is evident, then lubricate bearings.
6. Hold compression sleeve, **torque** nut in small increments to obtain bearing preload of 15–25 inch lbs., inspecting preload with suitable torque wrench after each adjustment.
7. Rotate tool to ensure bearings are seated, inspect preload and adjust as needed.
8. Mount gauge block part No. SP-6020 onto head of shaft part No. SP-526, install screw part No. SP-536 and securely tighten screw.
9. Install arbor part No. SP-6018 in housing side bearing bores and center arbor.
10. Install side bearing caps in respective position, insert .002 inch shim stock between each cap and arbor, then tighten cap bolts to specifications.
11. Insert progressively thicker shims between arbor and gauge block until fit of shim is snug but not excessively tight, then record shim thickness.
12. Inspect head of pinion for pinion depth modification code and select depth adjusting shim as follows. **To ensure proper tooth contact, pinion may be marked with a plus (+) or minus (–) code number, indicating in thousandths of an inch required modifications to "nominal" depth setting. It is essential that this modification code be factored when selecting pinion depth adjusting shim.**
    a. If pinion is marked with a minus (–) code, add that number of thousandths to dimension obtained in step 11 and select shim thickness equal to sum.
    b. If pinion is marked with a plus (+) code, subtract that number of thousandths from dimension obtained in step 11 and select shim thickness equal to remainder.
13. Remove gauging tool assembly from housing and bearings from tool.

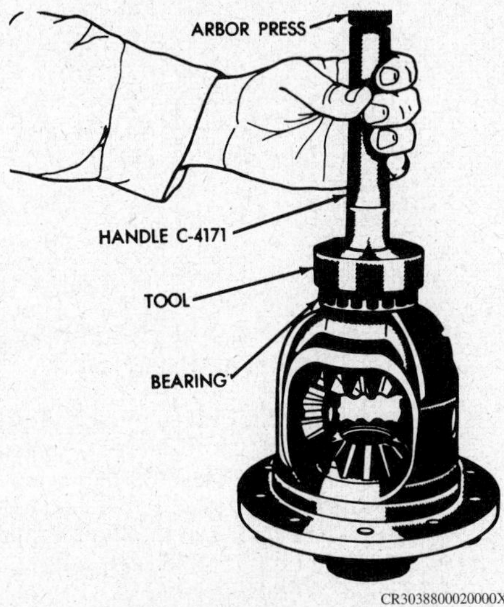

Fig. 12 Differential case side bearing installation

Drive Pinion Installation

1. Install bearing races, and bearing race shims if equipped, in housing as outlined in "Pinion Depth, Adjust."
2. Install selected depth adjusting shim on pinion.
3. Press rear bearing onto pinion using suitable spacer to ensure bearing is fully seated.
4. Install new collapsible spacer on pinion, lubricate pinion bearings, then insert pinion assembly into housing.
5. Install front pinion bearing, companion flange and forcing tool on pinion, **Fig. 20.**
6. Hold companion flange and tighten nut on forcing tool to seat front bearing on pinion shaft. **Care must be taken not to collapse spacer when seating front bearing on pinion shaft. Tighten tool only until endplay has been eliminated.**
7. Remove forcing tool and companion flange, then install new pinion seal using suitable driver.
8. Lubricate lips of pinion seal, then reinstall companion flange using forcing tool as outlined in steps 5 and 6.
9. Remove forcing screw, then install washer and new pinion nut.
10. Hold companion flange and tighten pinion nut to specifications, then inspect bearing preload using suitable torque wrench, **Fig. 7.** Bearing preload must be within specifications with pinion nut tightened to specifications. If bearing preload is greater than specified at minimum torque specification, or if preload is not even through full rotation, inspect pinion installation, replace collapsible spacer and repeat adjustment.
11. If bearing preload is less than specified, continue tightening nut in small increments, inspecting preload after each adjustment. **If specified preload is exceeded, spacer will be collapsed too far to be reused. Spacer must be replaced and adjustment procedure must be repeated. Do not loosen pinion nut to reduce preload.**

Exciter Ring

If required to replace exciter ring on models with anti-lock brakes, the following procedure should be performed after disassembly of the differential.

1. Remove exciter ring from case using suitable punch and hammer.
2. Heat new exciter ring using a heat lamp or immersing in a suitable hot fluid. Do not allow exciter ring to be heated past 300°F. **Do not use torch to heat exciter ring.**
3. Install exciter ring against shoulder of differential case.

Trac-Lok Differential Assemble

The clutch discs are replaceable as complete sets only. If one clutch disc pack is damaged, both packs must be replaced. Lubricate each component with gear lubricant before assembly.

1. Assemble clutch discs into packs and secure disc packs with retaining clips, **Fig. 21.**
2. Position assembled clutch disc packs

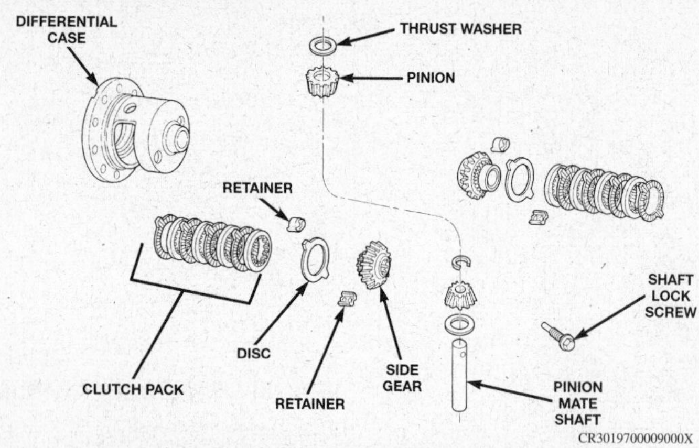

Fig. 13 Trac-Lok differential components

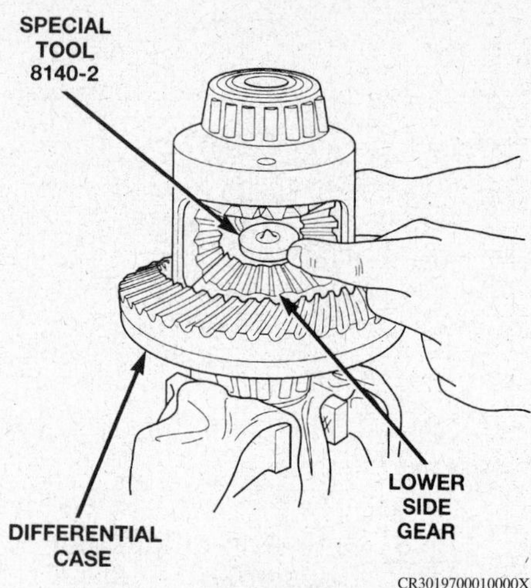

Fig. 14 Step plate tool installation

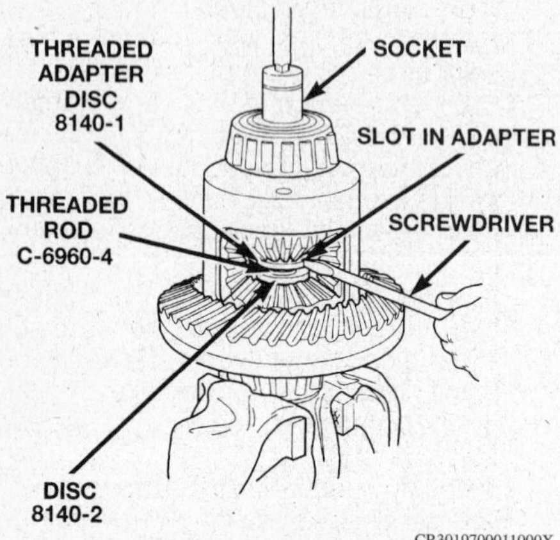

Fig. 15 Threaded adapter installation

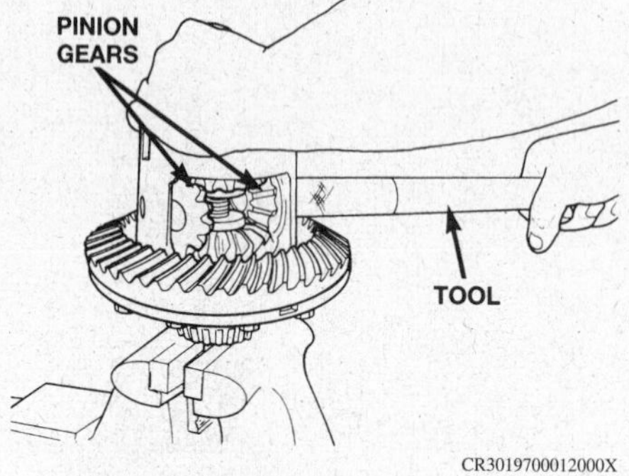

Fig. 16 Pinion gear removal

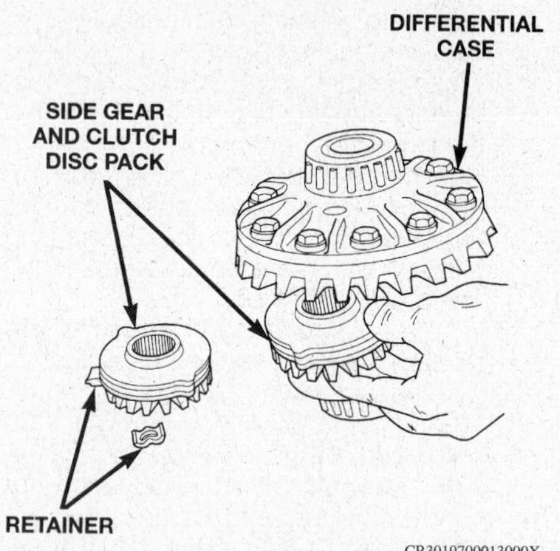

Fig. 17 Side gear & clutch disc removal

on side gear hubs.

3. Install clutch pack and side gear in ring gear side of differential case, **Fig. 22. Ensure clutch pack retaining clips remain in position and are seated in case pockets.**
4. Position differential case on side gear holding tool No. 8139, or equivalent.
5. Install lubricated step plate tool No. 8140-2, or equivalent, in lower side gear, **Fig. 23.**
6. Install upper side gear and clutch disc pack.
7. Hold assembly in position. Insert threaded adapter tool No. 8140-1, or equivalent, into top side gear.
8. Insert forcing screw tool No. 6960-4, or equivalent.
9. Tighten forcing screw tool to slightly compress clutch discs.
10. Place pinion gears in position in side gears and verify that pinion mate shaft holes are aligned.
11. Rotate case with turning bar tool No. 6960-2, or equivalent, until pinion mate shaft holes in pinion gears align with holes in case. It may be required to slightly tighten forcing screw in order to install pinion gears.
12. **Torque** forcing screw to 90 ft. lbs., maximum to compress belleville springs.
13. Lubricate and install thrust washers behind pinion gears and align washers with a small screw driver.
14. Insert mate shaft into each pinion gear to verify alignment.
15. Remove forcing screw, step plate and threaded adapter tools.
16. Install pinion gear mate shaft lock screw finger tight to hold shaft during differential installation.
17. Lubricate all differential components with hypoid gear lubricant.

Final Assembly & Adjustment

1. Coat side bearings, races and bearing adjusters with specified lubricant.
2. Place side bearing races over respective bearings, then install and support differential assembly in housing.
3. Install side bearing caps in proper locations, tighten top cap bolts to specifications and bottom bolts hand tight.
4. Tighten each bearing adjuster, **Fig. 6,** until side bearing endplay is reduced to zero, maintaining approximately .010 inch backlash between ring gear and pinion. **Side bearing caps will not always move directly with adjusters. In order to ensure accurate adjustment changes and to maintain proper gear mesh, seat bearings by oscillating drive pinion ½ turn in each direction, five to ten times, after each adjustment.**
5. Mount suitable dial indicator with plunger at righthand angle to ring gear tooth and contact button bearing against tooth, **Fig. 24.**
6. Hold pinion, rock ring gear back and forth and note backlash reading on dial indicator.
7. Inspect backlash at four evenly spaced positions around ring gear, index tooth at position where least backlash is observed and make all further inspects at this position. **Backlash variation of up to .003 inch between minimum and maximum readings is acceptable. If backlash variation exceeds .003 inch, inspect ring gear mounting, and ring gear and case, runout, and correct as needed.**
8. Loosen righthand adjuster and tighten lefthand adjuster until backlash is .003–.004 inch at indexed tooth with bearing adjusters torqued to 10 ft. lbs., seating side bearing races as outlined previously.
9. Tighten bearing cap to specifications.
10. **Torque** righthand adjusting nut to 70 ft. lbs., then seat bearings by tightening righthand adjuster and oscillating pinion to seat bearings until torque at righthand adjuster remains constant at 70 ft. lbs.
11. Measure backlash at indexed tooth. If backlash is not within specifications, continue tightening righthand adjuster and seating bearing races until proper

Fig. 18 Differential case runout inspection

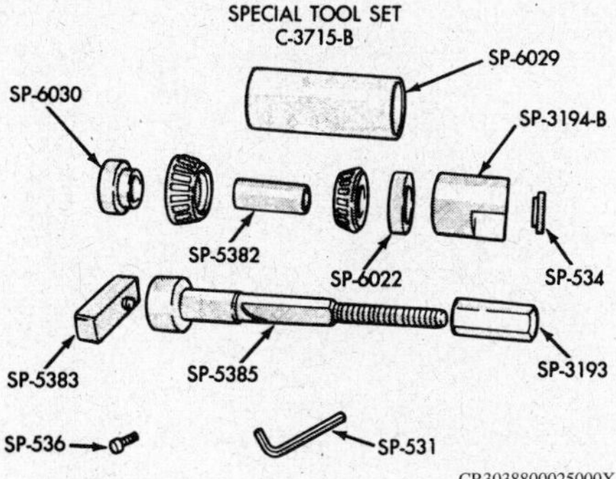

Fig. 19 Pinion depth gauge assembly.

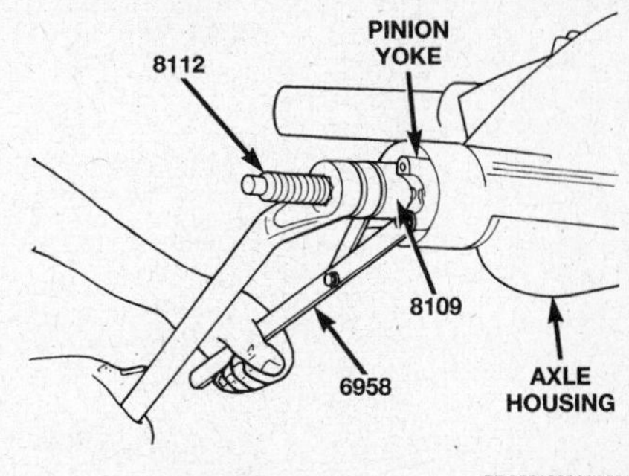

Fig. 20 Companion flange & front pinion bearing installation

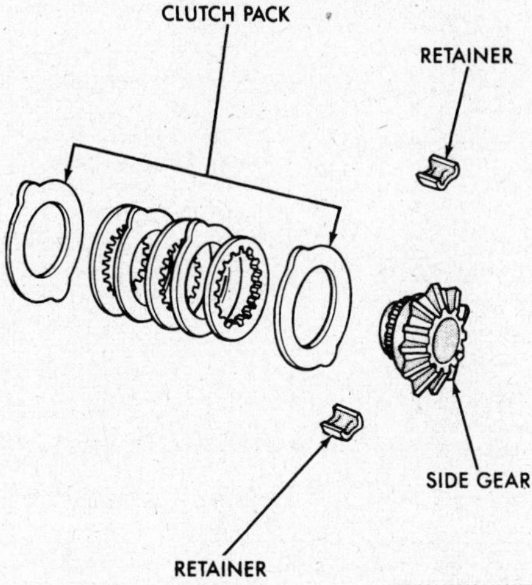

Fig. 21 Clutch disc pack

lash is obtained.

12. When proper backlash is obtained, inspect and adjust **torque** of lefthand bearing adjuster to 70 ft. lbs. **Torque** of lefthand bearing adjuster should be approximately 70 ft. lbs., after performing above procedures. If torque value is substantially less than 70 ft. lbs., loosen bearing caps and side bearing adjusters and repeat complete adjustment procedure in order to obtain proper side bearing preload at specified backlash.
13. Install adjuster locks ensuring locks are properly engaged in adjuster teeth, then **torque** lock bolts to 90 inch lbs.
14. If side bearings and thrust washers were replaced during "Differential Overhaul" inspect differential side gear clearance as follows:
    a. When measuring side gear clearance, inspect each gear independently.
    b. Install axle shafts, C-clip locks and pinion mate shaft.
    c. Measure each side gear clearance by inserting a matched pair of feeler gauge blades between gear and differential housing on opposite side of hub, **Fig. 25.**
    d. If side gear clearances does not exceed .005 inch. Inspect if shaft is contacting pinion gear mate shaft. Do not remove feeler gauges. If end of axle shaft is not contacting pinion gear mate shaft, side gear clearance is acceptable.
    e. If clearance is more than .005 inch (axle shaft not contacting mate shaft), record side gear clearance. Remove thrust washer and measure its thickness. Add washer thickness to recorded side gear clearance. Sum of gear clearance and washer thickness will determine required thickness of replacement thrust washer.
    f. In some cases, end of axle shaft will move and contact mate shaft when feeler gauge is inserted. C-clip lock is preventing side gear from sliding on axle shaft.
    g. If there is no side gear clearance, remove C-clip from axle shaft. Remove thrust washer, measure and record thrust washer thickness, then reinstall thrust washer. Assemble differential case without C-clip installed and measure side gear clearance.
    h. Compare both clearance measurements. If difference is less than .012 inch, add clearance recorded when C-clip was installed to thrust washer thickness measured. Sum will determine required thickness of replacement thrust washer.
    i. If clearance is .012 inch or greater, both side gears must be replaced (matched set) and clearance measurements repeated.
    j. If clearance continues to be .012 inch or greater, case must be replaced.
15. Coat coast and drive face of each ring gear tooth with suitable marking compound.
16. Apply braking force to differential case and turn pinion to rotate ring gear one full revolution in each direction. **If gears are not loaded, accurate contact pattern cannot be obtained.**

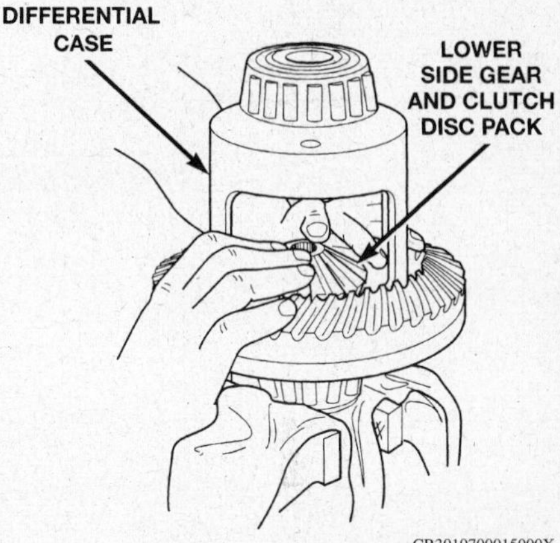

Fig. 22 Clutch discs & lower side gear installation

17. Contact pattern should be centered on ring gear teeth as outlined in **Fig. 26.**
18. If contact pattern is located at heel end (inside) of gear, pinion shim thickness should be increased to center pattern. If contact pattern is located at toe end (outside) of gear, decrease pinion shim thickness to center pattern. **Slight modifications in ring gear and pinion backlash may also be required to center contact pattern. However, backlash must be kept within specified limits in order to provide required operating clearance.**
19. Ensure bearing adjuster locks are properly installed, then install axle shafts, rear cover and propeller shaft, and fill axle with specified lubricant. **If RTV sealer is used to seal rear cover, apply a continuous bead of sealer to cover, 1/8 inch wide, circling all bolt holes.**
20. Install anti-lock brake sensor and tighten to specifications.

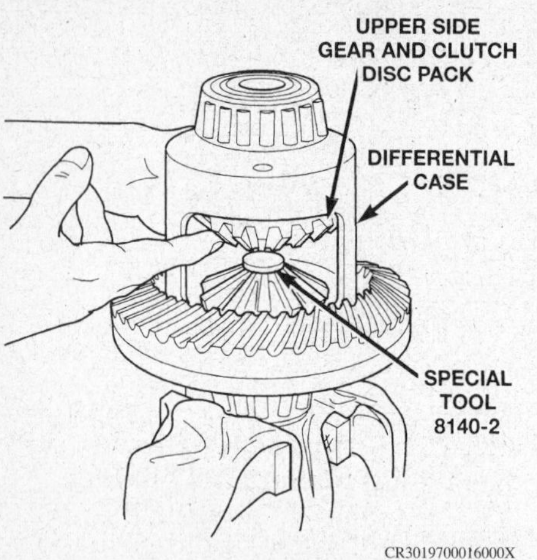

Fig. 23 Upper side gear & clutch disc pack installation

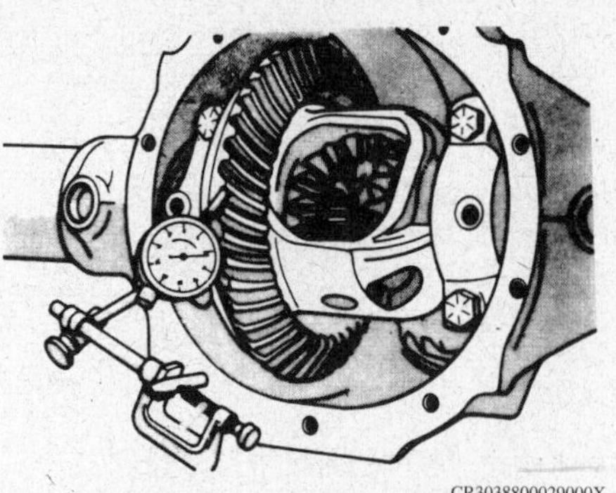

Fig. 24 Ring gear & pinion backlash inspection

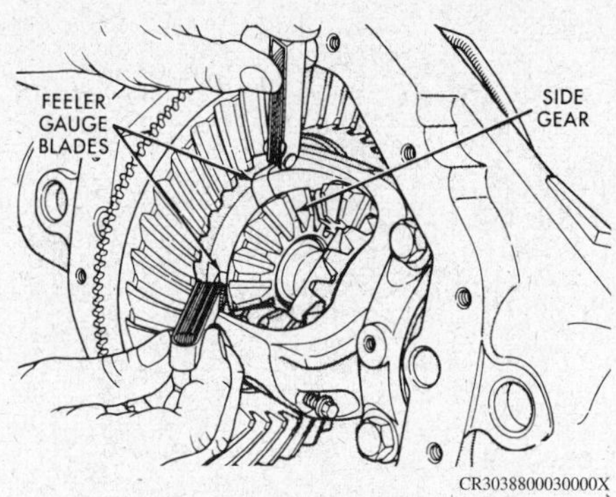

Fig. 25 Side gear clearance measurement

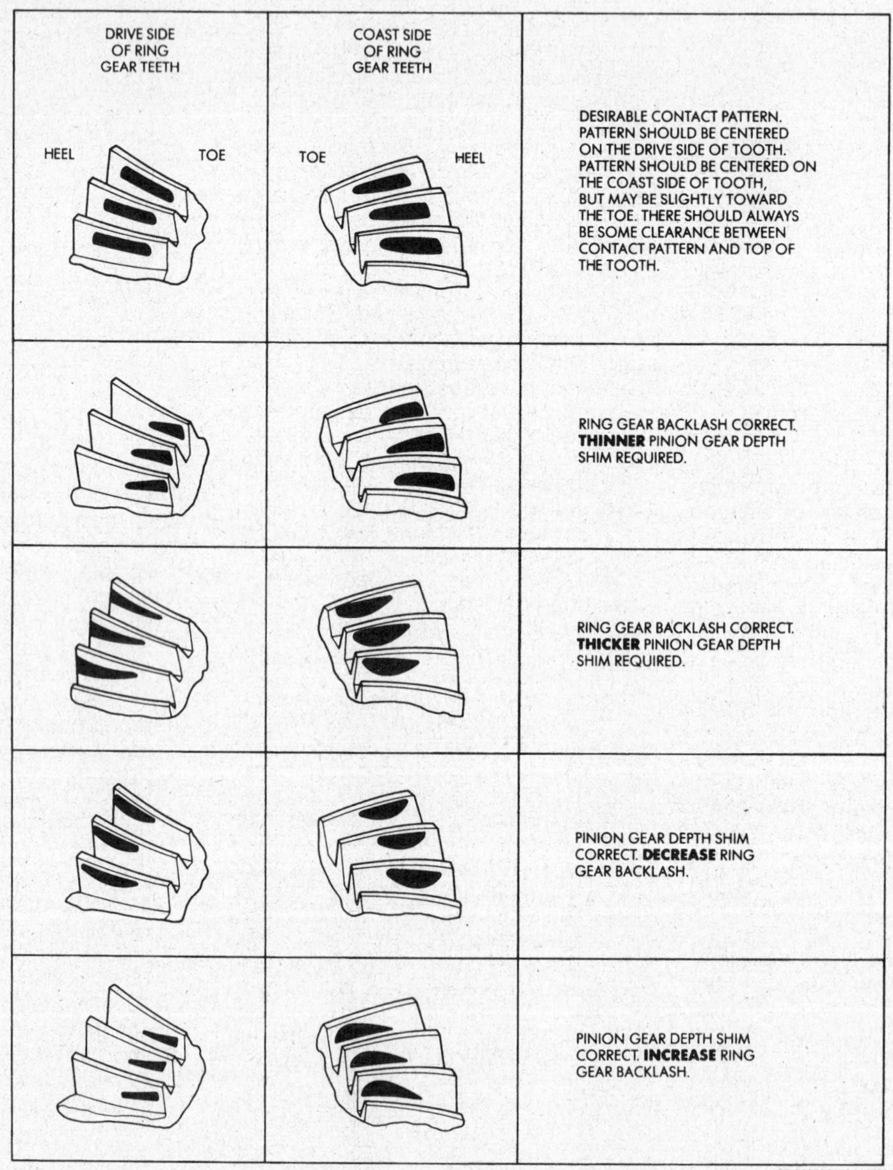

Fig. 26 Gear tooth contact inspection

DRIVE AXLE SPECIFICATIONS

Year	Ring Gear Size, Inch	Ring Gear & Pinion Backlash		Pinion Bearing Preload			Differential Bearing Preload		
		Method	Adjustment	Method	New Bearings, Inch Lbs.	Used Bearings, Inch Lbs.	Method	New Bearings, Inch Lbs.	Used Bearings, Inch Lbs.
DAKOTA & DURANGO									
2002–06	8¼	①	.005–.008	②	15–35	10–20	①	④	④
	9¼	①	.005–.008	②	③	③	①	④	④
FULL SIZE PICKUP									
2002–03	9¼	①	.005–.008	②	③	③	①	④	④
FULL SIZE VAN									
2002–03	8¼	①	.005–.008	②	15–35	10–20	①	④	④
	9¼	①	.005–.008	②	15–35	10–20	①	④	④
LIBERTY									
2002–06	8¼	①	.005–.008	—	10–30	10–20	①	④	④

① — Threaded adjuster.

② — Collapsible spacer.

③ — Original bearing, 10–20 inch lbs.; replacement bearing, 15–35 inch lbs

④ — Preload is correct when ring gear & pinion backlash is properly adjusted. .

TIGHTENING SPECIFICATIONS

Year	Component	Torque Ft. Lbs.
DAKOTA & DURANGO		
2002–06	ABS Sensor Bolt	18
	Backing Plate Bolt	48
	Bearing Cap Bolt	①
	Differential Cover Bolt	30
	Pinion Nut	210
	Ring Gear Bolt	②
	Threaded Adjusting Lock Screw	90③
FULL SIZE PICKUP		
2002–06	ABS Sensor Bolt	18
	Backing Plate Bolt	48
	Bearing Cap Bolt	100④
	Differential Cover Bolt	30
	Pinion Nut	210
	Ring Gear Bolt	115
FULL SIZE VAN		
2002–03	ABS Sensor Bolt	18
	Backing Plate Bolt	48
	Bearing Cap Bolt	①
	Differential Cover Bolt	30
	Pinion Nut	210
	Ring Gear Bolt	②
	Threaded Adjusting Lock Screw	90
LIBERTY		
2002–06	Adjuster Lock Screw	90③
	Axle Damper	45
	Bearing Cap Bolts	70
	Differential Cover Bolts	30
	Pinion Mate Shaft Screw	12
	Pinion Nut Minimum	210
	Ring Gear Bolts	75

① — 8¼, 70 ft. lbs.; 9¼, 100 ft. lbs.
② — 8¼, 75 ft. lbs.; 9¼, 115 ft. lbs.
③ — Inch lbs.
④ — With 216 axle bearing caps, 80 ft. lbs, pinion nut minimum 160 ft. lbs.

10½ & 11½ Inch DaimlerChrysler Drive Axles

INDEX

DISASSEMBLE

Pinion Gear, Ring Gear & Tone Ring

1. Remove differential from axle housing.
2. Place differential on plug tool No. 8888, or equivalent, then drive exciter ring off differential case with a hammer and punch, **Fig. 1.** Do not remove exciter ring if it is not being replaced.
3. Place differential case in a suitable soft jawed vise.
4. Remove ring gear bolts, then drive off ring gear using a soft hammer.
5. Hold pinion flange with flange wrench tool No. 8979, or equivalent, then remove pinion flange nut and washer, **Fig. 2.**
6. Remove pinion flange from pinion using pinion flange puller tool No. 8992, or equivalent, **Fig. 3.**
7. Remove pinion gear from housing using a hammer and pinion driver tool No. 8977, or equivalent, **Fig. 4.**
8. Remove pinion seal using a slide hammer or pry bar.
9. Remove and discard front pinion bearing.
10. Remove collapsible spacer from pinion shaft.
11. Remove rear pinion bearing using puller tool No. C-293-PA and adapter blocks tool No. 8879, or equivalents, **Fig. 5.**
12. Remove pinion depth shim from pinion gear shaft, then record thickness of shims.
13. Remove front pinion bearing cup from housing with a punch and hammer, then discard cup.
14. Remove rear pinion bearing cup from housing with a punch and hammer if bearing is going to be replaced.

Standard Differential

1. Remove lubricant fill hole plug from differential housing cover.
2. Remove differential housing cover draining fluid into suitable container.
3. Remove axle shafts.
4. Remove adjuster lock bolts, then the adjuster locks, **Fig. 6.**
5. Mark lefthand and righthand bearing caps for reference during installation.
6. Remove bearing cap bolts, then the bearing caps.
7. Loosen differential bearing adjusters using spanner wrench tool No. 8883, or equivalent, **Fig. 7.**
8. Remove differential case from housing.
9. Remove pinion shaft using a suitable hammer and punch from side with hole in pinion shaft, **Fig. 8.**
10. Rotate one pinion gear with thrust washer to differential window, then remove gear, **Fig. 9.**
11. Rotate other pinion gear with thrust washer to differential window, then remove gear.
12. Remove differential side gears and washers, **Fig. 10.**

Trac-Rite Differential

Mark all component locations for reference during installation.

1. Remove differential ring gear bolts.
2. Remove differential case cover locating screws, **Fig. 11.**
3. Remove differential case cover.
4. Remove side gear and thrust washer, **Fig. 12.**
5. Remove three pinion brake shoes, **Fig. 13.**
6. Remove six pinion gears, **Fig. 14.**
7. Remove remaining side gear thrust washer and spacer.
8. Remove remaining three pinion brake shoes.

CLEANING & INSPECTION

Standard Differential

Clean differential case and gears with light oil or lint free cloth. **Never use water, steam, kerosene or gasoline for cleaning.**

Trac-Rite Differential

1. Clean differential case and gears with light oil or lint free cloth. **Never use water, steam, kerosene or gasoline for cleaning.**
2. Minor corrosion, nicks or scratches can be smoothed with 400 grit emery cloth, then polished with a crocus cloth.
3. Inspect pinion gears teeth for chips and cracks, **Fig. 15.**
4. Inspect pinion gears shafts and brake shoes for scratches, flat spots or wear, **Fig. 15.**
5. Inspect side gears teeth for chips and cracks, **Fig. 16.**
6. Inspect pinion and side gear bores for scratches, **Fig. 17.**
7. If any damage is found, differential must be replaced as an assembly. Individual components can not be replaced separately.

ADJUSTMENTS

Pinion Depth

Measurements are taken with pinion bearing cups and pinion bearings installed

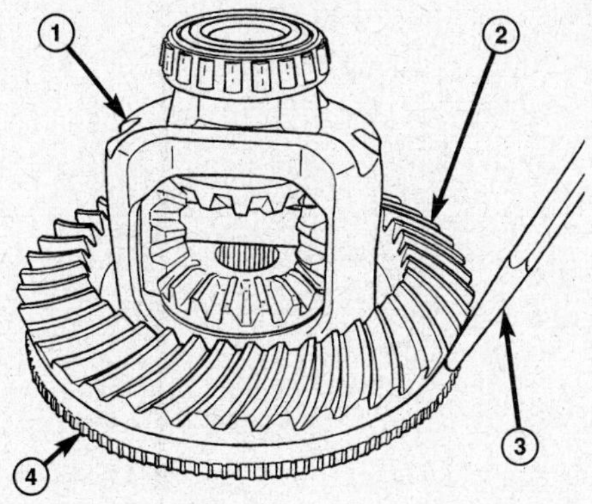

Fig. 1 Exciter ring

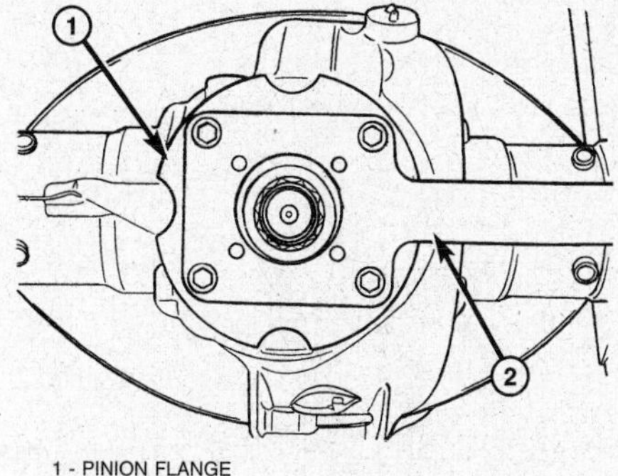

Fig. 2 Pinion flange wrench

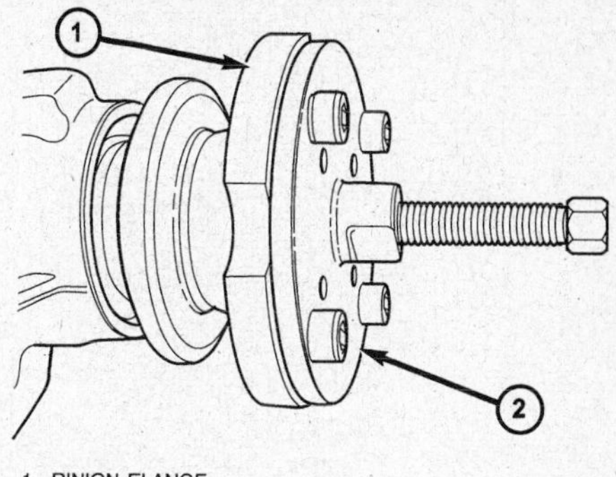

Fig. 3 Pinion flange puller

in the housing. Use pinion gauge set and dial indicator tool No. C-3339, or equivalent, to take measurements, **Fig. 18.**

1. Assemble pinion height block tool No. 6739, pinion block tool No. 8899, or equivalents, onto screw tool No. 6741, or equivalent, **Fig. 18.**
2. Insert assembled height gauge components, rear bearings and screw into housing through pinion bearings cups, **Fig. 19.**
3. Install front pinion bearing, then install cone nut tool No. 6740, or equivalent, hand tight.
4. Inspect tool rotating torque. Rotating torque should be 15–20 inch lbs.
5. Place arbor disc tool No. 6732 on arbor tool No. D-115-3, or equivalents, in position on housing side bearings cradles, **Fig. 20.**
6. Install differential bearings caps on arbor discs, then snug bearing cap bolts. Tighten bolts in a cross pattern to specifications.
7. Assemble dial indicator tool No. C-3339 into scooter block tool No. D-115-2, or equivalents, then secure set screw.
8. Position scooter block/dial indicator flush on pinion height block. Hold scooter block and zero dial indicator.
9. Slowly slide scooter block across pinion height block over to arbor, **Fig. 21.** Move scooter block till dial indicator crests arbor, then record highest reading.
10. Select shim equal to dial indicator reading.
11. Install select shim between rear pinion bearing and pinion gear head.

Differential Case Bearing Preload & Gear Backlash

Backlash is adjusted by moving the adjusters in and out or both. By moving the adjusters the case/ring gear will move closer or further away from pinion. In most cases this adjustment can be used to achieve the correct gear tooth pattern and set the case bearing preload.

1. Remove adjuster lock bolts and adjuster locks.
2. Loosen differential bearing caps.
3. Slide differential case toward pinion gear until gears make contact/zero backlash. If zero backlash cannot be obtained, turn pinion side adjuster until zero backlash is obtained.
4. Holding differential case toward pinion gear, then turn bearing adjusters with spanner wrench tool No. 8883, or equivalent, until they make contact with differential bearings/cups.
5. Back off ring gear side adjuster four holes to obtain initial ring gear backlash.
6. Install ring gear side adjuster lock and bolt. Do not tighten adjuster lock bolt at this time.
7. Tighten pinion gear side adjuster firmly against differential case bearing cup.
8. Rotate pinion several times to seat differential bearings.
9. Loosen pinion gear side adjuster until it is no longer in contact with bearing cup, then tighten it until it makes contact.
10. Tighten pinion gear side adjuster an additional six adjuster holes for new bearings or four adjuster holes for original bearings.
11. Install pinion gear side adjuster lock and bolt but do not tighten at this time.
12. Tighten bearing cap bolts to specifications.
13. Tighten adjuster lock bolts to specifications.
14. Measure ring gear backlash using dial indicator tool No. C-3339 and dial indicator stud tool No. L-4438, or equivalents, at eight points around drive side of ring gear. Backlash should be .003–.010 inch with preferred backlash of .005–.007 inch.
15. Backlash measurement should not vary more than .002 inch between measuring points. If measurement does vary, inspect gears for burrs, then the differential case flange and ring gear mounting.

Gear Tooth Contact Pattern

1. Wipe clean each tooth of ring gear, then apply gear marking compound to all ring gear teeth.
2. Verify bearing cap bolts are tightened to specifications.
3. Apply parking brakes to lightly create 10 ft. lbs., of pinion rotating torque.
4. Rotate pinion yoke four full revolutions in each direction.
5. Read gear tooth contact pattern as follows:
   a. Correct gear contact pattern, **Fig. 22.**
   b. Ring gear too far away from pinion gear, **Fig. 23.** Decrease backlash by moving ring closer to pinion gear using adjusters.
   c. Ring gear too close, **Fig. 24.** Increase backlash by moving ring away from pinion gear using adjusters.
   d. Ring gear too far away from pinion gear, **Fig. 25.** Decrease backlash by moving ring closer to pinion gear using adjusters.
   e. Ring gear too close to pinion gear, **Fig. 26.** Increase backlash by moving ring gear away from pinion using adjusters.
   f. Pinion gear is set too low, **Fig. 27.** Increase pinion gear height by increasing pinion depth shim thickness.
   g. Pinion gear is set too high, **Fig. 28.** Decrease pinion depth by decreasing pinion depth shim thickness.

ASSEMBLE

Pinion Gear, Ring Gear & Tone Ring

1. Install new front pinion bearing cup using installer tool No. 8960 and handle tool No. C-4171, or equivalents, **Fig. 29.**
2. Install new rear pinion bearing cup using installer tool No. 8959 and handle tool No. C-4171, or equivalents, **Fig. 30.**
3. Install pinion depth shim on pinion gear shaft, **Fig. 31.**
4. Install rear pinion bearing using installer tool No. MD-998805, or equivalent, and a suitable press.
5. Install new collapsible spacer, then lubricate pinion and bearings.

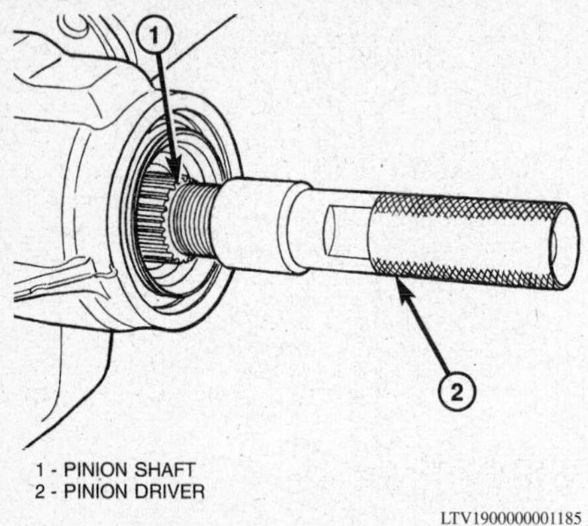

Fig. 4 Pinion driver

6. Install pinion into housing, then place front pinion bearing onto pinion shaft.
7. Draw pinion shaft into front bearing using installer tool No. 8981, or equivalent, **Fig. 32.**
8. Install new pinion seal using installer tool No. 8896 and handle tool No. C-4171, or equivalent.
9. Apply a light coat of teflon sealant to pinion flange splines.
10. Hold pinion and lightly tap pinion flange onto pinion until a few threads are showing.
11. Install pinion flange washer and new pinion nut.
12. Hold pinion flange with flange wrench tool No. 8979, then tighten nut until pinion end play is taken up.
13. Rotate pinion several times to seat bearings.
14. Measure pinion bearing rotating torque, then tighten pinion nut in small increments until rotating torque is within specifications.
15. Rotate pinion several times to verify pinion rotating torque.
16. Position ring gear on differential case, then install two new ring gear bolts.
17. Install remaining new ring gear bolts, then tighten alternately to seat ring gear.
18. Tighten ring gear bolts to specifications.
19. If exciter ring was removed, position differential assembly on plug tool No. 8888, or equivalent, then place exciter ring on differential.
20. Install exciter ring on differential case evenly using a hammer and a brass punch. Drive ring down until it is seated against ring gear.
21. Install differential into housing.
22. Verify ring gear backlash and gear contact pattern.
23. Ensure final rotating torque plus differential case bearing preload is within specifications.
24. Install axle shafts.

Standard Differential

If the same gears and thrust washers are being used, install them into their original locations.

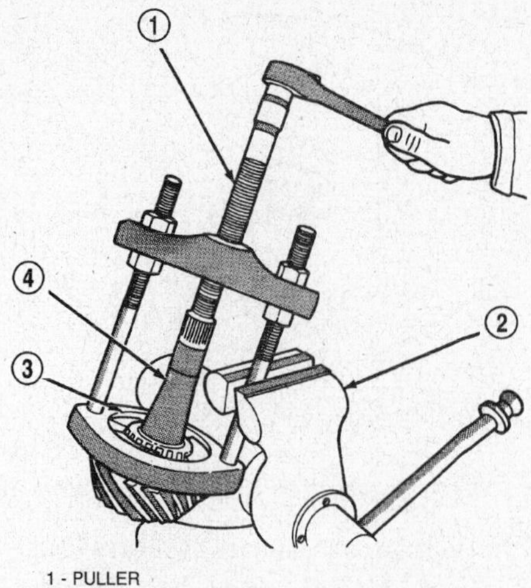

Fig. 5 Rear pinion bearing removal

1. Lubricate all differential components with axle lubricant.
2. Install differential side gears and thrust washers.
3. Install first pinion gear into differential window and side gears, then rotate gear to back of case.
4. Install other pinion gear and thrust washer, then rotate gears to align hole in pinion gears with hole in differential case.
5. Slide pinion shaft into case through pinion gears.
6. Tap pinion shaft to seat pinion shaft snap ring into case, **Fig. 33.**
7. Lubricate differential case bearings.
8. Install differential case with bearing cups into housing.
9. Install bearing caps and bolts finger tight. **Do not torque bearing cap bolts at this time.**
10. Slide differential case toward pinion gear until gears make contact/zero backlash.
11. If zero backlash cannot be obtained, turn pinion side adjuster until zero backlash is obtained.
12. Holding differential case toward pinion gear, turn bearing adjusters using spanner wrench tool No. 8883, or equivalent, until they make contact with differential bearings/cups.
13. Back off ring gear side adjuster four holes to obtain initial ring gear backlash.
14. Install ring gear side adjuster lock and bolt. Do not tighten adjuster lock bolt at this time.
15. Tighten pinion gear side adjuster firmly against differential case bearing cap.
16. Rotate pinion several times to seat differential bearings.

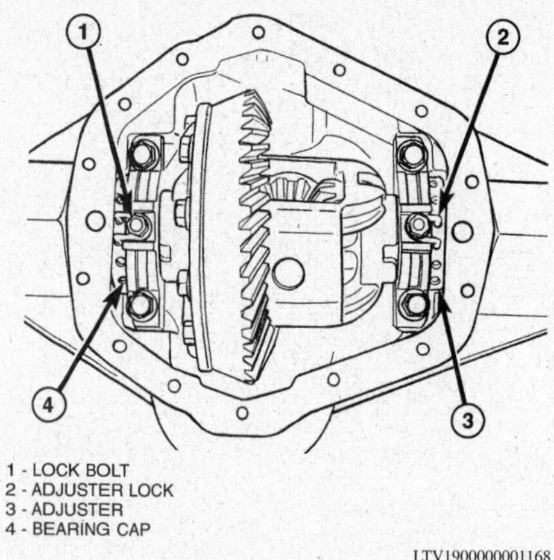

Fig. 6 Adjuster locks. Standard differential

17. Loosen pinion gear side adjuster until it is no longer in contact with bearing cup.
18. Tighten pinion gear side adjuster until it just makes contact with bearing cup.
19. Tighten pinion gear side adjuster an additional six holes for new bearings or four holes for original bearings.
20. Install pinion gear side adjuster lock and bolt. Do not tighten adjuster lock bolt at this time.
21. Tighten bearing cap bolts to specifications.
22. Tighten adjuster lock bolts to specifications.
23. Measure ring gear backlash and inspect gear tooth contact pattern as outlined under "Adjustments."
24. Install axle shafts.
25. Install differential housing gasket and cover.

Trac-Rite Differential

Install all components in their original locations.

1. Lubricate all gears and differential bores with differential lubricant.
2. Install one set of pinion brake shoes into case bores. Brake shoes can be installed upside down, but if installed wrong pinion gear will not fit.
3. Install side gear thrust washer, side gear and spacer, **Fig. 34.**
4. Install one set of pinion gears into bores next to brake shoes with pinion shaft facing up.
5. Install other side gear and thrust washer.
6. Install other set of pinion gears into brake shoes in case.
7. Install other set of brake shoes onto pinion gear shafts.
8. Install differential cover and location screws.
9. Install new ring gear bolts.

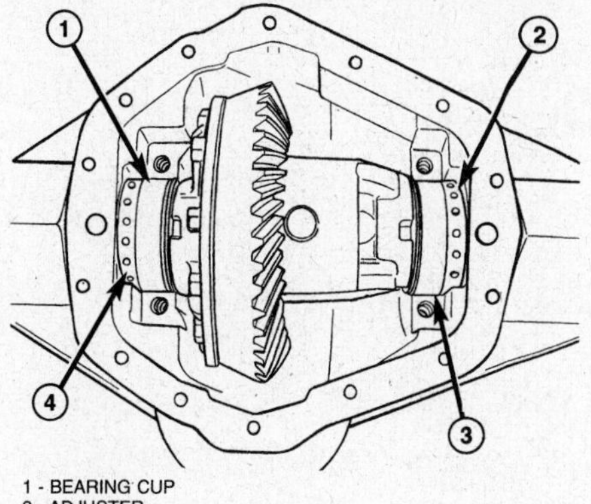

Fig. 7 Bearing adjusters. Standard differential

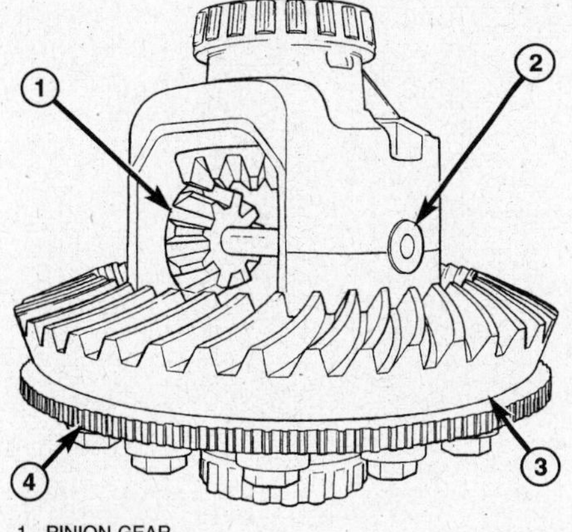

Fig. 8 Pinion shaft. Standard differential

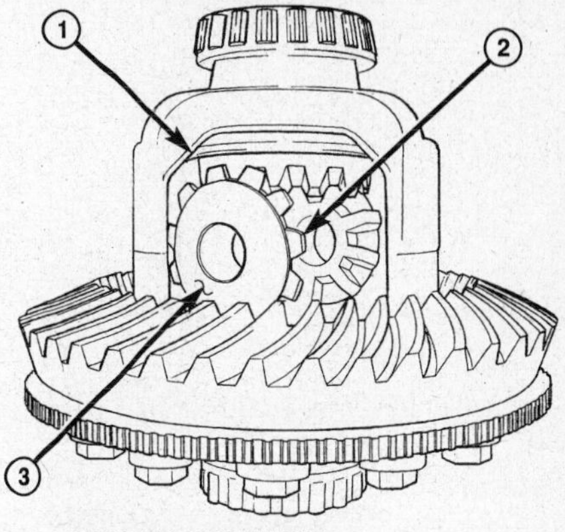

Fig. 9 Pinion gear. Standard differential

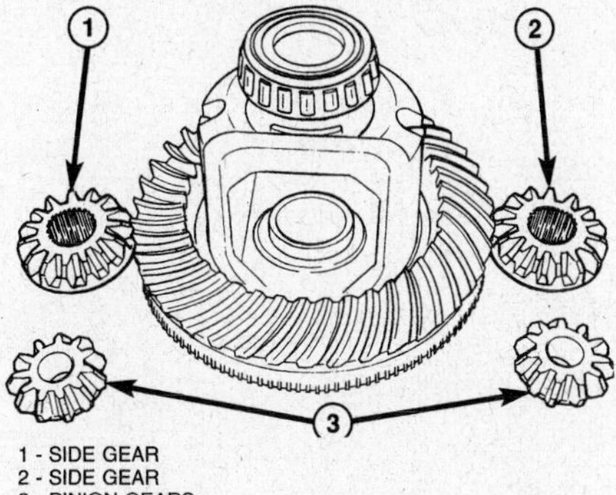

Fig. 10 Differential side gears. Standard differential

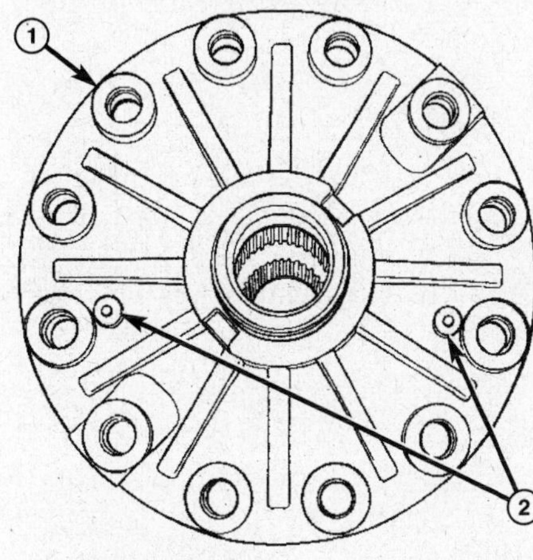

Fig. 11 Differential case cover locating screws. Trac-Rite differential

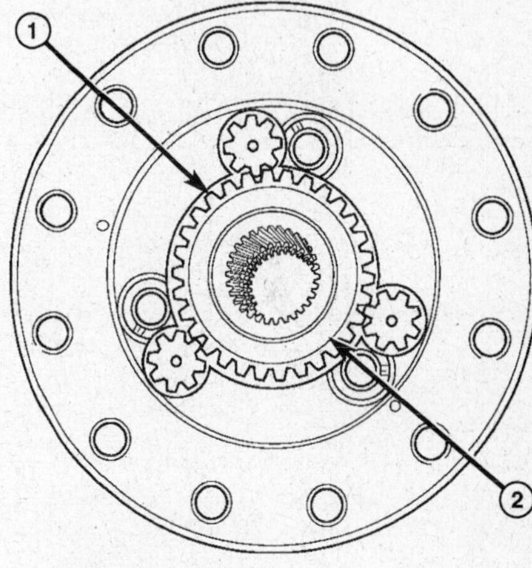

Fig. 12 Side gear & thrust washer. Trac-Rite differential

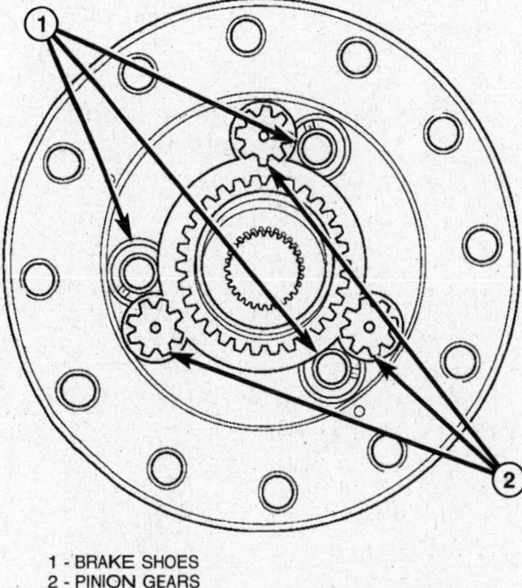

Fig. 13 Pinion brake shoes. Trac-Rite differential

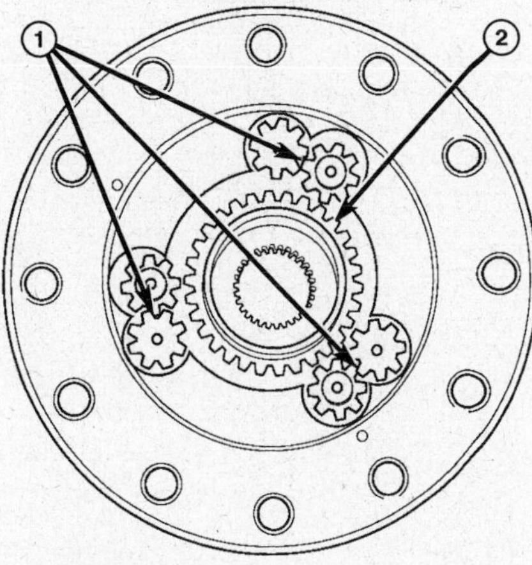

Fig. 14 Pinion gears. Trac-Rite differential

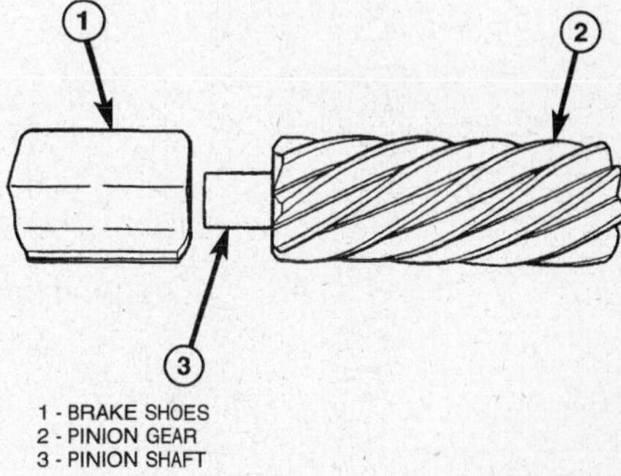

Fig. 15 Pinion gear & brake shoe. Trac-Rite differential

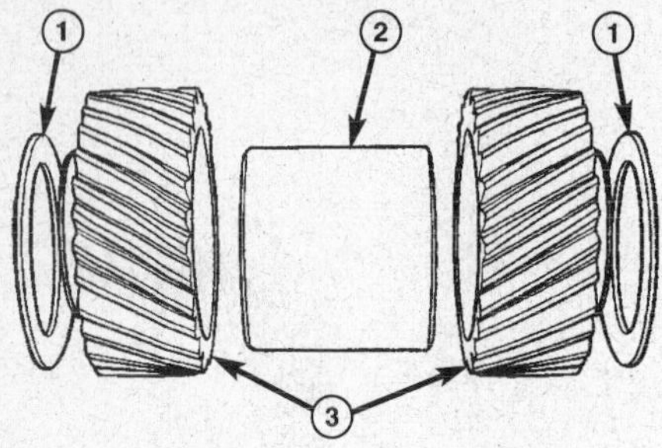
1 - THRUST WASHERS
2 - SPACER
3 - SIDE GEARS

LTV1900000001179

Fig. 16 Side gears. Trac-Rite differential

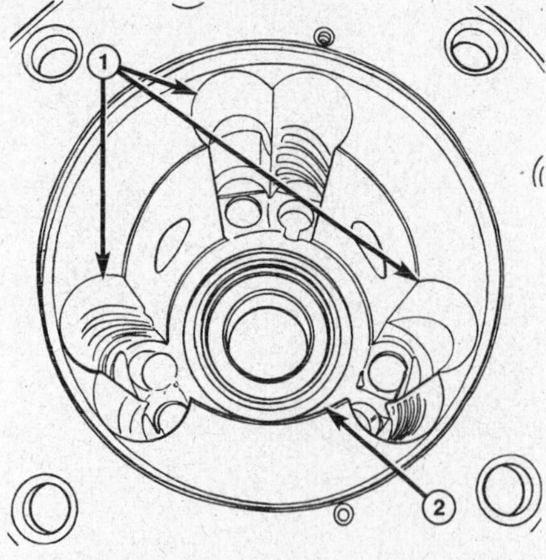
1 - PINION BORES
2 - SIDE GEAR BORE

LTV1900000001180

Fig. 17 Pinion/side gear bore. Trac-Rite Differential

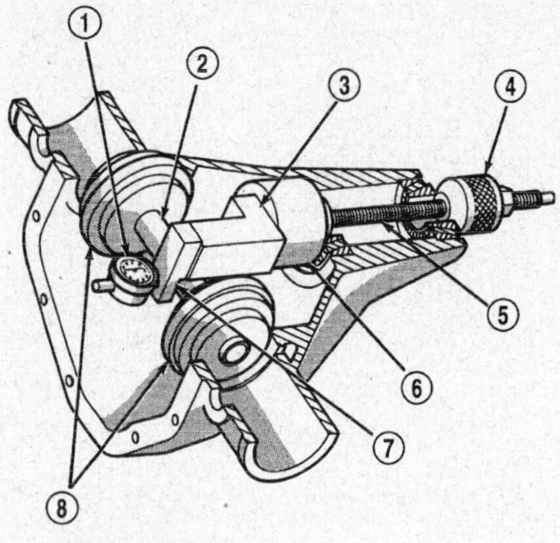
1 - DIAL INDICATOR
2 - ARBOR
3 - PINION HEIGHT BLOCK
4 - CONE
5 - SCREW
6 - PINION BLOCK
7 - SCOOTER BLOCK
8 - ARBOR DISC

LTV1900000001191

Fig. 18 Pinion gear depth gauge tools

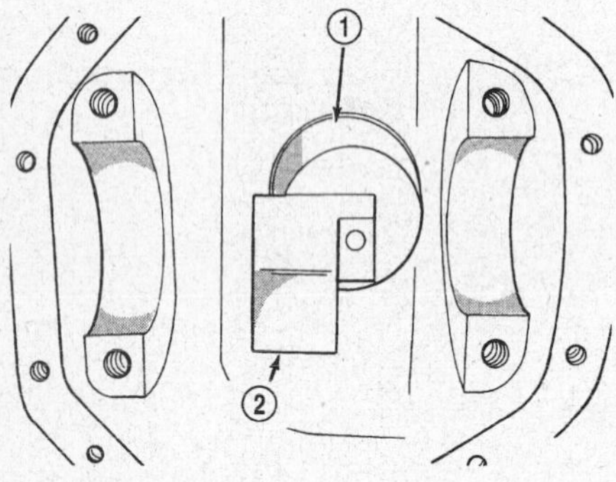
1 - PINION BLOCK
2 - PINION HEIGHT BLOCK

LTV1900000001192

Fig. 19 Pinion height block

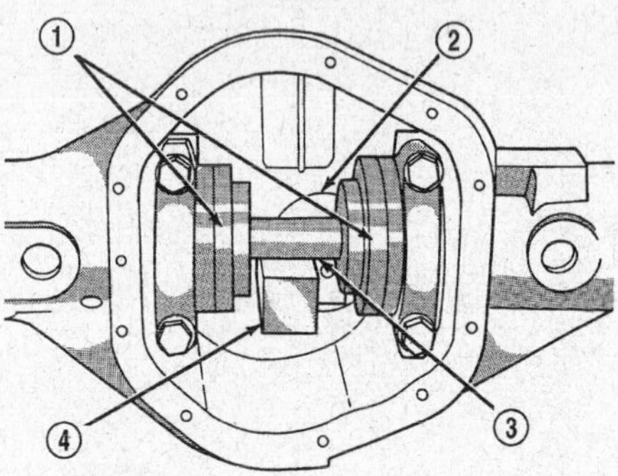
1 - ARBOR DISC
2 - PINION BLOCK
3 - ARBOR
4 - PINION HEIGHT BLOCK

LTV1900000001193

Fig. 20 Gauge tools in housing

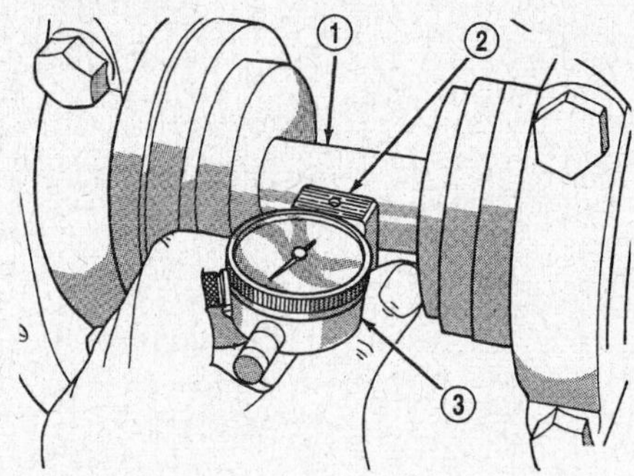
1 - ARBOR
2 - SCOOTER BLOCK
3 - DIAL INDICATOR

LTV1900000001194

Fig. 21 Pinion gear depth measurement

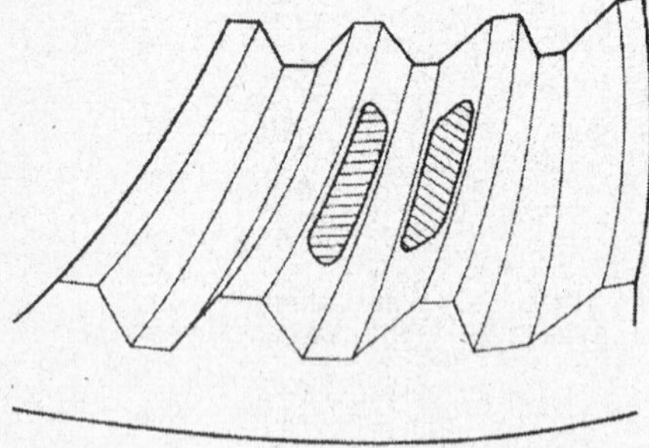
LTV1900000001195

Fig. 22 Correct contact pattern

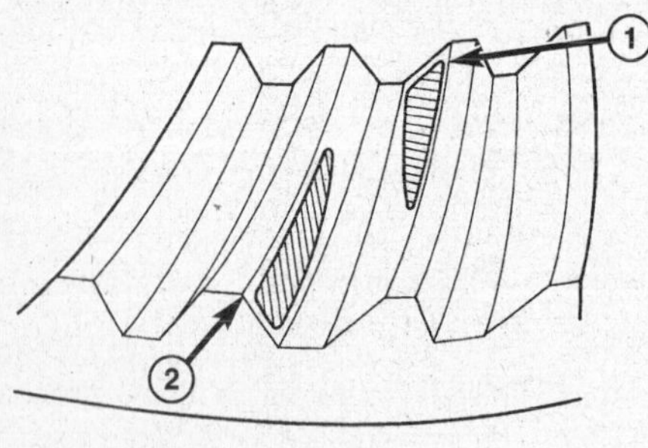
1 - COAST SIDE TOE
2 - DRIVE SIDE HEEL

LTV1900000001196

Fig. 23 Ring gear too far way

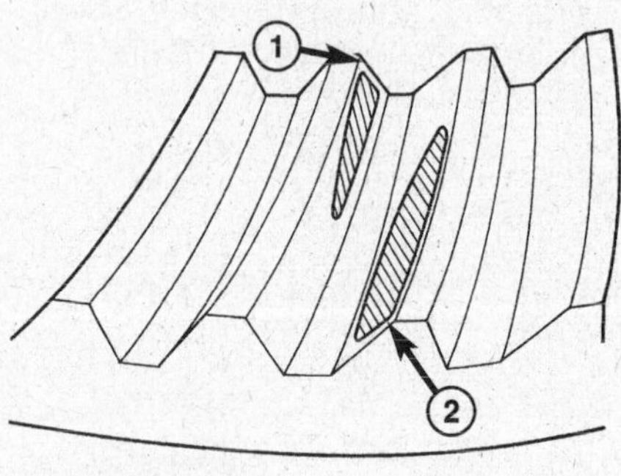
1 - DRIVE SIDE TOE
2 - COAST SIDE HEEL

LTV1900000001197

Fig. 24 Ring gear too close

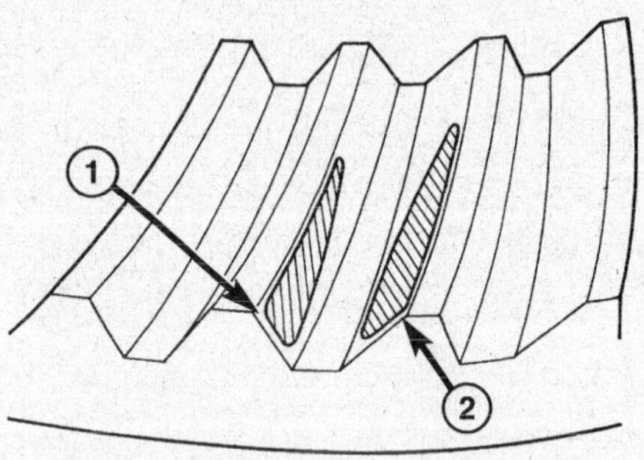
1 - DRIVE SIDE HEEL
2 - COAST SIDE HEEL

LTV1900000001198

Fig. 25 Ring gear too far away

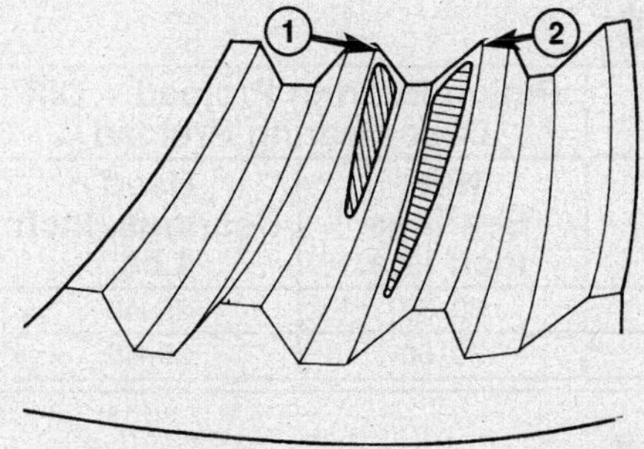

Fig. 26 Ring gear too close

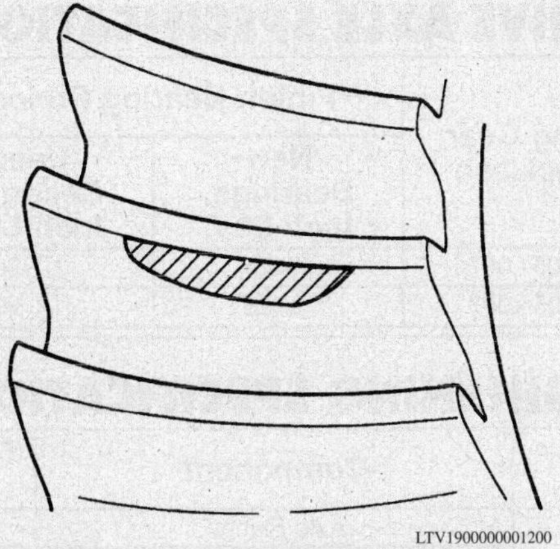

Fig. 27 Low pinion height

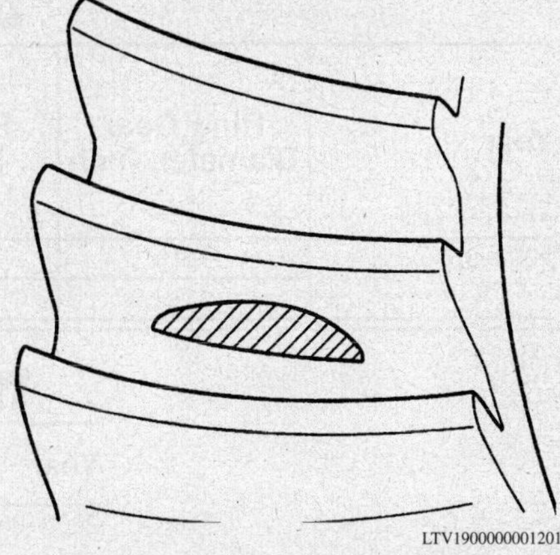

Fig. 28 High pinion height

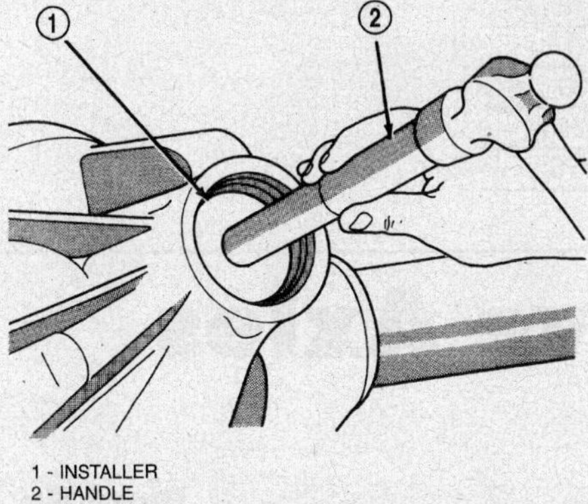

Fig. 29 Front pinion bearing cup

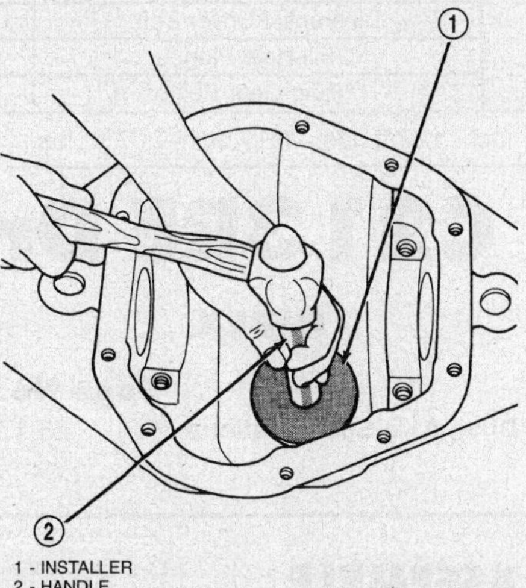

Fig. 30 Rear pinion bearing cup

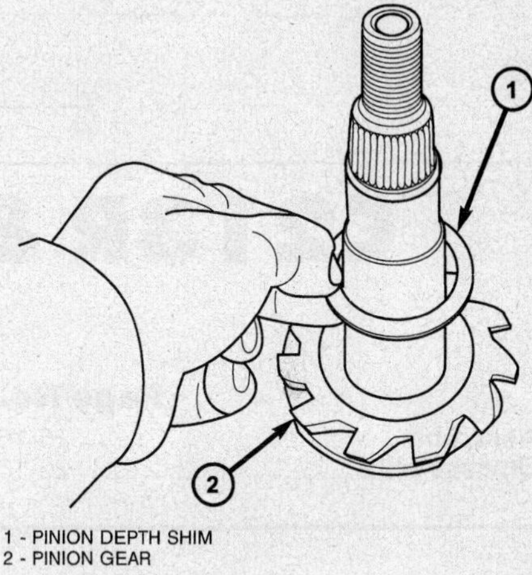

Fig. 31 Pinion depth shim

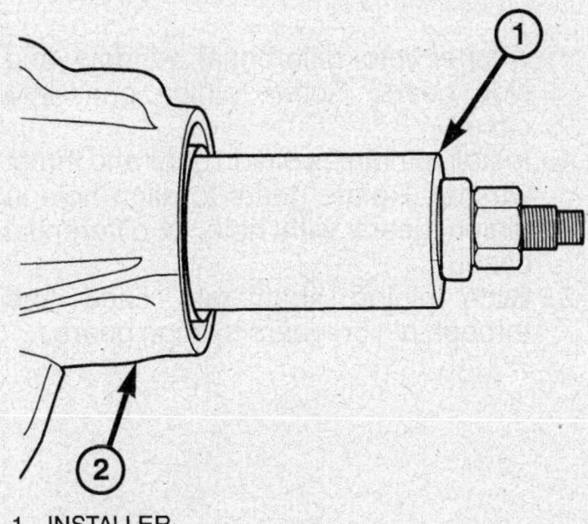

Fig. 32 Pinion gear installer

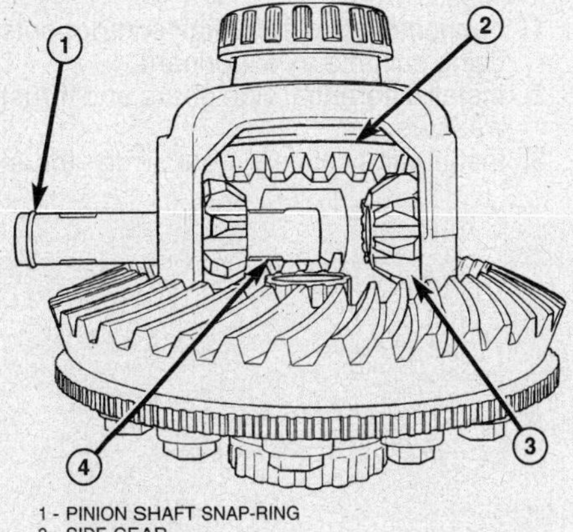

Fig. 33 Pinion shaft installation

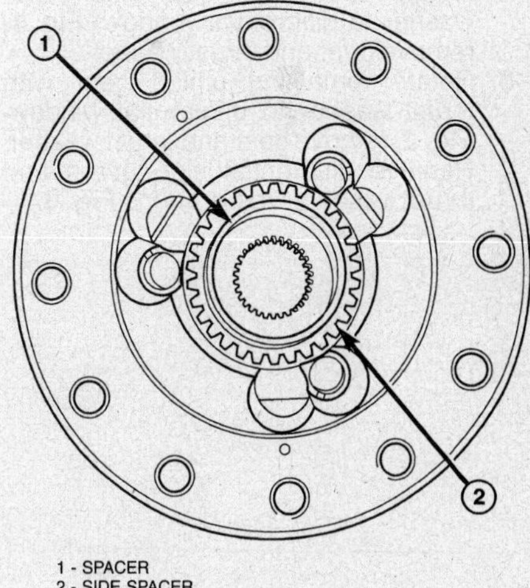

Fig. 34 Side gear & spacer. Trac-Rite differential

DRIVE AXLE SPECIFICATIONS

Year	Ring Gear Diameter, Inch	Ring Gear Backlash	Pinion Bearing Preload		Pinion Bearing Preload + Diff Case Bearing Preload	
			New Bearings, Inch Lbs.	Used Bearings, Inch Lbs.	New Bearings, Inch Lbs.	Used Bearings, Inch Lbs.
2003–06	10½	.005–.007	15–25	10–20	30–50	25–45
	11½	.005–.007	15–25	10–20	30–50	25–45

TIGHTENING SPECIFICATIONS

Year	Component	Torque Ft. Lbs.
2003–06	Axle Flange	95
	Axle Lock Bolt	18
	Bearing Cap Bolt	①
	Differential Cover Bolt	30
	Fill Hole Plug	24
	Ring Gear Bolt	175

① — 10½ inch, 122 ft. lbs.; 11½ inch, 207 ft. lbs.

C213R & C213RE Drive Axles

INDEX

DISASSEMBLE

1. Remove pinion mate shaft.
2. Rotate one pinion gear with thrust washer to differential window, **Fig. 1,** remove gear and thrust washer.
3. Rotate remaining pinion gear with thrust washer to differential window, **Fig. 2,** remove gear and thrust washer.
4. Remove differential side gears and thrust washers Nos. 1 and 2, **Fig. 3.**

ASSEMBLE

If same gears and thrust washwers are being used, install them into their original locations.

1. Lubricate all differential components using suitable axle lubricant.
2. Install differential side gears and thrust washers.
3. Install first pinion gear with thrust washer into differential window and side gears. Rotate pinion gear into case.
4. Install remaining pinion gear and thrust washer. Rotate gears to align hole in pinion gears with hole in differential case.
5. Slide pinion shaft into case and through pinion gears to align gears.

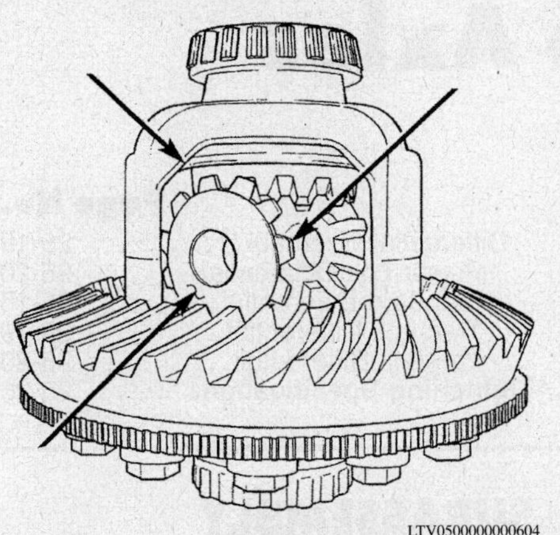

Fig. 1 Gear & thrust washer removal A

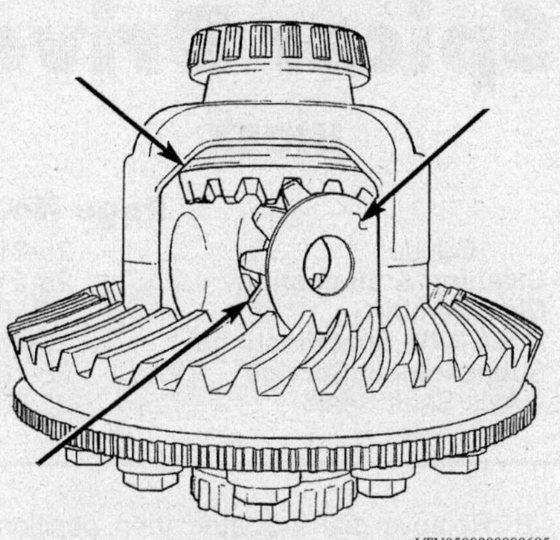

Fig. 2 Gear & thrust washer removal B

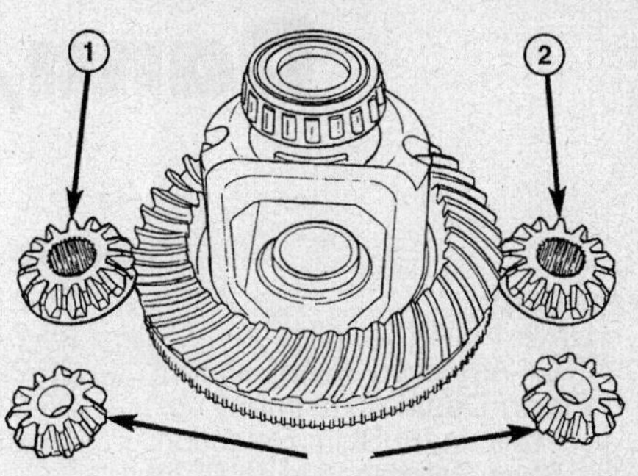

Fig. 3 Differential side gears & thrust washer removal

DRIVE AXLE SPECIFICATIONS

Model	Year	Ring Gear Diameter, Inch	Ring Gear Backlash, Inch	Pinion Gear Depth	Pinion Bearing Preload, Inch	Differential Bearing Preload	Side Gear Clearance	Case Runout, Inch
C213R & C213RE	2005–06	8.25	.005–.008	—	①	—	—	.003

① — Original bearings, 10–20 inch lbs.; New bearings, 15–35 inch lbs.

TIGHTENING SPECIFICATIONS

Year	Component	Torque Ft. Lbs
2005–06	Adjuster Lock Screw	96①
	Axle Flange Nuts	88
	Bearing Cap Bolts	100
	Differential Cover Bolts	30
	Pinion Nut Minimum	210
	Pinion Shaft Lock Screw	19
	Ring Gear Bolts	75

① — Inch lbs.

Dana/Spicer Drive Axles

INDEX

DISASSEMBLE

1. Raise and support vehicle, then disconnect propeller shaft from companion flange.
2. Remove differential housing cover, **Fig. 1,** then drain lubricant into suitable container and remove axle shafts as outlined in service section.
3. Remove RWAL brake sensor bolt and pull sensor from differential housing.
4. Clean housing and inner components, then inspect the following assembly adjustments to aid diagnosis and reassembly. Refer to "Final Assembly & Adjustment" for actual inspection procedures.
   a. Inspect ring gear and pinion tooth contact pattern using suitable marking compound. If contact pattern is not centered, inspect for improper backlash or pinion installation during inspection.
   b. Measure ring gear runout using suitable dial indicator. If runout exceeds .006 inch, inspect for improper ring gear mounting or faulty ring gear and/or case during inspection.
   c. Inspect ring gear and pinion backlash using suitable dial indicator. If gear set is to be reused, and contact pattern is acceptable, backlash should be adjusted to original value during final assembly to maintain established tooth contact.
   d. Inspect clearance between bearing and bearing cap, prying against case. If a .003 inch feeler gauge can be inserted between race and cap, inspect for spun side bearings.
5. Mark and remove differential bearing caps.
6. Install suitable case spreader and dial indicator on housing as outlined in **Fig. 2,** preloading indicator approximately ½ revolution. **Ensure mounting dowels are fully seated in housing and clamps are securing spreader in proper position.**
7. Zero dial indicator, then rotate spreader screw to spread housing .015 inch. **Do not spread housing more than .015 inch, as housing may become permanently distorted.**
8. Remove dial indicator, then position pry bars under ring gear bolt head and under differential case and remove differential assembly. **Remove spreader tool immediately after removing differential to avoid possibility of distorting housing or causing it to take a set.**
9. Measure pinion rotating torque (bearing preload) using suitable torque wrench. If preload is not within specifications, or if endplay is present, pinion must be disassembled for inspection.
10. Remove and discard pinion nut using suitable tool, **Figs. 3 and 4.**
11. Remove companion flange with suitable puller, then pry pinion seal from housing.
12. Remove dust cap from pinion gear, if equipped, then the pinion gear. Strike end of gear with a rawhide hammer to force pinion out of pinion rear bearing and housing. **Pinion bearing preload adjusting shims may remain on pinion shaft, stick to bearing remaining in housing or fall out. Tag and retain shims for assembly.**
13. Remove front bearing, seal, gasket and slinger from housing, as equipped.
14. **On model 194 and 198 axles,** remove pinion rear bearing as follows:
    a. Install bearing remover set No. J29721, or equivalent, on bearing and gear.
    b. Insert bearing remover adapters into remover base from top and position adapters 180° apart.
    c. Tighten remover tool forcing screw and remove bearing.
15. **On model 216 and 226 axles,** remove pinion rear bearing as follows:
    a. Install bearing removal tool Nos. J22921-1 or J23674, or equivalents, between bearing and pinion gear.
    b. Press bearing to remove.
16. **On model 248, 267 and 286 axles,** remove pinion rear bearing as outlined, **Fig. 5.**
17. **On all models,** inspect components as outlined in "Cleaning & Inspection" keeping components in order, and replace as needed. **Components that are to be reused must be installed in original position to ensure proper operation.**

SUBASSEMBLY SERVICE

Differential Overhaul

STANDARD DIFFERENTIAL

MODELS 194, 216, 226 & 248

1. Support differential case and remove and discard ring gear bolts, **Figs. 1, 6 and 7.**
2. Remove ring gear from case, tapping with soft faced hammer. **Do not pry gear from case as mounting surfaces will be damaged.**
3. Drive out pin securing differential pinion shaft, then remove shaft.
4. Rotate side gear to roll differential pinions from case, and remove pinions and thrust washers, noting installation position for assembly.
5. Remove side gears and thrust washers from case, noting installation position.
6. Remove differential case side bearings using tools outlined, **Fig. 8.**
7. Coat all components with specified lubricant prior to assembly. **Components that are to be reused should be installed in original position to ensure proper operation.**
8. Install side gears along with thrust washers in respective sides of case.
9. Install thrust washers on differential pinions using grease to adhere washers.
10. Position pinion assemblies in case 180° apart, then roll pinions into alignment with pinion shaft bores, ensuring thrust washers are in place.
11. Insert pinion shaft, aligning lockpin hole with hole in case, then secure shaft with new lockpin.
12. Support differential case, install ring gear and new ring gear bolts, then seat ring gear on case with suitable mallet.
13. Evenly tighten ring gear bolts to specifications.

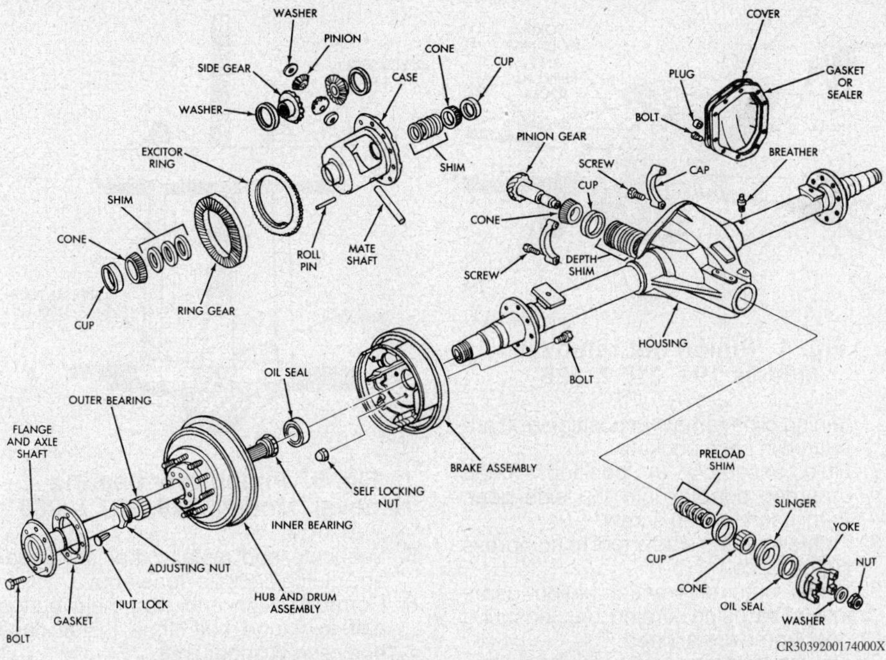

Fig. 1 Exploded view of models 248, 267 & 286

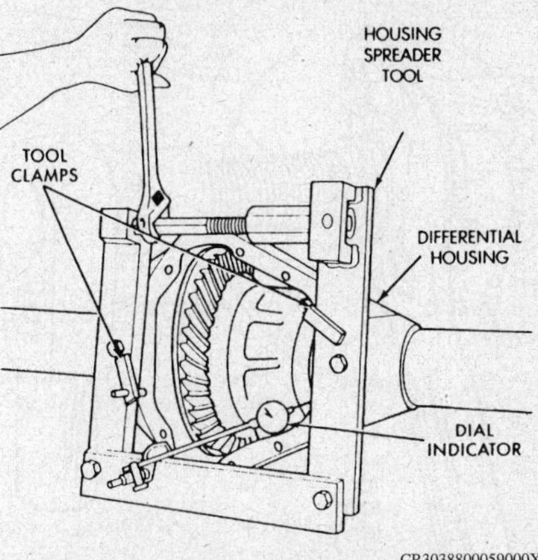

Fig. 2 Case spreader installation

14. Install differential side bearing using tools outlined, **Fig. 9.**
15. Install spreader tool and dial indicator on axle housing and spread case .015 inch as outlined during disassembly, then remove dial indicator. **Do not spread housing more than .015 inch as housing will be damaged. Leave spreader tool installed only long enough to perform required service to prevent permanent distortion.**
16. Mount differential in housing, install bearing caps, and tighten cap bolts hand tight, then remove spreader if installed.
17. Mount suitable dial indicator on housing with plunger bearing against back of ring gear, **Fig. 10.**
18. Pry differential case as far away from indicator as possible, inserting suitable lever between bearing race and housing.
19. Ensure indicator plunger is still in contact with gear, then zero indicator.
20. Pry differential toward indicator, as far as possible, then record dial indicator reading. **Repeat steps 19 through 21 until same reading is obtained each time. Recorded reading indicates shim thickness required to take up clearance between side bearings and housing. Shim pack thickness to be placed on bearing hubs between side bearings and case will be determined during "Final Assembly & Adjustment."**
21. Remove dial indicator, bearing caps and differential assembly from housing, keeping side bearing races in proper position for assembly.

MODELS 267 & 286

1. Support differential case and remove and discard ring gear bolts.
2. Remove ring gear from case, tapping with soft faced hammer. **Do not pry gear from case as mounting surfaces will be damaged.**
3. Drive out pin securing differential pinion shaft, then remove shaft.
4. Rotate side gear to roll differential pinions from case, and remove pinions and thrust washers, noting installation position for assembly.
5. Remove side gears and thrust washers from case, noting installation position.
6. Remove differential bearings using bearing removal tool Nos. DD-914-P, DD-914-8, DD-914-62, DD-914-7 and DD-914-42, or equivalents. Ensure adapter rings do not cause force on bearing races.
7. Coat all components with specified lubricant prior to assembly. **Components that are to be reused should be installed in original position to ensure proper operation.**
8. Install side gears along with thrust washers in respective sides of case.
9. Install thrust washers on differential pinions using grease to adhere washers.
10. Position pinion assemblies in case 180° apart, then roll pinions into alignment with pinion shaft bores, ensuring thrust washers are in place.
11. Insert pinion shaft, aligning lockpin hole with hole in case, then secure shaft with new lockpin.
12. Support differential case, install ring gear and new ring gear bolts, then seat ring gear on case with suitable mallet.
13. Evenly tighten ring gear bolts to specifications.
14. Place master gauge bearings tool No. D117, or equivalent, on case hubs.
15. Install spreader tool and dial indicator on axle housing and spread case .015 inch as outlined during disassembly, then remove dial indicator. **Do not spread housing more than .015 inch as housing will be damaged. Leave spreader tool installed only long enough to perform required service to prevent permanent distortion.**
16. Mount differential in housing, install bearing caps, and tighten cap bolts hand tight and remove spreader if installed.
17. Mount suitable dial indicator on housing with plunger bearing against back of ring gear, **Fig. 10.**
18. Pry differential case as far away from indicator as possible, inserting suitable lever between bearing race and housing.
19. Ensure indicator plunger is still in contact with gear, then zero indicator.
20. Pry differential toward indicator, as far as possible, then record dial indicator reading. **Repeat steps 18 through 20 until same reading is obtained each time. Recorded reading indicates shim thickness required to take up clearance between side bearings and housing. Shim pack thickness to be placed on bearing hubs between side bearings and case will be determined during "Final Assembly & Adjustment."**
21. Remove dial indicator, bearing caps and differential assembly from housing, keeping side bearing races in proper position for assembly.

TRAC-LOK DIFFERENTIAL

DISASSEMBLE

1. Mount one axle shaft in a vise with splined end facing upward. Do not allow end of shaft to extend more than 2¾ inch above top of vise, **Fig. 11.** This prevents shaft from fully entering side gear.
2. Mount differential case on axle shaft with ring gear bolt heads facing upward.
3. Remove ring gear bolts.
4. Loosen ring gear with a mallet.
5. Remove case from axle shaft, then the ring gear.
6. Remount differential case on axle shaft, then remove pinion gear mate shaft retaining roll pin.

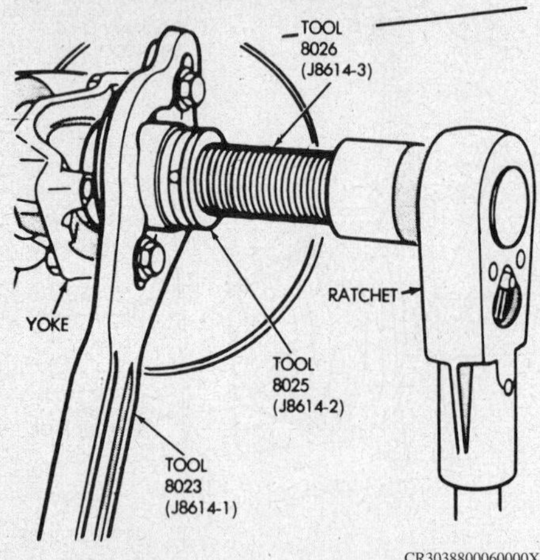

Fig. 3 Pinion nut & yoke removal. Models 194, 216 & 226

7. Remove pinion mate shaft with a suitable drift and hammer, **Fig. 12.The gear rotating tool No. J-23781, or equivalent, is required to perform following steps. Tool consists of three components: gear rotating tool, forcing screw and step plate.**
8. Install step plate in lower differential side gear.
9. Assemble threaded adapter into top side gear. Thread forcing screw into adapter until it becomes centered in adapter plate.
10. Position a screwdriver in slot of threaded adapter. This will prevent adapter from turning.
11. Tighten forcing screw tool enough to relieve clutch pack tension, then remove both pinion thrust washers.
12. Loosen forcing screw tool until clutch pack tension is relieved.
13. Insert turning bar in case. Rotate case with tool until pinion gears can be removed. Remove tools from case.
14. Remove top side gear and clutch pack, **Fig. 13.** Keep plates in correct order during removal.
15. Remove case from holding fixture. Remove remaining clutch pack.
16. Remove clutch pack retaining clips. Mark each clutch pack for installation reference.

ASSEMBLE

1. Lubricate differential gear teeth, thrust faces, splines and clutch discs and plates.
2. Assemble clutch packs, placing discs and plates in original position. Then, install retainer clips, **Fig. 12.**
3. Mount differential case on axle shaft.
4. Install clutch packs on differential side gears, then install one assembly in lower bore of case, **Fig. 14.** Ensure clutch pack retaining clips remain in position and are seated in case pockets.
5. Install step plate tool on clutch pack assembly. Apply a small amount of grease to centering hole of step plate.
6. Install remaining clutch pack and side gear, **Fig. 15.** Ensure clutch pack retaining clips remain in position and are seated in case pockets.

Fig. 4 Pinion nut removal. Models 194, 216 & 226

7. Hold assembly in position. Insert threaded adapter into top side gear, then insert forcing screw.
8. Tighten forcing screw tool to compress clutch discs.
9. Install both differential pinion gears into case using turning bar, ensuring gear bores are aligned.
10. Tighten forcing screw to compress conned plates. Install pinion gear thrust washers using a small screwdriver.
11. Remove threaded adapter, forcing screw, turning bar and step plate.
12. Install mate shaft into differential case, **Fig. 16,** then secure mate shaft with new roll pin. Stake roll pin to differential case.
13. Remove case from axle shaft.
14. Install ring gear as outlined for standard differential.

POWER-LOK DIFFERENTIAL

DISASSEMBLE

1. Mark case halves for installation reference.
2. Remove case retaining bolts, then remove button cover half, **Fig. 17.**
3. Remove pinion mate gear, side gear (clutch) ring and clutch pack shaft, **Fig. 18.** Keep these components with button cover half for correct installation.
4. Remove pinion mate gear, side gear (clutch) ring and clutch pack shaft, **Fig. 18.** Keep these components with flange cover half for correct installation.

ASSEMBLE

1. Mount one axle shaft in a vise with splined end facing upward. Do not allow end of shaft to extend more than 3 inches above top of vise, **Fig. 11.**
2. Assemble clutch packs into side gear plate in same position as removed.
3. Align plate ears and install assembled pack into flange half, **Fig. 19.** Ensure clutch plate lugs enter slots in case. Also ensure clutch pack bottoms out on case.
4. Install pinion mate shafts and pinion mate gears. Ensure shafts are correctly installed according to alignment marks.

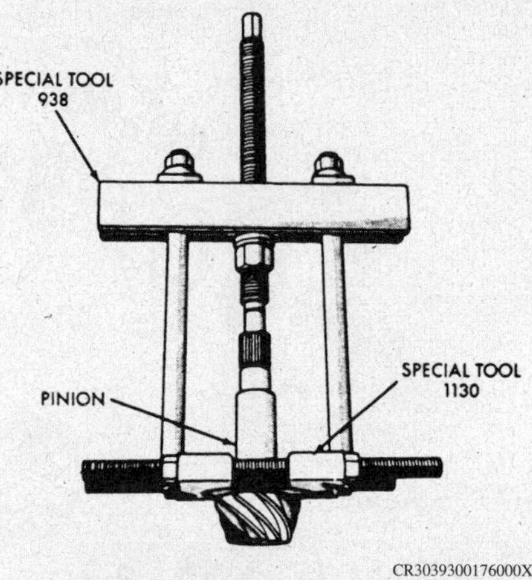

Fig. 5 Pinion rear bearing removal. Models 248, 267 & 286

5. Lubricate and install other side gear and clutch pack as done above.
6. Correctly align and assemble button half to flange half, then install case body screw finger tight.
7. Place case assembly onto axle shaft fixture. Install another axle shaft into opposite side gear. **Torque** case bolts alternately and evenly to 65–70 ft. lbs. Both axle shafts must be inserted fully on each side to align both splines. If bolt heads have seven radial lines stamped on head, **torque** these to 90–100 ft. lbs.
8. Remove differential assembly from axle shaft. Ensure pinion mate cross shaft is tight on ramp, clearance should not exceed .010 inch, being equal at all four shaft ends.

VARI-LOK DIFFERENTIAL

PLENUM

1. Remove bearing from ring gear side of differential case using tools outlined, **Fig. 20.**
2. Remove plenum from differential case hub. **Do not touch tuning reed under plenum. The metal is very sensitive and the unit will not operate properly if the reed valve is disturbed.**
3. Reverse procedure to install, noting the following:
   a. Install plenum with rubber seal toward differential case and raised metal tabs away from case.
   b. Install differential side bearing using tools outlined, **Fig. 21.**

Axle Shaft Seals

1. Remove hub bearings and axle shafts as outlined under "Disassemble."
2. Remove axle shaft seal from differential housing.
3. Clean inside perimeter of differential housing with fine crocus cloth or equivalent.
4. Reverse procedure to install using seal installer tool Nos. 5041–2, 8417, and 8411 or equivalents, **Fig. 22.**

CLEANING & INSPECTION

1. Wash all components in a suitable solvent and blow dry with compressed air, noting the following:
   a. Do not use a brush when cleaning bearings.
   b. Do not "spin dry" bearings, as they will be damaged.
   c. Lightly lubricate components after cleaning to retard corrosion.
   d. Keep all components in order to ensure proper assembly.
2. Inspect gears for cracks, chipped or broken teeth, wear or scoring. Replace gears that are damaged or excessively worn. **Ring gear and pinion must be replaced as an assembly. If differential pinions are faulty, they should be replaced as a set along with pinion shaft, not individually, to maintain proper backlash.**
3. Inspect RWAL exciter ring if equipped, for damage or distortion. Ring gear must be removed before exciter ring can be removed. Heat replacement exciter ring with a heat lamp or place in hot fluid, then position ring on differential case adjacent to flange.
4. Inspect differential case for cracks, damage, distortion, and worn or scored side gear bores and bearing surfaces. Replace case if damaged or scored.
5. Inspect axle housing for scored bearing mounting surfaces, cracks and distortion. Ensure housing is clean and free from foreign material.
6. Inspect bearing rollers and races for pitting, scoring, overheating and damage.
7. Mate each bearing with race and inspect operation.
8. Replace any bearing assembly that is damaged, excessively worn, or that fails to operate smoothly.
9. Inspect thrust washers and pinion shaft, and replace if damaged or worn.
10. Mount differential case in housing, adjust side bearings for zero preload and inspect runout using a suitable dial indicator, **Fig. 23.**
11. Replace case if ring gear mounting flange runout exceeds specification.

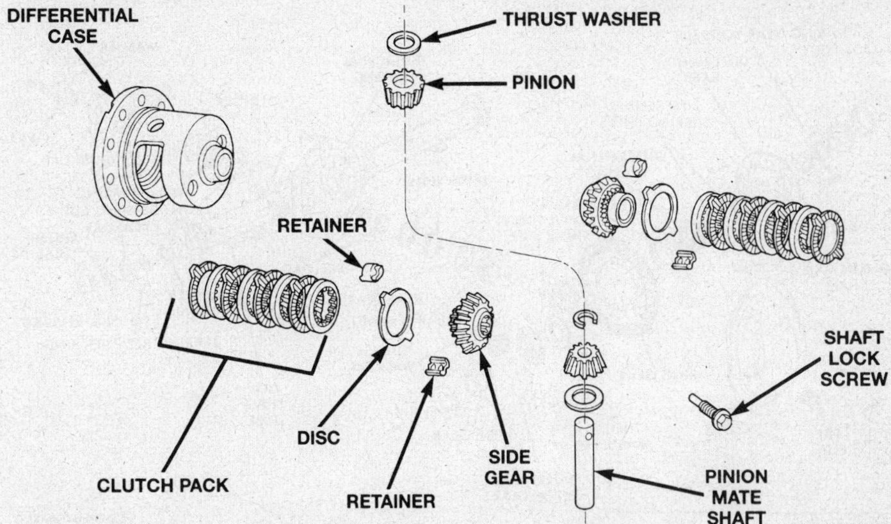

Fig. 6 Exploded view of differential. Model 194

ASSEMBLE

Pinion Depth Adjustment

If original ring gear and pinion, rear pinion bearing and housing are reused, original pinion depth adjusting shims can be reused to adjust pinion depth. However, if gear set, rear pinion bearing or housing are replaced, pinion depth adjusting shims must be selected in order to establish proper ring gear and pinion tooth contact. Several types of pinion depth gauging tools are available from a variety of manufacturers, and manufacturer's recommendations as to component selection and installation must be followed when using any depth gauging assembly. Procedures outlined use gauge tool set No. D-116, or equivalent, **Fig. 24,** or set No. 6730 and dial indicator tool No. C-3339, or equivalents. If no pinion depth gauge is available, preliminary shims can be selected as outlined, and final shim selection can be determined by performing gear tooth contact inspection outlined under "Final Assembly & Adjustment."

PRELIMINARY SHIM SELECTION

1. Inspect face of both new and old drive pinion for pinion depth modification code, **Fig. 25.** To ensure proper contact of ring gear and pinion teeth, pinion may be marked with a plus (+) or minus (–) code number. This number indicates in thousandths of an inch required modifications of nominal pinion depth. It is essential that this code number be factored when selecting pinion depth adjusting shims.
2. Measure thickness of shim pack removed from behind rear pinion bearing race and record thickness.
3. Refer to chart, **Fig. 26,** and select preliminary shim pack thickness by adding or subtracting indicated value from thickness of original shims. **If baffle is installed in assembly, thickness of baffle must be included in shim pack.**
4. Install selected shim pack behind rear pinion race as outlined in assembly procedures, then perform tooth contact inspection.
5. Adjust pinion shim thickness as needed, to obtain proper tooth contact.

SHIM SELECTION USING DEPTH GAUGE

1. Install master pinion block into pinion bore in housing, **Fig. 27.**
2. Install side bearing discs on arbor, then mount arbor assembly in housing ensuring arbor is centered and discs are seated in bearing bores.
3. Position pinion height block on pinion block and against arbor, **Fig. 28.**
4. Install gauge block and dial indicator on small step of pinion height block, ensuring gauge assembly is flat on height block, then zero dial indicator.
5. With dial indicator at zero, move gauge so that indicator plunger contacts arbor.
6. Move gauge assembly back and forth, recording indicator reading at highest point of contact. **Repeat steps 4 and 5 several times to ensure accurate reading.**
7. Indicator reading obtained in step 6 is proper shim thickness for "nominal" pinion.
8. Inspect face of drive pinion for modification code, outlined in preliminary shim selection and select pinion depth adjusting shims as follows:
   a. If pinion depth code is a plus (+) number, subtract that number of thousandths from dimension obtained in step 6 and select shim pack equal to remainder.
   b. If pinion depth code is a minus (–) number, add that number of thousandths to dimension obtained in step 6 and select shim pack equal to sum. **If baffle or oil slinger is used, thickness of these components must be included in shim pack.**

Drive Pinion Installation

1. Install selected pinion depth adjusting shims in rear pinion bearing bore in housing, then seat rear bearing race in housing using suitable driver.
2. Install front bearing race in housing using suitable driver.
3. Install oil slinger, if used, then press rear bearing onto pinion.
4. Insert pinion into housing, then install front bearing, oil slinger (if used), companion flange washer and nut. **Do not install preload shims or oil seal at this time.**
5. Ensure bearings are lubricated, then

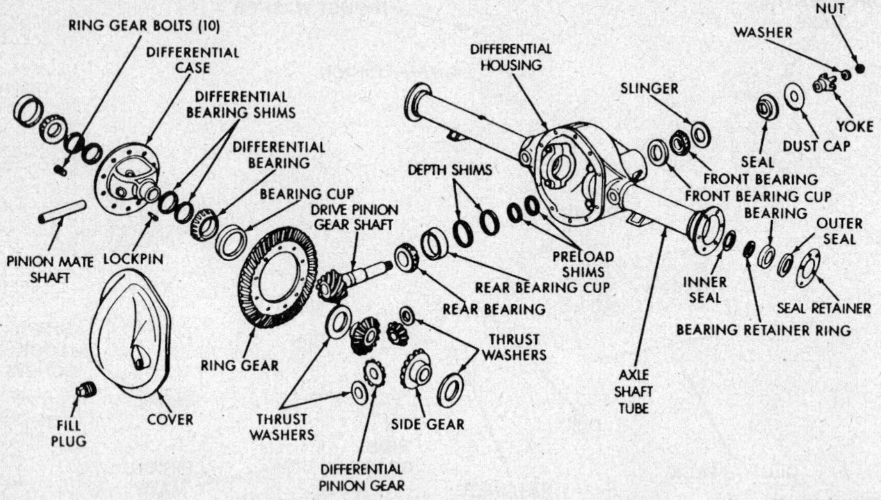

Fig. 7 Exploded view of differential. Models 216

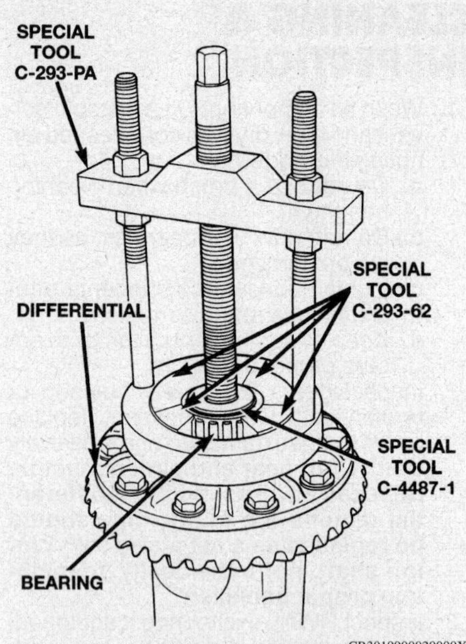

Fig. 8 Side bearing removal. Models 194, 216, 226 & 248

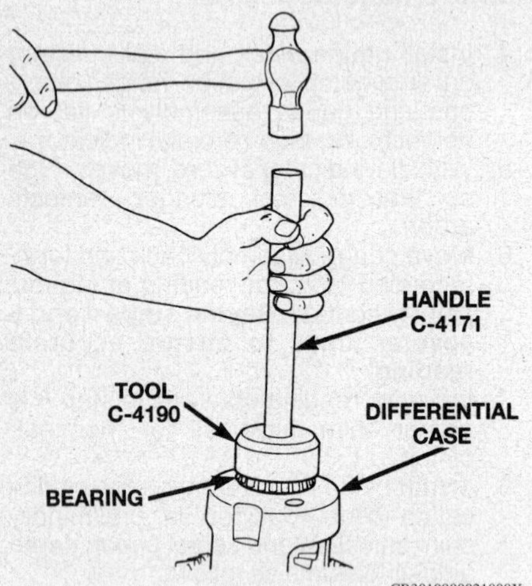

Fig. 9 Bearing replacement. Models 194, 216, 226 & 248

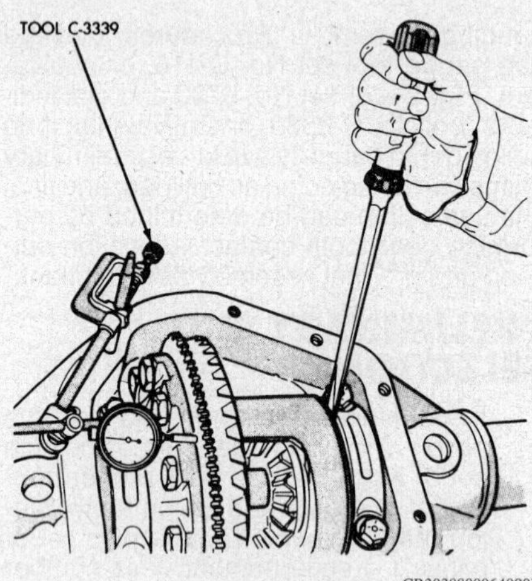

Fig. 10 Side bearing clearance inspection

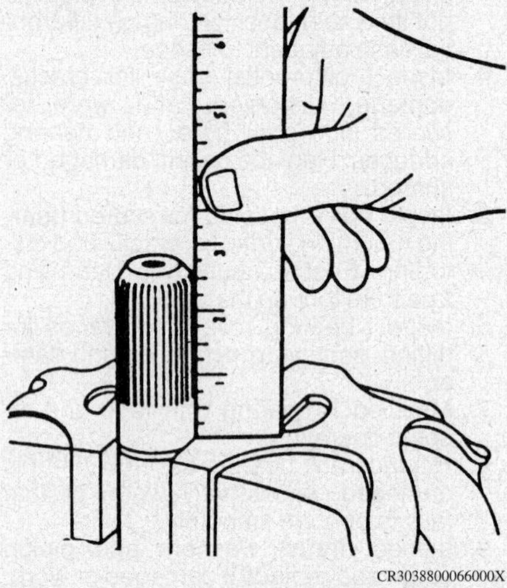

Fig. 11 Axle shaft measurement

torque nut in small increments until bearing preload is 10 inch lbs., rotating pinion and inspecting rotating torque with suitable torque wrench after each adjustment.

6. Inspect pinion depth adjustment as follows:
   a. Install arbor and disc assembly in bearing cap bores, then position height block on pinion face.
   b. Position gauge block and dial indicator assembly on small step of height block.
   c. Zero indicator, then slide gauge across or over arbor.
   d. Indicator should read within .002 inch of modification code etched on pinion at highest point.
   e. If reading is not within .002 inch of value on pinion, repeat shim selection.
7. When pinion depth has been verified, remove gauge tools, pinion nut, washer, companion flange and front bearing.
8. Install preload shims removed during disassembly on pinion shaft, then the front bearing and oil slinger, if used.
9. Install new seal in housing and coat seal lips with grease.
10. Install companion flange washer and pinion nut, then tighten pinion nut to specifications.
11. Measure pinion bearing preload (rotating torque) with suitable torque wrench.
12. If preload is not within specifications, add or subtract shims to obtain specified preload at specified pinion nut torque.

Final Assembly & Adjustment

1. Install differential assembly along with side bearings and races or master bearing gauges installed during overhaul.
2. Mount suitable dial indicator on housing with plunger bearing against back of ring gear, **Fig. 10.**
3. Push ring gear into contact with pinion, rocking gears to obtain proper mesh, then zero indicator with pressure still applied to ring gear.
4. Push ring gear away from pinion as far as possible, then record dial indicator reading. **Repeat steps 3 and 4 several times until same reading is obtained each time.**
5. Remove indicator and differential from housing.
6. Remove side bearings or master gauge bearings from case, then select side bearing shims as follows:
   a. Select shims equal to dial indicator reading obtained in step 4, and install this shim pack on case bearing hub behind ring gear.
   b. Subtract dial indicator reading obtained in step 4 from total side bearing clearance obtained in "Differential Overhaul" procedure, add .015 inch to remainder to establish preload, and select shim pack equal to sum.
   c. Install shim pack selected in step "b" on case hub on ring gear tooth side.

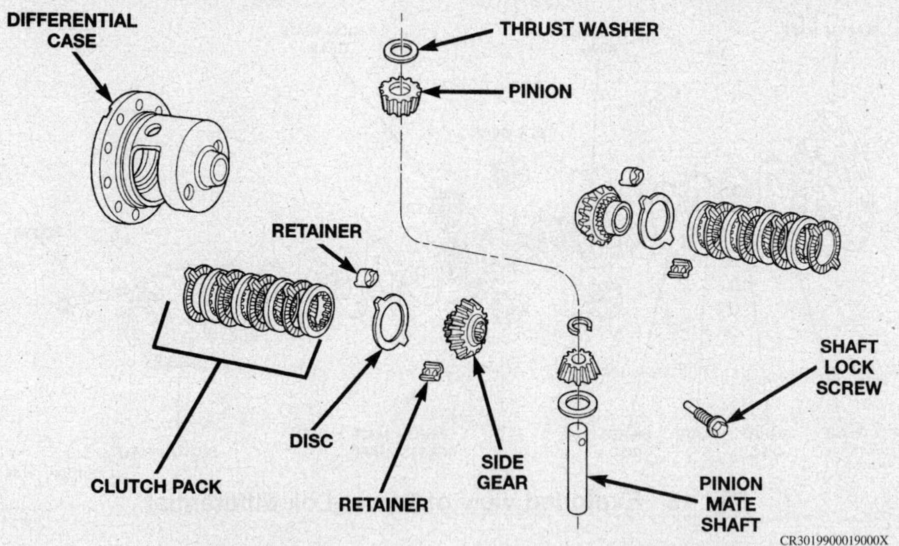

Fig. 12 Exploded view of Trac-Lok differential

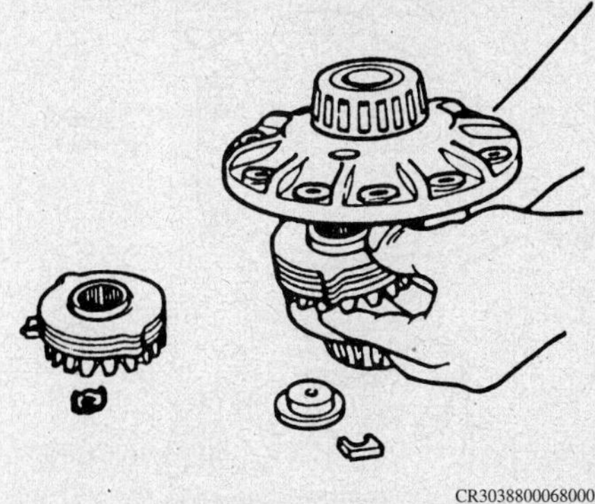

Fig. 13 Plate & disc separation. Trac-Lok differential

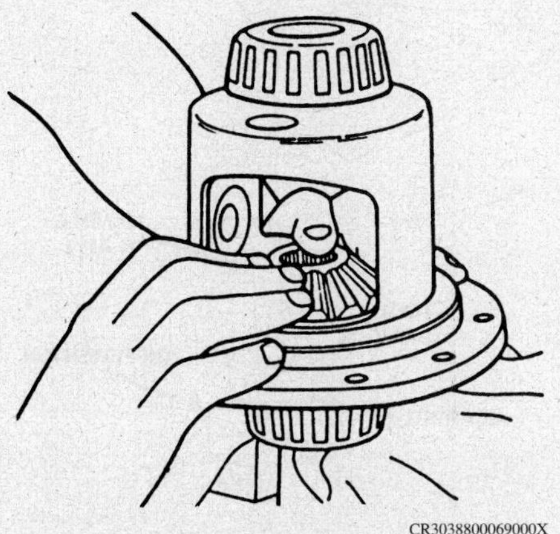

Fig. 14 First side gear & clutch pack assembly installation. Trac-Lok differential

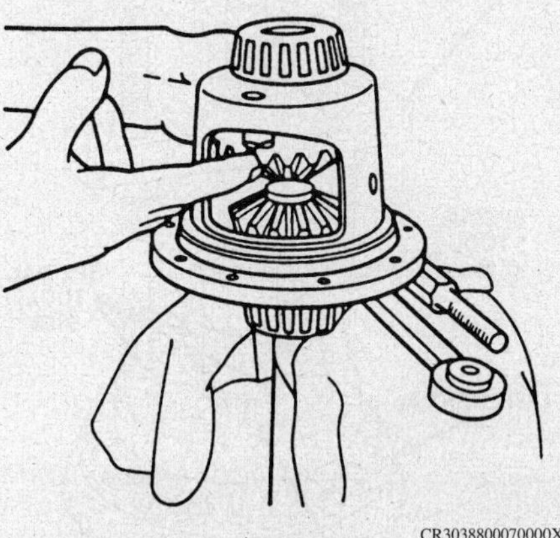

Fig. 15 Second side gear & clutch pack assembly installation. Trac-Lok differential

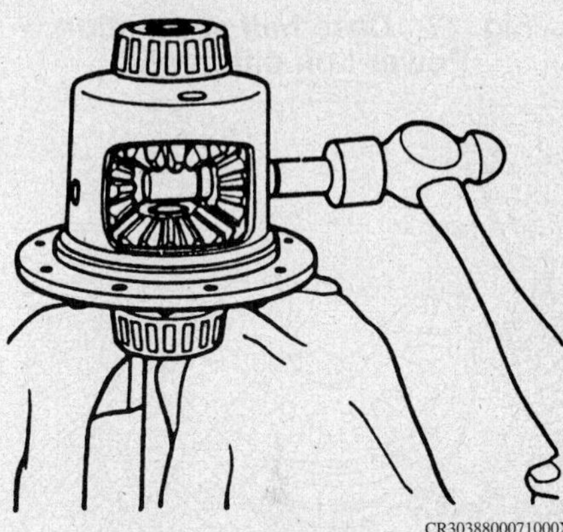

Fig. 16 Pinion mate shaft installation. Trac-Lok differential

7. Press side bearings onto differential case, ensuring shim packs are properly located between bearings and case.
8. Install inner axle shaft oil seal, if equipped.
9. Install spreader and dial indicator on housing, **Fig. 2,** as outlined during disassembly, then spread housing .015 inch. **Do not spread housing more than .015 inch or housing will be permanently distorted.**
10. Remove dial indicator, install differential case in housing, then remove spreader tool.
11. Install bearing caps in proper position and tap on ring gear to ensure case is seated.
12. Tighten bearing cap bolts to specifications.
13. Mount suitable dial indicator on housing with plunger at righthand angle to ring gear teeth, and contact bearing against heel of tooth, **Fig. 29.**
14. Hold pinion and rock ring gear back and forth, reading backlash from dial indicator.
15. If backlash is not within specifications, adjust as follows:
    a. Remove differential assembly from housing and side bearings from differential as previously outlined.
    b. If backlash is less than specified, increase thickness of shims on ring gear tooth side and decrease thickness of shims on opposite side by an equal mount. **Total shim thickness must remain constant when adjusting backlash in order to maintain previously established preload.**
    c. If backlash is greater than specified, decrease thickness of shims on ring gear tooth side and increase thickness of shims on opposite side by an equal amount.
16. Install selected shims, press bearings onto differential case, then reinstall case.
17. Coat drive and coast face of each ring gear tooth with suitable marking compound.
18. Apply braking force to differential case and turn pinion to rotate ring gear one full revolution in each direction. **Proper tooth contact pattern cannot be obtained unless gears are loaded.**
19. Contact pattern should be centered on ring gear teeth as outlined in **Fig. 30.**
20. Correct pinion shim thickness and/or backlash adjustment as needed to obtain proper contact pattern.
21. Reverse remaining disassembly procedures to complete assembly.

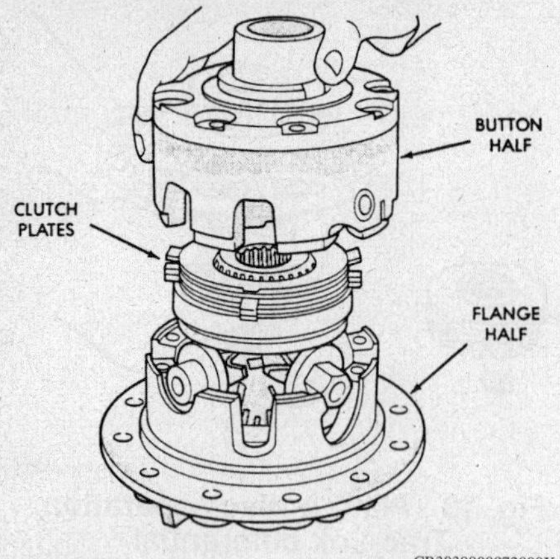

Fig. 17 Case half separation. Power-Lok differential

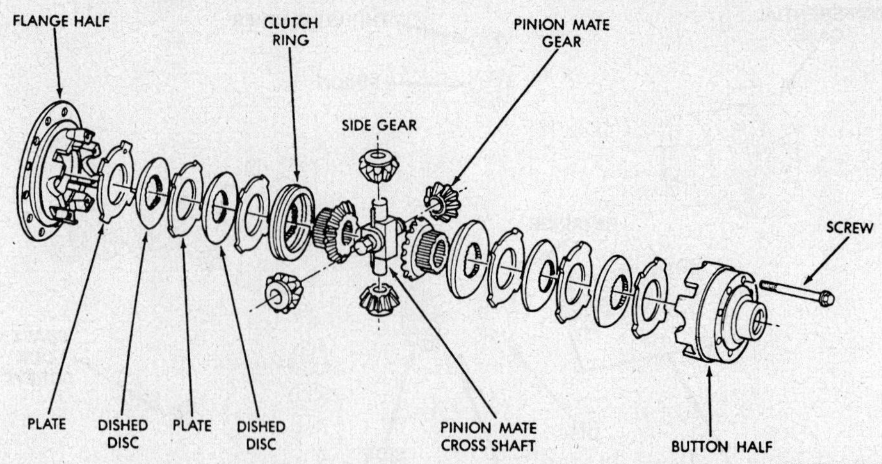

Fig. 18 Exploded view of Power-Lok differential

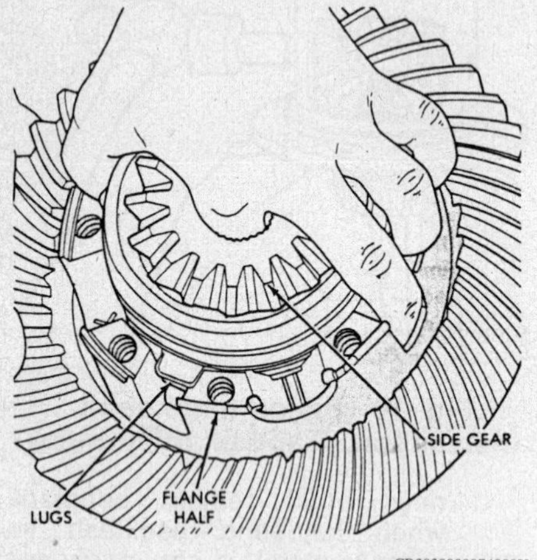

Fig. 19 Clutch pack installation. Power-Lok differential

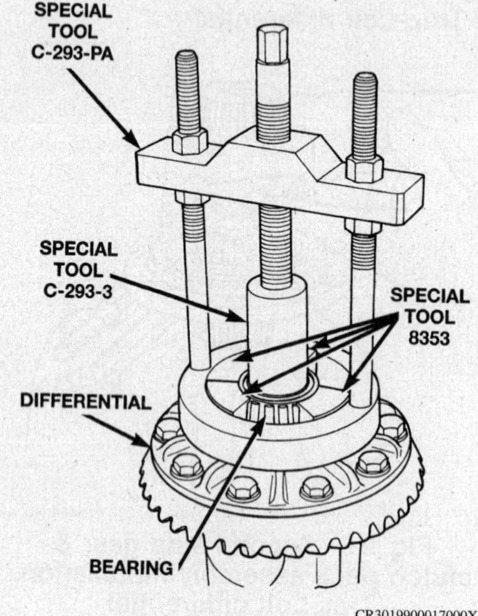

Fig. 20 Bearing removal. Vari-Lock differential

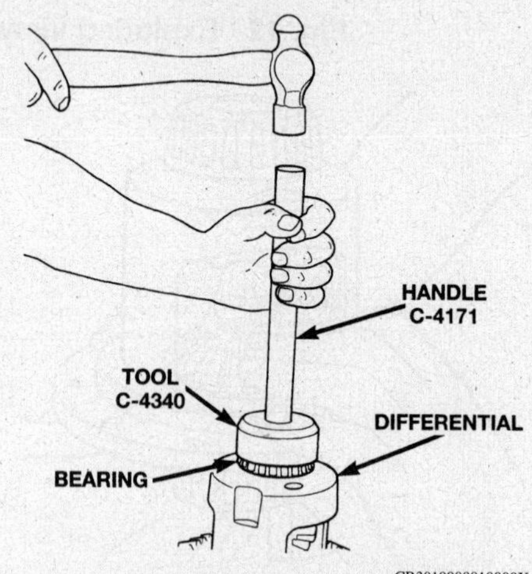

Fig. 21 Bearing installation. Vari-Lok differential

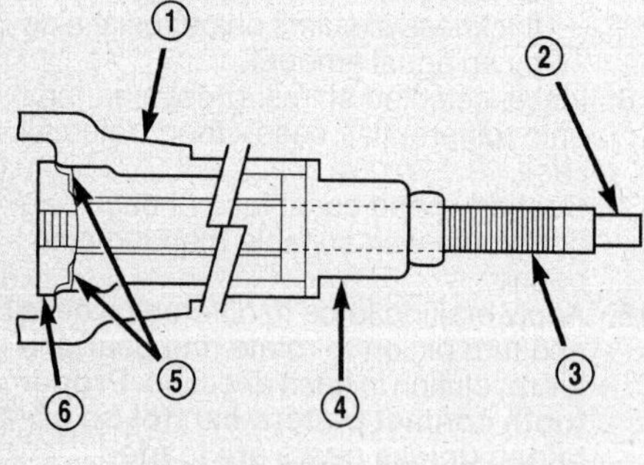

Fig. 22 Axle shaft seal installation

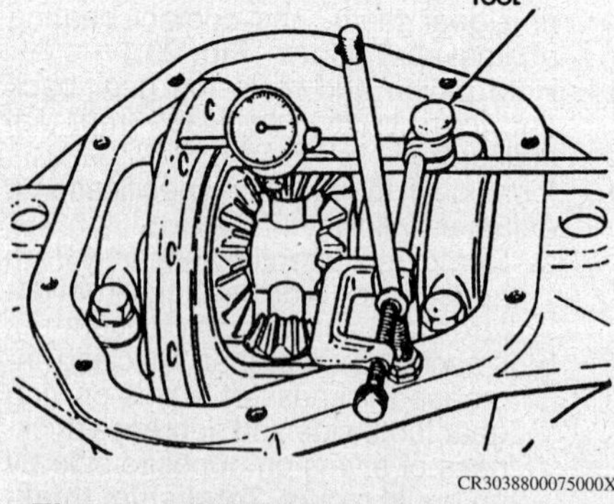

Fig. 23 Differential case runout inspection

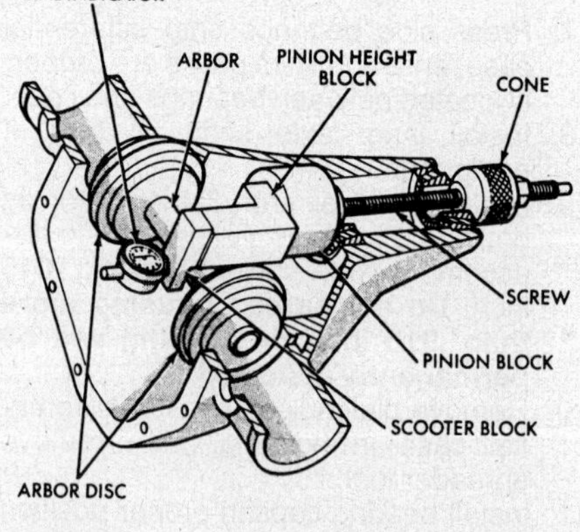

Fig. 24 Pinion depth gauge tool installation. Models 248, 267 & 286

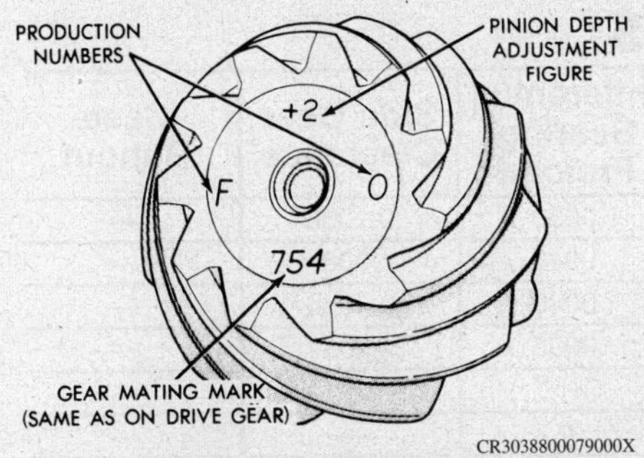

Fig. 25 Pinion depth modification code identification

Old Pinion Marking	New Pinion Marking (U.S. Standards)								
	−4	−3	−2	−1	0	+1	+2	+3	+4
+4	+0.008	+0.007	+0.006	+0.005	+0.004	+0.003	+0.002	+0.001	0
+3	+0.007	+0.006	+0.005	+0.004	+0.003	+0.002	+0.001	0	−0.001
+2	+0.006	+0.005	+0.004	+0.003	+0.002	+0.001	0	−0.001	−0.002
+1	+0.005	+0.004	+0.003	+0.002	+0.001	0	−0.001	−0.002	−0.003
0	+0.004	+0.003	+0.002	+0.001	0	−0.001	−0.002	−0.003	−0.004
−1	+0.003	+0.002	+0.001	0	−0.001	−0.002	−0.003	−0.004	−0.005
−2	+0.002	+0.001	0	−0.001	−0.002	−0.003	−0.004	−0.005	−0.006
−3	+0.001	0	−0.001	−0.002	−0.003	−0.004	−0.005	−0.006	−0.007
−4	0	−0.001	−0.002	−0.003	−0.004	−0.005	−0.006	−0.007	−0.008

CR3038800080000X

Fig. 26 Preliminary pinion depth adjusting shim selection chart

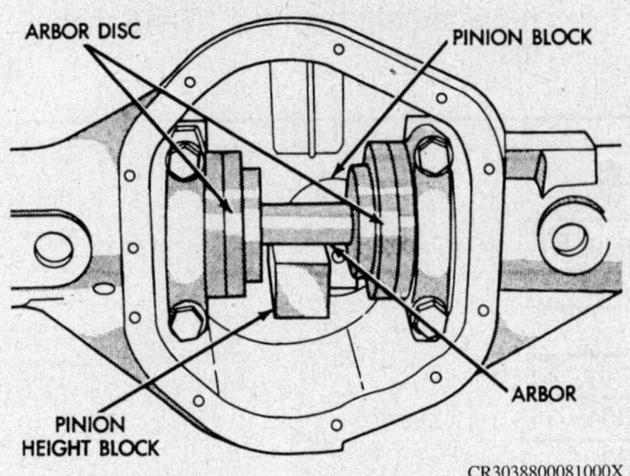

Fig. 27 Pinion block installation

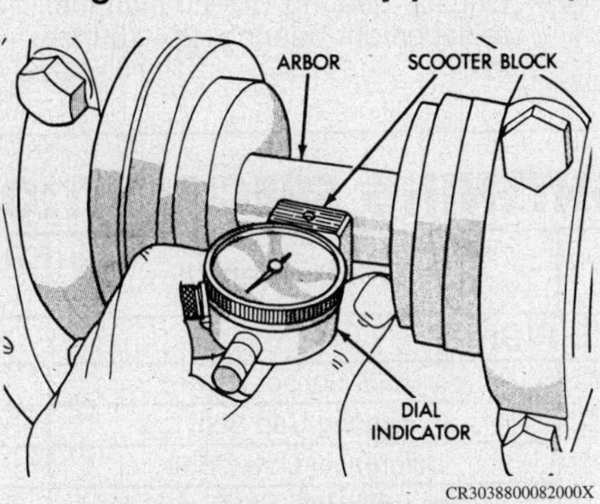

Fig. 28 Height block & dial indicator installation

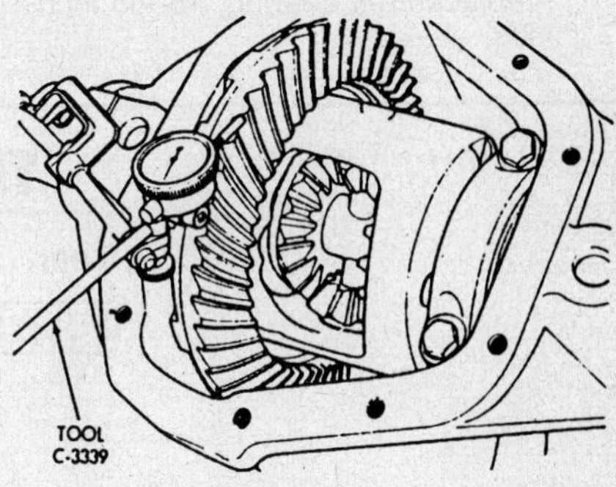

Fig. 29 Ring gear & pinion backlash inspection

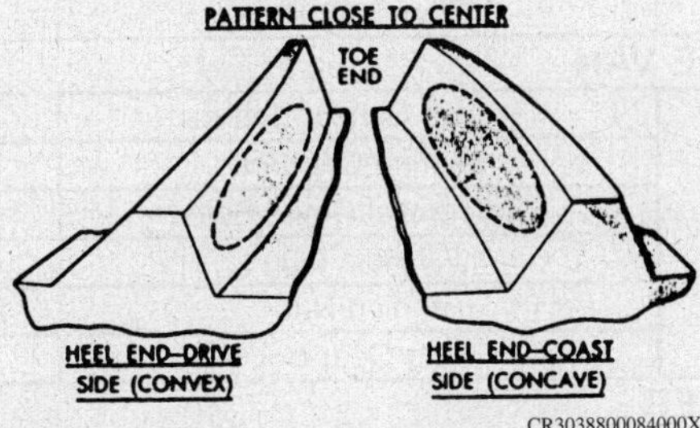

Fig. 30 Proper ring gear & pinion tooth contact

DRIVE AXLE SPECIFICATIONS

Model	Year	Ring Gear Diameter, Inch	Ring Gear Backlash	Pinion Gear Depth	Pinion Bearing Preload	Differential Bearing Preload	Side Gear Clearance	Case Runout
194	2002–06	7 9/16	.005–.008	3.813	①	.0050	0–.006	—
198	2002–04	7 4/5	.005–.008	3.625	①	.0040	.006	—
216	2002–06	8 1/2	.005–.008	4.312	①	.0040	0–.006	—
226	2002–04	8 9/10	.005–.008	4.312	②	.0005	.006	—
248	2002	9 3/4	.005–.008	5.000	③	—	—	—
267	2002	10 1/2	.005–.008	5.375	③	—	—	—
286	2002	11 1/4	.005–.008	5.812	③	—	—	—

① — Original bearing, 10–20 inch lbs.; replacement bearing, 15–35 inch lbs.

② — Original bearing, 10–20 inch lbs.; replacement bearing, 20–40 inch lbs.

③ — Original bearing, 10–20 inch lbs.; replacement bearing, 25–45 inch lbs.

TIGHTENING SPECIFICATIONS

Year	Component	Torque Ft. Lbs
FULL SIZE PICKUP		
2002	ABS Sensor Bolt	⑤
	Bearing Cap Bolt	80
	Differential Cover Bolt	30
	Fill Hole Plug	25
	Pinion Nut	②
	Power Lok Case Bolt	③
	Ring Gear Bolt	④
FULL SIZE VAN		
2002–03	ABS Sensor Bolt	18
	Bearing Cap Bolt	80
	Differential Cover Bolt	30
	Fill Hole Plug	25
	Pinion Nut	215–330
	Ring Gear Bolt	120–140
WRANGLER		
2002–06	ABS Sensor Bolt	⑥
	Bearing Cap Bolt	⑦
	Differential Cover Bolt	⑧
	Fill Hole Plug	25
	Pinion Nut	⑨
	Ring Gear Bolt	①

① — Model 194, 70–90 ft. lbs: model 198, 95–105 ft. lbs: models 216 & 226, 80 ft. lbs.
② — Model 216, 160–200 ft. lbs: models 248 & 267, 215–330 ft. lbs: model 286, 440–500 ft. lbs.
③ — Standard, 65–70 ft. lbs: heavy duty, 90–100 ft. lbs.
④ — Model 216, 70–90 ft. lbs: models 248 & 267, 120–140 ft. lbs: model 200–240 ft. lbs.
⑤ — Except model 216, 18 ft. lbs: models 216, 8 ft. lbs.
⑥ — Model 216, 18 ft. lbs: model 194, 6 ft. lbs: models 198 & 226, 70 inch lbs.
⑦ — Models 194 & 198, 57 ft. lbs: model 216, 80 ft. lbs: model 226, 63 ft. lbs.
⑧ — Model 216, 80 ft. lbs.
⑨ — Model 198, 210 ft. lbs: model 194, 200–350 ft. lbs: model 216, 180 ft. lbs.: model 226, 220–280 ft. lbs.

UNIVERSAL JOINTS

INDEX

SINGLE CARDAN

Individual components of Cardan universal joints are not serviceable. If components are worn or damaged, they must be replaced as an assembly.

Removal

Scribe or punch a reference mark on each component before removal of yoke from driveshaft for reassembly reference.

1. Remove driveshaft.
2. Tap outside of bearing cap to loosen snap ring using a suitable soft drift.
3. Remove snap rings from both sides of yoke.
4. Set yoke in an arbor press or vise with a socket whose inside diameter is large enough to receive bearing cap positioned beneath the yoke.
5. Position yoke with grease fitting, if equipped, facing up.
6. Place a socket with an outside diameter smaller than the upper bearing cap on upper bearing cap and press cap through yoke to release lower bearing cap, **Fig. 1.**
7. If bearing cap will not pull out of yoke by hand after pressing, tap yoke ear near bearing cap to dislodge cap.
8. To remove opposite bearing cap, turn yoke over and straighten cross in open hole.
9. Press on end of cross until remaining bearing cap can be removed.

Installation

During assembly, ensure alignment marks on link yoke and driveshaft yoke are properly aligned.

Ensure cross and bearing cap are straight during installation, otherwise, the bearing cap will score the walls of the yoke bore and damage may occur.

1. Apply suitable extreme pressure grease to inside of yoke bore to aid installation.
2. Position cross in yoke with its grease fitting, if equipped, facing up, **Fig. 2.**
3. Place a bearing cap over trunnion and align cap with yoke bore, **Fig. 3.**
4. Keep needle bearings upright in bearing assembly. Ensure needle bearings do not fall to bottom of cap.
5. Press bearing cap into yoke bore enough to install a snap ring, then install snap ring.
6. Repeat procedure to install opposite bearing cap.
7. If joint is stiff or binding, strike yoke with a soft hammer to seat needle bearings.
8. Add grease to fitting, if equipped, then install driveshaft.

DOUBLE CARDAN

Individual components of Cardan universal joints are not serviceable. If components are worn or damaged, they must be replaced as an assembly.

Removal

Scribe or punch a reference mark on each component before removal of yoke from driveshaft for reassembly reference.

1. Remove driveshaft.
2. Tap outside of bearing cap assembly to loosen snap ring using a suitable soft drift.
3. Remove all bearing cap snap rings.
4. Remove any grease fittings if equipped.
5. Set joint in an arbor press or vise with a socket whose inside diameter is large enough to receive bearing cap positioned beneath link yoke.
6. Place a socket with an outside diameter smaller than the upper bearing cap on the upper bearing cap.
7. Partially press one bearing cap from outboard side of link yoke enough to grasp the bearing cap with vise jaws, **Fig. 4.**
8. Grasp protruding bearing with jaws of vise.
9. Tap link yoke with mallet and drift to dislodge the bearing cap from yoke, **Fig. 5.**
10. Flip assembly and repeat procedure for opposite side.
11. Remove cross centering kit assembly and spring, **Fig. 6.**

Installation

During assembly, ensure alignment marks on link yoke and driveshaft yoke are aligned.

Ensure cross and bearing cap are straight during installation, otherwise, the bearing cap will score the walls of the yoke bore and damage may occur.

1. Apply suitable high pressure grease to inside of yoke bores to aid installation.
2. Fit a cross into driveshaft yoke.
3. Place a bearing cap over trunnion and align cap with yoke bore, **Fig. 7.**
4. Keep needle bearings upright in cap. Do not allow bearings to fall into bottom of cap.
5. Press bearing cap into yoke bore enough to install snap ring, **Fig. 8,** then install snap ring.
6. Flip driveshaft yoke and install bearing cap onto opposite trunnion. Install snap ring.
7. Fit link yoke on remaining two trunnions and press both bearing caps into place. Install snap rings.
8. Install centering kit assembly inside link yoke. Ensure spring is properly positioned.
9. Place two bearing caps on opposite trunnions of the remaining cross.
10. Fit open trunnions into link yoke bores and bearing caps into centering kit, **Fig. 9.**
11. Press remaining two bearing caps into position and install snap rings.
12. Tap snap rings to allow them to seat into grooves.
13. Flex joint beyond center. It should snap over-center in both directions when properly assembled.
14. Install driveshaft.

SERVICE NOTE

Service Recommendations

Before disassembling any universal joint, examine the assembly carefully and note the position of any grease fittings used. In addition, be sure to mark the yokes' relationship to the driveshaft so they may be reassembled in the same relative position. Failure to observe these precautions may produce improper vehicle operating conditions that will result in rapid component wear and failure.

When universal joints are disassembled for lubrication or inspection and the old components are to be installed again, special care must be exercised to avoid damage to universal joint spider or cross and bearing cups.

Lubrication

Lubrication of the CV joints should not be overlooked during the regular service intervals recommended by the manufacturer. Use only the recommended type of lubricant, which usually is lithium type chassis grease.

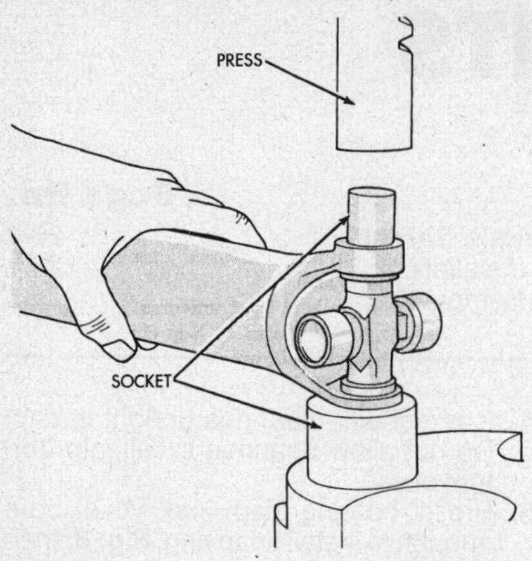

Fig. 1 Upper bearing cap removal. Single Cardan joint

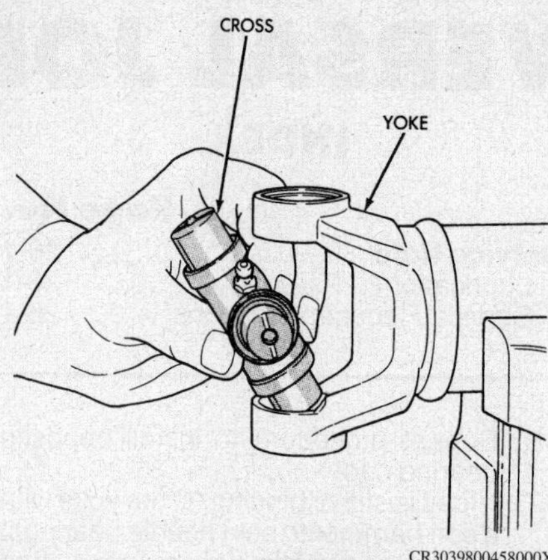

Fig. 2 Cross installation. Single Cardan joint

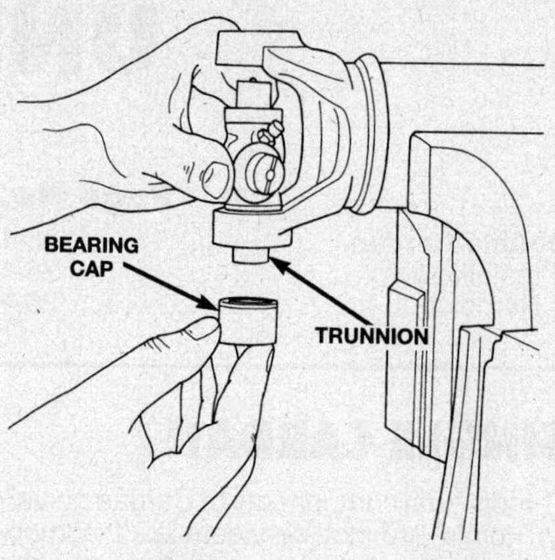

Fig. 3 Bearing cap installation. Single Cardan joint

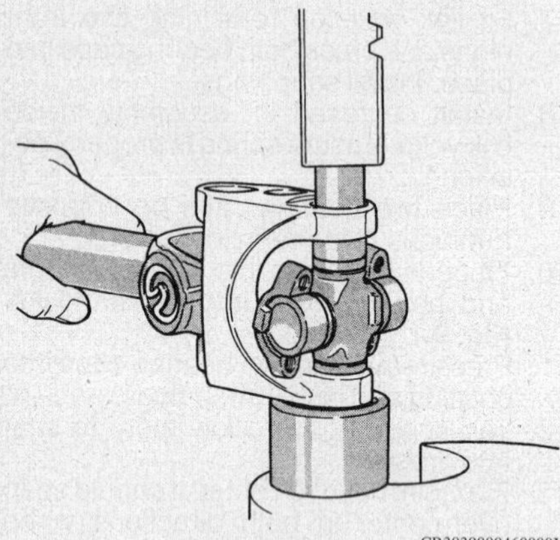

Fig. 4 Preliminary bearing removal. Double Cardan joint

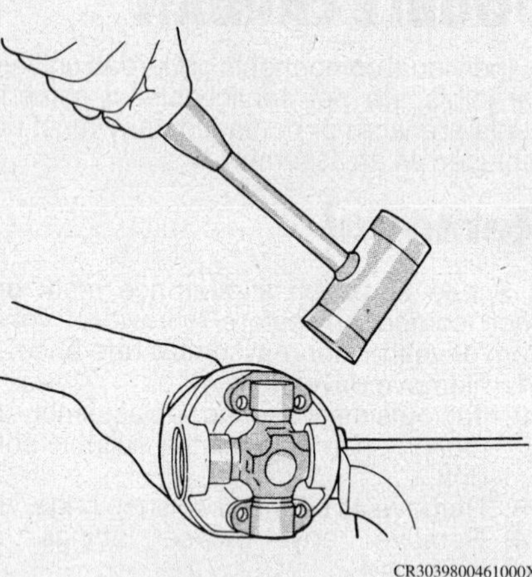

Fig. 5 Bearing removal. Double Cardan joint

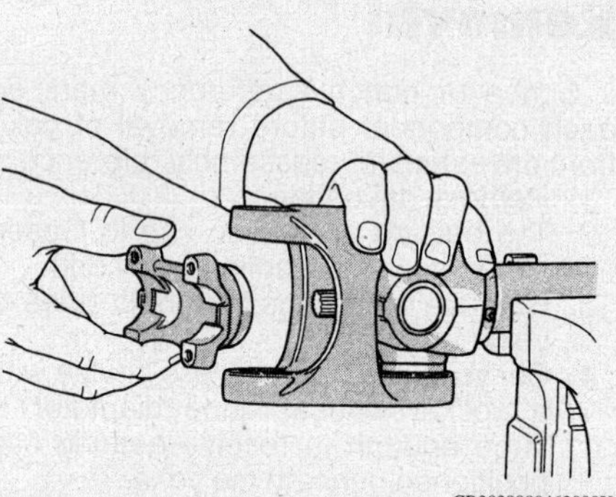

Fig. 6 Cross centering kit removal. Double Cardan joint

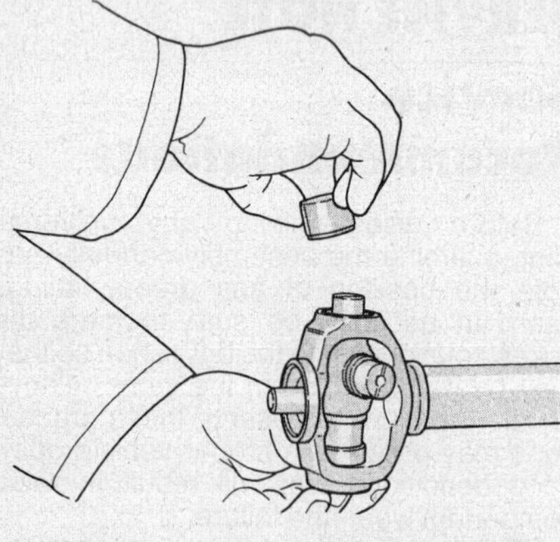

Fig. 7 Bearing cap & cross installation. Double Cardan joint

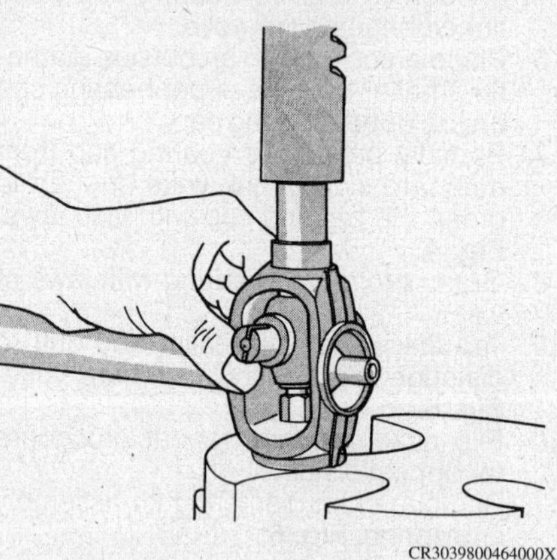

Fig. 8 Preliminary bearing cap installation. Double Cardan joint

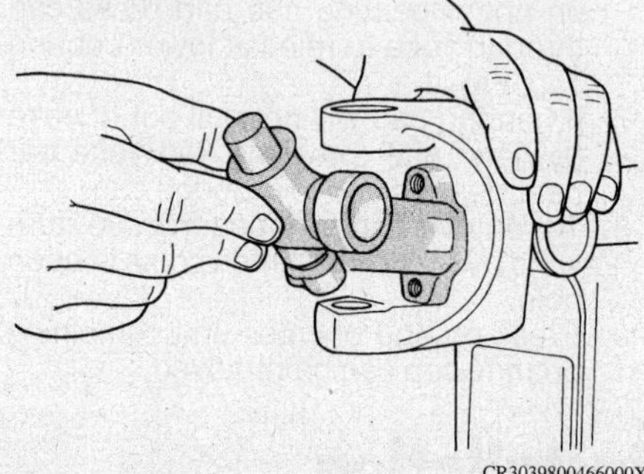

Fig. 9 Second cross installation. Double Cardan joint

ENGINE REBUILDING SPECIFICATIONS

NOTE: Refer To Engine Section In Individual Truck Chapters For Cylinder Head Tightening Information.

TABLE OF CONTENTS

DaimlerChrysler

INDEX

CYLINDER HEAD, VALVE GUIDE & VALVE SEATS

All Specifications Given In Inches Unless Otherwise Noted.

Engine Liter	Year	Cylinder Head Warpage Limit	Cylinder Head Height	Valve Guides		Valve Seats			
				Inside Diameter	Stem To Guide Clearance	Seat Angle, Deg.	Seat Width		Runout
							Intake	Exhaust	
2.4L	2002–06	.004	—	.2350–.2360	⑤	44½–45	.0350–.0510	.0350–.0510	.0020
2.5L	2002	②	—	.3130–.3140	.0010–.0030	44½	.0400–.0600	.0400–.0600	.0025
2.7L	2003–06	—	—	—	—	—	—	—	—
3.3L	2002–06	.008①	—	.2740–.2750	⑤	44½–45	.0570–.0780	.0570–.0780	.0030
3.5L	2004–06	—	—	—	⑧	45–45½	.0310–.0472	.0500–.0670	.0020
3.8L	2002–06	.008①	—	.2740–.2750	⑤	44½–45	.0570–.0780	.0570–.0780	.0030
3.9L	2002–03	①	—	.3130–.3140	.0010–.0030⑦	44¼–44¾	.0400–.0600	.0400–.0600	.0030
4.7L	2002–06	.002	—	.2747–.2756	④	44½–45	.0698–.0928	.0673–.0911	.0020
5.2L	2002–03	①	—	.3130–.3140	.0010–.0030⑦	44¼–44¾	.0400–.0600	.0600–.0800	.0030
5.7L	2003–06	—	—	—	⑨	44½–45	.0464–.0637	.0582–.0755	.0019
5.9L③	2002–03	①	—	.3740–.3750	⑦⑥	44¼–44¾	.0400–.0600	.0600–.0800	.0030
5.9L⑩	2002–06	.012	—	.2767–.2786	.0030	⑪	.0590–.0710	.0590–.0710	.0030
8.0L	2002–03	.010	—	.3130–.3140	.0010–.0030⑦	44½	.0400–.0600	.0400–.0600	.0030
8.3L	2004–06	—	—	.3130–.3140	.0010–.0030	44–44½	.0400–.0600	.0400–.0600	.0020

① — Length of span multiplied by .00075.

② — Not to exceed .0010 for any one inch of length; .0060 for any six inches of length or .0080 for total length.

③ — Gasoline engine.

④ — Intake, .008–.0028 inch; Exhaust, .0019–.0039 inch.

⑤ — Intake, .0010–.0025 inch; Exhaust, .0020–.0037 inch.

⑥ — Standard: intake, .0010–.0030; exhaust, .0020–.0040.

⑦ — Maximum allowable before reconditioning (inspect by rocking method), .0170 inch.

⑧ — Intake, .0009–.0026 inch; Exhaust, .0020–.0037 inch.

⑨ — Intake, .0008–.0025 inch; Exhaust, .0009–.0025 inch.

⑩ — Diesel engine.

⑪ — Intake, 30°; exhaust, 45°.

VALVE SPRINGS

All Specifications Given In Inches Unless Otherwise Noted.

Engine Liter	Year	Free Length	Maximum Straightness Deviation	Installed Height	Pressure, Pounds @ Inches	
					Closed	Open
2.4L	2002–06	1.9370	—	1.4960	③	④
2.5L	2002	1.8760	—	1.6400	71–79 @ 1.6400	202—218 @ 1.2160
2.7L	2003–06	—	—	—	—	—
3.3L	2002–06	⑤	—	1.6100–1.6800	84.6–95.6 @ 1.6500	194.2–215.8 @ 1.6500
3.5L	2004–06	⑥	—	1.4961	⑦	⑧
3.8L	2002–06	⑤	—	1.6100–1.6800	84.6–95.6 @ 1.6500	194.2–215.8 @ 1.6500
3.9L	2002–03	1.9670	—	1.6400	85 @ 1.6400	200 @ 1.2120
4.7L	2002	1.9134	—	②	70.92722–79.24515 @ 1.6099	176.6998–193.3357 @ 1.1670
	2003–06	1.9291	—	1.5795	70.3652–79.5824 @ 1.5795	174.4517–195.5838 @ 1.1370
5.2L	2002–03	1.9670	—	1.6400	85 @ 1.6400	200 @ 1.1212
5.7L	2003–06	2.189	—	1.8100	97.8 @ 1.771	242 @ 1.2830
5.9L①	2002–03	1.9670	—	1.6400	85 @ 1.6400	200 @ 1.2120
5.9L⑨	2002–06	1.8800	.059	—	76.4 @ 1.3900	—
8.0L	2002–03	1.9670	—	1.6400	85 @ 1.6400	200 @ 1.2120
8.3L	2004–06	2.1650	—	1.7500	120 @ 1.7500	280 @ 1.2070

① — Gasoline engine.

② — Intake, 1.613 inch; Exhaust, 1.606 inch.

③ — On 2002–04 models, 75 lbs., @ 1.496 inch; On 2005–06 models, 70 lbs., @ 1.496 inch.

④ — On 2002–04 models, 134 lbs., @ 1.172 inch; On 2005–06 models, 134 lbs., @ 1.152 inch.

⑤ — Type A, 2.0200 inch; Type B, 2.100 inch.

⑥ — Intake, 1.7195 inch; Exhaust w/yellow, 1.8543 inch; Exhaust w/white, 1.9015 inch.

⑦ — Intake, 69.5–80.5 lbs @ 1.4961 inch; Exhaust w/yellow, 71–79 lbs @ 1.1750 inch; Exhaust w/white, 80–90 lbs @ 1.4961 inch

⑧ — Intake, 188–204 lbs @ 1.1594 inch; Exhaust, 140–154 lbs @ 1.2390 inch.

⑨ — Diesel engine.

VALVES

All Specifications Given In Inches Unless Otherwise Noted.

Engine Liter	Year	Stem Diameter		Installed Height	Valve Recess	Maximum Tip Refinish	Face Angle, Deg.	Margin①		Valve Clearance	
		Intake	Exhaust					Intake	Exhaust	Intake	Exhaust
2.4L	2002–06	.2337–.2344	.2326–.2333	③	—	—	44½–45	.0470–.0660	.0380–.0510	—	—
2.5L	2002	.3110–.3120	.3110–.3120	—	—	.010	46½	—	—	.0010–.0030	.0010–.0030
2.7L	2003–06	—	—	—	—	—	—	—	—	—	—
3.3L	2002–06	.2718–.2725	.2718–.2725	—	—	—	45–45½	.0320–.0380	.0610–.0670	⑥	⑥
3.5L	2004–06	.2730–.2737	.2719–.2726	—	—	—	44½–45	.0329–.0459	.0567–.0697	⑥	⑥
3.8L	2002–06	.2718–.2725	.2718–.2725	—	—	—	45–45½	.0320–.0380	.0610–.0670	⑥	⑥
3.9L	2002–03	.3110–.3120	.3110–.3120	—	—	—	43¼–43¾	.0470	.0470	⑥	⑥
4.7L	2002–06	.2729–.2739	.2717–.2728	—	—	—	45–45½	—	—	.0008–.0028	.0019–.0039
5.2L	2002–03	.3110–.3120④	.3110–.3120④	—	—	②	43¼–43¾	.0470	.0470	⑥	⑥
5.7L	2003–06	.3120–.3130	.3120–.3130	—	—	—	45–45½	—	—	—	—
5.9L⑤	2002–03	.3720–.3730④	.3710–.3720④	—	—	②	43¼–43¾	.0470	.0470	⑥	⑥

Continued

VALVES—Continued

All Specifications Given In Inches Unless Otherwise Noted.

Engine Liter	Year	Stem Diameter		Instal-led Height	Valve Recess	Maxi-mum Tip Refinish	Face Angle, Deg.	Margin①		Valve Clearance	
		Intake	Ex-haust					Intake	Ex-haust	Intake	Exhaust
5.9L⑦	2002–06	.2752–.2760	.2752–.2760	—	—	—	⑧	.0310	.0310	.0060–.0150	.0150–.0300
8.0L	2002–03	.3110–.3120	.3110–.3120	1.870–1.895	—	—	45	.0470	.0470	⑥	⑥
8.3L	2004–06	.3110–.3120	.3110–.3120	—	—	—	45–45½	.0510	.0800	⑥	⑥

①— Minimum.
②— Valves may be ground to correct installed height unless they are equipped w/rotators. If valves are equipped w/rotators, do not grind stem tips.
③— Intake, 1.891; exhaust 1.889.
④— Standard diameter. Valve should be replaced if wear exceeds .002 inch.
⑤— Gasoline engine.
⑥— Hydraulic lash adjusters.
⑦— Diesel engine.
⑧— Intake, 30°; exhaust, 45°.

CAMSHAFT

All Specifications Given In Inches Unless Otherwise Noted.

Engine Liter	Year	Camshaft Journal Diameter	Camshaft Bearing Clearance	Camshaft Endplay	Lifter Bore Diameter	Lifter Diameter	Lifter To Bore Clearance
2.4L	2002–06	1.0220–1.0230	.0009–.0025	.0019–.0066	—	—	—
2.5L	2002	①	.0010–.0030	—	.9055–.9065	.9040–.9045	.0010–.0025
2.7L	2003–06	—	—	—	—	—	—
3.3L	2002–06	④	.0010–.0040	.0100–.0200	—	.9030–.9040	.0007–.0024
3.5L	2004–06	1.6905–1.6913	.0030–.0047	.0010–.0014	—	—	—
3.8L	2002–06	④	.0010–.0040	.0100–.0200	—	.9030–.9040	.0007–.0024
3.9L	2002–03	⑥	.0010–.0050	.0020–.0100	.9051–.9059	.9035–.9040	.0011–.210
4.7L	2002–06	1.0227–1.0235	.0010–.0026	.0030–.0079	—	—	—
5.2L	2002–03	⑧	.0010–.0050	.0020–.0100	.9051–.9059⑦	.9035–.9040⑦	.0011–.0024
5.7L	2003–06	⑨	⑩	.0031–.0114	.8444–.8435	—	—
5.9L⑤	2002–03	⑧	.0010–.0050	.0020–.0100	.9051–.9059⑦	.9035–.9040⑦	.0011–.0024
5.9L⑪	2002–06	③	—	.0040–.0182	—	—	—
8.0L	2002–03	③	②	.0050–.0150	.9048–.9059	.9035–.9040	.0008–.0024
8.3L	2004–06	2.0900–2.0910	.0020–.0040	.0050–.0150	—	.9035–.9040	.0005–.0017

①— No. 1, 2.029–2.030 inch; No. 2, 2.019–2.020 inch; No. 3, 2.009–2.010 inch; No. 4, 1.999–2.000 inch.
②— No. 1, 3, 4, 5 & 6, .001–.003 inch; No. 2, .0015–.0035 inch.
③— No. 1, 2.091–2.092 inch; No. 2, 2.075–2.076 inch; No. 3, 2.059–2.060 inch; No. 4, 2.043–2.044 inch; No. 5, 2.027–2.028 inch; No. 6, 1.917–1.918 inch.
④— No. 1, 1.9970–1.9990 inch; No. 2, 1.9809–1.9829 inch; No. 3, 1.9659–1.9679 inch; No. 4, 1.9499–1.9520 inch.
⑤— Gasoline engine.
⑥— No. 1, 1.998–1.999 inch; No. 2, 1.982–1.983 inch; No. 3, 1.951–1.952 inch; No. 4, 1.5605–1.5615 inch.
⑦— Oversize lifters (.008 inch) indicated by diamond stamping on top pad, front of engine, and a flat ground on outside surface of each oversize lifter bore.
⑧— No. 1, 1.998–1.999 inch; No. 2, 1.982–1.983 inch; No. 3, 1.967–1.968 inch; No. 4, 1.951–1.952 inch; No. 5, 1.5605–1.5615 inch.
⑨— No. 1, 2.290 inch; No. 2, 2.270 inch; No. 3, 2.260 inch; No. 4, 2.240 inch; No. 5, 1.720 inch.
⑩— Nos. 1, 3 & 5, .0015–.0030 inch; Nos. 2 & 4, .0019–.0035 inch.
⑪— Diesel engine.

ENGINE REBUILDING SPECIFICATIONS

CRANKSHAFT, BEARINGS & RODS

All Specifications Given In Inches Unless Otherwise Noted.

Engine Liter	Year	Crankshaft				Bearing Clearance			Connecting Rods	
		Main Bearing Journal Diameter	Connecting Rod Journal Diameter	Out Of Round All①	Taper All①	Main Bearings	Connecting Rod Bearings	Thrust Bearing	Pin Bore Diameter	Side Clearance
2.4L	2002–06	2.3620–2.3625	1.9680–1.9685	.0003	.0001	.0007–.0024	.0009–.0027	.0035–.0140	④	.005–.015
2.5L	2002	2.4996–2.5001	2.0934–2.0995	.0005	.0005	.0010–.0025	.0010–.0025	.0015–.0065	.9288–.9298	.0100–.0190
2.7L	2003–06	—	—	—	—	—	—	—	—	—
3.3L	2002–06	2.5190–2.5202	2.2827–2.2837	.0010	.0010	.0050–.0022	.0008–.0026	—	—	.0050–.0130
3.5L	2004–06	2.5190–2.5200	2.2820–2.2830	.0006	.0006	.0007–.0030	.0010–.0030	—	.9452–.9455	.0153
3.8L	2002–06	2.5190–2.5202	2.2827–2.2837	.0010	.0010	.0050–.0022	.0008–.0026	—	—	.0050–.0130
3.9L	2002–03	2.4995–2.5005	2.1240–2.1250	.0010	.0010	③	.0005–.0022	.0020–.0100	.9819–.9834	.0060–.0140
4.7L	2002–06	2.4996–2.5005	2.0076–2.0082	.0002	.0004	.0008–.0021	.0006–.0022	—	.0009–.0018	.0040–.0138
5.2L	2002–03	2.4995–2.5005	2.1240–2.1250	.0010	.0010	③	.0005–.0022	.0020–.0100	.9829–.9834	.0060–.0140
5.7L	2003–06	2.5585–2.5595	2.1250–2.1260	.0002	.0001	.0009–.0020	.0007–.0023	—	.9431–.9438	.0030–.0137
5.9L②	2002–03	2.8095–2.8105	2.1240–2.1250	.0010	.0010	③	.0005.–.0022	.0020–.0100	.9829–.9834	.0060–.0140
5.9L⑤	2002–06	3.2662	2.7150	.0020	.0005	.0047	.0035	.0040–.0170	1.5764	.0040–.0130
8.0L	2002–03	2.9995–3.0005	2.1240–2.1250	.0010	.0010	.0002–.0023	.0002–.0029	—	.9819–.9834	.0100–.0180
8.3L	2004–06	3.0008–3.0018	2.1256–2.1263	.0005	.0005	.0010–.0020	.0002–.0029	—	.9425–.9440	.0100–.0180

① — Maximum.
② — Gasoline engine.
③ — No. 1, .0005–.0015 inch; Nos. 2, 3 & 4, .0005–.0025 inch.
④ — Non-turbo models, .8252–.8260 inch; Turbo models, .8664–.8667 inch.
⑤ — Diesel engine.

PISTONS, PINS & RINGS

All Specifications Given In Inches Unless Otherwise Noted.

Engine Liter	Year	Piston Diameter (Std.)	Piston Clearance	Piston Pin Diameter	Piston Pin To Piston Clearance	Piston Ring End Gap①		Piston Ring Side Clearance	
						Comp.	Oil	Comp.	Oil
2.4L	2002–06	⑥	⑦	⑧	.00010–.00070	③	⑨	⑩	⑪
2.5L	2002	—	.0080–.0015	.9306–.9307	.00050–.00090	②	.0100–.0600	.0017–.0033	.0024–.0083
2.7L	2003–06	—	—	—	—	—	—	—	—
3.3L	2002–06	3.6600–3.6610	.0002–.0015	.9007–.9009	.00020–.00070	.0070–.0150	.0090–.0300	.0012–.0031	.0015–.0078
3.5L	2004–06	3.7780–3.7796	.0003–.0018	.9448–.9449	.00020–.00060	⑫	.0100–.0300	.0016–.0031	.0015–.0073
3.8L	2002–06	3.778–3.779	.0002–.0015	.9007–.9009	.00020–.00070	.0070–.0150	.0090–.0300	.0012–.0270	.0015–.0078
3.9L	2002–03	—	.0005–.0015	.9841–.9843	.00025–.00075	.0100–.0200	.0100–.0500	.0015–.0030	.0020–.0080
4.7L	2002–06	3.6605	—	.9454–.9456	.00040–.00080	⑬	.0099–.3000	⑭	.0070–.0091

Continued

PISTONS, PINS & RINGS—Continued

All Specifications Given In Inches Unless Otherwise Noted.

Engine Liter	Year	Piston Diameter (Std.)	Piston Clear-ance	Piston Pin Diameter	Piston Pin To Piston Clear-ance	Piston Ring End Gap①		Piston Ring Side Clearance	
						Comp.	Oil	Comp.	Oil
5.2L	2002–03	—	.0005–.0015	.9841–.9843	.00025–.00075	.0100–.0200	.0100–.0500	.0015–.0030	.0020–.0080
5.7L	2003–06	—	.0008–.0019	.9448–.9449	.00035–.00070	⑮	.0059–.0259	⑯	.0007–.0091
5.9L④	2002–03	—	.0005–.0015	.9845–.9848	.00025–.00075	⑤	.0100–.0500	.0016–.0033	.0020–.0080
5.9L⑰	2002–06	4.0110	.0015–.0093	1.5744	.00140	⑱	.0100–.0215	⑲	.0050
8.0L	2002–03	—	.0005–.0015	.9841–.9843	.00070–.00240	.0100–0200	.0150–.0550	.0029–.0038	.1020–.1080
8.3L	2004–06	4.0281–4.0288	.0010–.0022	.9425–.9440	.00040–.00090	⑳	.0100–.0300	.0016–.0033	.0018–.0079

① — Minimum.
② — Top ring, .0090–.0240 inch; second ring, .0190–.0380 inch.
③ — On Non-turbo models, top ring, .0098–.0200 inch; second ring, .0090–.0180 inch.; On turbo models, top ring, .0078–.0157 inch; second ring, .0070–.0150 inch.
④ — Gasoline engine.
⑤ — Standard: top, .0012–.0022 inch; second, .0022–.0031 inch.
⑥ — On Non-turbo models, 3.4431–3.4439 inch; On turbo models, 3.4424–3.4431 inch.
⑦ — On Non-turbo models, .0007–.0020 inch; On turbo models, .0018–.0025 inch.
⑧ — On Non-turbo models, .8252–.8260 inch; On turbo models, .8664–.8667 inch.
⑨ — On Non-turbo models, .0090–.0250 inch; On turbo models, .0050–.0250 inch.
⑩ — On Non-turbo models, .0011–.0031 inch; On turbo models, .0010–.0030 inch.
⑪ — On Non-turbo models, .0004–.0070 inch; On turbo models, .0010–.0060 inch.
⑫ — Top ring, .0080–.0140 inch.; 2nd ring, .0091–.0197 inch.
⑬ — Top ring, .0079–.0142 inch; second ring, .0146–.0249 inch.
⑭ — Top ring, .0020–.0037 inch; second ring, .0016–.0031 inch.
⑮ — Top ring, .0090–.0149 inch; second ring, .0137–.0236 inch.
⑯ — Top ring, .0007–.0026 inch; second ring, .0007–.0022 inch.
⑰ — Diesel engine.
⑱ — Top ring, .0140–.0177 inch; intermediate ring, .0334–.0452 inch.
⑲ — Upper need only inspection for damage; second ring, .0060 inch.
⑳ — Top ring, .0080–.0140 inch; second ring, .0220–.0310 inch.

CYLINDER BLOCK

All Specifications Given In Inches Unless Otherwise Noted.

Engine Liter	Year	Cylinder Bore Diameter (Std.)	Cylinder Bore Taper Max.	Cylinder Bore Out Of Round Max.	Cylinder Block Warpage Limit	Sleeve Protrusion	Combustion Deck Height
2.4L	2002–06	3.4446–3.4452	.0020	.0020	.008	—	—
2.5L	2002	3.8759–3.8775	.0010	.0010	.008	—	—
2.7L	2003–06	—	—	—	—	—	—
3.3L	2002–06	3.6610–3.6617	.0020	.0030	.004	—	—
3.5L	2004–06	3.7797–3.7803	.0020	.0030	.003	—	—
3.8L	2002–06	3.7792–3.7800	.0020	.0030	.004	—	—
3.9L	2002–03	3.9098–3.9122	.0010	.0010	—	—	—
4.7L	2002–06	3.6616–3.6622	.0020	.0030	—	—	—
5.2L	2002–03	3.9098–.309122	.0010	.0010	—	—	—
5.7L	2003–06	3.9170	.0005	.0003	—	—	—
5.9L①	2002–03	4.0000–4.0020	.0100	.0050	—	—	—
5.9L②	2002–06	4.0200	.0030	.0015	.003	.0000–.0019	③
8.0L	2002–03	4.0003–4.0008	.0050	.0030	—	—	—
8.3L	2004–06	4.0298–4.030	.0015	.0020	—	—	—

① — Gasoline engine.
② — Diesel engine.
③ — Standard height 12.7165 inch, block may be refaced twice in steps of .0039 inch.

OIL PUMP

All Specifications Given In Inches Unless Otherwise Noted.

Engine Liter	Year	Rotor Back-lash①	Rotor To Body Clear-ance	Rotor End-play②	Rotor Thickness (Minimum)		Outer Rotor Diameter (Min-imum)	Cover Flatness Variation (Max-imum)	Relief Spring Free Length	Relief Spring Pressure, Lbs. @ Inches
					Inner	Outer				
2.4L	2002–06	.0080	.0150	.0040	④	④	⑤	.0010	2.39	18–19 @ 1.600
2.5L	2002	—	.0020–.0040	.0040–.0080	—	—	—	—	—	—
2.7L	2003–06	—	—	—	—	—	—	—	—	—
3.3L	2002–06	.0080	.0150	.0040	.3010	.3010	3.148	.0030	1.95	19.5–20.5 @ 1.340
3.5L	2004–06	.0080	—	.0030	.5630	.5630	3.149	.0010	—	—
3.8L	2002–06	.0080	.0150	.0040	.3010	.3010	3.148	.0030	1.95	19.5–20.5 @ 1.340
3.9L	2002–03	.0080	.0140	.0040	.8250	.8250	2.469	.0015	1.95	20.5 @ 1.343
4.7L	2002–06	.4000	.0014–.0038	.0060	.4731	.4731	3.3829	.0010	—	—
5.2L	2002–03	.0080	.0140	.0040	.8250	.8250	2.469	.0015	—	—
5.7L	2003–06	.0038	.0090	—	—	—	—	—	—	—
5.9L③	2002–03	.0080	.0140	.0040	.8250	.8250	2.469	.0015	1.95	19.5–20. @ 5 1.343
5.9L⑥	2002–06	.0030–.0150	.0150	.0070	—	—	—	.0050	2.60	—
8.0L	2002–03	.0230	.0060	.0075	.5876	.5876	3.246	.0020	1.95	22.5–24.5 @ 1.343
8.3L	2004–06	.0068	.0030	.0030	.7440	.7440	3.246	.0030	—	—

① — Maximum inner to outer rotor tip clearance.
② — Measured between pump cover mounting surface & end of gear using straightedge & feeler gauge.
③ — Gasoline engine.
④ — On 2002–04 models, .3700 inch; On 2005–06 models, .4210 inch.
⑤ — On 2002–04 models, 3.148 inch; On 2005–06 models, 3.383 inch.
⑥ — Diesel engine.

Jeep

NOTE: Refer To "DaimlerChrysler" Section For 5.7L Engine Specifications.

INDEX

CYLINDER HEAD, VALVE GUIDE & VALVE SEATS

All Specifications Given In Inches Unless Otherwise Noted.

Engine Liter	Year	Cylinder Head Warpage Limit	Valve Guides		Valve Seats			
			Inside Diameter	Stem To Guide Clearance	Seat Angle, Deg.	Seat Width		Runout
						Intake	Exhaust	
2.4L	2002–06	.004	.2350–.2360	②	44½–45	.0350–.0510	.0350–.0510	.0020
2.5L	2002	.008	.3130–.3140	.0010–.0030	44½	.0400–.0600	.0400–.0600	.0025
2.8L④	2005–06	—	.2362–.2366	.0010–.0020	—	—	—	—
3.7L	2002–06	.002	—	①	44½–45	.0698–.0928	.0673–.0911	.0020
4.0L	2002–06	.008	.3130–.3140	.0010–.0030	44½	.0400–.0600	.0400–.0600	.0025
4.7L	2002–06	.002	.2747–.2756	③	44½–45	.0698–.0928	.0673–.0911	.0020
6.1L	2006	—	.3130–.3140	⑤	44½–45	.0464–.0637	.0582–.0755	.0019

① — Intake, .0008–.0028 inch; Exhaust, .0019–.0039 inch.

② — Intake, .0018–.0025 inch; Exhaust, .0029–.0037 inch.

③ — Intake, .0008–.0028 inch. Exhaust, .0019–.0039 inch.

④ — Diesel engine.

⑤ — Intake, .0008–.0025 inch; exhaust, .0010–.0028 inch.

VALVE SPRINGS

All Specifications Given In Inches Unless Otherwise Noted.

Engine Liter	Year	Free Length	Installed Height	Pressure, Pounds @ Inches	
				Closed	Open
2.4L	2002–06	1.9050	1.496	75.98 @ 1.49600	136 @ 1.1720
2.5L	2002	1.8760	1.640	71–79 @ 1.64000	202–218 @ 1.2160
2.8L⑥	2005–06	1.7810	1.496	—	—
3.7L	2002–06	②	1.579	③	④
4.0L	2002–06	1.8760	1.640	71–79 @ 1.64000	202–218 @ 1.2160
4.7L	2002–06	1.9134	①	70.92722–79.24515 @ 1.6099	176.6998–193.3357 @ 1.1670
4.7L HO	2002–03	1.9259	⑤	85.42740 @ 1.57950	231.5532 @ 1.1070
6.1L	2006	2.2560	⑦	⑧	⑨

① — Intake, 1.613 inch; Exhaust, 1.606 inch.

② — Intake, 1.926 inch; Exhaust, 1.961 inch.

③ — Intake, 81.15–87.67 lbs. @ 1.5795 inch; Exhaust, 87.67–96.66 lbs. @ 1.5795 inch.

④ — Intake, 221.2–233.8 lbs. @ 1.1.07 inch; Exhaust, 216.9–237.1 lbs. @ 1.107 inch.

⑤ — Intake, 1.613 inch. Exhaust, 1.606 inch.

⑥ — Diesel engine.

⑦ — Intake, 1.870 inch; exhaust, 1.772 inch.

⑧ — Intake, 90–108 @ 1.8700 inch; exhaust, 90–108 @ 1.7720 inch.

⑨ — Intake, 325.5 @ 1.3000 inch; exhaust, 325.5 @ 1.2200 inch.

ENGINE REBUILDING SPECIFICATIONS

VALVES

All Specifications Given In Inches Unless Otherwise Noted.

Engine Liter	Year	Stem Diameter	Maximum Tip Refinish	Face Angle, Deg.	Margin①
2.4L	2002–06	④	—	44½–45	⑤
2.5L	2002	.3110–.3120	.010	46½	—
2.8L⑥	2005–06	⑦	—	45¼–45	—
3.7L	2002–06	③	—	45–45½	—
4.0L	2002–06	.3110–.3120	.010	46½	—
4.7L	2002–06	②	.010	45–45½	—
6.1L	2006	.3120–.3130	—	⑧	—

① — Minimum.
② — Intake, .2727–.2739 inch. Exhaust, .2717–.2728 inch.
③ — Intake, .2729–.2739 inch; Exhaust, .2717–.2728 inch.
④ — Intake, .2337–.2344 inch; Exhaust, .2326–.2333 inch.
⑤ — Intake, .0470–.0660 inch. Exhaust, .0380–.0510 inch.
⑥ — Diesel engine.
⑦ — Intake, .2340–.2350 inch; exhaust, .2330–.2340 inch.
⑧ — Intake, 45½–46; exhaust, 45–45½.

CAMSHAFT

All Specifications Given In Inches Unless Otherwise Noted.

Engine Liter	Year	Camshaft Journal Diameter	Camshaft Bearing Clearance	Lifter Bore Diameter	Lifter Diameter	Lifter To Bore Clearance
2.4L	2002–06	1.0210–1.0220	.0027–.0030	—	—	—
2.5L	2002	①	.0010–.0030	.9055–.9065	.9040–.9045	.0010–.0025
2.8L②	2005–06	③	.0010–.0030	—	—	—
3.7L	2002–06	1.0227–1.0235	.0010–.0026	—	—	—
4.0L	2002–06	①	.0010–.0030	.9055–.9065	.9040–.9045	.0010–.0025
4.7L	2002–06	1.0227–1.0232	.0010–.0026	—	—	—
6.1L	2006	④	⑤	—	.8435–.8444	.0007–.0024

① — No. 1, 2.029–2.030 inch; No. 2, 2.019–2.020 inch; No. 3, 2.009–2.010 inch; No. 4, 1.999–2.000 inch.
② — Diesel engine.
③ — Front, 1.1790–1.180 inch, center and rear, 1.5450–1.5460 inch.
④ — No. 1, 2.2900 inch; No. 2, 2.2700 inch; No. 3, 2.2600 inch; No. 4, 2.2400 inch; No. 5, 1.7200 inch.
⑤ — Nos. 1, 3 & 5, .0015–.0030 inch; Nos. 2 & 4, .0019–.0035 inch.

CRANKSHAFT, BEARINGS & RODS

All Specifications Given In Inches Unless Otherwise Noted.

Engine Liter	Year	Crankshaft				Bearing Clearance			Connecting Rods	
		Main Bearing Journal Diameter	Connecting Rod Journal Diameter	Max. Out Of Round	Max. Taper	Main Bear.	Connect. Rod Bearings	Thrust Bearing	Pin Bore Diameter	Side Clearance
2.4L	2002–06	2.3620–2.3625	1.9680–1.9685	.0003	.0001	.0007–.0024	.0009–.0027	.0035–.0140	.8252–.8260	.0050–.0150
2.5L	2002	2.4996–2.5001	2.0934–2.0955	.0005	.0005	.0010–.0025	.0010–.0025	.0015–.0065	.9288–.9298	.0100–.0190
2.8L②	2005–06	—	—	—	—	—	—	—	—	—
3.7L	2002–06	2.4996–2.5005	2.2798–2.2792	.0002	.0004	.0001–.0013	.00024–.0017	—	—	.0040–.0138
4.0L	2002–06	①	2.0934–2.0955	.0005	.0005	.0010–.0025	.0010–.0025	.0015–.0065	.9288–.9298	.0100–.0190
4.7L	2002–06	2.4996–2.5005	2.0076–2.0082	.0002	.0004	.0008–.0021	.0004–.0019	—	.9467–.9463	.0040–.0138
6.1L	2006	2.5585–2.5595	2.1250–2.1260	.0002	.0001	.0009–.0020	.0007–.0029	—	.9431–.9438	.0030–.0137

① — Nos. 1–6, 2.4996–2.5001 inch; No. 7, 2.4980–2.4995 inch.

② — Diesel engine.

PISTONS, PINS & RINGS

All Specifications Given In Inches Unless Otherwise Noted.

Engine Liter	Year	Piston Clearance	Piston Pin Bore Diameter	Piston Pin Diameter	Piston Pin To Piston Clearance	Piston Ring End Gap		Piston Ring Side Clearance	
						Comp.	Oil	Comp.	Oil
2.4L	2002–06	.0009–.0022	—	.8660–.8662	.0002–.0080	①	.0098–.0250	.0011–.0031	.0040–.0070
2.5L	2002	.0008–.0015	.9312–.9315	.9306–.9307	.0005–.0009	②	.0100–.0600	.0017–.0033	.0024–.0083
2.8L⑥	2005–06	.0003–.0008	—	1.2590–1.2600	.0003–.0007	⑦	.0010–.0030	⑧	.0009–.0019
3.7L	2002–06	—	—	.944–.9456	.0002–.0005	④	.0099–.3000	⑤	.0007–.0091
4.0L	2002–06	.0008–.0015	.9312–.9315	.9306–.9307	.0005–.0009	②	.0100–.0600	.0017–.0033	.0024–.0083
4.7L	2002–06	.0008–.0020	—	.9454–.9456	.0004–.0008	.0146–.0249	.0099–.3000	③	.0007–.0091
6.1L	2006	.0009–.0020	—	.9843–.9844	.0002–.0006	⑨	.0079–.0210	⑩	.0007–.0091

① — Top ring, .0098–.0200 inch. Second ring, .0090–.0180 inch.

② — Top ring, .0090–.0240 inch. Second ring, .0190–.0380 inch.

③ — Top ring, .0020–.0037 inch. Second ring, .0016–.0031 inch.

④ — Top ring, .0079–.0142 inch. Second ring, .0146–.0249 inch.

⑤ — Top ring, .0020–.0037 inch. Second ring, .0016–.0031 inch.

⑥ — Diesel engine.

⑦ — Top ring, .0030–.0050 inch; second ring, .0020–.0040 inch.

⑧ — Top ring, .0110–.0170 inch; second ring, .0011–.0019 inch.

⑨ — Top ring, .0118–.0157 inch; second ring, .0137–.0236 inch.

⑩ — Top ring, .0007–.0026 inch; second ring, .0007–.0022 inch.

CYLINDER BLOCK

All Specifications Given In Inches Unless Otherwise Noted.

Engine Liter	Year	Cylinder Bore Diameter (Std.)	Cylinder Bore Taper Max.	Cylinder Bore Out Of Round Max.	Cylinder Block Warpage Limit
2.4L	2002–06	3.446–3.4452	.0020	.0020	.008
2.5L	2002	3.8759–3.8775	.0010	.0010	.008
2.8L①	2005–06	—	—	—	—
3.7L	2002–06	3.6616–3.6622	.0020	.0030	—
4.0L	2002–06	3.8759–3.8775	.0010	.0010	.008
4.7L	2002–06	3.6616–3.6622	.0020	.0030	—
6.1L	2006	4.0550	.0005	.0030	—

① — Diesel engine.

OIL PUMP

All Specifications Given In Inches Unless Otherwise Noted.

Engine Liter	Year	Rotor Backlash	Rotor To Body Clearance	Rotor Endplay②
2.4L	2002–06	.0080	.0150	.0040
2.5L	2002	①	.0020–.0040	.0040–.0080
2.8L③	2005–06	.0020–.0060	.0350–.0590	.0050–.0060
3.7L	2002–06	.0060①	.0014–.0038	—
4.0L	2002–06	①	.0020–.0040	.0040–.0080
4.7L	2002–06	①	.0020–.0040	.0040–.0080
6.1L	2006	.0060	.0038	.0090

① — Maximum inner to outer rotor tip clearance.
② — Measured between pump cover mounting surface & end of gear using straightedge & feeler gauge.
③ — Diesel engine.

FORD MOTOR COMPANY

FORD MOTOR COMPANY

FULL SIZE TRUCKS & VANS

NOTE: Refer To The Back Of This For The Manufacturer's Special Tool Suppliers.

INDEX OF SERVICE OPERATIONS

Specifications

GENERAL ENGINE SPECIFICATIONS

Year	Engine, Liter	Fuel System	Bore & Stroke	Compression Ratio	Horsepower @ RPM	Torque Ft. Lbs. @ RPM	Normal Oil Pressure, Lbs.
2002–03	4.2L	SFI	3.81 x 3.74	9.3	205 @ 4950	255 @ 3700	40–125⑤
	4.6L	SFI	3.55 x 3.54	9.0	220 @ 4500	290 @ 3250	20–45⑥
	5.4L②	SFI	3.55 x 4.16	9.0	260 @ 4500	350 @ 2500	20–45⑥
	5.4L③	SFI	3.55 x 4.16	9.5	300 @ 5000	355 @ 2750	20–45⑥
	5.4L②④	SFI	3.55 x 4.16	8.4	360 @ 4750	440 @ 3000	20–45⑥
	5.4L②④⑧	SFI	3.55 x 4.16	8.4	380 @ 4750	450 @ 3250	40–75⑩
	6.0L①	—	3.74 x 4.13	18.0	325 @ 3300	570 @ 2000	⑨
	6.8L	SFI	3.55 x 4.16	9.0	305 @ 4250	420 @ 3250	40–75⑩
	7.3L①	DI⑪	4.11 x 4.18	17.5	235 @ 2700	500 @ 1600	40–70⑦
2004–06	4.2L	SFI	3.81 x 3.74	9.3	205 @ 4950	255 @ 3700	40–125⑤
	4.6L	SFI	3.55 x 3.54	9.0	220 @ 4500	290 @ 3250	20–45⑥
	5.4L②	SFI	3.55 x 4.16	9.0	260 @ 4500	350 @ 2500	20–45⑥
	5.4L③	SFI	3.55 x 4.16	9.5	300 @ 5000	355 @ 2750	20–45⑥
	5.4L②④	SFI	3.55 x 4.16	8.4	360 @ 4750	440 @ 3000	20–45⑥
	5.4L②④⑧	SFI	3.55 x 4.16	8.4	380 @ 4750	450 @ 3250	40–75⑩
	6.0L①	—	3.74 x 4.13	18.0	325 @ 3300	570 @ 2000	⑨
	6.8L	SFI	3.55 x 4.16	9.0	305 @ 4250	420 @ 3250	40–75⑩

① — Diesel engine.
② — SOHC engine.
③ — DOHC engine.
④ — Supercharged.
⑤ — At normal operating temperature & 2500 RPM.
⑥ — At normal operating temperature & 1500 RPM.
⑦ — At normal operating temperature & 3300 RPM.
⑧ — SVT.
⑨ — Low, 10 psi @ 230°F oil temperature, high, 40 psi @ 230°F oil temperature.
⑩ — At normal operating temperature & 2000 RPM.
⑪ — Direct Injection (DI).

TUNE UP SPECIFICATIONS

Year & Engine	Spark Plug Gap	Ignition Timing BTDC: Firing Order ③	Ignition Timing BTDC: Man. Trans.	Ignition Timing BTDC: Auto. Trans.	Ignition Timing BTDC: Mark Location	Curb Idle Speed②: Man. Trans.	Curb Idle Speed②: Auto. Trans.	Fast Idle Speed②: Man. Trans.	Fast Idle Speed②: Auto. Trans.	Fuel Pump Pressure, psi.	Valve Lash, Inch
2002											
4.2L	.052–.056	⑥	10⑦	10⑦	⑪	⑧	⑧	⑧	⑧	④	⑨
4.6L	.052–.056	⑤	10⑦	10⑦	⑪	⑧	⑧	⑧	⑧	④	⑨
5.4L (Gasoline)	.052–.056	⑤	10⑦	10⑦	⑪	⑧	⑧	⑧	⑧	④	⑨
5.4L (NVG/LPG)	.052–.056	⑤	10⑦	10⑦	⑪	⑧	⑧	⑧	⑧	⑬	⑨
6.8L	.052–.056	①	10⑦	10⑦	⑪	⑧	⑧	⑧	⑧	④	⑨
2003–06											
4.2L	.052–.056	⑥	10⑦	10⑦	⑪	⑧	⑧	⑧	⑧	④	⑨
4.6L	.052–.056	⑤	⑩	⑩	⑪	⑧	⑧	⑧	⑧	50	⑨
5.4L DOHC	.052–.056	⑤	10⑦	10⑦	⑪	⑧	⑧	⑧	⑧	⑫	⑨
5.4L SOHC	.052–.056	⑤	⑩	⑩	⑪	⑧	⑧	⑧	⑧	55	⑨
6.8L	.052–.056	①	10⑩	10⑩	⑪	⑧	⑧	⑧	⑧	④	⑨

BTDC — Before Top Dead Center

D — Drive

N — Neutral

NGV — Natural Gas Vehicle

① — Equipped w/coil on plug ignition system. Cylinder numbering front to rear, righthand bank, 1, 2, 3, 4, 5; lefthand bank, 6, 7, 8, 9, 10. Firing order, 1-6-5-10-2-7-3-8-4-9.

② — When inspecting idle speed, set parking brake & block drive wheels.

③ — Before removing wires from distributor cap or coil unit, determine location of ignition wires, as position may have been altered from that outlined at end of this chart.

④ — Except F-150: engine running, 28–45 psi.; key on, engine off, 35–45 psi. F-150: engine running, 28–50 psi.; key on engine off, 35–45 psi.

⑤ — Equipped w/coil on plug ignition

system. Cylinder numbering front to rear, righthand bank, 1, 2, 3, 4; lefthand bank, 5, 6, 7, 8. Firing order, 1-3-7-2-6-5-4-8.

⑥ — Firing order, 1-4-2-5-3-6. Refer to **Fig. A,** for spark plug cable orientation at ignition coils.

⑦ — Equipped w/electronic distributorless ignition system and is not adjustable.

⑧ — Controlled by idle speed control motor.

⑨ — Equipped w/hydraulic lash adjusters.

⑩ — Controlled by PCM and not adjustable.

⑪ — Equipped w/crankshaft position sensor.

⑫ — Engine running, 28–45 psi. Key on, engine off, 35–45 psi.

⑬ — Locate vehicle in a well ventilated area away from heat, spark & flame producing equipment. Using extreme caution, connect a suitable natural gas approved fuel pressure gauge to the fuel pressure schraeder valve. Release fuel pressure in fuel injection supply manifold back to fuel tanks. Place ignition switch in On position, then start engine if possible. Place ignition switch in Off position. After 2 minutes, inspect fuel pressure reading on gauge.

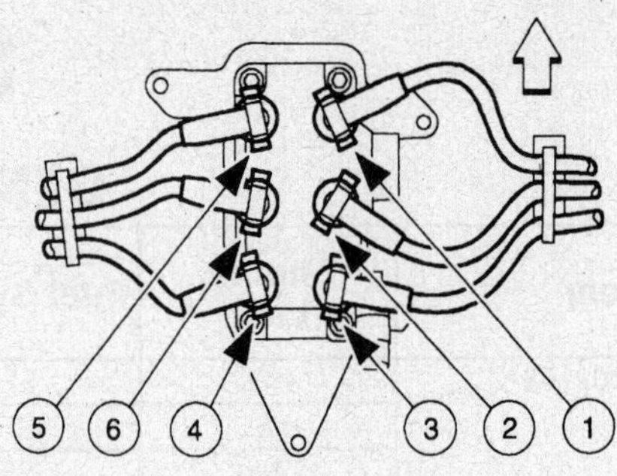

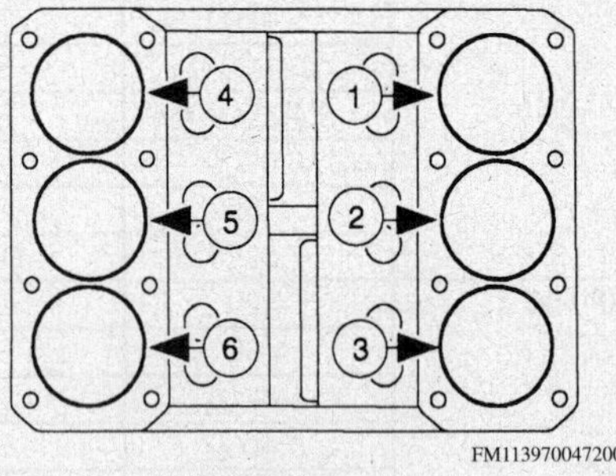

Fig. A

DIESEL ENGINE PERFORMANCE SPECIFICATIONS

Year	Engine, Liter	Compression Ratio	Firing Order, Fig.	Injection Timing (Static), BTDC	Injection Nozzle Opening Pressure, psi	Curb Idle Speed, RPM	Fast Idle Speed, RPM	Valve Clearance, Inch
2002–03	7.3L	17.5	A	①	②	①	①	—
2003–06	6.0L	18.0	A	①	—	—	—	—

BTDC — Before Top Dead Center

① — Controlled by PCM.

② — As high as 21,000 psi.

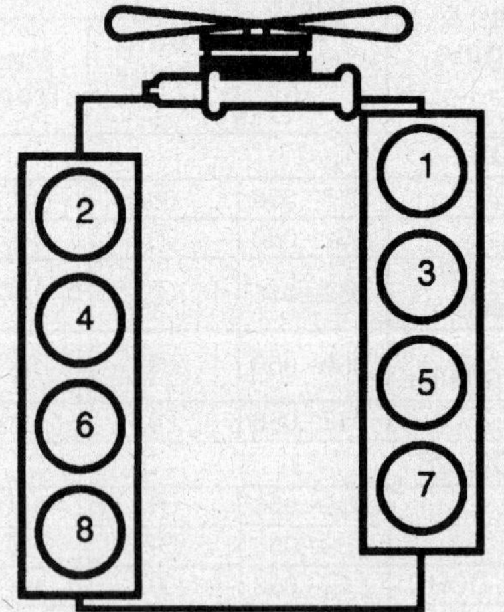

Fig. A

FRONT WHEEL ALIGNMENT SPECIFICATIONS

E-SERIES

Year	Model	Caster Angle, Degrees		Camber Angle, Degrees		Total Toe, Degrees①	
		Limits	Desired	Limits	Desired	Limits	Desired
2002	E150	⑤②	③②	-.25 to +.75④	+.25④	-.19 to +.31	+.06
	E250 & 350	⑤②	③②	0 to +1④	+.50④	-.19 to +.31	+.06
	E Super Duty	⑤②	③②	0 to +1④	+.50④	-.19 to +.31	+.06
	E550	+4.5 to +6.5	+5.5⑥	-.50 to +1⑦	+.25⑦	+.03 to +.09	+.06
2003–05	E150	⑥	③	-.25 to +.75	+.25	-.19 to +.85	+.06
	E250 & E350	⑧	③	-.25 to +.75	+.25	-.19 to +.85	+.06
	E Super Duty	③	③	-.50 to +.75	+.25	-.19 to +.85	+.06
	E550	+4.5 to +6.5	5.5	-.50 to +1	+.25	+.03 to +.09	+.06
2006	E150	⑧	③	-1.25 to +1.25	-.25	–.19 to +.31	+.06
	E250, E350 & E450	⑧	③	-1.25 to +1.25	-.25	–.19 to +.31	+.06

① — Toe-In (+). Toe-Out (-).
② — Split optimum range, -.5° (+/-1°).
③ — Lefthand side, +4.0°; Righthand side, +4.5°.
④ — Split optimum range, 0° (+/-.5°).
⑤ — Lefthand side, +1.25° to +6.75°; Righthand side, +1.75° to +7.25°.
⑥ — Split optimum range, 0° (+/-1°).
⑦ — Split optimum range, 0° (+/-.75°).
⑧ — Lefthand side, +1.25° to +6.75°; Righthand side, +1.75° to +7.25°.

EXCURSION

Year	Model	Caster Angle, Degrees		Camber Angle, Degrees		Total Toe, Degrees①	
		Limits	Desired	Limits	Desired	Limits	Desired
2002–03	2WD	+2 to +6②	+4②	-.38 to +1.62②	+.62②	-.22 to +.28	+.03
	4WD	+1.5 to +5.5②	+3.5②	-.75 to +1.25②	+.25②	-.22 to +.28	+.03
2004–05	2WD	+3 to +6②	+4.5②	-.38 to +1.62②	+.62②	-.22 to +.28	+.03
	4WD	+1.5 to +5.5②	③	-.75 to +1.25②	+.25②	-.22 to +.28	+.03

2WD — Two Wheel Drive
4WD — Four Wheel Drive
① — Toe-In (+). Toe-Out (-).
② — Split optimum range, 0° (+/-1°).
③ — LH, 3.50°; RH, 4.0°.

EXPEDITION & NAVIGATOR

Year	Model	Caster Angle, Degrees		Camber Angle, Degrees⑧		Total Toe, Degrees⑦	
		Limits	Desired	Limits	Desired	Limits	Desired
2002	2WD	①	②	-1 to +.40	-.3	-.19 to +.31	+.06
	4WD Less Air Suspension	③	④	-.90 to +.50	-.2	+.05 to +.55	+.30
	4WD w/Air Suspension⑨	⑤	⑥	⑩	⑪	-.05 to +.45	+.20
2003–06	Less Air Suspension	+4.3 to +6.3⑫	+5.3⑫	-1.05 to +.45⑬	-.3⑬	-.06 to +.34	+.14
	With Air Suspension	+4.5 to +6.5	+5.5⑫	⑭	-.6⑬	-.06 to +.34	+.14

2WD — Two Wheel Drive
4WD — Four Wheel Drive
① — Lefthand side, +5.1° to +7.1°; Righthand side, +5.6° to +7.6°. Split optimum range, -.5° (+/-.7°).
② — Lefthand side, +6.1°; Righthand side, +6.6°. Split optimum range, -.5° (+/-.7°).
③ — Lefthand side, +4.1° to +6.1°; Righthand side, +4.6° to +6.6°. Split optimum range, -.5° (+/-.7°).
④ — Lefthand side, +5.1°; Righthand side, +5.6°. Split optimum range, -.5° (+/-.7°).
⑤ — Lefthand side, +4° to +6°; Righthand side, +4.5° to +6.5°. Split optimum range, -.5° (+/-.7°).
⑥ — Lefthand side, +5°; Righthand side, +5.5°. Split optimum range, -.5° (+/-.7°).
⑦ — Toe-In (+). Toe-Out (-).
⑧ — Split optimum range, 0° (+/-.7°).
⑨ — These specifications are given w/vehicle at trim height settings. Apply parking brake, turn ignition On, place transmission range selector in Drive or Reverse & close all doors to activate trim height mode.
⑩ — Lefthand side, -.8° to 0°; Righthand side, -1.1° to +.3°. Split optimum range, 0° (+/-.7°).
⑪ — Lefthand & Righthand side, -.4°. Split optimum range, 0° (+/-.7°).
⑫ — Split optimum range, 0° (+/-1°).
⑬ — Split optimum range, 0° (+/-.75°).
⑭ — Navigator, -1.35° to +.15°; Expedition, -1.05° to +.45°.

FRONT WHEEL ALIGNMENT SPECIFICATIONS—Continued

FORD F150 & MARK LT

Year	Model	Caster Angle, Degrees		Camber Angle, Degrees		Total Toe, Degrees①	
		Limits	Desired	Limits	Desired	Limits	Desired
2002	2WD	②③	③④	-1 to +.4⑤	-.3⑤	-.19 to +.31⑥	+.06⑥
	4WD	⑦⑧	⑧⑨	-.8 to +.6⑩	-.1⑩	-.05 to +.45⑪	-.20⑪
	Lightning	—	③⑫	—	-.5⑤	-.35 to +.15	-.10
2003–04	2WD	②③	③④	-1 to +.4⑤	-.3⑤	-.12 to +.18⑥	+.06⑥
	4WD	⑦⑧	⑧⑨	-.8 to +.6	-.1	-.05 to +.25	.10
	Lightning	—	③⑫	—	-.5⑤	-.20 to +.10	-.05
2005–06	2WD	⑬	⑭	-1 to +.4⑤	-.3⑤	-.50 to +.35⑥	+.15⑥
	4WD	⑬	⑭	-1 to +.4⑤	-.3⑤	-.50 to +.35⑥	+.15⑥

2WD — Two Wheel Drive
4WD — Four Wheel Drive
① — Toe-In (+). Toe-Out (-).
② — Lefthand side, +5.2° to +7.2°; Righthand side, +5.7° to +7.7°.
③ — Split optimum range, -.5° (+/-.7°).
④ — Lefthand side, +6.2°; Righthand side, +6.7°.
⑤ — Split optimum range, 0° (+/-.7°).
⑥ — Split optimum range, .06° (+/-.25°).
⑦ — Lefthand side, +3.6° to +5.6°; Righthand side, +4.3° to +6.3°.
⑧ — Split optimum range, –.7° (+/-.7°).
⑨ — Lefthand side, +4.6°; Righthand side, +5.3°.
⑩ — Split optimum range, 0° (+/-.7°).
⑪ — Split optimum range, .2° (+/-.25°).
⑫ — Lefthand side, +6.7°; Righthand side, +7.2°.
⑬ — Lefthand side, +3.0° to +5.0°; Righthand side, +3.5° to +5.5°.
⑭ — Lefthand side, +4.0°; Righthand side, +4.5°.

F SUPER DUTY

Year	Model	Caster Angle, Degrees		Camber Angle, Degrees		Total Toe, Degrees①	
		Limits	Desired	Limits	Desired	Limits	Desired
2002–04	2WD	+2.00 to +6.00④	+4.00④	-.380 to +1.620④	+.62④	-.22 to +.28	+.03
	4WD	+1.50 to +5.50④	+3.50④	-.750 to +1.250④	+.25④	-.22 to +.28	+.03
	Motorhome Chassis	+4.13 to +5.13	+4.63	+.625 to +1.375	+1.00	②	③
2005–06	F250–350 2WD	+3.60 to +5.00	+3.80	-.130 to +1.370	+.62	+.15 to +.35	+.10
	F250 4WD⑤	+2.10 to +4.50	+3.30	–.600 to +.900	+.15	+.15 to +.35	+.10
	F250 4WD⑥	+1.30 to +4.90	+2.60	–.600 to +.000	+.15	+.15 to +.35	+.10
	F350 4WD⑤	+1.30 to +3.70	+2.50	–.600 to +.000	+.15	+.15 to +.35	+.10
	F350 4WD⑥	+.50 to +3.10	+1.80	–.600 to +.000	+.15	+.15 to +.35	+.10
	F450–550⑤	+1.00 to 3.40	+2.20	–.600 to +.000	+.15	+.15 to +.35	+.10
	F450–550⑥	+.60 to +3.30	+1.90	–.600 to +.000	+.15	+.15 to +.35	+.10
	Motorhome Chassis	+4.13 to +5.13	+4.63	+.625 to +1.375	+1.00	②	③

2WD — Two Wheel Drive
4WD — Four Wheel Drive
① — Toe-In (+). Toe-Out (-).
② — Toe-in .03 inch to .09 inch.
③ — Toe-in .06 inch.
④ — Split optimum range, 0° (+/-1°).
⑤ — Standard Suspension.
⑥ — Heavy duty suspension.

FLUID CAPACITIES & COOLING SYSTEM DATA

F-SERIES

Year	Model	Engine Liter	Cooling Capacity Qts.	Radiator Cap Relief Pres-sure, Lbs.	Engine Oil Refill Qts.①	Transmission Oil		Transfer Case Pts.	Drive Axle Oil	
						Manual Trans Pts.	Auto Trans. Qts.②		Front Pts.	Rear Pts.
2002	F150	4.2L	⑫	16	6⑱	7.4	④	4⑧	3.7	⑨
		4.6L	⑦	16	6⑱	7.4	④	4⑧	3.7	⑨
		5.4L	⑥	16	6⑱	7.4	④	4⑧	3.7	⑨
		5.4L SC	17③	16	6⑱	7.4	④	4⑧	3.7	⑨
	F Super Duty 250–550 & Motor Home Chassis	5.4L	26.4	16	6⑱	11.6	17.7	4⑧	⑩	⑳
		6.8L	28.5	16	6⑱	11.6	17.7	4⑧	⑩	⑳
		7.3L⑲	32.8	16	13⑤	11.6	17.7	4⑧	⑩	⑳
2003	F150	4.2L	17.3	16	6⑱	6.2	⑭	4⑧	3.5–3.7⑮	5.5⑪
		4.6L	19.4	16	6⑱	6.2	⑭	4⑧	3.5–3.7⑮	5.5⑪
		5.4L	19.4	16	6⑱	6.2	⑭	4⑧	3.5–3.7⑮	5.5⑪
	F Super Duty 250–550 & Motor Home Chassis	5.4L	26.4	⑯	6⑱	11.6	⑰	4⑧	5.9⑧	⑬
		6.0L⑲	27.5	⑯	15⑱	11.6	⑰	4⑧	5.9⑧	⑬
		6.8L	28.5	⑯	6⑱	11.6	⑰	4⑧	5.9⑧	⑬
		7.3L⑲	32.75	⑯	13⑤	11.6	⑰	4⑧	5.9⑧	⑬
2004–06	F150	4.2L	17.3	16	6⑱	6.2	⑭	4⑧	3.5–3.7⑮	5.5⑪⑳
		4.6L	20.7	16	6⑱	6.2	⑭	4⑧	3.5–3.7⑮	5.5⑪⑳
		5.4L	21.2	16	6⑱	6.2	⑭	4⑧	3.5–3.7⑮	5.5⑪⑳
	F Super Duty 250–550 & Motor Home Chassis	5.4L	26.4	⑯	6⑱	11.6	⑰	4⑧	6.4⑧	⑬
		6.0L⑲	27.5	⑯	15⑱	11.6	⑰	4⑧	6.4⑧	⑬
		6.8L	27.5	⑯	6⑱	11.6	⑰	4⑧	6.4⑧	⑬

SC — Supercharged
2WD — Two Wheel Drive
4WD — Four Wheel Drive
① — Add 1 qt. w/filter change.
② — Approximate. Make final inspection w/dipstick.
③ — Intercooler coolant, 42 qts.
④ — 2WD models w/4R100 trans., 17 qts. 4WD models w/4R100 trans., 17.7 qts. All models w/4R70W trans., 13.9 qts.
⑤ — Add 2 qts. w/filter change.
⑥ — 1 row, 23.9 qts., 2 row, 25.5 qts.
⑦ — 1 row, 20.6 qts., 2 row, 23.1 qts.
⑧ — Fill to bottom of filler plug hole.
⑨ — 8.80 & 9.75 inch rear axle S, 5.50 pts.; 10.25 inch axle 6.90 pts. these are approximate refills, fill to .25 inch below fill hole while on level surface.
⑩ — F250/350 Dana 50 Axle, 3.80 pts.; F-350/450/550 Dana 60 axle, 5.80 pts.
⑪ — 1/4 to 9/16 inch below filler hole.
⑫ — 1 row, 20.1 qts., 2 row 21.6 qts.
⑬ — Models w/Dana 80 conventional & Truetrac axles, 8.5 pts.; models w/Dana 80 Trac-Lok axle, first fill axle with .5 pint of additive friction modifier part No. C8AZ-19B546-A, or equivalent meeting Ford specification EST-M2C118-A, then add 8 pts. of suitable axle lubricant. Models w/Dana S135 axle, 24.5 pts. Models w/Ford 10.5 inch ring gear, fill to bottom of filler plug hole; models w/Trac-Lok axles, first fill axle with .5 pint of additive friction modifier part No. C8AZ-19B546-A, or equivalent meeting Ford specification EST-M2C118-A.
⑭ — 2WD vehicles w/4R100 trans., 17.1 qts.; 4WD vehicles w/4R100 trans., 17.7 qts.
⑮ — 3/8 inch below bottom of filler hole.
⑯ — Use individual readings listed on cap.
⑰ — With 20 plate oil-to-air cooler, 17.1 qts.; w/26 plates, 17.7 qts.
⑱ — Includes filter.
⑲ — Diesel engine.
⑳ — On models equipped w/10.25 inch ring gear, first fill axle with 7 ounces additive friction modifier XL-3 part No. EST-M2C118-A, or equivalent.

FLUID CAPACITIES & COOLING SYSTEM DATA—Continued

E-SERIES

Year	Engine Liter	Cooling System Capacity Qts.		Radiator Cap Relief Pressure, Lbs.	Engine Oil Refill Qts.	Auto. Trans. Qts.②	Drive Axle Oil
		Less A/C	With A/C				
2002–04	4.2L	23.3⑪	23.3⑪	16	6⑦	⑩	⑤
	4.6L	25③	25③	16	6⑦	⑩	⑤
	5.4L	29①	29①	16	6⑦	⑩	⑤
	6.0L⑨	27.5	27.5	⑫	15⑦	—	—
	6.8L	30.6⑧	30.6⑧	16	6⑦	⑩	⑤
	7.3L⑨	30⑥	30⑥	13	13④	⑩	⑤
2005–06	4.2L	17.6	23.3⑪	16	6⑦	⑩	⑤
	4.6L	25③	25③	16	6⑦	⑩	⑤
	5.4L	29①	29①	16	6⑦	⑩	⑤
	6.0L⑨	27.5	27.5	⑫	15⑦	⑬	⑤
	6.8L	30.6⑧	30.6⑧	16	6⑦	⑩	⑤

① — On models equipped w/auxiliary heater, 31 qts.
② — Approximate. Make final inspection w/dipstick.
③ — On models equipped w/auxiliary heater, 27.2 qts.
④ — Add 2 qts. w/filter change.
⑤ — Ford 8.8 & 9.75 inch conventional & Traction-Lok 5.5–5.8 pts.; Dana 9.75 inch, M60–IU, 6.3 pts.; Dana 10.5 inch, M70–2U, 6.6 pts.; Dana 10.5 inch, M70–1HD, 7.5 pts.; Dana 11.25 inch, Model 80, 8.25 pts.
⑥ — Add 2.6 qts. on models equipped w/auxiliary heater.
⑦ — Includes filter.
⑧ — On models equipped w/auxiliary heater, 32.8 qts.
⑨ — Diesel engine.
⑩ — 4R70W trans, 13.9 qts.; 4R100 except E Super Duty, 17 qts.; 4R100 E Super Duty, 17.7 qts.
⑪ — On models equipped w/auxiliary heater, 25.4 qts.
⑫ — Use individual readings listed on cap.
⑬ — w/4R70W & 4R75W trans, 13.6 qts.; w/ Torqshift trans, 19.2 qts.

EXCURSION

Year	Engine Liter	Cooling System Capacity Qts.	Radiator Cap Relief Pressure, Lbs.	Fuel Tank Gals.	Engine Oil Refill Qts.	Auto. Trans. Qts.①	Transfer Case Pts.	Drive Axle Oil	
								Front Pts.	Rear Pts.
2002	5.4L	26.4⑥	16	44	6⑤	⑧	4	5.9	⑦
	6.8L	28.5⑥	16	44	6⑤	⑧	4	5.9	⑦
	7.3L	32.8	16	44	13②	⑧	4	5.9	⑦
2003–05	5.4L	26.4	⑨	④	6⑤	③	4	5.9	⑦
	6.0L	27.5	⑨	④	16⑤	③	4	5.9	⑦
	6.8L	28.5	⑨	④	6⑤	③	4	5.9	⑦
	7.3L	32.75	⑨	④	13⑤	③	4	5.9	⑦

① — Approximate. Make final inspection w/dipstick.
② — Add 2 qts. w/filter change.
③ — With 20 plate oil-to-air cooler, 17.1 qts.; w/26 plates, 17.7 qts.
④ — Wide frame vehicles standard bed midship tank, 38 gals,; Wide frame vehicles short bed midship tank, 29 gals.; Narrow frame chassis cab aft-of-axle tank standard equipment, 40 gals.; Narrow frame chassis cab midship tank (optional), 19 gals.
⑤ — Includes filter.
⑥ — Models w/rear heater add 1.5 qts.
⑦ — Ford rear axle 7.0 pts., Dana 80 Conventional, 8.5 pts., Dana 80 trac-lok, 8.0 pts., Dana S135 rear axle, 24.5 pts.
⑧ — 2WD, 17.1 qts.; 4WD, 17.7 qts.
⑨ — Use individual readings listed on cap.

FLUID CAPACITIES & COOLING SYSTEM DATA—Continued

EXPEDITION

Year	Engine Liter	Cooling System Capacity Qts.	Radiator Cap Relief Pressure, Lbs.	Fuel Tank Gals.	Engine Oil Refill Qts.	Auto. Trans. Qts.①	Transfer Case Pts.	Drive Axle Oil	
								Front Pts.	Rear Pts.
2002	4.6L	⑦⑧	16	④	6⑥	③	4	3.7	5.8
	5.4L	⑧⑤	16	④	6⑥	③	4	3.7	5.8
2003–04	4.6L	⑨	16	28	6⑥	②	4	3.7	5.8
	5.4L	⑩	16	28	6⑥	②	4	3.7	5.8
2005–06	4.6L	⑨	16	28	6⑥	⑫	4	3.6	⑬
	5.4L	⑪	16	28	6⑥	⑫	3.8–4.2	3.6	⑬

DOHC — Dual Overhead Cam
SOHC — Single Overhead Cam
① — Approximate. Make final inspection w/dipstick.
② — 4R70W, 13.9 qts. 4R100, 15.9 qts.
③ — 4R70W, 13.9 qts. 4R100 2WD, 15.9 qts. 4R100 4WD, 16.4 qts.
④ — Expedition, 2WD vehicles less rear load leveling system, 26 gals.; 2WD vehicles w/rear load leveling system, 30 gals.; 4WD vehicles, 30 gals. Navigator, 30 gals.
⑤ — Less auxiliary heater, 1-row radiator, 23.9 qts.; w/2-row radiator, 25.5 qts.; w/auxiliary heater, 1-row radiator, 26.3 qts.; w/2-row radiator, 27.9 qts.
⑥ — Includes filter.
⑦ — Less auxiliary heater, 1-row radiator, 21.7 qts.; w/2-row radiator, 23 qts.; w/auxiliary heater, 1-row radiator, 22.9 qts.; w/2-row radiator, 24.8 qts.
⑧ — Up to 3.3 additional qts. may be required on models equipped w/auxiliary heater.
⑨ — Less auxiliray heater, 20.1 qts.; w/auxiliary heater 22.2 qts.
⑩ — Less auxiliary heater, 22.2 qts.; w/auxiliary heater 24.3 qts.
⑪ — Base radiator less auxiliary heater, 19.4 qts.; Heavy duty radiator less auxiliary heater, 19.7 qts.; Base radiator w/auxiliary heater, 20.7 qts.; Heavy duty radiator w/auxiliary heater, 20.9 qts.
⑫ — 4R70E & 4R75E trans, 13.9 qts.; 6HP26 trans, 9.5 qts.
⑬ — 4 pints plus 4 oz. Friction Modifier .9 in below fill hole.

LUBRICANT DATA

Year	Model	Lubricant Type						
		Transmission		Hydraulic Clutch Fluid	Transfer Case	Drive Axle	Power Steering	Brake System
		Manual	Automatic					
E-SERIES, EXCURSION & F-150, F-SUPER DUTY & MARK LT								
2002–04	Econoline	—	⑤	—	—	③	Mercon®	DOT 3
	Excursion	—	Mercon®	—	Mercon®	②	Mercon®	DOT 3
	F-150 & Mark LT	Mercon®	⑤	DOT 3	Mercon®	④	Mercon®	DOT 3
	F Super Duty 250–550 & Motorhome	⑦	Mercon®	DOT 3	Mercon®	⑥	Mercon®	DOT 3
2005–06	Econoline	—	⑤	—	—	③	Mercon®	DOT 3
	Excursion	—	Mercon®	—	Mercon®	②	Mercon®	DOT 3
	F-150 & Mark LT	Mercon®	⑤	DOT 3	Mercon®	④	Mercon®	DOT 3
	F Super Duty 250–550 & Motorhome	⑦	⑧	DOT 3	Mercon®	⑥	Mercon®	DOT 3
EXPEDITION & NAVIGATOR								
2002–04	All	—	⑤	—	Mercon®	①	Mercon®	DOT 3
2005–06	All	—	⑧	—	Mercon®	①	Mercon®	DOT 3

MERCON®, MERCON® V and MERCON® SP are not interchangeable transmission fluids.

PSF — Power Steering Fluid

① — Front, SAE 75W-90 gear lubricant, or equivalent meeting Ford specification WSP-M2C201-A. Rear, 75W-140 synthetic lube part No. F1TZ-19580-B, or equivalent synthetic gear lubricant meeting Ford specification WSL-M2C192-A. Add 4 oz. of friction modifier part No. C8AZ-19B546-A, or an equivalent meeting Ford specification EST-M2C118-A on models w/Traction-Lok axles.

② — Front, SAE 75W-90 gear lubricant, or equivalent meeting Ford specification WSP-M2C201-A. Rear, 75W-140 synthetic lube part No. F1TZ-19580-B, or equivalent synthetic gear lubricant meeting Ford specification WSL-M2C192-A. Add 8 oz. of friction modifier part No. C8AZ-19B546-A, or an equivalent meeting Ford specification EST-M2C118-A on models w/Traction-Lok axles.

③ — E-150 models w/Ford conventional & Traction-Lok axles use Motorcraft SAE 75W-140 Synthetic Rear Axle Lubricant part No. F1TZ-19580-B, or equivalent. Add 4 oz.

of friction modifier part No. C8AZ-19B546-A, or an equivalent meeting Ford specification EST-M2C118-A. E250–450 models w/Dana conventional & Traction-Lok axles use Motorcraft SAE 80W-90 Premium Rear Axle Lubricant, or equivalent. Add 6 oz. of friction modifier.

④ — Front, SAE 75W-90 gear lubricant, or equivalent meeting Ford specification WSP-M2C201-A. Rear, 75W-140 synthetic lube part No. F1TZ-19580-B, or equivalent synthetic gear lubricant meeting Ford specification WSL-M2C192-A.

⑤ — 4R70W trans., Mercon® V ATF; 4R100 trans., Mercon® ATF.

⑥ — Front, 75W-90 gear lubricant. Dana 135 rear axle, 80W-90 gear lubricant. Ford rear axle use Motorcraft SAE 75W-140 synthetic rear axle lubricant part No. F1TZ-19580-B, or an equivalent meeting Ford specification WSL-M2C192-A. For limited slip differential, add friction modifier C8AZ-19B546-A, or equivalent. Dana 80 rear axle, synthetic 75W-90 gear lubricant part No. 75W90-GLS, or an equivalent. Dana 135 rear axle, thermally stable 80W-90 gear lubricant meeting Ford specification WSP-M2C197-A.

⑦ — 5-speed trans., synthetic Mercon®; 6-speed trans., Mercon®.

⑧ — 4R70E, 4R75E & 6HP26 trans, MERCON® V ATF; Torqshift trans, MERCON® SP ATF.

Electrical

NOTE: On Air Bag Equipped Models, Refer To "Air Bag System Precautions" Located In The Front Of This Manual For System Disarming & Arming Procedures.

NOTE: Refer To "Computer Relearn Procedures" Located In The Front Of This Manual When Battery Power To The Computer Has Been Interrupted.

INDEX

PRECAUTIONS

Air Bag Systems

Refer to "Air Bag System Precautions" in the front of this manual for system disarming and arming procedures.

Battery Ground Cable

Prior to service, disconnect battery ground cable and isolate as required.

FUSE PANEL & FLASHER LOCATION

Excursion

The underhood fuse panel is located on the lefthand side of engine compartment. The interior fuse panel is located under lefthand side of instrument panel.

The flasher relay is located behind lefthand side of instrument panel.

Expedition, F-150, Mark LT & Navigator

The underhood fuse panel is located on the lefthand side of engine compartment. The interior fuse panel is located under lefthand side of instrument panel.

The flasher relay is located behind righthand side of the instrument panel.

E-Series

The underhood fuse panel is located at the lefthand front side of engine compartment. The interior fuse panel is located under lefthand side of instrument panel near kick panel.

The electronic flasher is located behind lefthand side of instrument panel.

F-SUPER DUTY

The underhood fuse panel is located on the lefthand side of engine compartment. The interior fuse panel is located under lefthand side of instrument panel.

The flasher relay is located behind lefthand side of instrument panel.

FUEL PUMP RELAY LOCATION

Except F-Super Duty

The fuel pump relay is in the engine compartment fuse panel.

F-Super Duty Series

The fuel pump relay is located behind the center of the instrument panel.

STARTER

REPLACE

1. **On models equipped with air suspension,** turn air suspension switch to Off position.
2. **On all models,** raise and support vehicle.
3. Remove starter terminal cover, then solenoid S terminal retaining nut and electrical connector.
4. Remove battery ground cable retaining from starter mounting stud, then the cable.
5. Remove solenoid B terminal retaining nut and electrical connector.
6. Remove starter motor mounting bolts and stud, then the starter motor.
7. Reverse procedure to install. **Torque** starter mounting stud and bolts to 18 ft. lbs.

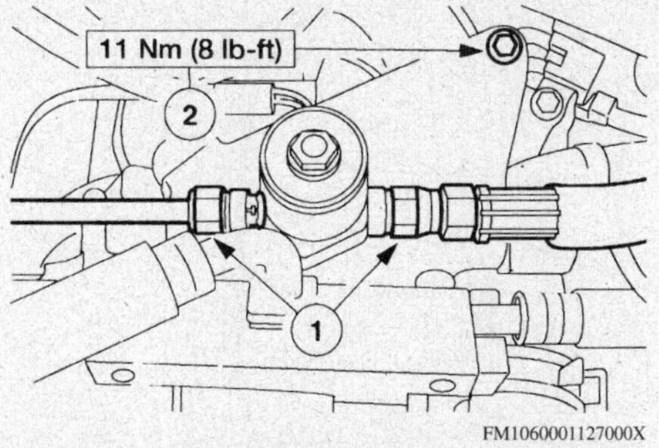

Fig. 1 Bi-fuel lock off solenoid. Excursion & F-Super Duty w/5.4L & 6.8L engines

ALTERNATOR

REPLACE

Single Alternator

ECONOLINE EXCEPT 215 AMP ALTERNATOR

1. Remove air cleaner assembly.
2. Disconnect wire harness connectors from voltage regulator.
3. Remove accessory drive belt.
4. Remove alternator mounting bolts, then the alternator.
5. Remove alternator fan shield, if equipped.
6. Reverse procedure to install.

ECONOLINE w/215 AMP ALTERNATOR

1. Remove air cleaner assembly.
2. Remove accessory drive belt.
3. Drain cooling system into suitable container.
4. Remove heater core tube from above alternator.
5. Position A/C manifold and tube aside.
6. Remove alternator attaching bolts, then the transmission dipstick.
7. Remove 3 electrical connectors located near alternator.
8. Rotate alternator counterclockwise.
9. Remove alternator electrical connectors, then the alternator.
10. Reverse procedure to install.

EXCURSION

6.0L ENGINE

1. Disconnect battery ground cable.
2. Remove upper fan shroud.
3. Rotate accessory drive belt tensioner clockwise, then remove drive belt from alternator pulley.
4. Disconnect electrical connectors from alternator.
5. Remove alternator mounting bolts, then the alternator.
6. Reverse procedure to install. **Torque** alternator mounting bolts to 35 ft. lbs.

5.4L, 6.8L & 7.3L ENGINES

1. Remove accessory drive belt.
2. **On models equipped with bi-fuel system,** proceed as follows:
   a. Disconnect LPG fuel tank relays. Residual pressure may be present.
   b. Position fuel selector switch to run on LPG, then operate vehicle until lamp is not illuminated. If vehicle is equipped with more than one LPG tank, repeat this step for remaining tanks.
   c. Repeat previous step to ensure all LPG is removed from fuel lines.
   d. Disconnect bi-fuel lines from fuel lock off solenoid, **Fig. 1,** then remove solenoid.
3. **On all models,** remove alternator bracket bolts.
4. Remove alternator attaching bolts, then the alternator.
5. Reverse procedure to install. To pressurize fuel system, reinstall fuel tank relays, then place fuel selector switch to run on LPG. Cycle ignition switch to run and repeat procedure for remaining fuel tank if required.

F150 & MARK LT

4.2L ENGINE

1. Rotate accessory drive belt tensioner counterclockwise, then position drive belt aside.
2. Disconnect alternator electrical connector.
3. Position alternator B+ terminal protective boot aside, remove nut, then disconnect B+ terminal connector.
4. Remove A/C line bracket mounting nut, then position bracket and line assembly aside.
5. Remove nut and position the alternator harness bracket aside.
6. Remove two alternator mounting studs and one bolt, then the alternator.
7. Reverse procedure to install. **Torque** mounting bolt and studs to 35 ft. lbs.

4.6L & 5.4L ENGINES LESS SUPERCHARGER

1. Remove the air cleaner inlet and outlet tubes.
2. Rotate accessory drive belt tensioner clockwise, then position drive belt aside.
3. Release alternator harness locator from alternator bracket.
4. Remove four alternator harness bracket mounting bolts, then the bracket.
5. Loosen two alternator mounting bolts and position alternator aside to access electrical connections.
6. Disconnect electrical connectors from alternator.

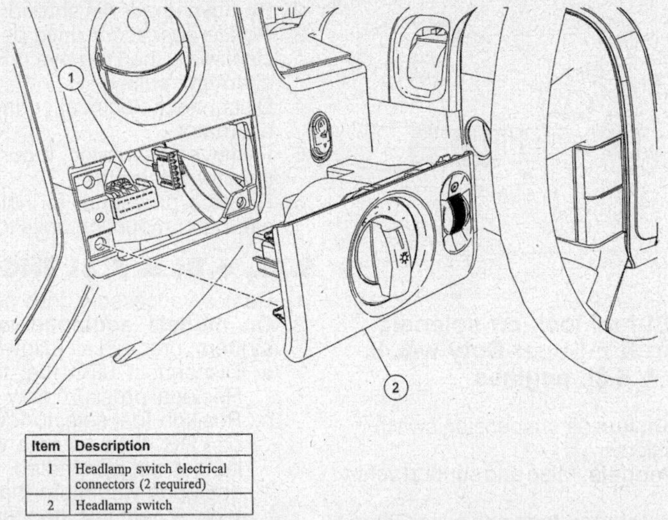

Item	Description
1	Headlamp switch electrical connectors (2 required)
2	Headlamp switch

LTV0500000000402

Fig. 2 Headlamp switch replacement. F-150 & Mark LT

7. Remove alternator assembly.
8. Reverse procedure to install, noting the following:
   a. **Torque** alternator mounting bolts to 18 ft. lbs.
   b. **Torque** harness bracket bolts to 89 inch lbs.

5.4L ENGINE w/SUPERCHARGER

1. Remove coolant overflow bottle and position aside.
2. Rotate belt tensioner clockwise and remove supercharger drive belt.
3. Remove air cleaner assembly.
4. Drain cooling system into suitable container.
5. Remove front air deflector, then the upper hose from radiator.
6. Remove fan and clutch using fan clutch holding tool No. T84T-6312-C and fan clutch wrench tool No. T93T-6312-B, or equivalents.
7. Remove fan shroud attaching screws, then the fan and shroud.
8. Raise and support vehicle.
9. Remove transmission cooler line shield.
10. Remove cooler line bracket, then the starter motor.
11. Install flywheel locking tool No. 303–673, or equivalent.
12. Remove auxiliary crankshaft supercharger pulley and brace, then the pulley adapter. **Pulley has lefthand threads.**
13. Remove accessory drive belt.
14. Remove accessory drive belt tensioner support bracket.
15. Remove alternator upper bracket, then the righthand lower alternator bolt.
16. Remove alternator to engine bracket, then the alternator from bracket.
17. Rotate alternator as required to access electrical connectors, then disconnect and remove alternator.
18. Reverse procedure to install.

SUPER DUTY

6.0L ENGINE

1. Disconnect battery ground cable.
2. Remove upper fan shroud.
3. Rotate accessory drive belt tensioner clockwise, then remove drive belt from alternator pulley.
4. Disconnect electrical connectors from alternator.
5. Remove alternator mounting bolts, then the alternator.
6. Reverse procedure to install. **Torque** alternator mounting bolts to 35 ft. lbs.

5.4L, 6.8L & 7.3L ENGINES

1. Remove accessory drive belt.
2. **On models equipped with bi-fuel system,** proceed as follows:
   a. Disconnect LPG fuel tank relays. Residual pressure may be present.
   b. Position fuel selector switch to run on LPG, then operate vehicle until lamp is not illuminated. If vehicle is equipped with more than one LPG tank, repeat this step for remaining tanks.
   c. Repeat previous step to ensure all LPG is removed from fuel lines.
   d. Disconnect bi-fuel lines from fuel lock off solenoid, **Fig. 1,** then remove solenoid.
3. **On all models,** remove alternator bracket bolts.
4. Remove alternator attaching bolts, then the alternator.
5. Reverse procedure to install. To pressurize fuel system, reinstall fuel tank relays, then place fuel selector switch to run on LPG. Cycle ignition switch to run and repeat procedure for remaining fuel tank if required.

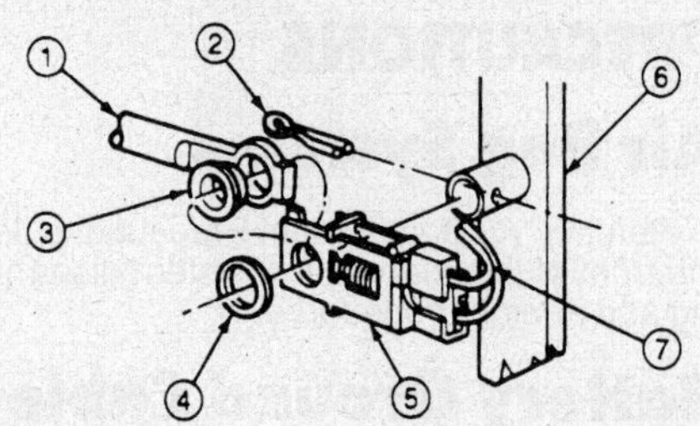

Item	Description
1	Power Brake Booster
2	Self-Locking Pin
3	Bushing
4	Spacer
5	Stoplamp Switch
6	Brake Pedal
7	Wiring

FM9049500050000X

Fig. 3 Stop light switch replacement

EXPEDITION & NAVIGATOR

2002–04

1. Remove air cleaner outlet tube assembly.
2. Drain cooling system into suitable container.
3. Remove front air deflector.
4. Remove upper radiator hose from radiator.
5. Remove overflow bottle from radiator.
6. Remove fan and clutch using fan pulley holding wrench tool No. T84T-6312-C and fan clutch wrench T93T-6312-A, or equivalents.
7. Remove fan shroud attaching bolts, then the fan and shroud.
8. Rotate belt tensioner clockwise, then remove accessory drive belt.
9. Remove alternator lower bolts.
10. Disconnect ignition harness retainer.
11. Remove remaining alternator bolts, then the alternator.
12. Reverse procedure to install.

2005–06

1. Release two engine retainers, then remove the engine cover.
2. Remove the air cleaner intake pipe.
3. Rotate accessory drive belt tensioner clockwise, then position drive belt aside.
4. Release alternator harness locator from alternator bracket.
5. Remove four alternator harness bracket mounting bolts, then the bracket.
6. Loosen two alternator mounting bolts and position alternator aside to access electrical connections.
7. Disconnect electrical connectors from alternator.
8. Remove alternator assembly.
9. Reverse procedure to install, noting the following:
   a. **Torque** alternator mounting bolts to 18 ft. lbs.
   b. **Torque** harness bracket bolts to 89 inch lbs.

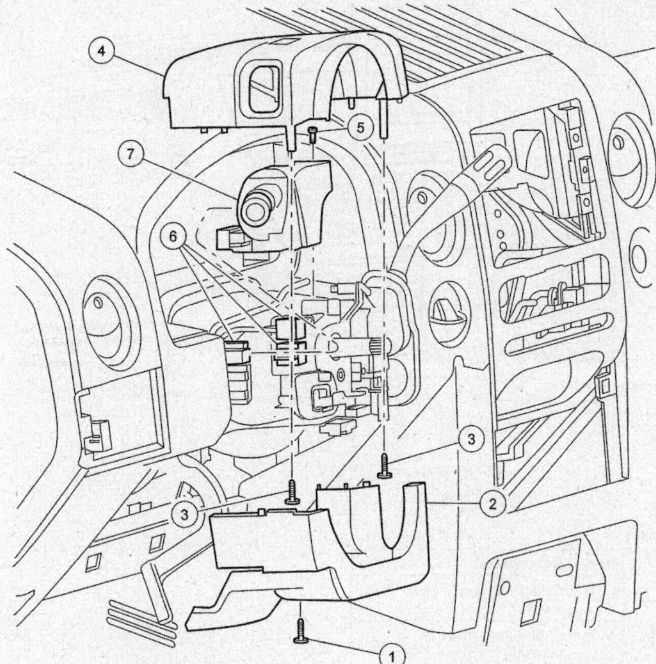

Item	Description
1	Lower steering column shroud screw
2	Lower steering column shroud
3	Upper steering column shroud screws (2 required)

Item	Description
4	Upper steering column shroud
5	Multi-function switch screw
6	Multi-function switch electrical connectors
7	Multi-function switch

LTV0500000000403

Fig. 4 Multi-function switch replacement. 2004–06

Dual Alternator

6.0L ENGINE

EXCURSION & F-SUPER DUTY

1. Disconnect battery ground cable and isolate.
2. Remove upper fan shroud.
3. Remove accessory drive belt.
4. Disconnect electrical connectors from upper alternator.
5. Remove upper alternator mounting bolts, then alternator.
6. Disconnect electrical connectors from lower alternator.
7. Remove lower alternator mounting bolts, then alternator.
8. Reverse procedure to install.

6.8L & 7.3L ENGINES

1. Remove air cleaner assembly.
2. Remove accessory drive belt.
3. Disconnect electrical connectors from upper alternator.
4. Remove alternator attaching bolts, then pull alternator forward and remove.
5. Raise and support vehicle.
6. Disconnect lower alternator electrical connectors.
7. Remove lower alternator attaching bolts, then pull alternator forward then down to remove.
8. Reverse procedure to install.

COIL PACK

REPLACE

1. Remove air cleaner assembly, if required.
2. Disconnect ignition coil electrical connection and radio ignition interference capacitor connector.
3. **Mark spark plug wire locations before removing them.** Squeeze locking tabs and disconnect ignition wires.
4. **On models equipped w/4.2L engine,** remove accelerator cable bracket nut, bolt and position bracket aside.
5. **On all models,** remove ignition coil nuts, then coil.
6. Reverse procedure to install.

COIL-ON-PLUG

REPLACE

1. Disconnect coil-on-plug electrical connector, then remove hold down bolt.
2. Remove coil-on-plug.
3. Reverse procedure to install.

IGNITION LOCK

REPLACE

1. Turn lock cylinder key to Run position.
2. Place suitable 1/8 inch diameter wire pin or small drift punch in hole in steering column shroud under ignition switch lock cylinder.

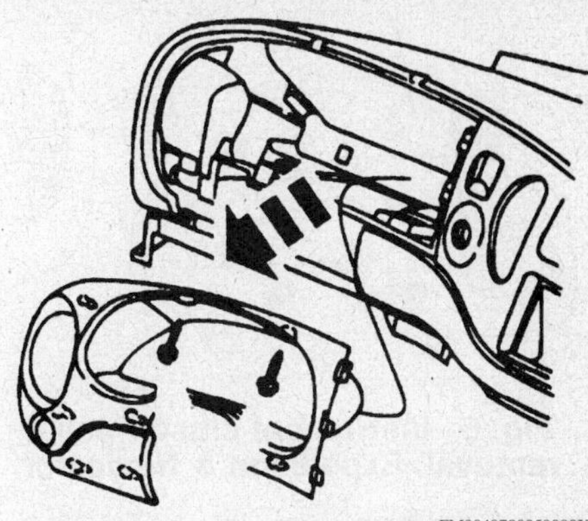

FM9049700059000X

Fig. 5 Instrument cluster panel removal. E-Series

3. Depress retaining pin while pulling out on ignition lock cylinder to remove from steering column.
4. To install lock cylinder, turn to Run position and depress retaining pin.
5. Insert ignition lock cylinder into steering column housing. Ensure ignition lock cylinder is fully seated and aligned in interlocking washer before turning key to Off position.
6. Rotate ignition lock cylinder to ensure proper mechanical operation in all positions.

IGNITION SWITCH

REPLACE

Expedition & Navigator

1. Remove steering wheel.
2. Remove lower steering column shroud screws, then shroud.
3. Remove upper steering column shroud screws, then shroud.
4. Remove multi-function switch bolt, push release then position switch aside.
5. Disconnect electrical connector from ignition switch.
6. Remove ignition switch.
7. Reverse procedure to install.

E-Series

1. Pull steering column opening cover off lower instrument panel, then locate ignition switch above driver side knee brace and steering column opening reinforcement.
2. Disconnect wiring harness from ignition switch, then remove ignition switch screws and switch.
3. Reverse procedure to install.

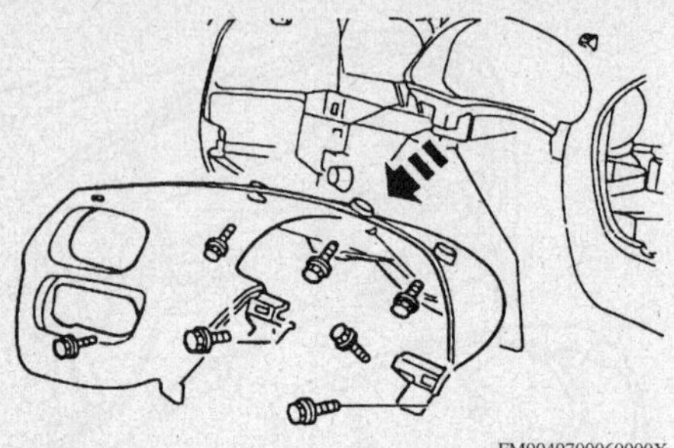

Fig. 6 Instrument cluster panel removal. Expedition & Navigator

Excursion, F-Super Duty, F-150 & Mark LT

1. Remove instrument panel steering column cover.
2. If equipped, remove tilt wheel lever.
3. Remove lower steering column shroud.
4. Remove ignition switch connector bolt, then disconnect ignition switch.
5. Remove ignition switch screws and ignition switch.
6. Reverse procedure to install.

HEADLAMP SWITCH

REPLACE

Expedition

1. Remove headlamp switch and bezel assembly using suitable flat blade screwdriver.
2. Disconnect electrical connectors.
3. Remove headlamp switch.
4. Reverse procedure to install.

Excursion, F-Super Duty

1. Remove headlamp switch from instrument panel.
2. Disconnect switch electrical connectors and remove switch.
3. Reverse procedure to install.

E-Series

1. Remove headlamp knob if required, then lefthand instrument panel finish panel two bolts.
2. Remove headlamp switch bolts, then disconnect switch electrical connector.
3. Reverse procedure to install.

F-150 & Mark LT

1. Remove headlamp switch and bezel assembly, **Fig. 2,** using suitable flat blade screwdriver.
2. Disconnect headlamp switch electrical connector.
3. Remove headlamp switch from bezel.
4. Reverse procedure to install.

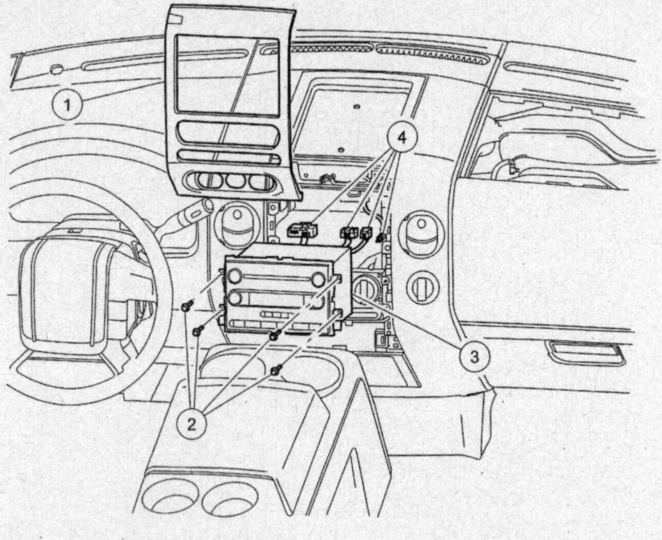

Item	Description
1	Center instrument panel finish panel
2	Audio unit screws (4 required)
3	Audio unit
4	Audio unit electrical connectors and antenna lead

LTV0500000000404

Fig. 7 Radio replacement. F-150 & Mark LT

Navigator

1. Remove instrument panel finish panel using suitable trim tool.
2. Release headlamp switch electrical connector retaining tabs, then the connector.
3. Remove two headlamp switch to finish panel retaining screws.
4. Remove headlamp switch.
5. Reverse procedure to install.

STOP LIGHT SWITCH

REPLACE

1. Lift locking tab, then disconnect electrical connector from switch, **Fig. 3.**
2. Remove hairpin retainer, then slide stop light switch, pushrod, nylon washers and bushings away from pedal and remove the switch from vehicle.
3. Reverse procedure to install. **Ensure stop light switch wires are of sufficient length to allow full travel of the brake pedal.**

MULTI-FUNCTION SWITCH

REPLACE

2002–03

1. Remove ignition lock cylinder as outlined under "Ignition Lock, Replace."
2. Remove tilt wheel lever if equipped.
3. Place gear selector lever to lowest position to allow access to steering column opening if required.
4. Release 4 clips, then remove steering column opening cover if required.
5. Remove upper and lower steering column shrouds.
6. Remove multi-function switch from steering column.
7. Reverse procedure to install.

2004–06

1. Place steering wheel in straight ahead position, then turn ignition switch to OFF position.
2. Remove steering wheel as outlined under "Steering Wheel, Replace."
3. Remove lower steering column shroud screw, **Fig. 4.**
4. Apply inward pressure to upper and lower shroud cover seam to separate them and remove lower shroud.
5. Remove two upper steering column shroud retaining screws, then the shroud.
6. Remove multi-function switch retaining screw, release tab, then position switch aside.
7. Disconnect multi-function switch electrical connector.
8. Remove multi-function switch.
9. Reverse procedure to install, noting the following:
   a. **Torque** driver air bag module to 80 inch lbs.
   b. **Torque** steering wheel bolt to 30 ft. lbs.

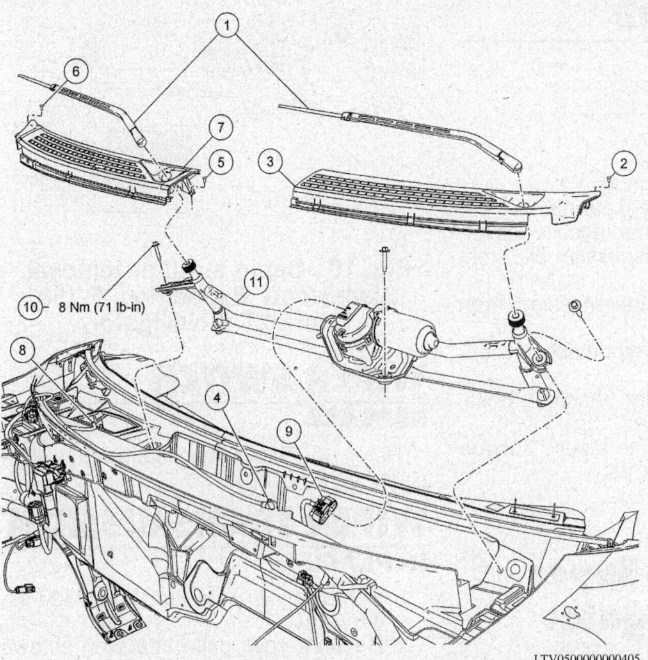

LTV0500000000405

Fig. 8 Cowl grille panel & wiper motor replacement (Part 1 of 2). F-150 & Mark LT

Item	Description
1	Wiper arms
2	Pin-type fastener
3	Left cowl grille panel
4	Windshield washer hose
5	Cowl panel grille screw
6	Pin-type fastener
7	Right cowl grille panel
8	Windshield washer hose
9	Windshield wiper motor electrical connector
10	Windshield wiper assembly bolts (3 required)
11	Windshield wiper assembly

LTV0500000000406

Fig. 8 Cowl grille panel & wiper motor replacement (Part 2 of 2). F-150 & Mark LT

STEERING WHEEL

REPLACE

1. Place front wheels in straight ahead position.
2. Remove driver air bag module to steering wheel attaching nuts.
3. Disconnect driver air bag module electrical connector, then remove driver air bag module.
4. Disconnect horn/speed control harness electrical connector from steering wheel.
5. **On all models except Expedition and Navigator,** remove and discard steering wheel attaching bolt.
6. **On Expedition and Navigator models,** remove steering wheel attaching bolt.
7. **On all models,** remove steering wheel using steering wheel puller tool No. T77F-4220-B1, or equivalent.
8. Reverse procedure to install. **Torque** to 23–32 ft. lbs.

INSTRUMENT CLUSTER

REPLACE

E-Series

1. Remove headlamp switch knob and bezel, then lefthand instrument panel finish panel, **Fig. 5.**
2. Remove instrument cluster bolts, then disconnect electrical connectors and transmission range indicator.
3. Remove cluster from vehicle.
4. Reverse procedure to install.

Expedition & Navigator

1. Upload module configuration data as outlined under "Module Configuration" in the front of this manual.
2. Remove headlamp switch as outlined under "Headlamp Switch, Replace."
3. Pry carefully to release four clips and remove steering column opening cover.
4. Remove instrument panel finish panel seven bolts and panel, **Fig. 6.**
5. Remove instrument cluster four bolts, then disconnect three electrical connectors and boost gauge vacuum line if equipped.
6. If equipped, remove transmission range indicator.
7. Reverse procedure to install. Upload module configuration data as outlined under "Module Configuration" in the front of this manual.

Excursion & F-Super Duty

1. Upload module configuration as outlined under "Module Configuration" in the front of this manual.
2. Remove radio, then lower steering wheel.
3. Remove cluster finish panel bolts, then pull back and position cluster finish panel out of the way.
4. Disconnect power point, headlight switch and passenger air bag module deactivation switch, if equipped.
5. Remove cluster finish panel.
6. Remove cluster screws and pull cluster out.
7. **On models equipped w/automatic transmission,** disconnect transmission range indicator by pushing in two clips and pull out transmission range indicator.
8. **On all models,** disconnect electrical connectors, then remove cluster.
9. Reverse procedure to install. Download module configuration as outlined under "Module Configuration" in the front of this manual.

F-150 & Mark LT

1. Upload module configuration as outlined under "Module Configuration" in the front of this manual.
2. Remove instrument cluster center finish panel.
3. Lower tilt steering column to lowest position.
4. Push in clips and disconnect transmission range indicator.
5. Remove four screws, then the instrument cluster.
6. Disconnect electrical connectors.
7. Reverse procedure to install. Upload module configuration data as outlined under "Module Configuration" in the front of this manual.

RADIO

REPLACE

E-Series

1. Insert radio removal tool No. T87P-19061-A, or equivalent, to radio face plate, then depress tool one inch to release radio clips, then pull radio from panel using tool.
2. Disconnect radio antenna lead cable and electrical connectors.
3. Reverse procedure to install.

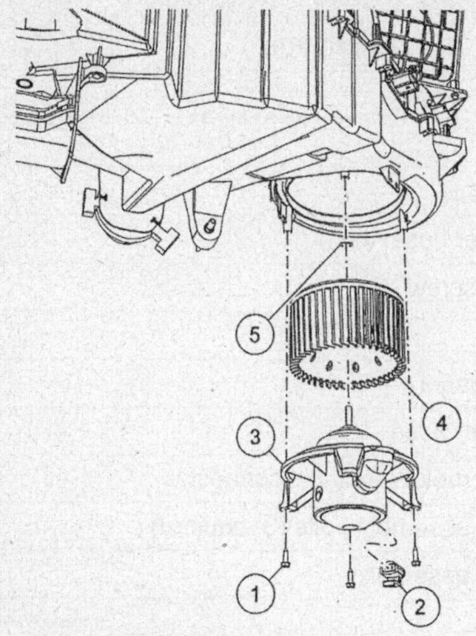

Item	Description
1	Blower motor screw (3 required)
2	Blower motor electrical connector
3	Blower motor
4	Blower motor wheel
5	Blower motor wheel clip

LTV0500000000407

Fig. 9 Blower motor replacement. F-150 & Mark LT

Expedition & Navigator

1. Carefully pry to release four clips and remove center instrument panel finish panel.
2. Insert radio removal tool No. T87P-19061-A, or equivalent, to radio face plate, then depress tool one inch to release radio clips, then pull radio from panel using tool.
3. Disconnect antenna and radio electrical connectors, then remove.
4. Reverse procedure to install.

Excursion & F-Super Duty

1. Insert radio removing tool No. T87P-19061-A, or equivalent, to radio face plate.
2. Pull outward on tools, then disconnect radio antenna lead and electrical connectors, then remove.
3. Reverse procedure to install.

F-150 & Mark LT

1. Remove center instrument panel finish panel, **Fig. 7.**
2. Disconnect finish panel electrical connectors.
3. Remove four mounting screws, then the radio.
4. Disconnect radio electrical connectors and antenna lead.
5. Reverse procedure to install.

WIPER MOTOR

REPLACE

E-Series

1. Remove wiper arms.
2. Raise and support hood.
3. Remove cowl top vent panels.
4. Remove dash panel access cover, then the wiper transmission clip from motor.
5. Disconnect wiper transmission from motor.
6. Disconnect wiper motor electrical connector.
7. Remove wiper motor attaching bolts, then the motor.
8. Reverse procedure to install. **Torque** motor to 62–89 inch lbs.

Expedition, Excursion, F-Super Duty & Navigator

FRONT

1. Remove windshield wiper pivot arm nut covers, nuts and arms.
2. Remove cowl top vent panels.
3. Remove hood struts and support hood.
4. Remove mounting arm and pivot shaft attaching bolts, then disconnect electrical connector.
5. Remove wiper motor bolts and motor from mounting arm and pivot shaft.
6. Reverse procedure to install.

REAR

1. Remove rear wiper cover, nut and wiper arm.
2. Remove upper liftgate trim panel, then the liftgate assist strap screws and strap.
3. Remove lower liftgate trim panel, then the liftgate water shield.
4. Disconnect wiper motor, then remove rear window wiper motor screws and wiper motor.
5. Reverse procedure to install.

F-150 & Mark LT

1. Pull upward on wiper arm pivot to lock arm in upper most position.
2. Pull outward on wiper arm retaining tab, then remove pivot arm.
3. Remove cowl grille panel, **Fig. 8.**
4. Disconnect windshield wiper motor electrical connector.
5. Remove three windshield wiper motor assembly mounting bolts.
6. Remove wiper motor transmission assembly.
7. Remove wiper transmission linkage retaining nut and transmission from motor.
8. Reverse procedure to install. **Torque** wiper motor mounting bolts to 71 inch lbs.

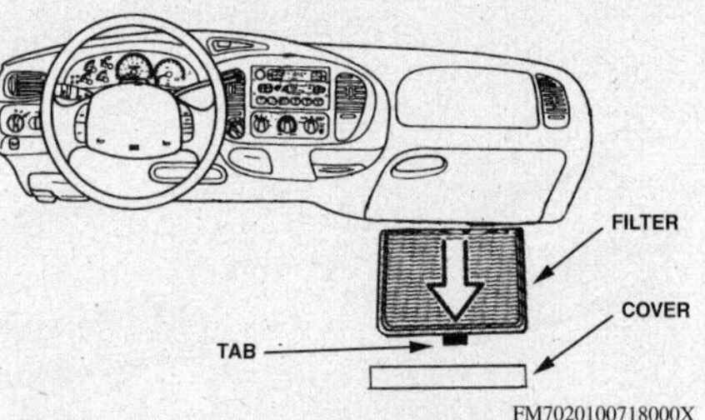

Fig. 10 Cabin air filter removal. Blackwood, Expedition, F-150, Mark LT & Navigator

WIPER SWITCH

REPLACE

Refer to "Multi-Function Switch, Replace" for procedure.

WIPER TRANSMISSION

REPLACE

1. Remove both wiper arm and blade assemblies.
2. Remove cowl grille attaching screws and raise the grille slightly.
3. Remove cowl grille.
4. Remove clip securing righthand and lefthand linkage and the retaining clip from wiper motor arm.
5. Remove pivot body to cowl panel attaching screws, then the arm and pivot shaft assembly.
6. Reverse procedure to install.

BLOWER MOTOR

REPLACE

E-Series

FRONT

1. Remove battery tray, if required.
2. **On models equipped with A/C,** remove three accumulator/drier mounting screws, then move accumulator drier aside.
3. **On all models,** disconnect electrical connector from blower motor.
4. Remove blower motor housing tube.
5. Remove four screws and retaining clip.
6. To ease removal, align flat spot on blower motor mounting plate with accumulator, then remove blower motor.
7. Remove retaining clip, then the blower motor wheel.
8. Reverse procedure to install.

REAR

1. Remove third, fourth and fifth bench seats as required.
2. Remove lefthand center bolster trim panel.
3. Remove quarter trim rear upper panel.
4. Remove lower rear body side trim panel.
5. Disconnect electrical connector.
6. Remove blower motor housing tube.
7. Remove mounting screws, then the blower motor.
8. Reverse procedure to install.

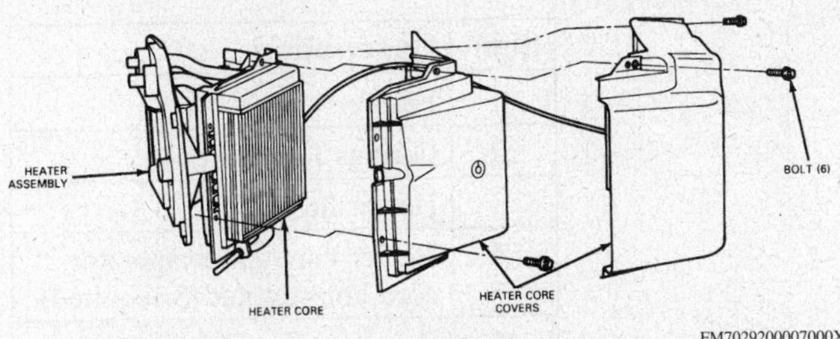

Fig. 11 Heater core replacement. E-Series

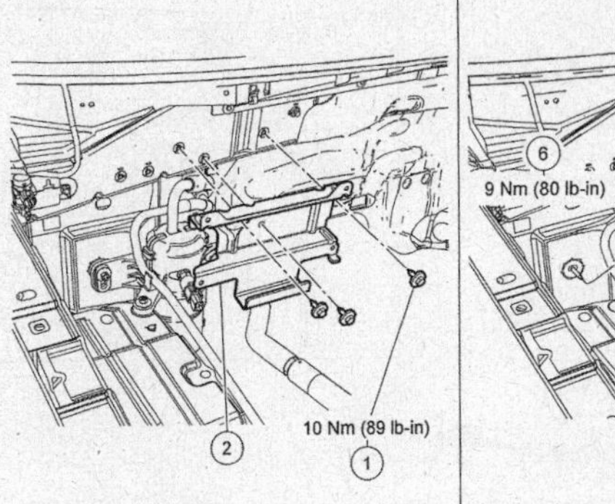

Item	Description
1	PCM bracket bolt (3 required)
2	PCM bracket
3	Suction accumulator outlet fitting nut
4	Suction accumulator inlet fitting
5	A/C cycling switch electrical connector
6	Suction accumulator bracket nut (2 required)
7	Suction accumulator
8	O-ring (4 required)

LTV0500000000410

Fig. 12 Suction accumulator removal. 2005–06 F-150 & Mark LT

Excursion & F-Super Duty

1. **On models equipped w/6.0L and 7.3L diesel engines,** disconnect connector from vacuum pump and remove pump bolts, pump and mounting bracket.
2. **On models equipped w/5.4L or 6.8L engines,** disconnect speed control servo and remove servo bolts and servo.
3. **On all models,** disconnect blower motor, then remove blower motor ventilation tube.
4. Remove blower motor screws and blower motor.
5. Reverse procedure to install.

Expedition & Navigator

2002

FRONT

1. Remove passenger side insulator panel.
2. Remove aftermarket air filter and mounting bracket, if equipped.
3. Disconnect retainer from motor mounting plate, then blower motor electrical connector.
4. Remove three blower motor cover screws and pry to release three tabs.
5. Remove three blower motor screws and blower motor.
6. Reverse procedure to install.

CENTER CONSOLE

1. Remove floor console, then the floor console support braces.
2. Remove motor duct screws and duct.
3. Remove blower motor assembly nuts and motor from bottom of console.
4. Disconnect harness connectors, then remove blower motor resistor connector, bolts and resistor.
5. Remove blower motor lower duct cover screws and duct cover.
6. Remove blower motor upper duct cover bolts and the upper duct cover.
7. Disconnect blower motor, then remove blower motor bolts and blower motor.
8. Reverse procedure to install.

2003–06

1. Remove righthand lower instrument panel insulator.
2. Remove righthand scuff plate.
3. **On Expedition models,** remove righthand lower A-pillar trim panel.
4. **On all models,** position carpet aside.
5. Disconnect blower motor electrical connector.
6. Remove blower motor screws, then the blower motor.
7. Reverse procedure to install.

F-150 & Mark LT

2002–04

1. Remove righthand lower insulator panel.
2. Remove aftermarket air filter and mounting bracket, if equipped.
3. Remove passenger side scuff plate.
4. Remove passenger side kick panel.
5. Disconnect electrical connector, then position carpet aside.
6. On EATC models:
   a. Disconnect aspirator tube and remove screw.
   b. Remove aspirator tube extension screws, then aspirator tube.
7. Disconnect electrical connector from blower motor.
8. Remove blower motor screws, then blower motor.
9. Reverse procedure to install.

2005–06

1. Remove righthand lower A-pillar trim panel, **Fig. 9.**
2. Position carpet below blower motor aside.
3. Disconnect blower motor electrical connector.
4. Remove three blower motor mounting screws.
5. Remove blower motor.
6. Remove blower motor wheel retaining clip, then the blower motor wheel.
7. Reverse procedure to install.

CABIN AIR FILTER

REPLACE

Blackwood, Expedition, F-150, Mark LT & Navigator

On these models, the cabin air filter is an option.

Under normal operating conditions the cabin air filter should be replaced 15,000 miles. In dusty areas change the cabin air filter more often.

1. From under passenger side of the instrument panel behind the glove compartment, remove the cabin air filter cover to the bottom of the heater plenum assembly attaching screws, then the cover, **Fig. 10.**
2. Grasp the cabin air filter element tab, then pull the filter element from the filter compartment.
3. Position the new cabin air filter element into the filter compartment with the tab facing toward the filter cover. Ensure the filter is firmly seated in the compartment.
4. Install the cabin air filter cover to the heater plenum assembly and secure with the attaching screws.

HEATER CORE

REPLACE

E-Series

STANDARD

1. Drain engine coolant into suitable container.

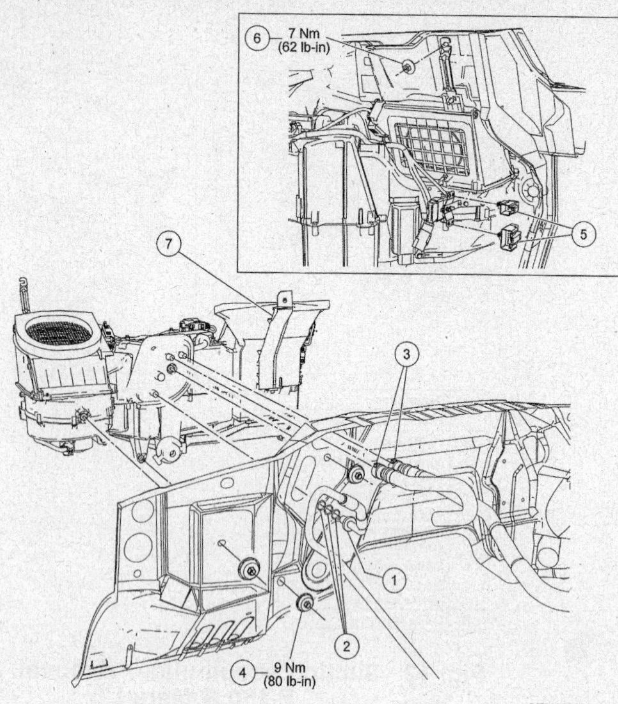

Fig. 13 Evaporator & heater core replacement (Part 1 of 2). 2005-06 F-150 & Mark LT

2. Disconnect quick disconnect heater hose couplings at heater core.
3. Plug heater hoses with suitable ⅝ or ¾ inch plugs.
4. Remove engine cover.
5. Remove instrument panel finish panel.
6. Remove heater core cover and discard heater core case seal.
7. Remove heater core using care to avoid spilling coolant.
8. Reverse procedure to install.

AUXILIARY

1. Drain coolant into a suitable container.
2. Remove rear bench seats, if equipped.
3. Remove lefthand center bolster trim panel, lefthand lower front trim panel, lefthand rear lower and upper trim panels, if equipped.
4. Remove heater core cover attaching screws, then remove, **Fig. 11.**
5. Disconnect heater hoses from core, then remove heater core and seal.
6. Reverse procedure to install.

Expedition & Navigator

2002

1. Drain coolant into suitable container.
2. Remove instrument panel as outlined under "Dash Panel Service" chapter.
3. **On models equipped with 5.4L engine,** remove junction block splash shield, cable ends from starter relay and junction block bracket.
4. **On all models,** compress holding tabs and disconnect heater hoses.
5. Remove A/C plenum demister adapter.
6. Disconnect vacuum line, heater core bracket and plenum chamber top.
7. Remove heater core.
8. Reverse procedure to install.

2003-06

1. Drain coolant into suitable container.
2. Recover A/C refrigerant as outlined under "Air Conditioning" chapter.
3. Remove instrument panel as outlined under "Dash Panel Service" chapter.
4. Remove rear footwell duct.
5. Disconnect PCM electrical connectors, then PCM and mounting bracket.
6. Disconnect heater hoses.
7. Disconnect A/C lines.
8. Disconnect vacuum lines and plenum chamber mounting bolts.
9. Remove plenum chamber assembly.
10. Remove dash seal, then heater core cover bolts and cover.
11. Remove heater core.
12. Reverse procedure to install.

Excursion & F-Super Duty

1. Drain coolant into a suitable container.
2. Disconnect heater hoses from heater core with heater hose disconnect tool No. T85T-18539-AH, or equivalent.
3. Disengage stops and lower the glove compartment door.
4. Remove electronic blend door actuator and bracket assembly.
5. Remove heater cover screws, then raise cover vertically to avoid damage to heater core housing.
6. Remove heater core.
7. Reverse procedure to install.

Item	Description
1	Fitting
2	O-rings (3 required)
3	Heater hoses
4	Heater core and evaporator core housing nut (3 required)
5	Harness electrical connectors
6	Air inlet duct bracket nut
7	Heater core and evaporator core housing

LTV0500000000409

Fig. 13 Evaporator & heater core replacement (Part 2 of 2). 2005-06 F-150 & Mark LT

F-150 & Mark LT

2002-04

1. Drain coolant into suitable container.
2. Recover A/C refrigerant as outlined under "Air Conditioning" chapter.
3. Remove instrument panel as outlined under "Dash Panel Service" chapter.
4. Compress holding tabs, then remove heater hoses at heater core.
5. Remove A/C plenum demister adapter.
6. Disconnect vacuum line and remove heater core bracket.
7. Remove plenum chamber top, then the heater core.
8. Reverse procedure to install.

2005-06

1. Drain coolant into suitable container.
2. Recover A/C refrigerant as outlined under "Air Conditioning" chapter.
3. Remove instrument panel as outlined under "Dash Panel Service" chapter.
4. Remove the suction accumulator, **Fig. 12.**
5. Disconnect evaporator core spring lock coupling.
6. Clamp off and disconnect two heater core quick disconnect fittings.
7. Remove heater core and evaporator core housing mounting nuts, **Fig. 13.**
8. Disconnect wire harness to housing electrical connectors.
9. Remove air inlet duct bracket nut.
10. Remove junction box mounting bolt, then position junction box aside.
11. Remove heater core and evaporator core housing mounting nuts.
12. Remove heater core and evaporator core housing assemblies.
13. Remove housing case retaining clips, then separate housing.
14. Remove heater core and or evaporator cores from housing.
15. Reverse procedure to install, noting the following:
    a. Install new O-ring seals.
    b. Lubricate refrigerant system with correct amount of clean PAG oil.
    c. **Torque** heater/evaporator housing mounting nuts to 80 inch lbs.

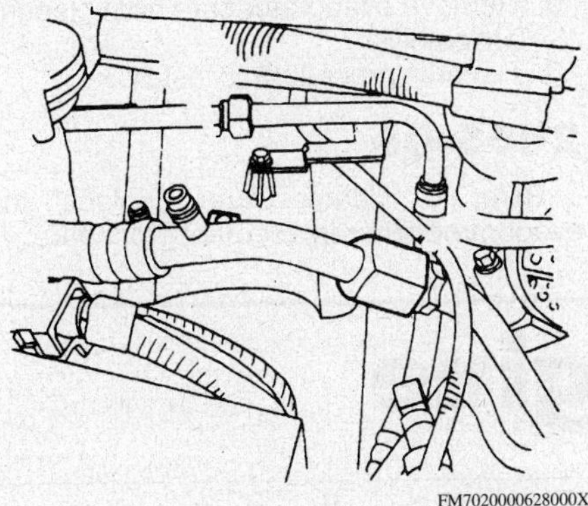

Fig. 14 Compressor suction line. Econoline w/standard A/C

d. **Torque** air inlet duct bracket nut to 62 inch lbs.
e. **Torque** suction accumulator bracket nuts to 80 inch lbs.

EVAPORATOR CORE

REPLACE

E-Series

STANDARD

1. Recover refrigerant as outlined under "Air Conditioning" chapter.
2. Remove battery tray.
3. Remove mounting screw and move oil fill pipe out of way.
4. Remove mounting screws and move windshield washer reservoir out of way.
5. Disconnect evaporator discharge line.
6. **On models equipped with standard A/C,** remove screw and compressor suction line, **Fig. 14,** then disconnect condenser to evaporator tube.
7. **On models equipped with auxiliary A/C,** disconnect suction accumulator/drier line spring lock connector, **Fig. 15.**
8. **On models equipped with 4.2L engine,** remove mounting screw, then move compressor discharge line isolator, out of way, **Fig. 16.**
9. **On all models,** disconnect compressor discharge line and condenser to evaporator tube.
10. Remove evaporator core housing support bracket.
11. Remove evaporator core cover, seal, then the evaporator. Use care to avoid damaging cooling fins while handling evaporator core.
12. Reverse procedure to install.

AUXILIARY

1. Remove rear heater and A/C assembly as follows:
   a. Recover refrigerant as outlined under "Air Conditioning" chapter.
   b. Drain cooling system into suitable container.
   c. Disconnect and plug heater hoses.
   d. Disconnect refrigerant line spring lock couplings.

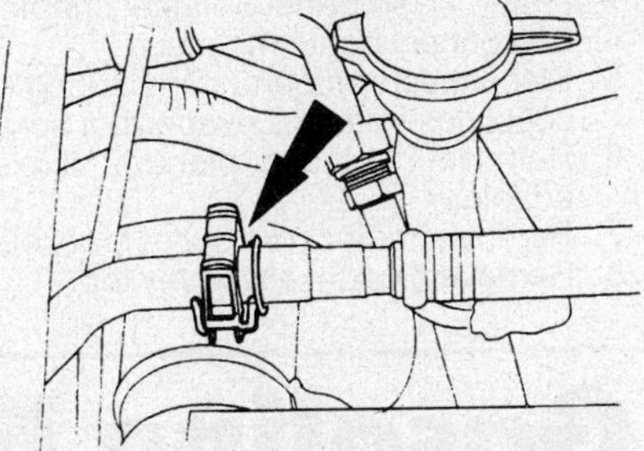

Fig. 15 Accumulator/drier line. Econoline w/auxiliary A/C

   e. Remove third, fourth and fifth seats as required.
   f. Remove lefthand bolster trim panels, quarter trim rear upper panel and lower rear body side trim panel.
   g. Remove heater air plenum chamber.
2. Position heater hoses out of way.
3. Remove evaporator case cover, then the evaporator core and seal.
4. Reverse procedure to install.

Expedition & Navigator

2002

1. Recover refrigerant as outlined under "Air Conditioning" chapter.
2. Drain coolant into suitable container.
3. Remove instrument panel as outlined under "Dash Panel Service" chapter.
4. Remove junction block with splash shield.
5. Disconnect cable ends.
6. Disengage connector, remove screws, then the junction block.
7. Disconnect heater hose couplings.
8. Disconnect refrigerant line spring lock connectors at A/C evaporator core.
9. Remove righthand side A/C plenum demister, heater core brackets and plenum assembly top.
10. Remove A/C evaporator core from plenum assembly.
11. Reverse procedure to install.

2003-06

1. Drain coolant into suitable container.
2. Recover A/C refrigerant as outlined under "Air Conditioning" chapter.
3. Remove instrument panel as outlined under "Dash Panel Service" chapter.
4. Remove rear footwell duct.
5. Disconnect PCM electrical connectors, then PCM and mounting bracket.
6. Disconnect heater hoses.
7. Disconnect A/C lines.
8. Disconnect vacuum lines and plenum chamber mounting bolts.
9. Remove plenum chamber assembly.
10. Remove dash panel seal.
11. Disconnect wiring harness from evaporator core cover.
12. Disconnect air inlet vacuum control motor vacuum connector.
13. Remove blower resistor or blower motor speed control and wire harness.

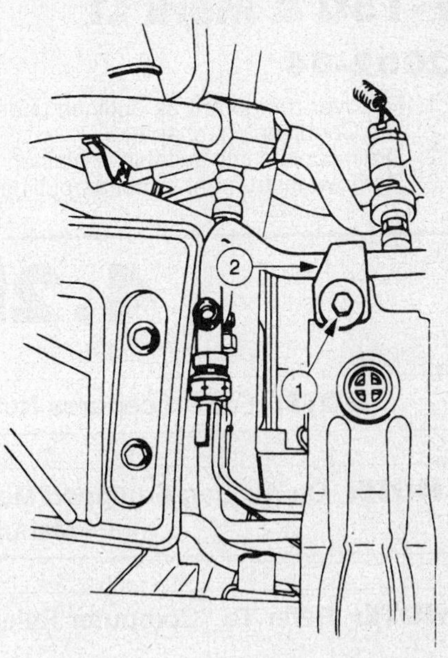

Fig. 16 Compressor discharge line isolator. Econoline w/4.2L engine

14. Remove four bottom evaporator core cover bolts.
15. Remove heater core cover bolts, then cover.
16. Remove five upper evaporator core cover bolts.
17. Remove all remaining evaporator core cover bolts, then evaporator core.
18. Reverse procedure to install.

Excursion & F-Super Duty

1. Recover refrigerant, then remove suction accumulator/drier.
2. Drain engine coolant into a suitable container.
3. **On models equipped with 6.0L & 7.3L diesel engine,** remove nuts and reposition manifold absolute pressure sensor and bracket.
4. **On models equipped with 5.4L and 6.8L engines,** remove nuts and reposition vapor management valve and bracket.
5. **On all models,** disconnect condenser to evaporator tube from A/C evaporator core.
6. **On models equipped with 6.0L & 7.3L diesel engine** loosen clamps and remove intercooler tube.
7. **On all models,** remove screws and remove evaporator core housing support bracket.
8. Disconnect heater hoses from heater core with heater hose disconnect tool No. T85T-18539-AH, or equivalent.
9. Remove eleven screws and release three retaining tabs.
10. Remove evaporator core cover and evaporator core.
11. Reverse procedure to install.

F-150 & Mark LT

2002-04

1. Recover refrigerant as outlined under "Air Conditioning" chapter.
2. Drain coolant into suitable container.
3. Remove instrument panel as outlined under "Dash Panel Service" chapter.
4. Disconnect heater hoses.
5. Disconnect refrigerant line spring lock couplings from A/C evaporator core.
6. Remove righthand plenum demister adapter.
7. Remove heater core outlet brackets.
8. Remove plenum assembly top.
9. Remove evaporator core from plenum assembly.
10. Reverse procedure to install.

2005-06

Refer to "Heater Core, Replace" for evaporator core replacement procedure.

4.2L Gasoline Engine

NOTE: For Procedures Not Found In This Section, Refer "4.6L & 5.4L SOHC Gasoline Engines."

NOTE: On Air Bag Equipped Models, Refer To "Air Bag System Precautions" Located In The Front Of This Manual For System Disarming & Arming Procedures.

NOTE: Refer To "Computer Relearn Procedures" Located In The Front Of This Manual When Battery Power To The Computer Has Been Interrupted.

INDEX

PRECAUTIONS

Air Bag Systems

Refer to "Air Bag System Precautions" in the front of this manual for system disarming and arming procedures.

Battery Ground Cable

Prior to service, disconnect battery ground cable and isolate as required.

Fuel System Pressure Relief

2002-03

The fuel system remains under high pressure even when the engine is not running. To avoid injury or fire, release pressure from the fuel system before disconnecting any fuel line. Proceed as follows:

1. Remove fuel tank cap to release residual fuel pressure from tank.
2. Connect fuel pressure gauge tool No. T80L-9974-B, or equivalent, to valve located on the fuel rail.
3. Gradually open testing kit valve to relieve fuel pressure in system. Drain fuel into suitable container or return to fuel tank.
4. To avoid unrequired fuel spillage and fire hazard, any time fuel lines are disconnected, ignition switch should be in Off position.
5. When repair is completed, turn ignition On and Off several times to pressurize fuel system. Do not start engine.
6. Inspect for fuel leaks at pressure regulator, fuel injectors and fuel fittings. Repair as required.

2004-06

1. Remove splash shield located on lefthand frame rail under driver's side door.
2. Disconnect fuel pump/tank sender harness electrical connector.
3. Start engine and allow it to idle until it stalls.
4. After engine stalls, crank engine for approximately five seconds to ensure fuel rail pressure has been released.
5. Turn ignition switch to OFF position.
6. After fuel system service is complete, connect electrical connector.
7. Reposition splash shield and install a new pushpin.
8. Cycle ignition switch and wait 3 seconds to pressurize fuel system. Inspect for leaks before starting engine.

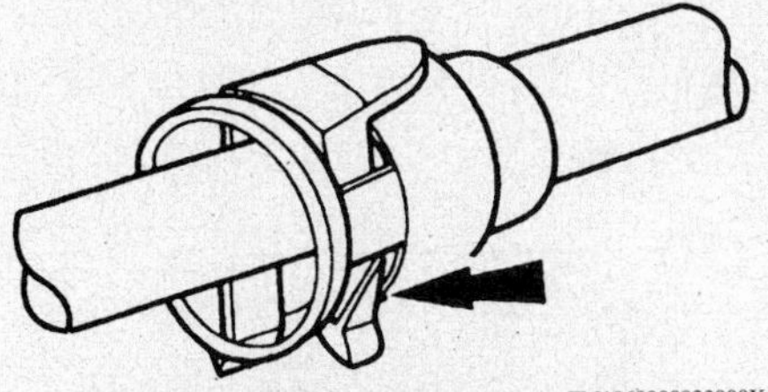

Fig. 1 R-clip connection

COMPRESSION PRESSURE

1. Warm engine to normal operating temperature, then remove spark plugs and set throttle plates to wide open position.
2. Install a suitable compression gauge in cylinder No. 1 spark plug hole.
3. Install an auxiliary starter switch in the starting circuit.
4. With key off, using auxiliary starter switch, crank engine at least five compression strokes and record highest reading.
5. Repeat test on each cylinder.
6. Indicated compression pressures are within specification if the lowest reading cylinder is within 75 percent of the highest reading, with a minimum of 101 psi.

QUICK DISCONNECT HOSES

Before disconnect quick connect fittings, ensure system pressure is relieved if applicable.

R-Clip

When working with R-clip type connections, **Fig. 1,** do not use tools to disconnect. Use of tools may deform clip components and could cause leaks.

To disconnect, bend shipping tab downward, **Fig. 1.** Spread R-clip and push clip into fitting. Separate fitting from tube.

To install, first inspect fitting and tube for damage and ensure connections are clean. Apply a light coat of clean 5W-30 motor oil to male end of tube. Insert R-clip into fitting. Align tube and fitting, then insert tube into fitting and push together until a click is heard. Pull on connection to ensure it is fully engaged.

Spring Lock

When working with spring lock type connections, **Fig. 2,** spring lock tool set No. T84L-19623-B, or equivalent, must be used to disconnect fittings. When connecting spring lock type fittings, inspect and clean both coupling ends. Lubricate fuel line O-ring seals with clean 5W-30 motor oil. When connection is made, pull on line to ensure it is fully engaged.

Vapor Tube

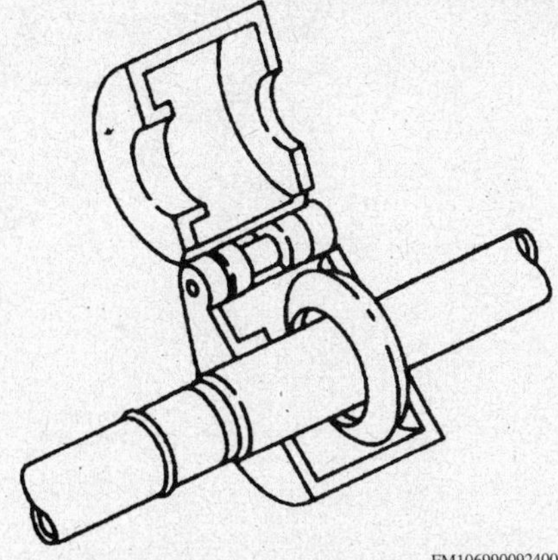

Fig. 2 Spring lock connection

To disconnect vapor tube connections, squeeze fitting (1) and disconnect vapor tube from fitting (2), **Fig. 3.** To connect, ensure fittings are clean and free from damage. Push tube onto fitting until it snaps into place. Pull on connection to verify fitting is secure.

Push Connect

To disconnect push connect fittings, first remove safety clip if equipped, then slide disconnect tool set No. T90T-9550-S into fitting, **Fig. 4.** Separate fittings, then remove disconnect tool.

ENGINE MOUNT

REPLACE

F150 & Mark LT

2002–04

1. Remove fan shroud.
2. Remove alternator.
3. Install three bar modular engine support bracket set on engine using the alternator mounting holes.
4. Raise and support vehicle.
5. Remove exhaust manifolds and oil dipstick tube.
6. Remove starter as outlined under "Starter, Replace" in the "Electrical" chapter.
7. Remove righthand and lefthand motor mount bolts.
8. Lower vehicle.
9. Raise engine with three bar engine support tool.
10. Raise and support vehicle.
11. Remove bolts, then the motor mounts.
12. Reverse procedure to install.

2005–06

Early build vehicles are equipped with an M14 through bolt. Late build vehicles are equipped with an M18 bolt.

1. Remove the lefthand and righthand engine support insulator through bolts, **Fig. 5.**
2. Remove righthand engine support insulator nuts and washers.
3. Remove A/C compressor and power steering pump bracket brace upper nut, then install lifting bracket tool No. T70P-6000, or equivalent, on bracket brace.
4. Support engine using a .39 inch (10 mm) spring link to connect engine lifting bracket to a suitable 3-Bar Engine Support.
5. Lift engine approximately 3 inches.
6. Remove engine mount to engine block mounting bolts, then the engine mount.
7. Reverse procedure to install.

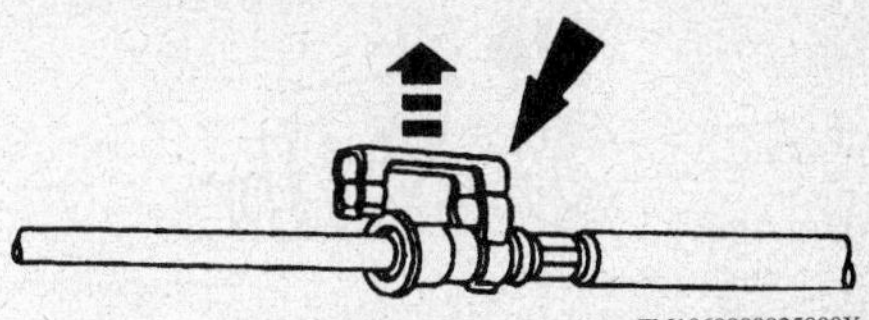

Fig. 3 Vapor tube connection

Econoline

1. Remove intake manifold as outlined under "Intake Manifold, Replace."
2. Remove fan shroud and engine cooling fan.
3. Remove retainers, then the front shield, **Fig. 6.**
4. Remove pipe bracket nut, **Fig. 7.**
5. Unclip wiring harnesses from retainers.
6. Remove pipe clamp stud bolts, **Fig. 8.**
7. Remove two transmission to engine bolts.
8. Install three bar engine support kit No. 303-F070, or equivalent, to support engine.
9. Raise and support vehicle.
10. If replacing righthand engine support insulator, remove starter.
11. Remove support insulator nuts, then lower vehicle.
12. Raise engine with three bar support tool.
13. Raise and support vehicle.
14. Remove insulator bolts, then the insulators from vehicle.
15. Reverse procedure to install.

Excursion & F-Super Duty

1. Partially drain radiator into a suitable container and disconnect upper radiator hose at radiator.
2. Remove air cleaner outlet tube, then accelerator cable snow shield.
3. Disconnect accelerator, speed control cables and return spring.
4. Remove accelerator cable bracket bolts and position bracket and cable aside
5. Disconnect PCV, brake booster and engine sensor control wiring harness.
6. Disconnect idle air control motor connector, bypass hose and heater hose.
7. Disconnect EGR transducer connector and throttle position sensor.
8. Disconnect EGR transducer vacuum lines and EGR valve to exhaust manifold tube fittings and remove tube.
9. Remove EGR transducer bracket and

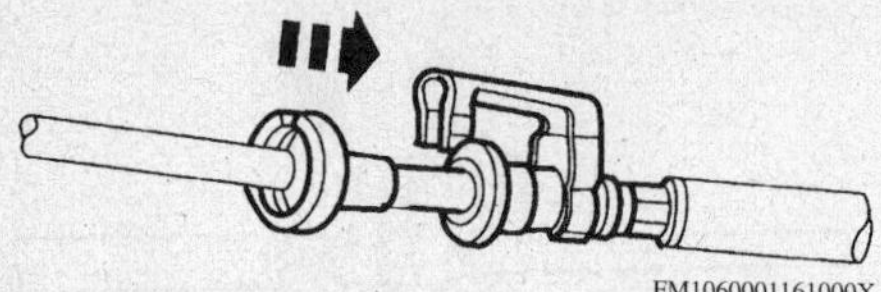

Fig. 4 Push connect fitting

disconnect EGR valve vacuum line.
10. Disconnect EVR solenoid and vacuum harness.
11. Remove throttle body adapter bolts, adapter and adapter gasket.
12. Remove two screws at top of fan shroud and position fan shroud toward engine.
13. Remove alternator, then install modular engine support to alternator mounting holes.
14. Raise and support vehicle, then remove engine mount nuts.
15. Lower vehicle, then raise engine using three bar engine support tool No. 303-F070, or equivalent, by inserting J-hook.
16. Raise and support vehicle.
17. If righthand engine mount is to be serviced, remove starter as outlined in "Starter Replace" in "Electrical" section.
18. Remove engine mounts.
19. Reverse procedure to install. Tighten to specifications.

ENGINE

REPLACE

F-150 & Mark LT

1. Remove vehicle hood.
2. **On models equipped with A/C,** recover refrigerant as outlined in "Air Conditioning" chapter.
3. **On all models,** drain cooling system into suitable container.
4. Relieve fuel system pressure as outlined under "Precautions."
5. Remove upper front air deflector.
6.
7. Remove upper intake manifold and manifold spacer assembly as outlined under "Intake Manifold, Replace."
8. Remove radiator, fan blade and shroud assembly.
9. Disconnect fuel pressure regulator vacuum connector and intake manifold runner control electrical connector.
10. Disconnect EGR valve vacuum connector.
11. Remove power steering pump reservoir and set aside.
12. Remove A/C hose manifold from compressor and position hoses aside.
13. Remove power steering pump bolts and position pump aside.
14. Remove fuel charging wiring harness.
15. Remove ignition coil and spark plug wires.
16. Disconnect two heater hoses.
17. Disconnect differential pressure feedback EGR system electrical connector and wiring harness pin type connector.

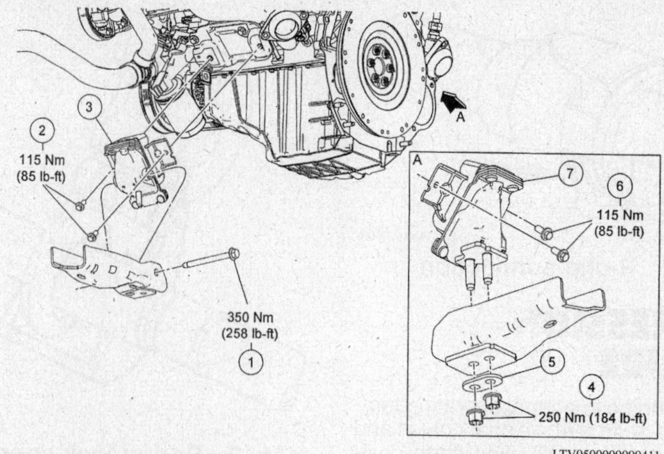

Fig. 5 Engine mount replacement (Part 1 of 2). 2005-06 F-150 & Mark LT

18. Remove exhaust manifold to EGR valve tube.
19. Remove crankcase ventilation hose.
20. Remove PCV valve/heater hose assembly.
21. Disconnect fuel tube spring lock couplings.
22. Remove fuel injectors and fuel injector supply manifold.
23. Raise and support vehicle.
24. **On models equipped with block heater,** disconnect block heater cable.
25. **On all models,** remove catalytic converter to exhaust manifold nuts.
26. Remove starter motor as outlined under "Starter, Replace" in "Electrical" section.
27. Remove transmission bolts.
28. **On models equipped with manual transmission,** remove clutch assembly.
29. **On all models,** remove engine support insulator through bolts.
30. Lower vehicle.
31. Remove engine from vehicle with suitable lifting device.
32. Reverse procedure to install.

E-Series

1. Remove engine cover.
2. Recover A/C refrigerant as outlined in "Air Conditioning" chapter.
3. Remove air cleaner assembly and throttle body inlet tube.
4. Remove radiator air deflector.
5. Remove radiator, fan shroud and fan.
6. Remove radiator inner grille, headlamps and side marker lamps.
7. Remove radiator grille opening panel reinforcement and front stone deflector.
8. Remove power steering cooler and auxiliary transmission cooler.
9. Remove transmission and power steering cooler mounting brackets.
10. Remove A/C condenser core.
11. Remove hood latch retaining bolts and position hood latch aside.
12. Remove power distribution box cover, then the nut and cable. Disengage routing clips and set battery feed wiring harness aside.
13. Remove bolts and position power steering reservoir aside.
14. Remove upper core support.
15. Remove screw, then disconnect wiring at front air bag sensor.
16. Disconnect wiring at horn and daytime running lamp module, then disengage harness routing clips and set harness aside.
17. Remove engine oil level dipstick and tube.
18. Remove lower intake manifold as outlined under "Intake Manifold, Replace."
19. Remove accessory drive belt.
20. Remove low pressure line from power steering pump.
21. Remove power steering pump mounting bolts, then set pump aside.
22. Disconnect degas bottle supply hose, oil cooler hoses and lower radiator hose.
23. Remove A/C manifold and tube assembly, then discard O-rings and cap lines to prevent contamination.
24. Disconnect A/C high pressure line from evaporator core.
25. Raise and support vehicle.
26. Drain engine oil into suitable container.
27. Remove starter motor as outlined under "Starter, Replace" in "Electrical" section.
28. Remove torque converter access cover.
29. Remove torque convertor to crankshaft nuts, rotate crankshaft to access nuts.
30. Remove lower transmission to engine mounting bolts.
31. Disconnect exhaust pipes at manifolds.
32. Remove shift cable routing bracket nuts, then the nuts for both engine mounts.
33. Lower vehicle.
34. Remove transmission oil level dipstick, discard O-ring.
35. Remove remaining transmission to engine mounting bolts.
36. Remove engine from vehicle.
37. Reverse procedure to install.

Item	Description
1	LH engine support insulator through bolt
2	LH engine support insulator bolts (2 required)
3	LH engine support insulator
4	RH engine support insulator nuts (2 required)
5	RH engine support insulator washer
6	RH engine support insulator bolts (2 required)
7	RH engine support insulator

LTV0500000000412

Fig. 5 Engine mount replacement (Part 2 of 2). 2005-06 F-150 & Mark LT

INTAKE MANIFOLD

REPLACE

Upper

1. Remove air cleaner assembly and engine cover.
2. Remove clip push pin, then the accelerator control splash shield.
3. Disconnect idle air control valve electrical connector, then remove idle air control valve assembly.
4. Disconnect accelerator and speed control cables at throttle body.
5. Disconnect accelerator and speed control cables at cable bracket.
6. Disconnect spark plug wire holders.
7. Remove 12 upper intake manifold bolts, then the upper intake manifold.
8. Reverse procedure to install, noting the following:
   a. Install new accelerator control splash shield clip push pin.
   b. Tighten upper intake manifold bolts in sequence, **Fig. 9,** in two steps.
   c. Step 1: **Torque** bolts to 53 inch lbs.
   d. Step 2: **Torque** bolts to 89 inch lbs.

Spacer Assembly

1. Remove upper intake manifold as previously outlined.
2. Disconnect throttle position sensor, brake booster vacuum line, vapor management valve and PCV valve hose.
3. Disconnect heater water hoses at intake manifold.
4. Disconnect intake manifold vacuum connector and EGR solenoid electrical and vacuum connectors.
5. Remove retaining nut at transmission oil level tube bracket and position out of way.
6. Remove eight bolts, then the intake manifold spacer assembly.
7. Reverse procedure to install, noting the following:
   a. Inspect manifold spacer gaskets and replace as required.

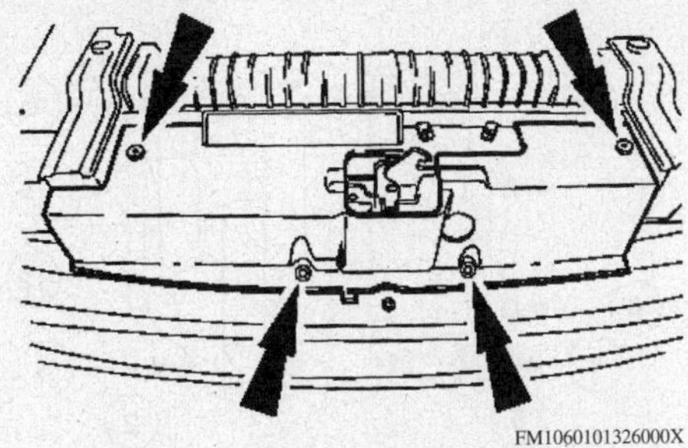

FM1060101326000X

Fig. 6 Front shield retainers. E-Series

   b. Tighten intake manifold spacer bolts in sequence, **Fig. 10,** in two steps.
   c. Step 1:**Torque** bolts to 53 inch lbs.
   d. Step 2: **Torque** bolts to 89 inch lbs.

Lower

1. Remove intake manifold spacer as outlined previously.
2. Disconnect EGR vacuum hose and EGR valve tube upper fitting.
3. Remove radiator hose from lower intake manifold.
4. Disconnect water bypass hose and heater hose.
5. Relieve fuel system pressure as outlined under "Precautions."
6. Disconnect fuel lines, fuel injector electrical connectors and fuel injector electrical harness from fuel injector supply manifold.
7. Disconnect IMRC electrical connector and fuel pressure regulator vacuum line.
8. Fuel charging and IMRC are removed with lower intake manifold.
9. Remove lower intake manifold bolts, then the lower intake manifold.
10. Reverse procedure to install, noting the following:
    a. Remove and discard all lower intake manifold gaskets and seals.
    b. Apply a bead of sealant to intake manifold front and rear seal mounting points, **Fig. 11,** then install front and rear seals.
    c. Install intake manifold gaskets and apply a bead of silicone sealant to areas indicated, **Fig. 12,** then install lower intake manifold.
    d. Lower intake manifold must be installed within fifteen minutes of applying sealer.
    e. **Torque** bolts in sequence, **Fig. 13,** in two stages, first to 44 inch lbs., then to 89 inch lbs.

EXHAUST MANIFOLD

REPLACE

Lefthand

1. Remove oil dipstick tube.
2. Raise and support vehicle.
3. Disconnect lefthand HO2S electrical connector.
4. Remove two three way catalytic converter to exhaust manifold nuts and disconnect Y-pipe from lefthand exhaust manifold.
5. Remove three lefthand exhaust manifold stud bolts.
6. Remove three lefthand exhaust manifold bolts, then the exhaust manifold.
7. Reverse procedure to install.

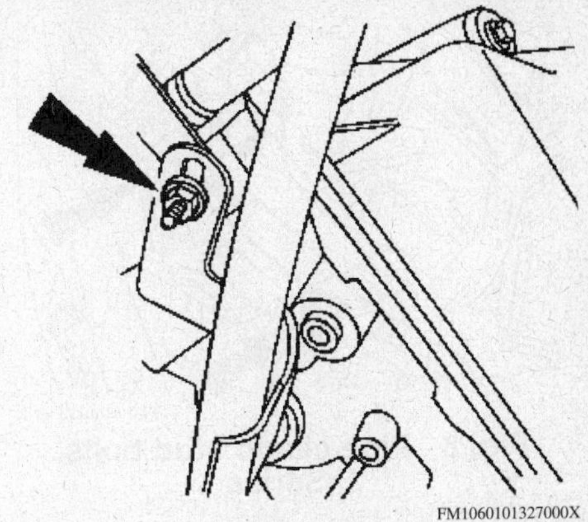

FM1060101327000X

Fig. 7 Pipe bracket mounting nut. E-Series

Righthand

1. Remove EGR valve to exhaust manifold tube.
2. Raise and support vehicle.
3. Disconnect righthand HO2S electrical connector.
4. Remove three righthand exhaust manifold stud bolts.
5. Remove three righthand exhaust manifold bolts, then the exhaust manifold.
6. Reverse procedure to install.

CYLINDER HEAD

REPLACE

1. Remove upper and lower intake manifolds as outlined under "Intake Manifold, Replace."
2. Remove lefthand and righthand valve covers.
3. Remove exhaust manifold as outlined under "Exhaust Manifold, Replace."
4. Remove and position power steering pump aside.
5. **On models equipped with A/C,** remove A/C compressor.
6. **On all models,** remove alternator.
7. Remove idler pulley and alternator bracket.
8. Remove six bolts, then the six rocker arms and pushrods.
9. If rocker arms and push rods are to be reused, mark component locations for installation reference.
10. Remove and discard the eight cylinder head bolts.
11. Remove cylinder head and gasket.
12. Reverse procedure to install, noting the following:
    a. Coat new cylinder head bolts with suitable engine oil.
    b. **Torque** bolts to 15 ft. lbs., in sequence, **Fig. 14.**

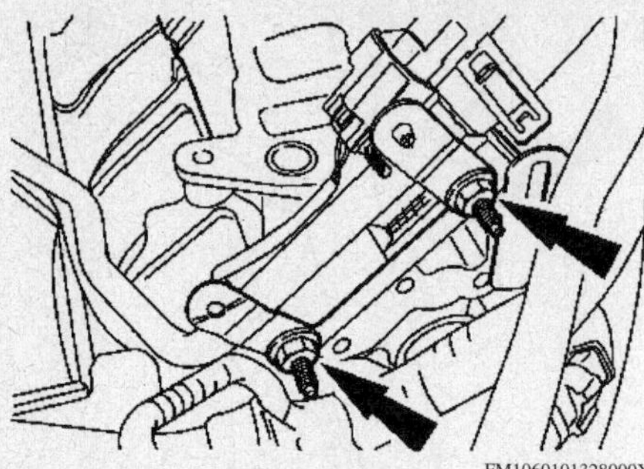

Fig. 8 Pipe clamp stud bolts. E-Series

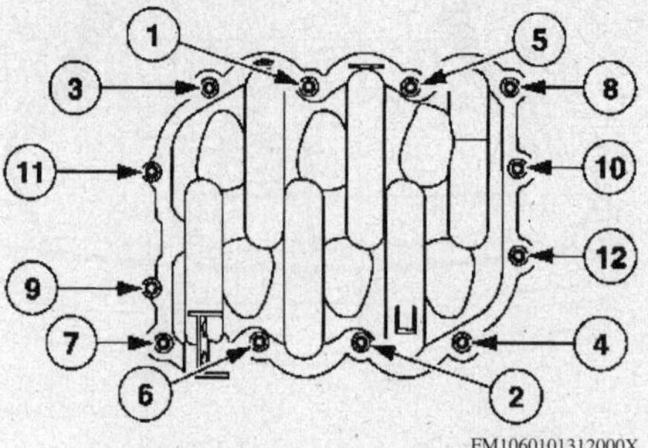

Fig. 9 Upper intake manifold tightening sequence

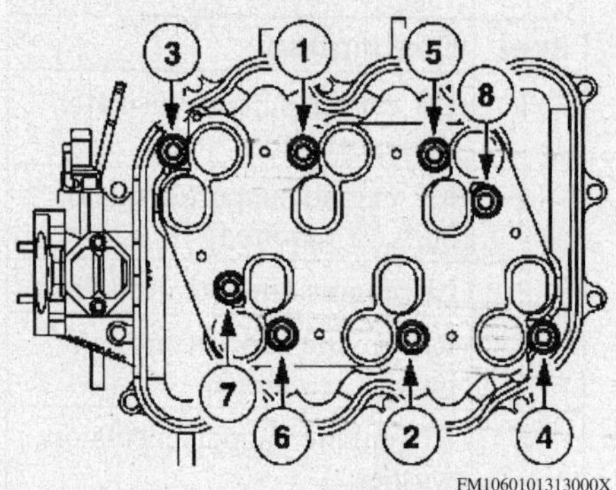

Fig. 10 Intake manifold spacer tightening sequence

c. **Torque** bolts to 30 ft. lbs., in sequence, **Fig. 14.**
d. **Torque** bolts to 37 ft. lbs., in sequence, **Fig. 14.**
e. **Loosen bolts one at a time in sequence. Do not loosen all bolts at the same time. Torque** short bolts to 18 ft. lbs., then an additional 180°. **Torque** long bolts to 33 ft. lbs., then an additional 180°.

VALVE LIFTERS

1. Drain cooling system into a suitable container.
2. Remove intake manifold as outlined under "Intake Manifold, Replace."
3. Remove rocker covers.
4. Remove rocker arm bolts, then the rocker arms.
5. Remove pushrods.
6. Remove two tappet guide plate bolts, then the tappet guide plate and retainer, **Fig. 15.**
7. Remove valve lifters.
8. Lubricate all valve lifters with engine oil prior to installation.
9. Reverse procedure to install.

FRONT COVER

REPLACE

E-Series

REMOVAL

1. Remove water pump as outlined under "Water Pump, Replace."
2. Raise and support vehicle.
3. Rotate crankshaft until damper timing mark aligns with top dead center indicator.
4. Mark crankshaft damper and pulley for alignment reference, then remove crankshaft pulley.
5. Remove crankshaft damper with suitable puller.
6. Disconnect wiring at crankshaft position sensor.
7. At front of oil pan, remove a retaining bolt from lefthand and righthand side of oil pan.
8. Lower vehicle.
9. Remove camshaft position sensor.
10. Disconnect EGR valve vacuum hose, then remove EGR valve tube upper fitting.
11. Remove nut and bolts, then the EGR valve and adapter assembly.
12. Remove camshaft synchronizer retaining bolt, then the synchronizer.
13. If oil pump driveshaft comes out with camshaft synchronizer, retrieve oil pump driveshaft before continuing with procedure. **Do not turn crankshaft or camshaft during removal and installation procedure or fuel system timing will be out of time with engine.**
14. Remove accessory drive belt idler pulley and tensioner.
15. Remove and discard water pump mounting studs.
16. Remove engine front cover and gasket.

INSTALLATION

1. Clean mating surfaces of oil pan and cylinder block using Metal Cleaner No. F4AZ-19A536-RA, or equivalent. Use care to ensure no debris fall into oil pan.
2. Apply a bead of Silicone Gasket and Sealant No. F6AZ-19562-A, or equivalent, at oil pump block seam.
3. Install engine front cover gasket.
4. Apply a second bead of sealant along edge of engine front cover gasket at oil pan block seam.
5. Apply a bead of sealant on oil pan flange.
6. Install front cover gasket, then apply sealant to oil pan.
7. Number 12 position is NOT part of the torque sequence.
8. Tighten front cover bolts in sequence, **Fig. 16,** in two stages. First, install studs and **torque** to 62 inch lbs., then **torque** stud bolts and nuts to 21 ft. lbs. New studs are supplied with Loctite thread locking compound on threads, ensure Loctite end of stud is installed in engine.
9. Install accessory drive belt tensioner and idler pulley.
10. A synchronizer alignment gauge must be used to install camshaft synchronizer assembly.
11. Install synchronizer alignment gauge tool No. 303–562, or equivalent, to camshaft by rotating tool until it engages in notch in camshaft synchronizer housing.
12. During installation, arrow on synchronizer alignment gauge will rotate clockwise as gear engages.
13. Install camshaft synchronizer housing assembly as outlined under, "Camshaft Position Sensor, Replace."
14. Install EGR valve, adapter plate, tube upper fitting and vacuum hose.
15. Install camshaft position sensor.
16. Raise and support vehicle.
17. Install oil pan retaining bolts.
18. Connect wiring at crankshaft position sensor.
19. Install crankshaft damper with suitable damper installation tool.
20. Align crankshaft pulley with marks made during disassembly, then install retaining bolts.
21. Lower vehicle.
22. Install water pump as outlined under "Water Pump, Replace."

F-150 & Mark LT

1. Drain cooling system into suitable container.
2. Remove air cleaner assembly.
3. Remove upper radiator hose, fan shroud and lower radiator hose.
4. Disconnect camshaft position sensor electrical connector.
5. Raise and support vehicle.
6. Remove oil pan drain plug and drain engine oil into suitable container.
7. Disconnect crankshaft sensor electrical connector.
8. Position engine wiring harness aside.
9. Remove power steering pump bracket bolts and nuts, then the power steering bracket.
10. Remove nuts and position A/C compressor aside.
11. Remove crankshaft pulley.
12. Remove bolts securing oil pan flange to front engine cover.
13. Remove Allen head bolt at engine front cover.
14. Lower vehicle.
15. Remove heater water outlet tube hoses.
16. Disconnect wiring harness from outlet tube and position aside.
17. Remove heater water outlet tube.
18. Remove camshaft position sensor.
19. Disconnect EGR valve vacuum hose, then remove EGR valve tube upper fitting.
20. Remove nut and bolts, then the EGR valve and adapter assembly.
21. Remove camshaft synchronizer retaining bolt, then the synchronizer.

22. Oil pump driveshaft may come out with camshaft synchronizer, if this happens, retrieve oil pump driveshaft before proceeding.
23. **Do not turn crankshaft or camshaft during removal and installation procedure or fuel system timing will be out of time with engine.**
24. Remove nuts and bolts, then the water pump.
25. Remove crankshaft front oil seal.
26. Remove stud bolts, bolts and cap screw, then the front cover.
27. Reverse procedure to install, noting the following:
    a. In order to prevent foreign material from contaminating engine block or engine front cover, it is required to seal coolant and oil passages of both components.
    b. Pack exposed portions of oil pan with shop towels.
    c. Plug oil and coolant passages.
    d. Clean gasket surfaces, remove any foreign material using compressed air.
    e. Remove shop towels from oil pan, remove plugs and seals from engine block and front cover.
    f. Install front cover gasket, then apply sealant to oil pan.
    g. Number 12 position is NOT part of the torque sequence.
    h. Tighten front cover bolts in sequence, **Fig. 16,** in two stages. First, install studs and **torque** to 62 inch lbs., then **torque** stud bolts and nuts to 21 ft. lbs. New studs are supplied with Loctite thread locking compound on threads, ensure Loctite end of stud is installed in engine.
    i. Install camshaft position sensor as outlined under "Camshaft Position Sensor, Replace."

TIMING CHAIN

REPLACE

1. Remove engine front cover as outlined under "Front Cover, Replace."
2. Remove camshaft position sensor drive gear.
3. Rotate crankshaft timing marks and keyways align, **Fig. 17.**
4. Compress timing chain tensioner and install suitable pin to hold tensioner.
5. Remove camshaft sprocket, crankshaft sprocket and timing chain as an assembly.
6. Reverse procedure to install.

CAMSHAFT

REPLACE

1. Remove valve lifters as outlined under "Valve Lifters."
2. Remove engine front cover as outlined under "Front Cover, Replace."
3. Remove camshaft key.
4. Remove engine dynamic balance shaft drive gear.
5. Remove two bolts from camshaft thrust plate, then the thrust plate.
6. Remove spacer, then the camshaft.

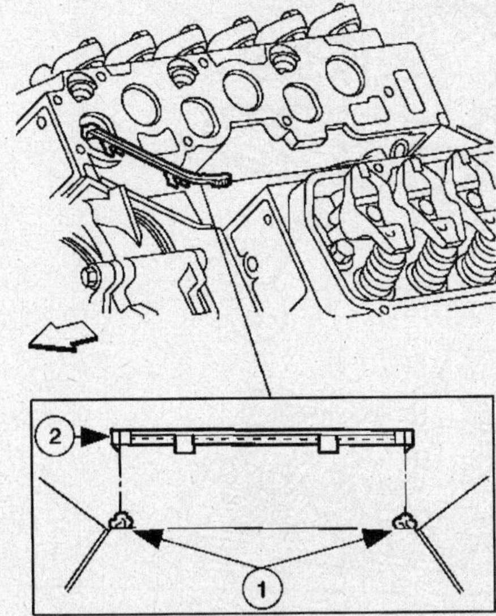

Fig. 11 Intake manifold sealant application

7. Reverse procedure to install.

CAMSHAFT POSITION SENSOR

REPLACE

1. Partially drain cooling system into suitable container.
2. Remove air cleaner assembly.
3. Remove bolt from heater water tube, then position aside.
4. Disconnect electrical connector from CMP.
5. Remove screws from CMP, then CMP.
6. Reverse procedure to install.

CRANKSHAFT SEAL

REPLACE

1. Remove crankshaft damper and pulley.
2. Remove front crankshaft seal using suitable seal removal tool, **Fig. 18.**
3. Reverse procedure to install, noting the following:
    a. Lubricate crankshaft seal lips with engine oil prior to installation.
    b. Use suitable front crankshaft seal installer as outlined, **Fig. 19.**

CRANKSHAFT REAR OIL SEAL

REPLACE

1. Remove transmission.
2. Remove six bolts, then the flywheel.
3. Use suitable rear crankshaft seal remover and slide hammer, "A," to remove seal, "B", **Fig. 20.**
4. Reverse procedure to install, noting the following:
    a. Lubricate crankshaft seal lips with engine oil prior to installation.
    b. Use suitable rear crankshaft seal installer, **Fig. 21.**

OIL PAN

REPLACE

E-Series

1. Drain cooling system.
2. Remove air cleaner assembly.
3. Remove upper radiator hose.
4. Remove fan using fan pulley holding wrench tool No. T84T-6312-C and fan clutch nut wrench tool No. T93T-6312-B, or equivalents.
5. Remove fan shroud attaching screws, then the fan with shroud.
6. Remove upper intake manifold as outlined under "Intake Manifold, Replace."
7. Remove dipstick tube support bracket to transmission bolt.
8. Raise and support vehicle.
9. Drain engine oil.
10. Loosen transmission mount nuts.
11. Disconnect exhaust system from righthand and lefthand exhaust manifolds.
12. Disconnect engine mounts from frame.
13. Position a suitable jack and block of wood under oil pan.
14. Raise engine at least 13 inches.
15. Support engine using suitable blocks of wood between engine mount bracket and exhaust manifolds.
16. Remove jack and block of wood from beneath oil pan.
17. Remove oil pan to transmission attaching bolts.
18. Remove remaining oil pan bolts, then the oil pan.
19. Reverse procedure to install, noting the following:
    a. Clean oil pan sealing area using Ford Metal Surface Cleaner F4AZ-19A536-RA, or equivalent.
    b. Apply silicone gasket and sealant F7AZ-19554-EA, or equivalent, as outlined in **Fig. 22.**
    c. **Torque** oil pan to 35–44 inch lbs, then to 79–106 inch lbs., in sequence outlined in **Fig. 23.**

F-150 & Mark LT

1. If equipped, turn air suspension switch off.
2. Raise and support vehicle.
3. Drain engine oil.
4. **On models equipped with 2WD,** remove engine as outlined under "Engine Replace."
5. **On models equipped with 4WD,** remove front differential.
6. **On all models,** remove oil pan to transmission bolts.
7. Remove fifteen bolts, then the oil pan.
8. Reverse procedure to install, noting the following:
    a. Clean and apply sealant to oil pan sealing areas.
    b. **Torque** oil pan to 44 inch lbs, then to 89 inch lbs., in sequence outlined in **Fig. 23.**

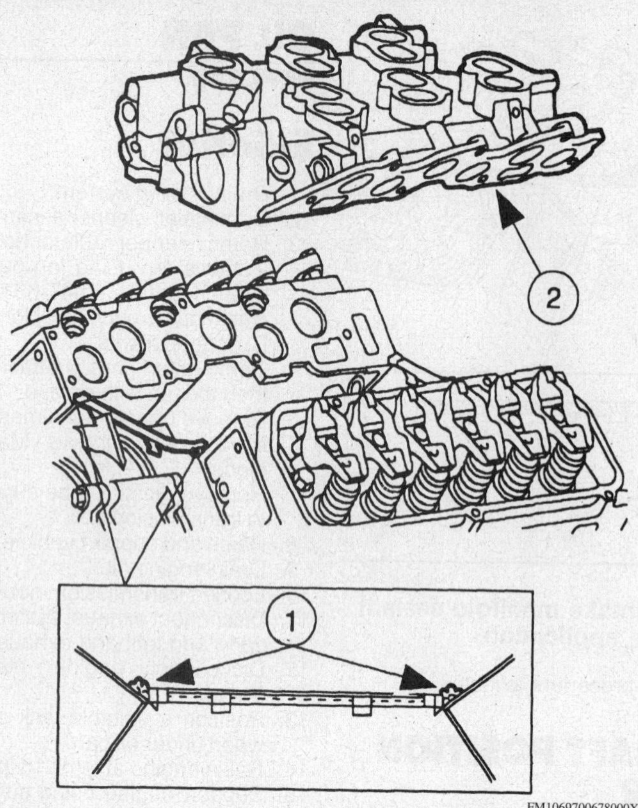

Fig. 12 Intake manifold gasket sealant application

OIL PUMP

REPLACE

1. Remove oil pan as outlined under "Oil Pan, Replace."
2. Remove oil filter.
3. Remove six oil pump attaching bolts, then the oil pump.
4. Reverse procedure to install.

OIL PUMP SERVICE

1. Remove oil pump as outlined under "Oil Pump, Replace."
2. Remove oil pump drive gear, "A", driven gear, "B", and O-ring, "C", **Fig. 24.**
3. Inspect all oil pump components, inspect the face of oil pump for flatness.
4. Remove engine front cover. Refer to "Front Cover, Replace.".
5. Remove the plug over oil pressure relief valve, **Fig. 25.**
6. Remove oil pressure relief valve ball and spring.
7. Clean and inspect ball and spring.
8. Reverse procedure to install.

BELT TENSION DATA

Drive belt tension is not adjustable. The drive belt tensioner automatically adjusts drive belt tension.

SERPENTINE DRIVE BELT

Belt Routing

Refer to **Figs. 26 and 27** for serpentine drive belt routing.

Belt, Replacement

1. Use drive belt tensioner pulley bolt to rotate drive belt tensioner counterclockwise and remove drive belt.
2. Remove belt, slowly release tensioner. **Do not allow tensioner to snap back, as damage may result.**
3. Reverse procedure to install.

Tensioner, Replacement

1. Remove drive belt as outlined under "Belt, Replacement."
2. Remove drive belt tensioner bolt and tensioner.
3. Reverse procedure to install.

THERMOSTAT

REPLACE

1. Partially drain cooling system into a suitable container.
2. Remove upper radiator hose, then the thermostat housing bolts.
3. Remove thermostat and paper gasket
4. Reverse procedure to install.

WATER PUMP

REPLACE

E-Series

1. Drain cooling system.
2. Remove air cleaner assembly.
3. Remove upper radiator air deflector.
4. Remove upper hose from radiator.
5. Remove fan and fan clutch from water pump pulley using fan pulley holding wrench tool No. T84T-6312-C and fan clutch nut wrench tool No. T93T-6312-B, or equivalents. **Fan clutch assembly has righthand threads.**
6. Remove fan shroud attaching bolts, then the shroud with fan.
7. Remove accessory drive belt.
8. Remove lower radiator hose from water pump.
9. Disconnect engine harness from water pump studs.
10. Remove A/C compressor support bracket and position aside.
11. Remove water pump pulley, then the bypass tube from water pump.
12. Remove water pump bolts, then the water pump.
13. Reverse procedure to install. Tighten water pump as outlined, **Fig. 28.**

F-150 & Mark LT

1. Remove air cleaner assembly.
2. Drain cooling system into a suitable container.
3. Remove front air deflector, then upper radiator hose from radiator.
4. Remove the engine cooling fan and the fan shroud.
5. Remove fan blade and clutch using fan clutch holding tool No. T84T-6312-C and fan clutch wrench tool No. T93T-6312-B, or equivalents.
6. Remove fan shroud attaching screws, then the fan, clutch and shroud.
7. Remove A/C compressor mounting bracket upper support bolt, **Fig. 29.**
8. Loosen A/C compressor mounting bracket lower support bolt. Position bracket and bolt forward until they contact power steering pump pulley.
9. Position A/C compressor mounting bracket aside.
10. Remove accessory drive belt, then the water pump pulley.
11. Remove upper radiator hose from water pump.
12. Remove four water pump attaching bolts, then the water pump.
13. Reverse procedure to install, noting the following:
    a. Lubricate water pump O-ring seal using suitable coolant.
    b. Install water pump and tighten bolts to specifications.
    c. Install water pump pulley and tighten specifications.

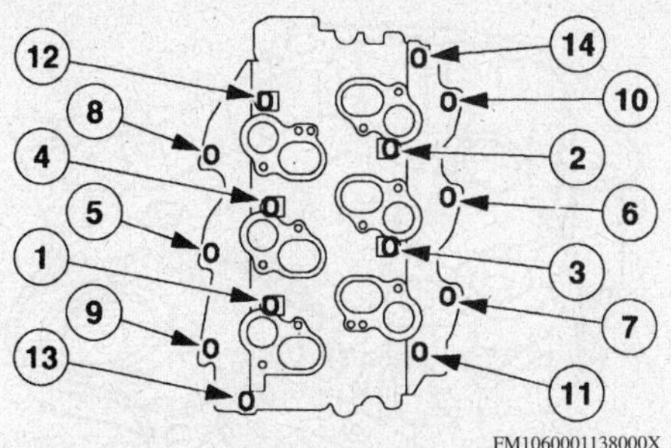

Fig. 13 Lower intake manifold bolt tightening sequence

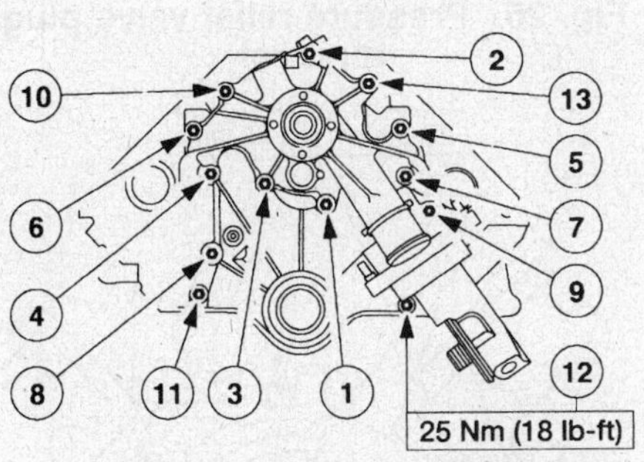

Fig. 16 Front cover tightening sequence. E-Series, F-150 & Mark LT

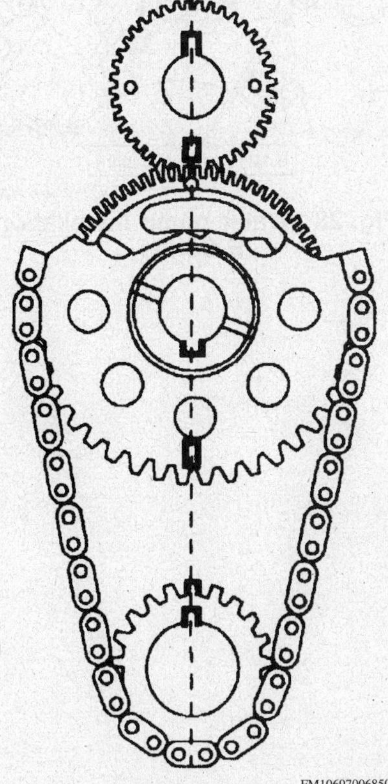

Fig. 17 Timing mark alignment

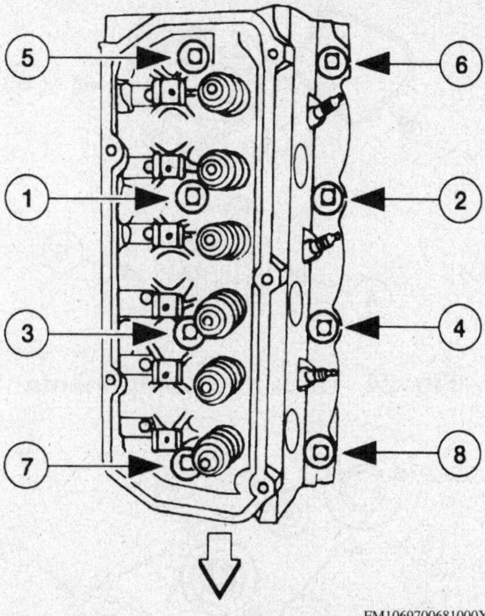

Fig. 14 Cylinder head tightening sequence

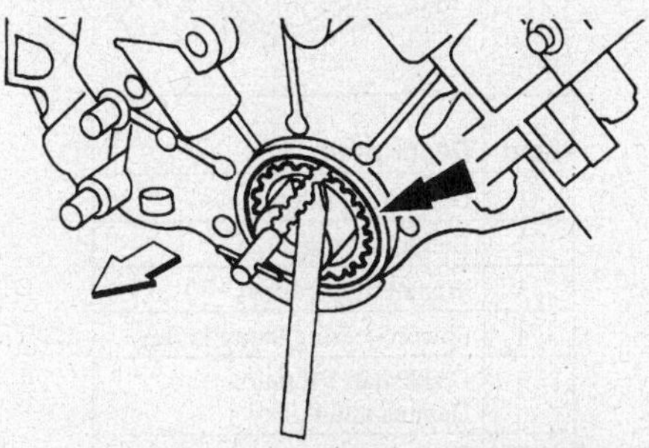

Fig. 18 Front crankshaft seal removal

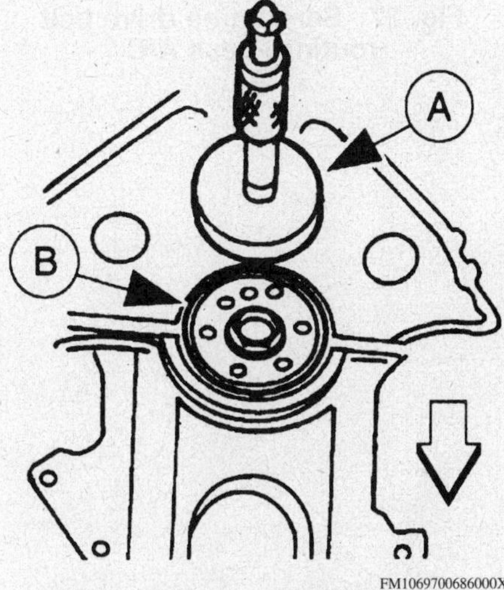

Fig. 20 Rear crankshaft seal removal

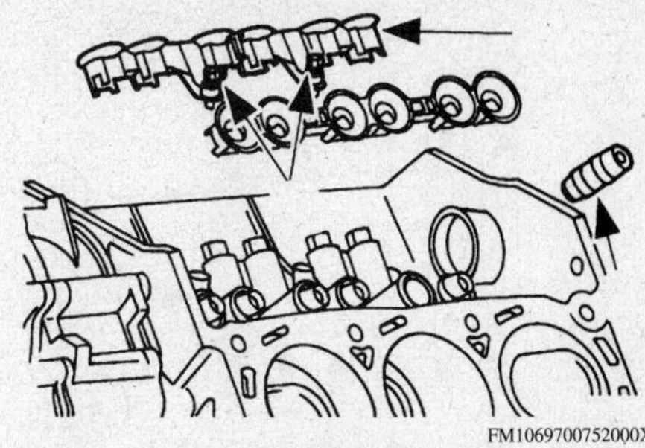

Fig. 15 Valve lifter guide plate removal

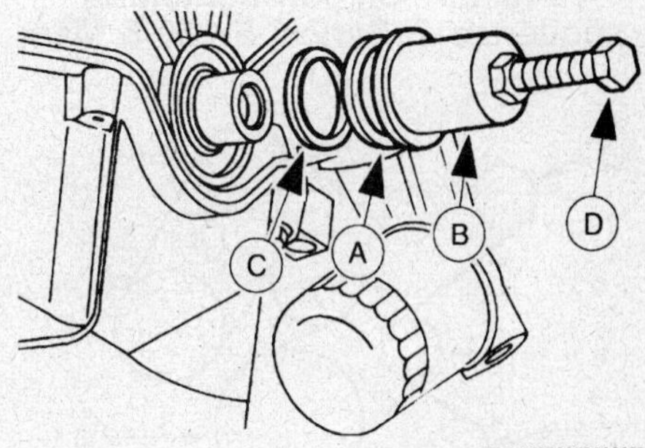

Fig. 19 Front crankshaft seal installation

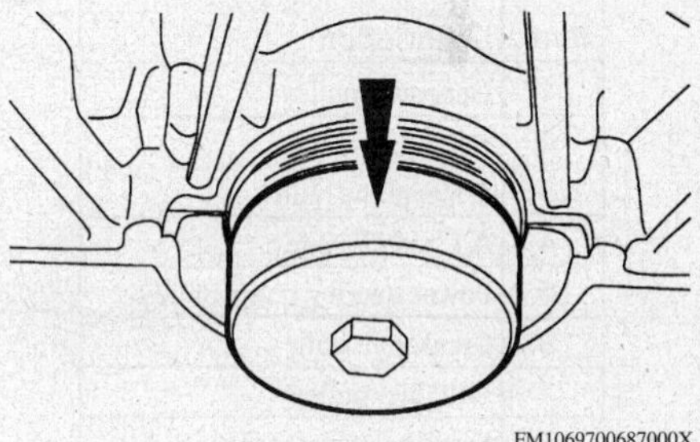

Fig. 21 Rear crankshaft seal installation

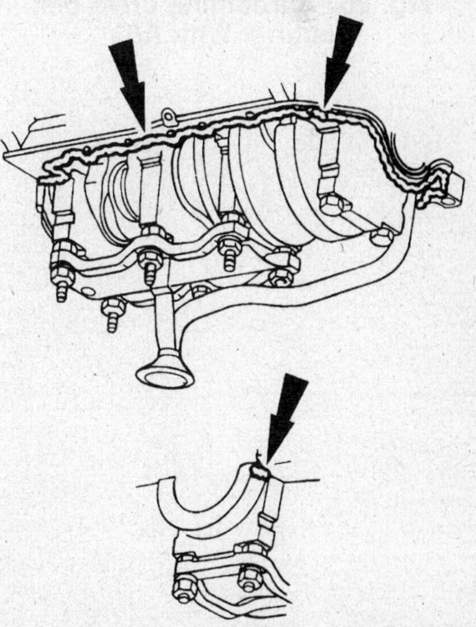

Fig. 22 Oil pan sealant application. E-Series, F-150 & Mark LT

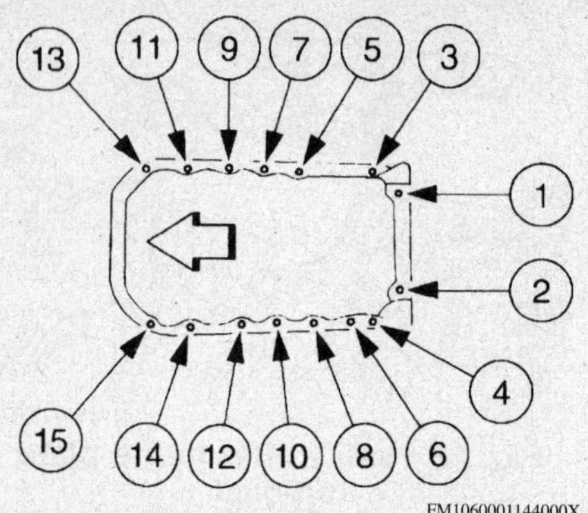

Fig. 23 Oil pan tightening sequence. E-Series, F-150 & Mark LT

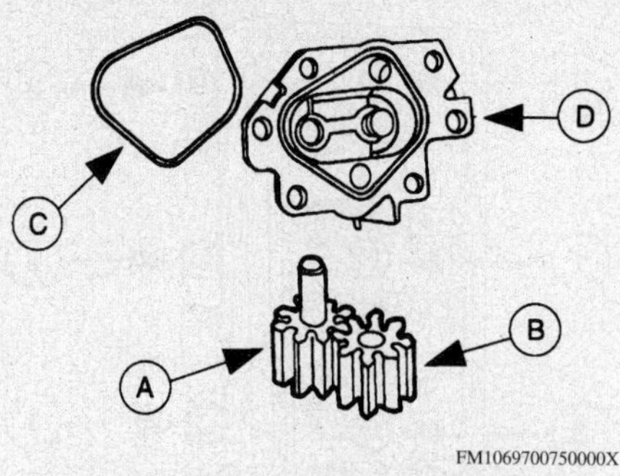

Fig. 24 Oil pump components

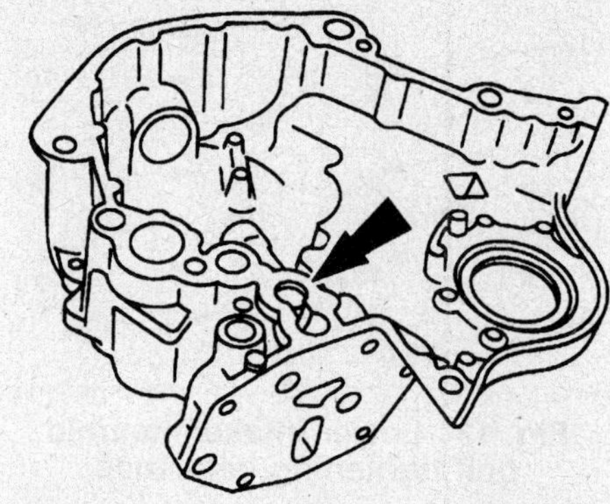

Fig. 25 Pressure relief valve plug removal

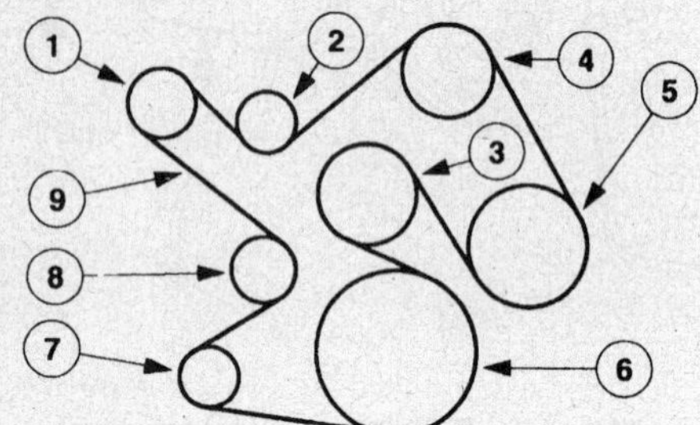

Item	Description
1	Generator pulley
2	Belt idler pulley
3	Water pump pulley
4	A/C clutch pulley
5	Power steering pump pulley
6	Crankshaft pulley
7	Belt idler pulley
8	Drive belt tensioner
9	Drive belt

FM1139700551000X

Fig. 26 Serpentine drive belt routing. With A/C

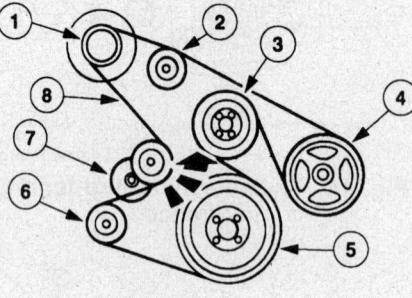

Item	Description
1	Generator Pulley
2	Belt Idler Pulley
3	Water Pump Pulley
4	Power Steering Pump Pulley
5	Crankshaft Vibration Damper and Pulley
6	Drive Belt Tensioner Pulley
7	Drive Belt Tensioner
8	Drive Belt

FM1069800518000X

Fig. 27 Serpentine drive belt routing. Less A/C

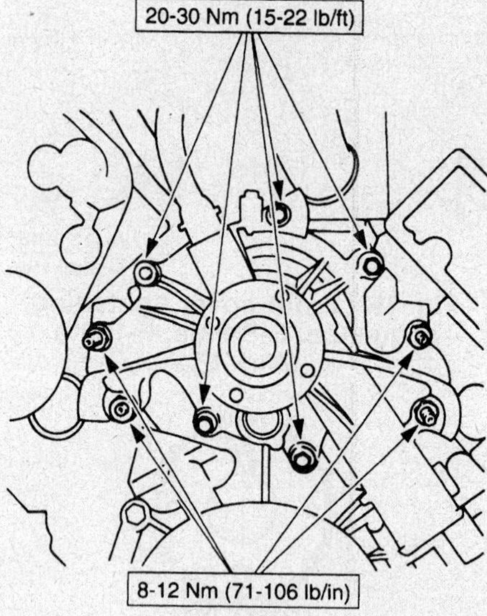

Fig. 28 Water pump installation. E-Series

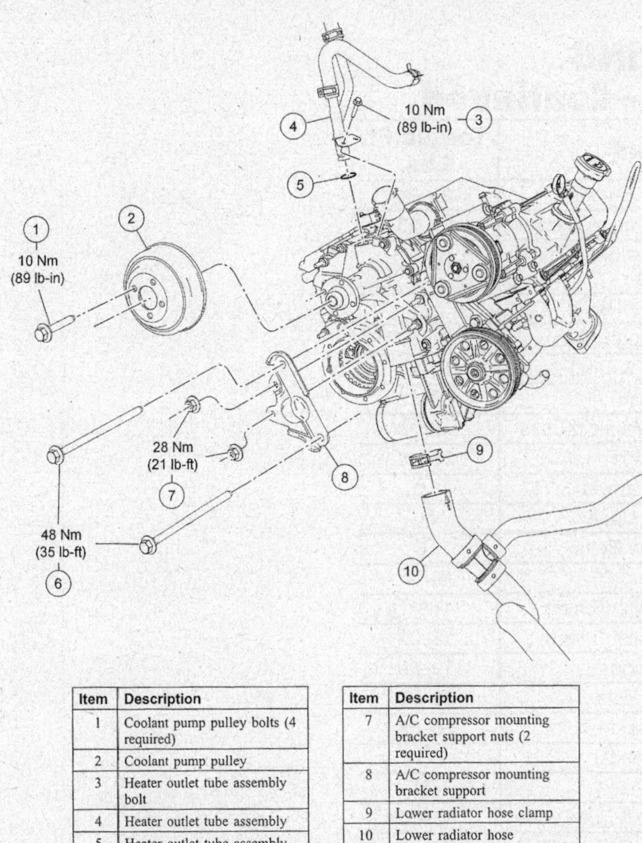

Item	Description
1	Coolant pump pulley bolts (4 required)
2	Coolant pump pulley
3	Heater outlet tube assembly bolt
4	Heater outlet tube assembly
5	Heater outlet tube assembly O-ring seal
6	A/C compressor mounting bracket support bolts (2 required)

Item	Description
7	A/C compressor mounting bracket support nuts (2 required)
8	A/C compressor mounting bracket support
9	Lower radiator hose clamp
10	Lower radiator hose

LTV0500000000413

Fig. 29 Water pump replacement (Part 1 of 2). F150 & Mark LT

Item	Description
11	Coolant pump bolts (3 required)
12	Coolant pump nuts (4 required)
13	Coolant pump bolt
14	Coolant pump stud bolt
15	Coolant pump
16	Coolant pump gasket

LTV0500000000414

Fig. 29 Water pump replacement (Part 2 of 2). F150 & Mark LT

TIGHTENING SPECIFICATIONS

Year	Component	Torque Ft. Lbs.
2002–06	A/C Compressor Bracket Bolts	30–40
	A/C Compressor Manifold Bolt	14–18
	Accelerator Cable Bracket Nut & Bolt	80①
	Accelerator Cable To Accelerator Cable Bracket Bolt	19–25①
	Alternator Bracket Long Bolts	31–39
	Alternator Bracket Short Bolt	18–22
	Alternator Mounting Nuts & Bolts	15–22
	Camshaft Position Sensor	27①
	Camshaft Position Sensor Drive Gear Bolt	30–36
	Camshaft Thrust Plate Bolt	72–120①
	Catalytic Converter To Exhaust Manifold Bolts	30
	Connecting Rod Bolts	⑦
	Crankshaft Damper Bolt	103–118
	Crankshaft Pulley Bolts	20–28
	Cylinder Head	③

Continued

TIGHTENING SPECIFICATIONS—Continued

Year	Component	Torque Ft. Lbs.
2002–06	EGR Valve Tube Fittings	25–34
	Engine Coolant Temperature Sensor	11–13
	Engine Dynamic Balance Shaft Thrust Plate Bolts	72–120①
	Engine Front Cover Bolts	②
	Engine Mount Through Bolts	51–67
	Exhaust Manifold Bolts & Stud Bolts	15–22
	Flywheel Bolts	56–59
	Fuel Injection Supply Manifold Bolts	80①
	Idler Pulley Bolt	36–46
	Intake Manifold, Lower	④
	Intake Manifold, Upper	④
	Main Bearing Cap Bolts	⑥
	Oil Filter	8–11
	Oil Filter Adapter Bolts (6 mm)	71–97①
	Oil Filter Adapter Bolts (8 mm)	15–22
	Oil Galley Plugs	19–29
	Oil Pan Baffle Nuts	30–37
	Oil Pan To Transmission Bolts	28–38
	Oil Pressure Sender	9–11
	Oil Pump	⑤
	Oil Pump Screen Cover & Tube Bolts	15–22
	Oil Pump Screen Cover & Tube Nuts	30–37
	Power Steering Pump Bolts	17–20
	Power Steering Reservoir Bolts	80–107①
	Power Steering Support Bracket Bolts	30–40
	Rocker Arm Bolts	23–29
	Rocker Cover Bolts	71–102①
	Thermostat Bolts	80①
	Timing Chain Tensioner Bolts	9–10
	Valve Lifter Guide Plate Bolts	96–120①
	Water Pump Bolts	15–22
	Water Pump Pulley Bolts	89①
	Water Pump Stud Bolts	15–22
	Water Temperature Indicator Sender Unit	11–13

①— Inch lbs.
②— E-Series, torque to 15–22 ft. lbs. On F-150, Mark LT & all 2002 models, refer to "Front Cover, Replace."
③— Refer to "Cylinder Head, Replace."
④— Refer to "Intake Manifold, Replace."
⑤— Refer to "Oil Pump, Replace."
⑥— First step, torque to 37 ft. lbs.; second step, an additional 120°.
⑦— First step, torque to 18 ft. lbs.; second step, torque to 33 ft. lbs.; third step, an additional 90–120°.

4.6L & 5.4L SOHC Gasoline Engines

NOTE: On Air Bag Equipped Models, Refer To "Air Bag System Precautions" Located In The Front Of This Manual For System Disarming & Arming Procedures.

NOTE: Refer To "Computer Relearn Procedures" Located In The Front Of This Manual When Battery Power To The Computer Has Been Interrupted.

INDEX

PRECAUTIONS

Air Bag Systems

Refer to "Air Bag System Precautions" in the front of this manual for system disarming and arming procedures.

Air Suspension System

On air suspension equipped vehicles, the air suspension service switch must be turned to the "Off" position before lifting or raising vehicle. The air suspension service switch is located behind righthand kick panel area.

Battery Ground Cable

Prior to service, disconnect battery ground cable and isolate as required.

Fuel System Pressure Relief

2002-03

The fuel system remains under high pressure even when the engine is not running. To avoid injury or fire, release pressure from the fuel system before disconnecting any fuel line. Proceed as follows:

1. Remove fuel tank cap to release residual fuel pressure from tank.
2. Connect fuel pressure gauge tool No. T80L-9974-B, or equivalent, to valve located on the fuel rail.
3. Gradually open testing kit valve to relieve fuel pressure in system. Drain fuel into suitable container or return to fuel tank.
4. To avoid unrequired fuel spillage and fire hazard, any time fuel lines are disconnected, ignition switch should be in Off position.
5. When repair is completed, turn ignition On and Off several times to pressurize fuel system. Do not start engine.
6. Inspect for fuel leaks at pressure regulator, fuel injectors and fuel fittings. Repair as required.

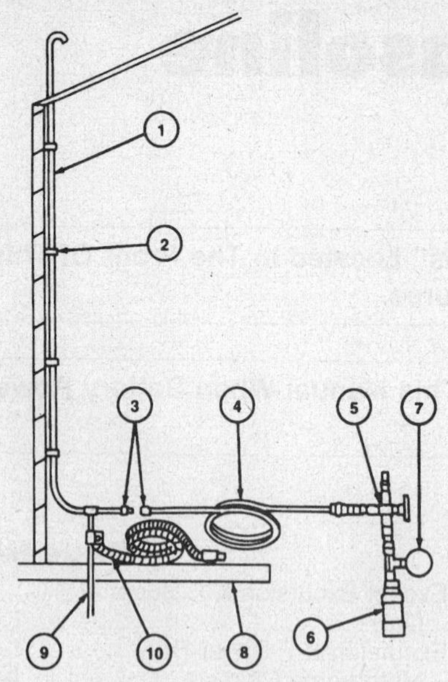

Item	Description
1	1/2 Inch Pipe
2	Vent Stack Support
3	Vent Stack Connectors
4	Rotunda Venting Hose
5	Rotunda Fuel Filter Neck Venting Kit
6	Fill Valve Connector
7	Gauge
8	Building Floor
9	Support/Grounding Rod
10	Grounding Cable

FM1029900308000X

Fig. 1 Typical vent stack installation

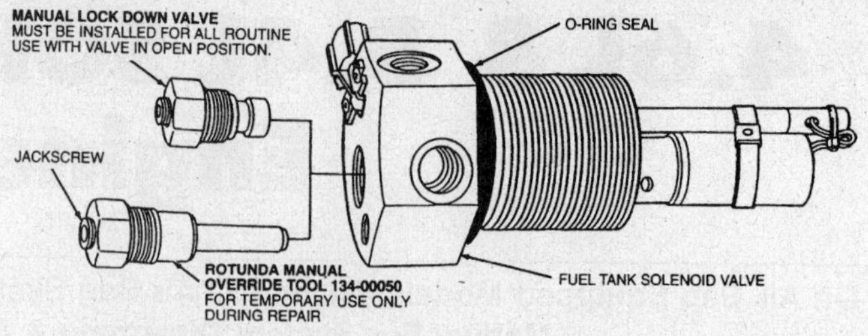

FM1029900309000X

Fig. 2 Fuel tank solenoid valve

Condition	Possible Source	Action
• Unable to Vent Fuel Tanks or Fuel Lines	• Damaged fuel tank solenoids. • Damaged lines or hoses. • Circuitry.	• GO to Pinpoint Test A.

FM1029900301000X

Fig. 3 NGV fuel tank solenoid valve symptom chart

2004–06

1. Remove splash shield located on left-hand frame rail under driver's side door.
2. Disconnect fuel pump/tank sender harness electrical connector.
3. Start engine and allow it to idle until it stalls.
4. After engine stalls, crank engine for approximately five seconds to ensure fuel rail pressure has been released.
5. Turn ignition switch to OFF position.
6. After fuel system service is complete, connect electrical connector.
7. Reposition splash shield and install a new pushpin.
8. Cycle ignition switch and wait 3 seconds to pressurize fuel system. Inspect for leaks before starting engine.

Fuel System Pressure Relief, Natural Gas Engine

When servicing any component of the fuel charging system, fuel pressure should be released using the following procedures.

When venting fuel system, venting into a vent stack is recommended, **Fig. 1.** If using a vent stack, ensure local regulations are followed. Before venting occurs, battery should be disconnected and isolated as required.

Natural gas O-rings are identified with a yellow stripe. Do not use unapproved O-rings.

Before performing pressure relief procedures, refer to "NGV Fuel Tank Solenoid Valve Test" to determine status of fuel tank solenoid valves.

If a manual override tool has been used to open fuel tank solenoid valve, solenoid valve must be replaced, Fig. 2.

Do not vent fuel tank unless tank or fuel tank solenoid valve is being replaced. Unrequired venting of good tanks will damage fuel tank solenoid valve.

Do not vent an entire fuel tank by using the fuel line venting procedure. Damage to the fuel supply manifold schraeder valve will result, with the possibility of personal injury or property damage.

NGV FUEL TANK SOLENOID VALVE TEST

Prior to relieving fuel pressure on NGV vehicles, the following diagnosis should be performed to determine whether or not the fuel tank solenoid valve is stuck open or closed.

1. Inspect fuel system and determine if any of the following apply:
   a. Damaged fuel tanks.
   b. Damaged fuel tank solenoid valve.
   c. Damaged lines or hoses.
   d. Damaged fuse or relay.
   e. Damaged power distribution box.
   f. Damaged, loose or corroded electrical connections.
2. If any of the preceding conditions were found during visual inspection, repair as required. If none of the preceding conditions were found during visual inspection, refer to symptom chart, **Fig. 3.** For pinpoint "A", except F-Series models, refer to **Fig. 4.** For pinpoint test "A" on F-Series models, refer to **Fig. 5.** If fuel tank requires pressure relief, refer to "Precautions."
3. If fuel tank solenoid valve requires replacement, refer to **MOTOR's "Domestic Engine Performance & Driveability Manual"** for procedure.

FUEL LINES, E-SERIES & F-SERIES

1. Connect ground cable tool No. 134–00121, or equivalent, to fuel supply manifold and to earth ground.
2. Turn in manual lockdown valve jackscrew on fuel tank solenoid valves.
3. When using fuel tester kit, ensure tester kit valve is closed. Connect fuel rail pressure test and venting kit tool No. 134–00116 and Rotunda venting hose assembly tool No. 134–00118, or equivalents to schrader valve on fuel supply manifold.
4. Connect venting hose to a suitable vent stack.
5. Remove fuel pump relay from power distribution box.
6. Connect wire sockets 87 and 30 in fuel pump relay socket of power distribution box using a jumper wire constructed of 6 inches of 18 gauge wire and two spade terminals.
7. Slowly open testing kit valve to relieve fuel pressure. Vent for 1 minute.
8. Close bleed valve and remove from vehicle.

NATURAL GAS FUEL TANK PRESSURE RELIEF

E-Series & F-Series w/Normally Operating Solenoid

1. Ensure all fuel tank solenoid valves are in locked down position.
2. Connect grounding cable tool No. 134–00121, or equivalent, to rear side of fuel fill valve at fuel line connection and earth ground.
3. Turn in manual lockdown valve jackscrew on fuel tank solenoid valves, **Fig. 6.**
4. Connect fuel filler neck venting kit tool No. 134–00117, or equivalent, to fuel filler valve.
5. Connect venting hose tool No. 134–00118, or equivalent, to fuel filler venting kit and vent stack.
6. Remove fuel pump relay from power distribution box.
7. Connect wire sockets 87 and 30 in fuel

TEST CONDITIONS	TESTDETAILS/RESULTS/ACTIONS
A1 CHECK THE MIDSHIP FUEL TANK FOR AN OPEN SOLENOID VALVE	
Note: The battery must be fully charged to carry out solenoid diagnostics. **Note:** Make sure that the manual lockdown valve jackscrew on the midship fuel tank solenoid valve is in the open (fully counterclockwise) position.	
1	
	2 Connect the grounding cable, the venting hose assembly and the fuel filler neck venting kit to the vent stack and the fuel fill valve assembly.
	3 Close the manual lockdown valve jackscrews on the forward and rear aft-axle fuel tank solenoid valves and the extended range fuel tank solenoid valve, if equipped. Tighten the jackscrews to 7-9 Nm (62-79 lb-in).
	4 Open the manual backflow valve on the fuel filler valve.
	5 Open the manual bleed valve on the fuel filler neck venting kit for 60 seconds.
	6 Close the manual bleed valve on the fuel filler neck venting kit.

FM1029900363010X

Fig. 4 Pinpoint Test A: Fuel Tank Solenoid Valve Diagnosis (Part 1 of 17). E-Series

TEST CONDITIONS	TESTDETAILS/RESULTS/ACTIONS
A1 CHECK THE MIDSHIP FUEL TANK FOR AN OPEN SOLENOID VALVE (Continued)	
	7 Observe the system pressure on the fuel filler neck venting kit gauge. • Is the pressure on the gauge 0 kPa (0 psi)? → **Yes** GO to **A3**. → **No** GO to **A2**.
A2 CHECK THE MIDSHIP FUEL TANK SOLENOID VALVE CIRCUIT 787 (PK/BK) FOR A SHORT TOVOLTAGE	
1 Midship Fuel Tank Solenoid Valve C348	
2 V	2 Measure the voltage between C348, circuit 787 (PK/BK) and ground. • Is the voltage 10 volts or greater? → **Yes** REPAIR circuit 787 (PK/BK). TEST the system for normal operation. If the vehicle is equipped with aft-axle fuel tanks, GO to **A6**. → **No** MARK the midship fuel tank solenoid valve as "Stuck Open"; the solenoid valve will be replaced after diagnostics are completed. If the vehicle is equipped with aft-axle fuel tanks, GO to **A6**; if not, INSTALL a new the midship fuel tank solenoid valve. TEST the system for normal operation.

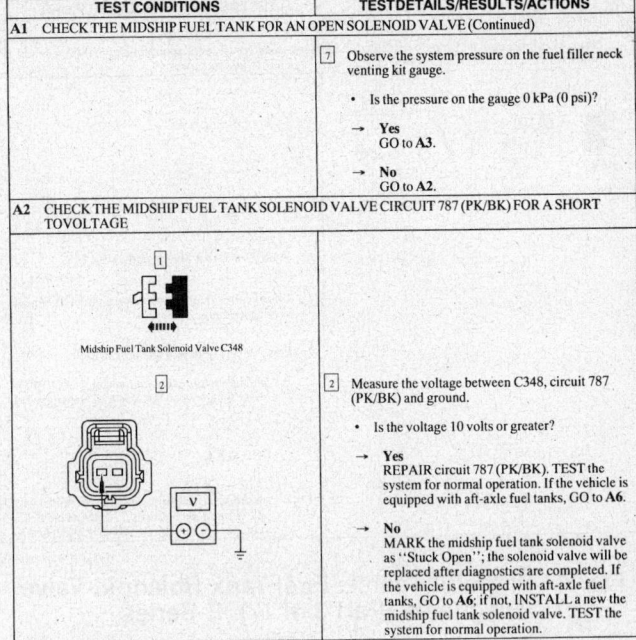

FM1029900363020X

Fig. 4 Pinpoint Test A: Fuel Tank Solenoid Valve Diagnosis (Part 2 of 17). E-Series

pump relay socket of power distribution box using a jumper wire constructed of 6 inches of 18 gauge wire and two spade terminals.

8. Slowly open manual lockdown valve jackscrew on fuel tank solenoid valve of fuel tank to be vented.
9. Slowly open manual backflow valve on fuel filler valve.
10. Observe gauge pressure of fuel filler neck venting kit. Pressure should be at tank pressure if fuel tank solenoid valve was identified as functioning normally.
11. Slowly open bleed valve on fuel filler neck venting kit and allow fuel tank to vent to atmosphere. Venting may take 1 hour or longer.
12. Close bleed valve on fuel filler neck venting kit and observe gauge pressure. Pressure should be 0 psi.
13. Remove fuel tank solenoid manual lockdown valve.
14. **Ensure jackscrew in manual override tool is retracted fully (counterclockwise) prior to installation into fuel tank solenoid valve. If tool is installed in vent position, fuel will be immediately released.**
15. Install manual override tool No. 134–00050, or equivalent, into fuel tank solenoid of tank to be vented.
16. Turn in manual override tool jackscrew until fuel flows.
17. Vent fuel tank until fuel flow stops, then close manual backflow valve on fuel filler valve.
18. Perform fuel line venting procedure as outlined under "Fuel Lines, Econoline & F-Series."
19. Remove manual override tool from fuel tank solenoid valve.
20. Install fuel tank solenoid manual lockdown valve and **torque** to 28–31 ft. lbs.
21. **Torque** manual lockdown valve jackscrew on fuel tank solenoid valve to 62–79 inch lbs.
22. Repeat procedure until all affected tanks are vented.

E-Series & F-Series w/Stuck Open Solenoid

1. Ensure all fuel tank solenoid valves are in locked down position.
2. Connect grounding cable tool No. 134–00121, or equivalent, to back side of fuel fill valve at fuel line connection and earth ground.
3. Turn in manual lockdown valve jackscrew on fuel tank solenoid valves, **Fig. 6.**
4. Connect fuel filler neck venting kit tool No. 134–00117, or equivalent, to fuel filler valve.
5. Connect venting hose tool No. 134–00118, or equivalent, to fuel filler venting kit and vent stack.
6. Slowly open manual lockdown valve jackscrew on fuel tank solenoid valve of fuel tank to be vented.
7. Slowly open manual backflow valve on fuel filler valve.
8. Ensure pressure reading on fuel filler neck venting kit is at tank pressure if fuel tank solenoid valve was identified as stuck open.
9. Slowly open bleed valve on fuel filler neck venting kit and allow contents of fuel tank to vent to atmosphere. Venting may take 1 hour or more.
10. Close bleed valve on fuel filler neck vent kit and ensure pressure reads 0 psi.
11. Remove fuel tank solenoid manual lockdown valve.
12. **Ensure jackscrew in manual override tool is retracted fully (counterclockwise) prior to installation into fuel tank solenoid valve. If tool is installed in vent position, fuel will be immediately released.**
13. Install manual override tool No. 134–00050, or equivalent, into fuel tank solenoid of tank to be vented.
14. Turn in manual override tool jackscrew until fuel flows.
15. Vent fuel tank until fuel flow stops.
16. Close manual backflow valve on fuel filler valve when tank is empty.
17. Perform fuel line vent procedure as outlined under "Fuel Lines, Econoline & F-Series."
18. Remove manual override tool from fuel tank solenoid valve.
19. Install fuel tank solenoid manual lockdown valve and **torque** to 28–31 ft. lbs.
20. **Torque** manual valve jackscrew to 62–79 inch lbs.
21. Repeat procedure until all affected tanks are vented.

E-Series & F-Series w/Stuck Closed Or Inoperative Solenoid

1. Ensure all fuel tank solenoid valves are in locked down position.
2. Connect grounding cable tool No. 134–00121, or equivalent, to back side of fuel fill valve at fuel line connection and earth ground.
3. Turn in manual lockdown valve jackscrew on fuel tank solenoid valves, **Fig. 6.**
4. Connect fuel filler neck venting kit tool No. 134–00117, or equivalent, to fuel filler valve.
5. Connect venting hose tool No. 134–00118, or equivalent, to fuel filler venting kit and vent stack.
6. Remove manual lockdown valve from fuel tank solenoid valve of fuel tank to be vented.
7. **Ensure jackscrew in manual override tool is retracted fully (counterclockwise) prior to installation into**

TEST CONDITIONS	TEST DETAILS/RESULTS/ACTIONS
A3 CHECK THE MIDSHIP FUEL TANK SOLENOID VALVE OPERATION	
Note: This procedure will supply power to the fuel tank solenoid valve for approximately 30-60 seconds. If time expires, cycle the START/STOP button on the scan tool to restore power.	
1 Midship Fuel Tank Solenoid Valve C348 · 2 Scan Tool · 3 · 4 Output Test Mode	5 Press the START button on the scan tool. 6 Observe the system pressure on the fuel filler neck venting kit gauge. 7 Press the STOP button on the scan tool. • Did the system pressure register 0 kPa (0 psi) on the gauge when the scan tool was triggered on? → **Yes** GO to **A4**. → **No** MARK the midship fuel tank solenoid valve as "Functions Normally." If the vehicle is equipped with aft-axle fuel tanks, GO to **A6**.

FM1029900363030X

Fig. 4 Pinpoint Test A: Fuel Tank Solenoid Valve Diagnosis (Part 3 of 17). E-Series

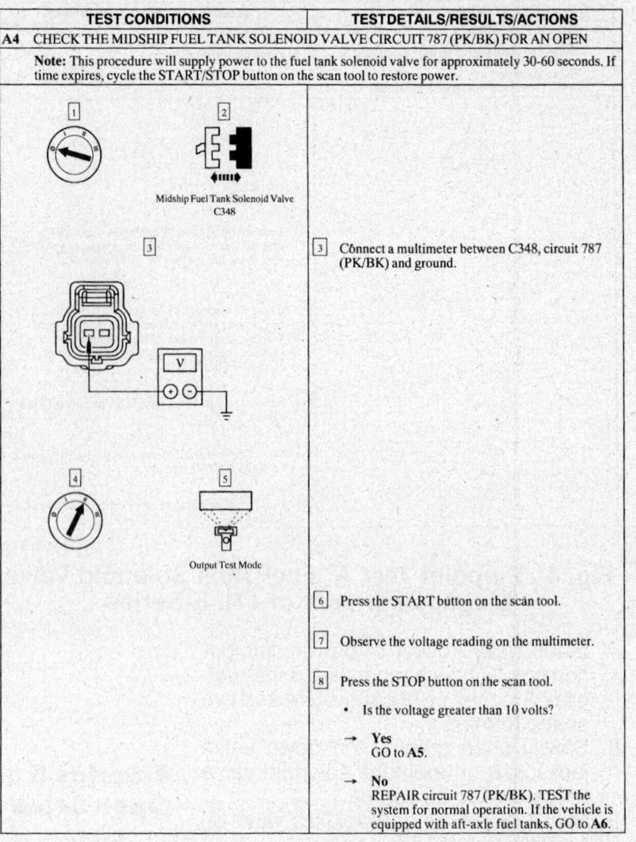

TEST CONDITIONS	TEST DETAILS/RESULTS/ACTIONS
A4 CHECK THE MIDSHIP FUEL TANK SOLENOID VALVE CIRCUIT 787 (PK/BK) FOR AN OPEN	
Note: This procedure will supply power to the fuel tank solenoid valve for approximately 30-60 seconds. If time expires, cycle the START/STOP button on the scan tool to restore power.	
1 · 2 Midship Fuel Tank Solenoid Valve C348	
3	3 Connect a multimeter between C348, circuit 787 (PK/BK) and ground.
4 · 5 Output Test Mode	6 Press the START button on the scan tool. 7 Observe the voltage reading on the multimeter. 8 Press the STOP button on the scan tool. • Is the voltage greater than 10 volts? → **Yes** GO to **A5**. → **No** REPAIR circuit 787 (PK/BK). TEST the system for normal operation. If the vehicle is equipped with aft-axle fuel tanks, GO to **A6**.

FM1029900363040X

Fig. 4 Pinpoint Test A: Fuel Tank Solenoid Valve Diagnosis (Part 4 of 17). E-Series

fuel tank solenoid valve. If tool is installed in vent position, fuel will be immediately released.

8. Install manual override tool No. 134–00050, or equivalent, into fuel tank solenoid of tank to be vented.
9. Turn in manual override tool jackscrew until fuel flows.
10. Slowly open manual backflow valve on fuel filler valve and ensure gauge pressure of fuel filler neck vent kit reads tank pressure.
11. Slowly open bleed valve on fuel filler neck venting kit and allow tank to vent to atmosphere until empty. Venting process may take 1 hour or more.
12. Close manual backflow valve on fuel filler valve when tank contents have been vented.
13. Vent fuel lines as outlined under "Fuel Lines, Econoline & F-Series."
14. Remove manual override valve from fuel tank solenoid valve.
15. Install solenoid lockdown valve and **torque** to 28–31 ft. lbs.
16. **Torque** lockdown valve jackscrew to 62–79 inch lbs.
17. Repeat procedure until all affected tanks are vented.

2000–03 E-Series & F-Series w/Normally Operating Solenoid

The jackscrew can be reached through vapor retaining cover access hole on models equipped with an extended range fuel tank.

1. **Torque** manual valve lockdown jackscrew to 62–79 inch lbs.
2. Vent fuel lines as outlined under "Fuel Lines, Econoline & F-Series."
3. Disconnect fuel fill line from fuel fill valve.
4. Connect fuel filler neck vent hose and adapter tool No. 134–00118, or equivalent, to fuel fill line.
5. Ensure all fuel tank solenoid valves are in locked down position.
6. Connect ground cable tool No. 134–00121, or equivalent, to fuel fill line connection and earth ground.
7. Install fuel filler neck vent kit tool No. 134–00117, or equivalent, to fuel vent hose and adapter.
8. Connect vent hose assembly to fuel filler neck venting kit and suitable vent stack.
9. Remove fuel pump relay from power distribution box.
10. Fabricate a jumper wire using six inches of 18 gauge wire and two spade terminals.
11. Connect fuel pump circuit 87 to 30 in power distribution box using jumper wire.
12. Slowly open manual lockdown valve jackscrew on fuel tank solenoid valve of fuel tank to be vented.
13. Ensure fuel filler neck vent kit gauge indicates tank pressure if solenoid was identified as normally operating.
14. Slowly open fuel filler neck vent kit bleed valve and vent fuel tank to atmosphere. Venting may take one hour or more.
15. Close bleed valve on fuel filler neck vent kit. Ensure gauge pressure indicates 0 psi.
16. Install fuel fill line to fuel fill valve.

2000–03 E-Series & F-Series w/Stuck Open Solenoid

The jackscrew can be reached through vapor retaining cover access hole on models equipped with an extended range fuel tank.

1. **Torque** manual valve lockdown jackscrew to 62–79 inch lbs.
2. Vent fuel lines as outlined under "Fuel Lines, Econoline & F-Series."
3. Disconnect fuel fill line from fuel fill valve.
4. Connect fuel filler neck vent hose and adapter tool No. 134–00118, or equivalent, to fuel fill line.
5. Ensure all fuel tank solenoid valves are in locked down position.
6. Connect ground cable tool No. 134–00121, or equivalent, to fuel fill line connection and earth ground.
7. Install fuel filler neck vent kit tool No. 134–00117, or equivalent, to fuel vent hose and adapter.
8. Connect vent hose assembly to fuel filler neck venting kit and suitable vent stack.
9. Slowly open manual lockdown valve jackscrew on fuel tank solenoid valve of fuel tank to be vented.
10. Ensure fuel filler neck vent kit gauge indicates tank pressure if solenoid was identified as stuck open.
11. Slowly open bleed valve on fuel filler neck vent kit and vent contents of fuel tank to atmosphere. Venting may take

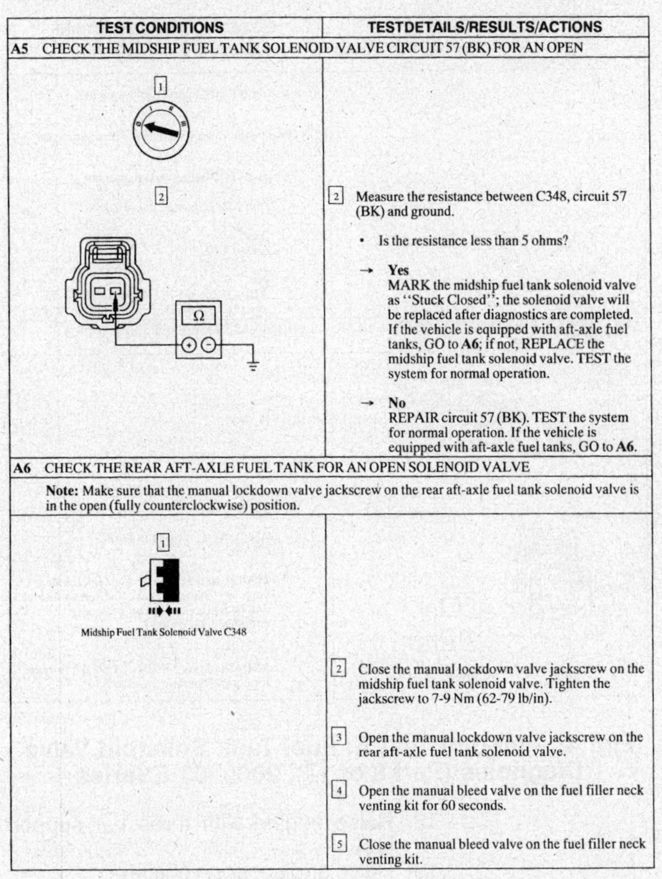

TEST CONDITIONS	TEST DETAILS/RESULTS/ACTIONS
A5 CHECK THE MIDSHIP FUEL TANK SOLENOID VALVE CIRCUIT 57 (BK) FOR AN OPEN	
1	
2	2 Measure the resistance between C348, circuit 57 (BK) and ground. • Is the resistance less than 5 ohms? → **Yes** MARK the midship fuel tank solenoid valve as "Stuck Closed"; the solenoid valve will be replaced after diagnostics are completed. If the vehicle is equipped with aft-axle fuel tanks, GO to **A6**; if not, REPLACE the midship fuel tank solenoid valve. TEST the system for normal operation. → **No** REPAIR circuit 57 (BK). TEST the system for normal operation. If the vehicle is equipped with aft-axle fuel tanks, GO to **A6**.
A6 CHECK THE REAR AFT-AXLE FUEL TANK FOR AN OPEN SOLENOID VALVE	
Note: Make sure that the manual lockdown valve jackscrew on the rear aft-axle fuel tank solenoid valve is in the open (fully counterclockwise) position.	
1 Midship Fuel Tank Solenoid Valve C348	2 Close the manual lockdown valve jackscrew on the midship fuel tank solenoid valve. Tighten the jackscrew to 7-9 Nm (62-79 lb/in). 3 Open the manual lockdown valve jackscrew on the rear aft-axle fuel tank solenoid valve. 4 Open the manual bleed valve on the fuel filler neck venting kit for 60 seconds. 5 Close the manual bleed valve on the fuel filler neck venting kit.

FM1029900363050X

Fig. 4 Pinpoint Test A: Fuel Tank Solenoid Valve Diagnosis (Part 5 of 17). E-Series

TEST CONDITIONS	TEST DETAILS/RESULTS/ACTIONS
A6 CHECK THE REAR AFT-AXLE FUEL TANK FOR AN OPEN SOLENOID VALVE (Continued)	
	6 Observe the system pressure on the fuel filler neck venting kit gauge. • Is the pressure on the gauge 0 kPa (0 psi)? → **Yes** GO to **A8**. → **No** GO to **A7**.
A7 CHECK THE REAR AFT-AXLE FUEL TANK SOLENOID VALVE CIRCUIT 787 (PK/BK) FOR A SHORT TO VOLTAGE	
1 Rear Aft-Axle Fuel Tank Solenoid Valve C354	
2	2 Measure the voltage between C354, circuit 787 (PK/BK) and ground. • Is the voltage 10 volts or greater? → **Yes** REPAIR circuit 787 (PK/BK). TEST the system for normal operation. GO to **A11**. → **No** MARK the rear aft-axle fuel tank solenoid valve as "Stuck Open"; the solenoid valve will be replaced after diagnostics are completed. GO to **A11**.
A8 CHECK THE REAR AFT-AXLE FUEL TANK SOLENOID VALVE OPERATION	
Note: This procedure will supply power to the fuel tank solenoid valve for approximately 30-60 seconds. If time expires, cycle the START/STOP button on the scan tool to restore power.	
1 2 3 4 Rear Aft-Axle Fuel Tank Solenoid Valve C354; Scan Tool; Output Test Mode	5 Press the START button on the scan tool.

FM1029900363060X

Fig. 4 Pinpoint Test A: Fuel Tank Solenoid Valve Diagnosis (Part 6 of 17). E-Series

one hour or more.

12. Close bleed valve on fuel filler neck vent kit. Ensure gauge pressure is 0 psi.
13. Remove fuel tank solenoid manual lockdown valve.
14. **Ensure manual override tool jackscrew is retracted fully counterclockwise prior to installation or fuel will be immediately released.**
15. Install manual override tool No. 134–00050, or equivalent, into fuel tank solenoid of tank to be vented.
16. Turn in manual override tool jackscrew until fuel flows.
17. Vent fuel tank until fuel flow stops.
18. Remove manual override tool from fuel tank solenoid valve.
19. Install fuel tank solenoid manual lockdown valve and **torque** to 28–31 ft. lbs.
20. **Torque** manual valve lockdown jackscrew to 62–79 inch lbs.
21. Repeat procedure for all affected fuel tanks.
22. Install fuel fill line to fuel fill valve.

2000–03 E-Series & F-Series w/Stuck Closed Or Inoperative Solenoid

The jackscrew can be reached through vapor retaining cover access hole on models equipped with an extended range fuel tank.

1. **Torque** manual lockdown valve jackscrew to 62–79 inch lbs.
2. Vent fuel lines as outlined under "Fuel Lines, Econoline & F-Series."
3. Disconnect fuel fill line from fuel fill valve.
4. Connect fuel filler neck vent hose and adapter tool No. 134–00118, or equivalent, to fuel fill line.
5. Ensure all fuel tank solenoid valves are in locked down position.
6. Connect ground cable tool No. 134–00121, or equivalent, to fuel fill line connection and earth ground.
7. Install fuel filler neck vent kit tool No. 134–00117, or equivalent, to fuel vent hose and adapter.
8. Connect vent hose assembly to fuel filler neck venting kit and suitable vent stack.
9. Remove manual lockdown valve from fuel tank solenoid valve of fuel tank to be vented.
10. **Ensure manual override tool jackscrew is retracted fully counterclockwise prior to installation or fuel will be immediately released.**
11. Install manual override tool No. 134–00050, or equivalent, into fuel tank solenoid of tank to be vented.
12. Slowly turn in manual override tool jackscrew until fuel flows.
13. Ensure fuel filler neck venting kit gauge indicates tank pressure.
14. Slowly open bleed fuel filler neck vent kit and vent contents of fuel tank to atmosphere. Venting may take one hour or more.
15. Vent fuel tank until fuel flow stops.
16. Remove manual override tool from fuel tank solenoid valve.
17. Install fuel tank solenoid manual lockdown valve.
18. **Torque** manual lockdown valve jackscrew on fuel tank solenoid valve.
19. Repeat procedure until all affected tanks are vented.
20. Install fuel fill line to fuel fill valve.

COMPRESSION PRESSURE

1. Ensure oil is at correct level and of correct viscosity and that battery is fully charged.
2. Run engine until operating temperature is reached.
3. Turn ignition switch to "OFF" position, then remove all spark plugs.
4. Place throttle plates to wide open position.
5. Install an auxiliary starter switch in starting circuit.
6. Install compression gauge in No. 1 cylinder.
7. Crank engine a minimum of five compression strokes and record highest reading using auxiliary starter switch.
8. Repeat test on each cylinder, cranking

TEST CONDITIONS	TEST DETAILS/RESULTS/ACTIONS
A8 CHECK THE REAR AFT-AXLE FUEL TANK SOLENOID VALVE OPERATION (Continued)	
	6 Observe the system pressure on the fuel filler neck venting kit gauge. 7 Press the STOP button on the scan tool. • Did the system pressure register 0 kPa (0 psi) on the gauge when the scan tool was triggered on? → **Yes** GO to **A9**. → **No** MARK the rear aft-axle fuel tank solenoid valve as "Functions Normally". GO to **A11**.
A9 CHECK THE REAR AFT-AXLE FUEL TANK SOLENOID VALVE CIRCUIT 787 (PK/BK) FOR AN OPEN	
Note: This procedure will supply power to the fuel tank solenoid valve for approximately 30-60 seconds. If time expires, cycle the START/STOP button on the scan tool to restore power.	
1 2 Rear Aft-Axle Fuel Tank Solenoid Valve C354	
3 V	3 Connect a multimeter between C354, circuit 787 (PK/BK) and ground.
4 5 Output Test Mode	

FM10299003630070X

Fig. 4 Pinpoint Test A: Fuel Tank Solenoid Valve Diagnosis (Part 7 of 17). E-Series

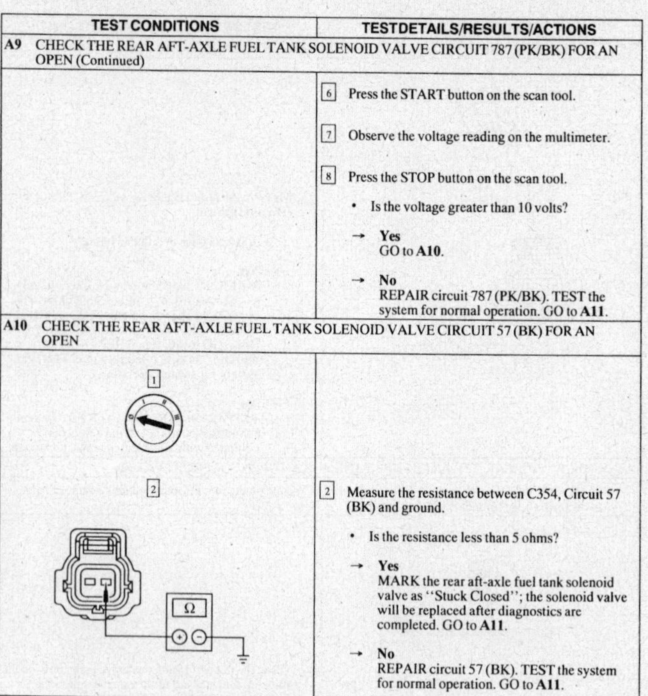

TEST CONDITIONS	TEST DETAILS/RESULTS/ACTIONS
A9 CHECK THE REAR AFT-AXLE FUEL TANK SOLENOID VALVE CIRCUIT 787 (PK/BK) FOR AN OPEN (Continued)	
	6 Press the START button on the scan tool. 7 Observe the voltage reading on the multimeter. 8 Press the STOP button on the scan tool. • Is the voltage greater than 10 volts? → **Yes** GO to **A10**. → **No** REPAIR circuit 787 (PK/BK). TEST the system for normal operation. GO to **A11**.
A10 CHECK THE REAR AFT-AXLE FUEL TANK SOLENOID VALVE CIRCUIT 57 (BK) FOR AN OPEN	
1	
2 Ω	2 Measure the resistance between C354, Circuit 57 (BK) and ground. • Is the resistance less than 5 ohms? → **Yes** MARK the rear aft-axle fuel tank solenoid valve as "Stuck Closed"; the solenoid valve will be replaced after diagnostics are completed. GO to **A11**. → **No** REPAIR circuit 57 (BK). TEST the system for normal operation. GO to **A11**.

FM10299003630080X

Fig. 4 Pinpoint Test A: Fuel Tank Solenoid Valve Diagnosis (Part 8 of 17). 2000–03 ESeries

engine same number of compression strokes as in previous step.

9. Compression is within specification if lowest reading cylinder is within 75 percent of highest reading cylinder.
10. If one or more cylinders read low, apply one tablespoon of suitable clean engine oil to top of pistons and repeat test. Interpret compression readings as follows:
    a. If compression improves drastically, piston rings are at fault.
    b. If compression does not improve, valves are sticking or not seating properly.
    c. If two adjacent cylinders are low and oil application does not improve compression, head gasket may be at fault.

ENGINE MOUNT

REPLACE

Expedition, F150, Mark LT & Navigator

1. Remove fan shroud.
2. Remove alternator.
3. Install three bar modular engine support bracket set on engine using the alternator mounting holes.
4. Raise and support vehicle.
5. **On Expedition models,** remove exhaust manifolds and oil dipstick tube.
6. **On all models,** remove starter.
7. Remove righthand and lefthand motor mount bolts.
8. Lower vehicle.
9. Raise engine with three bar engine support tool.
10. Raise and support vehicle.
11. Remove bolts, then the motor mounts.
12. Reverse procedure to install.

Econoline

1. Remove intake manifold as outlined under "Intake Manifold, Replace."
2. Remove fan shroud and engine cooling fan.
3. Remove retainers, then the front shield, **Fig. 6.**
4. Remove pipe bracket nut, **Fig. 7.**
5. Unclip wiring harnesses from retainers.
6. Remove pipe clamp stud bolts, **Fig. 8.**
7. Remove two transmission to engine bolts.
8. Install three bar engine support kit No. 303-F070, or equivalent, to support engine.
9. Raise and support vehicle.
10. If replacing righthand engine support insulator, remove starter.
11. Remove support insulator nuts, then lower vehicle.
12. Raise engine with three bar support tool.
13. Raise and support vehicle.
14. Remove insulator bolts, then the insulators from vehicle.
15. Reverse procedure to install.

Excursion & F-Super Duty

1. Partially drain radiator into a suitable container and disconnect upper radiator hose at radiator.
2. Remove air cleaner outlet tube, then accelerator cable snow shield.
3. Disconnect accelerator, speed control cables and return spring.
4. Remove accelerator cable bracket bolts and position bracket and cable aside
5. Disconnect PCV, brake booster and engine sensor control wiring harness.
6. Disconnect idle air control motor connector, bypass hose and heater hose.
7. Disconnect EGR transducer connector and throttle position sensor.
8. Disconnect EGR transducer vacuum lines and EGR valve to exhaust manifold tube fittings and remove tube.
9. Remove EGR transducer bracket and disconnect EGR valve vacuum line.
10. Disconnect EVR solenoid and vacuum harness.
11. Remove throttle body adapter bolts, adapter and adapter gasket.
12. Remove two screws at top of fan shroud and position fan shroud toward engine.
13. Remove alternator, then install modular engine support to alternator mounting holes.

TEST CONDITIONS	TEST DETAILS/RESULTS/ACTIONS
A11 CHECK THE FORWARD AFT-AXLE FUEL TANK FOR AN OPEN SOLENOID VALVE	
Note: Make sure that the manual lockdown valve jackscrew on the forward aft-axle fuel tank solenoid valve is in the open (fully counterclockwise) position.	
[1] Rear Aft-Axle Fuel Tank Solenoid Valve C354	
	[2] Close the manual lockdown valve jackscrew on the rear aft-axle fuel tank. Tighten the jackscrew to 7-9 Nm (62-79 lb/in).
	[3] Open the manual lockdown valve jackscrew on the forward aft-axle fuel tank solenoid valve.
	[4] Open the manual bleed valve on the fuel filler neck venting kit for 60 seconds.
	[5] Close the manual bleed valve on the fuel filler neck venting kit.
	[6] Observe the system pressure on the fuel filler neck venting kit gauge. • Is the pressure on the gauge 0 kPa (0 psi)? → **Yes** GO to **A13**. → **No** GO to **A12**.

FM1029900363090X

Fig. 4 Pinpoint Test A: Fuel Tank Solenoid Valve Diagnosis (Part 9 of 17). E-Series

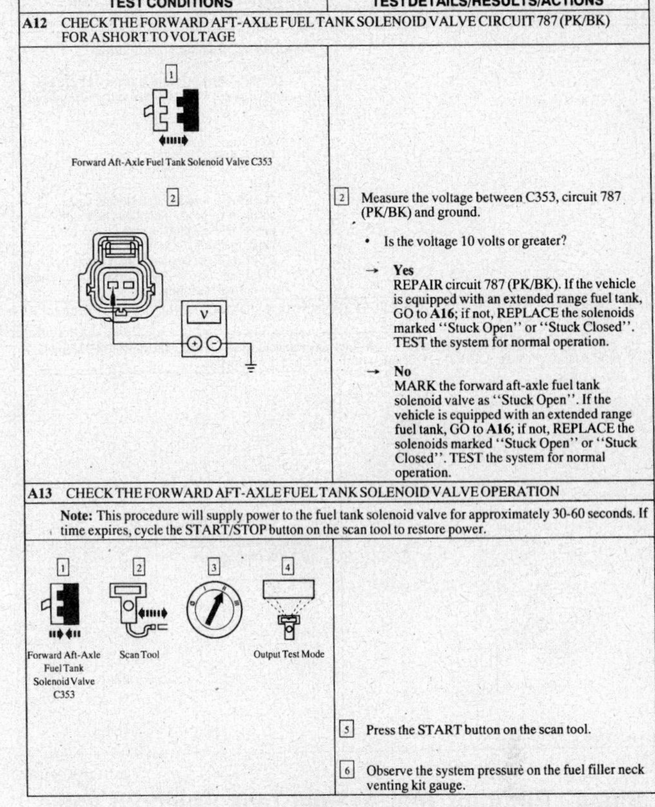

TEST CONDITIONS	TEST DETAILS/RESULTS/ACTIONS
A12 CHECK THE FORWARD AFT-AXLE FUEL TANK SOLENOID VALVE CIRCUIT 787 (PK/BK) FOR A SHORT TO VOLTAGE	
[1] Forward Aft-Axle Fuel Tank Solenoid Valve C353	
[2]	[2] Measure the voltage between C353, circuit 787 (PK/BK) and ground. • Is the voltage 10 volts or greater? → **Yes** REPAIR circuit 787 (PK/BK). If the vehicle is equipped with an extended range fuel tank, GO to **A16**; if not, REPLACE the solenoids marked "Stuck Open" or "Stuck Closed". TEST the system for normal operation. → **No** MARK the forward aft-axle fuel tank solenoid valve as "Stuck Open". If the vehicle is equipped with an extended range fuel tank, GO to **A16**; if not, REPLACE the solenoids marked "Stuck Open" or "Stuck Closed". TEST the system for normal operation.
A13 CHECK THE FORWARD AFT-AXLE FUEL TANK SOLENOID VALVE OPERATION	
Note: This procedure will supply power to the fuel tank solenoid valve for approximately 30-60 seconds. If time expires, cycle the START/STOP button on the scan tool to restore power.	
[1] Forward Aft-Axle Fuel Tank Solenoid Valve C353 [2] Scan Tool [3] [4] Output Test Mode	
	[5] Press the START button on the scan tool.
	[6] Observe the system pressure on the fuel filler neck venting kit gauge.

FM1029900363100X

Fig. 4 Pinpoint Test A: Fuel Tank Solenoid Valve Diagnosis (Part 10 of 17). E-Series

14. Raise and support vehicle, then remove engine mount nuts.
15. Lower vehicle, then raise engine using three bar engine support tool No. 303-F070, or equivalent, by inserting J-hook.
16. Raise and support vehicle.
17. If righthand engine mount is to be serviced, remove starter as outlined in "Starter Replace" in "Electrical" section.
18. Remove engine mounts.
19. Reverse procedure to install. Tighten to specifications.

ENGINE

REPLACE

Excursion & F-Super Duty

1. Recover A/C refrigerant as outlined under "Air Conditioning" chapter.
2. Remove radiator grille supports.
3. Remove A/C condenser core.
4. Remove radiator, fan shroud and engine cooling fan.
5. Disconnect main harness 42 pin and 16 pin connectors and bracket, **Fig. 7.**
6. Remove intake manifold as outlined under "Intake Manifold, Replace."
7. Disconnect lower radiator hose from oil cooler water inlet.
8. Remove bolts and position power steering pump aside.
9. Disconnect A/C cycling switch, remove harness from studs and position aside.
10. Disconnect suction hose at accumulator.
11. Disconnect heater hose.
12. Disconnect lefthand and righthand heated oxygen sensor connectors.
13. Remove A/C compressor.
14. Raise and support vehicle.
15. Remove front exhaust pipe nuts.
16. **On models equipped with manual transmission,** remove transmission and clutch.
17. **On all models,** drain engine oil into suitable container and remove oil bypass filter.
18. **On models equipped with automatic transmission,** remove starter motor, then remove transmission oil cooler line nuts and position cooler lines and bracket aside.
19. **On all models,** remove ground strap stud and position strap aside.
20. Remove nut and wiring bracket.
21. **On models equipped with automatic transmission,** remove flywheel inspection cover, access plug, **Fig. 8,** and torque converter nuts, then the four lower transmission to engine bolts.
22. **On all models,** lower vehicle.
23. Remove ground strap retaining nut and transmission filler tube.
24. Remove water heater tube.
25. **On models equipped with automatic transmissions,** remove upper transmission to engine bolts.
26. **On all models,** install suitable engine lifting device to engine.
27. Remove engine support insulator nuts, **Fig. 9.**
28. Support automatic transmission with suitable jack, then lift engine from vehicle.
29. Reverse procedure to install.

E-Series

1. Recover A/C refrigerant as outlined under "Air Conditioning" chapter.
2. Remove intake manifold as outlined under "Intake Manifold, Replace."
3. Remove front bumper.
4. Disconnect lower radiator hose from radiator.
5. Remove push pin retainers, then the splash shield.
6. Disconnect transmission cooler hoses and drain fluid into suitable container.
7. Disconnect exhaust system from exhaust manifolds.
8. Drain engine oil into suitable container, then remove oil filter.
9. Loosen threaded insert, then remove oil cooler from oil filter adapter.
10. Remove starter motor solenoid terminal cover.
11. Disconnect starter motor electrical connectors, then the starter motor.
12. Remove flexplate inspection cover.
13. Remove cylinder block opening cover.
14. Remove and discard torque converter to flexplate retaining nuts.
15. **On models equipped with 4R70W transmission,** disconnect shift cable and mounting bracket.
16. **On all models,** remove transmission to engine mounting bolts, **Fig. 10,** and position shifter cable support bracket, mounting bracket and cable aside
17. Remove righthand lower transmission to engine bolt.
18. Remove lower engine mounting nuts.

TEST CONDITIONS	TEST DETAILS/RESULTS/ACTIONS
A13 CHECK THE FORWARD AFT-AXLE FUEL TANK SOLENOID VALVE OPERATION (Continued)	
	7 Press the STOP button on the scan tool. • Did the system pressure register 0 kPa (0 psi) on the gauge when the scan tool was triggered on? → **Yes** GO to **A14**. → **No** MARK the forward aft-axle fuel tank solenoid valve as "Functions Normally". If the vehicle is equipped with an extended range fuel tank, GO to **A16**; if not, REPLACE the solenoids marked "Stuck Open" or "Stuck Closed". TEST the system for normal operation.
A14 CHECK THE FORWARD AFT-AXLE FUEL TANK SOLENOID VALVE CIRCUIT 787 (PK/BK) FOR AN OPEN	
Note: This procedure will supply power to the fuel tank solenoid valve for approximately 30-60 seconds. If time expires, cycle the START/STOP button on the scan tool to restore power.	
1 2 Forward Aft-Axle Fuel Tank Solenoid Valve C353 3 V	3 Connect a multimeter between C353, circuit 787 (PK/BK) and ground.

FM1029900363110X

Fig. 4 Pinpoint Test A: Fuel Tank Solenoid Valve Diagnosis (Part 11 of 17). E-Series

19. Disconnect power steering reservoir hose and power steering pressure tube at power steering pump and drain fluid into suitable container.
20. Remove nut and position transmission fluid cooler support bracket aside.
21. Lower vehicle.
22. Remove valance panel.
23. Disconnect upper radiator and degas hose from radiator.
24. Remove fan blade assembly and fan clutch. Large clutch assembly nut has righthand thread and must be rotated counterclockwise to remove.
25. Disconnect degas hose retainer from fan shroud.
26. Remove fan shroud, fan and fan clutch.
27. Remove radiator support brackets, then the radiator from vehicle.
28. Disconnect A/C pressure cutoff switch electrical connector.
29. Disconnect A/C compressor suction tube, then the condenser core refrigerant tubes.
30. Remove A/C condenser core.
31. Disconnect hood latch and position aside.
32. Remove bolts and position power steering reservoir aside.
33. Remove battery feed cable at power distribution box.
34. Position battery feed wiring harness aside.
35. Remove upper radiator support.
36. Remove air deflectors.
37. Position dash headlamp dash panel wiring harnesses aside.
38. Remove lower radiator support.
39. Disconnect lower radiator hose from oil filter adapter water inlet and position aside.
40. Rotate accessory drive belt tensioner clockwise to release belt tension, then remove drive belt.
41. Disconnect alternator electrical connectors and brackets, then remove alternator.
42. Remove engine oil filler tube support strap bolt.
43. Remove transmission fluid level dipstick.
44. Disconnect evaporative emission canister purge valve electrical connector.
45. Remove transmission fluid level dipstick tube.
46. Release wiring retainers from heater outlet tube bracket.
47. Disconnect hose from heater outlet tube, then remove heater outlet tube studs and heater outlet tube.
48. Disconnect transmission wiring harness and heated oxygen sensor connectors.
49. Remove upper transmission to engine mounting bolts, fuel line and lefthand HO2S brackets.
50. Install suitable engine lifting device, then remove engine from vehicle.
51. Reverse procedure to install.

Expedition & Navigator

Air suspension switch must be turned to Off position before raising vehicle. Failure to do so can result in unexpected inflation

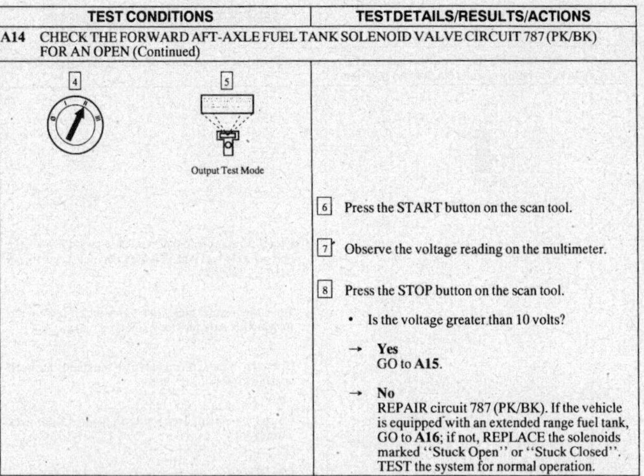

TEST CONDITIONS	TEST DETAILS/RESULTS/ACTIONS
A14 CHECK THE FORWARD AFT-AXLE FUEL TANK SOLENOID VALVE CIRCUIT 787 (PK/BK) FOR AN OPEN (Continued)	
4 5 Output Test Mode	6 Press the START button on the scan tool. 7 Observe the voltage reading on the multimeter. 8 Press the STOP button on the scan tool. • Is the voltage greater than 10 volts? → **Yes** GO to **A15**. → **No** REPAIR circuit 787 (PK/BK). If the vehicle is equipped with an extended range fuel tank, GO to **A16**; if not, REPLACE the solenoids marked "Stuck Open" or "Stuck Closed". TEST the system for normal operation.

FM1029900363120X

Fig. 4 Pinpoint Test A: Fuel Tank Solenoid Valve Diagnosis (Part 12 of 17). E-Series

or deflation of air springs which could result in shifting of vehicle during repair operation.

1. **On models equipped with air suspension,** turn air suspension switch to Off position.
2. **On all models,** remove intake manifold as outlined under "Intake Manifold, Replace."
3. Remove hood.
4. Remove engine air cleaner and position to gain access to mass air flow sensor. Disconnect mass air flow sensor electrical connector.
5. Drain coolant into suitable container.
6. Recover A/C refrigerant as outlined under "Air Conditioning" chapter.
7. Remove radiator and A/C condenser core.
8. Disconnect powertrain control module electrical connectors.
9. Disconnect main wiring harness connectors at firewall.
10. Remove powertrain control module and bracket, then remove ground wire, **Fig. 11.**
11. Disconnect evaporator tubes from manifold and evaporator.
12. Remove cable routing bracket from heater outlet tube mounting studs.
13. Remove wiring retainers from heater tube outlet bracket.
14. Disconnect hoses from heater outlet tube.
15. **On models equipped with 4.6L engines,** remove heater outlet tube upper and lower studs.
16. **On models equipped with 5.4L engines,** loosen heater outlet tube upper stud and remove lower stud.
17. **On all models,** remove heater outlet tube and discard seal.
18. Release wiring harness retainer from front cover stud, **Fig. 12.**
19. Disconnect alternator electrical connectors, then remove alternator.
20. Remove bolts and position power steering reservoir aside.
21. Disconnect transmission cooler tube and power steering hose brackets, **Fig. 13.**

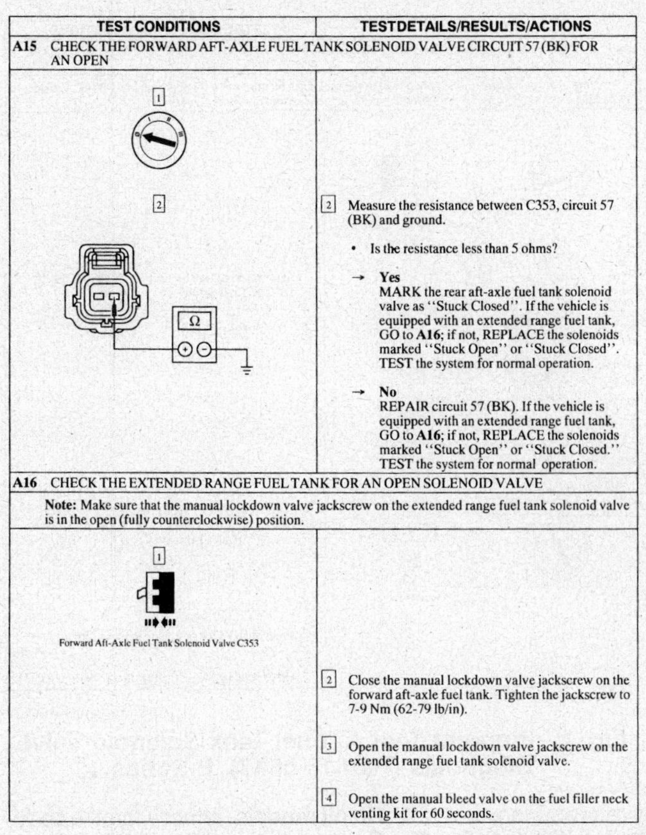

TEST CONDITIONS	TESTDETAILS/RESULTS/ACTIONS
A15 CHECK THE FORWARD AFT-AXLE FUEL TANK SOLENOID VALVE CIRCUIT 57 (BK) FOR AN OPEN	
1	
2	2 Measure the resistance between C353, circuit 57 (BK) and ground. • Is the resistance less than 5 ohms? → **Yes** MARK the rear aft-axle fuel tank solenoid valve as "Stuck Closed". If the vehicle is equipped with an extended range fuel tank, GO to **A16**; if not, REPLACE the solenoids marked "Stuck Open" or "Stuck Closed". TEST the system for normal operation. → **No** REPAIR circuit 57 (BK). If the vehicle is equipped with an extended range fuel tank, GO to **A16**; if not, REPLACE the solenoids marked "Stuck Open" or "Stuck Closed." TEST the system for normal operation.
A16 CHECK THE EXTENDED RANGE FUEL TANK FOR AN OPEN SOLENOID VALVE	
Note: Make sure that the manual lockdown valve jackscrew on the extended range fuel tank solenoid valve is in the open (fully counterclockwise) position.	
1 Forward Aft-Axle Fuel Tank Solenoid Valve C353	
	2 Close the manual lockdown valve jackscrew on the forward aft-axle fuel tank. Tighten the jackscrew to 7-9 Nm (62-79 lb/in). 3 Open the manual lockdown valve jackscrew on the extended range fuel tank solenoid valve. 4 Open the manual bleed valve on the fuel filler neck venting kit for 60 seconds.

FM1029900363130X

Fig. 4 Pinpoint Test A: Fuel Tank Solenoid Valve Diagnosis (Part 13 of 17). E-Series

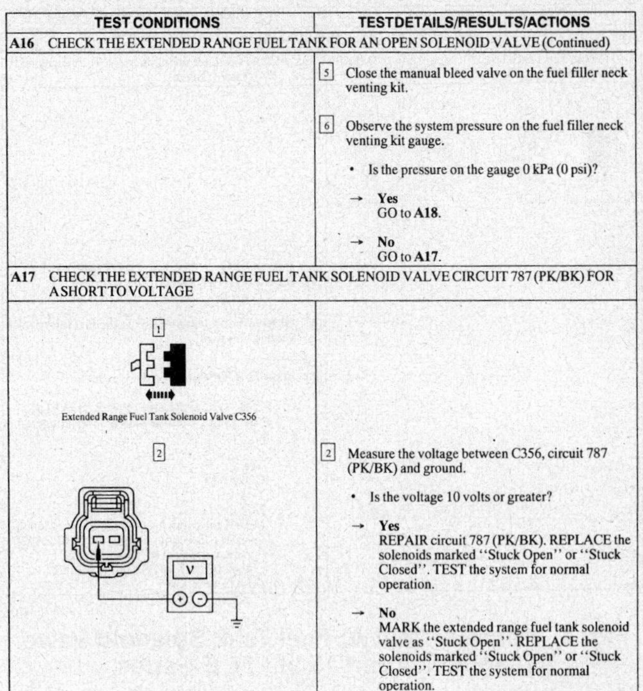

TEST CONDITIONS	TESTDETAILS/RESULTS/ACTIONS
A16 CHECK THE EXTENDED RANGE FUEL TANK FOR AN OPEN SOLENOID VALVE (Continued)	
	5 Close the manual bleed valve on the fuel filler neck venting kit. 6 Observe the system pressure on the fuel filler neck venting kit gauge. • Is the pressure on the gauge 0 kPa (0 psi)? → **Yes** GO to **A18**. → **No** GO to **A17**.
A17 CHECK THE EXTENDED RANGE FUEL TANK SOLENOID VALVE CIRCUIT 787 (PK/BK) FOR A SHORT TO VOLTAGE	
1 Extended Range Fuel Tank Solenoid Valve C356	
2	2 Measure the voltage between C356, circuit 787 (PK/BK) and ground. • Is the voltage 10 volts or greater? → **Yes** REPAIR circuit 787 (PK/BK). REPLACE the solenoids marked "Stuck Open" or "Stuck Closed". TEST the system for normal operation. → **No** MARK the extended range fuel tank solenoid valve as "Stuck Open". REPLACE the solenoids marked "Stuck Open" or "Stuck Closed". TEST the system for normal operation.

FM1029900363140X

Fig. 4 Pinpoint Test A: Fuel Tank Solenoid Valve Diagnosis (Part 14 of 17). E-Series

22. Remove power steering pump pulley with remover tool No. 211–016, or equivalent.
23. Disconnect power steering pressure hose, then remove power steering pump and position aside.
24. Raise and support vehicle.
25. Disconnect power steering pressure switch electrical connector.
26. Drain engine oil into suitable container.
27. Remove oil filter.
28. Disconnect lower radiator hose and degas bottle hose from oil filter adapter.
29. Disconnect exhaust manifold to EGR valve tube lower fitting and remove tube.
30. Disconnect crankshaft position sensor electrical connector and retainer.
31. Remove mounting bolts, then position A/C compressor aside.
32. Remove starter motor.
33. Remove transmission filler tube bolt.
34. Disconnect both heated oxygen sensor electrical connectors.
35. Remove exhaust manifold to converter Y-pipe nuts.
36. Remove righthand Y-pipe studs.
37. Disconnect shift cable and remove shift cable bracket.
38. Remove flexplate inspection cover.
39. Remove cylinder block opening cover, **Fig. 14.**
40. Remove and discard torque converter to flexplate nuts.
41. Remove lower transmission to engine bolts.
42. Remove righthand engine mount nut and lefthand engine mount through bolt.
43. Lower vehicle.
44. Support transmission with suitable jack.
45. **On models equipped with 4WD,** it may be required to reposition transfer case vent hose to access bolts.
46. **On all models,** remove upper transmission to engine bolts and wiring harness bracket.
47. Install suitable engine lifting device to engine, then remove engine from vehicle.
48. Reverse procedure to install.

F-150 & Mark LT

1. Remove intake manifold as outlined under "Intake Manifold, Replace."
2. Remove engine air cleaner and position aside to gain access to mass airflow sensor.
3. Disconnect mass airflow sensor electrical connector, then remove air cleaner assembly.
4. Remove A/C condenser core.
5. Disconnect climate control vacuum connector.
6. Remove mounting bolts and position power steering reservoir aside.
7. Disconnect exhaust manifold EGR valve tube lower fitting, then remove tube.
8. Disconnect alternator electrical connectors, then the alternator.
9. Disconnect engine electrical harnesses and position them aside.
10. Remove covers and connectors to gain access to starter relay connectors.
11. Disconnect starter relay electrical connectors and position wiring harness aside.
12. Remove electrical connector bracket.
13. Remove heater hoses from heater core.
14. Remove A/C compressor.
15. Raise and support vehicle.
16. Drain engine oil into suitable container.
17. Remove starter motor.
18. Remove A/C muffler bracket and position aside.
19. **On models equipped with manual transmission,** remove clutch disc and pressure plate.
20. **On models equipped with automatic transmission,** proceed as follows:
    a. Remove transmission cooler tubes from block mounted clip.
    b. Remove bolts and flexplate inspection cover
    c. Remove cylinder block opening cover, **Fig. 15.**
    d. Remove and discard torque converter to flexplate nuts.
    e. Remove lower transmission to engine mounting bolts.
    f. Remove nut, then the transmission fluid filler tube.
21. **On all models,** remove bolts and position power steering pump aside.
22. Disconnect oil pressure switch electrical connector.
23. Disconnect heated oxygen sensor electrical connectors.
24. Remove exhaust manifold to catalytic

TEST CONDITIONS	TESTDETAILS/RESULTS/ACTIONS
A18 CHECK THE EXTENDED RANGE FUEL TANK SOLENOID VALVE OPERATION	
Note: This procedure will supply power to the fuel tank solenoid valve for approximately 30-60 seconds. If time expires, cycle the START/STOP button on the scan tool to restore power.	
1 Extended Range Fuel Tank Solenoid Valve C356; 2 Scan Tool; 3; 4 Output Test Mode	5 Press the START button on the scan tool. 6 Observe the system pressure on the fuel filler neck venting kit gauge. 7 Press the STOP button on the scan tool. • Did the system pressure register 0 kPa (0 psi) on the gauge when the scan tool was triggered on? → **Yes** GO to **A19**. → **No** MARK the extended range fuel tank solenoid valve as "Functions Normally". REPLACE the solenoids marked "Stuck Open" or "Stuck Closed". TEST the system for normal operation.

FM1029900363150X

Fig. 4 Pinpoint Test A: Fuel Tank Solenoid Valve Diagnosis (Part 15 of 17). E-Series

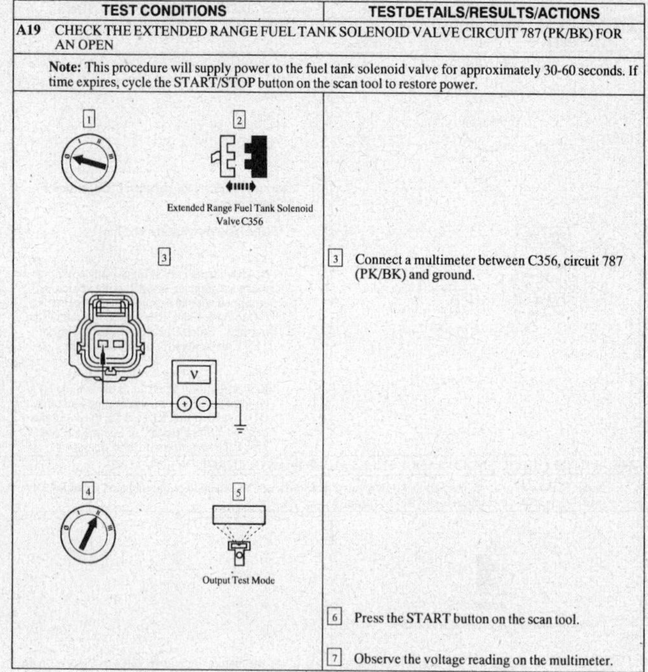

TEST CONDITIONS	TESTDETAILS/RESULTS/ACTIONS
A19 CHECK THE EXTENDED RANGE FUEL TANK SOLENOID VALVE CIRCUIT 787 (PK/BK) FOR AN OPEN	
Note: This procedure will supply power to the fuel tank solenoid valve for approximately 30-60 seconds. If time expires, cycle the START/STOP button on the scan tool to restore power.	
1; 2 Extended Range Fuel Tank Solenoid Valve C356; 3	3 Connect a multimeter between C356, circuit 787 (PK/BK) and ground.
4; 5 Output Test Mode	6 Press the START button on the scan tool. 7 Observe the voltage reading on the multimeter.

FM1029900363160X

Fig. 4 Pinpoint Test A: Fuel Tank Solenoid Valve Diagnosis (Part 16 of 17). E-Series

converter nuts, then position Y-pipe aside.
25. Remove righthand and lefthand motor mount bolts.
26. Remove oil filter and oil pressure switch.
27. Disconnect lower radiator hose from oil filter adapter.
28. Lower vehicle.
29. **On models equipped with automatic transmission,** support transmission with suitable jack, then remove upper transmission to engine bolts and wiring harness bracket.
30. **On all models,** release wiring retainers from heater outlet tube bracket.
31. Disconnect hoses from heater tube outlet, then remove heater outlet tube studs.
32. Remove heater outlet tube and discard seal.
33. Install suitable engine lifting device, then remove engine from vehicle.
34. Reverse procedure to install.

INTAKE MANIFOLD

REPLACE

Except Supercharged 5.4L Engine

1. Relieve fuel system pressure as outlined under "Precautions."
2. Remove air cleaner.
3. **On E-Series models,** remove engine cover.
4. **On all models,** drain cooling system.
5. Remove upper radiator hose.
6. Remove accelerator control splash shield.
7. Remove accelerator cable retaining bolt, then the accelerator cable from bracket.
8. Move throttle body cam forward, then slide accelerator cable from cam.
9. Remove throttle body return spring.
10. **On models equipped with speed control,** remove accelerator cable bracket bolt, then the cable from bracket.
11. **On all models,** disconnect intake manifold and throttle body vacuum hoses.
12. Remove brake booster vacuum hose bracket bolt, then the hose and bracket.
13. Disconnect fuel lines using fuel line disconnect tool Nos. D87L-9280-A and D87L-9280-B, or equivalents.
14. Disconnect TP sensor, EGR pressure transducer, EVR and IAC electrical connectors.
15. Disconnect EGR pressure transducer hoses.
16. Remove EGR tube.
17. Disconnect ECT, CHT jumper harness, and intake manifold tuning valve electrical connectors.
18. Disconnect VMV, EGR, EVR, and fuel pressure regulator vacuum connectors.
19. Disconnect lefthand and righthand fuel injector harness connectors.
20. Disconnect righthand and lefthand COP electrical connectors.
21. Remove lefthand and righthand COP retaining bolts, then the COPs.
22. Rotate drive belt tensioner, then remove belt.
23. Disconnect alternator electrical connectors.
24. Remove alternator retaining bolts, then the alternator.
25. **On Expedition and Navigator models,** remove power steering reservoir bracket bolts, then the power steering bracket.
26. Disconnect heater hose.
27. **On all models,** remove throttle body.
28. **On models equipped with 5.4L engine,** proceed as follows:
    a. Remove intake manifold attaching bolts, **Fig. 16.**
    b. Remove and discard gaskets.
29. **On all models,** reverse procedure to install, noting the following:
    a. Install new intake manifold gasket, then install upper intake manifold to lower intake manifold if equipped. Hand tighten bolts.
    b. Tighten lower intake manifold to specification using sequence outlined in **Figs. 17 and 18.**
    c. Install upper intake manifold and tighten to specification using sequence outlined in **Fig. 19.**

5.4L Supercharged Engine

1. Remove air cleaner outlet tube.
2. Disconnect IAC, then the TP sensor.
3. Disconnect IAC vent hose, then the throttle body vacuum hoses.
4. Disconnect throttle linkage, then remove throttle return spring from throttle lever.
5. Remove accelerator cable bracket and position aside.
6. Disconnect EGR valve vacuum line and tube.
7. Disconnect brake booster vacuum line.
8. Remove throttle body spacer tube from supercharger.
9. Remove accessory drive belts.
10. Drain supercharger coolant from super charger.
11. Remove supercharger coolant lines and position aside.

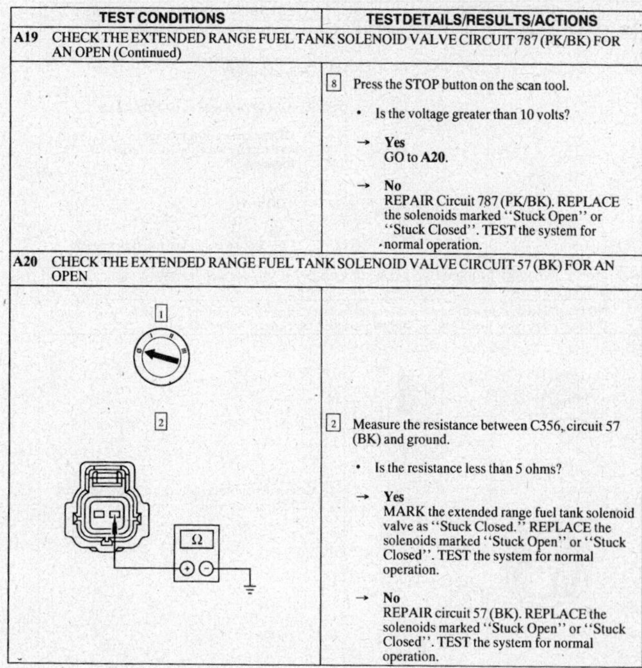

TEST CONDITIONS	TEST DETAILS/RESULTS/ACTIONS
A19 CHECK THE EXTENDED RANGE FUEL TANK SOLENOID VALVE CIRCUIT 787 (PK/BK) FOR AN OPEN (Continued)	
	8 Press the STOP button on the scan tool. • Is the voltage greater than 10 volts? → **Yes** GO to **A20**. → **No** REPAIR Circuit 787 (PK/BK). REPLACE the solenoids marked "Stuck Open" or "Stuck Closed". TEST the system for normal operation.
A20 CHECK THE EXTENDED RANGE FUEL TANK SOLENOID VALVE CIRCUIT 57 (BK) FOR AN OPEN	
1	
2	2 Measure the resistance between C356, circuit 57 (BK) and ground. • Is the resistance less than 5 ohms? → **Yes** MARK the extended range fuel tank solenoid valve as "Stuck Closed." REPLACE the solenoids marked "Stuck Open" or "Stuck Closed". TEST the system for normal operation. → **No** REPAIR circuit 57 (BK). REPLACE the solenoids marked "Stuck Open" or "Stuck Closed". TEST the system for normal operation.

FM1029900363170X

Fig. 4 Pinpoint Test A: Fuel Tank Solenoid Valve Diagnosis (Part 17 of 17). E-Series

TEST CONDITIONS	TEST DETAILS/RESULTS/ACTIONS
A1 CHECK THE REAR IN-BED FUEL TANK FOR AN OPEN SOLENOID VALVE **NOTE:** The battery must be fully charged to perform solenoid diagnostics. **NOTE:** Make sure that the manual lockdown valve jackscrew on the rear in-bed fuel tank solenoid valve is in the open (fully counterclockwise) position.	
1	2 Connect the grounding cable, the venting hose assembly and the fuel filler neck venting kit to the vent stack and the fuel fill valve assembly. 3 Close the manual lockdown valve jackscrew on the forward in-bed fuel tank solenoid valve. Tighten the jackscrews to 7-9 Nm (62-79 lb/in). 4 Close the manual lockdown valve jackscrew on the midship fuel tank solenoid valve, if equipped. Tighten the jackscrews to 7-9 Nm (62-79 lb/in). 5 Open the manual backflow valve on the fuel filler valve. 6 Open the manual bleed valve on the fuel filler neck venting kit for 60 seconds. 7 Close the manual bleed valve on the fuel filler neck venting kit.

FM1029900306010X

Fig. 5 Pinpoint Test A: Fuel Tank Solenoid Valve Diagnosis (Part 1 of 12). F-Series

12. Remove EGR vacuum regulator bracket and position aside.
13. Disconnect supercharger bypass valve actuator vacuum lines.
14. Remove supercharger attaching bolts and studs, **Fig. 20.**
15. Remove supercharger assembly, then the upper intake manifold.
16. Remove and discard charge air cooler bolts.
17. Remove charge air cooler and discard gasket.
18. Relieve fuel pressure as outlined under "Precautions."
19. Drain cooling system into a suitable container.
20. Disconnect thermostat housing bracket and position aside.
21. Disconnect upper radiator hose.
22. Disconnect PCV system. **Do not disconnect PCV hose system from intake manifold. PCV system cannot be installed to intake with intake installed to engine.**
23. Disconnect two radio interference capacitors and ground strap.
24. Disconnect remaining vacuum hoses from intake.
25. Disconnect IAT sensor, then the heater hoses.
26. Disconnect DPFE transducer hoses, then the fuel injectors.
27. Disconnect vapor management valve vacuum line.
28. Disconnect vacuum line near brake booster.
29. Remove fuel injection supply manifold, then disconnect ignition coil connectors.
30. Remove 8 ignition coils, then the alternator bracket.
31. Remove intake manifold and gaskets, **Fig. 21.**
32. Reverse procedure to install, noting the following:
    a. Ensure PCV hose is connected to intake.
    b. Tighten intake manifold to specifications in sequence as outlined in **Fig. 22.**
    c. Ensure new bolts are used when installing charge air cooler.
    d. Tighten supercharger and upper manifold to specifications in sequence as outlined in **Fig. 23.**

EXHAUST MANIFOLD

REPLACE

Excursion, E-Series, F-150, F-Super Duty & Mark LT

1. Raise and support vehicle.
2. Remove fender splash shield(s) as required.
3. If removing righthand exhaust manifold, proceed as follows:
    a. Remove catalytic converter to exhaust manifold nuts.
    b. Remove eight exhaust manifold nuts, then the exhaust manifold.
    c. Discard exhaust manifold gasket.
4. If removing lefthand exhaust manifold, proceed as follows:
    a. Remove brake booster vacuum hose bracket nut, then the bracket.
    b. Disconnect EGR pressure transducer hoses, then remove EGR tube.
    c. Remove catalytic converter to exhaust manifold nuts.
    d. Remove eight exhaust manifold nuts, then the exhaust manifold.
    e. Discard exhaust manifold gasket.
5. Reverse procedure to install, noting the following:
    a. Tighten to specification.
    b. Refer to **Figs. 24 and 25** for exhaust manifold tightening sequence.

Expedition & Navigator

1. If equipped, turn the air suspension switch off.
2. Disconnect battery ground.
3. Remove air cleaner outlet pipe.
4. Drain coolant system into suitable container.
5. Remove pin-type retainers, then upper air deflector.
6. Remove three bolts, then appearance cover mounting bracket.
7. Disconnect accelerator cable, speed control cable, and accelerator return spring.
8. Disconnect main vacuum harness, PCV hose, and IAC fresh air hose.
9. Disconnect IAC and TP sensor electrical connectors.
10. Disconnect EGR valve vacuum hose and EVAP canister purge valve hose.
11. Disconnect differential pressure feedback EGR electrical connector.
12. Remove brake booster bracket nut and vacuum line, then position aside.
13. Disconnect exhaust manifold to EGR valve tube and remove.
14. Remove four throttle body adapter bolts, then move slightly forward.
15. Disconnect heated throttle body hoses, throttle body adapter, and PCV hose.
16. Rotate belt tensioner clockwise and remove drive belt from alternator.

TEST CONDITIONS	TEST DETAILS/RESULTS/ACTIONS
A1 CHECK THE REAR IN-BED FUEL TANK FOR AN OPEN SOLENOID VALVE (Continued)	
	8 Observe the system pressure on the fuel filler neck venting kit gauge. • Is the pressure on the gauge 0 kPa (0 psi)? → **Yes** GO to **A3**. → **No** GO to **A2**.
A2 CHECK THE REAR IN-BED FUEL TANK SOLENOID VALVE CIRCUIT 787 (PK/BK) FOR A SHORT TO VOLTAGE	
1 Rear In-Bed Fuel Tank Solenoid Valve C316	
2	2 Measure the voltage between C316, Circuit 787 (PK/BK) and ground. • Is the voltage 10 volts or greater? → **Yes** REPAIR Circuit 787 (PK/BK). TEST the system for normal operation. GO to **A6**. → **No** MARK the rear in-bed fuel tank solenoid valve as "Stuck Open;" the solenoid valve will be replaced after diagnostics are completed. GO to **A6**.
A3 CHECK THE REAR IN-BED FUEL TANK SOLENOID VALVE OPERATION	
NOTE: This procedure will supply power to the fuel tank solenoid valve for approximately 30-60 seconds. If time expires, cycle the START/STOP button on the NGS Tester to restore power.	
1 Rear In-Bed Fuel Tank Solenoid Valve C316; 2 NGS Tester; 3; 4 Output Test Mode	5 Press the START button on the NGS Tester.

FM1029900306020X

Fig. 5 Pinpoint Test A: Fuel Tank Solenoid Valve Diagnosis (Part 2 of 12). F-Series

TEST CONDITIONS	TEST DETAILS/RESULTS/ACTIONS
A3 CHECK THE REAR IN-BED FUEL TANK SOLENOID VALVE OPERATION (Continued)	
	6 Observe the system pressure on the fuel filler neck venting kit gauge. 7 Press the STOP button on the NGS Tester. • Did the system pressure register 0 kPa (0 psi) on the gauge when the NGS Tester was triggered on? → **Yes** GO to **A4**. → **No** MARK the rear in-bed fuel tank solenoid valve as "Functions Normally." GO to **A6**.
A4 CHECK THE REAR IN-BED FUEL TANK SOLENOID VALVE CIRCUIT 787 (PK/BK) FOR AN OPEN	
NOTE: This procedure will supply power to the fuel tank solenoid valve for approximately 30-60 seconds. If time expires, cycle the START/STOP button on the NGS Tester to restore power.	
1; 2 Rear In-Bed Fuel Tank Solenoid Valve C316; 3	3 Connect a multimeter between C316, Circuit 787 (PK/BK) and ground.
4; 5 Output Test Mode	

FM1029900306030X

Fig. 5 Pinpoint Test A: Fuel Tank Solenoid Valve Diagnosis (Part 3 of 12). F-Series

17. Disconnect electrical connectors from alternator, remove lower alternator mounting bolts, then remove alternator.
18. Install tool No 303–639, or equivalent, to lower alternator mounting holes.
19. Remove fan shroud mounting bolts.
20. Remove righthand wheel and splash shield.
21. **On models equipped with 4WD,** remove lower engine skid and lower transmission skid shield.
22. **On all models,** remove the dual converter Y-pipe.
23. Remove lefthand engine mount bolt, righthand engine mount nut, and rear transmission mount nuts.
24. Index-mark driveshaft flange yoke to pinion flange, then remove bolts and support driveshaft to frame crossmember.
25. Install tool No. 303–F070, or equivalent, and raise engine.
26. If removing righthand exhaust manifold, proceed as follows:
    a. Remove eight exhaust manifold nuts, then exhaust manifold.
    b. Discard exhaust manifold gasket.
27. If removing lefthand exhaust manifold, proceed as follows:
    a. Remove heat shield bolts, then heat shield.
    b. Remove eight manifold nuts, then exhaust manifold.
    c. Discard exhaust manifold gasket.
28. Reverse procedure to install, noting the following:
    a. Tighten to specification.
    b. Refer to **Figs. 24 and 25** for exhaust manifold tightening sequence.

CYLINDER HEAD

REPLACE

2002

1. Remove valve covers as outlined under "Valve Cover, Replace."
2. Remove intake manifold as outlined under "Intake Manifold, Replace."
3. Remove timing chains as outlined under "Timing Chain, Replace."
4. Remove exhaust manifolds as outlined under "Exhaust Manifold, Replace."
5. Disconnect transmission fill tube from cylinder head if required.
6. **On Expedition, F-Series and Navigator models,** proceed as follows:
    a. Disconnect heater return tube.
    b. Remove wire harness retainer bracket.
    c. Remove lower stud bolt from heater supply tubes.
    d. Loosen top stud bolt, then move heater supply tube away from cylinder head.
    e. Slide heater tube back then remove.
    f. If removing lefthand cylinder head, remove oil dipstick and tube.
7. **On all models,** remove righthand and lefthand cylinder head retaining bolts and discard.
8. Install lifting handles tool No. T97T-6000-A, or equivalent, to cylinder heads if required.
9. Remove righthand and lefthand cylinder heads. **Use a plastic scraper to remove old gasket material to avoid damage to sealing surfaces.**
10. Reverse procedure to install, noting the following:
    a. **Cylinder head bolts must be replaced with new bolts.**
    b. Tighten cylinder heads bolts in three steps using sequence outlined, **Figs. 26 and 27.** First step, **torque** bolts to 27–31 ft. lbs.; second step, an additional 85–95°; third step, an additional 85–95.°

2003–06

1. Remove engine as outlined under "Engine, Replace."
2. Remove flexplate/flywheel and install engine on suitable engine stand.
3. Remove righthand engine mount.
4. Remove cylinder block drain plugs, and drain coolant into suitable container.
5. Disconnect radio interference capacitor, CHT sensor, CMP sensor, knock sensor, CKP sensor, and oil pressure switch electrical connectors.
6. Remove engine control sensor wiring harness.

TEST CONDITIONS	TEST DETAILS/RESULTS/ACTIONS
A4 CHECK THE REAR IN-BED FUEL TANK SOLENOID VALVE CIRCUIT 787 (PK/BK) FOR AN OPEN (Continued)	
	6 Press the START button on the NGS Tester. 7 Observe the voltage reading on the multimeter. 8 Press the STOP button on the NGS Tester. • Is the voltage greater than 10 volts? → **Yes** GO to **A5**. → **No** REPAIR Circuit 787 (PK/BK). TEST the system for normal operation. GO to **A6**.
A5 CHECK THE REAR IN-BED FUEL TANK SOLENOID VALVE CIRCUIT 57 (BK) FOR AN OPEN	
1 2	2 Measure the resistance between C316, Circuit 57 (BK) and ground. • Is the resistance less than 5 ohms? → **Yes** MARK the rear in-bed fuel tank solenoid valve as "Stuck Closed;" the solenoid valve will be replaced after diagnostics are completed. GO to **A6**. → **No** REPAIR Circuit 57 (BK). TEST the system for normal operation. GO to **A6**.

FM1029900306040X

Fig. 5 Pinpoint Test A: Fuel Tank Solenoid Valve Diagnosis (Part 4 of 12). F-Series

TEST CONDITIONS	TEST DETAILS/RESULTS/ACTIONS
A6 CHECK THE FORWARD IN-BED FUEL TANK FOR AN OPEN SOLENOID VALVE	
1 Rear In-Bed Fuel Tank Solenoid Valve C316	2 Close the manual lockdown valve jackscrew on the rear in-bed fuel tank solenoid valve. Tighten the jackscrew to 62-79 lb/in 3 Open the manual lockdown valve jackscrew on the forward in-bed fuel tank solenoid valve. 4 Open the manual bleed valve on the fuel filler neck venting kit for 60 seconds. 5 Close the manual bleed valve on the fuel filler neck venting kit. 6 Observe the system pressure on the fuel filler neck venting kit gauge. • Is the pressure on the gauge 0 kPa (0 psi)? → **Yes** GO to **A8**. → **No** GO to **A7**.

FM1029900306050X

Fig. 5 Pinpoint Test A: Fuel Tank Solenoid Valve Diagnosis (Part 5 of 12). F-Series

7. Remove both radio interference capacitors.
8. Remove crankcase ventilation tube from the lefthand valve cover.
9. Remove valve covers.
10. Remove front engine cover as outlined under "Front Cover, Replace."
11. Remove timing chain as outlined under "Timing Chain, Replace."
12. Remove exhaust manifolds as outlined under "Exhaust Manifold, Replace."
13. Remove oil dipstick tube.
14. Install tool No. 303–572, or equivalent, on both ends of cylinder head.
15. Remove hydraulic lash adjusters. **Hydraulic lash adjusters must be installed in their original location.**
16. Remove righthand and lefthand cylinder heads.
17. Reverse procedure to install, noting the following:
    a. **Cylinder head bolts must be replaced with new bolts.**
    b. Tighten cylinder heads bolts in three steps using sequence outlined, **Figs. 26 and 27.** First step, **torque** bolts to 27–31 ft. lbs.; second step, an additional 85–95°; third step, an additional 85–95.°

VALVE COVER

REPLACE

Left

1. Remove air cleaner.
2. **On Expedition, F-150, Mark LT and Navigator models,** proceed as follows:
    a. Remove power steering upper and lower bracket bolts and position bracket to side.
    b. Remove accelerator splash shield, then the accelerator cable from bracket.
    c. Move throttle body cam forward, then slide accelerator cable from cam.
    d. Remove throttle return spring.
    e. **On models equipped with cruise control,** remove cruise control cable from throttle body.
3. **On all models,** remove EGR valve to exhaust manifold tube as required.
4. **On E-Series models,** remove engine cover.
5. **On all models,** remove PCV tube from valve cover.
6. Disconnect EGR pressure transducer hoses from EGR tube, then remove tube.
7. **On models equipped with 5.4L engine** disconnect lefthand fuel injector CMP and COP electrical connections if required.
8. **On all models** remove wiring harness from valve cover studs and position to side.
9. Loosen valve cover bolts, then remove valve cover. **Valve cover bolts are part of valve cover and cannot be removed.**
10. Clean gasket mating surfaces.
11. Reverse procedure to install, noting the following:
    a. Apply silicone F6AZ-19562-AA, or equivalent, to two areas where front cover meets engine block. **Ensure valve cover is installed and tightened within four minutes of silicone application.**
    b. Tighten valve cover bolts in sequence, **Figs. 28 and 29.**

Right

EXCEPT EXCURSION & F-SUPER DUTY

1. Remove air cleaner.
2. **On E-Series models,** remove engine cover.
3. **On all models,** remove accelerator cable splash shield.
4. Remove PCV valve hose from valve cover.
5. **On E-Series models,** remove clamp and oil fill tube from valve cover.
6. **On all models,** disconnect righthand fuel injector and COP electrical connections, then position harness to side.
7. **On Expedition, F-150, Mark LT & Navigator models,** proceed as follows:
    a. Remove junction block splash shield.
    b. Disconnect two fuse block cable ends from starter relay.
    c. Remove mega fuses from junction block bracket.
    d. Disconnect 42-pin and 16-pin bulkhead connectors.
    e. Remove junction block bracket.
    f. Remove heater hose from heater supply tube.
    g. Remove heater hoses from heater core connection.
    h. Disconnect engine vacuum control connection.
    i. Raise and support vehicle.
8. **On models equipped with bi-fuel,** partially drain cooling system, then disconnect fuel charging cooling hoses.
9. **On all models,** disconnect A/C compressor and CKP electrical connections, position wiring harness to side as required.
10. Loosen valve cover bolts and remove valve cover. **Valve cover bolts are**

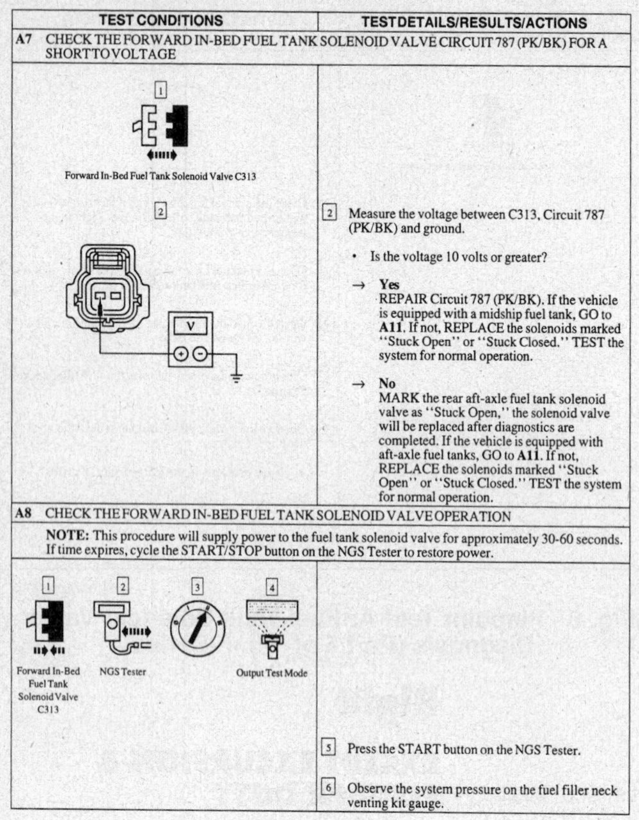

TEST CONDITIONS	TEST DETAILS/RESULTS/ACTIONS
A7 CHECK THE FORWARD IN-BED FUEL TANK SOLENOID VALVE CIRCUIT 787 (PK/BK) FOR A SHORT TO VOLTAGE	
1 Forward In-Bed Fuel Tank Solenoid Valve C313	
2	2 Measure the voltage between C313, Circuit 787 (PK/BK) and ground. • Is the voltage 10 volts or greater? → **Yes** REPAIR Circuit 787 (PK/BK). If the vehicle is equipped with a midship fuel tank, GO to **A11**. If not, REPLACE the solenoids marked "Stuck Open" or "Stuck Closed." TEST the system for normal operation. → **No** MARK the rear aft-axle fuel tank solenoid valve as "Stuck Open," the solenoid valve will be replaced after diagnostics are completed. If the vehicle is equipped with aft-axle fuel tanks, GO to **A11**. If not, REPLACE the solenoids marked "Stuck Open" or "Stuck Closed." TEST the system for normal operation.
A8 CHECK THE FORWARD IN-BED FUEL TANK SOLENOID VALVE OPERATION	
NOTE: This procedure will supply power to the fuel tank solenoid valve for approximately 30-60 seconds. If time expires, cycle the START/STOP button on the NGS Tester to restore power.	
1 Forward In-Bed Fuel Tank Solenoid Valve C313; 2 NGS Tester; 3; 4 Output Test Mode	5 Press the START button on the NGS Tester. 6 Observe the system pressure on the fuel filler neck venting kit gauge.

FM1029900306060X

Fig. 5 Pinpoint Test A: Fuel Tank Solenoid Valve Diagnosis (Part 6 of 12). F-Series

TEST CONDITIONS	TEST DETAILS/RESULTS/ACTIONS
A8 CHECK THE FORWARD IN-BED FUEL TANK SOLENOID VALVE OPERATION (Continued)	
	7 Press the STOP button on the NGS Tester. • Did the system pressure register 0 kPa (0 psi) on the gauge when the NGS Tester was triggered on? → **Yes** GO to **A9**. → **No** MARK the forward in-bed fuel tank solenoid valve as "Functions Normally." If the vehicle is equipped with a midship fuel tank, GO to **A11**. If not, REPLACE the solenoids marked "Stuck Open" or "Stuck Closed." TEST the system for normal operation.
A9 CHECK THE FORWARD IN-BED FUEL TANK SOLENOID VALVE CIRCUIT 787 (PK/BK) FOR AN OPEN	
NOTE: This procedure will supply power to the fuel tank solenoid valve for approximately 30-60 seconds. If time expires, cycle the START/STOP button on the NGS Tester to restore power.	
1; 2 Forward In-Bed Fuel Tank Solenoid Valve C313	
3	3 Connect a multimeter between C313, Circuit 787 (PK/BK) and ground.
4; 5 Output Test Mode	

FM1029900306070X

Fig. 5 Pinpoint Test A: Fuel Tank Solenoid Valve Diagnosis (Part 7 of 12). F-Series

part of valve cover and cannot be removed.

11. Clean gasket mating surfaces.
12. Reverse procedure to install, noting the following:
    a. Apply silicone F6AZ-19562-AA, or equivalent, to two areas where front cover meets engine block. **Ensure valve cover is installed and tightened within four minutes of silicone application.**
    b. Tighten valve cover bolts in sequence, **Figs. 30 and 31.**

EXCURSION & F-SUPER DUTY

1. Disconnect vacuum canister hose and position aside.
2. Remove nuts, then position EVAP canister purge valve, bracket, and heater hoses aside.
3. Disconnect PCV tube from valve cover.
4. Remove three suction accumulator bracket screws.
5. Remove eleven evaporative core screws, then remove evaporative core cover.
6. Disconnect righthand ignition coil electrical connectors.
7. Disconnect righthand fuel injector electrical connectors.
8. Release wiring harness routing clips from valve cover, then A/C compressor to condenser hose.
9. Lift fuel charging wiring off valve cover and position aside.
10. Loosen valve cover bolts and remove valve cover. **Valve cover bolts are part of valve cover and cannot be removed.**
11. Reverse procedure to install, noting the following:
    a. Apply a bead of silicone gasket sealer F7AZ-19554-EA, or equivalent, to two areas where front cover meets cylinder head.
    b. Tighten valve cover to specifications in sequence as outlined in **Fig. 31.**

VALVE ADJUSTMENT

These engines have overhead camshafts and there are no valve adjustments possible. A hydraulic lash adjuster provides automatic lash adjustment.

ROLLER FOLLOWER

REPLACE

1. Remove valve covers as outlined under "Valve Cover, Replace."
2. Position piston to bottom of stroke.
3. Install valve spring spacer tool No. T91P-6565-AH, or equivalent, between valve spring coils to prevent valve stem seal damage.
4. Compress valve spring and remove camshaft followers using valve spring compressor tool No. T97P-6565-AH, or equivalent.
5. Remove hydraulic lash adjuster. Repeat above procedure as needed.
6. Reverse procedure to install.

HYDRAULIC LASH ADJUSTERS

REPLACE

1. Remove camshaft roller followers as outlined in "Roller Follower, Replace."
2. Remove valve tappets.
3. Reverse procedure to install.

FRONT COVER

REPLACE

1. Remove valve covers as outlined under "Valve Cover, Replace."
2. Remove radiator as outlined under "Radiator, Replace."
3. Remove water pump as outlined under "Water Pump, Replace."
4. **On models equipped with coil pack,** disconnect ignition coil and radio capacitor connectors, then remove ignition coils and brackets.
5. **On all models,** raise and support vehicle.
6. Remove two top power steering pump bolts and one lower bolt, then position power steering pump to side.
7. Disconnect CKP sensor, then drain engine oil.
8. Remove front oil pan bolts.
9. Lower vehicle, then remove front oil seal as outlined under "Crankshaft Seal, Replace."

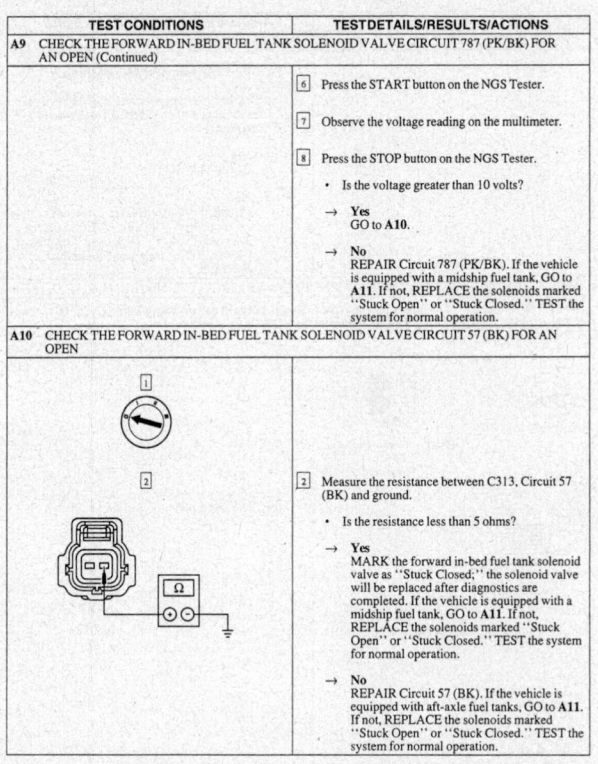

TEST CONDITIONS	TEST DETAILS/RESULTS/ACTIONS
A9 CHECK THE FORWARD IN-BED FUEL TANK SOLENOID VALVE CIRCUIT 787 (PK/BK) FOR AN OPEN (Continued)	
	6 Press the START button on the NGS Tester. 7 Observe the voltage reading on the multimeter. 8 Press the STOP button on the NGS Tester. • Is the voltage greater than 10 volts? → **Yes** GO to **A10**. → **No** REPAIR Circuit 787 (PK/BK). If the vehicle is equipped with a midship fuel tank, GO to **A11**. If not, REPLACE the solenoids marked "Stuck Open" or "Stuck Closed." TEST the system for normal operation.
A10 CHECK THE FORWARD IN-BED FUEL TANK SOLENOID VALVE CIRCUIT 57 (BK) FOR AN OPEN	
1 2 Ω	2 Measure the resistance between C313, Circuit 57 (BK) and ground. • Is the resistance less than 5 ohms? → **Yes** MARK the forward in-bed fuel tank solenoid valve as "Stuck Closed;" the solenoid valve will be replaced after diagnostics are completed. If the vehicle is equipped with a midship fuel tank, GO to **A11**. If not, REPLACE the solenoids marked "Stuck Open" or "Stuck Closed." TEST the system for normal operation. → **No** REPAIR Circuit 57 (BK). If the vehicle is equipped with aft-axle fuel tanks, GO to **A11**. If not, REPLACE the solenoids marked "Stuck Open" or "Stuck Closed." TEST the system for normal operation.

FM1029900306080X

Fig. 5 Pinpoint Test A: Fuel Tank Solenoid Valve Diagnosis (Part 8 of 12). F-Series

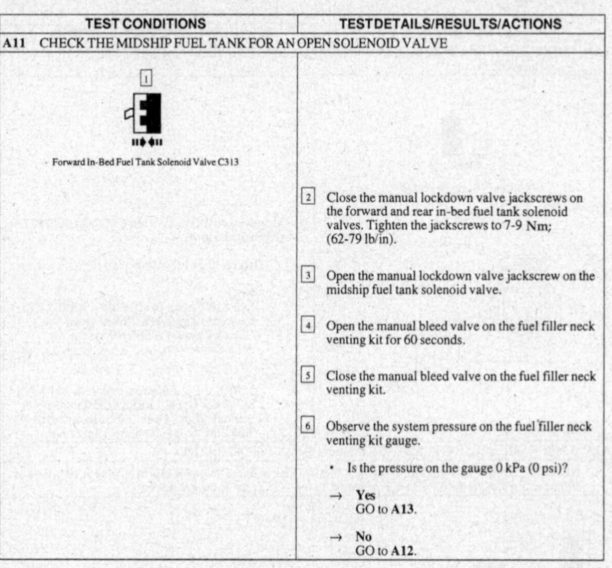

TEST CONDITIONS	TEST DETAILS/RESULTS/ACTIONS
A11 CHECK THE MIDSHIP FUEL TANK FOR AN OPEN SOLENOID VALVE	
1 Forward In-Bed Fuel Tank Solenoid Valve C313	2 Close the manual lockdown valve jackscrews on the forward and rear in-bed fuel tank solenoid valves. Tighten the jackscrews to 7-9 Nm; (62-79 lb/in). 3 Open the manual lockdown valve jackscrew on the midship fuel tank solenoid valve. 4 Open the manual bleed valve on the fuel filler neck venting kit for 60 seconds. 5 Close the manual bleed valve on the fuel filler neck venting kit. 6 Observe the system pressure on the fuel filler neck venting kit gauge. • Is the pressure on the gauge 0 kPa (0 psi)? → **Yes** GO to **A13**. → **No** GO to **A12**.

FM1029900306090X

Fig. 5 Pinpoint Test A: Fuel Tank Solenoid Valve Diagnosis (Part 9 of 12). F-Series

10. Disconnect CMP sensor electrical connector.
11. Remove drive belt idler pulley, then the front cover bolts.
12. Remove front cover, then the dowel from cylinder block.
13. Clean all gasket surfaces.
14. Reverse procedure to install, noting the following:
    a. Apply silicone F6AZ-19562-AA, or equivalent, to cylinder head to block surface and oil pan to block surface as outlined in **Fig. 32.** Ensure front cover is tightened within four minutes of silicone application.
    b. Install front cover, then install bolts and hand tighten.
    c. Refer to **Fig. 33** for tightening sequence.
    d. **Torque** bolts 1–7 to 15–22 ft. lbs., and bolts 8–15 to 30–40 ft. lbs.

TIMING CHAIN

REPLACE

With the timing chain removed, avoid turning the camshaft or crankshaft. If movement is required, exercise extreme caution to avoid valve damage caused by piston-to-valve contact.

4.6L VIN 6 & 5.4L Engines

REMOVAL

1. Remove front cover as outlined under "Front Cover, Replace."
2. Remove crankshaft sensor ring.
3. Place crankshaft keyway to 12 o'clock position, then install crankshaft holding tool No. T93P-6303-A, or equivalent.
4. Install and tighten camshaft holding tool No. T96T-6256-B, or equivalent, to both camshafts.
5. Remove timing chain tensioners, then the tensioner arms.
6. Remove crankshaft holding tool, then the righthand timing chain and crankshaft sprocket.
7. Remove lefthand timing chain and crankshaft sprocket.
8. Remove righthand and lefthand timing chain guides.

INSTALLATION

1. Compress timing chain tensioner plunger using a suitable vise. **Do not compress ratchet assembly.**
2. Push back and hold ratchet using a suitable screwdriver.
3. While holding ratchet mechanism, move ratchet arm back into tensioner housing.
4. Install a suitable clip to hole in tensioner housing to hold ratchet and plunger during installation.
5. If copper links of timing chain are not visible, mark 2 links on opposite ends of chain.
6. Install timing chain guides, **Fig. 34.**
7. Slightly loosen camshaft holding tools to allow a small amount of camshaft movement.
8. Rotate lefthand camshaft to 12 o'clock position using camshaft positioning tool No. T96T-6256-AR, or equivalent, **Fig. 35.**
9. Rotate righthand camshaft to 11 o'clock position using camshaft positioning tool, **Fig. 35.**
10. Tighten both camshaft holding tools to maintain proper camshaft position.
11. Place crankshaft in position as outlined in **Fig. 36. If crankshaft rotation is required, rotate counterclockwise only. Do not rotate past position outlined in Fig. 36.**
12. Remove crankshaft holding tool.
13. Install inner crankshaft sprocket with long hub facing outward.
14. Install lefthand timing chain to crankshaft sprocket. Align one copper or marked link with slot of crankshaft sprocket, **Fig. 37.**
15. Ensure upper half of timing chain is below tensioner guide dowel. If adjustment is required, use camshaft positioning tool.
16. Install lefthand timing chain to lefthand camshaft sprocket ensuring marked chain links and camshaft sprocket timing mark are aligned, **Fig. 37.**
17. Install righthand timing chain with sprocket. Ensure long hub of sprocket is facing inward and lower half of chain is positioned above dowel.
18. Adjust camshaft sprocket as required using camshaft positioning tool, then install timing chain to righthand camshaft sprocket. Ensure 2 marked links of chain are aligned with camshaft sprocket timing marks.
19. Ensure all timing marks are aligned as outlined in **Fig. 38.**
20. Install both timing chain tensioner arms to dowel pins.
21. Install chain tensioners and tighten to specifications.
22. Remove pins from chain tensioners.
23. Remove camshaft holding tools.
24. Install crankshaft sensor ring.
25. Install front cover as outlined under "Front Cover, Replace."

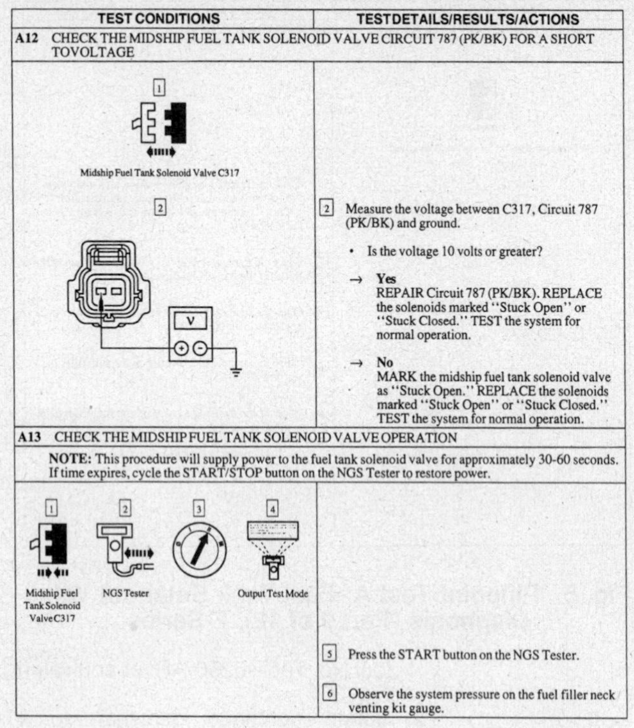

TEST CONDITIONS	TEST DETAILS/RESULTS/ACTIONS
A12 CHECK THE MIDSHIP FUEL TANK SOLENOID VALVE CIRCUIT 787 (PK/BK) FOR A SHORT TO VOLTAGE	
1 Midship Fuel Tank Solenoid Valve C317	
2 V	2 Measure the voltage between C317, Circuit 787 (PK/BK) and ground. • Is the voltage 10 volts or greater? → **Yes** REPAIR Circuit 787 (PK/BK). REPLACE the solenoids marked "Stuck Open" or "Stuck Closed." TEST the system for normal operation. → **No** MARK the midship fuel tank solenoid valve as "Stuck Open." REPLACE the solenoids marked "Stuck Open" or "Stuck Closed." TEST the system for normal operation.
A13 CHECK THE MIDSHIP FUEL TANK SOLENOID VALVE OPERATION	
NOTE: This procedure will supply power to the fuel tank solenoid valve for approximately 30-60 seconds. If time expires, cycle the START/STOP button on the NGS Tester to restore power.	
1 2 3 4 Midship Fuel Tank Solenoid Valve C317 NGS Tester Output Test Mode	
	5 Press the START button on the NGS Tester.
	6 Observe the system pressure on the fuel filler neck venting kit gauge.

FM1029900306100X

Fig. 5 Pinpoint Test A: Fuel Tank Solenoid Valve Diagnosis (Part 10 of 12). F-Series

TEST CONDITIONS	TEST DETAILS/RESULTS/ACTIONS
A13 CHECK THE MIDSHIP FUEL TANK SOLENOID VALVE OPERATION (Continued)	
	7 Press the STOP button on the NGS Tester. • Did the system pressure register 0 kPa (0 psi) on the gauge when the NGS Tester was triggered on? → **Yes** GO to **A14**. → **No** MARK the midship fuel tank solenoid valve as "Functions Normally." REPLACE the solenoids marked "Stuck Open" or "Stuck Closed." TEST the system for normal operation.
A14 CHECK THE MIDSHIP FUEL TANK SOLENOID VALVE CIRCUIT 787 (PK/BK) FOR AN OPEN	
NOTE: This procedure will supply power to the fuel tank solenoid valve for approximately 30-60 seconds. If time expires, cycle the START/STOP button on the NGS Tester to restore power.	
1 2 Midship Fuel Tank Solenoid Valve C317	
3 V	3 Connect a multimeter between C317, Circuit 787 (PK/BK) and ground.
4 5 Output Test Mode	

FM1029900306110X

Fig. 5 Pinpoint Test A: Fuel Tank Solenoid Valve Diagnosis (Part 11 of 12). F-Series

4.6L VIN W Engine

REMOVAL

1. Remove front cover as outlined under "Front Cover, Replace."
2. Remove crankshaft sensor ring from crankshaft.
3. Rotate crankshaft until both camshaft keyways are 90° from valve cover surface, **Fig. 39.** Ensure copper links are aligned with dots on camshaft sprocket.
4. Install camshaft positioning tool No. T91P-6256-A and camshaft positioning tool adapters tool No. T92P-6256-A, or equivalents to camshafts.
5. Remove timing chain tensioners, then the tensioner arms from dowel pins.
6. Remove timing chains and crankshaft sprockets.
7. Remove timing chain guides.

INSTALLATION

1. Compress timing chain tensioner plunger using a suitable vise. **Do not compress ratchet assembly.**
2. Push back and hold ratchet using a suitable screwdriver.
3. While holding ratchet mechanism, move ratchet arm back into tensioner housing.
4. Install a suitable clip to hole in tensioner housing to hold ratchet and plunger during installation.
5. If copper links of timing chain are not visible, mark 2 links on opposite ends of chain.
6. Install timing chain guides (1, 3) with bolts (2, 4), **Fig. 40.**
7. Install timing chains with crankshaft sprockets. Ensure lefthand inner sprocket is installed first and that sprocket hubs face each other. Align marked chain links with dot on crankshaft sprockets. Position chain over camshaft sprocket ensuring marked links are aligned with dot on camshaft sprocket.
8. After chains are installed, ensure marked links (A) of timing chain are aligned as outlined in **Fig. 41.**
9. Ensure camshaft sprocket keyway (A) is 90° from valve cover mounting surface (B), **Fig. 42.**
10. Install lefthand and righthand timing chain tensioner arms.
11. Install timing chain tensioners, then remove pins from tensioners.
12. Remove cam positioning tool and adapters from camshafts.
13. Install crankshaft sensor ring.
14. Install front cover as outlined under "Front Cover, Replace."

CAMSHAFT

REPLACE

Do not rotate crankshaft or camshaft with timing chains removed. Severe piston and valve damage will occur.

1. Remove valve covers as outlined under "Valve Covers, Replace."
2. Remove timing chain as outlined under "Timing Chain, Replace."
3. Remove camshaft roller followers as outlined under "Roller Followers" then on engines with bolt on sprockets remove bolt and sprockets.
4. **On models equipped with camshaft bolt,** remove camshaft sprocket bolt, then the camshaft sprocket.
5. **On all models,** remove thirteen camshaft bearing cap bolts and caps.
6. Remove camshafts from cylinder head.
7. Reverse procedure to install, noting the following:
   a. Lubricate camshaft journals and bearing caps with suitable clean engine oil.
   b. **Torque** camshaft bearing cap bolts to specifications in sequence, **Figs. 43 and 44.**

CRANKSHAFT SEAL

REPLACE

Front

1. Remove air cleaner, then drain cooling system.
2. Remove front air deflector.
3. Remove upper radiator hose and coolant overflow hose from radiator.
4. Remove fan blade and lefthand thread clutch using fan clutch holding tool No. T84T-6312-C and fan clutch wrench tool No. T93T-6312-B, or equivalents. **E-Series, Excursion and F-Super Duty fan clutch has righthand threads.**

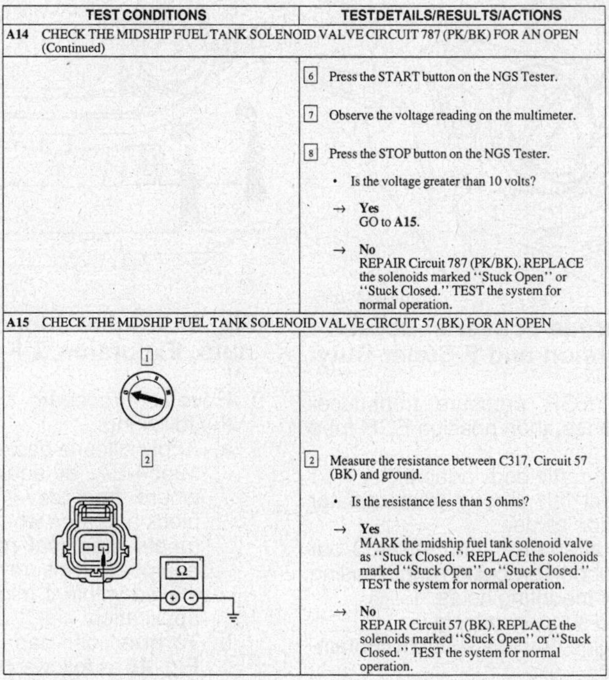

TEST CONDITIONS	TEST DETAILS/RESULTS/ACTIONS
A14 CHECK THE MIDSHIP FUEL TANK SOLENOID VALVE CIRCUIT 787 (PK/BK) FOR AN OPEN (Continued)	
	6 Press the START button on the NGS Tester. 7 Observe the voltage reading on the multimeter. 8 Press the STOP button on the NGS Tester. • Is the voltage greater than 10 volts? → **Yes** GO to **A15**. → **No** REPAIR Circuit 787 (PK/BK). REPLACE the solenoids marked "Stuck Open" or "Stuck Closed." TEST the system for normal operation.
A15 CHECK THE MIDSHIP FUEL TANK SOLENOID VALVE CIRCUIT 57 (BK) FOR AN OPEN	
1 2	2 Measure the resistance between C317, Circuit 57 (BK) and ground. • Is the resistance less than 5 ohms? → **Yes** MARK the midship fuel tank solenoid valve as "Stuck Closed." REPLACE the solenoids marked "Stuck Open" or "Stuck Closed." TEST the system for normal operation. → **No** REPAIR Circuit 57 (BK). REPLACE the solenoids marked "Stuck Open" or "Stuck Closed." TEST the system for normal operation.

FM1029900306120X

Fig. 5 Pinpoint Test A: Fuel Tank Solenoid Valve Diagnosis (Part 12 of 12). F-Series

5. Disconnect overflow hose from radiator.
6. Remove fan shroud, then the fan and shroud together.
7. Rotate drive belt tensioner, then remove supercharger drive belt and accessory drive belt as equipped.
8. Remove crankshaft pulley bolt.
9. Remove crankshaft pulley using crankshaft damper remover tool No. T58P-6316-D, or equivalent.
10. Remove front seal using front cover seal remover tool No. T74P-6700-A, or equivalent.
11. Reverse procedure to install, noting the following:
    a. Lubricate new seal using suitable 5W-30 motor oil and install using crankshaft seal replacer/aligner tool No. T88T-6701-A, or equivalent.
    b. Apply silicone F6AZ-19562-AA, or equivalent, to crankshaft pulley. Install pulley using crankshaft pulley installer tool No. T74P-6316-B, or equivalent.

Rear

REMOVAL

1. **On models equipped with automatic transmission,** remove transmission as outlined in **MOTOR's "Domestic Transmission, In-Vehicle Service" or "Transmission Service DVD."**
2. **On models equipped with manual transmission,** remove transmission as outlined in **MOTOR's "Domestic Transmission, In-Vehicle Service" or "Transmission Service DVD."**
3. **On all models,** remove flywheel.
4. **On models equipped with retainer plate,** remove oil pan as outlined under "Oil Pan, Replace."
5. **On all models,** remove two rear oil pan bolts if required.
6. Remove rear oil slinger using crankshaft slinger remover tool No. T95P-6701-AH, or equivalent.
7. Remove rear main seal using rear crankshaft seal remover tool No. T95P-6701-EH, or equivalent.
8. Remove seal retainer bolts, then the seal retainer.
9. Clean sealing surfaces.

INSTALLATION

1. Apply silicone F6AZ-19562-A, or equivalent, to rear oil seal retainer sealing surface.
2. Install rear oil seal retainer and tighten to specification using sequence outlined in **Fig. 45.** Ensure seal retainer is tightened within four minutes of silicone application.
3. Lubricate rear oil seal using suitable 50W motor oil, then install seal using rear crankshaft seal replacer tool No. T95P-6701-BH and rear crankshaft seal adapter tool No. T95P-6701-DH, or equivalents.
4. Install rear oil slinger using crankshaft seal adapter tool No. T95P-6701-DH, rear slinger replacer tool No. T95P-6701-CH, and seal replacer tool No. T95P-6701-BH, or equivalents.
5. Install oil pan as outlined under "Oil Pan, Replace."
6. **On models equipped with automatic transmission,** loosely install bolts in a circular, clockwise pattern, then tighten to specifications in sequence, **Figs. 46 and 47.**
7. **On models equipped with manual transmission,** tighten bolts to specifications.
8. **On models equipped with automatic transmission,** install transmission as outlined in **MOTOR's "Domestic Transmission, In-Vehicle Service" or "Transmission Service DVD."**
9. **On models equipped with manual transmission,** install transmission as outlined in **MOTOR's "Domestic Transmission, In-Vehicle Service" or "Transmission Service DVD."**

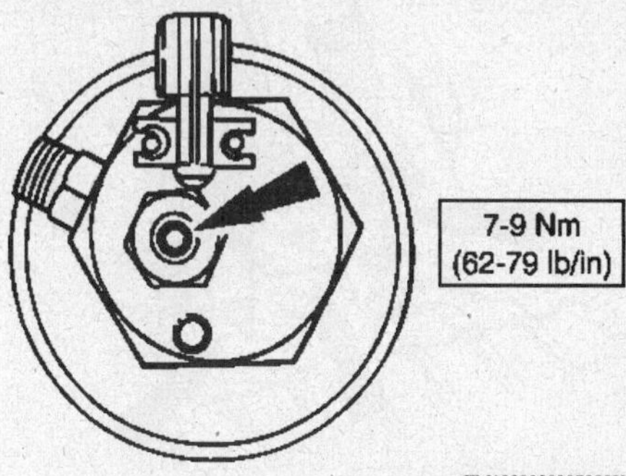

FM1029900307000X

Fig. 6 Fuel tank solenoid manual lockdown valve

OIL PAN

REPLACE

E-Series

1. Remove intake manifold as outlined under "Intake Manifold, Replace."
2. Remove air cleaner assembly, then the upper radiator hose.
3. Remove fan using fan pulley holding wrench tool No. T84T-6312-C and fan clutch nut wrench T93T-6312-B, or equivalents. **Fan has righthand threads.**
4. Remove fan shroud attaching bolts, then the fan with shroud.
5. Remove radiator air deflector.
6. Remove transmission filler tube from rear of righthand cylinder head.
7. Disconnect engine wiring harness from harness retainer.
8. Remove coolant tube stud bolts.
9. Remove two upper transmission to engine attaching bolts.
10. Install modular lifting bar tool No. 014-00073 and lift bar adapter tool No. 303-F694, or equivalent, to engine.
11. Install 3 bar engine support tool No. 303–F070, or equivalent, to modular lifting bar and support engine.
12. Raise and support vehicle.
13. Drain engine oil into a suitable container.
14. Remove oil filter, then the engine mount attaching nuts.
15. Remove flywheel inspection plate, then lower vehicle.
16. Raise engine 10¼ inches from crankshaft pulley to lower edge of No. 1 crossmember.
17. Raise and support vehicle.
18. Remove oil pan attaching bolts, then partially lower oil pan.

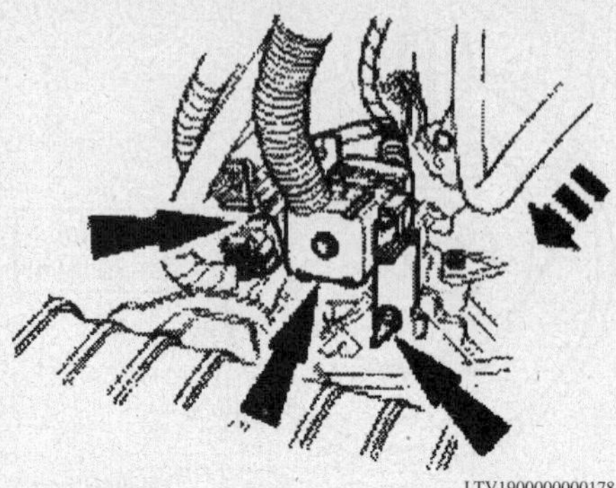

Fig. 7 42 pin and 16 pin connector. Excursion and F-Super Duty

19. Remove oil pump screen cover and tube, then the oil pan with screen and tube.
20. Reverse procedure to install, noting the following:
    a. Apply silicone gasket sealer F7AZ-19554-EA, or equivalent, to area where front cover meets engine block. Ensure oil pan is installed within 4 minutes of sealant application.
    b. Ensure O-ring is properly installed and undamaged.
    c. **Torque** oil pan in sequence, **Fig. 48** as follows; first step, 18 inch lbs.; second step, 15 ft. lbs.; third step, tighten an additional 90°.

F-150, Expedition, Mark LT & Navigator

2WD

1. Drain cooling system.
2. Remove radiator air deflector.
3. Remove air cleaner assembly.
4. Remove accelerator splash shield.
5. Disconnect throttle and cruise control cables.
6. Disconnect throttle return spring.
7. Remove accelerator cable bracket and position aside.
8. Disconnect vapor management valve.
9. Remove crankcase ventilation tube, then the IAC fresh air tube.
10. Disconnect EGR valve vacuum line, then the main vacuum harness.
11. Disconnect TP sensor, then the engine vacuum regulator.
12. Disconnect fuel pressure regulator and vapor management valve vacuum lines.
13. Remove brake booster vacuum line and bracket.
14. Disconnect fuel lines, then the IAC.
15. **On models equipped with 4.6L engine,** proceed as follows:
    a. Remove power steering fluid reservoir and position aside.
    b. Disconnect fuel injectors.
    c. Remove COP ignition coils if equipped.
    d. Disconnect heater hose from intake manifold.
16. **On all models,** disconnect EGR tube upper fitting, then loosen lower fitting.

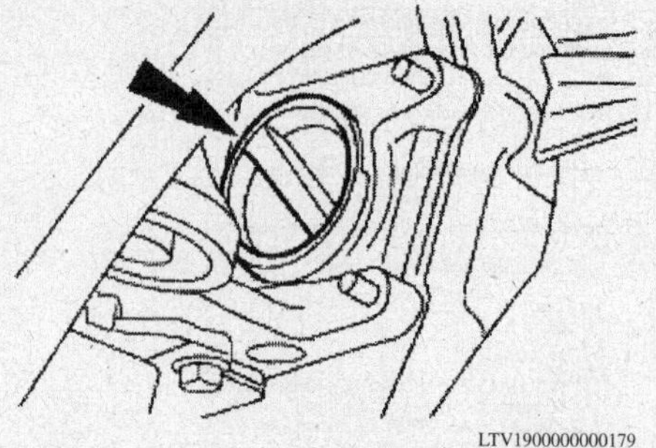

Fig. 8 Torque converter access plug. Excursion and F-Super Duty

17. Remove EGR pressure transducer vacuum lines, then position EGR tube aside.
18. Remove throttle body adapter.
19. Disconnect fan shroud from radiator and position aside.
20. Remove alternator, then install 3 bar engine support bracket to engine using alternator mounting holes.
21. Raise and support vehicle.
22. Drain engine oil into a suitable container.
23. **On models equipped with 5.4L engine,** disconnect electrical connections from starter.
24. **On all models,** remove lefthand and righthand motor mount bolts, then lower vehicle.
25. Install 3 bar engine support tool No. 303–F070, or equivalent, then raise engine.
26. Raise and support vehicle.
27. Remove oil pan attaching bolts, then partially lower oil pan.
28. Remove oil pump screen cover and tube, then the oil pan with screen and tube. **Oil pan gasket is reusable if not damaged during removal.**
29. Reverse procedure to install, noting the following:
    a. Apply silicone gasket sealer F7AZ-19554-EA, or equivalent, to area where front cover meets engine block. Ensure oil pan is installed within 4 minutes of sealant application.
    b. **Torque** oil pan in sequence, **Fig. 48** as follows; first step, 18 inch lbs.; second step, 15 ft. lbs.; third step, tighten an additional 60°.

4WD

1. Raise and support vehicle.
2. Drain engine oil into a suitable container.
3. Support front axle using suitable jack stands.
4. Remove front axle mount bolts, then the axle support bolts.
5. Remove axle support.
6. Remove righthand and lefthand axle housing mount bolts, then lower axle to allow clearance for oil pan removal.
7. Remove oil pan attaching bolts, then partially lower oil pan.
8. Remove oil pump screen cover and tube, then the oil pan with screen and tube. **Oil pan gasket is reusable if not damaged during removal.**

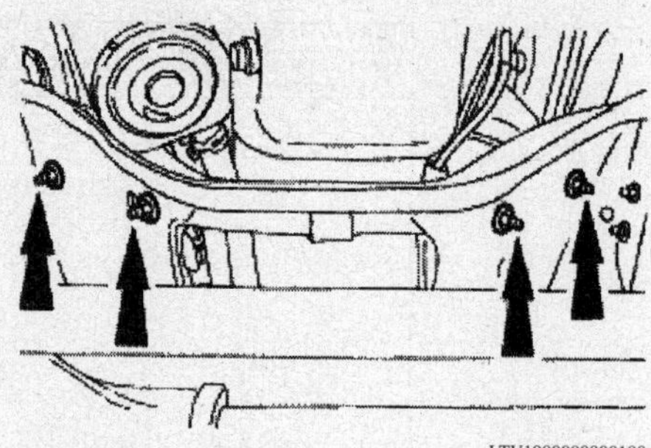

Fig. 9 Engine support insulator nuts. Excursion & F-Super Duty

9. Reverse procedure to install, noting the following:
    a. Apply silicone gasket sealer F7AZ-19554-EA, or equivalent, to area where front cover meets engine block and area where engine block meats rear seal retaining plate if equipped. Ensure oil pan is installed within 4 minutes of sealant application.
    b. **Torque** oil pan in sequence, **Fig. 48** as follows; first step, 18 inch lbs.; second step, 15 ft. lbs.; third step, tighten an additional 60°.

Excursion & F-Super Duty

1. Partially drain radiator and disconnect upper radiator hose at radiator.
2. Remove air cleaner outlet tube, then accelerator cable snow shield.
3. Disconnect accelerator and speed control cables and return spring.
4. Position accelerator cable bracket and cables aside.
5. Disconnect PCV, brake booster and engine sensor control wiring harness.
6. Disconnect idle air control motor and bypass hose.
7. Disconnect heater hose, EGR transducer, throttle position sensor and EGR transducer vacuum lines.
8. Disconnect exhaust manifold tube fittings and remove tube.
9. Remove EGR transducer bracket and EGR valve vacuum line.
10. Disconnect EVR solenoid and vacuum harness.
11. Remove throttle body four bolts, body adapter and adapter gasket.
12. Remove two screws at to of fan shroud and position fan shroud toward engine.
13. Remove alternator, then install modular engine support bracket on engine using alternator mounting holes.
14. Raise and support vehicle, then remove engine mount nuts.
15. If equipped, remove turbine shaft speed and output shaft sensors and install plugs in transmission.
16. Lower vehicle, then raise engine using a floor crane attached to support bracket.
17. Support engine using three bar engine support tool No. 303-F070, or equivalent. Support by inserting the J-hook.
18. Raise and support vehicle, then drain

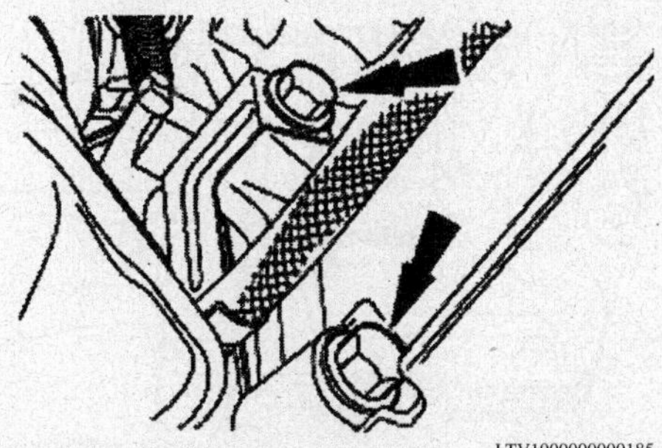

Fig. 10 Transmission to engine mounting bolts. E-Series

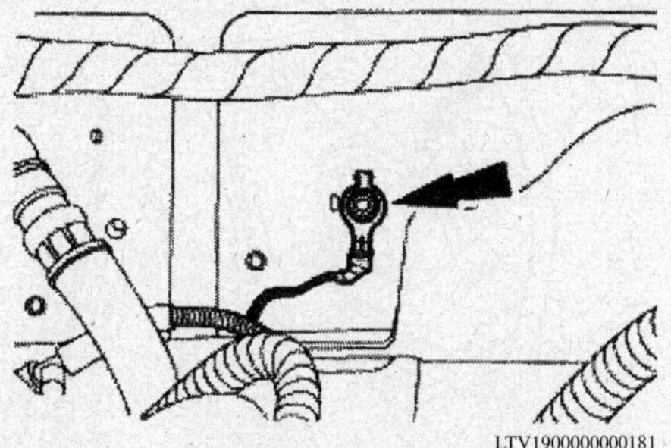

Fig. 11 Ground wire. Expedition & Navigator

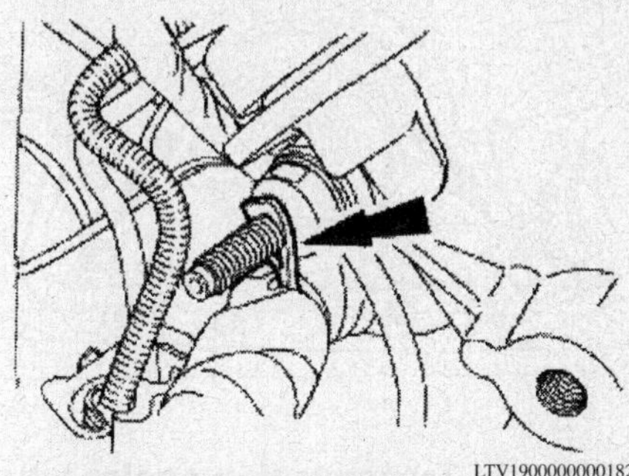

Fig. 12 Wiring harness retainer. Expedition & Navigator

engine oil and remove oil bypass filter.

19. Remove dual converter Y-pipe and flywheel inspection plate.
20. Install High Lift Transmission Jack 014-00942 and E40D Transmission Jack Adapter 014-00763, or equivalents.
21. Support transmission on oil pan rails only or internal transmission damage may occur.
22. Remove transmission mount nuts, then raise transmission.
23. Remove oil pan bolt and partially lower oil pan.
24. Remove two bolts from oil pump screen cover and tube and let them drop into the oil pan.
25. Remove rear bolt and oil pump screen cover and tube and let drop into oil pan.
26. Remove oil pan and oil pan gasket from rear of engine.
27. Clean mating surfaces and thoroughly clean oil pan.
28. Reverse procedure to install, noting the following:
    a. Apply silicone F6AZ-19562-AA, or equivalent, to front cover to block mating surface and rear seal retainer to block mating surface.
    b. Install oil pan and tighten to specification using sequence outlined in **Fig. 48.** Ensure oil pan is tightened within four minutes of silicone application.

OIL PUMP

REPLACE

1. Remove timing chain as outlined under "Timing Chain, Replace."
2. Remove oil pan as outlined under "Oil Pan, Replace."
3. **On models equipped with 4WD,** remove three oil pump screen and cover bolts, then the oil pump screen and cover.
4. **On all models,** remove oil pump bolts, then the oil pump.
5. Reverse procedure to install.

BELT TENSION DATA

The 4.6L and 5.4L gasoline engines are equipped with a serpentine drive belt and automatic tensioner.

SERPENTINE DRIVE BELT

Belt Routing

Refer to **Fig. 49** for serpentine drive belt routing.

Belt, Replacement

1. Use ½ square hole in drive belt tensioner pulley hub to rotate drive belt tensioner counterclockwise and remove drive belt.
2. Remove belt, slowly release tensioner. **Do not allow tensioner to snap back, as damage may result.**
3. Reverse procedure to install.

Tensioner, Replacement

1. Rotate drive belt tensioner counterclockwise and remove drive belt.
2. Remove belt, slowly release tensioner. **Do not allow tensioner to snap back, as damage may result.**
3. Reverse procedure to install.

COOLING SYSTEM BLEED

1. Add proper coolant mixture to degas bottle.
2. Move temperature blend selector to full warm position.
3. Run engine at normal operating temperature, at 2000 RPM, for five minutes.
4. Turn off engine and allow to cool
5. Add proper coolant mixture to degas bottle until coolant is between coolant fill level marks.

THERMOSTAT

REPLACE

1. Partially drain engine coolant into a suitable container, then remove upper radiator hose.
2. Remove thermostat bolts, housing, thermostat and O-ring.
3. Reverse procedure to install. Tighten bolt to specifications.

WATER PUMP

REPLACE

1. Drain cooling system into a suitable container.
2. Remove fan blade and lefthand thread clutch using fan clutch holding tool No. T84T-6312-C and fan clutch wrench tool No. T93T-6312-B, or equivalents.
3. Rotate drive belt tensioner, then remove drive belt.
4. Remove water pump pulley bolts, then the water pump pulley.
5. Remove water pump bolts, then the water pump.
6. Reverse procedure to install, noting the following:
    a. Install water pump and tighten to specification using sequence outlined in **Fig. 50.**
    b. Install water pump pulley and tighten to specification using sequence outlined in **Fig. 51.**

RADIATOR

REPLACE

Except Excursion & F-Super Duty

1. Drain cooling system.
2. Remove front air deflector if required.
3. Remove fan blade and lefthand thread clutch using fan clutch holding tool No. T84T-6312-C and fan clutch wrench tool No. T93T-6312-B, or equivalents.
4. Disconnect transmission fluid cooler lines from radiator.
5. Disconnect lower radiator hose as follows:
    a. Pry locking tab up and out of slot.
    b. Rotate and remove hose.
6. Remove upper radiator hose.
7. **On Expedition & Navigator models,** disconnect overflow hose from radiator.
8. Remove radiator attaching bolts and brackets.
9. Remove radiator.
10. Reverse procedure to install.

Fig. 13 Transmission cooler tube & power steering hose brackets. Expedition & Navigator

Excursion & F-Super Duty

PICKUP CHASSIS

1. Drain cooling system.
2. Remove degas bottle, then raise and support vehicle.
3. Remove lower radiator hose from radiator.
4. Lower vehicle, then remove upper hose from radiator.
5. Remove two pushpins and position radiator sight shield out of the way.
6. Remove bolts and righthand and lefthand upper radiator supports.
7. Remove insulators and degas bottle hose.
8. Remove fan blade clutch using fan clutch holding tool No. T84T-6312-C and fan clutch wrench tool No. T93T-6312-B, or equivalents.
9. Remove radiator.
10. Reverse procedure to install.

MOTORHOME CHASSIS

1. Drain coolant into a suitable container.
2. Gain access to engine compartment, then remove upper radiator hose from radiator.
3. Remove radiator overflow hose from radiator.
4. Remove fan shroud bolts and position fan shroud as far back as possible.
5. Raise and support vehicle.
6. Remove retaining strap from lower radiator hose and radiator support.
7. Remove degas bottle supply hose and lower radiator hose from radiator.
8. Remove two bolts and two nuts from power steering cooler.
9. Remove four bolts from radiator support, then support radiator and remove radiator bracket and position power steering cooler out of the way.
10. Lower radiator from vehicle.
11. Reverse procedure to install, noting the following:
    a. Extreme care must be taken to see that lower radiator tabs are properly seated in insulators. Upper and lower insulators must be in place.
    b. Replace lower hose retaining strap.

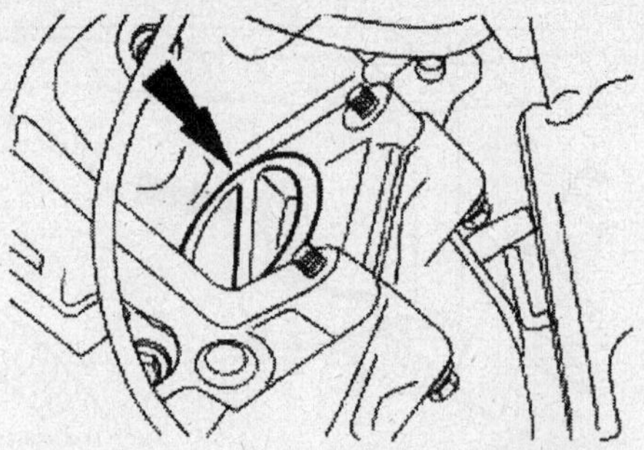

Fig. 14 Cylinder block opening cover. Expedition & Navigator

FUEL PUMP

REPLACE

Except Excursion & F-Super Duty

1. Relieve fuel pressure as outlined under "Precautions."
2. Raise and support vehicle.
3. Disconnect fuel filler tube from fuel tank.
4. Siphon fuel from filler tube into a suitable container.
5. Disconnect fuel tank filler vent tube from filler pipe.
6. Disconnect fuel pump electrical connector.
7. Place a suitable jack under fuel tank.
8. Remove skid plate if equipped.
9. Remove front and rear fuel tank straps.
10. Partially lower fuel tank, then disconnect evaporative emissions hoses.
11. Disconnect fuel pressure transducer if equipped.
12. Disconnect quick connect fittings as outlined under "Quick Disconnect Hoses" in the "4.2L Engine" section.
13. Lower fuel tank.
14. **On 2002 models equipped with fuel pump lockring,** remove locking retaining ring from fuel tank mounting flange using fuel tank locking wrench tool No. T86T-9275-A, or equivalent, and lift up on fuel pump sender flange to gain access to pump module.
15. **On 2003–06 models equipped with fuel pump lockring,** remove locking retaining ring from fuel tank mounting flange using fuel tank locking wrench tool No. 310–075, or equivalent, and lift up on fuel pump sender flange to gain access to pump module.
16. **On models equipped with fuel pump retaining bolts,** remove bolts around fuel pump.
17. **On all models,** remove any dirt accumulation from around fuel pump sealing area, then remove fuel pump.
18. Reverse procedure to install.

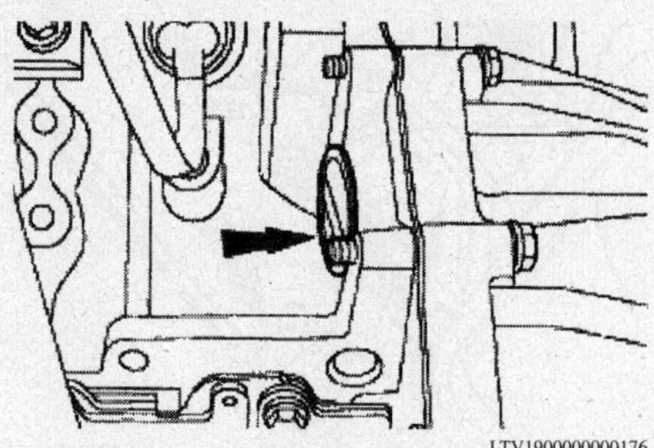

Fig. 15 Cylinder block opening cover. F-150 & Mark LT

Excursion & F-Super Duty

1. Relieve fuel pressure as outlined under "Precautions."
2. Drain fuel from tank, then raise and support vehicle.
3. Disconnect fuel tank filler pipe hose and filler pipe vent tube.
4. If equipped, remove skid plate.
5. Position jack under fuel tank and remove strap bolts.
6. Partially lower fuel tank and disconnect quick connect fittings as outlined under "Quick Disconnect Hoses" in the "4.2L Engine" section.
7. Clean area around fuel pump mounting area.
8. **On models equipped with fuel pump lockring,** remove locking retaining ring from fuel tank mounting flange using fuel tank locking wrench tool No. T97T-9275-A, or equivalent, and lift up on fuel pump sender flange to gain access to pump module.
9. **On models equipped with fuel pump retaining bolts,** remove bolts around fuel pump.
10. **On all models,** reach into tank to disconnect retaining latches by squeezing latches together while pushing down on module to release pump from mounting bracket in bottom of fuel tank.
11. Remove pump assembly and discard fuel pump mounting gasket.
12. Reverse procedure to install.

FUEL FILTER

REPLACE

1. Relieve fuel pressure as outlined under "Precautions."
2. Disconnect fuel lines from filter as outlined under "Quick Disconnect Hoses" in the "4.2L Engine" section.
3. Slide lines from fuel filter and remove.
4. Reverse procedure to install.

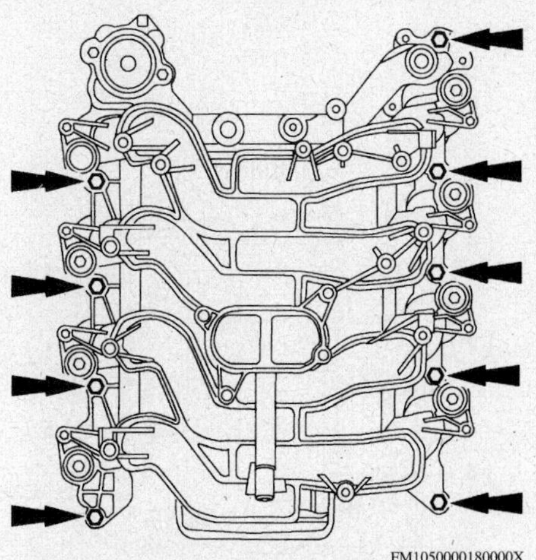

Fig. 16 Intake manifold removal. 5.4L non-supercharged engine

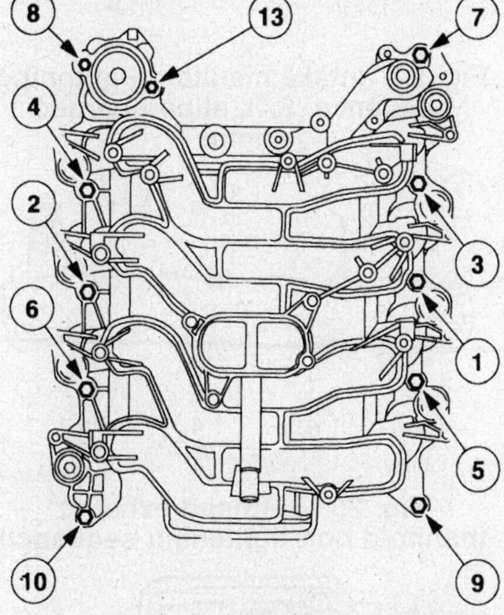

Fig. 19 Intake manifold tightening sequence. Expedition, F-Series & Mark LT w/5.4L non-supercharged engine

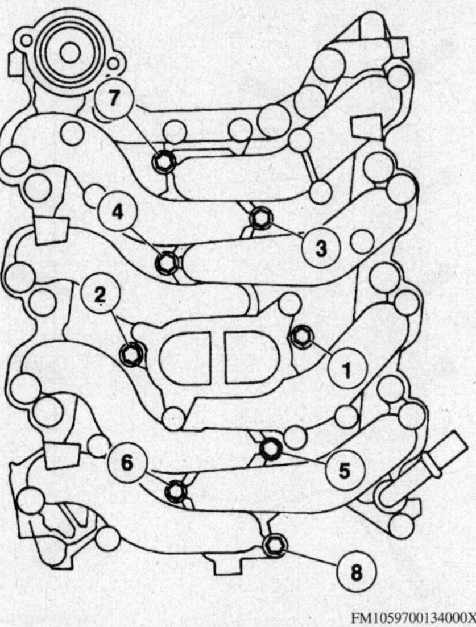

Fig. 17 Lower intake manifold tightening sequence. E-Series except 5.4L engine

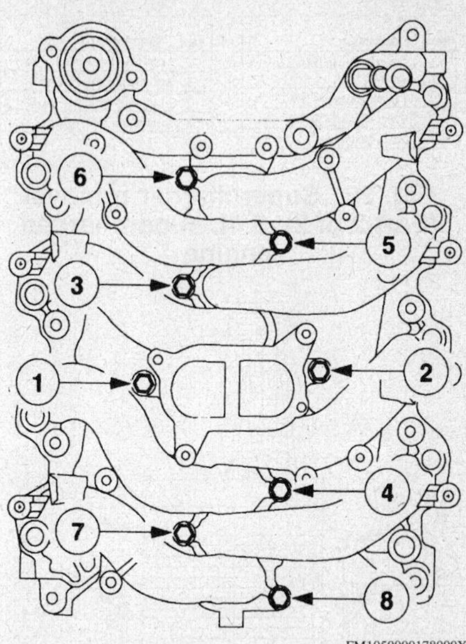

Fig. 18 Lower intake manifold tightening sequence. Expedition, F-Series & Mark LT w/4.6L engine

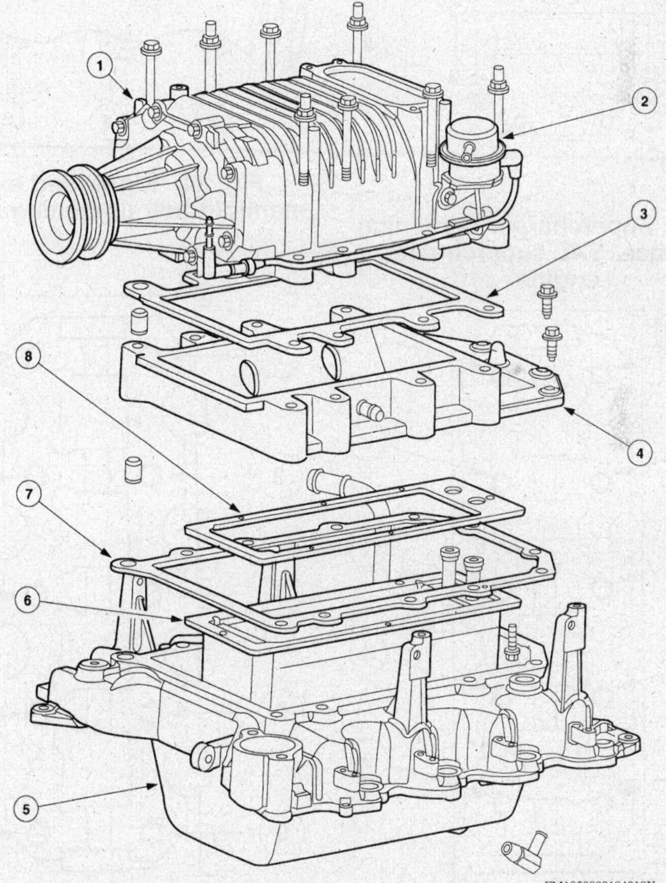

Fig. 20 Supercharger removal (Part 1 of 2). 5.4L supercharged engine

Item	Description
1	Supercharger and plenum assembly
2	Vacuum/actuator/valves
3	Upper intake manifold gasket
4	Intake manifold

Item	Description
5	Lower intake manifold gasket
6	Charge air cooler assembly
7	Lower intake manifold gasket
8	Charge air cooler gasket

FM1050000184020X

Fig. 20 Supercharger removal (Part 2 of 2). 5.4L supercharged engine

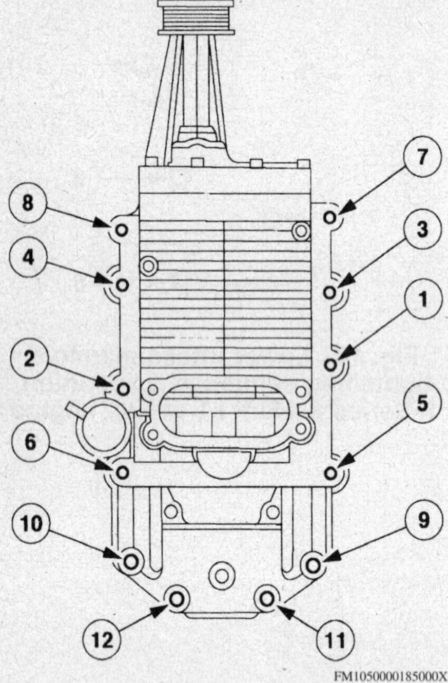

Fig. 23 Supercharger tightening sequence. 5.4L supercharged engine

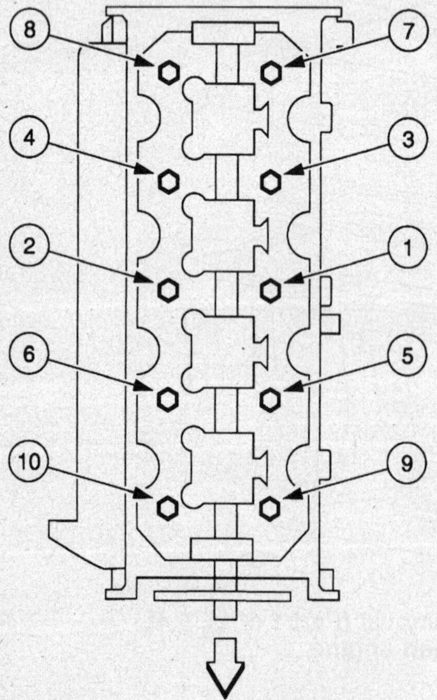

Fig. 26 Lefthand cylinder head tightening sequence

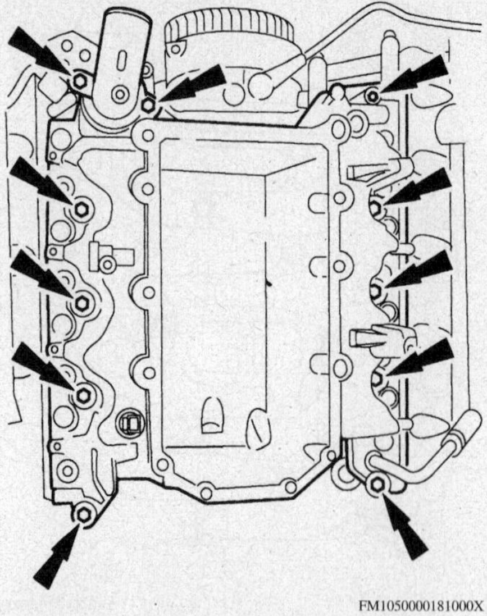

Fig. 21 Intake manifold removal. 5.4L supercharged engine

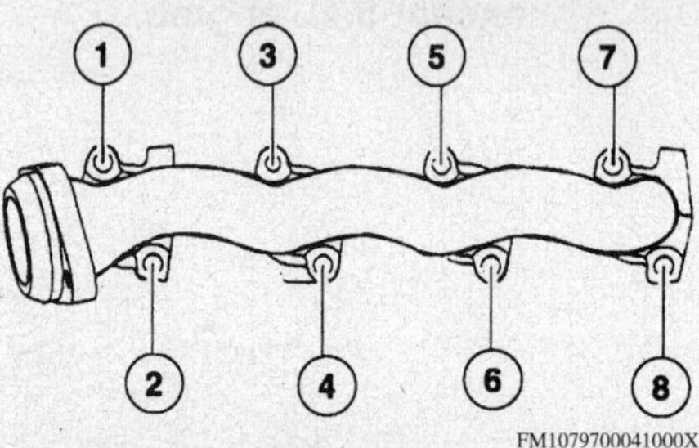

Fig. 24 Righthand exhaust manifold bolt tightening sequence

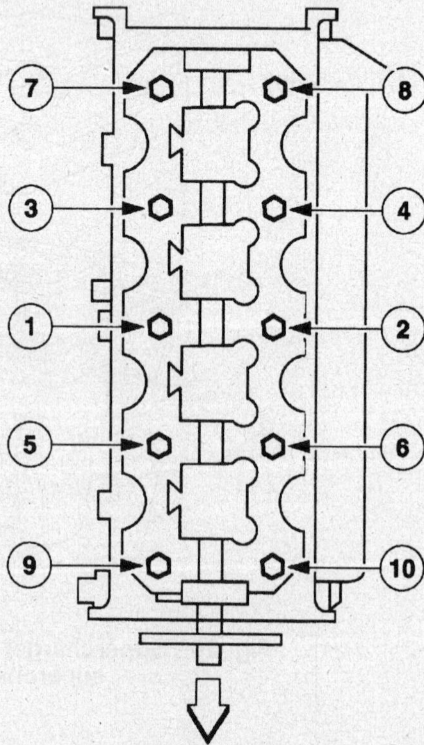

Fig. 27 Righthand cylinder head tightening sequence

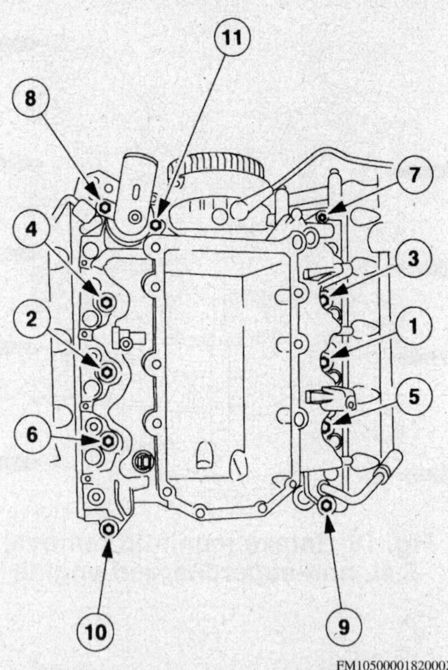

Fig. 22 Intake manifold tightening sequence. 5.4L supercharged engine

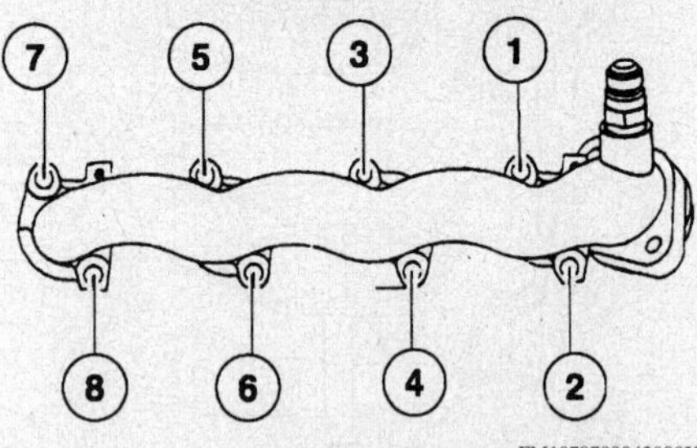

Fig. 25 Lefthand exhaust manifold bolt tightening sequence

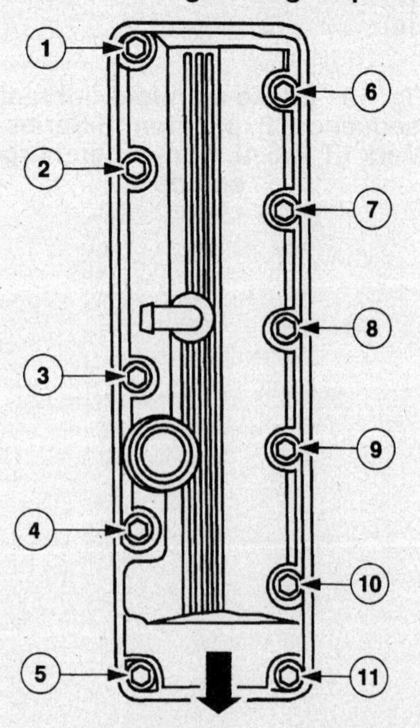

Fig. 28 Lefthand valve cover tightening sequence. 4.6L VIN W engine

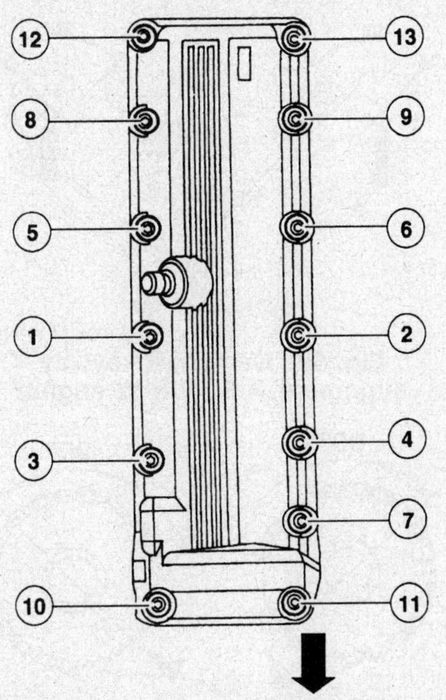

Fig. 29 Lefthand valve cover tightening sequence. 4.6L VIN 6 & 5.4L engine

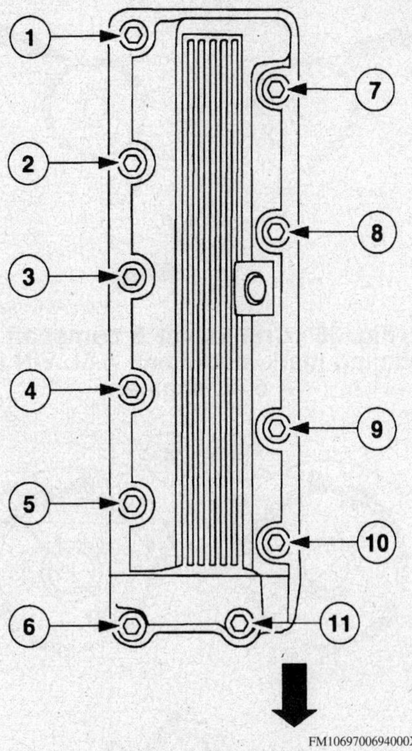

Fig. 30 Righthand valve cover tightening sequence. 4.6L w/VIN W engine

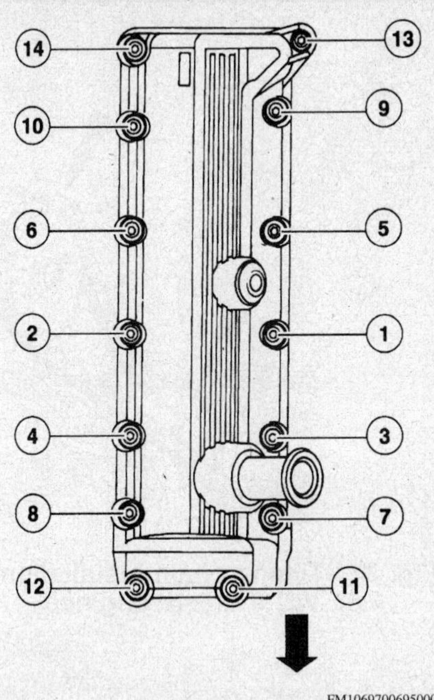

Fig. 31 Righthand valve cover tightening sequence. 4.6L w/VIN 6 & 5.4L engines

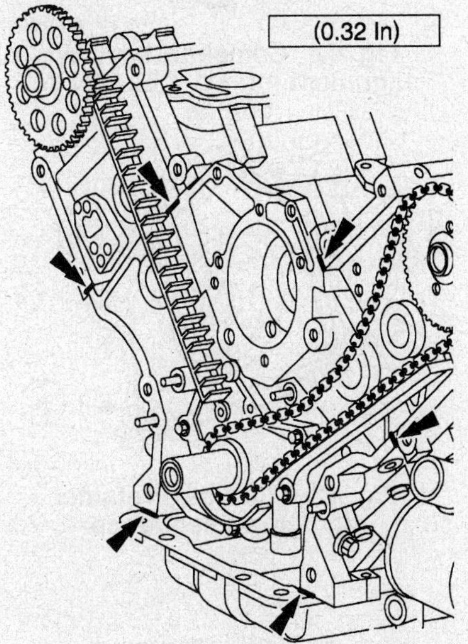

Fig. 32 Front cover silicone application

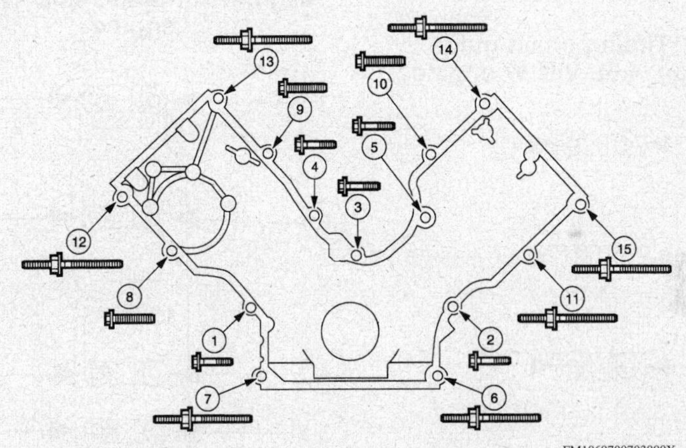

Fig. 33 Front cover tightening sequence

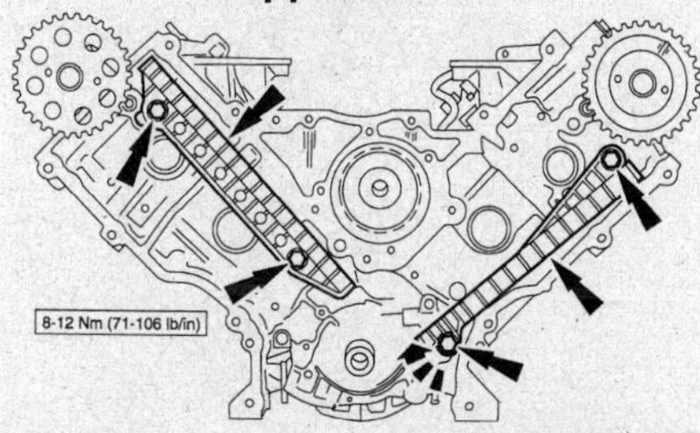

Fig. 34 Timing chain guide installation. 4.6L VIN 6 & 5.4L engines

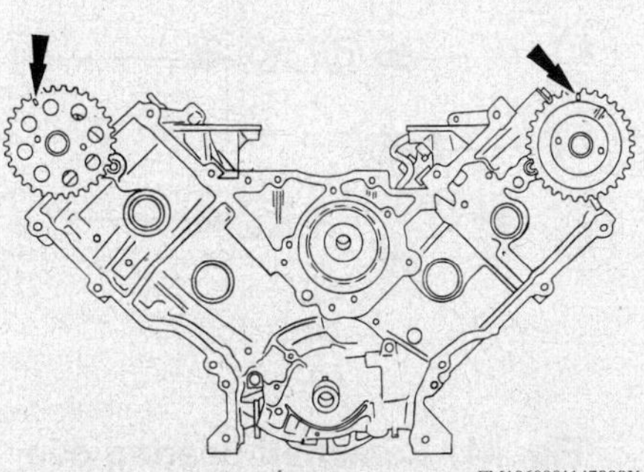

Fig. 35 Camshaft timing mark alignment. 4.6L VIN 6 & 5.4L engines

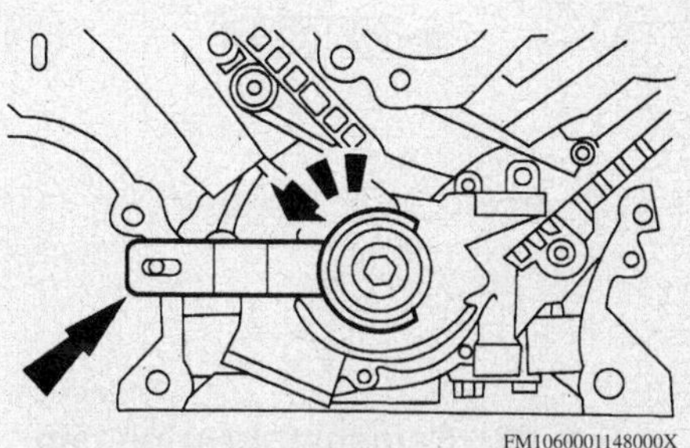

Fig. 36 Crankshaft alignment. 4.6L VIN 6 & 5.4L engines

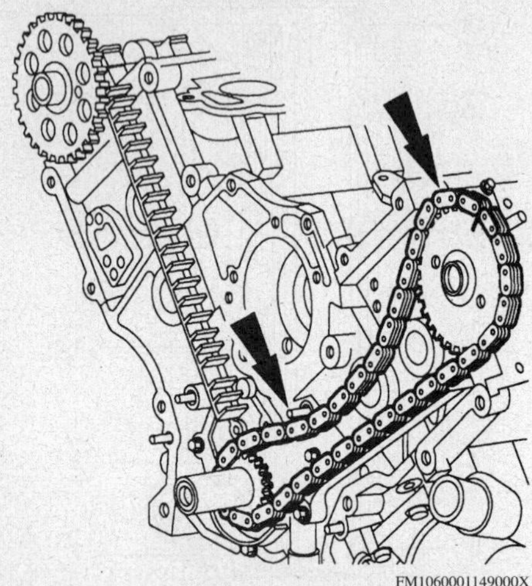

Fig. 37 Timing chain installation. 4.6L VIN 6 & 5.4L engines

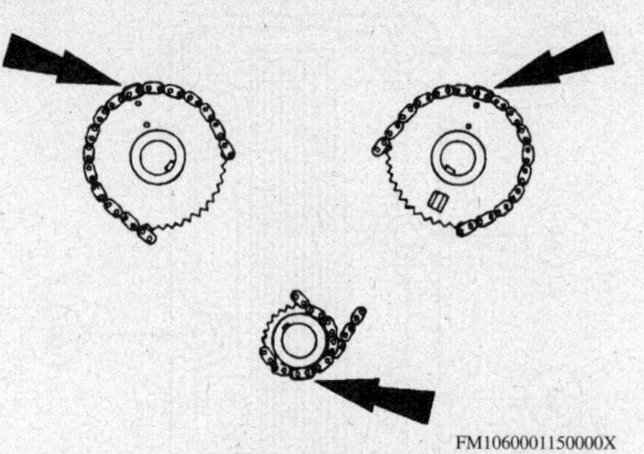

Fig. 38 Crankshaft & camshaft timing mark alignment. 4.6L VIN 6 & 5.4L engines

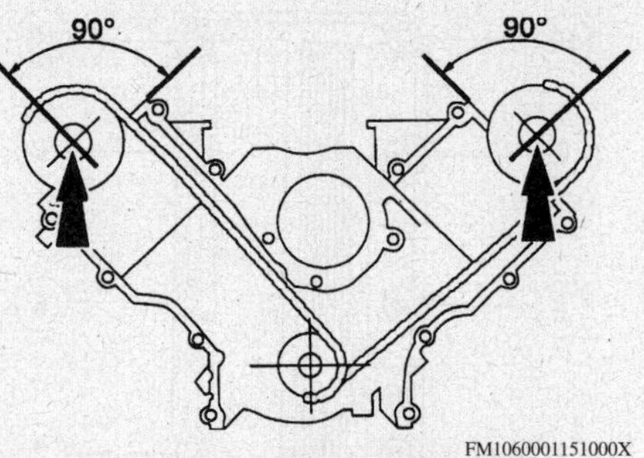

Fig. 39 Camshaft keyway alignment. 4.6L VIN W engine

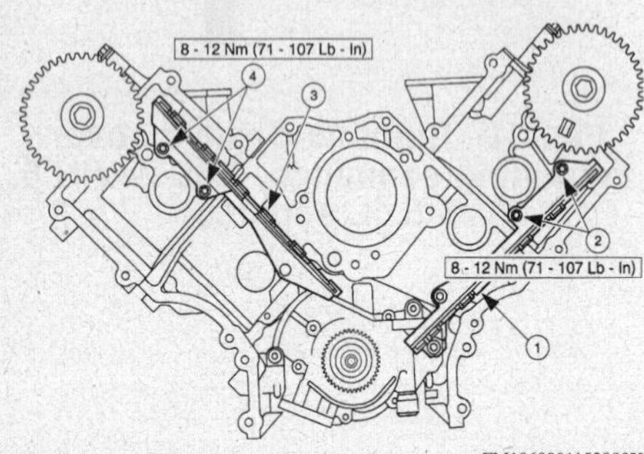

Fig. 40 Timing chain guide installation. 4.6L VIN W engine

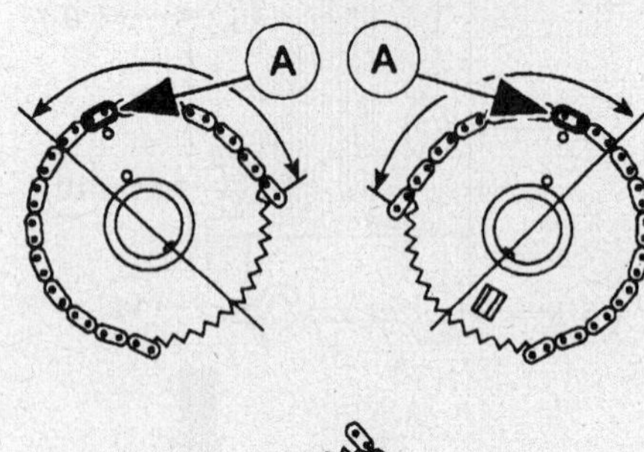

Fig. 41 Camshaft & crankshaft alignment marks. 4.6L VIN W engine

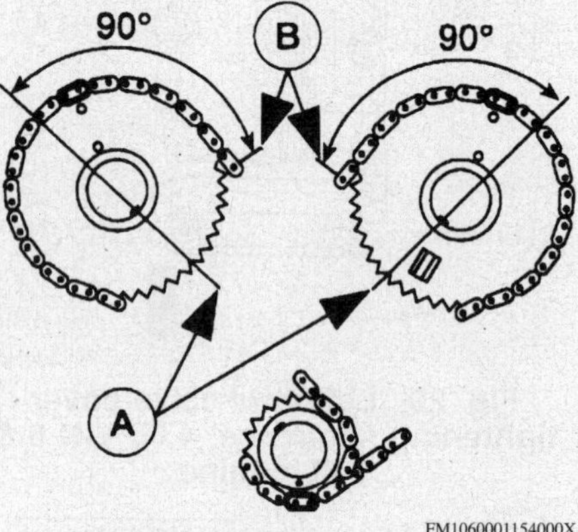

Fig. 42 Camshaft keyway alignment marks. 4.6L VIN W engine

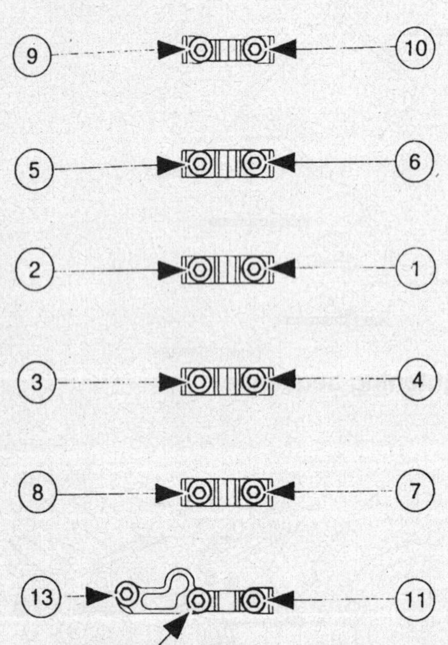

Fig. 43 Camshaft bearing cap tightening sequence. 4.6L VIN 6 & 5.4L engines

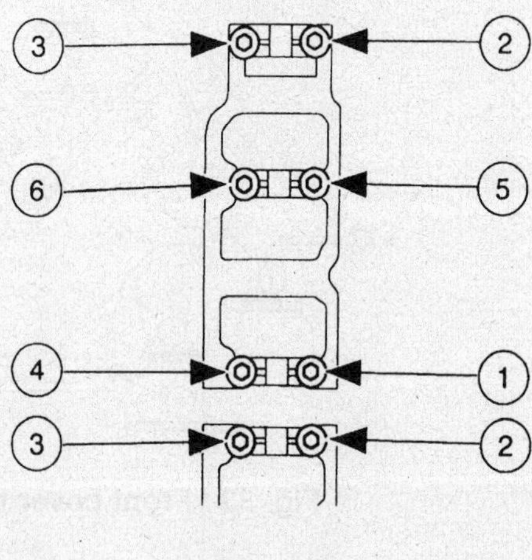

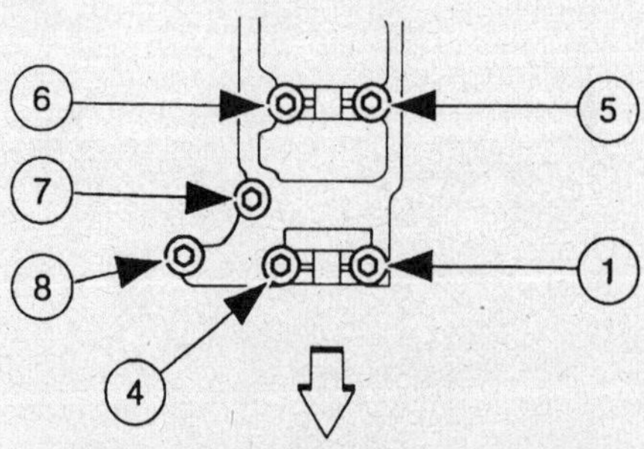

Fig. 44 Camshaft bearing cap tightening sequence. 4.6L VIN W engine

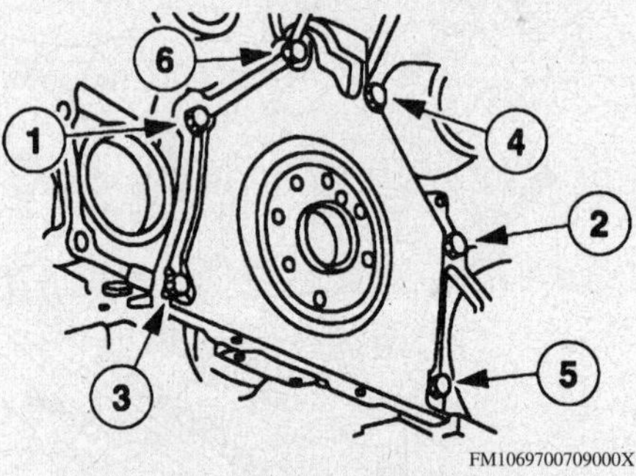

Fig. 45 Rear seal retainer tightening sequence

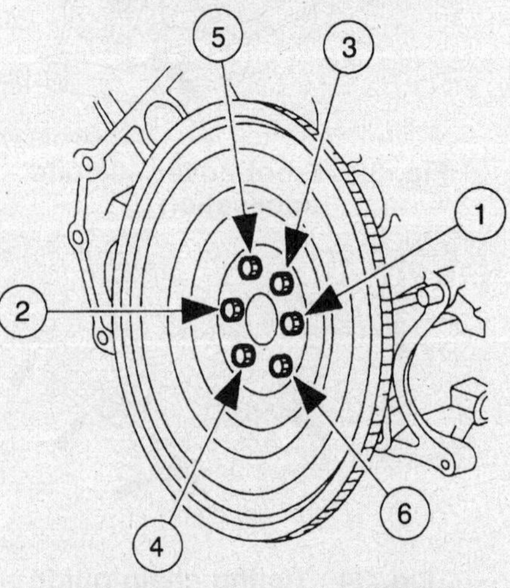

Fig. 46 Flywheel bolt tightening sequence. 4.6L VIN W engine

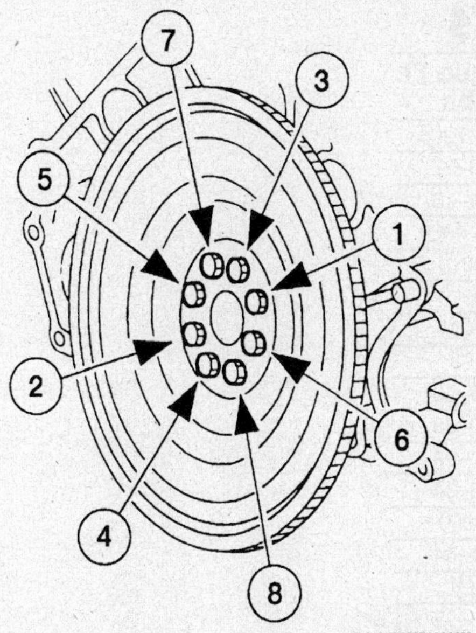

Fig. 47 Flywheel bolt tightening sequence. 4.6L VIN 6 & 5.4L engines

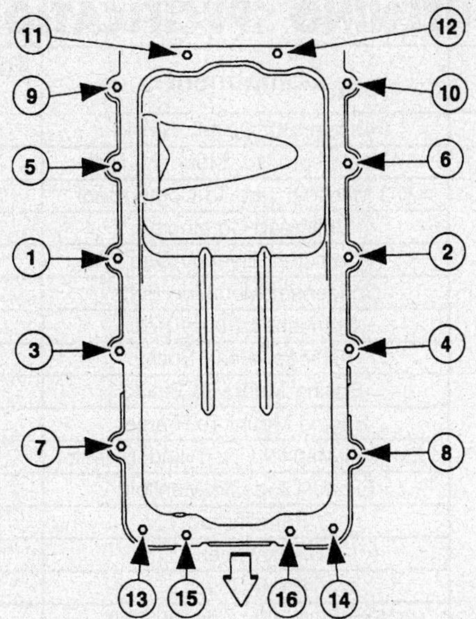

Fig. 48 Oil pan tightening sequence

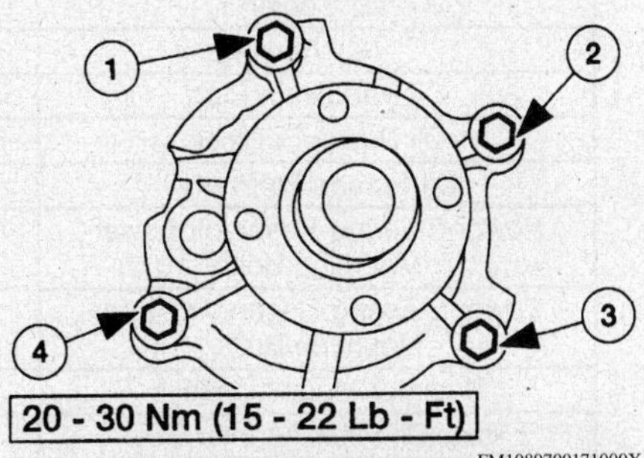

Fig. 50 Water pump tightening sequence

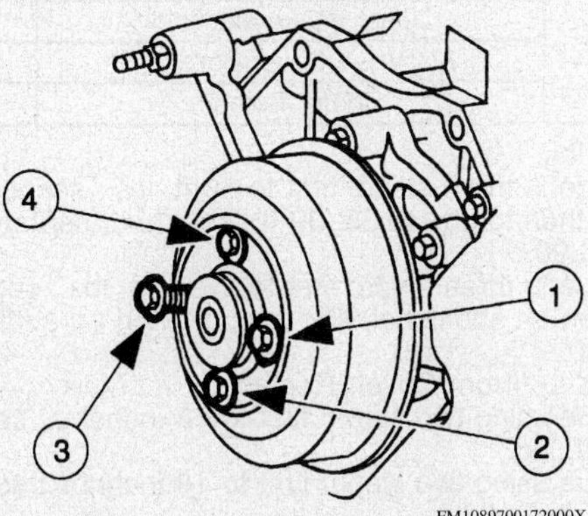

Fig. 51 Water pump pulley tightening sequence

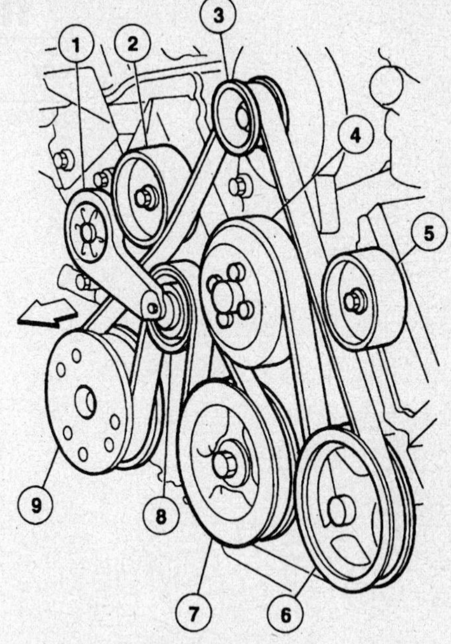

Item	Description
1	Drive Belt Tensioner
2	Belt Idler Pulley
3	Generator Pulley
4	Water Pump Pulley
5	Belt Idler Pulley
6	Power Steering Pump Pulley
7	Crankshaft Vibration Damper and Pulley
8	Drive Belt Tensioner Pulley
9	A/C Clutch Pulley (If Equipped)

FM1069800520000X

Fig. 49 Serpentine drive belt routing

TIGHTENING SPECIFICATIONS

Year	Component	Torque Ft. Lbs.
2002–06	Accelerator Splash Shield	53–72①
	A/C Compressor Mounting Bolt	18–22
	A/C Manifold Line To Compressor	14–18
	Bulkhead Connector	36–49①
	Camshaft Bearing Cap	80①
	Condenser Mounting Bolts	80①
	Crankshaft Pulley Bolt	②
	Cylinder Head Bolts	③
	Engine Mount To Block	39–53
	Engine Mount To Frame	50–68
	Exhaust Manifold To Cylinder Head	17–19
	Exhaust Pipe To Manifold	25–34
	Fan Shroud	80①
	Flywheel	54–64
	Front Cover	④
	Front Oil Filter Adapter Bolt	15–22
	Fuel Pump Mounting Bolts	80①
	Fuel Tank Strap	33–46
	Lower Intake Manifold	⑤
	Oil Cooler	41–44
	Oil Pan	⑥
	Oil Pan Drain Plug	8–12
	Oil Pump To Block	80①
	Oil Screen To Pump	80①
	Power Steering Reservoir Lower Mounting Bolts	26–33
	Power Steering Reservoir Upper Mounting Bolts	80①
	Radiator Mounting Bolts	18
	Rear Oil Filter Adapter Bolt	29–40
	Starter Relay Cable	48①
	Timing Chain Tensioner Bolts	15–22
	Transmission Cooler Lines	11–17
	Upper Intake Manifold	⑦
	Valve Cover Bolts	80①
	Water Pump	15–22

① — Inch lbs.
② — Torque in three steps: first to 66 ft. lbs.; second, loosen bolt, then torque to 35–39 ft. lbs.; third, tighten an additional 90.°
③ — Torque in three steps: first to 27-32 ft. lbs.; second, tighten an additional 90°; third, tighten an additional 85–90.°
④ — Refer to "Front Cover, Replace."
⑤ — Torque using two steps: first to 18 inch lbs.; second to 6–9 ft. lbs.
⑥ — Torque using two steps: first to 18 inch lbs.; second to 15 ft. lbs. +90.°
⑦ — Torque using two steps: first to 18 inch lbs.; second to 15–22 ft. lbs.

5.4L DOHC Gasoline Engine

NOTE: On Air Bag Equipped Models, Refer To "Air Bag System Precautions" Located In The Front Of This Manual For System Disarming & Arming Procedures.

NOTE: Refer To "Computer Relearn Procedures" Located In The Front Of This Manual When Battery Power To The Computer Has Been Interrupted.

INDEX

PRECAUTIONS

Air Bag Systems

Refer to "Air Bag System Precautions" in the front of this manual for system disarming and arming procedures.

Air Suspension Systems

Models equipped with automatic leveling systems should have power to this system shut off whenever vehicle is raised or when suspension system components are serviced. Failure to shut off this system could allow this system to operate during service procedures and cause vehicle to shift positions.

Battery Ground Cable

Prior to service, disconnect battery ground cable and isolate as required.

Fuel System Pressure Relief

2002-03

The fuel system remains under high pressure even when the engine is not running. To avoid injury or fire, release pressure from the fuel system before disconnecting any fuel line. Proceed as follows:

1. Remove fuel tank cap to release residual fuel pressure from tank.
2. Connect fuel pressure gauge tool No. T80L-9974-B, or equivalent, to valve located on the fuel rail.
3. Gradually open testing kit valve to relieve fuel pressure in system. Drain fuel into suitable container or return to fuel tank.
4. To avoid unrequired fuel spillage and fire hazard, any time fuel lines are disconnected, ignition switch should be in Off position.
5. When repair is completed, turn ignition On and Off several times to pressurize fuel system. Do not start engine.
6. Inspect for fuel leaks at pressure regulator, fuel injectors and fuel fittings. Repair as required.

2004-06

1. Remove splash shield located on lefthand frame rail under driver's side door.
2. Disconnect fuel pump/tank sender harness electrical connector.
3. Start engine and allow it to idle until it stalls.
4. After engine stalls, crank engine for approximately five seconds to ensure fuel rail pressure has been released.
5. Turn ignition switch to OFF position.
6. After fuel system service is complete, connect electrical connector.
7. Reposition splash shield and install a new pushpin.
8. Cycle ignition switch and wait 3 seconds to pressurize fuel system. Inspect for leaks before starting engine.

QUICK DISCONNECT HOSES

Refer to "Quick Disconnect Hoses" under "4.2L Engine" section.

ENGINE MOUNT

REPLACE

1. Remove lower intake manifold as outlined in "Intake Manifold, Replace."
2. Remove cooling fan, then the alternator.
3. Install three bar engine support tool No. 303-F070, or equivalent.
4. Raise and support vehicle.
5. Remove upper mount bolt.
6. Partially lower vehicle, then remove inner fenderwell.
7. Remove righthand side mount bolt.
8. Lower vehicle, then raise engine 2.5 inches.
9. Raise vehicle.
10. Remove remaining engine mount bolts, then the engine mount.
11. Reverse procedure to install. Tighten fasteners to specification.

ENGINE

REPLACE

1. Remove vehicle hood.
2. Drain coolant into suitable container.
3. Recover A/C refrigerant as outlined under "Air Conditioning" chapter.

4. Remove lower intake manifold as outlined under "Intake Manifold, Replace."
5. Disconnect powertrain control module electrical connectors, then the powertrain control module.
6. Disconnect auxiliary heater hoses at righthand side valve cover.
7. Disconnect heater hoses at heater core.
8. Disconnect A/C hoses from junction block.
9. Remove safety clips, then disconnect spring lock couplers at evaporator core.
10. Rotate accessory belt tensioner counterclockwise to remove tension from belt, then remove belt.
11. Disconnect alternator electrical connectors, then remove alternator.
12. Remove power steering pump pulley with removal tool No. 211–016, or equivalent.
13. Remove nuts, then disconnect transmission cooler tube and power steering hose brackets.
14. Disconnect power steering pressure hose, drain fluid into suitable container.
15. Remove mounting bolts, then position power steering pump out of way.
16. Disconnect EGR valve tube nut from lefthand exhaust manifold, then remove tube.
17. Remove engine noise shield.
18. Remove PCV valve and hose assembly.
19. Remove PCV tube assembly from vehicle.
20. Disconnect ground wire from body.
21. Disconnect vacuum hose, then remove vacuum harness.
22. Disconnect main engine harness electrical connector.
23. Raise and support vehicle.
24. Remove skid plate.
25. Working through righthand fenderwell, remove transmission filler tube to engine block bolt.
26. Disconnect heated oxygen sensor electrical connectors.
27. Disconnect dual converter Y-pipe.
28. Remove starter.
29. Disconnect A/C clutch electrical connector.
30. Remove mounting bolts and position A/C compressor aside.
31. Disconnect crankshaft position sensor electrical connector.
32. Remove oil filter.
33. Drain engine oil into suitable container.
34. Remove lower radiator hose.
35. Remove inspection plate, then the flexplate to torque converter nut access plug.
36. Mark one stud and flexplate for assembly reference.
37. Remove torque converter nuts.
38. Remove lower transmission to engine bolts.
39. Remove bolt from lefthand motor mount, then the nut from righthand motor mount.
40. Lower vehicle.
41. Support transmission with wood block and suitable floor jack.

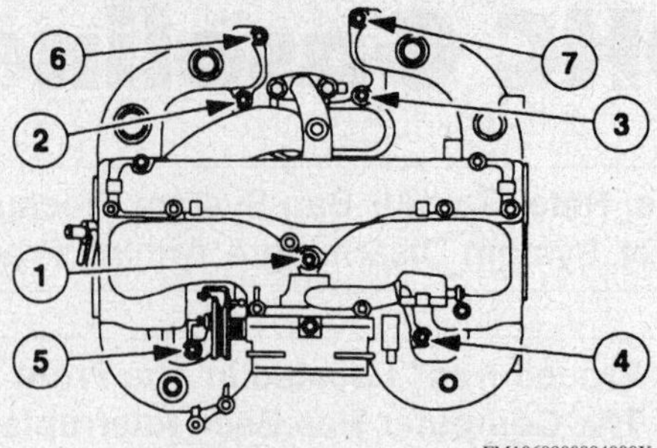

Fig. 1 Upper intake manifold bolt tightening sequence

42. **On models equipped with 4WD,** disconnect transfer case vent hose from bracket and position aside to gain access to upper transmission to engine bolts. Remove upper transmission to engine bolts.
43. **On all models,** install suitable engine lifting device to engine.
44. Remove engine from vehicle.
45. Reverse procedure to install.

INTAKE MANIFOLD

REPLACE

Upper

1. Remove air cleaner outlet tube.
2. Remove engine appearance cover.
3. Disconnect accelerator cable, speed control cable and return spring.
4. Remove cable bracket retaining bolts and position bracket aside.
5. Disconnect EVAP return line.
6. Disconnect Positive Crankcase Ventilation (PCV) tube from intake manifold.
7. Remove PCV valve from valve cover.
8. Disconnect PCV valve tube from water heated fitting, then remove tube assembly.
9. Disconnect coolant lines.
10. Disconnect electrical connector from communication valve.
11. Disconnect electrical connector from intake tuning valve.
12. Remove wiring harness shield bolts and clips, then the shield.
13. Remove balance tube from engine.
14. Remove and discard gaskets.
15. Disconnect throttle position sensor, then the idle air control motor.
16. Disconnect vacuum lines and electrical connector from EGR vacuum regulator.
17. Disconnect two hoses and electrical connector from differential feedback EGR.
18. Remove power steering reservoir bracket bolts and position aside.
19. Remove oil fill tube stud and position aside.
20. Disconnect brake booster vacuum line.
21. Disconnect vacuum line from EGR valve.
22. Remove EGR adapter retaining bolts.
23. Remove upper intake manifold retaining bolts, then the manifold.
24. Reverse procedure to install, noting the following:
    a. **Torque** intake manifold retaining bolts to 89 inch lbs., then an additional 90° using sequence outlined in **Fig. 1.**
    b. Tighten fasteners to specification.

Lower

1. Drain engine coolant into suitable container.
2. Remove upper intake manifold as previously outlined.
3. Disconnect fuel lines, engine water bypass hose and water temperature indicator sender electrical connector.
4. Disconnect upper radiator hose, heater water inlet hose and heated PCV water heated fitting inlet hose.
5. Remove four upper alternator support bracket bolts.
6. Disconnect eight fuel injectors.
7. Disconnect vacuum line from fuel injector pressure regulator and position aside.
8. Remove lower intake manifold retaining bolts, then the lower intake manifold.
9. Reverse procedure to install, noting the following:
    a. Lower intake manifold bolts should be hand tightened starting with positions 7–12, then 1–6.
    b. **Torque** lower intake manifold bolts to 89 inch lbs., then an additional 90° in sequence, **Fig. 2.**

EXHAUST MANIFOLD

REPLACE

Right

2002

1. Raise and support vehicle.
2. Remove four nuts from Y-pipe.
3. Partially lower vehicle.
4. Remove righthand front fender splash shield.
5. Remove starter cable harness bolt and position cable aside.
6. Remove exhaust manifold retaining nuts, then the exhaust manifold.
7. Reverse procedure to install. Tighten bolts to specification in sequence, **Fig. 3.**

2003

1. Remove lower intake manifold as outlined in "Intake Manifold, Replace."
2. Install tool No. 303–639, or equivalent, using alternator lower mounting bolts.
3. Install tool No. 303–F070, or equivalent, and support engine.
4. Remove starter, righthand wheel, and righthand fender splash shield.
5. Disconnect A/C compressor electrical connector.
6. Remove A/C compressor bolts and position compressor aside.
7. Disconnect HO2S electrical connectors.
8. Remove attaching nuts from righthand and lefthand Y-pipes.

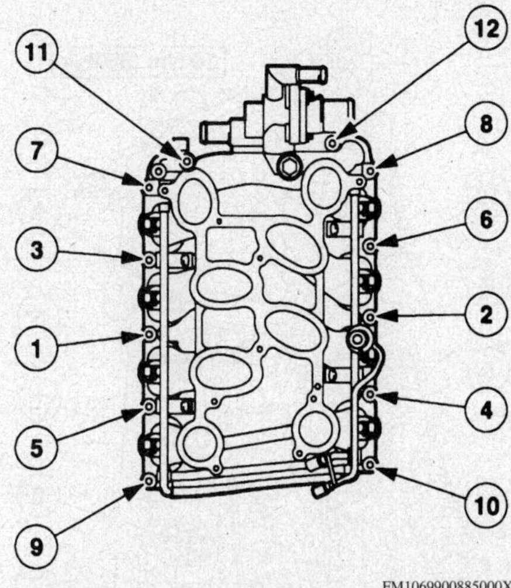

Fig. 2 Lower intake manifold bolts tightening sequence

9. Index-mark driveshaft yoke and pinion flange, then remove driveshaft bolts.
10. Support driveshaft and move aside.
11. Remove transmission to crossmember attaching nuts.
12. Remove bolt from lefthand motor mount.
13. Remove attaching nut from righthand motor mount.
14. Remove righthand motor mount from engine.
15. Raise engine approximately 2 inches.
16. Remove exhaust manifold retaining nuts, then the exhaust manifold.
17. Reverse procedure to install. Tighten bolts to specification in sequence, **Fig. 3.**

Left

1. Raise and support vehicle.
2. Remove attaching nuts from Y-pipe.
3. Partially lower vehicle.
4. Remove lefthand front fender splash shield.
5. Disconnect EGR to exhaust manifold tube.
6. Remove exhaust manifold retaining bolts, then the exhaust manifold.
7. Reverse procedure to install. Tighten bolts to specification in sequence, **Fig. 4.**

CYLINDER HEAD

REPLACE

2002

1. Remove valve covers as outlined under "Valve Cover, Replace."
2. Remove intake manifold as outlined under "Intake Manifold, Replace."
3. Remove timing chains as outlined under "Timing Chain, Replace."
4. Remove exhaust manifolds as outlined under "Exhaust Manifold, Replace."
5. Remove engine control sensor wiring from engine.

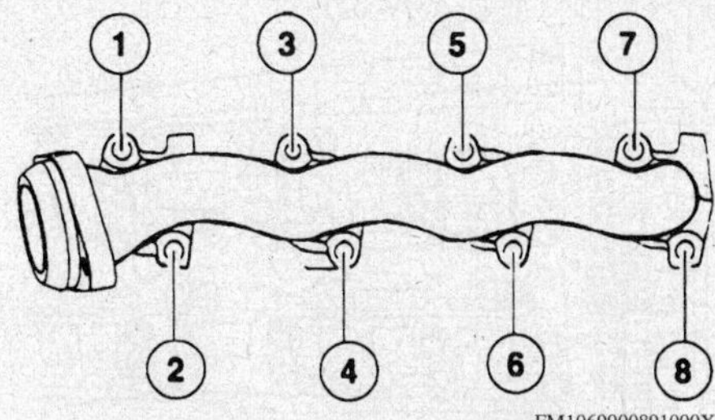

Fig. 3 Righthand exhaust manifold tightening sequence

6. Remove heater return tube, then the KS sensors.
7. Remove cylinder head attaching bolts, then the cylinder heads.
8. Reverse procedure to install, noting the following:
   a. **Cylinder head bolts should be replaced with new bolts.**
   b. Tighten cylinder heads bolts in three steps using sequence outlined, **Fig. 5.** First step, **torque** to 30 ft. lbs. Second step, tighten an additional 90°. Third step, tighten an additional 90°.

2003

1. Remove engine as outlined under "Engine, Replace."
2. Remove flexplate/flywheel and install engine on suitable engine stand.
3. Remove righthand engine mount.
4. Remove cylinder block drain plugs, and drain coolant into suitable container.
5. Disconnect radio interference capacitor, CHT sensor, CMP sensor, knock sensor, CKP sensor, and oil pressure switch electrical connectors.
6. Remove engine control sensor wiring harness.
7. Remove both radio interference capacitors.
8. Remove crankcase ventilation tube from the lefthand valve cover.
9. Remove valve covers.
10. Remove front engine cover as outlined under "Front Cover, Replace."
11. Remove timing chain as outlined under "Timing Chain, Replace."
12. Remove exhaust manifolds as outlined under "Exhaust Manifold, Replace."
13. Remove oil dipstick tube.
14. Install tool No. 303–572, or equivalent, on both ends of cylinder head.
15. Remove hydraulic lash adjusters. **Hydraulic lash adjusters must be installed in their original location.**
16. Remove righthand and lefthand cylinder heads.
17. Reverse procedure to install, noting the following:
   a. **Cylinder head bolts must be replaced with new bolts.**
   b. Tighten cylinder heads bolts in three steps using sequence outlined, **Fig. 5.** First step, **torque** to 30 ft. lbs. Second step, tighten an additional 90°. Third step, tighten an additional 90°.

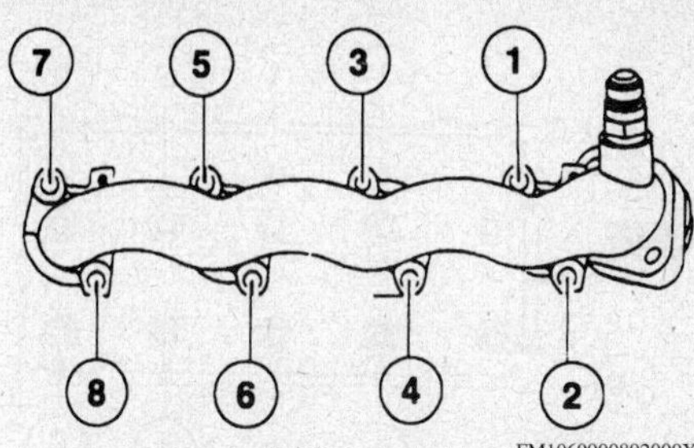

Fig. 4 Lefthand exhaust manifold tightening sequence

VALVE COVER

REPLACE

1. Remove upper intake manifold as outlined in this section.
2. **On lefthand side valve cover,** disconnect EGR tube from exhaust manifold and remove valve and tube assembly.
3. **On both sides,** remove ignition coil cover retaining bolts, then the cover.
4. Disconnect and remove four ignition coils.
5. Disconnect bulkhead wiring connectors.
6. Separate engine control wiring harness from valve cover studs.
7. Remove valve cover retaining bolts and studs, then the valve cover.
8. Reverse procedure to install, noting the following:
   a. Clean and inspect sealing surfaces.
   b. Apply Ford silicone gasket and sealant F7AZ-19554-EA, or equivalent, meeting Ford specification WSK-M2G343-A4 to cylinder head locations, **Fig. 6.**
   c. Tighten valve cover bolts to specification in sequence outlined in **Figs. 7 and 8.**
   d. Tighten fasteners to specification.

FRONT COVER

REPLACE

1. Remove valve covers as outlined in this section.
2. Remove cooling fan.
3. Remove water pump pulley retaining bolts, then the pulley.
4. Remove crankshaft pulley as outlined under "Crankshaft Seal, Replace."
5. Remove hose support.
6. Remove power steering pump bolts and position aside.
7. Remove A/C compressor bolts and position A/C compressor aside.
8. Disconnect Crankshaft Position (CKP) Sensor.
9. Drain engine oil.
10. Remove four front oil pan to front cover bolts.
11. Remove crankshaft front oil seal as outlined under "Crankshaft Seal, Replace."
12. Disconnect Camshaft Position (CMP) Sensor.
13. Remove belt idler pulley.

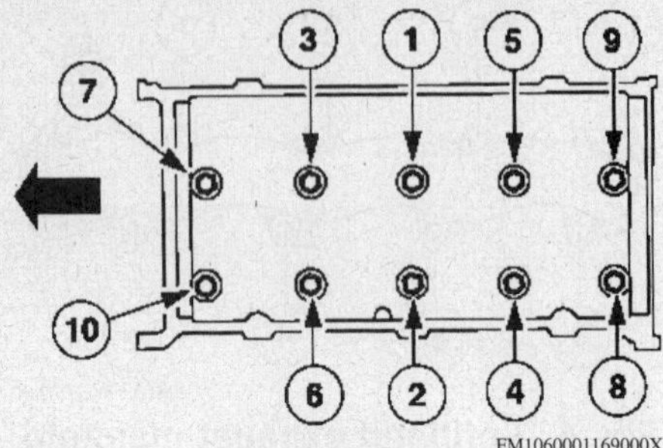

Fig. 5 Cylinder head tightening sequence

14. Remove engine front cover bolts and studs, then the engine front cover.
15. Reverse procedure to install, noting the following:
    a. Apply Ford silicone gasket and sealant F7AZ-19554-EA, or equivalent, meeting Ford specification WSK-M2G343-A4 to front cover, **Fig. 9.**
    b. **Torque** front cover bolts one through five to 18 ft. lbs., **Fig. 10.**
    c. **Torque** front cover bolts six and seven to 37 ft. lbs.
    d. **Torque** front cover bolts 11 through 15 to 18 ft. lbs.
    e. Tighten fasteners to specification.

TIMING CHAIN

REPLACE

With the timing chain removed, avoid turning the camshaft or crankshaft. If movement is required, exercise extreme caution to avoid valve damage caused by piston-to-valve contact.

Engine should only be rotated in a counterclockwise direction.

REMOVAL

1. Remove front cover as outlined under "Front Cover, Replace."
2. Remove crankshaft sensor ring.
3. Position crankshaft as outlined in **Fig. 11** using crankshaft holding tool No. T93P-6303-A, or equivalent.
4. Install camshaft positioning tool No. T93P-6256-A, or equivalents to camshafts.
5. Remove timing chain tensioners, then the tensioner arms.
6. Remove crankshaft holding tool.
7. Remove timing chains with crankshaft sprockets.
8. Remove timing chain guides.

INSTALLATION

1. Compress timing chain tensioner plunger using a suitable vise. **Do not compress ratchet assembly.**
2. Push back ratchet mechanism.
3. Position ratchet arm back into tensioner housing, then insert a suitable pin to tensioner to hold ratchet and plunger.
4. Place reference marks on two links of timing chains at opposite ends if copper links are not visible.
5. Install timing chain guides.

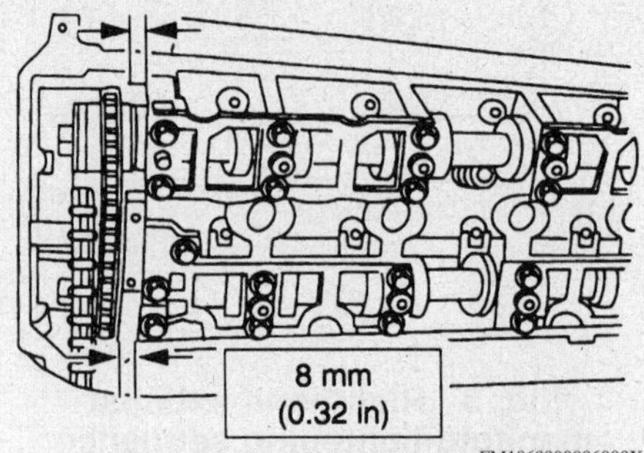

Fig. 6 Cylinder head sealant application points

6. Loosen camshaft holding tools to allow slight camshaft movement.
7. Rotate lefthand camshaft using a suitable camshaft positioning tool until timing mark is at 12 o'clock position, **Fig. 12.**
8. Rotate righthand camshaft using a suitable camshaft positioning tool until timing mark is at 11 o'clock position, **Fig. 12.**
9. Position crankshaft as outlined in **Fig. 11** using crankshaft holding tool No. T93P-6303-A, or equivalent.
10. Remove crankshaft holding tool.
11. Install inner crankshaft sprocket. Ensure long hub is facing outward.
12. Install lefthand timing chain to crankshaft sprocket. Align one marked link with slot on crankshaft sprocket.
13. Install lefthand timing chain to lefthand camshaft sprocket. Ensure 2 marked links and camshaft timing mark are aligned, **Fig. 13.**
14. Install righthand timing chain and sprocket. Ensure long hub of sprocket is facing inward and that marked link of chain and sprocket are aligned.
15. Install righthand timing chain to camshaft sprocket. Ensure 2 marked links of chain are aligned with camshaft sprocket timing mark.
16. Verify all timing marks are aligned properly.
17. Install righthand and lefthand chain tensioner arms, then the chain tensioners.
18. Remove pins from chain tensioners.
19. Remove camshaft holding tools.
20. Install crankshaft sensor ring.
21. Install front cover as outlined under "Front Cover, Replace."

ROLLER FOLLOWER

REPLACE

1. Remove valve cover as outlined under "Valve Cover, Replace."
2. Position piston of cylinder being worked on at bottom of stroke, ensuring camshaft is on base circle.
3. Compress valve spring using valve spring compressor tool No. T93P-6565-AR, or equivalent.
4. Remove roller follower.
5. Repeat steps 1–4 as required.
6. Reverse procedure to install.

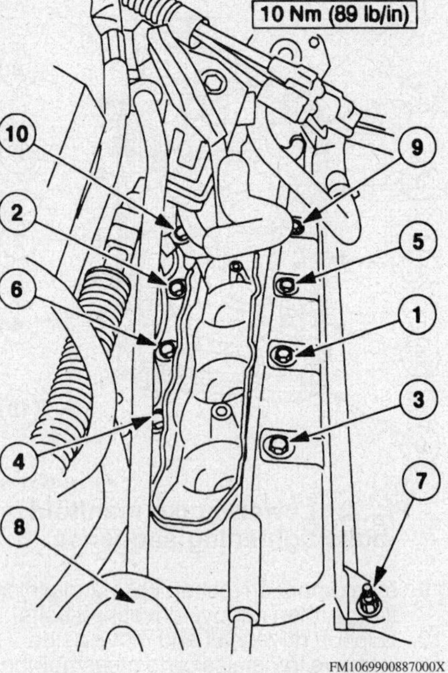

Fig. 7 Valve cover bolts tightening sequence (Righthand side). 5.4L DOHC engine

HYDRAULIC LASH ADJUSTER

REPLACE

1. Remove roller followers as outlined under "Roller Follower, Replace."
2. Remove lash adjusters from cylinder head.
3. Reverse procedure to install.

CAMSHAFT

REPLACE

1. Remove timing chain.
2. Remove hydraulic lash adjusters.
3. Remove camshaft sprocket retaining bolt, then the camshaft sprocket.
4. Compress tensioner and install a lock pin.
5. Remove bolt, washer and spacer.
6. Remove secondary timing chain and camshaft sprocket.
7. Remove tensioner bolts.
8. Remove camshaft bearing cap bolts, then the bearing caps. **Outer bolts on outer cam bearing cap (Exhaust) are longer and must be returned to same location or engine damage may occur.**
9. Remove camshafts.
10. Reverse procedure to install. **Torque** camshaft sprocket bolts to specification.

CRANKSHAFT SEAL

REPLACE

Front

REMOVAL

1. Remove crankshaft pulley as follows:

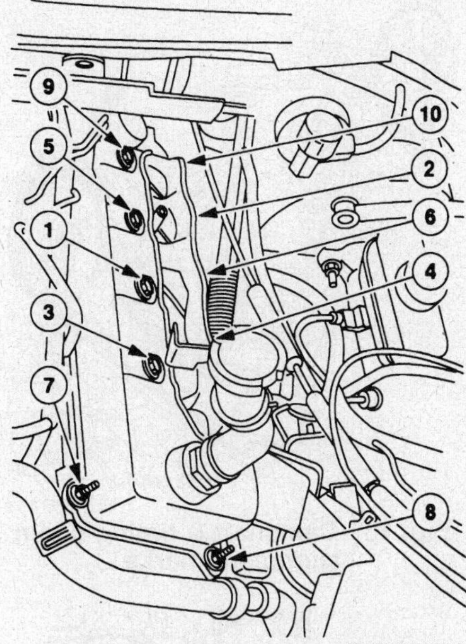

Fig. 8 Valve cover bolts tightening sequence (Lefthand side). 5.4L DOHC engine

a. Release drive belt tensioner, then remove drive belt.
b. Raise and support vehicle.
c. Remove crankshaft pulley center bolt.
d. Remove crankshaft pulley using crankshaft damper tool No. T58P-6316-D, or equivalent.

2. Remove front cover seal using front cover seal tool No. T74P-6700-A, or equivalent.

INSTALLATION

1. Lubricate engine front cover and front oil seal inner lip using Ford super premium SAE 5W-30 motor oil XO-5W30-QSP, or equivalent, meeting Ford specification WSS-M2C153-G.
2. Install front oil seal using crankshaft seal installer/aligner tool No. T88T-6701-A, or equivalent.
3. Install crankshaft pulley as follows:
   a. Apply silicone gasket and sealant F76AZ-19554-EA, or equivalent, meeting Ford specification WSK-M2G323-A4 to woodruff key slot.
   b. Install crank shaft pulley using crankshaft damper tool No. T74P-6316-B, or equivalent.
   c. **Torque** crankshaft pulley bolt to 66 ft. lbs, then loosen bolt one full turn.
   d. **Torque** crankshaft pulley bolt to 37 ft. lbs, then an additional 85–90.°

Rear

REMOVAL

1. Remove transmission as outlined in **MOTOR's "Domestic Transmission, In-Vehicle Service" or "Transmission Service DVD."**
2. Remove flywheel.
3. Remove crankshaft oil slinger using rear crankshaft slinger tool No. T95P-6701-AH and slide hammer tool No. T50T-100-A, or equivalents.
4. Remove crankshaft rear oil seal using rear crankshaft seal tool No. T95P-6701-EH and slide hammer, or equivalents.

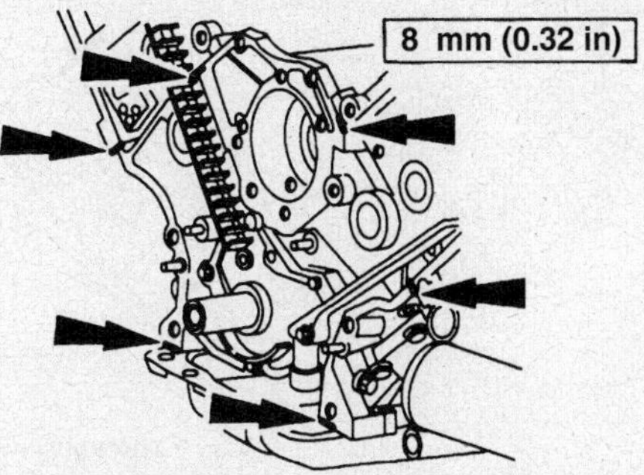

Fig. 9 Front cover sealant application location

INSTALLATION

1. Install crankshaft rear oil seal using rear crankshaft slinger tool No. T95P-6701-CH, or equivalent.
2. Install crankshaft oil slinger using rear crankshaft seal tool No. T95P-6701-BH and rear crankshaft seal adapter tool No. T95P-6701-DH, or equivalents.
3. Install flywheel.
4. Tighten flywheel to specifications in sequence as outlined in **Fig. 14.**

OIL PAN

REPLACE

2WD Models

2002

1. Remove lower intake manifold as outlined in this section.
2. Remove cooling fan.
3. Remove alternator.
4. Install three bar engine support tool No. 303-F070, or equivalent.
5. Raise and support vehicle.
6. Remove two bolts from engine mounts.
7. Drain engine oil.
8. Lower vehicle.
9. Raise engine 2.5 inches.
10. Raise and support vehicle.
11. Remove oil pan retaining bolts, then the oil pan.
12. Reverse procedure to install, noting the following:
    a. Clean mating surfaces.
    b. Apply Ford silicone gasket and sealant F7AZ-19554-EA, or equivalent, meeting Ford specification WSK-M2G323-A4 at rear oil seal retainer to cylinder block sealing surface. **Oil pan and gasket must be secured within four minutes or sealant must be removed and reapplied.**
    c. **Torque** oil pan bolts to 18 inch lbs, then 15 ft. lbs., and finally an additional 60° in sequence, **Fig. 15.**

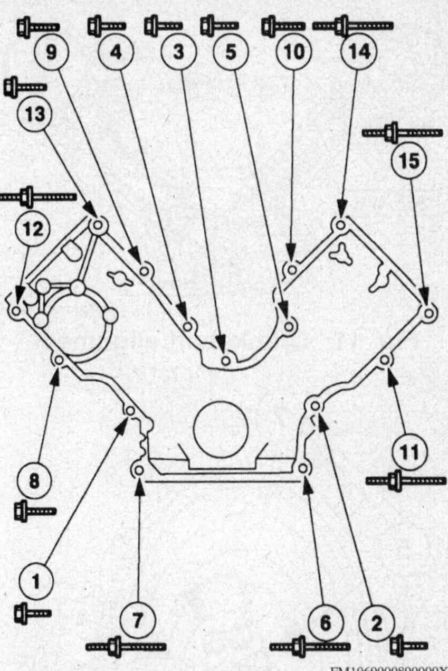

Fig. 10 Front cover bolt location

2003

1. Raise and support vehicle.
2. Drain engine oil into suitable container.
3. Remove frame crossmember bolts, then crossmember.
4. Remove and detach wire harness bracket.
5. Remove oil pan retaining bolts, then oil pan.
6. Reverse procedure to install, noting the following:
   a. Clean mating surfaces.
   b. Apply Ford silicone gasket and sealant F7AZ-19554-EA, or equivalent, meeting Ford specification WSK-M2G323-A4 at rear oil seal retainer to cylinder block sealing surface. **Oil pan and gasket must be secured within four minutes or sealant must be removed and reapplied.**
   c. **Torque** oil pan bolts to 18 inch lbs, then 15 ft. lbs., and finally an additional 60° in sequence, **Fig. 15.**

4WD MODELS

1. Raise and support vehicle.
2. Remove front drive axle assembly.
3. Drain engine oil.
4. Remove oil pan retaining bolts, then the oil pan.
5. Reverse procedure to install, noting the following:
   a. Clean mating surfaces.
   b. Apply Ford silicone gasket and sealant F7AZ-19554-EA, or equivalent, meeting Ford specification WSK-M2G323-A4 at rear oil seal retainer to cylinder block sealing surface. **Oil pan and gasket must be secured within four minutes or sealant must be removed and reapplied.**
   c. **Torque** oil pan bolts to 18 inch lbs, then 15 ft. lbs., and finally an additional 60° in sequence, **Fig. 15.**

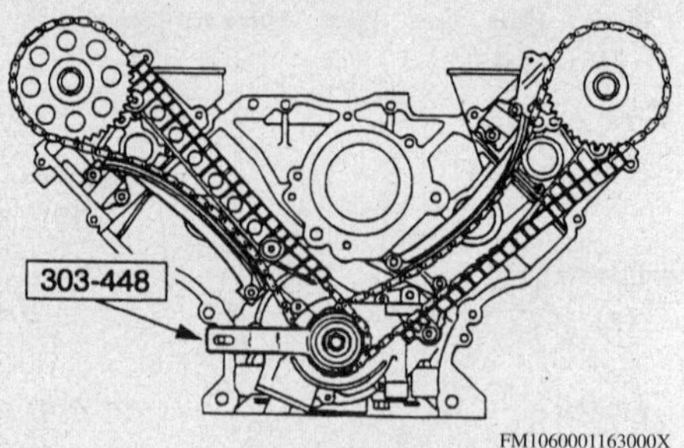

Fig. 11 Crankshaft alignment

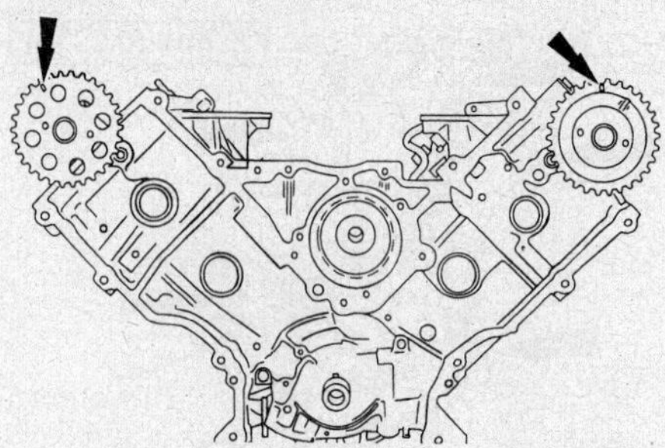

Fig. 12 Camshaft alignment marks

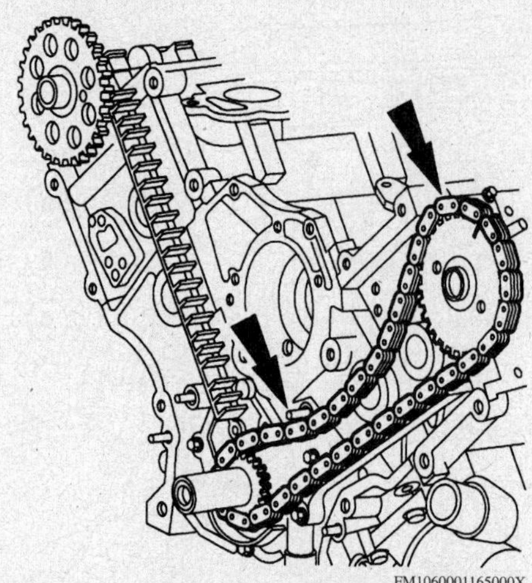

Fig. 13 Camshaft & timing chain alignment marks

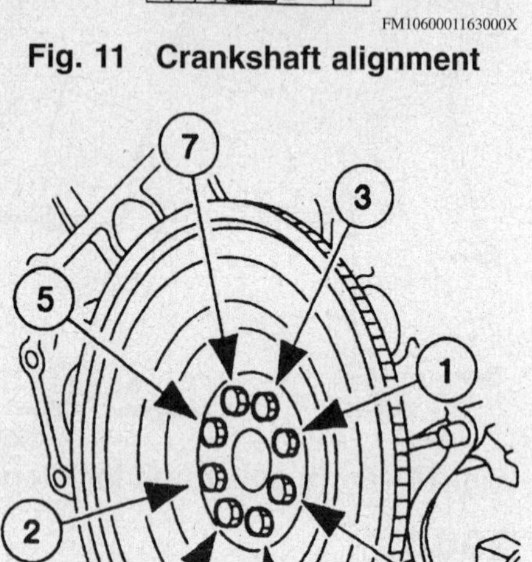

Fig. 14 Flywheel tightening sequence

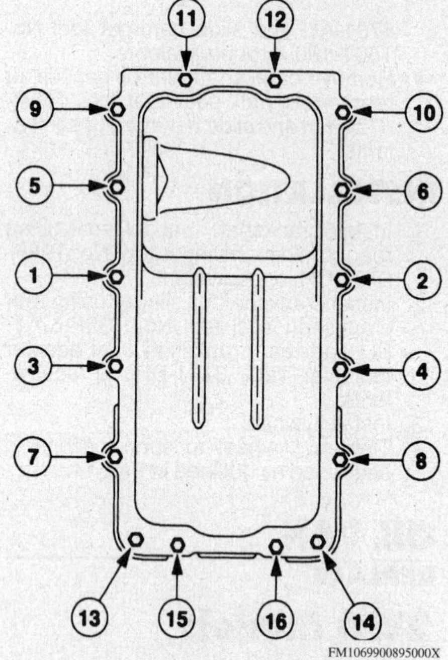

Fig. 15 Oil pan bolt tightening sequence

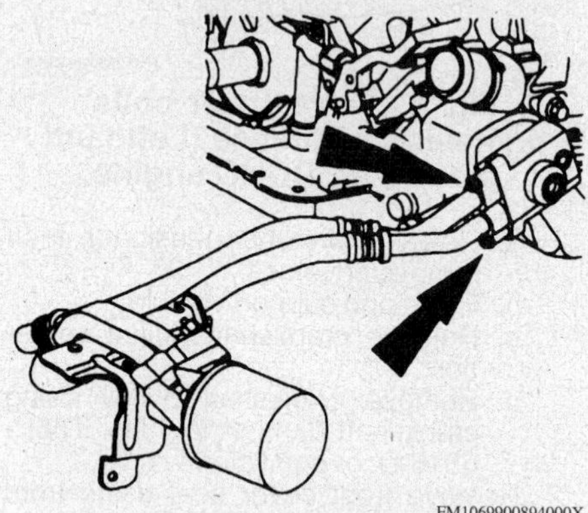

Fig. 16 Oil cooler replacement. 2WD models

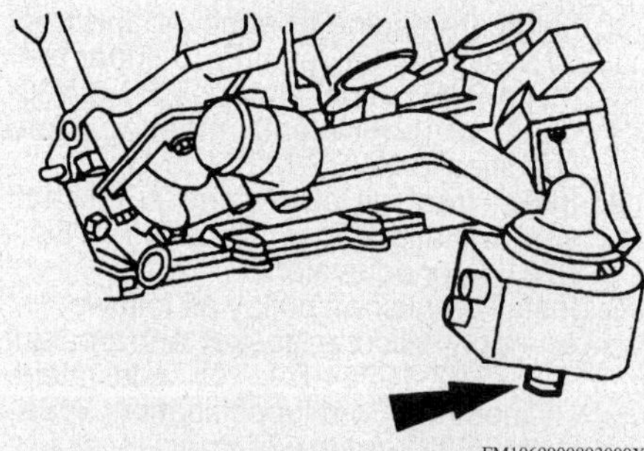

Fig. 17 Oil cooler replacement. 4WD models

OIL COOLER

REPLACE

2WD Models

1. Drain engine cooling system.
2. Remove bolts and position oil filter adapter lines aside.
3. Disconnect hoses.
4. Remove insert, then the oil cooler, **Fig. 16.**
5. Reverse procedure to install.

4WD Models

1. Drain engine cooling system.
2. Drain engine oil.
3. Remove oil bypass filter.
4. Disconnect coolant hoses from oil cooler.
5. Remove insert, then the oil cooler, **Fig. 17.**
6. Reverse procedure to install.

BELT TENSION DATA

Engine	Belt	
	New Lbs.	Used Lbs.
5.4L	110–120①	110–120①

① — Fixed belt application. Systems w/manually-adjusted centers which are bolted in place & considered fixed.

THERMOSTAT

REPLACE

1. Partially drain engine cooling system.
2. Disconnect upper radiator hose, heater water inlet hose and heated PCV inlet hose from water outlet pipe.
3. Remove water hose connection retaining bolts, then the water hose connection.
4. Remove thermostat and O-ring.
5. Reverse procedure to install. Install a new O-ring.

TIGHTENING SPECIFICATIONS

Year	Component	Torque Ft. Lbs.
2002–03	A/C Muffler Nut	18
	Accelerator Cable Bracket	89①
	Appearance Cover Bolts	89①
	Belt Idler Bolt	18
	Bulkhead Wiring Connector Bolts	44①
	Camshaft Sprocket Bolt	82–95
	Communication Valve Bolts	89①
	Crankshaft Pulley Bolt	②
	EGR Adapter Bolts	18
	EGR Valve Tube At Exhaust Manifold	18
	Engine Mount Bolts	59
	Exhaust Manifold Bolts	17–19
	Front Cover	④
	Hose Support Nut	18
	Ignition Coil Cover Bolts	89①
	Intake Manifold Bolts	⑤
	Oil Fill Tube Stud	89①
	Oil Pan Bolts	③
	Power Steering Pump Bolts	18
	Power Steering Reservoir Bracket	18
	Torque Converter Bolts	18
	Transmission Bellhousing Bolts	33
	Valve Cover Bolts	89①②
	Water Pump Pulley Bolts	18
	Wiring Harness Shield Bolts	89①

① — Inch lbs.

② — Refer to "Crankshaft Seal, Replace" for tightening procedure.

③ — Refer to "Oil Pan, Replace" for tightening procedure.

④ — Refer to "Front Cover, Replace" for tightening procedure.

⑤ — Refer to "Intake Manifold, Replace" for tightening procedure.

6.8L Gasoline Engine

NOTE: For Procedures Not Found In This Section, Refer "4.6L & 5.4L Gasoline Engines."

NOTE: On Air Bag Equipped Models, Refer To "Air Bag System Precautions" Located In The Front Of This Manual For System Disarming & Arming Procedures.

NOTE: Refer To "Computer Relearn Procedures" Located In The Front Of This Manual When Battery Power To The Computer Has Been Interrupted.

INDEX

PRECAUTIONS

Air Bag Systems

Refer to "Air Bag System Precautions" in the front of this manual for system disarming and arming procedures.

Air Suspension Systems

Models equipped with automatic leveling systems should have power to this system shut off whenever vehicle is raised or when suspension system components are serviced. Failure to shut off this system could allow this system to operate during service procedures and cause vehicle to shift positions.

Battery Ground Cable

Prior to service, disconnect battery ground cable and isolate as required.

Fuel Pressure Relief, Gasoline

The fuel system remains under high pressure even when the engine is not running. To avoid injury or fire, release pressure from the fuel system before disconnecting any fuel line. Proceed as follows:

1. Remove fuel tank cap to release residual fuel pressure from tank.
2. Connect fuel pressure gauge tool No. T80L-9974-B, or equivalent, to valve located on the fuel rail.
3. Gradually open testing kit valve to relieve fuel pressure in system. Drain fuel into suitable container or return to fuel tank.
4. To avoid unrequired fuel spillage and fire hazard, any time fuel lines are disconnected, ignition switch should be in Off position.
5. When repair is completed, turn ignition On and Off several times to pressurize fuel system. Do not start engine.
6. Inspect for fuel leaks at pressure regulator, fuel injectors and fuel fittings. Repair as required.

Fuel System Pressure Relief, Natural Gas Engines

Refer to "4.6L & 5.4L SOHC Engines."

QUICK DISCONNECT HOSES

Refer to "Quick Disconnect Hoses" under "4.2L Engine" section.

ENGINE MOUNT

REPLACE

E-Series

1. Remove intake manifold as outlined in "Intake Manifold, Replace."
2. Remove fan shroud and engine cooling fan.

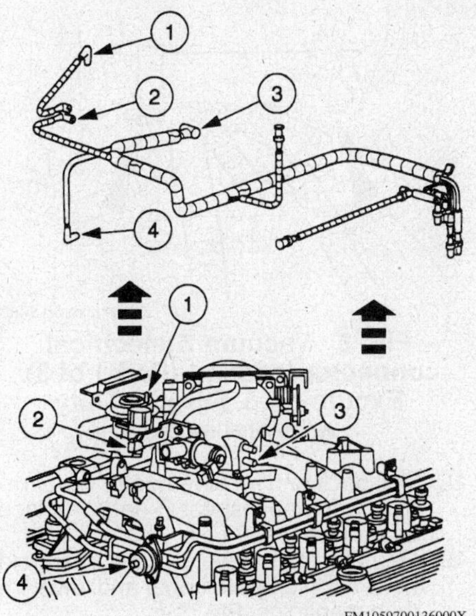

Fig. 1 Engine vacuum harness removal. E-Series

3. Remove radiator upper shield.
4. Remove transmission oil filler tube.
5. Detach wiring harness retainer.
6. Remove two transmission to engine bolts.
7. Install tool No. 303–F047, or equivalent, and 303–F694, or equivalent, then support engine.
8. Remove nuts retaining front engine support insulators (mount) to engine support brackets.
9. For righthand insulator remove starter motor.
10. Raise engine using engine support.
11. Remove engine support insulator bolts and remove insulators from vehicle.
12. reverse procedure to install. Tighten all nuts and bolts to specifications.

EXCURSION & F-SUPER DUTY SERIES

Refer to "4.6L & 5.4L SOHC Gasoline Engines" for this procedure.

ENGINE

REPLACE

E-Series

1. Recover refrigerant as outlined in "Air Conditioning" chapter.
2. Disconnect 42 pin and two 16 pin connectors, then remove nut and harness mounting bracket.
3. Remove intake manifold as outlined under "Intake Manifold, Replace."
4. Remove air deflector, radiator grille, radiator grille opening panel and upper and lower core supports.
5. Remove radiator as outlined under "Radiator, Replace."
6. Remove headlamps and side marker lamps.
7. Remove air conditioning condenser.
8. Remove drive belt.
9. Disconnect power steering reservoir

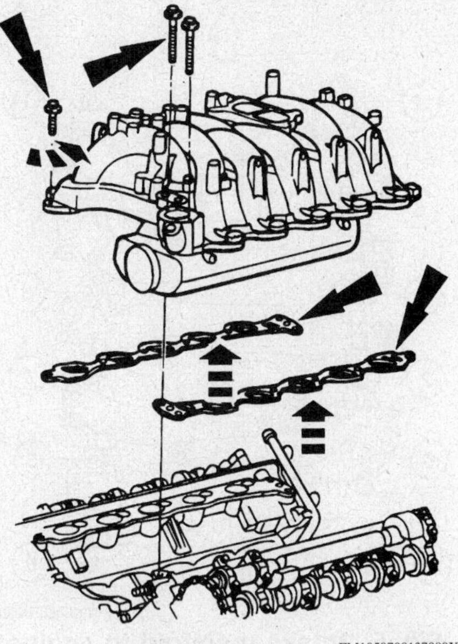

Fig. 2 Upper intake manifold removal. E-Series

hose at power steering pump and let drain into a suitable container.

10. Disconnect power steering pressure line.
11. Disconnect lower radiator hose at oil cooler water inlet, then position aside.
12. Disconnect suction hose at accumulator.
13. Disconnect transmission harness and lefthand and righthand heated O2 sensor connectors.
14. Raise and support vehicle.
15. Remove catalytic converter retaining nuts.
16. Drain engine oil and remove oil bypass filter.
17. Disconnect oil cooler hoses and set aside.
18. Loosen threaded shaft and remove oil cooler from oil filter adapter.
19. Remove starter, then the transmission to engine bolts.
20. Position shifter cable aside.
21. Remove and discard nuts retaining torque converter to flywheel.
22. Remove engine support insulator nuts.
23. Lower vehicle and install modular lifting bar tool No. 014-00073, or equivalent.
24. Remove nut retaining transmission oil filler tube, then the tube.
25. Support transmission with a suitable jack.
26. Remove engine from vehicle.
27. Reverse procedure to install.

Excursion & F-Super Duty Series

PICKUP CHASSIS

Refer to "4.6L & 5.4L SOHC Gasoline Engines" for this procedure.

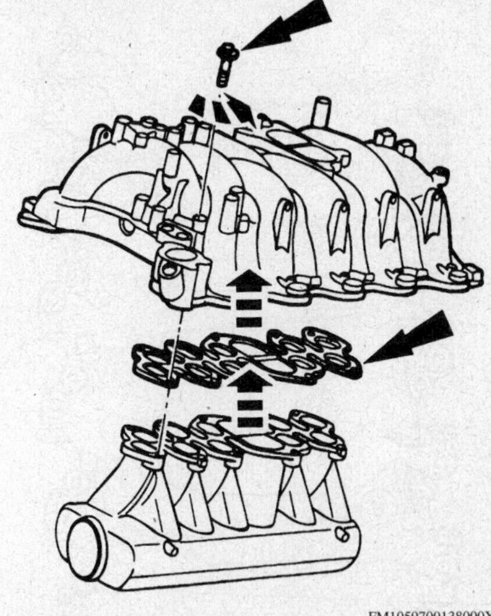

Fig. 3 Upper & lower intake manifolds. E-Series

MOTORHOME CHASSIS

1. Drain engine coolant into a suitable container.
2. Recover refrigerant as outlined in "Air Conditioning" chapter.
3. Remove grille opening panel, then remove transmission fluid level bolt and level indicators.
4. Disconnect air cleaner outlet tube from air cleaner assembly, then remove engine cover.
5. Remove air cleaner outlet tube, then accelerator cable snow shield.
6. Disconnect throttle control cable, speed control actuator cable and throttle return spring.
7. Remove accelerator cable bracket bolts and position bracket aside.
8. Disconnect upper radiator hose, then EGR vacuum line.
9. Disconnect fuel lines using fuel disconnect tool set 310-S039, or equivalent, and heated oxygen sensors.
10. Remove transmission fill tube nut, bolt and tube.
11. Disconnect heater hoses and all vacuum hoses.
12. Disconnect intake vacuum hoses.
13. Disconnect oil fill hose and alternator wiring.
14. Remove transmission to engine upper bolts.
15. Raise and support vehicle, then remove engine cooling fan and position fan in fan shroud.
16. Disconnect engine main wiring harness.
17. Disconnect lower radiator hose.
18. Remove drive belt, then power steering pump three bolts and position pump aside.
19. Remove A/C compressor, then disconnect crankshaft position sensor.
20. Remove starter and disconnect ground strap and cable bracket bolt and position cables forward.

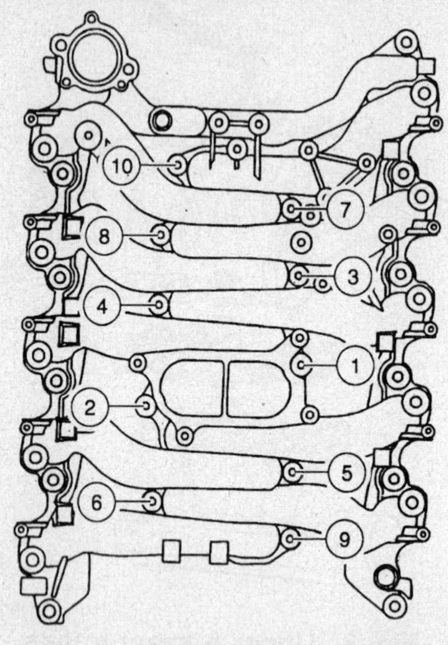

Fig. 4 Upper to lower intake manifold bolt tightening sequence

21. Cut transmission cooler tubes and remove rear portion of transmission cooler tubes.
22. Remove front axle and oil filter.
23. Remove transmission, then disconnect righthand front brake line.
24. Support engine, then remove twelve engine support bolts.
25. Lower engine until frame extensions are free of the crossmember.
26. Remove eight frame extension bolts and frame extensions.
27. Lower engine and remove righthand bolt and position capacitor aside.
28. Disconnect five righthand fuel injector connectors and five ignition coil connectors.
29. Disconnect idle air control motor connector and bypass hose.
30. Disconnect EGR transducer and throttle position sensor connectors.
31. Disconnect EGR transducer vacuum lines and remove EGR transducer bracket.
32. Remove EGR valve to exhaust manifold tube, then disconnect EGR valve vacuum line.
33. Disconnect EVR solenoid vacuum harness.
34. Remove EVR bracket bolt and bracket.
35. Disconnect five lefthand fuel injector connectors and water temperature indicator sender unit connector.
36. Remove five lefthand ignition coils.
37. Remove radio interference capacitor bolt and position capacitor aside.
38. Disconnect cylinder head temperature sensor and remove thermostat and housing.
39. Remove upper intake manifold and intake manifold gaskets. Discard intake manifold gaskets.
40. Clean all mating surfaces and install modular lifting bar tool No. 303-F047, or equivalent, to intake mounting holes.
41. Remove four engine mount nuts.

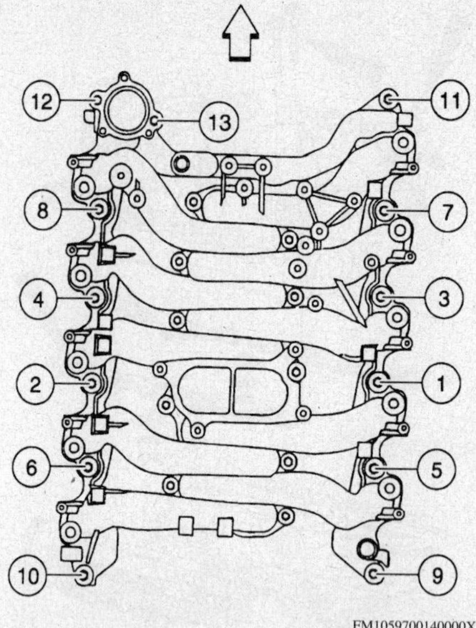

Fig. 5 Intake manifold to engine tightening sequence

42. Remove engine from second crossmember and engine mount assembly.
43. Reverse procedure to install.

INTAKE MANIFOLD

REPLACE

E-Series

REMOVAL

1. Drain coolant into suitable container.
2. Remove engine cover.
3. Remove engine vacuum harness, **Fig. 1.**
4. Remove throttle body as follows:
5. Remove accelerator cable splash shield.
6. Disconnect throttle body control linkage.
7. Remove three bolts retaining accelerator cable bracket to throttle body, throttle return spring from throttle bell crank and accelerator cable bracket.
8. Disconnect throttle position sensor connector.
9. Remove four throttle body bolts, then the throttle body.
10. Disconnect exhaust gas recirculation valve to exhaust manifold tube lower fitting.
11. Disconnect fuel injector electrical connectors.
12. Disconnect water temperature indicator sender unit electrical connectors.
13. Disconnect and remove coil and plug boots.
14. Remove drive belt.
15. Remove alternator as outlined under "Alternator, Replace" in "Electrical" section.
16. Remove two studs retaining heater water return tube.
17. Remove upper intake manifold bolts, upper intake and intake manifold gaskets, **Fig. 2.**

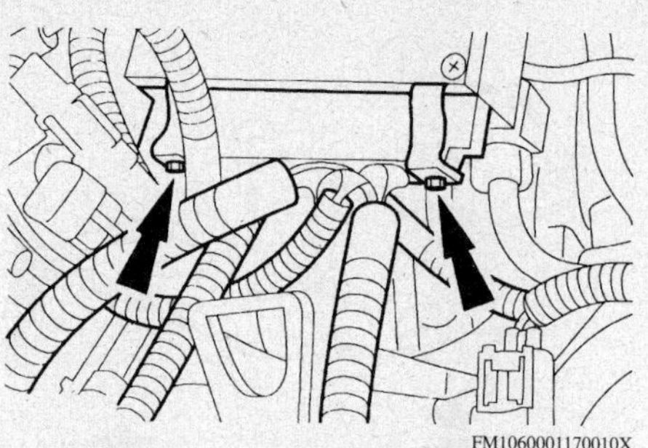

Fig. 6 Vacuum & electrical connector location (Part 1 of 3). Excursion & F-Super Duty w/bi-fuel system

18. Pull back and remove heater water return tube and inspect O-rings, replace as required.
19. Remove ten lower intake manifold bolts and separate upper and lower intake manifolds, **Fig. 3.**

INSTALLATION

1. Position lower intake manifold gasket and upper intake manifold on lower intake manifold and loosely install ten upper intake manifold bolts.
2. **Torque** intake manifold bolts in two steps; first to 18 inch. lbs., then to 6–9 ft. lbs., using sequence outlined, **Fig. 4.**
3. Install water return tube.
4. Install heater water return studs and tighten to specification.
5. Position upper intake manifold gaskets and intake manifold, and loosely install bolts.
6. **Torque** intake manifold bolts in two steps; first to 18 inch. lbs., then to 15–22 ft. lbs., using sequence, **Fig. 5.**
7. Install thermostat, then the throttle body.
8. Install heater water hose and position clamp
9. Connect water temperature indicator sending unit electrical connector.
10. Install alternator and drive belt.
11. Install coil and plug boots.
12. Connect five lefthand and five righthand injector electrical connectors.
13. Connect engine emission vacuum harness.
14. Connect EGR valve to exhaust manifold tube lower fitting.
15. Connect fuel lines, then the engine water outlet hose and position clamp.
16. Install air cleaner outlet tube.
17. Fill cooling system to specification.

EXCURSION & F-SUPER DUTY SERIES

Removal

1. Drain engine coolant into a suitable container.
2. Compress and slide hose clamp off water outlet hose.
3. Remove air cleaner outlet tube and accelerator cable snow shield.
4. Disconnect accelerator, speed control cables and return spring.
5. **On models equipped with bi-fuel,** proceed as follows:

Fig. 6 Vacuum & electrical connector location (Part 2 of 3). Excursion & F-Super Duty w/bi-fuel system

   a. Relieve fuel pressure as outlined under precautions.
   b. Disconnect fuel outlet line, then the vacuum and electrical connections outlined in **Fig. 6.**
   c. Disconnect fuel and coolant lines from compuvalve, then remove valve.
6. **On all models,** remove accelerator cable bracket bolts and position bracket aside.
7. Disconnect PCV, brake booster and engine sensor control wiring harness.
8. Remove capacitor bolt and position capacitor aside.
9. Disconnect vacuum lines from intake, then fuel injector and ignition coil connectors.
10. Disconnect idle air control motor, bypass hose and heater hose.
11. Disconnect EGR transducer and throttle position sensor.
12. Disconnect EGR transducer vacuum lines, then remove transducer bracket.
13. Position EGR valve to exhaust manifold tube aside.
14. Disconnect EGR valve vacuum line.
15. Disconnect EVR solenoid connector and vacuum hoses.
16. Remove throttle body bolts, throttle body adapter and gasket.
17. Remove EVR bracket bolts and bracket.
18. Disconnect water temperature indicator sender unit connectors, then remove alternator.
19. Remove ignition coil bolts and coils.
20. Disconnect fuel lines and vacuum connector from fuel pressure regulator.
21. Remove radio interference capacitor bolt and position capacitor aside.
22. Disconnect cylinder head temperature sensor, then remove thermostat and housing.
23. Remove upper intake manifold bolts and gasket. Discard intake gasket.
24. If required, remove fuel injection supply manifold.
25. Remove ten upper to lower intake bolts and separate. Discard gasket.
26. Clean all mating surfaces.

Installation

Ensure new copper washers are installed to compuvalve and that fuel system is properly inspected for leaks.

1. Position lower intake manifold gasket and upper intake manifold on lower intake manifold and loosely install ten upper intake manifold bolts.

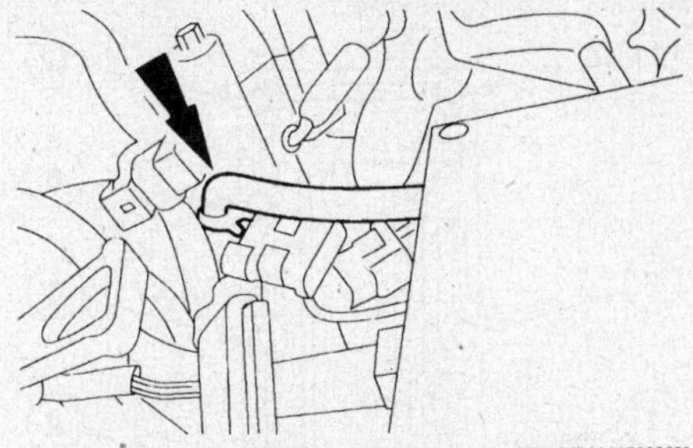

Fig. 6 Vacuum & electrical connector location (Part 3 of 3). Excursion & F-Super Duty w/bi-fuel system

2. **Torque** intake manifold bolts in two steps; first to 18 inch. lbs., then to 6–9 ft. lbs., using sequence outlined, **Fig. 4.**
3. If required, install fuel injector supply manifold.
4. Position thermostat and water outlet connector.
5. Position upper intake manifold gaskets and intake manifold, and loosely install bolts.
6. **Torque** intake manifold bolts in two steps; first to 18 inch. lbs., then to 15–22 ft. lbs., using sequence outlined, **Fig. 5.**
7. Connect engine sensor control wiring harness to cylinder head temperature sensor.
8. Install radio interference capacitor, then connect fuel lines and vacuum line to fuel injector supply manifold.
9. Install ten coils and bolts.
10. Install alternator and connect temperature indicator sending unit connector.
11. Connect fuel injector connectors and install EVR solenoid bracket.
12. Install throttle body adapter gasket, adapter. **Torque** bolts to 72–96 inch lbs., then tighten an additional 85–95.°
13. Connect EVR solenoid vacuum and connectors.
14. Connect EGR valve vacuum line, then install EGR valve to exhaust manifold tube.
15. Install EGR transducer bracket and bolt.
16. Connect vacuum lines to EGR transducer.
17. Connect EGR transducer and throttle position sensor connector.
18. Connect heater hose, idle air control motor and bypass hose.
19. Connect PCV, brake booster and engine control sensor wiring harness.
20. Install accelerator bracket, then connect accelerator and speed control cables and return spring.
21. Install accelerator cable snow shield.
22. Install air cleaner outlet tube and connect engine water outlet hose and position hose clamp.
23. Fill cooling system to specification.

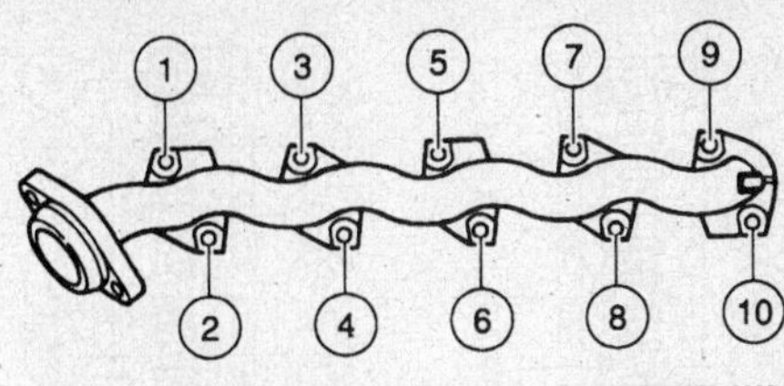

Fig. 7 Exhaust manifold tightening sequence

EXHAUST MANIFOLD

REPLACE

1. Raise and support vehicle.
2. Disconnect EGR to exhaust manifold tube lower fitting.
3. Remove three-way catalytic converter to exhaust manifold nuts.
4. Remove exhaust manifold nuts, then the exhaust manifold.
5. Clean and inspect exhaust manifold.
6. Reverse procedure to install and **torque** nuts in sequence, **Fig. 7** to specifications.

CYLINDER HEAD

REPLACE

Removal

1. Remove intake manifold as outlined under "Intake Manifold, Replace."
2. Remove timing chains as outlined under "Timing Chain, Replace."
3. **On E-Series models,** remove exhaust manifolds as outlined in "Exhaust Manifold, Replace."
4. **On all models,** compress and slide hose clamp back and remove heater water hose.
5. Install lifting handle tool No. T97T-6000-A, or equivalent.
6. Remove cylinder head bolts and cylinder head. **Cylinder head bolts must be replaced with new bolts. They are tighten to yield designed and cannot be reused.**
7. Clean and inspect mating surface of cylinder head. **Do not use metal scrapers, wire brushes, power abrasive discs or other abrasive means to clean aluminum retainer plate. These tools cause scratches and gouges, which make leak paths. Use a plastic scraping tool to remove all traces of old sealant.**

Installation

1. Rotate crankshaft to position keyway at 12 o'clock. **Do not turn crankshaft until otherwise instructed.**
2. Install head gasket over dowel pins.
3. Install cylinder heads on head gasket and loosely install cylinder head bolts.
4. **Torque** cylinder head bolts in three steps; first step to 27–32 ft. lbs., second step an additional 85–95,° third step rotate an additional 85–95° using sequence outlined, **Fig. 8.**
5. **On E-Series models,** install exhaust

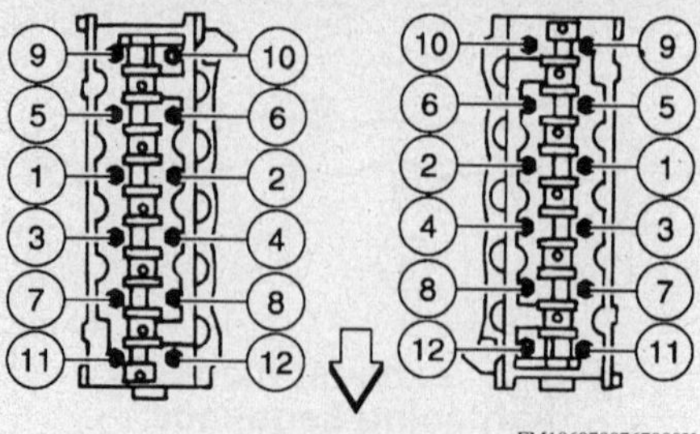

Fig. 8 Cylinder head tightening sequence

manifolds as outlined in "Exhaust Manifold, Replace."

6. **On all models,** install timing chains. Refer to "Timing Chain, Replace."
7. Install intake manifold. Refer to "Intake Manifold, Replace."

VALVE COVER

REPLACE

Left

REMOVAL

2002

1. **On E-Series models,** remove intake manifold as outlined under "Intake Manifold, Replace."
2. **On E-Series models,**disconnect fuel injector and coil connectors, then remove from valve cover studs as required.
3. **On all models** remove two nuts and valve cover attaching bolts.
4. Remove valve cover and gasket.

2003 E-SERIES

1. Remove engine cover.
2. Remove air cleaner assembly.
3. Disconnect crankcase vent tube from valve cover.
4. Remove nuts and bolts from oil dipstick tube, then position aside.
5. Disconnect five lefthand ignition coil electrical connectors.
6. Remove throttle clamp bolt.
7. Remove front and rear wiring harness brackets and position aside.
8. If equipped with rear auxiliary heat, the valve cover can be removed from front of vehicle.
9. Remove valve cover bolts. **The bolts are part of the valve cover and should not be removed.**
10. Remove valve cover and gasket.

EXCURSION, F-SUPER DUTY & MOTORHOME CHASSIS

1. Disconnect battery ground cable.
2. Remove engine air cleaner assembly.
3. Remove crankcase ventilation tube from valve cover.
4. Disconnect lefthand fuel injector electrical connectors and ignition coil electrical connectors.
5. Remove engine harness bracket nuts, then position bracket aside.
6. Lift fuel charging wiring off valve cover studs.

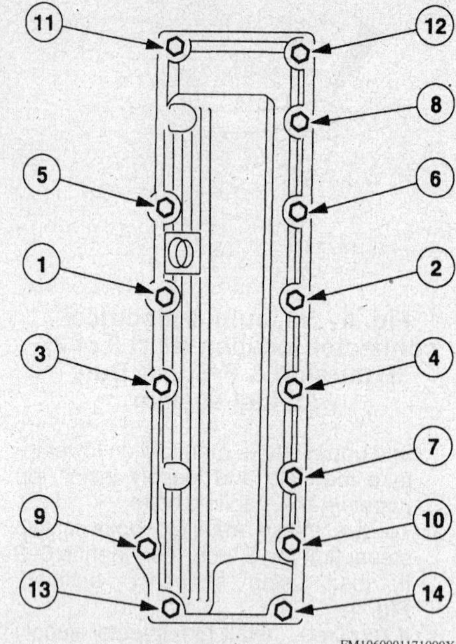

Fig. 9 Lefthand valve cover tightening sequence

7. Remove valve cover bolts. **The bolts are part of the valve cover and should not be removed.**
8. Remove valve cover and gasket.

INSTALLATION

1. Clean and inspect cylinder head mating surfaces. **Do not use metal scrapers, wire brushes, power abrasive discs or other abrasive means to clean aluminum retainer plate.**
2. Apply silicone in two places where engine front covers meets cylinder head.
3. Position valve cover and valve cover gasket on cylinder head and loosely install bolts and nuts.
4. Tighten nuts and bolts in sequence, **Fig. 9** to specifications.

Right

E-SERIES

REMOVAL

1. **On E-Series models,** remove intake manifold as outlined under "Intake Manifold, Replace."
2. **On all models** remove clamp and oil filler hose from valve cover.
3. Disconnect ventilation hoses, then the fuel injector and coil connectors from valve cover studs as required.
4. Remove valve cover bolts, then the valve cover and gasket.

INSTALLATION

1. Clean and inspect mating surfaces of cylinder head. **Do not use metal scrapers, wire brushes, power abrasive discs or other abrasive means to clean aluminum retainer plate.**
2. Apply silicone in two places where engine front covers meets cylinder head.
3. Position valve cover and valve cover gasket on cylinder head and loosely in-

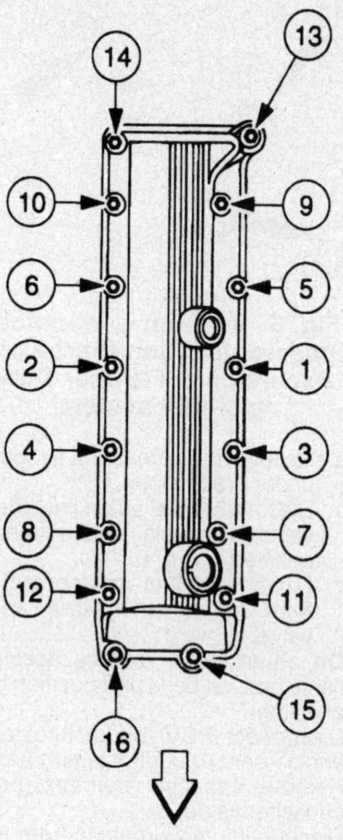

Fig. 10 Righthand valve cover tightening sequence. E-Series

stall bolts and nuts.

4. Tighten nuts and bolts in sequence, **Fig. 10,** to specifications.
5. Tighten nuts and bolts in sequence, **Fig. 11,** to specifications.
6. Install oil filler tube and clamp on valve cover.

EXCURSION & F-SUPER DUTY

1. Remove oil fill hose from valve cover.
2. Drain cooling system.
3. **On models equipped with bi-fuel,** remove compuvalve as outlined under "Intake Manifold, Replace."
4. **On all models,** disconnect fuel injector and ignition coil connectors.
5. Remove alternator, then install three bar engine support tool No. 303-F070.
6. Raise and support vehicle.
7. Remove righthand motor mounts, then lower vehicle.
8. Disconnect front heater hoses.
9. Disconnect vapor management valve vacuum hose, then the vacuum canister vacuum harness.
10. Lift fuel injector wiring from valve cover studs.
11. Raise engine using three bar engine support.
12. Remove valve cover attaching bolts, then the valve cover.
13. Reverse procedure to install, noting the following:
    a. Apply silicone and gasket sealant F7AZ-19554-EA, or equivalent, to corners where front cover meets cylinder head.

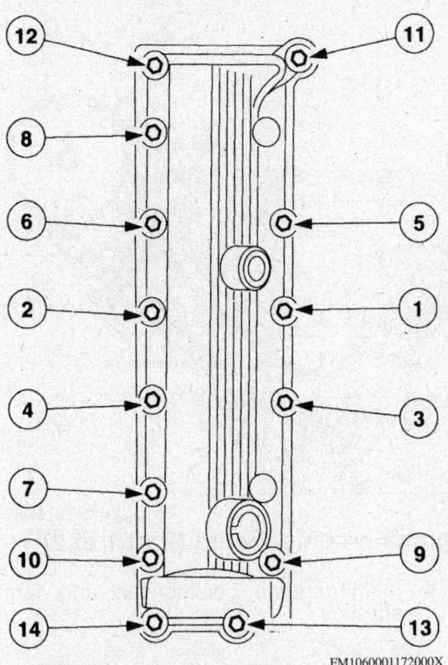

Fig. 11 Righthand valve cover tightening sequence. Excursion & F-Super Duty

b. Tighten valve cover to specifications in sequence as outlined in **Fig. 11.**

VALVE ADJUSTMENT

These engines have overhead camshafts and there are no valve adjustments possible. A hydraulic lash adjuster provides automatic lash adjustment.

FRONT COVER

REPLACE

1. Remove valve covers as outlined under "Valve Cover, Replace"
2. Remove radiator as outlined under "Radiator, Replace."
3. **On models equipped with bi-fuel,** remove compuvalve as outlined under "Intake Manifold, Replace."
4. **On all models,** disconnect camshaft position sensor.
5. Remove water pump as outlined under "Water Pump, Replace."
6. Raise and support vehicle.
7. Remove power steering pump bolts and position power steering pump aside, **Fig. 12. Only three bolts are required to secure power steering pump.**
8. Disconnect crankshaft position sensor electrical connector.
9. Drain engine oil into a suitable container.
10. Remove crankshaft front seal. Refer to "Crankshaft Seal, Replace."
11. Remove four front oil pan bolts, **Fig. 13.**
12. Remove idler pulley.
13. Lower vehicle and remove engine front cover fasteners.
14. Remove front cover from engine.

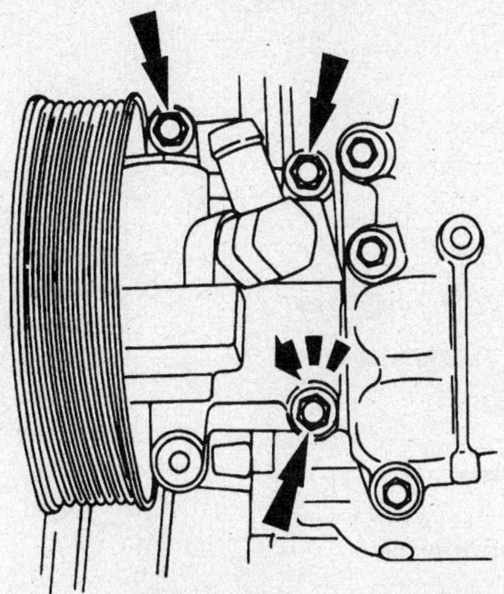

Fig. 12 Power steering pump removal

15. Reverse procedure to install, noting the following:
    a. Apply a bead of silicone along head to block surface and oil pan to block surface with silicone gasket and sealant No. F6AZ-19562-A, or equivalent.
    b. **Torque** engine front cover fasteners in two steps: first, fasteners 1–5 to 15–22 ft. lbs., then fasteners 6–15 to 30–41 ft. lbs., using sequence outlined, **Fig. 14.**
    c. **Torque** four front oil pan bolts in two steps; first to 15 ft. lbs., then rotate 60.°

TIMING CHAIN

REPLACE

With the timing chain removed, avoid turning the camshaft or crankshaft. If movement is required, exercise extreme caution to avoid valve damage caused by piston-to-valve contact.

Refer to **Fig. 15** for timing chain removal and installation.

REMOVAL

1. Remove front cover as outlined in "Front Cover, Replace."
2. Remove crankshaft sensor ring from crankshaft.
3. Remove six bolts retaining balance shaft bearing caps and remove bearing caps.
4. Remove balance shaft, **Fig. 16.**
5. Position crankshaft with keyway at 12 o'clock position.
6. Install camshaft holding tool No. T96T-6256-B, or equivalent, on camshafts.
7. Remove timing chain tensioner bolts and timing chain tensioner guides from dowel pins.
8. Remove lefthand and righthand timing chains and crankshaft sprockets.
9. Remove timing chain guides.

INSTALLATION

Timing chain procedures must be followed exactly or damage to valves and pistons will result.

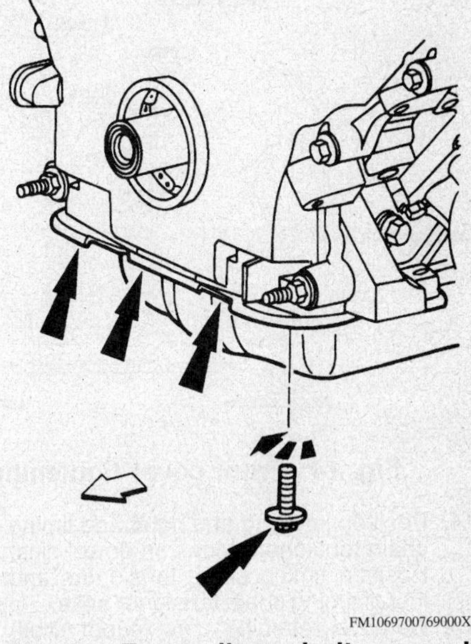

Fig. 13 Front oil pan bolt removal

Refer to **Fig. 15** for timing chain replacement.

1. Compress tensioner plunger, using an edge of a vice, **Fig. 17. Do not compress ratchet assembly. This will damage ratchet assembly.**
2. Push back and hold ratchet mechanism.
3. While holding ratchet mechanism, push ratchet arm back into tensioner housing.
4. Install a paper clip into hole in tensioner housing to hold ratchet assembly and plunger in during assembly, **Fig. 18.**
5. If copper links are not visible, mark two links on one end and one link on other end, and use as timing marks, **Fig. 19.**
6. Install timing chain guides.
7. Ensure crankshaft is in its proper position with crankshaft holding tool, and remove tool.
8. Install inner crankshaft sprocket with long hub facing outward.
9. Install inner camshaft timing chain on crankshaft.
10. Install timing chain on camshaft sprocket with two chain links and timing marks aligned, **Fig. 20. Ensure upper half of timing chain is below tensioner guide dowel. If required, use camshaft position tool to adjust.**
11. Install outer crankshaft sprocket and timing chain with long hub of crankshaft sprocket facing inward. **Ensure chain link and crankshaft sprocket timing marks are aligned and that the lower half of timing chain is positioned above dowel.**
12. Position timing chain on camshaft sprocket. Ensure two copper colored links align with camshaft sprocket timing marks.
13. Ensure proper alignment of all timing marks, **Fig. 21.**

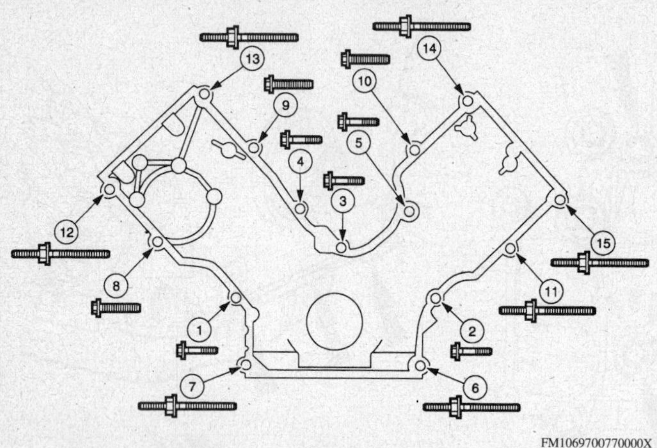

Fig. 14 Front cover tightening sequence

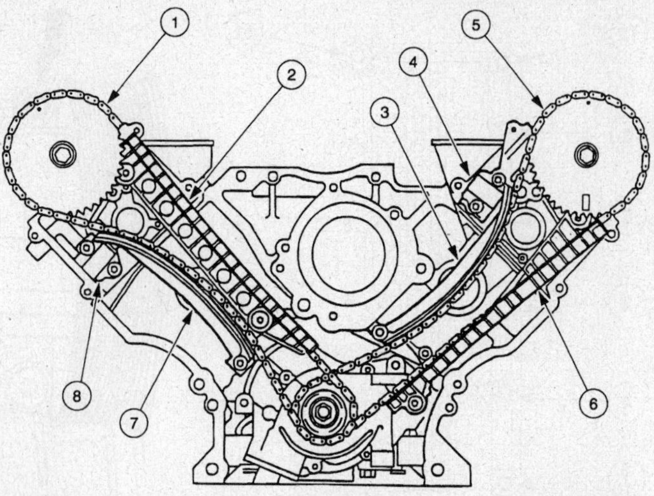

Fig. 15 Timing chain components (Part 1 of 2)

14. Position lefthand and righthand timing chain tensioner guides on dowel pins. Position timing chain tensioners and install timing chain tensioner bolts.
15. Remove retaining pins (paper clips) from righthand and lefthand timing chain tensioners.
16. Remove camshaft holding tools from camshaft.
17. Install crankshaft sensor ring on crankshaft.
18. Lubricate balance shaft journals with engine oil and position balance shaft on journals.
19. Align balance shaft timing marks as outlined in **Fig. 22.**
20. Install bearing caps, then the bolts and **torque** bolts in sequence outlined in **Fig. 23** to 6–9 ft. lbs.
21. Install front cover as outlined in "Front Cover, Replace."

CAMSHAFT

REPLACE

Removal

1. Remove intake manifold as outlined under "Intake Manifold, Replace."
2. Remove timing chains as outlined under "Timing Chain, Replace."
3. Remove six bolts retaining balance shaft bearing caps and remove bearing caps and balance shaft.
4. Compress valve springs and remove camshaft roller followers using valve spring compressor tool No. T91P-6565-A, or equivalent.
5. Place reference marks on camshafts and bearing caps for installation reference.
6. Remove camshaft bearing cap bolts, bearing caps and camshaft from cylinder head.

Installation

Use engine oil meeting ford specification WSS-M2C153-H (5W–20 weight oil) for installation purposes.

1. Lubricate camshaft journals.
2. Install camshaft and camshaft bearing caps onto cylinder head. Loosely install 11 bolts.
3. Tighten camshaft bearing cap bolts in sequence outlined in **Fig. 24** to specifications.
4. Install roller followers using valve spring compressor to compress valve springs.
5. Lubricate balance shaft journals with engine oil.
6. Position balance shaft on journals and align balance shaft timing marks, **Fig. 22.**
7. Position bearing caps and six bolts and **torque** in sequence outlined in **Fig. 23** to 6–9 ft. lbs.
8. Install intake manifold.
9. Install timing chains.

CRANKSHAFT SEAL

REPLACE

Removal

1. Remove engine cooling fan and fan shroud.
2. Remove drive belt.
3. Raise and support vehicle.
4. Remove crankshaft pulley bolt.
5. Remove crankshaft pulley using crankshaft damper remover tool No. T58P-6316-D, or equivalent.
6. Remove crankshaft front seal using front cover seal remover tool No. T74P-6700-A, or equivalent.

Installation

1. Lubricate engine front cover and crankshaft front seal inner lip with suitable engine oil.
2. Use crankshaft seal replacer tool No. T88T-6701-B1, or equivalent, and install crankshaft front seal into engine front cover.
3. Use crankshaft damper replacer tool No.T74P-6316-B, or equivalent, to install crankshaft pulley.
4. **Torque** crankshaft pulley in four steps; first to 66 ft. lbs., then loosen 360,° then to 35–39 ft. lbs., then rotate an additional 85–95.°
5. Lower vehicle and install drive belt.
6. Install engine cooling fan and fan shroud.

CRANKSHAFT REAR OIL SEAL

REPLACE

Removal

1. Remove transmission as outlined in **MOTOR's "Domestic Transmission, In-Vehicle Service" or "Transmission Service DVD."**
2. Remove flywheel bolts, then the flywheel.
3. Use rear crankshaft slinger remover tool No. T95P-6701-AH and slide hammer tool No. T50T-100-A, or equivalents, and remove crankshaft oil slinger.
4. Use rear crankshaft seal remover tool No. T95P-6701-EH, or equivalent, and a slide hammer to remove crankshaft rear oil seal.
5. **On models with retainer plate,** remove two rear oil pan bolts, crankcase rear oil seal retainer plate bolts and crankshaft rear oil seal retainer plate.
6. **On all models,** clean and inspect mating surfaces.

Installation

Do not use metal scrapers, wire brushes, power abrasive discs or other abrasive means to clean aluminum retainer plate. Use a plastic scraping tool to remove all traces of old sealant.

1. **On models with retainer plate,** proceed as follows:
   a. apply a bead of silicone gasket and sealant F6AZ-19562-A, or equivalent, around rear oil seal retainer sealing surface.
   b. Position crankshaft rear oil seal and retainer and install bolts.
   c. **Torque** rear oil seal retainer bolts and two oil pan bolts in two steps; first **torque** retainer plated bolts to

Item	Description
1	Timing Chain (RH)
2	Timing Chain Guide (RH)
3	Timing Chain Tensioner Arm (LH)
4	Timing Chain Tensioner (LH)
5	Timing Chain (LH)
6	Timing Chain Guide (LH)
7	Timing Chain Tensioner Arm (RH)
8	Timing Chain Tensioner (RH)

FM1069700777020X

Fig. 15 Timing chain components (Part 2 of 2)

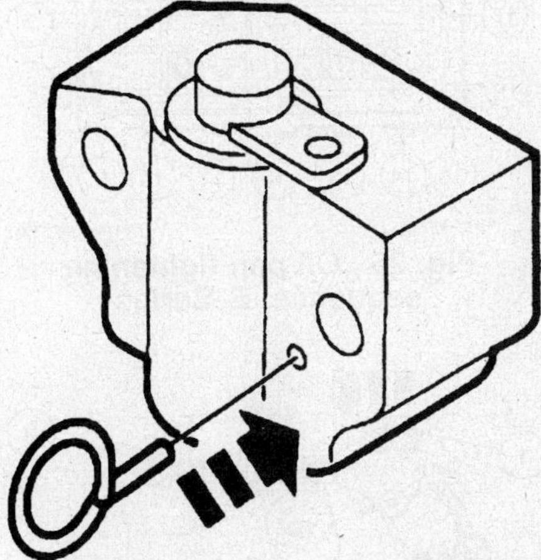

Fig. 18 Ratchet mechanism

72–108 inch lbs., then all pan bolts to 10–15 ft. lbs., then rotate 90.°

2. **On all models,** install rear crankshaft seal with rear crankshaft seal replacer tool No. T95P-6701-CH and rear crankshaft seal adapter tool No. T95P-6701-DH, or equivalents.
3. Install flywheel and flywheel bolts and tighten to specification.
4. Install transmission.

OIL PAN

REPLACE

E-Series

1. Remove intake manifold as outlined in "Intake Manifold, Replace."
2. Remove fan shroud and cooling fan.
3. Remove upper radiator shield retainers, then shield.
4. Remove nut retaining transmission filler tube at rear of righthand cylinder head and position tube aside.
5. Remove wiring harness retainer, then position wiring aside.
6. Remove two transmission to engine bolts.

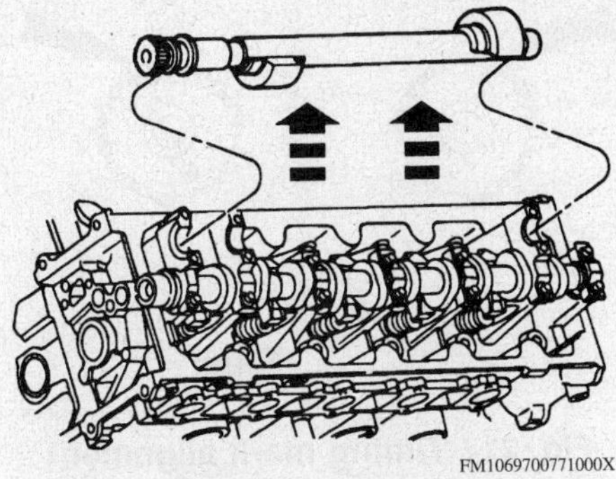

Fig. 16 Balance shaft removal

7. Install tool No. 303–F047, or equivalent, and support engine.
8. Raise and support vehicle.
9. Drain engine oil into a suitable container and remove oil filter.
10. Remove nuts retaining front engine mount insulator (mount) to front engine support bracket.
11. Remove flywheel inspection plate.
12. Raise engine to ideal working height using engine support.
13. Remove oil pan bolts and partially lower oil pan.
14. Remove two bolts and nut securing oil pump screen cover and tube and let drop into oil pan.
15. Remove oil pan and oil pan gasket from rear of engine.
16. Clean mating surfaces and thoroughly clean oil pan.
17. Reverse procedure to install, noting the following:
    a. **Torque** oil pump screen cover and tube bolts to 72–108 inch lbs.
    b. **Torque** oil pump screen cover and tube nut to 15–22 ft. lbs.
    c. **Torque** oil pan bolts in three steps; first to 18 inch lbs., then to 15 ft. lbs., then rotate 60° using sequence outlined, **Fig. 25.**
    d. **Torque** front engine support insulators to 50–68 ft. lbs.
    e. Fill engine with oil to specification.
    f. Fill cooling system to specification.

EXCURSION & F-SUPER DUTY SERIES

Refer to "4.6L & 5.4L SOHC Gasoline Engines" for removal procedure.

OIL PUMP

REPLACE

1. Remove engine front cover as outlined in "Front Cover, Replace."
2. Remove crankshaft sprockets as outlined in "Timing Chain, Replace."
3. Remove oil pan as outlined in "Oil Pan, Replace."
4. Remove oil pump and clean and inspect mating surfaces.
5. Reverse procedure to install and tighten oil pump bolts in sequence outlined in **Fig. 26** to specification.

BELT TENSION DATA

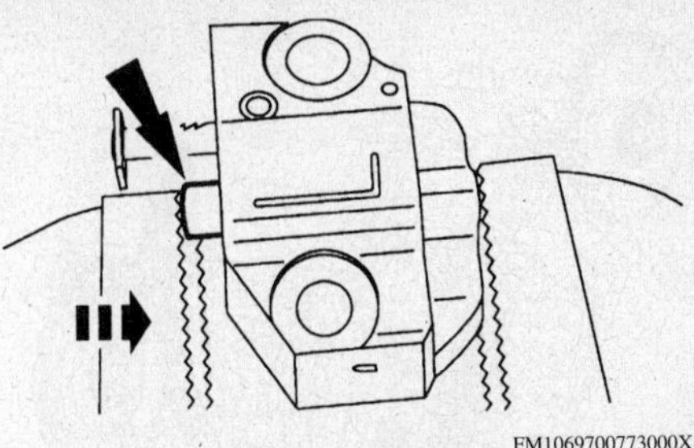

Fig. 17 Ratchet assembly tensioner plunger

Fig. 19 Copper link location

The drive belt tensioner will maintain correct belt tension if the correct length drive belt is on the engine. To verify that the drive belt tensioner is working properly, inspect to see that the belt length indicator mark on drive belt tensioner is between the minimum and maximum marks. Remove drive belt and rotate the tensioner from stop to stop to verify that the tensioner does not stick, grab or bind. If the tensioner exhibits any of these conditions, replace the tensioner.

RADIATOR

REPLACE

E-Series

1. Drain cooling system.
2. Remove air cleaner assembly, then the plastic rivet retainers and air deflector.
3. Remove upper and lower radiator hoses from radiator.
4. Disconnect overflow hose from radiator.
5. Remove fan and fan clutch from water pump pulley.
6. Remove radiator upper fan shroud attaching bolts and lift shroud off of radiator.
7. Remove underbody splash shield.
8. Compress transmission oil cooler line clamps, then disconnect coolant lines from radiator.
9. Remove radiator upper support bracket attaching bolts, then the support brackets.
10. Remove radiator from vehicle.
11. Reverse procedure to install.

Excursion & F-Super Duty Series

Refer to "4.6L & 5.4L SOHC Gasoline Engines" for removal procedure.

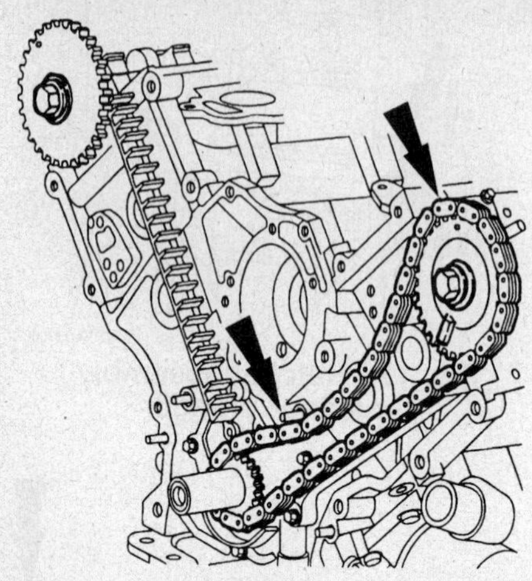
Fig. 20 Inner timing chain link location

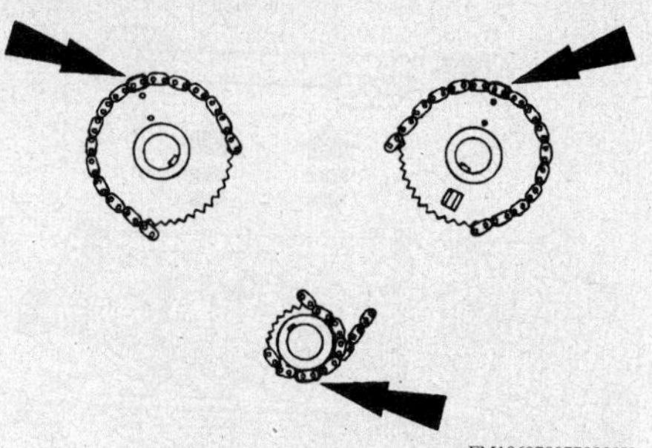
Fig. 21 Timing mark alignment

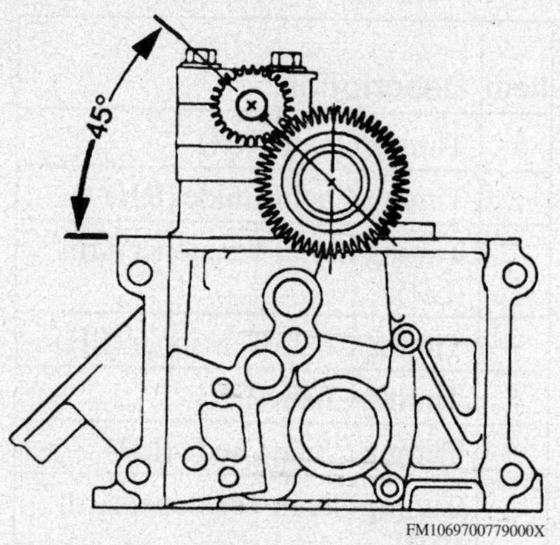

Fig. 22 Balance shaft timing marks

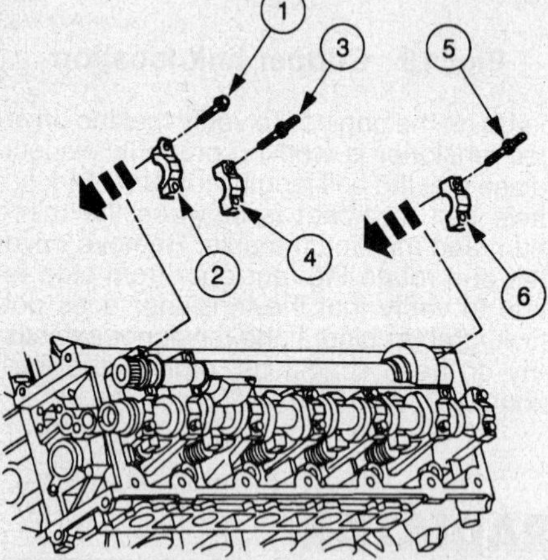

Fig. 23 Balance shaft bearing cap tightening sequence

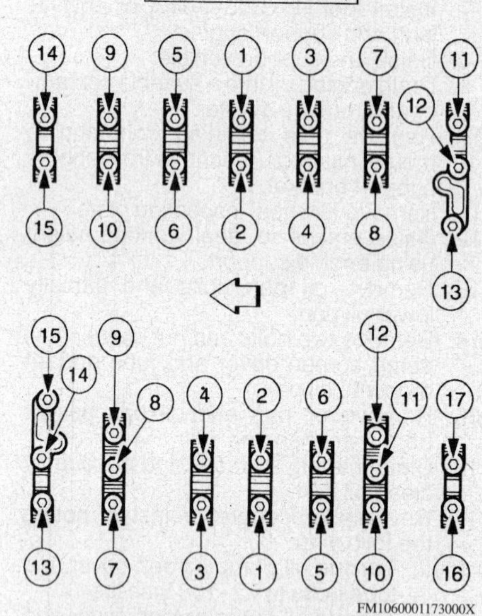

Fig. 24 Camshaft bearing cap tightening sequence

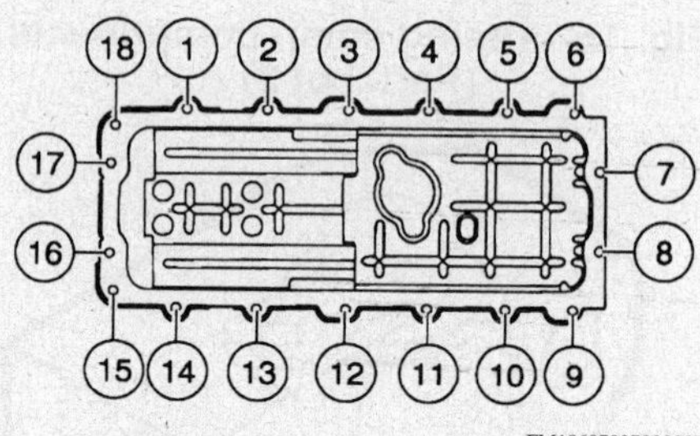

Fig. 25 Oil pan tightening sequence. E-Series

Fig. 26 Oil pump tightening sequence

TIGHTENING SPECIFICATIONS

Year	Description	Torque Ft. Lbs.
2002–06	Bolt Hex Flanged (Front Of Engine)	15–22
	Camshaft Bearing Cap Bolts	72–108①
	Crankshaft Pulley	④
	Coil Pack Bracket Bolts	15–22
	Cylinder Head	⑤
	EGR To Exhaust Manifold Tube Fittings	26–33
	Exhaust Manifold Nuts	17–20
	Flywheel Bolts	54–64
	Front Cover	③
	Idler Pulley Bolt	15–22
	Intake Manifold	②
	Motor Mount Pivot Bolts	50–68
	Motor Mount To Engine Bolts	38–52
	Oil Cooler Adapter	41–44①
	Oil Filter Assembly Bolts	15–22
	Oil Level Indicator Tube Bolt	72–108①
	Oil Pump Bolts	72–108①
	Power Steering Bolts (Lower)	15–20
	Power Steering Bolts (Upper)	15–20
	Rear Oil Seal Bolts	72–108①
	Valve Cover	72–108①
	Water Pump Bolts	15–22
	Water Pump Pulley Bolts	15–22

① — Inch lbs.
② — Refer to "Intake, Replace" for tighten procedure.
③ — Refer to "Front Cover, Replace" for tighten procedure.
④ — Refer to "Crankshaft, Replace" for tighten procedure.
⑤ — Refer to "Cylinder Head, Replace" for tighten procedure.

6.0L Diesel Engine

NOTE: On Air Bag Equipped Models, Refer To "Air Bag System Precautions" Located In The Front Of This Manual For System Disarming & Arming Procedures.

NOTE: Refer To "Computer Relearn Procedures" Located In The Front Of This Manual When Battery Power To The Computer Has Been Interrupted.

INDEX

PRECAUTIONS

Air Bag Systems

Refer to "Air Bag System Precautions" in the front of this manual for system disarming and arming procedures.

Battery Ground Cable

Prior to service, disconnect battery ground cable and isolate as required.

ENGINE MOUNT

REPLACE

Righthand

1. With transmission in neutral, raise and support vehicle.
2. Disconnect and cap engine vent hose and radiator overflow hose.
3. Remove bolts and position degas bottle aside.
4. Loosen clamps at charge air cooler and turbocharger, then remove charger air pipe.
5. Remove motor mount nuts, **Fig. 1.**
6. Install suitable lifting eye on front of engine, then raise with suitable lifting device.
7. Remove motor mount bolts, then the bracket to engine bolts.
8. Remove bracket and motor mount.
9. Reverse procedure to install.

Lefthand

1. With transmission in neutral position, raise and support vehicle.
2. Remove air cleaner assembly.
3. Disconnect and cap engine bent hose and radiator overflow hose.
4. Remove mounting bolts and position degas bottle aside.
5. Loosen clamps at charge air cooler and intake manifold, then remove charge air pipe.
6. Remove motor mount nuts.
7. Raise engine with suitable lifting device.
8. Remove motor mount bolts.
9. Remove bracket to engine bolts, then the bracket and motor mount.
10. Reverse procedure to install.

ENGINE

REPLACE

1. With transmission in neutral position, raise and support vehicle.
2. **On models equipped with manual transmission,** remove transmission and clutch assembly as outlined in **MOTOR's "Domestic Transmission, In-Vehicle Service" or "Transmission Service DVD."**
3. **On all models,** remove air cleaner assembly.
4. Drain coolant into suitable container.
5. Remove radiator.
6. Remove charge air cooler.
7. **On models equipped with air conditioning,** recover A/C refrigerant as

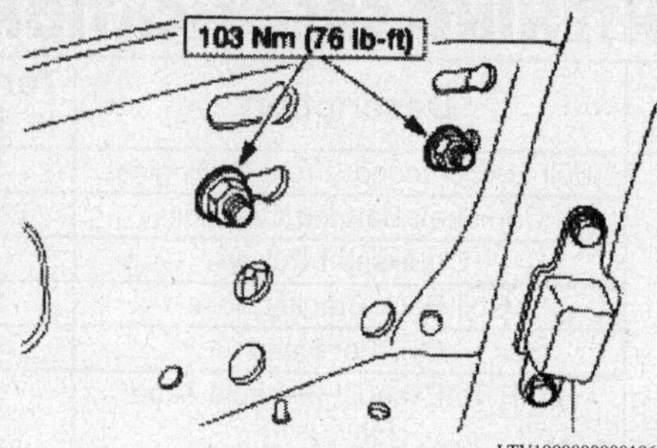

Fig. 1 Motor mount attaching nuts

outlined under "Air Conditioning" chapter, then remove condenser assembly.
8. **On all models,** remove parking lamp and headlamp assemblies
9. Remove radiator grille, radiator grille opening panel and upper radiator core supports.
10. Remove front bumper.
11. Disconnect transmission cooler hoses.
12. Remove transmission oil cooler.
13. Remove bolts and position power steering cooler aside.
14. Remove intake manifold as outlined under "Intake Manifold, Replace."
15. Disconnect heater hose at water pump.
16. Remove battery cable cover.
17. Remove nut, then position battery cable out of way.
18. Remove clips and disconnect fuel lines.
19. Remove lower radiator hose.
20. Remove power steering pump bolts and position pump aside.
21. Remove bolt and lefthand side ground cable, **Fig. 2.**
22. Remove nut and battery cable bracket.
23. Remove ground stud and ground cable, **Fig. 3.**
24. Disconnect glow plug electrical connectors, **Fig. 4.**
25. **On models equipped with air conditioning:**
    a. Disconnect A/C high pressure switch and A/C clutch electrical connectors.
    b. Remove air conditioning manifold lines from A/C compressor.
    c. Remove A/C compressor.
26. **On all models,** disconnect crankshaft position sensor electrical connector.
27. **On models equipped with automatic transmission,** remove transmission fluid dipstick and tube.
28. **On all models,** remove ground strap at back of righthand cylinder head.
29. Remove solenoid cap, then disconnect starter wiring.
30. Disconnect block heater electrical connector.
31. Position block heater and starter wiring harness out of way.
32. **On models equipped with automatic transmission,** remove torque converter cover, then the torque converter nuts.
33. **On all models,** remove bolts for turbocharger adapter pipe.
34. Remove righthand and lefthand motor mount nuts.
35. Loosen nuts at turbocharger adapter pipe flange.
36. **On models equipped with automatic transmission,** remove bell housing bolts.
37. **On all models,** remove turbocharger adapter pipe.
38. Remove fuel injection control module mounting bolts for access to module electrical connectors.
39. Disconnect electrical connectors, **Fig. 5,** then remove fuel injection control module.
40. Remove fuel injection control module bracket.
41. Remove lefthand rear valve cover stud.
42. Remove transmission cooler line bracket.
43. Secure turbocharger outlet pipe, **Fig. 6.**
44. Remove manufacturers lifting eye, **Fig. 7,** install lifting eye on righthand cylinder head, **Fig. 8.**
45. Install front lifting brackets, **Fig. 9.**
46. **On models equipped with automatic transmission,** support transmission with suitable jack.
47. **On all models,** install suitable engine lifting device to engine lifting brackets.
48. Raise engine enough to clear No. 1 crossmember, then pull engine forward and out of vehicle.
49. Reverse procedure to install.

INTAKE MANIFOLD

REPLACE

1. Remove lefthand battery.
2. Remove air cleaner assembly.
3. Remove cooling fan blade, clutch and shroud.
4. Remove upper radiator hose and coolant reservoir.
5. Remove turbocharger to charge air cooler tube.
6. Remove charge air cooler to engine tube.
7. Remove accessory drive belt.
8. Disconnect alternator electrical connectors.
9. Remove alternator.
10. Remove turbocharger and turbocharger pedestal as outlined under "Turbocharger, Replace."
11. Remove bolts and position heater hose tube aside. Remove and discard O-ring.
12. Disconnect manifold absolute pressure sensor.
13. Disconnect engine coolant vent hose.
14. Remove fuel injector driver module.
15. Disconnect powertrain control module electrical connectors.
16. Disconnect 12 pin and 8 pin electrical connectors, **Fig. 10.**
17. Disconnect wiring retainer, injector pressure regulator and injector control pressure sensor electrical connector, **Fig. 11.**
18. Disconnect EGR valve electrical connector.
19. Disconnect oil pressure and temperature sensors electrical connectors.

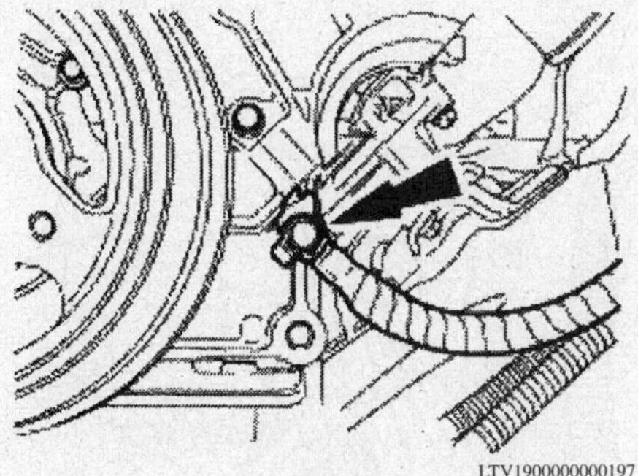

Fig. 2 Lefthand side ground cable

20. Disconnect throttle position control module electrical connector.
21. Disconnect throttle position sensor electrical connector.
22. Disconnect water temperature sensor electrical connector.
23. Disconnect intake air temperature sensor electrical connector.
24. Disconnect exhaust backpressure sensor retaining clip.
25. Disconnect camshaft position sensor and position wiring harness aside.
26. Disconnect fuel injector electrical connectors. Remove nut and fuel injector wiring harness.
27. Disconnect fuel line fittings, **Fig. 12.**
28. Remove oil filter housing, drain oil into suitable container.
29. Remove oil filter return tube.
30. Remove fuel line, discard sealing washers.
31. Remove turbocharger heat shield.
32. Pull EGR cooler clamp forward, twist and then slide EGR cooler hose rearward to remove.
33. Remove EGR cooler V-clamp and gasket.
34. Remove bolts, then the intake manifold.
35. Clean and inspect gaskets, replace as required.
36. Reverse procedure to install, noting the following:
    a. Install intake manifold gaskets, **Fig. 13.**
    b. Loosely install manifold and bolts, then tighten in sequence, **Fig. 14.**
    c. **Torque** bolts 9–16 to 96 inch lbs.
    d. **Torque** all bolts to 96 inch lbs.

CYLINDER HEAD

REPLACE

Removal

1. With transmission in neutral position, raise and support vehicle.
2. Drain engine oil into suitable container.
3. Remove intake manifold as outlined under "Intake Manifold, Replace."
4. Remove fuel injectors.
5. Remove turbocharger adapter pipe.
6. Remove glow plug bus bar and glow plugs.
7. Remove and discard crankcase to head tube assembly.
8. Remove and discard inner cylinder head bolts.

Fig. 3 Ground cable location

9. Remove eight bolts, then the rocker arm assemblies.
10. Mark eight valve bridges with permanent marker for installation reference.
11. Remove eight pushrods.
12. Remove outer cylinder head bolts, **Fig. 15.**
13. Install cylinder head lifting bracket No. 303–759, or equivalent and attache suitable lifting device.
14. With help of an assistant, remove cylinder head from vehicle.

Installation

1. Install new dowels in cylinder head, then install new press in place gasket, **Fig. 16.**
2. Install rocker arm carrier on cylinder head, **Fig. 17, torque** mounting bolts to 23 ft. lbs.
3. Apply anti-seize lubricant to exhaust manifold bolts.
4. Install exhaust manifold bolts and tighten in sequence, **Figs. 18 and 19** to 28 ft. lbs.
5. Install lifting bracket on cylinder head. Use care to avoid scratching blue compound on cylinder head gasket. Install gasket with part number facing upward.
6. Install new dowels and cylinder head gasket.
7. Install cylinder head with help of an assistant and suitable lifting device.
8. Install outer cylinder head bolts finger tight, **Fig. 20.**
9. Install eight pushrods with copper ends installed toward hydraulic rocker followers.
10. Install eight valve bridges.
11. Rotate crankshaft until damper locating dowel notch is in six o'clock position.
12. Install rocker arm assemblies.
13. Lightly lubricate cylinder head bolts with clean engine oil.
14. Install inner cylinder head bolts finger tight.
15. Tighten cylinder head bolts in following sequence:
    a. **Torque** bolts 1 through 10, **Fig. 21,** to 65 ft. lbs.
    b. **Torque** bolts 1, 3, 5, 7 and 9 to 85 ft. lbs.
    c. Turn bolts 1 through 10 in sequence, clockwise 90°.
    d. Turn bolts 1 through 10 in sequence, clockwise 90°.
    e. Turn bolts 1 through 10 in sequence, clockwise 90°.
    f. **Torque** bolts 11 through 15 to 18 ft. lbs.
    g. **Torque** bolts 11 through 15 to 23 ft. lbs.
16. Install new crankcase head tube assembly with new lower O-ring.
17. Install glow plugs and glow plug bus bar.
18. Install turbocharge adapter pipe.
19. Install fuel injectors and intake manifold.
20. Install new oil filter, then fill crankcase with clean engine oil.

Fig. 4 Glow plug electrical connectors

FUEL INJECTOR

REPLACE

1. Remove valve cover as outlined under "Valve Cover, Replace."
2. Disconnect fuel injector electrical connector.
3. Disconnect high pressure oil rail supply line at high pressure oil rail, **Fig. 22,** using removal tool No. 303–755, or equivalent.
4. Remove high pressure oil rail.
5. Push fuel injector electrical connector out of rocker arm carrier with suitable socket.
6. Remove bolt, fuel injector hold down and fuel injector, **Fig. 23.**
7. To prevent damage to engine, do not use air tools to remove fuel injectors. The clip that extracts the injector can dislodge and fall into oil drain hole.
8. If engine oil is found in engine coolant or engine coolant is found in combustion chambers, new injector sleeves may need to be installed.
9. If injector sleeves are needed, cylinder heads will need to be removed from vehicle.
10. Reverse procedure to install.

FUEL INJECTOR SLEEVE

REPLACE

Removal

Fuel injector sleeve is made of stainless steel. Lubrication of fuel injector sleeve removal tap is required. Excessive force will be needed to get tap started and damage to tap can occur without lubrication.

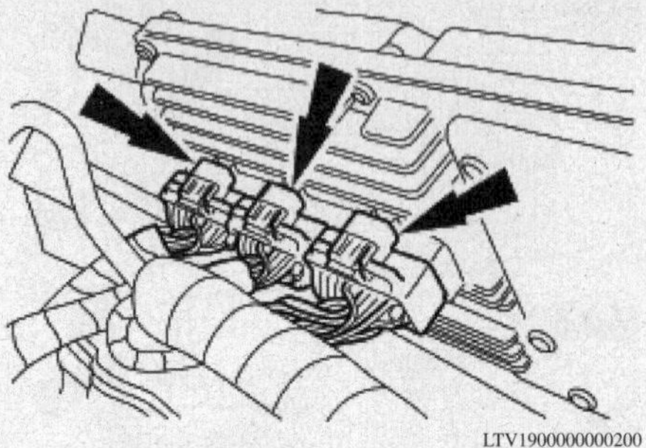

Fig. 5 Fuel injection control module electrical connectors

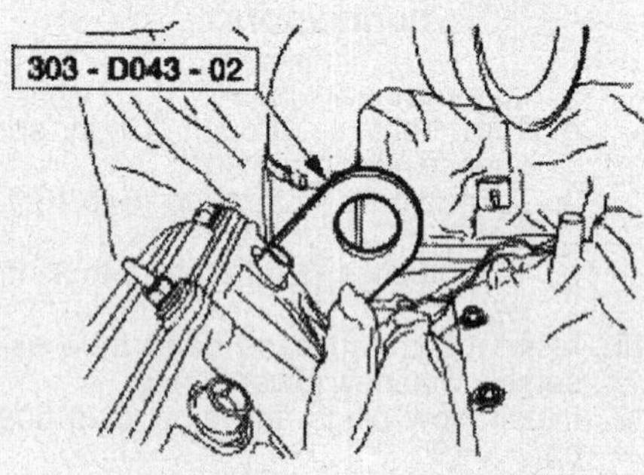

Fig. 8 Lifting eye installation, righthand cylinder head

1. Remove fuel injectors as outlined under "Fuel Injector, Replace."
2. Remove cylinder heads as outlined under "Cylinder Head, Replace."
3. Insert injector sleeve tap and injector sleeve tap pilot No. 303–768, or equivalent, into cylinder head fuel injector bore, **Fig. 24.**
4. Install fuel injector sleeve removal tool No. 100–0101, or equivalent, into threaded sleeve, **Fig. 25.**
5. Remove and discard sleeve.
6. Clean injector bores of deposits and hardened sealant using cleaning tool No. 303–DS110, or equivalent.
7. Remove fuel rail plug. Clean fuel gallery with a wire brush.
8. Use filtered compressed air to remove debris from gallery, then install fuel rail plug.

Installation

1. Verify injector bore is clean and dry.
2. Position fuel injector sleeve onto injector sleeve replacement tool No. 303–767, or equivalent.
3. Apply Threadlock 262, or equivalent to very bottom (smallest diameter) and very top (largest diameter) flat areas.
4. Position fuel injector sleeve into cylinder head fuel injector bore.
5. Seat fuel injector sleeve in bore with rubber mallet.
6. If any sealant gets inside of injector sleeve, it must be cleaned out before it hardens.
7. Install cylinder heads as outlined under "Cylinder Head, Replace."
8. Install fuel injectors as outlined under "Fuel Injector, Replace."

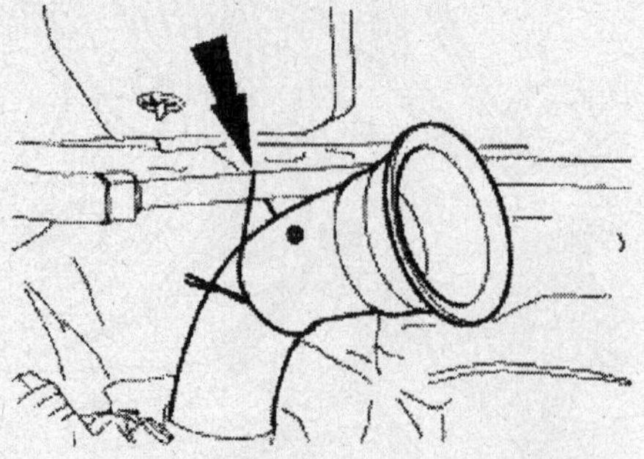

Fig. 6 Turbocharger outlet pipe

VALVE COVER

REPLACE

Righthand

1. Remove evaporator case as outlined under "Air Conditioning" chapter.
2. Loosen clamps at charge air cooler and turbocharger, then remove charge air tube.
3. Disconnect wiring retainer from valve cover stud.
4. Disconnect glow plug controller electrical connectors and wiring retainer.
5. Remove glow plug retainer.
6. **On models equipped with automatic transmission,** remove nut and position transmission fluid dipstick and tube aside.
7. **On all models,** mark position of valve cover bolts for installation reference.
8. Remove bolts, then the valve cover.
9. Reverse procedure to install.

Lefthand

1. Remove air cleaner assembly.
2. Remove bolts and position degas bottle aside.
3. Remove turbocharger inlet pipe mounting nuts and disconnect vent tube.
4. Loosen clamp and remove turbocharger inlet pipe.
5. Remove fuel injection control module mounting bolts and position module for access to electrical connectors.
6. Remove fuel injection control module and bracket.
7. Disconnect glow plug connector and position aside.
8. Remove nut and position oil dipstick and tube aside.
9. Mark position of valve cover bolts for installation reference.
10. Remove bolts, then the valve cover.
11. Reverse procedure to install.

ROCKER ARM & PUSHRODS

Removal

1. Remove cylinder head as outlined under "Cylinder Head, Replace."
2. Push down rocker arm, then pull out on bottom releasing ball, **Fig. 26.**

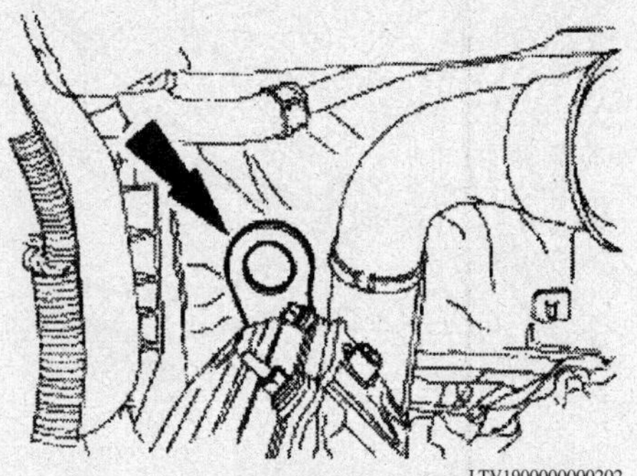

Fig. 7 Manufacturers lifting eye, righthand cylinder head

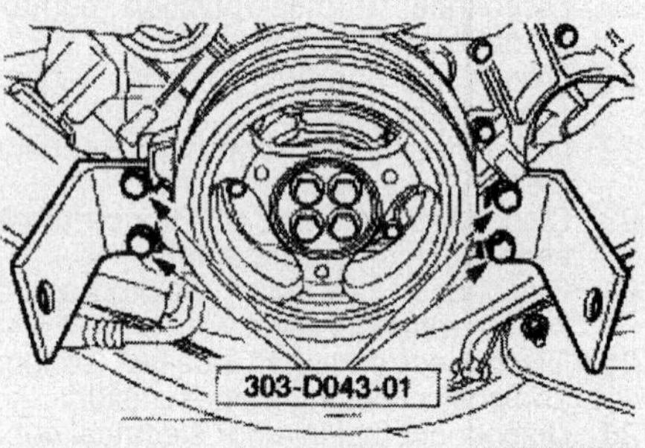

Fig. 9 Front lifting brackets installation

3. Remove steel ball from rocker arm.
4. Remove rocker arm clip from fulcrum plate.

Installation

1. Install rocker arm clip on fulcrum plate, **Fig. 27.**
2. Place steel ball in rocker arm cup, **Fig. 28,** and lubricate with clean engine oil.
3. Push down on rocker arm to compress clip.
4. Insert ball and release pressure. Verify free movement of rocker arm on fulcrum.

VALVE ADJUSTMENT

Valve lash is hydraulically controlled. Valve clearance is not adjustable.

CRANKSHAFT SEAL

REPLACE

Front

1. Remove cooling fan and accessory drive belt.
2. Remove and discard crankshaft vibration damper bolts, then remove damper.
3. Punch two holes in front crankshaft seal.
4. Remove seal using seal removal tool No. 303–D060, or equivalent.
5. Remove crankshaft damper wear sleeve, if equipped, with removal tool No. 303–762, or equivalent.
6. Reverse procedure to install, noting the following:

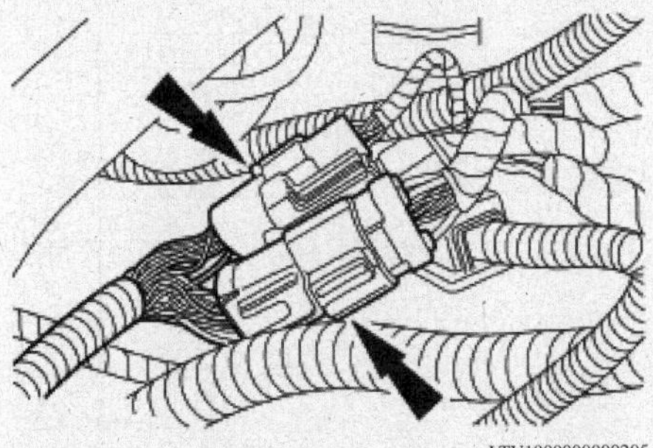

Fig. 10 12 pin and 8 pin electrical connectors

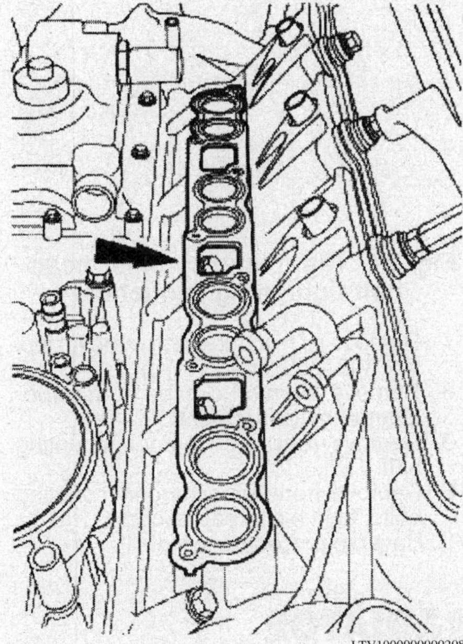

Fig. 13 Intake manifold gasket

a. Apply suitable threadlock compound to outer circumference of leading edge of crankshaft.
b. Install seal and wear sleeve with installation tool No. 303–761, or equivalent. New seal and sleeve must not be separated.

Rear

1. Remove transmission as outlined in **MOTOR's "Domestic Transmission In-Vehicle Service" or "Transmission Service DVD."**
2. Remove flexplate or flywheel.
3. Remove flywheel front adapter. Use care during removal to prevent damage to alignment dowel pin.
4. Remove rear seal with removal tool No. 100–001, or equivalent.
5. Remove crankshaft wear sleeve, if equipped, with removal tool No. 303–771, or equivalent.
6. Clean and inspect crankshaft sealing area.
7. Reverse procedure to install, noting the following:
   a. Crankshaft rear oil sleeve and wear sleeve are installed as an assembly.

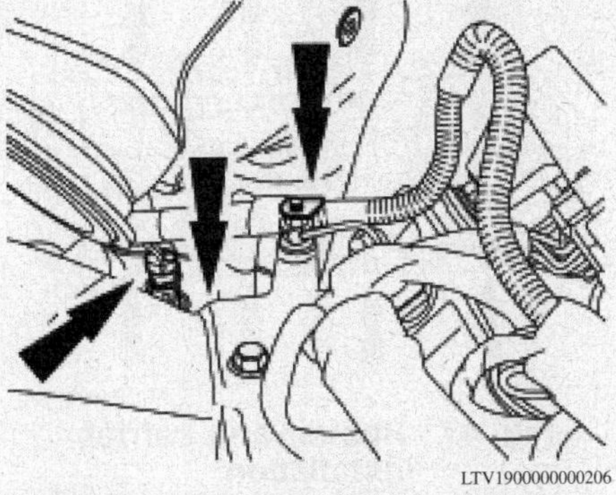

Fig. 11 Wiring retainer, injector pressure regulator & injector control pressure sensor electrical connectors

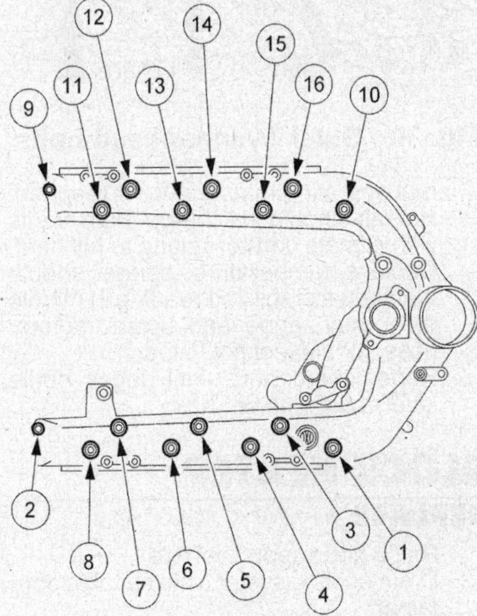

Fig. 14 Intake manifold bolt tightening sequence

b. Apply a bead of suitable threadlock compound around outer circumference of outer rear edge of secondary crankshaft flange.
c. Install seal with installation tool No. 303–770, or equivalent.
d. Install flexplate or flywheel. Snug all bolts to 44 inch lbs., then **torque** to 69 ft. lbs., in sequence, **Fig. 29.**

OIL PUMP

REPLACE

1. Remove crankshaft font oil seal as outlined under "Crankshaft Seal, Replace."
2. Remove bolts and gear rotor cover, **Fig. 30.** Remove and discard O-ring seal.
3. Mark inner and outer gear rotor for assembly reference.
4. Remove inner and outer gear rotors, **Fig. 31.**
5. Inspect oil pump components as outlined under "Oil Pump Service."

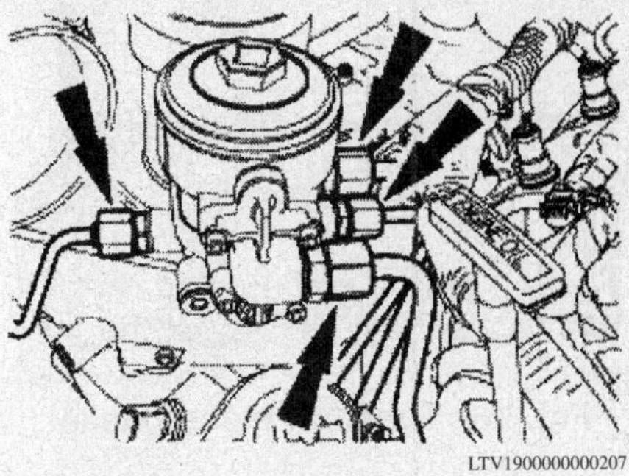

Fig. 12 Fuel line fittings

Fig. 15 Outer cylinder head bolts

6. Install gear rotor gears with marks pointing outward.
7. Lubricate inner gear with lithium assembly grease and install on crankshaft.
8. Lubricate outer gear rotor gear with lithium assembly grease and mesh with inner gear in oil pump housing.
9. Wipe off excessive assembly grease.
10. Install new O-ring seal, then the gear rotor cover and bolts.
11. Install crankshaft front oil seal and damper.

OIL PUMP SERVICE

1. Inspect oil pump for excessive metal particles, gouging, cracks or deep scratches.
2. Inspect oil pump inner and outer gear rotors for damage or excessive wear.
3. Measure height clearance between oil pump housing and inner and outer rotors with suitable straightedge, **Fig. 32.**
4. If measurement is not .001–.003 inch, install new gear rotor set.
5. Measure clearance between outer rotor and oil pump housing, **Fig. 33.**
6. If measurement is not .028–.032 inch, replace gear rotor set.

BELT TENSION DATA

Automatic tensioners are calibrated at the factory to provide correct amount of tension to belt. Belt wear is measured at the tensioner with the use of index marks incorporated into the tensioner, **Figs. 34 and 35.** Tension is correct if belt tensioner is within marks.

Fig. 16 Press in place gasket

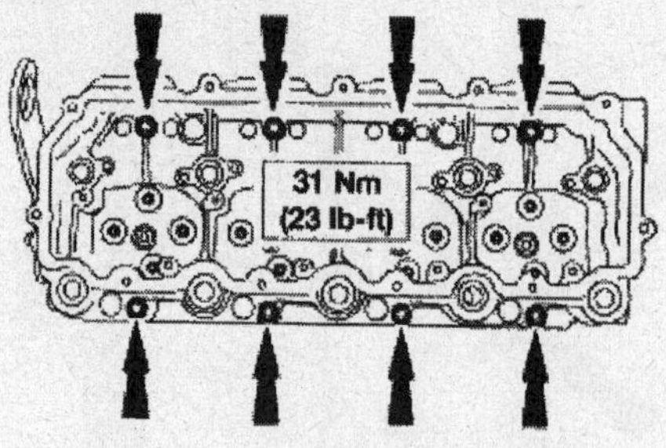

Fig. 17 Rocker arm carrier installation

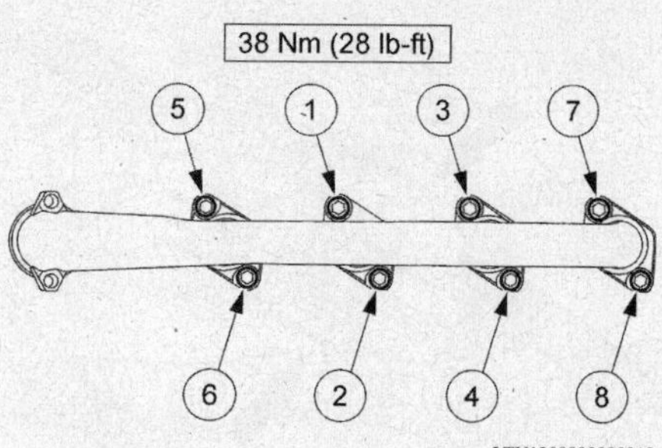

Fig. 18 Righthand exhaust manifold bolt tightening sequence

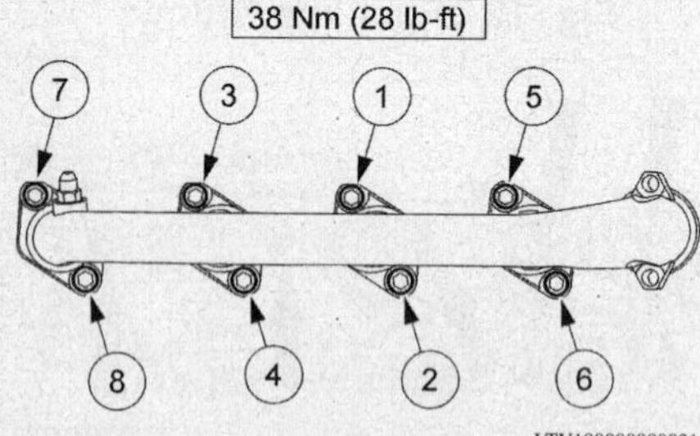

Fig. 19 Lefthand exhaust manifold bolt tightening sequence

Fig. 20 Outer cylinder head bolts

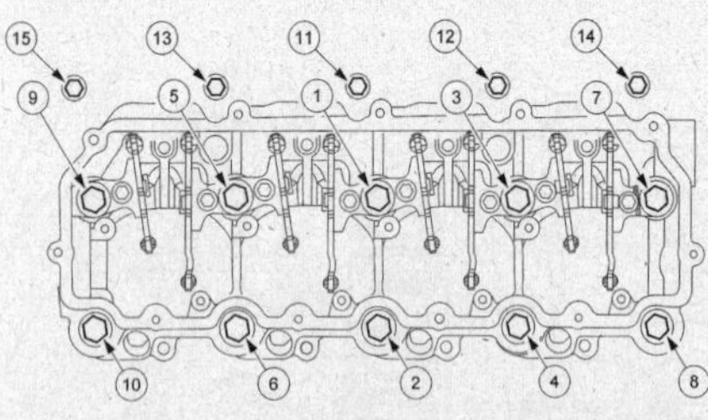

Fig. 21 Righthand cylinder head bolt tightening sequence

SERPENTINE DRIVE BELT

Belt Routing

Refer to **Figs. 36 and 37** for serpentine drive belt routing.

Belt Tensioner Replacement

1. Remove cooling fan, blade, clutch and shroud.
2. Remove accessory drive belt as outlined under "Belt Replacement."
3. Remove bolts and drive belt tensioner.

Belt Replacement

1. Remove cooling fan, blade, clutch and shroud.
2. **On models equipped with air conditioning,** rotate drive belt tensioner clockwise, then remove accessory drive belt.
3. **On models less air conditioning,** rotate drive belt tensioner counterclockwise, then remove accessory drive belt.
4. **On all models,** reverse procedure to install.

COOLING SYSTEM BLEED

1. Run engine until it reaches normal operating temperature (2000 RPM for five minutes).
2. Turn engine off and allow to cool.
3. Add correct engine coolant mixture to degas bottle until coolant level is between "Coolant Fill Level" marks.
4. Start engine and allow to idle until normal operating temperature is reached. Hot air should discharge from vents with climate control setting to full heat. Coolant temperature gauge should maintain a stabilized reading in middle of normal range and upper radiator hose should feel hot to touch.
5. Repeat procedure until degas bottle level is acceptable.

BLOCK HEATER

REPLACE

1. Raise and support vehicle.
2. Drain cooling system into suitable container.
3. Disconnect block heater electrical connector.
4. Remove block heater and discard O-ring.
5. Reverse procedure to install.

WATER PUMP

REPLACE

1. Drain cooling system into suitable container.
2. Remove cooling fan and clutch.
3. Remove accessory drive belt.
4. Remove water pump pulley, then the water pump.
5. Reverse procedure to install.

TURBOCHARGER

REPLACE

1. Remove turbocharger intake tube.
2. Disconnect charge air cooler pipe.
3. Disconnect two wiring harness push pins and position out of way.
4. Disconnect variable gate turbocharger electrical connector.
5. Remove oil supply tube from turbocharger and discard gasket.
6. Remove wire retainer from back of turbocharger.
7. Remove oil feed tube with removal tool No. 303–755, or equivalent.
8. Remove Marmon clamps from turbocharger outlet and inlet.
9. Remove rear turbocharger mounting bolt.
10. Remove front turbocharger mounting bolts, then the turbocharger.
11. Reverse procedure to install

RADIATOR

REPLACE

1. Raise and support vehicle.
2. Drain cooling system into suitable container.
3. Disconnect upper radiator hose and coolant overflow hose.
4. Remove cooling fan.
5. Disconnect lower radiator hose.
6. Disconnect transmission cooler tubes.
7. Remove radiator support brackets, then the radiator.
8. Reverse procedure to install.

FUEL PUMP

REPLACE

The fuel conditioning module contains the fuel pump, the fuel warmer and the fuel/water separator.

1. Raise and support vehicle.
2. Open fuel/water separator drain valve to release fuel pressure.
3. Disconnect electrical connectors from fuel pump, fuel warmer and fuel/water separator.
4. Remove and discard fuel hose retaining clips. Disconnect fuel hoses from fuel pump.
5. Remove mounting nuts, then the fuel conditioning module.
6. Reverse procedure to install.

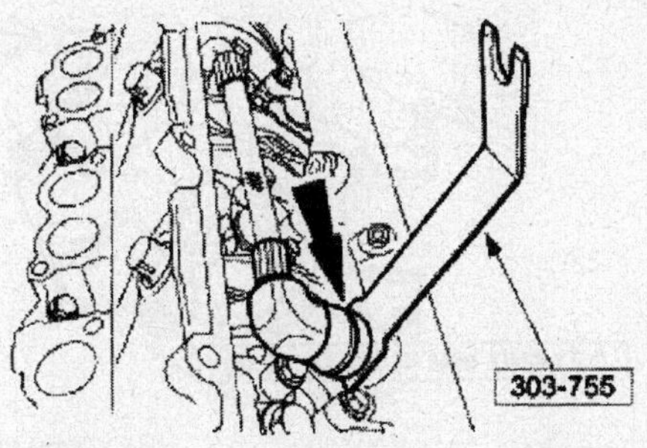

Fig. 22 High pressure oil rail supply line removal

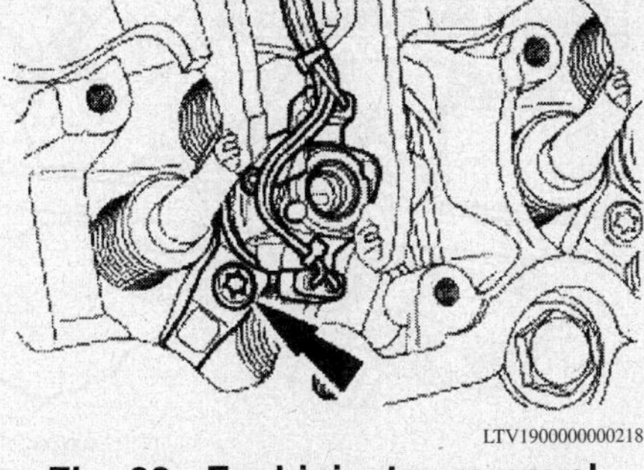

Fig. 23 Fuel injector removal

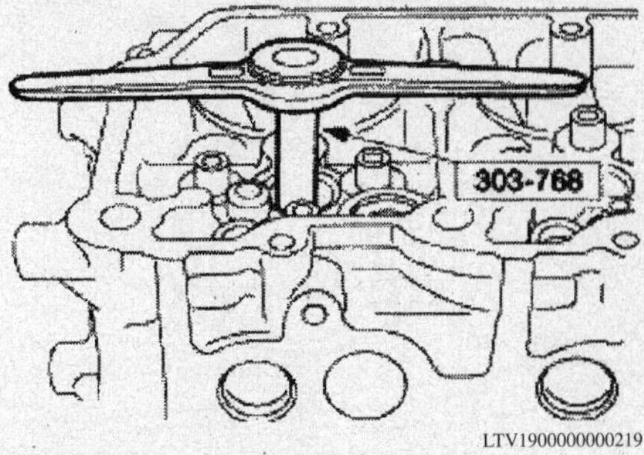

Fig. 24 Injector sleeve tap & pilot installation

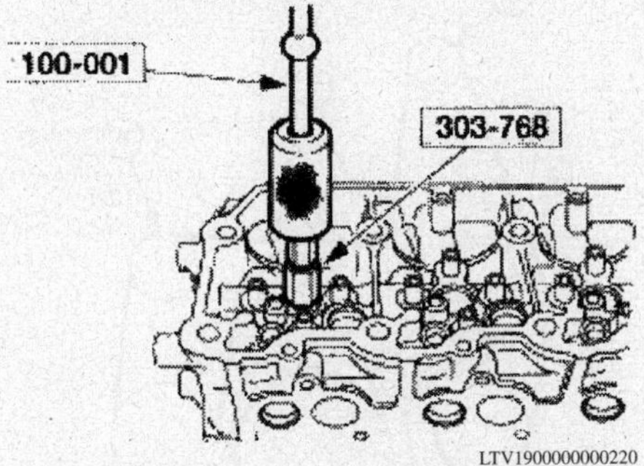

Fig. 25 Injector sleeve removal tool

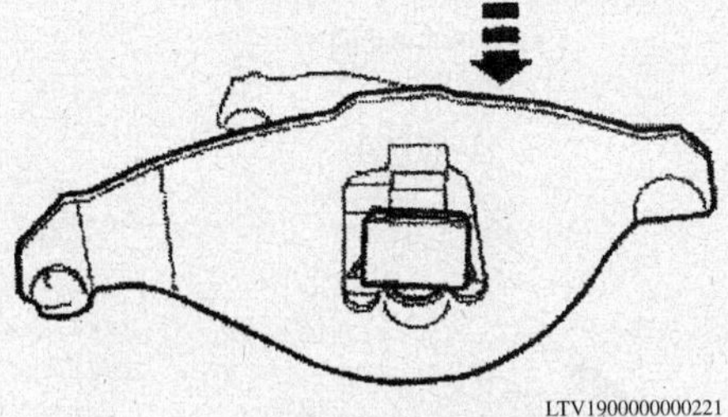

Fig. 26 Rocker arm removal

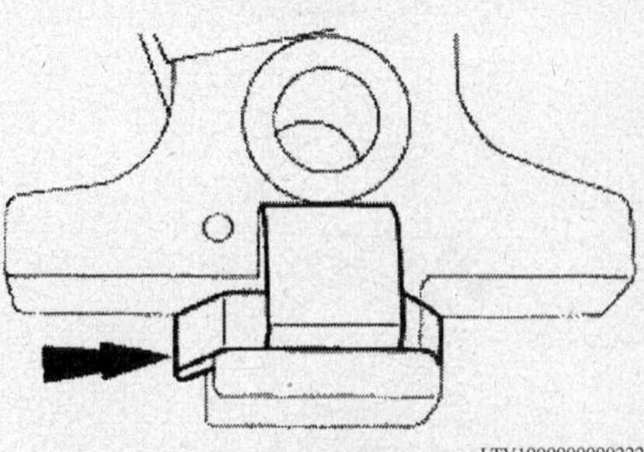

Fig. 27 Rocker arm clip installation

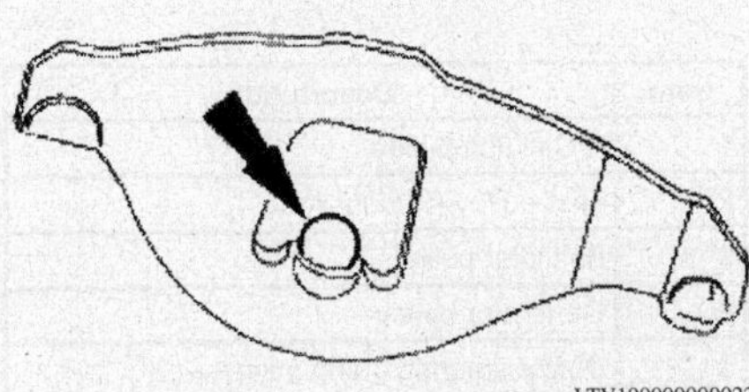

Fig. 28 Steel ball installation

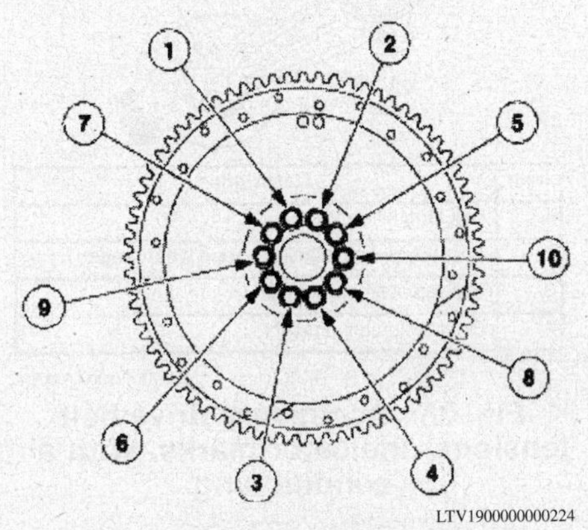

Fig. 29 Flywheel/flexplate tightening sequence

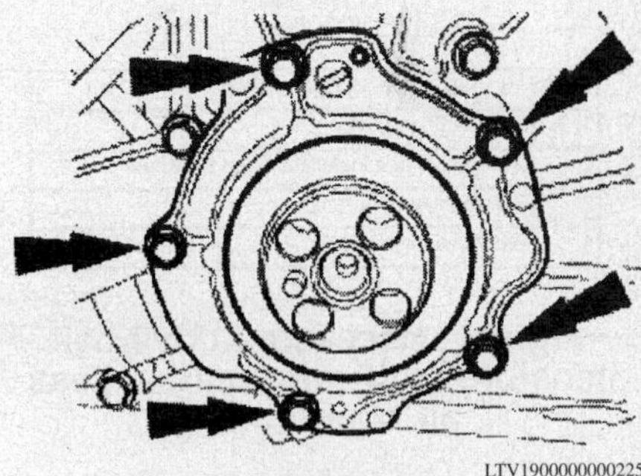

Fig. 30 Gerotor cover

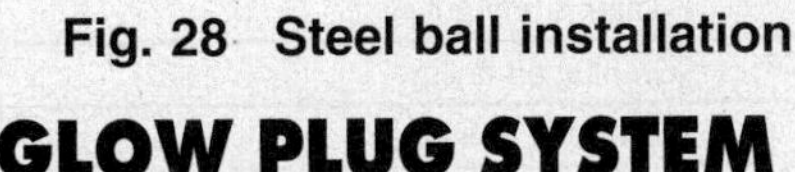

GLOW PLUG SYSTEM

Glow Plug, Replace

1. If servicing righthand glow plugs, remove evaporator core housing as outlined under "Air Conditioning" chapter.
2. Disconnect glow plug electrical connector.
3. Remove glow plug buss bar.
4. Remove glow plug.
5. Reverse procedure to install

Glow Plug Sleeve

REMOVAL

Glow plug sleeves are made of stainless steel. Lubrication of glow plug sleeve removal tap is required to prevent damage to tap.

1. Remove cylinder head as outlined under "Cylinder Head, Replace."
2. Insert glow plug sleeve removal tool No. 303–764, or equivalent, into threaded sleeve and tighten.
3. Use wrench to thread tool into sleeve until sleeve is extracted.
4. Clean glow plug bore with stiff wire brush. Use filtered compressed air to remove debris from glow plug recesses.

INSTALLATION

1. Verify glow plug bore is completely clean and dry.
2. Apply suitable threadlock compound to glow plug sleeve in two places, **Fig. 38.**
3. Install glow plug sleeve into glow plug bore until it bottoms out.
4. Clean glow plug sleeve after installation with nylon brush and solvent. Ensure threadlock sealant is cleaned out before it hardens.
5. Install cylinder head.
6. Install glow plugs and glow plug bus bar.
7. If removed, install evaporator core housing.

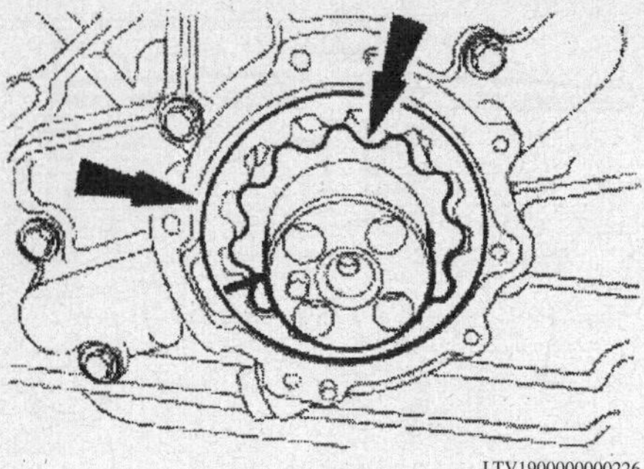

Fig. 31 Gear Rotors

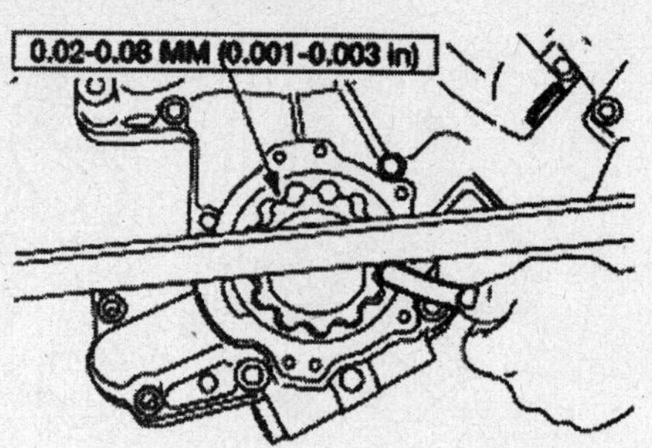

Fig. 32 Oil pump height clearance measurement

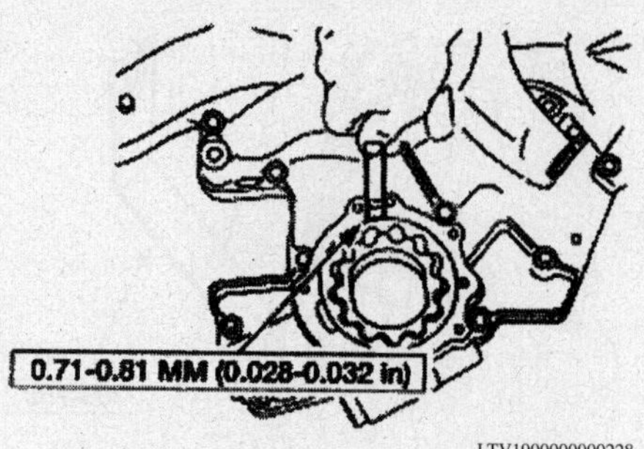

Fig. 33 Rotor to pump housing clearance measurement

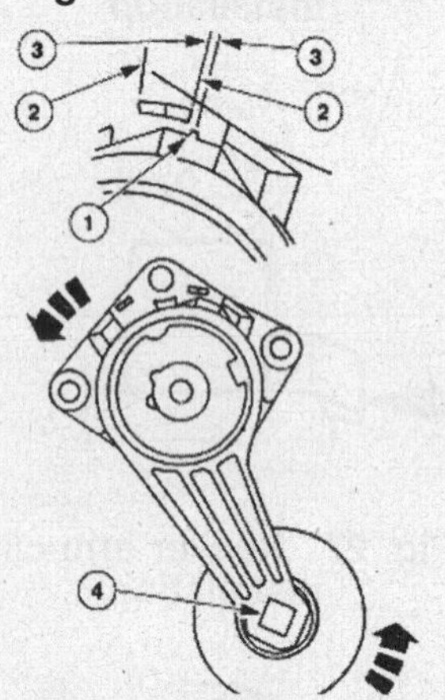

Item	Description
1	Belt length indicator
2	Acceptable belt installation and wear range
3	Belt replacement range
4	Belt tension relief point

Fig. 34 Accessory drive belt tensioner indicator marks. Less air conditioning

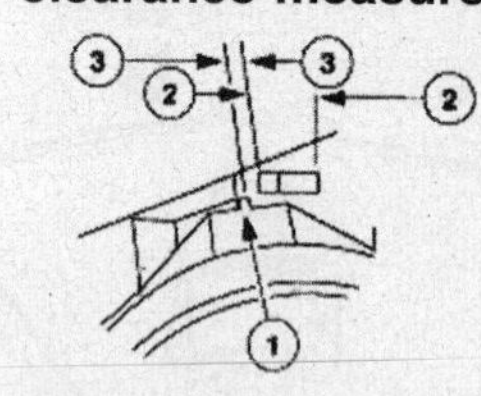

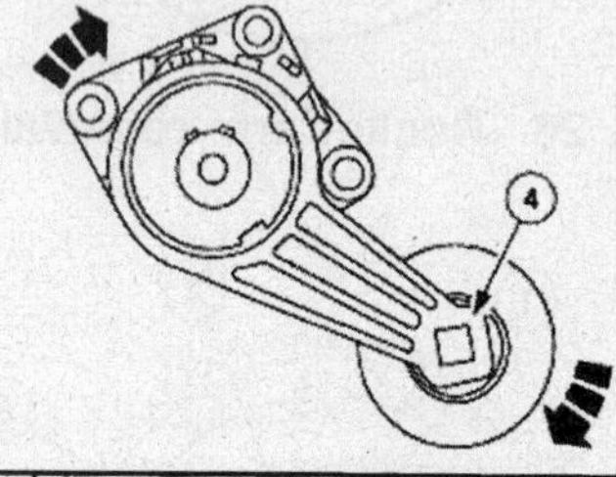

Item	Description
1	Belt length indicator
2	Acceptable belt installation and wear range
3	Belt replacement range
4	Belt tension relief point

Fig. 35 Accessory drive belt tensioner indicator marks. With air conditioning

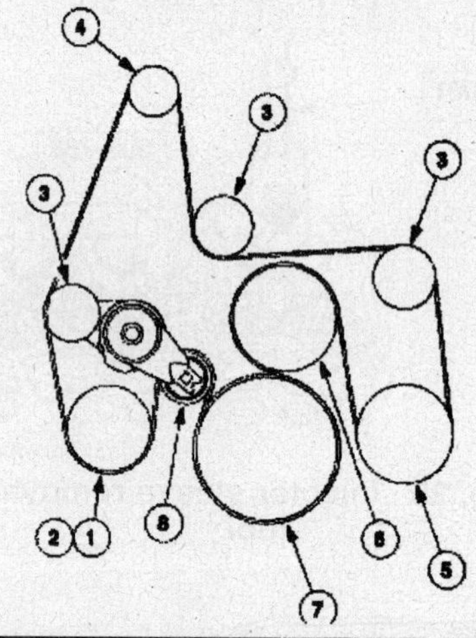

Item	Description
1	A/C clutch pulley
2	Idler pulley (without A/C)
3	Belt idler pulley
4	Generator pulley
5	Power steering pump pulley
6	Water pump pulley
7	Crankshaft pulley
8	Drive belt tensioner

Fig. 36 Serpentine drive belt routing. Single alternator

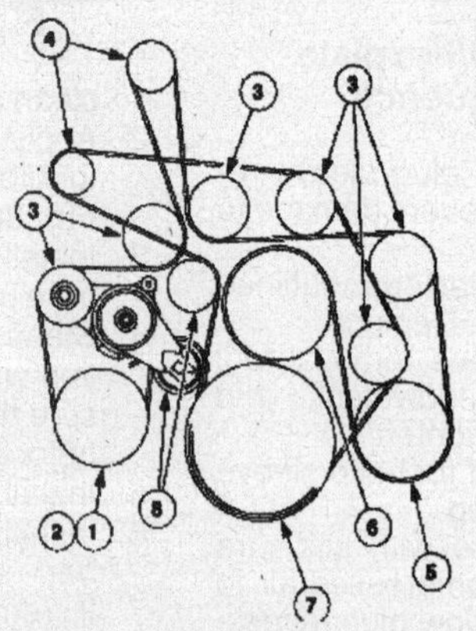

Item	Description
1	A/C clutch pulley
2	Idler pulley (without A/C)
3	Belt idler pulley
4	Generator pulley
5	Power steering pump pulley
6	Water pump pulley
7	Crankshaft pulley
8	Drive belt tensioner

Fig. 37 Serpentine drive belt routing. Dual alternator

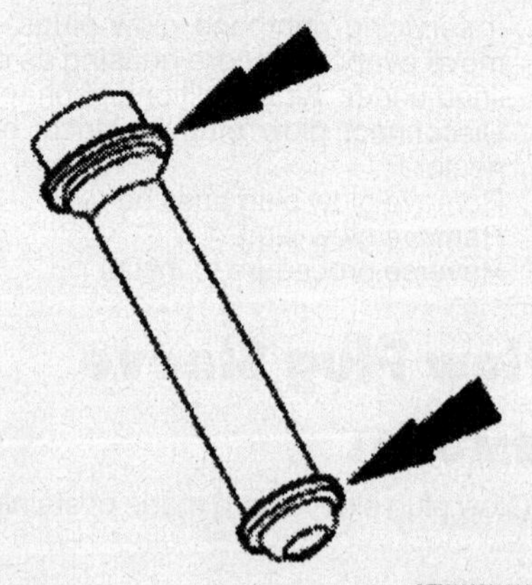

Fig. 38 Glow plug sleeve threadlock compound application areas

TIGHTENING SPECIFICATIONS

Year	Component	Torque Ft. Lbs.
2003	A/C Compressor	18
	A/C Manifold	15
	Air Inlet Duct Clamp	44①
	Alternator Mounting Bracket (Dual Alternators)	35
	Automatic Transmission Fill Tube	71①
	Battery Cable Nut	108①
	Battery Crossover Cable	108①
	Battery Ground Cable To Engine	35
	Belt Idler Pulley	35
	Belt Tensioner	18
	Cam Follower Mounting	120①
	Camshaft Position Sensor	96①
	Camshaft Thrust Plate	23
	Coolant Heater	30
	Cooling Fan Stator	30
	Crankcase Breather	62①
	Crankshaft Pulley (Dual Alternator)	35
	Crankshaft Position Sensor	96①
	Cylinder Head Bolt	②
	EGR Valve Mounting	120①
	EGR Valve V-Band Clamp	53①
	EGR Cooler Bolts (M8 x 16)	23
	EGR Cooler Coolant Supply Cover	89①
	EGR Cooler Stud Bolts (M6 x 55 x 20)	120①
	Engine Ground Strap	89①
	Exhaust Manifold Flange	28
	Exhaust Tube To Exhaust Manifold Flange	20
	Fan Clutch Hub	98
	Flywheel/Flexplate	69
	Fuel Filter Plug Assembly (Back Of Head)	20
	Fuel Injector Hold Down	24
	Fuel Supply & Return Tubes At Filter	32
	Glow Plugs	14
	High Pressure Oil Pump	18
	High Pressure Oil Pump Cover	96①
	High Pressure Oil Pump Discharge Tube	71①
	High Pressure Tube — Case To Head	33
	Intake Manifold Flange	96①

TIGHTENING SPECIFICATIONS—Continued

Year	Component	Torque Ft. Lbs.
2003	Intake Manifold Heat Shield	96①
	Motor Mount Nuts	83
	Oil Cooler Mounting (6mm)	89①
	Oil Cooler Mounting (8mm)	16
	Oil Filter Housing	11
	Oil Filter Return Tube (New Base)	44①
	Oil Filter Return Tube (Reinstallation)	27①
	Oil Pan (Lower)	120①
	Oil Pan (Upper)	120①
	Oil Pan Drain Plug	18
	Oil Pickup Tube Flange	120①
	Oil Pump Housing	71①
	Power Steering Cooler	96①
	Power Steering Pump	18
	Rocker Arm Fulcrum Plate	23
	Starter	18
	Starter Control Wire	53①
	Starter Positive Cable	108①
	Starter Solenoid Wire	53①
	Transmission Cooler	71①
	Transmission To Engine	35
	Turbocharger Down Pipe	30
	Turbocharger Exhaust Adapter V-Clamp	108①
	Turbocharger Flange To Exhaust/EGR Tube	20
	Turbocharger Mounting	28
	Turbocharger Oil Supply	18
	Turbocharger Pedestal	23
	Valve Cover Bolts & Studs	71①
	Water Pump	17
	Water Pump Pulley	23

①— Inch lbs.

②— Refer to "Cylinder Head, Replace" for toque specifications and procedure.

7.3L Diesel Engine

NOTE: On Air Bag Equipped Models, Refer To "Air Bag System Precautions" Located In The Front Of This Manual For System Disarming & Arming Procedures.

NOTE: Refer To "Computer Relearn Procedures" Located In The Front Of This Manual When Battery Power To The Computer Has Been Interrupted.

INDEX

PRECAUTIONS

Air Bag Systems

Refer to "Air Bag System Precautions" in the front of this manual for system disarming and arming procedures.

Battery Ground Cable

Prior to service, disconnect battery ground cable and isolate as required.

Fuel Injector Harness

Fuel injector harness red-striped wires carry 115 volts. If harness integrity is compromised, severe shock will occur.

COMPRESSION PRESSURES

1. Warm engine to normal operating temperature, then place ignition in Off position.
2. Remove alternator retaining bolt and electrical connectors and position aside.
3. Remove drive belt.
4. Remove alternator bracket retaining bolts, then the alternator and bracket.
5. Remove dipstick assembly and bracket.
6. Remove fuel injector wiring harness connector from valve cover gasket.
7. Remove valve covers.
8. Disconnect harness from glow plugs, then remove all glow plugs.
9. Install compression gauge into cylinder No. 1 glow plug hole.
10. Crank engine at least five compression strokes with ignition in Off position and record highest reading.
11. Repeat compression inspection on each cylinder, noting the following:
    a. Compression pressures are considered within specification if they are at least 350 psi and lowest cylinder is within 50 psi of highest.
    b. Variations exceeding specifications indicate an improperly seated valve or worn/broken piston rings.

ENGINE MOUNT

REPLACE

E-Series

1. Remove radiator assembly as outlined under "Radiator, Replace."
2. Recover A/C refrigerant as outlined under "Air Conditioning" chapter.
3. Remove air deflector retaining pins and deflector.
4. Disconnect condenser core refrigerant lines.
5. Remove two A/C condenser mounting brackets, then the condenser core.
6. Remove serpentine drive belt.
7. Remove turbocharger exhaust clamp.
8. Remove air cleaner assembly.
9. Loosen clamp and disconnect air inlet tube from resonator.
10. Remove turbocharger heat shield, then resonator.
11. Disconnect electrical connector and engine wiring from bracket, then remove engine wiring harness bracket.
12. Remove transmission fluid dipstick upper nut and lower bell housing bolt, then position transmission fluid dipstick aside.
13. Remove oil fill tube bolt.
14. Raise and support vehicle.
15. Remove bolt securing fuel lines, **Fig. 1.**
16. Remove nut and cable bracket, then stud bolt. Also remove bolt and transmission tube bracket, **Fig. 2.**
17. Install mounting brackets, **Fig. 3.**
18. Remove engine mounting nuts.
19. Loosen engine mount attaching bolts,

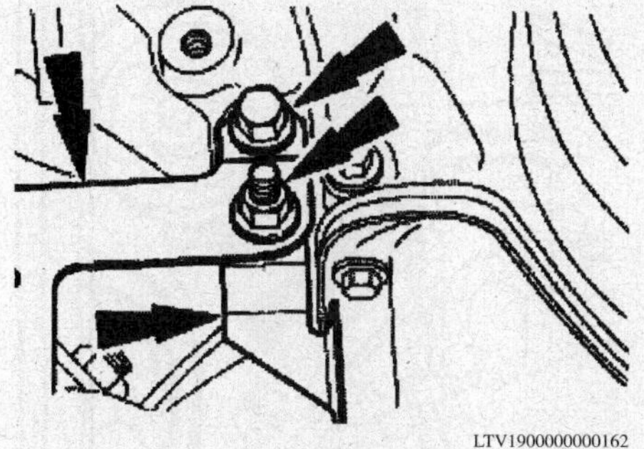

Fig. 1 Fuel line removal. E-Series

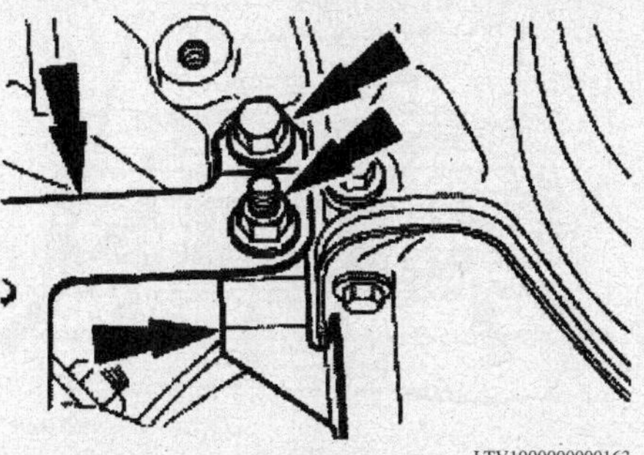

Fig. 2 Transmission bracket removal. E-Series

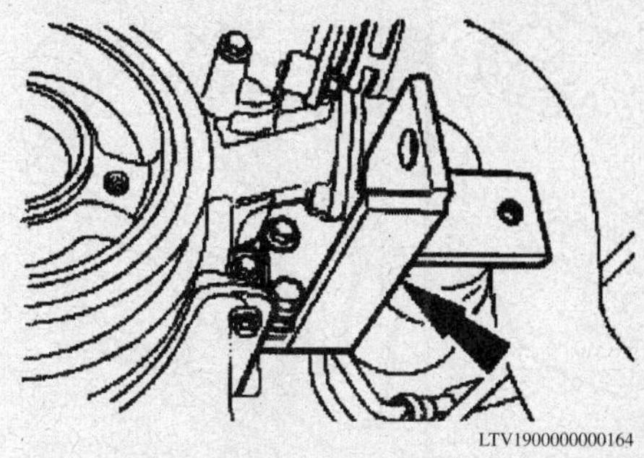

Fig. 3 Engine mounting bracket. E-Series

then lower vehicle.

20. Install tools No. D83T-6000-B and 014-00071, or equivalent.
21. Raise engine until studs clear cross-member. **Make sure turbocharger does not contact the cowl.**
22. Remove engine mounting bolts, then engine mounts.
23. Reverse procedure to install.

Excursion & F-Super Duty

1. Disconnect battery ground cables.
2. Remove air cleaner assembly, **for lefthand engine mount insulator.**
3. Disconnect MAP sensor hose.
4. Remove turbocharger to charge air cooler pipe.
5. Remove charge air cooler to engine pipe, **for lefthand engine mount insulator.**
6. Remove engine cover.
7. Disconnect heater hose and position aside.
8. Disconnect and remove glow plug controller.
9. Disconnect air warmer solenoid electrical connectors, then remove solenoid.
10. Disconnect high pressure oil hose using tool No. 303–625, or equivalent.
11. Drain fuel filter/water separator.
12. Disconnect fuel lines and position fuel lines out of the way.
13. Remove solenoid mounting bracket.
14. Install tool No. D94T-6000-C, or equivalent, **Fig. 4.**
15. Raise and support vehicle.
16. Remove engine mount insulator nuts.
17. Loosen engine mount insulator to cylinder block bolts.
18. Lower vehicle then using heavy duty floor crane tool No. 014-00071, or equivalent, raise engine.
19. Remove engine mount insulator bolts, then engine mount insulator.
20. Reverse procedure to install.

Rear

1. Remove engine mount to support assembly attaching bolt and locknut.
2. Remove engine mount to transmission housing attaching bolts and lockwashers.
3. Raise transmission, then remove mount and retainer.
4. Reverse procedure to install.

ENGINE

REPLACE

E-Series

1. Remove turbocharger.
2. Disconnect intake air warmer, map hose and electrical harness.
3. Remove turbocharger compressor manifold.
4. Remove bolts and turbocharger exhaust inlet Y-pipe.
5. Remove air inlet duct tube mounting bracket.
6. Drain coolant into suitable container.
7. Remove radiator.
8. Remove parking lamp and headlamp assemblies.
9. Recover A/C refrigerant as outline under "Air Conditioning" chapter.
10. Remove A/C condenser.
11. Remove radiator grille support.
12. Remove power steering reservoir.
13. Remove valance panel, **Fig. 5,** hood latch and radiator core supports.
14. Remove front bumper.
15. Remove accessory drive belt.
16. **On E-550 models,** disconnect vacuum hose and from oil filler tube.
17. **On all models,** remove oil filler tube.
18. **On models equipped with air conditioning,** disconnect A/C compressor electrical connector, air conditioning manifold and air conditioning manifold tube from tee block.
19. **On E-250–E-450 models,** disconnect vacuum pump hose.
20. **On all models,** disconnect power steering hoses.
21. Remove A/C compressor or idler pulley mounting bracket, **Fig. 6.**
22. **On models equipped with single alternator system,** disconnect alternator electrical connectors, accessory drive belt tensioner and alternator mounting bracket.
23. **On models equipped with dual alternator system,** proceed as follows:
    a. Disconnect lower alternator quick connector and push pins.
    b. Disconnect lower alternator electrical connector and push pins.
    c. Remove engine ground cables, **Fig. 7.**
    d. Remove lower alternator mounting bracket.
    e. Disconnect upper alternator electrical connector, then the upper alternator mounting bracket.
24. **On all models,** label and disconnect electrical leads.
25. Loosen nuts and position bracket out of way, **Fig. 8.**
26. Disconnect engine control sensor wiring, **Fig. 9.**
27. Remove retaining nuts and position bracket out of way, **Fig. 10.**
28. Disconnect lower radiator hose at water pump.
29. Disconnect heater supply hose.
30. **On models equipped with auxiliary heater,** disconnect heater hose on rear of lefthand cylinder head.
31. **On all models,** disconnect heater hose.
32. Disconnect maxi-fuse.
33. Disconnect fuel tubes.
34. Disconnect transmission sensor harness inline electrical connector, then the sensor harness.
35. Remove fuel tube retaining bolts, then install engine lift adapters No. 303–D099, or equivalent.
36. Raise and support vehicle.
37. Remove starter motor.
38. Remove engine mount nuts, **Fig. 11.**
39. Remove flywheel housing cover, then the torque converter to flywheel retaining nuts.
40. Remove oil filter.
41. Disconnect block heater.
42. Remove lower transmission to engine bolts.
43. Lower vehicle.
44. Remove transmission fluid dipstick and tube.
45. Remove transmission to engine bolts, **Fig. 12.**
46. Place suitable jack under transmission.
47. Attach suitable lifting device to engine, raise high enough to clear crossmember, then remove from vehicle.
48. Reverse procedure to install.

Excursion & F-Super Duty Series

On models equipped with manual transmission the transmission must be removed before engine can be removed.

1. Drain coolant into suitable container.
2. Recover A/C refrigerant as outlined under "Air Conditioning" chapter.
3. Remove air inlet duct and turbocharger.
4. Remove radiator, charge air cooler

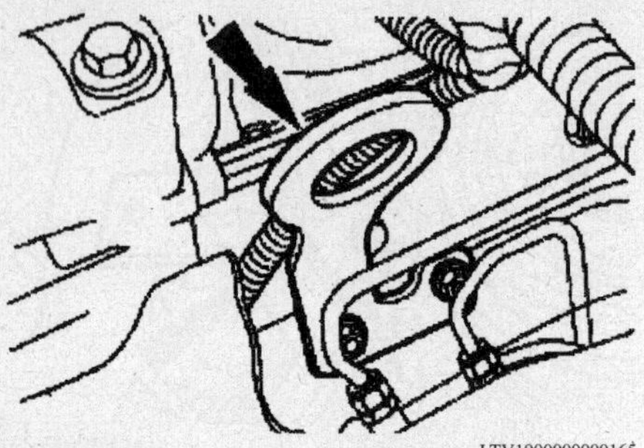

Fig. 4 Engine lifting eye. Excursion & F-Super Duty

and A/C condenser assembly.

5. Remove parking lamp and headlamp assemblies.
6. Remove radiator grille, radiator grille opening panel and upper and lower radiator core supports.
7. Remove front bumper and accessory drive belt.
8. Disconnect alternator, manifold absolute pressure sensor hose from turbocharger compressor manifold.
9. Remove compressor manifold clamps and compressor manifold.
10. **On models with dual alternators,** disconnect alternator and remove ground strap from righthand side of engine block.
11. **On all models,** disconnect A/C compressor connector, if equipped.
12. Disconnect A/C manifold lines from A/C compressor, if equipped.
13. Disconnect power steering lines.
14. **On models with single alternators,** remove ground cable from righthand side of engine block.
15. **On all models,** disconnect engine control sensor wiring and ground strap.
16. Disconnect heater return hose and heater supply hose.
17. Disconnect fuel lines using fuel line tool No. T90T-9550-S, or equivalent.
18. **On models with automatic transmission,** remove transmission sensor harness retaining bolt and harness.
19. **On all models,** fuel line retaining bolt must be removed before engine lift adapters can be install. Remove fuel line retaining bolt.
20. Install two engine lift adapters to fuel retaining bolt holes.
21. Install engine lifting eye tool No. D94T-6000-C, or equivalent, to cylinder head, if required.
22. Raise and support vehicle.
23. Remove starter motor and engine mount nuts.
24. **On models with automatic transmission,** remove flywheel housing cover and torque converter to flywheel retaining nuts.
25. **On all models,** remove oil filter and disconnect block heater.
26. **On models equipped with automatic transmission,** remove transmission to engine bolts.
27. **On all models,** lower vehicle and position a suitable jack under transmission.
28. Remove transmission fill tube.

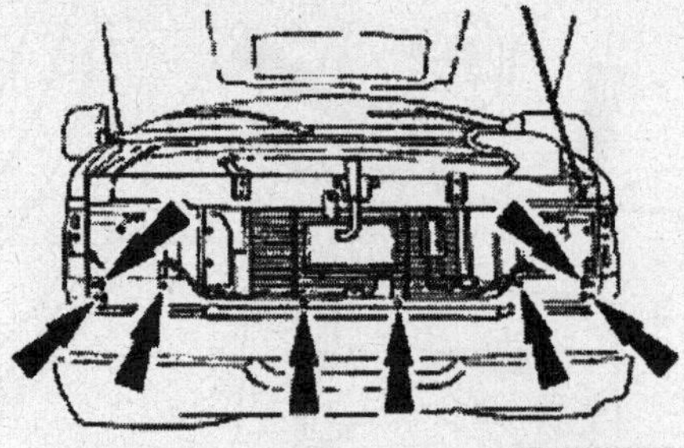

Fig. 5 Valance screw locations. E-Series

29. Install heavy duty floor crane tool No. 014–00071 and diesel engine lifting bracket tool No. D83T-6000-B, or equivalents on engine.
30. Raise engine high enough to clear No. crossmember and pull engine forward.
31. Remove engine lifting equipment from engine.
32. Remove flywheel and mount engine on a work stand, using engine mounting brackets D94T-6000-A, or equivalent.
33. Reverse procedure to install.

INTAKE MANIFOLD

REPLACE

The intake manifold on these engines are integral to the cylinder head and cannot be serviced.

EXHAUST MANIFOLD

REPLACE

1. Disconnect battery ground cable.
2. Remove engine cover.
3. Remove air cleaner assembly.
4. Remove oil dipstick tube and retaining screw, **righthand side only.**
5. Raise and support vehicle.
6. Remove two nuts and bolts retaining righthand or lefthand turbocharger exhaust inlet pipe to exhaust manifold.
7. Lower the vehicle.
8. Disconnect exhaust back pressure line from exhaust manifold.
9. Remove eight exhaust manifold bolts, then exhaust manifold.
10. Reverse procedure to install.

CYLINDER HEAD

REPLACE

E-Series

LEFTHAND

Fuel injector harness red-striped wires carry 115 volts. If harness integrity is compromised, severe shock will occur.

1. Remove console from engine cover.
2. Remove the instrument panel steering column cover.
3. Remove engine cover.
4. Disconnect oil pressure sensor.
5. Remove parking lamps and headlamps.

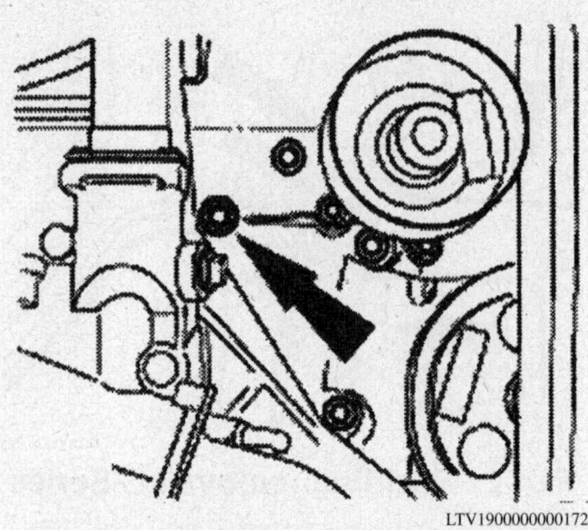

Fig. 6 A/C compressor or idler pulley mounting bracket. E-Series

6. Remove radiator as outlined under "Radiator, Replace."
7. Recover refrigerant as outlined under "Air Conditioning" chapter.
8. Remove air deflector.
9. Disconnect A/C lines from condenser.
10. Remove A/C condenser.
11. Remove radiator grille, grille opening and upper radiator support.
12. Remove turbocharger compressor manifold.
13. Remove accessory drive belt, then disconnect vacuum lines.
14. Disconnect power steering lines, then the A/C lines from compressor.
15. Remove compressor or idler pulley bracket.
16. Remove valve cover as outlined under "Valve Cover, Replace."
17. Remove rocker arms and pushrods as outlined under "Rocker Arms & Pushrods."
18. Remove fuel injectors as outlined under "Fuel Injector, Replace."
19. Disconnect fuel supply tubes from cylinder head.
20. Disconnect high pressure oil line using high pressure line disconnect tool No. 303–625 or equivalent.
21. Remove fuel tube nut from intake manifold stud.
22. Disconnect fuel return tube from cylinder head.
23. Remove fuel tube retaining clamp from cylinder head.
24. Disconnect exhaust pipe from manifold.
25. Remove cylinder head bolts.
26. Install cylinder head lifting tool No. D94T-6000–B or equivalent to cylinder head.
27. Remove cylinder head and gasket.
28. Inspect cylinder head and engine block for flatness.
29. Reverse procedure to install noting the following:
    a. Apply a small amount of suitable clean engine oil to new cylinder head bolt threads and flanges prior to installation.
    b. Install cylinder head bolts and **torque** to 65 ft. lbs., in sequence as outlined in **Fig. 13.**
    c. **Torque** cylinder head bolts to 85 ft. lbs., in sequence as outlined in **Fig. 13.**

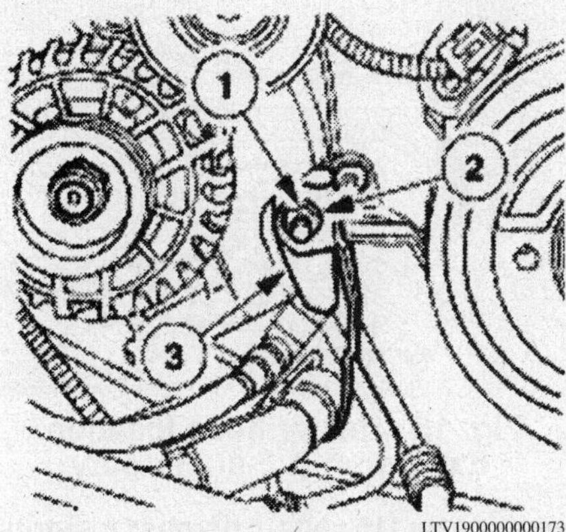

Fig. 7 Engine ground cable. E-Series

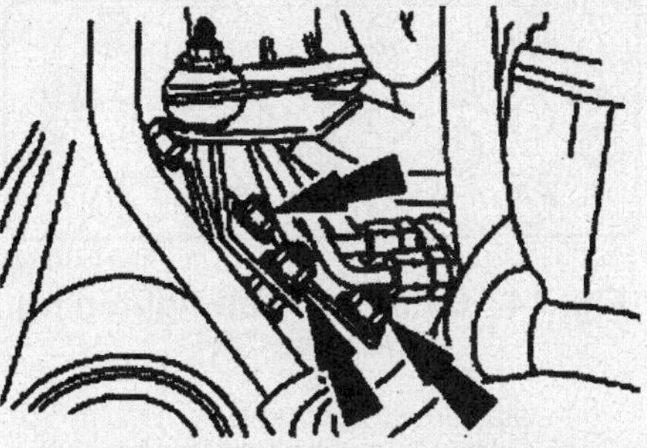

Fig. 8 Bracket mounting nuts. E-Series

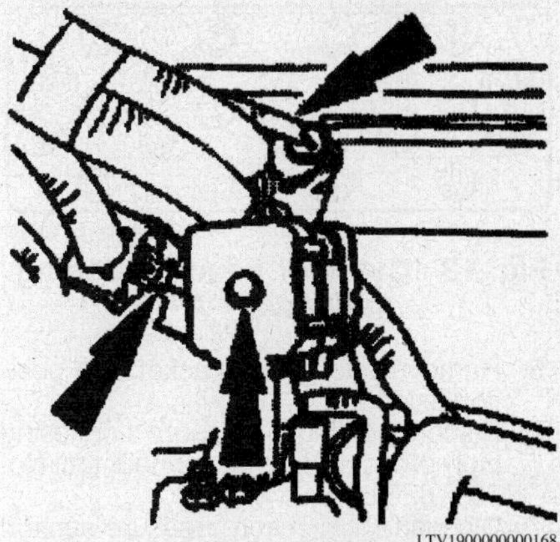

Fig. 9 Engine control sensor wiring. E-Series

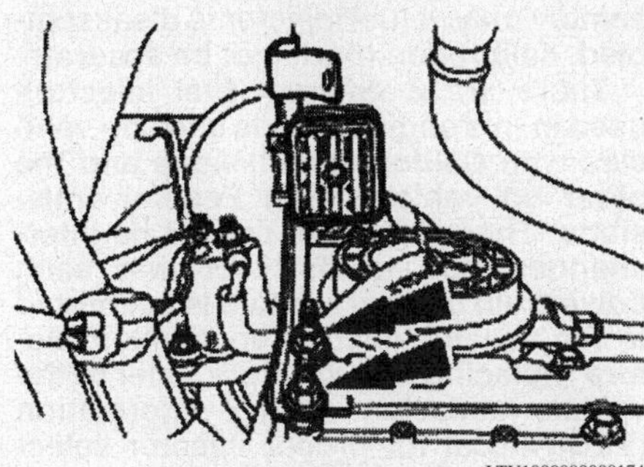

Fig. 10 Electrical mounting bracket. E-Series

Fig. 11 Engine mounting nuts. E-Series

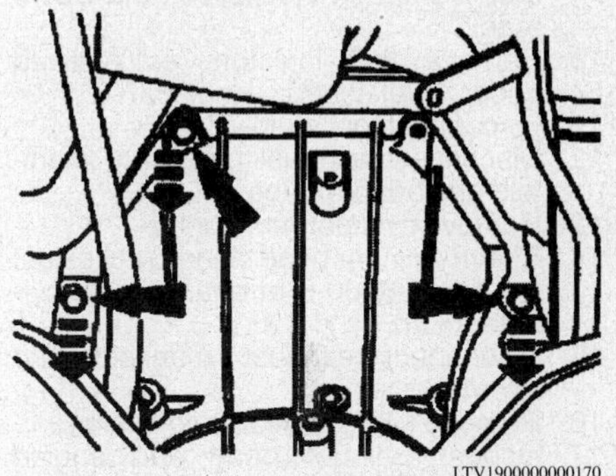

Fig. 12 Transmission to engine mounting bolts. E-Series

d. **Torque** cylinder head bolts to 95 ft. lbs., in sequence as outlined in **Fig. 14.**
e. Before rocker arm and pushrod installation, ensure timing mark on crankshaft vibration damper is at 11 O'clock position or engine damage may occur.
f. Ensure pushrods are installed with copper end up.

RIGHTHAND

Fuel injector harness red-striped wires carry 115 volts. If harness integrity is compromised, severe shock will occur.

1. Remove console from engine cover.
2. Remove the instrument panel steering column cover.
3. Remove engine cover.
4. Remove parking lamps and headlamps.
5. Remove radiator as outlined under "Radiator, Replace."
6. Recover refrigerant as outlined under "Air Conditioning" chapter.
7. Remove air deflector.
8. Disconnect A/C lines from condenser.
9. Remove A/C condenser.
10. Remove radiator grille, grille opening and upper radiator support.
11. Remove accessory drive belt as outlined under "Serpentine Drive Belt."
12. **On models equipped with dual alternators,** proceed as follows:
    a. Disconnect lower alternator electrical connectors.
    b. Remove engine ground cable.
    c. Remove upper and lower alternator bracket and alternator.
13. **On models equipped with single alternator,** remove alternator and bracket.
14. **On all models,** disconnect vacuum tube from righthand manifold.
15. Remove accessory drive belt tensioner.
16. Remove valve cover as outlined under "Valve Cover, Replace."
17. Remove rocker arms and pushrods as outlined under "Rocker Arms & Pushrods."
18. Disconnect fuel supply tube from rear of cylinder head.
19. Remove turbocharger compressor manifold.
20. Disconnect heater hose from righthand cylinder head.
21. Remove oil dipstick tube.
22. Remove fuel injectors as outlined under "Fuel Injector, Replace."
23. Remove high pressure oil pump supply tube from cylinder head.
24. Remove exhaust back pressure tube, then the glow plug relay bracket and relay.
25. Disconnect fuel return line from front of cylinder head.
26. Disconnect exhaust pipe from manifold.
27. Remove cylinder head bolts.
28. Install cylinder head lifting tool No. D94T-6000–B or equivalent to cylinder head.
29. Remove cylinder head and gasket.
30. Inspect cylinder head and engine block for flatness.
31. Reverse procedure to install noting the following:
    a. Apply a small amount of suitable clean engine oil to new cylinder head bolt threads and flanges prior to installation.
    b. Install cylinder head bolts and **torque** to 65 ft. lbs., in sequence as outlined in **Fig. 13.**
    c. **Torque** cylinder head bolts to 85 ft. lbs., in sequence as outlined in **Fig. 13.**
    d. **Torque** cylinder head bolts to 95 ft. lbs., in sequence as outlined in **Fig. 14.**
    e. Before rocker arm and pushrod installation, ensure timing mark on crankshaft vibration damper is at 11 O'clock position or engine damage may occur.
    f. Ensure pushrods are installed with copper end up.

Excursion & F-Super Duty

LEFTHAND

Fuel injector harness red-striped wires carry 115 volts. If harness integrity is compromised, severe shock will occur.

1. Remove turbocharger compressor manifold.
2. Remove air inlet duct and bracket.
3. Remove accessory drive belt as outlined under "Serpentine Drive Belt."
4. Disconnect power steering lines.

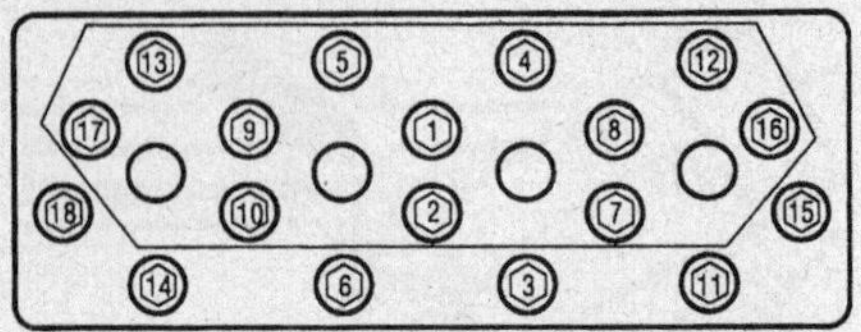

Fig. 13 Cylinder head tightening sequence "A"

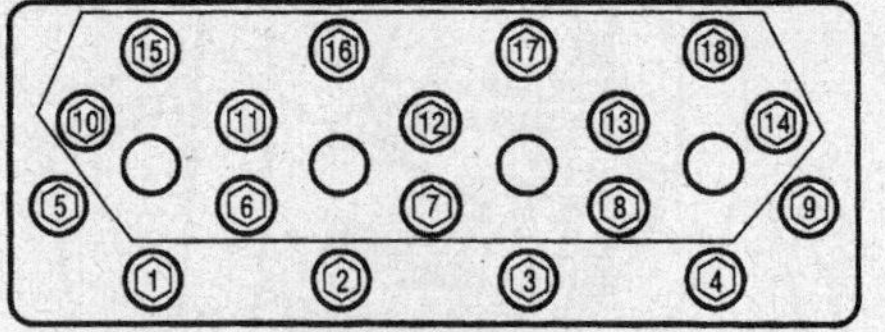

Fig. 14 Cylinder head tightening sequence "B"

5. Remove alternator bracket and position aside.
6. Disconnect high pressure line using high pressure line disconnect tool No. 303–625 or equivalent.
7. Disconnect injection pressure sensor.
8. Remove valve cover as outlined under "Valve Cover, Replace."
9. Remove rocker arms and pushrods as outlined under "Rocker Arms & Pushrods."
10. Remove fuel injectors as outlined under "Fuel Injector, Replace."
11. Disconnect fuel supply line.
12. Disconnect exhaust pipe from manifold and adapter tube.
13. Remove cylinder head bolts.
14. Attach cylinder head lifting bracket tool No. D94T-6000-B or equivalent to cylinder head.
15. Disconnect exhaust manifold and adapter pipe.
16. Remove cylinder head and gasket.
17. Inspect cylinder head and engine block for flatness.
18. Reverse procedure to install noting the following:
    a. Apply a small amount of suitable clean engine oil to new cylinder head bolt threads and flanges prior to installation.
    b. Install cylinder head bolts and **torque** to 65 ft. lbs., in sequence as outlined in **Fig. 13.**
    c. **Torque** cylinder head bolts to 85 ft. lbs., in sequence as outlined in **Fig. 13.**
    d. **Torque** cylinder head bolts to 95 ft. lbs., in sequence as outlined in **Fig. 14.**
    e. **Before rocker arm and pushrod installation, ensure timing mark on crankshaft vibration damper is at 11 O'clock position or engine damage may occur.**
    f. Ensure pushrods are installed with copper end up.

RIGHTHAND

Fuel injector harness red-striped wires carry 115 volts. If harness integrity is compromised, severe shock will occur.

1. Recover refrigerant as outlined under "Air Conditioning" chapter.
2. Remove turbocharger compressor manifold.
3. Remove accessory drive belt as outlined under "Serpentine Drive Belt."
4. **On models equipped with dual alternator system,** proceed as follows:
    a. Disconnect lower alternator electrical connectors.
    b. Remove engine ground cable from starter wire bracket.
    c. Remove lower alternator bracket.
5. **On all models,** remove A/C compressor bracket.
6. **On models equipped with single alternator system,** proceed as follows:
    a. Disconnect A/C compressor electrical connector.
    b. Remove glow plug relay and bracket.
7. **On models equipped with automatic transmission,** remove transmission dipstick tube.
8. **On all models,** remove valve cover as outlined under "Valve Cover, Replace."
9. Remove rocker arms and pushrods as outlined under "Rocker Arms & Pushrods."
10. Disconnect fuel supply line from cylinder head.
11. Disconnect heater hose, **Fig. 15.**
12. Remove fuel injectors as outlined under "Fuel Injector, Replace."
13. Disconnect high pressure line using high pressure line disconnect tool No. 303–625 or equivalent.
14. Remove exhaust backpressure tube.
15. Remove 2 nuts and bolts from turbocharger exhaust adapter tube.
16. Remove cylinder head bolts.
17. Install cylinder head lifting tool No. D94T-6000-B or equivalent to cylinder head.
18. Remove cylinder head and gasket.
19. Inspect cylinder head and engine block for flatness.
20. Reverse procedure to install noting the following:
    a. Apply a small amount of suitable clean engine oil to new cylinder head bolt threads and flanges prior to installation.
    b. Install cylinder head bolts and **torque** to 65 ft. lbs., in sequence as outlined in **Fig. 13.**
    c. **Torque** cylinder head bolts to 85 ft. lbs., in sequence as outlined in **Fig. 13.**
    d. **Torque** cylinder head bolts to 95 ft. lbs., in sequence as outlined in **Fig. 14.**
    e. **Before rocker arm and pushrod installation, ensure timing mark on crankshaft vibration damper is at 11 O'clock position or engine damage may occur.**
    f. Ensure pushrods are installed with copper end up.

FUEL INJECTOR

REPLACE

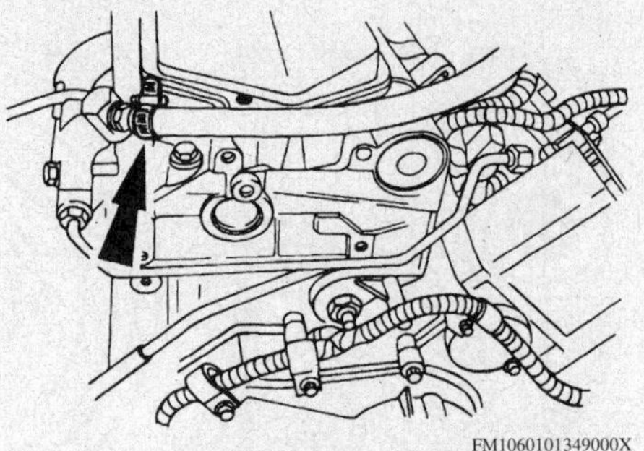

Fig. 15 Heater hose location. Excursion & F-super duty

Fuel injector harness red-striped wires carry 115 volts. If harness integrity is compromised, severe shock will occur.

The fuel injector is serviced as an assembly only. If fuel injector is disassembled, calibration of will not be accurate.

There are 2 different fuel injectors used in this engine. One is used on vehicles with California emissions and the other on vehicles with Federal emissions. These injectors cannot be interchanged due to the fact that each powertrain control module is calibrated to the specific injector application. Before replacing fuel injectors, refer to the vehicle emission control information (VECI) decal for proper injector selection.

1. Loosen fuel passage drain plugs and drain fuel from cylinder heads, **Fig. 16.**
2. Remove valve cover as outlined under "Valve Cover, Replace."
3. Remove fuel charging wiring as follows:
    a. Disconnect glow plug electrical connectors.
    b. Disengage clip and remove fuel injector wiring connectors, **Fig. 17.**
    c. Disconnect and remove electrical connectors from valve cover gaskets.
4. Remove oil drain plugs, **Fig. 18.**
5. Remove oil deflector from fuel injector hold down plate, **Fig. 19.**
6. Remove fuel injector outboard retaining bolts, **Fig. 20.**
7. Remove fuel injector from injector sleeve using fuel injector removal tool No. 303–491 or equivalent, **Fig. 21.**
8. Place removed fuel injectors into injector rack and protective sleeve tool No. D94T-9000-E or equivalent.
9. If replacing fuel injector sleeves, proceed as follows:
    a. Remove cylinder heads as outlined under "Cylinder Head, Replace."
    b. Place a suitable plastic cap or cork into injector sleeve to prevent damage to cylinder head.
    c. Insert injector sleeve tap and pilot tool No. D94T-9000-B or equivalent into fuel injector bore.
    d. Tighten injector sleeve tap 1½–2 turns.
    e. Attach impact slide hammer tool No. T50T-100-A or equivalent to tap pilot and remove fuel injector sleeve from cylinder head fuel injector bore.

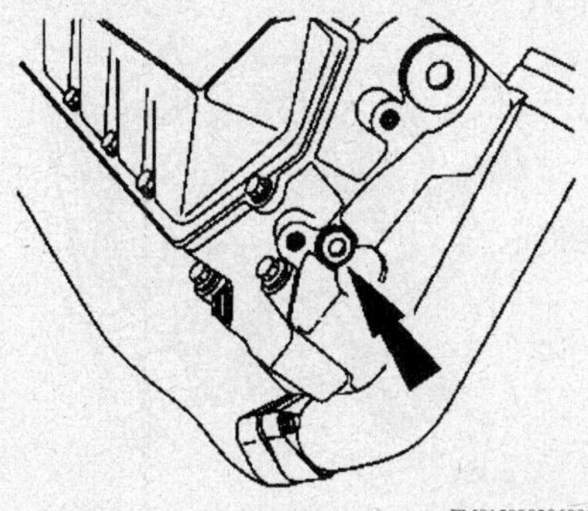

Fig. 16 Cylinder head fuel passage drain plug. E-Series

f. Remove sealant and debris from cylinder head fuel injector sleeve bore using injector sleeve brush tool No. D94T-9000-D or equivalent.

10. Reverse procedure to install noting the following:
    a. Apply Threadlock 620 or equivalent to fuel injector sleeve, **Fig. 22.**
    b. Install new fuel injector sleeve using injector sleeve replacer tool No. D94T-9000-C or equivalent.
    c. Install new O-rings to fuel injector and lubricate with clean engine oil.
    d. **Remove all fluid from cylinders before installing fuel injectors.**
    e. Install fuel injector to cylinder head. **Do not strike top of injector to seat in fuel injector bore.** Ensure fuel injector hold down plate is flush with cylinder head.
    f. Seat fuel injector to cylinder head using injector replacer tool No. 303–492 or equivalent.

VALVE COVER

REPLACE

Righthand

1. Remove engine cover.
2. Remove air cleaner assembly and air inlet tube.
3. Remove resonator bracket and resonator assembly.
4. Remove oil dipstick tube.
5. Disconnect fuel injector/glow plug nine pin electrical connector.
6. Remove nuts and resonator bracket.
7. Remove valve cover bolts, then the valve cover.
8. Disconnect four electrical leads from glow plugs.
9. Disconnect four electrical connectors from fuel injectors, then remove gasket.
10. Reverse procedure to install.

Lefthand

1. Remove air cleaner assembly.
2. Remove engine cover.
3. Remove oil fill tube.
4. Remove inlet duct, tube and bracket assembly.

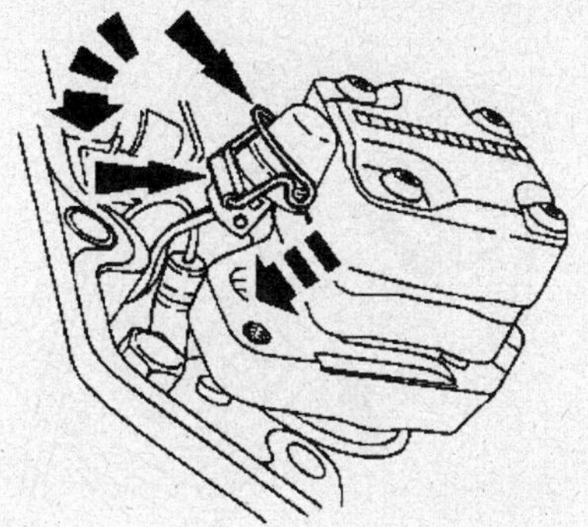

Fig. 17 Fuel injector harness removal

5. Disconnect fuel injector/glow plug electrical connector.
6. Remove valve cover bolts, then the valve cover.
7. Disconnect electrical connectors from fuel injectors and glow plugs, then remove valve cover gasket.
8. Reverse procedure to install.

ROCKER ARM & PUSHRODS

The lefthand engine mount isolator must be removed to provide clearance for the righthand side pushrod removal. The mounting nuts on the righthand engine mount must be removed to allow the engine to pivot while being lifted.

1. Remove righthand valve cover as outlined under "Valve Cover, Replace."
2. Disconnect A/C clutch wire connector.
3. Raise and support vehicle.
4. Raise engine with suitable jackstand to release pressure from engine mounts.
5. Remove righthand engine mount nuts.
6. Remove lefthand engine mount isolator.
7. Lower engine until oil pan rests on crossmember, remove jackstand and lower vehicle.
8. Remove 16 rocker arm bolts, eight rocker arm assemblies, then the pushrods.
9. Reverse procedure to install, noting the following:
    a. Lubricate pushrod ends with engine oil and install with copper end up.
    b. Rotate engine until mark on crankshaft damper is at 11 o'clock position, to prevent damage to timing components when installing intake rocker arms and exhaust rocker arms.

VALVE ARRANGEMENT

Front To Rear

Left ....I-E-I-E-I-E-I-E
Right..................................E-I-E-I-E-I-E-I

VALVE ADJUSTMENT

These engines use hydraulic lifters and there is no provision for adjustment.

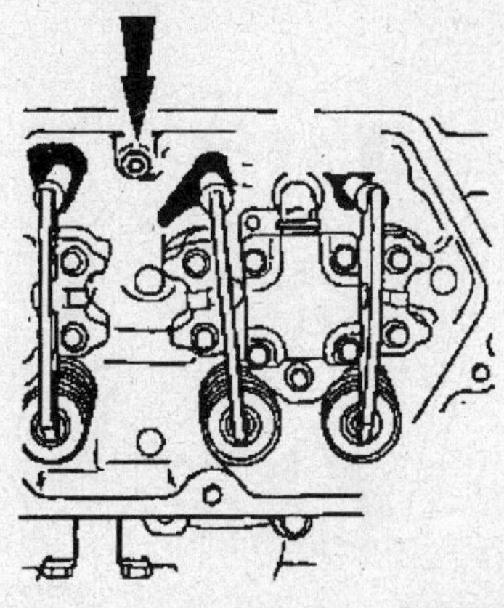

Fig. 18 Oil drain plug removal

VALVE GUIDES

If valve guides are damaged, or are larger than specifications allow, install repair insert as follows:

1. Drill out valve guide, then ream the drilled bore to correct size for insert sleeve.
2. Chill insert in dry ice, then carefully press insert in place.
3. Finish insert with reamer to specified valve guide diameter. **Reface valve seat after valve guide has been reamed, then, using a suitable scraping tool, break the sharp corner at top of valve guide.**

FRONT COVER

REPLACE

1. Remove engine as outlined under "Engine Replace."
2. Remove water pump.
3. Remove crankshaft damper bolt and washer.
4. Remove damper.
5. Remove high pressure oil pump reservoir.
6. Remove oil pump housing bolts, oil pump body plate and square cut O-ring.
7. Remove inner gerotor.
8. Remove oil pan, oil pump screen and cover.
9. Remove bolts retaining front header of oil cooler to engine front cover.
10. Remove front cover bolts, cover and gaskets.
11. Clean all mating surfaces, then reverse procedure to install, noting the following:
    a. Apply rubber silicone sealer to grooves in front cover, ensuring assembly within 15 minutes of silicone application to prevent premature hardening.

CAMSHAFT

REPLACE

1. Remove engine as outlined under "Engine, Replace."
2. Remove injection pump and adapter, intake manifold, valve lifters, engine front cover and fuel supply pump.

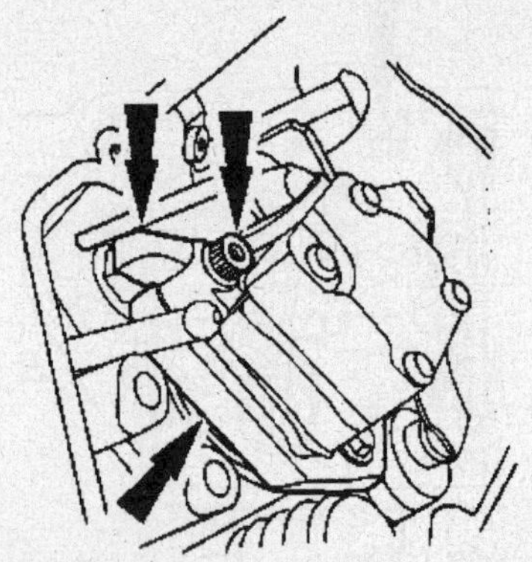

FM0159902863000X

Fig. 19 Oil deflector removal

3. Remove camshaft drive gear, fuel supply pump cam, spacer and thrust plate from camshaft, **Fig. 23.**
4. Remove camshaft using camshaft bearing set tool Nos. T65L-6250-A and Rotunda 14-0314, or equivalents.
5. Reverse procedure to install. Lubricate camshaft lobes with DOAZ-19584-A grease, or equivalent, and the journals with clean engine oil. Tighten camshaft Allen bolt to specifications.

PISTON & ROD ASSEMBLY

Assemble piston to rod so that connecting rod weight pad is installed on the opposite side of the piston as the relief pocket, **Fig. 24.** Install the piston into the cylinder so the piston relief pocket is on the camshaft side of the engine and the arrow on the piston top also faces the camshaft side of the engine, **Fig. 24.**

PISTONS, PINS & RINGS

Pistons are available in standard sizes and oversize of .003 inch.

MAIN BEARINGS

Tighten main bearing cap bolts in two steps; first step, **torque** to 76 ft. lbs.; second step, **torque** to 96 ft. lbs., using sequence **Fig. 25.**

LUBRICATION SYSTEM OIL FLOW

Refer to **Figs. 26 and 27** for lubrication system oil flow diagrams.

ENGINE OIL COOLER

REPLACE

1. Drain cooling system.
2. Remove fan shroud, then the fan and clutch assembly. The fan retaining nut has lefthand threads.
3. Raise and support vehicle.
4. Drain engine oil and remove oil filter. Do not reinstall drain plug.

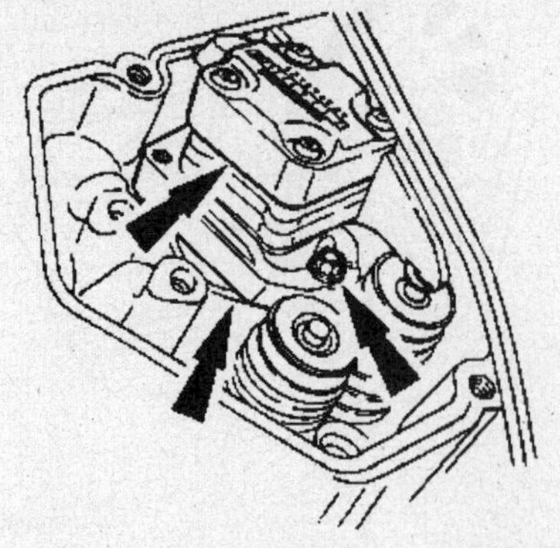

FM0159902864000X

Fig. 20 Fuel injector retaining bolts

5. Remove oil cooler attaching bolts and the oil cooler, **Fig. 28.**
6. Reverse procedure to install.

CRANKSHAFT SEAL

REPLACE

Front

REMOVAL

1. Remove radiator and drive belts, then raise and support vehicle.
2. Remove flywheel housing cover retainer screws and flywheel housing cover.
3. Remove crankshaft vibration damper, using crankshaft damper tool No. T79T-6316-A, or equivalent.
4. Remove crankshaft front seal using lube tube remover tool No. T86P-70001-A and impact hammer tool No. T59L-100-B, or equivalents.
5. Remove crankshaft damper wear ring as follows:
   a. Assemble step plate adapter, damper wear ring remover, bearing collet sleeve, remover tube and forcing screw to crankshaft vibration damper.
   b. Tighten forcing screw until crankshaft damper wear ring is pulled free from hub of crankshaft vibration damper.

INSTALLATION

1. Thoroughly clean crankshaft front seal mounting surface.
2. Coat new crankshaft front seal with multi-purpose grease.
3. If required, rotate front crank seal replacer tool No. T94T-6700-AH, or equivalent, to align with crankshaft key.
4. Install crankshaft front seal, using front crank seal replacer tool No. T94T-6700-AH, or equivalent, thread adapter, driver sleeve and driver/puller screw. Install crankshaft front seal until it is fully seated.
5. Install flywheel housing cover and screws and lower vehicle.
6. Install drive belts and radiator.
7. Inspect and refill engine oil.

FM0159902865000X

Fig. 21 Fuel injector removal

REAR

Removal

1. Remove transmission and flywheel.
2. Remove five crankshaft rear oil seal retaining bolts and crankshaft rear oil seal.
3. Clean crankshaft rear oil seal sealing surfaces.
4. If equipped with a crankshaft wear sleeve, use crankshaft rear wear ring remover tool No. T94T-6701-AH1, forcing screw tool No. T84T-7025-B, rear wear ring remover sleeve tool No. T94T-6701-AH2, or equivalents, to remove crankshaft rear wear sleeve.

Installation

1. Apply Silicone Rubber F4AZ-19562-B, or equivalent, meeting Ford specification ESE-M4G195-A or WSE-M4G323-A1 to rear oil seal retaining ring and five crankshaft rear oil seal retaining bolts.
2. Install crankshaft wear ring and crankshaft rear oil seal using crankshaft seal replacer tool No. T94T-6701-AH3, crankshaft seal replacer tool No. T94T-AH4 and if wear sleeve is to be replaced, driver sleeve tool No. T79T-6316-A4 and guide pins (part of T79T-6316-A), or equivalents.
3. Install five crankshaft rear oil seal retaining bolts. Tighten bolts to specification.
4. Remove installation tools and install flywheel and transmission.

OIL PUMP

REPLACE

1. Remove radiator, then raise and support vehicle.
2. Remove converter housing cover.
3. Prevent rotation of crankshaft with use of breaker bar.
4. Remove crankshaft damper.
5. Remove oil pump housing bolts, pump body plate and square cut O-ring.
6. Remove inner gerotor.
7. Clean and inspect oil pump assembly.
8. Reverse procedure to install, noting the following:
   a. Apply liberal amount of oil to gerotor pump.
   b. A new crankshaft seal must be installed.

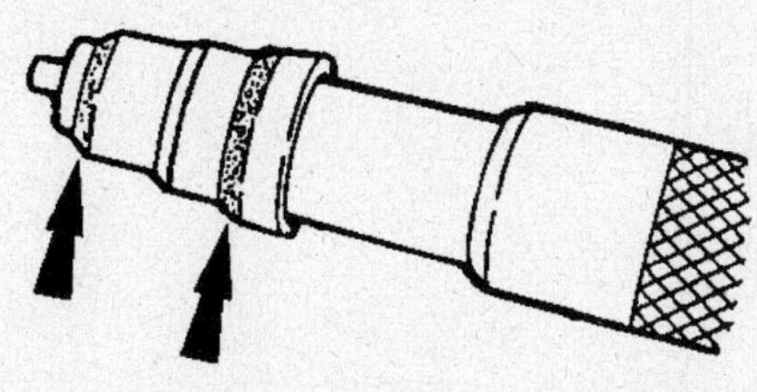

Fig. 22 Fuel injector sleeve Threadlock application points

HIGH PRESSURE OIL PUMP RESERVOIR

REPLACE

1. Loosen compressor manifold hose clamps, then remove compressor manifold.
2. Remove oil from high pressure oil pump reservoir using Rotunda vacuum pump tool No. 021-00037, or equivalent.
3. Remove cover plate and bolts at crankcase front cover.
4. Remove oil pump drive sprocket bolt and washer.
5. Remove high pressure oil pump.
6. Remove high pressure oil pump reservoir retaining bolts and position wiring harness aside.
7. Remove reservoir.
8. Disconnect wire connectors from sensors at top and back of reservoir.
9. Inspect oil pump drive sprocket backlash as follows:
   a. Mount dial indicator bracket tool No. D78P-4201-F and dial indicator tool No. D78P-4201-G, or equivalent.
   b. Zero dial indicator.
   c. Place dial indicator tip on drive sprocket tooth.
   d. Move drive sprocket by hand and record reading.
   e. If backlash reading exceeds .0055–.0101 inch, replace drive sprocket.
10. Reverse procedure to install. Tighten fasteners to specification.

BELT TENSION DATA

The automatic drive belt tensioner has no provision for adjustment and will be damaged if forced to travel beyond its operating range. New belt tension should be about 85 lbs.

SERPENTINE DRIVE BELT

Belt Routing

Refer to **Figs. 29 through 31** for serpentine drive belt routing.

Belt Replacement

1. Use ½ square hole in drive belt tensioner pulley hub to rotate drive belt tensioner and remove drive belt.
2. Remove belt, slowly release tensioner. **Do not allow tensioner to snap back, as damage may result.**
3. Reverse procedure to install.

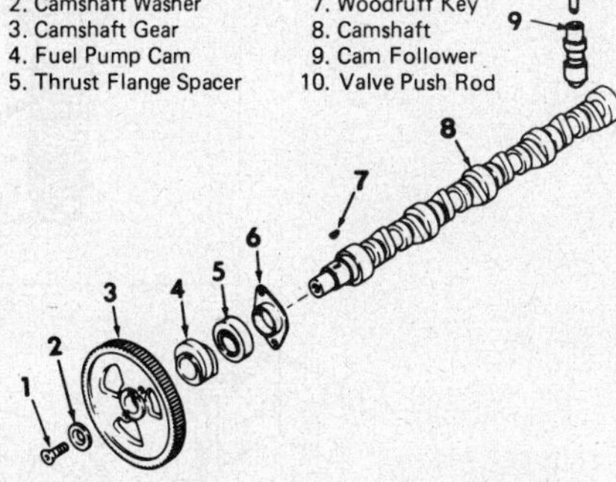

Fig. 23 Camshaft assembly

COOLING SYSTEM BLEED

Disconnect heater outlet hose at water pump to bleed air from the system. When coolant begins to flow, reconnect heater hose. Start engine and allow to warm up. Shut engine off and allow system to cool. Remove radiator cap and fill with coolant as needed.

THERMOSTAT

REPLACE

1. Drain radiator until level is below thermostat.
2. Remove drive belts.
3. Remove alternator and position aside.
4. Remove vacuum pump and bracket and position aside.
5. Remove all but lowest alternator/vacuum pump mounting casting bolt, loosen lowest bolt and pivot casting outward.
6. Remove water outlet housing attaching bolts, bend radiator hose upward and remove thermostat and gasket.
7. Reverse procedure to install.

WATER PUMP

REPLACE

1. Drain cooling system into suitable container.
2. Remove fan shroud, then the fan and clutch assembly. **The fan retaining nut has righthand threads turn nut counterclockwise.**
3. Remove drive belt, then the water pump pulley.
4. Disconnect heater hose from water pump, then remove heater hose fitting from pump.
5. Disconnect engine coolant temperature sensor.
6. Remove water pump inlet bolts and water pump inlet.
7. Remove water pump attaching bolts, then the pump.
8. Reverse procedure to install. Apply RTV sealer to two top and two bottom bolts, **Fig. 32.** Apply suitable pipe sealant to heater hose fitting. Tighten water pump attaching bolts to specifications.

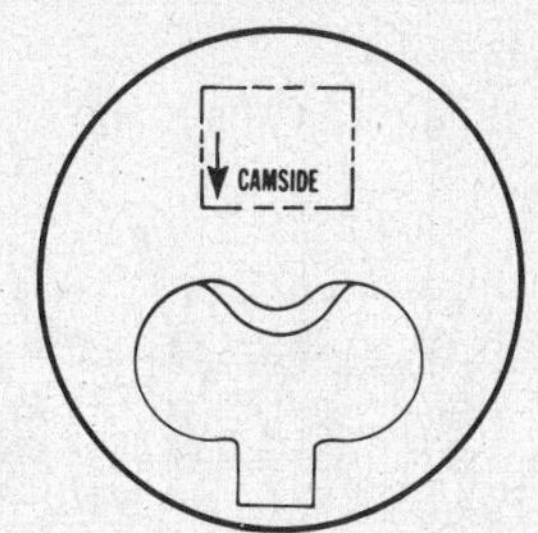

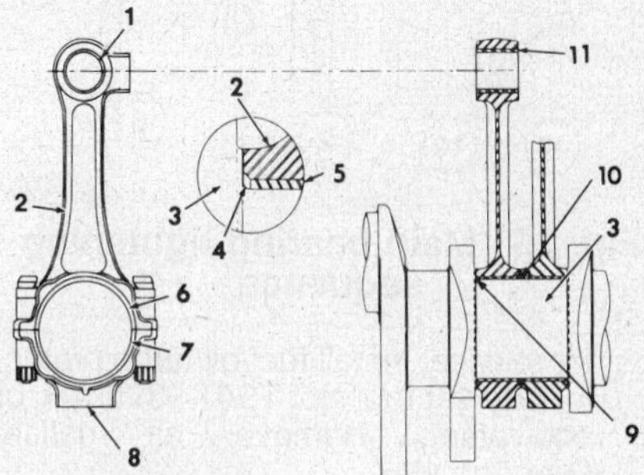

Fig. 24 Piston & rod assembly

TURBOCHARGER

REPLACE

E-Series

1. Remove engine cover and heat shield.
2. Remove four exhaust Y-pipe to turbo inlet adapter.
3. Remove exhaust outlet marmon clamp from turbocharger.
4. Loosen two bolts retaining turbocharger exhaust inlet pipe to lefthand exhaust manifold.
5. Loosen air inlet hose clamp at turbocharger. Disconnect hose and lay aside.
6. Loosen four intake manifold hose clamps and one clamp retaining compressor manifold to turbocharger.
7. Remove compressor manifold.
8. Remove four bolts retaining turbocharger pedestal assembly to cylinder block (righthand rear bolt cannot be completely removed).
9. Remove turbocharger assembly and disconnect electrical connectors.
10. If turbocharger is not being removed

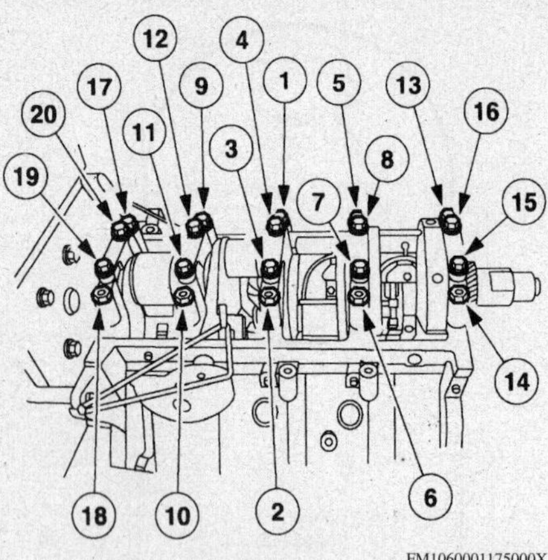

Fig. 25 Main bearing tightening sequence

for service, install fuel/oil/turbo protector cap set tool No. T94T-9395-AH, or equivalent. Remove oil gallery O-rings.

11. Reverse procedure to install. Tighten fasteners to specifications.

Excursion & F-Super Duty Series

1. Remove charge air cooler inlet and outlet ducts from compressor manifold.
2. Loosen turbocharger to compressor manifold marmon clamp, then remove compressor manifold.
3. Remove exhaust outlet pipe from turbocharger, then disconnect exhaust back pressure valve.
4. Remove air inlet tube.
5. Loosen marmon clamp and remove turbocharger. Marmon clamp cannot be removed with turbocharger in place.
6. Remove O-rings.
7. Reverse procedure to install.

RADIATOR

REPLACE

E-Series

1. Drain cooling system by removing radiator cap and opening draincock located at the lower rear corner of the radiator tank.
2. Remove rubber radiator overflow hose from radiator coolant recovery reservoir and disconnect it from radiator, **Fig. 33.**
3. Remove fan shroud attaching bolts.
4. Lift fan shroud back and drape it on fan.
5. Loosen upper and lower hose clamps at radiator and remove upper radiator hose and lower radiator from connectors.
6. Disconnect two automatic transmission oil cooling fans from radiator fittings, if equipped.
7. **On models equipped with E4OD transmission,** disconnect heated water bypass hose attached to lower tank.
8. **On all models,** remove four radiator attaching bolts.
9. Tilt radiator back about one inch and lift upward, clear of radiator support.
10. Lift fan shroud off of fan and remove from vehicle.
11. Reverse procedure to install.

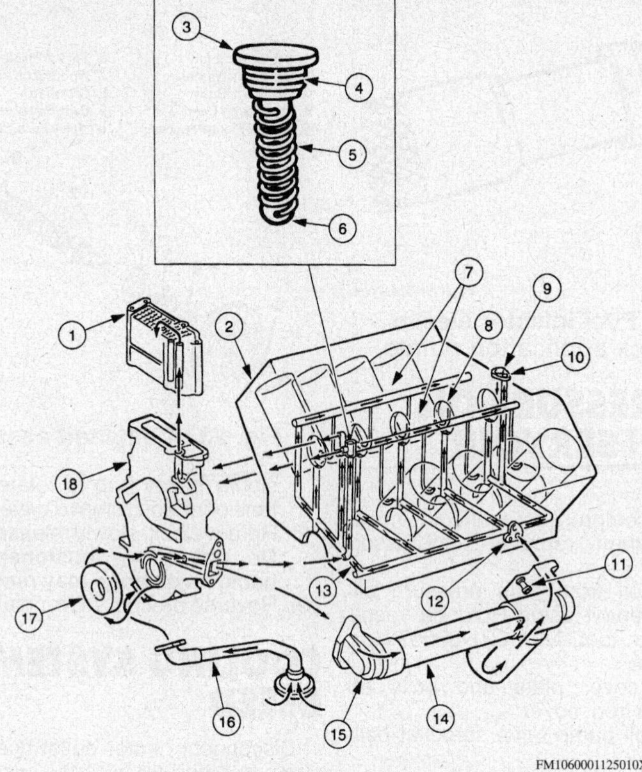

Fig. 26 Low pressure oil flow diagram (Part 1 of 2). 7.3L diesel engine

Excursion & F-Super Duty

Refer to "4.6L & 5.4L SOHC Gasoline Engines" for procedure.

FUEL PUMP

REPLACE

E-Series

1. Remove turbocharger as outlined under "Turbocharger, Replace."
2. Remove fuel line banjo fitting bolt at fuel pump.
3. Remove fuel line fittings at rear of cylinder heads.
4. Remove fuel line assembly.
5. Loosen three hose clamps at fuel pump fittings.
6. Disconnect water drain hose at fuel filter.
7. Remove fuel filter bolts and position fuel filter forward.
8. Remove two fuel pump bolts and lift fuel pump up and out of crankcase bore.
9. Remove fuel pump tappet from crankcase bore.
10. Reverse procedure to install.

Excursion & F-Super Duty

The electric fuel pump is located near lefthand frame rail.

1. Open fuel filter/water separator drain valve to release fuel pressure.
2. Raise and support vehicle.
3. Disconnect fuel pump harness connector.
4. Remove fuel pump retaining clip and discard, then disconnect fuel lines using fuel line disconnect tool No. T90T-9550-S, or equivalent.
5. Disconnect brake line from fuel pump bracket and remove pump mounting nuts and fuel pump.
6. Loosen pinch bolt and spread mounting bracket and remove fuel pump.
7. Reverse procedure to install.

FUEL FILTER

REPLACE

1. **On E-Series models,** remove turbocharger, baffle and air inlet crossover manifold.
2. **On all models,** place a suitable container at end of fuel filter/heater/water separator drain hose to catch fuel and open the drain.
3. Remove two capscrews securing fuel filter/heater/water separator base to cylinder block.

Item	Description
1	High-pressure oil pump reservoir
2	Cylinder block
3	Short circuit valve ball cap
4	O-ring
5	Spring
6	Check ball
7	Valve lifter oil galleries
8	Piston cooling oil jet
9	Turbocharger oil return gallery

Item	Description
10	Turbocharger oil supply gallery
11	Pressure relief/regulator valve
12	Oil filter bypass drain
13	Main oil gallery
14	Oil cooler
15	Oil cooler header
16	Oil pump screen cover and tube
17	Gerotor oil pump
18	Engine front cover

FM1060001125020X

Fig. 26 Low pressure oil flow diagram (Part 2 of 2). 7.3L diesel engine

Item	Description
9	Injection pressure regulator (IPR) valve

Item	Description
10	Engine front cover
11	High-pressure oil pump reservoir

FM1060001126020X

Fig. 27 High pressure oil flow diagram (Part 2 of 2). 7.3L diesel engine

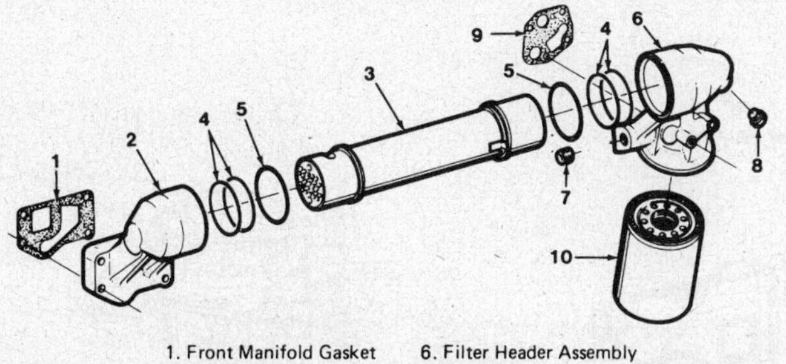

1. Front Manifold Gasket
2. Front Oil Cooler Adapter
3. Oil Cooler
4. "O" Ring
5. "O" Ring
6. Filter Header Assembly
7. Pipe Plug
8. Plug
9. Filter Header Gasket
10. Oil Filter

FM1098800009000X

Fig. 28 Exploded view of oil cooler. E-Series

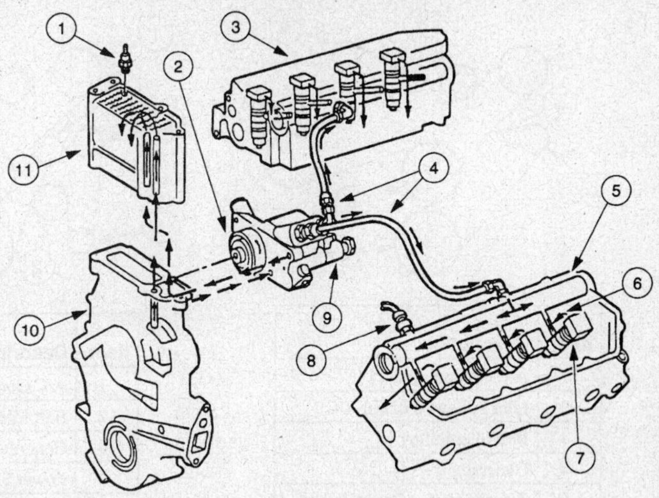

Item	Description
1	Oil pressure sensor
2	High-pressure oil pump
3	Cylinder head
4	High-pressure oil feed hoses
5	High-pressure oil rail

Item	Description
6	Injector oil feed galleries
7	Fuel injectors (8 req'd)
8	Injection control pressure (ICP) sensor

FM1060001126010X

Fig. 27 High pressure oil flow diagram (Part 1 of 2). 7.3L diesel engine

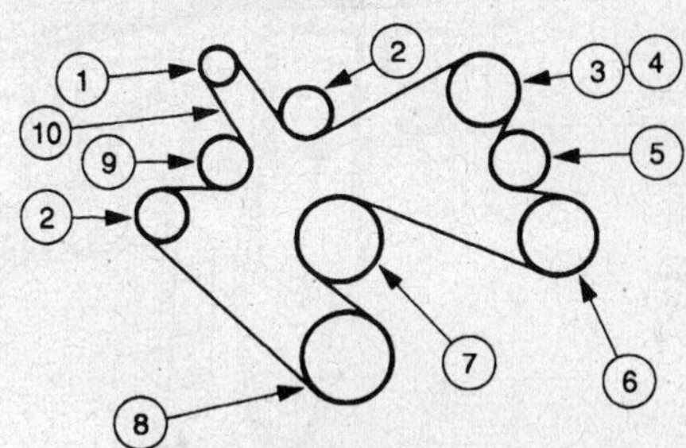

Item	Description
1	Generator Pulley
2	Belt Idler Pulley
3	Air Conditioner Pulley
4	Belt Idler Pulley (Without Air Conditioning Only)
5	Vacuum Pump Pulley
6	Power Steering Pump Pulley
7	Water Pump Pulley
8	Crankshaft Pulley
9	Drive Belt Tensioner
10	Drive Belt

FM1069500843000X

Fig. 29 Serpentine drive belt routing. E-Series

4. Remove drain hose, then fuel inlet hose located between fuel pump and fuel filter/heater/water separator assembly housing.
5. Remove fuel return hose from fuel pressure regulator valve, then two fuel supply hoses connecting regulator block to cylinder head fuel rails.
6. Loosen clamp at fuel pump end of hose connecting fuel filter/heater/water separator to inlet of high pressure stage of fuel pump.
7. Unclip wiring harness from righthand side of fuel filter/heater/water separator housing.
8. Disconnect water in fuel (WIF) sensor and fuel heater connectors.
9. Remove fuel filter/heater/water separator cap. The fuel filter element will come out with the cap, **Fig. 34.**
10. Remove and discard bevel gasket. Carefully clean mating surfaces.
11. Press on fuel filter element locking tabs to separate element from cap.
12. Reverse procedure to install.

GLOW PLUG SYSTEM

Description

The 7.3L diesel engine uses a glow plug system which preheats air in the combustion chamber to improve cold engine starting.

The glow plug system is electronically controlled by the Powertrain Control Module (PCM). The PCM energizes the intake manifold glow plugs when the ignition switch is turned On. It then determines how long the glow plugs will remain on according to engine oil temperature and barometric pressure. The intake manifold glow plugs are self-regulating and the PCM controls relay On time.

The system consists of eight intake manifold glow plugs, the glow plug control module, engine oil temperature sensor, barometric pressure sensor and PCM.

Replacement

1. Remove valve cover.
2. Disconnect glow plug electrical connector.
3. Remove intake manifold glow plug using suitable socket.
4. Clean and inspect glow plug for damage, replace if required.
5. Reverse procedure to install. Tighten glow plug to specifications.

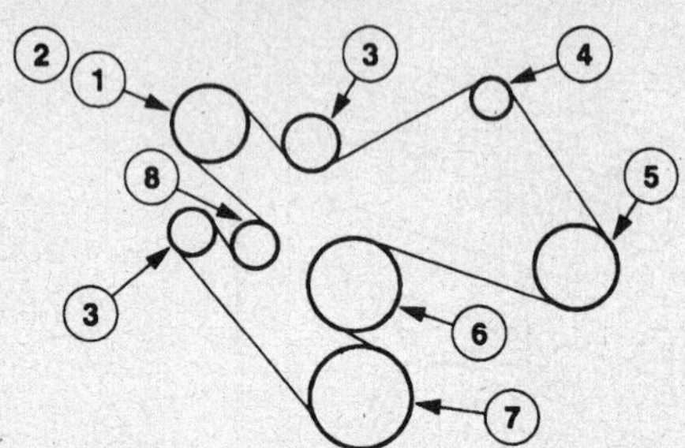

Item	Description
1	A/C Compressor
2	Idler Pulley (Without A/C)
3	Belt Idler Pulley
4	Generator
5	Power Steering Pump Pulley
6	Water Pump Pulley
7	Crankshaft Pulley
8	Drive Belt Tensioner

FM1069900844000X

Fig. 30 Serpentine drive belt routing. Excursion & F-Super Duty w/single alternator

Item	Description
1	A/C Compressor
2	Belt Idler Pulley
3	Generator
4	Power Steering Pump Pulley
5	Water Pump Pulley
6	Crankshaft Pulley
7	Drive Belt Tensioner

FM1069900845000X

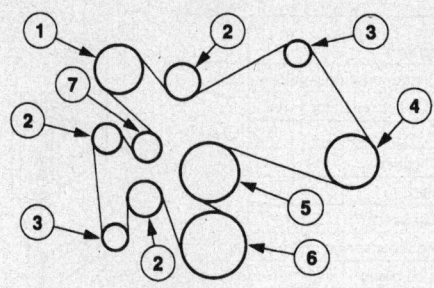

Fig. 31 Serpentine drive belt routing. Excursion & F-Super Duty w/dual alternator

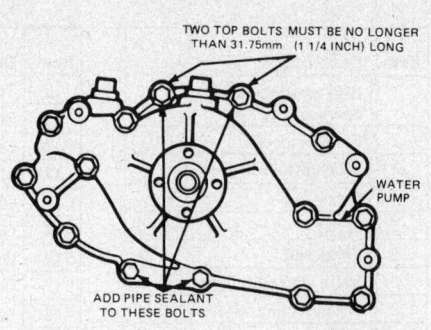

TWO TOP BOLTS MUST BE NO LONGER THAN 31.75mm (1 1/4 INCH) LONG

WATER PUMP

ADD PIPE SEALANT TO THESE BOLTS

FM1088800006000X

Fig. 32 Water pump installation

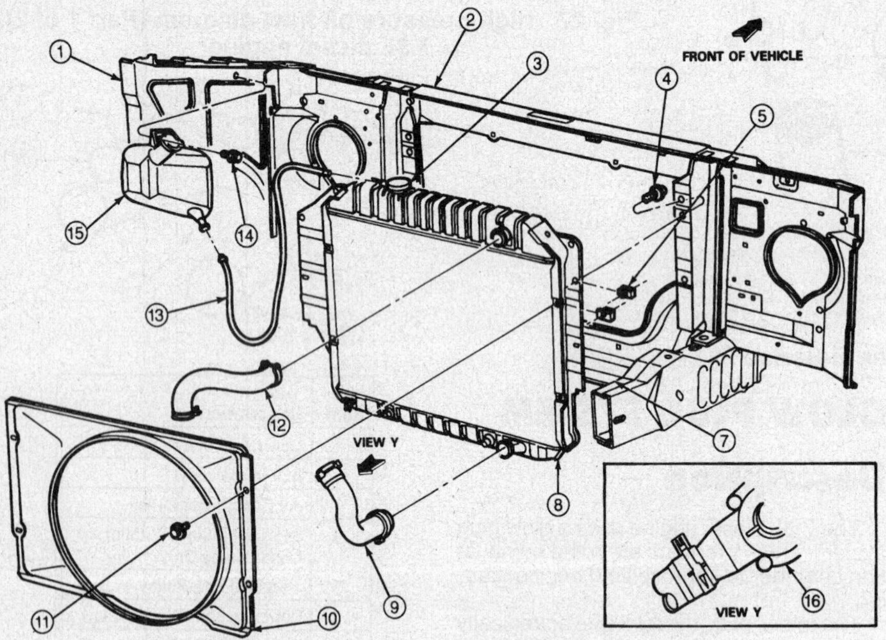

Item	Description
1	Radiator Support
2	Upper Radiator Support
3	Radiator Cap
4	Bolt M8 15-20 N·m (10-15 Ft-Lb)
5	U-Nut M8
6	U-Nut M6
7	Air Deflector
8	Radiator

Item	Description
9	Lower Radiator Hose
10	Fan Shroud
11	Bolt M6 6-8 N·m (53-71 In-Lb)
12	Upper Radiator Hose
13	Hose
14	Screw and Washer M6 Tap 6-8 N·m (53-71 In-Lb)
15	Radiator Coolant Recovery Reservoir
16	Water Pump

FM1089500097000X

Fig. 33 Radiator replacement. E-Series

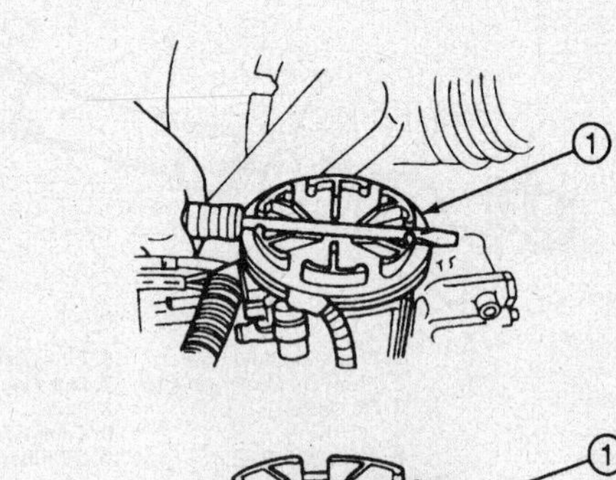

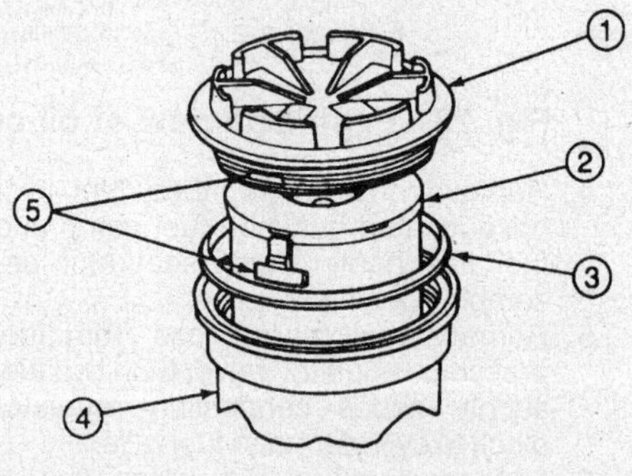

Item	Description
1	Fuel Filter Cap
2	Fuel Filter Element
3	Fuel Filter Bevel Cut Gasket
4	Fuel Filter Housing and Gland
5	Fuel Filter Element and Cap Locking Tabs

FM1029500286000X

Fig. 34 Fuel filter replacement

TIGHTENING SPECIFICATIONS

Year	Component	Torque Ft. Lbs.
2002–03	Connecting Rod Caps	③
	Cylinder Head	①
	Cylinder Head Oil Drain Plugs	53④
	Damper Bolt	212
	Exhaust Manifold	45
	Flywheel To Crankshaft	23–39
	Fuel Injector Outboard Retaining Bolts	10
	Glow Plug	14
	High Pressure Oil Pump Drive Sprocket Bolt	95
	Intake Manifold Cover	18
	Main Bearing Cap	②
	Oil Deflector	108④
	Rocker Arm Pedestal Attaching Bolt	20
	Turbocharger Exhaust Inlet Pipes To Exhaust Manifolds	21
	Turbocharger Pedestal To Engine Block Bolts	18
	Valve Cover	96④
	Valve Lever Post Bolt	20
	Water Housing Outlet (Thermostat To Crankshaft)	20
	Water Pump Attaching Bolts	⑤

① — Refer to “Cylinder Head, Replace” for tightening procedure.

② — Refer to “Main Bearings” for crankshaft main bearing bolt tightening.

③ — Torque in two steps as follows: first step, 53 ft. lbs., second step, 80 ft. lbs.

④ — Inch lbs.

⑤ — 35–46 ft. lbs.

Rear Axle & Suspension

INDEX

PRECAUTIONS

Air Suspension Systems

Models equipped with automatic leveling systems should have power to this system shut off whenever vehicle is raised or when suspension system components are serviced. Failure to shut off this system could allow this system to operate during service procedures and cause vehicle to shift positions.

System may be disabled with a switch located behind righthand kick panel.

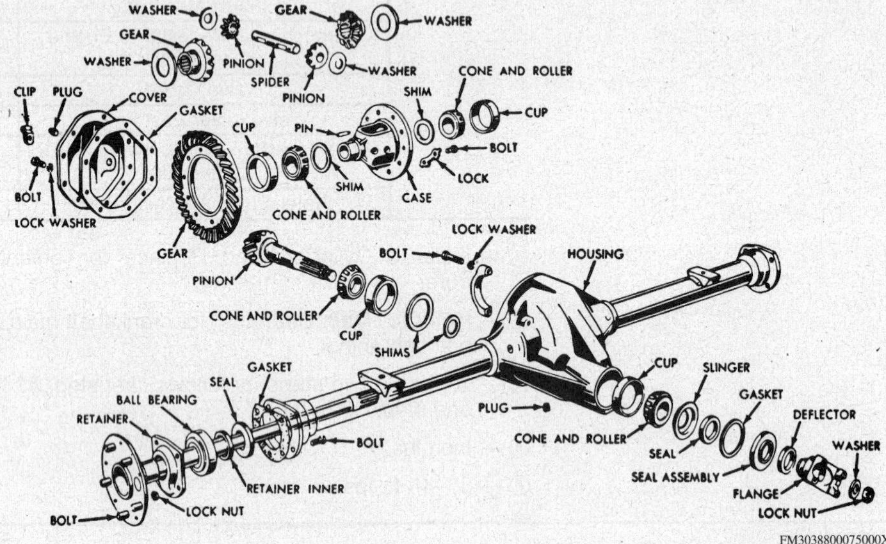

Fig. 1 Dana semi-floating integral housing hypoid rear axle

DANA/SPICER INTEGRAL AXLE

These rear axle, **Fig. 1,** is a semi-floating type, while the axle outlined in **Fig. 2** is of the full-floating type. The drive pinion of either axle is of the overhung design, mounted on preloaded tapered roller bearings. Sealing of the pinion shaft is accomplished by a spring-loaded seal on the companion flange. The flange is splined and secured to the pinion shaft by a nut.

The model outlined in **Fig. 3** is a front mounted removable one piece carrier full floating axle.

AXLE SHAFT, BEARING & OIL SEAL, REPLACE

FULL-FLOATING AXLE

1. Set park brake, then place drain pan under rear hub and remove rear axle shaft bolts and axle shaft.
2. Inspect O-ring from damage and axle shaft for cracked material around holes or oversized holes and replace if required.
3. Raise and support vehicle, then remove rear wheels.
4. Remove anchor plate, then using a suitable socket hub nut.
5. Remove outer rear wheel bearing and hub and rotor assembly.
6. Remove and discard rear hub seal.
7. Remove inner rear wheel bearing, then rear hub bolts and separate rear hub from rear disc brake rotor.
8. Remove inner bearing cup using inner bearing cup remover tool No. T88T-1175-B for Dana 80, inner hub bearing race remover tool No. 205-441 for S135 and driver handle tool No. T80T-4000-W, or equivalents.
9. Remove outer bearing cup using outer bearing cup remove tool No. T88T-1175-A for Dana 80, outer hub bearing race remover tool No. 205-443 for Dana S135 and drive handle tool No. T80T-4000-W, or equivalents.
10. Clean spindle of rear axle housing, all old grease and axle lubricant from rear hub and rear wheel bearings and cups.
11. Inspect bearing races and rollers for pitting, galling or erratic wear patterns. Inspect rollers for end wear and replace as required.
12. Reverse procedure to install, noting the following:
    a. For Dana 80, install rear bearing cups using bearing cup replacer tool No. T88T-1175-C and threaded drawbar tool No. T75T-1176-A, or equivalents.
    b. For Dana S135, install rear bearing cups using inner and outer hub bearing race installer tool Nos. 205-442 and 205-444, and driver handle tool No. T80T-4000-W, or equivalents
    c. Inspect for proper seating of new bearing cups by trying to insert a .0015 inch feeler gauge between cups and rear hub. The gauge should not enter beneath the cups. Inspect in several places to ensure cups are seated.

SEMI-FLOATING AXLE

1. Raise and support vehicle.
2. Remove wheel and brake drum.
3. Remove cover plate and discard gasket.
4. Remove differential pinion shaft lock screw and the shaft.
5. Remove C-clip from button end of shaft by pushing inward on other end.
6. Pull shaft from axle tube. Do not rotate differential side gears.
7. Remove and discard oil seal from axle tube.
8. Pull bearing from axle tube.

9. Lubricate new bearing and install in axle tube.
10. Lubricate and install new oil seal.
11. Insert shaft into axle tube, making sure splines engage side gears, then install C-clip and pull shaft outward until the clip locks.
12. Install pinion mate shaft, aligning lock-pin holes, and pinion gear side washers.
13. Install new lock screw and tighten to specifications.
14. Install cover plate and gasket. Tighten bolts to specifications.
15. Install wheel and drum assembly.
16. Remove supports and lower vehicle.

REAR AXLE ASSEMBLY, REPLACE

1. Set park brake and block front wheels.
2. Loosen, but do not remove rear lug nuts.
3. Raise and support rear of vehicle high enough so that it will clear axle assembly when removing it.
4. Remove rear wheels using wheel dolly tool No. 014-00030, or equivalent.
5. Release parking brake cable tension and disconnect cables at equalizer and anchor plate, then remove frame anchors and position parking brake cables aside.
6. Disconnect rear anti-lock sensor and release harness clip and position harness aside.
7. To maintain driveline balance, mark driveshaft components so they can be reinstalled in their original positions. Remove driveshaft.
8. Disconnect sway bar at sway links and shock absorbers at axle.
9. Disconnect brake hose and axle vent hose at crossmember. Plug brake hose and brake line and position hoses aside.
10. Support axle with a suitable floor jack, then remove U-bolt nuts, spring seat caps and U-bolts.
11. Carefully lower axle and remove from vehicle.
12. Reverse procedure to install. Bleed brake system when the installation is completed.

HUB & BEARING

REPLACE

1. **On models equipped with air ride suspension,** turn air suspension off as outlined under "Precautions."
2. **On all models,** raise and support vehicle.
3. Remove and discard rear halfshaft nut and washer, **Fig. 4.**
4. Separate outboard CV joint from wheel hub using suitable wheel hub puller.
5. Remove brake caliper mounting bolts, position caliper aside. Support caliper using suitable mechanic's wire.
6. Remove brake rotor.
7. Disconnect wheel speed sensor electrical connector, then the speed sensor harness from retainer.
8. Remove speed sensor harness mounting bolt.

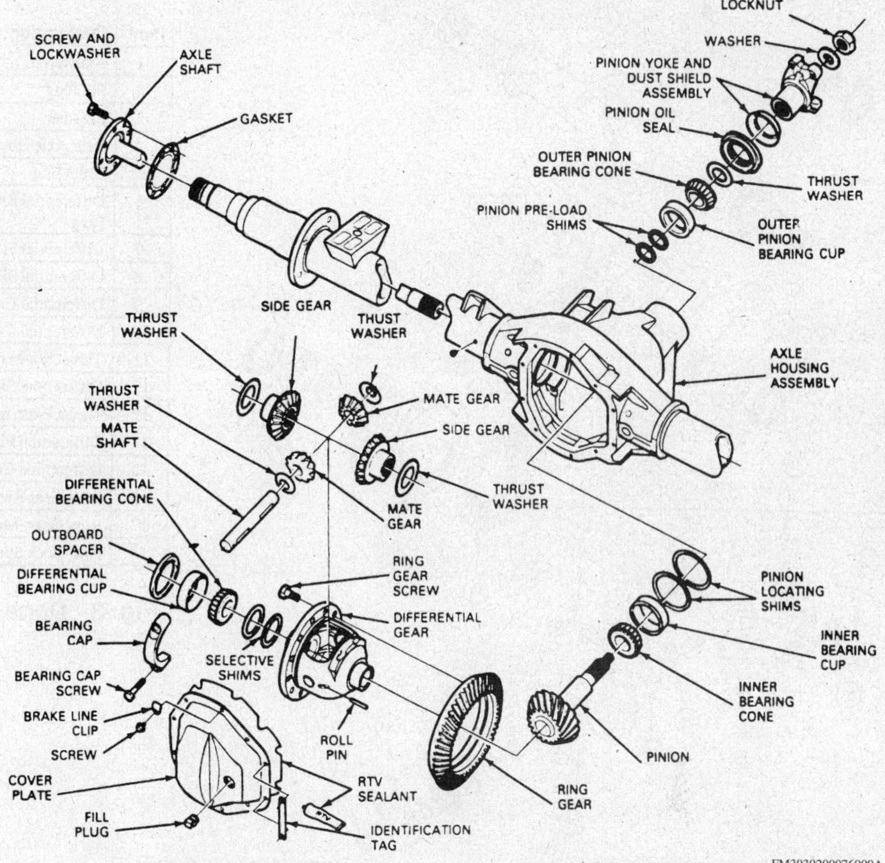

Fig. 2 Dana full-floating integral housing hypoid rear axle

9. Remove wheel bearing and hub assembly mounting bolts, wheel bearing assembly and speed sensor as an assembly. Ensure to route sensor wiring through access hole in brake shield.
10. Remove speed sensor mounting bolt and speed sensor from wheel bearing and hub assembly.
11. Reverse procedure to install.

FORD INTEGRAL CARRIER TYPE AXLE

On integral-type housing with hypoid gear design, **Figs. 5 and 6,** the center of the pinion sets below the centerline of the ring gear. The hypoid ring gear and pinion consists of a ring gear and an overhung drive pinion which is supported by 2 opposing tapered roller bearings. Drive pinion bearing preload is maintained by a drive pinion collapsible spacer on the drive pinion shaft and adjusted by the pinion nut.

The axle housing consists of a cast center section with 2 steel tube assemblies and a stamped differential housing cover. The differential housing cover uses silicone sealant as a gasket. The differential pinion shaft is retained by a threaded differential pinion shaft lock bolt assembled to the differential assembly. The differential assembly is mounted in the axle housing between 2 opposing differential bearings that are retained in the axle housing by removable differential bearing caps.

Differential bearing preload and differential ring and pinion backlash are adjusted by differential bearing shims located between the differential bearing cups and the axle housing. Axle identification is on an embossed metal tag bolted to the differential housing cover.

Axle Shaft, Bearing, Hub & Oil Seal, Replace

8.8 INCH AXLE

1. Set parking brake and loosen axle shaft bolts.
2. Raise and support rear of vehicle so that axle is parallel with floor.
3. Remove differential housing cover bolts, **Fig. 5,** then drain lubricant into suitable container.
4. Remove differential housing cover.
5. Remove disc brake caliper bolts, then using suitable mechanic's wire, position disc brake caliper aside.
6. Remove disc rotor.
7. Remove differential pinion shaft lock bolt, then discard bolt.
8. Remove differential pinion shaft.
9. Push inward on axle shafts and remove two U-washers, **Fig. 7.**
10. Remove axle shafts.
11. Remove axle seal using suitable seal removal tool No. T50T-100–A, or equivalent.

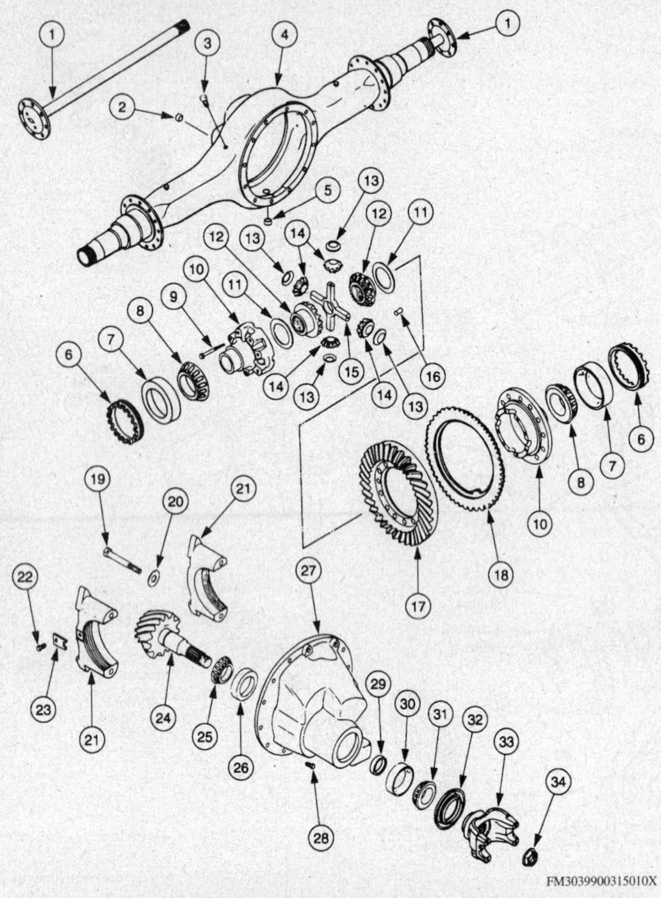

Fig. 3 Dana full-floating one piece carrier hypoid rear axle (Part 1 of 2)

Item	Description
1	Axle Shaft
2	Fill Plug
3	Breather
4	Rear Axle Housing
5	Drain Plug
6	Differential Bearing Adjusting Ring
7	Differential Side Bearing Cup
8	Differential Side Bearing Cone
9	Differential Case Bolt
10	Differential Case Half
11	Thrust Washer
12	Differential Side Gear
13	Thrust Washer
14	Differential Pinion Mate
15	Differential Cross Shaft
16	Ring Gear Rivet
17	Ring Gear (Matched Set)
18	Anti-Lock Speed Sensor Ring

Item	Description
19	Differential Bearing Cup Bolt
20	Washer
21	Differential Bearing Cap
22	Adjusting Ring Lock Bolt
23	Adjusting Ring Lock
24	Pinion (Matched Set)
25	Pinion Bearing Cone, Inner
26	Pinion Bearing Cup, Inner
27	Carrier Housing
28	Carrier Mounting Bolt
29	Pinion Preload Spacer (Selective)
30	Pinion Bearing Cup, Outer
31	Pinion Bearing Cone, Inner
32	Pinion Seal
33	Companion Flange
34	Pinion Hex Nut

FM3039900315020X

Fig. 3 Dana full-floating one piece carrier hypoid rear axle (Part 2 of 2)

12. Remove rear wheel bearing using suitable slide hammer and axle bearing removal tool No. T83T-1225-A, or equivalent. Ensure to avoid damaging axle shaft oil seal bore.
13. Reverse procedure to install, noting the following:
    a. Lubricate axle bearing with suitable axle lubricant.
    b. Install axle bearing using bearing installation tool No. T83T-1225–B and adapter tool No. T80T-4000–W, or equivalents.
    c. Lubricate lip of new axle shaft oil seal with suitable grease.
    d. Install axle seal using oil seal installation tool No. T83T-1175-A and adaptor tool No. T80T-4000-W, or equivalents.

9.75 & 10.25 INCH AXLES

1. Set parking brake and loosen axle shaft bolts.
2. Raise and support rear of vehicle so that axle is parallel with floor.
3. Remove differential housing cover bolts, **Fig. 6,** then drain lubricant into suitable container.
4. Remove differential housing cover.
5. Remove disc brake caliper bolts, then using suitable mechanic's wire, position disc brake caliper aside.
6. Remove disc rotor.
7. Remove differential pinion shaft lock bolt, then discard bolt.
8. Remove differential pinion shaft.
9. Push inward on axle shafts and remove two U-washers, **Fig. 7.**
10. Remove axle shafts.
11. Remove axle seal using suitable seal removal tool No. T50T-100-A, or equivalent.
12. Remove rear wheel bearing using suitable slide hammer and axle bearing removal tool No. T85T-1225-AH, or equivalent. Ensure to avoid damaging axle shaft oil seal bore.
13. Reverse procedure to install, noting the following:
    a. Lubricate axle bearing with suitable axle lubricant.
    b. Install axle bearing using bearing installation tool No. T80T-4000-X and adapter tool No. T80T-4000-W, or equivalents.
    c. Lubricate lip of new axle shaft oil seal with suitable grease.
    d. Install axle seal using oil seal installation tool No. T87T-1177-A and adaptor tool No. T80T-4000-W, or equivalents.

Axle Housing, Replace

1. Set parking brake and loosen axle shaft bolts.
2. Raise and support rear of vehicle so that axle is parallel with floor.
3. Remove differential housing cover bolts, then drain lubricant into suitable container.
4. Remove differential housing cover.
5. Remove disc brake caliper bolts, then using suitable mechanic's wire, position disc brake caliper aside.
6. Remove disc rotor.
7. Index mark driveshaft flange and pinion flange to ensure correct alignment during installation.
8. Remove four driveshaft to pinion flange mounting bolts.
9. Disconnect driveshaft centering socket yoke from pinion flange, then secure driveshaft aside using suitable wire or strap.
10. Disconnect anti-lock brake wheel sensor from axle.
11. Remove differential carrier vent hose.
12. Remove brake hose junction block retaining bolt.
13. Separate parking brake cables from axle housing.
14. Remove brake line bracket bolt, then remove brake line from brake line retaining clips.
15. Support axle assembly using suitable jack.
16. Remove lower shock absorber nuts and bolts.
17. Remove spring plate mounting nuts, two spring plate U-bolts, then remove the axle to spring retaining plate.
18. Lower axle housing from vehicle.
19. Reverse procedure to install.

Drive Pinion Flange & Drive Pinion Seal, Replace

1. Raise and support vehicle.
2. Remove disc brake caliper bolts, then using suitable mechanic's wire, position disc brake caliper aside. Disc

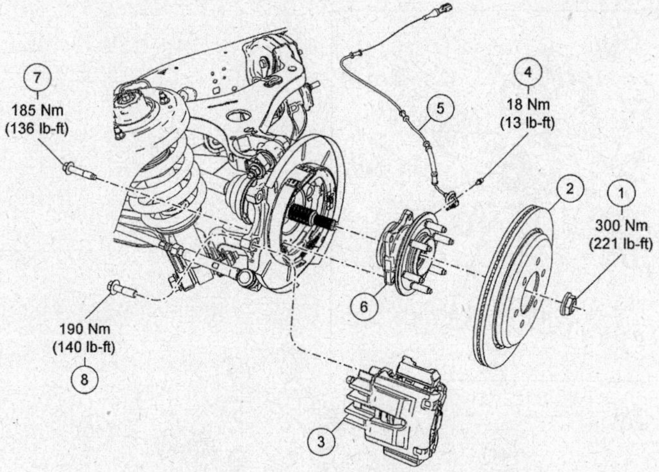

Item	Description
1	Halfshaft nut
2	Brake disc
3	Brake caliper assembly
4	Wheel speed sensor bolt
5	Wheel speed sensor
6	Wheel bearing and hub assembly
7	Wheel bearing and hub assembly bolt (4 required)
8	Brake caliper anchor plate bolt (2 required)

LTV0500000000428

Fig. 4 Rear hub & bearing replacement. Dana/ Spicer integral axle

brake calipers must be removed to prevent brake drag during drive pinion bearing preload adjustment.

3. Index mark driveshaft flange and pinion flange for correct alignment during installation.
4. Remove four driveshaft flange mounting bolts.
5. Disconnect driveshaft centering socket yoke from pinion flange.
6. Record torque required to maintain rotation of pinion gear through several revolutions using an inch lbs., torque wrench on pinion nut.
7. Hold pinion flange secure using holding fixture tool No. T78P-4851–A, or equivalent, then remove and discard pinion nut.
8. Index mark pinion flange in relation to drive pinion shaft, **Fig. 8,** to ensure correct alignment during installation.
9. Remove pinion flange using a two jaw puller tool No. D97L-4221–A, or equivalent.
10. Force upward on metal flange of drive pinion seal. Install gripping pliers and strike with a hammer until drive pinion seal is removed, **Fig. 9.**
11. Reverse procedure to install, noting the following:
    a. Lubricate new drive pinion seal with suitable grease.
    b. Install drive pinion seal using seal installation tool No. T83T-4676–A, or equivalent.
    c. Align pinion flange with drive pinion shaft, **Fig. 8.**
    d. Install and tighten new pinion flange nut using holding fixture tool No. T78P-4851–A, or equivalent, then remove holding fixture.
    e. Install drive pinion flange installation tool No. TOOL-4858–E, or equivalent.
    f. Rotate drive pinion through several revolutions, take frequent drive pinion bearing preload readings until original recorded drive pinion bearing preload reading is obtained.
    g. Install brake rotor, caliper and driveshaft.

TOE LINK

REPLACE

1. **On models equipped with air ride suspension,** turn air suspension off as outlined under "Precautions."
2. **On all models,** raise and support vehicle.
3. Remove toe link to wheel knuckle nut, **Fig. 10,** then separate toe link from wheel knuckle.
4. Remove toe link to frame nut, then the toe link.
5. Reverse procedure to install.

SHOCK ABSORBER

REPLACE

Except Expedition & Navigator

1. Raise and support rear of vehicle to a point where weight is relieved from rear springs and tires are still in contact with floor.
2. Remove lower attaching nut and bolt from shock absorber, **Fig. 11,** and swing lower end free of mounting bracket.
3. Remove upper mounting nut, then the shock absorber.
4. Reverse procedure to install.

Expedition & Navigator

1. **On models equipped with air ride suspension,** turn air suspension off as outlined under "Precautions."
2. **On all models,** raise and support vehicle.
3. Remove and discard shock and spring assembly upper nuts, **Fig. 12.**
4. Remove and discard shock and spring assembly lower nuts.
5. Remove shock absorber and spring assembly.
6. Index mark upper mount, spring and shock absorber for reference during installation.
7. Compress spring until tension is released from shock absorber using suitable spring compressor, **Fig. 13.**
8. While holding shock rod, remove upper nut and washer.
9. Remove upper mount, dust boot, insulator, then the coil spring.
10. Reverse procedure to install.

COIL SPRING

REPLACE

Except Expedition & Navigator

1. **On models equipped with air ride suspension,** turn air suspension off as outlined under "Precautions."
2. **On all models,** raise and support vehicle.
3. Remove wheel assembly, then the driveshaft.
4. Disconnect anti-lock wheel speed sensor.
5. Ensure parking brake is fully released, then disconnect rear parking brake cable and conduit from rear axle.
6. Remove rear calipers and place aside. Disconnect axle vent tube.
7. Disconnect stabilizer bar. Using a suitable jack support rear axle.
8. Remove lower shock nuts and bolts, then track bar bolt.
9. Remove upper and lower arm assembly to axle bolts.
10. Lower axle and remove coil springs.
11. Reverse procedure to install.

Expedition & Navigator

Refer to "Shock Absorber, Replace" for coil spring replacement procedure.

LEAF SPRING

REPLACE

E-Series

1. Raise rear of vehicle and support at frame. Support axle with a suitable jack.
2. Disconnect shock absorbers, **Fig. 14,** from lower mounts.
3. Remove two U-bolts and the U-bolt plate.
4. Lower axle assembly and remove upper and lower rear shackle bolts, then pull rear shackle assembly from bracket and spring.
5. Remove spring mounting nut and bolt, then lower spring assembly from vehicle.
6. Lower axle assembly and remove spring front bolt from hanger. Remove two attaching bolts from rear of spring, then lower spring assembly from vehicle.
7. Reverse procedure to install.

F-150 & Mark LT

1. Raise and support rear of vehicle to a point where weight is relieved from rear springs and tires are still in contact with floor.
2. Remove spring U-bolts, **Fig. 11,** and if equipped, the auxiliary spring and spacer.
3. Remove spring to bracket mounting nut and bolt from front of spring.
4. Remove upper and lower shackle mounting nuts and bolts from rear of spring, then lower spring and shackle assembly from vehicle.
5. Reverse procedure to install, noting the following:
   a. Tighten U-bolt nuts in 2 steps, using a cross pattern.
   b. **On light duty models,** step one, **torque** nuts to 22 ft. lbs.; Step two, **torque** nuts to 85 ft. lbs
   c. **On heavy duty models,** step one, **torque** nuts to 22 ft. lbs.; Step two, **torque** nuts to 184 ft. lbs

Excursion, F-250 & F-350

1. Raise rear of vehicle and support at frame. Support axle with a suitable jack.
2. Remove and discard U-bolt nuts and U-bolts, **Fig. 15,** then remove spring upper plate.
3. Remove and discard spring to front bracket bolt and flag nut.
4. Remove and discard shackle to rear bracket bolt and flag nut.
5. Remove rear spring assembly. If rear spring has an auxiliary spring and spacer, it is serviced as part of rear spring assembly.
6. Reverse procedure to install, noting the following:

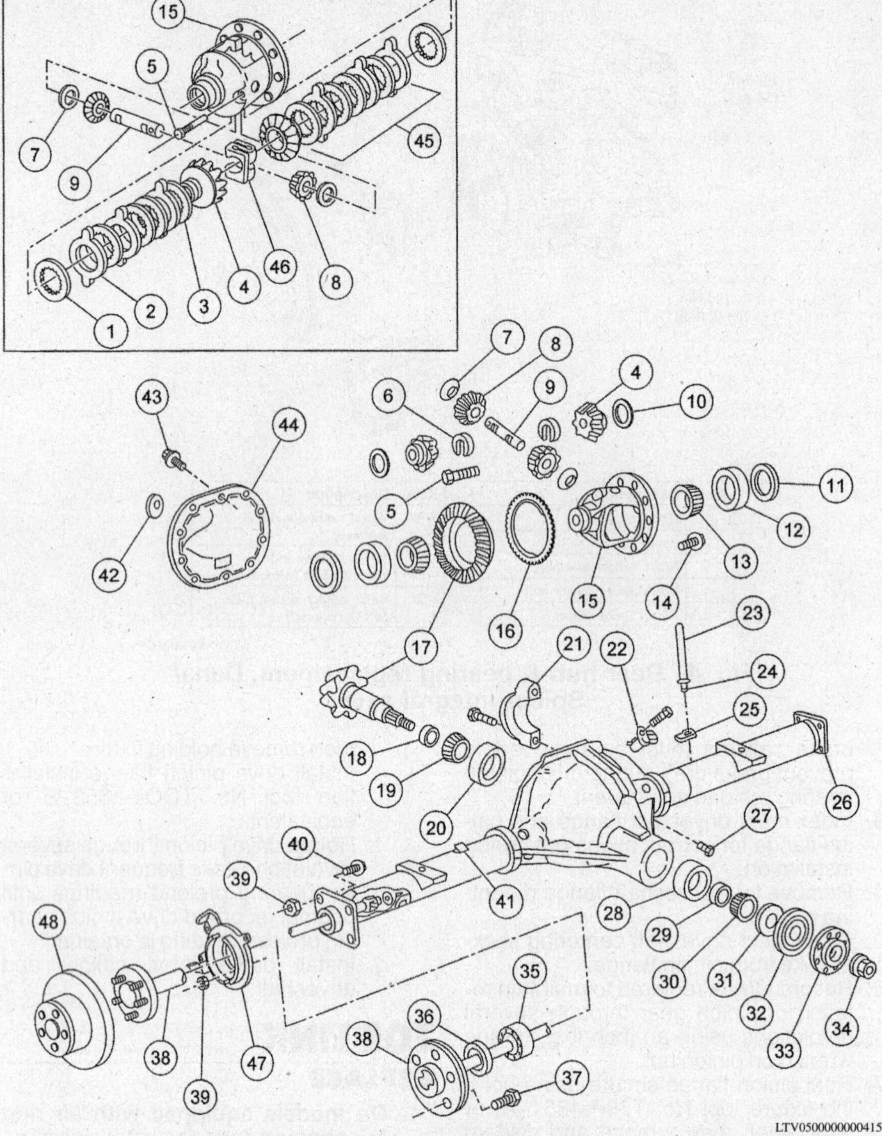

Fig. 5 Exploded view of Ford integral carrier type rear axle (Part 1 of 2). 8.8 Inch axle

   a. Tighten shackle to rear bracket bolt, with suspension at curb height.
   b. Tighten spring to front bracket bolt, with suspension at curb height.
   c. Tighten U-bolt nuts evenly in a cross pattern in four steps. Step one, **torque** nuts to 37 ft. lbs.; Step two, **torque** nuts to 74 ft. lbs.; Step three, **torque** nuts to 111 ft. lbs.; Step four, **torque** nuts to 148 ft. lbs.

F-450 & F-550

1. Raise rear of vehicle and support at frame. Support axle with a suitable jack.
2. Remove and discard U-bolt nuts, **Fig. 16,** then remove spring plate.
3. Remove and discard U-bolts.
4. Remove and discard spring to front bracket bolt and flag nut.
5. Remove and discard shackle to rear bracket bolt and flag nut.
6. Remove rear spring assembly.
7. Remove and discard spring to shackle nut and bolt, then remove the rear spring shackle.
8. Remove auxiliary spring nut, upper spring plate, auxiliary spring and auxiliary spring spacer.
9. Reverse procedure to install, noting the following:
   a. Tighten shackle to rear bracket bolt, with suspension at curb height.
   b. Tighten spring to front bracket bolt, with suspension at curb height.
   c. Tighten U-bolt nuts evenly in a cross pattern in four steps. Step one, **torque** nuts to 47 ft. lbs.; Step two, **torque** nuts to 148 ft. lbs.; Step three, **torque** nuts to 222 ft. lbs.; Step four, **torque** nuts to 295 ft. lbs.

Item	Description
1	Dished washer
2	Clutch plate
3	Clutch disc
4	Differential side gears (2 required)
5	Differential pinion shaft lock bolts
6	U-washer (2 required)
7	Differential pinion gear thrust washers (2 required)
8	Differential pinion gears (2 required)
9	Differential pinion shafts
10	Differential side gear thrust washer (2 required)
11	Differential bearing shim
12	Differential bearing cup (2 required)
13	Differential bearing (2 required)
14	Differential ring gear bolt (10 required)
15	Differential case
16	Anti-lock ring
17	Differential ring and pinion
18	Drive pinion bearing adjustment shim
19	Drive pinion bearing (2 required)
20	Drive pinion bearing cup—inner
21	Differential bearing cap (2 required) and differential bearing cap bolt (4 required)
22	Anti-lock speed sensor
23	Vent hose
24	Axle housing vent
25	Brake junction block
26	Axle housing
27	Filler plug
28	Drive pinion bearing cup (outer)
29	Drive pinion collapsible spacer
30	Drive pinion bearing (outer)
31	Drive pinion shaft oil slinger
32	Drive pinion seal
33	Pinion flange
34	Pinion nut
35	Rear wheel bearing (2 required)
36	Axle shaft oil seal (2 required)
37	Wheel stud (10 required)
38	Axle shafts (2 required)
39	Brake backing plate nuts (8 required)
40	Brake backing plate bolt (8 required)
41	Brake line clip
42	Axle identification tag (part
43	Differential housing cover bolt (10 required)
44	Differential housing cover
45	Differential clutch pack
46	Differential clutch spring
47	Rear wheel disc brake adapter (2 required)
48	Brake disc (2 required)

LTV0500000000416

Fig. 5 Exploded view of Ford integral carrier type rear axle (Part 2 of 2). 8.8 Inch axle

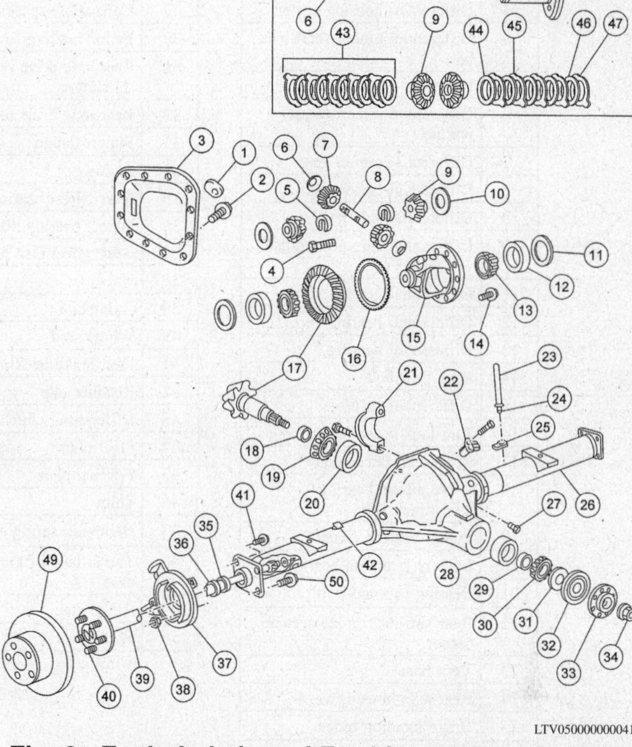

Fig. 6 Exploded view of Ford integral carrier type rear axle (Part 1 of 2). 9.75 & 10.25 Inch axles

CONTROL ARM

REPLACE

Lower

1. **On models equipped with air ride suspension,** turn air suspension off as outlined under "Precautions."
2. **On all models,** raise and support vehicle.
3. Remove and discard stabilizer bar link upper nut, **Fig. 17.** Use hex holding feature to prevent stud from turning while removing nut.
4. Remove shock absorber lower bolt and nut
5. Remove lower control arm front nut and bolt.
6. Remove lower control arm rear nut and bolt.
7. Remove lower control arm to wheel knuckle bolt, nut, then the lower control arm.
8. Reverse procedure to install.

Upper

1. **On models equipped with air ride suspension,** turn air suspension off as outlined under "Precautions."
2. **On all models,** raise and support vehicle.
3. Remove parking brake cable wireform bracket bolt.
4. Remove upper control arm to wheel knuckle nut and bolt, **Fig. 18.**
5. Remove upper control arm front mounting nut and bolt.
6. Remove the upper arm rear mounting nut, bolt, then the upper control arm assembly.
7. Reverse procedure to install.

KNUCKLE

REPLACE

1. **On models equipped with air ride suspension,** turn air suspension off as outlined under "Precautions."
2. **On all models,** raise and support vehicle.
3. Remove wheel bearing and hub assembly as outlined under "Hub & Bearing, Replace."
4. Remove parking brake shoe retaining clips, **Fig. 19,** adjuster spring, return spring, adjuster and parking brake shoes.
5. Depress tabs and disconnect parking brake cable from wheel knuckle.
6. Remove toe link to wheel knuckle mounting nut, then disconnect toe link from wheel knuckle.
7. Remove upper arm to wheel knuckle nut and bolt.
8. Remove lower arm to wheel knuckle nut, bolt and wheel knuckle.
9. Reverse procedure to install.

STABILIZER BAR

REPLACE

1. **On models equipped with air ride suspension,** turn air suspension off as outlined under "Precautions."
2. **On all models,** raise and support vehicle.
3. Remove and discard stabilizer bar link upper nuts, **Fig. 20.** Use hex holding feature to prevent stud from turning while removing nut.
4. Remove and discard stabilizer bar link lower nuts and two stabilizer bar links.
5. Remove four stabilizer bar bracket mounting nuts, two stabilizer bar brackets, then the stabilizer bar.
6. Reverse procedure to install.

Item	Description
1	Rear axle identification tag
2	Differential housing cover bolt
3	Differential housing cover
4	Differential pinion shaft lock bolt
5	U-washer
6	Differential pinion thrust washer
7	Differential pinion gear
8	Differential pinion shaft
9	Differential side gear
10	Differential side gear thrust washer
11	Differential bearing shim
12	Differential bearing cup
13	Differential bearing
14	Ring gear bolt
15	Differential case
16	Anti-lock speed sensor ring
17	Ring gear and pinion
18	Drive pinion bearing adjustment shim
19	Pinion bearing (inner)
20	Inner axle pinion bearing cup
21	Bearing cap and bolt
22	Rear anti-lock brake system sensor
23	Vent hose
24	Rear axle housing vent
25	Brake junction block

Item	Description
26	Rear axle housing
27	Filler plug
28	Outer pinion bearing cup
29	Collapsible spacer
30	Pinion bearing (outer)
31	Rear axle drive pinion shaft oil slinger
32	Rear axle drive pinion seal
33	Pinion flange
34	Pinion nut
35	Rear wheel bearing
36	Wheel bearing oil seal
37	Rear wheel disc brake adapter
38	Nut
39	Axle shaft
40	Wheel stud
41	Disc brake backing plate bolt
42	Retainer clip
43	Differential clutch pack
44	Steel plate
45	Friction plate
46	Shim
47	Belleville spring (part of
48	Thrust face of the differential case
49	Brake disc
50	Bolt

LTV0500000000418

Fig. 6 Exploded view of Ford integral carrier type rear axle (Part 2 of 2). 9.75 & 10.25 Inch axles

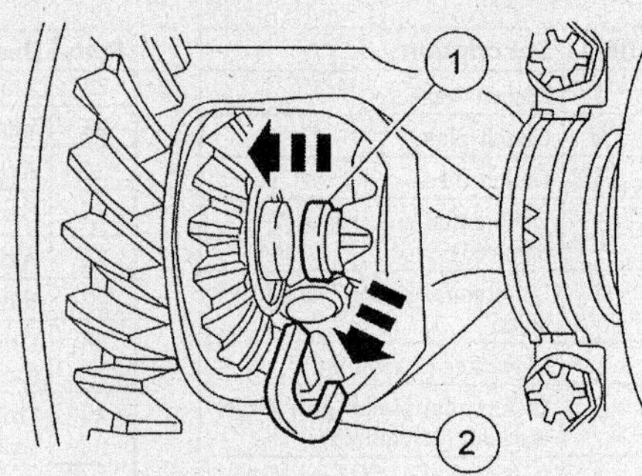

Fig. 7 Pinion shaft & U-washers removal

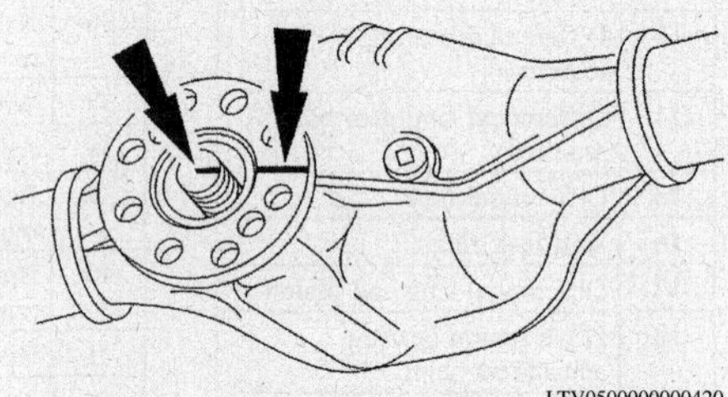

Fig. 8 Pinion flange and shaft alignment. Ford integral carrier type rear axle

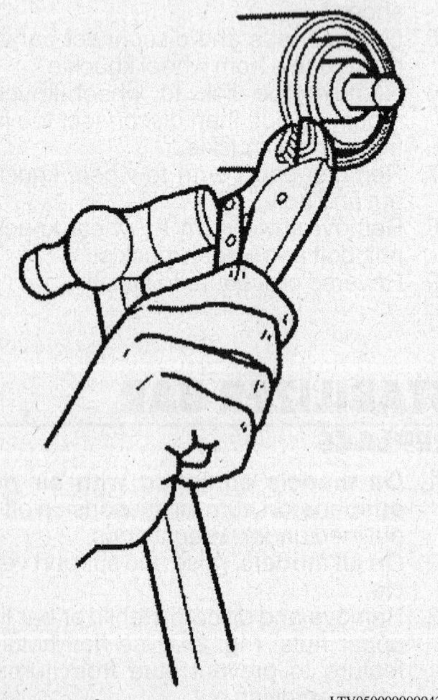

Fig. 9 Pinion seal removal. Ford integral carrier type rear axle

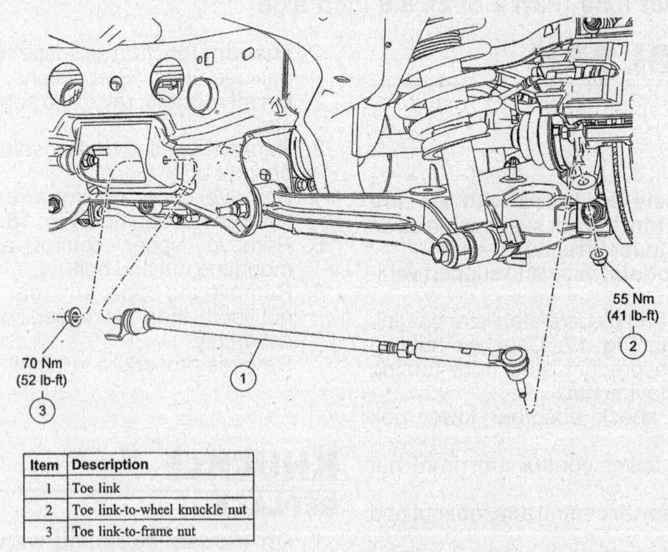

Item	Description
1	Toe link
2	Toe link-to-wheel knuckle nut
3	Toe link-to-frame nut

LTV0500000000429

Fig. 10 Toe link replacement

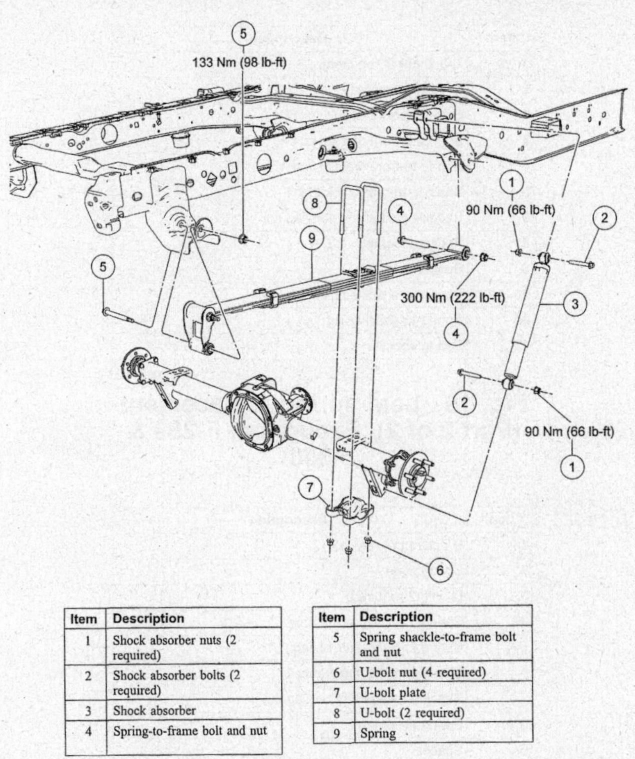

Item	Description
1	Shock absorber nuts (2 required)
2	Shock absorber bolts (2 required)
3	Shock absorber
4	Spring-to-frame bolt and nut

Item	Description
5	Spring shackle-to-frame bolt and nut
6	U-bolt nut (4 required)
7	U-bolt plate
8	U-bolt (2 required)
9	Spring

LTV0500000000422

Fig. 11 Exploded view of rear suspension. Except Expedition & Navigator

Item	Description
1	Shock absorber and spring assembly
2	Shock absorber lower nut
3	Shock and spring assembly upper nut (3 required)
4	Shock absorber lower bolt
5	Upper mount
6	Insulator
7	Dust boot
8	Shock rod nut
9	Shock absorber
10	Spring
11	Jounce bumper

LTV0500000000425

Fig. 12 Shock absorber & coil spring assembly replacement (Part 2 of 2). Expedition & Navigator

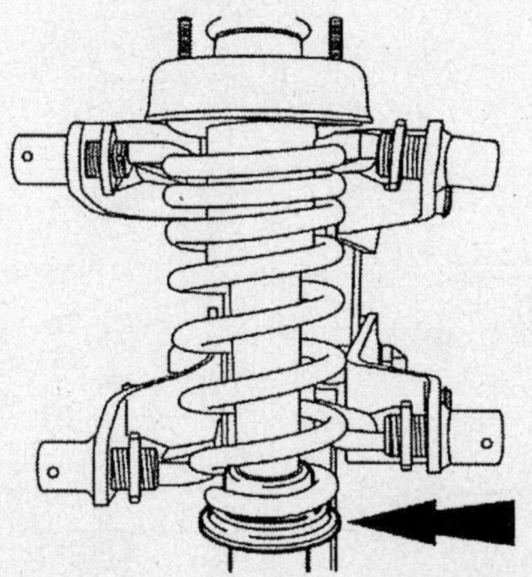

LTV0500000000426

Fig. 13 Coil spring replacement. Expedition & Navigator

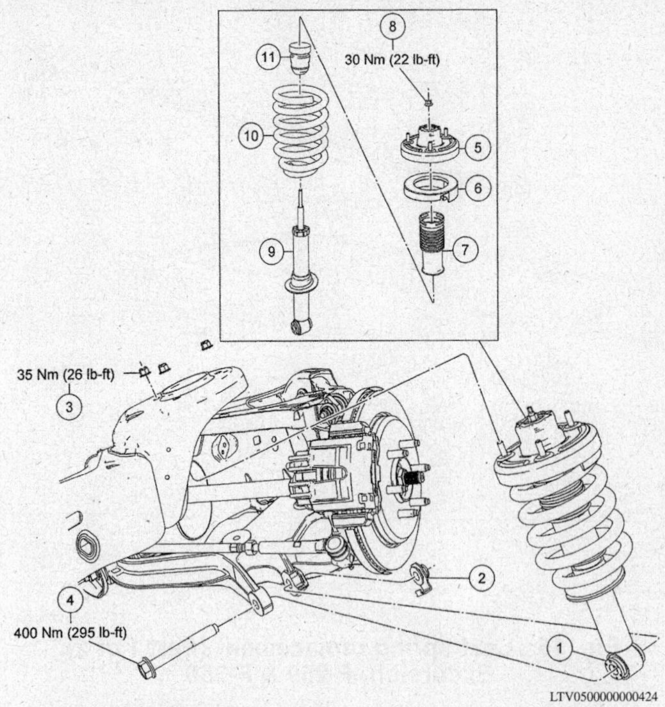

LTV0500000000424

Fig. 12 Shock absorber & coil spring assembly replacement (Part 1 of 2). Expedition & Navigator

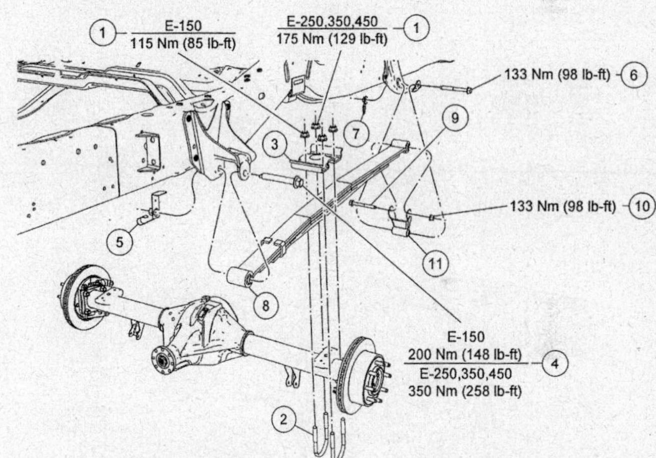

Item	Description
1	U-bolt nuts (4 required) (E-150)
1	U-bolt nuts (4 required) (E-250, E-350 and E-450)
2	U-bolt (2 required) (E-150)
2	U-bolt (2 required) (E-250, and E-350)
2	U-bolt (2 required) (E-350 chassis)
2	U-bolt (2 required) (E-450)
3	U-bolt plate
4	Leaf spring front bracket bolt (E-150)
4	Leaf spring front bracket bolt (E-250, E-350 and E-450)
5	Leaf spring front bracket flagnut (E-150)

Item	Description
5	Leaf spring front bracket flagnut (E-250 [RH only], E-350 [RH only] and E-450)
6	Leaf spring shackle-to-bracket bolt (E-150)
6	Leaf spring shackle-to-bracket bolt (E-250, E-350 and E-450)
7	Leaf spring shackle-to-bracket flagnut
8	Leaf spring
9	Leaf spring-to-shackle bolt (E-150)
9	Leaf spring-to-shackle bolt (E-250, E-350 and E450))
10	Leaf spring-to-shackle nut
11	Leaf spring shackle

LTV0500000000433

Fig. 14 Leaf spring replacement. E-Series

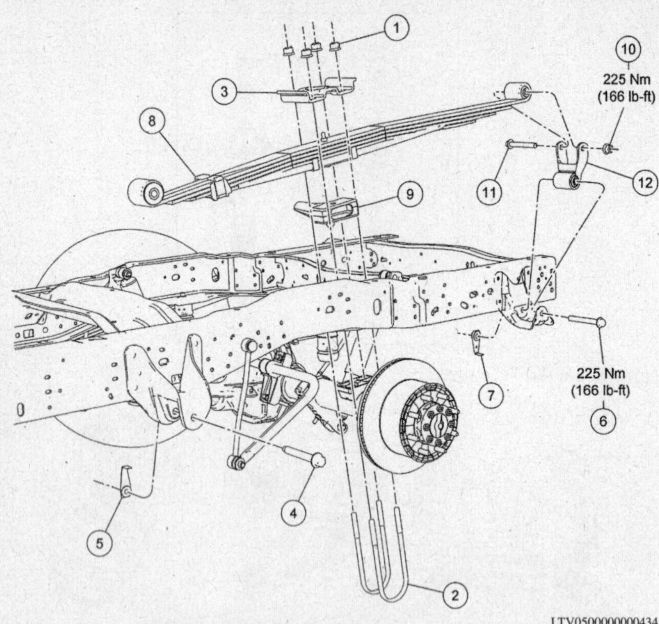

LTV0500000000434

Fig. 15 Leaf spring replacement (Part 1 of 2). Excursion, F-250 & F-350

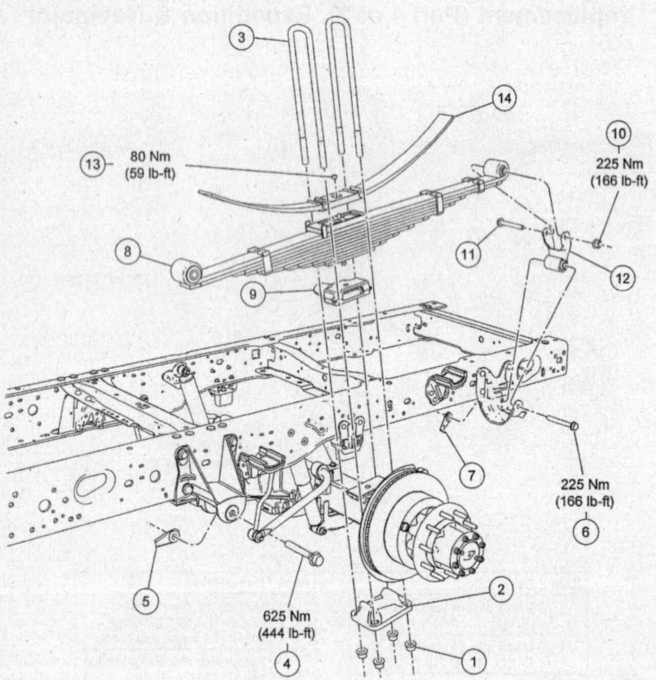

LTV0500000000436

Fig. 16 Leaf spring replacement (Part 1 of 2). F-450 & F-550

Item	Description
1	U-bolt nut (4 required)
2	U-bolt (2 required)
3	Spring upper plate
4	Spring-to-front bracket bolt
5	Spring-to-front bracket flag nut
6	Shackle-to-rear bracket bolt
7	Shackle-to-rear bracket flag nut
8	Spring assembly
9	Spacer
10	Spring-to-shackle bolt
11	Spring-to-shackle nut
12	Spring shackle

LTV0500000000435

Fig. 15 Leaf spring replacement (Part 2 of 2). Excursion, F-250 & F-350

Item	Description
1	U-bolt nut (4 required)
2	Spring plate
3	U-bolt (2 required)
4	Spring-to-front bracket bolt
5	Spring-to-front bracket flag nut
6	Shackle-to-rear bracket bolt
7	Shackle-to-rear bracket flag nut
8	Spring assembly
9	Spacer
10	Spring-to-shackle bolt
11	Spring-to-shackle nut
12	Spring shackle
13	Auxiliary spring nut
14	Auxiliary spring

LTV0500000000437

Fig. 16 Leaf spring replacement (Part 2 of 2). F-450 & F-550

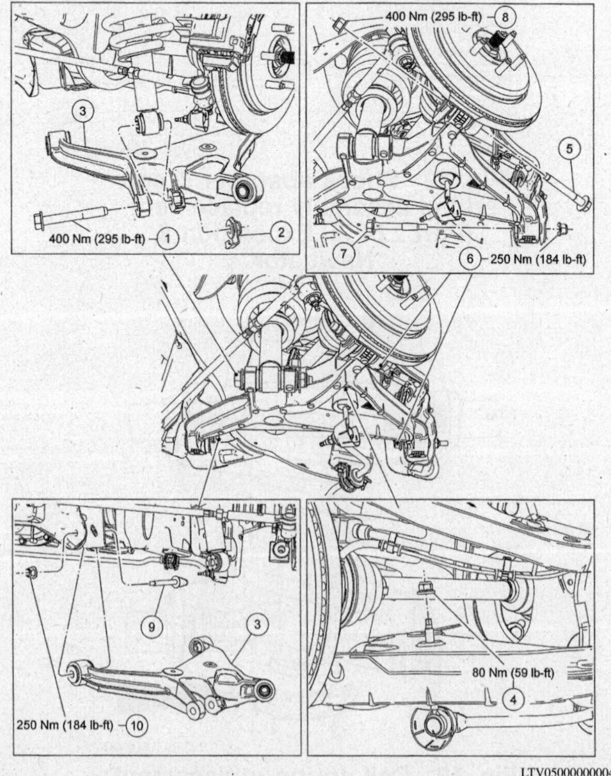

LTV0500000000431

Fig. 17 Lower control arm replacement (Part 1 of 2)

Item	Description
1	Shock absorber lower bolt
2	Shock absorber lower nut
3	Lower arm
4	Stabilizer bar link upper nut
5	Lower arm-to-wheel knuckle bolt
6	Lower arm forward nut
7	Lower arm forward bolt
8	Lower arm-to-wheel knuckle nut
9	Lower arm rearward bolt
10	Lower arm rearward nut

LTV0500000000432

Fig. 17 Lower control arm replacement (Part 2 of 2)

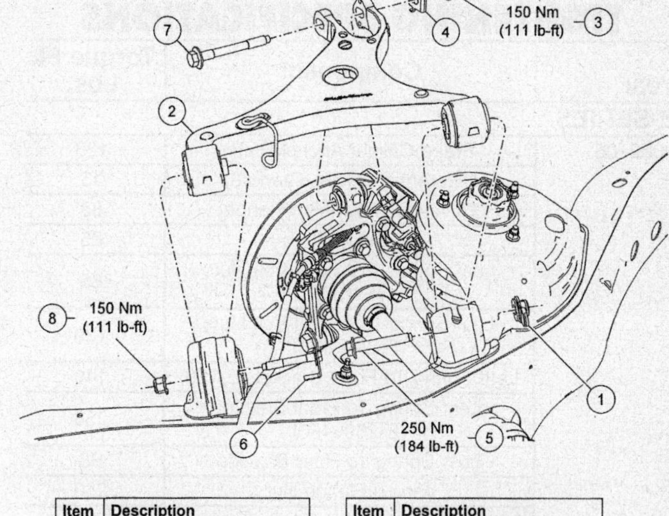

Item	Description
1	Upper arm rearward nut
2	Upper arm
3	Upper arm-to-wheel knuckle nut
4	Camber adjustment shim

Item	Description
5	Upper arm rearward bolt
6	Upper arm forward bolt
7	Upper arm-to-wheel knuckle bolt
8	Upper arm forward nut

LTV0500000000430

Fig. 18 Upper control arm replacement

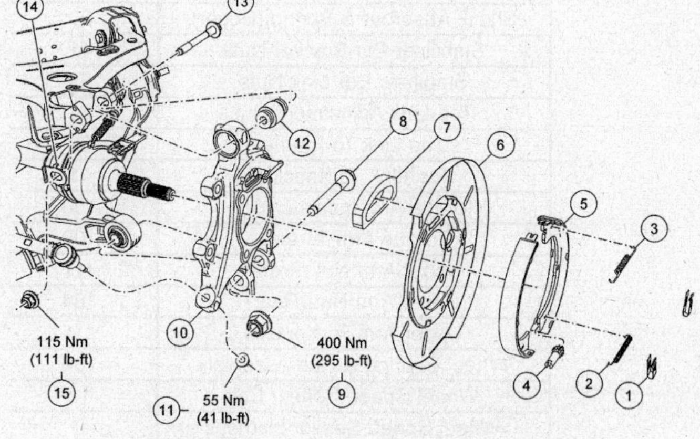

Item	Description
1	Parking brake shoe retaining clip (2 required)
2	Parking brake shoe adjuster spring
3	Parking brake shoe return spring
4	Parking brake shoe adjuster
5	Parking brake shoe (2 required)
6	Brake disc shield (part of
7	Shield gasket

Item	Description
8	Lower arm-to-wheel knuckle bolt
9	Lower arm-to-wheel knuckle nut
10	Wheel knuckle
11	Toe link-to-wheel knuckle nut
12	Wheel knuckle bushing
13	Upper arm-to-wheel knuckle bolt
14	Camber adjustment shim
15	Upper arm-to-wheel knuckle nut

LTV0500000000427

Fig. 19 Spindle knuckle replacement

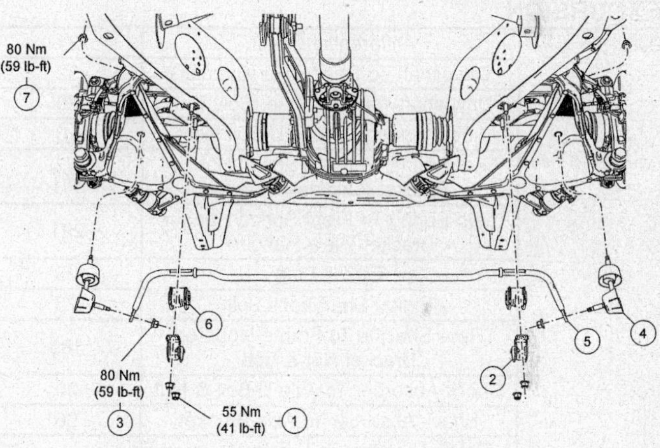

Item	Description
1	Stabilizer bar bracket nut (4 required)
2	Stabilizer bar bracket (2 required)
3	Stabilizer bar link lower nut (2 required)
4	Stabilizer bar link (2 required)

Item	Description
5	Stabilizer bar
6	Stabilizer bar bushing (2 required)
7	Stabilizer bar link upper nut (2 required)

LTV0500000000423

Fig. 20 Stabilizer bar replacement

TIGHTENING SPECIFICATIONS

Year	Component	Torque Ft. Lbs.
E-SERIES		
2002–06	Brake Caliper Anchor Plate	128
	Differential Cover (Grade 8)	45
	Driveshaft To Pinion Flange	83
	Fill Plug	25
	Leaf Spring To Axle U-Bolt Nuts (E-150)	85
	Leaf Spring To Axle U-Bolt Nuts (E-250–450)	129
	Leaf Spring To Front Bracket (E-150)	148
	Leaf Spring To Front Bracket (E-250–450)	258
	Leaf Spring To Rear Shackle	98
	Pinion Flange Nut	250
	Pinion Shaft Lock Bolt	20
	Shock Absorber (Lower)	52
	Shock Absorber (Upper)	30
	Stabilizer Bar Link (Lower)	21
	Stabilizer Bar Link (Upper)	52
	Stabilizer Bar Link To Stabilizer Bar	30
	Wheel Lug Nut (Single axle)	103
	Wheel Lug Nut (Dual Axle)	148
EXCURSION		
2002–05	Differential Cover	34
	Driveshaft To Rear Yoke (Circular)	82
	Driveshaft To Rear Yoke (Split Pin)	26
	Leaf Spring To Axle U-Bolt Nut	①
	Leaf Spring To Front Spring Hanger Bracket (Original Hanger)	277
	Leaf Spring To Front Spring Hanger Bracket (New Hanger)	221
	Oil Fill Plug	23
	Pinion Shaft Lock Bolt	23
	Rear Shackle To Frame Mounted Bracket Nut & Bolt	185
	Shock Absorber To Axle U-Bolt & Nut	30
	Shock Absorber To Axle Bracket	66
	Shock Absorber To Frame Mounted Bracket Nut	17
	Stabilizer Bar Retainer Bracket To Axle Bolt (Dana Axle)	30
	Stabilizer Bar Retainer Bracket To Axle Bolt (Ford Axle)	35
	Stabilizer Bar Link To Frame Nut	52
	Stabilizer Bar Link To Stabilizer Bar Nut	52
	Wheel Lug Nuts	148

TIGHTENING SPECIFICATIONS—Continued

Year	Component	Torque Ft. Lbs.
EXPEDITION & NAVIGATOR		
2002–06	Brake Caliper Anchor Plate	140
	Differential Cover	24
	Differential Pinion Shaft Lock Bolt	22
	Driveshaft Flex Coupler	111
	Driveshaft To Pinion Flange	83
	Halfshaft To Hub	221
	Lower Arm To Knuckle	295
	Lower Arm Front & Rear Nuts	184
	Oil Fill Plug	22
	Rear Axle Insulator Stud Nut	100
	Rear Axle Insulator Studs	30
	Shock Absorber Rod Nut	22
	Shock Absorber & Spring (Lower)	295
	Shock Absorber & Spring (Upper)	26
	Stabilizer Bar Bracket Nuts	41
	Stabilizer Bar Link Nuts	59
	Toe Link Adjustment Nut	85
	Toe Link To Frame	52
	Toe Link To Knuckle	41
	Torque Arm Insulator Bolt	100
	Torque Arm To Axle	100
	Upper Arm Nut (Front)	111
	Upper Arm Nut (Rear)	184
	Upper Arm To Knuckle	111
	Wheel Bearing & Hub Assembly	136
	Wheel Speed Sensor Bolt	13
	Wheel Speed Sensor Harness	11
	Wheel Lugs	150
F-150 & MARK LT		
2002–06	Brake Caliper Bolts	20
	Brake Hose Junction Block	13
	Brake Line Bracket	18
	Differential Pinion Shaft Lock Bolt	22
	Differential Cover	33
	Disc Brake Adapter Nuts	80
	Driveshaft Center Bearing	35
	Driveshaft Shield	18
	Driveshaft To Pinion Flange	76
	Oil Filler Plug	22
	Parking Brake Cable	18
	Shock Absorber Nut	66
	Shock Absorber To Axle Bracket (8.8 Inch Axle)	52
	Shock Absorber To Axle Bracket (9.75 & 10.25 Inch Axles)	66
	Spring Shackle To Frame	98
	Spring To Frame	222
	Spring To Shackle	98
	Spring U-Bolts	①

Continued

TIGHTENING SPECIFICATIONS—Continued

Year	Component	Torque Ft. Lbs.
F-250-550		
2002–06	Auxiliary Spring Nut	59
	Center Bearing	46
	Differential Cover (Dana 80 F-350)	35
	Differential Cover (Dana 80 F-450–550)	45
	Differential Cover (Ford Axle)	33
	Driveshaft To Axle Flange (Circular Yoke)	82–100
	Driveshaft To Axle Flange (Split-Pin-Yoke)	26
	Leaf Spring To Axle U-Bolt Nut	①
	Leaf Spring To Front Spring Hanger Bracket (F-250–350)	277
	Leaf Spring To Front Spring Hanger Bracket (F-450–550)	444
	Leaf Spring To Rear Shackle Bolt & Nut	166
	Oil Fill Plug (Dana 80)	25
	Oil Fill Plug (Dana S110 & S130)	40
	Oil Fill Plug (Ford Axle)	22
	Pinion Hex Nut (Dana S110 & S130)	832
	Pinion Shaft Lock Nut (Dana 80)	470
	Rear Shackle To Frame Mounted Bracket	166
	Reverse Slip Driveshaft Flange To Drivershaft Nut	301
	Shock Absorber To Axle Bracket U-Bolt	30
	Shock Absorber Nut (Lower)	66
	Shock Absorber Nut (Upper)	46
	Stabilizer Bar Bracket	30
	Stabilizer Bar Link Nut (Lower)	76
	Stabilizer Bar Link Nut (Upper)	46
	Wheel Lug Nuts	165

TIGHTENING SPECIFICATIONS—Continued

Year	Component	Torque Ft. Lbs.
MOTORHOME CHASSIS		
2002–06	Auxiliary Spring Nut	41
	Leaf Spring To Axle U-Bolt Nuts	258
	Leaf Spring To Front Spring Hanger Bracket	296
	Leaf Spring To Rear Shackle	184
	Rear Shackle To Frame Mounted Bracket	184
	Rear Spring Bracket To Frame	66
	Shock Absorber To Frame Mounted Bracket	258
	Shock Absorber To Axle Bracket	258
	Stabilizer Bar Bracket Bolt To Axle	59
	Stabilizer Bar Link	66
	Wheel Bolts (M14)	165
	Wheel Bolts (M22)	460

①— Refer to "Leaf Spring, Replace" for tightening procedure.

Front Suspension & Steering

NOTE: Refer To "Front Wheel Drive" For Service Procedures On Four Wheel Drive Models Not Covered In This Section.

NOTE: On Air Bag Equipped Models, Refer To "Air Bag System Precautions" Located In The Front Of This Manual For System Disarming & Arming Procedures.

INDEX

PRECAUTIONS

Air Bag Systems

Refer to "Air Bag System Precautions" in the front of this manual for system disarming and arming procedures.

Air Suspension Systems

Models equipped with automatic leveling systems should have power to this system shut off whenever vehicle is raised or when suspension system components are serviced. Failure to shut off this system could allow this system to operate during service procedures and cause vehicle to shift positions.

System may be disabled with a switch located behind righthand kick panel.

Battery Ground Cable

Prior to service, disconnect battery ground cable and isolate as required.

DESCRIPTION

2WD Models

E-SERIES

These models utilize an independent twin I-beam, coil springs, shock absorbers and a stabilizer bar, **Fig. 1.**

EXPEDITION & NAVIGATOR

These models incorporate a double wishbone (SLA), coil-over-shock, gas-filled shocks front suspension, **Fig. 2.**

EXCURSION

These models utilize an independent twin I-bean with stabilizer bar on the F-250 models, and a non-independent rigid axle with stabilizer bars on all other models, **Fig. 3.**

F SUPER DUTY

Super Duty models utilize an independent twin I-bean with stabilizer bar on the F-250 models, and a non-independent rigid axle with stabilizer bars on all other models, **Figs. 4 and 5.**

F-150 & MARK LT

These models incorporate a double wishbone (SLA), coil-over-shock, gas-filled shocks front suspension, **Fig. 6.**

MOTORHOME CHASSIS

Refer to **Figs. 7** for front suspension component diagrams.

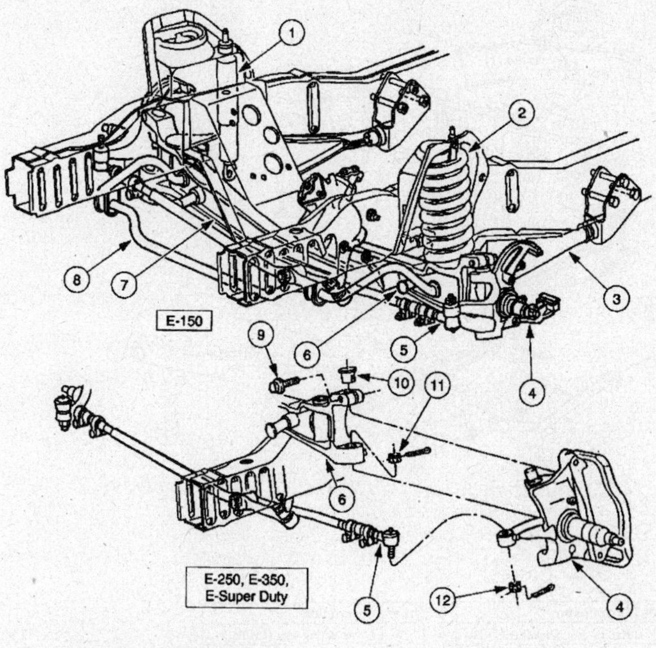

1. Shock absorber
2. Front coil spring
3. Radius arm
4. Front wheel spindle
5. Tie rod end
6. Front axle, lefthand
7. Front axle, righthand
8. Front stabilizer bar
9. Upper ball joint pinch bolt
10. Caster/Camber insert
11. Lower ball joint nut
12. Tie rod end to spindle nut

LTV1900000000187

Fig. 1 Front suspension components. E–Series w/2WD

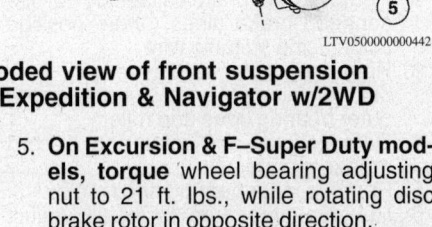

LTV0500000000442

Fig. 2 Exploded view of front suspension (Part 1 of 2). Expedition & Navigator w/2WD

4WD Models

E-SERIES

This independent front suspension **Fig. 8,** is a long spindle Short Arm/Long Arm (SLA) system, using frame mounted rubber bushed upper and lower control arms and radius arms combined with ball joints, attached to steering knuckles. Gas pressurized shock absorbers with torsion bars and a stabilizer bar are used to control front suspension movement.

EXPEDITION & NAVIGATOR

This independent front suspension **Fig. 9,** is a long spindle Short Arm/Long Arm (SLA) system, using frame mounted rubber bushed upper and lower control arms combined with ball joints, attached to steering knuckles. Gas pressurized shock absorbers with torsion bars and a stabilizer bar are used to control front suspension movement.

EXCURSION

These models utilize a non-independent rigid axle with stabilizer bars, **Fig. 10.**

F-150 & MARK LT

This independent front suspension **Fig. 11,** is a long spindle Short Arm/Long Arm (SLA) system, using frame mounted rubber bushed upper and lower control arms combined with ball joints, attached to steering knuckles. Gas pressurized shock absorbers with torsion bars and a stabilizer bar are used to control front suspension movement.

F-SUPER DUTY

These models utilize a non-independent rigid axle with stabilizer bars, **Fig. 12.**

WHEEL BEARING

ADJUST

2WD Models

EXCEPT MOTORHOME CHASSIS

1. Raise and support vehicle, then remove wheel and tire assembly.
2. Remove disc brake caliper and pads as outlined under "Disc Brakes" chapter.
3. Remove wheel bearing dust cap, locknut, adjusting nut washer and cotter pin.
4. **On Expedition, F-150, Mark LT & Navigator models, torque** wheel bearing adjusting nut to 30 ft. lbs., while rotating brake rotor counterclockwise, then back off two full turns.
5. **On Excursion & F–Super Duty models, torque** wheel bearing adjusting nut to 21 ft. lbs., while rotating disc brake rotor in opposite direction.
6. **On Expedition, F-150, Mark LT & Navigator models,** back off wheel bearing adjusting nut 175,° then **torque** to 17 inch lbs.
7. **On Excursion & F-Super Duty models,** back off wheel bearing adjusting nut 120–180,° then **torque** to 18 inch lbs. Required torque to rotate hub should be 18 inch lbs.
8. **On all models,** inspect endplay, .00025–.00500 inch should be indicated. Install dust cap, caliper, pads, then tire and wheel assembly.

MOTORHOME CHASSIS

1. Remove hub cap, gasket and cotter pin.
2. While rotating wheel, **torque** adjusting nut to 85 ft. lbs., to seat bearings.
3. Back off adjusting nut until loose.
4. Finger tighten adjusting nut. Final bearing adjustment end play must be within 0–.005 inch. Final adjustment must not result in a preloaded bearing.
5. If cotter pin hole lines up with slot in nut, insert and secure new cotter pin. If it does not, advance adjusting nut to align a slot with first available cotter pin hole. Insert and secure a new cotter pin.
6. Install new gasket and hub cap.

Item	Description
1	Upper arm RH/LH
2	Stabilizer bar bushing
3	Stabilizer bar bracket
4	Wheel knuckle RH/LH
5	Wheel bearing and hub
6	Lower arm RH/LH
7	Shock absorber
8	Coil spring
9	Shock absorber upper mount
10	Stabilizer bar link
11	Stabilizer bar

LTV0500000000443

Fig. 2 Exploded view of front suspension (Part 2 of 2). Expedition & Navigator w/2WD

4WD Models

On 4WD models, the wheel bearings are not adjustable.

WHEEL BEARING
REPLACE

2WD Models

1. Raise and support vehicle, then remove front wheels.
2. Remove front brake caliper, do not disconnect brake lines, then position aside using suitable wire.
3. Remove grease cap, cotter pin, locknut, adjusting nut and washer, then the outer bearing cone and roller.
4. Remove hub and rotor and discard grease retainer.
5. Remove inner bearing and roller.
6. Reverse procedure to install. Adjust bearings as outlined under "Wheel Bearings, Adjust."

4WD Models

The hub and bearing are replaced as an assembly, refer to "Hub & Bearing, Replace."

HUB & BEARING
REPLACE

4WD Models

1. Raise and support vehicle, then remove wheel.
2. Remove hub nut cotter pin and retainer, then the hub nut.
3. Remove brake rotor and caliper as outlined under "Disc Brakes" chapter.
4. **On Excursion and F-Super Duty models,** proceed as follows:
   a. Remove hub lock retainer ring.
   b. Remove axle shaft snap ring.
   c. Remove thrust washer.
5. **On models equipped with ABS,** remove the front brake rotor shield, then the wheel speed sensor.
6. **On all models,** remove hub and bearing mounting bolts, then pull hub and bearing assembly off axle spline and out of knuckle. **Axle spline into hub bearing is normally a slip fit, a puller should not be required.**
7. Reverse procedure to install.

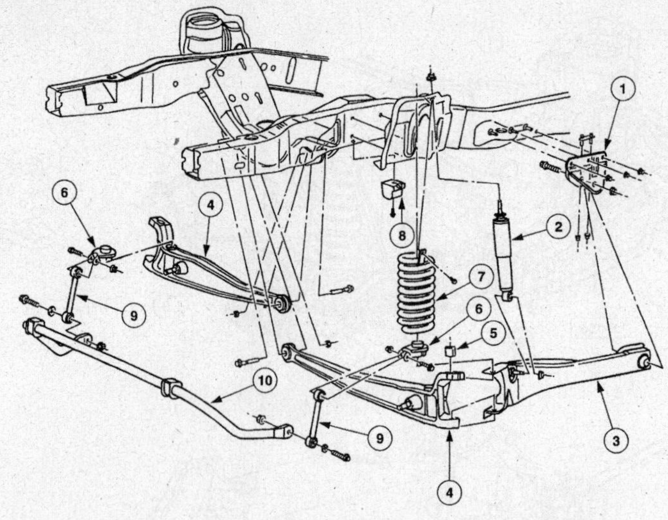

Item	Description
1	Radius arm bracket (LH/RH)
2	Shock absorber
3	Radius arm (LH/RH)
4	Front axle I-beam (LH/RH)
5	Upper ball joint adjuster
6	Lower spring seat (LH/RH)
7	Coil spring
8	Front axle jounce bumper
9	Front stabilizer bar link
10	Front stabilizer bar

LTV0500000000444

Fig. 3 Exploded view of front suspension (Part 1 of 3). Excursion w/2WD

DRIVESHAFT
REPLACE

1. Raise and support vehicle.
2. Index mark driveshaft to rear axle flange and at transfer case flange.
3. Remove and discard driveshaft flange bolts, **Figs. 13 and 14.**
4. Disconnect driveshaft flange from flange pilot using suitable pry bar.
5. **On models equipped with two piece driveshaft,** remove driveshaft center bearing support bolts.
6. **On all models,** remove driveshaft.
7. Reverse procedure to install.

BALL JOINT INSPECTION

1. Raise vehicle, then place a suitable support stand below the lower suspension control arm, then lower vehicle so that weight is supported on stand.
2. Adjust front wheel bearings as outlined under "Wheel Bearing, Adjust."
3. Inspect lower ball joint by grasping lower edge of tire and moving wheel in and out while observing lower spindle arm and lower portion of axle jaw. If movement exceeds 1/32 inch, **Figs. 15 and 16,** the lower ball joint must be replaced.
4. Inspect upper ball joint by grasping upper edge of tire and moving wheel in and out. If movement exceeds 1/32 inch, the upper ball joint must be replaced.

BALL JOINT
REPLACE

E-Series, Excursion, F-Super Duty & Motorhome Chassis

1. Remove steering knuckle and spindle as outlined under "Steering Knuckle, Replace."
2. Remove ball joint grease fitting.
3. Place steering knuckle with spindle in a suitable shop vice and holding fixture, then remove the lower ball joint snap ring.
4. Press ball joint from steering knuckle using, ball joint replacement C-frame and screw tool No. T74P-4638–C and ball joint removal adapter tool No. D89P- 3010–A, or equivalents, **Fig. 17.**
5. Reverse procedure to install, noting the following:
   a. Upper ball joint must be installed first.
   b. Install ball joints using, ball joint replacement C-frame and screw tool No. T74P-4638–C, ball joint installation adapter tool No. D89P-3010–A and receiving cup tool No. D84P-3395–A4, or equivalents,
   c. Install ball joint grease fitting.

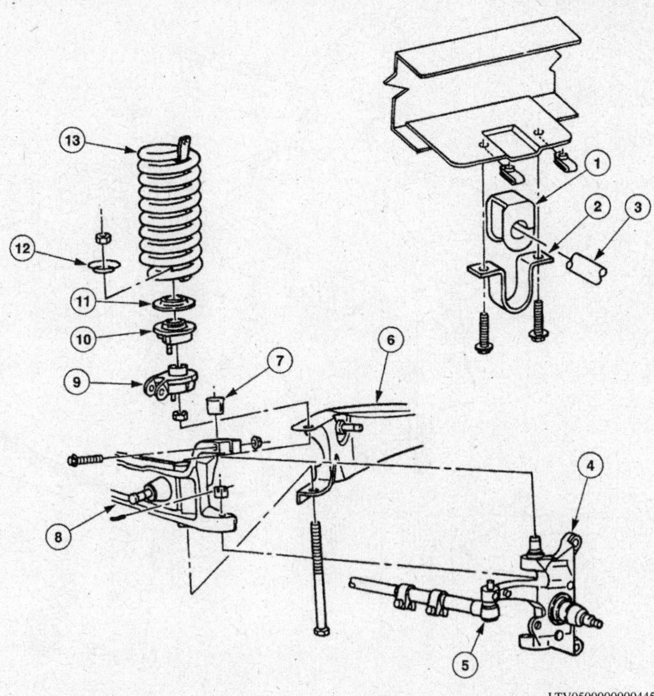

Fig. 3 Exploded view of front suspension (Part 2 of 3). Excursion w/2WD

Expedition, F-150, Mark LT & Navigator

The ball joint and control arm serviced as an assembly, refer to "Control Arm, Replace" for procedure.

COIL SPRING

REPLACE

E-Series, Excursion, F-Super Duty & Motorhome Chassis

The axle must be supported when replacing spring and not be permitted to hang by brake hose. If length of brake hose is not sufficient to permit spring replacement, it will be required to remove the disc brake caliper. Do not suspend caliper by brake hose, if removed.

1. Raise front and support vehicle, then remove wheels.
2. Support axle with a suitable jack.
3. Place matchmarks on all spring components for reference during assembly, **Fig. 18.**
4. Disconnect shock absorber(s) from lower mounting.
5. Remove spring upper retainer attaching bolts and the retainer, if equipped.
6. Remove spring lower retainer attaching nut and the retainer, as equipped.
7. Lower axle slowly and remove spring from vehicle.
8. Reverse procedure to install. Tighten to specification.

Expedition, F-150, Mark LT & Navigator

Refer to "Shock Absorber, Replace" for coil spring replacement procedures.

SHOCK ABSORBER

REPLACE

E-Series, Excursion, F-Super Duty & Motorhome Chassis

1. Raise and support vehicle, then remove wheels.
2. Disconnect shock absorber(s) from upper mounting, **Figs. 19 and 20.**
3. Disconnect shock absorber(s) from lower mounting, then compress shock(s) and remove from vehicle.
4. Reverse procedure to install.

F-150 & Mark LT

1. Raise and support vehicle, then remove wheels.
2. Remove and discard four upper shock absorber mount nuts, **Fig. 21.**
3. Remove and discard tie rod end nut, then separate tie-rod end from wheel spindle, using suitable tie rod puller.
4. Remove lower shock absorber/spring assembly mounting bolt, then the assembly.
5. Install shock absorber/spring assembly in suitable holding fixture.
6. Compress spring until tension is released from shock absorber.

Item	Description
1	Front stabilizer bar insulator
2	Front stabilizer bar retainer
3	Front stabilizer bar
4	Front spindle assembly
5	Tie-rod end
6	Radius arm (LH/RH)
7	Upper ball joint adjuster
8	Front axle I-beam (LH/RH)
9	Lower spring seat (with stabilizer bar)
10	Lower spring seat (without stabilizer bar)
11	Lower spring insulator
12	Lower spring retainer
13	Coil spring

LTV0500000000446

Fig. 3 Exploded view of front suspension (Part 3 of 3). Excursion w/2WD

7. While holding shock absorber rod, remove nut, upper mount, isolator and dust tube.
8. Carefully release spring compressor and remove coil spring from shock absorber.
9. Reverse procedure to install.

Expedition & Navigator

1. Raise and support vehicle, then remove wheels.
2. Remove and discard upper shock absorber/spring assembly mounting nuts, **Fig. 22.**
3. Remove and discard tie rod end nut, then separate tie-rod end from wheel spindle, using suitable tie rod puller.
4. Remove lower shock absorber/spring assembly mounting bolt, then the assembly.
5. Install shock absorber/spring assembly in suitable holding fixture.
6. Install shock absorber/spring assembly in suitable holding fixture.
7. Compress spring until tension is released from shock absorber.
8. While using hex feature to hold shock absorber rod, remove nut, upper mount, isolator and dust tube.
9. Carefully release spring compressor and remove coil spring from shock absorber.
10. Reverse procedure to install.

LEAF SPRING

REPLACE

1. Raise vehicle until weight is relieved from front spring with the front wheels still contacting floor. Support axle to prevent rotation.
2. Disconnect shock absorber lower end(s) from mounting(s).
3. **On models equipped with Dana 60 Monobeam axle,** remove tracking bar to righthand spring cap and tracking bar mounting bracket attaching bolts, as required.
4. **On all models,** remove front shackle to spring nut and bolt.

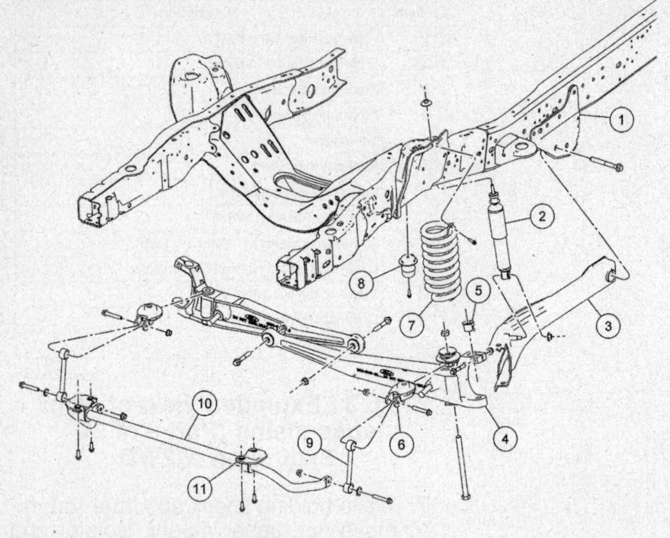

Item	Description
1	Radius arm bracket (LH/RH)
2	Shock absorber
3	Radius arm (LH/RH)
4	Front axle I-beam (LH/RH)
5	Upper ball joint adjuster
6	Lower spring seat (LH/RH)

Item	Description
7	Coil spring
8	Front axle jounce bumper
9	Front stabilizer bar link
10	Front stabilizer bar
11	Front suspension bar retainer

LTV0500000000447

Fig. 4 Exploded view of front suspension. F-250 & F-350

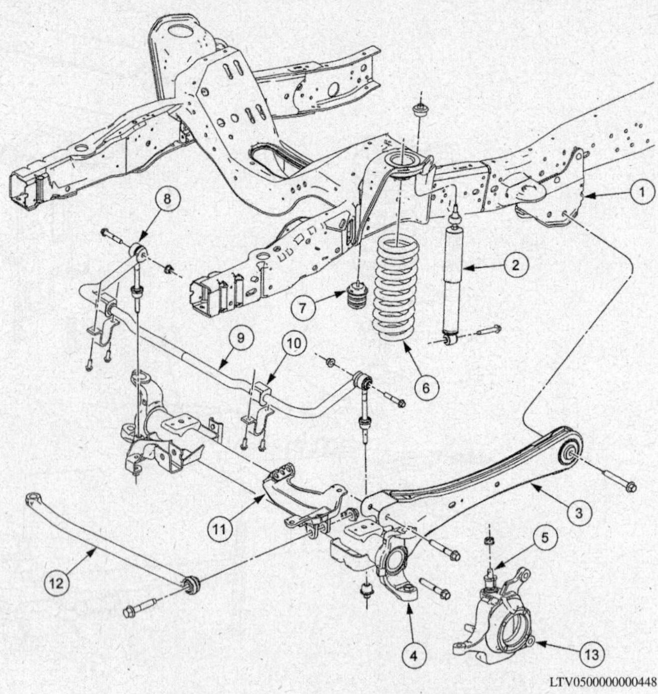

Fig. 5 Exploded view of front suspension (Part 1 of 2). F-450 & F-550

5. Remove rear hanger to spring nut and bolt.
6. Remove U-bolt nuts and jack bracket, then the U-bolts.
7. Remove spring from vehicle.
8. Reverse procedure to install. Tighten to specification.

CONTROL ARM

REPLACE

2WD Models

LOWER

1. Remove coil spring as outlined under "Coil Spring, Replace."
2. Remove control arm to frame mounting bolts, then the control arm.
3. Reverse procedure to install, noting the following:
   a. Install but do not final tighten control arm mounting bolts until vehicle weight is resting on suspension at curb height. This allows bushings to center in frame.
   b. Ensure coil spring is properly centered in control arm as outlined under "Coil Spring, Replace."
   c. Tighten to specification.

UPPER

1. Remove spindle as outlined under "Steering Knuckle, Replace."
2. Place match marks on upper control arm alignment cams and frame for later assembly reference.
3. Remove control arm to frame mounting bolts, then the control arm.
4. Reverse procedure to install, noting the following:
   a. Install but do not final tighten control arm mounting bolts until arm is connected to spindle, this allows bushings to center in frame.
   b. Align match marks for alignment cams.
   c. Tighten to specifications.

4WD Models

LOWER

1. Raise and support vehicle, then remove wheels.
2. Place assembly match marks on torsion bar adjustment components.
3. Remove torsion bar adjusters using torsion bar unloader/remover, tool No. T95T-5310-A with adapters, tool No. T96T-5310-A, or equivalents. Tighten tool to relieve pressure on torsion bar adjustment nut and bolt, then remove nut and bolt.
4. Back off torsion bar tool to relieve tension on torsion bar, then remove tool.
5. Remove torsion bar adjuster arm from torsion bar.
6. Reposition ABS wiring for clearance.
7. Disconnect stabilizer bar link from control arm, then the lower shock absorber mount.
8. Remove lower ball joint cotter pin and nut. Discard cotter pin.
9. Separate lower ball joint from steering knuckle using pitman arm puller, tool No. T64P-3590-F, or equivalent.
10. Remove lower control arm to frame mounting bolts, then the control arm with torsion bar.
11. Reverse procedure to install, noting the following:
    a. Install but do not final tighten control arm mounting bolts until vehicle weight is resting on suspension at curb height. This allows bushings to center in frame.

UPPER

1. Remove spindle as outlined under "Steering Knuckle, Replace."
2. Place match marks on upper control arm alignment cams and frame for later assembly reference.
3. Remove control arm to frame mounting bolts, then the control arm.
4. Reverse procedure to install, noting the following:
   a. Install but do not final tighten control arm mounting bolts until arm is connected to spindle, this allows bushings to center in frame.
   b. Align match marks for alignment cams.
   c. Tighten to specifications.

STEERING KNUCKLE

REPLACE

2WD Models

E-SERIES

1. Raise and support front of vehicle and remove front wheels.
2. Remove brake rotor and hub as outlined under "Disc Brakes" chapter.

Item	Description
1	Radius arm bracket (LH/RH)
2	Shock absorber
3	Radius arm (LH/RH)
4	Front axle
5	Upper ball joint adjuster
6	Front spring
7	Front axle jounce bumper
8	Stabilizer bar link
9	Stabilizer bar
10	Front stabilizer bar retainer
11	Track bar mounting bracket
12	Track bar
13	Wheel knuckle (LH/RH)

LTV0500000000449

Fig. 5 Exploded view of front suspension (Part 2 of 2). F-450 & F-550

3. Disconnect ABS sensors from knuckle, as equipped.
4. Position caliper aside, leaving brake lines attached. **Do not allow weight of caliper to hang on brake lines.**
5. Remove the brake dust shield, then the tie rod end cotter pin and nut. Discard cotter pin.
6. Remove tie rod end from spindle arm using pitman arm puller, tool No. T64P-3590-F, or equivalent.
7. Remove cotter pin, then the lower ball joint nut.
8. Place match marks on camber adjuster and suspension arm for later assembly alignment.
9. Remove the upper ball joint and camber adjuster pinch bolt, then lift out camber adjuster.
10. Separate ball joint and spindle from suspension arm. **Do not use "Pickle Fork" type ball joint separation tools.**
11. Remove steering knuckle from vehicle.
12. Reverse procedure to install.

EXPEDITION, F-150, MARK LT & NAVIGATOR

1. Raise and support vehicle, then remove wheel.
2. Place a suitable jack stand below lower control arm, then raise jack stand to relieve pressure from ball joints.
3. Remove brake rotor as outlined under "Disc Brakes" chapter, then remove disc brake shield.
4. Remove tie rod end cotter pin and nut, then separate tie rod from knuckle arm using pitman arm puller tool No. T64P-3590-F, or equivalent.
5. Disconnect ABS sensors from knuckle, as equipped.
6. Remove upper and lower ball joints cotter pins and nuts, then separate ball joints from knuckle using pitman arm puller tool No. T64P-3590-F, or equivalent.
7. Reverse procedure to install. Use new cotter pins.

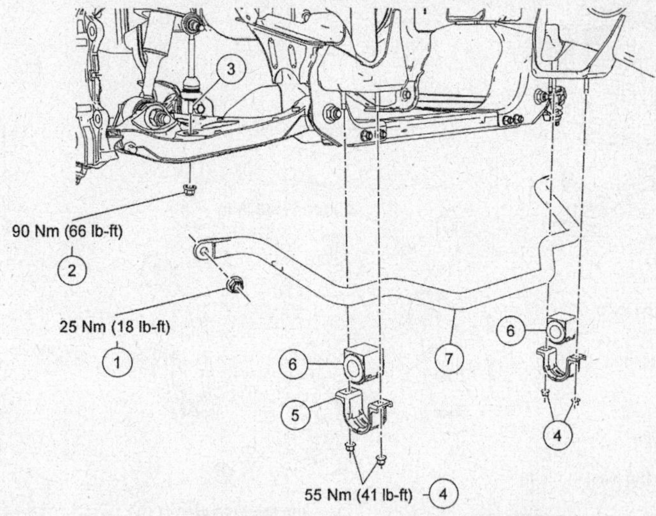

Fig. 6 Exploded view of front suspension (Part 1 of 4). F-150 & Mark LT w/2WD

EXCURSION, F-SUPER DUTY & MOTORHOME CHASSIS

REMOVAL

1. Remove hub and brake as outlined under "Wheel Bearing, Replace," then remove the disc rotor shield.
2. **On Motorhome Chassis models,** remove drag link joint cotter pin and nut, then separate drag link from knuckle using tie rod end remover, **Fig. 23,** tool No. 3290-D, or equivalent.
3. **On Excursion & F-Super Duty models equipped with 2WD,** remove steering link tie rod end cotter pin and nut, **Fig. 24,** then separate steering link from knuckle using tie rod end remover, tool No. 3290-D, or equivalent.
4. **On all models,** remove the kingpin (spindle pin) lockpin nut, then the lockpin.
5. Remove king pin grease plug caps, then using a suitable drift punch, drive king pin from knuckle.
6. Remove knuckle from axle. **Note assembly position of all seals, shims and bearings.**

INSTALLATION

Lubricate all components with a suitable long life grease prior to installation

1. Ensure mounting hole in axle and king pin bushings in knuckle are in good condition.
2. Install new king pin seal with metal backing facing up towards bushing in knuckle. **Do not distort seal case during installation.**
3. **On Motorhome Chassis models,** install new thrust bearing.
4. **On all models,** position knuckle on axle, then press knuckle upward tightly against axle and measure clearance between axle and knuckle at top of axle.
5. Select correct shim and install.
6. Position king pin with end marked with a T upward into knuckle, aligning lock pin cutout to hole in axle.
7. Tap king pin into place, align lock pin hole with cut out on pin.
8. Insert lock pin from rear to front, with flat towards king pin, then firmly drive in pin and install lock washer and nut. Tighten to specification.
9. Install upper and lower grease plug caps, then lubricate with a suitable long life grease until grease is seen at upper and lower junction of knuckle to axle.

4WD Models

EXPEDITION, F-150, MARK LT & NAVIGATOR

1. Raise and support vehicle, then remove wheel.
2. Place a suitable jack stand below lower control arm, then raise jack stand to relieve pressure from ball joints.
3. Remove brake rotor as outlined under "Disc Brakes" chapter, then remove disc brake shield.
4. Remove tie rod end cotter pin and nut, then separate tie rod from knuckle arm using pitman arm puller tool No. T64P-3590-F, or equivalent.
5. Disconnect ABS sensors from knuckle, as equipped.
6. Remove upper and lower ball joints cotter pins and nuts, then separate ball joints from knuckle using pitman arm puller tool No. T64P-3590-F, or equivalent.
7. Reverse procedure to install. Use new cotter pins.

EXCURSION & F-SUPER DUTY

1. Remove hub as outlined under "Hub & Bearing, Replace."
2. Remove spindle retaining nuts, then tap spindle loose from hub. Remove

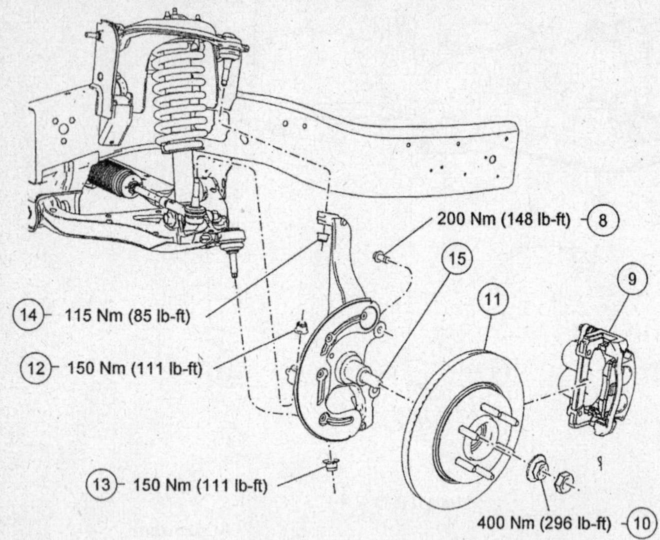

Item	Description
8	Brake caliper anchor plate bolt (2 required)
9	Brake caliper anchor plate assembly
10	Wheel hub nut (retainer/cotter pin)

Item	Description
11	Brake disc
12	Tie-rod end nut
13	Lower ball joint nut
14	Upper ball joint nut
15	Wheel spindle

LTV0500000000439

Fig. 6 Exploded view of front suspension (Part 2 of 4). F-150 & Mark LT w/2WD

23 150 Nm (111 lb-ft)
24
25
21
300 Nm (222 lb-ft) 19
300 Nm (222 lb-ft) 18
20
475 Nm (351 lb-ft) 16
17
22

Item	Description
16	Shock absorber lower nut
17	Shock absorber lower bolt
18	Lower arm-to-frame nut
19	Lower arm-to-frame nut
20	Lower arm-to-frame bolt
21	Lower arm-to-frame bolt
22	Lower arm

Item	Description
23	Upper arm-to-frame nut (2 required)
24	Upper arm-to-frame bolt (2 required)
25	Upper arm

LTV0500000000440

Fig. 6 Exploded view of front suspension (Part 3 of 4). F-150 & Mark LT w/2WD

disc brake shield as equipped.

3. Pull axle shaft from housing through knuckle. **Use caution not to damage seals in axle housing.**
4. Place match marks on axle housing and camber adjustment eccentric for later assembly reference.
5. Remove tie rod end cotter pin and nut, **Fig. 25,** then separate tie rod from knuckle steering arm using pitman arm puller, tool No. T64P-3490-F, or equivalent.
6. Remove upper ball joint nut and loosen lower ball joint nut. Strike upper ball joint stud with a heavy soft face mallet to loosen ball joints.
7. Remove lower ball joint nut and remove knuckle from yoke tube.
8. Remove camber adjuster bushing from tube and yoke assembly.
9. Reverse procedure to install.

STABILIZER BAR

REPLACE

1. Disconnect both ends of stabilizer bar from link assembly on frame bracket, **Fig. 26.**
2. Remove stabilizer bar attaching bolts and the stabilizer bar.
3. Reverse procedure to install.

RADIUS ARM

REPLACE

2WD Models

1. Remove coil spring as outlined under "Coil Spring, Replace."
2. Remove spring lower seat from radius arm, **Figs. 27 and 28.**
3. Remove radius arm and stabilizer bracket (if equipped) attaching nut and bolt from axle.
4. **On models except E-Series,** remove nut, rear washer, insulator and spacer from rear side of radius arm rear bracket.
5. **On all models,** remove radius arm from vehicle.
6. **On E-Series,** remove spacer, inner insulator and retainer from radius arm stud.
7. **On all models,** reverse procedure to install.

4WD Models

1. Raise and support vehicle under frame side rails.
2. Remove shock absorber to lower bracket attaching bolt and nut and separate shock from radius arm, **Figs. 27 and 28.**
3. Remove spring lower retainer attaching bolt(s) from inside coil spring.
4. Loosen axle pivot bolt.
5. Remove radius arm to frame bracket attaching nut, then the radius arm rear insulator and spacer (if equipped).
6. Lower axle and slide it forward. **The axle must be supported and not be permitted to hang by brake hose. If length of brake hose is not sufficient to provide adequate clearance, it will be required to remove the disc brake caliper. Do not suspend caliper by brake hose, if removed.**
7. Remove axle to radius arm bracket attaching screws, then the radius arm to axle attaching bolt and stud.
8. Move axle forward and remove radius arm from axle, then pull radius arm from frame bracket.
9. Reverse procedure to install.

POWER STEERING GEAR

REPLACE

E-Series

1. Place front wheels in straight ahead position and ignition switch in OFF position.
2. Remove power steering fluid from reservoir using suitable suction tool.
3. Remove bolt and disconnect intermediate shaft from steering gear, **Fig. 29.**
4. Disconnect power steering line fittings from steering gear.
5. Raise and support vehicle.
6. Remove and discard drag link cotter pin and nut.
7. Separate drag link from idler arm using suitable puller.
8. Remove power steering gear mounting bolts, then the gear.
9. Secure steering gear in suitable vise, then remove pitman arm to gear nut and lockwasher.
10. Remove pitman arm from steering gear sector shaft using pitman arm removal tool No. T74P-3044–A1, or equivalent.
11. Reverse procedure to install. Install new O-ring seals on power steering line fittings.

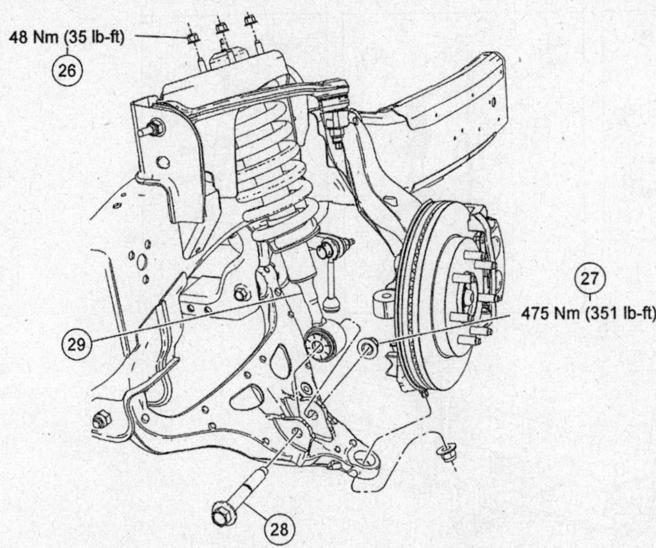

Item	Description
26	Shock absorber upper mount nuts (4 required)
27	Shock absorber lower nut
28	Shock absorber lower bolt
29	Shock absorber and spring assembly

LTV0500000000441

Fig. 6 Exploded view of front suspension (Part 4 of 4). F-150 & Mark LT w/2WD

LTV0500000000450

Fig. 7 Exploded view of front suspension (Part 1 of 4). Motorhome Chassis

Expedition, F-150, Mark LT & Navigator

1. Place front wheels in straight ahead position and ignition switch in OFF position.
2. Remove power steering fluid from reservoir using suitable suction tool.
3. Remove bolt and disconnect intermediate shaft from steering gear, **Fig. 30.**
4. Disconnect power steering line fittings from steering gear.
5. Raise and support vehicle.
6. Remove and discard drag link cotter pin and nut.
7. Separate drag link from idler arm using suitable puller.
8. Remove power steering gear mounting bolts, then the gear.
9. Secure steering gear in suitable vise, then remove pitman arm to gear nut and lockwasher.
10. Remove pitman arm from steering gear sector shaft using pitman arm renoval tool No. T74P-3044–A1, or equivalent.
11. Reverse procedure to install. Install new O-ring seals on power steering line fittings.

Excursion, F-Super Duty & Motorhome Chassis

New Teflon seals must be installed any time the power steering line fittings are disconnected.

1. Place front wheels in straight ahead position and ignition switch in OFF position.
2. Remove engine air cleaner.
3. Remove power steering fluid from reservoir using suitable suction tool.
4. Disconnect steering gear coupling shield from line fittings and slide shield upward on intermediate shaft.
5. Remove intermediate shaft to steering gear retaining bolt.
6. Disconnect power steering lines at gear assembly, **Fig. 31,** then discard Teflon seals.
7. Remove cotter pin retainer cap and drag link to sector shaft nut.
8. Disconnect drag link from sector shaft arm using suitable pitman arm removal tool.
9. Remove steering gear mounting bolts, then the steering gear.
10. Reverse procedure to install. Install Teflon seals on power steering line fittings using seal installation set tool No. D90P-3517–A, or equivalent.

POWER STEERING PUMP

REPLACE

E-Series, Expedition, F-150, Mark LT & Navigator

New Teflon seals must be installed any time the power steering line fittings are disconnected.

1. Remove air filter as required for removal clearance.
2. Remove as much fluid as possible from power steering pump remote reservoir.
3. Remove drive belt as outlined under the respective engine section in this chapter.
4. Place a suitable drain pan to catch remaining fluid, then remove reservoir line from power steering pump, **Fig. 32.**
5. **On Expedition, F-150, Mark LT and Navigator,** remove pressure line from steering gear.
6. **On all models,** remove upper pump mounting bolts.
7. Remove lower mounting bolt, then the steering pump.
8. Place pump in a suitable holding fixture, then using power steering pump pulley puller, tool No. T69L-10300-B, or equivalent, remove pull.

Item	Description
1	Front axle assembly
2	Drag link
3	Steering spindle drag link arm
4	Steering spindle arm (2 required)
5	Tie rod end (2 required)
6	Front wheel spindle stop (2 required)
7	Front wheel spindle (2 required)
8	Spindle pin cap (4 required)
9	Spindle pin seal (2 required)
10	Spindle bearing assembly (2 required)
11	Spindle pin locking bolt
12	Spindle shim
13	Spindle pin seal (2 required)
14	Spindle pin locking bolt
15	Spindle pin

LTV0500000000451

Fig. 7 Exploded view of front suspension (Part 2 of 4). Motorhome Chassis

9. **On F-150 and Mark LT models,** if required remove pressure hose from pump.
10. **On all models,** reverse procedure to install, noting the following.
    a. Install Teflon seals on power steering line fittings using seal installation set tool No. D90P-3517–A, or equivalent.
    b. Bleed system as outlined under "Power Steering."
    c. Place pulley into position on pump shaft, thread pulley installer, tool No. T91P-3A733-A, or equivalent, into pump shaft, then while holding shaft of tool tighten nut until tool bottoms on pump shaft.

Excursion & F-Super Duty

5.4L, 6.0L & 6.8L ENGINES

New Teflon seals must be installed any time the power steering line fittings are disconnected.

1. Remove as much fluid as possible from power steering pump remote reservoir.
2. Remove drive belt as outlined under the respective engine section in this chapter.
3. **On models equipped with 6.0L engine,** remove engine cooling fan as outlined in the "Electrical" section.
4. **On all models,** remove steering pump pulley using pullet removal tool No. T69L-3A733–A, or equivalent, **Fig. 33.**
5. Inspect pulley for paint marks in web area near hub. If there are 2 paint marks, discard pulley. If there is no paint or 1 paint mark, use a paint pencil to mark web area of pulley near hub.
6. Release clamp and disconnect fluid supply hose, **Fig. 34.**

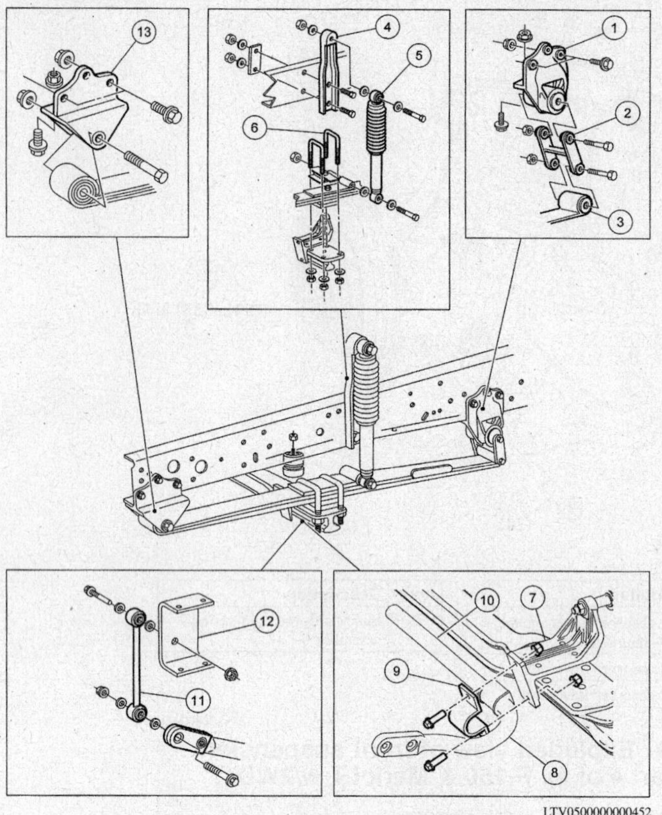

LTV0500000000452

Fig. 7 Exploded view of front suspension (Part 3 of 4). Motorhome Chassis

7. Disconnect pressure line to pump fitting. Discard Teflon seal.
8. Remove power steering pump mounting bolts, then the pump.
9. Reverse procedure to install. Install Teflon seals on power steering line fittings using seal installation set tool No. D90P-3517–A, or equivalent.

7.3L ENGINE

1. Remove drive belt, then air inlet tube.
2. Remove return hose, then place an pan under power steering pump and drain pump.
3. Remove pump pulley, then disconnect power steering high pressure line.
4. Remove pump bolts and pump.
5. Disconnect power steering oil cooler return hose.
6. Reverse procedure to install, noting the following:
    a. Use seal replacer set tool No. D90P-3517-A, or equivalent, to install a seal ring over a fitting.
    b. Fill and leak inspect system.

Motorhome Chassis

1. Remove as much fluid as possible from power steering pump or remote reservoir, as equipped.
2. Remove drive belt as outlined under the respective engine section in this chapter.
3. Place a suitable drain pan to catch remaining fluid, then remove fluid lines from power steering pump. **On some models it will be required to tag input and outlet to aid in installation.**
4. Remove pump mounting bracket to engine attaching bolts, then pump with bracket from engine.
5. Place pump into a suitable holding fixture, then using power steering pump pulley puller, tool No. T69L-10300-B, or equivalent, remove pulley.
6. Remove pump to bracket mounting bolts, then the pump from the bracket.
7. Remove pump pulley using steering pump pulley puller, tool No. T69L-10300-B, or equivalent. **On some models it may be required to remove radiator shroud for tool clearance.**
8. Reverse procedure to install. Place pulley into position on pump shaft, thread pulley installer, tool No. T91P-3A733-A, or equivalent, into pump shaft, then while holding shaft of tool tighten nut until tool bottoms on pump shaft.

Item	Description
1	Front spring shackle bracket
2	Front spring shackle
3	Front spring assembly
4	Front shock absorber bracket
5	Shock absorber
6	Front spring U-bolt
7	Stabilizer bar mounting bracket
8	Front stabilizer bar
9	Front stabilizer bar-to-axle clamp
10	Stabilizer bar insulator
11	Stabilizer bar link
12	Stabilizer bar link bracket
13	Front spring hanger bracket

LTV0500000000453

Fig. 7 Exploded view of front suspension (Part 4 of 4). Motorhome Chassis

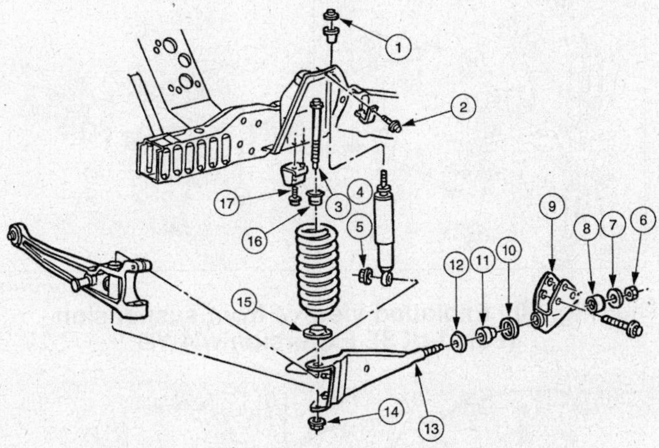

Item	Description
1	Shock absorber upper nut
2	Front spring upper retainer screw
3	Radius arm-to-front axle bolt, E150
4	Radius arm-to-front axle bolt, E250, E350, E-Super Duty
5	Shock absorber lower nut
6	Radius arm-to-rear bracket nut
7	Radius arm rear insulator washer

Item	Description
8	Radius arm rear insulator
9	Radius arm rear bracket
10	Radius arm spacer
11	Radius arm front insulator
12	Radius arm front insulator washer
13	Radius arm
14	Radius arm-to-front axle nut
15	Front spring insulator
16	Front spring lower retainer
17	Jounce bumper screw

LTV0500000000455

Fig. 8 Exploded view of front suspension (Part 2 of 2). E-Series w/4WD

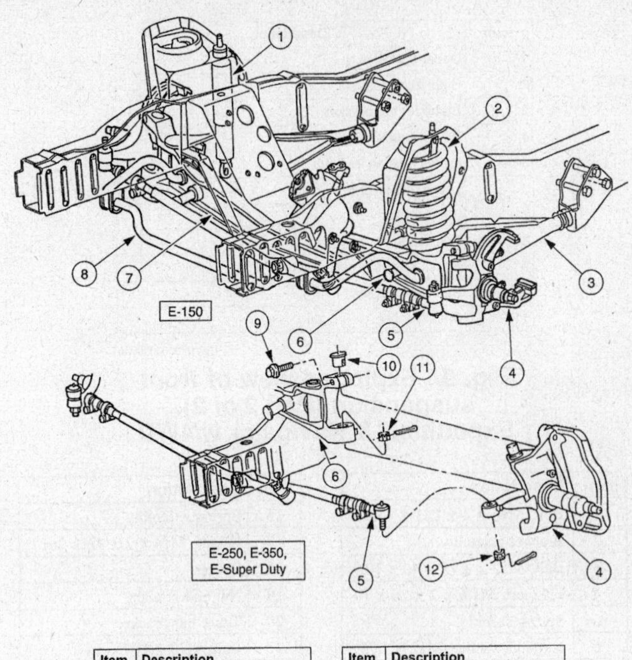

Item	Description
1	Shock absorber
2	Front coil spring
3	Radius arm
4	Front wheel spindle
5	Tie-rod end
6	Front axle (LH)

Item	Description
7	Front axle (RH)
8	Front stabilizer bar
9	Upper ball joint pinch bolt
10	Caster/camber insert
11	Lower ball joint nut
12	Tie-rod end-to-spindle nut

LTV0500000000454

Fig. 8 Exploded view of front suspension (Part 1 of 2). E-Series w/4WD

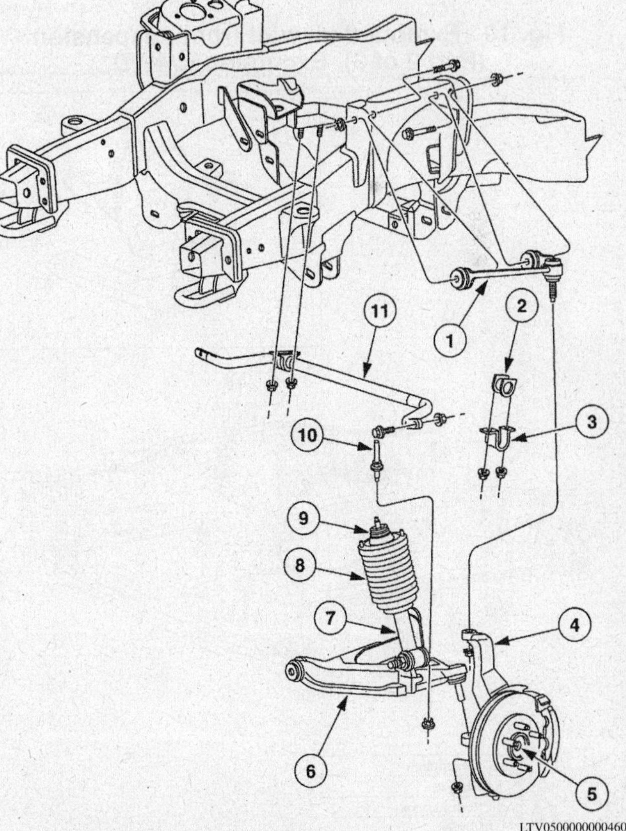

LTV0500000000460

Fig. 9 Exploded view of front suspension (Part 1 of 2). Expedition & Navigator w/4WD

Item	Description
1	Upper arm RH/LH
2	Stabilizer bar bushing
3	Stabilizer bar bracket
4	Wheel knuckle RH/LH
5	Wheel bearing and hub
6	Lower arm RH/LH
7	Shock absorber
8	Coil spring
9	Shock absorber upper mount
10	Stabilizer bar link
11	Stabilizer bar

LTV0500000000461

Fig. 9 Exploded view of front suspension (Part 2 of 2). Expedition & Navigator w/4WD

Item	Description	Item	Description
1	Bolt, M16 x 2 x 143 x 10.9	16	Spring assembly
2	Bracket assembly	17	U-bolt, M14 x 2 x 92 x 201
3	Bolt, M12 x 1.75 x 40 x 10.9	18	Spacer
4	Flag nut, M1.6 x 2 x 20 x 10	19	Nut and retainer
5	Spring shackle	20	Track bar bracket
6	Nut and washer, M12 x 1.75	21	Bolt, M20 x 100
7	Shock assembly	22	Track bar
8	Upper shock bracket	23	Spring cap
9	Nut and retainer	24	Bolt
10	Bolt, M12 x 1.75 x 80 x 10.9	25	Stabilizer bar retainer bracket
11	Nut, M12 x 1.75 x 13 x 10	26	Drive axle, Dana Model 50
12	Tow hook	27	Drive axle, Dana Model 60
13	Nut	28	Nut M14 x 2 x 15 x 10
14	Spring hanger	29	Stabilizer bar insulator
15	Bolt, M18 x 2.5 x 136 x 10.9	30	J-clip

LTV0500000000463

Fig. 10 Exploded view of front suspension (Part 2 of 3). Excursion w/4WD

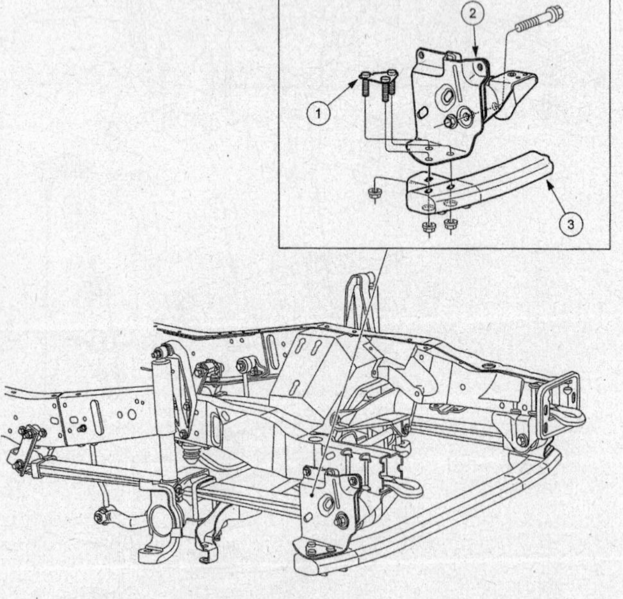

Item	Description
1	Bolt plate
2	Spring bracket
3	Blocker

LTV0500000000464

Fig. 10 Exploded view of front suspension (Part 3 of 3). Excursion w/4WD

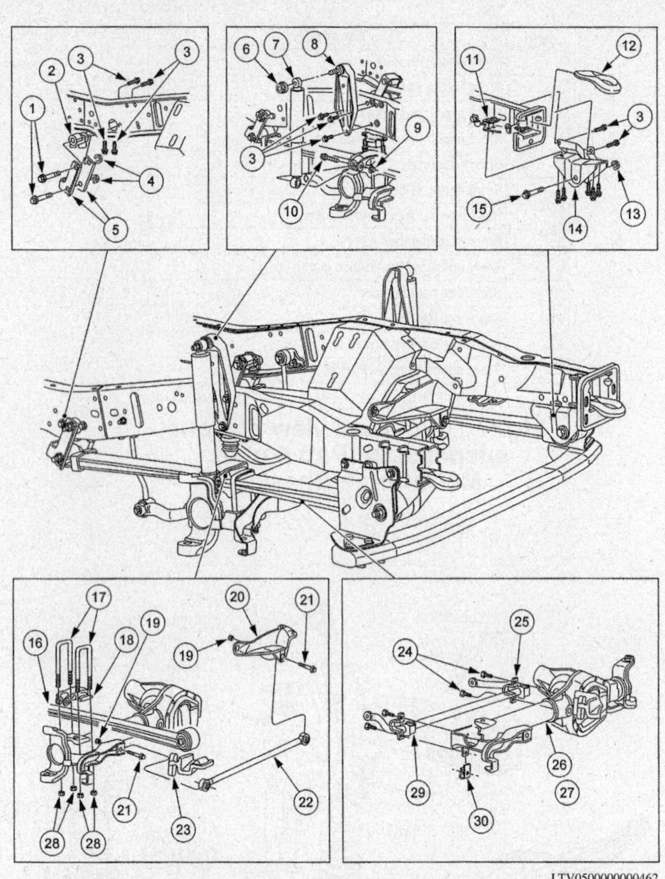

LTV0500000000462

Fig. 10 Exploded view of front suspension (Part 1 of 3). Excursion w/4WD

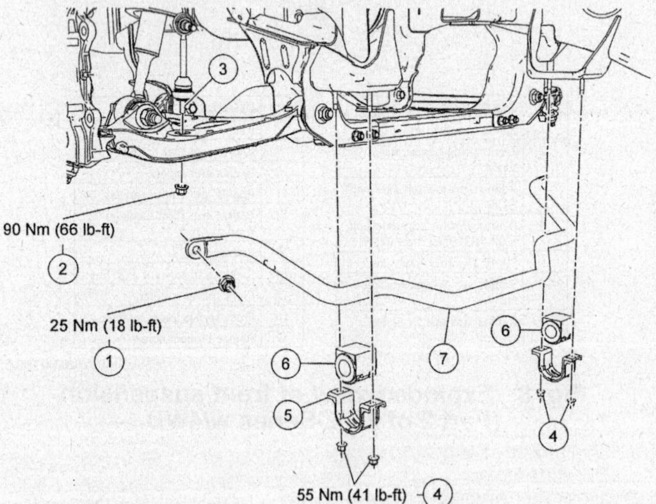

Item	Description	Item	Description
1	Stabilizer bar link upper nut (2 required)	5	Stabilizer bar bracket (2 required)
2	Stabilizer bar link lower nut (2 required)	6	Stabilizer bar bushings (2 required)
3	Stabilizer bar link (2 required)	7	Stabilizer bar
4	Stabilizer bar bracket nuts (4 required)		

LTV0500000000456

Fig. 11 Exploded view of front suspension (Part 1 of 4). F-150 & Mark LT w/4WD

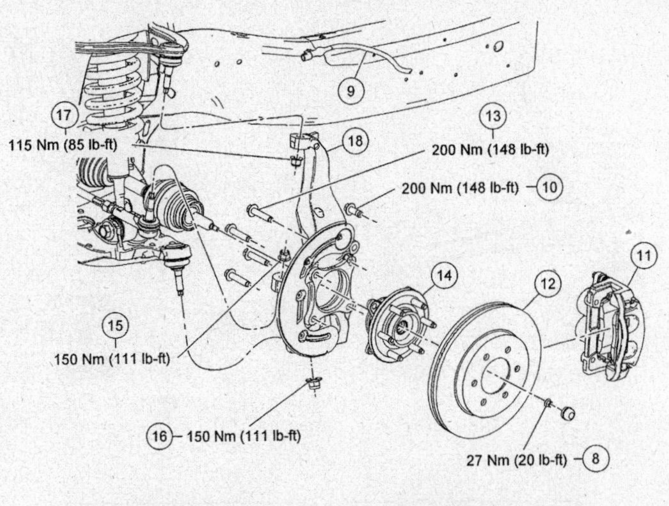

Item	Description
8	Halfshaft nut
9	Wheel speed sensor harness connector
10	Brake caliper anchor plate bolt (2 required)
11	Brake caliper, pads and anchor plate
12	Brake disc

Item	Description
13	Wheel hub bolt (4 required)
14	Wheel bearing and hub assembly
15	Tie-rod end nut
16	Lower ball joint nut
17	Upper ball joint nut
18	Wheel knuckle

LTV0500000000457

Fig. 11 Exploded view of front suspension (Part 2 of 4). F-150 & Mark LT w/4WD

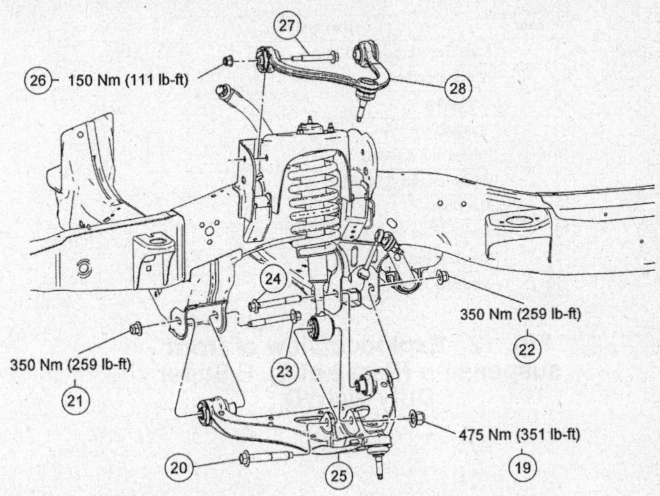

Item	Description
19	Shock absorber lower nut
20	Shock absorber lower bolt
21	Lower arm-to-frame nut
22	Lower arm-to-frame nut
23	Lower arm-to-frame bolt
24	Lower arm-to-frame bolt
25	Lower arm

Item	Description
26	Upper arm-to-frame nut (2 required)
27	Upper arm-to-frame bolt (2 required)
28	Upper arm

LTV0500000000458

Fig. 11 Exploded view of front suspension (Part 3 of 4). F-150 & Mark LT w/4WD

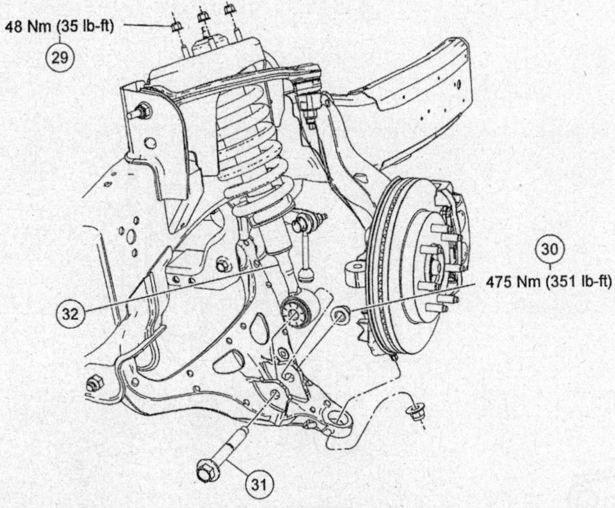

Item	Description
29	Shock absorber upper mount nut (3 required)
30	Shock absorber lower nut
31	Shock absorber lower bolt

Item	Description
32	Shock absorber and spring assembly

LTV0500000000459

Fig. 11 Exploded view of front suspension (Part 4 of 4). F-150 & Mark LT w/4WD

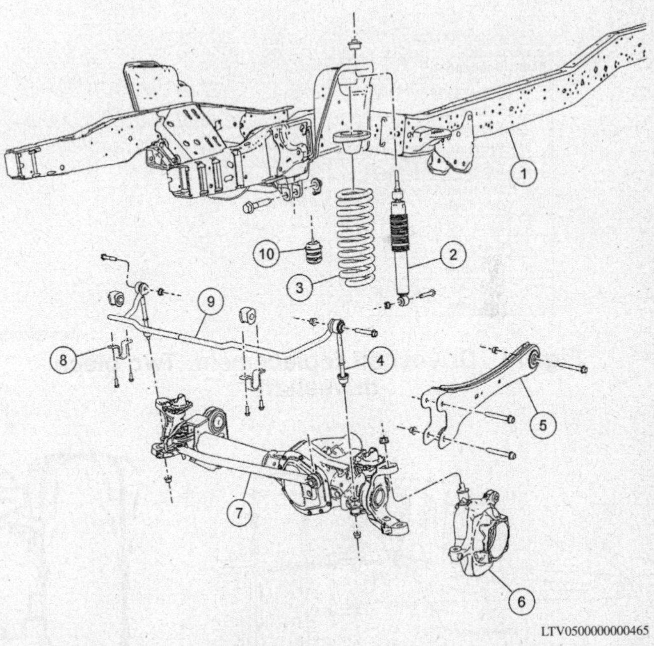

LTV0500000000465

Fig. 12 Exploded view of front suspension (Part 1 of 2). F-Super Duty w/4WD

Item	Description
1	Radius arm bracket (LH/RH)
2	Shock absorber
3	Coil spring
4	Stabilizer bar link
5	Radius arm (LH/RH)
6	Wheel knuckle (LH/RH)
7	Track bar
8	Stabilizer bar retainer
9	Stabilizer bar
10	Jounce bumper

LTV0500000000466

Fig. 12 Exploded view of front suspension (Part 2 of 2). F-Super Duty w/4WD

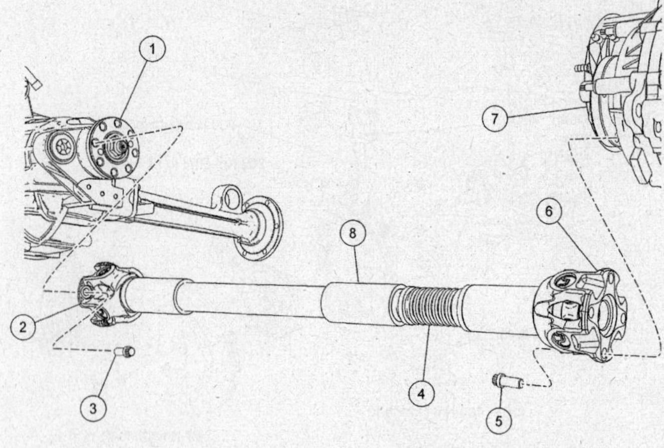

Item	Description
1	Pinion flange
2	Driveshaft flange
3	Driveshaft flange-to-pinion flange bolt
4	Driveshaft slip-yoke boot
5	Driveshaft flange-to-transfer case output flange bolt
6	Driveshaft flange

Item	Description
7	Transfer case output flange
8	Driveshaft

LTV0500000000474

Fig. 13 Drive shaft replacement. One piece driveshaft

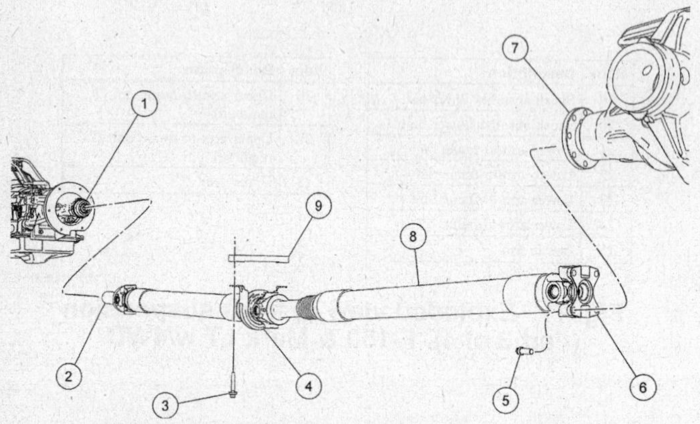

Item	Description
1	Transmission extension housing
2	Driveshaft slip yoke
3	Driveshaft center bearing bolt
4	Driveshaft center bearing
5	Driveshaft flange-to-pinion flange bolt
6	Driveshaft flange
7	Pinion flange
8	Driveshaft
9	Center bearing shim (if equipped)

LTV0500000000475

Fig. 14 Driveshaft replacement. Two piece driveshaft

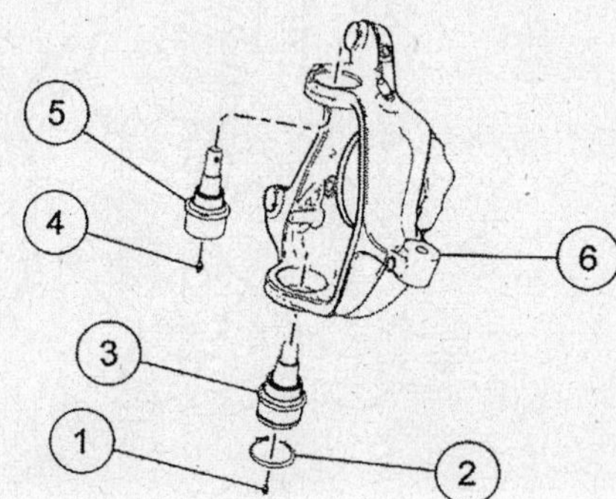

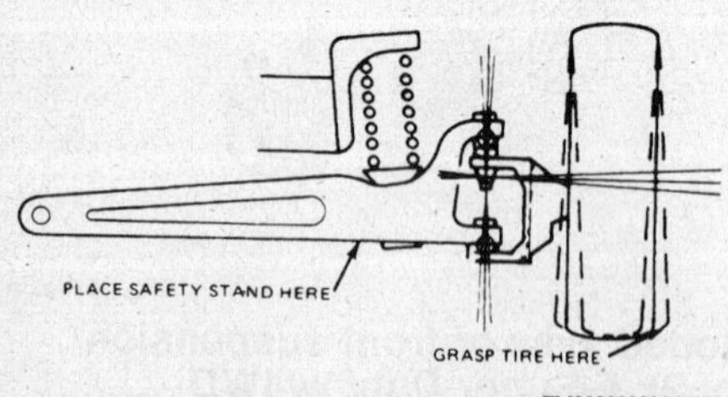

FM2028800005000X

Fig. 15 Ball joint inspection. E-Series, Excursion, F-Super Duty & Motorhome Chassis

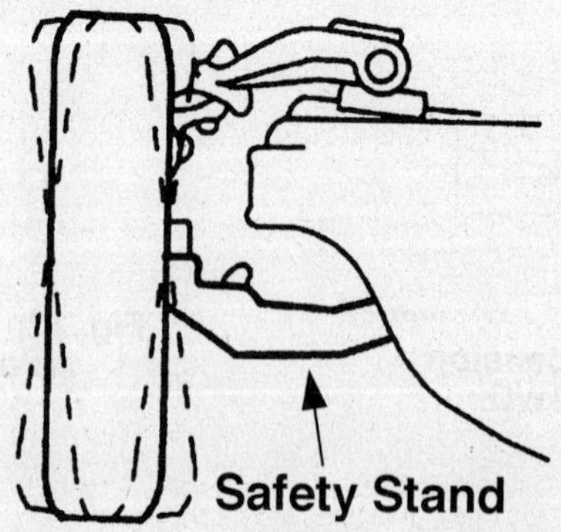

FM2029700127000X

Fig. 16 Ball joint inspection. Expedition, F-150, Mark LT & Navigator

Item	Description
1	Grease fitting
2	Snap ring
3	Lower ball joint
4	Grease fitting
5	Upper ball joint
6	Wheel knuckle

LTV0500000000467

Fig. 17 Lower & upper ball joint replacement. E-Series, Excursion, F-Super Duty & Motorhome Chassis

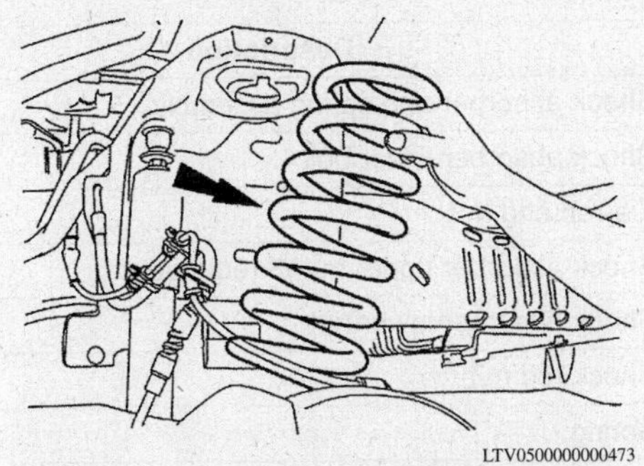

LTV0500000000473

Fig. 18 Front spring replacement. E-Series, Excursion, F-Super Duty & Motorhome Chassis

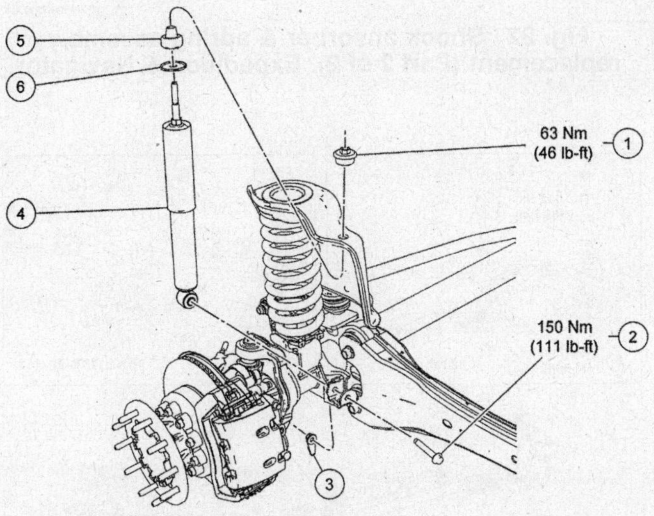

Item	Description
1	Upper nut and bushing (upper half)
2	Lower bolt
3	Lower flag nut
4	Shock absorber
5	Upper bushing (lower half)
6	Washer

LTV0500000000468

Fig. 20 Front shock absorber replacement. F-450 & F–550

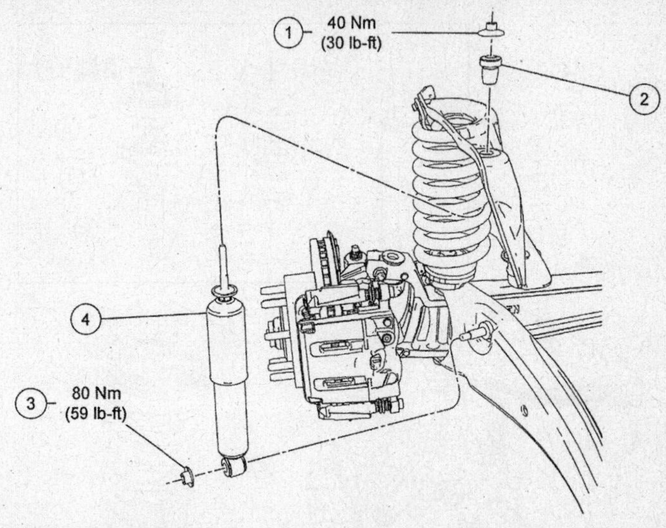

Item	Description	Item	Description
1	Upper nut and washer	3	Lower nut and washer
2	Upper bushing	4	Shock absorber

LTV0500000000469

Fig. 19 Front shock absorber replacement. E-Series, Excursion, F-250, F–350 & Motorhome Chassis

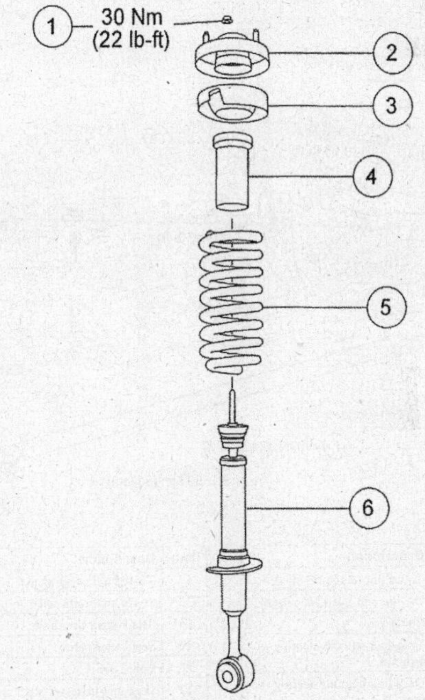

Item	Description
1	Shock absorber rod nut
2	Shock absorber upper mount
3	Isolator
4	Dust tube
5	Coil spring
6	Shock absorber

LTV0500000000470

Fig. 21 Exploded view of front shock absorber & Spring assembly. F-150 & Mark LT

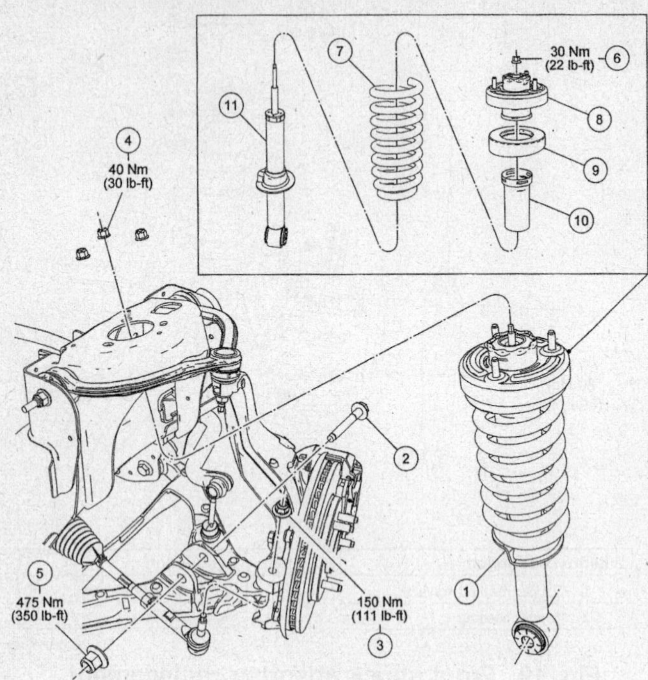

Fig. 22 Shock absorber & spring assembly replacement (Part 1 of 2). Expedition & Navigator

Item	Description
1	Shock absorber and spring assembly
2	Shock absorber lower bolt
3	Tie-rod end nut
4	Shock absorber upper nut (3 required)
5	Shock absorber lower nut
6	Shock rod nut
7	Spring
8	Upper mount
9	Insulator
10	Dust boot
11	Shock absorber

LTV0500000000472

Fig. 22 Shock absorber & spring assembly replacement (Part 2 of 2). Expedition & Navigator

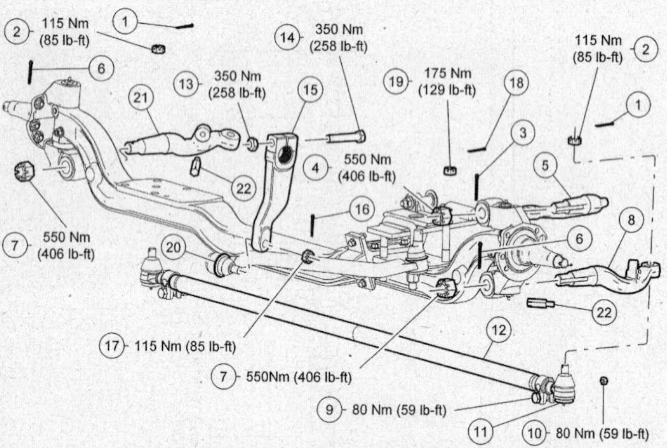

Item	Description
1	Cotter pin (2 required)
2	Tie-rod end nut (2 required)
3	Cotter pin
4	Drag link spindle steering arm nut
5	Drag link spindle steering arm
6	Cotter pin (2 required)
7	Spindle steering arm nut (2 required)
8	Spindle steering arm (LH)
9	Tie-rod adjusting sleeve clamp bolt (2 required)
10	Tie-rod adjusting sleeve clamp nut (2 required)
11	Tie-rod end (2 required)
12	Tie-rod adjusting sleeve
13	Sector shaft arm nut
14	Sector shaft arm bolt
15	Sector shaft arm
16	Cotter pin
17	Drag link-to-sector shaft arm nut
18	Cotter pin
19	Drag link-to-drag link spindle steering arm nut
20	Drag link
21	Spindle steering arm (RH)
22	Steering stop bolt (2 required)

LTV0500000000476

Fig. 23 Exploded view of Steering linkage. Motorhome Chassis

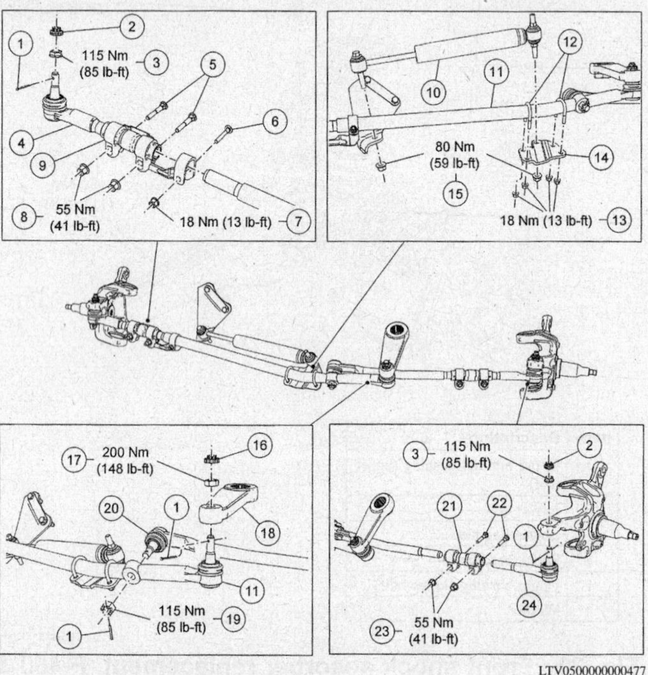

LTV0500000000477

Fig. 24 Exploded view of steering linkage (Part 1 of 2). Excursion & F-Super Duty w/2WD

Item	Description
1	Cotter pins (4 required)
2	Tie-rod end nut retainer caps
3	Outer tie-rod end-to-wheel spindle nuts (2 required)
4	RH outer tie-rod end
5	RH adjusting sleeve clamp bolts (2 required)
6	RH adjusting sleeve bracket bolt (part of 3281)
7	RH adjusting sleeve bracket nuts (part of 3281)
8	RH adjusting sleeve clamp nuts (2 required)
9	RH adjusting sleeve
10	Steering linkage damper
11	Drag link
12	Steering linkage damper U-bolts (2 required)
13	Steering linkage damper U-bolt nuts (4 required)
14	Steering linkage damper bracket
15	Steering linkage damper-to-bracket nuts (2 required)
16	Drag link-to-sector shaft arm nut retainer cap
17	Drag link-to-sector shaft arm nut
18	Sector shaft arm
19	Inner tie-rod end nut
20	Inner tie-rod end
21	LH adjusting sleeve
22	LH adjusting sleeve clamp bolts (2 required)
23	LH adjusting sleeve clamp nuts (2 required)
24	LH outer tie-rod end

LTV0500000000478

Fig. 24 Exploded view of steering linkage (Part 2 of 2). Excursion & F-Super Duty w/2WD

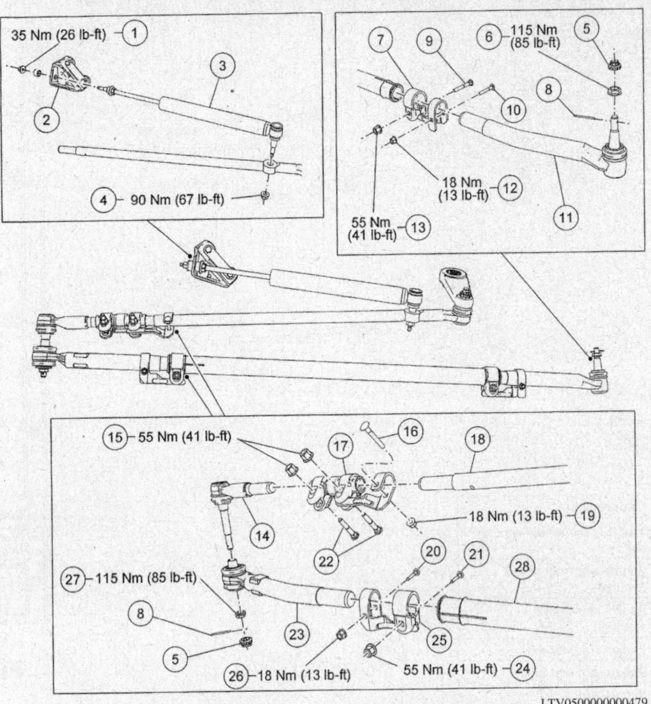

Fig. 25 Exploded view of steering linkage (Part 1 of 2). Excursion & F-Super Duty w/4WD

Item	Description
1	Steering linkage damper-to-bracket nut
2	Steering linkage damper bracket
3	Steering linkage damper
4	Steering linkage damper-to-drag link nut
5	Tie-rod end nut retainer cap
6	LH outer tie-rod end nut
7	LH adjusting sleeve clamp
8	LH adjusting sleeve clamp bolt
9	Cotter pin (2 required)
10	LH adjusting sleeve clamp bracket bolt
11	LH outer tie-rod end
12	LH adjusting sleeve clamp bracket nut
13	LH adjusting sleeve clamp bracket nut
14	Outer drag link
15	Drag link adjusting sleeve nuts (2 required)
16	Drag link adjusting sleeve clamp bracket bolt
17	Drag link adjusting sleeve
18	Inner drag link
19	Drag link adjusting sleeve clamp bracket nut
20	RH adjusting sleeve clamp bracket bolt
21	RH adjusting sleeve clamp bolt (part of 3281)
22	Drag link adjusting sleeve clamp bolts (2 required) (part of 3281)
23	Outer tie-rod end
24	RH adjusting sleeve clamp nuts
25	RH adjusting sleeve clamp
26	RH adjusting sleeve clamp bracket nut
27	RH outer tie-rod/drag link nut
28	Adjusting sleeve

LTV0500000000480

Fig. 25 Exploded view of steering linkage (Part 2 of 2). Excursion & F-Super Duty w/4WD

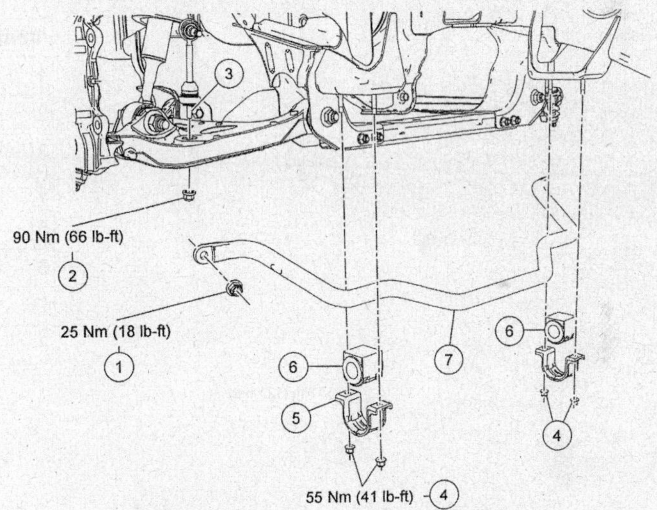

Item	Description
1	Stabilizer bar link upper nut (2 required)
2	Stabilizer bar link lower nut (2 required)
3	Stabilizer bar link (2 required)
4	Stabilizer bar bracket nuts (4 required)

Item	Description
5	Stabilizer bar bracket (4 required)
6	Stabilizer bar bushings (4 required)
7	Stabilizer bar

LTV0500000000481

Fig. 26 Stabilizer bar, busings & links replaced

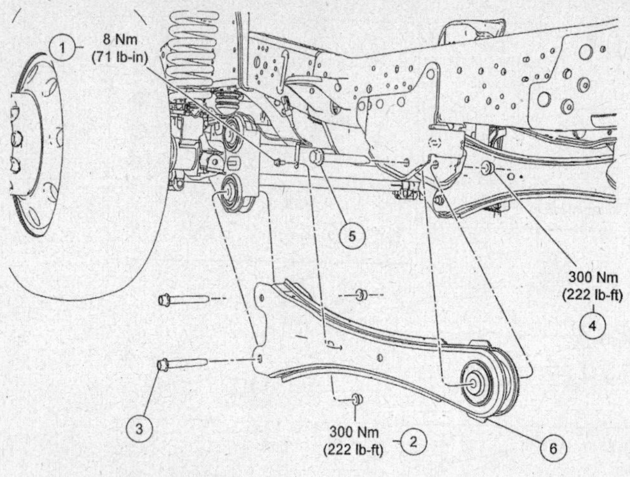

Item	Description
1	Wheel speed sensor harness bolt
2	Radius arm front nut (2 required)
3	Radius arm front bolt (2 required)
4	Radius arm rear nut
5	Radius arm rear bolt
6	Radius arm

LTV0500000000643

Fig. 27 Radius arm replacement. E-Series, Excursion, F-250 & F350

Step	Action	Value(s)	Yes	No
9	1. Disconnect the left front wheel speed sensor harness connector. 2. Test the left front wheel speed sensor signal circuit for an open or a short to ground. Did you find and correct the condition?	--	Go to Step 17	Go to Step 11
10	Test the left front wheel speed sensor supply voltage circuit for an open. Did you find and correct the condition?	--	Go to Step 17	Go to Step 11
11	1. Reconnect the wheel speed sensor harness connector. 2. At the EBCM harness connector, use a fused jumper wire to connect the left front wheel speed sensor supply voltage circuit to battery positive voltage. 3. Set-up the DMM to measure current flow (mA/A). 4. Connect the positive lead of the DMM to the left front wheel speed sensor signal circuit at the EBCM harness connector. 5. Connect the negative lead of the DMM to ground. Does the amperage measure within the specified range?	4-16 mA	Go to Step 15	Go to Step 13
12	1. Turn OFF the ignition. 2. Disconnect the EBCM harness connector. 3. Raise the vehicle so that the left front wheel is 2 cm (1 in) off of the floor. 4. At the EBCM harness connector, use a fused jumper wire to connect the left front wheel speed sensor supply voltage circuit to battery positive voltage. 5. Set-up the DMM to measure current flow (mA/A). 6. Connect the positive lead of the DMM to the left front wheel speed sensor signal circuit at the EBCM harness connector. 7. Connect the negative lead of the DMM to ground. 8. Slowly rotate the left front wheel by hand while observing the DMM. Does the amperage toggle from lower measurement to higher measurement within the specified ranges?	Low signal: 4-8 mA High signal: 12-16 mA	Go to Step 15	Go to Step 13
13	Inspect for poor connections at the harness connector of the left front wheel speed sensor. Did you find and correct the condition?	--	Go to Step 17	Go to Step 14

LTV0500000000642

Fig. 28 Radius arm replacement. F-450 & F-550

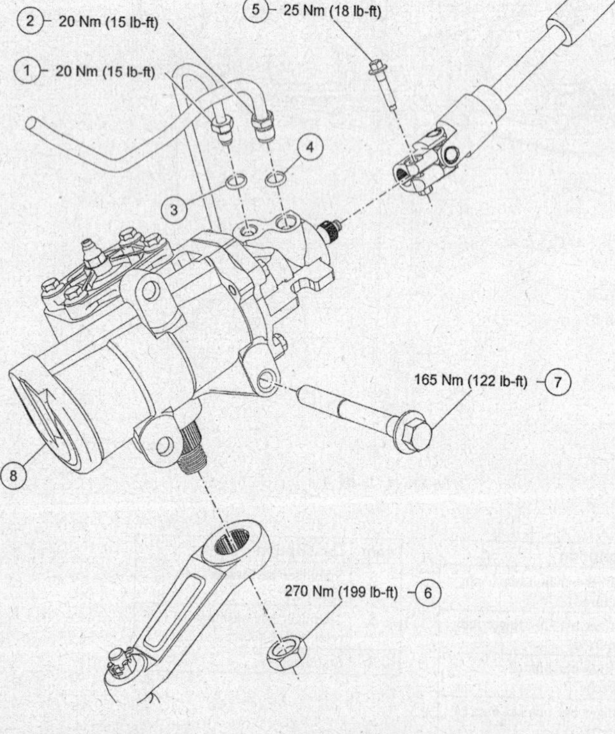

Item	Description
1	Power steering pump-to-steering gear fitting
2	Power steering gear-to-cooler line fitting
3	O-ring seal

Item	Description
4	O-ring seal
5	Intermediate shaft pinch bolt
6	Steering gear sector shaft arm-to-sector shaft nut
7	Steering gear bolt (3 required)
8	Steering gear

LTV0500000000646

Fig. 29 Power steering gear replacement (Part 1 of 2). E-Series

Item	Description
1	Power steering pump-to-steering gear fitting
2	Power steering gear-to-cooler line fitting
3	O-ring seal
4	O-ring seal
5	Intermediate shaft pinch bolt
6	Steering gear sector shaft arm-to-sector shaft nut
7	Steering gear bolt (3 required)
8	Steering gear

LTV0500000000647

Fig. 29 Power steering gear replacement (Part 2 of 2). E-Series

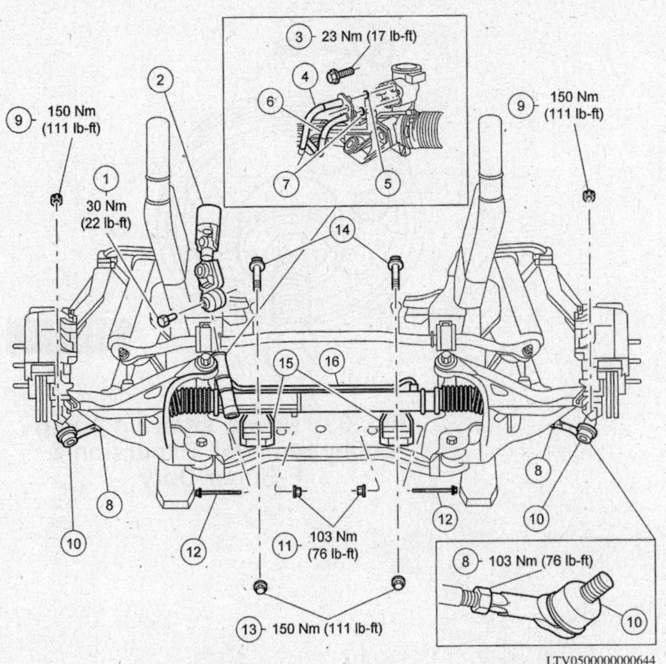

Fig. 30 Power steering gear replacement (Part 1 of 2), Expedition, F-150, Mark LT & Navigator

Item	Description
1	Lower steering column shaft-to-steering gear bolt
2	Lower steering column shaft
3	Power steering line clamp plate bolt
4	Power steering high pressure line
5	Power steering high pressure line O-ring seal
6	Power steering return line
7	Power steering return line O-ring seal
8	Outer tie-rod end lock nuts (part of 3280) (2 required)
9	Outer tie-rod end nuts (2 required)
10	Outer tie-rod ends (2 required)
11	Steering gear bracket-to-crossmember nuts (2 required)
12	Steering gear bracket-to-crossmember bolts (2 required)
13	Steering gear bracket-to-gear nuts (2 required)
14	Steering gear bracket-to-gear bolts (2 required)
15	Bracket
16	Steering gear

LTV0500000000645

Fig. 30 Power steering gear replacement (Part 2 of 2), Expedition, F-150, Mark LT & Navigator

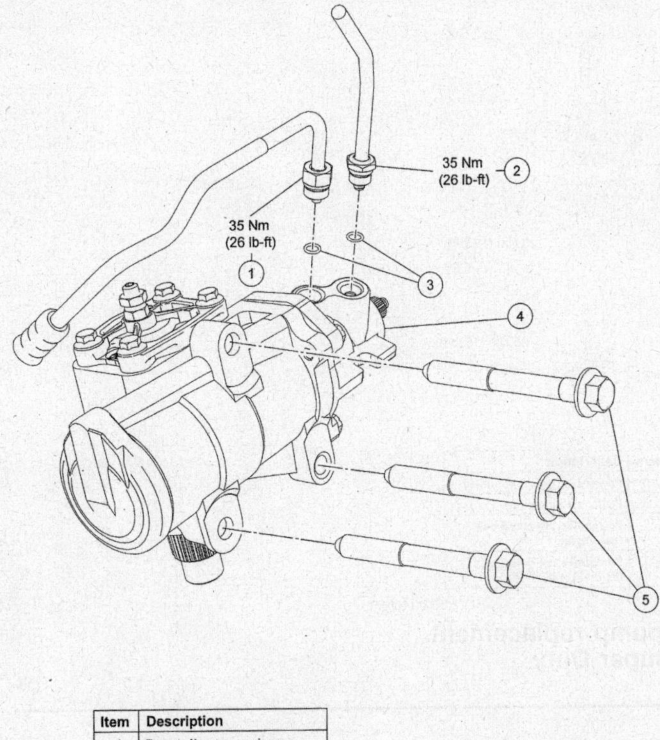

Item	Description
1	Return line-to-steering gear fitting
2	Pressure line-to-steering gear fitting
3	Seals (2 required) (F250/350)
3	Seal (2 required) (450/550)
4	Power steering gear
5	Steering gear bolts (3 required) (F250/350)
5	Steering gear bolts (3 required) (F450/550)

LTV0500000000648

Fig. 31 Power steering gear replacement. Excursion, F-Super Duty & Motorhome Chassis

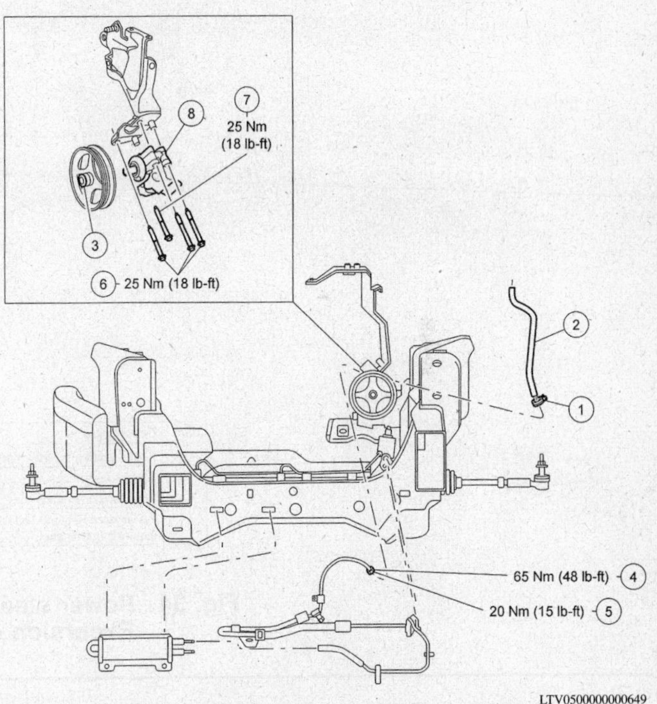

Fig. 32 Power steering pump replacement (Part 1 of 2). E-Series, Expedition, F-150, Mark LT & Navigator

Item	Description
1	Suction line-to-power steering pump clamp
2	Suction line
3	Power steering pump pulley
4	Pressure line fitting-to-pump (4.6L, 5.4L engines)
5	Pressure line fitting-to-pump (part of 3A719) (4.2L engine)
6	Power steering pump bolts (3 required)
7	Power steering pump bolt (4.2L engine)
8	Power steering pump

LTV0500000000650

Fig. 32 Power steering pump replacement (Part 2 of 2). E-Series, Expedition, F-150, Mark LT & Navigator

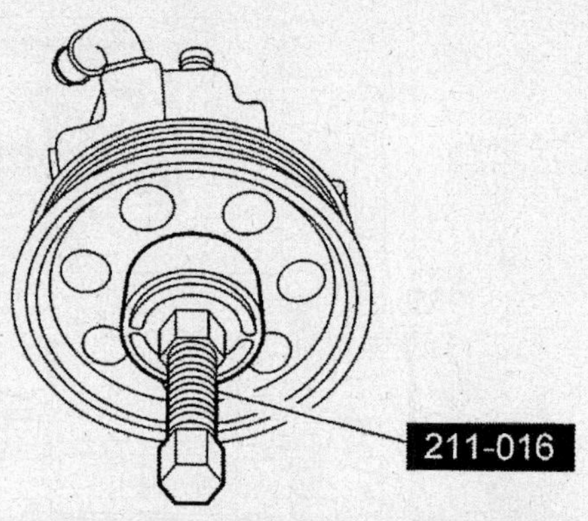

LTV0500000000652

Fig. 33 Power steering pump pulley removal. Excursion & F-Super Duty

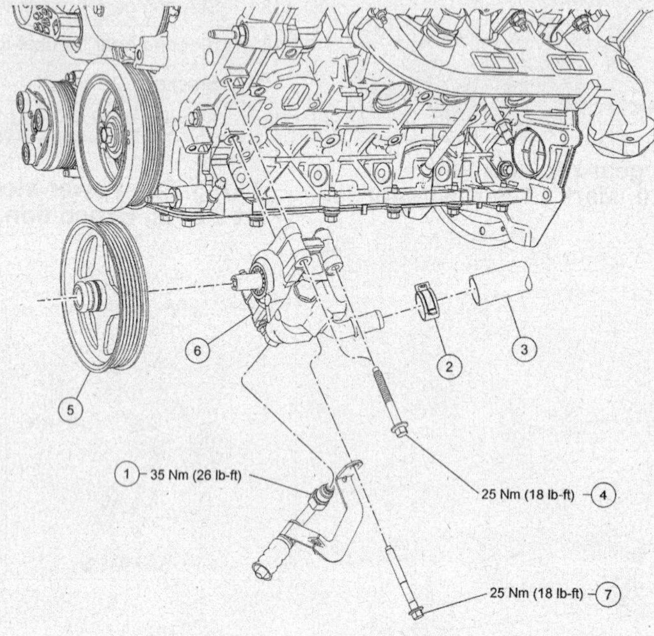

Item	Description
1	Power steering pressure line
2	Clamp
3	Power steering return hose
4	Power steering pump bolt (2 required) (gas engine)

Item	Description
5	Power steering pump pulley
6	Power steering pump
7	Power steering pump bolt (gas engine)
7	Power steering pump bolt (3 required) (diesel engine)

LTV0500000000651

Fig. 34 Power steering pump replacement. Excursion & F-Super Duty

TIGHTENING SPECIFICATIONS

Year	Component	Torque Ft. Lbs.
E-SERIES		
2002–06	Axle Pivot Nut	130
	Axle To Radius Arm Nut	221
	Brake Caliper	41
	Brake Caliper Anchor Plate	295
	Caster/Camber Insert Pinch Bolt	70
	Drag Link To Sector Shaft Arm	85
	Drag Link To Spindle Steering Arm	129
	Drag Link Spindle Steering Arm Nut	406
	Front Disc Brake Rotor Shield Bolts	84①
	Front Spring Upper Retainer Bolt	22
	Hub To Disc Extender	89
	Intermediate Shaft Pinch Bolt	35
	Jounce Bumper Screw	25
	Lower Ball Joint Nut	130
	Power Steering Pump Bolts	19
	Radius Arm To Rear Bracket Nut	89
	Sector Shaft Housing Bolt	55
	Shock Absorber Lower Nut	59
	Shock Absorber Upper Nut	30
	Spindle Steering Arm Nut	406
	Stabilizer Bar Bracket Bolt	20
	Steering Gear Bolts & Nuts	258
	Steering Gear Pressure Hose	26
	Steering Gear Return Hose	17
	Tie Rod End Adjusting Sleeve Bolts	59
	Tie Rod End To Drag Link	66
	Tie Rod End To Spindle Nut	85
	Wheel Bearing Adjusting Nut	②
EXCURSION w/2WD		
2002–06	Axle Pivot To Axle Pivot Bracket	130
	Axle Pivot Bracket To Frame	60
	Damper Bracket To Frame	67
	Drag Link	67
	Radius Arm Bracket To Frame	60
	Radius Arm Pivot Bolt To Bracket	221
	Radius Arm To Axle Nut	295
	Return Hose Fitting	26
	Sector Shaft Arm Nut	200
	Shock Absorber (Lower) Bolt	76
	Shock Absorber (Upper) Bolt	76
	Shock Absorber Upper Bracket	76
	Spring To Lower Seat	99
	Spring To Spring Shock	26–30
	Stabilizer Bar To Frame Bracket	35
	Stabilizer Bar To Lower Spring Seat	85
	Stabilizer Bar Link To Stabilizer Bar	85
	Steering Gear To Frame	59
	Steering Pump	19
	Steering Shaft Pinch Bolt	36
	Tie Rod Adjusting Sleeve	41
	Tie Rod End Nut	67
	Upper Ball Joint Nut	69
	Upper Spindle Pinch Bolt	60
	Wheel Hub To Knuckle	133

TIGHTENING SPECIFICATIONS—Continued

Year	Component	Torque Ft. Lbs.
EXCURSION w/4WD		
2002–06	Axle U-Bolts	99
	Damper Bracket To Frame	67
	Drag Link	67
	Driveshaft To Pinion Flange	76
	Jounce Bumper	30
	Lower Ball Joint	150
	Return Hose Fitting	26
	Sector Shaft Arm Nut	200
	Shackle Bracket	66
	Shock Absorber (Lower)	76
	Shock Absorber (Upper)	76
	Shock Absorber Upper Bracket	76
	Spring Hanger To Frame	76
	Spring To Shackle Nuts	185
	Spring To Spring Hanger	203
	Stabilizer Bar Bracket	35
	Stabilizer Bar Link To Bracket	80
	Stabilizer Bar To Link Nut	80
	Stabilizer Bar To Axle Bracket (Righthand Side Only)	41
	Stabilizer Bar To Spring (Lefthand Side Only)	41
	Steering Gear To Frame	59
	Steering Pump	19
	Steering Shaft Pinch Bolt	36
	Tie Rod Adjusting Sleeve	41
	Tie Rod End Nut	67
	Track Bar	406
	Upper Ball Joint Nut	69
	Wheel Hub To Knuckle	133
EXPEDITION & NAVIGATOR		
2002–06	Axle To Hub Nut	20
	Brake Caliper	24
	Brake Caliper Anchor Plate	148
	Brake Hose Bracket	10
	Disc Brake Shield	10
	Halfshaft To Axle Bolt	60
	Inner Tie Rod	81
	Intermediate Shaft To Gear	22
	Lower Control Arm To Frame	199
	Lower Ball Joint Nut	148
	Power Steering Fluid Cooler	96①
	Power Steering Fluid Reservoir	96①
	Pressure Line Bracket To Crossmember	80①
	Pressure Line Bracket To Engine	30
	Pressure Line Fitting	48
	Shock Absorber/Spring Rod Nut	22
	Shock Absorber/Spring Lower Nut	350
	Shock Absorber/Spring Upper Nuts	35
	Stabilizer Bar Bracket	41
	Stabilizer Bar Link (Lower)	66
	Stabilizer Bar Link (Upper)	18

Continued

TIGHTENING SPECIFICATIONS—Continued

Year	Component	Torque Ft. Lbs.
EXPEDITION & NAVIGATOR		
2002–06	Steering Gear Bracket To Gear	111
	Steering Gear Bracket To Crossmember	76
	Steering Pump	18
	Tie Rod End Castle Nut	111
	Tie Rod End Jam Nut	74
	Upper Control Arm	111
	Upper Ball Joint Nut	85
	Wheel Hub Nut	296
F-150 & MARK LT w/2WD		
2002–06	Brake Caliper	24
	Brake Caliper Anchor Plate	148
	Brake Hose Bracket	10
	Disc Brake Shield	10
	Inner Tie Rod	81
	Intermediate Shaft To Gear	22
	Lower Ball Joint Nut	111
	Lower Control Arm To Frame	259
	Power Steering Fluid Cooler	96①
	Power Steering Fluid Reservoir	96①
	Pressure Line Bracket To Crossmember	80①
	Pressure Line Bracket To Engine 4.2L & 4.6L Engines)	96①
	Pressure Line Bracket To Engine (5.4L Engine)	30
	Pressure Line Fitting To Pump (4.6L & 5.2L Engines	48
	Pressure Line Fitting To Pump (4.2L Engine)	15
	Skid Plate	18
	Shock Absorber/Spring Rod Nut	22
	Shock Absorber/Spring Lower Nut	350
	Shock Absorber/Spring Upper Nuts	30
	Stabilizer Bar Bracket	41
	Stabilizer Bar Link (Lower)	66
	Stabilizer Bar Link (Upper)	148
	Steering Gear Bracket To Gear	111
	Steering Gear Bracket To Crossmember	76
	Steering Pump	18
	Tie Rod End Castle Nut	111
	Tie Rod End Jam Nut	74
	Upper Control Arm	111
	Upper Ball Joint	111
F-150 & MARK LT w/4WD		
2002–06	Brake Caliper	24
	Brake Caliper Anchor Plate	148
	Brake Hose Bracket	10
	Disc Brake Shield	10
	Inner Tie Rod	81
	Halfshaft To Hub Nut	20
	Intermediate Shaft To Gear	22
	Lower Ball Joint Nut	111

TIGHTENING SPECIFICATIONS—Continued

Year	Component	Torque Ft. Lbs.
F-150 & MARK LT w/4WD		
2002–06	Lower Control Arm To Frame	259
	Power Steering Fluid Cooler	96①
	Power Steering Fluid Reservoir	96①
	Pressure Line Bracket To Crossmember	80①
	Pressure Line Bracket To Engine 4.2L & 4.6L Engines)	96①
	Pressure Line Bracket To Engine (5.4L Engine)	30
	Pressure Line Fitting To Pump (4.6L & 5.2L Engines	48
	Pressure Line Fitting To Pump (4.2L Engine)	15
	Skid Plate	18
	Shock Absorber/Spring Rod Nut	22
	Shock Absorber/Spring Lower Nut	350
	Shock Absorber/Spring Upper Nuts	30
	Stabilizer Bar Bracket	41
	Stabilizer Bar Link (Lower)	66
	Stabilizer Bar Link (Upper)	148
	Steering Gear Bracket To Gear	111
	Steering Gear Bracket To Crossmember	76
	Steering Pump	18
	Tie Rod End Castle Nut	111
	Tie Rod End Jam Nut	74
	Upper Control Arm	111
	Upper Ball Joint Nut	85
	Wheel Hub Assembly	148
F-SUPER DUTY w/2WD		
2002–06	ABS Sensor Retaining Bolt To Spindle	73①
	Axle Pivot Bolt Retainer Nut To Axle Pivot Bracket (F-250–350)	222
	Axle Pivot Bolt Retainer Nut To Axle Pivot Bracket (F-450–550)	295
	Axle Pivot Bracket Nut To Frame	30
	Brake Caliper Anchor Plate (F-250–350)	166
	Brake Caliper Anchor Plate (F-450–550)	295
	Disc Brake Rotor Shield	96①
	Lower Shock Absorber Retainer Nut	60
	Lower Spring Retainer Nut To Lower Spring Seat	98
	Radius Arm Front Nuts	295
	Radius Arm Rear Nuts	222
	Sector Shaft Arm Nut	350
	Shock Absorber Lower	59
	Shock Absorber Upper	30
	Stabilizer Bar Link (Lower) All	59
	Stabilizer Bar Link (Upper) F-450–550	111
	Stabilizer Bar Retainer Bracket To Frame	35
	Steering Damper Retainer Nut To Steering Damper Bracket	67

Continued

TIGHTENING SPECIFICATIONS—Continued

Year	Component	Torque Ft. Lbs.
F-SUPER DUTY w/2WD		
2002–06	Steering Gear Bolts (F250–350)	111
	Steering Gear Bolts (F250–350)	221
	Steering Pump	18
	Tie Rod End Retainer Nut To Spindle	67
	Track Bar	129
	Upper Spring Retainer Bolt To Spring/Shock Tower	26
	Upper Spindle Pinch Bolt Nut To Axle	60
	Wheel Hub Nut	133
F-SUPER DUTY w/4WD		
2002–06	Ball Joint	69
	Brake Caliper Anchor Plate (F-250–350)	166
	Brake Caliper Anchor Plate (F-450–550)	295
	Front Driveshaft To Pinion Flange	76
	Front Hub & Bearing To Knuckle	55
	Jounce Bumper	30
	Pressure Lines	26
	Sector Shaft Arm Nut	350
	Shackle Bracket To Frame	66
	Shock Absorber To Spring Spacer	76
	Shock Absorber Lower Nut	111
	Shock Absorber Upper Nut	46
	Stabilizer Bar To Axle Bracket	35
	Stabilizer Bar Lower Nut	59
	Stabilizer Bar To Link	85
	Stabilizer Bar Upper Nut	111
	Steering Gear Bolts (F250–350)	111
	Steering Gear Bolts (F450–450)	221
	Steering Pump	18
	Tie Rod End To Knuckle	53
	Track Bar Ball Joint	184
	Track Bar Bracket Nut	406
	Wheel Extension	130
	Wheel Hub Assembly	133

TIGHTENING SPECIFICATIONS—Continued

Year	Component	Torque Ft. Lbs.
MOTORHOME CHASSIS		
2002–03	Ball Joint	101
	Front Driveshaft To Pinion Flange	76
	Front Hub & Bearing To Knuckle	55
	Jounce Bumper	30
	Shackle Bracket To Frame	66
	Shock Absorber To Spring Spacer	76
	Shock Absorber Upper Nut	76
	Spring Hanger To Frame	76
	Spring To Axle U-Bolt	99
	Spring To Shackle	185
	Spring Shackle To Frame	185
	Spring To Spring Hanger	203
	Stabilizer Bar To Axle Bracket	35
	Stabilizer Bar To Frame	35
	Stabilizer Bar To Link	85
	Stabilizer Bar To Spring Spacer	35
	Tie Rod End To Knuckle	53
	Track Bar To Bracket	369
2004–06	Drag Link Nut	66
	Fluid Cooler Bracket	41
	Fluid Reservoir	18
	Intermediate Shaft To Steering Gear	35
	Lock Pin Nut	18
	Lower Shock Absorber Nut	260
	Sector Shaft Adjusting Screw	44①
	Sector Shaft Arm Nut	258
	Spindle Adapter Plate	66
	Spindle Lock Pin Nuts	60
	Spindle Pin Cap Bolt	12
	Spindle Steering Arm	424
	Spring Hanger Bracket To Frame	66
	Spring Hanger Nut	181
	Spring Shackle Nut	92
	Stabilizer Bar Link To Frame	66
	Stabilizer Bar To Axle	66
	Steering Gear Mounting Bolts	258
	Steering Gear Pressure Line	26
	Steering Pump Pressure Line	26
	Steering Gear Side Cover	118
	Tie Rod End Nut	66
	Track Bar	406
	U-Bolt Nuts	260
	Upper Shock Absorber Nut	260
	Wheel Bearing Adjusting Nut	②

①— Inch lbs.
②— Refer to "Wheel Bearing, Adjust" for procedure.

Front Wheel Drive

INDEX

AXLE

REPLACE

Expedition, F-150, Mark LT & Navigator

1. Ensure vehicle is in neutral, then raise and support vehicle.
2. Place match marks on front propeller shaft an differential flange for assembly reference.
3. Disconnect and support front propeller shaft. **Do not allow propeller shaft to hang free.**
4. Disconnect driveshaft to axle shaft flange bolts, then position driveshaft aside. **Support driveshaft, do not allow driveshaft to hang unsupported.**
5. Disconnect vacuum lines to axle disconnect motor, then support axle with a suitable lowering equipment.
6. Remove front differential bushing to support bolt, then the support to frame bolts.
7. Remove differential support, then the axle tube and differential cover bushing bolts.
8. Lower front axle from vehicle.
9. Reverse procedure to install. Tighten to specification.

Excursion & F-Super Duty

1. Raise and support vehicle.
2. Remove tire and wheels.
3. Remove brake calipers and pads.
4. Disconnect power vacuum hub hose from knuckle, then disconnect anti-lock brake sensor.
5. Disconnect steering damper at axle.
6. Disconnect steering linkage at steering knuckles and position aside.
7. Place index mark on driveshaft to companion flange for assembly reference.
8. Disconnect driveshaft from front axle and set aside. Wrap electrical tape around bearing caps to prevent loss of needle bearings.
9. Disconnect vent tube and plug fitting.
10. It is required to load suspension to remove trackbar.
11. Support axle with suitable jack, then lower vehicle enough to release tension on trackbar.
12. Remove U-bolts securing axle to axle springs.
13. Lower axle from vehicle.
14. Reverse procedure to install.

AXLE SHAFT

REPLACE

Expedition, F-150, Mark LT & Navigator

1. Raise and support vehicle, then remove wheels.
2. Remove cotter pin, retainer and hub nut.
3. Remove two caliper bolts, then lift front disc brake caliper off front anchor plate and position aside.
4. Remove upper ball joint cotter pin and nut.
5. Separate front wheel knuckle from front suspension upper arm using pitman arm puller tool No. T64P-3590-F, or equivalent..
6. Remove front halfshaft mounting bolts, then the front halfshafts.
7. Reverse procedure to install.

LOCKING HUB SERVICE

Excursion & F-Super Duty

1. Remove hub lock retainer ring, then pull outward on hub lock.
2. Reverse procedure to install, noting the following:
   a. Whenever front wheel hub, axle shaft or hub lock is removed and installed, front wheel end assemblies must be leak inspected to ensure sealing surfaces are intact.
   b. Disconnect wheel end vacuum hose, then connect vacuum pump tool No. D95L-7559-A, or equivalent, to vacuum fitting on wheel knuckle.
   c. Wheel end assembly must not leak more than .50 Hg inch in 30 seconds. Apply 15 Hg of vacuum to wheel end assembly and observe for 30 seconds.

TIGHTENING SPECIFICATIONS

Year	Component	Torque Ft. Lbs.
EXPEDITION, F-150, MARK LT & NAVIGATOR		
2002–06	Axle Tube Bushing Nut	85
	Brake Caliper Anchor Bolts	148
	Crossmember Bolts	66
	Differential Housing Bolts	24
	Driveshaft To Axle	26
	Driveshaft To Transfer Case	82
	Fill Plug	18
	Halfshaft Flange To Axle	60
	Lower Mounting Bushing	85
	Pinion Shaft lock Bolt	22
	Skid Plate	11
	Upper Mounting Bushing	85
	Wheel End Nut	20
EXCURSION & F-SUPER DUTY		
2002–06	Axle Housing Cover Fill Plug	23
	Axle Housing Cover Bolts	35
	Caliper To Anchor Plate	①
	Differential Bearing Cap Bolts	80
	Driveshaft to Axle Bolts	26
	Driveshaft To Transfer Case	82
	Knuckle To Upper Arm	66
	Stabilizer Bar Bolts	35
	Track Bar To Axle	129
	Trailing Arm To Axle Housing	221
	U-Bolt Nuts	99

① — Excursion, F250–350, 166 ft. lbs.; F-450–550, 295 ft. lbs.

Wheel Alignment

INDEX

PRELIMINARY INSPECTION

Inspect the following components, adjust, repair or replace as required prior to performing front wheel alignment.

1. Inflate tires to cold specifications.
2. Ensure front tires are of same size, ply rating and load rating.
3. Inspect for excessive wheel bearing endplay.
4. Inspect for worn or damaged spindle ball joints.
5. Inspect steering gear mounting bolts for proper torque.
6. Inspect radius arm or bent or damaged condition.
7. Inspect radius arm to frame bushings for looseness or wear.
8. Inspect for loose or broken shackles.
9. Inspect for distorted or split jounce bumper.
10. Inspect suspension components for wear or damage.
11. Inspect vehicle ride height as outlined under "Vehicle Ride Height."

FRONT WHEEL ALIGNMENT

On models not listed, the caster angle is designed into the axle and is not adjustable.

Caster & Camber

EXCURSION & F-SUPER DUTY w/4WD

The camber angle may be adjusted by means of mounting sleeves placed on the upper ball joint, **Fig. 1.** Four sleeves are available in ½° camber increments to allow a 3° range of adjustment from –1½° to +1½.°

E-SERIES 2WD w/BALL JOINTS

Caster and camber adjustment is possible with adjusters available in ½,° 1° and 1½° increments. Once adjuster is used to adjust both caster and camber. Refer to **Figs. 2 and 3** for adjuster replacement, then to **Fig. 4** for adjuster variations.

EXCURSION & F-SUPER DUTY w/2WD

The caster angle on models with leaf spring front suspension can be adjusted by inserting a shim between the spring and axle. Shims are available in increments of 0,° 1° and 2.° The 0° shim is used to adjust side to side ride height when an angled shim is installed on the opposite side of the axle.

EXPEDITION, F-150, MARK LT & NAVIGATOR

1. Remove alignment plate nuts and alignment plate, **Fig. 5.**
2. Install cams and upper arm adjusting nuts.
3. To increase caster, move front portion of front suspension upper arm outboard and move rear portion of front suspension upper arm inboard. To increase camber, move front suspension upper arm outboard equally.
4. To decrease caster, move front portion of front suspension upper arm inboard and move rear portion of front suspension upper arm outboard. To decrease camber, move front suspension upper arm inboard equally.
5. Tighten upper suspension arm cam nuts.

Toe-In, Adjust

Inspect the steering wheel spoke position when the front wheels are in the straight ahead position. If the spokes are not in the normal position, they can be adjusted while toe-in is being adjusted.

1. Loosen clamp bolts on each tie rod end sleeve.
2. Adjust toe-in. If steering wheel spokes are in their normal position, lengthen or shorten both rods equally to obtain specified toe-in. If spokes are not in normal position, make required rod adjustments to obtain specified toe-in and steering wheel spoke alignment. Refer to applicable "Wheel Alignment Specification Chart."

VEHICLE RIDE HEIGHT

Prior to inspecting and adjusting camber and caster, use the following procedure to inspect vehicle side to side lean.

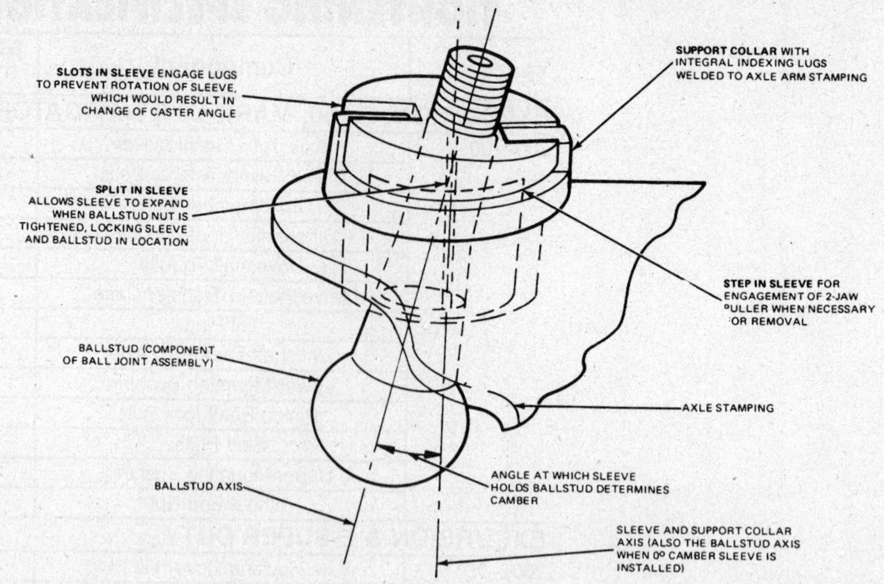

Fig. 1 Camber adjustment. Excursion & F-Super Duty w/4WD

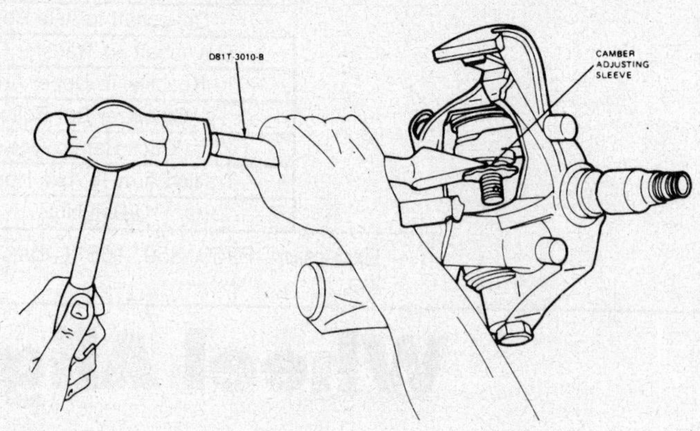

Fig. 2 Removing caster/camber adjustment sleeve. E-Series 2WD w/ball joints

1. Place vehicle on a flat, smooth surface.
2. Inspect for any excessive weight placed on any one corner of the vehicle.
3. Inspect all wheels and tires for correct size and inflation pressure.
4. Inspect front and rear spring part numbers and ensure front (left/right) and rear (left/right) springs have the same part number.
5. Jounce vehicle's front and rear suspensions to normalize static ride height.
6. Measure vehicle height at righthand and lefthand fender lip openings for both the front and rear dimensions, **Figs. 6 and 7.**
7. Calculate side to side differences for each dimension, maximum difference between righthand and lefthand sides is ⅝ inch on the front and ¾ inch on the rear.

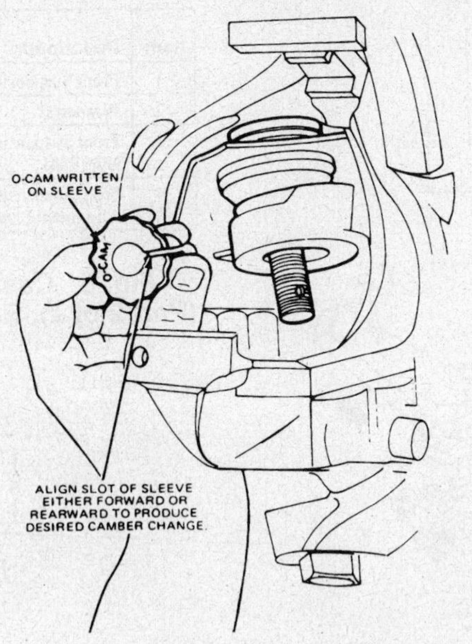

Fig. 3 Caster/camber adjustment. E-Series 2WD w/ball joints

Service Adjuster Type (Degrees)	Position Slot in Axle (Degrees)	LH Axle		RH Axle	
		Camber Change (Degrees)	Caster Change (Degrees)	Camber Change (Degrees)	Caster Change (Degrees)
1/2	0	−0.5	0	+0.5	0
1	0	−1.0	0	+1.0	0
1-1/2	0	−1.5	0	+1.5	0
1/2	45	−0.25	+0.25	+0.25	+0.25
1	45	−0.75	+0.75	+0.75	+0.75
1-1/2	45	−1.00	+1.00	+1.00	+1.00
1/2	90	0	+0.5	0	+0.5
1	90	0	+1.0	0	+1.0
1-1/2	90	0	+1.5	0	+1.5
1/2	135	+0.25	+0.25	−0.25	+0.25
1	135	+0.75	+0.75	−0.75	+0.75
1-1/2	135	+1.00	+1.00	−1.00	+1.00
1/2	180	+0.5	0	−0.5	0
1	180	+1.0	0	−1.0	0
1-1/2	180	+1.5	0	−1.5	0
1/2	225	+0.25	−0.25	−0.25	−0.25
1	225	+0.75	−0.75	−0.75	−0.75
1-1/2	225	+1.00	−1.00	−1.00	−1.0C
1/2	270	0	−0.5	0	−0.5
1	270	0	−1.0	0	−1.0
1-1/2	270	0	−1.5	0	−1.5
1/2	315	−0.25	−0.25	+0.25	−0.25
1	315	−0.75	−0.75	+0.75	−0.75
1-1/2	315	−1.00	−1.00	+1.00	−1.00

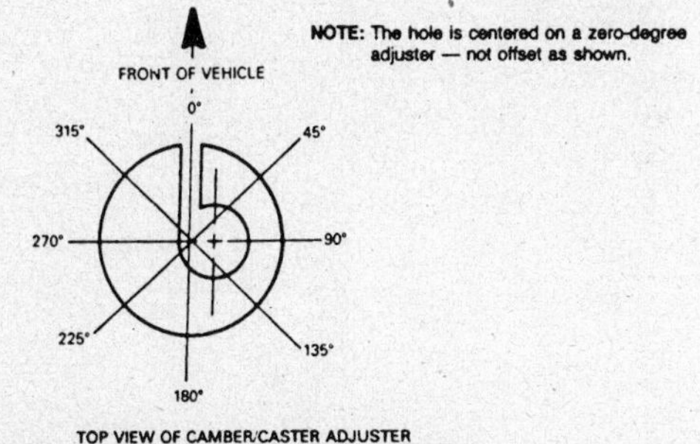

Fig. 4 Caster/camber variation chart

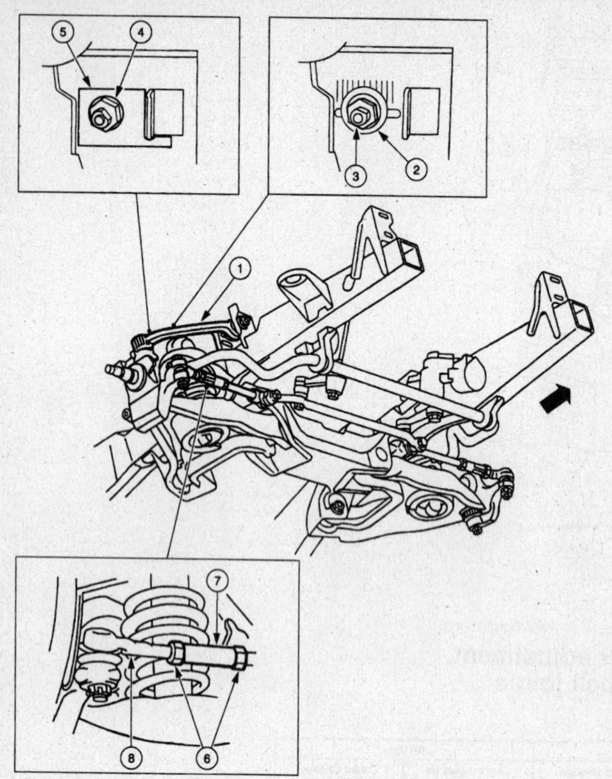

FM2049700055010X

Fig. 5 Caster & camber adjustment locations (Part 1 of 2). Expedition, F-150, Mark LT & Navigator

Item	Description
1	Front Suspension Upper Arm
2	Washer(s)
3	Front Suspension Upper Arm Nut (4x4)
4	Front Suspension Arm Alignment Plate Nut (4x2)
5	Front Suspension Arm Alignment Plate (4x2)
6	Toe Set Jam Nut
7	Front Wheel Spindle Tie Rod Adjusting Sleeve
8	Tie Rod End

FM2049700055020X

Fig. 5 Caster & camber adjustment locations (Part 2 of 2). Expedition, F-150, Mark LT & Navigator

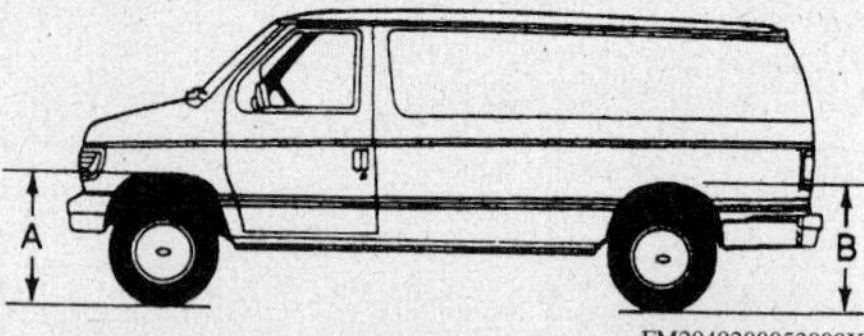

FM2049200053000X

Fig. 6 Vehicle side to side ride height measurement. E-Series

FM2049200054000X

Fig. 7 Vehicle side to side ride height measurement. Expedition, F-150, Mark LT & Navigator

ESCAPE & MARINER

NOTE: Refer To Back Of This Manual For Vehicle Manufacturer's Special Service Tool Suppliers.

INDEX OF SERVICE OPERATIONS

Specifications

GENERAL ENGINE SPECIFICATIONS

Year	Engine Liter	Fuel System	Bore & Stroke	Compres-sion Ratio	Net H.P. @ RPM	Maximum Torque Ft. Lbs. @ RPM	Normal Oil Pressure, Pounds
2002–04	2.0L	SMFI	3.34 x 3.46	9.6	127@5400	135@4500	54–80②
	3.0L	SMFI	3.50 x 3.13	10	201@5900	196@4700	45①
2005–06	2.3L	SMFI	3.44 x 3.70	9.7	151 @ 5750	154 @ 4250	29–39
	3.0L	SMFI	3.50 x 3.13	10	201@5900	196@4700	45①

①— Hot @ 448 RPM.

②— Hot @ 4000 RPM.

TUNE UP SPECIFICATIONS

Engine Liter	Spark Plug Gap, Inch	Ignition Timing, °BTDC				Curb Idle Speed		Fast Idle Speed		Fuel Pump Pres-sure, psi	Valve Cleara-nce, Inch
		Firing Order	Man. Trans.	Auto. Trans.	Mark Loc-ation	Man. Trans.	Auto. Trans.	Man. Trans.	Auto. Trans.		
2.0L	.051	①	③	③	④	⑤	⑤	⑤	⑤	65	⑥
2.3L	049–.053	①	③	③	④	⑤	⑤	⑤	⑤	65	⑧
3.0L	.052-.056	②	③	③	④	⑤	⑤	⑤	⑤	65	⑦

①— Cylinder numbering from front to rear of engine, 1-2-3-4. Firing order, 1-3-4-2.

②— Firing order, 1-4-2-5-3-6.

③— Non-adjustable.

④— Equipped w/crankshaft position sensor.

⑤— Idle speed controlled by an automatic idle speed control.

⑥— Intake valves, .004–.007 inch; exhaust valves, .010–.013 inch.

⑦— Equipped w/hydraulic lash adjusters (non-adjustable).

⑧— Intake valves, .008–.011 inch; exhaust valves, .010–.013 inch.

FRONT WHEEL ALIGNMENT SPECIFICATIONS

Year	Model	Caster Angle, Degrees		Camber Angle, Degrees		Total Toe, Inches	
		Limits	Desired	Limits	Desired	Limits	Desired
2002–04	V6	—	1.79	—	-.84	0 to .46	.23
	I4	—	1.79	—	-.48	-.31 to .15	-.08
2005–06	All	—	1.60	—	-1.00	0–.46	.23

REAR WHEEL ALIGNMENT SPECIFICATIONS

Year	Caster Angle, Degrees		Camber Angle, Degrees		Toe-In	Ball Joint Wear, Inch
	Limits	Desired	Limits	Desired		
2002–04	—	—	—	+.04	-.02 to +.02	①
2005–06	—	—	—	.75	-.10 to +.30	①

①— Refer to "Ball Joint Inspection" in "Front Suspension & Steering."

FLUID CAPACITIES & COOLING SYSTEM DATA

Engine	Coolant Capacity, Qts.		Coolant Type	Radiator Cap Pressure Relief Pressure, Lbs.	Thermo. Opening Temp., Degrees F.	Fuel Tank, Gals.	Engine Oil Refill, Qts.①	Transaxle Oil	
	Less A/C	With A/C						Man. Trans., Pts.	Auto Trans, Qts.
2.0L	6.5	6.5	②	13–18	194–201	15.3	4.5	③	—
2.3L	7.6	7.6	②	17–21	194–223	15	4.5	③	3.7
3.0L	10.5	10.5	②	17–21	183–210	16.	5.8	—	10

①— With filter change.
②— Use coolant No. E2FZ-19549-AA or equivalent meeting Ford specification. In Oregon, use coolant No. F5FZ-19549-CC, or equivalent, meeting Ford specification. In Canada, use coolant No. CXC-8-B, or equivalent, meeting Ford specification.
③— Fill the transaxle w/gear oil through the VSS opening until the full level on the VSS is reached.

LUBRICANT DATA

Year	Model	Lubricant Type					
		Transmission		Transfer Case	Rear Axle	Power Steering	Brake System
		Manual	Automatic				
2002–06	All	SAE 75W-90 Gear Oil	MERCON ATF	SAE 75W-140	SAE 75W-140	MERCON	DOT 3

Electrical

NOTE: On Air Bag Equipped Models, Refer To "Air Bag System Precautions" Located In The Front Of This Manual For System Disarming & Arming Procedures.

NOTE: Refer To "Computer Relearn Procedure" Located In The Front Of This Manual When Battery Power To The Computer Has Been Interrupted.

NOTE: Refer To "High-Voltage Traction Battery Systems Depowering" Located In The Engine Chapter Before Performing Any Diagnostics Or Repair On This Hybrid Vehicle.

INDEX

PRECAUTIONS

Air Bag Systems

Refer to "Air Bag System Precautions" in the front of this manual for system disarming and arming procedures.

Battery Ground Cable

Prior to service, disconnect battery ground cable and isolate as required.

FUSE PANEL & FLASHER LOCATION

The fuse panel is located at the drivers side lower kick panel.

FUEL PUMP RELAY LOCATION

The fuel pump relay is located in the battery junction box in the lefthand front engine compartment.

RELAY CENTER LOCATION

Relays are located in the battery junction box in the lefthand front engine compartment.

STARTER

REPLACE

2.0L Engine

1. Remove starter bolts, **Fig. 1.**
2. Raise and support vehicle.
3. **On models equipped with AWD,** disconnect exhaust system.
4. **On all models,** remove halfshaft support bracket bolts and nuts.
5. Remove battery cable and starter control electrical connector nuts, then the starter motor.
6. Reverse procedure to install.

2.3L Engine

1. Remove starter solenoid wire nut, **Fig. 2.**
2. Raise and support vehicle.
3. Remove battery cable and starter control electrical connector nuts.
4. Remove starter retaining stud bolts, then the starter motor.
5. Reverse procedure to install.

3.0L Engine

1. Remove air cleaner outlet tube and air cleaner assembly.
2. Drain cooling system into suitable container.
3. Disconnect four cooling system hoses, **Fig. 3,** then position thermostat aside.
4. Raise and support vehicle.
5. Remove attaching nuts and position starter solenoid cables aside.
6. Remove two bolts, then the starter motor.
7. Reverse procedure to install.

ALTERNATOR

REPLACE

2.0L Engine

1. Remove alternator drive belt.
2. Disconnect alternator electrical connectors.

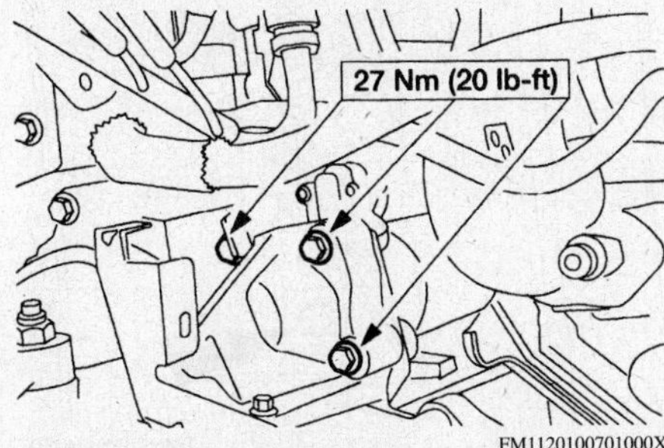

Fig. 1 Starter bolt locations. 2.0L engine

3. Remove lower alternator bolts.
4. Loosen but do not remove upper alternator bolt from engine. Insufficient clearance does not allow for removal of bolt.
5. Move alternator to rear of vehicle, then lift up and out of engine compartment.
6. Reverse procedure to install, ensuring upper mounting bolt is in place before installation.

2.3L Engine

1. Remove bolts and righthand lower splash shield.
2. Release tensioner and remove accessory drive belt.
3. Remove harness locators from top of alternator shield.
4. Remove alternator terminal nut, then position alternator B+ cable aside.
5. Disconnect alternator electrical connector, then remove alternator shield nut and lower air duct.
6. Remove harness locator and pin-type retainer from lower part of alternator shield.
7. Remove alternator bolts, stud nut and upper air duct.
8. Remove alternator from vehicle.
9. Reverse procedure to install.

3.0L Engine

1. Remove righthand front brake rotor.
2. Remove and discard righthand front axle wheel hub nut.
3. Release tie rod end from righthand steering knuckle using a suitable tie rod end removal tool.
4. Remove lower ball joint pinch bolt and nut, then release righthand lower ball joint from steering knuckle.
5. Separate righthand halfshaft from front wheel knuckle, using front hub removal tool No. 205-D070, or equivalent, then remove halfshaft.
6. Remove two intermediate shaft retainer nuts, then the righthand intermediate shaft.
7. Remove righthand lower splash shield screws and pin type retainers, then the splash shield.
8. Remove alternator drive belt.
9. Remove upper alternator mounting bolts, then the lower alternator mounting bolts and position alternator aside.
10. Remove alternator mounting bracket bolts, then the bracket.
11. Remove alternator electrical connectors.
12. Rotate alternator to gain clearance, then remove through opening in fenderwell.
13. Reverse procedure to install.

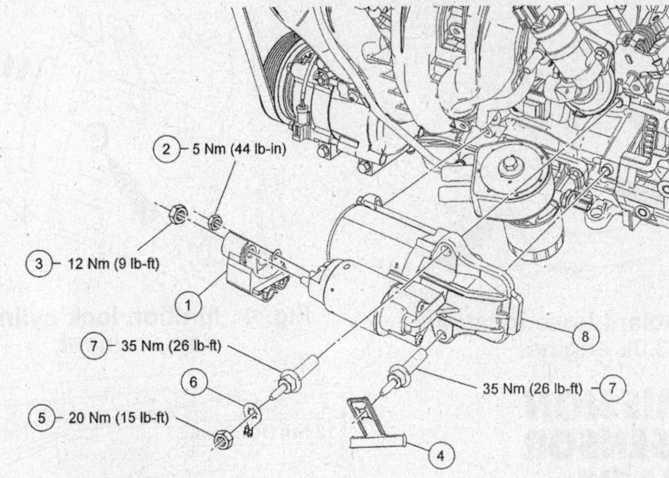

Item	Description
1	Starter motor solenoid terminal cover
2	Starter solenoid wire nut
3	Starter solenoid battery cable nut
4	Wiring harness retainer
5	Ground strap nut
6	Ground strap
7	Starter motor stud bolts (2 required)
8	Starter motor

LTV0500000000261

Fig. 2 Starter replacement. 2.3L engine

COIL-ON-PLUG

REPLACE

2.3L Engine

1. Disconnect ignition coil electrical connectors.
2. Remove bolts and ignition coils.
3. Reverse procedure to install. Apply a small amount of dielectric grease to inside of ignition coil boots before attaching to spark plugs.

3.0L Engine

These engines are equipped with individual coil on plug ignition coils.

RIGHTHAND COIL

1. Remove nuts, then the engine appearance cover.
2. Disconnect coil electrical connector and remove attaching bolt, then the ignition coil.
3. Reverse procedure to install.

LEFTHAND COIL

1. Remove upper intake manifold as outlined under "Intake Manifold, Replace" in the "3.0L Engine" section.
2. Disconnect ignition coil electrical connector and remove mounting bolt, then the ignition coil.
3. Reverse procedure to install.

COIL PACK

REPLACE

2.0L Engine

1. Disconnect ignition wires and electrical connectors from ignition coil.
2. Remove four mounting bolts, then the ignition coil.
3. Reverse procedure to install.

IGNITION LOCK

REPLACE

1. Remove upper and lower steering column shrouds.
2. Turn ignition key to On position.
3. Depress ignition lock cylinder release button with a small punch, **Fig. 4,** and pull ignition lock cylinder from housing.
4. Reverse procedure to install.

IGNITION SWITCH

REPLACE

1. Remove upper and lower steering column shrouds.
2. Disconnect ignition switch electrical connector.
3. Lower steering column to lowest position, depress ignition switch retaining tabs, then remove switch.
4. Reverse procedure to install.

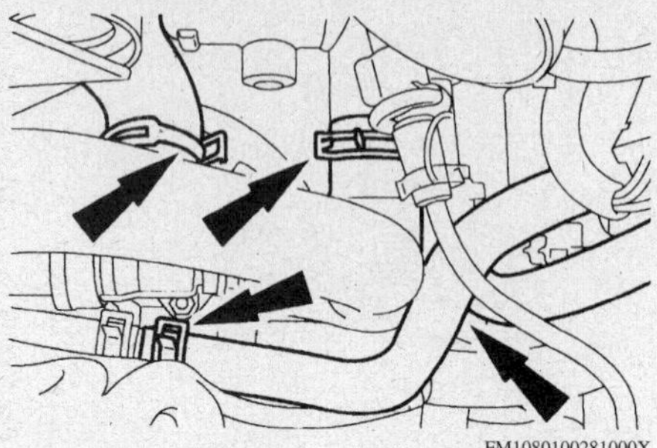
FM1080100281000X

Fig. 3 Coolant hose locations. 3.0L engine

TRANSMISSION RANGE SENSOR (AUTOMATIC TRANSMISSION)

REPLACE

1. Place transmission gear selector in Neutral position.
2. Remove battery and tray.
3. Disconnect breather tube and mass air flow sensor.
4. Remove air intake tube and air cleaner cover.
5. Remove air cleaner assembly.
6. Remove thermostat housing, if required, to gain access to transmission range sensor.
7. Disconnect transmission range sensor electrical connector.
8. Remove mounting bolts, then the transmission range sensor.
9. Reverse procedure to install.

PARK/NEUTRAL POSITION SWITCH (MANUAL TRANSMISSION)

REPLACE

1. Disconnect Park/Neutral switch electrical connector.
2. Remove Park/Neutral switch from transmission case.
3. Reverse procedure to install.

CLUTCH PEDAL POSITION SWITCH

REPLACE

1. Disconnect clutch pedal position switch electrical connector.
2. Remove switch locknut, then the switch.
3. Reverse procedure to install.

BRAKE PEDAL POSITION SWITCH

REPLACE

1. Disconnect brake pedal position switch electrical connector.
2. Rotate switch clockwise and remove from bracket.

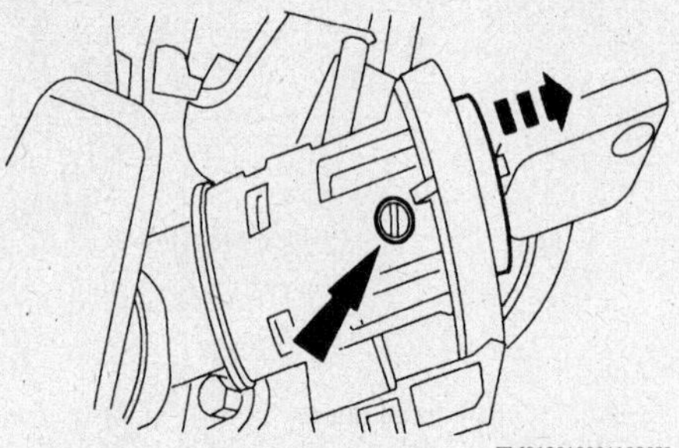
FM9120100811000X

Fig. 4 Ignition lock cylinder replacement

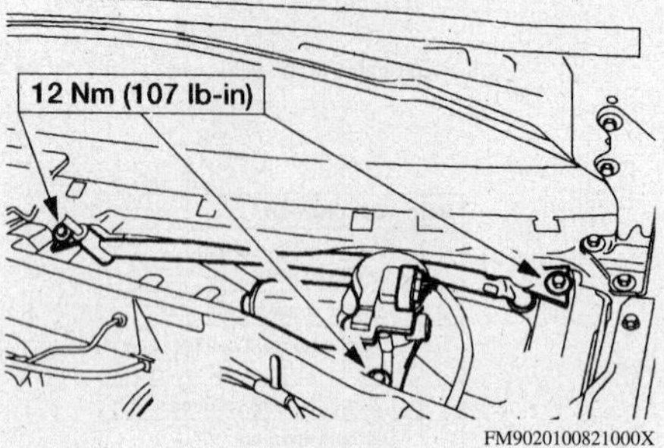

Fig. 6 Wiper arm and pivot shaft mounting bolts

3. Reverse procedure to install, noting the following:
   a. Initial installation of brake pedal position switch allows for one adjustment. If more adjustments are required, install a new switch.
   b. To unlock switch, rotate lock knob counterclockwise to stop.
   c. With engine running, fully depress and hold brake pedal.
   d. Position brake pedal position switch in bracket and rotate counterclockwise.
   e. Connect electrical connector and slowly release brake pedal.

MULTI-FUNCTION SWITCH

REPLACE

1. Remove upper and lower steering column shrouds.
2. Disconnect multi-function switch electrical connector and remove mounting screws, then the multi-function switch.
3. Reverse procedure to install.

STEERING WHEEL

REPLACE

1. Disarm air bag system as outlined under "Precautions."
2. Turn pinion shaft, **Fig. 5,** to release steering wheel from column shaft.
3. Partially remove steering wheel and disconnect electrical connector, then remove steering wheel.
4. Reverse procedure to install.

INSTRUMENT CLUSTER

REPLACE

Before removing instrument cluster module, it is required to retrieve and store module configuration information to a suitable scan tool. This information will be transferred to the new module once it is installed.

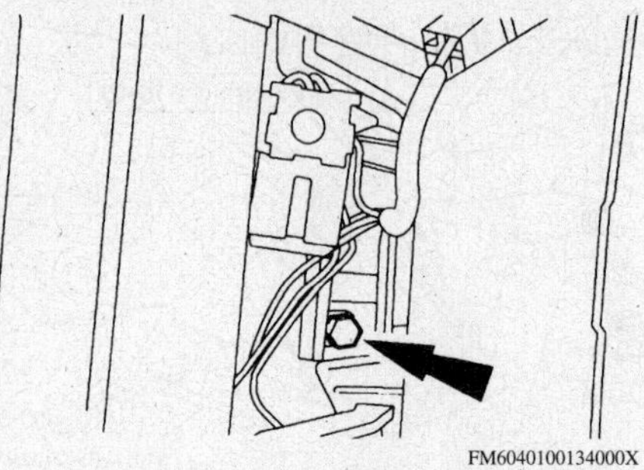
FM6040100134000X

Fig. 5 Pinion shaft location

1. Do not remove instrument cluster module from vehicle until diagnostic scan tool has retrieved module configuration information from module.
2. Select "Programmable Module Installation" on scan tool, then select "Retrieve Module Configuration."
3. Follow on screen prompts until all pertinent data has been retrieved and stored.
4. Loosen tilt lever and lower steering column.
5. Position transmission range selector down to provide access to instrument cluster finish panel and instrument cluster.
6. Remove instrument cluster finish panel.
7. Remove cluster attaching screws, then the instrument cluster.
8. Reverse procedure to install, noting the following:
   a. Once instrument cluster module is installed select "Programmable Module Installation" on the diagnostic scan tool.
   b. Select "Retrieve Module Configuration — Old ECU."
   c. Select "Restore Module Configuration — New ECU," then follow on screen prompts until module information is restored.
   d. Manually validate each customer preference item for correct settings.

RADIO

REPLACE

1. Insert audio unit removal tools No. 415-001, or equivalent, into holes in front of radio faceplate.
2. Pull outward on removal tools to release radio retaining clips, then remove radio from instrument panel.
3. Disconnect electrical connectors and antenna lead.
4. Reverse procedure to install.

WIPER MOTOR

REPLACE

Front

1. Remove wiper mounting arm and pivot shaft.

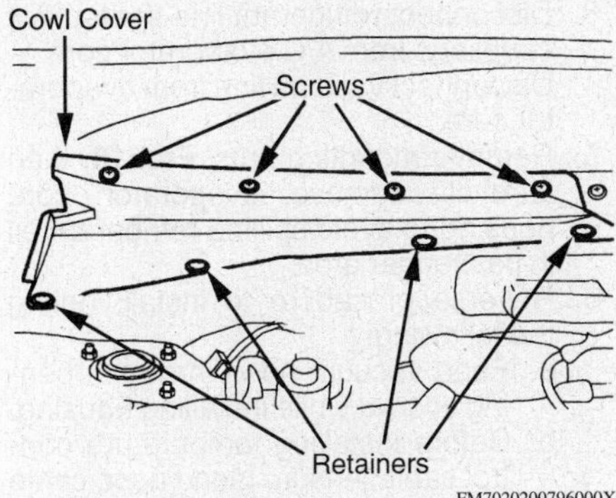

Fig. 7 Righthand side cowl cover removal. 2002–04

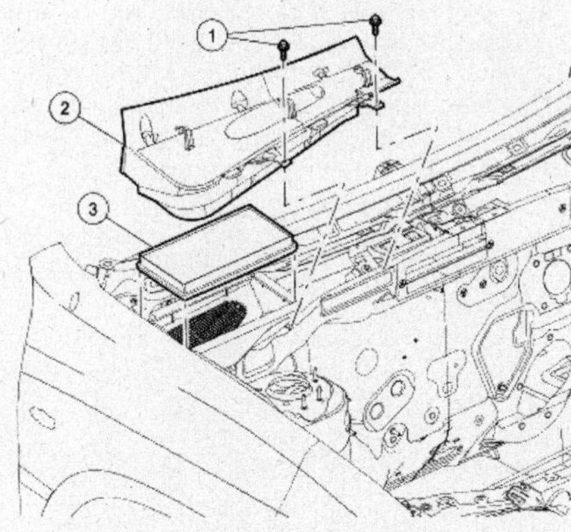

1. Water shield screws
2. Water shield
3. Cabin air filter

WCAF050000000026

Fig. 10 Water shields & cabin air filter replacement. 2005–06

2. Remove bolt and windshield wiper motor linkage.
3. Remove windshield wiper motor mounting bolts, then the wiper motor.
4. Reverse procedure to install.

Rear

1. Lift pivot arm to upright position, then slide wiper arm locking tab out.
2. Pull up and remove pivot arm.
3. Remove rear wiper motor shaft nut cover, then the shaft nut.
4. Open liftgate.
5. Remove rear wiper motor plastic cover.
6. Disconnect wiper motor electrical connector, remove mounting nut and bolt, then the rear wiper motor.
7. Reverse procedure to install.

WIPER SWITCH

REPLACE

1. Remove steering column shroud.
2. Remove wiper switch mounting screws and electrical connector, then the wiper switch.
3. Reverse procedure to install.

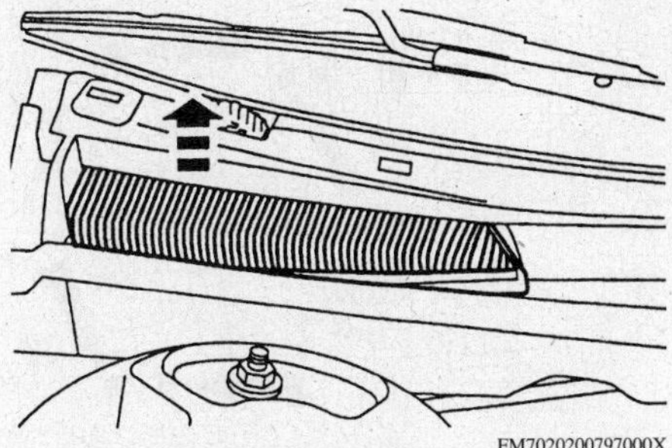

Fig. 8 Cabin air filter removal. 2002–04

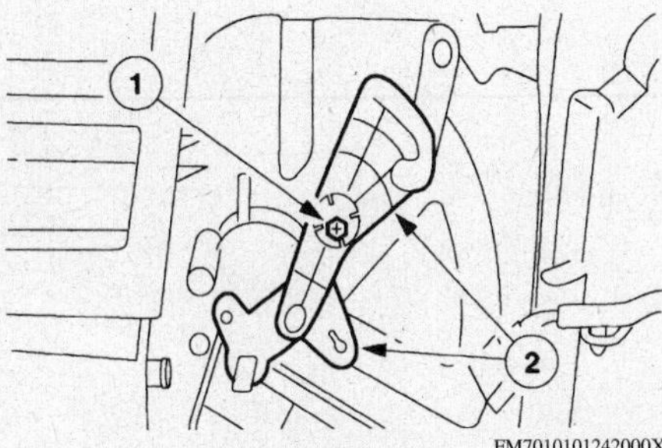

Fig. 11 Blending door lever replacement

WIPER TRANSMISSION

REPLACE

1. Remove wiper pivot arms.
2. Remove driver and passenger side cowl pin type retainers, screws and caps, then the cowl grilles.
3. Disconnect wiper motor electrical connector.
4. Remove wiper mounting arm and pivot shaft mounting bolts, **Fig. 6.**
5. Remove wiper motor mounting arm and pivot shaft assembly.
6. Reverse procedure to install.

BLOWER MOTOR

REPLACE

1. Remove righthand A-pillar trim panel.
2. Disconnect blower motor electrical connector.
3. Remove attaching screws, then the blower motor and cover.
4. Reverse procedure to install.

CABIN AIR FILTER

REPLACE

2002–04

Under normal operating conditions the cabin air filter should be replaced 15,000 miles. In dusty areas change the cabin air filter more often.

1. Open the hood.
2. Remove four caps from righthand side cowl cover retaining screws.
3. Remove four righthand side cowl cover retaining screws and four pin type retainers, then the cover, **Fig. 7.**
4. Pull rain shield rain up and out from cowl.

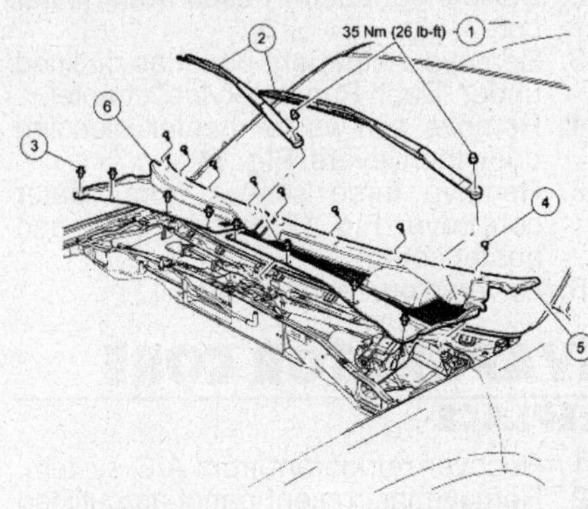

1. Wiper pivot arm nuts
2. Wiper pivot arms
3. Pin-type retainers
4. Cowl panel grille caps and screws LH cowl panel grille
5. RH cowl panel grille

WCAF050000000027

Fig. 9 Cowl panel removal. 2005–06

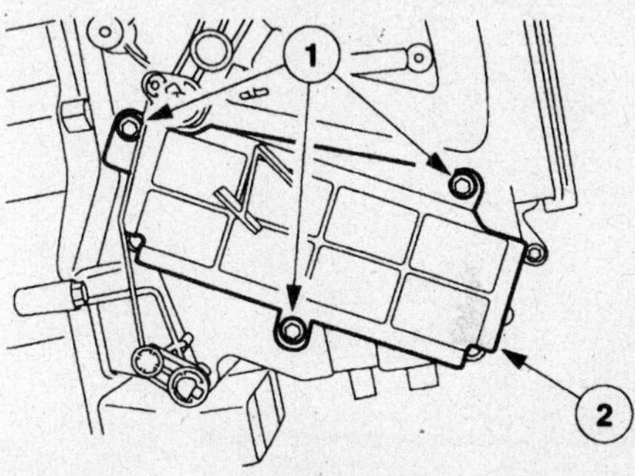

Fig. 12 Heater core cover removal

5. Remove cabin air filter element from filter housing, **Fig. 8.**
6. Position new cabin air filter element into filter housing. Ensure filter element is properly seated in housing.
7. Install rain shield. Ensure rain shield retaining clips are properly engaged.
8. Install righthand side cowl cover and secure with screws and retainers.
9. Close hood.

2005–06

Under normal operating conditions the cabin air filter should be replaced 15,000 miles. In dusty areas change the cabin air filter more often.

1. Remove two wiper pivot arms nuts, cowl panel grille pin-type retainers and cowl panel grille pin-type retainers, **Fig. 9.**
2. Remove lefthand and righthand wiper pivot arms and cowls, **Fig. 9.**
3. Remove two water shield screws and water shield, **Fig. 10.**
4. Remove cabin air filter, **Fig. 10.**
5. Reverse procedure to install.

HEATER CORE

REPLACE

1. Drain coolant into suitable container.

2. Disconnect heater hoses from heater core.
3. Remove instrument panel as outlined under "Dash Panel Service" chapter.
4. Remove screws for heater blending door, then levers, **Fig. 11.**
5. Remove three screws from heater core cover, **Fig. 12,** then the cover and heater core.
6. Reverse procedure to install.

EVAPORATOR CORE

REPLACE

1. Recover refrigerant from A/C system.
2. Remove instrument panel as outlined in "Dash Panel Service" chapter.

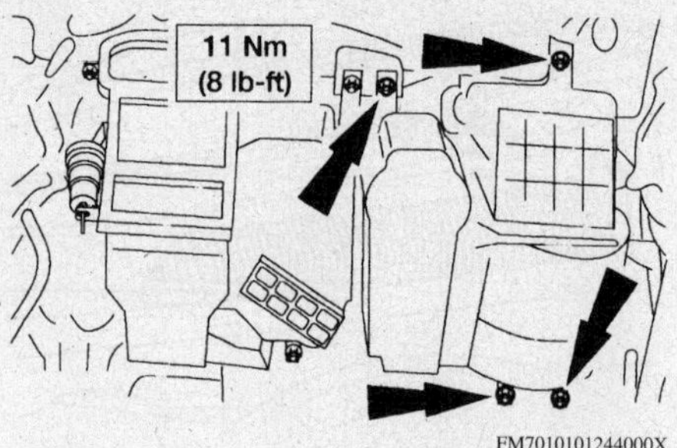

Fig. 13 Evaporator core housing nuts

3. Disconnect refrigerant line spring lock couplings from A/C evaporator core.
4. Disconnect vacuum line from evaporator core.
5. Remove mounting nuts, **Fig. 13,** then carefully remove evaporator core housing to avoid spilling refrigerant oil in passenger area.
6. Reverse procedure to install, noting the following:
   a. Feed vacuum hose through opening in cowl while installing housing.
   b. Before installing temperature control cable, ensure blend door, cable and temperature switch are properly positioned.

2.0L Engine

NOTE: On Air Bag Equipped Models, Refer To "Air Bag System Precautions" Located In The Front Of This Manual For System Disarming & Arming Procedures.

NOTE: Refer To "Computer Relearn Procedures" Located In The Front Of This Manual When Battery Power To The Computer Has Been Interrupted.

INDEX

PRECAUTIONS

Air Bag Systems

Refer to "Air Bag System Precautions" in the front of this manual for system disarming and arming procedures.

Battery Ground Cable

Prior to service, disconnect battery ground cable and isolate as required.

Fuel System Pressure Relief

1. Remove fuel pump relay from lefthand engine compartment relay panel.
2. Start engine and allow to run until engine stalls out.
3. After engine stalls, crank engine over two or three more times to ensure all fuel pressure has been released.
4. Turn ignition switch to Off position and install fuel pump relay.

COMPRESSION TEST

1. Remove fuel pump relay, start engine and allow to stall.
2. Remove spark plugs.
3. Install compression tester.
4. Install auxiliary starter switch.
5. With ignition switch in Off position, crank engine a minimum of five compression strokes and record highest reading.
6. Repeat test on all cylinders, cranking the engine the same amount of compression strokes.
7. The recorded compression pressures are considered within specification if lowest cylinder is within 75% of highest cylinder.
8. After test is complete, reset PCM.

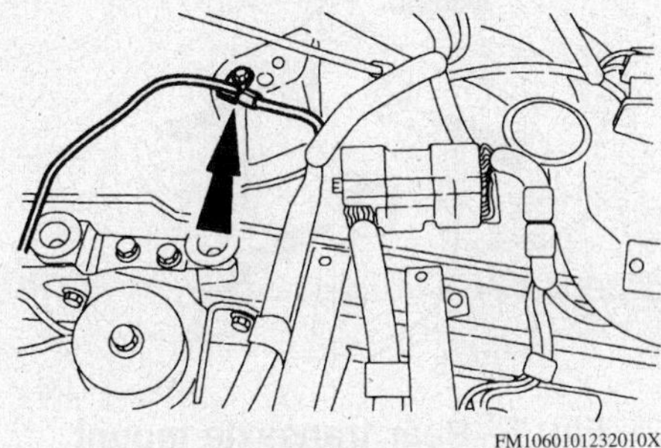

Fig. 1 Wire & connector removal (Part 1 of 3)

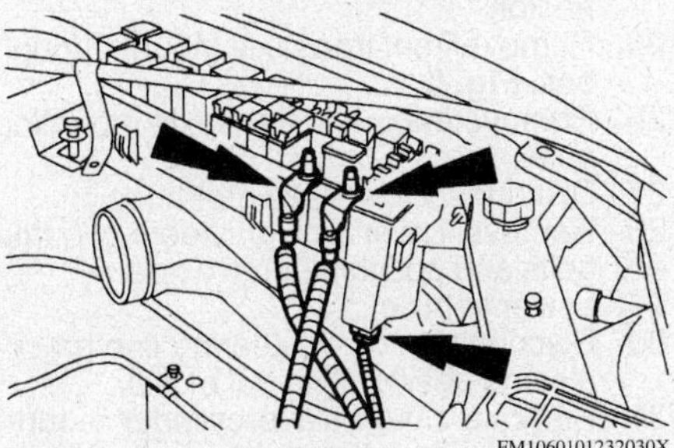

Fig. 1 Wire & connector removal (Part 3 of 3)

ENGINE MOUNT

REPLACE

1. Install engine support tool No. 303-F072, or equivalent, to support engine assembly.

Fig. 1 Wire & connector removal (Part 2 of 3)

2. Disconnect ground strap from engine mount.
3. Remove engine mount upper bracket.
4. Disconnect ground strap from power steering line bracket.
5. Remove power steering line bracket and set aside.
6. Remove three mounting bolts, then the motor mount.
7. Reverse procedure to install.

ENGINE

REPLACE

1. Remove hood.
2. Release fuel system pressure as outlined under "Fuel System Pressure Relief."
3. Remove battery tray and air cleaner assembly.
4. Drain engine coolant into suitable container.
5. Recover A/C refrigerant as outlined in "Air Conditioning" chapter.
6. Disconnect fuel line using a suitable fuel line removal tool.

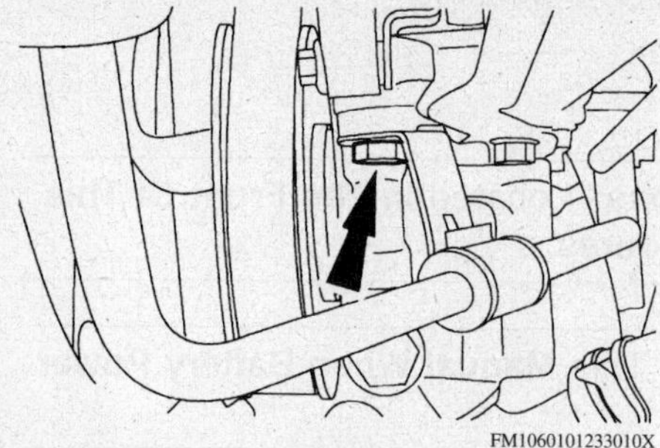

Fig. 2 Power steering line & pump bolts (Part 1 of 3)

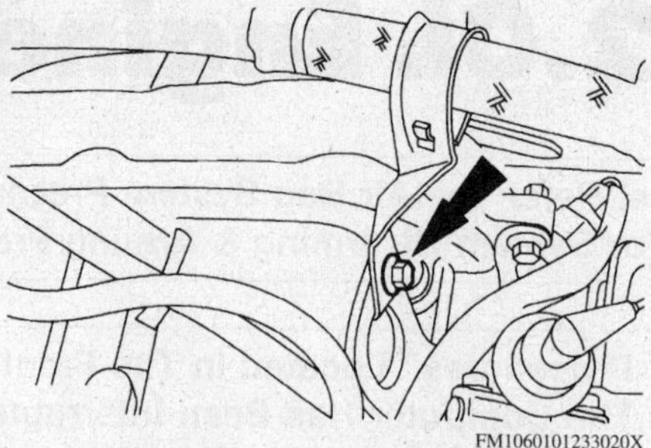

Fig. 2 Power steering line & pump bolts (Part 2 of 3)

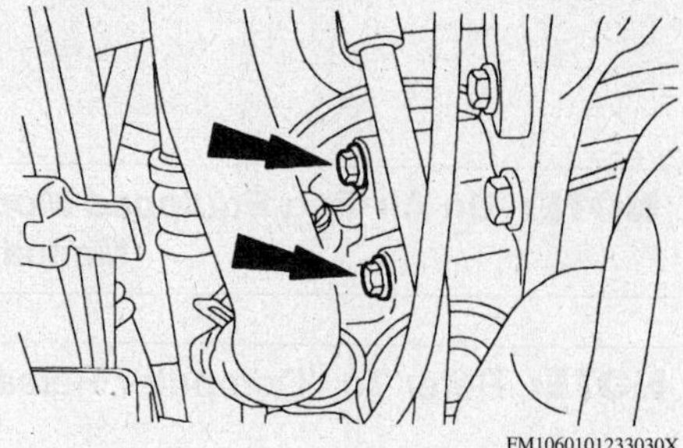

Fig. 2 Power steering line & pump bolts (Part 3 of 3)

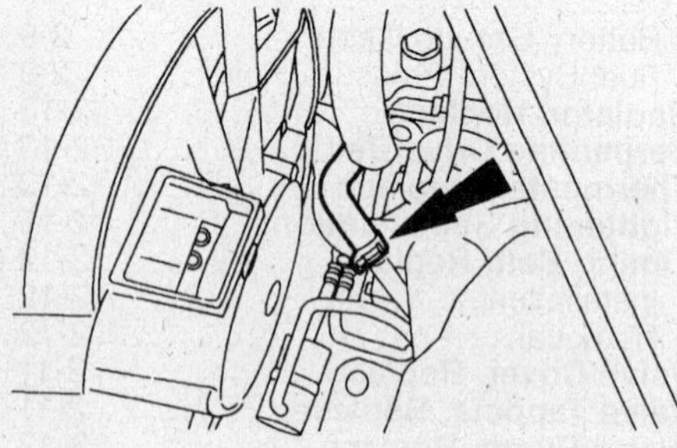

Fig. 3 Coolant hose location

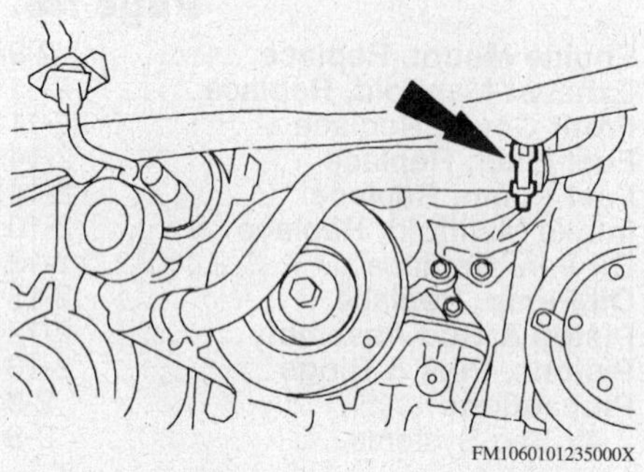

Fig. 4 Coolant hose location

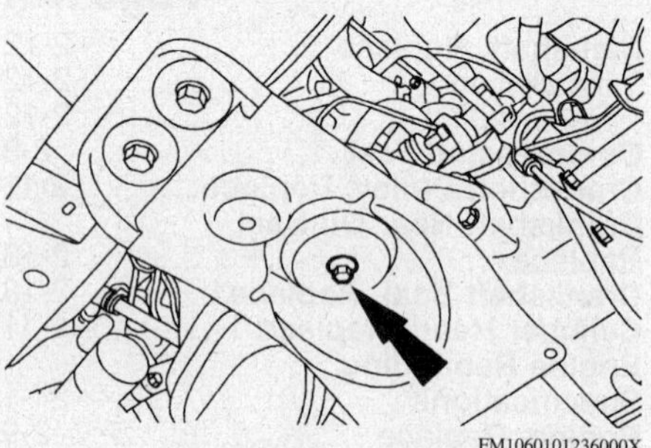

Fig. 5 Transaxle mount through bolt

Fig. 6 Lefthand transaxle mount

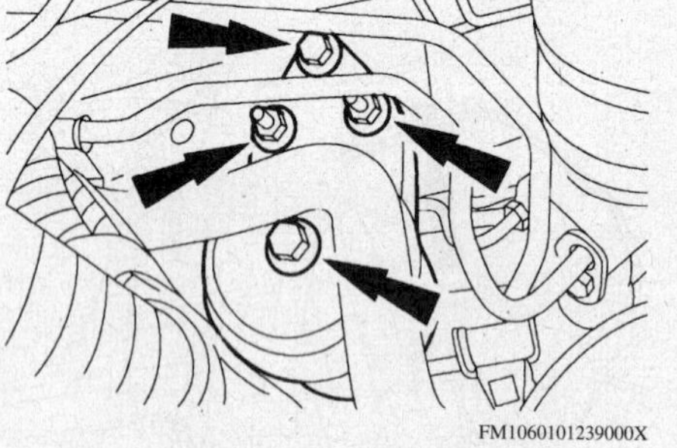

Fig. 7 Rear transaxle mount

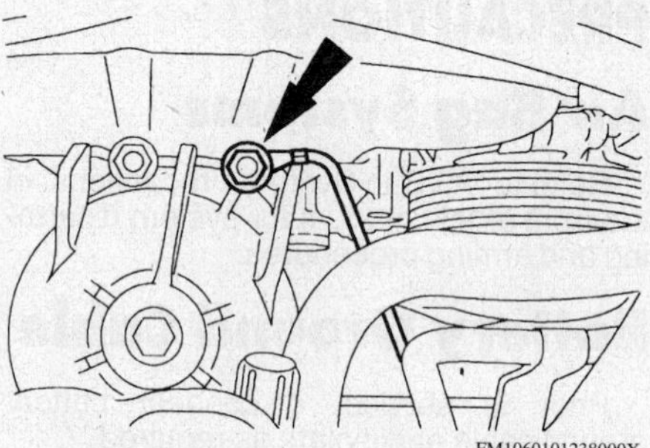

Fig. 8 Ground cable location

7. Disconnect throttle and speed control cables.
8. Disconnect EGR valve electrical connector and hoses.
9. Disconnect brake booster vacuum supply hose.
10. Disconnect powertrain control module wire harness and ground.
11. Disconnect ground wire, wire harness connector and power distribution box electrical connectors, **Fig. 1.**
12. Disconnect vacuum lines at evaporative emission canister.
13. Disconnect upper radiator hose.
14. Disconnect power steering line bracket bolts and upper power steering pump bolts, **Fig. 2.**
15. Disconnect coolant hose, **Fig. 3.**
16. Disconnect both heater hoses from heater core.
17. Remove speed control unit and position aside.
18. Remove catalytic converter.
19. Disconnect coolant hose, **Fig. 4.**
20. Remove A/C compressor.
21. Raise and support vehicle.
22. Remove halfshafts as outlined in "Front Wheel Drive Axles" chapter.
23. Remove halfshafts from transmission.
24. Disconnect block heater electrical connector.
25. Remove front transaxle mount through bolt, **Fig. 5.**
26. Remove engine to transaxle mounting bolts.
27. Disconnect lower radiator hose.
28. Remove lower power steering pump bolts and position pump aside.
29. Lower vehicle.
30. Disconnect power steering line brackets and position line out of way.
31. Remove clutch slave cylinder mounting bolts, then the clutch slave cylinder line from bracket and position slave cylinder aside.
32. Support engine with a suitable lifting device.
33. Remove rear transaxle mount and lefthand transaxle mount, **Figs. 6 and 7.**
34. Disconnect ground cable, **Fig. 8.**
35. Remove engine mount upper bracket.
36. Install suitable engine lifting device, then lift engine and transaxle from vehicle as an assembly.
37. Reverse procedure to install.

INTAKE MANIFOLD

REPLACE

1. Relieve fuel pressure as outlined under "Fuel System Pressure Relief."
2. Disconnect throttle position electrical connector.
3. Disconnect idle air control electrical connector, then unclip harness from bracket.
4. Disconnect main engine control sensor wiring and remove connector from mounting bracket.
5. Disconnect powertrain control module wire harness from bracket.
6. Disconnect brake booster vacuum supply hose and any remaining vacuum lines on intake manifold. Mark location of lines for installation reference.
7. Disconnect PCV vacuum line.
8. Disconnect knock sensor electrical connector.
9. Remove alternator.
10. Remove intake manifold bolts in sequence, **Fig. 9.**
11. Remove intake manifold.
12. Inspect intake manifold gaskets, replace as required.

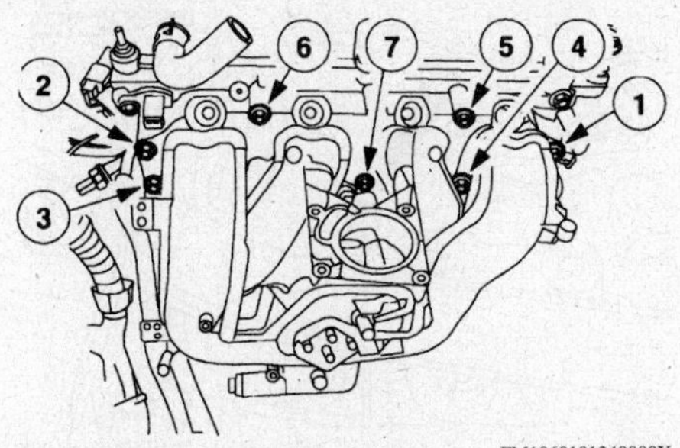

Fig. 9 Intake manifold bolt removal sequence

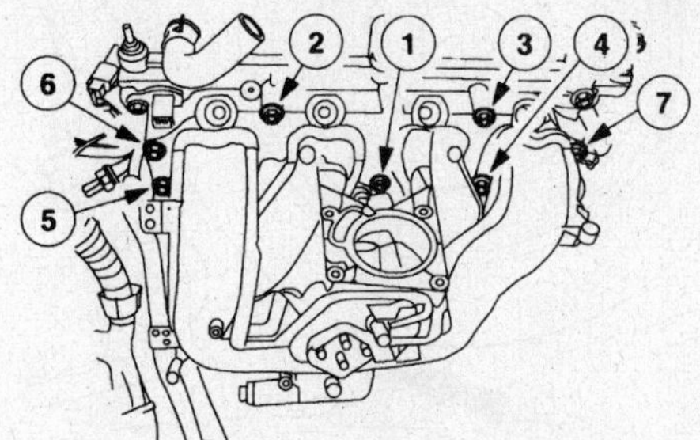

Fig. 10 Intake manifold bolt tightening sequence

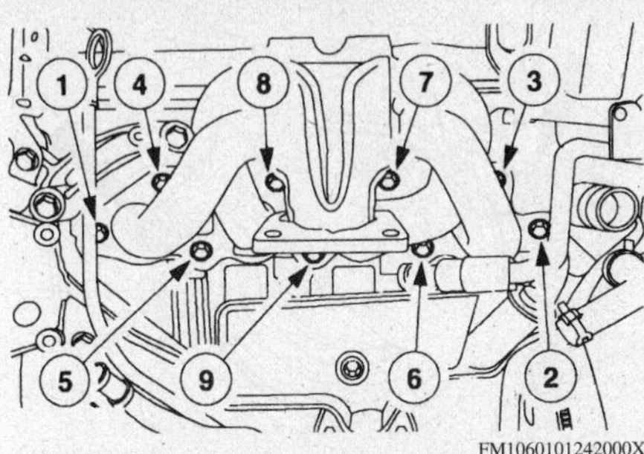

Fig. 11 Exhaust manifold bolt removal sequence

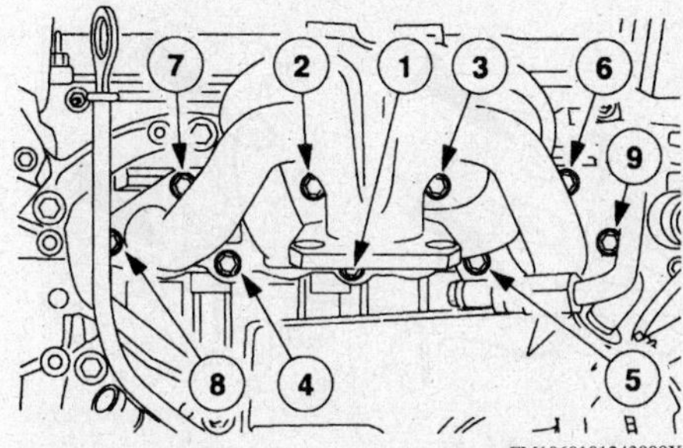

Fig. 12 Exhaust manifold bolt tightening sequence

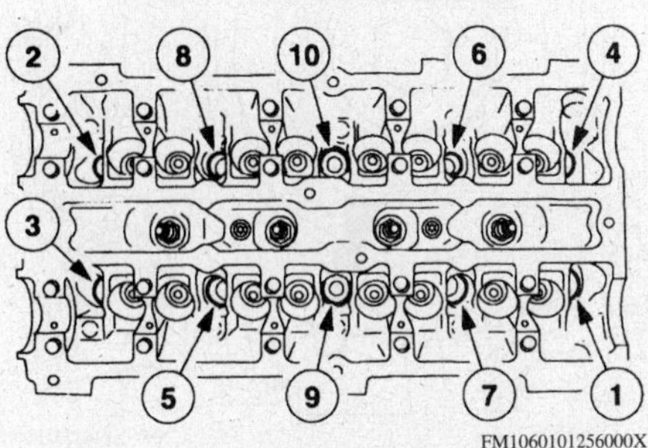

Fig. 13 Cylinder head bolt removal sequence

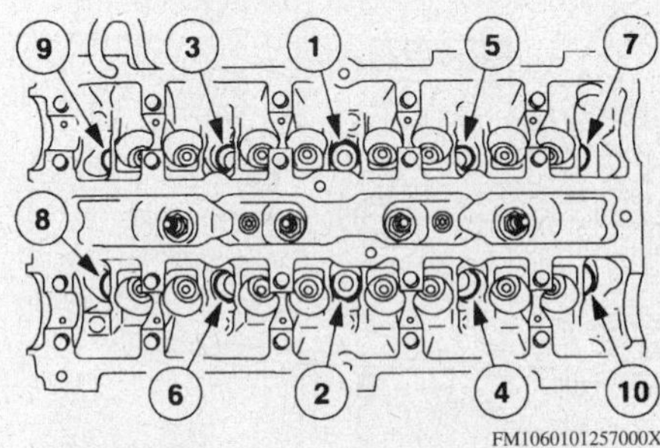

Fig. 14 Cylinder had bolt tightening sequence

13. Reverse procedure to install, tighten bolts in sequence, **Fig. 10,** to specification.

EXHAUST MANIFOLD

REPLACE

Do not work on aluminum engine components until engine is cold or damage to components may occur.

1. Raise and support vehicle.
2. Remove catalytic converter, then lower vehicle.
3. Remove oil dipstick and tube bracket bolt.
4. Remove nuts and bolts in sequence, **Fig. 11,** then the exhaust manifold.
5. Discard exhaust manifold gasket.
6. Reverse procedure to install, tighten exhaust manifold bolts in sequence, **Fig. 12,** to specification.

CYLINDER HEAD

REPLACE

1. Remove ignition coil bracket, thermostat housing and PCV tube.
2. Remove intake manifold as outlined in "Intake Manifold, Repalce."
3. Remove exhaust manifold as outlined in "Exhaust Manifold, Replace."
4. Remove power steering bracket retainers and position aside.
5. Remove timing belt covers, then the timing belt as outlined under "Timing Belt, Replace."
6. Remove valve tappets as outlined under "Valve Tappets, Replace."
7. Raise and support vehicle.
8. Install lower engine mount bracket that was removed.
9. Lower vehicle, install engine mount upper bracket.
10. Remove engine support tool installed during timing belt removal procedure.
11. Remove cylinder head bolts in sequence, **Fig. 13,** then the cylinder head.
12. Reverse procedure to install, noting the following:
    a. Cylinder head surfaces are soft metal. Do not use abrasive grinding discs to remove gasket materials, use only plastic scrapers. **Cylinder head bolts are torque to yield design, new bolts must be installed or damage to engine will occur.**
    b. Install new cylinder head gasket on cylinder block.
    c. Install cylinder head and tighten bolts in sequence, **Fig. 14,** in three stages.
    d. Stage 1: **Torque** bolts to 15 ft. lbs.; Stage 2: **Torque** bolts to 30 ft. lbs.; Stage 3: Tighten bolts an additional 90°.

VALVE COVER

REPLACE

1. Remove air cleaner outlet pipe.
2. Remove ignition wires from spark plugs.
3. Disconnect speed control actuator and accelerator cables.
4. Remove stud bolts and bolts, then the valve cover.
5. Inspect valve cover gasket and replace as required.
6. Reverse procedure to install.

VALVE TAPPETS

REPLACE

1. Remove camshafts as outlined under "Camshaft, Replace."
2. If camshafts and tappets are to be re-used, mark location of all components before removal.
3. Remove valve tappets from cylinder head bores.
4. Inspect tappets for excessive wear or damage, if excessive damage is noted, inspect camshaft lobes and journals. Replace components as required.
5. Reverse procedure to install, noting the following:
    a. Ensure valve tappets are installed in their original locations.
    b. Lubricate valve tappets with SAE 5W-20 motor oil, or equivalent, meeting Ford specification.

CRANKSHAFT PULLEY

REPLACE

1. Raise and support vehicle.
2. Remove righthand lower splash shield.
3. Loosen crankshaft pulley retaining bolt.
4. Remove accessory drive belt.
5. Remove crankshaft pulley bolt, then the crankshaft pulley.
6. Reverse procedure to install.

FRONT COVER

REPLACE

1. Raise and support vehicle.
2. Remove crankshaft pulley.
3. Remove bolts, **Fig. 15,** then the lower timing belt cover.
4. Lower vehicle.
5. Support engine with suitable engine support tool.
6. Remove ground strap and engine mount as outlined under "Engine Mount, Replace."
7. Remove motor mount studs.

Fig. 15 Lower timing cover bolt locations

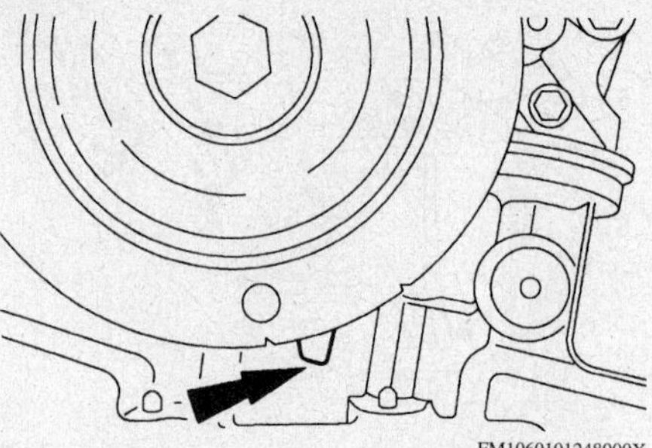

Fig. 16 Crankshaft pulley orientation

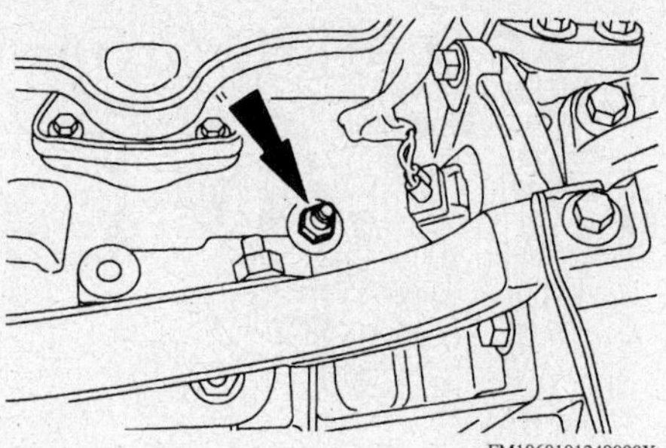

Fig. 17 Stud removal

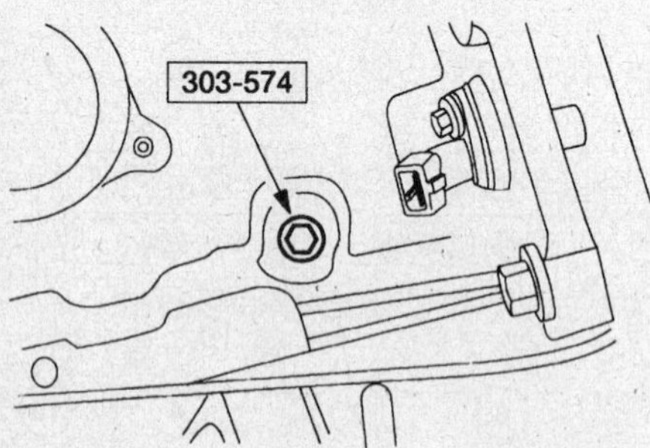

Fig. 18 Timing peg installation

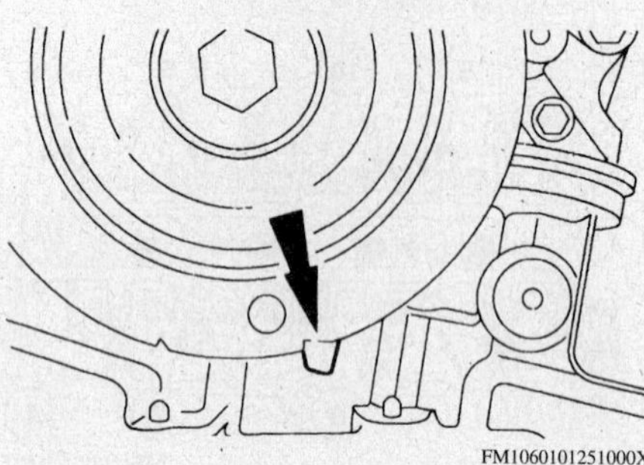

Fig. 19 Crankshaft pulley notch indexing

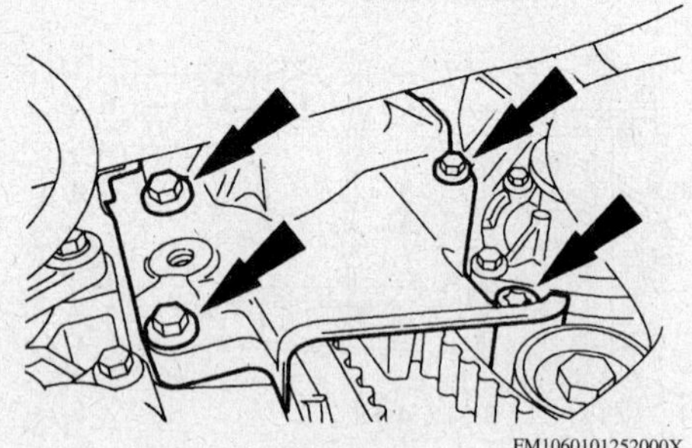

Fig. 20 Engine mount lower bracket

8. Remove bolts, then the upper timing belt cover.
9. Reverse procedure to install.

TIMING BELT

REPLACE

Removal

1. Remove valve cover as outlined under "Valve Cover, Replace."
2. Remove spark plugs.
3. Remove catalytic converter.
4. Remove coolant tube attaching nut and bolt, then position coolant tube aside.
5. Rotate crankshaft to just before top dead center of No. 1 cylinder, **Fig. 16.**
6. Remove stud, **Fig. 17.**
7. Install crankshaft TDC timing peg tool No. 303-574, or equivalent, **Fig. 18.**
8. Ensure second notch in crankshaft pulley, **Fig. 19,** is indexed to lower cylinder block.
9. Rotate crankshaft clockwise against peg tool to bring it to TDC for No. 1 cylinder.
10. Loosen water pump pulley bolts.
11. Remove front covers as outlined under "Front Cover, Replace."
12. Remove water pump pulley and accessory drive belt idler pulley.
13. Install camshaft alignment tool No. 303-465, or equivalent. Installation of alignment tool may require camshafts to be rotated clockwise slightly.
14. Raise and support vehicle.
15. Remove engine mount lower bracket, **Fig. 20.**
16. Loosen timing belt tensioner and allow to slide to bottom of it's travel.
17. If camshaft belt is to be reused, mark direction of rotation on belt prior to removal.
18. Slide timing belt off of camshaft and crankshaft sprockets.
19. Inspect for wear, replace as required.

Installation

1. Raise and support vehicle.
2. Slide crankshaft pulley onto crankshaft and confirm that crankshaft position is at TDC by rotating it clockwise against alignment peg.
3. Remove crankshaft pulley.
4. Lower vehicle.
5. Confirm that timing belt tensioner is installed correctly with tab positioned in slot in inner timing cover, **Fig. 21.**
6. Install timing belt onto sprockets, **Fig. 22.**
7. Rotate adjuster counterclockwise and align marks using a 6mm Allen wrench, **Fig. 23,** then tighten adjuster pulley bolt.
8. Raise and support vehicle.
9. Install front engine mount lower bracket.
10. Install accessory drive belt idler pulley.
11. Install water pump pulley, hand tighten bolts at this time.
12. Install timing belt covers, then tighten water pump pulley bolts.
13. Remove crankshaft TDC timing peg.
14. Install stud, **Fig. 17,** and coolant tubes.
15. Install catalytic converter.
16. Remove camshaft alignment timing tool.
17. Install valve cover and spark plugs.

CAMSHAFT

REPLACE

Removal

1. Remove timing belt as outlined under "Timing Belt, Replace."
2. Remove camshaft timing sprockets.
3. Verify valve clearance.
4. Loosen camshaft journal cap bolts in several two turn passes in sequence, **Fig. 24.**
5. Remove bolts, then the journal caps.
6. Inspect camshafts for wear or damage and replace as required.

Installation

Cylinder head camshaft journal caps are numbered on the outside flats to ensure they are reassembled in their proper order. Failure to place caps in their proper order may result in engine damage.

1. Front camshaft journal cap must be installed and tightened to specification within four minutes of applying sealer.
2. Coat sealing surface of front camshaft journal cap with Gasket Maker No. F8AZ-19B508-AB, or equivalent meeting Ford specifications.
3. Lubricate camshaft bearing surfaces with SAE 5W-20 motor oil, or equivalent.
4. Position camshafts and camshaft journal caps.
5. Install journal bolts and tighten in sequence, **Fig. 25,** in several two turn passes, to specification.
6. Verify valve clearance.
7. Install new camshaft front seals using camshaft seal replacement tool No. 303-464, or equivalent.
8. Install camshaft sprockets.

PISTON & ROD ASSEMBLY

PIP mark on pistons and squirt groove on connecting rods must be located on intake side of engine. The arrow on the piston must point toward the front of the engine.

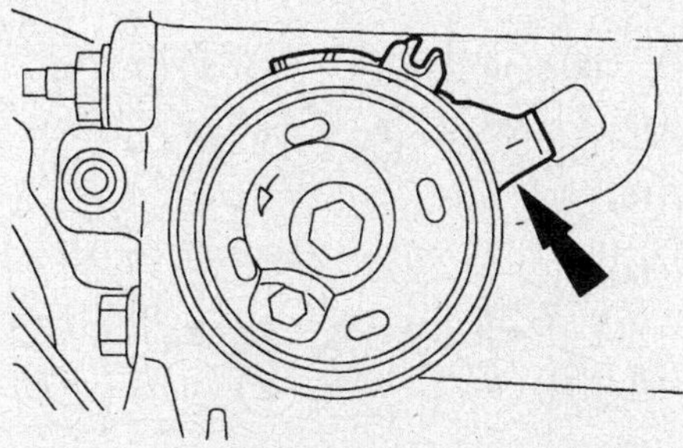

Fig. 21 Timing belt tensioner tab orientation

PISTONS, PINS & RINGS

Pistons and pins are a matched set and should not be interchanged. Pistons are precision fit and are divided into three categories within each size range based on their relative position within a range. A paint spot on the new piston indicates its position within the size range.

CRANKSHAFT SEAL

REPLACE

1. Remove timing belt as outlined under "Timing Belt, Replace."
2. Remove crankshaft sprocket and timing belt guide.
3. Remove front seal from oil pump using seal removal tool No. 303-409, or equivalent.
4. Reverse procedure to install.

CRANKSHAFT REAR OIL SEAL

REPLACE

1. **On models equipped with automatic transaxle,** remove transaxle as outlined in **MOTOR's "Domestic Transmission, In-Vehicle Service" or "Transmission Service DVD."**
2. **On models equipped with manual transaxle,** remove transaxle as outlined in **MOTOR's "Domestic Transmission, In-Vehicle Service" or "Transmission Service DVD."**
3. **On all models,** remove flywheel.
4. Remove crankshaft rear oil seal using oil seal removal tool No. 303-409, or equivalent.
5. Inspect rear crankshaft oil seal sealing surface for damage or excessive wear.
6. Reverse procedure to install, noting the following:
   a. Coat rear seal with SAE 5W-20 motor oil, or equivalent.
   b. Ensure rear seal is installed correctly and that edges of seal are not rolled over.
   c. Install rear oil seal, using seal installation tool No. 303-328 and oil seal pilot tool No. 303-329, or equivalents.

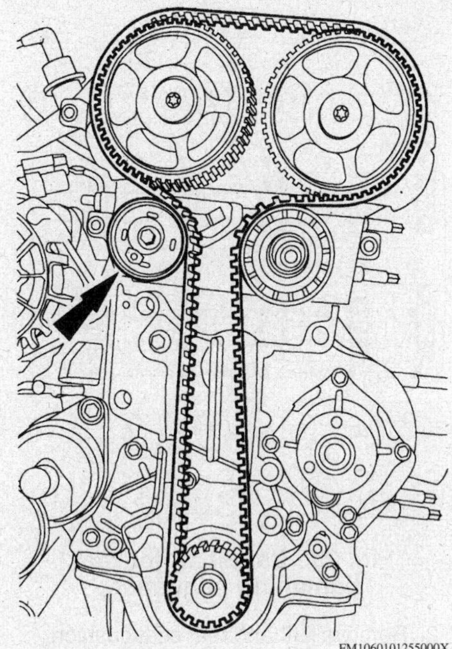

Fig. 22 Timing belt installation

OIL PAN

REPLACE

1. Remove catalytic converter.
2. Drain engine oil into suitable container, install drain plug.
3. Remove oil pan mounting bolts, then the oil pan.
4. Reverse procedure to install, noting the following:
   a. Do not use abrasive grinding discs to remove gasket material, oil pan surfaces are soft metal and damage may occur to surface.
   b. Clean and inspect sealing surfaces of oil pan and cylinder block with Metal Surface Cleaner No. F4AZ-19A536-RA, or equivalent.
   c. Ensure both surfaces are clean and dry.
   d. Oil pan must be installed within seven minutes of applying sealer.
   e. Apply a .1 inch bead of Silicone Gasket and Sealant No. F7AZ-19554-EA, or equivalent, to oil pan sealing surfaces.
   f. Install oil pan, tighten bolts in two stages, in sequence, **Fig. 26.**
   g. Stage 1: **torque** bolts to 53 inch lbs.; Stage 2: **torque** bolts to 91 inch lbs.

OIL PUMP

REPLACE

1. Remove oil pan as outlined under "Oil Pan, Replace."
2. Remove front timing covers, timing belt and sprockets as outlined under "Timing Belt, Replace."
3. Remove mounting bolts, then the oil pump assembly.
4. Remove and replace oil pump to cylinder block gasket.
5. Reverse procedure to install.

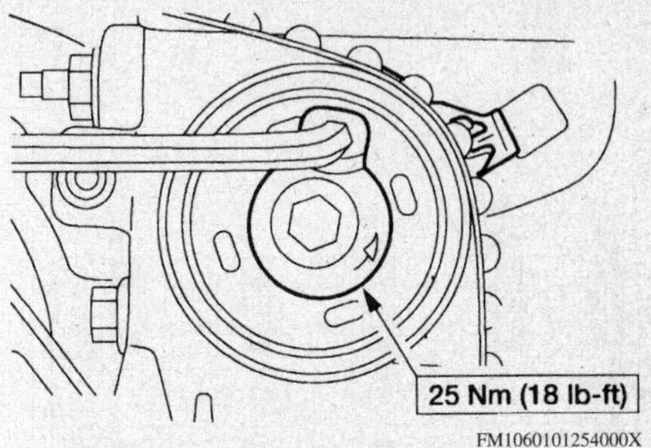

Fig. 23 Timing belt adjuster alignment marks

SERPENTINE DRIVE BELT

1. Raise and support vehicle, remove righthand front tire and wheel assembly.
2. Remove righthand front lower splash shield.
3. Rotate accessory drive belt tensioner clockwise, then remove accessory drive belt.
4. Reverse procedure to install.

THERMOSTAT

REPLACE

1. Drain engine coolant into suitable container.
2. Remove mounting bolts and separate water outlet adapter from thermostat housing.
3. Remove thermostat and O-ring.
4. Note that thermostat is indexed and must be installed with index marks aligned.
5. Reverse procedure to install.

WATER PUMP

REPLACE

1. Drain cooling system into suitable container.
2. Raise and support vehicle.
3. Remove righthand front tire assembly.
4. Remove splash shield.
5. Remove accessory drive belt and water pump pulley.
6. Remove water pump, clean and inspect sealing surfaces.
7. Reverse procedure to install.

RADIATOR

REPLACE

1. Raise and support vehicle.
2. Drain cooling system into suitable container.
3. Remove lower splash shields.
4. Disconnect lower radiator hose and degas return hose.
5. Lower vehicle.
6. Disconnect remaining coolant hose connections.
7. Disconnect upper radiator hose and degas supply hose.
8. Remove hood latch bolts and position latch aside.
9. Remove center support.

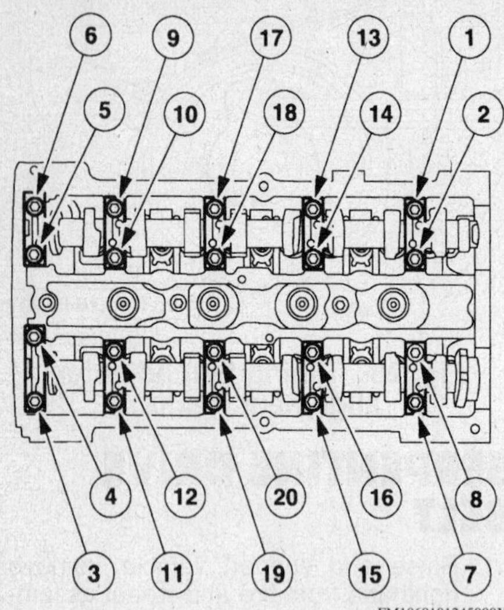

Fig. 24 Camshaft journal cap removal sequence

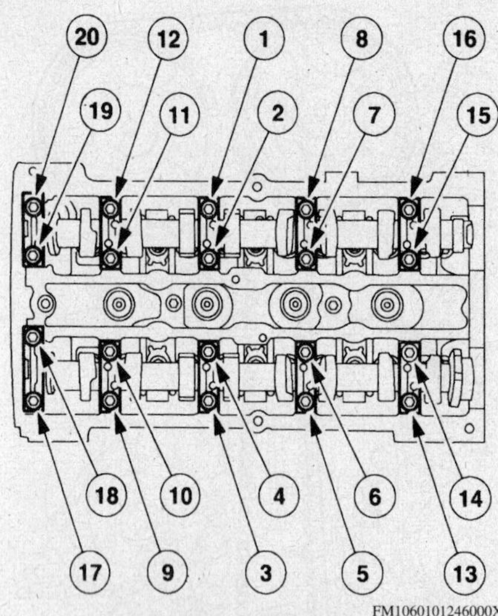

Fig. 25 Camshaft journal tightening sequence

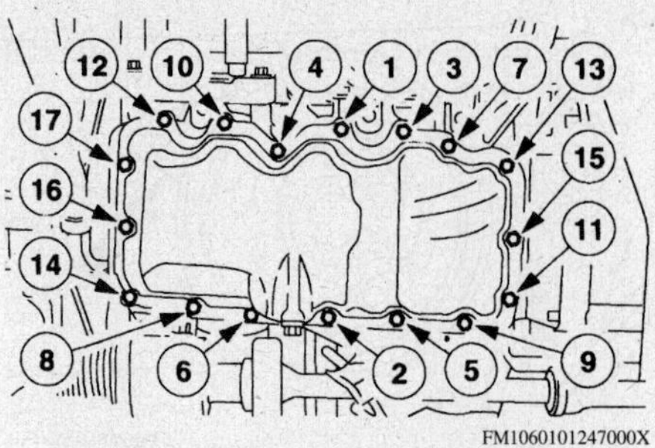

Fig. 26 Oil pan bolt tightening sequence

10. Remove upper bolts from cooling fan.
11. Remove upper radiator support brackets, then the radiator.
12. Reverse procedure to install.

FUEL PUMP

REPLACE

1. Relieve fuel system pressure as outlined under "Precautions."
2. Remove lefthand rear seat cushion.
3. Lift access cover on floor scuff plate, remove pin type retainers, then position carpet aside.
4. Remove fuel pump access cover.
5. Disconnect fuel pump electrical connectors.
6. Disconnect fuel vapor lines from fuel tank.
7. Remove gas cap.
8. Remove fuel pump module using fuel sender wrench tool No. 310-069 or equivalent, replace fuel pump mounting gasket.
9. Reverse procedure to install.

FUEL FILTER

REPLACE

1. Relieve fuel system pressure as outlined under "Precautions."
2. Place a suitable container under fuel lines, then disconnect fuel line to fuel filter.
3. Loosen clamp and remove fuel filter.
4. Reverse procedure to install.

TIGHTENING SPECIFICATIONS

Year	Component	Torque Ft. Lbs.
2002–04	A/C Compressor Bracket Bolts	18
	A/C Compressor Bracket Nuts	35
	Accessory Drive Belt Idler Pulley	35
	Alternator Bolts	33
	Alternator Lower Bracket Bolts/Nuts	35
	Alternator Upper Bracket Bolt	18
	Camshaft Cap Bolts	14
	Camshaft Sprocket Bolts	50
	Center Support	89③
	Cooling Fan To Radiator	89③
	Crankshaft Pulley Bolt	85
	Cylinder Head Bolts	①
	EGR Tube Bracket Bolt	46
	EGR Tube Nuts	46
	Exhaust Manifold Nuts And Bolts	12
	Engine Mount Lower Bracket Bolts	37
	Flywheel Bolts	83
	Front Transaxle Mount Through Bolt	66
	Hood Latch Nuts & Bolts	89③
	Intake Manifold Bolts/Nuts	13②
	Lefthand Transaxle Mount Bolts To Body	41
	Lefthand Transaxle Mount Bolt To Engine	66
	Lower Engine Mount Bracket Bolts	37
	Lower Engine Mount Bracket Studs	25
	Lower Timing Belt Cover Bolts	62③
	Oil Filter	12
	Oil Pan Drain Plug	18
	Oil Pump Screen Cover And Tube Bolts	89③
	Power Steering Pump Bolts	18
	Rear Transaxle Mount Bolts	41
	Starter Bolts	18
	Thermostat Housing Bolts	89③
	Timing Belt Idler Pulley	18
	Timing Belt Tensioner Bolt	18
	Valve Cover Bolts	80③
	Water Pump Bolts	89③
	Water Pump Pulley Bolts	89③

① — Refer to "Cylinder Head, Replace" for tightening procedure.

② — Refer to "Intake Manifold, Replace" for tightening procedure.

③ — Inch lbs.

2.3L Engine

NOTE: On Air Bag Equipped Models, Refer To "Air Bag System Precautions" Located In The Front Of This Manual For System Disarming & Arming Procedures.

NOTE: Refer To "Computer Relearn Procedures" Located In The Front Of This Manual When Battery Power To The Computer Has Been Interrupted.

NOTE: Refer To "High-Voltage Traction Battery Systems Depowering" Located In This Chapter Before Performing Diagnostics Or Repair On This Hybrid Vehicle.

INDEX

PRECAUTIONS

Air Bag Systems

Refer to "Air Bag System Precautions" in the front of this manual for system disarming and arming procedures.

Battery Ground Cable

Prior to service, disconnect battery ground cable and isolate as required.

High-Voltage Traction Battery Systems Depowering

The nominal high voltage traction battery (HVTB) voltage is 330 volts DC. The buffer zone must be set up. The high voltage traction battery and charging system contains high voltage components and wiring. High voltage cables and wiring are orange in color. High voltage insulated safety gloves and a face shield must be worn when carrying out any diagnostics on this vehicle. Failure to follow these instructions may result in severe personal injury or death.

Before carrying out any removal and installation procedures of the high voltage traction battery system, the high voltage traction battery must be depowered. The high voltage insulated safety gloves that are to be worn while working on the high voltage system should be of the appropriate safety and protection rating for use on the high voltage system. They must be inspected before use and must always be worn in conjunction with the leather outer glove. Any hole in the rubber insulating glove is a potential entry point for high voltage. Failure to follow these instructions may result in severe personal injury or death.

High voltage insulated safety gloves and a face shield must be worn when working with high voltage cables. The ignition switch must be OFF for a minimum of 5 minutes before removing high voltage cables. The buffer zone is required only when working with the high voltage system. Failure to follow these instructions may result in severe personal injury or death.

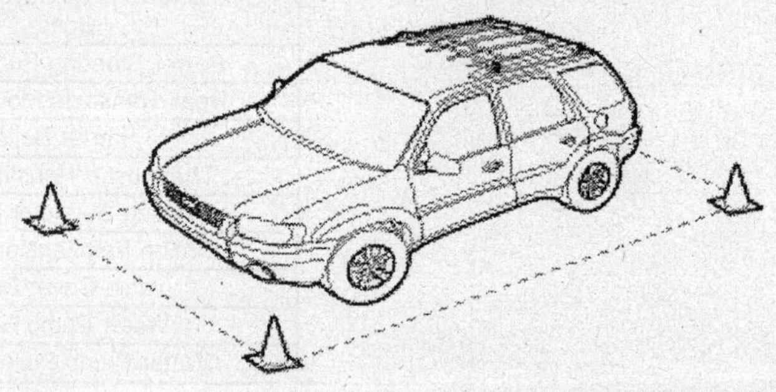

Fig. 1 Setting up a buffer zone

1. **Buffer zone is required only when working with high voltage system.** Set up buffer zone around vehicle as follows:
   a. Position vehicle in repair bay.
   b. Position four orange cones around corners of vehicle to mark off a 3 foot perimeter around vehicle, **Fig. 1.**
   c. Do not allow any unauthorized personnel into buffer zone during repairs involving high voltage system.
   d. Only personnel trained for repair on

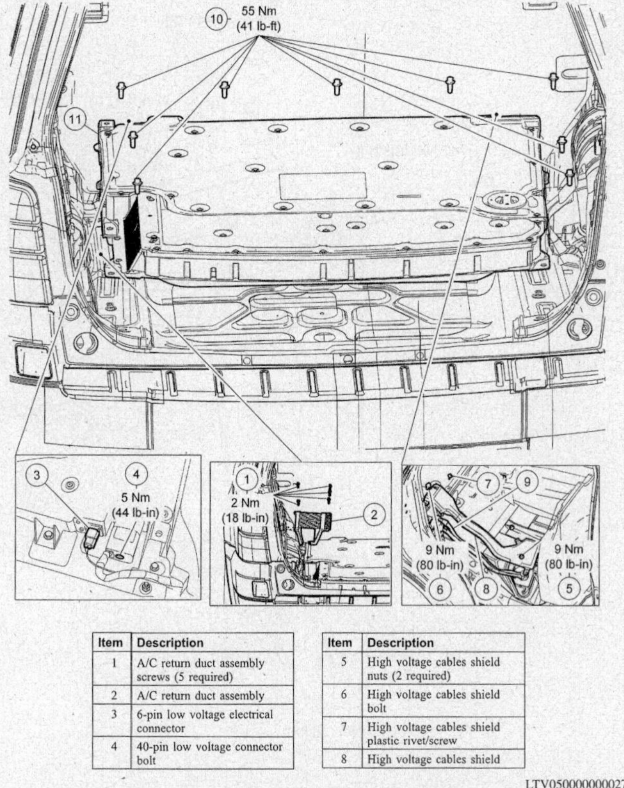

Item	Description
1	A/C return duct assembly screws (5 required)
2	A/C return duct assembly
3	6-pin low voltage electrical connector
4	40-pin low voltage connector bolt

Item	Description
5	High voltage cables shield nuts (2 required)
6	High voltage cables shield bolt
7	High voltage cables shield plastic rivet/screw
8	High voltage cables shield

LTV0500000000277

Fig. 2 Exploded view of high voltage traction battery (Part 1 of 2)

high voltage system are to be permitted in buffer zone.

2. Rotate service disconnect plug from lock position to unlock position.
3. Remove service disconnect plug, then place in servicing shipping position. **If service disconnect plug is left out and placed on bench or toolbox, dirt or other contaminants may enter HVTB which can cause damage.**
4. Insert service disconnect plug into servicing shipping position, this will disconnects HVTB.
5. Reverse procedure to connect.

Fuel System Pressure Relief

1. **On models except Hybrid,** remove fuel pump relay.
2. **On Hybrid models,** raise and support vehicle, then disconnect fuel pump driver module electrical connector.
3. **On all models,** start engine and allow to run until engine stalls out.
4. After engine stalls, crank engine for approximately five seconds to ensure fuel pressure has been released.
5. Turn ignition switch to OFF position.
6. **On models except Hybrid,** when fuel system service is complete, install fuel pump relay.
7. **On Hybrid models,** connect fuel pump driver module electrical connector.
8. **On all models,** it may take more than one key cycle to pressurize fuel system.
9. Cycle ignition key and wait three seconds to pressurize fuel system. Inspect for leaks before starting engine.
10. Start vehicle and inspect fuel system for leaks.

COMPRESSION PRESSURE

Except Hybrid

1. Ensure oil is of correct viscosity and at correct level, then operate vehicle until engine is at normal operating temperature.
2. Remove spark plugs.
3. Install compression tester.
4. Install auxiliary starter switch.
5. With ignition switch in Off position, crank engine a minimum of five compression strokes and record highest reading.
6. Repeat test on all cylinders, cranking the engine the same amount of compression strokes.
7. The recorded compression pressures are considered within specification if lowest cylinder is within 75% of highest cylinder.

Hybrid

The compression test requires cranking the engine a minimum of five compression strokes with the throttle plate in the wide-open position for each cylinder. The engine cranking diagnostic mode must be used to

Item	Description
9	High voltage cables electrical connector
10	High voltage traction battery bolts (9 required)
11	High voltage traction battery

LTV0500000000278

Fig. 2 Exploded view of high voltage traction battery (Part 2 of 2)

crank the engine and the brake/accelerator pedals must be used to position the throttle plate during the compression test.

The engine cranking diagnostic mode is a PCM strategy which is separate from the normal operating strategy. It allows the engine to crank in a similar fashion as a conventional vehicle with the fuel disabled. When in this mode, the PCM commands the TCM to spin the alternator, which cranks the engine with the speed between 900 and 1,200 RPM. The engine will crank as long as the traction battery state of charge (SOC) stays greater than 35%.

1. Ensure oil is of correct viscosity and at correct level, then operate vehicle until engine is at normal operating temperature.
2. Access traction battery control module (TBCM) and monitor traction battery SOC PID using Worldwide Diagnostic System (WDS) or equivalent.
3. If monitored PID displays SOC below 45%, start and idle engine with full A/C ON. When traction battery SOC exceeds 45%, engine cranking diagnostic mode can be activated.
4. Turn ignition switch to OFF position, then remove all spark plugs.
5. Install a compression gauge such as Compression Tester in No. 1 cylinder.
6. Apply parking brake, then place gear selector in PARK position. **Do not start engine.**
7. Turn key to ON position with engine OFF, then within five seconds of key in ON position, fully apply accelerator pedal and hold for ten seconds.
8. Within five seconds release accelerator pedal, then shift gear selector to NEUTRAL position and fully apply pedal.
9. Hold accelerator pedal fully applied for ten seconds, then release pedal and shift gear selector to PARK position.
10. If sequence is properly executed instrument cluster hazard indicator (red triangle) flashes once per second when gear selector is shifted to PARK position.
11. PCM exits engine cranking diagnostic mode when traction battery SOC drops below 35%, gear selector is shifted to any gear other than PARK or when ignition key is turned to OFF or ACC position.
12. **If ignition key stays in START position for 15 seconds or longer, PCM may set diagnostic trouble code**

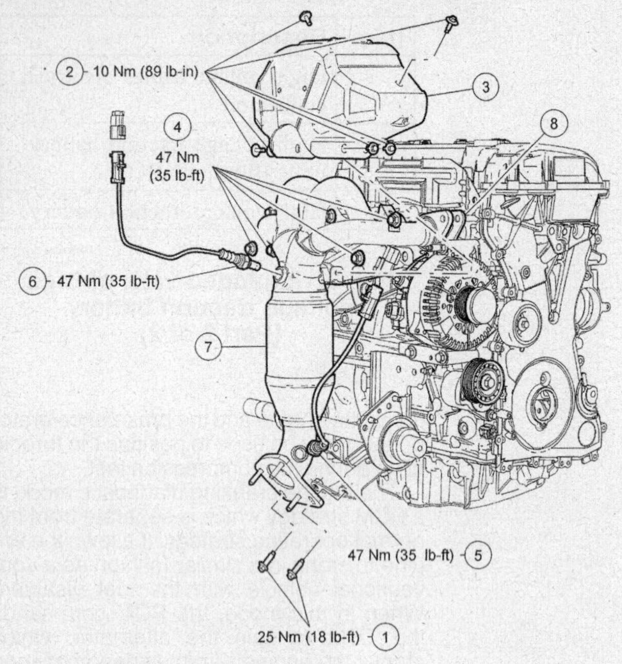

Item	Description
1	Catalytic converter bracket bolts (2 required)
2	Heat shield bolts (6 required)
3	Heat shield
4	Exhaust manifold nuts (7 required)
5	Catalyst monitor sensor
6	Heated oxygen sensor (HO2S)
7	Catalytic converter
8	Exhaust manifold gasket

LTV0500000000279

Fig. 3 Exploded view of exhaust manifold. Except Hybrid

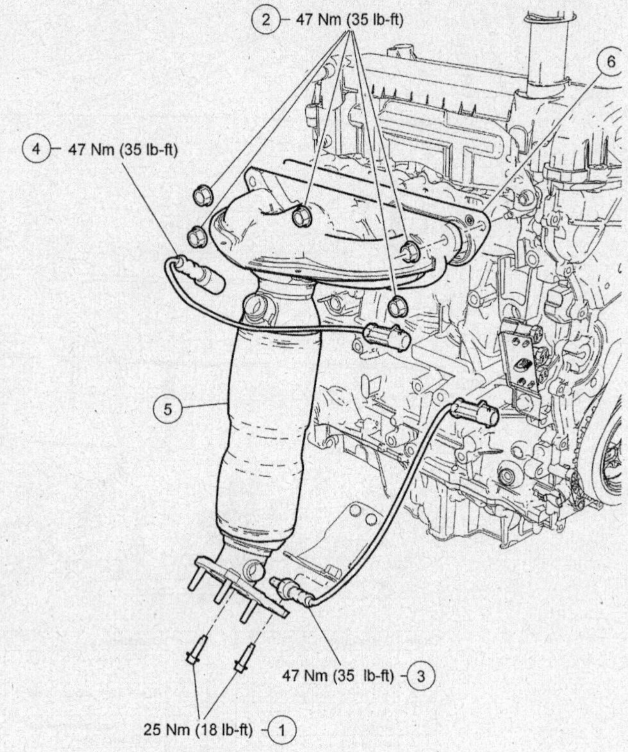

Item	Description
1	Catalytic converter bracket bolts (2 required)
2	Exhaust manifold nuts (7 required)
3	Catalyst monitor sensor
4	Heated oxygen sensor (HO2S)
5	Catalytic converter
6	Exhaust manifold gasket

LTV0500000000280

Fig. 4 Exploded view of exhaust manifold. Hybrid

(DTC) P2535. If brake pedal is not depressed and held prior to depressing accelerator pedal, throttle plate will fail to open.

13. Depress and hold brake pedal, then fully depress and hold accelerator pedal.
14. Turn key to START position and crank engine a minimum of five compression strokes, record highest reading and return key to ON position.
15. Release accelerator pedal, then the brake pedal.
16. Repeat test on each cylinder, cranking engine approximately same number of compression strokes.
17. Position key to OFF position to deactivate cranking diagnostic mode. Clear all DTCs.

ENGINE MOUNT

REPLACE

1. Raise and support vehicle, then drain cooling system into a suitable container.
2. Disconnect radiator to degas bottle hose from bottle, then the degas bottle to coolant bypass housing hose.
3. Remove retaining nuts, then bottle by lift up to disconnect bottle to radiator hose.
4. Install engine support tool No. 303-F072 or equivalent, to support engine assembly.
5. Remove engine mount bracket bolt, then raise engine .98 inch.
6. Remove remaining bolts, then the engine mount.
7. Reverse procedure to install.

ENGINE

REPLACE

Except Hybrid

1. Relieve fuel system pressure as outlined under "Precautions."
2. Remove battery tray and air cleaner assembly.
3. Drain engine coolant and engine oil into suitable containers.
4. Remove starter as outlined under "Starter, Repalce" in "Electrical" section.
5. Raise and support vehicle, then remove and discard exhaust catalytic converter and exhaust flexible pipe nuts.
6. Remove, then discard exhaust hanger and exhaust flexible pipe nuts.
7. Disconnect heated oxygen sensor and catalyst monitor sensor electrical connectors.
8. Remove bolts and righthand splash shield.
9. Rotate accessory drive belt tensioner clockwise and remove accessory drive belt.
10. Remove bolts and accessory drive belt tensioner.
11. Remove bolt, then press locking tab to release lower air duct from upper air duct.
12. Detach wire retainers from alternator shield, then remove nut and pin-type retainer and shield.
13. Remove halfshafts as outlined in "Front Wheel Drive Axles" chapter.
14. **On models equipped with automatic transaxle and 4WD,** remove transfer case as outlined under "Transfer Case" chapter.
15. **On models equipped with manual transaxle and 4WD,** remove bolts attaching driveshaft to transfer case and position driveshaft aside.
16. **On models less 4WD,** remove bolts

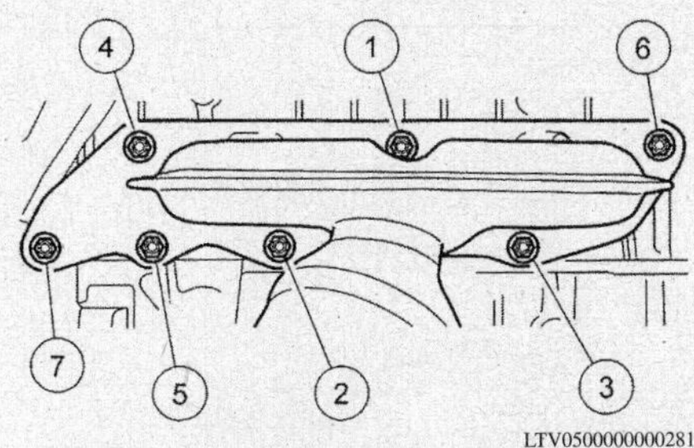

Fig. 5 Exhaust manifold nuts tightening sequence

and lateral support crossmember.

17. **On all models,** remove bolt and ground eyelet, then the power distribution box cover.
18. Remove nuts, then disconnect cables and electrical connector from power distribution box.
19. Remove bolt and disconnect ground strap and 42-pin electrical connector.
20. Detach wiring harness retainers from battery tray bracket and position wiring harness out of way.
21. **On models equipped with automatic transaxle,** proceed as follows:
    a. Disconnect transaxle electrical connector, then the shift cable from transaxle manual lever.
    b. Detach wiring harness pin-type retainer, remove bolts and position cable and bracket aside.
    c. Disconnect transmission range sensor electrical connector, then detach transaxle control harness from brackets.
    d. Disconnect front and rear transmission fluid cooler tubes, then the output shaft speed and turbine shaft speed sensor electrical connectors.
    e. Remove transmission fluid cooler retaining bracket bolt, then position fluid cooler tube aside.
    f. Remove bolt and OSS sensor, then detach transaxle control harness from retaining clip.
22. **On models equipped with manual transaxle,** proceed as follows:
    a. Disconnect clutch hydraulic tube fitting, then remove mounting bolt, detach spring clip and position tube aside.
    b. Remove retaining clips and disconnect transaxle control cable.
    c. Disconnect vehicle speed sensor electrical connector and pin-type retainer.
    d. Disconnect reversing lamp indicator switch and detach wiring harness retainers.
23. **On all models,** disconnect block heater electrical connector, then detach all block heater wiring harness retainers and position wiring harness aside.
24. Disconnect upper radiator and coolant vent hoses.
25. Remove nuts and coolant vent hose brackets, then position coolant vent hose aside.
26. Detach heater hose support strap from stud, then disconnect heater hoses from heater core.
27. Remove retainers and accelerator cable snow shield.
28. Disconnect accelerator and speed control cable from throttle body, then remove bolts from accelerator cable bracket.
29. Remove nut from the accelerator control cable bracket.
30. Remove nut from accelerator control cable bracket, then position accelerator control cable and bracket assembly aside.
31. Remove nut, then position power steering tube and bracket aside.
32. Disconnect vacuum supply tube, then the fuel vapor return tube, vacuum reservoir tube, fuel supply tube and retainer and position aside.
33. Detach electrical connector retainers, then disconnect powertrain control module connectors, remove nut and position harness aside.
34. Remove bolt and detach ground wire, then the power steering pump bolts.
35. Disconnect lower radiator hose from radiator, then the A/C compressor electrical connector and remove bolts and position A/C compressor aside.
36. Disconnect power steering pressure sensor electrical connector, **bolt under power steering pressure tube will remain with power steering pump.**

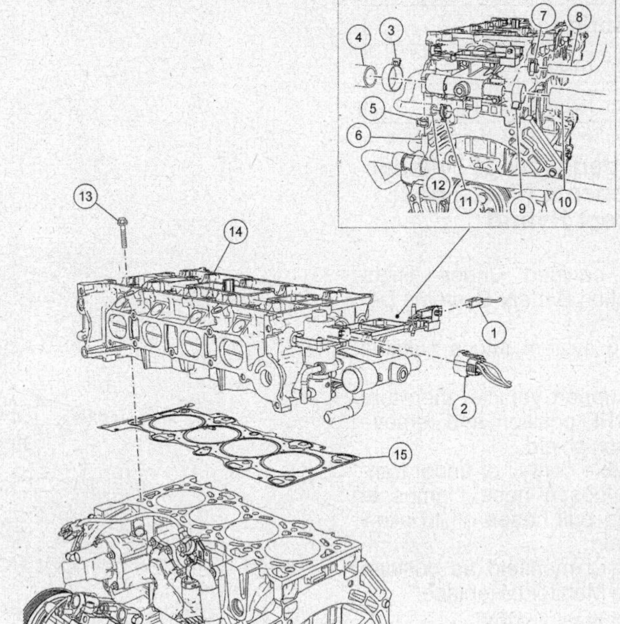

Item	Description
1	Radio ignition interference capacitor electrical connector
2	Exhaust gas recirculation (EGR) valve electrical connector
3	Upper radiator hose clamp
4	Upper radiator hose
5	EGR coolant tube clamp
6	EGR coolant hose (part of heater hose)

Item	Description
7	Engine coolant vent hose clamp
8	Engine coolant vent hose
9	Heater hose clamp
10	Heater hose
11	Bypass hose clamp
12	Bypass hose
13	Cylinder head bolt (10 required) (F7AZ-19554-EA)

LTV0500000000265

Fig. 6 Exploded view of cylinder head components (Part 1 of 2). Except Hybrid

37. Remove bolts and position power steering pump aside.
38. Remove front roll restrictor bolt, then bolts, nuts and engine support crossmember.
39. **Transaxle to engine bolts differ in length, match mark bolts for correct installation.** Remove transaxle to engine bolts.
40. Secure engine to lift table using engine support tool Nos. 014–00765 and 014–0001 or equivalents.
41. Remove engine mount bracket bolt, then the nuts and engine mount bracket.
42. Remove bolt from transaxle rear mount, then the lefthand transaxle mount.
43. Lower engine and transaxle from vehicle, then using engine crane and spreader bar, remove engine and transaxle from lift table.
44. Remove remaining engine to transaxle bolts, then separate engine and transaxle.
45. Reverse procedure to install.

Hybrid

1. Relieve fuel system pressure as outlined under "Precautions."
2. Disable vehicle high voltage electrical

Item	Description
14	Cylinder head
15	Cylinder head gasket

LTV0500000000266

Fig. 6 Exploded view of cylinder head components (Part 2 of 2). Except Hybrid

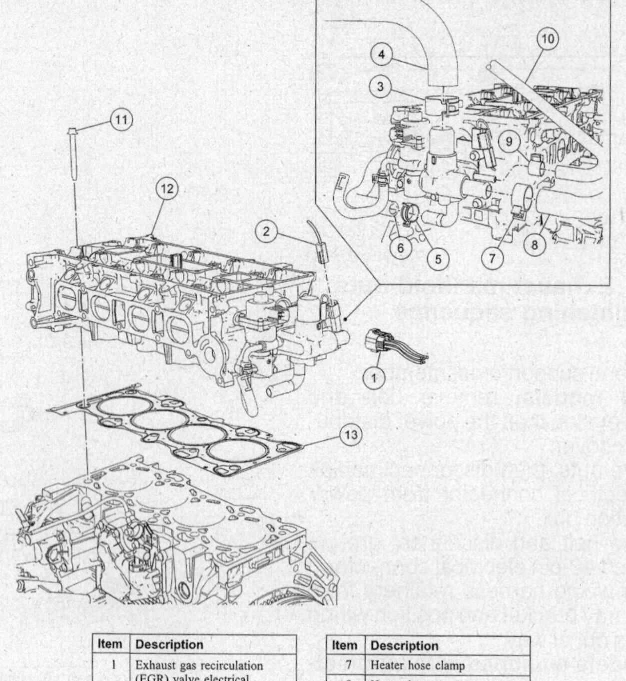

Item	Description	Item	Description
1	Exhaust gas recirculation (EGR) valve electrical connector	7	Heater hose clamp
2	Radio ignition interference capacitor electrical connector	8	Heater hose
3	Upper radiator hose clamp	9	Engine coolant vent hose clamp
4	Upper radiator hose	10	Engine coolant vent hose
5	Bypass hose clamp	11	Cylinder head bolt (10 required)
6	Bypass hose	12	Cylinder head
		13	Cylinder head gasket

LTV0500000000267

Fig. 7 Exploded view of cylinder head components. Hybrid

system as outlined under "High-Voltage Traction Battery Systems De-powering."

3. Drain cooling system into a suitable container.
4. Raise and support vehicle, then turn ignition to OFF position and remove lefthand splash shield.
5. Place a suitable container under transaxle, then loosen hose clamps at transaxle and pull hoses off to allow coolant to drain.
6. Remove intake manifold as outlined under "Intake Manifold, Replace."
7. Remove engine air cleaner.
8. Raise and support vehicle, then remove and discard exhaust catalytic converter and exhaust flexible pipe nuts.
9. Remove, then discard exhaust hanger and exhaust flexible pipe nuts.
10. Disconnect heated oxygen sensor and catalyst monitor sensor electrical connectors.
11. Remove and discard exhaust manifold nuts, then the catalytic converter from vehicle and discard exhaust manifold gasket.
12. Drain cooling system into a suitable container.
13. Disconnect radiator to degas bottle hose from bottle, then the degas bottle to coolant bypass housing hose.
14. Remove retaining nuts, then bottle by lift up to disconnect bottle to radiator hose.
15. Rotate accessory drive belt tensioner clockwise and remove accessory drive belt.
16. Remove halfshafts as outlined in "Front Wheel Drive Axles" chapter.
17. **On models equipped with 4WD,** remove transfer case as outlined under "Transfer Case" chapter.
18. **On models less 4WD,** remove bolts and lateral support crossmember.
19. Drain engine oil, then disconnect heater hoses from heater core.
20. Detach heater hose retaining clip from transaxle mount stud.
21. Disconnect upper radiator and coolant vent hoses, then electrical connectors from secondary air injection solenoid, transaxle mount control solenoid and purge valve.
22. Release powertrain control module connector and remove harness retaining nut.
23. Disconnect engine control harness electrical connectors and pin-type retainers.
24. Remove bolt and disconnect transaxle harness electrical connector.
25. Disconnect DC to DC converter electrical connector and pin-type retainer.
26. Disconnect and remove fuel supply tube and evaporative emissions tube.
27. Detach harness retainer clips, then route harness through radiator support into engine compartment.
28. Remove bolts and disconnect auxiliary coolant pump electrical connector, then position auxiliary coolant pump aside.
29. Remove bolts and transaxle control snow shield.
30. Release transaxle control cable from control lever, then remove nuts from transaxle control cable bracket.
31. Disconnect pin-type retainer and position the transaxle control cable aside.
32. Disconnect transaxle coolant temperature sensor electrical connector, pin-type retainer and transaxle coolant hoses.
33. Remove nut and ground cable, then the bolts and position motor electronics coolant pump aside.
34. Disconnect lower radiator hose from radiator, then the A/C compressor electrical connector and remove bolts and position compressor aside.
35. Remove front and rear roll restrictor bolts, then the nut, bolts and engine support crossmember.
36. Match mark bolts for correct installation, then remove transaxle to engine bolts.
37. **Due to weight of transaxle, mount powertrain securely to lift table,** using engine support tool Nos. 014–00765 and 014–0001 or equivalents, secure engine to lift table.
38. Remove nuts and engine mount bracket, then the righthand transaxle mount bracket nut.
39. Remove bolts and righthand transaxle mount bracket, then the bolt, nut and rear transaxle mount brace.
40. Remove nuts, bolt and rear transaxle mount, then lower engine and transaxle from vehicle.
41. Remove engine and transaxle from lift table using engine crane and spreader bar.
42. Disconnect high voltage wiring harness electrical connectors and position harness aside.
43. Remove remaining engine to transaxle bolts and separate engine and transaxle. **Due to packaging requirements correct bolt must be used at damper locations.**
44. **Damper contains a clutch which is designed to slip briefly during vehicle operation. It is essential that no grease, oil or cleaning solvents be allowed to contaminate slip clutch. Do not use grease on transmission input shaft. Should damper become contaminated, it must be replaced.**
45. Remove bolts and transaxle damper.
46. Reverse procedure to install.

HIGH VOLTAGE TRACTION BATTERY

REPLACE

The nominal high voltage traction battery (HVTB) voltage is 330 volts DC. The buffer zone must be set up. The high voltage traction battery and charging system contains high voltage components and wiring. High voltage cables and wiring are orange in color. High voltage insulated safety gloves and a face shield must be worn when carrying out any diagnostics on this vehicle. Failure to follow these instructions may result in severe personal injury or death.

Before carrying out any removal and installation procedures of the high voltage traction battery system, the high voltage traction battery must be depowered. The high voltage insulated safety gloves that are to be worn while working on the high voltage system should be of the appropriate safety and protection rating for use on the high voltage system. They must be inspected before use and must always be worn in conjunction with the leather outer glove. Any hole in the rubber insulating glove is a potential entry point for high voltage. Failure to follow these instructions may result in severe personal injury or death.

1. Disable vehicle high voltage electrical system as outlined under "High-Voltage Traction Battery Systems Depowering."
2. Remove rear cargo area carpet insert.
3. **When installing, tighten screws on HVTB first or an air flow loss to HVTB may occur.** Remove screws and A/C return duct assembly, **Fig. 2.**
4. Fold lefthand rear seat backrest down and disconnect 6-pin low voltage electrical connector.
5. Loosen bolt and disconnect 40-pin low voltage connector.
6. Fold righthand rear seat cushion forward, then remove two high voltage cables shield nuts. Access nuts through slotted opening in carpet.
7. Fold righthand rear seat backrest down and remove high voltage cables shield bolt, then the high voltage cables shield.
8. Press locking tab down, then rotate locking lever upward until aligning dowels are disengaged from locking lever to remove high voltage cables electrical connector.
9. **Attaching bolts have a conductive coating on them and are serrated under head flange. These features ground HVTB to vehicle, which is required for electro-magnetic compatibility. If a bolt(s) is lost or damaged, it must be replaced with identical type of bolt.**
10. Remove HVTB bolts. Two front lift points are eyelets on each front corner and rear lift point is beneath cap plug in center rear of HVTB.
11. Remove cap plug to expose center rear lifting attachment point, ensure to reinstall this plug during HVTB installation to avoid noise, vibration, and harshness issues.
12. Attach 3 M10 x 1.5 x 35 eyebolts to three HVTB lift points.
13. Ensure HVTB does not mar or damage interior panels during removal. There is only .23 inch clearance on each side and cover battery mounting brackets with protective padding.
14. Do not strike headliner with HVTB or floor crane during removal, then inspect HVTB tray drain grommet located in floor pan underneath HVTB. Replace it if required.
15. With an assistant, attach a chain or suitable lifting device to lift points and lift HVTB off 2 alignment dowels using a floor crane.
16. Remove HVTB from vehicle.
17. Reverse procedure to install.

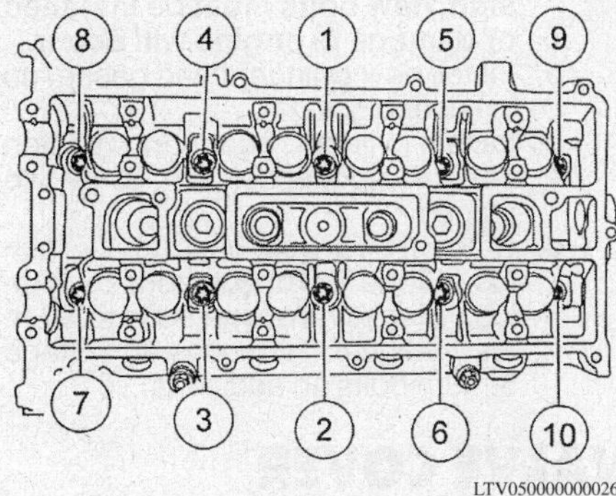

Fig. 8 Cylinder head bolts tightening sequence

INTAKE MANIFOLD

REPLACE

Except Hybrid

1. Relieve fuel system pressure as outlined under "Precautions."
2. Disconnect fuel supply tube quick connect coupling at fuel rail, then the fuel rail pressure and temperature vacuum tube and electrical connector.
3. Disconnect fuel injector electrical connectors.
4. Remove fuel rail bolts and detach wiring retainers from fuel rail, then the fuel rail and injectors as an assembly.
5. Remove fuel rail spacers, then fuel injector O-ring seals and discard seals.
6. Remove battery tray and air cleaner assembly and outlet pipe.
7. Remove upper snow shield, then detach accelerator and speed control cables from throttle body.
8. Disconnect throttle position sensor electrical connector, then remove bolts and throttle body.
9. Remove bolts and righthand splash shield, then bolts and oil dipstick tube.
10. Disconnect intake manifold vacuum hose and pin-type retainer, then position vacuum hose aside.
11. Disconnect power brake booster vacuum tube, then the fuel vapor return hose from intake manifold.
12. Remove bolts and position accelerator cable bracket aside, then disconnect idle air control motor electrical connector.
13. Disconnect swirl control valve and knock sensor electrical connectors.
14. Disconnect temperature manifold absolute pressure sensor and oil pressure sender electrical connector.
15. **Mark location of bolts to ensure they are installed in correct location.** Remove bolts and position intake manifold aside to access crankcase vent hose clamp and EGR tube.
16. Release clamp and disconnect crankcase vent hose, then remove exhaust gas recirculation tube.
17. Remove intake manifold and gaskets.
18. Reverse procedure to install.

Hybrid

1. Remove battery tray and air cleaner assembly and outlet pipe.
2. Disconnect coolant hoses from throttle body and plug coolant hoses.
3. Disconnect throttle body electrical connector, then remove bolts and electronic throttle body.
4. Relieve fuel system pressure as outlined under "Precautions."
5. Disconnect fuel supply tube quick connect coupling at fuel rail, then the fuel rail pressure and temperature vacuum tube and electrical connector.
6. Disconnect fuel injector electrical connectors.
7. Remove fuel rail bolts and detach wiring retainers from fuel rail, then the fuel rail and injectors as an assembly.
8. Remove fuel rail spacers, then fuel injector O-ring seals and discard seals.
9. Loosen clamp and disconnect the secondary air injection tube from air pump hose, then remove both splash shields.
10. Remove bolts and position motor electronics coolant pump aside, then disconnect AIR pump electrical connector.
11. Remove air pump, then the oil dipstick and tube.
12. Disconnect oil pressure sender, temperature manifold absolute pressure sensor, swirl control valve and intake manifold runner control actuator electrical connectors.
13. Disconnect block heater and knock sensor electrical connectors, then fuel vapor return hose from intake manifold and power brake booster vacuum tube.
14. **Match mark location of bolts ensure they are installed in correct location.** Remove bolts and position intake manifold aside to access crankcase vent hose clamp and EGR tube.
15. Release clamp and disconnect crankcase vent hose, then remove EGR tube.
16. Remove intake manifold and gaskets.
17. Reverse procedure to install.

EXHAUST MANIFOLD

REPLACE

1. Remove and discard exhaust catalytic

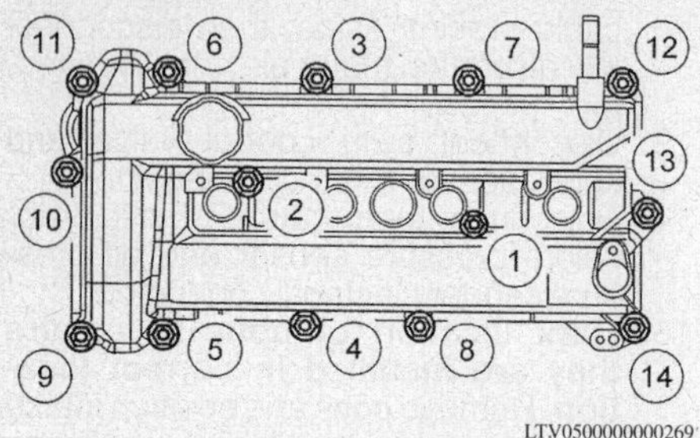

Fig. 9 Valve cover tightening sequence

converter and exhaust flexible pipe nuts, **Figs. 3 and 4.**

2. Remove exhaust hanger, then the exhaust flexible pipe and catalytic converter bracket bolts.
3. Remove heat shield bolts and heat shield,. **If installing a new converter, remove heated oxygen sensor and catalyst monitoring sensor for installation in new converter.**
4. Disconnect HO2S and catalyst monitoring sensor electrical connectors.
5. Remove exhaust manifold nuts, then the catalytic converter from vehicle. Discard exhaust manifold bolts gasket.
6. Reverse procedure to install noting the following:
   a. Inspect catalytic converter for warpage across manifold flange area.
   b. Position catalytic converter and tighten exhaust manifold nuts in sequence, **Fig. 5,** in two stages.
   c. Stage 1: **Torque** bolts to 47 ft. lbs.; Stage 2: **Torque** bolts to 47 ft. lbs.

CYLINDER HEAD

REPLACE

1. Relieve fuel system pressure as outlined under "Precautions."
2. Drain engine cooling system into a suitable container.
3. Remove camshafts as outlined under "Camshaft, Replace."
4. Remove Intake Manifold as outlined under "Intake Manifold, Replace."
5. Remove exhaust manifold as outlined under "Exhaust Manifold, Replace."
6. Disconnect radio ignition interference capacitor electrical connector.
7. Disconnect EGR valve electrical connector, then EGR coolant hose from valve.
8. Disconnect upper radiator hose, coolant bypass hose, heater hose and coolant vent hose from engine coolant outlet, **Figs. 6 and 7.**
9. Remove bolts and cylinder head, discard bolts.
10. Reverse procedure to install noting the following:
    a. Cylinder head surfaces are soft metal. Do not use abrasive grinding discs to remove gasket materials, use only plastic scrapers. **Cylinder head bolts are torque to yield design, new bolts must be installed or damage to engine will occur.**
    b. Install new cylinder head gasket on cylinder block.
    c. Install cylinder head and tighten bolts in sequence, **Fig. 8,** in five stages.
    d. Stage 1: **Torque** bolts to 44 inch lbs.; Stage 2: **Torque** bolts to 11 ft. lbs.; Stage 3: **Torque** bolts to 33 ft. lbs.; Stage 4: Turn bolts 90°; Stage 5: Turn bolts an additional 90°.

VALVE COVER

REPLACE

Except Hybrid

1. Disconnect ignition coil electrical connectors.
2. Remove bolts and ignition coils then disconnect crankcase vent hose.
3. Remove coolant vent tube bracket nuts, then position tube and brackets aside.
4. Disconnect camshaft position sensor and fuel rail pressure and temperature sensor electrical connector.
5. Disconnect cylinder head temperature sensor electrical connector, then the vacuum tube from intake manifold.
6. Remove accelerator cable bracket nuts, then position accelerator cable and brackets aside.
7. Remove power steering tube bracket nut, then position power steering tube and bracket aside.
8. Detach all of wiring harness retainers from valve cover studs and position harness aside.
9. Remove valve cover retainers, then the valve cover and gasket.
10. Reverse procedure to install noting the following:
    a. Clean and inspect sealing surfaces.
    b. Install valve cover, gasket and retainers.
    c. **Torque** retainers in sequence, **Fig. 9,** to 89 inch lbs.

Hybrid

1. Disconnect ignition coil electrical connectors.
2. Remove bolts and ignition coils.
3. Disconnect crankcase vent hose, then remove engine cover studs.
4. Disconnect camshaft position sensor and fuel rail pressure and temperature sensor electrical connector.
5. Disconnect cylinder head temperature sensor electrical connector.
6. Remove valve cover retainers, valve cover and gasket.
7. Reverse procedure to install noting the following:
   a. Clean and inspect sealing surfaces.
   b. Install valve cover, gasket and retainers.
   c. **Torque** retainers in sequence, **Fig. 9.**

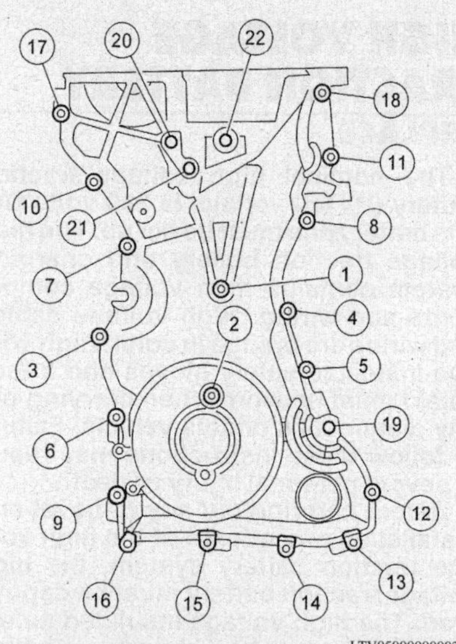

Fig. 10 Engine front cover tightening sequence

VALVE TAPPETS

REPLACE

1. Remove camshafts as outlined under "Camshaft, Replace."
2. If camshafts and tappets are to be reused, mark location of all components before removal.
3. Remove valve tappets from cylinder head bores.
4. Inspect tappets for excessive wear or damage, if excessive damage is noted, inspect camshaft lobes and journals. Replace components as required.
5. Reverse procedure to install, noting the following:
   a. Ensure valve tappets are installed in their original locations.
   b. Lubricate valve tappets with SAE 5W-20 motor oil, or equivalent, meeting Ford specification.

CRANKSHAFT PULLEY

REPLACE

1. Release tensioner and remove accessory drive belt.
2. Remove valve cover as outlined under "Valve Cover, Replace." **Failure to position No. 1 piston at TDC can result in damage to engine. Turn engine in normal direction of rotation only.**
3. Turn crankshaft clockwise to position No. 1 piston at TDC using engine crane and spreader bar using crankshaft pulley bolt. Hole in crankshaft pulley should be in 6 o'clock position.
4. **Camshaft timing slots are offset. If special tool cannot be installed, rotate crankshaft one complete revolution clockwise to correctly position camshafts.** Install special tool No. 303–465 or equivalent, in slots on rear of both camshafts.
5. Remove engine plug bolt, then install

holding tool Nos. 303–507, 205–072–02 and 205–126 or equivalents to crankshaft.
6. Remove crankshaft pulley bolt and washer, then the crankshaft pulley.
7. Reverse procedure to install noting the following:
   a. Install cylinder head and tighten bolts in two stages.
   b. Stage 1: **Torque** bolts to 74 ft. lbs.; Stage 2: Turn bolts an additional 90°.

FRONT COVER

REPLACE

1. Raise and support vehicle, then remove crankshaft pulley.
2. Remove crankshaft front oil seal using remover tool No. 303–406 or equivalent.
3. Remove bolts and coolant pump pulley, then the bolts and accessory drive belt tensioner.
4. **On models except Hybrid,** remove power steering pump retaining bolts and position pump aside.
5. **On all models,** disconnect CKP sensor electrical connector, then remove and discard CKP sensor.
6. Remove bolts and engine front cover.
7. Reverse procedure to install noting the following:
   a. Clean and inspect mounting surfaces of engine and front cover.
   b. Apply a .09 inch bead of silicone gasket and sealant to cylinder head and oil pan joint areas and front cover.
   c. Install engine front cover **torque** 8-mm bolts to 89 inch lbs., and 13-mm bolts to 35 ft. lbs., in sequence, **Fig. 10.**

TIMING CHAIN

REPLACE

1. Raise and support vehicle, then remove crankshaft pulley.
2. Remove crankshaft front oil seal using remover tool No. 303–406 or equivalent.
3. Remove bolts and coolant pump pulley, then the bolts and accessory drive belt tensioner.
4. **On models except Hybrid,** remove power steering pump retaining bolts and position pump aside.
5. **On all models,** disconnect CKP sensor electrical connector, then remove and discard CKP sensor.
6. Remove bolts and engine front cover.
7. Compress timing chain tensioner, then insert a paper clip into hole to retain tensioner, remove bolts and timing chain tensioner.
8. Remove righthand timing chain guides, **Fig. 11.**
9. Remove timing chain, **Fig. 12.**
10. Remove bolts and lefthand timing chain guide. **Do not rely on camshaft alignment plate to prevent camshaft rotation. Damage to tool or camshaft can occur.**
11. Remove bolts and camshaft sprockets, use flats on camshaft to prevent camshaft rotation.
12. Reverse procedure to install. **Torque** front cover in sequence as in **Fig. 10.**

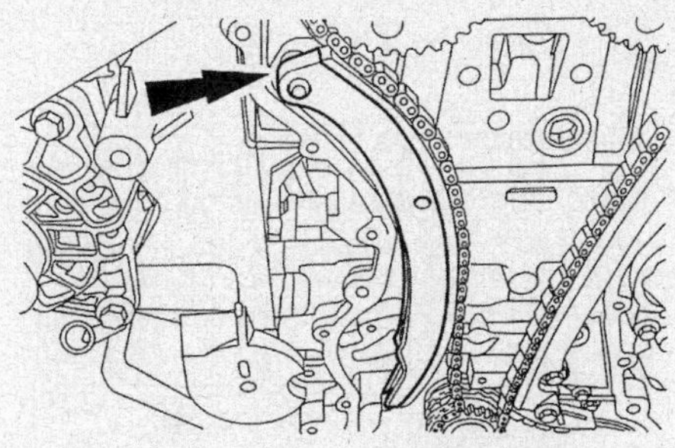

Fig. 11 Righthand timing chain guide removal

CAMSHAFT

REPLACE

Removal

Before removing the camshafts, measure the clearance of each valve at base circle, with the lobe pointed away from the tappet. Failure to measure all clearances prior to removing the camshafts will necessitate repeated removal and installation and wasted labor time.

1. Remove timing chain and sprockets as outlined under "Timing Chain, Replace."
2. Match mark position of camshaft lobes on No. 1 cylinder for assembly reference.
3. Loosen camshaft bearing cap bolts in sequence, **Fig. 13,** one turn at a time, until all tension is released.
4. Remove camshaft bearing caps, then the camshafts.

Installation

Install the camshafts with the alignment slots in the camshafts lined up so the Camshaft Alignment Plate can be installed without rotating the camshafts. Ensure the lobes on the No. 1 cylinder are in the same position as noted in the removal procedure. Rotating the camshafts when the timing chain is removed, or installing the camshafts 180° out of position can cause severe damage to the valves and pistons.

1. Lubricate camshaft journals and bearing caps with clean engine oil.
2. Install camshafts, bearing caps and replacement tool No. 303-465 or equivalent.
3. Install camshaft bearing cap bolts and tighten bolts in sequence, **Fig. 14,** in three stages.
4. Stage 1: Tighten bolts one turn at a time until finger tight; Stage 2: **Torque** bolts to 62 inch lbs.; Stage 3: **Torque** bolts to 12 ft. lbs.
5. Install timing chain and sprockets as outlined under "Timing Chain, Replace."

CRANKSHAFT SEAL

REPLACE

1. Release tensioner and remove accessory drive belt.
2. Remove valve cover as outlined under "Valve Cover, Replace." **Failure to position No. 1 piston at TDC can result in damage to engine. Turn engine in normal direction of rotation only.**
3. Turn crankshaft clockwise to position No. 1 piston at TDC using crankshaft pulley bolt. Hole in crankshaft pulley should be in 6 o'clock position.
4. **Camshaft timing slots are offset. If special tool cannot be installed, rotate crankshaft one complete revolution clockwise to correctly position camshafts.** Install special tool No. 303–465 or equivalent, in slots on rear of both camshafts.
5. Remove engine plug bolt, then install holding tool Nos. 303–507, 205–072–02 and 205–126 or equivalents to crankshaft.
6. Remove crankshaft pulley bolt and washer, then the crankshaft pulley.
7. **Do not damage engine front cover or crankshaft when removing seal.**
8. Remove crankshaft front oil seal using seal remover tool No. 303-409 or equivalent.
9. Reverse procedure to install, noting the following:
   a. Lubricate oil seal with clean engine oil.
   b. Install crankshaft front oil seal using installer tool No. 303-096 or equivalent.
   c. Install crankshaft pulley.

CRANKSHAFT REAR OIL SEAL

REPLACE

1. **On models equipped with automatic transaxle,** remove transaxle as outlined in **MOTOR's "Domestic Transmission, In-Vehicle Service" or "Transmission Service DVD."**
2. **On models equipped with manual transaxle,** remove transaxle as outlined in **MOTOR's "Domestic Transmission, In-Vehicle Service" or "Transmission Service DVD."**
3. **On all models,** remove flexplate or flywheel.
4. **If oil pan is not removed, damage to rear oil seal retainer joint can occur.** remove bolts and oil pan as outlined under "Oil Pan, Replace."
5. Remove bolts and crankshaft rear oil seal with retainer plate.
6. Reverse procedure to install, noting the following:
   a. Position crankshaft rear oil seal with retainer plate onto crankshaft using installer tool No. 303-328 or equivalent.
   b. Install crankshaft rear oil seal with retainer plate and bolts, tighten in sequence outlined in **Fig. 15** to 89 inch lbs.

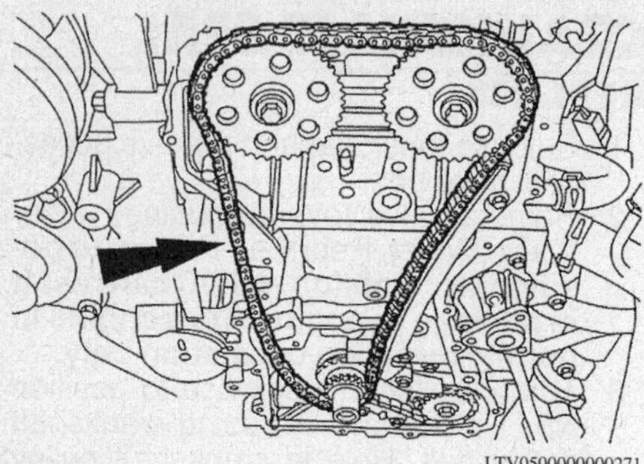

Fig. 12 Timing chain removal

OIL PAN

REPLACE

1. Drain engine oil into a suitable container.
2. Remove bolts and righthand splash shield, then the oil level indictor and oil dipstick tube.
3. Remove four lower engine front cover bolts, then the four oil pan to bell housing bolts, remaining bolts and oil pan.
4. Reverse procedure to install, noting the following:
   a. Install two rear oil pan bolts and finger tighten.
   b. Install four oil pan to bell housing bolts and tighten to 35 ft. lbs.
   c. Install four lower engine front cover bolts and tighten to 89 inch lbs.
   d. Install remaining oil pan bolts and tighten in sequence, **Fig. 16** to 18 ft. lbs.

OIL PUMP

REPLACE

1. Drain engine oil into a suitable container.
2. Remove bolts and righthand splash shield, then the oil level indictor and oil dipstick tube.
3. Remove four lower engine front cover bolts, then the four oil pan to bell housing bolts, remaining bolts and oil pan.
4. Remove bolts and oil pump screen and pickup tube.
5. Reverse procedure to install, noting the following:
   a. Install two rear oil pan bolts and finger tighten.
   b. Install four oil pan to bell housing bolts and tighten to 35 ft. lbs.
   c. Install four lower engine front cover bolts and tighten to 89 inch lbs.
   d. Install remaining oil pan bolts and tighten in sequence **Fig. 16,** to 18 ft. lbs.

SERPENTINE DRIVE BELT

1. Raise and support vehicle, remove righthand front tire and wheel assembly.

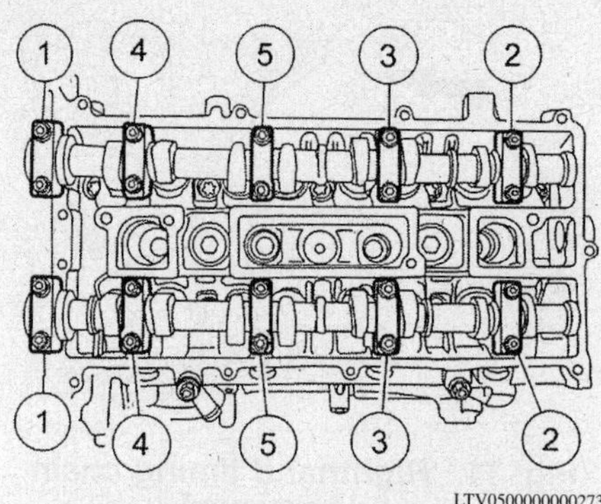

Fig. 13 Camshaft bearing cap bolts loosening sequence

2. Remove righthand front lower splash shield.
3. Rotate accessory drive belt tensioner clockwise, then remove accessory drive belt.
4. Reverse procedure to install.

COOLING SYSTEM BLEED

1. Add correct engine coolant mixture to degas bottle until coolant level is between "COOLANT FILL LEVEL" marks.
2. Select maximum heater temperature and blower motor speed settings.
3. Position control to discharge air at vents in instrument panel.
4. Start engine and allow to idle, while engine is idling feel for hot air at vents. **If air discharge remains cool and engine coolant temperature gauge does not move, engine coolant level is low in engine and must be filled. Stop engine, allow to cool and fill cooling system.**
5. Start engine and allow to idle until normal operating temperature is reached.
6. Hot air should discharge from vents, then engine coolant temperature gauge should maintain a stabilized reading in middle of NORMAL range and upper radiator hose should feel hot to touch.
7. Shut engine OFF and allow to cool, then inspect engine for coolant leaks.
8. Inspect engine coolant level in degas bottle and fill as required.

THERMOSTAT

REPLACE

The thermostat and thermostat housing are serviced as an assembly.

1. Raise and support vehicle, remove righthand front tire and wheel assembly.
2. Remove righthand front lower splash shield.
3. Rotate accessory drive belt tensioner clockwise, then remove accessory drive belt.

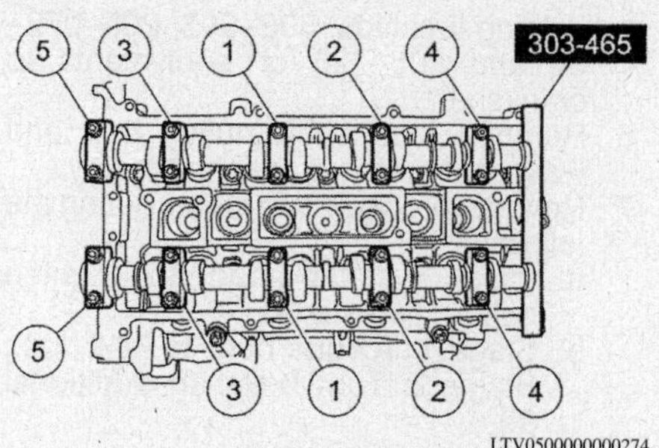

Fig. 14 Camshaft bearing cap bolts tightening sequence

4. Drain cooling system into a suitable container.
5. Disconnect heater hose and lower radiator hose at thermostat housing.
6. Reverse procedure to install. Fill and bleed cooling system as in "Cooling System Bleed."

WATER PUMP

REPLACE

1. Raise and support vehicle, remove righthand front tire and wheel assembly.
2. Remove righthand front lower splash shield.
3. Rotate accessory drive belt tensioner clockwise, then remove accessory drive belt.
4. Drain cooling system into a suitable container.
5. Remove bolts and coolant pump pulley.
6. Remove bolts and coolant pump. Discard O-ring seal.
7. Reverse procedure to install. Fill and bleed cooling system as in "Cooling System Bleed."

RADIATOR

REPLACE

Except Hybrid

1. Recover A/C refrigerant as outlined in "Air Conditioning" chapter.
2. Match mark hood latch position prior to removal of bolts.
3. Loosen hood latch nut, then remove hood latch bolts and position hood latch aside.
4. Detach wiring harness pin-type retainers, then remove radiator support bracket bolt.
5. Remove front impact severity sensor bolt.
6. Disconnect electrical connector and remove front impact severity sensor.
7. Remove pushpin retainers from front bumper bracket, then the front grille bolts.
8. Remove bolts and radiator brackets, then the center support lower bolt, nut and center support.

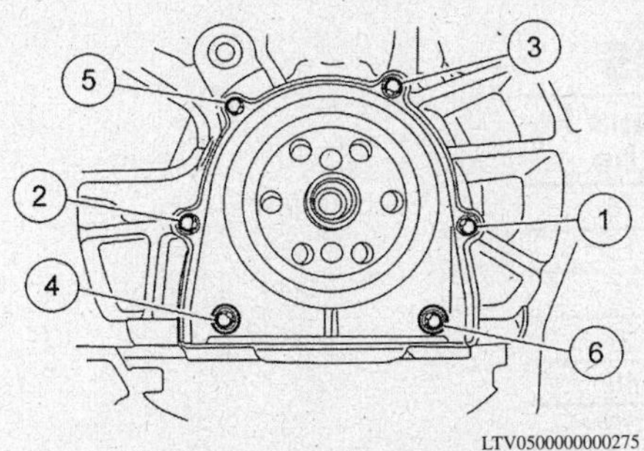

Fig. 15 Rear crankshaft rear oil seal tightening sequence

9. Disconnect cooling fan electrical connectors, then remove cooling fan bolts, motor and shroud.
10. Disconnect all hoses from radiator, then the transaxle cooling hoses from radiator.
11. Remove radiator from vehicle.
12. Reverse procedure to install. Fill and bleed cooling system as in "Cooling System Bleed."

Hybrid

1. Drain engine cooling system into a suitable container.
2. Remove lefthand splash shield, then place a suitable container below transaxle.
3. Loosen hose clamps at transaxle, then pull hoses off to allow coolant to drain.
4. Recover A/C refrigerant as outlined in "Air Conditioning" chapter.
5. Match mark hood latch position prior to removal of bolts.
6. Loosen hood latch nut, then remove hood latch bolts and position hood latch aside.
7. Detach wiring harness pin-type retainers, then remove radiator support bracket bolt.
8. Remove front impact severity sensor bolt.
9. Disconnect electrical connector and remove front impact severity sensor.
10. Remove bolts and radiator brackets, then disconnect hood switch electrical connector.
11. Remove relay box bracket bolts, then position relay box and bracket aside.
12. Remove center support lower bolt, then the center support lower bolt, nut and center support.
13. Remove bolts and position auxiliary coolant pump aside.
14. Disconnect cooling fan electrical connectors, then remove cooling fan bolts.
15. Remove lefthand cooling fan first, then slide the righthand cooling fan to lefthand side to remove.
16. Disconnect upper hose from motor electronics radiator, then remove motor electronics radiator to engine radiator bolts and position motor electronics radiator aside.
17. Remove A/C condenser to radiator bolts and position the A/C condenser aside.
18. Disconnect all hoses from radiator, then the transaxle cooling hoses from radiator.
19. Remove radiator from vehicle.
20. Reverse procedure to install. Fill and bleed cooling system as in "Cooling System Bleed."
21. Loosen the bleed screw and fill degas bottle with coolant until it begins to flow out of bleed hole. Then, close bleed screw.
22. Turn ignition to ON position to actuate motor electronics cooling pump and continue to fill degas bottle to correct level.
23. Most of MECS air bleeding occurs as a normal process at degas bottle through vent tube; very little occurs at bleed screw.
24. To bleed air from system, loosen bleed screw and allow air to escape while M/E coolant pump is operating.

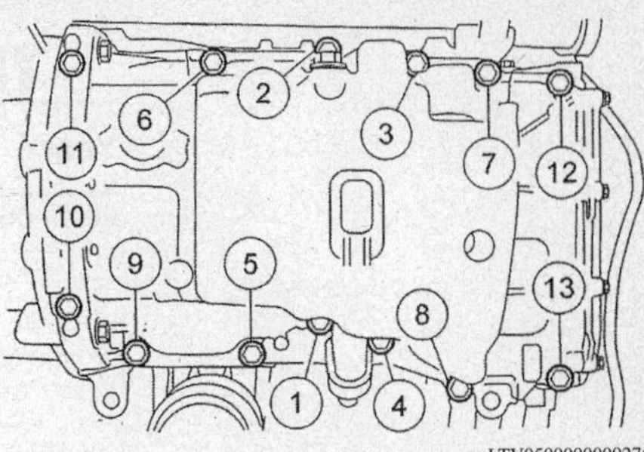

Fig. 16 Oil pan tightening sequence

FUEL PUMP

REPLACE

1. Remove fuel tank.
2. Remove any dirt that has accumulated around fuel pump attaching flange.
3. Remove fuel pump retaining ring using fuel tank lock ring wrench tool No. 310–075, or equivalent.
4. Remove fuel pump assembly.
5. Remove and discard fuel pump mounting gasket.
6. Reverse procedure to install.

FUEL FILTER

REPLACE

1. Relieve fuel system pressure as outlined in "Precautions."
2. Disconnect push connector and R-clip fittings at fuel filter.
3. Remove fuel filter from bracket.
4. Reverse procedure to install.

TIGHTENING SPECIFICATIONS

Year	Component	Torque Ft. Lbs.
2005–06	A/C Compressor	18
	A/C Manifold Tube	15
	Alternator Mounting	35
	Camshaft Bearing Caps	⑤
	Camshaft Sprocket	48
	Catalytic Converter To Cylinder Head	35
	Catalytic Converter Studs	13
	Crankshaft Position Sensor	62①
	Crankshaft Pulley	④
	Cylinder Head	②
	EGR Valve Assembly	18
	Engine Mount Bolts	41
	Engine Bracket To Engine Nut	66
	Engine Bracket To Mount Bolts	66
	Engine To Transmission	35
	Exhaust Manifold Studs	⑥
	Exhaust Flexible Pipe Nuts	18
	Fan Shroud	62①
	Front Cover	③
	High Voltage Cables Bracket Nut	71①
	High Voltage Cables Shield Nuts	80①
	High Voltage Cables Traction Battery Bolts	41
	Intake Manifold	13
	Knock Sensor	15
	Oil Drain Plug	21
	Oil Filter Adapter	18
	Oil Pan	⑦
	Oil Pressure Sensor	11
	Oil Pump Screen & Cover	89①
	Oil Pump Sprocket	18
	Power Steering Pressure Line Tube	15
	Power Steering Pump	18
	Starter Mounting	18
	Timing Chain Tensioner & Guides	89①
	Thermostat Housing	89①
	Valve Cover	⑧
	Water Pump	89①
	Water Pump Pulley	18

① — Inch lbs.

② — Refer to "Cylinder Head, Replace" for tightening procedure.

③ — Refer to "Front Cover, Replace" for tightening procedure.

④ — Refer to "Crankshaft Pulley, Replace" for tightening procedure.

⑤ — Refer to "Camshaft, Replace" for tightening procedure.

⑥ — Refer to "Exhaust Manifold, Replace" for tightening procedure.

⑦ — Refer to "Oil Pan, Replace" for tightening procedure.

⑧ — Refer to "Valve Cover, Replace" for tightening procedure.

3.0L Engine

NOTE: On Air Bag Equipped Models, Refer To "Air Bag System Precautions" Located In The Front Of This Manual For System Disarming & Arming Procedures.

NOTE: Refer To "Computer Relearn Procedures" Located In The Front Of This Manual When Battery Power To The Computer Has Been Interrupted.

INDEX

PRECAUTIONS

Air Bag Systems

Refer to "Air Bag System Precautions" in the front of this manual for system disarming and arming procedures.

Battery Ground Cable

Prior to service, disconnect battery ground cable and isolate as required.

Fuel System Pressure Relief

1. Remove shraeder valve cap at end of fuel injection supply manifold and attach fuel pressure gauge.
2. Position other end of fuel pressure gauge line into a suitable container.
3. Open manual valve slowly to relieve system pressure into container.

ENGINE MOUNT

REPLACE

1. Support engine using three bar engine support tools No. 303-F072, or equivalent.
2. Remove A/C line bracket bolt, **Fig. 1**, then position A/C lines out of way.
3. Remove engine support insulator nuts and bolts, **Fig. 2.**
4. Position power steering line and bracket aside, then remove insulator.
5. Reverse procedure to install.

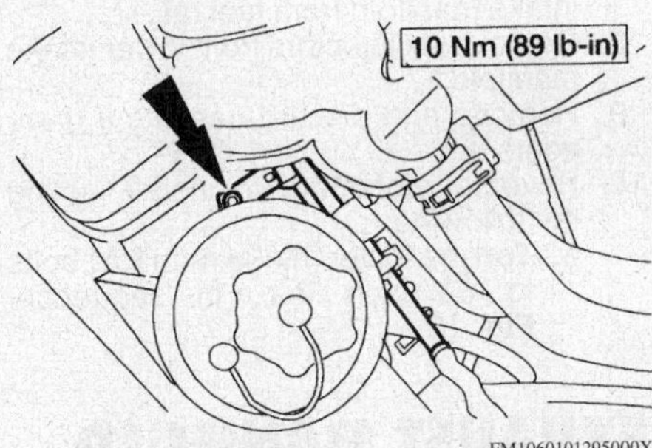

Fig. 1 A/C line bracket bolt

ENGINE

REPLACE

1. Remove battery tray and air cleaner outlet pipe.
2. Raise and support vehicle.
3. Remove lower radiator air deflectors.
4. Drain cooling system into suitable container.
5. Lower vehicle.
6. Relieve fuel system pressure as outlined under "Precautions."
7. Disconnect fuel line.
8. Remove water pump drive belt.
9. Disconnect accelerator and speed control cables.
10. Disconnect vapor management valve.
11. Disconnect powertrain control module.
12. Disconnect ground wire at firewall.
13. Disconnect coolant hoses and position thermostat housing and hose assembly aside.
14. Disconnect electrical connector from power distribution box, then remove power distribution box cover.
15. Remove nuts and cables from power distribution box, **Fig. 3.**
16. Disconnect transaxle linkage, **Fig. 4.**
17. Disconnect brake booster vacuum hose.
18. Disconnect vacuum line, **Fig. 5.**
19. Disconnect heater hoses from heater core.
20. Disconnect power steering return line.
21. Disconnect power steering pressure switch electrical connector and remove bracket bolt, then the power steering line.
22. Remove oil level dipstick.
23. Remove three way catalytic converter.
24. Recover A/C refrigerant as outlined under "Air Conditioning" chapter.
25. Remove A/C compressor.
26. Raise and support vehicle.
27. Remove both front tire and wheel assemblies.
28. Place index mark on pinion and yoke to rear of driveshaft.
29. Remove ground strap bolt located near catalytic converter.
30. Remove and discard driveshaft center bearing nuts.
31. Remove and discard front driveshaft to power take off bolts and washers.
32. Remove driveshaft.
33. Separate both lower ball joints.
34. Separate both tie rod ends from steering knuckle.
35. Separate both sway bar links from strut mount.
36. Separate both struts from steering knuckles.
37. Remove mounting bolt from both speed sensors and position aside.

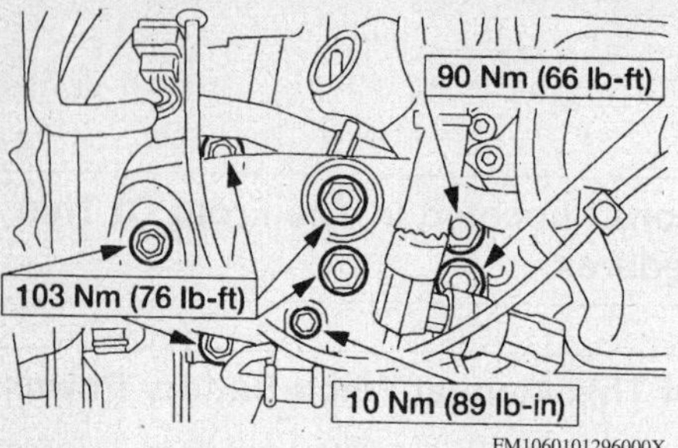

Fig. 2 Front, righthand engine support insulator mounting bolts & nuts

38. Remove both front brake calipers from steering knuckles.
39. Separate steering shaft from steering rack.
40. Remove transmission line bracket bolt, then both transmission oil cooler lines.
41. Remove torque converter inspection cover, then the four torque converter nuts.
42. Remove bolts, **Fig. 6.**
43. Disconnect block heater wiring, if equipped.
44. Position powertrain lift tool No. 014-00765, or equivalent, under vehicle.
45. Remove bolts and nuts, then the engine support bracket, **Fig. 7.**
46. Remove mounting bolts, then the transaxle support, **Fig. 8.**
47. Remove two rear subframe bolts and two subframe side nuts.
48. Remove four bolts from motor mount support, then raise vehicle to remove powertrain.
49. Reverse procedure to install.

INTAKE MANIFOLD

REPLACE

Upper

1. Remove crankcase ventilation tube, then loosen clamps and remove air cleaner outlet tube.
2. Remove engine appearance cover.
3. Disconnect throttle and speed control cables.
4. Disconnect throttle position sensor and idle air control sensor electrical connectors.
5. Disconnect EGR valve vacuum hose and EGR tube nut.
6. Disconnect EGR vacuum regulator valve electrical connector and vacuum hose.
7. Disconnect chassis vacuum hose, engine vacuum hose and PCV hose from back of intake manifold, **Fig. 9.**
8. Disconnect vapor management valve vacuum hose.
9. Disconnect two electrical connectors attached to lefthand side of upper intake manifold.
10. Disconnect power steering pressure sensor electrical connector.
11. Remove eight bolts, then the upper intake manifold.

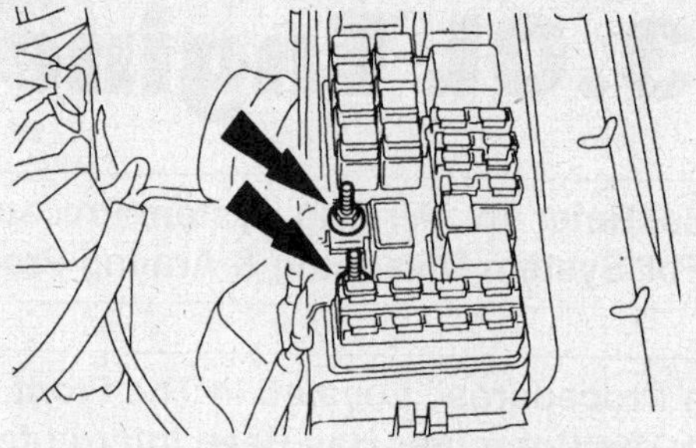

Fig. 3 Power distribution box cable locations

12. Reverse procedure to install, noting the following:
    a. Install new intake manifold gasket.
    b. **Torque** intake manifold bolts to 89 inch lbs., in sequence, **Fig. 10.**

Lower

1. Relieve fuel pressure as outlined under "Precautions."
2. Disconnect fuel line spring lock couplings.
3. Remove upper intake manifold.
4. Disconnect six fuel injector electrical connectors.
5. Disconnect fuel pressure damper vacuum line.
6. Remove mounting bolts, **Fig. 11,** then the lower intake manifold.
7. Remove four bolts and separate lower intake manifold from fuel rail.
8. Remove six injectors from lower intake manifold.
9. Remove and discard gaskets if damaged.
10. Reverse procedure to install, noting the following:
    a. **Torque** lower intake manifold bolts to 89 inch lbs., in sequence, **Fig. 12.**

EXHAUST MANIFOLD

REPLACE

Lefthand

1. Remove lefthand heated oxygen sensor.
2. Remove lower splash shield.
3. Remove exhaust crossover pipe and position aside.
4. Remove accessory drive belt.
5. Remove A/C compressor bolts and position aside.
6. Remove attaching nuts, then the exhaust manifold.
7. Discard gasket.
8. Reverse procedure to install, noting the following:
    a. Install new exhaust manifold gasket.
    b. **Torque** nuts to 15 ft. lbs., in sequence, **Fig. 13.**

Righthand

1. Remove EGR tube, alternator and righthand heated oxygen sensor.

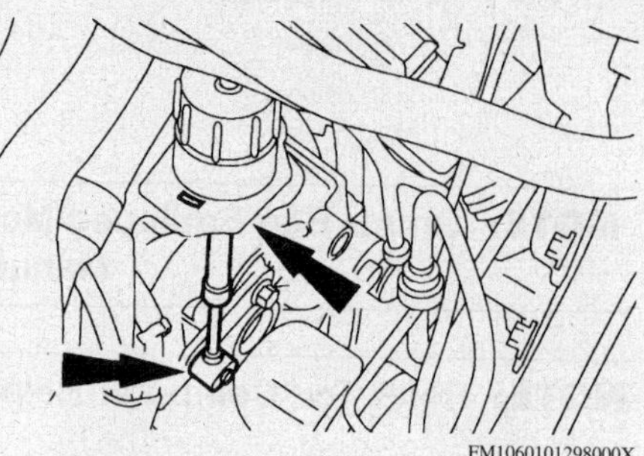

Fig. 4 Transaxle linkage

2. Remove righthand exhaust manifold, discard manifold gasket.
3. Reverse procedure to install, noting the following:
    a. Install new exhaust manifold gasket.
    b. **Torque** nuts to 15 ft. lbs., in sequence, **Fig. 14.**

CYLINDER HEAD

REPLACE

Lefthand

Cylinder head bolts are torque to yield design and must be replaced with new bolts.

1. Remove camshafts as outlined under "Camshaft, Replace" then the coolant bypass tube and exhaust manifold nuts.
2. Note position of camshaft followers for installation reference, then remove followers.
3. Note position of hydraulic lash adjusters for installation reference, then remove lash adjusters.
4. Remove cylinder head bolts in sequence, **Fig. 15.**
5. Clean and inspect sealing surfaces. Do not use power abrasive discs or metal scrapers to clean surfaces. Use plastic scraping tool and Metal Surface Cleaner No. F4AZ-19A536-RA, or equivalent.
6. Reverse procedure to install, noting the following:
    a. Position lefthand cylinder head and gasket, then install bolts in sequence, **Fig. 16.**
    b. Tighten bolts in six stages:
    c. Stage 1: **Torque** bolts to 30 ft. lbs.
    d. Stage 2: Tighten bolts an additional 90°.
    e. Stage 3: Loosen bolts one full turn.
    f. Stage 4: **Torque** bolts to 30 ft. lbs.
    g. Stage 5: Tighten an additional 90°.
    h. Stage 6: Tighten an additional 90°.
    i. Lubricate camshaft followers and hydraulic lash adjusters with SAE 5W-20 motor oil, or equivalent.
    j. Install exhaust manifold and tighten nuts in sequence as outlined under "Exhaust Manifold, Replace."

Righthand

Cylinder Head Bolts Are Torque To Yield Design And Must Be Replaced With New Bolts.

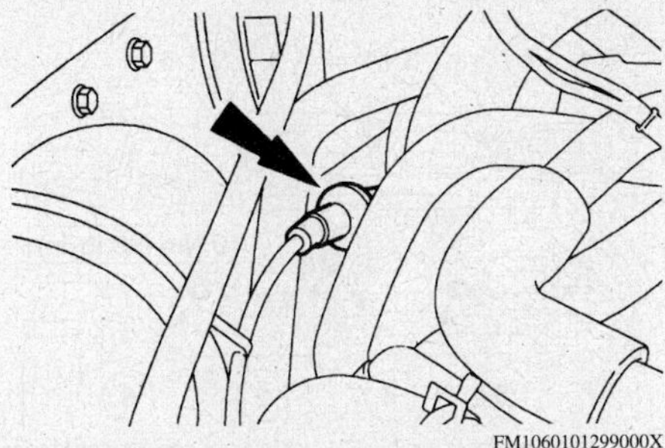

Fig. 5 Vacuum line location

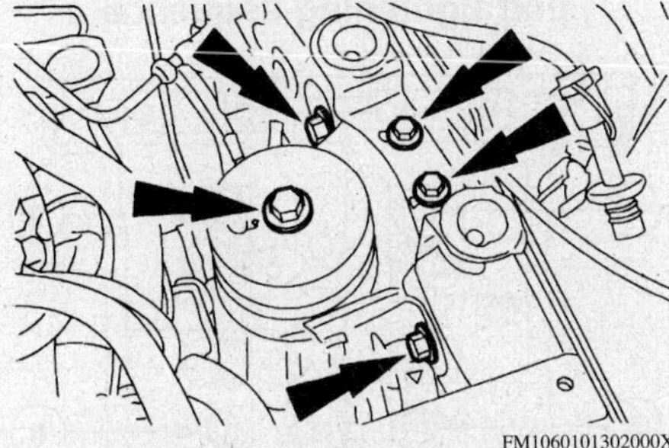

Fig. 8 Transaxle support

1. Remove coolant bypass tube, EGR tube and six nuts from exhaust manifold.
2. Remove camshafts as outlined under "Camshaft, Replace."
3. Remove camshaft followers and hydraulic lash adjusters as outlined under "Roller Followers & Hydraulic Lash Adjusters, Replace." Note location of followers and lash adjusters for installation reference.
4. Remove cylinder head bolts in sequence, **Fig. 17.**
5. Reverse procedure to install, noting the following:
   a. Do not use metal scrapers, wire brushes or power abrasive discs to clean cylinder head sealing surfaces. Clean all surfaces with Metal Surface Cleaner No. F4AZ-19A536-RA, or equivalent.
   b. Position cylinder head and gasket, install new cylinder head bolts and tighten in six stages, in sequence, **Fig. 18.**
   c. Stage 1: **Torque** all bolts to 30 ft. lbs.
   d. Stage 2: Tighten all bolts an additional 90°.
   e. Stage 3: Loosen all bolts one full turn.
   f. Stage 4: **Torque** all bolts to 30 ft. lbs.
   g. Stage 5: Tighten bolts 90°.
   h. Stage 6: Tighten bolts 90°.
   i. Lubricate camshaft followers and hydraulic lash adjusters with SAE 5W-20 motor oil, or equivalent.
   j. Install exhaust manifold nuts and tighten to specification, in sequence, as outlined under "Exhaust Manifold, Replace."

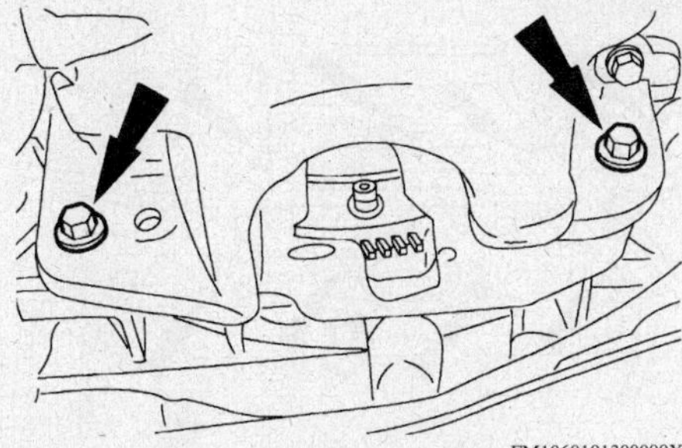

Fig. 6 Bolt locations

VALVE COVER

REPLACE

Lefthand

1. Remove engine appearance cover.
2. Disconnect crankcase ventilation tube for valve cover.
3. Disconnect electrical connectors and mounting bolts, then the ignition coils.
4. Disconnect wiring harness from valve cover studs.
5. Remove engine lift bracket.
6. Remove bolts and studs, then the lefthand valve cover.
7. Remove and discard valve cover gasket if damaged.
8. Reverse procedure to install, noting the following:
   a. Valve cover must be installed and bolts tightened within six minutes of applying sealer.
   b. Apply a dot of Silicone Gasket Sealant No. F7AZ-19554-EA, or equivalent, meeting Ford specification, to front cover to cylinder head joints.
   c. Position valve cover and install studs and bolts in sequence, **Fig. 19.**

Righthand

1. Remove upper intake manifold as outlined under "Intake Manifold, Replace."
2. Disconnect electrical connectors, remove mounting bolts, then remove ignition coils.
3. Remove wiring harness nuts, then disconnect oxygen sensor electrical connectors.
4. Disconnect radio ignition interference capacitor.
5. Disconnect crankcase ventilation tube from valve cover.
6. Remove bolts and studs, then the valve cover.
7. Inspect valve cover gasket, replace if damaged.
8. Reverse procedure to install, noting the following:
   a. Valve cover must be installed and bolts tightened within six minutes of applying sealant.
   b. Apply a 5mm dot of Silicone Gasket Sealant No. F7AZ-19554-EA, or equivalent, to front cover to cylinder head joints.
   c. Position valve cover and install bolt and studs.
   d. Tighten bolt and nuts to specification, in sequence, **Fig. 20.**

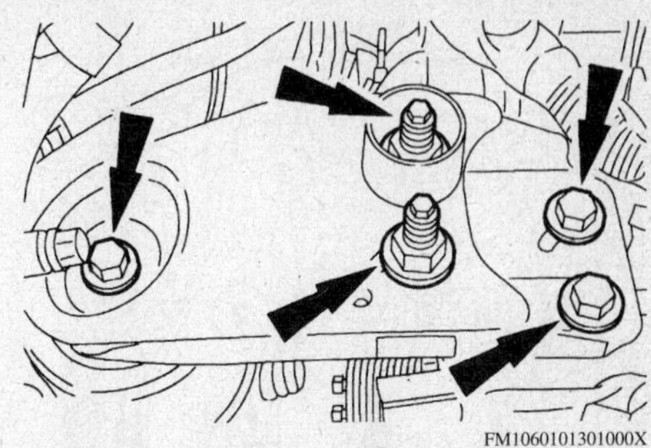

Fig. 7 Engine support bracket

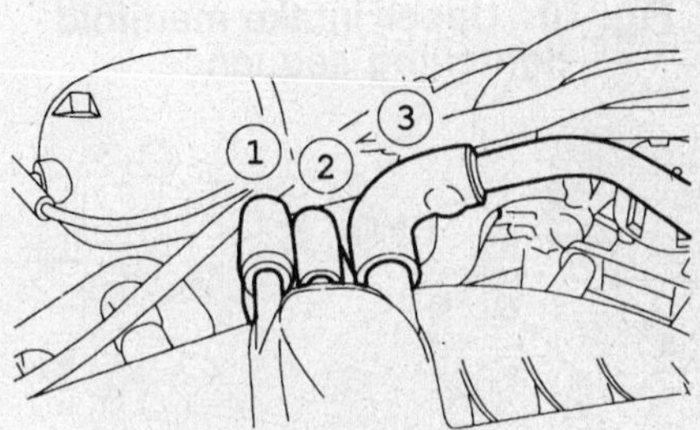

1. Chassis vacuum hose
2. Engine vacuum hose
3. Positive crankcase ventilation hose

FM1060101258000X

Fig. 9 Vacuum hose locations

ROLLER FOLLOWERS & HYDRAULIC LASH ADJUSTERS

REPLACE

1. Remove both valve covers as outlined under "Valve Cover, Replace"
2. Remove all spark plugs.
3. Raise and support vehicle, remove righthand front wheel.
4. Remove screws and pin type retainers, then the righthand front inner fender splash shield.
5. Rotate crankshaft until camshaft lobe is pointing directly away from follower.
6. Remove followers using valve spring compressor tool No. 303-473, or equivalent, **Fig. 21.**
7. Mark position of hydraulic lash adjusters to ensure proper location during assembly.
8. Remove hydraulic lash adjusters.
9. Inspect lash adjusters for scoring or uneven wear, replace as required.
10. Lubricate adjusters with SAE 5W-20 motor oil, or equivalent before installation.
11. Reverse procedure to install.

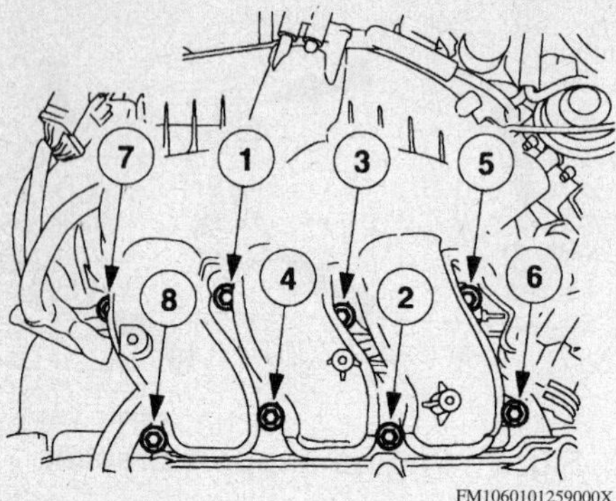

Fig. 10 Upper intake manifold tightening sequence

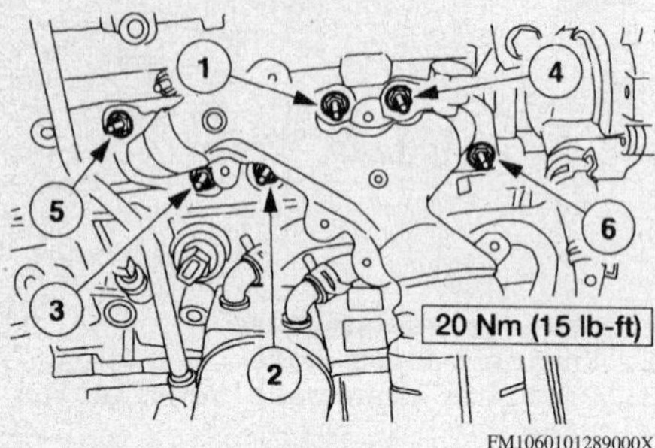

Fig. 13 Lefthand exhaust manifold tightening sequence

CRANKSHAFT DAMPER

REPLACE

Removal

1. Remove accessory drive belt.
2. Remove righthand front inner fender splash shield.
3. Remove torque converter inspection cover.
4. Install flywheel holding tool No. 303-544, or equivalent.
5. Remove crankshaft pulley bolt and washer.
6. Remove crankshaft damper using crankshaft damper removal tool No. 303-009, or equivalent.

Installation

1. Ensure all seal surfaces are free of dirt and oil.
2. Apply Silicone Gasket and Sealant No. F7AZ-19544-EA, or equivalent, to end of keyway slot.
3. Lubricate outside diameter sealing surface of crankshaft damper with SAE 5W-20 motor oil, or equivalent.
4. Install crankshaft damper using crankshaft damper installation tool No. 303-102, or equivalent.
5. Install crankshaft damper bolt and tighten in four stages:
   a. Stage 1: **Torque** bolt to 86 ft. lbs.
   b. Stage 2: Loosen 360°.
   c. Stage 3: **Torque** bolt to 37 ft. lbs.
   d. Stage 4: Tighten an additional 90°.
6. Remove flywheel holding tool, then install torque converter inspection cover.
7. Install righthand inner splash shield.
8. Install accessory drive belt.

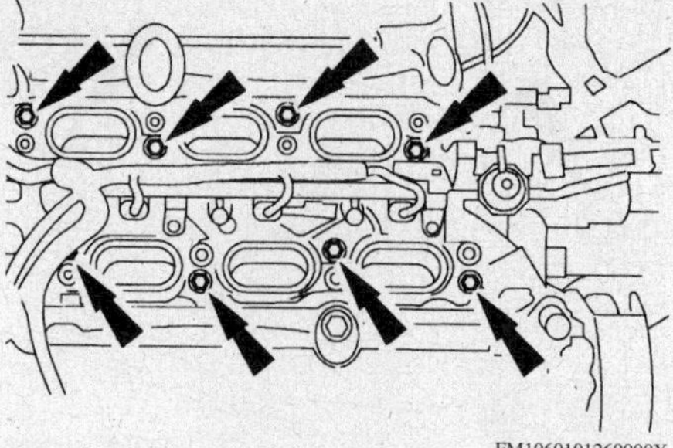

Fig. 11 Lower intake manifold mounting bolts

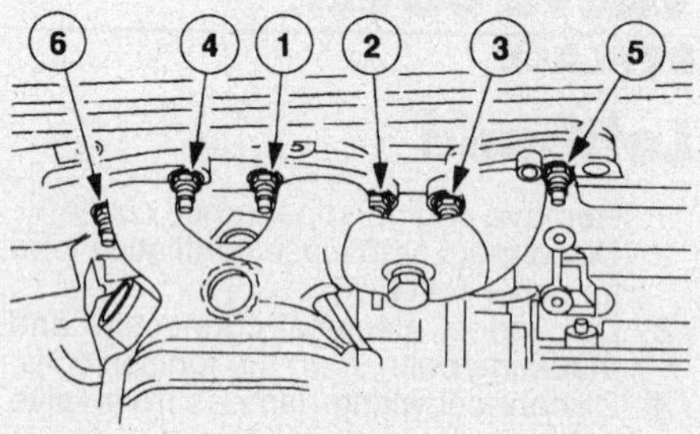

Fig. 14 Righthand exhaust manifold nut tightening sequence

FRONT COVER

REPLACE

Removal

1. Remove both valve covers as outlined under "Valve Cover, Replace."
2. Raise and support vehicle.
3. Remove oil pan.
4. Remove alternator, then the bolts and alternator bracket.
5. Remove bolt and camshaft position sensor.
6. Lower vehicle.
7. Remove radio ignition interference capacitor.
8. Remove front engine support insulator.
9. Raise and support vehicle.
10. Remove accessory belt tensioner.
11. Remove crankshaft pulley as outlined under "Crankshaft Damper, Replace."
12. Remove crankshaft position sensor.
13. With vehicle raised in air, remove front cover.

Installation

1. Clean all sealing surfaces with metal surface cleaner No. F4AZ-19A536-RA, or equivalent.
2. Install three new gaskets in front cover.
3. Apply a .24 inch diameter dot of Silicone gasket Sealer F7AZ-19554-EA, or equivalent, to cylinder block, lower cylinder block and cylinder head mating surfaces.
4. Position front cover and install studs and bolts in sequence, **Fig. 22.**
5. Note that fasteners No. 1, 3, 4, 8, 10, 11, 14, 15 and 16 are studs.
6. Install crankshaft position sensor and electrical connector.

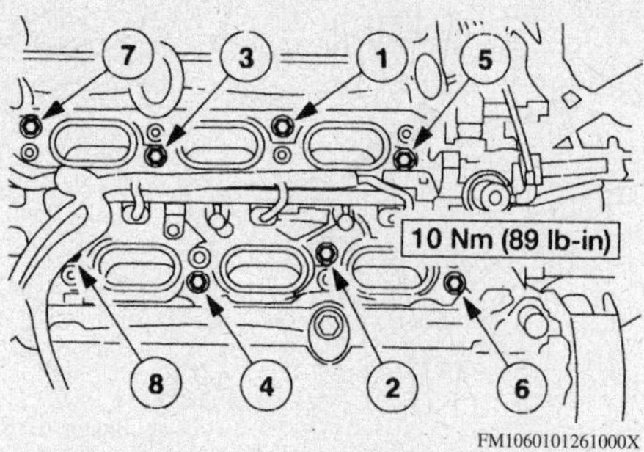

Fig. 12 Lower intake manifold bolt tightening sequence

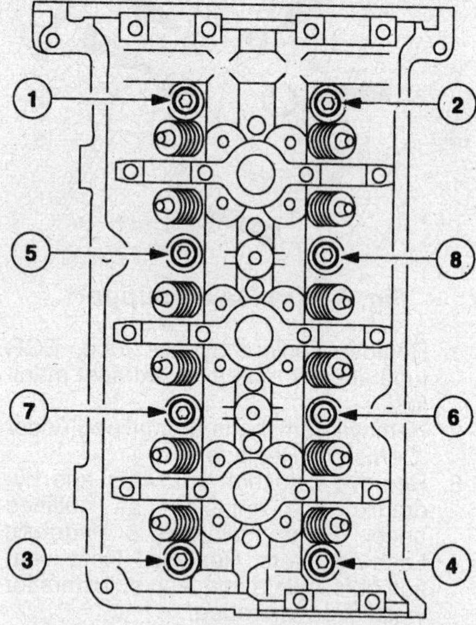

Fig. 15 Lefthand cylinder head bolt removal sequence

7. Install crankshaft pulley, accessory drive belt tensioner and alternator bracket.
8. Install alternator.
9. Install oil pan, then lower vehicle.
10. Install front engine support insulator.
11. Install radio ignition interference capacitor.
12. Install power steering pump and both valve covers.

TIMING CHAIN

REPLACE

Removal

The pulse wheel used in these engines is designed to be used in several different engines. When installing the pulse wheel, install with keyway in the slot stamped 20-25-34y-30m (color blue).

1. Remove engine front cover as outlined under "Front Cover, Replace."
2. Install crankshaft damper bolt.
3. Remove spark plugs.
4. Rotate crankshaft clockwise to position crankshaft keyway in 11 o'clock position and position camshafts in correct position, **Fig. 23.**
5. Rotate crankshaft clockwise 120° to 3

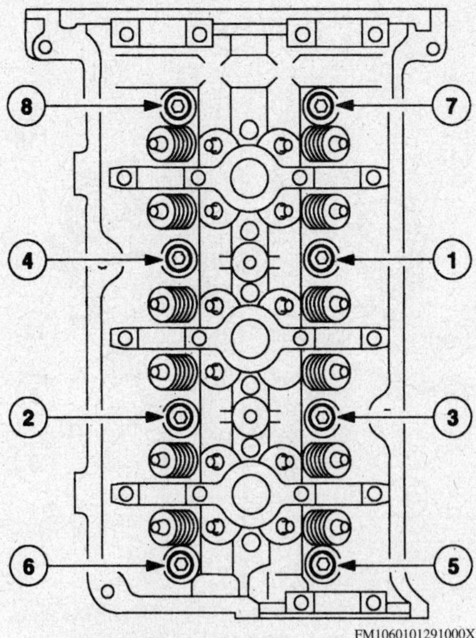

Fig. 16 Lefthand cylinder head bolt tightening sequence

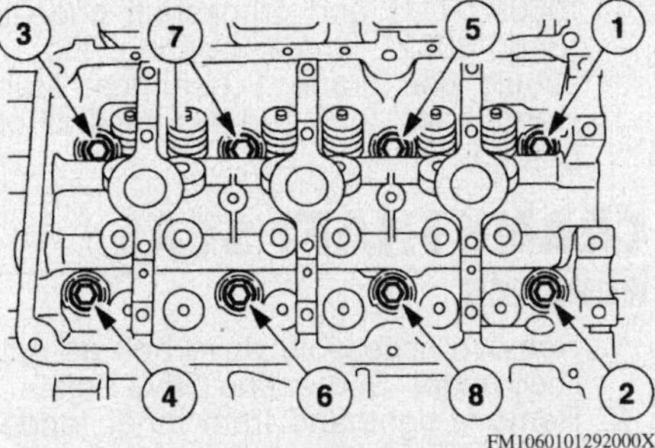

Fig. 17 Righthand cylinder head bolt removal sequence

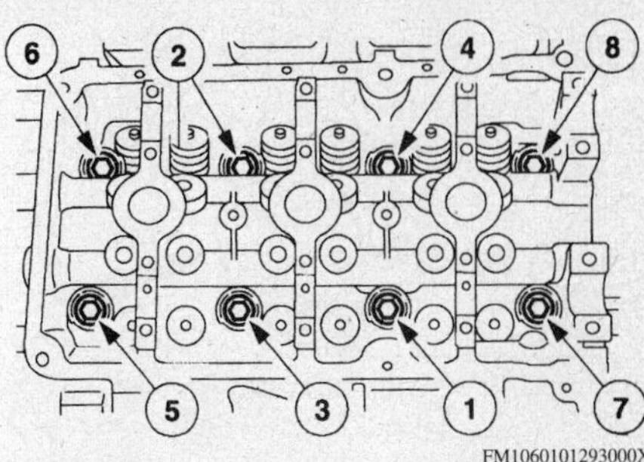

Fig. 18 Righthand cylinder head bolt tightening sequence

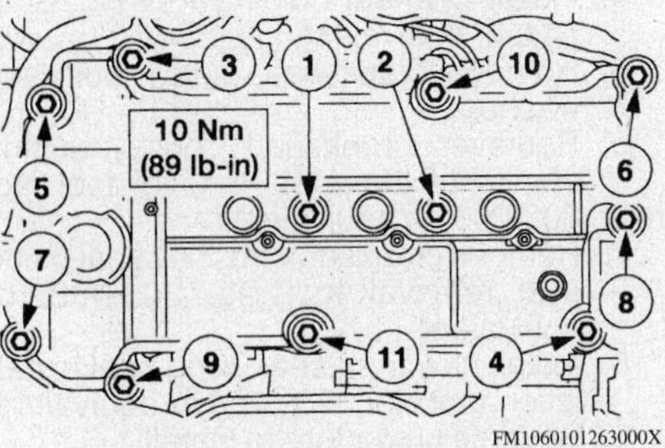

Fig. 19 Lefthand valve cover tightening sequence

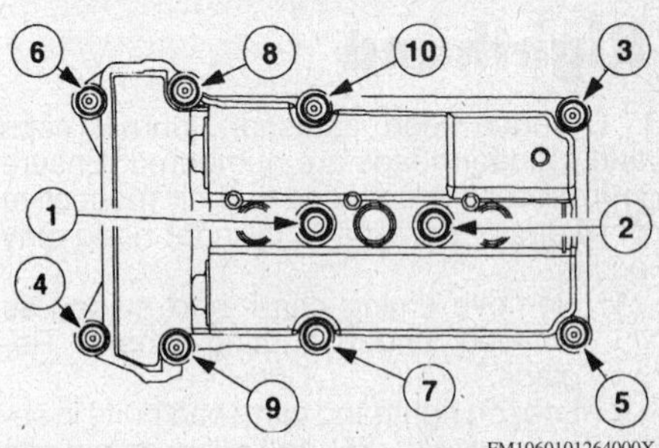

Fig. 20 Righthand valve cover tightening sequence

o'clock position, **Fig. 24,** to locate righthand camshafts in neutral position.

6. Ensure righthand camshafts are in neutral position, **Fig. 25.**
7. Remove righthand timing chain tensioner, tensioner arm and timing chain guide, then the timing chain.
8. Rotate crankshaft clockwise to position crankshaft keyway in 11 o'clock position, **Fig. 26,** so that camshafts are positioned in the neutral position.
9. Ensure lefthand camshafts are in neutral position, then mark link position if visible on crankshaft sprocket, **Fig. 27.**
10. Remove lefthand timing chain tensioner, tensioner arm and timing chain guide, then the timing chain.
11. Remove damper bolt and crankshaft sprockets.

Installation

1. Install crankshaft sprockets.
2. Position timing chain tensioner in a soft jawed vise.
3. Hold chain tensioner ratchet lock mechanism away from ratchet stem with a small pick.
4. During timing chain tensioner compression, do not release ratchet stem until tensioner piston is fully bottomed in it's bore or damage to ratchet stem will occur.
5. Slowly compress timing chain tensioner.
6. If timing marks on timing chain marks are not evident, us a permanent type marker to mark on righthand and lefthand timing chains.
7. Mark any link to use as the crankshaft timing mark, **Fig. 28.**
8. Count 29 links from the crankshaft timing mark and mark link as the exhaust camshaft sprocket timing mark.
9. Continue counting to 42 and mark that link as the intake camshaft sprocket timing mark.
10. Position timing chain guide and install bolts.
11. Install lefthand timing chain as follows:
    a. Position timing chain so that link No. 1 is positioned on the crankshaft timing mark, **Fig. 29.**
    b. Count twenty nine links from number one link and position this link on the exhaust camshaft sprocket, **Fig. 29.**
12. Continue counting to 42 and place this link on intake camshaft sprocket timing mark, **Fig. 29.**
13. Install lefthand timing chain tensioner and tensioner arm.
14. Install crankshaft damper bolt and rotate crankshaft keyway to 3 o'clock position, **Fig. 24.**
15. Ensure righthand camshafts are correctly positioned, **Fig. 25.**
16. Position righthand timing chain and chain guide, align marks on timing chain with marks on camshaft and crankshaft sprockets, **Fig. 30.**
17. Install righthand timing chain tensioner and tensioner arm.
18. Remove righthand and lefthand timing chain tensioner piston retaining wires.
19. Remove crankshaft damper bolt.
20. Install ignition pulse wheel with keyway in slot stamped "20-25-34Y-30M (Color Blue)."
21. Install spark plugs and engine front cover.

CAMSHAFT

REPLACE

Lefthand

Cylinder head camshaft journal caps and cylinder heads are numbered. Ensure journal caps are placed in their respective positions or damage to cylinder head may occur.

1. Remove water pump belt.
2. Remove timing chain and guides as outlined under "Timing Chain, Replace."
3. Remove water pump pulley using water pump pulley removal tool No. 303-S455, or equivalent.
4. Remove camshaft oil seal using seal removal tool No. 303-409, or equivalent.
5. Remove camshaft oil seal retainer.
6. Loosen lefthand camshaft cap bolts in sequence, **Fig. 31,** to allow camshafts to rise from cylinder head, then remove caps.
7. Remove camshafts.
8. Reverse procedure to install, noting the following:
    a. Lubricate camshafts with SAE 5W-20 motor oil, or equivalent, and carefully position camshafts into cylinder head.
    b. Align camshafts, **Fig. 32.**
    c. **Do not install camshaft journal thrust caps until all of the bearing caps have been installed, or damage to thrust caps may occur.**
    d. Lubricate bearing surfaces of camshaft bearing caps with SAE 5W-20 motor oil, or equivalent.
    e. Install bearing caps, loosely install bolts, **Fig. 33.**
    f. Lubricate bearing surfaces of camshaft bearing thrust caps with SAE 5W-20 motor oil, or equivalent.
    g. Install bearing thrust caps and loosely install bolts, **Fig. 34.**
    h. Tighten bolts to specification, in sequence, **Fig. 35.**

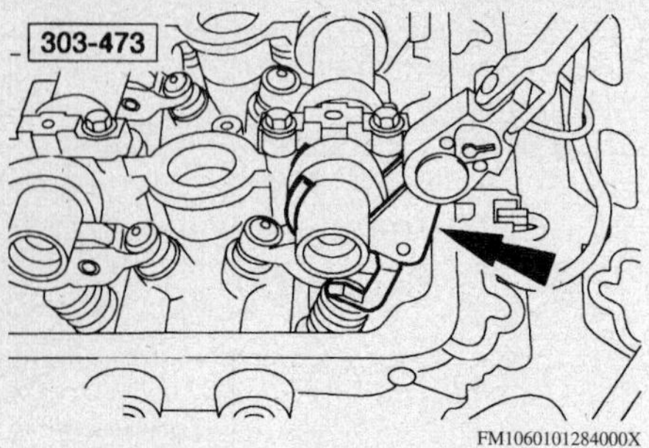

Fig. 21 Roller follower replacement

Righthand

Cylinder head camshaft journal caps and cylinder heads are numbered. Ensure journal caps are placed in their respective positions or damage to cylinder head may occur.

1. Remove timing chain and guides as outlined under "Timing Chain, Replace."
2. Loosen righthand camshaft bolts in sequence, **Fig. 36,** and allow camshafts to rise from cylinder head.
3. Remove camshaft caps, then the camshafts.
4. Reverse procedure to install, noting the following:
   a. Lubricate camshafts with SAE 5W-20 motor oil, or equivalent.
   b. Carefully position camshafts into cylinder head, then align camshafts, **Fig. 37.**
   c. **Do not install camshaft journal thrust caps until all of camshaft bearing caps have been installed, or damage to thrust caps may occur.**
   d. Lubricate bearing surfaces of camshaft bearing caps with SAE 5W-20 motor oil, or equivalent.
   e. Install bearing caps and loosely install bolts.
   f. Lubricate bearing surfaces of camshaft bearing thrust caps with SAE 5W-20 motor oil, or equivalent.
   g. Install bearing thrust caps and loosely install bolts, **Fig. 38.**
   h. Tighten all bolts to specification, in sequence, **Fig. 39.**

MAIN & ROD BEARINGS

1. Read code stamped on crankshaft flange.
2. Read code stamped on cylinder block rear face.
3. First two numbers after asterisk make up code for main journal No. 1 and next two numbers for main journal No. 2.
4. First two numbers after second asterisk make up code for main journal No. 3 and last two numbers for main journal No. 4.
5. Select bearing for each main journal using chart, **Fig. 40.**
6. Match block and crankshaft code with its corresponding column or row.
7. For example, if block code is *0609*0711* and crankshaft code is *8480*8082*, main bearing No. 1 should use grade 1 bearings. Main journals No. 2, 3 and 4 should all be grade 2.

CRANKSHAFT SEAL

REPLACE

1. Remove accessory drive belt as outlined under "Serpentine Drive Belt."
2. Remove righthand front inner fender splash shield.
3. Remove torque converter inspection cover.
4. Install flywheel holding tool No. 303-544, or equivalent.
5. Remove crankshaft pulley bolt and washer.
6. Remove crankshaft pulley using crankshaft damper removal tool No. 303-009, or equivalent.
7. Remove crankshaft front oil seal using seal removal tool No. 303-409, or equivalent.
8. Install new front seal using seal installation tool No. 303-335, or equivalent.
9. Reverse procedure to install.

CRANKSHAFT REAR OIL SEAL

REPLACE

1. Remove transaxle as outlined in **MOTOR's "Domestic Transmission, In-Vehicle Service" or "Transmission Service DVD."**
2. Remove flexplate.
3. Remove rear seal using rear crankshaft seal removal tool No. 303-519, or equivalent.
4. Reverse procedure to install, noting the following:
   a. Lubricate crankshaft rear oil lips with SAE 5W-20 motor oil, or equivalent.
   b. Install crankshaft rear oil seal using rear main seal replacement tool No. 303-178, or equivalent.

OIL PAN

REPLACE

1. Remove flexible exhaust pipe. Disconnect downstream catalyst monitor sensor.
2. Drain engine oil into suitable container, install new drain plug gasket and tighten plug to specification.
3. Remove mounting bolts, then the oil pan.
4. Reverse procedure to install, noting the following:
   a. Do not use power abrasive discs to clean oil pan sealing surfaces. Only use a plastic scraper to remove gasket material.
   b. Position new gasket on oil pan.
   c. Oil pan must be installed and it's bolts tightened within six minutes of applying sealant.
   d. Apply a small (.040 inch) diameter dot of Silicone Gasket and Sealer No. F7AZ-19554-EA, or equivalent, to areas indicated, **Fig. 41.**

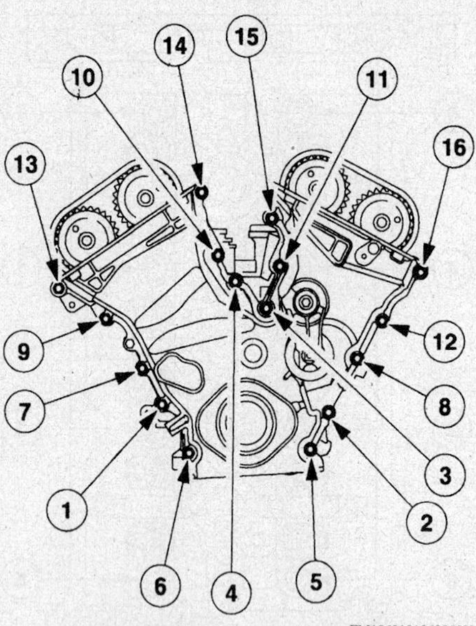

Fig. 22 Front cover bolt installation sequence

   e. Position oil pan and tighten oil pan bolts in sequence, **Fig. 42,** to specification.

OIL PUMP

REPLACE

1. Remove front cover as outlined under "Front Cover, Replace."
2. Remove timing chain, covers and gears, as outlined under "Timing Chain, Replace."
3. Remove oil pump screen cover and tube.
4. Remove damper bolts as outlined under "Crankshaft Damper, Replace" then the crankshaft sprockets.
5. Remove oil pump bolts in sequence, **Fig. 43.**
6. Reverse procedure to install, noting the following:
   a. **Torque** oil pump bolts to 89 inch lbs., in sequence, **Fig. 44.**

SERPENTINE DRIVE BELT

1. Raise and support vehicle.
2. Remove righthand front wheel and tire assembly.
3. Remove righthand front lower splash shield.
4. Rotate accessory drive belt tensioner clockwise, then remove belt.
5. Reverse procedure to install.

THERMOSTAT

REPLACE

1. Drain cooling system into suitable container.
2. Remove engine appearance cover.
3. Remove thermostat housing, then the thermostat and O-ring.
4. Clean and inspect sealing surfaces.
5. Reverse procedure to install.

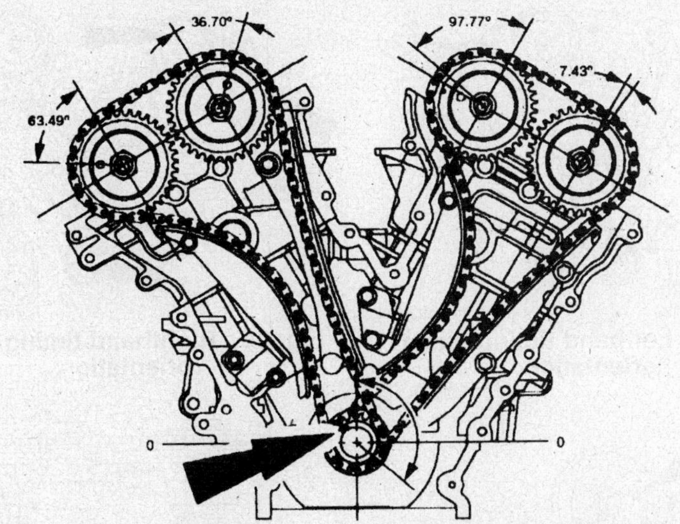

Fig. 23 Camshaft positioning

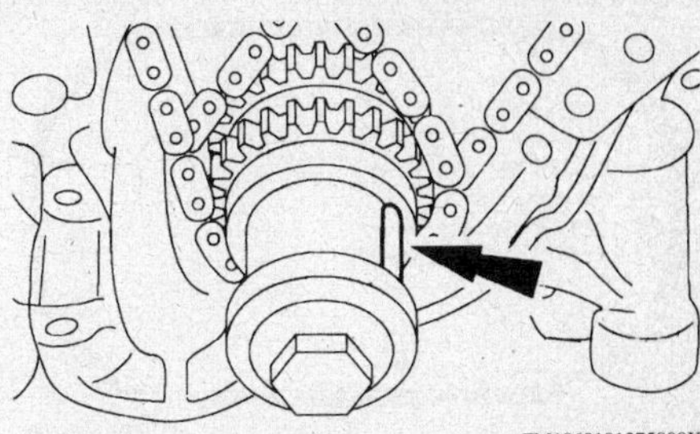

Fig. 24 Crankshaft orientation at 3 o'clock position

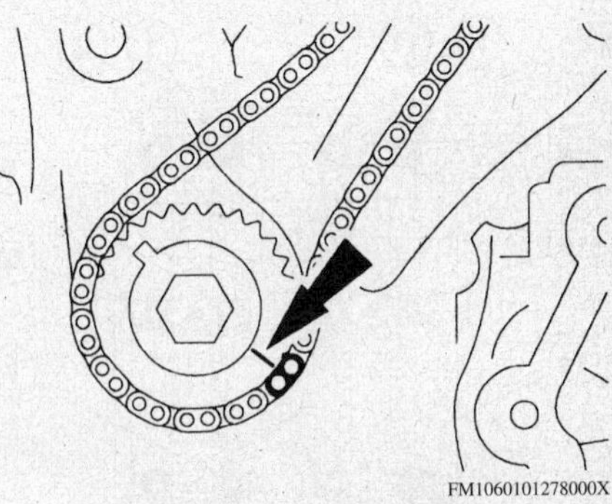

Fig. 27 Link position on crankshaft sprocket

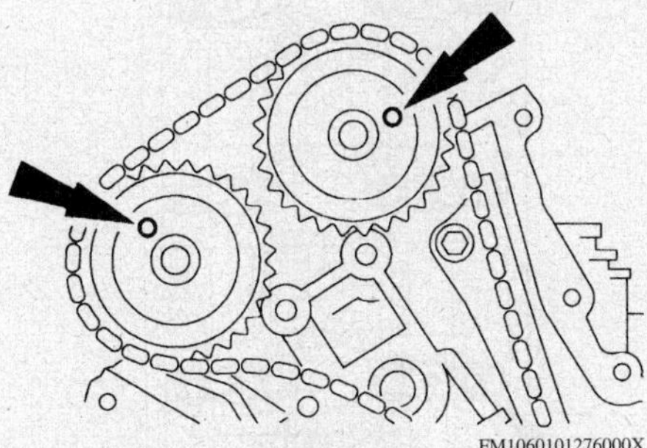

Fig. 25 Camshafts neutral position

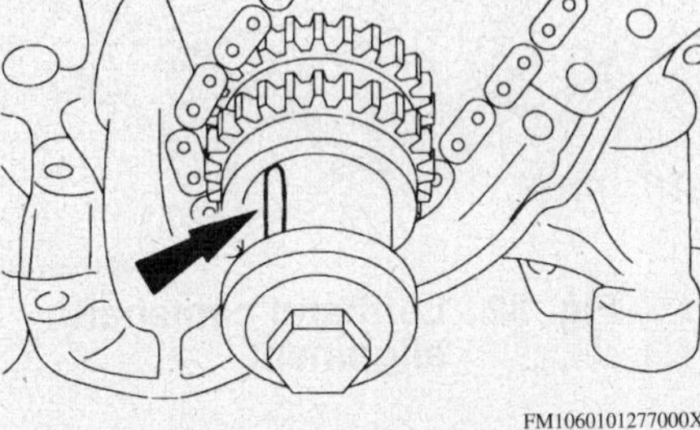

Fig. 26 Crankshaft keyway in 11 o'clock position

WATER PUMP

REPLACE

1. Drain cooling system into suitable container.
2. Remove air cleaner outlet tube.
3. Remove water pump belt tensioner.
4. Disconnect coolant hoses.
5. Remove water pump attaching bolts, then the water pump.
6. Separate water pump from water pump housing.
7. Clean and inspect sealing surfaces.
8. Reverse procedure to install.

RADIATOR

REPLACE

1. Raise and support vehicle.
2. Drain cooling system into suitable container.
3. Remove lower splash shields.
4. Disconnect lower radiator hose and high pressure transmission line.
5. Lower vehicle.
6. Disconnect transmission return line.
7. Disconnect upper radiator hose and degas supply hose.
8. Remove hood latch bolts and nuts and position hood latch aside.
9. Remove center support.
10. Remove cooling fan upper retaining bolts.
11. Remove upper radiator support brackets, then the radiator.
12. Reverse procedure to install.

FUEL PUMP

REPLACE

1. Relieve fuel system pressure as outlined under "Precautions."
2. Remove lefthand rear seat cushion.
3. Lift access cover on floor scuff plate, then remove pin type retainers and position carpet aside.
4. Remove fuel pump module access cover.
5. Disconnect fuel pump electrical connectors.
6. Disconnect fuel and vapor lines.
7. Remove gas cap.
8. Remove fuel pump module using fuel sender wrench tool No. 310-069, or equivalent.
9. Reverse procedure to install.

FUEL FILTER

REPLACE

1. Relieve fuel system pressure as outlined under "Precautions."
2. Place a suitable container below fuel lines, then disconnect lines.
3. Loosen fuel filter clamp and remove filter.
4. Reverse procedure to install.

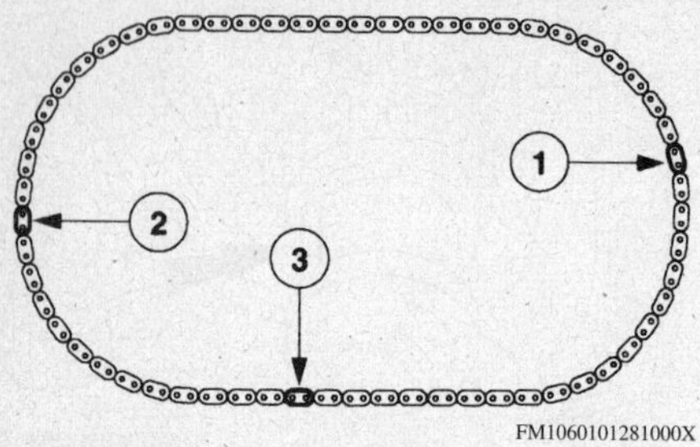

Fig. 28 Timing chain timing marks

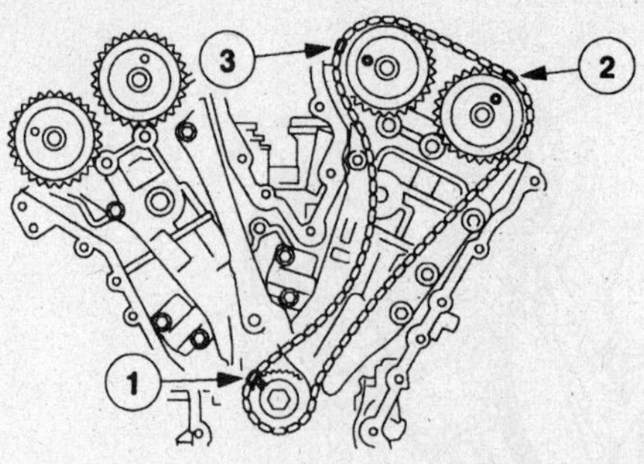

Fig. 29 Lefthand timing chain orientation

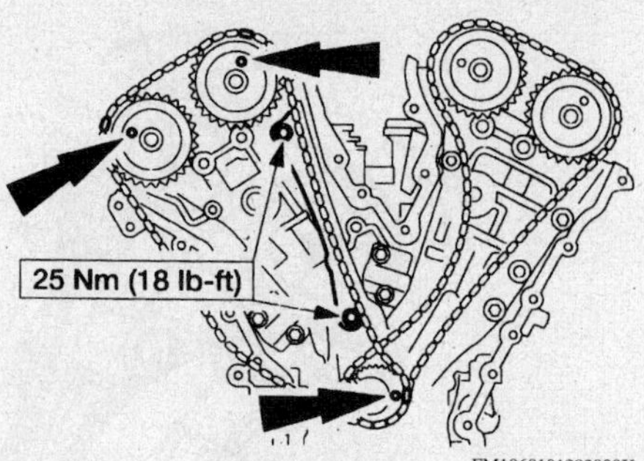

Fig. 30 Righthand timing chain orientation

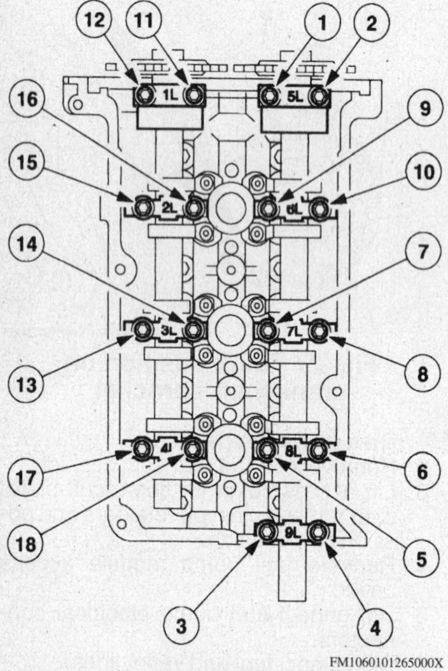

Fig. 31 Lefthand camshaft cap removal sequence

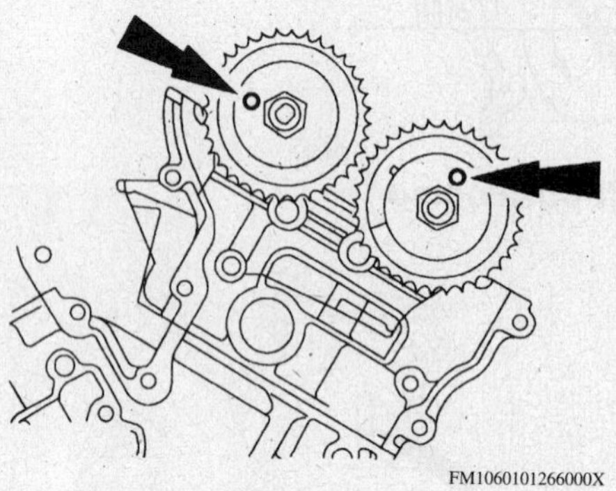

Fig. 32 Lefthand camshaft alignment

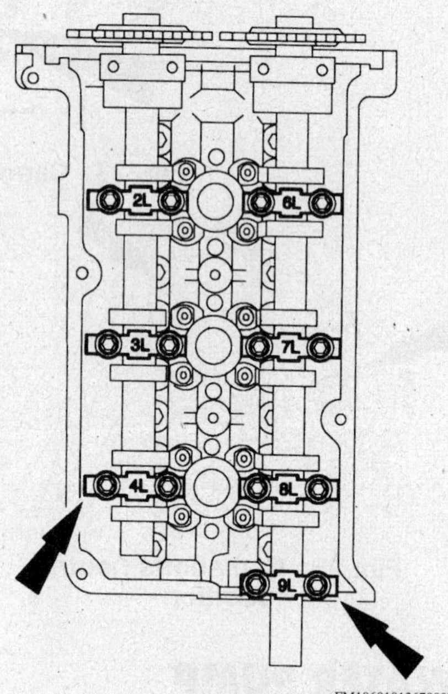

Fig. 33 Lefthand camshaft bearing cap installation

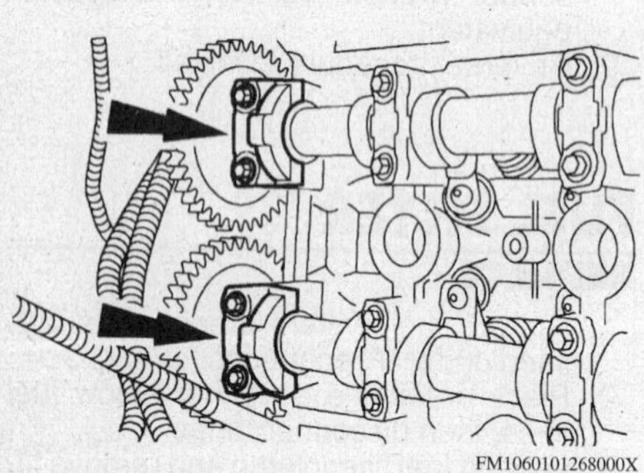

Fig. 34 Lefthand camshaft bearing thrust cap installation

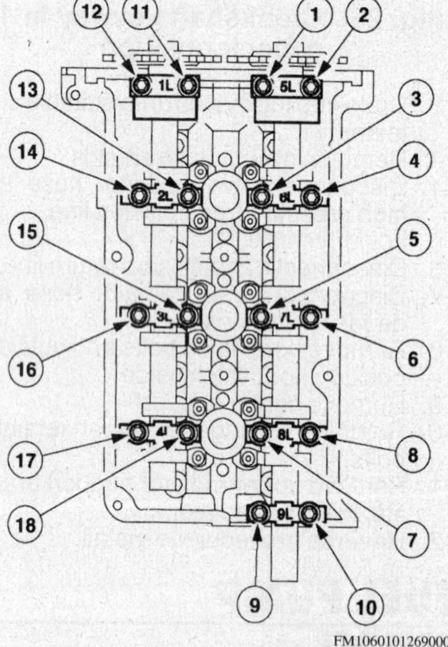

Fig. 35 Lefthand camshaft bolt tightening sequence

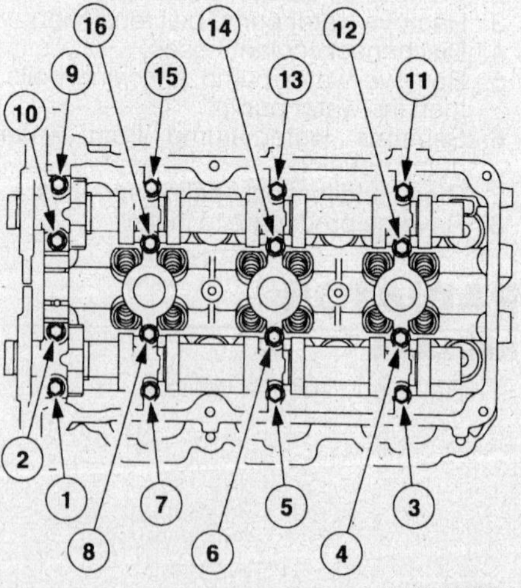

Fig. 36 Righthand camshaft cap removal sequence

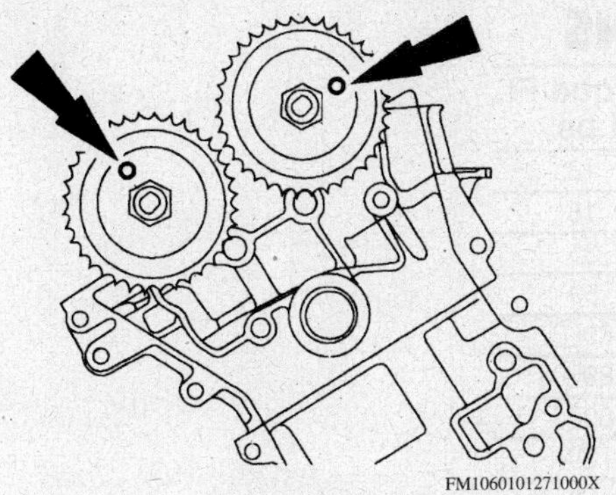

Fig. 37 Righthand camshaft alignment

Fig. 38 Righthand camshaft bearing thrust cap installation

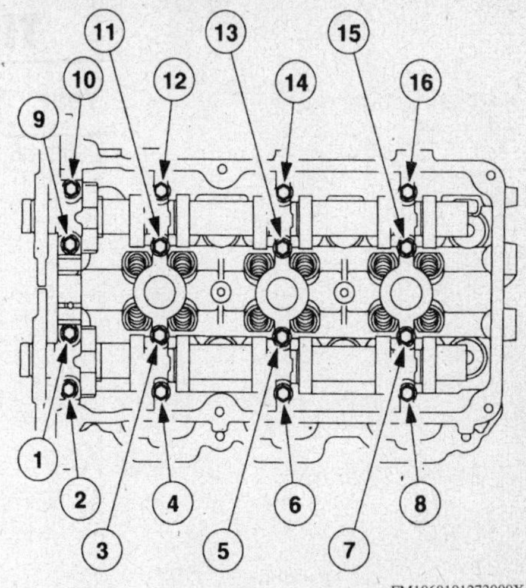

Fig. 39 Righthand camshaft bolt tightening sequence

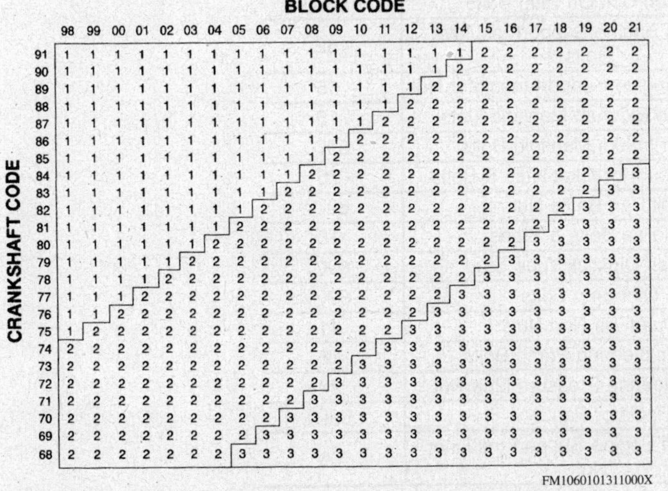

BLOCK CODE / CRANKSHAFT CODE

Crankshaft code	98	99	00	01	02	03	04	05	06	07	08	09	10	11	12	13	14	15	16	17	18	19	20	21
91	1	1	1	1	1	1	1	1	1	1	1	1	1	1	1	1	1	2	2	2	2	2	2	2
90	1	1	1	1	1	1	1	1	1	1	1	1	1	1	1	1	2	2	2	2	2	2	2	2
89	1	1	1	1	1	1	1	1	1	1	1	1	1	1	1	2	2	2	2	2	2	2	2	2
88	1	1	1	1	1	1	1	1	1	1	1	1	1	1	2	2	2	2	2	2	2	2	2	2
87	1	1	1	1	1	1	1	1	1	1	1	1	1	2	2	2	2	2	2	2	2	2	2	2
86	1	1	1	1	1	1	1	1	1	1	1	1	2	2	2	2	2	2	2	2	2	2	2	2
85	1	1	1	1	1	1	1	1	1	1	1	2	2	2	2	2	2	2	2	2	2	2	2	2
84	1	1	1	1	1	1	1	1	1	1	2	2	2	2	2	2	2	2	2	2	2	2	2	3
83	1	1	1	1	1	1	1	1	1	2	2	2	2	2	2	2	2	2	2	2	2	2	3	3
82	1	1	1	1	1	1	1	1	2	2	2	2	2	2	2	2	2	2	2	2	2	3	3	3
81	1	1	1	1	1	1	1	2	2	2	2	2	2	2	2	2	2	2	2	2	3	3	3	3
80	1	1	1	1	1	1	2	2	2	2	2	2	2	2	2	2	2	2	2	3	3	3	3	3
79	1	1	1	1	1	2	2	2	2	2	2	2	2	2	2	2	2	2	3	3	3	3	3	3
78	1	1	1	1	2	2	2	2	2	2	2	2	2	2	2	2	2	3	3	3	3	3	3	3
77	1	1	1	2	2	2	2	2	2	2	2	2	2	2	2	2	3	3	3	3	3	3	3	3
76	1	1	2	2	2	2	2	2	2	2	2	2	2	2	2	3	3	3	3	3	3	3	3	3
75	1	2	2	2	2	2	2	2	2	2	2	2	2	2	3	3	3	3	3	3	3	3	3	3
74	2	2	2	2	2	2	2	2	2	2	2	2	2	3	3	3	3	3	3	3	3	3	3	3
73	2	2	2	2	2	2	2	2	2	2	2	2	3	3	3	3	3	3	3	3	3	3	3	3
72	2	2	2	2	2	2	2	2	2	2	2	3	3	3	3	3	3	3	3	3	3	3	3	3
71	2	2	2	2	2	2	2	2	2	2	3	3	3	3	3	3	3	3	3	3	3	3	3	3
70	2	2	2	2	2	2	2	2	2	3	3	3	3	3	3	3	3	3	3	3	3	3	3	3
69	2	2	2	2	2	2	2	2	3	3	3	3	3	3	3	3	3	3	3	3	3	3	3	3
68	2	2	2	2	2	2	2	3	3	3	3	3	3	3	3	3	3	3	3	3	3	3	3	3

FM1060101311000X

Fig. 40 Crankshaft main bearing selection chart

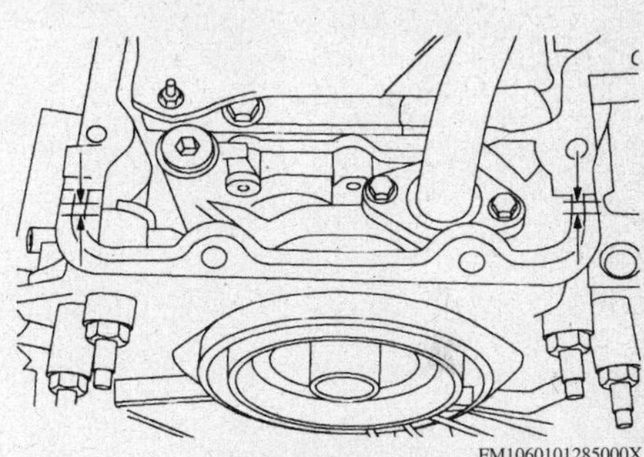

Fig. 41 Oil pan sealant location

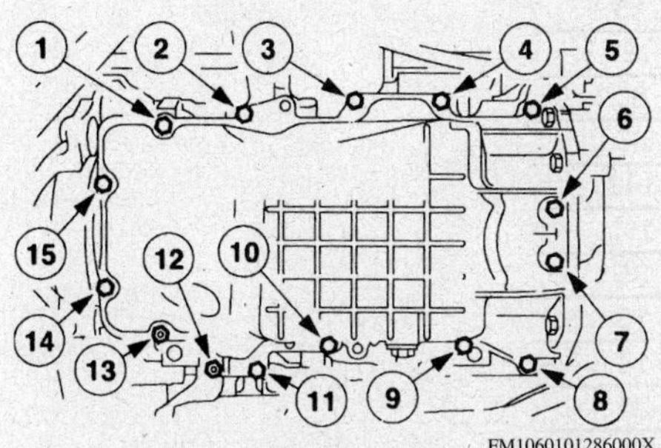

Fig. 42 Oil pan tightening sequence

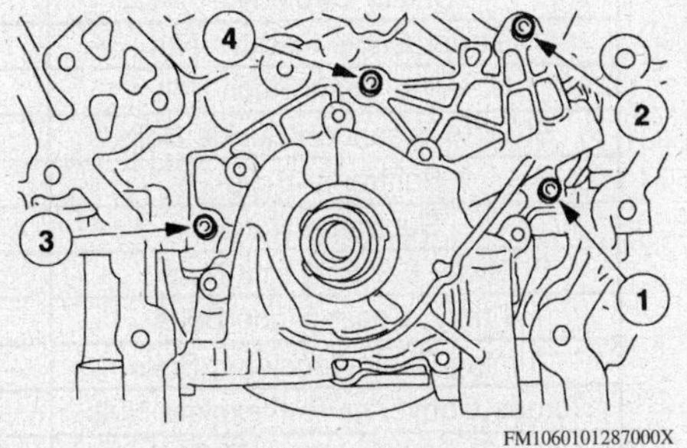

Fig. 43 Oil pump mounting bolt removal sequence

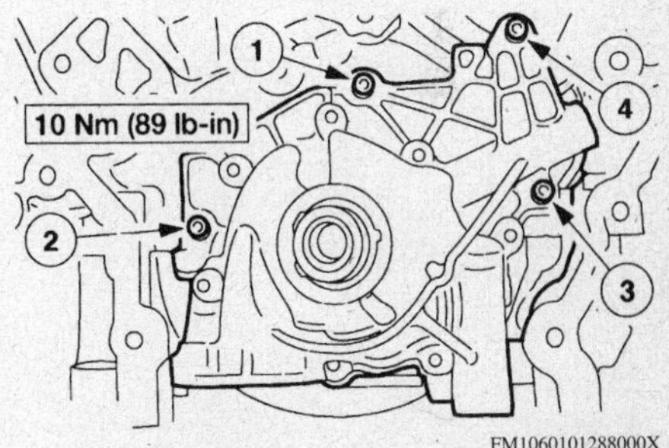

Fig. 44 Oil pump mounting bolt tightening sequence

TIGHTENING SPECIFICATIONS

Year	Component	Torque Ft. Lbs.
2002–06	A/C Compressor Bolts	18
	Accessory Drive Belt Tensioner	18
	Alternator Bolts & Studs	35
	Ball Joint Nuts	59
	Camshaft Cap Bolts	89①
	Camshaft Oil Seal Retainer	89①
	Camshaft Position Sensor	89①
	Crankshaft Damper Bolt	③
	Cylinder Head Bolts	②
	EGR Tube Nuts	30
	EGR Valve Bolts	18
	Flexplate Bolts	59
	Halfshaft Bracket Bolts	35
	Halfshaft Nuts	191
	Ignition Coil On Plug Bolts	53①
	Lefthand Engine Support Insulator Bolts	52
	Lefthand Engine Support Insulator Nut	66
	Lefthand Exhaust Manifold Nuts	15
	Lower Intake Manifold Bolts	89①
	Motor Mount Bracket Nuts & Bolts	76
	Oil Pan Baffle Nuts	89①
	Oil Pan Bolts & Studs	18
	Oil Pan Dipstick Tube Stud	89①
	Oil Pump Bolts	89①
	Outer Tie Rod Nuts	41
	Power Steering Pump Bolts	18
	Power Steering Pressure Line Nut	27
	Radiator Fan Bolt	89①
	Righthand Engine Support Insulator Nut	66
	Righthand Engine Support Insulator Through Bolt & Nut	89
	Righthand Exhaust Manifold Nuts	15
	Shifter Cable Nut	13
	Starter Cable Positive Nut	9
	Steering Shaft Pinch Bolt	30
	Strut To Steering Knuckle Bolts	85
	Subframe Bolts	148
	Subframe Nuts	111
	Sway Bar End Link Nuts	35
	Timing Chain Guide Bolts	18
	Timing Chain Tensioner Bolts	18
	Torque Converter To Flexplate Nuts	30
	Transaxle Mount Bolts	41
	Transaxle Mount Through Bolt	66
	Transaxle To Oil Pan Bracket Bolt	18
	Transaxle To Oil Pan Bracket Nuts	89①
	Upper Intake Manifold Bolts	89①
	Valve Cover Bolts & Studs	89①
	Water Pump Bolts	18
	Y-Pipe Nuts	30
	Y-Pipe To Exhaust Manifold Nuts	30

①— Inch lbs.

②— Refer to “Cylinder Head, Replace.”

③— Refer to “Crankshaft Damper, Replace.”

Rear Axle & Suspension

NOTE: On Air Bag Equipped Models, Refer To "Air Bag System Precautions" Located In The Front Of This Manual For System Disarming & Arming Procedures.

NOTE: Refer To "Computer Relearn Procedures" Located In The Front Of This Manual When Battery Power To The Computer Has Been Interrupted.

NOTE: Refer To "High-Voltage Traction Battery Systems Depowering" Located In The Engine Chapter Before Performing Any Diagnostics Or Repair On This Hybrid Vehicle.

INDEX

PRECAUTIONS

Air Bag Systems

Refer to "Air Bag System Precautions" in the front of this manual for system disarming and arming procedures.

Battery Ground Cable

Prior to service, disconnect battery ground cable and isolate as required.

DESCRIPTION

The rear axle assembly consists of an integral type housing hypoid gear design with the centerline of the pinion set below the centerline of the ring gear, a hypoid ring gear and pinion that consists of a ring gear and an overhung drive pinion which is supported by two opposed tapered roller bearings and a rear axle housing assembly which consists of a cast aluminum center section and a stamped steal rear differential housing cover. Pinion bearing preload is maintained by a drive pinion collapsible spacer on the pinion shaft and adjusted by the pinion nut. The differential case is a one piece design with two openings to allow for assembly of internal components and lubricant flow. The differential pinion shaft is retained by a threaded differential pinion shaft lock bolt assembled into the differential case. Differential bearing preload and ring gear backlash are adjusted by differential bearing shims located between the differential bearing cup and the rear axle housing.

REAR AXLE

REPLACE

1. Remove driveshaft.
2. Disconnect electrical connector, **Fig. 1.**
3. Drain differential fluid into suitable container.
4. Remove rear differential mass damper, **Fig. 2.**
5. Remove six bolts, then the rotary blade coupling, **Fig. 3.**
6. Remove rear halfshafts.
7. Remove axle assembly to front bracket bolts, **Fig. 4.**
8. Remove rear axle to side bracket bolts, **Fig. 5,** then the axle assembly.

REAR HALFSHAFT

REPLACE

1. Support rear wheel knuckles, then remove rear coil springs.
2. Remove nuts, then separate upper and lower ball joints.
3. Mark position of knuckle bolt and cam assembly for installation reference, then remove bolt and separate rear knuckle from vehicle.
4. Remove and discard rear halfshaft nuts.
5. Separate halfshafts from knuckles, **Fig. 6,** using front hub removal tool No. 205-D070, or equivalent,
6. Remove halfshafts using CV joint puller tool No. 205-241, **Fig. 7,** or equivalent.
7. Reverse procedure to install.

HUB & BEARING

REPLACE

2WD

1. Raise and support vehicle.
2. Remove rear wheel and tire assembly.
3. Remove brake drum.
4. Remove wheel hub nut.
5. Remove wheel hub using halfshaft installer tool No. 204-161, or equivalent, **Fig. 8.**
6. Press inner race from wheel hub.
7. Remove snap ring, then the wheel bearing from wheel knuckle using a suitable impact hammer and axle bearing removal tool No. 205-224, or equivalent.
8. Reverse procedure to install.

4WD

1. Raise and support vehicle.
2. Remove brake drums and brake shoes.
3. Remove rear halfshaft nut.
4. Loosen halfshaft from wheel hub using front hub removal tool No. 205-D070, or equivalent.
5. Remove wheel hub from rear knuckle using a suitable slide hammer tool.
6. Press inner wheel bearing race from wheel hub using suitable press tools.
7. **On models equipped with ABS,** remove ABS sensor bolt, then position ABS sensor aside.
8. **On all models,** remove parking brake cable bolt from wheel knuckle, then disconnect parking brake cable.
9. Disconnect rear brake line from wheel cylinder.
10. Support wheel knuckle.
11. Remove lower shock absorber nut.
12. Separate lower and upper ball joints from knuckle.
13. Note position of coil spring and insulator for installation reference.
14. Lower support under rear knuckle, then remove coil spring.
15. Mark position of rear adjustment cam notch, then remove wheel knuckle cam bolt.
16. Remove wheel knuckle cam, then the wheel knuckle.
17. Remove wheel bearing snap ring.

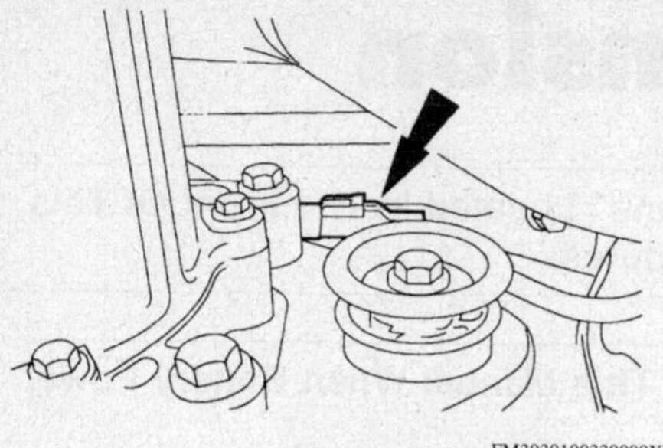
Fig. 1 Electrical connector location

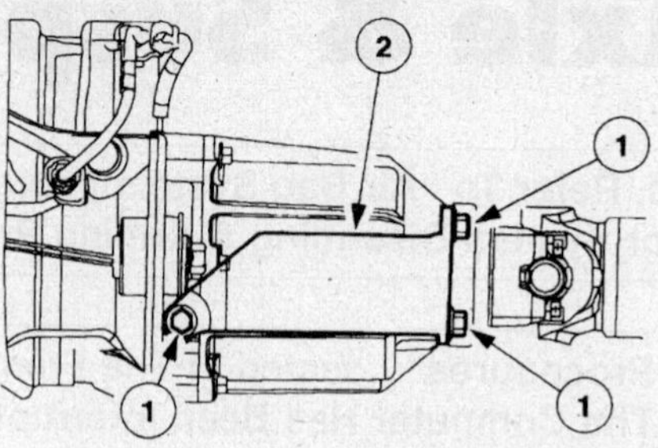

Fig. 2 Rear differential mass damper

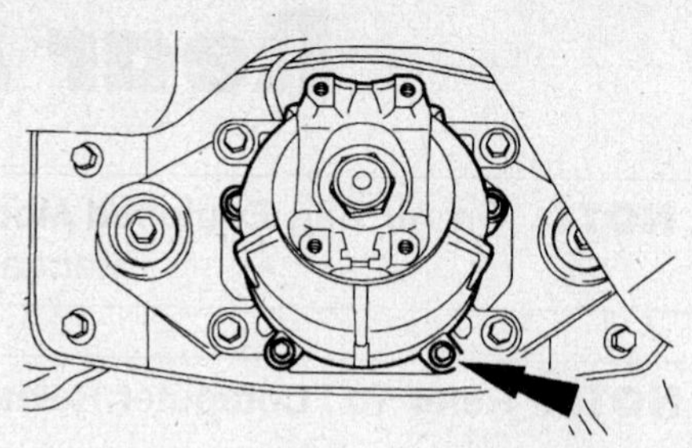
Fig. 3 Rotary blade coupling

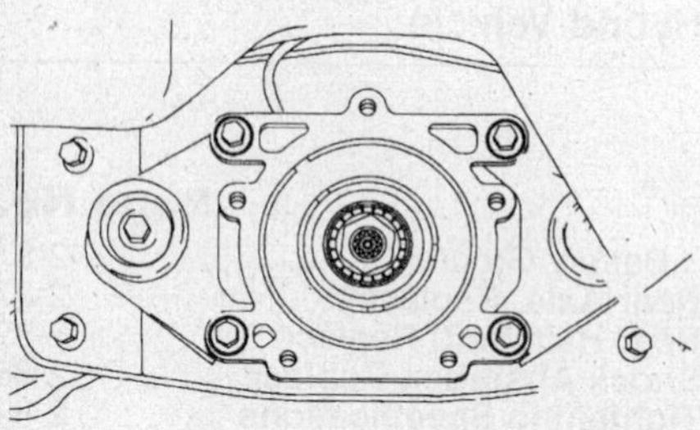
Fig. 4 Axle to front bracket bolts

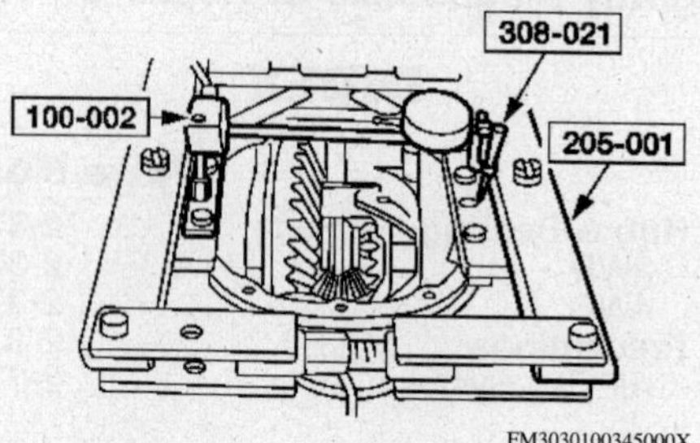

Fig. 5 Axle to side bracket bolts

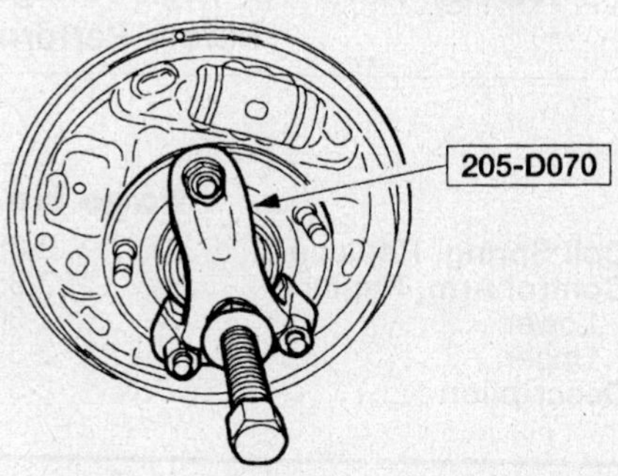

Fig. 6 Halfshaft & knuckle separation

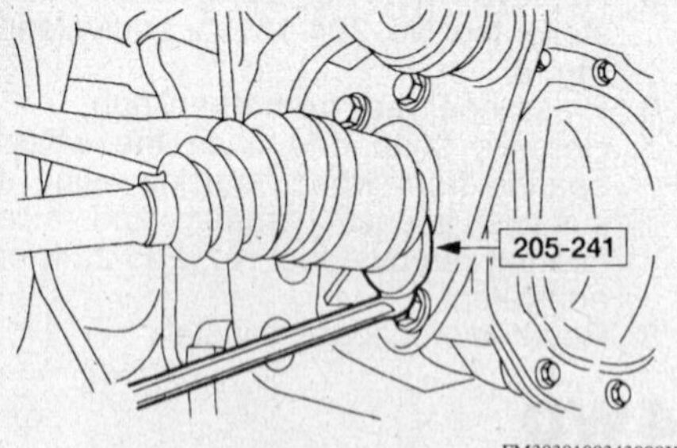

Fig. 7 Halfshaft removal procedure

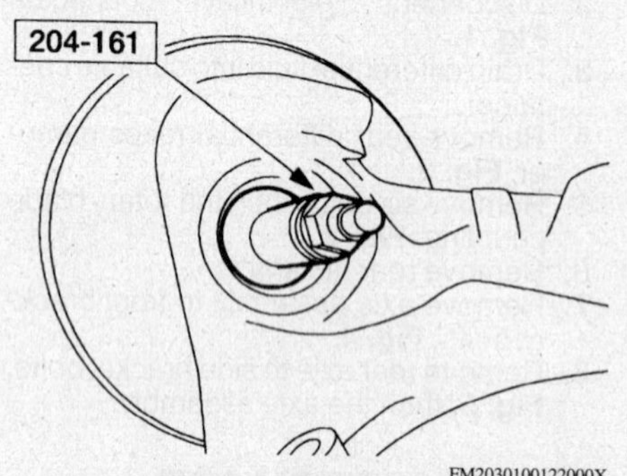

Fig. 8 Wheel hub removal. 2WD

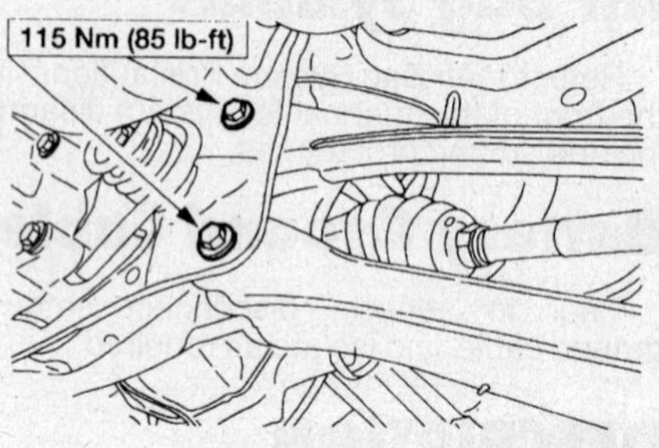

Fig. 9 Inside upper and lower arm bolts

18. Press outer wheel bearing race from wheel knuckle.
19. Reverse procedure to install.

SHOCK ABSORBER

REPLACE

1. Remove rear quarter trim panel, then the upper shock absorber nut.
2. Raise and support vehicle enough to relax suspension system.
3. Remove lower shock absorber nut, then the shock absorber.
4. Reverse procedure to install.

COIL SPRING

REPLACE

1. Raise and support vehicle.
2. Remove wheel and tire assembly.
3. Disconnect brake line from wheel cylinder.
4. **On models equipped with ABS,** remove ABS sensor mounting bolt and position sensor aside.
5. **On all models,** support rear wheel knuckle.
6. Loosen both inside upper and lower arm bolts, **Fig. 9.**
7. Remove lower shock nut and position shock aside.
8. Note position of spring insulator and spring for installation reference.
9. Lower support under wheel knuckle, then remove spring.
10. Reverse procedure to install.

CONTROL ARM

REPLACE

Lower

1. Raise and support vehicle.
2. Remove wheel and tire assembly.
3. Separate lower ball joint from knuckle.
4. Remove lower arm inner bolt, then the lower arm.
5. Reverse procedure to install.

Upper

1. Raise and support vehicle.
2. Remove wheel and tire assembly.
3. Separate upper ball joint from knuckle.
4. Remove upper arm inner bolt, then the upper arm.
5. Reverse procedure to install.

TIGHTENING SPECIFICATIONS

Year	Component	Torque Ft. Lbs.
2002–06	ABS Sensor Bolt	80①
	Ball Joint Nuts	85
	Brake Backing Plate Bolts	49
	Brake Line Nut	13
	Differential Housing Cover Retaining Bolt	17
	Differential Housing To Front Insulator Bracket Bolts	59
	Differential Housing To Side Insulator Bracket Bolts	59
	Lower Arm Inner Bolt	85
	Lower Ball Joint Nut	85
	Rear Axle Differential Rear Insulator Bolt	76
	Rear Axle Hub Nut	214
	Rear Differential Filler Plug	20
	Rear Differential Mass Damper Bolts	35
	Rotary Blade Coupling Bolts	24
	Shock Absorber Nut, Lower	85
	Shock Absorber Nut, Upper	13
	Upper Arm Inner Bolt	85
	Upper Ball Joint Nut	85
	Wheel Hub Nut	214
	Wheel Knuckle Cam Bolt	85

① — Inch lbs.

Front Suspension & Steering

NOTE: On Air Bag Equipped Models, Refer To "Air Bag System Precautions" Located In The Front Of This Manual For System Disarming & Arming Procedures.

NOTE: Refer To "Computer Relearn Procedures" Located In The Front Of This Manual When Battery Power To The Computer Has Been Interrupted.

NOTE: Refer To "High-Voltage Traction Battery Systems Depowering" Located In The Engine Chapter Before Performing Any Diagnostics Or Repair On This Hybrid Vehicle.

INDEX

PRECAUTIONS

Air Bag Systems

Refer to "Air Bag System Precautions" in the front of this manual for system disarming and arming procedures.

Battery Ground Cable

Prior to service, disconnect battery ground cable and isolate as required.

DESCRIPTION

The front suspension uses MacPherson struts, which attach to rearward facing L-shaped lower control arms. Springs and shocks are separately mounted to a dual-path upper-strut mount. The rack-and-pinion steering gear is mounted to a cross member.

HUB & BEARING

REPLACE

Install a new wheel bearing whenever a hub is removed.

1. Raise and support vehicle.
2. Remove front brake disc and front wheel hub.
3. Separate front tie rod from steering knuckle.
4. **On models equipped with ABS,** remove ABS sensor mounting bolt and position ABS sensor aside.
5. **On all models,** remove pinch bolt, then separate lower ball joint from steering knuckle.
6. Separate halfshaft from steering knuckle using front hub removal tool No. 205-D070, or equivalent.
7. Remove strut to steering knuckle bolts, then the steering knuckle.
8. Press hub from wheel bearing and knuckle, then press inner wheel bearing race from wheel hub.
9. Remove wheel bearing snap ring, then press outer wheel bearing race from steering knuckle.
10. Reverse procedure to install.

BALL JOINT INSPECTION

1. Raise and support vehicle to release load from front suspension.
2. Grasp upper and lower edges of tire and move wheel in and out from pivot centerline.
3. If excessive movement is felt while wheel is being moved, ball joint is worn.
4. If movement exceeds 1⁄32 inch, replace lower arm.

BALL JOINT

REPLACE

Lower ball joints are integrated into the lower control arm and cannot be replaced separately. If ball joint is damaged or excessively worn, replace the lower control arm.

LOWER CONTROL ARM

REPLACE

1. Raise and support vehicle.
2. Remove wheel and tire.
3. Remove pinch bolt, then separate ball joint from steering knuckle.
4. Support subframe with suitable support device.
5. Remove lower arm bolts, then the lower arm.
6. Reverse procedure to install.

STRUT

REPLACE

1. Raise and support vehicle.
2. Remove front wheel and tire assembly.
3. Disconnect brake hose grommet from bracket.
4. **On models equipped with ABS,** disconnect ABS harness from strut and spring assembly.
5. **On all models,** remove upper stabilizer bar link nut and position stabilizer bar link aside.
6. Remove strut to wheel knuckle bolts.
7. Support strut and spring assembly, then remove upper nuts.
8. Remove strut and spring assembly.
9. Reverse procedure to install.

STABILIZER BAR

REPLACE

1. Raise and support vehicle.
2. Remove front wheel and tire assemblies.
3. Remove four bolts, then the two stabilizer bar bushings.
4. Remove two stabilizer bar links lower nuts, then the stabilizer bar.
5. Reverse procedure to install.

TIE ROD

REPLACE

1. Turn ignition switch to unlocked position.
2. Raise and support vehicle.
3. Remove tire and wheel assembly.
4. Remove cotter pin and castellated nut from tie rod end.
5. Loosen tie rod jam nut.
6. Separate tie rod end from steering knuckle using suitable tie rod joint removal tool.
7. Remove tie rod end.
8. Reverse procedure to install, noting the following:
   a. Tighten tie rod jam nut to specification.
   b. Toe adjustment must be inspected after tie rod installation.

POWER STEERING GEAR

REPLACE

1. Remove rear transaxle insulator.
2. **On models equipped with automatic transaxle,** remove rear transaxle insulator bracket.
3. **On all models,** raise and support vehicle and remove front wheels.
4. **On models equipped with manual transmission,** remove rear transaxle insulator bracket.
5. **On all models,** remove tie rod cotter pins and nuts.
6. Release tie rod ends from steering knuckle.
7. Remove tie rod end jam nuts, then the tie rods.
8. Record number of turns required to remove each tie rod end, then remove tie rod ends for steering gear.
9. Slide steering gear coupling boot upward, then remove steering gear coupling pinch bolt.
10. Disconnect power steering pressure and return lines from steering rack. Drain excess fluid into suitable container, do not drop O-ring seals.
11. Remove power steering pressure and return line bracket bolts.
12. Remove two steering gear mounting bolts.
13. With mounting bolts removed, slide steering gear forward to separate steering coupling from steering gear shaft, then remove steering gear.
14. Reverse procedure to install.

POWER STEERING PUMP

REPLACE

2.0L & 2.3L Engines

1. Remove accessory drive belt.
2. Disconnect electrical connector at power steering pump.
3. Drain power steering fluid into suitable container.
4. Disconnect power steering pressure line.
5. Remove lower power steering pump bolts.
6. Remove power steering pressure line bracket bolt.
7. Disconnect power steering low pressure hose.
8. Remove bolts, then the power steering pump.
9. Reverse procedure to install.

3.0L Engine

1. Support engine.
2. Loosen power steering pump pulley bolt.
3. Remove drive belt.
4. Remove bolt, then the power steering pump pulley.
5. Drain power steering fluid into suitable container, then disconnect power steering low pressure hose.
6. Remove power steering pressure line bracket bolt, disconnect electrical connector, then disconnect power steering pressure line and position aside.
7. Remove ground wire from upper engine insulator bracket.
8. Remove nuts and bolts, then the upper insulator bracket.
9. Remove engine insulator.
10. Remove power steering pump bracket, then the power steering pump.
11. Reverse procedure to install.

TIGHTENING SPECIFICATIONS

Year	Component	Torque Ft. Lbs.
2.0L ENGINE		
2002–04	Inner Tie Rod To Steering Gear	81
	Power Steering Fluid Cooler Mounting Bolts	89①
	Power Steering Pressure Line Bracket To Engine	18
	Power Steering Pressure Line To Pump Fitting	48
	Power Steering Pressure & Return Line Retainer Plate To Gear Bolt	18
	Power Steering Pump Fluid Reservoir Mounting Bolts	89①
	Power Steering Pump Mounting Bolts	18
	Rear Transaxle Insulator Bracket Bolts	66
	Rear Transaxle Insulator Nuts & Bolts	66
	Steering Gear Mounting Bolts	93
	Steering Shaft Pinch Bolt	18
	Toe Rod End Jam Nut	35
	Tie Rod End Nut	41
2.3L ENGINE		
2004–06	Inner Tie Rod To Steering Gear	81
	Power Steering Fluid Cooler Mounting Bolts	89①
	Power Steering Pressure Line Bracket To Engine	18
	Power Steering Pressure Line To Pump Fitting	48
	Power Steering Line Clamp Plate	18
	Power Steering Pump Fluid Reservoir Mounting Bolts	71①
	Power Steering Pump Mounting Bolts	18
	Rear Transaxle Insulator Bracket Bolts	66
	Rear Transaxle Insulator Nuts & Bolts	66
	Steering Gear Mounting Bolts	85
	Steering Shaft Pinch Bolt	18
	Toe Rod End Jam Nut	35
	Tie Rod End Nut	41

TIGHTENING SPECIFICATIONS—Continued

Year	Component	Torque Ft. Lbs.
3.0L ENGINE		
2002–06	Engine Insulator Mounting Bolts & Nuts	41
	Ground Cable To Engine Insulator Bracket Nut	26
	Inner Tie Rod To Steering Gear	81
	Power Steering Pressure Line To Pump Fitting	48
	Power Steering Pump Bracket Mounting Nuts	89①
	Power Steering Pump Bracket To Pump Bolts	18
	Power Steering Pump Pulley Nut	36
	Power Steering Pressure & Return Line Retainer Plate To Gear Bolt	18
	Rear Transaxle Insulator Nuts & Bolts	66
	Rear Transaxle Insulator Bracket Bolts	66
	Steering Gear Mounting Bolts	93
	Steering Shaft Pinch Bolt	17
	Tie Rod End Jam Nut	35
	Tie Rod End Nut	41
	Upper Engine Insulator Bracket Nuts & Bolts	76

① — Inch lbs.

Wheel Alignment

NOTE: On Air Bag Equipped Models, Refer To "Air Bag System Precautions" Located In The Front Of This Manual For System Disarming & Arming Procedures.

NOTE: Refer To "Computer Relearn Procedures" Located In The Front Of This Manual When Battery Power To The Computer Has Been Interrupted.

NOTE: Refer To "High-Voltage Traction Battery Systems Depowering" Located In The Engine Chapter Before Performing Any Diagnostics Or Repair On This Hybrid Vehicle.

INDEX

PRECAUTIONS

Air Bag Systems

Refer to "Air Bag System Precautions" in the front of this manual for system disarming and arming procedures.

Battery Ground Cable

Prior to service, disconnect battery ground cable and isolate as required.

PRELIMINARY INSPECTION

1. Fill all fluids to specified levels.
2. Ensure spare tire and wheel assembly and related equipment are correctly stored.
3. Remove any excessive accumulation of mud, dirt or road deposits from chassis, wheels and underbody.
4. Retain all normal loads in vehicle.
5. Inflate all tires to specified pressures.
6. Inspect tires for excessive wear patterns (separation of treads or bulging).
7. Inspect vehicle attitude for evidence of overloading or sagging.
8. Inspect for worn or damaged steering or suspension components.
9. Inspect steering gear mounting bolts, tighten to specification.
10. Inspect wheel bearings for smooth movement, inspect wheel hub for damage or excessive wear.
11. Inspect strut and spring assemblies for excessive wear or damage.
12. Inspect shock absorbers for signs of oil leakage.
13. Road test vehicle to confirm customer concerns.

FRONT WHEEL ALIGNMENT

Camber & Caster Adjustment

1. Raise and support vehicle.
2. Remove front shock absorber upper mounting bracket nuts.
3. Push front shock absorber mounting bracket downward and turn it to desired position to set caster and camber, **Fig. 1.**
4. **Torque** front shock absorber upper mounting bracket nuts to 59 ft. lbs.

Front Toe Adjustment

1. Start engine and center steering wheel.
2. Turn engine off and lock steering wheel in position.
3. Inspect toe settings and adjust if required by loosening tie rod jam nuts and turning tie rod ends to obtain specified value.
4. **Torque** tie rod jam nuts to 41 ft. lbs.

Rear Toe Adjustment

1. Jounce vehicle to ensure suspension is in relaxed position.
2. Loosen righthand and lefthand rear suspension trailing arm bolts.
3. Turn righthand and lefthand adjusting cams simultaneously until toe is within specified range.
4. **Torque** suspension trailing arm bolts to 85 ft. lbs.

VEHICLE RIDE HEIGHT

Vehicle ride height should be inspected on a flat, level surface, preferably an alignment rack. Ensure tires are inflated to proper pressures and that all tires are of the same size. Measure distance from wheelhouse opening to center of wheel. Maximum right to left differential should not exceed .4 inch. Ride height can only be altered by installing new springs to obtain desired height differential.

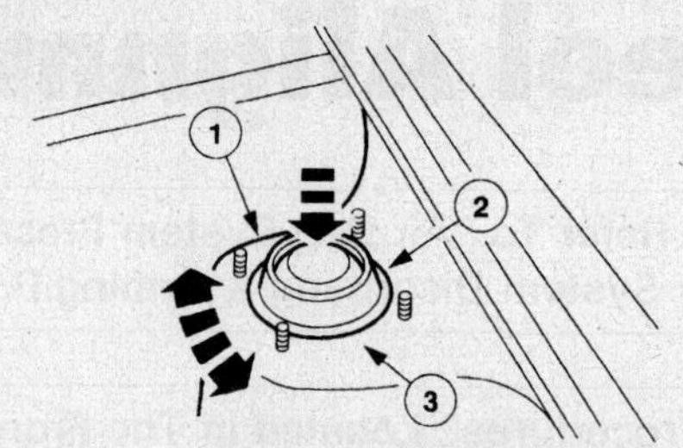

Direction Indicator	Difference From Standard Position	
	Camber Angle	Caster Angle
1	+30 Minutes	-30 Minutes
2	0°	-30 Minutes
3	+30 Minutes	0°

FM2020100183000X

Fig. 1 Caster & camber adjustment

AVIATOR, EXPLORER, MOUNTAINEER & RANGER

NOTE: Refer To Back Of This Manual For Vehicle Manufacturer's Special Service Tool Suppliers.

INDEX OF SERVICE OPERATIONS

Specifications

GENERAL ENGINE SPECIFICATIONS

Year	Engine Liter	Bore & Stroke	Fuel System	Compression Ratio	Net H.P. @ RPM	Maximum Torque, Ft. Lbs. @ RPM	Normal Oil Pressure, psi
2002–06	2.3L	3.44 x 3.70	EFI	9.7	143 @ 2550	154 @ 3750	29–39①
	3.0L	3.50 x 3.14	EFI	9.6	148 @ 4900	180 @ 3950	40–60②
	4.0L④	3.95 x 3.31	EFI	9.7	210 @ 5100	254 @ 3700	③
	4.0L⑤	3.95 x 3.31	EFI	9.7	210 @ 5150	248 @ 3000	③
	4.0L⑥	3.95 x 3.31	EFI	9.7	207 @ 5250	238 @ 3000	③
	4.6L⑦	3.55 X 3.54	EFI	9.8	292 @ 5750	300 @ 3950	75③
	4.6L⑧	3.55 X 3.54	EFI	9.8	300 @ 5750	320 @ 4500	75③

EFI — Electronic Fuel Injection

VIN — Vehicle Identification Number

① — At 2000 RPM w/engine @ normal operating temperature.

② — At 2500 RPM w/engine @ normal operating temperature.

③ — Minimum @ 2000 RPM.

④ — Explorer & Mountaineer.

⑤ — Explorer Sport & Explorer Sport Trac.

⑥ — Ranger.

⑦ — VIN code, W.

⑧ — VIN code, 8.

TUNE UP SPECIFICATIONS

The following specifications are published from the latest information available. This data should only be used in the absence of a decal affixed in the engine compartment.

Year & Engine	Spark Plug Gap	Ignition Timing BTDC			Curb Idle Speed②		Fast Idle Speed②		Fuel Pump Pressure, psi.	Valve Lash, Inch
		Firing Order ③	Man. Trans.	Auto. Trans.	Man. Trans.	Auto. Trans.	Man. Trans.	Auto. Trans.		
2002–06										
2.3L	.049–.053	①	10⑦	10⑦	④	④	④	④	60–65	⑨
3.0L	.042–.046	⑥	10⑦	10⑦	④	④	④	④	60–65	⑧
4.0L⑩	.061–.068	⑥	10⑦	10⑦	④	④	④	④	60–65	⑧
4.0L⑪	.061–.068	⑥	10⑦	10⑦	④	④	④	④	30–40	⑧
4.6L⑫	.052–.056	⑤	—	10⑦	—	④	—	④	30–40	⑧
4.6L⑬	.052–.056	⑤	—	10⑦	—	④	—	④	27–37	⑧

BTDC — Before Top Dead Center

VIN — Vehicle Identification Number

① — Cylinder numbering from front to rear, 1, 2, 3, 4. Firing order 1-3-4-2.

② — When inspecting idle speed, set parking brake & block drive wheels.

③ — Before removing wires from distributor cap or coil unit, determine location of ignition wires, as position may have been altered from that outlined at end of this chart.

④ — Controlled by Powertrain Control Module (PCM).

⑤ — Cylinder numbering from front to rear, righthand bank, 1-2-3-4; lefthand bank, 5-6-7-8. Firing order, 1-3-7-2-6-5-4-8.

⑥ — Cylinder numbering from front to rear, righthand bank, 1-2-3; lefthand bank, 4-5-6. Firing order 1-4-2-5-3-6.

⑦ — Not adjustable.

⑧ — Equipped w/hydraulic valve tappets.

⑨ — Intake, .008–.011 inch. Exhaust, .010–.013 inch.

⑩ — Explorer Sport, Explorer Sport Trac & Ranger.

⑪ — Explorer & Mountaineer.

⑫ — VIN code, W.

⑬ — VIN code, 8.

FRONT WHEEL ALIGNMENT SPECIFICATIONS

AVIATOR, EXPLORER & MOUNTAINEER

Year	Model	Caster Angle, Degrees		Camber Angle, Degrees		Total Toe, Degrees①	
		Limits	Desired	Limits	Desired	Limits	Desired
2002–05	All	②	③	-1.30 to +.30	-.50	-.15 to +.35	+.10
2006	All	+3.85 To +5.35	+4.60	-1.25 to +.25	-.50	-.10 to +.30	+.10

① — Toe-In (+). Toe-Out (–).

② — +LH, +4.1° to +6.1°; RH, +4.3° to +6.3°.

③ — LH, +5.1°; RH, +5.3°.

FRONT WHEEL ALIGNMENT SPECIFICATIONS—Continued

EXPLORER SPORT & SPORT TRAC

Year	Model	Caster Angle, Degrees②				Camber Angle, Degrees		Total Toe, Degrees①	
		LH		RH					
		Limits	Desired	Limits	Desired	Limits	Desired	Limits	Desired
2002	Explorer Sport	+2.95 to +4.95	+3.95	+3.35 to +5.85	+4.85	-1.20 to +.20	-.50	-.13 to +.37	+.12
2002–03	Explorer Sport	+2.15 to +4.15	+3.15	+2.65 to +4.65	+3.65	-1.20 to +.20	-.50	-.13 to +.37	+.12
2002–06	Sport Trac	+2.15 to +4.15	+3.15	+2.65 to +4.65	+3.65	-1.20 to +.20	-.50	-.13 to +.37	+.12

LH — Lefthand

RH — Righthand

① — Toe-In (+). Toe-Out (–).

② — Caster specifications assume a 0° frame angle. If vehicle's tail is higher than its nose, add frame angle to measured caster. If vehicle's tail is lower than its nose, subtract frame angle from measured caster. Compare total to specification.

RANGER

Year	Model	Caster Angle, Degrees		Camber Angle, Degrees		Total Toe, Degrees①	
		Limits	Desired	Limits	Desired	Limits	Desired
2002–06	2WD	②	+1.0	-1.2 to +.2	-.5	-.19 to +.31	.06
	4WD	③	+1.0	-1.2 to +.2	-.5	-.13 to +.37	.12

2WD — Two Wheel Drive
4WD — Four Wheel Drive
① — Toe-In (+). Toe-Out (–).

② — LH, +2.50° to +4.50°; RH, +2.90° to +4.90°.

③ — LH, +1.80° to +3.80°; RH, +2.50° to +4.50°.

VEHICLE RIDE HEIGHT SPECIFICATIONS

Year	Front, Inches①	Rear, Inches①	Ride Height Difference Side To Side, Inches	
			Front	Rear
EXPLORER & MOUNTAINEER				
2002–06	.32–.68②	.44–3.64③	.28	.32
EXPLORER SPORT				
2002–06	4.40–4.80④	4.80–5.60⑤	.60	.78
EXPLORER SPORT TRAC				
2002–06	4.40–4.80④	6.30–7.00⑤	.60	.78
RANGER w/2WD				
2002–06	3.90–4.20④	4.20–7.80⑤	.32	.80
RANGER w/4WD				
2002–06	3.30–3.90④	6.90–7.80⑤	.32	.80

① — See door sticker or inside of glove box for manufacturers original tire size specifications. If tires on vehicle do not match manufacturers original tire size & measurement is not within limits, it will be required to refer to the "Non-Standard Tire & Wheel Size Adjustment To Ride Height Specification & Tire Size Adjustment Charts" in the front of this manual for approximate changes in ride height specifications.

② — Measure front vehicle ride height, **Fig. A.**

③ — Measure rear vehicle ride height, **Fig. B.**

④ — Measure front vehicle ride height, **Fig. C.**

⑤ — Measure rear vehicle ride height models w/2WD, **Fig. D.** Measure rear vehicle ride height models w/4WD, **Fig. E.**

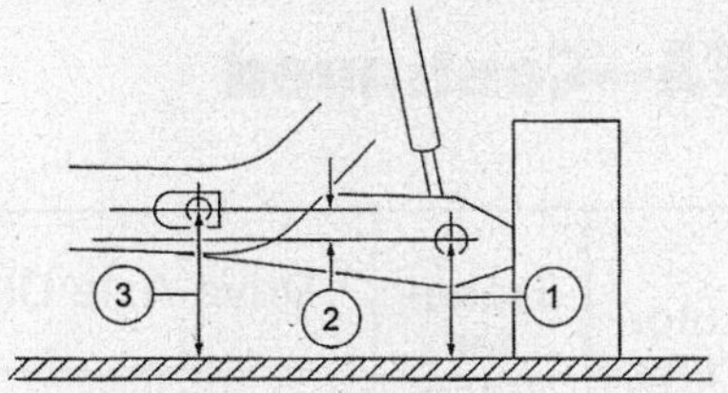

Item	Description
1	Distance between the ground and center of shock absorber lower bolt
2	Ride height = 3-1
3	Distance between the ground and the center of the lower arm inboard bolt

LTV0500000000653

Fig. A Front ride height measurement. Explorer & Mountaineer

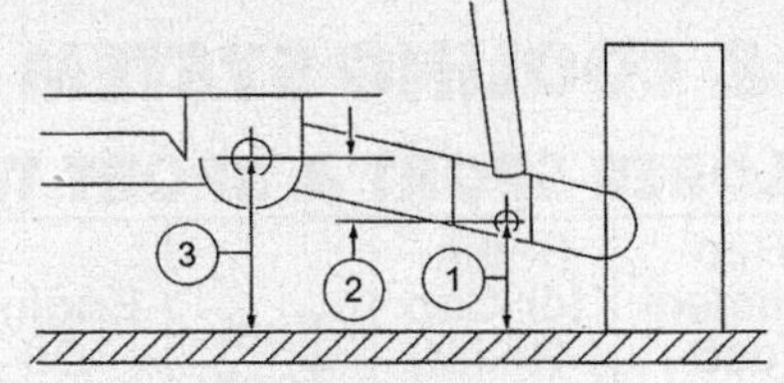

Item	Description
1	Distance between the ground and center of shock absorber lower bolt
2	Ride height = 3-1
3	Distance between the ground and the center of the lower arm inboard bolt

LTV0500000000654

Fig. B Rear ride height measurement. Explorer & Mountaineer

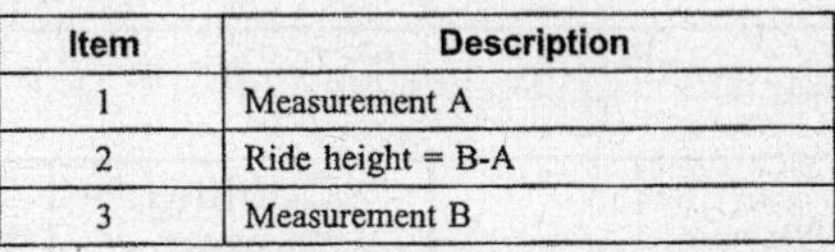

Item	Description
1	Measurement A
2	Ride height = B-A
3	Measurement B

LTV0500000000655

Fig. C Front ride height measurement. Explorer Sport, Sport Trac & Ranger

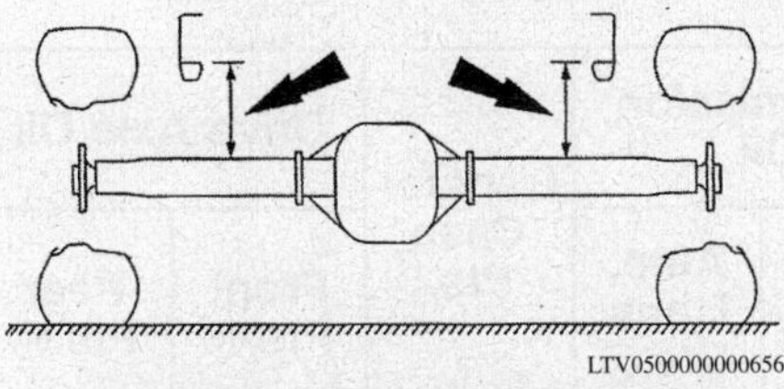

LTV0500000000656

Fig. D Rear ride height measurement. Explorer Sport, Sport Trac & Ranger w/2WD

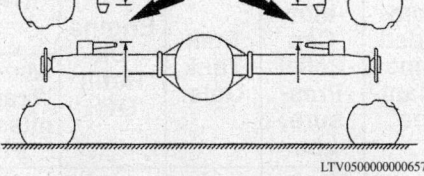

LTV0500000000657

Fig. E Rear ride height measurement. Explorer Sport, Sport Trac & Ranger w/4WD

FLUID CAPACITIES & COOLING SYSTEM DATA

AVIATOR, EXPLORER & MOUNTAINEER

Year	Engine Liter	Cooling System Capacity Qts.		Recom-mended Engine Coolant Type	Radiator Cap Relief Pres-sure, Lbs.	Fuel Tank Gals.	Engine Oil Refill Qts.	Transmission Oil		Drive Axle Oil	
		Less A/C	With A/C					Auto. Trans. Qts.②	Trans-fer Case Pts.	Front Pts.	Rear Pts.
2002–06	4.0L	12.2③	12.2③	④	18–22	22.5	5⑤	12.7	3⑥	2.7⑥	7⑥
	4.6L⑦	18.6①	18.6①	④	18–22	22.5	6.5⑤	12.7	3⑥	2.7⑥	7⑥
	4.6L⑧	18.6①	18.6①	④	18–22	22.5	6.5⑤	12.7	3⑥	2.7⑥	7⑥

VIN — Vehicle Identification Number

① — With auxiliary climate control, 15.7 qts.

② — Approximate. Make final inspection w/dipstick.

③ — With auxiliary climate control, 14 qts.

④ — Models with green coolant, Ethylene Glycol. Models with gold/yellow coolant, use coolant meeting Ford Motor Co. specification WSSM97B51–A1, or equivalent.

⑤ — Includes filter change.

⑥ — .38 inch below bottom of filler hole.

⑦ — VIN code, W.

⑧ — VIN code, 8.

FLUID CAPACITIES & COOLING SYSTEM DATA—Continued

EXPLORER SPORT & SPORT TRAC

Year	Model & Engine Liter	Cooling System Capacity Qts.		Recommended Engine Coolant Type	Radiator Cap Relief Pressure, Lbs.	Fuel Tank Gals.	Engine Oil Refill Qts.	Auto. Trans. Qts.②	Transfer Case Pts.	Drive Axle Oil	
		Less A/C	With A/C							Front Pts.	Rear Pts.
2002–03	Sport 4.0L	14	14	④	13–18	17.5	5①	③	2.6	3.6	5.5–5.8
2002–06	Sport Trac 4.0L	14	14	④	13–18	23	5①	③	2.5	3.6	5.3–5.5⑤

① — Includes filter change.

② — Approximate. Make final inspection w/dipstick.

③ — 2WD models, 10 qts.; 4WD models, 10.3 qts.

④ — Models with green coolant, Ethylene Glycol. Models with gold/yellow coolant, use coolant meeting Ford Motor Co. specification WSSM97B51–A1, or equivalent.

⑤ — .38 inch below bottom of filler hole.

RANGER

Year	Engine Liter	Cooling System Capacity Qts.		Recommended Engine Coolant Type	Radiator Cap Relief Pressure, Lbs.	Fuel Tank Gals.	Engine Oil Refill Qts.	Transmission Oil		Transfer Case Pts.	Drive Axle Oil	
		Less A/C	With A/C					Manual Transmission Pts.	Auto. Trans. Qts.②		Front Pts.⑩	Rear Pts.⑩
2002–06	2.3L	⑥	⑥	③	13–18	⑦	4.0⑧	5.6	9.9	2.5	2.7⑨	5⑨
	3.0L	①	①	③	13–18	⑦	4.5⑧	5.6	④	2.5	2.7⑨	5⑨
	4.0L	⑤	⑤	③	13–18	⑦	4.0⑧	5.6	④	2.5	2.7⑨	5⑨

① — Automatic trans., 14.8 qts.; Manual trans., 15.1 qts.

② — Approximate. Make final inspection w/dipstick.

③ — Models with green coolant, Ethylene Glycol, Models with gold/yellow coolant, use coolant meeting Ford Motor Co. specification WSSM97B51–A1, or equivalent.

④ — 2WD models, 10 qts.; 4WD models, 10.3 qts.

⑤ — Automatic transmission, 13.2 qts.; manual transmission., 13.7 qts.

⑥ — Automatic transmission, 10.9 qts.; manual transmission., 11.2 qts.

⑦ — Regular cab short wheelbase, 17 gals.; long wheelbase, 20 gals. Super Cab, 19.5 gals.

⑧ — Includes filter.

⑨ — On models equipped with Traction Lok, add 4 ounces of friction modifier part No. C8AZ-19B546–A, or equivalent.

⑩ — Approximate, ¼–9⁄16 below bottom of filler hole.

LUBRICANT DATA

AVIATOR, EXPLORER, MOUNTAINEER & RANGER

Year	Model	Lubricant Type						
		Transmission		Hydraulic Clutch Fluid	Transfer Case	Drive Axle	Power Steering	Brake System
		Manual	Automatic					
2002–06	Explorer & Mountaineer 4.0L	Mercon®	Mercon® V	DOT 3	Mercon®	②	Mercon®	DOT 3
	Explorer & Mountaineer 4.6L	Mercon®	Mercon® V	DOT 3	Mercon®	②	Mercon®	DOT 3
	Ranger	Mercon®	Mercon® V	DOT 3	Mercon®	80W-90①	Mercon®	DOT 3

PSF — Power Steering Fluid

① — On models w/limited slip differential, add 4 ounces of friction modifier C8AZ-19B546-A, or an equivalent meeting Ford specification EST-M2C118-A.

② — Front, SAE 75W-90 gear lubricant, or equivalent meeting Ford specification WSP-M2C201-A. Rear, 75W-140 synthetic lube part No. F1TZ-19580-B, or equivalent synthetic gear lubricant meeting Ford specification WSL-M2C192-A. Add 4 oz. of friction modifier part No. C8AZ-19B546-A, or an equivalent meeting Ford specification EST-M2C118-A on models w/Traction-Lok axles.

LUBRICANT DATA—Continued

EXPLORER SPORT & EXPLORER SPORT TRAC

Year	Model	Lubricant Type						
		Transmission		Hydraulic Clutch Fluid	Transfer Case	Drive Axle	Power Steering	Brake System
		Manual	Automatic					
EXPLORER SPORT								
2002–03	All	—	Mercon® V	—	Mercon®	①③	Mercon®	DOT 3
EXPLORER SPORT TRAC								
2002–03	All	—	②	—	Mercon®	①③	Mercon®	DOT 3
2004–06	All	—	②	—	Mercon®	④⑤	Mercon®	DOT 3

PSF — Power Steering Fluid

① — On models w/limited slip differential, add 4 ounces of friction modifier C8AZ-19B546-A, or an equivalent meeting Ford specification EST-M2C118-A.

② — E40D trans., Mercon ATF. 4R70W trans., Mercon® V ATF.

③ — Conventional front & rear axles, 80W-90 gear lubricant. On limited slip axle, 75W-140 synthetic gear lubricant part No. F1TZ-19580-B, or equivalent meeting Ford specification WSL-M2C192-A.

④ — Conventional front & rear axles, 80W-90 gear lubricant. On limited slip axle, SAE 75W-90 FEHP Fuel Efficient High Performance synthetic gear lubricant part No. XY-75W90-QFEHP, or equivalent meeting Ford specification ES-3W4W-19A508-AA.

⑤ — On models w/limited slip differential, add 4 ounces of friction modifier XL-7, or an equivalent meeting Ford specification ES-4L3W-M2C196-BA .

Electrical

NOTE: On Air Bag Equipped Models, Refer To "Air Bag System Precautions" Located In The Front Of This Manual For System Disarming & Arming Procedures.

NOTE: Refer To "Computer Relearn Procedures" Located In The Front Of This Manual When Battery Power To The Computer Has Been Interrupted.

INDEX

PRECAUTIONS

Air Bag Systems

Refer to "Air Bag System Precautions" in the front of this manual for system disarming and arming procedures.

Automatic Ride Control

On models equipped with automatic ride control, the automatic ride control service switch must be turned off before lifting vehicle. The service switch is located in the rear jack storage area.

Battery Ground Cable

Prior to service, disconnect battery ground cable and isolate as required.

FUSE PANEL & FLASHER LOCATION

The passenger compartment fuse panel is located behind the lower lefthand side of the instrument panel.

These vehicles use the same flasher both, turn signal and hazard indicators, in conjunction with the Smart Junction Box (SJB). The electronic combination turn signal/emergency flasher unit is located on the reverse side of the passenger compartment fuse panel.

FUEL PUMP RELAY LOCATION

The fuel pump relay is located on the rear lefthand side of the engine compartment in the engine compartment power distribution center.

RELAY CENTER LOCATION

The power distribution box is located in the engine compartment on the lefthand side inner fender, next to the power brake booster.

STARTER

REPLACE

Aviator, Explorer, Explorer Sport, Explorer Sport Trac & Mountaineer

1. Raise and support vehicle.
2. Remove starter motor electrical connectors.

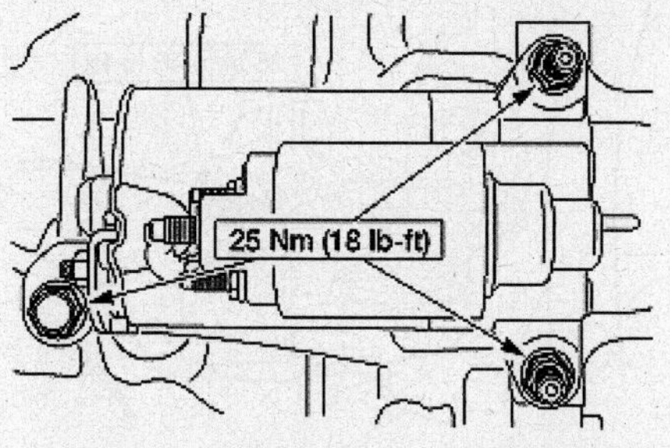

LTV1900000000234

Fig. 1 Starter mounting bolts. Ranger w/2.3L engine

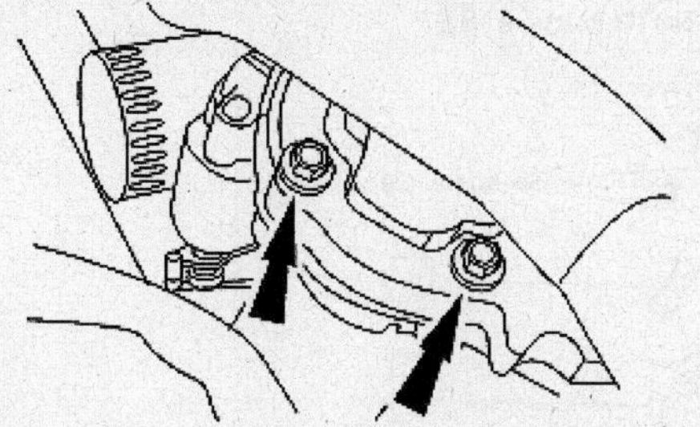

LTV1900000000235

Fig. 2 Starter motor mounting bolts. Ranger w/3.0L engine

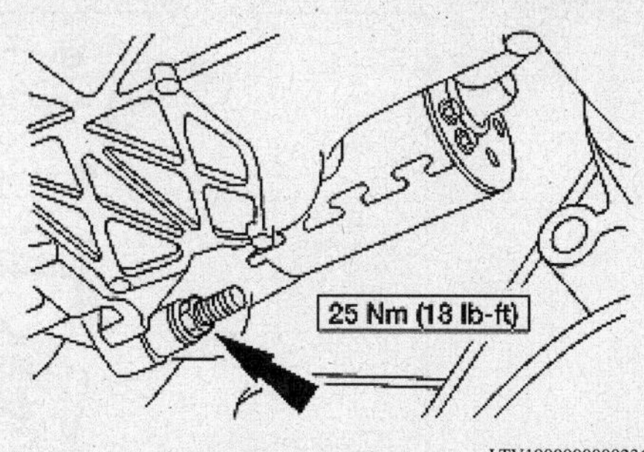

LTV1900000000236

Fig. 3 Lower starter mounting stud. Ranger w/3.0L engine

3. Remove upper and lower starter motor mounting bolts, then the starter motor.
4. Reverse procedure to install.

Ranger

2.3L ENGINE

1. Raise and support vehicle.
2. Remove lefthand front inner fender splash shield.
3. Remove protective cap from starter terminals, then the terminal nuts.
4. Remove ground cable retaining nut and position ground cable aside.
5. Remove starter mounting bolts, **Fig. 1,** then the starter.

3.0L & 4.0L ENGINES

1. Raise and support vehicle.
2. Remove bolts from starter, **Figs. 2 and 3,** then lower starter motor.
3. Remove wiring protective cap, then the wiring nuts and wiring.
4. Remove starter from vehicle.
5. Reverse procedure to install.

ALTERNATOR

REPLACE

Aviator, Explorer, Explorer Sport, Explorer Sport Trac & Mountaineer

Remove components in order listed, **Figs. 4 and 5.**

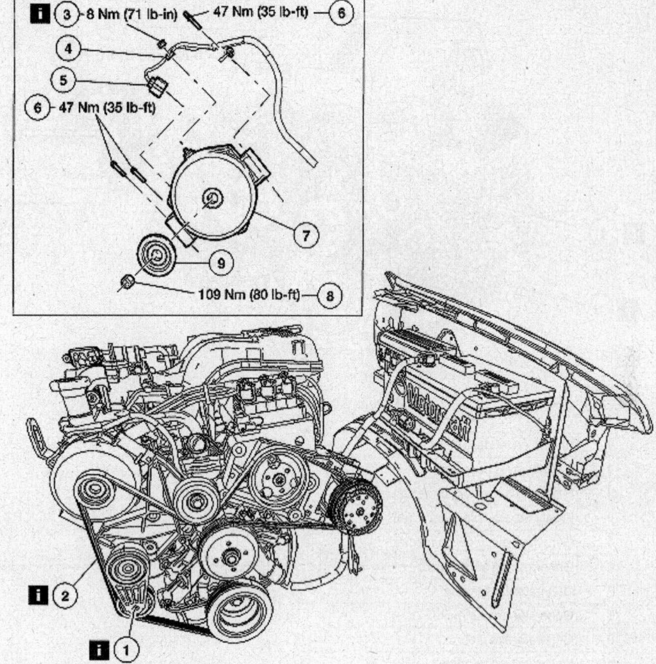

Item	Description
1	Front end accessory drive belt tensioner
2	Front end accessory drive belt
3	Generator B+ terminal nut
4	Generator B+ terminal (part of 14300)
5	Generator electrical connector (part of 14300)
6	Generator upper stud bolt and lower bolts
7	Generator
8	Generator pulley nut
9	Generator pulley

LTV1900000000297

Fig. 4 Alternator replacement. Aviator, Explorer, Explorer Sport, Explorer Sport Trac & Mountaineer w/4.0L engine

Ranger

1. Remove air cleaner outlet tube.
2. Remove accessory drive belt.
3. Remove alternator mounting bolts, **Figs. 6 through 8.**
4. Remove electrical connectors from alternator.
5. Remove alternator from vehicle.
6. Reverse procedure to install.

COIL PACK

REPLACE

2.3L Engine

1. Disconnect spark plug wires from ignition coils.
2. Disconnect engine control sensor electrical connector from ignition coil.
3. Remove four ignition coil retaining screws.
4. Remove ignition coil.
5. Reverse procedure to install. **Torque** ignition coil retaining screws to 60 inch lbs.

3.0L Engine

1. Disconnect fuel charging electrical connectors from ignition coil and radio interference capacitor.
2. Disconnect spark plug wires.
3. Remove two ignition coil nuts and top ignition coil mounting bracket nut.
4. Remove ignition coil and radio ignition interference capacitor if equipped.

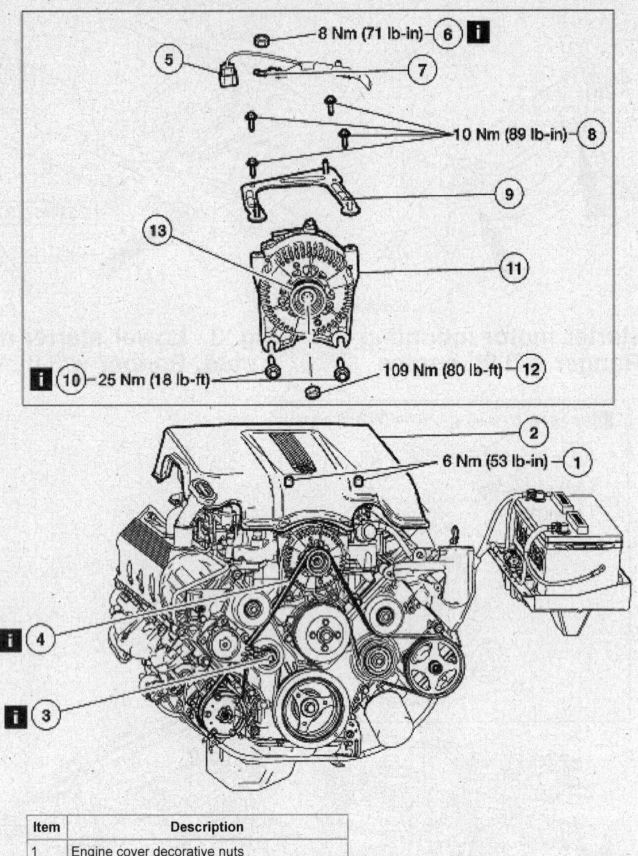

Item	Description
1	Engine cover decorative nuts
2	Engine cover assembly
3	Front end accessory drive belt tensioner
4	Front end accessory drive belt
5	Generator electrical connector
6	Generator B+ terminal nut
7	Generator B+ terminal
8	Generator bracket bolts
9	Generator bracket
10	Lower generator bolts
11	Generator
12	Generator pulley nut
13	Generator pulley

LTV1900000000298

Fig. 5 Alternator replacement. Aviator, Explorer & Mountaineer w/4.6L engine

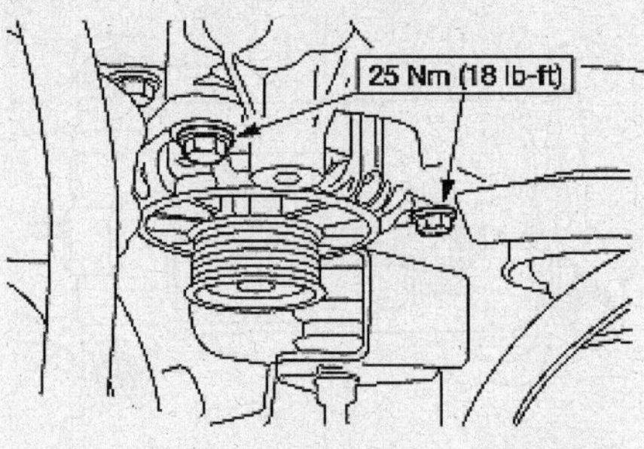

LTV1900000000237

Fig. 6 Alternator mounting bolts. Ranger w/2.3L engine

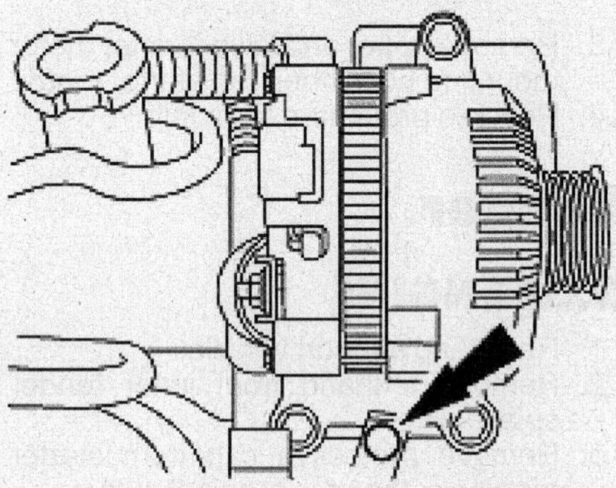

LTV1900000000238

Fig. 7 Alternator mounting bolts. Ranger w/3.0L engine

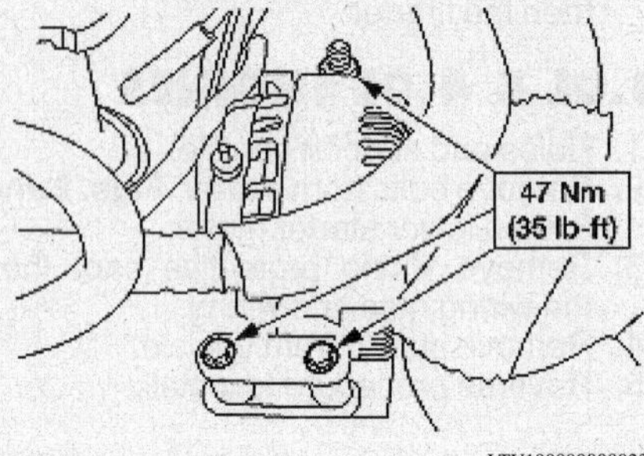

LTV1900000000239

Fig. 8 Alternator mounting bolts. Ranger w/4.0L engine

5. Remove EGR vacuum regulator solenoid from ignition coil if equipped.
6. Reverse procedure to install. **Torque** ignition coil mounting nuts to 12–14 lbs.

4.0L Engine

1. Disconnect ignition coil electrical connections.
2. Disconnect spark plug wires from ignition coil.
3. **On models equipped with A/C,** remove A/C tube to plenum bolt and move tube enough to gain access to ignition coil bolts.
4. **On all models,** remove ignition coil bolts and ignition coil.
5. Reverse procedure to install. **Torque** ignition coil bolts to 60 inch lbs.

4.6L Engine

1. Remove ignition coil on plug electrical connectors and retaining bolts.
2. Pull up on coil to disengage from spark plug, then remove from engine.
3. Apply dielectric compound to inside of coil boots.
4. Reverse procedure to install.

IGNITION LOCK

REPLACE

With Key

The following procedure applies to vehicles that have functional lock cylinders, ignition keys available for the vehicle, or ignition key numbers that are known and the proper key can be made.

1. Insert ignition key and turn to RUN position.
2. Access and depress ignition cylinder lock pin through steering column cover, **Fig. 9.**
3. Pull ignition cylinder from steering column.
4. Reverse procedure to install. Verify ignition cylinder operation.

Less Key

The following procedure applies to vehicles where the ignition lock is inoperative or lock cylinder cannot be rotated due to broken or missing ignition key and the key number is unknown, or the lock cylinder cap is damaged and/or broken so that lock cylinder cannot be rotated.

1. Remove steering wheel as outlined in "Steering Wheel, Replace."
2. Twist cap from ignition lock cylinder.

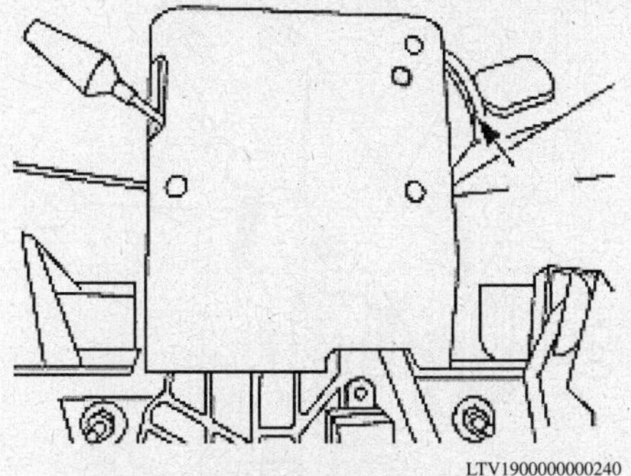

Fig. 9 Ignition switch lock cylinder release pin location

3. Remove upper and lower steering column covers to access lock cylinder retaining pin.
4. Drill out retaining pin using a suitable ⅛ inch drill bit.
5. Drill out center of lock cylinder until it is broken loose. Drilling distance should be approximately 1¾ inch.
6. Remove and discard ignition cylinder and drill shavings from steering column.
7. Remove bearing retainer, then the bearing and gear.
8. Ensure all drill shavings are removed from bearing, gear and steering column.
9. Reverse procedure to install. Verify ignition cylinder operation.

NEUTRAL SAFETY SWITCH

REPLACE

1. Raise and support vehicle.
2. Disconnect shift cable and fitting.
3. Disconnect harness connector, then remove manual lever nut and manual lever.
4. Remove mounting screws, then the switch.
5. Reverse procedure to install, noting the following:
   a. Use alignment tool No. T97L-70010-A, or equivalent, to properly align switch.
   b. **Torque** manual lever control nut to 30–40 ft. lbs.
   c. **Torque** mounting screws to 72–96 inch lbs.

HEADLAMP SWITCH

REPLACE

Aviator, Explorer, Explorer Sport, Explorer Sport Trac & Mountaineer

1. Remove instrument cluster finish panel.
2. Remove headlamp switch from cluster finish panel.
3. Reverse procedure to install.

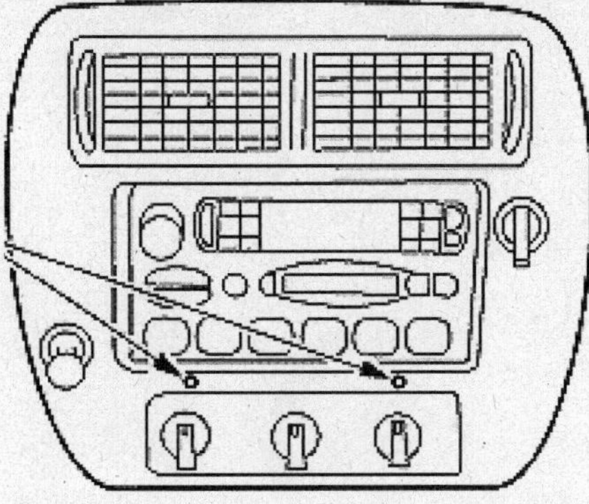

Fig. 10 Radio finish panel. Ranger

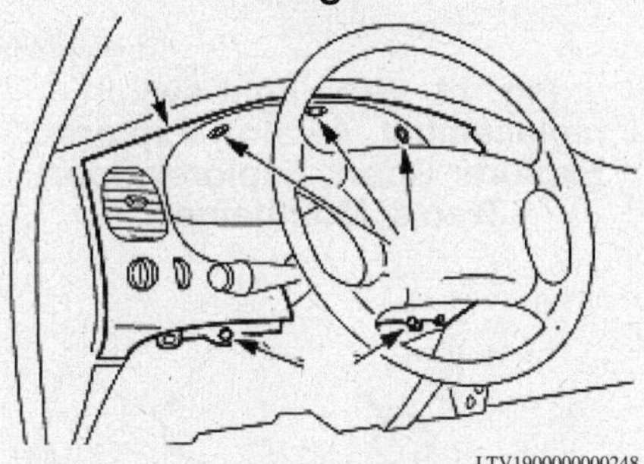

Fig. 12 Cluster finish panel. Ranger

Ranger

1. Remove radio finish panel, **Fig. 10.**
2. Disconnect and remove radio bezel assembly.
3. Remove lower instrument panel cover and reinforcement, **Fig. 11.**
4. **On models equipped with column gear shift,** position gear shift lever out of way.
5. **On all models,** pull out cluster finish panel, **Fig. 12,** remove electrical connectors, then remove finish panel.
6. Pull off and remove headlamp switch knob.
7. Remove screws, **Fig. 13,** then the headlamp switch.
8. Reverse procedure to install.

STOP LIGHT SWITCH

REPLACE

Aviator, Explorer, Explorer Sport, Explorer Sport Trac & Mountaineer

Do not pull or push on the brake pedal during removal and installation of the stoplamp switch.

1. Disconnect electrical connector from switch, **Fig. 14.**
2. Rotate the stoplamp switch 45° clockwise, then remove the stoplamp switch.
3. Reverse procedure to install.

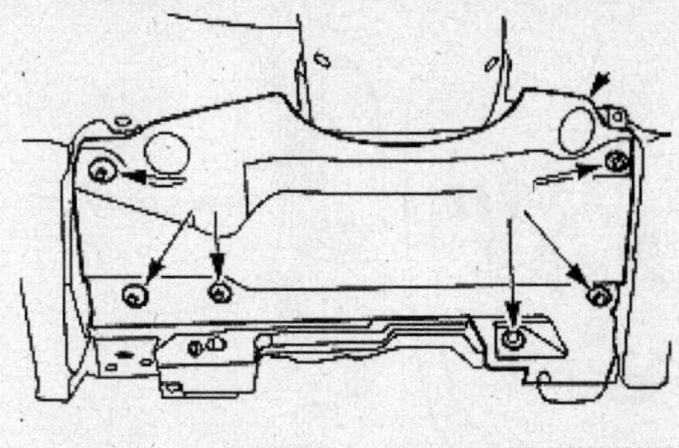

Fig. 11 Lower instrument panel reinforcement. Ranger

Ranger

1. Disconnect stoplamp switch electrical connector, **Fig. 15.**
2. Remove switch cover and self-locking pin.
3. Remove stoplamp switch from brake booster push rod and brake pedal assembly.
4. Remove spacer and stop lamp switch.
5. Reverse procedure to install.

BRAKE PEDAL POSITION SWITCH

REPLACE

1. Disconnect brake position switch electrical connector.
2. Remove self locking pin, spacer, **Fig. 16,** and brake pedal position switch.
3. Reverse procedure to install.

MULTI-FUNCTION SWITCH

REPLACE

Aviator, Explorer & Mountaineer

1. Remove two screws, **Fig. 17,** then the steering column opening cover.
2. Remove upper and lower steering column shrouds.
3. Disconnect multi-function switch electrical connector.
4. Remove two multi-function switch retaining screws, then the switch.
5. Reverse procedure to install.

Explorer Sport, Explorer Sport Trac & Ranger

1. Insert ignition key into ignition switch lock cylinder and turn to RUN position.
2. Push ignition switch lock cylinder release tab, **Fig. 18,** using suitable punch while pulling outward on ignition switch lock cylinder.
3. Twist tilt wheel handle and shank counterclockwise, then remove shank.
4. Remove upper and lower steering column shrouds.

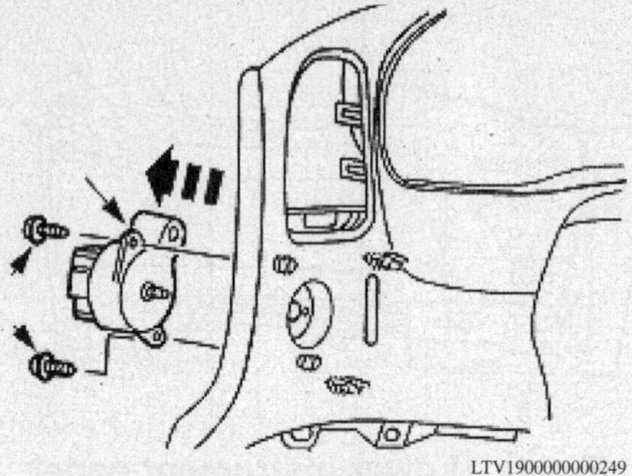

Fig. 13 Headlamp switch mounting. Ranger

5. Disconnect multi-function switch electrical connectors.
6. Remove multi-function switch retaining screws, then the switch.
7. Reverse procedure to install.

STEERING WHEEL

REPLACE

1. Disarm air bag system as outlined in "Precautions."
2. Center front wheels in straight ahead position.
3. Remove driver air bag module as outlined in "Passive Restraint Systems" chapter.
4. Disconnect horn and speed control electrical connectors.
5. Loosen but do not remove, steering wheel retaining bolt approximately 2–3 turns.
6. Install differential side bearing puller tool No. T77F-4220-B1, or equivalent, at the areas marked PULL near the loosened steering wheel retaining bolt. **Ensure air bag sliding contact does not get caught on steering wheel when lifting steering wheel off steering shaft.**
7. Pull steering wheel loose and remove differential side bearing puller tool.
8. Remove and discard original steering wheel bolt.
9. Remove steering wheel while routing wires from air bag sliding contact through steering wheel.
10. Reverse procedure to install, noting the following:
    a. Ensure alignment marks on steering wheel match alignment marks on steering shaft.
    b. **Torque** steering wheel bolt to 25–34 ft. lbs.
    c. **Torque** air bag module side retaining bolts to 6–96 inch lbs.

INSTRUMENT CLUSTER

REPLACE

Aviator, Explorer, Explorer Sport, Explorer Sport Trac & Mountaineer

1. Lower tilt steering wheel to lowest position.

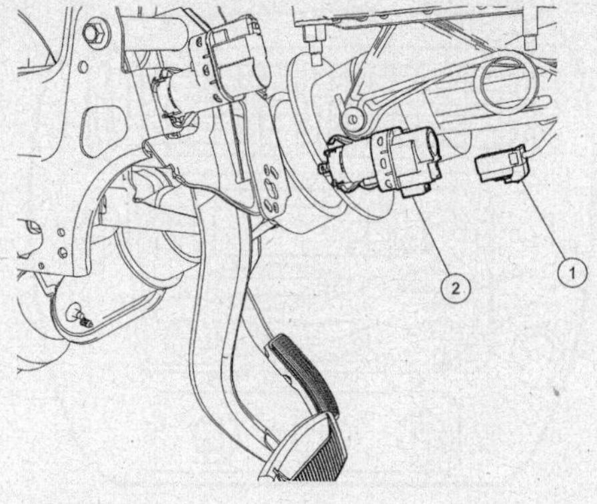

Item	Description
1	Stoplamp switch electrical connector
2	Stoplamp switch

LTV0500000000658

Fig. 14 Stop light switch replacement. Aviator, Explorer, Explorer Sport, Explorer Sport Trac & Mountaineer

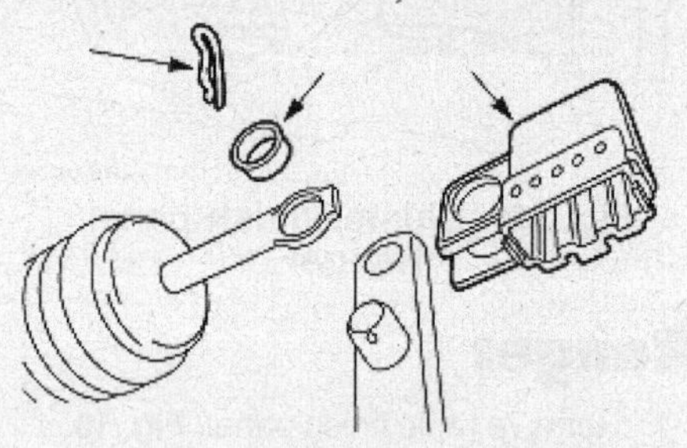

Fig. 16 Brake pedal position switch

2. Remove instrument cluster finish panel.
3. Remove components in order indicated, **Fig. 19.**
4. Reverse procedure to install.

Ranger

1. Remove screws and pull center instrument panel finish panel out from instrument panel, **Fig. 20.**
2. Disconnect electrical connectors, then remove radio and center instrument panel finish panel.
3. Remove hood latch release handle.
4. Remove instrument panel steering column covers and reinforcement, **Fig. 21.**
5. **On models equipped with column gear shift lever,** position gear shift lever aside.
6. **On all models,** remove screws, **Fig. 22,** then pull instrument cluster finish panel out from instrument panel.
7. Disconnect electrical connectors, then remove cluster finish panel.
8. Remove instrument cluster screws, **Fig. 23.**
9. **On models equipped with automatic transmission,** pull out cluster and remove transmission range indicator, **Fig. 24.**
10. **On all models,** disconnect remaining electrical connectors, then remove cluster from vehicle.
11. Reverse procedure to install.

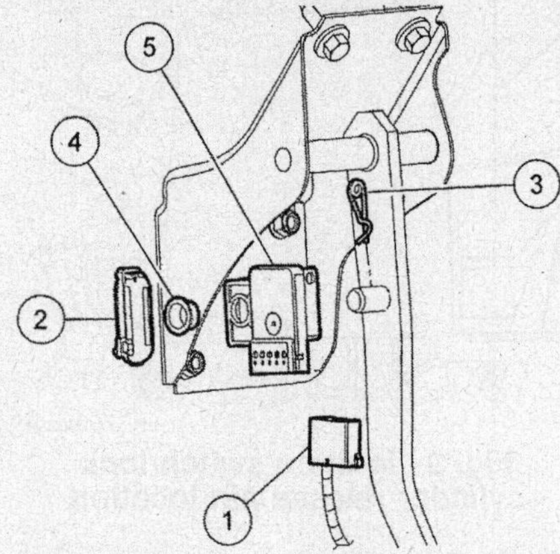

Item	Description
1	Stoplamp switch electrical connector
2	Stoplamp switch self-locking pin cover
3	Stoplamp switch self-locking pin
4	Stoplamp switch spacer
5	Stoplamp switch

LTV0500000000659

Fig. 15 Stop lamp switch replacement. Ranger

RADIO

REPLACE

1. Insert radio removal tool No. T87P-19061-A, or equivalent, into radio face plate, press in one inch to release retaining clips, then pull radio from instrument panel using tool as handles.
2. Disconnect electrical connectors and antenna lead.
3. If radio is being replaced, remove rear mounting bracket.
4. Reverse procedure to install, ensure rear mounting bracket engages track in instrument panel, then verify proper operation of radio.

WIPER MOTOR

REPLACE

Front

AVIATOR, EXPLORER, EXPLORER SPORT, EXPLORER SPORT TRAC & MOUNTAINEER

1. Lift lefthand wiper arm, pull out and release retainer tab, then remove wiper arm.
2. Disconnect washer hose from lefthand nozzle.

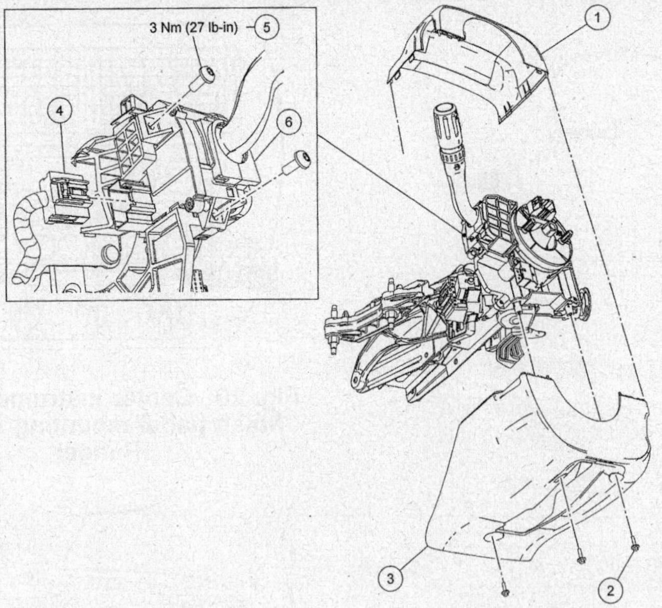

Item	Description
1	Upper steering column shroud
2	Steering column shroud screw (3 required)
3	Lower steering column shroud

Item	Description
4	Multi-function switch electrical connector
5	Multi-function switch screw (2 required)
6	Multi-function switch

LTV0500000000660

Fig. 17 Multi-function switch replacement. Aviator, Explorer & Mountaineer

3. Release spring retainers and remove cowl vent panel.
4. Remove wiper arm retaining clip from wiper motor.
5. Disconnect both windshield wiper arms and pivot shafts at motor.
6. Disconnect wiper motor electrical connector and ground strap.
7. Remove wiper motor.
8. Reverse procedure to install noting the following:
   a. **To avoid damage to wiper arm and retaining clip, ensure clip is fully seated on arm before installing on motor.**
   b. Install lefthand arm to motor, then the right.

RANGER

REMOVAL

1. Cycle windshield wipers until they are in straight up position, then turn ignition switch to Off position.
2. Disconnect the wiper motor electrical connector.
3. Remove righthand wiper arm and blade assembly, then the righthand pivot nut and allow linkage to drop into cowl.
4. Remove linkage access cover from righthand side of dash panel near wiper motor.
5. Release wiper motor retaining clip, then slide clip back until it clears nib on crank pin, and remove the clip. **The wiper motor retaining clip can be reached through the access cover opening.**
6. Remove wiper linkage from motor crank pin.
7. Remove motor attaching screws and the motor.

INSTALLATION

1. Install wiper motor and **torque** attaching screws to 10–14 ft. lbs.
2. Connect wiper motor electrical connector.
3. Install lefthand linkage arm to motor, then the right. **Ensure retaining clip is fully seated to righthand arm before installing to motor.**
4. Install righthand wiper pivot shaft and nut and **torque** to 84–120 inch lbs.
5. Turn ignition switch to On position, turn wiper switch Off so wiper motor will park, then turn ignition switch to Off position.
6. Install righthand linkage access cover, then the righthand wiper blade and arm assembly and inspect for proper operation.

Rear

1. Remove wiper arm and blade assembly.
2. Remove liftgate inner trim panel and water deflector.
3. Disconnect motor electrical connector.
4. Remove rear wiper motor.
5. Reverse procedure to install.

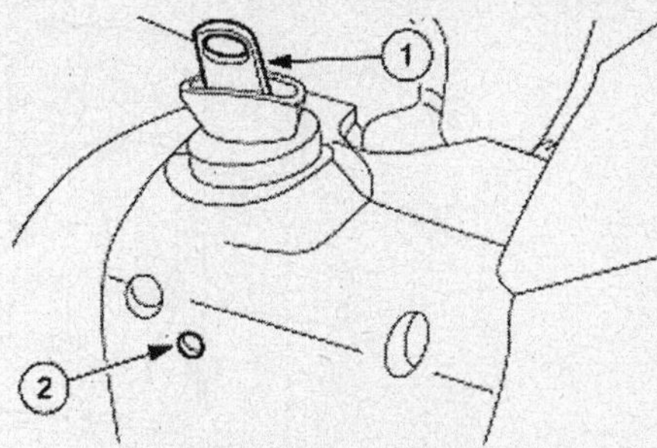

1. Ignition key & lock cylinder
2. Lock cylinder release tab access hole

LTV0500000000661

Fig. 18 ignition switch lock cylinder removal. Explorer Sport, Explorer Sport Trac & Ranger

WIPER SWITCH

REPLACE

Front

Refer to "Multi-Function Switch, Replace" for replacement procedures.

Rear

1. Remove ashtray and instrument cluster trim panel.
2. Remove switch mounting bezel containing switches, then disconnect switch electrical connector and remove switch.
3. Reverse procedure to install, verify wiper operation.

WIPER TRANSMISSION

REPLACE

Aviator, Explorer, Explorer Sport, Explorer Sport Trac & Mountaineer

1. Cycle wiper blades until they are in vertical position.
2. Remove wiper arms, then the cowl panel retaining screw.
3. Disengage cowl panel retaining clips and remove cowl panels.
4. Release wiper arm retaining clip from wiper motor.
5. Remove righthand and lefthand wiper pivot arms from motor.
6. Remove wiper linkage retaining nuts, then the mounting arm and pivot shafts.
7. Reverse procedure to install noting the following:
   a. **Torque** mounting arm retaining nuts to 108 inch lbs.
   b. **Install connecting clip to arm and ensure clip is fully seated before installing arm to motor.**

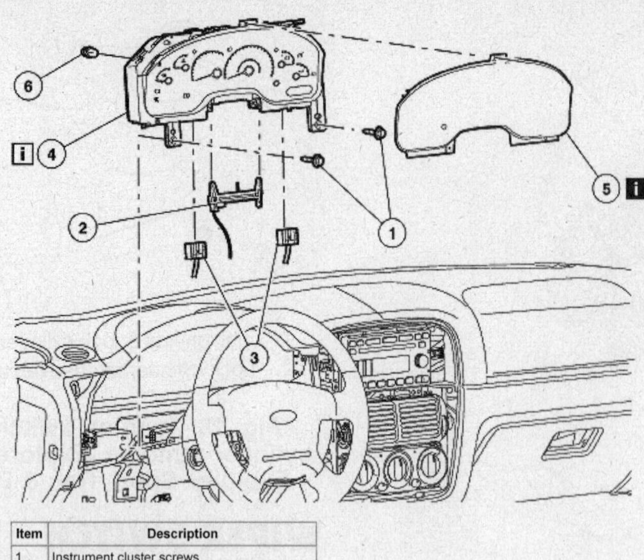

Item	Description
1	Instrument cluster screws
2	Transmission range indicator (if equipped)
3	Electrical connectors
4	Instrument cluster
5	Instrument cluster lens
6	Indicator bulbs (4 req'd)

Fig. 19 Instrument cluster replacement. Aviator, Explorer, Explorer Sport, Explorer Sport Trac & Mountaineer

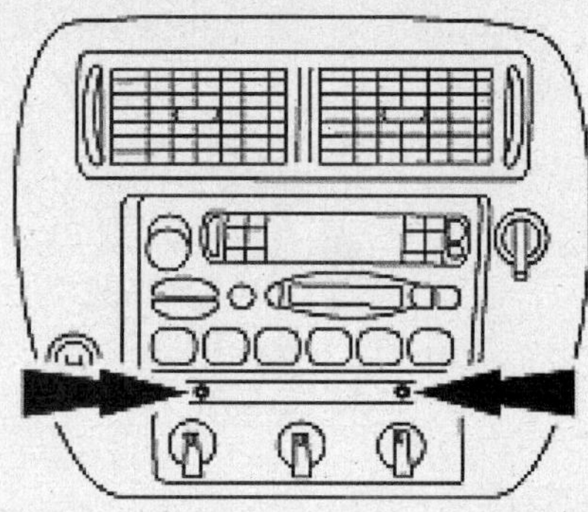

Fig. 20 Center instrument panel finish panel mounting screws. Ranger

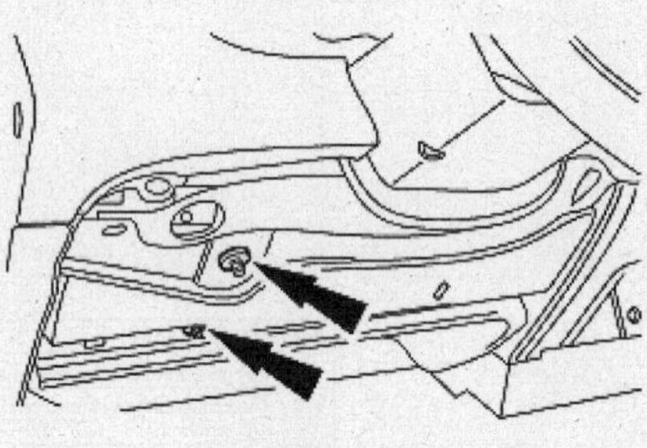

Fig. 21 Steering column opening cover reinforcement. Ranger

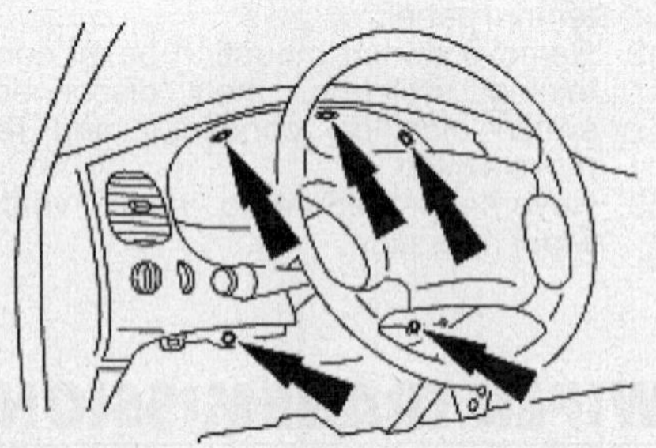

Fig. 22 Instrument panel cluster finish panel mounting screws. Ranger

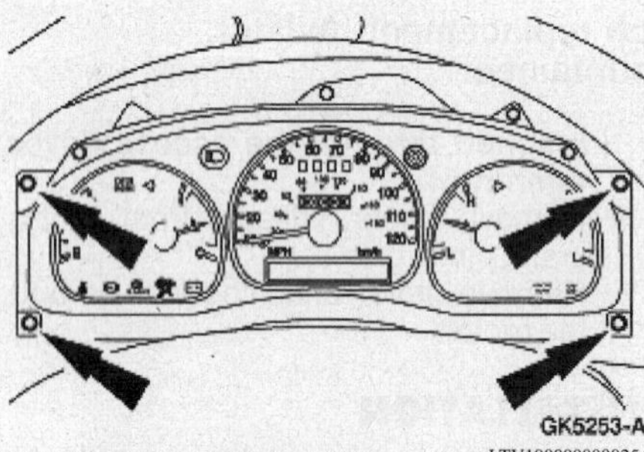

Fig. 23 Instrument cluster mounting screws. Ranger

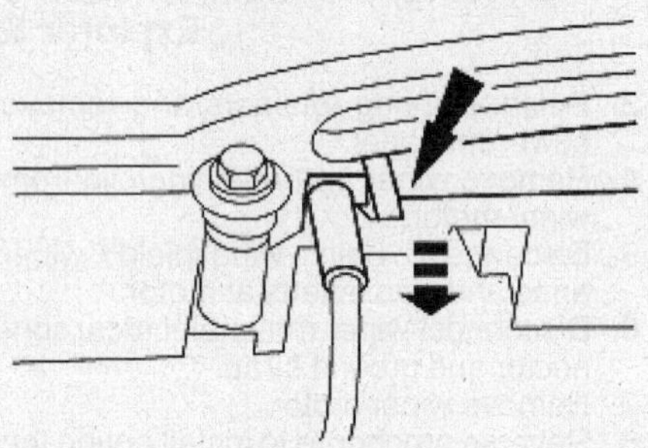

Fig. 24 Transmission range indicator. Ranger

c. Install lefthand arm to motor before righthand to ensure proper wiper motion.

Ranger

1. Cycle wiper blades until they are in vertical position.
2. Remove righthand and lefthand wiper arms.
3. Remove righthand cowl access cover.
4. Move power distribution box to side, then remove lefthand cowl access cover.
5. Reach through righthand cowl access cover and detach righthand wiper arm clip from motor.
6. Remove righthand and lefthand arms from motor.
7. Remove righthand and lefthand pivot arm nuts.
8. Remove wiper linkage through righthand access opening.
9. Reverse procedure to install. **Torque** pivot arm retaining nuts to 108 inch lbs. **Ensure retaining clip is fully seated on arm before installing to motor.**

BLOWER MOTOR

REPLACE

Front

AVIATOR, EXPLORER & MOUNTAINEER

1. Remove vacuum reservoir mounting screw, **Fig. 25,** then position reservoir aside.
2. Disconnect blower motor electrical connector.
3. Remove blower motor mounting screws, then the blower motor assembly.
4. Remove push clip, then the blower motor wheel.
5. Reverse procedure to install.

EXPLORER SPORT & EXPLORER SPORT TRAC

1. Remove air cleaner assembly.
2. Disconnect speed control servo electrical connector.
3. Remove servo mounting bolt, then position speed control servo aside.
4. Remove coolant expansion tank/windshield washer reservoir mounting bolts, then position reservoir aside.
5. Disconnect blower motor vent hose, **Fig. 26.**
6. Disconnect blower motor electrical connector.
7. Remove blower motor mounting screws, then the motor assembly.
8. reverse procedure to install.

RANGER

1. In engine compartment, remove speed control servo bracket, if equipped, and move servo to a secure location.
2. Remove windshield washer/coolant

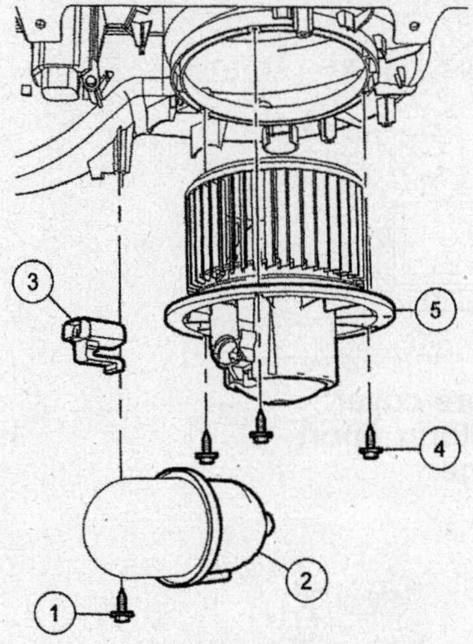

Item	Description
1	Vacuum reservoir screw
2	Vacuum reservoir
3	Blower motor electrical connector
4	Blower motor screw (3 required)
5	Blower motor

LTV0500000000662

Fig. 25 Front blower motor replacement. Aviator, Explorer & Mountaineer

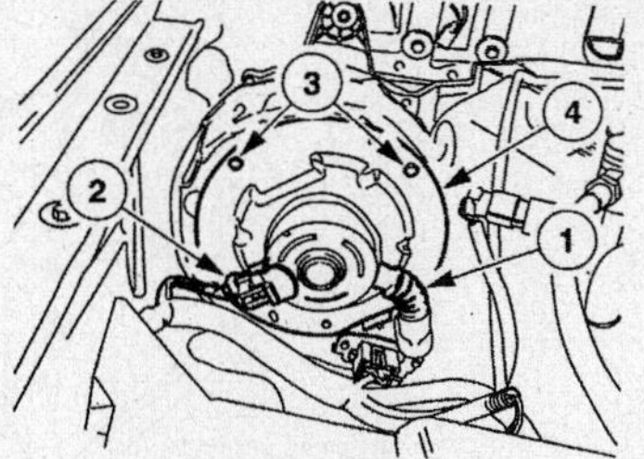

1. Vent hose
2. Electrical connector
3. Mounting screws
4. Blower motor

LTV0500000000663

Fig. 26 Front blower motor replacement. Explorer Sport & Explorer Sport Trac

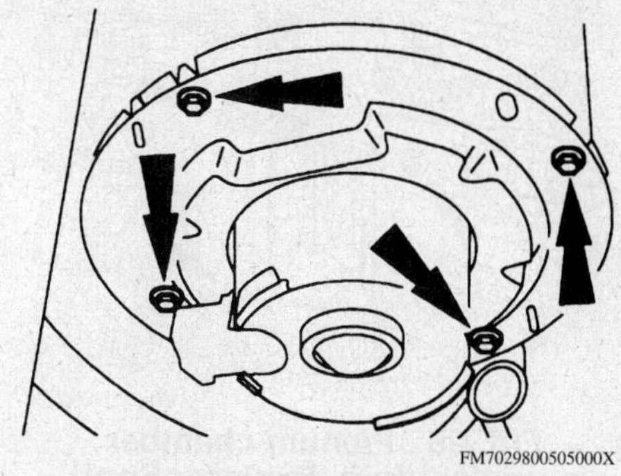

FM7029800505000X

Fig. 27 Blower motor replacement. Ranger

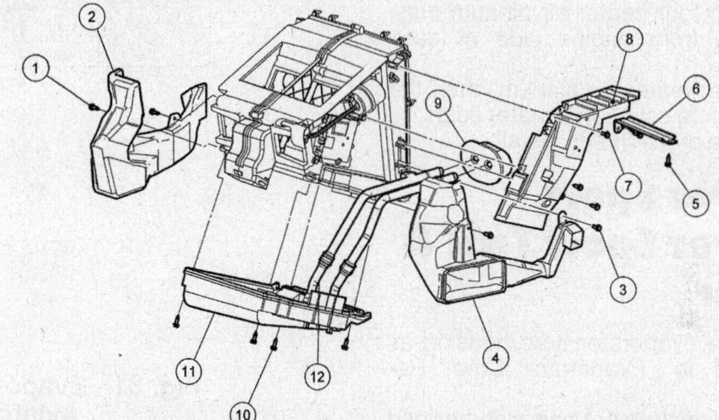

Item	Description
1	LH floor duct screw (2 required)
2	LH floor duct
3	RH floor duct screw (2 required)
4	RH floor duct
5	Housing brace screw (3 required)
6	Housing brace
7	Heater tube cover screw (3 required)
8	Heater tube cover
9	Heater tube seal
10	Heater core cover screw (4 required)
11	Heater core cover
12	Heater core

LTV0500000000668

Fig. 28 Heater core replacement. Aviator, Explorer & Mountaineer

bottle as required.

3. Disconnect A/C blower motor feed extension from blower motor and remove four screws retaining blower motor in evaporator housing, **Fig. 27.**
4. Remove blower motor and blower motor wheel as an assembly.
5. Reverse procedure to install.

Rear

1. Remove front seat center armrest.
2. Remove front floor console, utility tray and beverage holder.
3. Disconnect front console electrical connectors.
4. Remove front console mounting screws, then move console rearward to disengage rear mounting bracket.
5. Remove front console.
6. Remove rear console coin tray.
7. Remove screws, then the console insert.
8. Remove console lid to hinge mounting screws, then the lid.
9. Open rear cupholder and remove console rear finish panel screws.
10. Disengage retaining clips and remove rear finish panel.
11. Disconnect climate control assembly electrical connectors, disengage pin type harness retainer.
12. Disconnect air distribution door linkage from second row climate control assembly arm. Do not to bend second row climate control assembly arm.
13. Remove second row climate control assembly.
14. Remove rear air distribution duct retaining screws, then the distribution duct.
15. Remove nine console liner retaining screws, then the liner.
16. Remove rear console to floor tunnel mounting bolts.
17. Disconnect blower motor resistor electrical connector, pin type retainer, then remove blower motor resistor.
18. Slide console reinforcement rearward. Partially remove blower motor and air distribution duct assembly.
19. Disconnect blower motor electrical connector.
20. Remove blower motor from console air distribution duct.
21. Reverse procedure to install.

HEATER CORE

REPLACE

Aviator, Explorer & Mountaineer

1. Drain cooling system into suitable container.
2. Disconnect hoses from heater core. Plug hoses and core openings to prevent leakage of residual coolant.
3. Remove A/C evaporator housing as outlined in "Evaporator Core, Replace."
4. In passenger compartment, remove

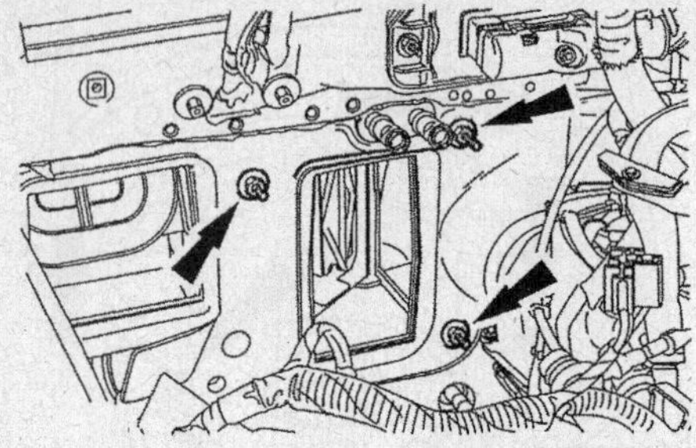

Fig. 29 Plenum chamber mounting nuts. Explorer Sport, Explorer Sport Trac & Ranger

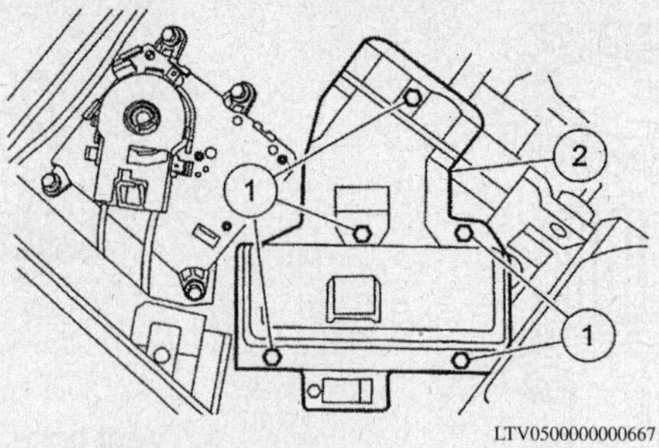

Fig. 30 Heater core cover. Explorer Sport, Explorer Sport Trac & Ranger

instrument panel as outlined in "Dash Panel Service" chapter.

5. Remove powertrain control module and heat sink.
6. Remove four heater air plenum nuts, **Fig. 28,** from engine side of dash panel.
7. Remove heater air plenum, then the heater core cover and heater core.
8. Reverse procedure to install.

Explorer Sport, Explorer Sport Trac & Ranger

1. Remove evaporator core housing as outlined in "Evaporator Core, Replace."
2. Remove instrument panel as outlined in "Dash Panel Service" chapter.
3. Remove powertrain control module.
4. Remove four nuts from engine side of dash panel, **Fig. 29,** then position plenum chamber on vehicle floor.
5. Remove heater core cover, **Fig. 30.**
6. Remove heater core.
7. Reverse procedure to install.

EVAPORATOR CORE

REPLACE

Aviator, Explorer & Mountaineer

Installation of a new accumulator is not required when repairing the air conditioning system except when there is physical evidence of contamination from a failed A/C compressor or damage to the accumulator. New O-ring seals lubricated in clean PAG oil must be installed before connecting any A/C fitting that has been disconnected.

1. Recover A/C refrigerant as outlined in "Air Conditioning" chapter.
2. Remove engine appearance cover.
3. Drain coolant into suitable container.
4. Remove instrument panel as outlined in "Dash Panel Service" chapter.
5. Remove remaining components in order listed, **Fig. 31.**
6. Reverse procedure to install.

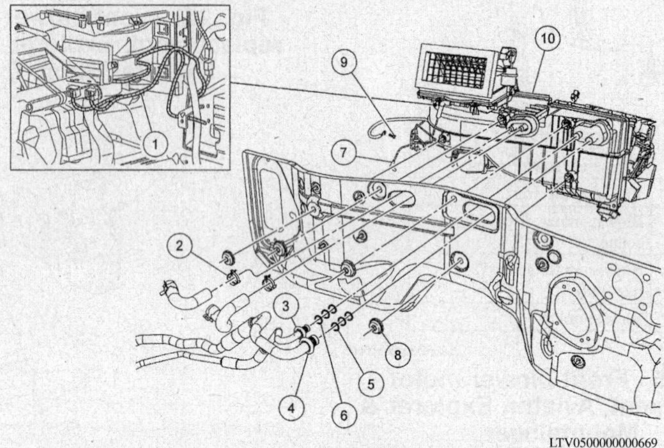

Fig. 31 Evaporator core replacement (Part 1 of 2). Aviator, Explorer & Mountaineer

Explorer Sport, Explorer Sport Trac & Ranger

Replacement of suction accumulator/drier is not required when repairing air conditioning system except when there is physical evidence of system contamination from a failed A/C compressor or damage to the suction accumulator/drier.

The evaporator core can not be serviced separately, it can only be serviced with the evaporator core housing assembly.

1. Recover A/C refrigerant as outlined in "Air Conditioning" chapter.
2. Drain coolant into suitable container.
3. Remove suction accumulator.
4. **On models equipped with 2.3L engine,** remove A/C compressor, engine oil dipstick and dipstick tube.
5. **On models equipped with 3.0L & 4.0L engines,** position coolant reservoir and windshield washer reservoir aside.
6. **On models equipped with speed control,** disconnect speed control servo electrical connector, remove bolt and disconnect cable from evaporator core housing. Position servo aside.
7. **On all models,** disconnect blower motor and blower motor resistor electrical connectors.
8. Disconnect heater hoses.
9. Disconnect pin type retainer and position windshield hose aside.
10. Disconnect heater control vacuum hose and vacuum supply hose near evaporator.
11. Disconnect condenser to evaporator line from evaporator core, discard O-ring seals.
12. Disconnect vacuum hose connector in passenger compartment at lower passenger side dash, **Fig. 32,** then remove nut.
13. Remove righthand wheel housing splash shield.
14. Remove nuts from evaporator core housing, then the housing, **Fig. 33.**
15. Reverse procedure to install, noting the following:
    a. Install correct amount of suitable refrigerant oil.
    b. Install new O-ring seals lubricated with suitable refrigerant oil.
    c. Lubricate coolant hoses with suitable lubricant or plain water as required to aid installation.

Item	Description
1	Wire harness
2	Heater hose clamps (2 required)
3	A/C line fitting
4	A/C line fitting
5	A/C line O-ring (3 required)
6	A/C line O-ring (3 required)
7	Vacuum connector
8	Heater core and evaporator core housing nuts (4 required)
9	Ground terminal bolt
10	Heater core and evaporator core housing

LTV0500000000670

Fig. 31 Evaporator core replacement (Part 2 of 2). Aviator, Explorer & Mountaineer

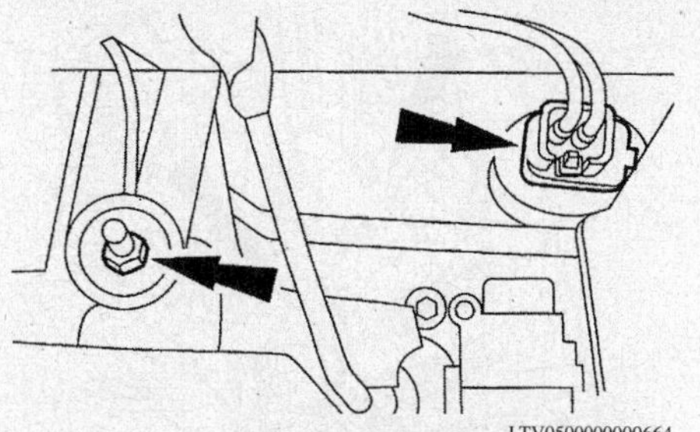

Fig. 32 Vacuum hose connector & nut. Explorer Sport, Explorer Sport Trac & Ranger

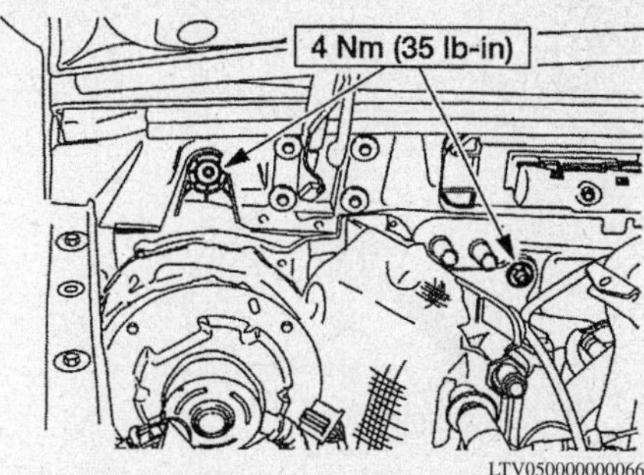

Fig. 33 Evaporator core housing mounting nuts. Explorer Sport, Explorer Sport Trac & Ranger

2.3L Engine

NOTE: On Air Bag Equipped Models, Refer To "Air Bag System Precautions" Located In The Front Of This Manual For System Disarming & Arming Procedures.

NOTE: Refer To "Computer Relearn Procedures" Located In The Front Of This Manual When Battery Power To The Computer Has Been Interrupted.

INDEX

PRECAUTIONS

Air Bag Systems

Refer to "Air Bag System Precautions" in the front of this manual for system disarming and arming procedures.

Battery Ground Cable

Prior to service, disconnect battery ground cable and isolate as required.

Fuel System Pressure Relief

1. Remove fuel cap to relieve tank pressure.
2. Remove cap from fuel pressure relief valve located on fuel line in upper right-hand corner of engine compartment, then release pressure from system using EFI pressure gauge tool No. T80L-9974-B, or equivalent.

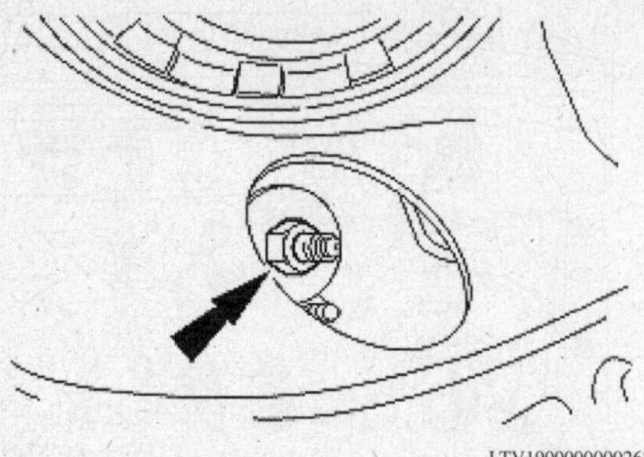

Fig. 1 Engine support insulator mounting nut location

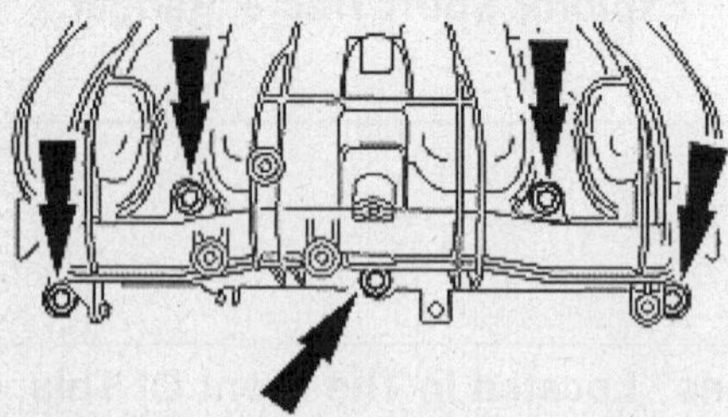

Fig. 4 Intake manifold mounting bolt locations

COMPRESSION PRESSURE

Compression pressure should be inspected with the engine at normal operating temperature, spark plugs removed and throttle plate in wide open position. Ensure battery is fully charged and oil is of proper viscosity. Apply parking brake and ensure transmission is in park or neutral. Crank the engine at least five compression strokes and record highest reading for each cylinder. The indicated compression pressures are considered within specification if the lowest reading cylinder is within 75 percent of the highest.

ENGINE MOUNT

REPLACE

1. Raise and support vehicle.
2. Remove front springs.
3. Remove pushpins and position righthand inner splash shield out of way.
4. Lower vehicle.
5. Remove clutch fan.
6. Remove righthand and lefthand insulator mounting nuts.
7. Install engine lifting eyes, 303–D030, or equivalent.
8. Raise engine with suitable three bar engine support tool.
9. Raise and support vehicle.
10. Remove nuts, **Fig. 1,** and engine support insulators.
11. Reverse procedure to install.

ENGINE

REPLACE

1. Relieve fuel system pressure as outlined in"Precautions."
2. Recover A/C refrigerant as outlined in "Air Conditioning" chapter.

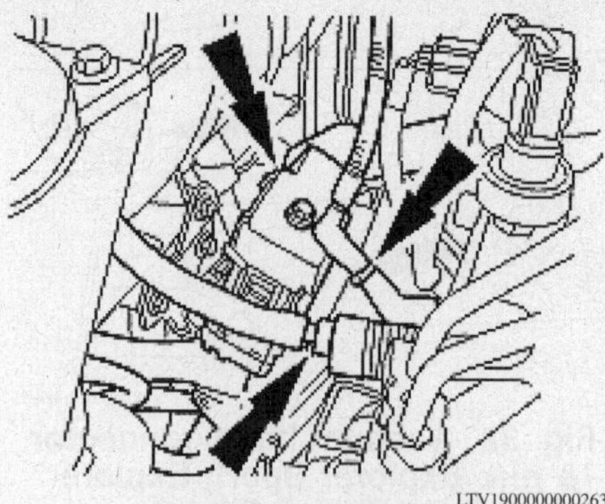

Fig. 2 42 pin electrical connector, VMV regulator supply hose & evaporative purge hose

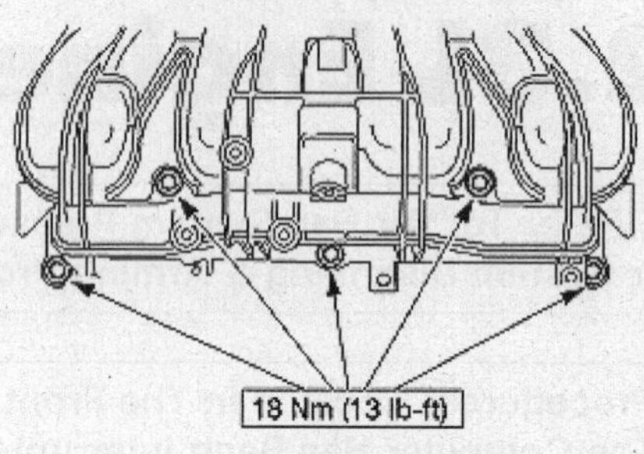

Fig. 5 Intake manifold bolt installation

3. Drain cooling system into suitable container.
4. Drain engine oil into suitable container.
5. Remove vehicle hood.
6. Remove accelerator control snow shield.
7. Remove air cleaner tube.
8. Remove upper and lower radiator hose.
9. Remove fan and shroud.
10. Disconnect powertrain control module electrical connector and position harness on engine.
11. Remove ground stud for PCM.
12. Remove heater hose assembly.
13. Disconnect vacuum hose to vacuum reservoir.
14. Disconnect engine to degas bottle bypass hose.
15. Disconnect degas bottle to engine supply hose.
16. Disconnect A/C compressor clutch electrical connector.
17. Disconnect mass air flow sensor electrical connector.
18. Disconnect A/C compressor manifold. Plug all lines and compressor ports.
19. Disconnect accelerator and speed control cables and position aside.
20. Disconnect power steering pressure switch electrical connector and power steering high pressure hose and position aside.
21. Remove fuel line clip, then disconnect fuel supply hose with removal tool No. 310–040, or equivalent.
22. Disconnect 42 pin electrical connector, VMV vacuum regulator solenoid supply hose and evaporative purge hose, **Fig. 2.**

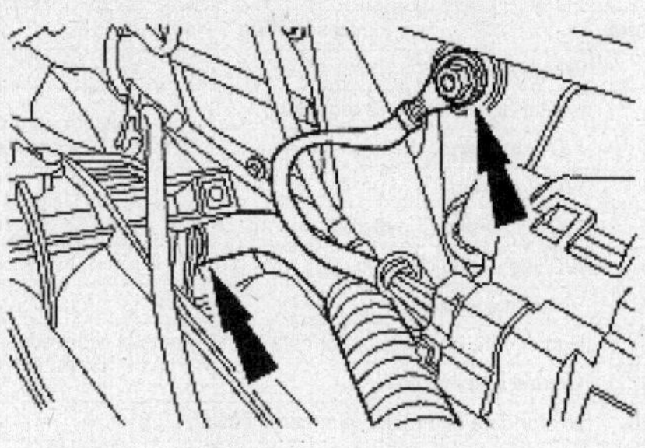

Fig. 3 Brake booster hose & engine ground strap

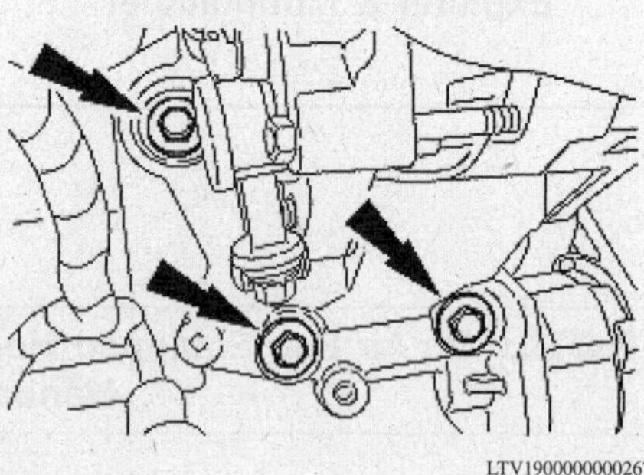

Fig. 6 Front end accessory drive (FEAD) mounting bolts

23. Disconnect brake booster hose and engine ground strap, **Fig. 3.**
24. Disconnect battery positive and negative cables and solenoid control wire at starter.
25. Remove starter wiring clamp bolt and position wiring harness out of way.
26. Raise and support vehicle.
27. Position righthand splash shield out of way.
28. Disconnect alternator electrical connectors.
29. Disconnect block electrical connector.
30. Disconnect front heated oxygen sensor.
31. **On models equipped with automatic transmission,** remove bolt retaining transmission cooling tubes to engine, remove bracket.
32. **On all models,** remove transmission dust shield.
33. Remove exhaust manifold to front pipe nuts.
34. Disconnect heated oxygen sensor electrical connector at rear of transmission.
35. Remove engine wiring harness bolts and position engine wiring harness out of way.
36. Disconnect oil pressure sensor electrical connector.
37. Remove engine oil filter.
38. Disconnect vehicle speed sensor, transmission range sensor, backup light switch and transmission electrical connectors.
39. Disconnect harness pushpins and position harness forward to engine.
40. Remove oil filter adapter.
41. Remove starter and starter dust shield.
42. **On models equipped with automatic transmission,** mark one stud and flexplate for assembly reference, then

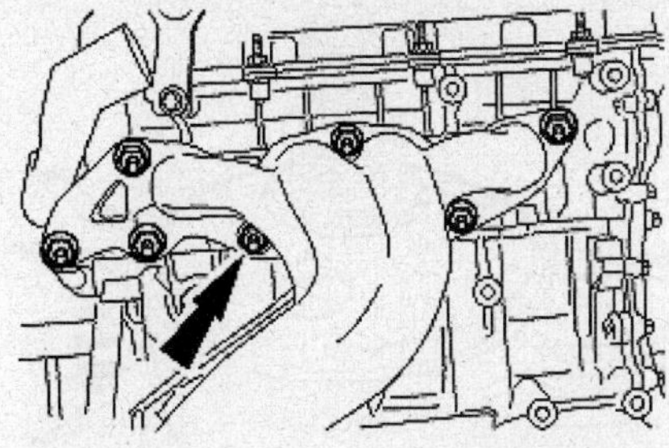

Fig. 7 Exhaust manifold mounting nuts

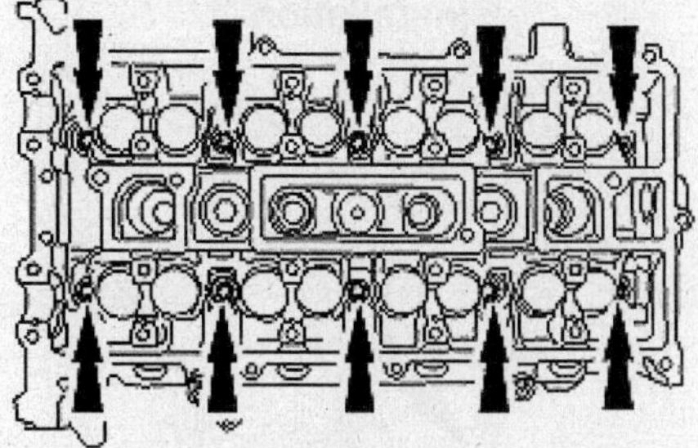

Fig. 10 Cylinder head bolt locations

remove torque converter nuts.

43. **On all models,** remove nine transmission to engine bolts. Leave two side bolts in until engine is ready to be removed.
44. Lower vehicle.
45. **On models equipped with automatic transmission,** remove transmission fluid dipstick and tube.
46. **On all models,** install suitable engine lifting bracket.
47. Support transmission with floor jack.
48. Support engine with suitable lifting device and spreader bar, then remove two side transmission to engine bolts.
49. Remove four engine support insulator nuts.
50. Remove engine from vehicle.
51. Reverse procedure to install.

INTAKE MANIFOLD

REPLACE

1. Remove accelerator control snow shield.
2. Remove air cleaner outlet tube.
3. Disconnect throttle cables from intake manifold.
4. Disconnect throttle position sensor electrical connector.
5. Disconnect manifold absolute pressure sensor electrical connector.
6. Disconnect vacuum hose and idle air control valve electrical connector.
7. Disconnect engine vacuum harness, brake booster hose and crankcase breather hose.
8. Disconnect engine wiring harness and position aside.
9. Remove EGR tube bracket bolt.
10. Disconnect swirl control valve electrical connector.
11. Disconnect fuel line from clip.

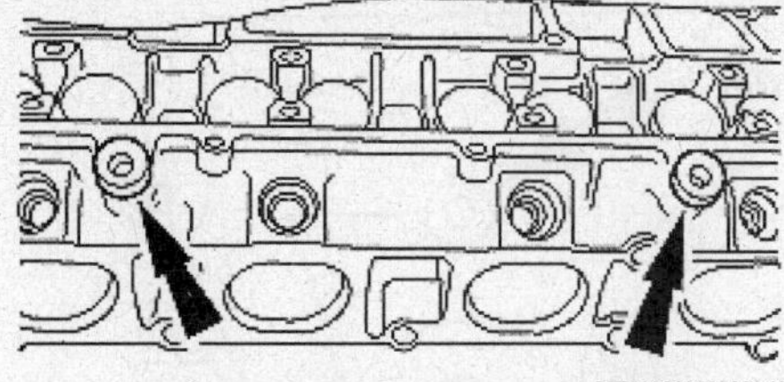

Fig. 8 Fuel injector supply manifold spacers

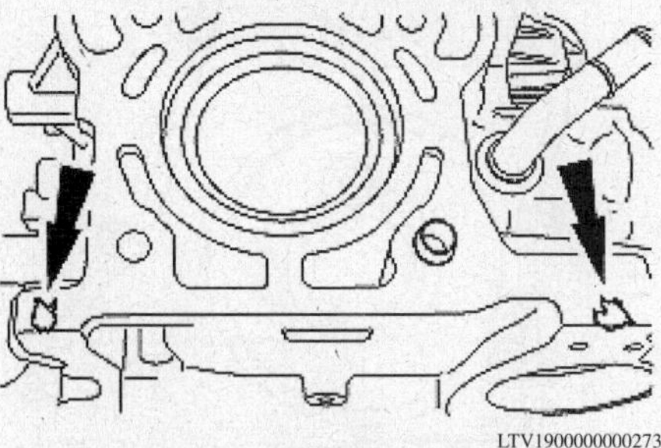

Fig. 11 Silicone sealant placement

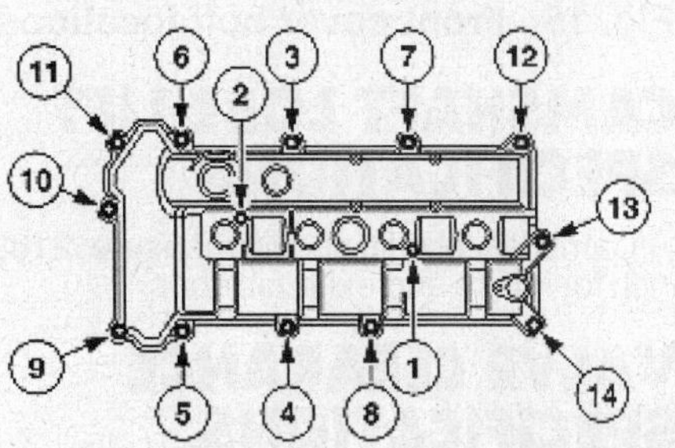

Fig. 13 Valve cover bolt tightening sequence

12. Remove bolts from EGR tube flange.
13. Disconnect 42 pin electrical connector from bracket and disconnect vapor purge hose.
14. Disconnect engine knock sensor electrical connector.
15. Remove wiring harness pushpin from bottom of intake manifold.
16. Disconnect fuel manifold vacuum hose.
17. Remove five bolts, **Fig. 4,** then the intake manifold.
18. Reverse procedure to install, noting the following:
    a. Inspect and install new intake manifold gaskets as required.
    b. Install intake manifold and five mounting bolts, **Fig. 5.**

EXHAUST MANIFOLD

REPLACE

1. Raise and support vehicle.
2. Remove exhaust flange nuts.
3. Lower vehicle.
4. Remove accessory drive belt.
5. Drain cooling system into suitable container.
6. Disconnect upper radiator hose and reservoir hose.
7. Remove A/C compressor.

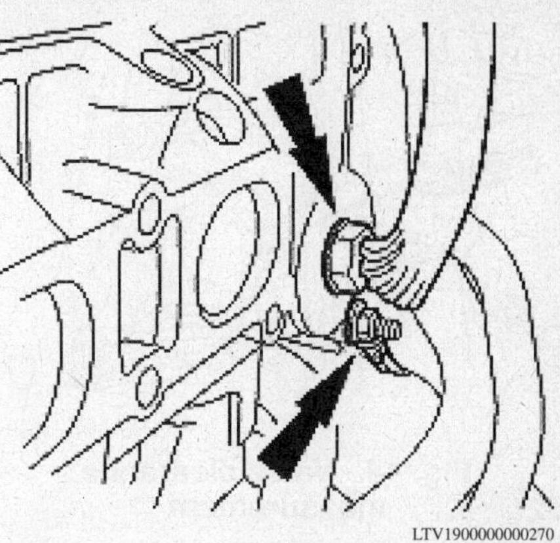

Fig. 9 EGR tube & ground strap

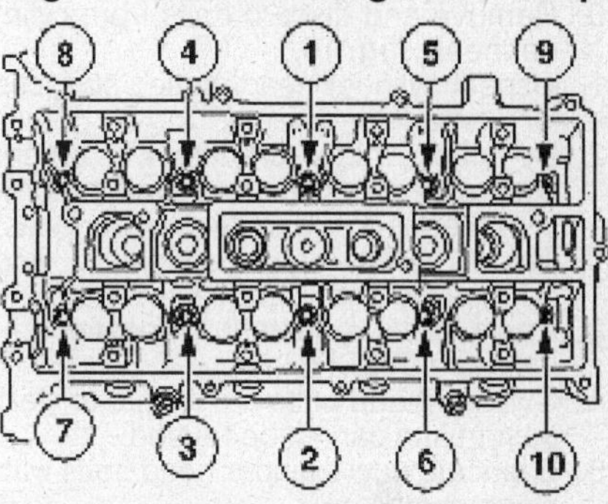

Fig. 12 Cylinder head bolt tightening sequence

8. Disconnect heater water hose.
9. Remove oil dipstick and tube.
10. Remove front radiator tube.
11. Raise and support vehicle.
12. Remove pushpins and position right-hand inner fender splash shield out of way.
13. Disconnect alternator electrical connectors.
14. Remove lower Front End Accessory Drive (FEAD) mounting bolts, **Fig. 6.**
15. Lower vehicle.
16. Remove upper mounting bolt and FEAD assembly.
17. Remove two nuts and position coolant tube out of way.
18. Remove nuts, then the exhaust manifold, **Fig. 7.**
19. Remove exhaust manifold gasket.
20. Reverse procedure to install.

CYLINDER HEAD

REPLACE

1. Remove camshafts as outlined in "Camshaft, Replace."
2. Remove exhaust manifold as outlined in "Exhaust Manifold, Replace."
3. Remove fuel injector supply manifold.
4. Remove fuel injector supply manifold spacers, **Fig. 8.**
5. Remove PCV hose clips.
6. Disconnect EGR tube and ground strap, **Fig. 9.**
7. Disconnect engine coolant temperature sender unit and EGR valve electrical connectors.
8. Disconnect EGR coolant hose and remove from hose bracket.

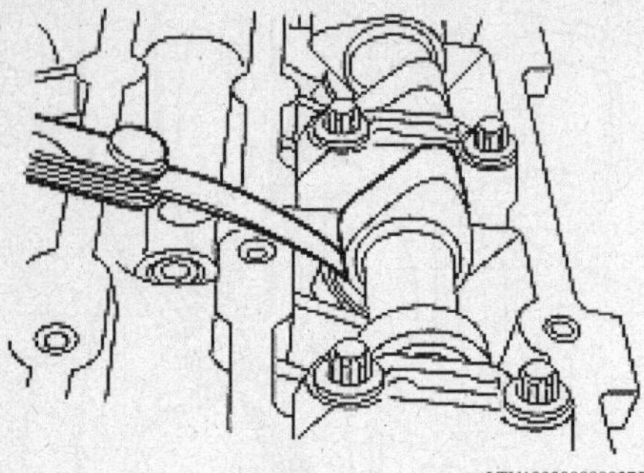

Fig. 14 Valve clearance measurement

9. Disconnect coolant bypass hose.
10. Remove and discard bolts from cylinder head, **Fig. 10.**
11. Inspect cylinder head mating surfaces for warpage or defects.
12. Do not use metal scrapers, wire brushes, power abrasive discs or other abrasive means to clean sealing surfaces. These tools cause scratches and gouges that may create leak paths.
13. Apply silicone sealant to locations illustrated, **Fig. 11.**
14. Cylinder head bolts are torque to yield design and cannot be reused.
15. Lubricate new cylinder head bolts with clean engine oil.
16. Install cylinder head with new gasket and bolts, tighten in sequence, **Fig. 12,** as follows:
    a. Stage 1: **Torque** bolts to 44 inch lbs.
    b. Stage 2: **Torque** bolts to 11 ft. lbs.
    c. Stage 3:**Torque** bolts to 33 ft. lbs.
    d. Stage 4: Tighten bolts 90°.
    e. Stage 5: Tighten bolts an additional 90°.
17. Reverse remaining procedures to install remaining components.

VALVE COVER

REPLACE

1. Remove intake manifold assembly as outlined in "Intake Manifold, Replace."
2. Position Cylinder Head Temperature sensor (CHT) boot aside.
3. Disconnect CHT sensor electrical connector.
4. Disconnect engine wiring harness from valve cover studs.
5. Remove spark plug wires, then disconnect ignition coil electrical connector.
6. Remove ignition coil.
7. Remove camshaft position sensor.
8. Remove crankcase ventilation tube.
9. Remove valve cover.
10. Reverse procedure to install, noting the following:
    a. Clean and inspect sealing surfaces.
    b. Install new gaskets as required.
    c. Install valve cover and bolts.
    d. **Torque** bolts to 89 inch lbs., in sequence, **Fig. 13.**

VALVE ARRANGEMENT

Front To Rear......................E-I-E-I-E-I-E-I

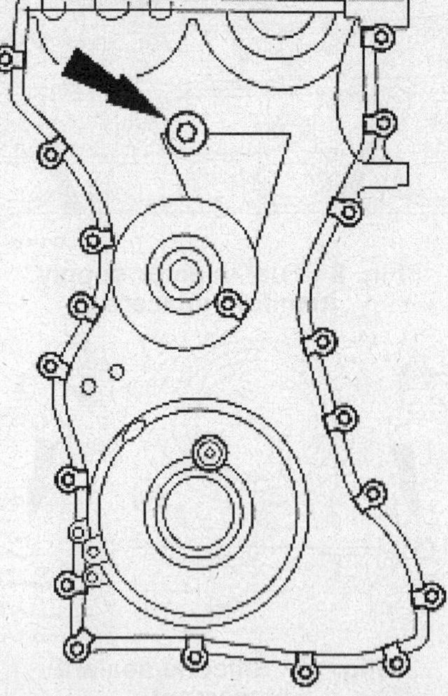

Fig. 15 Front cover bolt locations

CAMSHAFT LOBE LIFT SPECIFICATIONS

Camshaft lobe lift should measure .2163 inch for intake and exhaust lobes.

VALVE CLEARANCE SPECIFICATIONS

Valve clearance is .008–.011 inch for intake valves and .010–.013 inch for exhaust valves.

VALVE ADJUSTMENT

1. Remove valve cover as outlined in "Valve Cover, Replace."
2. Turn engine clockwise using crankshaft bolt.
3. Measure clearance with suitable feeler gauge, **Fig. 14.**
4. If clearance is not .008–.011 inch for intake valves and .010–.013 inch for exhaust valves, install new tappets as outlined in "Tappets, Replace" to obtain proper clearance.
5. Select tappets suing the following formula, tappet thickness equals measure clearance plus the base tappet thickness minus most desirable thickness.

VALVE TAPPETS

REPLACE

The crankshaft, crankshaft sprocket and pulley are fitted together by friction between the flange faces on each part. If the crankshaft pulley is loosened, the crankshaft sprocket is also loosened. **The engine must be timed each time the damper is removed or severe damage to engine may occur.**

1. Valve tappets are select fit and valve clearance must be inspected before removing tappets. Refer to "Valve Adjustment" for valve clearance measurement procedure.
2. Remove camshaft as outlined in "Camshaft, Replace."
3. Remove and replace valve tappets as required.

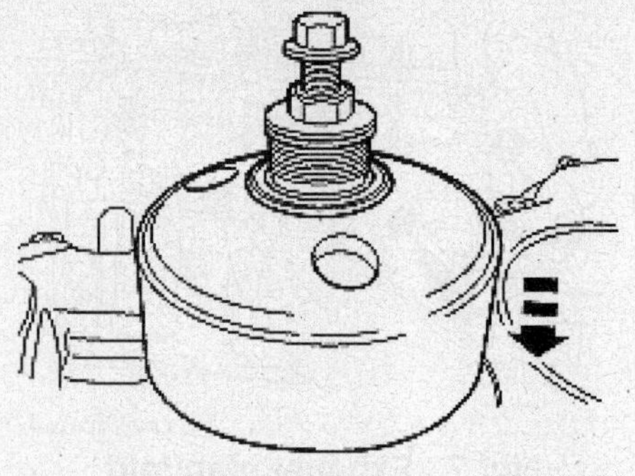

Fig. 16 Fan drive pulley installation

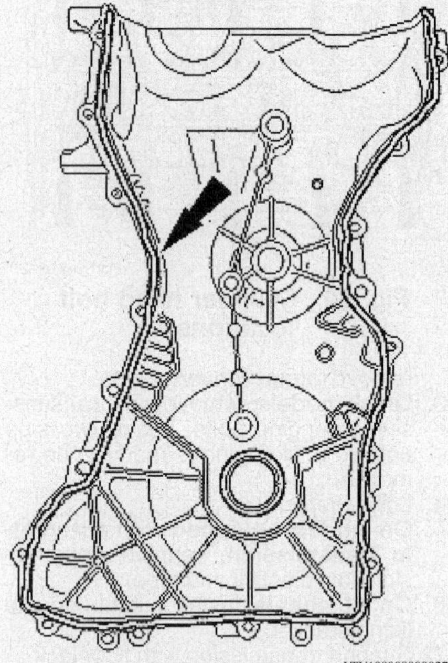

Fig. 17 Silicone gasket & sealant application

VALVE GUIDES

Valve guides are an integral part of the cylinder head. If valve stem to valve guide clearance exceeds specifications, ream valve guide to accommodate next oversize valve stem.

FRONT COVER

REPLACE

Removal

The crankshaft, crankshaft sprocket and pulley are fitted together by friction between the flange faces on each part. If the

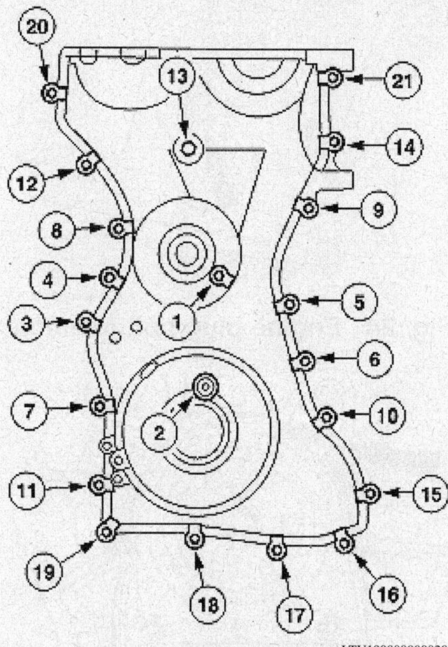

Fig. 18 Front cover bolt tightening sequence

crankshaft pulley is loosened, the crankshaft sprocket is also loosened. **The engine must be timed each time the damper is removed or severe damage to engine may occur.**

1. Remove crankshaft pulley as outlined in "Crankshaft Pulley, Replace."
2. Remove and discard crankshaft position sensor.
3. Remove accessory belt tensioner and water pump pulley.
4. Disconnect power steering pressure switch electrical connector.
5. Remove mounting bolt and position power steering pump aside.
6. If new cover is being installed, remove fan drive pulley with suitable three jaw puller.
7. There is one bolt behind cooling fan drive pulley that can be accessed by lining up one of the holes in fan drive pulley.
8. Remove bolts, **Fig. 15,** then the front cover.

Installation

The crankshaft, crankshaft sprocket and pulley are fitted together by friction between the flange faces on each part. If the crankshaft pulley is loosened, the crankshaft sprocket is also loosened. **The engine must be timed each time the damper is removed or severe damage to engine may occur.**

1. Install fan drive pulley if previously removed using a nut and bolt with flat washers, **Fig. 16.**
2. Clean and inspect front cover mating surfaces. Do not use metal scrapers, wire brushes or power abrasive discs.
3. Engine front cover must be installed and bolts tightened within four minutes of applying silicone gasket and sealant.
4. Apply a 2.5 mm bead of silicone gasket and sealant to cylinder head and oil pan joint areas. Apply a 2.5 mm bead of silicone gasket and sealant to front cover, **Fig. 17.**
5. Install front cover.
6. Tighten front cover bolts in sequence, **Fig. 18,** as follows:
   a. **Torque** 8 mm bolts to 89 inch lbs.
   b. **Torque** 10 mm bolts to 18 ft. lbs.
   c. **Torque** 13 mm bolts to 35 ft. lbs.
7. Connect power steering pump pressure switch.
8. Install water pump pulley and belt tensioner.
9. Install crankshaft pulley as outlined in "Crankshaft Pulley, Replace."
10. Install new crankshaft position sensor, do not tighten bolts at this time.
11. Adjust crankshaft position sensor alignment with tool supplied with new sensor, then tighten bolts.
12. Connect crankshaft position sensor electrical connector and wiring harness pin type connector.

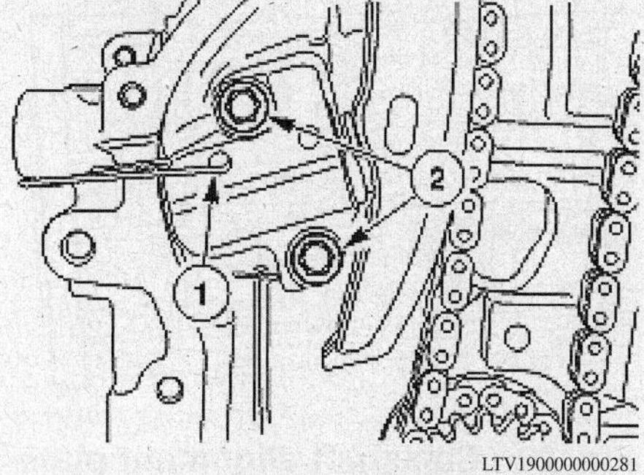

Fig. 19 Timing chain tensioner

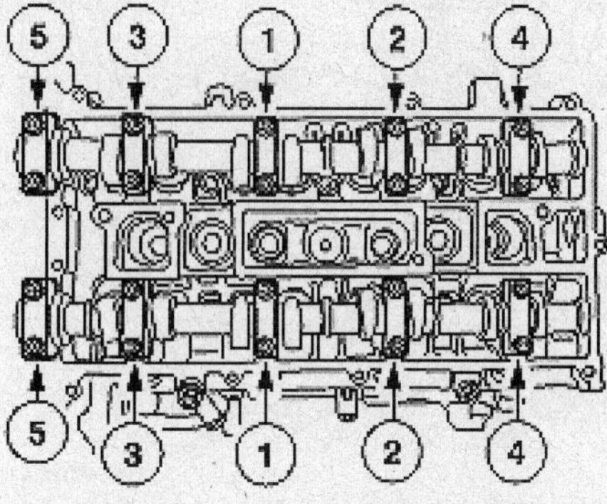

Fig. 21 Camshaft bearing cap bolt tightening sequence

TIMING CHAIN

REPLACE

The crankshaft, crankshaft sprocket and pulley are fitted together by friction between the flange faces on each part. If the crankshaft pulley is loosened, the crankshaft sprocket is also loosened. **The engine must be timed each time the damper is removed or severe damage to engine may occur.**

1. Remove engine front cover as outlined in "Front Cover, Replace."
2. Compress timing chain tensioner and insert paper clip into tensioner hole, **Fig. 19.**
3. Remove tensioner.
4. Remove righthand timing chain guide, then the timing chain.
5. Remove lefthand timing chain guide.
6. Reverse procedure to install.

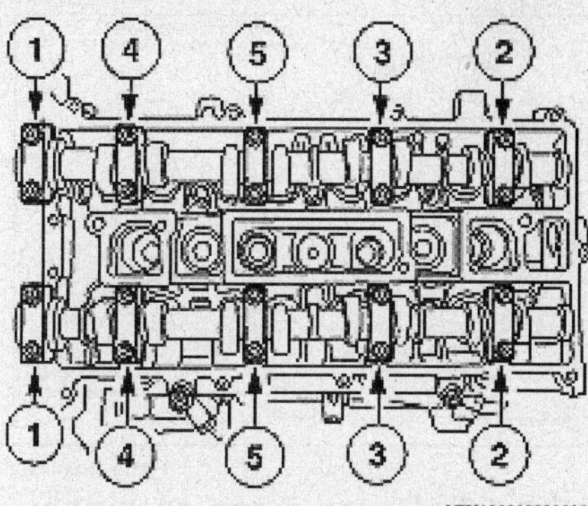

Fig. 20 Camshaft bearing cap bolt removal sequence

CAMSHAFT

REPLACE

The crankshaft, crankshaft sprocket and pulley are fitted together by friction between the flange faces on each part. If the crankshaft pulley is loosened, the crankshaft sprocket is also loosened. **The engine must be timed each time the damper is removed or severe damage to engine may occur.**

Removal

1. Install camshaft plate alignment tool No. 303–465, or equivalent.
2. Remove timing chain and sprockets as outlined in "Timing Chain, Replace."
3. Remove alignment tool.
4. Note position of lobes on No. 1 cylinder before removing camshafts for assembly reference.
5. Remove camshafts as follows:
   a. Loosen camshaft bearing bolts in sequence, **Fig. 20,** one turn at a time.
   b. Repeat first step until all tension is release from camshaft bearing caps.
   c. Remove camshaft bearing caps, then the camshafts.

Installation

Install camshafts with alignment slots in camshafts lined up so the camshaft alignment plate can be installed without rotating the camshafts. Ensure lobes on number one cylinder are in the same position as noted in removal procedure. Rotating camshafts when the timing chain is removed, or installing camshafts 180° out of position, can cause severe damage to valves and pistons.

1. Lubricate camshaft journals and bearing caps.
2. Tighten bolts in sequence, **Fig. 21,** in three stages.
   a. Stage 1: Tighten camshaft bearing cap bolts one turn at a time until tight.

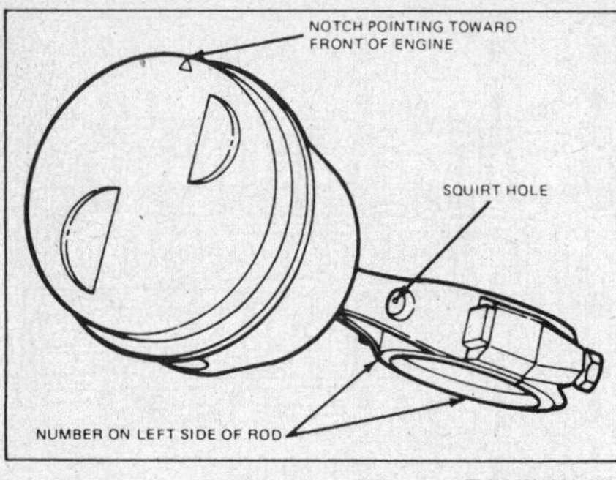

Fig. 22 Piston & rod assembly

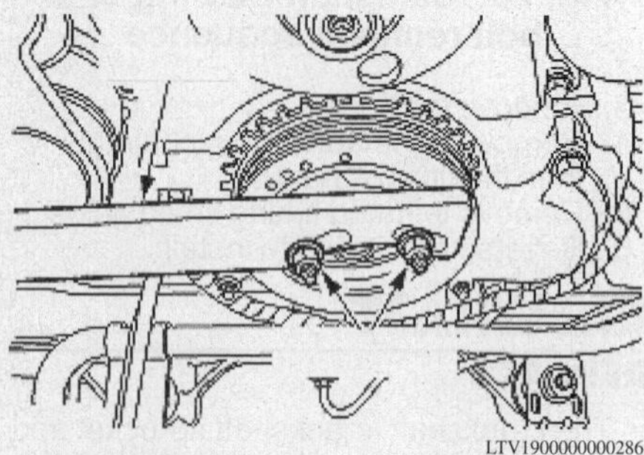

Fig. 25 Crankshaft timing peg alignment tool installation

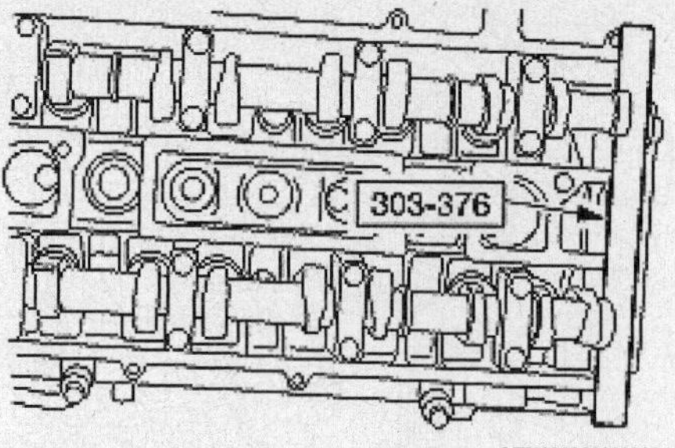

Fig. 23 Camshaft alignment plate tool installation

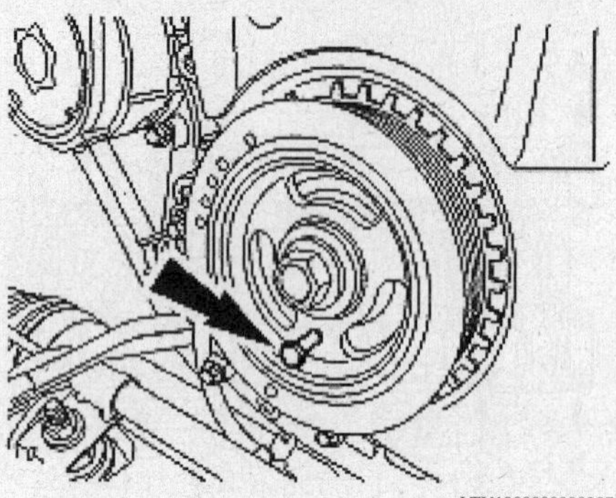

Fig. 26 Crankshaft to front cover bolt installation

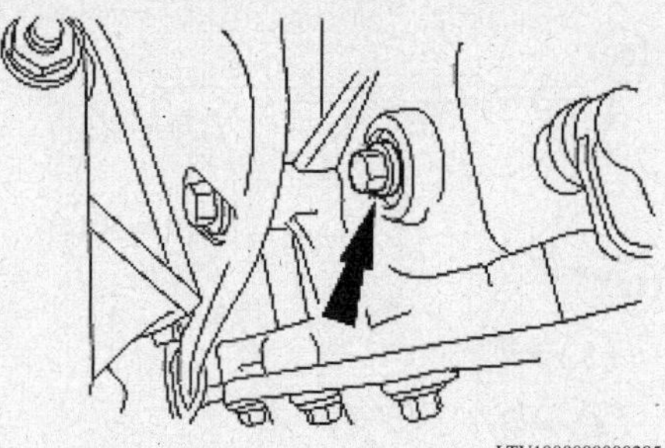

Fig. 24 Engine plug bolt location

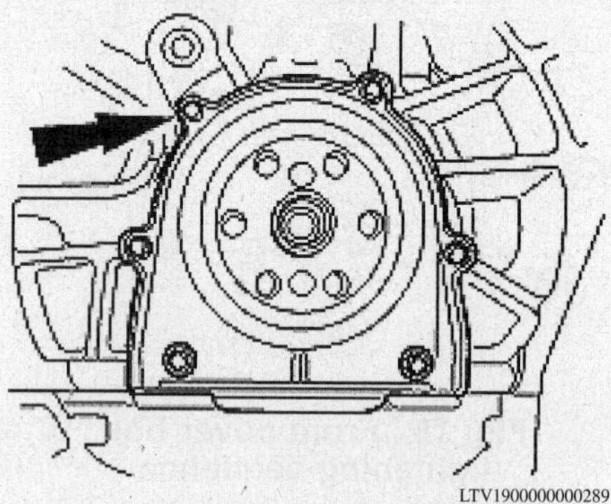

Fig. 27 Rear crankshaft seal retainer bolt locations

   b. **Torque** bolts to 62 inch lbs.
   c. **Torque** bolts to 12 ft. lbs.
3. Install camshaft drive gears hand tighten bolts.
4. Install timing chain and sprockets as outlined in "Timing Chain, Replace."

PISTON & ROD ASSEMBLY

Assemble rod to piston with arrow on top of piston facing front of engine and squirt hole on rod positioned as outlined in **Fig. 22.**

CRANKSHAFT PULLEY

REPLACE

Removal

1. Remove cooling fan, shroud and accessory drive belt.
2. Remove valve cover.
3. Turn crankshaft clockwise with crankshaft bolt, to position No. 1 piston at TDC.
4. Install camshaft alignment plate tool No. 303–376, or equivalent, in slots on rear of both camshafts, **Fig. 23.**
5. Camshaft alignment plate tool is for camshaft alignment only, using tool to prevent rotation can result in engine damage.
6. Remove engine plug bolt, **Fig. 24.**
7. Install crankshaft timing peg tool No. 303–507, or equivalent, **Fig. 25.**
8. Only turn engine in normal direction of rotation. Installing timing peg tool will prevent engine from being rotated in clockwise direction, but engine can still be rotated in counterclockwise direction.
9. Install drive pinion flange holding fixture No. 205–126, or equivalent.
10. Failure to hold crankshaft pulley in place during bolt loosening can cause damage to engine.
11. Remove and discard crankshaft pulley bolt and drive pinion holding fixture, then the crankshaft pulley.

Installation

1. Apply clean engine oil on seal area before installing pulley.
2. Install crankshaft pulley and hand tighten bolt. Hand tighten only or damage to front cover can occur.
3. Install a standard 6 mm x 18 mm bolt through crankshaft pulley and thread in into front cover, **Fig. 26.**
4. Failure to hold crankshaft pulley during tightening sequence can cause damage to engine front cover.
5. Tighten crankshaft pulley in two stages.
6. Stage 1: tighten bolt to 74 ft. lbs.
7. Stage 2: Rotate bolt an additional 90° (¼ turn).
8. Remove holding tools and crankshaft timing peg.
9. Turn engine two complete revolutions.
10. Install crankshaft timing peg tool No. 303–507, or equivalent.
11. Turn engine until No. 1 piston is at TDC.
12. Inspect position of crankshaft pulley using the 6 mm bolt, **Fig. 26.** If it is not possible to install bolt, correct engine timing.
13. Inspect position of camshafts with camshaft alignment plate tool No. 303–376, or equivalent. If it is not possible to install tool, correct engine timing.
14. Remove crankshaft pulley holding bolt and crankshaft timing peg tool.
15. Install engine plug bolt.
16. Install valve cover, drive belt, fan and shroud.

CRANKSHAFT SEAL

REPLACE

Front

1. Remove crankshaft pulley as outlined in "Crankshaft Pulley, Replace."
2. Pry crankshaft seal from front cover with suitable flat edged tool.
3. Lubricate new seal with clean engine oil.
4. Install seal with seal installation tool No. 303–096, or equivalent.
5. Install crankshaft pulley as outlined in "Crankshaft Pulley, Replace."

Rear

1. Remove transmission and flexplate/flywheel as outlined in **MOTOR's "Domestic Transmission, In-Vehicle Service" or "Transmission Service DVD."**
2. Remove seal retainer bolts, then the seal, **Fig. 27.**
3. Install new seal on crankshaft rear main oil seal installer tool No. 303–328, or equivalent.
4. Install crankshaft rear oil seal on crankshaft.
5. **Torque** bolts in sequence, **Fig. 28,** to 89 inch lbs.

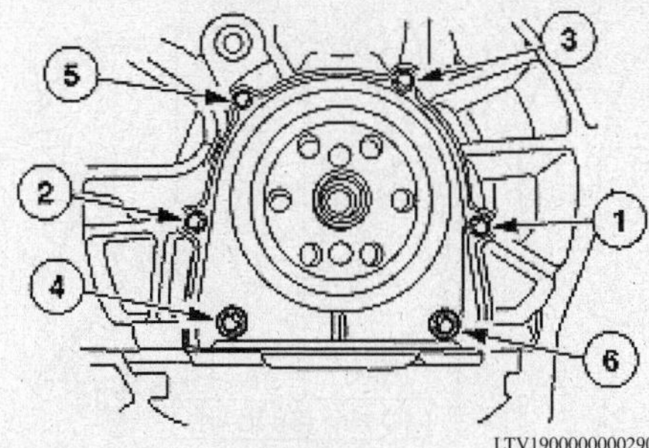

Fig. 28 Crankshaft rear oil seal bolt tightening sequence

OIL PAN

REPLACE

1. Drain crankcase, then remove engine assembly from vehicle as outlined in "Engine, Replace."
2. Position engine on a suitable engine stand. **Do not turn engine upside down with oil pan attached. Sludge and debris will fall into cylinders, pistons, and connecting rods possibly causing rapid wear.**
3. Remove oil level dipstick and tube.
4. Remove oil pan attaching bolts, then the oil pan, **Fig. 29.**
5. Clean and inspect all mating surfaces.
6. Oil pan must be installed and bolts tightened within four minutes of applying silicone gasket and sealant.
7. Apply a 2.5 mm bead of silicone gasket and sealant to oil pan.
8. Install oil pan.
9. **Torque** oil pan bolts in sequence, **Fig. 30,** to 18 ft. lbs.
10. Lubricate O-ring with clean engine oil. Install oil level dipstick and tube.
11. Install engine in vehicle as outlined in "Engine, Replace."

OIL PUMP

REPLACE

1. Remove oil pan as outlined in "Oil Pan, Replace."
2. Remove oil pump bolt, **Fig. 31,** then the oil pump.
3. Reverse procedure to install.

BELT TENSION DATA

No adjustments required; automatic tensioner gauges when belt should be replaced.

SERPENTINE DRIVE BELT

Belt Routing

Refer to **Figs. 32 and 33** for accessory drive belt routing.

Belt Replacement

1. Raise tensioner by turning counterclockwise, then remove belt.
2. Install new belt over pulleys, then raise

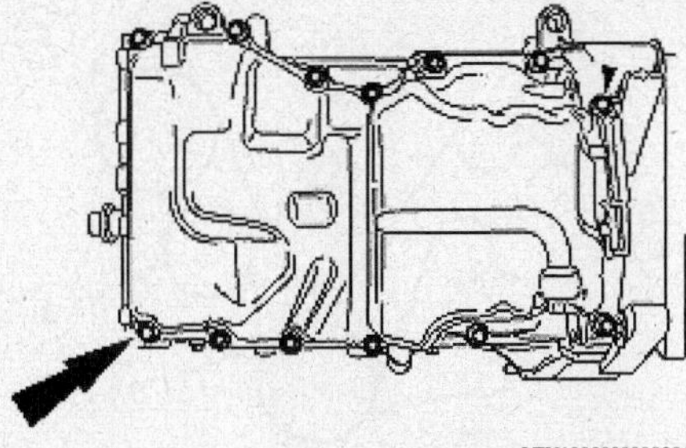

Fig. 29 Engine oil pan bolts

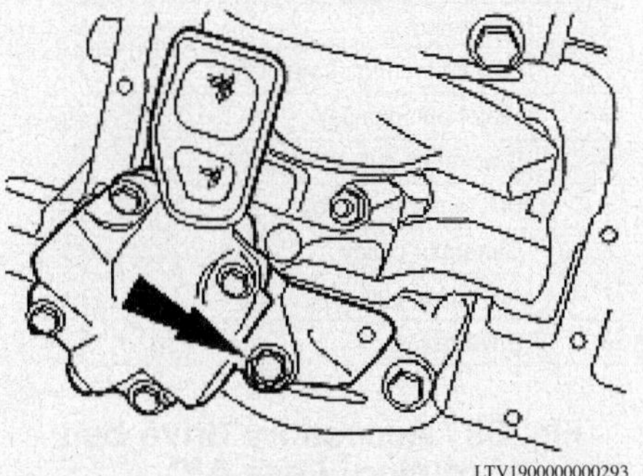

Fig. 31 Oil pump mounting bolt

tensioner and slide belt underneath. Release tensioner to rest pulley on belt.

COOLING SYSTEM BLEED

Partial Drain

1. Ensure radiator drain is fully closed.
2. Fill cooling system through degas bottle to ½ inch above maximum fill level.
3. Install degas bottle cap.
4. Start engine and hold at 2500 RPM for approximately eight minutes until thermostat opens.
5. Maintain 2500 RPM engine speed for an additional three minutes.
6. Increase engine speed to 4000 RPM and hold for five seconds.
7. Return engine speed to 2500 RPM and hold for an additional three minutes.
8. Stop engine and inspect for leaks.

Complete Drain

1. Install lower radiator hose and close radiator drain.
2. Fill cooling system through degas bottle to maximum fill level.
3. Start engine and run for approximately ten seconds at 2500 RPM to prime heater circuit then turn engine off.
4. Top off coolant level to ½ inch above maximum fill level.
5. Install degas bottle cap.
6. Start engine and hold at 2500 RPM for approximately eight minutes until thermostat opens.
7. Maintain 2500 RPM engine speed for an additional three minutes.
8. Increase engine speed to 4000 RPM for an additional three minutes.

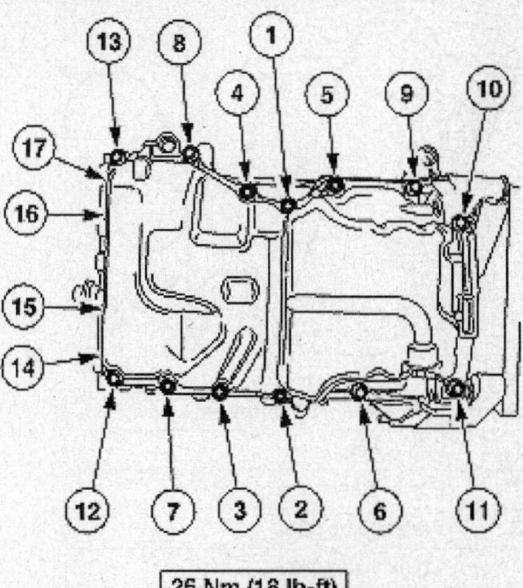

Fig. 30 Oil pan bolt tightening sequence

9. Return engine speed to 2500 RPM and hold for an additional three minutes.
10. Repeat previous two steps.
11. Stop engine and inspect for leaks.
12. Verify correct fluid level after engine cools for twenty minutes. To off degas bottle to "maximum" fill line.

THERMOSTAT

REPLACE

1. Drain cooling system into suitable container.
2. Disconnect radiator hose and electrical connector at thermostat housing.
3. Remove bolts, then the thermostat housing.
4. Reverse procedure to install.

WATER PUMP

REPLACE

1. Remove air cleaner outlet pipe.
2. Drain cooling system into suitable container.
3. Remove accessory drive belt.
4. Remove water pump pulley.
5. Remove water pump, **Fig. 34.**
6. Lubricate water pump O-ring with Merpol, or equivalent lubricant.
7. Reverse procedure to install.

RADIATOR

REPLACE

1. Drain cooling system into suitable container.
2. Disconnect coolant overflow hose from radiator and position away from radiator.
3. Disconnect upper radiator hose.
4. Remove cooling fan and shroud.
5. Disconnect lower radiator hose.
6. Remove upper mounting bolts, tilt radiator back and lift from vehicle.
7. Reverse procedure to install.

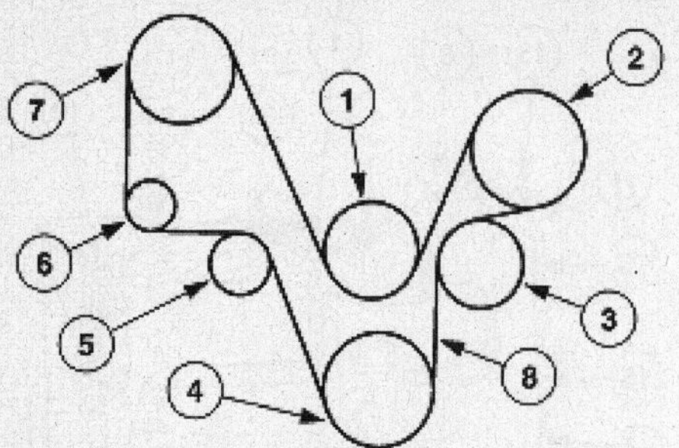

Item	Description
1	Fan pulley
2	Power steering pump pulley
3	Water pump pulley
4	Crankshaft pulley
5	Belt tensioner pulley
6	Generator pulley
7	A/C clutch pulley
8	Drive belt

LTV1900000000294

Fig. 32 Accessory drive belt routing. With A/C

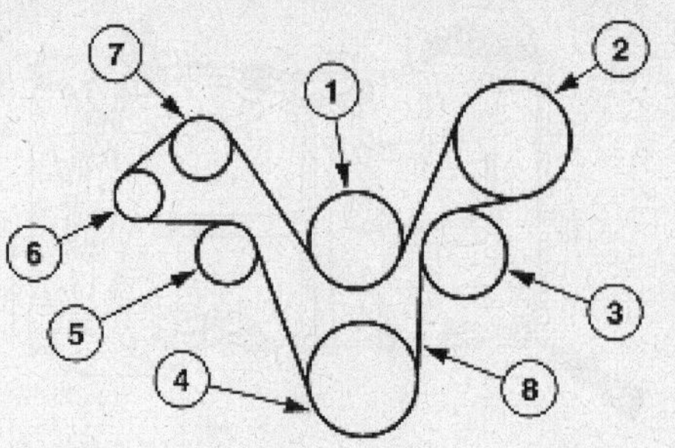

Item	Description
1	Fan pulley
2	Power steering pump pulley
3	Water pump pulley
4	Crankshaft pulley
5	Belt tensioner pulley
6	Generator pulley
7	A/C clutch pulley
8	Drive belt

LTV1900000000295

Fig. 33 Accessory drive belt routing. Less A/C

10 Nm (89 lb-in)

LTV1900000000296

Fig. 34 Water pump mounting bolts

FUEL PUMP

REPLACE

1. Remove fuel tank.
2. Remove any dirt that has accumulated around fuel pump attaching flange.
3. Remove fuel pump retaining ring using fuel tank lock ring wrench tool No. 310–075, or equivalent.
4. Remove fuel pump assembly.
5. Remove and discard fuel pump mounting gasket.
6. Reverse procedure to install.

FUEL FILTER

REPLACE

Early Build Vehicles

1. Relieve fuel system pressure as outlined in "Precautions."
2. Disconnect push connector and R-clip fittings.
3. Remove nut, then the fuel filter.
4. Reverse procedure to install.

Late Build Vehicles

1. Relieve fuel system pressure as outlined in "Precautions."
2. Disconnect push connector and R-clip fittings at fuel filter.
3. Remove fuel filter from bracket.
4. If required, remove nut and bracket.
5. Reverse procedure to install.

INERTIA SWITCH

The inertia switch, used on EFI engines, is located on the toe-board to the righthand of the transmission tunnel. Its purpose is to shut off fuel to the engine in the event of a vehicle collision. To reset switch, proceed as follows:

1. Turn ignition switch to Off position.
2. Inspect for leaking fuel in engine compartment, fuel lines and tank(s) and correct as required.
3. Push reset button on top of switch, then turn ignition switch On for several seconds.
4. Turn ignition switch Off, then inspect for and repair leaks as required.

TIGHTENING SPECIFICATIONS

Year	Component	Torque Ft. Lbs.
2002–06	A/C Compressor	18
	A/C Manifold Tube	15
	Alternator Mounting	18
	Alternator A/C Mounting Bracket Bolts	35
	Camshaft Bearing Caps	⑤
	Camshaft Sprocket	48
	Crankshaft Position Sensor	62①
	Crankshaft Pulley	④
	Cylinder Head	②
	EGR Outlet Tube At Cylinder Head	41
	EGR Outlet Tube At Intake Manifold	15
	EGR Tube Bracket	89①
	EGR Valve Assembly	18
	Engine Mounting Nuts	75
	Engine To Transmission	35
	Exhaust Manifold Studs	13
	Exhaust Manifold To Cylinder Head Nuts	40
	Exhaust Manifold To Exhaust Inlet Pipe Nuts	30
	Fan Shroud	62①
	Front Cover	③
	Intake Manifold	13
	Knock Sensor	15
	Oil Drain Plug	21
	Oil Filter Adapter	18
	Oil Pan	18
	Oil Pressure Sensor	11
	Oil Pump Screen & Cover	89①
	Oil Pump Sprocket	18
	Oil Pump To Engine	18
	Power Steering Pressure Line Tube	15
	Power Steering Pump	18
	Starter Mounting	18
	Timing Chain Tensioner & Guides	89①
	Timing Peg Plug	15
	Thermostat Outlet	89①
	Torque Converter To Flywheel	26
	Valve Cover	89①
	Water Pump	89①
	Water Pump Pulley	18

① — Inch lbs.

② — Refer to "Cylinder Head, Replace" for tightening procedure.

③ — Refer to "Front Cover, Replace" for tightening procedure.

④ — Refer to "Crankshaft Pulley, Replace" for tightening procedure.

⑤ — Refer to "Camshaft, Replace" for tightening procedure.

3.0L Engine

NOTE: On Air Bag Equipped Models, Refer To "Air Bag System Precautions" Located In The Front Of This Manual For System Disarming & Arming Procedures.

NOTE: Refer To "Computer Relearn Procedures" Located In The Front Of This Manual When Battery Power To The Computer Has Been Interrupted.

INDEX

PRECAUTIONS

Air Bag Systems

Refer to "Air Bag System Precautions" in the front of this manual for system disarming and arming procedures.

Battery Ground Cable

Prior to service, disconnect battery ground cable and isolate as required.

Fuel System Pressure Relief

METHOD 1

1. Remove fuel cap to relieve tank pressure.
2. Remove cap from fuel pressure relief valve located on fuel line in upper righthand corner of engine compartment, then release pressure from system using EFI pressure gauge tool No. T80L-9974-B, or equivalent..

ALTERNATE METHOD

Disconnect inertia fuel shutoff switch, located on the toe-board to the righthand of the transmission hump, then crank engine for 15–20 seconds to relieve fuel pressure.

COMPRESSION PRESSURE

Compression pressure should be inspected with the engine at normal operating temperature, spark plugs removed and throttle plate in wide open position. Crank the engine at least five compression strokes and record highest reading for each cylinder. Ensure battery is fully charged and oil is of proper viscosity. The indicated compression pressures are considered within specification if the lowest reading cylinder is within 75 percent of the highest.

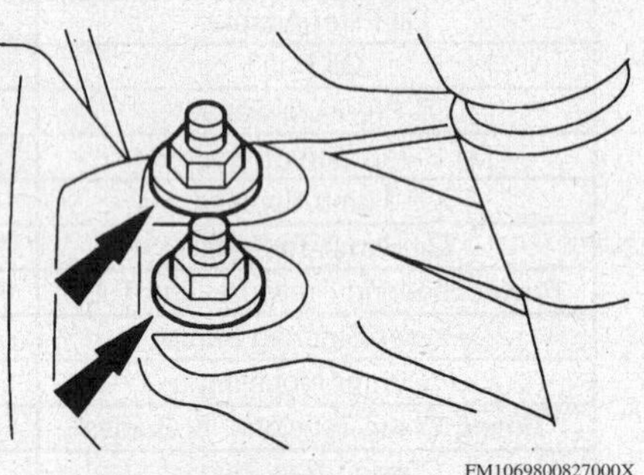

Fig. 1 Engine mount upper attaching nut removal

ENGINE MOUNT

REPLACE

Lefthand

1. Mark hood hinges and hood for alignment, then remove hood.
2. Remove fan and fan shroud.
3. Attach engine lift eyes, tool No. D81L–6001–D, or equivalent, to engine.
4. Remove engine mount attaching nuts, **Fig. 1.**
5. Raise and support engine using three bar engine support tool No. 014–00750 or equivalent.
6. Raise and support vehicle, then remove engine mount lower nut and mount, **Fig. 2.**
7. Reverse procedure to install. Tighten to specifications.

Righthand

1. Mark hood hinges and hood for alignment, then remove hood.
2. Remove fan attaching bolts and place fan into shroud cavity.
3. Remove fan shroud attaching bolts, then the fan and shroud.
4. Attach engine lift eyes, tool No. D81L–6001–D or equivalent, to engine.
5. Remove engine mount attaching nuts, **Fig. 1.**
6. Raise and support engine using three bar engine support tool No. 014–00750 or equivalent.
7. **On models equipped with 2WD,** remove righthand front spring.
8. **On models equipped with 4WD,** remove righthand front torsion bar.
9. **On all models,** remove engine mount lower nut and mount, **Fig. 2.**
10. Reverse procedure to install.

ENGINE

REPLACE

1. Relieve fuel system pressure as outlined in "Precautions."

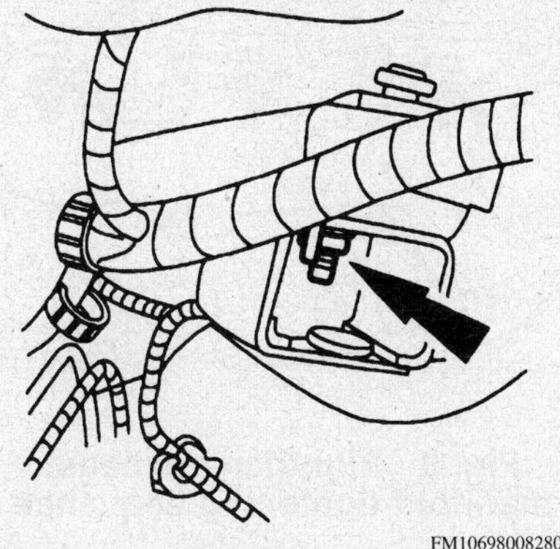

Fig. 2 Engine mount lower nut removal

2. drain cooling system into suitable container.
3. Remove radiator as outlined in "Radiator, Replace"
4. Remove air cleaner and intake duct assembly.
5. Disconnect upper and lower radiator hoses from radiator.
6. Loosen nut on fan clutch using Fan Clutch holding tool No. T84T-6312-C and Fan Clutch nut wrench tool No. T84T-6312-D, or equivalents, then remove assembled fan blade and clutch. **Fan clutch has lefthand threads. Nut must be turned clockwise for removal.**
7. Lift drive belt tensioner by rotating it, then remove accessory drive belt.
8. Recover refrigerant from A/C system, then disconnect liquid line at condenser and suction hose from accumulator.
9. Remove A/C hose assembly to compressor.
10. Plug all A/C openings to avoid dirt, foreign material and excess moisture from entering A/C system.
11. Remove A/C compressor mounting bracket with compressor and power steering pump still attached and set aside.
12. Disconnect heater hoses at intake manifold and water pump.
13. Remove dash panel ground cables from cylinder block.
14. Disconnect both fuel lines at chassis to engine connections.
15. Remove EGR tube and place kickdown cable to one side and secure as required.
16. Disconnect two delta PFE hoses from EGR valve to exhaust manifold tube.
17. If required, remove PFE sensor.
18. Disconnect MAF sensor electrical connector.
19. Disconnect PCM and ground strap from cowl.
20. Disconnect transmission harness connectors and remove oxygen sensors as required.
21. Remove throttle body snow shield, then disconnect accelerator cable and bracket and position aside.
22. Mark and disconnect all vacuum lines from rear of intake manifold.
23. Disconnect fuel charging wiring from engine control sensor wiring at righthand valve cover, then from oxygen sensor connectors.

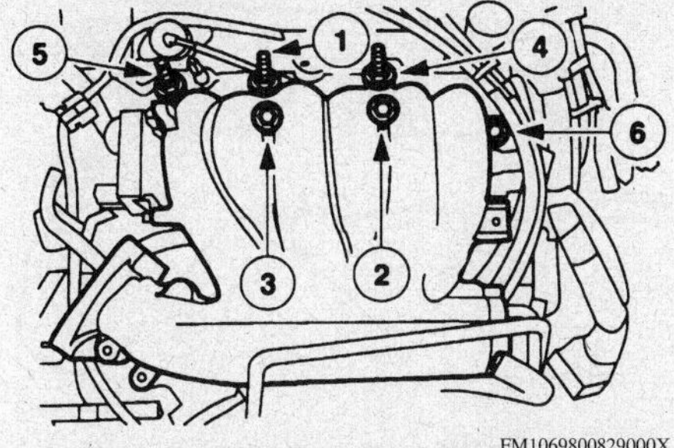

Fig. 3 Upper intake manifold tightening sequence

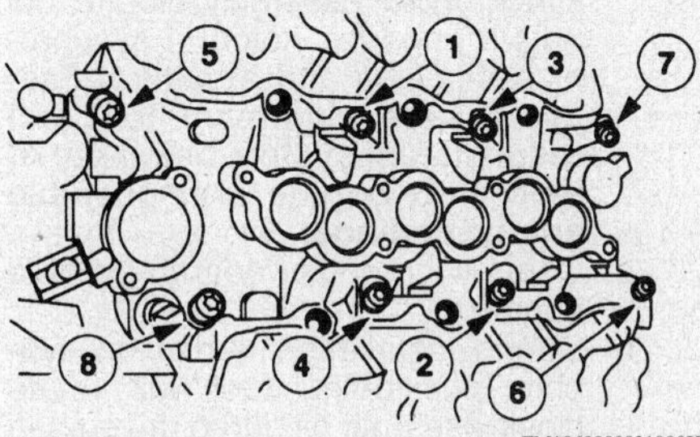

Fig. 5 Lower intake manifold tightening sequence

24. Place manual transmission in 4th gear or automatic transmission in Park.
25. Raise and support vehicle, then remove engine front support to crossmember attaching nuts.
26. Remove transmission oil cooler clip holding transmission cooling lines to righthand side of engine block.
27. Disconnect exhaust pipes at exhaust manifolds.
28. Disconnect battery to starter relay cable, then remove starter.
29. **On models equipped with manual transmission,** remove clutch housing attaching bolts with transmission, then disconnect clutch master cylinder at clutch housing.
30. **On models equipped with automatic transmission,** remove transmission housing cover and disconnect flywheel from torque converter.
31. **On all models,** remove converter housing to engine block bolts and adapter plate to converter housing bolt. Lower vehicle.
32. Attach a suitable engine lifting tool, then position jack under transmission. Raise engine slightly and carefully pull it from transmission. Lift engine out of engine compartment so engine rear plate is not bent or components damaged.
33. Reverse procedure to install. Tighten all nuts and bolts to specifications.

INTAKE MANIFOLD

REPLACE

Upper

1. Remove air cleaner outlet tube.

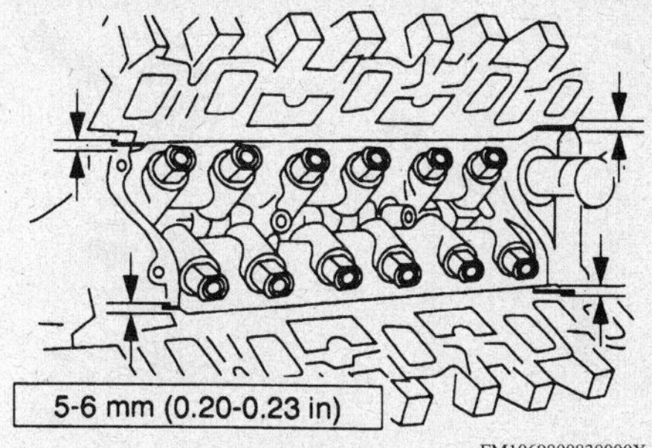

Fig. 4 Sealant application location

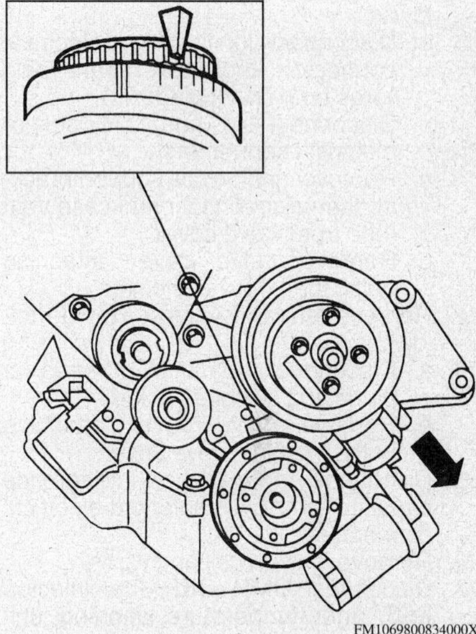

Fig. 6 TDC alignment marks

2. Disconnect accelerator cable and speed control actuator cable if equipped.
3. Disconnect TPS, IAC and EGR pressure transducer electrical connectors.
4. Remove EGR valve, then the intake vacuum connections.
5. Remove engine harness bracket from manifold.
6. Remove throttle body and gasket if required.
7. Remove ignition coil and position aside.
8. Remove EGR pressure transducer and disconnect EVAP hose.
9. Remove intake attaching studs and bolts.
10. Disconnect crankcase ventilation hose from bottom of intake.
11. Remove upper intake manifold and gasket.
12. Reverse procedure to install. Using sequence outlined **Fig. 3,** tighten bolts in two steps: First step, **torque** to 14 ft. lbs.; second step, **torque** to 18 ft. lbs.

Lower

1. Remove upper intake as outlined previously.
2. Drain cooling system into a suitable container.

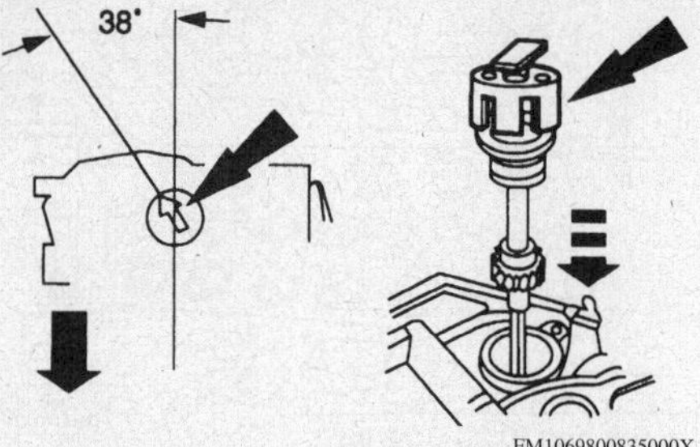

Fig. 7 Camshaft synchronizer installation

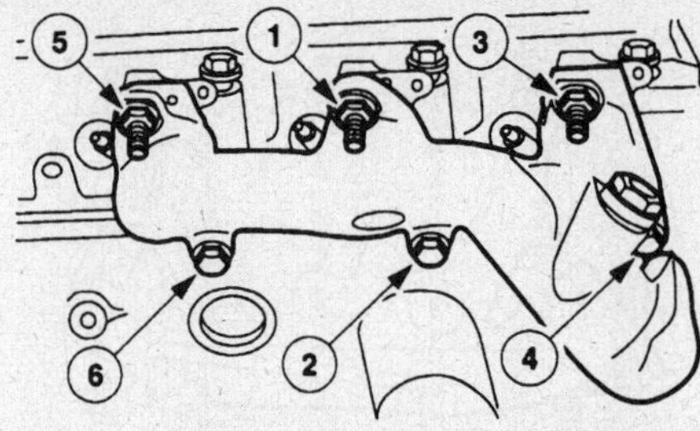

Fig. 8 Lefthand exhaust manifold tightening sequence

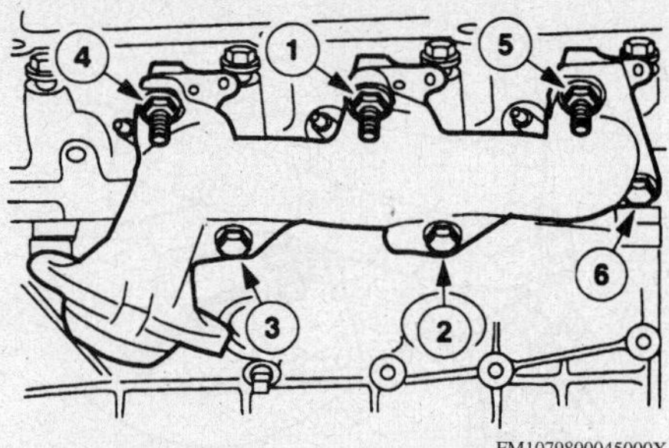

Fig. 9 Righthand exhaust manifold tightening sequence

3. Remove righthand valve cover as follows:
   a. Disconnect ignition coil electrical connector, then the spark plug wires from spark plugs.
   b. Disconnect IAT and MAF sensor electrical connectors.
   c. Remove ignition coil support bracket, then disconnect crankcase vent tube from valve cover.
   d. Remove valve cover attaching bolts, then the valve cover.
4. Remove lefthand valve cover as follows:
   a. Disconnect spark plug wires at plugs and set wires aside.
   b. Remove valve cover attaching bolts, then the valve cover.
5. Disconnect radio ignition interference capacitor and EGR solenoid electrical connectors.
6. Remove ignition coil and wires.
7. Disconnect CMP, CKP, fuel injector, ECT and temperature sending unit electrical connectors.
8. Relieve fuel pressure as outlined in "Precautions."
9. Disconnect fuel line.
10. Remove fuel injection supply manifold and fuel injectors.
11. Disconnect heater hoses and upper radiator hose.
12. Disconnect water bypass hose.
13. Remove thermostat housing.
14. Remove rocker arms and push rods. Ensure all are kept in order so each can be installed in original position.
15. Remove camshaft position sensor and synchronizer assembly if required.
16. Remove manifold attaching bolts, then the manifold and gaskets.
17. Reverse procedure to install noting the following:
   a. Apply suitable silicone gasket sealant at positions outlined in **Fig. 4.**
   b. When installing valve covers, apply suitable silicone gasket sealant at two points where lower intake meets cylinder head.
   c. **Torque** bolts to 21 ft. lbs., using sequence outlined in **Fig. 5.**
   d. If camshaft synchronizer assembly was removed, remove sensor from synchronizer assembly.
   e. Rotate engine until number 1 cylinder is at TDC of compression stroke and TDC mark is aligned as outlined in **Fig. 6.**
   f. Install synchro positioning tool No. 303–589 or equivalent on camshaft synchronizer assembly. Rotate tool until it engages notch in synchronizer housing and armature. **Failure to use alignment tool will result in fuel system being out of time with engine and possible engine damage.**
   g. Coat synchronizer gear in suitable engine oil.
   h. During installation, arrow on synchro positioning tool will rotate clockwise until oil pump drive shaft and cam gear engage. Install synchronizer assembly so that arrow on positioning tool is 38° from centerline of engine, **Fig. 7.**

EXHAUST MANIFOLD

REPLACE

Lefthand

1. Raise and support vehicle.
2. Remove exhaust pipe to manifold attaching nuts.
3. Lower vehicle, then disconnect EGR tube to manifold connection.
4. Remove dipstick tube attaching nut.
5. Remove exhaust manifold.
6. Reverse procedure to install. Using sequence outlined **Fig. 8, torque** bolts to 96 inch lbs., then to a final **torque** of 15–18 ft. lbs.

Righthand

1. Raise and support vehicle.
2. Remove oxygen sensor.
3. Remove exhaust pipe to manifold attaching nuts.
4. Lower vehicle, then remove coil support bracket.
5. Remove exhaust manifold attaching bolts, then the manifold and gasket.
6. Reverse procedure to install. Using sequence outlined **Fig. 9, torque** bolts to 96 inch lbs., then to a final **torque** of 15–18 ft. lbs.

CYLINDER HEAD

REPLACE

1. Drain cooling system into suitable container.
2. Remove intake tube from throttle body, then disconnect throttle linkage and cover.
3. Disconnect fuel lines, then mark and remove vacuum lines.
4. Disconnect upper radiator and heater hoses and position aside.
5. Recover refrigerant from A/C system, then disconnect liquid line at condenser and suction hose from accumulator.
6. Remove bolt securing A/C hose assembly to compressor housing, then remove hose assembly from vehicle.
7. Plug or cap all openings in A/C system to avoid dirt, foreign material and excess moisture from entering A/C system.
8. Remove exhaust manifold(s) as outlined in "Exhaust Manifold, Replace."
9. If removing lefthand cylinder head proceed as follows:
   a. Remove drive belt.
   b. Remove power steering pump bracket, pump, support and pressure hoses as an assembly, then set aside in a position to prevent leakage.
   c. Remove engine oil dipstick tube from exhaust manifold, then fuel line retaining bracket from front of cylinder head.
10. If removing righthand cylinder head, proceed as follows:
   a. Remove drive belt, then disconnect wiring from alternator.
   b. Remove alternator and bracket assembly from vehicle.
   c. Remove oil separator hose from rocker arm cover oil fill adapter.
11. Remove spark plugs.
12. Remove intake manifold as outlined in "Intake Manifold, Replace."
13. Remove rocker arms and pushrods in order so they can be installed in their original positions.
14. Remove cylinder head attaching bolts and the cylinder head.
15. Reverse procedure to install, noting the following:
   a. Refer to sequence outlined in **Fig. 10,** then tighten bolts in four steps: first step, **torque** to 59 ft. lbs.; second step, loosen bolts 1 full turn; third step, **torque** to 34–40 ft. lbs.; fourth step, **torque** to 63–73 ft. lbs.

VALVE ARRANGEMENT

FRONT TO REAR

The valves are in an alternated arrangement, intake/exhaust.

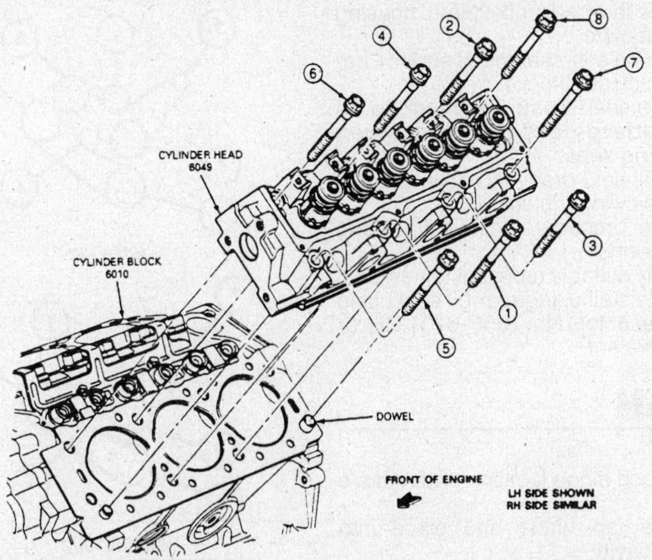

Fig. 10 Cylinder head bolt tightening sequence

VALVE CLEARANCE SPECIFICATIONS

Valve stem to guide clearance should be as follows: intake, .001–.0027 and exhaust, .0015–.0032 inch.

VALVE ADJUSTMENT

This engine uses hydraulic tappets which provide automatic lash adjustment. Clearance can be inspected by collapsing valve tappet and measuring clearance with a suitable feeler gauge. Specification for intake and exhaust is .088–.189 inch.

ROCKER ARMS

1. Remove upper intake manifold as outlined in "Intake Manifold, Replace.".
2. Drain cooling system into a suitable container.
3. Remove righthand valve cover as follows:
   a. Disconnect ignition coil electrical connector, then the spark plug wires from spark plugs.
   b. Disconnect IAT and MAF sensor electrical connectors.
   c. Remove ignition coil support bracket, then disconnect crankcase vent tube from valve cover.
   d. Remove valve cover attaching bolts, then the valve cover.
4. Remove lefthand valve cover as follows:
   a. Disconnect spark plug wires at plugs and set wires aside.
   b. Remove valve cover attaching bolts, then the valve cover.
5. Remove rocker arms and push rods. Ensure all are kept in order so each can be installed in original position.
6. Reverse procedure to install noting the following:
   a. When installing valve covers, apply suitable silicone gasket sealant at two points where lower intake meets cylinder head.
   b. Tighten to specifications.

VALVE GUIDES

Valve guides consist of holes bored in the cylinder head. For service, the guides can be reamed oversize to accommodate valves with oversize stems.

VALVE LIFT SPECIFICATIONS

Valve lift measured at zero lash, should be .402 inch on both intake and exhaust valves.

FRONT COVER

REPLACE

The front cover oil seal can be replaced without removing the front cover.

1. Remove water pump as outlined in "Water Pump, Replace."
2. Disconnect lower radiator hose.
3. Remove oil pan as outlined in "Oil Pan, Replace."
4. Remove CKP sensor.
5. Remove crankshaft pulley using puller tool No. T58P–6316–D or equivalent.
6. Remove front cover attaching bolts, then the front cover.
7. Reverse procedure to install noting the following:
   a. Tighten to specifications.
   b. Apply Teflon pipe sealant D8AZ–19954–A or equivalent to bolt locations outlined in **Fig. 11.**
   c. Install crankshaft pulley using installer tool No. T82L–6316–A or equivalent.

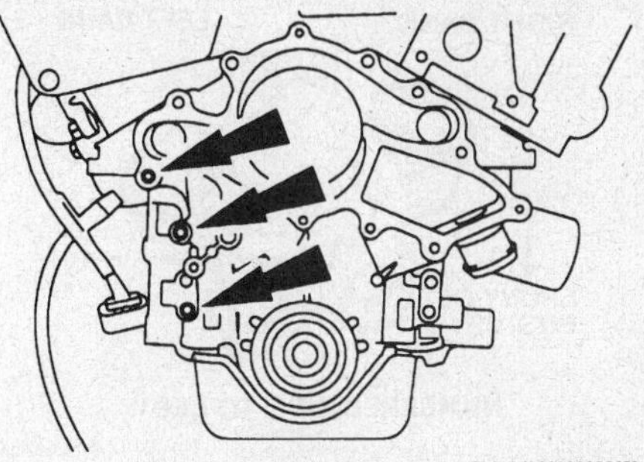

Fig. 11 Front cover bolt sealant location

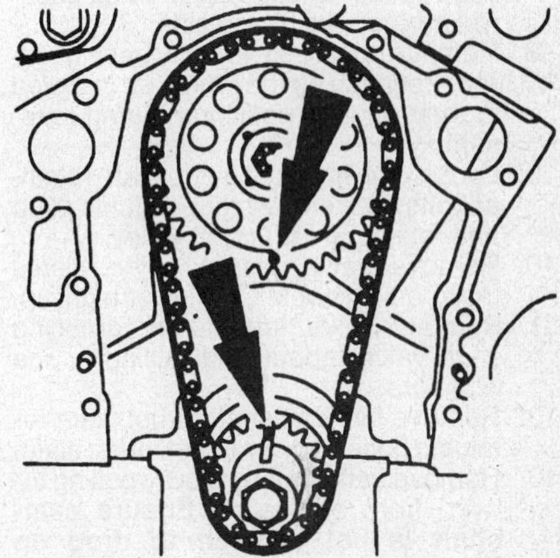

Fig. 12 Timing chain alignment marks

TIMING CHAIN

REPLACE

1. Remove engine front cover as outlined in "Front Cover, Replace," then set No. 1 piston to TDC.
2. Replace crankshaft pulley bolt, then turn crankshaft until timing marks on camshaft and crankshaft sprockets are aligned, **Fig. 12.**
3. Remove camshaft sprocket retaining bolt, then slide both sprockets and chain forward and remove as an assembly.
4. Reverse procedure to install, ensure timing marks are aligned as outlined in step 2.

CAMSHAFT

REPLACE

1. Rotate crankshaft to set No. 1 piston 0° at TDC on compression stroke.
2. Remove radiator as outlined in "Radiator, Replace."
3. Recover A/C refrigerant and remove A/C condenser core as outlined in "Air Conditioning" chapter.
4. Remove engine front cover as outlined in "Front Cover, Replace."
5. Remove timing chain/belt and sprockets as outlined in "Timing Chain, Replace."
6. Remove intake manifold and valve covers as outlined in "Intake Manifold, Replace."

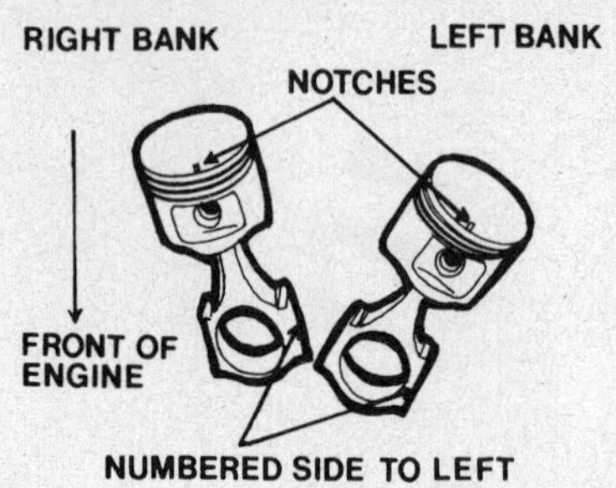

Fig. 13 Piston & rod assembly

7. Loosen rocker arm bolts enough to allow rocker arms to be lifted off pushrod and rotated to one side.
8. Remove pushrods. Identify each pushrod's location as they must be installed in their original positions during reassembly.
9. Loosen roller tappet guide plate retainer bolts and remove tappet guide plate and retainer from tappet valley.
10. Remove valve tappet guide plates from valve tappets by lifting straight up.
11. Remove valve tappets by grasping each valve tappet and pulling in line with bore.
12. Remove two camshaft thrust plate retaining bolts and camshaft thrust plate.
13. Remove camshaft by slowly pulling toward front of engine. **Ensure camshaft is not allowed to drop on bearing surface or cylinder block.**
14. Reverse procedure to install, noting the following:
    a. Lightly oil all bolt and stud threads before installing except those specified for special sealant.
    b. Clean all mating surfaces thoroughly.
    c. Inspect camshaft bearings for wear.
    d. Clean and inspect all components before installing.
    e. Install a suitable dial indicator to end of camshaft sprocket bolt.
    f. Push camshaft toward rear of engine, then zero dial indicator.
    g. Pull camshaft forward and release. If reading exceeds .007 inch, replace camshaft thrust plate and inspect again.
    h. **Do not replace camshaft sprocket bolt with a standard bolt or engine damage will occur.**

PISTON & ROD ASSEMBLY

Assemble rod to piston with notches on top of piston facing front of engine, **Fig. 13.**

CRANKSHAFT SEAL

REPLACE

Rear

1. Remove transmission assembly as outlined in **MOTOR's "Domestic Transmission, In-Vehicle Service" or "Transmission Service DVD."**
2. Remove flywheel or flexplate, housing and rear plate.
3. Place a hole in seal metal surface between cylinder blocks.
4. Remove seal. **Ensure damage to oil seal surface does not occur when removing seal.**
5. Clean oil seal groove in main bearing cap and cylinder block.
6. Reverse procedure to install, noting the following:
    a. Apply suitable lubricant to new seal and install using rear oil seal using replacer tool No. T95P-6701-BH, or equivalent.

OIL PAN

REPLACE

1. Mark hood hinge location and remove hood.
2. Remove fan blade and place into shroud cavity.
3. Remove fan shroud attaching bolts, then the fan and shroud.
4. Attach engine lifting eyes, tool No. D81L–6001–D or equivalent, to engine.
5. Remove engine mount attaching nuts.
6. Raise and support engine using three bar engine support kit tool No. D81L-6001–D or equivalent.
7. Raise and support vehicle.
8. Drain engine oil, then remove starter as outlined in "Starter, Replace" in "Electrical."
9. Remove oil pan attaching bolts, then the oil pan and gasket.
10. Reverse procedure to install noting the following:
    a. Apply a bead in two joints where engine block meets front cover and where block meets rear main bearing cap using a suitable silicone gasket and sealant.
    b. Tighten to specifications.

OIL PUMP

REPLACE

1. Remove oil pan as outlined in "Oil Pan, Replace."
2. Remove oil pickup screen and oil pump attaching bolts, then the oil pump and pump driveshaft.
3. Reverse procedure to install. Ensure oil pump is primed before installation.

OIL PUMP SERVICE

Individual oil pump components are not serviced. If any part of pump requires replacement, entire pump assembly must be replaced.

1. Inspect inside of pump housing, outer race and rotor for excessive wear or scoring.
2. Inspect mating surface of pump cover for excessive wear or scoring. Either of these conditions will necessitate replacement of pump.
3. Measure relief spring tension. Tension should be 9.1–10.1 lbs. at 1.11 inch.
4. Inspect relief valve piston for scores and ensure its free operation in bore.

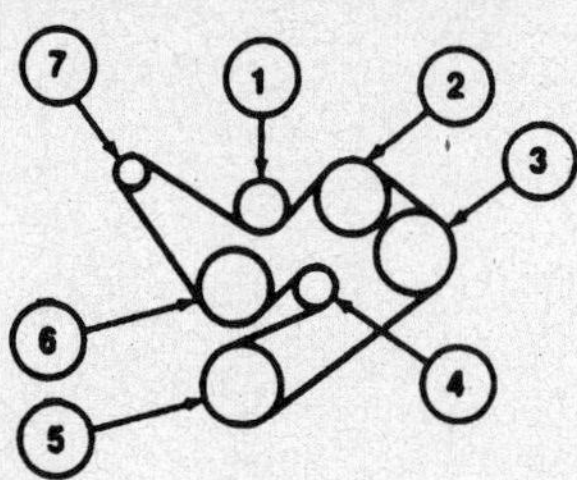

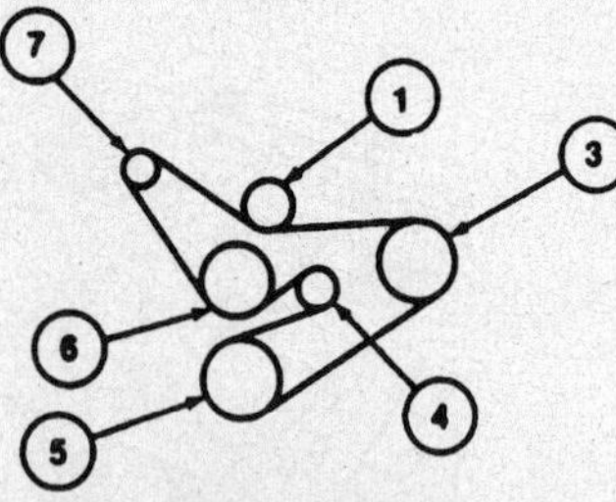

Item	Description
1	Belt Idler Pulley
2	A/C Compressor
3	Power Steering Pump Pulley
4	Drive Belt Tensioner
5	Crankshaft Pulley
6	Water Pump Pulley
7	Generator

FM1069700635000X

Fig. 14 Drive belt routing

5. Measure oil pump gear backlash. Ensure measurement is .008–.012 inch.
6. Measure oil pump gear height clearance. Ensure measurement is .0032–.0003 inch.
7. Measure driver shaft to housing clearance. Ensure measurement is .0019–.0005 inch.

BELT TENSION DATA

No adjustments are required; automatic tensioner gauges when belt should be replaced.

SEPARATED ACCESSORY DRIVE SYSTEM

Belt Routing

Refer to **Fig. 14** for drive belt routing.

Belt Replacement

1. Remove air outlet tube.
2. Rotate drive belt tensioner and remove drive belt.
3. Reverse procedure to install.

COOLING SYSTEM BLEED

1. Fill cooling system with a 50/50 mixture of coolant and water, then allow

several minutes for trapped air to escape (bubble out) and for coolant mixture to flow through the radiator.
2. Slide heater temperature and mode selection levers to maximum heat position.
3. Start engine and allow to idle until normal operating temperature is reached.
4. Shut engine off and allow to cool, then remove radiator cap and inspect coolant level. **Use caution when adding coolant to radiator to avoid hot coolant or steam blowing out from radiator.**

THERMOSTAT

REPLACE

1. Drain cooling system below level of thermostat, then disconnect heater return hose at thermostat housing.
2. Remove coolant outlet housing, then the thermostat.
3. Reverse procedure to install. Tighten outlet housing bolts to specifications.

WATER PUMP

REPLACE

1. Remove air cleaner outlet tube.
2. Remove fan and clutch assembly using fan clutch nut wrench tool No. T84T-6312-D or equivalent and fan clutch pulley holder tool No. T84T-6312-C, or equivalents. **Fan and clutch assembly retaining nut has lefthand threads and is removed by turning clockwise.**
3. Remove fan shroud, then the fan shroud and blade from vehicle.
4. Drain cooling system, then loosen water pump pulley bolts.
5. Rotate drive belt tensioner, then remove drive belt.
6. Remove water pump pulley, then the alternator electrical connectors.
7. Remove alternator and bracket as an assembly.
8. Disconnect crank position sensor wiring.
9. Remove heater hose at water pump and intake manifold.
10. Remove A/C compressor and support to side.
11. Remove belt tensioner if required, then the lower radiator hose.
12. Remove power steering pump bracket and support to side.
13. Remove water pump attaching bolts noting location, then the water pump assembly.
14. Reverse procedure to install.

RADIATOR

REPLACE

1. Drain cooling system.
2. Remove rubber radiator overflow hose from radiator, **Fig. 15.**
3. Remove two fan shroud attaching screws, then lift fan shroud out of lower retaining clips and drape over fan.
4. Loosen radiator upper and lower hose clamps, then remove upper and lower radiator hoses from radiator connectors.

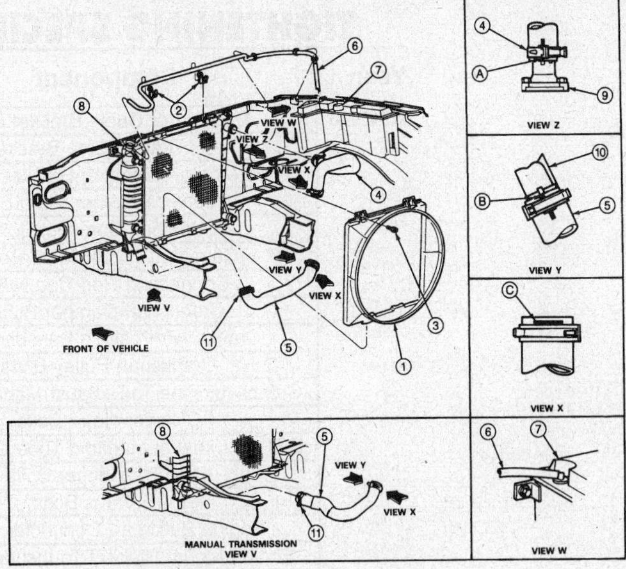

Item	Description
1	Fan Shroud
2	Radiator Overflow Tube Clip
3	Screw and Washer M6-1.0 x 27.5. Tighten to 6-8 N-m (53-71 In-Lb)
4	Upper Radiator Hose
5	Lower Radiator Hose
6	Radiator Overflow Hose
7	Overflow Reservoir
8	Radiator

Item	Description
9	Water Outlet
10	Water Pump
11	Clamp. Tighten to 2 N-m (18 In-Lb)
A	Arrow on Hose Must Align with Rib on Outlet ± 5°
B	Arrow on Hose Must Align with Rib on Water Pump ± 5°
C	Position Clamp to White Paint Stripe ± 5°

FM1089500100000X

Fig. 15 Radiator assembly

5. **On models equipped with automatic transmission:**
   a. Disconnect two transmission cooling lines from oil cooler fittings on radiator.
   b. Disconnect transmission cooler tube support bracket from bottom flange of radiator.
6. **On all models,** remove two radiator upper attaching screws.
7. Tilt radiator back approximately one inch and lift directly upward, clear of radiator support bracket and fan blade.
8. Lift fan shroud off of fan blade and remove it from vehicle.
9. Remove radiator lower support rubber insulators.
10. Reverse procedure to install. Tighten fasteners to specifications.

FUEL PUMP

REPLACE

When hairpin clips are removed, they must be replaced.

1. Relieve fuel system pressure as outlined in "Precautions," then remove fuel tank as follows:
   a. Drain fuel from tank, then loosen fill pipe clamp.
   b. Remove shield and bracket assembly to frame bolts, then remove assembly from vehicle.
   c. Remove fuel tank filler pipe, then suitably support fuel tank.
   d. Remove bolts and nuts from rear fuel tank support strap, then support strap. Repeat this step for front support strap.
   e. Lower fuel tank, then remove fuel feed hose and sender push connector.
   f. Remove fuel return hose at sender push unit push connector, then disconnect sender and fuel pump electrical connector.
   g. Remove fuel vapor hose from fuel vapor valve, then lower fuel tank from vehicle.
2. Remove any dirt that has accumulated around pump attaching flange.
3. Turn fuel tank sending unit lock retainer ring counterclockwise with Fuel Tank Lock Ring Wrench tool No. T90T-9275-A or T86T-9275-A, or equivalents, and remove fuel tank sending unit locking retainer ring.
4. Remove fuel pump and sender assembly, then pump mounting gasket. Discard old gasket.
5. Reverse procedure to install.

FUEL FILTER

REPLACE

1. Relieve fuel pressure as outlined in "Precautions."
2. Disconnect safety clips from fuel filter inlet and outlet lines.
3. Disconnect fuel line push connect fittings and remove filter using fuel line disconnect tool No. T90T–9550–S or equivalent.
4. Reverse procedure to install.

TIGHTENING SPECIFICATIONS

Year	Component	Torque Ft. Lbs.
2002–06	Accelerator Cable Bracket Bolts	89(1)
	A/C Bracket Line Bracket	89–106(1)
	Alternator Mounting Bracket Bolts	30–46
	Camshaft Retainer Plate Bolts	71–106(1)
	Camshaft Sprocket Bolt	40–51
	Camshaft Thrust Plate Bolts	71–106(1)
	Connecting Rod Cap Nuts	23–28
	Crankshaft Damper Bolts	93–121
	Crankshaft Position Sensor Bolts	71–106(1)
	Crankshaft Pulley Bolts	39–53
	Crossover Pipe To Exhaust Manifold Nuts	25–33
	Cylinder Head Bolts	(2)
	EGR to Exhaust Manifold Tube Connector	26–48
	EGR Transducer Bolts	71–106(1)
	EGR Valve Bolts	15–22
	Engine Bulkhead Connector Bolts	71–88(1)
	Engine Mount Bracket To Insulator Nuts	65–95
	Engine Insulator To Frame Nuts	71–94
	Exhaust Flange	30
	Exhaust Manifold To Cylinder Head Bolt/Studs	(3)
	Fan Shroud Bolts	54–70(1)
	Flexplate/Flywheel To Crankshaft	54–64
	Front Cover Bolts & Studs	15–22
	Fuel Injection Manifold Bolts	71–106(1)
	Fuel Line Bracket Nut	71–106(1)
	Lower Intake Manifold To Cylinder Head Bolts & Studs	(4)
	Main Bearing Cap Bolts	55–63
	Oil Dipstick Tube Stud	12–15
	Oil Pan Bolts	108(1)
	Oil Pressure Switch	15
	Oil Pump To Block Bolts	30–40
	Powertrain Control Module Connector Bolt	45–61(1)
	Powertrain Control Module Ground Strap Nut	80–106(1)
	Radiator Attaching Bolts	54–70(1)
	Rocker Arm Bolts	19–28
	Serpentine Belt Tensioner Bolts	30–45
	Spark Plug	96(1)
	Starter Motor Bolts	17–20
	Thermostat Housing	15–22
	Throttle Body Bolts	15–22
	Torque Convertor Access Plate Bolts	84–120(1)
	Torque Convertor Nuts	23–28
	Transmission Cooler Line Bracket Bolt	80–106(1)
	Transmission To Engine Bolts	29–37
	Transmission Insulator Nuts	73–97
	Upper Intake Manifold	(4)
	Valve Cover Studs and Bolts	108(1)
	Valve Tappet Retainer Bolts	89–123(1)
	Water Hose Connection Bolts	15–22
	Water Pump Pulley	17–20
	Water Pump To Front Cover	75–106(1)
	48 Pin Wire Harness	71–106(1)

(1)— Inch lbs.
(2)— Refer to "Cylinder Head, Replace" for tightening procedure.
(3)— Refer to "Exhaust Manifold, Replace" for tightening procedure.
(4)— Refer to "Intake Manifold, Replace" for tightening procedure.

4.0L SOHC Engine

NOTE: On Air Bag Equipped Models, Refer To "Air Bag System Precautions" Located In The Front Of This Manual For System Disarming & Arming Procedures.

NOTE: Refer To "Computer Relearn Procedures" Located In The Front Of This Manual When Battery Power To The Computer Has Been Interrupted.

INDEX

PRECAUTIONS

Air Bag Systems

Refer to "Air Bag System Precautions" in the front of this manual for system disarming and arming procedures.

Automatic Ride Control

On models equipped with automatic ride control, the automatic ride control service switch must be turned off before lifting vehicle. The service switch is located in the rear jack storage area.

Battery Ground Cable

Prior to service, disconnect battery ground cable and isolate as required.

Fuel System Pressure Relief

METHOD 1

1. Remove fuel cap to relieve tank pressure.
2. Remove cap from fuel pressure relief valve located on fuel line in upper righthand corner of engine compartment, then release pressure from system using EFI pressure gauge tool No. T80L-9974-B, or equivalent.

ALTERNATIVE METHOD

Disconnect inertia fuel shutoff switch, located on the toe-board to the righthand of the transmission hump, then crank engine for 15–20 seconds to relieve fuel pressure.

COMPRESSION PRESSURE

Compression pressure should be inspected with the engine at normal operating temperature, spark plugs removed and throttle plate in wide open position. Crank the engine at least five compression strokes and record highest reading for each cylinder. The indicated compression pressures are considered within specification if the lowest reading cylinder is within 75% of the highest.

ENGINE MOUNT

REPLACE

1. Remove upper radiator fan shroud.
2. Remove nuts from righthand side motor mount.
3. Raise and support vehicle.
4. Loosen transmission to crossmember nuts.
5. Remove both stabilizer bar bracket nuts.
6. **On models equipped with 4WD,** remove bolt from righthand side axle housing bushing.
7. **On models equipped with 4WD,** remove lefthand side lower axle housing bushing and lefthand side upper axle housing bushing.
8. **On all models,** remove lefthand front tire.
9. Remove righthand and lefthand lower mount nuts and washers.
10. Remove bolt from lefthand side motor mount.
11. Raise righthand side of engine with suitable jack until there is enough clearance to remove righthand motor mount, then remove mount.
12. Raise lefthand side of engine with suitable jack until there is enough clearance to remove lefthand motor mount, then remove mount.
13. Reverse procedure to install.

ENGINE

REPLACE

1. Mark hood hinges and hood for alignment, then remove hood.
2. Relieve fuel pressure as outlined in "Precautions"
3. Recover A/C system refrigerant as outlined in "Air Conditioning" chapter.
4. Remove radiator as outlined in"Radiator, Replace."
5. Remove air cleaner outlet tube.
6. Disconnect engine electrical connector, PCM electrical connector, and PCM ground, **Fig. 1.**
7. Disconnect engine ground strap at cowl.
8. Disconnect A/C high pressure switch connector, then the manifold line from compressor.
9. Disconnect fuel lines and heater hoses.
10. Raise and support vehicle.
11. Remove starter electrical connections, then the starter.
12. Drain engine oil into suitable container. Reinstall drain plug.

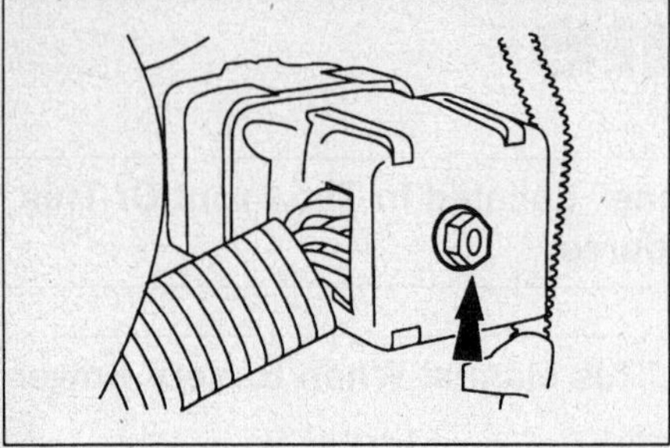
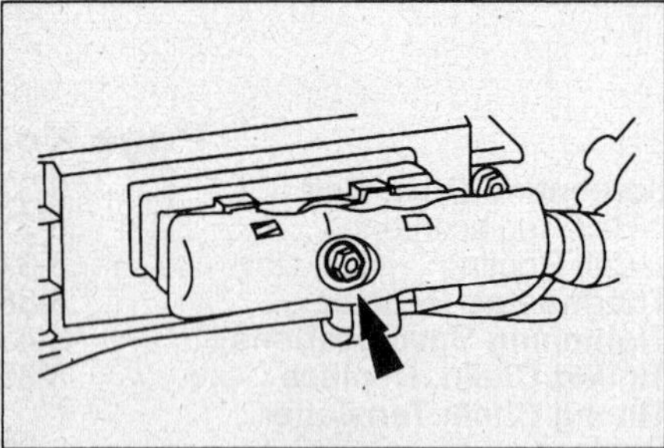
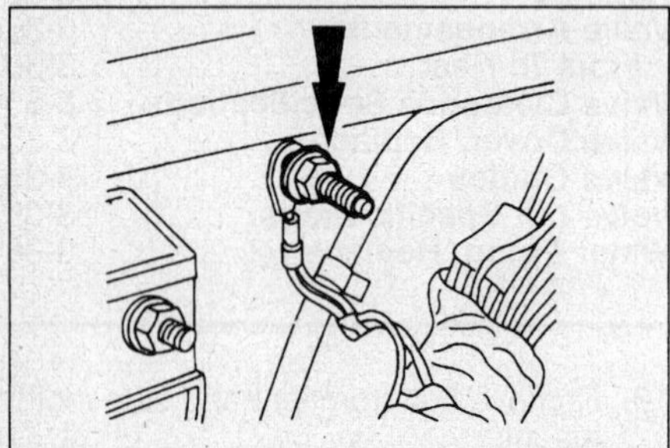

Fig. 1 PCM connector & ground locations

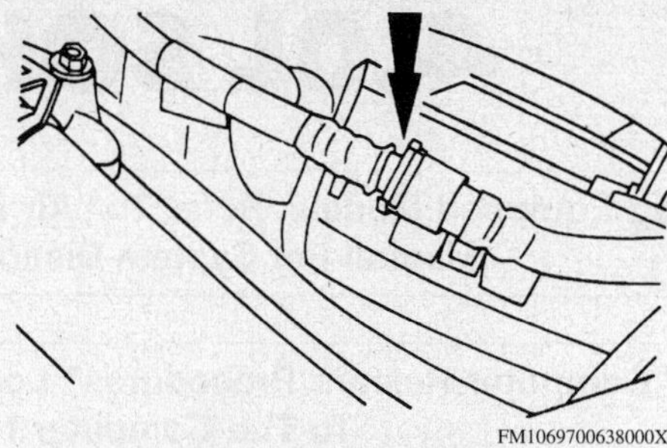

Fig. 2 Vapor management valve hose location

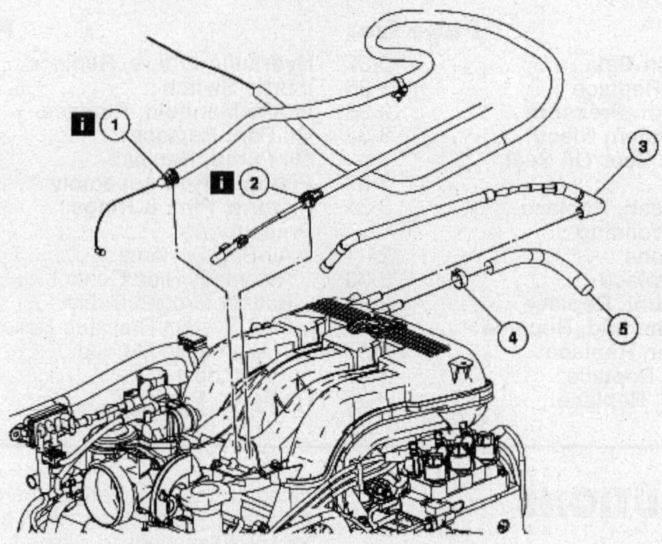

Item	Description
1	Accelerator cable Removal Note
2	Speed control cable Removal Note
3	Vacuum hose
4	Vacuum hose clamp
5	Vacuum hose

LTV1900000000521

Fig. 3 Intake manifold replacement (Part 1 of 4)

13. Disconnect both oxygen sensors and pipes from exhaust manifolds.
14. Disconnect electrical harness connector at transmission.
15. Disconnect transmission cooler line bracket and A/C line bracket and position aside.
16. Remove A/C line bracket and position to one side.
17. Disconnect power steering return and pressure hoses.
18. Disconnect vapor management valve hose connector, **Fig. 2.**
19. Remove transmission bolts, then lower vehicle.
20. Remove both motor mount nuts.
21. Carefully raise and remove engine.
22. Reverse procedure to install. Tighten all nuts and bolts to specifications.

INTAKE MANIFOLD

REPLACE

Refer to **Fig. 3** when performing the following procedure:

1. Remove air cleaner outlet pipe.
2. Remove accelerator and speed control cables.
3. Remove vacuum hoses from intake manifold.
4. Disconnect electrical connectors from throttle position sensor and idle air control valve.
5. Disconnect wiring harness retainers.
6. Remove EGR vacuum regulator and bracket.
7. Disconnect EGR tube upper fitting.
8. Remove PCV hose.
9. Remove eight intake manifold bolts, then the intake manifold.
10. Reverse procedure to install.

EXHAUST MANIFOLD

REPLACE

1. **On righthand exhaust manifold,** remove EGR recirculation tube.
2. **On both exhaust manifolds,** remove exhaust pipe to exhaust manifold nuts.
3. Remove exhaust manifold mounting nuts, then the exhaust manifold.
4. Reverse procedure to install.

CYLINDER HEAD

REPLACE

1. Remove lower intake manifold.
2. Remove camshaft roller followers.
3. Remove fan shroud and accessory drive belt.
4. Disconnect alternator wiring.
5. Remove drive belt tensioner.
6. Remove alternator mounting bracket.
7. Raise and support vehicle.
8. Remove bracket, **Fig. 4,** then lower vehicle.
9. Remove bolts and position accessory bracket aside, **Fig. 5.**
10. Remove coil bracket.
11. Disconnect crankshaft position sensor electrical connector, then remove wiring harness anchor and position harness aside.
12. Remove heater hose from thermostat housing.
13. Disconnect engine coolant temperature sensor electrical connector.
14. Disconnect EGR tube nut.
15. Position EGR bracket aside.
16. Remove upper and lower heater hoses.
17. Disconnect coolant bypass hose and position aside.
18. Remove thermostat housing.
19. Remove crankcase vent separator spring steel clip, then the separator.

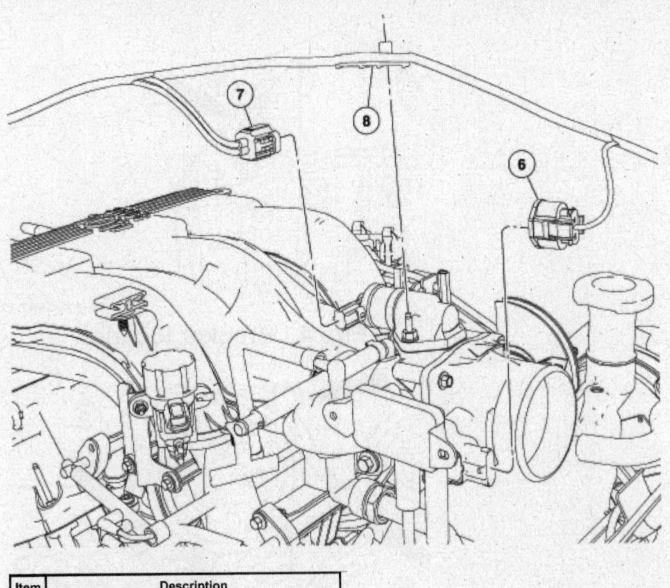

Item	Description
6	Throttle position (TP) sensor electrical connector
7	Idle air control (IAC) sensor electrical sensor
8	Wiring harness retainer

LTV1900000000522

Fig. 3 Intake manifold replacement (Part 2 of 4)

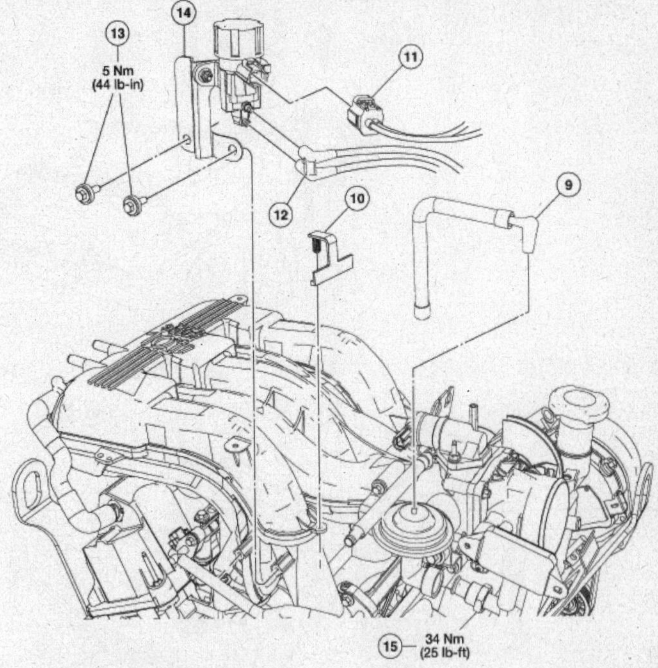

Item	Description
9	Vacuum hose
10	Wiring harness retainer
11	Exhaust gas recirculation (EGR) vacuum regulator solenoid electrical connector
12	Vacuum hoses
13	EGR vacuum regulator solenoid mounting bolts
14	EGR vacuum regulator solenoid mounting bracket
15	EGR tube upper fitting

LTV1900000000523

Fig. 3 Intake manifold replacement (Part 3 of 4)

20. Remove oil dipstick tube.
21. Remove exhaust manifolds as outlined in "Exhaust Manifold, Replace."
22. Remove lefthand hydraulic timing chain tensioner, **Fig. 6.**
23. Remove camshaft sprocket bolt and timing chain guide bolt, **Fig. 7.**
24. Hold timing chain and cassette with rubber band to aid in removal and to prevent chain from falling into cylinder head.
25. Remove lefthand camshaft sprocket from cassette.
26. Remove eight 12 mm bolts and two 8 mm bolts in sequence, **Fig. 8.**
27. Discard head gasket.
28. Remove righthand hydraulic timing chain tensioner as outlined in "Timing Chain, Replace."
29. Remove camshaft sprocket with gear removal tool No. 303–575, or equivalent.
30. Remove camshaft guide bolt, **Fig. 9.**
31. Hold chain and cassette with rubber band to aid in removal and prevent chain from falling into cylinder block, **Fig. 10.**
32. Remove righthand camshaft sprocket from cassette.
33. Remove two 8 mm bolts and eight 12 mm bolts from cylinder head in sequence, **Fig. 11.**
34. Discard head gasket.
35. Reverse procedure to install, noting the following:
    a. Install 12 mm bolts and tighten in sequence, **Fig. 12.**
    b. Install two 8 mm bolts, **Fig. 13.**
    c. **Torque** 12 mm bolts again, in sequence, **Fig. 12,** to 26 ft. lbs.
    d. Tighten all 12 mm bolts an additional 90°.
    e. Tighten all 12 mm bolts a final 90°.

VALVE COVER

REPLACE

1. Remove upper intake manifold as outlined in "Intake Manifold, Replace."
2. Disconnect spark plug wires.
3. If removing lefthand valve cover, proceed as follows:
    a. Remove two fuel line upper bracket bolts.
    b. Disconnect camshaft position sensor electrical connector.
    c. Disconnect differential pressure feedback transducer electrical connector and hoses.
    d. Disconnect engine electrical connector. Remove clip and slide electrical connector from valve cover.
    e. Disconnect coil pack electrical connectors.
4. If removing righthand valve cover, proceed as follows:
    a. Drain cooling system, then remove upper radiator hose.
    b. Remove two heater hose bracket bolts, then disconnect transmission dipstick tube.
5. Remove valve cover bolts, then the valve covers.
6. Reverse procedure to install, tighten all nuts and bolts to specification.

VALVE ARRANGEMENT

Front To Rear

Righthand Bank........................E-I-E-I-E-I
Lefthand Bank...........................I-E-I-E-I-E

VALVE LIFT SPECIFICATIONS

Intake valve lobe lift is .259 inch for intake and exhaust. Maximum allowable lobe lift loss is .005 inch.

VALVE CLEARANCE SPECIFICATIONS

Hydraulic lash adjusters are used in this engine. No provision for adjustment is provided.

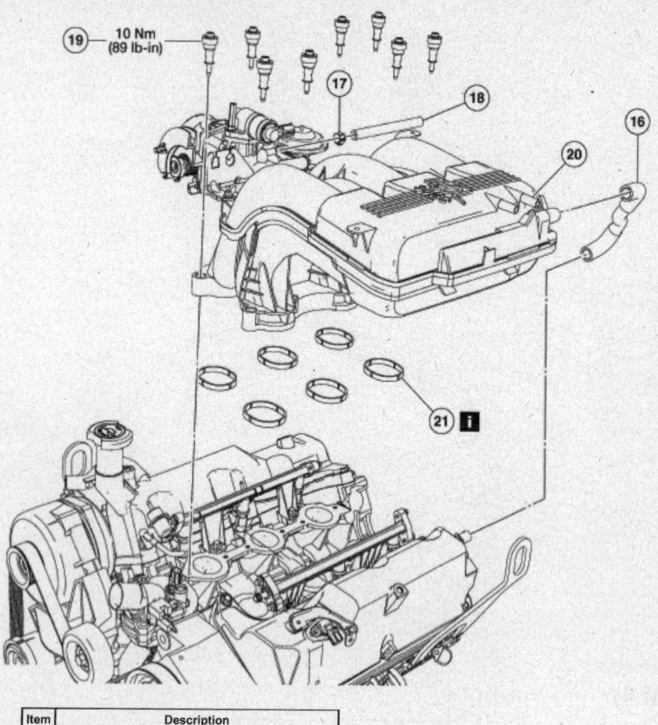

Item	Description
16	Positive crankcase ventilation (PCV) vacuum hose
17	Vacuum hose clamp
18	Vacuum hose
19	Intake manifold mounting bolts
20	Intake manifold
21	Intake manifold gaskets Removal Note

Fig. 3 Intake manifold replacement (Part 4 of 4)

Fig. 4 Bracket location

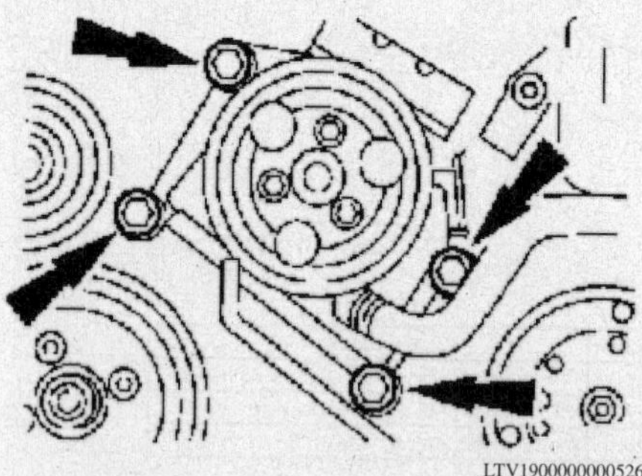

Fig. 5 Accessory bracket

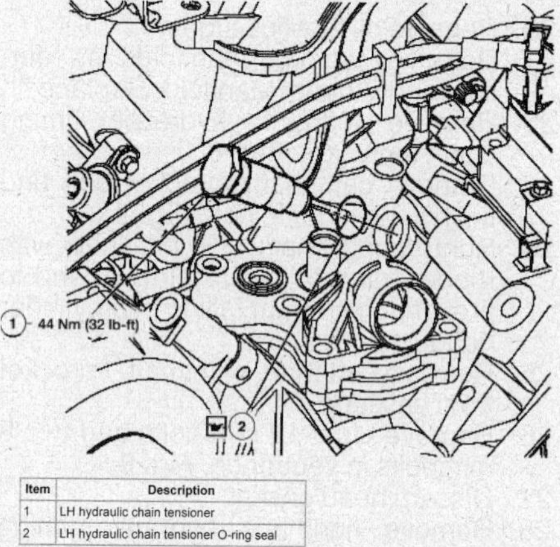

Item	Description
1	LH hydraulic chain tensioner
2	LH hydraulic chain tensioner O-ring seal

Fig. 6 Lefthand hydraulic timing chain tensioner

VALVE GUIDES

Valve guides consist of holes bored in the cylinder head. For service, the guides can be reamed oversize to accommodate valves with oversize stems.

HYDRAULIC LIFTERS

REPLACE

1. Remove valve covers as outlined in "Valve Cover, Replace."
2. Compress valve spring and remove camshaft follower using valve spring compressor tool No. T97T-6565-A, or equivalent.
3. Repeat procedure for remaining camshaft followers. **Ensure camshaft followers are installed in their original position.**
4. Remove hydraulic lash adjusters.
5. Reverse procedure to install.

FRONT COVER

REPLACE

1. Drain cooling system into suitable container.
2. Remove crankshaft pulley and front oil seal.
3. Remove front cover components in sequence, **Fig. 14.**
4. Apply silicone gasket and sealant in two places, **Fig. 15.**
5. Reverse procedure to install.

TIMING CHAIN

REPLACE

1. Remove engine from vehicle as outlined in"Engine, Replace."
2. Remove engine front cover as outlined in "Front Cover, Replace."
3. Remove timing chain and gear cassettes in sequence, **Fig. 16.**
4. Reverse procedure to install.

TIMING CHAIN TENSIONER

REPLACE

Refer to "Timing Chain, Replace" for timing chain tensioner replacement.

CAMSHAFT

REPLACE

Refer to **Figs. 17 and 18** when performing the following procedure:

1. Remove valve covers as outlined in "Valve Cover, Replace."
2. Remove cooling fan.
3. Remove hydraulic timing chain tensioner.
4. Rotate crankshaft until camshaft for cylinder being serviced is at base circle.
5. Mark each camshaft follower for installation reference.
6. Remove camshaft followers with removal tool No. 303–581, or equivalent.
7. Rotate crankshaft clockwise to position number one cylinder at TDC.
8. Remove retainer and position A/C manifold tube bracket aside.
9. **For righthand cylinder head,** install crankshaft TDC timing tool No. 303–573, or equivalent, to rear of righthand cylinder head, **Fig. 19.** Tighten two top clamp bolts to 89 inch lbs.
10. **For lefthand cylinder head,** install camshaft holding tools No. 303–578 and 303–564, or equivalents, to front of lefthand cylinder head and tighten two top clamp bolts to 89 inch lbs., **Fig. 20.**
11. **For both cylinder heads,** loosen camshaft sprocket bolt with tool No. 303–575, or equivalent.
12. Remove bolt and position camshaft sprocket aside.
13. Mark position of camshaft bearing

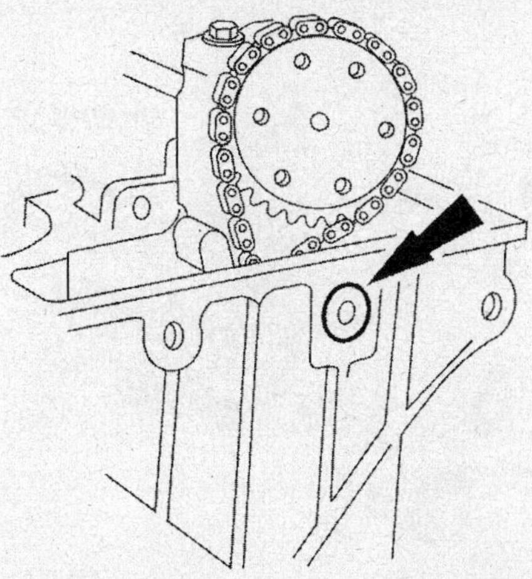

Fig. 7 Timing chain guide bolt

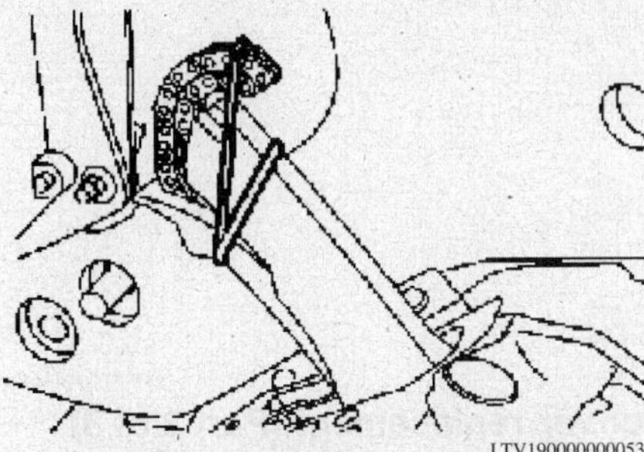

Fig. 10 Timing chain and cassette held with rubber band

caps for installation reference.

14. Remove camshaft bearing cap bolts in sequence, **Fig. 21.**
15. Reverse procedure to install, noting the following:
    a. Camshaft bearing caps must be installed in original locations.
    b. After installing bolts, inspect camshaft for free rotation.
    c. **Torque** all bolts in sequence, **Fig. 22,** in two stages.
    d. Stage 1: **Torque** bolts to 53 inch lbs.
    e. Stage 2: **Torque** bolts to 12 ft. lbs.

PISTON & ROD ASSEMBLY

Ensure arrow on piston dome faces front of engine.

PISTONS, PINS & RINGS

Pistons are available in standard sizes and oversizes.

CRANKSHAFT REAR OIL SEAL

REPLACE

1. Remove transmission assembly as outlined in **MOTOR's "Domestic Transmission, In-Vehicle Service" or "Transmission Service DVD."**

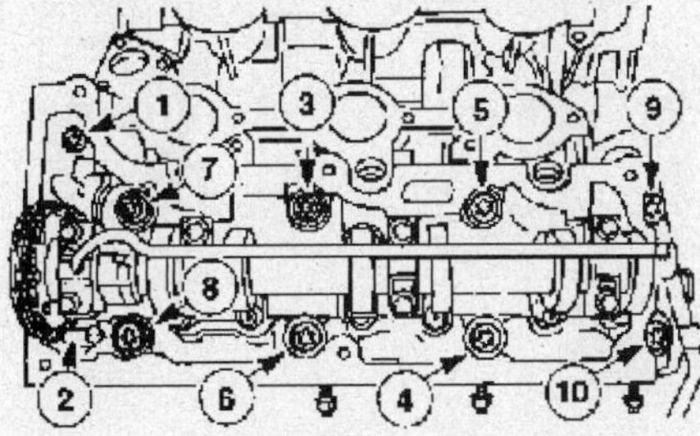

Fig. 8 Lefthand cylinder head bolt removal sequence

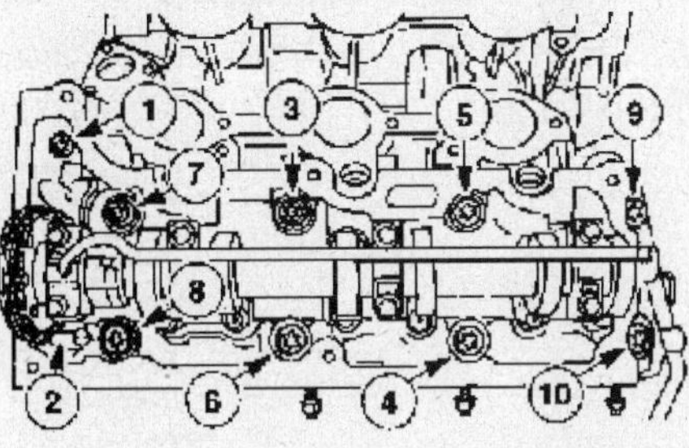

Fig. 11 Cylinder head bolt removal sequence

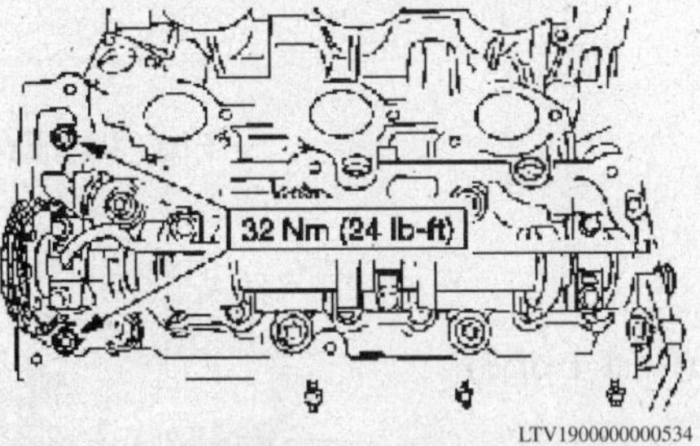

Fig. 13 8 mm cylinder head bolt installation

2. Remove flywheel or flexplate, housing and rear plate.
3. Remove rear crankshaft seal using rear crankshaft oil seal remover tool No. T92C-6700-CH, or equivalent. **Ensure oil seal surfaces are not damaged when removing seal.**
4. Reverse procedure to install, tighten all nuts and bolts to specifications.
    a. Tighten flywheel to specifications using sequence outlined in **Fig. 23.**
    b. Clean oil seal area before installing new seal.
    c. Apply suitable lubricant to new seal and install using rear oil seal replacer tool No. T95T-6701-A, or equivalent.

OIL PAN

REPLACE

1. Raise and support vehicle.
2. Remove upper air deflector.
3. Remove weatherstrip from upper core support.
4. Remove and discard screws from fan shroud.
5. Remove fan shroud and air cleaner outlet tube.
6. Install righthand lifting eye on engine.

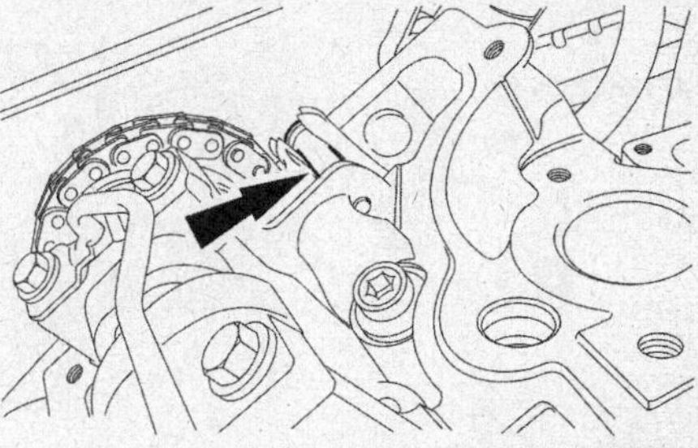

Fig. 9 Righthand camshaft guide bolt

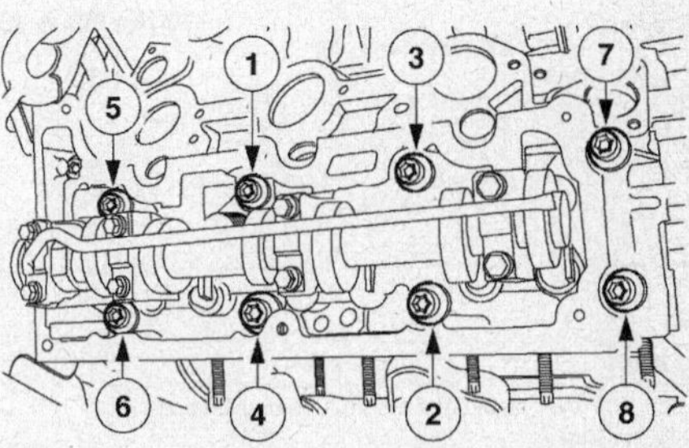

Fig. 12 12 mm cylinder head bolt tightening sequence

7. Install suitable three bar engine support tool.
8. Drain engine oil into suitable container.
9. **On models equipped with 2WD,** remove motor mount nuts.
10. **On models equipped with 4WD,** remove crossmember bolts, righthand motor mount nut and lefthand side through bolt and nut.
11. **On all models,** raise engine.
12. Remove components in sequence, **Fig. 24.**
13. Reverse procedure to install.

OIL PUMP

REPLACE

Refer to "Oil Pan, Replace" for oil pump replacement procedure.

BELT TENSION DATA

No adjustments required; automatic tensioner gauges when belt should be replaced.

SERPENTINE DRIVE BELT

Belt Routing

Refer to **Fig. 25** for serpentine drive belt routing.

Belt Replacement

1. Remove air cleaner outlet tube.
2. Rotate tensioner by turning counterclockwise, then remove belt.
3. Install new belt **Fig. 25,** then rotate tensioner and slide belt underneath, Release tensioner.

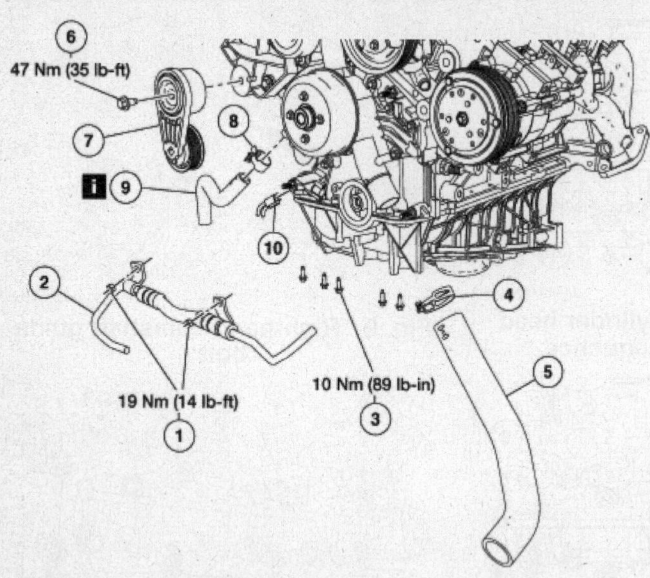

Item	Description
1	Power steering pressure tube bracket bolts (2 req'd)
2	Power steering pressure tube (position aside)
3	Oil pan-to-front cover bolts (5 req'd)
4	Lower radiator hose clamp
5	Lower radiator hose
6	Accessory drive belt tensioner bolt
7	Accessory drive belt tensioner
8	Clamp
9	Heater hose
10	Crankshaft position sensor electrical connector

LTV1900000000535

Fig. 14 Front cover replacement (Part 1 of 3)

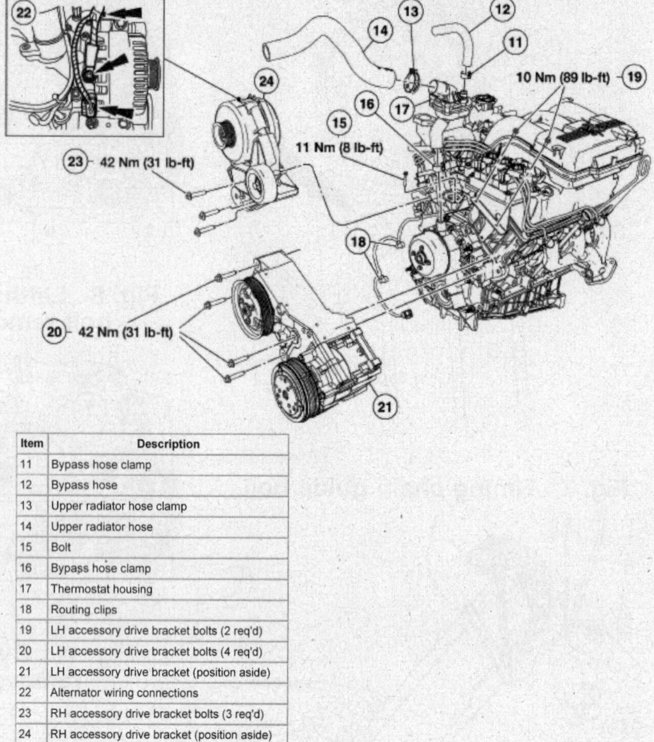

Item	Description
11	Bypass hose clamp
12	Bypass hose
13	Upper radiator hose clamp
14	Upper radiator hose
15	Bolt
16	Bypass hose clamp
17	Thermostat housing
18	Routing clips
19	LH accessory drive bracket bolts (2 req'd)
20	LH accessory drive bracket bolts (4 req'd)
21	LH accessory drive bracket (position aside)
22	Alternator wiring connections
23	RH accessory drive bracket bolts (3 req'd)
24	RH accessory drive bracket (position aside)

LTV1900000000536

Fig. 14 Front cover replacement (Part 2 of 3)

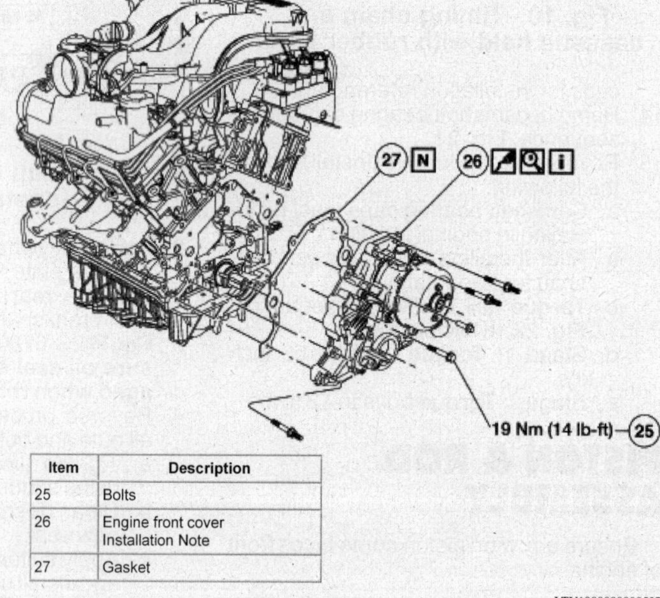

Item	Description
25	Bolts
26	Engine front cover Installation Note
27	Gasket

LTV1900000000537

Fig. 14 Front cover replacement (Part 3 of 3)

COOLING SYSTEM BLEED

1. Fill radiator through degas bottle until coolant level is at "Cold Fill" range mark.
2. Install pressure relief cap.
3. Set maximum heater temperature and blower motor speed settings. Position control to discharge air from A/C vents to instrument panel.
4. If air discharge remains cool and engine coolant temperature gauge does not move, engine coolant level is low and engine must be filled. Stop engine, allow to cool and fill cooling system.
5. Run engine until it reaches normal operating temperature.
6. Turn engine off and allow to cool.
7. Add more coolant to degas bottle until coolant level is at "Cold Fill" range mark.
8. Install pressure relief cap.
9. Start engine and allow to idle. While engine is idling, feel for hot air from A/C vents. Hot air should discharge from vents, engine temperature gauge should maintain a stabilized setting in the middle of the "Normal" range and upper radiator hose should be hot to touch.
10. Inspect coolant level in degas bottle and refill as required.
11. Repeat procedures as required.

THERMOSTAT

REPLACE

1. Drain cooling system into suitable container.
2. Remove components in sequence, **Fig. 26.**
3. Inspect thermostat housing gasket and thermostat housing cover gasket for damage. Replace as required.
4. Reverse procedure to install. Bleed cooling system.

WATER PUMP

REPLACE

1. Drain cooling system into suitable container.
2. Remove cooling fan.

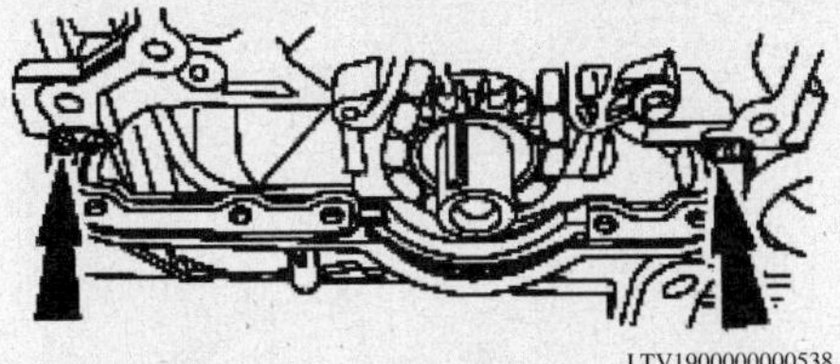

Fig. 15 Front cover silicone sealant application (Part 1 of 2)

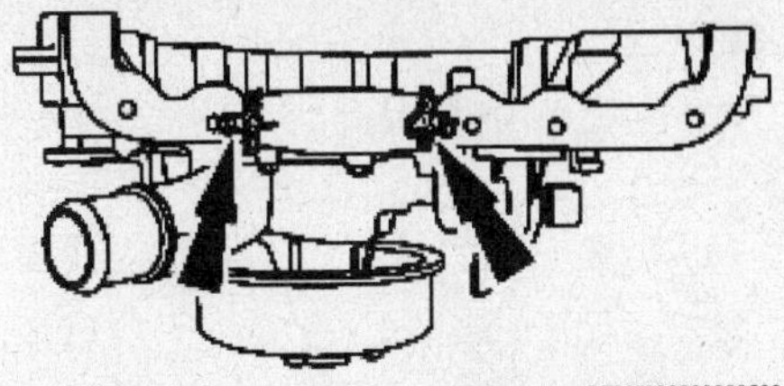

Fig. 15 Front cover silicone sealant application (Part 2 of 2)

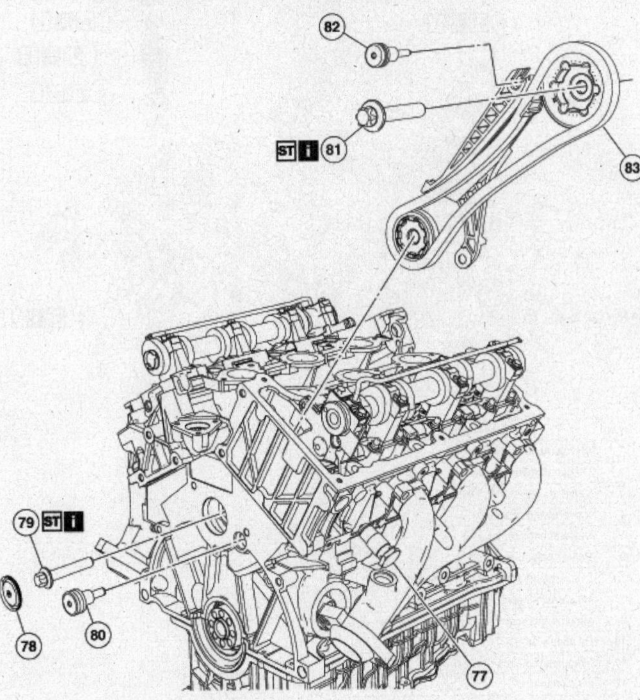

Item	Description
77	RH hydraulic timing chain tensioner
78	Jackshaft plug
79	Jackshaft sprocket bolt Disassembly Note
80	RH camshaft guide bolt
81	RH camshaft sprocket bolt Disassembly Note
82	RH camshaft guide bolt
83	RH camshaft drive cassette assembly

LTV1900000000540

Fig. 16 Timing chain replacement (Part 1 of 2)

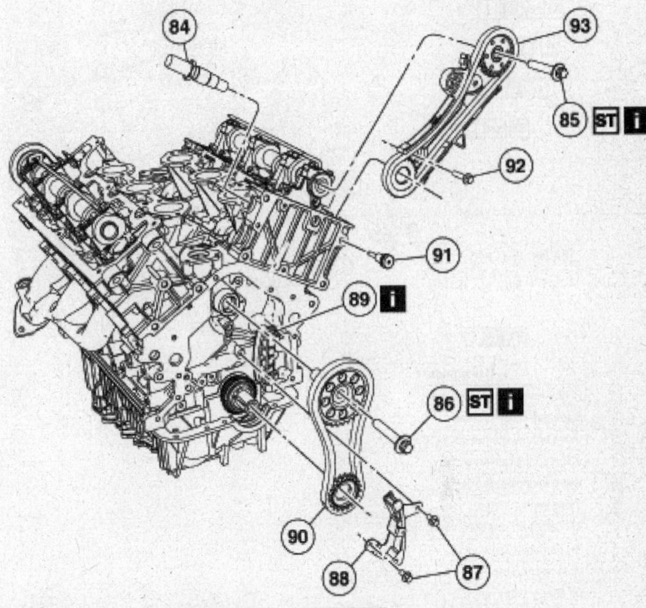

Item	Description
84	LH hydraulic timing chain tensioner
85	LH camshaft sprocket bolt
86	Jackshaft sprocket bolt
87	Primary tensioner bolts (2 req'd)
88	Primary chain tensioner
89	Primary chain guide Disassembly Note
90	Primary chain and sprocket assembly
91	Guide bolt
92	Guide bolt
93	LH camshaft drive cassette

LTV1900000000541

Fig. 16 Timing chain replacement (Part 2 of 2)

3. Remove accessory drive belt.
4. Remove components in sequence, **Fig. 27.**
5. Reverse procedure to install.

RADIATOR

REPLACE

1. Raise and support vehicle.
2. Drain cooling system into suitable container.
3. Remove components in sequence, **Fig. 28.**
4. Reverse procedure to install.

FUEL PUMP

REPLACE

To disconnect certain fuel lines, it may be required to use fuel line disconnect set No. T90T-9550-S, or equivalent.

1. Relieve fuel system pressure as outlined in "Precautions" then remove fuel tank as follows:
2. Drain fuel tank into suitable container, then loosen fill pipe clamp.
3. Remove shield and bracket assembly.
4. Remove fuel tank filler pipe, then suitably support fuel tank.
5. Remove front and rear fuel tank support straps.
6. Partially lower fuel tank, then remove fuel feed hose and sender push connector.
7. Remove fuel return hose at sender, then disconnect fuel pump electrical connector.
8. Remove fuel vapor hose from fuel vapor valve, then lower fuel tank from vehicle.
9. Remove any dirt that has accumulated around pump attaching flange.
10. **On models equipped with fuel pump lock ring,** turn fuel tank sending unit lock retainer ring counterclockwise with Fuel Tank Lock Ring Wrench tool No. T90T-9275-A or T86T-9275-A, or equivalent, and remove fuel tank sending unit locking retainer ring.
11. **On models less fuel pump lock ring,** remove fuel pump attaching bolts, then the fuel pump.
12. **On all models,** remove fuel pump, sender assembly and mounting gasket. Discard old gasket.

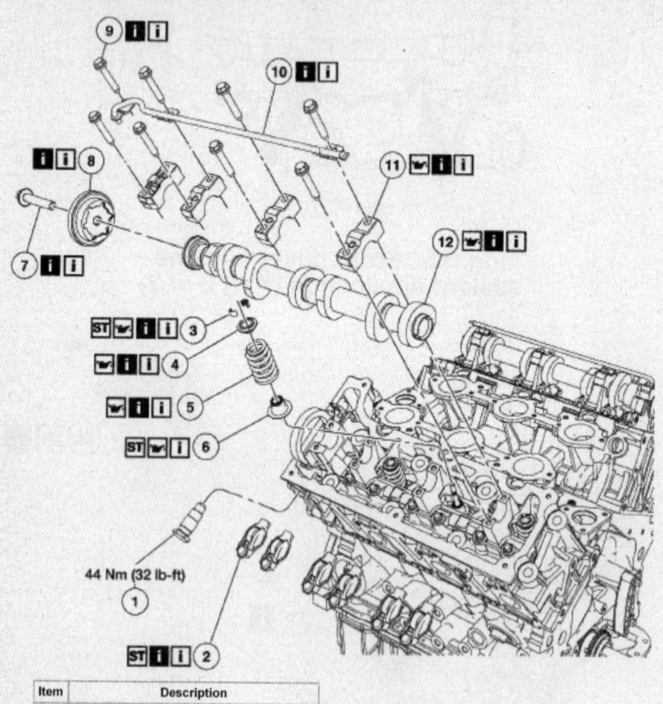

Item	Description
1	RH hydraulic chain tensioner
2	Camshaft roller follower
3	Valve spring retainer keys (12 req'd)
4	Valve spring retainers
5	Valve springs (6 req'd)
6	Valve seals (6 req'd)
7	RH camshaft sprocket mounting bolt
8	RH camshaft sprocket
9	Main bearing cap mounting bolts (8 req'd)
10	Oil supply tube
11	Main bearing caps (4 req'd)
12	RH camshaft

LTV1900000000542

Fig. 17 Righthand camshaft replacement

44 Nm (32 lb-ft)

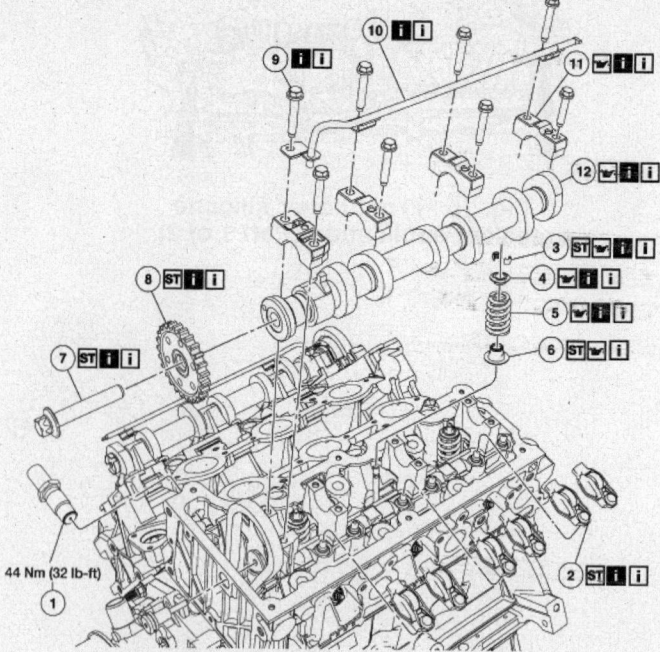

Item	Description
1	LH hydraulic chain tensioner
2	Camshaft roller follower
3	Valve spring retainer keys (12 req'd)
4	Valve spring retainers
5	Valve springs (6 req'd)
6	Valve seals (6 req'd)
7	LH camshaft sprocket mounting bolt
8	LH camshaft sprocket
9	Main bearing cap mounting bolts (8 req'd)
10	Oil supply tube
11	Main bearing caps (4 req'd)
12	LH camshaft

LTV1900000000546

Fig. 18 Lefthand camshaft replacement

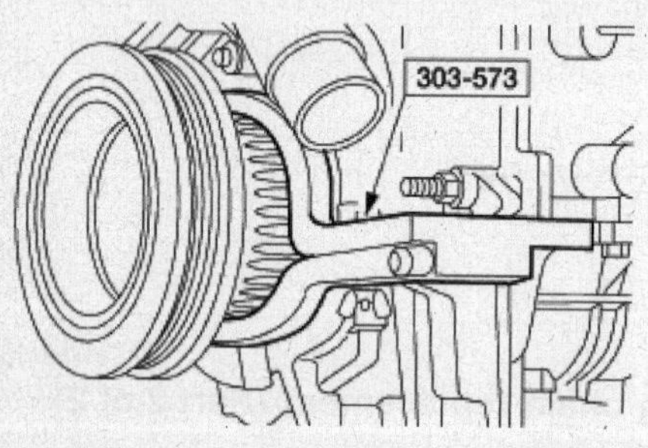

LTV1900000000543

Fig. 19 Crankshaft TDC timing tool installation

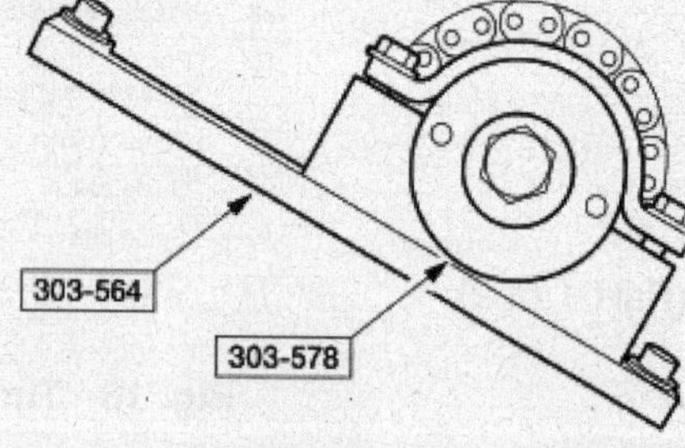

LTV1900000000547

Fig. 20 Lefthand camshaft holding tool installation

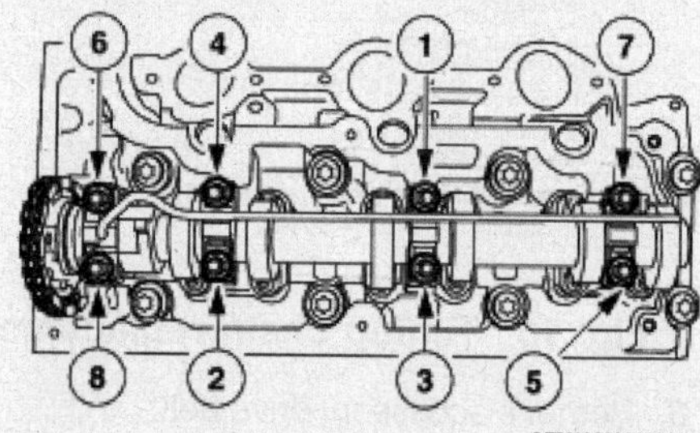

LTV1900000000544

Fig. 21 Camshaft bearing cap bolt removal sequence

FUEL FILTER

REPLACE

1. Relieve fuel system pressure as outlined in "Precautions."
2. Remove fuel line retainer clips.
3. Disconnect fuel lines from fuel filter using fuel line disconnect tool No. T90T-9550-S, or equivalent.
4. Remove fuel filter from support.
5. Install filter in bracket.
6. Install lines to fuel filter. Push until a click is heard indicating line is properly engaged.

INERTIA SWITCH

The inertia switch is located on the toeboard to the righthand of transmission tunnel. Its purpose is to shut off fuel to the engine in the event of a vehicle collision. To reset switch, proceed as follows:

1. Turn ignition switch to Off position.
2. Inspect for leaking fuel in engine compartment, fuel lines and tank(s) and correct as required.
3. Push reset button on top of switch, then turn ignition switch On and inspect for leaks.

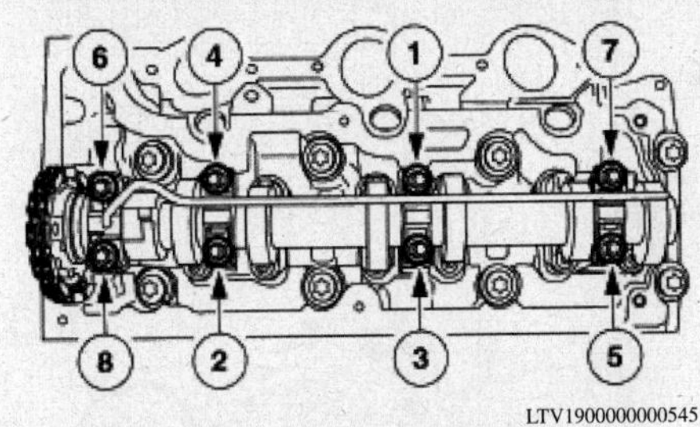

Fig. 22 Camshaft bearing cap bolt tightening sequence

Fig. 23 Flywheel tightening sequence

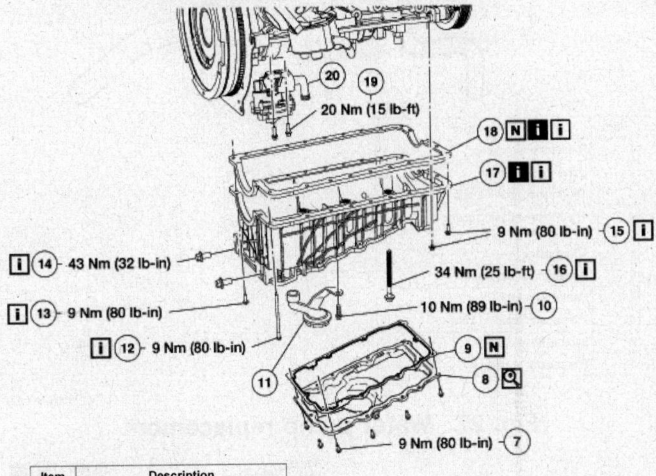

Item	Description
7	Oil pan bolt (12 required)
8	Oil pan
9	Oil pan gasket
10	Pickup tube bolt
11	Oil pump pickup tube
12	Lower block cradle bolt
13	Lower block cradle bolt
14	Lower block cradle bolt
15	Lower block cradle bolt
16	Lower block cradle bolt
17	Lower block cradle
18	Lower block cradle gasket
19	Oil pump bolt
20	Oil pump

LTV1900000000549

Fig. 24 Oil pan replacement (Part 2 of 2)

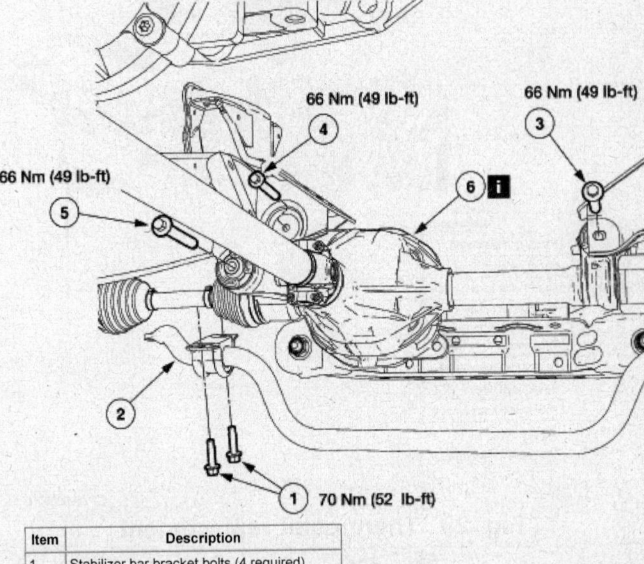

Item	Description
1	Stabilizer bar bracket bolts (4 required)
2	Stabilizer bar (position aside)
3	Axle housing bolt
4	Axle housing bolt
5	Axle housing bolt
6	Axle housing

LTV1900000000548

Fig. 24 Oil pan replacement (Part 1 of 2)

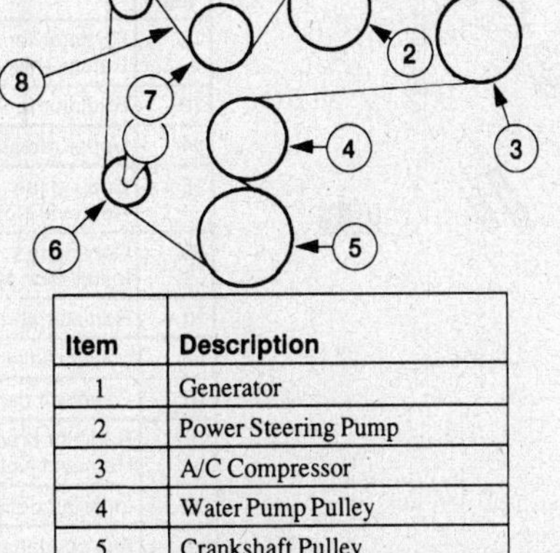

Item	Description
1	Generator
2	Power Steering Pump
3	A/C Compressor
4	Water Pump Pulley
5	Crankshaft Pulley
6	Drive Belt Tensioner
7	Belt Idler Pulley
8	Drive Belt

FM1069700646000X

Fig. 25 Serpentine drive belt routing

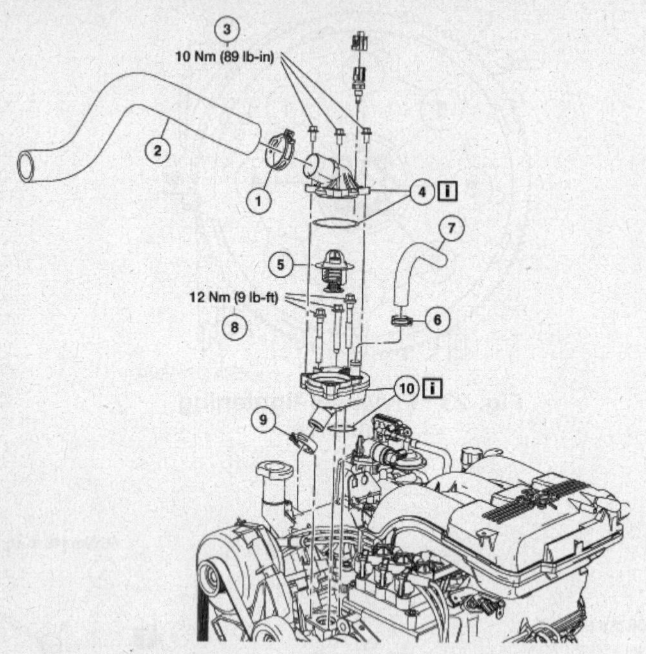

Item	Description
1	Radiator hose clamp
2	Upper radiator hose
3	Thermostat housing bolt
4	Thermostat housing cover Installation Note
5	Thermostat
6	Heater inlet tube clamp
7	Heater inlet tube
8	Thermostat housing bolt
9	Bypass hose clamp
10	Thermostat housing

LTV1900000000550

Fig. 26 Thermostat replacement

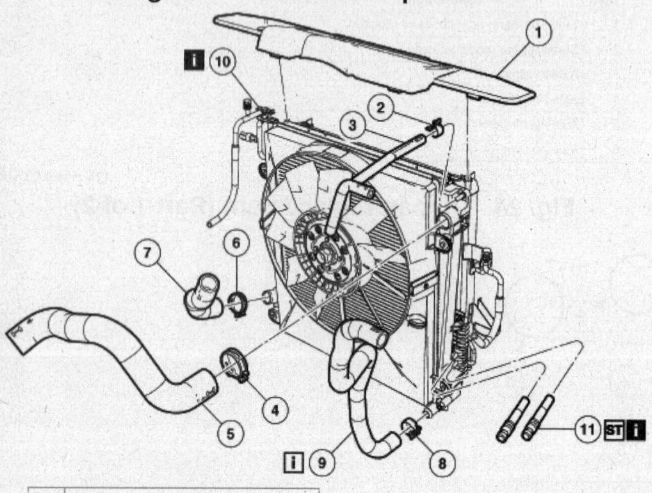

Item	Description
1	Coolant pump pulley bolts
2	Coolant pump pulley
3	Upper coolant pump bypass hose clamp
4	Coolant pump bypass hose
5	Heater hose clamp
6	Heater hose
7	Lower radiator hose clamp
8	Lower radiator hose
9	Coolant pump bolt (12 required)
10	Coolant pump

LTV1900000000552

Fig. 28 Radiator replacement (Part 1 of 2)

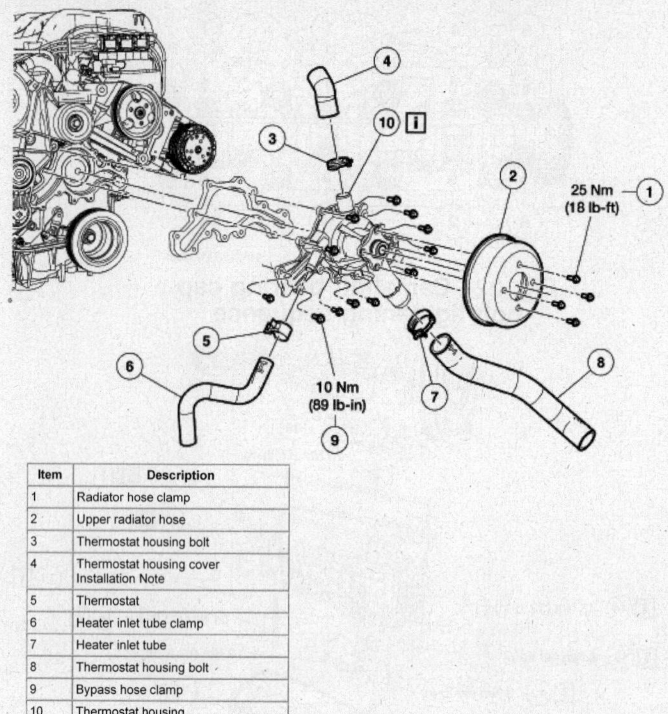

Item	Description
1	Radiator hose clamp
2	Upper radiator hose
3	Thermostat housing bolt
4	Thermostat housing cover Installation Note
5	Thermostat
6	Heater inlet tube clamp
7	Heater inlet tube
8	Thermostat housing bolt
9	Bypass hose clamp
10	Thermostat housing

LTV1900000000551

Fig. 27 Water pump replacement

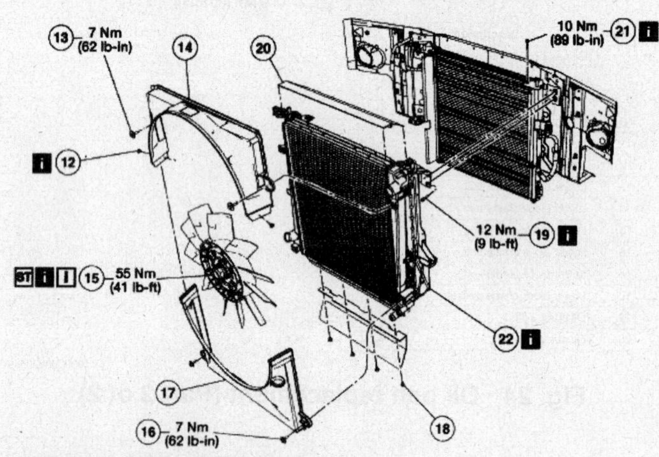

Item	Description
12	Radiator fan shroud screws (2 req'd) Removal Note
13	Radiator fan shroud bolt (2 req'd)
14	Upper radiator fan shroud
15	Cooling fan Removal Note
15	Cooling fan Installation Note
16	Radiator shroud bolt (2 req'd)
17	Lower radiator fan shroud
18	Lower air dam push pin (4 req'd)
19	Radiator bracket bolt (4 req'd) Removal Note
20	Inner air deflector
21	A/C condenser support bracket bolt Removal Note
22	Radiator Removal Note

LTV1900000000553

Fig. 28 Radiator replacement (Part 2 of 2)

TIGHTENING SPECIFICATIONS

Year	Component	Torque Ft. Lbs.
2002–06	A/C Compressor Manifold Bolt	15
	Accessory Drive Belt Tensioner	18
	Accessory Drive Belt Idler Pulley	35
	Alternator Bracket	31
	Balance Shaft Bolts	20
	Balance Shaft Guide Chain	89①
	Balance Shaft Tensioner	21
	Camshaft Bearing Cap	②
	Camshaft Sprocket Bolt	63
	Cassette Bolt, RH	9
	Cassette Bolt, LH	14
	Cylinder Head	③
	EGR Valve Bolts	15
	EGR Valve Tube	30
	EGR Vacuum Regulator Solenoid	89①
	Engine Front Cover	14
	Exhaust Manifold Nuts	16
	Exhaust Manifold To Exhaust Pipe	30
	Intake Manifold	89①
	Jackshaft Chain Guide	14
	Jackshaft Chain Tensioner	89①
	Jackshaft Thrust Plate	96①
	Knock Sensor	15
	Lower Engine Mount Bracket Bolts	59
	Lower Engine Mount Bracket Nuts	66
	Main Bearing Cap	72
	Motor Mount Through Bolt	76
	Oil Bypass Filter	10
	Oil Filter Adapter	42
	Oil Pan	80①
	Oil Pan Drain Plug	19
	Oil Pressure Sensor	10
	Oil Pump Bolts	14
	Oil Pump Drive Assembly	14
	Power Steering Pressure Line Nut	13
	Radiator Fan Shroud, Upper	62①
	Spark Plug	15
	Thermostat Housing	96①
	Torque Converter To Flywheel Nuts	35
	Transmission To Engine	35
	Upper Engine Mount Bracket Nuts	81
	Valve Cover	89①
	Water Pump	89①

① — Inch lbs.
② — Refer to "Camshaft, Replace" for tightening procedure.
③ — Refer to"Cylinder Head, Replace" for tightening procedure.

4.6L SOHC (Vin W) Engine

NOTE: On Air Bag Equipped Models, Refer To "Air Bag System Precautions" Located In The Front Of This Manual For System Disarming & Arming Procedures.

NOTE: Refer To "Computer Relearn Procedures" Located In The Front Of This Manual When Battery Power To The Computer Has Been Interrupted.

INDEX

PRECAUTIONS

Air Bag Systems

Refer to "Air Bag System Precautions" in the front of this manual for system disarming and arming procedures.

Battery Ground Cable

Prior to service, disconnect battery ground cable and isolate as required.

Fuel System Pressure Relief Procedure

Fuel in fuel system remains under high pressure even when engine is not running. Before servicing or disconnecting any of the fuel lines or fuel system components, the fuel system pressure must be relieved to prevent accidental spraying of fuel.

1. Remove schraeder valve cap, **Fig. 1**, from fuel rail.
2. Attach fuel system pressure gauge No. 310–012, or equivalent, to schraeder valve.
3. Open tool valve slowly and release fuel system pressure into suitable container.

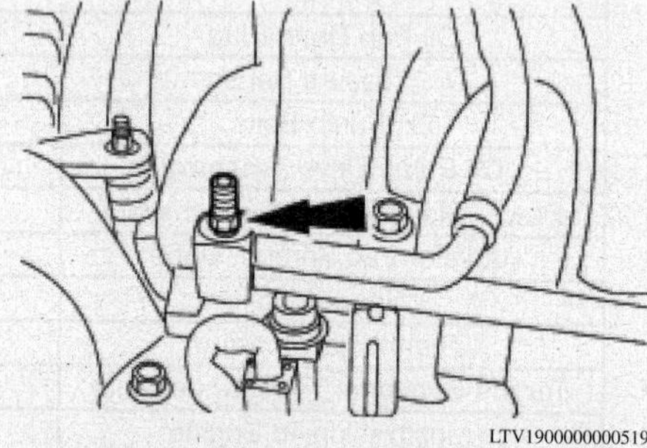

Fig. 1 Fuel system pressure release valve

COMPRESSION PRESSURE

1. Ensure oil in crankcase is of correct viscosity and at correct level and that battery is fully charged.
2. Set throttle plates wide open.
3. Install compression gauge in No. 1 cylinder.
4. Install auxiliary starter switch in starter circuit.
5. With ignition in Off position, crank engine a minimum of five compression strokes and record highest reading.
6. Note number of strokes required to obtain highest reading.
7. Repeat test on each cylinder, cranking engine approximately same number of compression strokes.
8. Compression pressures are considered within specification if lowest reading is at least 75% of highest reading.

ENGINE MOUNT

REPLACE

1. Raise and support vehicle.
2. Remove fan shroud.
3. Remove alternator.
4. Remove wiper cowling.
5. Remove exhaust gas recirculation system module and tube assembly.
6. Remove remaining components in order listed, **Fig. 2.**
7. Reverse procedure to install.

ENGINE

REPLACE

1. Remove vehicle hood.
2. Recover A/C refrigerant as outlined in "Air Conditioning" chapter.
3. Remove air cleaner assembly.
4. Remove evaporative emissions canister purge valve.
5. Remove cooling fan and shroud.
6. Relieve fuel system pressure as outlined in "Precautions."
7. Disconnect fuel hose spring coupling.
8. Remove starter motor.
9. Drain engine oil into suitable container.
10. Remove remaining components in order illustrated, **Fig. 3.**

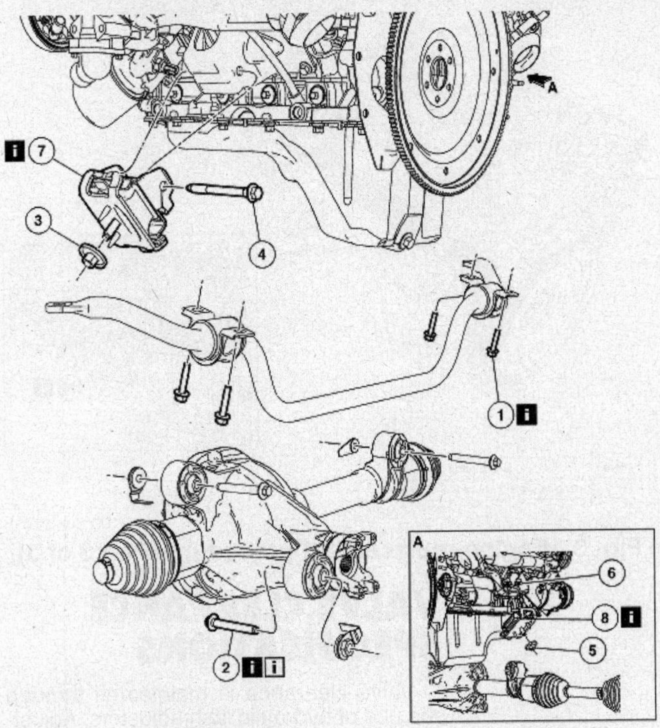

Item	Description
1	Stabilizer bar bracket bolts (4 req'd)
2	Front axle bolts (3 req'd) (if equipped)
3	LH engine support insulator nut
4	LH engine support insulator through-bolt
5	RH engine support insulator nut
6	RH engine support insulator nuts (2 req'd)
7	LH engine support insulator
8	RH engine support insulator

LTV1900000000301

Fig. 2 Engine mount replacement

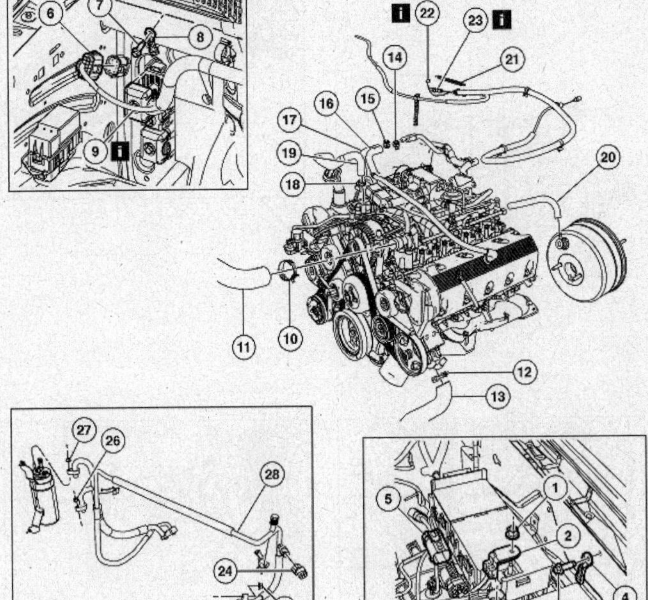

Item	Description
1	Terminal eyelet nut
2	Terminal eyelet
3	Ground strap bolt
4	Ground strap
5	Electrical connector
6	Electrical connector
7	Ground strap bolt
8	Ground strap
9	Engine electrical harness connector
10	Upper radiator hose clamp
11	Upper radiator hose
12	Lower radiator hose clamp
13	Lower radiator hose
14	Heater hose clamp
15	Heater hose clamp
16	Heater hose
17	Heater hose
18	Heater hose clamp
19	Heater hose
20	Brake booster vacuum hose
21	Throttle cable spring
22	Throttle cable assembly
23	Speed control cable
24	A/C electrical connector
25	A/C refrigerant tube nut
26	A/C refrigerant tube nut
27	A/C refrigerant tube nut
28	A/C refrigerant tube assembly

LTV1900000000302

Fig. 3 Engine replacement procedure (Part 1 of 3)

11. Install suitable three bar engine support tool and engine lifting bracket set No. 303–D074, or equivalent.
12. Remove transmission.
13. Disconnect lefthand HO2S harness from retainer.
14. Disconnect ATF cooler tubes from cooler and drain fluid into suitable container.
15. Remove ATF cooler tubes from vehicle.
16. Remove three bar engine support tool.
17. Attach spreader bar No. 303–D089, or equivalent to engine lifting brackets.
18. Lift engine from vehicle with suitable lifting device.
19. Reverse procedure to install.

INTAKE MANIFOLD

REPLACE

1. Drain cooling system into suitable container.
2. Release fuel system pressure as outlined in "Precautions."
3. Disconnect fuel line from fuel pressure manifold.
4. Remove components in order listed, **Fig. 4.**
5. Reverse procedure to install, noting the following:
   a. Clean and inspect all manifold mating surfaces.
   b. Install intake manifold mounting bolts and tighten in sequence, **Fig. 5,** to 18 ft. lbs.

EXHAUST MANIFOLD

REPLACE

Lefthand

1. Raise and support vehicle.
2. Remove lefthand inner fender well.
3. Remove components in order listed, **Fig. 6.**
4. When disconnecting steering gear from intermediate shaft, do not allow intermediate shaft to rotate or damage to clockspring can occur.
5. Reverse procedure to install, **torque** manifold nuts in sequence, **Fig. 7,** to 15 ft. lbs.

Righthand

1. Raise and support vehicle.
2. Remove righthand inner fender well.
3. Remove components in order listed, **Fig. 8.**
4. Reverse procedure to install, **torque** exhaust manifold nuts in sequence, **Fig. 9,** to 15 ft. lbs.

CYLINDER HEAD

REPLACE

1. Remove intake manifold as outlined in "Intake Manifold, Replace."

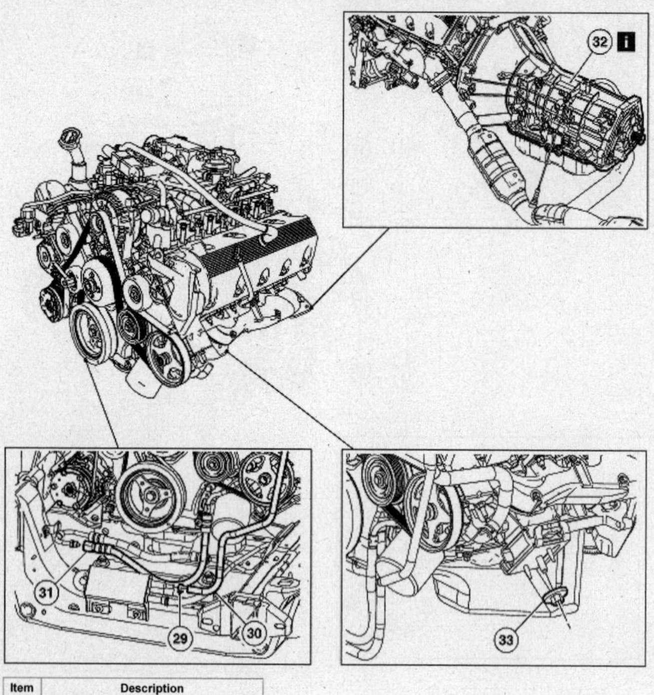

Item	Description
29	Power steering return hose clamp
30	Power steering return hose
31	Power steering pressure hose
32	Automatic transmission assembly
33	LH engine support insulator nut

LTV1900000000303

Fig. 3 Engine replacement procedure (Part 2 of 3)

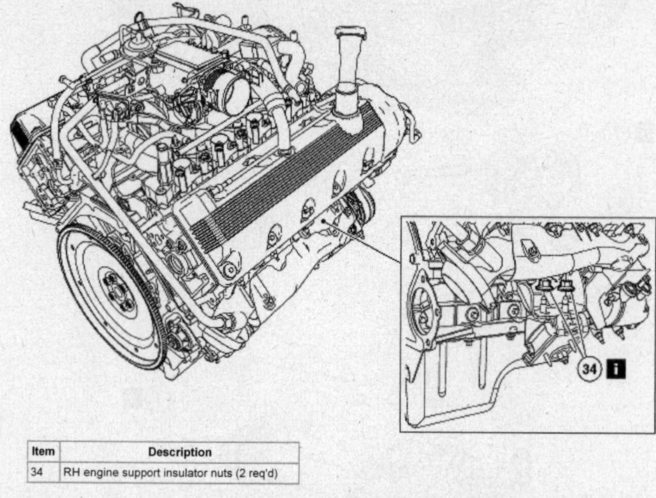

Item	Description
34	RH engine support insulator nuts (2 req'd)

LTV1900000000304

Fig. 3 Engine replacement procedure (Part 3 of 3)

2. Slide water heater tube back and remove. Discard O-ring.
3. Remove timing chains as outlined in "Timing Chains, Replace."
4. Remove exhaust manifolds as outlined in "Exhaust Manifold, Replace."
5. Remove cylinder head components in order listed, **Fig. 10.**
6. Cylinder head bolts must be discarded. Bolts are torque to yield design and cannot be reused.
7. Discard head gaskets and clean engine block surface with plastic scraper and metal surface cleaner.
8. Install new cylinder head gaskets on block dowel pins.
9. Install cylinder heads and loosely install cylinder head bolts.
10. Tighten all cylinder head bolts in sequence, **Figs. 11 and 12,** in six stages:
    a. **Torque** all bolts to 30 ft. lbs.
    b. Tighten an additional 90°.
    c. Back out all bolts one full turn (360°).
    d. **Torque** all bolts to 30 ft. lbs.
    e. Tighten 90°.
    f. Tighten an additional 90°.
11. Reverse procedure to install remaining components.

VALVE COVER

REPLACE

Righthand

1. Remove air cleaner outlet pipe.
2. Drain engine cooling system into suitable container.
3. Remove components in order, **Fig. 13.**
4. Reverse procedure to install, noting the following:
    a. If new gasket is being installed, apply instant adhesive completely around gasket groove in valve cover. Cover must be secured within four minutes of applying sealant.
    b. Apply silicone gasket sealant in two places where engine front cover meets cylinder head, **Fig. 14.**
    c. **Torque** valve cover bolts to 89 inch lbs., in sequence, **Fig. 15.**

Lefthand

1. Remove components in order, **Fig. 16.**
2. Reverse procedure to install, noting the following:
    a. If new gasket is being installed, apply instant adhesive completely around groove in valve cover.
    b. Valve cover must be installed within four minutes of applying sealant.
    c. Apply silicone gasket sealant in two places where engine front cover meets cylinder head, **Fig. 17.**
    d. **Torque** valve cover bolts to 89 inch lbs., in sequence, **Fig. 18.**

VALVE ARRANGEMENT

Front To Rear

Righthand Bank........................E-I-E-I-E-I
Lefthand Bank...........................I-E-I-E-I-E

VALVE CLEARANCE SPECIFICATIONS

Valve clearance is maintained through the use of hydraulic lash adjusters. Adjustment of valve lash is not possible.

VALVE GUIDES

If valve guides are not within the range specified, ream guides and fit with new valve with oversize stem or replace valve guide.

HYDRAULIC LIFTERS

REPLACE

1. Remove valve covers as outlined in "Valve Cover, Replace."
2. Remove cooling fan.
3. Remove any foreign material from spark plug wells with compressed air, then remove spark plugs.
4. Disconnect electrical connectors, bolts and ignition coils. Tilt coils away from fuel injection supply manifold to remove.
5. Rotate crankshaft until cam lobe is away from roller follower.
6. Install valve spring compressor spacer tool No. 303–382, or equivalent, between valve spring coils to prevent valve stem seal damage.
7. Mark position of followers and hydraulic lash adjusters for installation reference.
8. Compress valve springs with valve spring compressor tool No. 303–452, or equivalent.
9. Remove camshaft followers and hydraulic lifters.
10. Reverse procedure to install.

FRONT COVER

REPLACE

1. Drain cooling system into suitable container.
2. Remove crankshaft front seal.

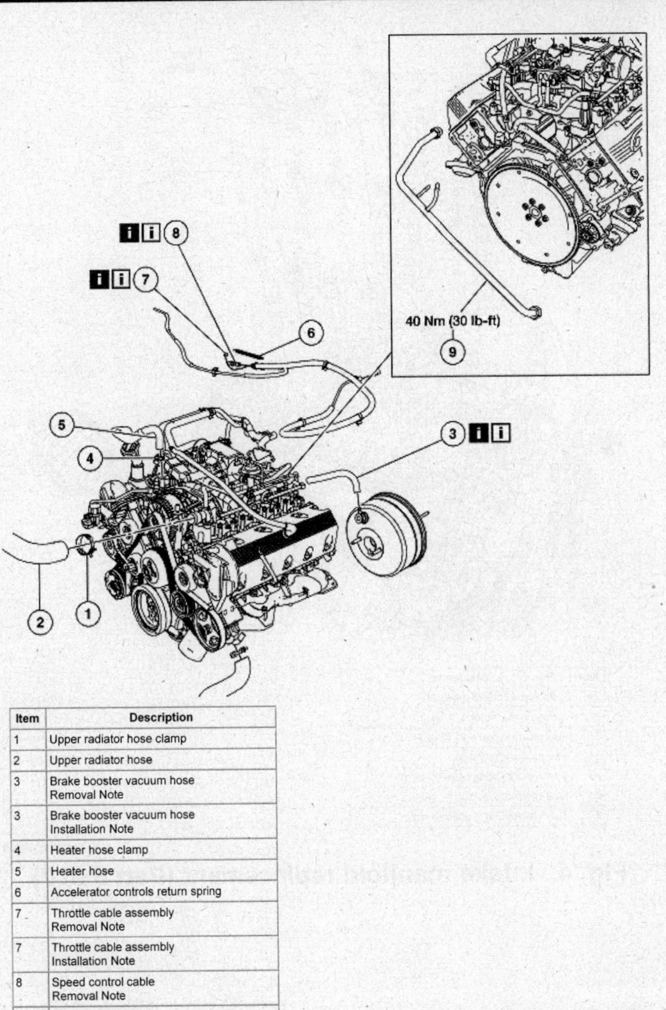

Item	Description
1	Upper radiator hose clamp
2	Upper radiator hose
3	Brake booster vacuum hose Removal Note
3	Brake booster vacuum hose Installation Note
4	Heater hose clamp
5	Heater hose
6	Accelerator controls return spring
7	Throttle cable assembly Removal Note
7	Throttle cable assembly Installation Note
8	Speed control cable Removal Note
8	Speed control cable Installation Note
9	Exhaust gas recirculation (EGR) tube

LTV1900000000305

Fig. 4 Intake manifold replacement (Part 1 of 7)

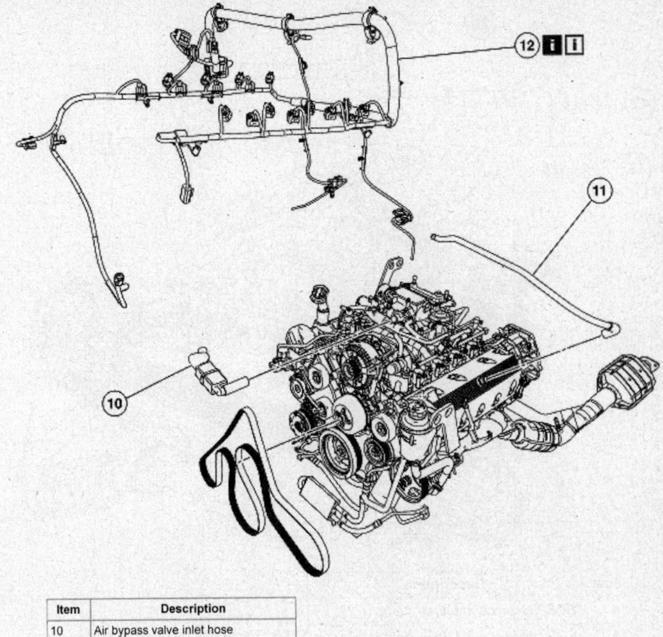

Item	Description
10	Air bypass valve inlet hose
11	Crankcase ventilation tube
12	Engine wiring harness
12	Engine wiring harness

LTV1900000000306

Fig. 4 Intake manifold replacement (Part 2 of 7)

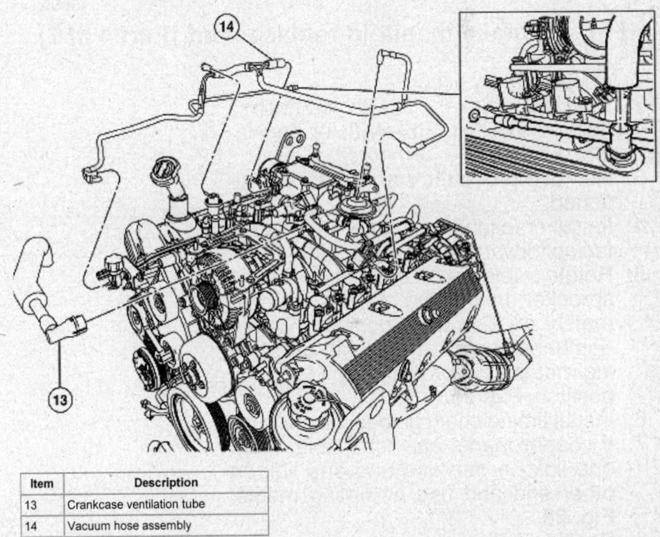

Item	Description
13	Crankcase ventilation tube
14	Vacuum hose assembly

LTV1900000000307

Fig. 4 Intake manifold replacement (Part 3 of 7)

3. Remove hydraulic roller followers as outlined in "Hydraulic Lifters, Replace."
4. Drain engine oil into suitable container.
5. Remove components in order listed, **Fig. 19.**
6. Remove front cover bolts in sequence, **Fig. 20.**
7. Reverse procedure to install, noting the following:
   a. Tighten four previously removed oil pan bolts in three stages, in sequence, **Fig. 21.**
   b. Stage 1: **Torque** bolts to 18 inch lbs.
   c. Stage 2: **Torque** bolts to 15 ft. lbs.
   d. Stage 3: Tighten all bolts an additional 60°.
   e. Apply silicone gasket sealant to front of engine, **Fig. 22.**
   f. If front cover is not secured to engine within four minutes of sealant application, sealant must be removed and sealing area cleaned with metal surface cleaner. Allow to dry, then reapply sealant.

TIMING CHAIN

REPLACE

Removal

1. Remove engine front cover as outlined in "Front Cover, Replace."
2. Remove timing chain and gears in sequence illustrated, **Fig. 23.**

Installation

Timing procedures must be followed exactly or piston and valve damage may occur to engine.

1. Rotate crankshaft counterclockwise only. Do not rotate past position outlined or severe damage to piston and/

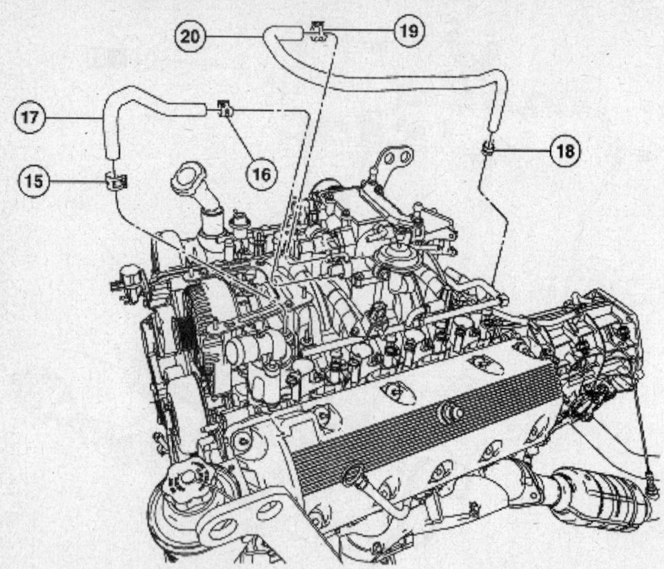

Item	Description
15	EGR valve coolant hose clamp
16	EGR valve coolant hose clamp
17	EGR valve coolant hose
18	EGR valve coolant hose clamp
19	EGR valve coolant hose clamp
20	EGR valve coolant hose

LTV1900000000308

Fig. 4 Intake manifold replacement (Part 4 of 7)

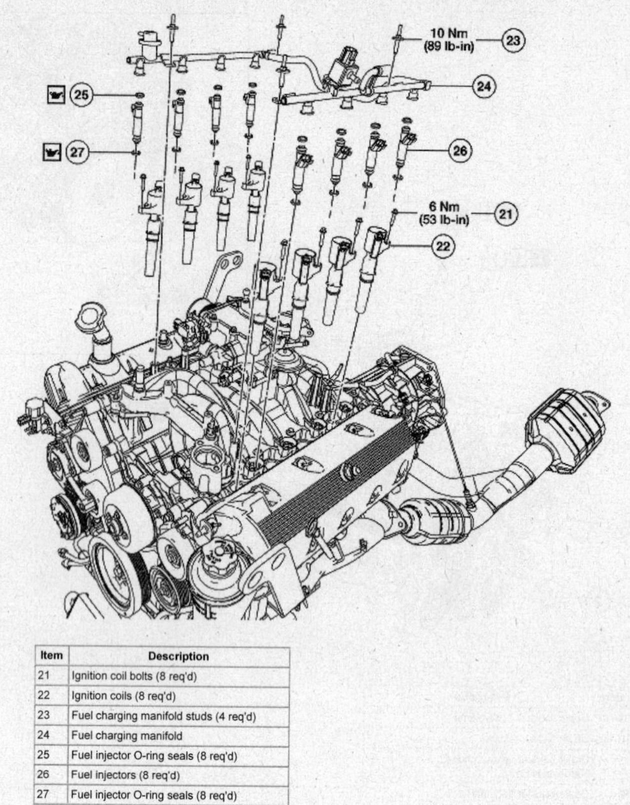

Item	Description
21	Ignition coil bolts (8 req'd)
22	Ignition coils (8 req'd)
23	Fuel charging manifold studs (4 req'd)
24	Fuel charging manifold
25	Fuel injector O-ring seals (8 req'd)
26	Fuel injectors (8 req'd)
27	Fuel injector O-ring seals (8 req'd)

LTV1900000000309

Fig. 4 Intake manifold replacement (Part 5 of 7)

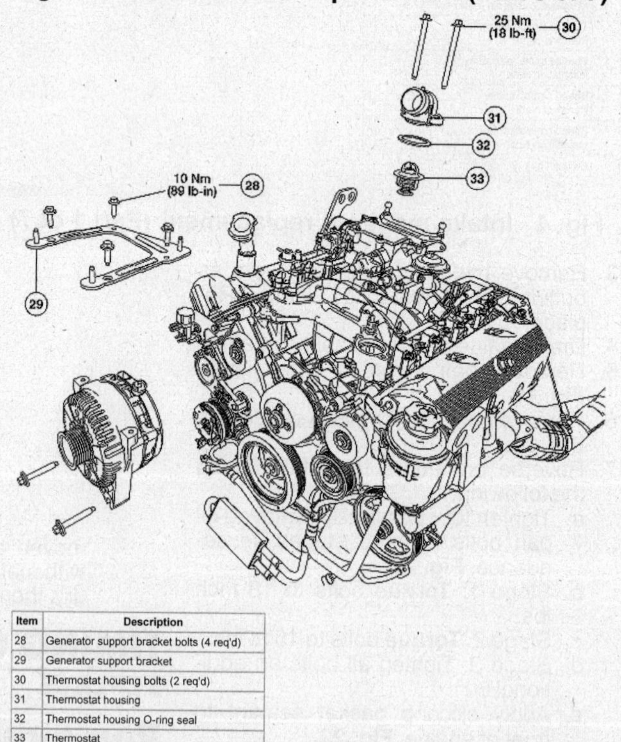

Item	Description
28	Generator support bracket bolts (4 req'd)
29	Generator support bracket
30	Thermostat housing bolts (2 req'd)
31	Thermostat housing
32	Thermostat housing O-ring seal
33	Thermostat

LTV1900000000310

Fig. 4 Intake manifold replacement (Part 6 of 7)

or valves may occur.

2. Position crankshaft with crankshaft holding tool No. 303–448, or equivalent, **Fig. 24.**
3. Remove tool after crankshaft is positioned.
4. Install crankshaft sprocket with flange facing forward, **Fig. 25.**
5. Rotate lefthand camshaft timing sprocket until timing mark is approximately at 12 o'clock position. Rotate righthand camshaft sprocket until timing mar is at approximately 11 o'clock position, **Fig. 26.**
6. Install timing chain guides, **Fig. 27.**
7. If copper marks are not visible, mark one link on one end and one link on other end and use as timing marks, **Fig. 28.**
8. Position lefthand (inner) timing chain on crankshaft sprocket, aligning copper link (marked) with timing mark on sprocket, **Fig. 29.** If required, adjust camshaft sprocket slightly to obtain timing mark alignment.
9. Position lefthand timing chain on camshaft sprocket. Ensure copper colored link (marked) aligns with camshaft sprocket timing mark, **Fig. 30.**
10. Compress lefthand timing chain tensioner with a suitable vise.
11. Install retaining clip on tensioner plunger, **Fig. 31.**
12. The lefthand timing chain tensioner has a bump near the dowel hole for identification.
13. Position lefthand timing chain tensioner arm on dowel pin and install lefthand tensioner, **Fig. 32.**
14. Remove retaining clip from lefthand tensioner.
15. Position righthand (outer) timing chain on crankshaft sprocket, aligning copper (marked) link with timing mark on sprocket, **Fig. 33.** If required, adjust camshaft sprocket slightly to obtain timing mark.

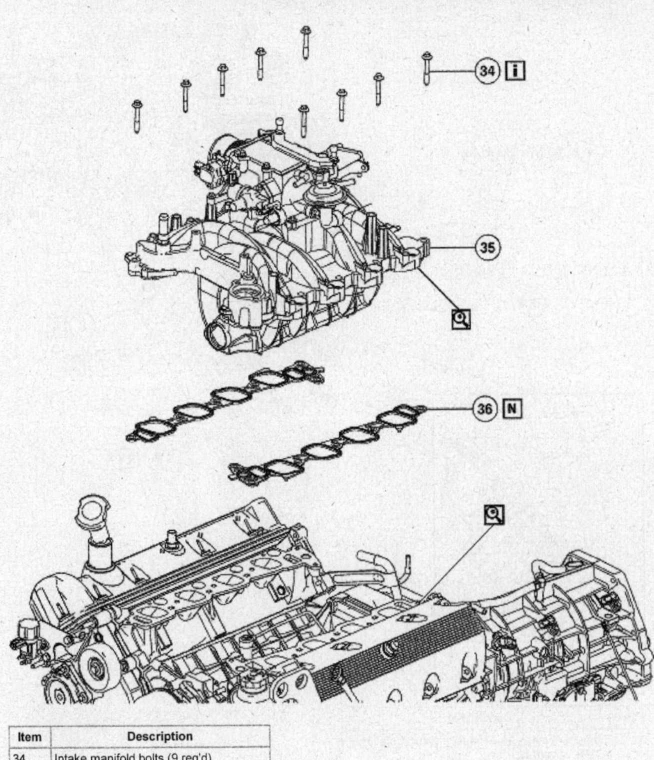

Item	Description
34	Intake manifold bolts (9 req'd)
35	Intake manifold
36	Intake manifold gasket

LTV1900000000311

Fig. 4 Intake manifold replacement (Part 7 of 7)

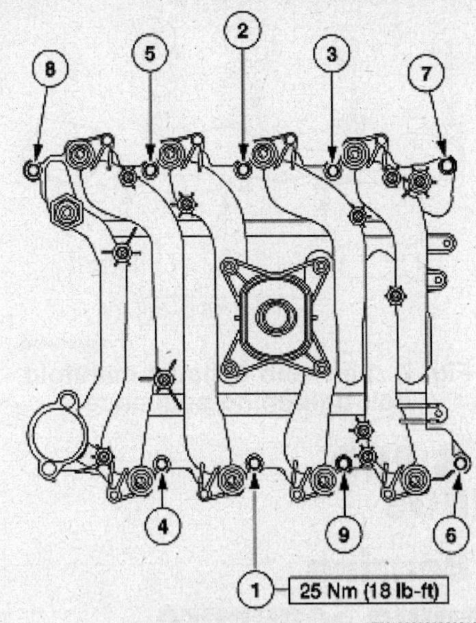

LTV1900000000312

Fig. 5 Intake manifold bolt tightening sequence

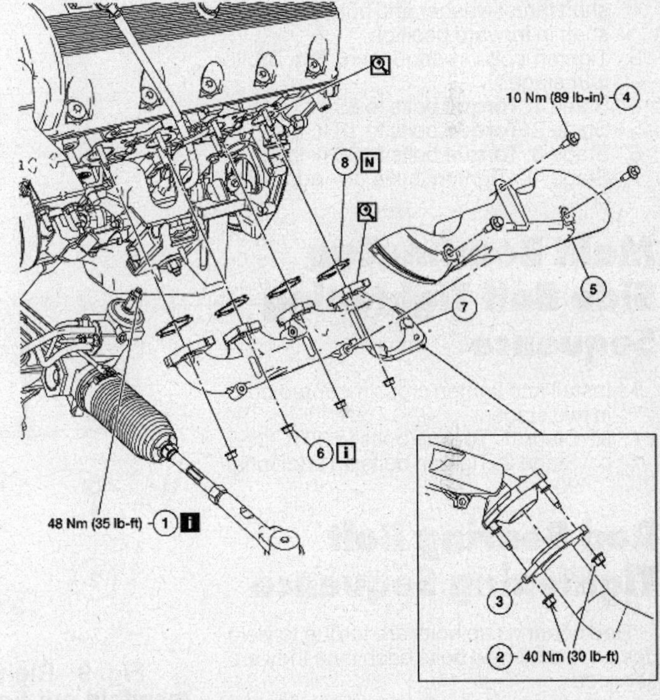

Item	Description
1	Steering gear shaft
2	Exhaust Y-pipe flange nuts (2 req'd)
3	Exhaust Y-pipe
4	Heat shield bolts (3 req'd)
5	Heat shield
6	Exhaust manifold nuts (8 req'd)
7	Exhaust manifold
8	Exhaust manifold gaskets

LTV1900000000313

Fig. 6 Lefthand exhaust manifold replacement

16. Position righthand timing chain on camshaft sprocket. Ensure copper colored link (marked), aligns with camshaft sprocket timing mark, **Fig. 34.**
17. Compress righthand timing chain tensioner with a suitable vise. Install plunger retaining clip.
18. Position righthand timing chain tensioner arm on dowel pin and install righthand tensioner, **Fig. 35.**
19. Remove retaining clip from righthand timing chain tensioner.
20. Verify correct alignment of all timing marks, **Fig. 36.**
21. Install crankshaft sensor ring on crankshaft.
22. Install front cover as outlined in “Front Cover, Replace.”

CAMSHAFT

REPLACE

1. Remove engine front cover as outlined in “Front Cover, Replace.”
2. Remove timing chains, gears and tensioners as outlined in “Timing Chain, Replace.”
3. Remove valve covers.
4. Remove camshaft components in sequence, **Fig. 37.**
5. Reverse procedure to install, noting the following:
   a. Lubricate camshaft bearing caps with clean engine oil.
   b. Install camshaft bearing caps and loosely install bolts.
   c. Tighten bolts in sequence, **Fig. 38,** to 89 inch lbs.
   d. Install camshaft gear spacer, then the sprocket.
   e. Tighten camshaft sprocket in two stages; Stage 1, **torque** sprocket bolt to 30 ft. lbs. Stage 2, tighten bolt an additional 90°.

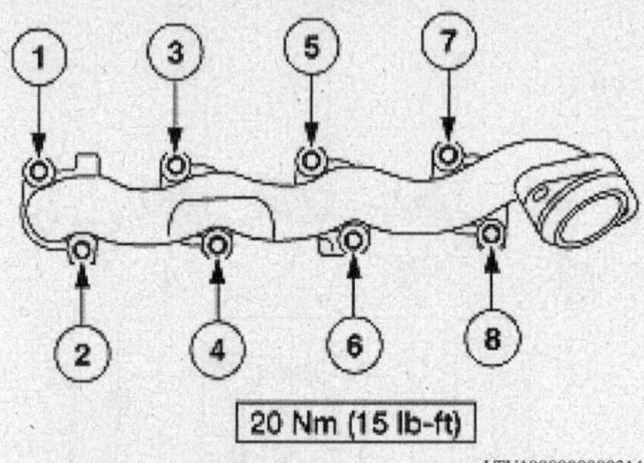

Fig. 7 Lefthand exhaust manifold bolt tightening sequence

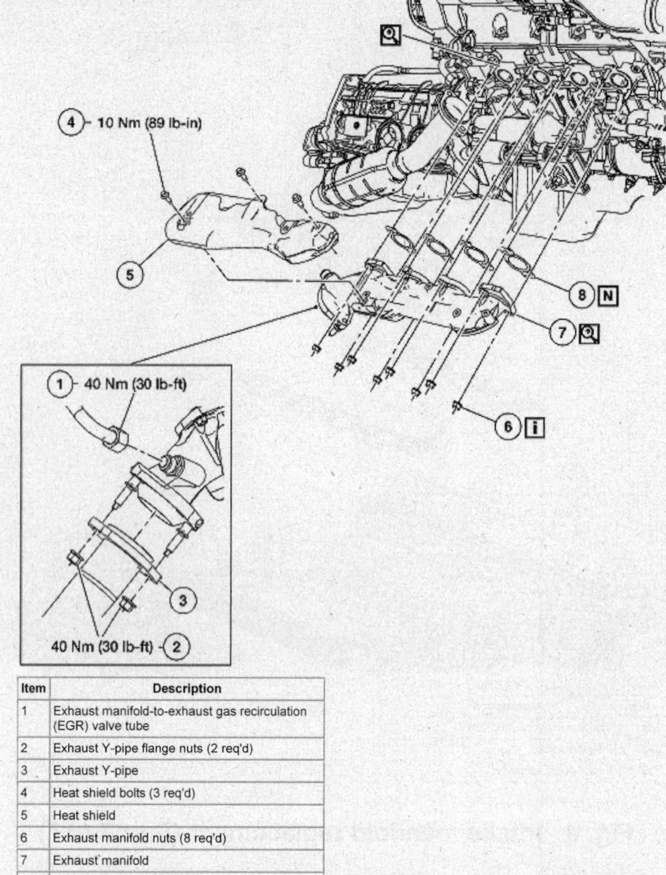

Item	Description
1	Exhaust manifold-to-exhaust gas recirculation (EGR) valve tube
2	Exhaust Y-pipe flange nuts (2 req'd)
3	Exhaust Y-pipe
4	Heat shield bolts (3 req'd)
5	Heat shield
6	Exhaust manifold nuts (8 req'd)
7	Exhaust manifold
8	Exhaust manifold gaskets

LTV1900000000315

Fig. 8 Righthand exhaust manifold replacement

MAIN & ROD BEARINGS

Main Bearing Tightening Sequence

1. Loosely install main bearing caps and bolts.
2. Push crankshaft forward to seat crankshaft thrust washer and hold the crankshaft in forward position.
3. Tighten bolts in sequence, **Fig. 39,** in four stages:
4. Stage 1: **Torque** bolts to 89 inch lbs.
5. Stage 2: **Torque** bolts to 18 ft. lbs.
6. Stage 3: **Torque** bolts to 30 ft. lbs.
7. Stage 4: Tighten bolts an additional 90°.

Main Bearing Cap Side Bolt Tightening Sequence

1. Install and tighten cross mounted bolts in two stages:
   a. Stage 1: **Torque** bolts to 30 ft. lbs.
   b. Stage 2: Tighten bolts an additional 90°.

Rod Bearing Bolt Tightening Sequence

Rod bearing cap bolts are torque to yield design. Install new bolts each time they are serviced.

1. Install connecting rod caps and bolts, then tighten in three stages:
   a. Stage 1: **Torque** bolts to 18 ft. lbs.
   b. Stage 2: **Torque** bolts to 33 ft. lbs.
   c. Stage 3: Tighten bolts an additional 90°.

CRANKSHAFT SEAL

REPLACE

Front

REMOVAL

1. Rotate accessory drive belt tensioner clockwise and remove drive belt.
2. Remove two bolts, then the lower radiator shroud.

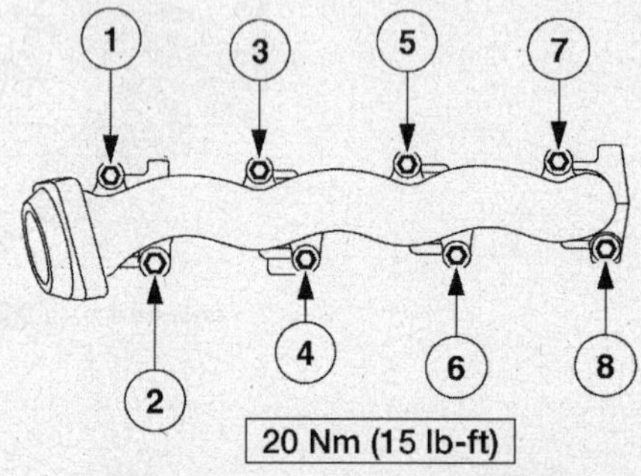

Fig. 9 Righthand exhaust manifold nut tightening sequence

3. Hold crankshaft pulley with suitable strap tool, then remove crankshaft pulley bolt.
4. Remove crankshaft vibration damper with removal tool No. 303–009, or equivalent.
5. Remove front crankshaft seal with seal removal tool No. 303–107, or equivalent.

INSTALLATION

1. Lubricate front cover and crankshaft front inner lip seal with clean engine oil.
2. Install crankshaft front seal with installation tools No. 303–102, 303–365 and 303–335, or equivalents.
3. Apply silicone gasket sealant to crankshaft woodruff key slot.
4. Install crankshaft pulley within four minutes of applying sealant.
5. Install crankshaft pulley using damper installation tool No. 303–102, or equivalent.
6. Tighten crankshaft pulley bolt in four stages:
   a. Stage 1: **Torque** bolt to 66 ft. lbs.
   b. Stage 2: Loosen bolt one full turn.
   c. Stage 3: **Torque** bolt to 37 ft. lbs.
   d. Tighten bolt an additional 90° without exceeding 148 ft. lbs.

Rear

REMOVAL

1. Remove transmission as outlined in **MOTOR's "Domestic Transmission, In-Vehicle Service" or "Transmission Service DVD."**
2. If rear seal retainer plate is being replaced, remove oil pan as outlined in "Oil Pan, Replace."
3. Remove components in sequence, **Fig. 40.**
4. Remove seal from retainer using removal tools No. 303–154 & 100–001, or equivalents.

INSTALLATION

1. Clean mating surfaces of oil seal retainer plate mating surfaces.
2. Apply a 4 mm bead of silicone gasket

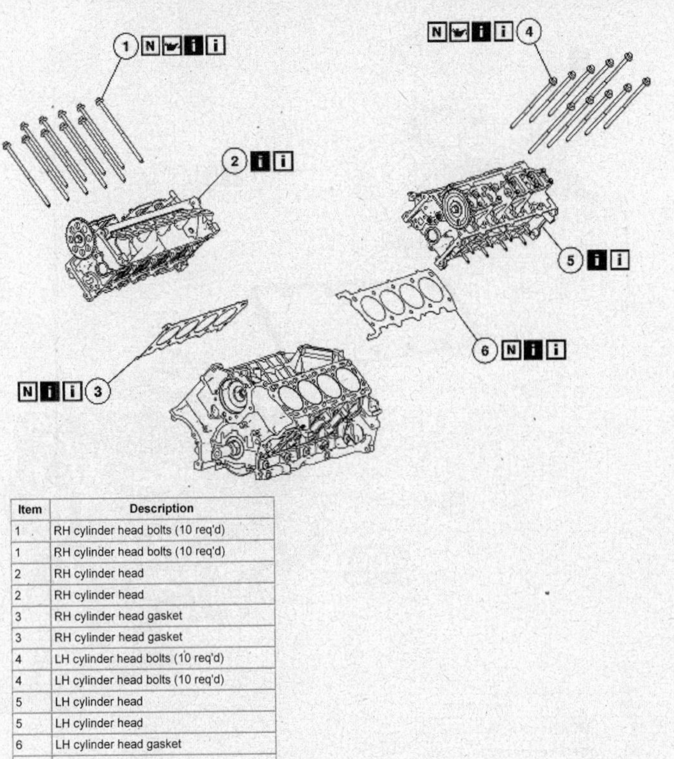

Item	Description
1	RH cylinder head bolts (10 req'd)
1	RH cylinder head bolts (10 req'd)
2	RH cylinder head
2	RH cylinder head
3	RH cylinder head gasket
3	RH cylinder head gasket
4	LH cylinder head bolts (10 req'd)
4	LH cylinder head bolts (10 req'd)
5	LH cylinder head
5	LH cylinder head
6	LH cylinder head gasket
6	LH cylinder head gasket

LTV1900000000317

Fig. 10 Cylinder head replacement

LTV1900000000318

Fig. 11 Lefthand cylinder head replacement

and sealant around rear oil seal retainer plate sealing surface, **Fig. 41.**

3. **Torque** bolts in sequence, **Fig. 42,** to 89 inch lbs.
4. Lubricate crankshaft rear oil seal with clean engine oil, then install crankshaft seal into retainer using installation tool No. 303–516, or equivalent.
5. Install crankshaft rear oil seal slinger with installation tool No. 303–517, or equivalent.
6. Install flexplate or flywheel bolts and tighten in crisscross pattern, **Fig. 43.**
7. Install transmission.

OIL PAN

REPLACE

Removal

1. Remove front drive axle as outlined in "Front Wheel Drive."
2. Remove front stabilizer as outlined in "Front Suspension & Steering."
3. Drain engine oil into suitable container.
4. Remove components in sequence, **Fig. 44.**
5. Remove and discard oil pan gasket.

Installation

1. Install components in reverse order of removal, **Fig. 44.**
2. Install front axle as outlined in "Front Wheel Drive."
3. Install front stabilizer as outlined in "Front Suspension & Steering."
4. Clean oil pan mating surfaces with suitable metal surface cleaner.

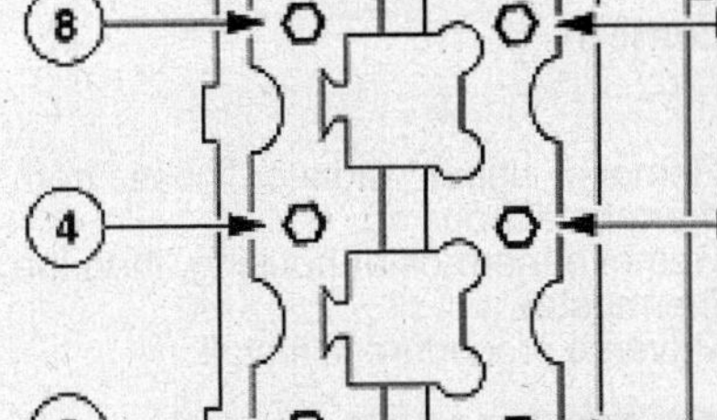

LTV1900000000319

Fig. 12 Righthand cylinder head replacement

5. Allow surfaces to dry before proceeding.
6. Apply silicone gasket and sealer in areas noted, **Fig. 45.**
7. Apply silicone gasket sealant in two additional places, **Fig. 46.**
8. Position new oil pan gasket and loosely install bolts.
9. Tighten bolts in three stages:
   a. Stage 1: **Torque** pan bolts to 18 inch lbs.
   b. Stage 2: **Torque** pan bolts to 15 ft. lbs.
   c. Stage 3: Tighten pan bolts an additional 60°.

OIL PUMP

REPLACE

1. Remove timing chains and gears as outlined in "Timing Chain, Replace."
2. Remove oil pan as outlined in "Oil Pan, Replace."
3. Remove components in sequence, **Fig. 44.**
4. Reverse procedure to install.

BELT TENSION DATA

This engine is equipped with an automatic drive belt tensioner. No adjustments are required.

SERPENTINE DRIVE BELT

Refer to **Fig. 47** for serpentine drive belt routing.

COOLING SYSTEM BLEED

1. Fill radiator through degas bottle with suitable coolant.

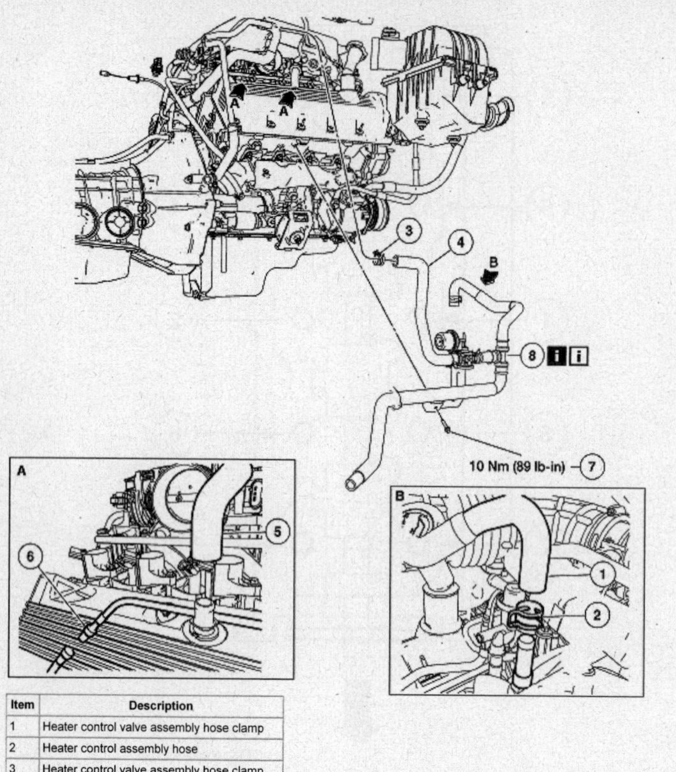

Item	Description
1	Heater control valve assembly hose clamp
2	Heater control assembly hose
3	Heater control valve assembly hose clamp
4	Heater control valve assembly hose
5	Crankcase ventilation hose
6	Vacuum hose
7	Heater control valve assembly bolt
8	Heater control valve assembly
8	Heater control valve assembly

LTV1900000000320

Fig. 13 Righthand valve cover replacement (Part 1 of 2)

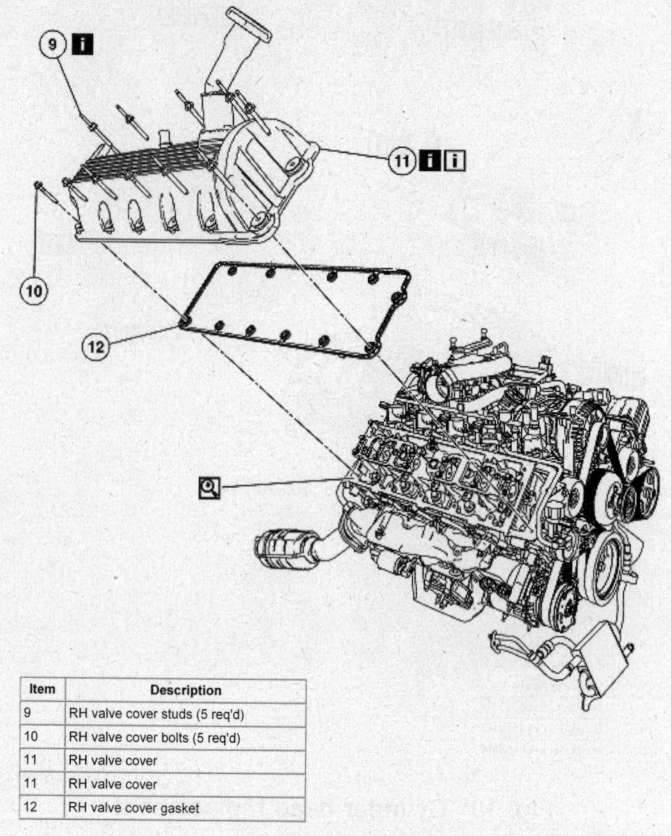

Item	Description
9	RH valve cover studs (5 req'd)
10	RH valve cover bolts (5 req'd)
11	RH valve cover
11	RH valve cover
12	RH valve cover gasket

LTV1900000000321

Fig. 13 Righthand valve cover replacement (Part 2 of 2)

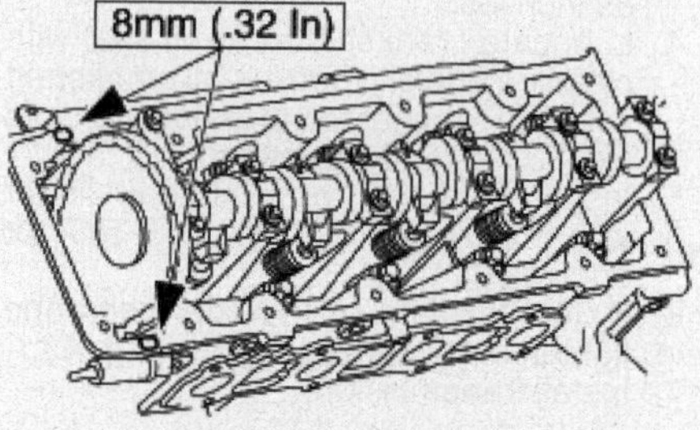

LTV1900000000482

Fig. 14 Righthand valve cover sealant application

2. Install pressure relief cap.
3. Select maximum heater temperature and blower motor speed settings. Position control to discharge air from A/C vents to instrument panel.
4. Run engine until normal operating temperature is achieved.
5. Turn off engine and allow to cool. When pressure has been released remove pressure relief cap.
6. Add coolant to degas bottle until coolant level is at"Cold Fill" range mark.
7. Install pressure relief cap.
8. Start engine and allow to idle. While idling, inspect for hot air from A/C vents. Coolant temperature gauge should read in middle of "Normal" range and upper radiator hose should feel hot to touch.
9. Inspect coolant level in degas bottle and top off as required.
10. Repeat refill procedure as required.

THERMOSTAT

REPLACE

1. Drain cooling system into suitable container.
2. Remove upper radiator hose from thermostat housing.
3. Remove thermostat housing, then the thermostat.
4. Reverse procedure to install.

WATER PUMP

REPLACE

1. Drain cooling system into suitable container.
2. Remove water pump pulley, then the water pump, **Fig. 48.**
3. Reverse procedure to install.

RADIATOR

REPLACE

Refer to "4.0L SOHC Engine" for radiator replacement procedure.

FUEL PUMP

REPLACE

1. Relieve fuel system pressure as outlined in "Precautions."
2. Remove fuel tank.
3. Install fuel tank sender wrench No. 310–059, or equivalent, onto fuel pump lock ring.
4. Remove fuel pump lock ring, then the fuel pump.
5. Reverse procedure to install.

FUEL FILTER

REPLACE

1. Relieve fuel system pressure as outlined in "Precautions."
2. Remove fuel filter shield.
3. Separate fuel line fittings with disconnect tool No. 310–S039, or equivalent.
4. Disconnect fuel lines from filter, then remove fuel filter.
5. Reverse procedure to install.

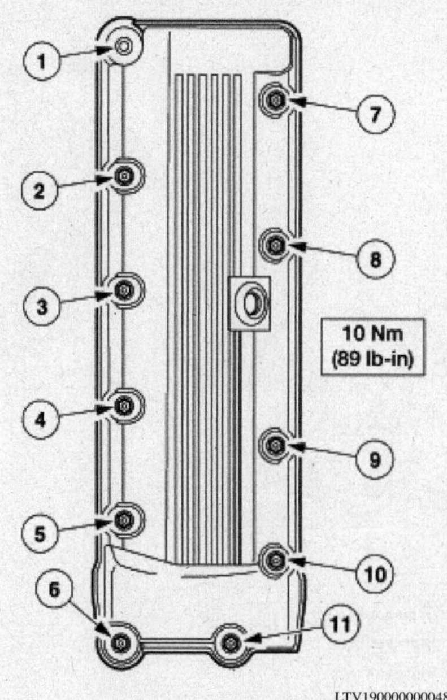

Fig. 15 Righthand valve cover bolt tightening sequence

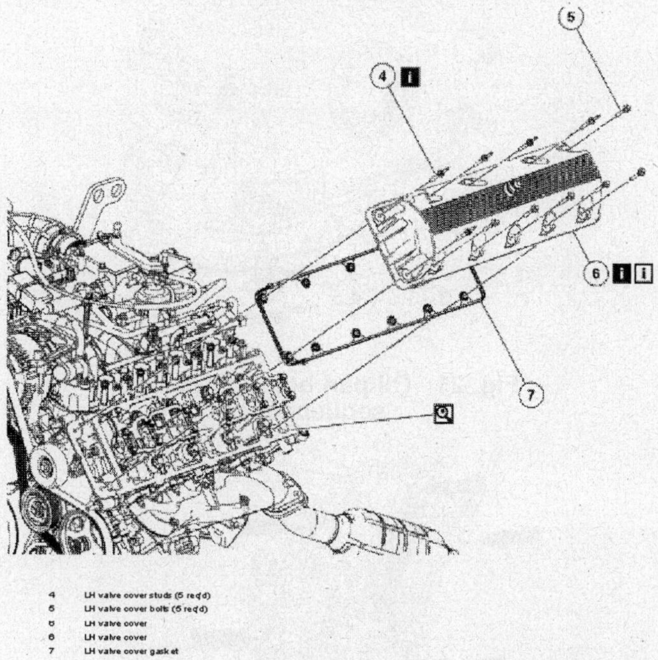

Fig. 16 Lefthand valve cover replacement (Part 2 of 2)

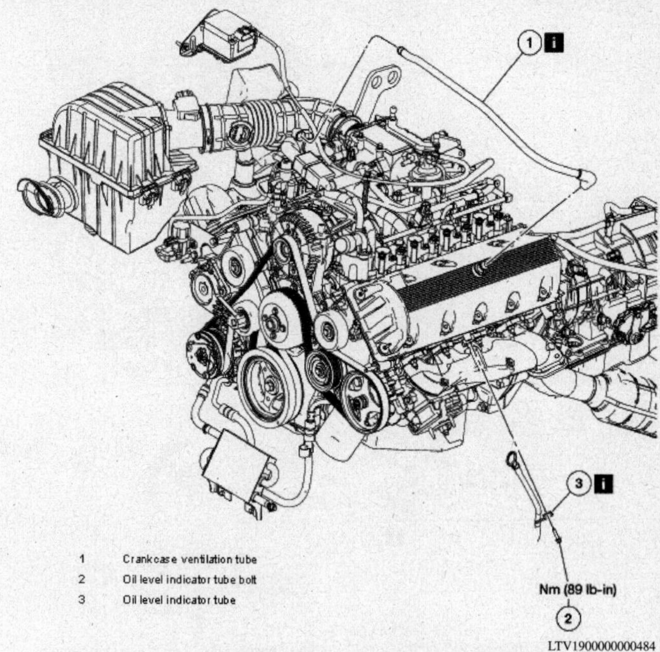

Fig. 16 Lefthand valve cover replacement (Part 1 of 2)

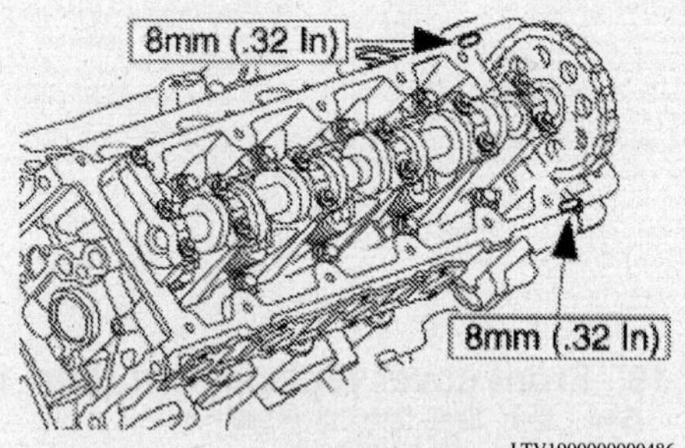

Fig. 17 Lefthand valve cover sealant application

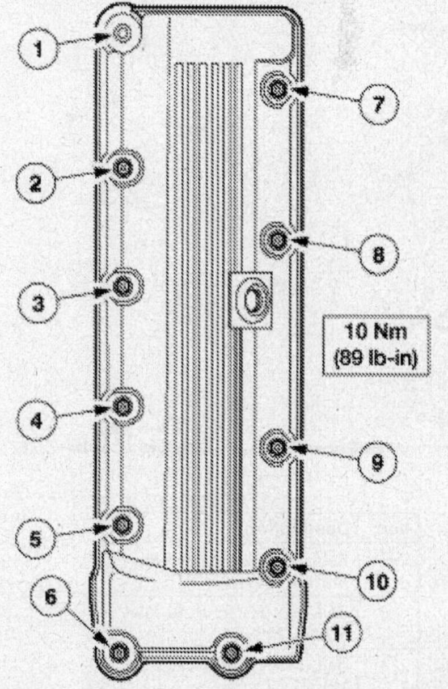

Fig. 18 Lefthand valve cover bolt tightening sequence

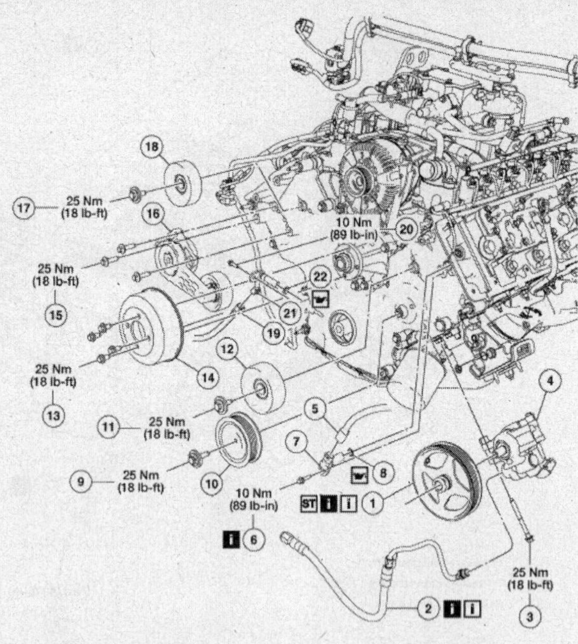

Item	Description
1	Power steering pump pulley
1	Power steering pump pulley
2	Power steering pressure hose
2	Power steering pressure hose
3	Power steering pump bolts (3 Req'd)
4	Power steering pump
5	Camshaft position (CMP) sensor electrical connector
6	CMP sensor bolt
7	CMP sensor
8	CMP O-ring seal
9	Accessory drive belt idler pulley bolt
10	Accessory drive belt idler pulley
11	Accessory drive belt idler pulley bolt

Item	Description
12	Accessory drive belt idler pulley
13	Coolant pump pulley bolts (4 req'd)
14	Coolant pump pulley
15	Accessory drive belt tensioner bolts (3 req'd)
16	Accessory drive belt tensioner
17	Accessory drive belt idler pulley bolt
18	Accessory drive belt idler pulley
19	Crankshaft position (CKP) sensor electrical connector
20	CKP sensor bolt
21	CKP sensor
22	CKP sensor O-ring seal

LTV1900000000488

Fig. 19 Front cover replacement (Part 1 of 2)

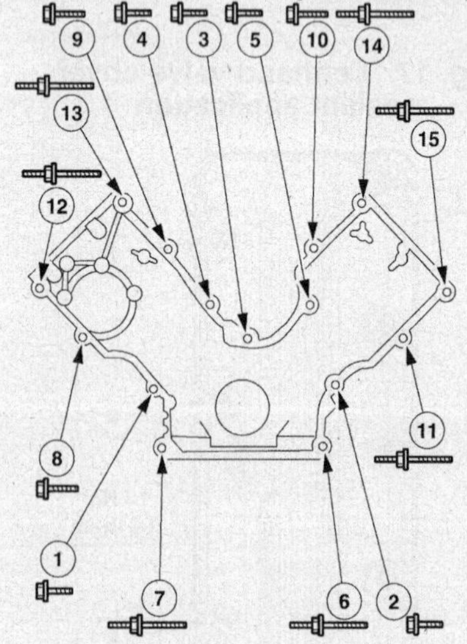

Item	Description
1	Bolt, Hex Flange Head Pilot, M8 x 1.25 x 53
2	Bolt, Hex Flange Head Pilot, M8 x 1.25 x 53
3	Bolt, Hex Flange Head Pilot, M8 x 1.25 x 53
4	Bolt, Hex Flange Head Pilot, M8 x 1.25 x 53

LTV1900000000491

Fig. 20 Front cover bolt removal sequence

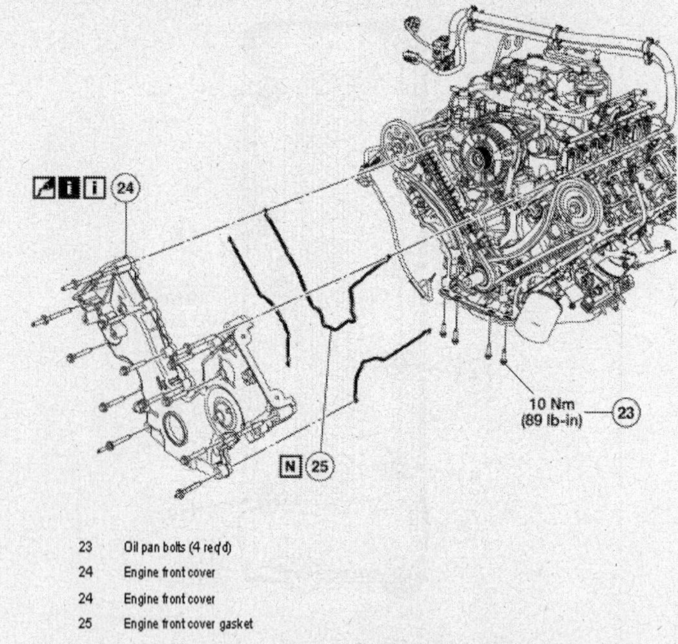

LTV1900000000489

Fig. 19 Front cover replacement (Part 2 of 2)

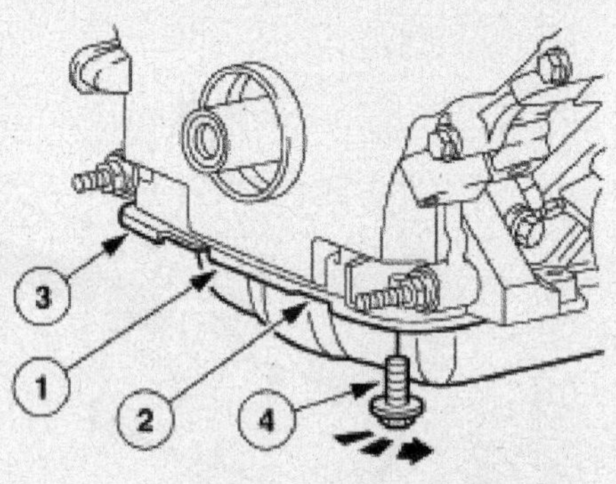

LTV1900000000492

Fig. 21 Oil pan bolt tightening sequence

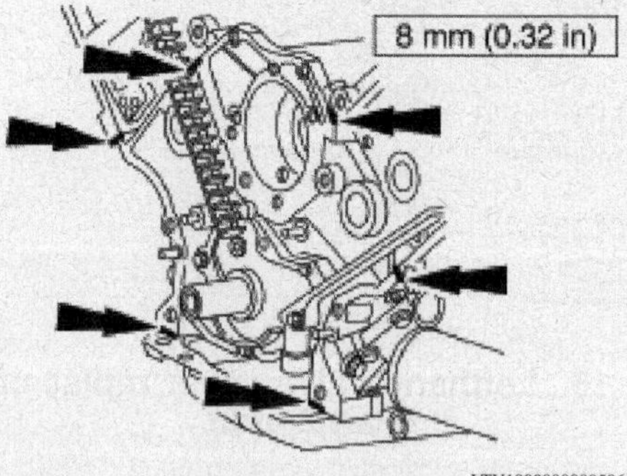

LTV1900000000506

Fig. 22 Silicone gasket sealant application

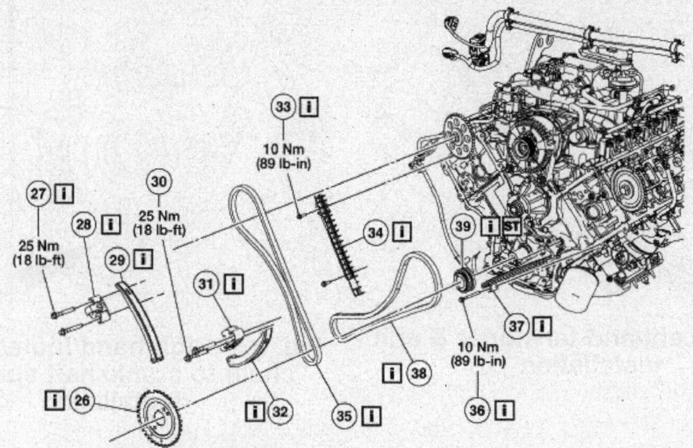

Item	Description
26	Crankshaft sensor ignition pulse ring
27	RH timing chain tensioner bolts (2 req'd)
28	RH timing chain tensioner
29	RH timing chain tensioner arm
30	LH timing chain tensioner bolts (2 req'd)
31	LH timing chain tensioner
32	LH timing chain tensioner arm
33	RH timing chain guide bolts (2 req'd)
34	RH timing chain guide
35	RH timing chain
36	LH timing chain guide bolts (2 req'd)
37	LH timing chain guide
38	LH timing chain
39	Crankshaft gear

LTV1900000000490

Fig. 23 Timing chain & gear replacement

LTV1900000000493

Fig. 24 Crankshaft positioning tool installation

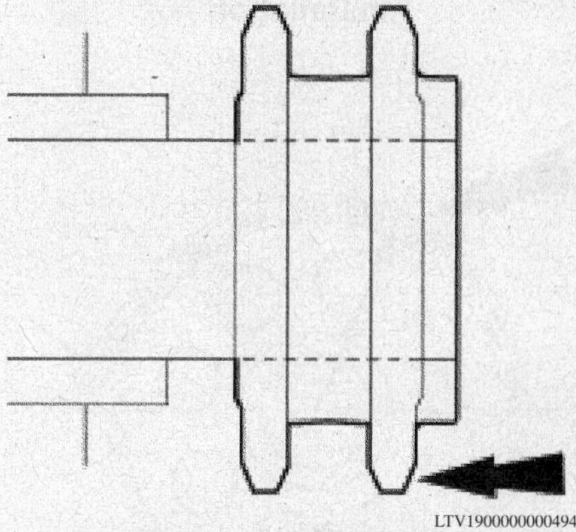

LTV1900000000494

Fig. 25 Crankshaft sprocket flange orientation

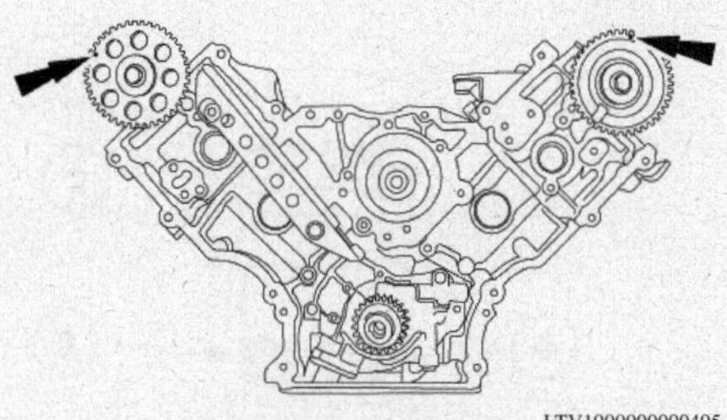

LTV1900000000495

Fig. 26 Camshaft sprocket alignment positions

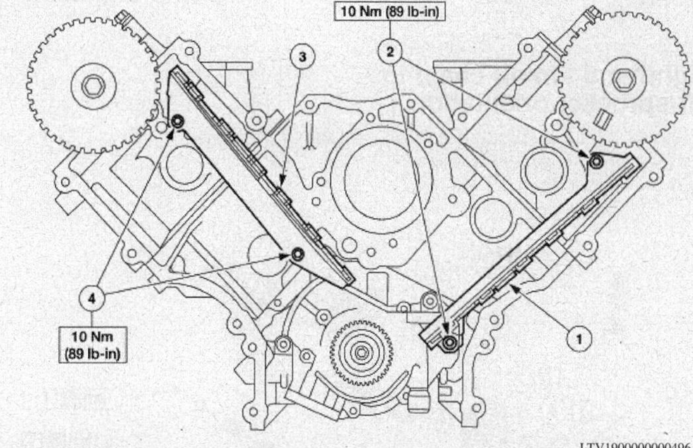

LTV1900000000496

Fig. 27 Timing chain guide installation

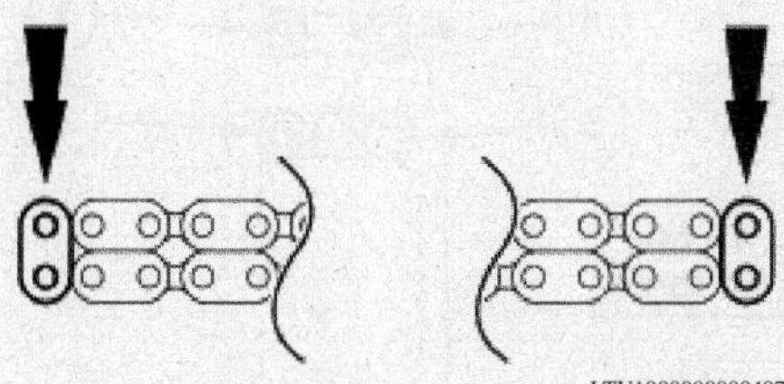

LTV1900000000497

Fig. 28 Timing chain marks

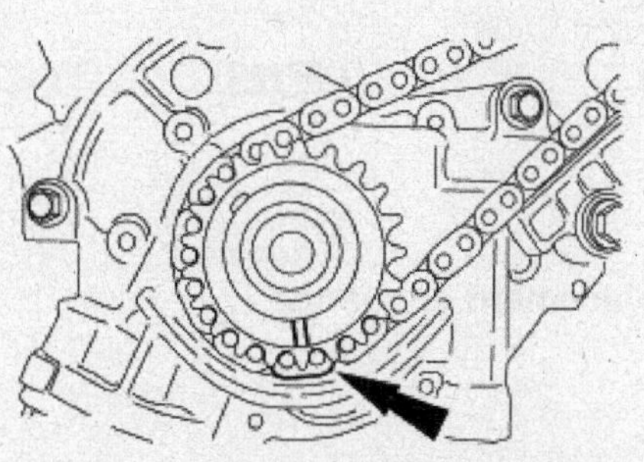

LTV1900000000498

Fig. 29 Lefthand (inner) timing chain to crankshaft sprocket installation

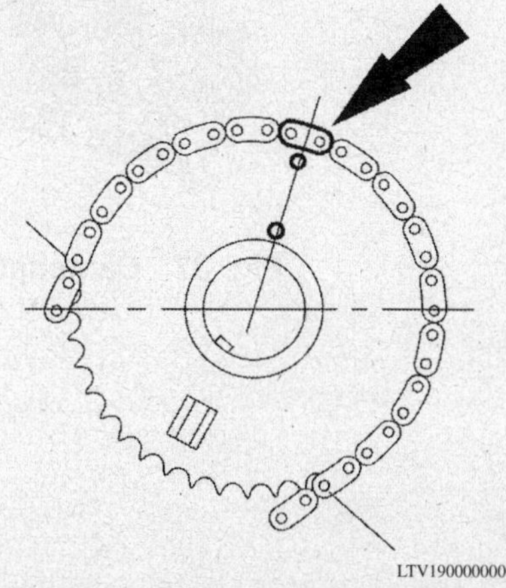

LTV1900000000499

Fig. 30 Lefthand timing chain to camshaft sprocket orientation

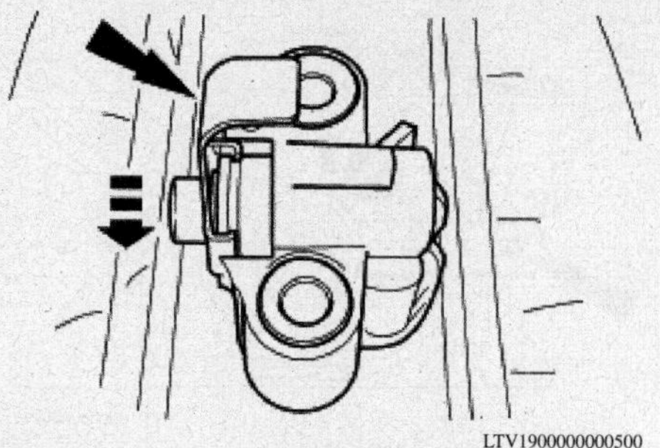

Fig. 31 Lefthand timing chain tensioner retaining clip installation

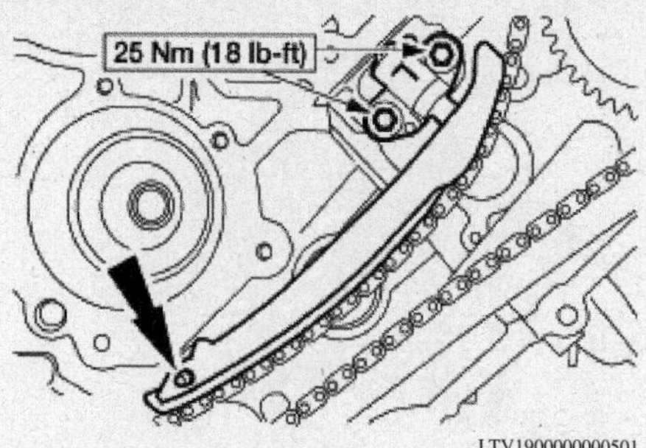

Fig. 32 Lefthand tensioner & arm installation

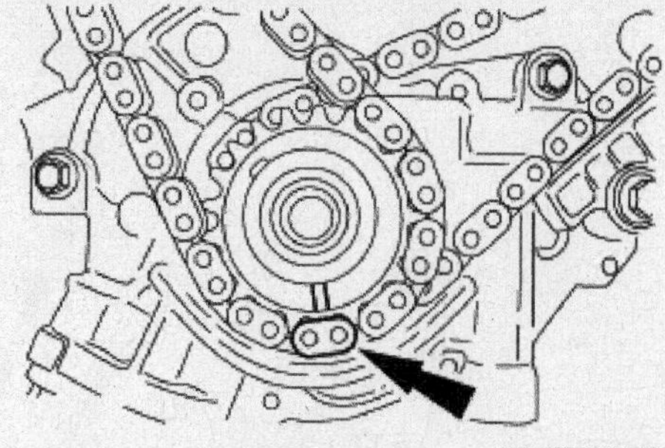

Fig. 33 Righthand (outer) timing chain to crankshaft sprocket installation

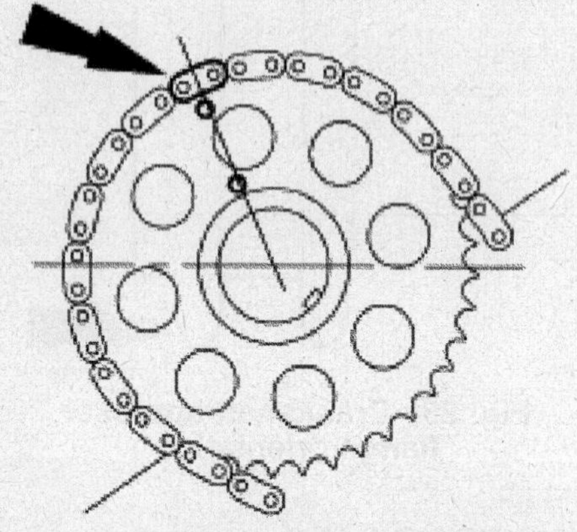

Fig. 34 Righthand timing chain to camshaft sprocket orientation

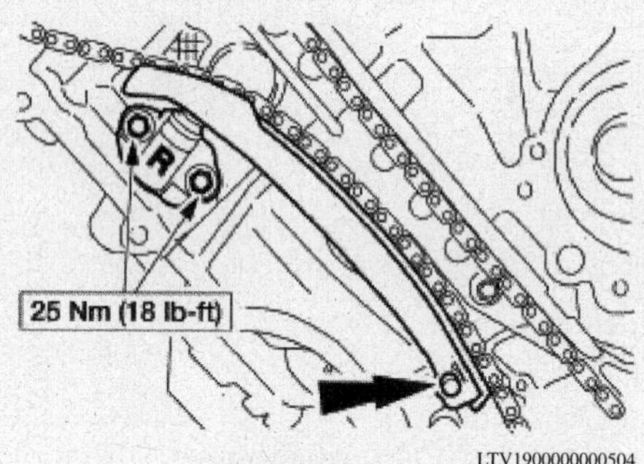

Fig. 35 Righthand tensioner & arm installation

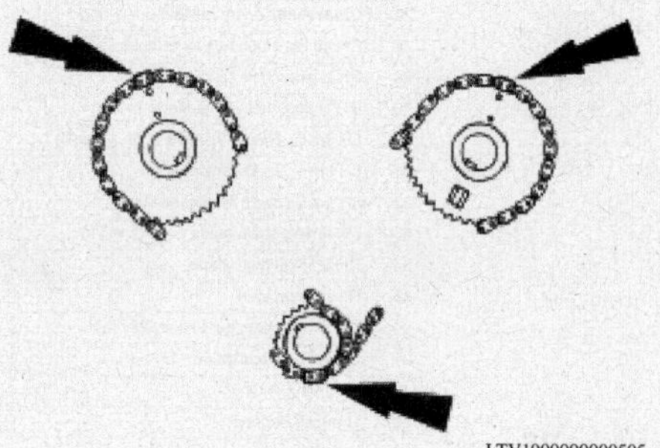

Fig. 36 Timing mark alignment

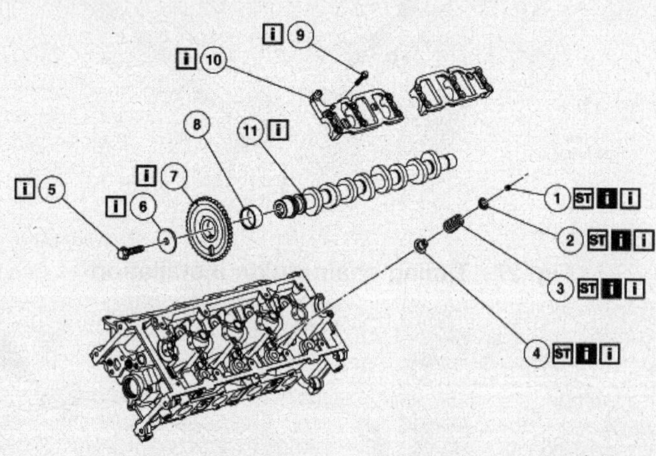

Fig. 37 Camshaft replacement sequence

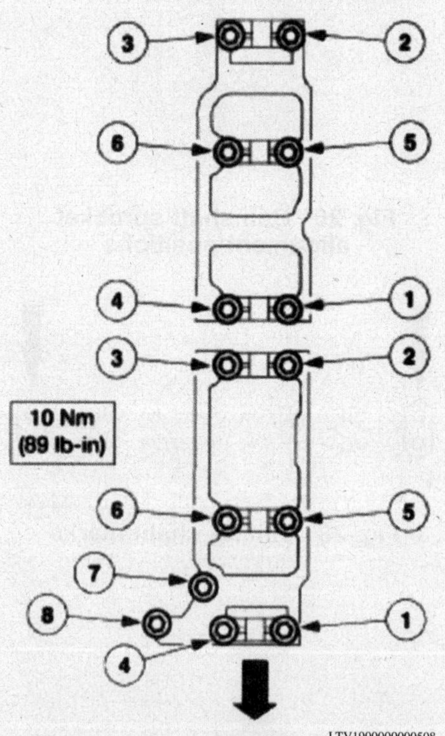

Fig. 38 Camshaft bearing cap installation

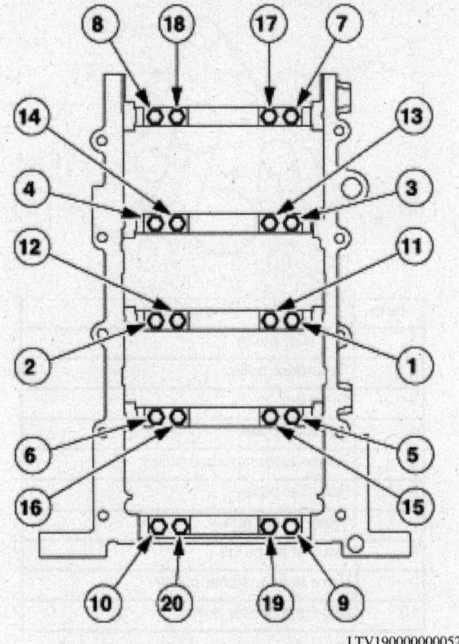

LTV1900000000520

Fig. 39 Main bearing bolt tightening sequence

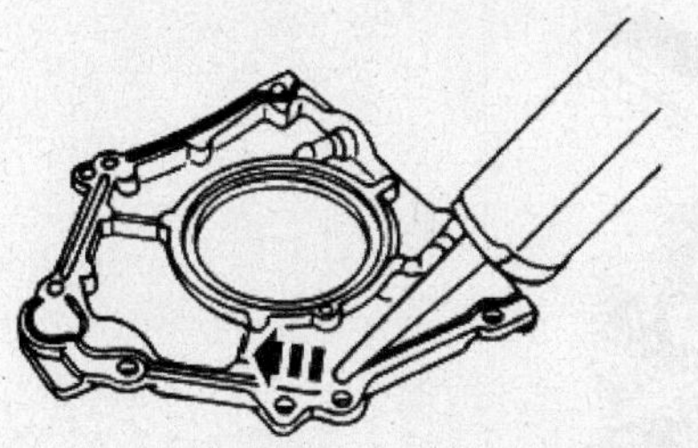

LTV1900000000510

Fig. 41 Rear crankshaft oil seal retainer silicone sealant & gasket application

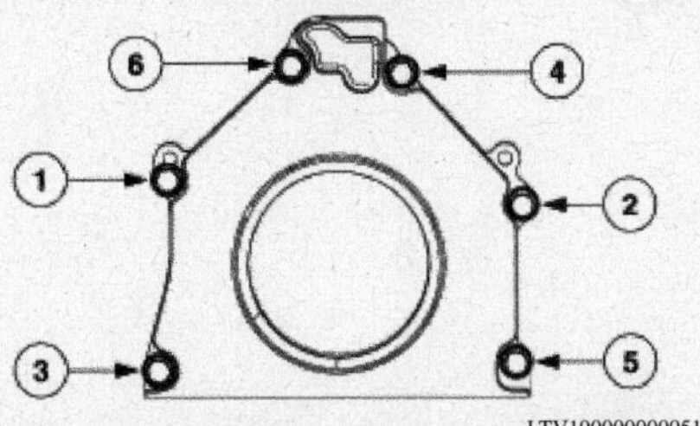

LTV1900000000511

Fig. 42 Crankshaft rear oil seal retainer plate bolt tightening sequence

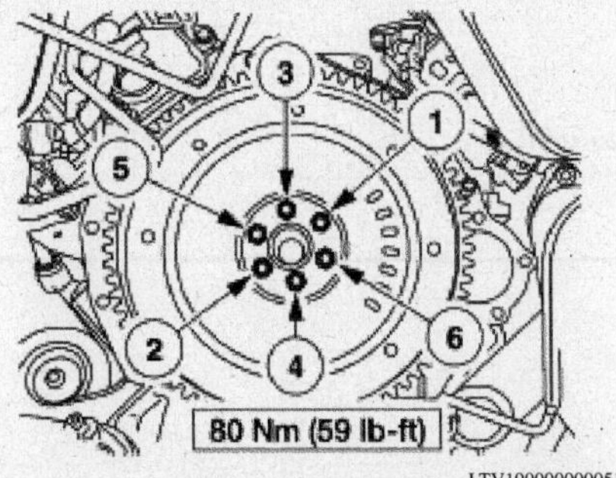

LTV1900000000512

Fig. 43 Flywheel/flexplate bolt tightening pattern

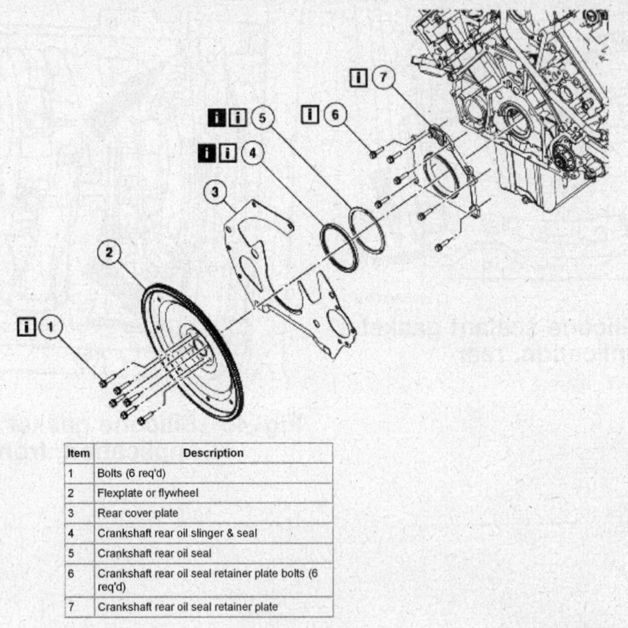

Item	Description
1	Bolts (6 req'd)
2	Flexplate or flywheel
3	Rear cover plate
4	Crankshaft rear oil slinger & seal
5	Crankshaft rear oil seal
6	Crankshaft rear oil seal retainer plate bolts (6 req'd)
7	Crankshaft rear oil seal retainer plate

LTV1900000000509

Fig. 40 Rear crankshaft oil seal replacement

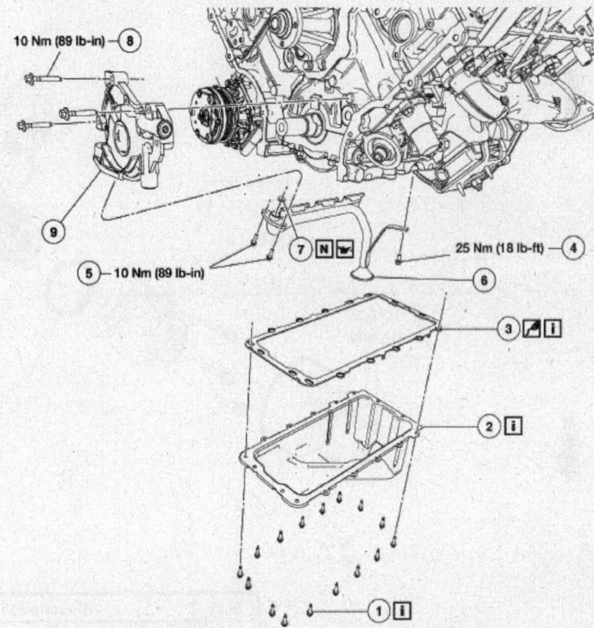

Item	Description
1	Oil pan bolts (16 req'd) Installation Note
2	Oil pan Installation Note
3	Oil pan gasket Installation Note
4	Oil pump screen and pickup tube bolt
5	Oil pump screen and pickup tube bolts (2 req'd)
6	Oil pump screen and pickup tube
7	Oil pump screen and pickup tube O-ring
8	Oil pump bolts (3 req'd)
9	Oil pump

LTV1900000000513

Fig. 44 Oil pan & pump replacement

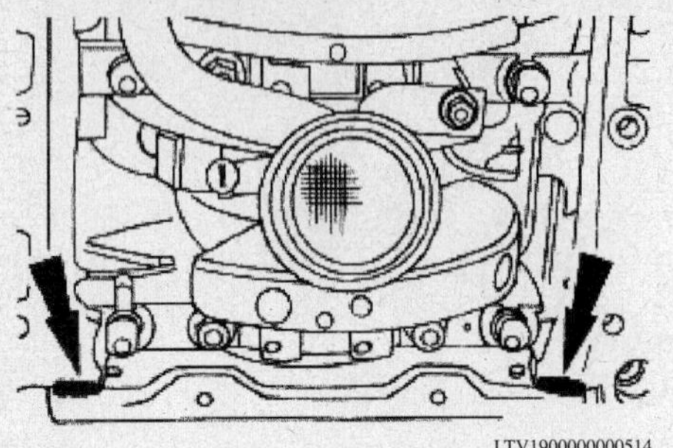

LTV1900000000514

Fig. 45 Silicone sealant gasket application, rear

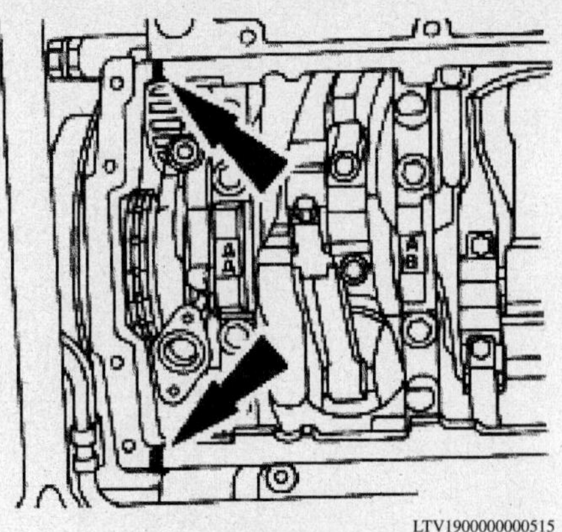

LTV1900000000515

Fig. 46 Silicone gasket & sealant application, front

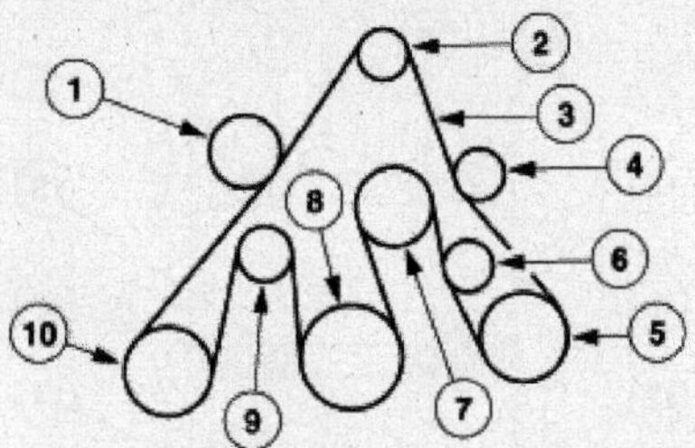

Item	Description
1	Belt idler pulley
2	Generator pulley
3	Drive belt
4	Belt idler pulley
5	Power steering pump pulley
6	Belt idler pulley
7	Water pump pulley
8	Crankshaft pulley
9	Drive belt tensioner pulley
10	A/C compressor pulley

LTV1900000000517

Fig. 47 Serpentine drive belt routing

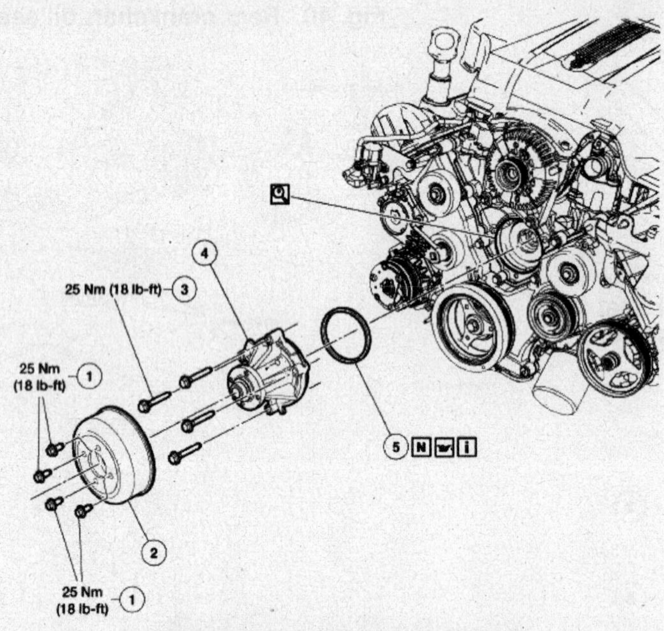

Item	Description
1	Coolant pump pulley bolts
2	Coolant pump pulley
3	Coolant pump bolts
4	Coolant pump
5	O-ring (part of 8501) Installation Note

LTV1900000000518

Fig. 48 Water pump replacement

TIGHTENING SPECIFICATIONS

Year	Component	Torque Ft. Lbs.
2003–06	Camshaft Bearing Cap	89①
	Camshaft Position Sensor	89①
	Camshaft Sprocket	②
	Cylinder Head Temperature Sensor	19
	Connecting Rod Bolts	③
	Crankshaft Damper Pulley	④
	Crankshaft Main Bearing Bolts	③
	Cylinder Head Bolts	⑤
	Drive Belt Idler Pulley	18
	Drive Belt Tensioner Pulley	18
	Engine Front Cover	18
	Exhaust Manifold Nuts	15
	Flexplate	59
	Fuel Injection Supply Manifold Bracket Bolts	89①
	Heater Return Tube Studs	30
	Heater Water Inlet Tube	11
	Ignition Coil	53①
	Intake Manifold	⑥
	Knock Sensor	15
	Motor Mount Nuts	52
	Motor Mount Through Bolts	76
	Oil Filter Adapter	18
	Oil Dipstick Tube	89①
	Oil Line Connector Adapter	18
	Oil Pan	⑦
	Oil Pan Drain Plug	10
	Oil Pressure Switch	89①
	Oil Pump Bolts	89①
	Power Steering Bracket Upper Bolts	89①
	Power Steering Bracket Lower Bolts	30
	Power Steering Pump	18
	Rear Main Oil Seal Retainer	18
	Spark Plugs	11
	Thermostat Housing	18
	Throttle Body Adapter	89①
	Timing Chain Guide	89①
	Timing Chain Hydraulic Tensioner	18
	Valve Cover	89①
	Water Pump	18
	Water Pump Pulley	18

①— Inch lbs.

②— Refer to "Camshaft, Replace" for tightening procedure.

③— Refer to "Main & Rod Bearings" for tightening procedure.

④— Refer to "Crankshaft Seal, Replace" for tightening procedure.

⑤— Refer to "Cylinder Head, Replace" for tightening procedure.

⑥— Refer to "Intake Manifold, Replace" for tightening procedure.

⑦— Refer to "Oil Pan, Replace" for tightening procedure.

4.6L SOHC (VIN 8) Engine

NOTE: For Procedures Not Found In This Section, Refer To "4.6L SOHC (VIN W) Engine" Section.

NOTE: On Air Bag Equipped Models, Refer To "Air Bag System Precautions" Located In The Front Of This Manual For System Disarming & Arming Procedures.

NOTE: Refer To "Computer Relearn Procedures" Located In The Front Of This Manual When Battery Power To The Computer Has Been Interrupted.

INDEX

PRECAUTIONS

Air Bag Systems

Refer to "Air Bag System Precautions" in the front of this manual for system disarming and arming procedures.

Battery Ground Cable

Prior to service, disconnect battery ground cable and isolate as required.

Fuel System Pressure Relief Procedure

Fuel in fuel system remains under high pressure even when engine is not running. Before servicing or disconnecting any of the fuel lines or fuel system components, the fuel system pressure must be relieved to prevent accidental spraying of fuel.

1. Remove schrader valve cap, **Fig. 1,** from fuel rail.
2. Attach fuel system pressure gauge No. 310–012, or equivalent, to schraeder valve.
3. Open tool valve slowly and release fuel system pressure into suitable container.

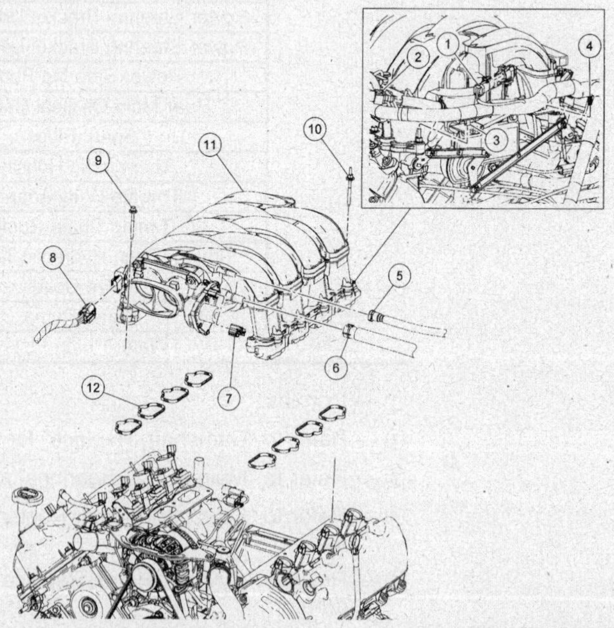

Fig. 1 Intake manifold replacement (Part 1 of 2)

Item	Description
1	Charge motion control valve (CMCV) electrical connector
2	Vacuum hose T-fitting
3	Wiring harness retainer
4	Wiring harness pin-type retainer
5	Evaporative emissions
6	Positive crankcase ventilation (PCV) tube
7	Electronic throttle body electrical connector
8	Throttle position (TP) sensor electrical connector
9	Intake manifold bolt (9 required)
10	Intake manifold stud bolt
11	Intake manifold
12	Intake manifold gasket (8 required)

ARM0400000000498

Fig. 1 Intake manifold replacement (Part 2 of 2)

COMPRESSION PRESSURE

1. Ensure oil in crankcase is of correct viscosity and at correct level and that battery is fully charged.
2. Set throttle plates wide open.
3. Install compression gauge in No. 1 cylinder.
4. Install auxiliary starter switch in starter circuit.
5. With ignition in Off position, crank engine a minimum of five compression strokes and record highest reading.
6. Note number of strokes required to obtain highest reading.
7. Repeat test on each cylinder, cranking engine approximately same number of compression strokes.
8. Compression pressures are considered within specification if lowest reading is at least 75% of highest reading.

ENGINE MOUNT

REPLACE

1. Raise and support vehicle.
2. Remove fan shroud.
3. Remove alternator.
4. Remove wiper cowling.
5. Remove exhaust gas recirculation system module and tube assembly.
6. Remove remaining components in order listed, **Fig. 2.**
7. Reverse procedure to install.

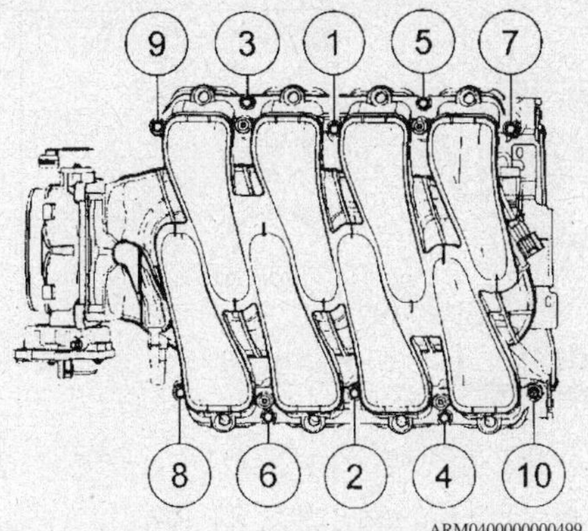

Fig. 2 Intake manifold tightening sequence

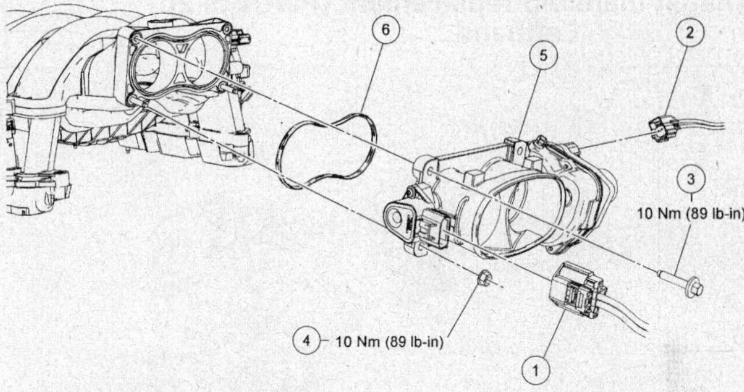

Item	Description
1	Electronic throttle control electrical connector
2	Throttle position (TP) sensor electrical connector
3	Throttle body bolts (2 required)
4	Throttle body nuts (2 required)
5	Throttle body
6	Throttle body gasket

ARM0400000000517

Fig. 3 Throttle body, TP sensor & electrical connectors

ENGINE

REPLACE

1. Remove vehicle hood.
2. Recover A/C refrigerant as outlined in "Air Conditioning" chapter.
3. Remove air cleaner assembly.
4. Remove evaporative emissions canister purge valve.
5. Remove cooling fan and shroud.
6. Relieve fuel system pressure as outlined in "Precautions."
7. Disconnect fuel hose spring coupling.
8. Remove starter motor.
9. Drain engine oil into suitable container.
10. Remove remaining components in order illustrated, **Fig. 3.**
11. Install suitable three bar engine support tool and engine lifting bracket set No. 303–D074, or equivalent.
12. Remove transmission.
13. Disconnect lefthand HO2S harness from retainer.
14. Disconnect ATF cooler tubes from cooler and drain fluid into suitable container.
15. Remove ATF cooler tubes from vehicle.
16. Remove three bar engine support tool.
17. Attach spreader bar No. 303–D089, or equivalent to engine lifting brackets.
18. Lift engine from vehicle with suitable lifting device.
19. Reverse procedure to install.

INTAKE MANIFOLD

REPLACE

1. Remove fuel pump relay.
2. Start engine and allow it idle until is stalls.
3. Crank engine for approximately five seconds to ensure fuel injection supply manifold pressure has been released.
4. Turn ignition switch to OFF position.
5. Disconnect crankcase vent tube from air cleaner outlet pipe.
6. Loosen two clamps and remove air cleaner outlet pipe.

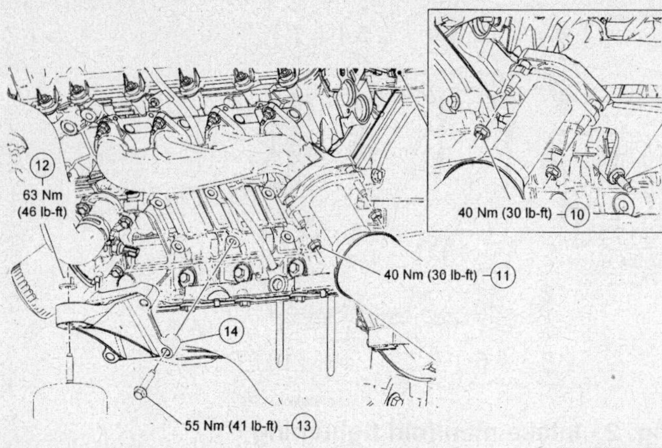

Fig. 4 Exhaust manifold replacement (Part 1 of 2). Lefthand

ARM0400000000518

Fig. 5 Alternator replacement (Part 1 of 2)

Item	Description
10	RH catalytic converter-to-exhaust manifold nuts (2 required)
11	LH catalytic converter-to-exhaust manifold nuts (2 required)
12	LH engine support insulator nut
13	LH engine support insulator bracket bolt (4 required)
14	LH engine support insulator bracket

ARM0400000000521

Fig. 4 Exhaust manifold replacement (Part 2 of 2). Lefthand

Item	Description
1	Pin-type retainer
2	Radiator sight shield
3	B+ terminal nut
4	B+ terminal cover
5	Generator electrical connector
6	Wiring harness pin-type retainer
7	Generator nut (2 required)
8	Generator bracket bolt (2 required)
9	Generator

ARM0400000000519

Fig. 5 Alternator replacement (Part 2 of 2)

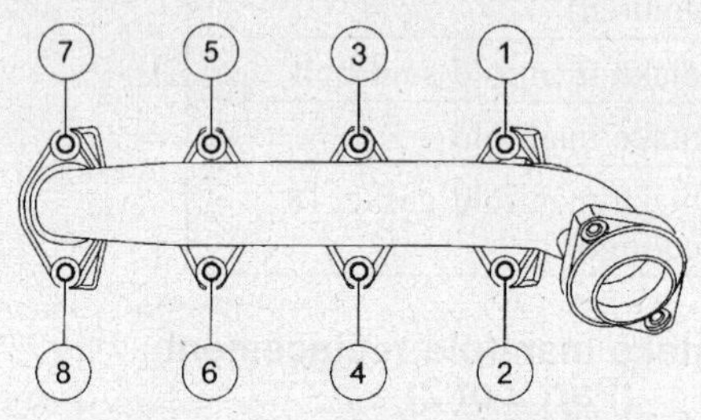

Fig. 6 Exhaust manifold tightening sequence. Lefthand

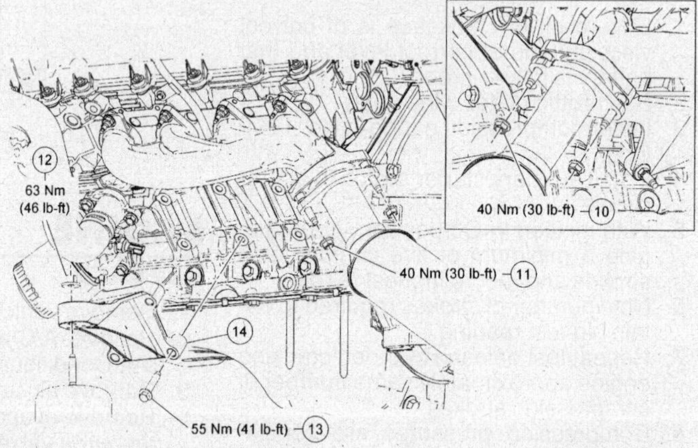

Fig. 7 Exhaust manifold replacement. Righthand

7. Disconnect fuel supply tube spring lock coupling.
8. Disconnect two retainers from fuel rail stud bolts and position wiring harness aside.
9. Disconnect fuel rail pressure and temperature sensor electrical connector and vacuum hose.
10. Disconnect eight fuel injection electrical connectors.
11. Remove four fuel rail stud bolts.
12. Remove fuel rail and injectors.
13. Disconnect Evaporative Emissions (EVAP) tube from intake manifold and position it aside, **Fig. 1.**
14. Disconnect Positive Crankcase Ventilation (PCV) tube from intake manifold and position it aside.
15. Disconnect Throttle Position (TP) sensor and electronic throttle body electrical connectors.
16. Disconnect Charge Motion Control Valve (CMCV) electrical connector.
17. Disconnect wiring retainers from intake manifold stud bolt and CMCV bracket. Position wiring harness aside.
18. Disconnect vacuum hose from T fitting.
19. Remove nine mounting bolts, stud bolt, intake manifold and gasket.
20. Reverse procedure to install, noting the following:
    a. Install new gasket.
    b. Tighten mounting bolts in sequence, **Fig. 2.**
    c. Install new upper and lower fuel injector O-ring seals lubricated with suitable, clean engine oil.

EXHAUST MANIFOLD

REPLACE

Lefthand

1. Raise and support vehicle.
2. Loosen clamp and disconnect air cleaner outlet pipe.
3. Disconnect Mass Air Flow (MAF) sensor electrical connector.
4. Remove mounting bolt and air cleaner. Ensure two rubber grommets are retained to feet.
5. Disconnect Throttle Position (TP) sensor and electronic throttle control electrical connectors, **Fig. 3.**
6. Remove mounting bolts, nuts and throttle body.
7. Disconnect lefthand Heated Oxygen Sensor (HO2S) electrical connector and wiring harness retainer.
8. Remove two righthand catalytic converter to exhaust manifold nuts, **Fig. 4.**

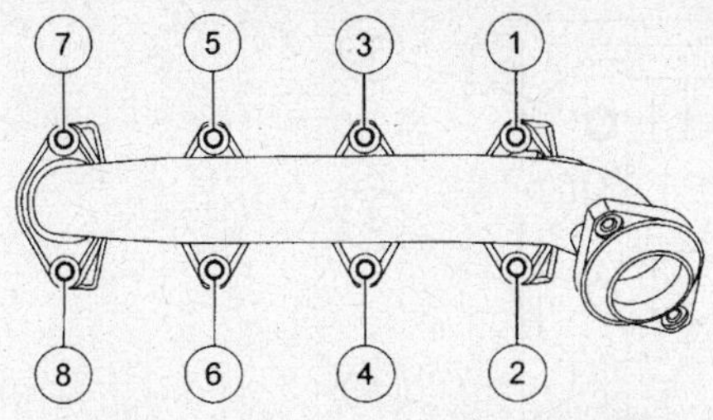

Fig. 8 Exhaust manifold tightening sequence. Righthand

9. Remove two lefthand catalytic converter-to-exhaust manifold nuts.
10. Remove fix pin-type retainers and radiator sight shield, **Fig. 5.**
11. Remove two outer bracket mounting bolts and two lower mounting nuts, then disconnect alternator electrical connector and pin-type retainer.
12. Position cover aside, then remove B+ terminal nut and alternator.
13. Support engine using suitable engine lifting brackets and three-bar engine support tools.
14. Remove lefthand and righthand engine support insulator nuts.
15. Raise engine approximately 1.57 inches.
16. Remove bolt and disconnect steering coupling. **Do not rotate steering wheel when steering column intermediate shaft is disconnected.**
17. Remove four bolts and lefthand engine support insulator bracket.
18. Remove eight nuts, exhaust manifold and gasket.
19. Reverse procedure to install, noting the following:
    a. Install new exhaust manifold gaskets.
    b. Tighten exhaust manifold mounting nuts in sequence, **Fig. 6.**

Righthand

1. Raise and support vehicle.
2. Loosen clamp and disconnect air cleaner outlet pipe.
3. Disconnect Mass Air Flow (MAF) sensor electrical connector.
4. Remove mounting bolt and air cleaner. Ensure two rubber grommets are retained to feet.
5. Disconnect Throttle Position (TP) sensor and electronic throttle control electrical connectors, **Fig. 3.**
6. Remove mounting bolts, nuts and throttle body.
7. Ensure anti-theft system is deactivated.
8. Raise and support vehicle.
9. Remove starter solenoid terminal cap.
10. Remove two terminal nuts and position wires aside.
11. Remove three mounting bolts and starter motor.
12. Disconnect lefthand Heated Oxygen Sensor (HO2S) electrical connector and wiring harness retainer.
13. Remove two righthand catalytic converter to exhaust manifold nuts, **Fig. 7.**
14. Remove two lefthand catalytic

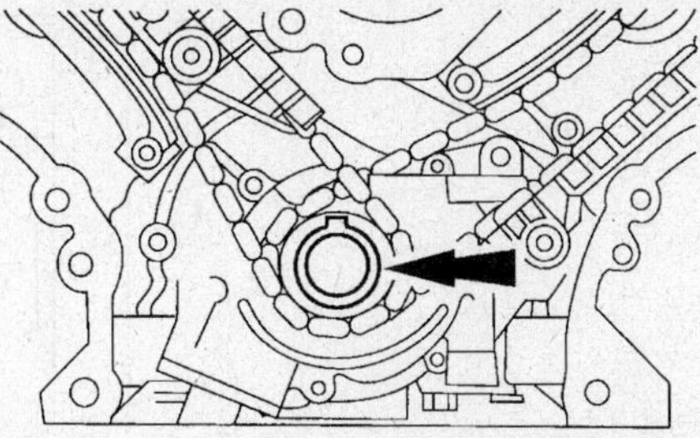

Fig. 9 Crankshaft keyway 12 o'clock position

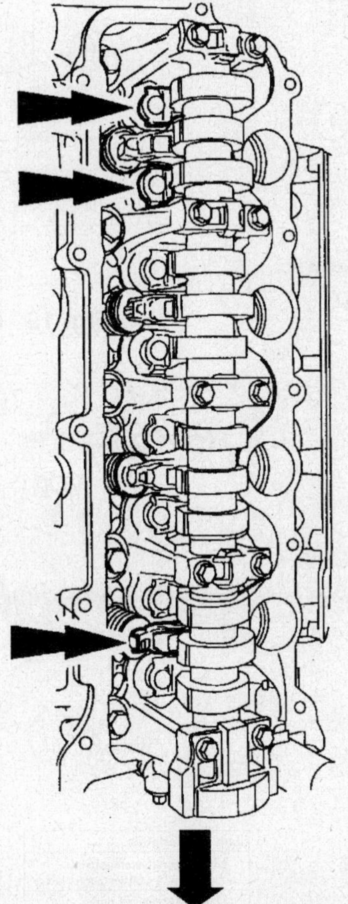

Fig. 11 Lefthand & righthand roller follower removal

converter-to-exhaust manifold nuts.

15. Remove six pin-type retainers and radiator sight shield, **Fig. 5.**
16. Remove two outer bracket mounting bolts and two lower mounting nuts, then disconnect alternator electrical connector and pin-type retainer.
17. Position cover aside, then remove B+ terminal nut and alternator.
18. Support engine using suitable engine lifting brackets and three-bar engine support tools.
19. Remove lefthand and righthand engine support insulator nuts.
20. Raise engine approximately 1.57 inches.

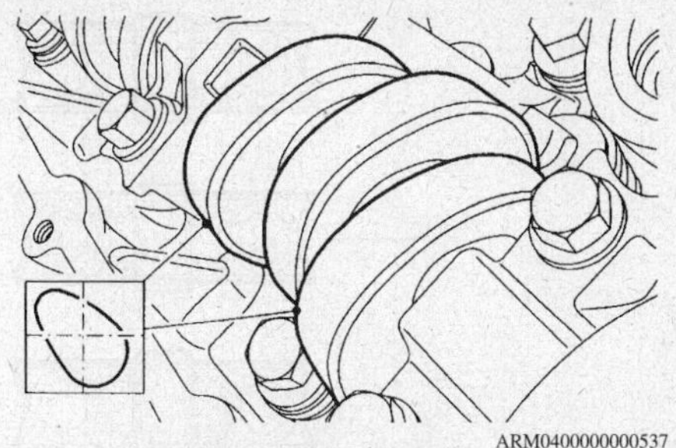

Fig. 10 Camshaft lobe positioning

21. Remove nut and ground wire from stud bolt.
22. **On models equipped with automatic transmission,** remove mounting nut and position transmission cooler tube bracket aside.
23. **On all models,** remove two bolts, two stud bolts and righthand engine support insulator bracket.
24. Remove eight nuts, exhaust manifold and gasket.
25. Reverse procedure to install, noting the following:
    a. Install new exhaust manifold gaskets.
    b. Tighten exhaust manifold mounting nuts in sequence, **Fig. 8.**

CYLINDER HEAD

REPLACE

1. Remove engine as outlined under "Engine, Replace."
2. Mount the engine on suitable work stand and remove special tools.
3. Disconnect lefthand and righthand Camshaft Position (CMP) sensor electrical connectors.
4. Disconnect lefthand and righthand Variable Camshaft Timing (VCT) solenoid electrical connectors.
5. Disconnect engine wiring harness pin-type retainers.
6. Remove mounting nut and righthand radio ignition interference capacitor.
7. Remove Positive Crankcase Ventilation (PCV) tubes from lefthand and righthand valve covers.
8. Disconnect ignition coils' electrical connectors.
9. Disconnect two engine wiring harness retainers from righthand and lefthand valve cover studs.
10. Disconnect engine wiring harness pin-type retainers.
11. Disconnect Cylinder Head Temperature (CHT) sensor electrical connector and jumper harness electrical connector pin-type retainer.
12. Disconnect Knock Sensor (KS) electrical connector and pin-type retainer.
13. Disconnect lefthand Heated Oxygen Sensor (HO2S) electrical connector.
14. Disconnect engine wiring harness retainer from stud bolt.
15. Disconnect engine oil pressure sensor electrical connector.
16. Remove engine wiring harness.
17. Remove oil filter.

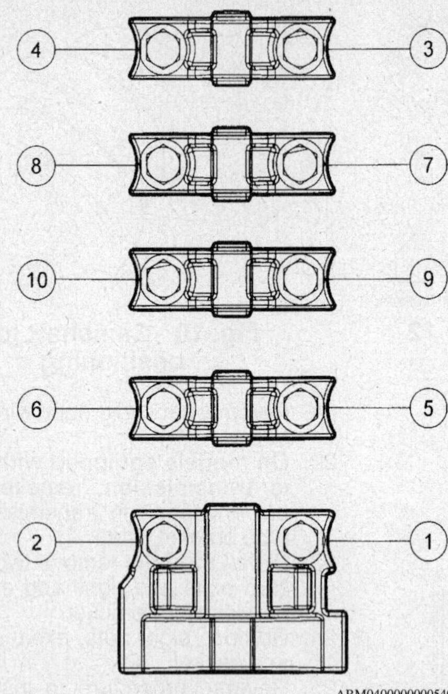

Fig. 12 Camshaft bearing cap removal sequence

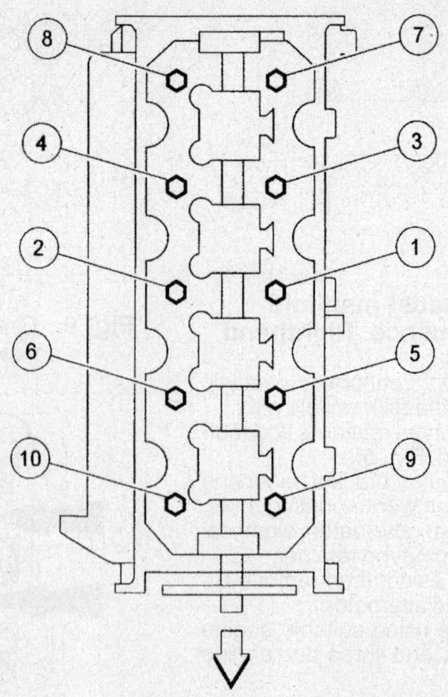

Fig. 13 Cylinder head tightening sequence

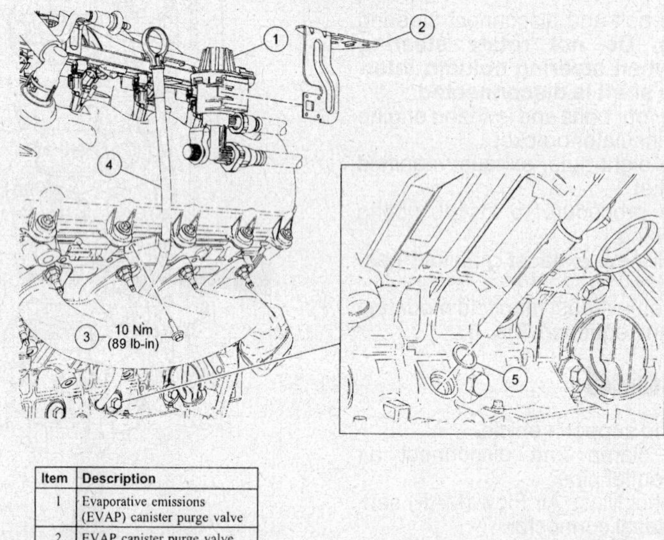

Item	Description
1	Evaporative emissions (EVAP) canister purge valve
2	EVAP canister purge valve bracket
3	Oil level indicator and tube bolt
4	Oil level indicator and tube
5	O-ring seal

ARM0400000000501

Fig. 14 Oil Dipstick tube replacement

18. Remove mounting bolt and oil dipstick tube.
19. Remove mounting bolts, then the lefthand and righthand CMP sensors.
20. Remove eight mounting bolts and ignition coils.
21. Loosen 29 mountings bolts and valve covers. **Mounting bolts are part of valve cover and should not be removed.**
22. Remove five mounting bolts, water pump pulley and righthand side accessory drive belt idler pulley.
23. Remove crankshaft pulley mounting bolt and washer.
24. Remove crankshaft pulley using suitable three-jaw puller tool.
25. Remove four oil pan-to-engine front cover mounting bolts.
26. Record front cover mounting bolt locations for installation alignment.
27. Remove mounting bolts and front cover.
28. Remove crankshaft sensor ring.
29. Position crankshaft keyway at 12 o'clock position, **Fig. 9,** noting the following:
    a. If camshaft lobes are not exactly positioned, **Fig. 10,** crankshaft will require one full additional rotation to 12 o'clock position.
    b. Cylinder No. 1 camshaft exhaust lobe must be coming up on exhaust stroke.
    c. Ensure positioning of two intake lobes and exhaust lobe on cylinder No. 1.
30. Mark components for installation into original locations.
31. Remove three roller followers from lefthand and righthand cylinder heads using valve spring compressor tool No. 303-1039, or equivalent, **Fig. 11. Do not allow valve keepers to fall off valve or valve may drop into cylinder.**
32. Rotate crankshaft clockwise and position crankshaft keyway at 6 o'clock position. **Do not move crankshaft past 6 o'clock position.**
33. Remove mounting bolts, then the lefthand and righthand timing chain tensioners and tensioner arms.
34. Remove righthand timing chain from camshaft and crankshaft sprockets.
35. Remove lefthand timing chain from the camshaft and crankshaft sprockets.
36. Remove two mounting bolts and both timing chain guides.
37. Remove mounting bolts, then the lefthand and righthand camshaft phaser sprocket using camshaft phase locking tool No. 303-1046, or equivalent. **Only use hand tools.**
38. Mark camshaft bearing caps for installation original locations.
39. Remove camshaft bearing caps bolts in sequence, **Fig. 12.**
40. **Remove front thrust camshaft bearing cap straight upward from bearing towers.** Remove remaining bearing caps.

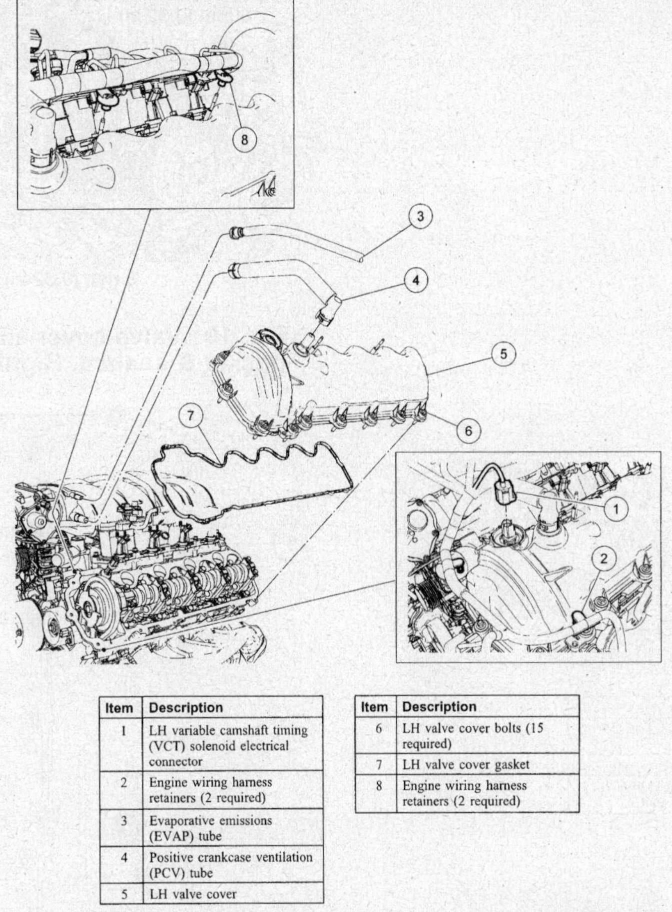

Item	Description
1	LH variable camshaft timing (VCT) solenoid electrical connector
2	Engine wiring harness retainers (2 required)
3	Evaporative emissions (EVAP) tube
4	Positive crankcase ventilation (PCV) tube
5	LH valve cover

Item	Description
6	LH valve cover bolts (15 required)
7	LH valve cover gasket
8	Engine wiring harness retainers (2 required)

Fig. 15 Valve cover replacement. Lefthand

41. Remove camshaft.
42. Mark components for installation into original locations.
43. Remove all remaining roller followers.
44. Remove hydraulic lash adjusters.
45. Install cylinder head remover/installer tool No. T97T-6000-A, or equivalent.
46. Remove eight mounting nuts and exhaust manifold.
47. Remove nut and ground strap from lefthand cylinder head stud bolt.
48. Remove stud bolt and coolant tube from righthand cylinder head.
49. Place suitable, clean shop towels over exposed engine cavities.
50. Remove 20 mounting bolts, cylinder heads and gaskets.
51. Reverse procedure to install, noting the following:
    a. **Ensure all coolant residue and foreign material are cleaned from block surface and cylinder bore.**
    b. **Do not use sealing aids (aviation cement, copper spray and glue).** Gasket must be installed dry.
    c. **Cylinder head bolts that are tighten-to-yield must be discarded and new bolts installed.**
    d. **Do not turn the crankshaft until instructed to do so.**
    e. Position cylinder head gaskets and cylinder heads over the dowels using cylinder head alignment pin tools No. SR-015486, or equivalent, and install cylinder head bolts loosely.
    f. **Torque** cylinder head bolts in sequence to 30 ft. lbs., **Fig. 13.**
    g. Tighten head bolts an additional 90° in sequence.
    h. Final tighten bolts an additional 90° in sequence.

VALVE COVER

REPLACE

Lefthand

1. Disconnect crankcase vent tube from air cleaner outlet pipe.
2. Loosen two clamps and remove air cleaner outlet pipe.
3. Disconnect ignition coil electrical connector.
4. Remove mounting bolts and ignition coil.
5. Raise and support vehicle.
6. Disconnect Evaporative Emissions (EVAP) canister purge valve from bracket and position it aside, **Fig. 14.**
7. Remove oil dipstick and tube mounting bolt.
8. Remove oil dipstick tube and O-ring.
9. Disconnect EVAP tube from Intake manifold, **Fig. 15.**

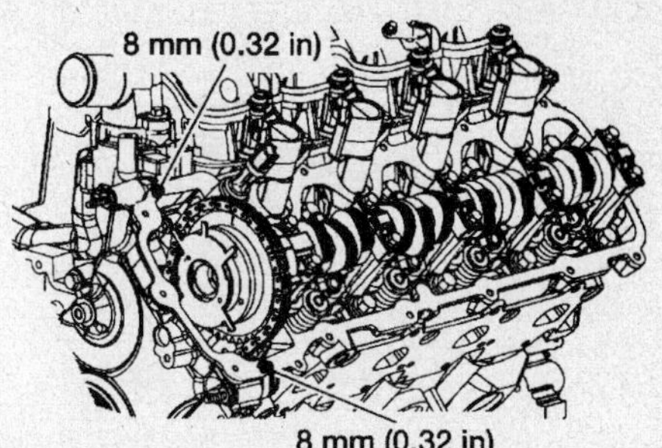

Fig. 16 Valve cover silicone gasket & sealant. Lefthand

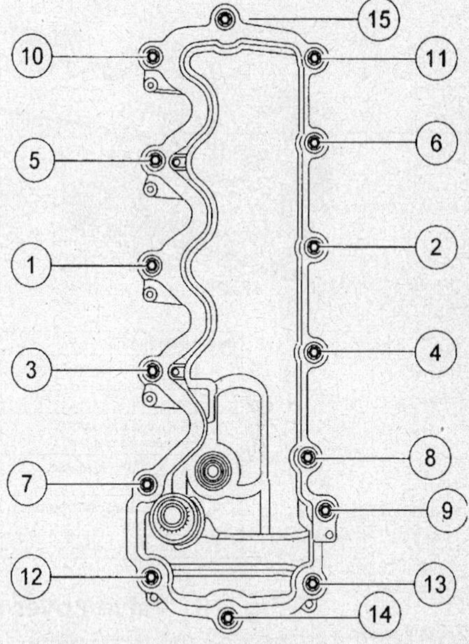

Fig. 17 Valve cover tightening sequence. Lefthand

10. Remove Positive Crankcase Ventilation (PCV) tube.
11. Disconnect Variable Camshaft Timing (VCT) solenoid electrical connector and two wiring harness pin-type retainers.
12. Disconnect two wiring harness retainers from valve cover stud bolts.
13. Loosen 15 mounting bolts, then remove valve cover and gasket. **Mounting bolts are part of valve cover and should not be removed.**
14. Clean cylinder head valve cover mating surfaces with suitable silicone gasket remover.
15. Clean valve cover gasket groove with soap and water, or suitable solvent.
16. Reverse procedure to install, noting the following:
    a. **Valve cover must be secured within four minutes of sealant application.**
    b. Apply .32 inch bead of suitable silicone gasket and sealant to where engine front cover meets cylinder head, **Fig. 16.**
    c. Tighten mounting bolts in sequence, **Fig. 17.**
    d. Lubricate new oil dipstick tube

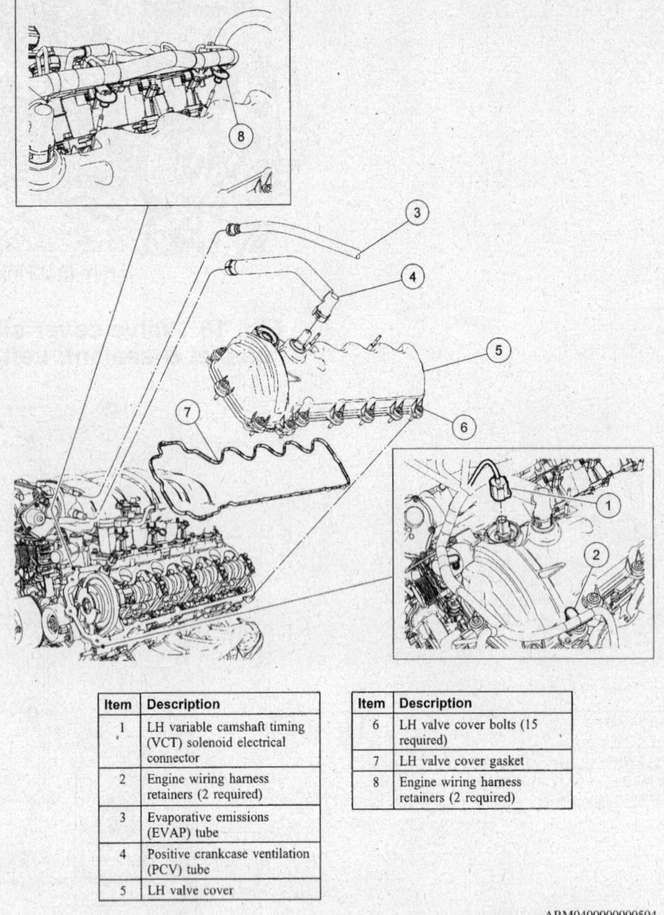

Item	Description
1	LH variable camshaft timing (VCT) solenoid electrical connector
2	Engine wiring harness retainers (2 required)
3	Evaporative emissions (EVAP) tube
4	Positive crankcase ventilation (PCV) tube
5	LH valve cover

Item	Description
6	LH valve cover bolts (15 required)
7	LH valve cover gasket
8	Engine wiring harness retainers (2 required)

ARM0400000000504

Fig. 18 Valve cover replacement. Righthand

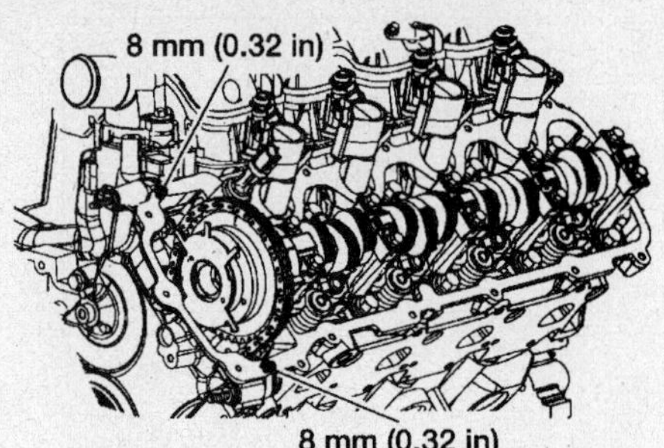

ARM0400000000505

Fig. 19 Valve cover silicone gasket & sealant. Righthand

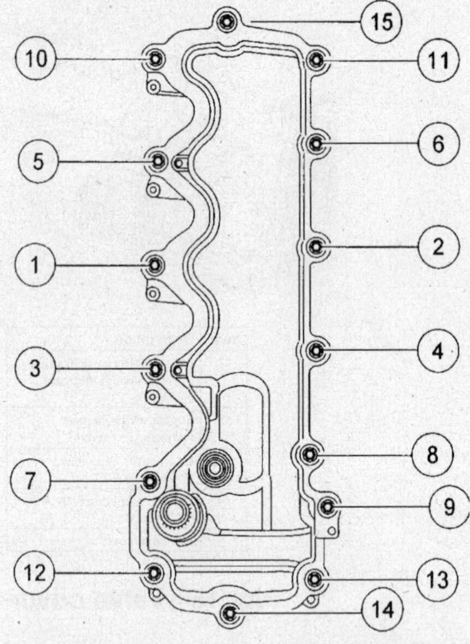

ARM0400000000506

Fig. 20 Valve cover tightening sequence. Righthand

O-ring seal with suitable, clean engine oil.

e. Apply light film of suitable silicone brake caliper great and dielectric compound to inside of coil boots.

Righthand

1. Disconnect ignition coil electrical connector.
2. Remove mounting bolts and ignition coil.
3. Disconnect two wiring harness retainers from valve cover stud bolts.
4. Disconnect Variable Camshaft Timing (VCT) solenoid electrical connector, **Fig. 18.**
5. Disconnect Positive Crankcase Ventilation (PCV) tube.
6. Disconnect four wiring harness retainers from valve cover stud bolts.
7. Loosen 14 mounting bolts, then remove valve cover and gasket. **Mounting bolts are part of valve cover and should not be removed.**
8. Clean cylinder head valve cover mating surfaces with suitable silicone gasket remover.
9. Clean valve cover gasket groove with soap and water, or suitable solvent.
10. Reverse procedure to install, noting the following:
    a. **Valve cover must be secured within four minutes of sealant application.**
    b. Apply .32 inch bead of suitable silicone gasket and sealant to where engine front cover meets cylinder head, **Fig. 19.**
    c. Tighten mounting bolts in sequence, **Fig. 20.**
    d. Apply light film of suitable silicone brake caliper great and dielectric compound to inside of coil boots.

CAMSHAFT LOBE LIFT SPECIFICATIONS

Engine	Intake, Inch	Exhaust, Inch
4.6L SOHC (VIN 8)	.217	.217

VALVE ADJUSTMENT

These engine are equipped with hydraulic valve lash adjusters. No valve adjustment is required.

HYDRAULIC LASH ADJUSTER

REPLACE

1. Remove camshafts as outlined under "Camshaft, Replace."
2. Rotate crankshaft until piston for valve being serviced is at top of stroke with intake and exhaust valves closed.
3. Compress spring and remove camshaft roller follower using valve spring compressor tool No. 303-1029, or equivalent.
4. Mark hydraulic lash adjusters for installation in original positions.
5. Remove hydraulic lash adjusters.
6. Reverse procedure to install.

CRANKSHAFT DAMPER

REPLACE

1. Raise and support vehicle.
2. Disconnect crankcase vent tube from air cleaner outlet pipe.
3. Loosen two clamps and remove air cleaner outlet pipe.
4. Rotate accessory drive belt tensioner clockwise with suitable belt tensioner release tool and remove belt.
5. Remove crankshaft pulley mounting bolt and washer.
6. Remove crankshaft pulley using suitable three-jaw puller tool.
7. Reverse procedure to install, noting the following:

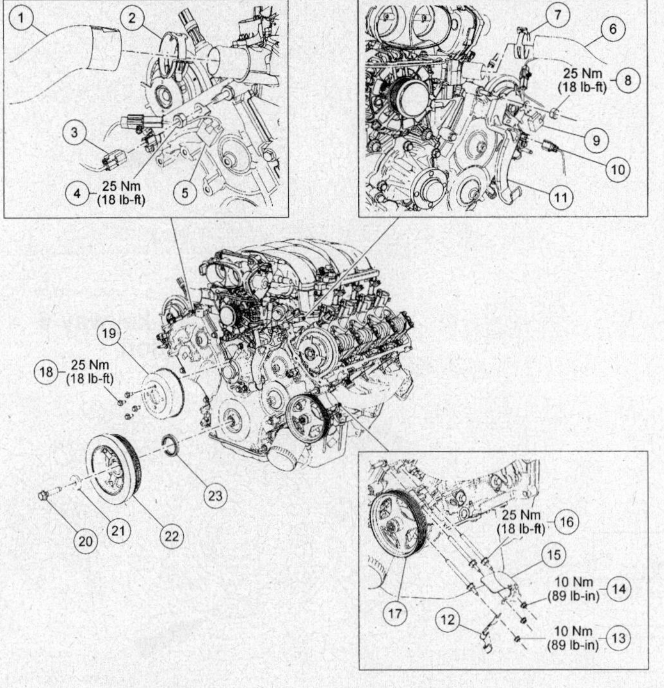

Item	Description
1	Coolant hose
2	Hose clamp
3	RH camshaft position (CMP) sensor electrical connector
4	RH radio ignition interference capacitor nut
5	RH radio ignition interference capacitor
6	Coolant hose

Item	Description
7	Hose clamp
8	LH radio ignition interference capacitor nut
9	LH radio ignition interference capacitor
10	LH CMP sensor electrical connector
11	J-bracket
12	Power steering tube retaining clip

ARM0400000000510

Fig. 21 Front cover replacement (Part 1 of 3)

Item	Description
13	Power steering tube retaining clip nut
14	Power steering pulley shield nut (2 required)
15	Power steering pulley shield
16	Power steering pump stud bolt (3 required)
17	Power steering pump

Item	Description
18	Coolant pump pulley bolts (4 required)
19	Coolant pump pulley
20	Crankshaft pulley bolt
21	Crankshaft pulley bolt washer
22	Crankshaft pulley
23	Crankshaft front oil seal

ARM0400000000511

Fig. 21 Front cover replacement (Part 2 of 3)

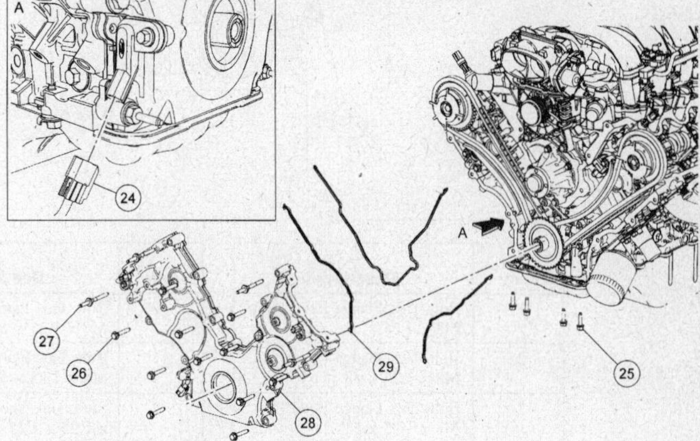

Item	Description
24	Crankshaft position (CKP) sensor electrical connector
25	Oil pan bolts (4 required)
26	Engine front cover bolts (11 required)
27	Engine front cover studs (4 required)
28	Engine front cover
29	Engine front cover gaskets (3 required)

ARM0400000000512

Fig. 21 Front cover replacement (Part 3 of 3)

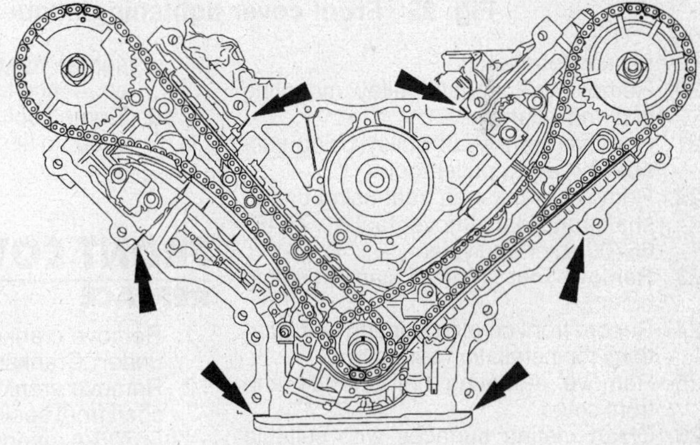

ARM0400000000515

Fig. 22 Front cover sealing

a. **Pulley must be secured within four minutes of sealant application.**
b. Apply suitable silicone gasket and sealant to crankshaft pulley Woodruff key slot.
c. Install crankshaft pulley using crankshaft vibration damper installer tool No. T74P-6316-B, or equivalent.
d. **Torque** next crankshaft pulley bolt to 66 ft. lbs.
e. Loosen crankshaft pulley bolt 360°.
f. **Torque** pulley bolt to 37 ft. lbs.
g. Tighten bolt an additional 90°.

FRONT COVER

REPLACE

1. Raise and support vehicle.
2. Drain engine oil into suitable container.
3. Drain engine coolant into suitable container.
4. Disconnect, then position upper and lower degas bottle hoses aside.
5. Remove two mounting bolts and degas bottle.
6. Rotate accessory drive belt tensioner clockwise with suitable belt tensioner release tool and remove belt.
7. Remove mounting bolt and righthand belt idler pulley.
8. Remove valve covers as outlined under "Valve Cover, Replace."
9. Disconnect two coolant hoses from crossover, **Fig. 21.**
10. Remove mounting nut and position righthand radio ignition interference capacitor aside.
11. Disconnect righthand Camshaft Position (CMP) sensor electrical connector.
12. Remove mounting nut and position lefthand radio ignition interference capacitor aside.
13. Remove J bracket from engine front cover stud bolt.
14. Disconnect lefthand CMP sensor electrical connector.
15. Remover four mounting bolts and water pump pulley.
16. Remove two mounting nuts and power steering pulley shield.
17. Remove wiring harness, retainer, nut and tube clip from power steering stud bolt.
18. Remove three stud bolts and support power steering pump aside.
19. Disconnect Crankshaft Position (CKP)

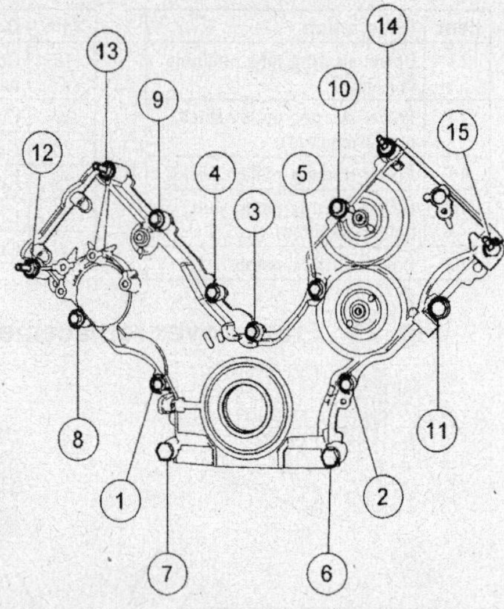

Item	Description
1	Bolt, Hex Flange Head Pilot, M8 x 1.25 x 53
2	Bolt, Hex Flange Head Pilot, M8 x 1.25 x 53
3	Bolt, Hex Flange Head Pilot, M8 x 1.25 x 53
4	Bolt, Hex Flange Head Pilot, M8 x 1.25 x 53
5	Bolt, Hex Flange Head Pilot, M8 x 1.25 x 53
6	Bolt, Hex Flange Head Pilot, M8 x 1.25 x 53
7	Bolt, Hex Flange Head Pilot, M8 x 1.25 x 53
8	Bolt, Hex Flange Head Pilot, M8 x 1.25 x 53
9	Bolt, Hex Flange Head Pilot, M8 x 1.25 x 53

Item	Description
10	Bolt, Hex Flange Head Pilot, M8 x 1.25 x 53
11	Bolt, Hex Flange Head Pilot, M8 x 1.25 x 53
12	Stud, Hex Shoulder Pilot, M8 x 1.25 x 1.25 x 91.1
13	Stud, Hex Shoulder Pilot, M8 x 1.25 x 1.25 x 91.1
14	Stud, Hex Shoulder Pilot, M8 x 1.25 x 1.25 x 91.1
15	Stud, Hex Shoulder Pilot, M8 x 1.25 x 1.25 x 91.1

ARM0400000000516

Fig. 23 Front cover tightening sequence

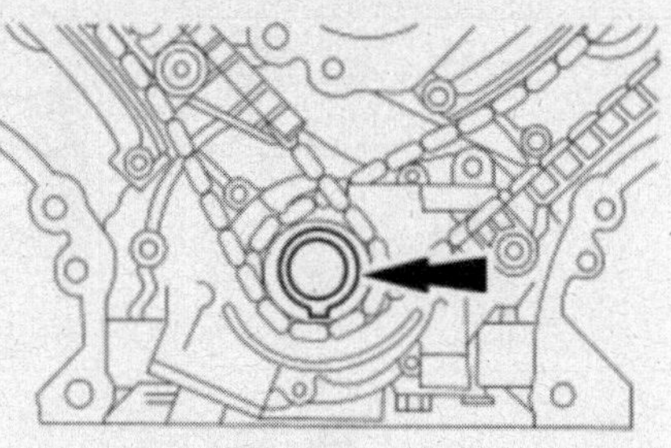

ARM0400000000542

Fig. 24 Crankshaft keyway 6 o'clock position

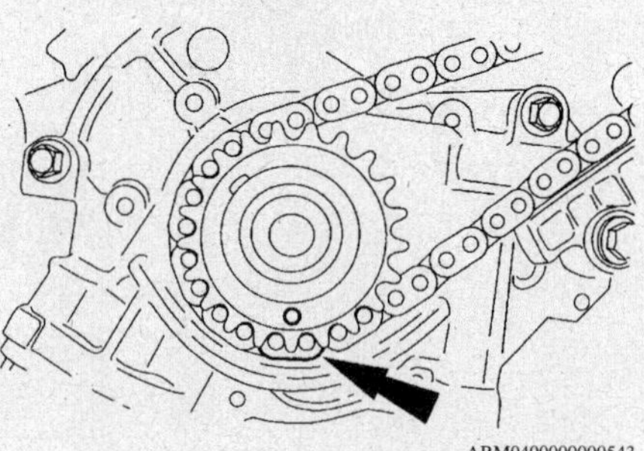

ARM0400000000543

Fig. 25 Lefthand timing chain & crankshaft sprocket alignment

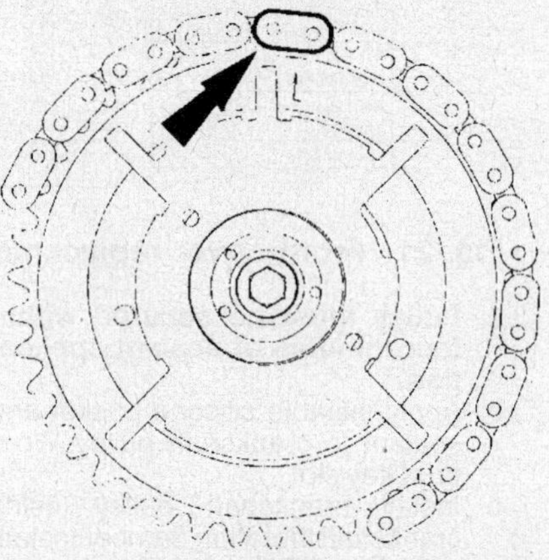

ARM0400000000544

Fig. 26 Lefthand timing chain & camshaft sprocket alignment

sensor connector.

20. Remove crankshaft pulley mounting bolt and washer.
21. Remove crankshaft pulley using suitable three-jaw puller tool.
22. Remove crankshaft seal using crankshaft front seal remover tool No. T74P-66700-A, or equivalent.
23. Remove four front oil pan mounting bolts.
24. Record front cover mounting bolt locations for installation alignment.
25. Remove mounting bolts, studs and front cover.
26. Clean mating surfaces with suitable silicone gasket remover.
27. Reverse procedure to install, noting the following:
    a. **Front cover must be secured within four minutes of sealant application.**
    b. Apply silicone gasket and sealant along cylinder head-to-cylinder block and oil pan-to-cylinder block surfaces, **Fig. 22.**
    c. Install new front cover gasket and tighten mounting bolts and studs in sequence to 15 ft. lbs., **Fig. 23.**
    d. Tighten bolts and studs an additional 60° in sequence.

FRONT COVER SEAL

REPLACE

1. Remove crankshaft pulley as outlined under "Crankshaft Damper, Replace."
2. Remove crankshaft seal using crankshaft front seal remover tool No. T74P-66700-A, or equivalent.
3. Reverse procedure to install, noting the following:
    a. Lubricate engine front cover and crankshaft front seal inner lip with suitable, clean engine oil.
    b. Install seal using crankshaft front seal installer tool No. 303-635, front cover seal installer tool No. T88T-6701-A and crankshaft vibration damper installer tool No. T74P-6316-B, or equivalents.

TIMING CHAIN

REPLACE

These engines have an interference fit design. If engine has jumped time cylinder heads must be removed to repair damage to valves and/or pistons.

At no time, when the timing chains are removed and the cylinder heads are installed, may the crankshaft and/or camshaft be rotated unless all rocker arms have been removed. Rotation may result in valve and/or piston damage.

Before loosening or tightening camshaft sprocket nuts and bolts, ensure camshaft positioning and locking devices are in place.

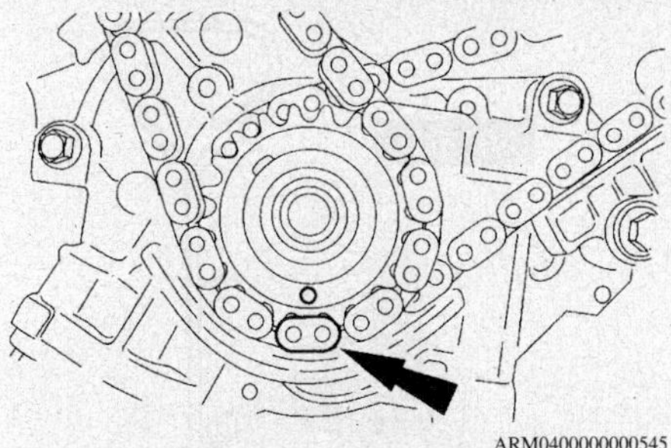

Fig. 27 Righthand timing chain & crankshaft sprocket alignment

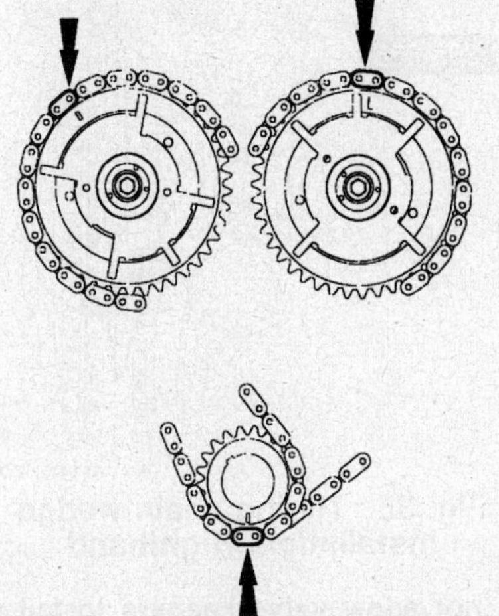

Fig. 30 Lefthand camshaft lobe positioning

Installation

1. Install camshafts as outlined under "Camshaft, Replace."
2. Install camshaft phaser sprockets and new mounting bolts finger tight.
3. **Torque** camshaft phaser sprocket bolts using camshaft phase locking tool No. 303-1046, or equivalent. to 30 ft. lbs. **Only use hand tools.**
4. Tighten sprocket bolts an additional 90°.
5. Install crankshaft sprocket, making sure the flange faces forward.
6. Rotate crankshaft to position crankshaft sprocket timing mark in 6 o'clock position, **Fig. 24.**
7. Compress tensioner plunger, using suitable vise.
8. Install suitable retaining clip to hold plunger in place.
9. If copper chain links are not visible, mark one link on one end and one link on other end and use as timing marks.
10. Install timing chain guides and four mounting bolts.
11. Position lower end of lefthand (inner) timing chain on crankshaft sprocket, aligning timing mark on outer flange of crankshaft sprocket with single copper (marked) link on chain, **Fig. 25.**
12. Ensure upper half of timing chain is below tensioner arm dowel.
13. Position lefthand timing chain on camshaft sprocket. Ensure camshaft sprocket timing mark is aligned with

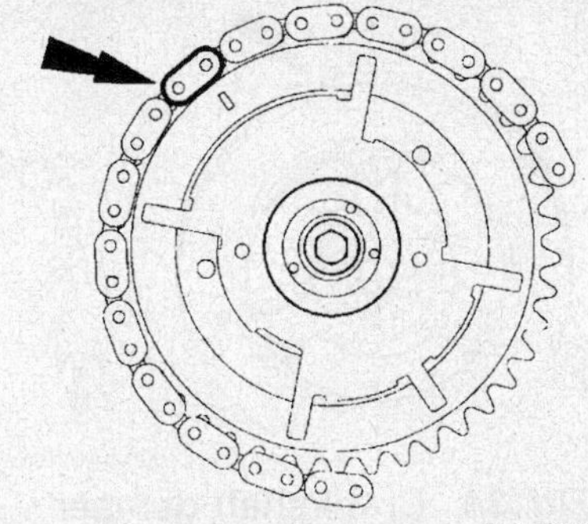

Fig. 28 Righthand timing chain & camshaft sprocket alignment

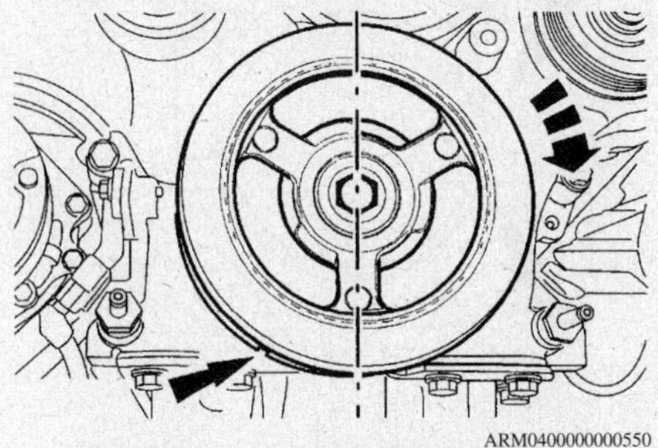

Fig. 31 Crankshaft damper position 6 o'clock position

copper (marked) chain link, **Fig. 26.**

14. Position lefthand timing chain tensioner arm on dowel pin, then install lefthand timing chain tensioner and mounting bolts. Lefthand timing chain tensioner arm has bump near dowel hole for identification.
15. Remove retaining clip from lefthand timing chain tensioner.
16. Position lower end of righthand (outer) timing chain on crankshaft sprocket, aligning timing mark on sprocket with single copper (marked) chain link, **Fig. 27.**
17. Lower half of timing chain must be positioned above tensioner arm dowel.
18. Position righthand timing chain on camshaft sprocket. Ensure camshaft sprocket timing mark is aligned with copper (marked) chain link, **Fig. 28.**
19. Position righthand timing chain tensioner arm on dowel pin, then install righthand timing chain tensioner and mounting bolts.
20. Remove retaining clip from righthand timing chain tensioner.
21. Righthand and lefthand camshaft phaser sprockets are similar. Righthand camshaft phaser sprocket has single timing mark to identify, while L timing mark identifies lefthand camshaft phaser sprocket. Ensure timing marks on sprockets align, **Fig. 29.**
22. Install crankshaft sensor ring.
23. Lubricate roller followers with suitable, clean engine oil.
24. Rotate engine to position camshaft lobes at base circle and install all camshaft roller followers.
25. Install engine front cover as outlined under "Front Cover, Replace."

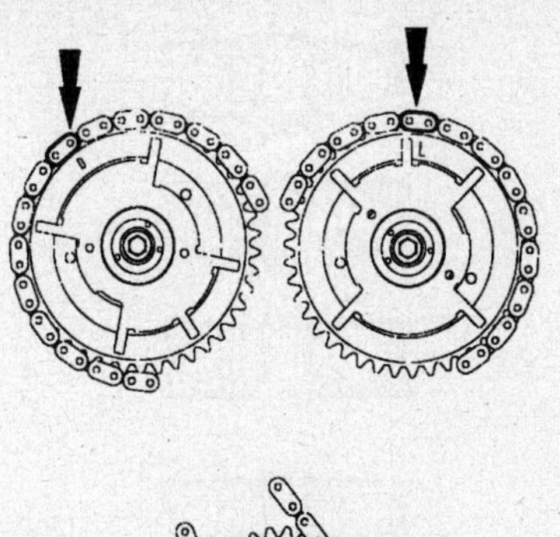

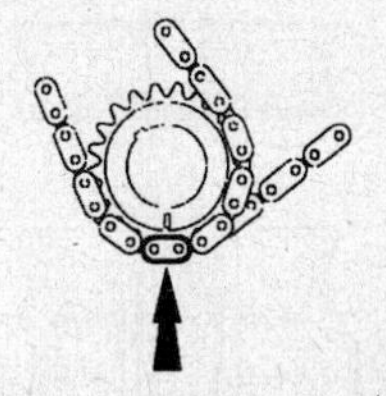

Fig. 29 Timing chain alignment

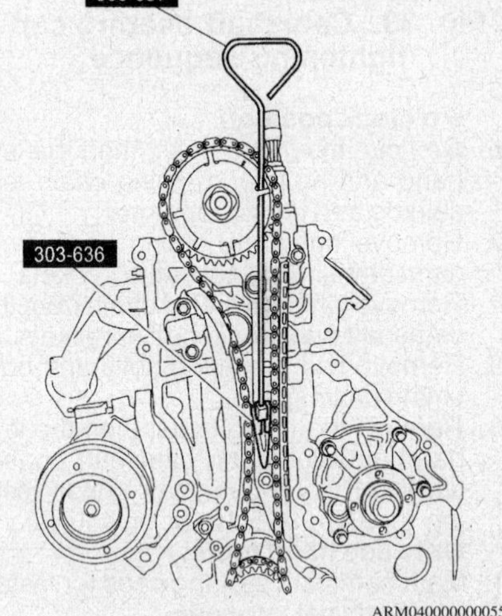

Fig. 32 Timing chain wedge installation. Lefthand

Removal

1. Remove engine front cover as outlined under "Front Cover, Replace."
2. Remove crankshaft sensor ring.
3. Position crankshaft keyway at 12 o'clock position, **Fig. 9,** noting the following:
   a. If camshaft lobes are not exactly positioned, **Fig. 10,** crankshaft will require one full additional rotation to 12 o'clock position.
   b. Cylinder No. 1 camshaft exhaust lobe must be coming up on exhaust stroke.
   c. Ensure positioning of two intake lobes and exhaust lobe on cylinder No. 1.
4. Remove three roller followers from lefthand and righthand cylinder heads using valve spring compressor tool No. 303-1039, or equivalent, **Fig. 11. Do not allow valve keepers to fall off valve or valve may drop into cylinder.**
5. Rotate crankshaft clockwise and position crankshaft keyway at 6 o'clock position. **Do not move crankshaft past**

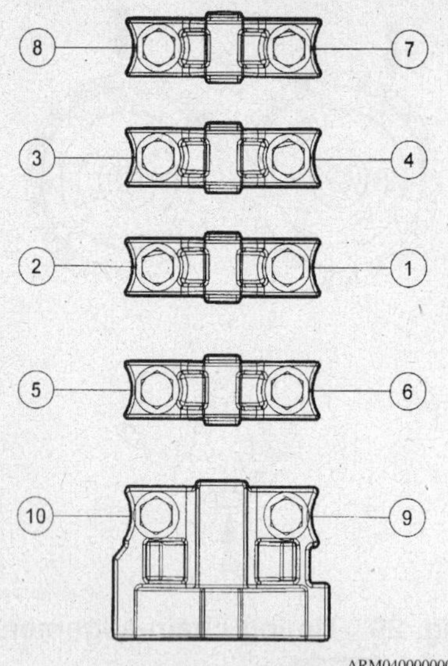

Fig. 33 Camshaft bearing cap tightening sequence

6 o'clock position.

6. Remove mounting bolts, then the lefthand and righthand timing chain tensioners and tensioner arms.
7. Remove righthand timing chain from camshaft and crankshaft sprockets.
8. Remove lefthand timing chain from the camshaft and crankshaft sprockets.
9. Remove two mounting bolts and both timing chain guides.
10. Remove mounting bolts, then the lefthand and righthand camshaft phaser sprocket using camshaft phase locking tool No. 303-1046, or equivalent. **Only use hand tools.**
11. Mark camshaft bearing caps for installation original locations.
12. Remove camshaft bearing caps bolts in sequence, **Fig. 12.**
13. **Remove front thrust camshaft bearing cap straight upward from bearing towers.** Remove remaining bearing caps.
14. Mark components for installation into original locations.
15. Remove all remaining roller followers.

CAMSHAFT

REPLACE

These engines have an interference fit design. If engine has jumped time cylinder heads must be removed to repair damage to valves and/or pistons.

At no time, when the timing chains are removed and the cylinder heads are installed, may the crankshaft and/or camshaft be rotated unless all rocker arms have been removed. Rotation may result in valve and/or piston damage.

Before loosening or tightening camshaft sprocket nuts and bolts, ensure camshaft positioning and locking devices are in place.

If removing both camshafts, righthand camshaft must be removed first.

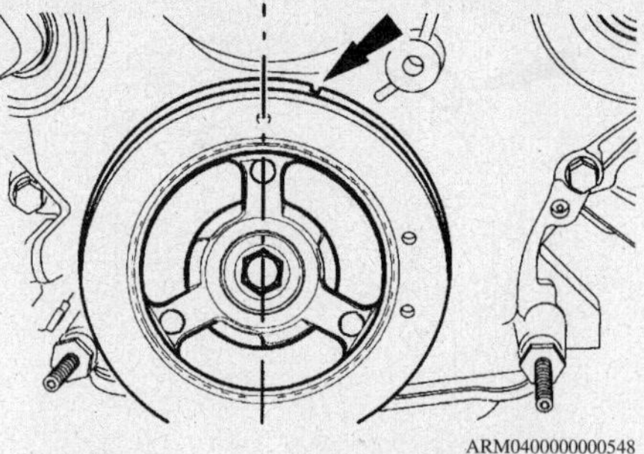

Fig. 34 Crankshaft damper position 12 o'clock position

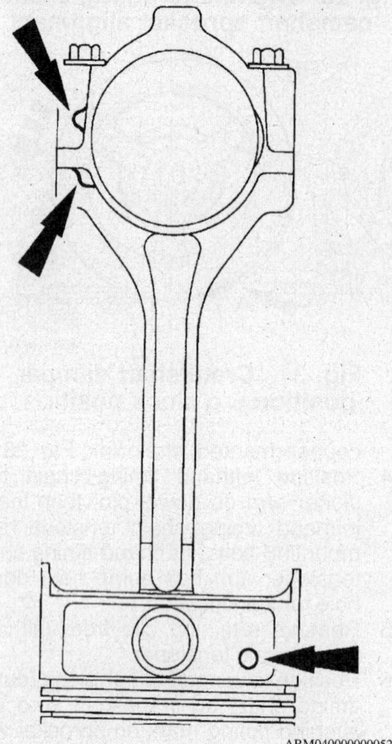

Fig. 36 Piston & connecting rod

Lefthand

1. Position crankshaft damper spoke at 12 o'clock position and timing mark indentation at 1 o'clock position, **Fig. 34.**
2. Remove lefthand valve cover as outlined under "Valve Cover, Replace."
3. Loosen and back off lefthand camshaft phaser bolt one full turn.
4. Disconnect lefthand Camshaft Position (CMP) sensor electrical connector.
5. Remove mounting bolt and lefthand CMP sensor.
6. If camshaft lobes are not exactly positioned, **Fig. 30,** crankshaft keyway will require one full additional rotation to 12 o'clock position.
7. Cylinder No. 5 cylinder must be coming up on exhaust stroke.
8. Ensure positioning of two intake lobes and exhaust lobe on cylinder No. 5.
9. Remove three roller followers from lefthand and lefthand cylinder heads using valve spring compressor tool No. 303-1039, or equivalent, **Fig. 11. Do not allow valve keepers to fall off valve or valve may drop into cylinder.**

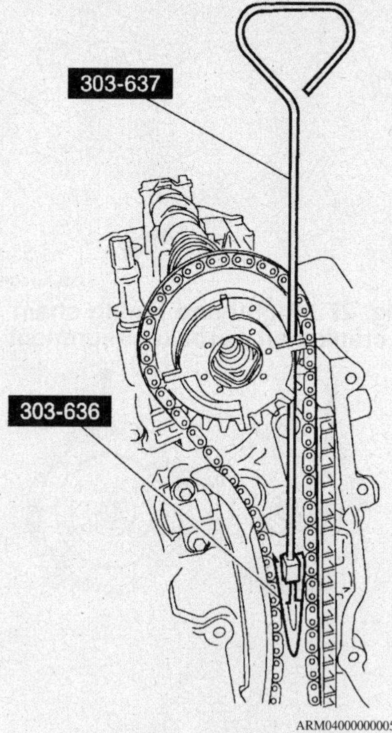

Fig. 35 Timing chain wedge installation. Righthand

10. Rotate crankshaft clockwise, as viewed from front, positioning crankshaft damper spoke at 6 o'clock position and timing mark indentation at 7 o'clock position, **Fig. 31. Crankshaft cannot be moved past 6 o'clock position once set.**
11. Install timing chain wedge tool No. 303-636 and handle tool No. 303-637, or equivalents, square to timing chain and engine block, **Fig. 32.**
12. **If timing chain wedge is removed or out of placement, engine front cover must be removed and engine must be timed.**
13. Mark timing chain and camshaft phaser sprocket for installation alignment.
14. Mark camshaft bearing caps for installation original locations.
15. Remove camshaft bearing caps bolts in sequence, **Fig. 12.**
16. **Remove front thrust camshaft bearing cap straight upward from bearing towers.** Remove remaining bearing caps.
17. Remove mounting bolt and withdraw camshaft from phaser sprocket leaving sprocket in place.
18. Reverse procedure to install, noting the following:
    a. Lubricate camshaft and camshaft journals with suitable, clean engine oil.
    b. Ensure camshaft phaser sprocket and timing chain scribe marks are still in alignment.
    c. **Do not allow roller followers to**

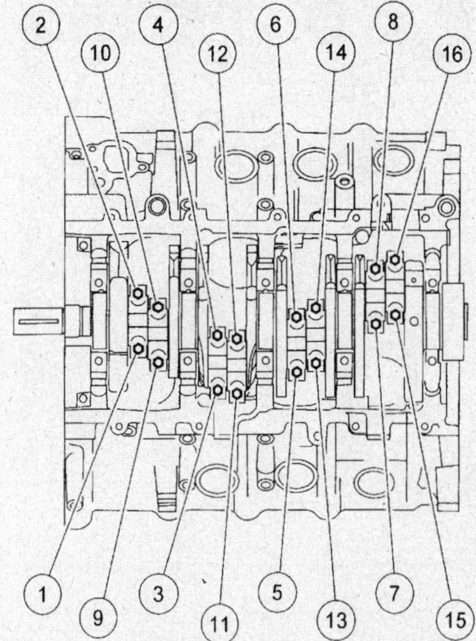

Fig. 37 Connecting rod bearing tightening sequence

move out of position when installing camshaft.

d. Install camshaft bearing caps in original locations.
e. Lubricate camshaft bearing caps with suitable, clean engine oil.
f. Position front camshaft bearing cap.
g. Position remaining camshaft bearing caps.
h. Install mounting bolts loosely.
i. Tighten mounting bolts in sequence, **Fig. 33.**
j. Remove special tools.

Righthand

1. Position crankshaft damper spoke at 12 o'clock position and timing mark indentation at 1 o'clock position, **Fig. 34.**
2. Remove righthand valve cover as outlined under "Valve Cover, Replace."
3. Loosen and back off righthand camshaft phaser bolt one full turn.
4. Disconnect righthand Camshaft Position (CMP) sensor electrical connector.
5. Remove mounting bolt and righthand CMP sensor.
6. If camshaft lobes are not exactly positioned, **Fig. 10,** crankshaft will require one full additional rotation to 12 o'clock position.
7. Cylinder No. 1 camshaft exhaust lobe must be coming up on exhaust stroke.
8. Ensure positioning of two intake lobes and exhaust lobe on cylinder No. 1.
9. Remove three roller followers from lefthand and righthand cylinder heads using valve spring compressor tool No.

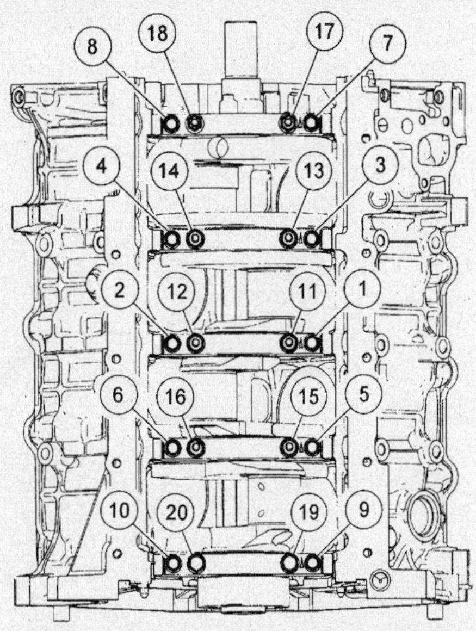

Fig. 38 Vertical main bearing cap tightening sequence

303-1039, or equivalent, **Fig. 11. Do not allow valve keepers to fall off valve or valve may drop into cylinder.**

10. Rotate crankshaft clockwise, as viewed from front, positioning crankshaft damper spoke at 6 o'clock position and timing mark indentation at 7 o'clock position, **Fig. 31. Crankshaft cannot be moved past 6 o'clock position once set.**
11. Install timing chain wedge tool No. 303-636 and handle tool No. 303-637, or equivalents, square to timing chain and engine block, **Fig. 35.**
12. **If timing chain wedge is removed or out of placement, engine front cover must be removed and engine must be timed.**
13. Mark timing chain and camshaft phaser sprocket for installation alignment.
14. Mark camshaft bearing caps for installation original locations.
15. Remove camshaft bearing caps bolts in sequence, **Fig. 12.**
16. **Remove front thrust camshaft bearing cap straight upward from bearing towers.** Remove remaining bearing caps.
17. Remove mounting bolt and withdraw camshaft from phaser sprocket leaving sprocket in place.
18. Reverse procedure to install, noting the following:
    a. Lubricate camshaft and camshaft journals with suitable, clean engine oil.
    b. Ensure camshaft phaser sprocket and timing chain scribe marks are still in alignment.
    c. **Do not allow roller followers to**

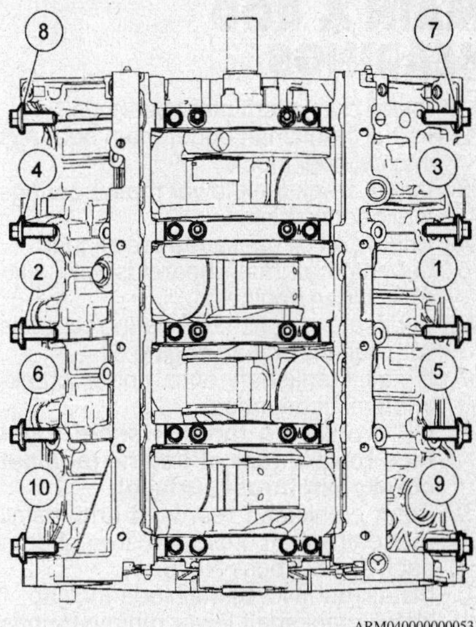

Fig. 39 Cross-mounted main bearing cap tightening sequence

move out of position when installing camshaft.

d. Install camshaft bearing caps in original locations.
e. Lubricate camshaft bearing caps with suitable, clean engine oil.
f. Position front camshaft bearing cap.
g. Position remaining camshaft bearing caps.
h. Install mounting bolts loosely.
i. Tighten mounting bolts in sequence, **Fig. 33.**
j. Remove special tools.

PISTON & ROD ASSEMBLY

The connecting rod must be installed into the connecting rod with identification markings toward the front, **Fig. 36.**

1. Lubricate piston and ring with suitable, clean engine oil.
2. Lubricate rod bearings with suitable, clean engine oil.
3. Install piston and connecting rod with upper connecting rod bearing in place using suitable piston ring compressor tool and connecting rod installer tools No. T93P-6136-A, or equivalent.
4. Once connecting rod is seated on crankshaft journal, remove special tools.
5. **The rod cap must be in same orientation as marked during disassembly.**
6. Position lower bearing and connecting rod , then install new bolts loosely.
7. **Torque** connecting rod bolts in sequence to 32 ft. lbs., **Fig. 37.**
8. Tighten bolts and additional 105° in sequence.

MAIN & ROD BEARINGS

1. Install crankshaft main bearings.
2. Install crankshaft upper main bearings into cylinder block.
3. Install crankshaft lower main bearings into bearing caps.
4. Ensure all oil passages are aligned.
5. Lubricate all main bearings with suitable, clean engine oil.
6. Lubricate crankshaft bearing journals with suitable, clean engine oil.
7. Install crankshaft onto upper crankshaft main bearings.
8. **Oil groove on thrust washer must face toward rear of engine (against crankshaft thrust surface).**
9. Push crankshaft rearward and install rear crankshaft upper thrust washer at back of main boss No. 5.
10. Install rear (No. 5) main bearing cap.
11. Install crankshaft lower main bearings into main bearing caps and lubricate them with suitable, clean engine oil.
12. Locate main bearing cap on cylinder block and, keeping cap as square as possible, alternately draw cap down evenly using cap fasteners.
13. Push crankshaft forward to seat crankshaft thrust washer. Hold crankshaft in forward position.
14. Install vertical main bearing cap nuts and bolts, then tighten in sequence, **Fig. 38.**
15. **Torque** 1–20 in sequence to 89 inch lbs.
16. **Torque** 1–10 in sequence to 18 ft. lbs.
17. **Torque** 11–20 in sequence to 30 ft. lbs.
18. Tighten 1–20 an additional 90° in sequence.
19. Install cross-mounted main bearing cap bolts and tighten in sequence, **Fig. 39.**
20. **Torque** in sequence to 30 ft. lbs.
21. Tighten an additional 90° in sequence.
22. Inspect crankshaft end play.
23. Ensure crankshaft torque-to-turn does not exceed 53 inch lbs.

CRANKSHAFT SEAL

REPLACE

1. Remove crankshaft pulley as outlined under "Crankshaft Damper, Replace."
2. Remove crankshaft seal using crankshaft front seal remover tool No. T74P-66700-A, or equivalent, **Fig. 40.**
3. Reverse procedure to install, noting the following:
   a. Lubricate engine front cover and crankshaft front seal inner lip with suitable, clean engine oil.
   b. Install seal using crankshaft front seal installer tool No. 303-635, front cover seal installer tool No. T88T-6701-A and crankshaft vibration damper installer tool No. T74P-6316-B, or equivalents.

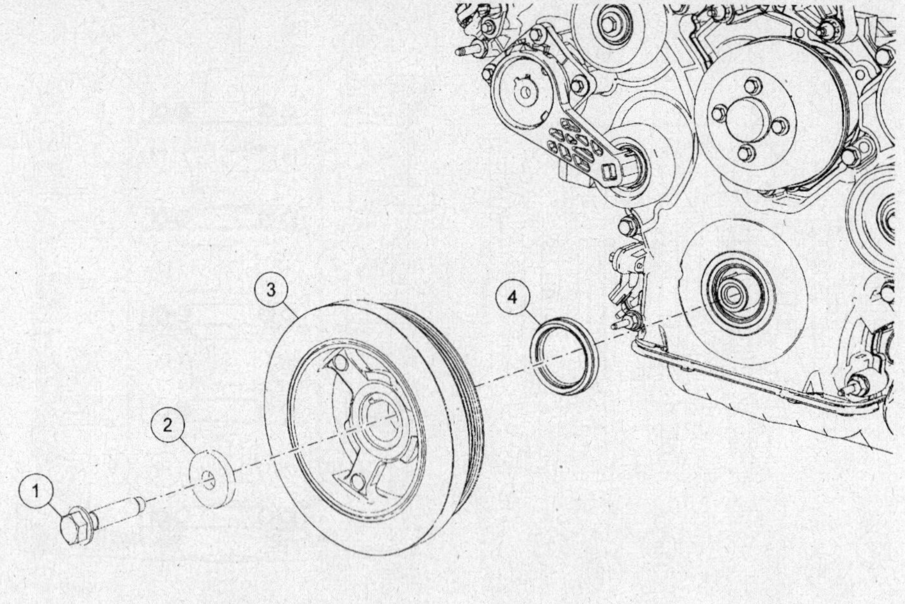

Item	Description
1	Crankshaft pulley bolt
2	Crankshaft pulley bolt washer
3	Crankshaft pulley
4	Crankshaft front oil seal

ARM0400000000513

Fig. 40 Front crankshaft seal replacement

CRANKSHAFT REAR OIL SEAL

REPLACE

1. Remove automatic transmission or manual transmission and clutch as outlined in **MOTOR's "Domestic Transmission, In-Vehicle Service" or "Transmission Service DVD."**
2. Remove six mounting bolts and flywheel/flexplate, **Fig. 41.**
3. Remove engine-to-transmission spacer plate.
4. Remove crankshaft oil slinger using crankshaft rear oil seal slinger remover tool No. T95P-6701-AH, or equivalent, and suitable impact slide hammer.
5. Remove crankshaft rear seal using crankshaft rear seal remover tool No. T95P-6701-EH, or equivalent, and suitable impact slide hammer.
6. Remove two oil pan-to-crankshaft rear seal retainer plate bolts.
7. Remove six mounting bolts and crankshaft rear seal retainer plate.
8. Clean sealing surfaces with suitable silicone gasket remover.
9. Reverse procedure to install, noting the following:
   a. **Rear crankshaft seal retainer plate must be secured within four minutes of sealant application.**
   b. Apply .16 inch bead of silicone gasket and sealant around crankshaft rear seal retainer plate sealing surface.
   c. Tighten mounting bolts in sequence, **Fig. 42.**
   d. Tighten flywheel/flexplate mounting bolts in sequence, **Fig. 43.**
   e. **Torque** retainer plate-to-oil pan bolts to 15 ft. lbs., then tighten an additional 60°.
   f. Lubricate crankshaft rear seal with suitable, clean engine oil, then install using crankshaft rear seal installer tools Nos. T95P-6701-BH and T95P-6701-DH, or equivalents.
   g. Install crankshaft rear oil slinger using crankshaft rear oil slinger tool No. T95P-6501-BH, crankshaft rear seal installer tools Nos. T95P-6701-BH and T95P-6701-DH, or equivalents.

OIL PAN

REPLACE

1. Raise and support vehicle.
2. Drain engine oil into suitable container.
3. Loosen clamp and disconnect air cleaner outlet pipe.
4. Disconnect Mass Air Flow (MAF) sensor electrical connector.
5. Remove mounting bolt and air cleaner. Ensure two rubber grommets are retained to feet.
6. Disconnect Throttle Position (TP) sensor and electronic throttle control electrical connectors, **Fig. 3.**
7. Remove mounting bolts, nuts and throttle body.
8. Remove six pin-type retainers and radiator sight shield, **Fig. 5.**
9. Remove two outer bracket mounting bolts and two lower mounting nuts, then disconnect alternator electrical connector and pin-type retainer.
10. Position cover aside, then remove B+ terminal nut and alternator.
11. Support engine using suitable engine

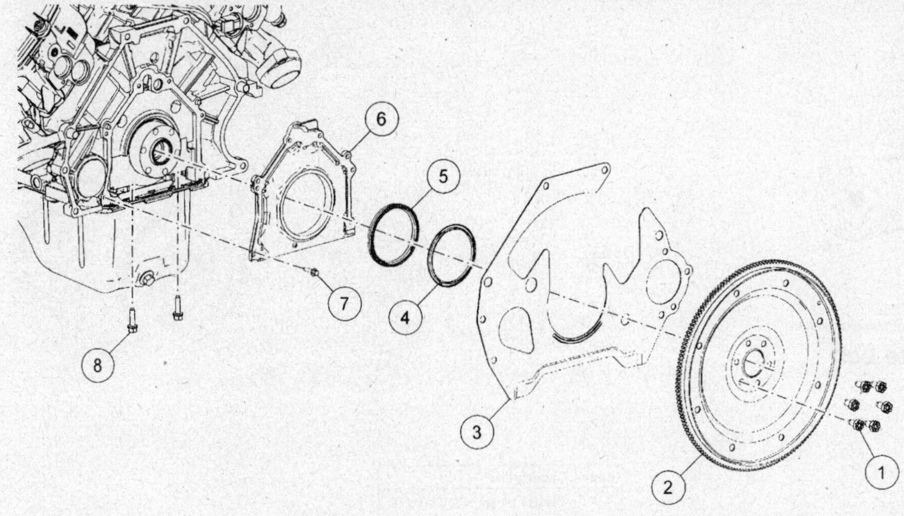

Item	Description
1	Flywheel/flexplate bolts (6 required)
2	Flywheel/flexplate
3	Engine-to-transmission spacer plate
4	Crankshaft oil slinger
5	Crankshaft rear seal

Item	Description
6	Crankshaft rear seal retainer plate
7	Crankshaft rear seal retainer plate bolts (6 required)
8	Oil pan bolts (2 required)

ARM0400000000514

Fig. 41 Crankshaft rear oil seal replacement

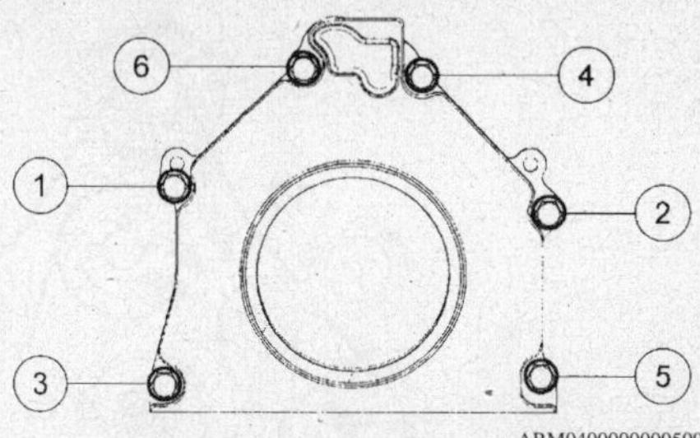

Fig. 42 Rear crankshaft seal retaining plate tightening sequence

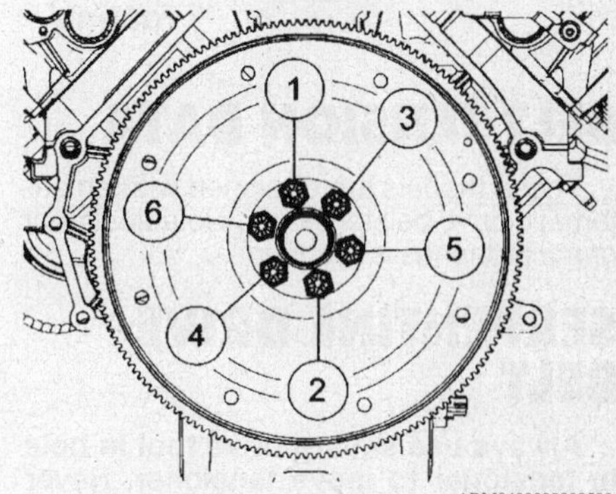

Fig. 43 Flywheel/flexplate tightening sequence

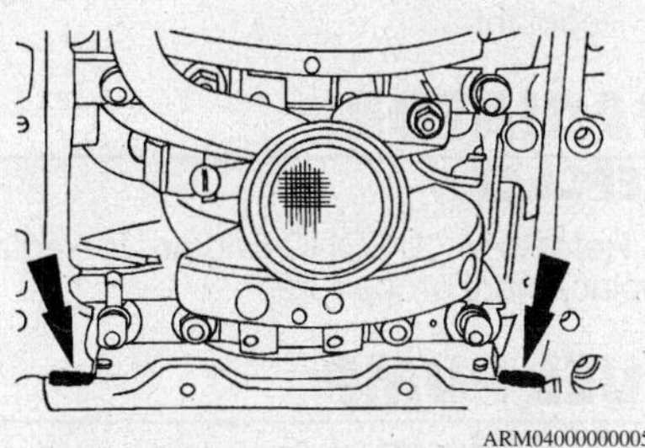

Fig. 44 Oil pan sealing (Part 1 of 2)

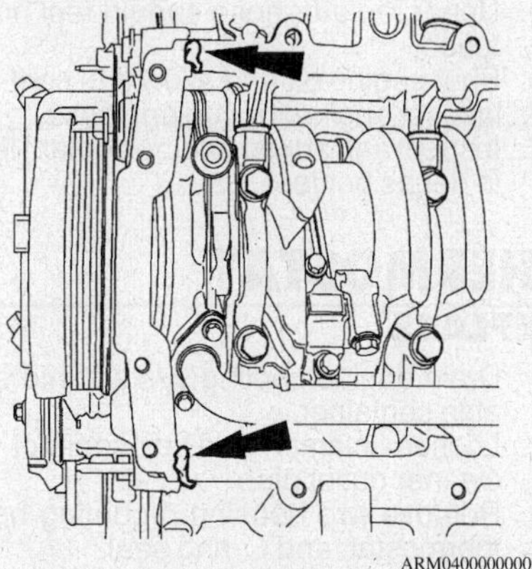

Fig. 44 Oil pan sealing (Part 2 of 2)

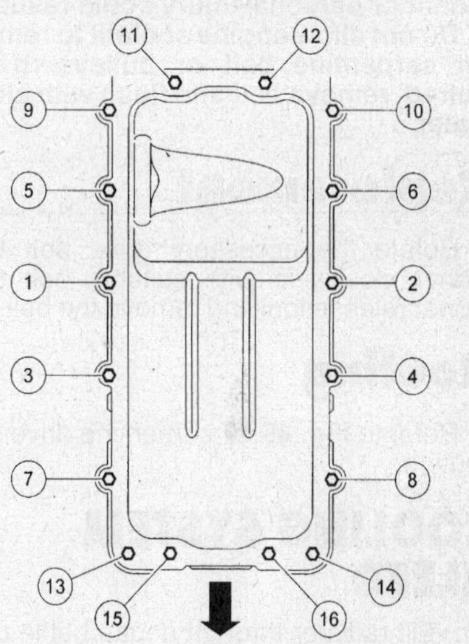

Fig. 45 Oil pan tightening sequence

lifting brackets and three-bar engine support tools.

12. Remove lefthand and righthand engine support insulator nuts.
13. Raise engine approximately 1.57 inches.
14. Position suitable adjustable jack stand under subframe.
15. Mark position of four subframe mounting nuts and four mounting bolts for installation alignment.
16. Remove subframe mounting nuts and bolts.
17. Lower subframe approximately 1.96 inches.
18. Disconnect oil temperature sensor electrical connector and two pin-type retainers.
19. Remove six mounting bolts, oil pan and gasket. **Oil pan gasket is reusable if it is not damaged.**
20. Reverse procedure to install, noting the following:
    a. Clean oil pan mating surface with suitable silicone gasket remover and metal surface prep.
    b. **Oil pan must be secured within four minutes of sealant application.**
    c. Apply silicone gasket and sealant at crankshaft rear seal retainer plate-to-cylinder block sealing surface, **Fig. 44.**
    d. Apply silicone gasket and sealant at engine front cover-to-cylinder block sealing surface, **Fig. 44.**
    e. Install gasket and the oil pan, then loosely install 16 mounting bolts.
    f. **Torque** oil pan mounting bolts in sequence to 18 inch lbs., **Fig. 45.**
    g. **Torque** pan mounting bolts in sequence to 15 ft. lbs.
    h. Tighten mounting bolts an additional 60° in sequence.

OIL PUMP

REPLACE

1. Remove oil pan as outlined under "Oil Pan, Replace."
2. Remove timing chain as outlined under "Timing Chain, Replace."
3. Remove mounting bolts, then the oil pump screen and pickup tube.
4. Remove three mounting bolts and oil pump.
5. Reverse procedure to install.

Fig. 46 Serpentine drive belt routing

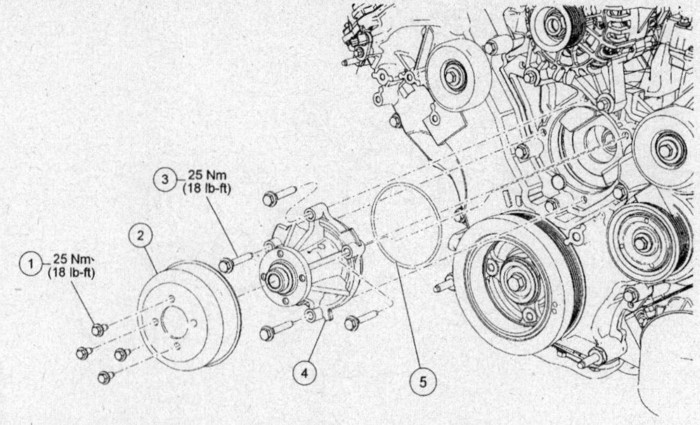

Item	Description
1	Coolant pump pulley bolts (4 required)
2	Coolant pump pulley
3	Coolant pump bolts (4 required)
4	Coolant pump
5	Coolant pump O-ring seal

ARM0400000000561

Fig. 47 Water pump replacement

BELT TENSION DATA

These models are equipped with an automatic drive belt tensioner. No adjustment or maintenance is required.

SERPENTINE DRIVE BELT

Always use square drive tool in hole in tensioner to move tensioner. Never pry on tensioner pulley. When releasing drive belt tensioner, never allow tensioner to snap back. Damage to tensioner or personal injury could result.

Do not allow engine coolant to remain on serpentine belt or pulleys. If required, remove belt and flush with clean water.

Replacement

Rotate the accessory drive belt tensioner clockwise with suitable belt tensioner release tool and remove the belt.

Routing

Refer to **Fig. 46** for serpentine drive belt routing.

COOLING SYSTEM BLEED

1. Fill radiator through degas bottle until the coolant level is between the COOLANT FILL LEVEL marks.
2. Select maximum heater temperature and blower motor speed settings.
3. Position control to discharge air at air conditioning vents in instrument panel.
4. Start engine and allow to idle.
5. While engine is idling, feel for hot air at air conditioning vents.
6. **If air discharge remains cool and engine coolant temperature gauge does not move, engine coolant level is low and must be filled. Stop engine, allow it to cool and fill cooling system.**
7. Allow engine to idle until normal operating temperature is reached. Hot air should discharge from air conditioning vents.
8. Engine coolant temperature gauge should maintain stabilized reading in middle of NORMAL range.
9. Upper radiator hose should feel hot to touch.
10. Shut engine off and allow it to cool.
11. Inspect engine for coolant leaks.
12. Inspect and adjust engine coolant level in degas bottle.

THERMOSTAT

REPLACE

1. Drain engine cooling system into suitable container.
2. Loosen clamp and disconnect air cleaner outlet pipe.
3. Remove two housing mounting bolts, thermostat. and O-ring seal.
4. Reverse procedure to install using new thermostat O-ring seal and lubricate with suitable, clean engine coolant.

WATER PUMP

REPLACE

1. Drain engine cooling system into suitable container.
2. Loosen clamp and disconnect air cleaner outlet pipe.
3. Loosen four coolant pump pulley bolts, **Fig. 47.**
4. Rotate accessory drive belt tensioner clockwise with suitable belt tensioner release tool and remove belt.
5. Remove four mounting bolts and water pump pulley.
6. Remove four mounting bolts, water pump and O-ring seal.
7. Reverse procedure to install, install new coolant pump O-ring seal and lubricate with suitable, clean engine coolant.

RADIATOR

REPLACE

Refer to "4.0L SOHC Engine" for radiator replacement procedure.

FUEL PUMP

REPLACE

1. Relieve fuel system pressure as outlined in "Precautions."
2. Remove fuel tank.
3. Install fuel tank sender wrench No. 310–059, or equivalent, onto fuel pump lock ring.
4. Remove fuel pump lock ring, then the fuel pump.
5. Reverse procedure to install.

FUEL FILTER

REPLACE

1. Relieve fuel system pressure as outlined in "Precautions."
2. Remove fuel filter shield.
3. Separate fuel line fittings with disconnect tool No. 310–S039, or equivalent.
4. Disconnect fuel lines from filter, then remove fuel filter.
5. Reverse procedure to install.

TIGHTENING SPECIFICATIONS

Year	Component	Torque Ft. Lbs.
2006	Air Cleaner	71①
	Air Cleaner Outlet Pipe	27①
	Air Conditioning Compressor	18
	Air Conditioning Condenser	89①
	Alternator, Lower	18
	Alternator, Upper	89①
	Alternator B+ Terminal	71①
	Alternator Support Bracket	89①
	Belt Idler Pulley	18
	Camshaft Bearing Cap	89①
	Camshaft Phaser Sprocket	⑧
	Catalytic Converter-To-Exhaust Manifold	30
	Coolant Crossover	89①
	Cooling Fan Motor & Shroud	80①
	Connecting Rod	⑥
	Crankshaft Pulley	②
	Crankshaft Rear Seal Retainer Plate	89①
	Crankshaft Rear Seal Retainer Plate To Oil Pan	③
	Cylinder Head	⑦
	Degas Bottle	71①
	Engine Support Insulator, Bolt	41
	Engine Support Insulator, Nut	46
	Exhaust Manifold	41
	Flywheel/Flexplate	59
	Front Cover	④
	Fuel Bundle Shield	62①
	Fuel Filter	44①
	Fuel Rail	89①
	Ground Wire	18
	Ignition Coil	44①
	Intake Manifold	89①
	Main Bearings	⑤
	Oil Dipstick Tube	89①
	Oil Pan	⑨
	Oil Pan Drain Plug	19
	Oil Pump	89①
	Oil Pump Screen & Pickup Tube-To-Oil Pump	89①
	Power Steering Pulley Shield	89①
	Power Steering Pump	18
	Power Steering Tube	89①
	Radiator Support Bracket	22
	Radio Ignition Interference Capacitor	18
	Steering Coupling	18
	Thermostat	89①
	Throttle Body	89①
	Timing Chain Guide	89①
	Timing Chain Tensioner	18
	Transmission Cooler Tube Bracket	18
	Valve Cover	89①
	Valve Cover Wiring Harness Bracket	30
	Water Pump	18
	Water Pump Pulley	18

① — Inch lbs.

② — Refer to "Crankshaft Damper, Replace" for tightening specifications and sequence.

③ — Refer to "Crankshaft Rear Oil Seal, Replace" for tightening specifications and sequence.

④ — Refer to "Front Cover, Replace" for tightening specifications and sequence.

⑤ — Refer to "Main & Rod Bearings" for tightening specifications and sequence.
⑥ — Refer to "Piston & Rod Assembly" for tightening specifications and sequence.
⑦ — Refer to "Cylinder Head, Replace" for tightening specifications and sequence.
⑧ — Refer to "Timing Chain, Replace" for tightening specifications and sequence.
⑨ — Refer to "Oil Pan, Replace" for tightening specifications and sequence.

Rear Axle & Suspension

NOTE: On Air Bag Equipped Models, Refer To "Air Bag System Precautions" Located In The Front Of This Manual For System Disarming & Arming Procedures.

INDEX

PRECAUTIONS

Air Bag Systems

Refer to "Air Bag System Precautions" in the front of this manual for system disarming and arming procedures.

Automatic Ride Control

On models equipped with automatic ride control, the automatic ride control service switch must be turned off before lifting vehicle. The service switch is located in the rear jack storage area.

Battery Ground Cable

Prior to service, disconnect battery ground cable and isolate as required.

DESCRIPTION

Semi-elliptic leaf type rear springs are used for the Explorer Sport, Explorer Sport Trac and Ranger rear axle suspensions. The forward end of each rear spring is attached to a bracket on the frame side member. The rear end of each rear spring is shackled to a bracket on the frame side member.

The Ranger rear axle is mounted below the rear spring, **Fig. 1.**The Explorer Sport and Sport Trac rear axle is mounted above the rear spring, **Fig. 2.**

The 2002–03 Explorer & Mountaineer utilizes an independent rear suspension and coil a springs system, **Fig. 3.**

REAR AXLE

REPLACE

Explorer & Mountaineer

1. Raise and support vehicle.
2. Remove rear wheel and tire assembly.
3. Place index mark on driveshaft flange and pinion flange for installation reference.
4. Remove driveshaft assembly.
5. Drain axle housing into suitable container.
6. Remove halfshafts as outlined under "Rear Halfshaft, Replace."
7. Support rear axle housing with suitable jack.
8. Disconnect speed sensor electrical connector.
9. Disconnect axle housing vent tube.
10. Remove upper axle housing bolts, then the lower axle housing bolt.
11. Lower axle housing from vehicle.
12. Reverse procedure to install.

Explorer Sport & Sport Trac

1. Release tension on parking brake cable.
2. Raise and support vehicle.
3. Remove rear wheel and tire assemblies.
4. Place index mark on driveshaft flange and pinion flange for installation reference.
5. Remove four bolts and position driveshaft aside.
6. Remove bolt and position brake hose junction block aside.
7. Disconnect parking brake cable and conduit at parking brake lever.
8. Disconnect vehicle speed sensor.
9. Remove bolt, then route parking brake cables and vehicle speed sensor wiring.
10. Disconnect vent hose.
11. Disconnect anti-wind up bar.
12. Remove rear brake disc calipers and attach to frame with wire.
13. Disconnect rear stabilizer bar at links.
14. Support rear axle assembly with suitable jack.
15. Remove lower nuts and bolts from shock absorbers.
16. Remove nuts and U-bolt.
17. Raise rear axle off springs and remove from vehicle.
18. Reverse procedure to install.

Ranger

1. Remove rear axles as outlined in "Rear Axle Shaft, Replace."
2. Place index mark on driveshaft flange and pinion flange for installation reference.
3. Remove four driveshaft bolts.
4. Disconnect driveshaft flange from rear axle pinion flange and position driveshaft aside.
5. Disconnect rear anti-lock brake sensor electrical connectors from sensors and position harness aside.
6. Disconnect vent hose from axle.
7. Separate brake lines from retaining clips on axle. Do not disconnect brake lines from brake hose junction block.
8. Disconnect brake hose junction block from differential housing.
9. Disconnect rear brake backing plates from axle and wire assemblies out of way.
10. Position suitable jack under differential housing and secure in place.
11. Remove nuts and bolts retaining shock

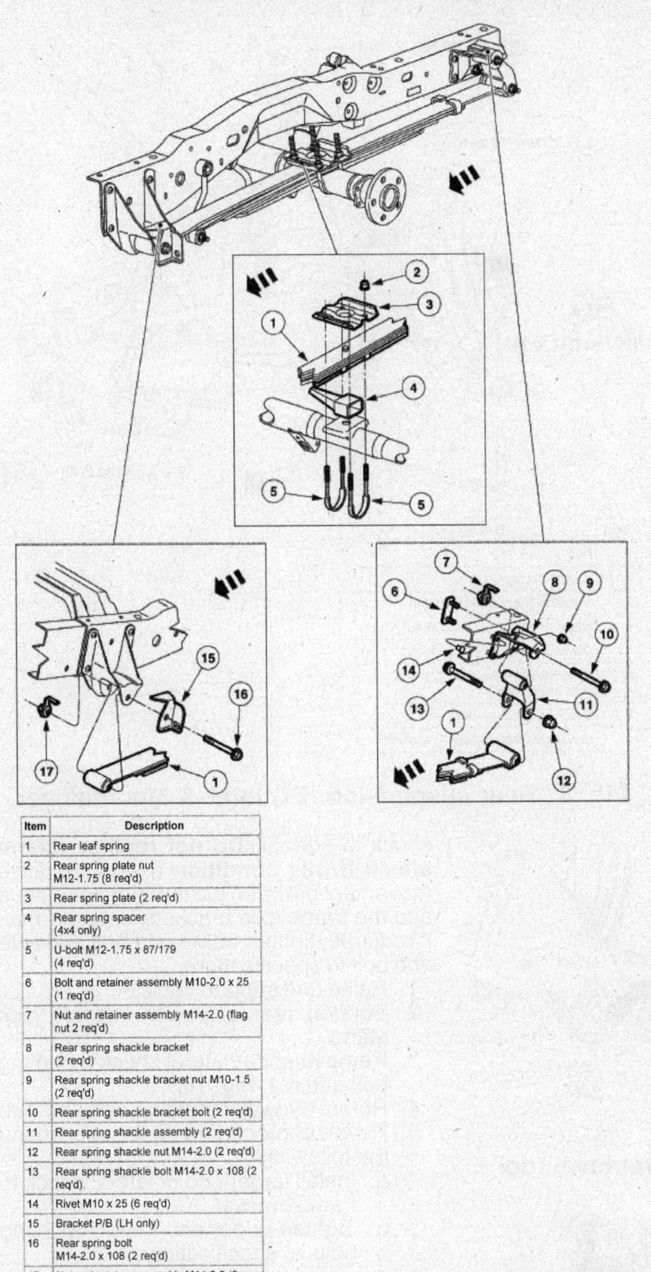

Item	Description
1	Rear leaf spring
2	Rear spring plate nut M12-1.75 (8 req'd)
3	Rear spring plate (2 req'd)
4	Rear spring spacer (4x4 only)
5	U-bolt M12-1.75 x 87/179 (4 req'd)
6	Bolt and retainer assembly M10-2.0 x 25 (1 req'd)
7	Nut and retainer assembly M14-2.0 (flag nut 2 req'd)
8	Rear spring shackle bracket (2 req'd)
9	Rear spring shackle bracket nut M10-1.5 (2 req'd)
10	Rear spring shackle bracket bolt (2 req'd)
11	Rear spring shackle assembly (2 req'd)
12	Rear spring shackle nut M14-2.0 (2 req'd)
13	Rear spring shackle bolt M14-2.0 x 108 (2 req'd)
14	Rivet M10 x 25 (6 req'd)
15	Bracket P/B (LH only)
16	Rear spring bolt M14-2.0 x 108 (2 req'd)
17	Nut and retainer assembly M14-2.0 (flag nut 2 req'd)

LTV1900000000554

Fig. 1 Rear suspension (Part 1 of 2). Ranger

Item	Description
1	Rear stabilizer bar to axle retainer (2 req'd)
2	Rear stabilizer bar assembly (1 req'd)
3	Rear stabilizer bar mounting bracket (1 req'd)
4	Rear stabilizer bar to axle retainer (2 req'd)
5	Rear stabilizer bar link assembly (2 req'd)
6	Flat washer M13-33 x 3.7 (2 req'd)
7	Rear stabilizer bar link nut M12-1.75 (2 req'd)
8	Rear stabilizer bar link nut and washer assembly M12-1.75 (2 req'd)
9	Rear stabilizer bar link bolt M12-1.75 (2 req'd)
10	Rear stabilizer bar to axle bolt (4 req'd)
11	Rear axle bumper retaining nut M10-1.5 (2 req'd)
12	Brake line bracket
13	Rear shock absorber upper retaining nut and washer assy M12-1.75 (2 req'd)
14	Rear axle bumper assembly (2 req'd)
15	Rear shock absorber lower retaining nut and washer assy M12-1.75 (2 req'd)
16	Rear shock absorber lower retaining bolt M12-1.75 x 70 (2 req'd)
17	Rear shock absorber (2 req'd)

LTV1900000000555

Fig. 1 Rear suspension (Part 2 of 2). Ranger

absorbers to axle.

12. Remove nuts, rear axle U-bolts and rear spring plates.
13. Lower rear axle from vehicle.
14. Reverse procedure to install, noting the following:
    a. If new retaining bolts for driveshaft to axle are not available, coat threads of original bolts with suitable threadlock compound.
    b. Drivehshaft flange fits tightly on rear axle pinion flange. To ensure flange seats squarely, tighten flange bolts in cross pattern.

REAR AXLE SHAFT

REPLACE

1. Raise and support vehicle, then remove rear wheel and tire assemblies.
2. Loosen bolts from differential housing cover, then drain fluid into suitable container.
3. Remove differential cover.
4. Remove rear brake discs or drums and backing plates.
5. Remove differential pinion shaft lock bolt, then the pinion shaft.
6. Push axle shaft inboard, then remove U-washer.
7. Do not damage rubber O-ring in U-washer groove.
8. Reinstall differential pinion shaft, install pinion shaft lock bolt finger tight.
9. Remove axle shaft.
10. Reverse procedure to install.

REAR HALFSHAFT

REPLACE

1. Raise and support vehicle.
2. Remove rear wheel and tire assemblies.
3. Remove rear calipers and position

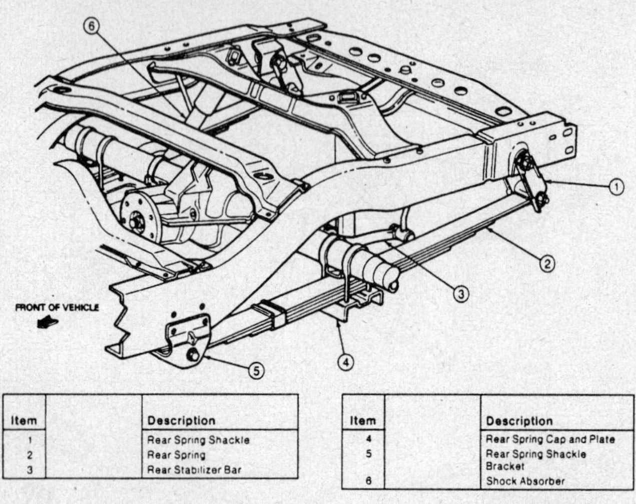

Item	Description
1	Rear Spring Shackle
2	Rear Spring
3	Rear Stabilizer Bar
4	Rear Spring Cap and Plate
5	Rear Spring Shackle Bracket
6	Shock Absorber

Fig. 2 Rear suspension. Explorer Sport & Sport Trac

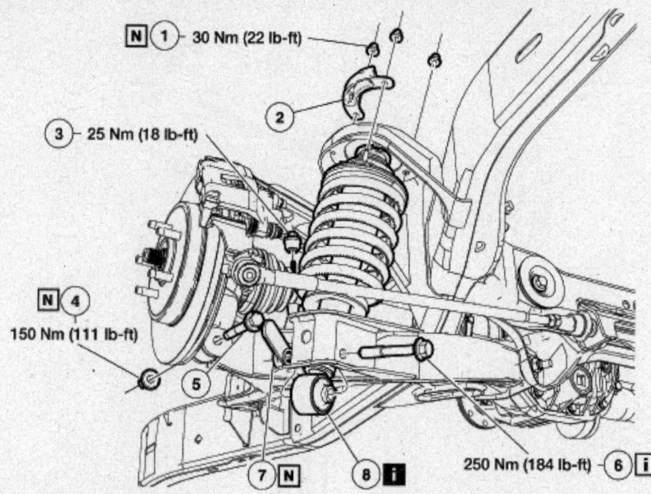

Item	Description
1	Nuts
2	Jounce bumper
3	Stabilizer link nut and grommet
4	Lower arm-to-wheel knuckle nut
5	Lower arm-to-wheel knuckle bolt
6	Shock absorber-to-lower arm bolt Installation Note
7	Shock absorber-to-lower arm flag nut
8	Shock absorber and spring assembly

LTV1900000000556

Fig. 3 Rear suspension. Explorer & Mountaineer

aside. Do not allow calipers to hang from hydraulic hoses.

4. Separate rear axle halfshaft outboard CV joint from hub with removal tool No. 205–502, or equivalent, **Fig. 4.**
5. Remove upper ball joint pinch bolt, toe link pinch bolt and sway bar stud nut.
6. Support rear suspension arm with wood stick approximately 18 inches long and 1 inch wide, **Fig. 5.**
7. Disengage inboard CV joint from differential side gear. Do not allow splines to touch axle shaft oil seal.
8. Before removing inboard CV joint, install halfshaft seal protector tool No. 205–506, or equivalent.
9. Remove CV inboard joint from differential, then the halfshaft from vehicle.
10. Reverse procedure to install.

STRUT

REPLACE

1. Raise and support vehicle.
2. Remove wheel and tire assembly.
3. Remove components in sequence, **Fig. 6.**
4. Compress spring with suitable spring compressor until tension is released from shock absorber.
5. Remove upper nut, then disassemble strut assembly, **Fig. 7.**
6. Reverse procedure to install.

SHOCK ABSORBER

REPLACE

1. Raise vehicle and support rear axle.
2. Remove lower attaching bolt and nut from shock absorber, then swing lower end free from mounting bracket.
3. Disconnect shock absorber from upper mounting, then remove shock from vehicle, **Figs. 8 and 9.**
4. Reverse procedure to install. Tighten shock absorber mounting bolts to specifications.

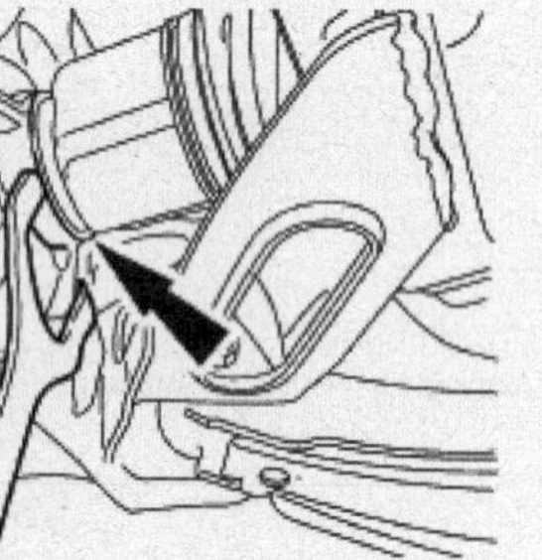

Fig. 4 Halfshaft removal tool

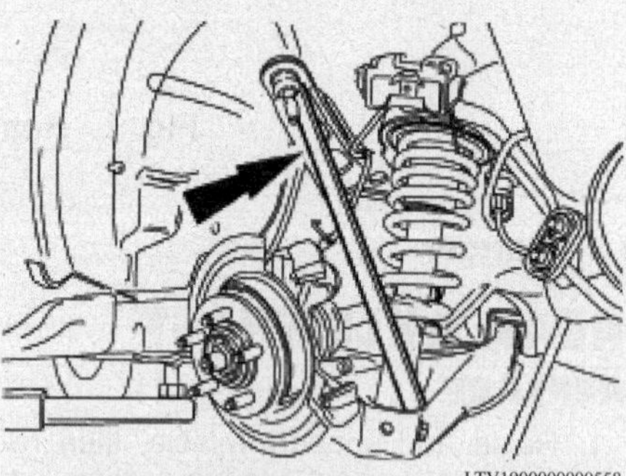

Fig. 5 Upper arm support

LATERAL SHOCK ABSORBER

REPLACE

Forward and rearward motion (relative movement between rubber shock bushing and metal sleeve) at each end of lateral shock is normal. **Do not replace lateral shock if this condition exists.** Relative movement between the metal shock sleeve and the frame/axle brackets is not normal. If required, tighten frame end bolt and axle end bolt to specifications.

1. Raise and support vehicle.
2. Support rear axle with suitable jack stand.
3. Remove upper lateral shock mounting bolt and nut, **Fig. 10.**
4. Remove lower mounting bolt and nut.
5. Reverse procedure to install, noting the following:
   a. Install larger end of lateral shock to frame bracket.
   b. Tighten upper and lower mounting bolts to specifications.

AIR SHOCK

REPLACE

Shock absorbers are charged with nitrogen gas. **Do not apply heat or attempt to open or puncture. On 4.0L models, place vehicle in AUTO. On 5.0L vehicles, place vehicle in NORMAL.**

Prior to replacing air shocks, connect a New Generation Star (NGS) tester to the data link connector. Select the RIDE CONTROL OUTPUT screen and turn on the following solenoids to vent the entire system of air and to lower vehicle to its lowest possible height: FRONT FIL, REAR FIL, GATE, and VENT.

1. Raise and support vehicle, then remove spare tire.
2. Use a suitable jack to support rear axle.

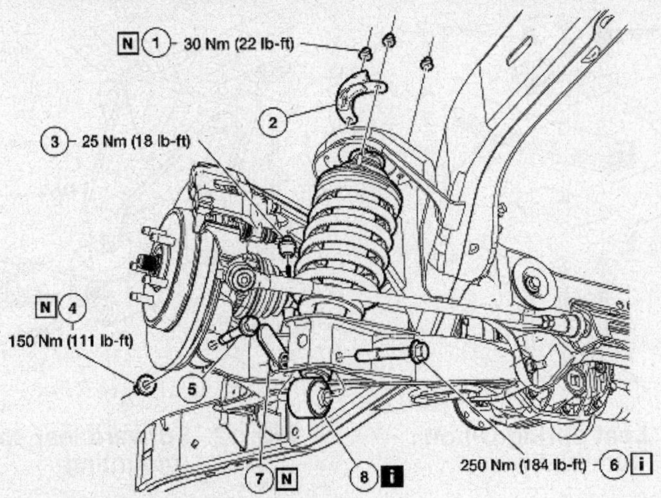

Item	Description
1	Nuts
2	Jounce bumper
3	Stabilizer link nut and grommet
4	Lower arm-to-wheel knuckle nut
5	Lower arm-to-wheel knuckle bolt
6	Shock absorber-to-lower arm bolt Installation Note
7	Shock absorber-to-lower arm flag nut
8	Shock absorber and spring assembly Removal Note

LTV1900000000560

Fig. 6 Rear shock & spring replacement

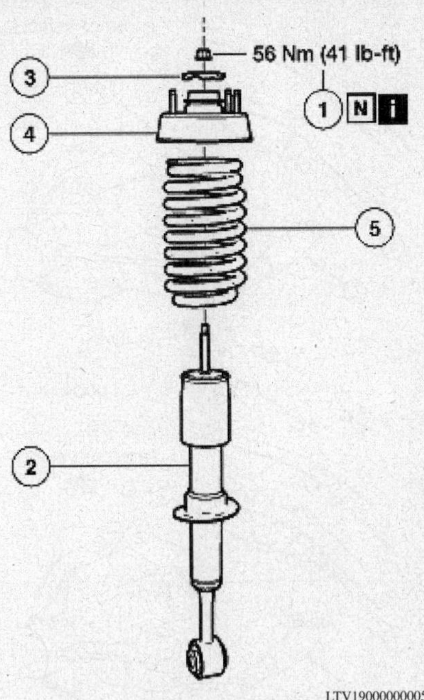

Fig. 7 Strut assembly replacement

3. Disconnect rear shock absorber electrical connector.
4. Push in red ring and remove air line.
5. Remove shock absorber lower retaining nut, then position shock aside.
6. Remove top attaching nuts, then the shock absorber.
7. Reverse procedure to install.

LEAF SPRING

REPLACE

1. Raise vehicle and remove rear wheels.
2. Support the rear axle.
3. Remove U-bolt nuts and the U-bolts, **Fig. 11.**
4. Remove spring to bracket attaching nut and bolt, **Fig. 12.**
5. Remove shackle to bracket attaching nuts and bolts, **Fig. 13,** then the spring and shackle assembly.
6. Reverse procedure to install.

STABILIZER BAR

REPLACE

1. Disconnect stabilizer bar from rear link, **Fig. 14.**
2. Remove mounting bracket U-bolt, then the mounting bracket, retainer and stabilizer bar.
3. Reverse procedure to install. The UP marking on the mounting bracket must be positioned as outlined in **Fig. 14.**

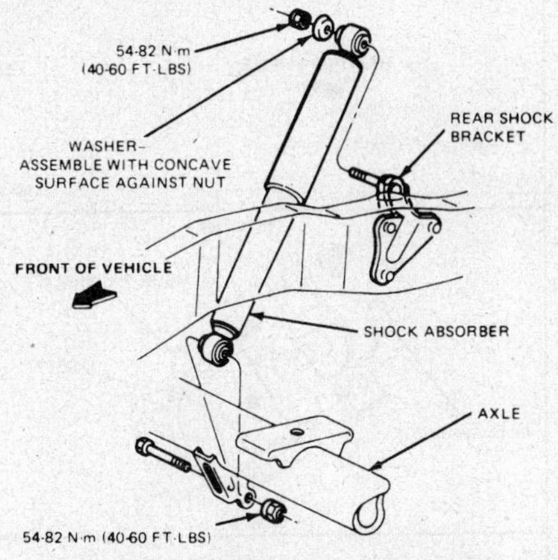

Fig. 8 Shock absorber replacement. Ranger

ANTI-WINDUP BAR

REPLACE

Some models are equipped with an anti-windup bar which is designed to counter rotational torque placed on the rear axle during braking and acceleration. It also reduces noise vibration and harshness caused by excessive driveline angles.

1. Remove parking brake cable, then the front anti-windup bar bolt.
2. Remove anti-windup bar to axle bolt, then the anti-windup bar.
3. Reverse procedure to install.

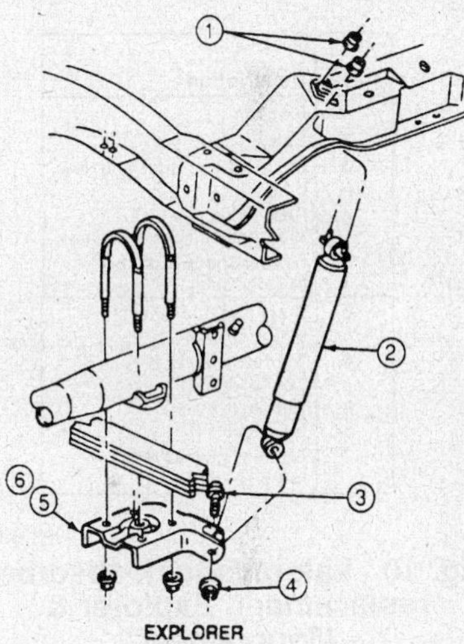

Item	Description
1	Nut
2	Shock Absorber
3	Bolt
4	Nut
5	Rear Spring Cap and Plate (RH)
6	Rear Spring Cap and Plate (LH)

FM2039500050000X

Fig. 9 Shock absorber replacement. Explorer Sport & Explorer Sport Trac

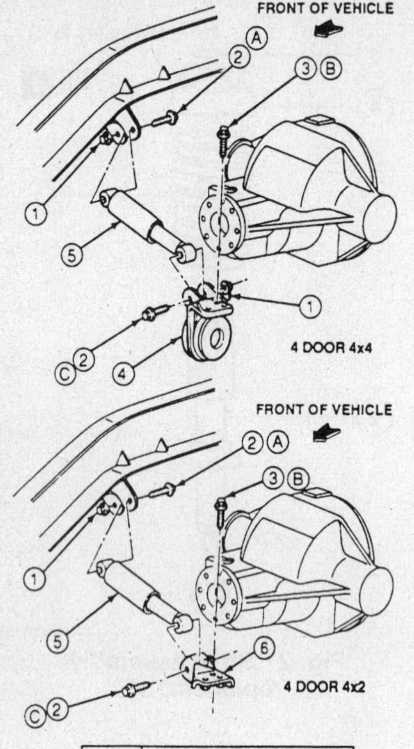

Item	Description
1	Flag Nut
2	Bolt
3	Bolt (Use Locktite® and New Bolt)
4	Rear Axle Drive Line Vibration Damper (4x4 Only)
5	Lateral Shock Absorber (4-Door Only)
6	Bracket, Shock Mount (4x2 — 4-Door)
A	Tighten to 53-72 N·m (39-53 Lb-Ft)
B	Tighten to 60-80 N·m (44-59 Lb-Ft)
C	Tighten to 68-92 N·m (50-68 lb-ft)

FM2039500051000X

Fig. 10 Lateral shock absorber replacement. Explorer & Mountaineer

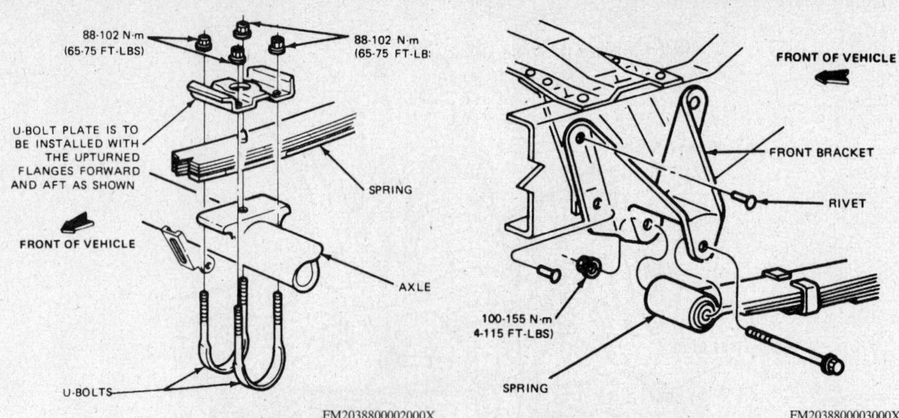

Fig. 11 Leaf spring U-bolt removal

Fig. 12 Forward leaf spring mounting

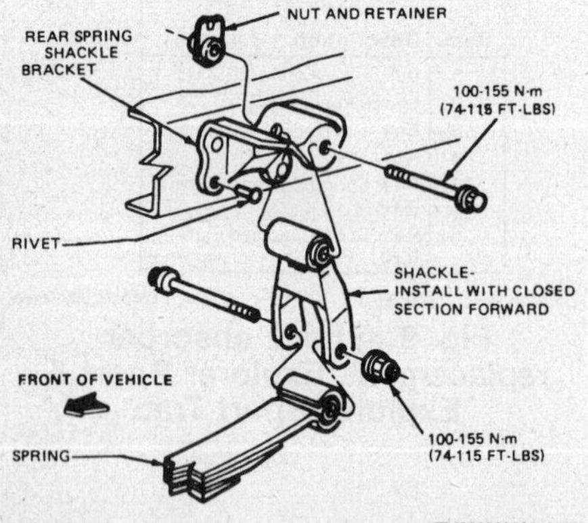

FM2038800004000X

Fig. 13 Rear leaf spring mounting

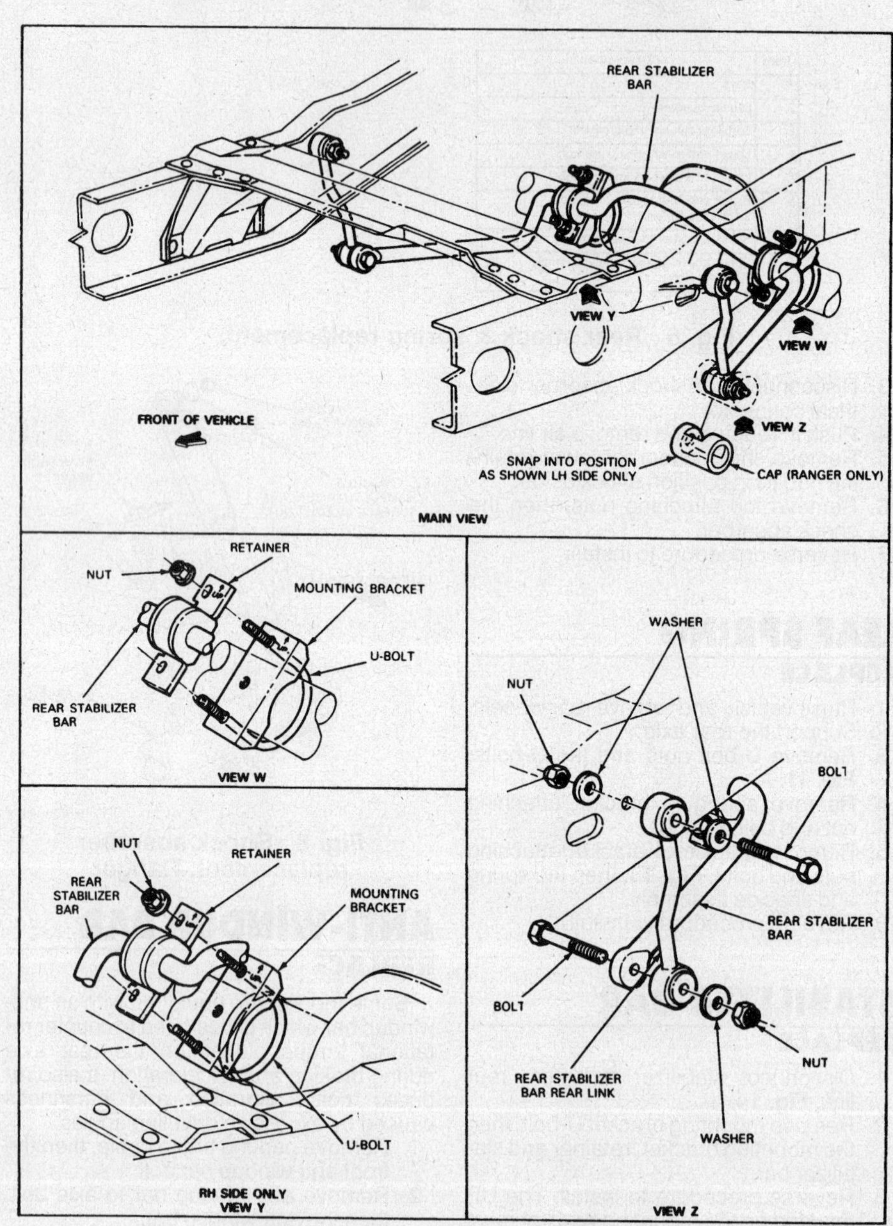

Fig. 14 Stabilizer bar replacement

TIGHTENING SPECIFICATIONS

Year	Component	Torque Ft. Lbs.
2002–06	Anti-Wind Up Bar Bolt	83–111
	Axle Cover Bolts	28–38
	Driveshaft Bolts	70–95
	Jounce Bumper Nut	15–21
	Oil Filler Plug	15–30
	Pinion Shaft Lock Bolt	15–30
	Rear Brake Hose	11–15
	Rear Spring Lower Bolt And Nut	74–97
	Rear Spring To Frame Bracket	55–77
	Rear Spring U-Bolt	65–76
	Rear Stabilizer Bar Bracket (Aviator, Explorer & Mountaineer)	35–41
	Rear Stabilizer Bar Bracket (Sport, Sport Trac & Ranger)	44–59
	Rear Stabilizer Bar To Link Nut (Aviator, Explorer & Mountaineer)	50–68
	Rear Stabilizer Bar To Link Nut (Ranger)	44–59
	Shock Absorber Lower (Aviator, Explorer & Mountaineer)	180–184
	Shock Absorber Lower (Sport, Sport Trac & Ranger)	44–59
	Shock Absorber Upper (Aviator, Explorer & Mountaineer)	45—59
	Shock Absorber Upper (Sport, Sport Trac & Ranger)	39–53
	Wheel Lug Nut	100

Front Suspension & Steering

NOTE: On Air Bag Equipped Models, Refer To "Air Bag System Precautions" Located In The Front Of This Manual For System Disarming & Arming Procedures.

INDEX

PRECAUTIONS

Air Bag Systems

Refer to "Air Bag System Precautions" in the front of this manual for system disarming and arming procedures.

Automatic Ride Control

On models equipped with automatic ride control, the automatic ride control service switch must be turned off before lifting vehicle. The service switch is located in the rear jack storage area.

Battery Ground Cable

Prior to service, disconnect battery ground cable and isolate as required.

DESCRIPTION

Ranger

SLA (SHORT ARM-LONG ARM)

The front suspension used on Ranger models is the new SLA suspension with rack and pinion power steering. This suspension uses coil springs on 2WD models and torsion bar on 4WD models, **Figs. 1 and 2.**

Explorer Sport & Explorer Sport Trac

The front suspension used on Explorer Sport and Explorer Sport Trac is the torsion bar long arm short arm type. The system primarily consists of upper and lower control arms with integral ball joints and bushings, **Figs. 3 and 4.**

Aviator, Explorer & Mountaineer

The front suspension used on Aviator, Explorer and Mountaineer is the Coil Spring Type. The system primarily consists of upper and lower control arms with integral ball joints and bushings, **Figs. 5 and 6.**

WHEEL BEARING

ADJUST

2WD Models

1. Raise and support front of vehicle.
2. Remove wheel cover, grease cap, cotter pin and locknut.
3. Loosen adjusting nut three turns, then lock wheel assembly in and out several times to push brake shoe and linings away from rotor.
4. While rotating rotor, **torque** spindle nut to 30 ft. lbs.
5. Loosen spindle nut two turns.
6. **Torque** spindle nut to 17–24 ft. lbs., while rotating rotor counterclockwise.
7. Loosen spindle nut ½ turn, then **torque** to 17 inch lbs.
8. Install nut retainer, cotterpin, and grease cap.

4WD MODELS

The front wheel bearings are non-adjustable.

FRONT WHEEL SPINDLE

REPLACE

2WD Models

RANGER

1. Raise and support vehicle.
2. Remove rotor as outlined in "Disc Brakes" chapter.
3. Remove brake rotor shield.
4. Support lower control arm using a suitable jack.
5. Remove upper shock absorber retaining nut, washer and bushing.
6. Remove upper ball joint retaining nut and pinch bolt.
7. Separate ball joint from spindle.
8. Remove lower shock absorber attaching nuts, then the shock.
9. Remove tie rod attaching nut, then the tie rod from spindle using pitman arm puller tool No. T64P–3590–F, or equivalent.
10. Compress coil spring using spring compressor tool No. D78P–5310–A or equivalent.
11. Remove lower ball joint attaching nut.
12. Separate ball joint from control arm

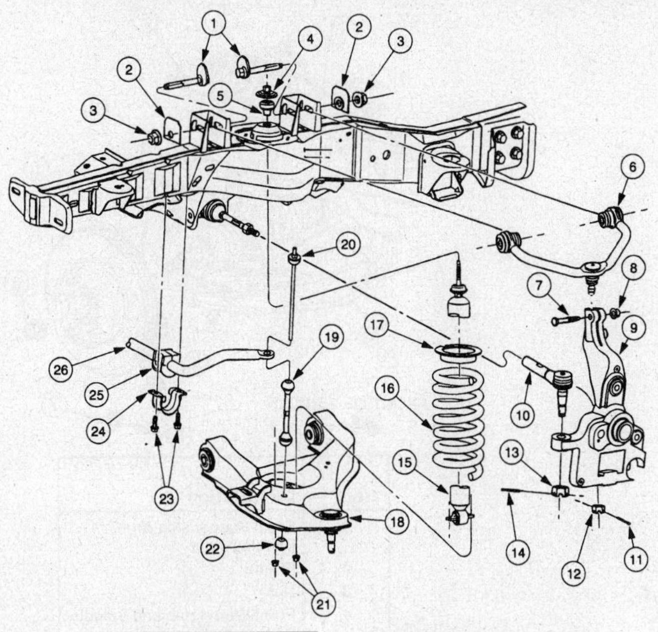

Item	Description
1	Front Suspension Upper Arm Cam Bolt (4 Req'd)
2	Front Suspension Upper Arm Cam Assy (2 Req'd)
3	Front Suspension Upper Arm Cam Assy Nut (2 Req'd)
4	Front Shock Absorber Upper Nut/Washer Assy (2 Req'd)
5	Front Shock Absorber Upper Bushing (2 Req'd)
6	Front Suspension Upper Arm (LH)
6	Front Suspension Upper Arm (RH)
7	Front Wheel Spindle Pinch Bolt (2 Req'd)
8	Front Wheel Spindle Pinch Bolt Nut
9	Front Wheel Spindle
10	Tie Rod End
11	Cotter Pin
12	Lower Ball Joint Castellated Nut (2 Req'd)

Item	Description
13	Tie Rod End Castellated Nut (2 Req'd)
14	Cotter Pin
15	Front Shock Absorber
16	Front Coil Spring
17	Front Spring Insulator
18	Front Suspension Lower Arm (LH)
18	Front Suspension Lower Arm (RH)
19	Front Stabilizer Bar Link
20	Front Stabilizer Bar Stud and Bushing Assy (2 Req'd)
21	Front Shock Absorber Lower Nut (4 Req'd)
22	Front Stabilizer Bar Nut and Washer Assy (2 Req'd)
23	Front Stabilizer Bar Mounting Bolts (4 Req'd)
24	Stabilizer Bar Bracket (2 Req'd)
25	Front Stabilizer Bar Bushing Assy (2 Req'd)
26	Front Stabilizer Bar

FM2029800142000X

Fig. 1 SLA suspension. Ranger w/2WD

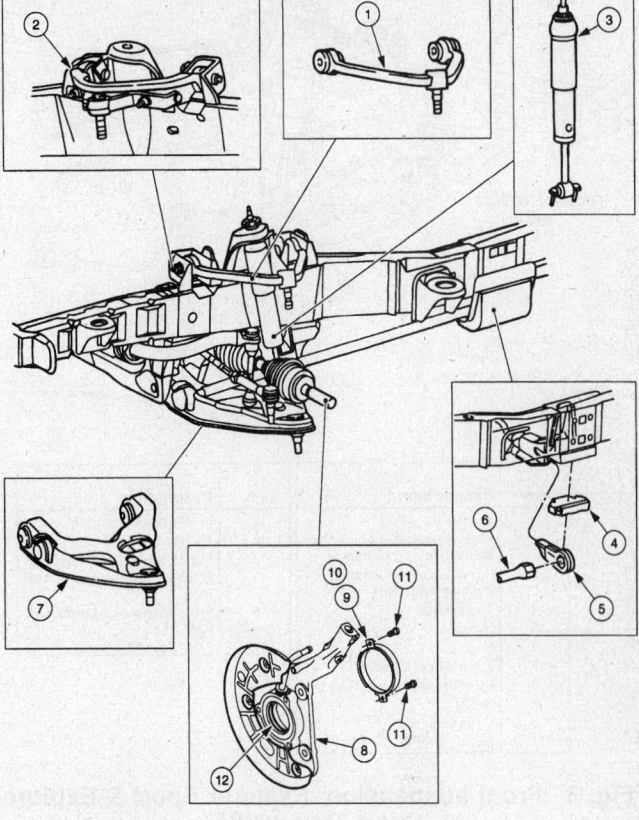

Item	Description
1	Upper Arm, Bushing and Joint Assy (LH)
2	Upper Arm, Bushing and Joint Assy (RH)
3	Shock Assy
4	Torsion Bar Adjuster Plate
5	Torsion Bar Adjuster
6	Torsion Bar (LH)

Item	Description
7	Lower Arm, Bushing and Joint Assy (LH)
8	Knuckle Assy
9	Protection Shield (RH)
10	Protection Shield (LH)
11	Screw (Self-Tapping)
12	Oil Seal

FM2029800143000X

Fig. 2 SLA suspension. Ranger w/4WD

using pitman arm puller tool No. T64P–3590–F or equivalent. Remove spindle.

13. Reverse procedure to install. Tighten to specifications and adjust wheel alignment.

EXPLORER SPORT & EXPLORER SPORT TRAC

1. Remove disc brake caliper, anchor plate, and brake rotor as outlined in "Disc Brakes" chapter.
2. Remove ABS sensor, then the tie rod retaining nut.
3. Separate tie rod from wheel spindle using a suitable pitman arm puller.
4. Unload torsion bar using torsion bar tool No. T95T-5310-A, or equivalent.
5. Support lower control arm using a suitable jack stand.
6. Remove pinch bolt and nut from spindle. **Before removing pinch bolt, support spindle to keep it from tilting to avoid possible damage.**
7. Remove lower ball joint nut.
8. Separate ball joint from spindle using a suitable pitman arm puller.

4WD Models

Refer to "Front Wheel Drive" section in this chapter for front wheel spindle replacement procedure.

AXLE I-BEAM

REPLACE

1. Remove front spindle as outlined in "Front Wheel Spindle, Replace."
2. Remove coil spring as outlined in "Coil Spring, Replace."
3. Remove stabilizer bar as outlined in "Stabilizer Bar, Replace."
4. Remove spring lower seat from radius arm, then the radius arm attaching bolt and nut.
5. Remove axle to frame pivot bracket bolt and nut.
6. Reverse procedure to install.

AXLE PIVOT BRACKET

REPLACE

2WD Models

1. Remove front spring, radius arm, wheel spindle and I-beam.
2. Remove four attaching nuts and two bolts and retainer assemblies. Remove axle pivot bracket, **Fig. 7.**
3. Reverse procedure to install. Position axle pivot bracket to frame and install forward and rearward bolts and retainer assemblies from inside of pivot bracket out through crossmember. Loosely install four nuts on outside of crossmember (two forward and two rearward). **Torque** nuts to 70–90 ft. lbs. Use nut part No. N8802073-S2 or

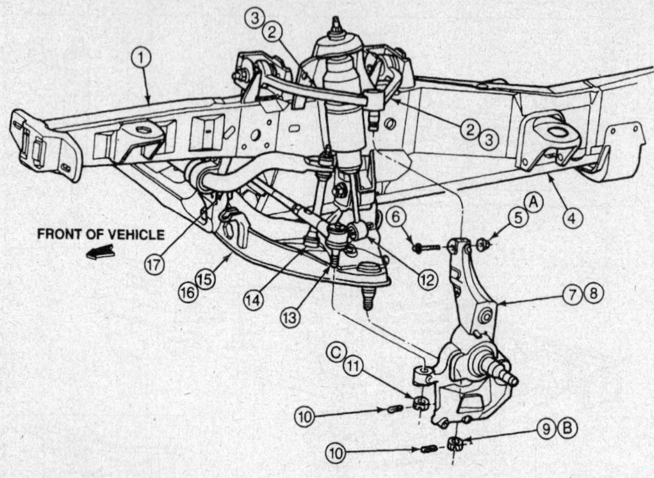

Item	Description
1	Frame
2	Front Suspension Arm Bushing Joint (LH Shown)
3	Front Suspension Arm Bushing Joint (RH)
4	Torsion Bar
5	Nut
6	Bolt
7	Front Wheel Spindle (RH)
8	Front Wheel Spindle (LH)
9	Nut
10	Cotter Pin
11	Nut

Item	Description
12	Front Shock Absorber
13	Tie Rod End
14	Front Stabilizer Bar Link
15	Front Suspension Lower Arm (RH)
16	Front Suspension Lower Arm (LH)
17	Front Stabilizer Bar

FM2029500118000X

Fig. 3 Front suspension. Explorer Sport & Explorer Sport Trac w/2WD

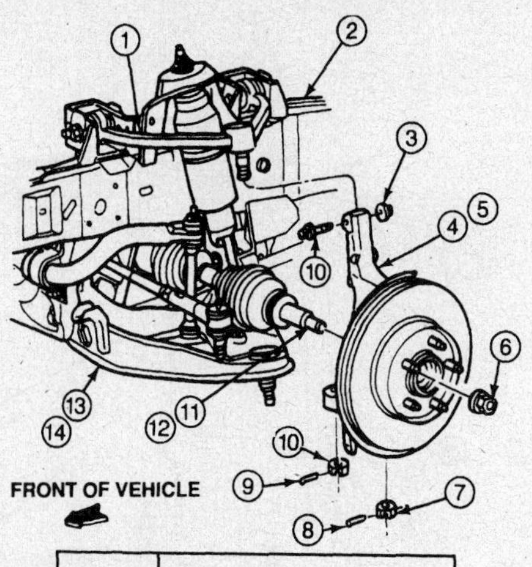

Item	Description
1	Front Suspension Arm Bushing Joint
2	Frame
3	Nut
4	Front Wheel Hub and Spindle (RH)
5	Front Wheel Hub and Spindle (LH)
6	Hub Washer and Nut Assembly
7	Nut
8	Cotter Pin
9	Cotter Pin
10	Nut
11	Front Wheel Driveshaft and Joint (RH)
12	Front Wheel Driveshaft and Joint (LH)
13	Front Suspension Lower Arm (RH)
14	Front Suspension Lower Arm (LH)

FM2029500119000X

Fig. 4 Front suspension. Explorer Sport & Explorer Sport Trac w/4WD

install one .20 inch thick hardened washer under each nut if a standard nut is used.

4WD Models

1. Raise and support vehicle on a frame hoist.
2. Position a suitable jackstand under axle arm near front axle pivot bracket. Lower hoist until jackstand contacts axle.
3. Remove bolt attaching axle to pivot bracket. Raise hoist and pry axle free from front axle pivot bracket if required.
4. On righthand axle pivot bracket, remove attaching nuts.
5. Remove upper and side bolts and retainers.
6. Remove and discard lower bolt and retainer.
7. Remove front axle pivot bracket from crossmember.
8. To remove lefthand pivot bracket, drill out rivets so that mounting holes in bracket and crossmember are 9⁄16 inch in diameter, then remove the bracket, **Fig. 8.**
9. Reverse procedure to install. Refer to **Figs. 8 and 9** for replacement hardware.

AXLE PIVOT BUSHING

REPLACE

2WD Models

1. Remove front coil spring as outlined in "Coil Spring, Replace."
2. For lefthand I-beam axle, remove axle pivot bolt and nut and pull lefthand I-beam axle down until bushing is exposed. For righthand I-beam axle, entire righthand I-beam axle must be removed. Refer to "Axle I-Beam, Replace."
3. Install forcing screw tool No. T78P-5638-A1, bushing remover tool No. T80T-5638-A2, spacer tool No. T82T-3006-A4 and receiver cup tool No. T78P-5638-A3, or equivalents, onto pivot bushing. Turn forcing screw and remove pivot bushing, **Fig. 10.**
4. Reverse procedure to install. Refer to **Fig. 11.** Lower vehicle and tighten pivot bushing and nut to specifications.

4WD Models

Refer to "Front Wheel Drive" section in this chapter for axle pivot bushing replacement procedure.

BALL JOINT INSPECTION

1. **On models equipped with I-Beam suspension,** place safety stands under I-Beam axle beneath coil spring.
2. **On models equipped with SLA and torsion bar suspension,** place safety stands under control arm.
3. **On all models,** grasp lower edge of tire and move wheel in and out, observe lower spindle arm and lower part of axle jaw.
4. If movement between lower spindle arm and lower spindle jaw is greater than 1⁄32 inch, replace lower ball joint.
5. Grasp upper edge of tire and move tire in and out, observe movement between upper spindle arm and upper part of axle jaw.
6. If movement is between upper part of axle jaw and upper spindle arm is greater than 1⁄32 inch, replace upper ball joint.

BALL JOINT

REPLACE

Aviator, Explorer, Explorer Sport, Explorer Sport Trac & Mountaineer

LOWER ARM

1. Raise and support vehicle, then remove front wheels.

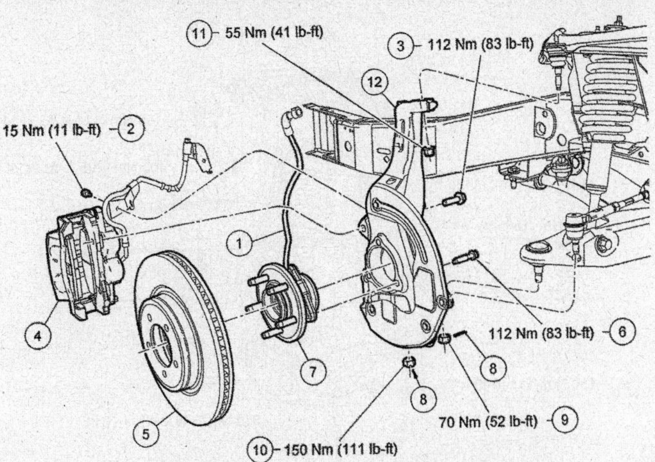

Item	Description
1	Speed sensor harness
2	Brake hose-to-wheel knuckle bolt
3	Anchor plate bolt (2 required)
4	Brake caliper, pads and anchor plate
5	Brake disc
6	Wheel hub-to-wheel knuckle bolt (3 required)

Item	Description
7	Wheel bearing and hub assembly
8	Cotter pins (2 required)
9	Tie-rod end-to-wheel knuckle nut
10	Lower ball joint-to-wheel knuckle nut
11	Upper ball joint-to-wheel knuckle nut
12	Wheel knuckle

LTV0500000000671

Fig. 5 Front suspension (Part 1 of 2). Aviator, Explorer & Mountaineer w/2WD

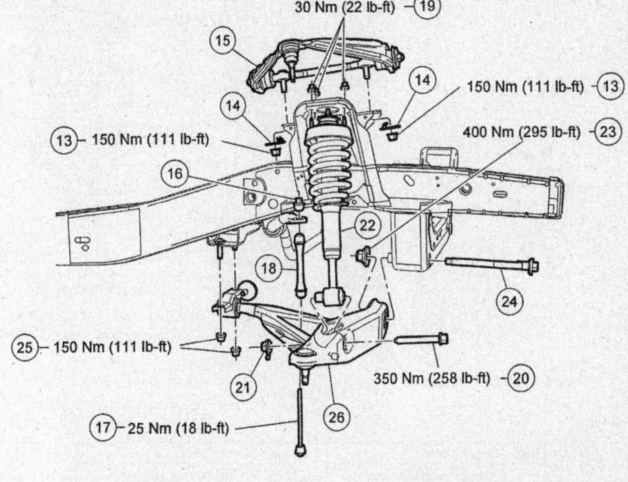

Item	Description
13	Upper arm-to-frame nuts (2 required)
14	Set shims (2 required)
15	Upper arm (RH/LH)
16	Nut and grommet
17	Stud
18	Stabilizer bar link
19	Shock absorber upper mount-to-frame nuts (3 required)
20	Shock absorber-to-lower arm bolt
21	Shock absorber-to-lower arm flag nut

Item	Description
22	Shock absorber and spring assembly
23	Lower arm-to-frame nut (forward mounting)
24	Lower arm-to-frame flag bolt (forward mounting)
25	Lower arm-to-frame nuts (rearward mounting) (2 required)
26	Lower Arm

LTV0500000000672

Fig. 5 Front suspension (Part 2 of 2). Aviator, Explorer & Mountaineer w/2WD

2. Remove stabilizer link nut, washer, and bushing.
3. Remove shock absorber to lower arm nuts.
4. Remove torsion bar as outlined in "Torsion Bar, Replace."
5. Remove lower ball joint nut, then using a suitable pitman arm puller, separate suspension arm from spindle.
6. Remove two front suspension lower arm bolts and nuts, then the suspension arm. **On 4WD models, ensure bushing joint, axle shaft and steering knuckle are supported before arm is removed.**
7. Reverse procedure to install, noting the following:
   a. When installing lower suspension arm, tighten pivot bolts until snug. Tighten to specification when installation procedure is complete.
   b. Ensure alignment is within specifications.

UPPER ARM

1. Raise and support vehicle, then remove front wheels.
2. Support lower control arm.
3. Remove pinch bolt and nut from front wheel spindle. **To avoid damage to spindle, ensure spindle is secured before removal of pinch bolt.**
4. Remove two upper control arm retaining nuts and bolts, then the upper arm.
5. Reverse procedure to install. Ensure alignment is within specifications.

Ranger

2WD MODEL LOWER ARM

1. Raise and support vehicle.
2. Remove brake rotor as outlined in "Disc Brakes" chapter.
3. Remove brake rotor shield.
4. Remove upper shock absorber nut, washer and bushing.
5. Remove lower shock attaching nuts, then the shock.
6. Remove stabilizer bar link, then compress coil spring using spring compressor tool No. D78P–5310–A or equivalent.
7. Remove lower ball joint attaching nut.
8. Separate ball joint from spindle using pitman arm puller tool No. T64P–3590–F or equivalent.
9. Remove lower arm nuts and bolt, then the arm and spring.
10. Reverse procedure to install noting the following:
   a. Ensure end of coil spring is over first hole and not visible in second hole, **Fig. 12.**
   b. Ensure lower arm nuts are not tightened until control arm is at curb position ride height.
   c. On righthand control arm, install rear bolt adjustment cam and nut in center of frame slot.
   d. Install ball joint cotter pin in outboard to inboard direction with pin fingers bent at righthand angles.

2WD MODEL UPPER ARM

1. Raise and support vehicle.
2. Remove disc brake rotor as outlined in "Disc Brakes" chapter.
3. Remove brake rotor shield.
4. Support control arm using a suitable jack.
5. Mark position of adjustment cams.
6. Remove upper ball joint attaching nut and pinch bolt.
7. Separate ball joint from spindle.
8. Remove upper arm attaching nuts and bolts, then the arm.
9. Reverse procedure to install noting the following:
   a. Tighten upper arm attaching nuts only when arm is at curb ride height position.
   b. Align marked position of adjustment cams.
   c. Tighten to specifications.

4WD MODELS

Refer to "Aviator, Explorer, Explorer Sport, Explorer Sport Trac & Mountaineer" for ball joint replacement.

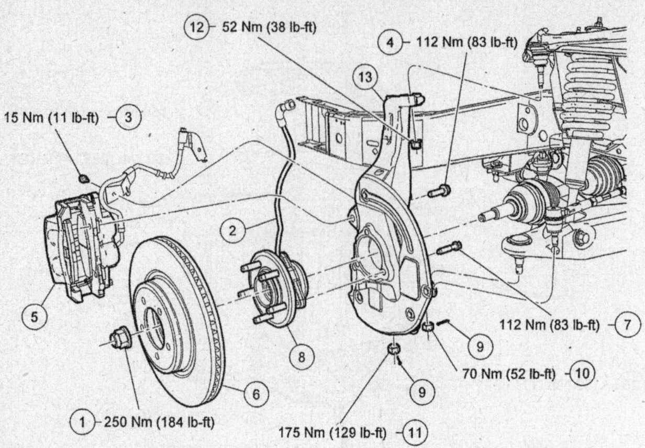

Item	Description
1	Axle-to-wheel hub nut
2	Speed sensor harness
3	Brake hose-to-wheel knuckle bolt
4	Anchor plate bolt (2 required)
5	Brake caliper, pads and anchor plate
6	Brake disc
7	Wheel hub-to-wheel knuckle bolt (3 required)

Item	Description
8	Wheel bearing and hub assembly
9	Cotter pins (2 required)
10	Tie-rod end-to-wheel knuckle nut
11	Lower ball joint-to-wheel knuckle nut
12	Upper ball joint-to-wheel knuckle nut
13	Wheel knuckle

LTV0500000000673

Fig. 6 Front suspension (Part 1 of 2). Aviator, Explorer & Mountaineer w/4WD

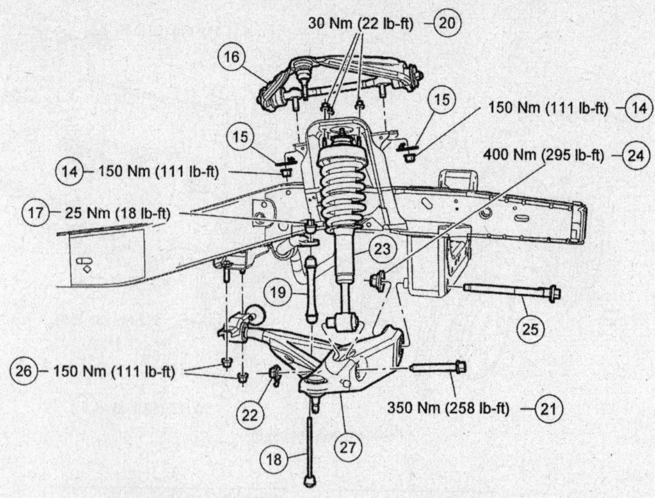

Item	Description
14	Upper arm-to-frame nuts
15	Set shims (2 required)
16	Upper arm (RH/LH)
17	Nut and grommet
18	Stud
19	Stabilizer bar link
20	Shock absorber upper mount-to-frame nuts (3 required)
21	Shock absorber-to-lower arm bolt
22	Shock absorber-to-lower arm flag nut

Item	Description
23	Shock absorber and spring assembly
24	Lower arm-to-frame nut (forward mounting)
25	Lower arm-to-frame flag bolt (forward mounting)
26	Lower arm-to-frame nuts (rearward mounting) (2 required)
27	Lower arm

LTV0500000000674

Fig. 6 Front suspension (Part 2 of 2). Aviator, Explorer & Mountaineer w/4WD

COIL SPRING

REPLACE

Aviator, Explorer, Mountaineer & Ranger

2WD MODELS

1. Raise and support vehicle.
2. Remove disc brake rotor as outlined in "Disc Brakes" chapter.
3. Remove brake rotor shield.
4. Remove upper shock absorber attaching nut, washer and bushing, then the lower nuts and shock absorber.
5. Remove stabilizer bar link attaching nut.
6. Compress coil spring using spring compressor tool No. D78P–5310–A or equivalent.
7. Remove lower ball joint attaching nut.
8. Separate ball joint from spindle using pitman arm puller T64P–3590–F or equivalent.
9. Position spindle aside and remove coil spring.
10. Reverse procedure to install noting the following:
    a. Ensure end of coil spring is over first hole and not visible in second hole, **Fig. 12.**
    b. Install ball joint cotter pin in outboard to inboard direction with pin fingers bent at righthand angles.

TORSION BAR

REPLACE

1. Raise and support vehicle.
2. Remove torsion bar cover plate.
3. Refer to **Fig. 13** and relieve torsion bar tension as follows:
    a. Install torsion bar tool No. T95T–5310–AR and adapter tool Nos. T96T–5310–AR or equivalents.
    b. Tighten torsion bar tool until torsion bar adjuster lifts off adjuster bolt.
    c. Remove torsion bar adjustment bolt and nut. **Torsion bar adjustment bolt is coated with dry adhesive and must be replaced if backed off or removed. Failure to follow this step may cause adjustment bolt to loosen and loss of vehicle alignment.**
    d. Loosen torsion bar adjustment tool until all tension is relieved from torsion bar.
4. Mark torsion bar and adjuster for installation reference.
5. Remove torsion bar insulator, then pull torsion bar from front suspension arm.
6. Reverse procedure to install. Ensure alignment is within specification.

SHOCK ABSORBER

REPLACE

1. Remove upper shock absorber retaining nut, **Fig. 14.**
2. Remove shock absorber lower attaching nuts. Slightly compress shock and remove.
3. Reverse procedure to install.

AIR SHOCK

REPLACE

Shock absorbers are charged with nitrogen gas. **Do not apply heat or attempt to open or puncture.**

Prior to replacing air shocks, connect a New Generation Star (NGS) tester to the data link connector. Select the RIDE CONTROL OUTPUT screen and turn on the following solenoids to vent the entire system of air and to lower vehicle to its lowest possible height: FRONT FIL, REAR FIL, GATE, and VENT.

Disconnect top of height sensor to prevent damage to sensor.

1. Raise and support vehicle.
2. Disconnect shock absorber electrical connector.
3. Push in red ring and remove air line.
4. Remove shock absorber lower retaining nuts.
5. Remove top attaching nut, then the shock absorber.
6. Reverse procedure to install.

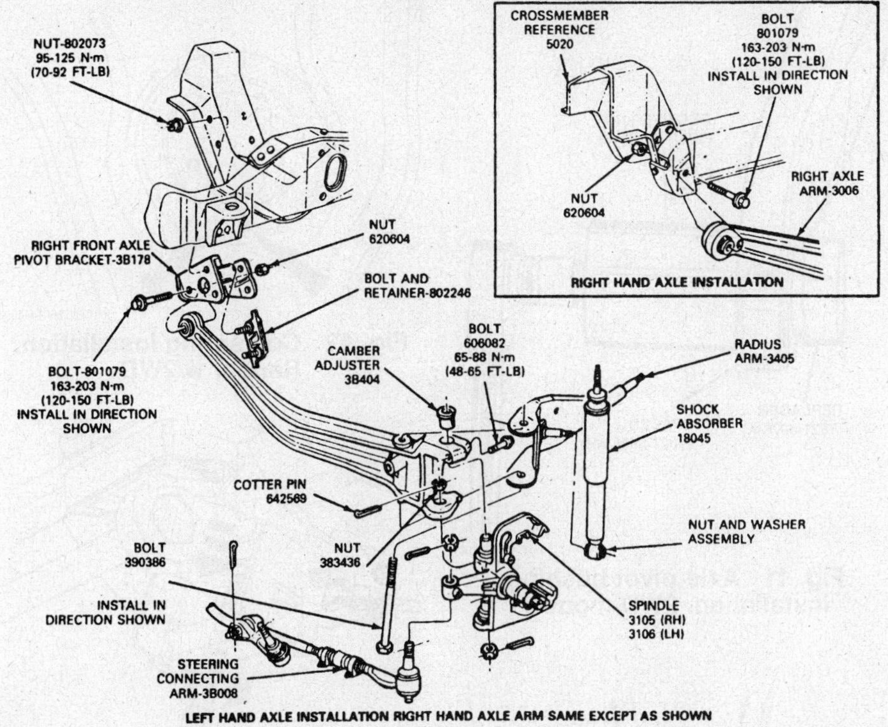

Fig. 7 Front I-beam axle assembly. 2WD Ranger

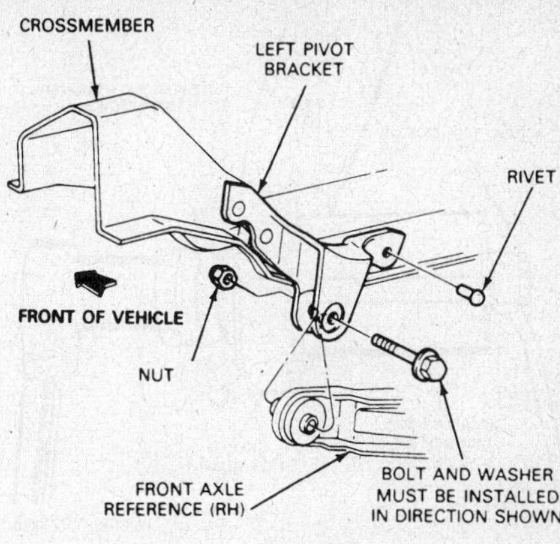

Fig. 8 Lefthand axle pivot bracket replacement. 4WD models

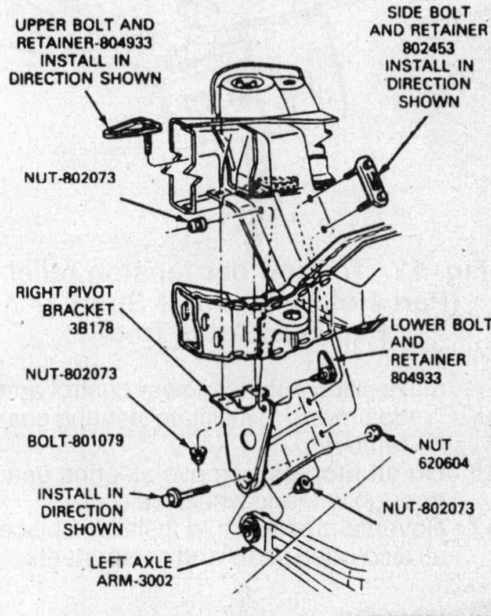

Fig. 9 Righthand axle pivot bracket replacement. 4WD models

STABILIZER BAR

REPLACE

1. Remove bolts and retainers from center and righthand end of stabilizer bar, **Fig. 15.**
2. Remove stabilizer bar to stabilizer link attaching nut, bolt and washer.
3. Remove stabilizer bar and bushings.
4. Reverse procedure to install.

RADIUS ARM

REPLACE

1. Raise and support front of vehicle. Support axle.
2. Disconnect lower end of shock absorber from shock lower bracket and remove front coil spring as outlined in "Coil Spring, Replace."
3. Loosen axle pivot bolt. Remove spring lower seat from radius arm. Remove nut and bolt from radius arm to axle and front bracket, **Figs. 16 and 17.**
4. Remove nut, rear washer and insulator from rear side of radius arm rear bracket and remove radius arm. Remove inner insulator and retainer from radius arm stud.
5. Reverse procedure to install.

RADIUS ARM INSULATOR

REPLACE

1. **On models equipped with 4WD,** remove coil spring as outlined in "Coil Spring, Replace," then remove front stabilizer bar link attachment, then rotate stabilizer bar out of way.
2. **On all models,** loosen axle pivot bolt and upper shock absorber pivot bolt and compress shock.
3. Remove nut and washer attaching radius arm to radius arm bracket. Remove outer insulator and spacer, **Fig. 17.**
4. Move radius arm and axle assembly forward out of radius arm bracket. Remove inner insulator and retainer.
5. Reverse procedure to install.

POWER STEERING GEAR

REPLACE

Aviator, Explorer, Explorer Sport, Explorer Sport Trac & Mountaineer

1. Place steering wheel in straight ahead position and turn ignition switch to OFF position.
2. Drain power steering fluid reservoir using a suitable suction device.
3. Raise and support vehicle.
4. Remove front wheel and tire assemblies.
5. Remove and discard lower arm to frame nuts, **Fig. 18.**
6. Remove steering gear mounting nuts and bolts.
7. Remove steering gear mounting bracket.
8. Remove and discard lower shaft to steering gear bolt.
9. Disconnect Variable Assist Power Steering (VAPS) switch electrical connector.
10. Remove power steering line clamp plate nut.
11. Remove power steering hoses from steering gear. Remove and discard O-rings.
12. Remove and discard tie rod end cotter pins and nuts.
13. Disconnect tie rod ends using tie rod end removal tool No. T74P-3044-A1, or equivalent.
14. Remove lefthand brake assembly mounting bolts, rotate assembly outward.
15. **On models equipped with 4WD,** proceed as follows:
    a. Remove lefthand lower shock absorber bolt.
    b. Remove stabilizer bar connecting link nut and disconnect link.
    c. Remove lefthand lower control arm to frame flag bolt.

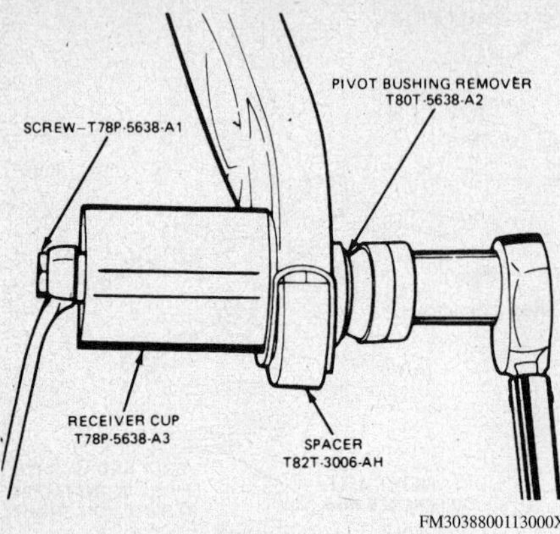

Fig. 10 Axle pivot bushing removal. 2WD models

Fig. 13 Torsion bar tension relief (Part 1 of 3). Explorer Sport & Explorer Sport Trac

d. Position lefthand lower control arm downward to facilitate steering gear removal.

16. **On all models,** remove steering gear through lefthand wheel well.
17. Reverse procedure to install. Replace all discarded seals and components.

Ranger

1. Position wheels in straight ahead position. Do not lock steering column.
2. Raise and support vehicle.
3. Remove front wheels.
4. **On models equipped with 4WD,** remove air deflector.
5. **On models equipped with power steering fluid cooler,** disconnect hoses from cooler and drain fluid into suitable container. Remove cooler attaching bolts, then the cooler.
6. **On all models,** remove tie rod to spindle attaching nuts, then tie rod from spindle using a suitable pitman arm puller.
7. **On models equipped with 4WD,** proceed as follows:
   a. Loosen lefthand outer tie rod jam nut and then remove tie rod. Count number of turns for installation reference.
   b. Remove stabilizer bar as outlined in

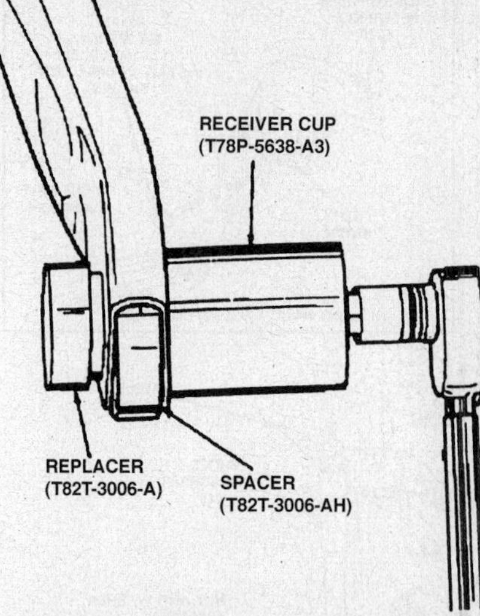
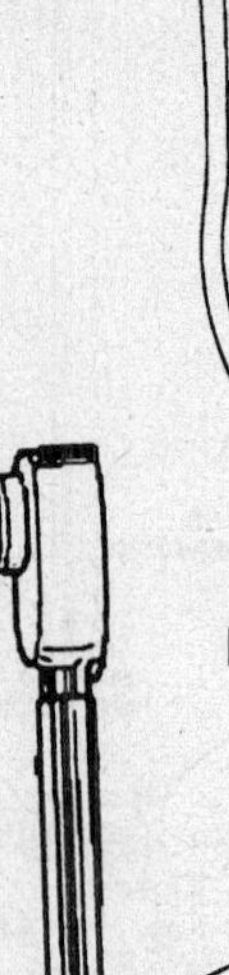

Fig. 11 Axle pivot bushing installation. 2WD models

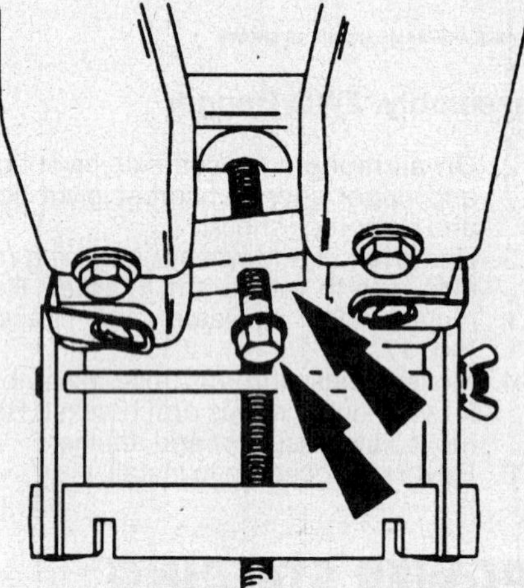
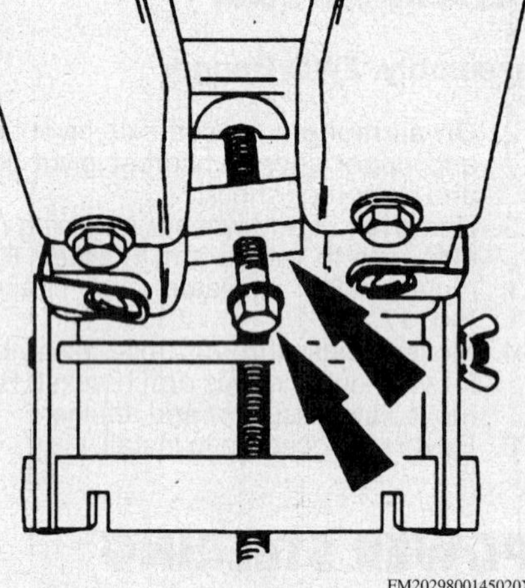

Fig. 13 Torsion bar tension relief (Part 2 of 3). Explorer Sport & Explorer Sport Trac

"Stabilizer Bar, Replace."

8. **On all models,** turn steering column shaft to gain access to pinch bolt, then remove bolt.
9. Lock steering column, then disconnect steering column shaft from gear. **Ensure steering wheel does not turn when lower column shaft is disconnected or clockspring damage may occur.**
10. Disconnect power steering hoses, then remove gear attaching nuts.
11. Remove mounting stud, nut, washer and stop assemblies. **Hold tops of stud bolts to avoid damage to power steering lines.**
12. **On models equipped with 2WD,** remove steering gear.

FM2029800144000X

Fig. 12 Coil spring installation. Ranger w/2WD

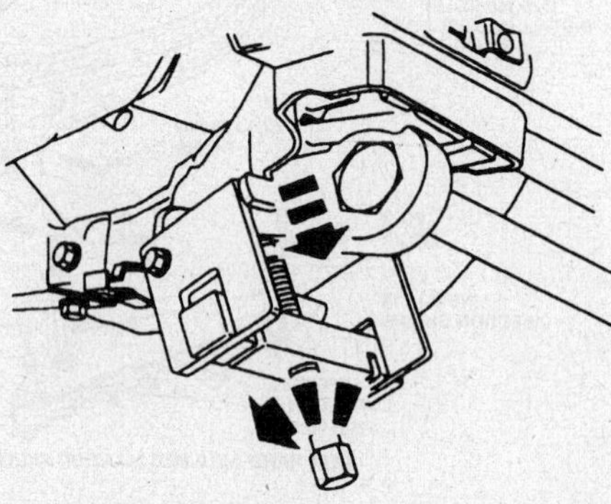

Fig. 13 Torsion bar tension relief (Part 3 of 3). Explorer Sport & Explorer Sport Trac

FM2029700123000X

Fig. 14 Shock absorber replacement

13. **On models equipped with 4WD,** proceed as follows:
    a. Rotate gear toward front of vehicle.
    b. Turn gear input shaft to righthand until stop is reached.
    c. Move steering gear to righthand as far as possible.
    d. Move lefthand tie rod forward to clear crossmember and remove gear from vehicle.
14. **On all models,** reverse procedure to install noting the following:
    a. Clean steering gear mounting surfaces.
    b. Inspect and adjust wheel alignment if required.

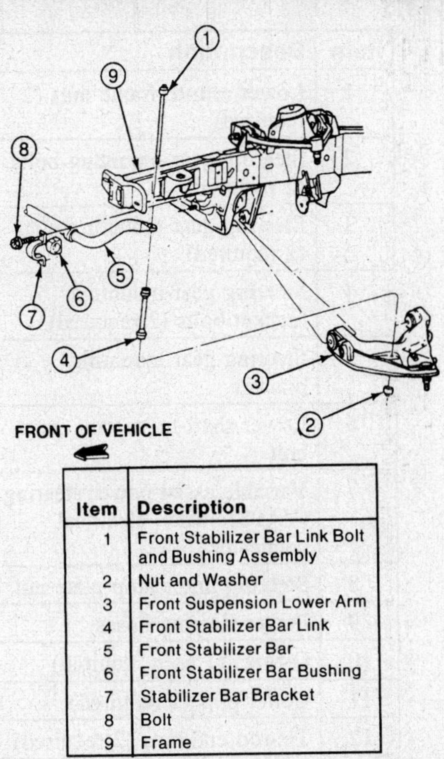

Item	Description
1	Front Stabilizer Bar Link Bolt and Bushing Assembly
2	Nut and Washer
3	Front Suspension Lower Arm
4	Front Stabilizer Bar Link
5	Front Stabilizer Bar
6	Front Stabilizer Bar Bushing
7	Stabilizer Bar Bracket
8	Bolt
9	Frame

Fig. 15 Stabilizer bar replacement

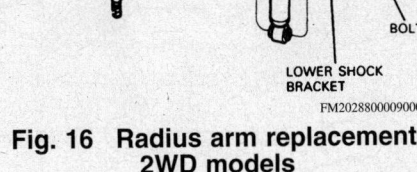

Fig. 16 Radius arm replacement. 2WD models

POWER STEERING PUMP

REPLACE

2.3, 3.0 & 4.0L Engines

1. Drain power steering fluid reservoir using a suitable suction device.
2. Remove cooling fan using wrench tool Nos. T84T-6312-C and T84T-6312-D, or equivalents, then remove fan and shroud.
3. Drain power steering pump reservoir, disconnect return hose at reservoir, then drain into suitable container.
4. Remove power steering pressure line.
5. Remove drive belt.
6. Remove oil dipstick tube, as required.
7. **On models equipped with 4.0L SOHC engine,** remove pulley attaching bolts, then the pulley.
8. **On all models,** remove power steering pump bracket support brace, if equipped.
9. Hold pulley and rotate tool nut counterclockwise to remove using power steering pump pulley removal tool No. T69L-10300-B, or equivalent. **Do not apply in and out pressure as internal thrust area damage may occur.**
10. Remove pump to bracket attaching bolts, then remove pump.
11. Reverse procedure to install.

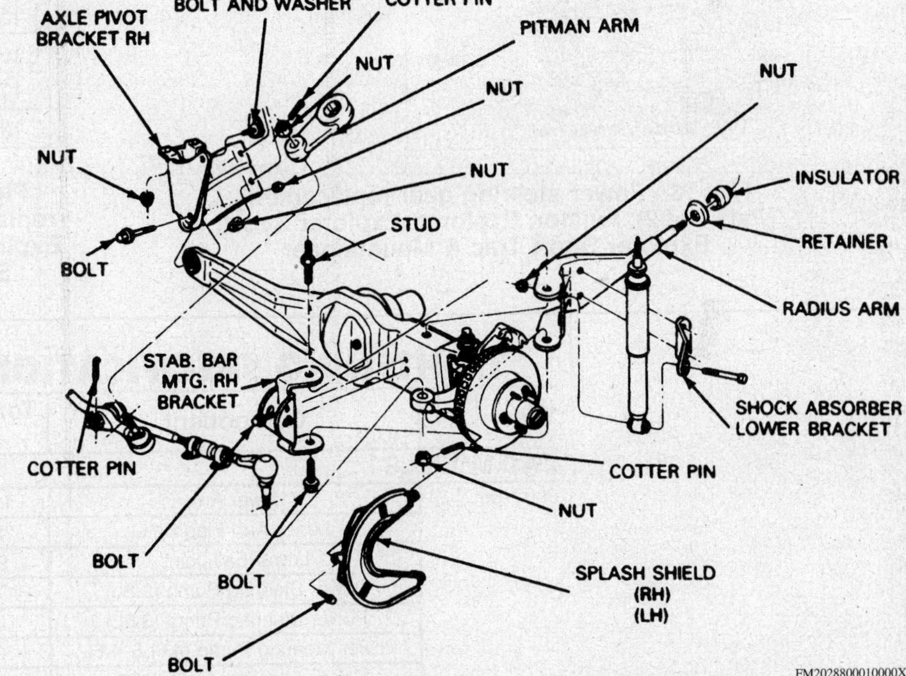

Fig. 17 Radius arm replacement. 4WD models

4.6L Engine

1. Remove power steering return hose at cooler and drain fluid into suitable container.
2. Remove power steering pressure hose at power steering pump and drain fluid into suitable container.
3. Remove drive belt.
4. Remove four power steering pump to pump support bolts.
5. Remove power steering pump.
6. Reverse procedure to install.

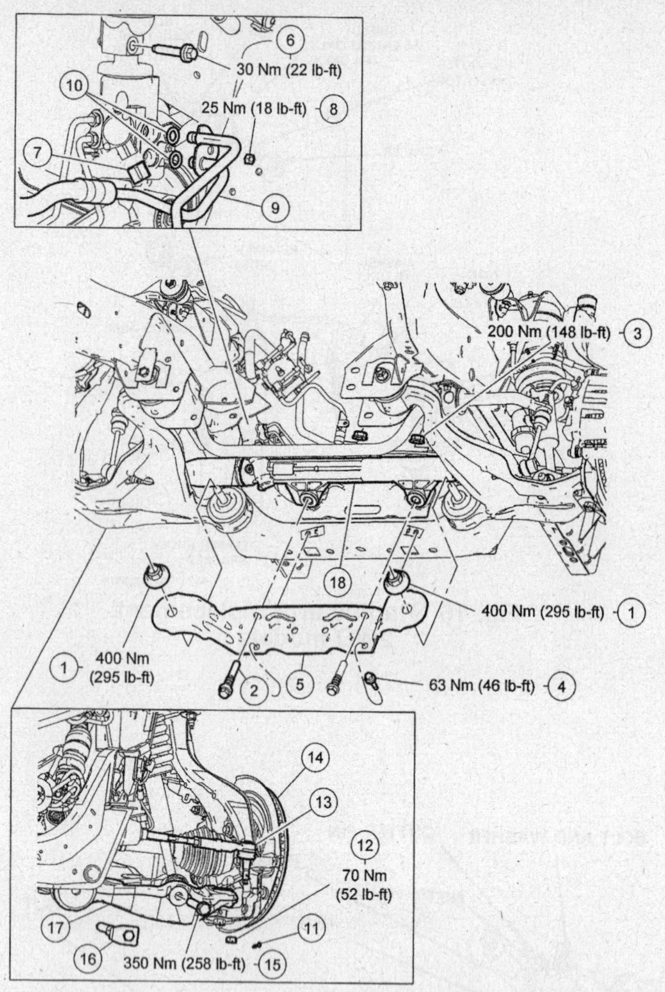

Fig. 18 Power steering gear replacement (Part 1 of 2). Aviator, Explorer, Explorer Sport, Explorer Sport Trac & Mountaineer

Item	Description
1	Lower arm-to-frame nuts (2 required)
2	Steering gear mounting bolts (2 required)
3	Steering gear mounting nuts (2 required)
4	Steering gear mounting bracket bolts (2 required)
5	Steering gear mounting bracket
6	Lower shaft-to-steering gear bolt
7	Variable assist power steering (VAPS) switch electrical connector
8	Steering line clamp plate nut
9	Power steering hoses
10	O-rings (1 each required)
11	Cotter pins (2 required)
12	Tie-rod end nuts (2 required)
13	Tie-rod end
14	LH brake assembly
15	Lower shock absorber bolt
16	Lower arm-to-frame flag bolt
17	Lower arm
18	Steering gear

LTV0500000000676

Fig. 18 Power steering gear replacement (Part 2 of 2). Aviator, Explorer, Explorer Sport, Explorer Sport Trac & Mountaineer

TIGHTENING SPECIFICATIONS

Year	Component	Torque Ft. Lbs.
2WD MODELS		
2002–06	Lower Arm	110–148
	Lower Arm Flag Bolt	282–295
	Lower Ball Joint	98–111
	Power Steering Pump (2.8L)	13–18
	Power Steering Pump (3.0L)	34–47
	Power Steering Pump (4.0L& 4.6L)	30–40
	Shock Absorber Lower Nuts	①
	Shock Absorber Upper Nuts	②
	Stabilizer Bar Link	15–18
	Stabilizer Bar Stud	③

Continued

TIGHTENING SPECIFICATIONS—Continued

Year	Component	Torque Ft. Lbs.
2WD MODELS		
2002–06	Stabilizer Bracket Bolts	30–52
	Steering Gear To Crossmember	111–148
	Tie Rod To Spindle Nut	48–52
	Torsion Bar Cover Plate	35–41
	Upper Arm Cam Bolt Nuts	96–111
	Upper Ball Joint Pinch Bolt	35–41
	Wheel Lug Nut	100
4WD MODELS		
2002–06	Caliper Anchor Plate To Knuckle	78–83
	Caliper To Anchor Plate	④
	Jounce Bumper To Frame	18–26
	Lower Ball Joint	111–129
	Lower Control Arm To Frame	111–148
	Power Steering Pump (2.8L)	13–18
	Power Steering Pump (3.0L)	34–47
	Power Steering Pump (4.0L & 4.6L)	30–40
	Shock Absorber Lower Nuts	①
	Shock Absorber Upper Nut	②
	Stabilizer Bar Bracket To Frame	⑤
	Stabilizer Bar Link	⑥
	Steering Gear To Crossmember	111–148
	Tie Rod End Nut	48–52
	Torsion Bar Cover Plate	35–41
	Upper Arm Pinch Bolt	35–41
	Upper Control Arm To Frame	98–111
	Wheel Lug Nut	100

① — Aviator, Explorer & Mountaineer, 258 ft. lbs.; Explorer Sport, Explorer Sport Trac, & Ranger, 18 ft. lbs.

② — Aviator, Explorer, Mountaineer & Ranger, 22 ft. lbs.; Explorer Sport & Explorer Sport Trac, 35 ft. lbs.

③ — Aviator, 66 ft. lbs.; Explorer & Mountaineer, 18 ft. lbs.

④ — Aviator, Explorer & Mountaineer, 155 ft. lbs.; Explorer Sport, Explorer Sport Trac & Ranger, 24 ft. lbs.

⑤ — Aviator, Explorer & Mountaineer, 46–52 ft. lbs.; Explorer Sport, Explorer Sport Trac, & Ranger, 30 ft. lbs.

⑥ — Aviator, 66 ft. lbs.; Explorer & Mountaineer, 18 ft. lbs.; Explorer Sport, Explorer Sport Trac, & Ranger, 18–30 ft. lbs.

Front Wheel Drive

NOTE: On Air Bag Equipped Models, Refer To "Air Bag System Precautions" Located In The Front Of This Manual For System Disarming & Arming Procedures.

INDEX

PRECAUTIONS

Air Bag Systems

Refer to "Air Bag System Precautions" in the front of this manual for system disarming and arming procedures.

Automatic Ride Control

On models equipped with automatic ride control, the automatic ride control service switch must be turned off before lifting vehicle. The service switch is located in the rear jack storage area.

Battery Ground Cable

Prior to service, disconnect battery ground cable and isolate as required.

AXLE

REPLACE

Aviator, Explorer & Mountaineer

1. Raise and support vehicle, then remove front wheel and tire assembly.
2. Remove front halfshafts as outlined under "Front Halfshaft, Replace."
3. Index mark front axle pinion flange, front driveshaft, front output shaft and front driveshaft constant velocity joint.
4. Remove and discard six CV joint mounting bolts and washers, **Fig. 1.**
5. Remove universal joint strap retaining bolts, then the universal joint straps and front driveshaft.
6. Position suitable hydraulic jack under front axle housing. Securely strap axle housing to jack.
7. Remove and discard axle assembly insulator bolts.
8. Lower axle to gain access to axle vent hose, then disconnect vent hose.
9. Lower axle assembly from vehicle.

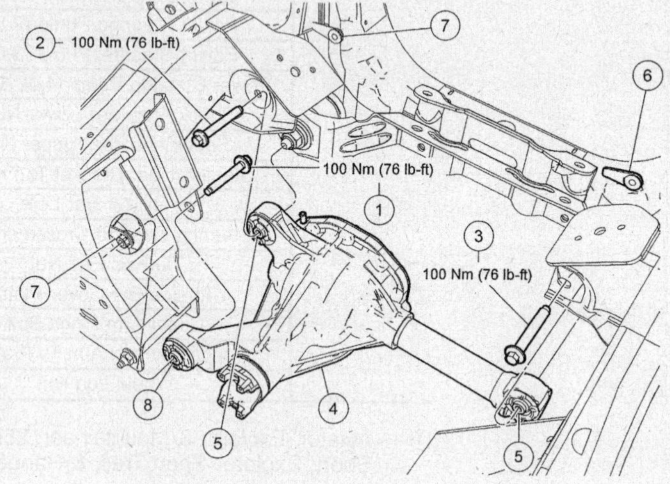

Item	Description
1	Axle assembly insulator bolt
2	Axle assembly insulator bolt
3	Axle assembly insulator bolt
4	Axle assembly
5	Axle assembly insulator bushing
6	Axle tube insulator bolt flag nut
7	Axle assembly insulator bolt elbow flag nut
8	Axle assembly insulator bushing

LTV0500000000679

Fig. 1 Axle replacement. Aviator, Explorer & Mountaineer

10. Reverse procedure to install. Install new fasteners.

Explorer Sport, Explorer Sport Trac & Ranger

1. Raise and support vehicle, then remove front wheel and tire assembly.
2. Remove front halfshafts as outlined under "Front Halfshaft, Replace."
3. Index mark front axle pinion flange, front driveshaft, front output shaft and front driveshaft constant velocity joint.
4. Remove front driveshaft mounting bolts, then the driveshaft.
5. Remove cotter pin and nut from each tie rod end.
6. Separate tie rod ends from steering knuckle using tie rod end removal tool No. TOOL-3290–D, or equivalent. **Remove adapter from ball end of tool. Apply a small amount of grease to tie rod stud and ball of tool.**
7. Unclip anti-lock wheel sensor wiring harnesses from locators.

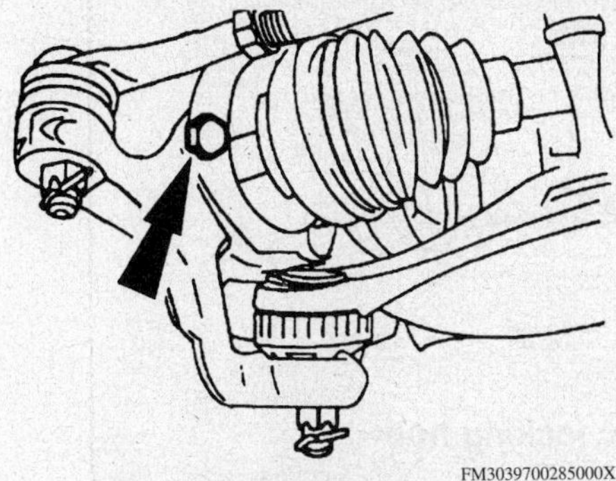

Fig. 2 Wheel hub removal. Explorer, Explorer Sport, Explorer Sport Trac & Mountaineer

Item	Description
1	Disc brake caliper
2	Front axle wheel end nut
3	Tie-rod nut
4	Stabilizer bar link nut
5	Upper ball joint nut
6	Halfshaft assembly

LTV0500000000678

Fig. 3 Front halfshaft replacement (Part 2 of 2)

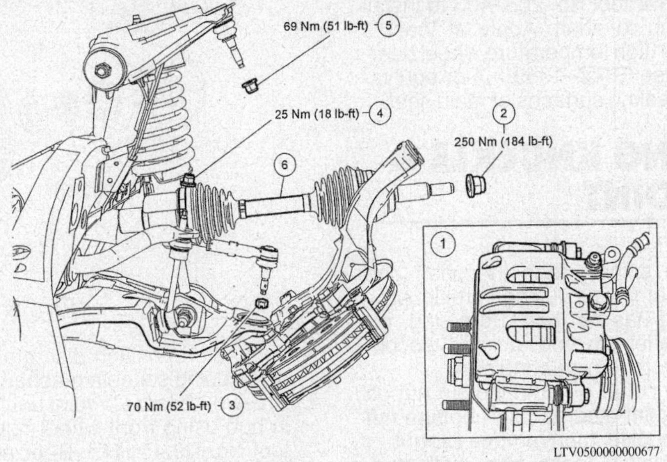

Fig. 3 Front halfshaft replacement (Part 1 of 2)

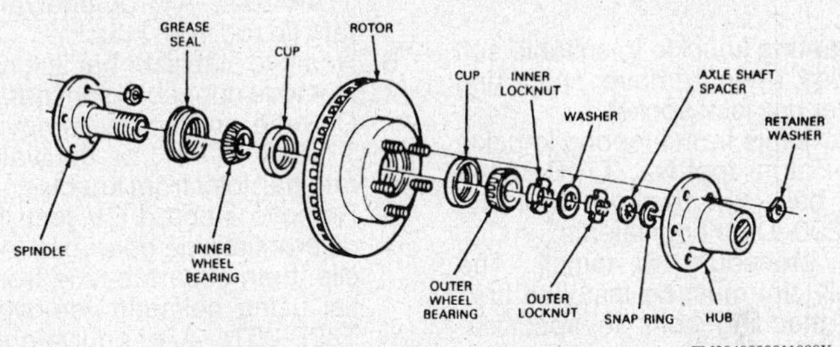

Fig. 4 Manual locking hub

8. Remove bolts retaining anti-lock sensor wiring harnesses to knuckles, then disconnect harness.
9. Support front suspension lower arm using suitable jack.
10. Remove shock absorber to lower control arm mounting bolts.
11. Remove upper ball joint pinch bolts, then disconnect ball joints from knuckles.
12. Support axle housing assembly using suitable hydraulic jack.
13. Remove axle housing to frame mounting bolts, the lower supporting jack and remove axle assembly.
14. Reverse procedure to install. Install new fasteners.

SPINDLE, SHAFT & JOINT ASSEMBLY

REPLACE

Aviator, Explorer, Explorer Sport, Explorer Sport Trac & Mountaineer

1. Remove caliper retaining bolts, then the caliper.
2. Remove caliper bracket retaining bolts, then the caliper bracket.
3. Remove brake rotor.
4. Remove dust shield.
5. Remove hub nut and washer assembly.
6. Remove ABS sensor.
7. A puller will not normally be required for next step. CV joint is a slip fit into wheel hub and bearing.
8. Remove three bolts, then the wheel hub, **Fig. 2. Do not over extend CV joint when removing hub and bearing assembly.**
9. Remove torsion bar as outlined in "Torsion Bar, Replace" in "Front Suspension & Steering."
10. Remove ABS sensor bracket bolt and reposition sensor wire to side.
11. Remove upper ball joint pinch bolt.
12. Remove tie rod castle nut.
13. Separate tie rod end from knuckle using a suitable pitman arm puller.
14. Remove lower ball joint castle nut, then using a suitable pitman arm puller, separate lower ball joint from knuckle.
15. Support front driveshaft with a suitable wire, then remove front wheel knuckle.
16. Reverse procedure to install.

Ranger

1. Raise and support vehicle.
2. Remove brake rotor as outlined in "Disc Brakes" chapter.
3. Install hub-lock removal clips, tool No. 205–404 or equivalent.
4. Install hub-lock puller, tool No. 205–405 or equivalent. Align puller with three slots in hub-lock. Tighten set screw finger tight.
5. Remove hub-lock using slide hammer tool No. T59L–100–B or equivalent.
6. Remove rotor shield.
7. Remove axle shaft retaining clip using a suitable pair of snap ring pliers.
8. Disconnect vacuum hose and ABS electrical connector if equipped.
9. Remove three wheel hub and bearing attaching bolts.
10. Remove wheel hub and bearing. **Hub and bearing are a slip fit design and should not require a puller for removal. If bearing retaining nut on wheel hub and bearing is removed, hub and bearing must be replaced.**
11. Remove O-rings from hub. **O-rings must be replaced or loss of four wheel drive operation and system contamination may result.**
12. Remove torsion bar as outlined in "Torsion Bar, Replace" in "Front Suspension & Steering."
13. Secure front axle shaft to prevent CV from overextending.
14. Remove tie rod end nut and lower ball joint attaching nut from spindle.
15. Separate ball joint and tie rod from spindle using a suitable pitman arm puller.
16. Remove upper control arm pinch bolt, then the steering knuckle. Knuckle seal should only be removed if it is damaged or fails leak test.
17. Reverse procedure to install. Use snap

ring sleeve tool No. 205–403 to install snap ring to shaft. Apply at least 3 grams of high temperature wheel bearing grease E8TZ–19590–A or equivalent to sealing surfaces of main seal.

STEERING KNUCKLE & BALL JOINT

REPLACE

1. Remove spindle then the shaft and joint assembly as outlined previously.
2. If tie rod has not been removed, remove cotter pin and nut and disconnect tie rod from steering arm.
3. Remove cotter pin and loosen nut on top ball joint stud. Loosen bottom nut inside knuckle, then remove top nut.
4. Break spindle loose from ball stud, then remove camber adjuster. Mark position of adjuster for assembly reference.
5. Install steering knuckle in suitable soft jawed vise, then remove snap ring from lower ball joint socket.
6. Press ball joints from steering knuckle using C-Frame tool No. T74P-3044–A1 with ball joint remover tool No. TOOL-3290–D, or equivalents.
7. Reverse procedure to install. The lower ball joint must be installed first. Tighten attaching bolts to specifications.

FRONT HALFSHAFT

REPLACE

1. Raise and support vehicle, then remove front wheel and tire assembly.
2. Remove and discard front axle wheel end nut, **Fig. 3.**
3. Remove disc brake caliper guide pin bolts, then position disc brake caliper aside using suitable mechanic's wire.
4. Press outboard CV joint until it is loose in hub using front wheel hub removal tool No. D93P-1175–B, or equivalent.
5. Remove tie rod nut, then using C-frame and screw removal tool No. T74P-3044–A1, or equivalent, separate tie rod from knuckle.
6. Remove stabilizer bar link nut.
7. Remove upper ball joint nut, then using C-frame and screw removal tool No. T74P-3044–A1, or equivalent, separate ball joint from knuckle.
8. Remove inboard CV joint housing to differential side gear axle retaining circlip, then separate axle from differential using halfshaft removal tool No. T89P-3514–A, or equivalent.
9. Remove halfshaft assembly from vehicle.
10. Reverse procedure to install. Install new circlip and fasteners.

FRONT DRIVESHAFT

REPLACE

Refer to "Axle, Replace" for front driveshaft replacement procedures.

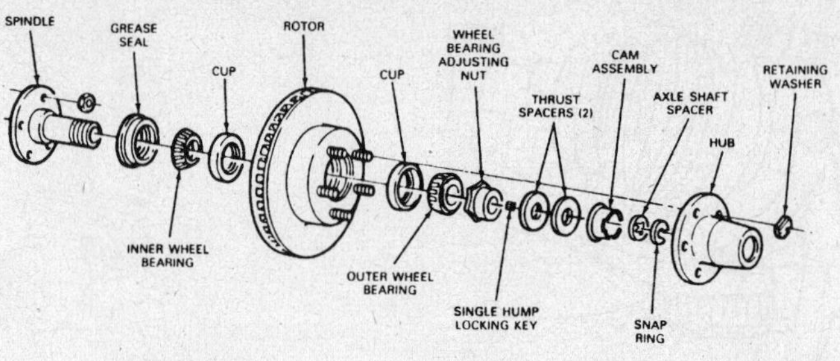

Fig. 5 Automatic locking hub

LOCKING HUB

REPLACE

To prevent damage to the spindle during removal, remove adjusting nut locking key from spindle keyway under adjusting nut prior to nut removal. A slight movement of the nut will loosen the locking key so that a magnet can be used for removal. During the front wheel bearing adjustment procedure, align the closest two holes in the wheel bearing adjusting nut with the center of the spindle keyway slot. Advance the nut to the next hole if required. To ensure proper wheel retention, install adjusting nut locking key in alignment with spindle keyway and insert into locknut holes. The double humped portion must be completely seated and flush with the locknut assembly.

1. Raise and support vehicle.
2. Remove wheel and tire assembly.
3. Remove lug nut stud retainer washers, then the locking hub assembly, **Figs. 4 and 5.**
4. Reverse procedure to install.

TIGHTENING SPECIFICATIONS

Year	Component	Torque Ft. Lbs.
2002–06	ABS Sensor	96–108①
	Anchor Plate	125–170
	Axle Stud	190–230
	Axle To Frame	45–59
	Bearing Cap Bolts	47–67
	Caliper Retaining Bolts	21–26
	Carrier Shear Bolt	75–95
	Carrier To Axle Arm Bolts	35–53
	Dust Shield	96–108①
	Front Axle Retainer Through Bolts	45–59
	Front Driveshaft U-Bolt Nuts	10–15
	Hub Nut	157–213
	Lower Ball Joint Nut	95–110
	Lower Shock Absorber To Radius Arm Nut	42–72
	Lower Spring Seat Nut	70–100
	Radius Arm Bracket Front Bolt	27–37
	Radius Arm Bracket Lower Bolt	160–220
	Ring Gear Bolts	70–90
	Tie Rod End	52–59
	Upper Ball Joint Nut	85–100
	Upper Ball Joint Pinch Bolt	30–41
	Wheel Lug Nuts	100

① — Inch lbs.

Wheel Alignment

NOTE: On Air Bag Equipped Models, Refer To "Air Bag System Precautions" Located In The Front Of This Manual For System Disarming & Arming Procedures.

INDEX

PRECAUTIONS

Air Bag Systems

Refer to "Air Bag System Precautions" in the front of this manual for system disarming and arming procedures.

Automatic Ride Control

On models equipped with automatic ride control, the automatic ride control service switch must be turned off before lifting vehicle. The service switch is located in the rear jack storage area.

Battery Ground Cable

Prior to service, disconnect battery ground cable and isolate as required.

PRELIMINARY INSPECTION

Inspect the following components, adjust, repair or replace as required prior to performing front wheel alignment.

1. Inflate tires to cold specifications.
2. Ensure front tires are of same size, ply rating and load rating.
3. Inspect for excessive wheel bearing endplay.
4. Inspect for worn or damaged spindle ball joints.
5. Inspect steering gear mounting bolts for proper torque.
6. Inspect radius arm or bent or damaged condition.
7. Inspect radius arm to frame bushings for looseness or wear.
8. Inspect suspension components for wear or damage.

FRONT WHEEL ALIGNMENT

Camber

Caster and camber are made by turning cams located on the upper control arm to frame attaching bolts. Vehicle is aligned at the factory with square caster/camber plates. If adjustment is needed, these plates must be replaced with four service cams. Caster split can be adjusted without replacing plates by using slider adjustment on the righthand upper front suspension arm bushing joint. Refer to **Fig. 1** when performing alignment.

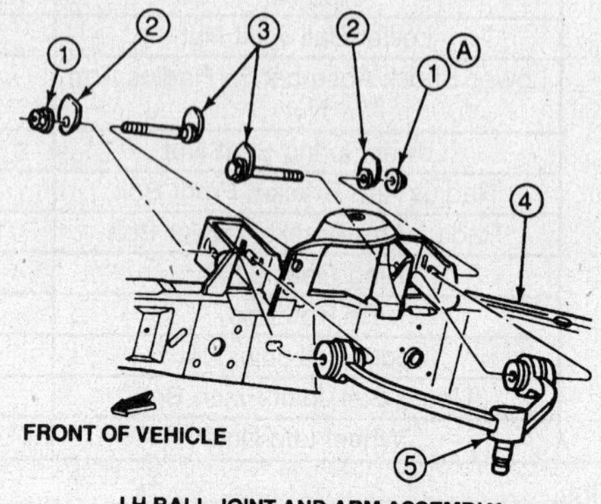

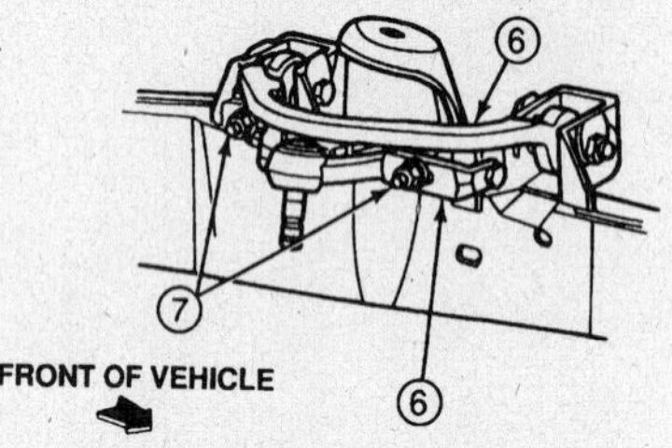

Item	Description
1	Nut
2	Front Suspension Upper Adjuster Cam (Service [Replacement] Cams Shown)
3	Front Suspension Upper Adjuster Cam Bolt
4	Frame
5	Front Suspension Arm Bushing Joint (LH)
6	Front Suspension Arm Bushing Joint (RH)
7	Nut (Part of 3084)

FM2049500052000X

Fig. 1 Front end alignment

1. Measure caster and camber.

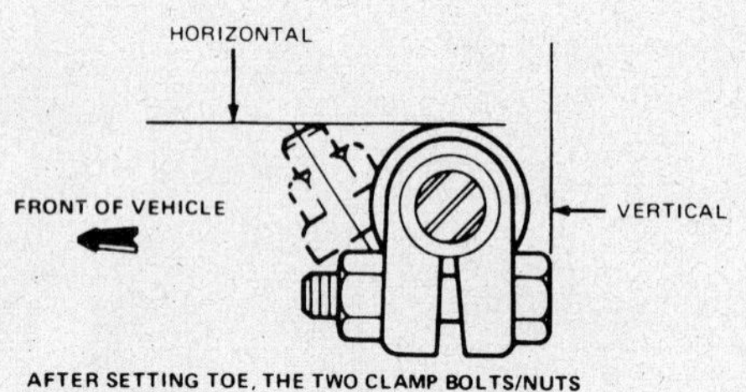

FM2048800016000X

Fig. 2 Toe-in adjustment

2. If adjustment to caster split is required, loosen two nuts on upper righthand front suspension arm bushing joint. Adjust slider bolt until caster split is within specification.
3. **Torque** nuts to 113 ft. lbs.
4. If adjustment is required to caster or camber, loosen cam bolt nuts and rotate cam bolt until alignment is within specification. **Torque** nuts to 113 ft. lbs.
5. Once optimal camber/caster alignment is achieved, reset front toe to specifications.

Caster

Caster and camber are adjusted with an adjuster, refer to "Camber" for procedure.

Toe-In

1. Loosen clamp bolts at each end of spindle connecting rod tube or inner tie rod, then rotate the sleeve or tie rod until correct toe alignment is obtained.
2. **On models equipped with adjusting sleeve,** center clamps between adjustment sleeve nibs, then position bolts horizontally with clamps nuts positioned as outlined in **Fig. 2.**
3. **On models equipped with inner tie rod adjustment,** tighten jam nut.
4. **On all models,** inspect toe-in adjustment, then inspect that steering wheel spokes are properly positioned and adjust as required.

FREESTAR & MONTEREY

NOTE: Refer To Back Of This Manual For Vehicle Manufacturer's Special Service Tool Suppliers.

INDEX OF SERVICE OPERATIONS

Specifications

GENERAL ENGINE SPECIFICATIONS

Year	Engine, Liter	Fuel System	Bore & Stroke	Comp. Ratio	Horsepower @ RPM	Torque Ft. Lbs. @ RPM	Normal Oil Pressure Lbs.①
2004–06	3.9L	SFI	3.8 x 3.4	9.27	194 @ 4500	243 @ 3750	40–125
	4.2L	SFI	3.8 x 3.8	9.35	201 @ 4250	263 @ 3650	40–125

① — At normal operating temperature & 2500 RPM.

TUNE UP SPECIFICATIONS

Year & Engine	Spark Plug Gap	Ignition Timing			Curb Idle Speed	Fast Idle Speed	Fuel Pump Pressure, psi.	Valve Lash, Inch
		Firing Order, Fig.	BTDC	Mark Location				
2004–06								
3.9L	.052–.056	A①	10	—	③	③	55	②
4.2L	.052–.056	A①	10	—	③	③	55	②

BTDC — Before Top Dead Center.

① — Firing order, 1-4-2-5-3-6. Refer to **Fig. A,** for spark plug cable orientation at ignition coil.

② — Equipped w/hydraulic valve tappets.

③ — Controlled by Powertrain Control Module (PCM).

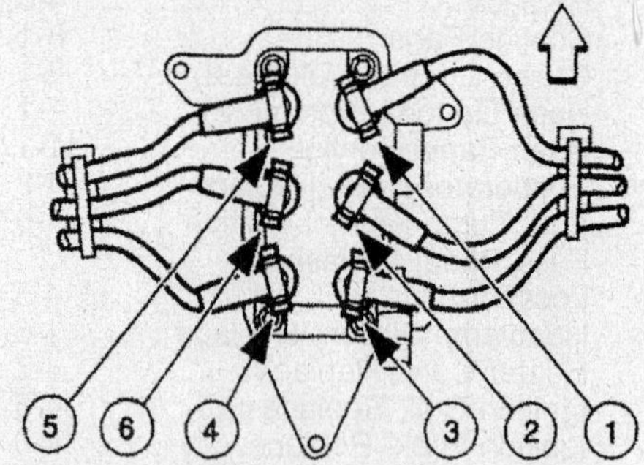

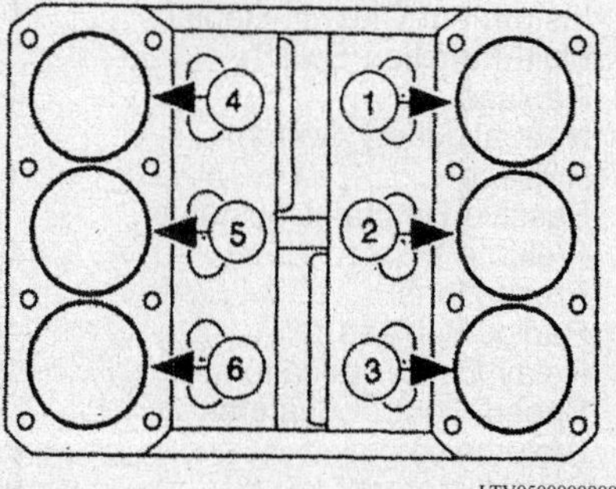

Fig. A

FRONT WHEEL ALIGNMENT SPECIFICATIONS

Year	Model	Caster Angle, Degrees		Camber Angle, Degrees		Total Toe, Degrees①	
		Limits	Desired	Limits	Desired	Limits	Desired
2004–06	All	+3.0 to +4.0	+3.5	-.96 to +.06	-.44	-.4 to +.1	-.15

① — Toe-In (+). Toe-Out (-).

REAR WHEEL ALIGNMENT SPECIFICATIONS

Year	Model	Camber Angle, Degrees		Total Toe, Degrees①	
		Limits	Desired	Limits	Desired
2004–06	All	-.83 to +.28	-.25	+.13 to +.27	+.07

① — Toe-In (+). Toe-Out (-).

VEHICLE RIDE HEIGHT SPECIFICATIONS

Year	Front, Inches①	Rear, Inches①	Ride Height Difference Side To Side, Inches	
			Front	Rear
2004–06	.37–1.18②	.39–6.37③	.28	.32

① — See door sticker or inside of glove box for manufacturers original tire size specifications. If tires on vehicle do not match manufacturers original tire size & measurement is not within limits, it will be required to refer to the "Non-Standard Tire & Wheel Size Adjustment To Ride Height Specification & Tire Size Adjustment Charts" in the front of this manual for approximate changes in ride height specifications.

② — Measure front vehicle ride height, **Fig. A.**

③ — Measure rear vehicle ride height, **Fig. B.**

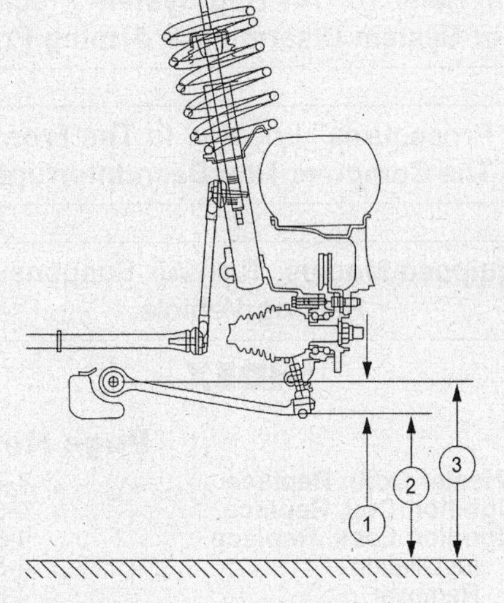

Item	Description
1	Ride height = B - A
2	Measurement A
3	Measurement B

LTV0500000000683

Fig. A Front ride height measurement

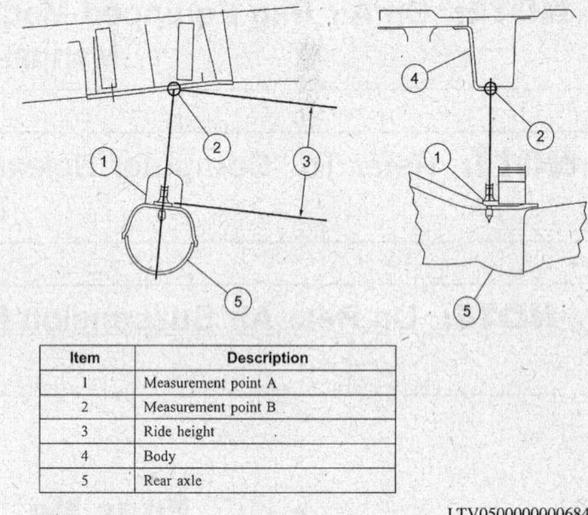

Fig. B Rear ride height measurement

FLUID CAPACITIES & COOLING SYSTEM DATA

Year	Engine Liter	Cooling System Capacity, Qts.		Recom-mended Engine Coolant Type	Radiator Cap Relief Pressure, Lbs.	Thermo Opening, Temp. °F	Fuel Tank, Gals.	Engine Oil Refill, Qts.①	Transaxle Oil, Qts.②
		Less A/C	With A/C						
2004–06	3.9L	15.0③	15.0③	④	14–18	188–195	26	5	12.25
	4.2L	15.0③	15.0③	④	14–18	188–195	26	5	12.25

①— Includes filter.
②— Approximate. Make final inspection w/dipstick.
③— Coolant capacity with rear auxiliary heater, 16.0 qts.
④— Motorcraft Premium Gold engine coolant, use coolant meeting Ford Motor Co. specification WSSM97B51–A1, or equivalent.

LUBRICANT DATA

Year	Model	Lubricant Type				
		Transaxle	Transfer Case	Rear Axle	Power Steering	Brake System
2004–06	All	Mercon® V	—	—	Mercon	DOT 3

Electrical

NOTE: On Air Bag Equipped Models, Refer To "Air Bag System Precautions" Located In The Front Of This Manual For System Disarming & Arming Procedures.

NOTE: Refer To "Computer Relearn Procedures" Located In The Front Of This Manual When Battery Power To The Computer Has Been Interrupted.

NOTE: On Rear Air Suspension Equipped Models, Turn Air Suspension Switch To "Off" Position Prior To Raising Vehicle.

INDEX

PRECAUTIONS

Air Bag Systems

Refer to "Air Bag System Precautions" in the front of this manual for system disarming and arming procedures.

Air Suspension Systems

Prior to raising vehicle, turn air suspension switch to "Off" position to prevent air suspension damage or vehicle from shifting on hoist.

Battery Ground Cable

Prior to service disconnect battery ground cable and isolate as required.

FUSE PANEL & FLASHER LOCATION

The main fuse panel may be found under the instrument panel to the lefthand side of the steering column under a plastic fuse panel cover. Additional fuses and circuit breakers may be found in the power distribution panel located on the lefthand front fender apron in the engine compartment.

These vehicles use the same flasher, both turn signal and hazard indicators in conjunction with the Smart Junction Box (SJB). The electronic combination turn signal/emergency flasher unit is located on the reverse side of the passenger compartment fuse panel.

RELAY CENTER LOCATION

Relays are contained in the battery junction box and in the central junction box located on the lefthand side of the engine compartment.

FUEL PUMP RELAY LOCATION

The fuel pump relay is located in the battery junction box.

STARTER

REPLACE

1. Raise and support vehicle.
2. Remove starter terminal cover, **Fig. 1**, then solenoid S terminal retaining nut and electrical connector.
3. Remove battery ground cable retaining from starter mounting stud, then the cable.
4. Remove solenoid B terminal retaining nut and electrical connector.
5. Remove starter motor mounting bolts and stud, then the starter motor.
6. Reverse procedure to install. **Torque** starter mounting stud and bolts to 21 ft. lbs.

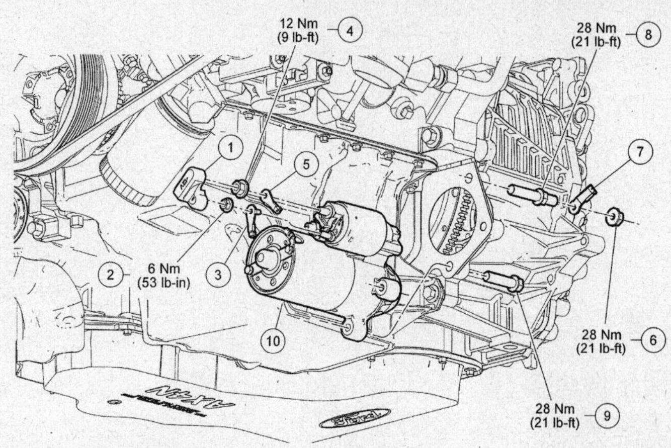

Item	Description
1	Starter motor solenoid terminal cover
2	Starter solenoid battery cable nut
3	Starter solenoid battery cable
4	Starter solenoid wire nut
5	Starter solenoid wire
6	Ground strap nut
7	Ground strap
8	Starter motor stud bolt
9	Starter motor bolt
10	Starter motor

LTV0500000000685

Fig. 1 Starter replacement

ALTERNATOR

REPLACE

1. Rotate accessory drive belt tensioner counterclockwise, then position drive belt aside.
2. Disconnect alternator electrical connector, **Fig. 2.**
3. Position alternator B+ terminal protective boot aside, remove nut, then disconnect B+ terminal connector.
4. Remove A/C line bracket mounting nut, then position bracket and line assembly aside.
5. Remove nut and position the alternator harness bracket aside.
6. Remove two alternator mounting studs and one bolt, then the alternator.
7. Reverse procedure to install. **Torque** mounting bolt and studs to 35 ft. lbs.

IGNITION COIL

REPLACE

1. Remove cowl panel grille, **Fig. 3.**
2. Disconnect windshield wiper motor electrical connector.
3. Remove cowl top panel retaining bolts, then the top panel.
4. Disconnect ignition coil electrical connector, **Fig. 4.**
5. Disconnect spark plug wires from ignition coil. Mark ignition wire locations for installation reference.
6. Remove three ignition coil mounting bolts, then the coil.
7. Reverse procedure to install. **Torque** coil mounting bolts to 62 inch lbs.

IGNITION LOCK

REPLACE

Removal

1. Turn ignition switch to Run position.
2. Insert a suitable ⅛ inch rod or pin through hole in column cover into lock housing and depress retaining pin.
3. Remove lock from housing.

Installation

1. Set lock cylinder to Run position.
2. Depress retaining pin, then install lock cylinder.
3. Ensure lock cylinder is fully seated before rotating lock, then rotate lock to Off position.
4. Rotate lock to all positions to ensure correct operation.

IGNITION SWITCH

REPLACE

1. Remove steering column cover and reinforcement.
2. Disconnect ignition switch electrical connector, **Fig. 5.**
3. Disconnect ignition switch electrical connector.
4. Remove ignition switch.
5. Reverse procedure to install. **Torque** ignition switch screws to 53 inch lbs.

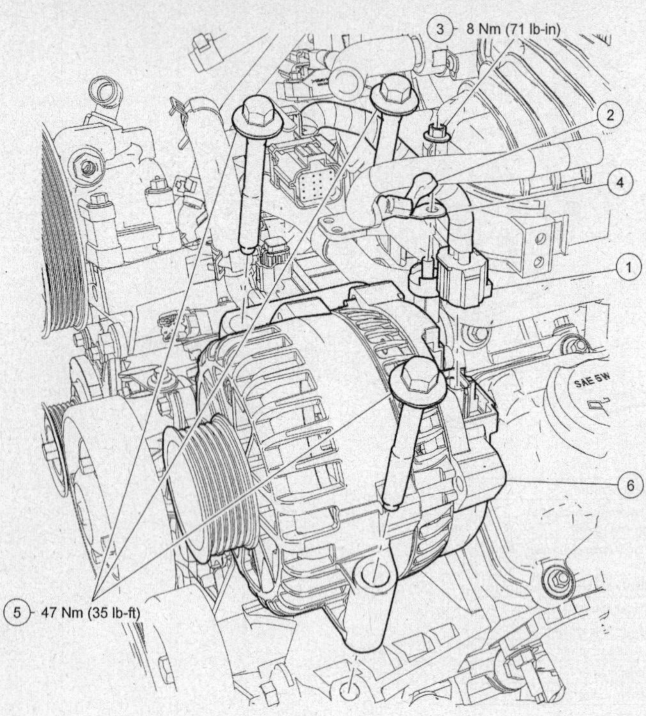

Item	Description
1	Generator electrical connector
2	Generator B+ cable boot
3	Generator B+ cable nut

Item	Description
4	Generator B+ cable
5	Generator bolts (3 required)
6	Generator

LTV0500000000686

Fig. 2 Alternator replacement

25 Nm (18 lb-ft) - 1

Item	Description
1	Windshield wiper arm nut (2 required)
2	RH windshield wiper arm
3	LH windshield wiper arm
4	Cowl panel grille push pin (4 required)
5	Cowl panel grille

LTV0500000000680

Fig. 3 Cowl panel grille replacement

NEUTRAL SAFETY SWITCH

REPLACE

Removal

The neutral safety switch is incorporated into the Digital Transaxle Range Sensor (TR) attached to the transaxle and connected to the manual control lever shaft.

1. Set parking brake.
2. Place transaxle range selector switch in neutral position.
3. Remove engine air cleaner assembly.
4. Disconnect electrical connector from range selector.
5. Disconnect shift cable and remove manual control lever.
6. Remove attaching bolts, then the digital transaxle range selector.

Installation

1. Shift transaxle into neutral position.
2. Install range sensor, loosely install bolts.
3. Align range sensor using alignment tool No. 307-351, or equivalent.
4. Install manual control lever and nut.
5. Connect shift cable and verify proper adjustment.
6. Connect digital range sensor electrical connector.
7. Install air cleaner assembly.

HEADLAMP SWITCH

REPLACE

1. Unclip headlamp switch trim bezel.
2. Disconnect electrical connectors, then remove switch from bezel.
3. Reverse procedure to install.

BRAKE PEDAL POSITION SWITCH

REPLACE

1. Disconnect brake pedal position switch electrical connector.
2. Remove self-locking pin and spacer, then the brake pedal position switch.
3. Reverse procedure to install.

MULTI-FUNCTION SWITCH

REPLACE

1. Remove ignition lock cylinder as outlined under "Ignition Lock, Replace."
2. Remove upper and lower steering column shrouds, **Fig. 6.**
3. Remove instrument cluster finish panel.
4. Disconnect electrical connects.
5. Remove mounting screws, then the multi-function switch.
6. Reverse procedure to install.

STEERING WHEEL

REPLACE

1. Disarm air bag system, then remove driver air bag module as outlined under "Air Bag System" chapter.
2. Through access cover hole, turn pinion shaft bolt to release steering wheel from column shaft.
3. Remove steering wheel using care not to damage wiring or connectors. Route wiring through small hole in back of steering wheel.
4. Reverse procedure to install, noting the following:
   a. Route wiring through hole in back of steering wheel.
   b. **Torque** pinion shaft bolt to 13 ft. lbs.

INSTRUMENT CLUSTER

REPLACE

1. Remove ignition lock cylinder as outlined under "Ignition Lock, Replace."
2. Tilt steering column to lowest position.
3. Remove upper and lower steering column shrouds.
4. Remove transmission range indicator cable attaching bolt, then position cable aside.
5. Remove instrument cluster finish panel, **Fig. 7.**
6. Remove two instrument cluster retaining screws.
7. Disconnect electrical connectors, then remove cluster assembly.
8. Reverse procedure to install.

RADIO

REPLACE

1. Turn ignition switch to Off position.
2. Remove instrument panel center finish panel, **Fig. 8.**
3. Remove four screws and audio unit.

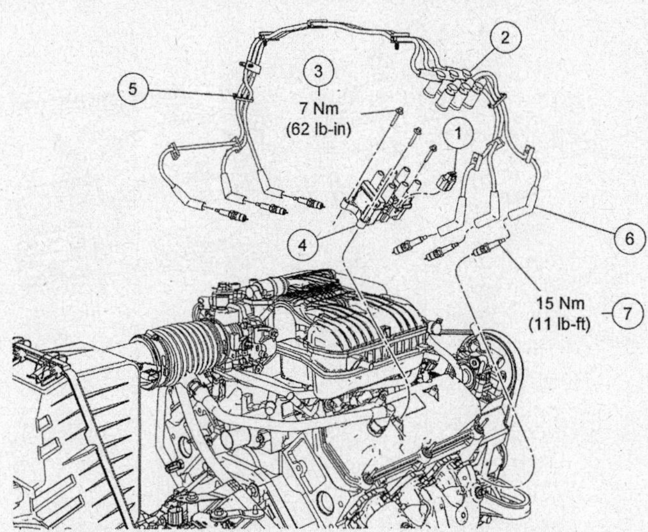

Item	Description
1	Ignition coil electrical connector
2	Spark plug wire-to-ignition coil (6 required)
3	Ignition coil bolt (3 required)
4	Ignition coil
5	Spark plug wire retainer

Item	Description
6	Spark plug wire-to-spark plug (6 required)
7	Spark plug (6 required)

LTV0500000000681

Fig. 4 Ignition coil replacement

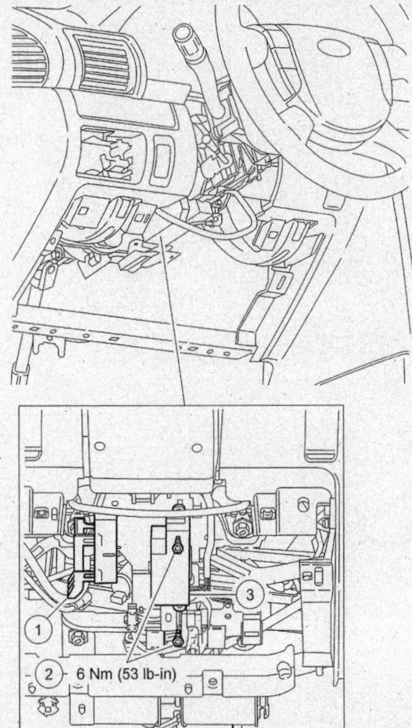

Item	Description
1	Ignition switch electrical connector
2	Ignition switch bolts (2 required)
3	Ignition switch

LTV0500000000687

Fig. 5 Ignition switch replacement

4. Slide radio from opening, then disconnect electrical connectors and antenna lead in cable.
5. Remove radio.
6. Reverse procedures to install.

WIPER MOTOR

REPLACE

Front

1. Remove windshield wiper arms.
2. Disconnect washer hose before removing cowl panel grille.
3. Remove pushpin type retainers and cowl panel grille.
4. Remove washer hose grommet from cowl panel and position washer hose aside.
5. Remove A/C air inlet filter.
6. Remove cowl panel bolts and position cowl panel aside.
7. Disconnect windshield wiper motor electrical connector.
8. Remove cowl panel from vehicle.
9. Remove four bolts and windshield wiper motor.
10. Reverse procedure to install, noting the following:
    a. **Torque** wiper arm pivot nuts to 11 ft. lbs.
    b. **Torque** windshield wiper to cowl panel bolts to 11 ft. lbs.
    c. **Torque** cowl panel bolts to 53 inch lbs.

Rear

1. Lift up wiper arm to pivot cap and remove nut from assembly, then raise arm to service position and rock arm to release from pivot shaft.
2. Remove interior lift gate trim panel.
3. Disconnect electrical connector at motor, **Fig. 9.**
4. Remove mounting screws, then the motor assembly from liftgate.
5. Reverse procedure to install, noting the following.
    a. **Torque** motor module to liftgate mounting screws to 89 inch lbs.
    b. Connect battery ground cable, then turn wiper On then Off to park system before installing wiper arms.
    c. Position arm to pivot shaft, then **torque** shaft nut to 15 ft. lbs.

BLOWER MOTOR

REPLACE

1. Lower glove compartment.
2. Remove glove compartment inner liner screws, then the liner.
3. Disconnect blower motor electrical connector, **Fig. 10.**
4. Remove three blower motor mounting screws, then the blower motor assembly.
5. Remove blower motor wheel clip.
6. Remove blower motor wheel.
7. Reverse procedure to install.

HEATER CORE

REPLACE

1. Drain engine coolant into suitable container.
2. Remove cowl top vent panel to allow clearance, then in engine compartment, disconnect heater hoses from core.
3. Remove ground strap from heater core tube, if equipped.
4. Remove center instrument panel, **Fig. 11,** support trim and cup holder.
5. Remove ash tray and cupholder.
6. **On models equipped with keyless entry,** disconnect wiring harness.
7. **On all models,** remove center instrument panel support brackets.
8. Disconnect climate control vacuum line connector.
9. Remove heater floor duct, then remove heater core cover.
10. Remove heater core from air box.
11. Reverse procedure to install, noting the following:
    a. **Torque** instrument panel to support bracket bolts to 108 inch lbs.
    b. Always use new heater core and core tube seals.
    c. Bleed cooling system as outlined in appropriate "Engine" section.

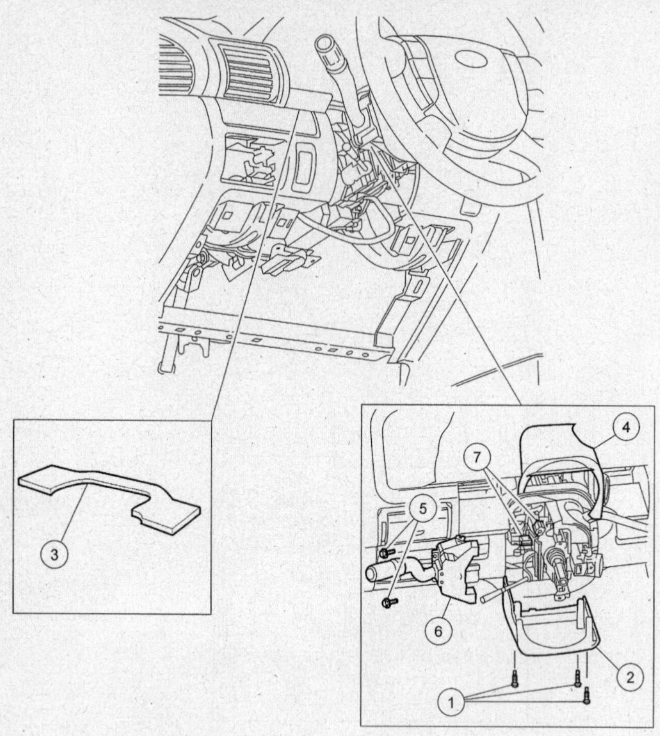

Item	Description
1	Lower steering column shroud screws (3 required)
2	Lower steering column shroud
3	Instrument cluster finish panel
4	Upper steering column shroud

Item	Description
5	Multi-function switch screws (2 required)
6	Multi-function switch
7	Multi-function switch electrical connectors

LTV0500000000688

Fig. 6 Multi-function switch replacement

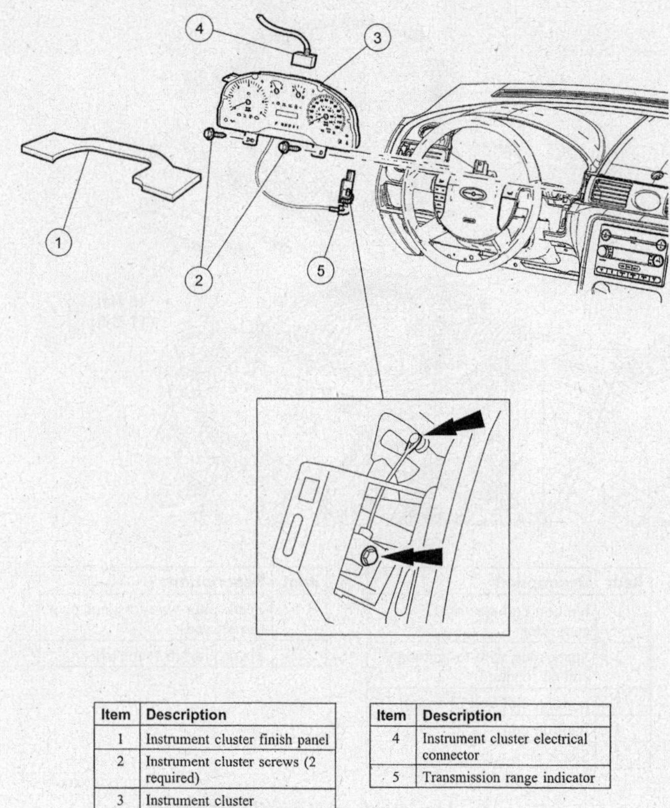

Item	Description
1	Instrument cluster finish panel
2	Instrument cluster screws (2 required)
3	Instrument cluster

Item	Description
4	Instrument cluster electrical connector
5	Transmission range indicator

LTV0500000000689

Fig. 7 Instrument cluster replacement

EVAPORATOR CORE

REPLACE

1. Remove heater core as outlined under "Heater Core, Replace."
2. Recover A/C system as outlined in the "Air Conditioning" chapter.
3. Remove wiper arm and pivot shaft.
4. Remove nuts and fresh air inlet duct.
5. Disconnect condenser to evaporator line fitting at evaporator core, then discard O-rings.
6. Disconnect evaporator core orifice fitting, then remove evaporator end of condenser to evaporator line and discard O-rings.
7. Remove evaporator core mounting screws, then the core from housing.
8. Reverse procedure to install. Lubricate all new O-rings with clean PAG oil.

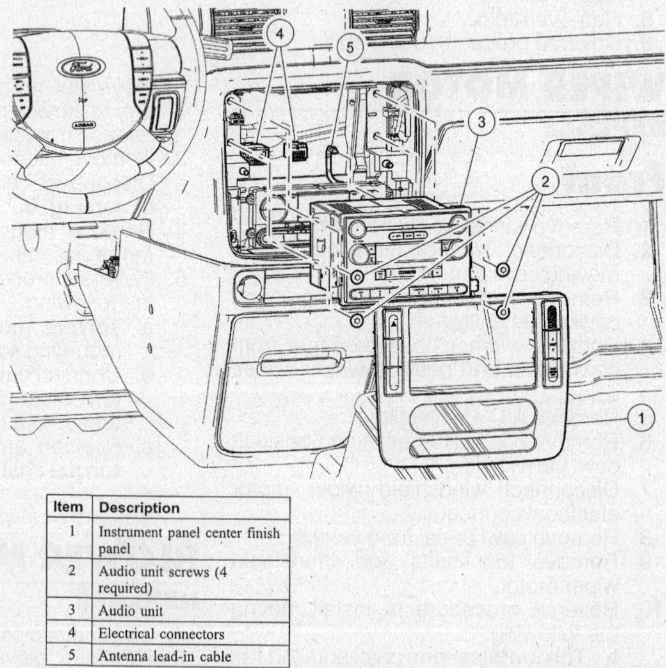

Item	Description
1	Instrument panel center finish panel
2	Audio unit screws (4 required)
3	Audio unit
4	Electrical connectors
5	Antenna lead-in cable

LTV0500000000690

Fig. 8 Radio replacement

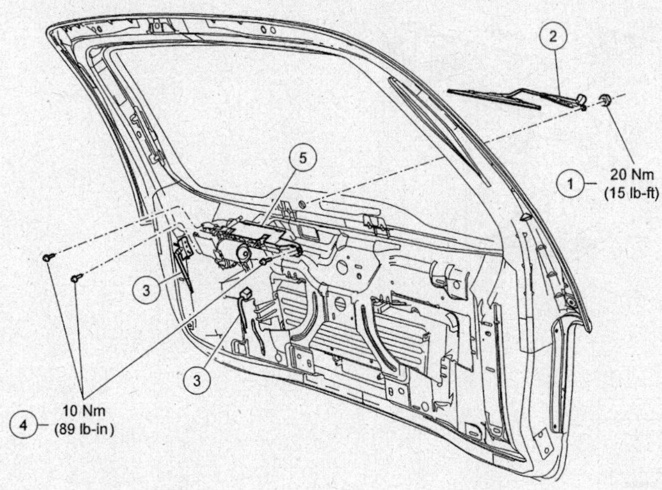

Item	Description
1	Rear wiper arm nut
2	Rear wiper arm
3	Electrical connectors
4	Screws (3 required)
5	Rear wiper module

LTV0500000000691

Fig. 9 Rear wiper motor replacement

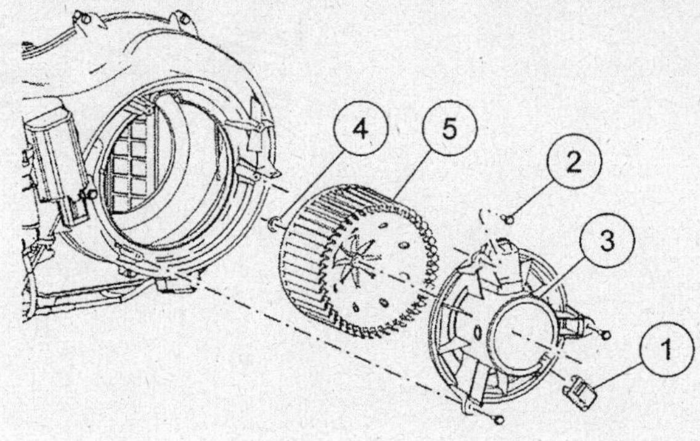

Item	Description
1	Blower motor electrical connector
2	Blower motor screw (3 required)
3	Blower motor
4	Blower motor wheel clip
5	Blower motor wheel

LTV0500000000692

Fig. 10 Blower motor replacement

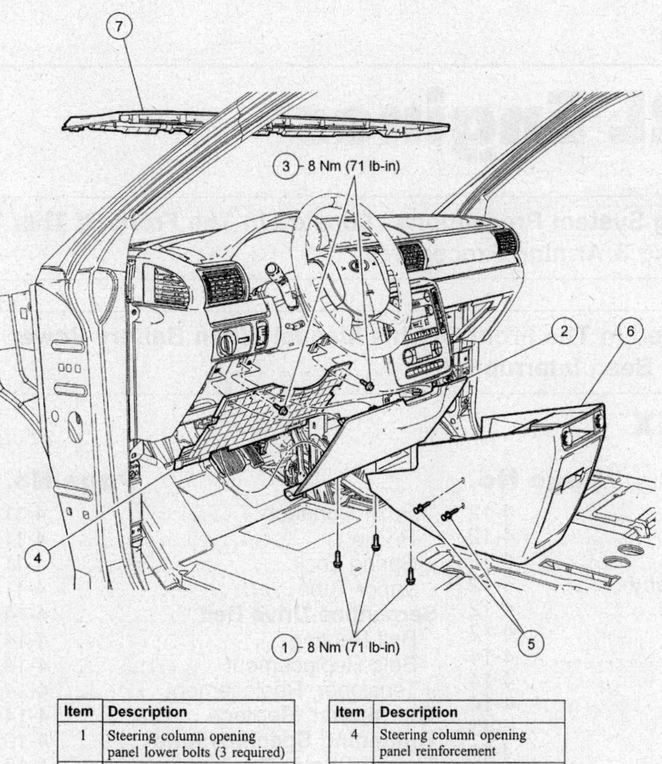

Item	Description
1	Steering column opening panel lower bolts (3 required)
2	Steering column opening panel cover
3	Steering column opening panel bolts (2 required)
4	Steering column opening panel reinforcement
5	Storage console pin-type retainers (4 required)
6	Storage console
7	Upper instrument panel finish panel

LTV0500000000693

Fig. 11 Heater core & instrument panel replacement (Part 1 of 3)

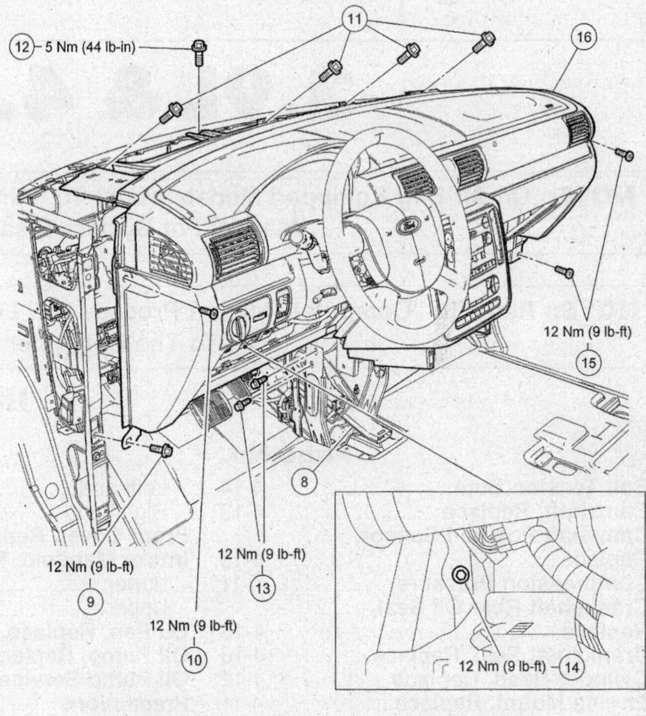

Item	Description
8	Rear seat floor duct adapter
9	LH lower instrument panel bolt
10	LH upper instrument panel bolt
11	Upper instrument panel bolts (4 required)
12	Instrument panel cowl bolt
13	Instrument panel support brace bolts (4 required)
14	LH instrument panel support bracket bolt
15	RH instrument panel bolts (2 required)
16	Instrument panel

LTV0500000000694

Fig. 11 Heater core & instrument panel replacement (Part 2 of 3)

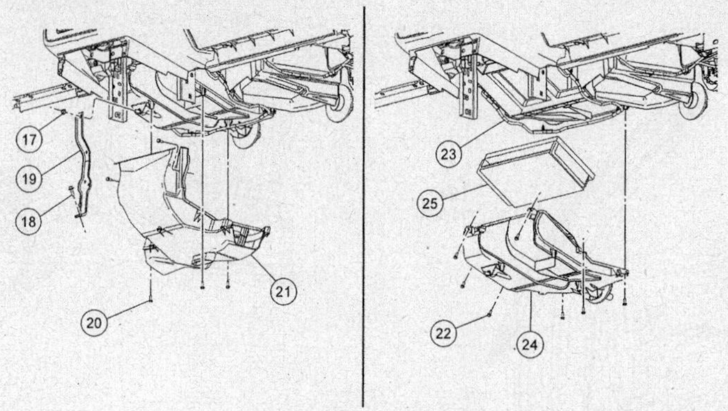

Item	Description
17	Heater core and evaporator core housing support brace nut
18	Heater core and evaporator core housing support brace bolt
19	Heater core and evaporator core housing support brace
20	Floor duct screw (4 required)
21	Floor duct
22	Heater core cover screw (7 required)
23	Wire harness
24	Heater core cover
25	Heater core

LTV0500000000695

Fig. 11 Heater core & instrument panel replacement (Part 3 of 3)

3.9L & 4.2L Engines

NOTE: On Air Bag Equipped Models, Refer To "Air Bag System Precautions" Located In The Front Of This Manual For System Disarming & Arming Procedures.

NOTE: Refer To "Computer Relearn Procedures" Located In The Front Of This Manual When Battery Power To The Computer Has Been Interrupted.

INDEX

PRECAUTIONS

Air Bag Systems

Refer to "Air Bag System Precautions" in the front of this manual for system disarming and arming procedures.

Battery Ground Cable

Prior to service, disconnect battery ground cable and isolate as required.

Fuel System Pressure Relief

The fuel system remains under high pressure even when the engine is not running. To avoid injury or fire, release pressure from the fuel system before disconnecting any fuel line. Proceed as follows:

1. Remove splash shield located on lefthand frame rail under driver's side door.
2. Disconnect fuel pump/tank sender harness electrical connector.
3. Start engine and allow it to idle until it stalls.
4. After engine stalls, crank engine for approximately five seconds to ensure fuel rail pressure has been released.
5. Turn ignition switch to OFF position.
6. After fuel system service is complete, connect electrical connector.
7. Reposition splash shield and install a new pushpin.
8. Cycle ignition switch and wait 3 seconds to pressurize fuel system. Inspect for leaks before starting engine.

COMPRESSION PRESSURE

1. Warm engine to normal operating temperature, then remove spark plugs and set throttle plates to wide open position.
2. Install a suitable compression gauge in cylinder No. 1 spark plug hole.
3. Install an auxiliary starter switch in the starting circuit.
4. With key off, using auxiliary starter switch, crank engine at least five compression strokes and record highest reading.
5. Repeat test on each cylinder.
6. Indicated compression pressures are within specification if the lowest reading cylinder is within 75 percent of the highest reading, with a minimum of 101 psi.

QUICK DISCONNECT HOSES

Before disconnect quick connect fittings, ensure system pressure is relieved if applicable.

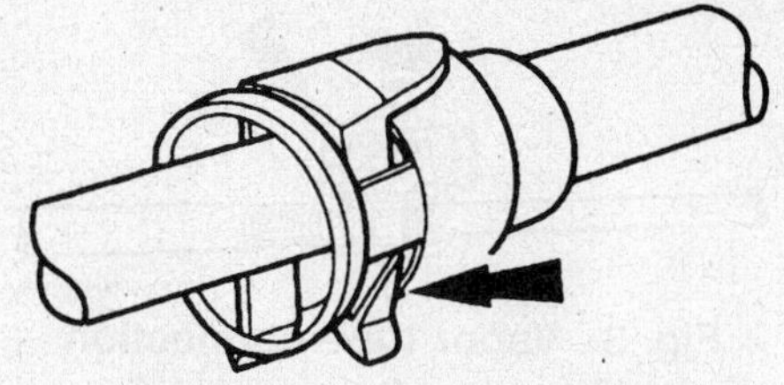

Fig. 1 R-clip connection

R-Clip

When working with R-clip type connections, **Fig. 1,** do not use tools to disconnect. Use of tools may deform clip components and could cause leaks.

To disconnect, bend shipping tab downward, **Fig. 1.** Spread R-clip and push clip into fitting. Separate fitting from tube.

To install, first inspect fitting and tube for damage and ensure connections are clean. Apply a light coat of clean 5W-30 motor oil to male end of tube. Insert R-clip into fitting. Align tube and fitting, then insert tube into fitting and push together until a click is heard. Pull on connection to ensure it is fully engaged.

Spring Lock

When working with spring lock type connections, **Fig. 2,** spring lock tool set No. T84L-19623-B, or equivalent, must be used to disconnect fittings. When connecting spring lock type fittings, inspect and clean both coupling ends. Lubricate fuel line O-ring seals with clean 5W-30 motor oil. When connection is made, pull on line to ensure it is fully engaged.

Vapor Tube

To disconnect vapor tube connections, squeeze fitting (1) and disconnect vapor tube from fitting (2), **Fig. 3.** To connect, ensure fittings are clean and free from damage. Push tube onto fitting until it snaps into place. Pull on connection to verify fitting is secure.

Push Connect

To disconnect push connect fittings, first remove safety clip if equipped, then slide disconnect tool set No. T90T-9550-S into fitting, **Fig. 4.** Separate fittings, then remove disconnect tool.

ENGINE MOUNT

REPLACE

Early build vehicles are equipped with an M14 through bolt. Late build vehicles are equipped with an M18 bolt.

1. Remove the lefthand and righthand engine support insulator through bolts, **Fig. 5.**
2. Remove righthand engine support insulator nuts and washers.
3. Remove A/C compressor and power steering pump bracket brace upper nut, then install lifting bracket tool No. T70P-6000, or equivalent, on bracket brace.
4. Support engine using a .39 inch (10 mm) spring link to connect engine lifting bracket to a suitable 3-Bar Engine Support.
5. Lift engine approximately 3 inches.
6. Remove engine mount to engine block mounting bolts, then the engine mount.
7. Reverse procedure to install.

ENGINE

REPLACE

1. Remove vehicle hood.
2. **On models equipped with A/C,** recover refrigerant as outlined in "Air Conditioning" chapter.
3. **On all models,** drain cooling system into suitable container.
4. Relieve fuel system pressure as outlined under "Precautions."
5. Remove upper front air deflector.
6. Remove upper intake manifold and manifold spacer assembly as outlined under "Intake Manifold, Replace."
7. Remove radiator, fan blade and shroud assembly.
8. Disconnect fuel pressure regulator vacuum connector and intake manifold runner control electrical connector.
9. Disconnect EGR valve vacuum connector.
10. Remove power steering pump reservoir and set aside.
11. Remove A/C hose manifold from compressor and position hoses aside.
12. Remove power steering pump bolts and position pump aside.
13. Remove fuel charging wiring harness.
14. Remove ignition coil and spark plug wires.
15. Disconnect two heater hoses.
16. Disconnect differential pressure feedback EGR system electrical connector and wiring harness pin type connector.
17. Remove exhaust manifold to EGR valve tube.
18. Remove crankcase ventilation hose.
19. Remove PCV valve/heater hose assembly.
20. Disconnect fuel tube spring lock couplings.
21. Remove fuel injectors and fuel injector supply manifold.
22. Raise and support vehicle.
23. **On models equipped with block heater,** disconnect block heater cable.
24. **On all models,** remove catalytic converter to exhaust manifold nuts.
25. Remove starter motor as outlined under "Starter, Replace" in "Electrical" section.
26. Remove transmission bolts.
27. **On models equipped with manual transmission,** remove clutch assembly.
28. **On all models,** remove engine support insulator through bolts.
29. Lower vehicle.
30. Remove engine from vehicle with suitable lifting device.
31. Reverse procedure to install.

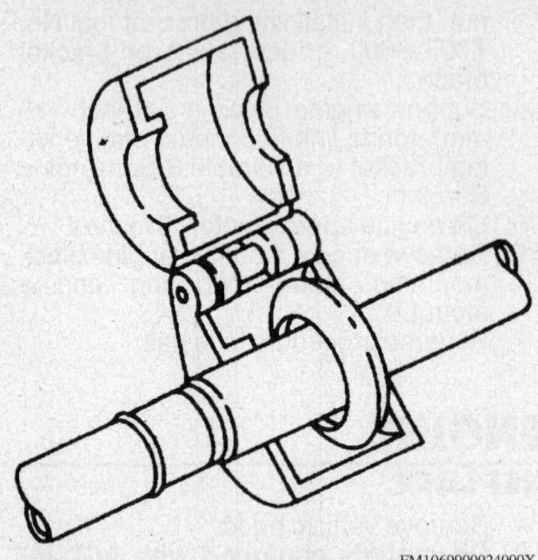

Fig. 2 Spring lock connection

INTAKE MANIFOLD

REPLACE

Lower

1. Disconnect EGR vacuum hose and EGR valve tube upper fitting.
2. Remove radiator hose from lower intake manifold, **Fig. 6.**
3. Disconnect water bypass hose and heater hose.
4. Relieve fuel system pressure as outlined under "Precautions."
5. Disconnect fuel lines, fuel injector electrical connectors and fuel injector electrical harness from fuel injector supply manifold.
6. Disconnect IMRC electrical connector and fuel pressure regulator vacuum line.
7. Fuel charging and IMRC are removed with lower intake manifold.
8. Remove lower intake manifold bolts, then the lower intake manifold.
9. Reverse procedure to install, noting the following:
   a. Remove and discard all lower intake manifold gaskets and seals.
   b. Apply a bead of sealant to intake manifold front and rear seal mounting points, **Fig. 7,** then install front and rear seals.
   c. Install intake manifold gaskets and apply a bead of silicone sealant to areas indicated, **Fig. 8,** then install lower intake manifold.
   d. Lower intake manifold must be installed within fifteen minutes of applying sealer.
   e. **Torque** bolts in sequence, **Fig. 9,** in two stages, first to 44 inch lbs., then to 89 inch lbs.

Upper

1. Remove air cleaner assembly and engine cover.
2. Remove clip push pin, **Fig. 10,** then the accelerator control splash shield.
3. Disconnect idle air control valve electrical connector, then remove idle air control valve assembly.
4. Disconnect accelerator and speed control cables at throttle body.
5. Disconnect accelerator and speed control cables at cable bracket.
6. Disconnect spark plug wire holders.
7. Remove 12 upper intake manifold bolts, then the upper intake manifold.
8. Reverse procedure to install, noting the following:
   a. Install new accelerator control splash shield clip push pin.
   b. Tighten upper intake manifold bolts in sequence, **Fig. 11,** in two steps.
   c. Step 1: **Torque** bolts to 53 inch lbs.
   d. Step 2: **Torque** bolts to 89 inch lbs.

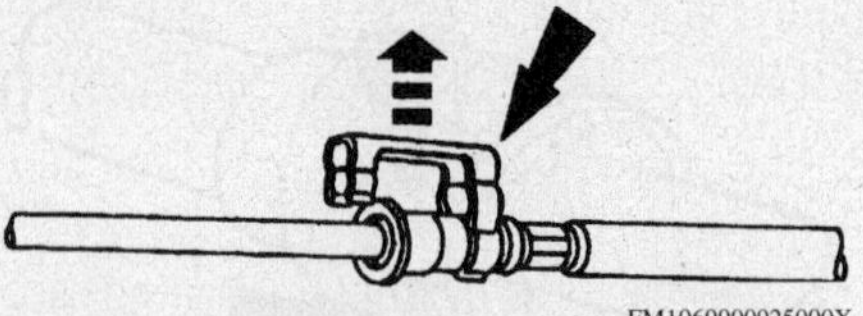

Fig. 3 Vapor tube connection

EXHAUST MANIFOLD

REPLACE

Lefthand

1. Remove oil dipstick tube.
2. Raise and support vehicle.
3. Disconnect lefthand HO2S electrical connector.
4. Remove two three way catalytic converter to exhaust manifold nuts and disconnect Y-pipe from lefthand exhaust manifold.
5. Remove three lefthand exhaust manifold stud bolts.
6. Remove three lefthand exhaust manifold bolts, then the exhaust manifold.
7. Reverse procedure to install.

Righthand

1. Remove EGR valve to exhaust manifold tube.
2. Raise and support vehicle.
3. Disconnect righthand HO2S electrical connector.
4. Remove three righthand exhaust manifold stud bolts.
5. Remove three righthand exhaust manifold bolts, then the exhaust manifold.
6. Reverse procedure to install.

CYLINDER HEAD

REPLACE

1. Remove upper and lower intake manifolds as outlined under "Intake Manifold, Replace."
2. Remove lefthand and righthand valve covers.
3. Remove exhaust manifold as outlined under "Exhaust Manifold, Replace."
4. Remove and position power steering pump aside.
5. **On models equipped with A/C,** remove A/C compressor.
6. **On all models,** remove alternator.
7. Remove idler pulley and alternator bracket.
8. Remove six bolts, then the six rocker arms and pushrods.
9. If rocker arms and push rods are to be reused, mark component locations for installation reference.
10. Remove and discard the eight cylinder head bolts.
11. Remove cylinder head and gasket.
12. Reverse procedure to install, noting the following:
   a. Coat new cylinder head bolts with suitable engine oil.
   b. **Torque** bolts to 15 ft. lbs., in sequence, **Fig. 12.**
   c. **Torque** bolts to 30 ft. lbs., in sequence, **Fig. 12.**
   d. **Torque** bolts to 37 ft. lbs., in sequence, **Fig. 12.**
   e. **Loosen bolts one at a time in sequence. Do not loosen all bolts at the same time. Torque** short bolts to 18 ft. lbs., then an additional 180°. **Torque** long bolts to 33 ft. lbs., then an additional 180°.

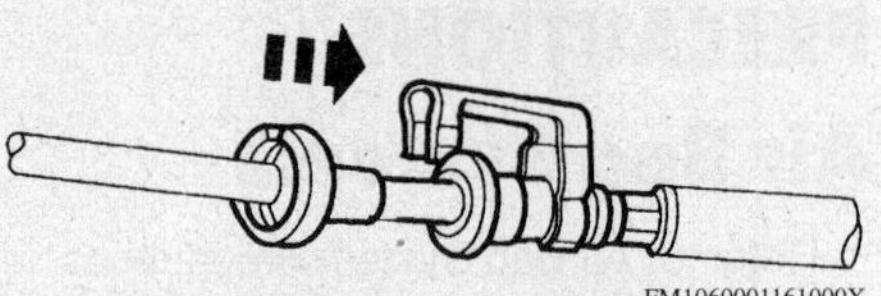

Fig. 4 Push connect fitting

VALVE LIFTERS

1. Drain cooling system into a suitable container.
2. Remove intake manifold as outlined under "Intake Manifold, Replace."
3. Remove rocker covers.
4. Remove rocker arm bolts, then the rocker arms.
5. Remove pushrods.
6. Remove two tappet guide plate bolts, then the tappet guide plate and retainer, **Fig. 13.**
7. Remove valve lifters.
8. Lubricate all valve lifters with engine oil prior to installation.
9. Reverse procedure to install.

FRONT COVER

REPLACE

1. Drain cooling system into suitable container.
2. Remove air cleaner assembly.
3. Remove upper radiator hose, fan shroud and lower radiator hose.
4. Disconnect camshaft position sensor electrical connector.
5. Raise and support vehicle.
6. Remove oil pan drain plug and drain engine oil into suitable container.
7. Disconnect crankshaft sensor electrical connector.
8. Position engine wiring harness aside.
9. Remove power steering pump bracket bolts and nuts, then the power steering bracket.
10. Remove nuts and position A/C compressor aside.
11. Remove crankshaft pulley.
12. Remove bolts securing oil pan flange to front engine cover.

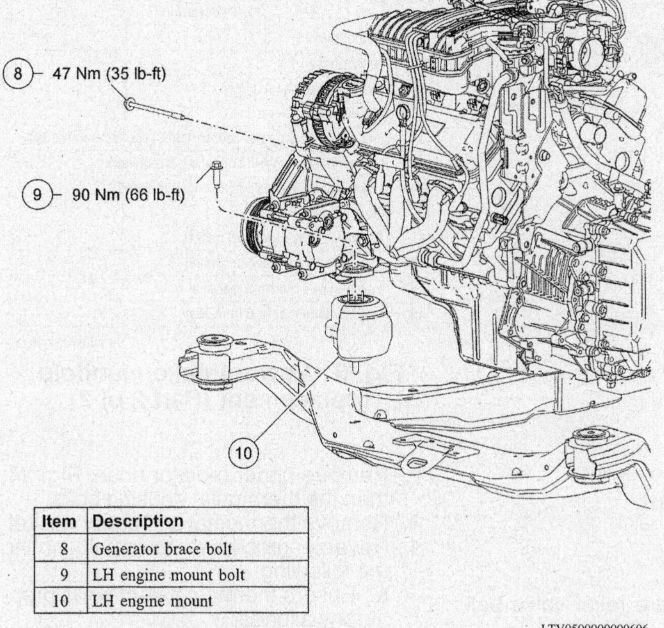

Item	Description
8	Generator brace bolt
9	LH engine mount bolt
10	LH engine mount

Fig. 5 Engine mount replacement (Part 1 of 2)

Item	Description
1	Engine roll restrictor bolt (2 required)
2	Engine roll restrictor
3	Transaxle support insulator nut

Item	Description
4	LH engine mount nut
5	RH engine mount nut
6	RH engine mount bolt
7	RH engine mount

LTV0500000000697

Fig. 5 Engine mount replacement (Part 2 of 2)

13. Remove Allen head bolt at engine front cover.
14. Lower vehicle.
15. Remove heater water outlet tube hoses.
16. Disconnect wiring harness from outlet tube and position aside.
17. Remove heater water outlet tube.
18. Remove camshaft position sensor.
19. Disconnect EGR valve vacuum hose, then remove EGR valve tube upper fitting.
20. Remove nut and bolts, then the EGR valve and adapter assembly.
21. Remove camshaft synchronizer retaining bolt, then the synchronizer.
22. Oil pump driveshaft may come out with camshaft synchronizer, if this happens, retrieve oil pump driveshaft before proceeding.
23. **Do not turn crankshaft or camshaft during removal and installation procedure or fuel system timing will be out of time with engine.**
24. Remove nuts and bolts, then the water pump.
25. Remove crankshaft front oil seal.
26. Remove stud bolts, bolts and cap screw, then the front cover.
27. Reverse procedure to install, noting the following:
    a. In order to prevent foreign material from contaminating engine block or engine front cover, it is required to seal coolant and oil passages of both components.
    b. Pack exposed portions of oil pan with shop towels.
    c. Plug oil and coolant passages.
    d. Clean gasket surfaces, remove any foreign material using compressed air.
    e. Remove shop towels from oil pan, remove plugs and seals from engine block and front cover.
    f. Install front cover gasket, then apply sealant to oil pan.
    g. Number 12 position is NOT part of the torque sequence.
    h. Tighten front cover bolts in sequence, **Fig. 14,** in two stages. First, install studs and **torque** to 62 inch lbs., then **torque** stud bolts and nuts to 21 ft. lbs. New studs are supplied with Loctite thread locking compound on threads, ensure Loctite end of stud is installed in engine.
    i. Install camshaft position sensor as outlined under "Camshaft Position Sensor, Replace."

TIMING CHAIN

REPLACE

1. Remove engine front cover as outlined under "Front Cover, Replace."
2. Remove camshaft position sensor drive gear.
3. Rotate crankshaft timing marks and keyways align, **Fig. 15.**
4. Compress timing chain tensioner and install suitable pin to hold tensioner.
5. Remove camshaft sprocket, crankshaft sprocket and timing chain as an assembly.
6. Reverse procedure to install.

CAMSHAFT

REPLACE

1. Remove valve lifters as outlined under "Valve Lifters."
2. Remove engine front cover as outlined under "Front Cover, Replace."
3. Remove camshaft key.
4. Remove engine dynamic balance shaft drive gear.
5. Remove two bolts from camshaft thrust plate, then the thrust plate.
6. Remove spacer, then the camshaft.
7. Reverse procedure to install.

CAMSHAFT POSITION SENSOR

REPLACE

1. Partially drain cooling system into suitable container.
2. Remove air cleaner assembly.
3. Remove bolt from heater water tube, then position aside.
4. Disconnect electrical connector from CMP.
5. Remove screws from CMP, then CMP.
6. Reverse procedure to install.

CRANKSHAFT SEAL

REPLACE

1. Remove crankshaft damper and pulley.
2. Remove front crankshaft seal, **Fig. 16.**
3. Reverse procedure to install, noting the following:
    a. Lubricate crankshaft seal lips with engine oil prior to installation.
    b. Use suitable front crankshaft seal installer as outlined in **Fig. 17.**

CRANKSHAFT REAR OIL SEAL

REPLACE

1. Remove transmission.
2. Remove six bolts, then the flywheel.
3. Use suitable rear crankshaft seal remover and slide hammer, "A," to remove seal, "B", **Fig. 18.**
4. Reverse procedure to install, noting the following:
    a. Lubricate crankshaft seal lips with engine oil prior to installation.
    b. Use suitable rear crankshaft seal installer, **Fig. 19.**

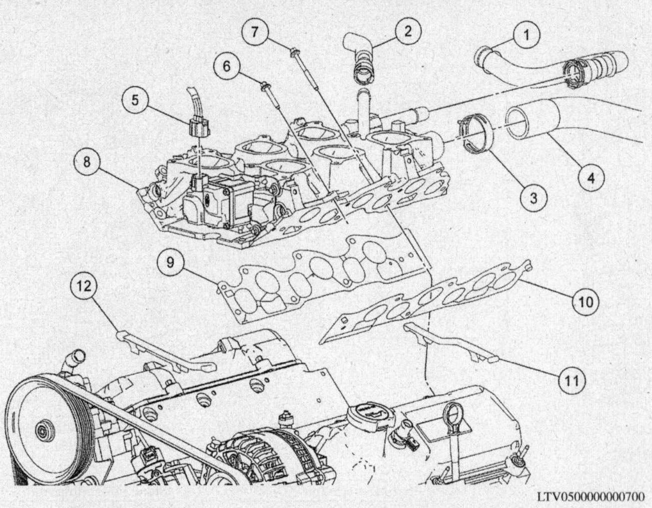

Fig. 6 Lower intake manifold replacement (Part 1 of 2)

Item	Description
1	Heater hose
2	Heater hose
3	Upper radiator hose clamp
4	Upper radiator hose
5	Intake manifold runner control (IMRC) electrical connector
6	Lower intake manifold bolt (short, 8 required)
7	Lower intake manifold bolt (long, 6 required)
8	Lower intake manifold
9	RH lower intake manifold gasket
10	LH lower intake manifold gasket
11	Lower intake manifold rear seal
12	Lower intake manifold front seal

LTV0500000000701

Fig. 6 Lower intake manifold replacement (Part 2 of 2)

OIL PAN

REPLACE

1. If equipped, turn air suspension switch off.
2. Raise and support vehicle.
3. Drain engine oil.
4. Remove oil pan to transmission bolts.
5. Remove fifteen bolts, then the oil pan.
6. Reverse procedure to install, noting the following:
   a. Clean and apply sealant to oil pan sealing areas.
   b. **Torque** oil pan to 44 inch lbs., then to 89 inch lbs., in sequence outlined in **Fig. 20.**

OIL PUMP

REPLACE

1. Remove oil pan as outlined under "Oil Pan, Replace."
2. Remove oil filter.
3. Remove six oil pump attaching bolts, then the oil pump.
4. Reverse procedure to install noting the following:
   a. Tighten oil pump mounting bolts in two steps in sequence, Fig. 21.
5. Step one, tighten bolts to 89 inch lbs.
6. Step two, tighten to 18 ft lbs.

OIL PUMP SERVICE

1. Remove oil pump as outlined under "Oil Pump, Replace."
2. Remove oil pump drive gear, "A", driven gear, "B", and O-ring, "C", **Fig. 21.**
3. Inspect all oil pump components, inspect the face of oil pump for flatness.
4. Remove engine front cover. Refer to "Front Cover, Replace."
5. Remove the plug over oil pressure relief valve, **Fig. 22.**
6. Remove oil pressure relief valve ball and spring.
7. Clean and inspect ball and spring.
8. Reverse procedure to install.

BELT TENSION DATA

Drive belt tension is not adjustable. The drive belt tensioner automatically adjusts drive belt tension.

SERPENTINE DRIVE BELT

Belt Routing

Refer to **Fig. 23** for serpentine drive belt routing.

Belt, Replacement

1. Use drive belt tensioner pulley bolt to rotate drive belt tensioner counterclockwise and remove drive belt.
2. Remove belt, slowly release tensioner. **Do not allow tensioner to snap back, as damage may result.**
3. Reverse procedure to install.

Tensioner, Replacement

1. Remove drive belt as outlined under "Belt, Replacement."
2. Remove drive belt tensioner bolt and tensioner.
3. Reverse procedure to install.

THERMOSTAT

REPLACE

1. Partially drain cooling system into a suitable container.
2. Remove upper radiator hose, **Fig. 24,** then the thermostat housing bolts.
3. Remove thermostat and paper gasket.
4. Reverse procedure to install, noting the following:
   a. Ensure thermostat vent pin is properly aligned.
   b. Tighten thermostat housing to engine bolts in two steps: Step one, **torque** bolts to 71 inch lbs.; Step two, tighten bolts an additional 60°.

WATER PUMP

REPLACE

1. Remove air cleaner assembly.
2. Drain cooling system into a suitable container.
3. Remove front air deflector, then upper radiator hose from radiator.
4. Remove the engine cooling fan and the fan shroud.
5. Remove fan blade and clutch using fan clutch holding tool No. T84T-6312-C and fan clutch wrench tool No. T93T-6312-B, or equivalents.
6. Remove fan shroud attaching screws, then the fan, clutch and shroud.
7. Remove A/C compressor mounting bracket upper support bolt, **Fig. 25.**
8. Loosen A/C compressor mounting bracket lower support bolt. Position bracket and bolt forward until they contact power steering pump pulley.
9. Position A/C compressor mounting bracket aside.
10. Remove accessory drive belt, then the water pump pulley.
11. Remove upper radiator hose from water pump.
12. Remove four water pump attaching bolts, then the water pump.
13. Reverse procedure to install, noting the following:
    a. Lubricate water pump O-ring seal using suitable coolant.
    b. **Torque** water pump bolts in sequence, **Fig. 26,** to 21 ft. lbs.
    c. Install water pump pulley.

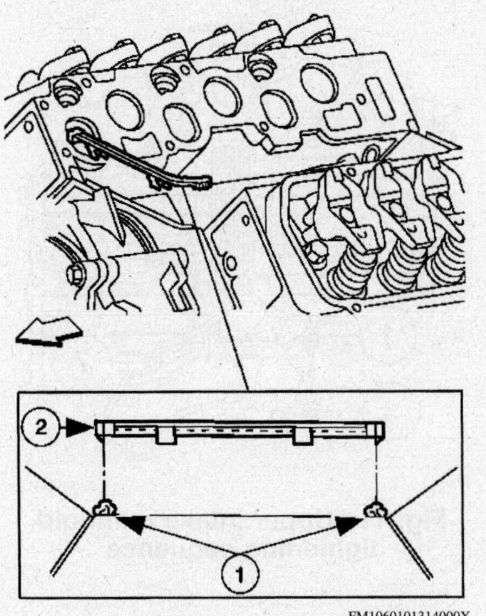

FM1060101314000X

Fig. 7 Lower intake manifold sealant application

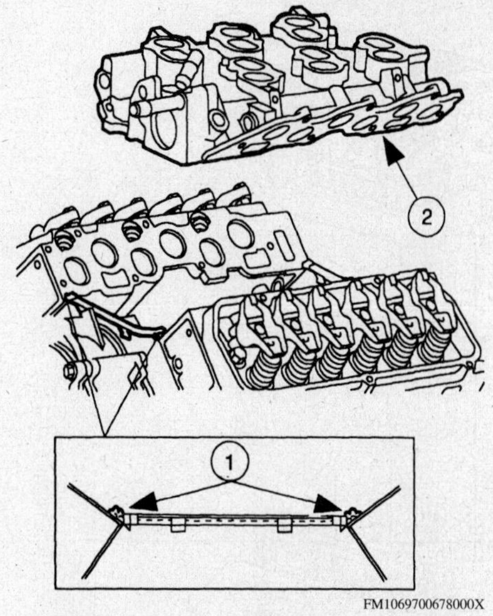

FM1069700678000X

Fig. 8 Lower intake manifold gasket sealant application. Lower intake manifold

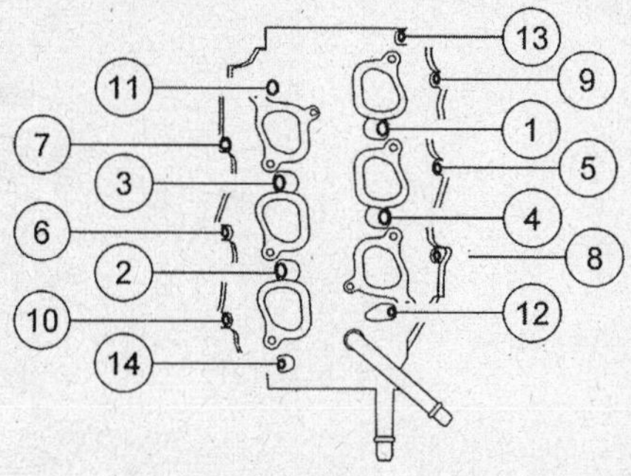

LTV0500000000699

Fig. 9 Lower intake manifold bolt tightening sequence. Lower intake manifold

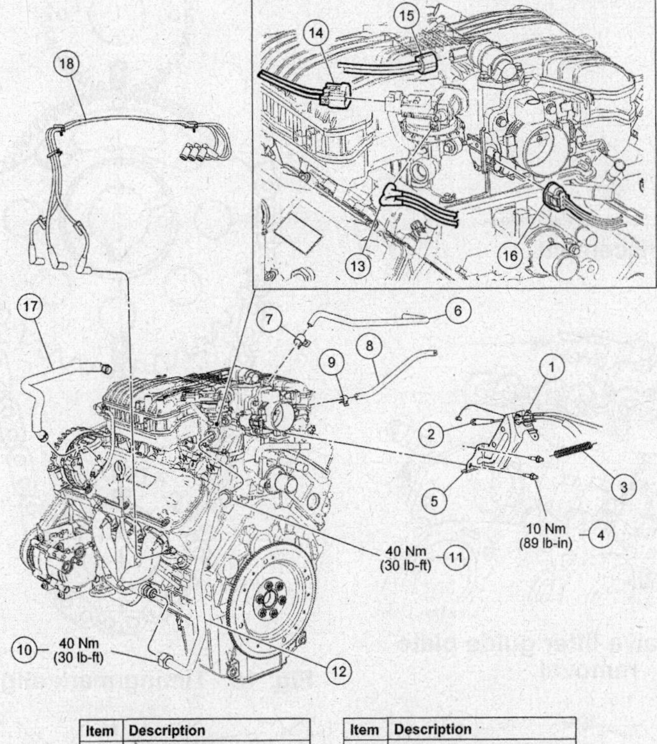

Item	Description
1	Accelerator cable
2	Speed control cable
3	Spring
4	Cable bracket stud bolt (2 required)
5	Cable bracket
6	Evaporative (EVAP) emission return tube
7	Clamp
8	Brake booster vacuum hose

Item	Description
9	Clamp
10	Exhaust gas recirculation (EGR) system module-to-exhaust manifold tube lower fitting
11	EGR system module-to-exhaust manifold tube upper fitting

LTV0500000000702

Fig. 10 Upper intake manifold replacement (Part 1 of 3)

Item	Description
1	Accelerator cable
2	Speed control cable
3	Spring
4	Cable bracket stud bolt (2 required)
5	Cable bracket
6	Evaporative (EVAP) emission return tube
7	Clamp
8	Brake booster vacuum hose
9	Clamp
10	Exhaust gas recirculation (EGR) system module-to-exhaust manifold tube lower fitting
11	EGR system module-to-exhaust manifold tube upper fitting
12	EGR system module-to-exhaust manifold tube
13	EGR system module vacuum connector
14	EGR system module electrical connector
15	Idle air control (IAC) electrical connector
16	Throttle position (TP) sensor electrical connector
17	Crankcase vent hose
18	LH spark plug wire assembly (with retainers)

LTV0500000000703

Fig. 10 Upper intake manifold replacement (Part 2 of 3)

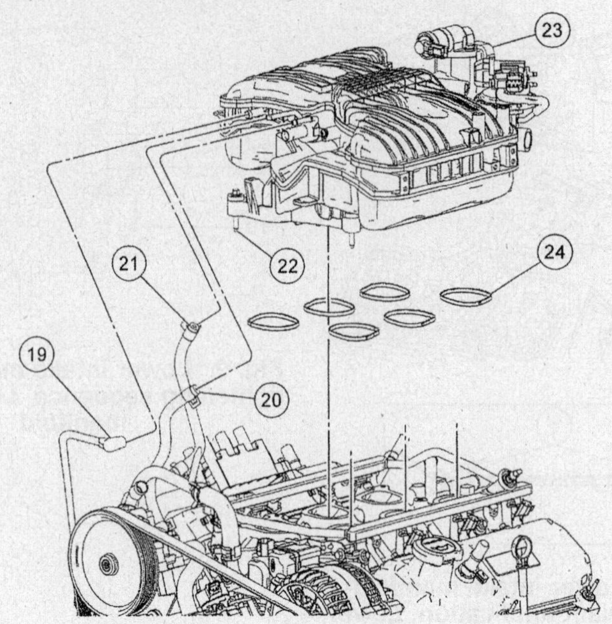

Item	Description
19	Upper intake manifold vacuum tube connector
20	Coolant inlet hose
21	Coolant outlet hose
22	Upper intake manifold bolt (8 required)
23	Upper intake manifold
24	Upper intake manifold gasket (6 required)

LTV0500000000704

Fig. 10 Upper intake manifold replacement (Part 3 of 3)

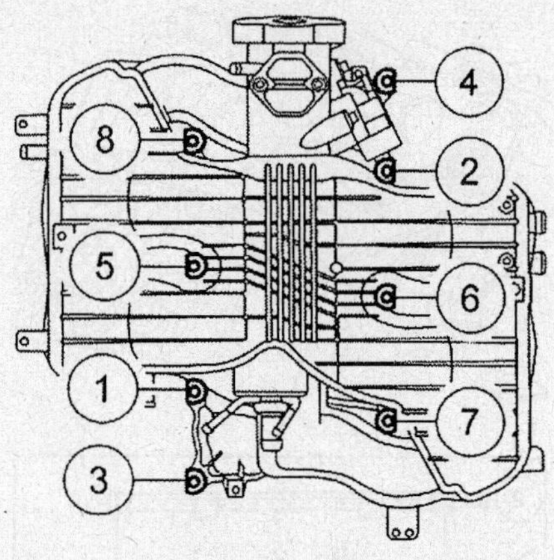

Fig. 11 Upper intake manifold tightening sequence

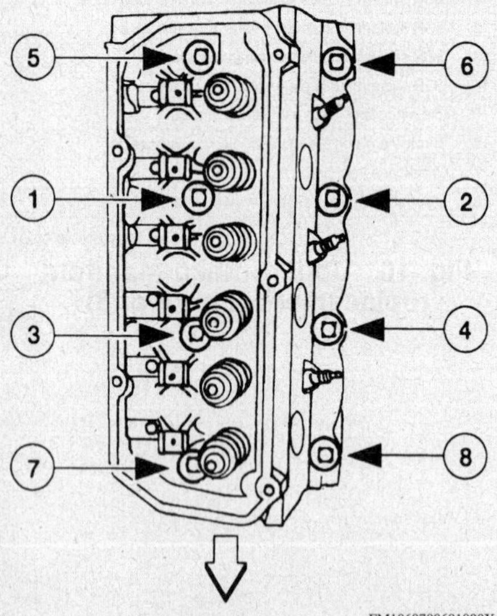

Fig. 12 Cylinder head tightening sequence

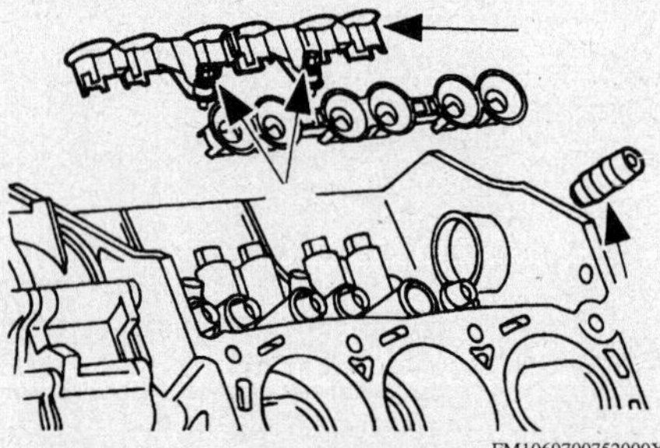

Fig. 13 Valve lifter guide plate removal

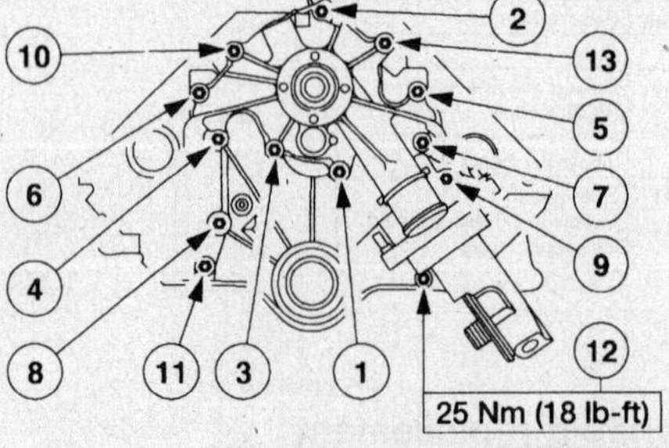

Fig. 14 Front cover tightening sequence

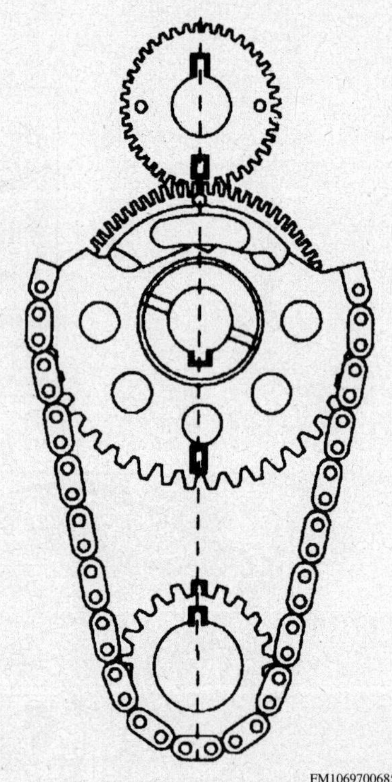

Fig. 15 Timing mark alignment

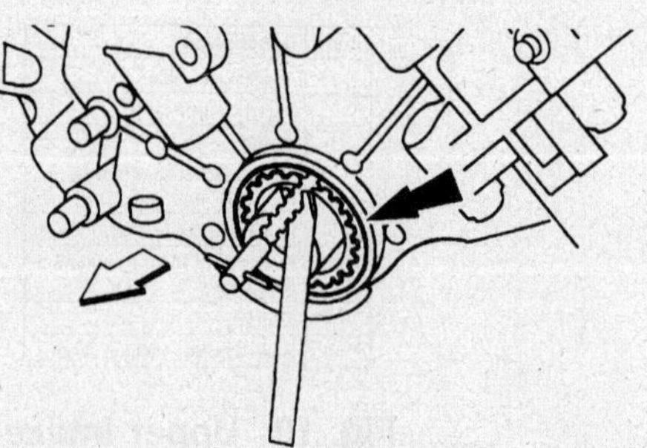

Fig. 16 Front crankshaft seal removal

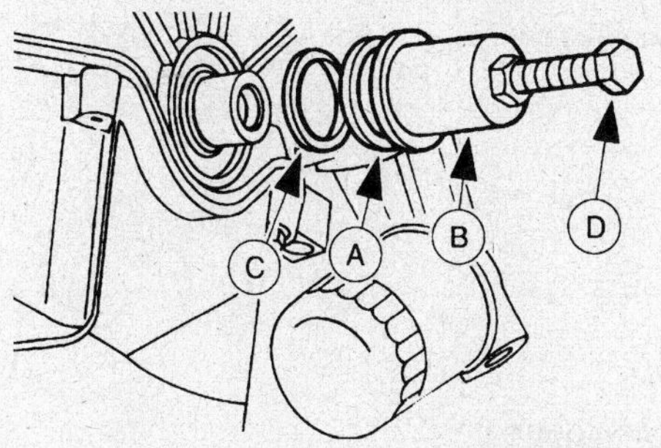

Fig. 17 Front crankshaft seal installation

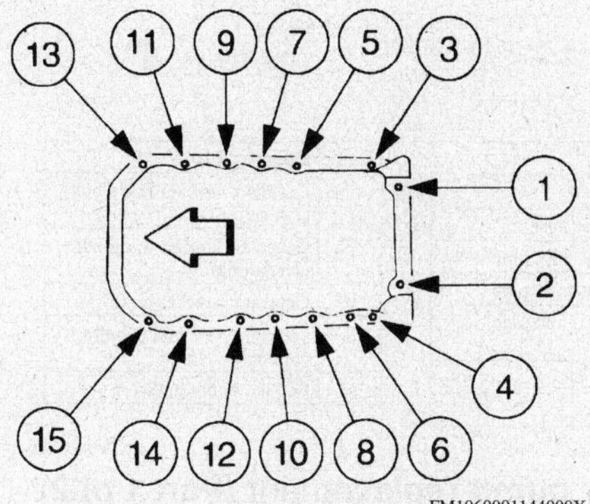

Fig. 20 Oil pan tightening sequence

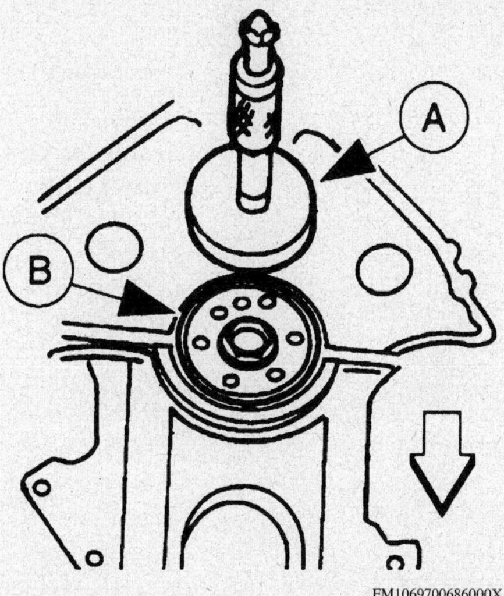

Fig. 18 Rear crankshaft seal removal

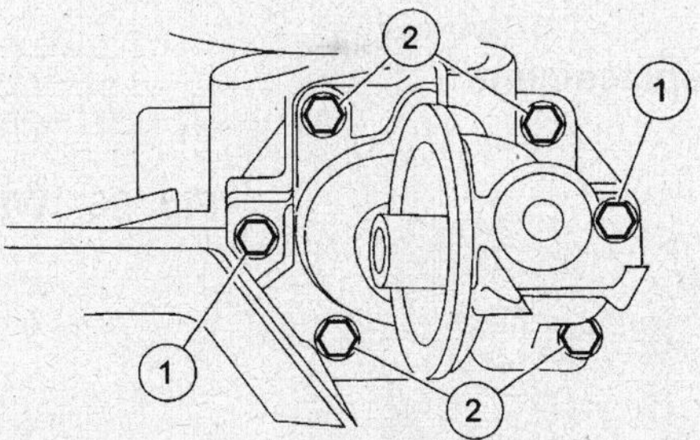

Fig. 21 Oil pump bolt tightening sequence

FM1069700687000X

Fig. 19 Rear crankshaft seal installation

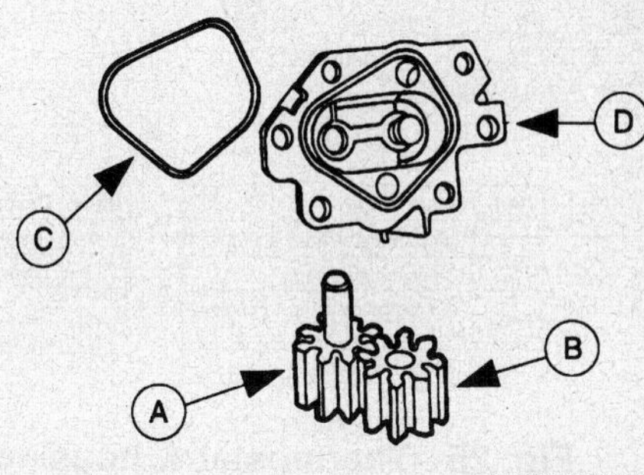

Fig. 22 Oil pump components

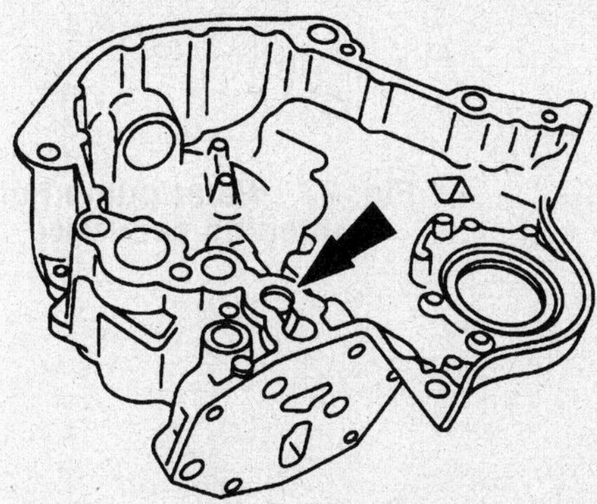

Fig. 23 Pressure relief valve plug removal

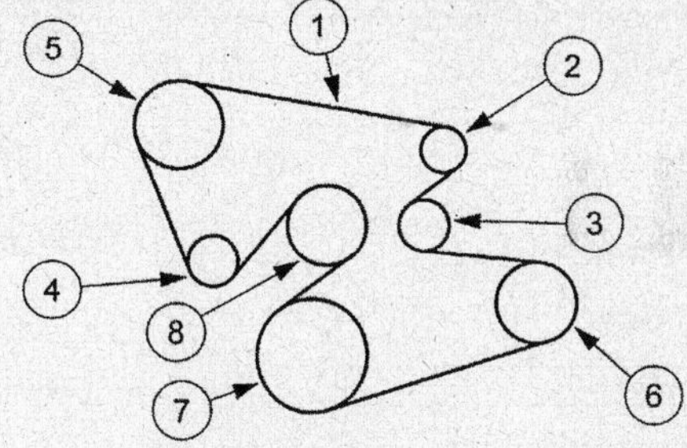

Item	Description
1	Drive belt
2	Generator pulley
3	Idler pulley
4	Drive belt tensioner
5	Power steering pump pulley
6	A/C clutch pulley
7	Crankshaft vibration damper pulley
8	Coolant pump pulley

LTV0500000000698

Fig. 24 Serpentine drive belt routing

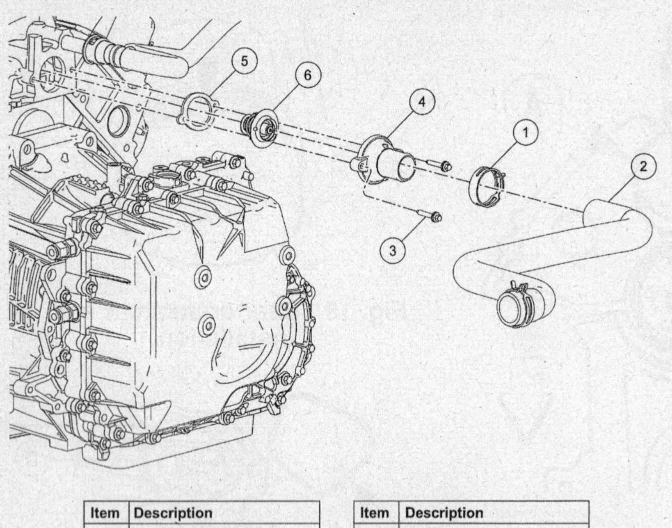

Item	Description
1	Upper radiator hose clamp
2	Upper radiator hose
3	Thermostat housing-to-engine bolts
4	Thermostat housing
5	Gasket
6	Thermostat

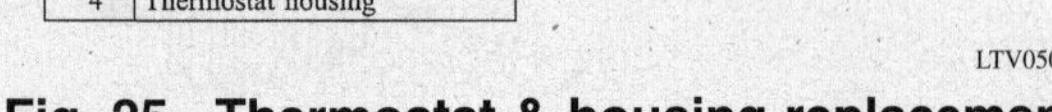

LTV0500000000706

Fig. 25 Thermostat & housing replacement

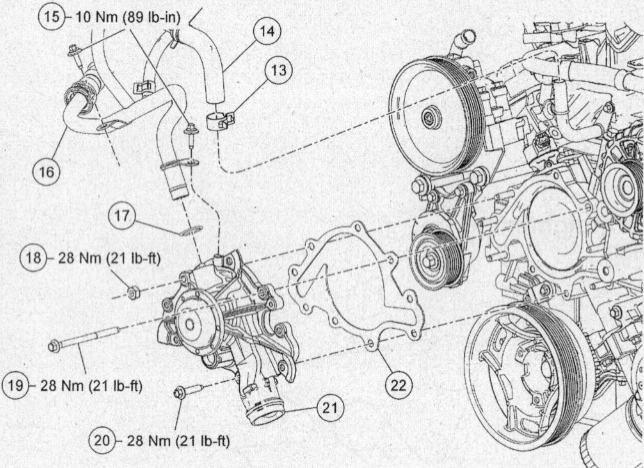

Item	Description
13	Clamp
14	Coolant bypass hose
15	Coolant pump outlet tube bolts
16	Coolant pump outlet tube
17	Coolant pump outlet tube O-ring seal
18	Coolant pump-to-engine front cover nut (5 required)
19	Coolant pump-to-engine front cover bolt
20	Coolant pump-to-engine front cover bolt (3 required)
21	Coolant pump
22	Coolant pump gasket

LTV0500000000708

Fig. 26 Water pump replacement (Part 2 of 2)

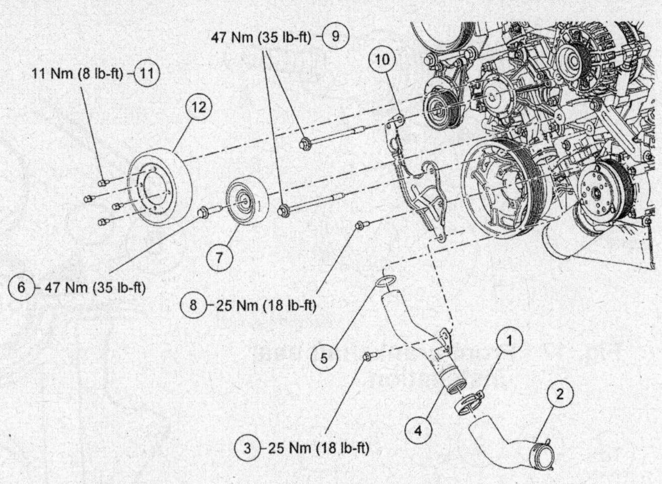

Item	Description
1	Clamp
2	Lower radiator hose
3	Coolant pump inlet pipe bolt
4	Coolant pump inlet pipe
5	Coolant pump inlet pipe O-ring seal
6	Idler pulley bolt
7	Idler pulley
8	Generator bracket brace bolt (2 required)
9	Generator bracket brace bolts (2 required)
10	Generator bracket brace
11	Coolant pump pulley bolt (4 required)
12	Coolant pump pulley

LTV0500000000707

Fig. 26 Water pump replacement (Part 1 of 2)

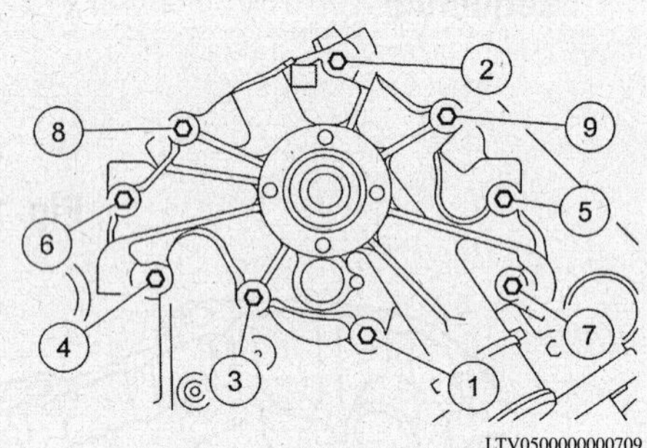

LTV0500000000709

Fig. 27 Water pump bolt tightening sequence

TIGHTENING SPECIFICATIONS

Year	Component	Torque Ft. Lbs.
2004–06	A/C Compressor Bracket Bolts	30–40
	A/C Compressor Manifold Bolt	14–18
	Accelerator Cable Bracket Nut & Bolt	80①
	Accelerator Cable To Accelerator Cable Bracket Bolt	19–25①
	Alternator Bracket Long Bolts	31–39
	Alternator Bracket Short Bolt	18–22
	Alternator Mounting Nuts & Bolts	15–22
	Camshaft Position Sensor	27①
	Camshaft Position Sensor Drive Gear Bolt	30–36
	Camshaft Thrust Plate Bolt	72–120①
	Catalytic Converter To Exhaust Manifold Bolts	30
	Connecting Rod Bolts	⑦
	Crankshaft Damper Bolt	103–118
	Crankshaft Pulley Bolts	20–28
	Cylinder Head	③
	EGR Valve Tube Fittings	25–34
	Engine Coolant Temperature Sensor	11–13
	Engine Dynamic Balance Shaft Thrust Plate Bolts	72–120①
	Engine Front Cover Bolts	②
	Engine Mount Through Bolts	51–67
	Exhaust Manifold Bolts & Stud Bolts	15–22
	Flywheel Bolts	56–59
	Fuel Injection Supply Manifold Bolts	80①
	Idler Pulley Bolt	36–46
	Intake Manifold, Lower	④
	Intake Manifold, Upper	④
	Main Bearing Cap Bolts	⑥
	Oil Filter	8–11
	Oil Filter Adapter Bolts (6 mm)	71–97①
	Oil Filter Adapter Bolts (8 mm)	15–22
	Oil Galley Plugs	19–29
	Oil Pan Baffle Nuts	30–37
	Oil Pan To Transmission Bolts	28–38
	Oil Pressure Sender	9–11
	Oil Pump	⑤
	Oil Pump Screen Cover & Tube Bolts	15–22
	Oil Pump Screen Cover & Tube Nuts	30–37
	Power Steering Pump Bolts	17–20
	Power Steering Reservoir Bolts	80–107①

TIGHTENING SPECIFICATIONS—Continued

Year	Component	Torque Ft. Lbs.
2004–06	Power Steering Support Bracket Bolts	30–40
	Rocker Arm Bolts	23–29
	Rocker Cover Bolts	71–102①
	Thermostat Bolts	80①
	Timing Chain Tensioner Bolts	9–10
	Valve Lifter Guide Plate Bolts	96–120①
	Water Pump Bolts	15–22
	Water Pump Pulley Bolts	89①
	Water Pump Bolts	⑧
	Water Temperature Indicator Sender Unit	11–13

①— Inch lbs.

②— Refer to "Front Cover, Replace."

③— Refer to "Cylinder Head, Replace."

④— Refer to "Intake Manifold, Replace."

⑤— Refer to "Oil Pump, Replace."

⑥— First step, torque to 37 ft. lbs.; second step, an additional 120°.

⑦— First step, torque to 18 ft. lbs.; second step, torque to 33 ft. lbs.; third step, an additional 90–120°.

⑧— Refer to "Water Pump, Replace."

Rear Axle & Suspension

NOTE: On Air Bag Equipped Models, Refer To "Air Bag System Precautions" Located In The Front Of This Manual For System Disarming & Arming Procedures.

NOTE: Refer To "Computer Relearn Procedures" Located In The Front Of This Manual When Battery Power To The Computer Has Been Interrupted.

NOTE: On Rear Air Suspension Equipped Models, Turn Air Suspension Switch To "Off" Position Prior To Raising Vehicle.

INDEX

PRECAUTIONS

Air Bag Systems

Refer to "Air Bag System Precautions" in the front of this manual for system disarming and arming procedures.

REAR AXLE

REPLACE

1. Raise and support vehicle, then remove wheels and tires.
2. Remove rear brake drums, then the rear anti-lock brake sensors.
3. Disconnect rear brake lines.
4. Disconnect parking brake cable and conduits from parking brake levers.
5. Disconnect parking brake cable and conduits from parking brake cable bracket, then pull parking brake cables and conduits from backing plates.
6. Support rear axle assembly, **Fig. 1**, with suitable lifting device.
7. Remove track bar from axle mounting bracket.
8. Remove rear shock absorber lower bolts.
9. Slowly lower rear axle from vehicle.
10. Reverse procedure to install.

HUB & BEARING

REPLACE

1. Raise and support vehicle, then remove rear tires.
2. Remove rear brake disc caliper mounting bolts, then position caliper aside using suitable mechanics wire.
3. Disconnect ABS wheel sensor connector.
4. Remove wheel hub and bearing bolts, **Fig. 2.**
5. Remove wheel hub and bearing assembly.
6. Reverse procedure to install.

WHEEL BEARING

ADJUST

The wheel bearing and hub assembly used on these models is a one piece assembly and is not adjustable.

SHOCK ABSORBER

REPLACE

1. Raise and support vehicle, then remove wheel and tire.
2. Place a suitable support under axle as close to shock as possible.
3. Lower vehicle or raise support to relieve tension on shock.
4. Remove upper and lower mounting bolts, then remove shock.
5. Reverse procedure to install, tighten bolts to specifications.

COIL SPRING

REPLACE

1. Raise and support vehicle, then remove wheel and tire.
2. Place a suitable support under axle as close to spring as possible.
3. Lower vehicle or raise support to relieve tension on shock.
4. Remove either a upper or lower shock mounting bolt, then raise vehicle or lower axle to relieve tension on spring.
5. Remove spring and insulator pads.
6. Reverse procedure to install. Ensure proper position of upper and lower insulator pad.

TRACK ROD

REPLACE

1. Raise and support vehicle.
2. Disconnect track arm from rear axle.
3. Disconnect track arm from frame mount, then remove track rod from vehicle.
4. Reverse procedure to install, tighten bolts to specifications.

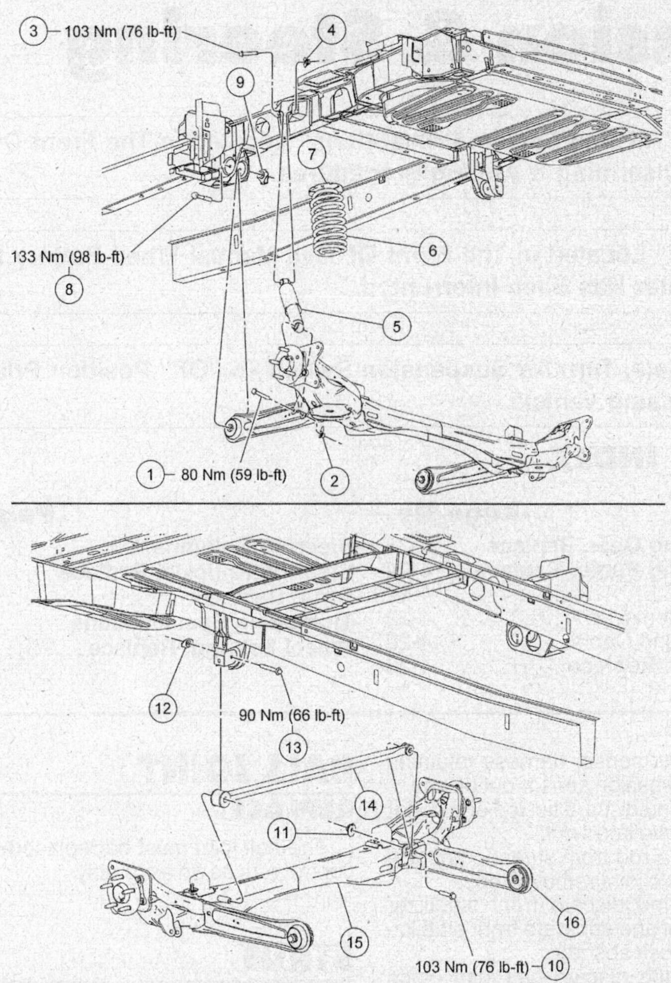

Fig. 1 Exploded view of rear axle assembly (Part 1 of 2)

Item	Description
1	Shock absorber-to-axle bolt
2	Shock absorber-to-axle flagnut
3	Upper shock absorber bolt
4	Upper shock absorber nut
5	Shock absorber
6	Coil spring
7	Spring insulator (2 required)
8	Trailing arm bolt (2 required)
9	Trailing arm nut (2 required)
10	Trackbar arm-to-axle bolt

Item	Description
11	Trackbar arm-to-axle nut
12	Trackbar arm-to-body bracket nut
13	Trackbar arm-to-body bracket bolt
14	Trackbar arm
15	Axle assembly
16	Trailing arm bushing

LTV0500000000711

Fig. 1 Exploded view of rear axle assembly (Part 2 of 2)

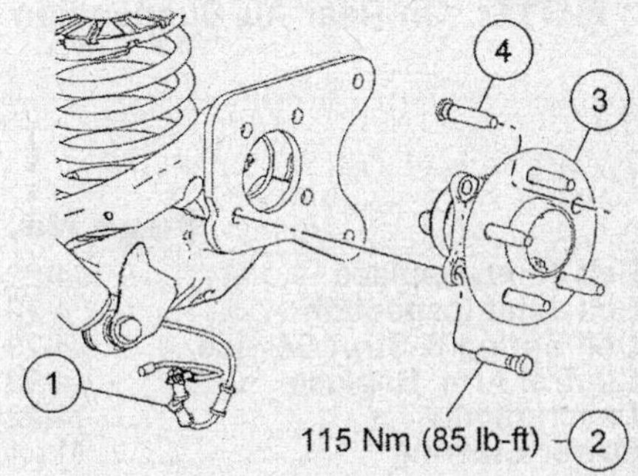

Item	Description
1	ABS sensor connector
2	Wheel hub and bearing assembly bolt
3	Wheel hub and bearing assembly
4	Wheel stud

LTV0500000000712

Fig. 2 Hub & bearing replacement

TIGHTENING SPECIFICATIONS

Year	Component	Torque Ft. Lbs.
2004–06	Anti-Lock Brake Sensor Bolt	40–78
	Brake Hose Bracket To Body	8–12
	Jounce Bumper To Axle	15–21
	Shock To Axle	50–68
	Shock To Frame	50–68
	Spindle & Brake Backing Plate To Axle	48–49
	Track Bar Retaining Bolts	50–68
	Trailing Arm To Frame	83–113
	Wheel Hub Retainer Nut	
	Wheel Lug Nuts	85–115

Front Suspension & Steering

NOTE: On Air Bag Equipped Models, Refer To "Air Bag System Precautions" Located In The Front Of This Manual For System Disarming & Arming Procedures.

NOTE: Refer To "Computer Relearn Procedures" Located In The Front Of This Manual When Battery Power To The Computer Has Been Interrupted.

NOTE: On Rear Air Suspension Equipped Models, Turn Air Suspension Switch To "Off" Position Prior To Raising Vehicle.

INDEX

PRECAUTIONS

Air Bag Systems

Refer to "Air Bag System Precautions" in the front of this manual for system disarming and arming procedures.

Battery Ground Cable

Prior to service disconnect battery ground cable and isolate as required.

DESCRIPTION

This suspension is of the gas filled McPherson strut type, **Fig. 1.** The strut top mount consists of a rubber insulated bearing and seat and coil spring insulator. The top mount is attached to the body side apron by three bolts. The lower part of the strut is mounted in the steering knuckle and is retained by a pinch bolt. A forged lower control arm is attached to the subframe and to the steering knuckle. A tension strut is connected to the lower control arm and to the forward part of the subframe.

WHEEL BEARING

REPLACE

The wheel hub and bearing are serviced as an assembly and cannot be repaired separately.

1. Raise and support vehicle, then remove wheel and tire.
2. Remove and discard front axle retainer nut.
3. Remove front brake rotor as outlined under "Disc Brakes" chapter, then remove rotor shield.
4. Remove anti-lock brake sensor retaining bolt and sensor harness retaining bolt, then position sensor out of way.
5. Remove and discard tie-rod end cotter pin and castellated nut.
6. Remove tie rod from steering knuckle with suitable joint removal tool.
7. Remove and discard front stabilizer bar link nut and separate front stabilizer front shock absorber.
8. Remove and discard ball joint pinch bolt and nut.
9. Place a suitable pry bar between front subframe and front suspension lower arm, then push down until lower ball joint is free of front wheel knuckle.
10. Press front driveshaft from wheel hub with press tool No. 204-069, or equivalent.
11. From back of steering knuckle, remove three mounting bolts, then remove wheel hub from knuckle. Wheel hub is a slip fit design and should not require a puller to remove.
12. Reverse procedure to install, noting the following. Apply a small amount of suitable thread locking compound to last five front wheel driveshaft joint threads prior to installing wheel hub retainer nut.

BALL JOINT INSPECTION

1. Raise vehicle until wheels fall to a full down position.
2. Grasp lower edge of tire and move wheel assembly in and out.
3. As wheel is being moved, observe lower end of knuckle and lower control arm. Any movement would indicate abnormal ball joint wear.
4. If movement is observed, replace lower control arm assembly.

BALL JOINT

REPLACE

The ball joint must be replaced with the control arm as an assembly.

STRUT

REPLACE

1. Place ignition switch in Off position and ensure steering wheel is not locked.
2. Remove hub nut and loosen three strut attaching nuts, then raise and support vehicle. Do not raise vehicle with lower control arm.
3. Raise and support vehicle, then remove front tires.
4. Remove brake caliper and wire it aside.
5. Remove brake rotor and tie rod end.
6. Remove stabilizer bar link nut, then remove link from strut.
7. Remove lower control arm to steering knuckle pinch nut and bolt, then slightly spread joint and remove lower control arm.
8. Press axle from hub using hub remover/installer tool Nos. T81P-1104-A, T81P-1104-C, T83P-1104-BH, T86P-1104-A1, or equivalents. Wire axle shaft to body to maintain level position. **Do not allow axle shaft to move outward. Over extension of the constant velocity (CV) joint could result in separation of internal components, which could cause CV joint failure.**
9. Remove strut to steering knuckle pinch bolt, then spread joint slightly and remove steering knuckle and hub assembly.
10. Remove anti-lock brake wheel speed sensor, if equipped.

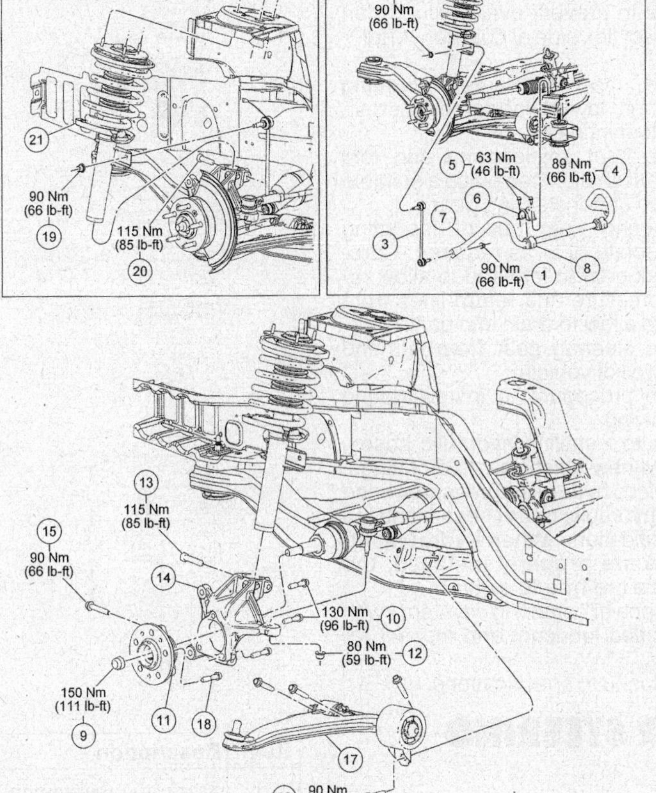

Fig. 1 Exploded view of front suspension (Part 1 of 2)

Item	Description	Item	Description
1	Stabilizer bar link nut	13	Wheel knuckle pinch bolt
2	Stabilizer bar link nut	14	Wheel knuckle (LH/RH)
3	Stabilizer bar links (2 required)	15	Lower ball joint stud-to-wheel knuckle bolt and nut
4	Subframe bolt	16	Lower arm bolts
5	Stabilizer bar bracket bolts	17	Lower arm (LH/RH)
6	Stabilizer bar bracket	18	Wheel stud
7	Stabilizer bar	19	Stabilizer bar link nut
8	Stabilizer bar bushing	20	Wheel knuckle pinch bolt
9	Axle shaft nut	21	Shock absorber
10	Wheel hub-to-wheel knuckle bolts (3 required)	22	Shock absorber upper mount-to-body nuts
11	Wheel bearing and hub assembly		
12	Tie-rod end-to-wheel knuckle nut		

LTV0500000000714

Fig. 1 Exploded view of front suspension (Part 2 of 2)

11. Remove strut attaching nuts, then remove strut assembly from vehicle.
12. Reverse procedure to install, noting the following:
    a. Tighten attaching nuts and bolts to specifications.
    b. With vehicle on ground, tighten hub nut to specification.
    c. Install new strut to knuckle bolt, control arm to knuckle bolt and nut, and tie rod nut.

COIL SPRING & STRUT SERVICE

1. Compress strut spring with coil spring compressor tool No. 014-00781, or equivalent.
2. Restrain strut shaft using a suitable 10 mm box wrench, then remove strut mounting nut with suitable 21 mm crow foot socket. Do not allow strut shaft to rotate.
3. Loosen compressor tool, **Fig. 2,** then remove strut top mount bracket assembly, bearing and seat assembly and spring, **Fig. 3.**
4. Reverse procedure to install.

CONTROL ARM

REPLACE

1. Place ignition switch in Off position and ensure steering wheel is not locked.
2. Raise and support vehicle.
3. Remove wheel and tire assembly.
4. Remove tension strut nut, then the dished washer.
5. Remove lower control arm to steering knuckle pinch nut and bolt, then slightly spread joint and separate ball joint from steering knuckle. **Do not use a hammer to separate suspension pieces.**
6. Remove lower control arm inner pivot bolt and nut, then the control arm.
7. Reverse procedure to install noting the following:
    a. Install new lower arm nut, pinch bolt and nut, and lower arm to subframe bolt and nut.
    b. Tighten all nuts and bolts to specifications.

STEERING KNUCKLE

REPLACE

1. Place ignition switch in Off position and ensure steering wheel is not locked.
2. Remove hub nut and loosen three strut attaching nuts, then raise and support vehicle. Do not raise vehicle with lower control arm.
3. Raise and support vehicle.
4. Remove wheel and tire assembly.
5. Remove brake caliper and wire it aside.
6. Remove brake rotor and tie rod end from knuckle.
7. Remove stabilizer bar link nut, then remove link from strut.
8. Remove lower control arm to steering knuckle pinch nut and bolt, then slightly spread joint and remove lower control arm from knuckle.
9. Press axle from hub using hub remover/installer tool Nos. T81P-1104-A, T81P-1104-C, T83P-1104-BH, T86P-1104-A1, or equivalents. Wire axle shaft to body to maintain level position. **Do not allow axle shaft to move outward. Over extension of the constant velocity (CV) joint could result in separation of internal components, which could cause CV joint failure.**
10. Remove rotor splash shield and anti-lock brake sensor, if equipped.
11. Remove strut to steering knuckle pinch bolt, then spread joint slightly and remove steering knuckle and hub assembly.
12. Reverse procedure to install.

STABILIZER BAR

REPLACE

1. Raise and support vehicle.
2. Remove stabilizer bar link to strut attaching nuts.
3. Remove stabilizer bar link to stabilizer bar attaching nuts.
4. Remove steering gear to subframe attaching bolts, then move steering gear off subframe.
5. Support subframe with suitable safety stands, then remove rear subframe attaching bolts. Lower rear part of subframe to gain access to stabilizer bar mounting brackets.
6. Remove mounting brackets, then the stabilizer bar.
7. Reverse procedure to install.

POWER STEERING GEAR

REPLACE

1. Remove steering shaft weather boot to dash panel attaching bolts.
2. Remove intermediate shaft to steering column shaft attaching bolts, **Fig. 4.**

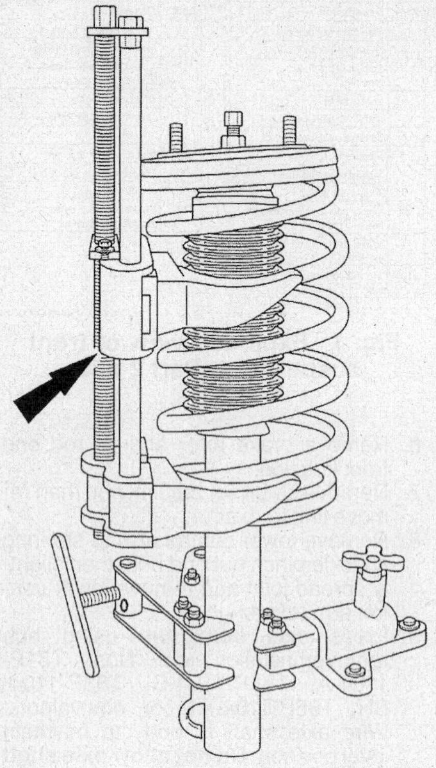

Fig. 2 Spring compressor installation

3. Move weather boot aside, then remove steering gear input shaft pinch bolt and remove intermediate shaft.
4. Raise and support vehicle.
5. Vehicle must be supported so that rear of subframe may be safely lowered.
6. Remove front wheels.
7. Remove tie rod ends from steering knuckles.
8. Remove front stabilizer bar.
9. Remove nuts from steering gear mounting bolts. **The gear mounting bolts are pressed into the steering gear housing and should not be removed during normal service procedures.**
10. With vehicle properly supported, place a suitable lifting device under subframe, so placed as to allow lowering of rear of subframe.
11. Place a suitable support on exhaust flex pipe to prevent over-flexing, then disconnect flex pipe at dual converter Y pipe.
12. Remove rear subframe mounting bolts, then lower subframe approximately four inches.
13. Remove heat shield band and fold down heat shield, then place a suitable drain pan under steering gear.
14. Lift steering gear out of mounting holes. Rotate gear as required. Carefully work gear to lefthand to allow removal pressure and return lines from gear and allow to drain into pan.
15. Remove steering gear from lefthand fender well of vehicle.
16. Reverse procedure to install, noting the following:
    a. Prior to installing hydraulic hoses, install new plastic seals on fittings.
    b. Tighten hydraulic pressure hose and hydraulic return hose fittings to specifications. **When hydraulic fittings are properly installed, the hoses are free to swivel.**
    c. Fill power steering system with specified lubricant and inspect for leaks.
    d. Set toe-in to specifications.

POWER STEERING PUMP

REPLACE

1. Remove drive belt as outlined under "Serpentine Drive Belt."
2. Remove alternator, if required.
3. Raise and support vehicle, then remove righthand front wheel.
4. Position a drain pan, then remove both hoses from power steering pump, **Fig. 5.**
5. Remove four pump mounting bolt (three front, one rear) and remove pump from vehicle.
6. Reverse procedure to install, noting the following:
    a. Prior to installing hydraulic hoses, install new plastic seals on fittings.
    b. Tighten steering pump attaching nuts to specification.
    c. Install power steering pulley using installer tool No. T65P-3A733-C, or equivalent.
    d. Tighten hydraulic pressure hose and hydraulic return hose fittings to specifications. **When hydraulic fittings are properly installed, the hoses are free to swivel.**
    e. Fill power steering system with specified lubricant and inspect for leaks.

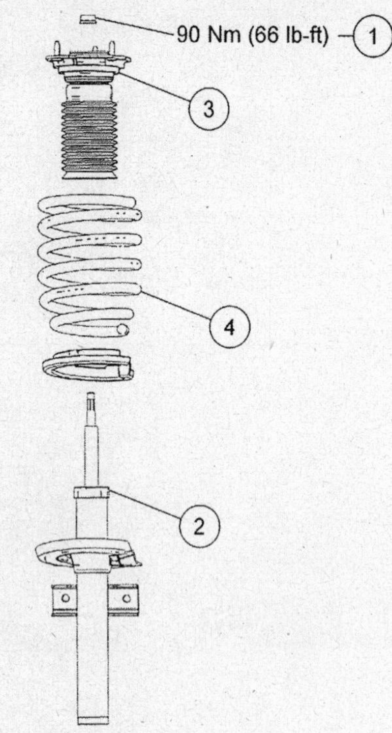

Item	Description
1	Shock absorber-to-upper mount nut
2	Shock absorber
3	Upper shock mount/bearing assembly
4	Coil spring

LTV0500000000715

Fig. 3 Exploded view of strut assembly

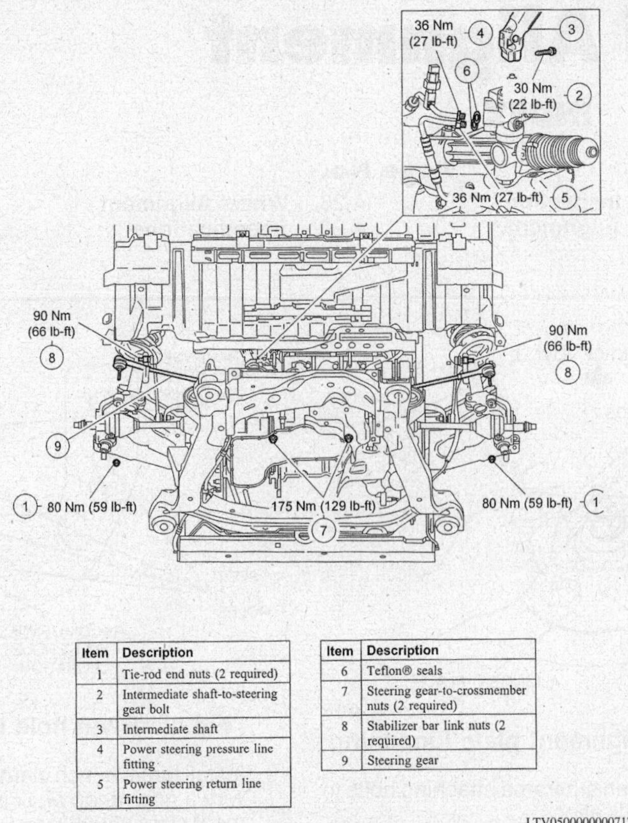

Item	Description
1	Tie-rod end nuts (2 required)
2	Intermediate shaft-to-steering gear bolt
3	Intermediate shaft
4	Power steering pressure line fitting
5	Power steering return line fitting

Item	Description
6	Teflon® seals
7	Steering gear-to-crossmember nuts (2 required)
8	Stabilizer bar link nuts (2 required)
9	Steering gear

LTV0500000000717

Fig. 4 Power steering gear replacement

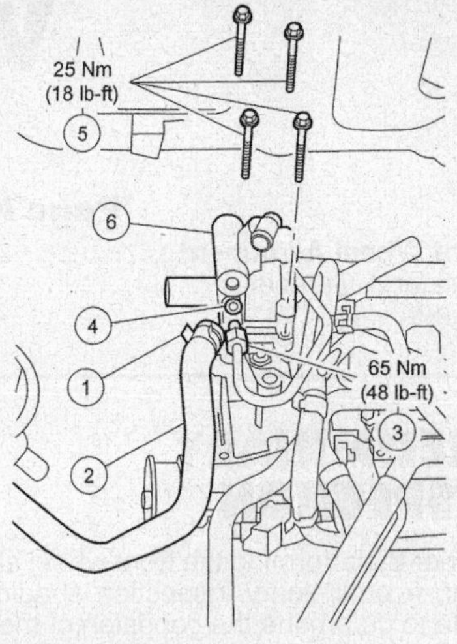

Item	Description
1	Power steering fluid reservoir-to-power steering pump hose lower clamp
2	Power steering fluid reservoir-to-power steering pump hose
3	Power steering pressure line-to-pump fitting
4	Teflon® seal
5	Power steering pump bolts (4 required)
6	Power steering pump

LTV0500000000718

Fig. 5 Power steering pump replacement

TIGHTENING SPECIFICATIONS

Year	Component	Torque Ft. Lbs.
2004–06	Ball Joint Pinch Bolt	46–52
	Bearing Mounting Bolts	85
	Boot To Firewall Nut	40–50①
	Control Arm To Subframe	85–97
	Front Axle Nut	170–202
	Front Caliper Mounting Bolt	73–97
	Front Strut Upper Mounting	26–30
	Front Suspension Tension Strut	85–97
	Intermediate Shaft To Column Pinch Bolt	30–40
	Intermediate Shaft To Gear Pinch Bolt	25–34
	Power Steering Line Fittings	26–33
	Power Steering Pump Mounting Bolts	15–24
	Pressure Line At Gear Fitting	15–25
	Pressure Line At Pump Fitting	10–15
	Pump Reservoir Fittings	25–34
	Return Line At Gear, Fitting	15–25
	Steering Gear To Crossmember Nut	85–100
	Strut Center Nut	40–46
	Stabilizer Bar Link	66–77
	Strut To Hub Pinch Bolt	85–97
	Tie Rod End Bolt	66–74
	Wheel Lug Nuts	85–105

① — Inch lbs.

Wheel Alignment

INDEX

PRELIMINARY INSPECTION

Prior to performing the front wheel alignment, a preliminary inspection should be made to determine the condition of the vehicle's suspension components. The following inspections and procedures should be made prior to performing front wheel alignment.

Do not attempt to adjust alignment by heating or bending suspension or steering components.

1. Vehicle must be level.
2. Inflate tires to specified pressure (cold).
3. Inspect vehicle ride height.
4. Inspect all suspension and steering components for looseness.
5. Inspect existing caster, camber, and toe settings prior to alignment.
6. Inspect all suspension fasteners for proper torque.
7. Alignment equipment must be capable of four wheel alignment.
8. Alignment rack must be leveled to 1⁄16 of an inch, side to side and front to rear and be equipped with wheel runout compensation.

FRONT WHEEL ALIGNMENT

Caster & Camber

1. Prior to aligning the front end, the subframe alignment must be inspected using the following procedure.
   a. Loosen subframe to body attaching bolts.
   b. Shift subframe if possible in the direction required to bring vehicle into alignment.

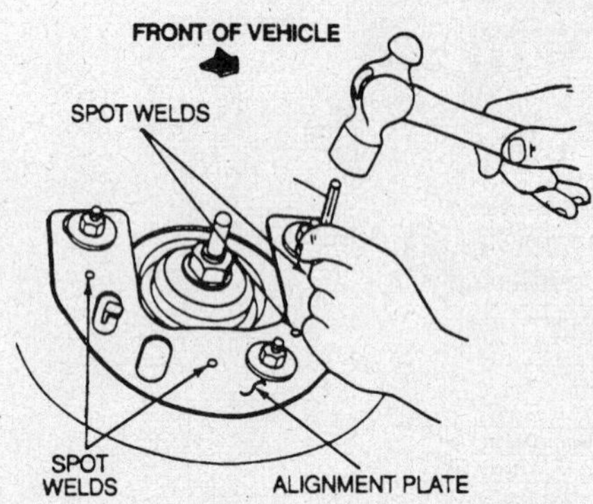

Fig. 1 Alignment plate loosening

   c. Tighten subframe attaching bolts to specifications.
   d. Inspect front alignment, if further adjustment is required use the following procedures.
2. Center punch spot welds on both strut alignment plates, then loosen strut attaching nuts, **Fig. 1.**
3. Remove spot welds using Rotunda Spot-Eze or equivalent. **Do not drill deeper than thickness of alignment plates.**
4. Remove strut attaching nuts, then the alignment plates.
5. Remove burrs from strut towers and alignment plates, then paint all exposed metal on strut towers and alignment plates.
6. Install alignment plates, then loosely install strut attaching nuts.
7. Align front end, then **torque** strut attaching nuts to 26–30 ft. lbs.
8. Drill three 1⁄8 inch holes as indicated in **Fig. 2,** through alignment plates and strut towers, then paint exposed metal. **Do not drill deeper than 3⁄8 inch into strut tower.**

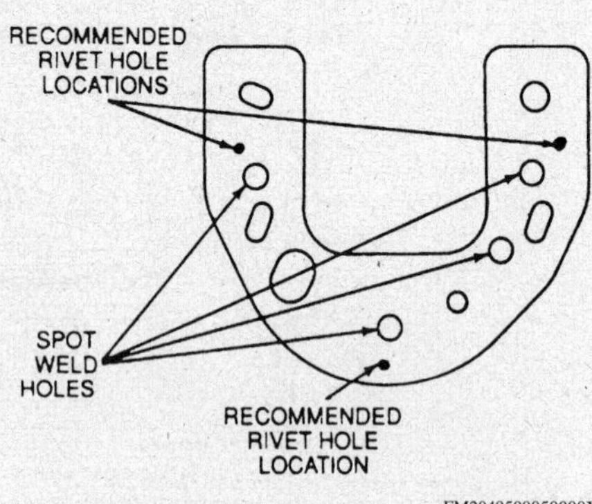

Fig. 2 Rivet hole location

9. Install three 1⁄8 inch diameter pop rivets with a grip range of 1⁄4 inch into alignment plate/strut tower.

Toe-In

To adjust toe-in, lock steering wheel in straight ahead position using suitable steering wheel holder. Loosen and slide off small outer clamps from steering boot to prevent boot from twisting during adjustment procedure. Loosen tie rod adjusting, then adjust lefthand and righthand tie rods until each wheel has 1⁄2 the desired total toe specification. Tighten tie rod adjusting nuts and install clamps. Remove steering wheel holding tool.

REAR WHEEL ALIGNMENT

The caster, camber and toe angles are factory set and cannot be adjusted. If rear wheel alignment is not to specifications, inspect suspension for faulty components.

VILLAGER

NOTE: Refer To Back Of This Manual For Vehicle Manufacturer's Special Tool Suppliers.

INDEX OF SERVICE OPERATIONS

Specifications

GENERAL ENGINE SPECIFICATIONS

Year	Engine, Liter	Fuel System	Bore & Stroke	Comp. Ratio	Horsepower @ RPM	Torque Ft. Lbs. @ RPM	Normal Oil Pressure, Lbs.
2002	3.3L	EFI	3.60 x 3.27	8.9	170 @ 4800	200 @ 2800	①

① — At idle, minimum 17 psi.; at 3200 RPM, 57–70 psi.

TUNE UP SPECIFICATIONS

Year	Engine, Liter	Spark Plug Gap, Inch	Ignition Timing, °BTDC			Curb Idle Speed, RPM	Fast Idle Speed, RPM	Fuel Pump Pressure, psi	Valve Lash
			Firing Order	Auto. Trans.	Mark Location, Fig. A				
2002	3.3L	.039–.043	⑤	15②	Damper	700–800①	①	③	④

BTDC — Before Top Dead Center

① — Controlled by idle air control-fast idle control.

② — With idle air control solenoid disconnected.

③ — Remove fuel pump relay from relay block, located on lefthand side of the engine compartment. Start engine & operate until engine stalls. Ensure fuel pressure has been released by cranking engine approximately 3 seconds. Place ignition switch in off position, then install fuel pump relay. Place shop towel over fuel hose connection between fuel line & fuel filter. Disconnect fuel hose & install a suitable fuel pressure test gauge between fuel line & filter. Start engine & inspect for fuel leakage at pressure test gauge connections. With engine idling, fuel pressure should be approximately 34 psi w/pressure regulator valve vacuum hose connected. With pressure regulator valve vacuum hose disconnected, fuel pressure should be approximately 37–43 psi.

④ — Equipped w/hydraulic valve tappets.

⑤ — Cylinder numbering from front of engine to rear, rear bank, 1, 3, 5; front bank, 2, 4, 6. Firing order 1-2-3-4-5-6

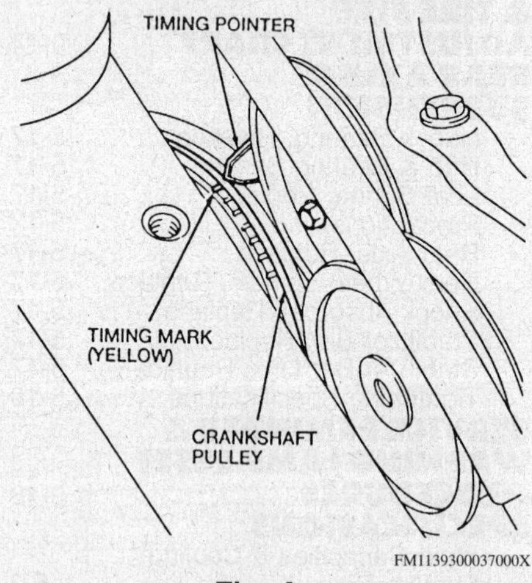

Fig. A

FRONT WHEEL ALIGNMENT SPECIFICATIONS

Year	Caster Angle, Degree①		Camber Angle, Degree①		Toe-In, Inch		Front Turning Angle, Degree①		Kingpin Inclination, Degree①	Ball Joint Wear Limit
	Limits	Desired	Limits	Desired	Limits	Desired	Inside	Outside		
2002	+.05 to +1.55	+.80	-.45 to +1.00	+.27	+.08 to +.16	+.08 to +.12	36–40	28–32	12.8 to 14.3	②

① — Caster, camber & kingpin inclination are preset at factory & cannot be adjusted.

② — Refer to "Ball Joint Inspection" in "Front Suspension & Steering."

REAR WHEEL ALIGNMENT SPECIFICATIONS

Year	Camber Angle, Degree		Toe-In, Inch	
	Limits	Desired	Limits	Desired
2002	-.25 to +.25	0	-.059 to +.059	0

FLUID CAPACITIES & COOLING SYSTEM DATA

Year	Engine, Liter	Coolant Capacity, Qts.		Coolant type	Radiator Cap Relief Pressure, Lbs.	Thermo Opening, Temp. °F	Fuel Tank, Gals.	Engine Oil Refill, Qts.①	Transaxle Oil, Qts.
		Less A/C	With A/C						
2002	3.3L	11.4②	11.4②	④	14.4–17.6	180	20	4.2③	8.25

① — Approximate; make final inspect w/dipstick.

② — With rear heater, 12.7 qts.

③ — Includes filter.

④ — For models w/green coolant use ethylene glycol. For models w/orange coolant, use coolant meeting Ford Motor Co. specification WSSM07B44D, or equivalent.

LUBRICANT DATA

Year	Model	Lubricant Type		
		Transaxle	Power Steering	Brake System
2002	All	Mercon® ATF	①	DOT 3

① — Premium power steering fluid meeting Ford specification No. ESW-M2C-33-F.

Electrical

NOTE: On Air Bag Equipped Models, Refer To "Air Bag System Precautions" Located In The Front Of This Manual For System Disarming & Arming Procedures.

NOTE: Refer To "Computer Relearn Procedures" Located In The Front Of This Manual When Battery Power To The Computer Has Been Interrupted.

INDEX

PRECAUTIONS

Air Bag Systems

Refer to "Air Bag System Precautions" in the front of this manual for system disarming and arming procedures.

Battery Ground Cable

Prior to service disconnect battery ground cable and isolate as required.

FUSE PANEL & FLASHER LOCATION

The fuse panel is located behind the lefthand side of the instrument panel, above the hood release lever, behind the fuse panel cover. The flasher module is located behind the lefthand side of instrument panel, on righthand side of steering column.

FUEL PUMP RELAY LOCATION

The fuel pump relay is located in the main lefthand engine compartment relay center, **Fig. 1.**

RELAY CENTER LOCATION

The main relay center is located in front of the battery on the lefthand side of the engine compartment. The secondary relay center is located on the lefthand side of the battery over the wheel housing.

STARTER

REPLACE

1. Remove air cleaner assembly.
2. Slide solenoid B terminal protective boot rearward and remove battery cable to B terminal nut.
3. Remove brush cable to M terminal nut.
4. Disconnect S terminal electrical connector.
5. Remove starter motor bolts, then motor.
6. Reverse procedure to install. **Torque** B terminal nut to 98 inch lbs., and starter motor bolts to 17–19 ft. lbs.

ALTERNATOR

REPLACE

1. Raise and support vehicle.
2. Remove engine splash shield.
3. Remove alternator adjuster bolt, then drive belt.
4. Remove two alternator to bracket attaching bolts and support alternator.
5. Disconnect alternator electrical connectors, then remove alternator from vehicle.
6. Reverse procedure to install, note following:
   a. **Torque** alternator to bracket attaching bolts to 19 ft. lbs.
   b. **Torque** alternator adjustment bolt to 14 ft. lbs.

DISTRIBUTOR

REPLACE

1. Set No. 1 piston to TDC of its compression stroke.
2. Mark spark plug wires for installation reference, then disconnect wires from distributor cap.
3. Remove two distributor cap attaching screws.
4. Disconnect ignition coil electrical connector from bracket.
5. Disconnect Camshaft Position (CMP) sensor electrical connector.
6. Remove distributor retaining bolt, then distributor from engine.
7. Remove rotor retaining screw, then rotor from distributor.
8. Reverse procedure to install, note following:
   a. If crankshaft position was changed with distributor removed, rotate crankshaft until No. 1 piston is at TDC of its compression stroke.
   b. Align mark on distributor shaft with protruding mark on distributor housing.
   c. **Torque** distributor retaining bolt to 12 ft. lbs.

IGNITION LOCK

REPLACE

1. Remove lower and upper steering column shrouds.
2. Turn ignition switch to ON position.
3. **On models equipped with non-functional ignition key lock switches,** groove heads of ignition lock with a

hammer and chisel, then remove ignition lock from column.

4. **On all ignition key lock switches,** remove two key-in reminder switch attaching screws, then key-in reminder switch from steering column.
5. Place suitable 1/8 inch wire pin or small drift punch in ignition lock cylinder access hole, then depress retaining pin while pulling lock cylinder rearward to remove. When removing ignition switch lock cylinder a small tension spring will pop out from beneath cylinder rod.
6. Reverse procedure to install, note following:
   a. **On models equipped with non-functional ignition key lock switches,** tighten ignition lock bolts until heads break off.
   b. **On all ignition key lock switches,** ensure lock cylinder is in ON position.
   c. Before installing ignition lock switch, ensure tension spring beneath lock cylinder is placed properly.
   d. Lock cylinder is fully seated in housing when pin snaps into access hole.

IGNITION SWITCH

REPLACE

1. Remove upper and lower steering column shrouds.
2. Remove ignition switch attaching screws, then pull switch from ignition switch cylinder.
3. Disconnect ignition switch harness connector and remove ignition switch assembly.
4. Reverse procedure to install.

DIGITAL TRANSMISSION RANGE (TR) SENSOR

REPLACE

1. Place shifter in NEUTRAL position.
2. Raise and support vehicle.
3. Remove engine splash shield attaching bolts, then splash shield from vehicle.
4. Remove shifter cable retaining nut, then shifter cable from manual lever.
5. Disconnect TR sensor attaching screws, then TR sensor.
6. Reverse procedure to install, adjust TR sensor as follows:
   a. Loosely install TR switch attaching screws.
   b. Place manual shift linkage rod in NEUTRAL position.
   c. Insert gear position sensor adjuster tool No. 307-250, or equivalent, between TR sensor and manual shift linkage rod alignment holes, **Fig. 2.**
   d. **Torque** TR sensor attaching screws to 27 inch lbs., and shift cable retaining nut to 80 inch lbs.
   e. Install shift control cable and verify engine will only start in PARK and NEUTRAL positions.

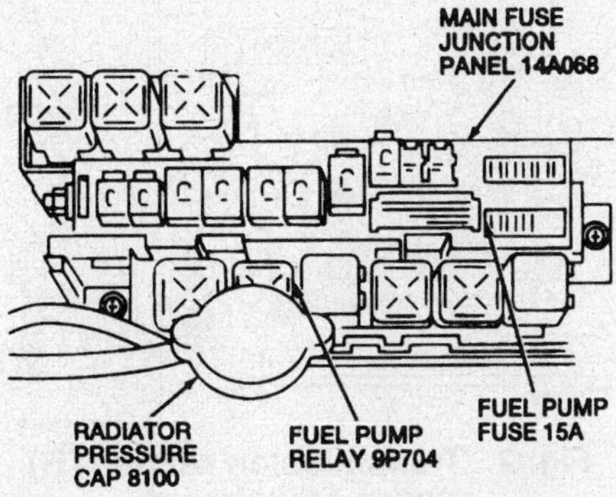

Fig. 1 Fuel pump relay location

HEADLAMP SWITCH

REPLACE

1. Gently pry headlamp switch panel away from instrument cluster trim panel.
2. Disconnect headlamp switch electrical connectors and remove headlamp switch panel.
3. Remove headlamp switch to switch panel attaching screws, then separate switch from panel.
4. Reverse procedure to install.

STOP LIGHT SWITCH

REPLACE

1. Depress switch electrical connector tabs, then disconnect electrical connector.
2. Loosen switch locknut, then remove switch.
3. Reverse procedure to install, note following:
   a. Measure distance between brake pedal stopper and threaded end of switch.
   b. Distance should be .012–.039 inch. If distance is not correct, loosen switch locknut and adjust switch until height is within specification.
   c. **Torque** switch locknut to 10–11 ft. lbs.

MULTI-FUNCTION SWITCH

REPLACE

1. Remove two steering column shroud retaining screws, then upper and lower steering column shrouds.
2. Remove two multi-function switch attaching screws.
3. Disconnect two multi-function switch electrical connectors, then remove switch.
4. Reverse procedure to install.

STEERING WHEEL

REPLACE

1. Remove driver air bag module as outlined in “Passive Restraint System” chapter.
2. Remove steering wheel retaining nut.
3. Remove steering wheel using gear and pulley puller tool No. D80L-522-A, or equivalent.
4. Reverse procedure to install. **Torque** steering wheel retaining nut to 25 ft. lbs.

INSTRUMENT CLUSTER

REPLACE

1. Block front wheels, then place steering column in its lowest position.
2. Place gearshift lever into 1 position.
3. Release two ashtray/cup holder locking tabs.
4. Disconnect electrical connector, then remove ashtray/cup holder from instrument panel.
5. Remove four console cover pin-type retainers, then console cover.
6. Remove instrument panel center finish panel attaching screws.
7. Disconnect electrical connector, then remove center finish panel from instrument panel.
8. Pry headlamp switch panel away from instrument panel cluster finish panel and position aside.
9. Remove instrument panel cluster finish panel attaching screws.
10. Disconnect electrical connector, then remove instrument panel cluster finish panel from instrument panel.
11. Disconnect transmission range indicator.
12. Remove instrument cluster attaching screws.
13. Disconnect cluster electrical connectors and remove cluster from instrument panel.
14. Reverse procedure to install.

RADIO

REPLACE

1. Release two ashtray/cup holder locking tabs.
2. Disconnect electrical connector, then remove ashtray/cup holder from instrument panel.
3. Remove four console cover pin-type retainers, then console cover.
4. Remove instrument panel center finish panel attaching screws.
5. Disconnect electrical connector, then remove center finish panel from instrument panel.
6. Remove radio to instrument panel attaching screws.
7. Pull radio unit away from instrument panel and disconnect antenna and electrical connectors.
8. Remove radio from instrument panel.
9. Reverse procedure to install.

WIPER MOTOR

REPLACE

Front

1. Remove wiper arms from pivot shafts.
2. Remove cowl pin-type retainers from front of cowl.
3. Remove cowl top vent panel attaching screws, then cowl from vehicle.

4. Disconnect wiper motor electrical connector.
5. Remove six mounting arm and pivot shaft attaching bolts.
6. Remove mounting arm and pivot shaft.
7. Remove wiper motor linkage retaining nut, then disconnect wiper linkage from wiper motor.
8. Disconnect wiper motor electrical connector.
9. Remove wiper motor attaching bolts, then wiper motor.
10. Reverse procedure to install.

Rear

1. Remove rear wiper arm and blade assembly.
2. Remove rear wiper motor shaft nut cover, then nut.
3. Remove outer collar and seal from liftgate.
4. Remove liftgate trim panel.
5. Remove rear courtesy lamps.
6. Carefully remove plastic weather barrier at adhesive areas.
7. Disconnect rear wiper electrical connector.
8. Remove wiper motor bracket bolts.
9. Remove wiper motor shaft inner collar, then wiper motor to bracket bolts.
10. Slide wiper motor connector from bracket, then motor.
11. Reverse procedure to install, note following:
    a. **Torque** wiper motor shaft to 54–70 inch lbs.
    b. **Torque** wiper motor bracket bolts to 54–61 inch lbs.
    c. **Torque** wiper motor to bracket bolts to 44 inch lbs.

WIPER TRANSMISSION
REPLACE

1. Mark alignment for reference during installation on end of wiper linkage, then remove front wiper motor as outlined under "Wiper Motor, Replace."
2. Remove each end of wiper linkage.
3. Remove two dust covers, then motor pivot shaft nut.
4. Remove pivot arm and dust cover.
5. Reverse procedure to install.

BLOWER MOTOR
REPLACE

Front

1. Release two ashtray/cup holder locking tabs.
2. Disconnect electrical connector, then remove ashtray/cup holder from instrument panel.
3. Remove four console cover pin-type retainers, then console cover.
4. Remove instrument panel center finish panel attaching screws.
5. Disconnect electrical connector, then remove center finish panel from instrument panel.

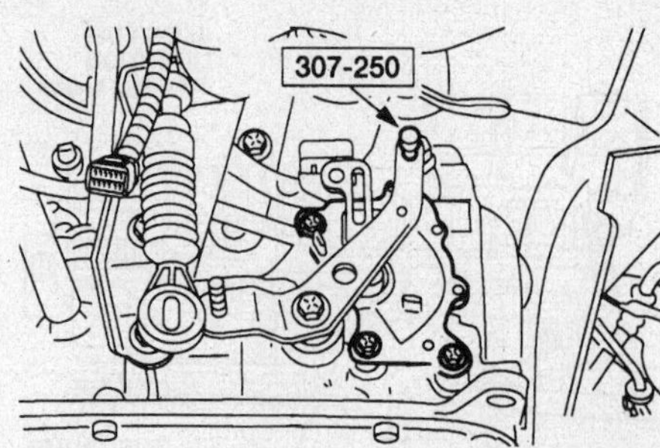

Fig. 2 Transmission range (TR) sensor adjustment

6. Open glove compartment, then release glove compartment stops and lower glove compartment.
7. Disconnect passenger air bag module electrical connector from access panel.
8. Remove passenger air bag module access panel.
9. Remove glover compartment attaching bolts and screws.
10. Disconnect glove compartment latch electrical connector, then remove glove compartment from instrument panel.
11. Remove instrument panel brace attaching bolts, then brace.
12. Disconnect blower motor hose.
13. **On models equipped with Electronic Automatic Temperature Control (EATC),** disconnect blower motor speed control electrical connector.
14. **On all models,** disconnect blower motor electrical connector.
15. Remove three blower motor attaching screws, then blower motor.
16. Reverse procedure to install.

Rear

1. Remove rear cargo shelf, then second row seat.
2. Move third row seat forward to second row seat position.
3. Remove cup holder from rear righthand side quarter trim panel.
4. Remove righthand side safety belt and shoulder belt anchor bolts from trim panel with a suitable T-50 Torx bit, or equivalent.
5. Remove sliding door and liftgate scuff plates.
6. Remove cargo net anchors using luggage hold down net retainer wrench tool No. 134-R0094, or equivalent.
7. Remove cargo shelf trim panel retaining screws, cargo shelf cups, then cargo shelf trim panel.
8. Remove righthand lower quarter trim panel pin-type retainers.
9. Disconnect power point electrical connector, then remove righthand lower quarter trim panel.
10. Remove rear package tray brace bolts.
11. Disconnect blower motor electrical connectors and air hose.
12. Remove blower motor attaching bolts, then blower motor.
13. Reverse procedure to install.

HEATER CORE
REPLACE

Front

1. Drain engine coolant, then disconnect heater hoses.
2. Remove A/C evaporator housing as outlined under "Evaporator Core, Replace."
3. Remove outboard seat riser trim cover pin-type connectors, then trim covers from front seats.
4. Remove seat belt buckle to seat attaching bolts from front seats, position belts aside.
5. Remove inboard seat riser trim cover pin-type connectors, then trim covers from front seats.
6. Position seat forward and remove rear seat track bolts.
7. Position seat rearward, then disconnect power seat module electrical connector.
8. Remove front seat track bolts, then front seats from vehicle.
9. Remove accelerator pedal stopper cover.
10. Remove front door skid plates, then righthand and lefthand kick panels.
11. Remove rear seat air flow duct bolts, rear seat air flow grilles, then position front floor carpet aside.
12. Remove rear heater duct cover attaching bolts, then cover.
13. Remove rear seat air flow duct attaching bolts and air flow duct.
14. Remove instrument panel center support bracket retaining nuts, then center support bracket.
15. Remove heater outlet floor duct.
16. Disconnect electronic door actuator motor electrical connector.
17. Remove heater and ventilation intake duct attaching bolts, then intake duct.
18. Remove upper and lower heater case retaining nuts, then heater case.
19. Remove heater core foam grommet.
20. Remove heater core attaching screws, then heater core support clip.
21. Remove heater core from heater case.
22. Reverse procedure to install.

Rear

Use the following procedure when replacing auxiliary heater core and/or evaporator core.

1. Drain engine coolant.
2. Discharge and recover refrigerant from A/C system as outlined in "Air Conditioning" chapter.
3. Remove center seats, then lefthand safety belt retractor and tongue lower anchor bolts.
4. Remove luggage hold down net retainers from quarter trim panel using suitable pliers. Use care to avoid damaging luggage hold down net retainers.

5. Pull up liftgate scuff plate to remove, then remove lefthand quarter trim panel center screw cover cap and screw.
6. Remove two lefthand quarter trim panel capped screws, then pull top of panel away from body side.
7. Disconnect rear climate control panel and rear radio control panel electrical connectors.
8. Release lefthand front lap belt guide from quarter trim panel and pass belt through trim panel.
9. Remove lefthand quarter trim panel.
10. Remove six rear air conditioning and heating assembly A/C outlet duct screws, then outlet duct from rear air conditioning and heating assembly.
11. Disconnect heater blower motor and blower motor resistor electrical connectors.
12. Disconnect rear temperature blend door actuator motor and rear vent door actuator motor electrical connectors.
13. Raise and support vehicle, then, using A/C spring lock coupling disconnect set tool No. T84L-19623-B, or equivalent, disconnect A/C tube lock coupling springs from under vehicle.
14. Loosen A/C hose clamps, then disconnect two water hoses from heater core.
15. Lower vehicle.
16. Remove air conditioning and heating assembly bolts, then heating assembly from vehicle.
17. Reverse procedure to install, note following:
    a. **Torque** lefthand quarter trim panel capped screws to 35 inch lbs.
    b. **Torque** lefthand quarter trim panel center screw to 18–26 inch lbs.
    c. **Torque** lefthand safety belt retractor and tongue lower anchor bolts to 28–33 ft. lbs.

EVAPORATOR CORE

REPLACE

Front

1. Discharge and recover A/C system refrigerant as outlined in "Air Conditioning" chapter.
2. Position power steering junction block aside.
3. Disconnect evaporator inlet and outlet line spring lock couplings inside engine compartment using A/C spring lock coupling disconnect tool No. T84L-19623-B, or equivalent.
4. Remove instrument panel as outlined in "Dash Panel Service" chapter.
5. Remove lower instrument panel brace attaching bolts, then lower instrument panel brace.
6. **On models equipped with Electronic Automatic Temperature Control (EATC),** proceed as follows:
    a. Disconnect blower motor speed control electrical connector.
    b. Remove speed control attaching bolts.
    c. Remove blower motor speed control.
7. **On all models,** disconnect temperature blend/panel bypass door actuator electrical connector.
8. Disconnect A/C blower motor to evaporator case cooling tube.
9. Remove A/C blower motor housing nut and screws.
10. Remove evaporator housing retaining nuts.
11. **On models equipped with EATC,** disconnect EATC temperature control hose from evaporator housing.
12. **On all models,** remove evaporator housing.
13. Reverse procedure to install.

Rear

1. Remove rear blower motor as previously outlined.
2. Disconnect evaporator line spring lock coupling using A/C spring lock coupling disconnect tool No. T84L-19623-B, or equivalent.
3. Disconnect A/C evaporator lines from expansion valves.
4. Disconnect evaporator case drain hose.
5. Remove evaporator case assembly attaching screws, then case assembly from vehicle.
6. Reverse procedure to install.

3.3L Engine

NOTE: On Air Bag Equipped Models, Refer To "Air Bag System Precautions" Located In The Front Of This Manual For System Disarming & Arming Procedures.

NOTE: Refer To "Computer Relearn Procedures" Located In The Front Of This Manual When Battery Power To The Computer Has Been Interrupted.

INDEX

PRECAUTIONS

Air Bag Systems

Refer to "Air Bag System Precautions" in the front of this manual for system disarming and arming procedures.

Battery Ground Cable

Prior to service disconnect battery ground cable and isolate as required.

Fuel System Pressure Relief

1. Remove lefthand engine compartment relay panel cover.
2. Remove fuel pump relay, then start engine.
3. After engine stalls, crank engine two more times to ensure pressure has been released.
4. Turn ignition to Off position, then install fuel pump relay.

COMPRESSION PRESSURE

When inspecting compression, the pressure should be 128–173 psi. The difference between any two cylinders should not exceed 14 psi.

ENGINE MOUNT

REPLACE

1. Raise and support vehicle.
2. Remove engine splash shields.
3. Remove heated oxygen sensor wire harness from frame clips.
4. Position a suitable screw-type jack under crankshaft pulley. Cover top of jack with a shop cloth to prevent any damage to pulley.
5. Remove righthand and lefthand engine support insulator through bolts and nuts.
6. Remove transverse member attaching bolts, then transverse member.
7. Remove righthand and lefthand engine support insulator attaching bolts and nuts.
8. Reverse procedure to install.

ENGINE

REPLACE

1. Relieve fuel system pressure as outlined under "Precautions."
2. Drain engine cooling system into suitable container.
3. Remove engine air cleaner outlet tube.
4. Remove oil drain plug and drain engine oil into suitable container, install drain plug.
5. Disconnect rear engine harness and Crank Position (CKP) sensor electrical connectors.
6. Disconnect starter motor wiring harness connector.
7. Disconnect valve body and vehicle speed sensor wiring harness connectors.
8. Disconnect emission MAP/BARO sensor electrical connector and vacuum line.
9. Disconnect vapor canister purge test port.
10. Remove fuel supply line bolts, then disconnect fuel supply and return lines.
11. Disconnect vapor canister purge vacuum line, then coolant temperature sensor electrical connector.
12. Disconnect A/C compressor electrical connectors.
13. Remove three ties holding wiring harness in place, then disconnect engine coolant temperature sensor connector.
14. Disconnect distributor electrical connector.
15. Remove main bulkhead wiring harness bolt, then disconnect main wiring harness connector.
16. Remove main bulkhead connector from bracket, then unclip front engine wiring harness from bracket.
17. Disconnect vacuum hose.
18. Disconnect throttle and speed control cables, then position cables aside.
19. Disconnect upper radiator hose from radiator.
20. Disconnect lower radiator hose from coolant crossover tube.
21. Remove engine ground cable bolt, then disconnect heater hoses.
22. Disconnect brake booster vacuum hose from bulkhead junction.
23. Loosen A/C drive belt tensioner bolt,

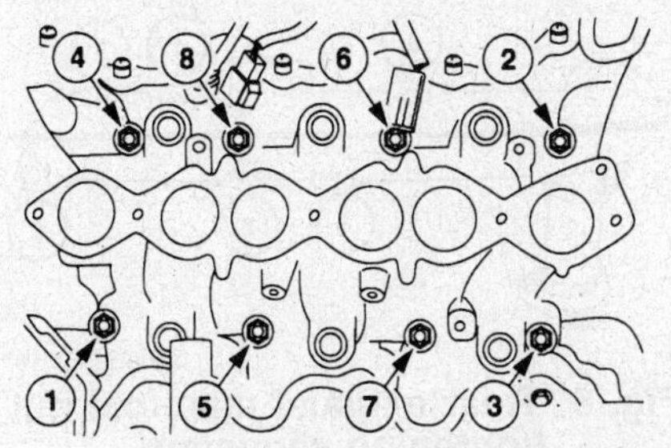

Fig. 1 Lower intake manifold bolt removal sequence

then remove A/C compressor drive belt.
24. Remove upper A/C compressor bolts.
25. Raise and support vehicle.
26. Remove wheel and tire, then lefthand and righthand splash shields.
27. Disconnect transaxle range sensor connector.
28. Remove shift cable nut, then shift cable from bracket and position aside.
29. Disconnect transaxle cooler lines from transaxle.
30. Disconnect oil pressure sender connector.
31. Remove B-terminal screw, then disconnect alternator connector.
32. Remove alternator wiring bracket screw.
33. **On models equipped with engine heater,** disconnect engine coolant heater connector.
34. **On all models,** disconnect heated oxygen sensor connector.
35. Loosen alternator drive belt lock bolt, then alternator adjustment bolt.
36. Loosen front and rear alternator to bracket bolts, then remove alternator drive belt.
37. Loosen belt tensioner lock bolt, then belt tensioner adjustment bolt.
38. Remove power steering drive belt.
39. Remove three power steering pump bolts, then rear power steering bracket bolt.
40. Remove lower A/C compressor bolts, then move A/C compressor aside.
41. Remove front exhaust pipe to manifold attaching bolts, then front exhaust bracket bolt.
42. Remove flexible pipe to catalytic converter retaining nuts.
43. Rotate flexible pipe to allow flange to clear catalytic converter bracket and remove flexible pipe.
44. Remove halfshafts as outlined in "Front Wheel Drive Axles" chapter.
45. Disconnect transaxle ground connector.
46. Position suitable engine lifting device under engine.
47. Remove rear transaxle support bracket nuts, then front transaxle support insulator through bolt.
48. Remove transverse member bolts.
49. Lower engine from vehicle.
50. Remove CKP sensor heat shield, then CKP sensor.
51. Remove starter motor attaching bolts, then starter motor.

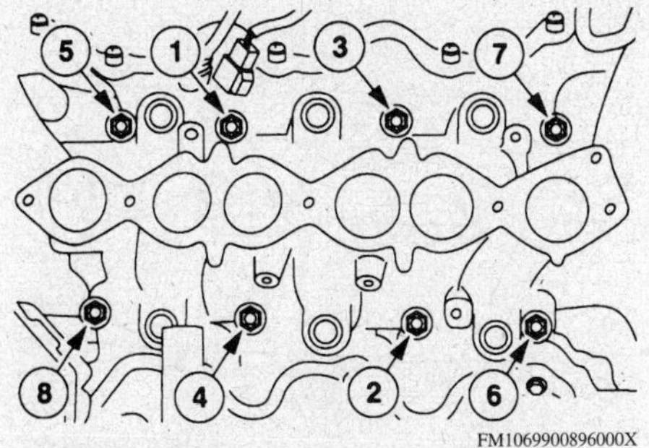

Fig. 2 Lower intake manifold bolt tightening sequence

52. Remove righthand transaxle to engine bracket and exhaust bracket bolts.
53. Remove lefthand transaxle to engine bracket bolts.
54. Remove lower transaxle to engine bolts, then transaxle inspection cover.
55. Remove transaxle to engine braces, then lefthand engine mount bolts.
56. Remove righthand engine mount attaching bolts, then transverse member.
57. Remove torque converter bolts.
58. Remove upper transaxle to engine bolts, then separate engine from transaxle.
59. Reverse procedure to install. Tighten all fasteners to specifications.

INTAKE MANIFOLD

REPLACE

Upper

1. Drain engine coolant into suitable container.
2. Remove air cleaner outlet tube.
3. Disconnect MAP/BARO sensor and MAP/BARO solenoid electrical connectors.
4. Disconnect following connectors:
   a. Throttle Position (TP) sensor.
   b. Throttle position switch.
   c. Idle speed control.
5. Remove hose clamp, then disconnect coolant hose.
6. Disconnect EVAP and fuel regulator vacuum hoses.
7. Unplug spark plug wires, then unclip retainer clips and position wires aside.
8. Disconnect vacuum reservoir hose.
9. Remove wire harness bolt, then position wire harness and bracket aside.
10. Disconnect speed control and accelerator cables.
11. Remove speed control and accelerator cable bracket attaching bolts, then position cables aside.
12. Disconnect brake booster check valve vacuum hose.
13. Disconnect EGR tube at EGR valve.
14. Disconnect fuel supply and return line bracket from EGR adapter plate.
15. Remove MAP/BARO solenoid vacuum hose.
16. Remove EGR adapter plate at bracket.
17. Remove PCV breather tube bracket.
18. Disconnect PCV breather hose at breather tube.

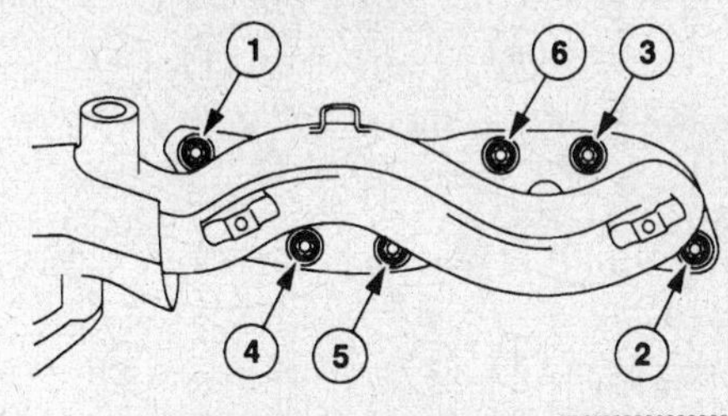

Fig. 3 Righthand exhaust manifold nut removal sequence

19. Disconnect EGR temperature sensor and EVAP purge solenoid connectors.
20. Remove upper intake manifold bolts, then reposition upper intake manifold to access underside of intake manifold.
21. Disconnect coolant and vacuum hoses.
22. Remove upper intake manifold stabilizer bracket.
23. Remove upper intake manifold.
24. Remove upper intake manifold gasket and discard.
25. Reverse procedure to install, note following:
   a. Ensure manifold gasket surfaces are clean and free of dirt, old gasket material and oil.
   b. Install new upper intake manifold gasket.
   c. Tighten all bolts to specification.

Lower

1. Relieve fuel system pressure as outlined under "Precautions."
2. Remove upper intake manifold.
3. Disconnect fuel injector connectors, then Engine Coolant Temperature (ECT) sensor connector.
4. Remove ground wire bolts.
5. Remove heated oxygen sensor (HO2S) wire harness from bracket, then disconnect HO2S connector.
6. Release breather hose clamp, then disconnect breather hose.
7. Remove wire harness retainer straps, then position breather hose and wire harness aside.
8. Disconnect water temperature indicator sender electrical connector.
9. Remove spark plug wire bracket attaching bolt, then bracket.
10. Disconnect fuel feed and fuel return lines.
11. Remove fuel injection supply manifold and insulators.
12. Remove upper radiator hose bracket attaching bolt.
13. Release upper radiator hose clamp, then position hose aside.
14. Remove upper timing belt cover bolt.
15. Remove coolant bypass hose at water hose connection.
16. Disconnect heater hose at heater hose pipe.
17. Remove lower intake manifold bolts and nuts in sequence, **Fig. 1.**
18. Remove lower intake manifold and gaskets. Discard gaskets.

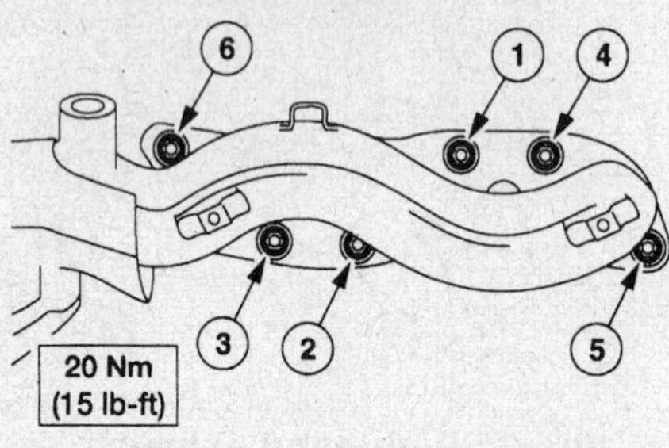

Fig. 4 Righthand exhaust manifold nut tightening sequence

19. Reverse procedure to install, note following:
    a. Ensure manifold gasket surfaces are clean and free of dirt, old gasket material and oil.
    b. **Torque** bolts in three steps: First step, 35 inch lbs.; second step, 80 inch lbs.; third step, 80 inch lbs., using sequence, **Fig. 2.**

EXHAUST MANIFOLD

REPLACE

Righthand Side

1. Disconnect battery junction box connectors.
2. Remove air cleaner assembly.
3. Remove battery junction box bolts, then unclip retainer and position junction box aside.
4. Remove exhaust heat shield attaching bolts, then heat shield.
5. Remove engine lifting eye bracket attaching bolts, then eye bracket.
6. Remove three lefthand exhaust manifold to righthand exhaust manifold nuts.
7. Disconnect EGR tube to EGR valve nut.
8. Raise and support vehicle, then remove EGR tube from manifold.
9. Remove exhaust manifold heat shield attaching bolts, then heat shield.
10. Remove exhaust manifold nuts in sequence, in two steps, **Fig. 3.**
11. Lower vehicle, then remove exhaust manifold.
12. Raise vehicle, then remove exhaust manifold gasket and discard.
13. Reverse procedure to install, note following:
    a. Clean gasket mating surface and install new gasket.
    b. Tighten manifold to specifications in sequence, **Fig. 4.**

Lefthand Side

GREEN STATES

1. Remove radiator fan motor and shroud as outlined in "Cooling Fans" chapter.
2. Disconnect heated oxygen sensor connector.
3. Remove exhaust manifold heat shield attaching bolts, then heat shield.
4. Loosen belt tensioner adjuster bolt,

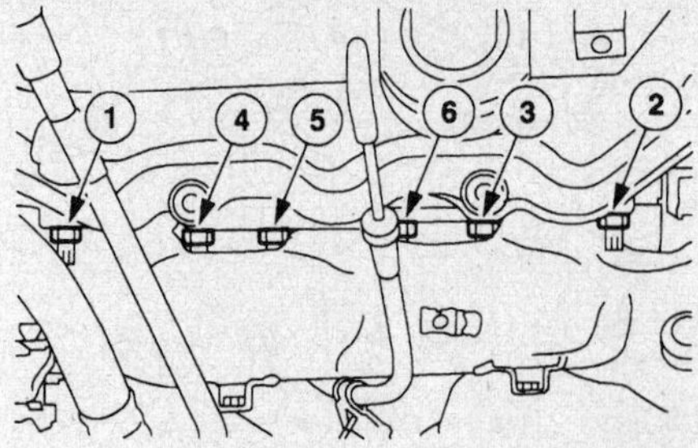

Fig. 5 Lefthand exhaust manifold nut removal sequence. Green state models

then remove A/C compressor drive belt.
5. Remove four A/C compressor bolts, then position A/C compressor aside.
6. Remove lefthand exhaust manifold nuts in sequence, in two steps, **Fig. 5.**
7. Raise and support vehicle, then remove engine splash shield.
8. Remove exhaust manifold to outlet pipe nuts.
9. Remove exhaust heat shield attaching bolts, then heat shield.
10. Remove engine lifting eye bracket from righthand exhaust manifold.
11. Remove three nuts and exhaust manifold, then gasket.
12. Reverse procedure to install, note following:
    a. Clean gasket mating surface and install new gasket.
    b. Tighten manifold in sequence, to specifications, **Fig. 6.**

FEDERAL

1. Remove radiator as outlined under "Radiator, Replace."
2. Remove exhaust manifold heat shield attaching bolts.
3. Position oil dipstick tube aside and remove heat shield
4. Remove engine lifting eye hook bracket from righthand exhaust manifold.
5. Remove three lefthand exhaust manifold to righthand exhaust manifold nuts.
6. Loosen tensioner bolt and belt tensioner adjuster bolt, then remove A/C compressor drive belt.
7. Remove A/C compressor bolts and position compressor aside.
8. Loosen lefthand exhaust manifold nuts in sequence **Fig. 7.**
9. Raise and support vehicle, then remove engine splash shield.
10. Disconnect heated oxygen sensor connector.
11. Remove lefthand exhaust manifold to outlet pipe bolts.
12. Remove exhaust system flex tube bracket bolt.
13. Lower vehicle, then remove exhaust manifold retaining nuts.
14. Remove exhaust manifold and manifold gasket.
15. Reverse procedure to install, note following:
    a. Clean gasket mating surface and install new gasket.

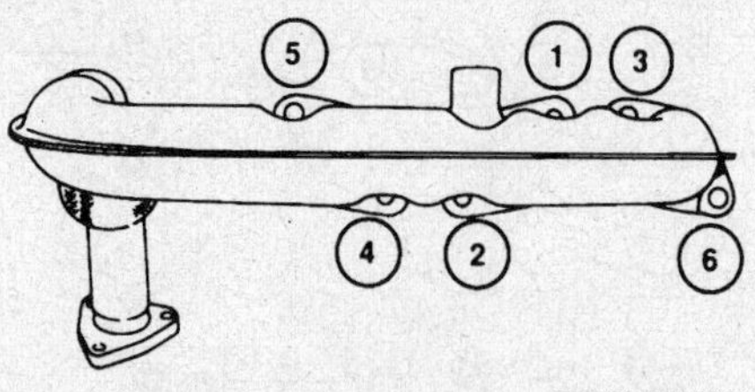

Fig. 6 Rear exhaust manifold nut tightening sequence

    b. Tighten manifold to specifications using tightening sequence, **Fig. 8.**

CYLINDER HEAD

REPLACE

Lefthand Side

REMOVAL

1. Remove lower intake manifold as outlined under "Intake Manifold, Replace."
2. Position coolant reservoir hose aside.
3. Disconnect upper transaxle cooler line, then relay box and position aside.
4. Raise and support vehicle, then remove engine splash shield.
5. Disconnect cooling fan electrical connector, then unclip wire harness from shroud.
6. Disconnect lower transaxle cooler line, then remove lower radiator hose.
7. Lower vehicle and remove radiator as outlined under "Radiator, Replace."
8. Remove distributor as outlined under "Distributor, Replace" in "Electrical" section.
9. Disconnect A/C high pressure switch and A/C compressor clutch connectors from compressor, then position wire harness aside.
10. Remove PCV breather hose and tube.
11. Remove water bypass hose clamp, then bypass hose.
12. Remove spark plugs.
13. Bring number one piston to TDC, then remove crankshaft pulley.
14. Raise and support vehicle, then remove transaxle fluid level indicator tube retaining bolt and position tube aside.
15. **On models equipped with Green state emissions,** remove exhaust heat shield.
16. **On all models,** remove lefthand exhaust manifold to righthand exhaust manifold nuts.
17. **On models equipped with Federal emissions,** proceed as follows:
    a. Disconnect HO2S electrical connector.
    b. Remove front exhaust pipe to manifold attaching bolts.
    c. Remove exhaust system flexpipe bracket bolt.
18. **On models equipped with Green state emissions,** remove front exhaust pipe to manifold attaching bolts.
19. **On all models,** remove timing belt as outlined under "Timing Belt, Replace."
20. Remove camshaft sprocket using A/C

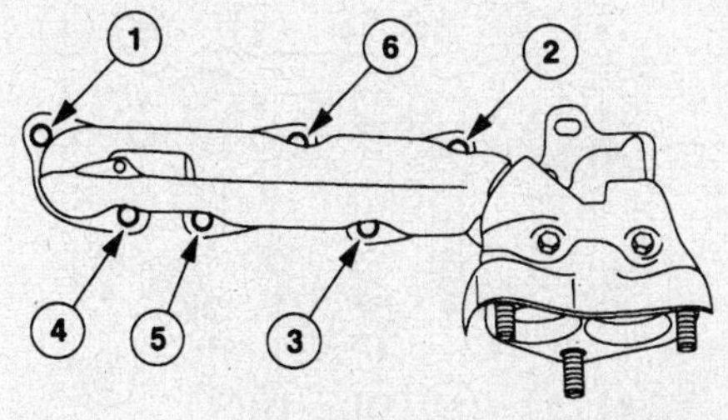

Fig. 7 Lefthand exhaust manifold nut removal sequence. Federal models

spring lock coupling disconnect tool No. T84L-19623-B, or equivalent, **Fig. 9.**

21. Remove four seal plate attaching bolts, then seal plate.
22. Remove engine lifting eye bracket from righthand exhaust manifold.
23. Disconnect heater core hose from coolant crossover tube.
24. Remove coolant and crossover tube and lower radiator hose.
25. **On models equipped with Federal emissions,** remove exhaust manifold heat shield.
26. **On all models,** remove A/C compressor mounting bolts, then position A/C compressor aside.
27. Remove two A/C mounting bracket attaching bolts.
28. Remove exhaust manifold as outlined previously.
29. Remove valve cover attaching bolts, then valve cover and gasket.
30. Remove rocker arm retaining bolts in two steps. **Loosening rocker arm shaft bolts in one step may distort or break rocker arm shaft.**
31. Remove rocker arm shafts and rocker arms.
32. Secure tappets in rocker arm shaft support with rubber bands, then remove shaft support and tappets as an assembly.
33. Remove cylinder head bolts in sequence, in two steps and discard, **Fig. 10. Ensure bolt marked No. 1 in removal sequence is removed prior to moving cylinder head. Cylinder head tab could break off if bolt is not removed. Do not reuse cylinder head bolts.**
34. Remove cylinder head and gasket, discard gasket.

INSTALLATION

1. Install cylinder head gasket, then cylinder head.
2. Cylinder head bolts located in positions 4, 7, 9, and 12 are 5.08 inches long, all other bolts are 4.24 inches long. **Cylinder head bolt washers must be installed with chamfered edge facing away from cylinder head surface.**
3. **Apply Super Premium SAE 5W-30, or equivalent, oil to threads and seating surfaces of cylinder head bolts.**
4. **Torque** cylinder head bolts in numbered sequence, first to 21 ft. lbs., then to 44 ft. lbs., using sequence outlined in **Fig. 11.**
5. Loosen cylinder head bolts completely in sequence, **Fig. 12.**
6. **Torque** cylinder head bolts to 89 inch lbs., in sequence, **Fig. 11.**
7. Install coolant crossover tube, then lower radiator hose.
8. Install lower intake manifold gaskets, then lower intake manifold.
9. **Torque** intake manifold bolts and nuts in three steps: first step, 35 inch lbs.; second step 13 ft. lbs.; third step 13 ft. lbs., using numbered sequence, **Fig. 2.**
10. Loosen lower intake manifold bolts and nuts completely in sequence, **Fig. 1.**
11. **Torque** cylinder head bolts to 21 ft. lbs., then to 44 ft. lbs., using sequence, **Fig. 11.**
12. **Torque** cylinder head bolt marked No. 1, **Fig. 10,** to 89 Inch lbs.
13. **Torque** intake manifold bolts and nuts in three steps: first step, 35 inch lbs.; second step 80 inch lbs.; third step 80 inch lbs., using numbered sequence, **Fig. 2.**
14. Install rocker arm shaft support and tappets.
15. **Set camshaft lobes so that valves are not lifted, tightening rocker arm shaft bolts with valves lifted can result in damage.**
16. Install rocker arm shafts and rocker arms, then install twelve bolts and tighten to specification in two steps. **Rocker arm shaft bolts must be tightened using a two step method.**
17. Install valve cover gasket, then valve cover.
18. Install exhaust manifold.
19. Install two A/C mounting bracket bolts, then A/C compressor.
20. Install exhaust manifold heat shield and oil dipstick tube.
21. Connect heater core hose to coolant crossover tube.
22. Install righthand exhaust manifold to engine lifting eye bracket.
23. Install seal plate.
24. Install righthand and lefthand camshaft sprockets and tighten to specification using holding tool No. 303-098, or equivalent.
25. Install timing belt and timing belt covers as outlined under "Timing Belt, Replace."
26. **On models equipped with Green State emissions,** install exhaust manifold to front exhaust pipe retaining nuts.
27. **On models equipped with Federal emissions,** install exhaust flex tube bracket bolt, exhaust manifold to front exhaust pipe bolts, then connect HO2S electrical connector.
28. **On all models,** install lefthand exhaust manifold to righthand exhaust manifold nuts.
29. **On models equipped with Green State emissions,** install exhaust heat shield.
30. **On all models,** install transaxle fluid level indicator tube bolt, then crankshaft pulley.
31. Install spark plugs.
32. **On models equipped with Federal emissions,** install exhaust manifold heat shield.
33. **On all models,** install water bypass hose.
34. Connect PCV breather hose and tube to valve cover.
35. Connect A/C compressor electrical connectors.
36. Install distributor as outlined under "Distributor, Replace" in "Electrical" section.
37. Connect heater hose to heater hose pipe.
38. Connect coolant bypass hose to water hose connection.
39. Install upper timing belt cover bolt, then connect upper radiator hose.
40. Install fuel injection supply manifold and insulators.
41. Connect fuel lines, then spark plug wire bracket bolt.
42. Connect water temperature indicator sender unit.
43. Position PCV breather hose and wire harness, then install new wire strap retainers.
44. Connect HO2S electrical connector.

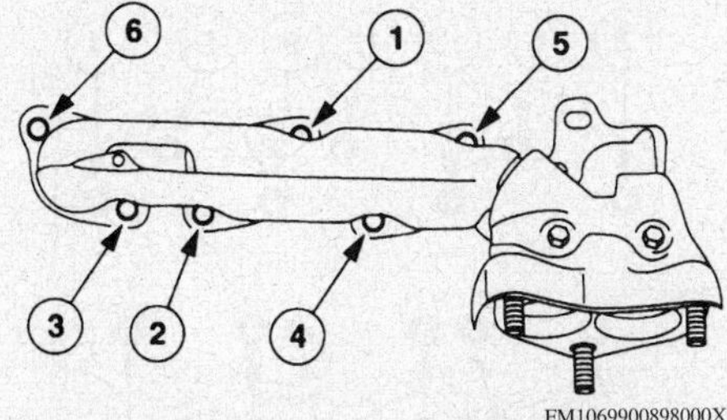

Fig. 8 Lefthand exhaust manifold nut tightening sequence. Federal

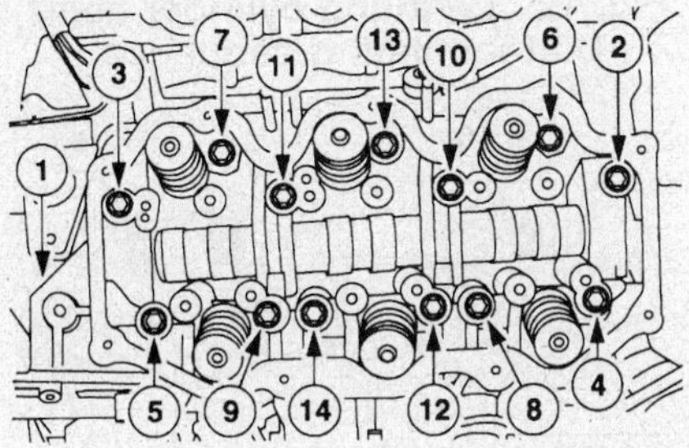

Fig. 10 Lefthand cylinder head bolt removal sequence

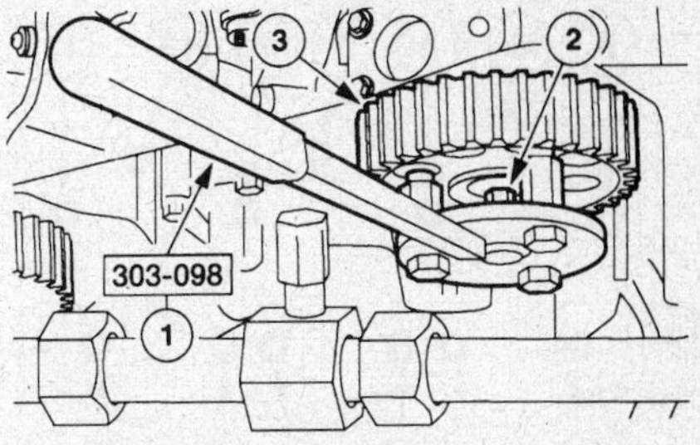

Fig. 9 Camshaft sprocket removal

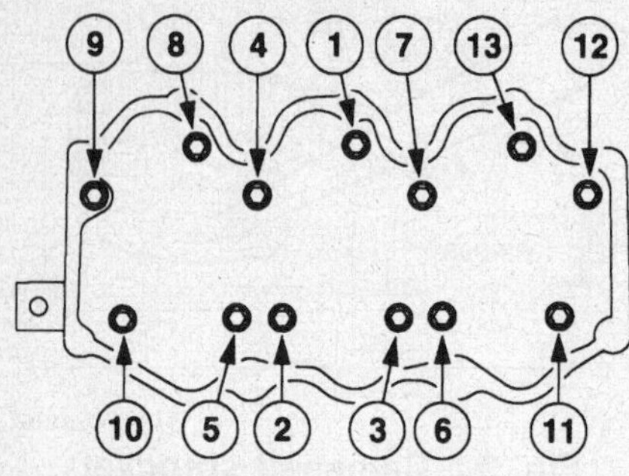

Fig. 11 Lefthand cylinder head bolt tightening sequence

45. Install ground wire bolts.
46. Connect fuel injector and ECT sensor electrical connectors.
47. Install radiator as outlined under "Radiator, Replace" then raise and support vehicle.
48. Connect lower radiator hose, then lower transaxle cooler line.
49. Connect wiring harness to fan shroud.
50. Install engine splash shield, then lower vehicle.
51. Install relay box, then connect upper transaxle cooler line.
52. Connect upper radiator hose.
53. Connect cooling fan electrical connector and clip wire harness to shroud.
54. Connect coolant reservoir hose.
55. Install upper intake manifold as outlined previously, then inspect ignition timing.

Righthand Side

REMOVAL

1. Remove lower intake manifold as outlined previously.
2. Remove distributor as outlined under "Distributor, Replace" in "Electrical" section.
3. Disconnect A/C high pressure switch and compressor clutch electrical connectors, then position wiring harness aside.
4. Remove PCV breather hose and tube.
5. Remove water bypass hose clamp, then water bypass hose.
6. **On models equipped with Federal emissions,** remove exhaust heat shield.
7. **On all models,** remove spark plugs.
8. Position No. 1 piston at TDC of its compression stroke, then remove crankshaft pulley.
9. Raise and support vehicle, then remove engine splash shield.
10. Remove transaxle fluid indicator tube retaining tube, position tube aside.
11. **On models equipped with Green State emissions,** remove exhaust heat shield.
12. **On all models,** remove lefthand exhaust manifold to righthand exhaust manifold nuts.
13. Remove six lower timing belt cover bolts.
14. Lower vehicle and remove A/C idler pulley and bracket attaching bolts,

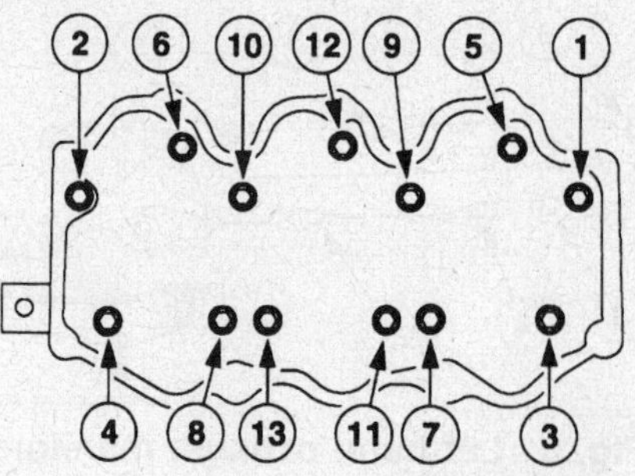

Fig. 12 Lefthand cylinder head bolt loosening sequence

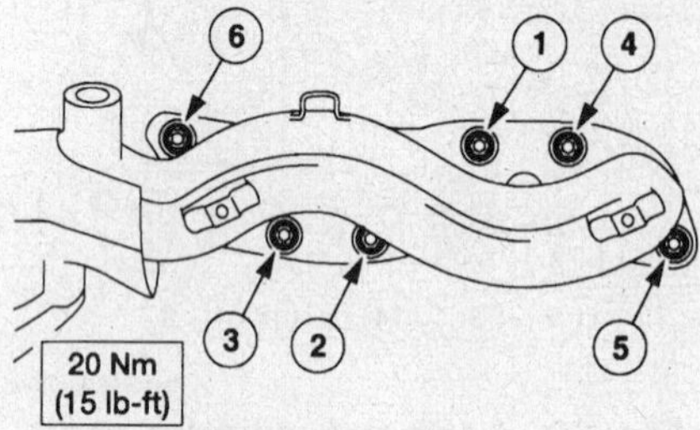

Fig. 14 Exhaust manifold nut installation sequence

then pulley and bracket.

15. Remove water pump pulley attaching bolts, then pulley.
16. Remove timing belt covers and timing belt as outlined under "Timing Belt, Replace."
17. Remove both camshaft sprockets using sprocket holding tool No. 303-098, or equivalent, **Fig. 9.**
18. Remove seal plate attaching bolts, then seal plate.
19. Remove righthand exhaust manifold to engine lifting eye bracket attaching bolt, then engine lifting eye bracket.
20. Disconnect heater core hose from coolant crossover tube.
21. Remove coolant and crossover tube and lower radiator hose.
22. Disconnect electrical connectors located above valve cover, then position wire harness aside.
23. Disconnect vacuum hoses from valve cover.
24. Remove upper intake manifold stabilizer bracket.
25. Remove valve cover attaching bolts, then valve cover.
26. Remove rocker arm retaining bolts in two steps. **Loosening rocker arm shaft bolts in one step may distort or break rocker arm shaft.**
27. Remove rocker arm shafts and rocker arms.
28. Secure tappets in rocker arm shaft support with rubber bands, then remove shaft support and tappets as an assembly.
29. Remove cylinder head bolts in sequence, in two steps and discard, **Fig. 13. Ensure bolt marked No. 1 in removal sequence is removed prior to moving cylinder head. Cylinder head tab could break off if bolt is not**

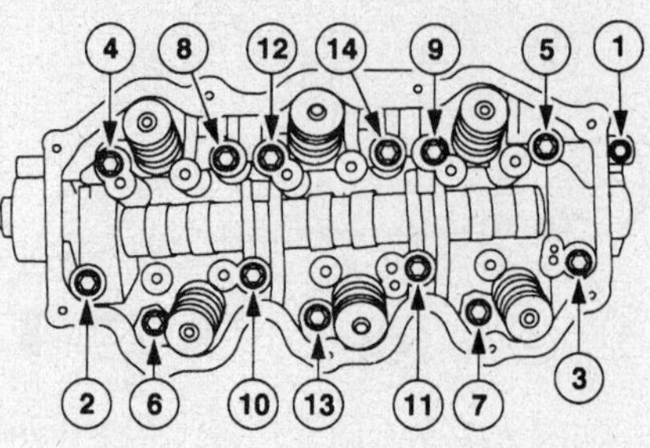

Fig. 13 Righthand cylinder head bolt removal sequence

removed. Do not reuse cylinder head bolts.

30. Remove cylinder head, then remove and discard cylinder head gasket.
31. Remove engine lifting eye hook bracket, then exhaust manifold heat shield.
32. Remove exhaust manifold nuts in sequence, in two steps, **Fig. 3.**
33. Remove exhaust manifold, then exhaust manifold gasket and discard.

INSTALLATION

1. Install exhaust manifold gasket, then exhaust manifold.
2. Install exhaust manifold nuts in sequence, **Fig. 14.**
3. Install cylinder head gasket, then cylinder head.
4. Cylinder head bolts located in positions 4, 7, 9, and 12 are 5.08 inches long, all other bolts are 4.24 inches long. **Cylinder head bolt washers must be installed with chamfered edge facing away from cylinder head surface.**
5. **Apply Super Premium SAE 5W-30, or equivalent, oil to threads and seating surfaces of cylinder head bolts.**
6. **Torque** cylinder head bolts first to 21 ft. lbs., then to 44 ft. lbs., using sequence, **Fig. 15.**
7. Loosen cylinder head bolts completely in sequence, **Fig. 16.**
8. **Torque** cylinder head bolts to 89 inch lbs., in sequence **Fig. 15.**
9. Install lower intake manifold gaskets, then lower intake manifold.
10. **Torque** intake manifold bolts and nuts in three steps: first step, 35 inch lbs.; second step 13 ft. lbs.; third step 13 ft. lbs., using sequence outlined in **Fig. 2.**
11. Loosen lower intake manifold bolts and nuts completely in sequence, **Fig. 1.**
12. **Torque** cylinder head bolts to 21 ft. lbs., then to 44 ft. lbs., using sequence outlined in **Fig. 15.**
13. **Torque** cylinder head bolt marked No. 1, **Fig. 13,** to 89 inch lbs.
14. **Torque** intake manifold bolts and nuts in three steps: first step, 35 inch lbs.; second step 80 inch lbs.; third step 80 inch lbs., using numbered sequence, **Fig. 2.**
15. Install rocker arm shaft support.
16. **Set camshaft lobes so that valves are not lifted. Tightening rocker arm shaft bolts with valves lifted can cause damage to valve components. Rocker arm shaft bolts must**

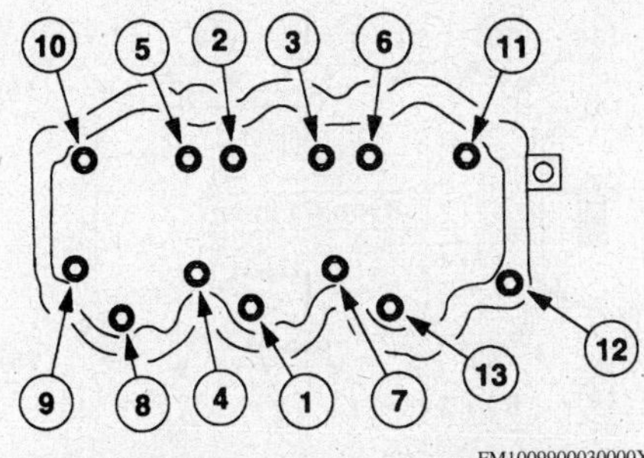

Fig. 15 Righthand cylinder head bolt tightening sequence

be tightened in a two step method.

17. Install rocker arm shafts and rocker arms.
18. Install valve cover gasket, then valve cover.
19. Install exhaust manifold nuts, then tighten to specification in numbered sequence, **Fig. 17.**
20. Install upper intake manifold stabilizer bracket.
21. Connect vacuum hoses to valve cover, then position wiring harness into valve cover clips.
22. Connect heater core hose to coolant crossover tube.
23. Install righthand exhaust manifold to engine lifting eye bracket.
24. Install seal plate.
25. Install righthand and lefthand camshaft sprockets using sprocket holding tool No. 303-098, or equivalent.
26. Install timing belt and cover as outlined under "Timing Belt, Replace."
27. Install water pump pulley.
28. Install A/C compressor idler pulley and bracket.
29. Install upper timing belt cover.
30. Install water pump pulley, then install A/C compressor idler pulley and bracket.
31. Raise and support vehicle, then install lower timing belt cover bolts.
32. Install lefthand exhaust manifold to righthand exhaust manifold nuts.
33. **On models equipped with Green State emissions,** install exhaust heat shield.
34. **On all models,** install transaxle fluid level indicator tube bolt.
35. Install crankshaft pulley, then spark plugs.
36. **On models equipped with Federal emissions,** install exhaust heat shield.
37. **On all models,** install water bypass hose.
38. Connect PCV breather hose and tube to valve cover.
39. Connect A/C compressor electrical connectors.
40. Install distributor assembly as outlined under "Distributor, Replace" in "Electrical" section.
41. Connect heater hose to heater hose pipe.
42. Connect coolant bypass hose to water hose connection.
43. Install upper timing belt cover bolt, then connect upper radiator hose.

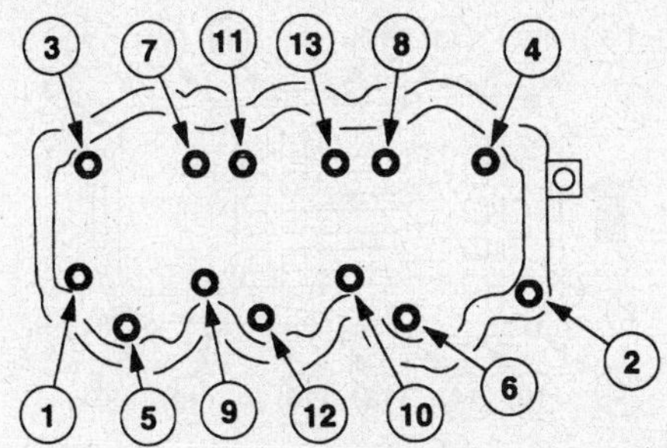

Fig. 16 Righthand cylinder head bolt loosening sequence

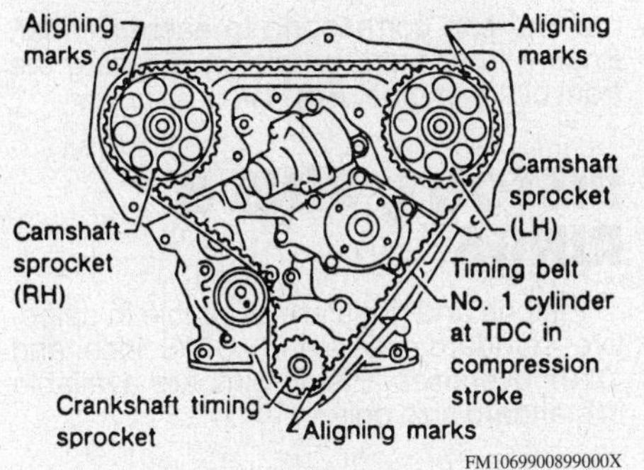

Fig. 18 Timing belt installation

44. Install fuel injection supply manifold and insulators.
45. Connect fuel lines, then spark plug wire bracket bolt.
46. Connect water temperature indicator sender unit electrical connector.
47. Position PCV breather hose and wire harness.
48. Connect HO2S electrical connector.
49. Install ground wire bolts.
50. Connect fuel injector and ECT sensor electrical connectors.
51. Install upper intake manifold as outlined previously, then inspect ignition timing.

VALVE COVER

REPLACE

Righthand Rear

1. Remove upper intake manifold as outlined under "Intake Manifold, Replace."
2. Disconnect PCV breather hose at valve cover.
3. Position wire harness aside.
4. Disconnect vacuum hoses at valve cover.
5. Remove valve cover.
6. Remove valve cover gasket and clean thoroughly.
7. Reverse procedure to install.

Lefthand Front

1. Disconnect heated oxygen sensor connector.
2. Remove PCV breather hose at valve cover.
3. Remove valve cover.

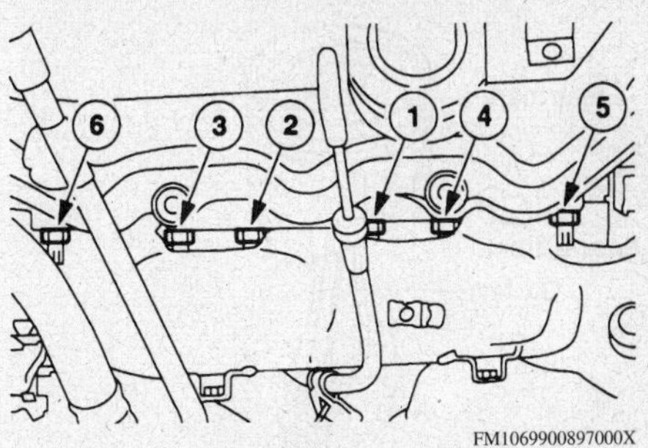

Fig. 17 Righthand exhaust manifold tightening sequence. Green state models

4. Remove valve cover gasket and clean thoroughly.
5. Reverse procedure to install.

ROCKER ARMS

REPLACE

1. Remove front or rear valve cover as required as outlined under "Valve Cover, Replace."
2. Loosen rocker arm shaft bolts in two steps. **Loosening rocker arm shaft bolts in one step may distort or break rocker arm shaft.**
3. Mark position of rocker arms for installation reference.
4. Secure tappets in rocker arm shaft support with rubber bands, then remove shaft support and tappets as an assembly.
5. Reverse procedure to install.

HYDRAULIC LIFTERS

REPLACE

1. Remove rocker arms and rocker arm shafts.
2. Remove rubber bands, then separate tappets from rocker arm assembly.
3. Lubricate all internal friction surfaces with suitable 5W-30 motor oil.
4. Reverse procedure to install.

TIMING BELT

REPLACE

1. Drain engine coolant into a suitable container.
2. Remove A/C drive belt.
3. Raise and support vehicle, then remove righthand side wheel assembly.
4. Remove engine splash shields and side splash shield.
5. Remove alternator and power steering drive belts.
6. Remove crankshaft pulley retaining bolt using pulley holding tool No. 303-D055, or equivalent, then crankshaft pulley.
7. Remove water pump pulley.
8. Remove lower timing belt cover.
9. Lower vehicle, then remove upper radiator hose.
10. Remove coolant bypass hose.
11. Remove A/C compressor idler pulley and bracket.
12. Unclip engine wiring harness and position aside.

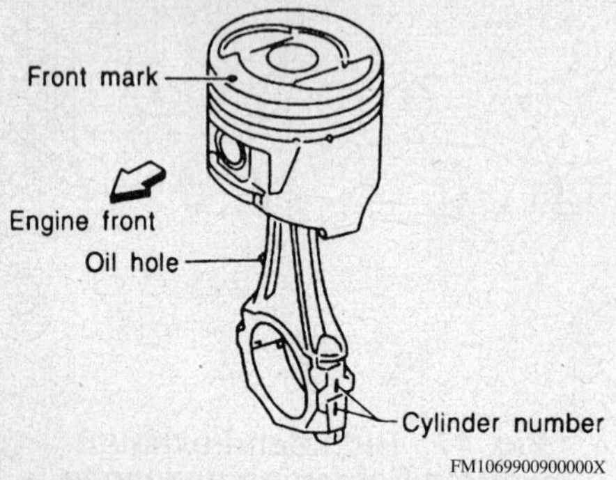

Fig. 19 Piston & rod assembly

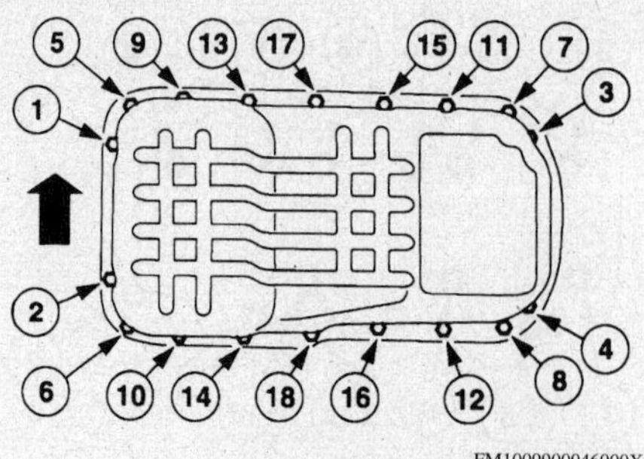

Fig. 20 Oil pan bolt removal sequence

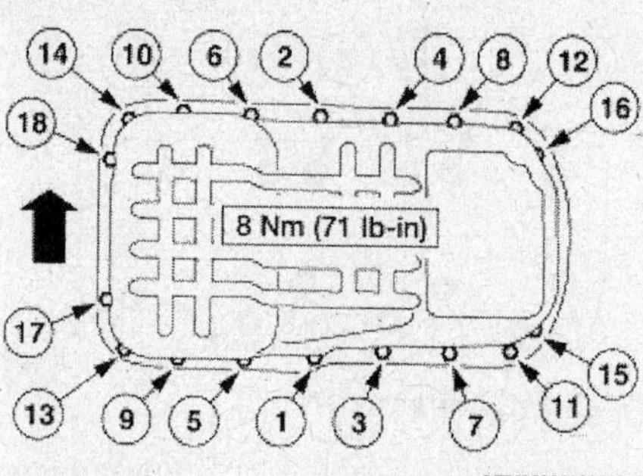

Fig. 21 Oil pan bolt tightening sequence

13. Disconnect vacuum reservoir vacuum hose.
14. Unclip main wire harness and position aside.
15. Remove spark plug wire from bracket, then remove wire harness bracket bolt and position bracket aside.
16. Remove PCV breather hoses and tube.
17. Remove seven upper timing cover attaching bolts, then upper and lower timing belt covers.
18. Rotate crankshaft until No. 1 piston is at TDC of its compression stroke.
19. Remove outer timing belt guide.
20. Loosen timing belt tensioner nut, then remove timing belt.
21. If timing belt is to be reused, mark direction of rotation.
22. Reverse procedure to install, note following:
    a. Ensure arrow on timing belt is pointing away from engine when installed.
    b. Align three white timing belt lines with punchmarks on camshaft and crankshaft sprockets, **Fig. 18.**
    c. Ensure camshaft timing marks are aligned with timing mark on seal plate and crankshaft sprocket timing mark is aligned with timing mark on oil pump.
    d. When installing timing belt, begin at crankshaft sprocket and move to camshaft sprocket in a counterclockwise direction.

CAMSHAFT

REPLACE

1. Remove timing belt as outlined under "Timing Belt, Replace."
2. Remove bolts, then camshaft endplate, discard gasket.
3. Remove camshaft thrust plate bolt using sprocket holding tool No. 303-098, or equivalent, then thrust plate.
4. Remove four seal plate attaching bolts, then seal plate.
5. Remove camshaft sprocket.
6. Remove camshaft through front of cylinder head.
7. Reverse procedure to install.

PISTON & ROD ASSEMBLY

When installing piston and rod assembly ensure numbers stamped on connecting rod and cap correspond to each cylinder. Ensure front mark on piston is facing the front of the engine, **Fig. 19.**

PISTONS, PINS & RINGS

Pistons and rings are available in selective standard sizes and .0098 inch and .0197 oversizes. Piston pins are available in standard size only.

MAIN & ROD BEARINGS

Main bearings are available in five different sizes. These sizes are identified by color as follows; black (.0715–.0717) inch, brown (.0717–.0719) inch, green (.0719–.0720) inch, yellow (.0720–.0722) inch, blue (.0722–.0723) inch.

Connecting rod bearings are available in the following four sizes; .0591–.0593 inch, .0607–.0609 inch, .0615–.0617 inch and .0641–.0642 inch.

CRANKSHAFT SEAL

REPLACE

Front

1. Remove timing belt as outlined under "Timing Belt, Replace."
2. Raise and support vehicle, then remove crankshaft sprocket.
3. Remove inner timing belt guide.
4. Remove crankshaft front oil seal, using seal removal tool No. 303-409, or equivalent.
5. Reverse procedure to install.

Rear

1. Remove transaxle as outlined in **MOTOR'S "Domestic Transmission, In-Vehicle Service" or "Transmission Service DVD."**
2. Remove flywheel and reinforcing plate attaching bolts, then flywheel and reinforcing plate from cylinder block.
3. Remove crankshaft rear oil seal using seal remover tool No. 303-409, or equivalent.
4. Reverse procedure to install. Apply suitable 5W-30 motor oil to seal.

OIL PAN

REPLACE

1. Remove oil level dipstick, then raise and support vehicle.
2. Remove engine splash shields.
3. Remove drain plug, then drain engine oil into a suitable container.
4. Install drain plug.
5. **On models equipped with Federal emissions,** proceed as follows:
    a. Disconnect heated oxygen sensor connector.
    b. Remove lefthand exhaust manifold to front exhaust pipe attaching bolts.
    c. Remove exhaust system flex tube bracket bolt.
6. **On models equipped with Green State emissions,** disconnect heated oxygen sensor harness.
7. **On all models,** position a screw type jack under crankshaft.
8. Remove lefthand engine support insulator through bolt.
9. Remove righthand engine support insulator through bolt and nut.
10. Remove transverse member.
11. **On models equipped with Green State emissions,** disconnect HO2S connector, then loosen exhaust outlet pipe nut and bolt and position pipe aside.
12. **On all models,** remove lefthand transaxle to engine brace.
13. Remove exhaust outlet pipe bracket.
14. Remove transaxle to engine separator plate.
15. Remove oil pan bolts in sequence, **Fig. 20.**
16. Remove oil pan and discard oil pan seals.
17. Reverse procedure to install, note following:
    a. Clean oil pan and mating surfaces thoroughly.
    b. Apply a bead of silicone gasket sealant F7AZ-19554-EA, or equivalent, to clean oil pan and cylinder block mating surfaces.
    c. Tighten oil pan bolts in sequence, **Fig. 21.**

OIL PUMP

REPLACE

1. Remove timing belt as outlined under "Timing Belt, Replace" then raise and

support vehicle.
2. Drain engine oil, then remove alternator bracket to oil pump bolt and position bracket aside.
3. Remove power steering pump bracket bolts and position pump aside, then remove crankshaft pulley as follows:
   a. Remove righthand splash shields, then use strap wrench tool No. D85L-6000-A or equivalent, to hold crankshaft pulley while removing pulley bolts.
   b. Install crankshaft damper remover tool No. T58P-6316-D, or equivalent, to crankshaft, then secure with capscrews from crankshaft damper removal tool No. T92C-6701-AH, or equivalent.
   c. Install forcing screw and tip from service kit tool No. T47P-6700-A or equivalent, into crankshaft damper remover, then pull crankshaft pulley off front of crankshaft.
   d. Remove crankshaft oil slinger and woodruff key.
4. Remove crankshaft timing belt sprocket, woodruff keys and crankshaft timing belt sprocket oil slinger.
5. Disconnect low oil pressure switch electrical connector, then remove oil filter adapter. Discard O-rings.
6. Remove oil pan as outlined under "Oil Pan, Replace" then oil pickup tube. Discard O-ring.
7. Remove oil pump bolts **Fig. 22,** then oil pump.
8. Reverse procedure to install. Install woodruff key, then crankshaft oil slinger with dished side facing away from engine block.

BELT TENSION DATA

Belt	Belt Deflection, Inches①	
	New	Used
A/C	.160–.240	.200–.280
Alternator	.256–.295	.295–.335
Power Steering	.310–.390	.390–.470

①— With 22 lbs. of pressure applied at midway point between pulleys.

THERMOSTAT

REPLACE

1. Drain cooling system into a suitable container, then remove upper radiator hose bracket bolt and bracket.
2. Disconnect coolant bypass hose from thermostat housing cover, then remove thermostat housing cover bolts and cover.
3. **On models equipped with A/C,** proceed as follows:
   a. Remove low pressure line hold-down bracket, then suction accumulator/drier bracket bolts and bracket.
   b. Position suction accumulator/drier and low pressure line aside.
4. **On all models,** remove water hose connection bolts, then water hose connection.

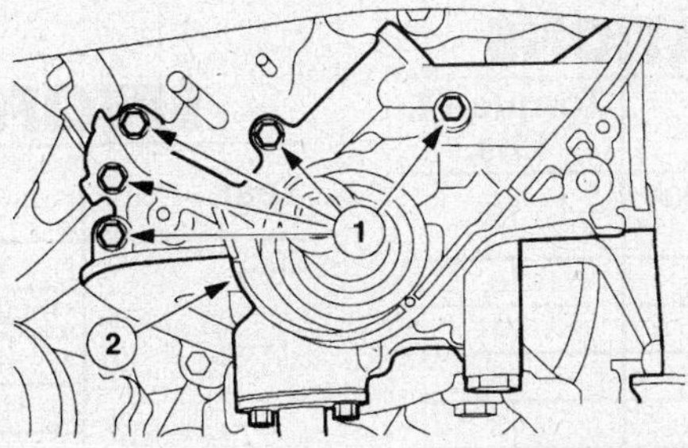

Fig. 22 Front view of oil pump

5. Remove thermostat from thermostat housing.
6. Reverse procedure to install, note following:
   a. Clean thermostat housing cover mating surface and groove.
   b. Apply a continuous .08–.12 inch wide bead of silicone sealant to inner surface and perimeter of thermostat housing cover.
   c. Fill cooling system, then bleed and inspect for leaks. **Wait at least 30 minutes for sealant to completely dry before filling engine coolant.**

WATER PUMP

REPLACE

1. Drain engine coolant into a suitable container.
2. Loosen A/C compressor drive belt tensioner bolt, then belt tension adjuster bolt.
3. Remove A/C compressor drive belt.
4. Raise and support vehicle, then remove righthand side wheel and tire assembly.
5. Remove lower engine splash shields, then splash shield from inside wheelwell.
6. Loosen alternator drive belt adjuster locking bolt.
7. Loosen front and rear alternator bracket bolts.
8. Loosen alternator drive belt adjuster bolt, then remove alternator drive belt.
9. Loosen power steering drive belt tensioner locknut.
10. Loosen power steering drive belt tensioner adjustment bolt, then remove drive belt.
11. Remove crankshaft pulley retaining bolt using pulley holding tool No. 303-D055, or equivalent, then crankshaft pulley.
12. Remove water pump pulley.
13. Remove 6 lower timing belt cover bolts, then lower vehicle.
14. Remove upper radiator hose, then coolant bypass hose.
15. Remove A/C compressor idler pulley and bracket, then position wire harness aside.
16. Disconnect vacuum reservoir vacuum hose.
17. Remove clip and move main wire harness aside.
18. Loosen wire harness bracket and position aside.
19. Remove PCV breather hose and tube.
20. Remove upper and lower timing belt covers.
21. Remove water pump attaching bolts, then pump. Note location of stud when removing pump.
22. Reverse procedure to install. Apply a bead of Silicone Gasket Sealant F7AZ-19554-EA, or equivalent, to water pump mating surface.

RADIATOR

REPLACE

1. Raise and support vehicle.
2. Drain engine cooling system.
3. Disconnect lower transmission cooler line, then lower radiator hose.
4. Disconnect wiring harness from fan shroud.
5. Lower vehicle and position relay box aside.
6. Position coolant reservoir hose aside, then disconnect cooling fan electrical connector.
7. Disconnect upper radiator hose, then upper transmission coolant line.
8. Remove radiator assembly bracket bolts, then radiator assembly.
9. Remove cooling fan assembly to radiator attaching bolts, then separate cooling fan from radiator.
10. Reverse procedure to install.

FUEL PUMP

REPLACE

1. Raise and support vehicle, then remove evaporative emission splash shield.
2. Support fuel tank with a suitable jack.
3. Remove fuel tank support strap bolt.
4. Remove hinge pin spring clip, then hinge pin.
5. Lower fuel tank. **While lowering tank, tip tank to avoid damage to fuel level sensor.**
6. Clean top of fuel tank.
7. Remove fuel pump bolts, then fuel pump.
8. Disconnect fuel temperature sensor connector.
9. Reverse procedure to install.

FUEL FILTER

REPLACE

In-Line Filter

1. Relieve fuel pressure as outlined under "Precautions."
2. Raise and support vehicle.
3. Remove fuel filter splash shield.
4. Disconnect fuel lines from fuel filter.
5. Remove fuel filter bracket nuts.
6. Reverse procedure to install. **Ensure fuel filter is replaced with arrow facing forward.**

Tank Filter

Refer to "Fuel Pump, Replace."

TIGHTENING SPECIFICATIONS

Year	Component	Torque Ft. Lbs.
2002	A/C Compressor Idler Pulley Bracket Bolts	15
	A/C Compressor Mounting Bolts	18
	A/C Drive Belt Tensioner Bolt	24
	A/C Mounting Bracket Bolts	38
	Alternator Drive Belt Lock Bolt	13
	Alternator To Bracket Bolts	19
	Battery Junction Box Bolt	44①
	Camshaft Sprocket Bolts	61
	Camshaft Thrust Plate Bolt	61
	CKP Sensor Heat Shield	10
	Connecting Rod Nuts	④
	Coolant Crossover Tube Bolts	18
	Coolant Crossover Tube Bracket Bolts	15
	Crankshaft Pulley Bolt	148
	Crankshaft Rear Oil Seal Retainer Plate Bolts	71①
	Cylinder Head Bolts	②
	Distributor Hold Down Bolt	12
	EGR Tube Nuts	29
	Engine Block Coolant Plug Bolts	29
	Engine Block Oil Adapter Cover Bolts	14
	Engine Ground Cable Bolt	35①
	Engine Lifting Eye Hook Bracket Bolt	19
	Engine Splash Shield Bolts	44①
	Engine Support Insulator Bolts	26
	Engine Support Insulator Through Bolts	61
	Engine Support Insulator To Transverse Member Bolts	61
	Engine To Transaxle Splash Shield Bolts	44①
	Exhaust Flex Tube Bracket Bolt	18
	Exhaust Manifold Nuts	15
	Exhaust Manifold To Outlet Pipe Bolts (Lefthand)	48
	Exhaust Outlet Pipe Bracket Bolts	26
	Flywheel Bolts	65
	Front Transaxle Support Insulator Through Bolt	36
	Fuel Injection Supply Manifold Bolts	19
	Fuel Line To Fuel Injection Supply Manifold Bolts	89①

TIGHTENING SPECIFICATIONS—Continued

Year	Component	Torque Ft. Lbs.
2002	Fuel Return Line Screw	9①
	Intake Manifold Bolts & Nuts (Lower)	③
	Intake Manifold Bolts (Upper)	89①
	Knock Sensor Bolt	22
	Lefthand Exhaust Manifold To Righthand Exhaust Manifold Nuts	15
	Main Bearing Cap Bolts	⑤
	Main Bulkhead Wiring Harness Electrical Connector Bolt	44①
	Oil Filter Adapter Bolts	18
	Oil Dipstick Tube Bracket Bolt	80
	Oil Pan Drain Plug	24
	Oil Pan Bolts	71①
	Oil Pump Bolts	10
	Oil Pump Screen Cover & Tube Bolts	14
	PCV Breather Tube Bracket Bolts	53①
	Power Steering Pump Bolts	13
	Power Steering Pump Bracket Bolts	24
	Power Steering Pump Drive Belt Tensioner Locknut	26
	Rear Transaxle Support Bracket Nuts	26
	Righthand Engine Support Insulator To Transverse Member Bolts	61
	Rocker Arm Shaft Bolts	15
	Short Oil Pump Bolts	62①
	Side Splash Shield Bolts	80①
	Spark Plugs	18
	Speed Control & Accelerator Cable Bracket Bolts	89①
	Starter Motor Bolts	18
	Timing Belt Tensioner Locknut	61
	Torque Converter Bolts	38
	Transaxle Shift Cable Nut	80①
	Transaxle To Engine Bolts	32
	Transaxle To Engine Bracket Bolts	26
	Transverse Member Bolts	61
	Valve Cover Screws	18①
	Water Pump Bolts	14
	Water Pump Pulley Bolts	89①
	Wheel Lug Nuts	80

① — Inch lbs.
② — Refer to "Cylinder Head, Replace" for procedure.
③ — Refer to "Intake Manifold, Replace" for procedure.
④ — Tighten in two steps; first step to 11 ft. lbs., second step to 30 ft. lbs.
⑤ — Tighten in three steps; first step to 22 ft. lbs., second step to 44 ft. lbs., third step to 66 ft. lbs.

Rear Axle & Suspension

NOTE: On Air Bag Equipped Models, Refer To "Air Bag System Precautions" Located In The Front Of This Manual For System Disarming & Arming Procedures.

NOTE: Prior To Performing Any Service Operations Listed In This Section, Consult The "Technical Service Bulletins" Section For Related Information.

INDEX

PRECAUTIONS

Air Bag Systems

Refer to "Air Bag System Precautions" in the front of this manual for system disarming and arming procedures.

Battery Ground Cable

Prior to service disconnect battery ground cable and isolate as required.

REAR AXLE

REPLACE

1. Raise and support vehicle.
2. Remove hub and bearing assembly as outlined under "Hub & Bearing, Replace."
3. Remove rear stabilizer bar as outlined under "Stabilizer Bar, Replace."
4. Support rear axle housing with jack stands.
5. Remove rear brake anti-lock sensor harnesses from axle clips.
6. Remove ABS sensor clip bolts, then clips.
7. Remove brake tubes and rear brake hoses from rear axle housing.
8. Remove two load sensor bracket bolts, then position load sensor aside.
9. Remove lower rear shock absorber nuts and washers, then position shock absorbers aside.
10. Remove rear spring U-bolt nuts.
11. Lower and remove rear axle housing.
12. Reverse procedure to install.

HUB & BEARING

REPLACE

1. Raise and support vehicle.
2. Remove wheel and tire assembly.
3. Remove brake drum, grease cap and cotter pin, **Fig. 1.** Discard cotter pin.
4. Remove hub/bearing assembly nut and washer, then hub/bearing assembly.
5. Reverse procedure to install.

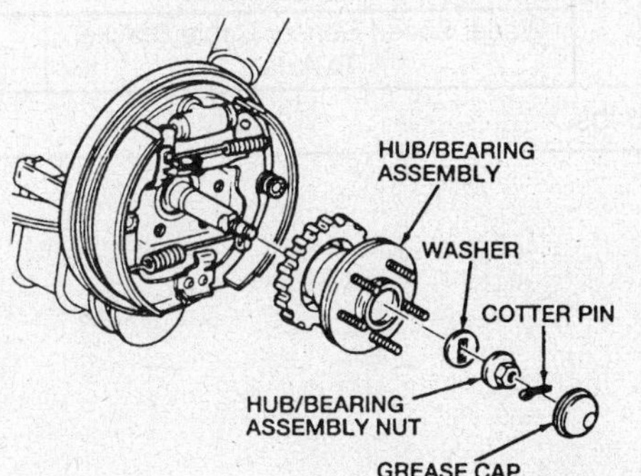

Fig. 1 Hub & bearing assembly

HUB & BEARING SERVICE

Rear wheel bearings and rear anti-lock sensor rings are integral and must be serviced as an assembly.

REAR WHEEL SPINDLE

REPLACE

1. Remove wheel hub and bearing assembly.
2. Remove backing plate attaching bolts, then backing plate.
3. Remove spindle.
4. Reverse procedure to install.

SHOCK ABSORBER

REPLACE

1. Raise and support vehicle, then remove wheel and tire assembly.
2. Place a suitable jack under axle housing.
3. Lower vehicle until tension on rear spring is relieved by floor jack or hoist.
4. Remove upper and lower shock absorber nuts and washers, then shock absorber.
5. Reverse procedure to install.

LEAF SPRING

REPLACE

1. Raise and support vehicle.
2. Support axle with floor jack or hoist.
3. Lower vehicle until tension on rear spring is relieved by floor jack or hoist.
4. Remove U-bolt nuts, washers, U-bolts, alignment bolt cover plate and U-bolt alignment cover plate.
5. Remove shackle nuts, shackle end plate and shackle.
6. Remove leaf spring front nut and bolt.
7. Raise vehicle until weight is removed from axle enough to easily remove leaf spring.
8. Reverse procedure to install.

STABILIZER BAR

REPLACE

1. Raise and support vehicle.
2. Hold stabilizer bar link studs with wrench and remove stabilizer bar to link nuts.
3. Disconnect stabilizer bar from link studs.
4. Loosen, but do not remove, upper stabilizer bar to axle bolts.
5. Remove lower stabilizer bar to axle bolts.
6. Slide stabilizer bar down until stabilizer bar mounting brackets clear loosened bolts and remove from rear axle.
7. Reverse procedure to install.

STABILIZER BAR LINK

REPLACE

1. Raise and support vehicle.
2. Hold stabilizer link with wrench and remove stabilizer to link nut.
3. Remove stabilizer bar from link.
4. Remove stabilizer to chassis bolts, then stabilizer bar links.
5. Reverse procedure to install.

TIGHTENING SPECIFICATIONS

Year	Component	Torque Ft. Lbs.
2002	Axle Bumper Stop	14
	Backing Plate Bolt	33
	Eye Bracket Bolts	14
	Hub & Bearing Assembly	178
	Leaf Spring Shackle Nuts	49
	Rear Spring Bolt Nuts	62
	Rear Spring Front Mounting Plate Nuts	49
	Rear Spring Front Nut	49
	Shock Absorber	26
	Stabilizer Bar To Axle	27
	Stabilizer Bar To Link	31
	Stabilizer Link To Chassis	14
	U-Bolt Nuts	62
	Wheel Lug Nuts	80
	Wheel Speed Sensor	15
	Wheel Speed Sensor Cable Bracket To Axle	35–44①

① — Inch lbs.

Front Suspension & Steering

NOTE: On Air Bag Equipped Models, Refer To "Air Bag System Precautions" Located In The Front Of This Manual For System Disarming & Arming Procedures.

INDEX

PRECAUTIONS

Air Bag Systems

Refer to "Air Bag System Precautions" in the front of this manual for system disarming and arming procedures.

Battery Ground Cable

Prior to service disconnect battery ground cable and isolate as required.

DESCRIPTION

The independent front suspension consists of McPherson struts riding in a heavy rubber spring seat. A forged steering knuckle bolts to bottom end of strut and also locates ball joint. A stabilizer bar connected to both control arms via stabilizer bar links controls vehicle's body lean while cornering. Each control arm attaches to a control arm gusset which is attached directly to the chassis.

WHEEL BEARING

ADJUST

Wheel bearing is not adjustable. If abnormal noise is indicated, bearing may require replacement. Noise will occur if bearing is dirty, worn or dry. Bearings are sealed and can not be cleaned or greased.

HUB & BEARING SERVICE

1. Remove steering knuckle as outlined under "Steering Knuckle, Replace."
2. Remove snap ring from knuckle assembly.
3. Press bearing out of steering knuckle using bearing puller attachment tool No. 205-D064, or equivalent.
4. Reverse procedure to install. Apply Threadlock part No. 262 E2FZ-19554-B, or equivalent, onto front bearing inner race.

BALL JOINT INSPECTION

1. Raise and support vehicle.
2. Grasp tire and rock wheel up and down, then side to side.
3. Inspect ball joint for any movement in control arm.
4. If movement is indicated, replace ball joint.

BALL JOINT

REPLACE

1. Raise and support vehicle.
2. Remove wheel and tire assembly.
3. Remove and discard cotter pin from ball joint shaft.
4. Loosen ball joint nut until it contacts outer CV joint.
5. Strike steering knuckle with a suitable hammer while pulling down on control arm until ball joint breaks free from steering knuckle.
6. Remove ball joint nut and ball joint to control arm nuts, **Fig. 1.**
7. Remove ball joint and three-stud shackle from control arm.
8. Reverse procedure to install.

COIL SPRING

REPLACE

1. Remove coil spring/strut assembly as outlined under "Strut, Replace."
2. Place assembly in suitable vise and remove strut nut cover.
3. Loosen, but do not remove, strut nut.
4. Compress coil spring using Rotunda McPherson Strut Compressor tool No. 014-00781, or equivalent.
5. Remove strut nut and rubber mounting block, **Fig. 2.**
6. Remove strut bearing seat and upper seat/dust boot assembly.
7. If required, remove dust boot by prying it from upper spring seat.
8. Remove coil spring from strut.
9. Slowly release tension from strut compressor.
10. Slide bump stopper off strut.
11. Reverse procedure to install.

CONTROL ARM

REPLACE

1. Raise and support vehicle.
2. Remove wheel and tire assembly.
3. Remove ball joint as outlined under "Ball Joint, Replace."
4. Remove stabilizer link to control arm nut, then stabilizer link shaft from control arm, **Fig. 1.**
5. Remove rear control arm bolts and mounting bracket.
6. Remove lower control arm nut.
7. Pull rear of control arm down and gently pry control arm forward and off gusset to remove.
8. Reverse procedure to install.

CONTROL ARM BUSHING

REPLACE

Front

1. Remove control arm as outlined under "Control Arm, Replace."
2. Position control arm on axle bearing/seal plate tool No. T75L-1165-B and axle bearing seal tool No. T75L-1165-DA, or equivalents.
3. Position control arm bushing tool No. T93P-5493-A, or equivalent, on front control arm bushing.
4. Press bushing out of control arm.
5. Reverse procedure to install.

Rear

1. Remove control arm as outlined under "Control Arm, Replace."
2. Position bearing pulling attachment tool No. D84L-1123-A, or equivalent, between control arm mounting bolt bushing and control arm flange.
3. Position suitable press rod or other suitable tool on control arm, then press bushing from arm.
4. Reverse procedure to install.

STEERING KNUCKLE

REPLACE

1. Raise and support vehicle.
2. Remove wheel and tire assembly.
3. Remove front brake caliper, then wire aside. It is not required to disconnect brake line.
4. Remove rotor and grease cap.
5. Remove steering knuckle/wheel hub assembly nut cotter pin.
6. Remove castle nut.
7. Remove steering knuckle/wheel hub nut.
8. Remove ball joint cotter pin from ball joint shaft. Loosen ball joint nut until it contacts outer CV joint.
9. Strike steering knuckle with hammer while pulling down on control arm until ball joint breaks free from steering knuckle, **Fig. 1.**
10. Remove ball joint nut, then separate ball joint from steering knuckle/wheel hub assembly.
11. Remove tie rod end from steering knuckle/wheel hub assembly.
12. Remove wheel speed sensor bolt.
13. Remove strut to steering knuckle/ wheel hub assembly nuts and bolts.
14. Remove strut to steering knuckle/ wheel hub assembly.
15. Use two-jaw puller tool No. D80L-1102-L, or equivalent, to separate half-shaft from steering knuckle/wheel hub assembly.
16. Remove steering knuckle/wheel hub assembly from vehicle.
17. Remove steering stop bolt, if required.
18. Reverse procedure to install.

STABILIZER BAR

REPLACE

1. Raise and support vehicle.
2. Remove stabilizer bar to stabilizer link nuts.
3. Remove stabilizer bar to control arm gusset nuts and bolts.
4. Remove stabilizer bar mounting brackets.
5. Gently pry stabilizer bar ends off stabilizer links and remove bar.
6. Reverse procedure to install.

STRUT

REPLACE

1. Place alignment mark on inside of strut mounting block and chassis strut tower.
2. Raise and support vehicle.
3. Remove wheel and tire assembly.

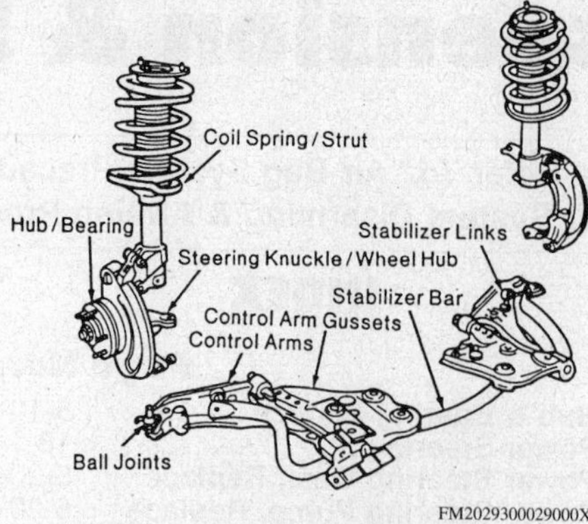

Fig. 1 Front suspension

4. Remove wheel speed sensor cable bracket bolts and position cable aside.
5. Remove brake hose U-clip and position aside.
6. Remove strut to steering knuckle/ wheel hub assembly nuts and bolts.
7. Separate strut from steering knuckle.
8. Remove mounting block nuts.
9. Remove coil spring/strut assembly from vehicle.
10. Reverse procedure to install.

TIE ROD END

REPLACE

Inner

Refer to "Power Steering Gears" in the "Power Steering" chapter for inner tie rod end replacement.

Outer

1. Raise and support vehicle.
2. Loosen tie rod end jam nut.
3. Separate tie rod end from steering knuckle.
4. Remove tie rod end from steering gear.
5. Reverse procedure to install. Align front end as outlined in "Wheel Alignment" section.

POWER STEERING GEAR

REPLACE

1. Raise and support vehicle, then remove wheel and tire assemblies.
2. Remove outer tie rod ends.
3. Remove engine support insulators as outlined under "Engine Mounts, Replace" in "3.3L Engine" section.
4. Loosen power steering fluid return line

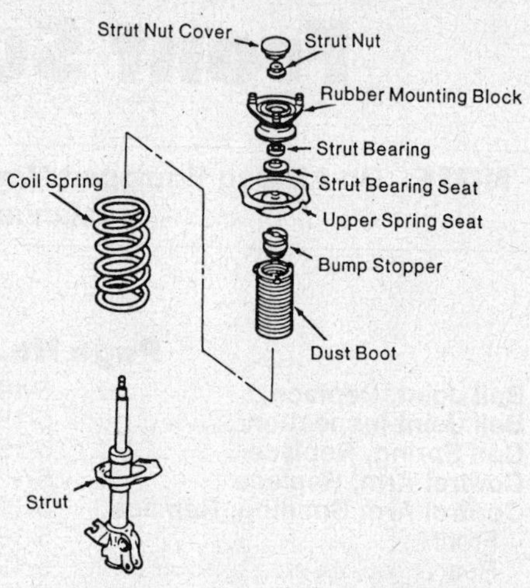

Fig. 2 Exploded view of strut assembly

clamp, then remove return line from steering gear.

5. Remove power steering pressure line from steering gear.
6. Remove steering gear dust seal clamp, then position gear dust seal aside.
7. Remove lower steering column shaft clamp bolt.
8. Remove catalytic converter flange nuts and exhaust bracket bolts, then position exhaust aside.
9. Remove steering gear bracket bolts.
10. Remove steering gear brackets and insulators, then steering gear.
11. Reverse procedure to install.

POWER STEERING PUMP

REPLACE

1. Raise and support vehicle.
2. Remove water pump and power steering pump drive belt.
3. Remove power steering pump pulley using strap wrench tool No. D85L-6000-A, or equivalent, to hold pulley while removing pulley nut.
4. Place drain pan under pump.
5. Remove hose connection bolt from pump. Place high-pressure hose and connection up out of way.
6. Remove pump inlet hose bolts and place hose up out of way.
7. Remove front bolts, then rear bolt.
8. Remove pump from vehicle.
9. Reverse procedure to install.

TIGHTENING SPECIFICATIONS

Year	Component	Torque Ft. Lbs.
2002	Ball Joint Nut	58
	Ball Joint To Control Arm Nuts	68
	Clamp Bolt	17–22
	Control Arm Gusset Bolts	98
	Control Arm Nuts	105
	Control Arm Rear Bolts	98
	Front Steering Pump Bolt	13
	Front Strut Damper Nut	51
	Front Strut Damper To Steering Knuckle Nuts	101
	Front Strut Damper Upper Mounting Bracket Nuts	35
	Hub Nut	203
	Junction Block Bolt	35①
	Junction Block/High-Pressure Line	15
	Power Steering Pressure Hose Connection Bolt	54
	Power Steering Pump Inlet Hose Bolts	13
	Power Steering Pump Pulley Nut	45
	Rear Steering Pump Bolt	13
	Stabilizer Bar To Gusset	27
	Stabilizer Bar To Stabilizer Link Nuts	34
	Stabilizer Link To Control Arm Nut	14
	Steering Gear Bolts	62
	Tie Rod End Jam Nut	45
	Tie Rod End Nut	26
	Upper High-Pressure Hose Bolt	43
	Upper Righthand Cooling Line Bolt	18–26①
	Wheel Lug Nuts	80
	Wheel Speed Sensor Bolts	19①
	Wheel Speed Sensor Cable Bracket Bolts	19①

① — Inch lbs.

Wheel Alignment

INDEX

PRELIMINARY INSPECTION

Inspect following components, adjust, repair or replace as required prior to performing front wheel alignment.

1. Inflate tires to cold specifications.
2. Ensure tires are of same size, ply rating and load rating.
3. Inspect for excessive wheel bearing endplay.
4. Inspect for worn or damaged ball joints.
5. Inspect steering gear mounting bolts for proper torque.
6. Inspect control arm for bent or damaged condition.
7. Inspect control arm to frame bushings for looseness or wear.
8. Inspect suspension components for wear or damage.
9. Inspect vehicle ride height as outlined under "Vehicle Ride Height."

Fig. 1 Vehicle ride height inspection locations & specifications

FRONT WHEEL ALIGNMENT

Caster & Camber

Caster and camber are preset at the factory and are not adjustable. If caster or camber angles are not within specifications, replace suspension components responsible for incorrect angles.

Toe-In

1. Loosen jam nuts at tie rod ends and release clips at small ends of steering gear boots. **Ensure boots are free on tie rods to prevent twisting.**
2. Turn tie rods in or out of ends an equal amount on each side to keep steering wheel centered.
3. Inspect front tracking. **Follow equipment manufacturers instructions.**
4. Double inspect toe-in.
5. **Torque** tie rod end jam nuts to 58–72 ft. lbs., and install clips.

KINGPIN

ADJUST

Kingpin inclination is preset at the factory and is not adjustable. If kingpin inclination is not within specifications, replace suspension components responsible for incorrect angles.

VEHICLE RIDE HEIGHT

Before inspecting vehicle ride height, ensure vehicle is on level ground and has no luggage or passenger load.

Refer to **Fig. 1** for vehicle ride height inspection locations and specifications. Ensure side to side difference does not exceed .4 inch.

WINDSTAR

NOTE: Refer To Back Of This Manual For Vehicle Manufacturer's Special Service Tool Suppliers.

INDEX OF SERVICE OPERATIONS

Specifications

GENERAL ENGINE SPECIFICATIONS

Year	Engine, Liter	Fuel System	Bore & Stroke	Comp. Ratio	Horsepower @ RPM	Torque Ft. Lbs. @ RPM	Normal Oil Pressure Lbs.
2002–03	3.8L	SFI	3.8 x 3.4	9.4	200 @ 4900	240 @ 3600	40–125

TUNE UP SPECIFICATIONS

Year	Engine	Spark Plug Gap	Ignition Timing			Curb Idle Speed①	Fast Idle Speed①	Fuel Pump Pressure, psi.	Valve Lash, Inch
			Firing Order ③	BTDC	Mark Location				
2002–03	3.8L	.052–.056	④	10⑤	—	⑥	⑥	⑦	②

BTDC — Before Top Dead Center.
① — When adjusting idle speed, set parking brake & chock drive wheels.
② — Equipped w/hydraulic valve tappets.
③ — Before removing wires from distributor cap or coil unit, determine location of ignition wires, as position may have been altered from that outlined at end of this chart.
④ — Cylinder numbering front to rear, righthand bank, 1, 2, 3; lefthand bank, 4, 5, 6. Firing order, 1-4-2-5-3-6. Refer to **Fig. A** for spark plug wire connections at ignition coil unit.
⑤ — Not adjustable.
⑥ — Controlled by idle air control system.
⑦ — Key on engine off, 35–45 psi. Key on engine running, 28–45 psi.

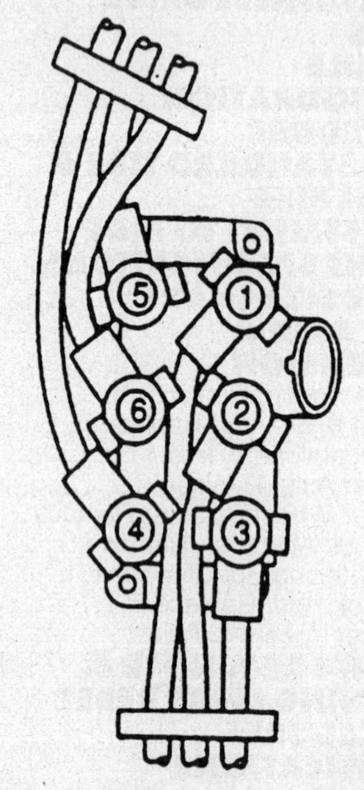

Fig. A

FRONT WHEEL ALIGNMENT SPECIFICATIONS

Year	Model	Caster Angle, Degrees②		Camber Angle, Degrees③		Total Toe, Degrees①		Front Wheel Turning Angles, Degrees	
		Limits	Desired	Limits	Desired	Limits	Desired	Outside wheel	Inside Wheel
2002–03	All	②	③	-.94 to +.06	-.44	-.4 to +.1	-.15	—	—

① — Toe-In (+). Toe-Out (-).

② — Caster difference, lefthand minus righthand, -5° (+0/-1°).

③ — Camber difference, lefthand minus righthand, 0° (+/-.5°).

REAR WHEEL ALIGNMENT SPECIFICATIONS

Year	Model	Camber Angle, Degrees		Total Toe, Degrees①	
		Limits	Desired	Limits	Desired
2002–03	All	-.6 to +.4	-.1	-.28 to +.4	-.06

① — Toe-In (+). Toe-Out (-).

FLUID CAPACITIES & COOLING SYSTEM DATA

Year	Engine Liter	Cooling System Capacity, Qts.		Recom-mend- ed Engine Coolant Type	Radiator Cap Relief Pressure, Lbs.	Thermo Opening, Temp. °F	Fuel Tank, Gals.	Engine Oil Refill, Qts.①	Transaxle Oil, Qts.②
		Less A/C	With A/C						
2002–03	3.8L	14.8③	14.8③	Ethylene Glycol	16	187	26	5.75	13.70

① — Includes filter.

② — Approximate. Make final inspection w/dipstick.

③ — Coolant capacity with rear heater, 15.9 qts.

LUBRICANT DATA

Year	Model	Lubricant Type				
		Transaxle	Transfer Case	Rear Axle	Power Steering	Brake System
2002–03	All	Mercon®	—	—	①	DOT 3

① — Type F trans. fluid or premium power steering fluid.

Electrical

NOTE: On Air Bag Equipped Models, Refer To "Air Bag System Precautions" Located In The Front Of This Manual For System Disarming & Arming Procedures.

NOTE: Refer To "Computer Relearn Procedures" Located In The Front Of This Manual When Battery Power To The Computer Has Been Interrupted.

NOTE: On Rear Air Suspension Equipped Models, Turn Air Suspension Switch To "Off" Position Prior To Raising Vehicle.

INDEX

PRECAUTIONS

Air Bag Systems

Refer to "Air Bag System Precautions" in the front of this manual for system disarming and arming procedures.

Air Suspension Systems

Prior to raising vehicle, turn air suspension switch to "Off" position to prevent air suspension damage or vehicle from shifting on hoist.

Battery Ground Cable

Prior to service disconnect battery ground cable and isolate as required.

FUSE PANEL & FLASHER LOCATION

The main fuse panel may be found under the instrument panel to the lefthand side of the steering column under a plastic fuse panel cover. Additional fuses and circuit breakers may be found in the power distribution panel located on the lefthand front fender apron in the engine compartment.

The electronic combination turn signal/ emergency flasher unit is located in the main fuse panel.

RELAY CENTER LOCATION

Relays are contained in the battery junction box and in the central junction box located on the lefthand side of the engine compartment.

FUEL PUMP RELAY LOCATION

The fuel pump relay is located in the battery junction box.

STARTER

REPLACE

1. Raise and support vehicle.
2. Disconnect starter cable, then disconnect solenoid connector by pulling on connector shell only, do not pull on wire.
3. Remove upper and lower starter bolts, then the starter.
4. Reverse procedures to install, noting the following:
   a. **Torque** starter bolts 15–20 ft. lbs.
   b. **Torque** starter cable to solenoid nut 84–120 inch lbs.

ALTERNATOR

REPLACE

1. Disconnect alternator harness.
2. Release tension on the drive belt using a suitable ½ in drive breaker bar or equivalent, inserted into automatic drive belt tensioner, then remove drive belt from alternator.
3. Remove three attaching bolts and alternator.
4. Reverse procedure to install, noting the following:
   a. **Torque** alternator bolts 30–41 ft. lbs.
   b. **Torque** alternator output terminal nut 84–96 inch lbs.

IGNITION COIL

REPLACE

1. Remove cowl panel.
2. Disconnect fuel charging wiring connectors from ignition coil and radio ignition interference capacitor.
3. Disconnect ignition wires.

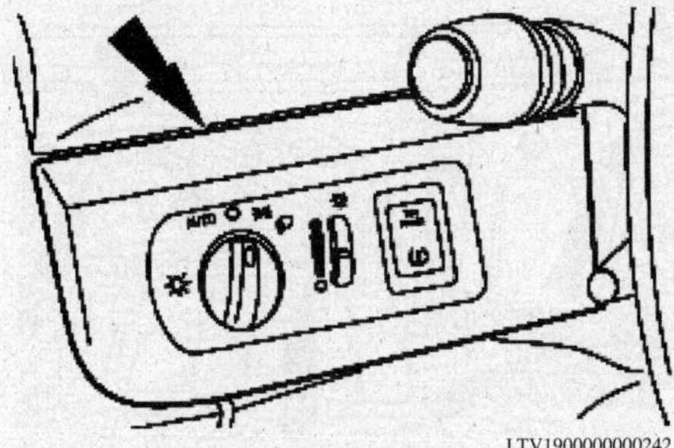

Fig. 1 Lefthand instrument panel finish panel

4. Remove ignition coil retaining screws.
5. Remove ignition coil and radio ignition interference capacitor.
6. Reverse procedure to install. **Torque** to 44–61 inch lbs.

IGNITION LOCK

REPLACE

Removal

1. Turn ignition switch to Run position.
2. Insert a suitable ⅛ inch rod or pin through hole in column cover into lock housing and depress retaining pin.
3. Remove lock from housing.

Installation

1. Set lock cylinder to Run position.
2. Depress retaining pin, then install lock cylinder.
3. Ensure lock cylinder is fully seated before rotating lock, then rotate lock to Off position.
4. Rotate lock to all positions to ensure correct operation.

IGNITION SWITCH

REPLACE

Refer to "Steering Columns" chapter in manual for ignition switch replacement procedures.

NEUTRAL SAFETY SWITCH

REPLACE

The neutral safety switch is incorporated into the Digital Transaxle Range Sensor (TR) attached to the transaxle and connected to the manual control lever shaft.

Removal

1. Set parking brake.
2. Place transaxle range selector switch in neutral position.
3. Remove engine air cleaner assembly.
4. Disconnect electrical connector from range selector.
5. Disconnect shift cable and remove manual control lever.
6. Remove attaching bolts, then the digital transaxle range selector.

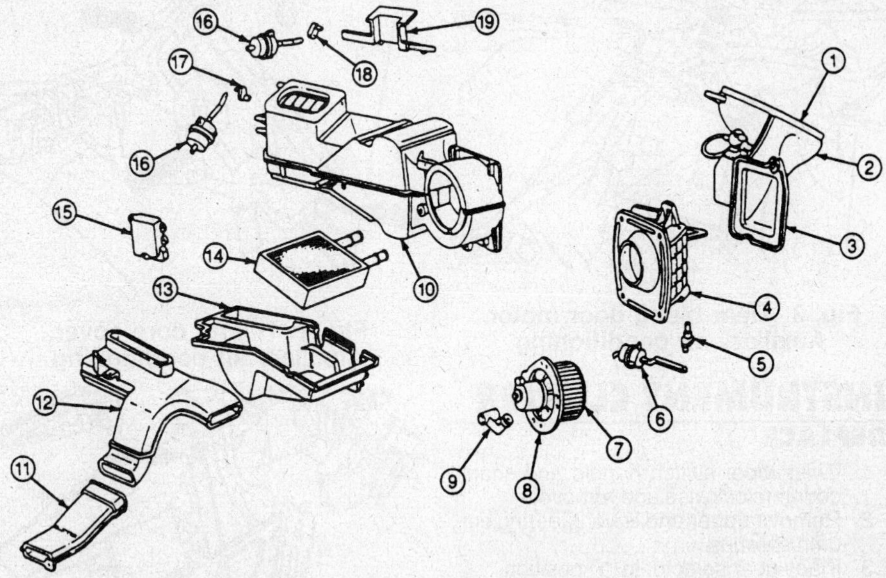

Item	Description
1	Outside Air Seal
2	Air Inlet Duct
3	Air Inlet Door Inner Seal
4	Recirculating Air Duct Assembly
5	Damper Door Shaft
6	Vacuum Control Motor
7	Blower Motor Wheel
8	Heater Blower Motor
9	Blower Motor Housing Tube
10	A/C Evaporator Housing, Lower
11	Rear Seat Air Flow Duct, Lower
12	Rear Seat Air Flow Duct, Upper
13	Heater Core Cover
14	Heater Core
15	Electronic Door Actuator Motor
16	Vacuum Control Motor
17	Windshield Defroster Door Shaft
18	Windshield Defroster Door Shaft
19	Windshield Defroster Duct

FM7029500234000X

Fig. 2 Air duct components

Installation

1. Shift transaxle into neutral position.
2. Install range sensor, loosely install bolts.
3. Align range sensor using alignment tool No. 307-351, or equivalent.
4. Install manual control lever and nut.
5. Connect shift cable and verify proper adjustment.
6. Connect digital range sensor electrical connector.
7. Install air cleaner assembly.

HEADLAMP SWITCH

REPLACE

1. Unclip headlamp switch trim bezel.
2. Disconnect electrical connectors, then remove switch from bezel.
3. Reverse procedure to install.

BRAKE PEDAL POSITION SWITCH

REPLACE

1. Disconnect brake pedal position switch electrical connector.
2. Remove self-locking pin and spacer, then the brake pedal position switch.
3. Reverse procedure to install.

MULTI-FUNCTION SWITCH

REPLACE

1. Twist tilt wheel handle and shank counterclockwise and remove.
2. Remove upper and lower steering column shrouds.
3. Disconnect electrical connects.
4. Remove mounting screws, then the multi-function switch.
5. Reverse procedure to install.

STEERING WHEEL

REPLACE

1. Disarm air bag system, then remove driver air bag module as outlined under "Air Bag System" chapter.
2. Through access cover hole, turn pinion shaft bolt to release steering wheel from column shaft.
3. Remove steering wheel using care not to damage wiring or connectors. Route wiring through small hole in back of steering wheel.
4. Reverse procedure to install, noting the following:
   a. Route wiring through hole in back of steering wheel.
   b. **Torque** pinion shaft bolt to 13 ft. lbs.

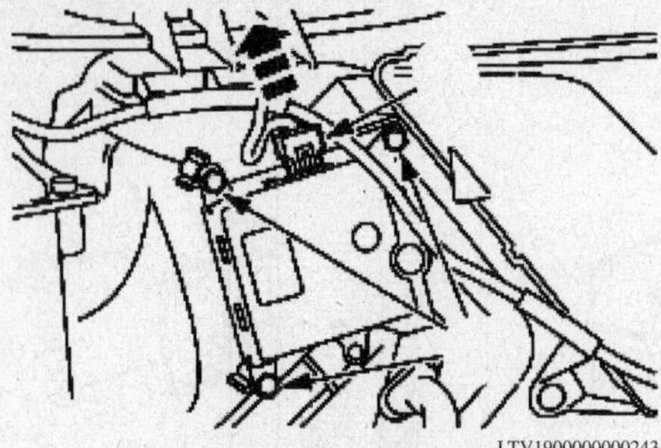
LTV1900000000243

Fig. 3 Rear blend door motor. Auxiliary air conditioning

INSTRUMENT CLUSTER

REPLACE

1. Twist wiper switch handle and shank counterclockwise and remove.
2. Remove upper and lower steering column shrouds.
3. Place gear selector in "1" position.
4. Remove lefthand instrument panel finish panel, **Fig. 1.**
5. Remove righthand instrument panel finish panel.
6. Remove steering column opening cover panel.
7. Remove instrument panel steering column cover reinforcement.
8. Loosen nuts and lower steering column approximately one inch.
9. Remove instrument panel cluster finish panel.
10. Remove transmission range indicator cable attaching bolt, then position cable aside.
11. Remove instrument cluster.
12. Reverse procedure to install.

RADIO

REPLACE

1. Insert radio removal tool No. T87P-19061-A, or equivalent, into radio face plate approximately one inch to release retaining clips.
2. Slide radio from opening, then disconnect wiring connectors.
3. Reverse procedures to install.

WIPER MOTOR

REPLACE

Front

1. Remove top cowl vent grille assembly.
2. Remove lower cowl top vent panel assembly.
3. Remove wiper motor mounting arm and pivot shaft.
4. Remove wiper motor linkage from motor.
5. Remove wiper motor.
6. Reverse procedure to install.

Rear

1. Lift up wiper arm to pivot cap and remove nut from assembly, then raise arm to service position and rock arm to release from pivot shaft.

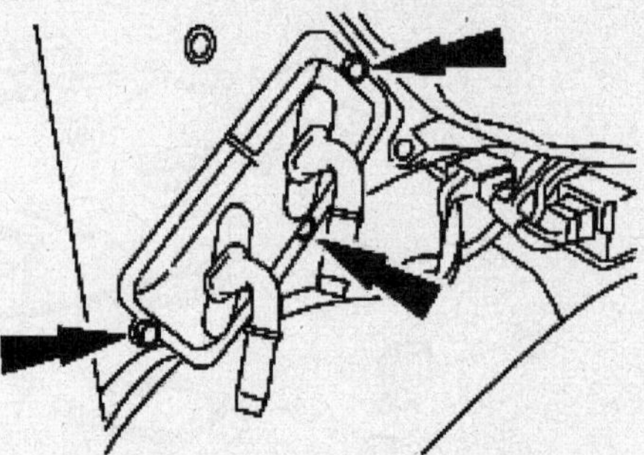
LTV1900000000244

Fig. 4 Heater core cover. Auxiliary air conditioning

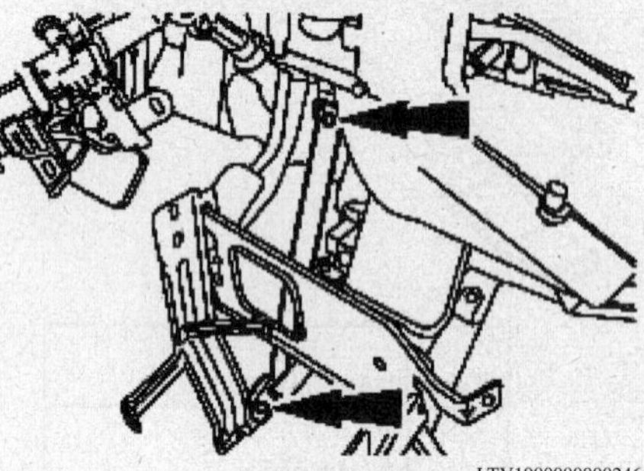
LTV1900000000246

Fig. 6 Air duct support brace assembly

2. Remove interior lift gate trim panel.
3. Disconnect electrical connector at motor.
4. Remove mounting screws, then the motor assembly from liftgate.
5. Reverse procedure to install, noting the following.
   a. **Torque** motor to liftgate mounting screws to 22–29 ft. lbs.
   b. Connect battery ground cable, then turn wiper On then Off to park system before installing wiper arms.
   c. Position arm to pivot shaft, then **torque** shaft nut to 22–29 ft. lbs.

BLOWER MOTOR

REPLACE

Main

1. Open and position glove box door aside.
2. Disconnect electrical connector and vent tube from blower assembly.
3. Remove retaining screws, then remove blower assembly from case, **Fig. 2.**
4. Remove push nut holding blower fan to shaft, then remove fan from shaft.
5. Reverse procedure to install.

Auxiliary

1. Remove second row passenger seat.
2. Remove pushpin retainers from lower edge of auxiliary heater and air conditioner cover, then pull cover out and up to remove.
3. Disconnect blower motor electrical connector, then remove four retaining screws from blower motor cover.
4. Remove blower motor.

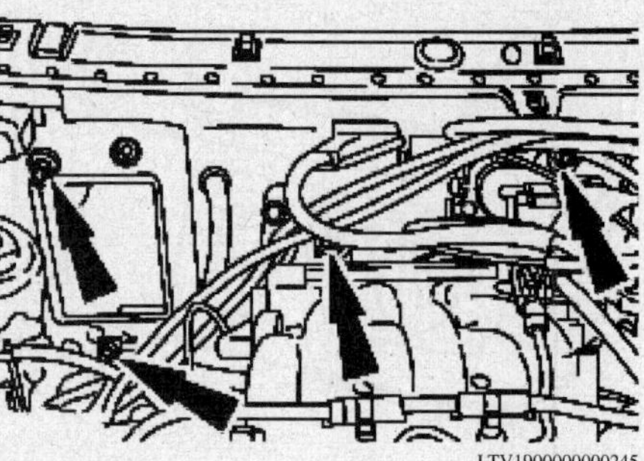
LTV1900000000245

Fig. 5 Evaporator mounting nuts

5. Remove push nut holding blower fan to shaft, then remove fan from shaft.
6. Reverse procedure to install.

HEATER CORE

REPLACE

Main

1. Drain cooling system into suitable container.
2. Remove cowl top vent panel to allow clearance, then in engine compartment, disconnect heater hoses from core.
3. Remove ground strap from heater core tube, if equipped.
4. Remove cassette box, center instrument panel support trim and cup holder.
5. Remove ash tray and cupholder.
6. Remove rear seat air flow ducts, **Fig. 2.**
7. **On models equipped with keyless entry,** disconnect wiring harness.
8. **On all models,** remove center instrument panel support brackets.
9. Disconnect climate control vacuum line connector.
10. Remove heater floor duct, then remove heater core cover.
11. Remove heater core from air box.
12. Reverse procedure to install, noting the following:
    a. Always use new heater core and core tube seals.
    b. Bleed cooling system as outlined in appropriate "Engine" section.

Auxiliary

1. Drain cooling system into suitable container.
2. Remove rear trim panels.
3. Disconnect rear heater hoses.
4. Remove rear blend door motor, **Fig. 3.**
5. Remove rear heater core cover, **Fig. 4.**
6. Remove heater core from housing.
7. Reverse procedure to install.

EVAPORATOR CORE

REPLACE

The A/C evaporator core is in unit with the heater and A/C evaporator housing and is replaced as an assembly.

1. Drain cooling system into suitable container.

2. Recover A/C system as outlined in "Air Conditioning" chapter.
3. Remove cowl top vent panel to allow clearance, then, in engine compartment, disconnect heater hoses from core, vacuum source hose, fresh air inlet duct and refrigerant lines attached to air duct assembly through firewall.
4. Remove instrument panel as outlined in "Dash Panel Service" chapter.
5. Disconnect vacuum and electrical connectors from air duct assembly.
6. In engine compartment, remove four nuts holding air duct assembly to firewall, **Fig. 5,** then inside vehicle, remove support brace holding air duct assembly, **Fig. 6.**
7. Remove air duct assembly from vehicle, then disconnect and remove components for transfer to new assembly.
8. Reverse procedure to install, noting the following:
   a. **When A/C housing assembly is removed, the suction accumulator/drier must be replaced. Refer to "Air Conditioning" chapter.**
   b. Always use new heater core and core tube seals.
   c. Bleed cooling system as outlined in appropriate "Engine" section.
   d. Recharge A/C as outlined in "Air Conditioning" chapter.
   e. **Torque** air duct to firewall and support brace nuts to 42–49 inch lbs.

3.8L Engine

NOTE: On Air Bag Equipped Models, Refer To "Air Bag System Precautions" Located In The Front Of This Manual For System Disarming & Arming Procedures.

NOTE: Refer To "Computer Relearn Procedures" Located In The Front Of This Manual When Battery Power To The Computer Has Been Interrupted.

NOTE: On Rear Air Suspension Equipped Models, Turn Air Suspension Switch To "Off" Position Prior To Raising Vehicle.

NOTE: Prior To Performing Any Service Operations Listed In This Section, Consult The "Technical Service Bulletins" Section For Related Information.

INDEX

PRECAUTIONS

Air Bag Systems

Refer to "Air Bag System Precautions" in the front of this manual for system disarming and arming procedures.

Air Suspension Systems

Prior to raising vehicle, turn air suspension switch to "Off" position to prevent air suspension damage or vehicle from shifting on hoist.

Battery Ground Cable

Prior to service disconnect battery ground cable and isolate as required.

Fuel System Pressure Relief

Fuel supply lines will remain pressurized for long periods of time after engine shut down. This pressure must be relieved before any service is attempted. A valve is provided on the fuel rail assembly for this purpose. To relieve system pressure, remove air cleaner assembly and connect pressure gauge tool No. T80L-9974-B, or equivalent, onto fuel valve on fuel rail assembly. To pressurize fuel system, proceed as follows:

1. Install pressure gauge tool No. T80L-9974-B, or equivalent, onto fuel rail pressure fitting.
2. Direct drain hose into a suitable container, then depress pressure relief button on tool.

COMPRESSION PRESSURE

Compression pressure should be inspected with the engine at normal operating temperature, spark plugs removed and a suitable compression pressure gauge installed. Crank the engine a minimum of five compression strokes and record the highest reading at each cylinder.

The indicated compression pressures are within specification if the lowest cylinder reading is within 75 percent of the highest cylinder reading.

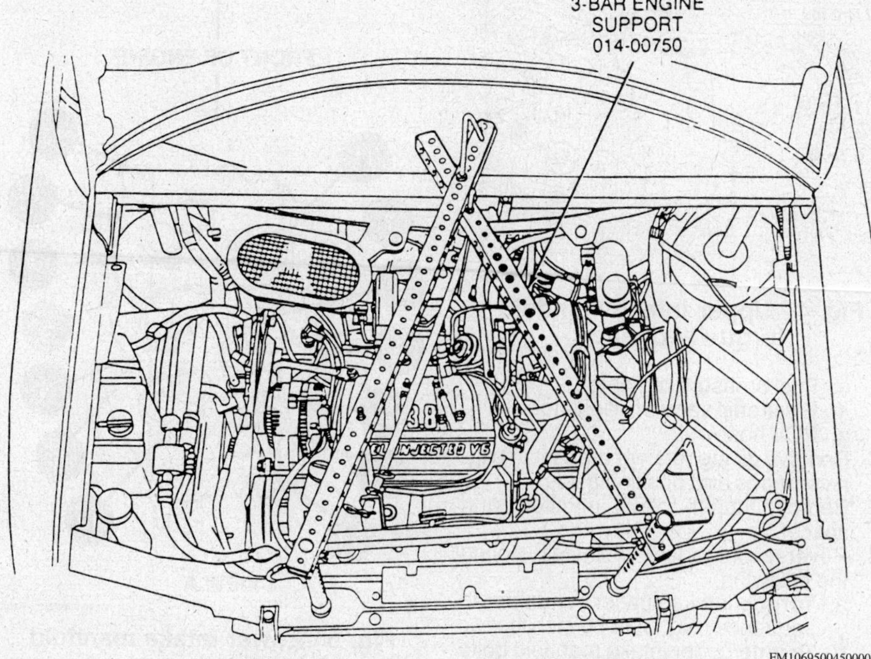

Fig. 1 Righthand front engine support fixture

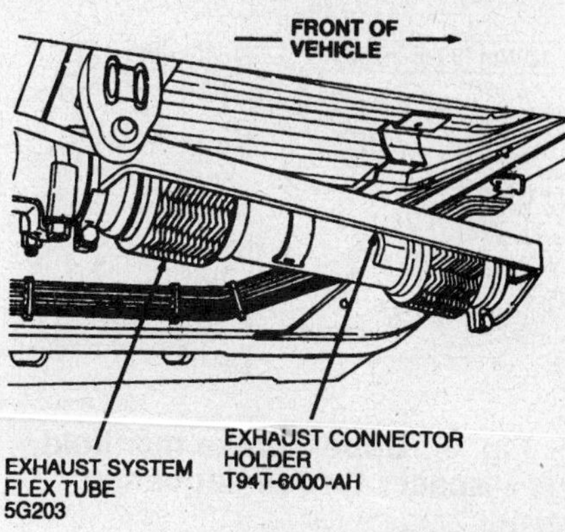

Fig. 2 Converter Y pipe removal

ENGINE MOUNT

REPLACE

Righthand Front

1. Relieve fuel system pressure as outlined under "Precautions."
2. Remove four bolts holding A/C compressor to bracket, then position aside without discharging system.
3. Remove mount upper attaching nut.
4. Install engine support fixture tool No. 014-00750, lifting bracket set tool No. 014-00794 and adapter kit tool No. 014-00792, or equivalents, to engine, **Fig. 1.**
5. Raise and support vehicle.
6. Remove front lower mount attaching nut.
7. Lower vehicle.
8. Lift engine about one inch using installed engine lifting equipment.
9. Raise and support vehicle, then remove engine mount.
10. Reverse procedure to install.

RIGHTHAND REAR

1. Raise and support vehicle.
2. Loosen righthand front and righthand rear upper motor mount attaching nuts.
3. Install engine support fixture tool No. 014-00750, lifting bracket set tool No. 014-00794 and adapter kit tool No. 014-00792, or equivalents, to engine, **Fig. 1.**
4. Raise and support vehicle.
5. Remove lower motor mount attaching nut, then motor mount.
6. Reverse procedure to install, tighten nuts and bolts to specifications.

LEFTHAND MOUNT & SUPPORT ASSEMBLY

1. Raise and support vehicle.
2. Remove lefthand front tire and wheel assembly, then support transaxle using suitable jack and block of wood.
3. Remove motor mount to support assembly attaching nuts.
4. Remove motor mount to frame through bolts, then raise transaxle enough to unload motor mount.
5. Remove support assembly to transaxle attaching bolts, then rotate the support assembly counterclockwise to allow removal of motor mount.
6. Reverse procedure to install, tighten nuts and bolts to specifications.

ENGINE

REPLACE

1. Relieve fuel system pressure as outlined under "Precautions."
2. Disconnect fuel hoses.
3. Recover A/C refrigerant as outlined in "Air Conditioning" chapter.
4. Drain cooling system into suitable container.
5. Remove cowl top vent panel.
6. Remove air cleaner assembly.
7. Remove upper radiator hose, then the heater hoses.
8. Disconnect transaxle oil cooler tubes using line disconnect tool No. T86P-77265-AH, or equivalent.
9. Remove A/C discharge and suction hoses at accumulator and secure to engine.
10. Remove accelerator cable mounting bracket.
11. Disconnect body ground at A/C accumulator bracket, if equipped.
12. Disconnect engine control sensor electrical connector, then remove bolt holding electrical harness bracket.
13. Disconnect and mark vacuum hoses and ground wire assembly.
14. Disconnect bulkhead electrical connector, then transaxle pressure switches.
15. Disconnect A/C high pressure and low pressure switches, if equipped.
16. Disconnect throttle control valve cable, if equipped.
17. Disconnect shift cable from transaxle.
18. Raise and support vehicle.
19. Drain engine oil and remove oil filter.
20. Remove wheel and tire assemblies.
21. Disconnect heated exhaust gas oxygen sensors.
22. Remove converter Y pipe retainer bolts, then install exhaust connector holder tool No. T94T-6000-AH, or equivalent, and remove converter Y pipe, **Fig. 2.**
23. Without disconnecting brake fluid lines, remove brake calipers, support and position aside.
24. Disconnect anti-lock brake wiring connectors at wheel sensors.
25. Disconnect starter motor wiring and secure to side.
26. Remove starter motor, then the engine rear plate and torque converter retaining nuts.
27. Remove nut securing battery cable support bracket to starter motor stud.
28. Disconnect power steering cooler lines, then the lower radiator hose at radiator.
29. Remove heater hoses to auxiliary heater, if equipped.
30. Remove dust boot from power steering rack pinion support by spreading integral tension ring and pushing upward.
31. Remove pinch bolt from intermediate shaft at power steering gear.
32. Remove intermediate shaft from steering gear.
33. Remove front stabilizer bar links from stabilizer bar.
34. Remove lower control arms from steering knuckles at ball joint.
35. Separate tie rods from steering knuckles.
36. Remove halfshafts from steering knuckles as outlined in "Front Wheel Drive Axles" chapter.

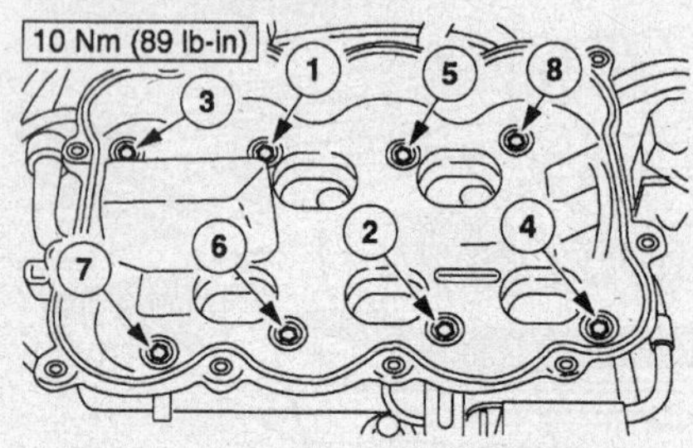

Fig. 3 Upper intake manifold spacer torque sequence

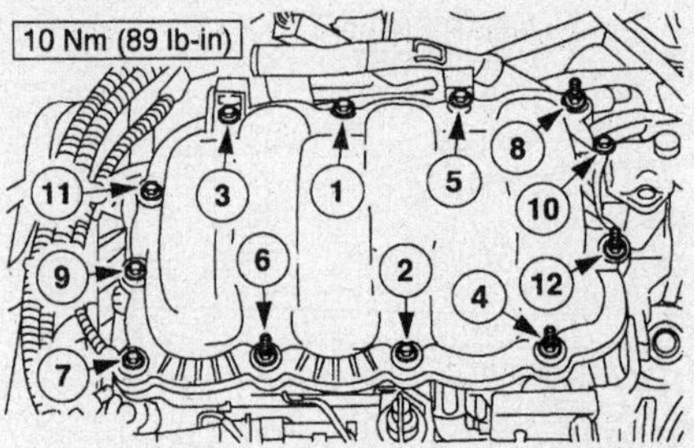

Fig. 4 Upper intake manifold torque sequence

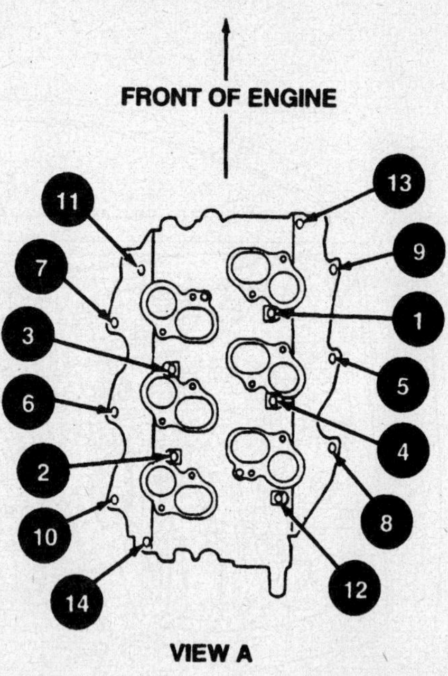

Fig. 5 Lower intake manifold tightening sequence

37. Support subframe, engine, and transaxle assembly using lift tool Nos. 014-00765 and 014-00766, or equivalent.
38. Remove four front subframe retaining bolts.
39. Disconnect power steering pressure hose from power steering pump.
40. Lower engine, transaxle, and subframe from vehicle.
41. Install engine lifting eyes, tool No. D81L-6001-D, or equivalent.
42. Install engine lift bracket set, tool No. 014-00793, or equivalent, to lifting eyes.
43. Support engine and transaxle using suitable jack stand.
44. Remove all engine and transmission mounts, then lift engine and transaxle from subframe.
45. Lower engine and transaxle. Support transaxle on a suitable surface, then remove engine to transaxle mounting bolts.
46. Place engine on a suitable work stand, then remove engine lifting tools.
47. Reverse procedure to install, noting the following:
    a. Tighten all nuts and bolts to specifications.
    b. Recharge A/C as outlined under "Air Conditioning" chapter.
    c. Bleed power steering as outlined under "Power Steering" chapter.
    d. Bleed cooling system as outlined under "Cooling System Bleed."
    e. Verify that front wheel alignment is within specifications.
    f. Inspect all fluid levels.

INTAKE MANIFOLD

REPLACE

Upper

1. Remove cowl top vent panel.
2. Remove air cleaner outlet tube.
3. Disconnect accelerator cable and speed control cable (if equipped) from throttle body.
4. Remove accelerator cable mounting bracket and position bracket and cables aside.
5. Disconnect the following:
    a. TPS.
    b. IAC.
    c. Evaporative emissions return tube.
    d. Brake booster vacuum hose.
    e. Fuel pressure regulator.
    f. Electronic vacuum regulator.
    g. PCV hose.
6. Remove wiring retainer bracket and ignition wires and position aside.
7. Remove upper intake manifold and spacer.
8. Reverse procedure to install, noting the following:
    a. **Torque** intake spacer in numbered sequence, **Fig. 3,** to 89 inch lbs.
    b. **Torque** upper intake manifold bolts in numbered sequence, **Fig. 4,** to 89 inch lbs.

Lower

1. Remove upper intake manifold as outlined in "Intake Manifold, Replace."
2. Relieve fuel system pressure as outlined under "Precautions."
3. Drain cooling system into suitable container, then disconnect upper radiator hose from thermostat housing, then coolant bypass hose from manifold.
4. Remove heater outlet hose.
5. Remove water bypass hose from lower intake manifold.
6. Remove wiring connectors for coolant temperature sending unit, engine coolant temperature sensor, and vacuum controls.
7. Disconnect vacuum control.
8. Remove fuel injectors and fuel supply manifold.
9. Disconnect valve assembly linkage from intake manifold runner control lever using suitable screwdriver.
10. Remove EGR valve and adapter.
11. Remove lower manifold attaching bolts and lower manifold. **It may be required to pry on front of lower manifold to break the seal. Ensure care is taken not to damage sealing surfaces.**
12. Reverse procedure to install, noting the following:
    a. Use only new intake gaskets and seals, use a suitable sealer on intake gaskets.
    b. Apply a ⅛ inch bead of silicone at each corner where cylinder head meets the block.
    c. Tighten manifold bolts in sequence to specifications, **Fig. 5.**
    d. Bleed cooling system as outlined under "Cooling System Bleed."

EXHAUST MANIFOLD

REPLACE

Lefthand Side

1. Remove oil dipstick tube support bracket, then disconnect spark plug wires.
2. Remove EGR tube.
3. Raise and support vehicle, then remove exhaust pipe to manifold attaching nuts, then lower vehicle.
4. Remove exhaust manifold attaching bolts, then the manifold.
5. Reverse procedure to install, noting the following:
    a. Lightly lubricate bolts and nuts with oil.
    b. Tighten all attaching bolts to specification.

Righthand Side

1. Remove cowl top vent panel.
2. Remove air cleaner assembly and outlet tube.
3. Disconnect spark plug wires.
4. Remove spark plugs.
5. Remove transmission dipstick tube and the thermactor downstream air tube as required.
6. Raise and support vehicle.
7. Remove exhaust pipe to manifold attaching nuts, then lower vehicle.
8. Remove exhaust manifold attaching bolts, then the manifold.
9. Reverse procedure to install, noting the following:
    a. Lightly lubricate bolts and nuts with oil.
    b. Tighten all attaching bolts to specifications.

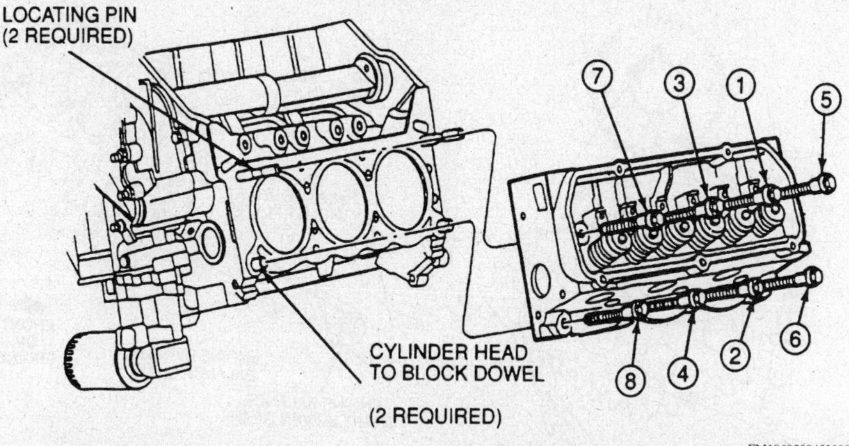

Fig. 6 Cylinder head bolt loosening & tightening sequence

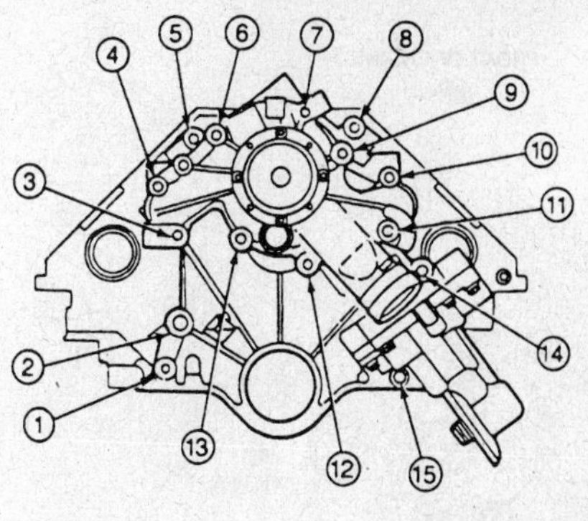

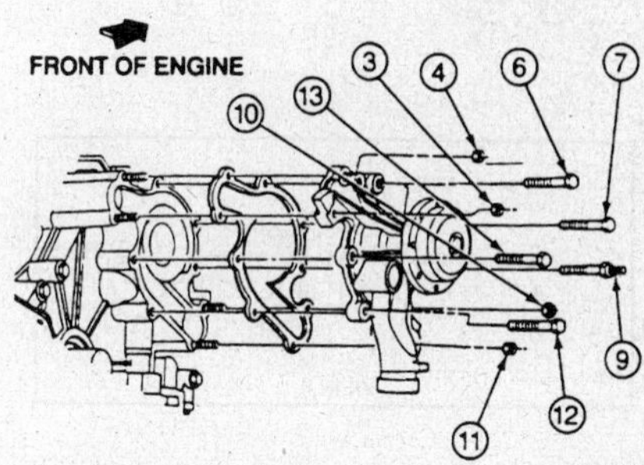

Fig. 7 Front cover torque sequence

CYLINDER HEAD

REPLACE

1. Remove intake manifold(s) as outlined under "Intake Manifold, Replace."
2. Remove exhaust manifold(s) as outlined under "Exhaust Manifold, Replace."
3. Remove valve cover(s) as outlined under "Valve Cover, Replace."
4. Remove drive belt.
5. When removing lefthand cylinder head, proceed as follows:
   a. Remove power steering pump and position aside, then remove oil fill cap.
   b. Remove alternator and bracket.
   c. Remove A/C compressor bracket mounting bolts. Leave hoses connected and position compressor aside.
6. When removing righthand cylinder head, proceed as follows:
   a. Remove drive belt tensioner.
   b. Remove PCV valve.
   c. Remove power steering line bracket, then the tensioner bracket and ignition coil.
7. Loosen rocker arm fulcrum attaching bolts enough to rotate rocker arm so pushrod can be removed. **Keep pushrods in order so they can be installed in original position.**
8. Loosen cylinder head bolts in multiple steps, in sequence, **Fig. 6,** then remove and discard cylinder head attaching bolts.
9. Remove cylinder head.
10. Reverse procedure to install, noting the following:
    a. Ensure proper location of gasket and head on locating dowels, always use new cylinder head bolts.
    b. Lightly oil all bolts except short cylinder head bolts.
    c. Apply suitable sealer to short cylinder head bolts.
    d. Tighten
    e. **Torque** bolts in sequence, **Fig. 6,** in three steps:
    f. Step 1: **Torque** bolts to 15 ft. lbs.
    g. Step 2: **Torque** bolts to 29 ft. lbs.
    h. Step 3: **Torque** bolts to 37 ft. lbs.
    i. Then, loosening only one bolt at a time, in sequence, **Fig. 6,** back each bolt off 2–3 turns.
    j. **Torque** long bolts to 33 ft. lbs., then an additional 180°. **Torque** short bolts to 18 ft. lbs., then an additional 180°.
    k. Tighten valve cover bolts to specifications.
    l. Bleed cooling system as outlined under "Cooling System Bleed."
    m. Seat each rocker arm fulcrum attaching bolt individually by first rotating crankshaft so that the matching lifter is on the base circle of the cam, then **torque** to 44 inch lbs. After all fulcrum bolts have been seated, **torque** all fulcrum bolts to 24 ft. lbs.

VALVE COVER

REPLACE

1. Disconnect spark plug wires from spark plugs and position aside, note location of ignition wire separators for assembly.
2. Remove upper intake manifold as outlined under "Intake Manifold, Replace."
3. If lefthand valve cover is to be removed proceed as follows:
   a. Remove the oil filler cap.
   b. Remove crankcase ventilation hose.
   c. Remove alternator harness at valve cover studs.
4. If righthand valve cover is to be removed proceed as follows:
   a. Remove the top cowl vent panel.
   b. Position air cleaner aside.
   c. Remove engine control wiring holder and cover.
   d. Remove PCV valve.
   e. Engine vacuum regulator.
5. Remove valve cover, note location of bolts and studs for assembly.
6. Reverse procedure to install.

VALVE ARRANGEMENT

Front To Rear

Righthand Side ....E-I-I-E-I-E
Lefthand Side ....E-I-E-I-I-E

CAMSHAFT LOBE LIFT SPECIFICATIONS

Exhaust ....**.259 inch**
Intake ....**.245 inch**

VALVE CLEARANCE SPECIFICATIONS

If any valve train component is replaced or if valve train components become intermixed, valve clearance will have to be inspected.

1. Apply pressure to the push rod side of the rocker arm until hydraulic lifter has bled down and bottomed out using a suitable pry bar.
2. Ensure clearance between valve stem and rocker arm is .085 and .185 inch.

VALVE ADJUSTMENT

This engine is equipped with hydraulic lifters. No adjustments are required.

HYDRAULIC LIFTERS

REPLACE

Before replacing hydraulic valve lifters for noisy operation, ensure the noise is not caused by improper rocker arm to stem clearance, worn rocker arms, pushrods or valve tips.

1. Disconnect spark plug wires from spark plugs and position aside.
2. Remove intake manifolds as outlined under "Intake Manifold, Replace."
3. Remove valve covers as outlined under "Valve Cover, Replace."
4. Loosen rocker arm fulcrum attaching bolts enough so rocker arm can be lifted off pushrod and rotated aside.

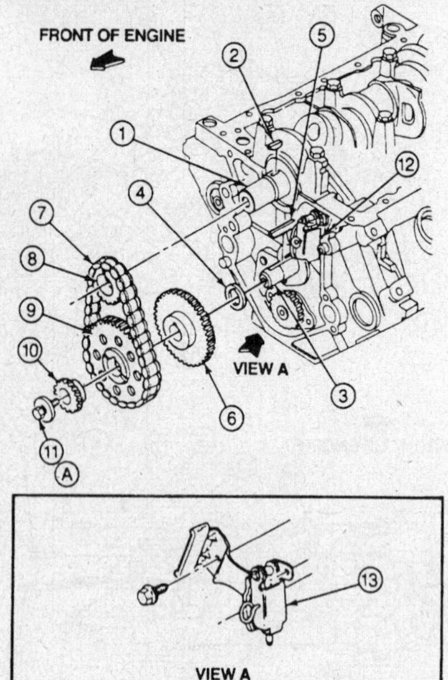

Item	Description
1	Crankshaft
2	Crankshaft Key
3	Camshaft
4	Camshaft Sprocket Spacer
5	Camshaft Sprocket Key
6	Engine Balance Shaft Drive Gear
7	Timing Chain
8	Crankshaft Sprocket
9	Camshaft Sprocket
10	Camshaft Position Sensor Drive Gear
11	Camshaft Sprocket Bolt
12	Timing Chain Vibration Damper
13	Timing Chain Vibration Damper
A	Tighten to 40-50 N·m (29.5-37 Ft-Lb)

FM1069500454000X

Fig. 8 Timing chain component location

5. Remove pushrods, tappet guide plates and retainers, then the lifters. Keep lifters and pushrods in order, so they can be installed in their original position.
6. Reverse procedure to install, noting the following:
   a. Lubricate lifters, pushrods and rocker arms with suitable lubricant.
   b. Tighten rocker arm fulcrum bolts as outlined under "Cylinder Head, Replace." **Prior to torquing bolts, ensure pushrods and rocker arms are fully seated.**

FRONT COVER

REPLACE

1. Remove engine as outlined under "Engine, Replace."
2. Remove drive belt, then the water pump pulley.
3. Disconnect heater hose outlet tube from water pump.

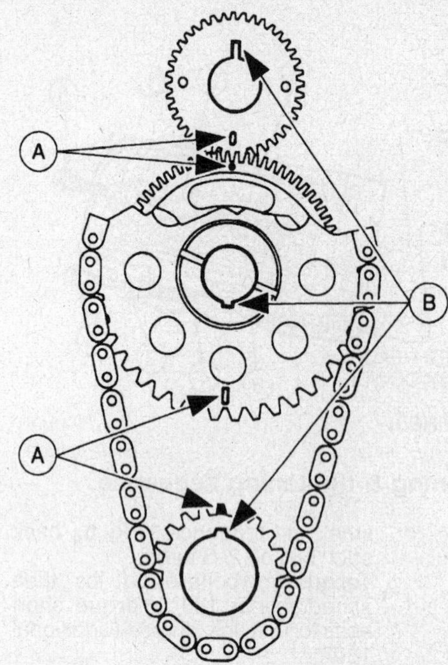

A. Crankshaft To Camshaft Timing Mark Alignment
B. Crankshaft, Camshaft & Balance Shaft Keyway Alignment

FM1139700479000X

Fig. 9 Timing mark alignment

4. Disconnect wire from CPS.
5. Disconnect lower radiator hose outlet tube from water pump.
6. Remove crankshaft pulley and damper using puller tool Nos. T58P-6316-D and adapter T82L-6316-B, or equivalents.
7. Remove oil filter.
8. Remove oil pan as outlined under "Oil Pan, Replace."
9. Remove front cover attaching bolts, **Fig. 7.** It is not required to remove water pump bolts to remove front cover.
10. Remove front cover and water pump as an assembly.
11. Separate water pump from front cover.
12. Reverse procedure to install, noting the following:
    a. Tighten front cover and water pump bolts in sequence, **Fig.7.** to specifications. Use suitable Loctite on bolt closest to oil filter flange.
    b. Always replace front seal when reusing front cover.
    c. Use a suitable silicone sealer on crankshaft key and keyway.

TIMING CHAIN

REPLACE

1. Remove front engine cover as outlined under "Front Cover, Replace."
2. Remove camshaft bolt and washer from end of camshaft.
3. Remove camshaft position sensor drive gear, camshaft sprocket, crankshaft sprocket and timing chain, **Fig. 8.**
4. Pry back ratchet mechanism, then install pin, **Fig. 8,** to relive tension on timing chain tensioner and remove tensioner.

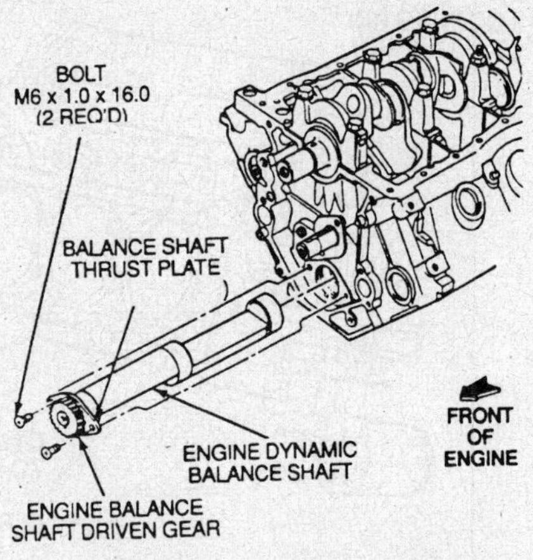

FM1069500456000X

Fig. 10 Balance shaft components

5. Reverse procedure to install, noting the following:
   a. Ensure balance shaft timing is correct as outlined under "Balance Shaft, Replace."
   b. Do not replace camshaft bolt with a standard bolt.
   c. Align timing chain and sprockets by placing No. 1 cylinder at TDC and crankshaft keyway to 12 o'clock position. Ensure timing marks on sprockets are positioned as indicated, **Fig. 9.**

CAMSHAFT

REPLACE

1. Remove front cover and timing chain as outlined under "Timing Chain, Replace."
2. Remove lifters as outlined under "Hydraulic Lifters, Replace."
3. Remove camshaft thrust plate.
4. Remove camshaft from front of engine, ensure not to damage bearings or lobes.
5. Reverse procedure to install, noting the following:
   a. Lubricate cam lobes and bearings with suitable lubricant.
   b. Ensure balance shaft timing is correct as outlined under "Balance Shaft, Replace."

BALANCE SHAFT

REPLACE

1. Remove front cover and timing chain as outlined under "Timing Chain, Replace."
2. Remove balance shaft thrust plate, **Fig. 10,** then balance shaft from front of engine.
3. Reverse procedure to install, noting the following:
   a. Lubricate balance shaft bearing journals with suitable lubricant.
   b. Ensure balance shaft timing marks are aligned.

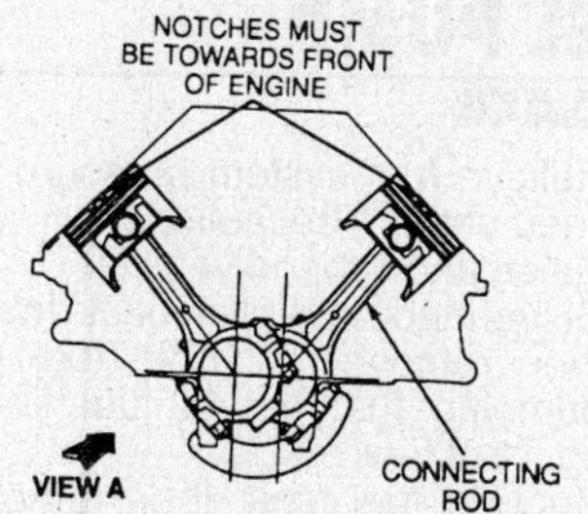

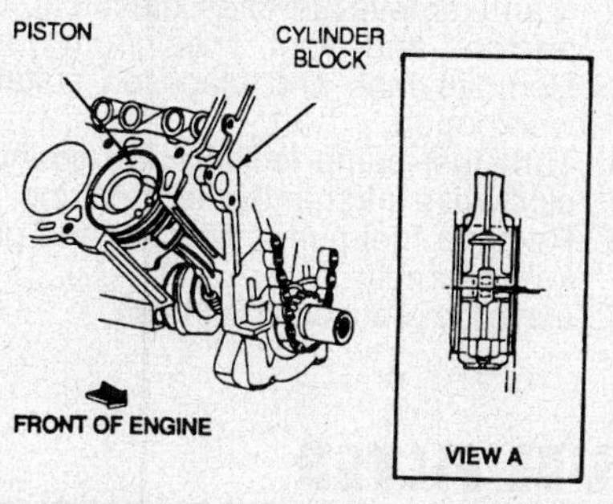

FM1069500457000X

Fig. 11 Piston alignment

PISTON & ROD ASSEMBLY

Assemble rod to piston with notch on piston dome on the same side as oil squirt hole on connecting rod. Assemble piston and rod assembly in engine with notch facing front of engine, **Fig. 11**.

CRANKSHAFT REAR OIL SEAL

REPLACE

1. Remove transaxle as outlined in **MOTOR's "Domestic Transmission, In-Vehicle Service" or "Transmission Service DVD."**
2. Remove flywheel and rear cover plate.
3. Punch hole in seal metal between seal lip and cylinder block. Using suitable slide hammer remove seal.
4. Coat crankshaft seal area and seal lip with engine oil, then install seal using seal installer tool No. T82L-6701-A, or equivalent.
5. Install rear cover plate, then the flywheel and transaxle.

OIL PAN

REPLACE

1. Relieve fuel system pressure as outlined under "Precautions."
2. Raise and support vehicle.
3. Drain crankcase into suitable container, then remove oil filter.
4. Remove dual converter Y pipe assembly using exhaust connector holder tool No. T94TY-6000-AH, or equivalent.
5. Remove starter motor, then torque converter housing cover.
6. Remove oil pan attaching bolts, then the oil pan.

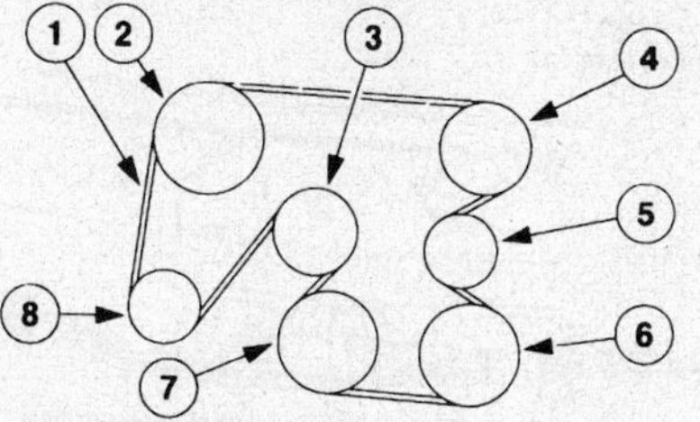

Item	Description
1	Drive belt
2	Power steering pump pulley
3	Water pump pulley
4	Generator pulley
5	Idler pulley
6	A/C clutch pulley
7	Crankshaft vibration damper pulley
8	Drive belt tensioner

FM1130000487000B

Fig. 12 Serpentine drive belt routing

7. Reverse procedure to install, noting the following:
   a. Use a suitable silicone sealant on clean dry surfaces, apply sufficient sealer to gaps where front cover and rear main housings meet block and pan to ensure an oil tight seal.
   b. Trial fit oil pan to ensure sufficient clearance exists to allow installation of oil pan without smearing or scraping off sealant.

OIL PUMP

REPLACE

1. Remove bolts holding oil pump and filter assembly to front engine cover, remove oil filter if required.
2. Disengage pump from front engine cover and pump drive shaft.
3. Reverse procedure to install, noting the following:
   a. Ensure proper engagement of oil pump drive shaft into pump.
   b. **Torque** four large oil pump to front cover bolts to 17–23 ft. lbs.
   c. **Torque** two smaller bolts to 72–96 inch lbs.

OIL PUMP SERVICE

1. Wash all components in suitable solvent, then dry with compressed air.
2. Ensure all dirt and particles are removed.
3. Inspect inner pump housing for wear or damage.
4. Inspect pump cover mating surface for wear, scuff marks are normal, if surface is worn or grooved, replace pump assembly.
5. Inspect rotor for nicks, burrs or score marks, remove imperfections with suitable oil stone.

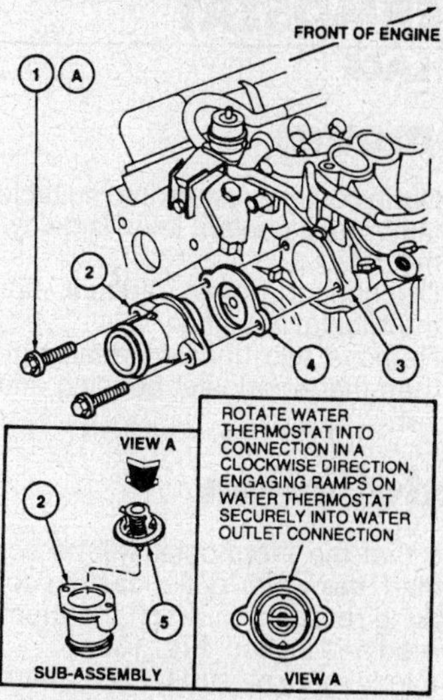

Item	Description
1	Bolt (2 Required)
2	Water Outlet Connection
3	Lower Intake Manifold
4	Water Outlet Connection Gasket
5	Water Thermostat
A	Tighten to 20-30 N-m (15-22 Ft-Lb)

FM1089500099000X

Fig. 13 Thermostat installation

BELT TENSION DATA

Belt tension is automatically maintained on this engine by an automatic tensioner. Therefore, no adjustment is required.

SERPENTINE DRIVE BELT

Belt Routing

Refer to **Fig. 12** for serpentine drive belt routing.

Belt Replacement

1. Rotate tensioner clockwise, then remove belt.
2. Reverse procedure to install.

COOLING SYSTEM BLEED

1. Slowly fill cooling system, allowing air to escape. Wait until coolant level has not dropped for at least five minutes, then install radiator cap to first notch.
2. Start and run engine until upper radiator hose is warm, indicating thermostat has opened, stop engine.
3. Carefully remove radiator cap, then slowly fill cooling system allowing air to escape. Wait until coolant level has not dropped for at least five minuets, then install radiator cap.
4. Fill coolant recovery bottle to Full Cold mark, then run engine until completely warmed up and top up coolant bottle to Full Warm mark.

THERMOSTAT

REPLACE

Removal

1. Drain cooling system into suitable container until coolant level is below thermostat.
2. Disconnect upper radiator hose at thermostat housing.
3. Remove two housing retaining bolts, then the thermostat housing and gasket.

Installation

So that the thermostat will be correctly installed, the water outlet casting contains a locking recess into which the thermostat is turned and locked, **Fig. 13.**

1. Clean gasket surface on thermostat housing and intake manifold, then position the thermostat in the housing, with the bridge section in the outlet casting.
2. Turn the thermostat clockwise to lock it in position.
3. Position new gasket and thermostat housing on the manifold, then install two retaining bolts.
4. Connect upper hose to housing, then fill cooling system with recommended coolant.
5. Start engine and inspect for leaks.

WATER PUMP

REPLACE

1. Drain cooling system into suitable container.
2. Remove drive belt as outlined under "Serpentine Drive Belt."
3. Raise and support vehicle, then remove lower radiator hose and hose tube from water pump.
4. Remove lower nuts from front and rear righthand motor mounts, then lower vehicle.
5. Remove alternator.
6. Disconnect power steering pressure line from pump using line disconnect tool set tool No. T90T-9550-S, or equivalent, then remove reservoir cap.
7. Disconnect water bypass and oil cooler hoses from heater outlet tube, then remove heater outlet tube from water pump.
8. Attach suitable lifting eye to front exhaust manifold, then using suitable lifting equipment raise front of engine approximately two inches.
9. Remove water pump pulley bolts and pulley.
10. Remove drive belt tensioner and pulley from power steering bracket.
11. Remove power steering pump bracket attaching bolts, then position bracket and pump aside.
12. Remove water pump attaching bolts, then the pump, **Fig. 7.**

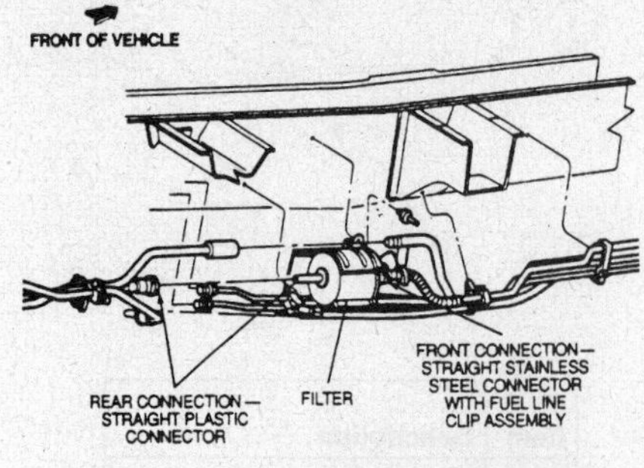

Fig. 14 Fuel filter location

13. Reverse procedure to install, noting the following:
    a. Use a suitable gasket adhesive to hold water pump gasket in place during assembly.
    b. **Coat threads of No. 1 water pump bolt with suitable sealer.**
    c. Tighten water pump bolts to specifications in sequence, **Fig. 7.**

RADIATOR

REPLACE

1. Drain cooling system into suitable container.
2. Remove fasteners holding grill panel to upper center reinforcement and fascia, then remove grill panel.
3. Remove righthand and lefthand headlamp and cornering lamp assemblies.
4. Disconnect and remove grill panel brackets from lower and upper center radiator supports.
5. Remove and position aside hood latch support brace from lower and upper center radiator supports.
6. Remove harness cover from upper center radiator support reinforcement.
7. Disconnect underhood lamp from upper center radiator support reinforcement.
8. Disconnect harness from cooling fan and shroud, then position aside from radiator and A/C condenser.
9. Disconnect and remove upper center reinforcement from radiator support.
10. Disconnect upper, lower and overflow hoses from radiator.
11. Disconnect oil cooler lines from radiator using line disconnect tool No. T86P-77265-AH, or equivalent. To prevent damage to O-ring seals, do not turn fittings in radiator.
12. Remove bolts and separate A/C condenser from radiator.
13. Lift radiator, shroud and cooling fan from vehicle as an assembly.
14. Separate cooling fan and shroud from radiator.
15. Reverse procedure to install, noting the following:
    a. Align stripe on hose with alignment rib on water outlets to prevent hose twisting.
    b. Bleed cooling system as outlined under "Cooling System Bleed."

FUEL PUMP

REPLACE

1. Relieve fuel system pressure as outlined under "Precautions."
2. Raise and support vehicle.
3. Disconnect fuel filler neck from tank, then remove fuel from fuel tank by pumping fuel out of fuel filler neck spout of tank.
4. Support fuel tank, then remove tank support straps. Lower fuel tank partially and remove fuel lines, electrical connectors and vent lines from tank. Remove tank and place on suitable workbench.
5. Turn fuel pump locking ring counterclockwise and remove locking ring.
6. Remove fuel pump, bracket and gasket assembly.
7. Reverse procedure to install.

FUEL FILTER

REPLACE

In-Tank Filter

The in-tank plastic sock fuel filter is part of the electric fuel pump assembly and cannot be serviced separately.

Inline Filter

1. Relieve fuel system pressure as outlined under "Precautions."
2. Disconnect outlet fitting using fuel line disconnect tool No. T90T-9550-S, or equivalent.
3. Remove clip from tube and inlet fitting by pulling gently on triangular end.
4. Separate fitting and hose assembly from fuel filter.
5. Remove filter from bracket, **Fig. 14.**
6. Reverse procedure to install.

TECHNICAL SERVICE BULLETINS

Chirping Noise During Normal Engine Operation

Some vehicles equipped with a 3.8L engine, may exhibit a chirping noise from the engine. This condition may be caused by flanges on the power steering pump pulley interfering with the front end accessory drive belt.

To correct this condition, replace power steering pump pulley with a revised pulley. The revised power steering pump pulley should be pressed flush with the pump shaft, within .10 inch. It is not required to remove power steering hose.

TIGHTENING SPECIFICATIONS

Year	Component	Torque Ft. Lbs.
2002–03	A/C Compressor	18
	Alternator Bracket	18
	Balance Shaft Thrust Plate	108②
	Camshaft Sprocket To Camshaft	46
	Camshaft Thrust Plate	108②
	Connecting Rod Nut	26
	Crankshaft Pulley & Damper Assembly	118
	Cylinder Head Bolts	①
	Drive Belt Tensioner	19
	EGR Valve To Intake Manifold	18
	Engine To Transaxle Bolts	37
	Exhaust Manifold	18
	Exhaust Pipe To Manifold	35
	Flywheel To Crankshaft	59
	Front Cover To Cylinder Block	18
	Fuel Injection Supply Manifold	89②
	Lefthand Engine Mount & Support Assembly Upper Nut & Lower Bolt	66
	Lower Intake Manifold To Cylinder Head	③
	Main Bearing Cap	37⑤
	Oil Dipstick Tube Support Bracket	89②
	Oil Pan Drain Plug	19
	Oil Pan To Cylinder Block	89②
	Oil Pump To Front Cover	④
	Power Steering Pump	35
	Radiator Mounting Bolts	18
	Righthand Front Engine Mount Nut	66
	Righthand Rear Engine Mount Nut	66
	Rocker Arm Cover To Cylinder Head	89②
	Rocker Arm Fulcrum To Cylinder Head	①
	Spark Plug To Cylinder Head	11
	Subframe Mounting Bolts	66
	Thermostat Housing Bolt	108②
	Throttle Body Nut	89②
	Torque Convertor To Drive Plate	27
	Upper Engine Mount Nut	66
	Upper Intake Manifold To Lower Intake Manifold	89②
	Valve Cover Attaching Bolts	89②
	Valve Lifter Guide Plate Bolt	108②
	Water Pump to Front Cover	18
	Water Pump Pulley Bolt	96②
	Wheel Lug Nuts	100

①— Refer to "Cylinder Head, Replace" for tightening procedure.
②— Inch lbs.
③— Refer to "Intake Manifold, Replace" for tightening procedure.
④— Refer to "Oil Pump, Replace" for tightening procedure.
⑤— Rotate an additional 115 to 125°.

Rear Axle & Suspension

NOTE: On Air Bag Equipped Models, Refer To "Air Bag System Precautions" Located In The Front Of This Manual For System Disarming & Arming Procedures.

NOTE: Refer To "Computer Relearn Procedures" Located In The Front Of This Manual When Battery Power To The Computer Has Been Interrupted.

NOTE: On Rear Air Suspension Equipped Models, Turn Air Suspension Switch To "Off" Position Prior To Raising Vehicle.

INDEX

PRECAUTIONS

Air Bag Systems

Refer to "Air Bag System Precautions" in the front of this manual for system disarming and arming procedures.

Air Suspension Systems

Prior to raising vehicle, turn air suspension switch to "Off" position to prevent air suspension damage or vehicle from shifting on hoist.

REAR AXLE

REPLACE

1. Raise and support vehicle, then remove wheels and tires.
2. Remove rear brake drums, then the rear anti-lock brake sensors.
3. Disconnect rear brake lines.
4. Disconnect parking brake cable and conduits from parking brake levers.
5. Disconnect parking brake cable and conduits from parking brake cable bracket, then pull parking brake cables and conduits from backing plates.
6. Support rear axle assembly with suitable lifting device.
7. Remove track bar from axle mounting bracket.
8. Remove rear shock absorber lower bolts.
9. Slowly lower rear axle from vehicle.
10. Reverse procedure to install.

HUB & BEARING

REPLACE

1. Raise and support vehicle, then remove rear tires.
2. Remove brake drum.
3. Remove hub cap grease seal.
4. Remove and discard rear wheel hub retainer nut and washer.
5. Remove wheel hub from rear wheel spindle.
6. Reverse procedure to install, noting the following:
   a. Use a new retainer nut and washer assembly.
   b. Thoroughly clean grease from surrounding areas.
   c. **Torque** new nut and washer assembly to 221 ft. lbs.

WHEEL BEARING

ADJUST

The wheel bearing and hub assembly used on these models is a one piece assembly and is not adjustable.

REAR WHEEL SPINDLE

REPLACE

1. Remove hub as outlined under "Hub & Bearing, Replace."
2. Remove anti-lock brake sensor, if equipped.
3. Remove brake line from wheel cylinder and parking brake cable from backing plate on models equipped with drum brakes.
4. Remove parking brake cable from parking brake cable bracket on models equipped with disc brakes.
5. Remove four nuts holding spindle and backing plate to trailing arm.
6. Drive out four studs holding backing plate to spindle, then separate spindle from backing plate.
7. Reverse procedure to install.

SHOCK ABSORBER

REPLACE

1. Raise and support vehicle, then remove wheel and tire.
2. Place a suitable support under axle as close to shock as possible.
3. Lower vehicle or raise support to relieve tension on shock.
4. Remove upper and lower mounting bolts, then remove shock.
5. Reverse procedure to install.

COIL SPRING

REPLACE

1. Raise and support vehicle, then remove wheel and tire.
2. Place a suitable support under axle as close to spring as possible.
3. Lower vehicle or raise support to relieve tension on shock.
4. Remove either a upper or lower shock mounting bolt, then raise vehicle or lower axle to relieve tension on spring.
5. Remove spring and insulator pads.
6. Reverse procedure to install. Ensure proper position of upper and lower insulator pad.

TRACK ROD

REPLACE

1. Raise and support vehicle.
2. Disconnect track arm from rear axle.
3. Disconnect track arm from frame mount, then remove track rod from vehicle.
4. Reverse procedure to install.

TIGHTENING SPECIFICATIONS

Year	Component	Torque Ft. Lbs.
2002–03	Anti-Lock Brake Sensor Bolt	80①
	Brake Hose Bracket To Body	80①
	Jounce Bumper To Axle	18
	Shock To Axle	59
	Shock To Frame	59
	Spindle & Brake Backing Plate To Axle	52
	Track Bar Retaining Bolts	59
	Trailing Arm To Frame	98
	Wheel Hub Retainer And Washer Assembly	221
	Wheel Lug Nuts	100

① — Inch lbs.

Front Suspension & Steering

NOTE: On Air Bag Equipped Models, Refer To "Air Bag System Precautions" Located In The Front Of This Manual For System Disarming & Arming Procedures.

NOTE: Refer To "Computer Relearn Procedures" Located In The Front Of This Manual When Battery Power To The Computer Has Been Interrupted.

NOTE: On Rear Air Suspension Equipped Models, Turn Air Suspension Switch To "Off" Position Prior To Raising Vehicle.

INDEX

PRECAUTIONS

Air Bag Systems

Refer to "Air Bag System Precautions" in the front of this manual for system disarming and arming procedures.

Air Suspension Systems

Prior to raising vehicle, turn air suspension switch to "Off" position to prevent air suspension damage or vehicle from shifting on hoist.

Battery Ground Cable

Prior to service disconnect battery ground cable and isolate as required.

DESCRIPTION

This suspension is of the gas filled McPherson strut type, **Fig. 1.** The strut top mount consists of a rubber insulated bearing and seat and coil spring insulator. The top mount is attached to the body side apron by three bolts. The lower part of the strut is mounted in the steering knuckle and is retained by a pinch bolt. A forged lower control arm is attached to the subframe and to the steering knuckle. A tension strut is connected to the lower control arm and to the forward part of the subframe.

WHEEL BEARING

REPLACE

The wheel hub and bearing are serviced as an assembly and cannot be repaired separately.

1. Raise and support vehicle, then remove wheel and tire.
2. Remove and discard front axle retainer nut.
3. Remove front brake rotor as outlined under "Disc Brakes" chapter, then remove rotor shield.
4. Remove anti-lock brake sensor retaining bolt and sensor harness retaining bolt, then position sensor out of way.
5. Remove and discard tie-rod end cotter pin and castellated nut.
6. Remove tie rod from steering knuckle with suitable joint removal tool.
7. Remove and discard front stabilizer bar link nut and separate front stabilizer front shock absorber.
8. Remove and discard ball joint pinch bolt and nut.
9. Place a suitable pry bar between front subframe and front suspension lower arm, then push down until lower ball joint is free of front wheel knuckle.
10. Press front driveshaft from wheel hub with press tool No. 204-069, or equivalent.
11. From back of steering knuckle, remove three mounting bolts, then remove wheel hub from knuckle. Wheel hub is a slip fit design and should not require a puller to remove.
12. Reverse procedure to install, noting the following. Apply a small amount of suitable thread locking compound to last five front wheel driveshaft joint threads prior to installing wheel hub retainer nut.

BALL JOINT INSPECTION

1. Raise vehicle until wheels fall to a full down position.
2. Grasp lower edge of tire and move wheel assembly in and out.
3. As wheel is being moved, observe lower end of knuckle and lower control arm. Any movement would indicate abnormal ball joint wear.
4. If movement is observed, replace lower control arm assembly.

BALL JOINT

REPLACE

The ball joint must be replaced with the control arm as an assembly.

STRUT

REPLACE

1. Place ignition switch in Off position and ensure steering wheel is not locked.
2. Remove hub nut and loosen three strut attaching nuts, then raise and support vehicle. Do not raise vehicle with lower control arm.
3. Raise and support vehicle, then remove front tires.
4. Remove brake caliper and wire it aside.

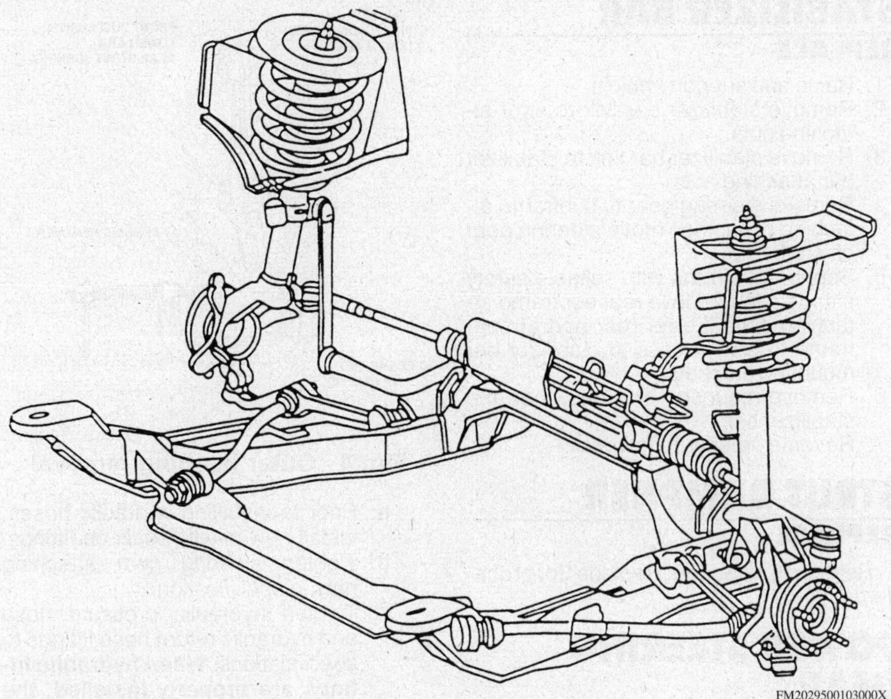

Fig. 1 Front suspension assembly

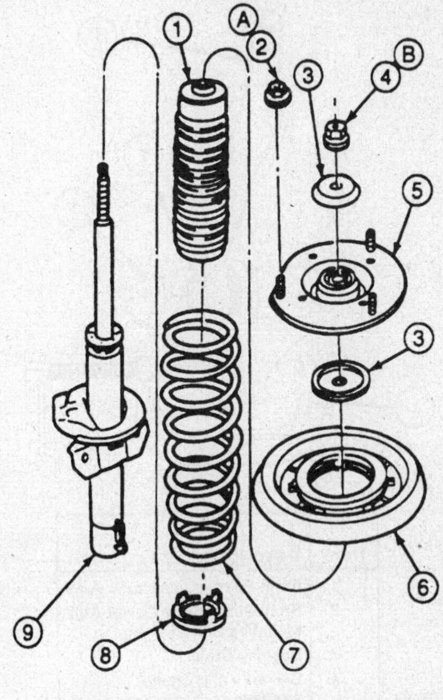

Item	Description
1	Dust Boot
2	Front Shock Absorber Mounting Bracket Nut (3 Req'd)
3	Washer
4	Front Shock Absorber Nut
5	Front Shock Absorber Mounting Bracket
6	Front Suspension Bearing and Seal
7	Front Coil Spring
8	Front Spring Insulator
9	Front Shock Absorber
A	Tighten to 35-40 N·m (25-30 Ft-Lb)
B	Tighten to 55-63 N·m (40-46 Ft-Lb)

FM2029500109000X

Fig. 2 Front strut components

5. Remove brake rotor and tie rod end.
6. Remove stabilizer bar link nut, then remove link from strut.
7. Remove lower control arm to steering knuckle pinch nut and bolt, then slightly spread joint and remove lower control arm.
8. Press axle from hub using hub remover/installer tool Nos. T81P-1104-A, T81P-1104-C, T83P-1104-BH, T86P-1104-A1, or equivalents. Wire axle shaft to body to maintain level position. **Do not allow axle shaft to move outward. Over extension of the constant velocity (CV) joint could result in separation of internal components, which could cause CV joint failure.**
9. Remove strut to steering knuckle pinch bolt, then spread joint slightly and remove steering knuckle and hub assembly.
10. Remove anti-lock brake wheel speed sensor, if equipped.
11. Remove strut attaching nuts, then remove strut assembly from vehicle.
12. Reverse procedure to install, noting the following:
    a. Tighten attaching nuts and bolts to specifications.
    b. With vehicle on ground, tighten hub nut to specification.
    c. Install new strut to knuckle bolt, control arm to knuckle bolt and nut, and tie rod nut.

COIL SPRING & STRUT SERVICE

1. Compress strut spring with coil spring compressor tool No. 014-00781, or equivalent.
2. Restrain strut shaft using a suitable 10 mm box wrench, then remove strut mounting nut with suitable 21 mm crow foot socket. Do not allow strut shaft to rotate.
3. Loosen compressor tool, then remove strut top mount bracket assembly, bearing and seat assembly and spring, **Fig. 2.**
4. Reverse procedure to install.

CONTROL ARM

REPLACE

1. Place ignition switch in Off position and ensure steering wheel is not locked.
2. Raise and support vehicle.
3. Remove wheel and tire assembly.
4. Remove tension strut nut, then the dished washer.
5. Remove lower control arm to steering knuckle pinch nut and bolt, then slightly spread joint and separate ball joint from steering knuckle. **Do not use a hammer to separate suspension pieces.**
6. Remove lower control arm inner pivot bolt and nut, then the control arm.
7. Reverse procedure to install noting the following:
    a. Install new lower arm nut, pinch bolt and nut, and lower arm to subframe bolt and nut.
    b. Tighten all nuts and bolts to specifications.

CONTROL ARM BUSHING

REPLACE

Inner

1. Remove control arm as outlined under "Control Arm, Replace."
2. Push bushing out of control arm using C frame tool No. T74P-3044-A1, cup tool No. T86P-5493-A3 and bushing remover tool No. T86P-5493-A5, or equivalents, **Fig. 3.**
3. Push bushing into control arm using C frame tool No. T74P-3044-A1 and bushing driver tool No. T86P-5493-A2, or equivalents.
4. Reverse procedure to install control arm, tighten bolts to specifications.

Outer

1. Remove control arm as outlined under "Control Arm, Replace."
2. Push bushing out of control arm using C frame tool No. T74P-3044-A1, bushing remover tool No. T86P-5493-A5, and cup tool No. T86P-5493-A3, or equivalents, **Fig. 4.**
3. Push bushing into control arm using C frame tool No. T74P-3044-A1, guide sleeve tool No. T86P-5493-A3 and bushing driver tool No. T86P-5493-A2,

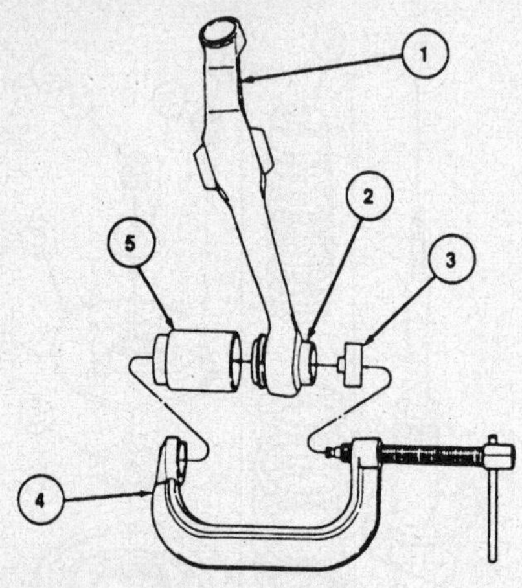

Item	Description
1	Front Suspension Lower Arm
2	Front Suspension Lower Arm Mounting Bolt Bushing
3	Bushing Driver
4	C-Frame and Clamp Assembly
5	Receiver Cup

FM2029500110000X

Fig. 3 Inner bushing removal

or equivalents.

4. Reverse procedure to install.

STEERING KNUCKLE

REPLACE

1. Place ignition switch in Off position and ensure steering wheel is not locked.
2. Remove hub nut and loosen three strut attaching nuts, then raise and support vehicle. Do not raise vehicle with lower control arm.
3. Raise and support vehicle.
4. Remove wheel and tire assembly.
5. Remove brake caliper and wire it aside.
6. Remove brake rotor and tie rod end from knuckle.
7. Remove stabilizer bar link nut, then remove link from strut.
8. Remove lower control arm to steering knuckle pinch nut and bolt, then slightly spread joint and remove lower control arm from knuckle.
9. Press axle from hub using hub remover/installer tool Nos. T81P-1104-A, T81P-1104-C, T83P-1104-BH, T86P-1104-A1, or equivalents. Wire axle shaft to body to maintain level position. **Do not allow axle shaft to move outward. Over extension of the constant velocity (CV) joint could result in separation of internal components, which could cause CV joint failure.**
10. Remove rotor splash shield and anti-lock brake sensor, if equipped.
11. Remove strut to steering knuckle pinch bolt, then spread joint slightly and remove steering knuckle and hub assembly.
12. Reverse procedure to install.

STABILIZER BAR

REPLACE

1. Raise and support vehicle.
2. Remove stabilizer bar link to strut attaching nuts.
3. Remove stabilizer bar link to stabilizer bar attaching nuts.
4. Remove steering gear to subframe attaching bolts, then move steering gear off subframe.
5. Support subframe with suitable safety stands, then remove rear subframe attaching bolts. Lower rear part of subframe to gain access to stabilizer bar mounting brackets.
6. Remove mounting brackets, then the stabilizer bar.
7. Reverse procedure to install.

STRUT DAMPNER

REPLACE

Refer to "Coil Spring, Replace" for procedures.

POWER STEERING GEAR

REPLACE

1. Remove steering shaft weather boot to dash panel attaching bolts.
2. Remove intermediate shaft to steering column shaft attaching bolts.
3. Move weather boot aside, then remove steering gear input shaft pinch bolt and remove intermediate shaft.
4. Raise and support vehicle.
5. Vehicle must be supported so that rear of subframe may be safely lowered.
6. Remove front wheels.
7. Remove tie rod ends from steering knuckles.
8. Remove front stabilizer bar.
9. Remove nuts from steering gear mounting bolts. **The gear mounting bolts are pressed into the steering gear housing and should not be removed during normal service procedures.**
10. With vehicle properly supported, place a suitable lifting device under subframe, so placed as to allow lowering of rear of subframe.
11. Place a suitable support on exhaust flex pipe to prevent over-flexing, then disconnect flex pipe at dual converter Y pipe.
12. Remove rear subframe mounting bolts, then lower subframe approximately four inches.
13. Remove heat shield band and fold down heat shield, then place a suitable drain pan under steering gear.
14. Lift steering gear out of mounting holes. Rotate gear as required. Carefully work gear to lefthand to allow removal pressure and return lines from gear and allow to drain into pan.
15. Remove steering gear from lefthand fender well of vehicle.
16. Reverse procedure to install, noting the following:

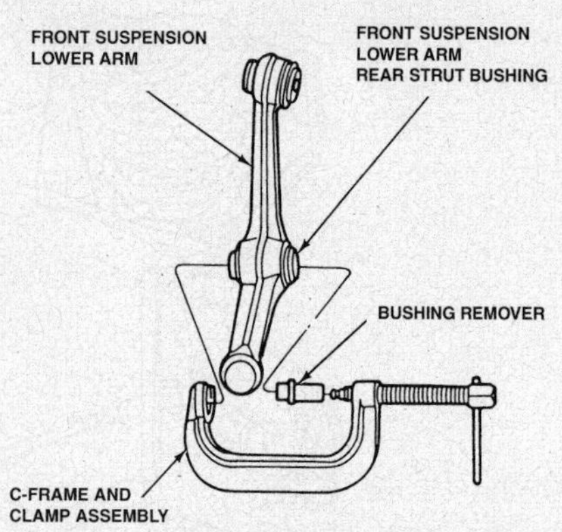

Fig. 4 Outer bushing removal

a. Prior to installing hydraulic hoses, install new plastic seals on fittings.
b. Tighten steering gear attaching nuts to specification.
c. Tighten hydraulic pressure hose and hydraulic return hose fittings to specifications. **When hydraulic fittings are properly installed, the hoses are free to swivel.**
d. Fill power steering system with specified lubricant and inspect for leaks.
e. Set toe-in to specifications.

POWER STEERING PUMP

REPLACE

1. Remove drive belt as outlined under "Serpentine Drive Belt."
2. Remove alternator, if required.
3. Raise and support vehicle, then remove righthand front wheel.
4. Remove power steering pulley using puller tool No. T69L-103000-B, or equivalent.
5. Position a drain pan, then remove both hoses from power steering pump.
6. Remove four pump mounting bolt (three front, one rear) and remove pump from vehicle.
7. Reverse procedure to install, noting the following:
   a. Prior to installing hydraulic hoses, install new plastic seals on fittings.
   b. Tighten steering pump attaching nuts to specification.
   c. Install power steering pulley using installer tool No. T65P-3A733-C, or equivalent.
   d. Tighten hydraulic pressure hose and hydraulic return hose fittings to specifications. **When hydraulic fittings are properly installed, the hoses are free to swivel.**
   e. Fill power steering system with specified lubricant and inspect for leaks.

TIGHTENING SPECIFICATIONS

Year	Component	Torque Ft. Lbs.
2002–03	Ball Joint Pinch Bolt	46
	Bearing Mounting Bolts	85
	Boot To Firewall Nut	44①
	Control Arm To Subframe	98
	Front Axle Nut	185
	Front Caliper Mounting Bolt	85
	Front Strut Upper Mounting	26
	Front Suspension Tension Strut	85
	Intermediate Shaft To Column Pinch Bolt	30
	Intermediate Shaft To Gear Pinch Bolt	30
	Power Steering Line Fittings	30
	Power Steering Pump Mounting Bolts	18
	Pressure Line At Gear Fitting	30
	Pressure Line At Pump Fitting	30
	Pump Reservoir Fittings	30
	Return Line At Gear, Fitting	30
	Stabilizer Bar Link	76
	Steering Gear To Crossmember Nut	98
	Strut Center Nut	43
	Strut To Hub Pinch Bolt	85
	Tie Rod End Nut	41
	Wheel Lug Nuts	95

① — Inch lbs.

Wheel Alignment

INDEX

PRELIMINARY INSPECTION

Prior to performing the front wheel alignment, a preliminary inspection should be made to determine the condition of the vehicle's suspension components. The following inspections and procedures should be made prior to performing front wheel alignment.

Do not attempt to adjust alignment by heating or bending suspension or steering components.

1. Vehicle must be level.
2. Inflate tires to specified pressure (cold).
3. Inspect vehicle ride height.
4. Inspect all suspension and steering components for looseness.
5. Inspect existing caster, camber, and toe settings prior to alignment.
6. Inspect all suspension fasteners for proper torque.
7. Alignment equipment must be capable of four wheel alignment.
8. Alignment rack must be leveled to 1/16 of an inch, side to side and front to rear and be equipped with wheel runout compensation.

FRONT WHEEL ALIGNMENT

Caster & Camber

1. Prior to aligning the front end, the subframe alignment must be inspected using the following procedure.
   a. Loosen subframe to body attaching bolts.
   b. Shift subframe if possible in the direction required to bring vehicle into alignment.

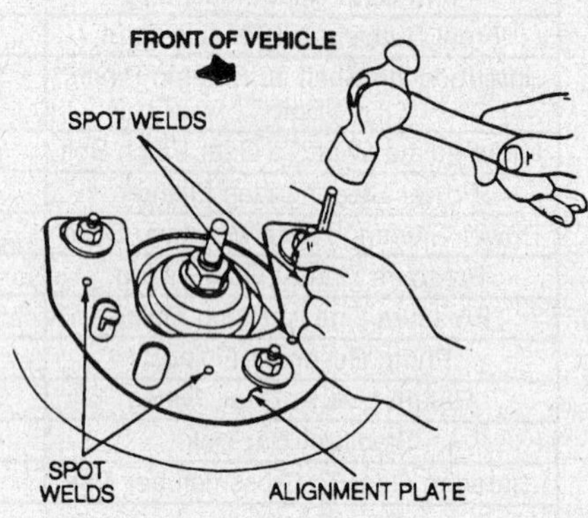

Fig. 1 Alignment plate loosening

   c. Tighten subframe attaching bolts to specifications.
   d. Inspect front alignment, if further adjustment is required use the following procedures.
2. Center punch spot welds on both strut alignment plates, then loosen strut attaching nuts, **Fig. 1.**
3. Remove spot welds using Rotunda Spot-Eze or equivalent. **Do not drill deeper than thickness of alignment plates.**
4. Remove strut attaching nuts, then the alignment plates.
5. Remove burrs from strut towers and alignment plates, then paint all exposed metal on strut towers and alignment plates.
6. Install alignment plates, then loosely install strut attaching nuts.
7. Align front end, then **torque** strut attaching nuts to 26–30 ft. lbs.
8. Drill three 1/8 inch holes as indicated in **Fig. 2,** through alignment plates and strut towers, then paint exposed metal. **Do not drill deeper than 3/8 inch into strut tower.**

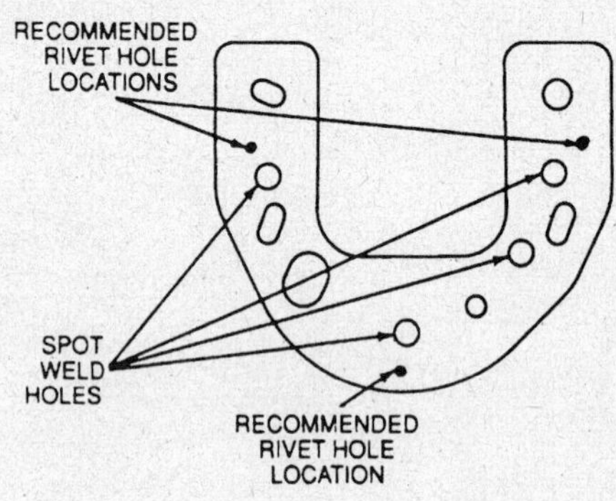

Fig. 2 Rivet hole location

9. Install three 1/8 inch diameter pop rivets with a grip range of 1/4 inch into alignment plate/strut tower.

Toe-In

To adjust toe-in, lock steering wheel in straight ahead position using suitable steering wheel holder. Loosen and slide off small outer clamps from steering boot to prevent boot from twisting during adjustment procedure. Loosen tie rod adjusting, then adjust lefthand and righthand tie rods until each wheel has 1/2 the desired total toe specification. Tighten tie rod adjusting nuts and install clamps. Remove steering wheel holding tool.

REAR WHEEL ALIGNMENT

The caster, camber and toe angles are factory set and cannot be adjusted. If rear wheel alignment is not to specifications, inspect suspension for faulty components.

AIR CONDITIONING

TABLE OF CONTENTS

System Testing

NOTE: On Air Bag Equipped Models, Refer To "Air Bag System Precautions" Located In The Front Of This Manual For System Disarming & Arming Procedures.

NOTE: Refer To "Computer Relearn Procedures" Located In The Front Of This Manual When Battery Power To The Computer Has Been Interrupted.

NOTE: Prior To Performing Any Service Operations Listed In This Section, Consult The "Technical Service Bulletins" In This Section For Related Information.

INDEX

PRECAUTIONS

Air Bag Systems

Refer to "Air Bag System Precautions" in the front of this manual for system disarming and arming procedures.

Battery Ground Cable

Prior to service disconnect battery ground cable and isolate as required.

System

R-134a is a hydro-fluorocarbon refrigerant that is non-corrosive, non-explosive, non-flammable, heavier than air and has a slight ether-like odor.

When recovered, R-134a must be recovered with an A/C recovery station designed specifically for R-134a. R134a is not compatible with R-12 or R-12 refrigerant oil. Liquid R-134a, at normal atmospheric pressures and temperatures, evaporates very rapidly and will freeze anything it contacts. Should any liquid refrigerant come in contact with skin or eyes, immediately flush eyes and/or skin with plenty of water for 15 minutes; call a doctor. Remove contaminated clothing and shoes.

Heat should not be applied to any part of the system as this could cause excessive A/C system pressure build-up. **To avoid a dangerous explosion, keep away from open flames, glowing metal surfaces, blow torch, steam cleaning and welding.** Ensure containers are never heated above 125°F.

When adding R-134a into refrigerant system, always keep tank in an upright position to prevent liquid R-134a from entering system and damaging compressor.

R-134a should not be mixed with air for leak testing or used with air above atmospheric pressure for any purpose. R-134a is combustible when mixed with high concentrations of air and higher pressures.

The A/C service port valves on R-134a systems are of the one-piece design. The top portion of the fitting is aluminum and is threaded into a steel body on the suction accumulator/drier or on the refrigerant line and sealed with an O-ring. Two special service tools have been developed to aid in servicing of the access gauge port valves. They are the high side A/C fitting socket tool No. D94L-19703-A, or equivalent, and low side A/C fitting socket tool No. D94L-19703-B, or equivalent. The high side fitting is the largest of the two valves. Both valves require special adapters to attach service equipment to the A/C system.

EXERCISE SYSTEM

When the air conditioner is not used regularly, particularly during cold months, it should be turned on for a few minutes once every two or three weeks while the engine is running to circulate the refrigerant in the A/C system.

PERFORMANCE TEST

Refrigerant system problems are diagnosed by inspecting refrigerant pressures and clutch cycle rate and times. Compare pressures and cycle time to charts outlined in **Fig. 1.** Conditional requirements for refrigerant systems tests must be satisfied to obtain accurate pressure readings. If findings do not fall between lines of respective charts, refer to **Fig. 2** to determine cause of improper readings.

After required repairs have been performed, take pressure readings while meeting conditional requirements to ensure problem has been corrected. Visual inspection of the system may determine some of the following problems: obstructed air passages, broken wires, loose or broken mounting brackets and refrigerant leaks. A refrigerant leak will usually appear as an oily residue at the leakage point in the system.

NORMAL CLUTCH CYCLE RATE PER MINUTE

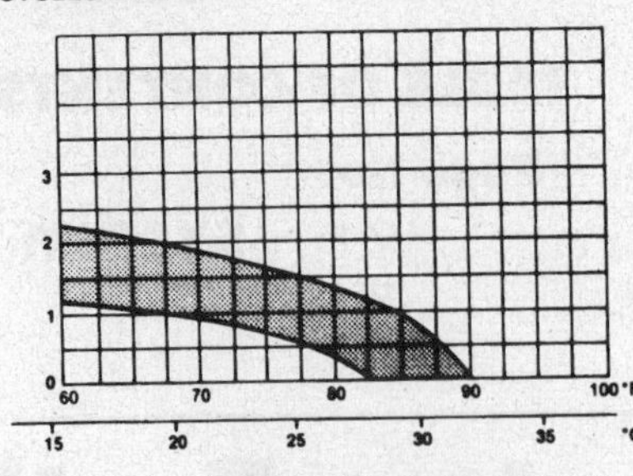

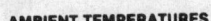

NORMAL CENTER REGISTER DISCHARGE TEMPERATURES

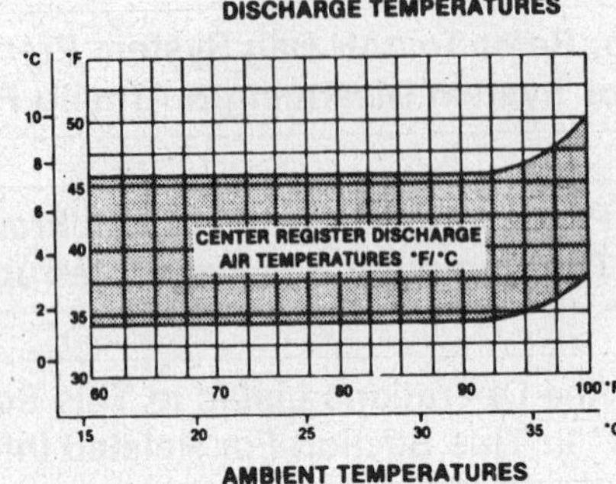

THESE CONDITIONAL REQUIREMENTS FOR THE FIXED ORIFICE TUBE CYCLING CLUTCH SYSTEM TESTS MUST BE SATISFIED TO OBTAIN ACCURATE PRESSURE READINGS.

- Stabilized in Car Temperatures @ 70°F to 80°F (21°C to 27°C)
- Maximum A/C (Recirculating Air)
- Maximum Blower Speed
- 1500 Engine RPM For 10 Minutes

NORMAL FIXED ORIFICE TUBE CYCLING CLUTCH REFRIGERANT SYSTEM PRESSURES

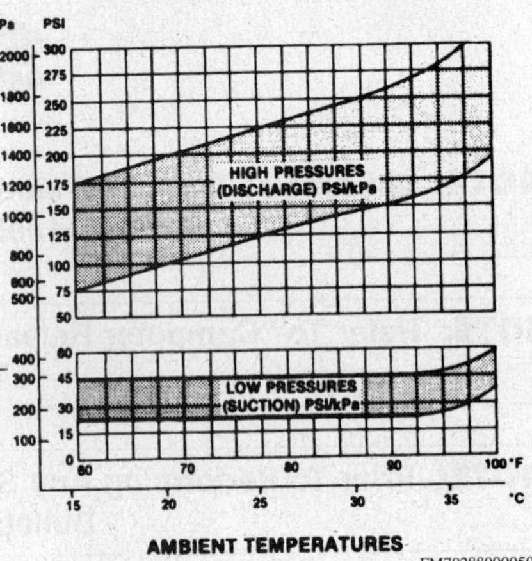

Fig. 1 Refrigerant system pressure & temperature charts (Part 1 of 2)

LEAK TEST

A/C Compressor

A/C COMPRESSOR MANIFOLD & TUBE LEAK TEST

1. **Torque** manifold bolt to 13–17 ft. lbs., then add refrigerant to system, if required.
2. Leak test manifold O-ring seals using Rotunda Halogen Leak Detector 023-R1003, or equivalent.
3. If no leaks are found, manifold O-ring seals are good.
4. If a leak is found at manifold and manifold bolt is **torque** to 13–17 ft. lbs., install new manifold O-ring seals, then repeat leak test.

EXTERNAL LEAK TEST

1. If compressor is on vehicle, discharge system, then remove compressor from vehicle.
2. Remove manifold bolt, then manifold from rear head of compressor. Install pressure test adapter on rear head of compressor using manifold bolt.
3. Connect high and low pressure lines of a R-134a manifold gauge set to corresponding fittings on pressure test adapter, then attach center hose of manifold gauge set to a suitable refrigerant container standing in an upright position.
4. Hand-rotate compressor shaft ten revolutions to distribute oil inside compressor.
5. Open low pressure gauge valve, then high pressure gauge valve and valve on refrigerant container to allow refrigerant vapor to flow into compressor.
6. Inspect for leaks at compressor shaft seal and compressor center seal using Rotunda R-134a Halogen Leak Detector 161–00010, or equivalent.
7. If a shaft seal leak is found, install a new shaft seal. If an external leak is found at center joint of compressor, install a new compressor assembly.
8. When leak test is completed, close manifold gauge valves (high and low) and valve on refrigerant container. Slowly remove gauge set hoses from pressure test fitting tool (allow refrigerant to escape from compressor).
9. Install compressor on vehicle, then leak test, evacuate and charge system.

DISCHARGING SYSTEM

System Flush

1. Discharge system as outlined in "Discharging System."
2. Disconnect refrigerant lines from heat exchanger(s) to be flushed.
3. Connect A/C flusher 219–00001 and A/C system flusher fitting kit 219–000020 or equivalents, to heat exchanger to be flushed. **Do not flush through A/C evaporator core orifice, mufflers or hoses. Internal plumbing and material make-up of these components make it impossible to correctly remove foreign or residual flushing solvent.**
4. Flush heat exchanger for a minimum of 15 minutes, using one gallon of flushing solvent part No. F4AZ-19570–A, or equivalent. Both solvent and filter are intended for one vehicle only.
5. Apply 90–125 psi pressurized air to component for a minimum of 30 minutes. Failure to remove all residual solvent can result in damage to system components.
6. Install a new A/C evaporator core orifice in any vehicle being serviced for compressor or desiccant failure.
7. Install new refrigerant hoses if clogged with foreign material, then connect heat exchanger being serviced.
8. Add refrigerant oil as required, refer to "A/C System Service."
9. Evacuate, leak test, and charge A/C system.
10. Inspect A/C system for normal operation.

SYSTEM EVACUATION

Vacuum Pump

Vacuum pumps suitable for removing air and moisture from A/C systems are commercially available. The pump should be capable of drawing the system down to 28–29½ inches Hg at sea level. For each 1000 foot increase in altitude, this specification should be decreased by 1 inch Hg. As an example, at 5000 feet elevation, only 23–24½ inches Hg can be obtained.

1. Connect suitable gauge manifold and discharge system as outlined previously. **System must be completely discharged prior to evacuation. If pressurized refrigerant is allowed to enter vacuum pump, the pump will be damaged.**
2. Connect hose from gauge manifold center port to vacuum pump inlet.
3. Fully open both gauge manifold hand valves.
4. Operate vacuum pump while observing low side compound gauge. If system does not "pump-down" to 28–29½

inches Hg (at sea level) within approximately five minutes, inspect connections and leak test system.

5. Continue to operate vacuum pump for 15–30 minutes, longer if system was open for an extended period of time, then close both manifold valves and stop pump.
6. Inspect ability of system to hold vacuum. Watch low side compound gauge and ensure reading does not rise at a rate faster than 1 inch Hg every four to five minutes.
7. If system fails to hold vacuum, inspect fittings and connections, and leak test system.
8. If system holds vacuum, charge system with refrigerant.

REFRIGERANT RECOVERY

The use of refrigerant recovery and recycling stations allows the recovery and reuse of refrigerant after contaminants and moisture have been removed.

When using a recovery or recycling station, follow the manufacturer's operating instructions, noting the following:

1. **Use extreme caution and observe all safety and service precautions related to use of refrigerants.**
2. Connect refrigerant recycling station hose(s) to vehicle A/C service port(s) and recovery station inlet fitting. Hoses used should have shutoff devices or check valves within 12 inches of hose ends to minimize introduction of air into recycling station.
3. Turn recycling station On to start recovery process. Allow recycling station to pump refrigerant from A/C system until station pressure gauge indicates vacuum.
4. After vehicle A/C system has been evacuated, close station inlet valve, if equipped.
5. Turn station Off. On some stations pump will automatically be turned Off by a low pressure switch.
6. Allow vehicle A/C system to remain closed for approximately two minutes. Observe vacuum level indicated on gauge. If pressure does not rise, disconnect recycling station hose(s).
7. If system pressure rises, repeat steps 3 through 6 until vacuum level remains stable for two minutes.
8. Service A/C system as required, then evacuate and recharge A/C system.

CHARGING SYSTEM

Refer to "Specifications" for refrigerant capacities.

1. Connect manifold gauge set or charging station. If low side service port is on receiver/drier, connect center hose to charging cylinder liquid port. If low side service port is on suction hose, connect center hose to charging cylinder GAS port.

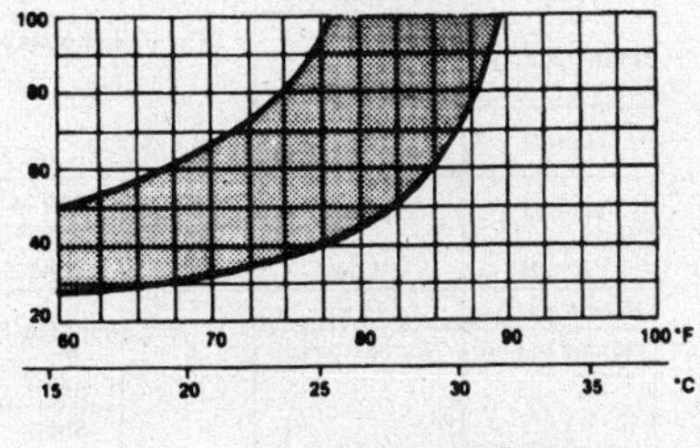

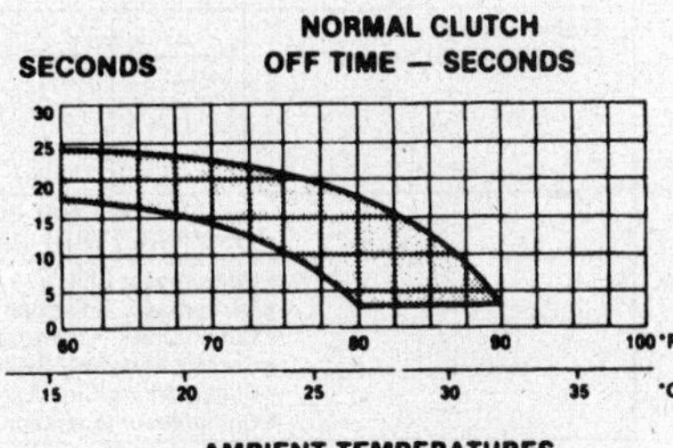

THESE CONDITIONAL REQUIREMENTS FOR THE FIXED ORIFICE TUBE CYCLING CLUTCH SYSTEM TESTS MUST BE SATISFIED TO OBTAIN ACCURATE CLUTCH CYCLE TIMING

- Stabilized In Car Temperatures @ 70°F to 80°F (21°C to 27°C)
- Maximum A/C (Recirculating Air)
- Maximum Blower Speed
- 1500 Engine RPM For 10 Minutes

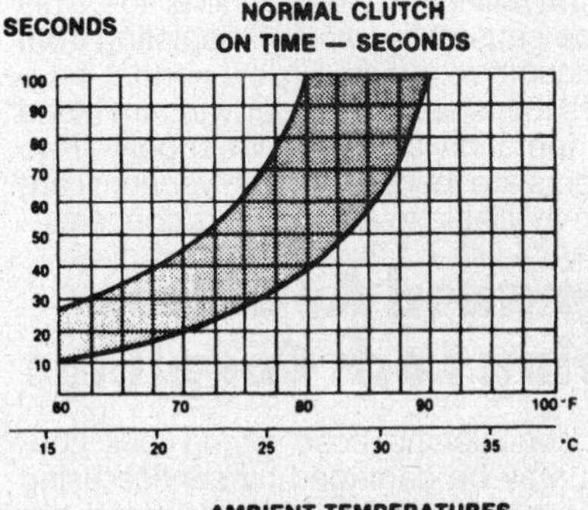

FM7028800005020X

Fig. 1 Refrigerant system pressure & temperature charts (Part 2 of 2)

2. Evacuate system using vacuum pump with second center hose connected to charging cylinder and open to gauge set. When system evacuated, close center valve and turn off pump.
3. Disconnect wire harness connector at clutch cycling pressure switch, if equipped. Install jumper wire across terminals of connector.
4. Open manifold gauge set low side valve and allow refrigerant to enter system. **Using small cans to charge systems is not recommended because level cannot be controlled accurately.**
5. When system stops drawing refrigerant in, close high side valve, start engine and set control lever to A/C position and blower switch to "HI" position to draw remaining refrigerant into system.
6. When specified weight of refrigerant is in system, close gauge set low pressure valve and refrigerant supply valve.
7. Remove jumper wire from clutch cycling pressure switch connector and connect connector to pressure switch, if equipped.
8. Operate system until pressures stabilize to inspect operation and system pressures. During high ambient temperatures, a high volume fan may be required to blow air through the radiator and condenser to cool engine and prevent excessive refrigerant system pressures.
9. When charging is complete and system operating pressures are normal, disconnect manifold gauge set from vehicle and install protective caps on service gauge port valves.

TECHNICAL SERVICE BULLETINS

A/C Condensation Drips Onto Passenger Floor

F-SERIES, MOUNTAINEER & RANGER

Condensation may drip onto passenger floor. This may be caused by the evaporator core not sealing properly and allowing air to carry condensation to heater plenum.

To correct this condition, use the following procedure to reseal evaporator core.

1. Verify concern, then inspect evaporator drain for proper flow and clear any obstructions.
2. Remove evaporator core as outlined in "Electrical" section of appropriate chassis chapter.
3. Adjust seal position to seal any gaps that will allow airfoil past any section other then the fin area. Refer to **Fig. 3** for suggested areas to be sealed.
4. Install evaporator core and verify repair.

A/C Coming Out Of Defrost Or Perceived A/C Cutting Out On Long Uphill Grade

2002 SUPER DUTY MOTORHOME

Some F53 motorhome chassis vehicles may exhibit A/C air coming from the defroster duct or a perceived A/C cutting out when travelling on a long uphill grade. This may be caused by vacuum depleting from the vacuum reservoir. Follow normal diagnostics to inspect for proper vacuum blend door operation and vacuum supply. If no problems are found, a revised vacuum canister is available to alleviate this concern.

Damaged A/C Hose Spring Lock Couplings

Air conditioning hose spring lock couplings may be damaged by service using small screwdrivers and similar metal objects to remove O-rings. The use of metal objects to remove O-rings can cause scratches across O-ring grooves, resulting in loss of refrigerant and repeat repair.

Use O-ring tool No. T71P-19703-C, a plastic toothpick, or equivalent tool to remove O-rings.

High (Discharge) Pressure	Low (Suction) Pressure	Clutch Cycle Time			Component – Causes
		Rate	On	Off	
High	High	Continuous Run			Condenser – Inadequate airflow
High	Normal to High				Engine overheating
Normal to High	Normal				Refrigerant overcharge (a) Air in refrigerant Humidity or ambient temperature very high (b)
Normal	High				Fixed orifice tube O-Rings leaking/missing
Normal	Normal	Slow or no cycle	Long or continuous	Normal or no cycle	Moisture in refrigerant system Excessive refrigerant oil
Normal	Low	Slow	Long	Long	Clutch cycling switch — Low cutout
Normal to Low	High	Continuous Run			Compressor — Low performance
Normal to Low	Normal to High				A/C suction line — Partially restricted or plugged (c)
Normal to Low	Normal	Fast	Short	Normal	Evaporator — Low or restricted airflow
			Short to very short	Normal to long	Condenser, fixed orifice tube, or A/C liquid line — Partially restricted or plugged
			Short to very short	Short to very short	Low refrigerant charge
			Short to very short	Long	Evaporator Core — Partially restricted or plugged
Normal to Low	Low	Continuous Run			A/C Suction Line — Partially restricted or plugged (d) Clutch Cycling Switch — Sticking closed
Erratic operation or Compressor not running		—	—	—	Clutch Cycling Switch — Dirty contacts or sticking open. High Pressure Switch — Dirty contacts or sticking open. Poor connection at A/C clutch connector, clutch cycling switch connector or high pressure switch. A/C electrical circuit erratic

ADDITIONAL POSSIBLE CAUSE COMPONENTS ASSOCIATED WITH INADEQUATE COMPRESSOR OPERATION:

- Compressor Clutch — Slipping
- Compressor Drive Belt — Loose
- Clutch Coil — Open, Shorted or Loose Mounting
- Control Assembly Switch — Dirty Contacts or Sticking Open
- Clutch Wiring Circuit — High Resistance. Open or Blown Fuse
- Compressor Operation Interrupted By Engine Computer

ADDITIONAL POSSIBLE CAUSE COMPONENTS ASSOCIATED WITH A DAMAGED COMPRESSOR:

- Clutch Cycling Switch — Sticking Closed or Compressor Clutch Seized
- High Pressure Switch — Sticking Closed
- Suction Accumulator/Drier — Refrigerant Oil Bleed Hole Plugged
- Refrigerant Leaks

(a) Compressor may make noise on initial run. This is slugging condition caused by excessive liquid refrigerant.

(b) Compressor clutch may not cycle in ambient temperatures above 27°C (80°F) depending on humidity conditions.

(c) Low pressure reading will be normal to high if pressure is taken at accumulator and if restriction is downstream of service access valve.

(d) Low pressure reading will be low if pressure is taken near the compressor and restriction is upstream of service access valve.

FM7028800007000X

Fig. 2 Refrigerant system pressure evaluation chart

Filtering Refrigerant After A/C Compressor Replacement

1. Recover refrigerant, then remove A/C compressor.
2. Install new A/C compressor, then the suction filter in hose between suction accumulator/drier and compressor. **Ensure suction filter is closed to compressor.**
3. Install pancake filter in liquid line between condenser and orifice tube, **Fig. 4.**
4. Remove a length of suction hose (close to compressor end) to accommodate suction filter and install filter using A/C clamps, then install O-rings on each filter tube on hose.
5. Charge refrigerant as outlined in "Charging System," then perform leak test as outlined in "Leak Test."
6. Set A/C control on "MAX" high blower and temperature control at full cold.
7. Start engine and let idle briefly, then gradually bring engine to 1200 RPM by running at lower RPM's for short periods, first at 800 RPM, then at 1000 RPM.
8. Set engine at 1200 RPM and run it for an hour with A/C system operating, then recover refrigerant.
9. Allow engine to cool sufficiently to remove fittings, flexible hoses and pancake filter from liquid line.
10. Discard pancake filter, then install liquid line back into system.
11. Charge refrigerant as outlined in "Charging System," then perform leak test as outlined in "Leak Test."
12. Ensure A/C system operates properly in all modes.

White Flakes Coming From A/C Vents

2002 EXPEDITION, F-150 & NAVIGATOR

Some vehicles may exhibit white flakes coming from the A/C vents when the blower motor is engaged. This may be caused by excessive amounts of brazing flux utilized in the manufacturing process of the evaporator.

Clean the A/C ducts through the registers and blow off the evaporator core through the blower motor opening using compressed air 90–150 psi, as follows:

1. Remove floor duct trim.
2. Connect vacuum cleaner to floor duct on drive side in such a way as to collect powder.
3. Tape off all other floor duct openings.
4. Connect two foot piece of flexible tubing to compressed air gun.
5. Close all instrument panel registers.
6. Place temperature setting in full cold, lace mode in floor/panel.
7. Turn on vacuum cleaner.
8. Open one register at a time and blow down through each duct for 30 seconds. Close each register before moving to next register.
9. Change mode to floor defrost.
10. Blow down each defroster duct for 30 seconds.
11. Alternate model door between floor and floor/defrost three times, giving door time to move between each change.
12. Turn off vacuum cleaner.
13. Change mode to full floor.
14. Ensure temperature is full cold.
15. Remove blower motor.
16. Turn on vacuum cleaner.
17. Reach into blower opening with tubing and proceed to clean core.
18. Blow core for a minimum of five minutes, utilizing a slow sweeping action.
19. Blow entire core face in up and down direction, then repeat moving from side to side.
20. Reassemble blower motor.
21. Operate A/C system with A/C on and blower motor on Max in each mode setting with temperature full cold then full warm. Stay in each mode position fro at least 30 seconds.
22. Disconnect vacuum cleaner, then reassemble floor duct trim.

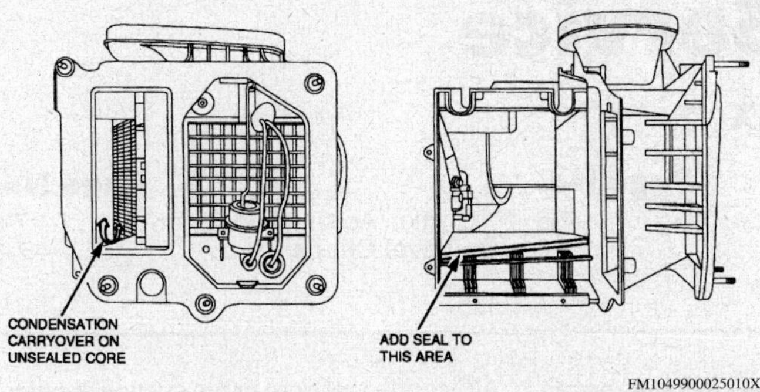

Fig. 3 Evaporator case sealing areas (Part 1 of 5). F-Series, Mountaineer & Ranger

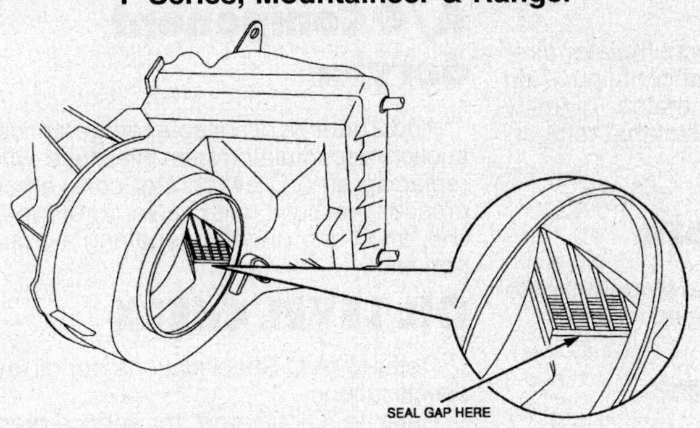

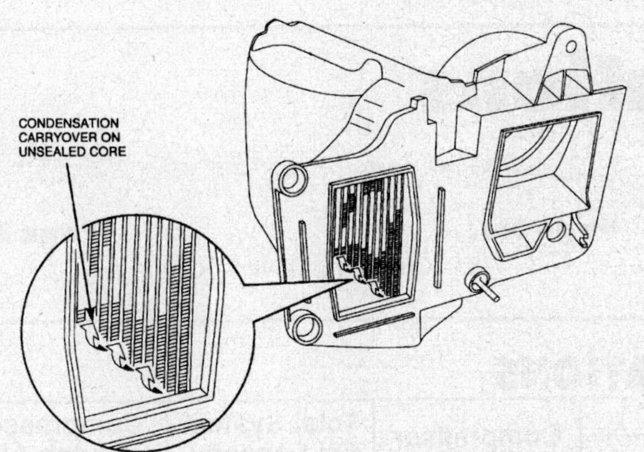

Fig. 3 Evaporator case sealing areas (Part 4 of 5). F-Series, Mountaineer & Ranger

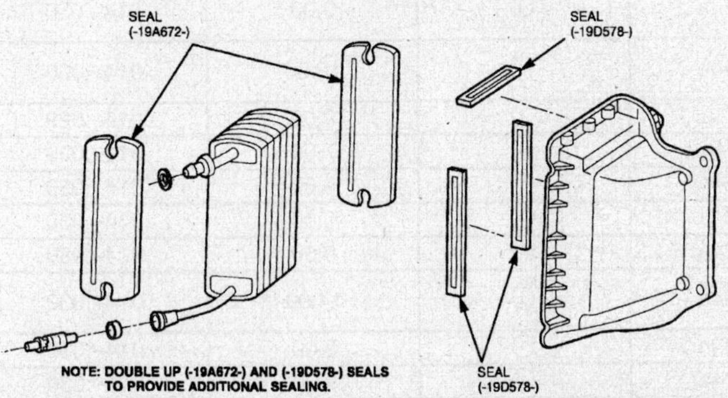

Fig. 3 Evaporator case sealing areas (Part 5 of 5). F-Series, Mountaineer & Ranger

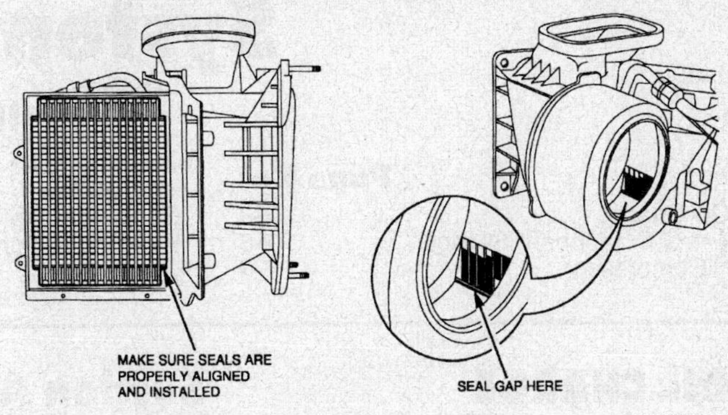

Fig. 3 Evaporator case sealing areas (Part 2 of 5). F-Series, Mountaineer & Ranger

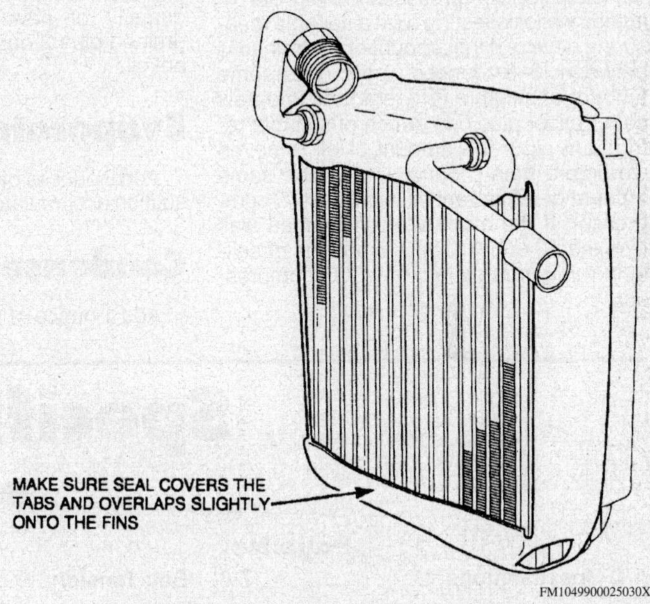

Fig. 3 Evaporator case sealing areas (Part 3 of 5). F-Series, Mountaineer & Ranger

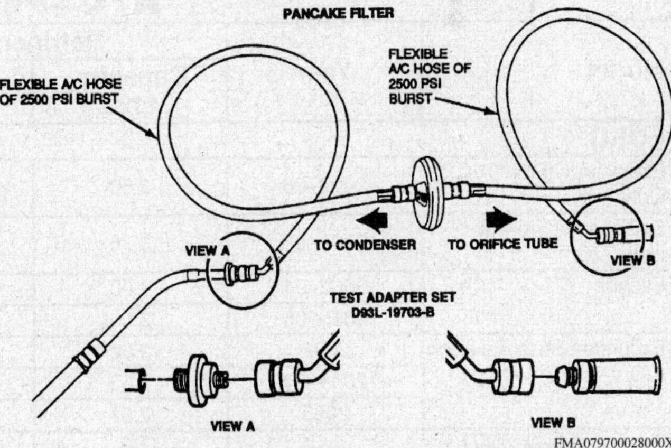

Fig. 4 Pancake filter installation

System Service

INDEX

OIL CHARGE

Compressor

Rotate A/C compressor six to eight revolutions while collecting oil in a suitable measuring device. If the amount of oil drained is between 3–5 ounces, pour the same amount of suitable refrigerant oil into new compressor plus one ounce of suitable refrigerant oil. If the amount of oil removed was more than 5 ounces, pour the same amount of refrigerant oil into new A/C compressor. If the amount of oil drained was less than 3 ounces, pour 3 ounces of suitable refrigerant oil into new A/C compressor.

Suction Accumulator/ Drier

Drill holes in bottom of accumulator/direr and drain oil into calibrated container. Add quantity of new oil to match quantity drained plus 2 ounces of suitable refrigerant oil.

Evaporator Core

Add 3 ounces of suitable refrigerant oil to suction accumulator/drier inlet tube.

Condenser Core

Add 1 ounce of suitable refrigerant oil to A/C condenser core or the suction accumulator drier inlet tube.

A/C Component Service

Add 2 ounces of suitable refrigerant oil to suction accumulator/drier inlet tube when replacing an A/C evaporator core, a compressor pressure relief valve, a refrigerant line, an O-ring or when repairing a charge port leak.

OIL LEVEL CHECK

Refer to "A/C Specifications" for oil level specifications.

Refer to "Oil Charge" for service procedures.

Specifications

INDEX

A/C SPECIFICATIONS

Model	Year	Refrigerant		Compressor Oil Viscosity	Total System Oil Capacity, Oz.	Compressor Clutch Air Gap, Inch
		Capacity, Lbs.	Type			
FORD						
E–Series w/Front A/C Only	2002–06	2.50	R-134a	①	9.00	.014–.030
E–Series w/Front & Rear A/C	2002–06	3.75	R-134a	①	13.00	.014–.030
Escape	2002–04	1.00	R134a	①	9.00	.014–.029
	2005–06	2.00	R134a	①	7.00	.014–.029
Excursion Less Auxiliary A/C	2002	2.62	R-134a	①	9.00	.014–.030
	2003–04	2.63	R-134a	①	9.00	.014–.030
	2005	2.81	R-134a	①	9.00	.014–.030
Excursion w/Auxiliary A/C	2002–05	4.25	R-134a	①	14.00	.014–.030
Expedition Less Auxiliary A/C	2002	2.31	R-134a	①	9.00	.014–.030
	2003–06	2.50	R-134a	①	9.00	.014–.030
Expedition w/Auxiliary A/C	2002	3.38	R-134a	①	11.00	.014–.030
	2003–06	3.62	R-134a	①	14.00	.014–.030

Continued

A/C SPECIFICATIONS—Continued

Model	Year	Refrigerant		Compressor Oil Viscosity	Total System Oil Capacity, Oz.	Compressor Clutch Air Gap, Inch
		Capacity, Lbs.	Type			
FORD						
Explorer Less Auxiliary A/C	2002	1.88	R-134a	①	9.00	.014–.030
	2003–04	2.00	R-134a	①	9.00	.014–.030
	2005–06	1.93	R-134a	①	9.00	.014–.030
Explorer w/Auxiliary A/C	2002–04	3.50	R-134a	①	13.00	.014–.030
	2005–06	2.93	R-134a	①	16.00	.014–.030
Explorer Sport & Sport Trac	2002–05	1.88	R-134a	①	9.00	.014–.030
Freestar Less Auxiliary A/C	2004–06	2.25	R-134a	①	10.00	.014–.030
Freestar w/Auxiliary A/C	2004–06	3.31	R-134a	①	12.00	.014–.030
Freestyle Less Auxiliary A/C	2005–06	1.81	R-134a	①	7.00	.014–.030
Freestyle w/Auxiliary A/C	2005–06	2.38	R-134a	①	9.00	.014–.030
F-Super Duty 250, 350, 450 & 550 Less Auxiliary A/C	2002–04	2.62	R-134a	①	9.00	.014–.030
F-Super Duty 250, 350, 450 & 550 w/Auxiliary A/C	2002–04	4.25	R-134a	①	14.00	.014–.030
F-Super Duty 250, 350, 450 & 550	2005–06	2.81	R-134a	①	9.00	.014–.030
F150	2002–04	2.06	R-134a	①	9.00	.014–.030
	2005–06	2.12	R-134a	①	8.00	.014–.030
F-53 Motorhome Chassis Less Auxiliary A/C	2002	2.62	R-134a	①	9.00	.014–.030
F-53 Motorhome Chassis w/Auxiliary A/C	2002	4.25	R-134a	①	14.00	.014–.030
Ranger 2.3L	2002	2.06	R-134a	①	9.00	.014–.030
Ranger 3.0L & 4.0L	2002	1.88	R-134a	①	9.00	.014–.030
Ranger	2003–06	2.06	R-134a	①	9.00	.014–.030
Windstar w/Front A/C Only	2002–03	2.75	R-134a	①	10.00	.014–.030
Windstar w/Front & Rear A/C	2002–03	3.50	R-134a	①	14.00	.014–.030
LINCOLN						
Aviator	2004–05	2.87	R-134a	①	14.00	.014–.030
Aviator Less Auxiliary A/C	2003	2.13	R-134a	①	9.00	.014–.030
Aviator w/Auxiliary A/C	2003	3.50	R-134a	①	13.00	.014–.030
Blackwood	2002	2.34	R-134a	①	9.00	.014–.030
LT	2006	2.12	R-134a	①	8.00	.014–.033
Navigator Less Auxiliary A/C	2002	2.31	R-134a	①	9.00	.014–.030
	2003–06	2.50	R-134a	①	9.00	.014–.030
Navigator w/Auxiliary A/C	2002	3.38	R-134a	①	11.00	.014–.030
	2003–06	3.62	R-134a	①	14.00	.014–.030
MERCURY						
Mariner	2006	2.00	R134a	①	7.00	.014–.029
Monterey Less Auxiliary A/C	2004–06	2.25	R-134a	①	10.00	.014–.030
Monterey w/Auxiliary A/C	2004–06	3.31	R-134a	①	12.00	.014–.030
Mountaineer Less Auxiliary A/C	2002	1.88	R-134a	①	9.00	.014–.030
	2003–04	2.00	R-134a	①	9.00	.014–.030
	2005–06	1.93	R-134a	①	9.00	.014–.030

Continued

A/C SPECIFICATIONS—Continued

Model	Year	Refrigerant		Compressor Oil Viscosity	Total System Oil Capacity, Oz.	Compressor Clutch Air Gap, Inch
		Capacity, Lbs.	Type			
MERCURY						
Mountaineer w/Auxiliary A/C	2002–04	3.50	R-134a	①	13.00	.014–.030
	2005–06	2.93	R-134a	①	16.00	.014–.030
Villager w/Front A/C Only	2002	2.00	R-134a	①	7.00	.014–.030
Villager w/Front & Rear A/C	2002	3.25	R-134a	①	10.00	.014–.030

① — PAG (Polyalkaline Glycol) compressor oil meeting Ford specification No. WSH-M1C-231-B.

CHARGING VALVE LOCATION

The high pressure service port is located in the A/C compressor to condenser discharge line. The low pressure service port is located in the evaporator to compressor suction line.

BELT TENSION

Compressor belt tension is automatically controlled by the automatic belt tensioner.

COOLING FANS

TABLE OF CONTENTS

Variable Speed Cooling Fans

INDEX

PRECAUTIONS

Do not operate engine until fan has first been inspected for cracks and/or separations. If a fan blade is found to be bent or damaged in any way, do not attempt to repair or reuse damaged part. Proper balance is essential in fan assembly operation. Balance cannot be ensured once a fan assembly has been found to be bent or damaged, and failure may occur during operation, creating an extremely dangerous condition. Always replace damaged fan assembly.

Air Bag Systems

Refer to "Air Bag System Precautions" in the front of this manual for system disarming and arming procedures.

Battery Ground Cable

Prior to service disconnect battery ground cable and isolate as required.

DESCRIPTION

The fan drive clutch is a fluid coupling containing silicone oil. Fan speed is regulated by the torque-carrying capacity of the silicone oil. The more silicone oil in the coupling, the greater the fan speed, and the less silicone oil, the slower the fan speed.

The fan drive clutch use is the coiled bimetallic thermostatic spring type, **Fig. 1.**

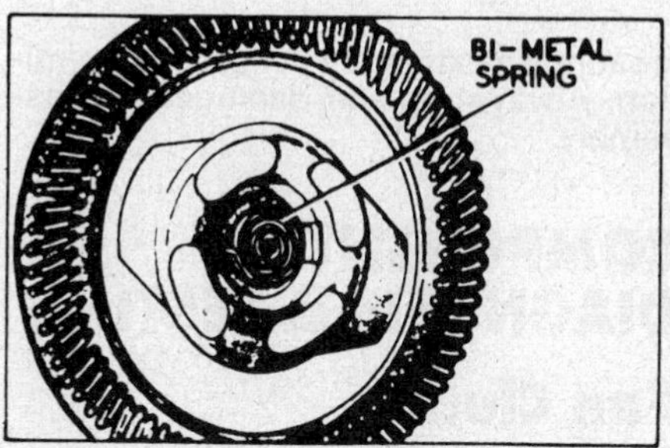

Fig. 1 Variable speed fan w/coiled bi-metallic thermostatic spring

The fan drive-clutch uses a heat-sensitive, coiled bi-metallic spring connected to an opening plate. This unit causes fan speed to increase with a rise in temperature and to decrease as temperature decreases.

TROUBLESHOOTING

Fan Drive Clutch Test

Do not operate the engine until the fan has been first inspected for possible cracks and separations.

Spin the fan blade by hand, a light resistance should be felt. If there is no resistance or very high resistance, the minimum and maximum fan speed must be inspected.

Run engine at a fast idle speed (1500 RPM) until normal operating temperature is reached. This can be done more quickly by blocking off the front of the radiator with cardboard. Regardless of temperatures, the unit must be operated for at least five minutes immediately before being tested.

Stop engine and, using a glove or a cloth to protect the hand, immediately inspect the effort required to turn the fan. If considerable effort is required, it can be assumed that the coupling is operating satisfactorily. If very little effort is required to turn the fan, the coupling is not operating properly and should be replaced.

The clutch fan may be tested while the vehicle is being driven. To inspect, disconnect the bi-metallic spring, **Fig. 2,** and rotate it 90° counterclockwise. This disables the temperature-controlled, free-wheeling feature and the clutch performs like a conventional fan. If this cures the overheating condition, replace the clutch fan.

Fan Clutch Noise

Fan clutch noise can sometimes be noticed when the clutch is engaged for maximum cooling. Clutch noise is also noticeable within the first few minutes after starting the engine while the clutch is redistributing the silicone fluid to its normal, disengaged operating condition after settling for long periods of time (over night). However, continuous fan noise or an excessive roar indicates the clutch assembly is

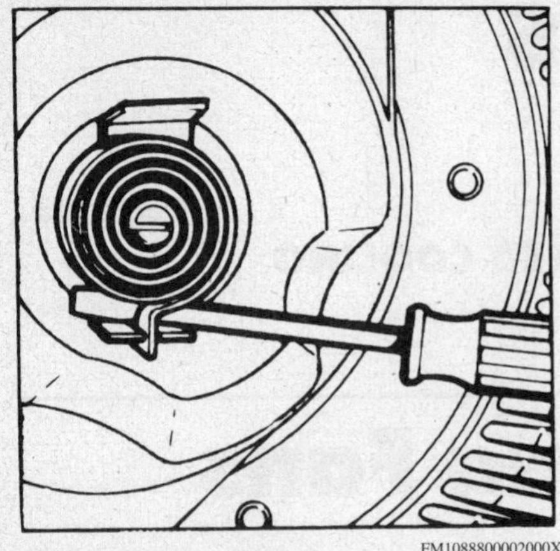

Fig. 2 Bi-metallic coiled spring removal

locked-up due to internal failure. This condition can be inspected by attempting to manually rotate the fan. If the fan cannot be rotated manually or there is a rough, abrasive feel as it is rotated, the clutch should be replaced.

Fan Looseness

Lateral movement can be observed at the fan blade tip under various temperature conditions because of the type of bearing used. This movement should not exceed 1/4 inch (6.5 mm) as measured at the fan tip. If this lateral movement does not exceed specifications, there is no cause for replacement.

Clutch Fluid Leak

Small fluid leaks do not generally affect the operation of the unit. These leaks generally occur around the area of the bearing assembly, but if the leaks appear to be excessive, engine overheating may occur. Inspect for clutch and fan free-wheeling by attempting to rotate fan and clutch assembly by hand five times. If no drag is felt, replace the clutch.

Fan Blade Inspection

Spin the fan blade by hand, a light resistance should be felt. If there is no resistance or very high resistance, the minimum and maximum fan speed must be inspected.

Place fan on flat surface with leading edge facing down. If the clearance between the fan blade touching surface and the opposite blade is more than .090 inch (2 mm), replace the fan. **Do not operate engine until fan has first been inspected for cracks and/or separations. If a fan blade is found to be bent or damaged in any way, do not attempt to repair or reuse damaged part. Proper balance is essential in fan assembly operation. Balance cannot be ensured once a fan assembly has been found to be bent or damaged, and failure may occur during operation,**

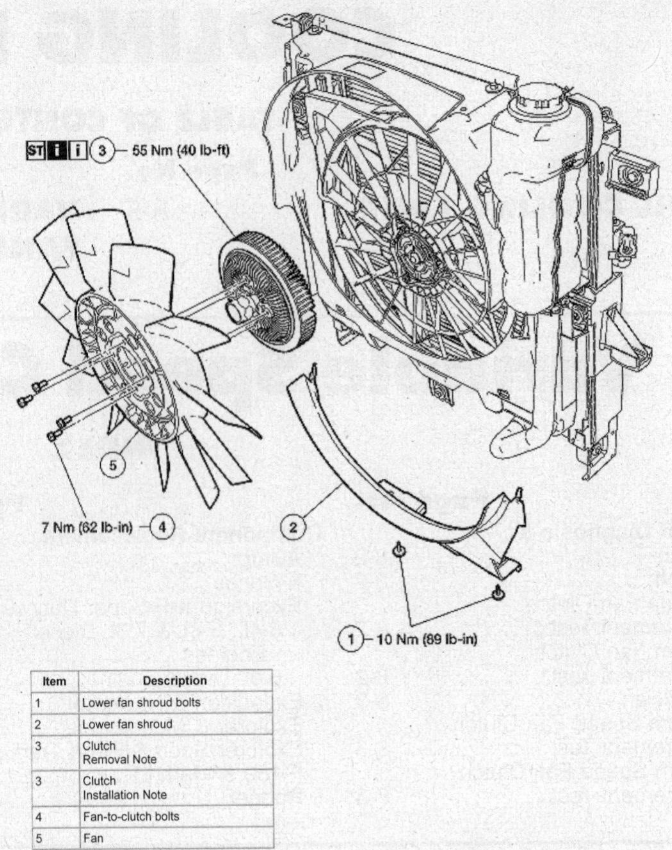

Item	Description
1	Lower fan shroud bolts
2	Lower fan shroud
3	Clutch Removal Note
3	Clutch Installation Note
4	Fan-to-clutch bolts
5	Fan

Fig. 3 Fan and clutch replacement. Aviator

creating an extremely dangerous condition. Always replace damaged fan assembly.

COMPONENT DIAGNOSIS & TESTING

Fan Clutch

MINIMUM FAN CLUTCH REQUIREMENT TEST

1. Mark water pump pulley, one of the fan blade retaining bolts and crankshaft pulley.
2. Connect tachometer to engine, then install throttle adjusting tool.
3. Connect Sun Strobe Light, or equivalent. This can be SLT-1 or SLT-2 Strobotach or an STA-1 Strobe Trigger adapter for Sun Distributor Test Stand. A Digital Photoelectric Tachometer 055-00108, or equivalent can also be used for this test.
4. Start engine and run approximately 1500 RPM until engine temperature has normalized.
5. Adjust engine speed to 2300 RPM.
6. Adjust strobe light to 3000 RPM and aim it at the water pump pulley. Adjust engine speed until light flashes and water pump pulley marks are synchronized.
7. Aim timing light at fan blade retaining bolts. Adjust strobe light until it is synchronized with marked fan retaining bolt (fan appears to stand still).
8. Fan speed must not be greater than specified fan test speed at water pump test speed.
9. Turn engine Off.
10. If fan speed was greater than specified fan test speed, inspect for proper components usage.
11. If correct components are used, replace fan clutch.

MAXIMUM FAN CLUTCH REQUIREMENT TEST

1. Follow steps 1–4 in minimum fan clutch requirement test.
2. Block off areas on each side of radiator in engine compartment and front of radiator grille. This will raise temperature of the air striking fan clutch and should cause fan to operate at maximum speed.
3. Place air conditioning selector, if so equipped, in maximum position and blower switch in high position.
4. Adjust strobe light to water pump test speed.
5. Start engine and adjust it until water pump pulley is synchronized with strobe light. This will be the engine testing speed.
6. Synchronized timing light with fan to fan clutch retaining bolt.
7. The fan speed must meet or exceed specified fan test speed at water pump test speed.
8. If fan speed was less than specified fan

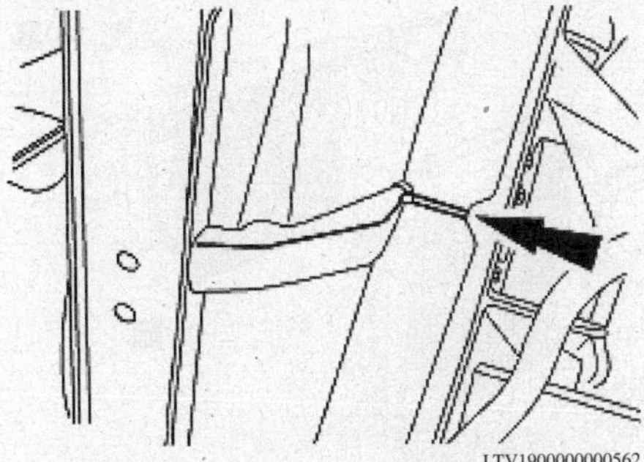

Fig. 4 Upper radiator shroud cutting locations. 6.0L Diesel

test speed, replace fan clutch.

Visctronic Fan

MINIMUM SPEED FAN CLUTCH REQUIREMENT TEST

1. Start engine.
2. Set visctronic drive fan duty cycle PID to 0 percent using suitable diagnostic scan tool.
3. Adjust engine speed to 1500 RPM until normal operating temperature is reached.
4. Increase engine speed to 3000 RPM for two minutes while reading the fan speed PID on diagnostic tool.
5. If fan speed is above 1500 RPM, replace visctronic fan clutch.

MAXIMUM SPEED FAN CLUTCH REQUIREMENT TEST

1. Start engine.
2. Set visctronic drive fan duty cycle PID to 100 percent using suitable diagnostic scan tool.
3. Adjust engine speed to 1500 RPM until normal operating temperature is reached.
4. Increase engine speed to 3000 RPM for two minutes while reading the fan speed PID on diagnostic tool.
5. If fan speed is less than RPM, replace visctronic fan clutch.

COMPONENT REPLACEMENT

Aviator

Use fan pulley holding wrench tool No. 303–239 and fan clutch nut wrench No. 303–240, or equivalents, when removing fan and clutch assembly, **Fig. 3.**

E-Series

The fan, fan clutch and shroud must be removed and installed together due to insufficient clearance to remove them separately.

1. Drain cooling system into suitable container.
2. Remove upper radiator air deflector.

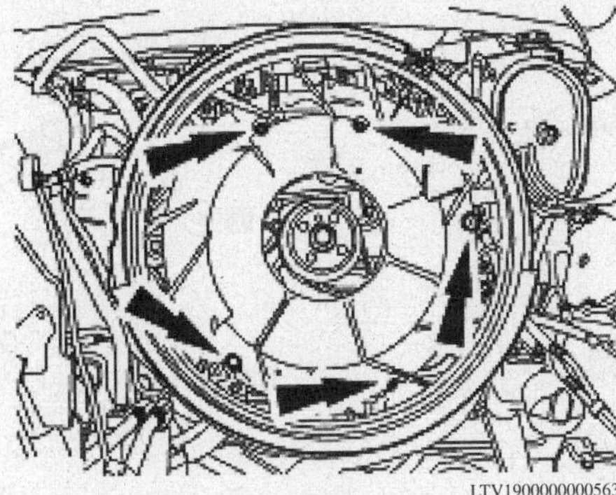

Fig. 5 Stator bolt locations. 6.0L Diesel

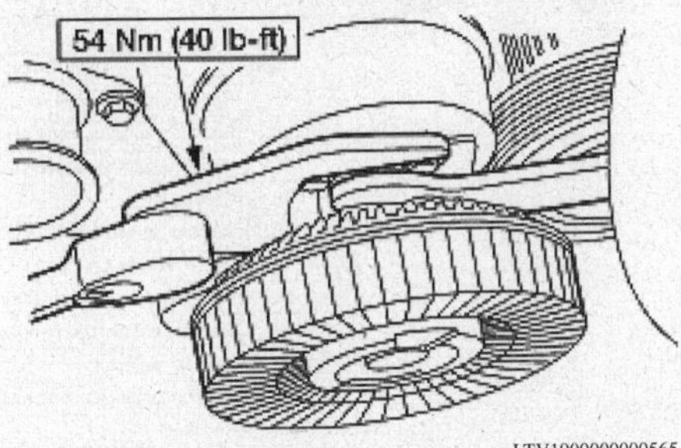

Fig. 7 Fan clutch wrench installation. Ranger w/4.0L engine

3. Remove air cleaner assembly.
4. Disconnect upper radiator hose from radiator.
5. Disconnect coolant degas bottle hose from shroud.
6. Loosen fan clutch with holding tool No. 303–239, or 303–478 and wrench No. 303–240, or equivalents. Clutch assembly has a righthand thread and must be rotated counterclockwise to remove it.
7. Carefully rotate fan and clutch assembly counterclockwise until assembly is free from water pump.
8. Disconnect retaining clips from fan shroud.
9. Raise and support vehicle.
10. Disconnect lower radiator hose retaining clamp from shroud.
11. Disconnect splash shield from shroud.
12. Lower vehicle.
13. Remove mounting bolts, then the fan, fan clutch and shroud. Use care when removing fan to avoid damaging radiator.
14. Reverse procedure to install.

F-150 & Mark LT

The fan, fan clutch and shroud must be removed and installed together due to insufficient clearance to remove them separately.

1. Drain cooling system into suitable container.
2. Remove air cleaner outlet pipe.
3. **On models equipped with supercharger,** remove supercharger degas bottle.
4. **On all models,** remove push pin type connectors, then the front air deflector.
5. Remove upper radiator from radiator.

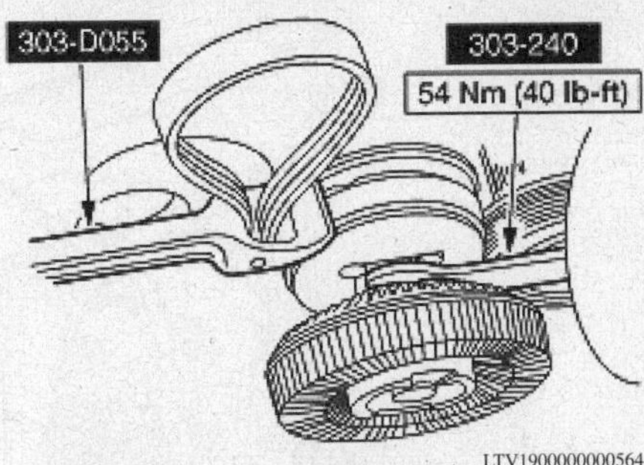

Fig. 6 Fan clutch strap wrench installation. Ranger w/2.3L & 3.0L engines

6. Remove degas bottle hose from radiator.
7. Hold water pump pulley steady with fan clutch holding wrench No. 303–239, or equivalent.
8. Remove ran blade with clutch hub nut wrench No. 303–240, or equivalent.
9. Remove screws from fan shroud.
10. Disconnect harness retaining pin type retainers from lefthand side of fan shroud.
11. Remove fan shroud and blade together.
12. Remove bolts and separate fan from clutch.
13. Reverse procedure to install.

Excursion & F-Super Duty

5.4L, 6.8L & 7.3L DIESEL ENGINES

1. Drain cooling system into suitable container.
2. Remove mounting bolts and position degas bottle out of way.
3. Remove upper radiator hose from radiator and position aside.
4. Clutch assembly nut has a righthand thread and must be rotated counterclockwise to remove.
5. Remove fan clutch from water pump using holding tool No. 303–239 or 303–478 and wrench No. 303–240 or 303–214, or equivalents.
6. Carefully position fan and fan clutch into shroud.
7. Remove fan shroud bolts, then the fan shroud, fan and clutch.
8. Reverse procedure to install.

6.0L DIESEL ENGINE

1. Remove air cleaner assembly.
2. Cut both sides of radiator shroud where indicated, **Fig. 4,** then remove upper shroud. Use care to avoid damaging radiator.
3. Disconnect cooling fan electrical connector. Unclip and position fan and wiring aside.
4. Loosen fan clutch with wrench tool No. 303–591, or equivalent.
5. Remove bolts from stator, **Fig. 5.**
6. Remove lower fan shroud.
7. Reverse procedure to install.

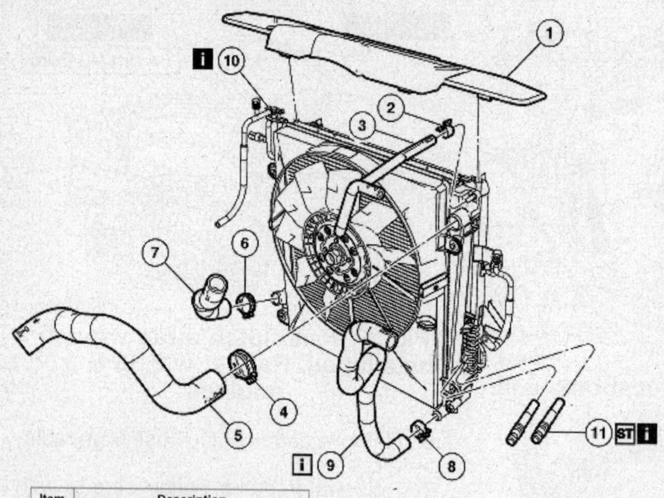

Item	Description
1	Upper air deflector
2	Upper degas bottle hose clamp
3	Upper degas bottle hose
4	Upper radiator hose clamp
5	Upper radiator hose
6	Lower radiator hose clamp
7	Lower radiator hose
8	Lower degas bottle hose clamp
9	Lower degas bottle hose
10	A/C tube
11	Transmission cooler lines Removal Note

LTV1900000000566

Fig. 8 Fan replacement (Part 1 of 2). Explorer & Mountaineer

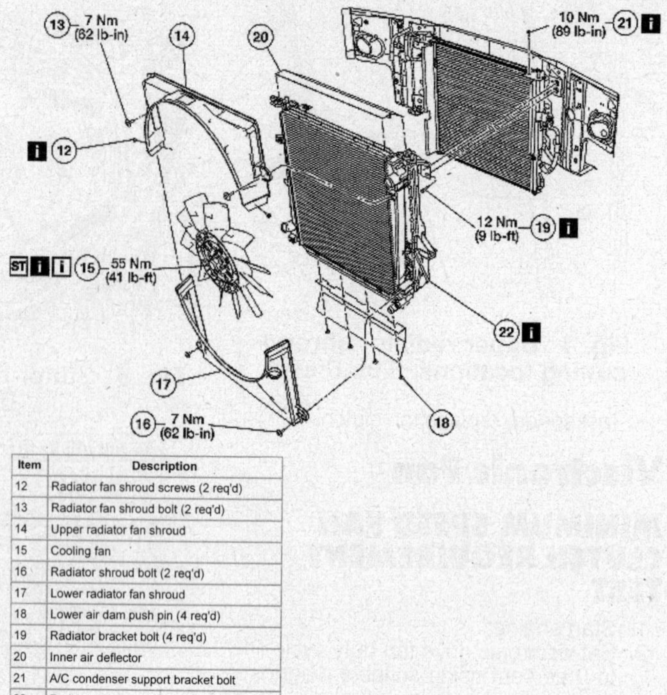

Item	Description
12	Radiator fan shroud screws (2 req'd)
13	Radiator fan shroud bolt (2 req'd)
14	Upper radiator fan shroud
15	Cooling fan
16	Radiator shroud bolt (2 req'd)
17	Lower radiator fan shroud
18	Lower air dam push pin (4 req'd)
19	Radiator bracket bolt (4 req'd)
20	Inner air deflector
21	A/C condenser support bracket bolt
22	Radiator

LTV1900000000567

Fig. 8 Fan replacement (Part 2 of 2). Explorer & Mountaineer

Ranger

2.3L ENGINE

1. Remove air cleaner outlet pipe.
2. Remove accessory drive belt.
3. Fan clutch nut has a lefthand thread and must be rotated clockwise to remove.
4. Loosen mechanical fan nut with strap wrench tool No. 303–D055 or equivalent, **Fig. 6.**
5. Remove fan and clutch assembly.
6. Reverse procedure to install.

3.0L & 4.0L ENGINES

1. Remove air cleaner outlet pipe.
2. Remove accessory drive belt.
3. Fan clutch nut has a lefthand thread and must be rotated clockwise to remove.
4. **On models equipped with 3.0L engine,** loosen mechanical fan nut with strap wrench tool No. 303–D055 or equivalent, **Fig. 6.**
5. **On models equipped with 4.0L engine,** remove fan blade and clutch assembly using fan clutch nut wrenches No. 303–239 and 303–240, **Fig. 7,** or equivalent.
6. **On all models,** remove fan blade and clutch assembly and let rest inside fan shroud.
7. Remove upper fan shroud bolts.
8. Lift fan shroud and fan blade and clutch assembly together and remove from vehicle.
9. Reverse procedure to install.

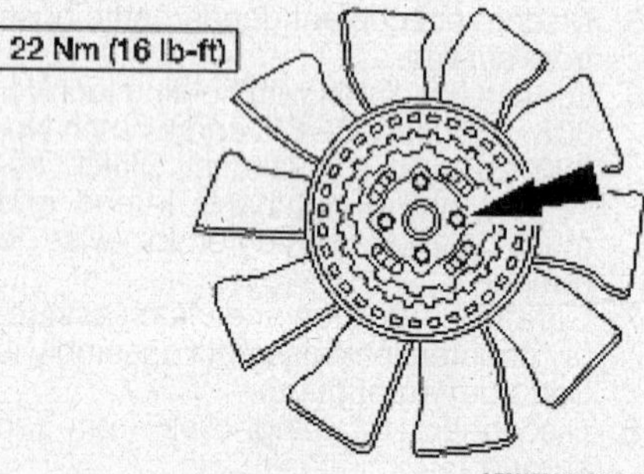

LTV1900000000568

Fig. 9 Fan blade mounting bolts. Explorer Sport & Sport Trac

Explorer & Mountaineer

1. Raise and support vehicle.
2. Remove components in sequence, **Fig. 8.**
3. Reverse procedure to install.

Explorer Sport & Sport Trac

1. Remove air cleaner outlet tube.
2. Remove fan shroud.
3. Remove fan mounting bolts, **Fig. 9,** then the fan.
4. Reverse procedure to install.

Expedition & Navigator

1. Remove air cleaner outlet pipe.
2. Disconnect mass air flow sensor electrical connector.
3. Remove outlet side of air cleaner.
4. Raise and support vehicle.
5. Remove skid plate.
6. Remove lower section of cooling fan shroud.
7. Lower vehicle
8. **On models equipped with 5.4L engine,** disconnect accelerator cable, speed control cable and return spring. Remove cable bracket and position bracket and cables out of way.
9. **On models equipped with 4.6L engine,** remove engine appearance cover bracket.
10. **On all models,** remove upper section of cooling fan shroud.
11. Remove fan blade and clutch using holding tool No. 303–239 and wrench tool No. 303–240, or equivalents.
12. Reverse procedure to install.

Electric Cooling Fans

NOTE: "Electrical Symbol & Wire Color Code Identification" Located In The Front Of This Manual May Be Used As An Aid When Using Wiring Circuits Found In This Section.

NOTE: Refer To "Computer Relearn Procedures" Located In The Front Of This Manual When Battery Power To The Computer Has Been Interrupted.

INDEX

PRECAUTIONS

Air Bag Systems

Refer to "Air Bag System Precautions" in the front of this manual for system disarming and arming procedures.

Battery Ground Cable

Prior to service disconnect battery ground cable and isolate as required.

High-Voltage Traction Battery Systems Depowering (Hybrid)

The nominal high voltage traction battery (HVTB) voltage is 330 volts DC. The buffer zone must be set up. The high voltage traction battery and charging system contains high voltage components and wiring. High voltage cables and wiring are orange in color. High voltage insulated safety gloves and a face shield must be worn when carrying out any diagnostics on this vehicle. Failure to follow these instructions may result in severe personal injury or death.

Before carrying out any removal and installation procedures of the high voltage traction battery system, the high voltage traction battery must be depowered. The high voltage insulated safety gloves that are to be worn while working on the high voltage system should be of the appropriate safety and protection rating for use on the high voltage system. They must be inspected before use and must always be worn in conjunction with the leather outer glove. Any hole in the rubber insulating glove is a potential entry point for high voltage. Failure to follow these instructions may result in severe personal injury or death.

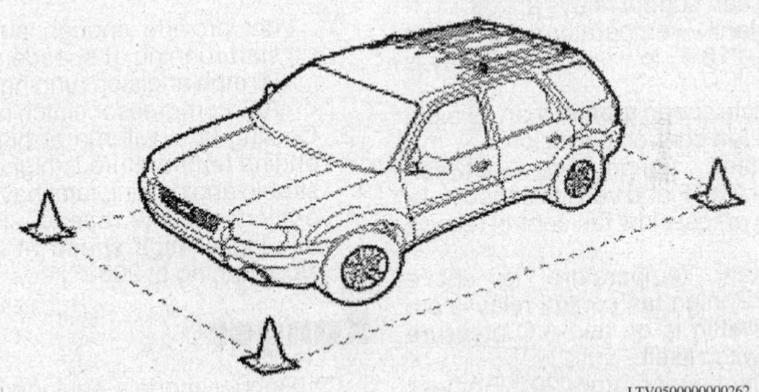

Fig. 1 Setting up a buffer zone

High voltage insulated safety gloves and a face shield must be worn when working with high voltage cables. The ignition switch must be OFF for a minimum of 5 minutes before removing high voltage cables. The buffer zone is required only when working with the high voltage system. Failure to follow these instructions may result in severe personal injury or death.

1. **Buffer zone is required only when working with high voltage system.** Set up buffer zone around vehicle as follows:
   a. Position vehicle in repair bay.
   b. Position four orange cones around corners of vehicle to mark off a three ft. perimeter around vehicle, **Fig. 1.**
   c. Do not allow any unauthorized personnel into buffer zone during repairs involving high voltage system.
   d. Only personnel trained for repair on high voltage system are to be permitted in buffer zone.
2. Rotate service disconnect plug from lock position to unlock position.
3. Remove service disconnect plug, then place in servicing shipping position. **If service disconnect plug is left out and placed on bench or toolbox, dirt or other contaminants may enter HVTB, which can cause damage.**
4. Insert service disconnect plug into servicing shipping position, this will disconnect HVTB.
5. Reverse procedure to connect.

DESCRIPTION

Escape, Freestar, Mariner & Monterey

The Freestar and Monterey cooling fans are controlled by 5 relays to provide 3 speeds. In all speeds, voltage is supplied to a specific cooling fan relay, which energizes the cooling fan motors based on cooling system temperature input from the cylinder head temperature (CHT) sensor and Powertrain Control Module (PCM), which energize the fans under the following conditions:

1. Engine cooling fans are turned on if the following conditions occur:
   a. Engine temperatures are higher than normal. Fans start running at 210°F and stop running at 204°F.

b. A/C is on and vehicle speed does not provide enough airflow. Fans start running at speeds at or below 60 mph and stop running at 65 mph.
c. A/C compressor clutch is engaged.

2. Cooling fans will run at high speed if engine temperature is higher than desirable and cooling fans have been operating at low speed. Fans start running at high speed at 225°F and stop running at 208°F.

Villager

The Villager cooling fan is installed on the rear of the radiator and uses a 2-speed electric motor mounted within the shroud. Three cooling fan relays (LO, HI 1 and HI 2) control operation of the fan. High fan control relay 2 (HI 2) is a safety relay, ensure cooling fan motor operation in the event of HI 1 relay failure. The fan control relays are located in the lefthand engine compartment relay panel. These relays govern fan under the following conditions:

1. With A/C switch in Off position:
   a. Coolant temperature of 201°F or less; fan control relays are off.
   b. Coolant temperature between 203–210°F; low fan control relay is on.
   c. Vehicle speed greater than 12 mph; high fan control relay is on.
   d. Coolant temperature between 212–219°F and vehicle speed is 12 mph or less; low fan control relay is on.
   e. Coolant temperature is above 221°F; high fan control relay is on.
2. If A/C switch is on and A/C pressure cutoff switch is off:
   a. Coolant temperature 201°F or less and vehicle speed at least 68 mph; fan control relays are off.
   b. Coolant temperature 201°F or less and vehicle speed 68 mph or less; low fan control relay is on.
   c. Coolant temperature between 203–219°F and vehicle speed 12 mph or less; low fan control relay is on.
   d. Coolant temperature between 203–219°F and vehicle speed at least 12 mph; high fan control relay is on.
   e. Coolant temperature above 221°F; high fan control relay is on.
3. If A/C switch is on and A/C pressure cutoff switch is on; high fan control relay is on.

Windstar

The Windstar fan control system consists of two 2-speed cooling fans. The fans are controlled by the constant control relay module (CCRM) and Powertrain Control Module (PCM), which energize the fans under the following conditions:

1. Engine cooling fans are turned on if the following conditions occur:
   a. Engine temperatures are higher than normal. Fans start running at 210°F and stop running at 204°F.
   b. A/C is on and vehicle speed does

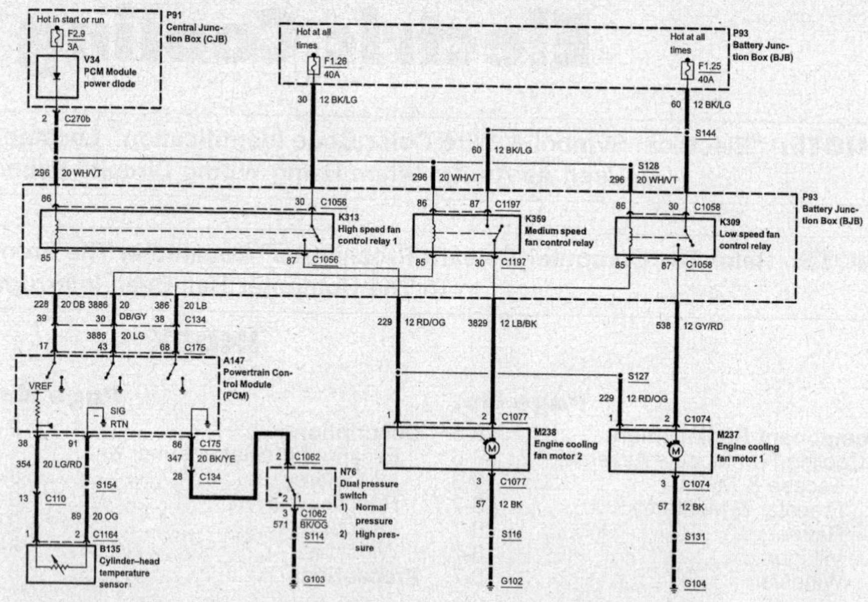

Fig. 2 Cooling fan wiring diagram. 2002–04 Escape w/2.0L engine

not provide enough airflow. Fans start running at speeds at or below 60 mph and stop running at 65 mph.
   c. A/C compressor clutch is engaged.
2. Cooling fans will run at high speed if engine temperature is higher than desirable and cooling fans have been operating at low speed. Fans start running at high speed at 225°F and stop running at 208°F.

Ranger

On Ranger models equipped with 2.3L engine, the cooling fans are controlled by 5 relays to provide 3 speeds. In all speeds, voltage is supplied to a specific cooling fan relay, which energizes the cooling fan motors based on cooling system temperature input from the cylinder head temperature (CHT) sensor and Powertrain Control Module (PCM). On Ranger models equipped with 3.0L and 4.0L engines, the cooling fans are controlled by 5 relays to provide 3 speeds. In all speeds, voltage is supplied to a specific cooling fan relay, which energizes the cooling fan motors based on cooling system temperature input from the Engine Coolant Temperature (ECT) sensor and Powertrain Control Module (PCM) which energize the fans.

SYSTEM DIAGNOSIS & TESTING

Wiring Diagrams

Refer to the wiring diagrams, **Figs. 2 through 10,** during diagnosis and testing procedures.

Symptom Charts

Refer to **Figs. 11 and 12** for electric cooling fan symptom charts.

COMPONENT REPLACEMENT

Cooling Fan Module Assembly

The engine cooling fan motor, fan blade and shroud cannot be serviced separately. The cooling fan module assembly is dynamically balanced when it is manufactured and should not be disassembled into component components. If assembly is serviced at component level balance could be adversely affected.

ESCAPE & MARINER

2002–04

1. Remove hood latch and position aside.
2. Remove center support upper and lower bolts, then the center support.
3. Disconnect lefthand fan electrical connector.
4. Remove lefthand and righthand upper radiator supports.
5. Tilt radiator forward for clearance.
6. Disconnect cooling fan electrical connectors.
7. Remove five lefthand cooling fan retaining bolts, then the cooling fan.
8. Remove righthand cooling fan retaining bolts, then the cooling fan.
9. Reverse procedure to install.

2005–06

1. Raise and support vehicle.
2. Drain engine coolant into suitable container.
3. Mark position of hood latch assembly, then remove mounting bolts and position latch aside.
4. Remove upper radiator support bracket, **Fig. 13.**
5. Disconnect front impact severity sensor electrical connector.

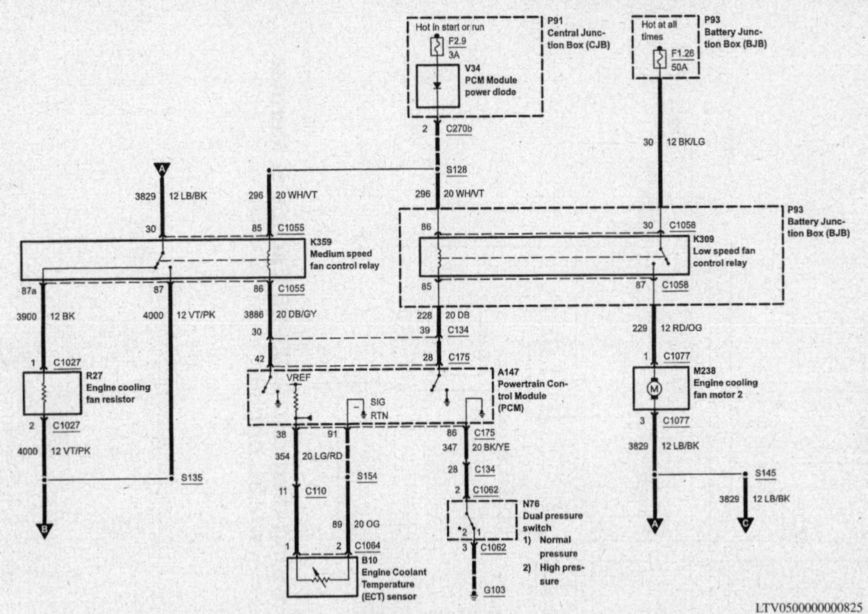

Fig. 3 Cooling fan wiring diagram (Part 1 of 2). 2002–04 Escape w/3.0L engine

6. Remove front impact severity sensor mounting bolt, then the sensor.
7. Remove two pushpin retainers from front bumper bracket.
8. Remove two front grille retaining bolts.
9. **On models equipped with 3.0L engine,** disconnect transmission cooler hose.
10. **On all models,** remove four bolts, then the two remaining radiator brackets.
11. Remove center support lower bolt and nut, then the support.
12. Disconnect cooling fan electrical connectors.
13. Remove two cooling fan bolts, then the cooling fan module assembly and shroud.
14. Reverse procedure to install. **Torque** radiator support bracket bolts to 89 inch lbs.

FREESTAR & MONTEREY

1. Raise and support vehicle.
2. Drain engine coolant into suitable container.
3. Remove pin type retainers, then the upper radiator sight shield, **Fig. 14.**
4. Disconnect cooling fan electrical connectors.
5. Disconnect harness retainers from fan shroud.
6. Disconnect upper radiator hose.
7. Tie radiator and condenser to upper radiator support separately. Allow two inches of slack in condenser wire to allow for movement.
8. Remove radiator alignment pins.
9. Disconnect radiator vent hose at radiator.
10. Disconnect degas bottle return hose.
11. Disconnect lower radiator hose.
12. Disconnect transmission cooler tube clips.
13. Push fluid cooler tube inward slightly, squeeze retaining clip, and with a slight twisting motion, pull fluid cooler tube out of connector.
14. Disconnect transmission cooler tube pin-type retainers.
15. Disconnect power steering tubes from both sides of radiator lower support.
16. Remove A/C muffler bracket bolts, then position assembly aside.
17. Remove power steering cooler mounting bolts, then position cooler aside.
18. Remove four bolts, lower radiator support and insulators.
19. Remove two radiator to condenser bolts.
20. Remove radiator.
21. Remove two cooling fan shroud to radiator bolts.
22. Remove cooling fan and shroud assembly.
23. Reverse procedure to install. **Torque** radiator support bracket bolts to 89 inch lbs.

RANGER

1. Remove air cleaner outlet pipe.
2. Disconnect cooling fan electrical connector, **Fig. 15.**
3. Remove power steering fluid reservoir mounting bolts, then position reservoir aside.
4. Remove two cooling fan shroud mounting bolts, then the fan and shroud assembly.
5. Reverse procedure to install. **Torque** fan shroud mounting bolts to 71 inch lbs.

WINDSTAR

1. Remove radiator as outlined in the "Engine" section of the "Windstar" chapter.
2. Remove clip from cooling fan blade.
3. Remove spacer plate, then the fan blade from motor.
4. Remove motor attaching bolts, then the fan motor.
5. Reverse procedure to install.

VILLAGER

1. Raise and support vehicle.
2. Disconnect wiring harness from fan shroud, then lower vehicle.
3. Position relay box aside.
4. Position coolant reservoir hose aside.
5. Disconnect cooling fan electrical connector.
6. Remove cooling fan assembly.
7. Reverse procedure to install, vehicle may need to be driven 10 miles or more to relearn the strategy.

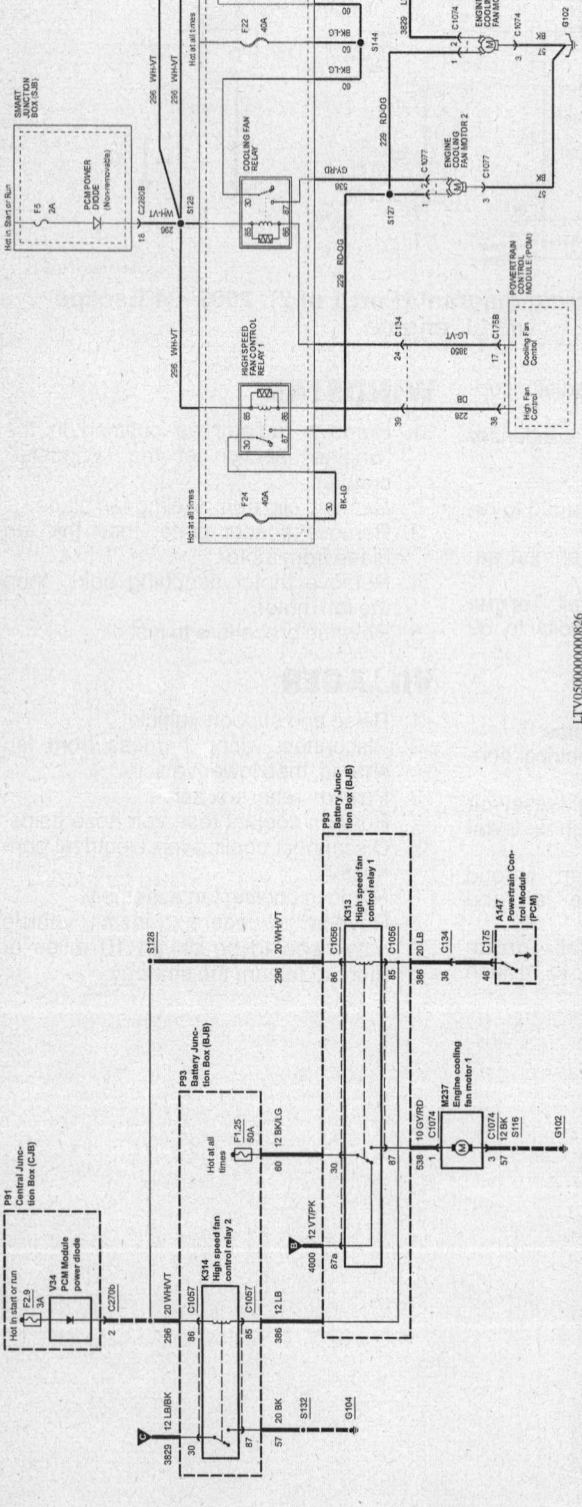

Fig. 3 Cooling fan wiring diagram (Part 2 of 2). 2002–04 Escape w/3.0L engine

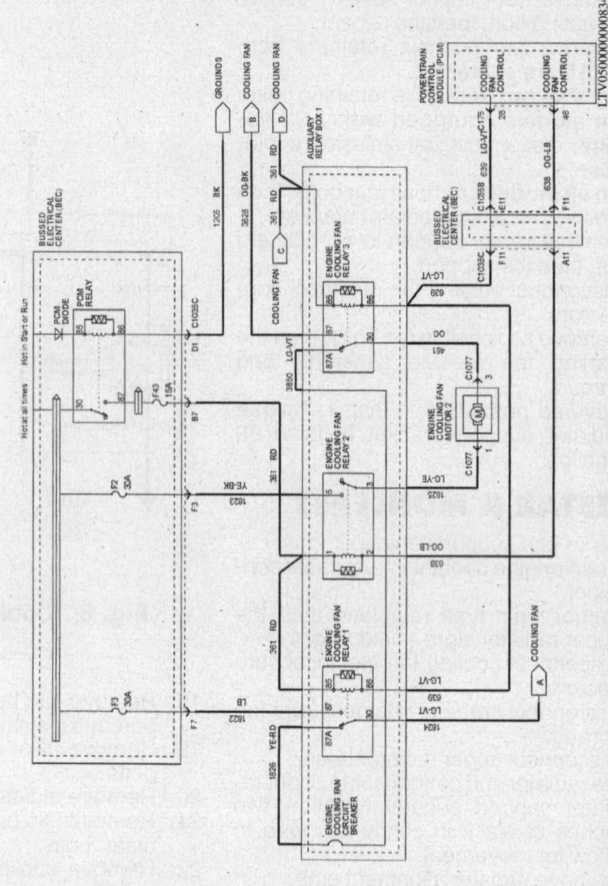

Fig. 4 Cooling fan wiring diagram. 2005–06 Escape & Mariner w/2.3L engine

Fig. 5 Cooling fan wiring diagram. 2005–06 Escape & Mariner W/3.0L engine

Fig. 6 Cooling fan wiring diagram (Part 1 of 3). Freestar & Monterey

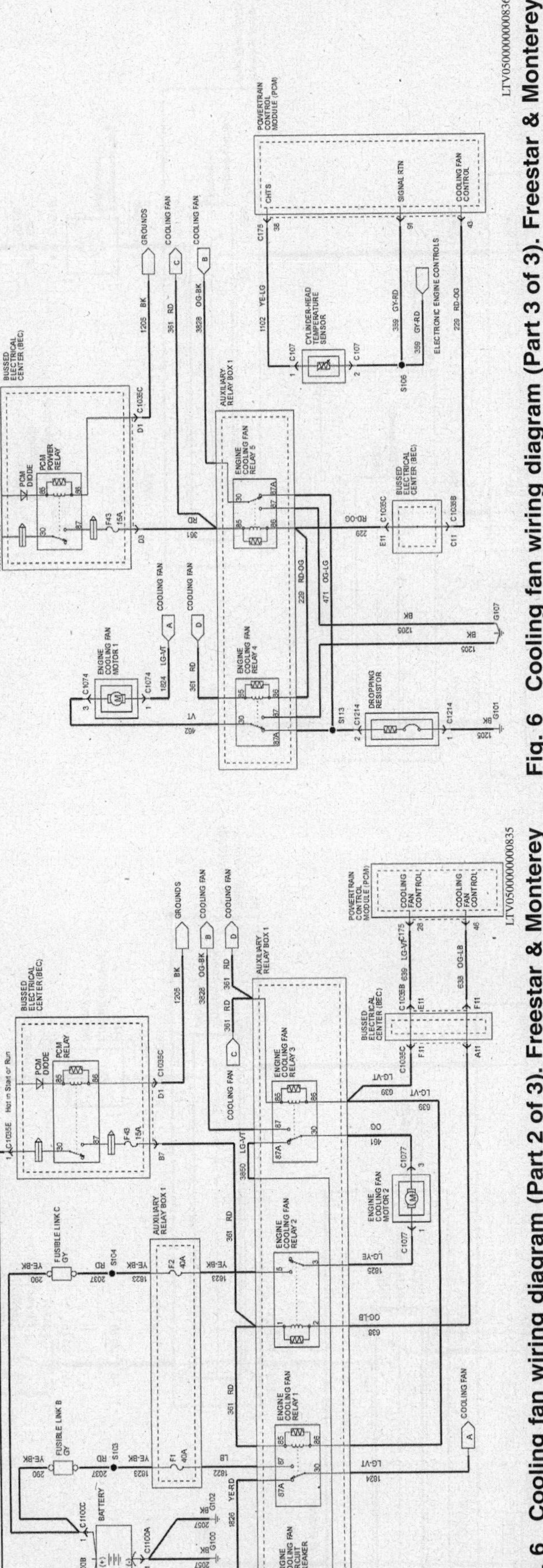

LTV0500000000835

Fig. 6 Cooling fan wiring diagram (Part 2 of 3). Freestar & Monterey

LTV0500000000836

Fig. 6 Cooling fan wiring diagram (Part 3 of 3). Freestar & Monterey

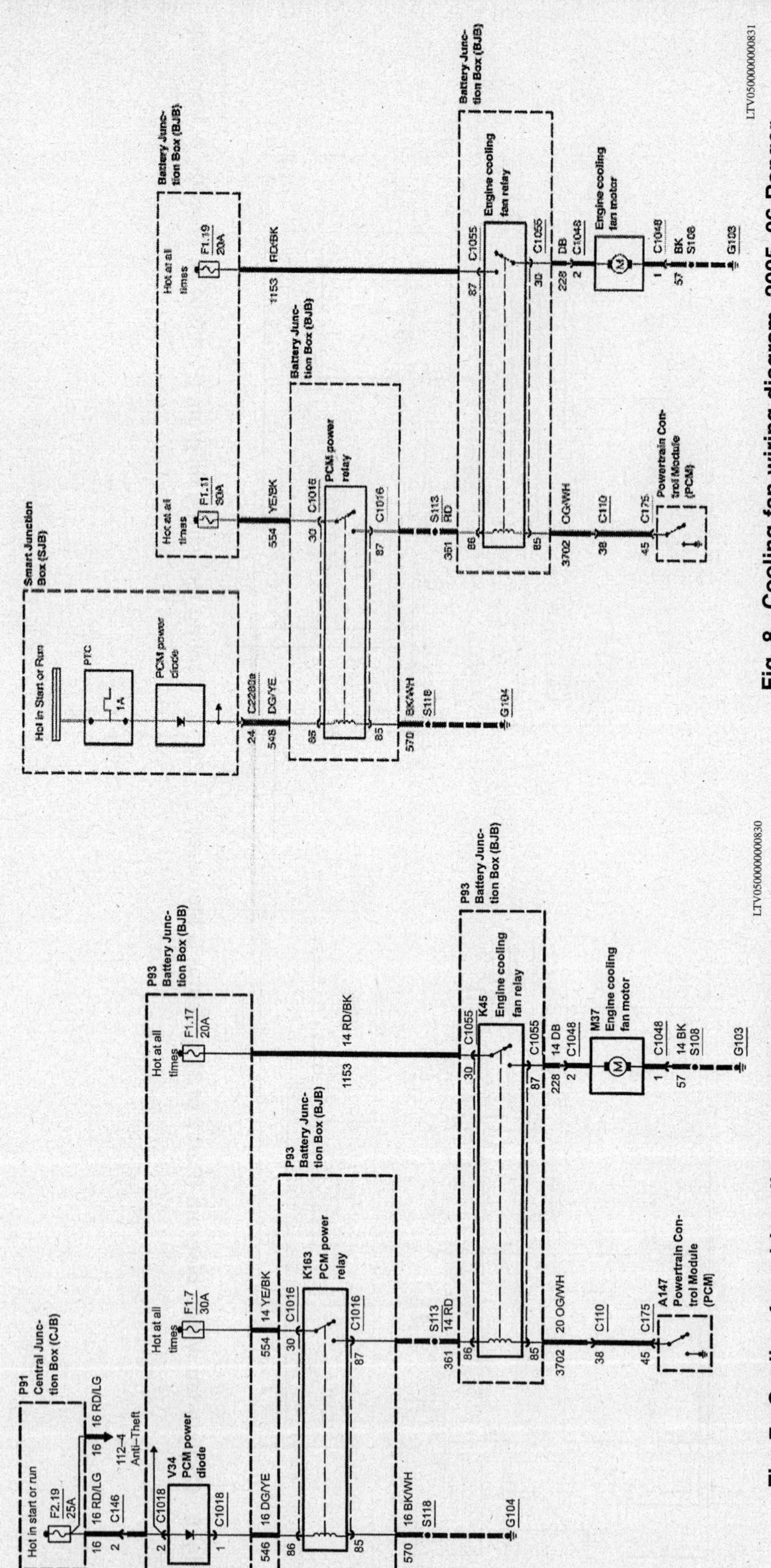

Fig. 7 Cooling fan wiring diagram. 2002–04 Ranger

Fig. 8 Cooling fan wiring diagram. 2005–06 Ranger

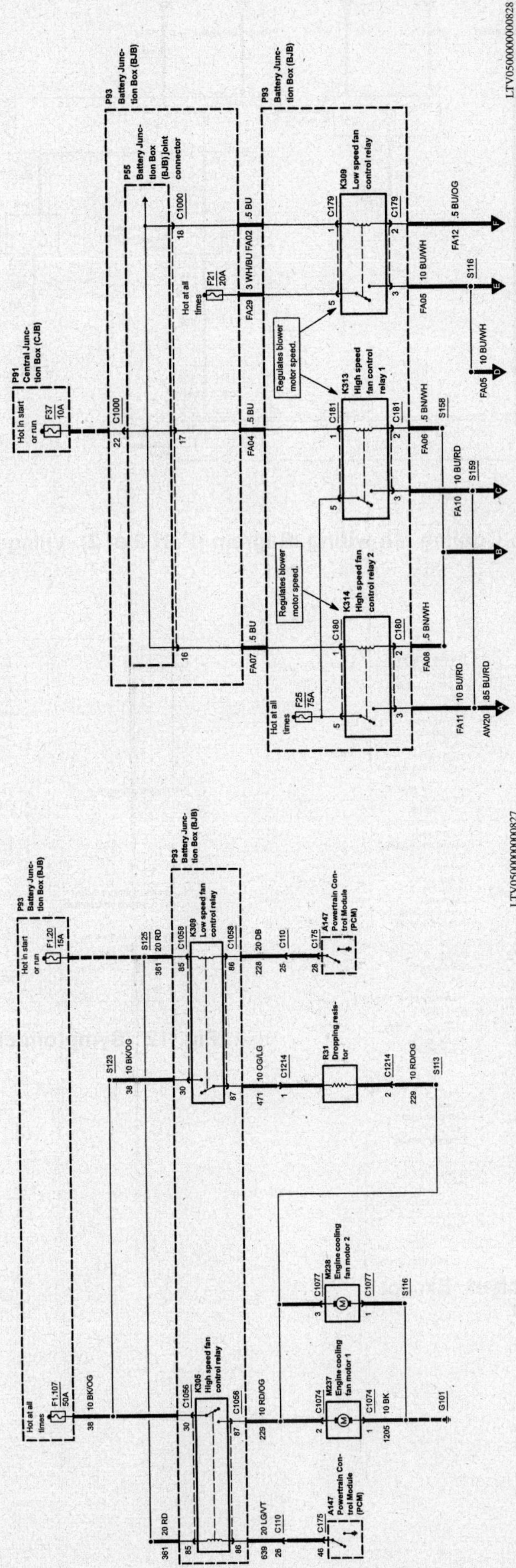

Fig. 9 Cooling fan wiring diagram. Windstar

Fig. 10 Cooling fan wiring diagram (Part 1 of 2). Villager

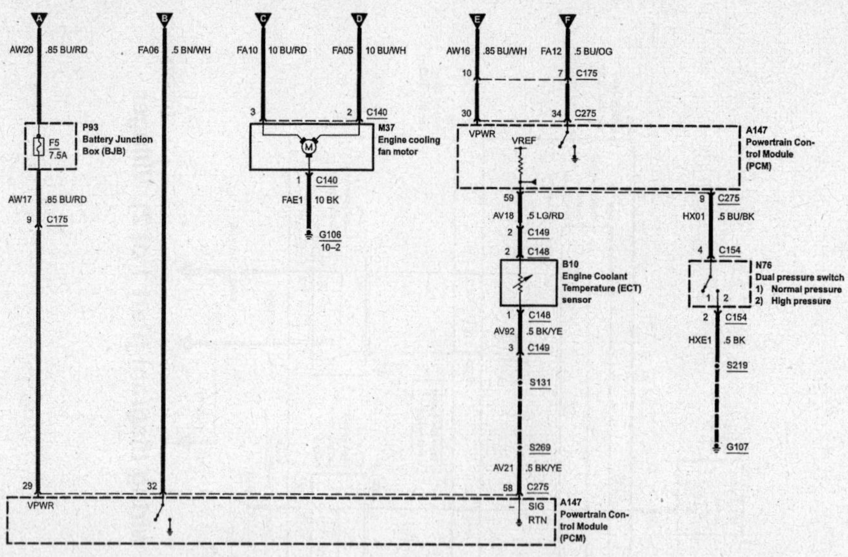

Fig. 10 Cooling fan wiring diagram (Part 2 of 2). Villager

Condition	Possible Sources
• Loss of engine coolant	• Radiator. • Thermostat housing assembly. • Coolant pump seal. • Radiator hoses. • Heater hoses. • Heater core. • Engine gaskets. • Degas bottle and hoses.
• The engine overheats	• Thermostat. • Low coolant fill. • Airlock in the system. • Coolant pump. • Internal engine coolant leak. • Radiator. • Radiator airflow obstruction. • Cooling fan. • Cooling fan wiring. • Pressure relief cap.
• The engine does not reach normal operating temperature	• Thermostat. • Low coolant fill.
• The block heater does not operate correctly	• Block heater power cable. • Block heater.
• Noisy cooling fan operation	• Foreign particle contamination. • Fan motor.
• The electric cooling fan(s) is inoperative in one or more speeds	• Fuses. • Circuitry. • Cooling fan motor. • Relay. • Cooling fan resistor.
• The electric cooling fan(s) stays on all the time	• Circuitry. • Relay(s).
• The electric cooling fan(s) incorrect operation	• Circuitry. • Relay(s).

LTV0500000000822

Fig. 11 Symptom chart. Except Ranger

Condition	Possible Sources
• Loss of coolant	• Radiator • Water pump seal • Radiator hoses • Heater hoses • Heater core • Engine gaskets • Degas bottle (2.3L) • Radiator coolant recovery reservoir bottle (3.0L and 4.0L)
• The engine overheats	• Thermostat • Coolant pump • Coolant • Radiator • Inoperative cooling fan • Pressure relief cap (2.3L) • Radiator cap (3.0L and 4.0L)
• The engine does not reach normal operating temperature	• Thermostat
• The block heater does not operate correctly	• Block heater power cable
	• Block heater

LTV0500000000823

Fig. 12 Symptom chart. Ranger

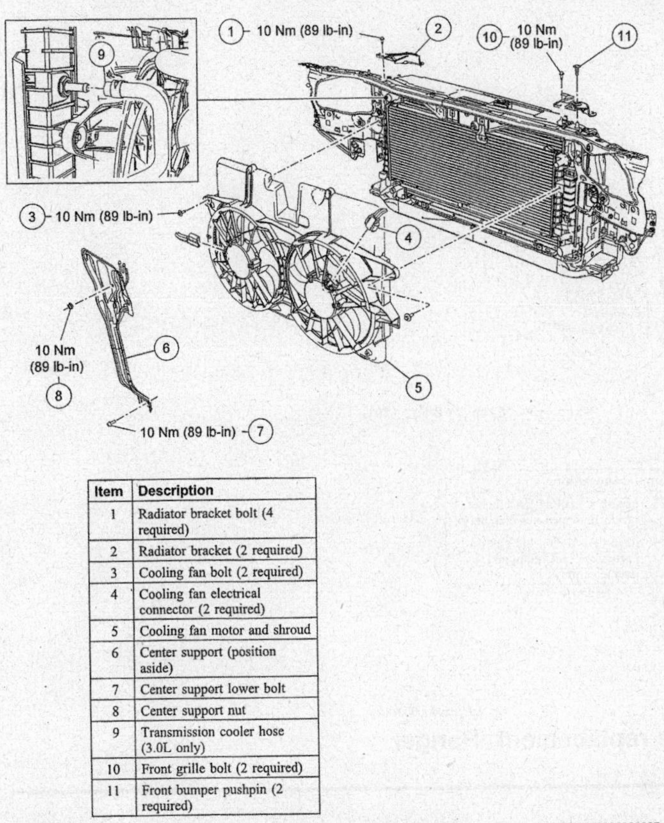

Item	Description
1	Radiator bracket bolt (4 required)
2	Radiator bracket (2 required)
3	Cooling fan bolt (2 required)
4	Cooling fan electrical connector (2 required)
5	Cooling fan motor and shroud
6	Center support (position aside)
7	Center support lower bolt
8	Center support nut
9	Transmission cooler hose (3.0L only)
10	Front grille bolt (2 required)
11	Front bumper pushpin (2 required)

LTV0500000000837

Fig. 13 Cooling fan module assembly replacement. 2005–06 Escape & Mariner

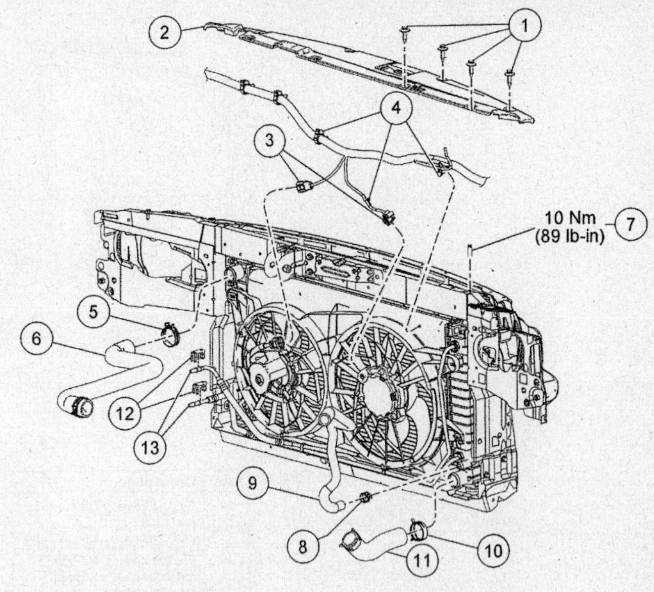

Item	Description
1	Pin-type retainers (8 required)
2	Upper radiator sight shield
3	Cooling fan electrical connectors
4	Harness retainers (3 required)
5	Clamp
6	Upper radiator hose
7	Radiator alignment pin (2 required)

Item	Description
8	Clamp
9	Degas bottle return hose
10	Clamp
11	Lower radiator hose
12	Transmission cooler tube clips
13	Transmission cooler tubes

LTV0500000000838

Fig. 14 Cooling fan module & radiator replacement (Part 1 of 2). Freestar & Monterey

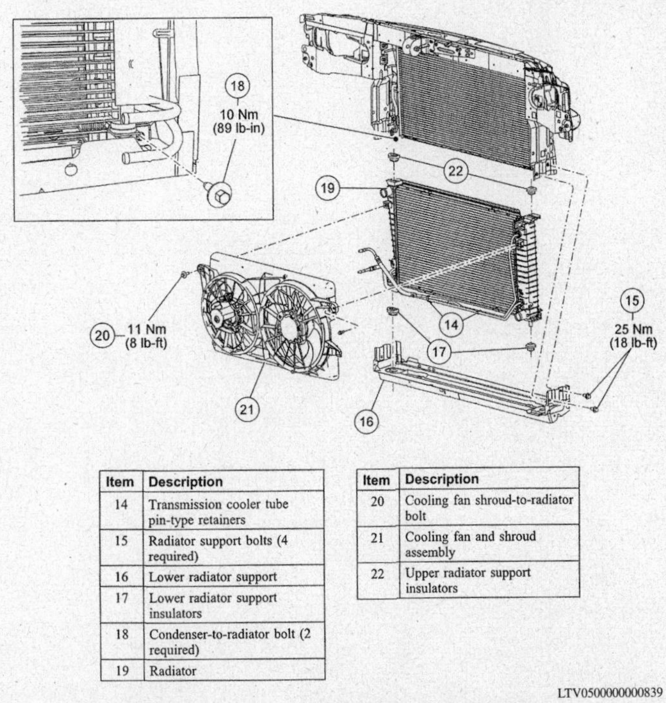

Item	Description
14	Transmission cooler tube pin-type retainers
15	Radiator support bolts (4 required)
16	Lower radiator support
17	Lower radiator support insulators
18	Condenser-to-radiator bolt (2 required)
19	Radiator

Item	Description
20	Cooling fan shroud-to-radiator bolt
21	Cooling fan and shroud assembly
22	Upper radiator support insulators

LTV0500000000839

Fig. 14 Cooling fan module & radiator replacement (Part 2 of 2). Freestar & Monterey

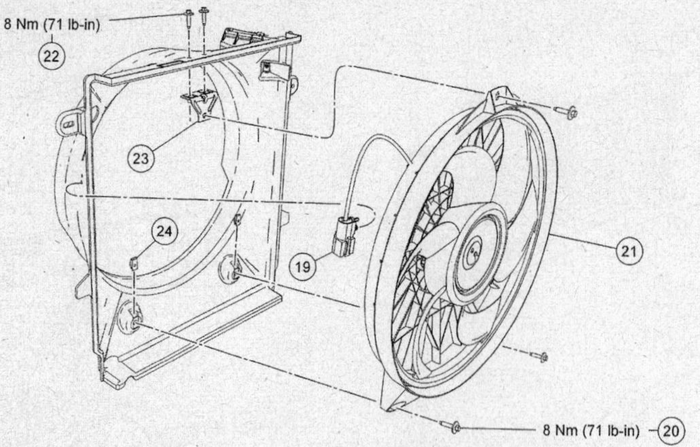

Item	Description
19	Electric cooling fan electrical connector (A/C equipped vehicles only)
20	Electric cooling fan bolt (3 required) (A/C equipped vehicles only)
21	Electric cooling fan (A/C equipped vehicles only)
22	Electric cooling fan bracket bolt (2 required) (A/C equipped vehicles only)

Item	Description
23	Electric cooling fan bracket (A/C equipped vehicles only)
24	Electric cooling fan nuts (3 required) (A/C equipped vehicles only)

LTV0500000000840

Fig. 15 Cooling fan module replacement. Ranger

STARTER MOTORS

TABLE OF CONTENTS

Mitsubishi Gear Reduction Starter Motor

INDEX

APPLICATION CHART

Year	Model
2002–03	E & F-Series w/7.3L Diesel Engine
2004–06	E & F Series w/6.0L Diesel Engine

PRECAUTIONS

Air Bag Systems

Refer to "Air Bag System Precautions" in the front of this manual for system disarming and arming procedures.

Battery Ground Cable

Prior to service, disconnect battery ground cable and isolate as required.

DESCRIPTION

These starters, **Fig. 1,** are 12 volt units that have the solenoid mounted on the starter housing. The solenoid is energized when the starter relay contacts are closed, causing the starter drive to engage with the flywheel ring gear, thereby starting the engine. An overrunning clutch in the drive protects the starter from excessive speeds once the engine starts. The current flows through the solenoid energizing coil until the solenoid plunger is at full travel, at which time the plunger closes a set of contacts that bypass the energizing coil, allowing the holding coil to keep the starter drive engaged and passing starting current to the starter.

The gear reduction starter motor is a compact design using an integral solenoid. With a gear reduction system, the starter motor is relatively small but still provides the torque required to crank the engine.

TROUBLESHOOTING

Refer to **Figs. 2 and 3** for starter motor troubleshooting chart.

DIAGNOSIS & TESTING

Armature Open Circuit Test

An open circuit in the armature can sometimes be detected by examining commutator for signs of burning. A spot burned on the commutator is caused by an arc formed every time a commutator segment connected to the open circuit winding passes under a brush.

Pinion Inspection

1. Connect starter using two switches and a battery, **Fig. 4.**
2. When switches K1 and K2 are closed, starter drive will be forced outward and motor will run. If switch K2 is opened, starter will stop turning with pinion in full out position.
3. Measure pinion end gap in this position, which should be .004–.100 inch.

Drive Pinion Test

Rotate pinion clockwise and counterclockwise. Pinion drive should freewheel in one direction and lock to armature shaft in other. If pinion operation is not as specified, it must be replaced.

Field Grounded Circuit Test

1. Measure insulation between yoke and field terminal using circuit tester. Circuit tester should show infinite resistance.
2. Ensure there is continuity between lead wires.

Starter Load Test

1. Connect test equipment as illustrated, **Fig. 5,** ensuring there is no current flowing through ammeter and heavy

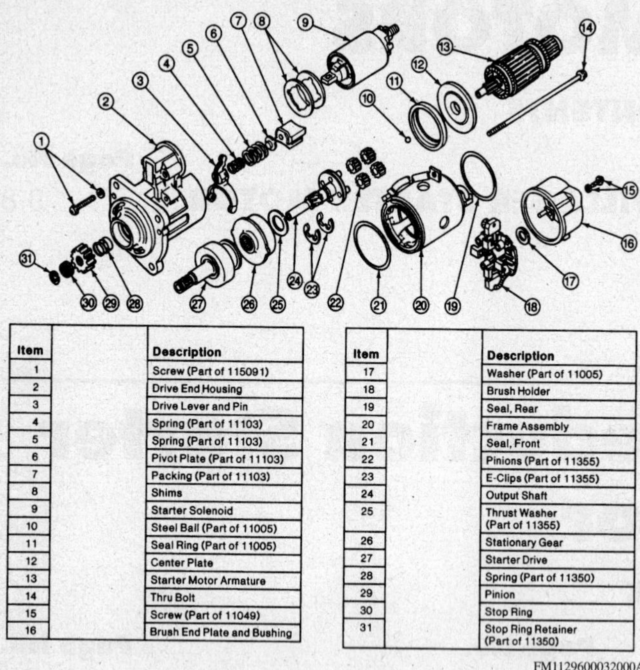

Item	Description
1	Screw (Part of 115091)
2	Drive End Housing
3	Drive Lever and Pin
4	Spring (Part of 11103)
5	Spring (Part of 11103)
6	Pivot Plate (Part of 11103)
7	Packing (Part of 11103)
8	Shims
9	Starter Solenoid
10	Steel Ball (Part of 11005)
11	Seal Ring (Part of 11005)
12	Center Plate
13	Starter Motor Armature
14	Thru Bolt
15	Screw (Part of 11049)
16	Brush End Plate and Bushing

Item	Description
17	Washer (Part of 11005)
18	Brush Holder
19	Seal, Rear
20	Frame Assembly
21	Seal, Front
22	Pinions (Part of 11355)
23	E-Clips (Part of 11355)
24	Output Shaft
25	Thrust Washer (Part of 11355)
26	Stationary Gear
27	Starter Drive
28	Spring (Part of 11350)
29	Pinion
30	Stop Ring
31	Stop Ring Retainer (Part of 11350)

FM1129600032000A

Fig. 1 Exploded view of Mitsubishi starter

Condition	Possible Sources
• The Engine Does Not Crank or the Relay Clicks	• Loose or corroded battery cable connections. • Undercharged battery. • Worn or damaged starter relay. • Faulty starter motor ground circuit. • Loose or corroded starter motor connections. • Worn or damaged starter motor.
• Engine Cranks Slowly	• Loose or corroded battery cable connections. • Undercharged battery. • Loose or corroded starter motor connections. • Worn or damaged starter motor.
• Unusual Starter Noise	• Starter motor improperly mounted. • Worn or damaged starter motor. • Improper starter drive engagement to flywheel.
• The Starter Spins but the Engine Does Not Crank	• Worn or damaged starter motor. • Damaged flywheel ring gear.

LTV0500000000293

Fig. 2 Troubleshooting chart. 2002–03

duty carbon pile rheostat portion of circuit.

2. Remove Fuse 17 from engine compartment fuse panel.
3. Disconnect push-on connectors at starter solenoid, then connect remote control starter switch from positive battery cable to starter solenoid S-terminal.
4. Crank engine with remote starter switch and determine exact reading on voltmeter.
5. Stop cranking engine, then reduce resistance of carbon pile until voltmeter indicates same reading as when engine was cranked. Ammeter should read 230–630 amps.

Starter No-Load Test

1. Ensure batteries are fully charged.
2. Connect a suitable alternator, regulator, battery and starter tester.
3. Connect a remote starter switch between starter solenoid S-terminal and battery positive.
4. Close remote starter switch. Pinion should shift to crank position and motor should run smoothly. While motor is running, record voltmeter and ammeter readings. Voltage should be greater than 11 volts and amperage should be 170 amps or less. If readings are not as specified, refer to **Fig. 6.**

Auxiliary Switch Test

1. Inspect switch for continuity.
2. If continuity exists, switch is open and must be replaced.

Feed Circuit Voltage Drop Test

This test is performed to determine if slow cranking is caused by high resistance in the starter motor circuit. It can only be performed with the starter motor mounted on the engine.

1. Disconnect wiring from fuel shutoff solenoid.
2. Connect positive lead from a suitable multi-meter to battery positive post. Connect negative lead to starter solenoid M-terminal.
3. Connect remote starter switch between starter solenoid S-terminal and positive battery post.
4. Press remote starter switch and record voltage reading.
5. Voltage reading should be .5 volt or less. A reading higher than .5 volt indicates high resistance.
6. Repeat test on starter solenoid B-terminal. If readings are higher than .5 volt, remove wiring from starter solenoid and clean connectors and terminals.
7. Install wires on starter and perform test again.
8. If the reading at the starter solenoid M-terminal is still higher than .5 volt or the reading at the B-terminal is lower, carry out the starter solenoid test. If no change is noted, install a new positive battery cable lead.

Starter Solenoid

Measure resistance between starter motor ground terminal and solenoid case using a suitable digital ohmmeter. If reading is not approximately .95 ohms, replace solenoid.

Condition	Possible Sources
• The engine does not crank and the relay does click	• Battery. • Fuse. • Starter motor/solenoid. • Ignition switch. • Circuit.
• The engine does not crank and the relay does not click	• Fuse. • Battery. • Starter relay. • Ignition switch. • Digital transmission range (TR) sensor. • Starter solenoid. • Circuit.
• The engine cranks slowly	• Battery. • Starter motor/solenoid. • Circuit.
• Unusual starter noise	• Starter mounting. • Starter motor. • Incorrect starter drive engagement.
• The starter spins but the engine does not crank	• Worn or damaged starter motor. • Damaged flywheel ring gear.

LTV0500000000294

Fig. 3 Troubleshooting chart. 2004–06

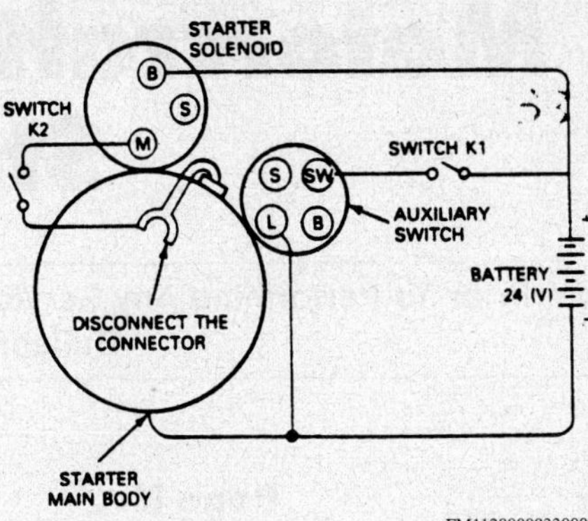

Fig. 4 Pinion travel inspection

Test Result	Probable Source	Action to Take
• Normal Current and Speed	• Cranking motor OK.	• RECHECK the battery, switches and wiring, including voltage drop tests, if cranking motor operation on the engine is slow or sluggish.
• Current Flow with Test Circuit Switch Open	• Solenoid contacts stuck closed.	• CARRY OUT the Starter Solenoid Component Test.
• Failure to Operate with Very Low or No Current	• Open solenoid winding. • Open field circuit. • Open armature coil(s) or high insulation between commutator bars. • Broken brush spring(s) or worn brushes.	• CARRY OUT the Starter Solenoid Component Test. • INSTALL a new starter motor. • INSTALL a new starter motor. • INSTALL a new starter motor.
• Failure to Operate with High Current	• Frozen bearing, or other damage to drivetrain. • Direct ground in terminals or fields.	• INSTALL a new starter motor. • INSTALL a new starter motor.
• Low Speed with High Current	• Excessive friction in bushings or gear reduction unit, bent armature shaft or loose pole shoe, bent driveshaft.	• INSTALL a new starter motor.

FM1129800719010X

Fig. 6 Starter no load test chart (Part 1 of 2)

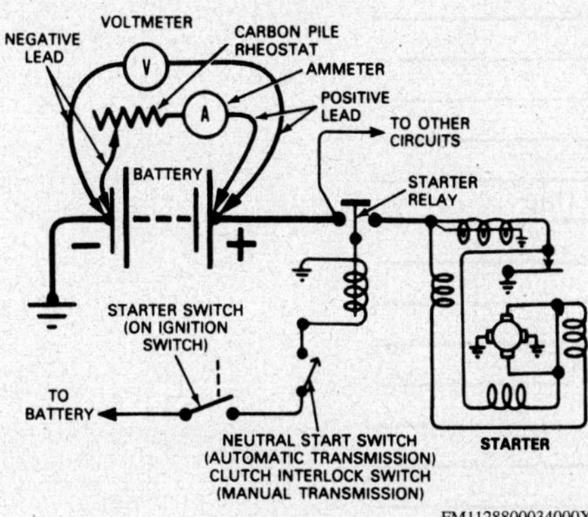

Fig. 5 Starter load test connections

Test Result	Probable Source	Action to Take
	• Shorted armature. • Grounded armature or fields.	• INSTALL a new starter motor. • INSTALL a new starter motor.
• Low Speed with Normal (or Low) Current	• High internal electrical resistance caused by poor connections, defective leads or dirty commutator. • Open solenoid winding. • Open field circuit. • Open field circuit. • Broken brush spring(s) or worn brushes.	• INSTALL a new starter motor. • CARRY OUT the Starter Solenoid Component Test. • INSTALL a new starter motor. • INSTALL a new starter motor. • INSTALL a new starter motor.
• High Speed with High Current	• Shorted fields.	• INSTALL a new starter motor.

FM1129800719020X

Fig. 6 Starter no load test chart (Part 2 of 2)

STARTER SPECIFICATIONS

Year	Starter, Inch Diameter	Ampere Draw Normal Load	Engine Cranking Speed RPM	Minimum Stall Torque @ 2.5 Volts Ft. Lbs.	No-Load Ampere @ 12 Volts	Brushes: Length Inch	Brushes: Wear Limit Inch	Brushes: Spring Tension Ounces
2002–03	3.4	230–630	150–200	27.5	170	.71	—	122
2004–06	—	365	185	55	155	—	—	—

Motorcraft Permanent Magnet Starter Motor

NOTE: Prior To Performing Any Service Operations Listed In This Section, Consult The "Technical Service Bulletins" Section For Related Information.

INDEX

APPLICATION CHART

Year	Model
2002–06	Aviator
	E-Series
	Escape
	Expedition
	Explorer
	Explorer Sport/Sport Trac
	Freestar
	Freestyle
	F-Series/Excursion
	LT
	Mariner
	Monterey
	Mountaineer
	Navigator
	Ranger
	Windstar

PRECAUTIONS

Air Bag Systems

Refer to "Air Bag System Precautions" in the front of this manual for system disarming and arming procedures.

Battery Ground Cable

Prior to service, disconnect battery ground cable and isolate as required.

DESCRIPTION

The starting system includes the permanent magnet gear reduction starter motor with solenoid actuated drive, **Fig. 1,** the battery, a remote control starter switch (part of the ignition switch), the park/neutral position switch (automatic transmission), Clutch Pedal Position (CPP) switch (manual transmission), the starter relay and heavy circuit wiring.

TROUBLESHOOTING

Refer to **Figs. 2 through 12** for starter motor troubleshooting charts.

DIAGNOSIS & TESTING

Voltage Drop Tests

The following test procedures will be performed with starter motor on the vehicle.

Ensure battery is in a fully charged state.

Make all multi-meter connections at the component terminal rather than the cable or wiring terminal.

There is a protective cap or boot over the battery input terminal which must be replaced after service has been completed. Always disconnect the battery ground cable before servicing the starter motor.

MOTOR FEED CIRCUIT

1. Disconnect inertia fuel shutoff (IFS) switch electrical connector.
2. Disconnect ignition coil electrical connector.
3. Connect a remote starter switch between starter solenoid S-terminal and battery positive post.
4. Connect positive lead of Rotunda digital multi-meter tool No. 73, or equivalent to battery positive post. Connect negative lead of multi-meter to starter solenoid M-terminal.
5. Engage remote starter switch. Multimeter reading should be .5 volts or less.
6. If voltage at M-terminal is greater than .5 volts, move multi-meter negative lead to starter solenoid B-terminal and repeat test.
7. If voltage reading at B-terminal is less than .5 volts, fault condition is either in connections at starter solenoid or the solenoid itself.
8. If voltage taken at starter solenoid B-terminal is greater than .5 volts, fault condition is either the positive battery cable connection or the cable itself.

MOTOR GROUND CIRCUIT

1. Disconnect inertia fuel shutoff (IFS) switch.

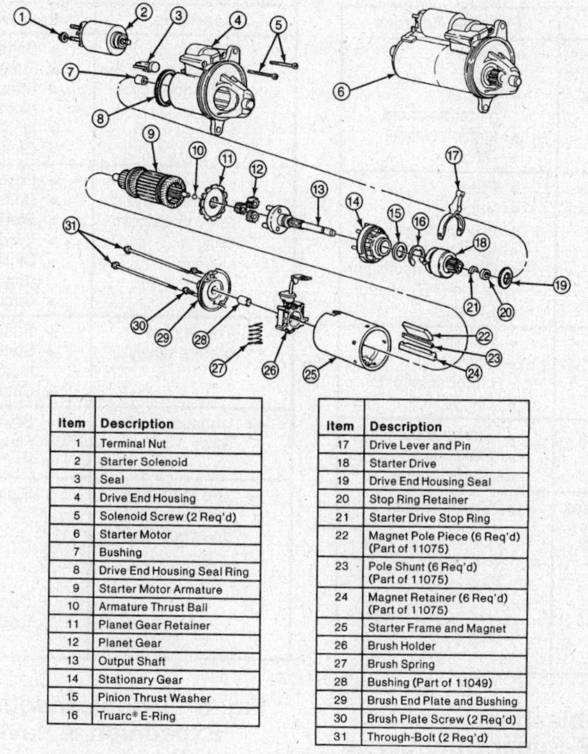

Item	Description
1	Terminal Nut
2	Starter Solenoid
3	Seal
4	Drive End Housing
5	Solenoid Screw (2 Req'd)
6	Starter Motor
7	Bushing
8	Drive End Housing Seal Ring
9	Starter Motor Armature
10	Armature Thrust Ball
11	Planet Gear Retainer
12	Planet Gear
13	Output Shaft
14	Stationary Gear
15	Pinion Thrust Washer
16	Truarc® E-Ring

Item	Description
17	Drive Lever and Pin
18	Starter Drive
19	Drive End Housing Seal
20	Stop Ring Retainer
21	Starter Drive Stop Ring
22	Magnet Pole Piece (6 Req'd) (Part of 11075)
23	Pole Shunt (6 Req'd) (Part of 11075)
24	Magnet Retainer (6 Req'd) (Part of 11075)
25	Starter Frame and Magnet
26	Brush Holder
27	Brush Spring
28	Bushing (Part of 11049)
29	Brush End Plate and Bushing
30	Brush Plate Screw (2 Req'd)
31	Through-Bolt (2 Req'd)

FM1129300036000X

Fig. 1 Exploded view of permanent magnet starter motor

Condition	Possible Sources
• The engine does not crank or relay clicks	• Battery. • Starter motor. • Starter motor relay. • Ignition switch. • Anti-theft system. • Circuitry.
• The engine cranks slowly	• Battery. • Starter motor. • Circuitry.
• Unusual starter noise	• Starter mounting. • Flywheel/ring gear. • Starter motor.
• The starter spins but the engine does not crank	• Starter motor. • Damaged flywheel/ring gear teeth.

LTV0500000000295

Fig. 2 Troubleshooting chart. Aviator

Condition	Possible Sources
• The engine does not crank and the relay does click	• Battery. • Fuse. • Starter motor/solenoid. • Ignition switch. • Circuit.
• The engine does not crank and the relay does not click	• Fuse. • Battery. • Starter relay. • Ignition switch. • Digital transmission range (TR) sensor (4.6L and 5.4L only). • Starter solenoid. • Circuit. • Powertrain control module (PCM).
• The engine cranks slowly	• Battery. • Starter motor/solenoid. • Circuit.
• Unusual starter noise	• Starter mounting. • Starter motor. • Flexplate. • Incorrect starter drive engagement.
• The starter spins but the engine does not crank	• Worn or damaged starter motor. • Damaged flexplate ring gear.

LTV0500000000296

Fig. 3 Troubleshooting chart. E-Series

2. Disconnect ignition coil connector.
3. Connect a remote starter switch between starter solenoid S-terminal and battery positive terminal.
4. Connect positive lead of Rotunda digital multi-meter tool No. 73, or equivalent to starter motor housing. **Connection must be clean and free of rust or grease.**
5. Connect negative lead of multi-meter to negative battery terminal.
6. Engage remote starter switch and read voltage, which should be .2 volts or less.
7. If voltage drop is greater than .2 volts, clean negative battery connections at battery and chassis. Also clean engine ground cable connections at cable mounting bracket.
8. If voltage drop is greater than .2 volts, determine which way current is flowing in cable. Connect multi-meter positive lead to end of cable nearest battery positive.
9. If voltage drop is still excessive, repair or replace battery ground cable.

Load Test

1. Connect Rotunda Starting and Charging Tester tool No. 078-00005, or equivalent. Ensure current is not flowing through ammeter and heavy duty carbon pile rheostat portion of circuit (rheostat at maximum counterclockwise position).
2. Disconnect push on S-terminal at starter relay, then connect remote control starter switch from positive battery terminal and S-terminal of starter relay.
3. Place transmission in Neutral or Park (automatic transmission) or fully depress clutch pedal (manual transmission), then crank engine with ignition turned Off. Record exact reading on voltmeter.
4. Stop cranking engine, then reduce carbon pile resistance until voltmeter indicates same reading as that obtained while starter cranked engine.
5. Ammeter will indicate starter current draw under normal load. Compare this value with value listed in specifications.

No-Load Test

The starter No-Load test will uncover such conditions as open or shorted windings or a rubbing armature. The starter can be tested, at no-load, on the test bench only.

1. Make test connections with Rotunda Starting and Charging Tester tool No. 078-00005, or equivalent. Ensure cables connected to starter are sufficient to carry high current flow (the same gauge wire as in vehicle).
2. Set rheostat at maximum counterclockwise position, ensuring no current flow through ammeter. Record exact reading on voltmeter.
3. Disconnect starter from battery, then reduce resistance of rheostat until voltmeter indicates same reading as that obtained while starter was running.
4. The ammeter will indicate starter no-load current draw. Refer to specifications for comparison.
5. Inspect for a rubbing armature, bent shaft, binding bearings, or shorts in armature and/or brushes if current exceeds specifications.

Solenoid Test

Inspect for continuity between S-terminal and M-terminal, and between S-terminal and ground (frame) using digital multi-meter tool No. 73, or equivalent. If there is no continuity, inspect for ice, dirt or foreign material preventing contact. Repair or replace solenoid as required.

Condition	Possible Sources
• The engine does not crank	• Battery • Fuse(s) • Starter motor • Circuitry • Starter motor relay • Anti-theft system • TR sensor
• The engine cranks slowly	• Battery • Starter motor • Circuitry
• Unusual starter noise	• Starter motor mounting • Starter motor • Incorrect starter drive engagement
• The starter spins but the engine does not crank	• Starter motor • Damaged flywheel/ring gear teeth

LTV0500000000297

Fig. 4 Troubleshooting chart. Escape & Mariner

Condition	Possible Sources
• The engine does not crank and the relay does click	• Battery. • Fuse. • Starter motor/solenoid. • Ignition switch. • Circuit.
• The engine does not crank and the relay does not click	• Fuse. • Battery. • Starter relay. • Ignition switch. • Digital transmission range (TR) sensor. • Circuit.
• The engine cranks slowly	• Battery. • Starter motor/solenoid. • Circuit.
• Unusual starter noise	• Starter mounting. • Flexplate. • Starter motor.
• The starter spins but the engine does not crank	• Starter motor. • Damaged flexplate teeth.

LTV0500000000301

Fig. 5 Troubleshooting chart. Excursion & F-Super Duty Series

Condition	Possible Sources
• The engine does not crank and the relay does click	• Battery. • Fuse. • Starter motor/solenoid. • Ignition switch. • Circuit.
• The engine does not crank and the relay does not click	• Fuse. • Battery. • Starter relay. • Ignition switch. • Digital transmission range (TR) sensor. • Circuit.
• The engine cranks slowly	• Battery. • Starter motor/solenoid. • Circuit.
• Unusual starter noise	• Starter mounting. • Flexplate. • Starter motor.
• The starter spins but the engine does not crank	• Starter motor. • Damaged flexplate teeth.

LTV0500000000298

Fig. 6 Troubleshooting chart. Expedition & Navigator

Condition	Possible Sources
• The engine does not crank	• Battery • Starter motor • Starter motor relay • Ignition switch • Damaged fuse • Anti-theft system • Circuitry
• The engine cranks slowly	• Battery • Starter motor • Circuitry
• Unusual starter noise	• Starter mounting • Flywheel/ring gear • Starter motor
• The starter spins but the engine does not crank	• Starter motor • Damaged flywheel/ring gear teeth

LTV0500000000299

Fig. 7 Troubleshooting chart. Explorer & Mountaineer

Condition	Possible Sources	Action
• The engine does not crank	• Battery. • Starter motor. • Starter motor relay. • Ignition switch. • CJB Fuse 24 (7.5A). • BJB Fuse 11 (50A). • Anti-theft system. • Circuitry.	• Go To Pinpoint Test A .
• The engine cranks slowly	• Battery. • Starter motor. • Circuitry.	• CARRY OUT the Starter Motor—Voltage Drop Test Component Test.
• Unusual starter noise	• Starter mounting. • Flywheel/ring gear. • Starter motor.	• Go To Pinpoint Test B .
• The starter spins but the engine does not crank	• Starter motor. • Flywheel/ring gear. • Damaged flywheel/ring gear teeth.	• INSPECT the starter motor mounting and engagement. INSTALL a new starter motor. • INSPECT the flywheel/ring gear for damaged, missing or worn teeth. REPAIR as necessary.

LTV0500000000300

Fig. 8 Troubleshooting chart. Explorer Sport/Sport Trac

Condition	Possible Sources
• The engine does not crank and the relay clicks	• Battery • Fuse • Starter motor/solenoid • Ignition switch (part of the key lock cylinder) • Circuit
• The engine does not crank and the relay does not click	• Fuse • Battery • Starter relay • Ignition switch • Digital transmission range (TR) sensor • Clutch pedal position (CPP) switch • Circuit
• The engine cranks slowly	• Battery • Starter motor/solenoid • Circuit
• Unusual starter noise	• Starter mounting • Flexplate or flywheel • Starter motor
• The starter spins but the engine does not crank	• Starter motor • Damaged flexplate or flywheel ring gear teeth

LTV0500000000302

Fig. 9 Troubleshooting chart. F-150 & LT

Condition	Possible Sources
• The engine does not crank	• Battery. • Bussed electrical center (BEC) fuse 4 (30A). • Smart junction box (SJB) fuse 21 (10A). • Starter motor. • Ignition switch. • Circuitry. • Starter motor relay. • Anti-theft system. • Digital transmission range (TR) sensor.
• The engine cranks slowly	• Battery. • Starter motor. • Circuitry.
• Unusual starter noise	• Starter motor mounting. • Starter motor. • Incorrect starter drive engagement.
• The starter spins but the engine does not crank	• Starter motor. • Damaged flexplate/ring gear teeth.

LTV0500000000303

Fig. 10 Troubleshooting chart. Freestar & Monterey

Condition	Possible Sources
• The engine does not crank	• Battery. • BJB Fuse 105 (30A) • CJB Fuse 19 (10A) • Starter motor. • Ignition switch. • Circuitry. • Starter motor relay. • Anti-theft system. • Digital TR sensor.
• The engine cranks slowly	• Battery. • Starter motor. • Ignition switch. • Circuitry.
• Unusual starter noise	• Starter motor mounting. • Starter motor. • Incorrect starter drive engagement.
• The starter spins but the engine does not crank	• Starter motor. • Damaged flywheel/ring gear teeth.

LTV0500000000305

Fig. 12 Troubleshooting chart. Windstar

Condition	Possible Sources
• The engine does not crank	• Battery • Fuse • Starter motor • Ignition switch • Circuitry • Starter motor relay • Clutch pedal position (CPP) switch • Anti-theft system, if equipped
• The engine cranks slowly	• Battery • Starter motor • Ignition switch • Circuitry
• Unusual starter noise	• Starter motor mounting • Starter motor • Incorrect starter drive engagement
• The starter spins but the engine does not crank	• Starter motor • Damaged flywheel/ring gear teeth

LTV0500000000304

Fig. 11 Troubleshooting chart. Ranger

STARTER SPECIFICATIONS

Year	Starter, Inch Diameter	Ampere Draw Normal Load	Engine Cranking Speed RPM	Minimum Stall Torque @ 5 Volts Ft. Lbs.	No-Load Ampere @ 12 Volts	Brushes		
						Length Inch	Wear Limit Inch	Spring Tension, Ounces
2002–06	4①	130–220①	140–220①	14.7①	60–80①	.66	—	65
	—	130–190②	200–250②	—	60–80②	—	—	—

①— Except Escape, Freestyle & Mariner.

②— Escape, Freestyle & Mariner.

Villager Starter Motor

INDEX

APPLICATION CHART

Year	Model
2002	Villager

PRECAUTIONS

Air Bag Systems

Refer to "Air Bag System Precautions" in the front of this manual for system disarming and arming procedures.

Battery Ground Cable

Prior to service, disconnect battery ground cable and isolate as required.

DESCRIPTION

When the solenoid is energized, a magnetic field is created in the solenoid windings. The iron plunger core is drawn into the solenoid coil, and a lever connected to the overrunning clutch engages the pinion drive gear to the flywheel ring gear. When the plunger is pulled all the way in, its contact disc closes the circuit between the battery and starter motor feed terminals. This sends current to the starter motor, **Figs. 1 and 2,** and the pinion drive gear cranks the flywheel to start the engine. When current flows to the starter motor, **Fig. 2,** the solenoid pull-in coil is bypassed and the hold-in coil keeps the pinion drive gear engaged with the flywheel until the ignition switch is released from the Start position. The starter uses a planetary gear reduction system to reduce internal torque.

TROUBLESHOOTING

Refer to **Fig. 3** for starter motor troubleshooting charts.

DIAGNOSIS & TESTING

On-Vehicle Inspection

Be aware that the heavy gauge battery input lead at the starter solenoid is "Electrically Hot" at all times. A protective cap or boot is provided over this terminal and must be replaced after servicing.

Always make connections with the digital multi-meter tool No. 73, or equivalent at the component terminal rather than at the wiring end connector. Making a connection at the wiring end connector could result in inaccurate readings since the meter will not pick up a high resistance between the connector and the component.

1. Determine state of charge using Rotunda Starting/Charging Tester tool No. 078-00005, or an equivalent test battery. Perform load test, then service or replace battery as required.
2. Disconnect inertia fuel shutoff (IFS) switch electrical connector.
3. If starter motor will not crank with a fully charged battery, connect positive lead of Rotunda digital multi-meter tool No. 73, or equivalent to S-terminal on starter solenoid, then the negative lead to starter motor housing.
4. Turn ignition to Start while reading voltmeter. **If solenoid is extremely hot, it may not function though voltage at S-terminal is eight volts or more. Allow solenoid to cool, then test again.**
5. If voltage at S-terminal is eight volts or more, there is a starter motor or high current circuit fault.

No-Load Test

1. Connect a fully charged battery, Rotunda Starting and Charging Tester tool No. 078-00005, or equivalent and a remote control starter switch to starter motor as illustrated in **Fig. 4.**
2. Engage remote starter switch. The starter motor should eject the pinion drive gear and run smoothly. If starter does not operate as specified, repair or replace as required.
3. While starter motor is running, read and record voltmeter and ammeter readings. Voltage should be greater than 11 volts and amperage should be no more than 90 amps.
4. If readings are not within specifications, replace starter motor.

Ground Circuit Test

Make all connections at the component terminal when performing this test procedure. Do not make connections at cable or wiring terminals.

A slow cranking condition may be caused by resistance in the ground or return portion of the cranking circuit. Test the voltage drop in the ground circuit as follows:

1. Disconnect coil wire from distributor cap, then connect a remote starter switch between starter solenoid S-terminal and the battery positive terminal.
2. Connect positive lead of Rotunda digital multi-meter tool No. 73, or equivalent to starter motor housing, then the meter negative lead to battery ground terminal. **The connection must be clean and free of rust and grease.**
3. Engage remote starter switch, then read voltage on lowest voltmeter scale, which should be .2 volts or less.
4. If voltage drop is greater than .2 volts, clean ground cable connections at battery and chassis, engine ground cable connections at front cover and engine mount bracket. If voltage reading is still excessive, repair or replace the battery ground cable or engine ground cables as required.
5. If battery and cables pass inspection but starter motor still cranks slowly or not at all, repair or replace starter motor as required.

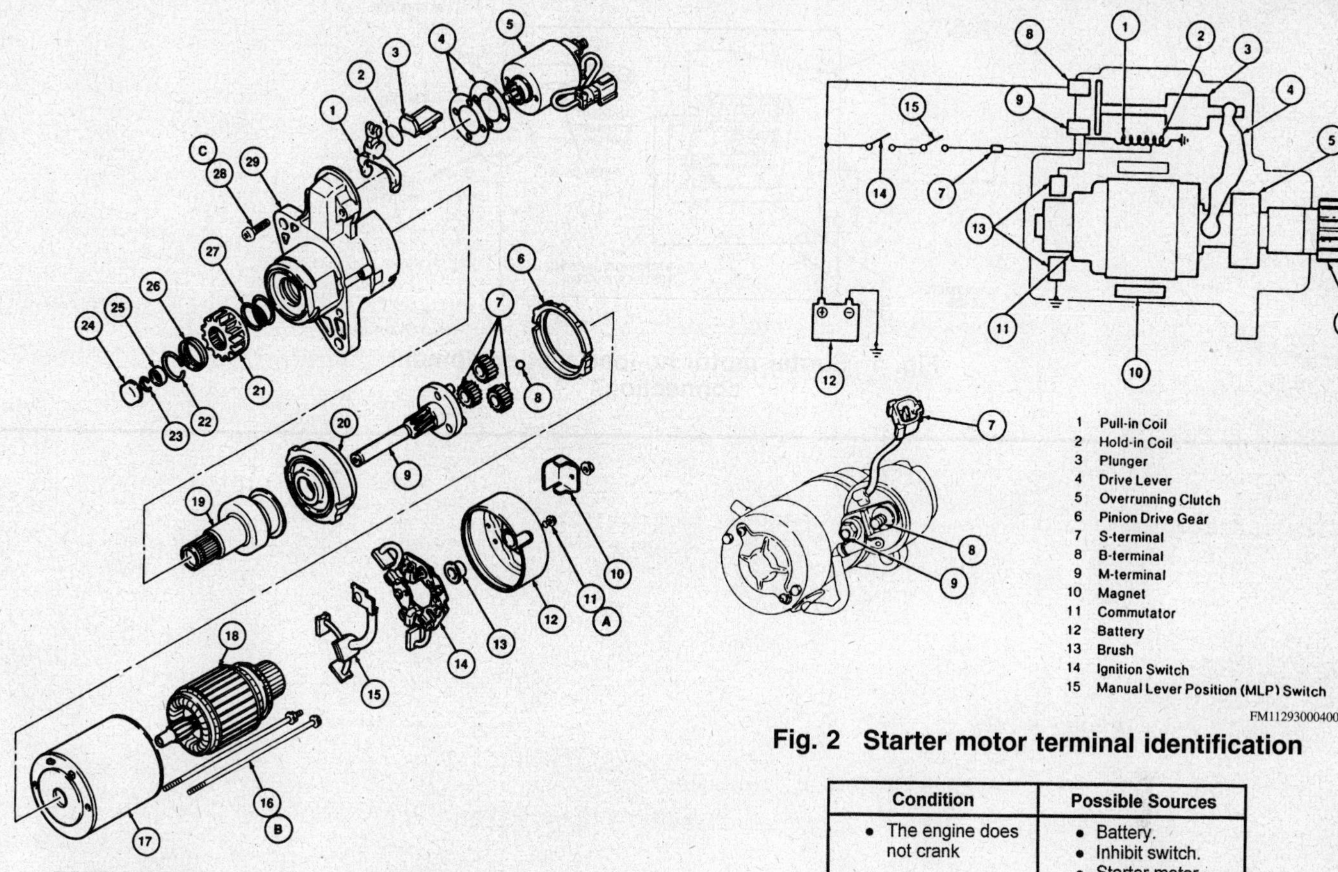

Fig. 2 Starter motor terminal identification

Item	Description
1	Drive Lever and Pin
2	Disc Plate
3	Dust Cover
4	Adjusting Plate
5	Starter Solenoid
6	Packing
7	Planet Gear
8	Ball Bearing
9	Output Shaft
10	Support Bracket
11	Brush Holder Screw (2 Req'd)
12	Brush End Plate
13	Bushing (Part of 11050)
14	Brush Holder
15	Brush Spring
16	Thru Bolt (2 Req'd)
17	Starter Frame
18	Starter Motor Armature
19	Starter Drive
20	Internal Gear

Item	Description
21	Pinion Drive Gear
22	Stop Ring
23	Stop Ring
24	Dust Cap
25	Stop Ring Retainer
26	Stop Ring Retainer
27	Pinion Drive Gear Spring
28	Starter Solenoid Screw (2 Req'd)
29	Drive End Housing
A	Tighten to 2.0-2.9 N·m (18-26 Lb-In)
B	Tighten to 6.9-8.8 N·m (61-78 Lb-In)
C	Tighten to 4.9-6.9 N·m (43-61 Lb-In)

FM1129800188000X

Fig. 1 Exploded view of starter motor

Condition	Possible Sources
• The engine does not crank	• Battery. • Inhibit switch. • Starter motor. • Ignition switch. • Circuitry. • TR sensor. • Anti-theft system, if equipped.
• The engine cranks slowly	• Battery. • Starter motor. • Circuitry.
• Unusual starter noise	• Starter motor mounting. • Starter motor. • Incorrect starter drive engagement.
• The starter spins but the engine does not crank	• Starter motor • Damaged flywheel/ring gear teeth.

LTV0500000000306

Fig. 3 Troubleshooting chart

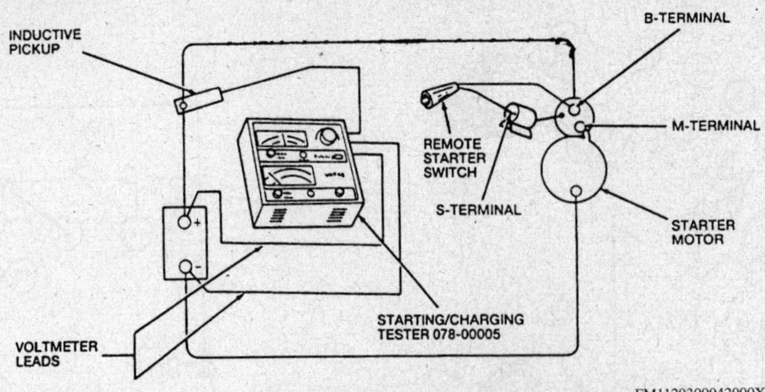

Fig. 4 Starter motor no-load test equipment connections

ALTERNATORS

NOTE: "Electrical Symbol & Wire Color Code Identification" Located In The Front Of This Manual May Be Used As An Aid When Using Wiring Circuits Found In This Section.

NOTE: Refer To "Computer Relearn Procedures" Located In The Front Of This Manual When Battery Power To The Computer Has Been Interrupted.

INDEX

APPLICATION CHART

Year	Model	Alternator Type
2002–06	Aviator	Ford Integral Regulator, Internal Fan
	E-Series	Internal Rear Mount
		Mitsubishi, Internal Fan
	Escape	Ford Integral Regulator, Internal Fan
	Excursion & F-Super Duty Series	Ford Integral Regulator, Internal Fan
		Mitsubishi, Internal Fan
	Expedition	Ford Integral Regulator, Internal Fan
	Explorer	Ford Integral Regulator, Internal Fan
	Freestar	Ford Integral Regulator, Internal Fan
	F-150	Ford Integral Regulator, Internal Fan
	Mariner	Ford Integral Regulator, Internal Fan
	Mark LT	Ford Integral Regulator, Internal Fan
	Monterey	Ford Integral Regulator, Internal Fan
	Mountaineer	Ford Integral Regulator, Internal Fan
	Navigator	Ford Integral Regulator, Internal Fan
	Ranger	Ford Integral Regulator, Internal Fan
	Villager	Mitsubishi, Internal Fan
	Windstar	Mitsubishi, Internal Fan

DESCRIPTION

Except Villager

A charge indicator lamp is used in the charging system, **Figs. 1 through 4.** System operation is as follows: when the ignition is turned On, a small electrical current flows through the lamp filament (turning lamp on) and through the alternator regulator to the alternator field. When the engine starts, the alternator field rotates and produces a voltage in the stator winding. When voltage at alternator stator terminal reaches approximately ½ system voltage, the regulator field relay closes. This puts the same voltage potential on both sides of the charge indicator lamp, causing it to go out. When the field relay has closed, current passes through the regulator "A" terminal and is metered to the alternator field.

When the engine starts, the alternator field rotates, causing the alternator to operate.

All vehicles, except those equipped with Integral Alternator/Regulator (IAR) charging systems, are equipped with electronic voltage regulators, **Figs. 1 and 2.** These solid state regulators are used in conjunction with other new components in the charging system, such as an alternator with a higher field current requirement, a warning indicator lamp shunt resistor and a new wiring harness with a new regulator connector.

On Windstar models, a powertrain control module (PCM) controlled "smart charge" charging system is used. The PCM determines the optimal voltage setpoint for the charging system and communicates this information to the voltage regulator. This system is unique because it features two unidirectional pulse-width modulated communication lines between the PCM and the alternator/regulator. The "GEN COM" line communicates the desired setpoint from the PCM to the voltage regulator. The "GEN MON" line reports alternator load conditions to the PCM. The third voltage regulator pin is the "A" circuit and is a dedicated battery voltage sense line.

Some models are equipped with an IAR charging system. This system has a solid state voltage regulator located in the rear of the alternator and is not replaceable. When replacing system components, note the following precautions:

1. Always use the proper alternator in the system.
2. Do not use an electromechanical regulator in an electronic system, as the wiring harness connector will not index properly with this type of regulator.
3. Electronic regulators are color coded for proper installation.
4. **On vehicles equipped with a warning indicator lamp,** a resistor is used

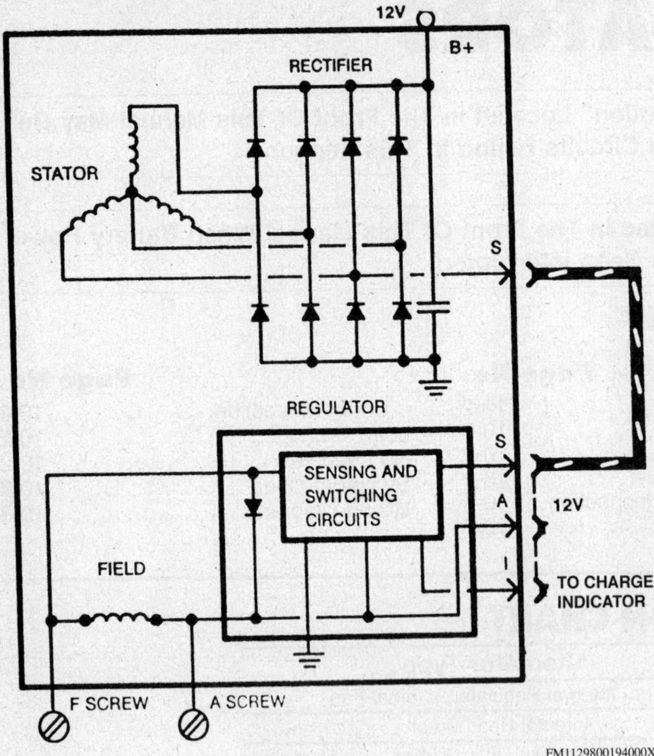

Fig. 1 Internal rear mount voltage regulator. Except Villager

Fig. 2 Internal rear mount voltage regulator. Except Villager

on the rear of the instrument cluster. Do not replace this resistor with the 15 ohm resistance wire used on previous systems.

On electronic systems with an indicator lamp, closing the ignition switch energizes the warning lamp and turns on the regulator output stage. The alternator receives maximum field current and is ready to generate an output voltage. As alternator rotor speed increases, the output and stator terminal voltages increase from zero to system regulation level determined by the regulator setting. When ignition switch is turned off, the solid state relay circuit turns the output stage off, interrupting current flow through the regulator so there is not a current drain on the battery.

Villager

The "B" terminal is connected internally to the rectifier bridge output, **Fig. 5.** Externally, the "B" terminal supplies alternator output (DC) to the electrical system. The alternator output charges the battery and operates the electrical accessories while the engine is running.

The "L" terminal is connected internally, through a network of integrated circuits, to the field coil. When the ignition is turned On, the field coil turns on the voltage regulator power transistor.

The "S" terminal is connected internally to the voltage regulator sensing circuit. Externally, the S terminal is connected to the ignition side of the ignition switch. The "S" terminal tells the voltage regulator how much alternator output is required.

The Integrated Circuit (IC) electronic voltage regulator is part of the rotor, brush and brush holder assembly. There is no voltage adjustment. The IC voltage regulator automatically reduces the regulated voltage when ambient temperature increases, so that the proper battery charging voltage is maintained.

DIAGNOSIS & TESTING

When performing diagnostic procedures on the charging system begin with the "No Load Test," "Load Test," and "Battery Drain Test." If system fails any of these tests, refer to "Wiring Diagrams" to inspect system wiring and connectors before replacing the alternator.

No Load Test

1. Turn off all electrical accessories.
2. Connect a suitable tachometer to engine.
3. Start engine and increase speed to 1500 RPM.
4. Voltmeter should increase to approximately 14.1–15 volts.
5. If voltage is satisfactory, perform "Load Test."
6. If voltage is higher than specified, refer to "Wiring Diagrams" to inspect system wiring and connectors.

Load Test

1. Connect suitable tachometer to engine.
2. With engine running, turn headlamps to high beam position and blower motor to maximum position.
3. Raise engine speed to 2000 RPM.
4. Voltmeter should indicate more than .5 volt above battery voltage.
5. If voltage is within specifications, charging system is operating properly.
6. If voltage is not as specified, refer to "Wiring Diagrams" to inspect system wiring and connectors.

Battery Drain Test

1. Disconnect battery ground cable.
2. Connect a suitable multi-meter between battery ground cable end and negative battery post.
3. Turn all electrical accessories off, then ensure ignition is Off.
4. Close all doors, then wait one minute for illuminated entry lamps to turn off.
5. Current reading should be less than 50 milliamps. If current reading is more than 50 milliamps, a current draw is indicated.
6. Remove fuses from fuse panel one at a time until cause of drain is located.

Bench Tests

ROTOR INSPECTION

1. Measure the resistance between slip rings, which should be 2.5–3.6 ohms. If reading is not as specified, replace rotor assembly.
2. Inspect for continuity between each slip ring and rotor core. If continuity exists, the rotor coil is shorted and should be replaced.
3. If rotor is good and is to be used again, clean the slip rings with fine emery

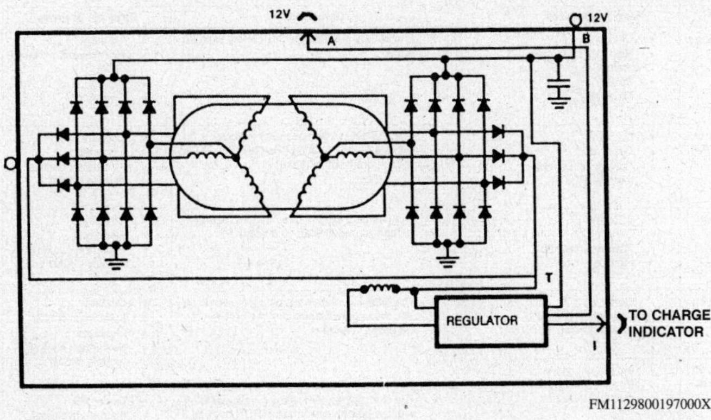

FM1129800197000X

Fig. 3 Internal alternator regulator. Except Villager

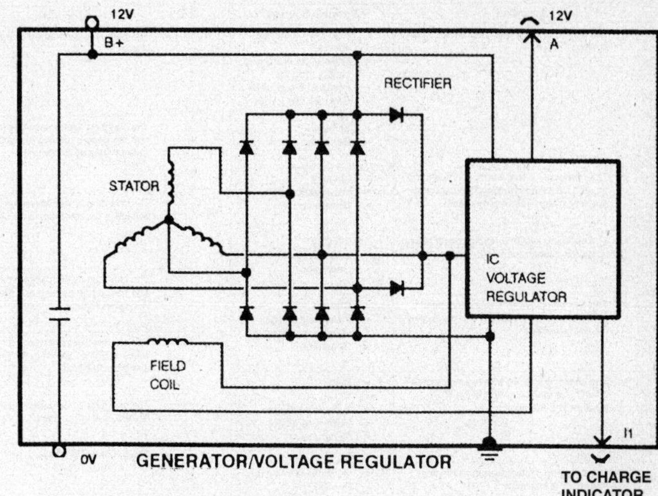

FM1129800196000X

Fig. 4 Internal alternator regulator. Except Villager

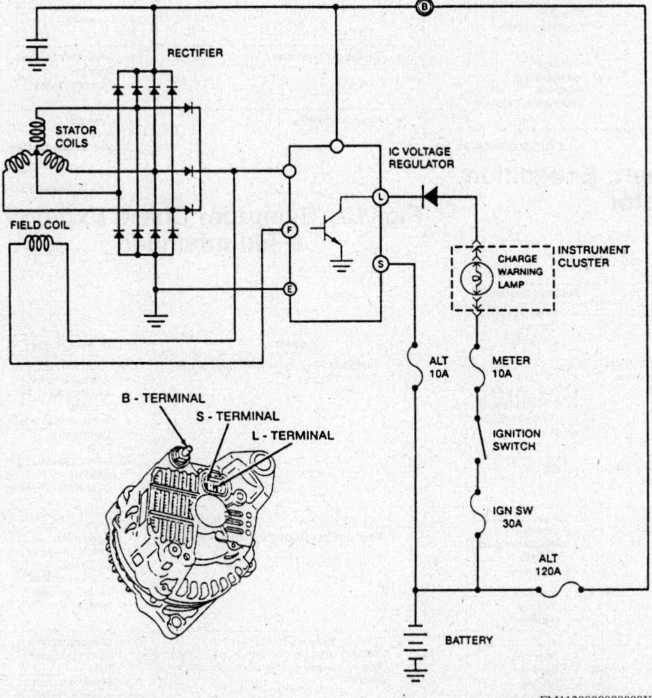

FM1128800008000X

Fig. 5 Alternator rear terminal circuits. Villager

Negative (Black)	Positive (Red)	Continuity
E	P_n, P_1, P_2, P_3	No
B	P_n, P_1, P_2, P_3	Yes
T	P_1, P_2, P_3	Yes
T	P_n	No
P_n, P_1, P_2, P_3	E	Yes
P_n, P_1, P_2, P_3	B	No
P_n, P_1, P_2, P_3	T	No

FM1129800199000X

Fig. 6 Rectifier assembly continuity inspection. Villager

Condition	Possible Sources
• The battery is discharged or battery voltage is low	• Circuitry. • High key-off current drain(s). • Battery. • Generator.
• The charging system warning indicator is ON with the engine running (the charging system voltage does not increase)	• Circuitry. • Generator.
• The charging system overcharges (battery voltage is greater than 15.5 volts)	• Circuitry. • Generator.
• The charging system warning indicator is ON with the engine running and the battery increases voltage	• Circuitry. • Instrument cluster. • Generator.
• The charging system warning indicator is OFF with the ignition switch in the RUN position and the engine off	• Bulb. • Circuitry. • Instrument cluster. • Generator.
• The charging system warning indicator flickers or is intermittent	• Fuse link(s). • Circuitry. • Generator.
• The generator is noisy	• Bolts or brackets. • Drive belt. • Generator. • Generator pulley.
• Radio interference	• Generator. • Circuitry. • Entertainment system.

LTV0500000000847

Fig. 7 Symptom Chart. Aviator

paper if they appear grooved or dark.

STATOR INSPECTION

1. Visually inspect the stator closely for signs of overheating. A burned spot usually indicates a shorted stator winding which should be replaced.
2. Inspect for continuity between the stator coil leads. No continuity between any two leads indicates an open winding. In this case the stator winding should be replaced.
3. Inspect for continuity between the three stator leads and the core. If continuity exists, a grounded stator winding is indicated, which should be replaced.

RECTIFIER ASSEMBLY INSPECTION

Inspect for continuity using Rotunda ohmmeter tool No. 059-00010, or equivalent by connecting the leads to the rectifier assembly as illustrated in **Fig. 6.** Replace rectifier assembly if any diode does not meet specifications in **Fig. 6.**

Symptom Chart

Refer to **Figs. 7 through 13** for symptom charts when diagnosing the charging system.

Wiring Diagrams

Refer to **Figs. 14 through 37** for wiring diagrams.

ADJUSTMENTS

Electronic Regulators

These regulators are factory calibrated and sealed and no adjustment is possible. If regulator calibration values are not within specifications, the regulator must be replaced.

Condition	Possible Sources
• The battery is discharged or battery voltage is low	• High key-off current drain(s) • Engine, generator and battery grounds • Positive battery cable • Generator B+ circuit high resistance • Battery • Generator
• The charging system warning indicator is on with the engine running (the charging system voltage does not increase)	• Circuitry • Voltage regulator • Generator
• The charging system overcharges (battery voltage is greater than 15.5 volts)	• Circuitry • Voltage regulator • Generator
• The charging system warning indicator is on with the engine running and the battery increases voltage	• Circuitry • Instrument cluster • Voltage regulator • Generator
• The charging system warning indicator is off with the ignition switch in the RUN position and the engine off	• Bulb • Circuitry • Instrument cluster • Voltage regulator • Generator
• The charging system warning indicator flickers or is intermittent	• Corroded terminal(s) • Fuse(s) • Fusible link(s) • Circuitry • Voltage regulator • Generator
• The generator is noisy	• Accessory drive belt • Loose bolts/brackets • Generator/pulley
• Radio interference	• Generator • Circuitry • In-vehicle entertainment system

LTV0500000000841

Fig. 8 Symptom Chart. E-Series, Excursion, F-Super Duty & Ranger

Condition	Possible Sources
• The battery is discharged or battery voltage is low	• Engine, battery and generator grounds • Positive battery cable • Circuitry • High key-off current drain(s) • Battery • Generator
• The charging system warning indicator is on with the engine running (the charging system voltage does not increase)	• Generator • Fusible links • Circuitry • Powertrain control module (PCM)
• The charging system overcharges (battery voltage is greater than 15.5 volts)	• Generator • Circuitry • Powertrain control module (PCM)
• The charging system warning indicator is on with the engine running and the battery increases voltage	• Generator • Instrument cluster • Powertrain control module (PCM)
• The charging system warning indicator is off with the ignition switch in the RUN position and the engine off	• Instrument cluster • Powertrain control module (PCM)
• The charging system warning indicator flickers or is intermittent	• Instrument cluster
• The generator is noisy	• Loose bolts/brackets • Drive belt • Generator/pulley
• Radio interference	• Generator • Wiring/routing • In-vehicle entertainment system

LTV0500000000842

Fig. 11 Symptom Chart. Escape, F-150, Freestar, Mariner, Mark LT & Monterey

Condition	Possible Sources
• The battery is discharged or battery voltage is low	• Circuitry • High key-off current drain(s) • Battery • Generator
• The charging system warning indicator is on with the engine running (the charging system voltage does not increase)	• Circuitry • Generator • Powertrain control module (PCM)
• The charging system overcharges (battery voltage is greater than 15.5 volts)	• Circuitry • Generator • Powertrain control module (PCM)
• The charging system warning indicator is on with the engine running and the battery increases voltage	• Generator • Powertrain control module (PCM)
• The charging system warning indicator is off with the ignition switch in the RUN position and the engine off	• Instrument cluster • Powertrain control module (PCM)
• The charging system warning indicator flickers or is intermittent	• Instrument cluster
• The generator is noisy	• Loose bolts/brackets • Drive belt • Generator/pulley
• Radio interference	• Generator • Wiring/routing • In-vehicle entertainment system

LTV0500000000844

Fig. 9 Symptom chart. Expedition & Navigator

Condition	Possible Sources
• The system overcharges (battery voltage is greater than 15.5 volts)	• BJB F9 (10A). • Circuitry. • Generator.
• The charging system warning indicator operates correctly but the battery voltage does not increase	• Circuitry. • BJB F9 (10A). • BJB F29 (140A). • Drive belt (8620). • Generator.
• The charging system warning indicator is on with the engine running and the battery voltage increases	• Circuitry.
• The charging system warning indicator is inoperative	• Circuitry. • Instrument cluster (10849). • Generator.
• The charging system indicator flickers or is intermittent	• Circuitry. • Generator.
• The generator is noisy	• Drive belt. • Generator. • Related components.
• Radio interference	• Generator. • Other components.
• The battery will not stay charged	• Battery drain. • Circuitry. • Battery. • Generator.

LTV0500000000846

Fig. 12 Symptom chart. Villager

Condition	Possible Sources
• The battery is discharged or battery voltage is low	• Circuitry • High key-off current drain(s) • Battery • Generator
• The charging system warning indicator is on with the engine running (the charging system voltage does not increase)	• Circuitry • Generator • Powertrain control module (PCM)
• The charging system overcharges (battery voltage is greater than 15.5 volts)	• Circuitry • Generator • Powertrain control module (PCM)
• The charging system warning indicator is on with the engine running and the battery increases voltage	• Circuitry • Instrument cluster • Generator • Powertrain control module (PCM)
• The charging system warning indicator is off with the ignition switch in the RUN position and the engine off	• Generator • Instrument cluster • Circuitry
• The charging system warning indicator flickers or is intermittent	• Fusible link(s) • Generator connections • Generator
• The generator is noisy	• Loose bolts/brackets • Drive belt • Generator/pulley
• Radio interference	• Generator • In-vehicle entertainment system

LTV0500000000843

Fig. 10 Symptom Chart. Explorer & Mountaineer

Condition	Possible Sources
• Charging system malfunction (high or low system voltage)	• A circuit 35 (OG/LB). • A circuit fuse link. • B+ circuit 36 (YE/WH). • B+ circuit fuse links. • Generator. • PCM • GEN-COM circuit 586 (RD/PK). • GEN-MON circuit 585 (VT).
• Dead battery or battery will not stay charged	• Generator. • Battery. • B+ Circuit. • High key-off load. • Loose, corroded terminal(s).
• Charging system warning indicator malfunctioning (light on with engine running, light off with key on engine off, light on with key off)	• Charging system warning indicator bulb. • Instrument cluster. • A circuit 35 (OG/LB). • Generator. • PCM.
• Generator is noisy	• Loose bolts/brackets. • Drive belt. • Generator.
• Radio interference	• Generator. • Wiring/routing. • In-vehicle entertainment system.

LTV0500000000845

Fig. 13 Symptom chart. Windstar

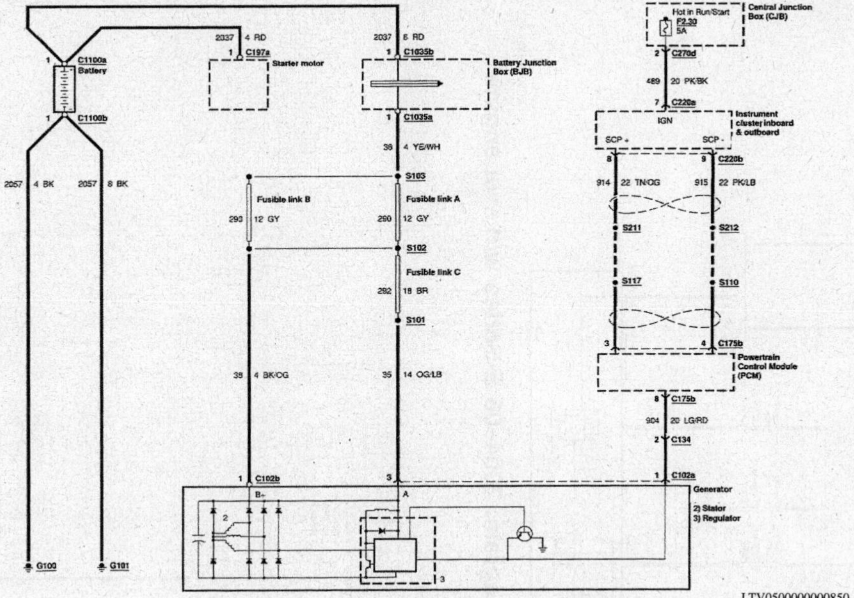

Fig. 14 Wiring diagram. Aviator

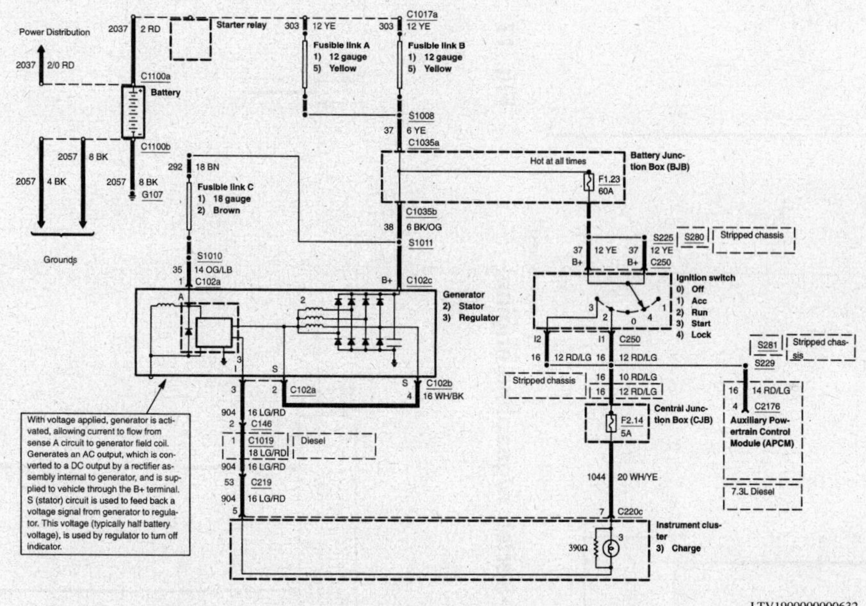

Fig. 15 Wiring diagram. 2002–03 E-Series w/single alternator

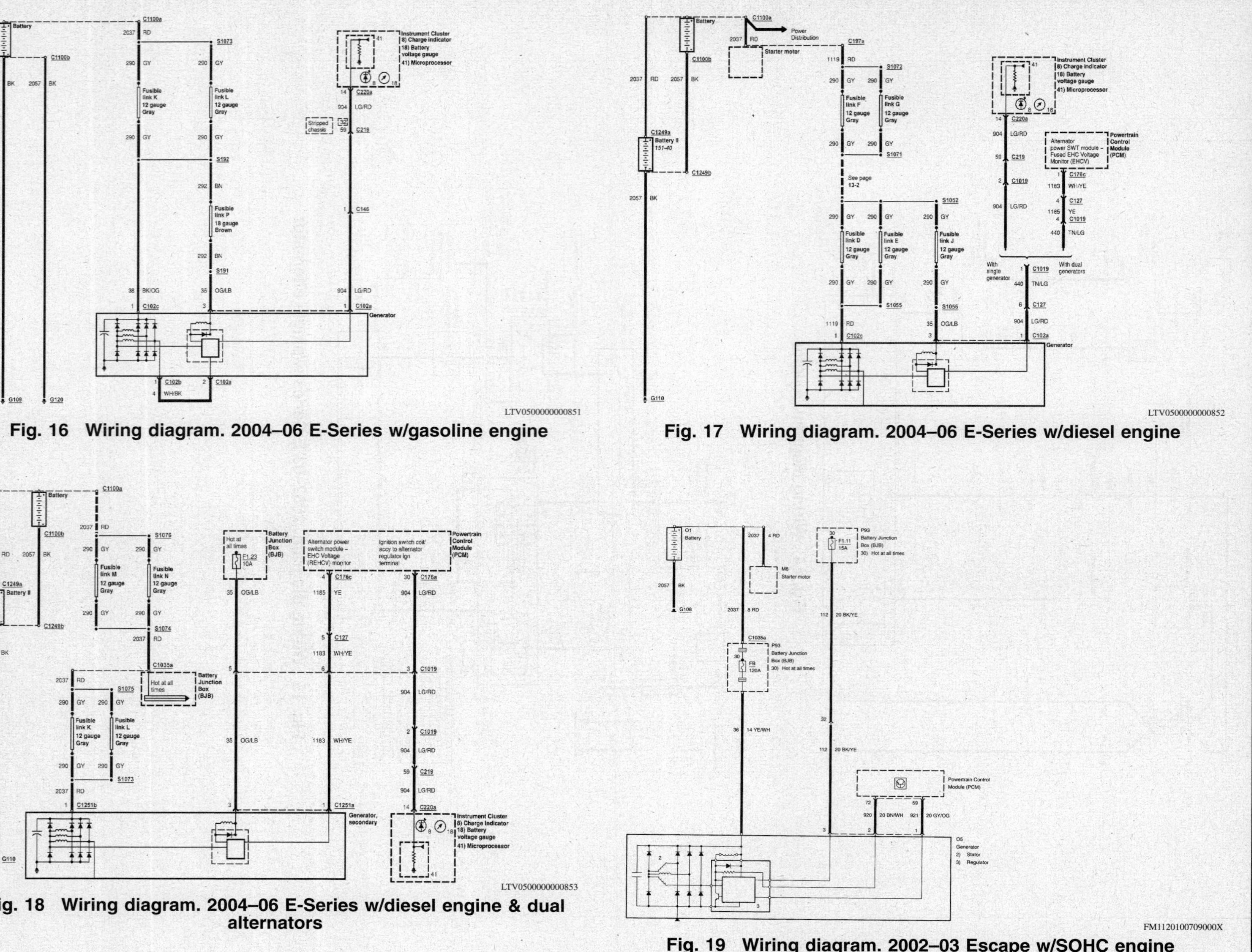

LTV0500000000851

Fig. 16 Wiring diagram. 2004–06 E-Series w/gasoline engine

LTV0500000000852

Fig. 17 Wiring diagram. 2004–06 E-Series w/diesel engine

LTV0500000000853

Fig. 18 Wiring diagram. 2004–06 E-Series w/diesel engine & dual alternators

FM1120100709000X

Fig. 19 Wiring diagram. 2002–03 Escape w/SOHC engine

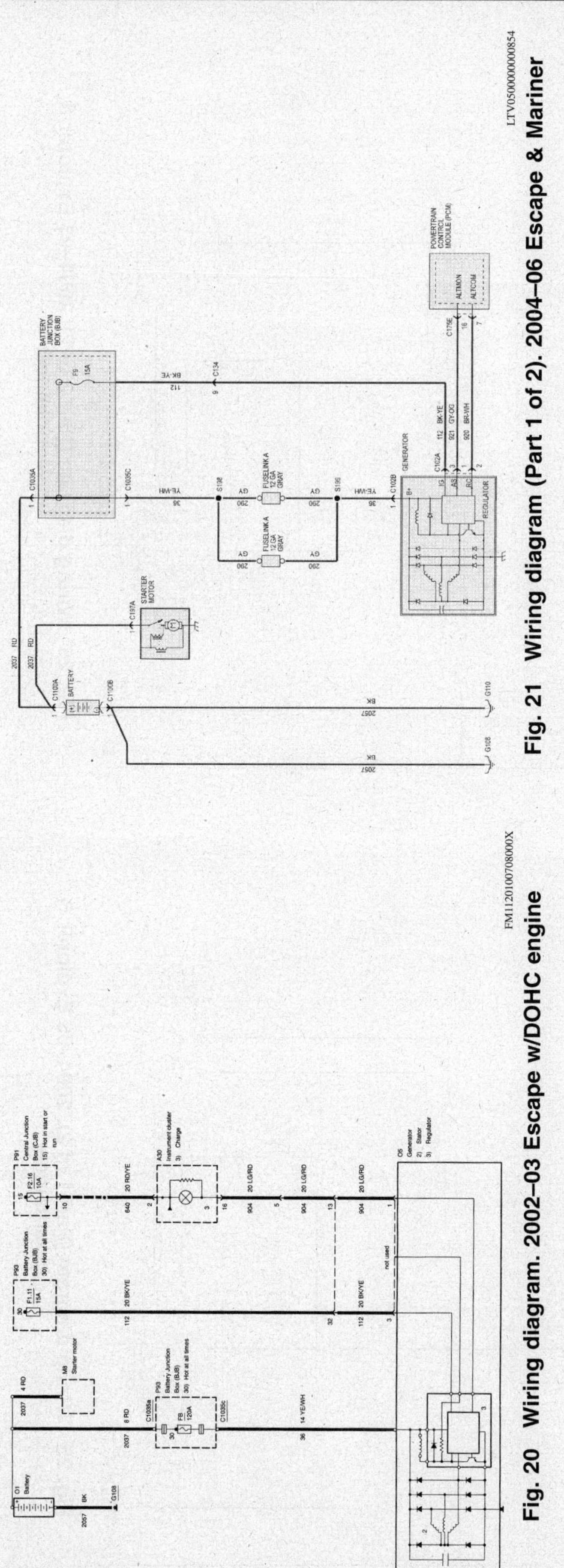

FM1120100708000X

Fig. 20 Wiring diagram. 2002–03 Escape w/DOHC engine

LTV0500000000854

Fig. 21 Wiring diagram (Part 1 of 2). 2004–06 Escape & Mariner

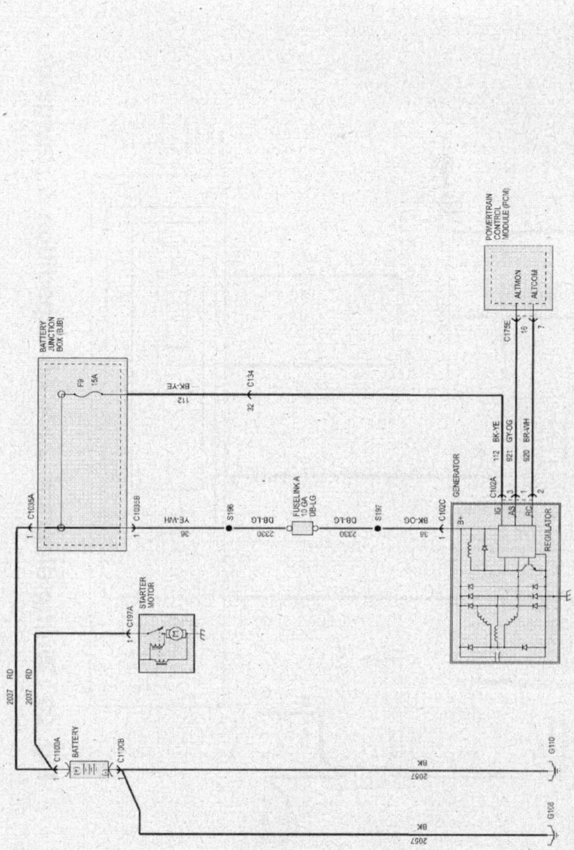

LTV0500000000855

Fig. 21 Wiring diagram. (Part 2 of 2) 2004–06 Escape & Mariner

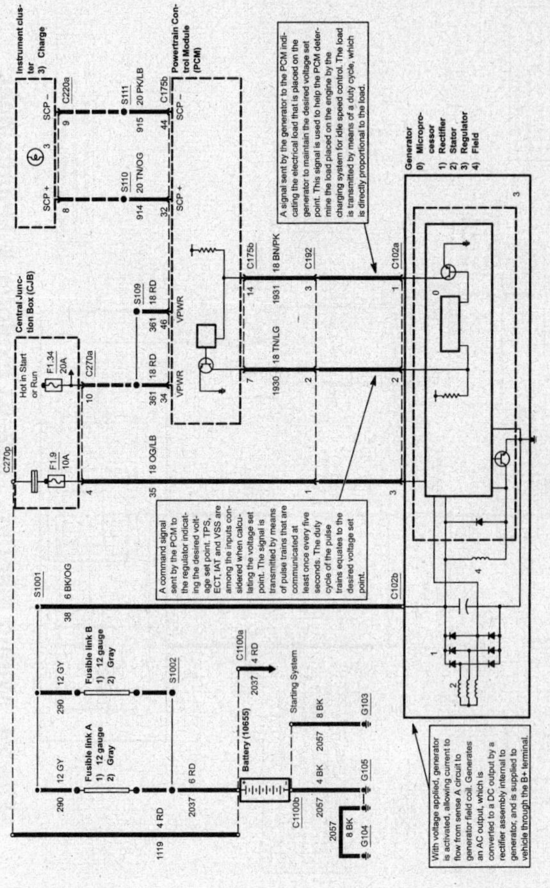

LTV1900000000635

Fig. 22 Wiring diagram. 2002–03 Expedition & Navigator

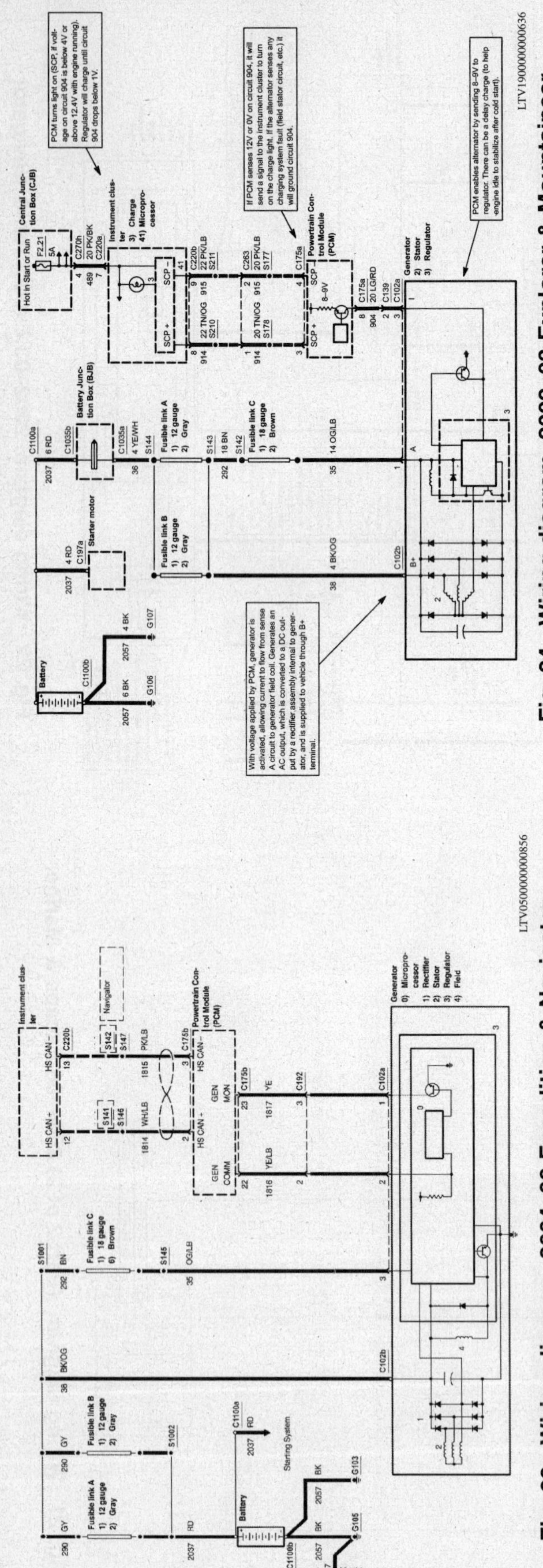

LTV1900000000636

Fig. 24 Wiring diagram. 2002–03 Explorer & Mountaineer

LTV0500000000856

Fig. 23 Wiring diagram. 2004–06 Expedition & Navigator

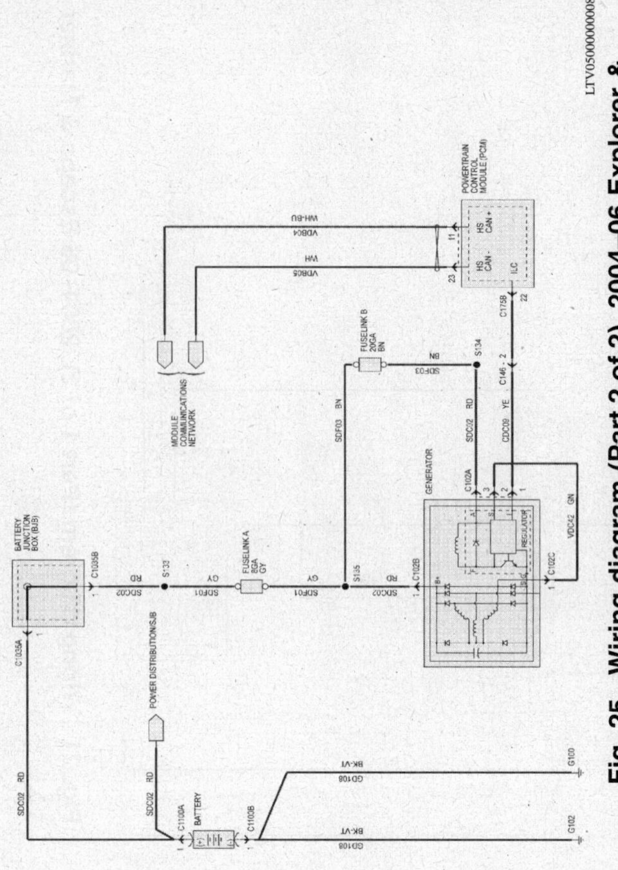

LTV0500000000858

Fig. 25 Wiring diagram (Part 2 of 2). 2004–06 Explorer & Mountaineer

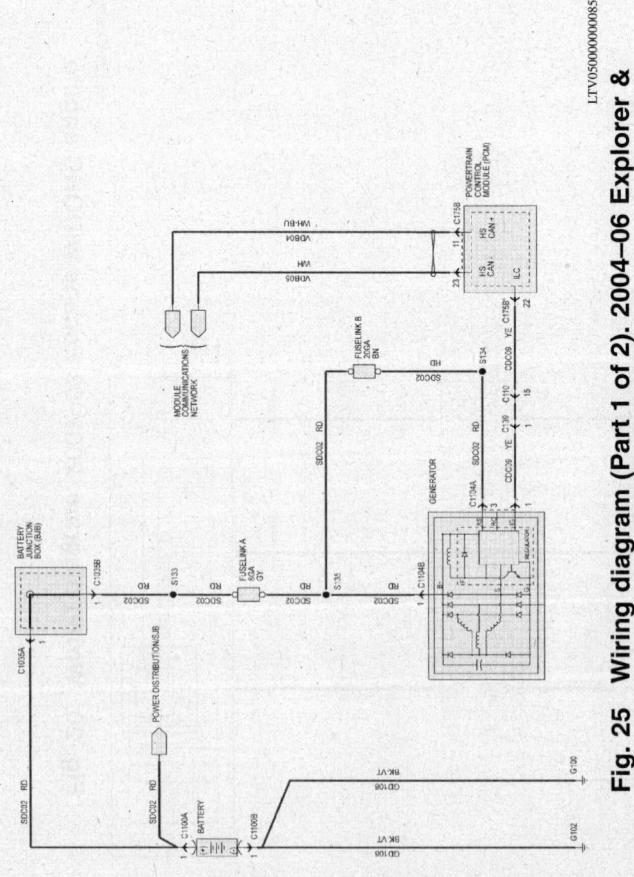

LTV0500000000857

Fig. 25 Wiring diagram (Part 1 of 2). 2004–06 Explorer & Mountaineer

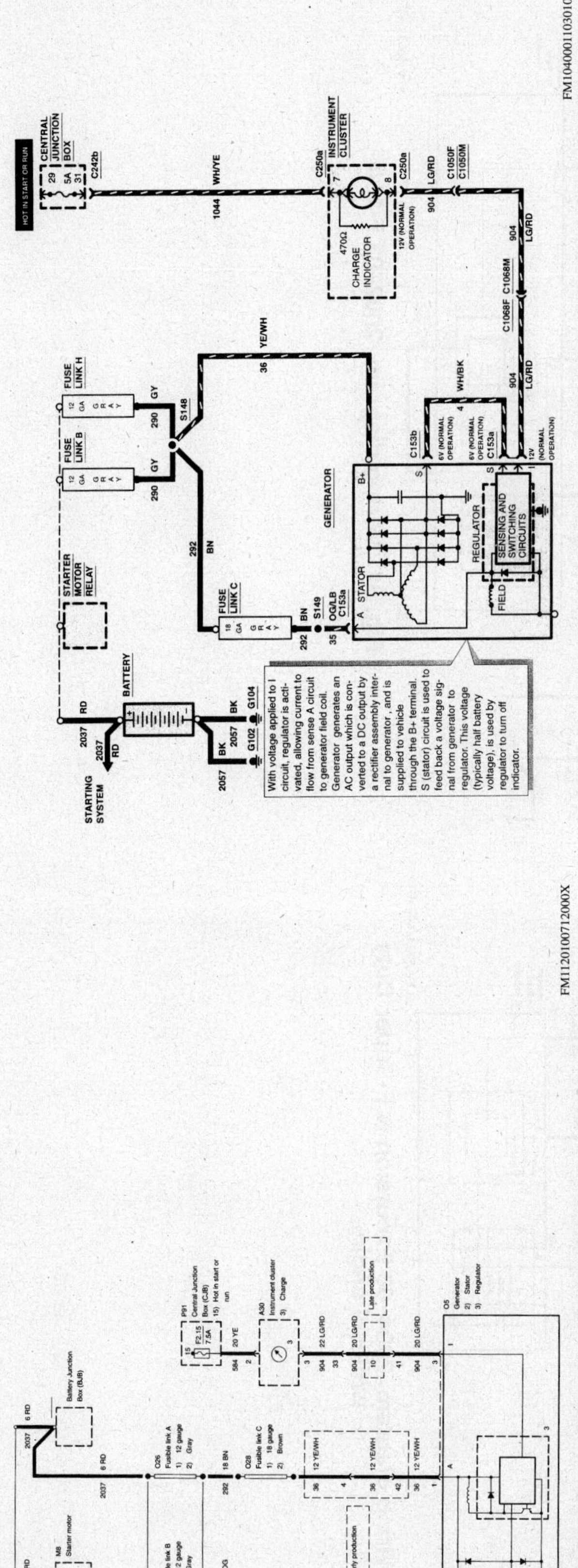

Fig. 26 Wiring diagram. Explorer Sport/Sport Trac

Fig. 27 Wiring diagram. 2002–03 Excursion & F-Super Duty w/gasoline engine

With voltage applied to I circuit, regulator is activated, allowing current to flow from B+ circuit to generator field coil. Generates an AC output which is converted to a DC output by a rectifier assembly internal to generator, and is supplied to vehicle through the B+ terminal.

LTV1900000000634

Fig. 28 Wiring diagram. 2002–03 Excursion & F-Super Duty w/single alternator

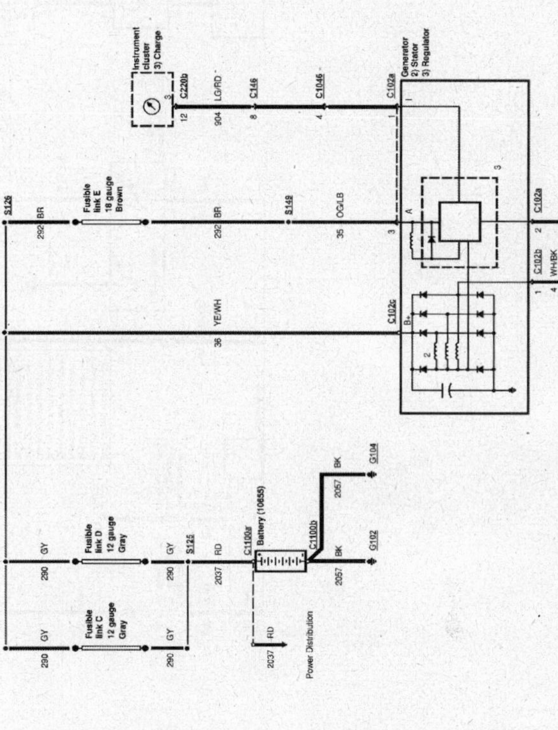

Fig. 29 Wiring diagram. 2004–06 Excursion & F-Super Duty w/gasoline engine

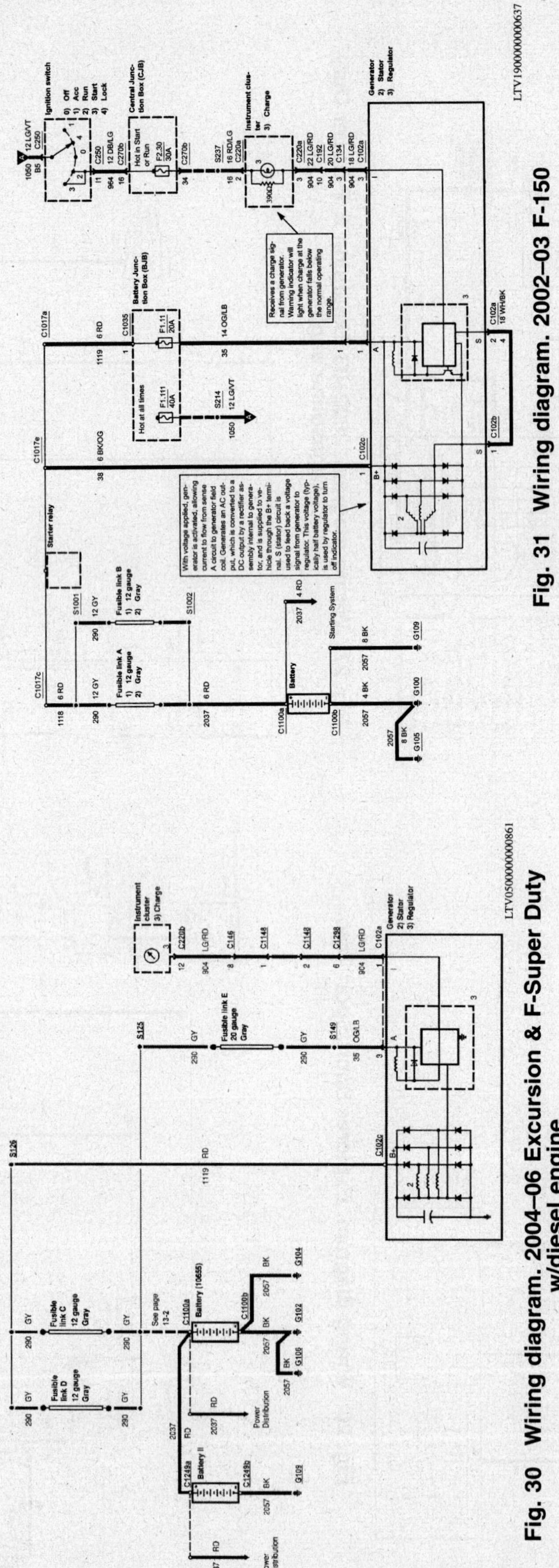

LTV1900000000637

Fig. 31 Wiring diagram. 2002–03 F-150

LTV0500000000861

Fig. 30 Wiring diagram. 2004–06 Excursion & F-Super Duty w/diesel engine

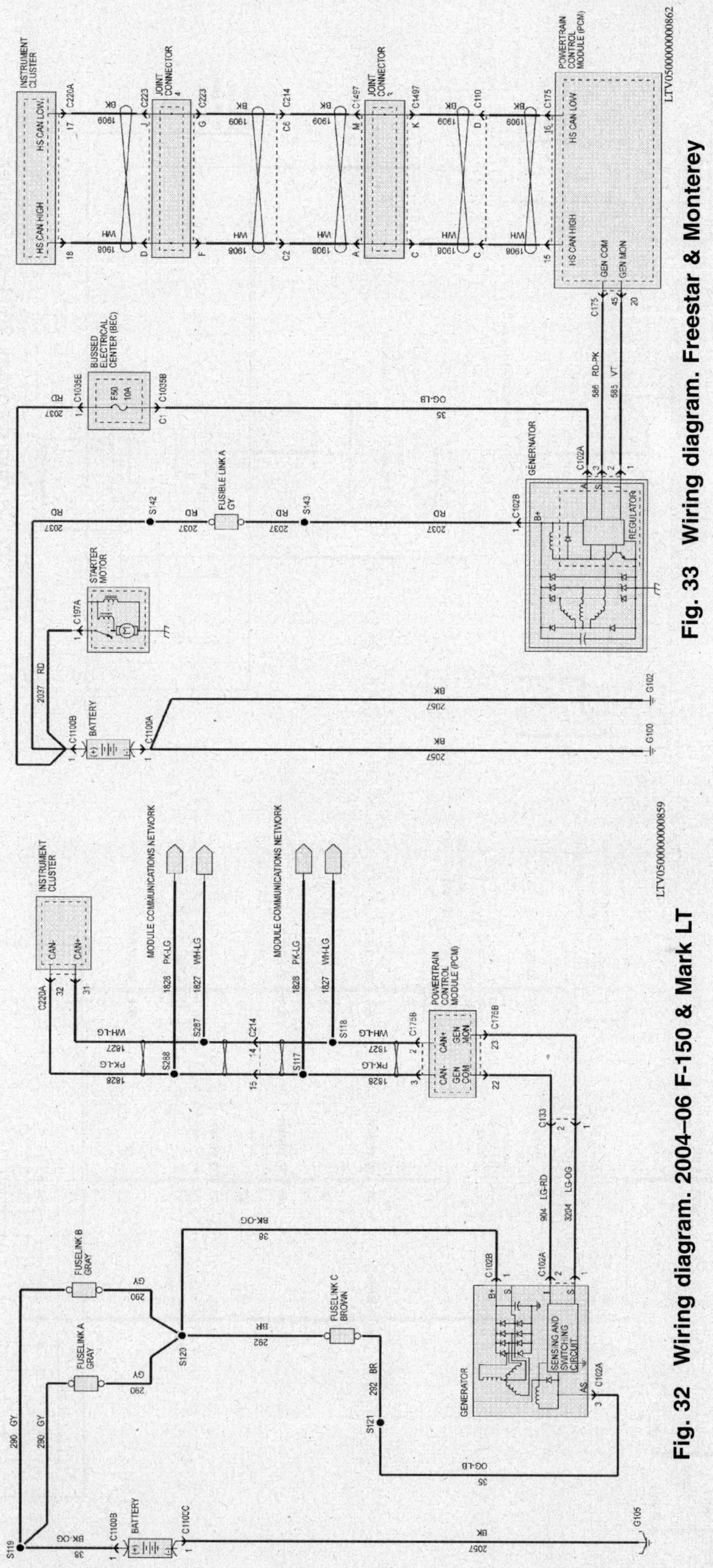

Fig. 32 Wiring diagram. 2004–06 F-150 & Mark LT

Fig. 33 Wiring diagram. Freestar & Monterey

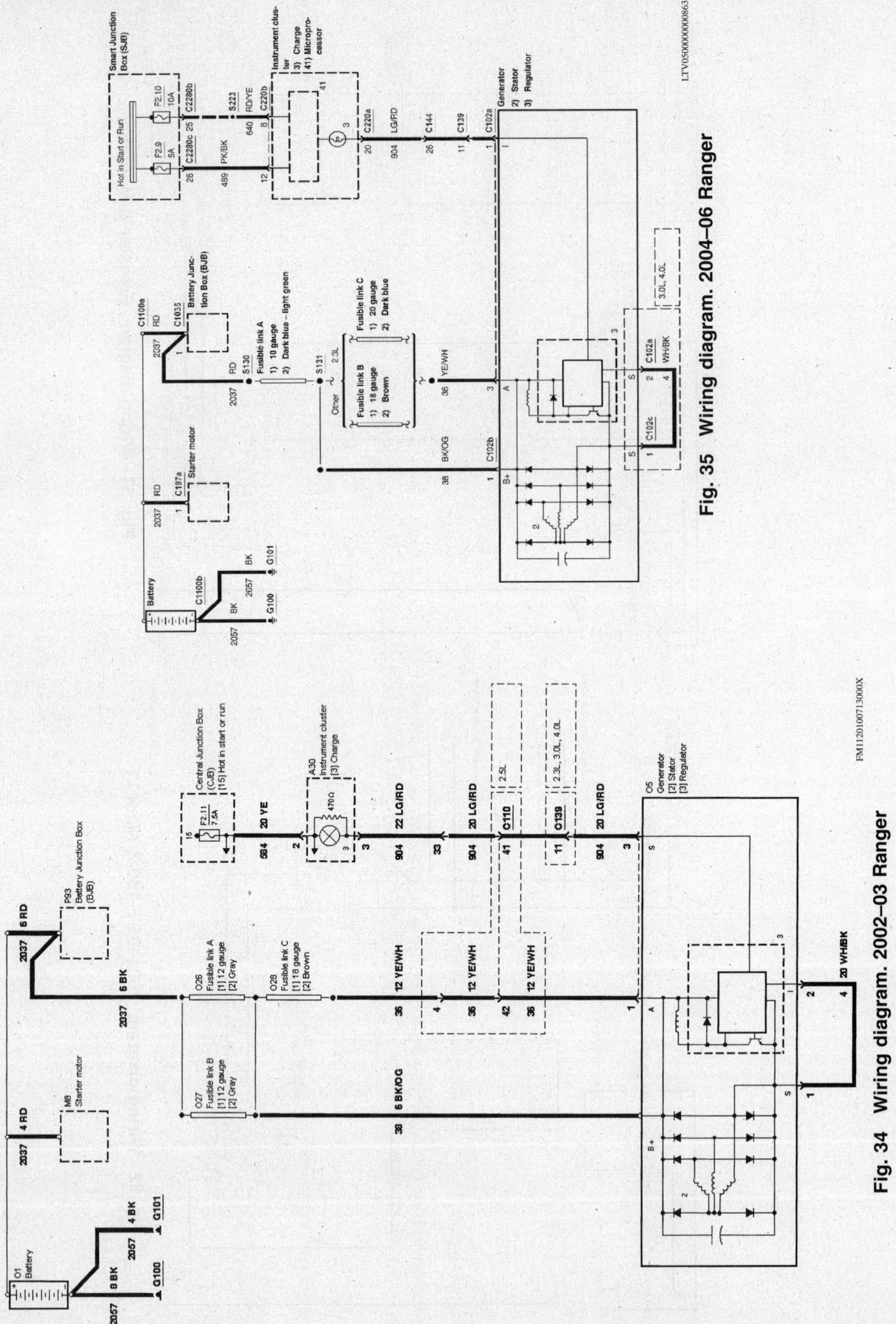

Fig. 35 Wiring diagram. 2004–06 Ranger

Fig. 34 Wiring diagram. 2002–03 Ranger

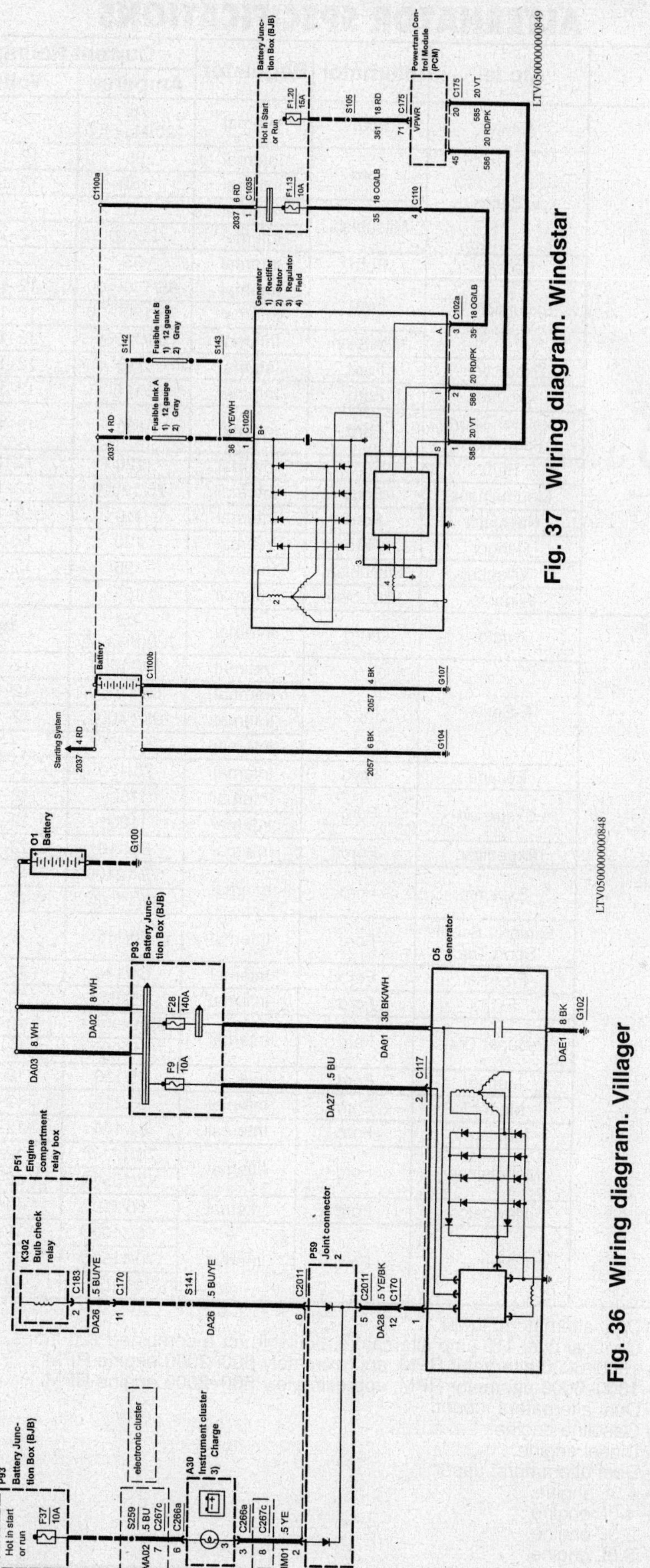

Fig. 37 Wiring diagram. Windstar

Fig. 36 Wiring diagram. Villager

ALTERNATOR SPECIFICATIONS

Year	Model	Alternator	Regulator	Current Rating	
				Amperes	Volts
2002–03	Aviator	Ford	Internal	76/ 120(Max.)③	12–15
	E-Series	Ford	Internal	95	12–15
			Internal	130	12–15
		Mitsubishi	Internal	110	12–15
			Internal	220②	12–15
	Escape	Ford	Internal	95	12–15
	Excursion & F-Super Duty	Ford	Internal	95/140⑤④	12–15
			Internal	75/120①④	12–15
		Mitsubishi	Internal	65/110④	12–15
	Expedition	Ford	Internal	110	12–15
	Explorer	Ford	Internal	75/120④	12–15
	Explorer Sport/ Sport Trac	Ford	Internal	130	12–15
	F-Series	Ford	Internal	120	12–15
	Mountaineer	Ford	Internal	75/120④	12–15
	Navigator	Ford	Internal	110	12–15
	Ranger	Ford	Internal	120	12–15
	Villager	MItsubishi	Internal	125	12–15
	Windstar	Mitsubishi	Internal	135	12–15
2004–06	Aviator	Ford	Internal	76/ 120(Max.)③	12
	E-Series	Ford	Internal	70/115⑥	12–15
			Internal	65/110⑦	12–15
			Internal	95/140⑧	12–15
			Internal	75/120①	12–15
	Escape	Ford	Internal	75/120	12–15
	Excursion	Ford	Internal	115⑥	12–15
			Internal	110⑦	12–15
	Expedition	Ford	Internal	65/110	12–15
	Explorer	Ford	Internal	70/121⑨	12–15
				82/135⑩	12–15
	Explorer Sport/ Sport Trac	Ford	Internal	70/115	12–15
	Freestar	Ford	Internal	84/144	12–15
	F-150	Ford	Internal	65/110	12–15
	F-Super Duty	Ford	Internal	95/140⑤④	12–15
				75/120①④	12–15
	Mariner	Ford	Internal	75/120	12–15
	Mark LT	Ford	Internal	65/110	12–15
	Monterey	Ford	Internal	84/144	12–15
	Mountaineer	Ford	Internal	70/121⑨	12–15
				82/135⑩	12–15
	Navigator	Ford	Internal	65/110	12–15
	Ranger	Ford	Internal	65/110⑪	12–15
				70/115⑫	12–15
				70/115⑨	12–15

① — Dual alternators, lower.
② — Optional dual 110 amp alternators available for a combined 220 amps.
③ — 1500–6000 alternator RPM, approximately 500–2000 engine RPM.
④ — 1800–6000 alternator RPM, approximately 500–2000 engine RPM.
⑤ — Dual alternators, upper.
⑥ — Gasoline engine.
⑦ — Diesel engine.
⑧ — Dual alternators, upper.
⑨ — 4.0L engine.
⑩ — 4.6L engine.
⑪ — 2.3L engine.
⑫ — 3.0L engine.

DASH PANEL SERVICE

NOTE: On Air Bag Equipped Models, Refer To "Air Bag System Precautions" Located In The Front Of This Manual For System Disarming & Arming Procedures.

NOTE: Refer To "Computer Relearn Procedures" Located In The Front Of This Manual When Battery Power To The Computer Has Been Interrupted.

NOTE: Refer To The "Electronic Instrumentation" Section In MOTOR's "Domestic Engine Performance & Driveability Manual" For Information Related To Electronic Instrumentation.

INDEX

PRECAUTIONS

Air Bag Systems

Refer to "Air Bag System Precautions" in the front of this manual for system disarming and arming procedures.

Battery Ground Cable

Prior to service disconnect battery ground cable and isolate as required.

DASH PANEL

REPLACE

Aviator

1. Place front seats in full forward position.
2. Remove floor console components in sequence, **Fig. 1.**
3. Remove passenger air bag as outlined in "Air Bag System" chapter.
4. Remove transmission selector lever.
5. Remove windshield side garnish molding and righthand cowl panel.
6. Remove steering column cover.
7. Remove instrument panel components in sequence, **Fig. 2.**
8. Reverse procedure to install.

E-Series

2002–03

1. Remove driver and passenger air bag modules as outlined in "Air Bag System" chapter.
2. Remove steering wheel and lower steering column trim moldings.
3. Remove steering column release lever by unscrewing from column.
4. Rotate ignition switch lock cylinder to Run position.
5. Press retaining pin of lock cylinder through access hole in lower steering column shroud using a suitable drift , then remove ignition switch lock cylinder.
6. **On all models except Commercial Chassis,** unsnap lower instrument panel steering column cover and remove six knee brace retaining bolts.
7. **On all models,** remove steering column support.
8. Disconnect PRNDL cable from steering actuator housing, then disconnect cable loop from shift tube hook.
9. Remove two screws, electrical connectors, then the multi-function switch.
10. Remove pinch bolt from steering column universal bolt.
11. Disconnect shift cable from selector lever pivot arm.
12. Remove shift cable from steering column lower mounting bracket by pushing tab on cable and sliding off of bracket.
13. Disconnect ignition switch.
14. Lower steering column bend bracket and disconnect electrical connectors.
15. While supporting steering column, remove four retaining nuts.
16. Remove steering column from vehicle.
17. Remove engine cover.
18. Remove instrument panel cowl top screws, **Fig. 3.**
19. Remove upper center instrument panel access panel.
20. Disconnect climate control vacuum harness connector.
21. Remove lefthand upper access panel, **Fig. 4.**
22. Remove instrument panel cowl top nut.
23. Remove instrument panel dash brace, **Fig. 5.**
24. From underhood, remove coolant reservoir mounting bolts and position aside.
25. Loosen bulkhead connector bolt, disconnect connector clips and remove bulkhead electrical connector.
26. Remove righthand side cowl trim panel.
27. Remove locking clip, then disconnect electrical connector from electronic crash sensor, **Fig. 6.**
28. Disconnect instrument panel cowl side wiring electrical connectors, **Fig. 7.**
29. Disconnect antenna cable from radio and unclip from instrument panel.
30. Remove righthand and lefthand side instrument panel bolts.
31. Pull instrument panel out and away from dash, then remove from vehicle.
32. Reverse procedure to install. Tighten fasteners to specifications.

2004–06

1. Remove engine cover.
2. Remove steering wheel and lower steering column trim moldings.
3. Remove driver and passenger air bag modules as outlined in "Air Bag System" chapter.
4. Release floor console storage bin locking tabs, then remove storage bin.
5. Working through floor console opening, push and hold locking clip while lifting upward on console and remove console.
6. Remove instrument panel cowl top screws, **Fig. 8.**
7. Remove upper center instrument panel access cover.
8. Disconnect climate control vacuum

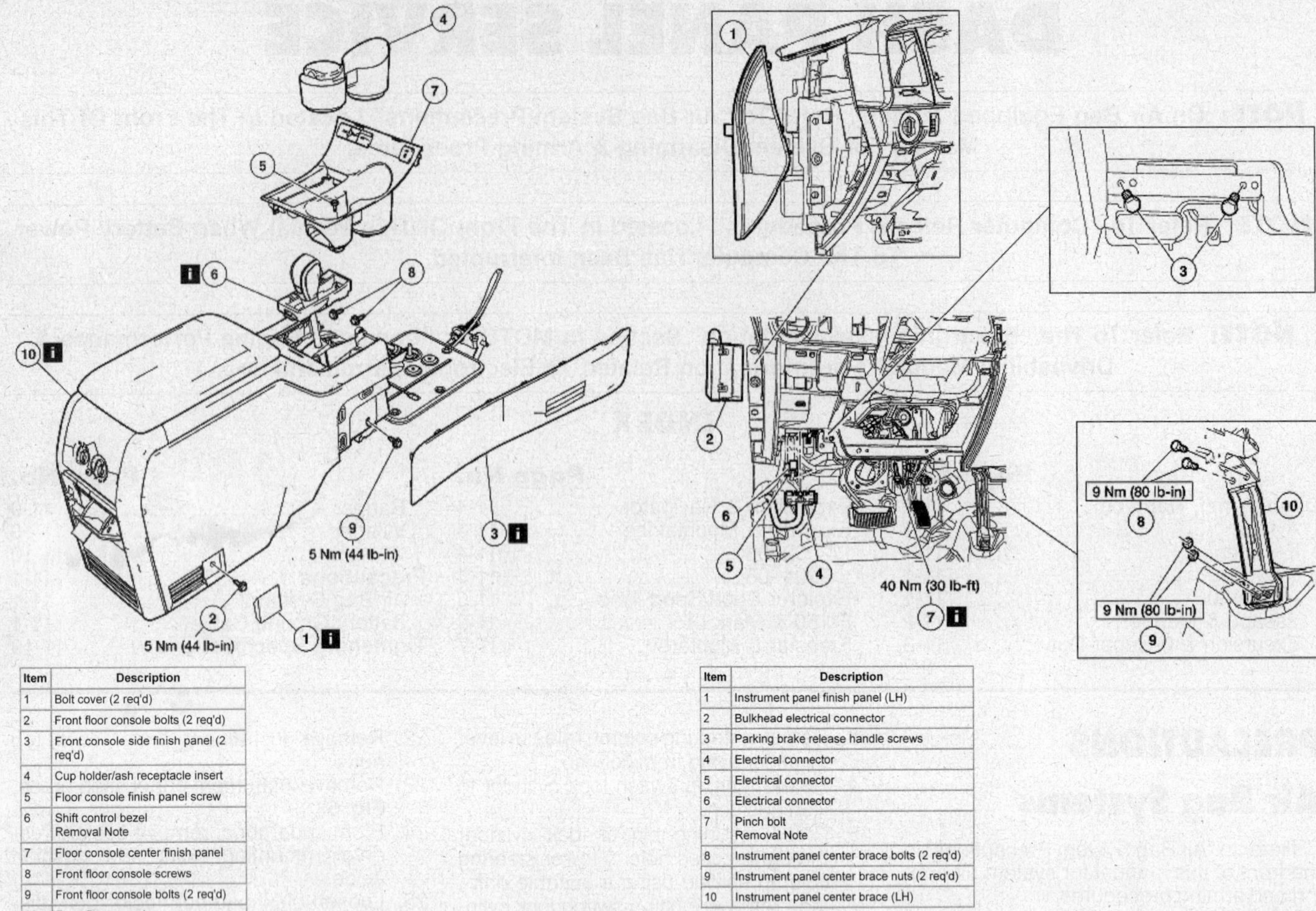

Item	Description
1	Bolt cover (2 req'd)
2	Front floor console bolts (2 req'd)
3	Front console side finish panel (2 req'd)
4	Cup holder/ash receptacle insert
5	Floor console finish panel screw
6	Shift control bezel Removal Note
7	Floor console center finish panel
8	Front floor console screws
9	Front floor console bolts (2 req'd)
10	Front floor console

LTV1900000000638

Fig. 1 Floor console replacement. Aviator

Item	Description
1	Instrument panel finish panel (LH)
2	Bulkhead electrical connector
3	Parking brake release handle screws
4	Electrical connector
5	Electrical connector
6	Electrical connector
7	Pinch bolt Removal Note
8	Instrument panel center brace bolts (2 req'd)
9	Instrument panel center brace nuts (2 req'd)
10	Instrument panel center brace (LH)

LTV1900000000639

Fig. 2 Instrument panel replacement (Part 1 of 3). Aviator

harness connector.

9. Remove lefthand upper instrument panel access covers.
10. Remove instrument panel cowl top nut.
11. Remove lefthand and righthand instrument panel knee bolsters.
12. Remove righthand instrument panel dash brace.
13. Disconnect DLC electrical connector, then remove DLC from lefthand dash brace.
14. Remove lefthand instrument panel dash brace.
15. Remove steering column pinch bolt, then separate intermediate shaft from column.
16. Disconnect steering column electrical connectors.
17. Disconnect transmission shifter cable.
18. Disconnect parking brake sensor electrical connector.
19. Remove coolant reservoir mounting bolts, then position reservoir aside.
20. Loosen bulkhead wiring connector bolt, disconnect bulkhead connector clips, then remove bulkhead connector.
21. Remove righthand A-pillar lower trim panel.
22. Disconnect righthand instrument panel cowl side wiring electrical connectors.
23. Disconnect antenna cable from radio and release cable locators from instrument panel.
24. Remove three lefthand instrument panel mounting bolts.
25. Remove instrument panel from vehicle through passenger side door.
26. Reverse procedure to install. **Torque** instrument panel to cowl bolts to 22 ft. lbs.

Escape & Mariner

1. Remove driver air bag module as outlined in "Air Bag System" chapter.
2. Remove pin-type retainers, then the two A-pillar lower trim panels.
3. Disconnect electrical connectors located by lefthand cowl.
4. Remove bolts, then position hood latch release handle aside, **Fig. 9.**
5. Remove pin-type retainers, then the utility compartment. Disconnect electrical connector.
6. Release clips, then remove screws and instrument panel steering column cover and column lower cover.
7. Disconnect shift cable from retaining bracket, then remove steering column coupler access cover.
8. Remove steering column coupler bolt and nut, then disconnect steering column coupler and electrical connectors.
9. Disconnect climate control vacuum harness connector.
10. Disconnect inline electrical connector.
11. Remove instrument panel center brace bolts, then the passenger air bag module.
12. Disconnect vacuum harness connector and temperature control cable from blend door shaft.
13. Press release tabs inward while raising glove compartment.
14. Disconnect blower motor electrical connector, then antenna cable inline connector.
15. Open A-pillar passenger assist handle covers, bolts and two pillar assist handles.
16. Remove two windshield side garnish mouldings, then the instrument panel cowl top cover and bolt.
17. Loosen tilt and lower steering column, then position transmission range selector lever down to provide access to instrument cluster and finish panel.
18. Remove screws, then the instrument cluster finish panel.
19. Remove screws, then the cluster and disconnect electrical connectors.
20. Through instrument cluster opening,

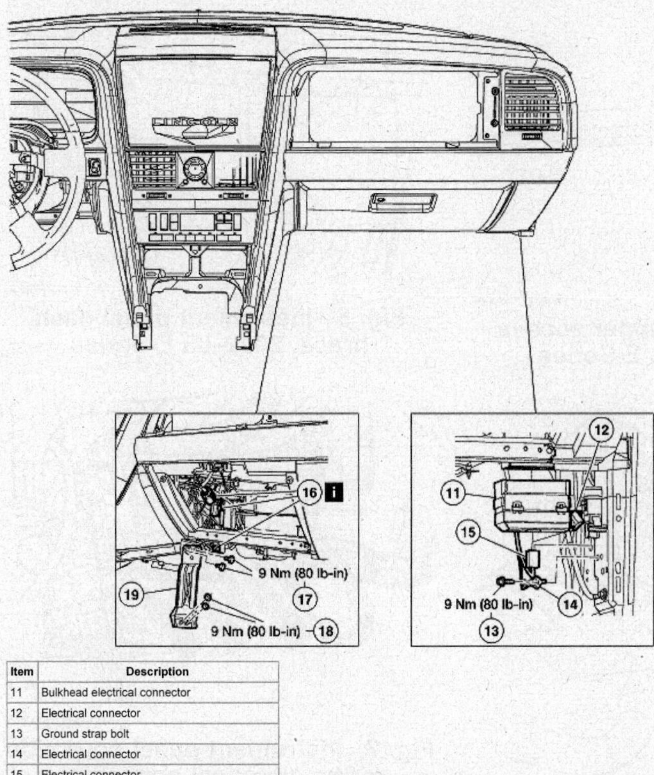

Item	Description
11	Bulkhead electrical connector
12	Electrical connector
13	Ground strap bolt
14	Electrical connector
15	Electrical connector
16	Electrical connectors Removal Note
17	Instrument panel center brace bolts (2 req'd)
18	Instrument panel center brace nuts (2 req'd)
19	Instrument panel center brace (RH)

LTV1900000000640

Fig. 2 Instrument panel replacement (Part 2 of 3). Aviator

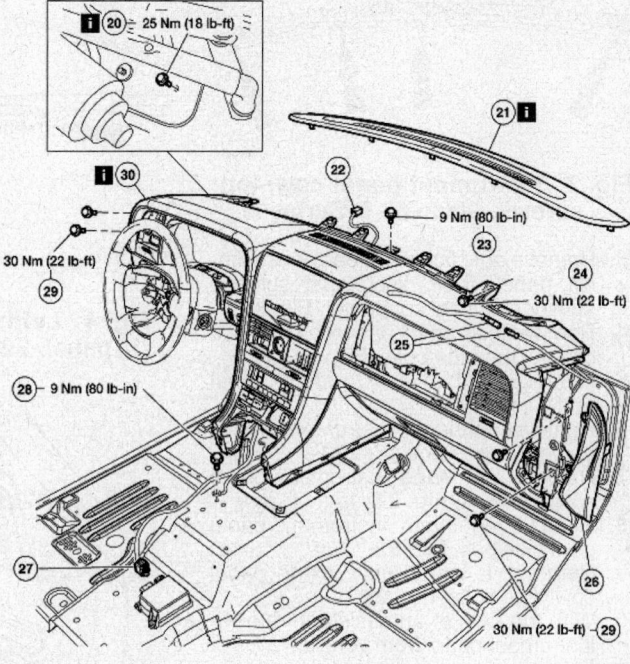

Item	Description
20	Instrument panel bolt
21	Instrument panel defroster grille
22	Electrical connector
23	Instrument panel bolt
24	Instrument panel bolt
25	Antenna cable lead
26	Instrument panel finish panel
27	Electrical connector
28	Ground strap bolt
29	Instrument panel bolts (4 req'd)
30	Instrument panel

LTV1900000000641

Fig. 2 Instrument panel replacement (Part 3 of 3). Aviator

remove instrument panel nut.

21. Remove instrument panel finish end panel.
22. Remove instrument panel cowl side bolts.
23. Remove instrument panel from vehicle.
24. Reverse procedure to install.

Excursion & F-Super Duty

1. Remove driver and passenger air bag modules as outlined in "Air Bag System" chapter.
2. **On Excursion models,** remove floor console.
3. **On models equipped with manual transmission,** remove four gearshift lever boot screws and position boot aside. Remove bolts, then the upper gearshift lever, **Fig. 10.**
4. **On all models,** disconnect electrical connectors, **Fig. 11,** and feed connectors into passenger compartment from engine compartment.
5. Disconnect central junction box cable at junction block, **Fig. 12.**
6. Release instrument panel harness from pedal bracket.
7. Release harness locator from powertrain control module bracket.
8. Remove righthand and lefthand scuff plates and A-pillar lower trim plates.
9. **On Excursion models,** disengage floor console wiring harness bracket locator and relocate harness from under carpet and heat duct, then position carpet aside.
10. **On all models,** position lefthand and righthand front door weatherstrips aside.
11. Remove antenna base, antenna cable will be removed with instrument panel.
12. Remove nuts, screws and pin type retainers, then position righthand front fender splash shield aside.
13. Unseat antenna cable grommet from dash panel. Route antenna cable into passenger compartment.
14. Remove instrument panel steering column cover. Use care to avoid damaging cover locating tab.
15. Remove bolt and release tab, **Fig. 13,** then position central junction box aside.
16. Disconnect central junction box electrical connectors, **Fig. 14.**
17. Disconnect inline electrical connector, **Fig. 15.**
18. Remove parking brake release handle nut and position parking brake handle aside.
19. Install central junction box into instrument panel.
20. Disconnect parking brake switch electrical connector.
21. Disconnect brake pedal position switch electrical connector.
22. **On models equipped with manual transmission,** disconnect clutch pedal position switch electrical connector.
23. **On all models,** through steering column opening, disconnect wiring harness electrical connector.
24. Disconnect adjustable pedal motor electrical connector.
25. Remove steering column shaft pinch bolt, then separate intermediate shaft from steering column, **Fig. 16.**
26. **On models equipped with automatic transmission,** disconnect cable from steering column shift tube lever, then from steering column bracket.
27. **On all models,** remove electronic crash sensor module cover, then remove locking clip and disconnect module electrical connector.
28. Disconnect blend door actuator harness connector.
29. Disconnect climate control vacuum harness connector.
30. Close glove compartment.
31. Disconnect righthand cowl electrical connectors, **Fig. 17.**
32. Remove righthand ground bolt and cowl side bolt cover.

Fig. 3 Instrument panel cowl top screws. 2002–03 E-Series

33. Remove auto lamp sunload sensor finish panel, then disconnect sunload sensor electrical connector, **Fig. 18.**
34. Remove instrument panel cowl top bolt covers, then the bolts, **Fig. 19.**
35. Remove lefthand instrument panel end finish panel.
36. Remove lefthand instrument panel center support bolt, **Fig. 20.**
37. Remove righthand instrument panel cowl side bolt, **Fig. 21.**
38. Remove righthand instrument panel cowl side bolt, **Fig. 22.**
39. Remove lefthand instrument panel cowl side bolts, **Fig. 23.**
40. With the help of an assistant, remove instrument panel from vehicle.
41. Reverse procedure to install.

Expedition & Navigator

Refer to **Figs. 24 and 25** when servicing the instrument panel on Expedition & Navigator models.

1. **On models equipped with adjustable pedals,** move pedals to full forward position.
2. **On models equipped with floor console,** remove floor console.
3. **On Navigator models,** remove driver air bag as outlined in "Air Bag System" chapter.
4. **On Expedition models,** remove steering wheel.
5. **On all models,** remove passenger air bag module as outlined in "Air Bag System" chapter.
6. Remove righthand instrument panel insulator, disconnect instrument panel insulator lamp.
7. Remove righthand and lefthand A-pillar lower trim panels.
8. Position lefthand and righthand door weatherstrip seals aside.
9. Remove lefthand and righthand assist handles.
10. Remove righthand and lefthand windshield garnish moldings by pulling inward at top then releasing lower hook.
11. Remove instrument panel steering column cover.
12. Remove bolts, then position hood release and parking brake release handles aside.
13. Remove steering column reinforcement panel, **Fig. 26.**
14. Disconnect lefthand instrument panel bulkhead connector.
15. Disconnect lefthand electrical connectors.
16. Remove bolts and position vehicle security module aside.
17. Remove bolts, **Fig. 27,** and position

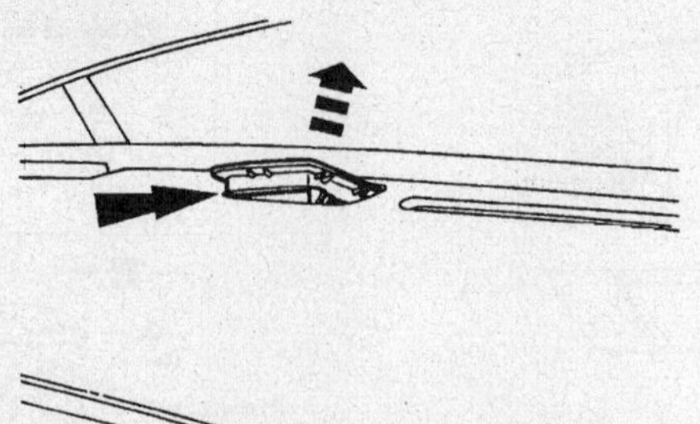

Fig. 4 Lefthand upper access panel. 2002–03 E-Series

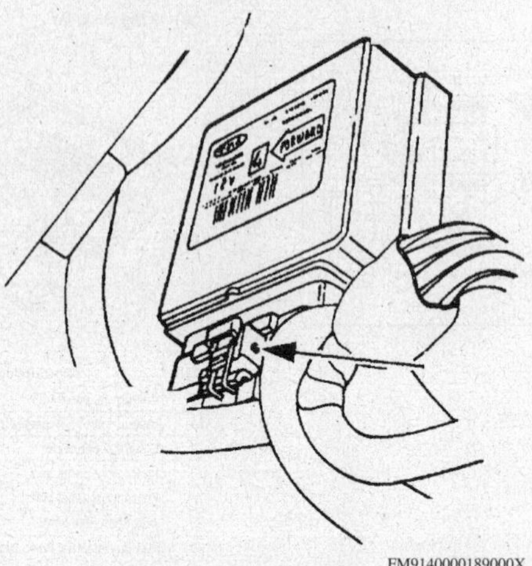

Fig. 6 Electronic crash sensor. 2002–03 E-Series

ground wires aside.

18. Disconnect cruise control deactivator and brake on/off switch electrical connectors.
19. Disconnect adjustable pedal motor electrical connectors.
20. **On Expedition models,** remove steering column shrouds, **Fig. 28,** and steering column shift cable, **Fig. 29,** then remove screw and position shift cable bracket aside.
21. **On all models,** secure steering wheel to prevent rotation or damage to clockspring may occur.
22. Remove pinch bolt and separate intermediate shaft from steering column.
23. Remove pin type retainers, then the valance panel.
24. Disconnect climate control head vacuum harness and electrical connector, **Fig. 30.**
25. Disconnect electronic automatic temperature control hose from evaporator case.
26. Remove righthand instrument panel side finish panel, then the righthand instrument panel electrical connectors, **Fig. 31.**
27. Remove instrument panel floor brace bolts, **Fig. 32.**
28. **On Navigator models,** remove bolts and position floor console bracket aside. Position carpet aside, then remove instrument panel floor braces, **Fig. 33,** and instrument panel defroster grille.
29. **On Expedition models,** position car-

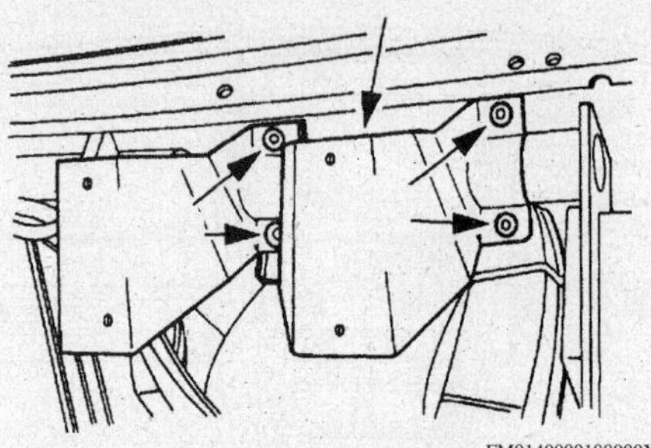

Fig. 5 Instrument panel dash brace. 2002–03 E-Series

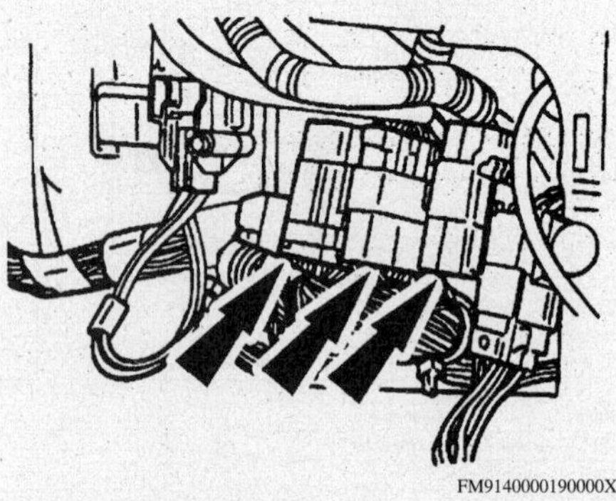

Fig. 7 Instrument panel cowl side wiring electrical connector. 2002–03 E-Series

pet aside, then remove instrument panel floor brace, **Fig. 34.** Remove instrument panel cowl bolt top covers.

30. **On all models,** remove instrument panel bolts, **Fig. 35.**
31. Remove lefthand, **Fig. 36,** and righthand, **Fig. 37,** instrument panel bolts.
32. With help of an assistant, remove instrument panel from vehicle. Two bullet connectors align instrument panel to bulkhead.
33. Reverse procedure to install.

Explorer & Mountaineer

2002–03

1. Remove driver and passenger air bag modules as outlined in "Air Bag System" chapter.
2. Remove A-pillar trim panels and righthand cowl side trim panel.
3. Remove instrument panel components in sequence, **Fig. 38.**
4. Reverse procedure to install.

2004–06

1. Remove driver and passenger air bag modules as outlined in "Air Bag System" chapter.
2. Remove front floor console pin type retainers, then release floor console front clips, **Fig. 39.**
3. Remove floor console trim ring.
4. Remove center finish panel retaining screws, disconnect electrical connectors, then remove finish panel.
5. Remove two front floor console forward bolts.

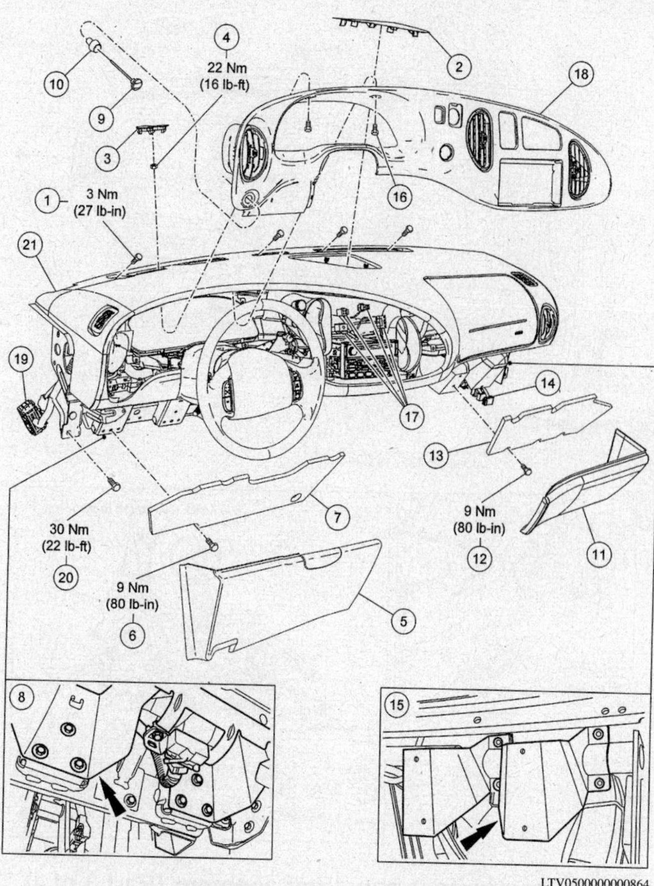

Fig. 8 Exploded view of instrument panel (Part 1 of 2). 2004–06 E-Series

Item	Description
1	Instrument panel cowl top bolt (4 required)
2	Upper center instrument panel access panel
3	Upper access panel
4	Nut
5	Steering column opening cover
6	Instrument panel LH knee bolster bolt (3 required)
7	Instrument panel LH knee bolster
8	Instrument panel LH dash brace
9	Headlamp switch knob
10	Headlamp switch bezel
11	Instrument panel finish panel
12	Instrument panel RH knee bolster bolt (3 required)
13	Instrument panel RH knee bolster
14	Electrical connectors
15	Instrument panel RH dash brace
16	Instrument cluster finish panel screw (2 required)
17	Instrument cluster finish panel electrical connectors
18	Instrument cluster finish panel
19	Instrument panel bulkhead connector
20	Instrument panel bolts (4 required)
21	Instrument panel

LTV0500000000865

Fig. 8 Exploded view of instrument panel (Part 2 of 2). 2004–06 E-Series

6. Position both front seats in full rearward position.
7. Remove two front floor console middle bolts.
8. Position both front seats in full forward position.
9. Remove two front floor console rear bolts.
10. Remove front console assembly.
11. Remove A-pillar and righthand cowl side trim panels, **Fig. 40.**
12. Remove instrument panel righthand and lefthand, side finish panels.
13. Remove instrument panel center finish panel and disconnect electrical connectors.
14. Remove steering column opening cover.
15. Remove upper and lower steering column shrouds.
16. Disconnect steering column electrical connectors.
17. Remove righthand side cowl panel and disconnect these components:
    a. Disconnect bulkhead electrical connector.
    b. Disconnect vacuum electrical connector.
    c. Disconnect inertia switch electrical connector.
    d. Disconnect two ground strap screws.
18. Open glove compartment and disconnect antenna lead-in cable.

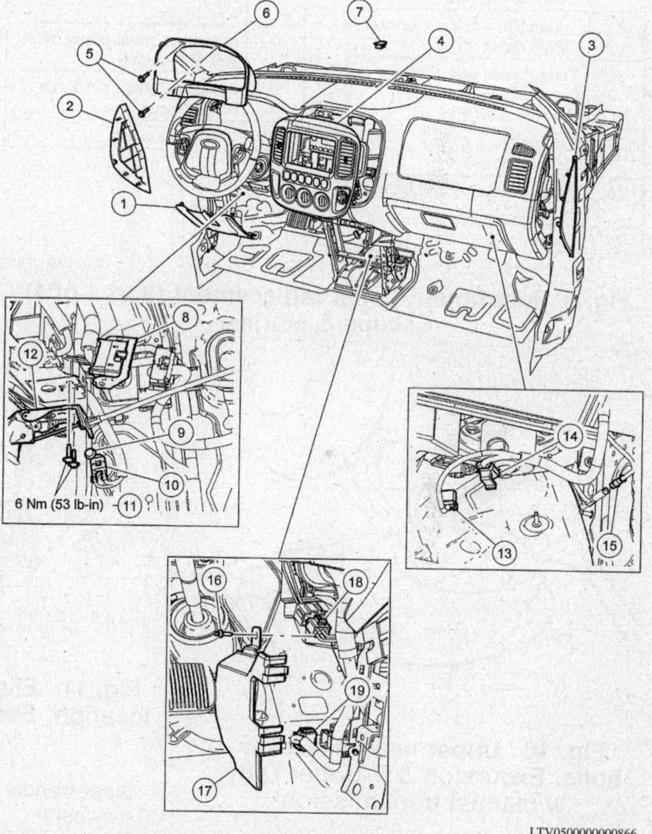

Fig. 9 Instrument panel replacement (Part 1 of 4). Escape & Mariner

19. Remove parking brake release handle.
20. Disconnect lefthand instrument panel bulkhead electrical connector.
21. Remove steering column shaft pinch bolt.
22. Disconnect lefthand and righthand adjustable pedal electrical connectors.
23. Disconnect brake light switch electrical connector.
24. Remove lefthand and righthand instrument panel center braces.
25. Remove six upper instrument panel mounting bolts.
26. Pinch thumb tab and pivot on large Restraint Control Module (RCM) electrical connector position assurance lever all the way back until it stops. Pull outward and disconnect large RCM electrical connector.

Item	Description
1	Instrument panel steering column opening cover
2	LH instrument panel end trim panel
3	RH instrument panel end trim panel
4	Instrument panel center trim panel
5	Cluster finish panel screw (2 required)
6	Cluster finish panel
7	Cowl top cover
8	Main electrical connector
9	Ground wire bolt
10	Ground wire
11	Hood release handle bolt (2 required)
12	Hood release handle
13	Blower motor resistor connector
14	Blower motor connector
15	Audio antenna connector
16	Cover panel pin-type retainer
17	Cover panel
18	Climate control vacuum harness connector
19	Restraint control module (RCM) electrical connector

LTV0500000000867

Fig. 9 Instrument panel replacement (Part 2 of 4). Escape & Mariner

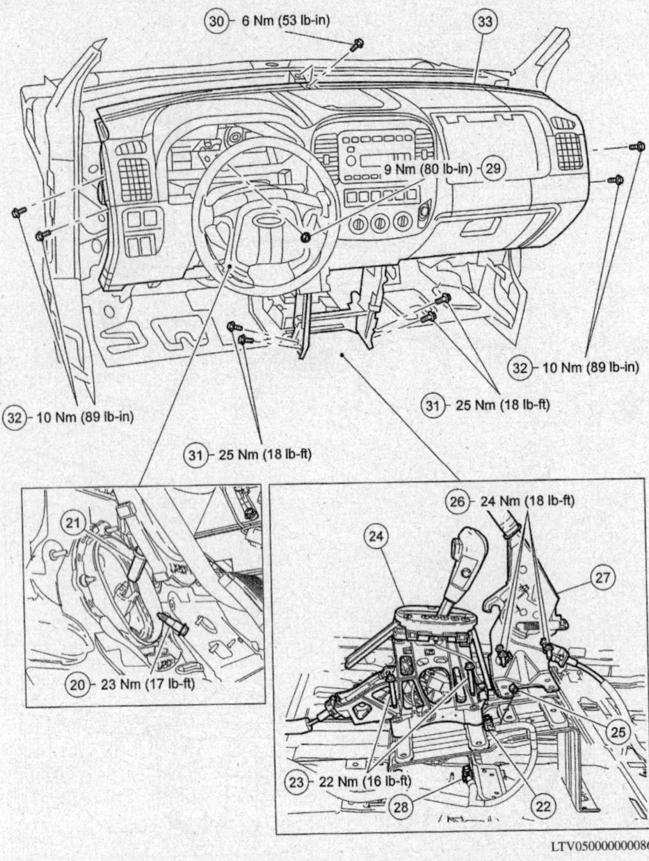

Fig. 9 Instrument panel replacement (Part 3 of 4). Escape & Mariner

Item	Description
20	Steering column pinch bolt
21	Intermediate shaft
22	Transmission selector lever electrical connector
23	Transmission selector lever bolt (4 required)
24	Transmission selector lever (automatic transmission shown/manual similar)
25	Parking brake control electrical connector
26	Parking brake control bolt (4 required)
27	Parking brake control
28	Electrical connector
29	Instrument panel cluster opening nut
30	Instrument panel cowl top bolt
31	Instrument panel center brace bolt (4 required)
32	Instrument panel cowl side bolt (4 required)
33	Instrument panel

LTV0500000000869

Fig. 9 Instrument panel replacement (Part 4 of 4). Escape & Mariner

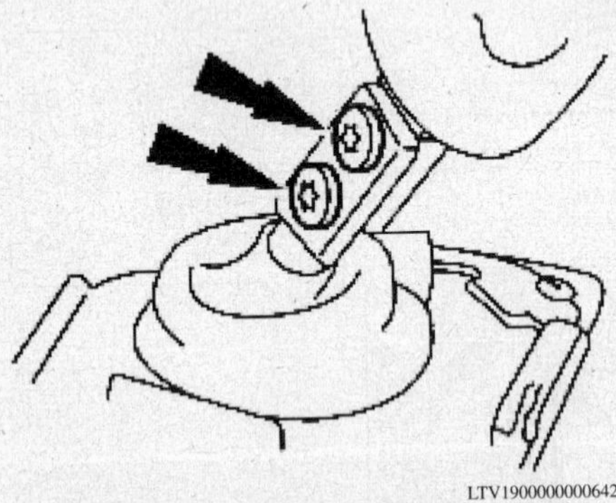

Fig. 10 Upper gearshift lever bolts. Excursion & F-Super Duty w/manual transmission

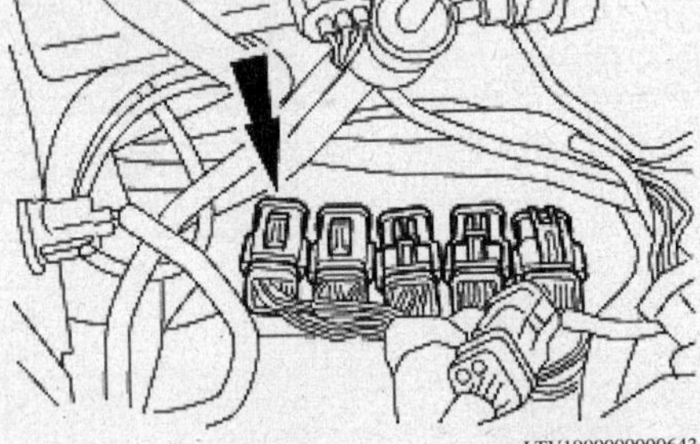

Fig. 11 Electrical connector location. Excursion & F-Super Duty

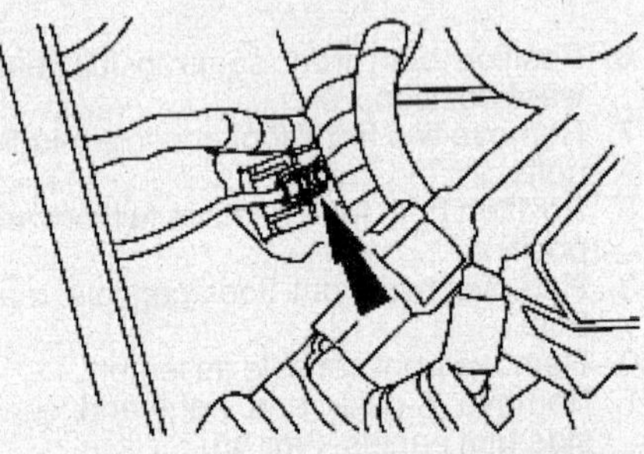

Fig. 12 Central junction box cable. Excursion & F-Super Duty

27. Disconnect center ground strap bolt.
28. Remove four lower instrument panel mounting bolts.
29. Remove instrument panel.
30. Reverse procedure to install.

Explorer Sport/Sport Trac

1. Remove driver air bag module as outlined in "Air Bag System" chapter.
2. Remove parking brake and hood release handle screws and position handles aside.
3. Remove instrument panel steering column cover and reinforcement, **Fig. 41.**
4. Disconnect shift cable from steering column, **Fig. 42.**
5. Disconnect upper intermediate steering shaft from steering column shaft.
6. Disconnect brake and clutch pedal position switch electrical connectors.
7. Remove both A-pillar lower trim panels.
8. Disconnect electrical connectors and ground wires on passenger side cowl panel, **Fig. 43.**
9. Disconnect battery junction box from bracket and position aside.
10. Disconnect bulkhead wiring harness connectors from inside engine compartment, **Fig. 44.**
11. Unclip bulkhead electrical connectors from dash panel.
12. Remove passenger air bag module as outlined in "Air Bag System" chapter.
13. Disconnect blend door actuator electrical connector, **Fig. 45.**
14. Disconnect climate control vacuum connector.
15. Disconnect antenna cable inline connector.
16. Press glove compartment release tabs inward while raising glove compartment.
17. Remove instrument panel defroster

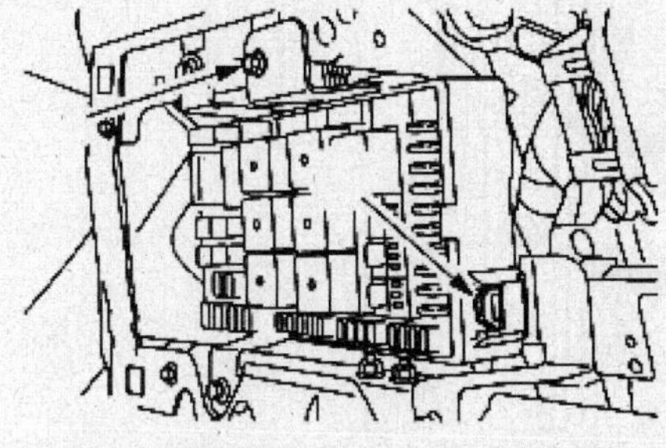

Fig. 13 Central junction box. Excursion & F-Super Duty

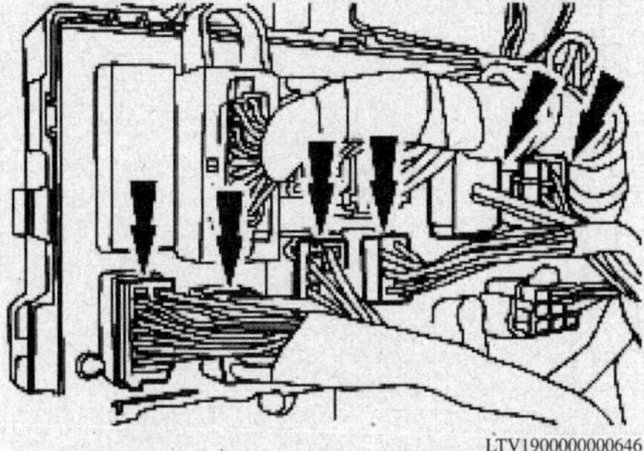

Fig. 14 Central junction box electrical connectors. Excursion & F-Super Duty

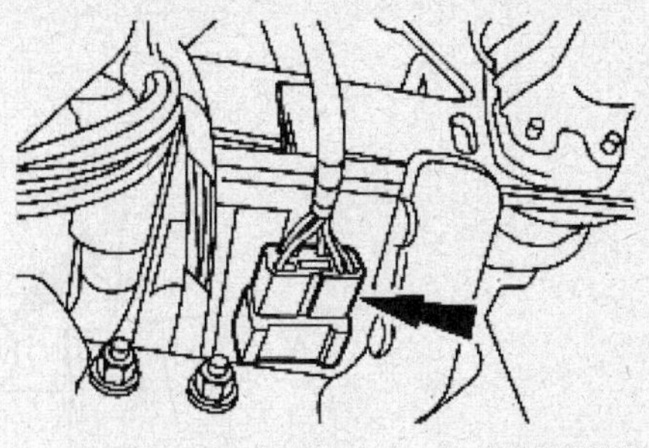

Fig. 15 Inline electrical connector. Excursion & F-Super Duty

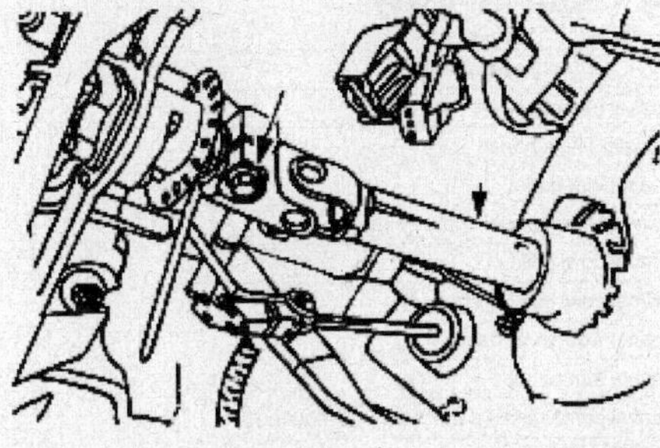

Fig. 16 Steering column shaft pinch bolt. Excursion & F-Super Duty

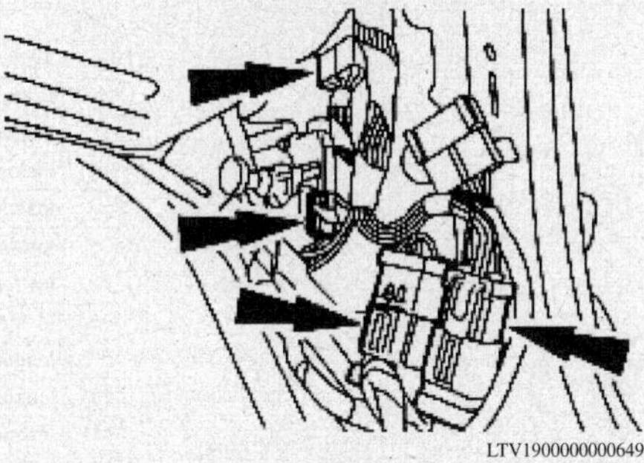

Fig. 17 Righthand cowl electrical connectors. Excursion & F-Super Duty

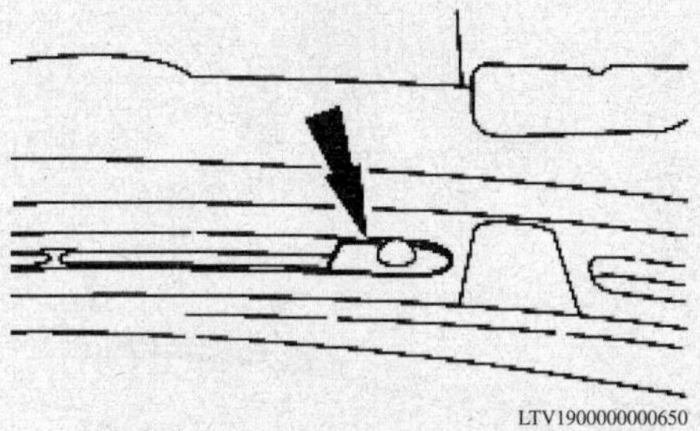

Fig. 18 Sunload sensor. Excursion & F-Super Duty

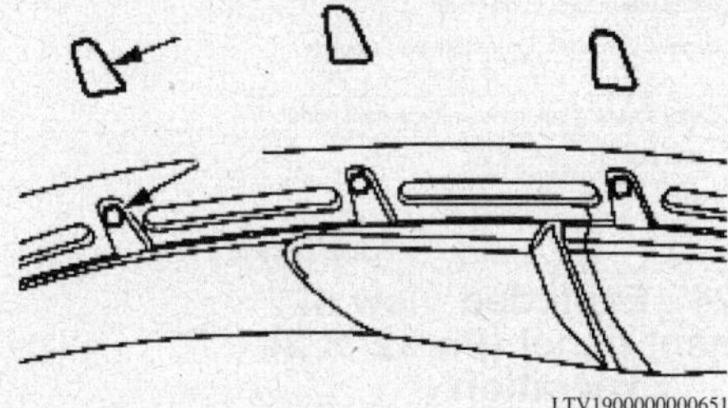

Fig. 19 Instrument panel cowl top bolts. Excursion & F-Super Duty

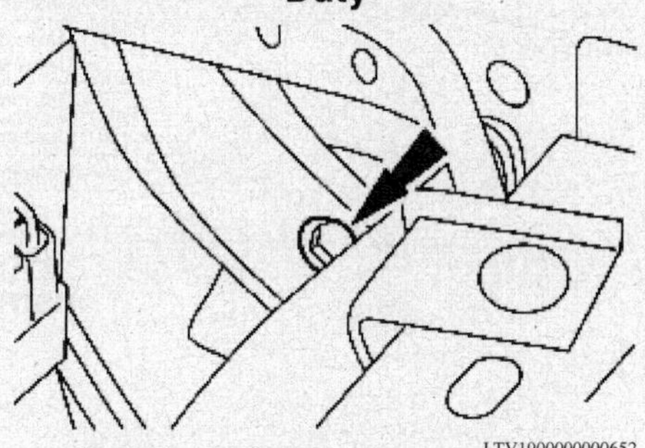

Fig. 20 Lefthand instrument panel center support bolt. Excursion & F-Super Duty

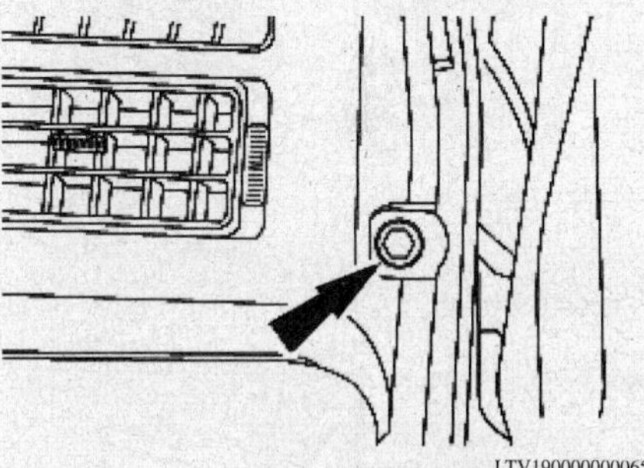

Fig. 21 Upper righthand instrument panel cowl side bolt. Excursion & F-Super Duty

opening grille.

18. Remove instrument panel cowl top bolts, **Fig. 46.**
19. **On models equipped with automatic transmission,** remove high series floor console and restraint control module cover.
20. **On models equipped with manual transmission,** remove gearshift lever handle and manual transmission consolette.
21. **On all models,** disconnect restraint control module and ground bolt, **Fig. 47.**
22. Remove instrument panel brace bolt from under steering column opening.
23. Remove two windshield side garnish moldings.
24. Remove passenger side instrument panel cowl side bolt.
25. Remove instrument panel fuse panel door.
26. Remove driver side instrument panel cowl side bolts.
27. Position instrument panel away from dash panel.
28. Disconnect instrument panel harness from body harness, **Fig. 48.**
29. With help of an assistant, remove instrument panel from vehicle.
30. Reverse procedure to install.

Freestar & Monterey

Refer to **Fig. 49** when replacing or servicing the instrument panel on these models.

1. Remove driver air bag module as outlined in "Air Bag System" chapter.
2. Position front seats rearward.
3. Remove lefthand and righthand A-pillar trim panels and cowl side trim panels.
4. Remove instrument panel steering column opening cover bolts, then the cover.
5. Remove two instrument panel steering column reinforcement bolts, then the reinforcement braces.
6. Remove two instrument panel to console pin type retainers.
7. Disconnect console electrical connectors.
8. Remove instrument panel console.
9. Remove defroster grille.
10. Disconnect electrical connectors located at lower center of instrument panel.
11. Disconnect electrical connectors located on lefthand side of instrument panel.
12. Disconnect Smart Junction Box (SJB) electrical connectors.
13. Remove intermediate steering shaft pinch bolt, then separate steering shaft.
14. Disconnect transmission shift cable.
15. Disconnect ground bolts located on righthand cowl.
16. Disconnect antenna lead-in cable.
17. Release tabs and lower glove compartment.
18. Remove glove compartment retaining screws, then the glove compartment.
19. Disconnect climate control electrical connector.
20. Disconnect blower motor electrical connector.

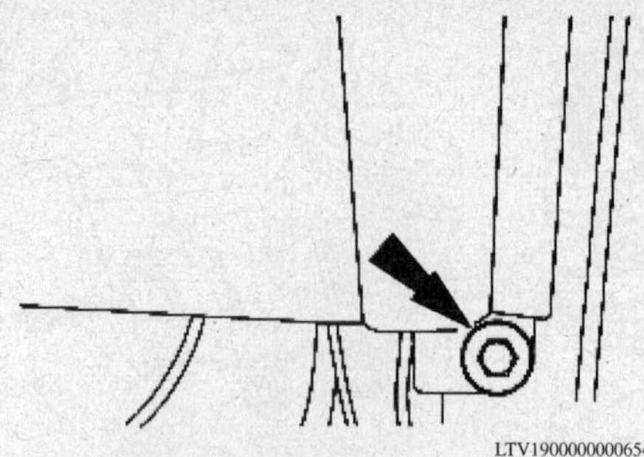

Fig. 22 Lower righthand instrument panel cowl side bolt. Excursion & F-Super Duty

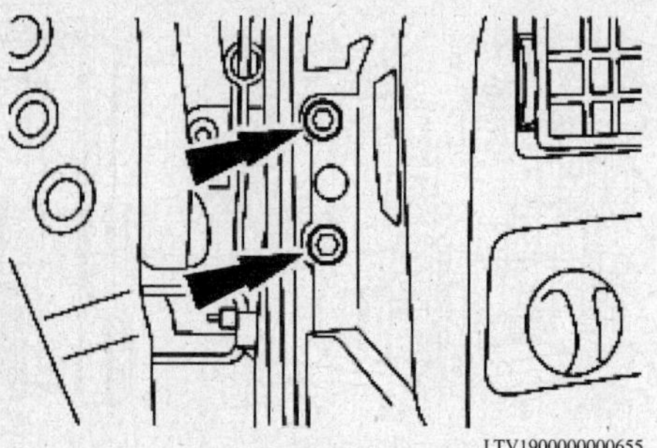

Fig. 23 Lefthand instrument panel cowl side bolts. Excursion & F-Super Duty

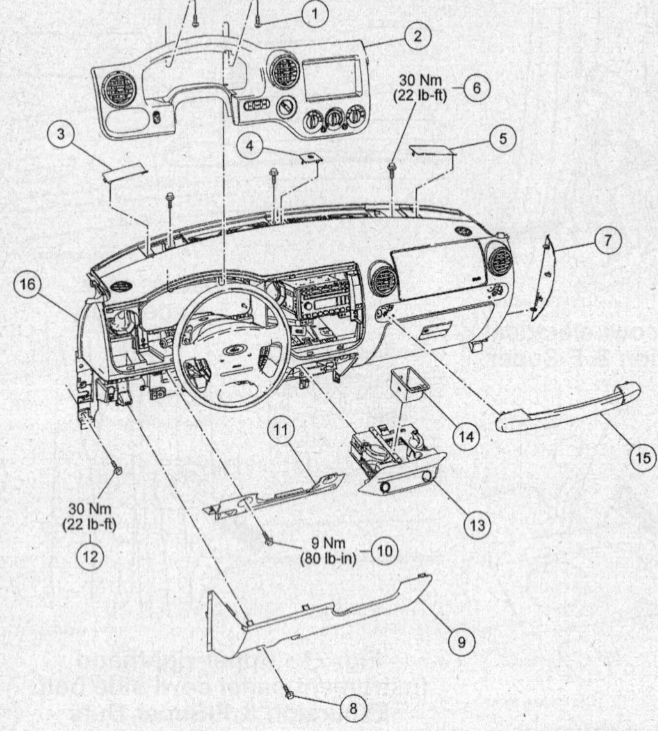

Fig. 24 Exploded view of instrument panel (Part 1 of 2). Expedition

Item	Description
1	Instrument panel trim panel
2	Instrument cluster finish panel
3	Instrument panel trim panel
4	Instrument cluster finish panel screw (6 required)
5	Instrument panel cowl grille
6	Instrument panel cowl bolt (3 required)
7	Instrument panel side finish panel
8	Instrument panel trim panel
9	Instrument panel center finish panel screw (2 required)
10	Instrument panel cover
11	Instrument panel center finish panel
12	Instrument panel ash tray cover
13	Instrument panel ash tray
14	Instrument panel steering column cover bolt (2 required)
15	Instrument panel steering column cover
16	Instrument panel column reinforcement panel bolt (4 required)
17	Instrument panel steering column reinforcement panel
18	Instrument panel bolt
19	Instrument panel

LTV0500000000871

Fig. 24 Exploded view of instrument panel (Part 2 of 2). Expedition

21. Disconnect main, heater servo, electronic air temperature and thermal resistor electrical connectors located behind glove compartment.
22. Remove lefthand and righthand instrument panel reinforcement bolts.
23. Remove four instrument panel center support bolts.
24. Remove instrument panel cowl reinforcement bolt.
25. Remove four instrument panel cowl, top mounting bolts.
26. Remove lefthand and righthand instrument panel cowl, side bolts
27. Remove instrument panel assembly from vehicle.
28. Reverse procedure to install.

F-150 & Mark LT

Refer to **Fig. 50** when replacing or servicing the instrument panel on these models.

1. **On models equipped with power seats,** move seats to full rearward position.
2. **On models equipped with adjustable pedal system,** move pedal to full forward position.
3. **On models equipped with manual transmission,** place transmission in second gear.
4. **On all models,** remove passenger air bag module as outlined in "Air Bag System" chapter.
5. Release mounting tabs and position battery junction box aside.
6. Remove bulkhead electrical connectors from inside of engine compartment.
7. Remove bulkhead connector seal, then unclip connectors from dash panel.
8. Remove lower instrument panel steering column cover.
9. Remove valance panel from center lower instrument panel.
10. Disconnect restraint control module electrical connector.
11. Disconnect electronic blend door actuator electrical connector and climate control head vacuum harness connector.
12. Remove righthand and lefthand front door scuff plates and A-pillar trim panels.
13. Remove alternative fuel control module, if equipped. Module is attached with Velcro.
14. Remove righthand and lefthand A-pillar passenger assist handles.
15. Remove righthand and lefthand windshield garnish moldings.
16. Disconnect brake pedal position switch electrical connector.
17. **On models equipped with adjustable pedals,** disconnect adjustable pedal motor electrical connectors.
18. **On models equipped with manual transmission,** disconnect Clutch Pedal Position (CPP) switch.
19. **On all models,** disconnect audio ground and GEM/CTM ground bolts.
20. Disconnect lefthand instrument panel wiring harness connectors.
21. Remove instrument panel steering column opening cover reinforcement.
22. Disconnect air bag sliding contact

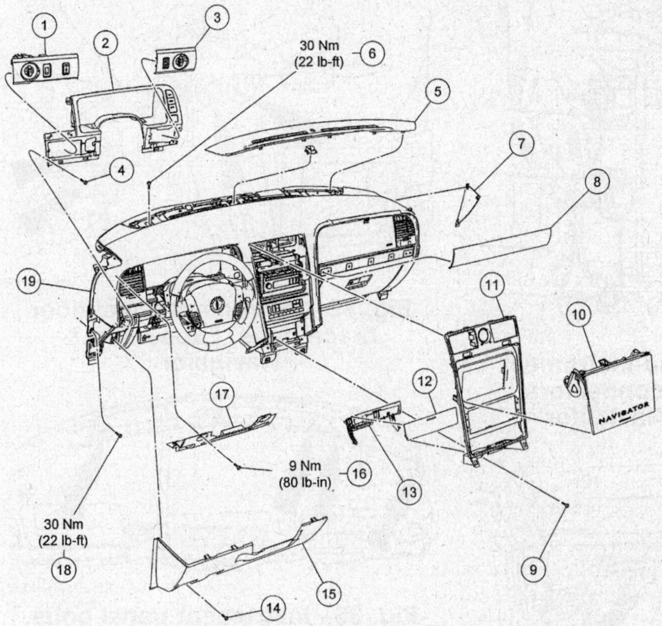

Fig. 25 Exploded view of instrument panel (Part 1 of 2). Navigator

Item	Description
1	Instrument cluster finish panel screw (2 required)
2	Instrument cluster finish panel
3	Instrument panel cowl top bolt cover
4	Instrument panel cowl top bolt cover
5	Instrument panel cowl top bolt cover
6	Instrument panel cowl bolt (3 required)
7	Instrument panel side finish panel
8	Instrument panel steering column cover bolt (2 required)
9	Instrument panel steering column cover
10	Instrument panel steering column reinforcement panel bolt (4 required)
11	Instrument panel steering column reinforcement panel
12	Instrument panel bolt (4 required)
13	Instrument panel cup holder
14	Instrument panel ash tray receptacle
15	Instrument panel assist handle
16	Instrument panel

LTV0500000000873

Fig. 25 Exploded view of instrument panel (Part 2 of 2). Navigator

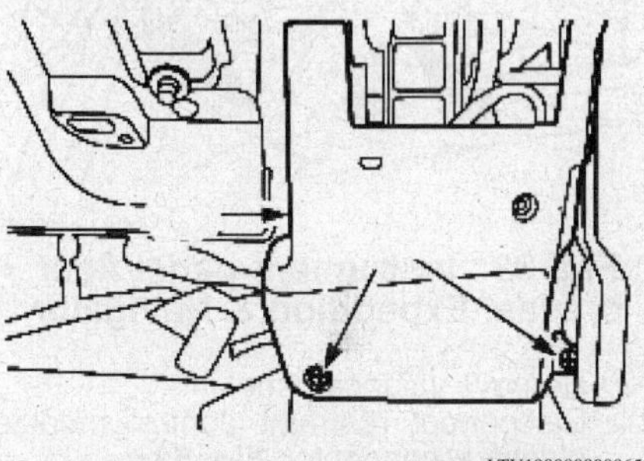

Fig. 28 Steering column shrouds. Expedition & Navigator

LTV1900000000656

Fig. 26 Steering column reinforcement panel. Expedition & Navigator

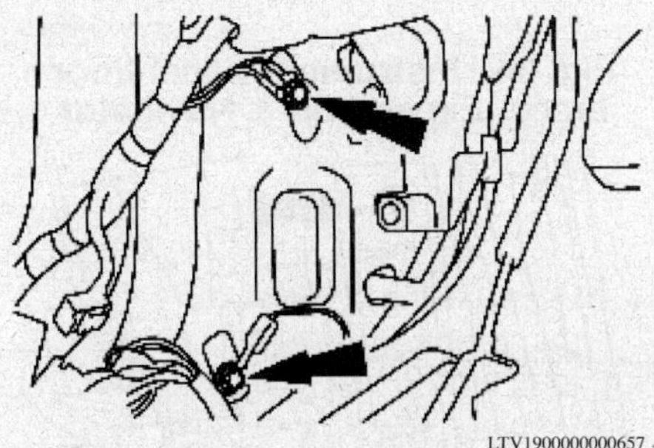

Fig. 27 Ground wires. Expedition & Navigator

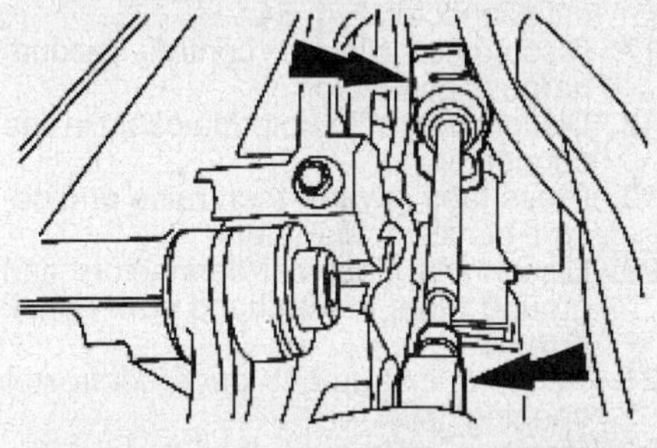

Fig. 29 Steering column shift cable. Expedition & Navigator

electrical connectors and anti-theft sensor electrical connector.

23. Disconnect all remaining electrical connectors on steering column.
24. **On models equipped with automatic transmission,** disconnect transmission range indicator from steering column.
25. **On all models,** remove mounting nuts, then lower steering column.
26. Remove instrument panel bolts through steering column opening.
27. Remove instrument panel reinforcement bolt located below lefthand corner of cigar lighter and power point.
28. Disconnect air bag diagnostic monitor electrical connector.
29. Disconnect inertia fuel shutoff switch electrical connector.
30. Remove righthand side ground bolts and main harness electrical connectors.
31. Disconnect climate control wiring harness connector.
32. Remove radio assembly and antenna lead in cable from instrument panel.
33. Remove instrument panel relay cover.
34. Disconnect autolamp sensor electrical connector, if equipped.
35. Remove glove compartment.
36. Remove passenger air bag module as outlined in "Air Bag System" chapter.
37. Remove instrument panel bolts through passenger air bag module opening.
38. Remove instrument panel bolt on relay bracket.
39. Remove instrument panel reinforcement bolt below lefthand corner of glove compartment.
40. Position carpet aside at righthand side floor, remove upper instrument panel floor brace bolt, then loosen panel brace bolts and nut.
41. Remove righthand and lefthand instrument panel cowl side nuts.
42. Remove instrument panel cowl top bolts.
43. Remove instrument panel from vehicle.
44. Reverse procedure to install.

Ranger

1. Remove steering column.
2. Remove screws and position parking brake release handle aside.
3. Disconnect brake pedal position switch electrical connector.
4. Disconnect clutch pedal position switch, if equipped.
5. Remove righthand and lefthand scuff plates.
6. Remove righthand and lefthand A-pillar lower trim panels.
7. Remove righthand and lefthand windshield side garnish moldings.
8. Remove instrument panel side finish panel.
9. Disconnect battery junction box from bracket and position aside.
10. Remove bulkhead wiring harness from inside engine compartment, **Fig. 51.**
11. Remove bulkhead connector insulator.
12. Unclip bulkhead electrical connectors from dash panel, **Fig. 52.**

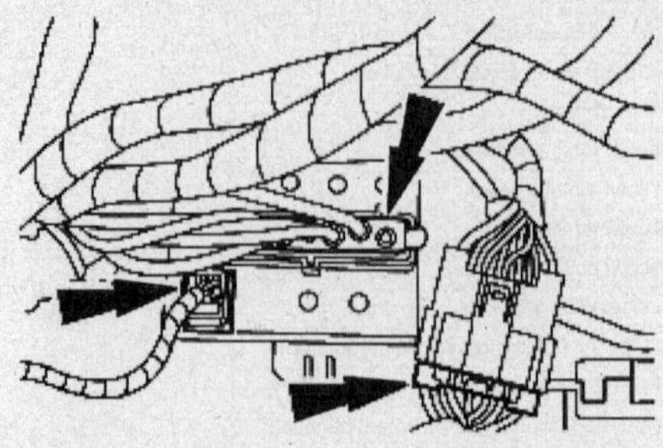

Fig. 30 Climate control head vacuum harness & electrical connector. Expedition & Navigator.

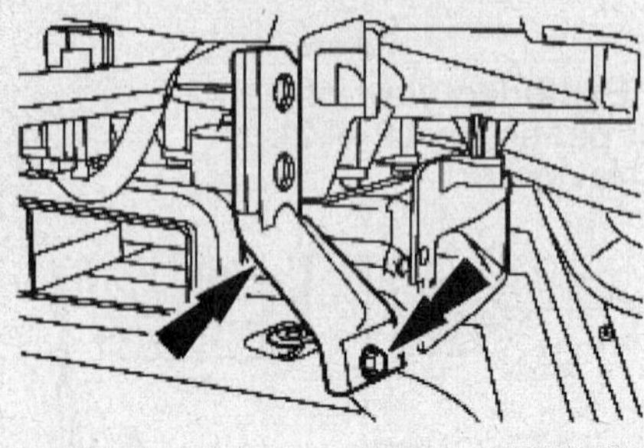

Fig. 33 Instrument panel floor braces. Expedition & Navigator

13. Remove valance panel.
14. Disconnect restraint control module electrical connector, **Fig. 53.**
15. Remove passenger air bag module as outlined in "Air Bag System" chapter.
16. Disconnect blend door actuator electrical connector, **Fig. 54.**
17. Disconnect climate control vacuum harness connector.
18. Disconnect radio antenna cable in line connector.
19. Press tabs inward, then raise and secure glove compartment.
20. Disconnect electrical connectors and ground wires at righthand cowl panel, **Fig. 55.**
21. Remove instrument panel defroster opening grille.
22. Remove instrument panel cowl top bolts, **Fig. 56.**
23. Remove instrument panel brace bolt under steering column, **Fig. 57.**
24. Remove righthand instrument panel cowl side bolt.
25. Remove lefthand instrument panel cowl side bolts.
26. Position instrument panel away from dash panel.
27. Disconnect instrument panel to body harness, **Fig. 58.**
28. With help of an assistant, remove instrument panel from vehicle.
29. Reverse procedure to install.

Villager

1. Remove driver's and passenger air bag module as outlined in "Air Bag System" chapter.
2. Remove instrument panel lower covers.

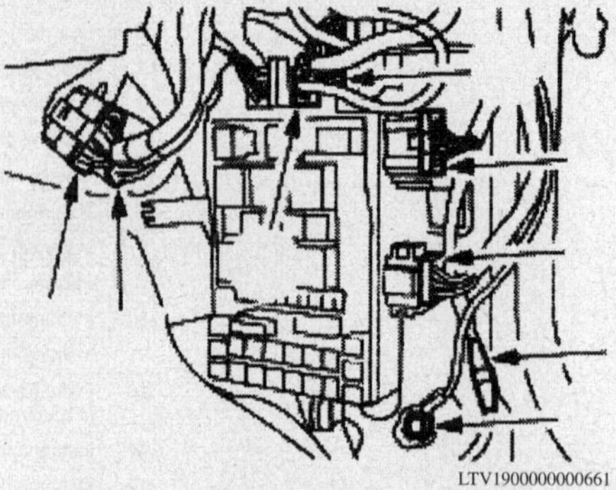

Fig. 31 Righthand instrument panel electrical connectors. Expedition & Navigator

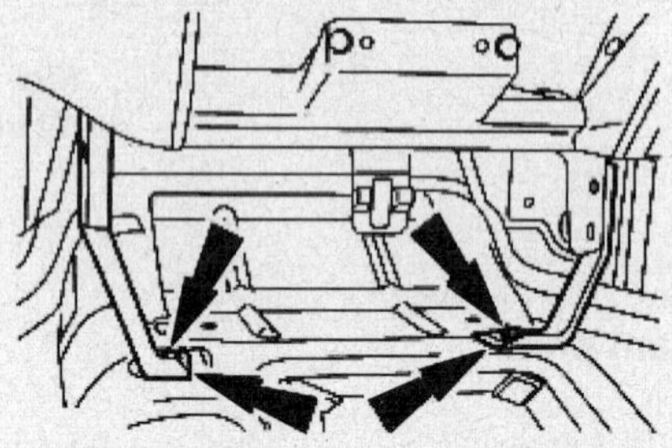

Fig. 34 Instrument panel floor brace. Expedition & Navigator

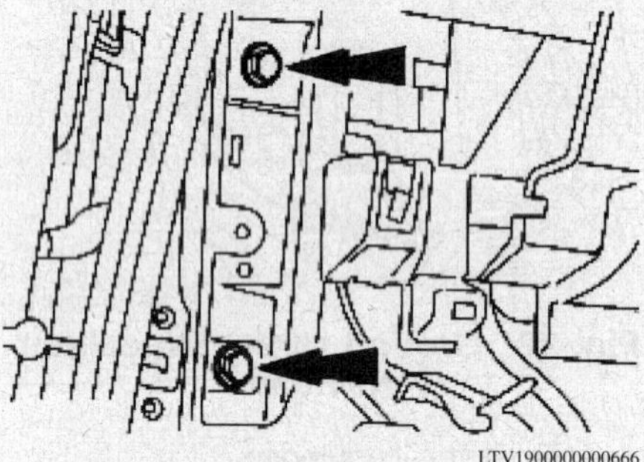

Fig. 36 Lefthand instrument panel bolts. Expedition & Navigator

3. Remove radio assembly and climate control assembly.
4. Remove CD changer, if equipped.
5. Disconnect light sensor amplifier harness electrical connector through glove compartment opening.
6. Remove instrument panel cluster finish panel, then the cluster assembly.
7. Remove instrument panel steering column cover and cover reinforcement, **Figs. 59 and 60.**
8. Remove lower heater duct.
9. Remove four nuts, then lower steering column.
10. Disconnect remote keyless entry electrical connector.
11. Disconnect lefthand instrument panel screw, **Fig. 61,** lefthand center instrument panel screw, **Fig. 62,** ashtray/cup holder bracket, **Fig. 63,** and righthand instrument panel screw, **Fig. 64.**
12. Remove instrument panel screw through passenger air bag module opening, **Fig. 65.**

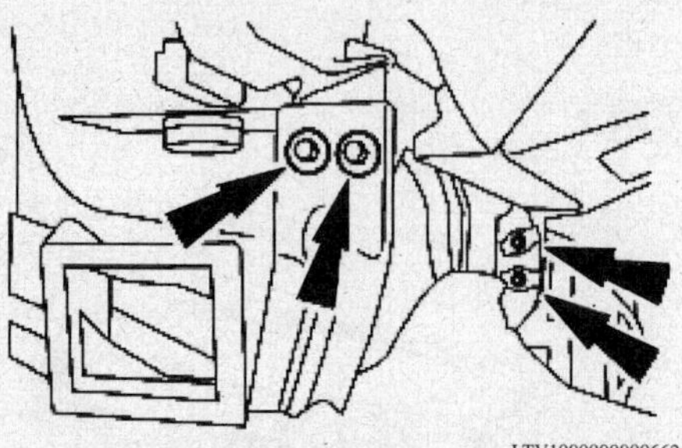

Fig. 32 Instrument panel floor brace bolts. Expedition & Navigator

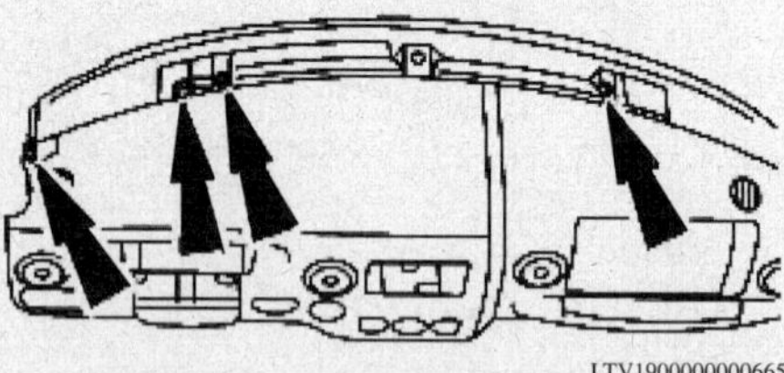

Fig. 35 Instrument panel bolts. Expedition & Navigator

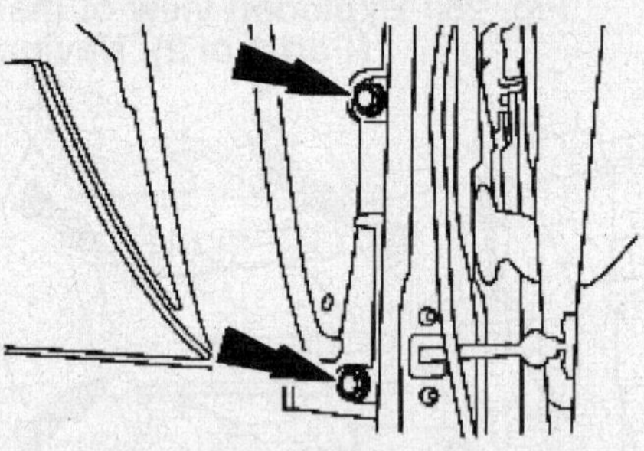

Fig. 37 Righthand instrument panel bolts. Expedition & Navigator

13. Remove instrument panel bolts through glove compartment opening, **Fig. 66.**
14. Remove lower righthand instrument panel screw, **Fig. 67.**
15. Remove instrument panel defroster opening grille assembly.
16. Remove righthand and lefthand windshield side garnish moldings.
17. Remove instrument panel cowl top screws and nuts, **Fig. 68.**
18. Remove instrument panel.
19. Reverse procedure to install. Tighten fasteners to specifications.

Windstar

1. Remove steering wheel.
2. Remove passenger air bag module as outlined in "Air Bag System" chapter.
3. Disconnect antenna inline connector.
4. Open glove compartment and remove righthand instrument panel reinforcement bolt, **Fig. 69,** then close glove compartment.
5. Remove utility compartment, then disconnect power point electrical connector.
6. Disconnect compact disc changer, if

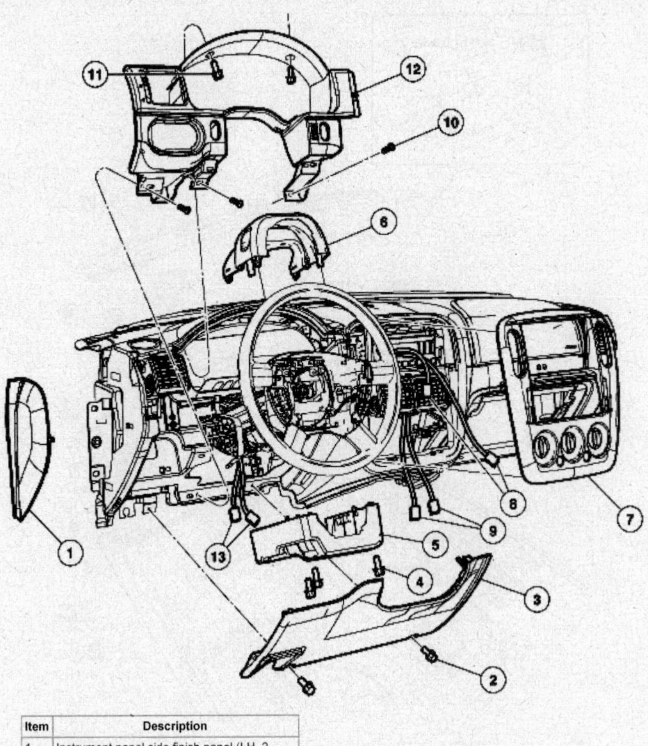

Item	Description
1	Instrument panel side finish panel (LH, 2 req'd)
2	Steering column opening cover screws (2 req'd)
3	Steering column opening cover
4	Lower steering column cover screws (3 req'd)
5	Lower steering column cover
6	Upper steering column cover
7	Instrument panel center finish panel
8	Center finish panel electrical connectors
9	Climate control electrical connectors
10	Instrument cluster finish panel screws (3 req'd)
11	Instrument cluster finish panel screws (2 req'd)
12	Instrument cluster finish panel
13	Steering column electrical connector

LTV1900000000668

Fig. 38 Instrument panel replacement (Part 1 of 4). 2002–03 Explorer & Mountaineer

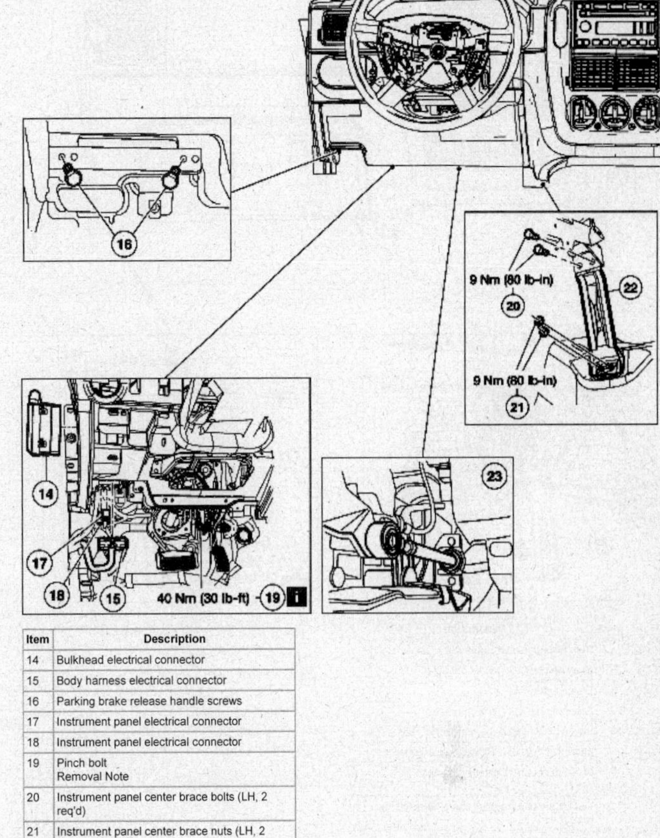

Item	Description
14	Bulkhead electrical connector
15	Body harness electrical connector
16	Parking brake release handle screws
17	Instrument panel electrical connector
18	Instrument panel electrical connector
19	Pinch bolt Removal Note
20	Instrument panel center brace bolts (LH, 2 req'd)
21	Instrument panel center brace nuts (LH, 2 req'd)
22	Instrument panel center brace (LH)
23	Transmission range indicator cable

LTV1900000000669

Fig. 38 Instrument panel replacement (Part 2 of 4). 2002–03 Explorer & Mountaineer

equipped, then release changer electrical connector.

7. Remove righthand and lefthand scuff plates.
8. Remove righthand and lefthand A-pillar lower trim panels.
9. Position righthand and lefthand door weatherstrip seals aside.
10. Remove righthand side ground bolts, **Fig. 70.**
11. Remove righthand and lefthand lower instrument panel insulators.
12. Remove instrument panel lower steering column opening cover and reinforcement.
13. Remove lefthand side wiring harness electrical connectors, **Fig. 71.**
14. Disconnect electronic crash sensor electrical connector, **Fig. 72.**
15. Disconnect automatic transmission shift cable from steering column shift tube, then the cable from bracket.
16. Remove pinch bolt, then separate intermediate shaft from steering column, **Fig. 73.**
17. Disconnect climate control harness electrical connector and vacuum harness connector.
18. Disconnect fuse panel electrical connectors.
19. Remove lefthand side panel reinforcement bolt, **Fig. 74,** and instrument panel center support bolts, **Fig. 75.**
20. Remove instrument panel defroster opening grille, then disconnect sunload sensor.
21. Remove top cowl bolts, **Fig. 76.**
22. Remove righthand and lefthand cowl side bolts, **Fig. 77.**
23. Remove instrument panel.
24. Reverse procedure to install. Tighten fasteners to specifications.

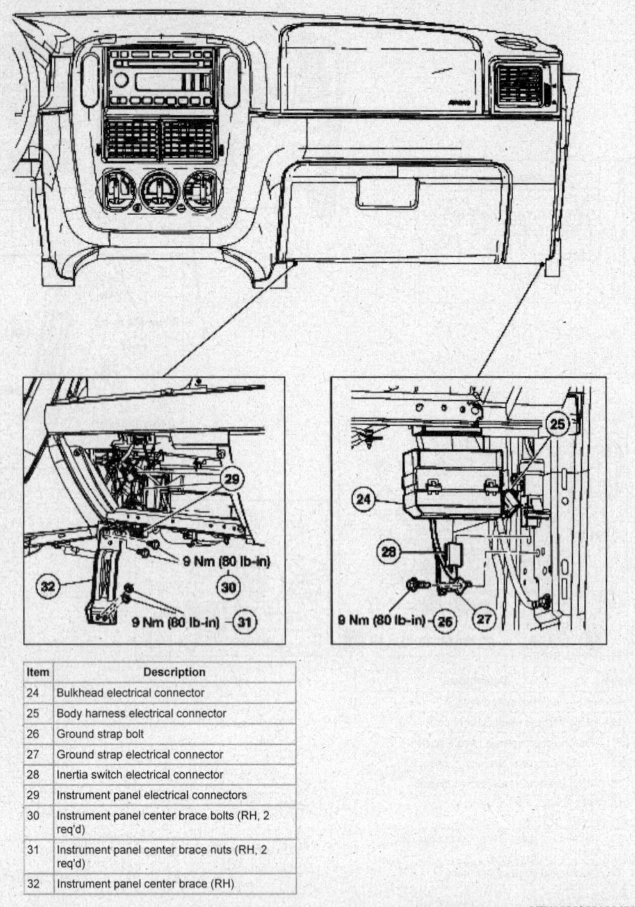

Item	Description
24	Bulkhead electrical connector
25	Body harness electrical connector
26	Ground strap bolt
27	Ground strap electrical connector
28	Inertia switch electrical connector
29	Instrument panel electrical connectors
30	Instrument panel center brace bolts (RH, 2 req'd)
31	Instrument panel center brace nuts (RH, 2 req'd)
32	Instrument panel center brace (RH)

LTV1900000000670

Fig. 38 Instrument panel replacement (Part 3 of 4). 2002–03 Explorer & Mountaineer

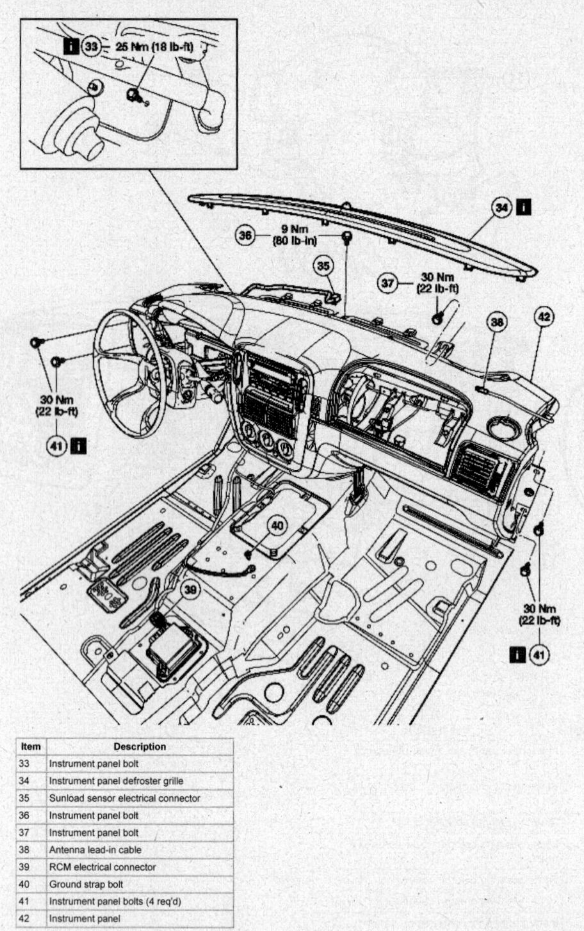

Item	Description
33	Instrument panel bolt
34	Instrument panel defroster grille
35	Sunload sensor electrical connector
36	Instrument panel bolt
37	Instrument panel bolt
38	Antenna lead-in cable
39	RCM electrical connector
40	Ground strap bolt
41	Instrument panel bolts (4 req'd)
42	Instrument panel

LTV1900000000671

Fig. 38 Instrument panel replacement (Part 4 of 4). 2002–03 Explorer & Mountaineer

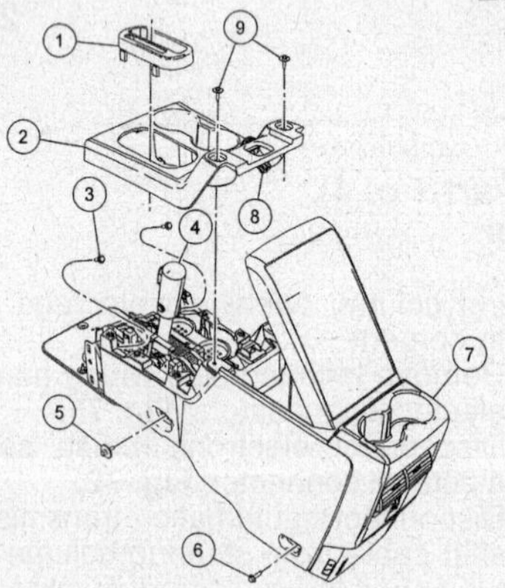

Item	Description
1	Front floor console trim ring
2	Front floor console center finish panel
3	Front floor console front bolt (2 required)
4	Floor shifter
5	Front floor console middle bolt (2 required)
6	Floor console rear bolt (2 required)
7	Floor console
8	Powerpoint electrical connector
9	Floor console center finish panel screws (2 required)

LTV0500000000874

Fig. 39 Front floor console replacement. 2004–06 Explorer & Mountaineer

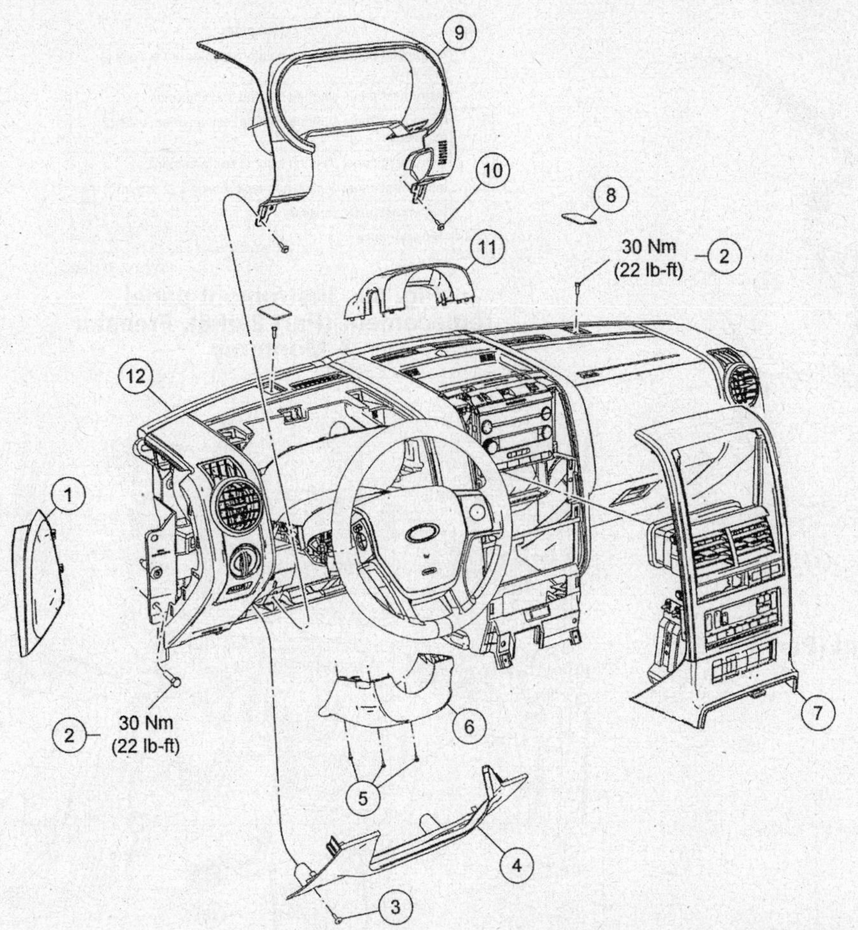

LTV0500000000875

Fig. 40 Exploded view of instrument panel (Part 1 of 2). 2004–06 Explorer & Mountaineer

Item	Description
1	Instrument panel side finish panels (2 required)
2	Instrument panel bolt (6 required)
3	Steering column opening cover screws (2 required)
4	Steering column opening cover
5	Steering column cover screws (3 required)
6	Lower steering column cover
7	Instrument panel center finish panel
8	Instrument panel cowl top bolt covers (2 required)
9	Instrument cluster finish panel
10	Instrument cluster finish panel screws (2 required)
11	Upper steering column cover
12	Instrument panel

LTV0500000000876

Fig. 40 Exploded view of instrument panel (Part 2 of 2). 2004–06 Explorer & Mountaineer

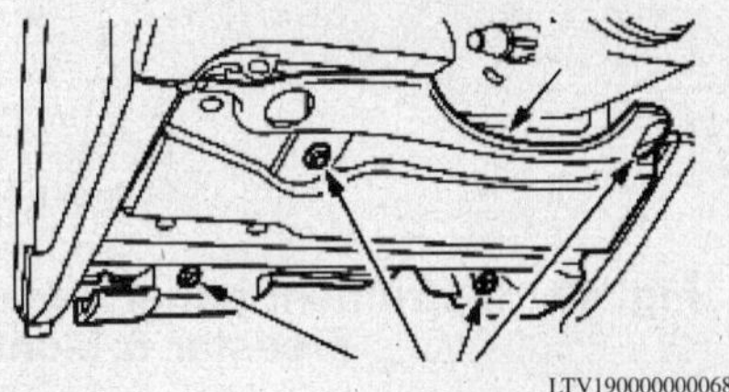

LTV1900000000680

Fig. 41 Steering column cover reinforcement. Explorer Sport/ Sport Trac

LTV1900000000681

Fig. 42 Shift cable. Explorer Sport/Sport Trac

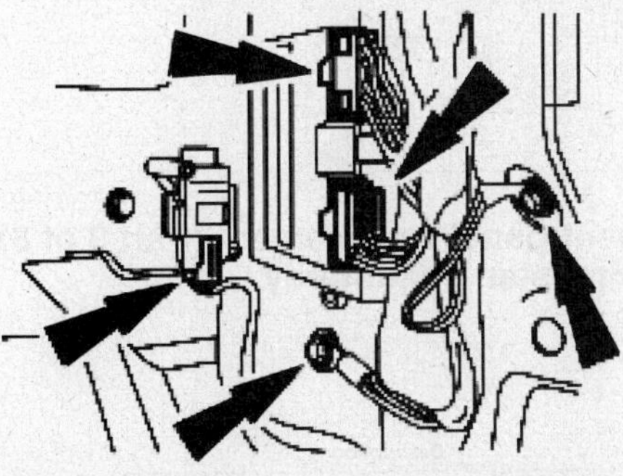

LTV1900000000682

Fig. 43 Electrical connectors and ground wires. Explorer Sport/ Sport Trac

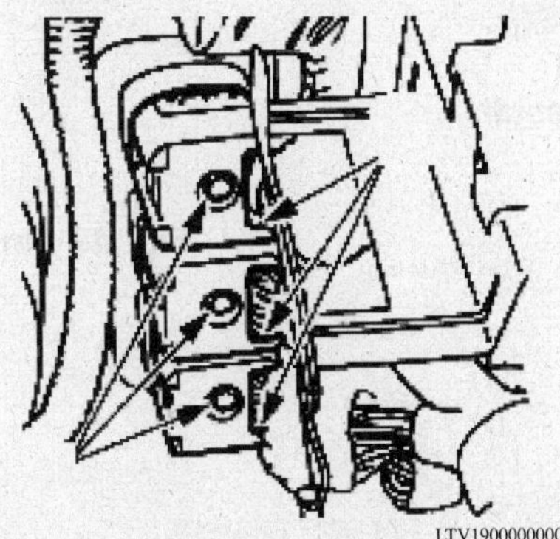

LTV1900000000683

Fig. 44 Bulkhead wiring harness connectors. Explorer Sport/Sport Trac

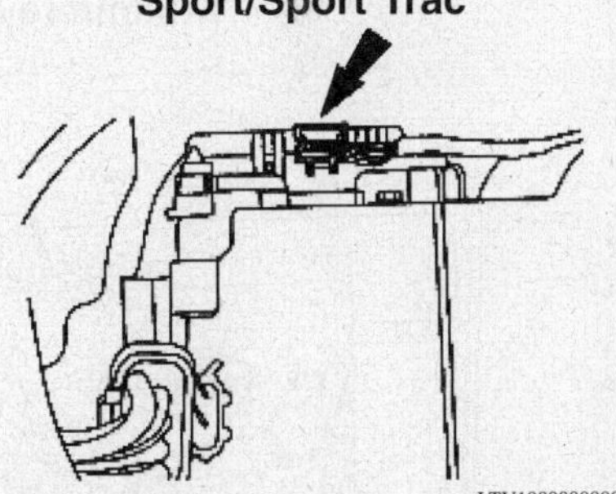

LTV1900000000684

Fig. 45 Blend door electrical connector. Explorer Sport/Sport Trac

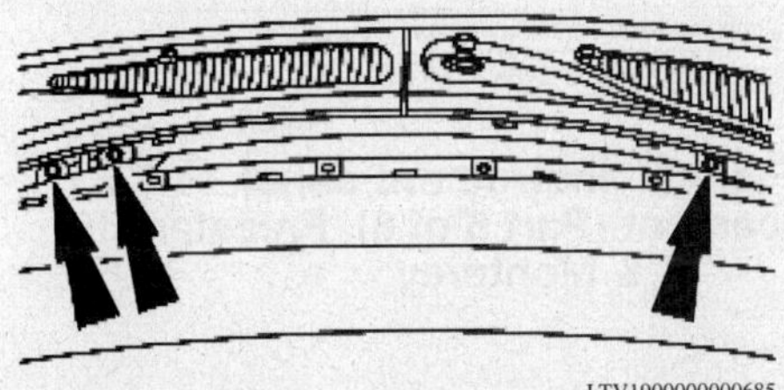

LTV1900000000685

Fig. 46 Instrument panel cowl top bolts. Explorer Sport/Sport Trac

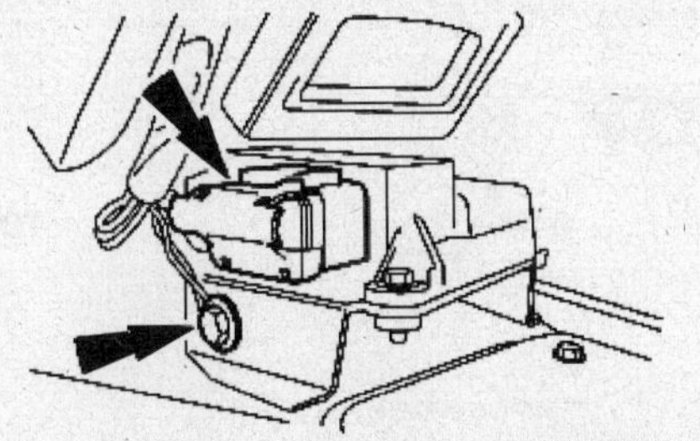

LTV1900000000686

Fig. 47 Restraint control module. Explorer Sport/Sport Trac

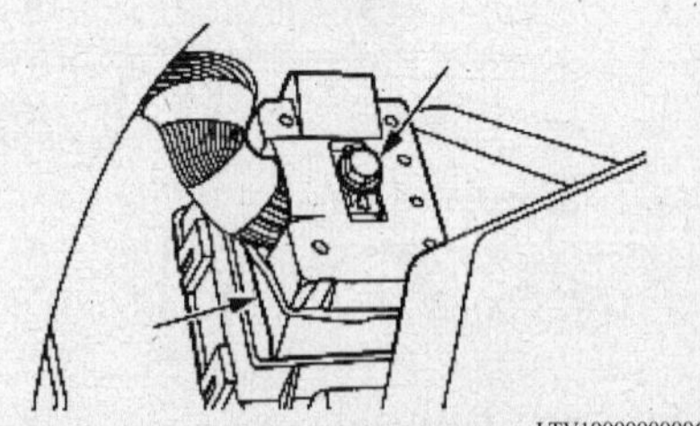

LTV1900000000687

Fig. 48 Instrument panel harness. Explorer Sport/Sport Trac

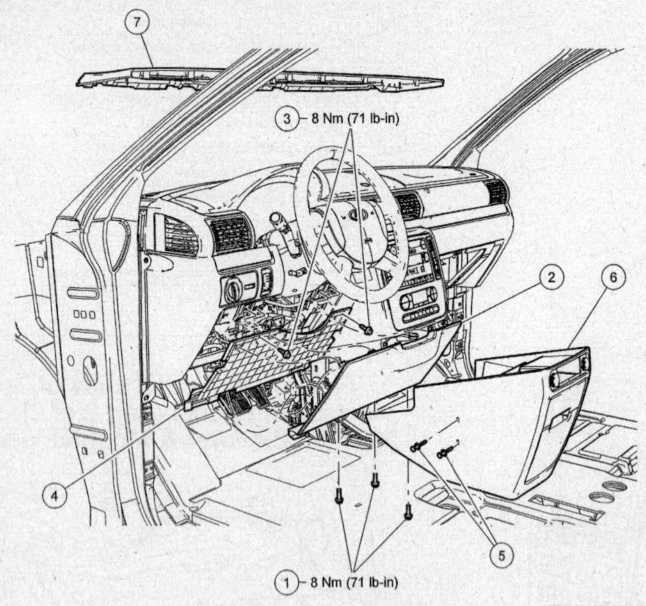

LTV0500000000964

Fig. 49 Instrument panel replacement (Part 1 of 8). Freestar & Monterey

Item	Description
8	Electrical connector
9	Restraint control module electrical connector
10	Electrical connector
11	Electrical connector
12	Electrical connector
13	Electrical connector
14	Electrical connector
15	Smart junction box electrical connector
16	Smart junction box electrical connector
17	Intermediate shaft pinch bolt
18	Intermediate shaft
19	Transmission shift cable

LTV0500000000967

Fig. 49 Instrument panel replacement (Part 4 of 8). Freestar & Monterey

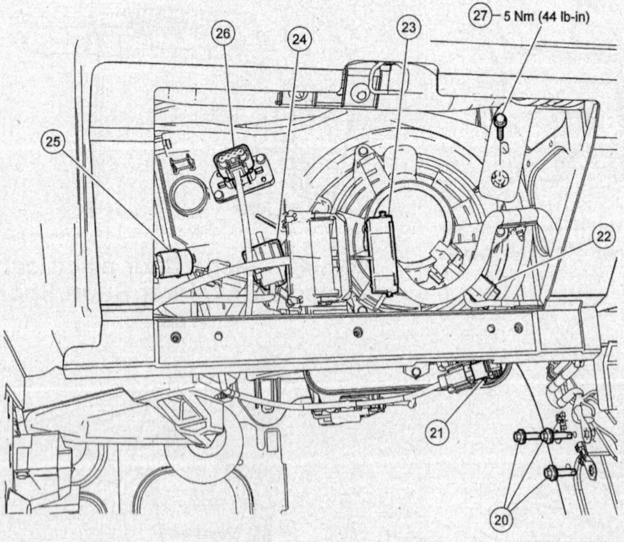

LTV0500000000968

Fig. 49 Instrument panel replacement (Part 5 of 8). Freestar & Monterey

Item	Description
1	Instrument panel steering column opening cover bolts (3 required)
2	Instrument panel steering column opening cover
3	Instrument panel steering column reinforcement bolts (2 required)
4	Instrument panel steering column reinforcement
5	Instrument panel console pin-type retainers (2 required)
6	Instrument panel console
7	Defroster grille

LTV0500000000965

Fig. 49 Instrument panel replacement (Part 2 of 8). Freestar & Monterey

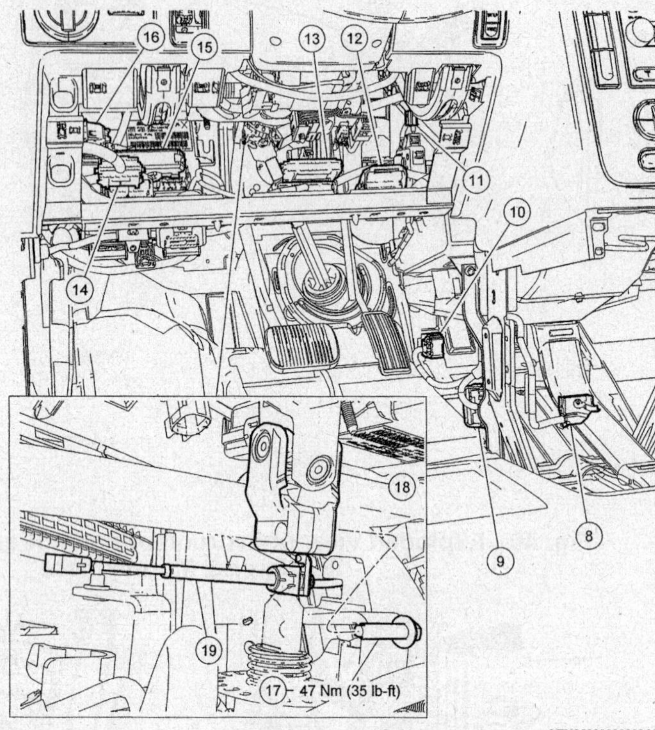

LTV0500000000966

Fig. 49 Instrument panel replacement (Part 3 of 8). Freestar & Monterey

Item	Description
20	Ground bolts
21	Climate control electrical connector
22	Blower motor electrical connector
23	Main electrical connector
24	Heater servo electrical connector
25	Electronic air temperature control air tube (if equipped)
26	Thermal resistor electrical connector (if equipped)
27	Instrument panel reinforcement bolt (RH)

LTV0500000000969

Fig. 49 Instrument panel replacement (Part 6 of 8). Freestar & Monterey

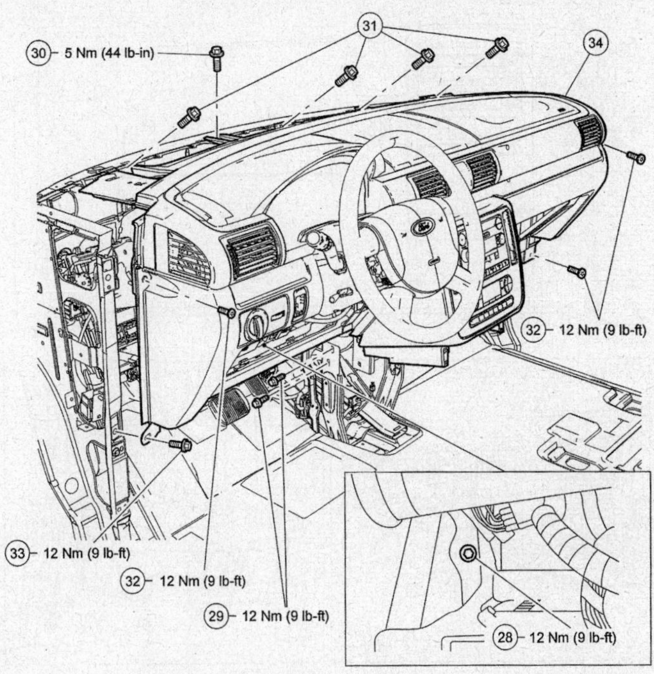

LTV0500000000970

Fig. 49 Instrument panel replacement (Part 7 of 8). Freestar & Monterey

Item	Description
28	Instrument panel reinforcement bolt (LH)
29	Instrument panel center support bolts (4 required)
30	Instrument panel cowl reinforcement bolt
31	Instrument panel cowl top bolts (4 required)
32	Instrument panel cowl side bolts (3 required)
33	Instrument panel cowl side bolt
34	Instrument panel

LTV0500000000971

Fig. 49 Instrument panel replacement (Part 8 of 8). Freestar & Monterey

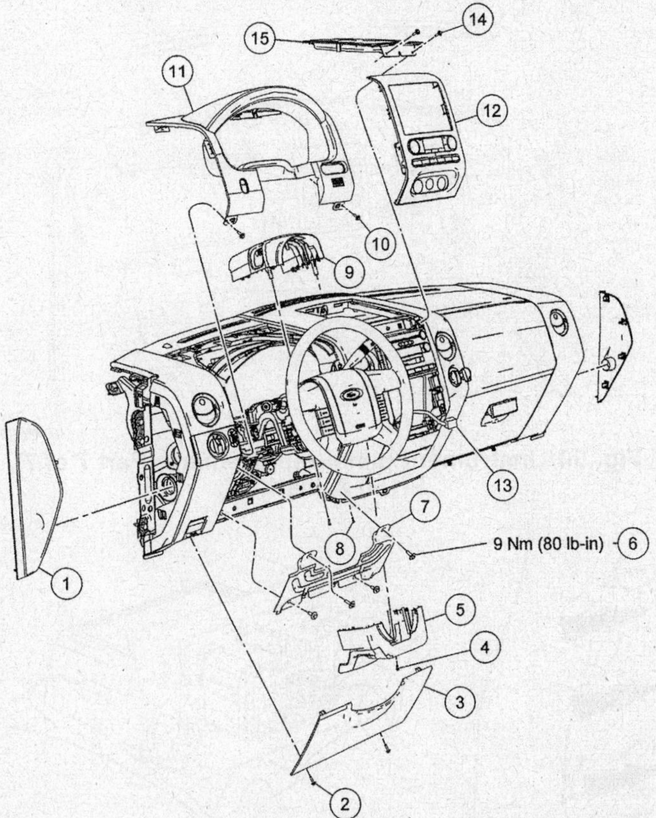

LTV0500000000877

Fig. 50 Instrument panel replacement (Part 1 of 7). F-150 & Mark LT

Item	Description
1	Instrument panel side finish panel (RH/LH)
2	Steering column opening trim screws (2 required)
3	Steering column opening trim
4	Lower steering column cover screw
5	Lower steering column cover
6	Steering column opening panel screws (4 required)
7	Steering column opening panel
8	Upper steering column cover screws (2 required)
9	Upper steering column cover
10	Instrument cluster finish panel screws (2 required)
11	Instrument cluster finish panel
12	Instrument panel center finish panel
13	Climate control electrical connector
14	Instrument cluster center finish panel screws (2 required)
15	Instrument cluster center finish panel

LTV0500000000878

Fig. 50 Instrument panel replacement (Part 2 of 7). F-150 & Mark LT

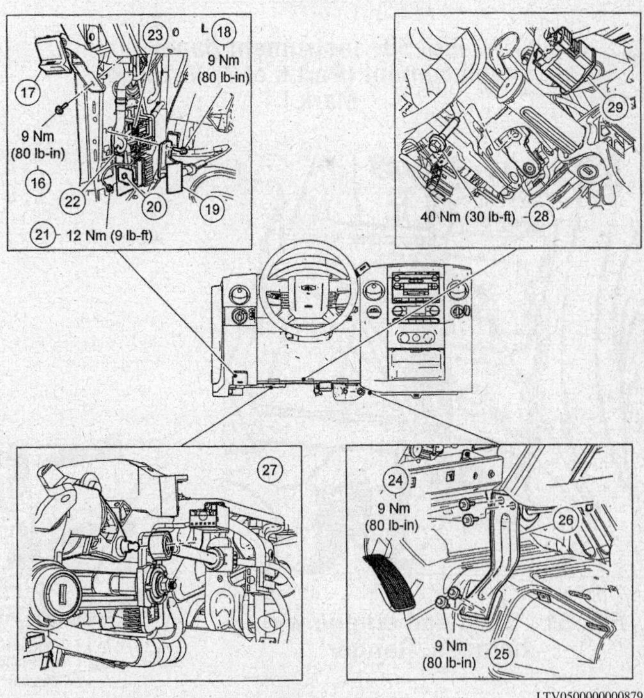

LTV0500000000879

Fig. 50 Instrument panel replacement (Part 3 of 7). F-150 & Mark LT

Item	Description
16	Parking brake release handle bolt
17	Parking brake release handle
18	Hood release handle bolt
19	Hood release handle
20	Electrical connector
21	Ground bolt
22	Electrical connector
23	Electrical connector
24	Center brace bolt (2 required)
25	Center brace bolt (2 required)
26	Center brace
27	Transmission range indicator cable
28	Pinch bolt
29	Electrical connector

LTV0500000000880

Fig. 50 Instrument panel replacement (Part 4 of 7). F-150 & Mark LT

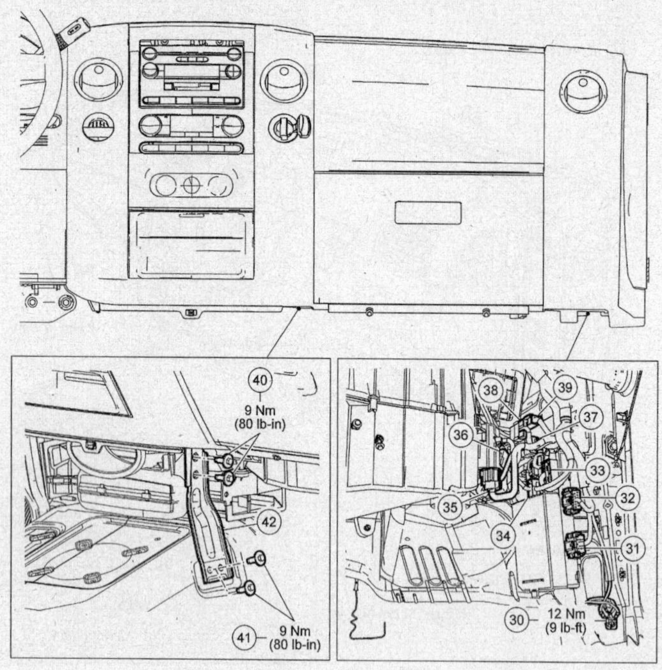

Fig. 50 Instrument panel replacement (Part 5 of 7). F-150 & Mark LT

Item	Description
30	Ground bolt
31	PDB B1 Electrical connector
32	PDB B2 Electrical connector
33	PDB L1 Electrical connector
34	PDB L2 Electrical connector
35	ETAC Electrical connector
36	Instrument panel electrical connector
37	Instrument panel electrical connector
38	Instrument panel electrical connector
39	Instrument panel electrical connector
40	Center brace bolt (2 required)
41	Center brace bolt (2 required)
42	Center brace

LTV0500000000962

Fig. 50 Instrument panel replacement (Part 6 of 7). F-150 & Mark LT

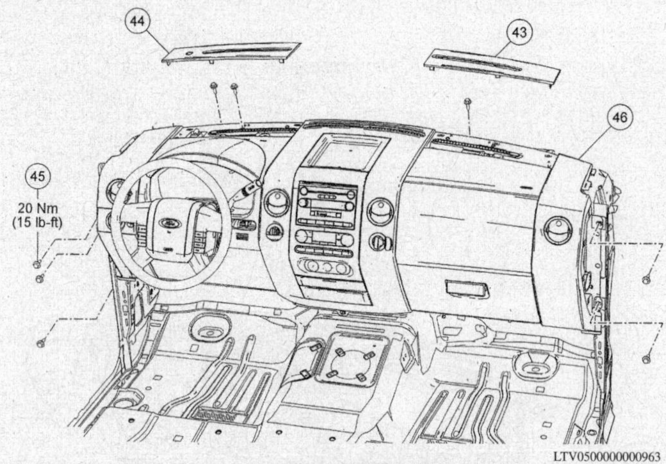

Fig. 50 Instrument panel replacement (Part 7 of 7). F-150 & Mark LT

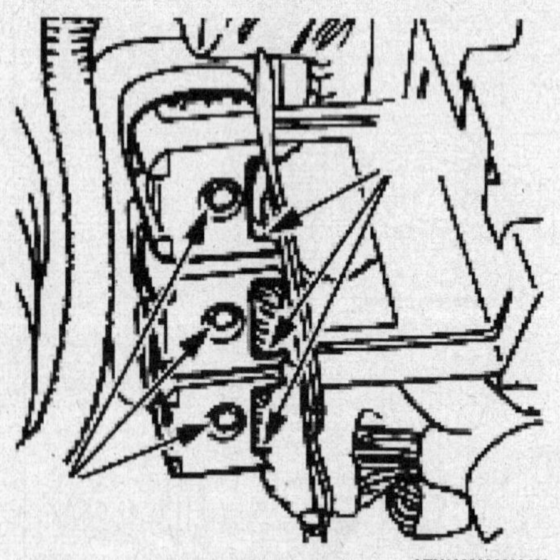

Fig. 51 Bulkhead engine wiring harness. Ranger

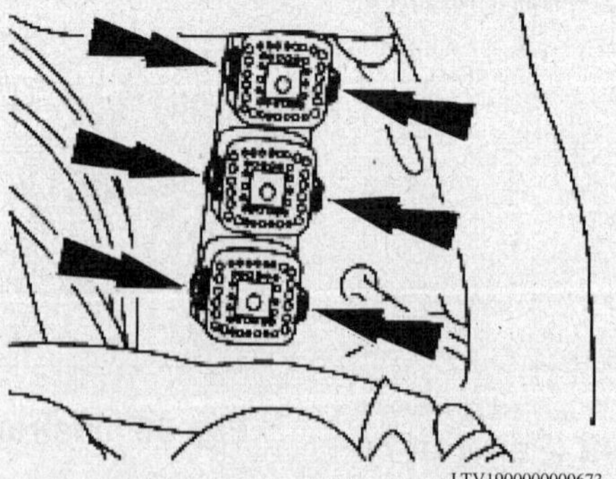

Fig. 52 Bulkhead electrical connectors retaining clips. Ranger

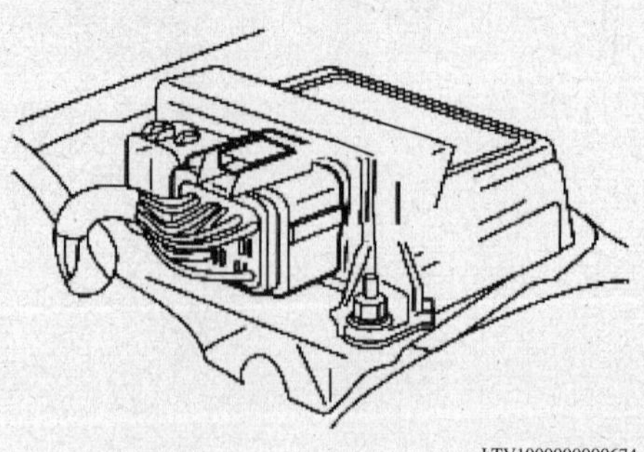

Fig. 53 Restraint control. Ranger

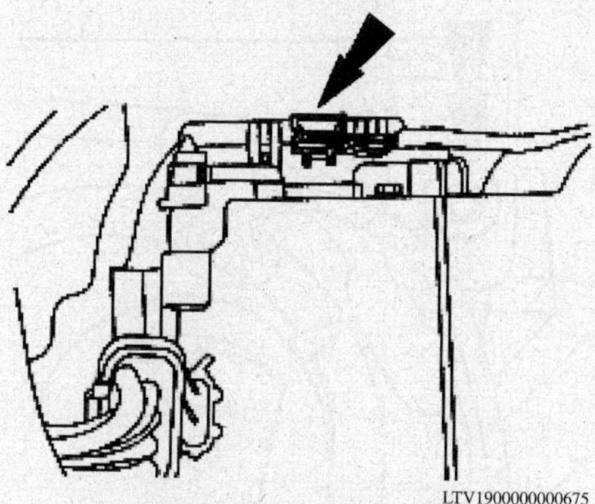

Fig. 54 Blend door actuator electrical connector. Ranger

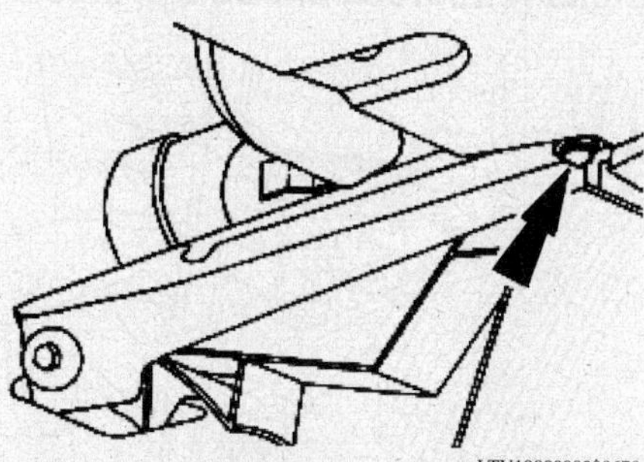

Fig. 57 Instrument panel brace bolt under steering column. Ranger

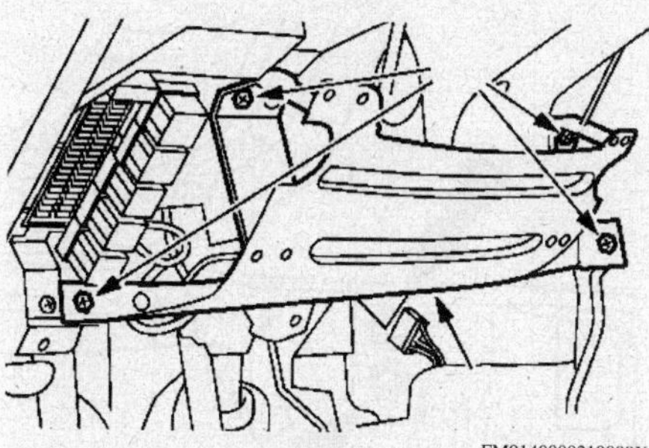

Fig. 60 Instrument panel cover reinforcement. Villager

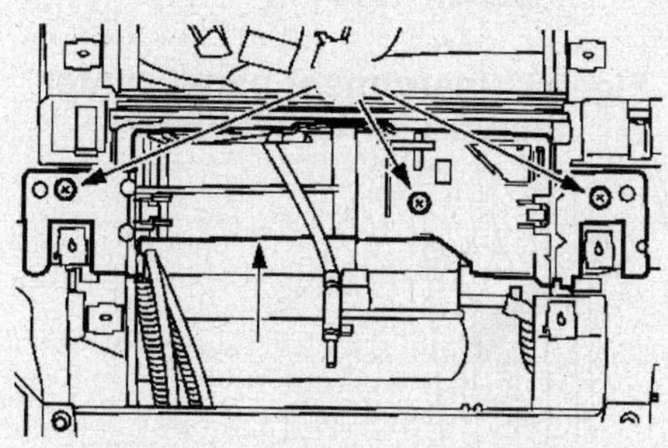

Fig. 63 Ashtray/cupholder bracket. Villager

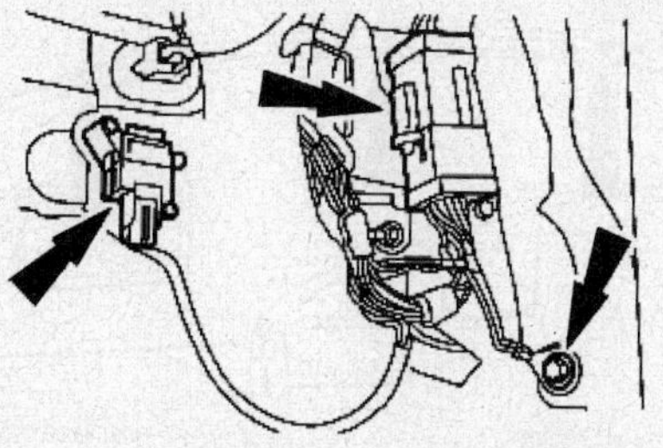

Fig. 55 Righthand cowl panel electrical connectors. Ranger

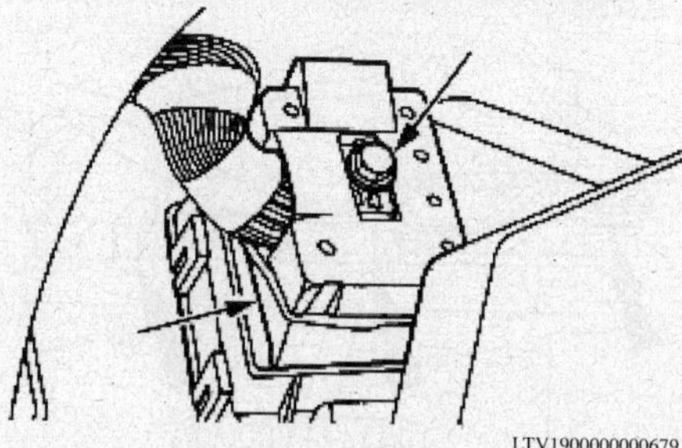

Fig. 58 Instrument panel to body harness connector. Ranger

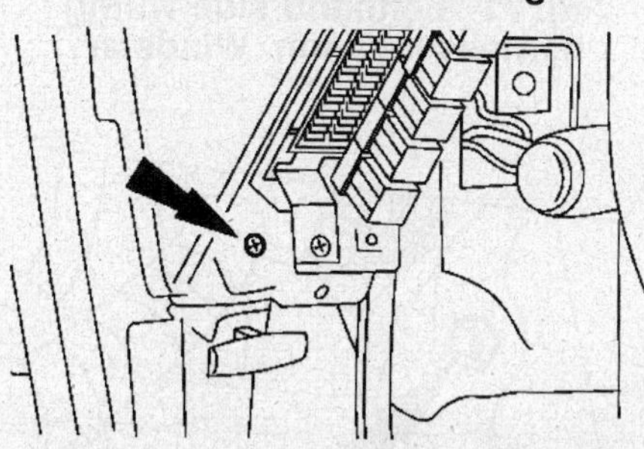

Fig. 61 Lefthand instrument panel screw. Villager

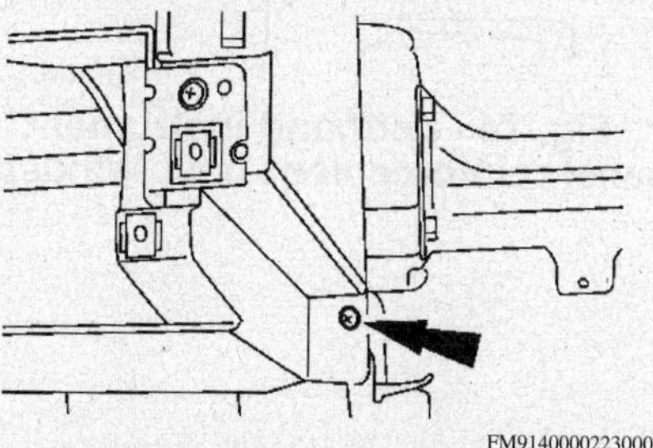

Fig. 64 Righthand instrument panel screw. Villager

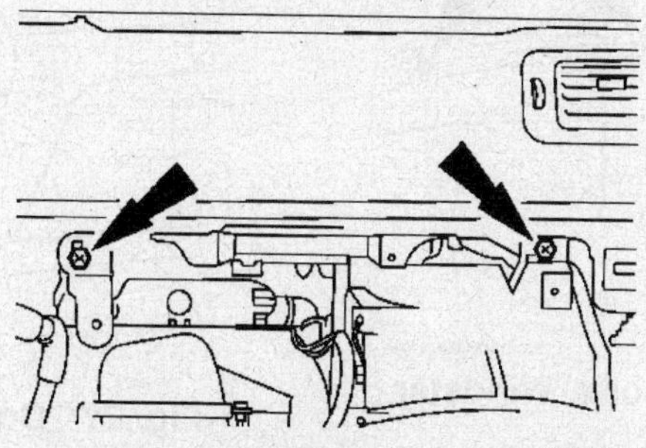

Fig. 66 Instrument panel bolts, glove compartment opening. Villager

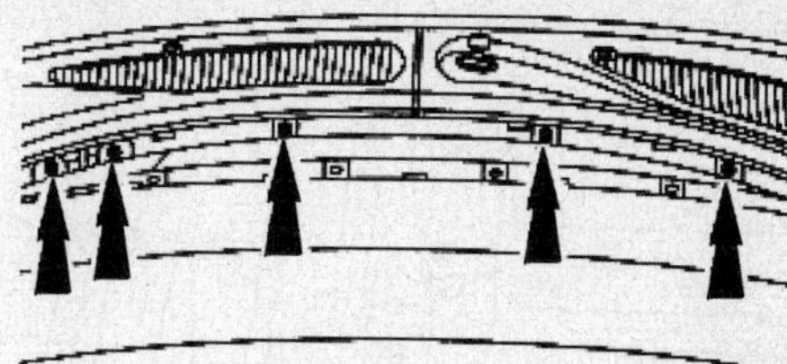

Fig. 56 Cowl top bolts. Ranger

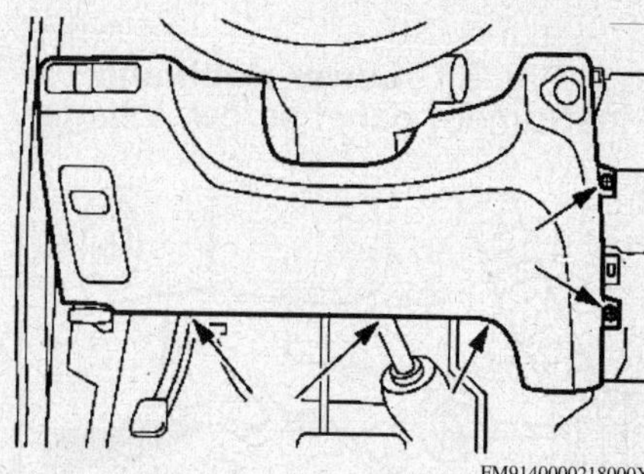

Fig. 59 Instrument panel steering column cover. Villager

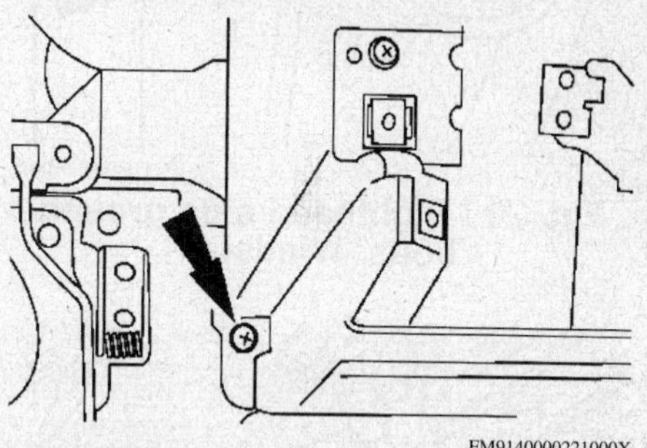

Fig. 62 Center, lefthand instrument panel screw. Villager

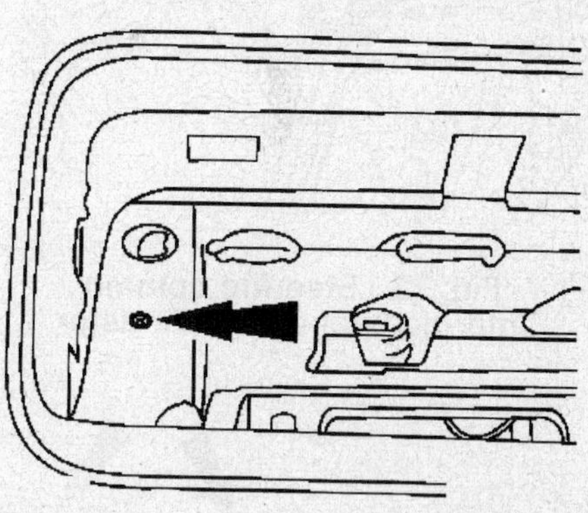

Fig. 65 Instrument panel screw, passenger air bag module opening. Villager

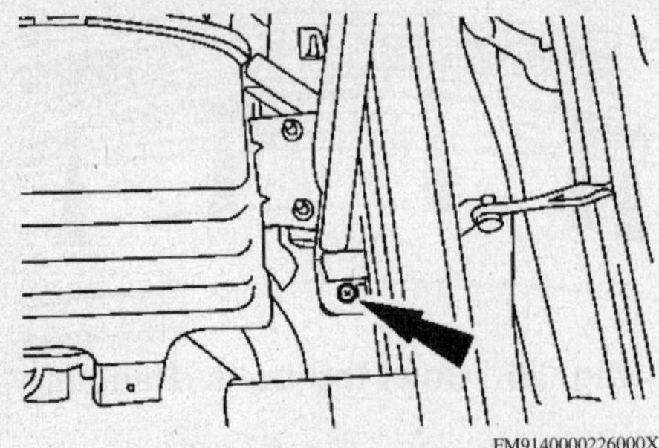

Fig. 67 Lower righthand instrument panel screw. Villager

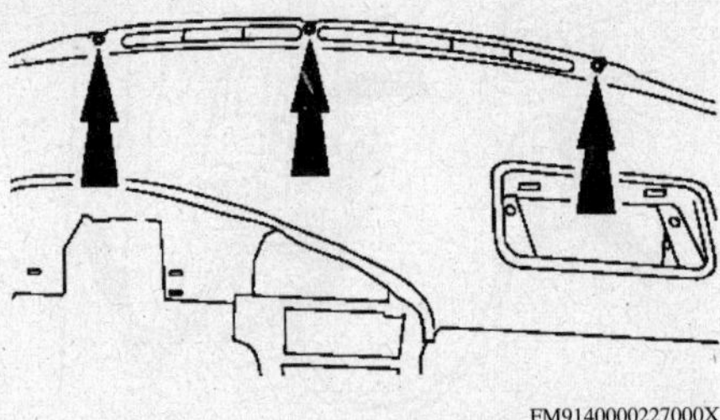

Fig. 68 Instrument panel top cowl nuts & screws. Villager

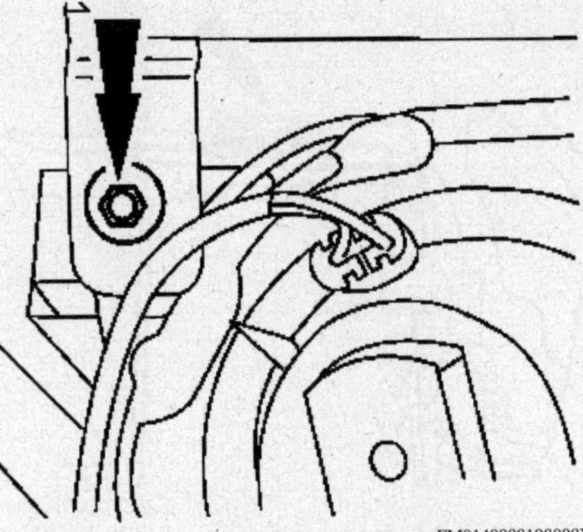

Fig. 69 Righthand instrument panel reinforcement bolt. Windstar

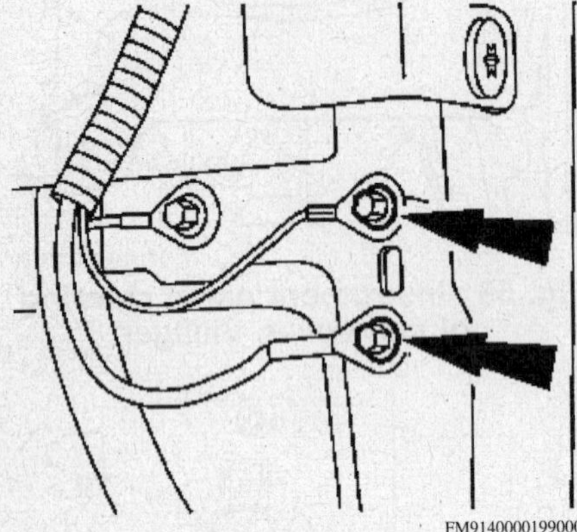

Fig. 70 Righthand side ground bolts. Windstar

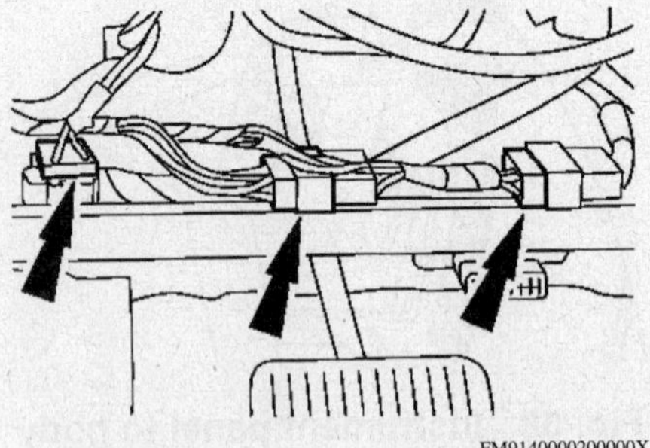

Fig. 71 Lefthand side wiring harness location. Windstar

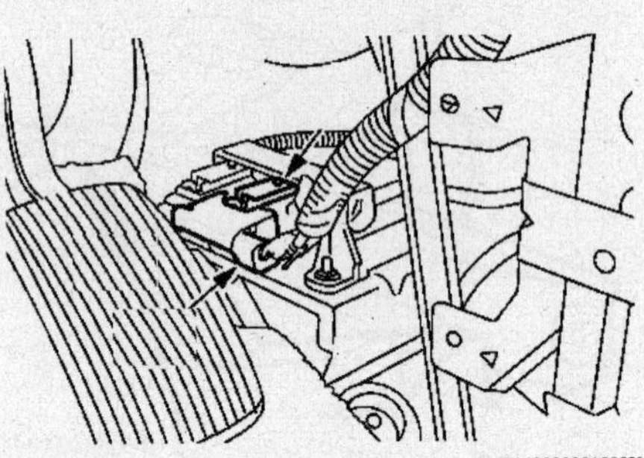

Fig. 72 Electronic crash sensor. Windstar

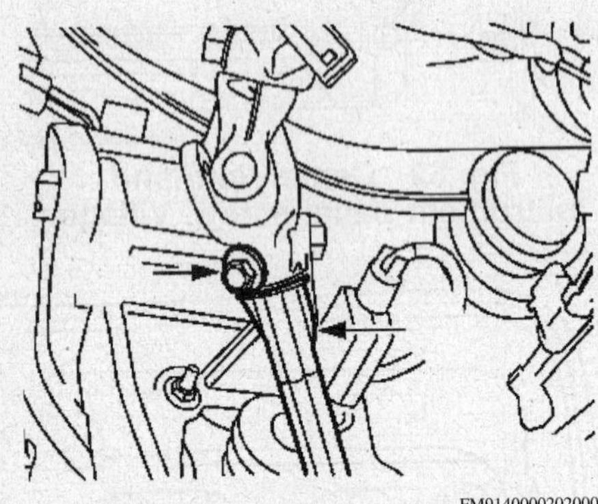

Fig. 73 Steering column intermediate shaft. Windstar

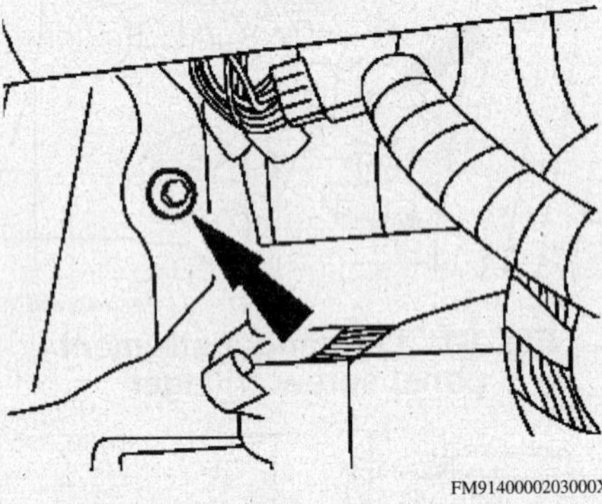

Fig. 74 Lefthand instrument panel reinforcement bolt. Windstar

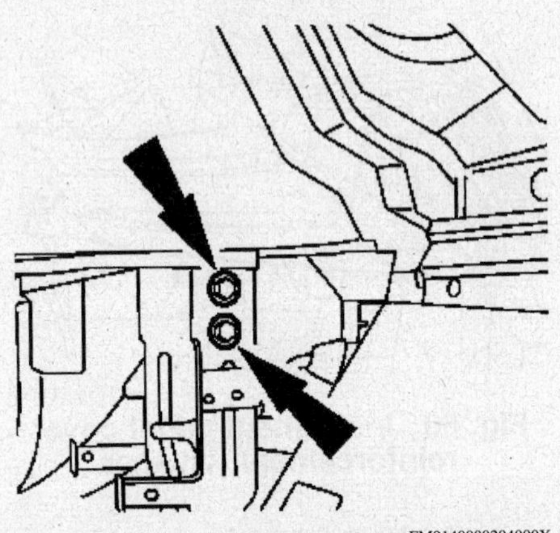

Fig. 75 Instrument panel center support bolts. Windstar

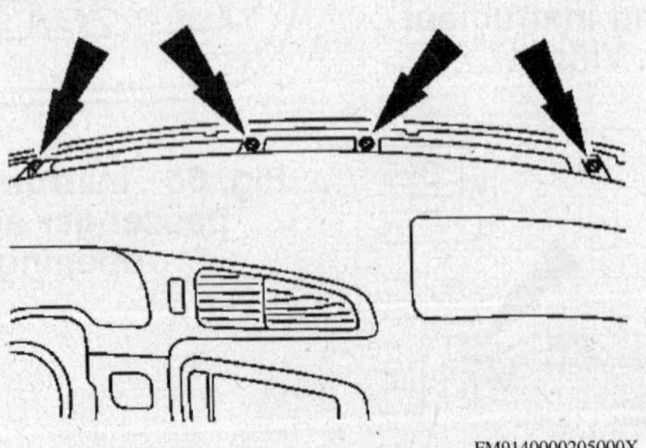

Fig. 76 Cowl top bolts. Windstar

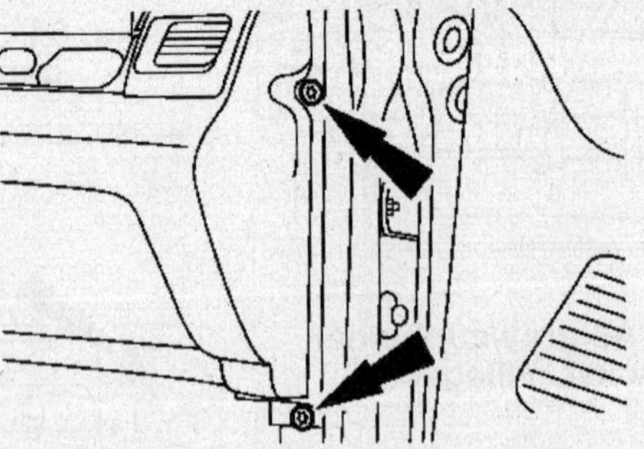

Fig. 77 Cowl side bolts. Windstar

TIGHTENING SPECIFICATIONS

Year/ Model	Component	Torque Ft. Lbs.
AVIATOR		
2003–06	Front Floor Console	44①
	Hood Release Handle	44①
	Instrument Panel Center Brace	80①
	Instrument Panel (Engine Compartment)	18①
	Instrument Panel (Side Cowl)	22
	Instrument Panel (Top Cowl)	22
	Intermediate Shaft Pinch Bolt	30
	Steering Column Cover	18①
E-SERIES		
2002–06	Floor Console	45①
	Instrument Panel Cowl Side	19–24
	Instrument Panel Cowl Top Screws	18–27①
	Instrument Panel Cowl Top Nuts	14–19
	Instrument Panel Dash Brace	62–89①
	Instrument Panel Finish	18–26①
	Instrument Panel Lower	18–27①
	Steering Column Opening Cover	18–27①
	Steering Column Support	10–12
ESCAPE & MARINER		
2002–06	Floor Console	53①
	Hood Latch Release Handle	53①
	Instrument Cluster Finish	27①
	Instrument Panel Center Brace	18
	Instrument Panel Cowl Side	80①
	Instrument Panel Cowl Top	53①
	Parking Brake Control	18
	Steering Column Pinch Bolt	17
EXCURSION		
2002–05	Floor Console	62①
	Instrument Panel Center Support	30
	Instrument Panel Cowl Side	30
	Instrument Panel Cowl Top	80①
	Instrument Panel Finish	24①
	Parking Brake Release Handle	90①
	Steering Column Shaft	35
EXPEDITION & NAVIGATOR		
2002–06	Front Floor Console Bracket To Floor	15
	Front Floor Console To Bracket (Expedition)	108①
	Front Floor Console To Bracket (Navigator)	62①
	Front Floor Console Rear Bolts (Expedition)	62①
	Hood Release Handle	80①
	Instrument Panel	22
	Instrument Panel Floor Brace	80①
	Instrument Panel Finish	21①
	Intermediate Shaft Pinch Bolt	22
	Steering Column Opening Cover	80①
	Steering Column Support	10

TIGHTENING SPECIFICATIONS—Continued

Year/ Model	Component	Torque Ft. Lbs.
EXPLORER & MOUNTAINEER		
2002–03	Floor Console	45–80①
	Instrument Panel	20–22
	Instrument Panel Cowl Top	20–22
	Instrument Panel Floor Brace	18–26①
	Instrument Panel Lower	30–39
	Steering Column Opening Cover	45–80①
	Steering Column Support	10–12
EXPLORER SPORT/SPORT TRAC		
2002–06	Bulkhead Wiring Connector	44①
	Instrument Panel Brace (Steering column opening)	80①
	Instrument Panel Cowl Side Bolts	22
	Instrument Panel Harness	44①
	Intermediate Steering Shaft Pinch Bolt	22
FREESTAR & MONTEREY		
2004–06	Floor Console Bin	18①
	Floor Console Bracket	18①
	Ground Bolts	27①
	Instrument Panel Center Support	108①
	Instrument Panel Cowl Side	108①
	Instrument Panel Cowl Top	27①
	Intermediate Shaft Pinch Bolt	35
F-SUPER DUTY		
2002–06	Floor Console Less Rear Video	44①
	Floor Console w/Rear Video	62①
	Instrument Panel Center Support	30
	Instrument Panel Cowl Side	30
	Instrument Panel Cowl Top	80①
	Instrument Panel Cowl Top (Center)	80①
	Instrument Panel Cowl Top (Lefthand)	80①
	Instrument Panel Cowl Top (Righthand)	27①
	Parking Brake Release Handle	89①
	Steering Column Shaft Pinch Bolt	35
	Steering Column Support	10
F-150 & MARK LT		
2002–06	Bulkhead Wiring Harness	44①
	Center Brace	80①
	Floor Console	53①
	Ground Bolts	108①
	Hood Release Handle	80①
	Instrument Panel	15
	Intermediate Shaft Pinch Bolt	30
	Parking Brake Release Handle	80①
	Steering Column Opening Cover	80①
RANGER		
2002–06	Center Arm Rest	108①
	Instrument Panel Cowl Top	22
	Instrument Panel Cowl Side	22
	Instrument Panel To Body Harness	44①
	Intermediate Shaft Pinch Bolt	21
	Steering Column Opening Cover	108①

Continued

DASH PANEL SERVICE

TIGHTENING SPECIFICATIONS—Continued

Year/ Model	Component	Torque Ft. Lbs.
VILLAGER		
2002	Glove Compartment	44①
	Instrument Panel	44①
	Instrument Panel Cowl	44①
	Instrument Panel Support Bracket	89①
	Steering Column	13

TIGHTENING SPECIFICATIONS—Continued

Year/ Model	Component	Torque Ft. Lbs.
WINDSTAR		
2002–03	Console Panel	16–23①
	Cowl Side	11
	Cowl Top	27
	Instrument Panel Center Support	108①
	Instrument Panel Reinforcement	11
	Intermediate Shaft Pinch Bolt	35

① — Inch lbs.

STEERING COLUMNS

NOTE: On Air Bag Equipped Models, Refer To "Air Bag System Precautions" Located In The Front Of This Manual For System Disarming & Arming Procedures.

NOTE: Refer To "Computer Relearn Procedures" Located In The Front Of This Manual When Battery Power To The Computer Has Been Interrupted.

INDEX

PRECAUTIONS

Air Bag Systems

Refer to "Air Bag System Precautions" in the front of this manual for system disarming and arming procedures.

Battery Ground Cable

Prior to service disconnect battery ground cable and isolate as required.

Steering Wheel & Column Service

When the steering column is installed in the vehicle it is not susceptible to damage through ordinary use; however, when it is removed, care must be taken during handling. Such actions as a sharp blow on the end of the steering shaft or shift levers, leaning on the column assembly or dropping of the assembly could loosen or shear the plastic shear joints or rivets used to maintain column rigidity. **Hammering, jolting or bumping on the steering shaft and gearshift tube must be avoided during all service operations. If the shear pins are broken, the controlled length of the telescoping design will be altered making these components unfit for further service. When removing the steering wheel, only a steering wheel puller designed for this purpose must be used.**

It is important that only the specified screws, bolts and nuts be used during the assembly procedure and tightened to specifications to ensure proper breakaway action of the column under impact. Avoid using excessively long bolts or fasteners as they may prevent a portion of the steering column from collapsing. When replacing fasteners, replace with ones of the same part number or equivalent.

When removing or installing the steering wheel, ignition switch, lock cylinder, turn signal switch, neutral start switch, or back-up light, refer to the appropriate vehicle chapter.

DESCRIPTION

Energy Absorbing Steering Columns

The energy absorbing function of the steering column allows the column to collapse at a controlled rate during a severe collision. The collapsing action reduces the possibility of the steering wheel being driven rearward towards the driver. If the driver is thrown forward into the steering wheel, the column can collapse even further at the same controlled rate, thereby reducing the force of impact.

Several designs of steering column jackets are used. There is the slip-tube design which is held together with plastic inserts or rivets that shear upon impact and allow the column to collapse. And there is the slotted or corrugated mesh design and bellows type design which shorten in length during impact.

The shift tube is a two piece design which is held together by injections of plastic that form the interconnecting inserts and shear pins. Under impact, there is a gradual paring away of the inserts by the knifelike edge in the adjoining tube section.

The steering shaft is a two piece assembly. The upper piece is solid and has a double flattened lower end. The lower piece is hollow and formed to fit over the double flattened section of the upper piece. The purpose of the double flattened section is to provide continued steering action even though the shaft is completely collapsed. Upon impact, the shear pins break off and the shaft gradually telescopes against resistance provided by the plastic injections.

The steering column mounting bracket prevents the column from being shifted towards the driver during impact. It uses two "breakaway capsules" that allow the mounting bracket to slip off its attaching points, allowing the steering column to compress or yield in a forward direction under a severe impact from the driver's end.

STEERING COLUMN

REPLACE

Aviator

1. Turn steering wheel to straight ahead position and ignition switch to lock position.
2. Deactivate supplemental restraint system as outlined in "Air Bag System" chapter.
3. If removing steering wheel, remove driver air bag module as outlined in "Air Bag System" chapter.
4. Remove clockspring as outlined in "Air Bag System" chapter.

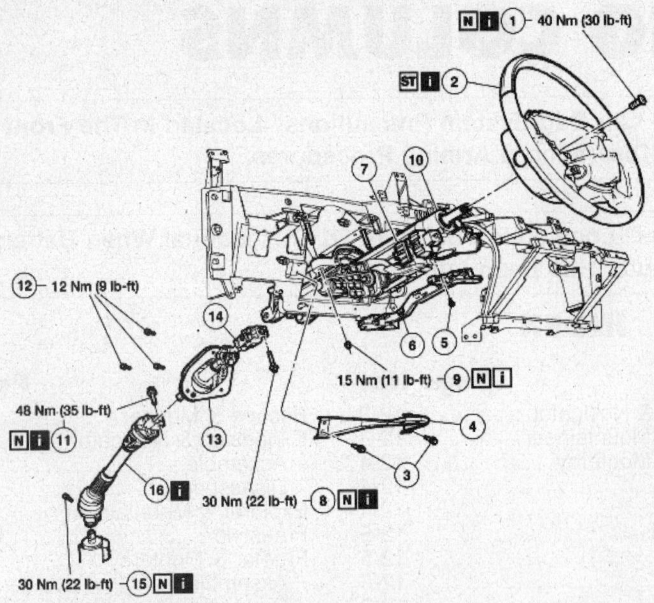

Item	Description
1	Steering wheel bolt
2	Steering wheel
3	Reinforcement screws
4	Reinforcement
5	Wiring shield-to-column screws (four required)
6	Wiring shield
7	Ignition switch electrical connector
8	Steering column shaft-to-steering column bolt
9	Steering column support-to-instrument panel nuts (4 required)
10	Steering column assembly
11	Lower shaft-to-upper shaft bolt
12	Dash seal bolts
13	Dash seal
14	Upper steering column shaft
15	Lower shaft-to-steering gear bolt
16	Lower steering column shaft

LTV1900000000688

Fig. 1 Steering column replacement. Aviator

5. Remove remaining components in sequence, **Fig. 1.**
6. Reverse procedure to install.

E-Series

1. Deactivate supplemental restraint system and remove clockspring as outlined in "Air Bag System" chapter.
2. **On commercial chassis vehicles,** remove nuts, **Fig. 2,** then the steering column support, **Fig. 3.**
3. **On all models,** remove transmission range indicator from steering column, **Fig. 4.**
4. Disconnect transmission shift cable loop from shift tube hook.
5. Remove multi-function switch from steering column.
6. Remove pinch bolt and disconnect intermediate shaft from steering column.
7. Disconnect shift cable from selector lever pivot arm.
8. Remove shift cable from steering column lower mounting bracket by pushing tab on cable and sliding cable off of bracket.
9. Disconnect ignition switch.
10. Lower steering column bend bracket and disconnect electrical connectors.
11. While supporting steering column, remove retaining nuts, **Figs. 5 and 6.**
12. Remove steering column from vehicle.
13. Reverse procedure to install, noting the following:
    a. **Torque** steering column retaining nuts to 11 ft. lbs.
    b. **On commercial vehicles, torque** intermediate shaft pinch bolt to 36 ft. lbs.
    c. **On all except commercial vehicles, torque** intermediate shaft pinch bolt to 18 ft. lbs.
    d. **On all models, torque** steering column support nuts to 13 ft. lbs.

Escape & Mariner

REMOVAL

1. Place front wheel in a straight ahead position.
2. Remove steering wheel as outlined in the "Electrical" section of the "Escape & Mariner" chapter.
3. Remove steering column upper and lower shroud attaching screws, then the shrouds from steering column.
4. Apply two strips of tape across air bag sliding contact to prevent accidental

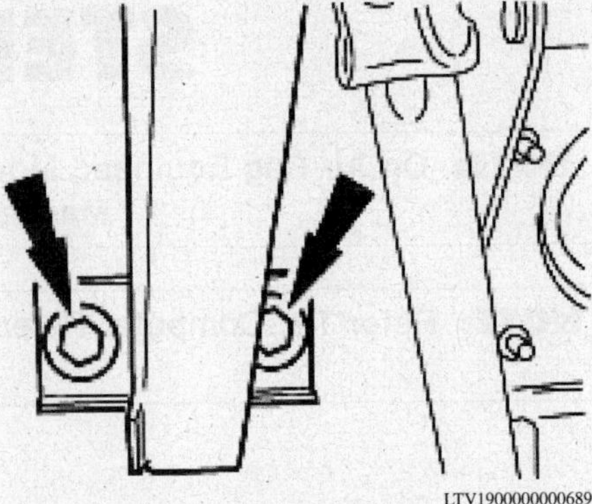

Fig. 2 Support nuts. E-Series commercial chassis

Fig. 3 Steering column support. E-Series commercial chassis

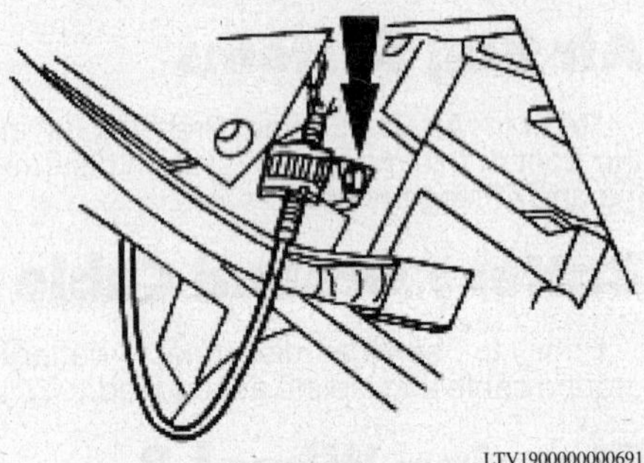

Fig. 4 Transmission range indicator. E-Series commercial chassis

rotation, then remove sliding contact retaining screws and contact, **Fig. 7.**

5. Disconnect multi-function switch assembly electrical connectors.
6. Disconnect selector lever shift cable from selector lever and bracket.
7. Disconnect passive anti-theft system (PATS) transceiver module electrical connector and pin type retainer **Fig. 8.**
8. Remove trim panel from under steering column.
9. Disconnect electrical connectors.
10. Position steering column shaft boot aside to gain access to flexible coupling.
11. Remove and discard pinch bolt/nut, then separate steering column shaft from flexible coupling.
12. While supporting column assembly, remove column assembly retaining nuts.

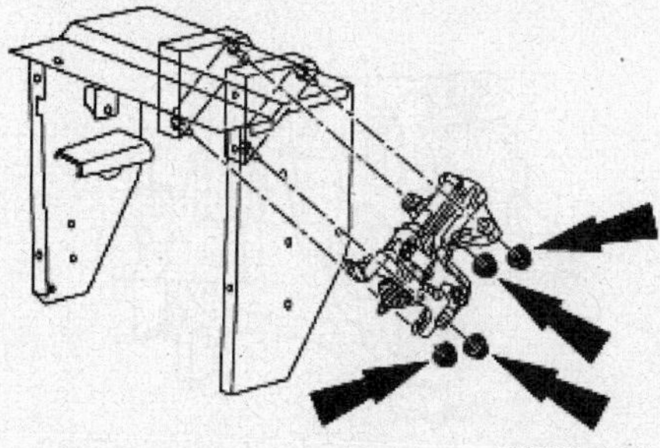

Fig. 5 Steering column retaining nuts. E-Series commercial chassis

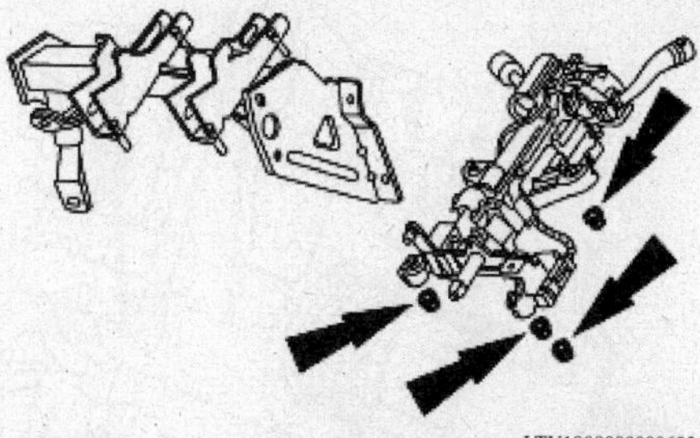

Fig. 6 Steering column retaining nuts. E-Series except commercial chassis

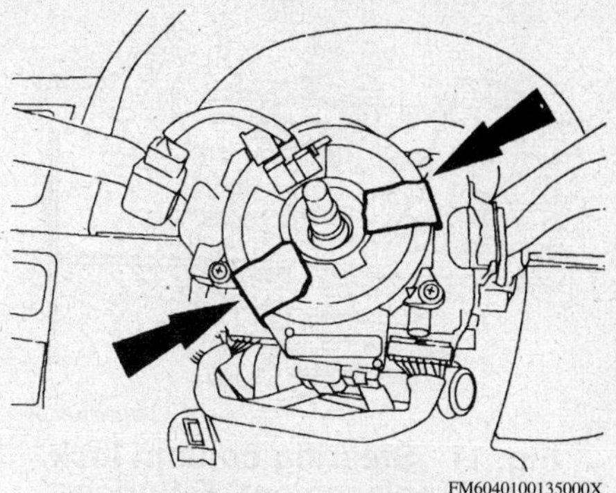

Fig. 7 Air bag sliding contact. Escape & Mariner

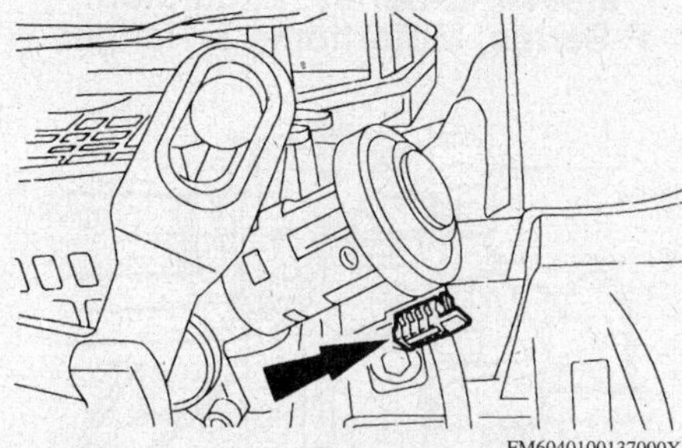

Fig. 8 Passive anti-theft system (PATS) transceiver module electrical connector. Escape & Mariner

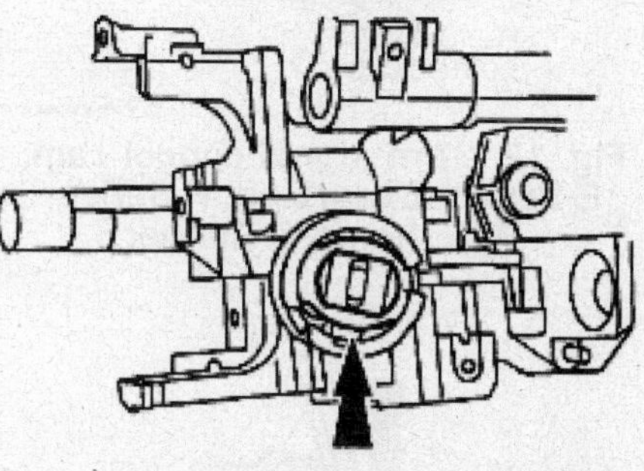

Fig. 9 Steering column bearing retainer. E-Series, Excursion, F-Series, Motorhome & Ranger

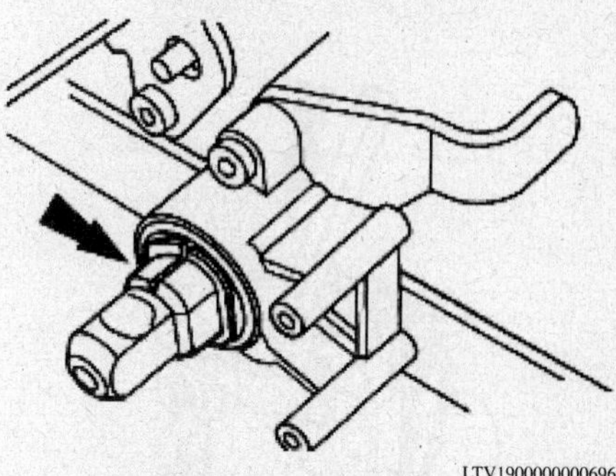

Fig. 10 Steering column bearing tolerance ring. E-Series, Excursion, F-Series, Motorhome & Ranger w/Automatic transmission

13. Remove steering column from vehicle.

INSTALLATION

1. **Torque** steering column assembly retaining nuts to 14 ft. lbs.
2. Install steering column support bolt and **torque** to 12 ft. lbs.
3. Connect steering column shaft to flexible coupling, install a new pinch bolt and nut and **torque** nut to 17 ft. lbs.
4. Position steering column shaft boot over steering column shaft flexible coupling.
5. Connect electrical connectors.
6. Replace steering column trim panel.
7. Connect passive anti-theft system (PATS) transceiver module electrical connector and pin type retainer, **Fig. 8.**
8. Connect selector lever shift cable to selector lever and bracket.
9. Connect multi-function switch assembly electrical connectors.
10. Install sliding contact and screws, then connect electrical connectors.
11. Remove tape from sliding contact.
12. Install lower and upper steering column shrouds.
13. Install steering wheel as outlined in the "Electrical" section of the "Escape & Mariner" chapter.
14. **Torque** pinion shaft to 11 ft. lbs.

Expedition & Navigator

1. Deactivate supplemental restraint system and remove clockspring as outlined in "Air Bag System" chapter.
2. Remove steering column cover and reinforcement.
3. Disconnect ignition switch electrical connector.
4. Remove electrical connector and push pin from steering column.
5. Disconnect PATS transceiver electrical connector.
6. **On models equipped with column shifter,** disconnect shift cable from column and bracket. Remove bolt, then disconnect transmission range indicator cable.
7. **On all models,** remove wiring conduit from steering column.
8. Remove pinch bolt, then disconnect intermediate shaft from steering column.
9. Remove steering column mounting nuts, the steering column. Discard mounting nuts.
10. Reverse procedure to install, noting the following:
    a. **Torque** intermediate shaft pinch bolt to 22 ft. lbs.
    b. **Torque** steering column support bracket to 11 ft. lbs.

Explorer & Mountaineer

1. Park vehicle with wheels in straight ahead position.
2. Remove steering wheel as outlined in "Steering Wheel, Replace" in appropriate chassis chapter.
3. Remove instrument panel steering column opening cover.
4. Disconnect multi-function switch, ignition switch and clockspring electrical connectors.
5. Disconnect key in switch electrical connector then the PATS electrical connector. .
6. Detach wiring harness retainer and position wiring harness aside.
7. Squeeze connector at sides and disconnect steering column adaptive load safety device electrical connector. Detach wiring retainer.
8. Remove and discard upper steering column shaft to steering column bolt.
9. Remove and discard steering column support bracket nuts and steering column.
10. Remove steering column from vehicle.
11. Reverse procedure to install, noting the following:
    a. **Torque** intermediate shaft pinch bolt to 22 ft. lbs.
    b. **Torque** steering column support bracket to 11 ft. lbs.

Excursion & F-Series

1. Position steering wheel in straight ahead position and ignition switch in Off position.
2. Deactivate supplemental restraint system and remove clockspring as outlined in "Air Bag System" chapter.
3. Remove multi-function switch.
4. Remove steering column cover reinforcement.
5. Disconnect ignition switch electrical connector.
6. **On models equipped with automatic transmission,** remove transmission range indicator from steering column, then disconnect shift cable.
7. **On all models,** remove steering column shaft pinch bolt.

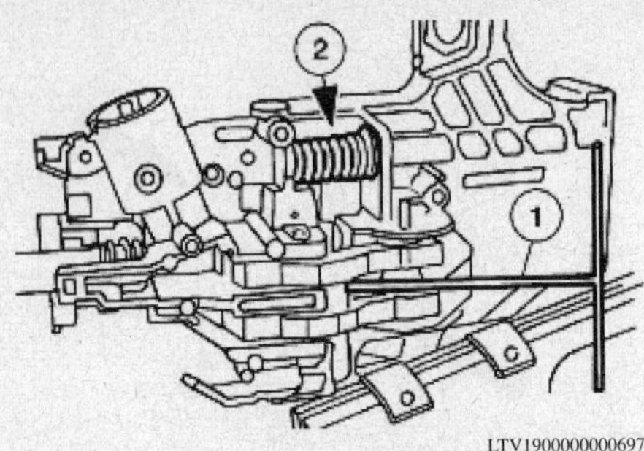

Fig. 11 Steering column lock lever replacement. E-Series, Excursion, F-Series, Motorhome & Ranger

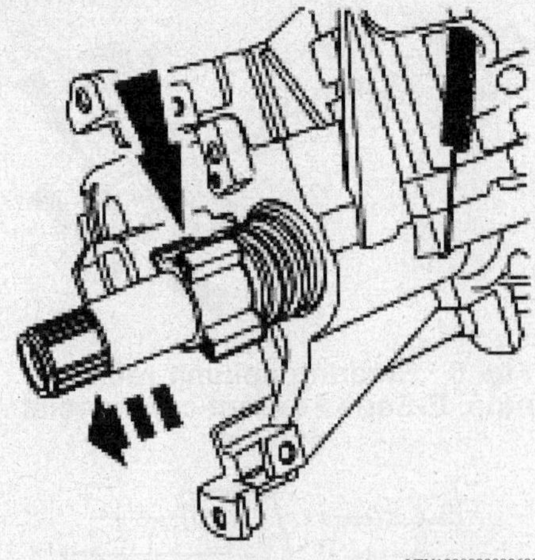

Fig. 12 Turn signal cancel cam. E-Series, Excursion, F-Series, Motorhome & Ranger

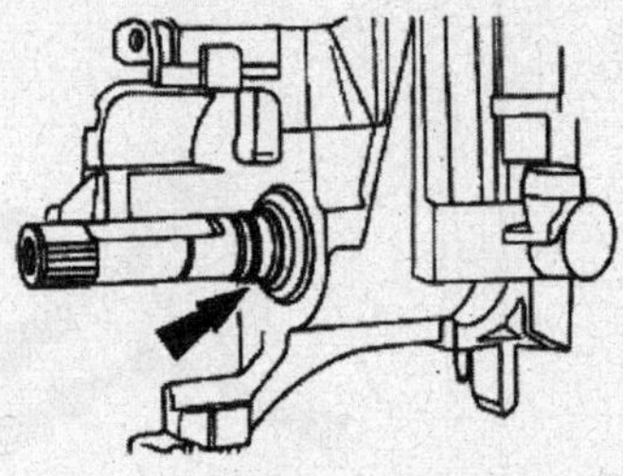

Fig. 13 Steering column bearing sleeve. E-Series, Excursion, F-Series, Motorhome & Ranger

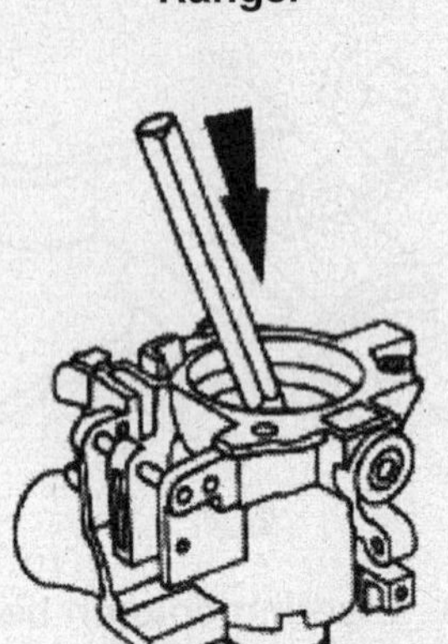

Fig. 14 Lock cylinder housing. E-Series, Excursion, F-Series, Motorhome & Ranger w/fixed steering column

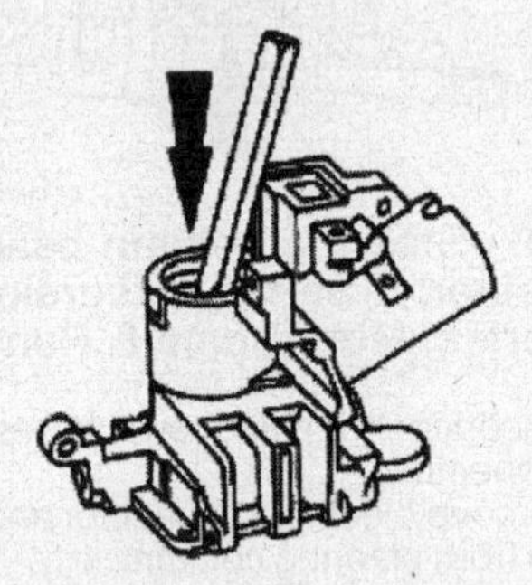

Fig. 15 Lock cylinder housing. E-Series, Excursion, F-Series, Motorhome & Ranger w/tilt steering column

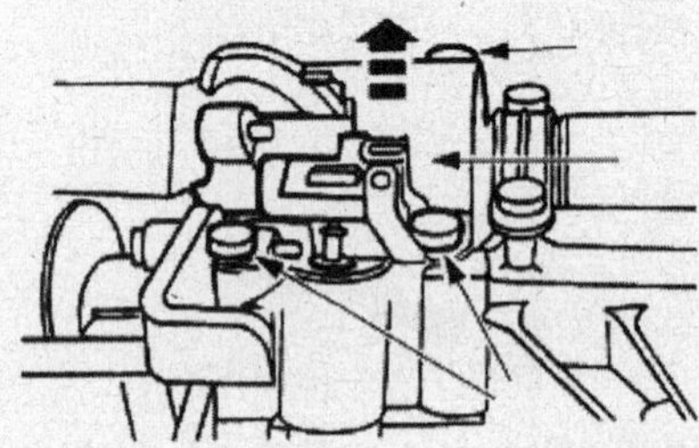

Fig. 16 Brake shift interlock solenoid. E-Series, Excursion, F-Series, Motorhome & Ranger w/automatic transmission

8. Remove steering column mounting nuts, then the steering column.
9. Reverse procedure to install, noting the following:
   a. **Torque** steering column cover reinforcement nuts to 11 ft. lbs.
   b. **Torque** ignition switch electrical connector to 108 inch lbs.
   c. **Torque** steering shaft pinch bolt to 35 ft. lbs.
   d. **Torque** steering column support nuts to 11 ft. lbs.

Freestar & Monterey

1. Position steering wheel in straight ahead position and ignition switch in Off position.
2. Deactivate supplemental restraint system as outlined in "Air Bag System" chapter.
3. Remove lower intermediate shaft to steering gear bolt.
4. Disconnect intermediate shaft from steering gear, then the transaxle shift cable.
5. Turn ignition key to RUN position, then using a suitable tool press ignition lock cylinder release button.
6. Remove ignition lock cylinder by pulling outward.
7. Remove lower and upper steering column shrouds.
8. Disconnect electrical connectors at base of steering column, then ignition switch electrical connector.
9. Remove transmission range indicator bolt and disconnect cable from steering column.
10. Remove lower steering column to instrument panel nuts and brace, then steering column to instrument panel nuts.
11. Remove column from vehicle.
12. Reverse procedure to install, noting the following:
    a. **Torque** intermediate shaft to steering gear bolt to 22 ft. lbs.
    b. **Torque** steering column to instrument panel nuts and brace to 11 ft. lbs.

Freestyle

1. Position steering wheel in straight ahead position and ignition switch in Off position.
2. Deactivate supplemental restraint system as outlined in "Air Bag System" chapter.
3. Remove steering column cover, then the instrument cluster finish panel and steering column upper shroud as an assembly.
4. Remove screws and lower steering column shroud, then the intermediate shaft to steering column bolt.
5. Disconnect intermediate shaft from steering column, then the multi-function switch electrical connectors.
6. Disconnect PATS transceiver electrical connector, then the wiring harness from steering column.
7. Remove steering column nuts, then the steering column.
8. Reverse procedure to install, noting the following:
   a. **Torque** intermediate shaft to steering column bolt to 18 ft. lbs.
   b. **Torque** steering column nuts to 13 ft. lbs.

LT

1. Park vehicle with wheels in straight ahead position.
2. Remove steering wheel as outlined in "Steering Wheel, Replace" in appropriate chassis chapter.
3. Remove instrument panel steering column opening cover.
4. Disconnect multi-function switch, ignition switch and clockspring electrical connectors.
5. Disconnect key in switch electrical connector then the PATS electrical connector. .
6. Detach wiring harness retainer and position wiring harness aside.
7. Squeeze connector at sides and disconnect steering column adaptive load

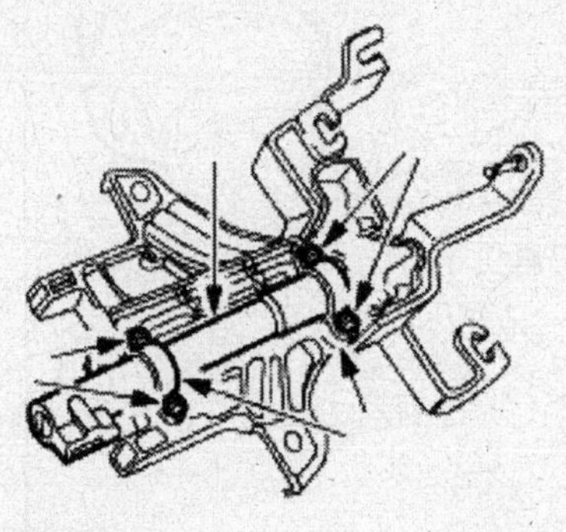

LTV1900000000703

Fig. 17 Shift tube replacement. E-Series, Excursion, F-Series, Motorhome & Ranger w/automatic transmission

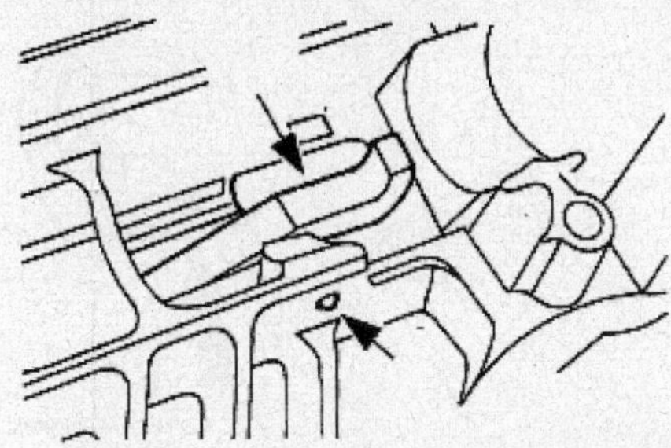

LTV1900000000706

Fig. 20 Steering column lock lever installation. E-Series, Excursion, F-Series, Motorhome & Ranger

safety device electrical connector. Detach wiring retainer.

8. Remove and discard upper steering column shaft to steering column bolt.
9. Remove and discard steering column support bracket nuts and steering column.
10. Remove steering column from vehicle.
11. Reverse procedure to install, noting the following:
    a. **Torque** intermediate shaft pinch bolt to 22 ft. lbs.
    b. **Torque** steering column support bracket to 11 ft. lbs.

Motorhome

Ensure front wheels are in the straight ahead position before performing the following procedure.

1. Unsnap steering wheel horn pad from steering wheel. Disconnect horn/speed control wire harness connector and remove steering wheel horn pad.
2. Remove steering wheel as outlined in "Steering Wheel, Replace" in the "Electrical" section of appropriate chassis chapter.
3. Remove four nylon push pins, then the steering column position control lever.
4. Remove steering column position control cover bracket.
5. Remove steering column release lever by

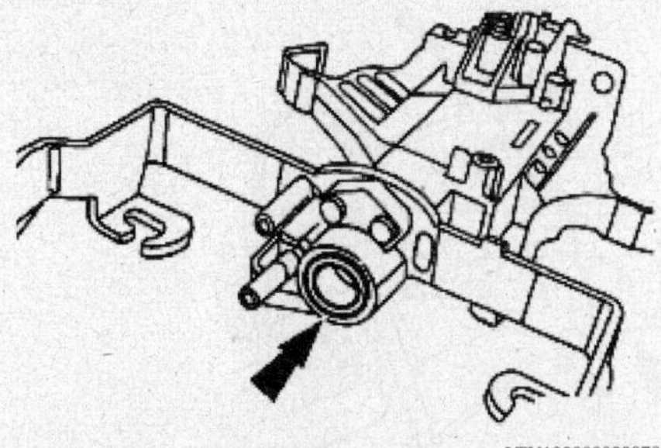

LTV1900000000704

Fig. 18 Lower steering column bearing and sleeve. E-Series, Excursion, F-Series, Motorhome & Ranger w/automatic transmission

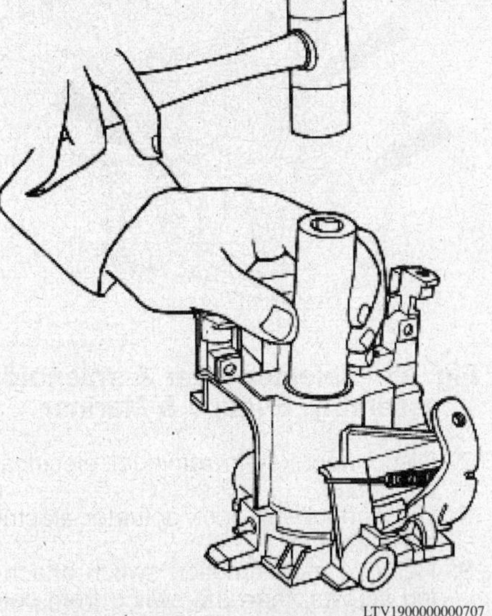

LTV1900000000707

Fig. 21 Upper steering column bearing installation. E-Series, Excursion, F-Series, Motorhome & Ranger w/automatic transmission & fixed steering

6. Remove steering column release lever by unscrewing it from steering column.
7. Insert ignition key, then turn to Run position.
8. Press ignition switch lock cylinder release pin through access hole using 1/8 inch drift, while pulling out ignition switch lock cylinder.
9. Remove three upper and lower steering column shroud retaining screws, then the upper and lower shroud.
10. Disconnect brake shift interlock and overdrive electrical connectors.
11. Remove multi-function switch screws, disconnect electrical connector, then the switch.
12. Remove ignition switch bolt, then disconnect ignition switch electrical connector.
13. **On models equipped with automatic transmission,** remove transmission range indicator bolt from the steering column, then disconnect cable and position cable aside.
14. **On all models,** remove intermediate shaft pinch bolt.

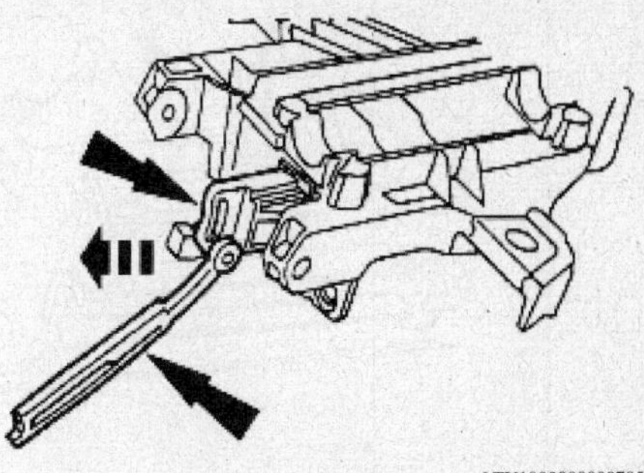

LTV1900000000705

Fig. 19 Upper and lower steering column lock actuator. E-Series, Excursion, F-Series, Motorhome & Ranger w/automatic transmission

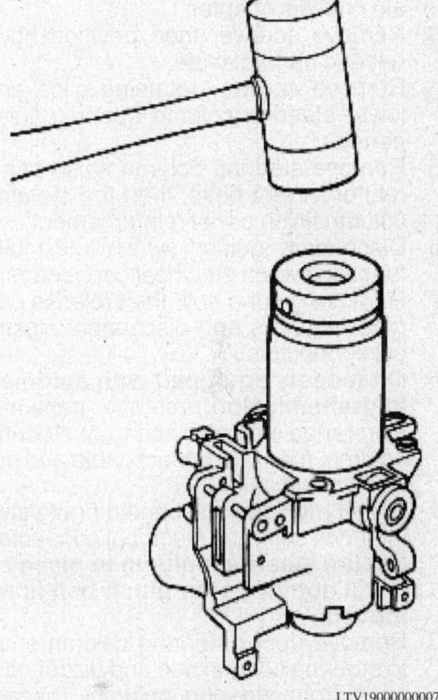

LTV1900000000708

Fig. 22 Upper steering column bearing installation. E-Series, Excursion, F-Series, Motorhome & Ranger w/automatic transmission & tilt steering

15. Remove four steering column retaining bolts, then the steering column.
16. Reverse procedure to install, noting the following:
    a. **Torque** steering column retaining bolts to 12 ft. lbs.
    b. **Torque** intermediate shaft pinch bolt to 36 ft. lbs.
    c. **Torque** ignition switch connector bolt 7–10 inch lbs.
    d. **Torque** multi-function switch to 18–26 inch lbs.
    e. **Torque** steering wheel bolt to 29 ft. lbs.

Ranger

1. Park vehicle with wheels in straight ahead position.
2. Remove steering wheel as outlined in

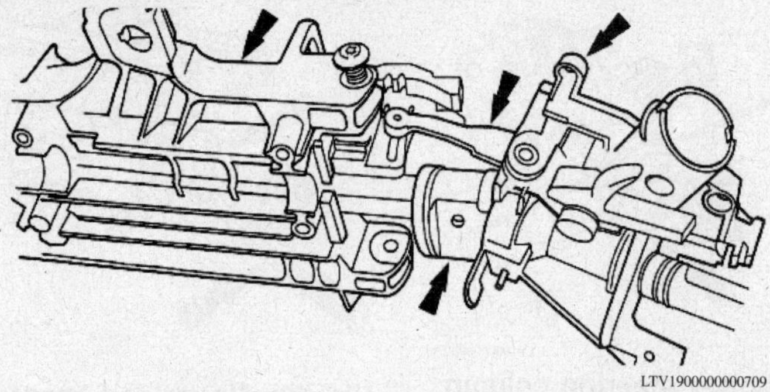

Fig. 23 Upper and lower steering column lock actuators. E-Series, Excursion, F-Series, Motorhome & Ranger w/automatic transmission

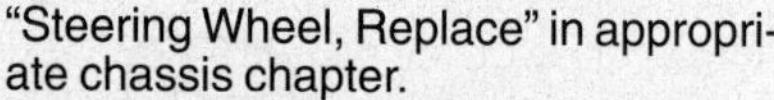

"Steering Wheel, Replace" in appropriate chassis chapter.

3. Remove screws, then position hood release handle aside.
4. Remove screws, retaining clips and lower steering column opening finish panel.
5. Remove steering column finish panel reinforcement bolts, then the steering column finish panel reinforcement.
6. Disconnect ignition switch and multi-function switch electrical connectors.
7. Remove ground bolt, then release pin-type retainers and disconnect electrical connectors.
8. **On models equipped with automatic transmission,** remove transmission range indicator bolt from steering column, then disconnect cable and position cable aside.
9. **On all models,** disconnect brake shift interlock solenoid electrical connector. **Secure steering column in place so it will not turn after pinch bolt is removed.**
10. Remove upper steering column shaft to steering column bolt and disconnect shaft from steering column. Discard bolt.
11. Remove steering column support bracket nuts and steering column.
12. Reverse procedure to install, noting the following:
    a. **Torque** intermediate shaft pinch bolt to 22 ft. lbs.
    b. **Torque** steering column support bracket to 11 ft. lbs.

Villager

1. Remove steering wheel as outlined in "Steering Wheel, Replace" in the "Electrical" section of appropriate chassis chapter.
2. Remove steering column shroud screws, then upper and lower steering column shrouds.
3. Remove instrument panel reinforcement bolts, then the instrument panel reinforcement.
4. Remove heater duct upper and lower screws, then the heater duct.
5. Loosen transmission range indicator cable retaining bolt, then position cable aside.
6. Disconnect driver air bag sliding contact connectors.

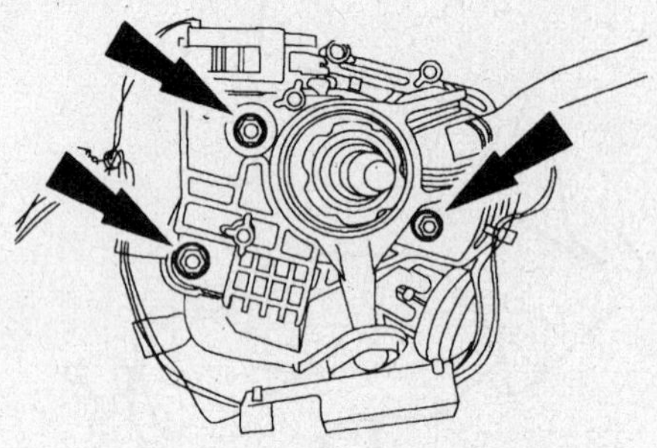

Fig. 25 Selector lever & solenoid assembly. Escape & Mariner

7. Disconnect key-in reminder electrical connector.
8. Disconnect shift lock actuator electrical connector.
9. Remove multi-function switch attaching screws, then the switch from column.
10. Remove overdrive cancel switch electrical connector.
11. Remove steering column clamp bolt, then the steering column mounting bracket nuts.
12. Remove transmission shift cable from ball socket, then slide cable housing from column.
13. Remove column from vehicle.
14. Reverse procedure to install, noting the following:
    a. **Torque** steering column clamp bolt to 20 ft. lbs.
    b. **Torque** steering column lower yoke clamp bolt to 32 ft. lbs.
    c. **Torque** steering column mounting bracket nuts to 12 ft. lbs.
    d. **Torque** steering column opening cover nuts to 20 ft. lbs.
    e. **Torque** steering wheel nut to 25 ft. lbs.

Windstar

1. Ensure front wheels are in straight ahead position.
2. Remove driver air bag module and clockspring assembly as outlined in "Air Bag System" chapter.
3. Remove multi-function switch.
4. Remove instrument panel steering column opening cover and reinforcement.
5. Remove ignition switch electrical connector.

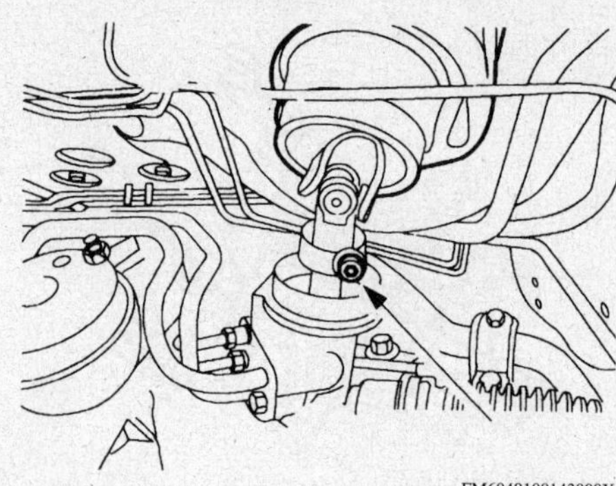

Fig. 24 Steering gear coupling. Escape & Mariner

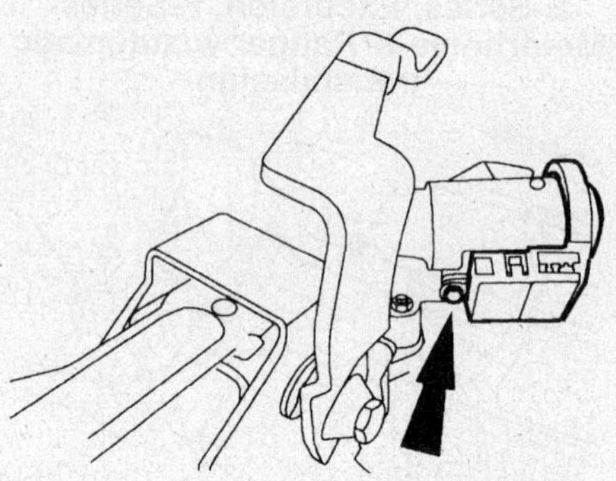

Fig. 26 Anti-theft system (PATS) transceiver module. Escape & Mariner

6. Remove transmission range indicator cable from steering column actuator housing.
7. Remove and discard steering column shaft pinch bolt, then disconnect coupler.
8. Disconnect transmission shift cable.
9. While supporting steering column, remove and discard four retaining nuts, then remove steering column.
10. Reverse procedure to install, noting the following:
    a. **Torque** steering column pinch bolt to 36 ft. lbs.
    b. **Torque** steering column mounting bolts to 12 ft. lbs.

STEERING COLUMN SERVICE

Aviator

The steering column tube is not serviceable and must be replaced as an assembly.

E-Series, Excursion, F-Series & Ranger

AUTOMATIC TRANSMISSION

DISASSEMBLE

1. Remove steering column as outlined in "Steering Column, Replace."
2. Note position of steering column lock

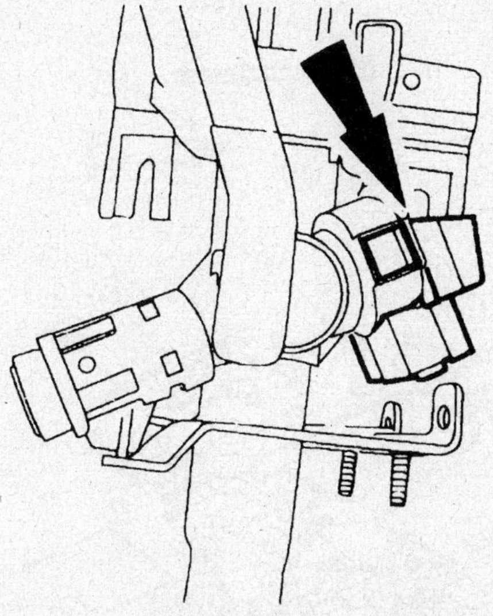

Fig. 27 Ignition switch. Escape & Mariner

gear, bearing and retainer for installation reference, then remove bearing retainer, **Fig. 9.**
3. Rotate clockwise 90° counterclockwise and remove steering column lock housing bearing.
4. Note position of keyhole and remove steering column lock gear.
5. **On models equipped with tilt column,** remove steering column lower bearing spring and sensor ring.
6. **On models equipped with fixed column,** remove snap ring from bottom of steering column shaft.
7. **On all models,** remove steering column bearing tolerance ring from steering column shaft, **Fig. 10.**
8. Remove two lock cylinder housing pivot screws.
9. Pry up on steering column locking levers using a fabricated tool, **Fig. 11.** On tilt steering columns, remove steering column position spring. Position spring is under tension and can release with great force.
10. Remove turn signal cancel cam, **Fig. 12.**
11. Remove steering column upper bearing snap ring and spring.
12. Remove steering column bearing sleeve, **Fig. 13.**
13. Slide steering column shaft in toward steering column lock cylinder housing. Slide steering column bearing tolerance ring off steering column shaft and remove shaft.
14. Remove steering column bearing from steering column lock cylinder housing, **Figs. 14 and 15.**
15. Remove brake shift interlock solenoid, **Fig. 16.**
16. Remove four mounting bolts and two shift tube clamps, then the shift tube, **Fig. 17.**
17. Remove transmission selector lever arm and support.
18. Remove spring from shift tube.
19. Drive out transmission shift selector lever pin from shift tube, then remove

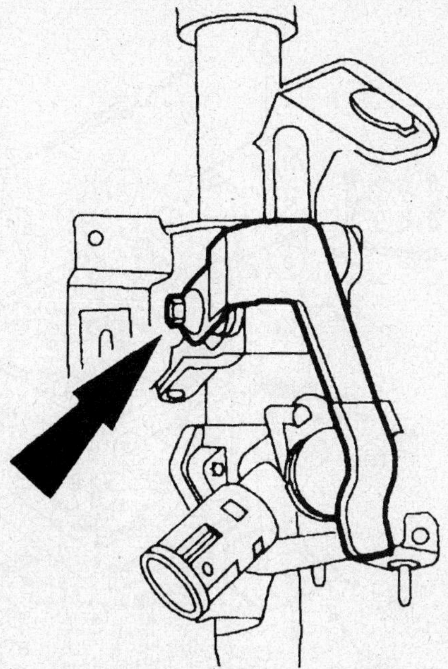

Fig. 28 Tilt column lever. Escape & Mariner

transmission shift selector lever.
20. Remove column shift selector lever plunger.
21. Remove two gearshift lever socket bushings and transmission control selector lever spring clip.
22. Drive out steering column lock lever pin, then remove steering column lock pawl.
23. Remove ignition switch.
24. Remove lower steering column bearing and sleeve, **Fig. 18.**
25. Remove steering column lower bearing retainer.
26. Remove upper & lower steering column lock actuator, **Fig. 19.**

ASSEMBLE

1. Use ignition lock grease to lubricate steering column lock actuators, then install actuators.
2. Coat steering lock pawl with ignition lock grease. Position lock pawl, then drive in steering column lever lock pin, **Fig. 20.**
3. Install steering column lower bearing retainer.
4. Install steering column bearing sleeve so inner race is visible when installed.
5. Install steering column bearing so "Up" marking is facing forward, toward engine.
6. Coat gearshift lever socket bushings with steering gear grease. Install transmission control selector lever spring clip and gearshift lever socket bushings on shift tube.
7. Coat column shift selector plunger with steering grease, then install.
8. Position transmission shift selector lever in shift tube.
9. Install gearshift lever pin in shift tube.
10. Coat end of gearshift selector tube spring with steering gear grease, then

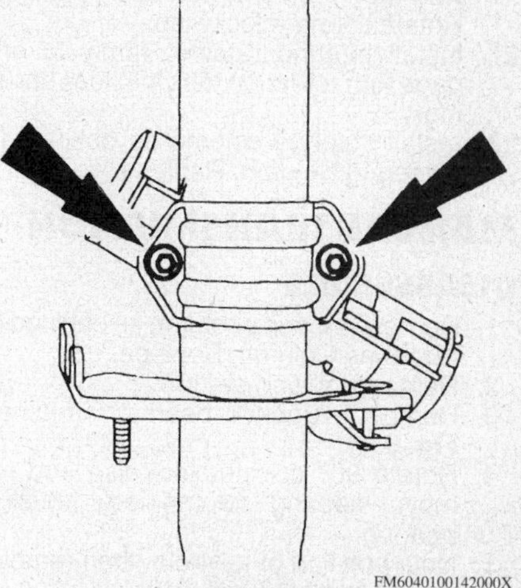

Fig. 29 Ignition lock cylinder housing. Escape & Mariner

install in shift tube.
11. Install transmission selector lever arm and support on shift tube. **Torque** bolts to 12 ft. lbs.
12. Install shift tube. **Torque** shift tube clamps to 80 inch lbs.
13. Position brake shift interlock solenoid and shift selector position insert. Install bolts and **torque** to 80 inch lbs.
14. Install upper steering column bearing on steering column lock cylinder housing using suitable bearing installer or socket, **Figs. 21 and 22.**
15. Position steering column shaft in steering column lock cylinder housing.
16. Install steering column bearing sleeve, bearing spring and snap ring.
17. Install turn signal cam with flat surface upwards. Push cam onto shaft until it makes contact with snap ring.
18. Install lock cylinder housing screws loosely and position steering actuator housing in vise.
19. Lubricate lock cylinder housing bushings with ignition lock grease. Position steering column lock cylinder housing and steering column shaft in steering actuator housing. Ensure upper and lower steering column lock actuators are aligned, **Fig. 23.**
20. Position steering column locking levers on steering actuator housing. Compress and install steering column position spring, if equipped.
21. Position lock cylinder housing and steering actuator housing, then **torque** lock cylinder housing screws to 17 ft. lbs.
22. Install steering column bearing tolerance ring.
23. **On models equipped with tilt column,** install sensor ring and lower bearing spring.
24. **On models equipped with fixed column,** install snap ring.
25. **On all models,** install ignition switch. Align ignition switch with slot and index mark on steering column. **Torque** bolts to 54 inch lbs.
26. Coat ignition lock gear with ignition lock grease then install with narrow section of keyhole in 1 o'clock position,

with tab inboard at 3 o'clock position. Rotate counterclockwise.

27. Install bearing retainer firmly to engage four retention tabs into lock housing.
28. Install steering column as outlined in "Steering Column, Replace."

MANUAL TRANSMISSION

DISASSEMBLE

1. Remove steering column as outlined in "Steering Column, Replace."
2. Remove ignition switch.
3. Remove upper bearing retainer, **Fig. 9.**
4. Rotate 90° counterclockwise and remove steering column lock housing bearing.
5. Note position of keyhole, then remove steering column lock gear.
6. **On models equipped with fixed steering column,** remove snap ring from bottom of steering shaft.
7. **On models equipped with tilt steering column,** remove steering column lower bearing support and the sensor ring.
8. **On all models,** remove steering column lower bearing tolerance ring from steering column shaft, **Fig. 10.**
9. **On models equipped with tilt steering column,** remove two lock cylinder housing pivot screws.
10. **On all models,** pry up on steering column lock lefthand levers using a shop fabricated tool, **Fig. 11.** If equipped with tilt column, remove steering gear position spring.
11. Remove turn signal cancel cam.
12. Remove snap ring, upper bearing spring and sleeve.
13. Slide steering shaft inward toward steering column lock cylinder, then slide steering column bearing tolerance ring off steering column shaft and remove shaft.
14. Remove steering column bearing with suitable punch, **Figs. 14 and 15.**
15. Remove steering column lower bearing and sleeve.
16. Remove steering column lower bearing retainer.
17. Remove upper steering column lock lever actuator and lower steering column lock lever actuator,

ASSEMBLE

1. Install steering column lock lever actuator, **Fig. 20.**
2. Install steering column lower bearing retainer.
3. Install steering column bearing and sleeve. "Up" marking on bearing must be facing upward.
4. Install steering column bearing in lock cylinder housing with suitable installer tool or socket, **Figs. 21 and 22.**
5. **On models equipped with tilt column,** install steering column bearing so inner race is visible when installed.
6. **On all models,** install steering column bearing tolerance ring on steering column shaft.
7. Install steering column bearing sleeve, spring and snap ring.

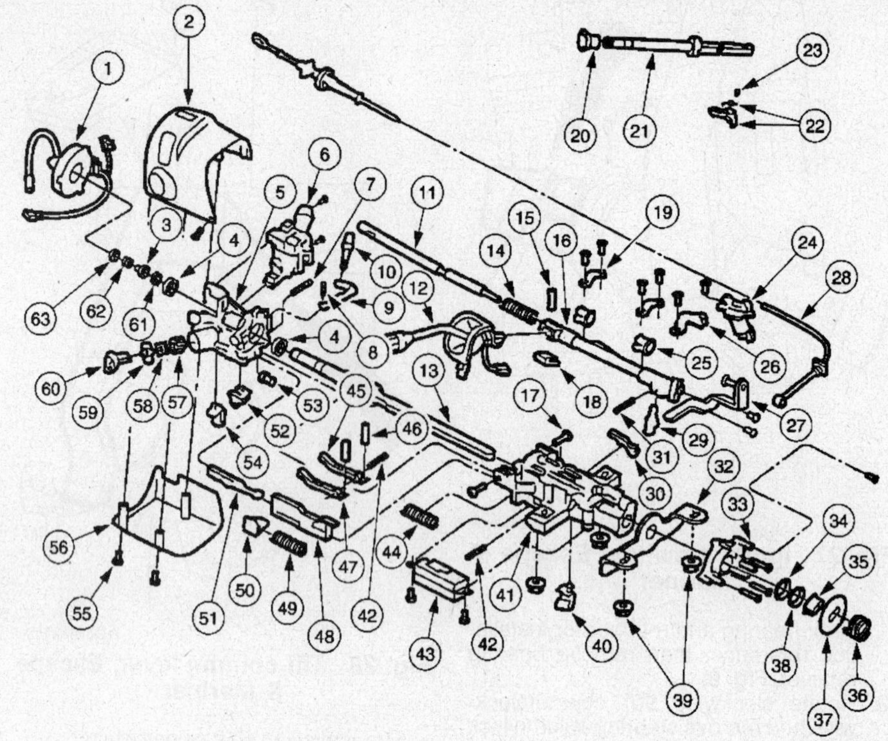

FM6040000127010X

Fig. 30 Exploded view of steering column (Part 1 of 2). Expedition & Navigator

1. Air Bag Sliding Contact
2. Upper Steering Column Shroud
3. Steering Column Bearing Sleeve
4. Steering Column Bearing
5. Steering Column Lock Cylinder Housing
6. Multi-Function Switch
7. Pin
8. Steering Column Release Lever Pin
9. Steering Column Release Lever
10. Tilt Wheel Handle & Shank
11. Column Shift Selector Lever Plunger
12. Gearshift Lever
13. Steering Column Shaft
14. Transmission Control Selector Spring
15. Gearshift Lever Pin
16. Shift Tube
17. Tilt Column Pivot Screw
18. Transmission Control Selector Lever Spring Clip
19. Gearshift Tube Bushing Clamp
20. Spacer (Fixed Column)
21. Steering Shaft (Fixed Column)
22. Lever Assembly (Manual Transmission)
23. Pin (Manual Transmission)
24. Brake Shift Interlock Solenoid
25. Gearshift Lever Socket Bushing
26. Transmission Shift Selector Position Insert
27. Transmission Selector Lever Arm & Support
28. Shift Cable & Bracket
29. Gearshft Lever
30. Steering Column Lock Pawl
31. Gearshift Lever Pin
32. Steering Column Instrument Panel Bracket
33. Steering Column Lower Bearing Retainer
34. Steering Column Bearing Sleeve
35. Steering Column Bearing Tolerance Ring
36. Steering Column Lower Bearing Spring
37. Sensor Ring
38. Steering Column Bearing Sleeve
39. Steering Column Retaining Nuts
40. Wiring Harness Retainer
41. Steering Actuator Housing
42. Steering Column Lock Lever Pin
43. Ignition Switch
44. Steering Column Position Spring
45. Steering Column Lock Lever
46. Steering Column Position Lock Spring
47. Steering Column Locking Lever
48. Lower Steering Column Lock Actuator
49. Steering Column Lock Spring
50. Steering Column lock Pawl
51. Upper Steering Column Lock Lever Actuator
52. Steering Column Lock Cam
53. Steering Column Tilt Flange Bumper
54. Wiring Harness Retainer
55. Shroud Screws
56. Lower Steering Column Shroud
57. Steering Column Lock Gear
58. Steering Column Lock Housing Bearing
59. Bearing Retainer
60. Ignition Switch Lock Cylinder
61. Steering Column Tolerance Ring
62. Steering Column Upper Bearing Spring
63. Snap Ring

FM6040000127020X

Fig. 30 Exploded view of steering column (Part 2 of 2). Expedition & Navigator

8. Install turn signal cam with flat surface facing upward.
9. Install lock cylinder screws loosely and position steering gear actuator housing in vise.
10. Lubricate lock cylinder housing screws and bushings with ignition lock grease.
11. Position steering column lock cylinder housing and steering column shaft on steering actuator housing. Ensure upper and lower steering column lock actuators are aligned, **Fig. 23.**
12. Position steering column locking levers on steering actuator housing.
13. **On models equipped with tilt column,** position lock cylinder housing and steering actuator housing, then tighten lock cylinder housing screws.
14. **On all models,** install steering column bearing tolerance ring.

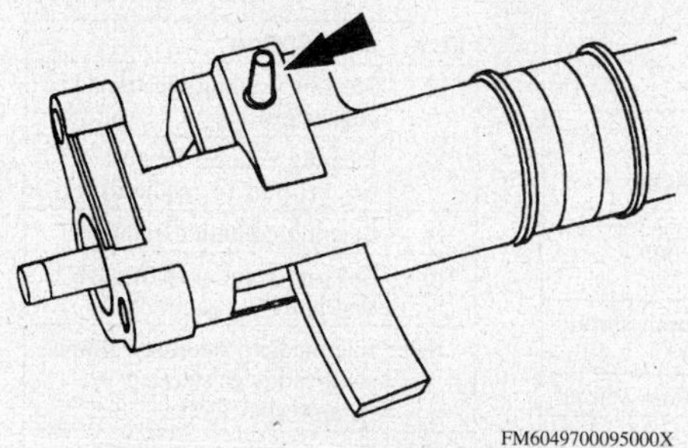

Fig. 31 Gearshift lever pin removal. Expedition & Navigator

15. **On models equipped with tilt column,** install sensor ring and lower bearing spring.
16. **On models equipped with fixed column,** install snap ring.
17. **On all models,** install ignition switch with slot and index mark on steering column aligned.
18. Coat steering column lock gear with ignition lock grease.
19. Install steering column lock gear with narrow section of keyhole in 1 o'clock position.
20. Install steering column lock housing bearing. Narrow section of keyhole should be in 1 o'clock position, with tab inboard at 3 o'clock position, then rotate counterclockwise.
21. Install steering column upper bearing retainer firmly to engage four retention tabs into lock cylinder.
22. Install steering column as outlined in "Steering Column, Replace."

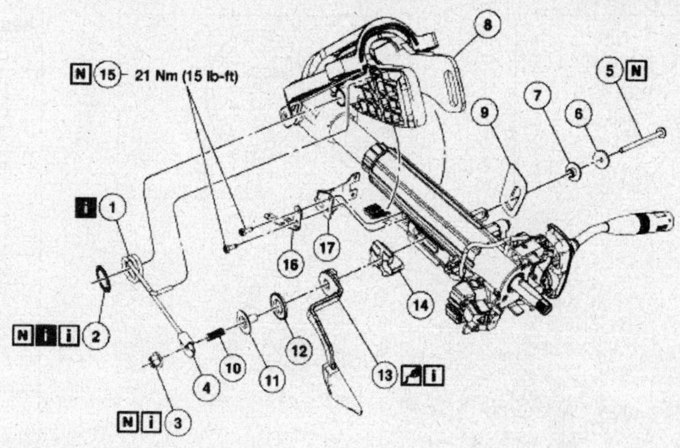

Item	Description
1	Tilt tension spring (release from hanger) Disassembly Note
2	Retainer clip Disassembly Note
2	Retainer clip Assembly Note
3	Nut Assembly Note
4	Spring hanger
5	Pin
6	Washer
7	Sleeve washer
8	Support/tilt bracket (pivot upward)
9	Bushing
10	Release lever spring
11	Sleeve washer
12	Bearing
13	Tilt lever Assembly Note
14	Clamp plate
15	Bolts
16	Harness retainer bracket
17	Shift cable bracket

LTV1900000000710

Fig. 32 Steering column components. Explorer & Mountaineer

Escape & Mariner

1. Position steering column shaft boot aside to gain access to flexible coupling.
2. Remove and discard pinch bolt and nut, then separate steering column shaft from flexible coupling.
3. Remove steering column shaft pin using a suitable punch, then the steering column shaft.
4. Remove steering gear coupling from flexible coupling and the pinch bolt from steering gear coupling, **Fig. 24.**
5. Remove screws and multi-function switch assembly.
6. Position multi-function switch and bracket aside.
7. Remove selector lever and solenoid assembly, **Fig. 25.**
8. Remove anti-theft system (PATS) transceiver module, **Fig. 26.**
9. Depress two tabs on ignition switch and remove switch, **Fig. 27.**
10. Turn ignition key to the ON position.
11. Depress ignition lock cylinder release button and pull out ignition lock cylinder.
12. Remove tilt column lever, **Fig. 28.**
13. Remove steering column mounting bracket.
14. Cut slots into heads of shear off bolts and remove shear off bolts and ignition lock cylinder, **Fig. 29.** Discard shear off bolts.
15. Reverse procedure to assemble, noting the following:
    a. **Torque** selector lever solenoid assembly bolts to 80 inch lbs.
    b. **Torque** tilt lever bolt to 108 inch lbs.
    c. **Torque** steering gear coupling pinch bolt to 30 ft. lbs.
    d. **Torque** steering column shaft coupling pinch bolt to 17 ft. lbs.
    e. **Torque** steering column support bracket nuts to 14 ft. lbs.
    f. **Torque** steering column mounting bracket bolts to 13 ft. lbs.
    g. **Torque** forward steering column support bolt to 12 ft. lbs.
    h. **Torque** steering wheel pinion shaft to 11 ft. lbs.
    i. **Torque** steering gear coupling bolt to 30 ft. lbs.

Expedition & Navigator

DISASSEMBLE

1. Remove steering column as outlined in "Steering Column, Replace" in this section.
2. Remove bearing retainer, steering column lock housing bearing and steering column lock gear as outlined in **Fig. 30.**
3. Remove shock absorber electronic steering sensor.
4. Remove upper bearing spring, then the sensor ring.
5. Remove bearing tolerance ring from steering column shaft, then the lock cylinder housing screws.
6. Pry up on locking levers and remove position spring. **The steering column position spring is under tension and may come out with great force.**
7. Remove bearing retainer, then the bearing spring and sleeve.
8. Slide steering column shaft in toward steering column lock cylinder housing and out, then slide bearing tolerance ring off the column shaft.
9. Remove steering column bearing from steering column lock cylinder housing.
10. Remove shift interlock solenoid, then the shift tube clamps and tube.

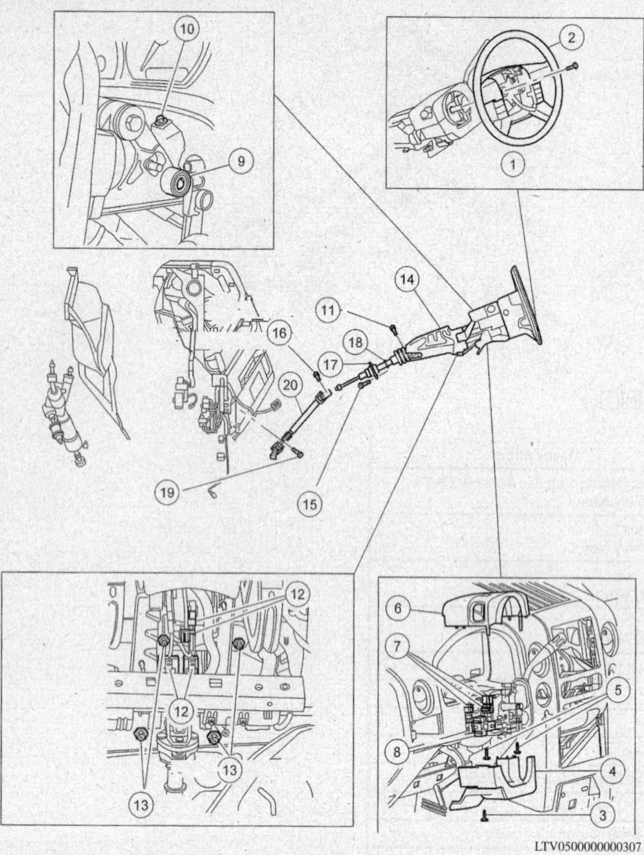

LTV0500000000307

Fig. 33 Steering column components (Part 1 of 2). LT

Item	Description
1	Steering wheel bolt
2	Steering wheel
3	Lower steering column shroud screw
4	Lower steering column shroud
5	Upper steering column shroud screws (2 required)
6	Upper steering column shroud
7	Multi-function switch electrical connectors
8	Ignition switch electrical connector
9	Shift cable (column shift only)
10	Shift cable screw (column shift only)
11	Intermediate steering column shaft-to-steering column shaft bolt

Item	Description
12	Steering column electrical connectors
13	Steering column support bracket nuts (4 required)
14	Steering column assembly
15	Steering column shaft dash seal bolts (2 required)
16	Intermediate steering column shaft-to-lower steering column shaft bolt
17	Dash boot bearing
18	Intermediate steering column shaft
19	Lower steering column shaft-to-steering gear bolt
20	Lower steering column shaft

LTV0500000000308

Fig. 33 Steering column components (Part 2 of 2). LT

11. Remove transmission selector lever arm, support, and plunger spring.
12. Drive out gearshift lever pin from shift tube, then remove gearshift lever as outlined in **Fig. 31.**
13. Remove column shift selector lever plunger, if bent, replace plunger.
14. Remove gearshift lever socket bushing and transmission control selector lever spring clip.
15. Remove ignition switch, then the lower column bearing.
16. Remove column lower bearing retainer.
17. Drive out steering column lock lever pin and remove lock pawl.
18. Remove upper and lower steering column lock actuators.

ASSEMBLE

1. Lubricate steering column lock actuators using steering gear grease XG-1-G or equivalent, then install lock actuators.
2. Position steering column lock pawl and drive lock pin into place.
3. Install lower bearing retainer and **torque** lower bearing retainer bolts to 84 inch lbs.
4. Install lower bearing, ensure inner race is visible.
5. Align ignition switch with slot and index mark on steering column and **torque** bolts to 55 inch lbs.
6. Install transmission control selector lever spring clip and gearshift lever socket bushings on shift tube, coat bushings with steering gear grease XG-1-G or equivalent.
7. Install column shift selector lever plunger and coat with steering gear grease XG-1-G or equivalent.
8. Position gearshift lever in shift tube and install lever pin.
9. Install gearshift selector tube spring in shift tube and coat with steering gear grease XG-1-G or equivalent.
10. Install transmission selector lever arm and support on shift tube, **torque** bolts to 10–12 ft. lbs.
11. Install shift tube and clamps and **torque** bolts to 84 inch lbs.
12. Install brake shift interlock solenoid and **torque** bolts to 84 inch lbs.
13. Install upper steering column bearing on steering column lock cylinder housing, then the large bearing into lock cylinder housing.
14. Install steering column bearing tolerance ring on shaft and position shaft in steering column lock cylinder housing.
15. Install steering column bearing sleeve, then the bearing spring and retainer.
16. Install lock cylinder housing screws loosely and position steering actuator housing in a vise.
17. Position steering column lock cylinder housing and steering column shaft on steering actuator housing, ensure upper and lower steering column lock actuators are aligned.
18. Install and compress position spring, then position steering column locking levers on actuator housing.
19. **Torque** lock cylinder housing screws to 14–19 ft. lbs.
20. Install bearing tolerance ring, then the sensor ring and bearing spring.
21. Install shock absorber electronic steering sensor and **torque** screws to 10–13 inch lbs.
22. Install lock gear, then the lock housing bearing and rotate clockwise.
23. Install upper bearing retainer.
24. Install steering column, then the steering wheel as outlined in "Steering Column, Replace."

Explorer & Mountaineer

The steering column tube is not serviceable and must be replaced as an assembly. For steering column component replacement, refer to **Fig. 32.**

LT

The steering column tube is not serviceable and must be replaced as an assembly. For steering column component replacement, refer to **Fig. 33.**

Freetar & Monterey

DISASSEMBLE

1. Remove steering column as outlined in "Steering Column, Replace" in this section.
2. Remove shift selector pin, then the shift selector lever assembly **Fig. 34.**
3. Remove steering column lock housing bearing snap ring and column housing bearing. **Carefully note position of steering column lock gear, bearing, and retainer prior to removal.**
4. Remove steering column lock gear, then the steering column lower bearing spring.
5. Remove bolts, rotation sensor and bracket.

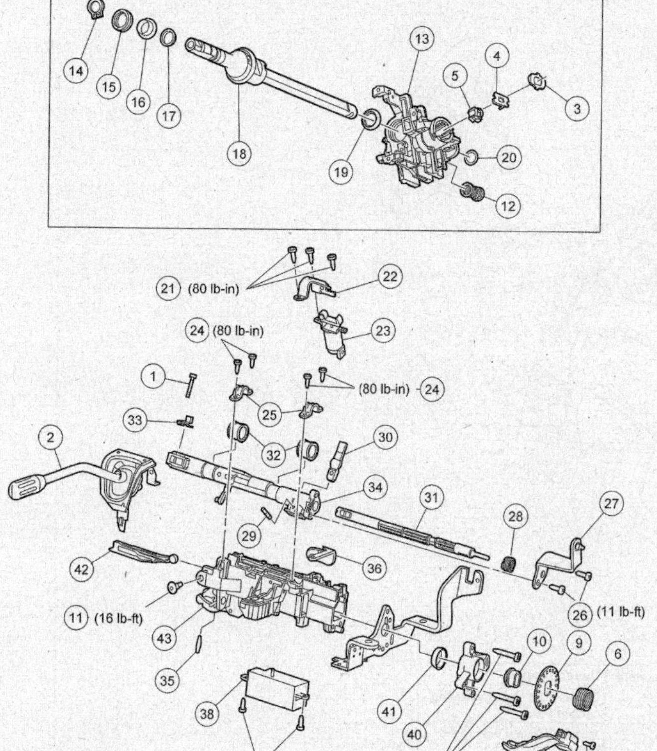

Fig. 34 Steering column components (Part 1 of 2). Freetar & Monterey

Item	Description
1	Shift selector pin
2	Shift selector lever assembly
3	Steering column lock housing bearing snap ring
4	Steering column lock housing bearing
5	Steering column lock gear
6	Steering column lower bearing spring
7	Rotation sensor bracket bolts (2 required)
8	Rotation sensor and bracket
9	Rotation sensor ring
10	Steering column bearing tolerance ring
11	Lock cylinder housing pivot screws (2 required)
12	Steering column position spring
13	Lock cylinder housing
14	Steering column upper bearing spring snap ring
15	Steering column upper bearing spring
16	Steering column bearing sleeve
17	Steering column bearing tolerance ring
18	Steering column shaft
19	Steering column bearing
20	Steering column bearing
21	Transmission shift position insert bolts (3 required)
22	Transmission shift position insert

Item	Description
23	Brake shift interlock solenoid
24	Shift tube clamp bolts (4 required)
25	Shift tube clamps (2 required)
26	Transmission shift arm bolts (2 required)
27	Transmission shift arm
28	Gearshift lever spring
29	Gearshift lever pin
30	Gearshift lever
31	Column shift selector lever plunger
32	Gearshift lever socket bushings (2 required)
33	Transmission control selector lever spring clip
34	Shift tube
35	Steering column lock lever pin
36	Steering column lock pawl
37	Ignition switch bolts (2 required)
38	Ignition switch
39	Steering column lower bearing retainer bolts (3 required)
40	Steering column lower bearing retainer
41	Steering column lower bearing
42	Steering column lock actuator
43	Steering column

LTV0500000000310

Fig. 34 Steering column components (Part 2 of 2). Freetar & Monterey

6. Remove rotation sensor ring, then the steering column bearing tolerance ring.
7. Remove lock cylinder housing pivot screws.
8. Release steering column locking levers and remove steering column position spring from steering column.
9. Remove lock cylinder housing, then the steering column upper bearing spring snap ring and ring.
10. Remove steering column bearing sleeve, then the steering column bearing tolerance ring.
11. Remove steering column shaft.
12. Remove upper and lower steering column bearings from lock cylinder housing.
13. Remove transmission shift position insert bolts, then the transmission shift position insert.
14. Remove brake shift interlock solenoid, then the shift tube clamp bolts.
15. Remove shift tube clamps, then the transmission shift arm bolts.
16. Remove transmission shift arm, then the gearshift lever spring.
17. Remove gearshift lever pin, then the gearshift lever.
18. Remove column shift selector lever plunger, then two gearshift lever socket bushings.
19. Remove transmission control selector lever spring clip, then shift tube.
20. Remove steering column lock lever pin, then the steering column lock pawl.
21. Remove ignition switch bolts, then the ignition switch.
22. Remove steering column lower bearing retainer bolts, then the steering column lower bearing retainer.
23. Remove steering column lower bearing, then the steering column lock actuator.

ASSEMBLE

1. Apply multi-purpose grease to contact surfaces of steering column lock actuator, then install steering column lock actuator.
2. Install steering column lower bearing. **UP position of bearing must be facing forward, toward engine. The numbering and description of components are for correct bearing orientation and not for an assembly order.**
3. Install steering column lower bearing and sleeve so that inner race is visible when installed.
4. Install steering column lower bearing retainer and bolts.
5. Align ignition switch with slot and index mark on steering column and install with bolts.
6. Apply multi-purpose grease to friction surfaces of steering column lock pawl, then install steering column lock pawl.
7. Install steering column lock lever pin, then the shift tube and transmission control selector lever spring clip.
8. Apply multi-purpose grease to friction surfaces of gearshift lever socket bushings, then install two gearshift lever socket bushings.
9. Apply multi-purpose grease to friction surfaces of column shift selector lever plunger, then install column shift selector lever plunger.
10. Install gearshift lever, **gearshift lever pin must be installed with tapered end up or first gear position may be blocked.**
11. Install gearshift lever pin and spring.
12. Install transmission shift arm bolts.
13. Install shift tube clamps with retaining bolts.
14. Install brake shift interlock solenoid, then the transmission shift position insert with bolts.
15. Install steering column upper bearing on steering column lock cylinder housing.
16. Install steering column lower bearing into steering column lock cylinder housing.
17. Install steering column shaft, then the steering column bearing tolerance ring.
18. Install steering column bearing sleeve,

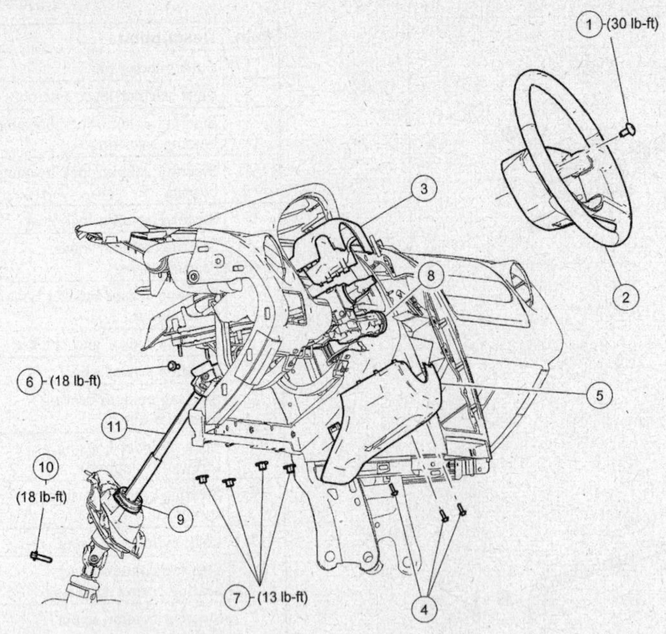

Item	Description
1	Steering wheel bolt
2	Steering wheel
3	Upper steering column shroud
4	Lower steering column shroud screw (3 required)
5	Lower steering column shroud

Item	Description
6	Intermediate shaft-to-steering column bolt
7	Steering column nuts (4 required)
8	Steering column
9	Intermediate shaft boot bearing clamp

LTV0500000000311

Fig. 35 Steering column components (Part 1 of 2). Freestyle

then the steering column upper bearing spring snap ring.

19. Release steering column locking levers, then install steering column position spring to steering column.
20. Install lock cylinder housing pivot screws, then the steering column bearing tolerance ring.
21. Install rotation sensor ring, then position rotation sensor bracket.
22. Install steering column lower bearing spring, then the steering column lock gear.
23. Install bearing retainer firmly to engage four retention tabs into lock housing using previously made index marks.
24. Install steering column lock housing bearing snap ring, then the shift selector lever assembly.
25. Install shift selector pin, then the steering column as outlined in "Steering Column, Replace" in this section.

Freestyle

The steering column tube is not serviceable and must be replaced as an assembly. For steering column component replacement, refer to **Fig. 35.**

Motorhome

Refer to **MOTOR's "Domestic Transmission, In-Vehicle Service" or "Transmission Service DVD"** for repair procedure.

Villager

The steering column tube is not serviceable and must be replaced as an assembly. For steering column component replacement, refer to **Fig. 36.**

Windstar

DISASSEMBLE

1. Remove overdrive on/off wiring harness from plastic harness retainer.
2. Unclip steering column opening gearshift lever seal from steering column.
3. Remove gearshift lever retaining pin, then the gearshift lever assembly.
4. **Note position of steering column lock gear, bearing and retainer for installation reference,** then remove snap ring.
5. Remove steering column lock housing bearing.
6. Remove steering column lock gear.
7. **On models equipped with fixed column,** proceed as follows:
   a. Remove steering column lower bearing ring, then the sensor ring.
   b. Remove steering column bearing tolerance ring from steering column shaft.
   c. Remove two lock cylinder housing pivot screws.
   d. Pry up on steering column locking levers. **Steering column position spring is under tension and can come free with great force.**
8. **On models equipped with tilt steering columns,** remove steering column position ring.
9. **On all models,** using a suitable flat blade screwdriver to pry up on flush surface of turn indicator cancel cam and remove.
10. Remove lock gear snap ring, then the steering column upper bearing spring.

11. Remove steering column bearing sleeve.
12. Move steering column shaft in toward steering column lock cylinder housing.
13. Move steering column bearing tolerance ring off shaft, then remove the shaft.
14. Remove steering column upper bearing from steering column lock cylinder housing.
15. **On models equipped with tilt steering columns,** use a suitable punch to remove steering column lower bearing from steering column lock cylinder housing.
16. **On all models,** remove two screws, then the plastic harness retainer.
17. Remove brake shift interlock solenoid, then the transmission shift position insert.
18. Remove four shift tube attaching bolts, two shift tube clamps, then the shift tube.
19. Remove two bolts, then the transmission shift arm assembly.
20. Remove spring, then drive out gearshift lever pin from shift tube.
21. Remove gearshift lever.
22. Remove and inspect column shift selector lever plunger.
23. Remove two gearshift lever socket bushings, then the transmission control selector lever spring clip.
24. Remove steering column lock lever pin, then the steering column lock pawl.
25. Remove ignition switch screws, then the ignition switch.
26. Remove steering column lower bearing and sleeve.
27. Remove lower bearing retainer bolts, then the steering column lower bearing retainer.
28. Remove steering column upper and lower lock actuator.

ASSEMBLE

1. Use ignition lock grease part No. FOAZ-19584-A, or equivalent, to lubricate steering column upper and lower lock actuator and lock pawl.
2. Install steering column upper and lower lock actuators.
3. Position steering column lock pawl, then drive in steering column lock lever pin.
4. Position steering column lower bearing retainer, then install bolts and **torque** to 80 inch lbs.
5. With "UP" position of bearing facing forward, install steering column lower bearing and sleeve so that inner race is visible when installed.
6. Align ignition switch with slot and index mark on steering column, **torque** screws to 54 inch lbs.
7. Lubricate gearshift lever socket bushings and column shift selector plunger using steering gear grease No. C3AZ-19578-A, or equivalent, then install transmission control selector lever.
8. Lubricate and install column shift selector lever plunger.
9. Position gearshift lever in shift tube, then install gearshift lever pin.
10. Lubricate and install gearshift selector tube in shift tube.
11. Position transmission selector lever arm and support, then install and **torque** bolts to 12 ft. lbs.
12. Position shift tube and shift tube clamps, install and **torque** bolts to 80 inch lbs.
13. Position brake shift interlock solenoid, install and **torque** bolts to 80 inch lbs.
14. Install upper bearing on steering column lock cylinder housing, in a manner that leaves inner race visible when installed.
15. Install lower bearing into steering column lock cylinder housing so that inner race is visible when installed.
16. Install steering column bearing tolerance ring on steering column shaft.
17. Install steering column bearing sleeve.
18. Install steering column upper bearing spring, then the snap ring.
19. Install turn indicator cancel cam.
20. Install lock cylinder housing screws loosely, then lubricate screws with Rust Penetrant and Inhibitor F-2AZ-19A501-A or equivalent.
21. Ensure upper and lower steering column lock actuators are aligned.
22. **On models equipped with tilt steering,** position steering column locking levers on steering actuator housing.
23. **On all models,** use shop fabricated tool to install and compress steering column position spring.
24. Position lock cylinder housing and steering actuator housing, then install and **torque** screws to 17 ft. lbs.
25. Install steering column bearing tolerance ring.
26. Install sensor ring, then the steering column lower bearing spring.
27. Install steering column lock housing bearing with narrow section of keyhole in 1 O'clock position and with tab in board at 3 O'clock position, then rotate counterclockwise.
28. Install bearing retainer, then install four retention tabs into lock housing.
29. Install gearshift lever assembly and install retaining pin.
30. Install steering column gearshift lever seal onto steering column.
31. Install overdrive on/off switch wiring harness to plastic harness retainer.

Item	Description
10	Intermediate shaft-to-steering gear bolt
11	Intermediate shaft

LTV0500000000312

Fig. 35 Steering column components (Part 2 of 2). Freestyle

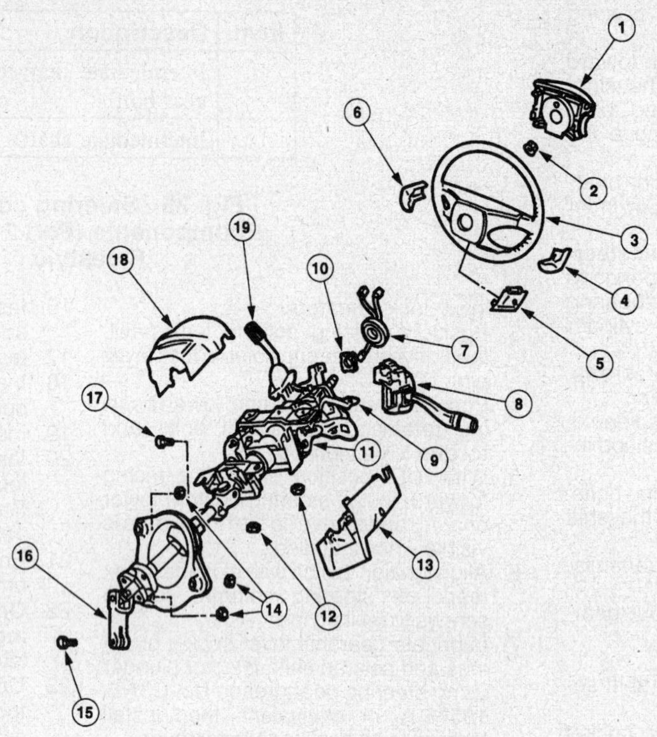

Item	Description
1	Driver side air bag module
2	Steering wheel nut
3	Steering wheel
4	Radio volume control cover
5	Air bag sliding contact electrical connector access panel
6	Cruise control cover
7	Air bag sliding contact
8	Multifunction switch
9	Tilt wheel lever
10	Turn indicator cancel cam
11	Steering column assembly

Item	Description
12	Steering column mounting bracket nuts (4 Req'd)
13	Lower column shroud
14	Steering column opening cover nuts (3 Req'd)
15	Steering column lower yoke bolt
16	Steering column lower yoke
17	Steering column clamp bolt
18	Upper column shroud
19	Gearshift lever

FM6049900107000X

Fig. 36 Exploded view of steering column. Villager

POWER STEERING

TABLE OF CONTENTS

Power Steering Pressure Specifications

Model	Minimum Relief Pressure, psi	Maximum Relief Pressure, psi	Minimum Flow, Gallons/Minute @ 750 psi ①	Maximum Free Flow @ 1500 RPM
Aviator	—	1740	⑤	—
Escape	1300	1480	1.16	—
E-Series	③	④	1.40	2.80–3.20
Excursion	1400	1530	1.40	2.80–3.20
Expedition	1300	1480	1.60	—
Explorer	1400	1530	1.15	2.50–2.90
Freestar	1450	1580	1.40	—
Freestyle	1450	1580	1.14	2.48
F-Super Duty	1750	1850	1.40	2.80–3.20
F-150	1300	1400	1.60	2.80–3.20
Mariner	1300	1480	1.16	—
Mark LT	1300	1400	1.60	2.80–3.20
Monterey	1450	1580	1.40	—
Motorhome (F-Super Duty)	②	②	1.60	—
Mountaineer	1400	1530	1.15	2.50–2.90
Navigator	1300	1480	1.60	—
Ranger	1300	1480	1.14	2.20–2.60
Ranger w/CII	1300	1480	.95	2.10–2.50
Villager	1067	1209	—	—
Windstar w/3.0L Engine	1300	1480	.95	—
Windstar w/3.8L Engine	1400	1530	1.40	—

① — Flow depends on pump model, engine RPM & pulley drive ratio. Engine RPM must be set to specification when inspecting pump minimum flow capacity.

② — 15,200 & 18,000 GVW relief pressure is 1799 psi; 20,500 GVW relief pressure is 2467 psi.

③ — 15,200 & 18,000 GVW minimum relief pressure is 1300 psi. 20,500 GVW relief pressure is 2465 psi.

④ — 15,200 & 18,000 GVW maximum relief pressure is 1430 psi. 20,500 GVW relief pressure is 2465 psi.

⑤ — Engine speed set at 2,100 RPM and power steering analyzer set at 50 psi.

Troubleshooting

INDEX

Condition	Possible Source
• Hard Steering or Lack of Assist	• Seized lower steering column shaft U-joints. • Damaged, fractured steering column bearing(s). • Power steering pump. • Suspension components. • Steering gear internal leakage.
• Excessive Steering Pump Noise	• Power steering pump.
• Excessive Steering Wheel Play	• Damaged, loose, or worn tie-rod end (3A130). • Loose, worn or damaged front wheel spindle tie-rod (3280). • Damaged/worn steering gear. • Loose, worn or damaged steering column bearing(s). • Loose, worn or damaged lower steering column shaft U-joint(s).
• Wander	• Unevenly loaded or overloaded vehicle. • Loose, worn or damaged front wheel spindle tie-rod. • Loose, worn or damaged tie-rod ends. • Loose or damaged steering gear mounting bolts. • Loose lower steering column shaft U-joint bolts. • Loose, worn or damaged lower steering column shaft U-joints. • Loose, worn or damaged steering column bearing(s). • Suspension components.

FM6029800318010X

Fig. 1 Troubleshooting chart (Part 1 of 2)

Condition	Possible Source
• Drift/Pull	• Unevenly loaded or overloaded vehicle. • Wheel alignment. • Loose, worn or damaged front wheel spindle tie-rod. • Loose, worn or damaged tie-rod ends. • Suspension components. • The steering gear valve effort out of balance. • Check the brake system for proper operation. • Improper frame/underbody alignment.
• Feedback	• Loose, worn or damaged front wheel spindle tie-rod. • Loose, worn or damaged tie-rod ends. • Loose or damaged steering gear insulators or bolts. • Loose lower steering column shaft U-joint bolts. • Loose suspension bushings, fasteners or ball joints. • Worn or damaged steering column bearing(s).
• Poor Returnability/Sticky Steering	• Binding lower steering column shaft U-joints. • Loose, worn or damaged front wheel spindle tie-rod. • Loose, worn or damaged tie-rod ends. • Suspension components. • Binding steering column bearing(s).
• Shimmy	• Loose, worn or damaged tie-rod end. • Loose, worn or damaged front wheel spindle tie-rod. • Suspension components.

FM6029800318020X

Fig. 1 Troubleshooting chart (Part 2 of 2)

Power Steering Pumps

INDEX

APPLICATION CHART

Model	Type
Aviator	—
Escape	—
E-Series	C111
Expedition	C111
Explorer w/4.0L Push Rod Engine	C11
Explorer w/4.0L SOHC & 5.0L Engines	C111
F-150	C111
Freestar	C111
Freestyle	C111
F-Super Duty Series & Excursion w/Diesel Engine	C11
F-Super Duty Series & Excursion w/Gasoline Engine	C111
Mark LT	C111
Mariner	—
Monterey	C111
Motorhome (F-Super Duty)	ZF
Mountaineer	C11
Navigator	C111
Ranger	C11
Villager	—
Windstar w/3.0L Engine	C11
Windstar w/3.8L Engine	C111

DIAGNOSIS & TESTING

System Pressure Test

C11

Do not touch flow meter during test procedure or severe burns or injury may occur.

1. Install power steering analyzer No. 211-F001, or equivalent, at high pressure port of power steering pump. Ensure power steering analyzer gate valve is in fully open position.
2. Place a digital thermometer in power steering pump reservoir.
3. Inspect power steering fluid level and top off as required.
4. Start engine and place transmission in neutral position. Set parking brake.
5. Start engine and raise temperature of power steering fluid by rotating steering wheel fully left to right several times.
6. Do not hold steering wheel against stops for more than three to five seconds at a time or damage to power steering pump will occur.
7. Set engine speed to 1500 RPM. Record flow rate and pressure readings.
8. If flow rate is below specified value, power steering pump may require service. Continue with test procedure.
9. If pressure reading is above maximum value specified, inspect power steering hoses for kinks or restrictions.
10. Partially close gate valve to obtain pressure of 750 psi, do not allow gate to remain closed for more than five seconds. Set engine speed to idle and record flow rate.
11. If flow is less than specified value, replace power steering pump.
12. Completely close and partially open gate valve three times. Record pressure relief valve actuation pressure reading.
13. If pressure does not meet specified value, replace power steering pump.
14. Set engine speed to 1500 RPM and record flow rate.
15. If flow rate varies by more than 3.785 liters/minute (1 gallon minute) from initial flow rate reading, replace power steering pump.
16. Set engine speed to idle.
17. Turn steering wheel from stop to stop and record flow rate and pressure readings at stops. Do not allow steering wheel to remain at stops for more than three to five seconds at a time or damage to power steering pump will occur.
18. Pressure readings at both stops should be approximately the same as maximum pump relief pressure.
19. Flow rate should drop below 1.9 liters/minute (.5 gallons minute).
20. If pressure does not reach maximum pump relief pressure or flow rate does not drop below specified value, excessive leakage is occurring. Repair or replace components as required.
21. Turn steering wheel slightly in both directions and release quickly while

watching pressure gauge.

22. Pressure reading should move from normal back pressure reading and snap back as steering wheel is released.
23. If pressure returns slowly or sticks, rotary valve in steering gear is sticking or steering column is binding. Inspect steering column and linkages.

C111 & ZF

On some models, the power steering pump high pressure port is inaccessible and the Power Steering Analyzer should be installed either at steering gear or at a point in the high pressure line between power steering pump and steering gear.

1. Install Power Steering Analyzer at high pressure port of power steering pump. Ensure Power Steering Analyzer gate valve is fully open.
2. Place a dial thermometer in power steering oil reservoir.
3. Inspect power steering fluid level and add if required.
4. Install a digital tachometer.
5. Start engine, place transmission in neutral and set parking brake. Raise power steering fluid temperature to 165–175°F by rotating steering wheel from stop to stop. **Do not hold at stop for more than three to five seconds.**
6. Set engine speed to 1500 RPM and record flow rate and pressure readings. If flow rate is below flow rate specification, power steering pump may require replacement. Continue with test. If pressure reading is above maximum pressure specification, then inspect hoses for kinks and restrictions.
7. Partially close gate valve to obtain 750 psi. Set engine speed at idle. Record flow rate. If flow rate is less than specified, replace pump.
8. Completely close and partially open gate valve three times. **Do not close for more than five seconds.** Record pressure relief valve actuation pressure reading. If pressure does not meet relief pressure specification, replace pump.
9. Set engine speed to 1500 RPM. Record flow rate. If flow rate varies more that one gallon a minute from initial flow rate reading, replace pump.
10. Set engine speed at idle. Turn steering wheel from stop to stop and record flow rate and pressure readings at stops.
11. Pressure reading at both stops should be nearly the same as maximum pump relief pressure. The flow rate should drop below .5 gallons a minute. If pressure does not reach maximum pump relief pressure or flow rate does not drop below specified value, excessive internal leakage is occurring. Repair or replace steering gear as required.
12. Turn steering wheel slightly in both directions and release quickly while watching pressure gauge. Pressure reading should move from normal back pressure reading and snap back as steering wheel is released. If pressure returns slowly or sticks, rotary valve in steering gear is sticking or steering column is binding. Inspect steering column and linkages before servicing the steering gear.

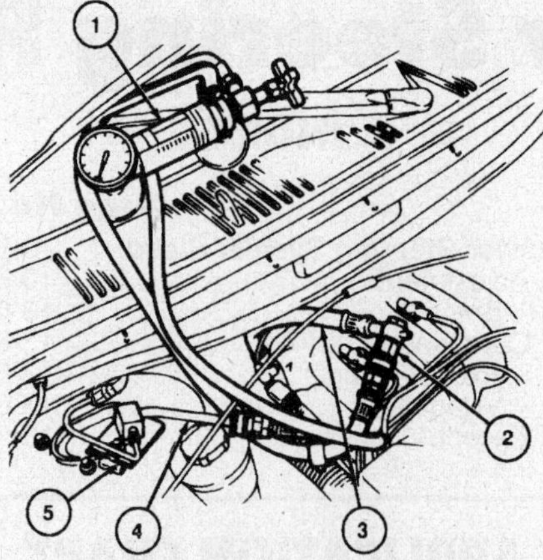

Item	Description
1	Rotunda Power Steering Analyzer
2	Power Steering System Analyzer Fitting
3	Power Steering Pressure Hose
4	Power Steering System Analyzer Fitting
5	Junction Block

FM6029800321000X

Fig. 1 Pressure analyzer hook up location

AVIATOR, ESCAPE & MARINER

1. Install Power Steering Analyzer at high pressure port of power steering pump. Make sure Power Steering Analyzer gate valve is fully open.
2. Place a dial thermometer in power steering oil reservoir.
3. Inspect power steering fluid level and add if required.
4. Install a digital tachometer.
5. Start engine, place transmission in neutral and set parking brake. Raise power steering fluid temperature to 165–175°F by rotating steering wheel from stop to stop. **Do not hold at stop for more than three to five seconds.**
6. Set engine to idle speed. Record free flow rate and pressure readings.
7. If flow rate is not within specified value, power steering pump may require repair. Continue with test procedure.
8. If back pressure reading is above maximum pressure specification, inspect power steering hoses for kinks or restrictions.
9. Partially close gate valve to obtain 740 psi. Set engine speed at idle. Record flow rate. If flow rate is less than specified, replace pump.
10. Completely close and partially open gate valve three times. **Do not close for more than five seconds.** Record pressure relief valve actuation pressure reading. If pressure does not meet relief pressure specification, replace pump.
11. Set engine speed to 1500 RPM. Record flow rate. If flow rate varies more that one gallon a minute from initial flow rate reading, replace pump.
12. Set engine speed at idle. Turn steering wheel from stop to stop and record flow rate and pressure readings at stops.
13. Pressure reading at both stops should be nearly the same as maximum pump relief pressure. The flow rate should drop below .5 gallons a minute. If pressure does not reach maximum pump relief pressure or flow rate does not drop below specified value, excessive internal leakage is occurring. Repair or replace steering gear as required.
14. Turn steering wheel slightly in both directions and release quickly while watching pressure gauge. Pressure reading should move from normal back pressure reading and snap back as steering wheel is released. If pressure returns slowly or sticks, rotary valve in steering gear is sticking or steering column is binding. Inspect steering column and linkages before servicing the steering gear.

VILLAGER

1. Raise and support vehicle.
2. Disconnect power steering pressure hose from junction block, letting power steering fluid to drain into a suitable container.
3. Connect Rotunda power steering analyzer tool No. 014-00207 with Power Steering Analyzer Fittings 014-00453, or equivalents between power steering pressure hose and junction block, **Fig. 1. Torque** fittings to 29–36 ft. lbs.
4. Place a thermometer in power steering oil reservoir.
5. Bleed system as follows:
   a. Inspect fluid level in power steering oil reservoir. Add fluid if required.
   b. Turn key On engine Off.
   c. Turn steering wheel fully left and right ten times.
   d. Inspect fluid level. If it had dropped, add fluid.
   e. Repeat steps 2 and 3 until fluid level stabilizes.
   f. Start engine and let it idle.
   g. Turn steering wheel fully left and right ten times.
   h. If foam is still present after repeating steps, inspect system for air leak.
   i. If fluid level has decreased, add fluid and repeat steps 7 and 8 until level does not change.
6. Leave engine running.
7. If required, turn steering wheel fully left and right several times to raise fluid temperature to 140–176°F.
8. To measure power steering pump output pressure, turn steering wheel to full right or left stop and increase engine speed to 1000 RPM.
9. Read pressure. The standard fluid pressure should be within 1109–1194 psi.
10. If fluid pressure is below standard pressure specification, slowly close

shutoff valve on the analyzer and inspect pressure.
11. If fluid pressure remains below standard pressure specification, the power steering pump is damaged. Repair or replace pump.
12. If fluid pressure reaches standard pressure specification, the steering gear is damaged. Repair or replace gear.
13. If fluid pressure is above standard pressure specification, inspect power steering pump flow control valve. Also inspect for crimped power steering lines. Replace if required.
14. Turn key Off and remove power steering analyzer and adapters.
15. Reconnect power steering pressure hose and tighten high pressure hose connections.
16. Bleed system as outlined in step 5.

POWER STEERING SYSTEM SERVICE

System Flush

EXCEPT VILLAGER

1. Disable ignition system.
2. Disconnect power steering return hose and plug reservoir.
3. Attach an extension hose between power steering return hose and an empty container.
4. Raise front wheels off the ground.
5. Inspect fluid level, if required fill to correct level with Multi-Purpose ATF XT-2-QDX, or equivalent.
6. Turn steering wheel from stop to stop while cranking engine until fluid exiting return hose is clear of all contamination and debris. **Do not crank engine for more than 15 seconds at a time. Allow starter to cool for one minute before cranking again.**
7. Add fluid to specified level and lower vehicle.
8. Disconnect extension hose from power steering return hose.
9. Remove plug and attach power steering return hose to reservoir.
10. Inspect fluid level and if required, fill to correct level.
11. Enable ignition system and start engine and turn steering wheel form stop to stop.
12. If power steering system is noisy and is the fluid is aerated it will required to purge the system.

VILLAGER

1. Leave all hoses connected, except power steering pressure hose located at steering gear.
2. Place pressure hose in suitable container, then fill oil reservoir with power steering fluid No. E6AZ-19582-AA, or equivalent.
3. Disconnect ignition coil electrical connection, then engage starter motor while pouring approximately two quarts of power steering fluid into reservoir. Place ignition in Off position after fluid has been added.
4. Connect pressure hose to steering gear and **torque** bolt to 11–18 ft. lbs.
5. Inspect oil level.
6. Engage starter motor and add fluid until level remains constant.
7. Connect ignition coil electrical connection, then cycle steering wheel left to right several times.

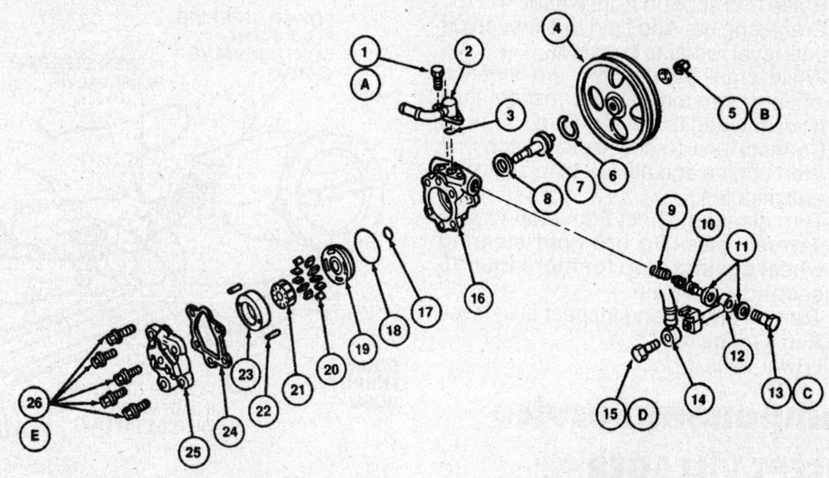

Item	Description
1	Power Steering Reservoir Pump Hose Bolt (2 Req'd)
2	Power Steering Reservoir Pump Hose Fitting
3	Power Steering Reservoir Pump Hose Fitting Seal
4	Power Steering Pump Pulley
5	Power Steering Pump Pulley Nut
6	Snap Ring
7	Power Steering Pump Rotor Shaft
8	Grease Seal
9	Power Steering Pump Flow Control Valve Spring
10	Power Steering Pump Valve
11	Power Steering Pressure Hose Connection Washers (2 Req'd)
12	Power Steering Pressure Hose Connection
13	Power Steering Pressure Hose Connection Bolt
14	Power Steering Pressure Hose
15	Lower Power Steering Pressure Hose Bolt

Item	Description
16	Power Steering Pump Housing, Front
17	Outer O-Ring
18	Inner O-Ring
19	Power Steering Pump Pressure Plate
20	Vane (10 Req'd)
21	Power Steering Pump Rotor
22	Guide Pin (2 Req'd)
23	Cam Ring
24	Rear Power Steering Pump Gasket
25	Power Steering Pump Housing, Rear
26	Power Steering Pump Rear Housing Bolts (5 Req'd)
A	Tighten to 14-18 N·m (10-13 Lb-Ft)
B	Tighten to 54-68 N·m (40-50 Lb-Ft)
C	Tighten to 69-78 N·m (51-58 Lb-Ft)

FM6029800314000X

Fig. 2 Exploded view of pump. Villager

POWER STEERING SYSTEM BLEED

EXCEPT VILLAGER

A whine heard from the power steering pump may be caused by air in the system.

1. Remove reservoir cap, inspect fluid level. If required, fill reservoir to correct level.
2. Tightly insert vacuum pump stopper part of tool No. D95L-7559-A, or equivalent, in place of reservoir cap.
3. Connect a short length of .25 inch plexiglass, steel or copper tubing to stopper cap.
4. Start vehicle, using tool No. D95L-7559-A, or equivalent, apply maximum vacuum of 20–25 inches Hg and maintain it for a minimum of three minutes with engine speed at idle.
5. Release vacuum and remove special tool.
6. Inspect fluid level and fill if required.
7. Install tool No. D95L-7559-A, or equivalent, apply maximum vacuum of 20–25 inches Hg.
8. Cycle steering wheel fully to left and right every 30 seconds from approximately five minutes.
9. Stop engine, release vacuum and remove tool.
10. Install reservoir cap.
11. Inspect for fluid leaks at all connections.

VILLAGER

1. Disconnect ignition coil electrical connection, then fill the oil reservoir to MAX mark.

2. Raise and support front wheel.
3. Crank engine. Add fluid to oil reservoir until level remains constant.
4. While cranking engine, turn steering wheel from stop to stop. Inspect fluid level and add fluid if required.
5. Connect ignition coil to distributor.
6. Start engine and allow it to idle for several minutes.
7. Turn steering wheel from stop to stop several times. **Do not hold steering wheel against stop for more than 15 seconds at a time.**
8. Turn off engine and inspect fluid level. Add as required.
9. Lower vehicle.

Component Service

EXCEPT VILLAGER

These power steering pumps are only serviceable as an individual assembly. If any components are damaged or worn, replace the entire pump assembly.

VILLAGER

DISASSEMBLE

1. Remove power steering pump.
2. Remove pressure hose connection bolt, pressure hose connection and two power steering pressure hose connection washers.
3. Remove pump valve spring, **Fig. 2.**
4. Remove five rear pump housing bolts.
5. Separate rear pump housing from front housing.
6. Use a screwdriver to remove snap ring from front housing.
7. Use a press to press rotor shaft from front housing.
8. Use Pulley shaft bearing replacement tool No. T92P-3504-MH, or equivalent and a press to press rotor shaft from bearing.
9. Use puller tool No. T58L-101-B, or equivalent to pull the grease seal from front pump housing.
10. Remove cam ring and rotor with vanes from rear housing.

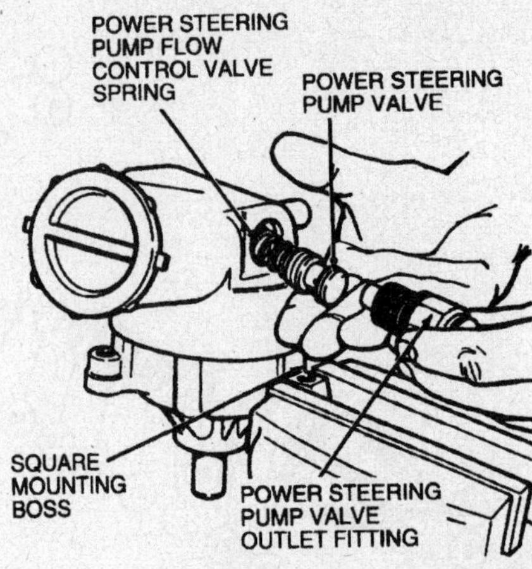

Fig. 3 Valve assembly removal

11. Remove two guide pins from rear housing.
12. Remove pump rotor with vanes from cam ring.
13. Remove vanes from pump rotor.

ASSEMBLE

1. Ensure pump rotor is placed in cam ring in proper direction so that the punch mark on the pump rotor faces front of the pump.
2. Place pump rotor in cam ring.
3. Ensure that the rounded portions of the vanes are on the outside of pump rotor and facing the cam ring.
4. Place vanes in pump rotor.
5. Install two guide pins in rear pump housing.
6. Position cam ring and pump rotor on rear housing in between two alignment pins.
7. Use a press and pulley shaft bearing replacement tool No. T92P-3504-MH, or equivalent to press pump rotor shaft onto the bearing.
8. Use Input shaft bearing/seal tool No. T65P-3534-A and Driver Handle T80T-4000-W, or equivalents, to install grease seal into front pump housing.
9. Use pulley shaft bearing replacement tool No. T92P-3504-MH and Driver Handle T80T-4000-W, or equivalents, to install pump rotor shaft into front pump housing.
10. Position rear pump housing and front pump housing together.
11. Install snap ring on front pump housing.
12. Install five rear pump housing bolts. **Torque** bolts to 23–31 ft. lbs.
13. Install pump flow control valve spring and pump valve.
14. Install pressure hose connection washers, hose connection and hose connection bolt. **Torque** connection bolt to 51–58 ft. lbs.
15. Install power steering pump.

Adjustments

SEALS

REMOVAL

1. Remove power steering pump.
2. Place pump assembly in a bench vise with soft jaws and remove pump valve outlet fitting, valve and flow control valve spring. Discard all seals, **Fig. 3.**
3. Remove fiberglass power steering oil reservoir by twisting side to side and lifting.
4. Discard O-ring seal on pump housing.

INSTALLATION

1. Install new O-ring seal on pump housing.
2. Apply petroleum jelly to reservoir O-ring seal and inside edge of the oil reservoir.
3. Place oil reservoir over the pump and align outlet fitting hole in the oil reservoir with hole in valve cover.
4. Place new O-ring seals on outlet fitting. Install flow control spring, valve and outlet fitting into power steering oil reservoir and cover. **Torque** fitting to 24–34 ft. lbs.
5. Install power steering pump.

Power Steering Gears

INDEX

PRECAUTIONS

Air Bag Systems

Refer to "Air Bag System Precautions" in the front of this manual for system disarming and arming procedures.

DESCRIPTION

E-Series, Excursion, Expedition, F-Super Duty & Navigator

The power steering unit, **Fig. 1.** is a torsion bar type hydraulic assisted system and utilizes a rotary style hydraulic valve.

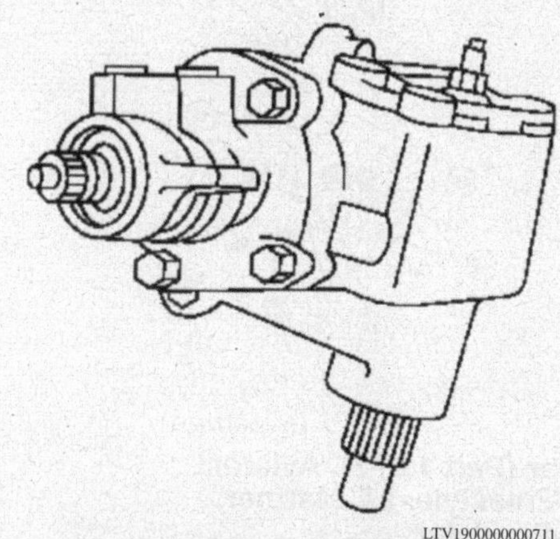

Fig. 1 Power steering gear. E-Series, Excursion, Expedition, F-Super Duty & Navigator

Internal valves directs pump flow and controls pressure to reduce steering effort during operation. The unit contains a rotary hydraulic fluid control valve integrated to the input shaft and a boost cylinder integrated with the rack.

Aviator, Escape, F-150, Freestar, Freestyle, LT, Mariner, Monterey & Windstar

This integral power steering gear contains a manual steering mechanism, hydraulic control valve and hydraulic power cylinder, **Fig. 2.**

Explorer, Mountaineer & Ranger

The Ford integral power rack and pinion steering gear incorporates a constant diameter rack, **Fig. 3.** The gear is mounted to the front of the crossmember underneath the vehicle. The gear and valve housings are combined in a one piece aluminum die casting and incorporates quick connect fittings for pressure and return lines to allow the lines to swivel.

The gear is a hydraulic mechanical unit that uses an integral piston and rack design to provide power assisted vehicle control.

Villager

The power steering gear is a typical rack and pinion design, **Fig. 4,** consisting of steering gear, pump, oil reserve, pressure hose, return hose, front wheel spindle tie rod and tie rod end.

POWER STEERING SYSTEM SERVICE

Adjustments

MESHLOAD

E-SERIES, EXCURSION, EXPEDITION, F-SUPER DUTY & NAVIGATOR

1. With engine Off, turn steering wheel from lock to lock at least once.
2. Remove driver air bag as outlined in "Air Bag System" chapter.
3. Raise and support vehicle.
4. Separate pitman arm from sector shaft with suitable pitman arm puller.
5. Lower vehicle but do not allow front wheels to touch ground.
6. Attach an inch lb. torque wrench to center bolt on steering wheel.
7. Rotate torque wrench 90° left to right and measure turning torque, **Fig. 5.**
8. If rotating torque is less than 13 inch lbs., hold sector shaft and loosen lock nut, **Fig. 6.**
9. Adjust sector shaft and inspect meshload adjustment.
10. Repeat as required to obtain proper meshload specification.
11. Hold sector shaft and **torque** locknut to 20–25 ft. lbs.
12. Install steering sector shaft arm drag link, then install castellated nut and **torque** to 57–76 ft. lbs.
13. Install cotter pin.
14. Lower vehicle and install driver air bag as outlined in "Air Bag System" chapter.

POWER STEERING SYSTEM BLEED

Refer to "Power Steering Pump" for system bleed procedures.

COMPONENT SERVICE

E-Series, Excursion, Expedition, F-Super Duty & Navigator

STEERING GEAR

DISASSEMBLE

The steering gear input shaft and seals cannot be repaired or replaced separately.

1. Secure steering gear in a suitable vise with indexing flat pointed down.
2. Rotate power steering gear input shaft and control from stop to stop and then center gear.
3. Remove steering gear sector shaft housing cover bolts.

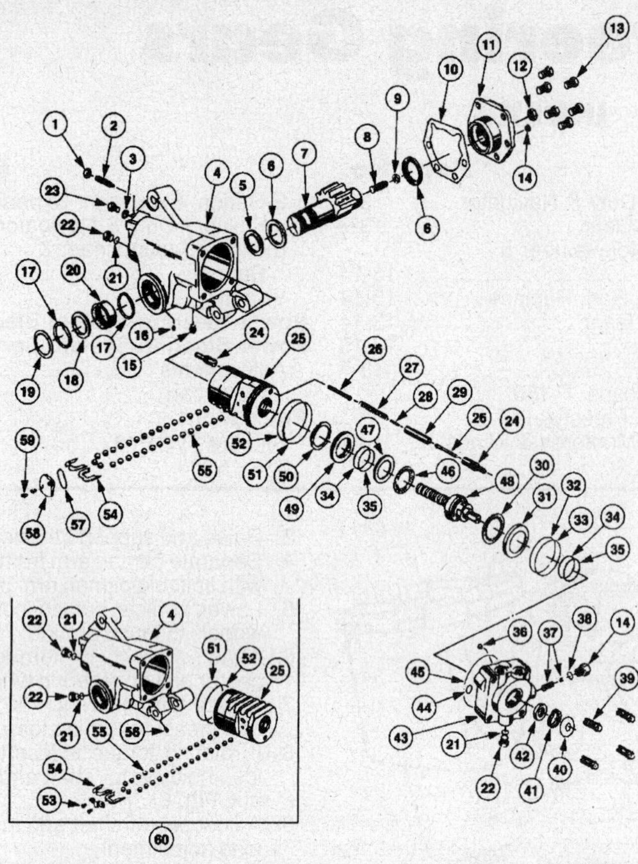

LTV1900000000814

Fig. 2 Power steering gear (Part 1 of 3). Aviator, Escape, F-150, Freestar, Freestyle, LT, Mariner, Monterey & Windstar

```
1. Service Sealing Jam Nut
2. Service Poppet Adjusting Screw
3. Washer (Stop Screw)
4. Housing
5. Washer (Spacer)
6. Seal, Output (2)
7. Sector Shaft
8. Adjusting Screw (Shaft)
9. Retainer (Adjusting Screw)
10. Gasket (Side Cover)
11. Side Cover and Bushing Assy
12. Sector Shaft Adjusting Screw Jam Nut
13. Special Bolts (Side Cover)
14. Relief Valve Cap/Vent Plug (Side Cover)
15. Plug (Auto Bleed)
16. Grease Fitting
17. Retaining Ring (2)
18. Dirt Seal
19. Dirt and Water Seal (Trunnion)
20. Roller Bearing
21. O-Ring (2) (Auxiliary Port Plug)
22. Auxiliary Port Plug (2)
23. Fixed Stop Screw (Poppet)
24. Poppet and Sleeve Assy (2)
25. Rack Piston
26. Poppet (2)
27. Poppet Spring
28. Spacer Rod
29. Push Tube
30. Ball Bearing Assy Valve Worm
```

LTV1900000000838

Fig. 2 Power steering gear (Part 2 of 3). Aviator, Escape, F-150, Freestar, Freestyle, LT, Mariner, Monterey & Windstar

```
31. Thrust Washer (Thick) (Alt.)
32. Seal Ring
33. O-Ring (Valve Housing)
34. Seal Ring (2)
35. O-Ring (2)
36. Check Ball (Float Valve Gear)
37. Relief Valve (2-Piece)
38. O-Ring (Relief Valve)
39. Bolts (4) (Valve Housing)
40. Dirt and Water Seal (Input)
41. Retaining Ring
42. Seal (Input Shaft)
43. Valve Housing
44. Seal Ring (Valve Housing)
45. Seal Ring (Valve Housing)
46. Thrust Bearing (2)
47. Thrust Washer (Thin)
48. Input Shaft, Valve, Worm Assy
49. Bearing Adjuster
50. Bearing Adjuster Lock Nut
51. Teflon° Seal Ring (Rack Piston)
52. O-Ring (Backup, Rack Piston)
53. Ball Return Guide Hex-Head Bolt (2)
54. Ball Return Guide Halves (2)
55. Balls
56. Bleed Screw
57. Seal (Ball Return Guide Cap)
58. Ball Return Guide Cap
59. Ball Return Guide Torx Screws (2)
60. Short V Construction Rack Piston
```

LTV1900000000839

Fig. 2 Power steering gear (Part 3 of 3). Aviator, Escape, F-150, Freestar, Freestyle, LT, Mariner, Monterey & Windstar

4. Tap on lower end of steering gear sector shaft, then remove shaft, **Fig. 7.**
5. Remove locknut from steering gear sector shaft adjustment screw, **Fig. 8.**
6. Hold steering gear sector shaft and rotate housing cover counterclockwise to remove.
7. Remove valve housing bolts and identification tag, **Fig. 9.**
8. Remove valve housing and piston assembly.
9. Remove and discard gasket, **Fig. 10.**
10. Remove steering gear ball return guide, then rotate piston over a suitable container and collect 28 steering gear worm balls.
11. Remove input shaft valve and housing assembly from piston. Remove and discard seal.
12. Install valve housing in bench mounted holding fixture, then loosen set screw.
13. Remove race nut with adjuster and locknut wrench No. 211-012, or equivalent, **Fig. 11.**
14. Remove input shaft and control from valve housing.
15. Rotate valve housing, then remove steering gear input shaft seal and dust seal, **Fig. 12.**
16. Remove input shaft snap ring, **Fig. 13.**
17. Rotate valve housing and remove bearing and power steering gear input shaft seal with removal tool No. 211-S005, or equivalent.
18. Remove valve housing from bench holding fixture.
19. Install steering gear housing in bench mounted holding fixture, then remove steering gear sector shaft dust seal from sector shaft seal bore, **Fig. 14.**
20. Remove snap ring and spacer, **Fig. 15.**
21. Remove sector shaft seal with puller tool No. 308-001, or equivalent, **Fig. 16.** Sector shaft bearing is not replaceable.

ASSEMBLE

The correct number of balls are required for proper steering gear operation. To ensure balls are inserted properly, rotate steering gear input worm gear and rack from one end of travel to other without allowing poppet adjuster to contact the valve housing or moving the valve housing pilot face more than 2 ¾ inches from input end of rack piston. If the steering gear input worm gear and rack cannot be rotated, reinstall balls. If the steering gear is installed with a steering gear input worm gear and rack that cannot rotate, the steering gear will not function correctly and steering gear failure can occur.

1. Lubricate sector shaft seal bore and seal **Fig. 17,** with multi-purpose grease DOAZ-19584-AA, or equivalent meeting Ford specifications ESB-M1C93B and ESR-M1C159-A, or equivalent.
2. Install sector shaft seal with installation tool No. 211-044, or equivalent, **Fig. 18.**
3. Install spacer, then the snap ring, **Fig. 19.**
4. Install sector shaft dust seal with raised lip toward installer tool No. 211-044, or equivalent. Lubricate dust seal with multi-purpose grease DOAZ-19584-AA, or equivalent meeting Ford specifications ESB-M1C93-B and ESR-M1C159-A, or equivalent.
5. Remove steering gear from bench mounted fixture.
6. Position input shaft bearing in valve housing and press into place with seal

installer tool No. 211-S005, or equivalent, **Fig. 20,** and a suitable hydraulic press.
7. Install input shaft bearing seal and press to seat with seal installer tool No. 211-S005, or equivalent.
8. Install input shaft snap ring, then the dust seal.
9. Mount valve housing in bench mounted holding fixture.
10. Install input shaft and control valve into housing.
11. Position power steering gear nut into valve housing.
12. **Torque** race nut to 55–90 ft. lbs., with adjuster and locknut wrench No. 211-012, or equivalent.
13. Install setscrew, **Fig. 21.**
14. Remove valve housing from bench mounted fixture and position piston on worm gear.
15. Install steering gear ball return guide on piston, **Fig. 22.** Hold guides until cap or clip is installed.
16. Failure to hold guides will result in trapped balls which can cause an accident. If ball guide becomes unseated at any time, remove balls and repeat procedure.
17. Rotate piston while holding steering gear ball return guide and install 28 ball bearings in opening in ball guide.
18. Install steering gear ball return guide clamp.
19. Install new gasket, then lubricate and install seal on piston, **Fig. 23.**
20. Install piston assembly into steering gear housing. Ensure oil passages in steering gear housing are aligned.
21. Rotate teeth so they are on same plane as steering gear sector shaft.
22. Loosely install valve housing bolts and identification.
23. Lubricate O-ring on sector shaft housing cover, **Fig. 24,** with multi-purpose grease DOAZ-19584-AA, or equivalent meeting Ford specifications ESB-M1C93-B and ESR-M1C159-A, or equivalent.
24. Rotate housing clockwise and install sector shaft into sector shaft housing.
25. Install sector shaft locknut. Do not tighten at this time, nut will be tightened during meshload adjustment.
26. Loosely install sector shaft housing bolts.
27. Install sector shaft and housing assembly.
28. **Torque** bolts, **Fig. 25,** to 45–55 ft. lbs., then **torque** opposite side bolts, **Fig. 26,** to 30–44 ft. lbs.

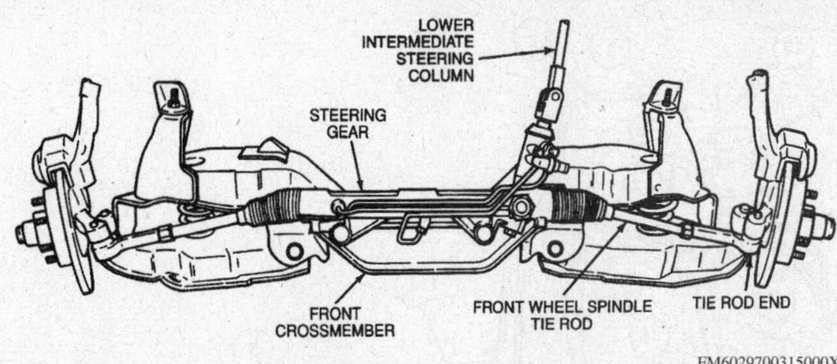

Fig. 3 Power rack & pinion gear. Explorer, Mountaineer & Ranger.

Aviator, Escape, F-150, Freestar, Freestyle, LT, Mariner, Monterey & Windstar

STEERING GEAR

DISASSEMBLE

Replace all of the seals and gaskets each time the steering gear is disassembled.

1. Place steering gear in a suitable vise and tighten jaws of vise on mounting flange or boss of housing. Do not clamp against body of steering gear.
2. Place suitable drain pan under steering gear, then unplug hydraulic ports on gear and drain fluid.
3. Rotate input shaft and valve worm assembly until timing mark on end of sector shaft is aligned with timing mark on end of housing trunnion, **Fig. 27.**
4. Remove any paint or corrosion from exposed area of sector shaft with fine grade emery cloth.
5. Remove dirt and water seal from housing trunnion with small screwdriver, **Fig. 28.**
6. Tape serrations and bolt groove of sector shaft with one layer of masking tape, **Fig. 29.** Tape must not extend onto diameter of sector shaft bearing.
7. Remove jam nut from sector shaft adjusting screw.
8. Remove side cover and sector shaft assembly as a unit from steering gear. Bolts that fasten side cover to housing are of a specially designed material and length. If replacing bolts use only exact replacement bolts.
9. Remove and discard sector shaft relief cap/vent plug. Remove reverse threaded sector shaft adjusting screw by turning clockwise, **Fig. 30,** through cover.
10. Clamp side cover in a vise. Place a standard ⅝ inch or 11⁄16 inch ⅜ inch drive socket in center of side cover.
11. Pry out seal with a rolling head pry bar using socket for support. Do not damage bore or bushing on gear when removing seal.
12. Inspect sector shaft assembly for damaged adjusting screw threads. Adjusting screw must rotate by hand with no perceptible end play.
13. Remove relief valve cap/vent cap, O-ring and two piece relief valve, **Fig. 31,** discard O-ring.
14. Remove and discard dirt and water seal from input shaft, **Fig. 32.**
15. Clean any paint or corrosion off of exposed area of input shaft with emery cloth.
16. Remove four Torx head bolts from valve housing.
17. Remove rack piston subassembly. The set position of poppet seat and sleeve assemblies must not be disturbed if poppets are not going to be replaced.
18. Remove and discard seal rings from valve housing.
19. Remove ball return guide halves by placing screwdriver between rack piston and guides, **Fig. 33.**
20. Steel balls are a matched set. If any are lost the set must be replaced.
21. Place rack piston on clean cloth to prevent steel balls from rolling, then remove balls from rack piston by rotating input shaft, valve and worm assembly until balls fall out.
22. Ensure all 32 balls have been removed.
23. Remove input shaft, valve worm and valve housing subassembly from rack piston, **Fig. 34.**
24. Cut and remove Teflon seal ring and

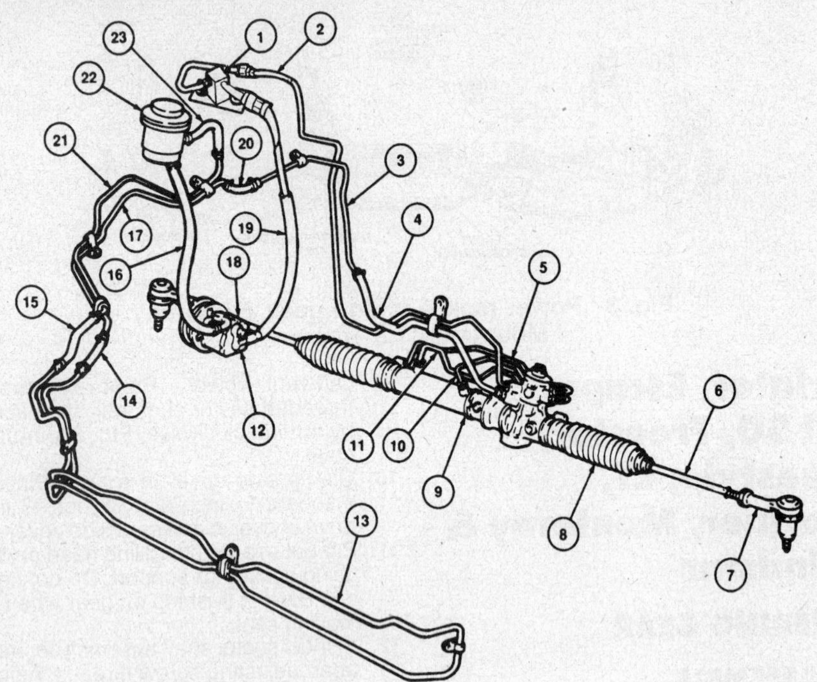

Item	Description
1	Junction Block / High-Pressure Line
2	Power Steering Pressure Switch
3	Intermediate Line C
4	Power Steering Return Hose
5	Breather Tube
6	Front Wheel Spindle Tie Rod
7	Tie Rod End
8	Front Suspension Steering Ball Stud Dust Seal
9	Steering Gear
10	Power Steering Left Turn Pressure Hose

Item	Description
11	Power Steering Right Turn Pressure Hose
12	Hose Connection
13	Power Steering Oil Cooler Tube
14	Intermediate Hose B
15	Intermediate Hose A
16	Power Steering Reservoir Pump Hose
17	Intermediate Line B
18	Power Steering Pump
19	Power Steering Pressure Hose
20	Intermediate Hose C
21	Intermediate Line A
22	Power Steering Oil Reservoir
23	Reservoir Return Hose

FM6029600216000X

Fig. 4 Power steering gear. Villager

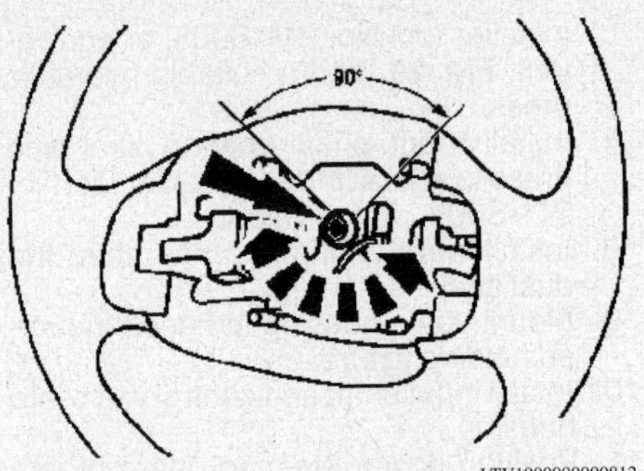

Fig. 5 Meshload measurement. E-Series, Excursion, Expedition, F-Super Duty & Navigator

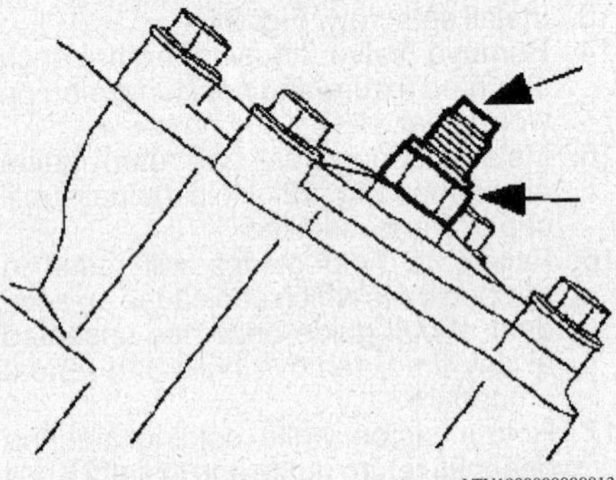

Fig. 6 Sector shaft locknut. E-Series, Excursion, Expedition, F-Super Duty & Navigator

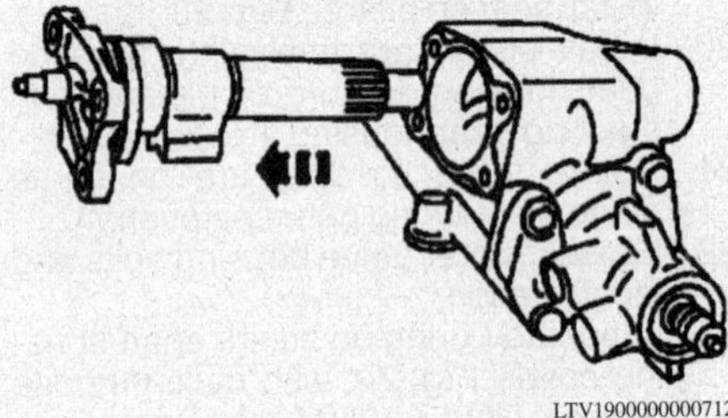

Fig. 7 Sector shaft replacement. E-Series, Excursion, Expedition, F-Super Duty & Navigator

O-ring from rack piston, **Fig. 35.**

25. Do not remove poppet adjuster seat and sleeve assemblies unless replacement of poppet components is required.
26. Push poppet stems, they should spring back. Push poppet seat, it should not move by hand. If components are bent or broken, or if poppet stems and seat do not perform as outlined, replace poppet components as outlined in "Poppet Components, Replace."
27. Inspect valve housing & worm screw subassembly for heat damage or bearing roughness, **Fig. 36.** Repair or replace as required.
28. Remove retaining ring that is closest to output end of housing trunnion, **Fig. 37.**
29. Remove and discard dirt seal from housing trunnion, **Fig. 38.**
30. Insert a screwdriver from trunnion end of housing and carefully push seal and spacer washer out of other end of housing, **Fig. 39.** Do not damage spacer washer or sealing area. Discard seal.
31. Inspect roller bearing in housing for brinelling or spalling and inspect retaining ring for damage. Replace as required.

INSPECTION

1. Wash all components in clean petroleum based solvent. Blow dry with compressed air.
2. Inspect housing cylinder bore. Some scoring is considered normal. If there is internal leakage greater than 1 gallon per minute, inspect for damaged seal before replacing housing.
3. Inspect housing faces for nicks that would prevent proper sealing. Replace gear housing if nicks are present and cannot be easily removed with fine tooth flat file without changing the dimension characteristics, or if depressions are located in a seal area.
4. Inspect teeth of rack piston for cracks and wear.
5. If a step is detected by running a fingernail horizontally across a tooth surface, rack piston, sector shaft and set of 32 service balls must be replaced.
6. Inspect internal ball track grooves of rack piston for brinelling (dents) or spalling (flaking). If either condition exists, replace rack piston, input shaft, worm valve assembly and set of balls as an assembly.
7. Inspect input shaft, worm valve assembly, ball track grooves, thrust bearing and ball bearing areas for the following:
   a. Brinelling or spalling.
   b. Nicks, cracks or abnormalities.
   c. Ridges or steps in surfaces.
   d. Discoloration from excessive heat.
8. If any of these conditions exist, replace input shaft, valve housing, valve worm

Fig. 8 Sector shaft adjustment screw locknut. E-Series, Excursion, Expedition, F-Super Duty & Navigator

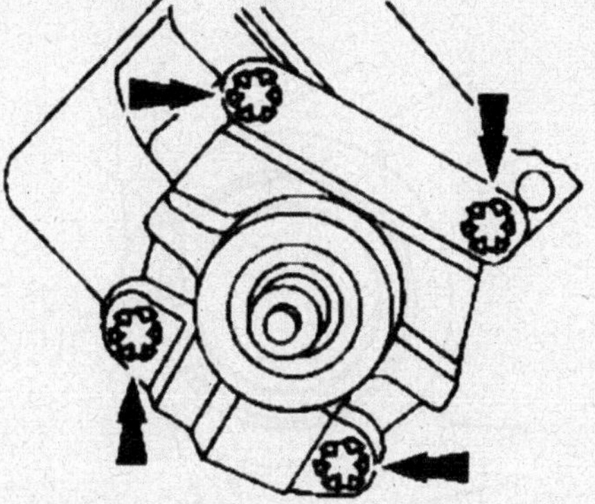

Fig. 9 Valve housing bolts. E-Series, Excursion, Expedition, F-Super Duty & Navigator

Fig. 10 Piston assembly gasket. E-Series, Excursion, Expedition, F-Super Duty & Navigator

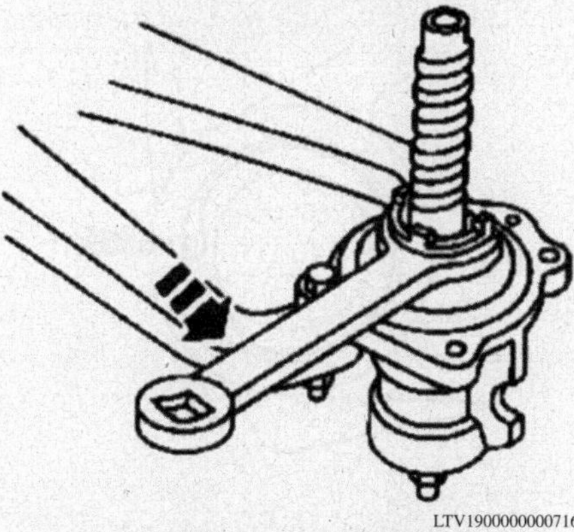

Fig. 11 Race nut replacement. E-Series, Excursion, Expedition, F-Super Duty & Navigator

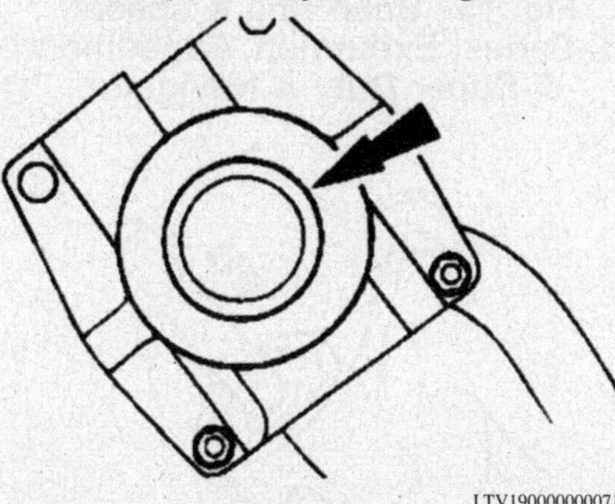

Fig. 12 Input shaft dust seal. E-Series, Excursion, Expedition, F-Super Duty & Navigator

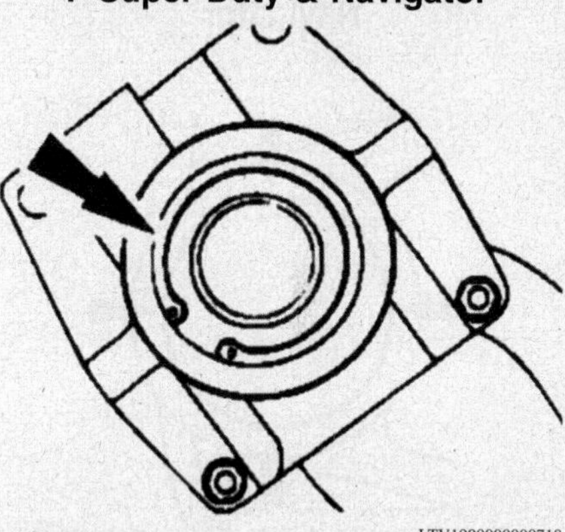

Fig. 13 Input shaft snap ring. E-Series, Excursion, Expedition, F-Super Duty & Navigator

assembly and set of balls as an assembly.

9. Replace rack piston if brinelling or spalling is found.
10. Replace housing only if internal leakage is greater than 1 gallon per minute.
11. Inspect face of housing for nicks that would prevent proper sealing. Replace housing if nicks cannot be easily removed without damaging housing.
12. Inspect face of housing for nicks that would prevent proper sealing. Replace housing if nicks cannot be easily removed with a fine tooth file.
13. Inspect side cover bushing for damage and inspect side cover bushing to sector shaft clearance. If damage exists or if clearance exceeds .008 inch, replace side cover and bushing assembly.
14. Inspect bearing, sealing and tooth contact surface areas on sector shaft for brinelling, spalling, nicks, grooves and twisted or damaged serrations.
15. Replace sector shaft if any of these conditions exist.

ASSEMBLE

1. Install new dirt seal into trunnion end of sector shaft bore of housing. Ensure seal is installed against bearing and lip of seal faces outward.
2. Install second retaining ring. Ensure ring is firmly seated in groove of housing.
3. Install washer into side cover of housing seal bore with small diameter piloted into retaining ring. A small dab of grease will hold washer in place.
4. Assemble a new seal onto bearing and seal tool so lip with garter spring is toward shoulder of tool.
5. Working from side cover side of housing, pilot the seal tool into washer and bearing and press into position with a force of 100–800 lbs., until seal is seated against washer, **Fig. 40.**
6. Pack area between dirt seal and pressure seal including roller bearing with high temperature front axle & wheel bearing grease No. E8TZ-19590-A, or equivalent meeting Ford specification ESA-M1C198-A.
7. Lightly oil new seal ring and assemble it in valve housing mounting face groove.
8. Install new backup O-ring and Teflon seal ring on rack piston, **Fig. 41.**
9. Place rack piston in housing piston bore with ball return guide holes facing upward.
10. Apply clean oil to cylinder bore.
11. Insert worm shaft into rack piston close to maximum depth, without valve housing making contact with poppet stem, **Fig. 42.**
12. Insert two 7⁄16-14 Ready Bolts through valve housing bolt holes and tighten into housing to support worm shaft, **Fig. 43.**
13. Line up rack piston ball guide holes with worm ball track grooves by rotating input shaft.
14. If a new piston or input shaft, valve, worm subassembly is being assembled, balls removed from unit must be discarded and a new service ball kit utilized.
15. Do not seat guides with a hammer. Damage to guides can result in subsequent lockup or loss of steering.
16. Compare new guides with guides removed from gear. Left guides are copper plated, right guides are unplated.
17. Assemble new ball return guide halves into rack piston until seated and rotate input shaft slightly if required, **Fig. 44.**
18. Hold ball return guides firmly in place and install as many steel balls as possible through hole in top of ball return.
19. Rotate input shaft to pull balls down and around ball track guide path.
20. Continue until correct number of balls (32) is in ball track guide path.
21. If ball return guide clip was used, install new guide clip. Line up holes in clip and on piston making sure clip is in complete contact with piston.

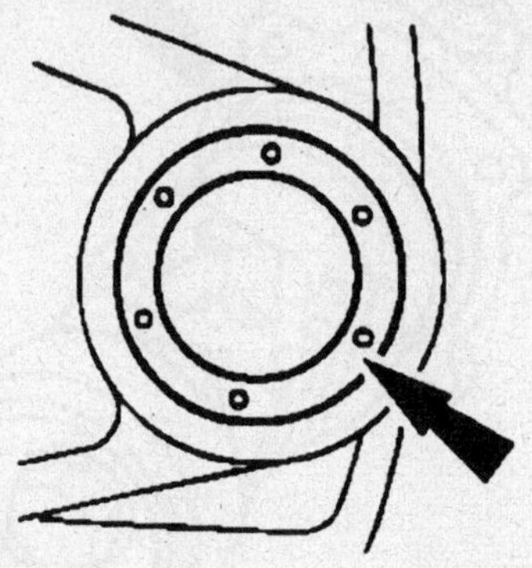

Fig. 14 Steering gear sector shaft dust seal. E-Series, Excursion, Expedition, F-Super Duty & Navigator

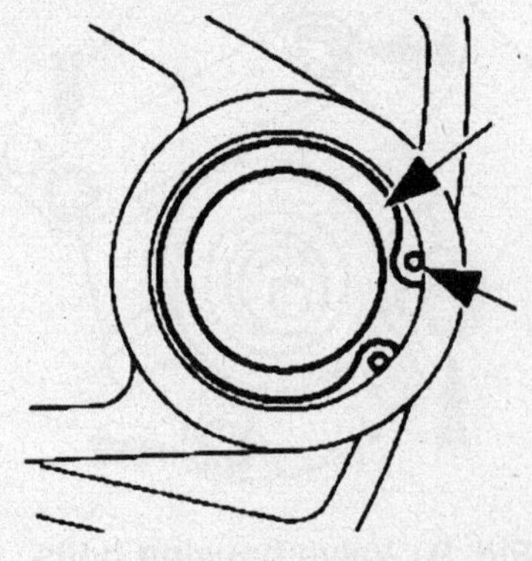

Fig. 15 Snap ring & spacer. E-Series, Excursion, Expedition, F-Super Duty & Navigator

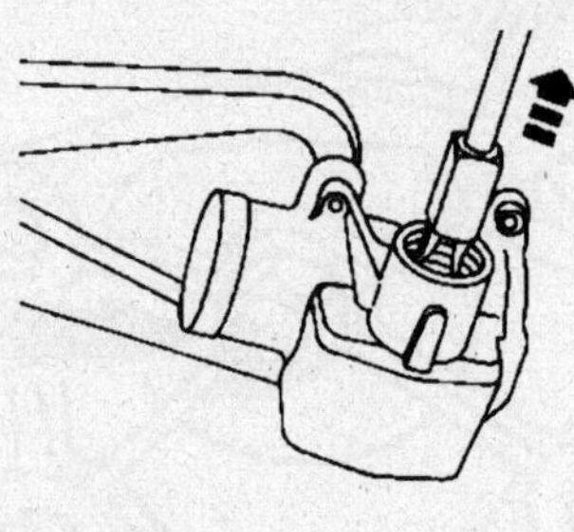

Fig. 16 Sector shaft seal replacement. E-Series, Excursion, Expedition, F-Super Duty & Navigator

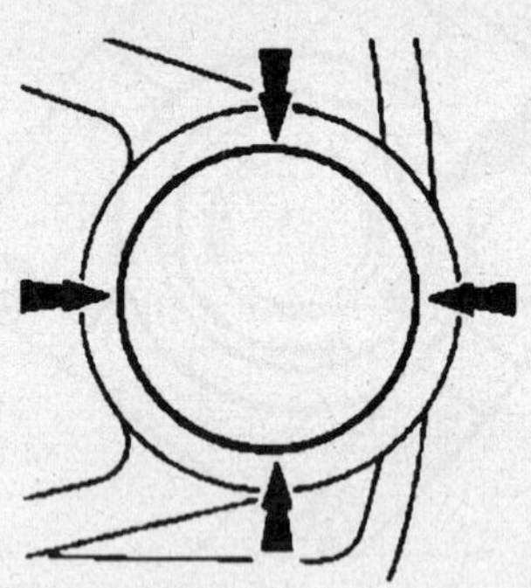

Fig. 17 Sector shaft seal bore lubrication. E-Series, Excursion, Expedition, F-Super Duty & Navigator

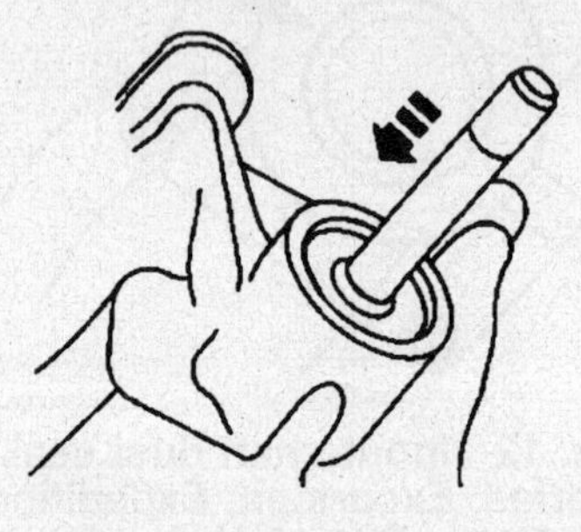

Fig. 18 Sector shaft seal installation. E-Series, Excursion, Expedition, F-Super Duty & Navigator

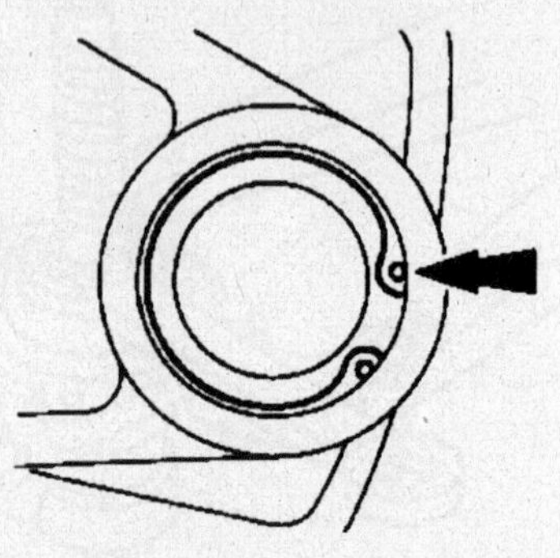

Fig. 19 Sector shaft seal snap ring installation. E-Series, Excursion, Expedition, F-Super Duty & Navigator

22. **Torque** guide clip bolts to 19 ft. lbs., then bend tabs of clip against bolt heads.
23. To ensure balls are properly installed, rotate wormshaft from one end of travel to other without allowing poppet adjuster to contact valve housing or moving valve housing pilot face more than 1 ½ inches from input end of rack piston.
24. If wormshaft cannot be rotated, reinstall balls.
25. If gear is equipped with ball return guide cap, lubricate new seal and install seal in cap groove.
26. Install cap so seal makes full contact with surface of piston, install two new cap bolts and **torque** to 14–22 ft. lbs.
27. Apply clean oil to Teflon seal ring on rack piston. Ensure there is a space of ⅜ to ½ inch between valve housing and poppet stem to prevent poppet contact at either end.
28. Remove previously installed Ready Bolts, then push rack piston assembly into housing with rack piston teeth toward sector shaft cavity.
29. Line up valve housing cylinder feed hole with gear housing feed hole.
30. Install four lubricated valve housing bolts into housing, **torque** bolts to 80 ft. lbs.
31. If gear is equipped with relief valve, assemble new O-ring on relief valve cap.
32. Assemble small end of tapered spring onto pin on relief valve cartridge and insert assembly (large end of tapered spring first) into relief valve cap cavity.
33. Install relief valve and **torque** to 30 ft. lbs.
34. Lightly oil DU bushing.
35. Grease and assemble new seal onto bearing and seal installation tool No. 211-S005, or equivalent, so side with garter spring is against shoulder of installation tool, **Fig. 45.**
36. Pilot tool into side cover with a force of 100–800 lbs. until it is firmly seated against bearing or bushing.
37. Lightly oil short bearing area of sector shaft.
38. Insert sector shaft into side cover subassembly and screw sector shaft adjusting screw counterclockwise into side cover until screw reaches solid height, **Fig. 46.**
39. Rotate adjusting screw clockwise one half turn so side cover will rotate freely on sector shaft.
40. Install sector shaft adjusting screw jam nut onto sector shaft adjusting screw a few threads. Final adjustment will be made later.
41. Press new vent plug into hole provided in side cover until plug is bottomed out, **Fig. 47.**
42. Apply clean grease to new side cover gasket to hold in place then install gasket on side cover.
43. Rotate input shaft to position rack piston so that space between second and third teeth is in center of sector shaft opening, **Fig. 48.**
44. Tape serrations and bolt groove of sector shaft with one layer of masking tape.
45. Install sector shaft and side cover assembly into gear housing. Ensure center tooth of sector shaft engages center space of rack piston.
46. Tighten side cover bolts in sequence, **Fig. 49,** until cover contacts housing.
47. **Torque** bolts to 119 ft. lbs.
48. Remove tape from sector shaft and pack end housing trunnion area at sector shaft with high temperature front

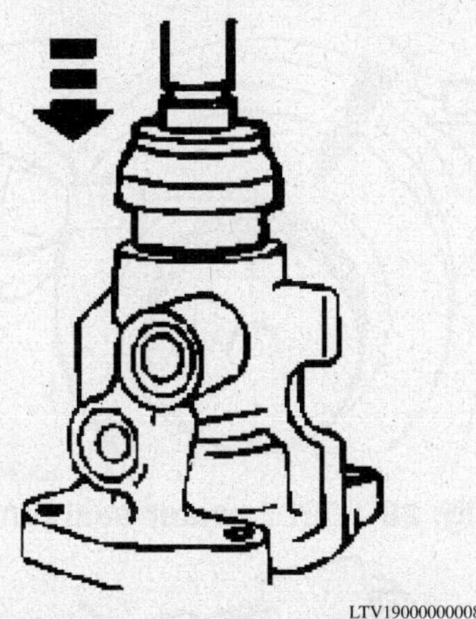

Fig. 20 Input shaft bearing installation. E-Series, Excursion, Expedition, F-Super Duty & Navigator

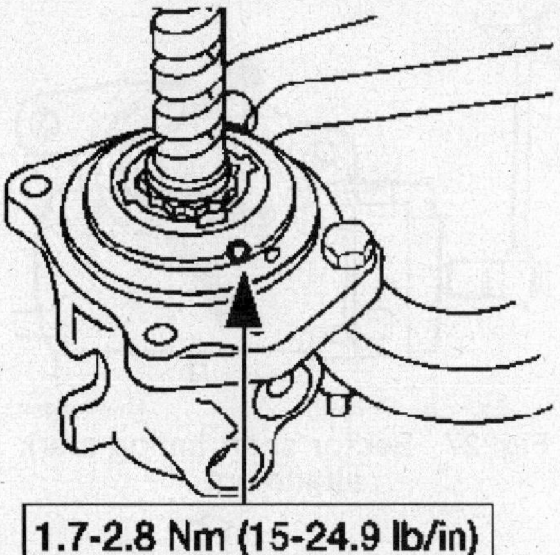

Fig. 21 Race nut set screw. E-Series, Excursion, Expedition, F-Super Duty & Navigator

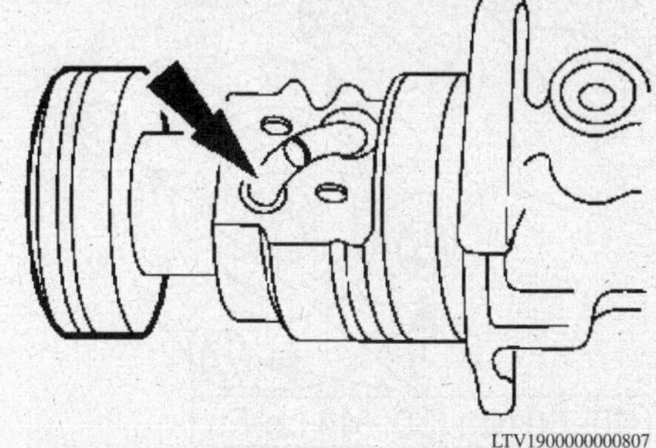

Fig. 22 Steering gear ball return guide. E-Series, Excursion, Expedition, F-Super Duty & Navigator

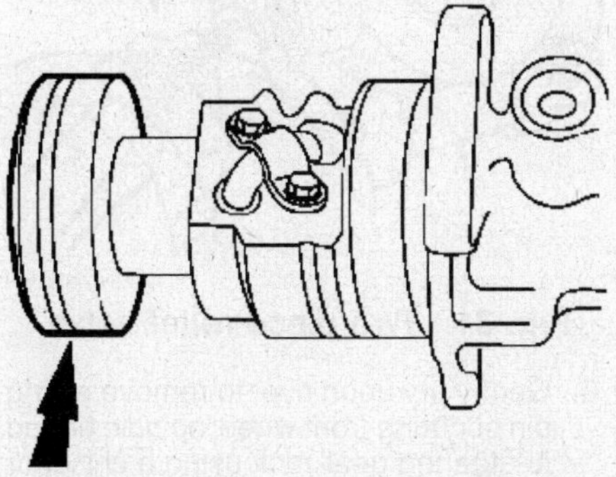

Fig. 23 Piston seal installation. E-Series, Excursion, Expedition, F-Super Duty & Navigator

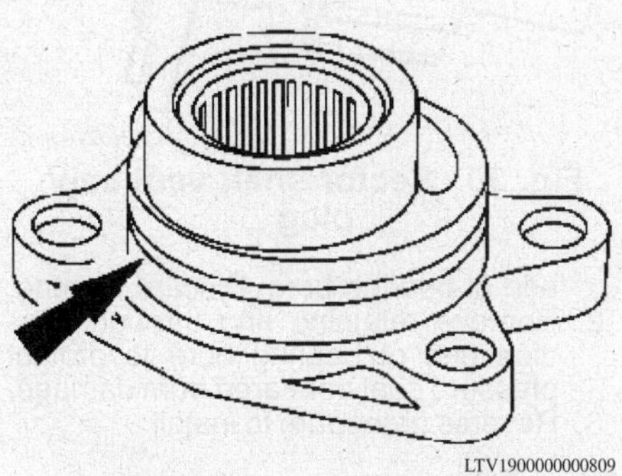

Fig. 24 Sector shaft housing O-ring lubrication. E-Series, Excursion, Expedition, F-Super Duty & Navigator

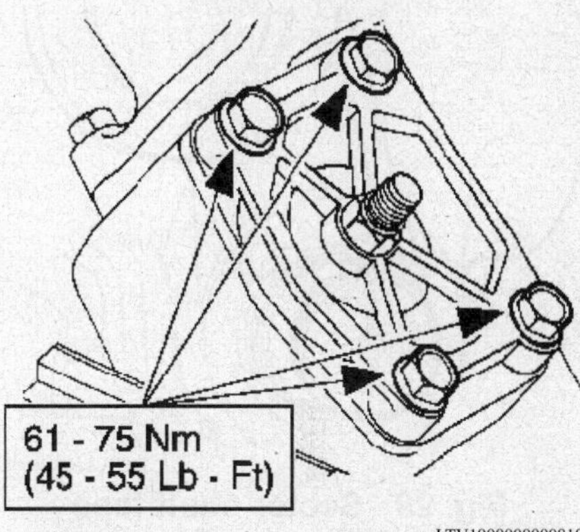

Fig. 25 Power steering gear upper bolt tightening. E-Series, Excursion, Expedition, F-Super Duty & Navigator

axle and wheel bearing grease E8TZ-19590-A, or equivalent meeting Ford specification ESA-M1C198-A.

49. Apply grease to new trunnion dirt seal and assemble it over sector shaft and into trunnion bore.
50. Pack end of valve housing around input shaft with high temperature front axle and wheel bearing grease E8TZ-19590-A, or equivalent meeting Ford specification ESA-M1C198-A.
51. Apply more of grease to inside of dirt and water seal and install over input shaft and seat in groove behind serrations and against valve housing.
52. Adjust steering gear meshload as outlined in "Adjustments."

POPPET COMPONENTS

REMOVAL

1. If poppet assemblies are to be removed for replacement or internally reset for fully automatic poppet adjustment after reinstallation, place rack piston in a soft jawed vise.
2. Slide poppet adjusting seat tool over seat of poppet adjuster seat and sleeve assembly and engage tool in slots in threaded sleeve, **Fig. 50.**
3. Hit end of tool firmly four or five times with a 2 lb. hammer to loosen Loctite sealer.
4. With ratchet applied to tool, turn one adjuster seat and sleeve assembly out of rack piston.
5. If engaging tangs won't stay in place while loosening, it may be required to hold it in place with an arbor press while loosening.
6. Remove two poppets, spring, spacer rod and push tube.
7. Reset one poppet adjuster seat and sleeve assembly for automatic poppet adjustment while it is in rack piston if one adjuster seat and sleeve assembly and poppets, spring, spacer rod and push tube are removed.
8. Remove remaining poppet seat and sleeve assembly as required.
9. Clean threads on poppet seat and sleeve assemblies using a suitable thread chaser.

INSTALLATION

1. Screw poppet seat and sleeve assembly loosely into it's threaded hole in rack piston for full thread length with slotted end in.
2. If one poppet seat and sleeve assembly was left in rack piston, it can be reset for automatic poppet adjustment by inserting a 3/8 inch diameter drill rod 6 inches long, down through poppet seat hole at opposite end of rack piston and against adjuster seat to press in seat until it bottoms against adjuster sleeve, **Fig. 51.**
3. Press adjuster seat into sleeve using 500–2500 lbs. force until shoulder on seat bottoms against sleeve, then remove adjuster seat and sleeve assembly from rack.
4. Carefully apply Loctite T Primer to threads in poppet holes and threads on seat and sleeve assemblies. Allow to dry for 10 minutes then carefully apply Loctite RC680 to same threads.
5. Place rack piston in soft jawed vise and turn one poppet adjuster seat and sleeve assembly with slotted end out, into poppet hole in one end of rack piston.
6. From other end of poppet hole in rack piston, Install one poppet, poppet spring, nylon spacer rod, push tube, other poppet and other poppet adjuster seat and sleeve assembly, **Fig. 52.**
7. Tighten both poppet adjuster seat and sleeve assemblies to specification with poppet adjusting seat tool and a suitable torque wrench.

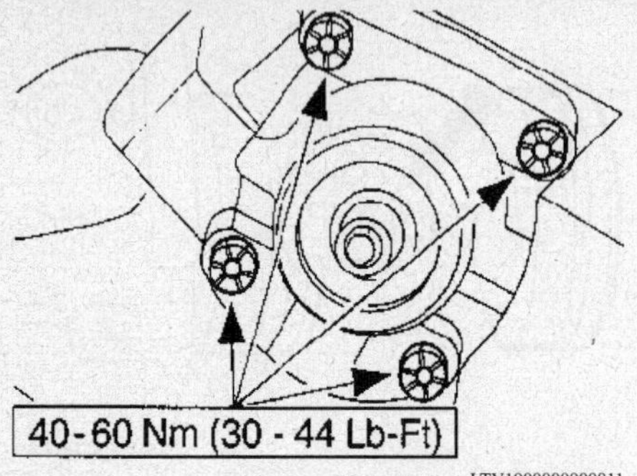

Fig. 26 Power steering gear lower bolt tightening. E-Series, Excursion, Expedition, F-Super Duty & Navigator

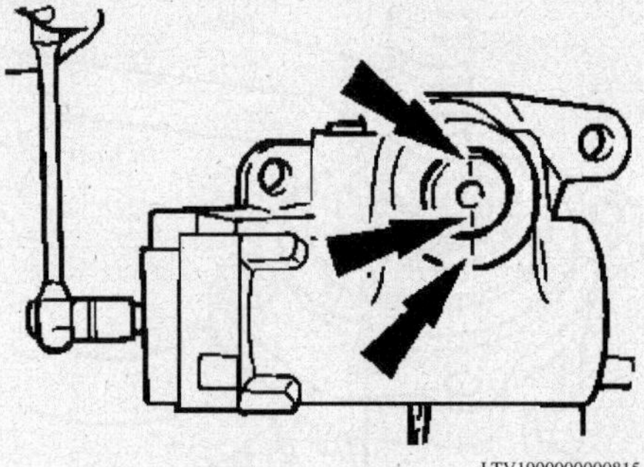

Fig. 27 Sector shaft timing mark alignment

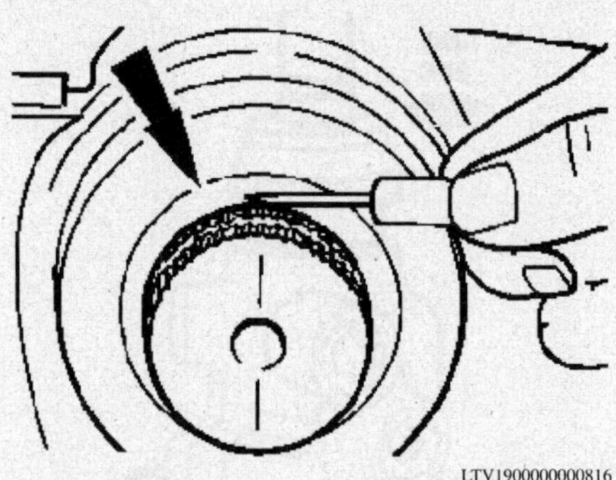

Fig. 28 Dirt & water seal removal

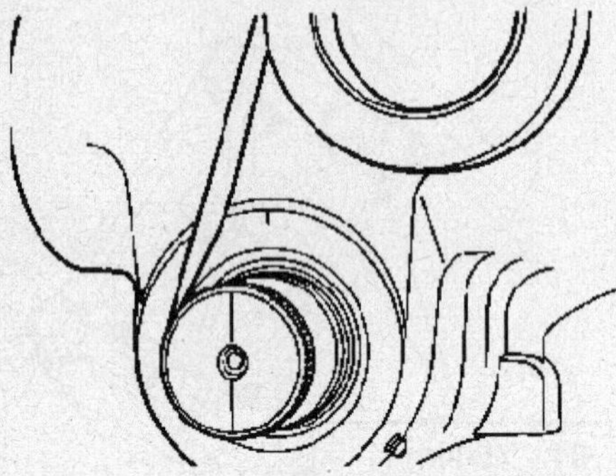

Fig. 29 Sector shaft tape placement

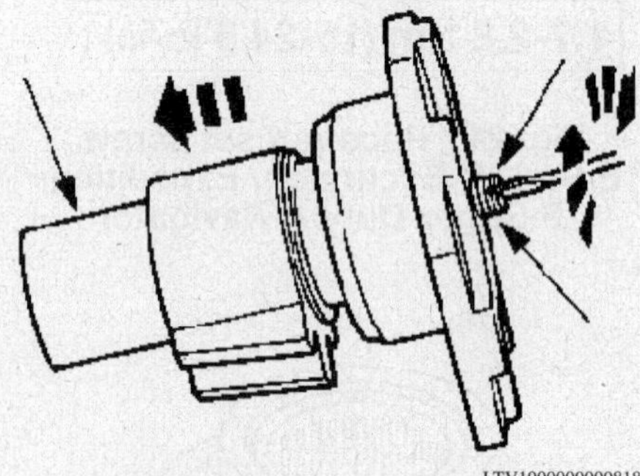

Fig. 30 Sector shaft vent cap/ plug

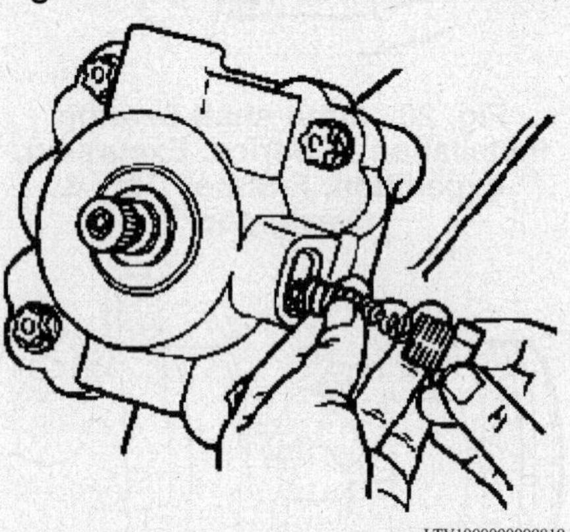

Fig. 31 Two piece relief valve

ADJUSTING SCREW & RETAINER

A service sector shaft will come assembled with adjusting screw and retainer.

1. Inspect sector shaft for bearing and sealing areas and sector teeth contact surfaces for brinelling, spalling or cracks.
2. Inspect for twisted or otherwise damaged serrations.
3. If any of these conditions exist, replace sector shaft.
4. Place sector shaft firmly in a soft jawed vise and unstake retainer, then turn retainer out of sector shaft pocket.
5. If required, remove adjusting screw. If adjusting screw is replaced, retainer must also be replaced.
6. If adjusting screw has been removed, coat expanded end of new adjusting screw with suitable wheel bearing grease and insert into recess in end of sector shaft.
7. Thread a new sector shaft screw retainer into sector shaft, tighten, then stake retainer in two slots provided.
8. Adjusting screw must rotate freely by hand with less than .002 inch end play.

HOUSING ROLLER BEARING OR RETAINING RING REPLACEMENT

1. Place bearing removal end of bearing and seal tool No. J37071, or equivalent, against side cover end of bearing and press roller bearing out of trunnion end of bearing bore. Discard bearing.
2. Remove retaining ring through trunnion end of bearing bore to protect pressure seal bore area from damage.
3. Reverse procedure to install.

Explorer, Mountaineer & Ranger

STEERING GEAR

There is no overhaul procedure available for this power steering gear. The gear must be replaced as an assembly.

INNER TIE ROD, REPLACE

REMOVAL

1. Unlock steering column by turning ignition key. Engage parking brake and raise and support the vehicle.
2. Clean any loose dirt or oil from steering gear and gear housing.
3. Loosen jam nut and keep flush with tie rod end.
4. Remove tie rod end cotter pin and castle nut.
5. Disconnect tie rod end from knuckle by using pitman arm puller tool No. T64-3590-F, or equivalent.
6. Mark threads at jam nut location.
7. Count number of turns to remove tie rod end from wheel spindle tie rod. Remove jam nut from front wheel spindle tie rod.
8. Remove left steering gear boot bellows if left front wheel spindle tie rod is being changed and both sides if right front wheel spindle tie rod is being changed.
9. Gently pry upon rivet to remove rolling pin securing front wheel spindle tie rod to steering gear rack using a chisel or Locknut pin remover tool No. D81P-3504-N, or equivalent. **Rivet has a steel core which will deform steering gear rack threads if it is not completely removed.**
10. Remove rivet using side cutters.

INSTALLATION

1. Clean steering gear housing, boot bellows interface to both outer and inner diameter.
2. Inspect all components and replace as required.
3. Replenish any grease which may have been removed from rack teeth, using steering gear grease C3AZ-19578-A, or equivalent.
4. Hold rack securely. **Torque** each tie rod to 40–50 ft. lbs., using a nut wrench or Rotunda socket.
5. Install pin using channel locks.
6. Inspect front wheel spindle tie rod end by moving spindle in various directions.
7. Apply steering gear grease C3AZ-19578-A, or equivalent, to front wheel spindle tie rod groove where boot bellows attach with a clamp to front wheel spindle tie rod. This allows for toe in adjustments without twisting bellows.
8. Install boot bellows and gear rack tube.
9. Inspect that boot is properly positioned over gear housing bead at large inner diameter and is in tie rod groove at the small inner diameter.

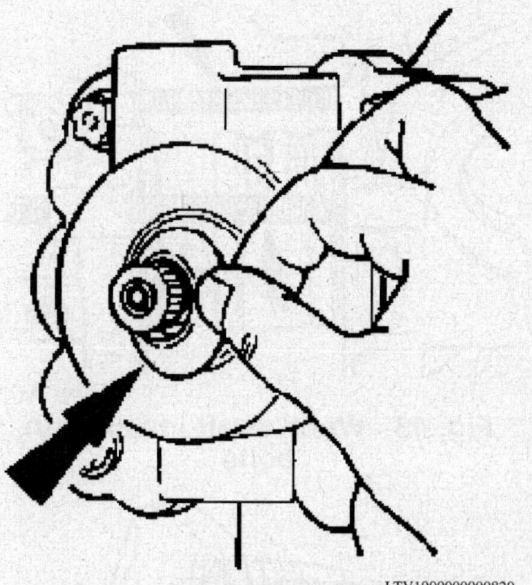
Fig. 32 Input shaft dirt & water seal

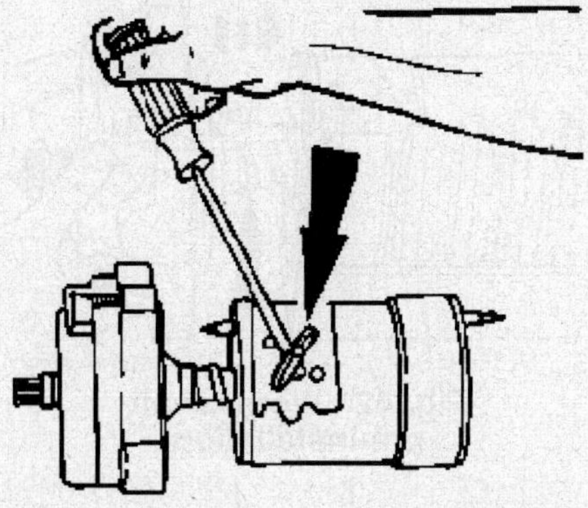
Fig. 33 Ball return guide removal

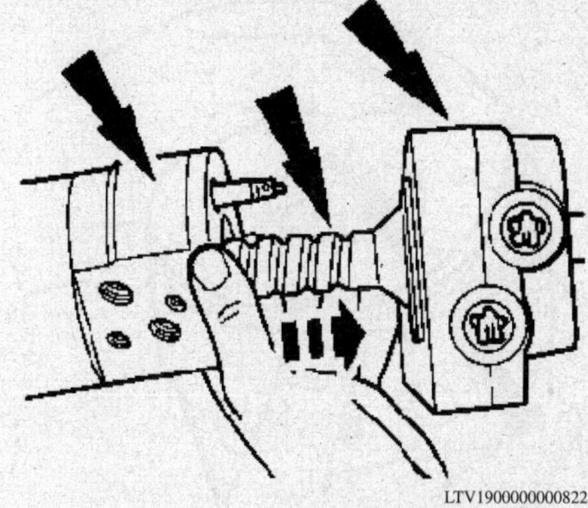
Fig. 34 Input shaft removal

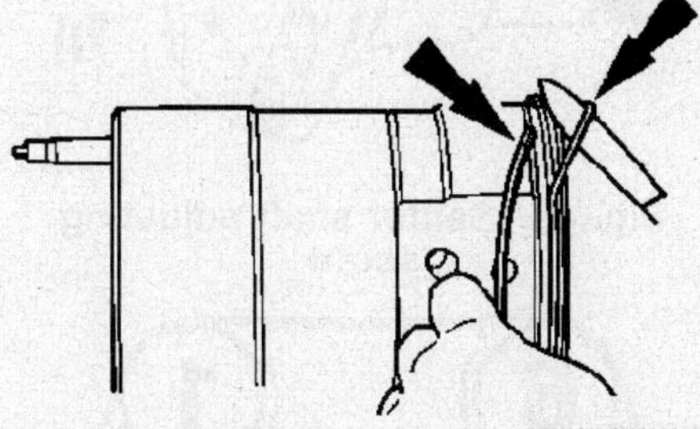
Fig. 35 Teflon rack piston seal removal

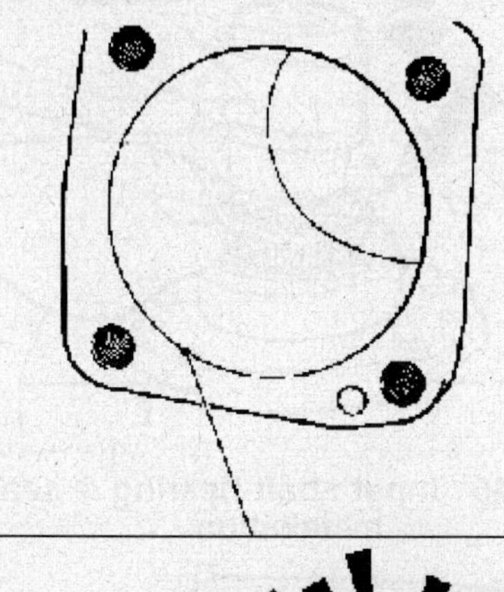

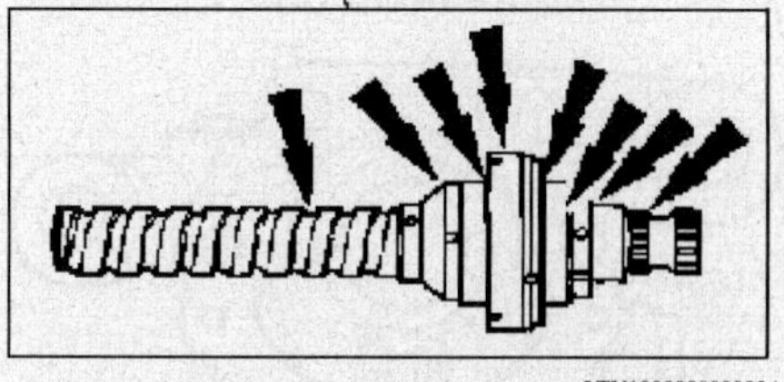
Fig. 36 Valve housing & worm screw subassembly inspection points

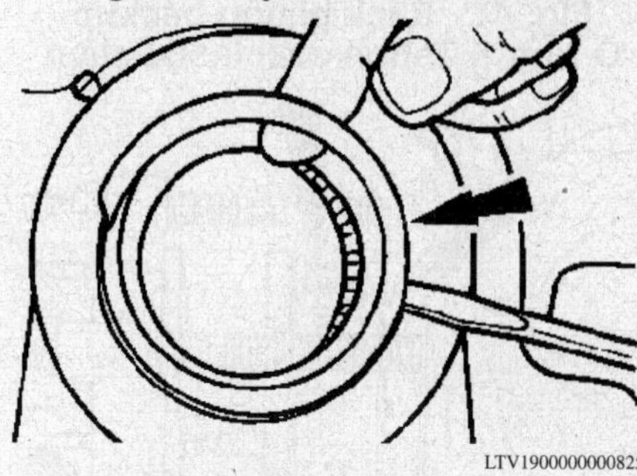
Fig. 37 Housing trunnion retaining ring

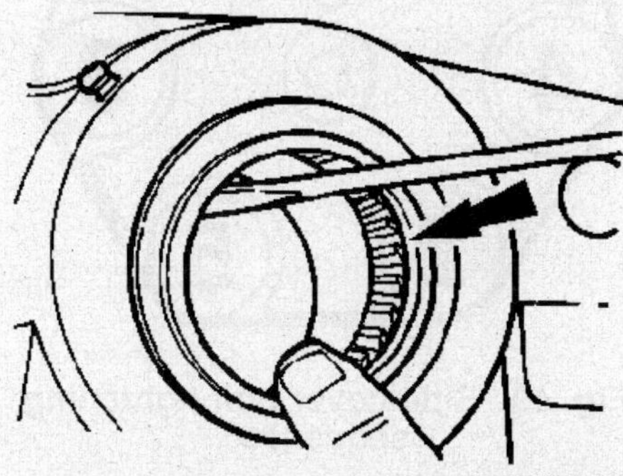
Fig. 38 Housing trunnion dirt seal

Fig. 39 Housing trunnion seal & washer removal

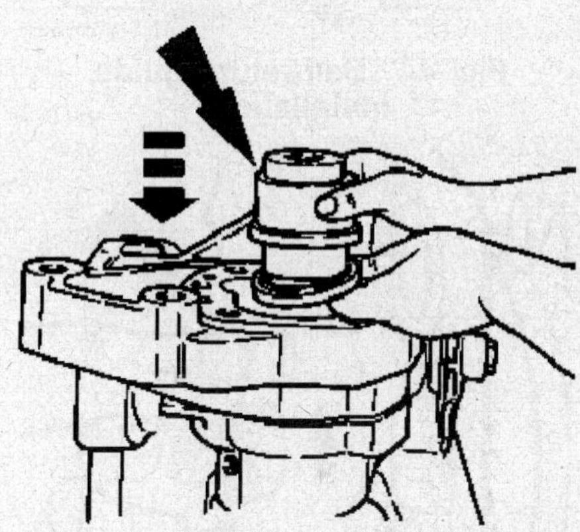
Fig. 40 Side cover bearing & seal installation

10. Inspect that boot bellows are not twisted and gear rack tube is securely inserted into vent nipple at both boots.
11. Install screw type clamps and **torque** to 20–30 inch lbs.
12. Install new clamp retaining bellows to front wheel spindle tie rod.
13. Apply disc brake caliper slide grease D7AZ-19590-A, or equivalent, to threads of front wheel spindle tie rod.
14. Count approximate turns recorded during removal. This approximates previous toe setting.
15. Connect outer tie rod to steering knuckle.
16. **Torque** jam nut against tie rod end to 35–50 ft. lbs.
17. **Torque** castle nut to knuckle to a minimum of 27 ft. lbs.
18. Continue to tighten castle nut to 52–73 ft. lbs.
19. Install new cotter pin.
20. Set toe to specifications.

Villager

The power steering gear is only serviceable as an assembly. The tie-rods and dust boots can be replaced. If any other components require service, replace as an assembly.

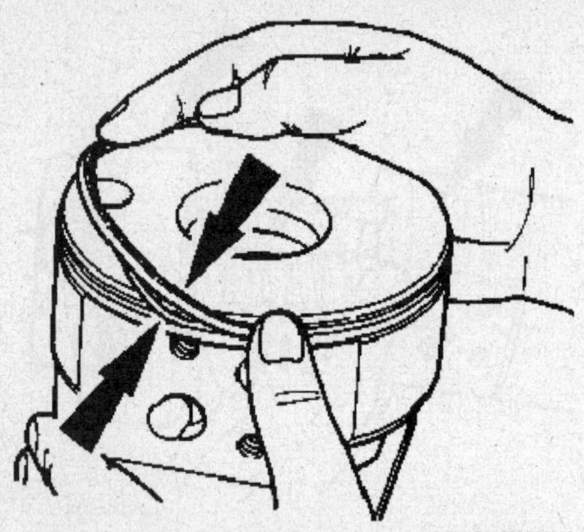

Fig. 41 Rack piston backup O-ring & Teflon seal installation

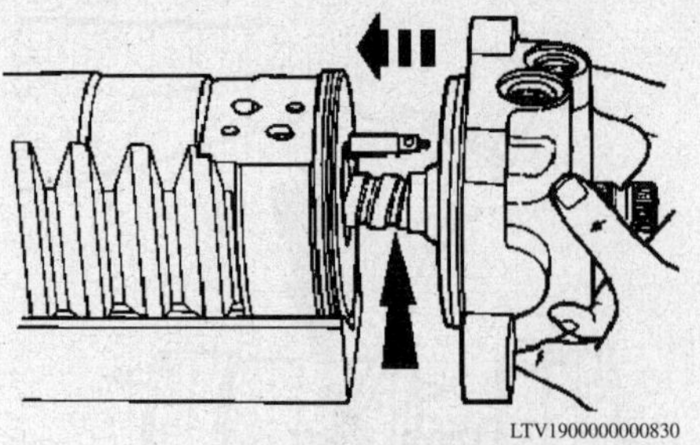

Fig. 42 Worm shaft pre-installation

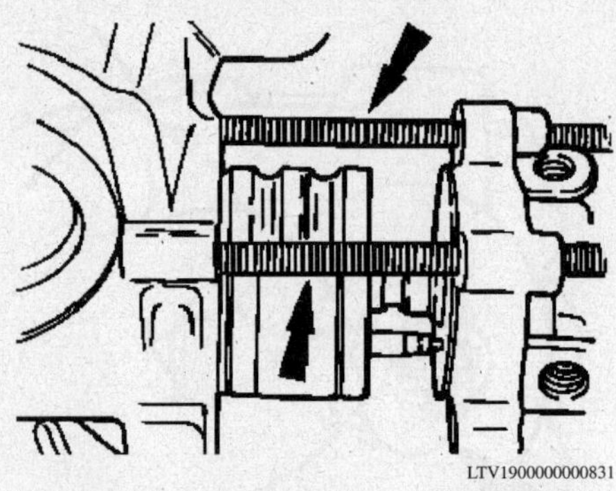

Fig. 43 Worm shaft installation bolts

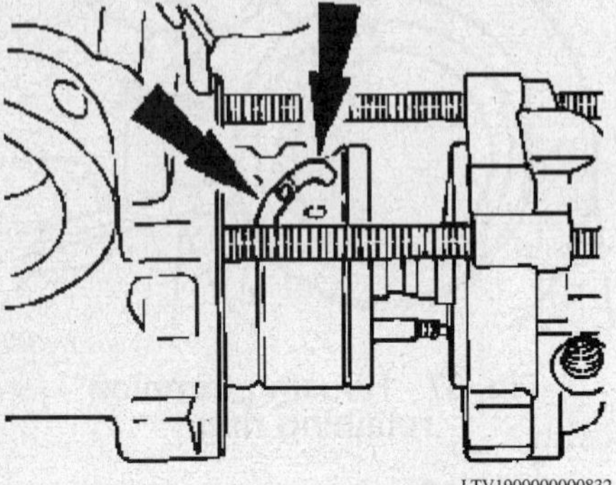

Fig. 44 Ball return guide installation

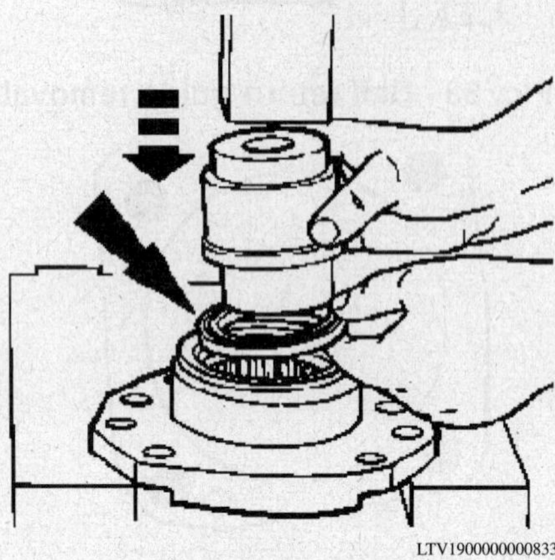

Fig. 45 Input shaft bearing & seal installation

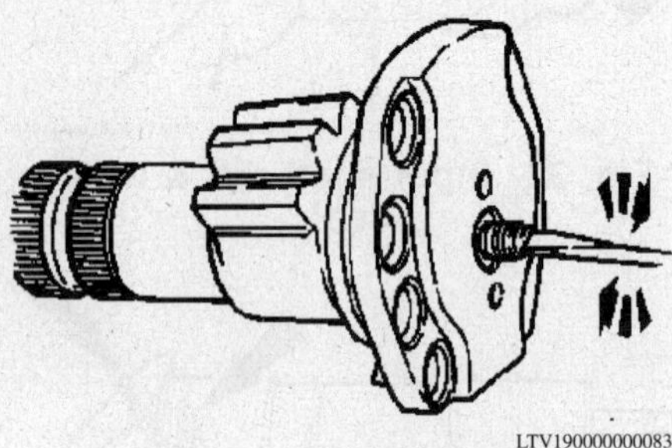

Fig. 46 Sector shaft adjusting screw

Fig. 47 Side cover vent plug

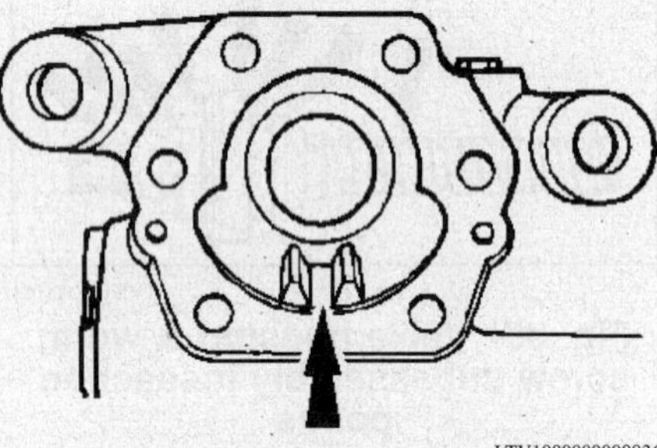

Fig. 48 Input shaft tooth centering

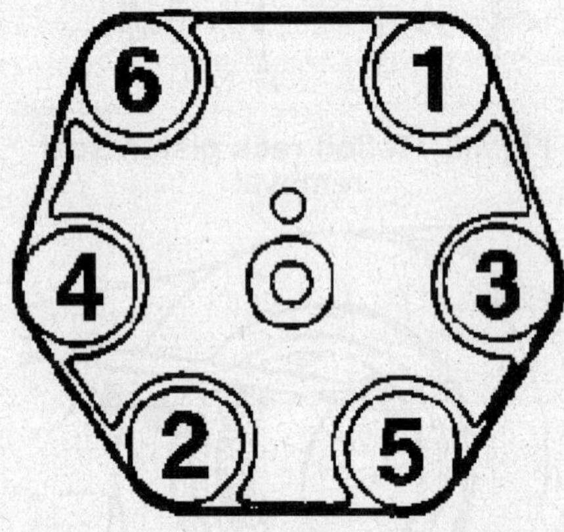

Fig. 49 Side cover bolt tightening sequence

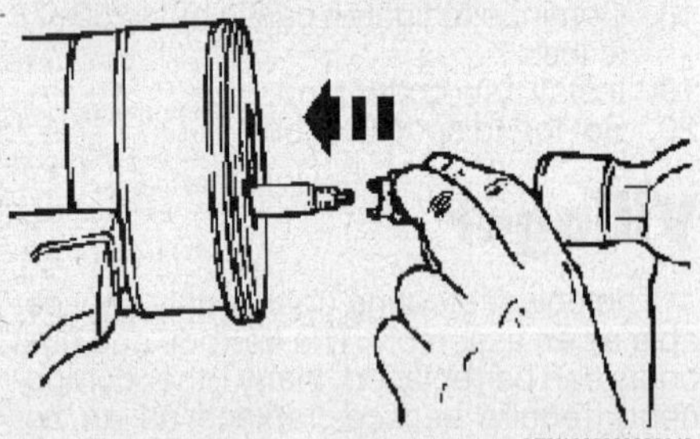

Fig. 50 Poppet adjusting seat tool. Aviator, Escape, F-150, Freestar, Freestyle, LT, Mariner, Monterey & Windstar

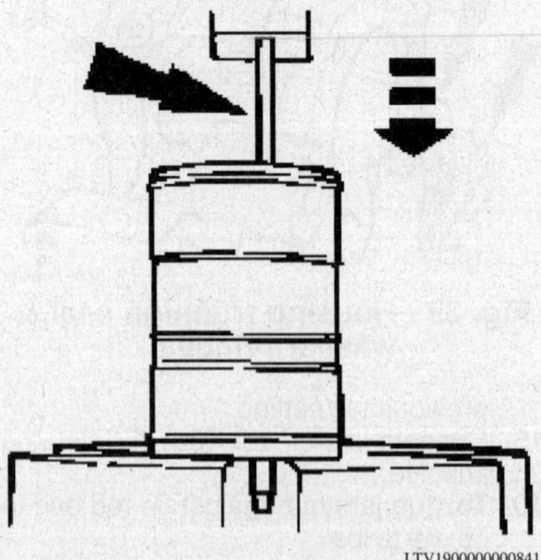

Fig. 51 Automatic poppet adjustment. Aviator, Escape, F-150, Freestar, Freestyle, LT, Mariner, Monterey & Windstar

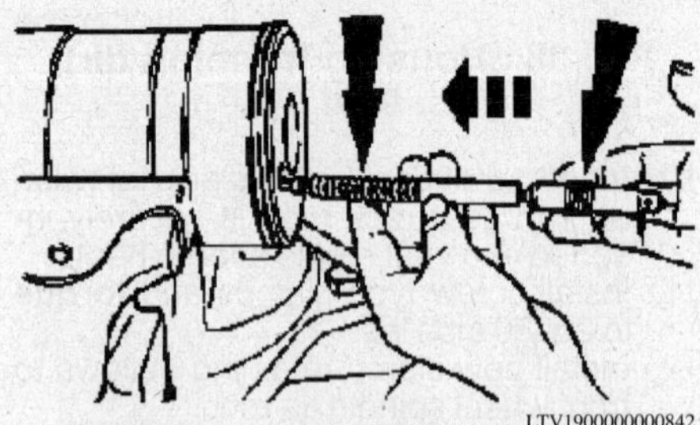

Fig. 52 Poppet installation. Aviator, Escape, F-150, Freestar, Freestyle, LT, Mariner, Monterey & Windstar

Electronic Variable Orifice (EVO) System

NOTE: On Air Bag Equipped Models, Refer To "Air Bag System Precautions" Located In The Front Of This Manual For System Disarming & Arming Procedures.

INDEX

PRECAUTIONS

Air Bag Systems

Refer to "Air Bag System Precautions" in the front of this manual for system disarming and arming procedures.

DESCRIPTION

The electronic variable orifice system, **Fig. 1,** is designed to vary the flow from the power steering pump based on vehicle speed and the rate of steering wheel rotation. The system provides full assist at low speed and minimum assist at high speed. In the event of system failure, full assist is provided.

DIAGNOSIS & TESTING

Parameter Identification (PID)

WITH AIR SUSPENSION

1. Connect New Generation Star Tester (NGS), or equivalent to data link connector below steering column.
2. Monitor PIDs STEER-A, STEER-B, and VSS-AS, then rotate steering wheel 90° left and right.
3. If either STEER-A or STEER-B PID do not toggle between high and low, go to test B.
4. Take vehicle for a test drive going 35 mph and comparing speedometer to VSS-AS output on scan tool.
5. If VSS-AS PID read within 5 mph of speedometer, end PID test.
6. Repeat test drive while monitoring generic electronic module (GEM) PID VSS-GEM.
7. If VSS-GEM PID reads within 5 mph of speedometer, repair circuit 679 (GY/BK).

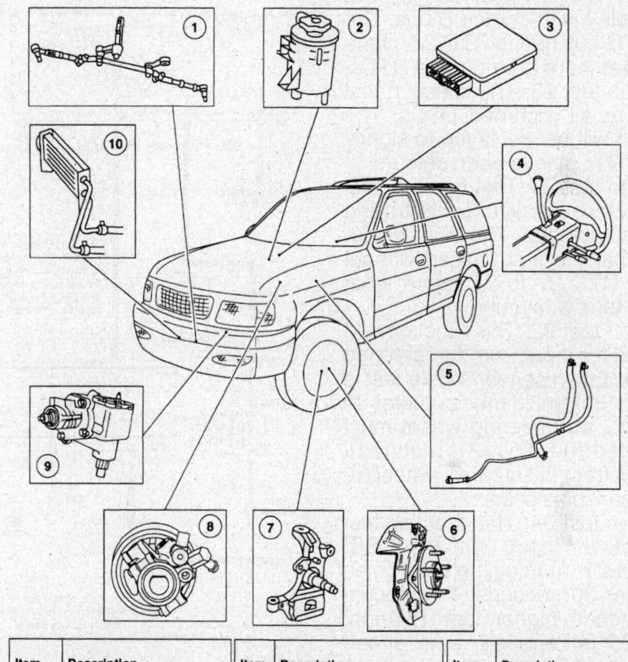

Item	Description
1	Steering Linkage
2	Power Steering Oil Reservoir
3	Air Suspension Control Module
3	Electronic Variable Orifice Control Module

Item	Description
4	Steering Wheel and Column Assembly
5	Power Steering Fluid Return Lines
6	Wheel Hub (4x4)
7	Front Wheel Spindle (4x2)

Item	Description
8	Power Steering Pump with EVO
9	Steering Gear
10	Power Steering Fluid Cooler

FM6029700251000X

Fig. 1 Component locations electronic variable orifice system

8. If VSS-GEM PID reading is not as specified, inspect transfer case.

Accessing Diagnostic Trouble Codes (DTCs)

LESS AIR SUSPENSION

1. Configure Super Star II Tester to FAST mode and EEC-IV/MCU.
2. Turn On and place Super STAR II Tester into HOLD mode.
3. Connect Super STAR II Tester to EVO diagnostic connector.
4. Turn ignition switch to RUN.
5. While Super STAR II Tester is in TEST mode, test will cycle through function test repeatedly.
6. Place Super STAR II Tester in TEST mode.
7. Run function test 21. Wait for number 21 to be displayed, then place Super STAR II Tester in HOLD mode for two

Function Test	Description
21	Read fault code?
23	Clear fault codes?
25	Carry out actuator test?
32	Carry out steering wheel rotation sensor test?
34	Carry out vehicle speed signal test?

FM6029900324000X

Fig. 2 Function test chart

seconds and then back to TEST mode.

8. If any diagnostic test codes are reported record them for test requirements to avoid misdiagnosis of the system.
9. Run each function test by placing Super STAR II Tester in HOLD mode for two seconds and then back to TEST mode. Each function test is the following, **Fig. 2.**
10. Retrieve, record and clear all DTCs.
11. The following function tests are used to retrieve DTCs, clear DTCs and run self diagnostics:
    a. Function test 21: This function test will display all recorded DTCs. The last DTC outlined is DTC 22, signifying that there are no more DTCs.
    b. Function test 23: This function test will clear all recorded DTCs. The DTC 24 will be displayed to signify that all DTCs have been deleted.
    c. Function test 25: This function test the electrical circuits for controlling the EVO actuator. The DTC 26 signifies that the test passed without errors. DTC 27 to 31 report what type of fault was found.
    d. Function test 32: This function test will look for input from the steering wheel rotation sensor. While test is running, before it times out after 30 seconds, the steering wheel must be rotated 90.° DTC 33 is reported if no input from the steering wheel rotation sensor is seen.
    e. Function test 34: This function test will look for input from the OSS. While test is running, before it times out after 30 seconds, the module must see a higher that 15 mph. DTC 35 is reported if no speed higher that 15 mph is seen.

WITH AIR SUSPENSION

There are two ways to access diagnostic trouble codes. On models less air suspension, use a Super Star II Tester or equivalent. On models equipped with air suspension, use New Generation Star (NGS) Tester or equivalent.

1. Connect a suitable scan tool to diagnostic connector located below steering wheel column.
2. Follow tool manufacture instructions to access diagnostic trouble codes.

DTC	Description	Pinpoint Test
20	Diagnostic mode entered.	—
22	End of fault codes.	—
24	Fault codes cleared.	—
26	Test passed.	—
27	Actuator open.	GO to Pinpoint Test E.
28	Actuator shorted.	GO to Pinpoint Test E.
29	Actuator high side shorted to ground.	GO to Pinpoint Test E.
30	Actuator high side or actuator low side shorted to power.	GO to Pinpoint Test E.
31	Actuator low side shorted to ground.	GO to Pinpoint Test E.
33	Steering wheel rotation not detected.	GO to Pinpoint Test F.
35	Vehicle speed greater than 24 km/h (15 mph) not detected.	GO to Pinpoint Test G.

FM6029900323000X

Fig. 3 Diagnostic trouble code interpretation

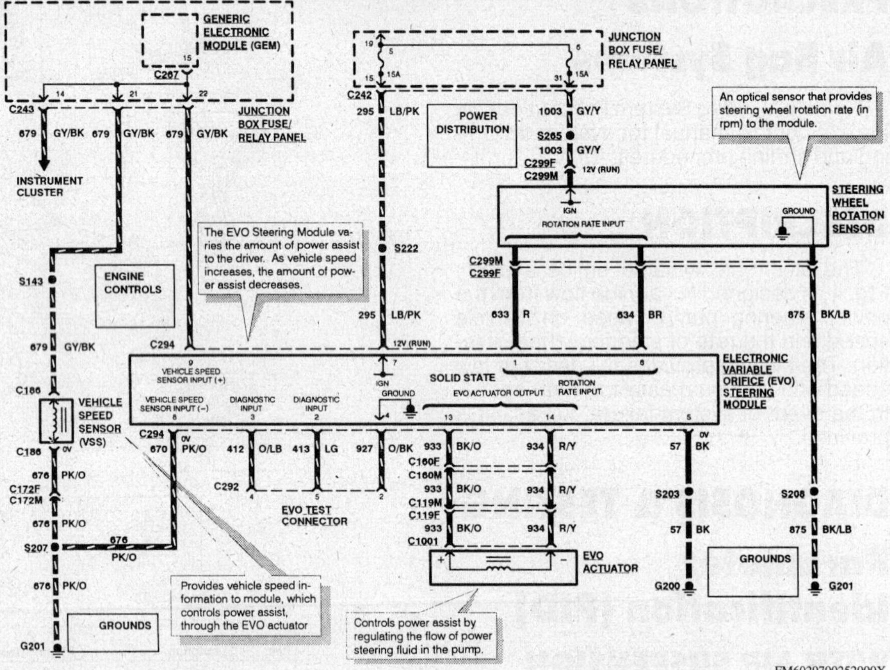

Fig. 4 Wiring diagram. Less air suspension

Diagnostic Trouble Code Interpretation

Refer to **Fig. 3** for diagnostic trouble interpretation.

Wiring Diagrams

Refer to **Figs. 4 and 5** for wiring diagrams.

Diagnostic Tests

Refer to **Fig. 6** for symptom chart and **Figs. 7 through 15** for pinpoint tests.

Clearing Diagnostic Trouble Codes

Connect a suitably programmed scan tool to Data Link Connector (DLC) and follow manufacturer's instructions.

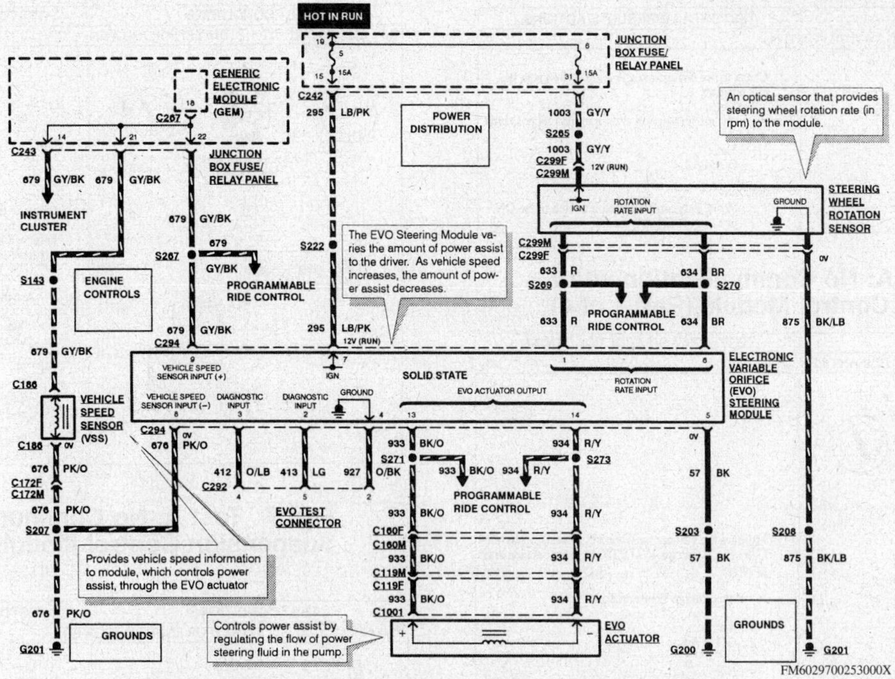

Fig. 5 Wiring diagram. With air suspension

Condition	Possible Source	Action
• No communication with the air suspension control module	• CJB Fuse 4 (15A), 6 (5A), 20 (5A). • Circuitry. • Air suspension control module.	• GO to Pinpoint Test A.
• No communication with the electronic variable orifice control module	• CJB Fuse 5 (15A). • Circuitry. • EVO control module.	• GO to Pinpoint Test B.
• Unable to enter self-test — with air suspension	• Air suspension control module.	• GO to Pinpoint Test C.
• Unable to enter self-test — without air suspension	• EVO control module.	• GO to Pinpoint Test D.
• Steering does not vary with vehicle speed	• Output shaft speed (OSS) sensor. • Circuitry. • EVO control module or air suspension control module.	• GO to Pinpoint Test G.
• Steering very difficult/very easy	• Power steering pump. • Power steering linkage. • Steering pivot. • Steering gear.	• GO to Pinpoint Test H.
• Steering does not vary with increased wheel rotation	• Power steering pump. • Power steering hose(s).	• GO to Pinpoint Test I.
• Engine stalls with high wheel rotation	• Powertrain control module (PCM).	• Diagnose idle control.

FM6029900322000X

Fig. 6 Symptom chart

DIAGNOSTIC CHART INDEX

Test	Code	Description	Page No.	Fig. No.
Test A	—	No Communication w/Air Suspension Control Module	13-20	7
Test B	—	No Communication w/Electronic Variable Orifice	13-20	8
Test C	—	Unable To Enter Self Test	13-21	9
Test D	—	Unable To Enter Self Test	13-21	10
Test E	27	Electronic Variable Orifice Control Valve Actuator Concern	13-21	11
	28	Electronic Variable Orifice Control Valve Actuator Concern	13-21	11
	29	Electronic Variable Orifice Control Valve Actuator Concern	13-21	11
	30	Electronic Variable Orifice Control Valve Actuator Concern	13-21	11
	31	Electronic Variable Orifice Control Valve Actuator Concern	13-21	11
	C1917	Electronic Variable Orifice Control Valve Actuator Concern	13-21	11
Test F	33	Steering Wheel Rotation Not Detected	13-22	12
Test G	—	Steering Does Not Vary w/Vehicle Speed	13-24	13
Test H	—	Steering Very Difficult/Very Easy	13-24	14
Test I	—	Steering Does Not Vary w/Increased Wheel Rotation	13-25	15

TEST CONDITIONS	TESTDETAILS/RESULTS/ACTIONS
A1 CHECK THE AIR SUSPENSION SWITCH POSITION	
	1 Check to see if the air suspension switch is in the ON position. • Is the air suspension switch in the ON position? → **Yes** GO to **A2**. → **No** PLACE the air suspension switch in the ON position. REPEAT the self-test.

FM6029900325010X

Fig. 7 Test A: No Communication w/Air Suspension Control Module (Part 1 of 4)

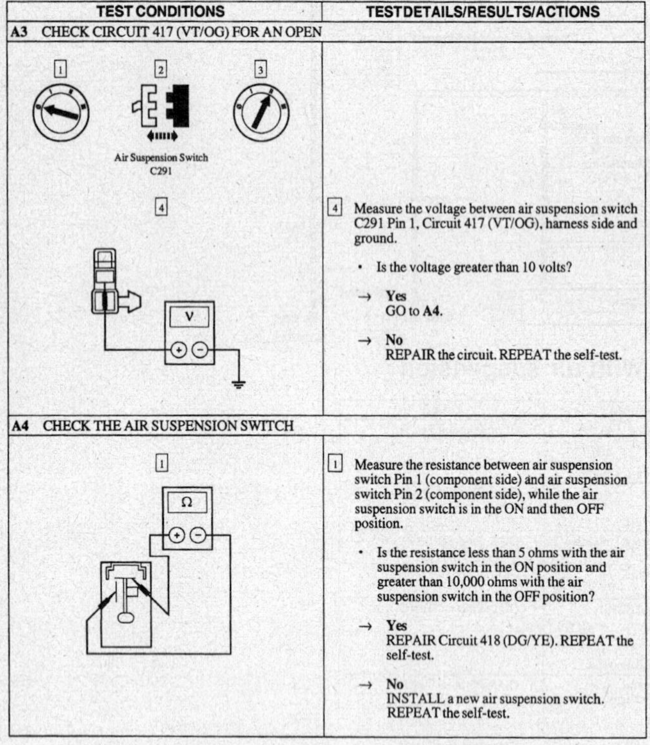

TEST CONDITIONS	TESTDETAILS/RESULTS/ACTIONS
A3 CHECK CIRCUIT 417 (VT/OG) FOR AN OPEN	
1 2 3 Air Suspension Switch C291	
4	4 Measure the voltage between air suspension switch C291 Pin 1, Circuit 417 (VT/OG), harness side and ground. • Is the voltage greater than 10 volts? → **Yes** GO to **A4**. → **No** REPAIR the circuit. REPEAT the self-test.
A4 CHECK THE AIR SUSPENSION SWITCH	
1	1 Measure the resistance between air suspension switch Pin 1 (component side) and air suspension switch Pin 2 (component side), while the air suspension switch is in the ON and then OFF position. • Is the resistance less than 5 ohms with the air suspension switch in the ON position and greater than 10,000 ohms with the air suspension switch in the OFF position? → **Yes** REPAIR Circuit 418 (DG/YE). REPEAT the self-test. → **No** INSTALL a new air suspension switch. REPEAT the self-test.

FM6029900325030X

Fig. 7 Test A: No Communication w/Air Suspension Control Module (Part 3 of 4)

TEST CONDITIONS	TESTDETAILS/RESULTS/ACTIONS
A5 CHECK CIRCUIT 432 (PK/LB), 57 (BK) AND 875 (BK/LB) FOR AN OPEN	
1	
	2 Place the air suspension switch in the OFF position.
3 Air Suspension Control Module C296	
4	4 Measure the resistance between air suspension control module C296 Pin 20, Circuit 432 (BK/PK), harness side and ground; and between air suspension control module C296 Pin 32, Circuit 57 (BK), harness side and ground. • Are the resistances less than 5 ohms? → **Yes** Diagnose module communications network. → **No** REPAIR Circuit 432 (BK/PK), Circuit 875 (BK/LB), and Circuit 57 (BK) as necessary. REPEAT the self-test.

FM6029900325040X

Fig. 7 Test A: No Communication w/Air Suspension Control Module (Part 4 of 4)

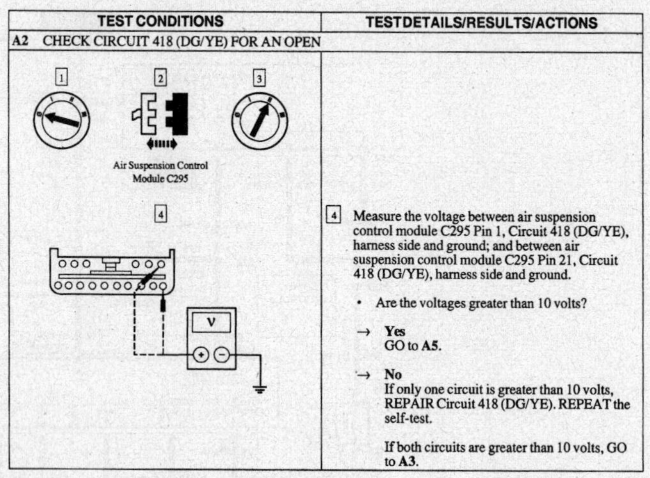

TEST CONDITIONS	TESTDETAILS/RESULTS/ACTIONS
A2 CHECK CIRCUIT 418 (DG/YE) FOR AN OPEN	
1 2 3 Air Suspension Control Module C295	
4	4 Measure the voltage between air suspension control module C295 Pin 1, Circuit 418 (DG/YE), harness side and ground; and between air suspension control module C295 Pin 21, Circuit 418 (DG/YE), harness side and ground. • Are the voltages greater than 10 volts? → **Yes** GO to **A5**. → **No** If only one circuit is greater than 10 volts, REPAIR Circuit 418 (DG/YE). REPEAT the self-test. If both circuits are greater than 10 volts, GO to **A3**.

FM6029900325020X

Fig. 7 Test A: No Communication w/Air Suspension Control Module (Part 2 of 4)

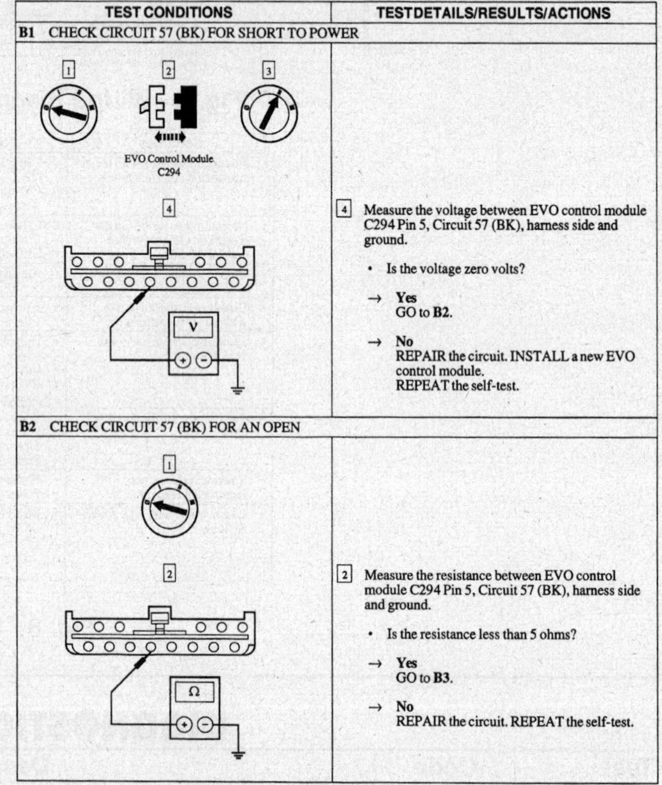

TEST CONDITIONS	TESTDETAILS/RESULTS/ACTIONS
B1 CHECK CIRCUIT 57 (BK) FOR SHORT TO POWER	
1 2 3 EVO Control Module C294	
4	4 Measure the voltage between EVO control module C294 Pin 5, Circuit 57 (BK), harness side and ground. • Is the voltage zero volts? → **Yes** GO to **B2**. → **No** REPAIR the circuit. INSTALL a new EVO control module. REPEAT the self-test.
B2 CHECK CIRCUIT 57 (BK) FOR AN OPEN	
1	
2	2 Measure the resistance between EVO control module C294 Pin 5, Circuit 57 (BK), harness side and ground. • Is the resistance less than 5 ohms? → **Yes** GO to **B3**. → **No** REPAIR the circuit. REPEAT the self-test.

FM6029900326010X

Fig. 8 Test B: No Communication w/Electronic Variable Orifice (Part 1 of 3)

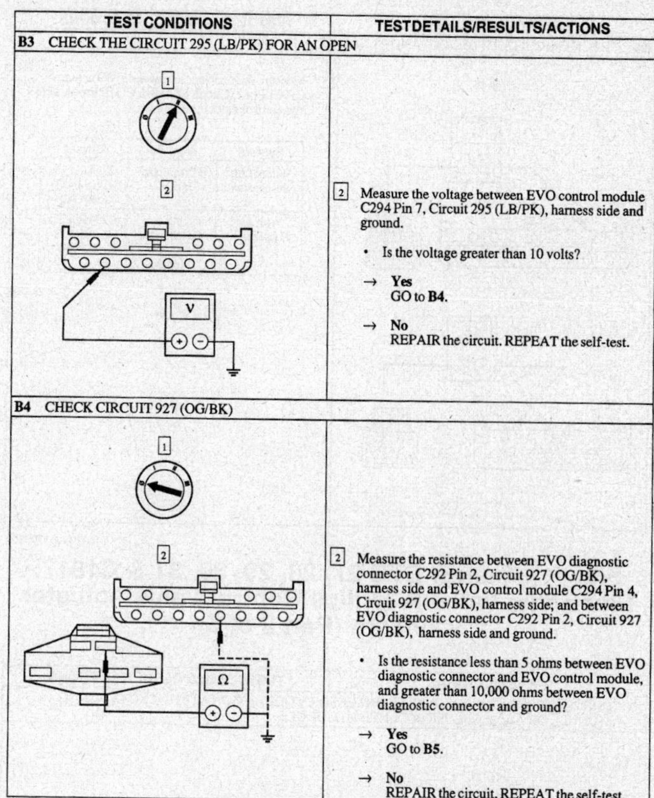

TEST CONDITIONS	TEST DETAILS/RESULTS/ACTIONS
B3 CHECK THE CIRCUIT 295 (LB/PK) FOR AN OPEN	
1	
2	2 Measure the voltage between EVO control module C294 Pin 7, Circuit 295 (LB/PK), harness side and ground. • Is the voltage greater than 10 volts? → **Yes** GO to **B4**. → **No** REPAIR the circuit. REPEAT the self-test.
B4 CHECK CIRCUIT 927 (OG/BK)	
1	
2	2 Measure the resistance between EVO diagnostic connector C292 Pin 2, Circuit 927 (OG/BK), harness side and EVO control module C294 Pin 4, Circuit 927 (OG/BK), harness side; and between EVO diagnostic connector C292 Pin 2, Circuit 927 (OG/BK), harness side and ground. • Is the resistance less than 5 ohms between EVO diagnostic connector and EVO control module, and greater than 10,000 ohms between EVO diagnostic connector and ground? → **Yes** GO to **B5**. → **No** REPAIR the circuit. REPEAT the self-test.

FM6029900326020X

Fig. 8 Test B: No Communication w/Electronic Variable Orifice (Part 2 of 3)

TEST CONDITIONS	TEST DETAILS/RESULTS/ACTIONS
C1 CHECK THE COMMUNICATIONS TO THE AIR SUSPENSION CONTROL MODULE	
	1 Check the communication to the air suspension control module. • Does NGS Tester communicate with the air suspension control module? → **Yes** INSTALL a new air suspension control module. REPEAT the self-test. → **No** GO to Pinpoint Test A.

FM6029900327000X

Fig. 9 Test C: Unable To Enter Self Test. With Air Suspension

TEST CONDITIONS	TEST DETAILS/RESULTS/ACTIONS
D1 CHECK THE COMMUNICATIONS TO THE EVO CONTROL MODULE	
	1 Check the communication to the EVO control module. • Does NGS Tester communicate with the EVO control module? → **Yes** INSTALL a new EVO control module. REPEAT the self-test. → **No** GO to Pinpoint Test B.

FM6029900328000X

Fig. 10 Test D: Unable To Enter Self Test. Less Air Suspension

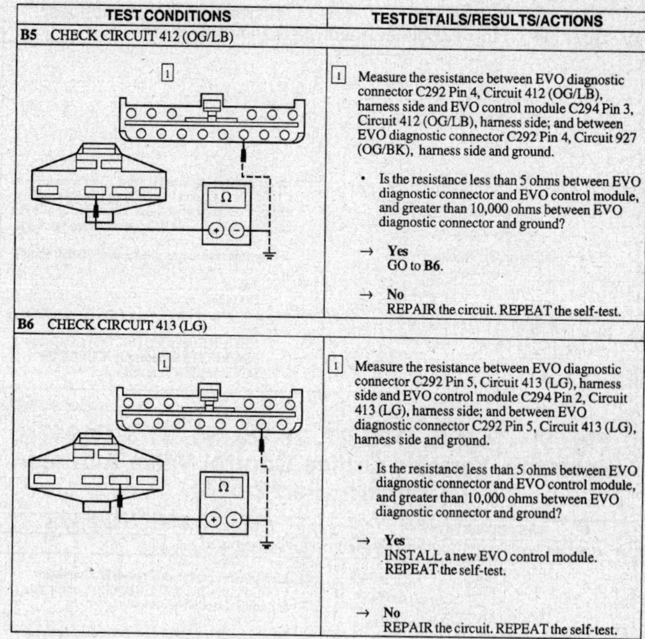

TEST CONDITIONS	TEST DETAILS/RESULTS/ACTIONS
B5 CHECK CIRCUIT 412 (OG/LB)	
1	1 Measure the resistance between EVO diagnostic connector C292 Pin 4, Circuit 412 (OG/LB), harness side and EVO control module C294 Pin 3, Circuit 412 (OG/LB), harness side; and between EVO diagnostic connector C292 Pin 4, Circuit 927 (OG/BK), harness side and ground. • Is the resistance less than 5 ohms between EVO diagnostic connector and EVO control module, and greater than 10,000 ohms between EVO diagnostic connector and ground? → **Yes** GO to **B6**. → **No** REPAIR the circuit. REPEAT the self-test.
B6 CHECK CIRCUIT 413 (LG)	
1	1 Measure the resistance between EVO diagnostic connector C292 Pin 5, Circuit 413 (LG), harness side and EVO control module C294 Pin 2, Circuit 413 (LG), harness side; and between EVO diagnostic connector C292 Pin 5, Circuit 413 (LG), harness side and ground. • Is the resistance less than 5 ohms between EVO diagnostic connector and EVO control module, and greater than 10,000 ohms between EVO diagnostic connector and ground? → **Yes** INSTALL a new EVO control module. REPEAT the self-test. → **No** REPAIR the circuit. REPEAT the self-test.

FM6029900326030X

Fig. 8 Test B: No Communication w/Electronic Variable Orifice (Part 3 of 3)

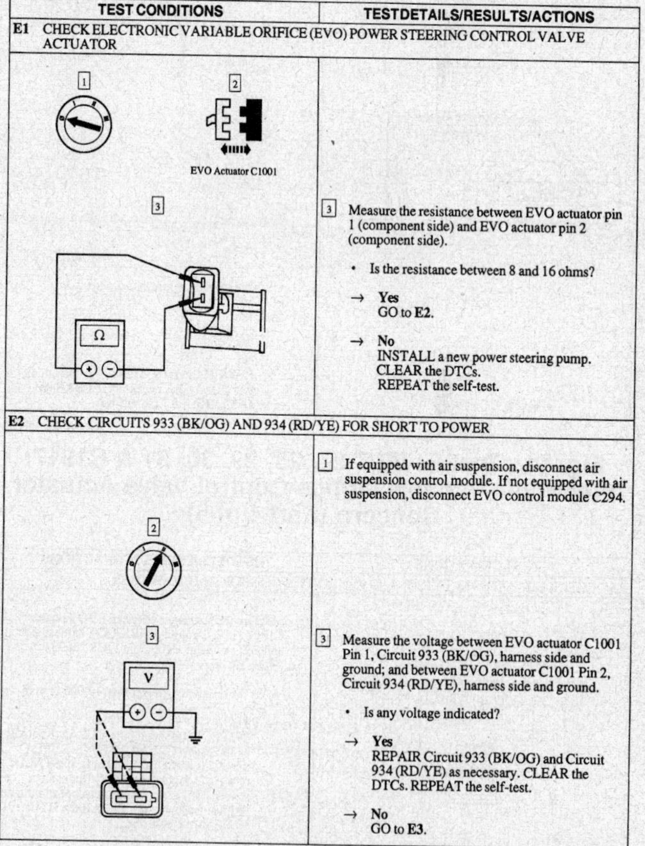

TEST CONDITIONS	TEST DETAILS/RESULTS/ACTIONS
E1 CHECK ELECTRONIC VARIABLE ORIFICE (EVO) POWER STEERING CONTROL VALVE ACTUATOR	
1 2	
3	3 Measure the resistance between EVO actuator pin 1 (component side) and EVO actuator pin 2 (component side). • Is the resistance between 8 and 16 ohms? → **Yes** GO to **E2**. → **No** INSTALL a new power steering pump. CLEAR the DTCs. REPEAT the self-test.
E2 CHECK CIRCUITS 933 (BK/OG) AND 934 (RD/YE) FOR SHORT TO POWER	
	1 If equipped with air suspension, disconnect air suspension control module. If not equipped with air suspension, disconnect EVO control module C294.
2	
3	3 Measure the voltage between EVO actuator C1001 Pin 1, Circuit 933 (BK/OG), harness side and ground; and between EVO actuator C1001 Pin 2, Circuit 934 (RD/YE), harness side and ground. • Is any voltage indicated? → **Yes** REPAIR Circuit 933 (BK/OG) and Circuit 934 (RD/YE) as necessary. CLEAR the DTCs. REPEAT the self-test. → **No** GO to **E3**.

FM6029900329010X

Fig. 11 Test E: DTC 27, 28, 29, 30, 31 & C1917: Electronic Variable Orifice Control Valve Actuator Concern (Part 1 of 5)

TEST CONDITIONS	TEST DETAILS/RESULTS/ACTIONS
E3 CHECK CIRCUITS 933 (BK/OG) AND 934 (RD/YE) FOR SHORT TO GROUND	
1 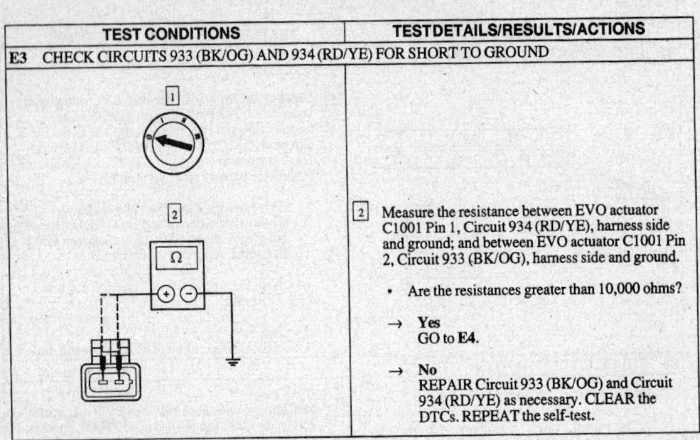 2	2 Measure the resistance between EVO actuator C1001 Pin 1, Circuit 934 (RD/YE), harness side and ground; and between EVO actuator C1001 Pin 2, Circuit 933 (BK/OG), harness side and ground. • Are the resistances greater than 10,000 ohms? → **Yes** GO to **E4**. → **No** REPAIR Circuit 933 (BK/OG) and Circuit 934 (RD/YE) as necessary. CLEAR the DTCs. REPEAT the self-test.

FM6029900329020X

Fig. 11 Test E: DTC 27, 28, 29, 30, 31 & C1917: Electronic Variable Orifice Control Valve Actuator Concern (Part 2 of 5)

TEST CONDITIONS	TEST DETAILS/RESULTS/ACTIONS
E4 CHECK CIRCUITS 933 (BK/OG) AND 934 (RD/YE) FOR OPENS (Continued)	
2	2 Measure the resistance between EVO actuator C1001 Pin 1, Circuit 934 (RD/YE), harness side and control module as follows:

System	Module	Circuit
Without Air Suspension	EVO Control Module	C294 Pin 14, Circuit 934 (RD/YE)
With Air Suspension	Air Suspension Control Module	C295 Pin 26, Circuit 934 (RD/YE)

• Is the resistance less than 5 ohms?

→ **Yes** GO to **E5**.

→ **No** REPAIR Circuit 933 (BK/OG) and circuit 934 (RD/YE) as necessary. CLEAR the DTCs. REPEAT the self-test.

FM6029900329040X

Fig. 11 Test E: DTC 27, 28, 29, 30, 31 & C1917: Electronic Variable Orifice Control Valve Actuator Concern (Part 4 of 5)

TEST CONDITIONS	TEST DETAILS/RESULTS/ACTIONS
E5 CHECK CIRCUITS 933 (BK/OG) AND 934 (RD/YE) FOR SHORTING TOGETHER	
1	1 Measure the resistance between EVO actuator C1001 Pin 2, Circuit 933 (BK/OG), harness side and EVO actuator C1001 Pin 1, Circuit 934 (RD/YE), harness side. • Is the resistance greater than 10,000 ohms? → **Yes** INSPECT connector pins. CLEAN/REPAIR as necessary. CLEAR the DTCs. REPEAT the self-test. If DTC 35 repeats, INSTALL a new EVO control module (without air suspension) or air suspension control module (with air suspension). CLEAR the DTCs. REPEAT the self-test. → **No** REPAIR Circuits 933 (BK/OG) and 934 (RD/YE) as necessary. CLEAR the DTCs. REPEAT the self-test.

FM6029900329050X

Fig. 11 Test E: DTC 27, 28, 29, 30, 31 & C1917: Electronic Variable Orifice Control Valve Actuator Concern (Part 5 of 5)

TEST CONDITIONS	TEST DETAILS/RESULTS/ACTIONS
E4 CHECK CIRCUITS 933 (BK/OG) AND 934 (RD/YE) FOR OPENS	
1 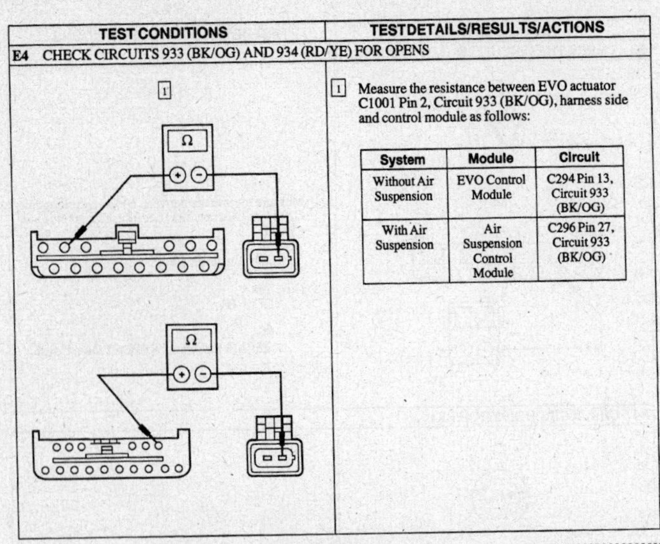	1 Measure the resistance between EVO actuator C1001 Pin 2, Circuit 933 (BK/OG), harness side and control module as follows:

System	Module	Circuit
Without Air Suspension	EVO Control Module	C294 Pin 13, Circuit 933 (BK/OG)
With Air Suspension	Air Suspension Control Module	C296 Pin 27, Circuit 933 (BK/OG)

FM6029900329030X

Fig. 11 Test E: DTC 27, 28, 29, 30, 31 & C1917: Electronic Variable Orifice Control Valve Actuator Concern (Part 3 of 5)

TEST CONDITIONS	TEST DETAILS/RESULTS/ACTIONS
F1 CHECK STEERING WHEEL ROTATION SENSOR MODULATION AT THE EVO CONTROL MODULE OR AIR SUSPENSION CONTROL MODULE	
1	
	2 If equipped with air suspension, disconnect air suspension control module C295. If not equipped with air suspension, disconnect EVO control module C294.
3	
	4 Place the 73 Digital Multimeter in the diode check position.

FM6029900330010X

Fig. 12 Test F: DTC 33: Steering Wheel Rotation Not Detected (Part 1 of 7)

TEST CONDITIONS	TEST DETAILS/RESULTS/ACTIONS
F1 CHECK STEERING WHEEL ROTATION SENSOR MODULATION AT THE EVO CONTROL MODULE OR AIR SUSPENSION CONTROL MODULE (Continued)	
5 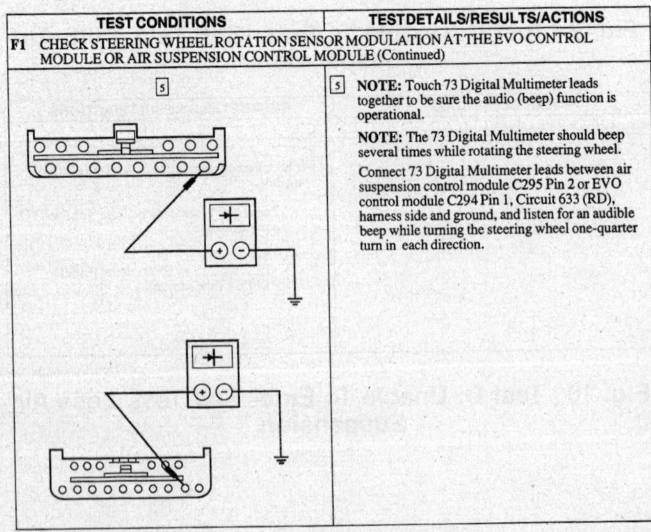	5 **NOTE:** Touch 73 Digital Multimeter leads together to be sure the audio (beep) function is operational. **NOTE:** The 73 Digital Multimeter should beep several times while rotating the steering wheel. Connect 73 Digital Multimeter leads between air suspension control module C295 Pin 2 or EVO control module C294 Pin 1, Circuit 633 (RD), harness side and ground, and listen for an audible beep while turning the steering wheel one-quarter turn in each direction.

FM6029900330020X

Fig. 12 Test F: DTC 33: Steering Wheel Rotation Not Detected (Part 2 of 7)

TEST CONDITIONS	TEST DETAILS/RESULTS/ACTIONS
F1 CHECK STEERING WHEEL ROTATION SENSOR MODULATION AT THE EVO CONTROL MODULE OR AIR SUSPENSION CONTROL MODULE (Continued)	
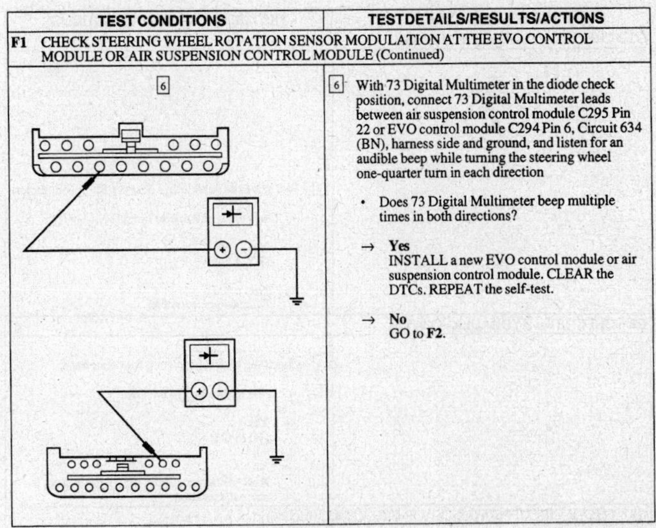 6	6 With 73 Digital Multimeter in the diode check position, connect 73 Digital Multimeter leads between air suspension control module C295 Pin 22 or EVO control module C294 Pin 6, Circuit 634 (BN), harness side and ground, and listen for an audible beep while turning the steering wheel one-quarter turn in each direction • Does 73 Digital Multimeter beep multiple times in both directions? → **Yes** INSTALL a new EVO control module or air suspension control module. CLEAR the DTCs. REPEAT the self-test. → **No** GO to **F2**.

FM6029900330030X

Fig. 12 Test F: DTC 33: Steering Wheel Rotation Not Detected (Part 3 of 7)

TEST CONDITIONS	TEST DETAILS/RESULTS/ACTIONS
F4 CHECK CIRCUITS 633 (RD) AND 634 (BN) FOR SHORT TO POWER	
1	1 Measure the voltage between steering wheel rotation sensor C299 Pin 2, Circuit 633 (RD), harness side and ground; and between steering wheel rotation sensor C299 Pin 3, Circuit 634 (BN), harness side and ground. • Is the voltage greater than 10 volts? → **Yes** REPAIR Circuit 633 (RD) and 634 (BN) as necessary. CLEAR the DTCs. REPEAT the self-test. → **No** GO to **F5**.
F5 CHECK CIRCUITS 633 (RD) AND 634 (BN) FOR SHORT TO GROUND	
1 2	2 Measure the resistance between steering wheel rotation sensor C299 Pin 2, Circuit 633 (RD), harness side and ground; and between steering wheel rotation sensor C299 Pin 3, Circuit 634 (BN), harness side and ground. • Is the resistance greater than 10,000 ohms? → **Yes** GO to **F6**. → **No** REPAIR Circuit 633 (RD) or Circuit 634 (BN). CLEAR the DTCs. REPEAT the self-test.

FM6029900330050X

Fig. 12 Test F: DTC 33: Steering Wheel Rotation Not Detected (Part 5 of 7)

TEST CONDITIONS	TEST DETAILS/RESULTS/ACTIONS
F2 CHECK STEERING WHEEL ROTATION SENSOR FOR VOLTAGE AND GROUND	
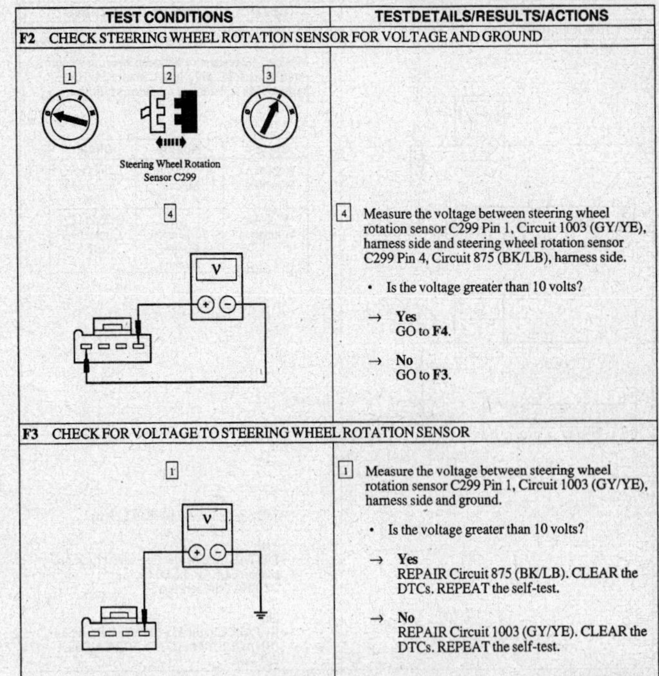	4 Measure the voltage between steering wheel rotation sensor C299 Pin 1, Circuit 1003 (GY/YE), harness side and steering wheel rotation sensor C299 Pin 4, Circuit 875 (BK/LB), harness side. • Is the voltage greater than 10 volts? → **Yes** GO to **F4**. → **No** GO to **F3**.
F3 CHECK FOR VOLTAGE TO STEERING WHEEL ROTATION SENSOR	
1	1 Measure the voltage between steering wheel rotation sensor C299 Pin 1, Circuit 1003 (GY/YE), harness side and ground. • Is the voltage greater than 10 volts? → **Yes** REPAIR Circuit 875 (BK/LB). CLEAR the DTCs. REPEAT the self-test. → **No** REPAIR Circuit 1003 (GY/YE). CLEAR the DTCs. REPEAT the self-test.

FM6029900330040X

Fig. 12 Test F, DTC 33: Steering Wheel Rotation Not Detected (Part 4 of 7)

TEST CONDITIONS	TEST DETAILS/RESULTS/ACTIONS
F6 CHECK CIRCUITS 633 (RD) AND 634 (BN) FOR OPEN	
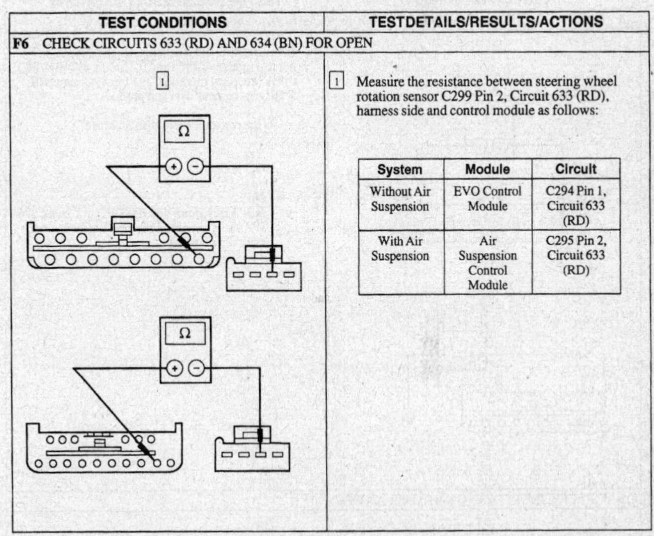 1	1 Measure the resistance between steering wheel rotation sensor C299 Pin 2, Circuit 633 (RD), harness side and control module as follows:

System	Module	Circuit
Without Air Suspension	EVO Control Module	C294 Pin 1, Circuit 633 (RD)
With Air Suspension	Air Suspension Control Module	C295 Pin 2, Circuit 633 (RD)

FM6029900330060X

Fig. 12 Test F: DTC 33: Steering Wheel Rotation Not Detected (Part 6 of 7)

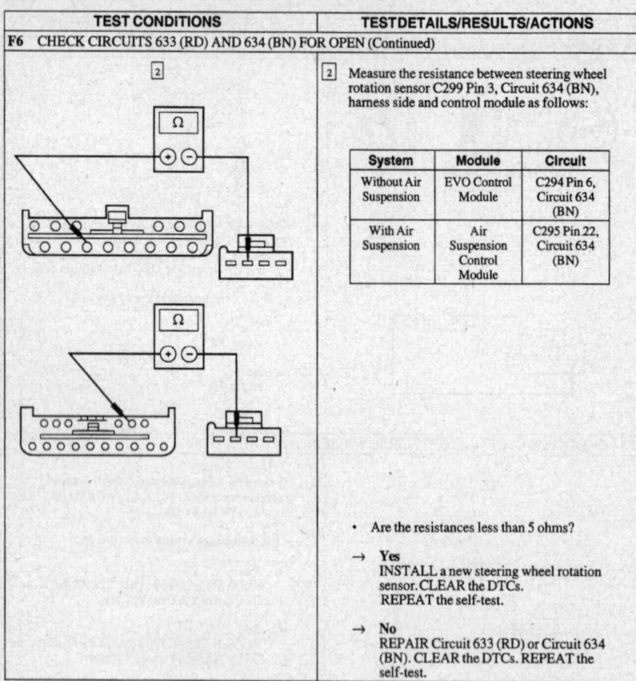

TEST CONDITIONS	TEST DETAILS/RESULTS/ACTIONS
F6 CHECK CIRCUITS 633 (RD) AND 634 (BN) FOR OPEN (Continued)	
2	2 Measure the resistance between steering wheel rotation sensor C299 Pin 3, Circuit 634 (BN), harness side and control module as follows:

System	Module	Circuit
Without Air Suspension	EVO Control Module	C294 Pin 6, Circuit 634 (BN)
With Air Suspension	Air Suspension Control Module	C295 Pin 22, Circuit 634 (BN)

- Are the resistances less than 5 ohms?

→ **Yes**
INSTALL a new steering wheel rotation sensor. CLEAR the DTCs. REPEAT the self-test.

→ **No**
REPAIR Circuit 633 (RD) or Circuit 634 (BN). CLEAR the DTCs. REPEAT the self-test.

FM6029900330070X

Fig. 12 Test F: DTC 33: Steering Wheel Rotation Not Detected (Part 7 of 7)

TEST CONDITIONS	TEST DETAILS/RESULTS/ACTIONS
G3 CHECK CIRCUIT 676 (PK/OG) OR CIRCUIT 432 (BK/PK) FOR AN OPEN (Continued)	
3	3 Measure the resistance between air suspension control module C296 Pin 20, Circuit 432 (BK/PK), or EVO control module C294 Pin 8, Circuit 676 (PK/OG), harness side and ground. • Is the resistance less than 5 ohms? → **Yes** GO to **G4**. → **No** REPAIR Circuit 432 (BK/PK) or Circuit 676 (PK/OG) as necessary. TEST the system for normal operation.
G4 CHECK CIRCUIT 679 (GY/BK) FOR AN OPEN	
1 PCM C174	2 Connect EEC-V 104-Pin Breakout Box.

FM6029900331020X

Fig. 13 Test G: Steering Does Not Vary w/Vehicle Speed (Part 2 of 3)

TEST CONDITIONS	TEST DETAILS/RESULTS/ACTIONS
G1 CHECK SPEEDOMETER OPERATION	
1	2 Test drive the vehicle and observe the speedometer. • Does the speedometer operate? → **Yes** GO to **G2**. → **No** Diagnose speedometer
G2 CHECK THE HYDRAULIC SYSTEM	
	1 Check the hydraulic system for concerns. • Is the hydraulic system OK? → **Yes** GO to **G3**. → **No** REPAIR as necessary. TEST the system for normal operation.
G3 CHECK CIRCUIT 676 (PK/OG) OR CIRCUIT 432 (BK/PK) FOR AN OPEN	
1	2 If equipped with air suspension, disconnect air suspension control module C295 and C296. If not equipped with air suspension, disconnect EVO control module C294.

FM6029900331010X

Fig. 13 Test G: Steering Does Not Vary w/Vehicle Speed (Part 1 of 3)

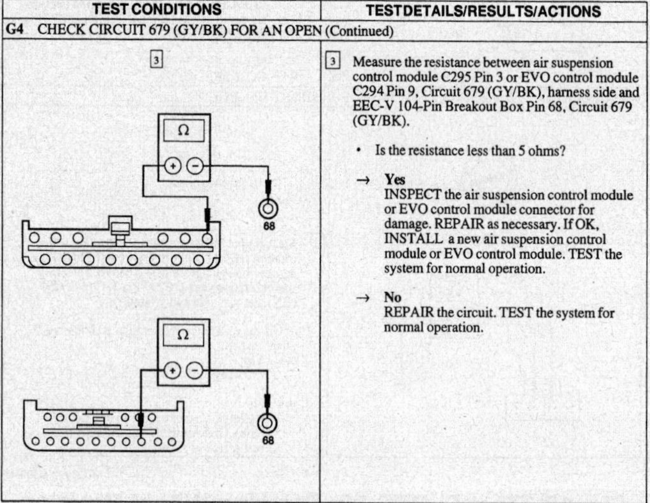

TEST CONDITIONS	TEST DETAILS/RESULTS/ACTIONS
G4 CHECK CIRCUIT 679 (GY/BK) FOR AN OPEN (Continued)	
3	3 Measure the resistance between air suspension control module C295 Pin 3 or EVO control module C294 Pin 9, Circuit 679 (GY/BK), harness side and EEC-V 104-Pin Breakout Box Pin 68, Circuit 679 (GY/BK). • Is the resistance less than 5 ohms? → **Yes** INSPECT the air suspension control module or EVO control module connector for damage. REPAIR as necessary. If OK, INSTALL a new air suspension control module or EVO control module. TEST the system for normal operation. → **No** REPAIR the circuit. TEST the system for normal operation.

FM6029900331030X

Fig. 13 Test G: Steering Does Not Vary w/Vehicle Speed (Part 3 of 3)

TEST CONDITIONS	TEST DETAILS/RESULTS/ACTIONS
H1 CHECK THE POWER STEERING PUMP	
1	2 Check the power steering pump for leaks by rotating the steering wheel (3600) while observing the power steering pump (3A674).

FM6029900332010X

Fig. 14 Test H: Steering Very Difficult/Very Easy (Part 1 of 3)

TEST CONDITIONS	TEST DETAILS/RESULTS/ACTIONS
H1 CHECK THE POWER STEERING PUMP (Continued)	
	[3] Carry out the Pump Flow and Pressure Test. Go to Pump Flow and Pressure Test. • Is the power steering pump OK? → **Yes** GO to **H2.** → **No** INSTALL a new power steering pump. TEST the system for normal operation.
H2 CHECK THE STEERING LINKAGE	
	[1] Visually check the steering linkage while an assistant rotates the steering wheel from stop to stop. • Does the steering linkage move smoothly from stop to stop? → **Yes** GO to **H3.** → **No** INSTALL a new steering linkage component(s). TEST the system for normal operation.
H3 CHECK THE STEERING PIVOT	
[1]	[2] Check the ball joints for binding, lack of lubrication or worn surfaces. • Are the steering pivot points OK? → **Yes** GO to **H4.** → **No** LUBRICATE components as necessary. INSTALL new ball joint(s) if worn. TEST the system for normal operation.

FM6029900332020X

Fig. 14 Test H: Steering Very Difficult/Very Easy (Part 2 of 3)

POWER STEERING SYSTEM BLEED

Refer to "Power Steering Pump" section for system bleed procedure.

COMPONENT SERVICE

Control Module, Replace

1. Remove center instrument panel around radio, then steering column cover trim panel.
2. Remove headlamp switch as outlined in "Electrical" section of chassis chapter.
3. Remove left side instrument panel finish panel as outlined in "Dash Panel Service" chapter.
4. Remove instrument cluster panel, disconnect module electrical connectors and remove control module mounting bracket screws, **Fig. 16.**
5. Reverse procedure to install. Vehicle may need to be driven 10 or more miles to relearn strategy.

TEST CONDITIONS	TEST DETAILS/RESULTS/ACTIONS
H4 CHECK THE STEERING GEAR	
	[1] Visually check the steering gear operation while an assistant rotates the steering wheel from stop to stop. [2] Check the steering gear mounting fasteners for loose bolts. • Is the steering gear OK? → **Yes** If the condition still exists. REFER to the Symptom Chart. → **No** REPAIR as necessary. TEST the system for normal operation.

FM6029900332030X

Fig. 14 Test H: Steering Very Difficult/Very Easy (Part 3 of 3)

TEST CONDITIONS	TEST DETAILS/RESULTS/ACTIONS
I1 CHECK THE POWER STEERING PUMP	
[1]	[2] Check the power steering pump for leaks by rotating the steering wheel while watching the power steering pump. [3] Carry out the power steering Pump Flow and Pressure Test. Go to Pump Flow and Pressure Test. • Is the power steering pump OK? → **Yes** INSPECT for kinked lines or hoses from the power steering pump. INSTALL new lines or hoses as necessary. TEST the system for normal operation. → **No** INSTALL a new power steering pump; TEST the system for normal operation. GO to Pinpoint Test H.

FM6029900333000X

Fig. 15 Test I: Steering Does Not Vary w/Increased Wheel Rotation

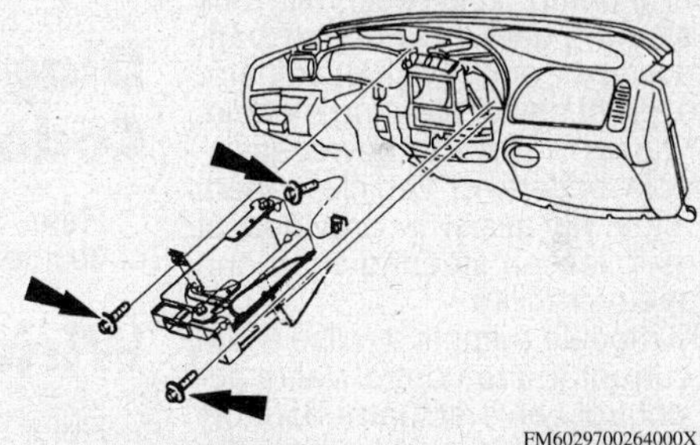

Fig. 16 Control module removal. Expedition & Navigator

Variable Assist Power Steering System (VAPS)

NOTE: On Air Bag Equipped Models, Refer To "Air Bag System Precautions" Located In The Front Of This Manual For System Disarming & Arming Procedures.

INDEX

PRECAUTIONS

Air Bag Systems

Refer to "Air Bag System Precautions" in the front of this manual for system disarming and arming procedures.

DESCRIPTION

The power steering system consists of a power steering pump, fluid reservoir, rack and pinion steering gear, fluid cooler, variable assist power steering (VAPS) actuator and variable assist power steering module. The system varies the level of power assistance available based on vehicle speed. Full power steering assist is provided at lower speeds to lessen steering effort and increase maneuverability.

The VAPS module outputs a pulse width modulated current to the control valve actuator. The control valve actuator controls the hydraulic valve which determines the amount of hydraulic assist provided. Vehicle speed is provided to the VAPS module by the powertrain control module.

TROUBLESHOOTING

Refer to **Fig. 1** for steering system troubleshooting procedures.

Condition	Possible Sources	Action
• No communication with the air suspension module	• Circuit(s). • Air suspension control module.	• GO to Pinpoint Test A.
• Steering system noise	• Low fluid level. • Fluid aeration. • Steering gear. • Power steering pump. • Loose or damaged steering linkage. • Loose or damaged suspension component(s). • Steering column. • Steering column boot bearing. • Intermediate shaft. • Loose dash boot seal.	• GO to Pinpoint Test C.

LTV0500000001122

Fig. 1 Steering system troubleshooting (Part 1 of 3)

DIAGNOSIS & TESTING

Accessing Diagnostic Trouble Codes

Connect a suitably programmed scan tool to Data Link Connector (DLC) and follow manufacturer's instructions.

Diagnostic Trouble Code Interpretation

Refer to **Fig. 2** for diagnostic trouble code interpretation.

Wiring Diagram

Refer to **Fig. 3** for wiring diagram.

Pinpoint Tests

Refer to **Figs. 4 through 9** for diagnostic pinpoint tests.

Clearing Diagnostic Trouble Codes

Connect a suitably programmed scan tool to Data Link Connector (DLC) and follow manufacturer's instructions.

Component Tests

STEERING LINKAGE

1. **Excessive vertical motion of studs relative to sockets may indicate excessive wear.** With vehicle on ground and parking brake applied, start engine.
2. Have an assistant rotate steering wheel back and forth 360°, then watch for relative motion of studs in steering linkage ball sockets and for loose steering gear mounting.
3. With key ON engine OFF and front wheels raised off ground, grasp wheel at front and rear and watch for excessive play or binding in joints while trying to steer wheels.
4. Install new components if required, tighten any worn, damaged or loose components.

TURNING EFFORT

Ensure the front wheels are correctly aligned and tire pressure is correct before inspecting steering effort.

1. Park vehicle on dry concrete and set parking brake, then insert a thermometer into power steering fluid reservoir.
2. **Do not hold steering wheel against stops for more than 3 to 5 seconds at a time. Damage to power steering pump can occur.** Idle engine for two to three minutes, then turn steering wheel from stop to stop several times to warm fluid to 122 - 140°F.
3. With engine running, attach spring scale to rim of steering wheel.

Condition	Possible Sources	Action
• Steering is very difficult/very easy	• Seized intermediate shaft U-joints. • Damaged, fractured steering column bearing(s). • Steering gear. • Power steering pump. • Power steering hoses. • Binding dash boot seal	• GO to Pinpoint Test D.
• Excessive steering wheel play	• Steering gear. • Steering column. • Steering column intermediate shaft. • Steering linkage. • Ball joints.	• GO to Pinpoint Test E.
• Steering system drift/pull/wander	• Tire pressure. • Wheel alignment. • Steering gear. • Unevenly loaded vehicle. • Steering column intermediate shaft. • Frame alignment.	• CORRECT the vehicle loading as necessary. GO to Pinpoint Test F.
• Feedback	• Loose, worn or damaged tie rod. • Loose, worn or damaged tie-rod ends. • Loose or damaged steering gear insulators or bolts. • Loose lower steering column shaft U-joint bolts. • Loose suspension bushings, fasteners or ball joints. • Worn or damaged steering column bearing(s).	• GO to Component Tests, Tie-Rod Articulation Torque in this section. • GO to Component Tests, Steering Linkage in this section. • INSTALL new steering gear insulators or bolts if necessary, or TIGHTEN the bolts as needed. • INSTALL new bolts or TIGHTEN the bolts. • INSTALL new components as necessary. • INSTALL new steering column bearing(s).
• Poor returnability/sticky steering	• Binding lower steering column shaft U-joints. • Loose, worn or damaged tie rod. • Loose, worn or damaged tie-rod ends. • Suspension components. • Binding steering column bearing(s). • Binding dash boot seal.	• INSTALL a new lower steering column shaft. • GO to Component Tests, Tie-Rod Articulation Torque in this section. • GO to Component Tests, Steering Linkage • INSPECT Suspension. • INSTALL new steering column bearing(s).

LTV0500000001123

Fig. 1 Steering system troubleshooting (Part 2 of 3)

Condition	Possible Sources	Action
• Shimmy	• Loose, worn or damaged tie-rod end. • Loose, worn or damaged tie rod. • Suspension components.	• GO to Component Tests, Steering Linkage • GO to Component Tests, Tie-Rod Articulation Torque • DIAGNOSE suspension.

LTV0500000001124

Fig. 1 Steering system troubleshooting (Part 3 of 3)

DTC	Description
B1317	Battery Voltage High
B1318	Battery Voltage Low
B1342	ECU is Defective
B2477	Module Configuration Failure
C1445	Vehicle Speed Signal Circuit Failure
C1897	Steering VAPS Circuit Loop Failure
U1950	VAP Communication BUS Fault

LTV0500000001125

Fig. 2 Diagnostic trouble code interpretation

4. Measure pull required to turn the steering wheel one complete revolution in each direction. Turning effort specification should be 4.7 lbs. for Navigator and 5.9 lbs for Expedition.

PUMP FLOW & PRESSURE

Refer to "Power Steering Pump" for system Flow and pressure test procedures.

TIE ROD TORQUE

This inspection may be done with the steering gear on or off the vehicle.

1. Disconnect tie-rod end from front wheel knuckle, then move front wheel knuckle tie rod back and forth three times.
2. Hook a spring scale over tie rod, tie-rod end or threaded portion of front wheel knuckle tie rod, and measure force required to move front wheel knuckle tie rod.
3. If force required to move front wheel knuckle tie rod does not meet specifications which are Navigator, 35 inch lbs., Expedition 44 inch lbs., install a new front wheel knuckle tie rod.

STEERING GEAR VALVE

1. With vehicle in motion, place transmission in NEUTRAL and turn engine OFF, if vehicle does not pull with engine OFF, repair or install a new steering gear.
2. If vehicle pulls with engine OFF, switch right side front wheel to left side of vehicle and left side front wheel to right side of the vehicle.
3. If vehicle pulls to opposite side, switch front wheels with rear wheels keeping them on same side of vehicle.
4. If vehicle pull direction does not change, inspect front suspension components, wheel alignment and frame alignment.

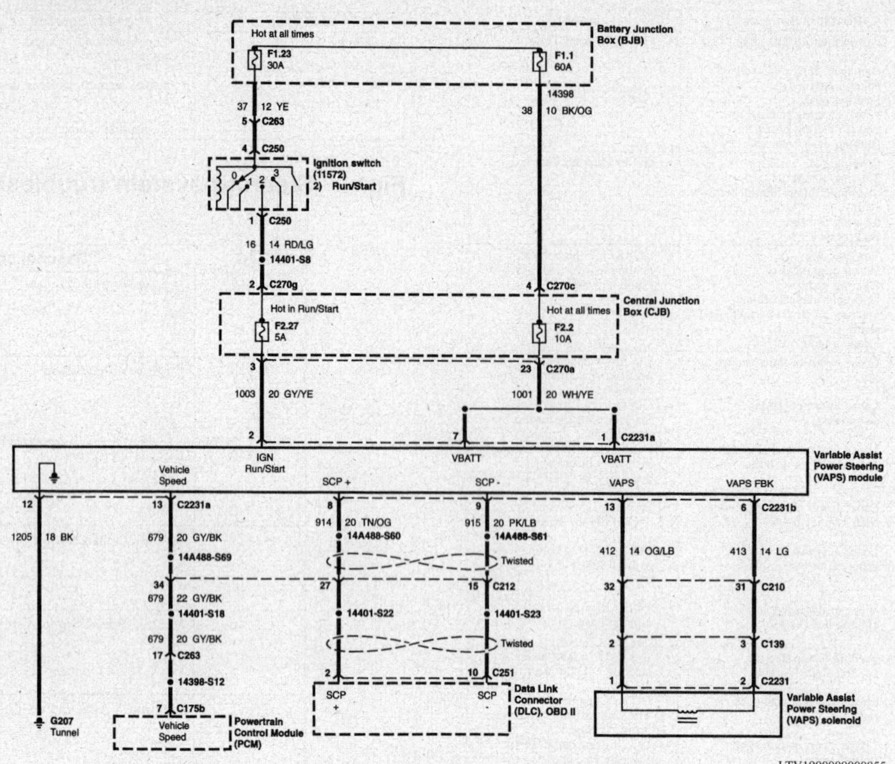

Fig. 3 Wiring diagram

DIAGNOSTIC CHART INDEX

	Test Step	Result / Action to Take
A1	CHECK CIRCUITS 1003 (GY/YE) AND 1524 (DB) FOR AN OPEN	
	• Key in OFF position. • Disconnect: Air Suspension Control Module C2131a. • Key in ON position. • Measure the voltage between the following air suspension control module C2131a pins, harness side and ground: Pin 1 — Circuit 1524 (DB) Pin 4 — Circuit 1003 (GY/YE) Pin 15 — Circuit 1524 (DB) • Are the voltages greater than 10 volts?	**Yes** GO to A2. **No** VERIFY CJB fuses 30 (25A) and 27 (5A) are OK. If OK, REPAIR the affected circuit(s) for an open. TEST the system for normal operation.
A2	CHECK CIRCUIT 875 (BK/LB) FOR AN OPEN	
	• Key in OFF position.	

LTV0500000001126

Fig. 4 Test A: No Communication w/Air Suspension Control Module (Part 1 of 2)

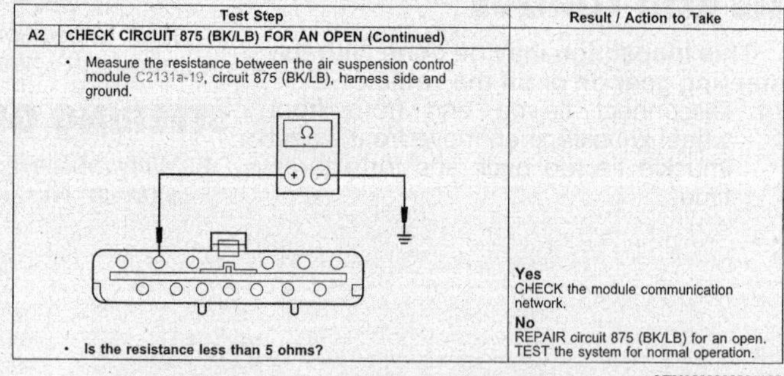

	Test Step	Result / Action to Take
A2	CHECK CIRCUIT 875 (BK/LB) FOR AN OPEN (Continued)	
	• Measure the resistance between the air suspension control module C2131a-19, circuit 875 (BK/LB), harness side and ground. • Is the resistance less than 5 ohms?	**Yes** CHECK the module communication network. **No** REPAIR circuit 875 (BK/LB) for an open. TEST the system for normal operation.

LTV0500000001127

Fig. 4 Test A: No Communication w/Air Suspension Control Module (Part 2 of 2)

	Test Step	Result / Action to Take
B1	CHECK CIRCUITS 412 (OG/LB) AND 413 (LG) FOR SHORT TO VOLTAGE	
	• Disconnect: Air Suspension Control Module C2131b. • Disconnect: VAPS Actuator C120. • Key in ON position.	

LTV0500000001128

Fig. 5 Test B: DTC 1897 - Steering VAPS Circuit Loop Failure (Part 1 of 3)

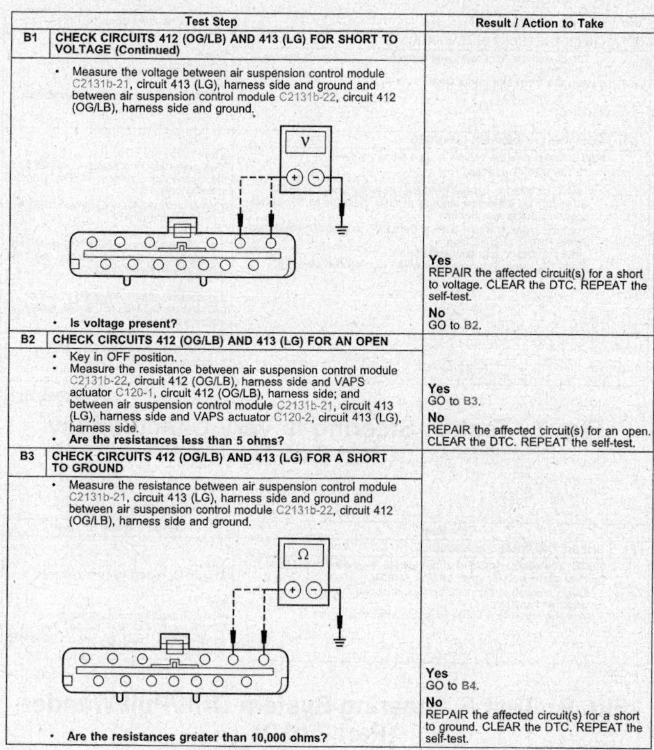

	Test Step	Result / Action to Take
B1	**CHECK CIRCUITS 412 (OG/LB) AND 413 (LG) FOR SHORT TO VOLTAGE (Continued)**	
	• Measure the voltage between air suspension control module C2131b-21, circuit 413 (LG), harness side and ground and between air suspension control module C2131b-22, circuit 412 (OG/LB), harness side and ground. • **Is voltage present?**	**Yes** REPAIR the affected circuit(s) for a short to voltage. CLEAR the DTC. REPEAT the self-test. **No** GO to B2.
B2	**CHECK CIRCUITS 412 (OG/LB) AND 413 (LG) FOR AN OPEN**	
	• Key in OFF position. • Measure the resistance between air suspension control module C2131b-22, circuit 412 (OG/LB), harness side and VAPS actuator C120-1, circuit 412 (OG/LB), harness side; and between air suspension control module C2131b-21, circuit 413 (LG), harness side and VAPS actuator C120-2, circuit 413 (LG), harness side. • **Are the resistances less than 5 ohms?**	**Yes** GO to B3. **No** REPAIR the affected circuit(s) for an open. CLEAR the DTC. REPEAT the self-test.
B3	**CHECK CIRCUITS 412 (OG/LB) AND 413 (LG) FOR A SHORT TO GROUND**	
	• Measure the resistance between air suspension control module C2131b-21, circuit 413 (LG), harness side and ground and between air suspension control module C2131b-22, circuit 412 (OG/LB), harness side and ground. • **Are the resistances greater than 10,000 ohms?**	**Yes** GO to B4. **No** REPAIR the affected circuit(s) for a short to ground. CLEAR the DTC. REPEAT the self-test.

LTV0500000001129

Fig. 5 Test B: DTC 1897 - Steering VAPS Circuit Loop Failure (Part 2 of 3)

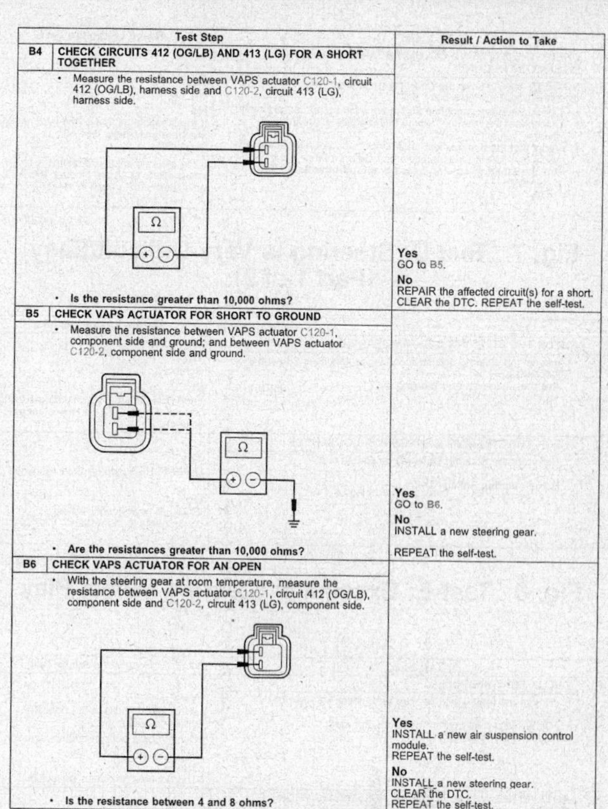

	Test Step	Result / Action to Take
B4	**CHECK CIRCUITS 412 (OG/LB) AND 413 (LG) FOR A SHORT TOGETHER**	
	• Measure the resistance between VAPS actuator C120-1, circuit 412 (OG/LB), harness side and C120-2, circuit 413 (LG), harness side. • **Is the resistance greater than 10,000 ohms?**	**Yes** GO to B5. **No** REPAIR the affected circuit(s) for a short. CLEAR the DTC. REPEAT the self-test.
B5	**CHECK VAPS ACTUATOR FOR SHORT TO GROUND**	
	• Measure the resistance between VAPS actuator C120-1, component side and ground; and between VAPS actuator C120-2, component side and ground. • **Are the resistances greater than 10,000 ohms?**	**Yes** GO to B6. **No** INSTALL a new steering gear. REPEAT the self-test.
B6	**CHECK VAPS ACTUATOR FOR AN OPEN**	
	• With the steering gear at room temperature, measure the resistance between VAPS actuator C120-1, circuit 412 (OG/LB), component side and C120-2, circuit 413 (LG), component side. • **Is the resistance between 4 and 8 ohms?**	**Yes** INSTALL a new air suspension control module. REPEAT the self-test. **No** INSTALL a new steering gear. CLEAR the DTC. REPEAT the self-test.

LTV0500000001130

Fig. 5 Test B: DTC 1897 - Steering VAPS Circuit Loop Failure (Part 3 of 3)

	Test Step	Result / Action to Take
C1	**CHECK FOR MECHANICAL NOISE**	
	• Test drive the vehicle to verify the steering system noise. • **Does the steering system make a clunk noise?**	**Yes** CHECK for loose, worn or damaged tie-rod ends. REFER to Component Tests, Steering Linkage in this section. CHECK for loose or worn steering gear isolators (if applicable). INSTALL new isolators if necessary. If the noise is from the steering column, CHECK the steering column intermediate shaft for grounding through the body and REPAIR as necessary. If the noise is from the steering column boot bearing, INSTALL a new steering column boot bearing. If the noise is from the suspension components, INSTALL new suspension components as necessary. If the noise is from loose, worn or damaged intermediate shaft U-joint(s), INSTALL a new lower steering column shaft. **No** If a squeak is present in the steering column, REPAIR the steering column mountings or ALIGN the steering column as necessary. For all other concerns, GO to C2.

LTV0500000001131

Fig. 6 Test C: Steering System Noise (Part 1 of 3)

	Test Step	Result / Action to Take
C2	**VERIFY THE CONCERN**	
	NOTE: Make sure the vehicle is on a flat dry surface, the transmission is in PARK and the windows are rolled up. **NOTE:** Some power steering noise is expected. If in doubt of the acceptability of the noise level, evaluate another vehicle of the same model and powertrain. • Key in START position. • Turn the steering wheel 1/2 turn off-center to the RIGHT then 1/2 turn off-center to the LEFT. • **Is the power steering noisy?**	**Yes** If a grunt noise is present, VERIFY the steering column boot is OK and the exhaust system is not grounding out. If a moan is present, VERIFY that the tie-rod ends and ball joints are OK. GO to C3. **No** If a squeal is present, INSPECT and INSTALL a new engine drive belt or belt tensioner as necessary. If the steering system noise is a hiss or whistle, INSPECT the steering column boot at the dash panel. REPAIR or INSTALL a new boot as necessary. INSPECT the steering gear input shaft and valve for wear or damage. INSPECT the power steering gear, intermediate shaft and power steering lines and hoses for grounding to the body and REPAIR as necessary. INSPECT for openings or missing plugs in the instrument panel cowl and REPAIR as necessary. If there are no missing plugs or openings in the cowl, grounded power steering gear, intermediate shaft or power steering lines or hoses, GO to C6.
C3	**CHECK FOR A COLD START NOISE**	
	NOTE: Some noise during an extremely cold start (-25.5°C [-14°F]) is normal and should improve as the steering system warms up, usually within 60 seconds. • Key in START position. • Verify the noise condition. • **Is the noise present only during cold start up?**	**Yes** CHECK for contamination in the power steering reservoir screen. FLUSH the power steering system as necessary. TEST the system for normal operation. **No** GO to C4.
C4	**INSPECT THE POWER STEERING FLUID**	
	• Key in OFF position. • With the engine OFF, inspect the power steering fluid for aeration. • **Is the power steering fluid foamy or aerated?**	**Yes** GO to C5. **No** PURGE the power steering system. If a whine or moan is still present, INSTALL a new power steering pump. If a grunt is still present, INSTALL a new power steering gear.

LTV0500000001132

Fig. 6 Test C: Steering System Noise (Part 2 of 3)

	Test Step	Result / Action to Take
C5	**CHECK THE POWER STEERING FLUID LEVEL WITH THE ENGINE ON AND OFF**	
	NOTE: Record the vacuum level when the pump noise occurs with no steering input. Vacuum level should be greater than 10 in-Hg with the CII pump and 15 in-Hg with the CIII pump. • Key in START position. • With the engine running, inspect the power steering fluid level. • Key in OFF position. • With the engine OFF, inspect the power steering fluid level. • **Does the power steering fluid level change with the engine off?**	**Yes** PURGE the power steering system. **No** GO to C6.
C6	**CHECK THE POWER STEERING PUMP**	
	NOTE: Do not turn the steering wheel to either the right or left stop. Power steering relief noise will occur and is normal at the stop positions. • Key in START position. • With the engine running, rotate the steering wheel 90 degrees to the left then 180 degrees to the right. • **Does the frequency of the hiss change between the LEFT and RIGHT positions?**	**Yes** INSTALL a new power steering gear. **No** INSTALL a new power steering pump.

LTV0500000001133

Fig. 6 Test C: Steering System Noise (Part 3 of 3)

	Test Step	Result / Action to Take
D1	CHECK THE STEERING COLUMN BEARINGS AND THE INTERMEDIATE SHAFT	
	NOTE: Be sure to keep the clockspring centered when disconnecting the intermediate shaft. • Check the steering column and intermediate shaft for grounding. • Disconnect the steering column intermediate shaft at the steering column. • Verify that the intermediate shaft U-joints do not bind and move freely and that the steering column bearing rotates freely. • **Are the steering column bearing and intermediate shaft U-joints OK?**	**Yes** GO to D2. **No** If the steering column or the intermediate shaft are grounding, REPAIR as necessary. If the steering column bearings or the intermediate shaft are binding. INSTALL a new intermediate shaft or steering column.

LTV0500000001134

Fig. 7 Test D: Steering Is Very Difficult/Easy (Part 1 of 2)

	Test Step	Result / Action to Take
E1	CHECK THE STEERING COLUMN BEARING	
	• Inspect the steering column mounting fasteners and bearing for looseness. • **Are the fasteners and bearing OK?**	**Yes** GO to E2. **No** TIGHTEN the steering column mounting fasteners or INSTALL a new steering column.
E2	CHECK THE STEERING LINKAGE FOR LOOSENESS	
	• Carry out the Steering Linkage component test. • **Is the steering linkage OK?**	**Yes** DIAGNOSE suspension components. **No** INSTALL new steering linkage components as necessary.

LTV0500000001136

Fig. 8 Test E: Excessive Steering Wheel Play

	Test Step	Result / Action to Take
F1	CHECK FOR TIRE PULL	
	• Rotate the front wheel and tire assemblies side-to-side. • Carry out a road test on a smooth, flat road. • **Does the vehicle drift/pull?**	**Yes** If the vehicle pulls in the opposite direction, GO to F2. If the vehicle pulls in original direction, GO to F3. **No** The concern has been corrected.
F2	ROTATE THE WHEEL AND TIRE ASSEMBLIES FRONT TO REAR	
	• Rotate the wheel and tire assemblies front to rear. • Carry out a road test on a smooth, flat road. • **Does the vehicle drift/pull?**	**Yes** GO to F3. **No** The concern has been corrected.
F3	CHECK THE STEERING COLUMN INTERMEDIATE SHAFT	
	NOTE: Be sure to keep the clockspring centered when disconnecting the intermediate shaft. • Check the steering column and intermediate shaft for grounding. • Disconnect the steering column intermediate shaft at the steering column. • Inspect the steering column intermediate shaft U-joints for looseness or wear. • **Are the steering column intermediate shaft U-joints OK?**	**Yes** GO to F4. **No** INSTALL a new steering column intermediate shaft.
F4	CHECK THE STEERING GEAR MOUNTING	
	• Check the steering gear mounts for looseness or wear. • **Are the steering gear mounts OK?**	**Yes** GO to F5. **No** INSTALL new steering gear mount(s).
F5	CHECK THE STEERING GEAR	
	• Carry out the Steering Gear Valve component test. • **Is the steering gear valve OK?**	**Yes** GO to F6. **No** REPAIR or INSTALL a new steering gear.
F6	CHECK THE SUSPENSION COMPONENTS	
	• Check for loose or worn suspension components. • **Are the suspension components OK?**	**Yes** GO to F7. **No** INSTALL new suspension component(s).

LTV0500000001137

Fig. 9 Test F: Steering System Drift/Pull/Wander (Part 1 of 2)

POWER STEERING SYSTEM BLEED

Refer to "Power Steering Pump" for system bleed procedure.

COMPONENT SERVICE

Variable Assist Power Steering Module

Refer to **Fig. 10** for module removal sequence.

	Test Step	Result / Action to Take
D2	CHECK THE FRONT BALL JOINTS	
	• Check that the front ball joints move freely and are not binding or sticking. • **Are the front ball joints OK?**	**Yes** GO to D3. **No** INSTALL new ball joint(s) as necessary.
D3	MONITOR ENGINE RPM CHANGES	
	NOTE: Make sure the vehicle is on a flat dry surface. • Key in START position. • ⚠ **CAUTION: Do not hold the steering wheel at the stops for an extended amount of time. Damage to the power steering pump can occur.** Turn the steering wheel once to the LEFT stop position and then to the RIGHT stop position. • Note the engine rpm during the turns. • **Does the engine rpm change when turning the steering wheel?**	**Yes** If no power steering assist is present and the engine rpm changes, INSTALL a new steering gear. If left-to-right variation is present, INSTALL a new steering gear. If no power steering assist is present and the engine rpm does not change, INSTALL a new power steering pump. If excessive effort is required in one or both directions, INSTALL a new power steering pump. **No** CARRY OUT the Pump Flow and Pressure Test.

LTV0500000001135

Fig. 7 Test D: Steering Is Very Difficult/Easy (Part 2 of 2)

	Test Step	Result / Action to Take
F7	CHECK THE WHEEL ALIGNMENT	
	NOTE: The vehicle will tend to pull toward the side with the least positive caster and the most positive camber. • Using a suitable alignment system, measure the wheel alignment settings. • **Are the alignment settings within specifications?**	**Yes** CHECK for correct frame alignments. **No** ADJUST the alignment angles to specifications. DO NOT exceed the specifications. TEST the system for normal operation.

LTV0500000001161

Fig. 9 Test F: Steering System Drift/Pull/Wander (Part 2 of 2)

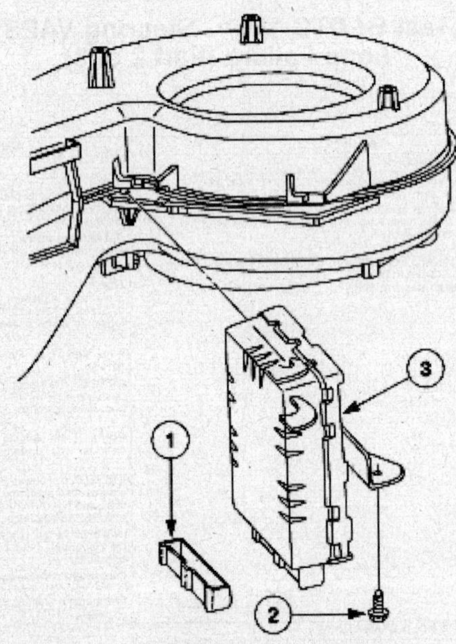

Item	Description
1	VAPS module electrical connector
2	VAPS module bolt
3	VAPS module

LTV1900000000856

Fig. 10 VAPS module replacement

Electric Power Assist Steering System

NOTE: On Air Bag Equipped Models, Refer To "Air Bag System Precautions" Located In The Front Of This Manual For System Disarming & Arming Procedures.

INDEX

PRECAUTIONS

Air Bag Systems

Refer to "Air Bag System Precautions" in the front of this manual for system disarming and arming procedures.

DESCRIPTION

The electrical power assist steering system consists of power steering control module, electric motor, torque sensor, rack and pinion steering gear.

The electrical power steering system provides power steering assist to the driver by replacing the conventional hydraulic valve system with an electric motor coupled to the steering gear. The motor is controlled by an electronic control unit that senses the steering effort through the use of a torque sensor mounted between the steering column shaft and the steering gear. Steering assist is provided in proportion to the steering input effort and vehicle speed.

TROUBLESHOOTING

Refer to **Fig. 1** for steering system troubleshooting procedures.

Condition	Possible Sources	Action
• No communication with the power steering control module	• Circuitry. • Fuse(s). • Power steering control module. • Smart junction box (SJB).	• GO to Pinpoint Test E.
• The steering is very difficult/very easy	• Circuitry. • Seized intermediate shaft U-joints. • Damaged, fractured steering column bearing(s). • Ball joints. • Strut bearing plate. • Binding dash boot seal. • Smart junction box (SJB). • Power steering control module. • Torque sensor. • Steering gear motor. • Steering gear.	• GO to Pinpoint Test H.
• Steering system noise	• Loose or damaged steering linkage. • Loose or damaged suspension component(s). • Steering column. • Steering column boot bushing. • Intermediate shaft. • Loose dash boot seal. • Power steering control module. • Steering gear.	• GO to Pinpoint Test I.
• Excessive steering wheel play	• Steering column. • Steering column bearings. • Steering column intermediate shaft. • Steering linkage. • Ball joints. • Strut bearing plate. • Steering gear.	• GO to Pinpoint Test J.
• Steering system drift/pull/wander	• Tire pressure. • Wheel alignment. • Unevenly loaded vehicle. • Steering column intermediate shaft. • Strut bearing plate. • Frame alignment. • Power steering control module. • Steering gear.	• CORRECT the vehicle loading as necessary. • GO to Pinpoint Test K.

LTV0500000001138

Fig. 1 Steering system troubleshooting (Part 1 of 2)

DIAGNOSIS & TESTING

Accessing Diagnostic Trouble Codes

Connect a suitably programmed scan tool to Data Link Connector (DLC) and follow manufacturer's instructions.

Diagnostic Trouble Code Interpretation

Refer to **Fig. 2** for diagnostic trouble code interpretation.

Wiring Diagram

Refer to **Fig. 3** for wiring diagram.

Pinpoint Tests

Refer to **Figs. 4 through 10** for diagnostic pinpoint tests.

Clearing Diagnostic Trouble Codes

Connect a suitably programmed scan tool to Data Link Connector (DLC) and follow manufacturer's instructions.

Condition	Possible Sources	Action
• Feedback	• Loose, worn or damaged tie-rod.	• GO to Component Test, Tie-Rod Articulation Torque
	• Loose, worn or damaged tie-rod ends.	• GO to Component Test, Steering Linkage
	• Loose or damaged steering gear insulators or bolts.	• TIGHTEN the bolts as needed. INSTALL new steering gear insulators or bolts if necessary.
	• Loose steering column shaft U-joint or pinch bolts.	• TIGHTEN the bolts as needed. INSTALL a new steering column shaft U-joint and bolts.
	• Loose suspension bushings, fasteners, ball joints or strut bearing plate (if applicable).	• INSTALL new suspension components as necessary.
	• Worn or damaged steering column bearing(s).	• INSTALL a new steering column.
	• Excessive steering gear wear.	• INSTALL a new steering gear.
• Poor returnability/sticky steering	• Binding lower steering column shaft U-joints.	• INSTALL a new steering column U-joint.
	• Loose, worn or damaged front wheel knuckle tie-rod.	• GO to Component Test, Tie-Rod Articulation Torque
	• Loose, worn or damaged tie-rod ends.	• GO to Component Test, Steering Linkage
	• Suspension components.	• DIAGNOSE suspension.
	• Binding steering column bearing(s). • Binding dash boot seal.	• INSTALL a new steering column.
• Shimmy	• Loose, worn or damaged tie-rod end.	• GO to Component Test, Steering Linkage
	• Loose, worn or damaged tie rod.	• GO to Component Test, Tie-Rod Articulation torque
	• Suspension components.	• DIAGNOSE suspension.

LTV0500000001139

Fig. 1 Steering system troubleshooting (Part 2 of 2)

DTCs	Description	Source
B1317	Battery Voltage High	Power Steering Control Module
B1318	Battery Voltage Low	Power Steering Control Module
B1342	ECU is Faulted	Power Steering Control Module
B2277	Electric Power Steering Motor Malfunction	Power Steering Control Module
B2278	Steering Shaft Torque Sensor Malfunction	Power Steering Control Module
B2477	Module Configuration Failure	Power Steering Control Module
C1778	Power Steering Failure	Power Steering Control Module
C2791	Power Steering Motor Wire Open	Power Steering Control Module
C2792	Electric Power Steering Motor Wire Short to Battery	Power Steering Control Module
C2793	Electric Power Steering Motor Wire Short to Ground	Power Steering Control Module
C2794	Electric Power Steering Motor Overheat Protection	Power Steering Control Module
U1900	CAN Communication Bus Fault - Receive Error	Power Steering Control Module

LTV0500000001140

Fig. 2 Diagnostic trouble code interpretation (Part 1 of 2)

Component Tests

STEERING LINKAGE

1. With vehicle on ground and parking brake applied, start engine.
2. Have an assistant rotate steering wheel back and forth 360°, then watch for relative motion of studs in steering linkage ball sockets and for loose steering gear mounting.
3. With engine off, steering wheel unlocked, and front wheels raised off ground, grasp wheel at front and rear and watch for excessive play or binding in joints while trying to steer wheels.
4. Grasp inner tie-rod boot at inner tie-rod socket and inspect for movement of socket relative to steering gear.
5. Install new components if required, tighten any worn, damaged or loose components.

TURNING EFFORT

Ensure the front wheels are correctly aligned and tire pressure is correct before inspecting steering effort.

1. Park vehicle on dry concrete and set parking brake.
2. With engine running, attach spring scale to rim of steering wheel.
3. Measure pull required to turn the steering wheel one complete revolution in each direction. Turning effort specification should be 6.75 lbs.

TIE ROD TORQUE

This inspection may be done with the steering gear on or off the vehicle.

1. Disconnect tie-rod end from front wheel knuckle, then move front wheel knuckle tie rod back and forth three times.
2. Hook a spring scale over tie rod, tie-rod end or threaded portion of front wheel knuckle tie rod, and measure force required to move front wheel knuckle tie rod.
3. If force required to move front wheel knuckle tie rod does not meet specifications which is 9-27 inch lbs, install a new front wheel knuckle tie rod.

DTCs	Description	Source
B1317	Battery Voltage High	Power Steering Control Module
B1318	Battery Voltage Low	Power Steering Control Module
B1342	ECU is Faulted	Power Steering Control Module
B2277	Electric Power Steering Motor Malfunction	Power Steering Control Module
B2278	Steering Shaft Torque Sensor Malfunction	Power Steering Control Module
B2477	Module Configuration Failure	Power Steering Control Module
C1778	Power Steering Failure	Power Steering Control Module
C2791	Power Steering Motor Wire Open	Power Steering Control Module
C2792	Electric Power Steering Motor Wire Short to Battery	Power Steering Control Module
C2793	Electric Power Steering Motor Wire Short to Ground	Power Steering Control Module
C2794	Electric Power Steering Motor Overheat Protection	Power Steering Control Module
U1900	CAN Communication Bus Fault - Receive Error	Power Steering Control Module

LTV0500000001141

Fig. 2 Diagnostic trouble code interpretation (Part 2 of 2)

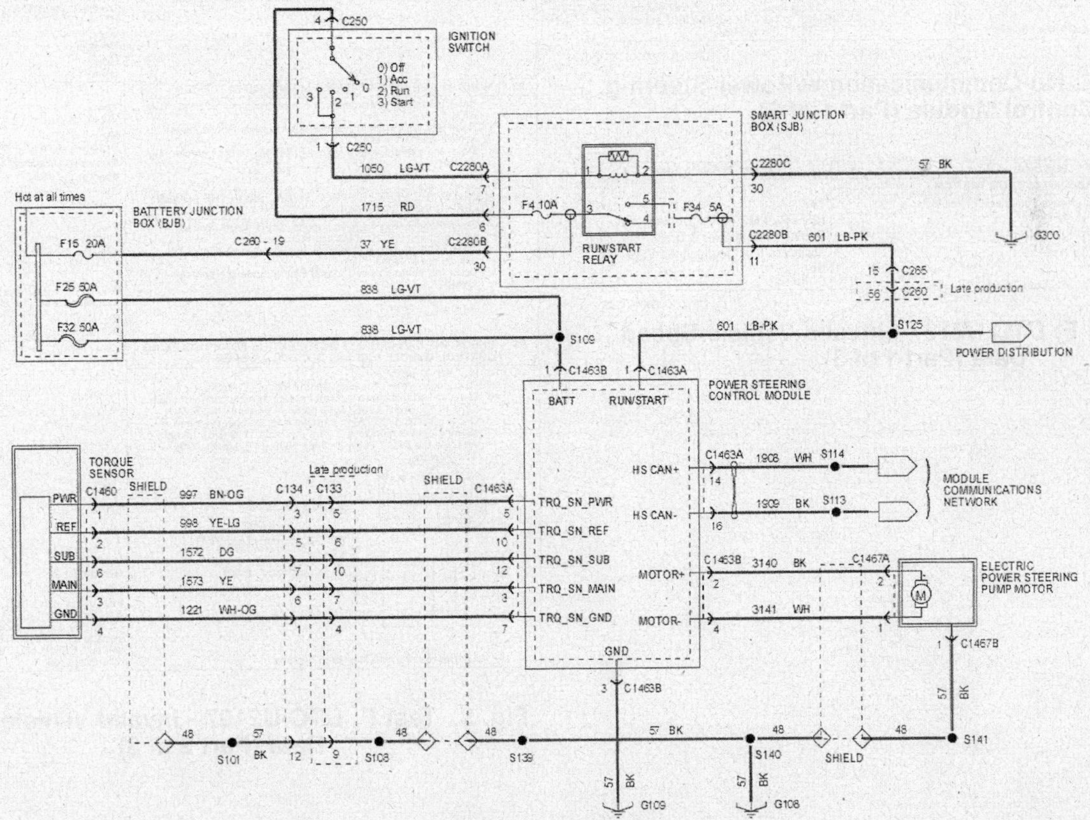

Fig. 3 Wiring diagram

DIAGNOSTIC CHART INDEX

Test Step	Result / Action to Take
E1 CHECK THE POWER STEERING CONTROL MODULE CIRCUIT 838 (LG/VT) FOR VOLTAGE • Key in OFF position. • Disconnect: Power Steering Control Module C1463b. • Measure the voltage between power steering control module C1463b-1, circuit 838 (LG/VT), harness side and ground. • **Is the voltage greater than 10 volts?**	**Yes** GO to E2. **No** INSPECT BJB fuses 25 (50A) and 32 (50A), if OK, REPAIR circuit 838 (LG/VT) for an open. CLEAR the DTCs. CYCLE the ignition switch to the OFF position for 3 seconds. REPEAT the self-test.
E2 CHECK THE POWER STEERING CONTROL MODULE CIRCUIT 601 (LB/PK) FOR VOLTAGE • Disconnect: Power Steering Control Module C1463b. • Key in ON position. • Measure the voltage between power steering control module C1463b-1, circuit 601 (LB/PK), harness side and ground. • **Is the voltage greater than 10 volts?**	**Yes** GO to E3. **No** INSPECT SJB fuse 34 (5A), if OK, REPAIR circuit 601 (LB/PK) for an open. CLEAR the DTCs. CYCLE the ignition switch to the OFF position for 3 seconds. REPEAT the self-test.

LTV0500000001143

Fig. 4 Test E: No Communication w/Power Steering Control Module (Part 1 of 2)

Test Step	Result / Action to Take
F1 CHECK THE RECORDED DTCs FROM THE TCM • Check the recorded results from the TCM self-test. • **Are any TCM DTCs recorded?**	**Yes** REFER to MOTOR's "Domestic Engine Performance & Driveability Manual " to diagnose VSS. **No** GO to F2.

LTV0500000001145

Fig. 5 Test F: DTC U2197 - Invalid Vehicle Speed Data (Part 1 of 3)

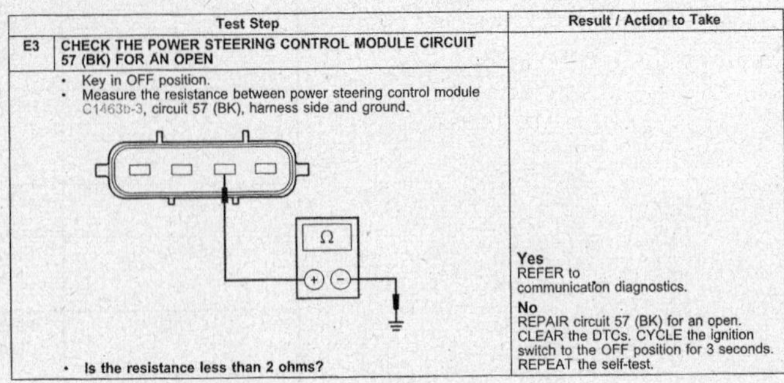

Test Step	Result / Action to Take
E3 CHECK THE POWER STEERING CONTROL MODULE CIRCUIT 57 (BK) FOR AN OPEN • Key in OFF position. • Measure the resistance between power steering control module C1463b-3, circuit 57 (BK), harness side and ground. • **Is the resistance less than 2 ohms?**	**Yes** REFER to communication diagnostics. **No** REPAIR circuit 57 (BK) for an open. CLEAR the DTCs. CYCLE the ignition switch to the OFF position for 3 seconds. REPEAT the self-test.

LTV0500000001144

Fig. 4 Test E: No Communication w/Power Steering Control Module (Part 2 of 2)

Test Step	Result / Action to Take
F2 CHECK THE RECORDED DTCs FROM THE POWER STEERING CONTROL MODULE **NOTE:** To clear DTCs, it is necessary to cycle the ignition switch to the OFF position for 3 seconds. • Check the recorded results from the power steering control module self-test. • **Are any power steering control module DTCs recorded?**	**Yes** REPAIR all other power steering control module DTCs before continuing diagnosis of DTC U2197. REFER to the Power Steering Control Module Diagnostic Trouble Code (DTC). CLEAR the DTCs. CYCLE the ignition switch to the OFF position for 3 seconds. REPEAT the self-test. **No** GO to F3.
F3 MONITOR THE VEHICLE SPEED SIGNAL PID IN THE TCM • Enter the following diagnostic mode on the diagnostic tool: TCM PID. • Road test the vehicle at various speeds while monitoring the vehicle speed signal PID. • **Does the vehicle speed signal PID indicate the vehicle speed?**	**Yes** GO to F4. **No** REFER to MOTOR's "Domestic Engine Performance & Driveability Manual" to diagnose the VSS.
F4 MONITOR THE VEHICLE SPEED SIGNAL PID IN THE POWER STEERING CONTROL MODULE • Enter the following diagnostic mode on the diagnostic tool: Power Steering Control Module PID. • Road test the vehicle at various speeds while monitoring the vehicle speed signal PID. • **Does the vehicle speed signal PID indicate the vehicle speed?**	**Yes** CLEAR the DTCs. CYCLE the ignition switch to the OFF position for 3 seconds. If DTC U2197 is retrieved again, GO to F6. If no DTCs are retrieved the system is operating correctly at this time. **No** GO to F5.
F5 CHECK THE CAN CIRCUITS BETWEEN THE POWER STEERING CONTROL MODULE AND THE DLC FOR AN OPEN • Key in OFF position. • Disconnect: Power Steering Control Module C1463b. • Measure the resistance between power steering control module C1463b-14, circuit 1908 (WH), harness side and the DLC C251-6, circuit 1908 (WH), harness side; and between power steering control module C1463b-16, circuit 1909 (BK), harness side and the DLC C251-14, circuit 1909 (BK), harness side. • **Are the resistances less than 5 ohms?**	**Yes** GO to F6. **No** REPAIR circuit(s) 1908 (WH) and/or 1909 (BK) for an open. CLEAR the DTCs. CYCLE the ignition switch to the OFF position for 3 seconds. REPEAT the self-test. CARRY OUT the data link diagnostics test.

LTV0500000001146

Fig. 5 Test F: DTC U2197 - Invalid Vehicle Speed Data (Part 2 of 3)

	Test Step	Result / Action to Take
F6	CHECK FOR CORRECT POWER STEERING CONTROL MODULE OPERATION	
	• Disconnect all the power steering control module connectors. • Check for: — corrosion. — pushed-out pins. • Connect all power steering control module connectors and make sure they are seated correctly. • Operate the system and verify that the concern is still present. • **Is the concern still present?**	**Yes** INSTALL a new power steering control module. CLEAR the DTCs. CYCLE the ignition switch to the OFF position for 3 seconds. REPEAT the self-test. **No** The system is operating correctly at this time. The concern may have been caused by a loose or corroded connector. CLEAR the DTCs. CYCLE the ignition switch to the OFF position for 3 seconds. REPEAT the self-test.

LTV0500000001147

Fig. 5 Test F: DTC U2197 - Invalid Vehicle Speed Data (Part 3 of 3)

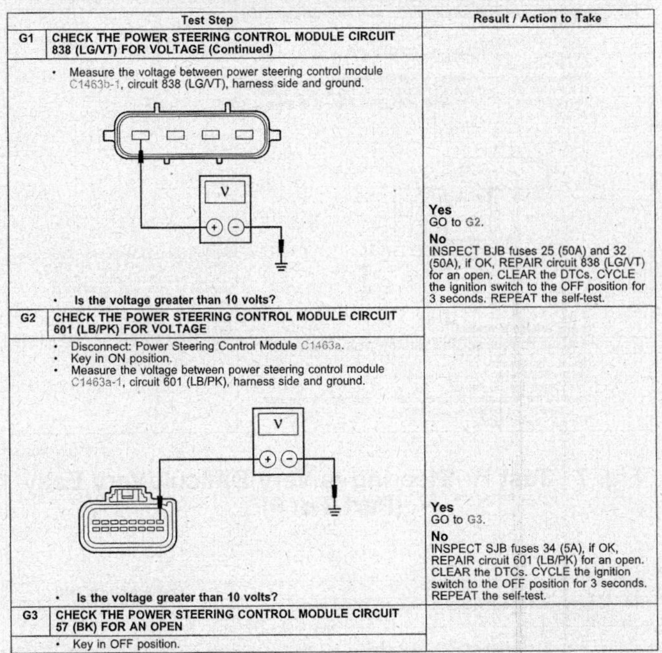

	Test Step	Result / Action to Take
G1	CHECK THE POWER STEERING CONTROL MODULE CIRCUIT 838 (LG/VT) FOR VOLTAGE (Continued)	
	• Measure the voltage between power steering control module C1463b-1, circuit 838 (LG/VT), harness side and ground. • **Is the voltage greater than 10 volts?**	**Yes** GO to G2. **No** INSPECT BJB fuses 25 (50A) and 32 (50A), if OK, REPAIR circuit 838 (LG/VT) for an open. CLEAR the DTCs. CYCLE the ignition switch to the OFF position for 3 seconds. REPEAT the self-test.
G2	CHECK THE POWER STEERING CONTROL MODULE CIRCUIT 601 (LB/PK) FOR VOLTAGE	
	• Disconnect: Power Steering Control Module C1463a. • Key in ON position. • Measure the voltage between power steering control module C1463a-1, circuit 601 (LB/PK), harness side and ground. • **Is the voltage greater than 10 volts?**	**Yes** GO to G3. **No** INSPECT SJB fuses 34 (5A), if OK, REPAIR circuit 601 (LB/PK) for an open. CLEAR the DTCs. CYCLE the ignition switch to the OFF position for 3 seconds. REPEAT the self-test.
G3	CHECK THE POWER STEERING CONTROL MODULE CIRCUIT 57 (BK) FOR AN OPEN	
	• Key in OFF position.	

LTV0500000001149

Fig. 6 Test G: DTC C1778 - Power Steering Failure (Part 2 of 4)

	Test Step	Result / Action to Take
G5	CHECK THE STEERING GEAR MOTOR FOR AN OPEN	
	• Measure the resistance between power steering motor C1467a-2, circuit 3140 (BK), component side and power steering motor C1467a-1, circuit 3141 (WH), component side. • **Is the resistance less than 2 ohms?**	**Yes** GO to G6. **No** INSTALL a new steering gear. REFER to Section 211-02. CLEAR the DTCs. CYCLE the ignition switch to the OFF position for 3 seconds. REPEAT the self-test.
G6	CHECK FOR CORRECT POWER STEERING CONTROL MODULE OPERATION	
	• Disconnect all the power steering control module connectors. • Check for: — corrosion. — pushed-out pins. • Connect all power steering control module connectors and make sure they are seated correctly. • Operate the system and verify if the concern is still present. • **Is the concern still present?**	**Yes** INSTALL a new power steering control module. REFER to Section 211-02. CLEAR the DTCs. CYCLE the ignition switch to the OFF position for 3 seconds. REPEAT the self-test. **No** The system is operating correctly at this time. The concern may have been caused by a loose or corroded connector. CLEAR the DTCs. CYCLE the ignition switch to the OFF position for 3 seconds. REPEAT the self-test.

LTV0500000001151

Fig. 6 Test G: DTC C1778 - Power Steering Failure (Part 4 of 4)

	Test Step	Result / Action to Take
G1	CHECK THE POWER STEERING CONTROL MODULE CIRCUIT 838 (LG/VT) FOR VOLTAGE	
	• Key in OFF position. • Disconnect: Power Steering Control Module C1463b.	

LTV0500000001148

Fig. 6 Test G: DTC C1778 - Power Steering Failure (Part 1 of 4)

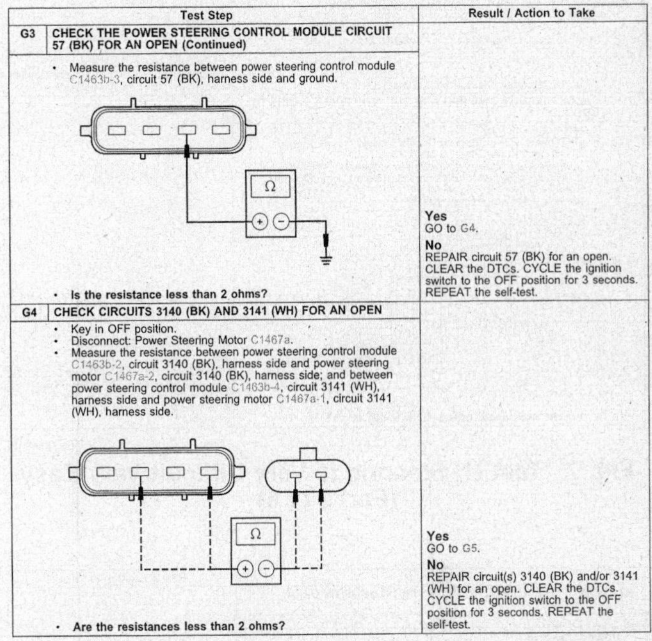

	Test Step	Result / Action to Take
G3	CHECK THE POWER STEERING CONTROL MODULE CIRCUIT 57 (BK) FOR AN OPEN (Continued)	
	• Measure the resistance between power steering control module C1463b-3, circuit 57 (BK), harness side and ground. • **Is the resistance less than 2 ohms?**	**Yes** GO to G4. **No** REPAIR circuit 57 (BK) for an open. CLEAR the DTCs. CYCLE the ignition switch to the OFF position for 3 seconds. REPEAT the self-test.
G4	CHECK CIRCUITS 3140 (BK) AND 3141 (WH) FOR AN OPEN	
	• Key in OFF position. • Disconnect: Power Steering Motor C1467a. • Measure the resistance between power steering control module C1463b-2, circuit 3140 (BK), harness side and power steering motor C1467a-2, circuit 3140 (BK), harness side; and between power steering control module C1463b-4, circuit 3141 (WH), harness side and power steering motor C1467a-1, circuit 3141 (WH), harness side. • **Are the resistances less than 2 ohms?**	**Yes** GO to G5. **No** REPAIR circuit(s) 3140 (BK) and/or 3141 (WH) for an open. CLEAR the DTCs. CYCLE the ignition switch to the OFF position for 3 seconds. REPEAT the self-test.

LTV0500000001150

Fig. 6 Test G: DTC C1778 - Power Steering Failure (Part 3 of 4)

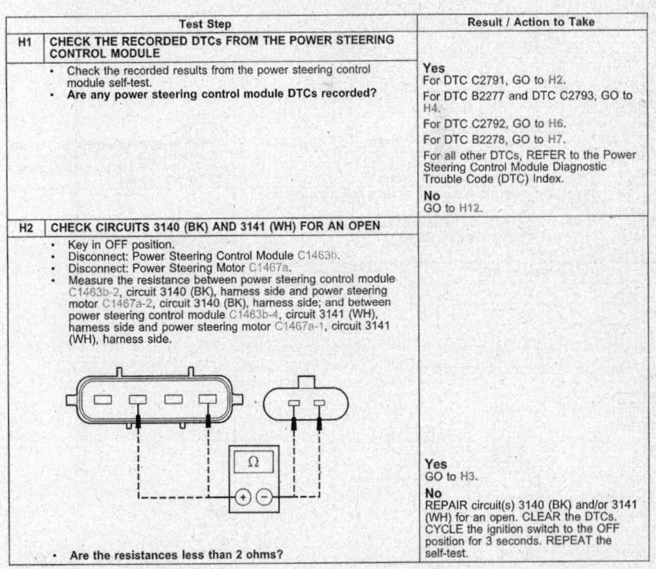

	Test Step	Result / Action to Take
H1	CHECK THE RECORDED DTCs FROM THE POWER STEERING CONTROL MODULE	
	• Check the recorded results from the power steering control module self-test. • **Are any power steering control module DTCs recorded?**	**Yes** For DTC C2791, GO to H2. For DTC B2277 and DTC C2793, GO to H4. For DTC C2792, GO to H6. For DTC B2278, GO to H7. For all other DTCs, REFER to the Power Steering Control Module Diagnostic Trouble Code (DTC) Index. **No** GO to H12.
H2	CHECK CIRCUITS 3140 (BK) AND 3141 (WH) FOR AN OPEN	
	• Key in OFF position. • Disconnect: Power Steering Control Module C1463b. • Disconnect: Power Steering Motor C1467a. • Measure the resistance between power steering control module C1463b-2, circuit 3140 (BK), harness side and power steering motor C1467a-2, circuit 3140 (BK), harness side; and between power steering control module C1463b-4, circuit 3141 (WH), harness side and power steering motor C1467a-1, circuit 3141 (WH), harness side. • **Are the resistances less than 2 ohms?**	**Yes** GO to H3. **No** REPAIR circuit(s) 3140 (BK) and/or 3141 (WH) for an open. CLEAR the DTCs. CYCLE the ignition switch to the OFF position for 3 seconds. REPEAT the self-test.

LTV0500000001152

Fig. 7 Test H: Steering Is Very Difficult/Very Easy (Part 1 of 6)

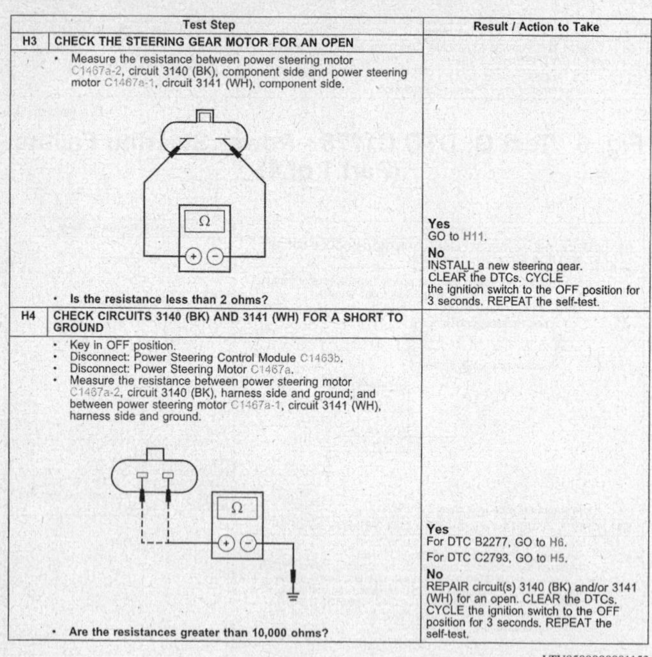

Step	Test Step	Result / Action to Take
H3	**CHECK THE STEERING GEAR MOTOR FOR AN OPEN** • Measure the resistance between power steering motor C1467a-2, circuit 3140 (BK), component side and power steering motor C1467a-1, circuit 3141 (WH), component side. • Is the resistance less than 2 ohms?	**Yes** GO to H11. **No** INSTALL a new steering gear. CLEAR the DTCs. CYCLE the ignition switch to the OFF position for 3 seconds. REPEAT the self-test.
H4	**CHECK CIRCUITS 3140 (BK) AND 3141 (WH) FOR A SHORT TO GROUND** • Key in OFF position. • Disconnect: Power Steering Control Module C1463b. • Disconnect: Power Steering Motor C1467a. • Measure the resistance between power steering motor C1467a-2, circuit 3140 (BK), harness side and ground; and between power steering motor C1467a-1, circuit 3141 (WH), harness side and ground. • Are the resistances greater than 10,000 ohms?	**Yes** For DTC B2277, GO to H6. For DTC C2793, GO to H5. **No** REPAIR circuit(s) 3140 (BK) and/or 3141 (WH) for an open. CLEAR the DTCs. CYCLE the ignition switch to the OFF position for 3 seconds. REPEAT the self-test.

LTV0500000001153

Fig. 7 Test H: Steering Is Very Difficult/Very Easy (Part 2 of 6)

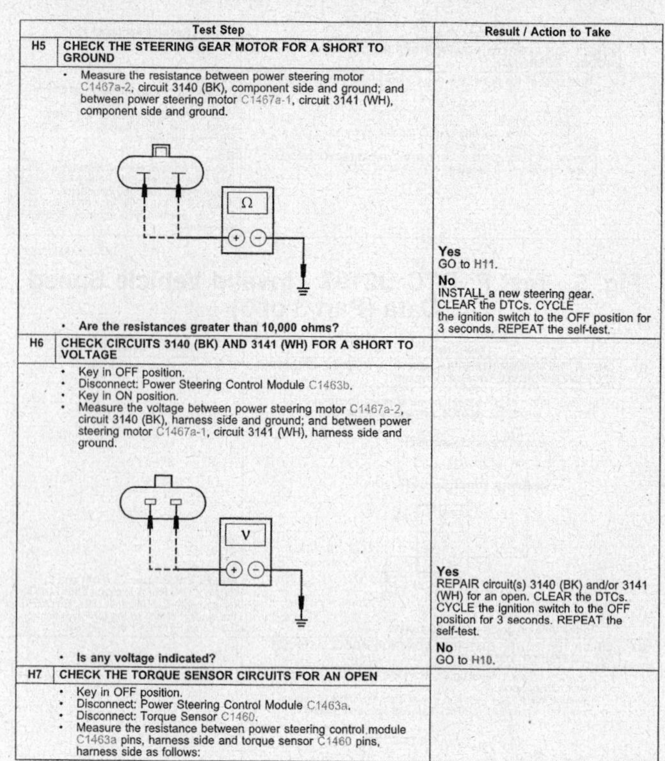

Step	Test Step	Result / Action to Take
H5	**CHECK THE STEERING GEAR MOTOR FOR A SHORT TO GROUND** • Measure the resistance between power steering motor C1467a-2, circuit 3140 (BK), component side and ground; and between power steering motor C1467a-1, circuit 3141 (WH), component side and ground. • Are the resistances greater than 10,000 ohms?	**Yes** GO to H11. **No** INSTALL a new steering gear. CLEAR the DTCs. CYCLE the ignition switch to the OFF position for 3 seconds. REPEAT the self-test.
H6	**CHECK CIRCUITS 3140 (BK) AND 3141 (WH) FOR A SHORT TO VOLTAGE** • Key in OFF position. • Disconnect: Power Steering Control Module C1463b. • Key in ON position. • Measure the voltage between power steering motor C1467a-2, circuit 3140 (BK), harness side and ground; and between power steering motor C1467a-1, circuit 3141 (WH), harness side and ground. • Is any voltage indicated?	**Yes** REPAIR circuit(s) 3140 (BK) and/or 3141 (WH) for an open. CLEAR the DTCs. CYCLE the ignition switch to the OFF position for 3 seconds. REPEAT the self-test. **No** GO to H10.
H7	**CHECK THE TORQUE SENSOR CIRCUITS FOR AN OPEN** • Key in OFF position. • Disconnect: Power Steering Control Module C1463a. • Disconnect: Torque Sensor C1460. • Measure the resistance between power steering control module C1463a pins, harness side and torque sensor C1460 pins, harness side as follows:	

LTV0500000001154

Fig. 7 Test H: Steering Is Very Difficult/Very Easy (Part 3 of 6)

Step	Test Step	Result / Action to Take
H7	**CHECK THE TORQUE SENSOR CIRCUITS FOR AN OPEN (Continued)**	

Power Steering Control Module Pin	Torque Sensor Pin	Circuit
C1463a-5	C1460-1	997 (BN/OG)
C1463a-10	C1460-2	998 (YE/LG)
C1463a-12	C1460-6	1572 (DG)
C1463a-3	C1460-3	1573 (YE)
C1463a-7	C1460-4	1221 (WH/OG)

• Are the resistances less than 5 ohms?

Yes
GO to H8.
No
REPAIR the affected circuit(s) for an open. CLEAR the DTCs. CYCLE the ignition switch to the OFF position for 3 seconds. REPEAT the self-test.

Step	Test Step	Result / Action to Take
H8	**CHECK THE TORQUE SENSOR CIRCUITS FOR A SHORT TO GROUND** • Measure the resistance between torque sensor C1460 pins, harness side and ground as follows:	

Torque Sensor Pin	Circuit
C1460-1	997 (BN/OG)
C1460-2	998 (YE/LG)
C1460-3	1573 (YE)
C1460-6	1572 (DG)

• Are the resistances greater than 10,000 ohms?

Yes
GO to H9.
No
REPAIR the affected circuit(s) for a short to ground. CLEAR the DTCs. CYCLE the ignition switch to the OFF position for 3 seconds. REPEAT the self-test.

LTV0500000001155

Fig. 7 Test H: Steering Is Very Difficult/Very Easy (Part 4 of 6)

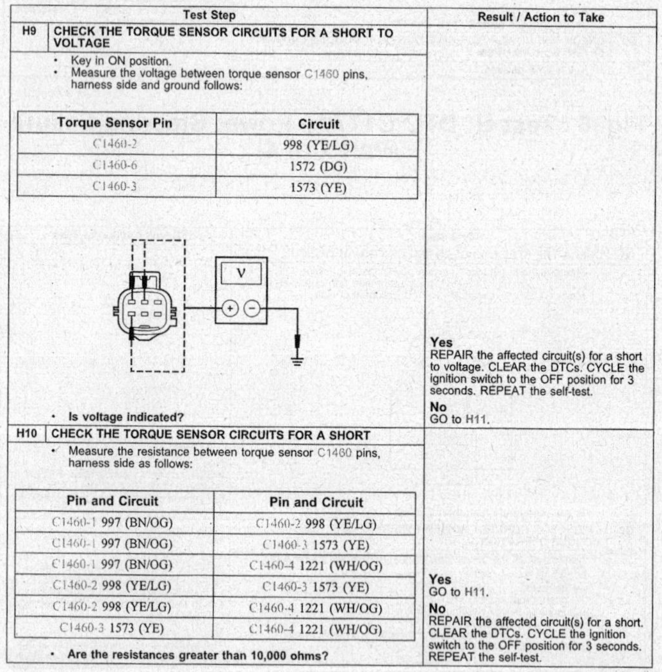

Step	Test Step	Result / Action to Take
H9	**CHECK THE TORQUE SENSOR CIRCUITS FOR A SHORT TO VOLTAGE** • Key in ON position. • Measure the voltage between torque sensor C1460 pins, harness side and ground follows:	

Torque Sensor Pin	Circuit
C1460-2	998 (YE/LG)
C1460-6	1572 (DG)
C1460-3	1573 (YE)

• Is voltage indicated?

Yes
REPAIR the affected circuit(s) for a short to voltage. CLEAR the DTCs. CYCLE the ignition switch to the OFF position for 3 seconds. REPEAT the self-test.
No
GO to H11.

Step	Test Step	Result / Action to Take
H10	**CHECK THE TORQUE SENSOR CIRCUITS FOR A SHORT** • Measure the resistance between torque sensor C1460 pins, harness side as follows:	

Pin and Circuit	Pin and Circuit
C1460-1 997 (BN/OG)	C1460-2 998 (YE/LG)
C1460-1 997 (BN/OG)	C1460-3 1573 (YE)
C1460-1 997 (BN/OG)	C1460-4 1221 (WH/OG)
C1460-2 998 (YE/LG)	C1460-3 1573 (YE)
C1460-2 998 (YE/LG)	C1460-4 1221 (WH/OG)
C1460-3 1573 (YE)	C1460-4 1221 (WH/OG)

• Are the resistances greater than 10,000 ohms?

Yes
GO to H11.
No
REPAIR the affected circuit(s) for a short. CLEAR the DTCs. CYCLE the ignition switch to the OFF position for 3 seconds. REPEAT the self-test.

LTV0500000001156

Fig. 7 Test H: Steering Is Very Difficult/Very Easy (Part 5 of 6)

	Test Step	Result / Action to Take
H11	**CHECK FOR CORRECT POWER STEERING CONTROL MODULE OPERATION**	
	• Disconnect all the power steering control module connectors. • Check for: — corrosion. — pushed-out pins. • Connect all power steering control module connectors and make sure they are seated correctly. • Operate the system and verify if the concern is still present. • **Is the concern still present?**	**Yes** INSTALL a new power steering control module. CLEAR the DTCs. CYCLE the ignition switch to the OFF position for 3 seconds. REPEAT the self-test. If the condition still remains, INSTALL a new steering gear. CLEAR the DTCs. CYCLE the ignition switch to the OFF position for 3 seconds. REPEAT the self-test **No** The system is operating correctly at this time. The concern may have been caused by a loose or corroded connector. CLEAR the DTCs. CYCLE the ignition switch to the OFF position for 3 seconds. REPEAT the self-test.
H12	**CHECK THE STEERING COLUMN BEARINGS AND THE INTERMEDIATE SHAFT**	
	NOTE: Be sure to keep the clockspring centered when disconnecting the intermediate shaft. • Check the steering column and intermediate shaft for grounding. • Disconnect the steering column intermediate shaft U-joint at the steering gear. • Verify that the intermediate shaft U-joints do not bind and move freely and that the steering column bearing rotates freely. • **Are the steering column bearing and intermediate shaft U-joints OK?**	**Yes** GO to H13. **No** If the steering column or the intermediate shaft is grounding, REPAIR as necessary. If the steering column bearings or the intermediate shaft are binding, INSTALL a new steering column.
H13	**CHECK THE FRONT BALL JOINTS AND UPPER STRUT BEARING**	
	• Verify that the front ball joints and upper strut bearing move freely and are not binding or sticking. • **Are the front ball joints and upper strut bearing OK?**	**Yes** INSTALL a new steering gear. **No** INSTALL new ball joints or an upper strut bearing as necessary.

LTV0500000001157

Fig. 7 Test H: Steering Is Very Difficult/Very Easy (Part 6 of 6)

	Test Step	Result / Action to Take
J1	**CHECK THE STEERING COLUMN BEARING**	
	• Inspect the steering column mounting fasteners and bearings for looseness. • **Are the fasteners and bearings OK?**	**Yes** GO to J2. **No** TIGHTEN the steering column mounting fasteners or INSTALL a new steering column.
J2	**CHECK THE STEERING LINKAGE FOR LOOSENESS**	
	• Carry out the steering linkage component test. Refer to Component Tests in this section. • **Is the steering linkage OK?**	**Yes** DIAGNOSE suspension. **No** INSTALL new steering linkage as necessary.

LTV0500000001159

Fig. 9 Test J: Excessive Steering Wheel Play

	Test Step	Result / Action to Take
I1	**CHECK FOR MECHANICAL NOISE**	
	• Test drive the vehicle to verify the steering system noise. • **Does the steering system make a clunking noise when rotating the steering wheel from left to right?**	**Yes** CHECK for loose, worn or damaged tie-rod ends. If the noise is from the steering column, CHECK the steering column intermediate shaft for grounding through the body and REPAIR as necessary. If the noise is from the steering column boot bushing, INSTALL a new steering column boot bushing. If the noise is from the suspension components, INSTALL new suspension components as necessary. If the noise is from loose, worn or damaged intermediate shaft U-joint(s), INSTALL a new steering column coupling. **No** If a squeak is present in the steering column, REPAIR the steering column mountings or ALIGN the steering column as necessary. For all other concerns, GO to I2.
I2	**VERIFY THE CONCERN**	
	NOTE: Make sure the vehicle is on a flat, dry surface, the transmission is in PARK and the windows are rolled up. **NOTE:** Some power steering noise is expected. If in doubt of the acceptability of the noise level, evaluate another vehicle of the same model and powertrain. • Key in START position. • Turn the steering wheel one-half turn off-center to the right, then one-half turn off-center to the left. • **Is the power steering noisy?**	**Yes** If a grunting noise is present, VERIFY the steering column boot is OK and the exhaust system is not grounding out. If a moan is present, VERIFY the tie-rod ends and ball joints are OK. INSTALL a new steering gear. **No** If the steering system noise is a hiss or whistle, INSPECT the steering column boot at the dash panel. REPAIR or INSTALL a new boot as necessary. INSPECT the steering gear input shaft for wear or damage. INSPECT the power steering gear and intermediate shaft and repair as necessary. INSPECT for openings or missing plugs in the instrument panel cowl and repair as necessary. If there are no missing plugs or openings in the cowl or a grounded power steering gear or intermediate shaft, INSTALL a new steering gear.

LTV0500000001158

Fig. 8 Test I: Steering System Noise

	Test Step	Result / Action to Take
K1	**CHECK FOR TIRE PULL**	
	• Rotate the front wheel and tire assemblies side-to-side. Refer to Section 204-04. • Carry out a road test on a smooth, flat, dry road. • **Does the vehicle drift/pull?**	**Yes** If the vehicle pulls in the opposite direction, GO to K2. If the vehicle pulls in the original direction, GO to K3. **No** The concern has been corrected.
K2	**ROTATE THE WHEEL AND TIRE ASSEMBLIES FRONT TO REAR**	
	• Rotate the front wheel and tire assemblies from the front to the rear. Refer to Section 204-04. • Carry out a road test on a smooth, flat, dry road. • **Does the vehicle drift/pull?**	**Yes** GO to K3. **No** The concern has been corrected.
K3	**CHECK THE STEERING COLUMN INTERMEDIATE SHAFT**	
	NOTE: Be sure to keep the clockspring centered when disconnecting the intermediate shaft. • Check the steering column and intermediate shaft for grounding. • Disconnect the steering column intermediate shaft at the steering column. • Inspect the steering column intermediate shaft U-joints for looseness or wear. • **Are the steering column intermediate shaft U-joints OK?**	**Yes** GO to K4. **No** INSTALL a new steering column.
K4	**CHECK THE STEERING GEAR MOUNTING**	
	• Check the steering gear mounts for looseness or wear. • **Are the steering gear mounts OK?**	**Yes** GO to K5. **No** INSTALL new steering gear mounts.
K5	**CHECK THE SUSPENSION COMPONENTS**	
	• Check for loose or worn suspension components. • **Are the suspension components OK?**	**Yes** GO to K6. **No** INSTALL new suspension components.
K6	**CHECK THE WHEEL ALIGNMENT**	
	NOTE: The vehicle will tend to pull toward the side with the least positive caster and the most positive camber. • Using a suitable alignment system, measure the wheel alignment settings. • **Are the alignment settings within specifications?**	**Yes** GO to K7. **No** ADJUST the alignment angles to specifications. DO NOT exceed the specifications. TEST the system for normal operation.
K7	**VERIFY THE FRAME ALIGNMENT**	
	• Check for correct frame alignments. • **Are the frame alignment settings within specifications?**	**Yes** INSTALL a new steering gear. TEST the system for normal operation. If the condition still remains, INSTALL a new power steering control module. **No** ALIGN the frame to specifications.

LTV0500000001160

Fig. 10 Test K: Steering System Drift/Pull/Wander

POWER STEERING SYSTEM BLEED

Refer to "Power Steering Pump" for system bleed procedure.

COMPONENT SERVICE

Power Steering Control Module, Replace

1. Remove air cleaner assembly, then the battery junction box bracket nuts on strut tower and position BJB aside.
2. Disconnect power steering control module electrical connectors.
3. Remove power steering control module nuts, then ground cable bolt and nuts from inside vehicle.
4. Remove power steering control module from vehicle.
5. Reverse procedure to install. Tighten power steering control module bolts and nuts to 17 ft. lbs.

DISC BRAKES

INDEX

PRECAUTIONS

Do not spill brake fluid on painted surfaces. If brake fluid is spilled on surfaces, wash off immediately.

Always inspect brake fluid level prior to servicing brake system If brake fluid level is low, clean reservoir cap and sealing area before removing cap, then top up fluid top proper level. Prior to performing any brake system diagnosis, ensure brake warning indicator system is functional.

INSPECTION

Brake Linings

Remove both front wheels and inspect the brake discs, calipers and linings. (Wheel bearings should be inspected at this time and repacked if required).

Do not get any oil or grease on the linings. It is recommended that both front wheel sets be replaced whenever a respective shoe and lining is worn or damaged. Inspect and, if required, replace rear brake linings also.

If the caliper is cracked or fluid leakage through the casting is evident, it must be replaced as a unit.

Brake Roughness

The most common cause of brake chatter on disc brakes is a variation in thickness of the disc. If roughness, vibration and/or pedal pulsation are encountered during vehicle operation, the disc may have excessive thickness variation. To inspect for this condition, measure the disc at twelve points with a micrometer at a radius approximately one inch from edge of disc. If thickness measurements vary more than specifications allow, the disc should be replaced with a new one.

Excessive lateral runout of braking disc may cause a "knocking back" of the pistons, possibly creating increased pedal travel and vibration when brakes are applied.

Before inspecting runout, wheel bearings should be adjusted. Be sure to make adjustments according to recommendations given in the individual truck chapters.

Brake Disc Service

Servicing of disc brakes is extremely critical due to close tolerances required in machining the brake disc to ensure proper brake operation.

Maintenance of these close controls on friction surfaces is required to prevent brake roughness. In addition, surface finish must be non-directional and maintained at a micro-inch finish. This close control of the rubbing surface finish is required to avoid pulls and erratic performance and promote long lining life and equal lining wear of both lefthand and righthand brakes.

In light of the foregoing remarks, refinishing of the rubbing surfaces should not be attempted unless suitable precision equipment, capable of measuring in micro-inches (millionths of an inch) is available.

To inspect runout of a disc, mount a suitable dial indicator on a convenient part (steering knuckle, tie rod, disc brake caliper housing) so that the plunger of the dial indicator contacts the disc at a point one inch from the outer edge. If the total indicated runout exceeds specifications, install a new disc.

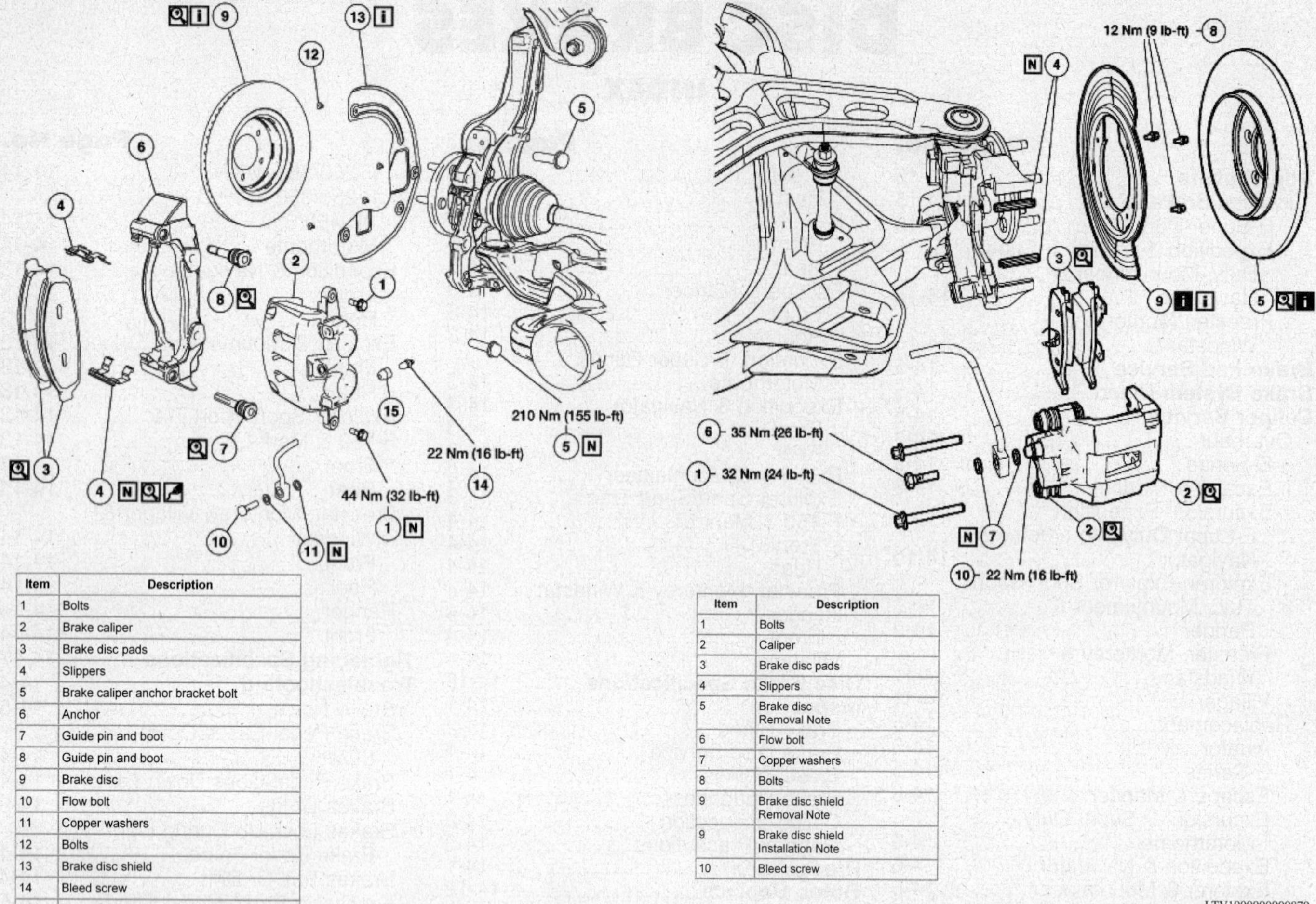

Item	Description
1	Bolts
2	Brake caliper
3	Brake disc pads
4	Slippers
5	Brake caliper anchor bracket bolt
6	Anchor
7	Guide pin and boot
8	Guide pin and boot
9	Brake disc
10	Flow bolt
11	Copper washers
12	Bolts
13	Brake disc shield
14	Bleed screw
15	Bleed screw cap

Fig. 1 Front disc brake system. Aviator

Item	Description
1	Bolts
2	Caliper
3	Brake disc pads
4	Slippers
5	Brake disc Removal Note
6	Flow bolt
7	Copper washers
8	Bolts
9	Brake disc shield Removal Note
9	Brake disc shield Installation Note
10	Bleed screw

Fig. 2 Rear disc brake system. Aviator

General Precautions

1. Grease or any other foreign material must be kept off the caliper, surfaces of the disc and external surfaces of the hub, during service procedures. Handling brake disc and calipers should be done in a way to avoid deformation of the disc and nicking or scratching brake linings.
2. If inspection reveals rubber piston seals are worn or damaged, they should be replaced immediately.
3. During removal and installation of a wheel assembly, exercise care so as not to interfere with or damage the caliper splash shield, the bleeder screw or the transfer tube, (if equipped).
4. Front wheel bearings should be adjusted to specifications.
5. Be sure vehicle is centered on hoist before servicing any of the front end components to avoid bending or damaging the disc splash shield on full righthand or lefthand wheel turns.
6. Before the vehicle is moved after any brake service work, be sure to obtain a firm brake pedal.
7. The assembly bolts of the two caliper housings (if equipped) should not be disturbed unless the caliper requires service.

Caliper Inspection

Should it become required to remove the caliper for installation of new components, clean all components in denatured alcohol, wipe dry using lint-free cloths. Using an air hose, blow out drilled passages and bores. Inspect dust boots for punctures or tears. If punctures or tears are evident, new boots should be installed upon reassembly.

Inspect piston bores in both housings for scoring or pitting. Bores that show light scratches or corrosion can usually be cleaned with crocus cloth. However, bores that have deep scratches or scoring may be honed, provided the diameter of the bore is not increased more than .002 inch. If the bore does not clean up within this specification, a new caliper housing should be installed (black stains on the bore walls are caused by piston seals and will do no harm).

When using a hone, be sure to install the hone baffle before honing bore. The baffle is used to protect the hone stones from damage. Use extreme care in cleaning calipers after honing. Remove all dust and grit by flushing caliper with denatured alcohol. Wipe dry with clean lint-free cloth and then clean a second time in the same manner.

Brake Bleed

The disc brake hydraulic system can be bled manually or with pressure bleeding equipment. On vehicles with disc brakes the brake pedal will require more pumping and frequent inspecting of fluid level in master cylinder during bleeding operation.

Never use brake fluid that has been drained from hydraulic system when bleeding the brakes. Be sure the disc brake pistons are returned to their normal positions and that the shoe and lining assemblies are properly seated. Before driving the vehicle, inspect brake operation to be sure that a firm pedal has been obtained.

DESCRIPTION

Aviator

FRONT

The Aviator utilizes a dual piston front brake caliper and a single piston rear brake caliper. The caliper floats on two guide pins that are bolted to the caliper and extend into the caliper anchor, **Fig. 1.**

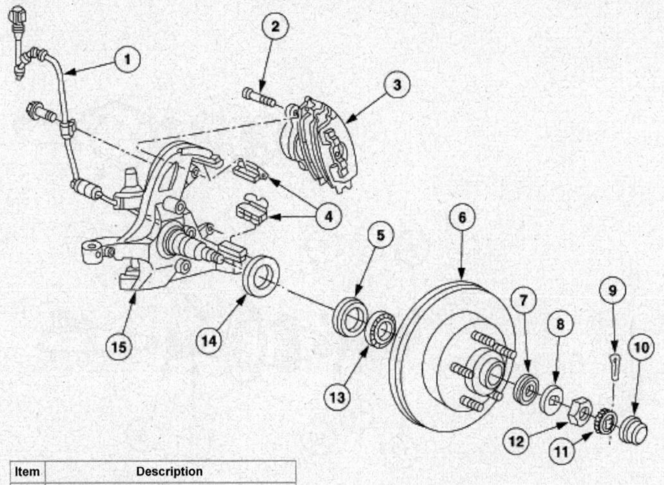

Item	Description
1	Front brake anti-lock sensor
2	Disc brake caliper bolt
3	Disc brake caliper
4	Disc brake pad anti-rattle clip
5	Grease seal
6	Brake disc and hub
7	Front wheel bearing
8	Front wheel outer bearing retainer washer
9	Cotter pin
10	Hub grease cap
11	Nut retainer
12	Spindle nut
13	Front wheel bearing
14	Front brake splash shield gasket
15	Front wheel spindle

LTV1900000000861

Fig. 3 Front disc brake system. E-150

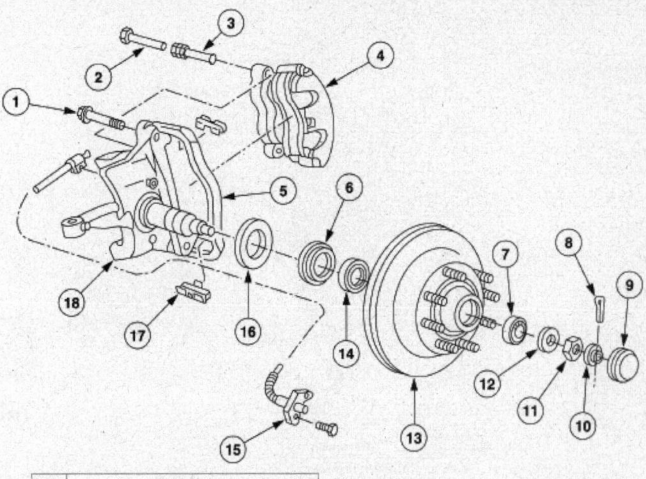

Item	Description
1	Anchor bracket-to-spindle bolt
2	Disc brake caliper bolt
3	Caliper bolt sleeve
4	Disc brake caliper
5	Front disc brake caliper anchor plate
6	Wheel hub grease seal
7	Front wheel bearing
8	Cotter pin
9	Hub grease cap
10	Nut retainer
11	Spindle nut
12	Front wheel outer bearing retainer washer
13	Brake disc and hub
14	Bearing cone and roller
15	Front brake anti-lock sensor
16	Front brake splash shield gasket
17	Disc brake pad anti-rattle clip
18	Front wheel spindle

LTV1900000000862

Fig. 4 Front brake system. E-250 & E-350 w/single rear wheel

REAR

The rear disc brake system utilizes a single piston brake caliper. The mechanical parking brake system uses a drum in hat system within the rear brake disc, **Fig. 2.**

E-Series

FRONT

The disc brake caliper is a pin slider, single piston design on the E-150 models and a pin slider dual piston design on the E-250, E-350, E-450 & E-550 models, **Figs. 3 through 5.**

REAR

E-Series vehicles equipped with dual rear wheels, utilize a dual piston rear disc brake system. The system uses a vented-cast, drum in hat rear brake disc, **Figs. 6 through 8.**

Escape & Mariner

FRONT

The front disc brake system includes the brake caliper, **Fig. 9,** disc brake pads, anchor plate, and brake disc. The brake caliper is a single piston floating design. The caliper is mounted to the anchor plate by caliper guide bolts. The brake caliper slides, or floats, on the caliper guide bolts. The disc brake is a cast, ventilated type disc.

REAR

The rear disc brake system includes the brake caliper, **Fig. 10,** brake pads and brake disc. The brake caliper is a single piston floating design. The brake caliper is mounted to the anchor plate by caliper guide bolts. The brake caliper slides, or floats, on the caliper guide bolts. The brake disc is a cast, non-ventilated type rotor.

Excursion, F-Super Duty & Motorhome

The front brake disc caliper mounts to a caliper anchor plate which bolts to the front wheel spindle. The caliper is a dual piston, pin slider type with a fluid inlet at the center of the housing, **Fig. 11.**

Expedition & Navigator

FRONT

The front brake caliper bolts to the front caliper plate which is attached to the front wheel spindle or knuckle. The caliper is a dual piston, pin slider type, **Figs. 12 and 13.**

REAR

The rear brake caliper is a single piston design. The brake disc is a vented, full cast, drum in hat type, **Fig. 14.**

Explorer & Mountaineer

These models utilize a front dual piston and rear single piston caliper system, **Figs. 15 and 16.**

Explorer Sport/Sport Trac

On 2WD vehicles, the disc brake caliper bolts to the spindle assembly. The disc and hub is an integrally cast assembly. On 4WD vehicles, the front disc brake caliper bolts to the front knuckle assembly and utilizes a separate brake disc which attaches to the

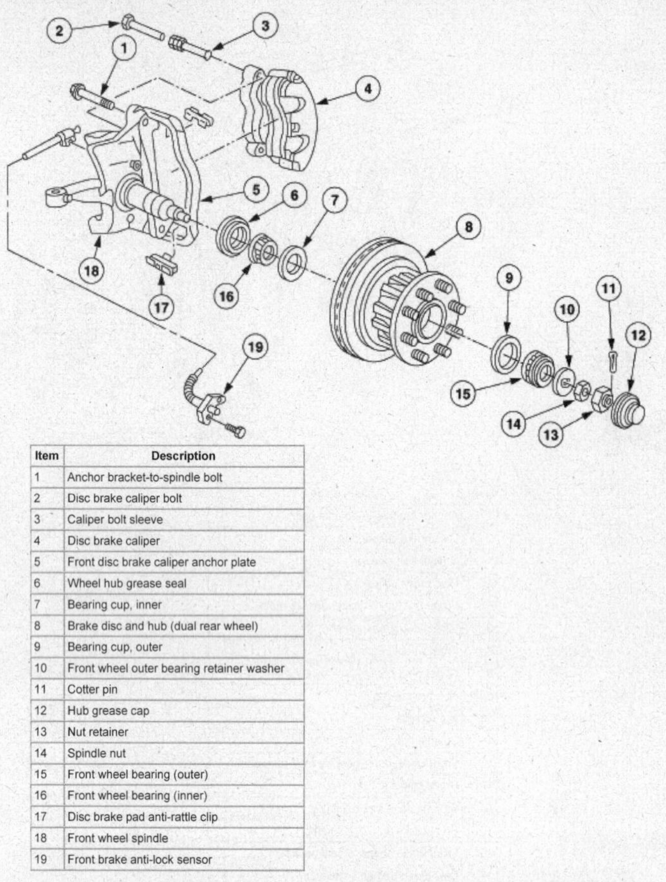

Item	Description
1	Anchor bracket-to-spindle bolt
2	Disc brake caliper bolt
3	Caliper bolt sleeve
4	Disc brake caliper
5	Front disc brake caliper anchor plate
6	Wheel hub grease seal
7	Bearing cup, inner
8	Brake disc and hub (dual rear wheel)
9	Bearing cup, outer
10	Front wheel outer bearing retainer washer
11	Cotter pin
12	Hub grease cap
13	Nut retainer
14	Spindle nut
15	Front wheel bearing (outer)
16	Front wheel bearing (inner)
17	Disc brake pad anti-rattle clip
18	Front wheel spindle
19	Front brake anti-lock sensor

LTV1900000000863

Fig. 5 Front disc brake system. E-350, E-450 & E-550 w/dual rear wheel

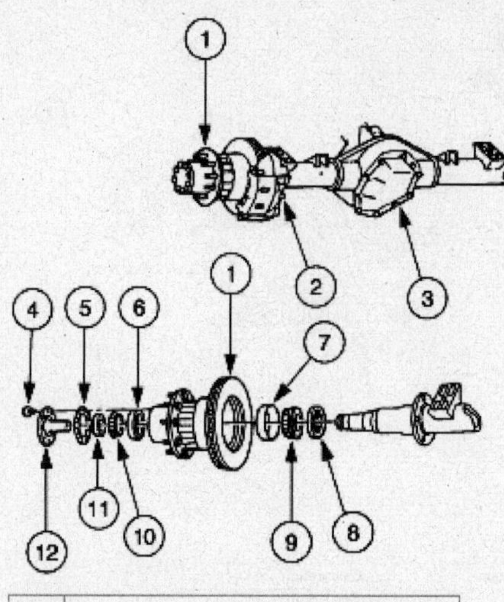

Item	Description
1	Rear brake disc and hub assembly
2	Rear disc brake caliper
3	Dana full-floating axle — Model 80
4	Axle shaft-to-rear hub bolt
5	Rear wheel gasket
6	Outer bearing cup
7	Inner bearing cup
8	Inner hub seal
9	Rear wheel bearing inner cone and roller
10	Rear wheel bearing outer cone and roller
11	Wheel bearing lock nut
12	Axle shaft

LTV1900000000880

Fig. 6 Rear disc brake system. E-Series w/dual rear wheels

knuckle assembly. Both vehicles use a dual piston, pin slider type caliper, **Figs. 17 and 18.**

F-150 & Mark LT

FRONT

The front brake disc caliper is a two piston, sliding pin type caliper that mounts to the front wheel knuckle or spindle, **Figs. 12 and 13.**

REAR

The rear brake disc system utilizes a solid, full cast, drum in hat brake disc, **Fig. 19.** The caliper is a single piston design with a riveted spring clip that secures it to either the rear disc brake caliper or the rear disc brake caliper housing.

Ranger

FRONT

The front brake disc caliper is a dual piston pin slider style caliper that bolts to front wheel knuckle or spindle, **Figs. 20 and 21.**The caliper has a fluid inlet at the center of the caliper housing. On 2WD vehicles, the brake disc and hub are an integrally cast assembly. On 4WD vehicles, a separate brake disc attaches to the wheel hub.

Villager

These models use a pin slider caliper type system, **Fig. 22,** in which the caliper slides on two pins attached to the spindle assembly.

Freestar, Monterey & Windstar

These models use a pin slider caliper type system, **Fig. 23.**

TROUBLESHOOTING

Brakes Pull Or Drift

1. Tire air pressure.
2. Wheel alignment.
3. Brake pads, shoes or linings.
4. Brake or suspension components.

Red Brake Warning Indicator Always On

1. Instrument cluster.
2. Warning indicator circuit.
3. Parking brake.
4. Brake fluid level.

Brake Pedal Goes Down Fast

1. Brake fluid level.
2. Air in system.
3. Brake master cylinder fault.
4. Normal RABS or ABS function.

Brake Pedal Eases Down Slowly

1. Air in system.
2. Brake master cylinder fault.
3. Normal RABS or ABS function.

Brakes Lock Up During Light Brake Pedal Force

1. Disc or drum brake component.
2. Parking brake component.
3. Anti-lock brake control system.
4. Fluid control valve.

Excessive Or Erratic Brake Pedal Travel

1. Leak in hydraulic system.
2. Air in system.
3. Disc brake caliper.

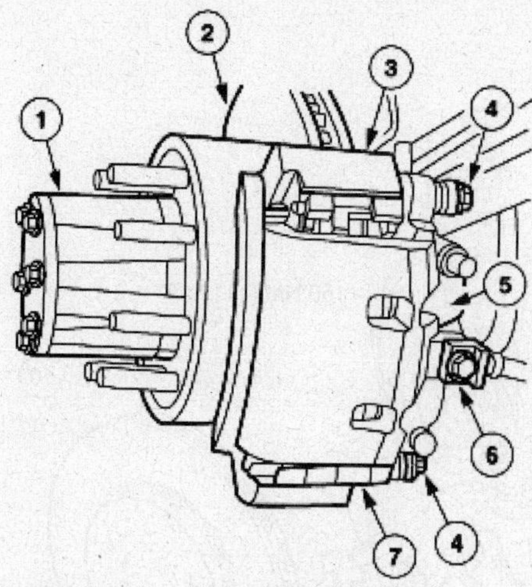

Item	Description
1	Hub
2	Brake disc
3	Caliper anchor plate
4	Caliper pin bolts
5	Caliper
6	Brake hose
7	Stainless steel slippers

LTV1900000000881

Fig. 7 Rear disc brake caliper components. E-Series w/dual rear wheels

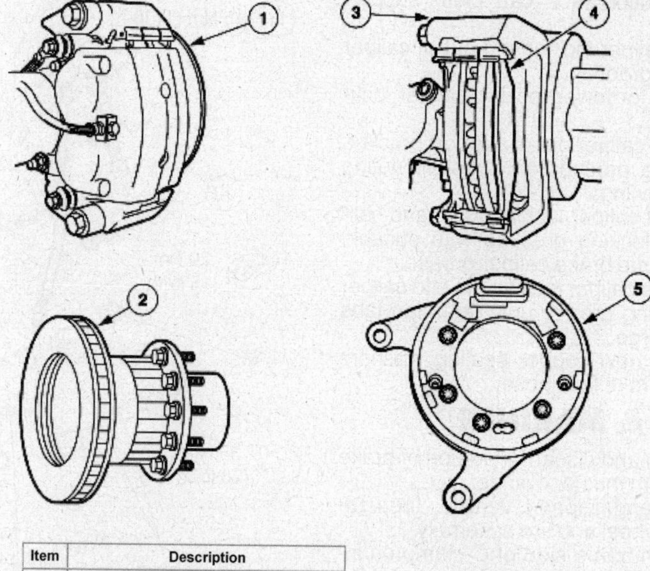

Item	Description
1	Rear disc brake caliper
2	Rear brake disc and hub assembly
3	Rear disc brake caliper anchor plate
4	Brake pads
5	Rear wheel disc brake adapter

LTV1900000000882

Fig. 8 Rear disc brake system, disc components. E-Series w/dual rear wheels

4. Drum brake components.
5. Brake booster to brake master cylinder push rod adjustment.
6. Brake master cylinder.

Brakes Drag

1. Parking brake component.
2. Disc brake caliper.
3. Drum brake component.
4. Brake booster to brake master cylinder push rod adjustment.
5. Brake master cylinder.

Excessive Brake Pedal Effort

1. Power brake booster.
2. Power brake booster check valve.
3. Power brake booster hose.

Brake Noise

Disc or drum brake component.

BRAKE SYSTEM BLEED

Refer to "Hydraulic Brakes" for brake system bleed procedure.

BRAKE PAD SERVICE

1. Remove and discard a portion of brake fluid from master cylinder.
2. Raise and support vehicle, then remove wheel and tire assembly.
3. Unclip speed sensor wiring from brake hose.
4. Remove caliper as outlined in "Caliper Service" leaving brake hose connected.
5. Secure caliper with wire so that caliper is not hanging with weight on brake hose.
6. Remove pads.
7. Reverse procedure to install.

CALIPER SERVICE

Replacement

AVIATOR

FRONT

1. Raise and support vehicle.
2. Remove front tire and wheel assemblies.
3. Remove components in sequence, **Fig. 1.**
4. Reverse procedure to install.

REAR

Refer to **Fig. 2,** and remove rear brake components in sequence listed.

E-SERIES

FRONT

E-150, E-250, E-350 & E-450

1. Raise and support vehicle, remove front tire and wheel assemblies.
2. Unclip speed sensor wiring from front brake hose.
3. Disconnect and plug front brake caliper hose from caliper. Discard copper sealing rings.
4. Remove two disc caliper mounting bolts, then the caliper, **Fig. 24.**
5. Reverse procedure to install, noting the following:
   a. Fill rubber caliper sleeve boots with caliper grease.
   b. Install new copper sealing washers.
   c. Bleed system and inspect for proper operation.

E-550

1. Raise and support vehicle, remove front tire and wheel assemblies.
2. Remove and plug caliper hose. Discard copper sealing washers.
3. Remove brake caliper pin bolts, **Fig. 25,** then lift caliper from anchor plate.
4. Reverse procedure to install.

REAR

E-150, E-250, E-350 & E-550

1. Raise and support vehicle, remove wheel and tire assembly.
2. Remove caliper pin bolts.
3. Remove brake hose flow bolt. Remove and discard copper washers.
4. Remove rear brake disc caliper.
5. Reverse procedure to install.

E-450

1. Raise and support vehicle, remove rear wheel and tire assemblies.
2. Remove brake hose flow bolt, discard copper washer sealing rings.
3. Set notched end of brake caliper pin removal tool No. 206–D004, or equivalent at 45° angle against end of upper caliper locking pin.
4. Tap tool to squeeze caliper locking pin

so retention tabs can clear support bracket.
5. Drive caliper locking pin out of caliper locking groove.
6. Repeat for lower locking caliper locking pin.
7. Tilt rear caliper out of support bracket.
8. Reverse procedure to install, noting the following:
   a. Coat caliper locking keys and caliper locking grooves with suitable silicone brake caliper grease.
   b. Drive caliper locking pin into caliper locking groove until retention tabs emerge.
   c. Use new copper sealing washers on brake fluid hose.

ESCAPE & MARINER

1. Syphon and discard a portion of brake fluid from master cylinder.
2. Raise and support vehicle, then remove wheel and tire assembly.
3. Position frame side of C-clamp on inboard side of disc brake caliper. **Do not place clamp frame over front brake hose.**
4. Position screw side of C-clamp on outboard brake shoe and lining, then tighten C-clamp until there is enough clearance to remove caliper.
5. Remove front brake hose flow bolt, then disconnect and plug front brake hose. Discard copper washers.
6. Remove two caliper slide pins.
7. Slide brake shoe and lining out of front disc brake caliper anchor plate.
8. Remove caliper anchor plate from front wheel hub and spindle.
9. Reverse procedure to install, noting the following:
   a. Tighten nuts and bolts to specification.
   b. Use new copper washers.
   c. Fill brake fluid reservoir and bleed brake system as outlined in "Hydraulic Brakes" chapter.

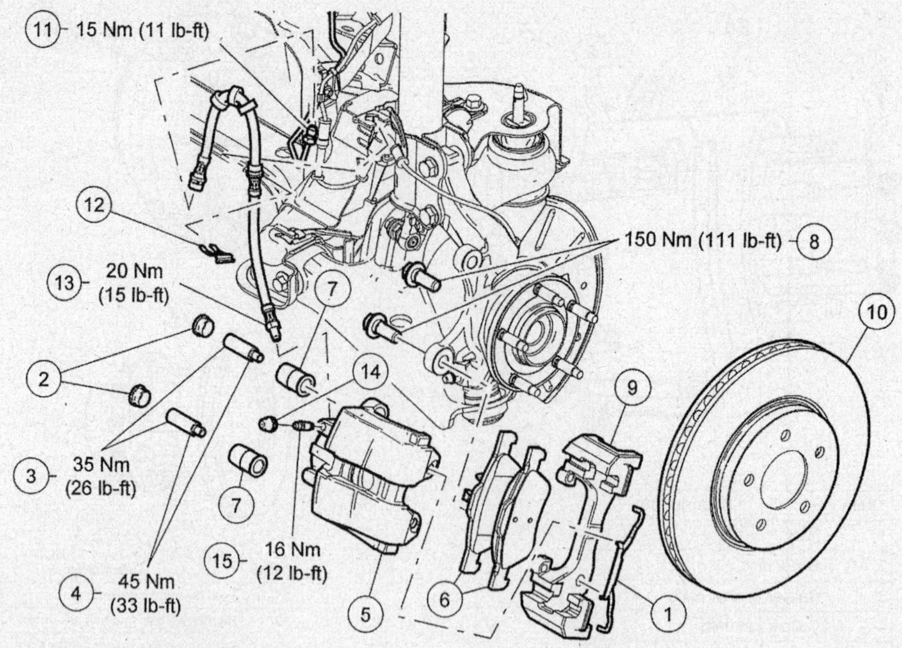

Item	Description
1	Brake caliper clip
2	Brake caliper dust boot caps (2 required)
3	Brake caliper guide bolts (disc-drum system) (2 required)
4	Brake caliper guide bolts (4-wheel disc brake system) (2 required)
5	Brake caliper (RH/LH)
6	Brake pads (kit)
7	Brake caliper dust boots (2 required)

Item	Description
8	Brake caliper anchor plate bolts (2 required)
9	Brake caliper anchor plate
10	Brake disc
11	Brake line fitting nut
12	Brake caliper jounce hose retaining clip
13	Brake caliper jounce hose
14	Bleeder screw cap
15	Bleeder screw

LTV0500000000972

Fig. 9 Exploded view of front disc brake system. Escape & Mariner

EXCURSION, F-SUPER DUTY & MOTORHOME

1. Raise and support vehicle.
2. Remove wheel and tire assembly.
3. Remove front brake hose bolt, then disconnect front brake hose.
4. Remove and discard copper washers, plug front brake hose to prevent fluid loss and contamination.
5. Remove disc caliper pin bolts.
6. Lift front caliper from front disc brake caliper anchor plate.
7. Reverse procedure to install, noting the following:
   a. Use new copper washers when installing front brake hose.
   b. Top up fluid and bleed brake system.
   c. Inspect for leaks and proper system operation.

EXPEDITION & NAVIGATOR

FRONT

1. Raise and support vehicle, then remove tire and wheel assembly.
2. Remove brake pads as outlined in "Brake Pad, Replace."
3. Disconnect and plug front brake hose.
4. Remove brake caliper mounting bolts, then the caliper.
5. Reverse procedure to install.

REAR

1. Raise and support vehicle, remove tire and wheel assemblies.
2. Remove bolt and disconnect fluid hose from caliper, discard copper sealing washers.
3. Remove caliper mounting bolts, then the caliper.
4. Reverse procedure to install.

EXPLORER & MOUNTAINEER

FRONT

1. Remove and discard a portion of brake fluid from master cylinder.
2. Raise and support vehicle, then remove wheel and tire assembly.
3. Use a C-clamp to move piston back into its bore as follows:
   a. Position frame of C-clamp on inboard side of disc brake caliper. Do not place clamp frame over front brake hose.
   b. Position C-clamp screw on outboard brake shoe and lining.
   c. Compress C-clamp only enough to give removal clearance for disc brake caliper.
4. Remove front brake hose flow bolt, then disconnect and plug front brake hose. Discard copper washers.
5. **Use care to retain as much of original caliper slide pin grease as possible.** From inboard side of disc brake caliper, remove two caliper slide pins.
6. Slide brake shoe and lining out of front disc brake caliper anchor plate.
7. Remove two caliper anchor plate bolts, then front disc brake caliper anchor plate from front wheel hub and spindle.
8. Reverse procedure to install, noting the following:
   a. Tighten two caliper anchor plate bolts to specification.
   b. Tighten caliper slide pins to specification.
   c. Use new copper washers.
   d. Tighten flow bolt to specification.

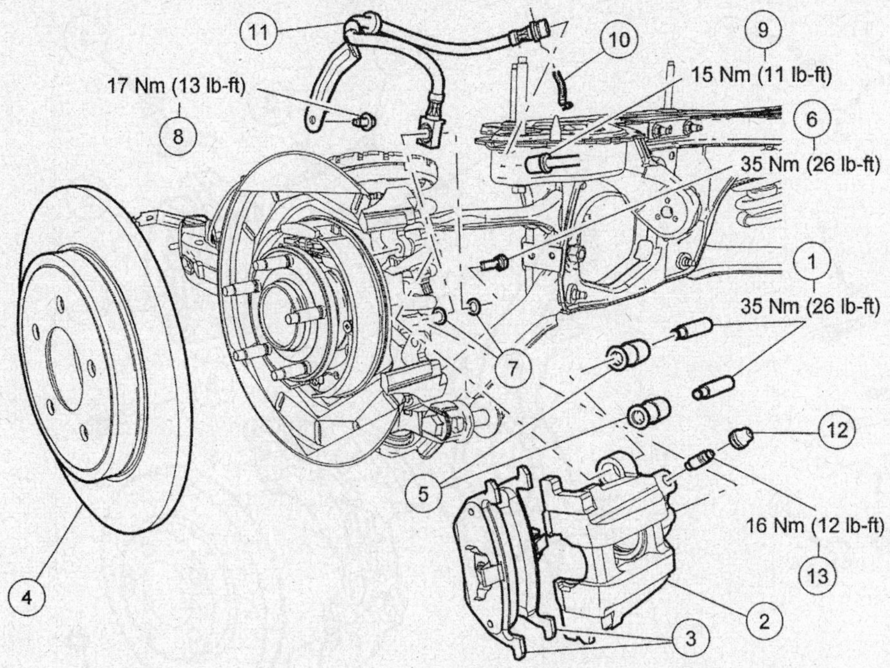

Item	Description
1	Brake caliper guide bolts (2 required)
2	Brake caliper (RH/LH)
3	Brake pads
4	Brake disc
5	Brake caliper guide bolt bushings (2 required)
6	Brake caliper jounce hose flow bolt
7	Copper washers (2 required)

Item	Description
8	Brake caliper jounce hose bracket bolt
9	Brake line fitting nut
10	Brake caliper jounce hose retaining clip
11	Brake caliper jounce hose (RH/LH)
12	Bleeder screw cap
13	Bleeder screw

LTV0500000000973

Fig. 10 Exploded view of rear disc brake system. Escape & Mariner

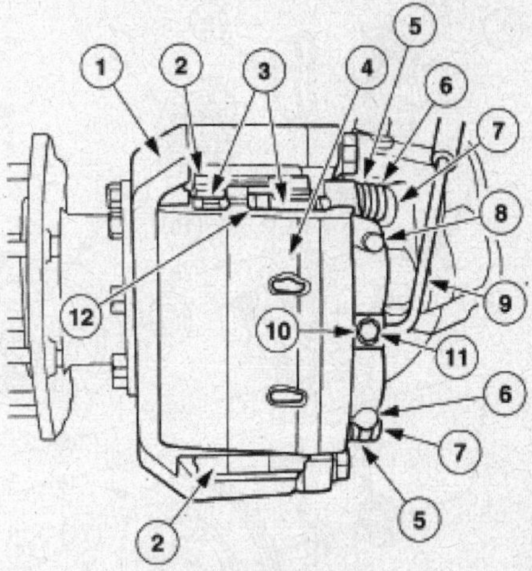

Item	Description
1	Front disc brake caliper anchor plate
2	Stainless steel slippers
3	Pads
4	Disc brake caliper
5	Guide pin boot
6	Guide pin
7	Caliper bolt
8	Bleeder screw and bleeder screw cap assembly
9	Front brake hose
10	Brass washer
11	Flow bolt
12	Front disc brake rotor

LTV1900000000871

Fig. 11 Front brake caliper components. Excursion, F-Super Duty & Motorhome

REAR

1. Remove and discard sufficient brake fluid from master cylinder reservoir.
2. Raise and support vehicle, then remove wheel and tire assembly.
3. Remove rear brake hose to caliper flow bolt and washers. Discard washers.
4. **Do not press against brake shoe and lining spring clip. To avoid damage to spring clip, compress piston only enough to free caliper (about 1⁄16 inch).**
5. Position C-clamp frame on inboard side on rear caliper housing. Position clamp screw on outboard brake shoe and lining backing plate. Tighten c-clamp to press caliper piston into caliper bore enough to release pressure on shoe.
6. Remove c-clamp, then two caliper bolts.
7. Pull caliper off rear wheel brake adapter.
8. Reverse procedure to install, noting the following:
   a. Tighten caliper slide pins to specification.
   b. Use new copper washers.
   c. Tighten flow bolt to specification.

EXPLORER SPORT/SPORT TRAC

1. Raise and support vehicle, remove front tire and wheel assemblies.
2. Remove front brake hose bolt. Do not clamp brake hose, hose can be damaged.
3. Disconnect and plug front brake caliper hose, discard copper sealing washers.
4. Remove brake caliper mounting bolts, then the caliper.
5. Replace copper sealing washers.
6. Reverse procedure to install.

F-150 & MARK LT

FRONT

1. Raise and support vehicle, remove front tire and wheel assemblies.
2. Remove front brake hose bolt, then disconnect and plug hose fitting from caliper. Discard copper sealing washers.
3. Remove two brake caliper mounting bolts, then the caliper.
4. Reverse procedure to install.

REAR

1. Raise and support vehicle, remove rear wheel and tire assemblies.
2. Remove brake hose fitting from caliper, remove and discard copper sealing washers and plug hose.
3. Drain remaining fluid into suitable container.
4. Do not remove guide pins or guide pin boots. Pins and boots are sealed for life and are not repairable.
5. Remove rear caliper bolts, then the caliper and anchor plate.
6. Reverse procedure to install, noting the following:
   a. Ensure stainless steel shoe slippers are correctly positioned. Install new slippers if worn or damaged.
   b. When installed, locator notch on brake pads will be located at upper end of rear disc brake caliper.

RANGER

REMOVAL

1. Raise and support vehicle, remove front tire and wheel assemblies.
2. **On models equipped with 2WD,** remove front brake rotor.
3. **On models equipped with 4WD,** remove hub grease cap, cotter pin, nut retainer and spindle nut, outer bearing retainer washer and bearing, then the brake disc and hub.
4. **On all models,** remove inner grease

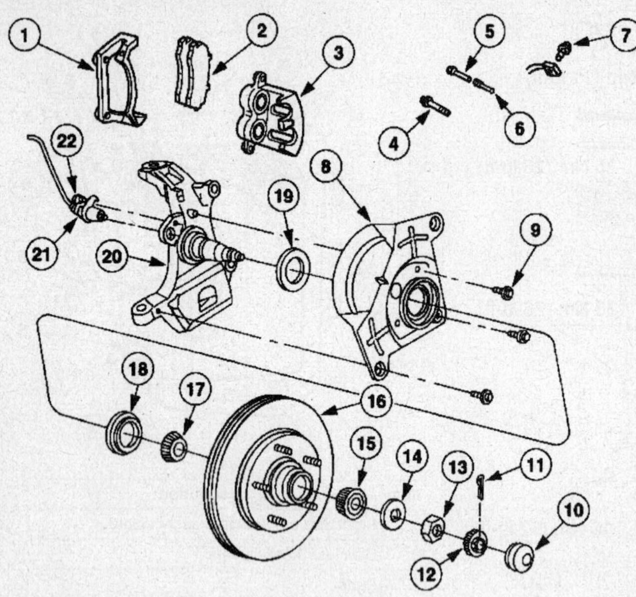

1. Front Disc Brake Caliper Anchor Plate
2. Pads
3. Disc Brake Caliper
4. Front Disc Brake Caliper Anchor Plate Bolt (2 Req'd)
5. Disc Brake Caliper Bolt (2 Req'd)
6. Disc Brake Caliper Locating Pin (2 Req'd)
7. Front Brake Hose
8. Brake Disc Shield
9. Screws (3 Req'd)
10. Hub Grease Cap
11. Cotter Pin
12. Nut Retainer
13. Spindle Nut
14. Front Wheel Outer Bearing Retainer Washer
15. Front Wheel Bearing Outer
16. Brake Disc and Hub
17. Bearing Cone and Roller Inner
18. Wheel Hub Grease Seal
19. Front Brake Splash Shield Gasket
20. Front Wheel Spindle
21. Anti-Lock Brake Sensor
22. Anti-Lock Brake Sensor Bolt

LTV1900000000858

Fig. 12 Front disc brake system. Expedition, F-150, Mark LT & Navigator w/2WD

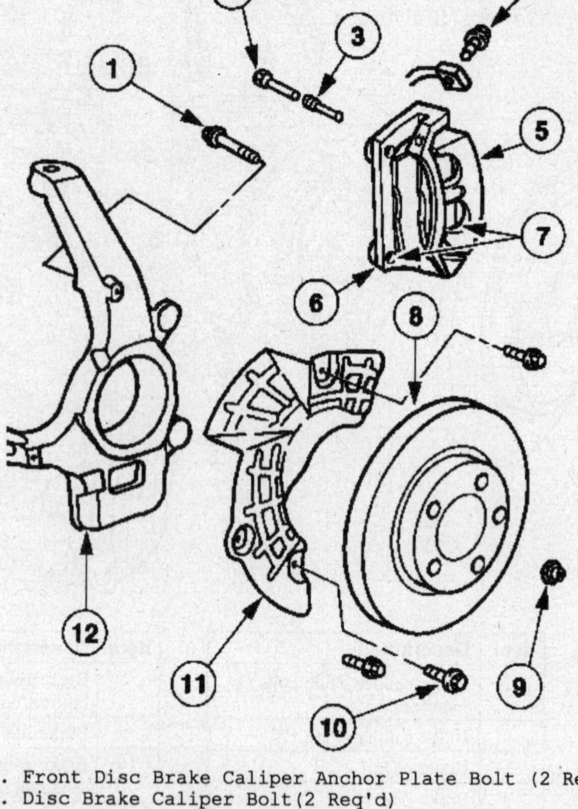

1. Front Disc Brake Caliper Anchor Plate Bolt (2 Req'd)
2. Disc Brake Caliper Bolt(2 Req'd)
3. Caliper Slide Pin (2 Req'd)
4. Front Brake Hose
5. Disc Brake Caliper
6. Front Disc Brake Caliper Anchor Plate
7. Pads
8. Brake Disc
9. Front Axle Wheel Hub Retainer
10. Screw (3 Req'd)
11. Brake Disc Shield
12. Front Wheel Knuckle

LTV1900000000859

Fig. 13 Front disc brake system. Expedition, F-150, Mark LT & Navigator w/2WD

seal and bearing.

5. Resurface brake hub if required with hub mounted brake lathe.

INSTALLATION

1. **On models equipped with 2WD,** proceed as follows:
   a. Install inner bearing then install new inner grease seal.
   b. Position brake disc and hub on spindle.
   c. Install outer wheel bearing and retainer washer.
   d. Install spindle nut while rotating brake disc and hub.
   e. Loosen spindle nut.
   f. **Torque** spindle nut to 17 inch lbs., while rotating brake disc and hub.
   g. Install nut retainer, cotter pin and grease cap.
   h. Install front caliper and anchor plate.
2. **On models equipped with 4WD,** install rotor, caliper and anchor plate.

VILLAGER & WINDSTAR

1. Remove brake fluid from brake master cylinder until fluid level in reservoir is half full.
2. Raise and support vehicle, then remove wheel and tire assembly.
3. Disconnect brake flex hose by removing banjo bolt. Discard old crush washer.
4. Remove caliper locating pins/bolts, then the caliper from rotor.
5. Reverse procedure to install, noting the following:
   a. Lubricate caliper locating pins with suitable silicone dielectric compound.
   b. Install new banjo bolt copper crush washer.
   c. Tighten locating pins, brake flex hose banjo bolt and wheel lug nuts to specifications.

Overhaul

ESCAPE & MARINER

DISASSEMBLE

1. Remove caliper and brake pads as outlined in "Caliper Service." Place a wood block in caliper jaws to avoid damage to caliper pistons when they are forced out of caliper bores.
2. Apply low pressure to force caliper pistons out of caliper bore using a rubber nosed air nozzle at brake fluid inlet port.
3. If caliper piston is difficult to remove, tap gently around piston housing with a suitable hammer. If caliper piston cannot be removed, replace caliper.
4. Pry caliper piston dust boots out of caliper bores using a suitable tool. Discard dust boots.
5. Remove and discard caliper piston seals from caliper bores.

CLEANING & INSPECTION

Clean all metal components with brake cleaner, then clean out and dry grooves and passageways with compressed air. Ensure caliper bore and component pieces are thoroughly clean.

Inspect cylinder bore and piston for damage or excessive wear. Replace piston if signs of pitting, scoring or cracks are evident.

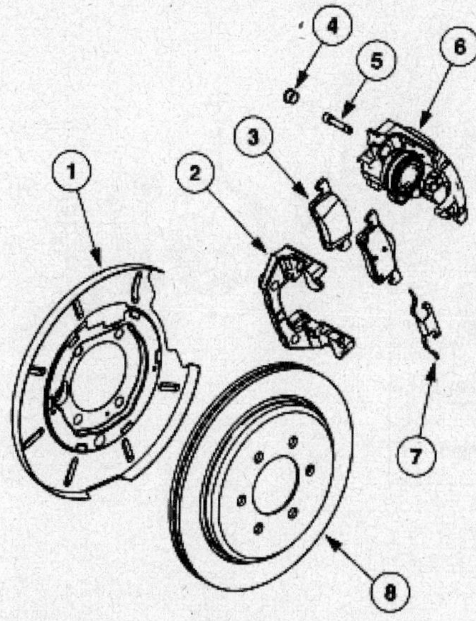

Item	Description
1	Brake disc shield
2	Brake caliper anchor plate
3	Brake pads
4	Cap
5	Brake caliper bolt
6	Brake caliper
7	Anchor housing spring
8	Brake disc

LTV1900000000883

Fig. 14 Rear brake disc system. Expedition & Navigator

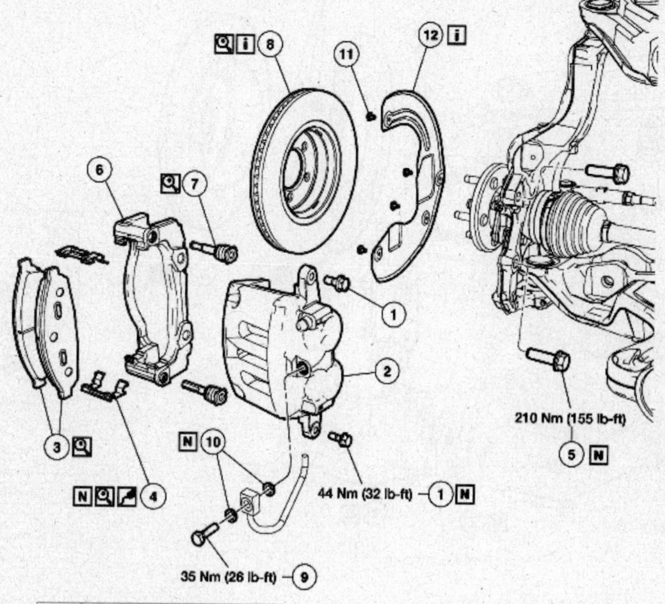

Item	Description
1	Bolts
2	Brake caliper
3	Brake disc pads
4	Slippers
5	Bolts
6	Anchor plate
7	Guide pin and boot
8	Brake disc
9	Flow bolt
10	Copper washers
11	Bolts
12	Brake disc shield (LH/RH)

LTV1900000000875

Fig. 15 Front disc brake system. Explorer & Mountaineer

ASSEMBLE

1. Apply a film of clean brake fluid to new caliper piston seal, then install into cylinder bore. Ensure seal does not become twisted and is firmly seated in groove.
2. Install new dust boot by setting flange squarely in outer groove of caliper bore.
3. Coat piston with brake fluid, then install into cylinder bore. Spread dust boot over piston as it is installed. Seat dust boot in piston groove, behind pressed on steel ring.
4. Install caliper and pads as outlined in "Caliper Service."

E-SERIES

Do not hone brake calipers, pistons are not available for honed caliper bores.

FRONT

1. Raise and support vehicle and remove front tire and wheel assemblies.
2. Remove front caliper as outlined in "Caliper, Replace."
3. Drain remaining brake fluid from caliper into suitable container.
4. Place a block of wood between caliper bridge and caliper piston.
5. Apply low air pressure to fluid port on caliper and force piston out of caliper.
6. Remove wood block and caliper piston.
7. Discard caliper piston seals and dust boots, **Figs. 26 and 27.**
8. Inspect caliper bore for pitting, scoring and damage, replace as required.
9. Install new piston seals and dust boots.
10. Lubricate piston boot, piston seals, caliper piston and caliper bore with clean brake fluid.
11. Install caliper piston into caliper housing. Use care to ensure piston does not become cocked in caliper bore.
12. Press caliper piston into caliper bore with even pressure.
13. Install caliper, bleed brake system and inspect for proper operation.

REAR

1. Raise and support vehicle, remove rear wheel and tire assemblies.
2. Remove caliper assembly.
3. Drain remaining fluid into suitable container.
4. Place a block of wood between caliper piston and caliper bridge.
5. Apply moderate air pressure to release piston from caliper.
6. Remove wood block and caliper piston.
7. Discard piston seal and dust boot.
8. Lubricate caliper piston bore, piston seal, caliper piston and dust boot with clean brake fluid.
9. Install caliper piston seal, then the dust boot using installation tool No. 206–053 and adapter No. 205–153, or equivalents.
10. Install caliper piston.
11. Install caliper, bleed brake system and inspect for proper brake caliper functioning.

EXPLORER, EXPLORER SPORT/SPORT TRAC, MOUNTAINEER & RANGER

FRONT

Disassemble

1. Remove caliper and brake pads as previously outlined.
2. Place a wood block in between caliper piston and caliper bridge.
3. Apply low pressure to force caliper pistons out of caliper bores.
4. Pry caliper piston dust boots out of caliper bores. Discard caliper piston dust boots.
5. Remove and discard caliper piston seals from caliper bores.

Cleaning & Inspection

Clean all metal components with brake cleaner, then clean out and dry grooves and passageways with compressed air. Ensure caliper bore and component pieces are thoroughly clean.

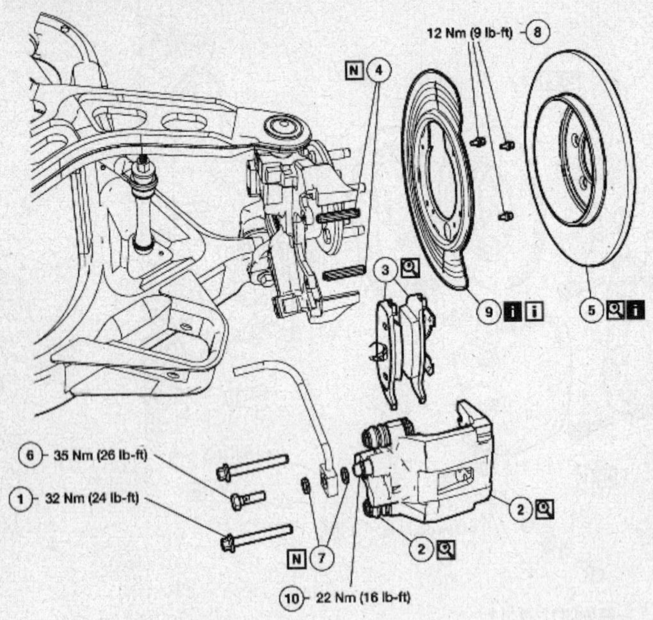

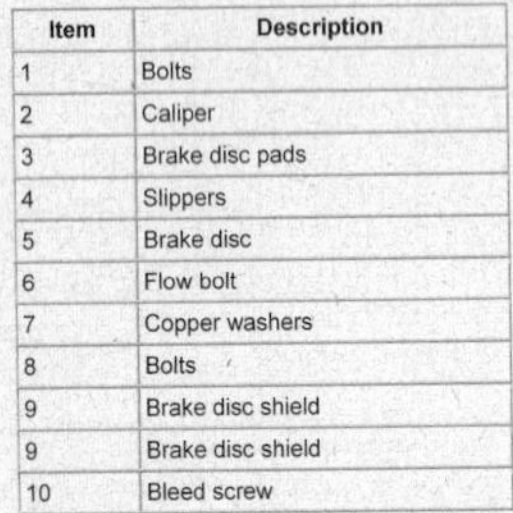

Item	Description
1	Bolts
2	Caliper
3	Brake disc pads
4	Slippers
5	Brake disc
6	Flow bolt
7	Copper washers
8	Bolts
9	Brake disc shield
9	Brake disc shield
10	Bleed screw

LTV1900000000876

Fig. 16 Rear disc brake system. Explorer & Mountaineer

Item	Description
1	Front brake anti-lock sensor
2	Front wheel spindle
3	Brake disc shield
4	Bolt
5	Grease seal
6	Front wheel bearing
7	Brake disc and hub
8	Front wheel bearing
9	Front wheel outer bearing retainer washer
10	Hub spindle nut
11	Cotter pin
12	Nut retainer
13	Hub grease cap
14	Disc brake caliper
15	Front disc brake caliper anchor plate
16	Caliper anchor plate bolts
17	Disc brake caliper bolt

LTV1900000000877

Fig. 17 Front disc brake system. Explorer Sport/ Sport Trac w/2WD

Inspect cylinder bore and piston for damage or excessive wear. Replace piston if signs of pitting, scoring or cracks are evident.

Assemble

1. Lubricate caliper bores, new piston seals and caliper pistons with clean brake fluid.
2. Install new piston seals into caliper bore seal grooves. Make sure seals are not twisted and are fully seated.
3. Install caliper pistons into caliper bores past piston seals. use a rocking, twisting motion and use care not to distort piston seals.
4. After caliper pistons are past the piston seals, press caliper pistons about ⅔ inch into caliper bores.
5. Install new dust boots on caliper pistons using Piston Dust Seal Replacer T92P-2588-AH and Driver Handle T80T-4000-W, or equivalents to seat dust boots into caliper bores. Make sure dust boots are fully seated into caliper bore grooves. After installation, dust boots should not extend beyond the face of caliper piston.
6. After installing dust boots, press caliper pistons to bottom of caliper bores.
7. Install caliper slide pin dust boots into caliper anchor plate. Make sure boots are fully seated in grooves.
8. Install caliper slide pins into caliper slide pin boots. Make sure caliper slide pin boots are seated in grooves in caliper slide pins.
9. Expel air from caliper slide pin boots and make sure caliper slide pins are fully coated with lubricant.
10. Install caliper and pads as previously outlined.

REAR

1. Raise and support vehicle, remove rear wheel and tire assemblies.
2. Remove caliper and secure in suitable vise.
3. Place a block of wood between caliper piston and caliper bridge.
4. Force caliper piston from caliper using low air pressure. Apply moderate air pressure in short bursts to prevent uncontrolled release of caliper piston.
5. Remove piston and wood block.
6. Replace seals and dust boots.
7. Coat all seals and O-rings with clean brake fluid.
8. Install dust boot into caliper with installation tool No. 206–053 and adapter No. 205–153, or equivalents.
9. Install new caliper seal in caliper bore groove.
10. Apply moderate air pressure to caliper while pushing piston into bore. Ensure caliper piston does not become cocked in bore.
11. Install caliper assembly, bleed system and inspect for proper functioning.

EXCURSION, EXPEDITION, F-SUPER DUTY, MOTORHOME & NAVIGATOR

FRONT

Disassemble

1. Remove caliper and brake pads as previously outlined, then drain brake fluid from cylinders.
2. Secure caliper in a suitable soft-jawed vise, then place a suitable block of wood between caliper bridge and cylinders. Apply low air pressure to fluid port in caliper to remove pistons. Apply only enough air pressure to ease piston out of bore.
3. Remove wood block and pistons, then the piston seals and boots, **Fig. 28.** Discard piston seals and boots.

Inspection

If caliper assembly is leaking, replace piston assemblies. If cylinder bores are excessively scored or corroded, replace caliper assembly.

Do not hone cylinder bores, piston assemblies are not available for honed cylinder bores.

Assemble

1. Lubricate new piston seals with heavy

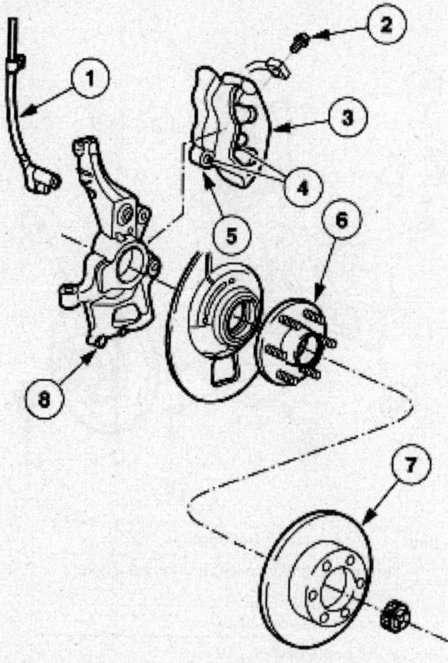

Item	Description
1	Front brake anti-lock sensor
2	Front brake hose bolt
3	Disc brake caliper
4	Pads
5	Front disc brake caliper anchor plate
6	Wheel hub
7	Brake disc
8	Front wheel knuckle assembly

LTV1900000000878

Fig. 18 Front disc brake system. Explorer Sport/Sport Trac w/4WD

duty brake fluid, then install into cylinder bore seal grooves.
2. Apply a film of clean brake fluid to cylinder bores.
3. Lubricate retaining lips of new dust boots with clean brake fluid, then install into boot retaining grooves in cylinder bores.
4. Apply a film of clean brake fluid to pistons, then insert pistons into dust boots and start them into cylinders by hand until they are beyond piston seals.
5. Place a suitable wood block over one piston and press into cylinder being careful not to cock piston in cylinder bore. Repeat procedure for second piston.
6. Install caliper and pads as previously outlined in "Caliper Service."

REAR

1. Raise and support vehicle.
2. Remove rear brake disc caliper.
3. Drain remaining brake fluid into suitable container.
4. Secure rear caliper in a vise.
5. Place a block of wood between caliper bridge and caliper piston.
6. Apply low air pressure to fluid port to force out caliper piston.
7. Remove wood block and caliper piston.
8. Do not hone cylinder bore, pistons are not available for hone cylinder bores.
9. Remove and discard piston seal and dust boot.
10. Lubricate cylinder bore, piston seal, caliper piston and dust boot with clean brake fluid.
11. Install dust boot with installer tool No. 206–053 and adapter No. 303–224, or equivalents.
12. Place caliper in a suitable vise.
13. Place piston squarely against dust boot. While applying shop air into brake caliper, push piston squarely into brake caliper bore.
14. Install rear brake caliper and bleed brake system.

VILLAGER

DISASSEMBLE

1. Remove caliper and brake pads as previously outlined, then open bleeder screw and drain any remaining brake fluid from caliper. After draining, close bleeder screw.
2. Position shop towels between caliper housing and piston, then apply air pressure through brake hose fitting to force piston from its bore. **Apply only enough air pressure to ease piston out of bore.**
3. Remove piston, then the dust seal. Discard dust seal.
4. Use a suitable plastic or wooden pick to remove piston seal from bore and discard.

CLEANING & INSPECTION

1. Inspect caliper bore, caliper piston and piston seal groove for cuts, deep scratches, pitting and presence of foreign materials.
2. Caliper piston and caliper bore may be lightly polished with crocus cloth but if deep scratches remain, replace caliper.
3. Piston seal groove in caliper must not have deep scratches that would prevent piston seal from working properly.

ASSEMBLE

1. Lubricate new piston seal with brake fluid and install in groove in bore, then lubricate piston bore and piston with brake fluid.
2. Install new dust seal on piston, then the piston into piston bore.
3. Use piston dust seal replacer tool No. T92P-2588-AH, or equivalent, and handle tool No. 80T-400-W, or equivalent, to seat seal in caliper.
4. Install caliper and pads as previously outlined in "Caliper Service."

FREESTAR, MONTEREY & WINDSTAR

DISASSEMBLE

1. Remove caliper and brake pads as previously outlined. Cushion piston impact by inserting a wooden block or shop towel between piston(s) and housing, then apply air pressure to fluid port in caliper.
2. If piston is seized and cannot be forced from caliper, tap lightly around caliper piston while applying air pressure.
3. Remove dust boot from and rubber piston seal from caliper and discard it.

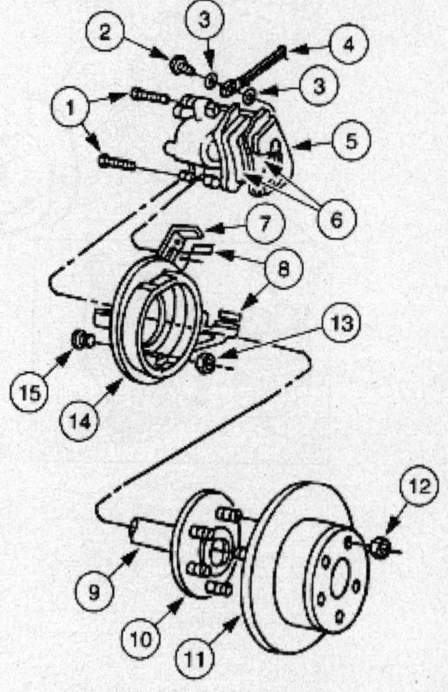

Item	Description
1	Brake caliper bolt
2	Flow bolt
3	Copper washer (2 req'd)
4	Rear wheel brake hose
5	Rear disc brake caliper
6	Brake pads
7	Adapter assy
8	Shoe slippers
9	Axle shaft
10	Wheel stud (5 req'd)
11	Brake disc
12	Keeper nut
13	Rear wheel disc brake adapter nut
14	Rear wheel disc brake adapter
15	Rear wheel disc brake adapter bolt

LTV1900000000884

Fig. 19 Rear disc brake system. F-150 & Mark LT

CLEANING & INSPECTION

Clean all metal components with suitable brake cleaner, then clean out and dry grooves and passageways with compressed air. Ensure caliper bore and component pieces are thoroughly clean.

Inspect cylinder bore and piston for excessive scoring or corrosion, replace as required.

ASSEMBLE

1. Lubricate caliper pistons, bores and seals before assembly with suitable brake fluid.
2. Install piston seal into caliper bore, then the piston boot on piston.

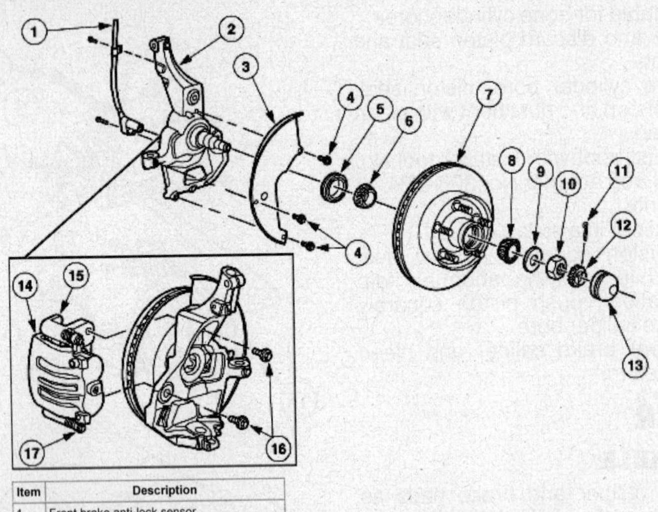

Item	Description
1	Front brake anti-lock sensor
2	Front wheel spindle (LH/RH)
3	Brake disc shield (LH/RH)
4	Bolt
5	Grease seal
6	Front wheel bearing
7	Brake disc and hub
8	Front wheel bearing
9	Front wheel outer bearing retainer washer
10	Hub spindle nut
11	Cotter pin
12	Nut retainer
13	Hub grease cap
14	Disc brake caliper
15	Front disc brake caliper anchor plate
16	Caliper anchor plate bolt
17	Disc brake caliper bolts

LTV1900000000873

Fig. 20 Front disc brake system. Ranger w/2WD

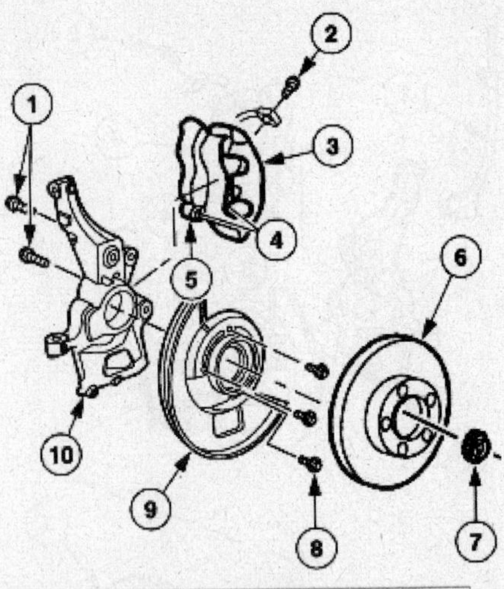

Item	Description
1	Front disc brake caliper anchor plate bolt (2 req'd)
2	Front brake hose bolt
3	Disc brake caliper
4	Pads
5	Front disc brake caliper anchor plate
6	Brake disc
7	Front axle wheel hub retainer
8	Bolt (3 req'd)
9	Brake disc shield
10	Front wheel knuckle

LTV1900000000874

Fig. 21 Front disc brake system. Ranger w/4WD

3. Start caliper piston into bore by hand to ensure correct alignment.
4. When installing caliper piston back into bore, use wood block or another flat stock, like an old pad between c-clamp and piston. Do not apply c-clamp directly to caliper piston surface. This can result in damage to piston. Be sure piston is not cocked.
5. Make sure dust boot is tight in boot groove on caliper piston and in caliper.
6. Install caliper and pads as previously outlined.

ROTOR

REPLACE

Aviator

FRONT

1. Raise and support vehicle.
2. Remove front tire and wheel assemblies.
3. Remove front brake components in sequence, **Fig. 1.**
4. Reverse procedure to install.

REAR

Refer to **Fig. 2** and remove rear brake components in sequence listed.

Escape & Mariner

1. Remove disc brake caliper and anchor plate as outlined in "Caliper Service."
2. Remove rotor
3. Reverse Procedure to install. Tighten all nuts and bolts to specification.

E-Series

FRONT

Refer to **Figs. 3 through 5** and remove components in sequence listed.

REAR

Removal

1. Remove disc brake caliper, refer to "Caliper Service."
2. Remove axle shafts as outlined in "Rear Axle & Suspension" in chassis chapter.
3. Lift lock washer tab from slot in outer lock nut, **Figs. 6 through 8.**
4. Remove outer lock nut using Front Wheel Bearing Spanner tool No. D78T-1197–A or equivalent.
5. Lift lock washer tab from inner lock nut.
6. Remove outer rear wheel pinion nut locking washer.
7. Remove inner lock nut using Front Wheel Bearing Spanner tool No. D78T-1197–A or equivalent.
8. Remove inner rear wheel pinion nut locking washer.
9. Remove outer rear wheel bearing cone and roller.
10. Protect rear axle spindle threads with cardboard tubing, tape or equivalent.
11. Remove rear hub and rotor assembly.
12. With rotor facing upward, secure rear hub and rotor assembly in a soft jaw vice.
13. Remove rotor to hub bolts, then the rotor from rear hub.

Installation

1. Position rotor on hub.
2. Install rotor to hub bolts and tighten to specification.
3. Carefully position rear hub and rotor assembly on rear axle spindle.
4. Install outer rear wheel bearing cone and roller.
5. Install inner rear wheel pinion nut locking washer, engaging washer tab into keyway in rear axle spindle
6. Install inner lock nut with Front Wheel Bearing Spanner tool No. D78T-1197-A or equivalent.
7. Seat bearings by **torquing** inner lock nut to 50–60 ft. lbs.
8. Back off inner lock nut 90°.
9. **Torque** inner lock nut to 30–40 ft. lbs., while turning rear hub and rotor assembly.
10. Back off inner lock nut 135–150°.
11. Install lock washer with flat side inboard, noting relative position of flat tabs to six slots in inner lock nut.
12. Tighten inner lock nut until one of the tabs aligns with a slot.
13. Bend tab a minimum of 30° to fully engage slot.
14. Install outer lock nut and **torque** to 65 ft. lbs., then additionally until one of

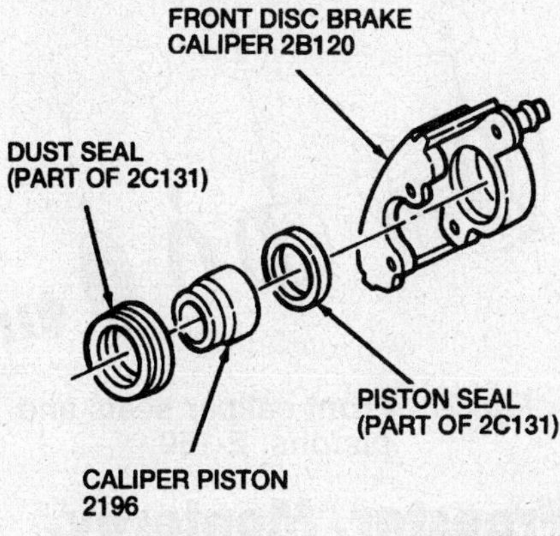

Fig. 22 Exploded view of pin slider caliper type system. Villager

eight L-shaped tabs on lock washer aligns with one of the six slots on outer lock nut.

15. Mount Dial Indicator with magnetic base tool No. D78P-4201-B or equivalent, to measure end play of rear hub. Endplay should be .001–.010 inch.
16. Bend L tab of lock washer a minimum of 60° over outer lock nut, to full engage slot.
17. Install axle shaft and disc brake caliper.

Expedition & Navigator

FRONT

REMOVAL

1. Raise and support vehicle, then remove wheel and tire assembly.
2. Remove caliper assembly as outlined in "Caliper Service."
3. **On models equipped with 4WD,** remove rotor.
4. **On models equipped with 2WD,** remove hub grease cap, cotter pin, nut retainer, spindle nut, outer bearing retainer washer and rotor.

INSTALLATION

1. **On models equipped with 4WD,** position rotor on hub.
2. **On models equipped with 2WD,** proceed as follows:
   a. Install new wheel bearing and hub grease seal.
   b. Position hub and rotor on spindle and install outer wheel bearing, outer wheel bearing retainer washer and spindle nut.
   c. **Torque** spindle nut to 30 ft. lbs.
   d. Back nut off two turn.
   e. **Torque** spindle nut to 17–24 ft. lbs., while rotating rotor counterclockwise.
   f. Loosen spindle nut 175°, then **torque** nut to 17 inch lbs.
   g. Install retainer and new cotter pin and grease cap.
3. **On all models,** install disc brake caliper and anchor bracket bolts, then tighten to specifications.
4. Install wheel and tire assembly, tighten wheel nuts to specifications.
5. Lower vehicle, inspect brake fluid level and brake operation.

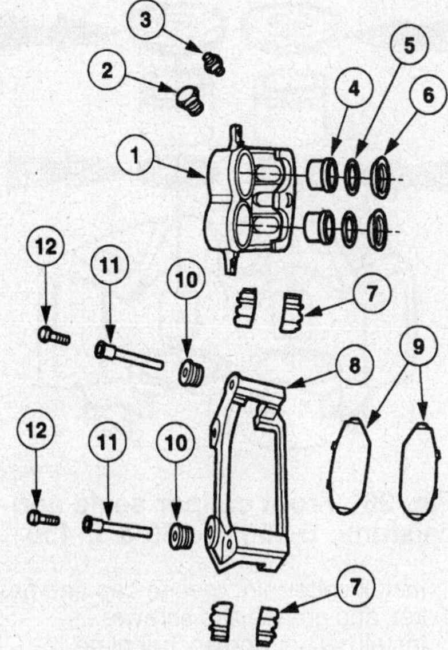

Item	Description
1	Disc brake caliper (RH)
1	Disc brake caliper (LH)
2	Bleeder screw cap
3	Bleeder screw
4	Caliper piston
5	Piston seal (part of 6175)
6	Piston dust boot (part of 6175)
7	Shoe slipper (4 req'd)
8	Front disc brake caliper anchor plate (RH)
8	Front disc brake caliper anchor plate (LH)
9	Brake pads
10	Guide pin boot
11	Guide pin (part of 2L527)
12	Caliper bolt (part of 2L527)

FM4079800111000X

Fig. 23 Exploded view of pin slider caliper type system. Freestar, Monterey & Windstar

REAR

1. Raise and support vehicle.
2. Remove rear wheel and tire assemblies.
3. Remove rear brake caliper anchor plate bolts. It is not required to disconnect rear brake hose.
4. Remove anchor plate and caliper as an assembly.
5. Remove brake disc.
6. Reverse procedure to install.

Explorer & Mountaineer

FRONT

1. Raise and support vehicle.
2. Remove tire and wheel assemblies.

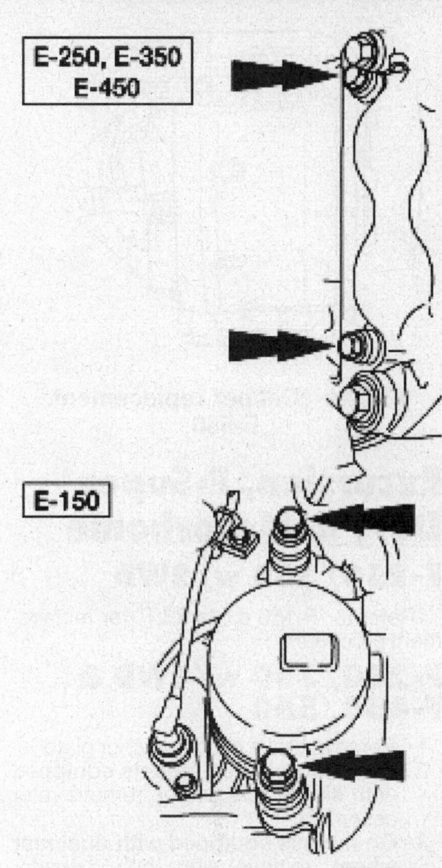

Fig. 24 Front caliper mounting bolt locations. E-150, E-250, E-350 & E-450

3. Remove brake components in sequence, **Fig. 15.**
4. Reverse procedure to install.

REAR

Refer to **Fig. 16** and remove rear brake components in sequence illustrated.

Explorer Sport/Sport Trac

Refer to **Figs. 17 and 18** and remove components in sequence listed.

F-150 & Mark LT

FRONT

Refer to **Figs. 12 and 13** and remove components in sequence listed.

REAR

It is not required to remove hydraulic brake line when replacing caliper.

1. Raise and support vehicle, remove rear wheel and tire assemblies.
2. Remove caliper assembly.
3. Remove rear brake disc. If brake disc binds on parking brake shoe and linings, remove adjustment hole access plug and retract parking brake shoes.
4. Reverse procedure to install.

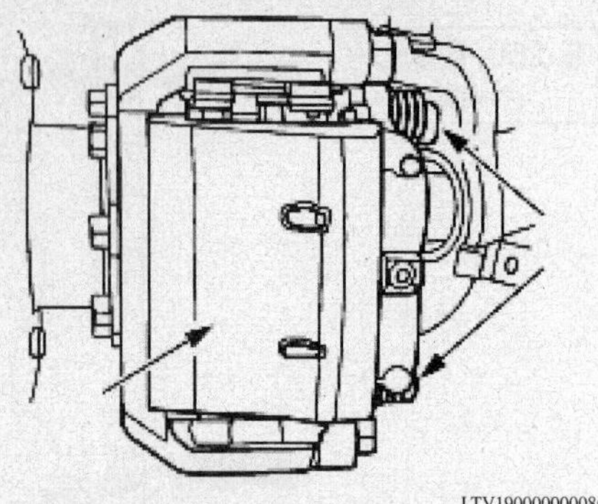

Fig. 25 Caliper replacement. E-550

Excursion, F-Super Duty & Motorhome

F-250/350 w/2WD

Refer to "F-150 & Mark LT" for replacement procedure.

F-250/350 w/4WD & F-450/550

1. Remove brake caliper anchor plate
2. **On F-250 & F-350 models equipped with single real wheel,** remove rotor assembly.
3. **On models equipped with dual rear wheel,** remove eight hub extender nuts, hub plate and rotor.
4. If excessive force must be used to remove brake rotor, inspect lateral runout before installation.
5. Reverse procedure to install.

MOTORHOME

Removal

1. Raise and support vehicle, remove front tire and wheel assemblies.
2. Remove brake disc caliper and anchor plate.
3. Remove hub grease cap, cotter pin, spindle nut, outer wheel nearing retainer and bearing, grease cap and gasket, then the hub & rotor.
4. Clean, inspect and resurface rotor as required.
5. Remove wheel hub grease seal and inner wheel bearing.

Installation

1. Lubricate wheel bearing with suitable grease meeting Ford specification ESA-M1C75–B, or equivalent.
2. Install inner bearing and new inner grease seal.
3. Position hub and rotor on spindle.
4. Install bearing, retaining washer and spindle nut.
5. While rotating brake hub and rotor, tighten spindle nut.
6. Loosen spindle nut until loose.
7. **Torque** spindle nut to 18 inch lbs., while rotating brake hub and rotor.
8. Bearing endplay should be less than .005 inch.

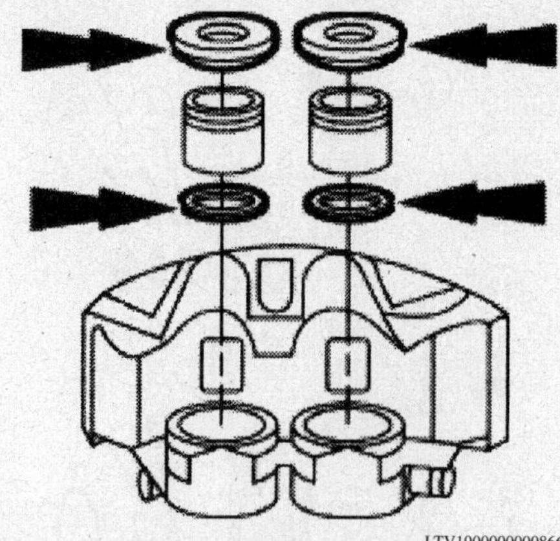

Fig. 26 Front caliper seals and pistons. E-250, E-350 & E-450

9. Install cotter pin, grease cap and gasket, and grease cap screws.
10. Install caliper and anchor plate.

Ranger

FRONT

Removal

1. Remove sufficient brake fluid from master cylinder reservoir.
2. Raise and support vehicle, then remove tire and wheel assembly.
3. Remove disc brake caliper as outlined in "Caliper Service".
4. **On models equipped with 2WD,** remove hub grease cap, cotter pin, nut retainer, hub spindle nut and front outer wheel bearing washer, then remove outer wheel bearing and rotor.
5. **On models equipped with 4WD,** remove rotor retaining screw, then rotor.

Installation

1. **On models equipped with 4WD,** install rotor on front hub, then rotor retaining screw tightening to specifications.
2. **On models equipped with 2WD,** install front disc brake hub and rotor on spindle.
3. **On all models,** install front wheel bearing.
4. Install bearing retainer washer and spindle nut. Tighten hub nut as follows:
   a. **Torque** hub spindle nut to 17–25 ft. lbs., while rotating front disc brake hub and rotor.
   b. Back off 120–180°, then **torque** to 18–20 inch lbs.
5. While holding position of hub spindle nut, install retainer, cotter pin and hub grease cap.
6. Install disc brake caliper and anchor plate assembly, then tighten bolts to specifications.
7. Install tire and wheel assembly, tighten wheel nuts to specifications.
8. Lower vehicle and inspect brake fluid level.

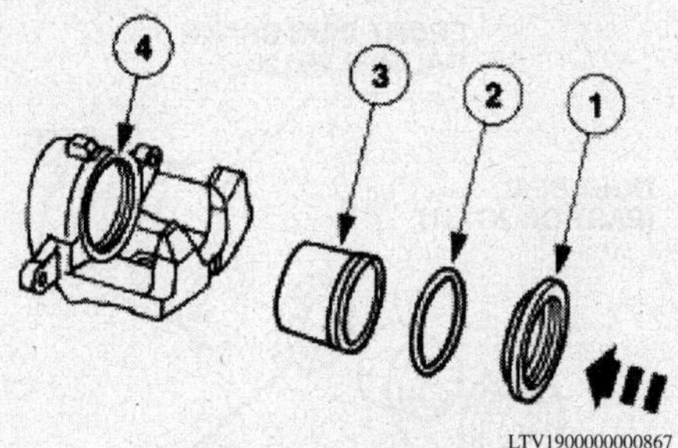

Fig. 27 Front caliper seals and pistons. E-150

Freestar, Monterey, Villager & Windstar

FRONT

REMOVAL

1. Raise and support vehicle.
2. Remove tire and wheel assembly.
3. Remove caliper anchor bracket bolts and caliper, as outlined in "Caliper Service."
4. Remove disc brake rotor from hub assembly, noting the following:
   a. If excessive force is required for removal apply rust penetrant to hub assembly and rotor mating surfaces.
   b. Strike rotor between studs with plastic hammer to loosen from hub.
   c. If rotor still cannot be removed, use 2–3 Jaw Puller tool No. D80L-1013-A, or equivalent to pull rotor from hub.

INSTALLATION

Prior to installation clean rust from hub and rotor mounting area. Failure to do so may result in high lateral runout causing roughness and vibration. When installing new rotor, remove protective coating with suitable solvent.

1. Apply a light coating of silicone dielectric compound part No. D7AZ-19A331-A, or equivalent, to pilot diameter of rotor.
2. Install rotor on hub assembly.
3. Install disc brake caliper and caliper anchor bracket bolts and tighten to specifications.
4. Inspect total indicated runout.
5. Install wheel and tire assembly on front hub, then tighten wheel hub nuts in star pattern to specifications.
6. Lower vehicle, then pump brake pedal to seat brake lining prior to moving vehicle.

REAR

1. Remove caliper, refer to "Caliper Service." It is not required to remove the rear brake hose.
2. Remove the adjustment hole access plug from the rear wheel disc brake shield.
3. Contract the parking brake shoes by turning the parking brake adjuster.

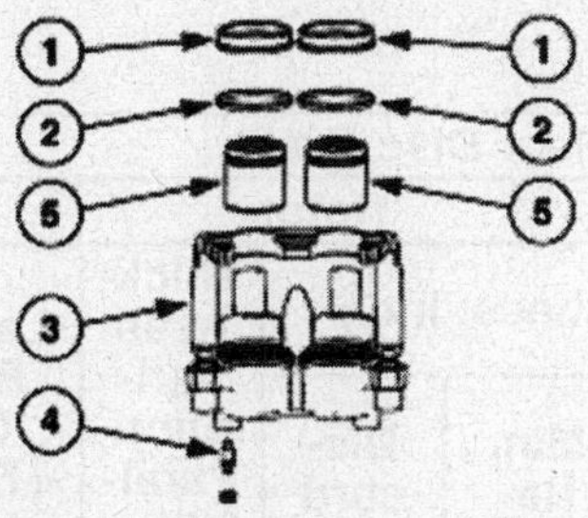

Item	Description
1	Piston boot
2	Piston seal
3	Disc brake caliper
4	Bleeder screw
5	Caliper piston

LTV1900000000860

Fig. 28 Exploded view of front caliper. Excursion, Expedition, F-Super Duty, Motorhome & Navigator

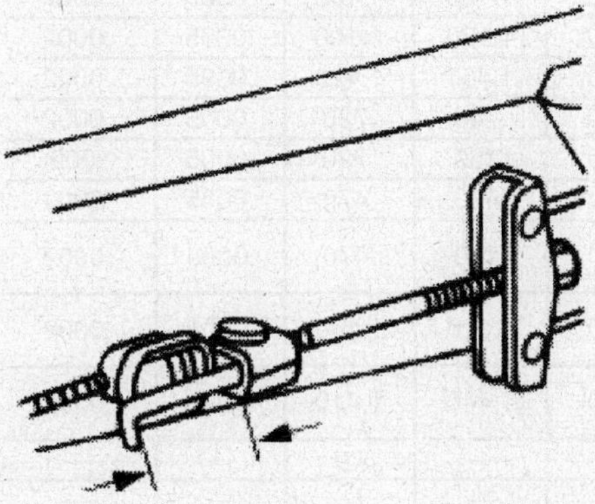

LTV1900000000868

Fig. 31 Exposed length of cinch strap. E-250

4. Remove press-on keeper nuts from rear disc brake rotor.
5. Remove rear disc brake rotor from hub.
6. Reverse procedure to install.

ADJUSTMENTS

Parking Brake

EXPEDITION, EXPLORER, F-SUPER DUTY, MOUNTAINEER & NAVIGATOR

REAR DISC

1. Remove rear disc brake rotor as outlined in "Rotor, Replace."
2. Measure inside diameter of parking brake drum using brake adjustment gauge tool No. D81L-1103-A, or equivalent, **Fig. 29.**
3. Adjust parking brake shoe to .020 inch

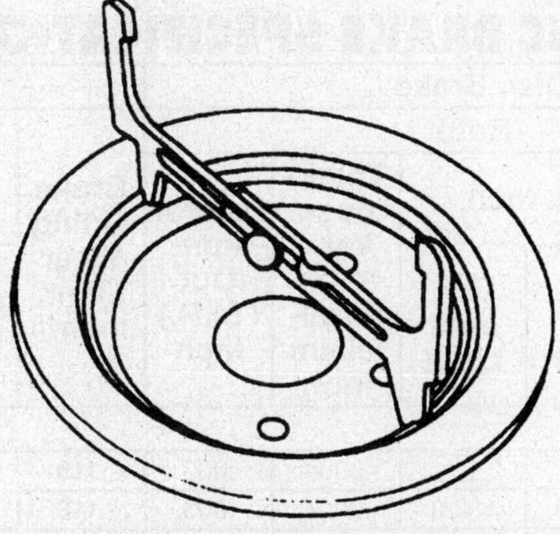

FM4059500011000X

Fig. 29 Parking brake drum inside diameter inspection. Expedition, Explorer, F-Super Duty, Mountaineer & Navigator

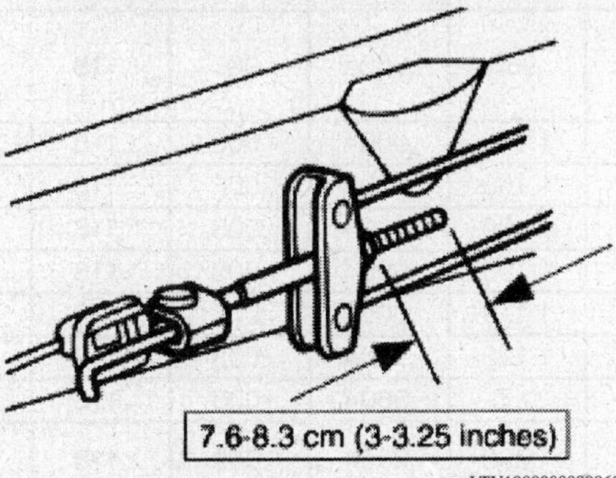

LTV1900000000869

Fig. 32 Tension limiter adjustment. E-250

(.508 mm) less than drum measurement, **Fig. 30.**

4. Reverse procedure to install.

E-SUPER DUTY

E-250 w/TENSION LIMITER

1. Loosen tension limiter nut to end of tension limiter threads.
2. Depress brake pedal to last detent position (17 clicks).
3. Measure and record exposed length of cinch strap, **Fig. 31.**
4. Tighten tension limiter nut to obtain 3–3.25 inches as measured from end of tension limiter threads to beginning of hex portion of tension limiter nut, **Fig. 32.**
5. Ensure adjustment has caused cinch strap to slip minimum specified length from length recorded previously.
6. If cinch strap has not slipped as specified, tighten tension limiter nut additional amount to achieve specified slippage, **Fig. 33.**
7. Release parking brake control.
8. Depress to floor and release parking brake control two times.
9. Inspect to ensure parking brake is applied and released fully.

E-450 & E-550

1. Raise and support vehicle.

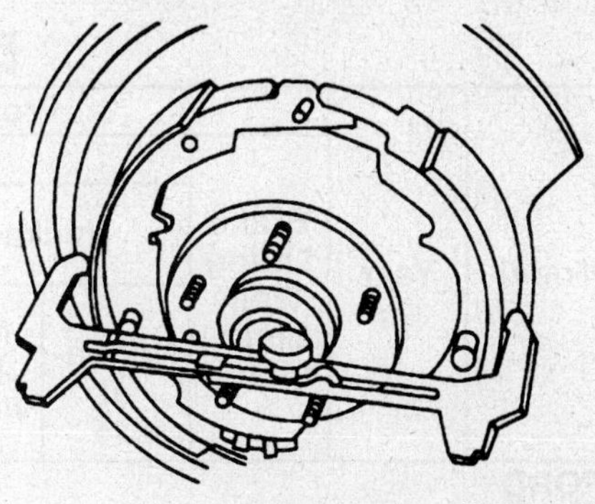

FM4059500012000X

Fig. 30 Parking brake shoe & lining inspection. Expedition, Explorer, F-Super Duty, Mountaineer & Navigator

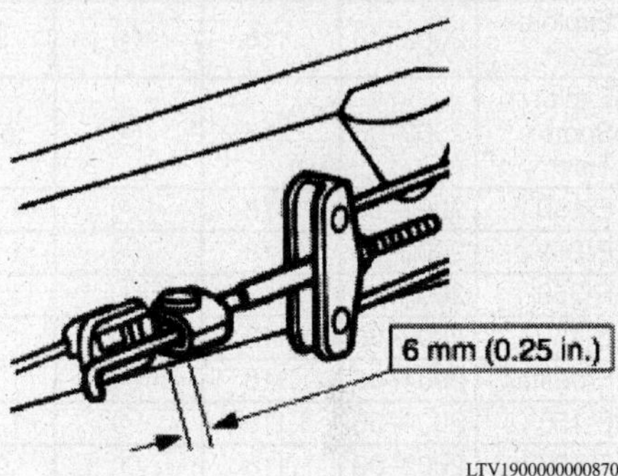

LTV1900000000870

Fig. 33 Cinch strap slippage. E-250

2. Remove clevis pin and disconnect adjusting clevis from parking brake lever.
3. Loosen jam nut several turn and position parking brake lever in applied position.
4. Tighten or loosen adjusting clevis until adjusting clevis hole lines up with parking brake lever hole, then loosen adjusting clevis .5 inch.
5. Install clevis pin through adjusting clevis and parking brake lever.
6. Install locking pin in clevis pin and tighten jam nut to specification.
7. Lower vehicle and test parking brake.

FREESTAR, MONTEREY & WINDSTAR

1. Raise and support vehicle.
2. At inboard side of rear wheel disc brake adapter, remove rubber plug from parking brake adjuster access hole.
3. Insert a suitable tool into adjuster access hole and expand parking brake adjuster while turning the tire until resistance is felt.
4. Back off parking brake adjuster one turn.
5. Repeat steps for other rear wheel.
6. Lower vehicle and test parking brake.
7. Pull up on parking brake control and listen to clicks from pawl in parking brake control. Resistance should be felt after five clicks.

DISC BRAKE SPECIFICATIONS

Model	Year	Front Disc Brake						Rear Disc Brake					
			Rotor						Rotor				
			Thickness, Inch						Thickness, Inch				
		Brake Lining Wear Limit, Inch②	Nominal	Min. Refinish	Discard Limit	Thickness Variation Parallelism Inch	Lateral Run-Out (T.I.R.) Inch	Brake Lining Wear Limit, Inch②	Nominal	Min. Refinish	Discard Limit	Thickness Variation Parallelism Inch	Lateral Run-Out (T.I.R.) Inch
FORD													
Escape	2002–06	.118	⑤	④	③	.0004	.003	.118	⑤	.450	.430	.0005	.0002
Excursion	2002–05	.118	⑤	1.440	1.410	.0004	.003	.118	⑤	1.120	1.100	.0005	.0002
Expedition	2002–04	.118	⑤	1.110	1.060	.0004	.003	.118	⑤	.770	.740	.0005	.0002
	2005–06	.079	⑤	1.110	1.060	.0004	.003	.118	⑤	.770	.740	.0005	.0002
Explorer	2002–06	.118	⑤	1.150	1.120	.0002	.005	.118	⑤	.450	.430	.0005	.0002
Explorer Sport	2002–03	.118	⑤	.980	.960	.0002	.005	.118	⑤	.450	.430	.0005	.0002
Explorer Sport Trac	2002–05	.118	⑤	.980	.960	.0002	.005	.118	⑤	.450	.430	.0005	.0002
E-150	2002–06	.118	⑤	1.170	1.140	.0004	.003	.118	⑤	.820	.800	.0005	.0002
E-250	2002–06	.118	⑤	1.120	1.100	.0004	.003	.118	⑤	1.120	1.100	.0005	.0002
E-350	2002–06	.118	⑤	1.120	1.100	.0004	.003	.118	⑤	1.120	1.100	.0005	.0002
E-450	2002–06	.118	⑤	1.120	1.100	.0004	.003	.118	⑤	1.450	1.420	.0005	.0002
Freestar	2004–06	.118	⑤	1.140	1.110	.0004	.003	.118	⑤	.740	.720	.0005	.0002
F-150	2004–06	.118	⑤	1.146	1.122	.0004	.003	.118	⑤	.750	.720	.0005	.002
F-150 LD	2002–03	.118	⑤	.980	.965	.0004	.003	.118	⑤	.490	.470	.0005	.0002
F-150 HD	2002–03	.118	⑤	1.110	1.090	.0004	.003	.118	⑤	.490	.470	.0005	.0002
F-250– & F-350	2002–06	.118	⑤	1.440	1.410	.0004	.003	.118	⑤	1.120	1.100	.0005	.0002
F-450 & F-550	2003–06	.118	⑤	1.440	1.410	.0004	.003	.118	⑤	1.440	1.410	.0005	.0002
Ranger	2002–06	.118	⑤	.990	.960	.0004	.003	.118	—	—	①	—	—
Windstar	2002–03	.118	⑤	1.000	.970	.0004	.003	.118	—	—	①	—	—
LINCOLN													
Aviator	2003–06	.118	⑤	1.060	1.040	.0004	.003	.118	⑤	.450	.430	.0005	.0002
Mark LT	2006	.118	⑤	1.146	1.122	.0004	.003	.118	⑤	.750	.720	.0005	.0002
Navigator	2002–04	.118	⑤	1.110	1.060	.0004	.003	.118	⑤	.770	.740	.0005	.0002
	2005–06	.079	⑤	1.110	1.060	.0004	.003	.118	⑤	.770	.740	.0005	.0002
MERCURY													
Mariner	2005–06	.118	⑤	④	③	.0004	.003	.118	⑤	.450	.430	.0005	.0002
Monterey	2004–06	.118	⑤	1.140	1.110	.0004	.003	.118	⑤	.740	.720	.0005	.0002
Mountaineer	2002–03	.118	⑤	1.150	1.120	.0004	.003	.118	⑤	.450	.430	.0005	.0002
Villager	2002	.118	⑤	.960	.940	.0004	.003	.118	—	—	①	—	—

LD — Light Duty
HD — Heavy Duty
2WD — Two Wheel drive
4WD — Four Wheel Drive
① — Discard thickness is stamped on rotor.

② — Above rivet head or backing plate. Original equipment type brake lining.

③ — Base brake system, .860 inch; Four wheel disc brake system, .950 inch.

④ — Base brake system, .880 inch; Four wheel disc brake system, .970 inch.

⑤ — Not specified by manufacturer.

TIGHTENING SPECIFICATIONS

Year	Component	Torque Ft. Lbs.
AVIATOR		
2003–05	Brake Booster	18
	Brake Master Cylinder	18
	Front Caliper Bleed Screw	120①
	Front Caliper Bolt	20
	Front Caliper Anchor Plate	155
	Parking Brake Control	15
	Parking Brake Release Bracket	
	Rear Caliper Bleed Screw	16
	Rear Caliper Bolt	20
E-SERIES		
2002–06	Caliper Support Bracket To Rear Axle Flange Nuts	74–100
	Front Anchor Plate Bolts	14–191
	Front Brake Hose Bolt	22–30
	Front Caliper Bolts (E-150)	22–26
	Front Caliper Bolts (E-250, E-350 & E-Super Duty)	16–30
	Parking Brake Adjustment Clevis	14–20
	Rear Brake Disc To Hub	94
	Rear Caliper Anchor Bolts (E-550)	296
	Rear Caliper Bleeder Screw (E-550)	11
	Rear Caliper Flow Bolt (E-450)	26
	Rear Caliper Flow Bolt (E-550)	37
	Rear Caliper Pin Bolts (E-250, E-350)	27
	Rear Caliper Pin Bolts (E-550)	41
	Rear Caliper Support Bracket (E-250, E-350)	100
	Rear Caliper Anchor Plate (E-250, E-350)	128
	Rear Caliper Support Bracket (E-450)	87
	Rotor Shield Bolts	80①
ESCAPE & MARINER		
2002–06	Brake Caliper Anchor Plate Bolts	111
	Brake Caliper Bolts	26
	Brake Line To Caliper	15
	Wheel Lug Nut	100
EXCURSION, F-SUPER DUTY & MOTORHOME		
2002–06	Caliper Bleeder Screw	13–18
	Caliper Pin Bolt	42
	Front Brake Hose Bolt	26
	Front Caliper Anchor Plate Bolt (F-250 & F-350)	166
	Front Caliper Anchor Plate Bolt (F-450, F-550 & Motorhome)	295
	Front Disc Rotor Shield	98
	Front Wheel Hub Extender Nuts	130
	Rear Caliper Anchor Bolts (F-250 & F-350)	128
	Rear Caliper Anchor Bolts (F-450 & F-550)	295
	Rear Rotor Shield Bolts (F-250 & F-350)	80①
	Rear Rotor Shield Bolts (F-450 & F-550)	12
	Rear Rotor To Hub Bolts	94
	Rear Wheel Disc Brake Adapter (F-250, F-350 & F-550 w/Dana Axle)	100
	Rear Wheel Disc Brake Adapter (F-250 & F-350 w/Ford Axle)	150

Continued

TIGHTENING SPECIFICATIONS—Continued

Year	Component	Torque Ft. Lbs.
EXPEDITION, F-150, MARK LT & NAVIGATOR		
2002–06	Anti-Lock Brake Sensor Screws	80①
	Axle Hub Nut	295
	Brake Hose Bolt	23–29
	Caliper Bleeder Screws	12–18
	Front Caliper Bolts	26–47
	Front Disc Brake Caliper Anchor Plate Bolts	125–148
	Front Disc Brake Rotor Shield Screws	80①
	Rear Caliper Bolts	26–47
	Rear Wheel Disc Brake Adapter Bolts	40
	Wheel Lugs Nuts	83–112
EXPLORER, MOUNTAINEER & RANGER		
2002–06	Axle Nut	170–208
	Caliper Anchor Plate Bolts	74–96
	Caliper slide Pin Bolts	21–26
	Flow Bolt	29
	Hub Spindle Nut	②
	Rotor Shield Retaining Bolts	7–10
	Speed Sensor Clamp Bolt	53–62①
	Speed Sensor Spindle Bolt	61–90①
	Wheel Lug Nuts	85–115
EXPLORER SPORT/SPORT TRAC		
2002–06	Caliper Bleed Screw	15
	Front Brake Hose Bolt	23–29
	Front Caliper Anchor Plate	72–97
	Front Caliper Mounting	21–26
	Front Disc Shield	84–120①
	Rear Caliper Mounting	24
	Rear Wheel Disc Adapter	80
FREESTAR & MONTEREY		
2004–06	Brake Calipers	24
	Brake Master Cylinder Lines	13
	Caliper Bleeder Screw	89①
	Wheel Lugs	100
VILLAGER		
2002	Axle Nut	174–231
	Brake Flex Hose Banjo Bolt	12–14
	Brake Line Flare Nut	11–13
	Brake Lines At Master Cylinder	13
	Brake Load Sensor Proportioning Valve Eye Bracket Bolts	14
	Brake Pedal Adjustment Rod Nut	14
	Caliper Mounting Bolt	18–25
	Driveshaft Nut	174–231
	Front Caliper Bleeder Screw	15
	Hub Retaining Nut	174–231
	Wheel Cylinder Bleeder Screw	71①
	Wheel Lug Nuts	72–87
WINDSTAR		
2002–03	Brake Master Cylinder Tube Fitting	14
	Caliper Bleeder Screw	108–160①
	Cruise Switch	10–14
	Wheel Cylinder Bleeder Screw	11

① — Inch lbs.
② — Refer to "Rotor, Replace."

DRUM BRAKES

TABLE OF CONTENTS

E-Series, F-150 & Ranger

INDEX

PRECAUTIONS

When working on or around brake assemblies, care must be taken to prevent breathing asbestos dust, as many manufacturers incorporate asbestos fibers in the production of brake linings. During routine service operations, precautions should be taken to minimize exposure. Do not sand or grind brake linings unless suitable local exhaust ventilation equipment is used to prevent excessive asbestos exposure.

1. Wear a suitable respirator approved for asbestos dust use during all repair procedures.
2. When cleaning brake dust from brake components, use a vacuum cleaner with a highly efficient filter system. If a suitable vacuum cleaner is not available, use a water soaked rag. Do not use compressed air or dry brush to clean brake components.
3. Keep work area clean, using same equipment as for cleaning brake components.
4. Properly dispose of rags and vacuum cleaner bags.
5. Do not smoke or eat while working on brake systems.

INSPECTION

Brake Drums

Any time brake drums are removed for brake service, braking surface diameter should be inspected with a suitable micrometer at several points to determine if they are within the safe oversize limit stamped on the brake drum outer surface. If braking surface diameter exceeds specifications, the drum must be replaced. If braking surface diameter is within specifications, drums should be cleaned and inspected for cracks, scores, deep grooves, taper, out of round and heat spotting. If drums are cracked or heat spotted, they must be replaced.

Minor scores should be removed with sandpaper. Grooves and large scores can only be removed by machining with special equipment, as long as the braking surface is within specifications stamped on brake drum outer surface. Any brake drum sufficiently out of round to cause vehicle vibration or noise while braking, or showing taper should also be machined, removing only enough stock to true up the brake drum.

After a brake drum is machined, wipe braking surface diameter with a suitable cloth soaked in denatured alcohol. If one brake drum is machined, the other should also be machined to the same diameter to maintain equal braking forces.

Brake Linings & Springs

Inspect brake linings for excessive wear, damage, oil, grease or brake fluid contamination. If any of the above conditions exist, brake linings should be replaced. Do not attempt to replace only one set of brake shoes; they should be replaced as an axle set only to maintain equal braking forces. Examine brake shoe webbing, hold-down and return springs for signs of overheating indicated by a slight blue color. If any component exhibits signs of overheating, replace hold-down and return springs with new ones. Overheated springs lose their pull and could cause brake linings to wear out prematurely. Inspect all springs for sags, bends and external damage, and replace as required.

Inspect hold-down retainers and pins for bends, rust and corrosion. If any of the above conditions exist, replace retainers and pins.

Backing Plate

Inspect backing plate shoe contact surface for grooves that may restrict shoe movement and cannot be removed by lightly sanding with emery cloth or other suitable abrasive. If backing plate exhibits above condition, it should be replaced. Also inspect for signs of cracks, warping and excessive rust, indicating need for replacement.

Adjuster Mechanism

Inspect all components for rust, corrosion, bends and fatigue. Replace as required. On adjuster mechanism equipped

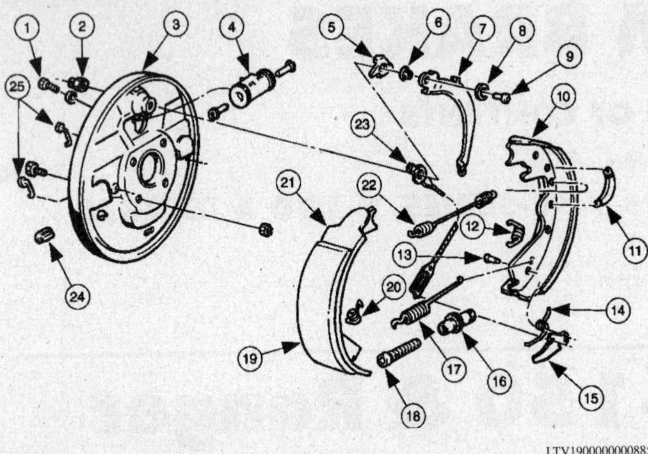

Fig. 1 Heavy duty rear drum brakes (Part 1 of 2)

Item	Description
1	Wheel Cylinder-to-Backing Plate Bolt (2 Req'd)
2	Lock Nut
3	Brake Backing Plate
4	Rear Wheel Cylinder
5	Brake Shoe Anchor Pin Guide Plate
6	Parking Brake Link Spring
7	Parking Brake Lever
8	Parking Brake Lever Pin Retainer
9	Parking Brake Lever Bolt
10	Rear Brake Shoe and Lining, Secondary
11	Cable Guide
12	Brake Shoe Hold-Down Spring
13	Adjusting Lever Pin
14	Adjusting Lever Return Spring
15	Brake Shoe Adjusting Lever
16	Brake Shoe Adjusting Screw Nut
17	Brake Shoe Adjusting Screw Spring
18	Brake Adjuster Screw
19	Shoe Lining (Part of 2200)
20	Brake Shoe Hold-Down Spring
21	Rear Brake Shoe and Lining, Primary
22	Brake Shoe Retracting Spring
23	Brake Shoe Adjusting Lever Cable
24	Brake Adjusting Hole Cover
25	Brake Shoe Hold-Down Spring Pin

LTV1900000000886

Fig. 1 Heavy duty rear drum brakes (Part 2 of 2)

with adjuster cable, inspect cable for kinks, fraying or elongation of eyelet and replace as required.

Parking Brake Cable

Inspect parking brake cable end for kinks, fraying and elongation, and replace as required. Use a small hose clamp to compress clamp where it enters backing plate to remove.

BRAKE SERVICE

Drum brakes are available in standard versions or in heavy duty versions. Refer to **Figs. 1 and 2** for component locations when performing the following procedures.

Removal

STANDARD DUTY

1. Raise and support vehicle, remove rear wheel and tire assemblies.
2. Remove and discard spring nut.
3. If brake drum is rusted to axle shaft pilot diameter, tap center of brake drum between wheel studs.
4. Pull brake drum off of axle.
5. If brake drums will not come off, sing a screwdriver, move brake shoe adjusting lever off of brake adjusting screw, then loosen brake adjuster to allow drum to release.
6. Remove long brake shoe retracting screw, then the short one.
7. Disconnect brake shoe adjusting lever cable and guide.
8. Remove adjusting lever return spring and brake shoe adjusting lever.
9. Remove brake shoe adjusting screw spring.
10. Remove brake adjuster screw assembly.
11. Remove brake shoe anchor pin guide plate, parking brake strut and parking brake lever pin retainer. Parking brake link spring and spring retainer will come off with parking brake strut.
12. Remove brake hold down springs, then remove rear brake shoes and linings.
13. Remove brake shoe hold down spring pins.
14. Pull back parking brake cable spring and disconnect parking brake lever.
15. Inspect components as outlined under "Inspection."

HEAVY DUTY

1. Raise and support vehicle, remove rear tire and wheel assemblies.
2. Remove and discard spring nut.
3. If brake drum is rusted to axle shaft pilot diameter, tap center of brake drum between wheel studs.
4. Pull brake drum off of axle.
5. If brake drums will not come off, using a screwdriver, move brake shoe adjusting lever off of brake adjusting screw, then loosen brake adjuster to allow drum to release.
6. Inspect brake components as outlined under "Inspection."
7. Remove brake shoe retracting spring.
8. Remove parking brake lever bolt lock nut at back of backing plate, then the parking brake lever bolt.
9. Remove parking brake rear cable and conduit from parking brake lever.
10. Disconnect brake shoe adjusting lever cable from adjusting lever.
11. Remove brake shoe adjusting lever cable and guide.
12. Remove adjusting lever return spring and brake shoe adjusting lever.
13. Remove brake shoe adjusting screw spring.
14. Remove brake adjuster screw assembly.
15. Remove brake shoe anchor pin guide plate.
16. Remove brake shoe hold down springs and pins.
17. Remove brake shoes and linings.
18. Inspect components as outlined under "Inspection."

Installation

STANDARD DUTY

1. Compress parking brake cable spring and attach parking brake lever.
2. Clean and lubricate backing plate with silicone brake caliper grease and dielectric compound No. D7AZ-19A331–A, or equivalent meeting Ford specification ESE-M1C171–A.
3. Attach parking brake lever to rear brake shoe and lining and secure parking brake lever pin retainer.
4. Position brake shoes and linings on backing plate, then install hold down spring pins and springs.
5. Install parking brake link spring and retainer.
6. Install parking brake strut.
7. Install brake shoe anchor pin guide plate.
8. Place brake shoe adjusting lever cable over anchor pin with crimped side in.
9. Install short brake shoe retracting spring.
10. Ensure brake shoe adjusting cable is positioned in cable groove guide.
11. Install long brake shoe retracting spring.
12. To prevent incorrect installation, socket end of each adjuster screw is stamped with a "R" or "L."
13. Apply silicone brake caliper grease and dielectric compound No. D7AZ-19A331–A, or equivalent meeting Ford

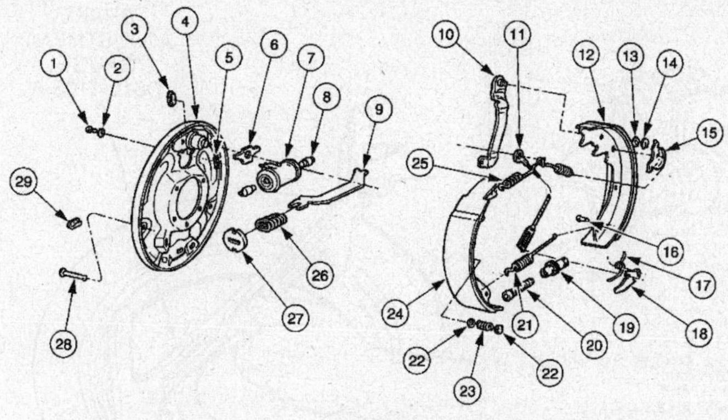

LTV1900000000887

Fig. 2 Standard rear drum brakes (Part 1 of 2)

1. Wheel Cylinder-to-Backing Plate Bolt
2. Washer
3. Inspection Hole Cover
4. Brake Backing Plate
5. Lining Inspection Hole
6. Anchor Pin Guide Plate
7. Rear Wheel Cylinder
8. Wheel Cylinder Brake Shoe Link
9. Parking Brake Strut
10. Parking Brake Lever
11. Brake Shoe Adjusting Lever Cable
12. Rear Brake Shoe and Lining, Secondary
13. Washer
14. Parking Brake Lever Pin Retainer
15. Cable Guide
16. Adjusting Lever Pin
17. Adjusting Lever Return Spring
18. Brake Shoe Adjusting Lever
19. Brake Shoe Adjusting Screw Nut
20. Brake Adjuster Screw
21. Brake Shoe Adjusting Screw Spring
22. Brake Shoe Hold-Down Spring Cup
23. Brake Shoe Hold-Down Spring
24. Rear Brake Shoe and Lining, Primary
25. Brake Shoe Retracting Spring, Short
26. Parking Brake Link Spring
27. Parking Brake Spring Retainer
28. Brake Shoe Hold-Down Spring Pin
29. Brake Adjusting Hole Cover

LTV1900000000888

Fig. 2 Standard rear drum brakes (Part 2 of 2)

specification ESE-M1C171–A to brake adjuster screw assembly components.

14. Install brake adjuster screw into brake shoe adjusting screw nut to end of threads, then loosen one half turn.
15. Install brake shoe adjusting screw socket on brake shoe adjusting screw nut.
16. Position brake adjuster screw assembly, then install brake shoe adjusting screw spring.
17. Position brake shoe adjusting lever cable.
18. Position adjusting lever return spring and brake shoe adjusting lever.
19. Hook brake shoe adjusting lever cable to brake shoe adjusting lever.
20. Pull brake shoe adjusting lever cable and ensure brake shoe adjusting lever rotates brake shoe adjuster assembly.
21. Release brake shoe adjusting lever cable and ensure brake shoe adjusting lever advances to next notch on brake shoe adjusting screw nut.
22. Install brake drum.
23. Adjust brakes.
24. Install wheel and tire assemblies, then lower vehicle.

HEAVY DUTY

1. Lubricate backing plate friction points with silicone brake caliper grease and dielectric compound No. D7AZ-19A331–A, or equivalent meeting Ford specification ESE-M1C171–A.
2. Position rear brake shoes on backing plate.
3. Install brake shoe hold down spring pins and springs.
4. Install brake shoe anchor pin guide plate.
5. To prevent incorrect installation, socket end of each adjuster screw is stamped with a "R" or "L."
6. Apply silicone brake caliper grease and dielectric compound No. D7AZ-19A331–A, or equivalent meeting Ford specification ESE-M1C171–A to brake adjuster screw assembly components.
7. Install brake adjuster screw into brake shoe adjusting screw nut to end of threads, then loosen one half turn.
8. Install adjusting screw socket on adjusting screw nut.
9. Position brake adjuster screw assembly.
10. Install brake shoe adjusting screw spring and brake shoe adjusting lever.
11. Install cable guide.
12. Position adjusting lever return spring and brake shoe adjusting lever.
13. Hook brake shoe adjusting lever cable to brake shoe adjusting lever.
14. Pull brake shoe adjusting lever cable and ensure brake shoe adjusting lever rotates brake shoe adjuster assembly.
15. Release brake shoe adjusting lever cable and ensure brake shoe adjusting lever advances to next notch on brake shoe adjusting screw nut.
16. Attach parking brake rear cable and conduit to parking brake lever.
17. Position parking brake lever, then install brake lever bolt and nut.
18. Install brake shoe retracting spring.
19. Install brake drum, then adjust brakes.
20. Install wheel and tire assemblies, then lower vehicle.

PARKING BRAKE w/REAR DISC

F-Super Duty

1. Raise and support vehicle, remove tire and wheel assemblies.
2. Remove rear brake disc rotor.
3. Disconnect rear parking brake cable at parking brake cable equalizer.
4. Disconnect parking brake cable at parking brake lever.
5. Remove outboard brake shoe retaining spring.
6. Remove brake shoe adjusting screw spring, brake shoe hold down springs and brake adjuster screw.
7. Remove parking brake shoe and linings along with inboard brake shoe retracting spring.
8. Reverse procedure to install.

Expedition, Explorer, F-150, F-250, Mountaineer & Navigator

1. Pull front parking brake cable and conduit, then insert a 5/32 inch drill bit or equivalent into hole in pedal linkage to hold cable in relaxed position.
2. Raise and support vehicle, remove rear wheel and tire assemblies.
3. **On F-150 models,** remove square cut O-ring from hub.
4. **On all models,** remove rear brake caliper and disc.
5. Remove brake shoe retracting spring and adjusting screw spring.
6. Remove brake adjuster and rear brake shoe hold down springs.
7. Remove rear brake shoes and linings along with inboard brake shoe retracting spring.
8. Reverse procedure to install.

E-Series

1. Raise and support vehicle, remove rear wheel and tire assemblies.
2. Remove caliper and anchor plate.
3. Remove axle shaft.
4. Remove hub nut with suitable socket wrench.

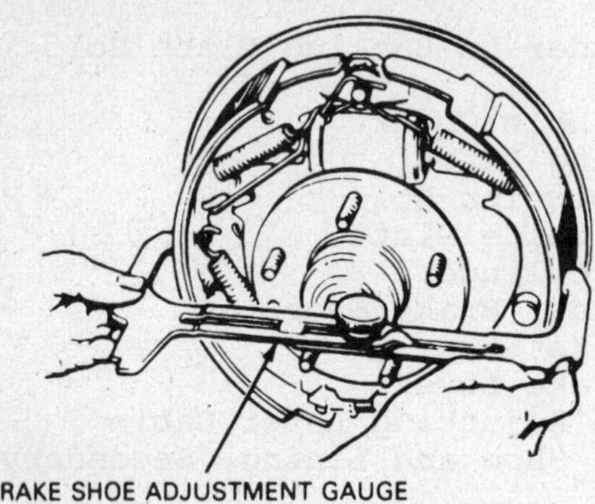

Fig. 3 Brake lining clearance inspection

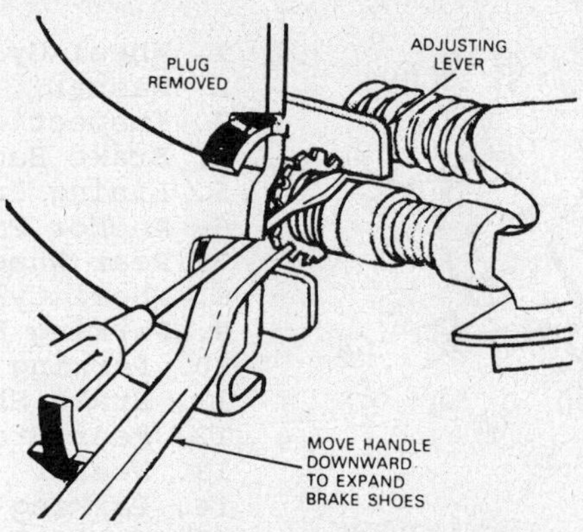

Fig. 4 Rear drum brake adjustment

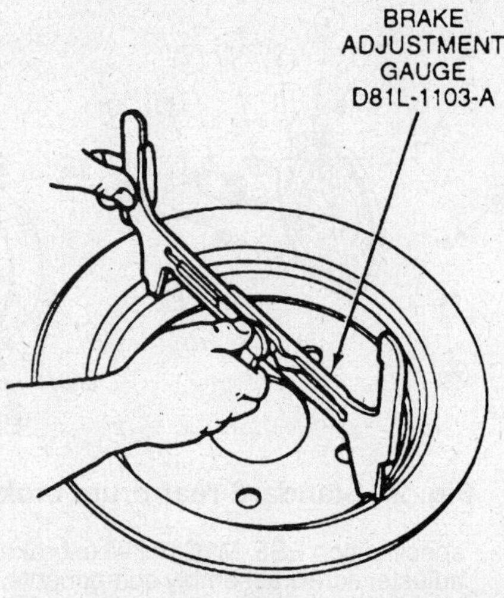

Fig. 5 Parking brake drum inside diameter measurement. Expedition, Explorer, F-150, F-250, Mountaineer & Navigator

5. Remove outer wheel bearing.
6. Remove rear hub and brake disc assembly.
7. Remove brake shoe retracting spring and brake shoe hold down springs.
8. Pull primary shoe forward and out, then pull secondary shoe rearward and remove parking brake shoes as an assembly.
9. Remove brake shoe inner retracting spring.
10. Remove brake adjuster screw and spring.
11. Reverse procedure to install.

ADJUSTMENTS

Service Brake

The rear brake shoes adjust automatically when the vehicle is driven in reverse and the brakes are applied sharply several times. Manual adjustment is required only when brake shoes are replaced. When adjusting rear brakes, ensure parking brake is properly adjusted and adjuster is operating freely.

DRUMS REMOVED

1. With drums removed, clean areas where shoes contact backing plate, then apply suitable lubricant to contact areas. Ensure lubricant does not contaminate linings.
2. Adjust gauge to inside diameter of brake drum using suitable brake shoe adjusting gauge.
3. Reverse tool and adjust shoes until they contact gauge. Ensure gauge is parallel to vehicle and at centerline of axle, **Fig. 3.** Holding automatic adjusting lever aside, rotate adjusting screw as required.
4. Install drums, wheels and retaining nuts, then complete adjustment by applying brakes several times while driving vehicle in reverse.

DRUMS INSTALLED

1. Raise and support rear of vehicle.
2. Remove cover from adjusting hole located at bottom of backing plate.
3. Rotate adjusting screw star wheel with brake adjustment tool No. D81L-1103-C, or equivalent, until brake shoes are locked against drum using suitable small screwdriver to hold adjusting lever away from star wheel, **Fig. 4.**
4. Back-off brake adjusting screw approximately 10–12 notches so that brake drum rotates freely without drag. If brake drum does not rotate freely, remove drum and clean and inspect drum brake components.
5. After adjusting both drum brakes, lower vehicle and apply brakes several times to position brake shoes.
6. Road test vehicle to ensure brakes operate properly.

Parking Brake Except Rear Disc

These models are equipped with a self-adjusting parking brake system. No manual adjustment is required.

Parking Brake w/Rear Disc

EXPEDITION, EXPLORER, F-150, F-250, MOUNTAINEER & NAVIGATOR

1. Remove rear disc brake rotor as outlined in “Disc Brakes” chapter.
2. Measure inside diameter of parking brake drum using tool No. D81L-1103-A brake adjustment gauge, or equivalent, **Fig. 5.**
3. Adjust parking brake shoe to .020 inch less than drum measurement using parking brake adjuster screw.
4. Reverse procedure to install.

TIGHTENING SPECIFICATIONS

Year	Component	Torque Ft. Lbs.
2002–06	Backing Plate	40–50
	Bleeder Screw	60–72①
	Brake Tube	11–15
	Brake Line To Wheel Cylinder	11–14
	Front Parking Brake Clamp	11–14
	Front Master Cylinder Brake Line	17–20
	Lefthand Rear Brake Hose Bracket Bolt	120–144①
	Parking Brake Cable & Conduit Clip	11–14
	Parking Brake Cable Support	32
	Parking Brake Control	13–17
	Parking Brake Control Release Handle	26①
	Parking Brake Remote Release	19–25①
	Parking Brake Signal Switch	18–27①
	Parking Brake To Extension Housing	25–42
	Parking Brake Warning Indicator	12–20①
	Rear Brake Line	11–14
	Rear Disc Brake Caliper Bleeder Screw	12–18
	Rear Disc Brake Caliper Hose Bolt	29
	Rear Master Cylinder Brake Line	11–14
	Wheel Cylinder	9–13
	Wheel Lug Nuts	100

① — Inch lbs.

Escape, Mariner, Villager & Windstar

INDEX

PRECAUTIONS

When working on or around brake assemblies, care must be taken to prevent breathing asbestos dust, as many manufacturers incorporate asbestos fibers in the production of brake linings. During routine service operations, precautions should be taken to minimize exposure. Do not sand or grind brake linings unless suitable local exhaust ventilation equipment is used to prevent excessive asbestos exposure.

1. Wear a suitable respirator approved for asbestos dust use during all repair procedures.
2. When cleaning brake dust from brake components, use a suitable vacuum cleaner with a highly efficient filter system. If a suitable vacuum cleaner is not available, use a suitable water soaked rag. Do not use compressed air or dry brush to clean brake components.
3. Keep work area clean, using same equipment as for cleaning brake components.
4. Properly dispose of rags and vacuum cleaner bags.
5. Do not smoke or eat while working on brake systems.

INSPECTION

Brake Drums

Any time brake drums are removed for brake service, braking surface diameter should be inspected with a suitable micrometer at several points to determine if they are within the safe oversize limit stamped on the brake drum outer surface. If braking surface diameter exceeds specifications, the drum must be replaced. If braking surface diameter is within specifications, drums should be cleaned and inspected for cracks, scores, deep grooves, taper, out of round and heat spotting. If drums are cracked or heat spotted, they must be replaced.

Minor scores should be removed with sandpaper. Grooves and large scores can only be removed by machining with special equipment, as long as the braking surface is within specifications stamped on brake drum outer surface. Any brake drum sufficiently out of round to cause vehicle vibration or noise while braking, or showing taper should also be machined, removing only enough stock to true up the brake drum.

After a brake drum is machined, wipe braking surface diameter with a cloth soaked in denatured alcohol. If one brake drum is machined, the other should also be machined to the same diameter to maintain equal braking forces.

Brake Linings & Springs

Inspect brake linings for excessive wear, damage, oil, grease or brake fluid contamination. If any of the above conditions exist, brake linings should be replaced. Do not attempt to replace only one set of brake shoes; they should be replaced as an axle set only to maintain equal braking forces. Examine brake shoe webbing, hold-down and return springs for signs of overheating indicated by a slight blue color. If any component exhibits signs of overheating, replace hold-down and return springs with new ones. Overheated springs lose their pull and could cause brake linings to wear out prematurely. Inspect all springs for sags, bends and external damage, and replace as required.

Inspect hold-down retainers and pins for bends, rust and corrosion. If any of the above conditions exist, replace retainers and pins.

Backing Plate

Inspect backing plate shoe contact surface for grooves that may restrict shoe movement and cannot be removed by lightly sanding with emery cloth or other suitable abrasive. If backing plate exhibits above condition, it should be replaced. Also inspect for signs of cracks, warping and excessive rust, indicating need for replacement.

Adjuster Mechanism

Inspect all components for rust, corrosion, bends and fatigue. Replace as required. On adjuster mechanism equipped with adjuster cable, inspect cable for kinks, fraying or elongation of eyelet and replace as required.

Parking Brake Cable

Inspect parking brake cable end for kinks, fraying and elongation, and replace as required. Use a small hose clamp to compress clamp where it enters backing plate to remove.

BRAKE SERVICE

Escape & Mariner

1. Raise and support vehicle.
2. Remove rear tire and wheel assemblies.
3. Remove brake drum retaining clips, if equipped.
4. If brake drums will not come off, move brake shoe adjusting lever of brake adjuster screw, then loosen brake shoe adjuster nut.
5. Remove brake dust and dirt from assemblies with brake/clutch service vacuum.
6. If new shoes are to be installed, resurface rear brake drums.
7. Remove parking brake cable from parking brake cable lever.
8. Remove hold down clips and pins.
9. Remove lower spring.
10. Pull bottom of brake shoe forward, then release upper return spring.
11. Remove self adjuster lever and spring assembly.
12. Remove horseshoe clip and parking brake lever.
13. Reverse procedure to install.

Villager

1. Raise and support vehicle.
2. Remove rear tire and wheel assemblies.
3. Loosen rear brake adjuster, then remove rear drum.
4. Remove upper and lower retracting springs.
5. Remove self adjuster.

6. Remove two hold down springs and retainers.
7. Remove parking brake lever clip and parking brake lever.
8. Reverse procedure to install.

Windstar

1. Raise and support vehicle.
2. Remove rear wheel and tire assemblies.
3. If brake drum is rusted to axle shaft pilot diameter, tap center of brake drum between wheel studs.
4. If brake drum will not come off, move brake shoe adjusting lever off of brake adjuster screw with suitable screwdriver.
5. Loosen brake adjustment screw with suitable brake adjustment tool.
6. Remove brake drum.
7. Remove brake shoe adjusting screw spring.
8. Remove brake adjuster lever and screw.
9. Remove brake shoe hold down spring and retracting spring.
10. Remove rear brake shoes and linings.
11. Remove and discard parking brake lever clip, then remove brake shoes from parking brake lever.
12. Reverse procedure to install.

ADJUSTMENTS

Service Brake

1. Raise and support vehicle. Ensure parking brake is released.
2. Remove rubber access plug from backing plate.
3. Slowly rotate rear wheel while gradually increasing length of adjuster assembly by rotating adjusting screw using brake adjustment tool No. D91L-1103-C, or equivalent.
4. Increase adjuster assembly length until brake shoes contact brake drum.

Parking Brake

1. Start engine and depress brake pedal several times while vehicle is moving in reverse.
2. Stop engine, then turn cable adjustment nut until parking brake pedal stroke is 11–12 notches when depressed with force of 44 lbs.

TIGHTENING SPECIFICATIONS

Year	Component	Torque Ft. Lbs.
ESCAPE & MARINER		
2002–06	Brake Backing Plate	49
	Brake Line To Rear Wheel Cylinder Fitting	10
	Parking Brake Cable Bracket Bolt	16
	Rear Wheel Cylinder Bolts	108①
	Wheel Cylinder Bolts	108①
	Wheel Cylinder Bleeder Screws	71①
	Wheel Lug Nuts	98
VILLAGER & WINDSTAR		
2002–03	Backing Plate	51–67
	Bleeder Screw	12
	Brake Line Flare Nut	13
	Brake Load Sensor	14
	Opening Cover	27–35①
	Parking Brake Control, Bolts	12–17
	Parking Brake Control, Nuts	71–97①
	Parking Brake Lever	71–88①
	Parking Brake Release	18–27①
	Warning Indicator	19–20
	Wheel Cylinder Bolts	12

① — Inch lbs.

Drum Brake Specifications

Model	Year	Brake Lining Wear Limit, Inch②	Brake Drum Inside Diameter, Inches		
			Nominal	Maximum Refinish	Maximum Inside Diameter (Discard Limit)①
FORD					
Escape	2002–06	.040	9.000	9.050	9.060
Explorer Sport	2002	.030	11.000	11.060	11.090
Explorer Sport Trac	2002	.030	11.000	11.060	11.090
E-150	2002–06	.030	11.030	11.090	11.120
E-250	2002–03	.030	12.000	12.060	12.090
E-350	2002–03	.030	12.125	12.185	12.210
F-150	2002–03	.030	11.030	11.090	11.120
Mariner	2005–06	.040	9.000	9.050	9.060
Ranger	2002–06	.040	9.000	9.050	9.060
Windstar	2002–03	.150	9.843	9.902	③
MERCURY					
Villager	2002	.059	9.840	9.060	9.090

DRW — Dual Rear Wheels

SRW — Single Rear Wheels

① — Maximum brake drum inside diameter (discard limit) is stamped on drum.

② — Above rivet head or shoe. Original equipment type brake linings.

③ — Discard limit is stamped on drum.

HYDRAULIC BRAKE SYSTEMS

NOTE: Prior To Performing Any Service Operations Listed In This Section, Consult The "Technical Service Bulletins" Section For Related Information.

INDEX

DESCRIPTION

Master Cylinder

The master cylinder consists primarily of a hydraulic cylinder, primary and secondary hydraulic pistons and a single or dual chamber fluid reservoir. The front brakes are connected to the primary outlet port(s) and are actuated by the primary piston assembly. The rear brakes are connected to the secondary outlet port and are actuated by the secondary piston assembly.

Hydraulic Control Valves

COMBINATION VALVE

This multi-function hydraulic control unit consists primarily of a pressure differential valve, brake lamp warning switch and a proportioning valve. A pressure differential shuttle and/or metering valve are also incorporated with some valve applications.

The metering valve delays front disc brake effectiveness until the rear brake shoes contact the brake drums. The proportioning valve regulates rear hydraulic system pressure to prevent rear brake lockup. The pressure differential valve senses hydraulic system pressure and will activate the brake lamp warning switch if a pressure loss occurs. The pressure differential shuttle bypass feature provides full rear brake application if front hydraulic system pressure is significantly reduced.

INTEGRAL BYPASS PROPORTIONING VALVE

This multi-function hydraulic control unit consists primarily of a proportioning valve, pressure differential valve with a shuttle bypass feature and a brake lamp warning switch. The proportioning valve is integral with the recessed cartridge type master cylinder, which eliminates a need for additional tubing and connection points.

HEIGHT SENSING PROPORTIONING VALVE

This valve, used with some hydraulic brake systems, regulates hydraulic pressure to the rear brakes according to vehicle load. It is commonly located on a crossmember and is activated through a linkage system that is connected to the rear axle housing cover. Pressure from a loaded vehicle on the linkage lever will cause the height sensing valve to increase hydraulic pressure to the rear brakes or, if the vehicle's load is reduced, hydraulic pressure to the rear brakes is reduced.

HYDRAULIC CONTROL UNIT (HCU)

The anti-lock brake hydraulic control unit, (HCU), consists of normally open solenoid valves and a pressure accumulator. If the ABS senses that wheel lockup is about to occur, the solenoid valve will pulse closed preventing more fluid from entering that wheel circuit. If at the next inspection the ABS system determines wheel lockup is going to occur, the solenoid valve will open allowing pressure to bleed into the HCU accumulator. After the affected wheel circuit returns to vehicle speed, all solenoids return to their normal position.

Bendix Hydro-Boost Brake Booster

This brake booster is hydraulically operated, receiving its power from the power steering system. The power steering pump provides fluid pressure to operate both the booster and the power steering gear. This fluid pressure provides a variable power assist that is regulated by brake pedal application pressure.

The Hydro-Boost also has a reserve system (compressed gas accumulator) that is designed to store sufficient fluid under pressure to provide at least two brake applications in the event that fluid flow from the power steering pump is not available. Brakes can also be applied manually if reserve system is depleted.

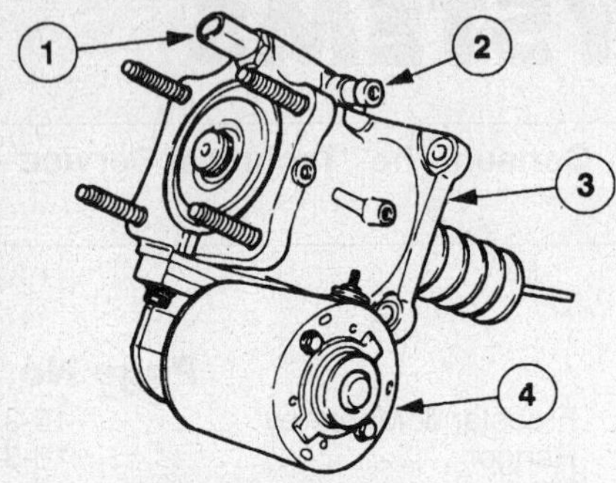

Item	Description
1	Flow Switch Contact Assy
2	Outlet Return Port
3	Hydro-Max Booster
4	Electric Pump and Motor Assy

FM4039900024000X

Fig. 1 Hydro-Max brake booster

Bendix Hydro-Max Brake Booster

The Hydro-Max power brake system, **Fig. 1,** is composed of a hydraulically powered booster, a mini-master cylinder, a reserve system electric motor pump, a relay, an electric monitor and an integral pressure differential switch.

ADJUSTMENTS

Master Cylinder Pushrod

Refer to "Adjustments" in "Power Brake Units" section for pushrod adjustment procedures.

DIAGNOSIS & TESTING

Refer to "Diagnosis & Testing" in "Power Brake Units" for testing procedures.

COMPONENT REPLACEMENT

Master Cylinder

AVIATOR

Remove components in sequence illustrated, **Fig. 2.**

E-SERIES

1. Drain brake master cylinder with suitable suction device.
2. Remove coolant reservoir.
3. **On models equipped with Hydro Boost,** remove three power distribution box bracket bolts and position box aside.

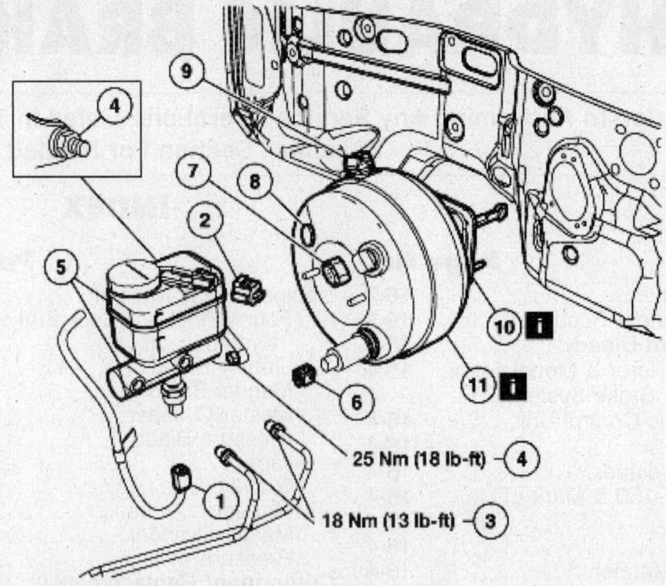

Item	Description
1	Connector
2	Brake fluid level warning switch electrical connector
3	Brake tube fittings
4	Brake master cylinder nut (2 req'd)
5	Brake master cylinder/reservoir assembly
6	Brake booster solenoid electrical connector (vehicles equipped with Stability Assist)
7	Brake booster transducer electrical connector (vehicles equipped with Stability Assist)
8	Brake booster vacuum fitting
9	Electrical harness connector bracket
10	Brake booster nuts (4 req'd)
11	Brake booster assembly

LTV1900000000910

Fig. 2 Master cylinder & brake booster replacement (Part 1 of 2). Aviator

4. **On all models,** remove speed control deactivator switch.
5. Disconnect fluid level sensor connector.
6. Remove and discard master cylinder mounting nuts.
7. Disconnect master cylinder brake tubes.
8. Remove master cylinder cylinder.
9. Reverse procedure to install, noting the following:
   a. **Torque** master cylinder mounting nuts to 18 ft. lbs.
   b. Bleed brake system as outlined under "Brake System Bleed."

EXCURSION & F-SUPER DUTY

Do not depress brake pedal while fluid supply line is disconnected. The inlet pressure port check ball may dislodge which will result in a non-functional backup system.

WITH HYDRO-MAX

1. Remove support bracket and nut.
2. Disconnect brake lines.
3. Remove ground wire nut and ground wire.
4. Remove master cylinder mounting nuts, then the master cylinder.
5. Reverse procedure to install, noting the following:
   a. **Torque** master cylinder mounting nuts to 28 ft. lbs.
   b. **Torque** ground wire nut to 15 ft. lbs.
   c. **Torque** brake line flare nuts to 19 ft. lbs.
   d. Bleed brake system as outlined under "Brake System Bleed."

LESS HYDRO MAX

1. Remove air cleaner housing.
2. Disconnect fluid level sensor electrical connector.
3. Disconnect brake pressure switch.
4. Disconnect brake lines.
5. **On models equipped with Hydro-Boost,** remove bolts retaining power steering tubes to bracket.
6. **On all models,** remove master cylinder mounting nuts.
7. **On models equipped with Hydro-Boost,** remove power steering tube retaining bracket.
8. **On all models,** remove master cylinder.
9. Reverse procedure to install, noting the following:

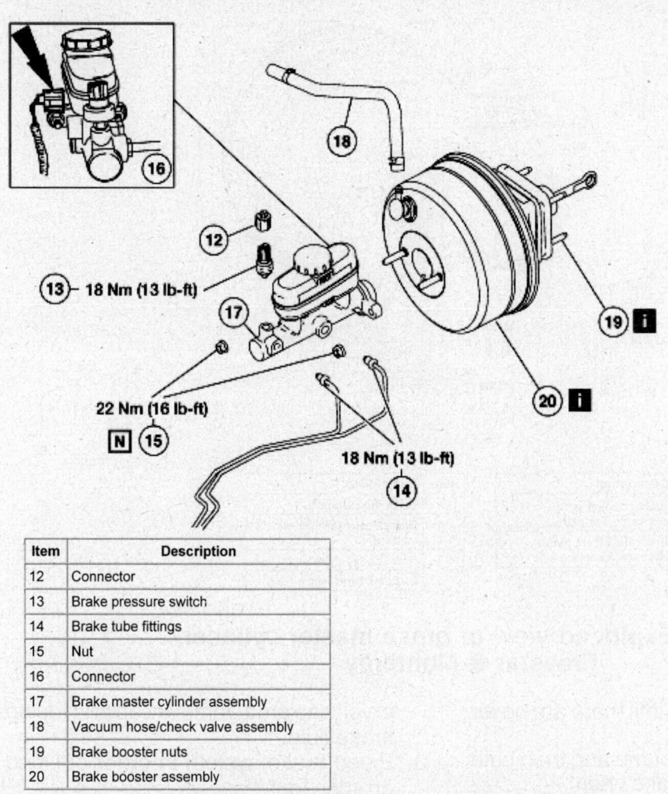

Item	Description
12	Connector
13	Brake pressure switch
14	Brake tube fittings
15	Nut
16	Connector
17	Brake master cylinder assembly
18	Vacuum hose/check valve assembly
19	Brake booster nuts
20	Brake booster assembly

Fig. 2 Master cylinder & brake booster replacement (Part 2 of 2). Aviator

a. **Torque** master cylinder mounting nuts to 20 ft. lbs.
b. **Torque** brake line flare nuts to 19 ft. lbs.
c. Bleed brake system as outlined under "Brake System Bleed."

ESCAPE & MARINER

1. Disconnect brake fluid level warning switch electrical connector, **Fig. 3.**
2. Drain brake master cylinder reservoir using a suitable suction device.
3. **On models equipped with manual transmission,** disconnect clutch master cylinder supply line.
4. **On all models,** disconnect brake fluid lines from master cylinder, then plug all open ports.
5. Remove and discard master cylinder mounting nuts.
6. Remove master cylinder from booster.
7. Reverse procedure to install, noting the following:
   a. If a new brake master cylinder reservoir is being installed, be sure to install new seals. Lubricate them with clean brake fluid.
   b. Transfer brake master cylinder reservoir if a new master cylinder is being installed.
   c. Fill master cylinder reservoir to proper level, then bleed brake system as outlined under "Brake System Bleed."
   d. Install new master cylinder mounting nuts, then **torque** to 13 ft. lbs.
   e. **On models equipped with manual transmission,** bleed clutch master cylinder.

EXPEDITION, EXPLORER, EXPLORER SPORT & SPORT/TRAC, F-150, MARK TL, MOUNTAINEER & NAVIGATOR

1. Disconnect low fluid warning switch electrical connector.
2. **On models equipped with cruise control,** disconnect brake pressure switch electrical connector.
3. **On all models,** disconnect and plug brake fluid lines and master cylinder ports.
4. Remove master cylinder retaining nuts, then the master cylinder.
5. Reverse procedure to install, noting the following:
   a. Adjust pushrod length. Refer to "Adjustments" in "Power Brake Units" section for pushrod adjustment procedures.
   b. **On all models except Explorer, Explorer Sport & Sport/Trac, torque** master cylinder mounting nuts to 17–21 ft. lbs.
   c. **On Explorer, Explorer Sport & Sport/Trac models, torque** master cylinder mounting nuts to 17 ft. lbs.
   d. **On all models,** ensure brake fluid lines are tightened securely.
   e. Fill master cylinder reservoir to proper level, then bleed brake system as outlined under "Brake System Bleed."

Item	Description
1	Brake fluid level warning switch electrical connector
2	Brake line fitting nuts

Item	Description
3	Master cylinder nuts (2 required)
4	Brake master cylinder assembly

LTV0500000000974

Fig. 3 Exploded view of brake master cylinder. Escape & Mariner

FREESTAR & MONTEREY

1. Remove air cleaner assembly.
2. Drain brake fluid reservoir using suitable suction device.
3. Disconnect brake pressure switch electrical connector, **Fig. 4.**
4. Disconnect brake fluid level switch electrical connector.
5. Disconnect brake line fittings. Cap brake line and plug master cylinder ports.
6. Remove master cylinder mounting nuts, then the master cylinder.
7. Reverse procedure to install, noting the following:
   a. **Torque** master cylinder mounting nuts to 18 ft. lbs.
   b. **Torque** brake line fittings to 13 ft. lbs.
   c. Fill master cylinder reservoir to proper level, then bleed brake system as outlined under "Brake System Bleed."

RANGER

1. Disconnect brake fluid level warning switch.
2. **On models equipped with cruise control,** disconnect brake pressure switch.
3. **On all models,** disconnect two brake lines, plug lines and ports on master cylinder.
4. Remove wiring retainer clip from master cylinder.
5. Remove mounting nuts, then the master cylinder.
6. Reverse procedure to install, noting the following:
   a. **Torque** master cylinder mounting nuts to 17 ft. lbs.
   b. **Torque** master cylinder brake line flare nuts to 13 ft. lbs.
   c. Bleed brake system as outlined under "Brake System Bleed."

VILLAGER

1. Disconnect brake fluid level switch electrical connector.
2. Remove brake master cylinder reservoir bolts.
3. Remove dampening valve.
4. Remove brake master cylinder and brake master cylinder reservoir.
5. Loosen clamps, then remove brake master cylinder reservoir hoses from brake master cylinder.
6. Reverse procedure to install, noting the following:
   a. Adjust pushrod length. Refer to "Adjustments" in "Power Brake Units" section for pushrod adjustment procedures.
   b. **Torque** master cylinder mounting nuts to 11 ft. lbs.
   c. Fill master cylinder reservoir to proper level, then bleed brake system as outlined under "Brake System Bleed."

WINDSTAR

1. Remove air cleaner assembly.
2. Disconnect speed control switch electrical connector.
3. Disconnect fluid level sensor electrical connector.
4. Disconnect brake fluid lines.
5. Remove wiring bracket nut, then position aside.
6. Remove brake master cylinder nuts, then master cylinder.
7. Reverse procedure to install, noting the following:
   a. Adjust pushrod length. Refer to "Adjustments" in "Power Brake Units" section for pushrod adjustment procedures.
   b. **Torque** master cylinder mounting nuts to 23 ft. lbs.
   c. Fill master cylinder reservoir to proper level, then bleed brake system as outlined under "Brake System Bleed."

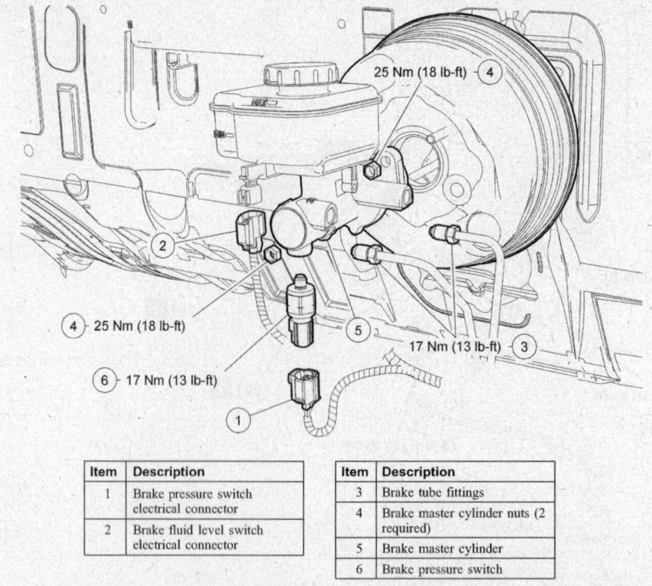

Item	Description
1	Brake pressure switch electrical connector
2	Brake fluid level switch electrical connector

Item	Description
3	Brake tube fittings
4	Brake master cylinder nuts (2 required)
5	Brake master cylinder
6	Brake pressure switch

Fig. 4 Exploded view of brake master cylinder. Freestar & Monterey

POWER BRAKE UNIT SERVICE

The Hydro-Boost and Hydro-Max power brake boosters are serviced as complete units. No disassembly procedures are provided.

BRAKE SYSTEM BLEED

Aviator, Explorer & Mountaineer

MASTER CYLINDER

1. Connect one end of a clear flexible hose to master cylinder bleeder screw. Submerge other end in a container partially filled with suitable brake fluid.
2. Have an assistant pump and then hold firm pressure on brake pedal.
3. Open master cylinder bleeder screw until brake fluid flows into container.
4. When fluid stops flowing, close bleeder screw.
5. Repeat procedure until there are no air bubbles in fluid.
6. Have an assistant pump and then hold firm pressure on brake pedal.
7. Loosen a master cylinder tube fitting at anti-lock brake hydraulic control unit.
8. When fluid stops flowing from fitting, tighten fitting.
9. Repeat procedure until there are no air bubbles in fluid.
10. Repeat bleed procedure on master cylinder tube fitting.

CALIPER

1. Connect one end of a clear flexible hose to caliper bleed screw. Place other end in a container partially filled with suitable brake fluid.
2. Have an assistant pump and then hold firm pressure on brake pedal.
3. Open caliper bleeder screw until brake fluid flows into container.
4. When fluid stops flowing, close bleeder screw.
5. Repeat procedure until there are no bubbles in brake fluid.

ANTI-LOCK BRAKE SYSTEM HYDRAULIC CONTROL UNIT

This procedure is only required when a new hydraulic control unit is installed.

1. Connect a suitable scan tool to system and follow scan tool ABS system bleed instructions.
2. Perform caliper bleed procedure starting at righthand rear caliper.

E-Series, F-150 & Mark LT

MANUAL

1. Connect suitable scan tool to DLC located under dash, and follow on screen procedure.
2. Clean all dirt from master cylinder reservoir cap area, remove cap and top up brake fluid.
3. Bleed brake system in order outlined on scan tool.
4. Attach a rubber hose to bleeder screw.
5. Have an assistant pump and hold pressure on brake pedal.
6. Loosen bleeder screw until a stream of brake fluid comes out.
7. While assistant maintains pressure on brake pedal, tighten bleeder screw.
8. Repeat until clear, bubble free fluid comes from bleeder screw.
9. Repeat procedure for remaining bleeder screws.

PRESSURE

1. Clean all dirt from master cylinder reservoir cap area, remove cap and top up brake fluid.
2. Install bleeder adapter into master cylinder.
3. Bleed longest line first.
4. Attach rubber hose to righthand rear brake bleeder and submerge free end in container partially filled with clean brake fluid.
5. Open valve on bleeder tank.
6. Open bleeder screw and leave open until bubble free brake fluid comes from bleeder, then close bleeder.
7. Continue bleeding brake system going from lefthand rear to righthand front and ending with lefthand front.
8. Close bleeder tank valve. Remove adapter and reinstall reservoir cap.

Escape & Mariner

ANTI-LOCK BRAKES

Bleeding the hydraulic control unit (HCU) is only required when removing or installing the HCU or master cylinder, or when opening the lines to the HCU. Carrying out the system bleed function drives trapped air from the HCU. Subsequent bleeding removes air from the brake hydraulic system through the bleeder screws.

1. Connect suitable diagnostic scan tool.
2. Access "System Bleed Function." Go to Tool Tab-Chassis-Braking-ABS Service Bleed and follow directions on scan tool.
3. Manually bleed brake hydraulic system as outlined under "Manual Bleed."
4. Repeat procedure carrying out a total of two diagnostic tool cycles and two manual bleed cycles.

MANUAL BLEED

1. Fill master cylinder with suitable brake fluid.
2. Attach a rubber hose to rear bleeder screw and submerge free end in a container partially filled with suitable brake fluid.
3. Have an assistant pump brake pedal ten times and hold pressure on pedal.
4. Loosen bleeder screw until fluid flow stops. Maintain pressure on brake pedal and tighten brake bleeder screw.
5. Repeat until bubble free fluid flows from system.
6. Continue bleeding system going in order from righthand rear wheel to lefthand rear wheel then to righthand front wheel and ending with lefthand front wheel.

GRAVITY BLEED

1. Fill brake master cylinder with suitable brake fluid.
2. Attach hose to brake bleeder screw, place suitable drain pan below bleeder screw.
3. Loosen bleeder screw and allow system to bleed until bubble free brake fluid flows.
4. Tighten bleeder screw.
5. Continue bleeding system going from righthand rear wheel to lefthand rear wheel, then to righthand front wheel and ending with lefthand front wheel.

Excursion, Explorer Sport/Sport Trac, Freestar, F-Super Duty, Monterey, Motorhome, Ranger & Windstar

MANUAL BLEED

1. Clean all dirt from and remove brake master cylinder filler cap, then fill master cylinder with suitable brake fluid.
2. Place box end wrench on righthand rear bleeder screw, then attach rubber drain tube to bleeder screw. Submerge other end of hose in a container partially filled with suitable brake fluid.
3. Have an assistant pump and hold pressure on brake pedal.
4. Loosen brake bleeder until stream of brake fluid comes out.
5. While assistant maintains pressure on brake pedal, tighten brake bleeder screw.
6. Repeat until clear, bubble free fluid comes out.
7. Continue bleeding system, going in order from lefthand rear bleeder screw to righthand front bleeder screw, ending with lefthand front bleeder screw.

PRESSURE BLEED

1. Clean all dirt from reservoir cap, then remove and fill reservoir with suitable brake fluid.
2. Install bleeder adapter to brake master cylinder reservoir and attache bleeder tank hose to fitting on adapter.
3. Bleed longest line first.
4. Open valve on bleeder tank.
5. Loosen righthand rear bleeder screw and leave open until clear, bubble free brake fluid flows, then tighten bleeder screw.
6. Continue bleeding rear of system, going in order from lefthand rear bleeder screw to righthand front bleeder screw, ending with lefthand front bleeder screw.
7. Close bleeder tank valve, remove tank hose and adapter.

Expedition & Navigator

MASTER CYLINDER

When a new master cylinder has been installed, or the system has been emptied or partially emptied, the master cylinder should be primed.

IN VEHICLE

1. Disconnect brake master cylinder outlet tubes.
2. Install short tubes with ends submerged in brake master cylinder reservoir, then fill master cylinder reservoir with clean, suitable brake fluid.
3. Have an assistant pump brake pedal until clear fluid flows from both brake tubes without air bubbles.
4. Remove short tubes and install brake outlet tubes.
5. Bleed each tube at master cylinder as follows:
   a. Have an assistant pump brake pedal and then hold pressure on pedal.
   b. Loosen rear most brake line at master cylinder until a stream of brake fluid comes out. Have assistant maintain pressure on pedal, then tighten brake line fitting.
   c. Repeat until clear bubble free fluid comes out of each line fitting.

BENCH

1. Support brake master cylinder body in a vise and fill master cylinder reservoir with suitable brake fluid.
2. Install short tubes with ends submerged in brake fluid reservoir.
3. Slowly depress primary piston until clean fluid flows from both brake lines without air bubbles.
4. Remove brake tubes.

FOUR WHEEL ANTI-LOCK BRAKE SYSTEM

This procedure must be performed if a new hydraulic control unit has been installed. Performing the NGS program routine drives trapped air from the otherwise inaccessible lower section of the four wheel ABS valve into the upper sections where subsequent bleedings from the bleeder screws can remove the air.

1. Connect a clear rubber hose to righthand rear brake bleeder screw, submerge other end of hose in a container partially filled with brake fluid.
2. Have assistant pump brake pedal and hold pressure on pedal.
3. Loosen bleeder screw until stream of fluid comes out, then tighten bleeder screw.
4. Repeat procedure until clear, bubble free fluid comes from bleeder screw.
5. Repeat procedure for lefthand rear, righthand front and finally lefthand front.
6. Connect suitable scan tool to DLC under dash, follow on screen prompts and perform brake bleed procedure.
7. Repeat conventional brake bleed procedure.
8. Repeat as required.

GRAVITY BLEED

1. Fill master cylinder with suitable brake fluid.
2. Place box end wrench on righthand rear bleeder screw.
3. Attach a rubber drain hose to bleeder screw and submerge free end of hose into a container partially filled with suitable brake fluid.
4. Open bleeder screw and leave open until clear bubble free fluid flows.
5. Tighten bleeder screw.
6. Repeat procedure for lefthand rear caliper, righthand front caliper and finally the lefthand front caliper.

MANUAL BLEED

1. Fill master cylinder with suitable brake fluid.
2. Place box end wrench on righthand rear bleeder screw.
3. Attach a rubber drain hose to bleeder screw and submerge free end of hose into a container partially filled with suitable brake fluid.
4. Have an assistant pump and hold pressure on brake pedal.
5. Open bleeder screw and leave open until clear bubble free fluid flows.

6. Tighten bleeder screw.
7. Repeat procedure for lefthand rear caliper, righthand front caliper and finally the lefthand front caliper.
8. If required, bleed master cylinder.

PRESSURE BLEED

1. Clean all dirt from around master cylinder cap, remove cap and fill reservoir with clean, suitable brake fluid.
2. Install bleeder adapter to master cylinder.
3. Place box end wrench on righthand rear bleeder screw.
4. Attach a rubber drain hose to bleeder screw and submerge free end of hose into a container partially filled with suitable brake fluid.
5. Open bleeder screw and leave open until clear bubble free fluid flows.
6. Tighten bleeder screw.
7. Repeat procedure for lefthand rear caliper, righthand front caliper and finally the lefthand front caliper.

Villager

MASTER CYLINDER

1. Disconnect brake master cylinder outlet tubes.
2. Install short tubes with ends submerged in brake master cylinder reservoir, then fill master cylinder reservoir with clean, suitable brake fluid.
3. Have an assistant pump brake pedal until clear fluid flows from both brake tubes without air bubbles.
4. Remove short tubes and install brake outlet tubes.
5. Bleed each tube at master cylinder as follows:
   a. Have an assistant pump brake pedal and then hold pressure on pedal.
   b. Loosen brake line at master cylinder until a stream of brake fluid comes out. Have assistant maintain pressure on pedal, then tighten brake line fitting.
   c. Repeat until clear bubble free fluid comes out of each line fitting.

PRESSURE

1. Clean outside of master cylinder reservoir.
2. Remove reservoir cap, fill with suitable brake fluid, then attach brake bleeder adapter to reservoir.
3. Attach rubber hose to righthand rear bleeder screw.
4. Open valve on bleeder tank.
5. Loosen bleeder screw and leave open until clear bubble free fluid flows, then close bleeder and remove rubber hose.
6. Continue bleeding system going from lefthand rear to righthand front and finally to lefthand front.
7. Close bleeder tank valve, remove hose and adapter.
8. Top up brake fluid reservoir.

GRAVITY

1. Fill master cylinder with suitable brake fluid.
2. Attach rubber drain hose to righthand rear brake bleeder, submerge free end of hose in a container partially filled with clean brake fluid.
3. Loosen righthand rear bleeder screw and leave open until clear, bubble free fluid flows, then close.
4. Ensure master cylinder fluid lever remains full.
5. Continue bleeding system going from lefthand rear to righthand front and lastly to lefthand front.
6. Fill master cylinder reservoir and install cap.

MANUAL

1. Fill master cylinder with suitable brake fluid.
2. Attach rubber drain hose to righthand rear brake bleeder, submerge free end of hose in a container partially filled with clean brake fluid.
3. Have an assistant pump brake pedal ten times, then hold firm pressure on pedal.
4. Loosen righthand rear bleeder screw and leave open until clear, bubble free fluid flows, then close.
5. Have assistant maintain pressure on pedal.
6. Ensure master cylinder fluid lever remains full.
7. Continue bleeding system going from lefthand rear to righthand front and lastly to lefthand front.
8. Fill master cylinder reservoir and install cap.

POWER BRAKE UNITS
Bendix Vacuum Brake Booster

INDEX

DESCRIPTION

The single and tandem vacuum boosters, **Figs. 1 and 2,** are self contained vacuum hydraulic power braking units. These are vacuum suspended units that use vacuum and atmospheric pressure for their power.

On models equipped with gasoline engines, vacuum is supplied through a fitting in the intake manifold. On models equipped with diesel engines, vacuum is supplied through a vacuum pump.

The three basic elements of the booster are the vacuum power chamber, mechanically actuated booster check valve and a hydraulic dual master cylinder which supplies hydraulic pressure to the brake system.

The vacuum power chamber consists of a front and rear shell, diaphragm plate, hydraulic pushrod and vacuum diaphragm return spring.

The mechanically actuated booster check valve controls degree of power brake application in accordance with foot pressure applied to valve operating rod through brake pedal linkage. This valve is integral with the vacuum power diaphragm.

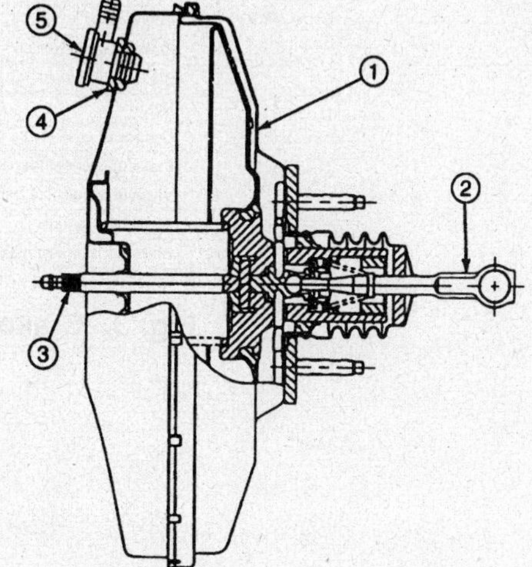

Item	Description
1	Power Brake Booster
2	Brake Pedal Push Rod
3	Master Cylinder Push Rod
4	Grommet
5	Power Brake Booster Check Valve

FM4039900017000X

Fig. 1 Single vacuum booster

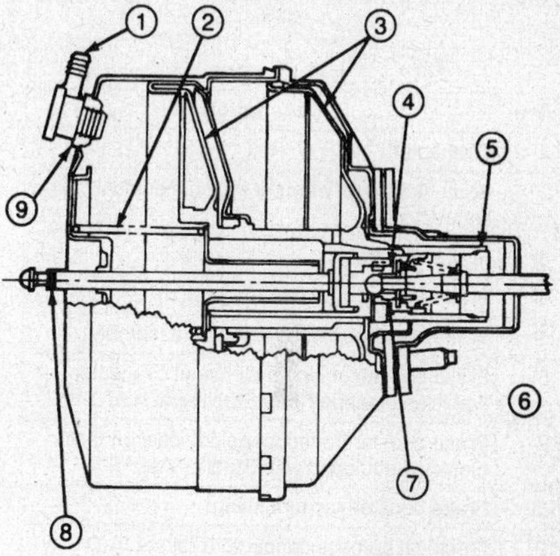

Item	Description
1	Power Brake Booster Check Valve
2	Return Spring
3	Tandem Power Diaphragms
4	Vacuum Port Closed — Brakes On
5	Filter (Air Inlet)
6	Brake Pedal Push Rod
7	Atmospheric Port Open — Brakes On
8	Master Cylinder Push Rod
9	Check Valve Grommet

FM4039900018000X

Fig. 2 Tandem vacuum booster

BRAKE BOOSTER

REPLACE

Aviator

Refer to **Fig. 3** and remove components in sequence illustrated. Use new nuts when installing brake booster.

Excursion & F-Super Duty

1. Remove air cleaner housing, if required.
2. Remove brake master cylinder attaching nuts.
3. Position brake master cylinder aside.
4. Disconnect booster vacuum hose.
5. Disconnect power distribution box auxiliary relay and set aside.
6. Remove fuse panel cover.
7. Remove brake pedal position switch self-locking pin.
8. Remove brake pedal position switch and brake booster pushrod from brake pedal pin.
9. Remove power brake booster nuts.
10. Remove power brake booster.
11. Reverse procedure to install. **Torque** booster mounting nuts to 16–21 ft. lbs.

Escape & Mariner

1. Remove brake master cylinder as outlined under "Hydraulic Brake Systems."
2. Remove Brake Pedal Position (BPP) switch.
3. Remove speed control deactivator switch.
4. Remove brake pedal push rod cotter pin and washer.
5. Remove four power brake booster pushrod bracket nuts, **Fig. 4.**
6. Disconnect brake pedal pushrod.
7. **On models equipped with 3.0L engine,** disconnect evaporative emission canister purge valve and position it aside.
8. **On all models,** disconnect brake booster vacuum hose.
9. Remove brake booster.

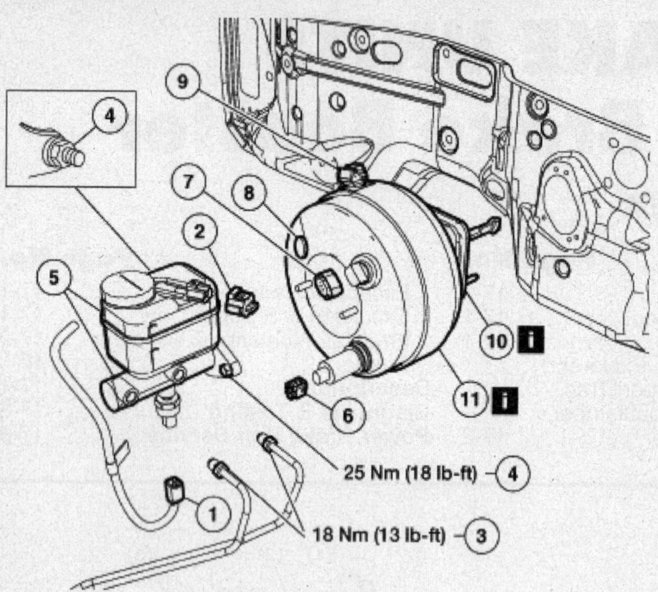

Item	Description
1	Connector
2	Brake fluid level warning switch electrical connector
3	Brake tube fittings
4	Brake master cylinder nut (2 req'd)
5	Brake master cylinder/reservoir assembly
6	Brake booster solenoid electrical connector (vehicles equipped with Stability Assist)
7	Brake booster transducer electrical connector (vehicles equipped with Stability Assist)
8	Brake booster vacuum fitting
9	Electrical harness connector bracket (IVD only)
10	Brake booster nuts (4 req'd)
11	Brake booster assembly

LTV1900000000912

Fig. 3 Brake booster replacement (Part 1 of 2). Aviator

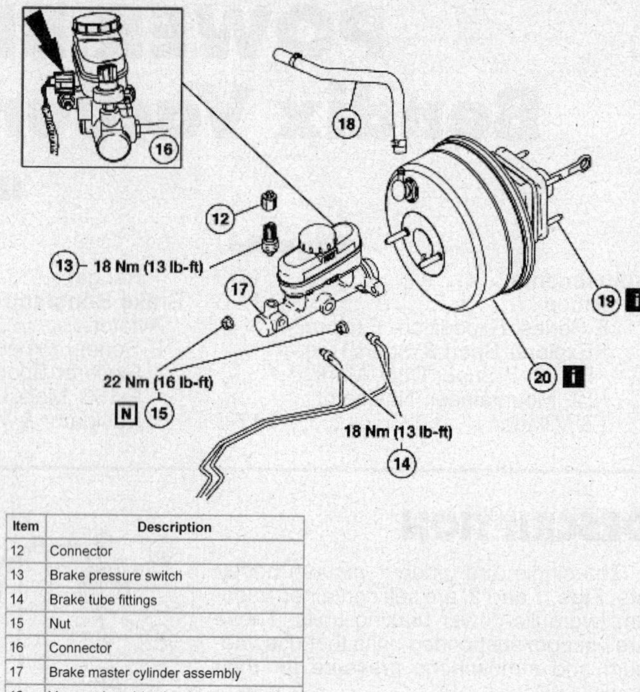

Item	Description
12	Connector
13	Brake pressure switch
14	Brake tube fittings
15	Nut
16	Connector
17	Brake master cylinder assembly
18	Vacuum hose/check valve assembly
19	Brake booster nuts
20	Brake booster assembly

LTV1900000000913

Fig. 3 Brake booster replacement (Part 2 of 2). Aviator

10. Reverse procedure to install, noting the following:
    a. **Torque** new master cylinder mounting nuts to 13 ft. lbs.
    b. **Torque** booster mounting nuts to 17 ft. lbs.

E-Series, Expedition, Explorer, Explorer Sport & Sport/Trac, F-150, Mark LT, Mountaineer, Navigator & Villager

1. Remove brake master cylinder as outlined under "Hydraulic Brake Systems."
2. Disconnect vacuum hose from power brake booster.
3. Remove brake pedal spring clip, clevis pin and stop lamp switch self-locking pin.
4. Slide stop lamp switch, booster pushrod and bushing off brake pedal pin.
5. **On models equipped with firewall sound insulator,** remove sound insulator.
6. **On all models,** remove booster mounting nuts, then the booster.
7. **On Villager models,** before installing booster, adjust pushrod to approximately 4¾ inches, **Fig. 5.**
8. **On Expedition, F-150, Mark LT and Navigator models,** adjust brake booster to master cylinder pushrod length to .980–.995 inch, **Fig. 6.**
9. **On Explorer, Explorer Sport and Sport/Trac and Mountaineer models,** adjust brake booster to master cylinder pushrod length to .990–1.000 inch.
10. **On E-Series models,** pushrod length is not adjustable.
11. **On all models,** reverse procedure to install, noting the following:
    a. Vacuum hose must be pushed onto booster fitting at least one inch.
    b. **On E-Series, torque** booster mounting nuts to 19–26 ft. lbs.
    c. **On Explorer, Expedition, F-150, Mark LT, Mountaineer and Navigator models, torque** booster mounting nuts to 16–21 ft. lbs.
    d. **On Explorer Sport and Sport/Trac models, torque** booster mounting nuts to 15–20 ft. lbs.
    e. **On Villager models, torque** booster mounting nuts to 11 ft. lbs.

Freestar, Monterey & Windstar

1. Remove air cleaner assembly.
2. Remove brake master cylinder as outlined under "Hydraulic Brake Systems."
3. Disconnect brake booster check valve vacuum hose, **Fig. 7.**
4. Disconnect speed control and accelerator cables.
5. Remove wiring harness retaining bracket.
6. Remove cable bracket bolts, then position bracket aside.
7. Remove speed control module bolts, then position module aside.
8. Remove instrument closeout panel bolts, then the panel.
9. Remove stop lamp switch self-locking pin.
10. Slide stoplight switch, booster pushrod and bushing off brake pedal pin.
11. Remove brake booster mounting nuts, then the booster.
12. Reverse procedure to install, noting the following:
    a. **Torque** booster mounting nuts to 18 ft. lbs.
    b. **Torque** cable bracket bolts to 89 inch lbs.
    c. **Torque** speed control module bolts to 108 inch lbs.

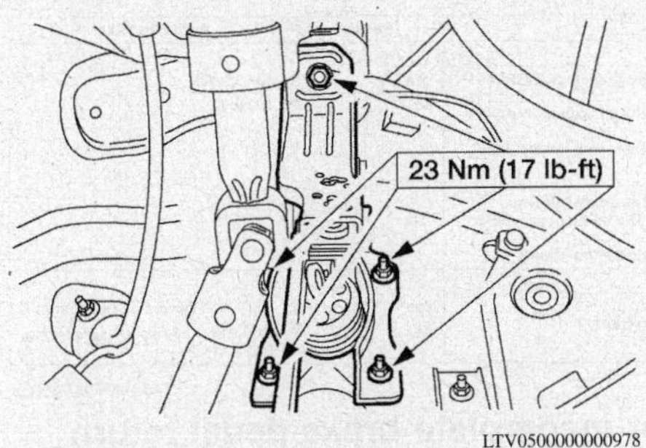

Fig. 4 Brake booster bolt locations. Escape & Mariner

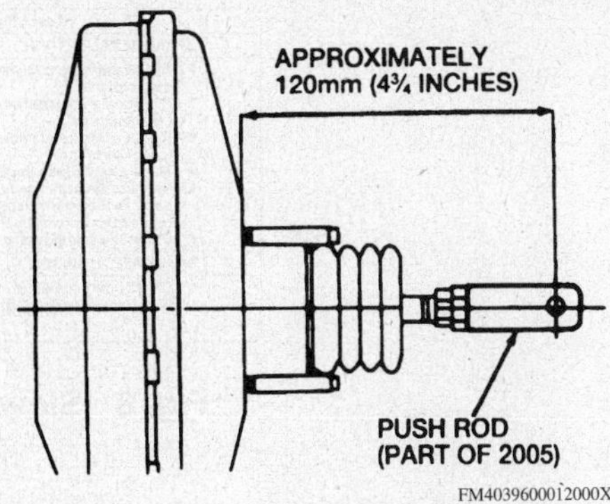

Fig. 5 Pushrod adjustment. Villager

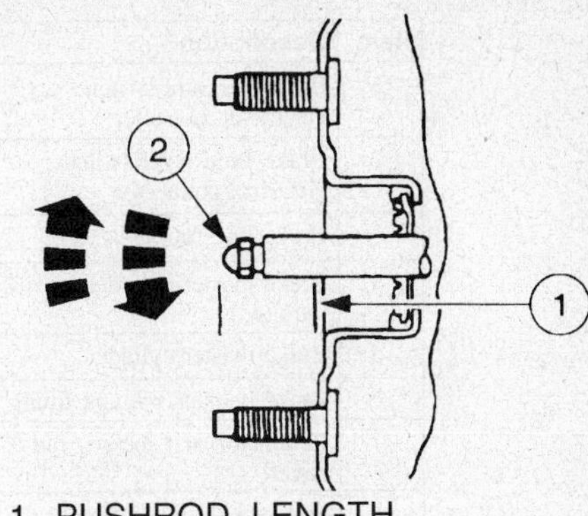

1. PUSHROD LENGTH MEASUREMENT
2. ADJUSTER NUT

FM4039700026000X

Fig. 6 Pushrod adjustment. Expedition, F-150, Mark LT & Navigator

Ranger

1. Remove brake master cylinder as outlined under "Hydraulic Brake Systems."
2. Disconnect power brake booster hose.
3. Remove self-locking brake pedal to booster pushrod pin.
4. Remove stop lamp switch, booster pushrod and bushing from brake pedal pin.
5. Remove the firewall sound insulator.
6. Support booster as required.
7. Remove booster mounting nuts, then the booster.
8. Reverse procedure to install, noting the following:
   a. Before installing booster, adjust booster to master cylinder pushrod length to .980–.995 inch, **Fig. 6.**
   b. **Torque** booster mounting nuts to 15–20 ft. lbs.

DIAGNOSIS & TESTING

Refer to **Figs. 8 and 9** for pinpoint tests on power brake booster.

ADJUSTMENTS

Pushrod

E-SERIES, EXPEDITION, EXPLORER, EXPLORER SPORT & SPORT/TRAC, F-150, F-SUPER DUTY, MARK LT, MOUNTAINEER, NAVIGATOR, & VILLAGER

Refer to "Brake Booster, Replace" for pushrod adjustment.

RANGER

To measure pushrod adjustment, use a suitable gauge and position it against the master cylinder mounting surface as illustrated in **Fig. 10.** Adjust pushrod screw by turning it until the end just touches inner edge of gauge slot.

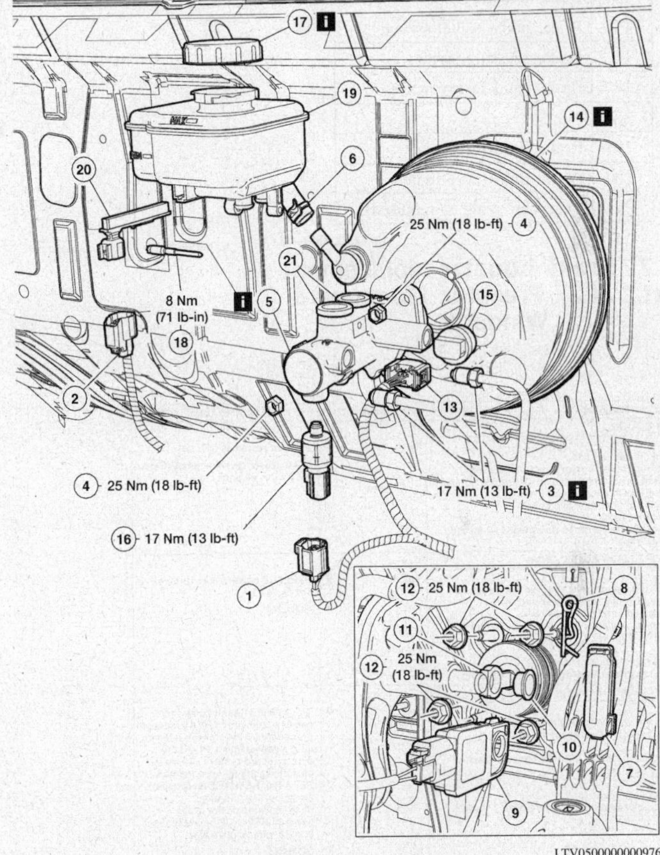

Fig. 7 Brake booster replacement (Part 1 of 2). Freestar, Monterey & Windstar

POWER BRAKE UNIT SERVICE

The Bendix vacuum brake booster unit is serviced as a complete unit. No disassembly procedures are provided.

Item	Description
1	Brake pressure switch electrical connector
2	Brake fluid level switch electrical connector
3	Brake line fittings
4	Brake master cylinder nuts (2 required)
5	Brake master cylinder
6	Brake booster vacuum fitting
7	Redundant self locking pin cover
8	Self locking clip
9	Brake pedal position switch
10	Bushing
11	Brake booster rod
12	Brake booster nuts
13	Brake pedal travel switch electrical connector
14	Brake booster
15	Brake pedal travel switch
16	Brake pressure switch
17	Brake fluid reservoir cap
18	Pin
19	Brake fluid reservoir
20	Brake fluid level switch
21	Reservoir seals (2 required)

LTV0500000000977

Fig. 7 Brake booster replacement (Part 2 of 2). Freestar, Monterey & Windstar

	Test Step	Result	▶	Action to Take
N2	SYSTEM INSPECTION			
	• Key off. • Reconnect the vacuum line. • Inspect power brake booster check valve, rubber grommet and all vacuum plumbing for cracks, holes, bad connections or missing clamps. • Push down on brake pedal and hold. • Key on, engine running. • **Does the brake pedal move downward when the engine is started?**	Yes No	▶ ▶	Vacuum system is OK. GO to **N3** for diesel engines. GO to **N4** for gas engines.
N3	VACUUM DROP CHECK, DIESEL ONLY			
	• Key off. • Disconnect the vacuum line and connect a vacuum gauge with a T-fitting to the lower part of dash-mounted plastic check valve. • Key on, engine running at idle until vacuum reaches 57-70 kPa (17-21 in-Hg). • Key off. • Observe vacuum gauge for 1 minute. • **Does vacuum pressure drop more than 1 in-Hg?**	Yes No	▶ ▶	REPLACE power brake booster check valve. GO to **N4**.
N4	COMPONENT ISOLATION CHECK			
	• Key off. • Reconnect the vacuum gauge to the same point as in Step N1, but leave the rest of the system connected. • Key on, engine running at idle until vacuum reaches 57-70 kPa (17-21 in-Hg). • Key off. • Observe vacuum gauge for 1 minute. • **Does vacuum pressure drop more than 1 in-Hg?**	Yes No	▶ ▶	DISCONNECT each component one at a time and REPEAT the test procedures in **N4** until the leaking component is found. PLUG the disconnected vacuum line while performing the test procedures. REPAIR or REPLACE as required. On diesel engines with dash-mounted power brake booster, REPLACE power brake booster check valve also. GO to **N5**.
N5	BOOSTER LEAK CHECK			
	• Key on. • Run engine until vacuum pressure reaches 57-70 kPa (17-21 in-Hg). • Key off. • Push down on the brake pedal and hold for a few seconds and release. • **Does the vacuum drop to 0 kPa (0 in-Hg)?**	Yes No	▶ ▶	REPLACE power brake booster. System checks OK. REMOVE vacuum gauge and RECONNECT all vacuum lines.

FM4039900020020X

Fig. 9 Excessive pedal effort (Part 2 of 2)

	Test Step	Result	▶	Action to Take
L1	BRAKE PEDAL RETURN			
	• Run engine at fast idle while making several brake applications. • Pull brake pedal rearward with approximately 44.5N (10 lbs.) force. • Release the brake pedal and measure the distance to the toe board. • Make a hard brake application. • Release the brake pedal and measure the brake pedal to toe board distance. The brake pedal should return to its original position. • **Did brake pedal return to original position?**	Yes No	▶ ▶	Vehicle OK. GO to **L2**.
L2	BRAKE PEDAL BINDING			
	• Check brake pedal for sticking or binding. • **Is the brake pedal operating freely?**	Yes No	▶ ▶	REPLACE power brake booster. CORRECT any sticking or binding. REPEAT **L2**.

FM4039900023000X

Fig. 8 Slow or incomplete brake pedal return

	Test Step	Result	▶	Action to Take
N1	VACUUM CHECK			
	• Disconnect vacuum booster hose from booster. • Connect Rotunda Vacuum/Pressure Tester 164-R0253 or Rotunda Vacuum Tester 014-R1054 or equivalent to the vacuum hose with a T-fitting. • Key on, engine running. Allow engine to reach normal operating temperature. • Record the vacuum pressure. • **Is the vacuum reading 57-70 kPa (17-21 in-Hg)?**	Yes No	▶ ▶	GO to **N2**. TUNE UP or REPAIR engine as required.

FM4039900020010X

Fig. 9 Excessive pedal effort (Part 1 of 2)

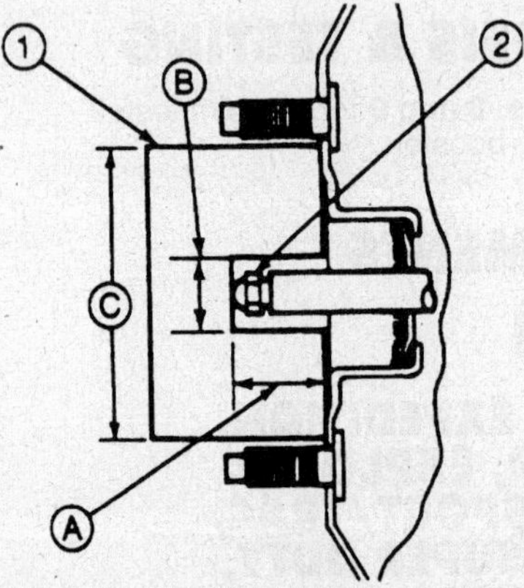

Item	Description
1	Gauge Block
2	Adjustment Screw
A	24.89-25.27mm (0.980-0.995 In.)
B	19.05mm (3/4 In.)
C	74.61mm (2-15/16 In.)

FM4099500011000X

Fig. 10 Pushrod adjustment. Ranger

VACUUM PUMPS

INDEX

PRECAUTIONS

Air Bag Systems

Refer to "Air Bag System Precautions" in the front of this manual for system disarming and arming procedures.

Battery Ground Cable

Prior to service, disconnect battery ground cable and isolate as required.

DESCRIPTION

On models equipped with diesel engines, vacuum available to operate the vacuum booster brake is insufficient, therefore vacuum is supplied from a vacuum pump located on the left side of the engine. This pump is driven by a single belt off the alternator.

VACUUM PUMP

REPLACE

Excursion & F-Super Duty

1. Disconnect electrical connector, **Fig. 1,** from vacuum pump.
2. Remove vacuum pump bracket mounting bolts, **Fig. 2.**
3. Disconnect vacuum hose, **Fig. 3,** and remove pump and bracket.
4. Remove three ISO mounts, then remove pump from bracket.
5. Reverse procedure to install, **torque** mounting bolts to 80–106 inch lbs.

E-Series

1. Remove vacuum pump drive belt.
2. Disconnect vacuum hose from vacuum pump.
3. Remove mounting bolts, then the vacuum pump.
4. Reverse procedure to install, **torque** vacuum pump mounting bolts to 18–23 ft. lbs.

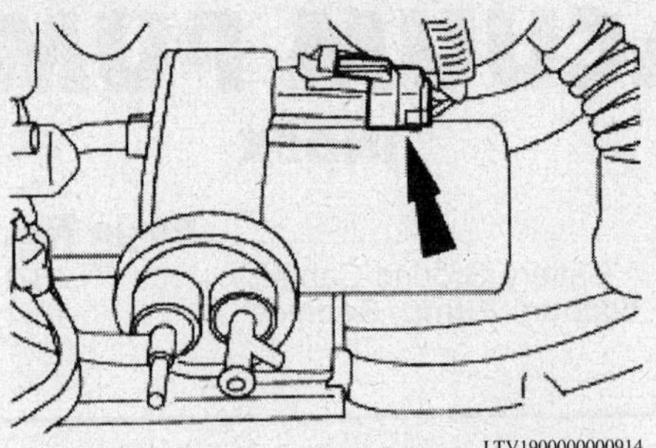

Fig. 1 Vacuum pump electrical connector. Excursion & F-Super Duty

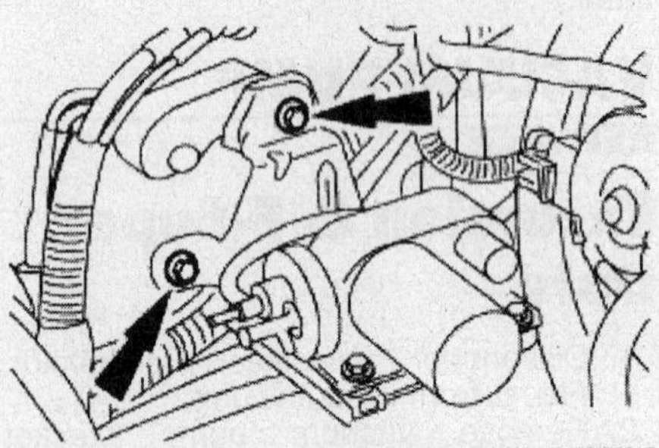

Fig. 2 Vacuum pump mounting bracket bolts. Excursion & F-Super Duty

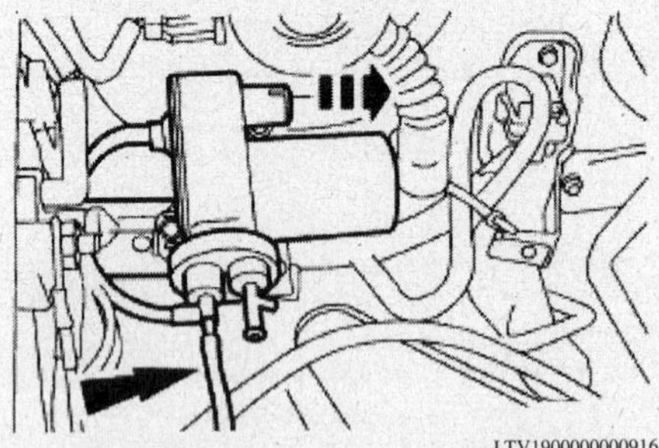

Fig. 3 Vacuum pump hose removal. Excursion & F-Super Duty

TRANSFER CASES

NOTE: See Individual Truck Chapters For Transfer Case Adjustment & Removal Procedures.

TABLE OF CONTENTS

Application Chart

Model	Transfer Case
2002–03	
Aviator	Torque On Demand Transfer Case
Escape	Escape Electronic Shift Transfer Case
Excursion	NP271
Expedition	Borg Warner 4406
Explorer	Borg Warner 4411
Explorer Sport/Sport Trac	Borg Warner 1354
F-Super Duty	NP271
F-150	Borg Warner 4406
Mountaineer	Borg Warner 4411
Navigator	Borg Warner 4406
Ranger	Borg Warner 1354
2004–06	
Aviator	Torque On Demand Transfer Case
Excursion	NP271
Escape	Escape Electronic Shift Transfer Case
Expedition	Borg Warner 4406
Explorer	Borg Warner 4411
Explorer Sport Trac	Borg Warner 1354
F-Super Duty	NP271
F-150	Borg Warner 4406
Mark LT	Borg Warner 4406
Mountaineer	Borg Warner 4411
Navigator	Borg Warner 4406
Ranger	Borg Warner 1354

Borg Warner 4406

NOTE: On Air Bag Equipped Models, Refer To "Air Bag System Precautions" Located In The Front Of This Manual For System Disarming & Arming Procedures.

NOTE: "Electrical Symbol & Wire Color Code Identification" Located In The Front Of This Manual May Be Used As An Aid When Using Wiring Circuits Found In This Section.

NOTE: Refer To "Computer Relearn Procedures" Located In The Front Of This Manual When Battery Power To The Computer Has Been Interrupted.

INDEX

PRECAUTIONS

Air Bag Systems

Refer to "Air Bag System Precautions" in the front of this manual for system disarming and arming procedures.

Battery Ground Cable

Prior to service, disconnect battery ground cable and isolate as required.

MAINTENANCE

Fluid Check

1. Raise and support vehicle.
2. Locate and remove drain fill plug on transfer case.
3. Fill transfer case with Mercon multipurpose XT-2-QDX ATF, or equivalent to specifications.

Fluid Change

1. Raise and support vehicle.
2. Locate and remove drain plug on transfer case and drain fluid into a suitable container.
3. Install drain plug and tighten to specifications.
4. Locate and remove fill plug on transfer case.
5. Fill transfer case with Mercon multipurpose XT-2-QDX ATF, or equivalent to specifications.

DESCRIPTION

The Borg Warner 4406 manual and electronic shift on the fly transfer cases are a three-piece magnesium design. Under normal conditions the unit is in 2H, but when desired, operator may shift into 4H or 4L. The operator may shift from 2H to 4H or from 4H to 2H at any speed up to 55 mph. Vehicle speed must be less than 5 mph, brake applied and transmission in neutral to shift into 4L.

The transfer case is equipped with an electromagnetic clutch which is located inside the case. This clutch is used to spin up the front driveline when shifting from 2WD to 4x4 mode at speed.

The mechanical shift on the fly (MSOF) transfer case is manual shift 4WD system that allows operator to choose between two different 4x4 modes as well as 2WD. When the manual shift lever is moved, this activates the 4WD indicator switch, 4WD electric clutch relay and electromagnetic clutch. When front and rear output shafts are synchronized, the spring loaded lock-up collar mechanically engages mainshaft hub to drive sprocket. Finally, the front axle collar is engaged and the electromagnetic clutch is deactivated.

The electronic shift on the fly (ESOF) transfer case is an electronic shift 4x4 system that allows the operator to choose between two different 4x4 modes as well as 2WD. When the control switch on the instrument panel is turned, the GEM recognizes that a shift has been requested and activates electromagnetic and the relays which power transfer case shift motor. When motor reaches desired position, as determined by the contact plate position inputs to GEM, power to shift relays and motors will be removed. When front and rear output shafts are synchronized, the spring loaded lock-up collar mechanically engages mainshaft hub to drive sprocket. Finally, the front axle collar is engaged and the electromagnetic clutch is deactivated.

The automatic 4WD (A4WD) transfer case uses an electronic shift 4x4 system that allows the operator to choose between three different 4x4 modes.

DIAGNOSIS & TESTING

For transfer case diagnosis and testing procedures refer to **MOTOR's "Domestic Transmission, In-Vehicle Service"** or **"Transmission Service DVD."**

DISASSEMBLE

On the manual shift transfer case place selector in neutral position for disassembly.

1. **On models equipped with manual shift,** remove 4WD indicator switch.
2. **On all models,** secure transfer case using holding fixture tool No. T57L-500-B, or equivalent.
3. Remove coil wire from electric shift motor electrical connector, then the vehicle speed sensor.
4. **On models equipped with electrical shift,** remove shift motor retaining bolts, then the motor.
5. **On all models,** remove six extension housing retaining bolts, then the housing.
6. Remove speedometer gear spacer, then push speedometer drive gear toward transfer case.
7. Remove steel ball, then the speedometer drive gear.
8. Remove rear output shaft snap ring. Lift up on shaft while removing snap ring.
9. Remove transfer case retaining bolts. Bolts are self tapping and it is normal to find metal shavings while removing cover.
10. Remove transfer case cover. Use pry bosses to separate cover from case.
11. Remove three coil to cover retaining nuts, then the cover.
12. Remove front output shaft bearing using slide hammer tool No. D80L-100-D and Bearing Cup Remover tool No. T77F-1102-A, or equivalents.
13. Remove rear output shaft bearing

using slide hammer tool No. D80L-100-D and bearing cup remover tool No. T77F-1102-A, or equivalents.
14. Remove shift collar hub snap ring from rear output shaft, then the shift collar hub.
15. Remove coil housing.
16. Remove lockup hub, then the shift fork and spring.
17. Remove spacer, then the drive chain and sprocket assembly.
18. Remove magnet from its slot in case, then the oil pump and output shaft as an assembly.
19. Remove shift fork shaft, then the shift fork and reduction shaft.
20. **On models equipped with electrical shift,** remove electrical shift cam assembly. **Do not disassemble shift cam assembly.**
21. **On all models,** remove input seal using seal remover tool No. T92C-6700-CH, or equivalent.
22. Remove front planet carrier snap ring, then the planet carrier.
23. Remove ring gear snap ring, then the ring gear.
24. Remove front output shaft snap ring, then the output shaft.
25. Remove front yoke to flange seal using bearing cup remover tool No. T77F-1102-A and slide hammer tool No. D80L-100-D, or equivalents.
26. Remove front planet carrier bearing snap ring, then the bearing using bearing cup replacer tool No. T73T-1202-A and slide hammer tool No. D80L-100-D, or equivalents.
27. Remove front output shaft bearing using slide hammer tool No. D80L-100-D and bearing cup remover tool No. T77F-1102-A, or equivalents.
28. **On models equipped with manual shift,** proceed as follows:
    a. Access shift lever set screw through 4WD indicator switch hole.
    b. Remove shift lever (from outside of case), shift cam and spring.
    c. Remove shift lever seal using collet tool No. D80L-100-S and slide hammer from blind hole puller set tool No. D80L-100-A, or equivalents.
29. **On models equipped with electrical shift,** remove electrical shift motor seal using collet tool No. D80L-100-S and slide hammer from blind hole puller set tool No. D80L-100-A, or equivalents.

ASSEMBLE

1. **On models equipped with electrical shift,** install electric shift motor seal using seal replacer tool No. T96T-7127-B, or equivalent.
2. **On models equipped with manual shift,** proceed as follows:
    a. Install shift lever seal using seal replacer tool No. T96T-7127-B, or equivalent.
    b. Install shift lever (from outside case), shift cam and spring.
    c. Access shift lever set screw through 4WD indicator hole. Tighten screw to specifications.
3. **On all models,** install front output shaft bearing using drive handle tool No. T80T-4000-W and bearing replacer tool No. T77J-7025-K, or equivalents.
4. Install front carrier bearing using dust shield replacer tool No. T88C-5493-CH and driver handle tool No. T80T-4000-W, or equivalents.
5. Install front planet carrier bearing snap ring. then the front yoke to flange seal using seal replacer tool No. T96T-7127-A, or equivalent.
6. Install front output shaft, then the snap ring.
7. Install ring gear, then the snap ring.
8. Install front planet carrier, then the snap ring.
9. Install input seal using seal replacer tool No. T96T-7127-A and seal protector tool No. T96T-7127-C, or equivalents.
10. **On models equipped with electrical shift,** install electric shift cam assembly.
11. **On all models,** install shift fork and reduction hub, then the shift fork shaft.
12. Install oil pump onto output shaft, then install assembly into case.
13. Install magnet into its slot in case.
14. Install drive chain and sprocket assembly, then the spacer.
15. Install lockup hub and shift fork and spring.
16. Install coil housing, then the shift collar hub. Install shift collar hub snap ring onto rear output shaft.
17. Install rear output shaft bearing using center bearing replacer tool No. T77J-7025-K and drive handle tool No. T80T-4000-W, or equivalents.
18. Install coil. Tighten coil retaining nuts to specifications.
19. Coat mating surfaces of case and cover with a small bead of black non-acid cure silicone rubber E7TZ-19562, or equivalent, meeting Ford specification ESL-M4G273-A.
20. Position two transfer case halve and tighten bolts in sequence. Tighten bolts to specifications.
21. Install rear output shaft snap ring. Lift up on output shaft while installing snap ring.
22. Slide speedometer gear onto output shaft until it touches case, then position steel ball.
23. Lift up on speedometer gear, then install gear spacer.
24. Apply a small bead of black non-acid cure silicone rubber E7TZ-19562, or equivalent, meeting Ford specification ESL-M4G273-A, to case cover and extension housing mating surfaces.
25. Position brown clutch coil wire through its hole in extension housing, then install housing retaining bolts. Tighten bolts to specifications.
26. Install vehicle speed sensor and tighten retaining bolt to specifications.
27. **On models equipped with electrical shift,** install transfer case shift motor. Tighten bolts to specifications.
28. **On all models,** install coil wire into shift motor electrical connector.
29. **On models equipped with manual shift,** install 4WD indicator switch.

TIGHTENING SPECIFICATIONS

Year	Component	Torque Ft. Lbs.
2002–06	Coil Nuts	89①
	Drain Plug	11
	Fill Plug	11
	Front Driveshaft Shield Nuts	13
	Output Speed Sensor Bolt	44①
	Shift Motor Bolts	89①
	Transfer Case Bolts	18
	Transfer Case Extension Housing Bolts	18
	Transmission To Transfer Case Bolts	35

① — Inch lbs.

Borg Warner 4411

NOTE: On Air Bag Equipped Models, Refer To "Air Bag System Precautions" Located In The Front Of This Manual For System Disarming & Arming Procedures.

NOTE: "Electrical Symbol & Wire Color Code Identification" Located In The Front Of This Manual May Be Used As An Aid When Using Wiring Circuits Found In This Section.

NOTE: Refer To "Computer Relearn Procedures" Located In The Front Of This Manual When Battery Power To The Computer Has Been Interrupted.

INDEX

PRECAUTIONS

Air Bag Systems

Refer to "Air Bag System Precautions" in the front of this manual for system disarming and arming procedures.

Battery Ground Cable

Prior to service, disconnect battery ground cable and isolate as required.

MAINTENANCE

Fluid Check

1. Raise and support vehicle.
2. Remove transfer case fill plug, **Fig. 1.**
3. Inspect oil level to ensure level is just below fill plug.
4. Add Mercon fluid as required.
5. Replace transfer case fill plug and **torque** to 11 ft. lbs.

Fluid Change

1. Raise and support vehicle.
2. Remove transfer case drain plug, **Fig. 1,** and drain transfer case fluid into suitable container.
3. Replace transfer case drain plug and **torque** to 11 ft. lbs.
4. Remove transfer case fill plug.
5. Add Mercon fluid to just below fill plug opening.
6. Replace fill plug and **torque** to 11 ft. lbs.

DIAGNOSIS & TESTING

For transfer case diagnosis and testing procedures refer to **MOTOR's "Domestic Transmission, In-Vehicle Service" or "Transmission Service DVD."**

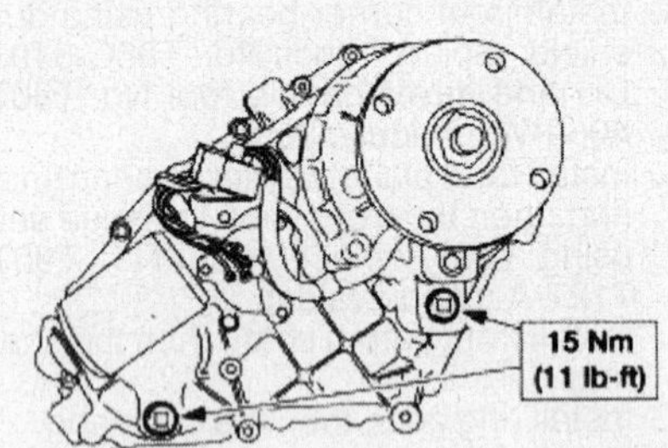

Fig. 1 Transfer case fill and drain plug

DISASSEMBLE

Refer to **Fig. 2** when disassembling transfer case.

1. Remove mounting bolts and case vibration dampner.
2. Remove mounting bolt and heat shield.
3. Mount transaxle on suitable work bench using holding fixture tool No. T57L-500-B, or equivalent.
4. Mark rear output flange and shaft for assembly alignment.
5. Remove rear output shaft mounting nut using drive pinion flange holding fixture tool No. T78P-4851-A, or equivalent.
6. Remove rear output flange and shaft yoke washer.
7. Remove oil seal using bushing remover tool No. 1175-AC, or equivalent, and suitable slide hammer.
8. Disconnect connect interlock and remove coil wire pin.
9. Remove mounting bolts, then the front and rear output shaft speed sensors.
10. Remove four mounting bolts and shift motor.
11. Inspect tone wheel teeth.
12. Remove 17 case mounting bolts.
13. Remove clutch coil mounting nuts.
14. Separate transfer case halves using case pry bosses.
15. Remove front output shaft rear and rear output shaft support bearings using suitable slide hammer.
16. Remove thrust bearing.
17. Remove cam and coil housing.
18. Remove steel balls and apply cam.
19. Remove wave spring and snap ring.
20. Remove clutch pack, noting the following:
    a. **Do not separate clutch pack.** Keep tension of pack while removing.
    b. Set pack on bench in same position as installed in case.
21. Remove tone wheel.
22. Remove drive chain and sprockets as an assembly.
23. Remove and clean oil pan magnet.
24. Remove thrust washer.
25. Remove oil pump and rear output shaft as an assembly. **Do not disassembly pump.**
26. Remove electric shift cam. **Do not disassembly electric shift cam.**
27. Remove reduction shift fork and high-low collar as an assembly.
28. Remove shift rail.
29. Remove oil seal using oil seal remover tool No. T92C-6700-CH, or equivalent.
30. Expand snap ring and remove front planetary gear set.
31. Remove snap ring and ring gear.
32. Remove output shaft bushing and bearing using suitable drift and hammer.
33. Remove snap ring and planetary gear carrier support bearing using bearing puller tool No. D84L-1123-A, or equivalent, and suitable press.
34. Remove dampner snubber.
35. Hold front output shaft and flange, then remove snap ring and assembly.

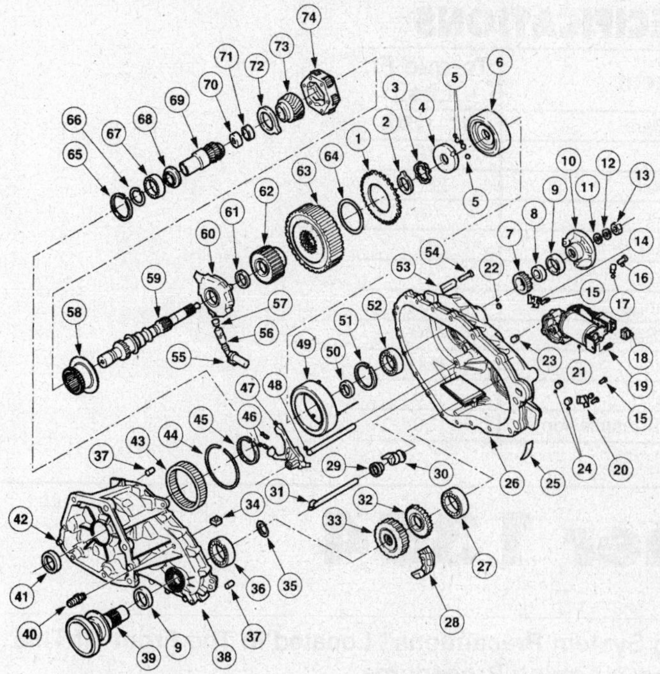

Item	Description
1	Armature
2	Snap ring
3	Wave spring
4	Apply cam
5	Ball

Item	Description
6	Cam and coil housing assembly
7	Tone wheel (upper)
8	Spacer
9	Oil seal

FM3040200425010X

Fig. 2 Exploded view of transfer case (Part 1 of 2)

Item	Description
10	Rear output flange
11	Oil seal
12	Output shaft yoke washer
13	Shaft nut
14	Speed sensor (rear output shaft)
15	Bolt
16	Bolt (3 req'd)
17	J-clip
18	Connector interlock (part of 7G360)
19	Bolt (hex-head)
20	Speed sensor (front output shaft)
21	Transfer case shift motor
22	Hex nut (3 req'd)
23	Shifter shaft seal
24	Drain/fill plug
25	Identification decal (part of 7005)
26	Cover (with dampener snubber) (serviced separately)
27	Bearing (front output shaft rear)
28	Drive chain
29	Torsion spring
30	Electric shift cam assembly
31	Shift shaft
32	Tone wheel (lower)
33	Driven sprocket (30T)
34	Oil pan magnet
35	Snap ring
36	Bearing
37	Dowel pins (2 req'd) (part of 7003)
38	Case assembly
39	Output shaft and flange (front)
40	Breather barb
41	Input seal

Item	Description
42	Spiral pin (part of 7005)
43	Ring gear
44	Snap ring
45	Snap ring
46	Shift fork facing (2 req'd)
47	Reduction shift fork
48	Shift rail
49	Clutch coil assembly
50	Thrust bearing
51	Snap ring
52	Bearing (rear output shaft support)
53	Identification tag (part of 7A195)
54	Bolt— hex-head (M10 x 1.5 x 30.0) (17 req'd)
55	Oil strainer
56	Pump hose
57	Hose clamp
58	High-low collar
59	Rear output shaft
60	Pump assembly
61	Thrust washer
62	Drive sprocket (30T)
63	Clutch pack assembly
64	Insulator washer
65	Snap ring
66	Snap ring
67	Bearing (planetary gear carrier support)
68	Carrier thrust washer
69	Input shaft
70	Bearing
71	Output shaft bushing (part of 7017)
72	Thrust plate
73	Sun gear
74	Front planetary gear set assembly

FM3040200425020X

Fig. 2 Exploded view of transfer case (Part 2 of 2)

36. Remove oil seal using bearing cap remover tool No. T77F-1102-A, or equivalent.
37. Remove front output shaft support bearing using stator bearing remover tool No. T94P-7701-KH, or equivalent, and suitable slide hammer.
38. Remove shifter shaft seal.

ASSEMBLE

Refer to **Fig. 2** when assembling transfer case.

1. Install shift shaft seal using valve steam oil seal installer tool No. T90P-6510-AH, or equivalent.
2. Press front output shaft support bearing into case using differential bearing cup installer tool No. T88C-7700-FH, and adapter handle tool No. T80T-4000-W, or equivalents.
3. Install oil seals using input shaft oil seal installer tool No. T90T-7127-H, or equivalent.
4. Install front output shaft, flange and snap ring.
5. Install ring gear and snap ring.
6. Install dampner snubber.
7. Install bushing and bearing using input shaft bearing installer tool No. T83T-7025-C, or equivalent, and suitable press. **Do not crush bearing cage.**
8. Install planetary gear carrier support bearing using suitable press.
9. Install snap ring.
10. Expand snap ring, then install front planetary gear set and snap ring.
11. Install shift rail.
12. Install reduction shift fork and high-low collar as an assembly.
13. Install electric shift cam.
14. Install pump and rear output shaft as an assembly.
15. Install thrust washer.
16. Install oil pan magnet into case slot.
17. Install drive chain and sprockets as an assembly.
18. Install tone wheel.
19. Install clutch pack, noting the following:
    a. **Do not separate clutch pack.** Keep tension on pack.
    b. Ensure thrust washer tabs hold lower clutch pack in place.
20. Install new snap ring.
21. Install wave spring.
22. Install apply cam and steel balls.
23. Install cam and coil housing.
24. Install thrust bearing.
25. Press front output shaft rear and rear output shaft support bearings into case using wheel hub bearing cup installer tool No. T73T-1202-A and handle adapter tool No. T80T-4000-W, or equivalents.
26. Install clutch coil and mounting nuts.
27. Ensure transfer case mating surfaces are clean, then apply ⅛ inch bead of suitable sealant to mating surfaces.
28. Position transfer case halves together and tighten mounting bolts in star pattern.
29. Install tone wheel.
30. Install oil seal using input shaft oil seal installer tool No. T90T-7127-B, or equivalent.
31. Align index marks, then install output flange, oil seal, washer and nut.
32. Tighten nut using drive pinion flange holding fixture tool No. T78T-4851-A, or equivalent.
33. Install front and rear out shaft speed sensors. Ensure sensors seat flat against boss.
34. Apply ⅛ inch bead of suitable sealant to mating surfaces and install transfer case shift motor.
35. Install coil wire pin and connector interlock.
36. Install heat shield and mounting bolts.
37. Install dampner and mounting bolts.

TIGHTENING SPECIFICATIONS

Year	Component	Torque Ft. Lbs.
2002–03	Breather Barb	71–123①
	Case	18
	Clutch Coil	88①
	Dampner	16
	Drain Plug	11
	Fill Plug	11
	Output Flange	262
	Shaft Speed Sensor	44①
	Shift Motor	89①
	Skid Plate	18
	Transfer Case To Transmission	30

① — Inch lbs.

Borg Warner 1354

NOTE: On Air Bag Equipped Models, Refer To "Air Bag System Precautions" Located In The Front Of This Manual For System Disarming & Arming Procedures.

NOTE: "Electrical Symbol & Wire Color Code Identification" Located In The Front Of This Manual May Be Used As An Aid When Using Wiring Circuits Found In This Section.

NOTE: Refer To "Computer Relearn Procedures" Located In The Front Of This Manual When Battery Power To The Computer Has Been Interrupted.

INDEX

PRECAUTIONS

Air Bag Systems

Refer to "Air Bag System Precautions" in the front of this manual for system disarming and arming procedures.

Battery Ground Cable

Prior to service, disconnect battery ground cable and isolate as required.

MAINTENANCE

Fluid Check

1. Raise and support vehicle.
2. Locate and remove drain fill plug on transfer case.
3. Fill transfer case with Mercon multi-purpose XT-2-QDX ATF, or equivalent, to specifications.

Fluid Change

1. Raise and support vehicle.
2. Locate and remove drain plug on transfer case and drain fluid into a suitable container.
3. Install drain plug and tighten to specifications.
4. Locate and remove fill plug on transfer case.
5. Fill transfer case with Mercon multi-purpose XT-2-QDX ATF, or equivalent to specifications.

DESCRIPTION

The four wheel drive system is an electronic shift 4x4 system that allows the operator to choose between three modes. The operator can switch 4x4 HIGH modes at any speed. To engage or disengage 4x4 LOW the vehicle speed must be less than 3 mph, the brake depressed and transmission must be in Neutral.

The shift motor sense plate, a part of electronic shift motor, informs the generic electronic module (GEM) of transfer case shift motor and contact plates A, B, C and D position. The electronic shift motor is externally mounted at rear of transfer case and drives a rotary cam which moves the mode fork and range fork within the transfer case between the 4x4 HIGH, 4x4 LOW and 2WD range positions.

DIAGNOSIS & TESTING

For transfer case diagnosis and testing procedures refer to **MOTOR's "Domestic Transmission, In-Vehicle Service" or "Transmission Service DVD."**

DISASSEMBLE

Refer to **Fig. 1** when disassembling transfer case.

1. Remove and discard rear output shaft

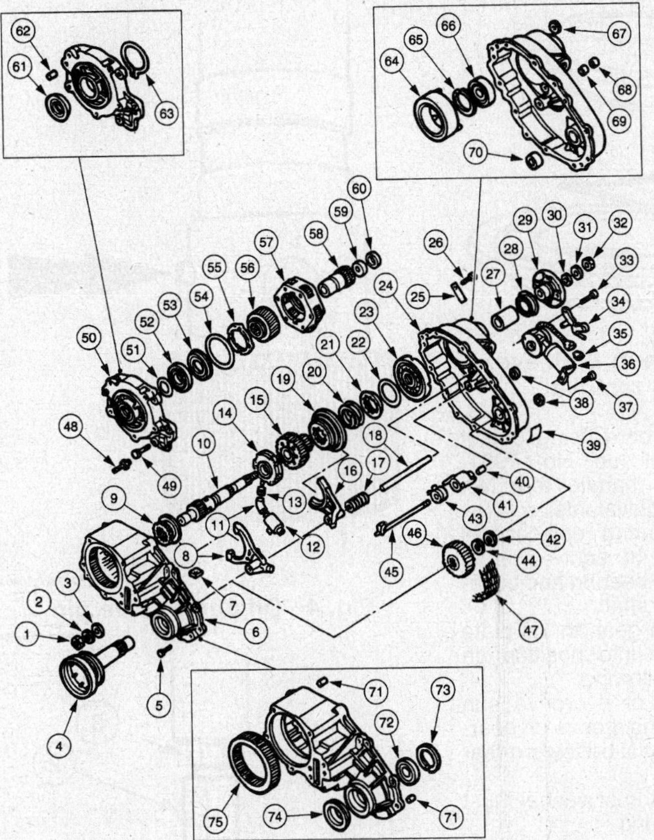

FM3049800228010X

Fig. 1 Exploded view of electronic shift transfer case (Part 1 of 2)

Item	Description
1	Shaft Nut
2	Output Shaft Yoke Washer
3	Oil Seal
4	Cupped CV Flange
5	Bolt
6	Case
7	Oil Pan Magnet
8	Shift Fork
9	First Gear
10	Rear Output Shaft
11	Hose Coupling
12	Oil Strainer
13	Hose Clamp
14	Pump Assy
15	Drive Sprocket
16	Lockup Fork
17	Lockup Return Spring
18	Shift Rail
19	Lockup Collar
20	Sleeve Return Spring
21	Output Shaft Hub
22	Snap Ring
23	Clutch Housing
24	Case
25	Identification Tag (Part of 7005)
26	Bolt
27	Sleeve (Part of 7061)
28	Yoke to Flange Seal
29	Rear Output Flange
30	Oil Seal
31	Output Shaft Yoke Washer
32	Shaft Nut
33	Bolt (Hex-Head)
34	Bracket
35	Wire Connector Spacer (Part of 7G360)
36	Transfer Case Shift Motor
37	Bolt (Hex-Head)
38	Pipe Plug

Item	Description
39	Broadcast Code Decal (Part of 7005)
40	Spacer
41	Electric Shift Cam
42	Snap Ring
43	Spring (Torsion)
44	Thrust Washer
45	Shift Shaft
46	Driver Sprocket
47	Drive Chain
48	Breather Barb
49	Bolt
50	Main Drive Gear Bearing Retainer
51	Snap Ring
52	Bearing
53	Output Shaft Thrust Washer
54	Snap Ring
55	Thrust Plate
56	Overdrive Sun Gear
57	Front Planet
58	Input Shaft
59	Bearing
60	Output Shaft Bearing
61	Yoke to Flange Seal
62	Spiral Pin (Part of 7050)
63	Snap Ring
64	Coil Assy (Clutch)
65	Snap Ring
66	Bearing
67	Nut (Hex)
68	Shifter Shaft Seal
69	Bearing (Sleeve) (Self-Lubricating)
70	Gear Bearing
71	Dowel Pin (Part of 7005)
72	Bearing
73	Snap Ring
74	Yoke to Flange Seal
75	Ring Gear

FM3049800228020X

Fig. 1 Exploded view of electronic shift transfer case (Part 2 of 2)

nut. Output shaft nut has a self locking feature and must be replaced once removed.

2. Remove output shaft yoke washer and rear output flange. Use slide hammer tool No. D80L-100-D and seal remover tool No. T92C-6700-CH, or equivalents, to remove yoke to flange seal.
3. Remove spacer, then shift motor as follows:
   a. Disconnect harness connector.
   b. Remove two harness to transfer case shift motor retaining bolts, then remove brown wire from harness to shift motor.
   c. Remove rear mounting bolt. Note position of triangular shaft extending out of rear of case.
   d. Remove remaining front bolt and transfer case shift motor.
4. Remove front and rear, front case to rear case retaining bolts. Ensure front case is facing downward and rear is facing upward.
5. Insert a breaker bar between pry bosses and separate front and rear case.
6. Remove all traces of RTV sealant from both cases, then remove output shaft bearing snap ring.
7. From outside of case, drive out rear output shaft bearing using driver handle tool No. T80T-4000-W and bearing puller tool No. T77F-1102-A, or equivalents.
8. Remove front output shaft needle bearing using slide hammer and puller collet tool No. D80L-100-T, or equivalent.
9. Remove nyloc nuts retaining clutch coil assembly to rear case, then pull assembly along with O-rings and brown wire from case.
10. Remove lockup return spring from boss on fork, then remove clutch housing from output shaft.
11. Remove 2W-4W lockup and 2W-4W shift fork assembly, **Fig. 2,** then pull out shift shaft rail.
12. Remove internal snap ring, then pull lockup hub and sleeve return spring from collar, **Fig. 3.**
13. Remove helical cam from front case.
14. Remove external snap ring and thrust washer that retains driven sprocket to front output shaft.
15. Remove chain, driven sprocket and drive sprocket as an assembly, then remove oil pan magnet from slot in front of case bottom.
16. Remove output shaft and oil pump as an assembly.
17. Do not pound or use force to remove pump. Rotate pump to align cover keyway to pin of output shaft and pull pump straight out.
18. Measure and record oil pump drive pin height above diameter of output shaft, **Fig. 4,** then remove pin from shaft.
19. Remove snap ring retaining front output shaft, then output shaft.
20. Remove high-low range shift fork and collar as an assembly.
21. Turn front case over, then remove six bolts retaining main drive gear bearing retainer to front case.
22. Remove main drive gear bearing retainer, input shaft and front planet as an assembly.
23. Expand tangs of large snap ring and remove main drive gear assembly from bearing, **Fig. 5.**
24. Use slide hammer and seal remover tool No. T96T-7127-A, or equivalent, to remove input yoke to flange seal from main drive gear bearing retainer.
25. Remove ring gear from front case half using a press.
26. Remove internal snap ring retaining front output shaft ball bearing, then remove bearing.
27. Remove front yoke to flange seal using slide hammer.

SUBASSEMBLY SERVICE

Main Drive Gear

1. Remove snap ring retaining input shaft bearing from input shaft.
2. Invert main drive gear assembly and pull input shaft out of bearing and planetary.
3. Remove internal snap ring, thrust washer, thrust plate and sun gear from main gear assembly.
4. Reverse procedures to assemble.

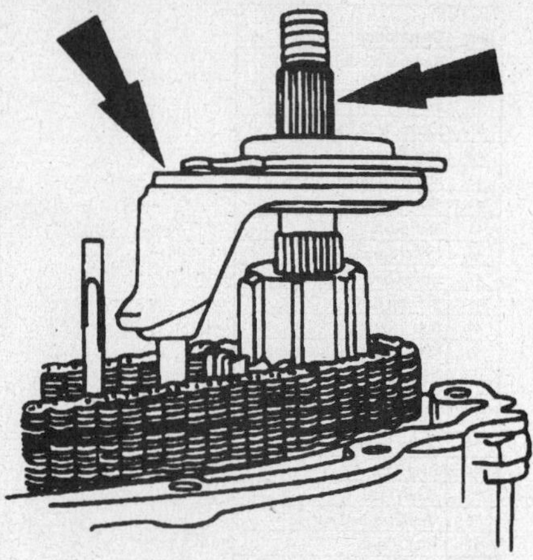

Fig. 2 2W-4W lock-up & shift fork removal

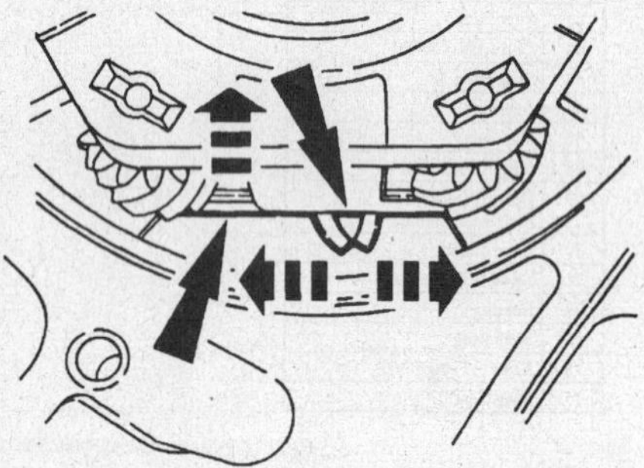

Fig. 5 Main drive assembly removal

Input Shaft

Bushing and needle bearing in input shaft must be replaced as a set.

1. Position input shaft on Axle Bearing/ Seal Plate and use Pinion Bearing Cone Replacer as a spacer, **Fig. 6.**
2. Insert input shaft bearing remover tool No. T83T-7025-C, or equivalent, into input shaft.
3. Tighten actuator pin until it stops, then press bearing and bushing out together using a suitable press.
4. Reverse procedures to assemble.

ASSEMBLE

Prior to assembly, lubricate all components with Mercon multi-purpose automatic transmission fluid WSP-M2C185-A, or equivalent.

1. Drive bearing into front output case bore using output shaft seal replacer tool No. T96T-7127-B and drive handle tool No. T80T-4000-W, or equivalents, then install retaining internal snap ring.
2. Install front yoke flange seal using output shaft seal replacer tool No. T96T-7127-B and drive handle tool No. T80T-4000-W, or equivalents.
3. Align serrations on outside of ring gear to serrations previously cut in front case bore. Using a press, install ring gear.
4. Install input yoke to flange seal into

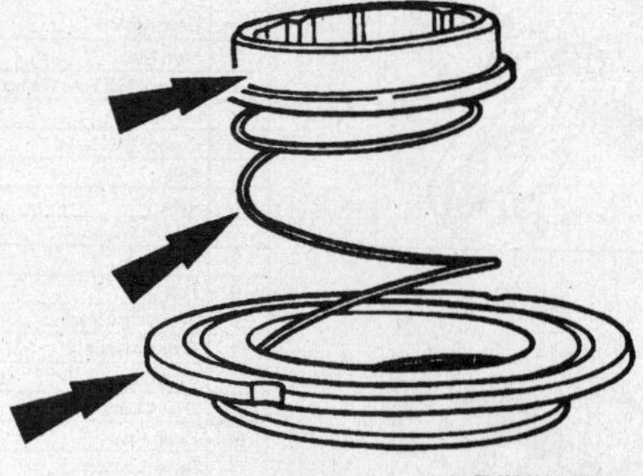

Fig. 3 Lock-up hub & sleeve return spring removal

mounting adapter bore using output shaft seal replacer tool No. T96T-7127-B and drive handle tool No. T80T-4000-W, or equivalents.

5. Use Input shaft bearing replacer tool No. T83T-7025-C, or equivalent, to press a new needle bearing and bushing into end of input shaft.
6. Slide overdrive sun gear, thrust plate and thrust washer into position on input shaft noting following:
   a. Recessed face of overdrive sun gear and snap ring groove on bearing outer race must be toward rear of transfer case.
   b. Stepped face of thrust washer must face toward bearing.
7. Press bearing over input shaft, then install external snap ring to input shaft.
8. Install internal snap ring to planetary carrier.
9. Place tanged snap ring in mounting adapter groove, **Fig. 7.**
10. Place input shaft and front planet in main drive gear bearing retainer.
11. Expand tanged snap ring while pushing inward until front planet and input shaft are seated in main drive gear bearing retainer. Inspect installation by holding main drive gear bearing retainer by hand and carefully tapping face of input shaft against a wooden block to ensure snap ring is engaged.
12. install a bead of RTV gasket sealant on surface of front case. Use non-acid cure silicone rubber E7TZ-19562-A, or equivalent, meeting Ford specification ESL-M4G273-A.
13. Position main drive gear bearing retainer on front case. Tighten bolts to specifications.
14. Mount transfer case front on holding fixture tool No. T57L-500-B, or equivalent.
15. Ensure nylon wear pads are installed on shift fork and snapped securely into place, **Fig. 8.**
16. Install high-low collar as an assembly into front planet.
17. Press pin into rear output shaft pinhole to previously measured height. If a measurement was not taken during disassembly, install pin to height of .40 inch.
18. Install oil pump onto rear of output shaft noting following:
   a. Do not remove plastic insert from bore of new pump. Discard it after it

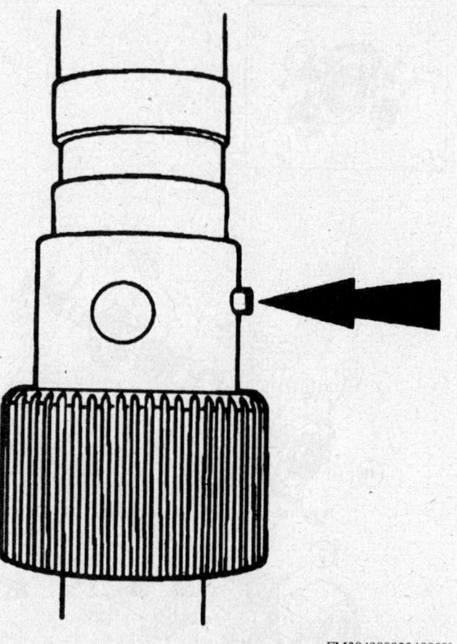

Fig. 4 Oil pump drive pin

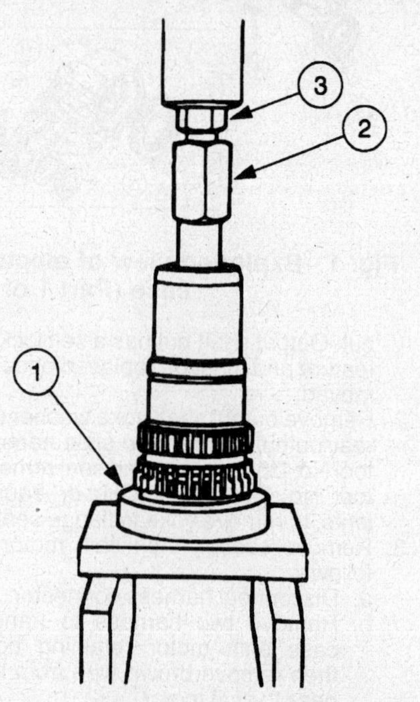

Fig. 6 Input shaft bushing & bearing removal

slides out during pump installation.
   b. If a new pump is used, slide pump housing slot onto pin of output shaft with retaining arm of cover toward rear of case.
   c. While turning output shaft, prime pump through oil filter pickup tube or housing inlet hole with clean ATF.
19. If oil pump does not turn freely, realign cover keyway to pin of rear output shaft and jiggle pump until it fully seats and rotates freely.
20. Install output shaft and oil pump in input shaft, then install oil pan magnet in slot in front case just above oil filter leg.
21. Install front output shaft in front case,

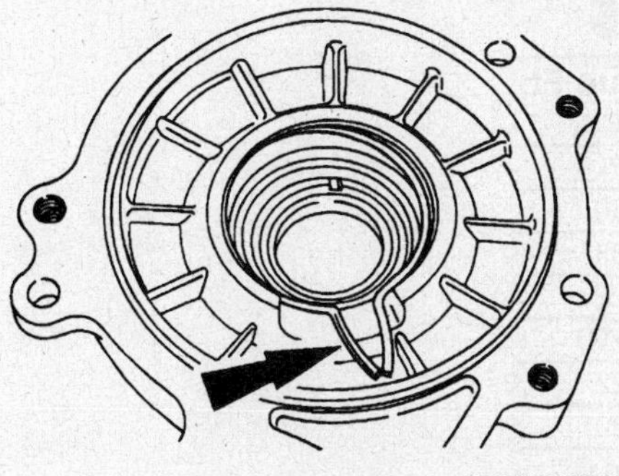

Fig. 7 Mounting adapter snap ring installation

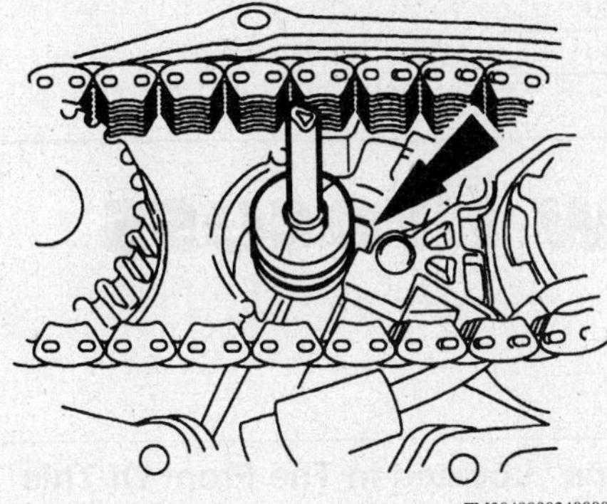

Fig. 10 Torsion spring position

then install retaining snap ring.

22. Assemble 2W-4W lockup assembly as follows:
    a. Install sleeve return spring into bore of lockup collar with large end installed first.
    b. Place lockup hub over spring and install lockup hub into lockup collar.
23. Press down and install internal snap ring on lockup assembly.
24. Install chain, drive sprocket and driven sprocket as an assembly over output shaft. Driven sprocket must be installed with marking REAR facing toward rear case.
25. Install thrust washer and external snap ring over thrust washer to retain driven sprocket.
26. Install helical cam and slide drive tang between torsion spring tangs as far as it will go, **Fig. 9.**
27. Install pin on tang end of helical cam into hole in front case.
28. Position torsion spring tangs so that they are pointing toward top side of transfer case and just touching high-low shift fork, **Fig. 10.**
29. Install shift rail through high-low shift fork and ensure rail is seated in front case bore.
30. Install 2W-4W shift fork to 2W-4W lockup, then install lockup and shift fork over input shaft and onto shift rail.
31. Triangular shaft will be in two wheel high position at final assembly. After 2W-4W shift fork is released, ensure

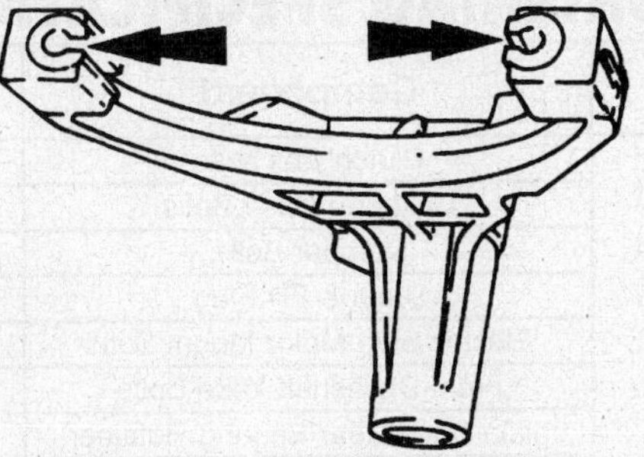

Fig. 8 Nylon wear pads installation

2W-4W fork roller bushing is resting on top surface of helical cam and not into an inside track.

32. Lift 2W-4W shift fork slightly while holding shift rail down, then rotate helical cam track into high-low fork roller bushing by turning cam, **Fig. 11.**
33. Install clutch housing on output shaft with cavity side or notches facing rear case.
34. Drive output shaft needle bearing onto rear cover bore with front shaft needle bearing replacer tool No. T83T-7025-C and drive handle tool No. T80T-4000-W, or equivalents.
35. Install rear output bearing in rear case bore using Output Shaft Bearing Replacer and Drive Handle, then install internal snap ring that retains bearing to rear case.
36. Apply a small bead of non-acid cure silicone rubber E7TZ-19562-A, or equivalent, meeting Ford specification ESL-M4G273-A to base of clutch coil studs and grommet. Clutch must be installed within 15 minutes of application of silicone or sealant. If possible, allow one hour before filling case to allow silicone to cure.
37. Install clutch coil from inside rear case. Tighten bolts to specifications.
38. Install lockup return spring to shift rail and shift fork with spring mounted in a vertical position.
39. Install rear output yoke to flange seal using drive handle and seal install tool No. T96T-7127-A, or equivalent.
40. Coat mating surface of front case with a bead of non-acid cure silicone rubber E7TZ-19562-A, or equivalent, meeting Ford specification ESL-M4G273-A. Clutch must be installed within 15 minutes of application of silicone or sealant. If possible, allow one hour before filling case to allow silicone to cure.
41. Assemble cases as follows:
    a. Align output shaft with rear case output shaft bore.
    b. Align helical cam with rear case motor bore.
    c. Align rear case so that spring boss engages lockup return spring and shift rail.
42. Install front and rear bolts retaining

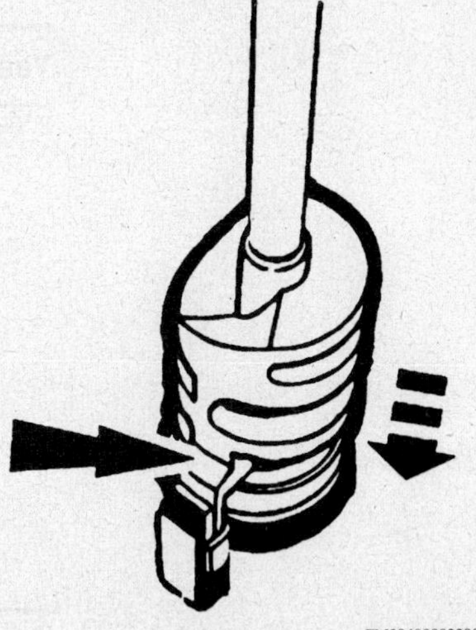

Fig. 9 Helical cam installation

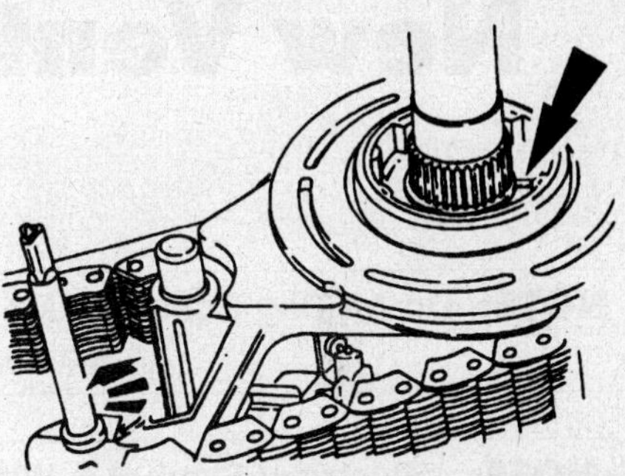

Fig. 11 Helical cam track positioning

case halves and tighten to specifications.

43. If shaft will not stay in 4H position, rotate shaft counterclockwise to 2H position. During motor installation, rotate transfer case shift motor counterclockwise until transfer case shift motor is aligned with mounting hole.
44. Install transfer case shift motor as follows:
    a. Apply a small bead of non-acid cure silicone rubber E7TZ-19562-A, or equivalent, meeting Ford specification ESL-M4G273-A to motor housing base.
    b. Install shift motor onto case, then attach front and rear mounting bolts. Tighten bolts to specifications.
    c. Instal brown wire from harness to shift motor.
    d. Install two bolts retaining harness to shift motor.
    e. Connect harness connector.
45. Install spacer into rear case bore, then the rear output flange, washer and nut. Tighten nut to specifications.
46. Refer to "Lubricant Data Charts" for fluid type and quantity. Install fill plug.

TIGHTENING SPECIFICATIONS

Year	Component	Torque Ft. Lbs.
2002–03	Clutch Coil Nuts	97①
	Cover To Case Bolts	30
	Damper Bolts	35
	Drain & Fill Plug	22
	Electric Shift Motor Mount Bolts	97①
	Front Driveshaft Yoke Bolts	22
	Main Drive Gear Bearing Retainer	30
	Motor Bracket Bolt	97①
	Motor Bracket Nuts	35①
	Rear Driveshaft Flange Bolts	76
	Rear Output Driveshaft Nut	275
	Skid Plate To Frame Bolt	20
	Transfer Case To Transmission	46

① — Inch lbs.

New Venture Gear/New Process 271

NOTE: On Air Bag Equipped Models, Refer To "Air Bag System Precautions" Located In The Front Of This Manual For System Disarming & Arming Procedures.

NOTE: "Electrical Symbol & Wire Color Code Identification" Located In The Front Of This Manual May Be Used As An Aid When Using Wiring Circuits Found In This Section.

NOTE: Refer To "Computer Relearn Procedures" Located In The Front Of This Manual When Battery Power To The Computer Has Been Interrupted.

INDEX

PRECAUTIONS

Air Bag Systems

Refer to "Air Bag System Precautions" in the front of this manual for system disarming and arming procedures.

Battery Ground Cable

Prior to service, disconnect battery ground cable and isolate as required.

MAINTENANCE

Fluid Check

1. Raise and support vehicle.
2. Locate and remove drain fill plug on transfer case.
3. Fill transfer case with Mercon multi-purpose XT-2-QDX ATF, or equivalent to specifications.

Fluid Change

1. Raise and support vehicle.
2. Locate and remove drain plug on transfer case and drain fluid into a suitable container.
3. Install drain plug and tighten to specifications.
4. Locate and remove fill plug on transfer case.
5. Fill transfer case with Mercon multi-purpose XT-2-QDX ATF, or equivalent to specifications.

DESCRIPTION

The New Venture Gear transfer cases are either manual or electric shift. These transfer cases are specifically designed to withstand high engine torque loads under all modes of operation. When in the 4x4 mode of operation, torque is transferred from the main input shaft through a high load capacity chain link belt to the transfer case front output shaft. The front output driveshaft then transfers this torque to the front differential.

DIAGNOSIS & TESTING

For transfer case diagnosis and testing procedures refer to **MOTOR's "Domestic Transmission, In-Vehicle Service" or "Transmission Service DVD."**

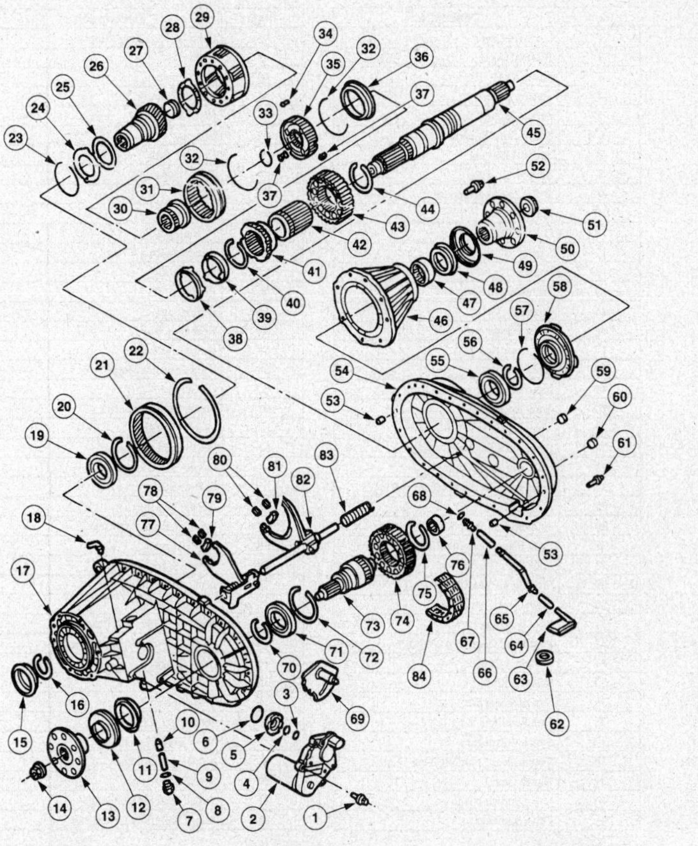

FM3049900296010X

Fig. 1 Cross-sectional view of transfer case (Part 1 of 2). Electronic shift

Item	Description
1	Bolt
2	Gearmotor Encoder Assy
3	Plastic Retainer
4	O-Ring Motor Seal
5	Motor Adapter
6	O-Ring Support Seal
7	Poppet Screw
8	O-Ring Seal
9	Spring
10	Poppet
11	Front Output Seal
12	Slinger
13	Front Flange
14	Hex Lock Nut
15	Input Seal
16	Input Bearing Retaining Ring
17	Front Half Case
18	Vent
19	Ball Bearing, Front Input
20	Front Input Bearing Retaining Ring
21	Annulus Gear
22	Annulus Retaining Ring
23	Lock Plate Retaining Ring
24	Lock Plate
25	Front Input Gear Thrust Washer
26	Input Gear
27	Pilot Bearing
28	Rear Input Gear Thrust Washer
29	Planetary Carrier Assy
30	Range Shift Sleeve
31	Synchronizer Sleeve
32	Synchronizer Spring
33	Hub Retaining Ring
34	Synchronizer Strut
35	Synchronizer Hub
36	Outer Ring
37	Synchronizer Strut
38	Middle Ring
39	Inner Ring
40	Clutch Gear Retaining Ring
41	Clutch Gear
42	Drive Sprocket Hub

Item	Description
43	Drive Sprocket
44	Sprocket Retaining Ring
45	Mainshaft
46	Rear Retainer
47	Needle Bearing
48	Rear Output Seal
49	Slinger
50	Rear Flange
51	Nut
52	Retainer Bolt
53	Bushing Dowel
54	Rear Half Case
55	Ball Bearing
56	Retaining Ring
57	Retaining Ring
58	Oil Pump Assy
59	Fill Plug
60	Drain Plug
61	Rear Case Bolt
62	Chip Collector Magnet
63	Oil Screen
64	Lower Tube Connector
65	Lower Oil Tube
66	Upper Tube Connector
67	Upper Oil Tube
68	O-Ring Seal
69	Sector Assy
70	Front Oil Pump Retaining Ring
71	Front Oil Pump Ball Bearing
72	Retaining Ring
73	Front Output Shaft
74	Driven Sprocket
75	Sprocket Retaining Ring
76	Needle Bearing
77	Range Fork Assy
78	Range Shift Fork End Pad
79	Range Shift Fork Center Pad
80	Mode Fork End Pad
81	Mode Fork Center Pad
82	Mode Fork Assy
83	Mode Spring
84	Drive Chain

FM3049900296020X

Fig. 1 Cross-sectional view of transfer case (Part 2 of 2). Electronic shift

DISASSEMBLE

Refer to **Figs. 1 and 2** during disassembly of transfer case.

All nuts, bolts and retaining rings are to be discarded and replaced with new components.

1. **On models equipped with electric shift,** remove gearmotor encoder assembly.
2. **On models equipped with manual shift,** remove three-position switch.
3. **On all models,** remove drain and fill plugs. **Do not use air tools to remove plugs.**
4. Remove companion flange nut using companion flange holding tool No. T78P-4851-A, or equivalent, to prevent flange from turning.
5. Remove companion flange using flange remover tool No. 205-076, or equivalent.
6. Remove slinger from front flange and rear flange if replacement is required.
7. Remove rear output seal using converter seal remover tool No. T94P-77001-BH, or equivalent.
8. Remove rear retainer mounting bolts.
9. Remove rear retainer using transfer case housing spreader tool No. 308-396, or equivalent.
10. Remove needle bearing using front pump bushing remover tool No. 307-016 and driver handle tool No. T80T-4000-W, or equivalents, with suitable press.
11. Disconnect oil tube and remove oil pump assembly.
12. Remove retaining ring by install rear output shaft snap ring protector sleeve tool No. 308-404, or equivalent, and lifting shaft up.
13. Remove and case bolts.
14. Separate case halves using transfer case housing spreader tool No. 308-396, or equivalent.
15. Remove oil tube.
16. Remove ball bearing retaining ring.
17. Remove ball bearing using rear output bearing remover tool No. 205-138, or equivalent, driver handle and a suitable press.
18. Remove needle bearing using blind hole puller set tool No. D80L-100-A, or equivalent, and slide hammer.
19. Remove chip collector magnet.
20. Remove driven and drive sprockets' retaining rings.
21. Remove mode spring, then the sprockets and chain as an assembly.
22. Remove mainshaft and mode fork as an assembly.
23. Slide mode fork and synchronizer sleeve off of mainshaft and separate components.
24. Place mainshaft in suitable soft jawed vise with threaded end up.
25. Remove clutch gear, then the retaining ring and synchronizer hub.
26. **On models equipped with electric shift,** remove outer, middle and inner rings.
27. **On all models,** remove drive sprocket hub.
28. Inspect all of components for wear and damage, then the mode fork pads for wear.
29. Rotate sector assembly to 4-wheel high position for easy removal.
30. Remove range fork assembly and range shift sleeve, then inspect range fork pads.
31. Remove input seal using converter seal remover tool No. T94P-77001-BH, or equivalent.
32. Remove retaining ring using input gear snap ring protector sleeve tool No. 308-406, or equivalent.
33. Remove planetary assembly.
34. Remove input bearing retaining ring.
35. Remove front input bearing using pinion bearing cup installer tool No. 205-140, or equivalent and suitable press.
36. Remove front output seal using converter seal remover tool No. T94P-77001-BH, or equivalent.
37. Remove retaining ring using front output shaft snap ring protector sleeve tool No. 308-405, or equivalent.
38. Remove sleeve and front output shaft.
39. Remove front output ball bearing retaining ring.
40. Remove front output ball bearing using rear axle seal installer tool No. 205-155, or equivalent driver handle and suitable press.
41. Remove lock plate retaining ring and lift out input gear.

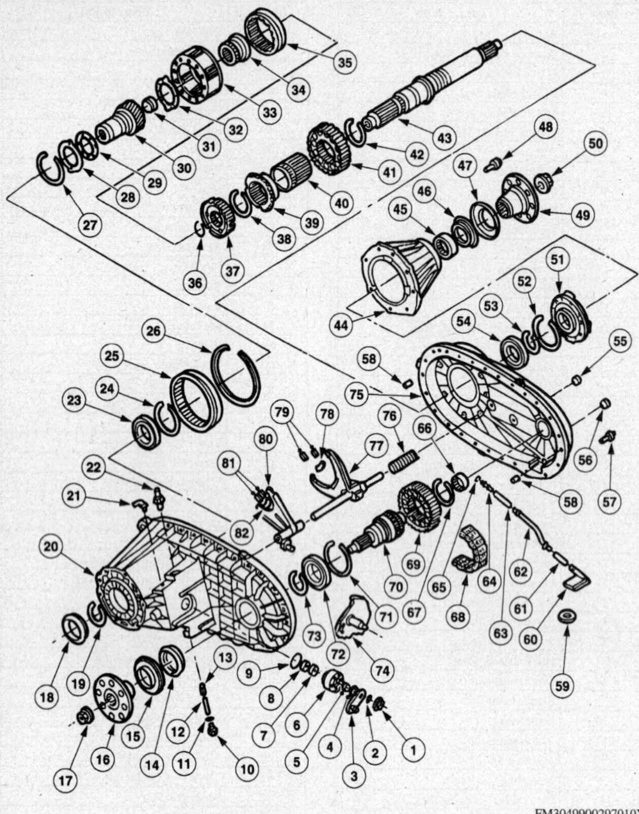

Fig. 2 Cross-sectional view of transfer case (Part 1 of 2). Manual shift

Item	Description
1	Locknut, Lever
2	Washer, Lever
3	Lever ASM
4	Spacer, Lever
5	Sector Support Seal
6	Sector Shaft Support
7	Support Bearing
8	Support Bearing
9	O-Ring Sector Support
10	Poppet Screw
11	O-Ring Seal
12	Spring
13	Poppet
14	Front Output Seal
15	Slinger
16	Front Flange
17	Hex Lock Nut
18	Input Seal
19	Input Bearing Retaining Ring
20	Front Half Case
21	Vent
22	Precision 3 Position Switch
23	Ball Bearing, Front Input
24	Front Input Bearing Retaining Ring
25	Annular Gear
26	Annulus Retaining Ring
27	Lock Plate Retaining Ring
28	Lock Plate
29	Front Input Gear Thrust Washer
30	Input Gear
31	Pilot Bearing
32	Rear Input Gear Thrust Washer
33	Planetary Carrier Assy
34	Range Shift Sleeve
35	Synchronizer Sleeve
36	Hub Retaining Ring
37	Synchronizer Hub
38	Clutch Gear Retaining Ring
39	Clutch Gear
40	Drive Sprocket Hub
41	Drive Sprocket

Item	Description
42	Sprocket Retaining Ring
43	Mainshaft
44	Rear Retainer
45	Needle Bearing
46	Rear Output Seal
47	Slinger
48	Retainer Bolt
49	Rear Flange
50	Nut
51	Oil Pump Assy
52	Retaining Ring
53	Retaining Ring
54	Ball Bearing
55	Fill Plug
56	Drain Plug
57	Rear Case Bolt
58	Dowel Bushing
59	Chip Collector Magnet
60	Oil Screen
61	Lower Tube Connector
62	Lower Oil Tube
63	Upper Tube Connector
64	Upper Oil Tube
65	O-Ring Seal
66	Needle Bearing
67	Sprocket Retaining Ring
68	Drive Chain
69	Driven Sprocket
70	Front Output Shaft
71	Retaining Ring
72	Front Oil Pump Ball Bearing
73	Front Oil Pump Retaining Ring
74	Sector Assy
75	Rear Case Half
76	Mode Spring
77	Mode Fork Assy
78	Mode Fork Center Pad
79	Mode Fork End Pad
80	Range Fork Assy
81	Range Shift Fork End Pad
82	Range Shift Fork Center Pad

FM3049900297020X

Fig. 2 Cross-sectional view of transfer case (Part 2 of 2). Manual shift

42. Remove lock plate, then the front and rear input gear thrust washers.
43. Inspect gear teeth and thrust washers for wear and damage.
44. Replace planetary gear assembly, if required.
45. Remove poppet assembly, then disassemble poppet screw, spring and poppet.
46. **On models equipped with manual shift,** remove locknut, washer, lever, spacer and sector assembly.
47. **On models equipped with electric shift,** remove plastic retainer and O-ring, then the sector assembly.
48. **On all models,** remove sector shaft support (motor adapter for electric shift transfer case) using sector shaft nut socket tool No. 308-407, or equivalent.
49. Remove support O-ring seal.

ASSEMBLE

1. Install new support O-ring seal.
2. Install sector shaft support (motor adapter for electric shift transfer case) using sector shaft nut socket tool No. 308-407, or equivalent. Before installing, coat threads with pipe sealant with Teflon No. D8AZ-19554-A, or equivalent.
3. Install sector assembly.
4. **On models equipped with electric shift,** install plastic retainer and O-ring.
5. **On models equipped with manual shift,** install spacer, lever, washer and locknut.
6. **On all models,** assemble poppet screw, spring and poppet, then install assembly. **If poppet spring is being replaced, like color spring must be used.**
7. Install rear and front input gear thrust washers.
8. Install lock plate with stamped letter E facing outward.
9. Place input gear into planetary carrier assembly, then install new lock plate retaining ring.
10. Install new front input bearing using bearing installer tool No. 308-412 and driver handle tool No. T80T-4000-W, or equivalents, and suitable press, then the new bearing retainer ring.
11. Position planetary assembly into front case and install new retaining ring using input gear snap ring protector sleeve tool No. 308-406, or equivalent.
12. Install new input seal using input shaft seal installer tool No. 308-408, or equivalent, and driver handle.
13. Install new front output ball bearing using suitable bearing installer, driver handle and press.
14. Install new front output ball bearing retaining ring.
15. Position front output shaft in front case and install new retaining ring using front output shaft snap ring protector sleeve tool No. 308-405, or equivalent.
16. Install new front output seal using output shaft seal installer tool No. 308-403, or equivalent, and drive handle.
17. Install new slinger on front flange using output flange slinger installer tool No. 308-399 and pilot tool No. 308-400, or equivalents.
18. Install front flange and new mounting nut while using companion flange holding tool No. T78P-4851-A, or equivalent, to prevent flange from turning.
19. Rotate sector assembly to 4-wheel high position for easy installation.
20. Position range fork assembly and range shift sleeve in front case, then the drive sprocket hub onto mainshaft.
21. **On models equipped with electric shift,** position inner ring onto drive sprocket, middle ring onto inner ring and outer ring onto middle ring.
22. **On all models,** position and rotate synchronizer hub until it drops into installed position. Install new retaining ring.
23. Assemble mode fork, shift rail and synchronizer sleeve. Thin side of synchronizer sleeve must face up.
24. Install mode fork and shift rail assembly into front case. Ensure to bottom shift rail in case.
25. Install mainshaft. **Install mainshaft assembly so synchronizer strut bears against one of synchronizer sleeve teeth.**
26. Install clutch gear.
27. Install drive sprocket, driven sprocket and drive chain as an assembly.
28. Install mode spring.

29. Install new drive and driven sprockets' retaining rings.
30. Install new ball bearing using suitable bearing installer, driver handle and press, then the new ball bearing retaining ring.
31. Install new needle bearing using front output shaft rear bearing installer tool No. 308-401, or equivalent, driver handle and suitable press. **Identification numbers must face driver while installing.**
32. Install chip collector magnet and oil tube.
33. Clean both case mating surfaces with metal surface cleaner No. F4A3-19A536-RA, or equivalent.
34. Apply .08 inch diameter bead of silicone rubber No. F4AZ-19562-B, or equivalent, to joint face of case. Bead must be on inside of bolt holes, toward inside of case.
35. Position rear case half onto front case half and use crisscross pattern when tightening case bolts to specifications. **Do not install two new dowel bolts until next step.**
36. Install new dowel bolts at each end of case.
37. Install new retaining ring using rear output shaft snap ring protector sleeve tool No. 308-404, or equivalent.

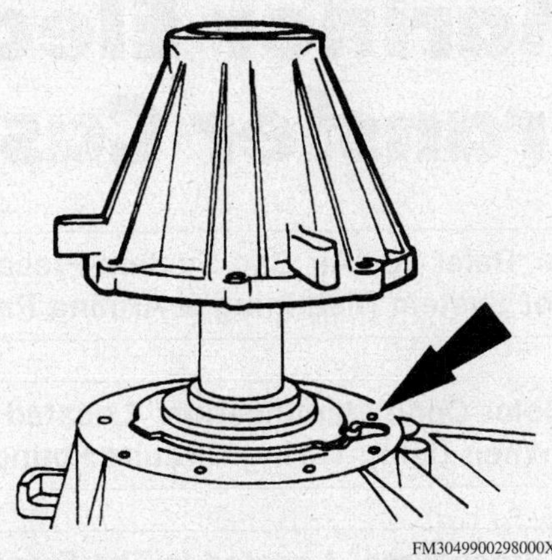

Fig. 3 Rear retainer replacement

38. Ensure O-ring is in oil pump pickup inlet.
39. Slide oil pump assembly onto mainshaft and connect oil tube.
40. Install new needle bearing using extension housing needle bearing installer tool No. 308-402, or equivalent, driver handle and suitable press. Identification numbers must face driver while installing.
41. Clean case and rear retainer mating surfaces with metal surface cleaner No. F4A3-19A536-RA, or equivalent.
42. Apply bead of silicone rubber No. F4AZ-19562-B, or equivalent, to rear retainer joint face. Bead must be on inside of all but one of bolt holes, **Fig. 3.**
43. Position rear retainer onto rear case and install new mounting bolts.
44. Install new rear output seal using suitable outer shaft seal installer.
45. Install new slinger if previously removed using output flange slinger installer tool No. 308-399 and pilot tool No. 308-400, or equivalents.
46. Install rear flange and new nut while using companion flange holding tool No. T78P-4851-A, or equivalent, to prevent flange from turning.
47. Install drain and fill plugs. **Do not use air tools.**
48. Apply coat of multi-purpose grease No. DOAZ-19584-AA, or equivalent, to motor adapter.
49. **On models equipped with electric shift,** install gearmotor encoder assembly.
50. **On models equipped with manual shift,** install three-position switch.
51. **On all models,** tighten lever nut to specifications.

TIGHTENING SPECIFICATIONS

Year	Component	Torque Ft. Lbs.
2002–06	Case At Dowel	18
	Drain Plug	20
	Fill Plug	20
	Front Output	165
	Poppet Screw	15
	Rear Output	186
	Sector Support	23
	Shift Lever	15
	Shift Motor	15
	Three-Position Indicator Switch	20
	Transmission Case	23
	Transfer Case Mount	37

Escape & Mariner Electronic Shift Transfer Case

NOTE: On Air Bag Equipped Models, Refer To "Air Bag System Precautions" Located In The Front Of This Manual For System Disarming & Arming Procedures.

NOTE: "Electrical Symbol & Wire Color Code Identification" Located In The Front Of This Manual May Be Used As An Aid When Using Wiring Circuits Found In This Section.

NOTE: Refer To "Computer Relearn Procedures" Located In The Front Of This Manual When Battery Power To The Computer Has Been Interrupted.

INDEX

PRECAUTIONS

Air Bag Systems

Refer to "Air Bag System Precautions" in the front of this manual for system disarming and arming procedures.

Battery Ground Cable

Prior to service, disconnect battery ground cable and isolate as required.

MAINTENANCE

Fluid Check

The transfer case is lubricated for life and should not be inspected unless a leak is suspected or a repair is required.

1. Raise and support vehicle.
2. Remove filler plug.
3. Fluid level must be even with the bottom of the filler hole.
4. Add fluid as required and tighten fill plug to specifications.

Fluid Change

1. Raise and support vehicle.
2. Remove drain plug and drain transfer case fluid into a suitable container.
3. Install drain plug and remove fill plug.
4. Fill transfer case with SAE 75W-140 synthetic gear lubricant, or equivalent.
5. Apply sealant to fill plug and tighten to specification.

DESCRIPTION

The transfer case system consists of a power transfer unit, rear propeller shaft, coupling device and rear axle. The power transfer unit is a gearbox that attaches to a transaxle. The righthand fail-safe passes through the transfer case and engages the differential side gear as in normal TX applications. The transfer case provides power to the rear propshaft through a helical gear spline coupled to the transaxle differential case, a helical gear drop (idler gear) and hypoid/helical ring gear assembly and pinion set.

The front-wheel drive transaxle utilizes a transfer case unit to transfer power through a driveshaft and universal joints to the rotary blade coupling (RBC) mounted to the rear differential.

DIAGNOSIS & TESTING

For transfer case diagnosis and testing procedures refer to **MOTOR's "Domestic Transmission, In-Vehicle Service" or "Transmission Service DVD."**

DISASSEMBLE

Repair of the transfer case is limited to seals, gaskets and output flange on automatic transaxle vehicles only. If any internal components fail, the transfer case must be replaced.

HALFSHAFT SEAL

REPLACE

Lefthand (Inner)

1. Remove transfer case. Refer to **MOTOR's "Domestic Transmission, In-Vehicle Service" or "Transmission Service DVD."**
2. Remove lefthand halfshaft seal using slide hammer tool No. 100–001 and seal removal tool No. 308–428, or equivalents.
3. Clean and remove any foreign material from inside driven gear and cavity.
4. Install new seal using seal installation tool No. 308–429 and adapter handle 303–224, or equivalents.

Righthand

1. Remove transfer case. Refer to **MOTOR's "Domestic Transmission, In-Vehicle Service" or "Transmission Service DVD."**
2. Remove three transfer case heat shield mounting bolts, **Fig. 1**, then the heat shield.
3. Remove halfshaft seat dust shield.
4. Remove seal using suitable flat blade screwdriver.
5. Clean and remove any foreign material from inside driven gear and cavity.
6. Install seal using halfshaft seal installation tool No. 205–155 and adapter handle tool No. 303–224, or equivalents.
7. Press halfshaft dust shield firmly to snap it into position.
8. Install heat shield.

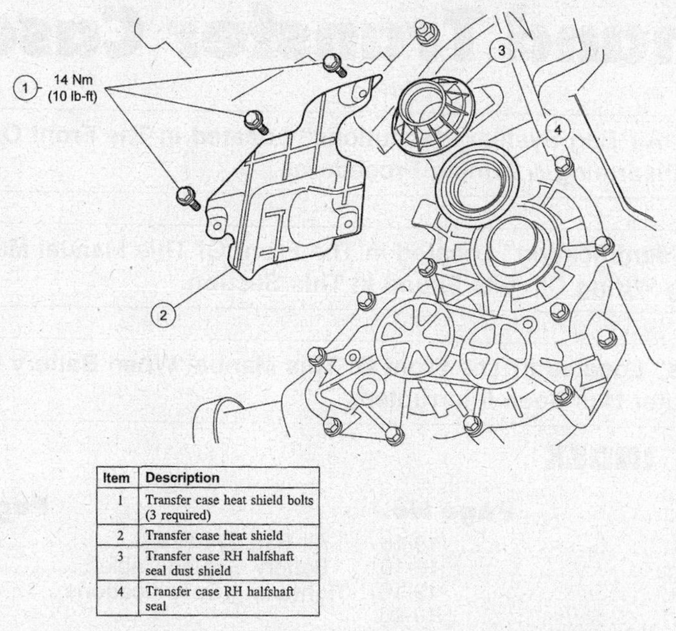

Item	Description
1	Transfer case heat shield bolts (3 required)
2	Transfer case heat shield
3	Transfer case RH halfshaft seal dust shield
4	Transfer case RH halfshaft seal

Fig. 1 Righthand halfshaft seal replacement

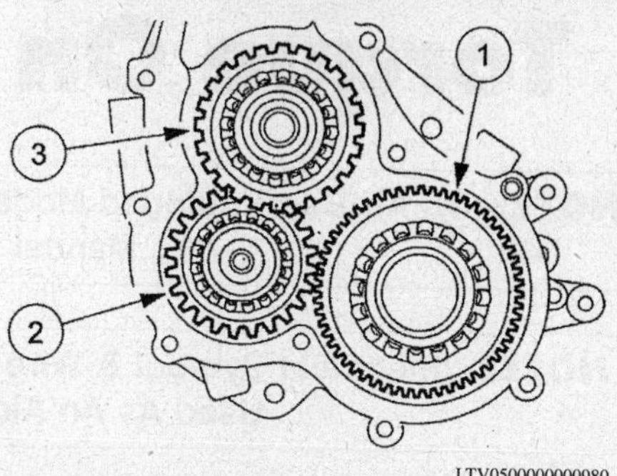

Fig. 2 Idler, drive & driven gears removed

REAR OUTPUT SHAFT OIL SEAL

REPLACE

1. Remove transfer case. Refer to **MOTOR's "Domestic Transmission, In-Vehicle Service" or "Transmission Service DVD."**
2. Remove output shaft flange retaining nut, then the flange.
3. Remove transfer case output shaft seal using suitable flat blade screwdriver.
4. Clean and remove any foreign material from inside drive gear and cavity.
5. Install new seal using PTO drive gear seal installation tool No. 308–430, or equivalent.

REAR OUTPUT SHAFT FLANGE DUST SHIELD

REPLACE

1. Remove transfer case. Refer to **MOTOR's "Domestic Transmission, In-Vehicle Service" or "Transmission Service DVD."**
2. Remove output shaft flange retaining nut, then the flange.
3. Remove dust shield using dust flange remove/install tool No. 308–432, or equivalent.
4. Install dust flange using dust flange remove/install tool No. 308–432, or equivalent.
5. Install output shaft flange.

DRIVEN GEAR SEAL

REPLACE

1. Remove transfer case, refer to **MOTOR's "Domestic Transmission, In-Vehicle Service" or "Transmission Service DVD."**
2. Remove two bolts, then the transfer case vent tube.
3. Remove and discard dust shield.
4. Remove transfer case cover mounting bolts, then the cover.
5. Remove gears, **Fig. 2,** drive gear (1), idler gear (2) and driven gear (3).
6. Remove inner seal using suitable flat blade screwdriver.
7. Clean transfer case sealing surfaces.
8. Install new seal using seal driver tool No. 308–427, or equivalent.
9. Install drive gear using a slight rotation to prevent damaging transfer case inner halfshaft seal.
10. Install idler gear and driven gear.
11. Install transfer case cover. Torque bolts in a cross pattern to 24 ft. lbs.
12. Install a new dust shield.
13. Install transfer case vent tube.

TIGHTENING SPECIFICATIONS

Year	Component	Torque Ft. Lbs.
2002–06	Drain Plug	89①
	Fill Plug	12
	Transfer Case Cover	24
	Transfer Case Heat Shield	10
	Transfer Case Vent Tube	22

① — Inch lbs.

Torque On Demand Transfer Case

NOTE: On Air Bag Equipped Models, Refer To "Air Bag System Precautions" Located In The Front Of This Manual For System Disarming & Arming Procedures.

NOTE: "Electrical Symbol & Wire Color Code Identification" Located In The Front Of This Manual May Be Used As An Aid When Using Wiring Circuits Found In This Section.

NOTE: Refer To "Computer Relearn Procedures" Located In The Front Of This Manual When Battery Power To The Computer Has Been Interrupted.

INDEX

PRECAUTIONS

Air Bag Systems

Refer to "Air Bag System Precautions" in the front of this manual for system disarming and arming procedures.

Battery Ground Cable

Prior to service, disconnect battery ground cable and isolate as required.

MAINTENANCE

Fluid Check

1. Raise and support vehicle.
2. Remove fill plug and inspect fluid level. Level should be just below filler hole.
3. Top up fluid with XT-5–QM, or equivalent, Mercon V approved fluid, as required
4. Replace fill plug.

Fluid Change

1. Raise and support vehicle.
2. Remove transfer case drain plug, **Fig. 1.**
3. Drain fluid into suitable container.
4. Replace drain plug and **torque** to 13 ft. lbs.
5. Remove transfer case fill plug, fill fluid level to just below drain plug.

DESCRIPTION

These models use a one speed, all wheel drive system that utilizes a fully automatic, torque on demand transfer case without a shift motor. Warnings are displayed through the instrument cluster message center. The message center also allows the user to enable and disable the all wheel drive function. The message center communicates with the four wheel drive control module through the universal asynchronous receiver-transmitter UBP network. The four wheel drive control module is located in the center console, between the drive and passenger front seats.

DIAGNOSIS & TESTING

For transfer case diagnosis and testing procedures refer to **MOTOR's "Domestic Transmission, In-Vehicle Service" or "Transmission Service DVD."**

DISASSEMBLE

1. Secure transfer case to bench with holding fixture 307-003, or equivalent.
2. Remove dampener.
3. Remove drain plug and drain fluid, reinstall drain plug.
4. Place index mark on rear output flange and upper output shaft for installation reference.
5. Remove components in sequence illustrated, **Fig. 2,** noting the following:
   a. Hold output shaft flange in place with holding fixture No. 205-126, or equivalent, then remove output shaft flange nut.
   b. Remove output flange oil seal with removal tool No. 307-00, or equivalent and suitable slide hammer.
   c. Remove interlock connector then remove coil wire pin from connector with suitable connector pin extraction tool.
   d. Separate transfer case halves at transfer case pry bosses.
   e. When removing or installing clutch pack assembly, do not separate clutch pack assembly. Keep tension on clutch pack and set on bench in same position as located in transfer case. Thrust washer in lower clutch pack uses tabs to hold it in place.
   f. Remove drive chain, driven sprocket and drive sprocket as an assembly.
   g. Remove rear output shaft, pump assembly and input shaft as an assembly.

ASSEMBLE

Refer to **Fig. 2** and assemble transfer case in reverse sequence noting the following:

1. Hold rear output flange in position with holding tool No. 205-126, or equivalent, then install output flange nut.
2. Apply a ⅛ inch bead of silicone sealant to transfer case mating surfaces. Too much silicone will plug fluid filter and cause premature transfer case failure.
3. Tighten transfer case bolts in a star pattern.
4. Install drive chain, driven sprocket and drive sprocket as an assembly.
5. Install rear output shaft, pump assembly and input shaft as an assembly.

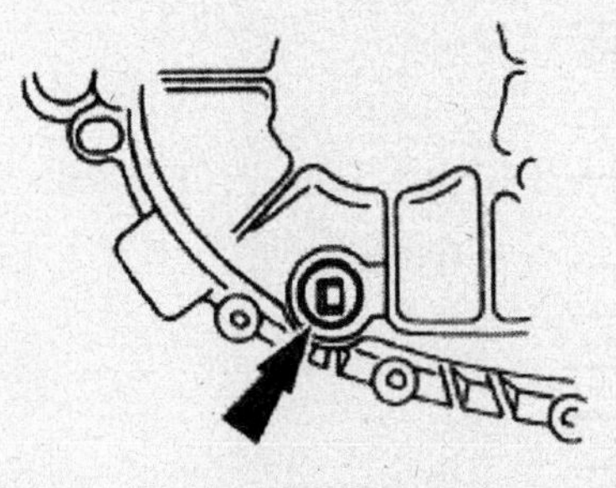
LTV1900000000920

Fig. 1 Transfer case drain plug

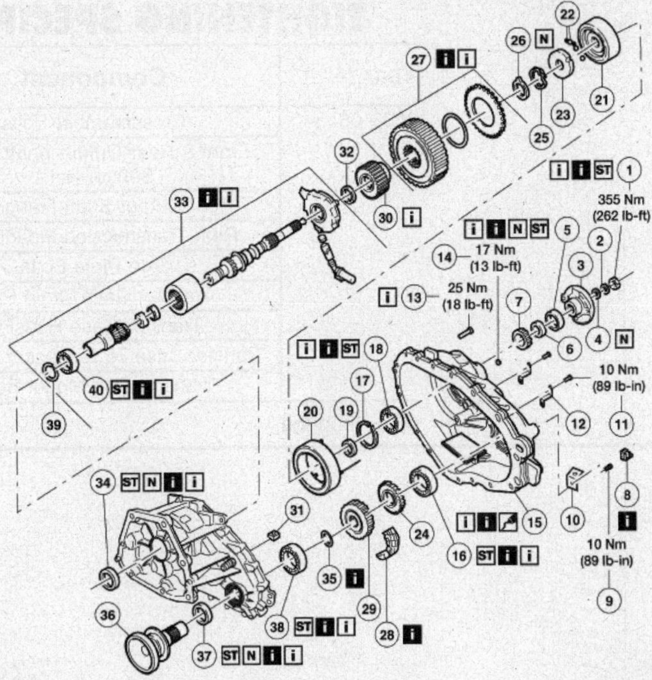

LTV1900000000931

Fig. 2 Exploded view of transfer case (Part 1 of 3)

Item	Description
1	Output flange shaft nut
2	Output shaft yoke washer
3	Rear output flange
4	Oil seal
5	Output flange oil seal
6	Spacer
7	Tone wheel
8	Connector interlock
9	Bolt (hex-head)
10	Bracket
11	Bolt (hex-head)
12	J-clip
13	Transfer case bolt - hex-head (M10 x 1.5 x 30.0)
14	Hex nut
15	Transfer case cover gear
16	Bearing (front output shaft rear)
17	Snap ring
18	Bearing (rear output shaft support)
19	Thrust Bearing
20	Clutch coil assembly

LTV1900000000932

Fig. 2 Exploded view of transfer case (Part 2 of 3)

Item	Description
21	Cam and coil housing assembly
22	Ball
23	Apply cam
24	Tone wheel (lower)
25	Wave spring
26	Snap ring
27	Clutch pack assembly
28	Drive chain Disassembly Note
29	Driven sprocket (30T)
30	Drive sprocket (30T)
31	Oil pan magnet
32	Thrust washer
33	Rear output shaft
34	Input shaft oil seal
35	Front output shaft snap ring
36	Output shaft and flange (front)
37	Front output shaft oil seal
38	Front output shaft support bearing
39	Snap ring
40	Input shaft support bearing

LTV1900000000933

Fig. 2 Exploded view of transfer case (Part 3 of 3)

TIGHTENING SPECIFICATIONS

Year	Component	Torque Ft. Lbs.
2003–06	Crossmember Bolts	46
	Front & Rear Output Shaft Speed Sensor Bolts	89①
	Rear Output Shaft Flange Nut	262
	Rear Transmission Mount Nuts	72
	Skid Plate Bolts	18
	Transfer Case Drain Plug	13
	Transfer Case Housing	18
	Transfer Case To Extension Housing	30
	Transmission Mount Bolts	66

① — Inch lbs.

FRONT WHEEL DRIVE AXLES

INDEX

HALFSHAFT

REPLACE

Escape & Mariner

2002 ESCAPE

1. Raise and support vehicle, remove front tire and wheel.
2. Remove brake disc.
3. Remove and discard front axle wheel hub nut.
4. Remove cotter pin, then the tie rod nut.
5. Remove tie rod end with removal tool No. 211-105, or equivalent.
6. Remove lower ball joint pinch bolt and nut, then separate ball joint from steering knuckle.
7. Separate halfshaft from steering knuckle with removal tool No. 205-D070, or equivalent.
8. Pull front steering knuckle out and away from halfshaft, then remove halfshaft from vehicle.
9. Reverse procedure to install, noting the following:
   a. Ensure retainer clip snaps into position when installing halfshaft.
   b. Position driveshaft and joint so splines line up with differential side gear splines, then push into place.
   c. Position halfshaft into front steering knuckle with front hub replacement tool No. 205-D069, or equivalent.
   d. **Torque** lower ball joint pinch bolt to 52 ft. lbs.
   e. **Torque** tie rod end nut to 41 ft. lbs.
   f. **Torque** front axle wheel hub nut to 214 ft. lbs.

MARINER & 2003–06 ESCAPE

1. Raise and support vehicle, remove front tire and wheel.
2. Remove and discard front axle wheel hub nut.
3. Remove clip attaching brake hose to front suspension.
4. Remove lower pinch bolt and nut, then separate lower control arm from steering knuckle.
5. Separate halfshaft from steering knuckle with removal tool No. 205-D070, or equivalent.
6. Remove halfshaft from differential with removal tool No. 205-241, **Fig. 1**, or equivalent.

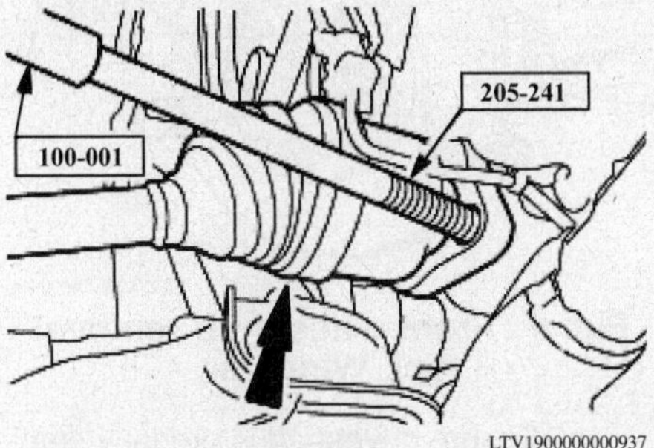

Fig. 1 Halfshaft removal tool. Mariner & 2003–06 Escape

7. Reverse procedure to install, noting the following:
   a. Ensure driveshaft circlip snaps into position when installing driveshaft.
   b. Position front wheel driveshaft and joint so splines line up with differential side gear splines. Push driveshaft and joint into position.
   c. Position halfshaft into steering knuckle with installation tool No. 204-161, or equivalent.
   d. **Torque** lower ball joint pinch bolt and nut to 52 ft. lbs.
   e. **Torque** new front axle wheel hub nut to 214 ft. lbs.
   f. Inspect and top up transaxle fluid as required.

Freestar & Monterey

1. Raise and support vehicle, remove front tire and wheel.
2. Remove front brake anti-lock sensor harness from clip, then the caliper bolts and position disc brake caliper aside.
3. Remove front axle wheel end nut and washer. **Front axle wheel end nut is a torque prevailing design nut. Do not reuse this nut.**
4. Remove lower pinch bolt and nut, then separate lower control arm from steering knuckle.
5. Separate halfshaft from steering knuckle with removal tool No. 205-D070, or equivalent.
6. Remove halfshaft from differential with removal tool No. 205-241, or equivalent.
7. Reverse procedure to install, noting the following:
   a. Install a new circlip every time halfshaft is removed from transaxle.
   b. Start one end of circlip in groove and work circlip over halfshaft and into groove to prevent circlip from overexpanding.
   c. **Torque** lower ball joint pinch bolt and nut to 47 ft. lbs.
   d. **Torque** new front axle wheel hub nut to 111 ft. lbs.

Freestyle

LEFTHAND

1. Raise and support vehicle, then remove front tire and wheel.
2. Remove and discard front axle wheel end nut and washer.
3. Remove caliper bolts and position disc brake caliper aside.
4. Separate halfshaft from hub using tool No. 205–D070 or equivalent.
5. Remove and discard lower ball joint nut, then disconnect lower control arm.
6. Remove half shaft from transaxle using special tool Nos. 100–011 and 205–290 or 205–241 or equivalents.
7. Reverse procedure to install, noting the following:
   a. Install a new circlip every time halfshaft is removed from transaxle.
   b. Start one end of circlip in groove and work circlip over halfshaft and into groove to prevent circlip from overexpanding.
   c. **Torque** new ball joint nut to 59 ft. lbs.
   d. **Torque** new front axle wheel hub nut to 184 ft. lbs.

RIGHTHAND

1. Raise and support vehicle, then remove front tire and wheel.
2. Remove and discard front axle wheel end nut and washer.
3. Remove caliper bolts and position disc brake caliper aside.
4. Seperate halfshaft from hub using tool No. 205–D070 or equivalent.
5. Remove and discard lower ball joint nut, then disconnect lower control arm.

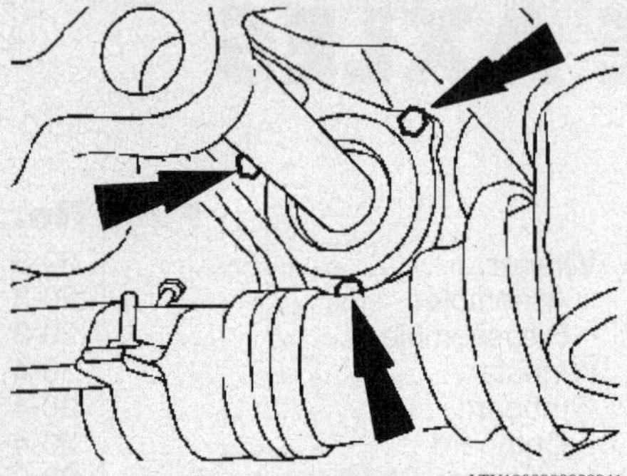

Fig. 2 Support bearing bolts. Villager

6. Remove two halfshaft bearing nuts, then the halfshaft.
7. Reverse procedure to install, noting the following:
   a. **Torque** halfshaft bearing nuts to 20 ft. lbs.
   b. **Torque** new ball joint nut to 59 ft. lbs.
   c. **Torque** new front axle wheel hub nut to 184 ft. lbs.

Villager

LEFTHAND

1. Raise and support vehicle, remove tire and wheel assemblies.
2. Remove cotter pin, then the front hub nut and washer.
3. Remove stabilizer link nut.
4. Remove cotter pin and nut, then separate lower ball joint from steering knuckle.
5. Separate halfshaft from transaxle.
6. Separate outer CV joint from steering knuckle with removal tool No. 205D070, or equivalent.
7. Remove halfshaft from vehicle.
8. Reverse procedure to install, noting the following:
   a. Ensure driveshaft bearing retainer circlip snaps into position in differential side gear.
   b. **Torque** ball joint nut to 58 ft. lbs.
   c. **Torque** stabilizer link nut to 50 ft. lbs.
   d. **Torque** hub nut to 203 ft. lbs.

RIGHTHAND

1. Raise and support vehicle, remove front tire and wheel.
2. Remove cotter pin, then the wheel hub nut and washer.
3. Remove stabilizer link nut.
4. Remove cotter pin and lower ball joint nut, then separate lower ball joint from steering knuckle.
5. Remove support bearing bolts, **Fig. 2,** then separate halfshaft from transaxle.
6. Use care to ensure pry bar does not damage transaxle case, oil seal, driveshaft or boot.
7. Separate outer CV joint from steering knuckle with removal tool No. 205D070, or equivalent.
8. Remove halfshaft from vehicle.
9. Reverse procedure to install, noting the following:

Fig. 3 Anti lock sensor harness clip. Windstar

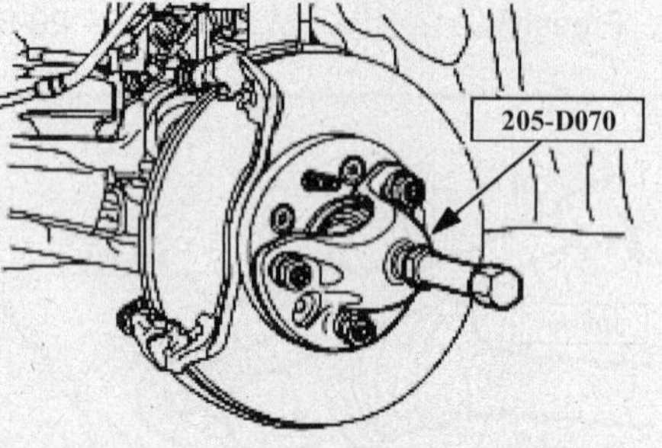

Fig. 5 Front wheel hub removal tool. Windstar

   a. Ensure driveshaft is properly seated in differential side gear. Driveshaft bearing retainer clip will snap into side gear groove when properly seated.
   b. **Torque** stabilizer link nut to 50 ft. lbs.
   c. **Torque** lower ball joint nut to 58 ft. lbs.
   d. **Torque** wheel hub nut to 203 ft. lbs.

Windstar

REMOVAL

Do not begin this procedure unless the following components are available: new front axle wheel end nut, new lower ball joint pinch bolt and nut and new retainer circlip. Do not reuse these components, their torque retention capabilities diminish during removal.

1. Raise and support vehicle, remove tire and wheel assembly.
2. Insert a suitable steel rod in brake disc to prevent halfshaft from turning while removing front axle wheel end nut.
3. Remove wheel end nut and washer, then the steel rod from brake disc.
4. Remove caliper mounting bolts and position caliper aside. Remove brake pads or tape in place.
5. Do not allow caliper to hang from hydraulic hose.
6. Remove front brake anti-lock sensor harness from clip, **Fig. 3.**
7. Remove lower ball joint pinch bolt and nut. It may be required to drive bolt out of knuckle with suitable punch and hammer.
8. Position end of pry bar outside bushing pocket to avoid damage to bushing, **Fig. 4.**
9. Use care to prevent damaging front driveshaft joint boot.

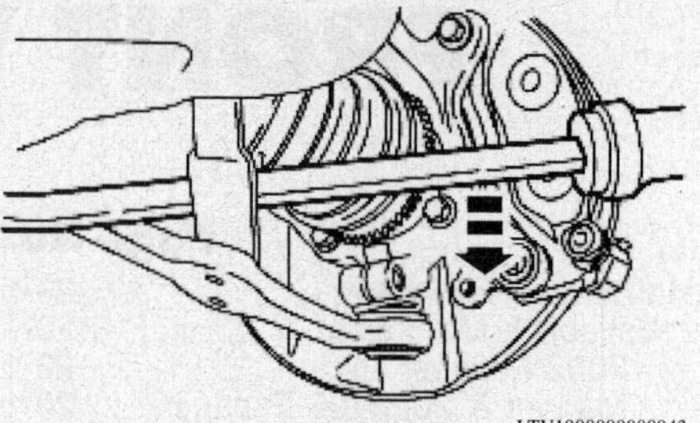

Fig. 4 Pry bar positioning. Windstar

10. Pry down and separate front suspension lower control arm from steering knuckle.
11. Press front driveshaft outer CV joint from wheel hub until it is loose with removal tool No. 205-D070, or equivalent, **Fig. 5.**
12. Never use a hammer to separate front wheel driveshaft from wheel hub.
13. Rotate wheel knuckle rearward, while pulling it outward at bottom and remove front wheel driveshaft joint from hub.
14. Separate inboard CV joint from transaxle with suitable pry bar. Use care to avoid damaging differential seal.
15. Remove driveshaft from vehicle.

INSTALLATION

Always install new circlip each time halfshaft is removed from vehicle.

1. Lubricate differential seal with Mercon V automatic transmission fluid XT-5-QM, or equivalent meeting Mercon V specifications.
2. Install new circlip on righthand halfshaft. Start at one end in groove and work circlip over shaft and into groove to prevent clip from over expanding.
3. Align inboard CV joint housing splines with differential side gear splines or output shaft splines, and push CV joint inward until circlip seats in differential side gear or inboard CV joint housing
4. If required, use a non metallic mallet to aid in seating circlip. Tap only on outboard front wheel driveshaft joint.
5. Align front wheel driveshaft joint splines and wheel hub splines, then push joint into wheel hub as far as possible.
6. Install washer and old nut. Seat front driveshaft joint in hub with old nut, then remove and discard nut.
7. Connect lower ball joint to steering knuckle. Install new pinch bolt and nut and **torque** to 46 ft. lbs.
8. Insert a suitable steel rod in brake disc to prevent disc rotation while installing new front axle wheel end nut.
9. Apply a small patch of Loctite 242, or equivalent thread locking compound, to last five driveshaft joint threads, **Fig. 6.**
10. **Torque** new front axle wheel end nut to 184 ft. lbs., in a continuous rotation. Stopping rotation during installation will cause nylon lock to set incorrectly and provide incorrect torque readings.
11. Remove steel rod from brake disc.

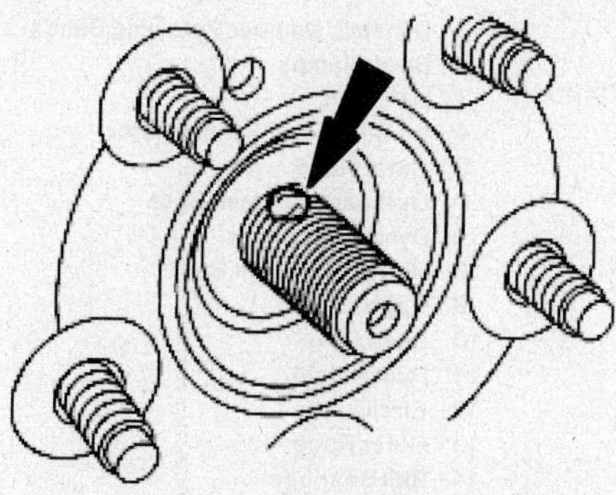

Fig. 6 Driveshaft joint thread locking compound placement. Windstar

12. Install brake caliper **torque** mounting bolts to 41 ft. lbs.
13. Install front anti lock sensor harness in clip.
14. Install tire and wheel assembly.
15. Lower vehicle. Inspect transaxle fluid level and top up as required.

INTERMEDIATE SHAFT

Replace

ESCAPE & MARINER

1. Remove righthand halfshaft as outlined in "Halfshaft, Replace."
2. Remove two inner halfshaft bearing retainer nuts, **Fig. 7**, then the intermediate shaft.
3. Reverse procedure to install.

HALFSHAFT SERVICE

Escape & Mariner

DISASSEMBLE

1. Remove halfshaft.
2. Secure halfshaft in suitable vise with protective jaw covers.
3. Remove inboard halfshaft boot clamps, then slide halfshaft boot off of CV joint housing.
4. Separate tripod joint from CV joint housing. If original tripod joint is going to be installed, mark joint and halfshaft for installation reference.
5. Remove snap ring from outer edge of tripod joint.
6. Slide tripod joint off of shaft.
7. Remove inner snap ring.
8. Remove inboard halfshaft boor from halfshaft.
9. Remove two outboard halfshaft boot clamps.
10. Slide boot back to expose outboard CV joint.
11. Separate outer CV joint from axle shaft by tapping on joint with soft faced hammer.
12. Remove and discard halfshaft bearing retainer clip.
13. Slide outboard halfshaft boot off of halfshaft.

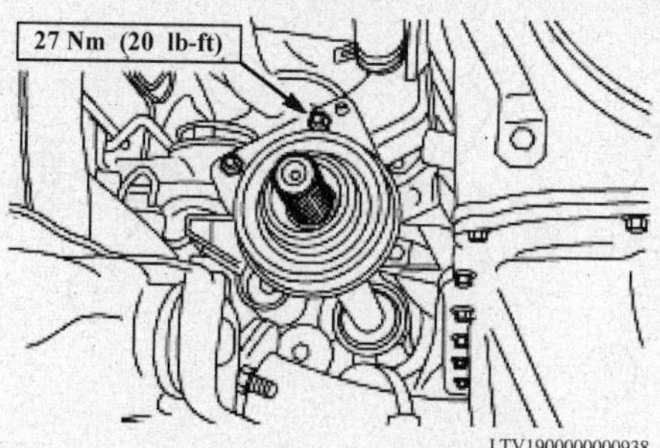

Fig. 7 Intermediate shaft retaining nuts. Escape & Mariner

ASSEMBLE

1. Clean all components.
2. Lubricate outboard CV joint with Ford high temperature constant velocity joint grease E43Z-19590-A, or equivalent meeting Ford specification ESP-M1C207-A.
3. Install outboard halfshaft boot.
4. Install new halfshaft shaft bearing retainer circlip
5. Install outer CV joint by tapping into position with soft faced hammer.
6. Remove any excess grease on mating surfaces and slide outboard halfshaft boor forward onto outboard CV joint.
7. Remove any trapped air in outboard halfshaft boot using a cloth covered screwdriver, **Fig. 8,** after adjusting outboard halfshaft boot spacing.
8. Install new halfshaft boot clamps and crimp with installation tool No. 205-343.
9. Position inboard halfshaft boot, then the axle snap ring.
10. Install tripod joint on halfshaft and the outer snap ring.
11. Lubricate the three tripod joint needle bearings with Ford high temperature constant velocity joint grease No. E43Z-19590-A, or equivalent meeting Ford specification ESP-M1C207A.
12. Fill tripod joint housing with Ford high temperature constant velocity joint grease No. E43Z-19590-A, or equivalent meeting Ford specification ESP-M1C207A.
13. Position tripod housing on tripod joint.
14. Position inboard halfshaft boot and clamp.
15. Remove any trapped air in joint with a cloth covered screwdriver, **Fig. 8.**
16. Crimp new CV boot clamps with installation tool No. 205-343, or equivalent.

Freestar & Monterey

Halfshaft assemblies are not repairable and must be replaced if worn or damaged.

Freestyle

The halfshafts are not serviced. If the halfshafts are worn or damaged, install new components.

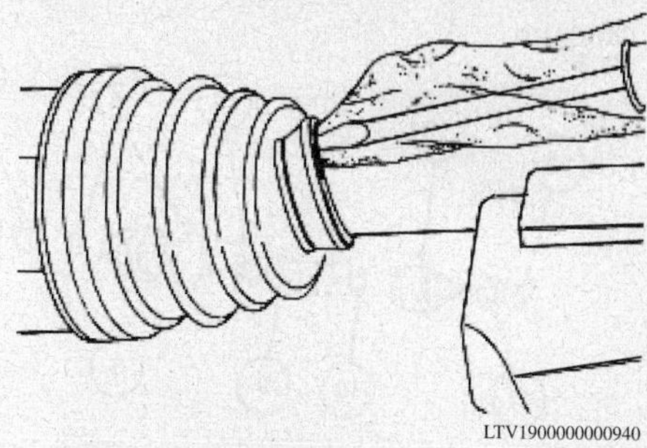

Fig. 8 Trapped air removal procedure. Escape & Mariner

Villager

DISASSEMBLE

Refer to **Figs. 9 and 10** when performing repair procedures on these halfshafts.

1. Place halfshaft in vise equipped with protective jaw caps to prevent damage to any machined components.
2. Do not remove wheel speed sensor rotors. Using boot clamp pliers tool No. D87P-1090-A, or equivalent, remove boot clamps and discard.
3. If these procedure are being performed to replace damaged boot, inspect grease for contamination by rubbing grease between two fingers. If there is any gritty feeling, CV joint must be disassembled, cleaned and inspected.
4. If grease is not contaminated and CV joint has been operating satisfactorily, replace only boot and add required amount of specified lubricant.
5. Slide inboard CV joint boot back, then clean grease out of joint assembly and boot.
6. Slide outer race off halfshaft, then remove six ball bearings from cage.
7. Clean ball bearing in solvent.
8. Remove snap ring from end of halfshaft.
9. Remove inner race using two-jaw puller tool No. D80L-1002-L, or equivalent.
10. Slide cage off shaft. **If boot is to be reinstalled, wrap halfshaft splines with tape before removing boot.**
11. Slide inboard CV joint boot off halfshaft.
12. If required to replace outboard CV joint boot on righthand halfshaft, slide outboard CV joint boot off halfshaft.
13. If required to replace outboard CV joint boot on lefthand halfshaft, remove dynamic damper as follows:
    a. Pry up dynamic damper retaining bands, then remove bands with pliers.
    b. Pull damper off shaft.

ASSEMBLE

The outboard and inboard CV joint boots

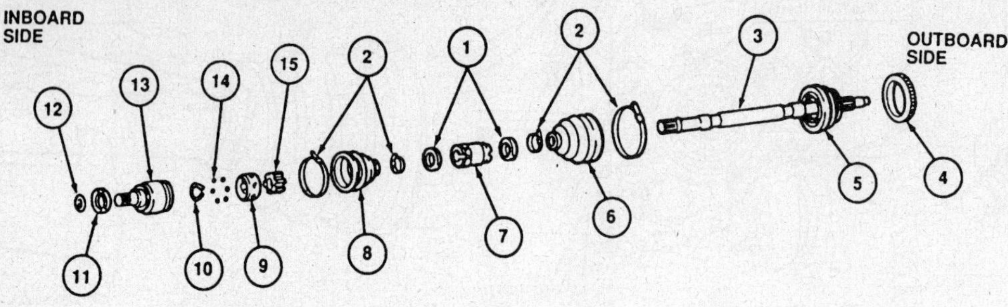

Fig. 9 Exploded view of lefthand halfshaft assembly. Villager

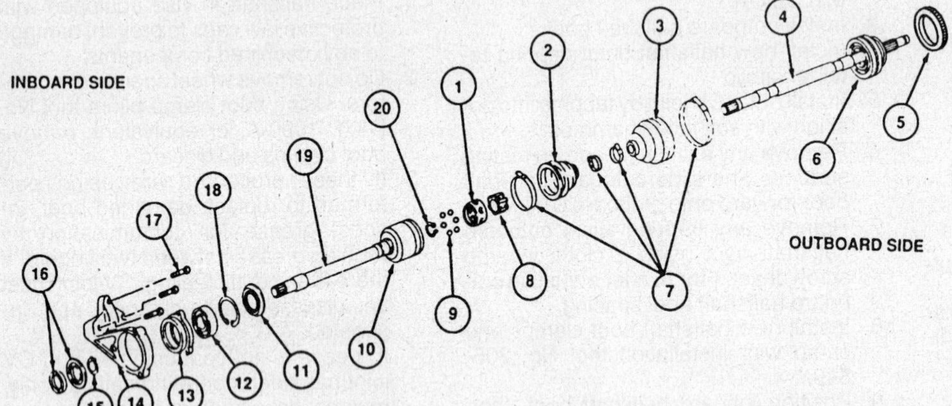

Fig. 10 Exploded view of righthand halfshaft assembly. Villager

are different. Failure to correctly install the boot on the proper end of the halfshaft could lead to premature boot and/or CV joint wear. Inboard CV joint boot measurement at large end is 3.99–4.07 inches. Outboard CV joint boot measurement is 3.39–3.46 inches.

1. Wrap halfshaft splines with tape before installing CV boots, then slide outboard CV joint boot on halfshaft.
2. Fill outboard CV joint boot with 6.17–6.88 ounces of Constant Velocity Joint Grease part No. E2FZ-19590-B (ESP-M1C187-A), or equivalent.
3. Position boot on outboard CV joint assembly. Ensure boot is fully seated in shaft grooves and outer race.
4. Insert dulled screwdriver blade between boot and outer race to allow trapped air to escape.
5. Install two new boot clamps around boots in clockwise direction using boot clamp pliers tool No. D87P-1090-A, or equivalent. **Tighten boot clamps securely, but not to point where boot clamp bridge is cut or damage to boot could occur.**
6. If dynamic damper on lefthand halfshaft was removed, slide dynamic damper on halfshaft and install new retaining bands. Use pliers to pull retaining bands tight, then bend locking tabs to secure bands in place.
7. Slide inboard CV joint boot onto halfshaft.
8. Gently tap inner race on shaft.
9. Slide cage on halfshaft, then using snap ring pliers, seat snap ring on end of halfshaft.
10. Fill inboard CV joint boot with 7.41–8.29 ounces of High-Temperature Constant Velocity Joint Grease part No. E43Z-19590-A (ESP-M1C207-A), or equivalent.
11. Install six ball bearings into cage. Lubricate with small amount of specified lubricant to secure ball bearings in cage.
12. Slide outer race onto end of halfshaft, over ball bearings.
13. Position boot on inboard CV joint assembly. Ensure boot is fully seated in shaft grooves and outer race.
14. Install two new boot clamps around boots in clockwise direction using boot clamp pliers tool No. D87P-1090-A, or equivalent. **Tighten boot clamps securely, but not to point where boot clamp bridge is cut or damage to boot could occur.**
15. Work CV joint through its full range of travel at various angles. The joint should flex, extend and compress smoothly.

Windstar

INBOARD

1. Remove driveshaft boot clamps.
2. Separate front wheel driveshaft joint boot from inboard CV joint housing.
3. Inspect CV joint grease for contamination by rubbing it between two fingers. Any gritty feeling indicates contamination.
4. If assembly is worn or damaged, it must be replaced. Component pieces cannot be replaced.
5. Reverse procedure to install.

OUTBOARD

REMOVAL

Do not mix or substitute driveshaft components from other driveshafts. Halfshaft components are matched by the manufacturer during production.

1. Clamp halfshaft assembly in a suitable vise.

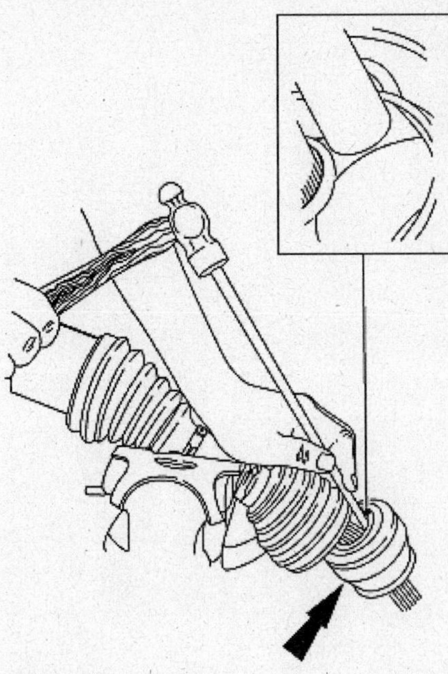

Fig. 11 Outer CV joint removal. Windstar

2. Remove boot clamps. Separate driveshaft boot from driveshaft joint.
3. Inspect CV grease for contamination. If grease is contaminated, proceed as follows:
   a. Give a sharp tap with a brass drift and a hammer to the inner bearing race, **Fig. 11,** to dislodge CV joint circlip.
   b. Remove and discard circlip, remove stop ring if worn or additional halfshaft disassembly is required.
   c. Remove CV boot from shaft.
4. If installing new anti-lock brake sensor indicator, proceed as follows:
   a. Position wheel sensor installer tool No. 206-072, **Fig. 12,** or equivalent, on suitable press bed.
   b. Place front wheel driveshaft joint on tool.
   c. Press anti-lock brake sensor indicator off of CV joint and discard sensor, **Fig. 13.**

INSTALLATION

1. Position wheel speed sensor tool on suitable press bed, then place anti-lock sensor ring on tool, **Fig. 14.**

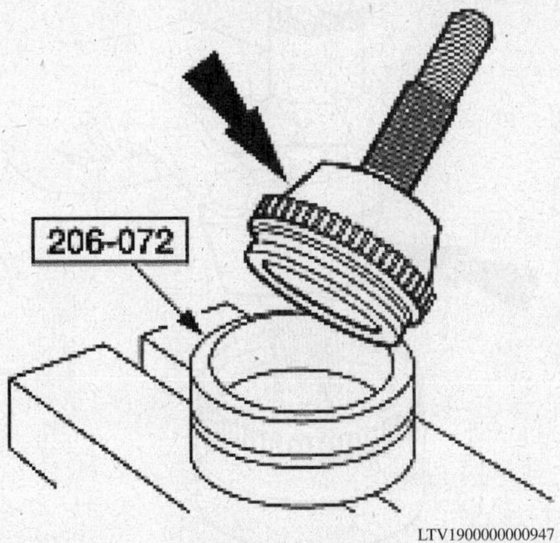

Fig. 12 Wheel speed sensor installation tool

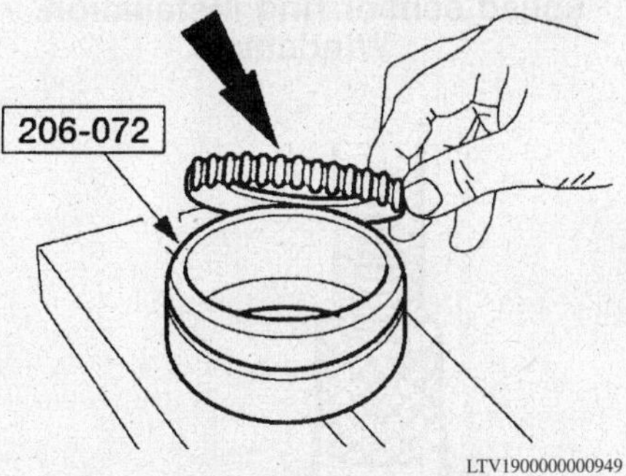

Fig. 14 Anti-lock sensor ring installation. Windstar

2. Position front wheel driveshaft joint in special tool, **Fig. 15.**
3. Place steel plate across front wheel driveshaft joint back face, **Fig. 16.**
4. Press anti-lock brake sensor indicator onto driveshaft joint. Installation is complete when joint bottoms out on installation tool.
5. Install clamp and driveshaft joint boot. Ensure joint boot seats in boot groove.
6. Install clamps as tight as possible by hand.
7. Position boot clamp installation tool No. 205-343, or equivalent, on clamp ear and tighten tool through bolt until tool closes completely.
8. Install stop ring, ensure ring seats in groove.

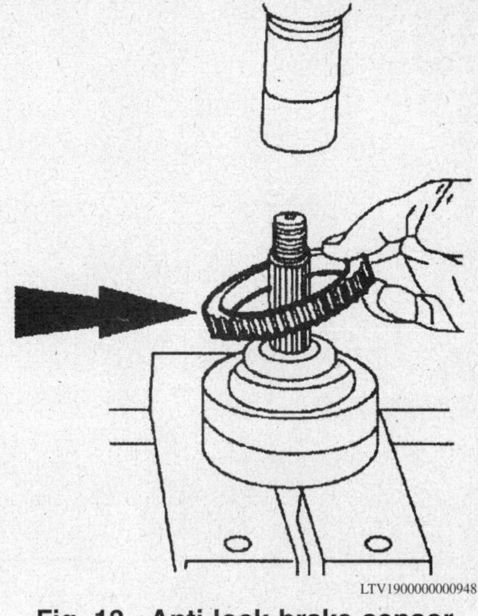

Fig. 13 Anti-lock brake sensor replacement

9. Install a new circlip. Start one end in groove and work circlip over shaft and into groove to avoid over expanding clip.
10. Righthand and lefthand halfshafts use different types of grease.
11. **On righthand halfshaft,** fill driveshaft joint with 6.3 ounces of Ford high temperature constant velocity joint grease E43Z-19590-A, or equivalent meeting Ford specification ESP-M1C207-A. Spread remaining grease inside CXV joint boot.
12. **On lefthand halfshaft,** fill driveshaft joint with 6.3 ounces of GKN Thermax Grease M-3020, or equivalent. Spread remaining grease inside CV joint boot.
13. **On both halfshafts,** tap CV joint onto interconnecting shaft with a nonmetallic hammer. Ensure joint has locked onto shaft by attempting to pull joint off of shaft.
14. Remove all excess grease from joint external surfaces and boot mating surfaces.
15. Seat driveshaft joint boot in groove, install clamp as tight as possible by hand.
16. Tighten clamp with boot clamp tool No. 205-343, or equivalent.

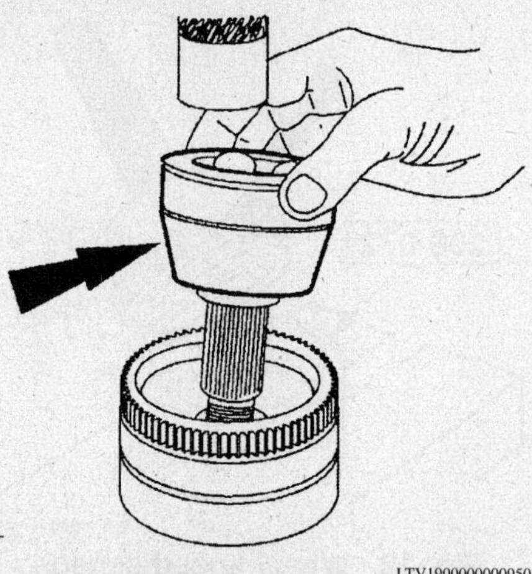

Fig. 15 Driveshaft joint to wheel speed sensor ring installation. Windstar

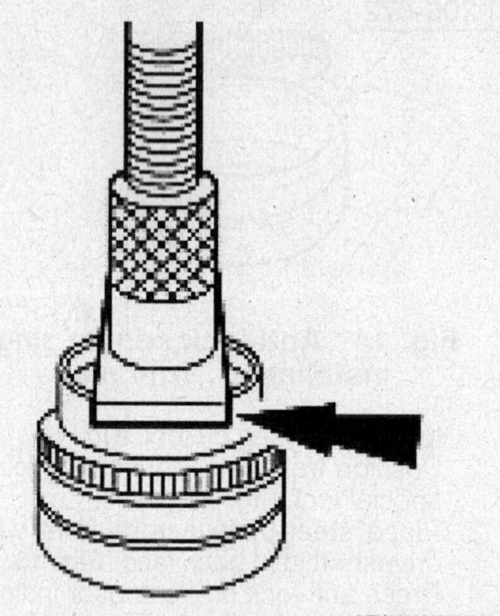

Fig. 16 Press tool placement. Windstar

ALL-WHEEL DRIVE SYSTEMS

INDEX

PRECAUTIONS

Inspection

While inspecting boots, watch for indentations (dimples) in boot convolutions. If an indentation is observed, it must be removed. Refer to "CV Joint Boot Indentation Removal."

The outboard CV joint boot uses a keyway vent between interconnection shaft and boot under the small clamp. A small amount of grease leakage at this vent is normal.

The CV joint boot will sweat during normal operation, causing a light film of grease to show on the outside of boot. This condition is normal.

1. Inspect boots for evidence of cracks, tears or splits.
2. Inspect underbody for any indication of grease splatter in vicinity of CV joint boots.
3. Ensure wheel hub retaining nut is correctly tightened.

DESCRIPTION

The All-Wheel Drive system has Constant Velocity (CV) joints at the outboard end of each axle shaft. A plunged CV joint is at the inboard end, **Fig. 1.**

The inboard CV joint is fastened by four bolts that insert through the joint and thread into the circular flange of the axle.

The outboard CV joint stub shaft is splined into the wheel hub and secured with a torque nut. CV joints are lube-for-life with special CV joint grease and require no periodic lubrication. CV joint boots, however, should be periodically inspected and replaced immediately if damage or grease leakage is evident. Continued operation will result in joint failure due to contamination or loss of grease.

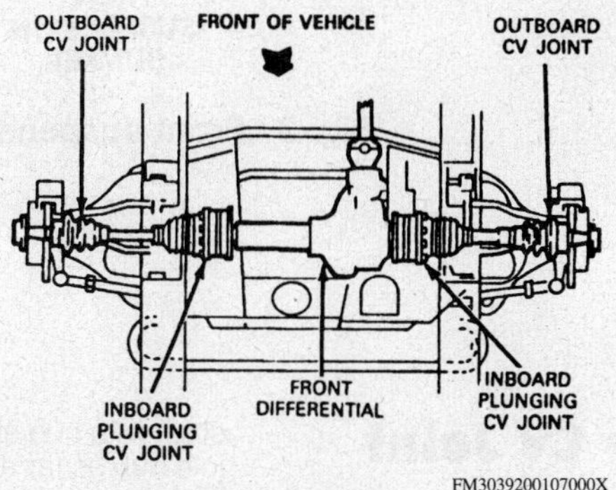

Fig. 1 All-wheel drive system components

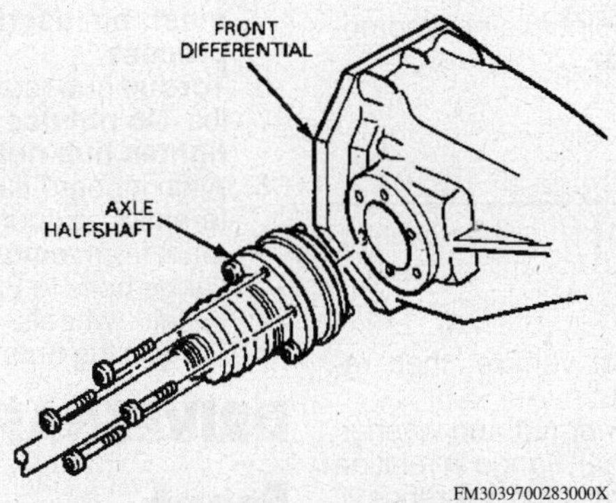

Fig. 2 Front halfshaft removal

TROUBLESHOOTING

Noise & Vibration In Turns

1. Cut or damaged boots resulting in insufficient or contaminated grease in outboard CV.
2. Loose CV joint boot clamps.
3. Other components contacting halfshaft assembly.
4. Worn, damaged or improperly installed wheel bearings.

Vibration At Highway Speeds

Halfshafts are not balanced and do not contribute to rotational vibration disturbances.

1. Out of balance front wheels or tires.
2. Out of round front tires.
3. Out of balance front of rear driveshaft.

Shudder Or Vibration During Acceleration

1. Excessively worn or damaged outboard CV joint.
2. Excessively high CV joint operating angles caused by improper ride height.

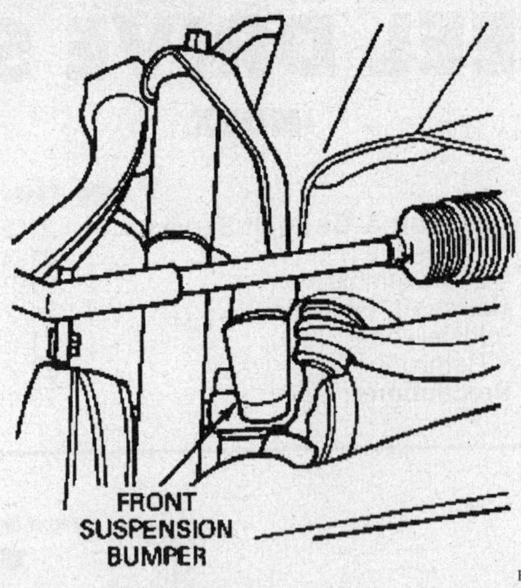

Fig. 3 Front suspension bumper replacement

Halfshaft Or CV Joint Pull Out

1. Differential improperly positioned.
2. Frame rail or strut tower out of position or damaged.
3. Front suspension components worn or damaged.
4. Inboard universal joint retainer improperly seated or loose.

HALFSHAFT

REPLACE

Removal

1. Raise and support vehicle, then remove front wheels.
2. Remove hub retainer nut and washer.
3. Mark differential shaft flange in relation to halfshaft for installation reference.
4. Remove four bolts and disconnect halfshaft inboard joint from differential axle shaft flange, **Fig. 2. Only four of six bolts hold CV to axle shaft.**
5. Support end of shaft with suitable length of wire to prevent damage to outboard CV joint.
6. Loosen shock absorber attachment on lower control arm and position to side.
7. Remove suspension bumper, **Fig. 3.**
8. Remove outer CV joint from hub using hub replacement tool Nos. T81P-1104-C, T81P-1104-A, T83P-1104-BH and T86P-1104-A, or equivalents. **After halfshafts have been removed, vehicle must not be driven or rolled with vehicle weight supported by hub bearing.**

Installation

1. Align splines of outboard CV joint stub shaft with hub splines, then push shaft into hub as far as possible.
2. Temporarily fasten brake rotor to hub with washers and two lug nuts.
3. Install steel rod to rotor to prevent hub from turning during CV installation.
4. Install washer, then manually thread retainer nut onto halfshaft as far as possible. **A new hub retainer nut must be used during installation process.**
5. **Torque** hub retainer nut to 170–209 ft. lbs. **Do not use power or air tools to tighten hub nut.**
6. Align inboard flange of halfshaft to differential output flange using index mark from removal procedure. **Torque** flange bolts to 22–30 ft. lbs.
7. Install wheels and lower vehicle. **Torque** lug nuts to 85–115 ft. lbs.

DRIVESHAFT

Front

REMOVAL

1. Mark driveshaft and axle companion flanges as well as driveshaft boot and transfer case front output for reference during installation.
2. Release driveshaft boot clamp with boot clamp pliers tool No. D87P-1090-A, or equivalent, and free boot from transfer case.
3. Remove axle snubber from beneath pinion, then the front driveshaft to front axle companion flange bolts.
4. Remove transmission mount stud nuts from front crossmember, then raise transfer case so transmission mount studs are almost out of front crossmember.
5. Slide driveshaft front flange between front axle and starter motor, then, when front flange has cleared, slide boot and splined yoke out of transfer case front output.
6. Remove front driveshaft.

INSTALLATION

1. Ensure transfer case is raised so transmission mount studs are almost out of front crossmember, then align marks made at removal and slide boot and splined yoke assembly into transfer case front output.
2. Slide driveshaft front flange between front axle and starter motor, then remove snubber from crossmember rear lateral support, located below axle pinion.
3. Lower transfer case so transmission studs are in original positions, then **torque** transmission mount nuts to 33–38 ft. lbs.
4. Align companion flanges as marked during removal, then install bolts and **torque** to 22–30 ft. lbs.
5. Position axle snubber on crossmember just below axle pinion, then install fasteners and **torque** to 17–24 ft. lbs.
6. Install boot clamp using boot clamp pliers tool No. D87P-1090-A, or equivalent.

HALFSHAFT & CV JOINT SERVICE

Disassemble

1. Clamp halfshaft in suitable vise, **Fig. 4. Do not allow vise jaws to contact boot or its clamp.**
2. Cut inner boot clamps using suitable side cutters, then remove clamps, pull larger boot end from joint.
3. Remove inboard CV joint assembly bolts, then separate spacer and grease cap from joint assembly.

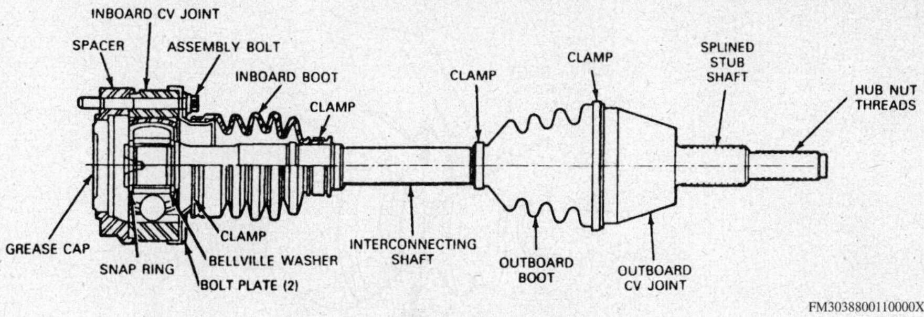

Fig. 4 Halfshaft assembly

4. Remove interconnecting shaft end to CV joint cage snap ring and discard, remove joint from shaft.
5. Remove and discard shaft belleville washer, then remove and discard inner boot.
6. Cut outer boot clamps using suitable side cutters, then remove outboard shaft and boot from vise pull outer boot from shaft and discard.
7. Clean all components in suitable components solvent.
8. Inspect CV joints for excessive wear, pitting, rust and broken components. Replace inboard joint or outboard joint and shaft assembly as required.

Assemble

1. Slide new outer boot over shaft. Fill CV joint area around balls with 2.8 ounces of constant velocity joint grease No. E2FZ-19590-B, or equivalent, then spread 1.4 ounces of grease evenly inside large boot.
2. Assemble outer boot onto outboard shaft and joint assembly, ensure boot is seated in boot grooves, then tighten clamps using suitable crimping pliers. **If clamp is overtightened, damage to boot or clamp may occur.**
3. Slide new inner boot over shaft. Slide belleville washer onto shaft end, ensure proper orientation.
4. Assemble inboard CV joint to interconnecting shaft spline until resting on belleville washer, then install snap ring.
5. Evenly spread 1.4 ounces of CV joint grease No. E2FZ-19590-B, or equivalent, inside inner boot, install inner boot, ensure boot is seated in boot grooves, then tighten clamps using suitable crimping pliers. **Do not overtighten clamp, damage to boot or clamp may occur.**
6. Fill spacer and grease cap with 1.4 ounces of CV joint grease No. E2FZ-19590-B, or equivalent, ensure not to contaminate bolt holes with grease.
7. Install spacer to CV joint end pilot, then the bolts, **torque** to 19–25 ft. lbs., work inboard joint few times to spread grease evenly within joint.

CV JOINT BOOT INDENTATION REMOVAL

Indentations or dimples in outboard CV boots may occur due to improper handling during storage or service of halfshafts.

Inspect boot for any sign of grease leakage in dimple which would indicate a cut. Replace boot if cut or other damage exists.

1. Grasp dimpled convolution on either side of dimple using forefinger and thumb of each hand, **Fig. 5.**
2. Pull convolution by moving hands in opposite directions, dimple should pop out.
3. If dimple does not pop out or if it dimples again, remove one clamp and allow internal and external air pressure to equalize.

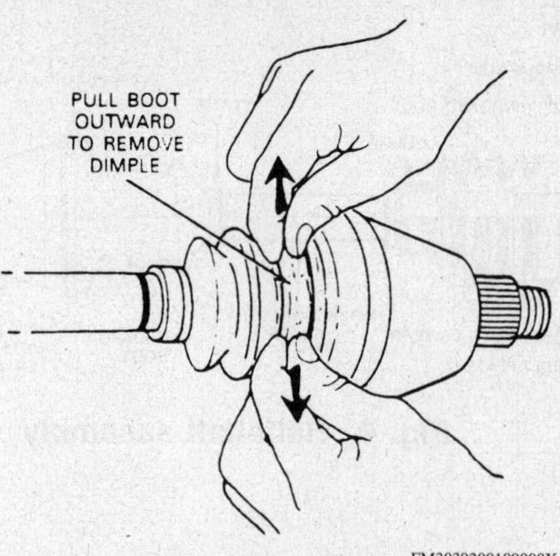

Fig. 5 Boot indentation removal

DRIVE AXLES

NOTE: Refer To "Front Wheel Drive Axles" Chapter For Escape, Freestar, Mariner, Monterey, Villager & Windstar Front Axle Service.

TABLE OF CONTENTS

Application Chart

Model	Year	Drive Axle
FRONT DRIVE AXLES		
Aviator	2003–05	Dana/Spicer Model 35
Expedition	2002–06	Ford Aluminum 8.8 Inch Ring Gear
Explorer	2002–04	Dana/Spicer Model 35
	2005–06	Dana/Spicer Model 30
Explorer Sport/Sport Trac	2002–03	Dana/Spicer Model 35
Excursion	2002–06	Dana/Spicer Model 50 & 60
F-Super Duty Series	2002–06	Dana/Spicer Model 50 & 60
F-150	2002–06	Ford Aluminum 8.8 Inch Ring Gear
Mountaineer	2002–03	Dana/Spicer Model 35
	2005–06	Dana/Spicer Model 30
Navigator	2002–06	Ford Aluminum 8.8 Inch Ring Gear
Ranger	2002–06	Dana/Spicer Model 35
REAR DRIVE AXLES		
Aviator	2003–05	Ford Aluminum 8.8 Inch Ring Gear
Escape	2002–06	Dana/Spicer Model 174
E-Series	2002–06	Dana/Spicer Model 60-1U
		Dana/Spicer Model 70-2U
		Dana/Spicer Model 80
		Ford Integral Carrier Axle w/8.8 Inch Ring Gear
		Ford 9.75 Inch Ring Gear w/Semi Floating Axle
Excursion	2002–06	Dana/Spicer Model S135
		Dana/Spicer Model 80
		Dana/Spicer Model S135
		Dana/Spicer Model S110
		Ford Integral Carrier Axle w/10.5 Inch Ring Gear
Expedition	2002–06	Ford Integral Carrier Axle w/8.8 Inch Ring Gear
		Ford 9.75 Inch Ring Gear w/Semi Floating Axle
Explorer	2002–03	Ford Integral Carrier Axle w/8.8 Inch Ring Gear
Explorer Sport/Sport Trac	2002–03	Ford Integral Carrier Axle w/8.8 Inch Ring Gear
		Dana/Spicer Model 35
F-150	2002–06	Ford Integral Carrier Axle w/8.8 Inch Ring Gear
		Ford 9.75 Inch Ring Gear w/Semi Floating Axle
		Ford 10.25 Inch Ring Gear w/Semi Floating Axle
F-Super Duty	2002–06	Dana/Spicer Model 80
		Dana/Spicer Model S110
		Dana/Spicer Model S135
Mariner	2002–06	Dana/Spicer Model 174

Continued

Model	Year	Drive Axle
REAR DRIVE AXLES		
Mark LT	2002–06	Ford Integral Carrier Axle w/8.8 Inch Ring Gear
		Ford 9.75 Inch Ring Gear w/Semi Floating Axle
		Ford 10.25 Inch Ring Gear w/Semi Floating Axle
Mountaineer	2002–06	Ford Integral Carrier Axle w/8.8 Inch Ring Gear
Navigator	2002–03	Ford Integral Carrier Axle w/8.8 Inch Ring Gear
		Ford 9.75 Inch Ring Gear w/Semi Floating Axle
Ranger	2005–06	Ford Integral Carrier Axle w/7.5 Inch Ring Gear
		Ford Integral Carrier Axle w/8.8 Inch Ring Gear
		Ford Integral Carrier Axle w/8.8 Inch Ring Gear High Torque

Dana/Spicer Front Drive Axles

INDEX

IDENTIFICATION

Refer to **Fig. 1** for axle identification number location and description.

DESCRIPTION

Model 30 & 35

The Dana models 30 and 35 are equipped with a hypoid design gearset that consists of a differential ring gear and a drive pinion gear. Two opposed pinion bearings support the drive pinion gear in the differential housing.

The differential case is a one piece design with two openings to allow for assembly of the internal components and lubricant flow. Two opposed differential bearings support the differential assembly in the differential housing. Removable differential bearing caps retain the differential assembly in the differential housing.

On these axles, the inboard front halfshaft joint is repairable. The side shaft assembly (interconnecting shaft and outboard CV joint) is not repairable, other than the boot. Install a new assembly if components are damaged or worn.

Models 50 & 60

The Dana models 50 and 60 are equipped with a hypoid gear design with the centerline of the pinion set below the centerline of the ring gear, a conventional differential case, full floating axle shafts, a cast center section with two steel tubes and a stamped axle housing cover.

DISASSEMBLE

Models 30 & 35

1. For front axle removal procedures refer to **MOTOR's "Domestic Transmission, In-Vehicle Service" or "Transmission Service DVD."**
2. Remove front axle dampener from axle to frame bracket, if equipped.
3. Mount axle assembly onto holding fixture tool No. 307-003 (T57L-500-B), or equivalent.
4. Place an approved drain pan under axle.
5. Remove differential housing cover bolts, then the cover, **Fig. 2.** Allow lubricant to drain.
6. Remove axle shafts as outlined in "Front Wheel Drive Axles" chapter.
7. Note all matched numbers or letters stamped on both differential bearing caps and differential housing. These must align during assembly.
8. Remove bearing cap bolts, then the caps.
9. Install housing spreader adapter tool No. 205-356, or equivalent with bolt threads engaged at least ½ inch.
10. Install differential carrier spreader tool No. 205-001, clutch housing gauge tool No. 308-021 and dial indicator gauge with holding fixture tool No. 100-002, or equivalent as illustrated in **Fig. 3.**
11. Spread differential housing to specification as follows:
    a. Adjust dial indicator to zero.
    b. Tighten spreader screw to spread differential housing to specification, **Fig. 4. Do not exceed .015 inch.**
    c. Remove dial indicator setup and clutch housing alignment adapter tool.
12. Remove differential assembly from axle housing as follows:
    a. Position suitable wooden blocks to avoid damaging axle housing.
    b. Carefully lever differential assembly upward using suitable pry bars.
    c. Remove differential assembly from axle housing.
13. Remove spreader tool.
14. Measure pinion bearing preload using a suitable inch lb. torque wrench. Record this measurement.
15. Mark alignment of pinion flange to pinion stem.
16. Remove flange nut while holding flange in place with fixture tool No. 205-126, or equivalent.
17. Hold pinion inside differential housing.
18. Remove pinion from differential housing using a soft-face hammer. Never use a metal hammer on pinion.
19. Remove pinion seal using seal remover tool No. 307-309, or equivalent and a suitable slide hammer.
20. Remove drive pinion shaft oil slinger and pinion bearing.
21. Remove outer and inner drive pinion bearing cups by tapping alternately on each side of cups to prevent them from cocking in bore.
22. Remove pinion bearing using bearing remover tool No. 205-055, or equivalent and a suitable press.
23. Remove pinion position shim from differential pinion gear. Measure pinion position shim thickness with a micrometer. Record this measurement.
24. Remove and discard differential ring gear mounting bolts.
25. Separate ring gear from differential

case using a suitable drift that will bottom out in the bolt holes.
26. Drive out pinion shaft roll pin.
27. Remove pinion shaft.
28. Rotate pinion gears to differential case window, then remove gears and pinion thrust washers. Avoid letting upper side gear fall out of case bore after removing pinion gears.
29. Remove differential side gears and thrust washers.
30. Assemble drive pinion/differential carrier tool No. 205-D036, or equivalent, then position it onto a differential bearing.
31. Remove bearing using tool No. 205-D036. Repeat procedure for opposite side.

Models 50 & 60

1. Remove front axle shaft assemblies as outlined under "Front Wheel Drive" in "Full Size Trucks & Vans" chapter.
2. Remove front axle assembly as outlined under "Front Wheel Drive" in "Full Size Trucks & Vans" chapter.
3. Remove differential housing cover and drain fluid into suitable container.
4. Clean gasket material from differential housing and cover.
5. Clean internal components and inspect for wear or damage.
6. Rotate gears and inspect for roughness.
7. Inspect teeth of ring gear for scoring, nicks, wear or chips.
8. Measure ring gear and pinion backlash at three equally spaced points with suitable dial indicator, **Fig. 5.**
9. Backlash tolerance must be between .005–.008 inch and cannot vary by more than .002 inch between points inspected.
10. Make corrections for high or low backlash during assembly by changing differential bearing selective shim thickness.
11. Stamp identifying markings on differential bearing caps and differential housing for installation reference. Remove bearing caps.
12. Spread differential housing .015 inch with differential carrier spreader No. 205-001, or equivalent, **Fig. 6.** Do not spread differential more than specified.
13. Remove differential with two pry bars using vehicle to avoid damaging ring gear and pinion.
14. Rotate pinion with an inch pound torque wrench, **Fig. 7.** Record torque required to maintain rotation of pinion through several revolutions.
15. Install drive pinion flange holding tool No. 205-012, or equivalent, **Fig. 8,** then remove and discard nut and washer.
16. Remove flange with removal tool No. 205-018, or equivalent, **Fig. 9.**
17. Tap pinion through outer bearing with soft faced hammer. Remove pinion through rear of differential housing.

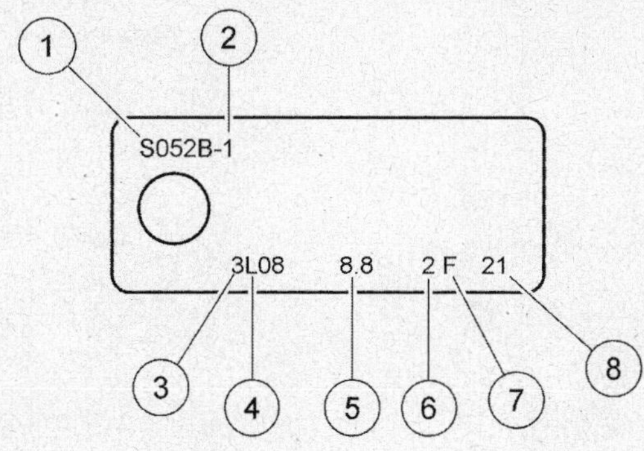

Item	Description
1	Plant code
2	Denotes interchangeability affected internally
3	Axle ratio
4	Denotes Traction-Lok®
5	Ring gear diameter (in)
6	Build year
7	Build month
8	Build day

LTV0500000000981

Fig. 1 Dana/Spicer front drive axle identification

18. Remove and discard pinion seal.
19. Remove oil slinger and differential pinion bearing.
20. Remove outer and inner pinion bearing cups and oil baffle.
21. Drive inner axle seals out of differential housing through axle tubes, discard seals.
22. **On model 60 axles,** remove and discard collapsible spacer.
23. **On all models,** remove differential pinion bearing with removal tool No. 205-D036, or equivalent, **Fig. 10.**
24. Remove drive pinion position shim. Discard shim if bent or nicked, measure shim thickness before discarding.
25. Thoroughly clean and inspect all components. Discard complete differential if wear is visible on all components.
26. Discard both differential pinion gears and both side gears if any one of these gears are worn or damaged.
27. Inspect flange lugs for damage. End of flange that contacts bearing cone as well as nut counterbore and seal contact area must be smooth and nick free.
28. Verify that differential and pinion bearing bores are smooth. Remove any nicks or burrs from mounting surfaces of differential housing.

SUBASSEMBLY SERVICE

Differential Case

MODELS 30 & 35

DISASSEMBLE

1. Place differential case in a suitable vise, then drive out lockpin that retains pinion mate shaft to case.
2. Remove pinion mate shaft using a suitable drift, then rotate pinion mate gears and side gears until pinion mate gears turn to opening of case.
3. Remove pinion mate gears and spherical washers behind gears, then lift out side gears and thrust washers.
4. Inspect all components and machined surfaces of case. **If excessive wear is visible on all components, it is suggested that complete differential case assembly be replaced. If any one gear is to be replaced, the gears must be replaced as a set.**

ASSEMBLE

1. Apply a suitable multi-purpose long life lubricant to side gear thrust washers, hub, thrust face of side gears, pinion mate gears and spherical washers.
2. Hold side gears in place in case, then install pinion mate gears and spherical washers.
3. Rotate side gears and pinion mate

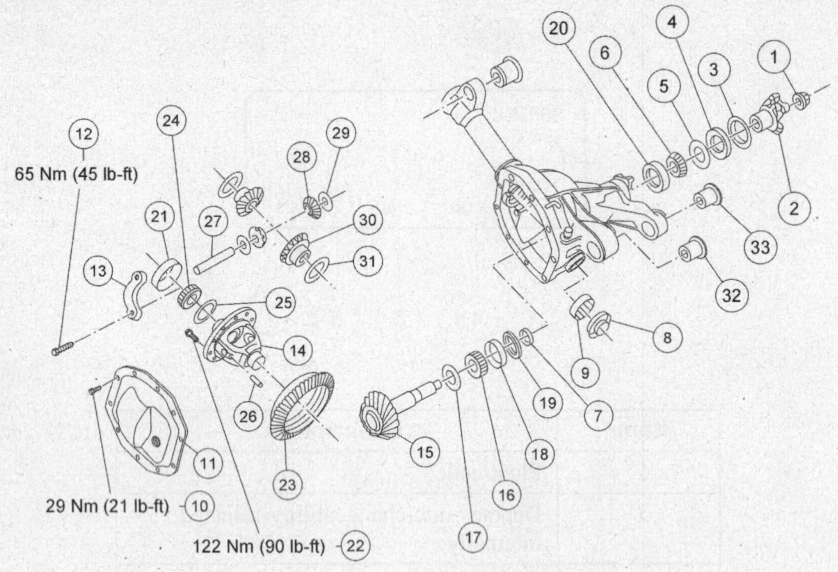

Item	Description
1	Pinion nut and washer
2	Pinion flange
3	Drive pinion oil seal deflector
4	Drive pinion oil seal
5	Drive pinion shaft oil slinger
6	Outer pinion bearing

Item	Description
7	Drive pinion collapsible spacer
8	Axle shaft oil seal (2 required)
9	Axle shaft bearing (2 required)
10	Differential cover bolts (10 required)

LTV0500000000982

Fig. 2 Exploded view of front axle (Part 1 of 2). Models 30 & 35

Item	Description
11	Differential cover
12	Differential bearing cap bolt (4 required)
13	Differential bearing cap
14	Differential case
15	Pinion gear
16	Inner pinion bearing
17	Drive pinion position shim
18	Inner pinion bearing cup
19	Oil baffle
20	Outer pinion bearing cup
21	Differential bearing cup (2 required)
22	Differential ring gear bolt (8 required)
23	Differential ring gear
24	Differential bearing (2 required)
25	Differential bearing shim
26	Differential pinion shaft roll pin
27	Differential pinion shaft
28	Differential pinion gear (2 required)
29	Differential pinion gear thrust washer (2 required)
30	Differential side gears (2 required)
31	Differential side gear thrust washer (2 required)
32	Axle insulator (2 required)
33	Axle insulator

LTV0500000000983

Fig. 2 Exploded view of front axle (Part 2 of 2). Models 30 & 35

gears until holes in washers and pinion mate gears align with holes in case.

4. Insert pinion mate shaft into case, ensuring lockpin hole in shaft aligns with lockpin holes in case.
5. Insert lockpin, then peen some metal of case over pin to lock it into place.

MODELS 50 & 60

DISASSEMBLE

1. Remove differential bearings and shims as follows:
   a. Place differential case in a vise with soft jaws.
   b. Remove differential bearing using pinion and carrier bearing puller tool No. D81L-4220-A, or equivalent, **Fig. 11.**
   c. Wire shims, bearing cone and cup together. Mark which side components are removed from for assembly.
   d. Repeat procedure on opposite side.
2. Remove ring gear as follows:
   a. Place differential case into a vise with soft jaws.
   b. Remove and discard all but four of retaining bolts. Leave four loosely assembled bolts spaced apart from each other.
   c. Tap each bolt head alternately with a soft faced hammer to loosen ring gear.
   d. Remove remaining ring gear bolts, then the ring gear.
3. Drive out differential pinion shaft lock pin using a small drift.
4. Remove differential pinion shaft.
5. Remove differential pinion gears and thrust washers and differential side gears and thrust washers.
6. Inspect components as follows:
   a. Replace complete differential if excessive wear is visible.
   b. Replace differential pinion and side gears as a set, if required.
   c. Ensure differential bearing bores are smooth.
   d. Remove any nicks or burrs from mounting surfaces of axle housing.

ASSEMBLE

1. Place differential case into a vise with soft jaws.
2. Apply high temperature 4×4 front axle and wheel bearing lubricant E8TZ-19590, or equivalent, meeting Ford specification ESA-M1C198-A to following components:
   a. Side gear thrust washers.
   b. Side gear hubs and thrust faces.
   c. Pinion thrust washers.
   d. Pinion gears.
3. Lubricate gears with premium rear axle lubricant part No. XY-80W90-QL, or an equivalent meeting Ford specification WSP-M2C197-A.
4. Install gears into differential case, noting the following:
   a. Install and hold side gears and thrust washers in case.
   b. Install pinion gears and thrust washers.
   c. Rotate gears until pinion shaft bore in case and gears align.
   d. If gears cannot be rotated by hand, install axle shaft into side gear and turn shaft with pipe wrench.
   e. Use a drift to align pinion shaft bores, if required.
5. Install differential pinion shaft. Ensure lock pin bore in case and pinion shaft are aligned.
6. Install differential pinion shaft lock pin, then peen case metal over lock pin in two places 90° from slot in lock pin.
7. Assemble ring gear to differential case, then alternately and evenly tighten bolts to specification.
8. Install differential bearings after calculating proper amount of differential bearing shims required. Refer to "Models 50 & 60" under "Disassemble."

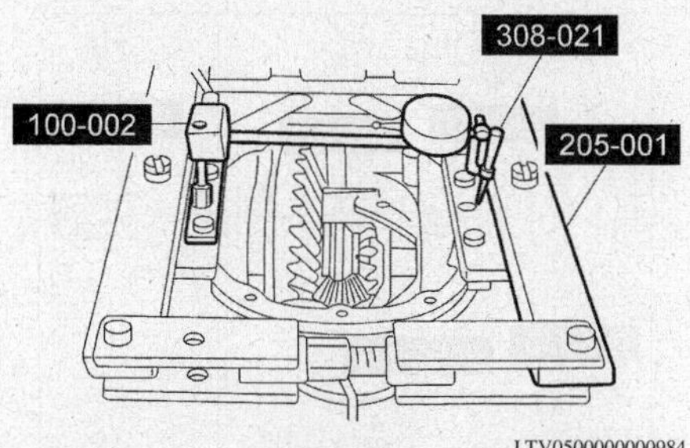

Fig. 3 Tool setup for spreading differential. Models 30 & 35

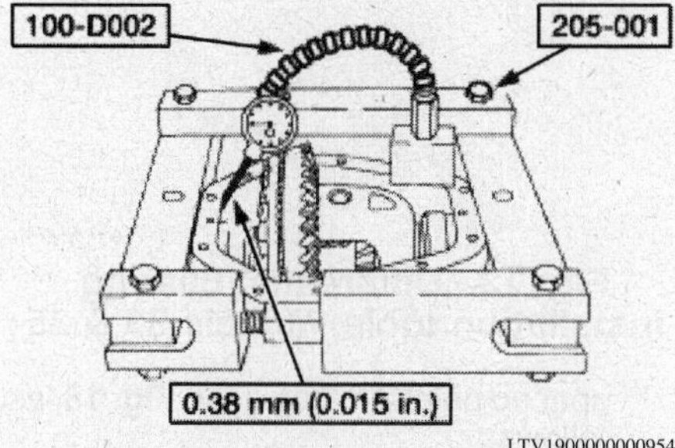

Fig. 6 Differential spreader installation. Models 50 & 60

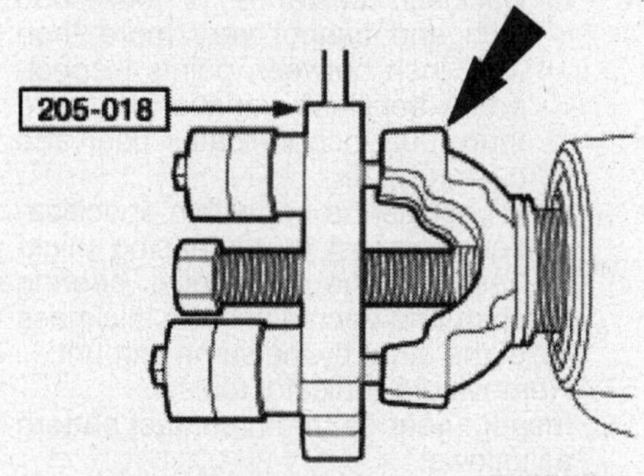

Fig. 9 Drive pinion flange removal tool. Models 50 & 60

ASSEMBLE

Models 30 & 35

1. Lubricate differential side gear thrust washers and gears with SAE 80W-90 premium axle lubricant part No. XY-80W90-QL, or an equivalent meeting Ford specification WSP-M2C197-A, then assemble them.
2. Position side gear and thrust washer assemblies in differential case.
3. Lubricate differential pinion thrust washers and pinion gears, then assemble them.
4. Engage pinion gears between side gears.
5. Rotate pinion gears and align them with pinion shaft bore.
6. Install differential pinion shaft and roll pin.
7. Always install new differential pinion bearings when installing new differential drive pinion bearing cups. Lubricate cups as required.

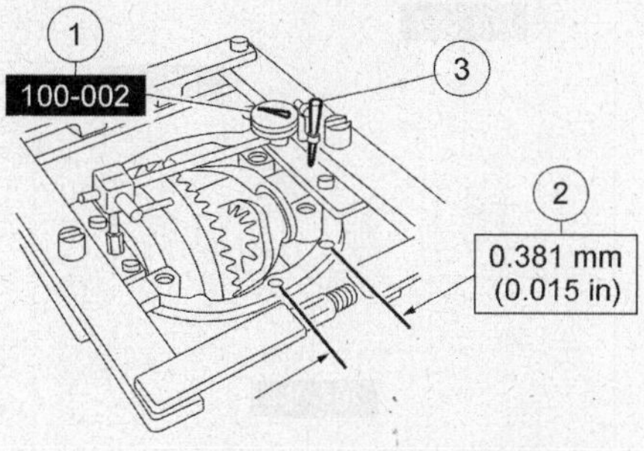

Fig. 4 Spreading differential. Models 30 & 35

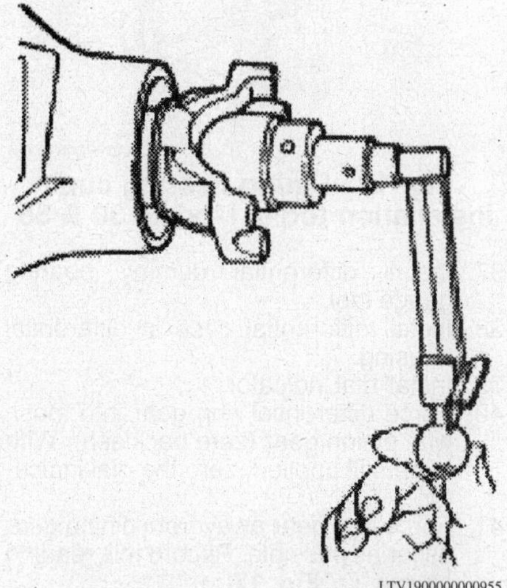

Fig. 7 Pinion bearing torque preload. Models 50 & 60

8. Install pinion bearing cups using installer tool Nos. 205-014, 205-054 and drawbar tool No. 205-098, or equivalents as illustrated, **Fig. 12.**
9. Spread a light film of axle lubricant on differential pinion bearings.
10. Assemble tools or their equivalents and components in differential housing in sequence illustrated, **Fig. 13:**
    a. Screw tool No. 205-109.
    b. Aligning adapter tool No. 205-093.
    c. Inner differential pinion bearing.
    d. Gauge disc tool No. 205-303.
    e. Gauge block tool No. 205-110.
    f. Outer differential pinion bearing.
    g. Handle tool No. 205-111 onto screw.
    h. **Torque** handle to 15–30 inch lbs.
11. Offset gauge block to obtain an accurate reading, then rotate several half turns to ensure differential pinion bearings seat properly and position gauge block as illustrated, **Fig. 14.**
12. Install gauge tube and paper shipping tags tool No. 205-D034, or equivalent as illustrated, **Fig. 15.**
13. Install differential bearing caps. **Torque** bolts to 45 ft. lbs.
14. Measure between gauge block and gauge tube using a feeler gauge, or a flat, clean drive pinion position shim.

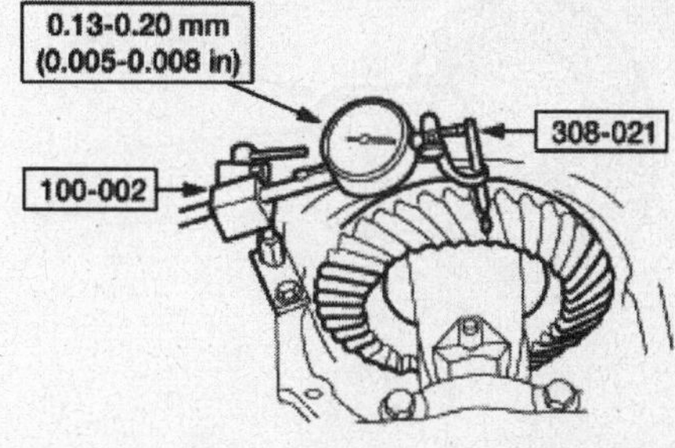

Fig. 5 Ring gear & pinion backlash measurement. Models 50 & 60

LTV1900000000956

Fig. 8 Drive pinion flange holding fixture. Models 50 & 60

LTV1900000000958

Fig. 10 Differential pinion bearing removal. Models 50 & 60

Record measurement. **Selecting a shim that is too thick results in deep tooth contact at final assembly. Do not attempt to force gauge or shim between gauge block and gauge tube. A slight drag indicates proper selection.**

15. Remove tools after determining proper shim thickness.
16. Select proper thickness drive pinion position shim, available in thicknesses of .030 inch to .052 inch in .002 increments. If installing a new gear set, observe plus (+), minus (–), or zero (0) etching on both original and new drive pinion, and adjust thickness of new shim as specified in, **Fig. 16.**
17. Install a new collapsible spacer.
18. Install differential pinion bearing and front drive pinion shaft oil slinger.
19. Install pinion seal using installer tool No. 205-133, or equivalent.
20. Lightly lubricate pinion gear splines.

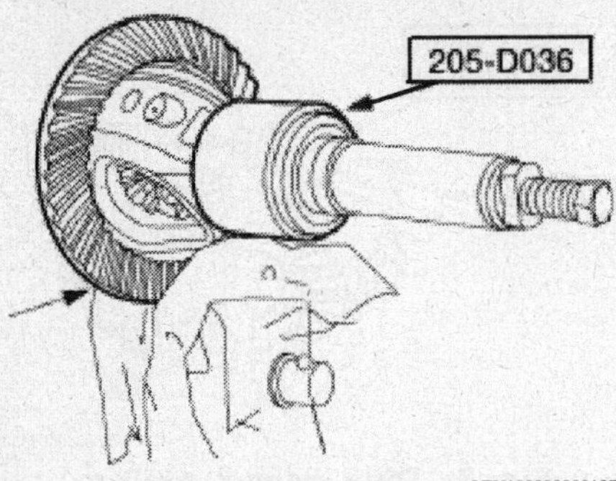

Fig. 11 Differential bearing removal tool. Models 50 & 60

21. Install pinion gear in differential housing.
22. Align index marks, then install pinion flange. Do not use a metal hammer or power tools. Use a plastic hammer to tap on a tight fitting flange.
23. Install new nut and hand tighten.
24. **Do not loosen the nut to reduce preload.** Install a new collapsible spacer and nut if preload reduction is required. Proceed as follows:
    a. Remove holding tool before taking differential pinion bearing preload reading, but use it to hold pinion flange while tightening nut to set preload.
    b. Rotate pinion occasionally to ensure differential pinion bearings are seating properly. Take frequent differential pinion bearing preload readings by rotating pinion with a suitable inch lb., torque wrench.
    c. If installing new differential pinion bearings, tighten nut to specifications.
    d. If installing original differential pinion bearings, final preload reading must be five inch lbs., greater than initial reading taken during disassembly.
25. Install differential dummy bearing gauge tool No. 205-247, or equivalent.
26. Install differential case in differential housing.
27. Force differential case as far as possible away from indicator.
28. Position dial indicator tool No. 100-002, or equivalent with indicator tip on machined surface and adjust it to measure full travel. With force still applied, set indicator to zero.
29. Force differential case as far as possible in opposite direction.
30. Record total end play reading on Line "A," **Fig. 17.**
31. Remove dial indicator.
32. Remove differential case.
33. Use a fine, flat file to remove any burrs and nicks from ring gear mounting surface.
34. Position ring gear and differential case. Start two or three new bolts to align holes in ring gear and case. **Do not use old bolts.**
35. Install ring gear using a suitable press.
36. Install remaining new bolts. Tighten to specifications.

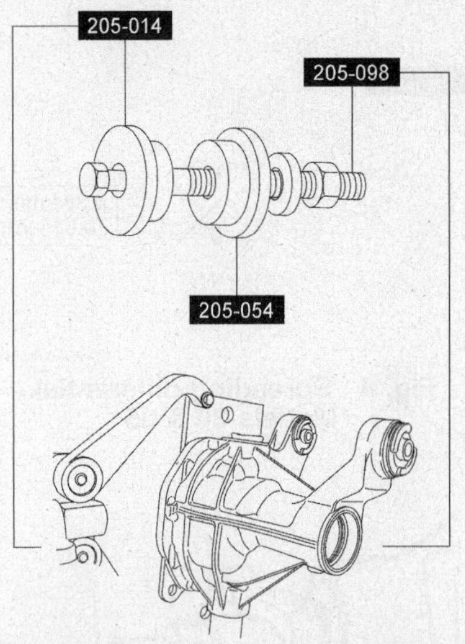

Fig. 12 Pinion bearing cup installation tools. Models 30 & 35

37. Install differential dummy bearing gauge tool.
38. Install differential case in differential housing.
39. Install dial indicator.
40. Force differential ring gear into mesh with pinion gear (zero backlash). With force still applied, zero the dial indicator.
41. Force ring gear away from pinion gear as far as possible. Record this reading on line "D," **Fig. 17.**
42. Remove dial indicator.
43. Remove differential case.
44. Remove differential dummy bearing gauge tool.
45. Fill in worksheet, then select proper differential shims, available in .003 inch, .005 inch, .010 inch and .030 inch thicknesses.
46. Install differential shims and bearings using a suitable press.
47. Install differential carrier spreader tool No. 205-001, clutch housing gauge tool No. 308-021 and dial indicator gauge with holding fixture tool No. 100-002, or equivalents as illustrated in, **Fig. 3.**
48. Tighten spreader screw to spread differential housing to specification, **Fig. 4. Do not exceed .015 inch.**
49. Remove dial indicator setup and clutch housing alignment adapter tool.
50. Push differential case downward to fully seat differential bearing cups in differential housing.
51. Position differential bearing cups on differential bearings.
52. Lower the differential case into place.
53. Install differential bearing caps in their original positions. Tighten bolts hand tight.
54. Remove remaining tools.
55. **Torque** bolts to 45 ft. lbs. Ensure differential case rotates freely.
56. Measure backlash at three equally

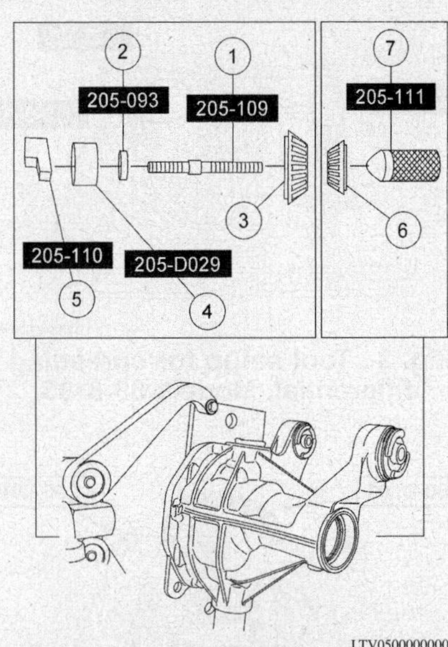

Fig. 13 Differential bearing installation tools. Models 30 & 35

spaced points on ring gear, **Fig. 18,** as follows:
    a. Rotate ring gear without turning pinion gear. Record this measurement.
    b. Backlash tolerance is .005–.008 inch and cannot vary more than .002 inch between points inspected. A backlash variation of more than .002 inch indicates gear and case runout.
    c. If backlash is not within specifications, correct by increasing thickness of one differential bearing shim and decreasing the thickness of the other by the same amount.
57. Remove dial indicator tools.
58. Inspect gear set tooth contact pattern as follows:
    a. Paint gear teeth with suitable gear marking compound. A mixture too wet will smear and run. A mixture too dry will not press out from between teeth.
    b. With a suitable box wrench levering on ring gear bolts, rotate ring gear several complete revolutions in both directions or until a clear tooth contact pattern appears.
    c. Certain gear tooth contact pattern types on ring gear indicate improper adjustment. This can be corrected by adjusting ring gear or pinion.
    d. Desirable ring gear tooth patterns must have a drive pattern on drive side ring gear well centered on tooth and a coast pattern on coast side ring gear well centered on tooth.
    e. There must be clearance between pattern and top of tooth and no hard lines where pressure is high.
    f. Contact pattern along length is indicated as toward heel or toe of differential ring gear, **Fig. 19.**
    g. Acceptable ring gear tooth patterns

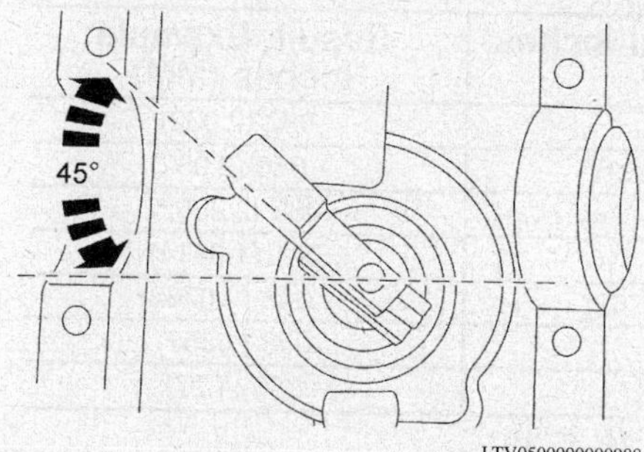

Fig. 14 Gauge block positioning. Models 30 & 35

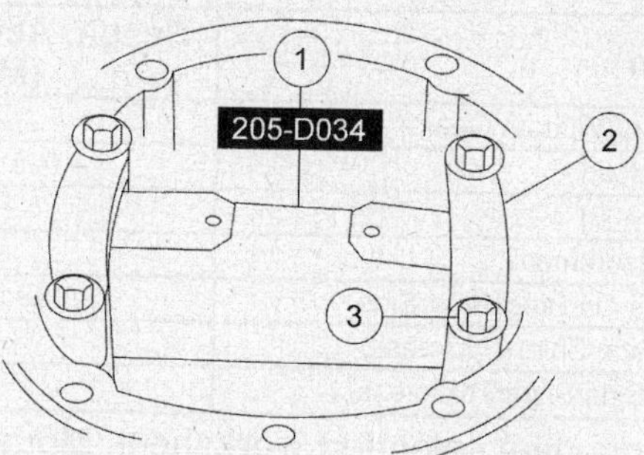

Fig. 15 Gauge tube installation

mm	inch
1.35	0.053
1.40	0.055
1.45	0.057
1.50	0.059
1.55	0.061
1.60	0.063
1.65	0.065
1.70	0.067
1.75	0.069
1.80	0.071
1.85	0.073

LTV0500000000990

Fig. 16 Shim thickness table. Models 30 & 35

for all axles are illustrated in, **Fig. 20.**

h. Pattern contacting more toward heel, **Fig. 21.**
i. , **Fig. 22.**
j. Pattern contacting more toward toe, **Fig. 23.**

59. Install axle shafts as outlined in "Front Drive Axles" chapter.
60. All machined mating surfaces of differential housing and housing cover must be clean and free of lubricant before applying new silicone sealant. Cover inside of differential housing before cleaning machined surface to prevent contamination.
61. Apply a continuous bead of clear silicone rubber sealant part No. D6AZ-19562-AA, or an equivalent meeting Ford specification ESB-M4G92-A to differential housing cover.
62. Install differential housing cover within 15 minutes of applying silicone or an application of new sealant will be required.
63. Install axle assembly as outlined under "Front Wheel Drive" in "Aviator, Explorer, Mountaineer & Ranger" chassis chapter.
64. Allow sealant one hour to cure before filling axle with lubricant.

Models 50 & 60

1. Coat seal axle tube mating surfaces with lubricant.
2. Place axle shaft oil seals onto installation tool, then position tool assembly into differential housing, **Fig. 24.** Lengthen tool as required until both seals start evenly in axle tubes.
3. Continue to lengthen tool until both step plates bottom out against housing.
4. Install dummy bearing set No. 205-D046 or 205-D047, or equivalents, then position differential assembly in housing.
5. Repeat the following procedure until there is a consistent reading:
   a. Determine total thickness of differential bearing shims to install on differential case hubs, less the preload. Record this measurement as total case end play.
   b. Install clutch housing gauge tool No. 308-021 and dial indicator gauge and holding tool No. 100-002, or equivalents, **Fig. 25.**
   c. Locate tip of dial indicator on flat surface of one of ring gear bolt spot faces.
   d. Force ring gear as far as possible toward dial indicator, then zero gauge.
   e. Force ring gear as far as it will go in other direction, then record reading.
6. Remove differential case with tool from differential housing. Do not remove tools from differential case hubs.
7. Install inner oil baffle and bearing cups with bearing cup tools No. 205-139 and 205-140 for Model 50 axles and tools No. 205-B006-B1 and 205-006-B2 for model 60 axles.
8. Install tool No. 205-098, or equivalent, to seat cups. Remove tool after seating.
9. If feeler gauge can fit between a cup and bottom of it's bore at any point around cup, remove and reseat cup.
10. Apply a light film of oil to pinion bearing before assembling tools, then position adapter tools as illustrated, **Figs. 26 and 27.**
11. **Torque** tool to 15–30 inch lbs., **Fig. 28.**
12. Rotate tool several turns to seat pinion bearings
13. Position tool as outlined, **Fig. 29,** then install bearing caps and bolts.
14. **Torque** bolts to 80 ft. lbs.
15. Measure and record gap between tools using feeler gauge or flat clean drive pinion position shims. Do not attempt to force gauge or shims between tools. A slight drag indicates a correct selection.
16. Remove tools after making shim selection.
17. Differential ring gear and pinion are only available as a matched set. Matching numbers on bottom of pinion and ring gear are used for verification.
18. Shim pinion gear as follows:
    a. If reusing old differential ring gear and pinion, measure and record old drive pinion position shim thickness and select a new shim of same dimension.
    b. If installing a new differential ring gear and pinion, adjust shim thickness to compensate for difference between two figures etched on both ends of pinions.
    c. For example: a pinion etched with m + 8 (+3) requires .003 inch less shimming than a pinion etched "0." To increase mounting distance by amount etched in pinion, subtract .003 inch from drive pinion shim selected for installation.
    d. A pinion etched m - 8 (-3), requires .003 inch more shimming than a pinion etched "0." Add .003 inch to drive pinion position shim selected for installation to decrease pinion mounting distance by amount etched in pinion.
    e. Refer to **Fig. 30** for pinion marking cross referencing.
    f. Install correct thickness shim on pinion.
19. Install differential pinion bearing with installation tool No. 205-004 or 205-092, or equivalents, and a suitable press.
20. **On model 50 axles,** position a new collapsible spacer inside differential housing before installing pinion bearing and oil slinger.
21. **On all models,** install differential pinion bearing and oil slinger.
22. Lightly coat pinion seal lip with lubricant, then install pinion oil seal with suitable seal driver.
23. **On model 60 axles,** install new collapsible collar, **Fig. 31.**
24. **On all models,** insert pinion into differential housing and seat inner bearing into bearing cup.
25. Lightly coat flange splines and seal mating area with lubricant, then install flange with new washer and nut ensuring alignment marks made previously are matched.
26. Use drive pinion flange holding tool No. 205-012, or equivalent, to prevent flange from turning while tightening nut.
27. Rotate pinion occasionally to ensure bearings are seating correctly.
28. Never back off pinion nut to reduce preload. If preload reduction is required, install a new collapsible spacer and pinion nut.
29. Take frequent pinion bearing torque preload readings.
30. If installing a new differential pinion bearing, tighten pinion nut to a rotating torque of 15–30 inch lbs.

Line	Item	Result, Actual Inches (MM)	Result, Example Inches (MM)
A	Total Endplay Reading (Without Gears)	—	.080 (2.032)
B	Add Preload	+.008 (.2032)	+.080 (2.032)
C	Total (A + B)	—	.088 (2.2352)
D	Endplay Measurement	—	.041 (1.0414)
E	Subtract Shim Thickness On Ring Gear Side	–.003 (–.0762)	–.003 (–.0762)
F	Total D–E (Ring Gear Side Shim Thickness)	—	.038 (.9652)
G	Total F–C (Drive Pinion Side Shim Thickness)	—	.050 (1.27)

Fig. 17 Differential bearing shim selection worksheet. Models 30 & 35

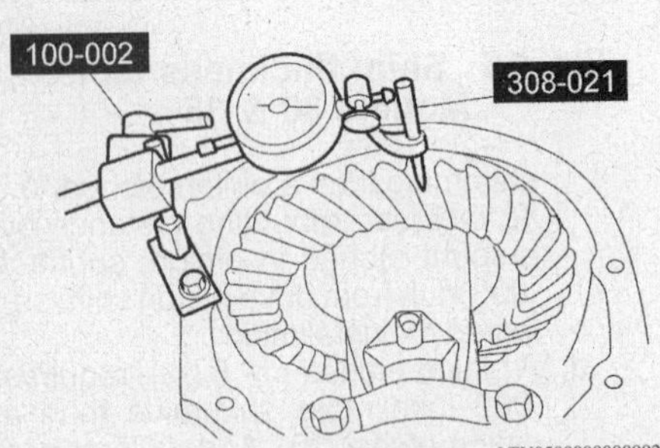

Fig. 18 Ring gear backlash measurement. Models 30 & 35

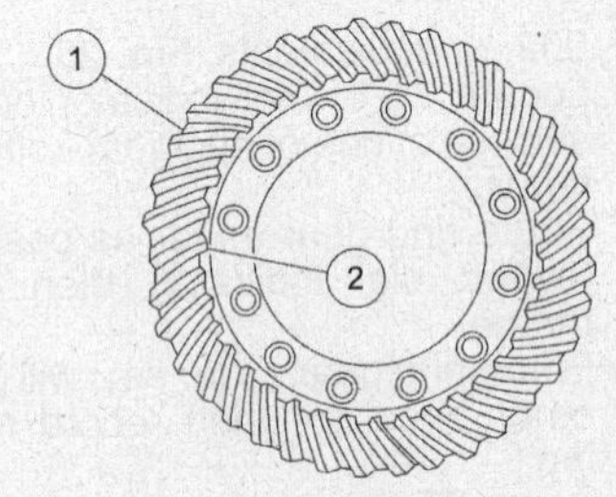

Item	Description
1	Heel
2	Toe

LTV0500000000997

Fig. 19 Ring gear heel & toe locations. Models 30 & 35

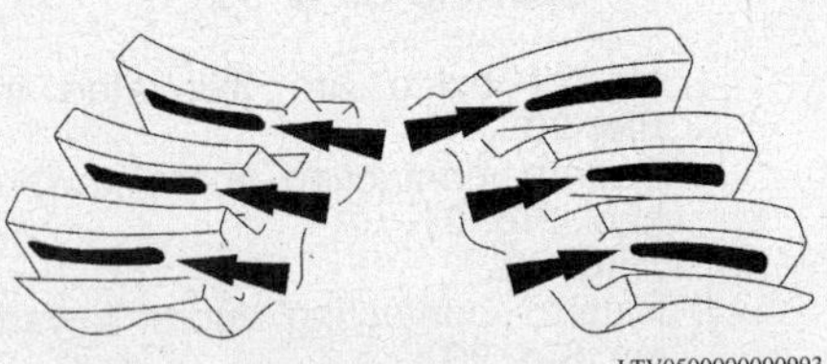

Fig. 20 Acceptable ring gear tooth patterns. Models 30 & 35

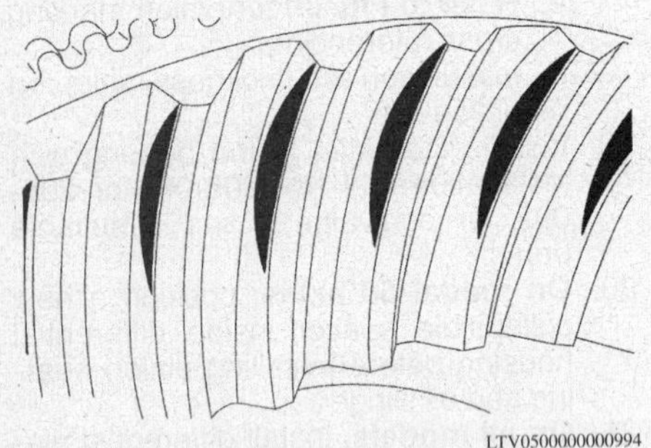

Fig. 21 Pattern contacting more toward heel. Models 30 & 35

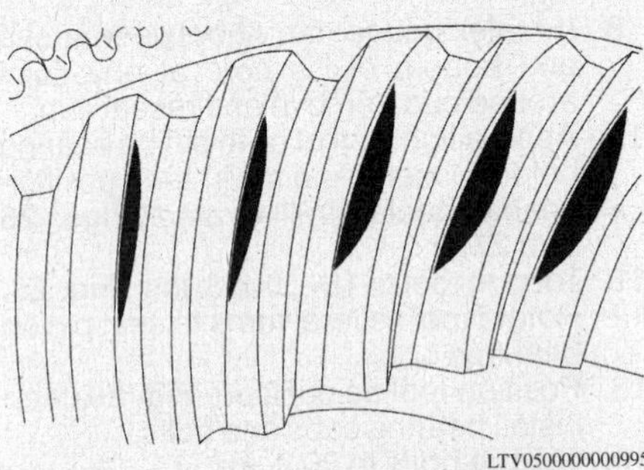

Fig. 22 Pattern contacting in center of tooth. Models 30 & 35

Fig. 23 Pattern contacting more toward toe. Models 30 & 35

31. If installing original pinion bearings, the final reading must be 5 inch lbs., more than the initial reading taken during disassembly.
32. Position differential case in differential housing with tool No. 205-D046 for model 50 axles and tool No. 205-D047 for model 60 axles.
33. Determine total thickness of differential bearing shims to install under ring gear side of differential case. Record this measurement, as the shims thickness required for ring gear side of differential case.
34. Position dial indicator and mounting tools as illustrated, **Figs. 32 and 33.**
35. Rock ring gear to allow teeth of gears to mesh.
36. With pressure still applied, zero the dial indicator.
37. Force ring gear away from pinion, record reading.
38. Remove differential case from housing, then remove tools.
39. Place required thickness of differential bearing shims on ring side gear of case. For example, if a reading of .045 inch was recorded previously, install .045 inch shims on ring gear side of differential case.
40. Install differential bearing, **Fig. 34.**
41. Subtract shim thickness measurement recorded for ring gear side of differential case from total case end play measurement taken at beginning of assembly procedure. Then add .015 inch to total. This is the total amount of differential bearing shims to install under differential bearing on drive pinion side of differential case.
42. Place differential shims on drive pinion side of differential case, then install bearing.
43. Position differential bearing cups on bearings.
44. Spread differential case .015 inch with spreader tool No. 205-001, or equivalent, **Fig. 6.**
45. Seat differential into housing with soft faced hammer, then remove special tools.
46. Match positioning letters on differential bearing caps, then install caps.
47. Measure backlash at three equally spaced points.
48. Adjust backlash, **Fig. 5,** by moving shims from one side of differential case to other.
49. Correct for high backlash by moving ring gear toward pinion, correct for low backlash by moving ring gear away from pinion.
50. Backlash must be .005–.008 inch and the three measurements cannot vary by more than .002 inch. Backlash variation of more than .002 inch, indicates gear/case runout.
51. Inspect gear tooth contact
52. Apply a ⅛ to ¼ inch bead of silicone sealer to differential housing sealing area.
53. Install differential cover within 15 minutes of applying sealant
54. Install differential housing cover bolts and **torque** to 35 ft. lbs.

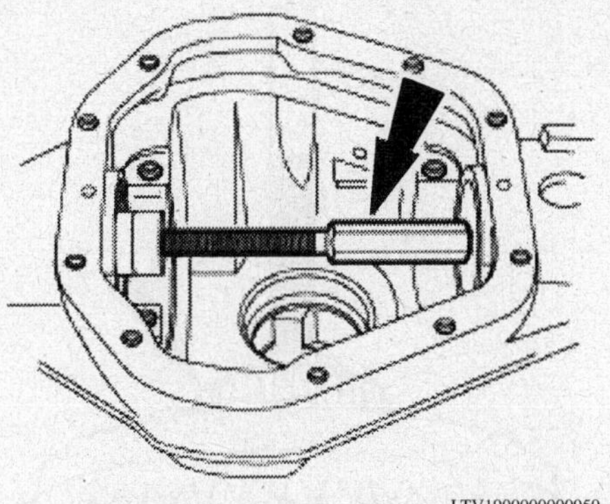

LTV1900000000959

Fig. 24 Axle shaft oil seal installation. Models 50 & 60

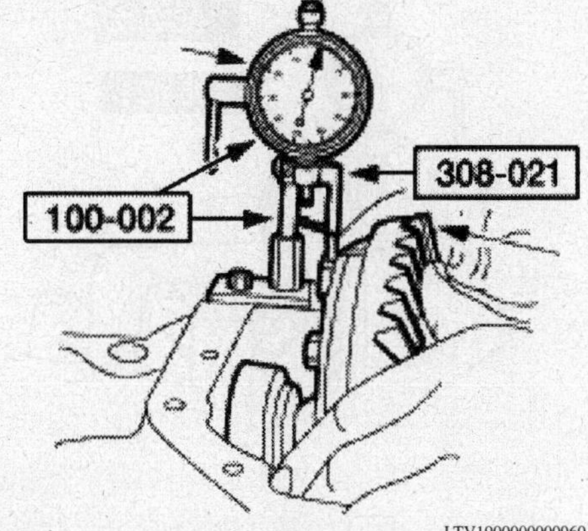

LTV1900000000960

Fig. 25 Dial indicator installation. Models 50 & 60

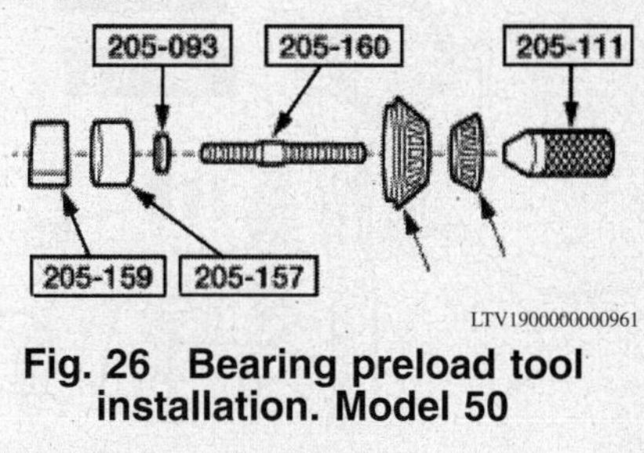

LTV1900000000961

Fig. 26 Bearing preload tool installation. Model 50

Model 60

205-105 205-160 205-111

205-159 205-125

LTV1900000001362

Fig. 27 Bearing preload tool installation. Model 60

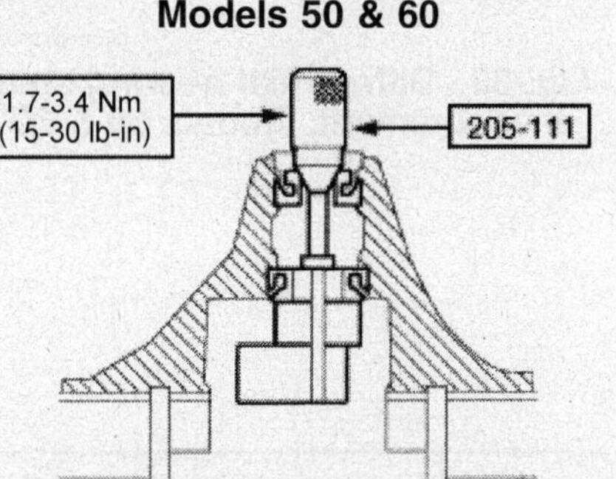

LTV1900000001363

Fig. 28 Bearing preload tool torque in place. Models 50 & 60

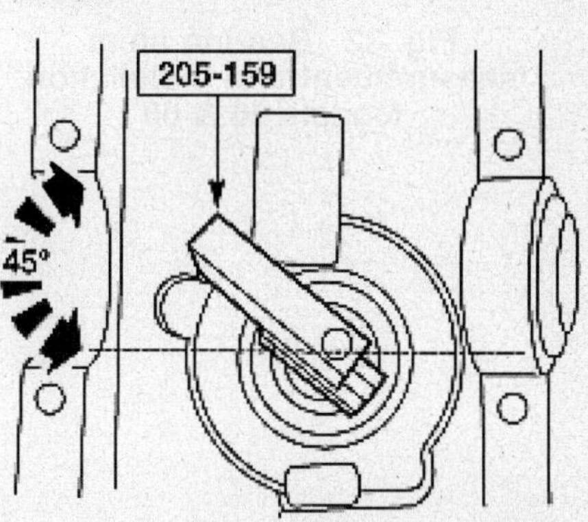

LTV1900000001364

Fig. 29 Tool orientation. Models 50 & 60

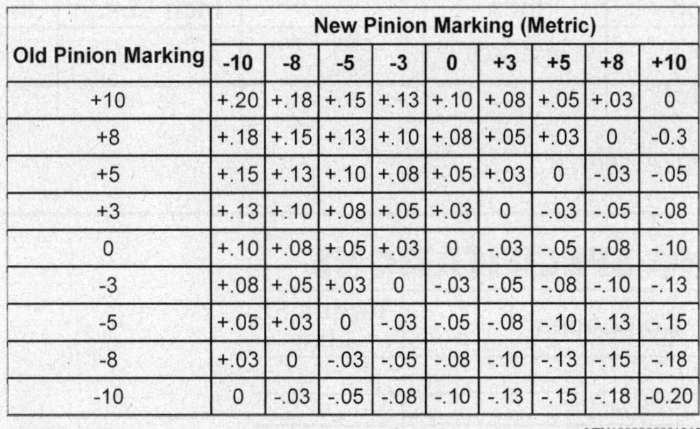

Old Pinion Marking	New Pinion Marking (Metric)								
	-10	-8	-5	-3	0	+3	+5	+8	+10
+10	+.20	+.18	+.15	+.13	+.10	+.08	+.05	+.03	0
+8	+.18	+.15	+.13	+.10	+.08	+.05	+.03	0	-0.3
+5	+.15	+.13	+.10	+.08	+.05	+.03	0	-.03	-.05
+3	+.13	+.10	+.08	+.05	+.03	0	-.03	-.05	-.08
0	+.10	+.08	+.05	+.03	0	-.03	-.05	-.08	-.10
-3	+.08	+.05	+.03	0	-.03	-.05	-.08	-.10	-.13
-5	+.05	+.03	0	-.03	-.05	-.08	-.10	-.13	-.15
-8	+.03	0	-.03	-.05	-.08	-.10	-.13	-.15	-.18
-10	0	-.03	-.05	-.08	-.10	-.13	-.15	-.18	-0.20

LTV1900000001365

Fig. 30 Pinion marking cross reference. Models 50 & 60

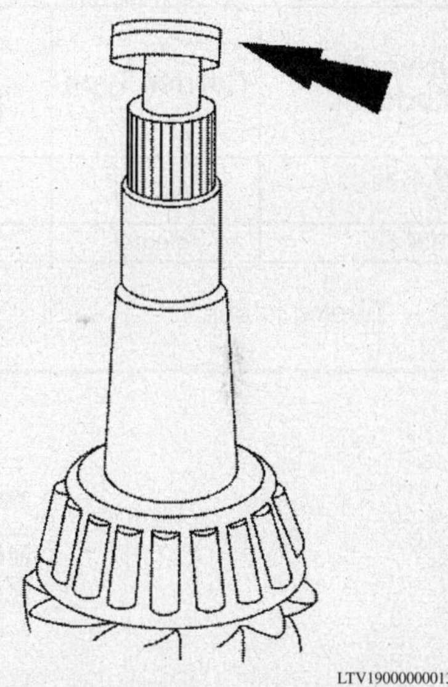

LTV1900000001366

Fig. 31 Collapsible spacer installation. Model 60 axles

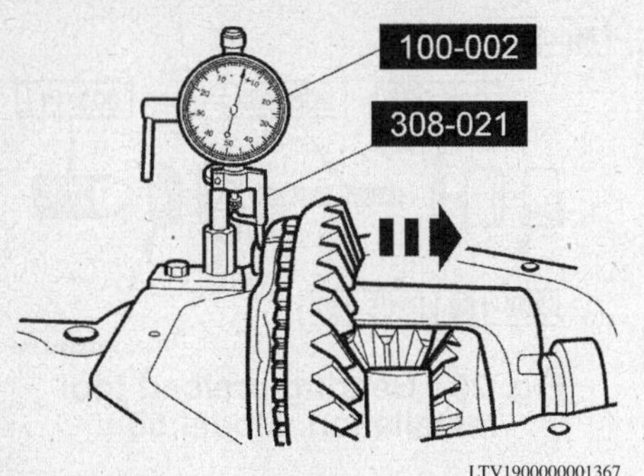

Fig. 32 Bearing shim measurement tool installation. Models 50 & 60

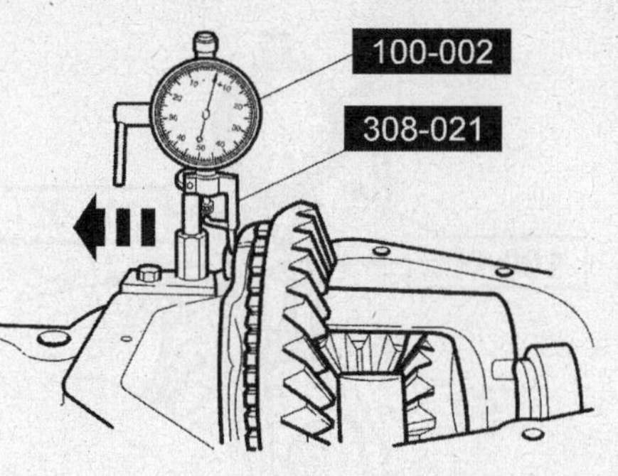

Fig. 33 Differential bearing shim measurement. Models 50 & 60

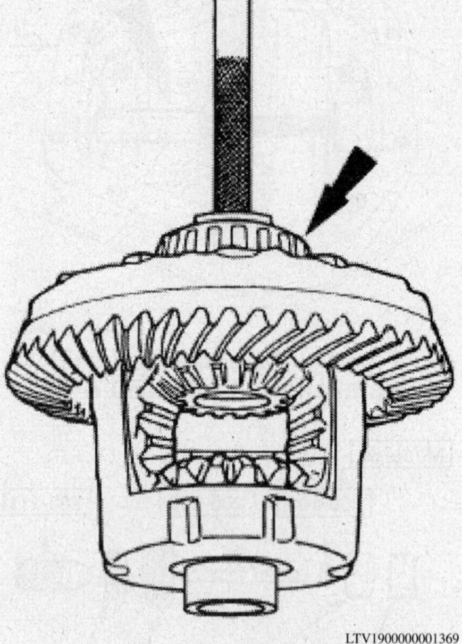

Fig. 34 Differential bearing installation. Models 50 & 60

DRIVE AXLE SPECIFICATIONS

Drive Axle Model	Carrier Type	Ring Gear & Pinion Backlash			Pinion Bearing Preload		
		Method	New Bearings, Inch	Used Bearings, Inch	Method	New Bearings, Inch Lbs.①	Used Bearings, Inch Lbs.①
30 & 35	Integral	Shims	②	.005–.008	Collapsible Spacer	15–30②	15–35②
50 & 60	Integral	Shims	②	—	Shims	15–30	—

① — Turning torque. ② — Refer to "Assemble."

TIGHTENING SPECIFICATIONS

Year	Component	Torque Ft. Lbs.
MODELS 30 & 35		
2002–03	Cover Bolts	16
	Differential Bearing Cap Bolts	45
	Ring Gear Bolts	80
	U-Joint Retainer To Flange Bolt	14
MODEL 35-IS		
2002–06	Differential Bearing Cap Bolts	47–67
	Differential To Axle Arm Bolts	35–53
	Pinion Shaft Nut	200–350
	Ring Gear Bolts	70–90
	Yoke Nut	200–350
MODELS 50 & 60		
2002–06	Axle Housing Cover	35
	Bearing Cap Bolts	80
	Pinion Nut	160–500
	Ring Gear Bolts (Model 50)	101
	Ring Gear Bolts (Model 60)	135

Ford Front Drive Axles

NOTE: Prior To Performing Any Service Operations Listed In This Section, Consult The "Technical Service Bulletins" Section For Related Information.

INDEX

IDENTIFICATION

Refer to **Fig. 1** for axle identification number location and description.

DESCRIPTION

The front axle, **Figs. 2 and 3,** is an integral type housing, hypoid gear design with the centerline of the pinion set above the centerline of the ring gear. The hypoid gear set consists of a ring gear and an overhung drive pinion supported by two opposed tapered roller bearings. Pinion bearing preload is maintained by the differential drive pinion collapsible spacer on the drive pinion shaft and adjusted by the pinion nut.

The rear axle consists of a cast aluminum differential and axle housing, with a cast aluminum cover. An extension tube is bolted to the righthand side of the axle housing to allow offset mounting of the differential and still allow the use of equal length driveshafts.

An electronically controlled, vacuum operated, dog type axle disconnect is mounted in a cast in housing on the righthand side of the differential housing. This allows the differential to be disconnected from the front wheels during 2WD operation without the need of gear type locking hubs.

DISASSEMBLE

It is recommended that the ring gear backlash, endplay and runout be measured and recorded prior to disassembly, to be used as aids during assembly procedures.

Refer to exploded views of front drive axle, **Figs. 2 and 3,** during the following procedures.

1. With axle removed and drained, remove differential cover.
2. Mount axle in overhaul fixture tool No. T57L-500-B, or equivalent. **Ensure sufficient thread engagement of bolts into aluminum case to prevent case damage.**
3. Pull back boot on axle disconnect vacuum motor. Remove snap ring then the vacuum motor from the actuator arm and case.
4. Remove righthand axle extension and disconnect as follows:
   a. Remove retaining bolts of righthand axle extension, then the extension.
   b. Remove thrust washer, then lift out cluster gear.
   c. Rotate axle disconnect actuator arm to lift shift collar up, then remove collar from shift fork.
   d. Use a suitable pin punch to drive out shift fork roll pin, then pull lever and shaft from case and remove shift fork.
5. Rotate differential carrier case to expose lefthand axle snap ring, then remove snap ring and pull axle from case.
6. Install case spreader adapters tool Nos. T93P-4000-A (righthand) and T96T-4000-A (lefthand), or equivalents to case. **Ensure sufficient thread engagement of bolts into aluminum case to prevent case damage.**
7. Attach case spreader tool No. T4000-E, or equivalent to adapters, then install a suitable dial gauge with brackets to spreader, **Fig. 4.**
8. Spread case with spreader tool .030 inch, then remove dial gauge set.
9. Place match marks on differential bearing caps, then remove the caps.
10. Insert suitable pry bars into differential case, then, prying against spreader tool only, lift differential from case, **Fig. 5.**
11. Place match marks on pinion driveshaft flange and pinion shaft for later assembly alignment.
12. Install counterhold handle tool No. T78P-4851-A, or equivalent to flange, then, while holding flange to prevent rotation, loosen pinion nut, but do not remove it.
13. Remove counterhold handle then, using puller tool No. D80L-1002-L, or equivalent, pull flange loose from shaft.
14. Remove puller tool, then the pinion nut and flange from pinion shaft.
15. Tap pinion shaft from case using a suitable soft face hammer while supporting pinion gear inside case.
16. Pry differential seals from case using caution not to damage aluminum case.
17. Remove inner bearing race from case using slide hammer of blind hole puller set tool No. D80L-100-A with bearing cup puller tool No. T77F-1102-A, or equivalents. **The lubrication baffle behind pinion bearing race is not normally removed. If removal is required, tap from case using a suitable punch.**
18. Remove outer pinion bearing from case using a suitable drift punch.
19. Place differential carrier into a suitable soft jaw vise, or equivalent holding fixture, then remove bolts retaining ring gear to carrier.
20. Tap ring gear from carrier using a suitable drift punch that will bottom in bolt holes of ring gear.
21. Remove bearing from pinion shaft using puller set tool No. D81L-4220-A, or equivalents. Measure and record thickness of pinion bearing shim for later assembly reference.
22. Remove side bearings from differential carrier using puller set tool No. D81L-4220-A, or equivalents.

SUBASSEMBLY SERVICE

Differential Carrier

DISASSEMBLE

1. Remove pinion shaft lock bolt, then pinion shaft from differential case. Discard lock bolt.
2. Rotate pinion gears to opening in differential carrier, then remove gears and thrust washers.
3. Lift out differential side gears and thrust washers.
4. Inspect components for chips, scratches, galling, cracks or wear. Repair or replace as required.

ASSEMBLE

During assembly procedures lubricate all components with a suitable differential fluid. Refer to "Specifications" for fluid type.

1. Insert differential side gear thrust washers, then side gears into carrier.

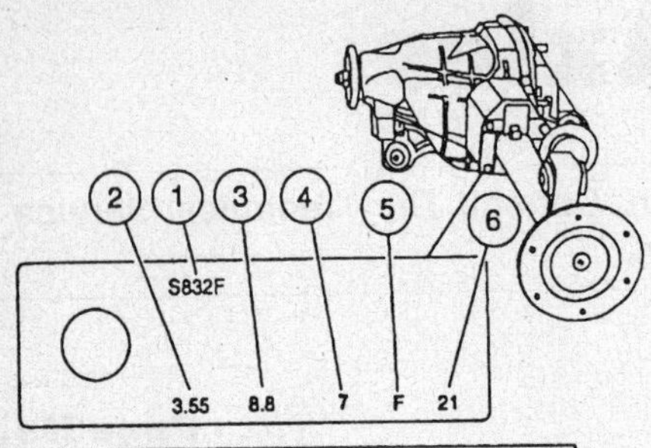

Item	Description
1	Plant Code
2	Axle Ratio
3	Ring Gear Diameter
4	Build Year
5	Build Month
6	Build Day

FM3039700286000X

Fig. 1 Front axle identification

2. Insert differential pinion gears with thrust washers into carrier, then rotate into position.
3. Align pinion gears and thrust washers with pinion gear shaft hole, then insert pinion gear shaft.
4. Install new pinion gear shaft lock bolt, then tighten to specification.

Righthand Axle Extension & Disconnect

DISASSEMBLE

1. Position axle extension tube in a suitable holding fixture, then remove disconnect clutch gear snap ring and gear from axle shaft. Discard snap ring.
2. Remove clutch gear thrust washers from extension tube. Note position of thrust washers.
3. Pull axle shaft from extension tube, then using suitable pry tools, remove axle seal from housing.
4. Inspect condition of dust shield on axle shaft, if damaged pry loose from shaft, using caution not to damage bearing or seal surfaces of shaft.
5. Remove needle bearings from tube using slide hammer of blind hole puller set tool No. D80L-100-A with bearing cup puller tool No T77F-1102-A, or equivalents.
6. Remove axle housing vent tube assembly, then clean sealing compound from all surfaces.
7. Pull pilot bearing from axle cluster gear shaft using blind hole puller set tool No. D80L-100-A, or equivalent.
8. Inspect components for chips, scratches, galling, cracks or wear. Repair or replace as required.

ASSEMBLE

1. Install axle shaft dust shield using press tool No. T96T-3A379-A, or equivalent.
2. Drive inner, then outer axle bearings into extension tube using properly sized end of needle bearing replacing mandrel tool No. T96T-1244-A, or equivalent. Tool will bottom on housing when bearing is properly positioned
3. Drive axle seal into extension tube until flush using seal driver tool No. T96T-1102-A, or equivalent.
4. Insert axle into extension housing, then position clutch gear thrust washers and clutch gear onto axle shaft and install new snap ring.
5. Install vent tube assembly into extension housing, tighten to specifications.
6. Insert bearing into axle cluster gear shaft using pilot bearing driver tool No. T96T-3N106-A, or equivalent.

Item	Description
1	LH Front Axle Shaft
2	Snap Ring
3	Front Axle Differential and Carrier Assembly
4	Bushing (2 Req'd)
5	Fill Plug
6	Front Axle Housing Cover
7	Front Axle Housing Cover Bolts (10 Req'd)
8	Drain Plug (With Magnet)
9	Gasket (Silicone)
10	Front Axle Actuator Motor Assembly
11	RH Front Axle Shaft
12	Front Axle Shaft Dust Deflector
13	Front Axle Shaft Dust Seal
14	Axle Shaft Bearing Assembly (Outer)
15	RH Front Axle Housing Tube
16	Front Axle Housing Vent
17	RH Front Axle Housing Tube to Differential Bolts (4 Req'd)
18	Front Axle Ratio Tag
19	Axle Shaft Bearing Assembly (Inner)
20	Thrust Washers (3 Req'd)
21	Front Axle Cluster Gear
22	E-Ring
23	Clutch Shaft Rod Boot
24	Manual Shaft Retaining Pin
25	Front Axle Shaft Shift Lever

FM3039700287000X

Fig. 2 Exploded view of front drive disconnect for 8.8 inch ring gear drive axle

ASSEMBLE

Bearings to be used in final assembly must be used for measurement procedures. Mark and maintain bearing installed position during adjustment and assembly procedures.

1. If pinion bearing lubrication baffle was removed, tap new baffle into position.
2. Pull new pinion bearing outer races into case using bearing race inserting set tool No. T67P-4616-A, or equivalent.
3. Lightly lubricate bearing races prior to performing measurements.
4. Assemble pinion depth gauge set tool No. T96P-4020-A, or equivalent, into case as illustrated in **Figs. 6 through 8.** Place paper shipping tags, or equivalent between mandrel and bearing caps before tightening to specifications as illustrated in **Fig. 8.**
5. Measure clearance between gauge block and mandrel using pinion bearing shims. Shims must be clean and flat.
6. Place shim selected for zero clearance aside for pinion shaft assembly.
7. Remove pinion depth gauge set from housing.
8. Place selected shim onto pinion shaft, then press inner pinion bearing onto shaft using bearing replacer tool No.

T53T-4621-C, or equivalent.

9. Install new collapsible spacer onto pinion shaft.
10. Install pinion shaft outer bearing and oil slinger into case, then drive new seal into case using driver tool No. T79P-4676-A, or equivalent.
11. Lubricate all components, then install pinion shaft into case.
12. Install driveshaft flange to pinion shaft, if reusing old pinion and flange, align match marks made on disassembly.
13. Install pinion nut and washer to pinion shaft, then counterhold bar tool No. T78P-4851-A, or equivalent to driveshaft flange. **Do not use air tools or allow shaft to turn while tightening. If pinion nut must be loosened, a new collapsible sleeve must be installed.**
14. Without loosening pinion nut, **torque** in several steps to 217 ft. lbs. Measure at each step to ensure a turning torque of 16–29 inch lbs.
15. Install master bearings tool Nos. T93P-4222-A (lefthand) and T93P-4222-B (righthand), or equivalents to differential carrier on righthand and lefthand sides as marked.
16. Install carrier with master bearings into case. **Do not install bearing caps.**
17. Install a suitable dial indicator with brackets positioned to allow measurement of total side play, **Fig. 9.**
18. Measure then record total side play measurement as Line "A," then remove dial indicator and carrier from case and master bearings from carrier.
19. Place ring gear into position on carrier, loosely install three bolts to act as guides during press operation, then supporting ring gear, press carrier into position.
20. Tighten ring gear retaining bolts to specifications, then remove three adjacent bolts.
21. Install master bearings to differential carrier to righthand and lefthand sides as marked, then carrier into case with area of three removed bolts down. **Do not install bearing caps.**
22. Install a suitable dial indicator with brackets, positioned to measure side play.
23. Fully engage ring gear into pinion gear (zero clearance) using a rocking and pushing motion, then zero the dial indicator.
24. Pull ring gear as far as possible away from pinion gear, record this measurement as Line "B," then remove dial indicator and carrier from case and master bearings from carrier.
25. Subtract Line "A" from Line "B" and record difference as Line "C."
26. Install base of bearing preload measurement set tool T93P-4220-A, or equivalent into a suitable vise, then the bearing marked to be lefthand carrier bearing into tool.
27. Measure total bearing thickness using a suitable depth gauge, record this as Line "D" lefthand bearing height.
28. Repeat procedure with righthand carrier bearing, record result as Line "D" Righthand Bearing Height.

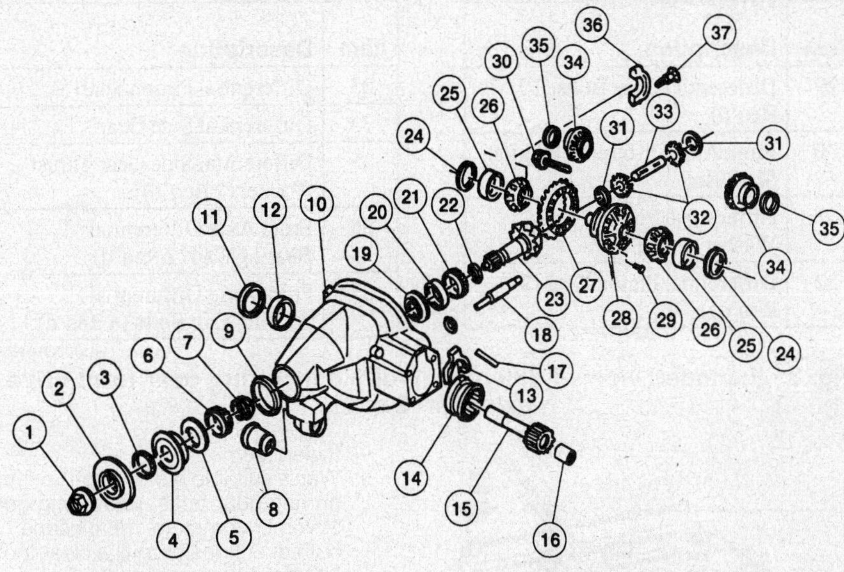

Item	Description
1	Pinion Nut
2	Axle Companion Flange
3	Drive Pinion Oil Seal Deflector
4	Front Drive Axle Pinion Oil Seal
5	Slinger
6	Differential Pinion Bearing
7	Differential Drive Pinion Collapsible Spacer
8	Bushing
9	Differential Drive Pinion Bearing Cup
10	Front Axle Differential 8.8 Carrier
11	Driveshaft Inner Dust Seal
12	Front Axle Shaft Bearing Assembly
13	Front Drive Axle Shift Fork
14	Coupler Cluster Gear
15	Front Axle Cluster Gear Shaft

Item	Description
16	Front Axle Shaft Pilot Bearing Assembly
17	Manual Shaft Retaining Pin
18	Front Drive Axle Shaft Shift Lever Shaft
19	Front Axle Pinion Bearing Oil Baffle
20	Axle Pinion Bearing Cup
21	Differential Pinion Bearing
22	Drive Pinion Bearing Adjustment Shim
23	Front Drive Axle Pinion Gear
24	Differential Bearing Shim (2 Req'd)
25	Differential Bearing Cup (2 Req'd)
26	Differential Bearing (2 Req'd)
27	Front Drive Axle Ring Gear
28	Differential Case

FM3039700288010X

Fig. 3 Exploded view of differential for 8.8 inch ring gear front drive axle (Part 1 of 2)

29. Subtract lefthand bearing height from the master bearing thickness of .8695 inch and record result as Line "E" (lefthand).
30. Repeat procedure for righthand bearing and record result as Line "E" (righthand).
31. To select lefthand side carrier bearing shim, proceed as follows:
    a. Add figure recorded as Line "B" to figure recorded as Line "E" (lefthand) and record result.
    b. From result, subtract backlash standard dimension of .0060 inch and record result as Initial Shim Size (lefthand).
    c. From shim selection table, **Fig. 10,** select a shim and round off as required.
    d. Mark shim as Final Shim (lefthand) and place aside.
32. To select righthand carrier bearing shim, proceed as follows:
    a. Add figure recorded as Line "C" to figure recorded as Line "E" (righthand) and record result.
    b. Add backlash/preload standard figure of .020 inch to result and record result as Initial Shim Size (righthand).
    c. From shim selection table, **Fig. 10,** select a shim and round off as required.
    d. Mark shim as Final Shim (righthand) and place aside.
33. Remove dial indicator, then differential carrier from case.
34. Remove master bearings from differential carrier, then install three removed ring gear bolts and tighten to specification.
35. Press bearings as marked onto lefthand and righthand sides of carrier using suitable press tool.

Item	Description
29	Differential Case Bolts (10 Req'd)
30	Front Axle Differential Pinion Shaft Bolt
31	Differential Pinion Thrust Washer (2 Req'd)
32	Differential Pinion Gear (2 Req'd)

Item	Description
33	Differential Pinion Shaft
34	Differential Side Gear
35	Differential Side Gear Thrust Washer (2 Req'd)
36	Front Axle Differential Bearing Cap (2 Req'd)
37	Front Axle Differential Bearing Cap Bolts (4 Req'd)

FM3039700288020X

Fig. 3 Exploded view of differential for 8.8 inch ring gear front drive axle (Part 2 of 2)

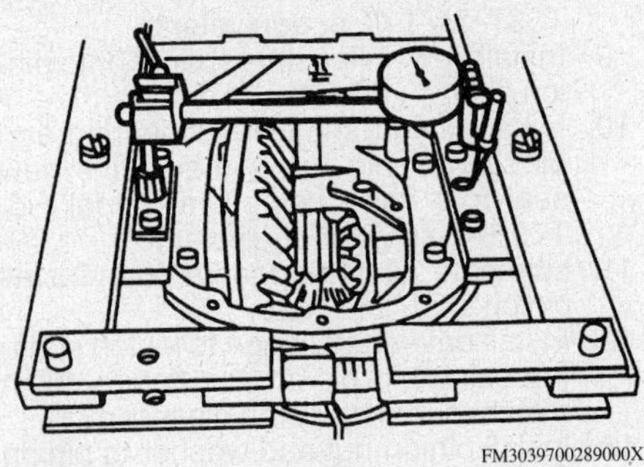

FM3039700289000X

Fig. 4 Case spreader fixture installation

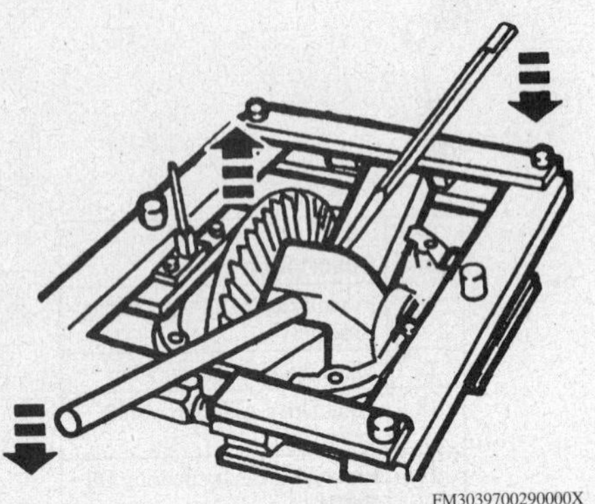

FM3039700290000X

Fig. 5 Differential case removal

36. Mount case spreader as outlined under "Disassemble" then spread case .030 inch.
37. Place a light coat of grease on one side of carrier bearing shim to hold shim in place, then place shim into position as marked.
38. Place carrier with bearing into place in case, then install bearing caps in to position, noting match marks made as disassembly.
39. Prior to releasing case spreader, tighten carrier bearing cap bolts to specification.
40. Release, then remove case spreader, then install a suitable dial indicator with brackets positioned to measure ring gear backlash.
41. Measure backlash at a minimum of four points on ring gear (approximately 90° apart), then average results for measurement.
42. Refer to "Drive Axle Specifications" for proper backlash.
43. To correct backlash, refer to table, **Fig. 11,** for the amount of shim change required. **Whenever shim thickness is changed on one side, the opposite side must be changed a corresponding amount to maintain overall total shim thickness.**
44. Inspect gear set tooth contact pattern as follows:
    a. Paint gear teeth with suitable gear marking compound. A mixture too wet will smear and run. A mixture too dry will not press out from between teeth.
    b. With a suitable box wrench levering on ring gear bolts, rotate ring gear several complete revolutions in both directions or until a clear tooth contact pattern appears.
    c. Certain gear tooth contact pattern types on ring gear indicate improper adjustment. This can be corrected by adjusting ring gear or pinion.
    d. Desirable ring gear tooth patterns must have a drive pattern on the drive side ring gear well centered on the tooth and a coast pattern on the coast side ring gear well centered on the tooth.
    e. There must be clearance between the pattern and top of tooth and no hard lines where pressure is high.
    f. Acceptable ring gear tooth patterns for all axles are illustrated in **Fig. 12.**
    g. Proper backlash with a thinner pinion position shim required is illustrated in **Fig. 13.**
    h. Proper backlash with a thicker pinion position shim required is illustrated in **Fig. 14.**
    i. Proper pinion position shim that requires less backlash is illustrated in **Fig. 15.**
    j. Proper pinion position shim that requires more backlash is illustrated in **Fig. 16.**
45. Install a new O-ring seal to the disconnect shift lever shaft and lubricate with a suitable silicone grease.
46. Install disconnect shift fork into case, then install shift lever through case and into fork.
47. Align roll pin hole in lever shaft and fork, then install the roll pin.
48. Rotate shift lever to allow selector gear to be installed into fork, then install and engage axle clutch gear shaft to selector gear and differential side gear.
49. Place axle clutch gear shaft into position, then place a bead of suitable silicone sealer on flange of axle extension housing. **Do not allow sealer to extrude into axle housing during assembly.**
50. Install axle extension tube to differential housing, ensure pilot of axle shaft is properly engaged into bearing of axle clutch gear shaft.
51. Install extension tube bolts, then tighten to specification.
52. Install lefthand axle into case and through differential side gear, install new snap ring.
53. Connect axle disconnect vacuum motor to case and shift arm, ensure boot is properly installed.
54. Install a suitable vacuum pump to disconnect motor and operate system while rotating differential to ensure proper operation.
55. Place a bead of suitable silicone sealer on differential cover. **Do not allow sealer to extrude into axle housing during assembly.**
56. Install cover, then tighten cover bolts to specification.
57. Refer to "Specifications" for axle fluid amount and type.

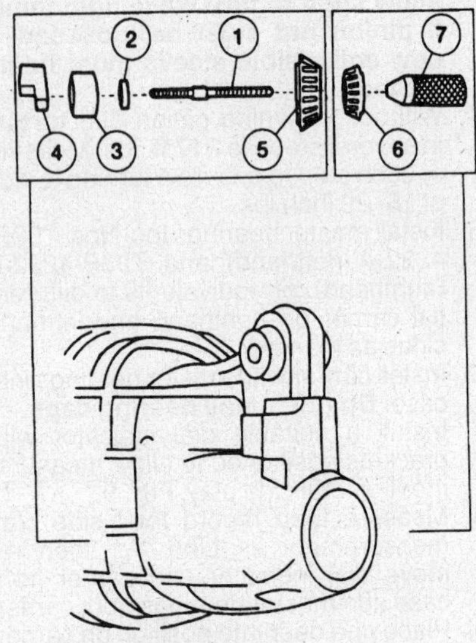

1 Position Screw.
2 Position Aligning Adapter.
3 Position Gauge Disc.
4 Position Gauge Block.
5 Position the differential pinion bearing
6 Position the differential pinion bearing
7 Thread on Driver Handle.

FM3039700291000X

Fig. 6 Pinion depth gauge set installation

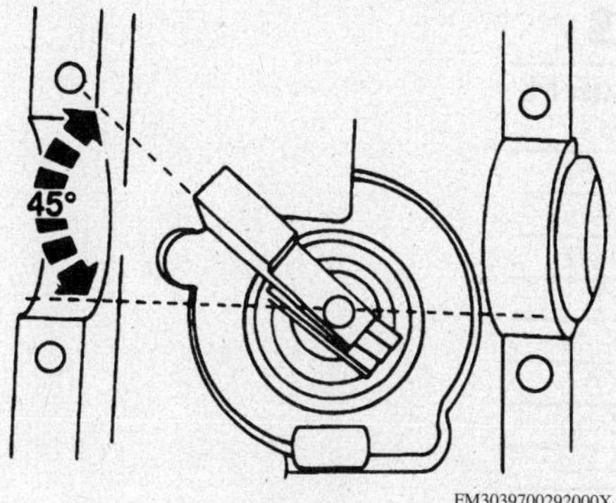

Fig. 7 Pinion depth gauge set position

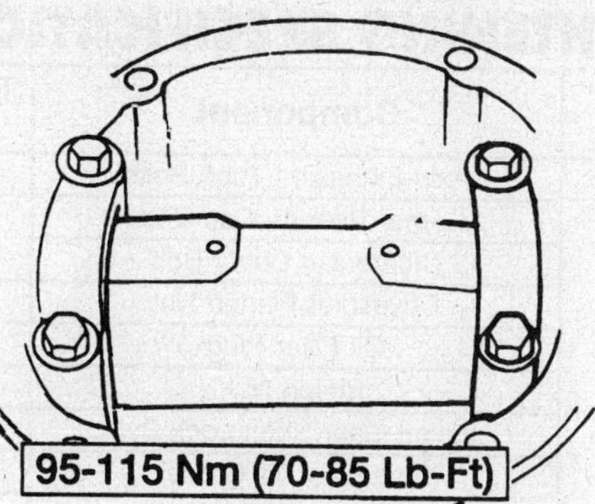

Fig. 8 Pinion depth mandrel installation

FM3039700294000X

Fig. 9 Differential case total side play measurement

Numbers of Stripes and Color Code	Dimension A	
	mm	Inch
2— C-COAL	7.7978— 7.8105	0.3070— 0.3075
1— C-COAL	7.7470— 7.7597	0.3050— 0.3055
5— BLU	7.6962— 7.7089	0.3030— 0.3035
4— BLU	7.6454— 7.6581	0.3010— 0.3015
3— BLU	7.5946— 7.6073	0.2990— 0.2995
2— BLU	7.5458— 7.5565	0.2970— 0.2975
5— PINK	7.4422— 7.4549	0.2930— 0.2935
4— PINK	7.3914— 7.4041	0.2910— 0.2915
3— PINK	7.3406— 7.3533	0.2890— 0.2895
2— PINK	7.2898— 7.3025	0.2870— 0.2875
1— PINK	7.2390— 7.2517	0.2850— 0.2855
5— GRN	7.1882— 7.2009	0.2830— 0.2835
4— GRN	7.1374— 7.1501	0.2810— 0.2815
3— GRN	7.0866— 7.0993	0.2790— 0.2795
2— GRN	7.0358— 7.0485	0.2770— 0.2775
1— GRN	6.9850— 6.9977	0.2750— 0.2755
5— WH	6.9342— 6.9469	0.2730— 0.2735
4— WH	6.8834— 6.8961	0.2710— 0.2715
3— WH	6.8326— 6.8453	0.2690— 0.2695
2— WH	6.7818— 6.7945	0.2670— 0.2675
1— WH	6.7310— 6.7437	0.2650— 0.2655
5— YEL	6.6802— 6.6929	0.2630— 0.2635
4— YEL	6.6294— 6.6421	0.2610— 0.2615
3— YEL	6.5786— 6.5913	0.2590— 0.2595
2— YEL	6.5278— 6.5405	0.2570— 0.2575
1— YEL	6.4770— 6.4897	0.2550— 0.2555
5— ORNG	6.4262— 6.4389	0.2530— 0.2535
4— ORNG	6.3754— 6.3881	0.2510— 0.2515
3— ORNG	6.3246— 6.3373	0.2490— 0.2495
2— ORNG	6.2738— 6.2865	0.2470— 0.2475
1— ORNG	6.2223— 6.2357	0.2450— 0.2455
2— RED	6.1722— 6.1849	0.2430— 0.2335
1— RED	6.1214— 6.1341	0.2410— 0.2415

FM3039700295000X

Fig. 10 Side play shim selection table

Backlash Change Required		Thickness Change Required	
mm	Inch	mm	Inch
0.025	0.001	0.050	0.002
0.050	0.002	0.050	0.002
0.076	0.003	0.101	0.004
0.101	0.004	0.152	0.006
0.127	0.005	0.152	0.006
0.152	0.006	0.203	0.008
0.177	0.007	0.254	0.010
0.203	0.008	0.254	0.010
0.228	0.009	0.304	0.012
0.254	0.010	0.355	0.014
0.279	0.011	0.355	0.014
0.304	0.012	0.406	0.016
0.330	0.013	0.457	0.018
0.335	0.014	0.457	0.018
0.381	0.015	0.508	0.020

FM3039700296000X

Fig. 11 Backlash shim change table

FM3039700357000X

Fig. 12 Acceptable ring gear tooth patterns

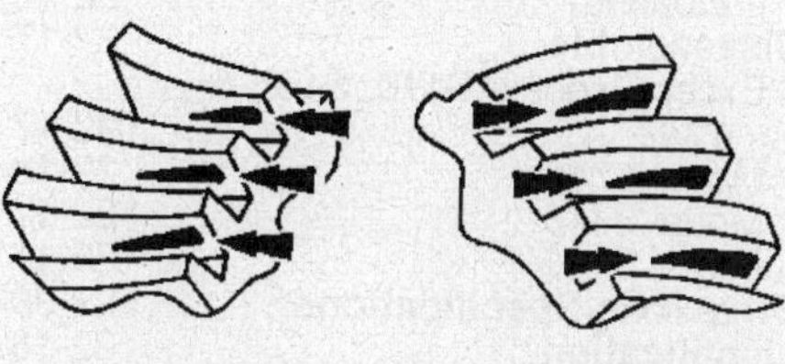

Fig. 13 Proper backlash requiring thinner pinion shim

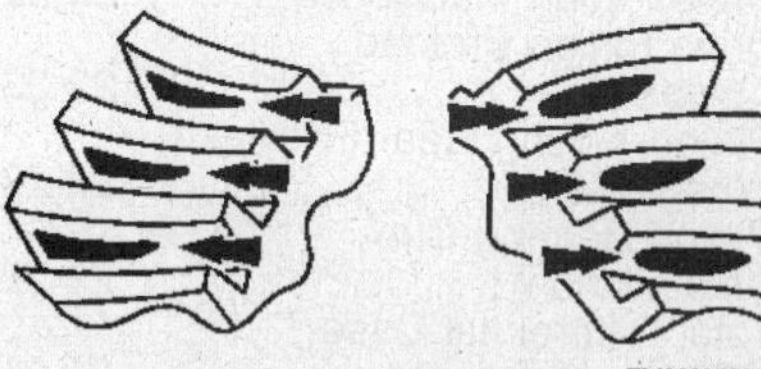

Fig. 14 Proper backlash requiring thicker pinion shim

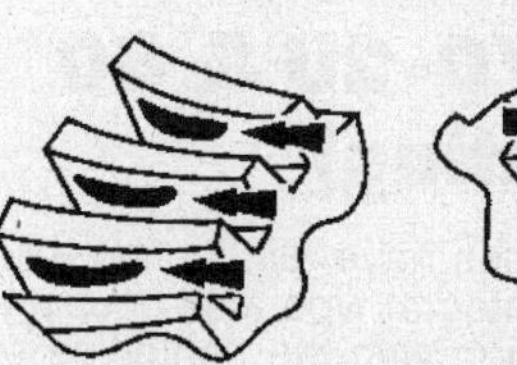

Fig. 15 Proper pinion position shim requiring less backlash

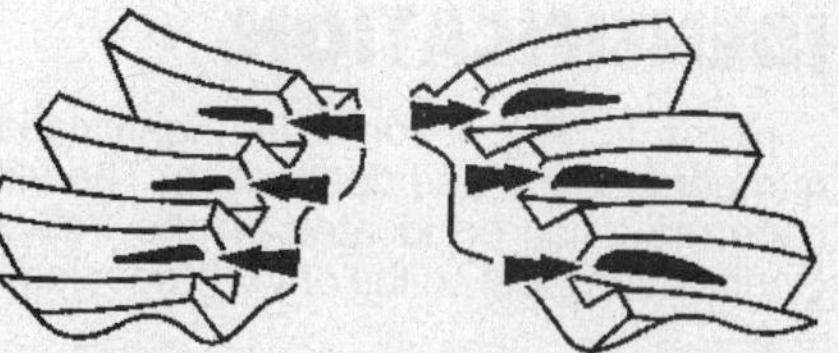

Fig. 16 Proper pinion position shim requiring more backlash

DRIVE AXLE SPECIFICATIONS

Drive Axle Model	Carrier Type	Ring Gear & Pinion Backlash, Inches			Pinion Bearing Preload		
		Method	New Bearings	Used Bearings	Method	New Bearings	Used Bearings
All	Integral	Shims	.008–.013	.008–.013	Collapsible Spacer	①	①

① — Refer to "Assemble."

TIGHTENING SPECIFICATIONS

Year	Component	Torque Ft. Lbs.
2002–06	Axle Extension Tube Bolts	50–57
	Carrier Bearing Cap Bolts	70–85
	Differential Cover Bolt	20–27
	Driveshaft Flange Nut	①
	Oil Filler Plug	15–22
	Pinion Nut	①
	Pinion Gear Shaft Lock Bolt	15–30
	Ring Gear To Carrier	70–84
	Vent Assembly	12–19
	Yoke Nut	①

① — Refer to "Assemble."

Dana/Spicer Rear Drive Axles

NOTE: **Prior To Performing Any Service Operations Listed In This Section, Consult The "Technical Service Bulletins" Section For Related Information.**

INDEX

IDENTIFICATION

Refer to **Fig. 1** for axle identification number location and description. The axle code may also be located on the Vehicle Certification label on the driver's door jamb.

DESCRIPTION

Model 60-1U (Semi-Floating)

This rear axle has semi-floating axle shafts, retained in the rear axle by U-washers positioned in a groove on the splined end of the axle shaft. These U-washers also fit into a machined recess in the differential side gears within the differential case. The axle shaft rides on one straight roller bearing at the outboard end.

Models 70-2U & 80 (Full Floating)

These rear axles have full floating axle shafts, with an integral type axle housing, hypoid gear design with the centerline of the pinion set below the centerline of the ring gear. The axle shaft is retained by bolts attached to the hub. The rear hub rides on two opposed tapered bearings at the outboard end of the rear axle housing. The axle housing consists of a cast center section with two steel tubes.

Model S110

The Model S110 differential consists of a hypoid design differential ring gear and pinion. The unit features a two bearing overhung pinion mounting and full floating axle shafts. It is available as a conventional differential assembly or as a Truetrac limited slip differential assembly.

Model S135 (Full Floating)

The Model S135 rear axle consists of a hypoid design ring gear and pinion, a two bearing overhung pinion mounting, full floating axle shafts, HLSA steel axle housing and a front mounted, removable one piece carrier.

Model 174

The Dana Model 174 axle has a ring gear diameter of 6.85 inches. Those equipped with Anti-Lock Brake System (ABS) include an anti-lock speed sensor ring located on the halfshaft outer joints.

This axle features a hypoid ring gear and pinion which consists of a ring gear and an overhung drive pinion which is supported by two opposed tapered roller bearings.

The axle housing assembly consists of a cast aluminum center section which must be spread in order to remove the differential case. The stamped-steel rear differential housing cover does away with a gasket and instead uses a silicone sealant.

The halfshafts are retained in the differential case by a driveshaft bearing retainer circlip that is located on the inboard CV joint stub shaft pilot bearing housing. The driveshaft bearing retainer circlip engages a step in the differential side gear when each halfshaft is installed.

Differential bearing preload and ring gear backlash are adjusted by differential bearing shims located between the differential bearing cup and the rear axle housing.

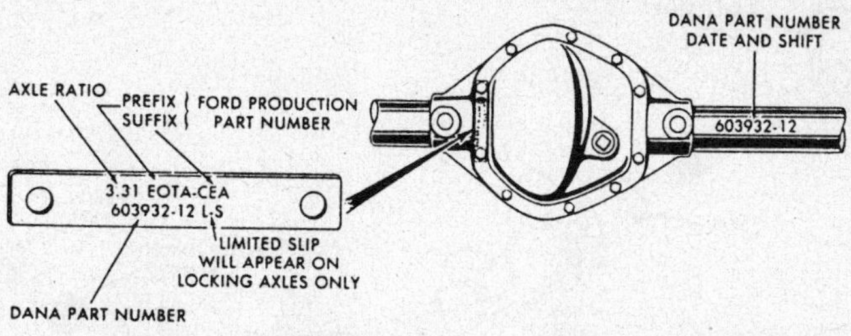

Fig. 1 Rear drive axle identification

DISASSEMBLE

Except Models S110, S135 & 174

For differential case disassembly on models 70-1HD and 70-2U with Power-Lok limited slip differential, refer to "Subassembly Service."

When changing ratios on Models 60 and 70 series axles, changing the differential case, ring gear and drive pinion may be required.

1. Remove axle assembly from vehicle as outlined under "Rear Axle & Suspension" in appropriate chassis chapter.
2. Remove axle shafts as outlined under "Rear Axle & Suspension" in appropriate chassis chapter.
3. Remove cover plate and drain lubricant, then clean all gasket surfaces.
4. Remove bearing caps. Note matched numbers or letters stamped on the cap and carrier assembly. These numbers or letters must be matched during assembly. These numbers may either be stamped vertically, horizontally or, in some instances, both vertically and horizontally.
5. Mount spreader tool No. 4000-E, or equivalent onto carrier assembly.
6. Position a dial indicator onto carrier, then spread housing. **Do not spread housing more than .015 inch.**
7. Remove differential case from carrier, **Figs. 2 through 4.** It may be required to pry case from carrier with suitable pry bars. **Use care to avoid damaging machined surfaces.**
8. Remove and tag bearing cups to indicate which side of carrier they were removed from, then remove spreader tool from case. **Models 60, 70 and 80 series axles use spacers installed outboard of each bearing cup, remove and tag for reference during assembly.**
9. Remove differential case bearings from case using tool No. D81L-4220-A, or equivalent. Place tool in a vise when removing bearing. Turn case over and remove other bearing in same manner.
10. Wire shims, bearing cup, bearing and spacer, if applicable, together and identify from which side of differential case they were removed. If any shims are damaged, replace with new shims. **It is recommended that bearings be replaced.**
11. Place a few shop towels over a vise to prevent ring gear teeth from being nicked after it is free from case assembly. Remove ring gear bolts, leaving four bolts loosely assembled 90° apart. Tap each bolt head alternately with a rawhide or plastic hammer to loosen ring gear from case. Remove case and ring gear from vise. **If applicable, use care not to damage exciter ring when removing ring gear. Whenever removing ring gear bolts, discard and replace with new bolts upon assembly.**
12. If applicable or required, remove exciter ring using a soft-faced hammer, then discard ring.
13. Replace differential case in vise, then drive out lockpin that retains pinion mate shaft to case.
14. Remove pinion mate shaft using a suitable drift, then rotate side gears until pinion mate gears turn to opening of case.
15. Remove pinion mate gears and spherical washers behind gears, then lift out side gears and thrust washers.
16. Inspect all components, including machined surfaces of case. **If excessive wear is visible on all components, it is suggested that complete differential case assembly be replaced. If any one gear are to be replaced, they are to be replaced as a set.**
17. Turn nose of carrier upward, hold end yoke or flange with a suitable pinion flange holding tool, then remove pinion nut and washer from pinion shaft.
18. Remove end yoke or flange using a suitable yoke remover and perform inspection. Replace yoke or flange if they show any signs of wear.
19. Remove drive pinion by tapping on drive pinion shaft using a rawhide or plastic hammer. **Catch pinion to prevent damage to pinion teeth. Gear teeth may have sharp edges, use care when handling gear to prevent personal injury. On spline end of pinion there are bearing preload shims. Collect shims and keep together for reassembly. Model 70 axles may also use a pinion preload spacer with preload shims, preload spacer must be assembled in sequence outlined in Fig. 5,** or unit failure may occur.
20. Remove drive pinion oil seal from carrier using a suitable bearing cup puller and a slide hammer.
21. Remove outer pinion bearing cone and outer oil slinger.
22. Turn nose of carrier downward and remove outer pinion bearing cup using a suitable pinion bearing cup remover and driver handle. Locate driver on back edge of cup and drive cup out of bore.
23. Remove inner pinion bearing cup and baffle using a suitable pinion bearing cup remover and driver handle. **Shims are located between bearing cup and carrier bore and may also include an oil baffle. If shims and/or baffle are bent or nicked, replace. Wire shim stacks together and measure each. If stack has to be replaced, replace with same thickness.**
24. Remove inner pinion bearing from drive pinion using tool No. D81L-4220-A, or equivalent.

Model S110

1. Steam clean axle assembly.
2. Set parking brake and chock rear wheels.
3. Remove bottom two differential carrier bolts and drain fluid into suitable container.
4. Disconnect rear anti-lock brake sensor electrical connector, if equipped.
5. Place index marks on driveshaft, then disconnect driveshaft and set aside.
6. Loosen pinion hex nut if drive pinion disassembly is required.
7. Remove axle shaft bolts, **Fig. 6,** then the axle shaft.
8. Remove all but top two carrier bolts, **Fig. 7,** note length and position of bolts, then discard bolts.
9. Position a suitable jack under carrier.
10. Secure differential carrier to jack.
11. Remove and discard remaining retaining bolts.
12. Use slots to separate carrier from axle housing, then lower from vehicle.
13. Clean all components with suitable solvent

Model S135

1. Remove carrier assembly and mount in a suitable stand, **Fig. 8.**
2. If ring gear and pinion are to be used again, measure and record backlash noting the following:
   a. Measure backlash in four equally spaced positions around ring gear

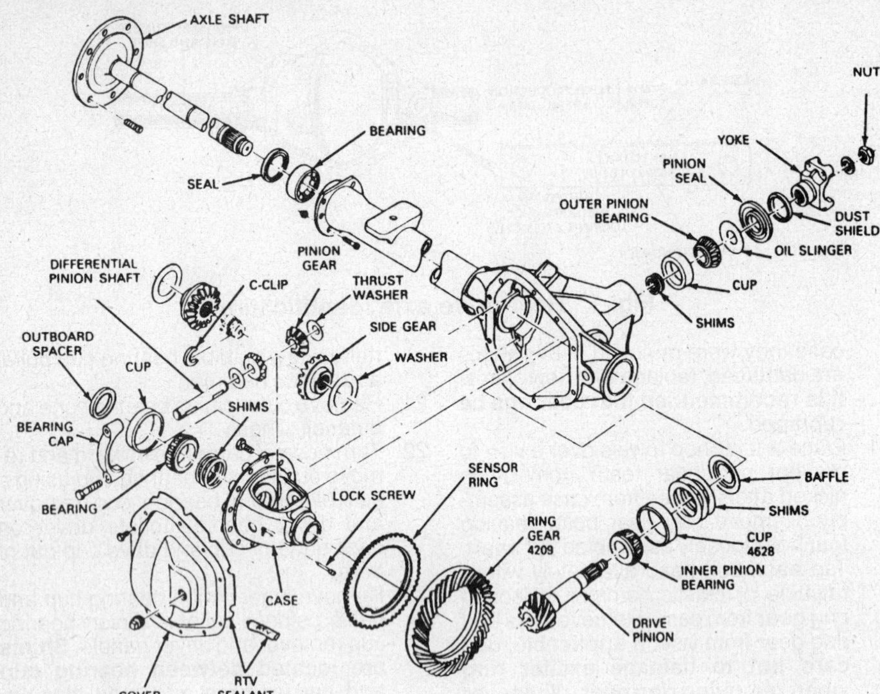

Fig. 2 Exploded view of Model 61-1U semi-floating rear axle

using a dial indicator.

b. Backlash should be within .002 inch from specification scribed in ring gear.

3. Remove anti-lock brake sensor.
4. Remove adjusting lock rings.
5. Place a reference mark on one differential bearing cap and leg for assembly.
6. Loosen four differential bearing cap retaining bolts.
7. Relieve bearing preload by loosening each differential bearing adjusting ring.
8. Remove differential bearing cap retaining bolts, bearing caps and adjusting rings.
9. Lift differential subassembly out of carrier using endless lifting sling tool No. D87L-1000-A, or equivalent.
10. Place a reference mark on differential case halves for assembly.
11. Remove differential case retaining bolts, then separate case halves.
12. Remove thrust washer and differential side gear, then the cross shaft with pinion mates and thrust washers.
13. Remove differential side gear and thrust washer.
14. Remove differential side bearings using a suitable puller, if required.
15. If pinion/ring gear requires replacement, proceed as follows:
    a. Center punch each ring gear rivet. **Do not use a chisel to remove rivet heads. Use a soft hammer.**
    b. Drill rivet heads to proper depth, **Fig. 9**, using a 9/16 inch drill bit.
    c. Separate ring gear from case half.
    d. Drive out remaining rivet portions using a punch.
    e. Separate ring gear from case half.
16. Clean and dry components

Model 174

1. Remove axle assembly as outlined under "Rear Axle & Suspension" in "Escape & Mariner" chassis chapter.
2. Mount axle assembly on a suitable bench using holding fixture tool No. 307-003, or equivalent.
3. Remove halfshaft bearings and seals using bearing cup remover tool No. 308-125 and slide hammer tool No. 100-001, or equivalent.
4. Note all matched numbers or letters stamped on both differential bearing caps and differential housing. These must align during assembly.
5. Remove differential bearing cap bolts, then the caps.
6. Spread axle housing using differential carrier spreader tool No. 205-001 and housing spreader tool No. 205-136, or equivalent to specification as illustrated in **Fig. 10. Do not exceed .10 inch.**
7. Remove differential case and tag bearing cups to indicate which side of carrier they came from.
8. Remove tools.
9. Remove drive pinion nut using socket tool No. 205-175 and nut remover tool No. 205-503, or equivalent. Ensure drive pinion does not fall out of axle case. Pinion nut is staked in pinion shaft groove. There may be metal remaining in groove which must be removed.
10. Remove drive pinion, collapsible spacer and inner and outer drive pinion bearings. Discard collapsible spacer and pinion nut.
11. Remove outer drive pinion bearing cup using bearing remover tool No. 205-249 (T86T-4628-BH) and handle tool No. 205-153, or equivalent.
12. Remove inner drive pinion bearing cup and oil baffle. Discard baffle.
13. Remove differential case bearings and shims using step plate tool No. 205-D016 and puller tool No. 205-D036, or equivalent. Tag bearing cups and cones together to indicate which side of carrier they came from. Discard any damaged shims.
14. Remove and discard differential ring gear mounting bolts.
15. Remove ring gear.
16. Remove differential pinion shaft lockpin, then the shaft.
17. Note location of pinion gears, side gears and thrust washers to assure assembly in same locations.
18. Rotate pinion gears and pinion gear thrust washers to window and remove them.
19. Remove side gears and thrust washers.
20. Remove drive pinion bearing and drive pinion position shim using step plate tool No. 205-D016 and puller tool No. 205-D036, or equivalent.

SUBASSEMBLY SERVICE

Model 70-2U

DISASSEMBLE

1. Scribe a mark between the differential case halves to be used during assembly. Also, mark the pinion mate shafts and corresponding ramps for assembly in original locations.
2. Clamp differential assembly in a soft jaw vise.
3. Loosen but do not remove the case half retaining bolts, **Fig. 11.**
4. Place assembly on bench with the ring gear half down and remove case half retaining screws.
5. Remove the cover half of the case.
6. Remove upper mate shaft, side gear, side gear ring and clutch pack. Retain components with cover half of case so they can be installed in original position.
7. Remove lower mate shaft, side gear, side gear ring and clutch pack from drive gear case half.

ASSEMBLE

1. Place side gear ring from ring gear half of case on a pinion flange or other suitable fixture so the case is approximately four inches above bench.
2. Lubricate clutch plates and assemble clutch pack on side gear ring.
3. Place ring gear side of case over clutch pack and side gear ring. Ensure the clutch plate lugs enter the slots in the case and that the case bottoms on the clutch pack.
4. Invert the assembly. Hold assembly together while inverting.
5. Install the ring gear case half side gear in side gear ring.
6. Install axle shaft spacer in cross shaft.
7. Install the ring gear case half pinion mate shaft and pinions on the side gear ring.

8. Install the cover half pinion mate shaft and pinions.
9. Place side gear on pinions, then the side gear ring on side gear.
10. Assemble clutch pack on side gear ring, aligning clutch pack lugs.
11. Install cover half of case over assembly, aligning the marks made during disassembly.
12. Install the case half retaining bolts, turning the bolts to engage a few threads only.
13. Insert axle shaft into assembly and align the splines of the side gears and side gear rings. With the axle shafts in position, tighten case half retaining bolts to specifications.
14. Remove axle shafts.
15. If the differential has been assembled properly, each pinion mate cross shaft should be tight on its ramp. However, if clearance is present, it should not exceed .010 inch and be equal at all four cross shaft ends.

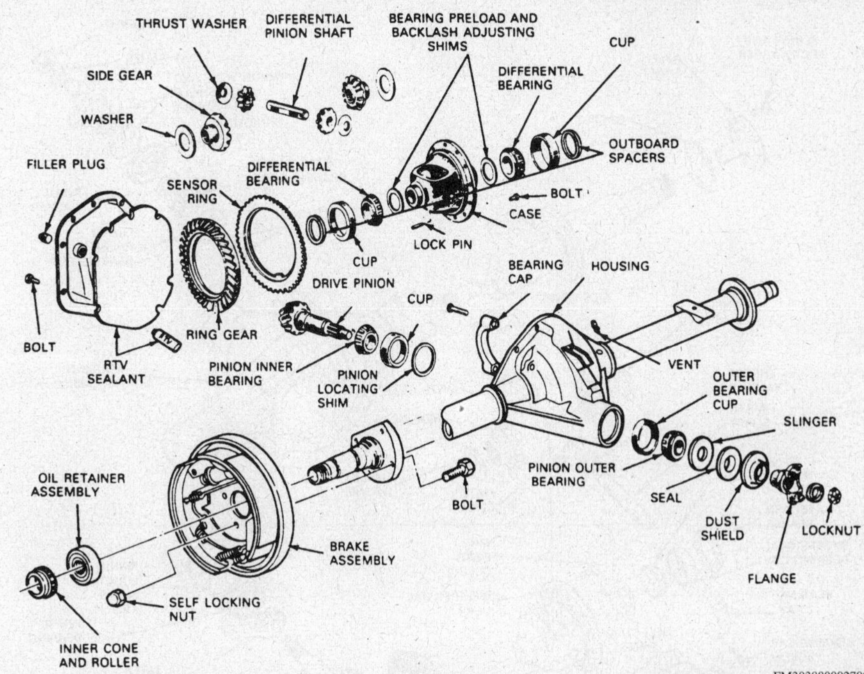

Fig. 3 Exploded view of Model 61-1U, 70-1HD & 70-2U full-floating rear axles

Model 60-1U

DISASSEMBLE

1. Place one axle shaft in vise, splined end up, so that splines do not extend more than three inches above jaws of vise.
2. Mount differential case on axle shaft.
3. Remove roll pin retaining cross pin using a suitable drift, then drive out cross pin with hammer and drift, **Fig. 12.**
4. Position step plate into bottom side gear and lubricate centering hole of step plate.
5. Position gear rotating tool into top side gear.
6. Lubricate threads of forcing screw and thread screw into gear rotating tool, guiding forcing screw into step plate.
7. Tighten forcing screw securely, then, using a piece of .030 inch shim or gauge stock, push out differential spherical washers.
8. Loosen forcing screw momentarily, then tighten forcing screw until a very slight movement of the differential pinion gears is seen.
9. Slide pawl of gear rotating tool between two side gear teeth and pull handle so top side gear rotates, rotating differential pinion gears. Remove differential pinion gears through large openings in case. **When attempting to rotate side gear, it may be required to tighten or loosen forcing screw to permit gear movement.**
10. Manually hold top side gear and clutch pack in case and remove forcing screw, then the gear rotating tool.
11. Remove top side gear and clutch pack, keeping plates and discs in exact order.
12. Turn case so that ring gear side faces up, easing step plate, side gear and clutch pack out of case.
13. Remove retainer clips from clutch packs, keeping discs and plates in exact order.

ASSEMBLE

1. Install side gears and thrust washers in proper order.
2. Lubricate thrust face of side gear and plates and discs with suitable lubricant and assemble plates and discs to side gear splines.
3. Assemble retainer clips to ears of plates, ensure clips are completely assembled or seated onto ears of plates.
4. Assemble clutch pack and side gear into case, ensure clutch pack stays assembled to side gear splines and that retainer clips are completely seated into pockets of case.
5. Manually retain clutch pack in case, position case on bench and assemble step plate into side gear, applying small amount of lubricant into centering hole of step plate.
6. Assemble remaining clutch pack and side gear, ensure clutch pack stays assembled to side gear splines and that retainer clips are completely seated into pockets of case.
7. Position gear rotating tool into top side gear, manually hold side gear and rotating tool in position, insert forcing screw down through top of case, and thread screw into rotating tool until screw contacts step plate.
8. Position case onto axle shaft by aligning splines of side gear with splines of shaft.
9. Position differential pinion gears opposite one another through openings in case, ensure holes of gears are aligned, manually retain gears in position, and tighten forcing screw so that side gears move away from differential pinion gears.
10. Hold differential pinion gears in place and insert pawl of rotating tool between two side gear teeth, then pull on handle so that top side gear rotates and allows differential pinion gears to rotate and enter into case. **It may be required to slightly tighten or loosen forcing screw to permit gear movement.**
11. Put on tool until handle hits case, then remove pawl from between gear teeth and position handle and pawl. Repeat this step until holes of differential pinion gears are perfectly aligned with holes of case.
12. Lubricate both sides of pinion spherical washers with suitable lubricant.
13. Tighten forcing screw to obtain installation clearance for spherical washers.
14. Install spherical washers, ensure holes of washers and gears are perfectly aligned with holes of case, then remove forcing screw, rotating tool and step plate.
15. Install pinion shaft in differential case, then the cross shaft locking pin.

Model 80

Do not unbolt case halves without running a suitable bolt, washers and wing nut lengthwise through center of differential assembly, Fig. 13, or preloaded springs may pop loose and cause serious injury.

1. Remove eight retaining bolts from upper case half, **Fig. 14,** then lift upper case half off and remove differential assembly.
2. Remove case thrust washers, then unscrew differential retaining bolt, washers and wing nut. **The springs are under load and may cause injury if proper precautions are not taken.**
3. Inspect central driver and clutch assemblies for worn teeth, then inspect

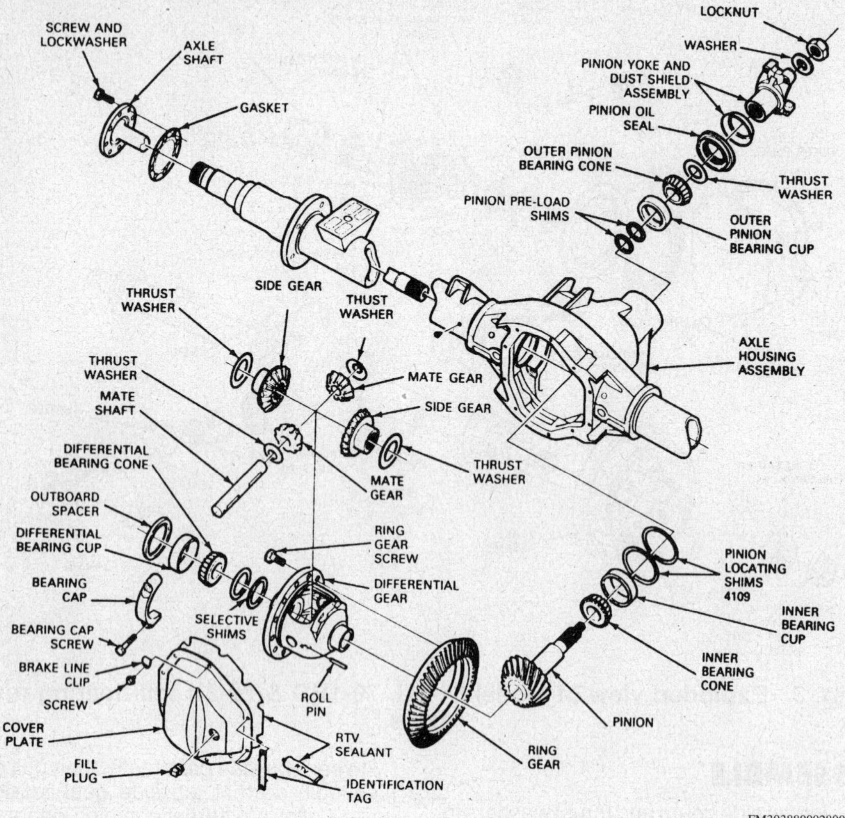

Fig. 4 Exploded view of Model 80 full-floating rear axle

hold ring, side gears, springs, thrust blocks, bevel springs and spring retainers for wear or damage. Replace as required.

4. Reverse procedure to assemble, noting the following:
   a. Place assembly in a suitable press and compress the springs, the run bolt, washers and wing through assembly and tighten securely.
   b. Install thrust washes into case so oil groove is visible.
   c. **Torque** case bolts to 76–80 ft. lbs.

Model S135

DRIVE PINION

DISASSEMBLE

1. Remove pinion hex nut.
2. Remove companion flange using a suitable puller. **Do not hammer on companion flange.**
3. Remove pinion seal.
4. Press pinion through outer pinion bearing using a suitable press.
5. Remove pinion preload spacer.
6. If gear set is to be reused, remove inner pinion bearing using a suitable puller.
7. If replacing bearings, remove outer and inner pinion bearing cups.
8. Clean and dry components.

INSPECTION

Inspect companion flange for grooves in sealing surface caused by contamination. If grooves are detectable with a fingernail, repair flange with a CR approved sleeve or replace the flange.

ASSEMBLE

1. Press inner portion bearing onto pinion using a suitable press.
2. Press inner and outer pinion bearing cups into carrier until seated, noting the following:
   a. Ensure bearing cups have completely seated in bearing bores using a .0015 inch feeler gauge.
   b. Lubricate bearing cups and cones.
3. Seat pinion bearing on pinion as follows:
   a. Position 6 x 6 x 6 inch block of wood under pinion.
   b. Place original pinion preload spacer onto pinion.
   c. Place outer pinion bearing onto pinion.
   d. Seat outer bearing onto pinion using a suitable press.
4. Install companion flange using yoke installer thread sleeve tool No. 205-436, yoke installer tube tool No. 205-435 and yoke installer drive nut tool No. 205-437, or equivalents.
5. Install pinion hex nut and tighten to specification.
6. Measure turning torque, noting the following:
   a. Take measurements every fourth revolution.
   b. If turning torque is not 10–40 inch lbs., proceed to next step. If turning torque is as specified, proceed to step 8.
7. Adjust pinion bearing preload by replacing pinion bearing preload spacer, noting the following:
   a. Increase preload by installing a thinner spacer and decrease preload by installing a thicker spacer.
   b. Pinion preload spacers are available in sizes from .286–.315 inch.
   c. Measure replacement spacer before installing it.
   d. On a flat surface, sand next thicker size spacer with emery cloth to appropriate thickness to obtain a closer adjustment.
   e. A .001 inch change in spacer thickness will change torque rate 30 inch lbs.
8. Remove pinion hex nut.
9. Remove companion flange using a suitable puller. **Do not hammer companion flange.**
10. Install pinion seal using pinion seal driver tube tool No. 205-440 and pinion seal driver tool No. 205-439, or equivalents. **Turning torque of 15–45 inch lbs., is acceptable with pinion seal installed.**
11. Install companion flange using yoke installer thread sleeve tool No. 205-436, yoke installer tube tool No. 205-435 and yoke installer drive nut tool No. 205-437, or equivalents.
12. Apply Loctite to pinion threads and install new pinion hex nut. Tighten nut to specifications.

Model S110

DRIVE PINION

DISASSEMBLE

1. Remove hex nut.
2. Remove pinion yoke with removal tool No. 205-433, or equivalent.
3. Remove pinion seal.
4. Position block of wood under pinion to avoid damage to gear teeth, then press pinion through outer bearing, **Fig. 15,** and remove pinion.
5. Measure and record pinion preload spacer thickness. Set spacer aside for use in assembly.
6. If reusing gear set, remove inner pinion bearing with a suitable puller.
7. If new bearings are being installed, remove outer and inner pinion bearing cups.
8. Clean and dry components as required. Use only emulsion cleaners or petroleum based cleaning solvent. Alkaline cleaning solutions will damage machined surfaces.
9. Inspect pinion flange for grooves in sealing surface caused by contamination. If grooves are detectable with fingernail, repair flange with CR-approved sleeve or install new flange.

ASSEMBLE

1. Press inner pinion bearing onto pinion with suitable driver.
2. Press inner and outer pinion bearing cups into carrier until seated.
3. Use a .0015 inch feeler gauge to verify cups have fully seated.
4. Lubricate bearing cups and cones.
5. Seat outer pinion bearing on pinion.

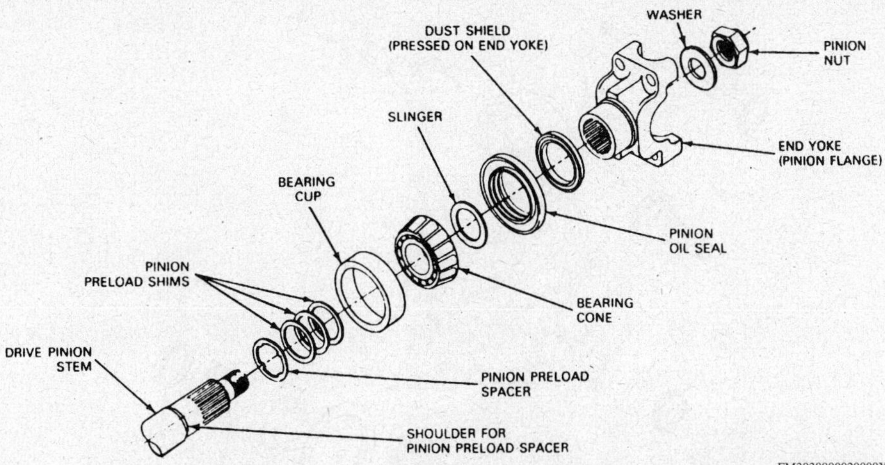

Fig. 5 Exploded view of pinion preload spacer & shims. Model 70 type full-floating rear axle

6. Seat inner pinion bearing into cup as follows:
   a. Position a 6 x 6 x 6 inch wood block under pinion, **Fig. 16.**
   b. Place original pinion preload spacer onto pinion.
   c. Place outer pinion bearing onto pinion.
   d. Press outer bearing onto pinion.
7. Do not install pinion seal at this time.
8. Install pinion flange.
9. **Torque** pinion flange hex nut to 832 ft. lbs.
10. Measure rotating torque. Take torque measurements every fourth revolution.
11. If bearing preload torque is not 20–40 inch lbs., refer to "Pinion Bearing Preload Adjustment"."
12. Remove pinion flange hex nut, then remove pinion flange with removal tool No. 205-433, or equivalent.
13. Install pinion seal with seal installer tool No. 205-S438, or equivalent.
14. A rotational torque of 15–45 inch lbs., is acceptable with seal installed.
15. Install pinion flange.
16. Apply stud and bearing mount compound to pinion threads and install new hex nut. **Torque** nut to 832 ft. lbs.

PINION BEARING PRELOAD ADJUSTMENT

1. Adjust pinion bearing preload by installing new pinion bearing preload spacer:
   a. To increase preload, install a thinner spacer, to decrease preload, install a thicker spacer.
   b. Always measure new spacer before installing.
   c. A .001 inch change in spacer thickness will change torque rate approximately 30 inch lbs.
   d. If close adjustment is needed, sand spacer with emery cloth to obtain a closer adjustment.
   e. Repeat procedures until rotational torque is within specification.

CASE & RING GEAR

Truetrac differential assembly is non-repairable. Discard entire assembly if it is worn or damaged.

Refer to **Figs. 17 through 19** when performing the following procedures:

1. Mount carrier housing in suitable repair stand.
2. If reusing differential ring gear and opinion, measure and record backlash before disassembling. Measure backlash in four equally spaced positions around differential gear, **Fig. 20.**
3. Remove rear anti-lock brake sensor.
4. Remove adjusting ring cotter pins.
5. Loosen but do not remove six bearing cap bolts.
6. Loosen each differential bearing adjusting ring, **Fig. 21,** to relieve bearing preload.
7. Remove bolts, bearing caps and adjusting rings.
8. Carefully lift differential subassembly out of carrier.
9. Inspect bearing surfaces for pitting, wear and overheating.
10. Remove differential side bearings if worn or damaged, **Fig. 22.**
11. Remove ring gear bolts.
12. Place differential assembly in a suitable press supported on ring gear, **Fig. 23.**
13. Press arbor will press on pinion cross shaft to separate ring gear from differential. Do not use more than 3 tons of pressure to release ring gear from differential case.
14. If required, remove anti-lock speed sensor ring. If removed, discard sensor ring.
15. Clean and dry all components.
16. On conventional differentials, remove side gear.
17. Remove differential pinion cross shaft lock pin, **Fig. 24,** then the pinion cross shaft.
18. Remove inner side gear and thrust washer.

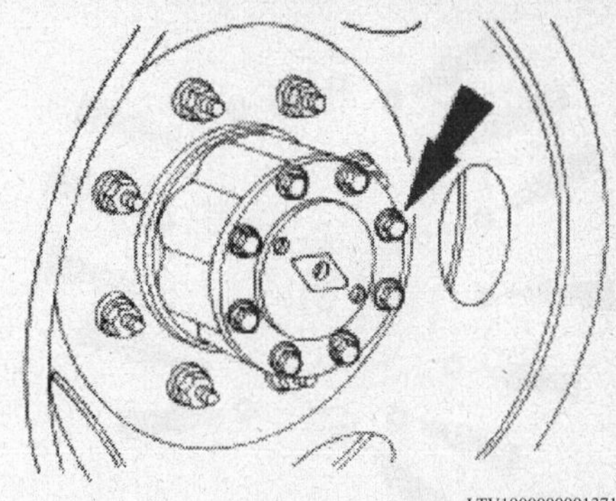

Fig. 6 Axle shaft bolts. Model S110

ASSEMBLE

Except Model S110, S135 & 174

TOTAL DIFFERENTIAL CASE ENDPLAY INSPECTION

1. Apply a suitable multi-purpose long life lubricant to side gear thrust washers, hub, thrust face of side gears, pinion mate gears and spherical washers.
2. Hold side gears in place in case, then install pinion mate gears and spherical washers.
3. Rotate side gears until holes in washers and pinion mate gears align with holes in case. **If gears cannot be rotated by hand, install an axle shaft into side gear spline and use a pipe wrench to turn shaft.**
4. Use a drift to align holes, then insert pinion mate shaft and drive into case to remove drift, ensuring lockpin hole in shaft aligns with lockpin holes in case.
5. Insert lockpin, then peen some metal of case over pin to lock it into place. **The semi-float shaft riding bearing design uses a lockpin that is installed using a 12 point socket. Use a new lockpin and assemble finger tight. This prevents differential side gears and differential pinion mate gears from rotating inside case and dropping out when servicing the carrier section. A new lockpin should be installed after assembling the axle shafts.**
6. If applicable, install exciter ring as follows:
   a. Align tab in exciter ring with slot in differential case, then thread two ring gear bolts through case into ring gear to ensure bolt hole alignment. **Tab on exciter ring must be aligned with slot in differential case.**
   b. Press exciter ring and ring gear onto differential case. Ring gear acts as a pilot for exciter ring.
   c. Apply threadlock and sealer part No. E0AZ-19554-AA, or equivalent to new ring gear bolts.
7. Attach ring gear to differential case using new bolts, then tighten bolts alternately and evenly to specifications.

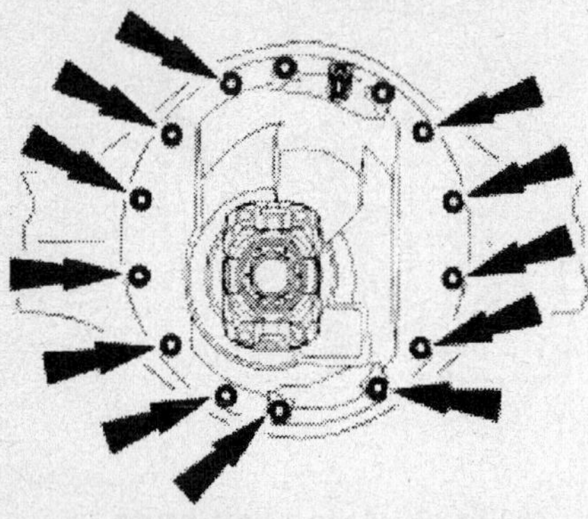

Fig. 7 Differential carrier to axle retaining bolt. Model S110

8. Clean trunnions on differential and install bearings onto differential case. Remove all burrs and nicks from hubs so bearings rotate freely.
9. Place differential case into carrier (without pinion). Differential case should move freely in carrier assembly. Position a suitable dial indicator against differential case flanges. Locate tip of indicator on flat surface of one ring gear bolt, **Fig. 25.** Force differential case toward dial indicator as far as possible and zero dial indicator with force still applied. Dial indicator should have a minimum of .200 inch. Force differential case away from dial indicator as far as it will go. Repeat this procedure until same reading is obtained. Record dial indicator reading as measurement "A" on a work sheet for calculating ring gear backlash and differential bearing preload shims. This reading indicates amount of shims needed behind differential side bearings to take up total clearance between differential bearing cup and carrier. This reading will be used during "Pinion & Ring Gear Backlash Inspection" in this section.
10. Remove differential case from carrier. Do not remove differential case bearings at this time.

DRIVE PINION INSTALLATION

Two separate adjustments affect drive pinion and ring gear tooth contact: pinion depth and pinion to ring gear backlash.

Pinion depth is controlled by a pinion locating shim pack installed between drive pinion inner bearing cup and carrier housing. This shim pack and inner oil slinger controls the position of the pinion. Adding shims moves pinion toward ring gear and removing shims moves pinion away from ring gear.

Pinion to ring gear backlash is controlled by preload shims located between the differential bearing cup and carrier. This adjustment will be outlined during "Carrier Assembly" procedures.

On the button of each drive pinion is marked a plus (+), a minus (–) or a zero (0), **Fig. 26.** These markings indicate the position for each gear set. The position is determined by amount of shims between inner pinion bearing cup and carrier bearing bore. Any pinion depth change is made by changing amount of shims.

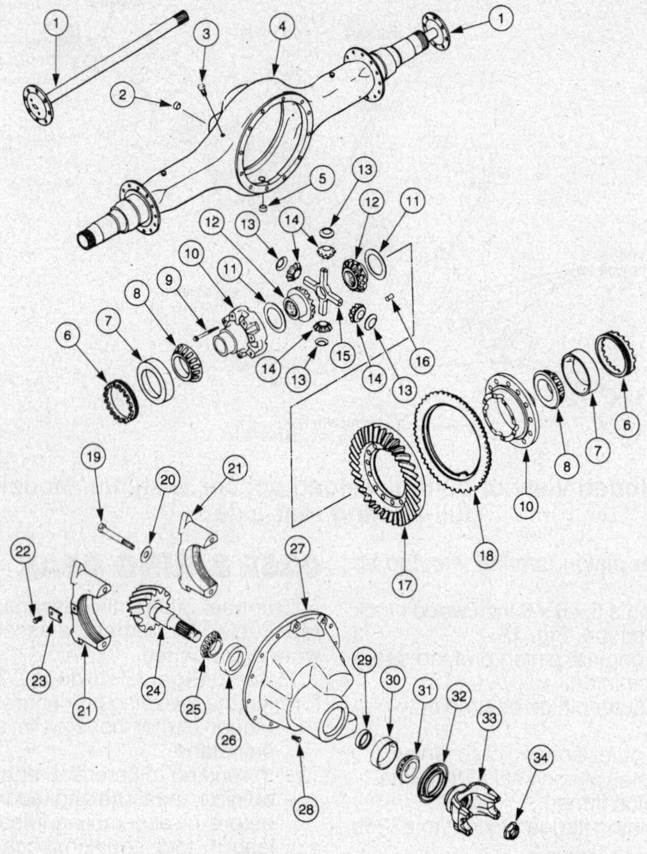

Fig. 8 Exploded view of model S135 rear axle (Part 1 of 2)

If the original gear set is being used, measure the slinger and each shim separately and add each shim measurement to total original measurement. Replace old shims with new shims that equal this measurement, if required.

If a new gear set is being used, notice the plus (+), minus (–) or zero (0) etchings on both original and new drive pinion and add or subtract shims according to charts in **Figs. 27 and 28** to compensate for differences between old and new pinion.

PINION BEARING CUP INSTALLATION

1. Place inner and outer pinion bearing cups into carrier bore.
2. Place suitable inner and outer bearing cup replacer tools on their respective cups, **Fig. 29.**
3. Install a suitable threaded drawbar into replacer tools, then tighten drawbar to install cups in their bores.

DEPTH GAUGE INSPECTION

1. Refer to **Fig. 30** for proper tools for particular axle assemblies. **If any gauge surfaces become nicked, high spots must be removed with a medium India oilstone to ensure no erroneous readings.**
2. Place a new inner pinion bearing over proper aligning adapter and insert into pinion bearing retainer assembly. Place outer pinion bearing into bearing cup in carrier and assemble handle onto screw and hand tighten. Note that 3/8 inch square drive in handle is to be used for obtaining proper pinion bearing preload. To preload bearings, **torque** handle to 20–40 inch lbs.
3. Center proper gauge tube into differential bearing bore, install bearing caps and tighten to specifications.
4. Select thickest feeler gauge that will enter between gauge tube and gauge block. Insert feeler gauge directly along gauge block to ensure a proper reading. Feeler gauge fit between gauge tube and gauge block should be a slight drag type feeling.
5. After proper feeler gauge feel is obtained, thickness of feeler gauge used to obtain slight drag-type feel is the thickness of shims required, provided new pinion gear is marked with a zero (0). If new pinion gear is marked with a plus (+) reading, the plus (+) amount stamped on pinion gear must be subtracted from thickness dimension obtained in preceding step. If new pinion gear is marked with a minus (–) reading, the minus (–) amount stamped on pinion gear must be added to thickness dimension obtained in preceding step. Also, you must use exact same new inner pinion bearing that was used

Item	Description
1	Axle Shaft
2	Fill Plug
3	Breather
4	Rear Axle Housing
5	Drain Plug
6	Differential Bearing Adjusting Ring
7	Differential Side Bearing Cup
8	Differential Side Bearing Cone
9	Differential Case Bolt
10	Differential Case Half
11	Thrust Washer
12	Differential Side Gear
13	Thrust Washer
14	Differential Pinion Mate
15	Differential Cross Shaft
16	Ring Gear Rivet
17	Ring Gear (Matched Set)
18	Anti-Lock Speed Sensor Ring

Item	Description
19	Differential Bearing Cup Bolt
20	Washer
21	Differential Bearing Cap
22	Adjusting Ring Lock Bolt
23	Adjusting Ring Lock
24	Pinion (Matched Set)
25	Pinion Bearing Cone, Inner
26	Pinion Bearing Cup, Inner
27	Carrier Housing
28	Carrier Mounting Bolt
29	Pinion Preload Spacer (Selective)
30	Pinion Bearing Cup, Outer
31	Pinion Bearing Cone, Inner
32	Pinion Seal
33	Companion Flange
34	Pinion Hex Nut

FM3039900327020X

Fig. 8 Exploded view of model S135 rear axle (Part 2 of 2)

to obtain this dimension.

6. Remove inner pinion bearing cup and install proper thickness of shims into carrier bore, then reinstall bearing cup and oil slinger and/or baffle, if required.
7. Press bearing onto pinion as illustrated in **Fig. 31. If a baffle and/or slinger is used, replace with a new one upon assembly and measure as part of the shim stack.**

DRIVE PINION PRELOAD INSPECTION

1. Assemble preload shims and slinger, if applicable, onto pinion, then install pinion gear into carrier housing.
2. Install outer pinion bearing and oil slinger, if applicable.
3. Install end yoke or flange, washer and new pinion nut on pinion shaft and tighten to specifications.
4. Place a suitable inch lb. torque wrench on pinion nut and measure pinion rotational torque, which should be 20–40 inch lbs.
5. To increase preload, remove shims. To decrease preload, add shims.
6. With drive pinion at proper preload, remove pinion nut, washer and end yoke or flange.
7. Coat drive pinion oil seal with suitable hypoid gear lubricant, or equivalent, then install drive pinion oil seal using suitable oil seal replacer. **After installation, ensure garter spring did not pop out. If garter spring pops out, remove and replace seal.**
8. Install end yoke or flange with a suitable pinion flange replacer, then the washer and nut and tighten to specifications.

PINION & RING GEAR BACKLASH INSPECTION

1. Place differential case into position in carrier (differential case bearings should still be installed).
2. Force differential case away from drive pinion gear until it is completely seated against cross bore face of carrier. Position a dial indicator so indicator tip rests on a ring gear bolt head, **Fig. 25.** Zero dial indicator.
3. Force ring gear against pinion gear. Rock ring gear slightly to ensure gear teeth are in contact, then force ring gear away from pinion gear, ensuring dial indicator returns to zero. Repeat this procedure until dial indicator reading is the same. This reading should be recorded as measurement "B" and reveals amount of shims required between differential case and differential bearing on ring gear side.
4. Assemble shim pack for ring gear side to measurement "B."
5. Subtract measurement "B" from measurement "A" obtained in "Total Differential Case Endplay Inspection" in this section to obtain measurement "C." Measurement "C" equals amount of shims required between differential case and bearing on side opposite of ring gear.
6. Assemble shim pack for side opposite of ring gear to measurement "C" plus (+) .015 inch.
7. Remove differential case from carrier, then the bearings from case.
8. Place required amount of shims on hub of ring gear side of differential case, then install bearing and drive bearing onto hub using a suitable differential side bearing replacer.
9. Place required amount of shims on hub of differential case opposite of ring gear side, then install bearing. Place a suitable step plate on ring gear side bearing to protect bearing, then drive bearing opposite of ring gear side onto hub using differential side bearing replacer.

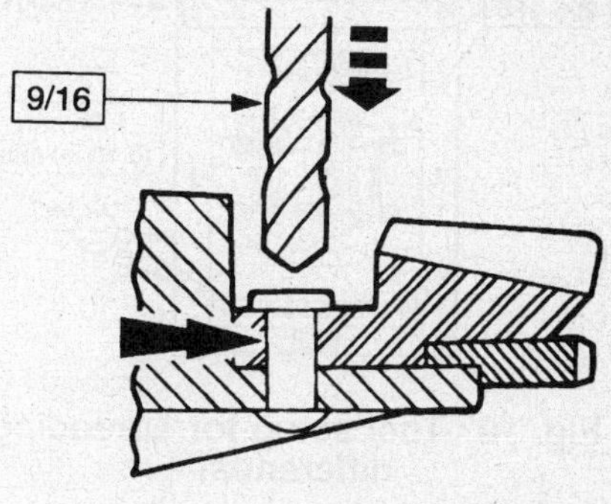

FM3039900328000X

Fig. 9 Ring/pinion gear rivet removal. Model S135

10. Install differential bearing cups onto bearings.
11. Mount spreader tool Nos. T4000-E and T80T-4000-B, or equivalents onto carrier assembly.
12. Position a dial indicator onto carrier, then spread the housing. **Do not spread housing more than .015 inch.**
13. Install differential case into carrier. **If required, use a rawhide or plastic hammer to seat case in carrier bore. With partial and non-hunting/partial ring gear and pinion sets, align marks on ring gear and drive pinion, if applicable. Use care not to nick teeth of ring gear or pinion.**
14. Remove spreader and dial indicator.
15. Install bearing caps and bolts, ensuring letters or numbers stamped on caps correspond in both position and direction with letters or numbers stamped into carrier, then tighten bolts to specifications.
16. Install dial indicator on case, **Fig. 32.**
17. Measure ring gear and pinion backlash at three equally spaced points on ring gear. Backlash tolerance is .005–.009 inch and cannot vary more than .003 inch between the three points.
18. If backlash is high, ring gear must be moved closer to pinion by moving shims to ring gear side from opposite side.
19. If backlash is low, ring gear must be moved away from pinion by moving shims from ring gear side to opposite side.
20. Inspect gear set tooth contact pattern as follows:
    a. Paint gear teeth with suitable gear marking compound. A mixture too wet will smear and run. A mixture too dry will not press out from between teeth.
    b. With a suitable box wrench levering on ring gear bolts, rotate ring gear several complete revolutions in both directions or until a clear tooth contact pattern appears.
    c. Certain gear tooth contact pattern types on ring gear indicate improper adjustment. This can be corrected by adjusting ring gear or pinion.
    d. Desirable ring gear tooth patterns must have a drive pattern on the drive side ring gear well centered

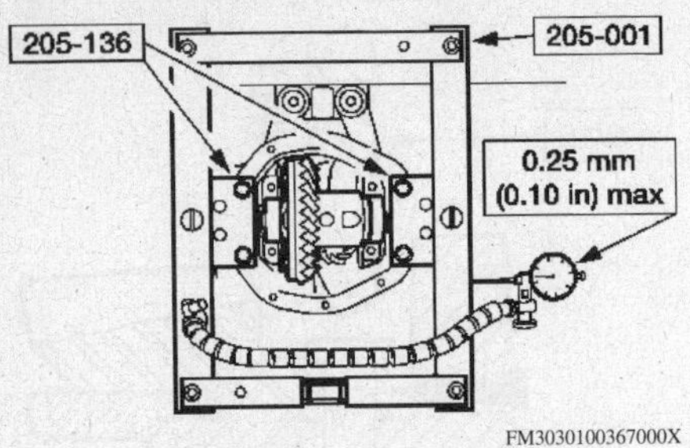

Fig. 10 Tool setup for spreading differential

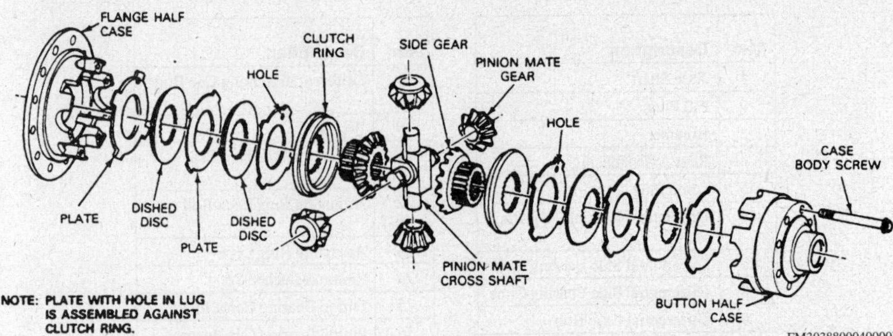

Fig. 11 Exploded view of Power-Lok locking differential. Model 70-2U

on the tooth and a coast pattern on the coast side ring gear well centered on the tooth.

e. There must be clearance between the pattern and top of tooth and no hard lines where pressure is high.
f. Acceptable ring gear tooth patterns for all axles are illustrated in **Fig. 33.**
g. Proper backlash with a thinner pinion position shim required is illustrated in **Fig. 34.**
h. Proper backlash with a thicker pinion position shim required is illustrated in **Fig. 35.**
i. Proper pinion position shim that requires less backlash is illustrated in **Fig. 36.**
j. Proper pinion position shim that requires more backlash is illustrated in **Fig. 37.**

21. Install new cover gasket and cover plate, then the mounting bolts and tighten to specifications.

Model S110

1. If removed previously, install new anti-lock speed sensor ring with a dead blow hammer, then press into position.
2. Install inner side gear thrust washer and inner side gear.
3. Align pinion gear cross shaft with pin hole vertical position.
4. Lightly lubricate all mating surfaces with clean axle lubricant.
5. Install first pinion gear thrust washer and pinion gear on pinion cross shaft.
6. Install second pinion gear and pinion gear thrust washer on differential cross shaft.
7. Install differential cross shaft lock pin.
8. Install outer side gear.
9. Align ring gear and differential case bolt holes. Install bolts finger tight.
10. Press differential assembly half on ring gear half with suitable press and press tools.
11. Install ring gear bolts, **torque** to 150 ft. lbs.
12. Install ring gear side carrier bearing and differential side carrier bearing.
13. Carefully position differential assembly into carrier housing.
14. Position differential bearing caps on differential.
15. Apply Threadlock 262, or equivalent, to bolt threads and install bolts. Tighten bolts just enough to eliminate visible space between bearing cap and leg bolt, do not torque bolts at this time.
16. Install differential bearing adjusting rings and adjust both rings until there is zero end play and some backlash between differential ring gear and pinion. Ensure adjusting ring tooth aligns so installation of adjusting cotter pin is possible.
17. Adjusting ring tooth must always align so installation of adjusting ring cotter pin is visible.
18. Loosen adjusting ring on tooth side of differential ring gear one tooth, and tighten opposite adjusting ring one tooth. Repeat until backlash is at zero.
19. Set backlash to specifications.
20. Inspect differential ring gear and pinion backlash in four equally spaced positions around differential ring gear.
21. If backlash tolerance varies by more than .003 inch between four positions, remove differential and determine cause.
22. **Torque** differential bearing cap bolts to 140 ft. lbs., then reinspect backlash measurement.
23. Install adjusting cotter pins.
24. Install rear anti-lock brake sensor.
25. Apply a continuous bead of Ford Gasket Maker onto axle housing mounting flange and around each bolt hole.
26. Thread two studs into axle housing to prevent rotation of carrier once it makes contact with gasket material.
27. Position carrier into axle housing using two studs to align carrier and housing.
28. Install new carrier housing bolts, remove studs and replace with new bolts.
29. **Torque** differential carrier housing bolts to 150 ft. lbs.
30. Install axle shafts.

Model S135

1. Inspect components as follows:
   a. Inspect bearing surfaces for pitting, wear and overheating.
   b. Inspect differential case machine surfaces.
   c. Inspect thrust washers for scoring and cracking.
   d. Inspect gears for pitting, scoring, wear and damage. **Replace all gears in sets.**
   e. Inspect shafts for nicks and scores.
2. Assemble ring gear to differential case half as follows:
   a. Install a new anti-lock speed sensor ring, if required.
   b. Align tab on sensor ring with notch in case flange.
   c. Bolt ring gear to case half in three places, 120° apart.
3. Press anti-lock speed sensor ring on case flange, if installing a new sensor ring.
4. Install rivets using a suitable press and riveting fixture, noting the following:
   a. Compress rivets before removing bolts from ring gear and case half to prevent ring gear runout.
   b. Apply 45–50 tons of force on each rivet.
5. Press differential side bearings on differential case halves and place bearing cups on bearings.
6. Install gear assembly as follows:
   a. Lightly lubricate all mating surfaces with axle lubricant.
   b. Position thrust washer and differential side gear into case half.
   c. Position differential cross shaft with pinion mates and thrust washers into case half.
   d. Position differential side gear and thrust washer on differential pinion mates.
7. Align reference marks on differential case halves and install retaining bolts. Tighten bolts to specification.
8. Position differential subassembly into carrier using endless lifting sling tool No. D87L-1000-A, or equivalent.
9. Install differential bearing caps as follows:
   a. Position bearing cap onto leg.
   b. Apply threadlock part No. E2FZ-19554-B, or equivalent meeting Ford specification WSK-M2G351-A6 to bolts threads, then install bolts.
   c. Tighten bolts enough to eliminate visible space between bearing cap and leg.
10. Install differential bearing adjusting rings as follows:
    a. Align differential assembly within bearing bores before applying preload.
    b. Tighten both adjusting rings until there is zero endplay and some backlash between ring gear and pinion.
    c. Ensure adjusting ring tooth aligns so installation of adjusting ring lock is possible.
11. Set backlash at zero as follows:

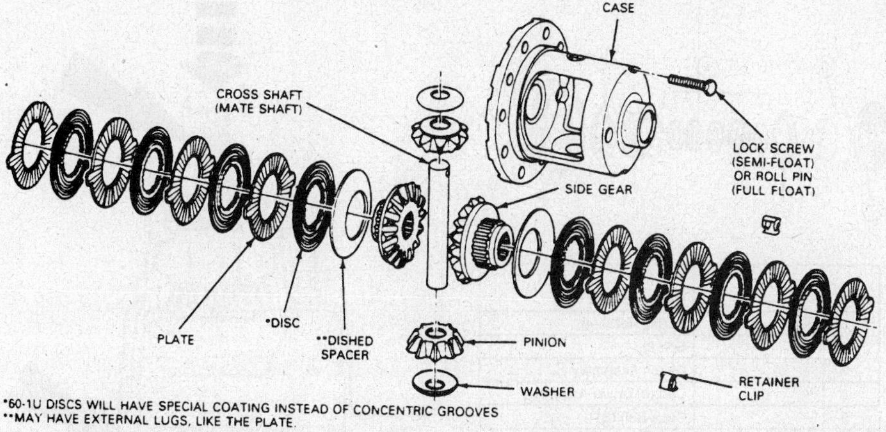

Fig. 12 Exploded view of Trac-Lok locking differential. Model 61-1U

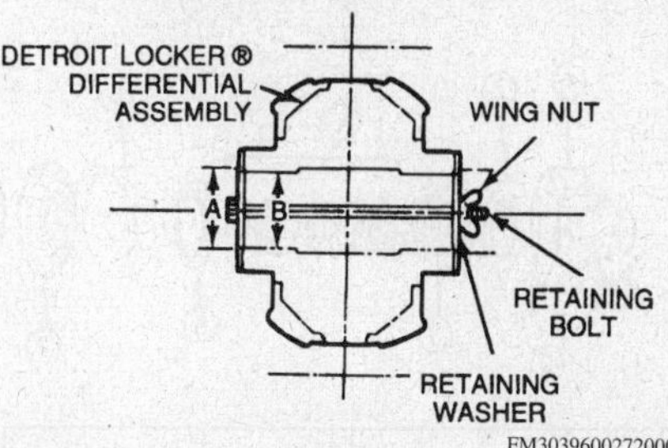

Fig. 13 Detroit Locker differential bolt, nut & washer installation

a. Loosen adjusting ring on tooth side of ring gear one tooth.
b. Tighten opposite adjusting ring one tooth.
c. Repeat process until backlash is zero.

12. Set backlash and bearing preload to specification, noting the following:
    a. If a new matched set is installed, set backlash to specification scribed in ring gear.
    b. If original matched set is installed, set backlash to specification recorded prior to disassembly.
    c. Tighten adjusting ring on tooth side of ring gear until backlash is within specification.
13. Inspect ring gear and pinion backlash in four equally spaced points on ring gear, noting the following:
    a. Backlash should be .002 inch from backlash scribed in ring gear.
    b. If backlash tolerance varies more than .003 inch between four points, remove differential and inspect components for damage.
14. Tighten differential bearing cap bolts to specifications, then measure backlash once again.
15. Install adjusting ring locks and tighten to specifications.
16. Inspect gear set tooth contact pattern as follows:
    a. Paint gear teeth with suitable gear marking compound. A mixture too wet will smear and run. A mixture too dry will not press out from between teeth.
    b. With a suitable box wrench levering on ring gear bolts, rotate ring gear several complete revolutions in both directions or until a clear tooth contact pattern appears.
    c. Certain gear tooth contact pattern types on ring gear indicate improper adjustment. This can be corrected by adjusting ring gear or pinion.
    d. Desirable ring gear tooth patterns must have a drive pattern on the drive side ring gear well centered on the tooth and a coast pattern on the coast side ring gear well centered on the tooth.
    e. There must be clearance between the pattern and top of tooth and no hard lines where pressure is high.
    f. Acceptable ring gear tooth patterns for all axles are illustrated in **Fig. 33.**
    g. Proper backlash with a thinner pinion position shim required is illustrated in **Fig. 34.**
    h. Proper backlash with a thicker pinion position shim required is illustrated in **Fig. 35.**
    i. Proper pinion position shim that requires less backlash is illustrated in **Fig. 36.**
    j. Proper pinion position shim that requires more backlash is illustrated in **Fig. 37.**
17. Install rear anti-lock brake sensor.
18. Install carrier assembly.

Model 174

1. Apply a suitable dry film lubricant to drive pinion bearing cup bore.
2. Install a new oil baffle using cup replacer tool No. 205-054 (T71P-4616-A), or equivalent.
3. Install inner and outer drive pinion bearing cups using handle tool No. 205-111, screw tool No. 205-109, alignment adapter tool No. 205-104, gauge disc tool No. 205-204 and gauge block tool No. 205-100, or equivalents as illustrated in **Fig. 38. Preload bearings to 27 inch lbs.**
4. Position gauge block tool No. 205-110, or equivalent as illustrated in **Fig. 39.**
5. Rotate handle tool several half turns to properly seat drive pinion bearings.
6. Install gauge tube tool No. 205-108, or equivalent.
7. Install bearing caps. Tighten bolts to specifications.
8. Measure and record clearance between gauge tube and gauge block.
9. If drive pinion is marked with a plus (+) reading, this amount must be subtracted from thickness measured. If pinion is marked with a minus (–) reading, this amount must be added to thickness measured.
10. Select and inspect proper drive pinion position shim as required.
11. Install drive pinion position shim and bearing onto pinion using plate tool No. 205-090, cone replacer tool No. 205-011, or equivalent and a suitable press.
12. Install a new collapsible spacer. **Do not use old spacer.**
13. Install drive pinion and a new nut using socket tool No. 205-175 and nut remover tool No. 205-503, or equivalent.
14. Rotate pinion counterclockwise until all endplay is removed, then **torque** nut to 180 ft. lbs.
15. If rotational torque is less than specification, tighten pinion nut in small increments until it is within specification. **Do not torque nut more than 500 ft. lbs., or collapsible spacer will be damaged.** If rotating torque is higher than specification, collapsible spacer has been compressed too far and must be replaced.
16. Rotate pinion 10 revolutions before taking a rotating torque reading. Torque may exceed maximum specification when tightening pinion nut to remove initial endplay. Once endplay is removed and collapsible spacer has begun to collapse, the torque should drop into specified range.
17. Measure pinion rotational torque and adjust as required.
18. Install differential case into axle housing using master bearing set tool No. 205-207A, or equivalent.
19. Seat differential case away from pinion, then push differential case toward pinion while measuring and recording differential case total endplay. Repeat until an identical reading is obtained twice.
20. Observe location of tools to ensure installation on same side of differential case for next measurement with ring gear installed.
21. Remove differential case and tools.
22. Rotate pinion gears and pinion gear thrust washers to pinion shaft hole in differential case.
23. Apply high performance SAE 80W-90 rear axle lubricant part No. F1TZ-19580-B, or an equivalent meeting Ford specification WSP-M2C197-A to pinion gears, side gears and thrust washers. If using original components, install them in same locations.
24. Install pinion shaft and lockpin.
25. Install ring gear with new bolts in an alternate and even pattern. Tighten to

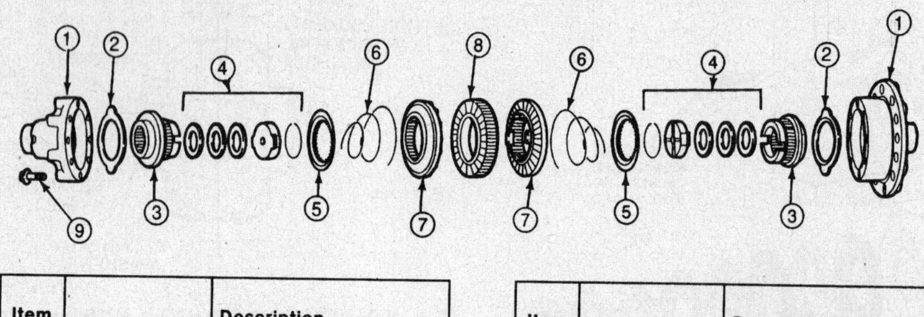

Item		Description
1	—	Case Assembly
2	—	Thrust Washer
3	—	Side Gear
4	—	Preload Dampener Kit

Item		Description
5	—	Spring Retainer
6	—	Spring
7	—	Clutch Assembly
8	—	Central Driver Assembly
9	—	Case Bolt (8)

FM3039600273000X

Fig. 14 Exploded view of Detroit Locker locking differential. Model 80

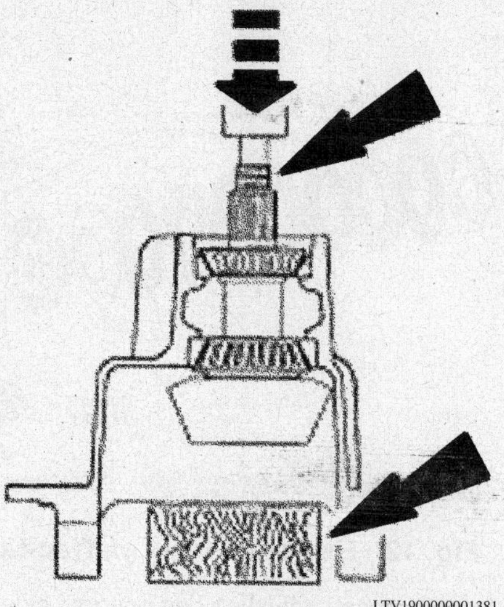

LTV1900000001381

Fig. 15 Pinion removal. Model S110

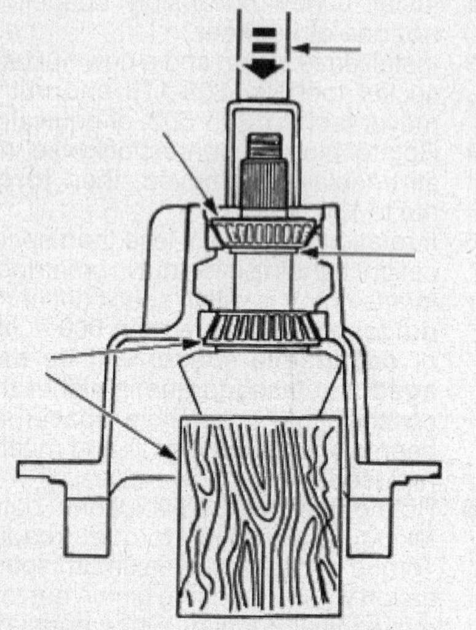

LTV1900000001382

Fig. 16 Pinion bearing replacement. Model S110

specifications.

26. Install differential case into axle housing with tools on same ends of case as noted earlier.
27. Seat differential case away from pinion, then push differential case toward pinion while measuring and recording differential case total endplay. Repeat until an identical reading is obtained twice.
28. Remove differential case and tools.
29. Determine proper differential case bearing shims as follows:
    a. Measure and record total differential case endplay with ring gear removed.
    b. Measure and record total differential case endplay with ring gear installed.
    c. Subtract calculation in Step "b" from Step "a."
    d. Total shims required for ring gear side of case is Step "b" + .003 inch.
    e. Total shims required for opposite side of ring gear is Step "c" + .010 inch.
30. Measure width of tools used on ends of differential case and select proper case bearing shims. If tools do not measure .713–.715 inch, the numbers in Step One will be overstated by difference measured on each tool. The number in Step Two will be overstated by difference measured on tool. Adjustments to shim pack will be required in order to prevent excessive bearing preloads.
31. Install differential case bearings and proper shims using handle tool No. 205-153 and bearing replacer tool No. 205-206, or equivalent.
32. Spread axle housing using differential carrier spreader tool No. 205-001 and housing spreader tool No. 205-136, or equivalent to specification as illustrated in **Fig. 10. Do not exceed .10 inch.**
33. Install differential case.
34. Removal tools.
35. Install bearing caps. Tighten bolts to specifications.
36. Measure ring gear backlash at three equally spaced points on ring gear. If reading is high, ring gear must be moved closer to pinion by moving shims to ring gear side from opposite side. If readings are low, ring gear must be moved away from pinion by moving shims from ring gear side to opposite side.
37. Position axle assembly with pinion stem facing upward.
38. Measure and record total turning torque required to rotate drive pinion and adjust as required. Total turning torque should be drive pinion rotational torque plus 6–10 inch lbs. If torque is too high, subtract an equal amount of shims from each side of differential case. If torque is too low, add an equal amount of shims to both sides of case.
39. Lubricate needle bearings prior to installation with premium long life grease part No. XG-1-C, or an equivalent meeting Ford specification ESA-M1C75-B.
40. Install halfshaft bearings using bearing replacer tool No. 205-195 and handle tool No. 205-153, or equivalent.
41. Install halfshaft seals using seal installer tool No. 205-350 and handle tool No. 205-153, or equivalent.
42. Install axle assembly as outlined under "Rear Axle & Suspension" in "Escape & Mariner" chassis chapter.

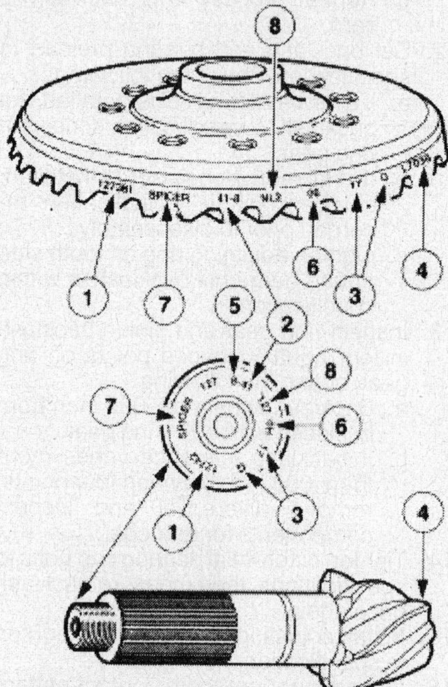

Item	Description
1	Part number
2	Number of ring gear teeth
3	Manufacturing date
4	Matching gear set number
5	Number of pinion teeth
6	Date code
7	Genuine Dana Spicer parts
8	Heat code

LTV1900000001373

Fig. 17 Differential gear set identification. Model S110

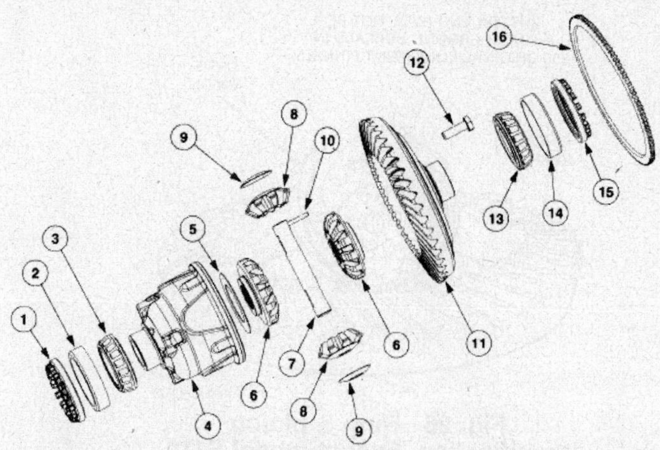

Item	Description
1	Differential bearing adjusting ring
2	Differential side bearing cup
3	Differential side bearing cone
4	Differential case (conventional differential)
5	Differential side gear thrust washer
6	Differential side gear (conventional differential)
7	Differential pinion shaft
8	Differential pinion gear
9	Differential pinion thrust washer
10	Differential pinion shaft pin (conventional differential)
11	Differential ring gear
12	Differential ring gear bolt
13	Differential side bearing cone
14	Differential side bearing cup
15	Differential bearing adjusting ring
16	Anti-lock speed sensor ring

LTV1900000001374

Fig. 18 Exploded view of differential assembly. Model S110

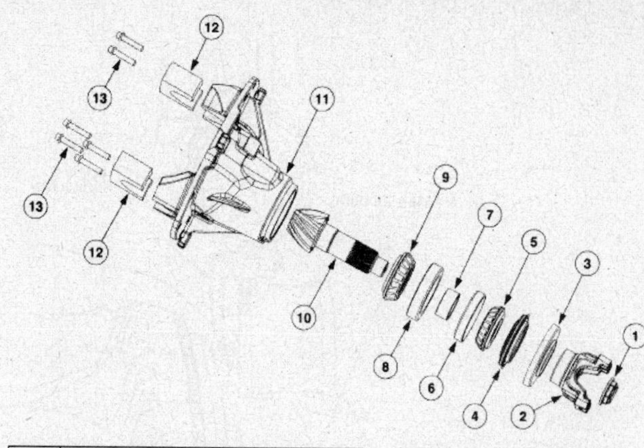

Item	Description
1	Pinion hex nut
2	Pinion yoke
3	Pinion oil seal slinger
4	Pinion oil seal
5	Outer pinion bearing
6	Outer pinion bearing cup
7	Pinion preload spacer (selective)
8	Inner pinion bearing cup
9	Inner pinion bearing
10	Rear axle drive pinion
11	Carrier housing
12	Differential bearing caps
13	Differential bearing cap bolts

LTV1900000001375

Fig. 19 Exploded view of pinion assembly. Model S110

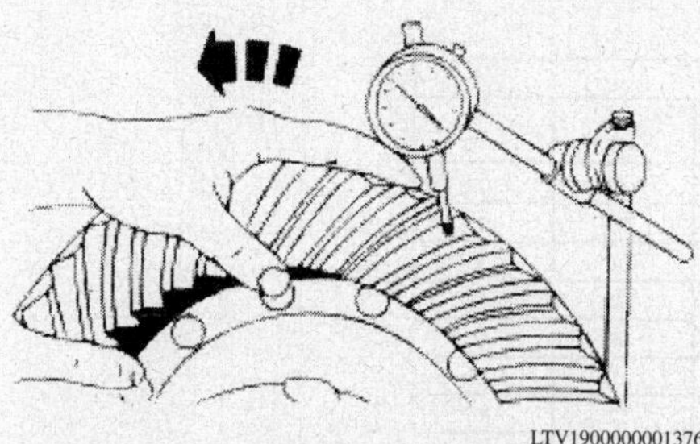

LTV1900000001376

Fig. 20 Backlash measurement. Model S110

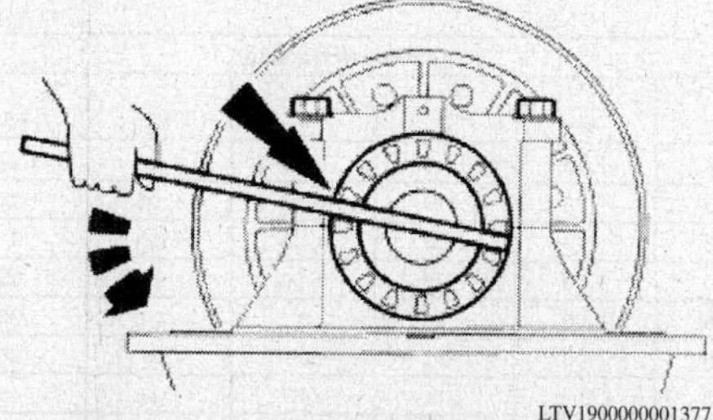

LTV1900000001377

Fig. 21 Differential bearing adjusting ring loosening. Model S110

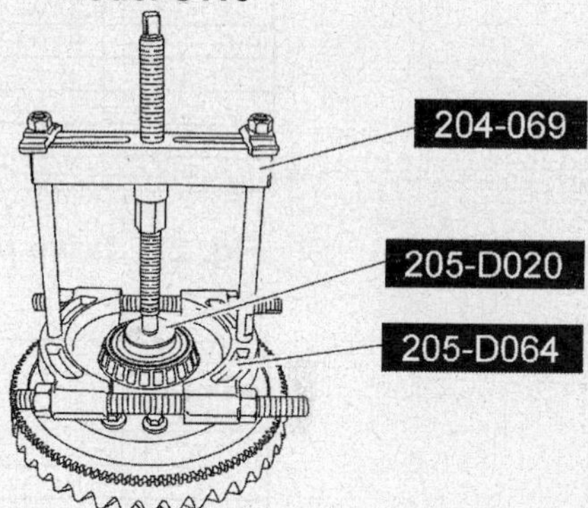

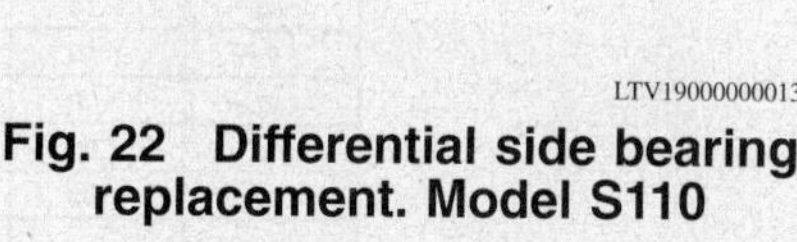

LTV1900000001378

Fig. 22 Differential side bearing replacement. Model S110

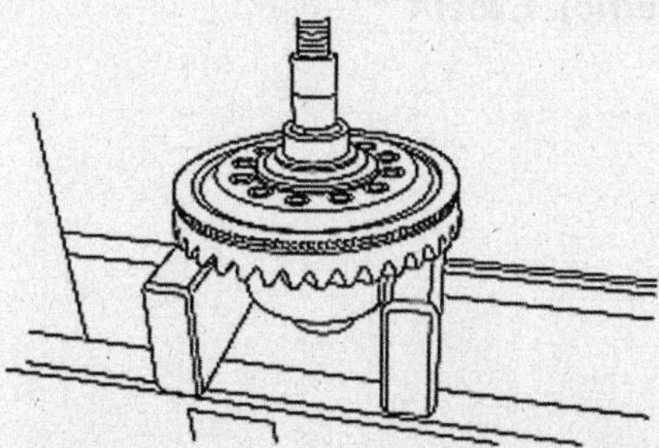

LTV1900000001379

Fig. 23 Separating ring gear from differential carrier. Model S110

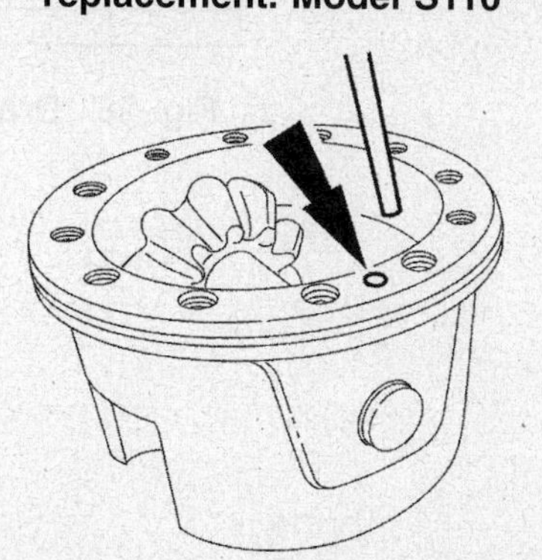

LTV1900000001380

Fig. 24 Pinion cross shaft lock pin removal. Model S110

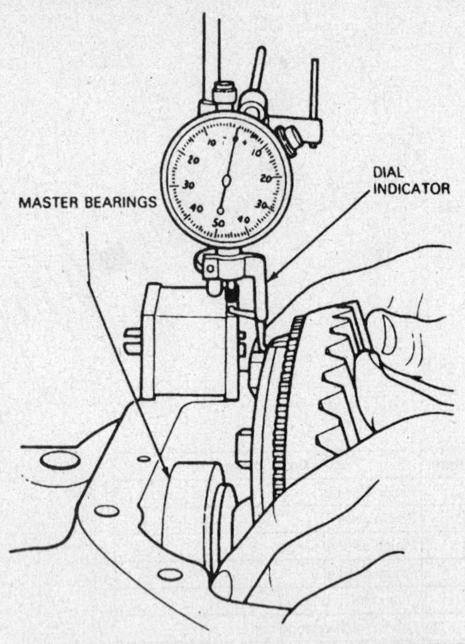

Fig. 25 Total differential case endplay inspection. Except model S135 & 174

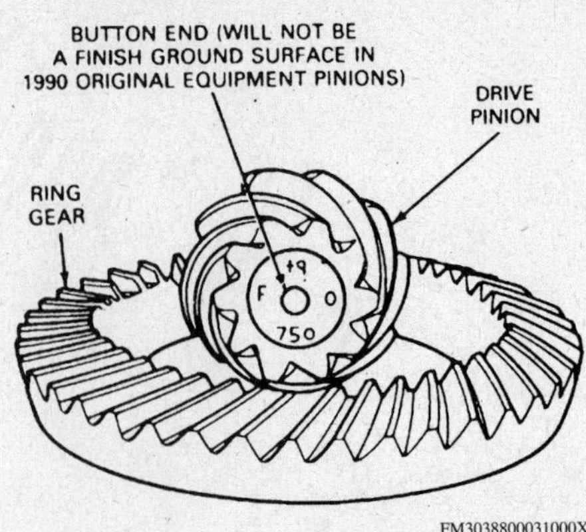

Fig. 26 Ring & pinion identification. Except model S110, S135 & 174

Old Pinion Marking	New Pinion Marking								
	-4	-3	-2	-1	0	+1	+2	+3	+4
+4	+0.008	+0.007	+0.006	+0.005	+0.004	+0.003	+0.002	+0.001	0
+3	+0.007	+0.006	+0.005	+0.004	+0.003	+0.002	+0.001	0	-0.001
+2	+0.006	+0.005	+0.004	+0.003	+0.002	+0.001	0	-0.001	-0.002
+1	+0.005	+0.004	+0.003	+0.002	+0.001	0	-0.001	-0.002	-0.003
0	+0.004	+0.003	+0.002	+0.001	0	-0.001	-0.002	-0.003	-0.004
-1	+0.003	+0.002	+0.001	0	-0.001	-0.002	-0.003	-0.004	-0.005
-2	+0.002	+0.001	0	-0.001	-0.002	-0.003	-0.004	-0.005	-0.006
-3	+0.001	0	-0.001	-0.002	-0.003	-0.004	-0.005	-0.006	-0.007
-4	0	-0.001	-0.002	-0.003	-0.004	-0.005	-0.006	-0.007	-0.008

FM3038800034000X

Fig. 27 Drive pinion adjusting shim thickness chart (English). Except model S110, S135 & 174

Old Pinion Marking	New Pinion Marking								
	-10	-8	-5	-3	0	+3	+5	+8	+10
+10	+.20	+.18	+.15	+.13	+.10	+.08	+.05	+.03	0
+8	+.18	+.15	+.13	+.10	+.08	+.05	+.03	0	-.03
+5	+.15	+.13	+.10	+.08	+.05	+.03	0	-.03	-.05
+3	+.13	+.10	+.08	+.05	+.03	0	-.03	-.05	-.08
0	+.10	+.08	+.05	+.03	0	-.03	-.05	-.08	-.10
-3	+.08	+.05	+.03	0	-.03	-.05	-.08	-.10	-.13
-5	+.05	+.03	0	-.03	-.05	-.08	-.10	-.13	-.15
-8	+.03	0	-.03	-.05	-.08	-.10	-.13	-.15	-.18
-10	0	-.03	-.05	-.08	-.10	-.13	-.15	-.18	-.20

FM3038800035000X

Fig. 28 Drive pinion adjusting shim thickness chart (Metric). Except model S110, S135 & 174

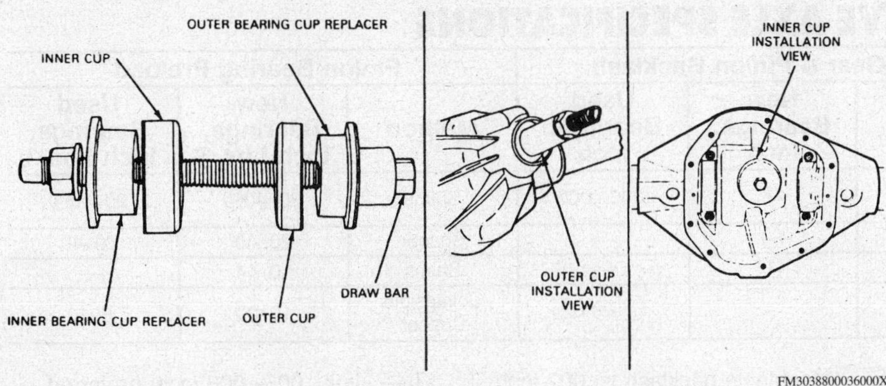

Fig. 29 Inner & outer pinion cup installation tools. Except model S110, S135 & 174

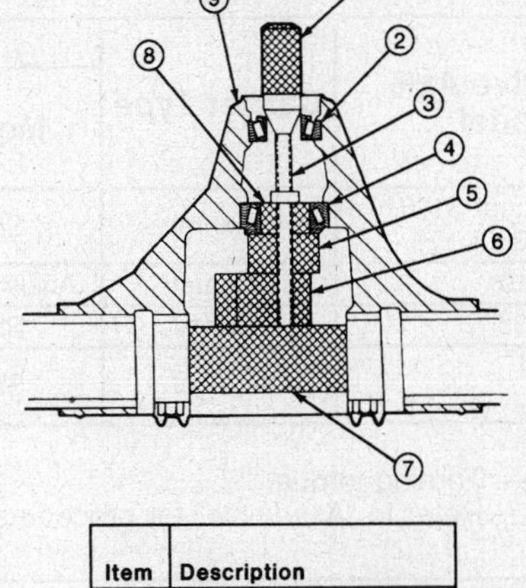

Item	Description
1	Handle
2	Differential Pinion Bearing
3	Screw
4	Differential Pinion Bearing
5	Gauge Disc
6	Gauge Block
7	Gauge Tube
8	Aligning Adapter
9	Rear Axle Housing

FM3038800037000X

Fig. 30 Depth gauge tool selection. Except model S110, S135 & 174

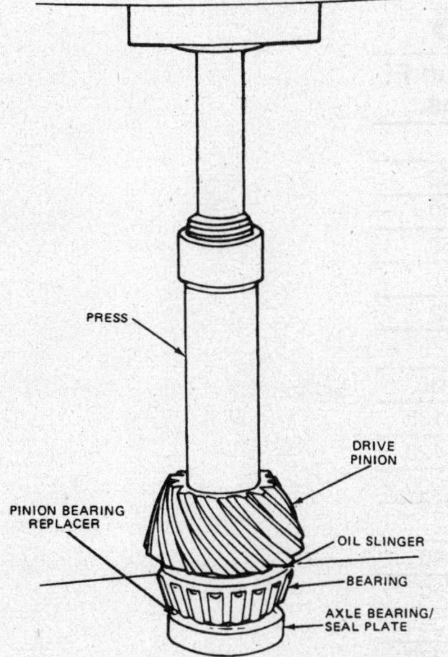

Fig. 31 Bearing installation on drive pinion. Except model S110, S135 & 174

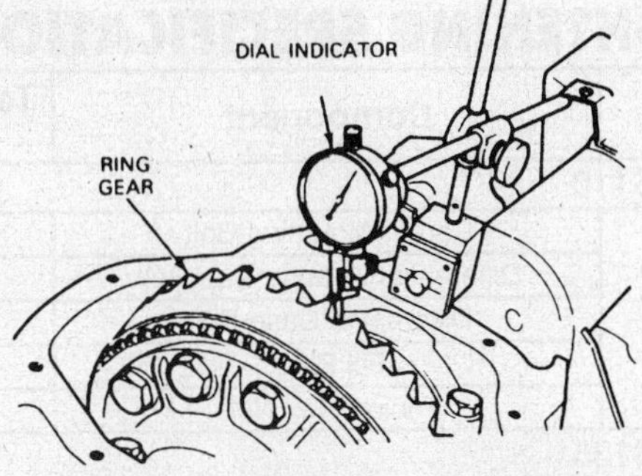

Fig. 32 Ring gear & pinion backlash inspection. Except model S110, S135 & 174

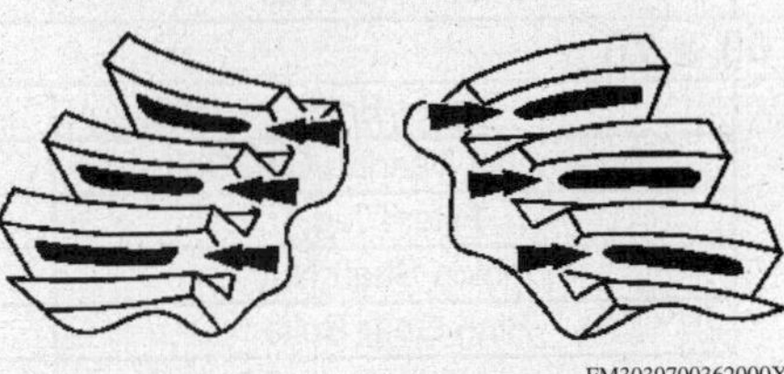

Fig. 33 Acceptable ring gear tooth patterns

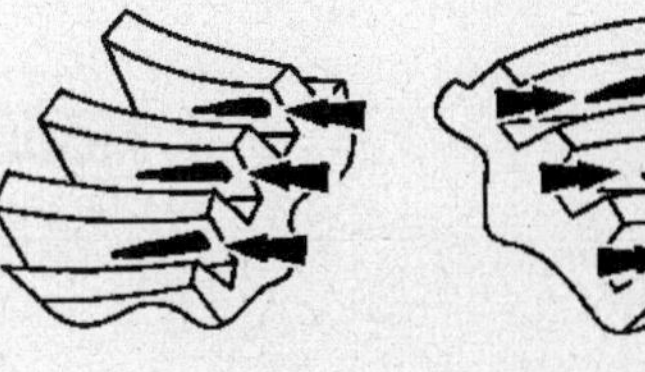

Fig. 34 Proper backlash requiring thinner pinion shim

Fig. 35 Proper backlash requiring thicker pinion shim

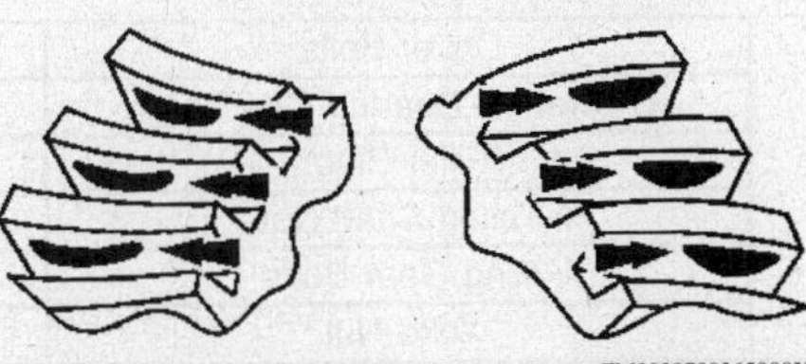

Fig. 36 Proper pinion position shim requiring less backlash

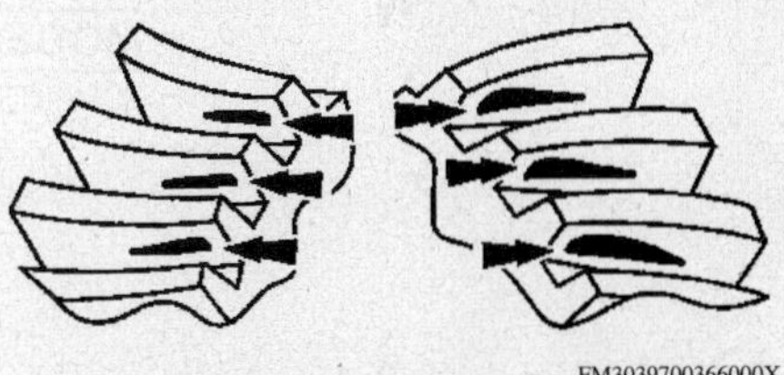

Fig. 37 Proper pinion position shim requiring more backlash

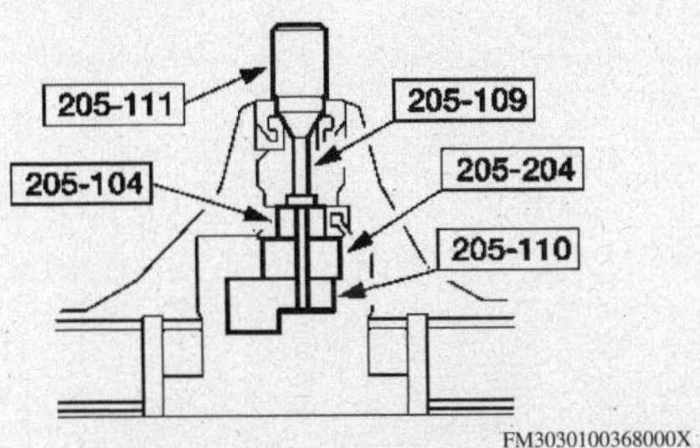

Fig. 38 Inner & outer drive pinion bearing cup installation

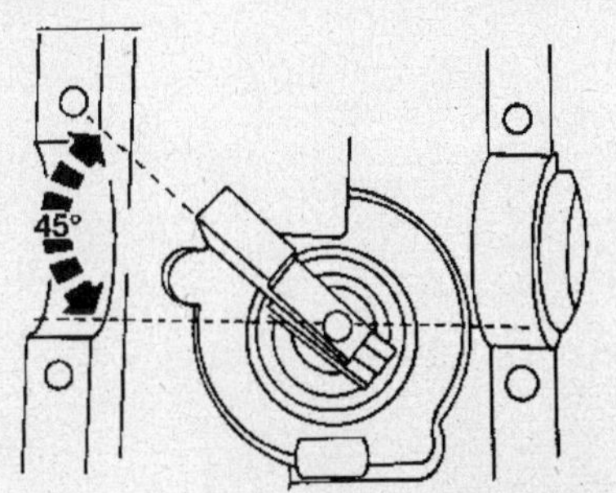

Fig. 39 Gauge block positioning

DRIVE AXLE SPECIFICATIONS

Drive Axle Model	Carrier Type	Ring Gear & Pinion Backlash			Pinion Bearing Preload		
		Method	New Bearings, Inch	Used Bearings, Inch	Method	New Bearings, Inch Lbs.①	Used Bearings, Inch Lbs.①
Except S110, S135 & 174	Integral	Shims	—	.005–.008	Shims	20–40②	20–40②
S110	Integral	Adjusting Ring	③	—	Spacer	20–40	20–40
S135	Integral	Shims	③	—	Shims	10–14	—
174	Intergal	Shims	—	④	Collapsible Spacer	15–30	6–10

① — Turning torque.
② — Refer to "Assemble" for procedure.
③ — Acceptable backlash is .002 inch from backlash scribed in ring gear.
④ — Limit, .005–.008 inch; preferred, .006 inch.

TIGHTENING SPECIFICATIONS

Year	Component	Torque Ft. Lbs.
MODEL S110		
2002–06	Carrier Mounting Bolt	150
	Differential Bearing Cap Bolt	140
	Differential Case Bolt	150
	Fill Plug	40
	Pinion Hex Nut	832
MODEL S135		
2002–06	Adjusting Ring Lock	20–30
	Differential Bearing Cap Bolts	115–135
	Differential Case Half Bolts	100–120
	Pinion Hex Nut	700–900
MODELS 60 & 70		
2002–06	Cover Bolts	30–40
	Differential Bearing Cap Bolts	80–90
	Filler Plug	15–25
	Pinion Shaft Nut	250–270
	Ring Gear Bolts	①
	U-Joint Bolts	15–20
	Yoke Nut	250–270
MODEL 80		
2002–06	Cover Bolts	30–40
	Differential Bearing Cap Bolts	80–90
	Filler Plug	15–25
	Pinion Shaft Nut	440–500
	Ring Gear Bolts	200–240
	Yoke Nut	440–500

① — Grade 8 bolts, 100–120 ft. lbs.; grade 9 bolts, 125–135 ft. lbs.

Ford Rear Drive Axle

NOTE: Prior To Performing Any Service Operations Listed In This Section, Consult The "Technical Service Bulletins" Section For Related Information.

INDEX

IDENTIFICATION

Refer to **Figs. 1 and 2** for axle identification number location and description.

DESCRIPTION

The rear axle is an integral type housing, hypoid gear design with the centerline of the pinion set below the centerline of the ring gear. The hypoid gear set consists of a ring gear and an overhung drive pinion supported by two opposed cone and roller bearings. Pinion bearing preload is maintained by the differential drive pinion collapsible spacer on the drive pinion shaft and adjusted by the pinion nut. The rear axle housing consists of a cast center section with two steel tube assemblies and a stamped axle housing cover.

DISASSEMBLE

7.5, 8.8, 9.75 & 10.25 Inch Ring Gear

1. Remove differential housing cover, **Figs. 3 through 7,** and allow lubricant to drain into an approved container.
2. Remove axle shafts as outlined in "Rear Axle & Suspension" section. **Avoid damaging shaft oil seals.**
3. Wipe all lubricant from internal working components, then visually inspect for wear or damage.
4. Inspect ring gear teeth for signs of scoring, abnormal wear, nicks or chips.
5. Rotate differential case and inspect for any roughness. This would indicate damaged bearings or gears.
6. Position dial indicator and bracket tool No. 100-002, or equivalent into space provided between ABS speed sensor ring and ring gear, then measure ring gear back face runout, which should be .000–.004 inch.
7. Mark position of bearing caps because arrows may not be visible. These caps must be returned to original locations and positions.
8. Remove four bearing cap bolts, then the two bearing caps.
9. **Do not to allow differential case to fall. Place a wood block between a suitable pry bar and rear axle housing to protect machined surface from damage.**
10. Remove differential case from rear axle housing using pry bars and wooden blocks.
11. Remove and discard differential pinion shaft lock bolt.
12. Remove differential pinion shaft.
13. **On models equipped with 8.8, 9.75 or 10.25 inch ring gear,** proceed as follows:
    a. Measure ring gear backlash using dial indicator, which should be .012–.015 inch.
    b. Do not use contact pattern as a guide to inspect for noise. Inspect for proper gear set assembly using pinion depth gauge tool to determine proper pinion shim required to ensure acceptable running condition.
14. **On models equipped with 7.5 inch ring gear,** test ring gear runout as follows:
    a. Install dial indicator and bracket tool No. 100-002, or equivalent.
    b. Zero the indicator, then rotate ring gear and record reading.
    c. If reading exceeds .003 inch, inspect for improper ring gear bolt tightening or dirt between ring and case.
15. **On all models,** if reading still exceeds .003 inch, diagnose ring gear runout as follows:
    a. Remove ring gear by inserting a suitable punch in bolt holes, then carefully driving off ring gear and ABS speed sensor ring if required. **The sensor ring cannot be used again after removal.**
    b. Place differential assembly in carrier casting.
    c. Install .265 inch shim on lefthand side as guide.
    d. Install lefthand bearing cap and tighten bolts finger tight.
    e. Install progressively larger shims on righthand side until largest shim selected can be assembled with a slight drag feel. **Apply pressure toward lefthand side to ensure bearing cup is seated.**
    f. Install righthand side bearing cap and tighten differential bearing cap bolts to specifications, then rotate assembly to ensure free rotation.
    g. Measure runout of differential case flange with dial indicator. If runout is within .003 inch, install new ring and pinion gear. If runout exceeds specifications, trouble is due to either a damaged case or worn bearings.
    h. Remove differential case from carrier and the differential bearings from case.
    i. Install new differential bearings on case hubs and install differential assembly in carrier less ring gear.
    j. Measure case runout. If runout is within .003 inch, use new bearings

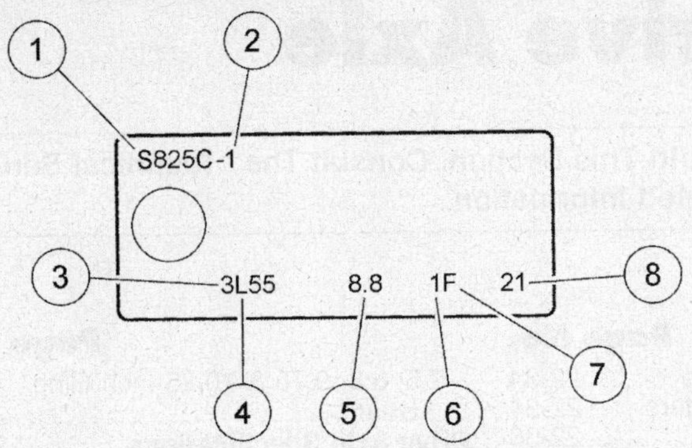

Item	Description
1	Plant code
2	Denotes interchangeability affected internally
3	Axle ratio
4	Denotes Traction-Lok®
5	Ring gear diameter (inch)
6	Build year
7	Build month
8	Build day

LTV0500000000998

Fig. 1 Rear drive axle identification

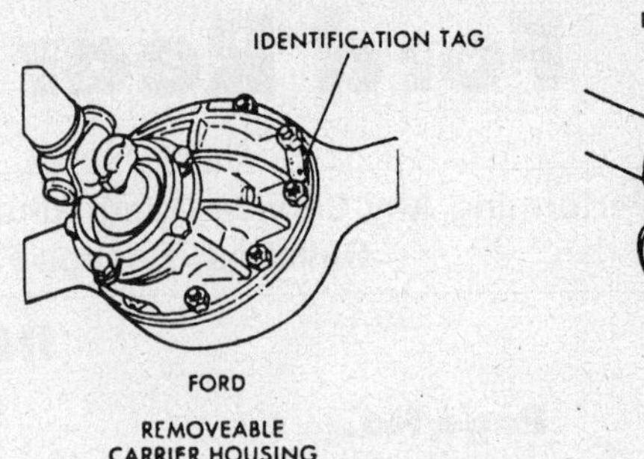

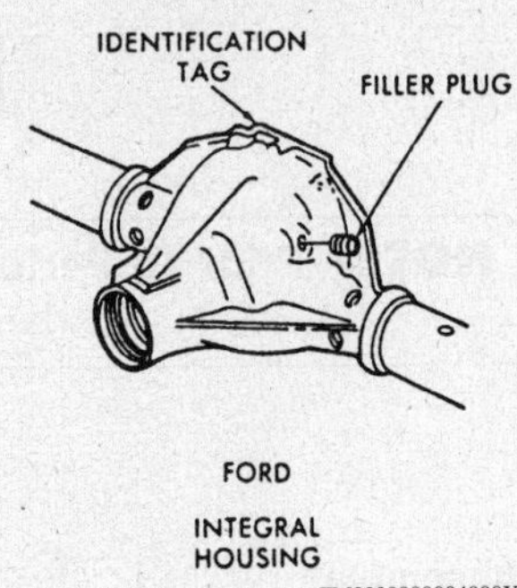

FM3038800004000X

Fig. 2 Carrier type identification

for reassembly. If runout is still excessive, case is damaged and must be replaced.

16. Insert a suitable punch in bolt holes, then carefully drive off ring gear and ABS speed sensor ring if required. **The sensor ring cannot be used again after removal.**
17. Mark relationship of driveshaft end yoke and axle companion flange for proper assembly, then disconnect driveshaft at rear axle universal joint.
18. Install a suitable inch pound torque wrench on pinion nut and tighten as required to maintain rotation of pinion through several turns.
19. Hold companion flange and remove pinion nut using suitable tools.
20. Clean area around oil seal and place drain pan under seal.
21. Mark relationship of companion flange to pinion shaft for proper assembly, then, using suitable puller, remove companion flange.
22. Remove pinion oil seal using suitable tool.
23. Mark one differential bearing cap to ensure proper positioning of caps during assembly. **Do not interchange lefthand and righthand bearing caps.**
24. Loosen differential bearing cap bolts and bearing caps, noting direction of triangles on bearing caps for proper assembly.
25. Pry differential case, bearing cups and shims out until they are loose in bearing caps, then remove bearing caps and pry differential assembly from carrier. **When using pry bar, place a wood block between pry bar and axle housing to protect casting face from damage.**
26. Drive pinion out of front bearing cone using a suitable mallet and remove through rear of carrier casting.
27. Remove pinion rear cone and roller bearing assembly using suitable tools, then, using micrometer, measure and record thickness of shim found under bearing cone.
28. Remove damaged pinion bearing cups from carrier by tapping alternately with brass drift on opposite sides of cups to prevent cups from cocking in casting.

10.5 Inch Ring Gear

CONVENTIONAL ONE-PIECE DIFFERENTIAL CASE

1. Remove differential case, **Fig. 8.**
2. Remove ring gear bolts.
3. Insert a punch into bolt holes and drive ring gear off.
4. Remove anti-lock speed sensor ring. **This part cannot be reused once removed.**
5. Remove differential bearings, if required.
6. Remove differential pinion shaft lock bolt, then the pinion shaft.
7. Rotate and remove differential pinion gears and thrust washers.
8. Remove differential side gears and thrust washers.

CONVENTIONAL TWO-PIECE DIFFERENTIAL CASE

1. Remove differential case, **Fig. 8.**
2. Remove ring gear bolts.
3. Insert a punch in bolt holes and drive off ring gear.
4. Remove anti-lock speed sensor ring, if required. **Sensor ring cannot be reused once removed.**
5. Position differential holding tool, tool No. 205-447, or equivalent in a vise.
6. Place differential case on holding tool.
7. Place reference marks on case halves for assembly.
8. Install companion flange holding tool No. T78P-4851-A, or equivalent on differential case and loosen case bolts.
9. Remove differential case bolts.
10. Remove righthand side differential case half and side gear.
11. Remove differential pinion shaft and pinion gears.
12. Remove lefthand differential side gear and side gear thrust washers.

TRACTION-LOK ONE-PIECE DIFFERENTIAL CASE

1. Remove differential case, **Fig. 9.**
2. Remove differential pinion shaft lock bolt, then the pinion shaft.
3. Remove ring gear and anti-lock speed sensor ring, if required. **Anti-lock sensor ring cannot be reused once removed.**
4. Install Traction-Lok torque tool set No. 205-447, or equivalent in a vise.
5. Install differential case on tool.
6. Install step plate tool No. D80L-630-8, or equivalent in bottom side gear bore. Apply small amount of grease to step plate centering hole.
7. Install nut in upper differential side gear and hold in position while installing hex screw.
8. Tighten hex head screw until contact is made with step plate.
9. Insert a dowel bar in hole of nut, then tighten forcing screw to force differential side gear away from pinion gears.
10. Insert limited slip differential rotator tool No. T86T-4205-A, or equivalent in pinion shaft bore.

11. Turn differential case to walk differential pinion gears and pinion thrust washers out to case windows. **Differential pinion thrust washers cannot be removed independently of pinion gears.**
12. Remove differential pinion gears and pinion thrust washers.
13. Remove differential side gears and clutch packs. Side gears and clutch packs must be installed in original positions.

TRACTION-LOK TWO-PIECE DIFFERENTIAL CASE

1. Remove differential case, **Fig. 9.**
2. Remove ring gear bolts.
3. Insert a punch in bolt holes and drive ring gear off.
4. Remove anti-lock speed sensor ring, if required. **Anti-lock speed sensor ring cannot be reused once removed.**
5. Remove differential bearings, if required.
6. Place Traction-Lok torque tool set No. 205-447, or equivalent in a suitable vise.
7. Place differential case on tool set.
8. Place reference marks on case halves for assembly.
9. Remove differential case retaining bolts.
10. Remove righthand differential case half and side gear.
11. Remove differential pinion shaft and pinion gears.
12. Remove differential pinion gears from pinion shaft.
13. Remove both differential side gears and clutch packs from each case half.
14. Remove Belleville spring and shim from clutch packs.

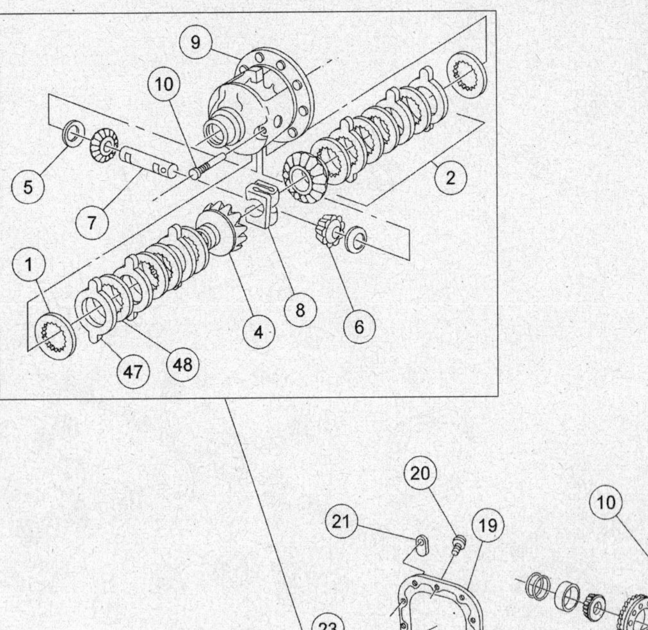

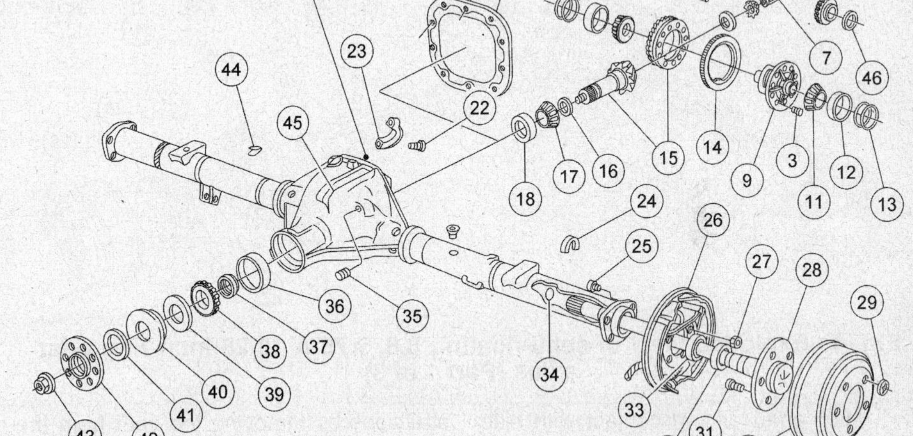

Fig. 3 Exploded view of 7.5 inch ring gear axle

SUBASSEMBLY SERVICE

Standard Differential

1. Remove pinion gears and thrust washers, rotating as required to align with windows.
2. Remove side gears and thrust washers.
3. Remove and discard ring gear attaching bolts, then press ring gear off of case. Models equipped with anti-lock brakes incorporate an exciter ring located on the ring gear. Removal of this ring is not required when removing ring gear. But care should be taken when removing ring gear assembly.
4. Remove differential bearings from case using a suitable puller.
5. Install differential bearings on case using suitable press.
6. Install ring gear on case, then coat bolts with suitable locking compound and tighten to specifications.

Clutch Type Traction-Lok Limited Slip Differential

Overhaul procedures for this limited slip differential, **Fig. 10,** are the same as for "Ford Traction-Lok Differential."

Ford Traction-Lok Differential

DISASSEMBLE

1. Remove pinion shaft lock screw and pinion shaft.
2. Push axle shafts inward and remove C-clips from axle shafts. Remove axle shafts.
3. Remove preloaded "S" shaped spring, **Fig. 11. Use caution when removing "S" shaped spring since it is under tension.**
4. Rotate pinion gears and thrust washers until they can be removed through access hole using 12 inch socket extension inserted into tool No. T80P-4205-A, or equivalent, **Fig. 12.**
5. Remove lefthand and righthand side gears, clutch packs and shims, **Fig. 10.** Note order of removal for reference during assembly.

INSPECTION

1. Visually inspect clutch packs, side gears, pinion gears and pinion shaft for damage or wear and replace as required.
2. Place each clutch pack without shims into tool No. T80P-4946-A, or equivalent, **Fig. 13.** Tighten nut to specifications. Determine thickness of new shims by inserting thickest feeler gauge blade possible between clutch pack and tool, **Fig. 14.**

ASSEMBLE

1. Apply suitable lubricant to clutch plates, then install lefthand side gear, clutch pack and new shim into differential case. Repeat procedure for righthand side.
2. Install pinion gears and thrust washers

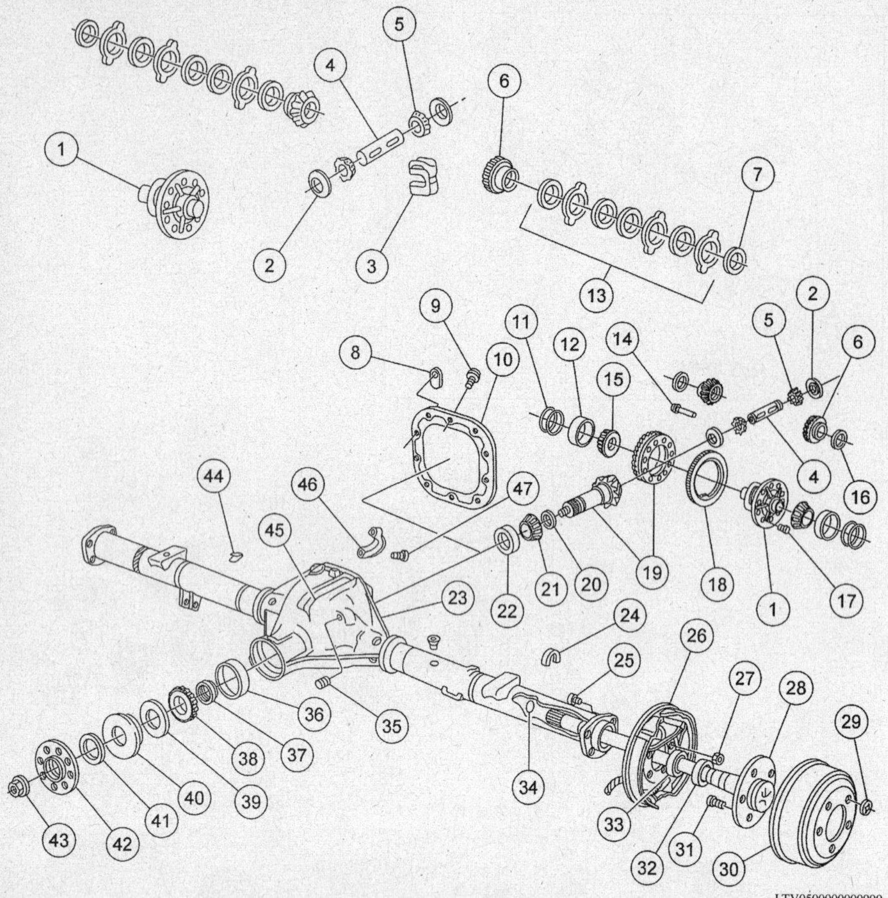

Fig. 4 Exploded view of semi-floating 8.8, 9.75 & 10.25 inch ring gear axles (Part 1 of 3)

Item	Description
1	Differential cases
2	Differential pinion thrust washers
3	Differential clutch spring
4	Differential pinion shafts
5	Differential pinion gears
6	Differential side gears
7	Rear axle differential clutch shim
8	Rear axle identification tag
9	Differential housing cover bolt
10	Differential housing cover
11	Differential bearing shim
12	Differential bearing cup
13	Differential clutch pack
14	Differential pinion shaft lock bolt
15	Differential bearing
16	Differential side gear thrust washer
17	Case bolt
18	Anti-lock speed sensor ring
19	Differential ring gear and pinion
20	Drive pinion bearing adjustment shim
21	Pinion bearing (inner)
22	Pinion bearing cup
23	Differential housing
24	U-washer
25	Bolt
26	Drum brake assembly
27	Brake backing plate nut
28	Axle shaft
29	Retainer
30	Brake drum
31	Wheel stud
32	Wheel bearing oil seal
33	Rear wheel bearing

LTV0500000001000

Fig. 4 Exploded view of semi-floating 8.8, 9.75 & 10.25 inch ring gear axles (Part 2 of 3)

180° apart and in contact with side gears.

3. Align gears with pinion shaft bore, **Fig. 11,** using 12 inch socket extension inserted in pinion shaft rotator.
4. Install "S" shaped preload spring into differential using soft faced hammer.
5. Install axle shafts and secure with C-clip.
6. Install pinion shaft. Apply Loctite, or equivalent, onto pinion shaft lock bolt, then tighten to specifications.

CLEANING & INSPECTION

Thoroughly clean all components. Do not soak or wash synthetic seals in cleaning solvents. Use only clean solvent to wash bearings. Oil bearings immediately after cleaning to prevent rusting. A visual inspection of components will detect any major wear or damage. Clean inside of carrier and carrier housing before rebuilding and assembling components.

If water is present in the axle or fluid loss is noted, the cause may be a plugged axle vent. Ensure the axle vent is clear of all obstructions by removing the vent from the axle and inspecting it. If the vent is plugged, place in a suitable vise and drill out the vent using a 3/16 inch drill bit. Install the vent and vent hose, ensuring entire vent hose is clear of obstructions.

Gears

Examine drive pinion and ring gear teeth for scoring or signs of excessive wear. Worn gears cannot be rebuilt to correct a noisy condition. Gear scoring and flaking are the result of excessive shock loading or the use of improper lubricant. Scored gears cannot be reused.

Examine teeth and thrust surfaces of differential gears. Wear on hub of differential side gears may cause a chucking noise known as chuckle, when the vehicle is operated at low speeds. Wear of splines, thrust surfaces or thrust washers may contribute to excessive drive line backlash.

Bearing Cups

Inspect bearing cups for rings, galling or erratic wear patterns. The bearing cups must be solidly seated. Inspect by attempting to insert .0015 inch feeler gauge between cups and bottoms of bores.

Cone & Roller Assemblies

When operated in the cups, the cone and roller assemblies must turn without any roughness. Examine roller ends for wear.

Differential Bearing Adjusters

Test fit of bearing adjusters in their threads with bearing caps installed. Ensure bearing caps are on sides that they were machined to fit. The faces of the adjusters that contact the bearing cups must be smooth and square. Examine threads in carrier if their fit is not proper and replace any adjuster with a damaged face or threads.

34	Rear axle shaft O-ring
35	Filler plug
36	Pinion bearing cup (outer)
37	Drive pinion collapsible spacer
38	Pinion bearing (outer)
39	Rear axle drive pinion shaft oil slinger
40	Rear axle drive pinion seal
41	Drive pinion oil seal deflector
42	Pinion flange
43	Pinion nut
44	Rear axle brake line clip
45	Anti-lock speed sensor
46	Bearing cap
47	Bearing cap bolt

LTV0500000001001

Fig. 4 Exploded view of semi-floating 8.8, 9.75 & 10.25 inch ring gear axles (Part 3 of 3)

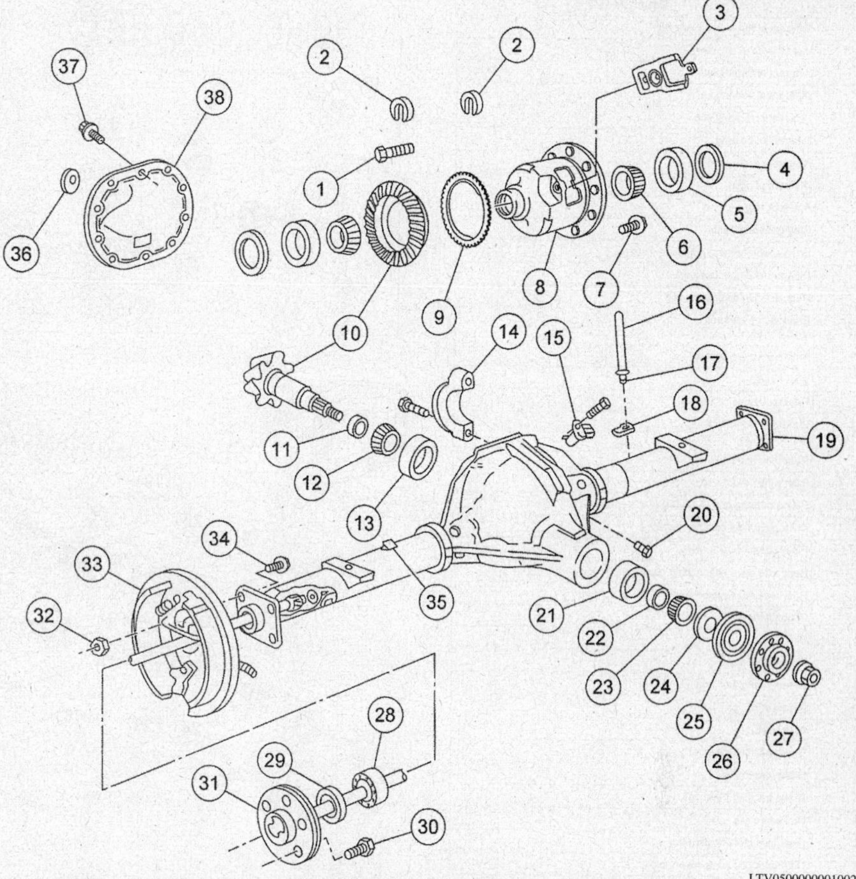

LTV0500000001002

Fig. 5 Exploded view of high torque 8.8 inch ring gear axle (Part 1 of 2)

Companion Flange

Be sure that flat machined surfaces and the bearing cup sockets of the flange have not been damaged in removing driveshaft or in removing flange from axle. The edge of the flange that contacts the oil slinger or pinion front bearing must be smooth. Roughness aggravates backlash noises and causes wear on the slinger with a resultant loss in drive pinion bearing preload. The seal surface should be perfectly smooth or leakage will result.

Pinion Retainer

Inspect visually for damage. Ensure pinion bearing cups are seated. Ensure there are no chips or burrs on mounting flange. Clean all lubricant passages. If pinion bearing cups were removed, examine bores in retainer carefully. Any nicks or burrs in these bores must be removed to permit proper seating of cups.

Carrier Housing

Inspect visually for damage. Ensure differential bearing bores are smooth and that threads are not damaged. Remove any nicks or burrs from mounting surfaces of housing. Only repairs to cast axle housing and the "puddle-welded" area of the housing are approved. They should be made as follows:

1. Clean surfaces to be repaired by grinding or rotary filing to a clean bright metal finish. Clean repair area thoroughly. Metallic plastic will not stick to a dirty or oily surface. Chamfer or undercut the hole or porosity to a greater depth than the rest of the cleaned surface. Solid metal must surround the hole. Openings larger than 1/4 inch should not be repaired with metallic plastic. They can be drilled, tapped and plugged using common tools.
2. Mix metallic plastic base and hardener according to manufacturer's instructions. Stir thoroughly until uniform.
3. Apply repair mixture with suitable clean tool, forcing epoxy into hole or porosity.
4. Allow repair mixture to harden. Heat cure with a 250 watt lamp placed 10 inches from repaired surface or air dry for 10–12 hours at temperatures above 50° F.
5. Sand or grind repaired area to blend with general contour of surrounding surface.
6. Paint the surface to match the rest of the axle housing.

Differential Case

Ensure the hubs where bearings mount are smooth. Inspect fit of differential gears in the counterbores. Carefully examine thrust washers, which may be damaged when bearings are removed. If differential bearing assemblies do not seat firmly on hubs, failure is certain. Ensure mating surfaces of the two components of case and the face of the ring gear attaching flange are smooth and free from nicks and burrs.

Ring Gear Runout

Models equipped with anti-lock brakes incorporate a multi-tooth exciter ring which is pressed on the differential case located behind the ring gear assembly. Do not remove exciter ring to measure ring gear runout. A space is provided between the exciter ring and ring gear to measure ring gear runout.

If ring gear runout during disassembly exceeded specifications, the condition may be caused by a warped gear or distorted or damaged case or foreign matter trapped between differential case halves or under ring gears.

To determine cause of excessive runout, assemble differential case without ring gear, then inspect as follows:

1. Install case in differential carrier without ring gear attached.
2. Install bearing caps and adjuster nuts, then tighten cap bolts to specifications.
3. Tighten adjuster nuts to center differential side bearing.
4. Mount a suitable dial indicator, then measure runout of case flange and ring gear pilot.
5. If runout at either point is excessive, install a new differential case.
6. If runout is within specification, the ring gear is out of specification.
7. **On models equipped with locking differential case,** when performing this inspection, the four compression springs within the case should be temporarily removed. This will prevent a false runout reading due to distortion caused by springs forcing the case apart.

Item	Description
1	Differential thrust plate lock bolt
2	U-washers
3	Differential thrust plate
4	Differential bearing shim
5	Differential bearing cup
6	Differential bearing
7	Ring gear bolt
8	Differential case
9	Anti-lock ring
10	Ring gear and pinion
11	Drive pinion bearing adjustment shim
12	Differential pinion bearing
13	Rear axle pinion bearing cup
14	Bearing cap and bolt (part of 4010)
15	Anti-lock speed sensor
16	Vent hose
17	Rear axle housing vent
18	Brake junction block (part of 4022)
19	Rear axle housing
20	Filler plug
21	Pinion bearing cup — (outer)
22	Drive pinion collapsible spacer
23	Pinion bearing — (outer)
24	Rear axle drive pinion shaft oil slinger
25	Rear axle drive pinion seal
26	Pinion flange
27	Pinion nut
28	Rear wheel bearing
29	Wheel bearing oil seal
30	Wheel stud
31	Axle shaft
32	Brake backing plate nut
33	Brake assembly
34	Brake backing plate bolt
35	Brake line clip
36	Rear axle identification tag
37	Differential housing cover bolt
38	Differential housing cover

LTV0500000001003

Fig. 5 Exploded view of high torque 8.8 inch ring gear axle (Part 2 of 2)

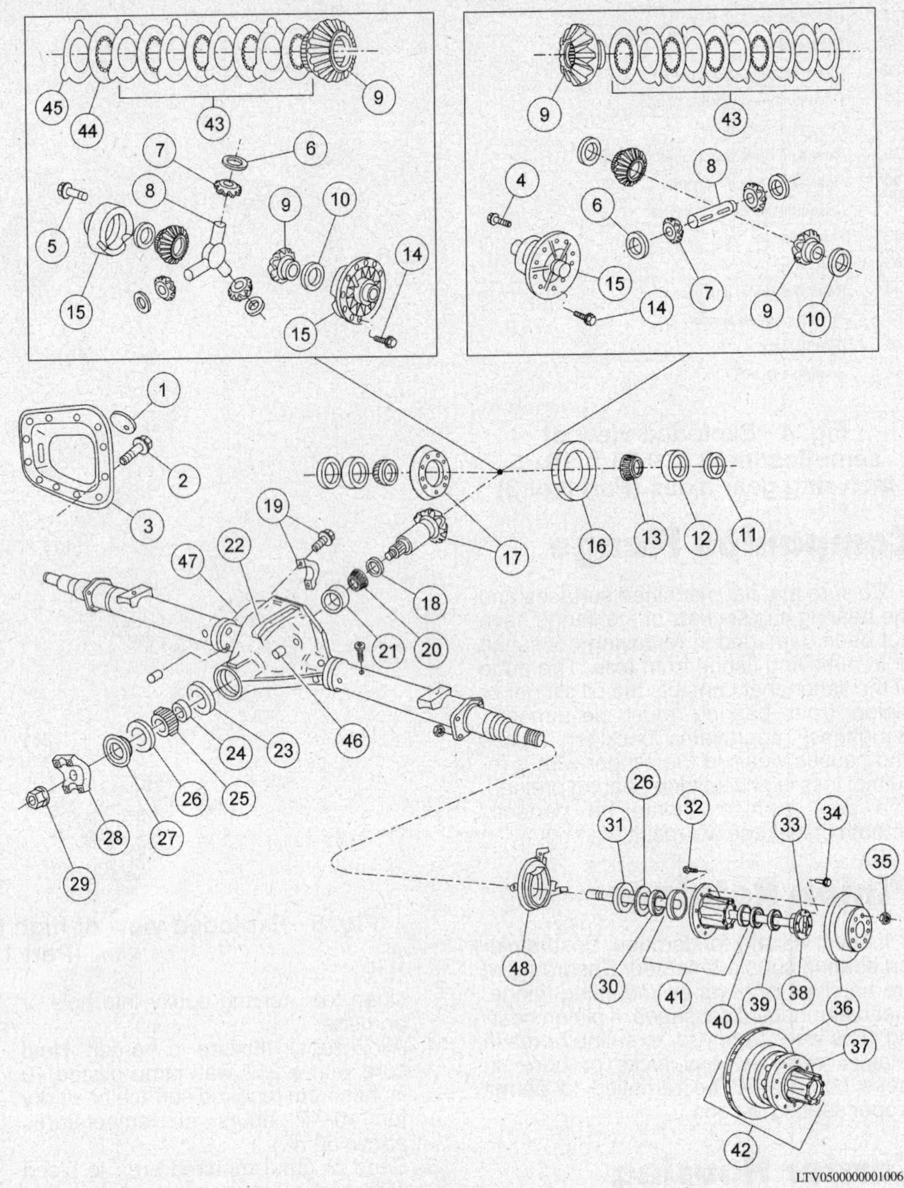

Fig. 6 Exploded view of Traction-Lok 10.5 inch ring gear axle (Part 1 of 2)

ASSEMBLE

7.5, 8.8, 9.75 & 10.25 Inch Ring Gear

1. If removed, install new bearing cups using suitable tool. Ensure cups are properly seated in their bores. If a .0015 inch feeler gauge can be inserted between a cup and the bottom of its bore at any point around cup, the cup is not properly seated. Whenever cups are replaced, the cone and roller assembly should also be replaced.
2. Assemble appropriate aligning adapter, gauge disc and gauge block to screw using proper rear axle pinion depth gauge tool.
3. Place rear pinion bearing over aligning disc and insert it into rear pinion bearing cup and assemble tool handle to screw. Roll assembly back and forth a few times to seat bearings while tightening tool handle by hand. **Torque** tool handle to 20 ft. lbs. **The gauge block must be offset 45° to obtain accurate reading.**
4. Center gauge tube into differential bearing bore, then install bearing caps, torquing bolts to specifications. Select thickest shim that will enter between gauge tube and gauge block. Insert shim directly along gauge block to ensure a proper reading. The shim fit should be a slight drag type feel. **Shims used for gauging must be flat to obtain proper feel.**
5. Place selected shim(s) on pinion and press pinion bearing cone and roller assembly until it is firmly seated on shaft. **The same rear pinion bearing used in this procedure must be used in final assembly of axle. Ensure press load is not applied to bearing cage.**
6. Inspect splines on pinion shaft to be sure that they are free of burrs. If burrs are evident, remove them with a fine crocus cloth, working in a rotational motion, then wipe pinion clean.
7. Place collapsible spacer on pinion shaft against rear bearing.
8. Working from rear of axle housing, install drive pinion assembly into housing pinion shaft bore.
9. Install front cone and roller and the oil slinger on pinion shaft.
10. Clean oil seal seat surface, then, using suitable seal installation tool, install seal in carrier and pack lips of seal with suitable lubricant. **Installation without proper tool may result in early seal failure. If seal becomes cocked during installation, remove it and install new one.**
11. Apply small amount of suitable lubricant to companion shaft splines, align mark on companion flange with mark

Item	Description
1	Rear axle identification tag
2	Differential housing cover bolt
3	Differential housing cover
4	Differential pinion shaft lock bolt
5	Differential case bolt
6	Differential pinion thrust washer
7	Differential pinion gear
8	Differential pinion shaft
9	Differential side gear
10	Differential side gear thrust washer
11	Differential bearing shim
12	Differential bearing cup
13	Differential bearing
14	Ring gear bolt
15	Differential case
16	Anti-lock speed sensor ring
17	Ring gear and pinion
18	Drive pinion bearing adjustment shim
19	Bearing cap and bolt
20	Pinion bearing (inner)
21	Inner axle pinion bearing cup
22	RABS sensor
23	Outer pinion bearing cup

Item	Description
24	Collapsible spacer
25	Pinion bearing (outer)
26	Rear axle drive pinion shaft oil slinger
27	Rear axle drive pinion seal
28	Pinion flange
29	Pinion nut
30	Rear wheel bearing inner cone and roller
31	Wheel bearing oil seal
32	Lug bolt
33	Axle shaft
34	Axle shaft nut
35	Lug nut
36	Rear disc brake rotor
37	Rear hub
38	Gasket
39	Bearing
40	Hub and bearing cup
41	Rear brake hub and drum (DRW only)
42	Differential clutch pack
43	Rear axle differential clutch shim
44	Differential clutch spring
45	Filler plug
46	Rear axle housing
47	Brake adapter plate

LTV0500000001007

Fig. 6 Exploded view of Traction-Lok 10.5 inch ring gear axle (Part 2 of 2)

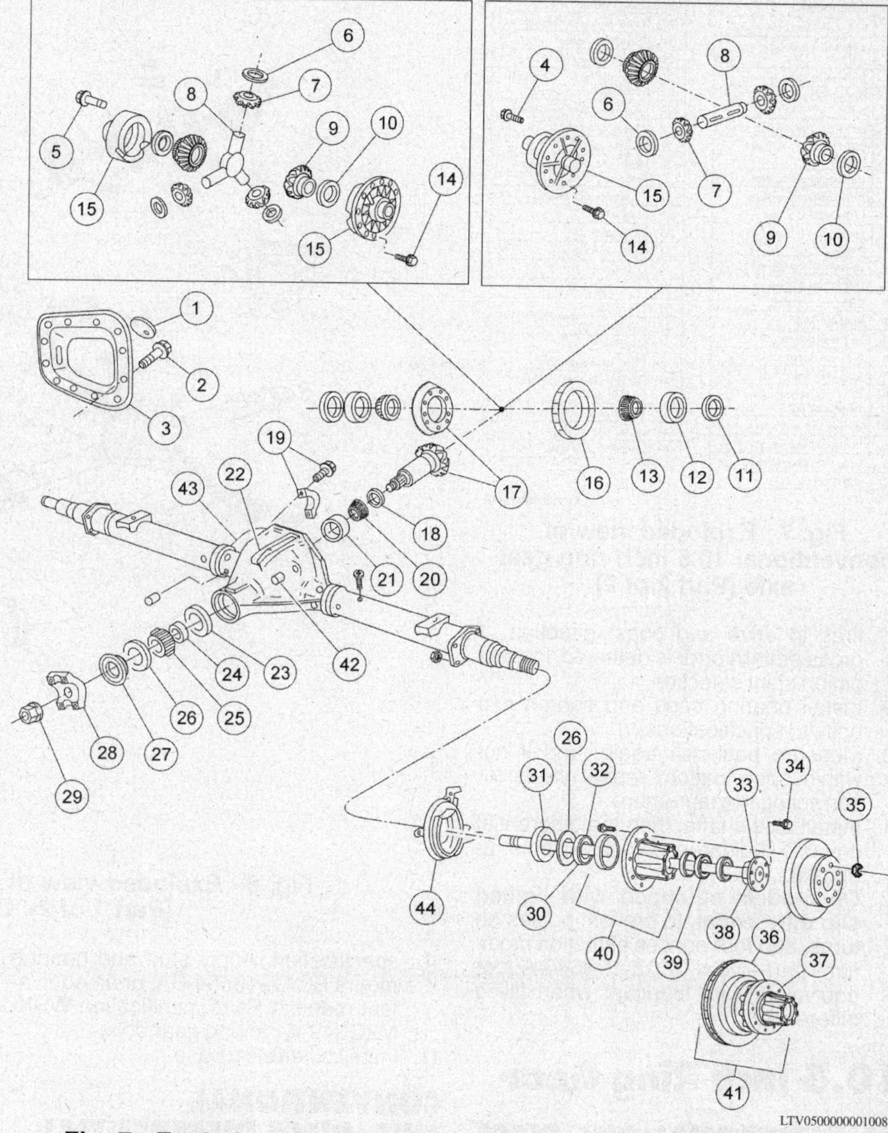

LTV0500000001008

Fig. 7 Exploded view of conventional 10.5 inch ring gear axle (Part 1 of 2)

on pinion shaft, install flange and install new nut on pinion shaft. **If a new companion flange is being installed, disregard scribe mark on pinion shaft. The companion flange must never be hammered on or installed with power tools.**

12. Hold companion flange with suitable tool and tighten pinion nut to specifications, rotating pinion occasionally to ensure proper bearing seating. Take frequent pinion bearing preload readings until original recorded preload reading is obtained.
13. If original recorded preload is lower than 8–13 inch lbs., for original bearings or 16–29 inch lbs., for new bearings, tighten pinion nut to specifications. If preload is higher than specification, tighten to original reading as recorded. **Under no circumstances should pinion nut be backed off to reduce preload. If reduced preload is required, a new collapsible pinion spacer and pinion nut must be installed.**
14. Apply suitable lubricant to new wheel bearing and install bearing into housing using suitable tool.
15. Pack lips of seal with suitable lubricant and install axle shaft seal using suit able seal installation tool. **Installation of bearing or seal assembly without proper tool may result in early bearing or seal failure. If seal becomes cocked in bore during installation, remove it and install new one.**
16. Place differential case subassembly in carrier.
17. Install a .265 inch shim on lefthand side.
18. Install lefthand bearing cap and tighten bolts finger tight.
19. Install progressively larger shims on righthand side until largest shim selected can be assembled with a slight drag feel. Apply pressure towards lefthand side to ensure bearing cup is seated.
20. Install righthand side bearing cap and tighten cap bolts to specifications.
21. Rotate assembly to ensure free rotation.
22. Measure ring gear and pinion backlash, noting the following:
    a. If backlash is .008–.015 inch, proceed to preload shimming steps in this procedure.
    b. If backlash is zero, add .020 inch to righthand side and subtract .020 inch from lefthand side.
    c. If backlash is not zero and not .008–.015 inch, proceed to next step.
23. Measure backlash again, noting the following:
    a. If backlash is not within specification, correct backlash by increasing thickness of one shim and decreasing thickness of other shim by same amount.
    b. If backlash is within specification, continue to next step.
24. Install shim and bearing caps, torquing cap bolts to specifications.
25. Rotate assembly several times to ensure proper seating of differential bearings.
26. Measure backlash again, noting the following:
    a. If backlash is not within specification, correct backlash by increasing thickness of one shim and decreasing thickness of other shim by same amount.
    b. If backlash is within specification, continue to next step.
27. Increase both lefthand and righthand shim sizes by .006 inch and install for proper differential bearing preload. Ensure shims are fully seated and assembly turns freely.
28. Obtain tooth mesh contact pattern using white marking compound. Pattern legibility can be improved by connecting driveshaft and rotating both

Item	Description
1	Rear axle identification tag
2	Differential housing cover bolt
3	Differential housing cover
4	Differential pinion shaft lock bolt
5	Differential case bolt
6	Differential pinion thrust washer
7	Differential pinion gear
8	Differential pinion shaft
9	Differential side gear
10	Differential side gear thrust washer
11	Differential bearing shim
12	Differential bearing cup
13	Differential bearing
14	Ring gear bolt
15	Differential case
16	Anti-lock speed sensor ring
17	Ring gear and pinion
18	Drive pinion bearing adjustment shim
19	Bearing cap and bolt
20	Pinion bearing (inner)
21	Inner axle pinion bearing cup
22	RABS sensor

Item	Description
23	Outer pinion bearing cup
24	Collapsible spacer
25	Pinion bearing (outer)
26	Rear axle drive pinion shaft oil slinger
27	Rear axle drive pinion seal
28	Pinion flange
29	Pinion nut
30	Rear wheel bearing inner cone and roller
31	Wheel bearing oil seal
32	Lug bolt
33	Axle shaft
34	Axle shaft nut
35	Lug nut
36	Rear disc brake rotor
37	Rear hub
38	Gasket
39	Bearing
40	Hub and bearing cup
41	Rear brake hub and drum (DRW only)
42	Filler plug
43	Rear axle housing
44	Brake adapter plate

LTV0500000001009

Fig. 7 Exploded view of conventional 10.5 inch ring gear axle (Part 2 of 2)

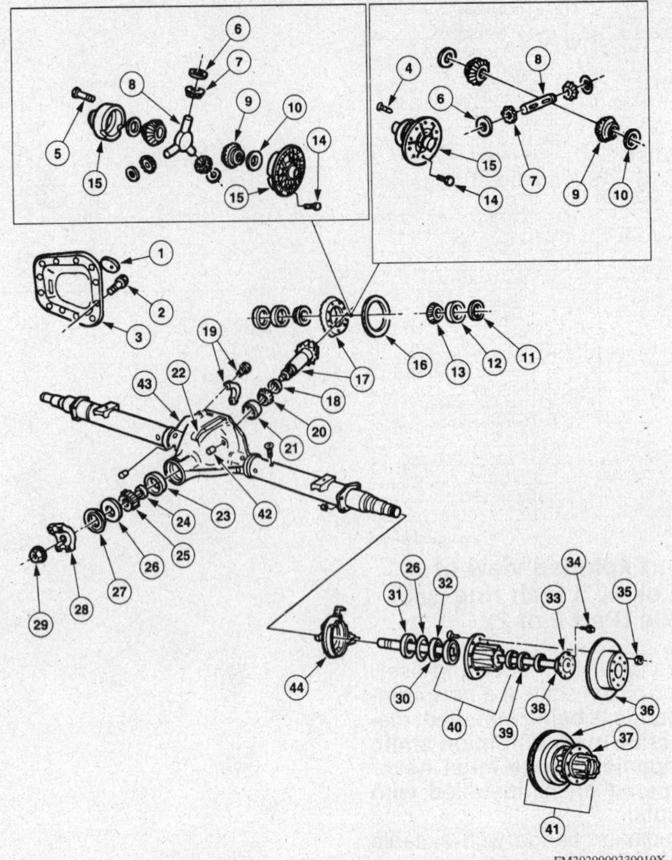

Fig. 8 Exploded view of 10.5 inch ring gear axle (Part 1 of 2). Conventional

tires in drive and coast direction. If gross pattern error is detected, inspect pinion shim selection.

29. Install bearing caps and tighten cap bolts to specifications.
30. Measure backlash again, and if not within specification, repeat steps for correcting measurement.
31. Install axle shafts, then the differential cover. Fill differential with suitable lubricant.
32. **On models equipped with limited slip differential,** to prevent noises on turns, add four ounces of friction modifier part No. C8AZ-19B546-A, or equivalent with lubricant when filling differential.

10.5 Inch Ring Gear

CONVENTIONAL ONE-PIECE DIFFERENTIAL CASE

1. Lubricate differential side gear thrust washers and side gear journals with premium long life grease part No. XG-1-C, or an equivalent meeting Ford specification ESA-M1C75-B.
2. Place differential side gear thrust washers on differential side gears.
3. Place differential side gears into position.
4. Assemble differential pinion thrust washers and pinion gears. Lubricate with premium long life grease part No. XG-1-C, or equivalent.
5. Install pinion gears opposite of side gears.
6. Install differential bearings using differential side bearing replacer tool No. D81T-4221-A, or equivalent.
7. Rotate pinion gears to align pinion shaft bore.
8. Install pinion shaft, then the new pinion shaft lock bolt. Tighten bolt to specification.
9. Press new anti-lock speed sensor ring and ring gear on differential case.
10. Install ring gear bolts and tighten to specification. Apply stud and bearing mount EOAZ-19554-BA, or an equivalent meeting Ford specification WSK-M2G349-A1 to ring gear bolts.
11. Install differential case.

CONVENTIONAL TWO-PIECE DIFFERENTIAL CASE

1. Place lefthand differential case half (ring gear side) on differential holder tool No. 205-447, or equivalent.
2. Lubricate differential side gears and thrust washers with premium long life grease part No. XG-1-C, or an equivalent meeting Ford specification ESA-M1C75-B.
3. Lubricate differential pinion gears, pinion gear thrust washers and pinion shaft with premium long life grease.
4. Install lefthand differential side gear.
5. Install differential pinion shaft and pinion gears.
6. Place righthand differential case half with reference marks aligned.
7. Install differential case retaining bolts.
8. Tighten case retaining bolts to specifications using companion flange holder tool No. 205-447, or equivalent to keep case from turning.
9. Press on new anti-lock speed sensor ring, if required.
10. Install ring gear on differential case.
11. Install ring gear bolts and tighten to specification. Apply stud and bearing mount EOAZ-19554-BA, or an equivalent meeting Ford specification WSK-M2G349-A1 to ring gear bolts.
12. Install differential case.

TRACTION-LOK ONE-PIECE DIFFERENTIAL CASE

1. Lubricate each steel clutch plate and soak all friction plates in additive friction modifier part No. C8AZ-19B546-A, or an equivalent meeting Ford specification EST-M2C118-A for at least 15 minutes.
2. Assemble differential clutch packs on respective differential side gears.
3. Clamp bolt head of Traction-Lok clutch gauge (with mandrel) tool No. T80P-4946-A, or equivalent in a vise.
4. Install differential clutch pack and side gear on gauge. Do not include shim or Belleville spring.
5. Position Traction-Lok gauge (less mandrel) tool No. 205-135, or equivalent on top of differential clutch pack.
6. Install Traction-Lok clutch gauge (less mandrel) over disc and clutch pack.
7. Install nut of gauge over top.
8. Select thickest feeler gauge blade that will enter between tool and clutch pack. This reading will be thickness of new clutch shim.
9. Select new clutch shim, **Fig. 15.**
10. Position shim and Belleville spring on differential clutch pack. Belleville

spring must face up and against thrust face of differential case.

11. Install clutch packs with shims, Belleville springs and side gears into differential case.
12. Assemble forcing screw, nut and step plate to differential case as follows:
    a. Position step plate in bottom side gear bore.
    b. Position nut in top side gear bore and hold in place.
    c. Install hex head screw and tighten it two turns after it contacts bottom step plate.
13. Lubricate both sides of differential pinion thrust washers with Motorcraft synthetic rear axle lubricant F1TZ-19580-B, or an equivalent meeting Ford specification WSL-M2C192-A.
14. Ensure differential pinion gears are 180° apart so they will align properly with pinion shaft bore.
15. Position differential pinion gears and pinion thrust washers in window of differential case so they mesh with side gear teeth.
16. Insert rotating handle into pinion shaft bore and turn differential case. Rotate differential case until pinion mating shaft holes are lined up exactly with holes in pinion gears.
17. Loosen forcing screw and remove step plate and nut from side gear bores.
18. Install differential pinion shaft in differential case. Install new differential pinion shaft lock bolt.
19. Measure turning torque as follows:
    a. Install Traction-Lok torque tool set with ½ drive hole tool No. 205-446, or equivalent, **Fig. 16.**
    b. If original clutch plates are used, initial breakaway torque should be 20 ft. lbs.
    c. Rotating torque to keep differential side gear turning with new clutch plates may vary.
20. Install ring gear and anti-lock speed sensor ring, if removed, on differential case. Tighten bolts to specification.
21. Install differential case.

Item	Description
1	Rear Axle Identification Tag
2	Axle Housing Cover Bolt
3	Axle Housing Cover
4	Differential Pinion Shaft Lock Bolt
5	Differential Case Bolt
6	Differential Pinion Thrust Washer
7	Differential Pinion Gear
8	Differential Pinion Shaft
9	Differential Side Gear
10	Differential Side Gear Thrust Washer
11	Differential Bearing Shim
12	Differential Bearing Cup
13	Differential Bearing
14	Ring Gear Bolt
15	Differential Case
16	Anti-Lock Speed Sensor Ring
17	Ring Gear and Pinion
18	Drive Pinion Bearing Adjustment Shim
19	Bearing Cap and Bolt
20	Pinion Bearing— (Inner)
21	Inner Axle Pinion Bearing Cup

Item	Description
22	RABS Sensor
23	Outer Pinion Bearing Cup
24	Collapsible Spacer
25	Pinion Bearing (Outer)
26	Rear Axle Drive Pinion Shaft Oil Slinger
27	Rear Axle Drive Pinion Seal
28	Rear Axle Companion Flange
29	Pinion Nut
30	Rear Wheel Bearing Inner Cone and Roller
31	Inner Wheel Bearing Oil Seal
32	Lug Bolt
33	Axle Shaft
34	Axle Shaft Nut
35	Lug Nut
36	Rear Disc Brake Rotor
37	Rear Hub
38	Gasket
39	Bearing
40	Hub and Bearing Cup
41	Rear Brake Hub and Drum (DRW Only)
42	Filler Plug
43	Rear Axle Housing
44	Brake Adapter Plate

FM3039900330020X

Fig. 8 Exploded view of 10.5 inch ring gear axle (Part 2 of 2). Conventional

TRACTION-LOK TWO-PIECE DIFFERENTIAL CASE

1. Lubricate each clutch disc and soak clutch friction plate for 15 minutes in additive friction modifier part No. C8AZ-19B546-A, or an equivalent meeting Ford specification EST-M2C118-A.
2. Assemble differential clutch packs on respective side gears. Do not include shims and Belleville springs.
3. Clamp bolt head of Traction-Lok clutch gauge (with mandrel) tool No. T80P-4946-A, or equivalent in a vise.
4. Install differential clutch pack and side gear on gauge. Do not include shim or Belleville spring.
5. Position Traction-Lok gauge (less mandrel) tool No. 205-135, or equivalent on top of differential clutch pack.
6. Install Traction-Lok clutch gauge (less mandrel) over disc and clutch pack.
7. Install nut of gauge over top.
8. Select thickest feeler gauge blade that will enter between tool and clutch pack. This reading will be thickness of new clutch shim.
9. Select proper shim size and remove gauge.
10. Place selected shim and Belleville spring on clutch pack. Dished or concave side of Belleville spring must be face up and against face of differential case.
11. Install differential side gear and clutch pack into lefthand case half.
12. Position lefthand differential case half on Traction-Lok torque tool set tool No. 205-447, or equivalent.
13. Lubricate differential pinion gears, pinion gear thrust washers and pinion shaft with premium long life grease part No. XG-1-C, or an equivalent meeting Ford specification ESA-M1C75-B.
14. Install differential pinion gears in differential pinion shaft.
15. Install differential pinion shaft and pinion gears.
16. Install righthand differential clutch pack and side gear into righthand case half.
17. Position righthand differential case half with reference marks aligned.
18. Install differential case retaining bolts and tighten to specification.
19. Measure turning torque to rotate one differential side gear as follows:
    a. Install Traction-Lok torque tool set with ½ drive hole tool No. 205-446, or equivalent, **Fig. 16.**
    b. Initial breakaway torque, if original clutch plates are used, should be 20 ft. lbs.
    c. Rotating torque to keep differential side gear turning with new clutch plates may vary.
20. Install ring gear. Tighten bolts to specification.
21. Install anti-lock speed sensor ring on differential case, if required.
22. Install differential case.

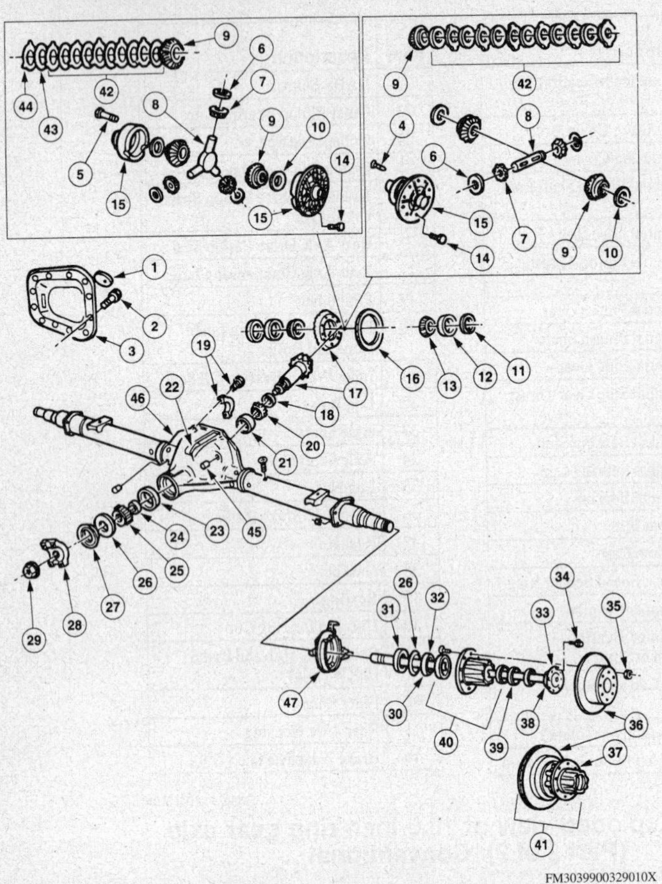

FM3039900329010X

Fig. 9 Exploded view of 10.5 inch ring gear axle (Part 1 of 2). Traction-Lok

Item	Description
1	Rear Axle Identification Tag
2	Axle Housing Cover Bolt
3	Axle Housing Cover
4	Differential Pinion Shaft Lock Bolt
5	Differential Case Bolt
6	Differential Pinion Thrust Washer
7	Differential Pinion Gear
8	Differential Pinion Shaft
9	Differential Side Gear
10	Differential Side Gear Thrust Washer
11	Differential Bearing Shim
12	Differential Bearing Cup
13	Differential Bearing
14	Ring Gear Bolt
15	Differential Case
16	Anti-Lock Speed Sensor Ring
17	Ring Gear and Pinion
18	Drive Pinion Bearing Adjustment Shim
19	Bearing Cap and Bolt
20	Pinion Bearing— (Inner)
21	Inner Axle Pinion Bearing Cup
22	RABS Sensor
23	Outer Pinion Bearing Cup

Item	Description
24	Collapsible Spacer
25	Pinion Bearing (Outer)
26	Rear Axle Drive Pinion Shaft Oil Slinger
27	Rear Axle Drive Pinion Seal
28	Rear Axle Companion Flange
29	Pinion Nut
30	Rear Wheel Bearing Inner Cone and Roller
31	Inner Wheel Bearing Oil Seal
32	Lug Bolt
33	Axle Shaft
34	Axle Shaft Nut
35	Lug Nut
36	Rear Disc Brake Rotor
37	Rear Hub
38	Gasket
39	Bearing
40	Hub and Bearing Cup
41	Rear Brake Hub and Drum (DRW Only)
42	Differential Clutch Pack
43	Rear Axle Differential Clutch Shim
44	Differential Clutch Spring
45	Filler Plug
46	Rear Axle Housing
47	Brake Adapter Plate

FM3039900329020X

Fig. 9 Exploded view of 10.5 inch ring gear axle (Part 2 of 2). Traction-Lok

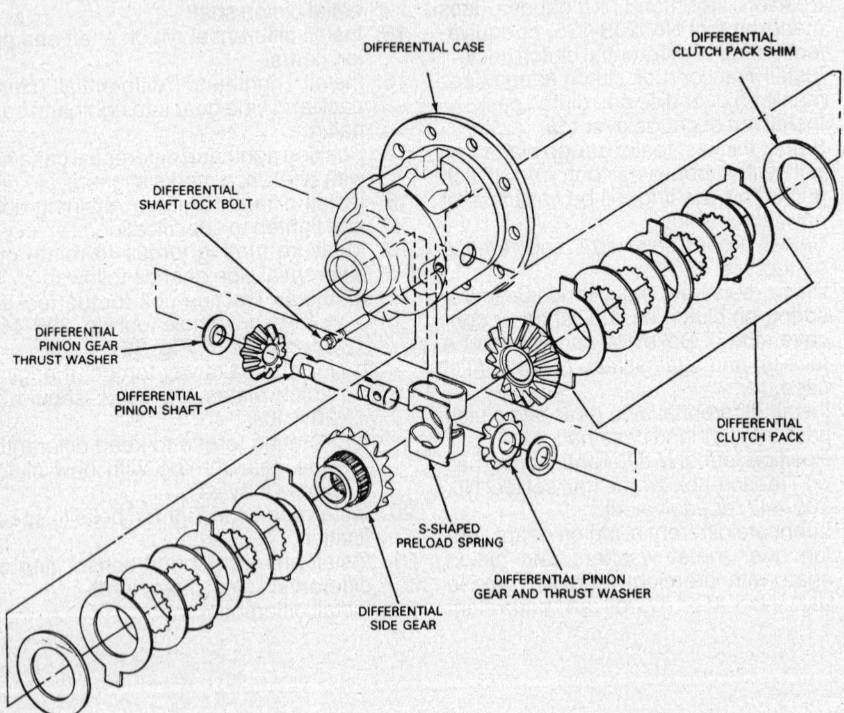

FM3038800044000X

Fig. 10 Exploded view of Traction-Lok differential

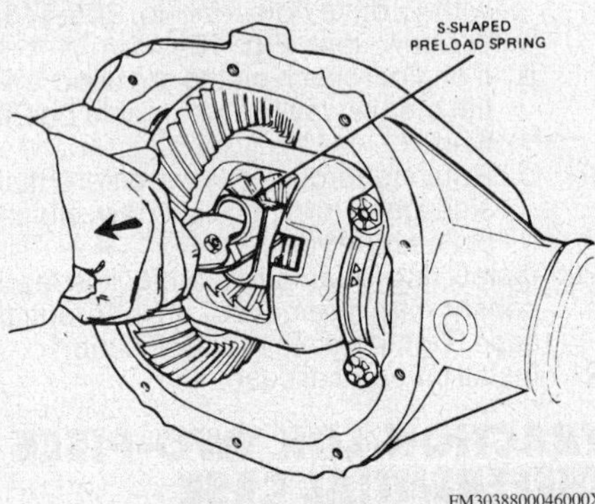

FM3038800046000X

Fig. 11 S-shaped preload spring removal

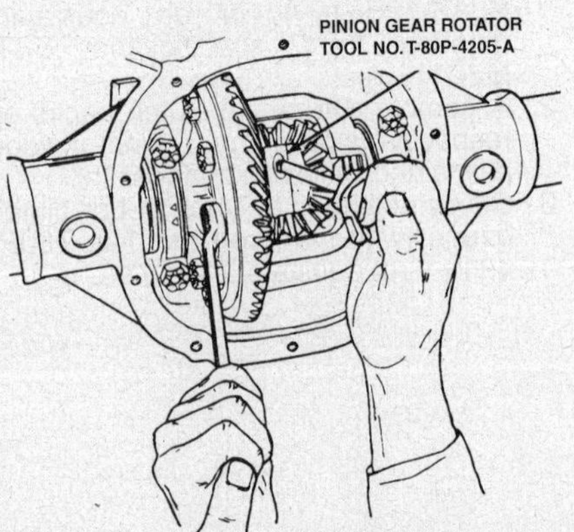

FM3038800045000X

Fig. 12 Pinion gear replacement

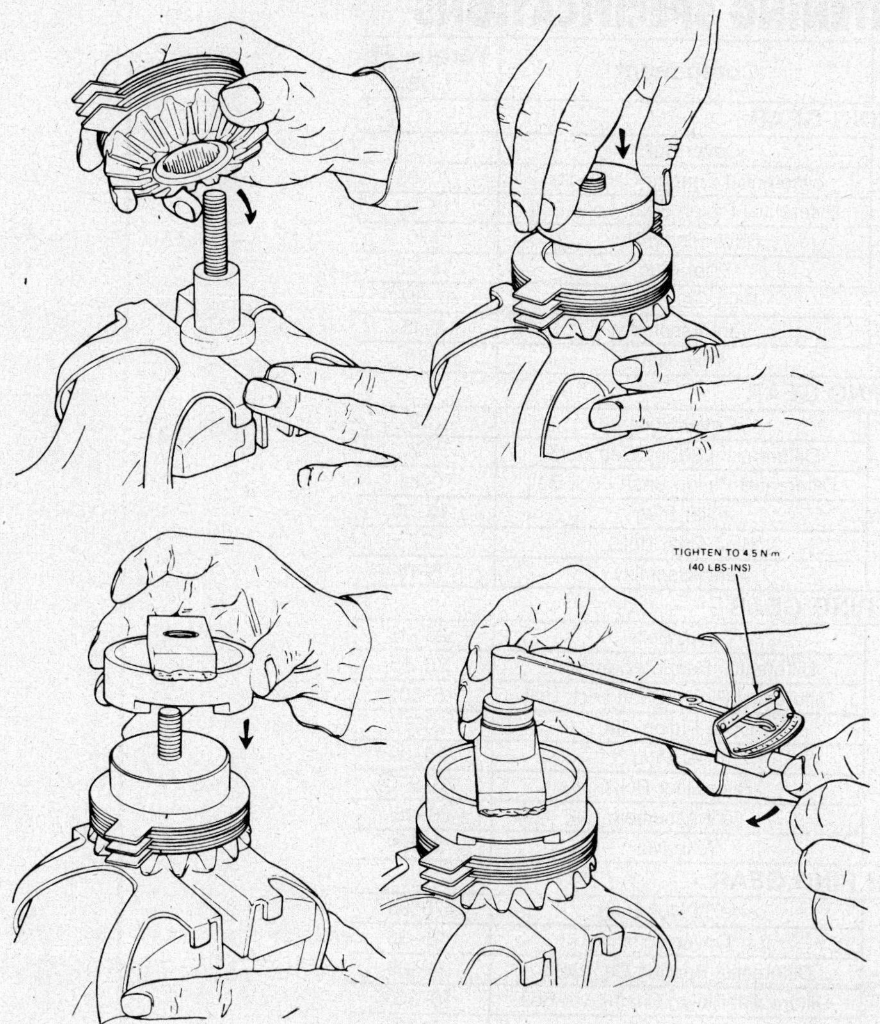

Fig. 13 Clutch pack shim thickness measurement tool installation

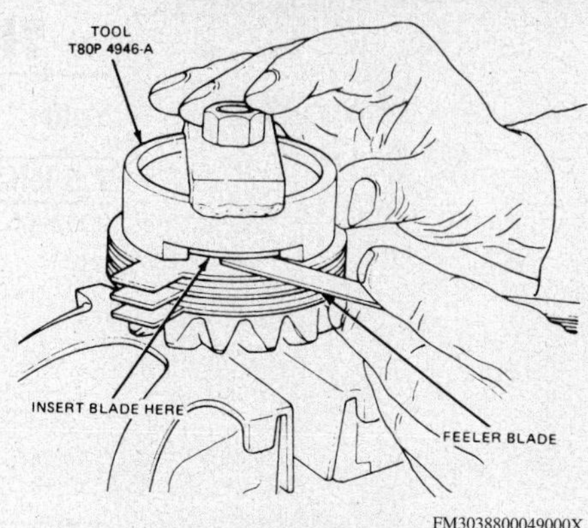

Fig. 14 Shim thickness measurement

Part Number	Description
F75Z-4A324-DA	0.030 Inch
F75Z-4A324-EA	0.035 Inch
F75Z-4A324-FA	0.040 Inch
F75Z-4A324-GA	0.045 Inch
F75Z-4A324-HA	0.050 Inch
F75Z-4A324-JA	0.055 Inch
F75Z-4A324-KA	0.060 Inch

FM3039900331000X

Fig. 15 Clutch shim application chart. Traction-Lok one-piece differential case

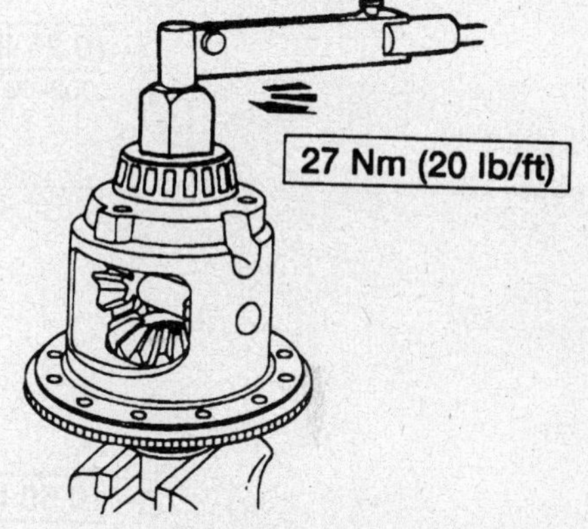

Fig. 16 Traction-Lok torque tool set installation. Traction-Lok differential case

DRIVE AXLE SPECIFICATIONS

Drive Axle Model	Carrier Type	Ring Gear & Pinion Backlash			Pinion Bearing Preload		
		Method	New Bearings, Inch	Used Bearings, Inch	Method	New Bearings, Inch Lbs.①	Used Bearings, Inch Lbs.①
All	Integral	Shims	—	②	Collapsible Spacer	16–29	8–14

① — Turning torque.

② — Preferred, .012–.015 inch; minimum, .008–.015 inch.

TIGHTENING SPECIFICATIONS

Year	Component	Torque Ft. Lbs.
7.5 INCH RING GEAR		
2002–06	Cover Bolts	①
	Differential Bearing Cap Bolts	70–85
	Differential Pinion Shaft Lock Bolt	15–30
	Drive Pinion Nut	170
	Filler Plug	15–30
	Ring Gear Bolts	70–85②
	Vent Assembly	8–15
	Yoke Nut	170
8.8 INCH RING GEAR		
2002–06	Cover Bolts	33
	Differential Bearing Cap Bolts	77
	Differential Pinion Shaft Lock Bolt	②22
	Filler Plug	15–30
	Ring Gear Bolts	77
	Vent Assembly	8–15
9.75 INCH RING GEAR		
2002–06	Cover Bolts	28–38
	Differential Bearing Cap Bolts	70–85
	Differential Pinion Shaft Lock Bolt	15–30②
	Drive Pinion Nut	217③
	Filler Plug	15–30
	Ring Gear Bolts	70–85②
	Vent Assembly	8–15
	Yoke Nut	217③
10.25 INCH RING GEAR		
2002–06	Axle To Hub Bolts	70–85
	Cover Bolts	25–35
	Differential Bearing Cap Bolts	80–95
	Differential Pinion Shaft Lock Bolt	15–30②
	Drive Pinion Nut	217③
	Filler Plug	15–30
	Hub Nut	55–65④
	Ring Gear Bolts	100–120②
	Vent Assembly	8–15
	Yoke Nut	217③
10.50 INCH RING GEAR		
2002–06	Differential Case Bolts	90
	Pinion Shaft Lock Bolt	23
	Ring Gear Bolts	100–120

① — With plastic cover, replace cover & bolts & torque to 15–20 ft. lbs.; with steel cover, torque to 25–35 ft. lbs.
② — Coat bolt threads w/Loctite part No. E0AZ-19554-AA, or equivalent.
③ — If pinion bearing preload exceeds specification before torque is obtained, replace collapsible spacer.
④ — Back off six clicks (1/6 turn).

UNIVERSAL JOINTS

INDEX

CONSTANT VELOCITY (CV)

The CV type joint incorporates an outer bearing retainer and flange, spring, cap, circlip, inner bearing assembly and a wire ring. The inner bearing assembly incorporates a bearing cage, six ball bearings and an inner race, **Fig. 1.**

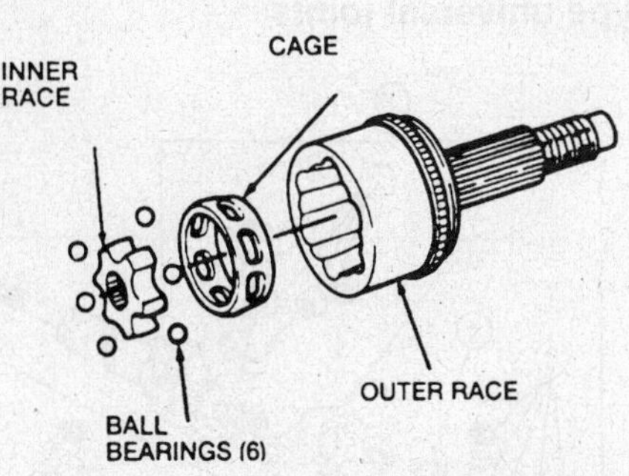

Fig. 1 Constant velocity (CV) joint

CROSS & ROLLER

Less Universal Joint Replacement Tool

DISASSEMBLE

1. Remove snap rings (or retainer plates) that retain bearings in yoke and driveshaft, **Fig. 2.**
2. Place U-joint in a vise.
3. Select a wrench socket with an outside diameter slightly smaller than the U-joint bearings. Select another wrench socket with an inside diameter slightly larger than the U-joint bearings.
4. Place the sockets at opposite bearings in the yoke so smaller socket becomes a bearing pusher and the larger socket becomes a bearing receiver when the vise jaws come together. Close vise jaws until both bearings are free of yoke and remove bearings from the cross or spider.
5. If bearings will not come all the way out, close vise until bearing in receiver socket protrudes from yoke as much as possible without using excessive force. Then remove from vise and place that portion of bearing which protrudes from yoke between vise jaws. Tighten vise to hold bearing and drive yoke off with a suitable soft hammer.
6. To remove opposite bearing from yoke, replace in vise with pusher socket on exposed cross journal with receiver socket over bearing cup. Then tighten vise jaws to press bearing back through yoke into receiving socket.
7. Remove yoke from driveshaft and again place protruding portion of bearing between vise jaws. Then tighten vise to hold bearing while driving yoke off bearing with a suitable soft hammer.
8. Turn spider or cross 1/4 turn and use the same procedure to press bearings out of driveshaft.

ASSEMBLE

1. If old components are to be reassembled, pack bearing cups with universal joint grease. Do not fill cups completely or use excessive amounts, as over-lubrication may damage seals during reassembly. Use new seals.
2. If new components are being installed, inspect new bearings for adequate grease before assembling.
3. With the pusher (smaller) socket, press one bearing part way into driveshaft. Position spider into the partially installed bearing. Place second bearing into driveshaft. Fasten driveshaft in vise so that bearings are in contact with faces of vise jaws. Some spiders are provided with locating lugs which must face toward driveshaft when installed.
4. Press bearings all the way into position and install snap rings or retainer plates.
5. Install bearings in yoke in same manner. When installation is completed, inspect U-joint for binding or roughness. If free movement is impeded, correct the condition before installation in vehicle.

With Universal Joint Replacement Tool

DISASSEMBLE

1. Place driveshaft in a vise, using care to avoid damaging it.
2. Remove bearing retaining snap rings. Some universal joints use injected nylon retainers in place of snap rings. During servicing, the snap rings supplied with the replacement universal joint assembly must be used.
3. Position tool on shaft and press bearing out of yoke, **Fig. 3.** If bearing cannot be pressed all the way out, remove it using vise grips or channel lock pliers or position driveshaft as outlined and strike center yoke with a suitable hammer, **Fig. 4.** Mark yoke and shaft to ensure they will be reassembled in their same relative positions.
4. Reposition tool so that it presses on the spider in order to press other bearing from opposite side of flange.
5. If used, remove flange from spider.

ASSEMBLE

1. Start new bearing into yoke, then position spider into yoke and press bearing until it is 1/4 inch below surface.
2. Remove tool and install a new snap ring.
3. Start new bearing in opposite side of yoke, then install tool and press on bearing until opposite bearing contacts snap ring.
4. Remove tool and install remaining snap ring.

DOUBLE CARDAN

The double Cardan type joint, **Fig. 5,** incorporates two universal joints, a centering socket yoke and center yoke at one end of the shaft. A single universal joint, **Fig. 6,** is used at the other end.

Disassemble

1. Remove all bearing cap retainers.
2. Mark bearing caps, spiders, propeller shaft yoke, link yoke and socket yoke for assembly alignment reference, **Fig. 5.**
3. Remove bearing caps attaching spider to propeller shaft yoke as follows:
   a. Use a 5/8 inch socket to drive the bearing cap and a 1 1/16 inch socket to receive the opposite bearing cap as it is driven out.
   b. Place a 5/8 inch socket on one bearing cap and a 1 1/16 inch socket on opposite bearing.
   c. Position assembly in vise so vise jaws bear directly against sockets.
   d. Tighten vise to press first bearing cap out of link yoke.
   e. Loosen vise, reposition sockets and press opposite bearing cap out of link yoke.

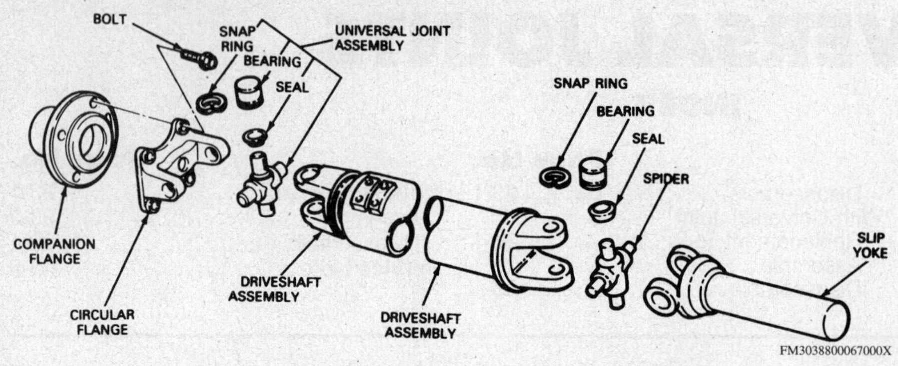

Fig. 2 Cross & roller type universal joints

Fig. 3 Bearing cap removal (with special tool)

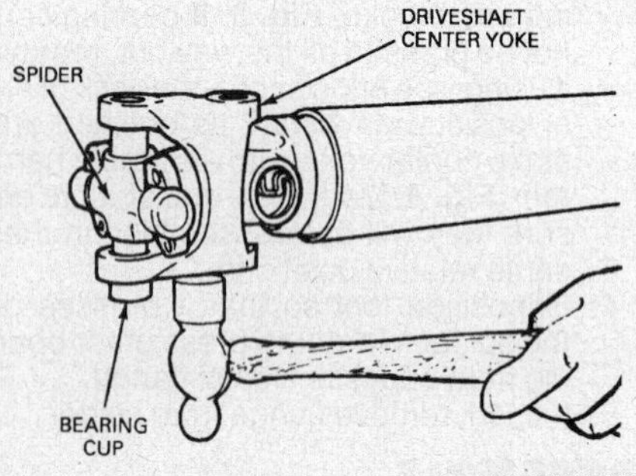

Fig. 4 Bearing cap removal (less special tool)

4. Disengage propeller shaft yoke from link yoke.
5. Remove bearing caps attaching front spider to propeller shaft as outlined in Step 3 above.
6. Remove front spider from yoke.
7. Remove bearing caps attaching rear spider to link yoke as outlined in Step 3 above and remove spider and socket yoke from link yoke.
8. Clean all components in solvent and wipe dry. Inspect assembly for damage or wear. If any component is worn or damaged, the entire assembly must be replaced.

Assemble

When assembling universal joint, ensure to align spiders and yokes according to marks made during disassembly.

1. Lubricate all bearings and contact surfaces with lithium base chassis grease.
2. Install bearing caps on yoke ends of rear spider and secure caps with tape, **Fig. 5.**
3. Assemble socket yoke and rear spider.
4. Position rear spider in link yoke and install bearing caps. Press caps into yoke using 5/8 inch socket until bearing cap retainer grooves are exposed.
5. Install rear spider-to-link yoke bearing cap retainers.
6. Position front spider in propeller shaft yoke and install bearing caps. Press caps into yoke using a 5/8 inch socket until bearing cap retainer grooves are exposed.

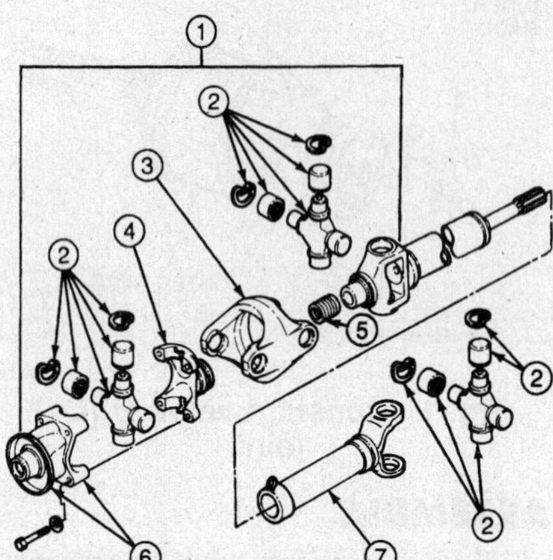

Item	Description
1	Double Cardan Assembly
2	U-Joint Assembly
3	Driveshaft Center Yoke
4	Driveshaft Centering Socket Yoke
5	Centering Spring
6	Transfer Case Yoke (Flange)
7	Driveshaft Slip Yoke

FM3038800069000X

Fig. 5 Exploded view of double Cardan assembly

7. Install front spider-to-propeller shaft yoke bearing cap retainers.
8. Install thrust washer and socket spring in ball socket bearing bore, if removed.
9. Install thrust washer on ball socket bearing boss (located on propeller shaft yoke), if removed.
10. Align ball socket bearing boss on propeller shaft yoke with ball socket bearing bore and insert boss into bore.
11. Align front spider with link yoke bearing cap bores and install bearing caps. Press caps into yoke using a 5/8 inch socket until bearing cap retainer grooves are exposed.
12. Install front spider-to-link yoke bearing cap retainers.

SERVICE NOTE

Before disassembling any universal joint, examine the assembly carefully and note the position of the grease fitting (if used). Also, ensure to mark the yokes with relation to the propeller shaft so they may be reassembled in the same relative position. Failure to observe these precautions may produce rough vehicle operation, which results in rapid wear and failure of components and place an unbalanced load on transmission, engine and rear axle.

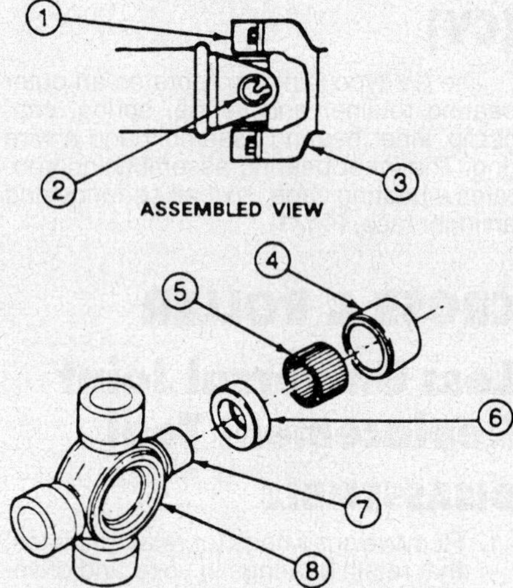

Item	Description
1	Bearing Strap Type
2	Snap Ring Type
3	Companion (Universal Joint) Flange
4	Bearing Cup
5	Needle Rollers
6	Grease Seal
7	Trunnion
8	Spider
9	U-Joint Assembly (Items 4, 5, 6, 7, 8)

FM3039500251000X

Fig. 6 U-joint assembly

ENGINE REBUILDING SPECIFICATIONS

NOTE: Refer To Engine Section In Individual Truck Chapters For Cylinder Head Tightening Information.

INDEX

CYLINDER HEAD, VALVE GUIDE & VALVE SEATS

All specifications given in inches unless otherwise noted.

Engine Liter	Year	Cylinder Head Warpage Limit	Valve Guides			Valve Seats			
			Inside Diameter Std.①	Stem To Guide Clearance		Seat Angle①	Seat Width		Runout
				Intake	Exhaust		Intake	Exhaust	
2.0L	2002–04	⑤	.2386	.00060–.00250	.00060–.00250	45.00°	—	—	.0014
2.3L	2003–06	—	.2160–.2180	.00090	.00110	45.00°	.0380–.0720	.0380–.0720	.0010
3.0L⑦	2002–06	.007	.2762–.2772	.00100–.00270	.00150–.00320	45.00°	.0780–.0980	.0780–.0980	.0030
3.0L②	2002–06	⑤	.2360–.2370	.00070–.00270	.00170–.00370	44.75°	.0430–.0550	.0550–.0660	.0010
3.3L	2002	.004	③	.00080–.00210	.00120–.00190	45.00°	.0689	.0670	—
3.8L	2002–03	.007	.2760–.2770	.00070–.00270	.00180–.00370	44.75°	.0600–.0800	.0600–.0800	.0030
3.9L	2002–06	.007	.2760–.2770	.00080–.00270	.00180–.00370	44.75°	.0600–.0800	.0600–.0800	.0020
4.0L ③	2002–06	.004	.2756–.2762	.00100–.00200	.00100–.00300	45.00°	.0600–.0940	.0500–.0830	.0020
4.2L	2002–06	.007	.2760–.2770	.00080–.00270	.0080–.0037	44.75°	.0600–.0800	.0600–.0800	.0020
4.6L	2002–06	—	.2773–.2762	.00080–.00270	.01800–.00370	44.51–45.01°	.0748–.0827	.0748–.0827	.0019
5.4L	2002–06	—	.2762–.2773	.00080–.00270	.00180–.00370	45.50°	.0512–.0591	.0748–.0827	.0010
6.0L⑥	2003–06	.004	.2760–.2770	.00550	.00550	④	.0580–.0880	.0710–.1010	.0150
6.8L	2002–06	—	.2761–.2773	.00070–.00270	.00170–.00370	44.50–45.00°	.0748–.0826	.0748–.0826	.0009
7.3L⑥	2002–03	.004	.3141–.3151	.00550	.00550	④	.0650–.0950	.0650–.0950	.0020

① — Specifications given are for intake & exhaust.

② — Escape & Mariner w/DOHC engine.

③ — Intake, .2756–.2763 inch; Exhaust; .3150–.3154 inch.

④ — Intake, 30°; exhaust, 37.5°.

⑤ — .002 inch for each six inches of length.

⑥ — Diesel engine.

⑦ — Ranger & Windstar.

VALVE SPRINGS

All specifications given in inches unless otherwise noted.

Engine Liter	Year	Free Length		Out Of Square Limit	Installed Height		Pressure, Lbs. @ Inches			
							Closed		Open	
		Intake	Ex-haust		Intake	Exhaust	Intake	Exhaust	Intake	Exhaust
2.0L	2002–04	1.701	1.701	—	1.3460	1.3460	④	②	—	—
2.3L	2003–06	1.768	1.768	—	1.4920	1.4920	38.6670	38.6670	97.032 @ .3500	93.338 @ .0291
3.0L⑨	2002–06	1.890	1.890	—	1.6500–1.7360	1.6500–1.7360	65 @ 1.5800	65 @ 1.5800	180 @ 1.1600	180 @ 1.1600
3.0L⑦	2002–06	1.840	1.840	2.5%	1.5700	1.5700	54 @ 1.5700	54 @ 1.5700	156 @ 1.1800	156 @ 1.1800
3.3L	2002	⑥	⑥	③	1.7360	1.7360	⑧	⑧	—	—
3.8L	2002–03	—	—	—	1.6200	1.6200	79 @ 1.6200	79 @ 1.6200	224 @ 1.1600	224 @ 1.1600
3.9L	2002–06	1.996	1.996	—	1.6200	1.6200	79 @ 1.6200	79 @ 1.6200	224 @ 1.1600	224 @ 1.1600
4.0L	2002–06	1.700	1.700	—	1.5690–1.6010	1.5900–1.6010	—	—	203–225 @ 1.4130–1.4455	203–225 @ 1.4130–1.4455
4.2L	2002–06	1.996	1.996	—	1.6200	1.6200	79 @ 1.6200	79 @ 1.6200	224 @ 1.1600	224 @ 1.1600
4.6L	2002–06	1.9508	1.9508	2°	1.5630-1.5866	1.5630-1.5866	55 @ 1.5740	55 @ 1.5740	132 @ 1.1020	132 @ 1.1020
5.4L	2002–06	2.10	2.10	2.0°	1.6654–1.6890	1.6654–1.6890	67.8923 @ 1.6756	67.8923 @ 1.6756	170.855 @ 1.1339	170.855 @ 1.1339
6.0L①	2003–06	2.045	2.045	—	—	—	—	—	—	—
6.8L	2002–06	1.977	1.977	2.5°	—	—	65 @ 1.5700	65 @ 1.5700	150 @ 1.1000	150 @ 1.1000
7.3L①	2002–03	1.925–2.225	1.925–2.225	.078⑤	1.7670	1.8330	71–79 @ 1.8330	71–79 @ 1.8330	206–220 @ 1.3520	206–220 @ 1.3520

① — Diesel engine.
② — 94.94 lbs. @ 1.0275 inch.
③ — With damper removed.
④ — 82.1 lbs. @ .988 inch.
⑤ — Inch.
⑥ — Inner valve spring, 1.736 inches; outer spring, 2.016 inches.
⑦ — Escape & Mariner w/DOHC engine.
⑧ — Inner valve spring, 57.3 lbs. @ .9840 inch; outer spring, 117.7 lbs. @ 1.1810 inches.
⑨ — Ranger & Windstar.

VALVES

All specifications given in inches unless otherwise noted.

Engine Liter	Year	Stem Diameter Std.		Installed Height	Maximum Tip Refin-ish	Face Angle	Margin①		Valve Clearance
		Intake	Exhaust				Intake	Exhaust	
2.0L	2002–04	.2374	.2374	1.3460	—	45.000°	—	—	③
2.3L	2003–06	.2153–.2159	.2151–.2157	—	—	45.000°	—	—	—
3.0L⑥	2002–06	.2744–.2752	2739–.2747	④	.0100	44.000°	1/32	1/32	.0880–.1890
3.0L⑩	2002–06	.2350–.2358	.2343–.2350	1.5700	—	45.500°	—	—	.0190–.0430⑨
3.3L	2002	.2742–.2748	.3136–.3138	—	⑪	45.000°	.0453–.0571	.0531–.0650	—
3.8L	2002–03	.2738–.2751	.2728–.2741	④	—	45.675°	—	—	—
3.9L	2002–06	.2746–.2754	.2735–.2744	1.6200	—	45.675°	—	—	.0886–.1886⑫
4.0L	2002–06	.2740–.2750	.270–.2740	④	—	45.000°	—	—	—
4.2L	2002–06	.2746–.2754	.2735–.2744	1.6200	—	45.675°	—	—	.0886–.1886⑫
4.6L	2002–06	.2746–.2754	.2736–.2744	—	—	45.250–45.750°	—	—	—
5.4L	2002–06	.2746–.2754	.2736–.2744	—	—	45.250–45.750°	—	—	—
6.0L②	2003–06	.2720–.2740	.2720–.2740	—	—	⑧	—	—	—
6.8L	2002–06	.2746–.2750	.2736–.2740	—	—	44.750–45.250°	—	—	—

Continued

VALVES—Continued

All specifications given in inches unless otherwise noted.

Engine Liter	Year	Stem Diameter Std.		Installed Height	Maximum Tip Refinish	Face Angle	Margin①		Valve Clearance
		Intake	Exhaust				Intake	Exhaust	
7.3L②	2002–03	.3118–.3125	.3118–.3125	⑤	.0100	⑧	.0660	.0540	.1850⑦

① — Minimum.
② — Diesel engine.
③ — Intake, .0043–.0070 inch; exhaust, .0106–.0133 inch.
④ — Refer to "Installed Height" under "Valve Springs" specification.
⑤ — Valve head recession relative to deck surface: intake, .0460–.0580 inch; exhaust, .0520–.0640 inch.
⑥ — Ranger & Windstar.
⑦ — Collapsed tappet clearance measured between valve tip and rocker arm.
⑧ — Intake 30.0°; exhaust 37.5°.
⑨ — With cylinder @ top dead center, hold steady pressure on lifter until fully collapsed to measure clearance.
⑩ — Escape & Mariner w/DOHC engine.
⑪ — Less than .008 inch.
⑫ — With tappet collapsed.

CAMSHAFT

All specifications given in inches unless otherwise noted.

Engine Liter	Year	Camshaft					Lifter Bore Diameter	Lifter Diameter Std.	Lifter to Bore Clearance
		Journal Diameter	Bearing Inside Diameter	Bearing Clearance	Endplay	Runout Max.			
2.0L	2002–04	1.0221–1.0227	—	.0007–.0027	.0031–.0086	—	—	—	—
2.3L	2003–06	.9820–.9830	—	.0010–.0030	.0030–.0090	.0010	—	—	—
3.0L④	2002–06	2.0074–2.0084	2.0094–2.0104	.0010–.0030	.0010–.0070	.0020	.8752–.8767	.8740	.0007–.0027
3.0L③	2002–06	1.0600–1.0610	1.0620–1.0630	.0010–.0029	.0010–.0064	—	—	.6290–.6294	.0007–.0027
3.3L	2002	—	⑤	.0024–.0059	.0012–.0024	.0040	.6304–.6309	.6278–.6282	.0017–.0026
3.8L	2002–03	2.0670–2.0740	2.0525–2.0535	.0010–.0030	.0010–.0060	—	—	.8738–.8745	.0007–.0027
3.9L	2002–06	2.0505-2.0515	—	.0010–.0030	.0010–.0060	.0005	—	.8738–.8745	.0007–.0027
4.0L	2002–06	1.0990–1.1010	1.1020–1.1040	.0020–.0040	.0003–.007	.0020	—	—	—
4.2L	2002–06	2.0505-2.0515	—	.0010–.0030	.0010–.0060	.0005	—	.8738–.8745	.0007–.0027
4.6L	2002–06	1.0605–1.0615	1.0625–1.0635	.0010–.0030	.0035–.0075	.0020	—	—	—
5.4L	2002–06	1.0605–1.0615	1.0625–1.0635	.0010–.0030	.001–.0075	.0012	—	—	—
6.0L①	2003–06	2.4400–2.4410	2.4430–2.4460	.0015–.0060	.0020–.0080	—	—	—	—
6.8L	2002–06	1.0605–1.0615	1.0625–1.0635	.0001–.0030	.0010–.0074	.0035②	—	—	—
7.3L①	2002–03	2.0990–2.1000	2.1020–2.1050⑥	.0020–.0060	.0020–.0080	—	.9220–.9250	.9209–.9217	.0011–.0034

① — Diesel engine.
② — Indicator measurement on all journals when supported on front and rear journals.
③ — Escape & Mariner w/DOHC engine.
④ — Ranger & Windstar.
⑤ — Righthand front three & lefthand middle three, 1.8504–1.8514 inches. Lefthand & righthand rear, 1.6732–1.6742 inches. Lefthand front, 1.8898–1.8907 inches.
⑥ — Front bearing installation recess into block, .0200–.0500 inch.

CRANKSHAFT, BEARINGS & RODS

All specifications given in inches unless otherwise noted.

Engine Liter	Year	Crankshaft Journals				Bearing Clearance			Connecting Rod	
		Main Bearing Journal Diameter	Connecting Rod Journal Diameter	Max Taper	Runout Limit	Main Bearings	Connecting Rod Bearings	Thrust Bearing	Side Bearing Clearance	Pin Bore Diameter
2.0L	2002–04	2.2827–2.2835	1.8461–1.8500	—	—	.0004–.0028	.0006–.0028	—	—	.81060–.81140
2.3L	2003–06	2.0460–2.0470	1.9670–1.9680	—	—	.0007–.0013	.0010–.0020	—	—	.82500–.82600
3.0L③	2002–06	2.5190–2.5198	2.1253–2.1261	.00060	.00200	.0005–.0023	.0009–.0027	.0040–.0080	.0060–.0140	.91190–.91240
3.0L②	2002–06	2.4670–2.4790	1.9670–1.9680	—	—	.0009–.0017	.0010–.0025	—	.0039–.0118	.82700–.82800
3.3L	2002	④	1.9667–1.0675	.00020	.00390	—	—	—	.0079–.0138	.82610–.82650
3.8L	2002–03	2.5190–2.5198	2.3103–2.3111	.00030	.00200	.0010–.0014	.0010–.0014	—	.0047–.0192	④
3.9L	2002–06	2.5190–2.5198	2.3103–2.3111	.00060	.00200	.0005–.0023	.0086–.0027	.0005–.0023	.0047–.0192	.90315–.90472
4.0L	2002–06	2.2430–2.2440	2.1250–2.1260	.00030	.00200	.0005–.0020	.0005–.0020	.0005–.0020	.0036–.0106	.94300–.94400
4.2L	2002–06	2.5190–2.5198	2.3103–2.3111	.00060	.00200	.0005–.0023	.0086–.0027	.0005–.0023	.0047–.0192	.90315–.90472
4.6L	2002–06	2.4803	2.0861–2.0867	.0006	.00200	.0011–.0026	.0010–.0027	.0011–.0026	.0006–.0177	.86400–.86500
5.4L	2002–06	2.6576–2.6568	2.0859–2.0867	.00020	.00030	.0009–.0019	.0010–.0025	—	.0049–.0187	.86650–.86670
6.0L①	2003–06	3.1500–3.1880	2.7160–2.7170	—	—	.0080–.0034	—	—	.0120–.0240	—
6.8L	2002–06	2.6567–2.6577	2.0859–2.0867	.00020	.00200	.0009–.0019	.0010–.0025	.0030–.0148	—	.86660–.86670
7.3L	2002–03	3.1228–3.1236	2.4980–2.4990	.00015	.00100	.0018–.0046	.0015–.0045	.0025–.0085	.0120–.0240	1.43200–1.43300

① — Diesel engine.
② — Escape & Mariner w/DOHC engine.
③ — Ranger & Windstar.
④ — 2002, .90315–.90472 inch; 2003, .8465 inch.

PISTONS, PINS & RINGS

All specifications given in inches unless otherwise noted.

Engine Liter	Year	Piston Diameter Std.⑬	Piston Clearance	Piston Pin Bore Diameter	Piston Pin Diameter Std.	Pin to Piston Bore Clearance	Piston Rings			
							End Gap①		Side Clearance	
							Comp.	Oil	Comp.	Oil
2.0L	2002–04	㉙	.001400–.002500	—	㉚	.00040–.00060	—	—	—	—
2.3L	2003–06	⑦	.000900–.001700	—	.82660–.82680	.00030–.00060	⑧	.0070–.0270	—	—
3.0L⑨	2002–06	④	.001200–.003200	.909200–.911200	.91190–.91240	.00020–.00050	.0100	.0100	.0016–.0037	⑭
3.0L㉛	2002–06	③	.000500–.000900	827000–.827200	.82740–.82790	.00000–.00010	⑥	.0060–.0250	.0012–.0031	—
3.3L	2002	⑯	⑳	.825500–.826000	.82560–.82610	.00020–.00070	㉑	0079–.0272	㉒	.0006–.0073
3.8L	2002–03	㉓	.000710–.001730	.906060–.0906220	.90550–.90560	.00043–.00071	㉔	.0059–.0255	.0011–.0031	—
3.9L	2002–06	㉗	.000710–.001730	.906060–.906220	.90551–.90563	.00043–.00071	⑪	.0059–.0064	.0011–.0031	—

Continued

PISTONS, PINS & RINGS—Continued

All specifications given in inches unless otherwise noted.

Engine Liter	Year	Piston Diameter Std.⑬	Piston Clearance	Piston Pin Bore Diameter	Piston Pin Diameter Std.	Pin to Piston Bore Clearance	Piston Rings			
							End Gap①		Side Clearance	
							Comp.	Oil	Comp.	Oil
4.0L⑱	2002–06	3.9520–3.9528	.001200–.002000	.945000	㉕	.00040–.00060	㉖	—	.0020–.0030	—
4.2L	2002–06	㉗	.000710–.001730	.906060–.906220	.90551–.90563	.00043–.00071	⑪	.0059–.0064	.0011–.0031	—
4.6L	2002–06	⑤	.000500–.001000	.866000–.866300	.86600–.86610	.00020–.00040	.0100–.0200	.0060–.0260	—	.0500
5.4L	2002–06	⑰	.001000–.001800	.866500–.866700	.86620–.86630	.00020–.00050	⑩	.0059–.0256	—	—
6.0L②	2003–06	3.737–3.738	.001700–.003600	—	1.3385–1.3387	.00050–.00090	⑮	.0090–.0190	—	—
6.8L	2002–06	3.5500	.000100–.000900	.867200–.867700	.86660–.86670	.00030–.00090	⑲	.0050–.0250	—	—
7.3L②	2000–03	4.1045–4.1050	.004400–.005700	1.308600	1.30790–1.30810	.00030–.00070	㉘	.0120–.0240	⑫	—

① — Minimum.
② — Diesel engine.
③ — Coated pistons, measure 90° from pin bore, 1.7 inches down from top of piston; grade 1, 3.5035–3.5043 inch; grade 2, 3.5038–3.5048 inch; grade 3, 3.5043–3.5051 inch.
④ — Coded red, 3.5024–3.5031 inches; coded blue, 3.5035–3.5041 inches; and coded yellow, 3.5045–3.5051 inches.
⑤ — Coded red, 3.550–3.551 inches; coded blue, 3.5507–3.5515 inches; coded yellow, 3.5513–3.5521 inches.
⑥ — Top ring, .0039–.0098 inch; 2nd ring, .0106–.0165 inch.
⑦ — Type 1, 3.444–3.445; Type 2, 3.445–3.446; Type 3, 3.444–3.446.
⑧ — Top ring, .006–.012 inch; second ring, .012–.018 inch.
⑨ — Ranger & Windstar.
⑩ — Top ring, .0051–.0110 inch; 2nd ring, .0098–.0150 inch.
⑪ — Top compression ring gap, .00098–.00161 inch: bottom compression ring gap , .00149–.0025 inch.
⑫ — Second compression ring only .0020–.0040 inch.
⑬ — Measured at the piston pin bore centerline at 90° to the pin.
⑭ — Snug fit.
⑮ — Top compression, .011–.021 inch; second compression, .055–.065 inch.
⑯ — Grade No. 1; 3.4238–3.4242 inches, Grade No. 2; 3.4242–3.4246 inches, Grade No. 3; 3.4246–3.4250 inches.
⑰ — Grade 1, 3.5498–3.5502 inch; Grade 2, 3.5502–3.5506 inch; Grade 3, 3.5506–3.5510 inch.
⑱ — SOHC engine.
⑲ — Top compression .0100–.0200 inch; bottom compression, .0180–.0280 inch.
⑳ — No. 3 & 4 cylinders, .0006–.0010 inch. Except No. 3 & 4 cylinders, .0010–.0018 inch.
㉑ — Top compression, .0083–.0213 inch. Second compression, .0197–.0272 inch.
㉒ — Top compression, .0009–.0043 inch. Second compression, .0012–.0040 inch.
㉓ — Coded red, 3.8103–3.8108 inches; coded blue, 3.8108–3.8113 inches; coded yellow, 3.8113–3.8118 inches.
㉔ — Top compression, .0066–.0129 inch; second compression, .0059–.0255 inch.
㉕ — Coded red, .9446–.9447 inch. Coded blue, .9447–.9449 inch.
㉖ — Top compression, .008–.018 inch; second compression, .018–.028 inch.
㉗ — Coded red, 3.8103–3.8108 inches. Coded blue, 3.8108–3.8113 inches. Coded yellow, 3.8113–3.8118 inches.
㉘ — Top compression, .0138–.0240 inch; second compression, .0618–.0720 inch.
㉙ — Standard, 3.3369–3.3375; Oversize, 3.3468–3.3473.
㉚ — White, .8119–.8120 inch; red, .8120–.8121 inch; blue, .8121–.8122 inch.
㉛ — Escape & Mariner w/DOHC engine.

CYLINDER BLOCK

All specifications given in inches unless otherwise noted.

Engine Liter	Year	Bore Diameter Std.	Out Of Round Service Limit	Taper Service Limit	Deck Warpage Service Limit	Main Bearing Bore Diameter Std.
2.0L	2002–04	③	.0010	.0005	—	2.2840–2.2850
2.3L	2003–06	3.4440–3.4450	.0003	—	.0040	2.2440–2.2450
3.0L②	2002–06	3.5040	.0020	.0020	.0030	2.7120–2.7130
3.0L④	2002–06	⑥	.0007	.0008	—	2.6770–2.6780
3.3L	2002	⑦	.0004	.0006	.0040	⑧
3.8L	2002–03	3.8100	.0020	.0020	.0040	2.7130
4.0L	2002–06	3.9530	.0010	.0010	.0040	2.3870
4.2L	2002–06	3.8100	.0050	.0020	.0030	2.7120–2.7130
4.6L	2002–06	3.5510	.0008	.0002	—	2.8500–2.8510

Continued

CYLINDER BLOCK—Continued

All specifications given in inches unless otherwise noted.

Engine Liter	Year	Bore Diameter Std.	Out Of Round Service Limit	Taper Service Limit	Deck Warpage Service Limit	Main Bearing Bore Diameter Std.
5.4L	2002–06	⑤	.0008	.0002	—	2.8500–2.8510
6.0L①	2003–06	3.7401–3.7402	.0020	.0030	.0010	3.3854–3.3862
6.8L	2002–06	3.5520	.0005	.0010	—	2.8500–2.8530
7.3L ①	2002–03	4.1096–4.1103	.0020	.0030	.0040	3.1228–3.1236

① — Diesel engine.

② — Ranger & Windstar.

③ — 2002 models, Grade 1 bore, 3.3386–3.3390 inch; grade 2 bore, 3.3390–3.3394 inch; grade 3, 3.3394–3.3398 inch. 2003 models, standard bore, 3.3389–3.3395 inch; oversize bore, 3.3488–3.3492 inch.

④ — Escape & Mariner w/DOHC engine.

⑤ — Grade 1, 3.5512–3.5516 inch; Grade 2, 3.5516–3.5520 inch; Grade 3, 3.5520–3.5524 inch.

⑥ — Grade 1 bore, 3.5039–3.5043 inch; grade 2 bore, 3.5043–3.5047 inch; grade 3 bore 3.5047–3.5051 inch.

⑦ — No. 3 & 4 cylinders, grade 1, 3.6024–3.6026 inches. No. 3 & 4 cylinders, grade 2, 3.6026–3.6027 inches. No. 3 & 4 cylinders, grade 3, 3.6027–3.6029 inches. No. 3 & 4 cylinders, grade 4, 3.6029–3.6031 inches. No. 3 & 4 cylinders, grade 5, 3.6031–3.6033 inches. No. 3 & 4 cylinders, grade 6, 3.6033–3.6035 inches. Except No. 3 & 4 cylinders, grade 1, 3.6024–3.6027 inches. Except No. 3 & 4 cylinders, grade 2, 3.6027–3.6031 inches. Except No. 3 & 4 cylinders, grade 3, 3.6031–3.6035 inches.

⑧ — Grade 0, 2.6238–2.6242 inches. Grade 1, 2.6242–2.6245 inches. Grade 2, 2.6245–2.6249 inches.

OIL PUMP

All specifications given in inches unless otherwise noted.

Engine Liter	Year	Rotor Backlash	Rotor To Body Clearance	Rotor End Clearance ①	Maximum Cover Flatness Variation	Driveshaft To Pump Body Clearance	Relief Valve To Body Clearance	Relief Spring Pressure Lbs. @ Inches
2.0L	2002–04	⑧	—	—	—	—	—	—
2.3L	2003–06	—	—	—	—	—	—	—
3.0L⑥	2002–06	.0080–.0120	⑦	—	④	.0005–.0019	.0017–.0029	9.10–10–1 @ 1.10
3.0L⑤	2002–06	⑧	—	—	—	—	—	—
3.3L	2002	—	—	—	—	—	—	—
3.8L	2002–03	.0080–.0120	.00200–.00550	.00050–.00550	—	③	.0017–0029	15.2–17.1 @ 1.200
3.9L	2002–06	.0080–.0120	—	—	—	.0015–.0030	.0029–.0017	15.1–17.2 @ 1.200
4.0L	2002–06	—	—	.00060–.00170	④	.0007–.0012	.0007–.0012	45–49 @ 1.390
4.2L	2002–06	.0080–.0120	—	—	—	.0015–.0030	.0029–.0017	15.1–17.2 @ 1.200
4.6L	2002–06	—	—	—	—	—	—	—
5.4L	2002–06	—	—	—	—	—	—	—
6.0L②	2003–06	—	.02800–.03200	.00100–.00300	—	—	—	—
6.8L	2002–06	—	—	—	—	—	—	—
7.3L②	2002–03	—	.02800–.03200	.00100–.00300	—	—	—	—

① — Measured between pump cover mounting surface & end of gear using suitable straightedge & feeler gauges.

② — Diesel engine.

③ — Driver shaft, .0015–.0030 inch; idler shaft, .0005–.0017 inch.

④ — Pump should be replaced if cover is damaged, scored or worn.

⑤ — Escape & Mariner w/DOHC engine.

⑥ — Ranger & Windstar.

⑦ — Oil pump gear radial clearance, (idler & driver), .0055–.0020 inch.

⑧ — Not a service item. Replace as an assembly.

GENERAL MOTORS CORPORATION

GENERAL MOTORS CORPORATION

AVALANCHE, ESCALADE EXT, SIERRA, SILVERADO & SSR

NOTE: Refer To The Rear Of This Manual For Vehicle Manufacturer's Special Tool Suppliers.

INDEX OF SERVICE OPERATIONS

Specifications

GENERAL ENGINE SPECIFICATIONS

Year	Engine	Engine VIN Code	Fuel System	Bore & Stroke, Inch	Compres-sion Ratio	Horse-power@ RPM	Torque, Ft. Lbs. @ RPM	Normal Oil Pressure, psi
2002	4.3L	W	Central SFI	4.00 X 3.48	9.2	200 @ 4600	260 @ 2800	③
	4.8L	V	SFI	3.78 X 3.27	9.5	270 @ 5200	285 @ 4000	④
	5.3L	T	SFI	3.78 X 3.62	9.5	285 @ 5200	325 @ 4000	④
	6.0L	U	SFI	4.00 X 3.62	9.4	300 @ 4800	355 @ 4000	④
	6.6L	1	Direct Electronic Fuel Injection	4.06 x 3.90	17.5	300 @ 3100	520 @ 1800	①
	8.1L	G	SFI	4.25 x 4.37	9.1	340 @ 4200	455 @ 3200	②
2003–06	4.3L	W	Central SFI	4.00 X 3.48	9.2	200 @ 4600	260 @ 2800	③
	4.8L	V	SFI	3.78 X 3.27	9.5	270 @ 5200	285 @ 4000	④
	5.3L	T	SFI	3.78 X 3.62	9.5	285 @ 5200	325 @ 4000	④
	6.0L	U	SFI	4.00 X 3.62	9.4	300 @ 4800	355 @ 4000	④
	6.6L	1	Direct Electronic Fuel Injection	4.06 x 3.90	17.5	300 @ 3100	520 @ 1800	①
	8.1L	G	SFI	4.25 x 4.37	9.1	340 @ 4200	455 @ 3200	②

SFI — Sequential Fuel Injection.

① — Minimum: 14psi @ idle; 42psi @ 1800 RPM.

② — Minimum: 5 psi @ 1000 RPM; 10 psi @ 2000 RPM.

③ — Minimum: 6 psi @ 1000 RPM; 18 psi @ 2000 RPM; 24 psi @ 4000 RPM.

④ — Minimum: 6 psi @ 1000 RPM; 18 psi @ 2000 RPM; 24 @ 4000 RPM.

TUNE UP SPECIFICATIONS

The following specifications are published from the latest information available. This data should only be used in the absence of a decal affixed in the engine compartment.

Year & Engine①	Spark Plug Gap	Ignition Timing BTDC				Curb Idle Speed⑥		Fast Idle Speed⑥		Fuel Pump Pres-sure psi.	Valve Lash, Inch
		Firing Order, Fig. ③	Man. Trans.	Auto. Trans.	Mark Lo-cation	Man. Trans.	Auto. Trans.	Man. Trans.	Auto. Trans.		
4.3L	.060	A	④	④	⑧	⑦	⑦	⑦	⑦	55–62⑨	②
4.8L	.060	⑤	④	④	⑧	⑦	⑦	⑦	⑦	55–62⑨	②
5.3L	.060	⑤	④	④	⑧	⑦	⑦	⑦	⑦	55–62⑨	②
6.0L	.060	⑤	④	④	⑧	⑦	⑦	⑦	⑦	55–62⑨	②
8.1L	.060	⑤	④	④	⑧	⑦	⑦	⑦	⑦	55–62⑨	②

BTDC — Before Top Dead Center

D — Drive

N — Neutral

① — The eighth digit of VIN denotes engine code.

② — Equipped w/hydraulic valve lifters.

③ — Before removing wires from distributor cap or coil unit, determine location of ignition wires, as position may have been altered from that outlined at end of this chart.

④ — Not adjustable.

⑤ — Firing order, 1-8-7-2-6-5-4-3.

⑥ — When inspecting idle speed, set parking brake & block drive wheels.

⑦ — Equipped w/Idle Speed Control (ISC) motor or Idle Air Control (IAC) valve.

⑧ — Equipped w/crankshaft position sensor.

⑨ — Wrap shop towel around engine compartment fuel pressure fitting. Connect suitable fuel pressure gauge to fuel pressure fitting. Turn ignition to On position & note fuel pressure reading.

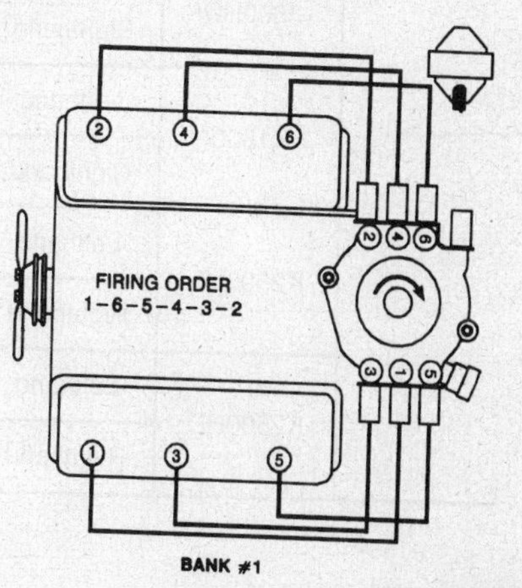

Fig. A

DIESEL ENGINE PERFORMANCE SPECIFICATIONS

Year	Engine	Firing Order	Injection Timing	Idle Speed, RPM	
				Curb	Fast
2002–06	6.6L	1-2-7-8-4-5-6-3	—	①	①

① — Refer to emission control information label located in engine compartment.

FRONT WHEEL ALIGNMENT SPECIFICATIONS

Jounce vehicle three times prior to inspecting alignment to eliminate false geometry readings.

Year/ Model	Series	Side	Caster Angle, Degrees		Camber Angle, Degrees		Total Toe, Degrees①		Ball Joint Wear Limit⑧
			Limits	Desired	Limits	Desired	Limits	Desired	
2002–03									
Avalanche & Escalade EXT	C1500 w/16" tires	Lefthand	+2.90 to +4.90⑤	+3.90⑤	-.25 to +.75③	+.25③	-.10 to +.30	+.10	.08
		Righthand	+3.70 to +5.70⑤	+4.70⑤	-.25 to +.75③	+.25③	-.10 to +.30	+.10	.08
	C1500 w/17" tires	Lefthand	+3.10 to +5.10⑦	+4.10⑦	-.25 to +.75③	+.25③	-.10 to +.30	+.10	.08
		Righthand	+3.70 to +5.70⑦	+4.70⑦	-.25 to +.75③	+.25③	-.10 to +.30	+.10	.08
	K1500 w/17" tires	Lefthand	+3.80 to +5.80	+4.80	-.25 to +.75③	+.25③	-.10 to +.30	+.10	.08
		Righthand	+3.50 to +5.50	4.50⑥	-.25 to +.75③	+.25③	-.10 to +.30	+.10	.08
	C & K 2500	Lefthand	+3.50 to +5.50④	+4.50④	-.25 to +.75③	+.25③	-.10 to +.30	+.10	.08
		Righthand	+3.75 to +5.75④	+4.75④	-.25 to +.75③	+.25③	-.10 to +.30	+.10	.08
Sierra & Silverado Except Crew Cab	C1500	Lefthand	+2.5 to +4.5②	+3.5②	-.25 to +.75③	+.25③	-.10 to +.30	+.10	.08
		Righthand	+3.00 to +5.00②	+4.00②	-.25 to +.75③	+.25③	-.10 to +.30	+.10	.08
	C2500LD	Lefthand	+3.50 to +5.50④	+4.50④	-.25 to +.75③	+.25③	-.10 to +.30	+.10	.08
		Righthand	+3.75 to +5.75④	+4.75④	-.25 to +.75③	+.25③	-.10 to +.30	+.10	.08
	C2500HD	Lefthand	+3.25 to +5.25②	+4.25②	-.25 to +.75③	+.25③	-.10 to +.30	+.10	.08
		Righthand	+3.75 to +5.75②	+4.75②	-.25 to +.75③	+.25③	-.10 to +.30	+.10	.08
	C3500/ 3600HD	Lefthand	+3.25 to +5.25②	+4.25②	-.25 to +.75③	+.25③	-.10 to +.30	+.10	.08
		Righthand	+3.75 to +5.75②	+4.75②	-.25 to +.75③	+.25③	-.10 to +.10	+.10	.08
	K1500	Lefthand	+2.5 to +4.5②	+3.50②	-.25 to +.75③	+.25③	-.10 to +.10	+.10	.08
		Righthand	+3.50 to +5.50②	+4.50②	.25 to +.75③	+.25③	-.10 to +.10	+.10	.08
	K2500LD	Lefthand	+3.25 to +5.25②	+4.50②	-.25 to +.75③	+.25③	-.10 to +.30	+.10	.08
		Righthand	+3.75 to +5.75②	+4.75②	-.25 to +.75③	+.25③	-.10 to +.30	+.10	.08
	K2500HD	Lefthand	+3.00 to +5.00②	+4.00②	-.25 to +.75③	+.25③	-.10 to +.30	+.10	.08
		Righthand	+3.75 to +5.75②	+4.75②	-.25 to +.75③	+.25③	-.10 to +.30	+.10	.08

Continued

FRONT WHEEL ALIGNMENT SPECIFICATIONS

Jounce vehicle three times prior to inspecting alignment to eliminate false geometry readings.

Year/ Model	Series	Side	Caster Angle, Degrees		Camber Angle, Degrees		Total Toe, Degrees①		Ball Joint Wear Limit⑧
			Limits	Desired	Limits	Desired	Limits	Desired	
2002–03									
Sierra & Silverado Except Crew Cab	K3500/ 3600HD	Lefthand	+3.00 to +5.00②	+4.00②	-.25 to +.75③	+.25③	-.10 to +.30	+.10	.08
		Righthand	+3.75 to +5.75②	+4.75②	-.25 to +.75③	+.25③	-.10 to +.30	+.10	.08
Sierra & Silverado w/Crew Cab	C1500	Lefthand	+3.50 to +5.50④	+4.50④	-.25 to +.75	+.25	-.10 to +.30	+.1	.08
		Righthand	+3.75 to +5.75④	+4.75④	-.25 to +.75③	+.25③	-.10 to +.30	+.1	.08
	C2500HD	Lefthand	+3.25 to +5.25②	+4.25②	-.25 to +.75③	+.25③	-.10 to +.30	+.1	.08
		Righthand	+3.75 to +5.75②	+4.75②	-.25 to +.75③	+.25③	-.10 to +.30	+.1	.08
	C3500/ 3600HD	Lefthand	+3.25 to +5.25②	+4.25②	-.25 to +.75③	+.25③	-.10 to +.30	+.10	.08
		Righthand	+3.75 to +5.75②	+4.75②	-.25 to +.75③	+.25③	-.10 to +.30	+.10	.08
	K1500	Lefthand	+3.25 to +5.25②	+4.50②	-.25 to +.75③	+.25	-.10 to +.30	+.10	.08
		Righthand	+3.75 to +5.75②	+4.75②	-.25 to +.75③	+.25③	-.10 to +.30	+.10	.08
	K2500HD	Lefthand	+3.00 to +5.00②	+4.00②	-.25 to +.75③	+.25③	-.10 to +.30	+.10	.08
		Righthand	+3.75 to +5.75②	+4.75②	-.25 to +.75③	+.25③	-.10 to +.30	+.10	.08
	K3500/ 3600HD	Lefthand	+3.00 to +5.00②	+4.00②	-.25 to +.75③	+.25③	-.10 to +.10	+.10	.08
		Righthand	+3.75 to +5.75②	+4.75②	-.25 to +.75③	+.25③	-.10 to +.30	+.10	.08
2004–06									
Avalanche	C1500⑨	Lefthand	+2.90 to +4.90⑤	+3.90⑤	-.25 to +.75③	+.25③	-.10 to +.30	+.10	.08
		Righthand	+3.70 to +5.70⑤	+4.70⑤	-.25 to +.75③	+.25③	-.10 to +.30	+.10	.08
	C1500⑫	Lefthand	+3.10 to +5.10⑦	+4.10⑦	-.25 to +.75③	+.25③	-.10 to +.30	+.10	.08
		Righthand	+3.70 to +5.70⑦	+4.70⑦	-.25 to +.75③	+.25③	-.10 to +.30	+.10	.08
	K1500⑨	Lefthand	+2.60 to +4.60⑤	+3.60⑤	-.25 to +.75③	+.25③	-.10 to +.30	+.10	.08
		Righthand	+3.40 to +5.40⑤	+4.40⑤	-.25 to +.75③	+.25③	-.10 to +.30	+.10	.08
	C & K 2500	Lefthand	+3.50 to +5.50④	+4.50④	-.25 to +.75③	+.25③	-.10 to +.30	+.10	.08
		Righthand	+3.75 to +5.75④	+4.75④	-.25 to +.75③	+.25③	-.10 to +.30	+.10	.08
Escalade	C1500	Lefthand	+2.90 to +4.90⑤	+3.90⑤	.00 to +1.00③	+.50③	-.10 to +.30	+.10	.08
		Righthand	+3.70 to +5.70⑤	+4.70⑤	.00 to +1.00③	+.50③	-.10 to +.30	+.10	.08
	K1500⑫	Lefthand	+2.80 to +4.80⑥	+3.80⑥	-.25 to +.75③	+.25③	-.10 to +.30	+.10	.08
		Righthand	+3.50 to +5.50⑥	+4.50⑥	-.25 to +.75③	+.25③	-.10 to +.30	+.10	.08
	K1500⑮	Lefthand	+3.10 to +5.10⑳	+4.10⑳	-.60 to +.40③	-.10③	-.10 to +.30	+.10	.08
		Righthand	+4.10 to +6.10⑳	+5.10⑳	-.60 to +.40③	-.10③	-.10 to +.30	+.10	.08

Continued

FRONT WHEEL ALIGNMENT SPECIFICATIONS

Jounce vehicle three times prior to inspecting alignment to eliminate false geometry readings.

Year/ Model	Series	Side	Caster Angle, Degrees		Camber Angle, Degrees		Total Toe, Degrees①		Ball Joint Wear Limit⑧
			Limits	Desired	Limits	Desired	Limits	Desired	
2004–06									
Sierra & Siverado	C1500⑨	Lefthand	+1.55 to +3.55⑩	+2.55⑩	-.35 to +.85⑪	+.25⑪	-.10 to +.30	+.10	.08
		Righthand	+1.80 to +3.80⑩	+2.80⑩	-.35 to +.85⑪	+.25⑪	-.10 to +.30	+.10	.08
	C1500 ⑮	Lefthand	+2.75 to +4.75⑭	+3.75⑭	-.70 to +.50⑪	-.10⑪	-.10 to +.30	+.10	.08
		Righthand	+3.05 to +5.05⑭	+4.05⑭	-.70 to +.50⑪	-.10⑪	-.10 to +.30	+.10	.08
	C1500HD⑨	Lefthand	+2.50 to +4.50⑩	+3.50⑩	-.35 to +.85⑪	+.25⑪	-.10 to +.30	+.10	.08
		Righthand	+2.75 to +4.75⑩	+3.75⑩	-.35 to +.85⑪	+.25⑪	-.10 to +.30	+.10	.08
	C2500 LD	Lefthand	+2.50 to +4.50⑩	+3.50⑩	-.35 to +.85⑪	+.25⑪	-.10 to +.30	+.10	.08
		Righthand	+2.75 to +4.75⑩	+3.75⑩	-.35 to +.85⑪	+.25⑪	-.10 to +.30	+.10	.08
	C3500/3600	Lefthand	+1.80 to +3.80⑯	+2.80⑯	-.35 to +.85⑪	+.25⑪	-.10 to +.30	+.10	.08
		Righthand	+2.15 to +4.15⑯	+3.15⑯	-.35 to +.85⑪	+.25⑪	-.10 to +.30	+.10	.08
	C & K 1500⑫	Lefthand	+1.30 to +3.30⑬	+2.30⑬	-.35 to +.85⑪	+.25⑪	-.10 to +.30	+.10	.08
		Righthand	+1.55 to +3.55⑬	+2.55⑬	-.35 to +.85⑪	+.25⑪	-.10 to +.30	+.10	.08
	C & K 2500 HD	Lefthand	+2.25 to +4.25⑩	+3.25⑩	-.35 to +.85⑪	+.25⑪	-.10 to +.30	+.10	.08
		Righthand	+2.50 to +4.50⑩	+3.50⑩	-.35 to +.85⑪	+.25⑪	-.10 to +.30	+.10	.08
	K1500⑨	Lefthand	+1.60 to +3.60⑭	+2.60⑭	-.35 to +.85⑪	+.25⑪	-.10 to +.30	+.10	.08
		Righthand	+1.90 to +3.90⑭	+2.90⑭	-.35 to +.85⑪	+.25⑪	-.10 to +.30	+.10	.08
	K1500⑫	Lefthand	+1.30 to +3.30⑩	+2.30⑩	-.35 to +.85⑪	+.25⑪	-.10 to +.30	+.10	.08
		Righthand	+1.55 to +3.55⑩	+2.55⑩	-.35 to +.85⑪	-.25⑪	-.10 to +.30	+.10	.08
	K1500⑮	Lefthand	+1.65 TO +3.65⑭	+2.65⑭	-.35 to +.85⑪	+.25⑪	-.10 to +.30	+.10	.08
		Righthand	+1.95 to + 3.95⑭	+2.95⑭	-.35 to +.85⑪	+.25⑪	-.10 to +.30	+.10	.08
	K1500 HD	Lefthand	+2.25 to +4.25⑩	+3.25⑩	-.35 to +.85⑪	+.25⑪	-.10 to +.30	+.10	.08
		Righthand	+2.50 to +4.50⑩	+3.50⑩	-.35 to +.85⑪	+.25⑪	-.10 to +.30	+.10	.08

Continued

FRONT WHEEL ALIGNMENT SPECIFICATIONS

Jounce vehicle three times prior to inspecting alignment to eliminate false geometry readings.

Year/ Model	Series	Side	Caster Angle, Degrees		Camber Angle, Degrees		Total Toe, Degrees①		Ball Joint Wear Limit⑧
			Limits	Desired	Limits	Desired	Limits	Desired	
2004–06									
Sierra & Siverado	K2500 LD	Lefthand	+2.25 to +4.25⑩	+3.25⑩	-.35 to +.85⑪	+.25⑪	-.10 to +.30	+.10	.08
		Righthand	+2.15 to +4.15⑩	+3.15⑩	-.35 to +.85⑪	+.25⑪	-.10 to +.30	+.10	.08
	K3500/ 3600⑰	Lefthand	+1.80 to +3.80⑯	+2.80⑯	-.35 to +.85⑪	+.25⑪	-.10 to +.30	+.10	.08
		Righthand	+2.15 to +4.15⑯	+3.15⑯	-.35 to +.85⑪	+.25⑪	-.10 to +.30	+.10	.08
	K3500/ 3600⑱	Lefthand	+2.15 to +4.15⑲	+3.15⑲	-.35 to +.85⑪	+.25⑪	-.10 to +.30	+.10	.08
		Righthand	+2.65 to +4.65⑲	+3.65⑲	-.35 to +.85⑪	+.25⑪	-.10 to +.30	+.10	.08
SSR	All	Lefthand	+3.65 to +4.85㉑	+4.25㉑	-1.10 to +.10⑪	-.50⑪	-.10 to +.30	+.10	.08
		Righthand	+3.65 to +4.85㉑	+4.25㉑	-1.10 to +.10⑪	-.50⑪	-.10 to +.30	+.10	.08

① — Toe-In (+). Toe-Out (–).
② — Cross caster (L-R), –1° to +0, preferred, –5°
③ — Cross camber (L-R), –.5° to +.5°, preferred, 0°
④ — Cross caster (L-R), –.75° to +.25°, preferred, –.25°
⑤ — Cross caster (L-R), –1.3° to –.3°, preferred, –.8°.
⑥ — Cross caster (L-R), –1.2° to –.2°, preferred, –.7°.
⑦ — Cross caster (L-R), –1.1° to –.1°, preferred, –.6°.
⑧ — Refer to "Ball Joint Inspection" in "Front Suspension & Steering" section for inspection procedure.
⑨ — With 16 inch tires.
⑩ — Cross camber (L-R), –1.00° to +.50°, preferred, –.25°.
⑪ — Cross camber (L-R), –.6° to +.6°, preferred, 0°.
⑫ — With 17 inch tires.
⑬ — Cross caster (L-R), –.90° to +.60°, preferred, –.15°.
⑭ — Cross caster (L-R), –1.05° to +.45°, preferred, –.30°.
⑮ — With 20 inch tires.
⑯ — Cross caster (L-R), –1.1° to +.4°, preferred, –.35°.
⑰ — With dual rear wheels.
⑱ — Less dual rear wheels.
⑲ — Cross caster (L-R), –1.25° to +.25°, preferred, –.5°.
⑳ — Cross caster (L-R), –1.5° to -.5°, preferred, -1.0°.
㉑ — Cross caster (L-R), –.6° to +.6°, preferred, 0°.

FLUID CAPACITIES & COOLING SYSTEM DATA

Year/Model	Engine Liter	Cooling System Capacity, Qts.		Coolant Type	Radiator Cap Relief Pressure, Lbs.	Thermo. Opening Temp. °F	Fuel Tank Gals.	Engine Oil Refill Qts.③	Transmission Oil		Transfer Case Pts.	Drive Axle Oil	
		Less A/C	With A/C						Man. Trans. Pts.	Auto. Trans. Qts. ①		Front Pts.	Rear Pts.
2002–03													
Avalanche	5.3L	16.5	16.5	②	15	195	31	6.0	—	⑦	4	⑰	⑱
	8.1L	24	25	②	15	195	37	6.5	—	⑦	4	⑰	⑱
Escalade EXT	6.0L	—	17	②	15	195	31	6.0	—	⑦	4	⑩	⑨
Sierra & Silverado	4.3L	⑥	⑥	②	15	195	⑮	4.5	⑭	⑦	⑯	⑰	⑱
	4.8L	⑤	⑤	②	15	195	⑮	6.0	⑭	⑦	⑯	⑰	⑱
	5.3L	13.4	14.9	②	15	195	⑮	6.0	⑭	⑦	⑯	⑰	⑱
	6.0L	15.2	14.8	②	15	195	⑮	6.0	⑭	⑦	⑯	⑰	⑱
	6.6L⑧	④	④	②	15	180	⑮	8.0	12.6	⑪	⑯	⑰	⑱
	8.1L	⑬	⑬	②	15	195	⑮	6.5	12.6	⑪	⑯	⑰	⑱
2004–06													
Avalanche	5.3L	16.7	16.7	②	15	195	31	6.0	—	⑦	4	3	⑱
	8.1L	27	27	②	15	195	37	6.5	—	⑦	4	3.6	⑱
Escalade EXT	6.0L	—	16.2	②	15	195	31	6.0	—	⑦	4	⑩	⑨

Continued

FLUID CAPACITIES & COOLING SYSTEM DATA—Continued

Year/Model	Engine Liter	Cooling System Capacity, Qts.		Coolant Type	Radiator Cap Relief Pressure, Lbs.	Thermo. Opening Temp. °F	Fuel Tank Gals.	Engine Oil Refill Qts.③	Transmission Oil		Transfer Case Pts.	Drive Axle Oil	
		Less A/C	With A/C						Man. Trans. Pts.	Auto. Trans. Qts. ①		Front Pts.	Rear Pts.
2004–06													
Sierra & Silverado	4.3L	—	16.5	②	15	195	⑮	4.5	⑭	⑦	⑯	⑩	⑱
	4.8L	—	16.8	②	15	195	⑮	6.0	⑭	⑦	⑯	⑩	⑱
	5.3L	—	16.8	②	15	195	⑮	6.0	⑭	⑦	⑯	⑩	⑱
	6.0L	—	16.7	②	15	195	⑮	6.0	⑭	⑫	⑯	⑩	⑱
	6.6L⑧	—	27	②	15	180	⑮	10.0	12.6	⑲	⑯	⑩	⑱
	8.1L	—	27	②	15	195	⑮	6.5	12.6	⑲	⑯	⑩	⑱
SSR	6.0L	—	13.7	②	15	195	25	6.0	7.4	⑫	—	—	⑨

① — Approximate, make final inspection w/dipstick.

② — 50/50 mixture water and GM Goodwrench DEX-COOL or Havoline DEX-COOL coolant.

③ — Includes filter.

④ — M/T, 20.7 qts.; A/T, 20.3 qts.

⑤ — M/T, 13.7 qts.; A/T, 13.4 qts.

⑥ — M/T, 12.9 qts.; A/T, 12.6 qts.

⑦ — 4L60-E, pan removal, 5 qts., overhaul, 11.2 qts.; 4L80-E, pan removal, 7.7 qts., overhaul, 13.5 qts.

⑧ — Diesel engine.

⑨ — 8.6 inch ring gear, 4.2 pts.; 9.5 inch ring gear, 5.5 pts.; 10.5 inch ring gear, 5.5 pts.; 11.5 inch ring gear, 7.66 pts.

⑩ — 8.25 inch ring gear, 3 pts.; 9.25 inch ring gear, 3.65 pts.

⑪ — Pan removal, 7.4 qts., overhaul, 12.7 qts.

⑫ — 4L80-E pan removal, 7.7 qts., overhaul, 13.5 qts.; Allison 1000 pan removal, 7.4 qts., overhaul, 12.7 qts.

⑬ — M/T, 21.1 qts.; A/T, 20.7 qts.

⑭ — New Venture 3500 trans, 4.8 pts.; 4500 trans, 8 pts.; 6 speed, 12.6 pts.

⑮ — Short bed models, 26 gals.; long bed models, 34 gals.; chassis-cab models, side tank 22 gals., rear tank 30 gals.

⑯ — NVG 149, 4.8 pts.; NVG 236, 246, NV261 & 263, 4 pts.

⑰ — Front Axle 8.25 inch, 3.5 pts.; 9.25 inch, 3.7 pts.

⑱ — 8.6 inch ring gear, 4.3 pts.; 9.5 inch ring gear, 5.5 pts.; 9.75 inch ring gear, 6 pts.; 10.5 inch ring gear, 5.5 pts., 11.5 inch ring gear, 7.66 pts.

⑲ — Pan removal, 5 qts., overhaul, 11 qts.

LUBRICANT DATA

Year	Model	Lubricant Type						
		Transmission		Hydraulic Clutch Fluid	Transfer Case	Drive Axle	Power Steering	Brake System
		Manual	Automatic					
2002–05	All	75W-85 GL-4	Dexron III	DOT 3	Dexron III	②	①	DOT 3
2006	All	75W-85 GL-4	Dexron VI	DOT 3	③	②	①	DOT 3

① — Power steering fluid GM part No. 1050017, or equivalent.

② — Front S4WD, 80W-90; Front F4WD, 75W-90; Rear 75W-90 synthetic.

③ — NVG 149, NVG 261 & NVG 263 transfer cases, Dexron III: NVG 246 transfer case, Auto-Trak II transfer case fluid, GM part No. 12378508, or equivalent.

Electrical

NOTE: On Air Bag Equipped Models, Refer To "Air Bag System Precautions" Located In The Front Of This Manual For System Disarming & Arming Procedures.

NOTE: Refer To "Computer Relearn Procedures" Located In The Front Of This Manual When Battery Power To The Computer Has Been Interrupted.

INDEX

PRECAUTIONS

Air Bag Systems

Refer to "Air Bag System Precautions" in the front of this manual for system disarming and arming procedures.

Battery Ground Cable

Prior to service disconnect battery ground cable and isolate as required.

Radio Security System

If the Theftlock system is active when battery power is interrupted, the customers security code must be entered to restore proper function of the radio. Use the following procedure to unlock a secured radio after a power loss. Do not wait more than 15 seconds between steps.

1. Theftlock is engaged if radio is inoperable and "LOC" appears with ignition in On position.
2. Obtain customers' code number.
3. Press "MIN" button and "000" will appear on display.
4. Press "MIN" again until last two digits displayed agree with security code.
5. Press "HR" button until first 1 or 2 digits agree with security code.
6. Press "AM-FM" to select code entered. "SEC" will display indicating radio is now operable and secure.
7. If incorrect code is entered, "SEC" will display and radio will be inoperable.
8. Radio will remain inoperable until correct code is displayed. Repeat steps until correct code is entered. If correct code cannot be obtained, contact Delco technical assistance.

FUSE PANEL & FLASHER LOCATION

Except 2500HD & 3500HD

The body junction block is located under the lefthand side of the instrument panel near the lefthand kick panel.

The instrument panel junction block is located in the lower righthand side of the instrument panel.

The instrument panel fuse block is located on the lower lefthand side of the instrument panel.

The underhood fuse block is located on the lefthand side of the engine compartment near the battery.

The rear lamps junction block is located in the front of the rear bumper on the crossmember.

The hazard and turn signal flasher is located behind the lefthand side of the instrument panel, on the instrument panel fuse block.

2500HD & 3500HD

The instrument panel fuse block is located at the lefthand end of the instrument panel, near the lefthand front door jamb switch.

The underhood fuse block is located in the lefthand rear side of the engine compartment, on the fender.

The hazard and turn signal flasher is located behind the lefthand side of the instrument panel, on the instrument panel fuse block.

FUEL PUMP RELAY LOCATION

The fuel pump relay is located on the left-hand side of the engine compartment, inside the underhood fuse block

RELAY CENTER LOCATION

Except 2500HD & 3500HD

The Underhood Bussed Electrical Center (UBEC) contains the engine compartment relays and is mounted on the lefthand wheelhouse, near the battery. The convenience center is located just below the left-hand side of the instrument panel.

2500HD & 3500HD

The underhood fuse block contains the engine compartment relays and is located in the lefthand rear side of the engine compartment, on the fender. The convenience center contains interior relays and is located under the lefthand side of the instrument panel, on the bulkhead.

STARTER

REPLACE

4.3L Engine

1. Raise and support vehicle.
2. Remove starter motor mounting bolts.
3. Disconnect starter positive battery cable and wiring harness.
4. Remove starter.
5. Reverse procedure to install, noting the following:
   a. **Torque** starter mounting bolts to 32 ft. lbs.
   b. **Torque** cable and wiring harness mounting nut to 80 inch lbs.

4.8L, 5.3L & 6.0L Engines

1. Remove mounting bolts and engine shield, as required.
2. Remove mounting bolts and oil pan skid plate, as required.
3. Remove righthand transmission cover bolt.
4. Remove front axle mounting bracket nut, then position front axle mounting bracket bolt until tip is flush with support bushing. **DO NOT remove bolt.**
5. Remove mounting bolts and slide starter forward until it clears transmission.
6. Disconnect oil level sensor electrical connector.
7. Remove starter solenoid nut and lead from stud.
8. Remove starter lead nut and the positive cable from starter stud.
9. Remove starter.

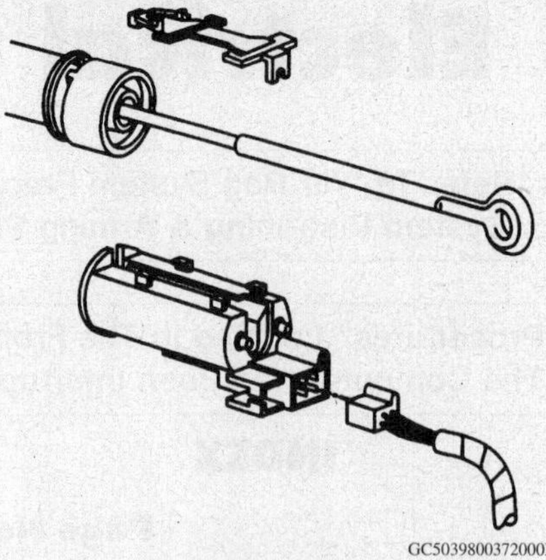

Fig. 1 Clutch start switch removal

10. Reverse procedure to install, noting the following:
    a. **Torque** starter lead nut to 80 inch lbs.
    b. **Torque** starter solenoid nut 30 inch lbs.
    c. **Torque** starter mounting bolts 37 ft. lbs.
    d. **Torque** front axle mounting bracket nut 70 ft. lbs.
    e. **Torque** transmission cover bolt 80 inch lbs.
    f. **Torque** oil pan skid plate bolts to 15 ft. lbs.
    g. **Torque** engine shield bolts to 15 ft. lbs.

6.6L Engine

1. Raise and support vehicle, then remove righthand front tire and wheel assembly.
2. Remove righthand front fender wheelhouse inner panel.
3. Remove starter motor battery positive cable, then the solenoid wires.
4. Remove mounting bolts and starter motor.
5. Reverse procedure to install, noting the following:
   a. **Torque**starter motor mounting bolts to 58 ft. lbs.
   b. **Torque** starter solenoid nut to 30 inch lbs.
   c. **Torque** starter battery positive cable nut to 80 inch lbs.

8.1L Engine

1. Raise and support vehicle.
2. Disconnect starter battery positive cable and wiring harness.
3. Remove starter mounting bolts, washers, shims, starter and heat shield.
4. Reverse procedure to install, noting the following:
   a. **Torque** starter shield bolts to 35 inch lbs.
   b. **Torque** starter mounting bolts to 37 ft. lbs.
   c. **Torque** battery positive cable to 89 inch lbs.
   d. **Torque** ignition switch wires to solenoid to 18 inch lbs.

ALTERNATOR

REPLACE

1. Remove air inlet duct, as required.
2. Disconnect terminal plug and battery lead connections from back of alternator.
3. Remove upper fan shroud mounting bolts and fan shroud.
4. Remove accessory drive belt using suitable 3/8 inch drive wrench to rotate tensioner arm counterclockwise.
5. Remove mounting bolts and alternator.
6. Reverse procedure to install, noting the following:
   a. **Torque** alternator mounting bolts to 37 ft. lbs.
   b. **Torque** battery lead mounting nut to 80 inch lbs.

COIL PACK

REPLACE

4.3L Engine

1. Remove air cleaner.
2. Disconnect coil electrical connectors.
3. Remove ignition coil to distributor wire.
4. Remove ignition coil bracket to intake manifold mounting studs.
5. Remove ignition coil and bracket.
6. Drill and punch out ignition coil to bracket rivets.
7. Separate ignition coil.
8. Reverse procedure to install. **Torque** ignition coil bracket to intake manifold studs to 96 inch lbs.

4.8L, 5.3L & 6.0L Engines

1. Disconnect spark plug wires at ignition coils.
2. Disconnect ignition coil harness connector.
3. Remove mounting bolts and ignition coil.
4. Reverse procedure to install. **Torque** mounting bolts to 71 inch lbs.

8.1L Engine

1. Disconnect ignition coil harness connector.
2. Remove mounting bolts and ignition coil.
3. Reverse procedure to install. **Torque** mounting bolts to 106 inch lbs.

IGNITION LOCK

REPLACE

1. Remove steering wheel as outlined under "Steering Wheel, Replace."
2. Remove tilt lever by pulling it out of steering column.
3. Remove lower steering column trim cover mounting screws.
4. Remove lower steering column trim cover by tilting it down and sliding back to disengage locking tabs.

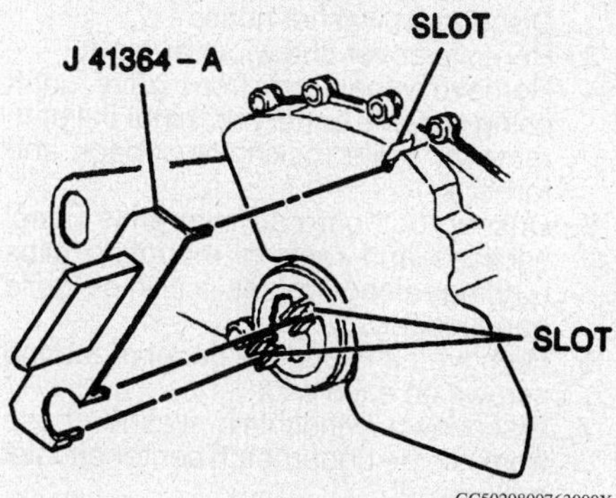

Fig. 2 Neutral safety switch installation

5. Remove mounting screws and upper steering column trim cover.
6. Turn ignition lock cylinder to START position.
7. Insert tip of suitable awl into ignition lock cylinder access hole, then push down and hold ignition lock cylinder retaining pin.
8. Release ignition lock cylinder to RUN position and remove ignition lock cylinder by pulling it away from steering column.
9. Reverse procedure to install, noting the following:
   a. **Torque** lower steering column trim cover mounting screws to 31 inch lbs.
   b. **Torque** upper steering column trim cover mounting screws to 13 inch lbs.

IGNITION SWITCH

REPLACE

1. **On models equipped with automatic transmission,** apply parking brake and move shift lever all way down to last gear.
2. **On all models,** tilt steering wheel to full down position.
3. Remove instrument cluster trim bezel by pulling rearward on corners.
4. Remove mounting screws and knee bolster by unsnapping top.
5. Remove steering wheel as outlined under "Steering Wheel, Replace."
6. Remove tilt lever by pulling it out of steering column.
7. Remove lower steering column trim cover mounting screws.
8. Remove lower steering column trim cover by tilting it down and sliding back to disengage locking tabs.
9. Remove mounting screws and upper steering column trim cover.
10. Disconnect steering column electrical connectors.
11. Remove wire harness assembly from steering column and wire harness strap.
12. Slide two turn signal and multifunction switch connectors out of bulkhead connector.
13. Remove lock module key alarm connector by rotating connector 90° and pull key alarm connector out of lock module.

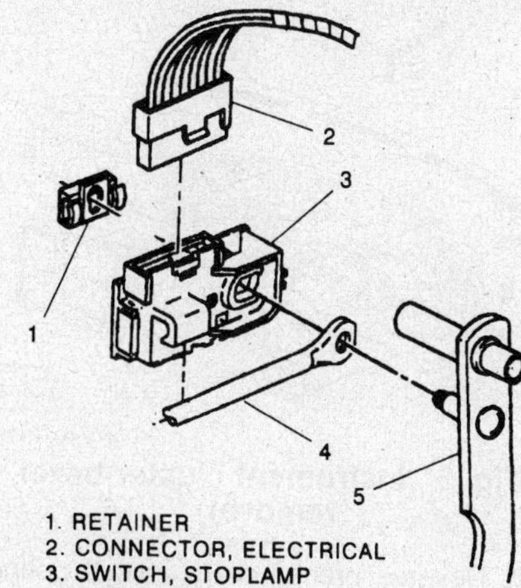

Fig. 3 Stop lamp switch removal

14. Remove passkey connector from lock module assembly.
15. **On models equipped floor shifters,** remove electric park lock connector.
16. **On all models,** remove ignition switch from lock module using switch connector release tool No. J-42759, or equivalent.
17. Reverse procedure to install, noting the following:
    a. **Torque** lower steering column trim cover mounting screws to 31 inch lbs.
    b. **Torque** upper steering column trim cover mounting screws to 13 inch lbs.
    c. **Torque** knee bolster screws to 18 inch lbs.

CLUTCH START SWITCH

REPLACE

1. Remove plastic retaining tabs from clutch start switch.
2. Remove clutch start switch from push rod, **Fig. 1.**
3. Disconnect switch electrical connector.
4. Reverse procedure to install.

NEUTRAL SAFETY SWITCH

REPLACE

Removal

1. Apply parking brake.
2. Shift transmission into neutral position, then raise and support vehicle.
3. **On models equipped with 4WD,** remove front propeller shaft as outlined in "Front Wheel Drive" section.
4. **On all models,** remove transmission control to manual mounting nut and lever.
5. Disconnect park/neutral safety switch electrical connector.
6. Remove two mounting bolts and park/neutral safety switch.

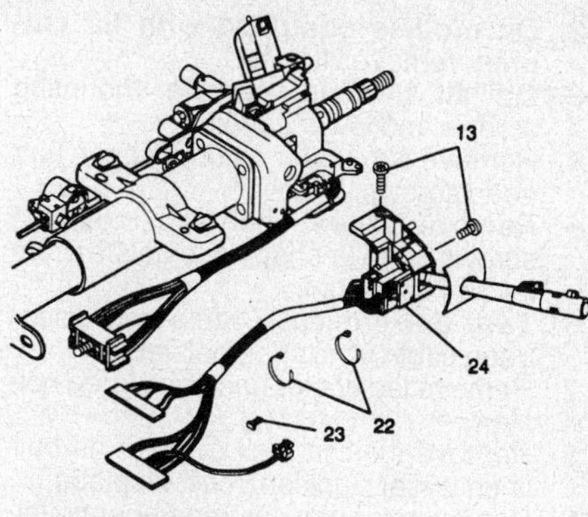

Fig. 4 Multi-Function switch removal

Installation

1. Install adjustment tool No. J-41364-A, or equivalent, onto park/neutral safety switch. Ensure two slots on switch are lined up with lower two tabs on tool, **Fig. 2.**
2. Rotate tool until upper locator pin is lined up with slot on top of switch.
3. Install switch to transmission.
4. Install park/neutral switch to transmission mounting bolts. **Torque** bolts to 18 ft. lbs.
5. Remove adjusting tool.
6. Connect park/neutral safety switch electrical connector.
7. Install transmission control lever to manual shaft and install nut. **Torque** control lever nut to 18 ft. lbs.
8. **On models equipped with 4WD,** install front propeller shaft as outlined in "Front Wheel Drive" section.

HEADLAMP SWITCH

REPLACE

1. Remove instrument cluster bezel, refer to "Instrument Cluster, Replace."
2. Disconnect electrical connector from switch.
3. Remove headlamp switch by unsnapping it from instrument cluster bezel.
4. Reverse procedure to install.

STOP LIGHT SWITCH

REPLACE

1. Remove push rod retainer from brake pedal pin, **Fig. 3.**
2. Unsnap stop lamp switch from pushrod.
3. Disconnect electrical connector from stop lamp switch.
4. Reverse procedure to install.

MULTI-FUNCTION SWITCH

REPLACE

1. Remove steering wheel as outlined under "Steering Wheel, Replace."

2. **On models equipped with tilt column,** remove tilt lever.
3. **On all models,** remove mounting screws and lower cover.
4. Remove two upper column cover Torx head screws.
5. Remove knee bolster mounting screws, then unsnap knee bolster from instrument panel.
6. Twist brake release cable and disengage cable from knee bolster.
7. Remove lap cooler hose and knee bolster.
8. Remove ignition lock cylinder as outlined under "Ignition Lock, Replace."
9. Remove steering column upper cover.
10. Remove two wiring harness straps from steering column wiring harness, **Fig. 4.**
11. Disconnect steering column bulkhead connector from vehicle wiring harness.
12. **On models equipped with column shift,** remove axial position assurance connector from BTSI actuator.
13. **On all models,** remove grey and black multi-function switch connectors from column bulkhead connector.
14. Remove mount screws and multi-function switch.
15. Reverse procedure to install.

TURN SIGNAL SWITCH

REPLACE

Refer to "Multi-Function Switch, Replace" for replacement procedures.

DIMMER SWITCH

REPLACE

Refer to "Multi-Function Switch, Replace" for replacement procedures.

STEERING WHEEL

REPLACE

Except 2500HD & 3500HD

1. Turn ignition switch to ON position.
2. Turn steering wheel 90° so side of SIR module is at 12 o'clock position.
3. Insert suitable screwdriver into access hole and push leaf spring to release air bag module notched pin.
4. Turn steering wheel 180° and repeat previous step.
5. Tilt air bag module top rearward and disconnect SIR lead wire from clips.
6. Disconnect Connector Position Assurance retainer from connector. Disconnect SIR connector.
7. Remove air bag module.
8. Remove horn contact plate mounting screws and plunger from steering wheel.
9. Mark steering wheel to steering shaft alignment for installation.
10. Remove steering wheel nut.
11. Remove steering wheel using steering wheel puller tool No. J-1859-A, or equivalent.

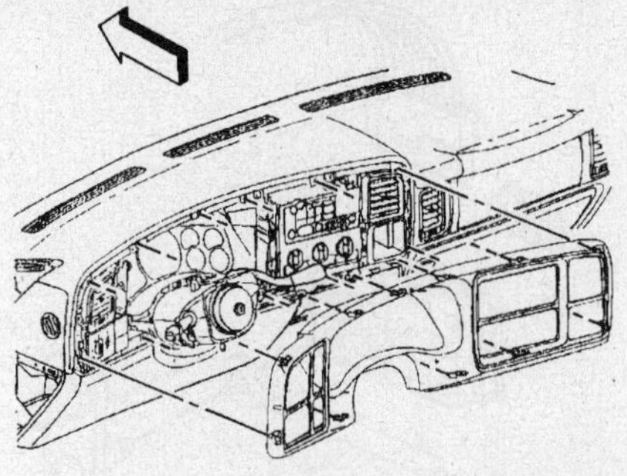

Fig. 5 Instrument cluster bezel removal

12. Reverse procedure to install, noting the following:
    a. **Torque** steering wheel nut to 30 ft. lbs.
    b. **Torque** horn contact plate mounting screws to 50 inch lbs.

2500HD & 3500HD

1. Pull horn pad four corners from steering wheel.
2. Disconnect ground wire and horn wire.
3. Mark steering wheel to steering shaft alignment for installation.
4. Remove steering wheel mounting nut.
5. Remove steering wheel using steering wheel puller tool No. J-1859-A, or equivalent.
6. Reverse procedure to install. **Torque** steering wheel nut to 30 ft. lbs.

INSTRUMENT CLUSTER

REPLACE

1. Engage parking brake lever.
2. Move gear shift lever and tilt steering wheel to lowest positions.
3. Remove bezel by pulling rearward on clips , **Fig. 5.**
4. Remove instrument panel cluster mounting screws, **Fig. 6.**
5. Disconnect instrument panel cluster electrical harness connectors.
6. Remove instrument panel cluster by tilting bottom of cluster outward.
7. Reverse procedure to install. **Torque** mounting screws to 18 inch lbs.

RADIO

REPLACE

1. Remove instrument cluster trim bezel as outlined under "Instrument Cluster, Replace."
2. Release radio assembly lock tabs using suitable screwdriver.
3. Slide radio rearward away from instrument panel and disconnect electrical connectors.
4. Remove radio.
5. Reverse procedure to install.

WIPER MOTOR

REPLACE

1. Mark position of wiper blade on windshield for installation alignment.
2. Disconnect washer hose.
3. Remove cover and wiper arm nut.
4. Remove wiper arm from drive shaft using suitable battery terminal puller to remove, while rocking arm back and forth.
5. Unsnap outboard air inlet grille panel sections and remove mounting clips running along center air inlet grille panel edges.
6. Remove air inlet grille panel mounting screws on each end.
7. Disconnect windshield washer hose from nozzle underneath center air inlet grille panel.
8. Remove air inlet grille panel.
9. Remove four mounting bolts and reinforcement panel.
10. Disconnect wiper motor electrical connector.
11. Remove two mounting bolts and wiper transmission.
12. Remove drive link from wiper motor crank arm using wiper transmission separator tool No. J-39232, or equivalent.
13. Remove two mounting bolts and wiper motor.
14. Reverse procedure to install, noting the following:
    a. **Torque** wiper motor mounting bolts to 89 inch lbs.
    b. **Torque** transmission mounting bolts to 80 inch lbs.
    c. **Torque** reinforcement panel mounting bolts to 80 inch lbs.
    d. **Torque** air inlet grille panel mounting screws to 18 inch lbs.
    e. **Torque** wiper arm nut to 18 ft. lbs.

WIPER SWITCH

REPLACE

Refer to "Multi-Function Switch, Replace" for replacement procedures.

BLOWER MOTOR

REPLACE

Except 2500HD & 3500HD

1. Remove hush panel from under right-hand side of instrument panel.
2. Disconnect blower relay/resistor electrical connector.
3. Remove blower motor insulating cover mounting screws.
4. Disconnect blower motor electrical connector, then remove insulating cover.
5. Pull blower motor retaining tab down and turn motor counterclockwise to disengage retaining tab,
6. Remove blower motor.
7. Reverse procedure to install.

2500HD & 3500HD

1. Remove knee bolster from under left-hand side of instrument panel.
2. Remove knee bolster reinforcement and knee deflector bracket.

3. Remove tubular tie bar from under steering column.
4. Remove steering column trim panels.
5. Disconnect transmission control cable from steering column.
6. Disconnect steering column wiring harness from connectors.
7. Remove upper to lower steering column shaft mounting bolt.
8. Remove upper and lower steering column support bracket mounting nuts.
9. Lower steering column.
10. Rotate steering column so shift lever clears instrument panel opening, then remove column.
11. Remove glove compartment door passenger air bag module bracket mounting bolts.
12. Remove left and righthand lower instrument panel pivot bolts.
13. Remove instrument panel center support bolt and pivot instrument panel downward.
14. Remove glove compartment to instrument panel carrier mounting screws.
15. Remove glove compartment.
16. Remove passenger door sill plate front screw.
17. Remove passenger door hinge pillar trim panel.
18. Disconnect PCM electrical connectors.
19. **On models equipped with diesel engine,** remove PCM and PCM mounting bracket.
20. **On all models,** disconnect blower motor electrical connectors.
21. Remove righthand lower instrument panel support.
22. Remove blower motor cover and cooling tube.
23. Remove blower motor flange screws.
24. Remove blower motor and fan.
25. Reverse procedure to install.

HEATER CORE
REPLACE

Except 2500HD & 3500HD

1. Drain cooling system into suitable container.
2. Recover refrigerant as outlined under "Air Conditioning."
3. Disconnect heater hoses.
4. Remove accumulator.
5. Remove instrument panel carrier as outlined "Dash Panel Service."
6. Remove HVAC module drain hose.
7. Disconnect electrical harnesses and ground connections as needed.
8. Remove HVAC module mounting nuts and screws.
9. Remove HVAC module and set on bench.
10. Remove heater core cover screws and cover.
11. Remove heater core.
12. Reverse procedure to install. **Torque** HVAC module mounting nuts to 84 inch lbs., and bolts to 35 inch lbs.

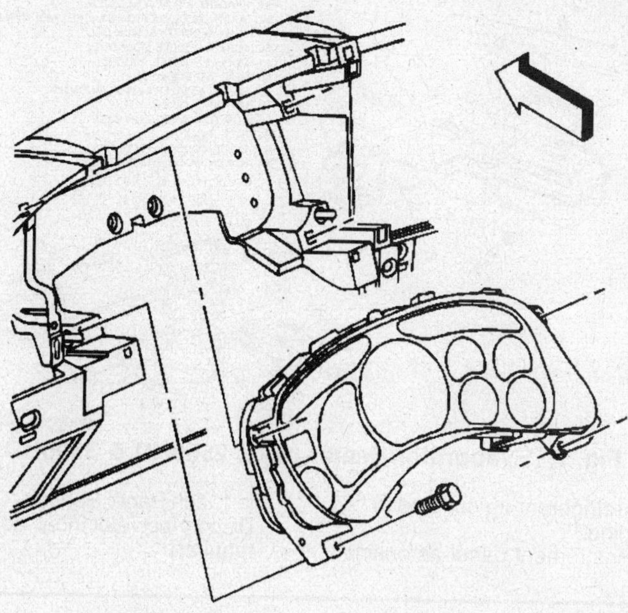

Fig. 6 Instrument cluster removal

2500HD & 3500HD

1. Remove knee bolster from under lefthand side of instrument panel.
2. Remove knee bolster reinforcement and knee deflector bracket.
3. Remove tubular tie bar from under steering column.
4. Remove steering column trim panels.
5. Disconnect transmission control cable from steering column.
6. Disconnect steering column wiring harness from connectors.
7. Remove upper to lower steering column shaft mounting bolt.
8. Remove upper and lower steering column support bracket mounting nuts.
9. Lower steering column.
10. Rotate steering column so shift lever clears instrument panel opening, then remove column.
11. Remove glove compartment door and passenger air bag module bracket mounting bolts.
12. Remove left and righthand lower instrument panel pivot bolts.
13. Remove instrument panel center support bolt and pivot instrument panel downward.
14. Remove glove compartment to instrument panel carrier mounting screws.
15. Remove glove compartment.
16. Remove passenger door sill plate front screw.
17. Drain cooling system into suitable container, then remove seven lower cover plate mounting screws.
18. Remove lower cover plate, then the heater hoses from core tubes, **Fig. 7.**
19. Disconnect electrical connectors.
20. Remove center floor air distribution duct, then the PCM and PCM mounting bracket.
21. Remove hinge pillar trim panels and blower motor cover.
22. Remove blower as outlined under "Blower Motor, Replace."
23. Remove heater core and bracket to case mounting screws, then the heater core.
24. Reverse procedure to install.

EVAPORATOR CORE
REPLACE

Except 2500HD & 3500HD

1. Drain cooling system into suitable container.
2. Recover refrigerant as outlined in "Air Conditioning."
3. Disconnect heater hoses.
4. Remove accumulator.
5. Remove instrument panel as outlined in "Dash Panel Service."
6. Remove HVAC module drain hose.
7. Disconnect electrical harnesses and ground connections as needed.
8. Remove HVAC module mounting nuts and screws.
9. Remove HVAC module and set on bench.
10. Remove HVAC module screws and separate HVAC module.
11. Remove evaporator core.
12. Reverse procedure to install. **Torque** HVAC module mounting nuts to 84 inch lbs., and bolts to 35 inch lbs.

2500HD & 3500HD

1. Drain cooling system into suitable container.

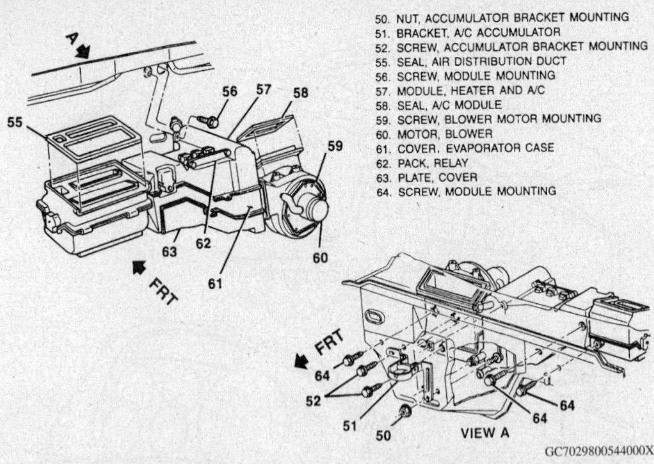

Fig. 7 Evaporator/Heater case. 2500HD & 3500HD

2. Recover refrigerant as outlined in "Air Conditioning."
3. Remove instrument panel as outlined in "Dash Panel Service."
4. Disconnect electrical connectors, as required.
5. Remove center floor air distribution duct.
6. **On models equipped with diesel engine,** remove PCM and mounting tray.
7. **On all models,** remove left and right-hand hinge pillar trim panels.
8. Remove blower motor as outlined under "Blower Motor, Replace."
9. Remove coolant recovery reservoir.
10. Disconnect heater hoses from heater core.
11. Disconnect evaporator tubes from evaporator core.
12. Remove bracket and accumulator, **Fig. 7.**
13. Remove mounting bolts and evaporator case.
14. Remove evaporator cover mounting screws.
15. Remove evaporator by pulling down and outward.
16. Reverse procedure to install.

4.3L Gasoline Engine

NOTE: On Air Bag Equipped Models, Refer To "Air Bag System Precautions" Located In The Front Of This Manual For System Disarming & Arming Procedures.

NOTE: Refer To "Computer Relearn Procedures" Located In The Front Of This Manual When Battery Power To The Computer Has Been Interrupted.

NOTE: Prior To Performing Any Service Operations Listed In This Section, Consult The "Technical Service Bulletins" Section For Related Information.

INDEX

PRECAUTIONS

Air Bag Systems

Refer to "Air Bag System Precautions" in the front of this manual for system disarming and arming procedures.

Battery Ground Cable

Prior to service disconnect battery ground cable and isolate, as required.

Radio Security System

If the Theftlock system is active when battery power is interrupted, the customers security code must be entered to restore proper function of the radio. Use the following procedure to unlock a secured radio after a power loss. Do not wait more than 15 seconds between steps.

1. Theftlock is engaged if radio is inoperable and "LOC" appears with ignition in On position.
2. Obtain customers' code number.
3. Press "MIN" button and "000" will appear on display.
4. Press "MIN" again until last two digits displayed agree with security code.
5. Press "HR" button until first 1 or 2 digits agree with security code.
6. Press "AM-FM" to select code entered. "SEC" will display indicating radio is now operable and secure.
7. If incorrect code is entered, "SEC" will display and radio will be inoperable.
8. Radio will remain inoperable until correct code is displayed. Repeat steps until correct code is entered. If correct code cannot be obtained, contact Delco technical assistance.

Fuel System Pressure Relief

1. Disconnect battery ground cable.
2. Loosen fuel filler cap to relieve fuel tank pressure.
3. Connect pressure gauge tool No. J-34730-1A, or equivalent, to fuel pressure connection. Wrap suitable shop towel around fitting while connecting gauge.
4. Install bleed hose of gauge into suitable container.
5. Open gauge valve to bleed fuel system pressure.
6. Small amount of fuel may remain in system, to prevent fuel spillage wrap suitable shop towel around any fuel line fittings before disconnecting.

COMPRESSION PRESSURE

When inspecting compression, the lowest cylinder must be within 70% of the highest and no cylinder should be less than 100 psi. Perform compression test with engine at operating temperature, all spark plugs removed and throttle wide open.

ENGINE MOUNT

REPLACE

1. Remove three engine mount to engine mount frame bracket mounting bolts.
2. Raise and support vehicle.
3. Remove oil pan skid plate.
4. If removing righthand side mount, remove starter as outlined in "Electrical" section.
5. If replacing lefthand mount, remove oil filter.
6. Raise and support engine using suitable jack on square tab at rear of engine block. **Do not use jack under oil pan, any sheet metal or crankshaft pulley.** Raise engine only enough to remove frame side mount.
7. Remove engine mount bracket and engine bolts, then the mount.
8. Remove two engine mount frame bracket through-bolts and bracket, as required.
9. Reverse procedure to install.

ENGINE

REPLACE

1. Drain engine coolant into suitable container.
2. Recover A/C refrigerant.
3. Raise and support vehicle.
4. Remove oil pan skid plate and engine shield.
5. Remove starter as outlined in "Electrical" section.
6. Remove transmission cover.
7. Remove starter cables and transmission cooler lines bracket mounting bolt.
8. Loosen catalytic converter pipe mounting nuts and remove exhaust pipes from manifolds
9. Remove battery cables mounting bolts from oil pan.
10. Disconnect Crankshaft Position sensor electrical connector and remove harness from retainer.
11. Disconnect low oil level sensor electrical connector then remove wire harness from retainer.
12. Remove engine battery ground and ground cables mounting bolt.
13. **On models equipped with automatic transmission,** remove torque converter to flywheel bolts through starter opening.
14. **On all models,** remove engine to transmission bolts.
15. Lower vehicle.
16. Move hood hinge bolts service position.
17. Separate MAF/IAT sensor and air inlet tube by loosening hose clamp.
18. Disconnect PCV hose from air cleaner outlet duct.
19. Remove mounting wing nut, then the air inlet tube and resonator from throttle body by pivoting tube and resonator upward until hinge clip releases from throttle body lip.
20. Position inlet hose clamp at radiator, then remove inlet hose rosebud clips from fan shroud and air cleaner outlet duct.
21. Remove inlet hose from radiator and position aside.
22. Remove retainers, mounting bolts and upper fan shroud.
23. Remove fan blade using fan clutch remover and installer tool No. J-41240, or equivalent.
24. Remove lower fan shroud by lifting up to disengage retaining clips.
25. Remove drive belt by installing suitable 3/8 inch drive wrench on tensioner arm and rotate arm counterclockwise. Slowly release tension on arm.
26. Remove radiator inlet and outlet hoses.
27. Remove accelerator and cruise control cables from throttle shaft and cable bracket.
28. Remove engine wiring harness clip from accelerator control cable bracket.
29. Remove accelerator control cable bracket with accelerator control and cruise control cables from throttle body.
30. Move and secure accelerator control and cruise control cables out of way.
31. Disconnect A/C hoses from compressor and accumulator.
32. Remove crossover pipe from secondary air injection pipe.
33. Remove AIR pipe from lefthand exhaust manifold and AIR pump.
34. Remove AIR pipe from righthand exhaust manifold.
35. Disconnect A/C pressure switch, A/C compressor clutch and Exhaust Gas Recirculation valve electrical connectors, then the alternator battery positive cable.
36. Disconnect fuel meter body, Idle Air Control motor, Throttle Position sensor and Engine Coolant Temperature sensor electrical connectors.
37. Disconnect EVAP canister purge solenoid valve, Manifold Absolute Pressure sensor, Ignition Control Module and ignition coil electrical connectors.
38. Disconnect engine oil pressure gauge sensor, distributor and Knock Sensor electrical connectors.
39. Remove engine wiring harness bracket to intake manifold studs' mounting nuts.
40. Remove engine wiring harness clip to battery positive cable junction block bracket mounting bolt.
41. Remove battery positive cable junction block from power steering pump mounting bracket.
42. Move battery positive and negative cables aside.
43. Remove ground wire to stud mounting nut at rear of righthand cylinder head.
44. Remove engine wiring harness bracket mounting stud at rear of righthand cylinder head.
45. Remove engine wiring harness bracket to EVAP canister purge solenoid valve stud mounting nut.
46. Remove ground strap and ground wire mounting bolt at rear of lefthand cylinder head.
47. Move engine wiring harness aside.

48. Remove engine and cowl heater hoses.
49. Remove distributor cap.
50. Disconnect fuel pipes at rear of engine.
51. Disconnect EVAP purge canister solenoid valve hose.
52. Disconnect power brake booster vacuum hose from engine and vacuum brake booster.
53. Loosen power steering pump rear bracket mounting nut.
54. Remove power steering pump rear bracket mounting nut.
55. Remove power steering pump mounting bracket mounting bolts and nut.
56. Slide power steering pump mount bracket off of stud and set aside with power steering pump and A/C compressor attached.
57. Remove thermostat water outlet.
58. Remove EGR valve inlet pipe from intake and exhaust manifold.
59. Remove righthand rear lower intake manifold bolts and instal engine lift bracket tool No. J-41427, or equivalent, marked RIGHT REAR.
60. Remove lefthand front lower intake manifold bolts. Install engine lift bracket tool No. J-41427, or equivalent, marked LEFT FRONT with arrow pointing to front of engine.
61. Attach suitable lifting device to engine lift brackets.
62. Remove engine motor mount to frame bracket bolts.
63. Support transmission with suitable jack.
64. Remove engine.
65. Reverse procedure to install. Install new accelerator control cable.

INTAKE MANIFOLD

REPLACE

It is not required to remove the upper intake manifold in order to remove the lower intake manifold.

Upper

1. Separate MAF/IAT sensor and air inlet tube by loosening hose clamp.
2. Disconnect PCV hose from air cleaner outlet duct.
3. Remove air inlet tube and resonator mounting wing nut.
4. Remove air inlet tube and resonator from throttle body by pivoting them upward until hinge clip releases from throttle body lip.
5. Remove accelerator cable from cable routing bracket, then from throttle body lever.
6. Disconnect cruise control cable from throttle shaft and accelerator cable bracket at side of throttle body.
7. Remove engine wiring harness clip from accelerator control cable bracket.
8. Remove accelerator control cable bracket with accelerator and cruise control cables from throttle body.
9. Move and secure accelerator and cruise control cables out of way.
10. Disconnect secondary air injection crossover pipe from AIR pipe, then remove AIR crossover pipe.
11. Disconnect A/C compressor clutch, A/C pressure switch and EGR valve electrical connections:
12. Disconnect Throttle Position sensor, Idle Air Control motor and fuel meter body electrical connections.
13. Disconnect Manifold Absolute Pressure sensor and EVAP canister purge solenoid valve electrical connections.
14. Remove two engine wiring harness bracket to upper intake manifold studs' mounting nuts .
15. Remove engine wiring harness bracket from studs.
16. Remove engine wiring harness bracket to EVAP canister purge solenoid valve stud mounting nut.
17. Remove mounting nut and ground wire from engine wiring harness bracket stud at rear of righthand cylinder head.
18. Remove engine wiring harness bracket stud.
19. Move engine wiring harness and brackets aside.
20. Disconnect the Evaporative Emission purge pipe and solenoid electrical connector.
21. Remove mounting nuts, engine wiring harness bracket and purge solenoid.
22. Remove PCV valve hose form intake manifold and valve rocker arm cover.
23. Disconnect power brake booster vacuum hose from intake manifold.
24. Remove accelerator control cable bracket from intake manifold and throttle body.
25. Disconnect chassis fuel pipes at engine compartment pipes.
26. Loosen fuel pipes at bellhousing stud clip.
27. Remove mounting nuts, then the injector fuel inlet and outlet pipe retainer nuts.
28. Remove rear fuel pipe bracket mounting bolt.
29. Remove fuel pipes by pulling straight up on pipes.
30. Remove O-rings from both ends of fuel feed and return pipes. Discard O-rings.
31. Remove studs, upper intake manifold and gasket. Discard gasket.
32. Reverse procedure to install, nothing the following:
    a. Lubricate new PCV valve cover, power brake booster vacuum tube fitting and fuel meter body O-rings with clean engine oil.
    b. Install new upper intake manifold to lower intake manifold gasket.

Lower

1. Drain cooling system into suitable container.
2. Separate MAF/IAT sensor assembly and air inlet tube by loosening hose clamp.
3. Disconnect PCV hose from air cleaner outlet duct.
4. Remove air inlet tube and resonator mounting wing nut.
5. Remove air inlet tube and resonator from throttle body by pivoting air inlet tube and resonator upward until hinge clip releases from throttle body lip.
6. Remove accelerator cable from cable routing bracket and throttle body lever.
7. Disconnect cruise control cable from throttle shaft and accelerator cable bracket at side of throttle body.
8. Remove engine wiring harness and clip from accelerator control cable bracket.
9. Remove accelerator control cable bracket with accelerator and cruise control cables from throttle body.
10. Move and secure accelerator control cable bracket with cables out of way.
11. Disconnect Secondary Air Injection crossover pipe from AIR pipe assemblies, then remove AIR crossover pipe.
12. Disconnect EVAP canister purge solenoid valve, Manifold Absolute Pressure sensor, Ignition Control Module and ignition coil electrical connectors.
13. Disconnect A/C pressure switch(es), A/C compressor clutch, Exhaust Gas Recirculation valve and alternator battery positive cable electrical connectors.
14. Disconnect fuel meter body, Throttle Position sensor, Idle Air Control motor and Engine Coolant Temperature sensor electrical connectors.
15. Remove nut holding engine wiring harness bracket to EVAP purge solenoid valve stud.
16. Remove nut holding ground wire to engine wiring harness bracket stud at rear of righthand cylinder head.
17. Remove stud holding engine wiring harness bracket.
18. Remove two nuts holding engine wiring harness bracket to upper intake manifold studs.
19. Remove engine wiring harness bracket from studs.
20. Move engine wiring harness with brackets aside.
21. Remove radiator inlet hose from thermostat housing.
22. Remove water pump inlet hose from intake manifold.
23. Remove engine heater hoses.
24. Remove distributor as outlined under "Electrical" section.
25. Disconnect chassis fuel pipes at engine compartment pipes.
26. Loosen fuel pipes at bellhousing stud clip.
27. Remove mounting nuts, then the injector fuel inlet and outlet pipe retainer nuts.
28. Remove rear fuel pipe bracket mounting bolt.
29. Remove fuel pipes by pulling straight up on pipes.
30. Remove O-rings from both ends of fuel feed and return pipes. Discard O-rings.
31. Disconnect PCV valve hose assembly from intake manifold and valve rocker arm cover.
32. Disconnect power brake booster vacuum hose from intake manifold.
33. Disconnect hose to EVAP canister purge solenoid valve.
34. Remove spark plug wire harness retainer from EGR valve inlet pipe.
35. Remove clamp bolt, then the for EGR

valve inlet pipe from intake and exhaust manifolds.

36. Remove drive belt as outlined under "Serpentine Drive Belt."
37. Loosen power steering pump rear bracket side nut.
38. Remove power steering pump rear bracket front nut.
39. Remove power steering pump mounting bracket bolts and nut.
40. Leave A/C compressor and power steering pump on bracket.
41. Slide power steering pump mounting bracket forward to access bolt at front of intake manifold.
42. Remove ECT sensor wire connector from engine wiring harness bracket.
43. Remove mounting bolts and lower intake manifold.
44. Remove and discard lower intake manifold gaskets.
45. Reverse procedure to install, noting the following:
    a. Apply .157 inch patch of adhesive No. 12346141, or equivalent, to cylinder head side of lower intake manifold gasket at each end.
    b. Lower intake manifold gasket must be installed while adhesive is still wet.
    c. Use gasket locator pins to properly seat lower intake manifold gasket on cylinder head.
    d. Apply .197 inch bead of adhesive to front and rear top of engine block. Extend adhesive bead .50 inch onto each lower intake manifold gasket.
    e. **Torque** lower intake manifold mounting bolts to 27 inch lbs., in sequence, **Fig. 1.**
    f. **Torque** mounting bolts to 106 inch lbs., in sequence.
    g. Final **torque** bolts to 11 ft. lbs., in sequence.

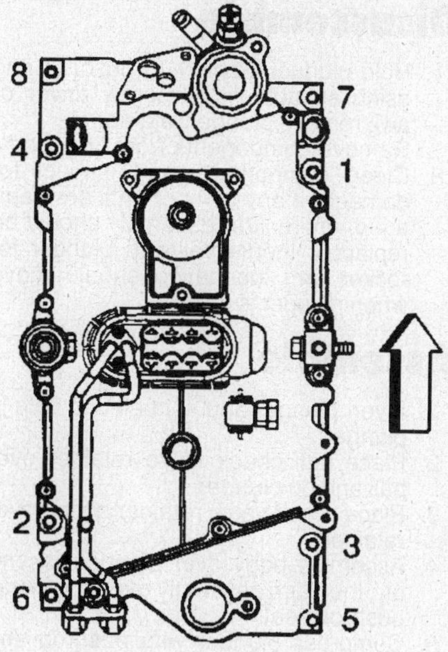

Fig. 1 Intake manifold tightening sequence

Righthand

1. Raise and support vehicle.
2. Remove righthand exhaust manifold pipe nuts.
3. Lower vehicle.
4. Separate MAF/IAT sensor assembly and inlet tube by loosening hose clamp.
5. Disconnect PCV hose from air cleaner outlet duct.
6. Remove air inlet tube and resonator mounting wing nut.
7. Remove air inlet tube and resonator from throttle body by pivoting air inlet tube and resonator upward until hinge clip releases from throttle body lip
8. Remove Secondary Air Injection pipe assembly.
9. Disconnect spark plug wires from spark plugs.
10. Remove spark plug wires from retainers.
11. Remove mounting bolts and exhaust manifold.
12. Remove and discard exhaust manifold gaskets.
13. Remove mounting bolts and spark plug wire shield.
14. Reverse procedure to install. Apply threadlock No. 12345493, or equivalent, to exhaust manifold mounting bolts threads.

EXHAUST MANIFOLD

REPLACE

Lefthand

1. Raise and support vehicle.
2. Remove exhaust manifold pipe nuts.
3. Lower vehicle.
4. Remove Secondary Air Injection pipe assembly.
5. Disconnect spark plug wires from spark plugs.
6. Remove spark plug wires from wire retainers.
7. Disconnect EGR valve inlet pipe from exhaust manifold.
8. Disconnect ECT sensor electrical connector.
9. Remove mounting bolts, stud and exhaust manifold.
10. Remove and discard exhaust manifold gaskets.
11. Remove bolts and spark plug wire shield.
12. Reverse procedure to install. Apply threadlock No. 12345493, or equivalent, to mounting bolts and studs.

CYLINDER HEAD

REPLACE

Removal

1. Remove intake and exhaust manifolds as outlined under "Intake Manifold, Replace." and "Exhaust Manifold, Replace."
2. Remove power steering pump pulley.
3. Recover refrigerant as outlined in "Air Conditioning" chapter and remove compressor.
4. Disconnect power steering pump electrical connector, then remove pump mounting nuts and bolts from bracket front.
5. Remove bracket front nut and slide power steering pump and bracket off stud. Remove stud.
6. Remove alternator as outlined under "Electrical."
7. Remove bolts and nut from alternator bracket front and slide bracket off stud. Remove stud.
8. Remove wiring harness, clip and coolant sensor wire.
9. Remove valve cover.
10. Disconnect wires, then remove spark plugs.
11. Remove rocker arms and pushrods.
12. Remove mounting bolts, then the cylinder head.

Installation

1. Inspect gasket surfaces on heads and block for nicks or heavy scratches. Block bolt and cylinder head mounting bolt threads must be clean, as dirt will affect bolt holding power.
2. **On engines equipped with steel gasket,** coat both sides of gasket with suitable sealer.
3. **On engines equipped with composition steel/asbestos type gasket,** do not use sealer.
4. **On all models,** place new gasket in position over dowel pins with bead up.
5. Install cylinder head over locating pins and gasket.
6. Coat cylinder head bolt threads with suitable sealer and install bolts hand tight.
7. **Torque** mounting bolts to 22 ft. lbs., in sequence, **Fig. 2.**
8. Tighten short bolts Nos.. 2, 3, 6, 7, 10 and 11 an additional 55° using suitable torque angle meter.
9. Tighten medium bolt Nos. 12 and 13 an additional 65°.
10. Tighten long bolts Nos. 1, 4, 5, 8 and 9 an additional 75°.
11. Install push rods and rocket arms, then the valve covers.
12. Install bracket and alternator, then the bracket and power steering pump.
13. Install air conditioning compressor.
14. Install exhaust and intake manifolds as outlined under "Exhaust Manifold, Replace." and "Intake Manifold, Replace."

VALVE COVER

REPLACE

Lefthand

1. Remove engine cover.
2. Remove PCV valve from cover and set it aside.
3. Disconnect and remove Engine Coolant Temperature (ECT) gauge sensor connector from bracket.

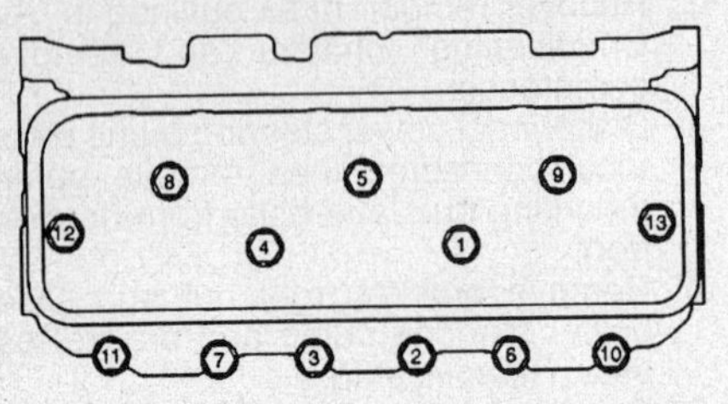

Fig. 2 Cylinder head tightening sequence

4. Disconnect spark plug wires from distributor cap.
5. Remove rear spark plug wire harness retainer from EGR valve inlet pipe bracket.
6. **On models equipped with air conditioning,** remove auxiliary evaporator tube from air conditioning compressor.
7. **On all models,** remove mounting bolts, grommets, valve cover and gasket. Discard grommets and gasket.
8. Reverse procedure to install.

Righthand

1. Remove engine cover.
2. Disconnect spark plug wires from distributor cap.
3. Remove PCV tube from valve cover and air inlet duct.
4. Position engine wiring harness aside.
5. Remove oil fill tube to alternator and drive belt tensioner bracket mounting screw.
6. Remove oil fill tube.
7. Remove valve cover and gasket.
8. Reverse procedure to install.

VALVE ARRANGEMENT

Front To Rear

Lefthand Side .... **E-I-E-I-I-E**
Righthand Side .... **E-I-I-E-I-E**

VALVE LIFTERS

Hydraulic valve lifters do not normally require periodic adjustment, **Fig. 3.** However, if the cylinder head or valve train requires service and/or lifter noise is excessive, adjust valves as outlined. Servicing the lifters requires that care and cleanliness be exercised in the handling of components.

Removal

1. Remove lower intake manifold as outlined under "Intake Manifold, Replace."
2. Remove rocker arms as outlined under "Rocker Arms, Replace" then the pushrods.
3. Remove mounting bolts and valve lifter pushrod guide.
4. Remove valve lifters. If lifter is stuck use valve lifter tool No. J-3049-A, or equivalent.

Disassemble

1. Hold plunger down with pushrod and using suitable small screw driver or awl, remove plunger retainer.
2. Remove components from lifter body.
3. Clean components and inspect for damage. If any components are damaged, entire lifter assembly should be replaced. Inertia valve in plunger for rocker arm lubrication should move when plunger is shaken.

Assemble

1. Invert plunger and set ball into hole in plunger.
2. Place ball check valve retainer over ball and on plunger.
3. Place check valve retainer spring over retainer.
4. Assemble body over plunger assembly, then turn assembly over and install pushrod seat.
5. Compress plunger with pushrod and install retainer.
6. Compress plunger to open oil holes and fill plunger with engine oil. Work plunger up and down and refill.

Installation

1. Apply suitable lubricant No. 12345501, or equivalent, to valve lifter rollers.
2. Install valve lifters.
3. Install mounting bolts and valve lifter pushrod guide.
4. Tighten pushrod guide bolts.
5. Install pushrods and rocker arms as outlined under "Rocker Arms, Replace."
6. Install lower intake manifold as outlined under "Intake Manifold, Replace."

VALVE CLEARANCE SPECIFICATIONS

Correct valve lash is .0010–.0037 inch.

VALVE ADJUSTMENT

Initial Adjustment

1. With engine in position to fire No. 1 cylinder, adjust the following valves:
   a. Exhaust Nos. 1, 5 and 6; intake Nos. 1, 2 and 3.
   b. Back off adjusting nut until lash is felt, (when pushrod can be rotated by hand), then tighten nut until lash is eliminated.
   c. After zero lash is obtained, tighten nut an additional one full turn.
2. Turn crankshaft one complete revolution, which will bring engine in position to fire cylinder No. 4.
3. With engine in this position, adjust the following valves:
   a. Exhaust Nos. 2, 3 and 4; intake Nos. 4, 5 and 6.
   b. After zero lash is obtained, tighten nut an additional one full turn.

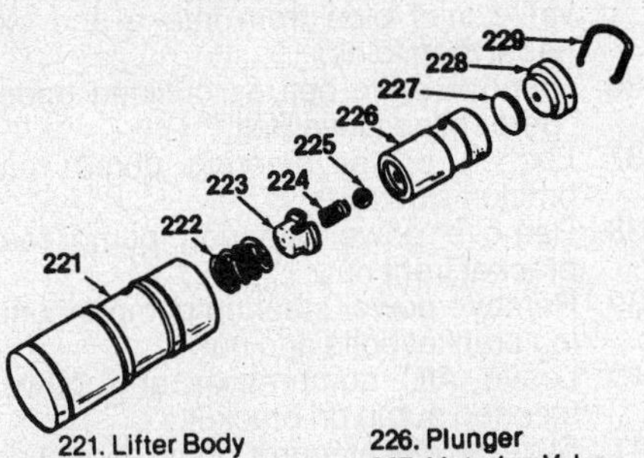

Fig. 3 Hydraulic valve lifter

Final Adjustment

1. Warm engine operating temperature and remove valve cover.
2. With engine running at idle speed, back off valve rocker arm nut until rocker arm starts to clatter.
3. Turn rocker arm nut down slowly until clatter just stops. This is zero lash position.
4. Turn nut down an additional ¼ turn, then pause 10 seconds until engine runs smoothly.
5. Repeat ¼ turns, pausing 10 seconds each time, until nut has been turned an additional one full turn from zero lash.
6. This preload adjustment must be done slowly to allow lifter to adjust itself to prevent possibility of interference between intake valve head and top of piston, which might result in internal damage and/or bent pushrods. Noisy lifters should be replaced.
7. Install valve cover, with new gasket.

PUSH RODS

When a replacement pushrod has a paint stripe at one end, this painted end must be installed in contact with the rocker arm. To provide durability a hardened insert is incorporated in the rocker arm end of these pushrods.

VALVE GUIDES

Valve guides in these engines are an integral part of the head and, therefore, cannot be removed. For service, guide holes can be reamed oversize to accommodate one of several service valves with oversize stems.

Inspect the valve stem clearance of each valve (after cleaning) in its respective valve guide. If the clearance exceeds the service limits of .004 inch on the intake or .005 inch on the exhaust, ream the valve guide to accommodate the next oversize diameter valve stem.

Select the reamer for the smallest oversize which will provide a clean straight bore through the valve guide. After reaming, a new seat should be cut into the head to ensure perfect seating of the new valve.

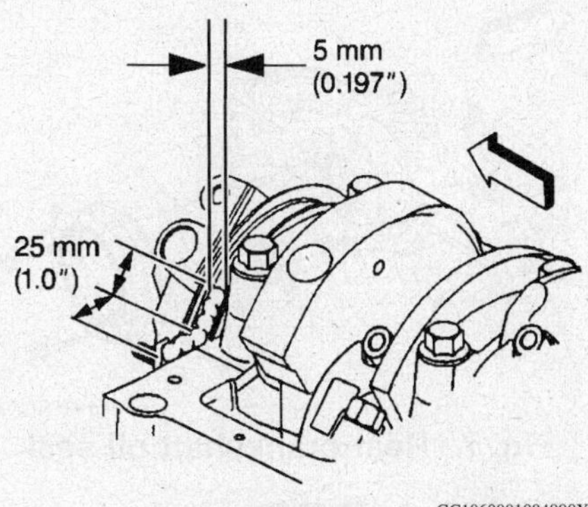

Fig. 4 Front cover adhesive installation

VALVE SEATS

1. Inspect valve margin. Exhaust valve may be refaced if margin is more than .05 inch thick before grinding.
2. Reface pitted exhaust valves on suitable valve refacing machine.
3. Replace valve if margin is less than .05 inch thick after grinding.
4. If valve face has been ground, it may be required to shim valve spring to obtain proper spring installed height.
5. Inspect for loose valve seat in cylinder head. Valve seat has an interference fit to cylinder head.
6. Clean valve guide bores using suitable tool.
7. A valve guide bore that is oversized must be repaired or replaced prior to valve seat grinding.
8. Inspect valve seats. Valve seats should be concentric to .0021 inch total indicator reading.
9. If valve seat has to be ground, it may be required to shim valve spring to attain proper spring installed height.

HYDRAULIC LIFTERS

REPLACE

Removal

1. Remove cylinder head and gasket as outlined under "Cylinder Head, Replace."
2. Remove valve lifter guide bolts and guides, as required.
3. Remove valve lifters using lifter pliers tool No. J-3049-A, or equivalent.
4. Remove valve lifters from guide.
5. Organize or mark components for installation reference.

Installation

1. Lubricate valve lifters and lifter bores with clean engine oil.
2. Insert valve lifters into lifter guides, aligning flat area on top of lifter with flat area in lifter guide bore, then push lifter completely into guide bore.
3. Install valve lifters and guide into engine block.
4. Install valve lifter guide bolt.

CRANKSHAFT DAMPER

REPLACE

1. Remove drive belt as outlined under "Serpentine Drive Belt."
2. Remove air cleaner and air intake duct.
3. Remove coolant reservoir.
4. Remove engine and transmission oil dipstick at alternator bracket mounting bolt.
5. Remove engine oil fill tube at alternator bracket mounting bolt.
6. Move oil dipstick tubes and oil fill tube away from fan shroud.
7. Remove upper fan shroud mounting bolts from top of radiator.
8. Remove upper to lower fan shroud mounting bolts.
9. Push radiator intake hose aside for clearance.
10. Remove upper fan shroud.
11. Remove fan and clutch.
12. Remove crankshaft damper using crankshaft balancer remover tool No. J-23523-F, or equivalent.
13. Reverse procedure to install.

FRONT COVER

REPLACE

The engine front cover gasket is reusable.

1. Remove crankshaft damper as outlined under "Crankshaft Damper, Replace."
2. Remove water pump as outlined under "Water Pump, Replace."
3. Remove oil pan as outlined under "Oil Pan, Replace."
4. Remove the Crankshaft Position (CKP) sensor from front cover.
5. Remove mounting bolts, front cover and gasket.
6. Reverse procedure to install, noting the following:
   a. Apply .197 inch bead of adhesive part No. 12346141, or equivalent, in inch long to engine front cover to engine block junction at oil pan, **Fig. 4.**

TIMING CHAIN

REPLACE

Removal

1. Remove front cover as outlined under "Front Cover, Replace."
2. Remove Crankshaft Position (CKP) sensor reluctor ring.
3. Install 7/16-20 x 1 inch bolt into crankshaft end. **Install bolt with same threads as crankshaft, but do not use crankshaft balancer bolt or bolt longer than 1 inch.**
4. Align timing marks before removing timing chain, **Fig. 5.**
5. Rotate crankshaft until timing marks on both sprockets line up and cylinder No. 4 is at top dead center (TDC) of compression stroke.
6. Remove bolts, camshaft sprocket and camshaft timing chain.

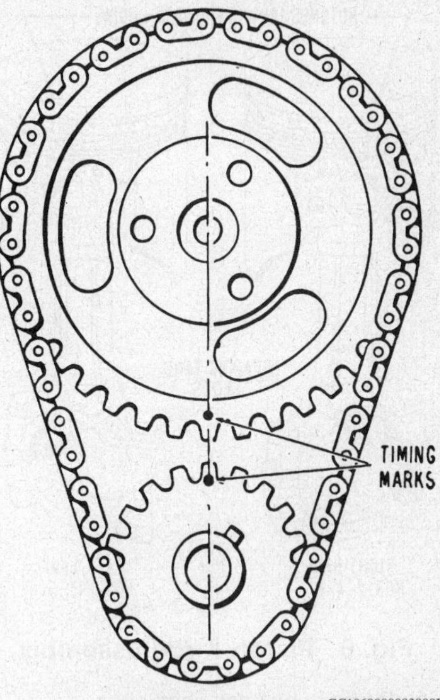

Fig. 5 Timing mark alignment

7. Remove crankshaft sprocket using crankshaft gear remover tool No. J-5825-A, or equivalent.
8. Remove crankshaft balancer key.

Installation

1. Install crankshaft balancer key into crankshaft keyway. Key should be parallel to crankshaft or with slight incline.
2. Install crankshaft sprocket using crankshaft sprocket installer tool No. J-5590, or equivalent.
3. Rotate crankshaft until crankshaft sprocket alignment mark is at 12 o'clock position.
4. Install camshaft sprocket and camshaft timing chain. **Install camshaft sprocket with alignment mark at 6 o'clock position.**
5. Ensure camshaft and crankshaft timing marks are aligned, **Fig. 5. Do not use hammer to install camshaft sprocket.**
6. Tighten camshaft sprocket mounting bolts.
7. Install CKP sensor reluctor ring by aligning ring keyway with crankshaft balancer key.
8. Remove bolt from crankshaft end.
9. Install front cover as outlined under "Front Cover, Replace."

CAMSHAFT

REPLACE

Depending on vehicle and engine application, the grille, engine cover, radiator and condenser may have to be removed.

1. Remove intake manifold as outlined under "Intake Manifold, Replace."
2. Remove pushrods and valve lifters as outlined under "Valve Lifters."
3. Remove timing chain as outlined under "Timing Chain, Replace."

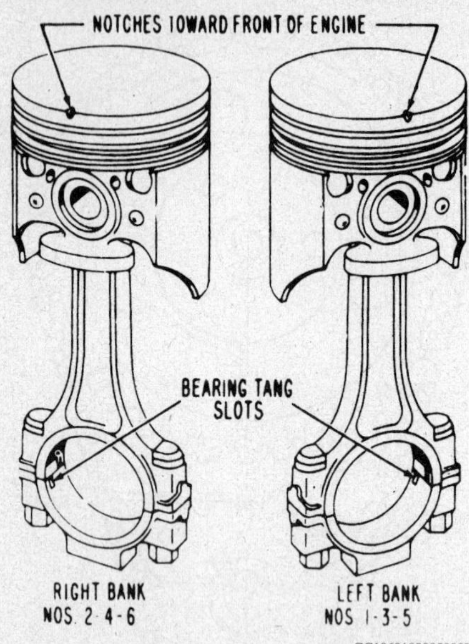

Fig. 6 Piston & rod assembly

4. Remove balance shaft gear.
5. Install two or three 5⁄16-18 x 4–5 inch bolts into holes, then pull camshaft out of cylinder block.
6. Reverse procedure to install.

BALANCE SHAFT

REPLACE

Depending on vehicle and engine application, the grille, engine cover, radiator and condenser may have to be removed.

Removal

1. Remove valve lifter pushrod guide.
2. Hold camshaft sprocket with suitable wrench and loosen and remove balance shaft driven gear mounting bolt and washer.
3. Remove timing chain as outlined under "Timing Chain, Replace."
4. Place suitable wrench onto balance shaft near front bearing and remove driven gear mounting bolt.
5. Remove balance shaft driven gear.
6. Remove mounting bolts and balance shaft retainer.
7. Remove mounting bolts and balance shaft retainer.
8. Remove balance shaft using suitable soft-faced hammer. **Do not remove bearing.**

Installation

1. Apply clean engine oil part No. 12345610, or equivalent, to balance shaft front bearing.
2. Install balance shaft using balance shaft installer tool No. J-36996 and universal driver handle tool No. J-8092, or equivalent.
3. Install balance shaft retainer and tighten mounting bolts.
4. Install balance shaft driven gear.
5. Apply threadlock part No. 12345382, or equivalent, to balance shaft driven gear bolt threads.
6. Install balance shaft driven gear mounting bolt using suitable wrench to secure shaft. Place wrench onto shaft near front bearing.
7. Tighten balance shaft driven gear mounting. Remove wrench.
8. Rotate balance shaft by hand to ensure there is clearance between shaft and valve lifter pushrod guide. If shaft does not rotate freely, ensure front bearing retaining ring is seated on case.
9. Install balance shaft drive gear. **Do not install camshaft sprocket bolts at this time.**
10. Rotate engine camshaft so balance shaft drive gear timing mark is at 12 o'clock position.
11. Remove balance shaft drive gear.
12. Rotate balance shaft so balance shaft driven gear timing mark is at 6 o'clock position.
13. Position balance shaft drive gear onto camshaft.
14. Ensure balance shaft drive gear and balance shaft driven gear timing marks are aligned.
15. Install camshaft timing chain and the camshaft sprocket as outlined under "Camshaft, Replace."
16. Install crankshaft position reluctor ring and front cover.
17. Install valve lifter pushrod guide.

PISTON & ROD ASSEMBLY

When assembling the piston and connecting rod, the mark on the top of the piston must point to the front of the engine block. The lefthand bank connecting rods should have the flange face toward the front of the engine block. The righthand bank connecting rods should have the flange face toward the rear of the engine block. The piston pin has an interference fit into the connecting rod and is full floating in the piston. The space compression ring end gaps should be 120° apart and the oil ring end gaps should be a minimum of 90° apart. Assemble the pistons to the connecting rods, **Fig. 6.**

PISTONS, PINS & RINGS

A .001 inch oversize piston is available for service use so proper clearances can be obtained for slightly worn cylinder bores requiring only light honing. In addition, oversizes of .020 inch, .030 inch and .040 inch are available. If the cylinders have less than .005 inch taper or wear, they can be reconditioned with a hone and fitted with the .001 inch oversize piston.

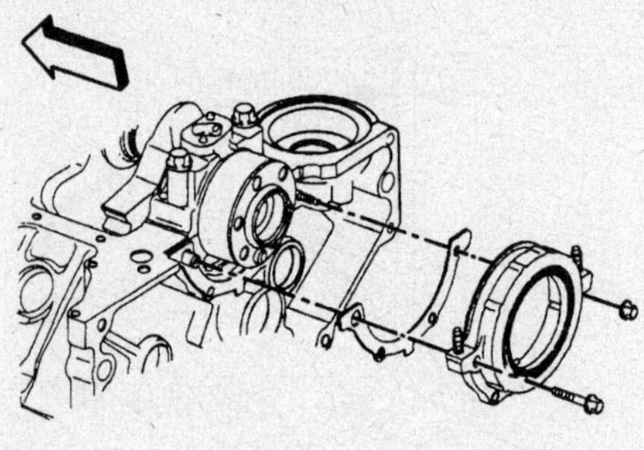

Fig. 7 Rear crankshaft oil seal

MAIN & ROD BEARINGS

Main Bearings

Shell type bearings are used and if worn excessively, should be replaced. No attempt should be made to shim, file or otherwise take up worn bearings.

Main bearings are available in standard and undersizes of .001, .002, .009, .010 and .020 inch.

INSTALLATION

1. Install crankshaft bearings.
2. Apply clean engine oil to bearings and journals.
3. Install crankshaft.
4. Install crankshaft bearings into caps.
5. Apply clean engine oil to bearings.
6. Install crankshaft bearing caps in original positions and with arrow in direction of front of engine block.
7. Install crankshaft bearing cap bolts and studs.
8. Thrust crankshaft rearward to set and align crankshaft thrust bearings and caps.
9. Thrust crankshaft forward to align rear faces of crankshaft thrust bearings.
10. Ensure crankshaft bearing caps are fully seated in engine block crankshaft bearing cap channel and are centered on engine block bulkheads.
11. **Torque** crankshaft bearing cap bolts and studs to 15 ft. lbs.
12. **On models equipped with two bolt caps,** tighten crankshaft bearing cap bolts and studs an additional 73° using electronic torque angle meter tool No. J-36660-A, or equivalent.
13. **On models equipped with four bolt caps,** proceed as follows:
    a. Tighten bearing cap outboard bolts an additional 43° using electronic torque angle meter tool No. J-36660-A, or equivalent.
    b. Tighten bearing cap inboard bolts and studs an additional 73° using electronic torque angle meter tool.

Rod Bearings

Connecting rod bearing inserts are available in standard size and undersizes of .001 inch, .002 inch, .010 inch and .020

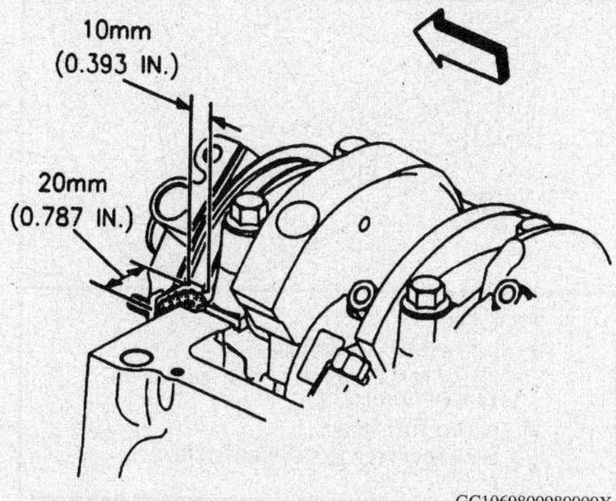

Fig. 8 Oil pan sealer installation

inch. The bearings can be replaced without removing the rod assembly by removing the cap and replacing the upper and lower halves of the bearing.

CRANKSHAFT REAR OIL SEAL

REPLACE

Removal

1. Raise and support vehicle.
2. Remove transmission as outlined under **MOTOR's "Domestic Transmission, In-Vehicle Service."**
3. Remove flywheel or flex plate, as required.
4. Remove rear oil seal using suitable tool inserted into access notches and carefully prying seal from housing, **Fig. 7.**

Installation

1. Apply 2–3 drops of clean engine oil to rear oil seal housing bore, outside diameter of flywheel pilot flange, crankshaft seal surface and crankshaft rear oil seal O.D.
2. Apply one drop of clean engine oil to flywheel locator pin O.D.
3. **Do not allow oil or any other lubricants to contact seal lip surface of rear oil seal.**
4. Remove rear oil seal sleeve.
5. Install rear oil seal near to flush and square to crankshaft rear oil seal housing using rear main seal installer tool No. J-35621-B, or equivalent.
6. Install flywheel and transmission.

OIL PAN

REPLACE

1. Raise and support vehicle.
2. Drain engine oil into a suitable container, then remove oil filter.
3. Remove oil cooler lines and adapter.
4. Remove oil pan skid plate.
5. Remove crossbar.
6. Remove battery cable brackets' mounting bolts and oil pan.
7. Remove starter motor as outlined under "Electrical" section.
8. Remove starter opening shield.

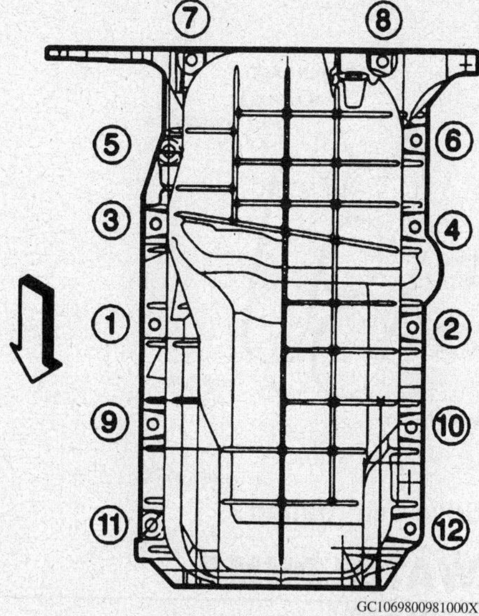

Fig. 9 Oil pan bolt tightening sequence

9. Remove starter positive cable and transmission oil cooler line bracket from oil pan.
10. Disconnect low oil level sensor electrical connector.
11. Remove oil pan rear nuts access plugs.
12. Remove engine oil level sensor. Discard sensor.
13. Remove mounting bolts and crankshaft rear oil seal mounting nuts.
14. Remove oil pan and gasket.
15. Reverse procedure to install, noting the following:
    a. Apply .197 inch wide bead of sealant part No. 12346141, or equivalent, to front cover block joint 1 inch in both directions from corners, **Fig. 8.**
    b. Apply .197 inch wide bead of sealant to rear crankshaft seal for 1 inch in both directions from four corners.
    c. Ensure clearance between three oil pan to transmission contacts points is less than .01 inch.
    d. Tighten oil pan bolts in sequence, **Fig. 9.**

OIL PUMP

REPLACE

1. Remove oil pan as outlined under "Oil Pan, Replace."
2. remove pump to rear main bearing cap nut, then the pump and extension shaft.
3. Reverse procedure to install.

OIL PUMP SERVICE

1. Remove oil pump as outlined under "Oil Pump, Replace."
2. Remove pump cover screws and pump cover, **Figs. 10.**
3. Mark gear teeth so they can be assembled with same teeth indexing.
4. Remove drive gear, idler gear and shaft.
5. Remove pressure regulator valve retaining pin, pressure regulator valve and related components.

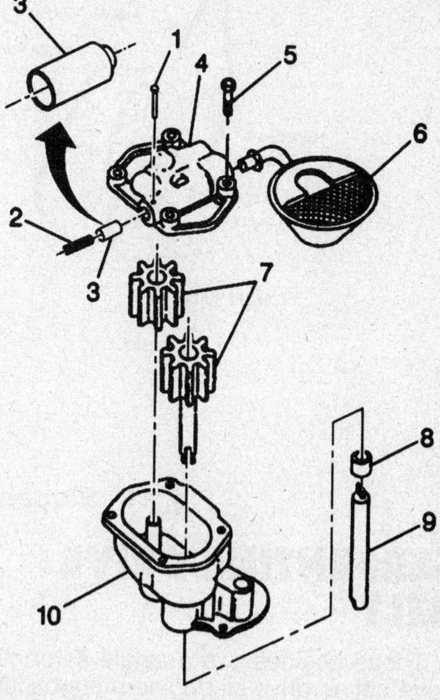

Fig. 10 Oil pump

6. If pickup screen and pipe require replacement, mount pump in suitable soft-jawed vise and extract pipe from pump.
7. Wash components in cleaning solvent and dry with compressed air.
8. Inspect pump body and cover for cracks and excessive wear.
9. Inspect pump gears for damage or excessive wear.
10. Inspect drive gear shaft for looseness in pump body.
11. Inspect inside of pump cover for wear that would allow oil to leak past ends of gears.
12. Inspect pickup screen and pipe for damage to screen, pipe or relief grommet.
13. Inspect pressure regulator valve for proper fit in pump housing.
14. Reverse procedure to assemble, nothing the following:
    a. Turn driveshaft by hand to inspect for smooth operation.
    b. **Pump gears and body are not serviced separately. If pump gears or body are damaged or worn, pump should be replaced.**
    c. **If pickup screen was removed, it should be replaced with new one as loss of press fit condition could result in air leak and loss of oil pressure.**

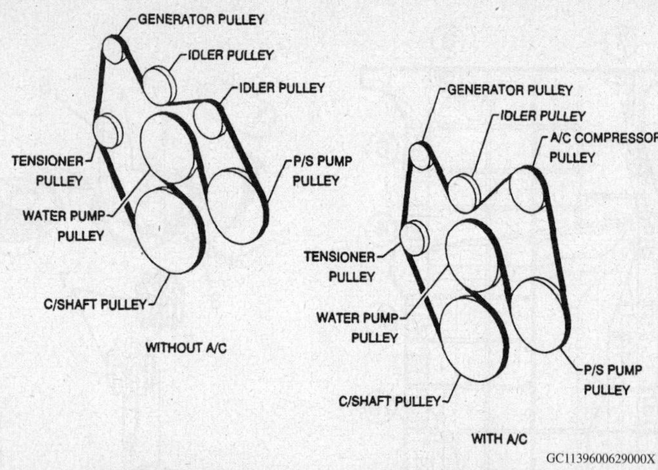

Fig. 11 Serpentine drive belt routing

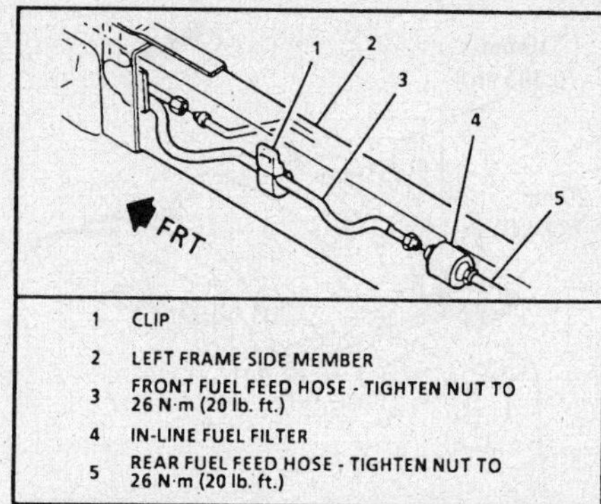

Fig. 12 Fuel filter replacement

SERPENTINE DRIVE BELT

These engines use a single serpentine drive belt to drive all engine-mount accessories. All belt drive accessories are rigidly mounted with belt tension maintained by a spring loaded automatic tensioner.

1. Rotate tensioner counterclockwise using suitable ½ inch breaker bar with socket placed on tensioner pulley axis bolt.
2. Remove belt from pulleys.
3. Route new belt as outlined, **Fig. 11.**
4. Rotate tensioner pulley axis bolt counterclockwise and slip belt over tensioner using suitable breaker bar and socket.
5. Release tensioner. Tensioner is spring loaded and will return to original position when released.

COOLING SYSTEM BLEED

These engines do not require a specified bleed procedure. After filling cooling system, run engine to operating temperature with radiator/pressure cap off. Air will then be automatically bled through cap opening.

THERMOSTAT

REPLACE

1. Remove engine cover, air cleaner and air inlet duct, as required.
2. Drain cooling system into suitable container until radiator coolant level is below thermostat.
3. Remove radiator hose at coolant outlet.
4. Remove thermostat housing mounting bolts and ground wire, if applicable.
5. Remove thermostat housing, thermostat and gasket.
6. Reverse procedure to install.

WATER PUMP

REPLACE

1. Drain cooling system into suitable container.
2. Remove air cleaner, duct and coolant recovery reservoir.
3. Remove upper fan shroud, fan and clutch.
4. Remove accessory drive belt(s).
5. Remove water pump pulley mounting bolts.
6. Disconnect lower radiator and upper bypass hoses from pump.
7. Remove four mounting bolts, water pump and two gaskets.
8. Reverse procedure to install.

RADIATOR

REPLACE

1. Drain cooling system into suitable container.
2. Disconnect MAF/IAT sensor harness connector.
3. Separate MAF/IAT sensor and air inlet tube by loosening hose clamp.
4. Remove inlet hose from support, radiator and thermostat housing. Remove radiator inlet hose.
5. Remove outlet hose from surge tank, water pump and radiator. Remove radiator outlet hose.
6. Remove retainers, mounting bolts and upper fan shroud.
7. Remove fan and clutch using fan clutch wrench tool No. J-41240, or equivalent.
8. Remove lower fan shroud by lifting up to disconnect from clips on radiator and remove.
9. Remove surge tank hose.
10. Remove engine oil cooler line's plastic cap from connector by pulling back along pipe.
11. Release open ends of retaining ring from connector fitting using suitable small pick type tool, or screwdriver.
12. Rotate retaining ring out of position on connector fitting, then remove ring completely. Discard retaining ring clip.
13. Remove pipe from connector fitting by pulling outward on pipe.
14. Disconnect oil cooler line retaining clip at fan shroud.
15. Remove oil cooler line from radiator.
16. Raise and support vehicle.
17. Remove underbody protective shields.
18. Remove junction block bolts, clip bolt and oil cooler lines. Discard gasket.
19. Pull transmission oil cooler lines' plastic cap back from quick connect fitting and remove them from clips.
20. Remove two cooling lines to transmission retaining rings.
21. Pull on open ends of retaining ring in order to rotate retaining ring around quick connect fitting until it is of fitting using suitable bent tip screwdriver. Discard retaining ring.
22. Pull cooling lines straight out from quick connect fittings.
23. Remove cooling lines from radiator and from auxiliary oil cooler.
24. Lower vehicle.
25. Remove radiator mounting bolts.
26. Tilt radiator towards engine and remove it by pulling from support.
27. Reverse procedure to install.

FUEL PUMP

REPLACE

1. Drain fuel tank into suitable container.
2. Remove fuel tank.
3. Remove fuel sender by turning cam lock counterclockwise using fuel tank sending unit wrench tool No. J-44402, or equivalent.
4. Remove fuel pump from sender.
5. Reverse procedure to install.

FUEL FILTER

REPLACE

1. Remove fuel filler cap, then disconnect fuel feed nuts, **Fig. 12.**
2. Remove clamp bolt, filter and clamp, then clamp from filter.
3. Reverse procedure to install.

TIGHTENING SPECIFICATIONS

Year	Component	Torque/Ft. Lbs.
2002–06	Accelerator Control Cable Bracket	80–106①
	Air Conditioning Compressor	37
	Air Conditioning Compressor Bracket	37
	Air Conditioning Hose Bracket	35
	Air Conditioning Tensioner	37
	AIR Bracket	71①
	AIR Pipe To Exhaust Manifold, Nuts	18
	AIR Pipe To Exhaust Manifold, Studs	45
	Alternator	37
	Alternator Mounting Bracket	30
	Alternator Rear Bracket	37
	Belt Tensioner	37
	Connecting Rod	⑦
	Coolant Temperature Gauge Sensor	15
	Crankshaft Bearing Cap	②
	Crankshaft Damper	③
	Crankshaft Oil Deflector	18
	Crankshaft Position Sensor	18
	Crossbar	74
	Cylinder Head	④
	Distributor Clamp	18
	EGR Valve Inlet Pipe	18
	Engine Lift Bracket Tool	41
	Engine Mount Through Bolt	55
	Engine Mount Through Bolt, Nut	46
	Engine Oil Cooler Line Fitting	18
	Engine Oil Level Sensor	115①
	Engine Shield	15
	Engine Wiring Harness Bracket, Lefthand Nut	106①
	Engine Wiring Harness Bracket, Righthand Nut	88①
	EVAP Purge Solenoid Mounting	106①
	Exhaust Crossover Pipe	25
	Exhaust Manifold	⑤
	Exhaust Manifold AIR Pipe	45①
	Exhaust Manifold Heat Shield	80①
	Exhaust Pipe	48
	Fan Clutch	17
	Fan Shroud	72①
	Flywheel	74
	Front Engine Mount	44

TIGHTENING SPECIFICATIONS—Continued

Year	Component	Torque/Ft. Lbs.
2002–06	Fuel Pipe Bracket, Rear Bolt	53①
	Fuel Pipe Bracket, Rear Nut	27①
	Fuel Pipe Fitting	21
	Fuel Pipes To Bellhousing Stud	18
	Ground Wire	12
	Hood	18
	Ignition Coil	22①
	Intake Manifold, Lower	⑧
	Intake Manifold, Upper	⑥
	Main Bearing Cap	②
	Oil Cooler Line Clamp	80①
	Oil Cooler Line Clip	53①
	Oil Cooler Fitting	18
	Oil Filter	15
	Oil Filter Adapter	15
	Oil Dipstick Tube	18
	Oil Level Sensor	15
	Oil Pan, Bolt	18
	Oil Pan, Nut	18
	Oil Pan Drain Plug	18
	Power Steering Bracket	30
	Power Steering Pump, Bolt	37
	Power Steering Pump, Nut	30
	Propeller Shaft	15
	Rear Engine Mount, Nut	40
	Rear Engine Mount, Bolt	35
	Rear Engine Mount to Crossmember	33
	Rear Engine Mount To Transmission	44
	Spark Plugs	22
	Spark Plug Wire Shield	80①
	Starter	35
	Transmission, Automatic	34
	Transmission, Manual	35
	Transmission Fluid Cooler Line	19
	Transmission To Oil Pan	35
	Thermostat Housing	18
	Torsional Damper	70
	Transmission Cover	96①
	Engine Wiring Harness Bracket	18

①— Inch lbs.
②— Refer to "Main & Rod Bearings."
③— First pass to 37 ft. lbs.; final pass, tighten an additional 140°.
④— Refer to "Cylinder Head, Replace."
⑤— First pass to 11 ft. lbs.; final pass to 22 ft. lbs.
⑥— First pass, 44 inch lbs.; final pass, 80 inch lbs.
⑦— First pass to 15 ft. lbs.; final pass, tighten additional 60°.
⑧— Refer to "Intake Manifold, Replace."

4.8L, 5.3L & 6.0L Gasoline Engines

NOTE: On Air Bag Equipped Models, Refer To "Air Bag System Precautions" Located In The Front Of This Manual For System Disarming & Arming Procedures.

NOTE: Refer To "Computer Relearn Procedures" Located In The Front Of This Manual When Battery Power To The Computer Has Been Interrupted.

INDEX

PRECAUTIONS

Air Bag Systems

Refer to "Air Bag System Precautions" in the front of this manual for system disarming and arming procedures.

Battery Ground Cable

Prior to service disconnect battery ground cable and isolate, as required.

Radio Security System

If the Theftlock system is active when battery power is interrupted, the customers security code must be entered to restore proper function of the radio. To unlock a secured radio after power loss, proceed as follows:

1. "LOC" appears with ignition in On position.
2. Press "NM" and "000" will appear on display.
3. Press "NM" again to make last two digits agree with security code.
4. Press "HR" to make first 1 or 2 digits agree with security code.
5. Press "AM-FM" to select code entered. "SEC" will show on display indicating radio is now operable and secure.
6. If incorrect code is entered eight times, "INOP" will display. In order to reenter code, ignition must be left on for one hour before code can be entered and only three more chances to enter code are available before display reads "INOP."

Fuel System Pressure Relief

Prior to service, fuel pressure must be relieved by disconnecting the fuel line fittings. A small amount of fuel may still be released when the fuel line is disconnected. To reduce the chance of injury, cover the fitting(s) to be disconnected with a shop towel. Place towel in an approved container when the procedure is complete.

COMPRESSION PRESSURE

When inspecting compression, the lowest cylinder must be within 70% of the highest and no cylinder should be less than 100 psi. Perform compression test with engine at operating temperature, all spark plugs removed and throttle wide open.

ENGINE MOUNT

REPLACE

1. Raise and support vehicle.
2. Remove engine mount-to-engine mount bracket bolts.
3. Remove mounting bolts and engine shield.
4. Raise and support engine using adjustable screw type jack stands. **Do not raise and/or support engine by oil pan or crankshaft balancer.**
5. Remove mounting bolts and mount.
6. Reverse procedure to install.

ENGINE

REPLACE

1. Open hood and lace fender covers over both fenders.
2. Remove hinge bolts, raise hood until vertical and install bolts until snug.
3. Recover air conditioning refrigerant.
4. Remove drive belt as outlined under "Serpentine Drive Belt."
5. Raise and support vehicle.
6. Remove righthand front tire and wheel assembly, then the inner fender skirt.
7. Remove A/C compressor discharge and suction hoses. Discard sealing washers and cap all of openings.
8. Disconnect compressor electrical connections.

9. Remove A/C compressor mounting bolts. Lower righthand bolt will stay with compressor because of lack of clearance.
10. Remove A/C compressor from bracket through fender well. Remove A/C compressor from bottom on rear-wheel-drive 2500 series vehicles, only.
11. Remove mounting nut and bolt, support baffle and lower radiator support.
12. Disconnect clamps, then remove radiator inlet and outlet hoses from water pump.
13. Remove heater hoses.
14. Loosen mounting bolt and remove intake manifold sight shield.
15. **On models equipped with 6.0L engine,** loosen mounting bolts and remove righthand fuel rail cover.
16. **On all models,** unsnap cruise control cable from throttle body lever, then remove it from bracket. Remove clip from sight shield retainer.
17. Unsnap accelerator control cable from throttle body lever, then remove it from bracket. Remove clip from sight shield retainer.
18. Remove mounting bolts and upper intake manifold sight shield retainer.
19. Disconnect Evaporative emissions canister purge solenoid and alternator electrical connectors.
20. Remove engine harness bracket nut.
21. Position throttle body vent inlet hose clamp aside.
22. Remove radiator vent inlet hose from throttle body.
23. Slide boot down revealing terminal stud, then remove mounting nut from terminal stud and alternator cable.
24. Disconnect main coil harness and fuel injector electrical connectors on lefthand side.
25. Disconnect main coil harness, fuel injectors and Exhaust Gas Recirculation valve electrical connectors.
26. Disconnect Throttle Position sensor and Idle Air Control valve electrical connectors.
27. Disconnect Manifold Absolute Pressure sensor and Knock Sensor electrical connectors.
28. Remove harness ground bolt.
29. Position harness ground and battery ground aside from block.
30. Disconnect coolant temperature sensor and electronic variable orifice switch electrical connectors.
31. Remove harness ground bolt at righthand rear of engine block.
32. Position harness ground and auxiliary battery ground aside.
33. Remove harness ground bolt at lefthand rear of engine block.
34. Position harness ground and engine ground strap aside.
35. Disconnect oil pressure and Camshaft Position sensors electrical connectors.
36. Unclip engine harness clips.
37. Remove battery cable junction block from bracket.
38. Remove EVAP purge solenoid vent tube end from solenoid, then remove EVAP tube end from vapor pipe.
39. Disconnect fuel pipes.
40. Raise and support vehicle.
41. Disconnect Crankshaft Position sensor, engine oil level sensor and coolant heater electrical connectors.
42. Remove battery cable channel bolt, slide channel pin out of oil pan tab, gather all branches of engine wiring harness and position aside.
43. Lower vehicle.
44. Remove rear power steering pump-to-engine block bolt, and alternator bracket mounting bolts. Position bracket aside.
45. Remove vacuum brake booster hose.
46. Remove ignition coils for proper fit of engine lifting brackets.
47. Install engine lifting brackets tools No. J-41798, or equivalent, to cylinder heads.
48. Remove left and righthand engine mount-to-engine mount bracket bolts.
49. Raise and support vehicle.
50. Remove mounting bolts and engine shield.
51. Remove mounting bolts and oil pan skid plate.
52. Drain engine oil into suitable container.
53. Remove starter motor as outlined in "Electrical" section.
54. Remove catalytic converter.
55. Remove mounting bolt and positive battery cable clip.
56. **On models equipped with automatic transmission,** proceed as follows:
    a. Remove flywheel to torque converter bolts.
    b. Remove mounting nut and transmission oil dipstick tube.
    c. **On models equipped with 4L80-E automatic transmission,** remove righthand side mounting bolt and stud, then the converter cover bolts.
    d. **On all models,** remove mounting bolt/studs.
    e. Separate engine from automatic transmission.
    f. Hold torque converter by installing converter holding strap tool No. J-21366, or equivalent.
57. **On models equipped with manual transmission,** proceed as follows:
    a. Remove concentric slave cylinder clutch line using clutch line removal tool No. J-42371, or equivalent.
    b. Remove righthand side mounting stud.
    c. Remove mounting bolt/studs.
    d. Separate the transmission from engine.
    e. Mark flywheel and clutch pressure plate lug for installation alignment.
    f. Remove mounting bolts, clutch pressure plate and disc.
58. **On all models,** lower vehicle.
59. Install suitable engine hoist to engine lifting brackets.
60. Support transmission using suitable floor jack.
61. Remove engine. **Avoid breaking MAP sensor locating tabs.**
62. Reverse procedure to install.

INTAKE MANIFOLD

REPLACE

1. **On models equipped with Electronic Throttle Control (ETC),** proceed as follows:
    a. Partially drain cooling system into suitable container.
    b. Disconnect Intake Air Temperature sensor harness connector.
    c. Remove air intake duct.
    d. Disconnect throttle actuator motor and Throttle Position sensor harness connectors.
    e. Disconnect crankcase ventilation hose from throttle body.
2. **On models less Electronic Throttle Control (ETC),** proceed as follows:
    a. Remove air intake duct.
    b. Disconnect accelerator and cruise control cables from throttle body.
    c. Disconnect vacuum hose from throttle body.
    d. Disconnect Throttle Position (TP) sensor and Idle Air Control (IAC) valve harness connectors.
    e. Disconnect coolant hose from throttle body and vapor vent pipe.
3. **On all models,** remove engine sight shield.
4. Disconnect accelerator and cruise control cables from cable bracket and throttle body.
5. Remove upper engine wire harness mounting nut.
6. Disconnect EVAP purge solenoid electrical connector.
7. Position upper engine wire harness aside.
8. Identify connectors to their corresponding injectors to ensure correct sequential injector firing order after installation.
9. Pull top portion of injector connectors up. **Do not pull past top of white portion.**
10. Release connectors from injector by pushing tab on lower side.
11. Disconnect fuel feed and return pipes from fuel rail.
12. Disconnect fuel pressure regulator vacuum line.
13. Loosen crossover tube to righthand fuel rail mounting screw.
14. Disconnect Manifold Absolute Pressure (MAP) sensor, Knock (KS) Sensor and EGR valve electrical connectors.
15. Remove knock sensor harness electrical connector from intake manifold. Set harness aside.
16. Remove EGR pipe to intake manifold, cylinder head and exhaust manifold mounting bolts, then the EGR pipe, valve and gasket.
17. Remove vacuum brake booster hose from rear of intake manifold.
18. Remove PCV hose with valve.
19. Remove MAP sensor from intake manifold.
20. Remove mounting bolts and accelerator control cable bracket .
21. Remove EVAP purge solenoid vent tube end.
22. Squeeze connect fitting retainer and remove VEEP tube end from the vapor pipe.
23. Remove mounting bolt, EVAP purge solenoid and isolator.

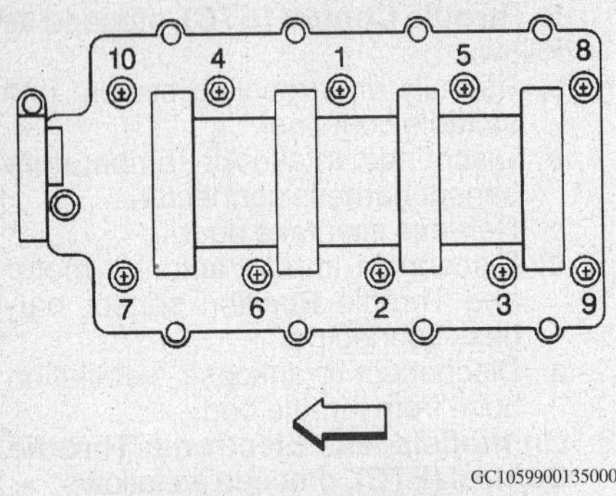

Fig. 1 Intake manifold bolt tightening sequence

24. Remove mounting bolts, intake manifold and gaskets. Discard gaskets.
25. Reverse procedure to install, noting the following:
    a. Install new intake manifold-to-cylinder head gaskets.
    b. Apply .20 inch band of threadlock part No. 12345382, or equivalent, to intake manifold bolts' threads.
    c. Using sequence, **Fig. 1, torque** intake manifold mounting bolts to 44 inch lbs., then to 89 inch lbs.

EXHAUST MANIFOLD

REPLACE

Lefthand

1. Raise and support vehicle.
2. Remove mounting nuts and separate exhaust pipe from manifold.
3. Lower vehicle and remove spark plugs.
4. Remove air injection reaction center pipe bolt.
5. Loosen hose clamps and remove hose.
6. Remove AIR pipe, nuts, studs and gasket.
7. Remove spark plugs' ignition wires.
8. Remove exhaust manifold bolts, manifold and gasket. Discard gasket.
9. Reverse procedure to install.

Righthand

1. Raise and support vehicle.
2. Remove mounting nuts and separate exhaust pipe from manifold.
3. Lower vehicle and remove spark plugs.
4. Remove EGR valve, gasket and bolts.
5. Remove EGR pipe bolt from intake manifold.
6. Remove EGR pipe bolts and gasket from exhaust manifold.
7. Remove EGR pipe bolts from cylinder head.
8. Remove EGR pipe from intake manifold.
9. Remove O-ring seal from EGR pipe. Discard gasket and O-ring seal.
10. Remove AIR pipe, nuts and gasket from righthand exhaust manifold.
11. Remove exhaust manifold, bolts and gasket. Discard gasket.
12. Reverse procedure to install.

CYLINDER HEAD

REPLACE

Lefthand

1. Remove alternator and mounting bracket as outlined under "Electrical" section.
2. Remove intake manifold as outlined under "Intake Manifold, Replace."
3. Remove coolant air bleed pipe bolts and pipe. Remove and discard gaskets.
4. Remove exhaust manifold as outlined under "Exhaust Manifold, Replace."
5. Remove pushrods as outlined under "Rocker Arms & Pushrods, Replace."
6. Remove cylinder head bolts and discard M11 bolts.
7. Remove cylinder head and gasket. Discard gasket.
8. Reverse procedure to install, noting the following:
    a. Apply .20 inch band of threadlock part No. 12345382, or equivalent, to threads of M8 cylinder head bolts.
    b. Using sequence, **Fig. 2,** tighten M11 bolts in three steps: First step, **torque** bolts to 22 ft. lbs.; second step, tighten bolts an additional 90°; third step, tighten bolt Nos. 1–8 an additional 90°, then tighten bolt Nos. 9 and 10 an additional 50°.
    c. **Torque** M8 bolts to 22 ft. lbs., beginning with center bolts and working outward.

Righthand

1. Remove mounting and oil dipstick tube.
2. Remove intake manifold as outlined under "Intake Manifold, Replace."
3. Remove exhaust manifold as outlined under "Exhaust Manifold, Replace."
4. Remove pushrods as outlined under "Rocker Arms & Pushrods, Replace."
5. Remove cylinder head bolts. Discard M11 bolts.
6. Remove cylinder head and gasket. Discard gasket.
7. Reverse procedure to install, noting the following:
    a. Using sequence, **Fig. 2,** tighten M11 bolts in three steps: First step, **torque** bolts to 22 ft. lbs.; second step, tighten bolts an additional 90°; third step, tighten bolt Nos. 1–8 an additional 90°, then tighten bolt Nos. 9 and 10 an additional 50°.
    b. **Torque** M8 bolts to 22 ft. lbs., beginning with center bolts and working outward.

VALVE COVER

REPLACE

1. Remove ignition coil as outlined under "Electrical" section.
2. Remove PCV valve and hose from lefthand side valve cover.
3. Remove oil fill cap and tube from righthand side valve cover.

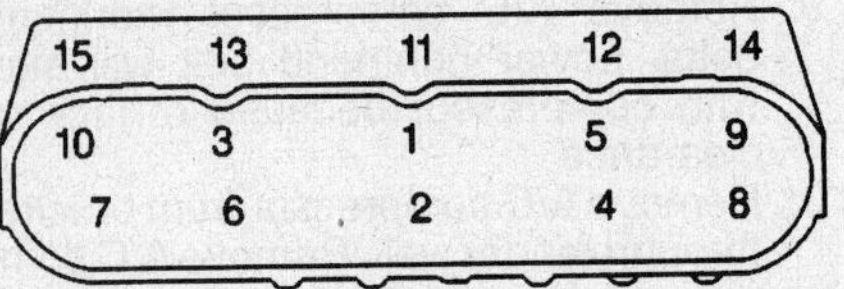

Fig. 2 Cylinder head tightening sequence

4. Remove mounting bolts, covers and gaskets. Discard gaskets.
5. Reverse procedure to install.

VALVE ARRANGEMENT

Front To Rear

Left Side ....I-E-I-E-I-E-I-E
Right Side ....E-I-E-I-E-I-E-I

VALVE ADJUSTMENT

Valve lash is net build and no valve adjustment is required on these models.

PUSH RODS

Removal

1. Remove valve cover as outlined under "Valve Cover, Replace."
2. Remove bolts and rocker arms.
3. Remove rocker arm pivot support.
4. Remove pushrods.

Installation

1. Lubricate rocker arms and pushrods with clean engine oil.
2. Lubricate flange of rocker arm bolts with clean engine oil.
3. Install valve rocker arm pivot support.
4. Install pushrods. Ensure pushrods are seated properly in valve lifter sockets.
5. Install rocker arms and bolts, but do not tighten bolts at this time. Ensure pushrods seat properly to ends of rocker arms.
6. Rotate crankshaft until piston No. 1 is at top dead center of compression stroke with crankshaft and camshaft sprocket marks aligned.
7. With engine in No. 1 firing position, tighten exhaust rocker arm bolts 1, 2, 7 and 8, then intake rocker arm bolts 1, 3, 4 and 5 to specifications.
8. Rotate crankshaft 360,° then tighten exhaust rocker arm bolts 3, 4, 5 and 6, then intake rocker arm bolts 2, 6, 7 and 8 to specifications.
9. Install valve cover as outlined under "Valve Cover, Replace."

HYDRAULIC LIFTERS

REPLACE

1. Remove cylinder head and gasket as outlined under "Cylinder Head, Replace."
2. Remove mounting bolts and valve lifter guide.
3. Remove valve lifters using lifter pliers tool No. J-3049-A, or equivalent.

4. Remove valve lifters from guide. Keep lifters in order, to ensure they are installed in their original position.
5. Reverse procedure to install. Lubricate valve lifter with clean engine oil.

CRANKSHAFT DAMPER

REPLACE

Removal

1. Remove drive belt as outlined under "Serpentine Drive Belt."
2. Remove upper fan shroud.
3. Remove engine cooling fan.
4. Remove starter motor as outlined under "Electrical" section.
5. Install flywheel holder tool No. J-42386-A, or equivalent.
6. Remove crankshaft damper bolt.
7. Remove crankshaft damper using puller tool Nos. J-41816 and J-41816-2, or equivalents.

Installation

1. Install damper onto end of crankshaft.
2. Install damper using crankshaft damper installation tool No. J-41665, or equivalent.
3. Remove damper installation tool and install crankshaft damper bolt.
4. Remove crankshaft damper bolt and measure for correctly installed damper. Nose of crankshaft should be recessed .094–.176 inch into damper bore.
5. If damper is not installed properly, repeat installation procedure.
6. Tighten new crankshaft damper.
7. Remove flywheel holder tool.

FRONT COVER

REPLACE

Removal

1. Remove water pump as outlined under "Water Pump, Replace."
2. Remove the crankshaft balancer as outlined under "Crankshaft Damper, Replace."
3. Remove oil pan-to-front cover mounting bolts.
4. Remove mounting bolts, front cover and gasket. Discard gasket.

INSTALLATION

1. Apply .20 inch bead of sealant No. 12378190, or equivalent, .80 inch long to oil pan to engine block junction.
2. Install new gasket and front cover.
3. Install mounting bolts until snug. **Do not overtighten.**
4. Install oil pan-to-front cover bolts until snug. **Do not over tighten.**
5. Install front and rear cover alignment tool No. J 41476, or equivalent, to front cover. Align tapered legs with machined alignment surfaces on front cover.
6. Install crankshaft balancer bolt until snug. **Do not overtighten.**
7. Tighten oil pan to front cover and front cover mounting bolts.
8. Remove alignment tool.
9. Install new crankshaft front oil seal.
10. Install water pump.

FRONT COVER SEAL

REPLACE

1. Remove crankshaft damper as outlined under "Crankshaft Damper, Replace."
2. Remove crankshaft front oil seal.
3. Reverse procedure to install, noting the following:
   a. Lubricate outer edge of new oil seal and front cover seal bore with clean engine oil.
   b. Install seal into front cover using front oil seal installer tool No. J-41478, or equivalent.

TIMING CHAIN

REPLACE

Removal

1. Remove oil pump as outlined under "Oil Pump, Replace."
2. Rotate crankshaft until timing marks on crankshaft and camshaft sprockets are aligned.
3. Remove mounting bolts, camshaft sprocket and timing chain.
4. Remove crankshaft sprocket using crankshaft sprocket puller tool Nos. J-41558, J-41816-2 and J-8433-1, or equivalents.
5. Remove crankshaft key.

Installation

1. Install key into keyway, if necessary.
2. Install crankshaft sprocket onto front of crankshaft. Align crankshaft key with crankshaft sprocket keyway.
3. Install sprocket onto crankshaft until fully seated against crankshaft flange using sprocket installer tool No. J-41665, or equivalent.
4. Rotate crankshaft sprocket until alignment mark is in 12 o'clock position.
5. Install camshaft sprocket and timing chain.
6. Align camshaft sprocket locating pin with camshaft sprocket alignment hole.
7. Position camshaft sprocket alignment mark in the 6 o'clock position.
8. Rotate camshaft or crankshaft sprockets to align timing marks.
9. Install camshaft sprocket mounting bolts.

CAMSHAFT

REPLACE

1. Raise hood to servicing position as outlined under "Engine, Replace."
2. Remove radiator support as outlined under "Engine, Replace."
3. Remove timing chain as outlined under "Timing Chain, Replace."
4. Remove valve lifters as outlined under "Valve Lifters, Replace."
5. Remove mounting bolt and camshaft sensor .
6. Remove mounting bolts and camshaft retainer.
7. Install three M8-1.25 x 4.0 inch bolts in camshaft front bolt holes.
8. Rotate and pull camshaft out of engine block using bolts as handle.
9. Remove bolts from front of camshaft.
10. Reverse procedure to install, noting the following:
    a. If camshaft replacement is required, valve lifters must also be replaced.
    b. Lubricate camshaft journals and bearings with clean engine oil.
    c. Install retainer plate with sealing gasket facing engine block.
    d. Lubricate camshaft sensor seal with clean engine oil.

PISTON & ROD ASSEMBLY

When assembling the piston and connecting rod, the mark on the top of the piston must point to the front of the engine block. Lefthand bank connecting rods should have the flange face toward front of engine block. Righthand bank connecting rods should have flange face toward rear of the engine block. The piston pin has an interference fit into the connecting rod and is full floating in the piston. Space compression ring end gaps a minimum of one inch apart and oil ring end gaps a minimum of 90° apart.

PISTONS, PINS & RINGS

A .001 inch oversize piston is available so proper clearance can be obtained for slightly worn cylinder bores requiring light honing, only. If the cylinder have less than .005 inch taper or wear, they can be reconditioned with a hone and fitted with the .001 inch oversize piston.

In addition, oversizes of .020, .030 and .040 inch are available.

MAIN & ROD BEARINGS

Main Bearings

Shell type bearings are used and if worn excessively, should be replaced. No attempt should be made to shim, file or otherwise take up worn bearings.

Main bearings are available in standard and undersides of .001, .002, .009, .010 and .020 inch.

Bearing caps must be installed in proper location and direction.

1. Install crankshaft bearing caps with bearings into engine block.
2. Start M10 bolts and bolt/studs.
3. Tap bearing caps into place suitable plastic-faced hammer.
4. Install new M8 bearing cap side bolts.

5. **Torque** inner M10 bearing cap bolts to 15 ft. lbs., in sequence. **Fig. 3.**
6. Tap crankshaft rearward, then forward to align thrust bearings using suitable plastic faced hammer.
7. Tighten inner M10 bolts an additional 80° in sequence using torque angle meter tool No. J-36660-A, or equivalent.
8. **Torque** outer M10 bolts/studs to 60 inch lbs., then tighten an additional 53°, in sequence.
9. **Torque** bearing cap side M8 bolts to 18 ft. lbs.

CRANKSHAFT REAR OIL SEAL

REPLACE

Removal

1. Remove transmission as outlined under **MOTOR's "Domestic Transmission, In-Vehicle Service."**
2. Remove mounting bolts and flywheel.
3. Remove crankshaft rear oil sea from rear cover.

Installation

Do not lubricate the oil seal inside diameter or the crankshaft surface.

1. Remove flywheel spacer.
2. Lubricate outside diameter of oil seal with clean engine oil. **DO NOT allow oil or other lubricants to contact seal surface.**
3. Lubricate rear cover oil seal bore with clean engine oil. **DO NOT allow oil or other lubricants to contact crankshaft surface.**
4. Install tapered cone tool No. J 41479, or equivalent, and mounting bolts onto crankshaft rear.
5. Tighten bolts until snug. **Do not overtighten.**
6. Install rear oil seal onto tapered cone and push seal to rear cover bore.
7. Thread tool rod into tapered cone until tool contacts oil seal.
8. Align oil seal into tool.
9. Rotate tool handle tool clockwise until seal enters rear cover and bottoms into cover bore.
10. Remove tool and install flywheel. Tighten flywheel mounting bolts in three steps: First step, **torque** to 15 ft. lbs.; second step, **torque** to 37 ft. lbs.; third step, **torque** to 74 ft. lbs.
11. Install transmission as outlined under **MOTOR's "Domestic Transmission, In-Vehicle Service."**

OIL PAN

REPLACE

1. **On models equipped with 4WD,** remove front differential as outlined in "Front Wheel Drive Axles" section.
2. **On all models,** remove starter motor as outlined in "Electrical" section.
3. Remove mounting bolts and engine shield.

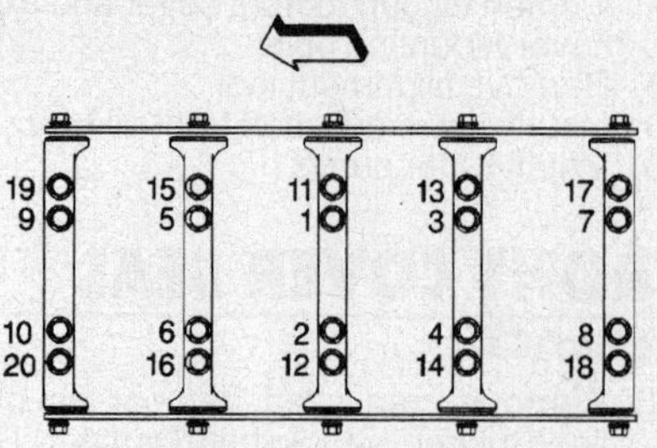

Fig. 3 Main bearing cap tightening sequence

4. Remove mounting bolts and oil pan skid plate.
5. Remove mounting bolts and crossbar.
6. Remove mounting bolt and transmission cover.
7. Drain engine oil into suitable container and remove engine oil filter.
8. Install drain plug and oil filter until snug.
9. **On models equipped with 4L60-E automatic transmission,** remove righthand side transmission mounting bolt and stud, then the bottom lefthand side mounting bolt.
10. **On models equipped with the 4L80-E automatic transmission,** remove transmission converter cover bolts.
11. **On models equipped with manual transmission,** remove two bottom bellhousing bolts.
12. **On all models,** disconnect oil level sensor electrical connector.
13. Remove battery cable channel bolt and slide channel pin out of oil pan tab.
14. Remove wiring harness and positive battery cable clips.
15. Remove engine oil cooler lines from positive battery cable clip.
16. Remove positive battery cable clip bolt and clip.
17. Remove mounting bolts and oil pan.
18. Drill out oil pan gasket retaining rivets and remove gasket. Discard gasket and rivets.
19. Reverse procedure to install, noting the following
    a. It is not required to rivet new gasket to oil pan.
    b. Apply .20 inch bead of sealant No. 12378190, or equivalent, .8 inch long to engine block.
    c. Apply sealant directly onto tabs of front and rear cover gaskets that protrudes into the oil pan surface.

OIL PUMP

REPLACE

1. Remove oil pan as outlined under "Oil Pan, Replace."
2. Remove front cover as outlined under "Front Cover, Replace."
3. Remove mounting bolt, nuts and oil pump screen with O-ring seal. Discard seal
4. Remove mounting nuts and crankshaft oil deflector.
5. Remove mounting bolts and oil pump.
6. Reverse procedure to install.

SERPENTINE DRIVE BELT

Routing

Refer to **Fig. 4** for serpentine drive belt routing.

Replacement

1. Rotate tensioner clockwise to release belt tension using suitable wrench, then remove belt.
2. Route belt over pulleys except belt tensioner.
3. Rotate tensioner to released position and slide belt over tensioner pulley.
4. Ensure belt has correct groove tracking around each pulley.

COOLING SYSTEM BLEED

These engines do not require a specified bleed procedure. After filling cooling system, run engine to operating temperature with radiator/pressure cap off. Air will then be automatically bled through cap opening.

THERMOSTAT

REPLACE

1. Remove radiator outlet hose.
2. Remove mounting bolts, then the water pump inlet.
3. Remove thermostat from water pump.
4. Reverse procedure to install.

WATER PUMP

REPLACE

1. Drain engine coolant into suitable container.
2. Loosen throttle body Mass Air Flow/Intake Air Temperature (MAF/IAT) sensor air cleaner outlet duct clamps, then remove air cleaner outlet duct.
3. **On models equipped with 6.0L engine,** remove engine sight shield.
4. **On all models,** remove radiator vent inlet hose from clips.
5. Remove water pump inlet hose.
6. Remove upper fan shroud as outlined under "Engine, Replace."
7. Remove fan using fan clutch remover and installer tool No. J-41240, or equivalent.
8. Remove accessory drive belt as outlined under "Serpentine Drive Belt."
9. Remove water pump outlet, surge tank outlet hose and heater inlet hoses.
10. Remove mounting bolts and water pump pulley.
11. Remove mounting bolts, water pump and gaskets. Discard gaskets.
12. Reverse procedure to install. Use new gaskets and tighten mounting bolts.

RADIATOR

REPLACE

1. Drain radiator coolant into suitable container.
2. Remove upper and lower radiator hoses.
3. Remove mounting bolts and lower fan shroud.
4. Remove engine vent hose and surge take hose.
5. Disconnect engine oil cooler lines. Cap lines.
6. Disconnect transmission fluid cooler lines.
7. Remove radiator mounting bolts.
8. Tilt radiator towards engine, then pull up to remove it from support.
9. Reverse procedure to install.

FUEL PUMP

REPLACE

1. Release fuel system pressure as outlined under "Precautions."
2. Drain fuel tank into suitable container.
3. Remove fuel tank.
4. Remove fuel sender by turning cam lock counterclockwise using tool No. J-39765, or equivalent.
5. Remove fuel pump from sender.
6. Reverse procedure to install.

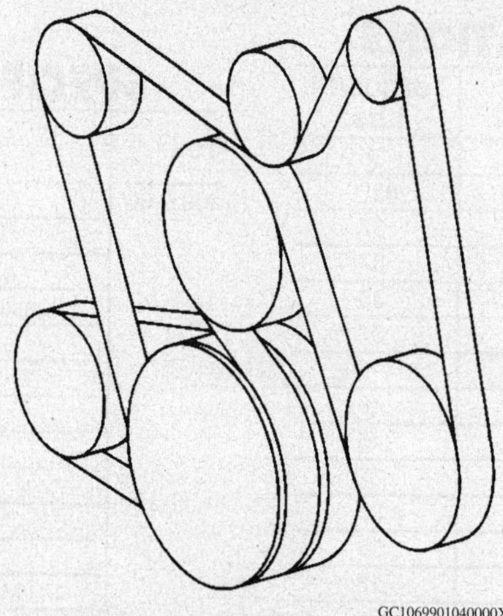

Fig. 4 Serpentine drive belt routing

FUEL FILTER

REPLACE

1. Release fuel system pressure as outlined under "Precautions."
2. Remove fuel filler cap, then disconnect fuel feed nuts.
3. Remove clamp bolt, filter and clamp.
4. Remove clamp from filter.
5. Reverse procedure to install.

TIGHTENING SPECIFICATIONS

Year	Component	Torque/Ft. Lbs.
2002–06	Alternator Bracket	37
	Accelerator Control Cable Bracket	89(1)
	Air Conditioning Compressor	37
	Air Conditioning Compressor Bracket	37
	Air Conditioning Hose Bracket	35
	Air Conditioning Tensioner	37
	AIR Bracket	71(1)
	AIR Pipe To Exhaust Manifold, Nuts	18
	AIR Pipe To Exhaust Manifold, Studs	45
	Alternator & Power Steering Bracket	37
	Belt Idler Pulley	37
	Camshaft Retainer	18
	Camshaft Sensor	18
	Camshaft Sprocket	26
	Clutch Pressure Plate	52(14)
	Connecting Rod	(9)
	Coolant Temperature Gauge Sensor	15
	Crankshaft Bearing Cap	(2)
	Crankshaft Damper	(3)
	Crankshaft Oil Deflector	18
	Crankshaft Position Sensor	18
	Crossbar	74
	Cylinder Head	(4)
	Cylinder Head Coolant Plug	15
	Cylinder Head Core Hole Plug	15
	Drive Belt Idler Pulley	37
	Drive Belt Tensioner	37
	Engine Block Coolant Drain Plugs	44
	Engine Oil Cooler Line Fitting	18
	Engine Oil Level Sensor	115(1)
	Engine Shield	15
	Engine Wiring Harness Bracket	89(1)
	EGR Valve	(6)
	EGR Valve Inlet Pipe Intake Manifold	18
	EGR Valve Inlet Pipe Exhaust Manifold	22
	EGR Valve Pipe To Cylinder Head	37
	EGR Valve Pipe To Exhaust Manifold	20
	EGR Valve Pipe To Intake Manifold	89(1)
	Exhaust Crossover Pipe	25
	Exhaust Manifold AIR Pipe	45(1)
	Exhaust Manifold	(7)
	Exhaust Manifold Heat Shield	80(1)
	Exhaust Pipe	48
	EVAP Purge Solenoid	89(1)
	Fan Clutch	17
	Fan Shroud	72(1)
	Flywheel	(5)
	Front Cover	18
	Front Differential Carrier Shield	26
	Fuel Rail	89(1)
	Fuel Rail Cover	80(1)
	Fuel Rail Crossover Tube	34(1)
	Fuel Rail Stop Bracket	37
	Hood	18
	Ignition Coil	22(1)

TIGHTENING SPECIFICATIONS—Continued

Year	Component	Torque/Ft. Lbs.
2002–06	Intake Cover	89(1)
	Intake Cover Bracket	45(1)
	Ignition Coil To Bracket	106(1)
	Ignition Coil Bracket To Valve Cover	106(1)
	Intake Manifold	(8)
	Intake Manifold Wiring Harness	89(1)
	Knock Sensors	15
	Main Bearing Cap	(2)
	MAF Sensor Clamp	27–44(1)
	Motor Mount	37
	Motor Mount Bracket	48
	Motor Mount, Lower To Upper	37
	Motor Mount, Through Bolt	68
	Motor Mount, Upper	37
	Oil Cooler Line Clamp	80(1)
	Oil Cooler Line Clip	53(1)
	Oil Cooler Fitting	18
	Oil Filter	22
	Oil Filter Fitting	40
	Oil Dipstick Tube	18
	Oil Level Sensor	15
	Oil Pan Baffle	106(1)
	Oil Pan Closeout Cover	80(1)
	Oil Pan Drain Plug	18
	Oil Pan To Block & Front Cover	18
	Oil Pan To Rear Cover	106(1)
	Oil Pan Skid Plate	15
	Oil Pressure Sensor	15
	Oil Pump To Engine Block	18
	Oil Pump Cover	106(1)
	Oil Pump Relief Valve Plug	106(1)
	Oil Pump Screen	18
	Oil Pump Screen To Oil Pump	106(1)
	Oil Transfer Cover	106(1)
	Power Steering Pump	37
	Power Steering Pump Bracket	37
	Propeller Shaft	15
	Radiator Shroud	71(1)
	Rear Cover	18
	Spark Plugs (Aluminum Cylinder Heads)	(10)
	Spark Plugs (Iron Cylinder Heads)	(11)
	Starter Cover	15
	Radiator Support	52
	Rear Engine Mount, Bolt	35
	Rear Engine Mount, Nut	40
	Rear Engine Mount, Bolt	35
	Rear Engine Mount to Crossmember	33
	Rear Engine Mount To Transmission	44
	Throttle Body	89(1)
	Torque Converter	46
	Transmission, Automatic	34
	Transmission, Manual	35
	Transmission Fluid Cooler Line	19
	Transmission To Oil Pan	41
	Universal Lift Bracket	15

Continued

TIGHTENING SPECIFICATIONS—Continued

Year	Component	Torque/Ft. Lbs.
2002–06	Valley Cover	106①
	Valve Lifter Guide	106①
	Valve Rocker Arm	22
	Valve Rocker Arm Cover	106①
	Vapor Vent Pipe	106①
	Water Inlet Housing	11
	Water Pump	⑫
	Water Pump Cover	11
	Water Pump Pulley	⑬

①— Inch lbs.
②— Refer to "Main & Rod Bearings."
③— First pass, to 37 ft. lbs.; final pass, tighten an additional 140°.
④— Refer to "Cylinder Head, Replace."
⑤— Refer to "Crankshaft Rear Oil Seal, Replace"
⑥— First pass, 90 inch lbs.; final pass, 20 ft. lbs.
⑦— First pass, 11 ft. lbs.; final pass, 18 ft. lbs.
⑧— Refer to "Intake Manifold, Replace."
⑨— First pass, to 15 ft. lbs.; final pass, tighten additional 60°.
⑩— Spark plugs in new aluminum cylinder heads, 15 ft. lbs.; all subsequent installations, 11 ft. lbs.
⑪— Spark plugs in new iron cylinder heads, 22 ft. lbs.; all subsequent installations, 11 ft. lbs.
⑫— First pass, 11 ft. lbs.; final pass, 22 ft. lbs.
⑬— First pass, 90 inch lbs.; final pass, 18 ft. lbs.
⑭— Tighten clutch pressure plate bolts in star pattern and evenly over three increments with fourth increment to 52 ft. lbs.

6.6L Diesel Engine

NOTE: On Air Bag Equipped Models, Refer To "Air Bag System Precautions" Located In The Front Of This Manual For System Disarming & Arming Procedures.

NOTE: Refer To "Computer Relearn Procedures" Located In The Front Of This Manual When Battery Power To The Computer Has Been Interrupted.

INDEX

PRECAUTIONS

Air Bag Systems

Refer to "Air Bag System Precautions" in the front of this manual for system disarming and arming procedures.

Battery Ground Cable

Prior to service disconnect battery ground cable and isolate as required.

COMPRESSION PRESSURE

1. Remove fuel solenoid fuse.
2. Disconnect glow plug wires, then remove all glow plugs.
3. Install compression gauge adaptor tool No. J-26999-10, or equivalent.
4. Connect compression gauge tool No. J-26999, or equivalent.
5. Crank engine, allowing six "puffs" per cylinder.
6. Lowest cylinder compression reading should be within 80 percent of the highest cylinder. No cylinder compression reading should be less than 380 psi.
   a. Normal compression builds quickly and evenly to specified compression on each cylinder. Readings should be in the 380–400 psi range.
   b. Leaking compression is low on the first stroke, then tends to build up on following strokes, but does not reach normal range.

ENGINE MOUNT

REPLACE

1. Raise and support vehicle.
2. **On lefthand motor mount,** remove lefthand front tire and wheel.
3. **On righthand motor mount,** remove righthand front tire and wheel.
4. **On either motor mount,** remove pushpins holding wheelhouse inner panel, then the inner panel from wheelhouse.
5. Remove engine mount to engine mount frame bracket attaching bolts.
6. Remove oil pan skid plate and engine protection shield.
7. **On 2WD models equipped with automatic transmission,** remove oil cooler line bracket attaching bolt, then position line and bracket aside.
8. **On models equipped with 2WD,** place a suitable jack under ground wire bolt boses, then raise engine enough to separate engine mount from engine mount bracket.
9. **On models equipped with 4WD,** attach a suitable chain to alternator and power steering pump mounting brackets, then using a suitable lifting device, raise engine enough to separate engine mount from engine mount bracket.
10. **On all models,** remove engine mount to engine attaching bolts.
11. Remove engine mount frame bracket through bolts.
12. Remove engine mount frame bracket, then the engine mount.
13. Reverse procedure to install.

ENGINE

REPLACE

1. Recover A/C refrigerant as outlined in "Air Conditioning."
2. Raise hood to service position by moving hood hinge bolts to service position.
3. Remove upper intake manifold sight shield retaining bolt, then the shield from intake manifold.
4. Drain engine coolant from radiator and engine block.
5. Remove air cleaner outlet duct from air cleaner and turbocharger.
6. Disconnect MAF sensor, A/C pressure cycling pressure switch and surge tank switch electrical connectors, **Fig. 1.**
7. Remove engine wiring harness clips from accumulator, wheelhouse inner panel and engine bracket.
8. Remove air cleaner assembly and bracket, then the surge tank.
9. Raise and support vehicle, then remove front tires and wheels.
10. Remove lefthand and righthand wheelhouse inner panels.
11. Lower vehicle.

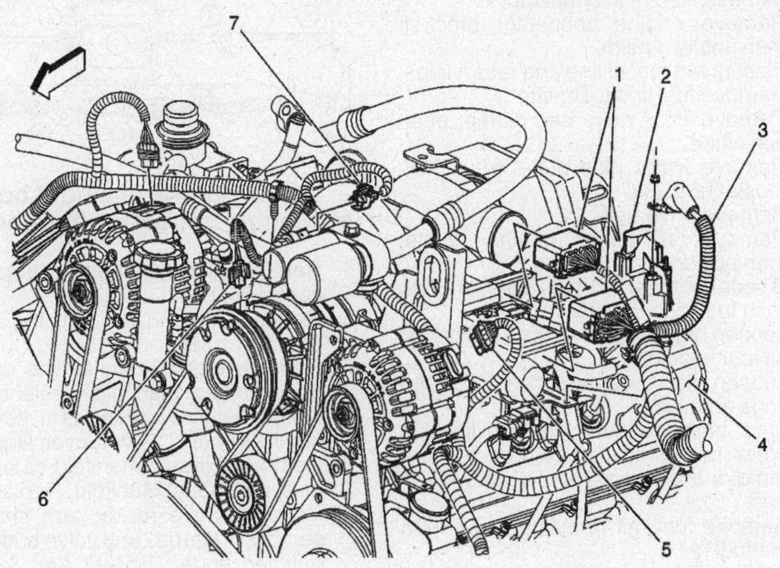

(1) Inlines to Engine Harness Connectors-C107,C108
(2) Engine Glow Plug Relay
(3) Glow Plug Harness
(4) Diesel Engine-6.6L
(5) Generator Connector
(6) AC Compressor Clutch Connector
(7) AC High Pressure Switch Connector

GC1060101160000X

Fig. 1 Engine harness & connectors

12. Loosen both charged air cooler outlet duct to intake manifold tube hose clamps, then twist hose from outlet duct and intake manifold tube. **Do not use screwdriver or other tool to remove hose, damage to the hose could occur.**
13. Remove radiator inlet hose from engine.
14. Remove upper and lower fan shrouds, then the outlet hose from radiator.
15. Disconnect outlet heater hose from outlet radiator hose.
16. Remove hose clips from frame, then the outlet hose from engine.
17. Remove outlet heater hose to alternator bracket retaining bolt.
18. Remove heater hose to fuel filter mounting bracket retaining nut, then the heater hose from engine. Position and secure hose aside.
19. Remove upper radiator support, then the radiator.
20. Remove charged air cooler and A/C condenser.
21. Disconnect alternator harness, A/C refrigerant switch and A/C compressor clutch electrical connectors.
22. Remove engine harness retaining clip from A/C compressor bracket.
23. Disconnect battery cable to alternator connector.
24. **On models equipped with auxiliary alternator,** disconnect battery cable to alternator connector.
25. **On all models,** remove battery cable harness clip from bracket.
26. Remove battery cable junction block to power steering pump retaining bolt, then position and secure battery cables aside.
27. Disconnect both fuel injection control module harness connectors.
28. Remove engine wire harness from retainer.
29. Disconnect fuel lines from engine, then remove fuel line bracket from upper valve rocker arm cover stud. Position and secure fuel lines aside.
30. Remove power supply cable from glow plug relay.
31. Rotate drive belt tensioner using a suitable ⅜ inch drive wrench, then remove drive belt.
32. Remove suction hose from accumulator.
33. Remove A/C compressor mounting bolts, then the compressor with hoses attached. Position and secure aside.
34. Move wiring harness to lefthand side of vehicle. Position and secure aside.
35. Remove power steering front bracket to power steering pump and A/C compressor mounting bracket attaching bolts.
36. Remove PCV oil separator from bracket.
37. Remove PCV separator bracket and fuel bleed valve.
38. Remove right idler pulley, then the alternator mounting bracket.
39. Disconnect inlet heater hose from heater core inlet.
40. Remove ground wires from rear of lefthand cylinder head.
41. Raise and support vehicle.
42. Remove oil pan skid plate and engine protection shield from under engine.
43. Remove battery ground cable and engine wiring harness from lefthand side of engine.
44. Remove battery cable channel retainer to lower crankcase attaching bolts.
45. Disconnect engine coolant heater electrical connector.
46. Remove starter motor attaching bolts and starter motor.
47. Remove nut holding battery cable bracket to righthand side of lower crankcase.
48. Remove bolt holding auxiliary battery ground cable and engine wiring harness ground wires to righthand side of engine. Position and secure battery cables aside.
49. Raise and support vehicle, then drain engine oil.
50. Remove exhaust pipe to exhaust outlet clamp.
51. **On models equipped with 4WD,** remove lower oil pan.
52. **On models equipped with automatic transmission,** proceed as follows:
    a. Mark flywheel and torque convertor relationship for installation reference.
    b. Remove torque convertor bolts through starter opening.
    c. Remove transmission oil line clip.
    d. Remove transmission fluid fill tube bracket retaining nuts.
53. **On all models,** remove transmission to engine attaching bolts and nuts. Note location of studs and any brackets attached to studs.
54. Lower vehicle, then working through wheelhouse opening, remove engine mount to frame bracket bolts.
55. Lower vehicle.
56. Install engine lift brackets tool No. J 36857, or equivalent to rear of lefthand cylinder head and front of righthand cylinder head.
57. Attach a suitable lifting device to lift brackets. Engine will have to be angled to remove, use a suitable load positioning sling to angle engine.
58. Raise engine off engine mounts, then remove lefthand and righthand engine mount frame brackets.
59. Remove engine from vehicle.
60. Reverse procedure to install.

INTAKE MANIFOLD

REPLACE

Left

1. Remove turbocharger assembly as outlined under "Turbocharger, Replace."
2. Remove fuel cap.
3. Remove PCV hose and clamp, then the turbo hose and clamp.
4. Remove banjo bolt from fuel junction block.
5. Remove fuel lines from fuel junction block.
6. Remove fuel junction block attaching bolts, then the junction block.

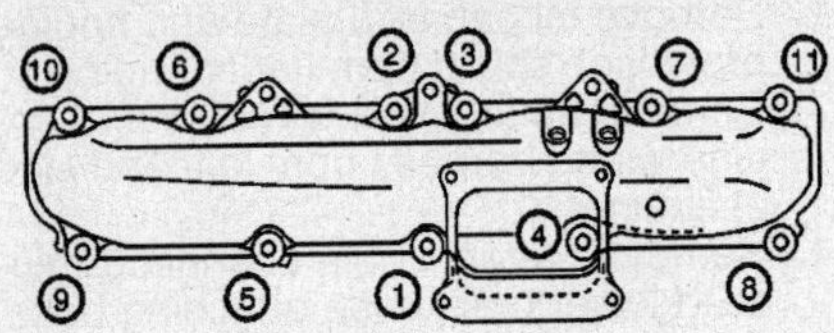

Fig. 2 Intake manifold bolt tightening sequence (lefthand)

7. Remove large tie wraps from fuel injector control module, then disconnect control module harness connectors.
8. Remove fuel lines from fuel injector control module.
9. Remove fuel injector control module mounting bolts, then the control module from valve cover.
10. Remove insulators between control module and bracket.
11. Remove fuel lines from fuel filter.
12. Remove fuel filter attaching bolts, then the fuel filter.
13. Disconnect high pressure fuel rail line from fuel junction block.
14. Loosen high pressure injection lines at all four injectors.
15. Loosen high pressure lines at four fittings on fuel rail.
16. Mark high pressure injection lines in order for installation reference, then remove lines from fuel rail and injectors.
17. Remove fuel rail retaining bolts, then the fuel rail.
18. Remove intake manifold tube retaining bolts and nuts.
19. Remove intake manifold tube and gaskets from intake manifold.
20. Remove intake manifold attaching bolts and nuts, then the intake manifold.
21. Reverse procedure to install, noting the following:
    a. Apply a ⅛ inch wide bead of sealer part No. 12378521, or equivalent, to sealing surface of intake manifold.
    b. **Torque** intake manifold attaching bolts and nuts to 15 ft. lbs., using sequence outlined in **Fig. 2.**

Right

1. Remove turbocharger assembly as outlined under "Turbocharger, Replace."
2. Drain engine coolant, then remove upper radiator hose.
3. Remove bolt holding positive battery cable junction box and bracket. Position and secure junction box and bracket aside.
4. Remove fuel cap.
5. Remove banjo bolt from fuel junction block.
6. Remove fuel lines from fuel junction block.
7. Remove fuel junction block attaching bolts, then the junction block.
8. Disconnect both glow plug relay connectors, then remove glow plug relay bracket.
9. Disconnect 40-pin and 24-pin engine harness electrical connectors.
10. Remove engine connector bracket, then position aside.
11. Disconnect fuel in line and return lines.
12. Remove fuel line L-Bracket.
13. Remove PCV hose and clamp, position aside.
14. Remove water pipe outlet from thermostat housing.
15. Remove drive belt.
16. Remove A/C pump attaching bolts, then position pump aside.
17. Disconnect fuel rail high pressure line from fuel junction block.
18. Loosen high pressure injection lines at all four injectors.
19. Loosen high pressure lines at four fittings on fuel rail.
20. Mark high pressure injection lines in order for installation reference, then remove lines from fuel rail and injectors.
21. Remove fuel rail retaining bolts, then the fuel rail.
22. Remove intake manifold tube retaining bolts and nuts.
23. Remove intake manifold tube and gaskets from intake manifold.
24. Remove intake manifold attaching bolts and nuts, then the intake manifold.
25. Reverse procedure to install, noting the following:
    a. Apply a ⅛ inch wide bead of sealer part No. 12378521, or equivalent, to sealing surface of intake manifold.
    b. **Torque** intake manifold attaching bolts and nuts to 15 ft. lbs., using sequence outlined in **Fig. 3.**

EXHAUST MANIFOLD

REPLACE

1. Raise and support vehicle.
2. Remove exhaust pipe heat shield retaining bolts, then position heat shield aside.
3. Remove exhaust pipe to exhaust manifold attaching bolts.
4. Lower vehicle and remove lefthand wheelhouse inner panel.
5. Remove left tire and wheel.
6. Remove charged air cooler outlet duct.
7. Remove exhaust manifold heat shield retaining bolts, then the heat shield.
8. Remove exhaust manifold attaching bolts and nuts, then the manifold and gasket.
9. Reverse procedure to install, noting the following. **Torque** manifold bolts to 25 ft. lbs., using sequence outlined in **Fig. 4.**

CYLINDER HEAD

REPLACE

1. Drain engine coolant.
2. **On lefthand cylinder head,** remove lefthand wheelhouse inner panel.
3. **On righthand cylinder head,** remove righthand wheelhouse inner panel.
4. **On either cylinder head,** remove turbocharger as outlined under "Turbocharger, Replace."

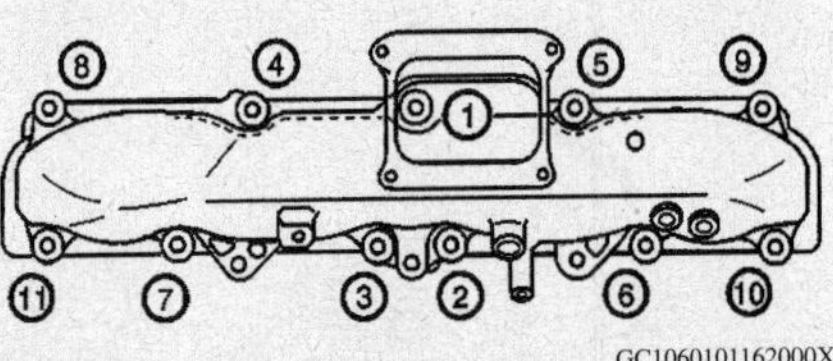

Fig. 3 Intake manifold bolt tightening sequence (righthand)

5. Remove turbocharger charged air cooler inlet duct.
6. Remove thermostat housing crossover.
7. Remove intake manifold as outlined under "Intake Manifold, Replace."
8. Remove valve rocker arm cover as outlined under "Valve Cover, Replace."
9. Remove exhaust manifold as outlined under "Exhaust Manifold, Replace."
10. Remove valve rocker arm shaft assembly, pushrods and valve bridges as outlined under "Rocker Arm & Pushrods."
11. Remove glow plugs.
12. Remove fuel injector return pipe eye bolts and washers, then the fuel injector return pipe assembly.
13. Remove fuel injector bracket bolts.
14. Remove fuel injector and brackets using injector removal tool No. J 44639, or equivalent.
15. Remove injector bracket pins.
16. Remove cylinder head bolts in sequence, **Fig. 5.**
17. Remove cylinder head from cylinder block.
18. Reverse procedure to install, noting the following:
    a. Cylinder head gasket thickness is determined by piston head projection from cylinder block deck surface.
    b. To determine piston head projection, zero dial indicator tool No. J 26900-12, or equivalent, to cylinder deck surface, **Fig. 6.**
    c. Place dial indicator pointer on top of centerline of piston. For an accurate measurement, ensure pointer is directly over centerline of piston.
    d. Rotate engine to roll piston through TDC while noting maximum reading.
    e. Position dial indicator pointer on second piston measuring point, then rotate engine to roll piston through TDC while noting maximum reading.
    f. Repeat steps "b" through "e" on each piston.
    g. Calculate average value of piston projection for each cylinder and obtain maximum projection for bank of cylinders.
    h. Compare piston projection to projection value outlined in **Fig. 7,** then select gasket that compares with projection value.
    i. Using numbered sequence outlined in **Fig. 8,** tighten cylinder head M12 bolts in three steps: first step, **torque** bolts to 37 ft. lbs.; second step, **torque** bolts to 59 ft. lbs.; third

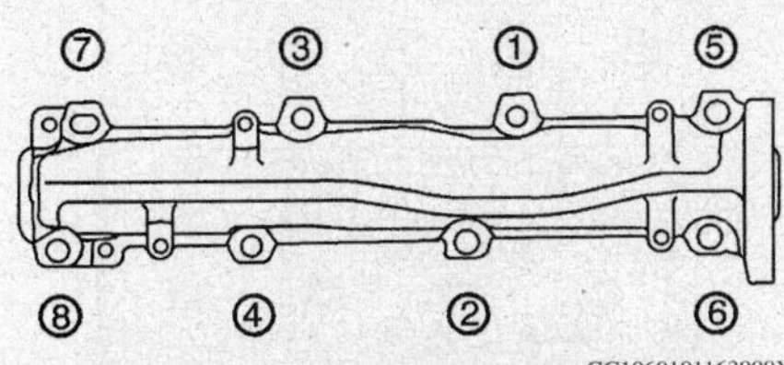

Fig. 4 Exhaust manifold bolt tightening sequence

step, tighten bolts an additional 150°.

j. **Torque** M8 bolts to 18 ft. lbs.

ROCKER ARM & PUSHRODS

1. Remove upper and lower valve rocker arm covers as outlined under "Valve Cover, Replace."
2. Loosen valve clearance lock nuts on each rocker arm.
3. Loosen valve clearance adjusting screw on each rocker arm to relieve tension on valve train.
4. Loosen rocker arm shaft assembly bolts in sequence, **Fig. 9.** Leave bolts in rocker arm shaft brackets.
5. Remove valve bridge pins, valve bridges and pushrods.
6. Reverse procedure to install, noting the following:
   a. Lubricate valves, valve bridge stem, valve bridge, valve bridge pins, rocker arm shaft bolt threads, tops of pushrods and rocker arms with clean engine oil.
   b. **Torque** rocker arm shaft assembly bolts to 30 ft. lbs., using sequence outlined in **Fig. 10.**

VALVE COVER

REPLACE

Upper Left

1. Remove upper intake manifold sight shield.
2. Drain engine coolant.
3. Remove charge air cooler inlet duct to turbocharger charge air cooler outlet.
4. Remove battery cable to alternator retaining nut.
5. **On models equipped with auxiliary battery** disconnect battery cable from auxiliary battery.
6. **On all models,** remove battery cable harness clip from bracket.
7. Remove battery cable junction block to power steering pump attaching bolt.
8. Position and secure battery cable aside.
9. Disconnect fuel hoses, then remove fuel hose bracket to upper valve rocker arm cover retaining nut.
10. Remove large tie wraps from fuel injector control module, then disconnect control module harness connectors.
11. Remove fuel lines from fuel injector control module.
12. Remove fuel injector control module

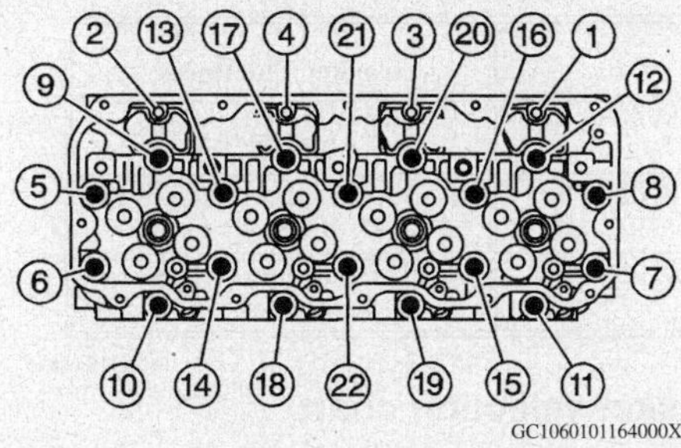

Fig. 5 Cylinder head bolt removal sequence

mounting bolts, then the control module from valve cover.

13. Remove insulators between control module and bracket.
14. Remove radiator inlet hose from water outlet tube.
15. Remove wiring harness bracket from thermostat housing.
16. Disconnect turbocharger coolant hose from turbocharger bypass valve.
17. Remove turbocharger bypass valve and sealing washer from water outlet tube.
18. Remove water outlet tube to valve rocker arm cover retaining bolts.
19. Remove water outlet tube to thermostat housing attaching bolt, then the outlet tube.
20. Remove glow plug relay bracket from upper valve cover.
21. Remove auxiliary alternator.
22. Disconnect PCV hose from valve cover.
23. Remove fuel injector pipes.
24. Remove upper valve cover attaching bolts, then the upper valve cover.
25. Reverse procedure to install, noting the following:
    a. If installing a new valve cover, remove injector line fittings, screws, PCV diaphragm and spring from old valve cover. Install components into new cover.
    b. If installing old valve cover, remove sealant from cover sealing surfaces.
    c. Apply a ⅛ inch bead of high bead sealant part No. 12378521, or equivalent, to valve cover sealing surface.
    d. Apply a bead of high bead sealant part No. 12378521, or equivalent, to area under injector wire harness on lower valve rocker cover surface.
    e. **Torque** valve cover bolts to 71 inch lbs., using sequence outlined in **Fig. 11.**

Upper Right

1. Remove upper intake manifold sight shield.
2. Remove air cleaner outlet duct from air cleaner and turbocharger. Cover turbocharger opening with tape.
3. Loosen charged air cooler outlet duct to intake manifold tube hose, then using a twisting motion, remove hose from intake manifold tube and pipe.

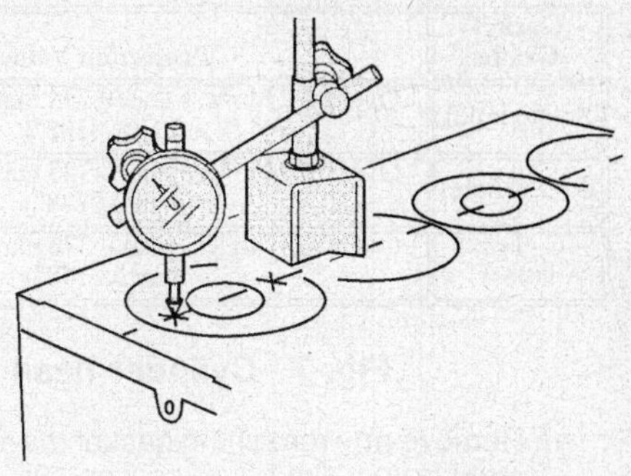

Fig. 6 Piston projection measurement

Cover opening on intake manifold tube and pipe with tape.

4. Remove outlet heater hose to alternator mounting bracket retaining bolts.
5. Remove fuel filter mounting bolts.
6. Disconnect fuel injection control module electrical connectors, then remove module from valve cover.
7. Position outlet heater hose aside and disconnect PCV hose from rocker arm cover.
8. Remove fuel injector lines.
9. Remove upper valve cover retaining bolts, then the valve cover.
10. Reverse procedure to install, noting the following:
    a. If installing a new valve cover, remove injector line fittings, screws, PCV diaphragm and spring from old valve cover. Install components into new cover.
    b. If installing old valve cover, remove sealant from cover sealing surfaces.
    c. Apply a ⅛ inch bead of high bead sealant part No. 12378521, or equivalent, to valve cover sealing surface.
    d. Apply a bead of high bead sealant part No. 12378521, or equivalent, to area under injector wire harness on lower valve rocker cover surface.
    e. **Torque** valve cover bolts to 71 inch lbs., using sequence outlined in **Fig. 11.**

Lower

1. Remove upper valve cover as outlined under "Valve Cover, Replace."
2. Disconnect injector wiring harness connectors.
3. Remove injector harness bracket bolts for both injector harnesses.
4. Remove encapsulated injector wire terminal nuts from each injector.
5. Remove both injector harnesses.
6. Remove lower valve rocker arm cover bolts, then the lower valve rocker arm cover.
7. Remove gasket and bolt grommets from valve cover.
8. Reverse procedure to install, noting the following:

Gasket Grade	Projection Value	Gasket Thickness
A (No hole)	Over 0.223 to less than 0.274 mm (0.0088 to less than 0.0108")	0.90 to 1.00 mm (0.0354 to 0.0394")
B (One hole)	Over 0.274 to less than 0.325 mm (0.0108 to less than 0.0128")	0.95 to 1.05 mm (0.0374 to 0.0413")
C (Two holes)	Over 0.325 to less than 0.376 mm (0.0128 to less than 0.0148")	1.00 to 1.10 mm (0.0394 to 0.0433")

GC1060101168000X

Fig. 7 Cylinder head gasket selection chart

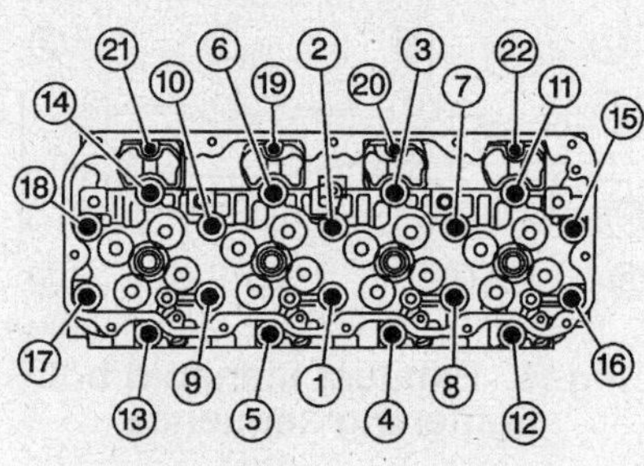

Fig. 8 Cylinder head bolt tightening sequence

a. Remove any remaining gasket material from valve cover sealing surfaces.
b. **Torque** valve cover bolts to 89 inch lbs., using sequence outlined in **Fig. 12.**

VALVE ADJUSTMENT

1. Remove engine harness clip from PCM cover.
2. **On models equipped with an automatic transmission,** proceed as follows:
   a. Remove Transmission Control Module (TCM) cover bolts, then lift TCM cover up and off of fan shroud.
   b. Loosen TCM electrical connector retaining bolts, then disconnect TCM electrical connectors.
   c. Remove TCM and cover and position connectors aside.
3. **On all models,** remove inlet hose from radiator and position aside.
4. Remove fan shroud plastic retainers, fan shroud attaching bolts and the fan shroud.
5. Remove drive belt, then the fan clutch.
6. Remove left and right upper valve covers as outlined under "Valve Cover, Replace."
7. Rotate engine in normal direction until No. 1 piston (right side front) is at TDC of compression stroke. Align mark on crankshaft balancer with pointer on engine, **Fig. 13.**
8. Loosen valve clearance adjustment screws for valves outlined in **Fig. 14.**
9. Insert a feeler gauge between tip of rocker arm and valve bridge.
10. Adjust valve clearance to .0112 inch with engine cold, then tighten adjusting screws.
11. Rotate engine in normal direction until No. 1 piston (right side front) is at TDC of the exhaust stroke. Align mark on crankshaft balancer with pointer on engine, **Fig. 13.**
12. Loosen valve clearance adjustment screws for valves outlined in **Fig. 15.**
13. Insert a feeler gauge between tip of rocker arm and valve bridge.
14. Adjust valve clearance to .0112 inch with engine cold, then tighten adjusting screws.
15. Install rocker arm covers, fan clutch and fan shroud.

VALVE LIFTERS

REPLACE

1. Remove cylinder head as outlined under "Cylinder Head, Replace."
2. Remove valve lifter guide hold down bracket bolts, then the hold down brackets.
3. Remove valve lifter guides and lifters.
4. Reverse procedure to install, noting the following:
   a. Clean lifter with suitable cleaning solvent and air dry.
   b. Measure roller protrusion from valve lifter body, **Fig. 16.** Protrusion should be .0354–.0394 inch, if protrusion is less than .0354 inch, replace lifter.
   c. Inspect lifter and roller for any scuffing or wear, replace as required.

CRANKSHAFT DAMPER

REPLACE

1. Raise and support vehicle.
2. Remove right front fender wheelhouse panel.
3. Remove starter motor and position aside.
4. Install flywheel holding tool No. J 44643, or equivalent, into starter opening to prevent engine from turning.
5. Lower vehicle.
6. Remove engine harness clip from PCM cover.
7. **On models equipped with an automatic transmission,** proceed as follows:
   a. Remove Transmission Control Module (TCM) cover bolts, then lift TCM cover up and off of fan shroud.
   b. Loosen TCM electrical connector retaining bolts, then disconnect TCM electrical connectors.
   c. Remove TCM and cover and position connectors aside.
8. **On all models,** remove inlet hose from radiator and position aside.
9. Remove upper fan shroud plastic retainers, fan shroud attaching bolts and the fan shroud.
10. Holding fan clutch in position, remove fan blade.
11. Lift lower fan shroud upward to disengage from clips, then remove lower fan shroud from vehicle.
12. Remove crankshaft damper (balancer) retaining bolt, then the damper.
13. Reverse procedure to install.

FRONT COVER

REPLACE

1. Remove upper intake manifold sight shield.
2. Drain engine coolant from radiator and cylinder block.
3. Remove right front fender wheelhouse panel.
4. Remove engine harness clip from PCM cover.
5. **On models equipped with an automatic transmission,** proceed as follows:
   a. Remove Transmission Control Module (TCM) cover bolts, then lift TCM cover up and off of fan shroud.
   b. Loosen TCM electrical connector retaining bolts, then disconnect TCM electrical connectors.
   c. Remove TCM and cover and position connectors aside.
6. **On all models,** remove inlet hose from radiator and position aside.
7. Remove upper fan shroud plastic retainers, attaching bolts and the fan shroud.
8. Remove drive belt, then the fan clutch.
9. Remove oil fill tube, then the thermostat housing crossover.
10. Remove crankshaft front oil seal as outlined under "Crankshaft Seal, Replace."
11. Remove water pump as outlined under "Water Pump, Replace."
12. Disconnect camshaft sensor electrical connector.
13. Remove camshaft sensor retaining bolt, then the sensor.
14. Disconnect crankshaft position sensor electrical connector.
15. Remove crankshaft position sensor mounting bolt and the sensor.
16. Remove crankshaft position sensor spacer mounting bolts, then the spacer.
17. Remove upper oil pan to front cover attaching bolts.
18. Remove bracket bolts and bracket for turbocharger outlet coolant pipe.
19. Remove front cover attaching bolts, then the front cover using seal cutter tool No. J 37228, or equivalent, to separate cover from cylinder block.
20. Reverse procedure to install, noting the following:
    a. Apply a ⅛ inch bead of high bead sealant part No. 12378521, or equivalent, to sealing surface between front cover and engine block, **Fig. 17.**
    b. Apply a ⅛ inch bead of high bead sealant part No. 12378521, or equivalent, to sealing surface between front cover and oil pan.
    c. Lubricate new front cover O-ring with clean engine oil.

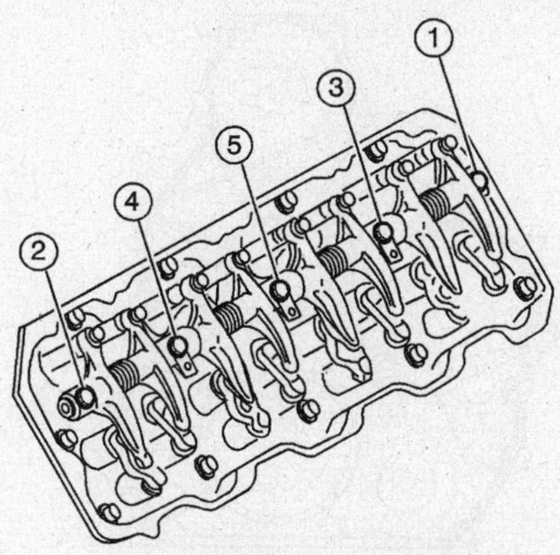

Fig. 9 Rocker arm shaft assembly bolt loosening sequence

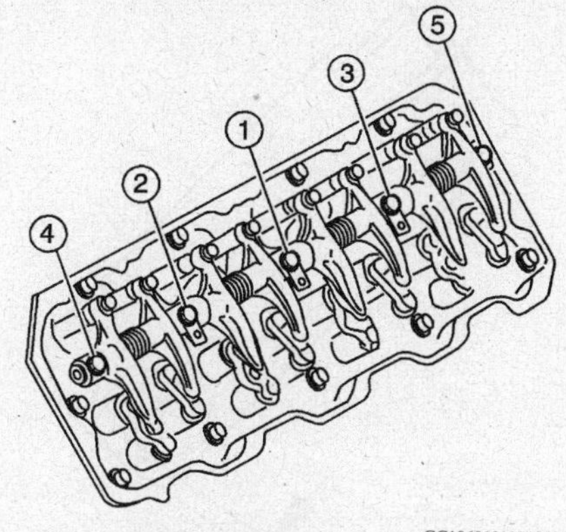

Fig. 10 Rocker arm shaft assembly bolt tightening sequence

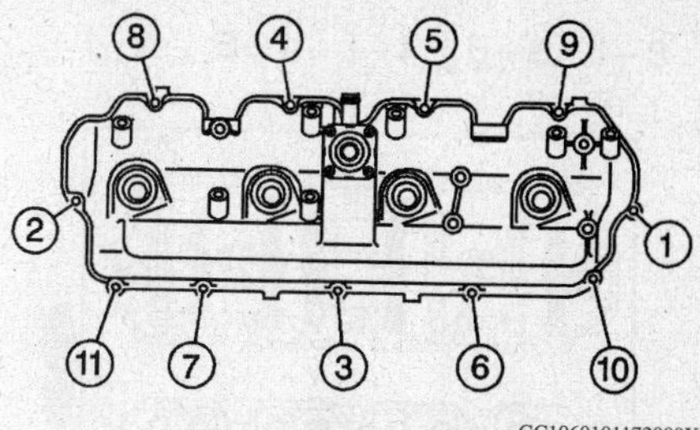

Fig. 11 Upper valve cover bolt tightening sequence

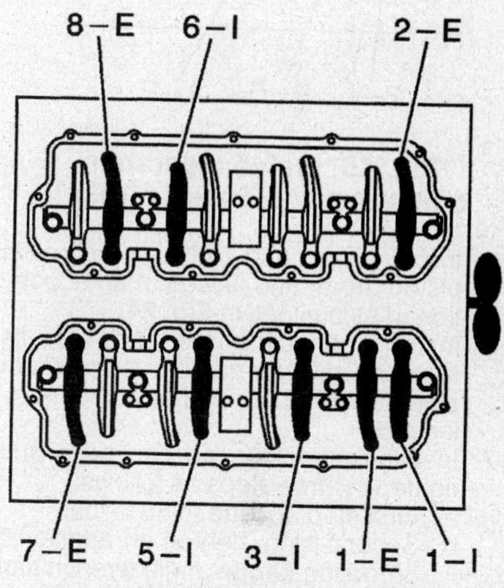

Fig. 14 Valve clearance adjustment (compression stroke)

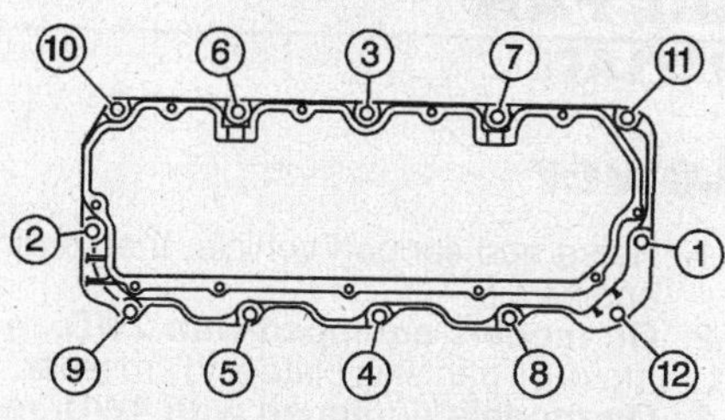

Fig. 12 Lower valve cover bolt tightening sequence

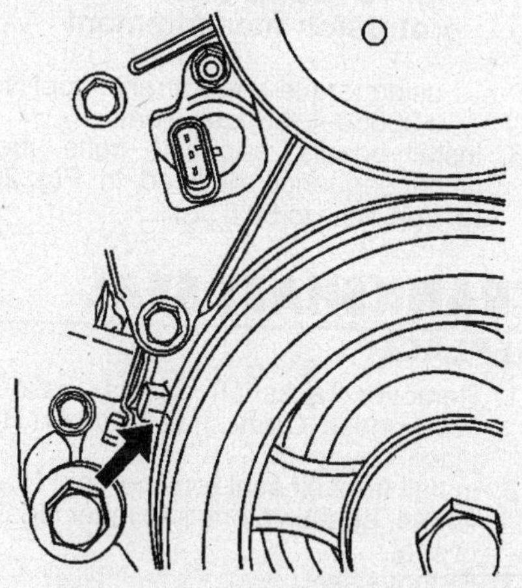

Fig. 13 TDC alignment mark

CAMSHAFT RELUCTOR

REPLACE

1. Remove engine front cover as outlined under "Front Cover, Replace."
2. Remove oil pump driven gear retaining nut and oil pump driven gear, **Fig. 18.**
3. Remove oil pump drive gear and crankshaft reluctor assembly, **Fig. 19. Do not remove crankshaft reluctor from oil pump drive gear. Reluctor is timed to gear and once removed the correct timing is lost.**
4. Remove camshaft reluctor retaining screws, then the camshaft reluctor.
5. Reverse procedure to install.

CRANKSHAFT RELUCTOR & OIL PUMP DRIVE GEAR

REPLACE

1. Remove engine front cover as outlined under "Front Cover, Replace."
2. Remove oil pump driven gear retaining nut and oil pump driven gear, **Fig. 18.**
3. Remove oil pump drive gear and crankshaft reluctor assembly.
4. Remove crankshaft reluctor to oil pump drive gear retaining bolts, then separate reluctor from drive gear.
5. Reverse procedure to install, noting the following:
   a. Install knock pins into oil pump drive gear to a height of .177–.217 inch (4.5–5.5 mm), **Fig. 20.**
   b. Ensure reluctor is aligned on oil pump drive gear knock pins.

CAMSHAFT

REPLACE

1. Remove lefthand and righthand cylinder heads as outlined under "Cylinder Head, Replace."
2. Remove valve lifter as outlined under "Valve Lifters."
3. Remove charged air cooler.
4. Recover A/C refrigerant as outlined in "Air Conditioning."
5. Remove A/C condenser.
6. Remove starter motor as outlined under "Starter Motor, Replace" in "Electrical" section.
7. Install flywheel holding tool No. J 44643, or equivalent, in starter motor opening.
8. Remove engine front cover as outlined under "Front Cover, Replace."
9. Remove oil pump driven gear retaining nut and oil pump driven gear, **Fig. 18.**
10. Remove oil pump drive gear and crankshaft reluctor assembly, **Fig. 19. Do not remove crankshaft reluctor from oil pump drive gear. Reluctor is timed to gear and once removed the correct timing is lost.**
11. Mount a suitable dial indicator on front of engine as outlined in **Fig. 21,** measure camshaft endplay. Endplay should be .002–.008 inch. If endplay exceeds .008 inch, replace camshaft gear or camshaft thrust plate.
12. Remove camshaft reluctor retaining screws and camshaft reluctor from camshaft gear.
13. Loosen camshaft gear bolt, then remove camshaft thrust plate bolts through openings in gear.
14. Remove camshaft with gear attached.
15. Remove camshaft gear attaching bolts, then separate gear from camshaft.
16. Reverse procedure to install, noting the following:
    a. Align camshaft gear to crankshaft gear as outlined in **Fig. 22.**
    b. Apply threadlocker part No. 12345493, or equivalent, to threads of camshaft thrust plate bolts.

PISTON & ROD ASSEMBLY

1. Select connecting rod bearing from chart, **Fig. 23.**
2. Position crankshaft so connecting rod journal is opposite piston and connecting rod assembly being installed.
3. Install connecting rod bearing inserts, then lubricate insert surface with clean engine oil.
4. Lubricate cylinder wall and piston rings with clean engine oil.

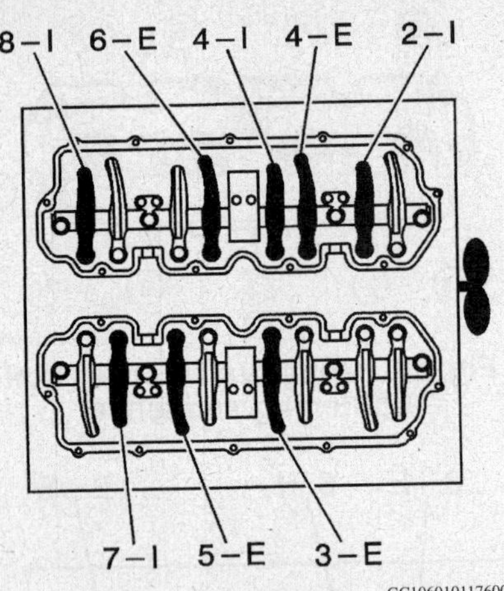

Fig. 15 Valve clearance adjustment (exhaust stroke)

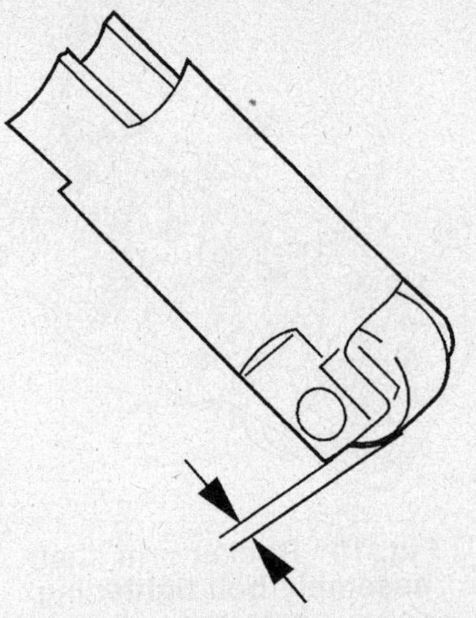

Fig. 16 Valve lifter roller protrusion measurement

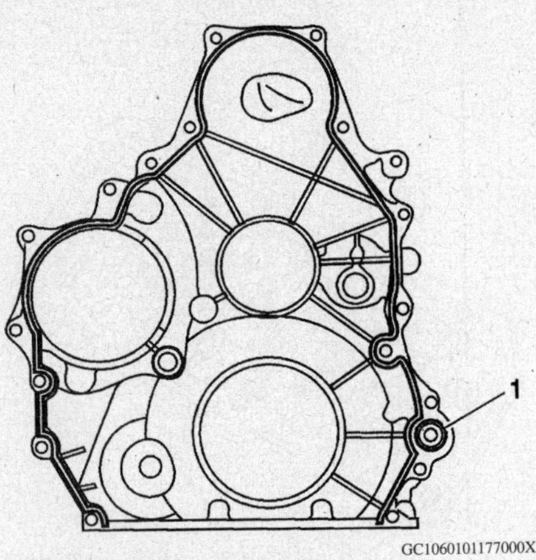

Fig. 17 Front cover sealant application

5. Install piston and rod assembly with piston front and inside marks positioned as outlined in **Fig. 24.**
6. Install connecting rod cap with its stamped cylinder number aligned with stamped cylinder number on connecting rod.
7. Install connecting rod cap bolts and tighten in three steps as follows:
   a. First step, **torque** to 36 ft. lbs.
   b. Second step, tighten an additional 30° using torque angle wrench tool No. J 36660-A, or equivalent.
   c. Third step, tighten an additional 30° using torque angle wrench tool No. J 36660-A, or equivalent.

MAIN & ROD BEARINGS

Shell type bearings are used and if worn excessively, should be replaced. No attempt should be made to shim, file or otherwise take up worn bearings.

Main bearings are available in standard and undersides, refer to **Fig. 25** for main bearing selection.

1. Install upper crankshaft bearings into cylinder block. Bearing halves that are being inserted into main bearing saddle have a wide groove and oil hole in center of bearing, **Fig. 26.**
2. Install lower crankshaft bearings into cylinder block. Bearing halves that are being inserted into crankshaft main bearing caps do not have a wide groove or oil hole in center of bearing, **Fig. 27.**
3. Lubricate crankshaft bearing surfaces with clean engine oil, then install crankshaft.
4. Install No. 5 crankshaft bearing cap with lower thrust bearing, then the four remaining crankshaft bearing caps.
5. Install bearing cap bolts, then using sequence outlined in **Fig. 28,** tighten bolts in three steps as follows:
   a. First step, **torque** bolts to 72 ft. lbs.
   b. Second step, **torque** bolts to 97 ft. lbs.
   c. Third step, tighten an additional 30° using torque angle wrench tool No. J 36660-A, or equivalent.
6. Install bearing cap side bolts, then using sequence outlined in **Fig. 29, torque** bolts to 58 ft. lbs.

CRANKSHAFT SEAL

REPLACE

1. Remove crankshaft damper as outlined under "Crankshaft Damper, Replace."
2. Install front oil seal remover tool No. J 44644, or equivalent, into inner sleeve of seal.
3. Remove seal.
4. Reverse procedure to install.

CRANKSHAFT REAR OIL SEAL

REPLACE

1. Remove transmission as outlined under **MOTOR's "Domestic Transmission, In-Vehicle Service."**
2. Remove starter motor as outlined under "Starter Motor, Replace" in "Electrical" section.
3. Install flywheel holding tool No. J 44643, or equivalent, then remove flywheel to crankshaft attaching bolts and the flywheel.
4. Remove rear oil seal using seal removal tool No. J 44641, or equivalent.
5. Reverse procedure to install, noting the following:
   a. Coat crankshaft surface with clean engine oil.
   b. Lightly coat sealing area of new seal with engine oil or grease.
   c. Do not scratch or nick sealing edge.
   d. Use rear crankshaft oil seal installer tool No. J 44642, or equivalent.
   e. Using sequence outlined in **Fig. 30,** tighten flywheel bolts in three steps: First step, **torque** to 58 ft. lbs.; second step, tighten an additional 60°; third step, tighten an additional 60°. Ensure final tightening **torque** is at least 266 ft. lbs.

OIL PAN

REPLACE

Lower

1. Raise and support vehicle, then drain engine oil.
2. **On models equipped with 2WD,** remove oil pan skid plate and crossbar.
3. **On models equipped with 4WD,** remove crossbar.
4. **On all models,** disconnect oil level sensor electrical connector.
5. Remove lower oil pan attaching bolts and nuts.
6. Separate lower oil pan from crankcase, then remove lower oil pan.
7. Remove oil level sensor to oil retaining clip, then the sensor from oil pan.
8. Reverse procedure to install, noting the following:
   a. Inspect pan mating surface for dents or distortion.
   b. Apply ⅛ inch bead of sealant part No. 12378521, or equivalent, to oil pan mating surface.

Upper

1. Remove oil dipstick.
2. **On models equipped with 4WD,** remove differential carrier as outlined under "Differential Carrier, Replace" in "Front Wheel Drive" section.
3. **On all models,** remove transmission as outlined under **MOTOR's "Domestic Transmission, In-Vehicle Service."**
4. Remove starter motor as outlined under "Starter Motor, Replace" in "Electrical" section.
5. Install flywheel holding tool No. J 44643, or equivalent, then remove flywheel to crankshaft attaching bolts and the flywheel.
6. Remove battery cable bracket to upper oil pan attaching bolts. Position and secure cables aside.
7. **On models equipped with 4WD,** remove engine flywheel housing to upper oil pan bolts denoted by triangles outlined in **Fig. 31.**

Fig. 18 Oil pump driven gear removal

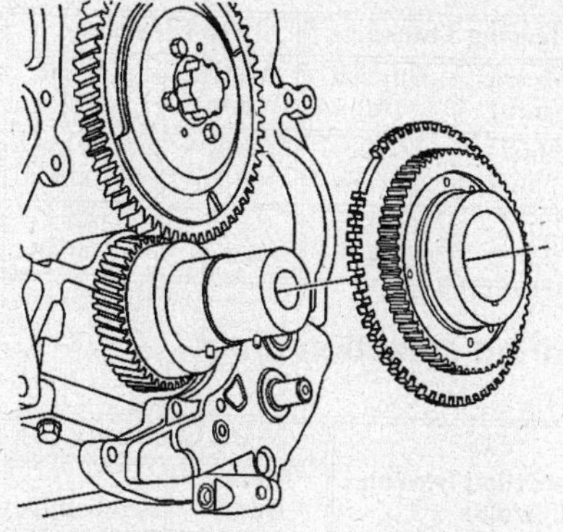

Fig. 19 Oil pump drive gear & crankshaft reluctor assembly removal

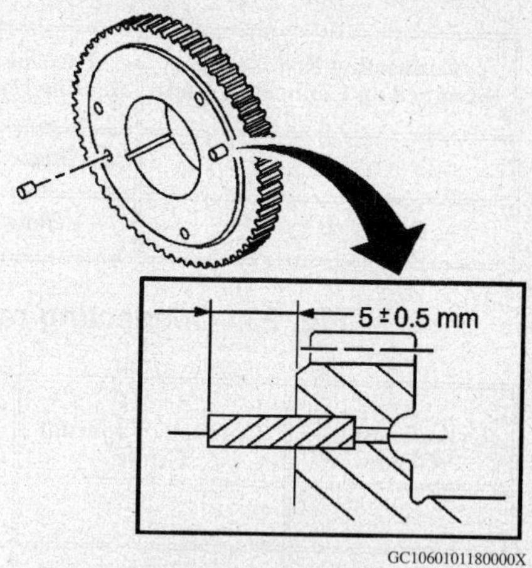

Fig. 20 Oil pump drive gear knock pin installation

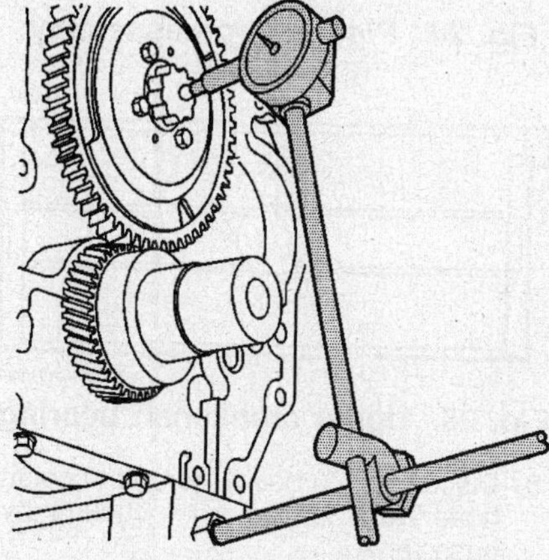

Fig. 21 Camshaft endplay measurement

8. **On models equipped with 2WD,** remove flywheel housing to engine block bolts, then the housing from engine.
9. **On all models,** remove upper oil pan bolts and brackets. Mark location of bracket bolts on oil pan for installation reference.
10. Separate upper oil pan from engine block.
11. **On models equipped with 4WD,** oil dipstick tube must be removed while lowering upper oil pan.
12. **On models equipped with 2WD,** oil pump pipe and screen retaining bolts have to be removed to remove upper oil pan. Remove upper oil pan and oil pump pipe.
13. **On all models,** reverse procedure to install, noting the following:
    a. Inspect upper oil pan for cracks, then the mating surfaces for damage or distortion.
    b. Apply 1/8 inch bead of sealant part No. 12378521, or equivalent, to oil pan mating surface.
    c. **Torque** oil pan bolts to 15 ft. lbs., using sequence outlined in **Fig. 32.**

OIL PUMP

REPLACE

1. Remove front cover as outlined under "Front Cover, Replace."
2. Remove upper oil pan as outlined under "Oil Pan, Replace."
3. Remove oil pump pipe and screen assembly retaining bolts and nuts.
4. Remove pipe and screen assembly, then the gasket.
5. Block crankshaft from turning using a suitable wooden handle, then remove oil pump drive gear nut and drive gear.
6. Remove crankshaft reluctor as outlined under "Crankshaft Reluctor & Oil Pump Drive Gear, Replace."
7. Remove oil pump retaining bolts, oil pump and O-ring seal.
8. Reverse procedure to install.

OIL PUMP SERVICE

1. Remove oil pump gear cover bolts and the cover.
2. Inspect clearance between gear teeth and oil pump housing using a suitable feeler gauge, **Fig. 33.** If clearance is less than .0049 inch or more than .0087 inch, replace oil pump.
3. Inspect clearance between side of gear and cover using a suitable feeler gauge and straightedge, **Fig. 34.** If clearance is less than .0025 inch or more than .0043 inch, replace oil pump.
4. Install cover and cover retaining bolts.

SERPENTINE DRIVE BELT

1. Rotate tensioner to release belt tension using a 1/2 inch breaker bar with a 5/8 inch socket placed on tensioner pulley, then remove belt.
2. Route belt over all pulleys except belt tensioner. Refer to **Fig. 35** for correct serpentine drive routing.
3. Rotate tensioner to released position and slide belt over tensioner pulley.
4. Ensure belt has correct groove tracking around each pulley.

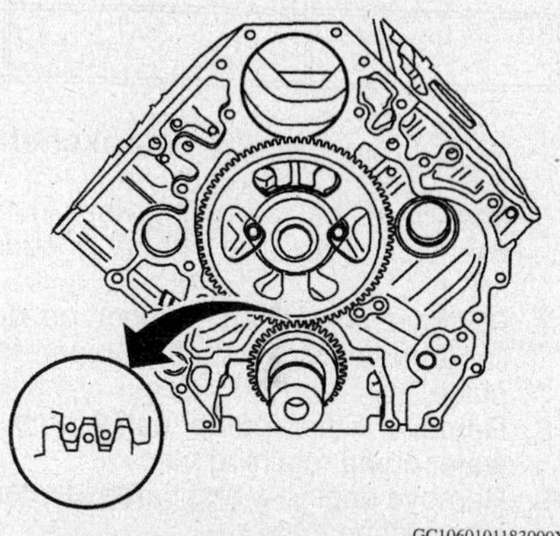

Fig. 22 Camshaft gear & crankshaft gear alignment

COOLING SYSTEM BLEED

This engine does not require a specified bleed procedure. After filling cooling system, run engine to operating temperature with radiator/pressure cap off. Air will automatically bleed through the cap opening.

THERMOSTAT

REPLACE

1. Drain cooling system.
2. Remove water outlet tube, then the fuel line bracket attaching bolt.
3. Remove thermostat housing cover retaining bolts, then the cover.
4. Remove thermostats and seals.
5. Reverse procedure to install.

WATER PUMP

REPLACE

1. Remove lefthand front fender wheelhouse inner panel
2. Drain engine coolant from radiator and engine block.
3. Remove thermostat housing crossover.
4. Remove drive belt as outlined under "Serpentine Drive Belt."
5. Remove upper fan shroud.
6. Remove fan clutch attaching bolts

Connecting Rod Grade (Stamped on Connecting Rod)	Use This Bearing Color	Bearing Thickness		Oil Clearance	
		Metric (mm)	English (in)	Metric (mm)	English (in)
A	Green	2.007 - 2.013	0.0790 - 0.0793	0.037 - 0.076	0.0015 - 0.0030
B	Yellow	2.011 - 2.017	0.0792 - 0.0794	0.037 - 0.076	0.0015 - 0.0030

GC1060101191000X

Fig. 23 Connecting rod bearing selection chart

Cylinder Block Grade	Crankshaft Journal Grade	Identification Bearing Color	Oil Clearance	
			Metric (mm)	English (in)
1	1	Black	0.041-0.068	0.0016-0.0027
1	2	Brown	0.039-0.065	0.0015-0.0026
2	1	Blue	0.043-0.070	0.0017-0.0028
2	2	Black	0.041-0.068	0.0016-0.0027

GC1060101192000X

Fig. 25 Crankshaft bearing selection chart

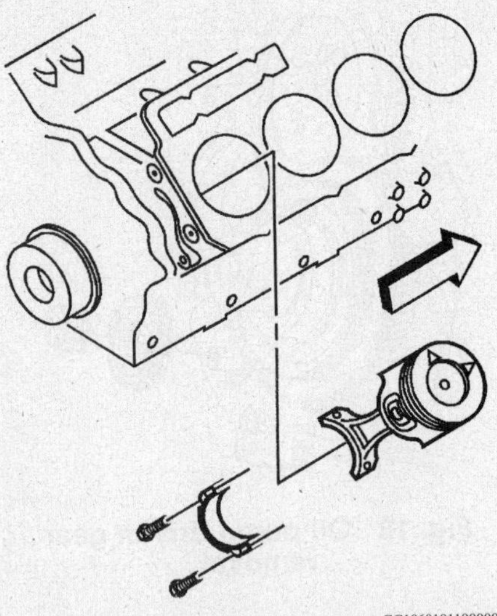

GC1060101190000X

Fig. 24 Piston & rod assembly installation

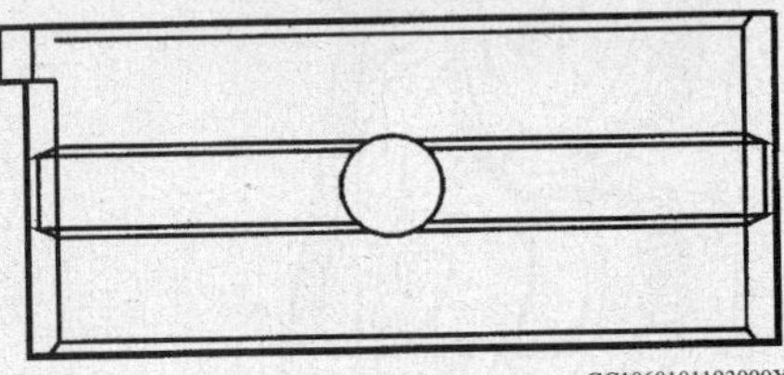

GC1060101193000X

Fig. 26 Upper crankshaft bearing

from rear of fan using fan clutch wrench tool No. J 41240-5A, or equivalent.

7. Remove crankshaft damper as outlined under "Crankshaft Damper, Replace."
8. Remove water pump outlet pipe to water pump retaining nuts.
9. Remove engine wiring harness retainer from inner stud.
10. Remove water pump attaching bolts, then the water pump, **Fig. 36.**
11. Reverse procedure to install.

RADIATOR

REPLACE

1. Drain coolant.
2. Remove radiator air upper baffle retainers, then the upper air baffle, **Fig. 37.**
3. Remove inlet and outlet hoses from radiator.
4. Lift lower fan shroud upward to disengage from clips, then remove lower fan shroud from vehicle.
5. Remove surge tank hose from radiator
6. Remove and discard radiator quick connect fittings as follows:
   a. Pull caps back along pipe, then holding one leg of retaining clip gently pull other end of clip from quick connect fitting with a small pick-type tool, **Fig. 38.**
   b. Rotate retaining clip out of quick connect fitting.
   c. Remove and discard retaining clip.
   d. Repeat procedure for all radiator quick connect fittings.
7. Gently pull transmission cooler pipes straight out of quick connect fittings.
8. Remove radiator retaining bolts, then the radiator from vehicle.
9. Reverse procedure to install.

TURBOCHARGER

REPLACE

1. Raise hood to service position by moving hood hinge bolts to service position.
2. Raise and support vehicle.
3. Remove exhaust pipe to exhaust outlet clamp.
4. **On models equipped with automatic transmission,** remove transmission fluid fill tube to bell housing attaching nuts, then position and secure fill tube to righthand side of vehicle.
5. **On all models,** remove lefthand exhaust heat shield to lower dash panel attaching nuts.
6. Remove lefthand exhaust pipe heat shield bolts, then position aside.
7. Remove lefthand exhaust pipe to manifold attaching bolts, then discard gasket.
8. Remove righthand exhaust pipe to manifold attaching bolts, then discard gasket.
9. Remove exhaust outlet shield lower attaching bolt.
10. Lower vehicle and remove upper intake manifold sight shield.
11. Drain engine coolant.
12. Remove air cleaner outlet duct from air cleaner and turbocharger.
13. Loosen both charged air cooler outlet duct hose clamps, then the hose from charge air cooler duct to intake manifold tube.
14. Remove charged air cooler inlet duct to turbocharger cool air outlet hose from turbocharger.
15. Disconnect A/C compressor clutch and A/C cutout switch electrical connectors.
16. Remove drive belt as outlined under "Serpentine Drive Belt."
17. Remove A/C compressor mounting bolts, then position and secure compressor and hoses aside.
18. Disconnect turbocharger inlet coolant hose from turbocharger coolant bypass valve.
19. Disconnect PCV hose from left valve rocker arm cover and position hose aside.
20. Remove wire connector from intake heater, then remove intake heater relay.
21. Remove three heat shield to turbocharger retaining bolts, then the heat shield.
22. Remove remaining exhaust outlet heat shield attaching bolts, then the heat shield.
23. Remove exhaust outlet retaining bolts and nuts, then position outlet aside to access turbocharger bolts.
24. Remove and discard exhaust outlet gasket, **Fig. 39.**
25. Remove righthand exhaust pipe to turbocharger bolts, then the exhaust pipe and gasket. Discard gasket.
26. Position exhaust outlet aside to access lefthand exhaust pipe.
27. Remove lefthand exhaust pipe heat shield, then the exhaust pipe and gasket from turbocharger. Discard gasket.
28. Remove turbocharger oil supply hose eye bolt and washers, then position oil supply hose aside, **Fig. 40.**
29. Remove turbocharger oil drain pipe retaining nuts from flywheel housing.
30. Remove turbocharger mounting bolts, then the turbocharger with oil drain pipe attached.
31. Reverse procedure to install.

Fig. 27 Lower crankshaft bearing

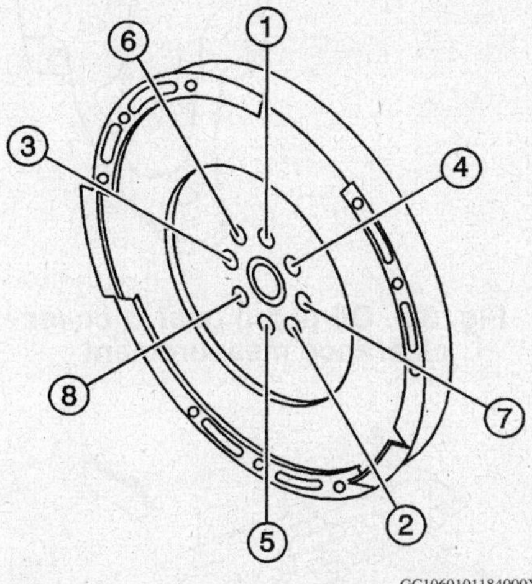

Fig. 30 Flywheel bolt tightening sequence

FUEL PUMP

REPLACE

1. Loosen fuel filler cap to relieve fuel system pressure.
2. Raise and support vehicle.
3. Disconnect transfer pump electrical connector.
4. Clean fuel pipe connections and surrounding area to prevent fuel contamination.
5. Disconnect both fuel pipes from pump.
6. Slide pump from frame mounted bracket, then cap lines to prevent contamination.
7. Reverse procedure to install.

INJECTION PUMP

REPLACE

1. Remove air intake duct, then drain engine coolant.
2. Remove upper and lower fan shrouds.
3. Remove fan blade from fan clutch.
4. Remove drive belt as outlined under "Serpentine Drive Belt."
5. Remove drive belt tensioner bolt, then the tensioner.
6. Remove positive battery cable junction box and bracket retaining bolt, then position box and bracket aside.
7. Remove A/C compressor and power steering pump mounting bolts, then with hoses attached position compressor and pump aside.
8. Remove oil filler tube.
9. Remove A/C compressor and power steering pump bracket mounting bolts, then the bracket from engine block.

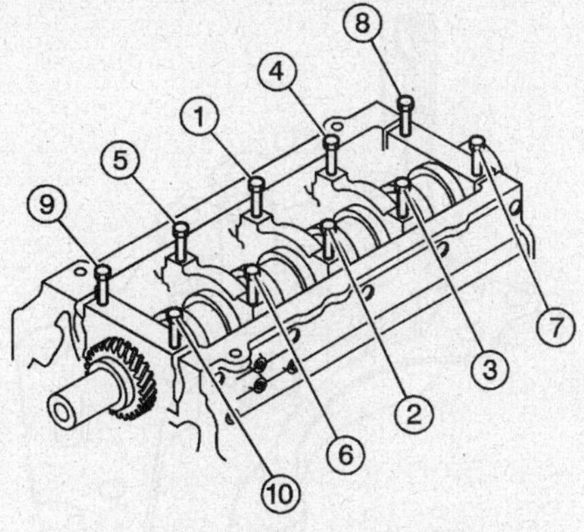

Fig. 28 Bearing cap bolt tightening sequence

10. Remove alternator and thermostat housing bracket.
11. Disconnect wiring, then remove fuel test port.
12. Remove PCV catch tank from bracket and bolt holding lower line, position tank and line aside.
13. Remove alternator bracket, then the turbo cooling return hose.
14. Remove upper radiator hose from outlet pipe, then the bracket support bracket from valve cover and position aside.
15. Remove wiring support bracket retaining bolt from thermostat housing.
16. Remove two ground wires from engine block and disconnect the following electrical connectors:
    a. Injection pump connector.
    b. PDU module connectors.
    c. Fuel filter assembly connectors.
    d. MAP sensor connector.
    e. Camshaft sensor connector.
    f. Crankshaft sensor connector.
17. Flip wire harness and harness tray towards back and set aside.
18. Remove heater pipe bolt and disconnect temperature sensor electrical connector from thermostat housing.
19. Remove air intake and water crossover pipes.
20. Remove hose to turbo water feed line.
21. Disconnect all high pressure fuel lines, then remove supply pipe and hose from fuel injection pump and function blocks.
22. Remove function block.
23. Disconnect fuel pressure regulator harness connector.
24. Remove fuel return hose from injection pump.
25. Remove fuel injection pump to engine block and front cover attaching bolts.
26. Remove fuel injection pump by using two suitable screwdrivers to lift pump towards rear of engine, keep pump straight during removal.
27. Reverse procedure to install.

FUEL FILTER

REPLACE

1. Install a suitable hose onto fuel filter housing water drain, then drain as

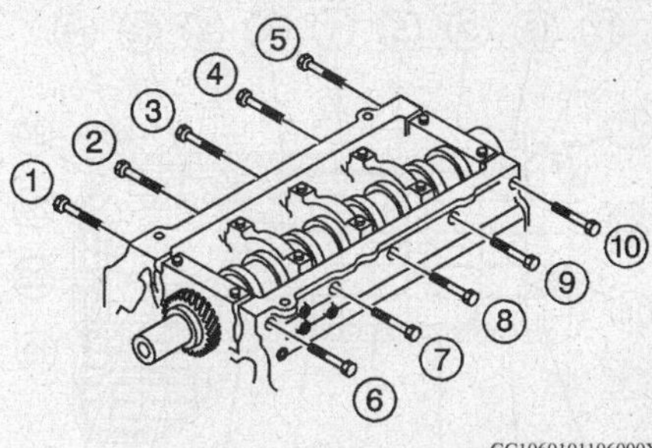

Fig. 29 Bearing cap side bolt tightening sequence

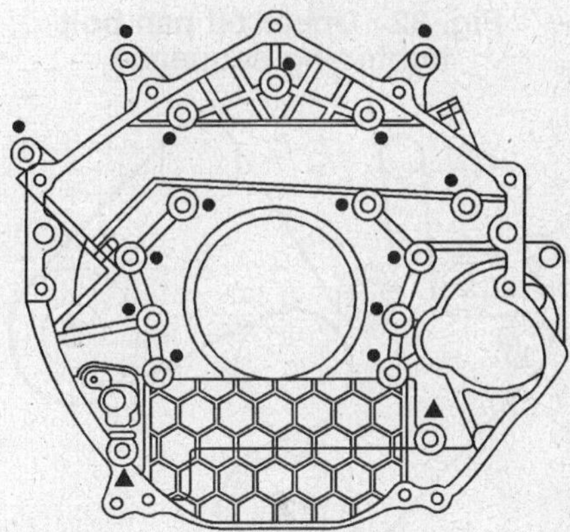

Fig. 31 Flywheel housing to upper oil pan bolts. Models w/4WD

much fuel as possible from housing.

2. Spin fuel filter housing from water in fuel sensor.
3. Reverse procedure to install.

GLOW PLUG SYSTEM

Description

The system consists of an glow plug relay (Federal emissions) or controller (California emissions) assembly, glow plugs, fuel heater and a Wait To Start lamp.

System Operation

Normal system operation is as follows:

1. Key-On/Engine Not Running and at room temperature:
2. Glow plugs energize (turn on) for approximately 1–16 seconds.
3. If engine is cranked during or after above sequence, glow plugs may cycle on and off after engine control switch is returned from the crank position, whether engine starts or not. Engine does not have to be operating to terminate glow plug cycling.
4. Glow plug initial on time will vary based on system voltage and temperature.

System Diagnosis

Refer to **Fig. 41** for glow plug system circuit diagnosis.

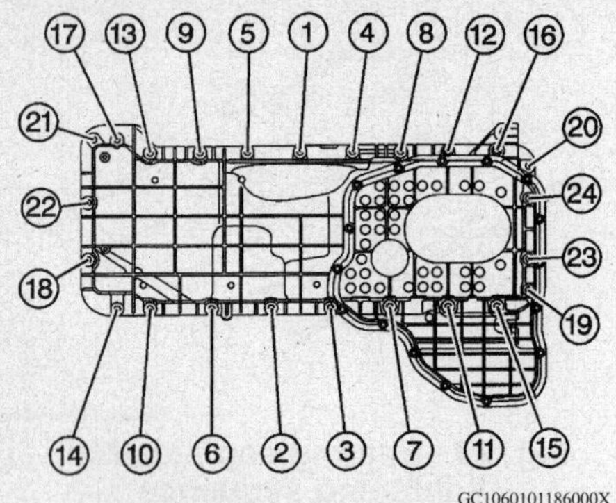

Fig. 32 Upper oil pan bolt tightening sequence

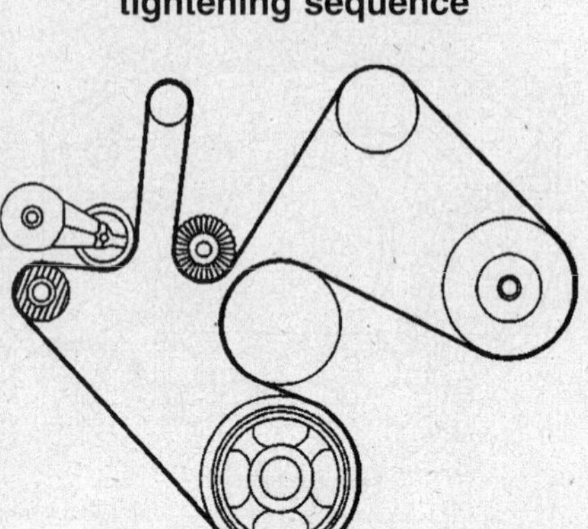

Fig. 35 Serpentine drive belt routing

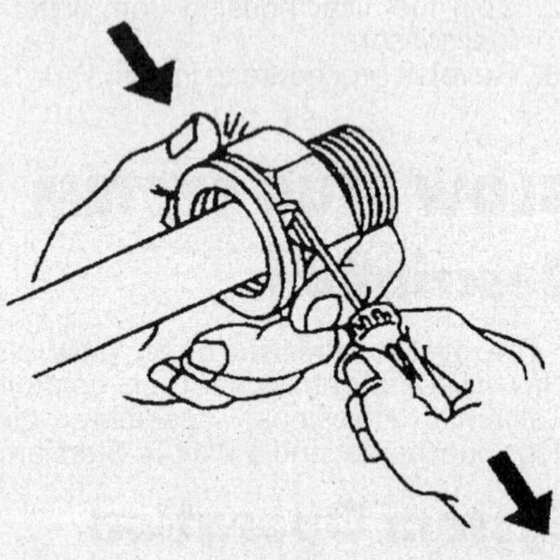

Fig. 38 Quick connect fitting removal

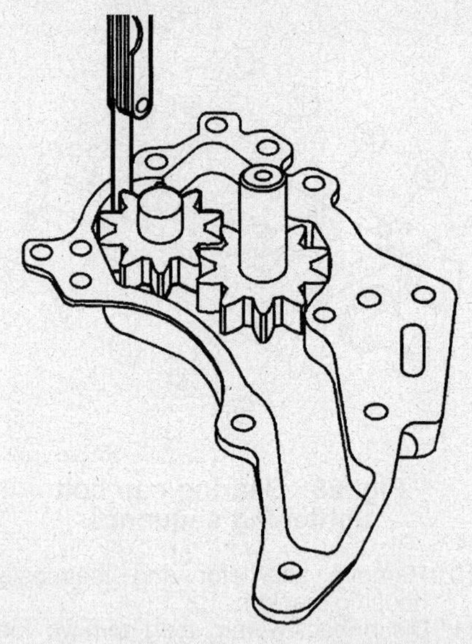

Fig. 33 Oil pump gear & housing clearance measurement

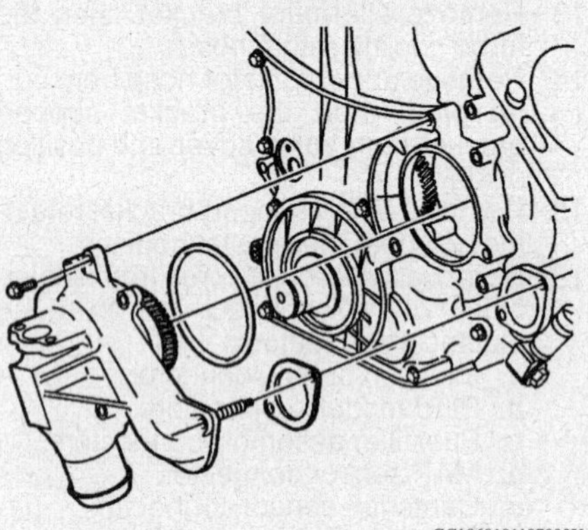

Fig. 36 Water pump removal

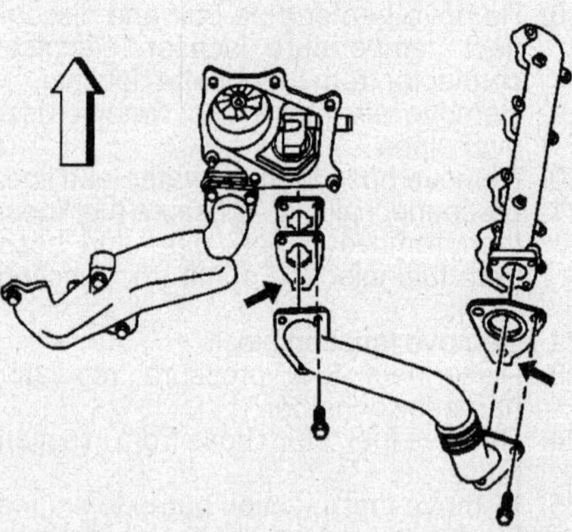

Fig. 39 Exhaust pipe removal

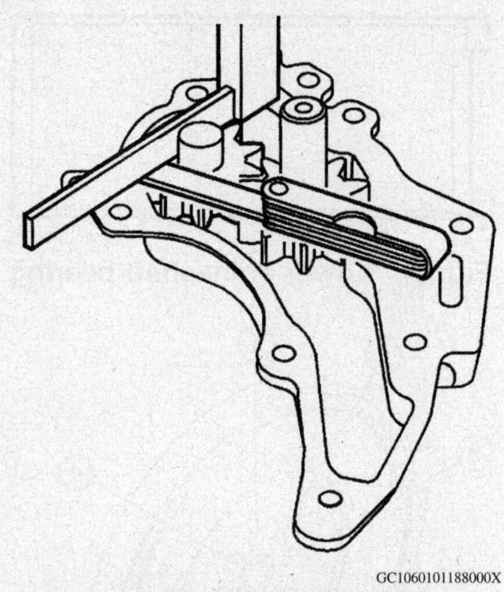

Fig. 34 Oil pump gear & cover clearance measurement

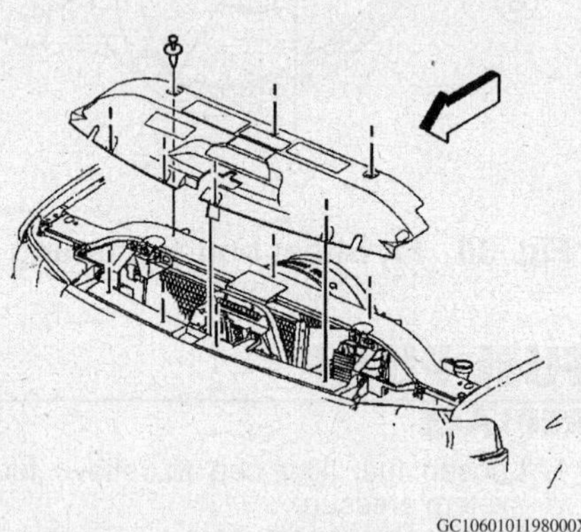

Fig. 37 Radiator upper baffle removal

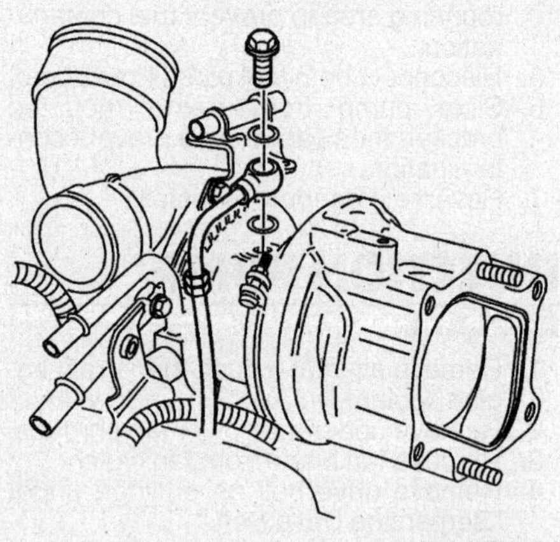

Fig. 40 Turbocharger removal

Circuit Description

The glow plug system is used to assist in providing the heat required to begin combustion during engine starting at cold ambient temperatures. The glow plugs are heated before and during cranking, as well as during the engine operation. The engine control module (ECM) controls the glow plug ON times by monitoring coolant temperatures and glow plug voltage. This system check will check the glow plugs and the glow plug feed circuit coming from the relay/controller.

Diagnostic Aids

If the glow plug relay or controller is stuck in the ON position, check for proper operation of the glow plugs. When the glow plugs are commanded ON by the scan tool, an internal PCM timer protects the glow plugs from damage by cycling them ON for 3 seconds and then OFF for 12 seconds. Most glow plug system failures are covered by DTC P0380. If no DTCs are stored, the vehicle is hard to start and white smoke is present during cranking or after the vehicle is started, the most likely cause of failure is the glow plugs.

Test Description

The numbers below refer to the numbers on the diagnostic table.

1. This step will make sure the Diagnostic System Check-Engine Controls is performed.
2. This step will make sure there are no other DTCs stored that will affect the operation of the glow plug system.
3. This step will check each glow plug for an open.
4. This step will check each glow plug feed circuit for an open.

Step	Action	Yes	No
1	Are DTCs P0117, P0118, P0380 stored as history or current codes?	Go to Diagnostic Trouble Code (DTC) List	Go to Step 3

GC1060101200010X

Fig. 41 Glow plug system diagnosis (Part 1 of 2)

Step	Action	Yes	No
2	1. Turn OFF the ignition. 2. Disconnect all the glow plugs. 3. With a test lamp connected to battery voltage, probe the spade terminal on each glow plug. Do all glow plugs illuminate the test lamp?	Go to Step 3	Go to Step 8
3	1. Turn ON the ignition, with the engine OFF. 2. Verify the glow plugs are still disconnected. 3. Probe each glow plug supply voltage circuit with a test lamp connected to ground. 4. With a scan tool, command the glow plugs ON. Does each circuit illuminate the test lamp?	Go to Step 4	Go to Step 9
4	Does the test lamp illuminate all the time for each glow plug terminal (even when the glow plugs are not commanded ON)?	Go to Step 5	Go to Step 10
5	1. Disconnect the glow plug supply voltage connection from the glow plug relay. 2. Probe each glow plug terminal with a test lamp connected to ground. Does the test lamp illuminate for all terminals?	Go to Step 6	Go to Step 7
6	Repair the short to voltage on the glow plug supply voltage circuit. Did you complete the repair?	Go to Step 10	--
7	Replace the glow plug relay/controller. Did you complete the replacement?	Go to Step 10	--
8	Replace all glow plugs that do not turn ON the test lamp. Did you complete the replacement?	Go to Step 10	--
9	Repair open in each circuit that does not turn ON the test lamp? Did you complete the repair?	Go to Step 10	--
10	Operate vehicle within the conditions under which system was noted. Does system operate properly?	System OK	Go to Step 1

GC1060101200020X

Fig. 41 Glow plug system diagnosis (Part 2 of 2)

TIGHTENING SPECIFICATIONS

Year	Component	Torque Ft. Lbs.
2002–06	A/C Compressor Mounting Bolt	37
	Auxiliary Alternator Bracket Mounting Bolt	37
	Auxiliary Alternator Mounting Bolt	37
	Auxiliary Battery To Engine Ground Bolt	25
	Bell Housing	30
	Bypass Pipe To Water Pump Bolt	15
	Camshaft Gear	173
	Camshaft Position Sensor Bolt	89②
	Camshaft Reluctor Bolt	80②
	Camshaft Thrust Plate	17
	Charged Air Cooler Bolts	15
	Clutch Bolts	30
	Connecting Rod Cap Nuts	①
	Coolant Duct To Flywheel Housing Nuts	15
	Coolant Duct To Flywheel Housing Nuts	15
	Cooling Fan Pulley Bolts	30
	Crankshaft Balancer Bolt	278
	Crankshaft Bearing Cap Bolts	③
	Crankshaft Damper	278
	Crankshaft Position Sensor	89②
	Crankshaft Reluctor Bolt	71②
	Crossbar Bolts	74
	Cylinder Block Coolant Drain Plugs	13
	Cylinder Head	④
	Drive Belt Tensioner Bolt	30
	Engine Coolant Heater	18
	Engine Coolant Temperature Sensor	24
	Engine Front Cover To Engine Block	15
	Engine Mount To Engine	44
	Engine Mount To Frame Bracket	50
	Engine Mount Through Bolt	55
	Engine Protection Shield	15
	Engine Oil Level Sensor	80②
	Engine Wiring Harness Ground Wire Bolt	25
	Exhaust Heat Shield	80②
	Exhaust Manifold	25
	Exhaust Manifold Pipe Clamp	30
	Exhaust Outlet Heat Shield	71②
	Exhaust Outlet Bolt	39
	Exhaust Pipe Bolts	39
	Fan Shroud	53②
	Flywheel	⑤
	Flywheel Housing To Engine Block	72
	Flywheel Housing To Upper Oil Pan	37
	Front Cover To Block	15
	Fuel Filter Bracket	15
	Fuel Hose Bracket To Valve Cover	15
	Fuel Injector Control Module	89②
	Fuel Rail Assembly	18
	Fuel Return Pipe Eye Bolt	11
	Fuel Supply Pump Assembly To Cylinder Block	15
	Glow Plugs	13
	Glow Plug Relay Bracket	15
	Ground Strap To LH Cylinder Head	18
	Hood Hinge Bolts	18

TIGHTENING SPECIFICATIONS—Continued

Year	Component	Torque Ft. Lbs.
2002–06	Hydraulic Lifter Guide Plate Clamp	19
	Idler Pulley	32
	Inlet Heater Pipe To Thermostat Housing	15
	Injector Bracket	37
	Injector Harness Bracket	80②
	Intake Heater	37
	Intake Manifold	⑥
	Intake Manifold Tube	80②
	Injection Pump	15
	Injection Pump Gear	17
	Injection Pump High Pressure Lines	40
	Lifting Bracket	40
	Main Bearing Cap Bolts	④
	Oil Fill Adapter Bolt	47
	Oil Fill Neck Nuts	17
	Oil Gallery Plugs	25
	Oil Pan	⑦
	Oil Pan Drain Plug	62
	Oil Pressure Relief Valve	30
	Oil Pump	15
	Oil Pump Cover	15
	Oil Pump Driven Gear	74
	Oil Pump Pipe & Screen	18
	Outlet Heater Hose Bracket To Fuel Filter Bracket	80②
	Outlet Heater Hose Bracket To Alternator Mounting Bracket	18
	PCV Diaphragm Cover	35②
	Power Steering Pump Front Bracket To Pump Mounting Bracket	34
	Power Steering Pump Mounting Bracket	34
	Power Steering Pump To Front Bracket	37
	Power Steering Pump To Rear Bracket	37
	Radiator Bolts	18
	Rocker Arm Cover	71⑧
	Starter Motor	58
	Thermostat Housing Bolts	15
	Thermostat Housing Crossover Bolts	15
	Torque Converter To Flywheel	44
	Transmission To Engine Studs/Nuts	37
	Turbocharger Bolt	80
	Turbocharger Coolant Bypass Valve	44
	Turbocharger Coolant Outlet Pipe Bracket To MAP Sensor Nut	80②
	Turbocharger Coolant Outlet Pipe Bracket To Front Cover	15
	Turbocharger Heat Shield	80②
	Turbocharger Inlet Duct To Turbocharger	80②
	Turbocharger Oil Supply Hose Eye Bolts	31
	Turbocharger Oil Return Pipe	15
	Upper Intake Manifold Sight Shield	80②
	Valve Adjusting Screw Nut	16
	Valve Lifter Guide Hold-Down Bolt	97②
	Valve Rocker Arm Cover	71⑧
	Valve Rocker Arm Shaft Bracket Bolt	30

Continued

TIGHTENING SPECIFICATIONS—Continued

Year	Component	Torque Ft. Lbs.
2002–06	Water Outlet Tube To Thermostat Housing Crossover	15
	Water Outlet Tube To Valve Rocker Arm Cover	15
	Water Pump To Engine	15
	Water Pump To Water Pump Housing	15
	Water Pump Outlet Pipe To Water Pump	18

① — Refer to "Piston & Rod Assembly" for tightening procedure.

② — Inch lbs.

③ — Refer to "Main & Rod Bearings" for tightening procedure.

④ — Refer to "Cylinder Head, Replace" for tightening procedure.

⑤ — Refer to "Crankshaft Rear Oil Seal, Replace" for tightening procedure.

⑥ — Refer to "Intake Manifold, Replace" for tightening procedure.

⑦ — Refer to "Oil Pan, Replace" for tightening procedure.

⑧ — Tighten two times.

8.1L Gasoline Engine

NOTE: For Procedures Not Found In This Section, Refer To The "8.1L Gasoline Engine" Section Located In The "Express, Savana & P Series" Chapter.

NOTE: On Air Bag Equipped Models, Refer To "Air Bag System Precautions" Located In The Front Of This Manual For System Disarming & Arming Procedures.

NOTE: Refer To "Computer Relearn Procedures" Located In The Front Of This Manual When Battery Power To The Computer Has Been Interrupted.

NOTE: Prior To Performing Any Service Operations Listed In This Section, Consult The "Technical Service Bulletins" In This Section For Related Information.

INDEX

PRECAUTIONS

Air Bag Systems

Refer to "Air Bag System Precautions" in the front of this manual for system disarming and arming procedures.

Battery Ground Cable

Prior to service disconnect battery ground cable and isolate.

Fuel System Pressure Relief

Always release residual fuel system pressure prior to disconnecting fuel lines or hoses.

1. Loosen fuel filler cap.
2. Remove fuel injector sight shield.
3. Connect suitable fuel pressure gauge to fuel pressure valve and install bleed hose into suitable container.
4. Open valve and bleed system pressure.

COMPRESSION PRESSURE

When inspecting compression, the lowest cylinder must be within 70% of the highest and no cylinder should be less than 100 psi. Perform compression test with engine at operating temperature, all spark plugs removed and throttle wide open.

ENGINE MOUNT

REPLACE

1. Support engine assembly with suitable jack stands.
2. Remove front engine mount through bolt and nut.
3. Raise engine enough to access engine mount.
4. Remove engine mount assembly mounting bolts, nuts and washers.
5. Remove engine mount assembly from front lefthand side of engine.
6. Reverse procedure to install.

ENGINE

REPLACE

1. Raise hood, then support hood assembly at front and rear.
2. Place protective covering over cowl and fenders.
3. Remove hood ground strap, then disconnect hood lamp electrical connector.
4. Remove hood hinge to hood link assembly attaching bolt.
5. Lower and support hood.
6. Remove outboard sections from each end of cowl vent grill panel.
7. Remove pivot bolts, then the hood assembly.
8. Relieve fuel system pressure as outlined under "Precautions."
9. Remove air intake duct from throttle body, then the air cleaner assembly.
10. Disconnect ignition wires from coils.
11. Remove ignition coil attaching bolts, then the coils from valve rocker arm covers.
12. Disconnect fuel supply lines from rear of engine.
13. Drain cooling system and recover A/C refrigerant as outlined in "Air Conditioning" chapter.
14. Remove A/C compressor from mounting bracket and position aside.
15. Rotate drive belt tensioner arm with a suitable 3/8 inch drive and remove drive belt.
16. Remove fan clutch from water pump.
17. Remove radiator from vehicle.
18. Disconnect throttle body actuator control electrical connectors.
19. Disconnect engine vacuum lines. Mark lines for installation reference.
20. Disconnect EGR valve electrical connector, then remove EGR valve and adapter.
21. Remove alternator from mounting

bracket and position aside.
22. Disconnect engine electrical harness and position aside.
23. Raise and support vehicle.
24. Remove hydraulic hoses from power steering pump.
25. **On models equipped with 4WD,** proceed as follows:
    a. Remove transfer case shield.
    b. Remove propeller shaft boot clamp at transfer case.
    c. Remove bolts and yoke retainers from front axle pinion yoke.
    d. Disconnect propeller shaft from front axle pinion yoke. Wrap bearing caps with suitable tape to prevent loss of bearing rollers. **Do not attempt to remove shaft by pounding on yoke ears or using a tool between yoke and universal joint. Injection joints may fracture and cause premature failure.**
26. **On all models,** remove ground wires from engine block.
27. Remove starter motor, then the flywheel inspection cover.
28. Remove torque converter to flywheel bolts.
29. Remove exhaust pipe to manifold retaining bolts, then the exhaust pipe from manifold.
30. Remove transmission to engine attaching bolts.
31. **On models equipped with auxiliary oil cooler,** remove cooler lines from cylinder block.
32. **On all models,** lower vehicle.
33. Support transmission with a suitable jack.
34. Attach engine lifting brackets tool No. J 36857, or equivalent, to rear of right cylinder head and front of left cylinder head.
35. Remove engine mount through bolts.
36. Remove engine from vehicle using suitable lifting device.
37. Remove engine oil fill tube, then the oil dipstick and tube.
38. Remove alternator mounting bracket from cylinder block.
39. Remove A/C compressor and power steering mounting bracket from cylinder head.
40. Reverse procedure to install.

INTAKE MANIFOLD

REPLACE

1. Remove EGR pipe, EGR valve and adapter.
2. Remove mounting bolt and sight shield.
3. Disconnect MAP sensor electrical connector, then remove mounting bolt and MAP sensor.
4. Disconnect EVAP purge solenoid, TP sensor and ETC electrical connectors.
5. Remove engine wiring harness bracket studs and position wiring harness aside.
6. Remove secondary Air Injection (AIR) crossover pipe.
7. Disconnect fuel injector electrical connectors. Mark fuel injector electrical connectors for installation reference.
8. Remove fuel rail mounting bolts.

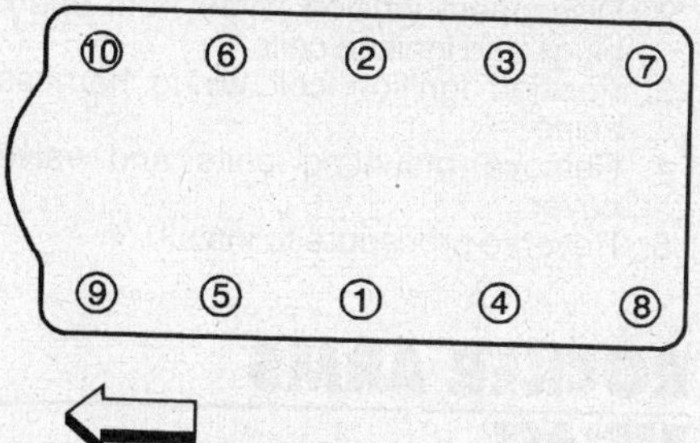

Fig. 1 Intake manifold bolt tightening sequence

9. Carefully remove fuel rail from intake manifold. Cap fittings and holes to prevent contamination.
10. Remove intake manifold to cylinder head mounting bolts.
11. Remove intake manifold, gaskets and seals from cylinder head.
12. Reverse procedure to install, noting the following:
    a. Apply thread locking material part No. 12346004, or equivalent, to threads of intake manifold bolts.
    b. Using sequence indicated in **Fig. 1,** tighten intake manifold bolts in three steps: First step, **torque** bolts to 18 inch lbs.; second step, **torque** bolts to 88 inch lbs.; third step, **torque** bolts to 106 inch lbs.

EXHAUST MANIFOLD

REPLACE

Lefthand

1. Remove secondary air injection pipe nut from fuel injection rail stud.
2. Remove secondary air injection pipe bolts from exhaust manifold.
3. Disconnect secondary air injection pipe from air injection pump pipe and remove secondary injection pipe.
4. Remove ignition wires from spark plugs and ignition coils.
5. Raise and support vehicle.
6. Remove mounting bolts, nuts and exhaust manifold heat shield.
7. Remove exhaust pipe to exhaust manifold mounting nuts.
8. Remove mounting nuts, center bolt, exhaust manifold and gasket.
9. Reverse procedure to install.

Righthand

1. Remove oil dipstick and tube from engine block.
2. Remove secondary air injection pipe nut from fuel injection rail stud.
3. Remove secondary air injection pipe bolts from exhaust manifold.
4. Disconnect secondary air injection pipe from air injection pump pipe and remove secondary injection pipe.
5. Remove secondary air injection pump pipe from cylinder head.
6. Remove ignition wires from spark plugs and ignition coils.
7. Remove EGR pipe bolts from EGR adapter plate.
8. Remove mounting nuts from exhaust manifold, bracket bolt and EGR pipe.
9. Raise and support vehicle.
10. Remove mounting bolts, nuts and exhaust heat shield.
11. Remove exhaust pipe to exhaust manifold mounting nuts.
12. Remove mounting bolts, nuts, exhaust manifold and gasket.
13. Reverse procedure to install.

CYLINDER HEAD

REPLACE

Lefthand

1. Drain cooling system into suitable container.
2. Relieve fuel system pressure as outlined under "Precautions."
3. Remove engine wiring harness and position aside.
4. Disconnect engine ground straps.
5. Rotate drive belt tensioner arm with suitable ⅜ inch drive and remove drive belt.
6. Remove coolant reservoir tank, air cleaner and fan shroud.
7. Remove heater hose pipe from alternator and oil fill tube from support bracket.
8. Remove support bracket from alternator bracket.
9. Remove mounting bolts and alternator from mounting bracket.
10. Remove accessory mounting bracket from engine block.
11. Remove intake manifold from cylinder heads as outlined under "Intake Manifold, Replace."
12. Remove water crossover pipe and bypass hose.
13. Remove drive belt tensioner bolt and tensioner.
14. Remove valve rocker arm cover as outlined under "Valve Cover, Replace."
15. Remove rocker arm as outlined under "Rocker Arm, Replace."
16. Remove pushrods from cylinder head. Keep pushrods in order, to ensure they are installed in original position.
17. Remove spark plugs from cylinder head.
18. Remove exhaust manifold as outlined under "Exhaust Manifold, Replace."
19. Remove mounting bolts, cylinder head and gasket.
20. Reverse procedure to install. Using sequence indicated in **Fig. 2,** tighten bolts as follows:
    a. **Torque** bolts to 22 ft. lbs., in sequence,
    b. **Torque** bolts to 22 ft. lbs., in sequence, again.
    c. Tighten bolts an additional 120° in sequence using torque angle wrench tool No. J-36660-A, or equivalent.
    d. Tighten bolts 1, 2, 3, 6, 7, 9, 10, 11, 14, 16 and 17 an additional 60° in sequence.
    e. Tighten bolts 4, 5, 12 and 13 an additional 30° in sequence.
    f. Tighten bolts 15 and 18 an additional 45°.

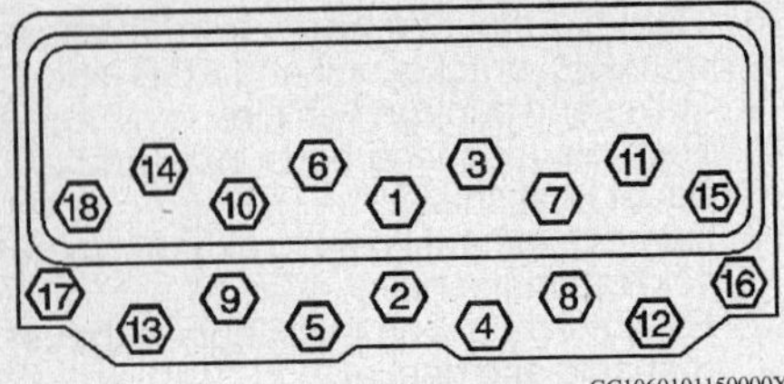

Fig. 2 Cylinder head tightening sequence

Righthand

1. Drain cooling system into suitable container.
2. Relieve fuel system pressure as outlined under "Precautions."
3. Remove engine wiring harness and position aside.
4. Disconnect engine ground straps.
5. Rotate drive belt tensioner arm with suitable ⅜ inch drive and remove drive belt.
6. Remove intake manifold from cylinder heads as outlined under "Intake Manifold, Replace."
7. Remove support bracket from alternator bracket.
8. Remove mounting bolts and alternator from mounting bracket.
9. Remove accessory mounting bracket from engine block.
10. Remove water crossover pipe and bypass hose.
11. Remove drive belt tensioner bolt and tensioner.
12. Remove valve rocker arm cover as outlined under "Valve Cover, Replace."
13. Remove rocker arm as outlined under "Rocker Arm, Replace."
14. Remove pushrods from cylinder head. Keep pushrods in order, to ensure they are installed in original positions.
15. Remove spark plugs from cylinder head.
16. Remove exhaust manifold as outlined under "Exhaust Manifold, Replace."
17. Remove mounting bolts, cylinder head and gasket.
18. Reverse procedure to install. Using sequence indicated in **Fig. 2,** tighten bolts as follows:
    a. **Torque** bolts to 22 ft. lbs., in sequence,
    b. **Torque** bolts to 22 ft. lbs., in sequence, again.
    c. Tighten bolts an additional 120° in sequence using torque angle wrench tool No. J-36660-A, or equivalent.
    d. Tighten bolts 1, 2, 3, 6, 7, 9, 10, 11, 14, 16 and 17 an additional 60° in sequence.
    e. Tighten bolts 4, 5, 12 and 13 an additional 30° in sequence.
    f. Tighten bolts 15 and 18 an additional 45°.

VALVE COVER

REPLACE

1. Remove air cleaner from throttle body.
2. Disconnect ignition wires from spark plugs and ignition coils.
3. Position ignition coil wiring harness aside.
4. Remove mounting bolts and valve cover.
5. Reverse procedure to install.

ROCKER ARMS

REPLACE

1. Remove valve rocker arm cover as outlined under "Valve Cover, Replace."
2. Remove rocker arm mounting nuts from cylinder head.
3. Remove rocker arms from cylinder head. Keep rocker arms in order, to ensure they are installed in original positions.
4. Reverse procedure to install.

HYDRAULIC LIFTERS

REPLACE

1. Remove intake manifold as outlined under "Intake Manifold, Replace."
2. Remove valve rocker covers as outlined under "Valve Cover, Replace."
3. Remove rocker arm as outlined under "Rocker Arms, Replace."
4. Remove pushrods from cylinder block. Keep pushrods in order, to ensure they are installed in original positions.
5. Remove mounting bolts, retainer and valve lifter guides.
6. Remove lifters one at time. Keep lifters in order, to ensure they are installed in original positions.
7. Reverse procedure to install. Lubricate valve lifter with clean engine oil.

CRANKSHAFT DAMPER

REPLACE

1. Remove upper fan shroud from radiator.
2. Rotate drive belt tensioner arm with suitable ⅜ inch drive and remove drive belt.
3. Raise and support vehicle.
4. Remove lower fan shroud from radiator.
5. Remove fan clutch from water pump.
6. Remove drive belt pulley from damper.
7. Disconnect starter motor electrical connectors.
8. Remove mounting bolts and starter motor.
9. Install flywheel holding tool No. J-42847, or equivalent, in place of starter.
10. Remove crankshaft bolt and washer from end of crankshaft.
11. Install crankshaft balancer protector button tool No. J-42846, or equivalent, onto end of crankshaft.
12. Remove crankshaft damper using crankshaft balancer puller tool No. J-38416, or equivalent.
13. Reverse procedure to install.

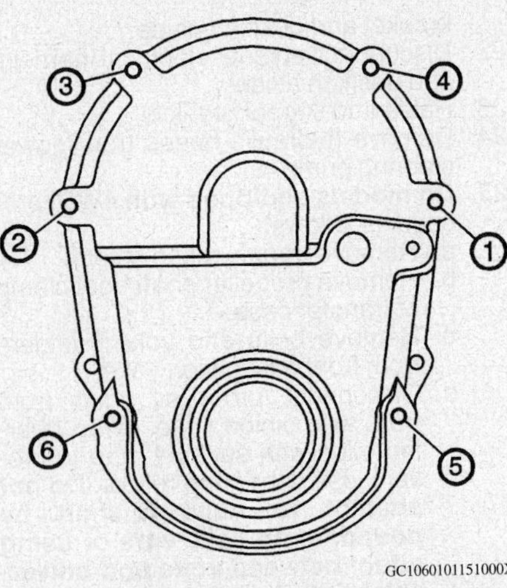

Fig. 3 Front cover bolt tightening sequence

FRONT COVER

REPLACE

1. Rotate drive belt tensioner arm with suitable ⅜ inch drive and remove drive belt.
2. Remove fan clutch from water pump.
3. Remove water pump as outlined under "Water Pump, Replace."
4. Disconnect electrical connector, then remove mounting bolt and camshaft position sensor.
5. Raise and support vehicle.
6. Remove crankshaft damper as outlined under "Crankshaft Damper, Replace."
7. Remove oil dipstick.
8. Drain engine oil from crankcase into suitable container.
9. Loosen remove oil pan mounting bolts. **Do not remove mounting bolts.**
10. Lower pan as required to allow clearance for front cover removal.
11. Remove mounting bolts, front cover and gasket.
12. Reverse procedure to install, noting the following:
    a. **Torque** front cover mounting bolts to 54 inch lbs., in sequence, **Fig. 3,**
    b. Final **torque** mounting bolts to 106 inch lbs., in sequence.
    c. Lubricate camshaft position sensor O-ring with clean engine oil.
    d. **Torque** oil pan mounting bolts to 18 ft. lbs., in sequence, **Fig. 4.**

TIMING CHAIN

REPLACE

1. Drain engine coolant into suitable container and remove coolant reservoir from radiator.
2. Remove crankshaft damper as outlined under "Crankshaft Damper, Replace."
3. Align timing marks on camshaft and crankshaft gears, **Fig. 5.**
4. Remove camshaft sprocket mounting bolts.

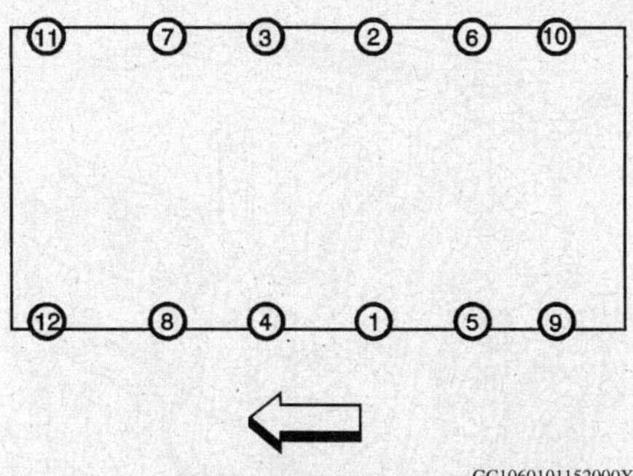

Fig. 4 Oil pan bolt tightening sequence

5. Remove timing chain and camshaft sprocket.
6. Reverse procedure to install. Align timing marks, **Fig. 5.**

CAMSHAFT

REPLACE

1. Remove air intake duct from throttle body.
2. Remove upper grill baffle from top of grill.
3. Rotate grill retainers ¼ turn counterclockwise with a suitable Phillips screwdriver.
4. Remove grill to latch support attaching screw.
5. Unsnap grill ends from fender, then remove grill from front of vehicle.
6. Recover A/C refrigerant from A/C system, then remove radiator and A/C condenser.
7. Remove intake manifold as outlined under "Intake Manifold, Replace."
8. Remove valve lifters as outlined under "Hydraulic Lifters, Replace."
9. Remove timing chain and camshaft sprocket as outlined under "Timing Chain, Replace."
10. Remove camshaft retainer attaching bolts, then the retainer.
11. Install three 81.25 X 100 mm bolts into camshaft. Using bolts as a handle, carefully pull camshaft out of cylinder block.
12. Reverse procedure to install. Coat camshaft lobes, journals and bearings with clean engine oil.

CRANKSHAFT SEAL

REPLACE

1. Remove crankshaft damper as outlined under "Crankshaft Damper, Replace."
2. Remove crankshaft front cover oil seal from front cover.
3. Reverse procedure to install. Coat oil seal with clean engine oil.

CRANKSHAFT REAR OIL SEAL

REPLACE

Removal

1. Remove transmission as outlined under **MOTOR's "Domestic Transmission, In-Vehicle Service."**
2. Remove flywheel to crankshaft mounting bolts and flywheel.
3. Install guide pins of crankshaft rear seal puller tool No. J-43320, or equivalent, into crankshaft, **Fig. 6.**
4. Insert self-drilling sheet metal screws through tool and into oil seal in crisscross pattern.
5. Tighten center bolt of tool to remove seal from crankshaft.

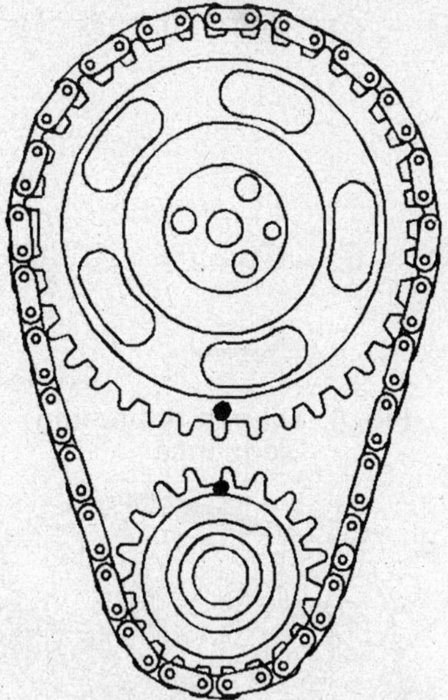

Fig. 5 Timing mark alignment

Installation

1. Apply light coat of clean engine oil onto seal.
2. Install seal onto rear seal installer tool No. J-42849, or equivalent.
3. Position seal installer tool onto crankshaft and thread mounting screws into tapped holes of crankshaft.
4. Tighten screws until seal is installed squarely over crankshaft.
5. Tighten center bolt on installation tool until it bottoms.
6. Remove tool, then install flywheel and transmission as outlined under **MOTOR's "Domestic Transmission, In-Vehicle Service."**

OIL PAN

REPLACE

1. Remove oil dipstick and tube from engine.
2. Raise and support vehicle, then drain engine oil.
3. **On models equipped with 4WD,** proceed as follows:
   a. Remove transfer case shield.
   b. Remove propeller shaft boot clamp at transfer case.
   c. Remove bolts and yoke retainers from front axle pinion yoke.
   d. Disconnect propeller shaft from front axle pinion yoke. Wrap bearing caps with suitable tape to prevent loss of bearing rollers. **Do not attempt to remove shaft by pounding on yoke ears or using a tool between yoke and universal joint. Injection joints may fracture and cause premature failure.**
4. **On all models,** disconnect starter motor electrical connectors, then remove starter motor attaching bolts and starter motor.
5. Remove flywheel inspection cover.
6. Remove oil cooler line retainer from retaining bracket.
7. Disconnect oil level sensor switch electrical connector, then remove switch from oil pan.
8. Remove oil pan attaching bolts, then the oil pan from cylinder block.
9. Reverse procedure to install, noting the following:
   a. Apply RTV sealer part No. 12345739, or equivalent, to front cover block joint and crankshaft rear seal block joint.
   b. Apply RTV sealer part No. 12345739, or equivalent, for approximately one inch in both directions at each corner of oil pan.
   c. Apply sealant part No. 12346286, or equivalent, to front and rear crankshaft bearing caps, on both left and right sides, **Fig. 7.**
   d. **Torque** oil pan bolts to 18 ft. lbs., in sequence, **Fig. 8.**

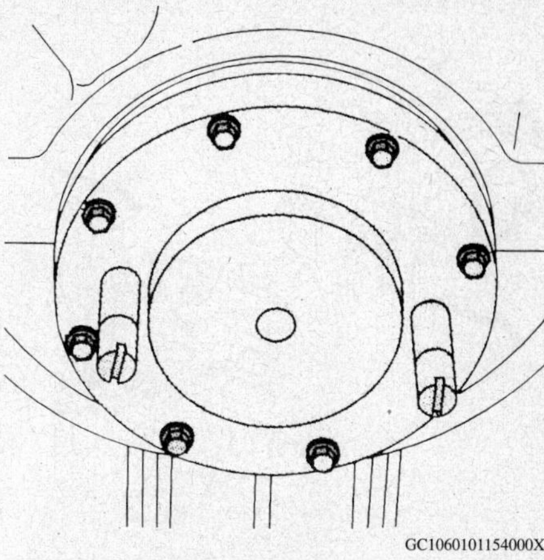

Fig. 6 Crankshaft rear oil seal removal

OIL PUMP

REPLACE

1. Remove oil pan as outlined under "Oil Pan, Replace."
2. Remove oil pump to rear crankshaft bearing cap retaining bolt.
3. Remove oil pump, driveshaft and retainer from rear crankshaft bearing.
4. Separate oil pump, driveshaft and retainer, then discard retainer.
5. Reverse procedure to install. Install new retainer.

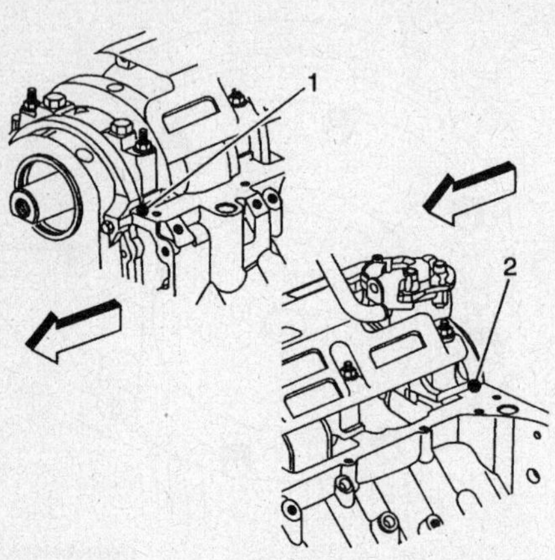

Fig. 7 Crankshaft bearing cap sealant application

SERPENTINE DRIVE BELT

1. Rotate tensioner counterclockwise using suitable 3/8 inch breaker bar.
2. Remove belt from pulleys.
3. Route new belt as outlined, **Figs. 9 and 10.**
4. Rotate tensioner pulley axis bolt counterclockwise using suitable breaker bar and socket and slip belt over tensioner, then release tensioner.

COOLING SYSTEM BLEED

1. Remove cap from surge tank.
2. Remove bleed screw from top of thermostat housing.
3. Pour coolant into surge tank and watch for coolant flowing from bleed screw.
4. When coolant flow is constant, close bleed screw and continue to fill coolant until it reaches proper level.
5. Install surge tank cap.

THERMOSTAT

REPLACE

1. Drain cooling system into suitable container until radiator coolant level is below thermostat.
2. Remove radiator hose from coolant outlet.
3. Remove mounting bolts, thermostat housing, thermostat and gasket.
4. Reverse procedure to install.

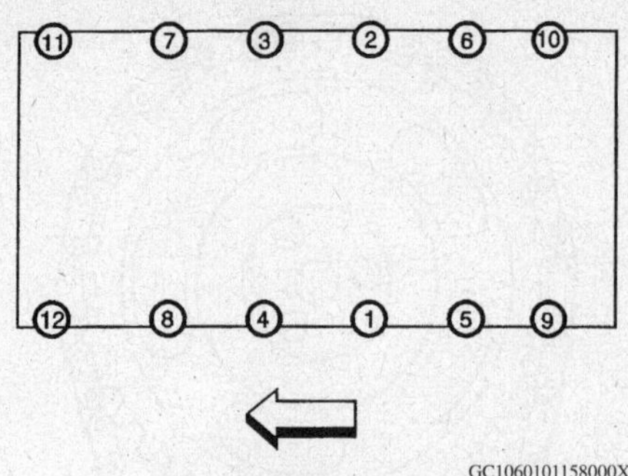

Fig. 8 Oil pan tightening sequence

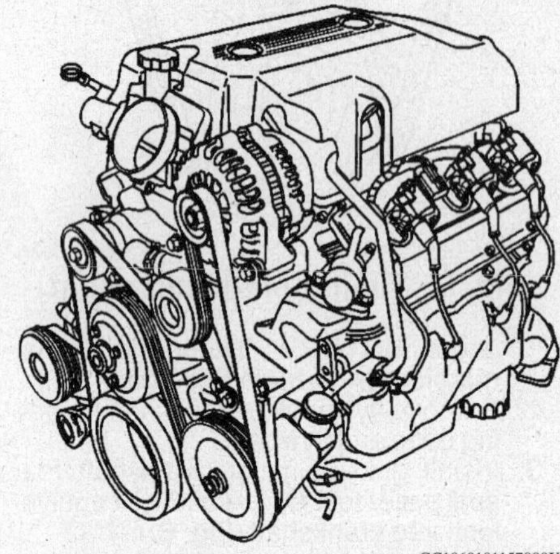

Fig. 10 Serpentine drive belt routing. With air conditioning

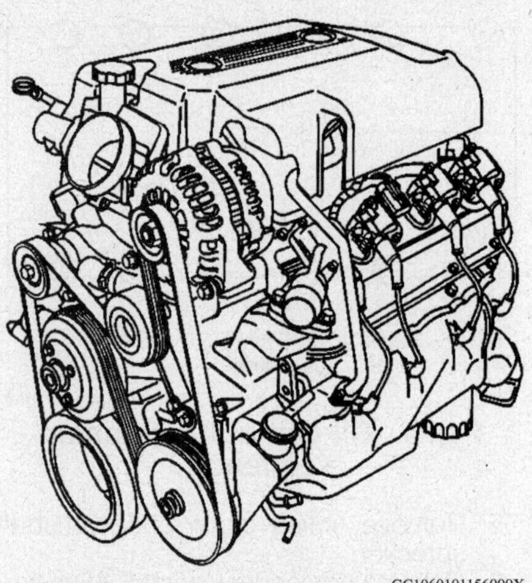

Fig. 9 Serpentine drive belt routing. Less air conditioning

WATER PUMP

REPLACE

1. Drain cooling system into suitable container.
2. Remove upper fan shroud and drive belt.
3. Remove fan, fan clutch and pulley from water pump.
4. Disconnect lower radiator and upper bypass hoses from pump.
5. Remove mounting bolts, water pump and two gaskets.
6. Reverse procedure to install.

RADIATOR

REPLACE

Refer to "4.8L, 5.3L & 6.0L Gasoline Engines" section for radiator replacement procedures.

FUEL PUMP

REPLACE

Refer to "4.8L, 5.3L & 6.0L Gasoline Engines" section for fuel pump replacement procedures.

FUEL FILTER

REPLACE

Refer to "4.8L, 5.3L & 6.0L Gasoline Engines" section for fuel filter replacement procedures.

TIGHTENING SPECIFICATIONS

Year	Component	Torque, Ft. Lbs.
2002–06	Air Injection Pipe Bolt	19
	Air Injection Pipe Nut	106①
	Air Injection Pump Pipe Bolt	37
	Air Injection Pump Pipe Nut	106①
	Camshaft Retainer Bolt	106①
	Crankshaft Balancer (Damper) Bolt	110
	Crankshaft Position Sensor Bolt	106①
	Cylinder Head Bolts	④
	Drive Belt Tensioner Bolt	37
	EGR Vacuum Regulator Bracket Bolt	22
	EGR Valve Bolt	22
	EGR Valve Pipe Bracket Bolt	22
	EGR Valve Pipe Nut	22
	Engine Mount Bolt	44
	Engine Mount Nut	33
	Flywheel Cover	106①
	Flywheel Housing Bolt (Countersunk)	44
	Flywheel Housing Bolt (Hex Head)	50
	Front Cover	⑤
	Fuel Rail Bolt	89①
	Fuel Rail Stud	18
	Ignition Coil Bolt	106①
	Ignition Coil Wiring Harness Bolt	106①
	Intake Manifold	③
	Oil Pan Bolt	②
	Oil Pan Drain Plug	21
	Oil Pressure Gauge Sensor	22
	Throttle Body Nut	89①
	Throttle Body Stud	106①
	Transmission Convertor Cover Bolts	106①
	Valve Cover	106①
	Water Crossover Pipe Bolt	37
	Water Pump Bolt	37
	Water Pump Pulley Bolt	19

① — Inch lbs.
② — Refer to "Oil Pan, Replace" for tightening procedure.
③ — Refer to "Intake Manifold, Replace" for tightening procedure.
④ — Refer to "Cylinder Head, Replace" for tightening procedure.
⑤ — Refer to "Front Cover, Replace" for tightening procedure.

Rear Axle & Suspension

INDEX

REAR AXLE

REPLACE

Avalanche, Escalade, Sierra & Silverado

1. Raise and support vehicle. Support rear axle using suitable jack.
2. Drain axle fluid into suitable container.
3. Mark driveshaft to flange, disconnect driveshaft and tie driveshaft to side rail or crossmember.
4. Tape bearing cups to prevent loss of rollers.
5. Remove wheel and brake drum or hub and drum.
6. Disconnect parking brake cable from lever and brake flange plate.
7. Disconnect and cap hydraulic brake lines from connectors.
8. Remove shock absorbers from axle brackets, **Fig. 1.**
9. Disconnect vent line from vent fitting.
10. Remove height sensing and brake proportional valve brackets.
11. Remove nuts, washers, U-bolts, spring plates, spacers and axle.
12. Reverse procedure to install.

SSR

1. Raise and support vehicle, then remove wheel and tire asssemblies.
2. Support rear axle with suitable jack stands.
3. Disconnect rear axle vent tube.
4. Disconnect propeller shaft from pinion yoke.
5. Remove left and right rear parking brake cables from rear axle.
6. Remove brake calipers as outlined in "Disc Brakes" chapter.
7. Remove stabilizer shaft from rear axle.
8. Remove coil springs as outlined under "Coil Springs, Replace."
9. Disconnect rear axle tie rod end from rear axle.
10. Disconnect lower and upper control arms from rear axle.
11. Remove rear axle from vehicle.
12. Reverse procedure to install.

REAR AXLE SHAFT

REPLACE

1. Raise and support vehicle, then remove tire and wheel assembly.
2. Remove axle shaft mounting bolts
3. Tap axle shaft flange lightly using suitable soft-faced hammer to loosen shaft.
4. Remove axle shaft by twisting flange using suitable locking pliers.
5. Remove gasket and RTV.
6. Reverse procedure to install. Install new gasket and RTV.

HUB & BEARING

REPLACE

1. Raise and support vehicle.
2. Remove axle shaft as outlined under "Rear Axle Shaft, Replace."
3. Remove retaining ring and key.
4. Remove adjusting nut and washer.
5. Remove hub and drum.
6. Remove oil seal.
7. **On models equipped with 8 ½ 9 ½ and 10 ½ inch ring gears,** proceed as follows:
   a. Remove inner bearing and cup using suitable drill.
   b. Remove retaining ring using suitable snap ring pliers.
8. **On models equipped with 11 inch ring gear,** proceed as follows:
   a. Lay drum on suitable flat surface, then place suitable shop towel under drum to catch inner bearing and seal.
   b. Remove bearing cup and seal using suitable drift.
   c. Remove retaining ring using suitable snap ring pliers.
9. **On all models,** drive outer bearing and cup from hub using bearing remover tool Nos. J-8092 and J-24426, or equivalents.
10. Reverse procedure to install.

WHEEL BEARING

ADJUST

Ensure brakes are completely released and do not drag. Inspect wheel bearing play by grasping the tire at the top and pulling and pushing back and forth, or by using a pry bar under the tire. If the wheel bearings are properly adjusted, movement of the brake drum in relation to the brake flange plate will be barely noticeable and the wheel will turn freely. If the movement is excessive, adjust the bearings.

8 ½, 9 ½ & 10½ INCH RING GEARS

1. Raise and vehicle until wheel is free to spin.
2. Remove axle shaft as outlined under "Axle Shaft, Replace."
3. Clean adjusting nut and threads.
4. Remove retaining ring and key.
5. **Torque** adjusting nut to 50 ft. lbs., while turning drum in opposite direction.
6. Ensure inner bearing roller assembly is seated against spindle shoulder.
7. Loosen adjusting nut ¼ turn, then **torque** adjusting nut to 13 ft. lbs.
8. Align closest adjusting nut slot with keyway in axle spindle.
9. Install key into keyway and adjusting nut slot.
10. Install retaining ring and axle shaft.

11 INCH RING GEAR

1. Raise and vehicle until wheel is free to spin.
2. Remove axle shaft as outlined under "Axle Shaft, Replace."
3. **Torque** adjusting nut to 50 ft. lbs., while rotating hub in opposite direction.
4. Ensure bearing cones are seated and in contact with spindle shoulder.
5. Loosen adjusting nut, then tighten nut while rotating hub.
6. Loosen adjusting nut, then **torque** nut to 35 ft. lbs., while rotating hub.
7. Loosen adjusting nut 135–150°.
8. Install lock washer, then bend one tang of retaining washer over flat on adjusting nut to minimum of 30°.
9. Install outer mounting nut and **torque** to 65 ft. lbs.
10. Bend one tang of retaining washer over flat of outer nut to minimum of 60°.
11. Add wheel bearing grease to bearings, then install axle shaft as outlined under "Rear Axle Shaft, Replace."

SHOCK ABSORBER

REPLACE

1. Raise and support vehicle.
2. Support rear axle using suitable jack.
3. Remove mounting nuts and disconnect shock absorber from upper mounting bracket.
4. Remove lower mounting nuts and shock absorber.
5. Reverse procedure to install.

COIL SPRING

REPLACE

1. Raise and support vehicle.
2. Support rear axle using suitable jack.
3. Remove stabilizer shaft link retaining nut from frame
4. Remove lower shock absorber nut and bolt from rear axle.
5. Lower rear axle until springs are fully unloaded.
6. Remove coil spring and insulators.
7. Reverse procedure to install.

LEAF SPRING

REPLACE

1. Raise and support vehicle.
2. Support rear axle using suitable jack.
3. Remove U-bolt nuts and washers.
4. Remove anchor plate.
5. Remove U-bolts and spacer.
6. Loosen shackle to spring nut.
7. Remove shackle to rear bracket mounting nut, washer and bolt.
8. Remove spring to front bracket, nut, washers and bolt.
9. Remove spring.
10. Reverse procedure to install.

CONTROL ARM

REPLACE

Lower

1. Raise and support vehicle.
2. Support rear axle at curb height using suitable jack.
3. Remove lower control arm retaining nuts and bolt.
4. Remove lower control arm from vehicle.
5. Reverse procedure to install.

Upper

1. Raise and support vehicle.
2. Support rear axle at ride height using suitable jack.
3. Remove upper control arm retaining nut and bolt from frame bracket.
4. Remove upper control arm retaining nut and bolt from axle bracket.
5. Remove upper control arm from vehicle.
6. Reverse procedure to install.

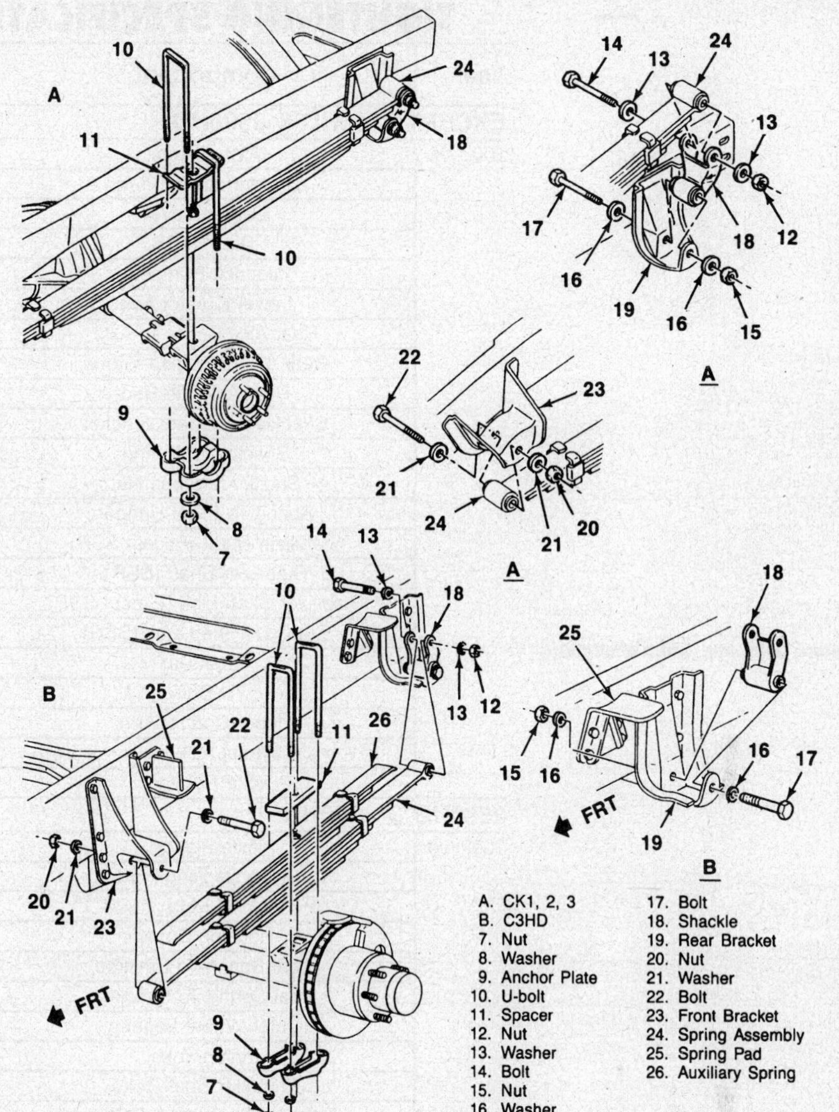

Fig. 1 Exploded view of axle components. Avalanche, Escalade, Sierra & Silverado

TIE ROD

REPLACE

SSR

1. Raise and support vehicle.
2. Support rear axle with suitable jack stands.
3. Remove rear axle tie rod to axle mounting bolt and nut.
4. Remove rear axle tie rod to frame mounting bolt and nut, then the tie rod from vehicle.
5. Reverse procedure to install.

STABILIZER SHAFT

REPLACE

SSR

1. Raise and support vehicle, then remove tire and wheel assembly.
2. Remove stabilizer shaft links to stabilizer shaft retaining nuts.
3. Disconnect stabilizer shaft links from stabilizer shaft.
4. Remove stabilizer shaft insulator clamp mounting nuts.
5. Remove insulator clamps, then the stabilizer shaft.
6. Reverse procedure to install.

REAR AXLE BRACE

REPLACE

SSR

1. Raise and support vehicle.
2. Support rear axle with suitable jack stands.
3. Remove rear axle brace to axle mounting bolt and nut.
4. Remove rear axle brace to frame mounting bolt and nut, then the brace from vehicle.
5. Reverse procedure to install.

TIGHTENING SPECIFICATIONS

Year	Component	Torque/Ft. Lbs.
EXCEPT 2500HD & 3500HD		
2002–06	Axle Flange	②
	Brake Backing Plate	103
	Carrier Cover	30
	Drain Plug	24
	Jounce Bumper	24
	Lower Control Arm	89
	Rear Axle Brace To Axle	144
	Rear Axle Brace To Frame	70
	Rear Axle Tie Rod	144
	Shackle To Frame Bracket	70
	Shackle To Spring	70
	Shock Absorber, Nut	70
	Spring To Front Hanger	92
	Stabilizer Shaft (Except SSR)	24
	Stabilizer Shaft (SSR)	55
	Stabilizer Shaft Link (Except SSR)	48
	Stabilizer Shaft Link (SSR)	66
	Track Bar	77
	U-Bolt	①
	Upper Control Arm	77
	Wheel Axle Hub	52
	Yoke Retainer	19
2500HD & 3500HD		
2002–06	Axle Flange	15
	Brake Backing Plate	78
	Fill Plug	24
	Housing Cover	35
	Leaf Spring To Bracket	306
	Leaf Spring To Shackle	157
	Outer Wheel Bearing	65
	Pinion Yoke	470
	Propeller Shaft Yoke	70
	Propeller Shaft Yoke Retainer	27
	Shackle To Bracket	157
	Shock Absorber, Lower	52
	Shock Absorber, Upper	11
	Stabilizer Link	17
	Stabilizer Shaft	24
	U-Bolt To Spring	187
	Vent Hose	17

① — Less washers, 101 ft. lbs; w/washers, 53 ft. lbs.

② — 8.5 inch, 9.5 inch & 10.5-inch, 115 ft. lbs.; 11.5-inch, 148 ft. lbs.

Front Suspension & Steering

NOTE: Refer To "Computer Relearn Procedures" Located In The Front Of This Manual When Battery Power To The Computer Has Been Interrupted.

INDEX

PRECAUTIONS

Battery Ground Cable

Prior to service disconnect battery ground cable and isolate, as required.

Radio Security System

If the Theftlock system is active when battery power is interrupted, the customers security code must be entered to restore proper function of the radio. Use the following procedure to unlock a secured radio after a power loss. Do not wait more than 15 seconds between steps.

1. Theftlock is engaged if radio is inoperable and "LOC" appears with ignition in On position.
2. Obtain customers' code number.
3. Press "MIN" button and "000" will appear on display.
4. Press "MIN" again until last two digits displayed agree with security code.
5. Press "HR" button until first 1 or 2 digits agree with security code.
6. Press "AM-FM" to select code entered. "SEC" will display indicating radio is now operable and secure.
7. If incorrect code is entered, "SEC" will display and radio will be inoperable.
8. Radio will remain inoperable until correct code is displayed. Repeat steps until correct code is entered. If correct code cannot be obtained, contact Delco technical assistance.

WHEEL BEARING

ADJUST

1. Raise and support vehicle.
2. Remove cap from hub/disc.
3. Remove cotter pin.
4. **Torque** adjusting nut to 12 ft. lbs., while turning wheel forward by hand, this will seat bearing.
5. Back off adjusting nut one flat. If hole in spindle lines up with slot in nut, insert cotter pin. If hole and slot do not line up, back nut off until hole and slot align. Do not back nut off more than one additional flat.
6. Install cotter pin.

HUB, BEARING & SEAL

REPLACE

2500HD & 3500HD

2WD MODELS

1. Remove brake caliper as outlined in "Disc Brakes" chapter.
2. Remove retainer/cap, then the cotter pin, nut, and washer, **Fig. 1.**
3. Remove wheel hub/rotor. Pull hub/rotor free from spindle ensuring outer wheel bearing comes free.
4. Remove inner wheel bearing and pry out seal.
5. Remove races using suitable brass drift to drive out each race.
6. Reverse procedure to install, noting the following:
   a. Place hub/rotor on wheel stud remover tool No. J-9746-02, or equivalent.
   b. Rest assembly on suitable press bars.
   c. Press outer bearing race into position using suitable 3-inch diameter bar, or equivalent.
   d. Remove wheel stud remover tool and use 3-inch diameter bar, or equivalent, to press inner bearing race into position.
   e. Use suitable high-temperature front wheel bearing grease to lubricate bearings.
   f. Apply thin film of grease to steering knuckle spindle at outer wheel bearing seat and at inner wheel bearing seat, shoulder and seal seat.
   g. Apply small amount of grease inboard of each wheel bearing retainer/cap.
   h. Fill each wheel bearing cone and roller assembly full of grease. Use suitable cone-type grease machine that forces grease into bearing.
   i. Put additional grease outboard of inner wheel bearing.
   j. Install new seal using suitable seal installer or block. Ensure seal is flush with hub/rotor flange.
   k. Lubricate seal lip with thin layer of grease.
   l. Tighten nut as outlined under "Wheel Bearing, Adjust."

4WD MODELS

1. Remove brake caliper and rotor as outlined under "Disc Brakes" chapter.
2. Remove drive axle nut and washer.
3. Remove nut and disconnect tie rod end from knuckle.
4. Remove hub and bearing assembly using suitable puller.
5. Lay hub and bearing assembly on hub bolt outboard side.
6. Remove halfshaft as outlined under "Front Wheel Drive Axles" chapter.
7. Remove mounting bolts and splash shield.
8. Support lower control arm with suitable jack stand.
9. Remove nut and upper ball joint from the knuckle using ball joint separator tool No. J-36607, or equivalent.
10. Remove nut and lower ball joint from the knuckle using ball joint separator tool.
11. Remove knuckle and seal.
12. Reverse procedure to install, noting the following:
    a. Install seal using steering knuckle seal installer tool No. J-36605, or equivalent.
    b. Tighten nuts to align cotter pin. **Do not tighten more than 1/6 turn.**
    c. Install new cotter pins.

Except 2500HD & 3500HD

1. Remove brake rotor as outlined in "Disc Brakes" chapter.
2. Remove wheel speed sensor and brake hose mounting bracket bolt from steering knuckle.
3. Disconnect wheel speed sensor electrical connection.
4. **On models equipped with 4WD,** proceed as follows:
    a. Remove cover, mounting wheel driveshaft nut and washer.
    b. Disconnect wheel driveshaft from wheel hub and bearing.
5. **On all models,** remove mounting bolts, wheel hub and bearing, then the splash shield.
6. Remove wheel speed sensor mounting bolt.
7. Reverse procedure to install. Replace O-ring seal.

BALL JOINT INSPECTION

1. Wipe ball joints clean and inspect seals for damage. If seals are damaged, replace ball joint.
2. Adjust wheel bearings as outlined under "Wheel Bearing, Adjust."
3. Raise and support vehicle.
4. Place suitable dial indicator against spindle to measure vertical movement.
5. Pry between lower control arm and outer race using suitable pry bar while reading dial indicator.
6. If dial indicator reading is more than .08 inch, replace ball joint.

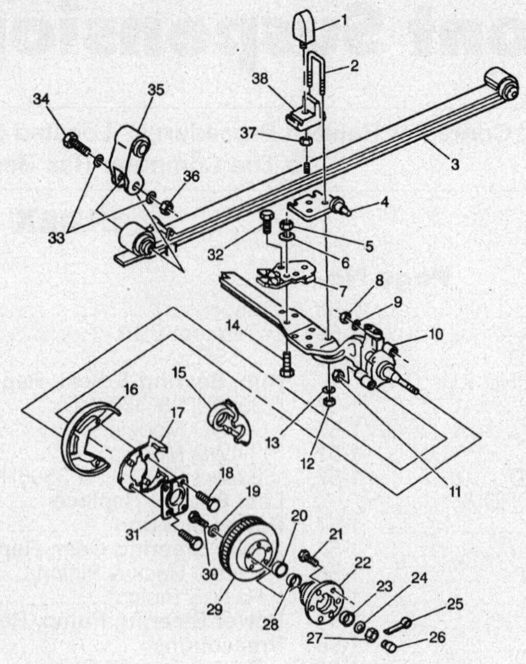

(1) Front Spring Spacer Cushion
(2) Front Spring U-bolt
(3) Front Spring
(4) Spring Spacer
(5) Front Stabilizer Bracket Nut
(6) Front Stabilizer Bracket Washer
(7) Front Stabilizer Bracket
(8) Steering Knuckle Nut
(9) Steering Knuckle Washer
(10) Steering Knuckle
(11) Steering Knuckle Nut
(12) Front Spring U-bolt Nut
(13) Front Spring U-bolt Washer
(14) Front Stabilizer Bracket Bolt
(15) Brake Caliper
(16) Splash Shield
(17) Anchor Plate
(18) Splash shield Bolt
(19) Wheel Hub Rotor Bolt Washer
(20) Bearing Seal
(21) Wheel Hub Bolt
(22) Wheel Hub
(23) Hub Outer Bearing
(24) Washer
(25) Retainer Cap Cotter Pin
(26) Retainer Cap
(27) Wheel Bearing Nut
(28) Inner Bearing
(29) Hub Rotor
(30) Wheel Hub Rotor Bolt

GC2029300026000X

Fig. 1 Exploded view of front suspension. 2500HD & 3500HD

BALL JOINT

REPLACE

Lower

2500HD & 3500HD

2WD

1. Raise and support vehicle, then remove wheel and tire assembly.
2. Raise control arm with suitable floor jack. **Floor jack must remain under lower control arm during removal and installation to retain control arm in position.**
3. Remove brake caliper as outlined in "Disc Brakes" chapter.
4. Remove cotter pin and nut, **Fig. 2.**
5. Break ball joint loose from knuckle using ball joint separator tool No. J-23742, or equivalent.
6. Remove lower control arm from knuckle. Place suitable wooden block between frame and upper control arm to block knuckle assembly out of way.
7. Guide lower control arm out of splash shield with suitable screwdriver while lifting upper control arm with suitable pry bar.
8. Remove lower ball joint from lower control arm using ball joint remover and installer tool No. J-9519-D, or equivalent.
9. Reverse procedure to install. Apply 1/4 inch bead of Loctite 680, or equivalent, evenly to ball joint serrations prior to installation.

4WD

1. Raise and support vehicle, then remove wheel and tire assembly.
2. Raise control arm with suitable floor jack. **Floor jack must remain under lower control arm during removal and installation to retain control arm in position.**
3. Remove halfshaft as outlined in "Front Wheel Drive Axles" chapter.
4. Remove brake caliper as outlined in "Disc Brakes" chapter.
5. Remove cotter pin and nut, **Fig. 2.**
6. Break ball joint loose from knuckle using ball joint/tie rod end separator

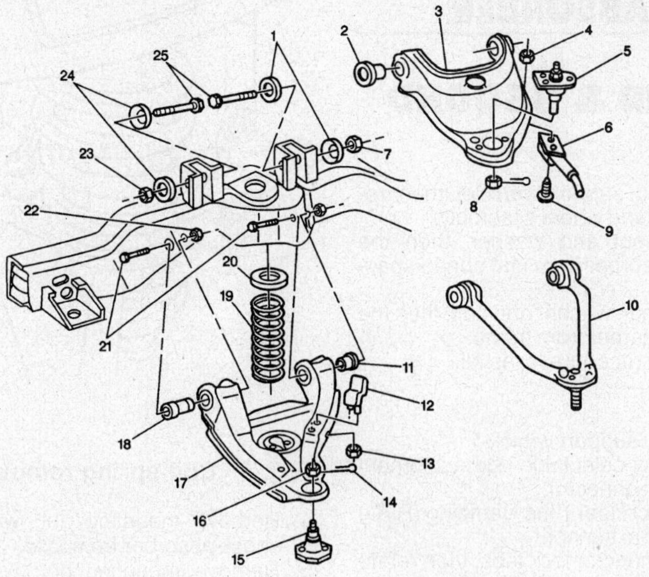

(1) Cam
(2) Upper Control Arm Bushing
(3) Upper Control Arm
(4) Nut
(5) Upper Ball Joint
(6) Brake Hose Bracket
(7) Upper Control Arm to Frame Nut
(8) Upper Ball Joint Nut
(9) Brake Hose Bracket Screw
(10) Upper Control Arm
(11) Lower Control Arm Bushing
(12) Lower Control Arm Bumper
(13) Lower Control Arm Bumper Nut
(14) Lower Ball Joint Cotter Pin
(15) Lower Ball Joint
(16) Lower Ball Joint Nut
(17) Lower Control Arm
(18) Lower Control Arm Bushing
(19) Front Coil Spring
(20) Front Coil Spring Upper Insulator
(21) Lower Control Arm to Frame Bolts
(22) Lower Control Arm to Frame Nut
(23) Upper Control Arm to Frame Nut
(24) Cams
(25) Upper Control Arm to Frame Bolts

GC2028800024000X

Fig. 2 Control arms & components. 2500HD & 3500HD

tool No. J-39549, or equivalent.
7. Remove lower control arm from knuckle. Place suitable wooden block between frame and upper control arm to block knuckle assembly out of way.
8. Guide lower control arm out of splash shield with suitable screwdriver while lifting upper control arm with suitable pry bar.
9. Remove lower ball joint from lower control arm using ball joint remover and installer tool No. J-41435, or equivalent.
10. Reverse procedure to install. Apply ¼ inch bead of Loctite 680, or equivalent, evenly to ball joint serrations prior to installation.

EXCEPT SSR, 2500HD & 3500HD

2WD MODELS

1. Raise and support vehicle, then remove tire and wheel assembly.
2. Disconnect Real Time Damping (RTD) link rod from sensor.
3. Remove front coil spring as outlined under "Coil Spring, Replace."
4. Remove lower control arm mounting nuts, washers and bolts.
5. Remove nut and disconnect the ball joint stud from steering knuckle using ball joint separator tool No. J-43631, or equivalent.
6. Remove lower control arm.
7. Secure lower control arm in suitable bench vice.
8. Remove rivets and lower ball joint.
9. Reverse procedure to install.

4WD MODELS

1. Raise and support vehicle, then remove tire and wheel assembly.
2. Disconnect Real Time Damping (RTD) link rod from sensor.
3. Remove stabilizer shaft links from lower control arm.
4. Remove shock absorber lower mounting nut and bolt.
5. Remove torsion bars.
6. Remove halfshaft as outlined in "Front Wheel Drive Axles" chapter.
7. Remove nut and disconnect the ball joint stud from steering knuckle using ball joint separator tool No. J-43631, or equivalent.
8. Remove lower control arm mounting nuts, washers and bolts.
9. Remove lower control arm.
10. Secure lower control arm in suitable bench vice.
11. Remove lower ball joint rivets
12. Remove ball joint from lower control arm using suitable press.
13. Reverse procedure to install.

SSR

1. Raise and support vehicle, then remove wheel and tire assembly
2. Remove steering knuckle as outlined under "Steering Knuckle, Replace."
3. Remove lower ball joint flange with a suitable chisel.
4. Install ball joint separation tool No. J 34874, or equivalent, to lower ball joint and control arm.
5. Remove lower ball joint from control arm.
6. Reverse procedure to install.

Upper

2500HD & 3500HD

1. Raise and support vehicle.
2. Support control arm using suitable jack. **Jack must remain under control arm spring seat during removal and installation to retain spring and control arm in position.**
3. Remove wheel and tire assembly.
4. Remove brake caliper as outlined in "Disc Brakes" chapter.
5. Remove wheel speed sensor.
6. Remove upper ball joint rivets.
7. Remove cotter pin.
8. Remove stud nut from upper ball joint.
9. Break stud loose using ball joint separator tool No. J-23742, or equivalent.
10. Remove tool and pull stud away from knuckle.
11. Remove upper ball joint
12. Reverse procedure to install.

EXCEPT SSR, 2500HD & 3500HD

1. Raise and support vehicle, then remove tire and wheel assembly.
2. Disconnect Real Time Damping (RTD) link rod from sensor.
3. Remove brake hose and the wheel speed sensor brackets mounting bolt.
4. **On models equipped with 4WD,** remove halfshaft as outlined in "Front Wheel Drive Axles" chapter.
5. **On all models,** remove upper ball joint mounting nut. Discard nut.
6. Disconnect upper control arm from steering knuckle using ball joint separator tool No. J-43631, or equivalent.
7. Remove upper control arm mounting nuts, bolts and adjustment cams.
8. Remove upper control arm.
9. Remove upper ball joint using suitable press.
10. Reverse procedure to install.

SSR

1. Raise and support vehicle, then remove tire and wheel assembly.
2. Remove steering knuckle as outlined under "Steering Knuckle, Replace."
3. Remove upper ball joint retaining clip and boot.
4. Remove upper ball joint from upper control arm using joint separator tool No. J-9519, or equivalent.
5. Reverse procedure to install.

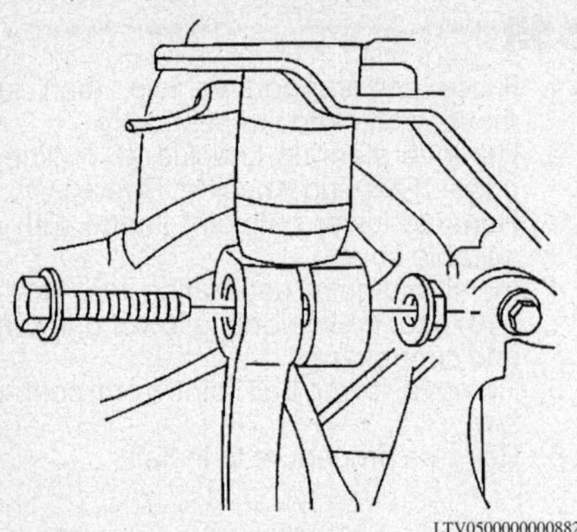

Fig. 3 Shock absorber pinch bolt & nut. SSR

COIL SPRING

REPLACE

Except SSR

1. Raise and support vehicle, then remove engine protection shield.
2. **On 2500 models,** remove frame cross bar.
3. **On all models,** remove tire and wheel assembly.
4. Remove shock absorber as outlined under "Shock Absorber, Replace."
5. Remove front stabilizer shaft link.
6. Install coil spring replacement tool No. J-23028-15, or equivalent using outboard locating tab on 1500 series models and inboard locating tab on 2500 series.
7. Attach retaining hook to control arm and tighten wing nut to eliminate freeplay.
8. Securely attach coil spring replacement tool No. J-23028-01, or equivalent, to suitable transmission jack.
9. Relieve spring tension from lower control arm pivot bolts by raising jack.
10. Remove lower control arm pivot bolt nuts, then rear and front pivot bolts.
11. Slowly lower transmission jack to unload front coil spring.
12. Remove coil spring and insulator.
13. Reverse procedure to install.

SSR

1. Remove shock module assembly as outlined under "Shock Absorber, Replace."
2. Remove shock module yoke to shock absorber pinch bolt and nut, **Fig. 3.**
3. Spread shock module yoke with a suitable flat-bladed tool.
4. Remove shock module yoke from shock module assembly.
5. Install coil spring compressor tool No. J 45400, or equivalent, onto coil spring. Install pieces of heater hoses to coil spring where compressor tool contacts spring, **Fig. 4.**
6. Compress spring and remove shock absorber upper retaining nut.
7. Remove shock absorber and coil spring from shock module.
8. Reverse procedure to install.

SHOCK ABSORBER

REPLACE

2500HD & 3500HD

2WD

1. Raise and support vehicle, then remove tire and wheel assembly.
2. Remove nut and washer, then the shock absorber from leaf spring spacer.
3. Remove nut, washer and bolt, then the shock absorber from frame.
4. Reverse procedure to install.

4WD

1. Raise and support vehicle.
2. Disconnect selectable ride equipment electrical connector.
3. Disconnect Real Time Damping (RTD) link rod from sensor.
4. Grasp connector lock tabs, then rotate them counterclockwise until connector is unlocked.
5. Disconnect connector from tennon by firmly pulling it up.
6. Hold tennon end with suitable wrench while removing nut.
7. Remove upper insulator. **Do not discard plastic pilot ring.**
8. Remove lower control arm shock absorber mounting bolts.
9. Remove shock absorber through lower control arm from below.
10. Reverse procedure to install.

Except SSR, 2500HD & 3500HD

1. Raise and support vehicle, then remove tire and wheel assembly.
2. Remove mounting nut and washer, then shock absorber from leaf spring spacer.
3. Remove mounting nut, washer and bolt, then the shock absorber from frame.
4. Reverse procedure to install.

SSR

1. Remove shock module assembly upper retaining nuts.
2. Raise and support vehicle, then remove wheel and tire assembly.
3. Remove shock module yoke to lower control arm retaining nut.
4. Remove shock module yoke from lower control arm using ball joint separation tool No. J 24319, or equivalent, **Fig. 5.**
5. Remove shock module from vehicle.
6. Reverse procedure to install.

LEAF SPRING

REPLACE

1. Raise and support vehicle.
2. Support axle separately to eliminate any load on springs.
3. Remove tire and wheel assembly.

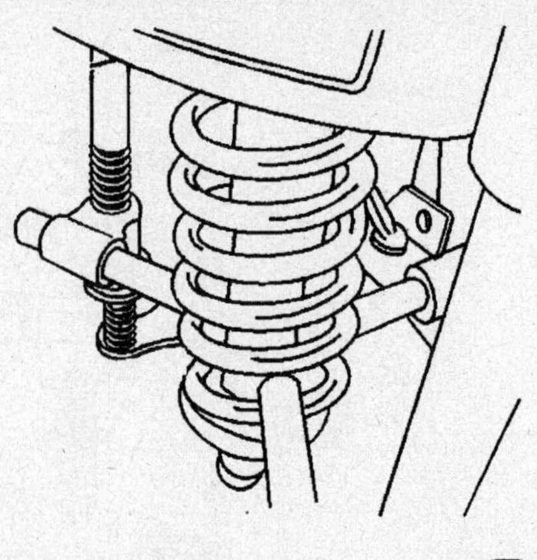

Fig. 4 Coil spring removal. SSR

4. Remove mounting nut, washer and shock absorber from axle.
5. Remove mounting nut, washer and stabilizer link from shaft using wheel stud and tie rod remover tool No. J-6627-A, or equivalent, to separate stabilizer shaft from link.
6. Remove mounting nut, retainer and insulator, then the stabilizer link from axle. Pull link free from axle. **Do not lose other insulator and retainer.**
7. Remove mounting nuts, washers and U-bolts.
8. Remove spacer and spring spacer.
9. Remove leaf spring from axle.
10. Remove mounting nut, washers and bolt, then separate spring from rear shackle.
11. Remove mounting nut, washers and bolt, then separate spring from front hanger.
12. Remove leaf spring from frame by pulling back and out.
13. Reverse procedure to install.

CONTROL ARM

REPLACE

Lower

2WD MODELS

EXCEPT SSR

1. Raise and support vehicle, then remove tire and wheel assembly.
2. Disconnect Real Time Damping (RTD) link rod from sensor.
3. Remove front coil spring as outlined under "Coil Spring, Replace"
4. Remove lower control arm mounting nuts, washers and bolts.
5. Remove lower ball joint stud nut.
6. Disconnect lower ball joint stud from the steering knuckle using ball joint separator tool No. J-43631, or equivalent.
7. Remove the lower control arm.
8. Reverse procedure to install.

SSR

1. Raise and support vehicle, then remove tire and wheel assembly.
2. Remove outer tie rod to steering knuckle retaining nut, then separate tie rod from steering knuckle using ball joint separation tool No. J 24319, or equivalent.
3. Remove stabilizer shaft link lower retaining nut, then separate link from lower control arm.
4. Remove shock module yoke to control arm mounting nut.
5. Remove shock module yoke from lower control arm using ball joint separation tool No. J 24319, or equivalent, **Fig. 5.**
6. Remove lower ball joint to steering knuckle retaining nut, then separate ball joint from steering knuckle using joint separation tool No. J 43631, or equivalent.
7. Remove lower control arm to lower control arm bracket mounting nuts.
8. Remove lower control arm to lower control arm bracket mounting bolts.
9. Remove lower control arm.
10. Reverse procedure to install.

4WD MODELS

1. Raise and support vehicle, then remove tire and wheel assembly
2. Disconnect Real Time Damping (RTD) link rod from sensor.
3. Remove stabilizer shaft links from lower control arm.
4. Remove shock absorber lower mounting nut and bolt.
5. Remove torsion bars.
6. Remove wheel drive shaft as outlined in "Front Wheel Drive Axles" chapter.
7. Remove lower ball joint stud nut.
8. Disconnect lower ball joint stud from steering knuckle using ball joint separator tool No. J-43631, or equivalent.
9. Remove mounting nuts, washers, bolts and lower control arm.
10. Reverse procedure to install.

Upper

EXCEPT SSR

1. Raise and support vehicle, then remove tire and wheel assembly.
2. Disconnect Real Time Damping (RTD) link rod from sensor.
3. Remove brake hose and the wheel speed sensor brackets mounting bolt.
4. Remove wheel drive shaft as outlined in "Front Wheel Drive Axles" chapter.
5. Remove upper ball joint nut . Discard nut.
6. Disconnect upper control arm from steering knuckle using ball joint separator tool No. J-43631, or equivalent.
7. Remove upper control arm mounting nuts, adjustment cams and mounting bolts.
8. Remove upper control arm.
9. Reverse procedure to install.

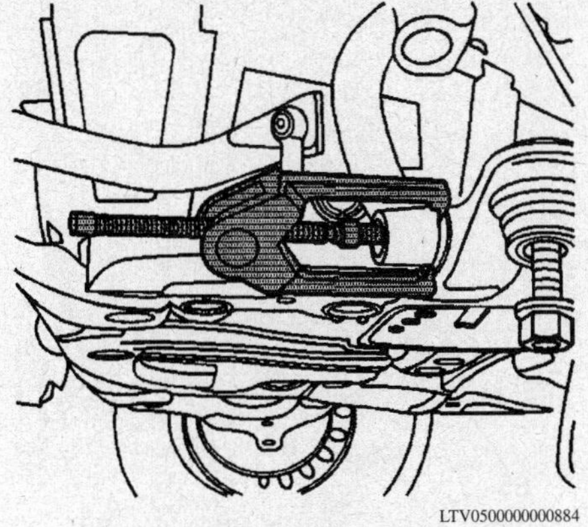

Fig. 5 Shock module yoke removal. SSR

SSR

1. Raise and support vehicle, then remove wheel and tire assembly.
2. Remove upper ball joint to control arm pinch bolt and nut.
3. Separate upper control arm from steering knuckle.
4. Disconnect ABS wheel speed harness from upper control arm.
5. Remove upper control arm mounting bolts, then the upper control arm.
6. Reverse procedure to install.

STEERING KNUCKLE

REPLACE

2500HD & 3500HD

1. Raise and support vehicle, then remove tire and wheel assembly.
2. Remove brake caliper as outlined in "Disc Brakes" chapter.
3. Remove hub and rotor.
4. Remove mounting bolts, washers and nuts, then the anchor plate, splash shield and steering arm. Steering arm hangs by rods.
5. Remove mounting bolts and washers, then separate anchor plate from splash shield.
6. Separate steering arm from tie rod and pitman arm.
7. Remove mounting bolts, washers and stabilizer bracket.
8. Remove gaskets and steering knuckle caps.
9. Remove mounting nut, washer and lock pin.
10. Remove steering knuckle king pin using suitable drift to drive out king pin. Spacers and bushings will also come out.
11. Remove steering knuckle.
12. Remove dust seal, shim and thrust bearing.
13. Reverse procedure to install, noting the following:
    a. Ream new bushings to between 1.1804–1.1820 inches after installation.
    b. Prelube thrust bearing and king pin.

Except SSR, 2500HD & 3500HD

1. Raise and support vehicle, then remove tire and wheel assembly.
2. Remove wheel hub and bearing as outlined under "Hub, Bearing & Seal, Replace."
3. Disconnect Real Time Damping link rod from sensor, as required.
4. **On models equipped with 2WD,** support lower control arm with suitable jack.
5. **On models equipped with 4WD,** unload torsion bars.
6. **On all models,** disconnect outer tie rod from knuckle.
7. Remove brake hose bracket mounting bolt.
8. Remove mounting nut and separate upper ball joint from steering knuckle using ball joint separating tool No. J-43631, or equivalent.
9. Remove mounting nut and separate lower ball joint from steering knuckle using ball joint separating tool.
10. Remove steering knuckle.
11. Reverse procedure to install.

SSR

1. Raise and support vehicle, then remove wheel and tire assembly.
2. Remove wheel hub and bearing assembly.
3. Remove outer tie rod end to steering knuckle retaining nut, then separate tie rod end from steering knuckle using ball joint remover tool No. J 43631, or equivalent.
4. Remove brake hose bracket retaining bolts, then the bracket from steering knuckle.
5. Disconnect ABS wheel speed sensor wiring harness from steering knuckle bracket.
6. Remove upper control arm to steering knuckle pinch bolt and nut, then separate control arm from steering knuckle.
7. Remove lower ball joint to steering knuckle retaining nut, then separate ball joint from steering knuckle using ball joint remover tool No. J 43631, or equivalent.
8. Remove steering knuckle from vehicle.
9. Reverse procedure to install.

STABILIZER BAR

REPLACE

Except 3500HD

1. Raise and support vehicle.
2. Remove nut from link bolt, **Fig. 6.**
3. Remove link bolt.
4. Remove spacer, mounting bolts, bracket and stabilizer shaft.
5. Remove bushing.
6. Reverse procedure to install.

3500HD

1. Raise and support vehicle, then remove tire and wheel assembly.
2. Remove mounting nut and washer, then the stabilizer bar from stabilizer link.
3. Separate stabilizer link from stabilizer end using wheel stud and tie rod remover tool No. J-6627-A, or universal steering linkage puller tool No. J-24319-B, or equivalent.
4. Remove mounting nuts, washers, clamp bolts and clamps, then the stabilizer bar from axle.
5. Remove insulator from stabilizer shaft.
6. Remove mounting nut, retainer and insulator, then the stabilizer link from frame bracket. Another insulator and retainer will come off of link.
7. Reverse procedure to install. Tighten nut until distance between each insulator retainer is 1.5 inches.

TIE ROD END

REPLACE

Except 2500HD & 3500HD

1. Raise and support vehicle, then remove tire and wheel assembly.
2. Remove ball stud cotter pin and nut.
3. Loosen adjuster clamp nut.
4. Remove tie rod end using steering linkage puller tool No. J-26813-B, or equivalent.
5. Remove outer tie rod from inner tie rod sleeve.
6. Reverse procedure to install. Use steering linkage installer tool No. J-29194, or equivalent.

2500HD & 3500HD

1. Before removing tie rod end, record the following:
   a. Number of threads visible on tie rod.
   b. Position of tie rod end clamps.
   c. Direction from which clamp bolts are installed.
2. Tie rod adjuster tube components may be rusted. Apply suitable penetrating oil between clamp and tube.
3. Rotate clamps until they move freely.
4. Remove cotter pin from tie rod end ball joint. Discard cotter pin.
5. Remove nut from tie rod ball joint.
6. Remove tie rod ball joint using steering linkage puller tool No. J-26813-B, or equivalent.
7. Loosen tie rod tube clamp nut and remove tie rod from the tube.
8. Reverse procedure to install.

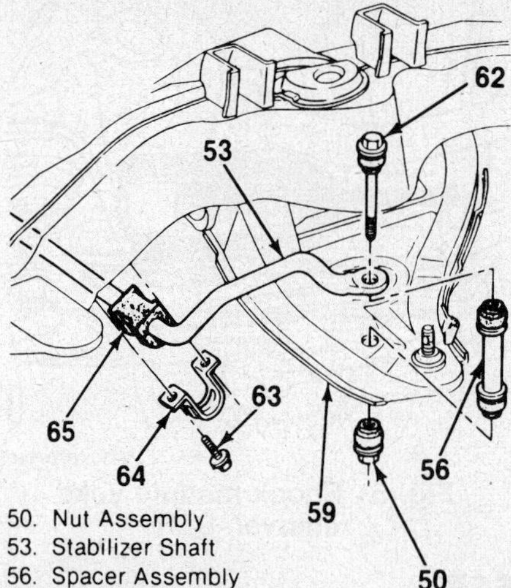

Fig. 6 Stabilizer shaft components. Except 3500HD

POWER STEERING GEAR

REPLACE

Except Rack & Pinion

1. Place suitable drain pan below steering gear.
2. Remove steering gear hoses.
3. Raise hoses up to prevent oil drainage. Cap or tape hose ends and gear fittings ends.
4. Place front wheels in straight ahead position, then lock steering column by placing steering column anti-rotation pin tool No. J-42640, or equivalent, through steering column access hole.
5. Remove steering gear shield.
6. Mark relationship of upper to lower intermediate shaft and lower shaft to steering gear input shaft for installation reference.
7. Remove upper to lower shaft connection mounting nut and bolt, then the lower shaft coupler mounting bolt.
8. Slide lower intermediate shaft towards dash panel to clear lower shaft coupler clear from input shaft.
9. Remove intermediate shaft by sliding it down upper shaft.
10. Raise and support vehicle.
11. Remove relay rod nut from pitman arm ball stud. Discard nut.
12. Remove relay rod from pitman arm ball stud using universal steering linkage puller tool No. J-24319-01, or equivalent.
13. Remove pitman arm nut and washer.
14. Mark pitman arm shaft for proper installation alignment.
15. Remove pitman shaft nut or pinch bolt.
16. Remove pitman arm from shaft using pitman arm puller tool No. J-6632-01, or equivalent. **Do not hammer on pitman arm, shaft or puller.**.
17. Remove mounting bolts and steering gear.
18. Reverse procedure to install. Install pitman arm ball stud using steering linkage installer tool No. J-29193, or equivalent.

Rack & Pinion

1. Raise and support vehicle.
2. Place a suitable drain pan under vehicle.
3. Remove left and right outer tie rod to steering knuckle retaining nuts.
4. Separate tie rod ends from steering knuckles using ball joint separator tool No. J 24319, or equivalent.
5. Remove crossmember brace attaching bolts, then the crossmember brace from frame.
6. Remove rear lower control arm bracket to frame mounting bolts.
7. Remove steering gear crossmember mounting bolts, then the steering gear crossmember.
8. Remove lower intermediate shaft to power steering gear input shaft pinch bolt.
9. Disconnect the lower intermediate shaft from the power steering gear.
10. Remove power steering hose assembly to power steering gear retaining bolt.
11. Remove power steering hose assembly from power steering gear.
12. Support power steering gear.
13. Remove power steering gear mounting bolts, then the power steering gear from vehicle.
14. Reverse procedure to install.

POWER STEERING PUMP

REPLACE

1. Remove serpentine drive belt as outlined under "Serpentine Drive Belt."
2. Place suitable drain pan under power steering pump, then disconnect hoses from pump. Plug pump ports and hoses.
3. Remove pulley using power steering pump pulley remover tool No. J-25034-C, or equivalent.
4. Disconnect electrical connector from EVO actuator.
5. Remove front and rear mounting bolts, then the pump.
6. Reverse procedure to install.

TIGHTENING SPECIFICATIONS

Year	Component	Torque/Ft. Lbs.
EXCEPT SSR, 2500HD & 3500HD		
2002–06	Ball Joint, Lower	52
	Ball Joint Stud, Lower	74
	Frame Cross Bar	74
	Lower Control Arm	107
	Pivot Bolt	107
	Power Steering Pump	37
	Power Steering Pump Hose	20
	Shock Absorber Lower Control Arm, Bolt	18
	Shock Absorber Lower Nut (4WD)	37
	Shock Absorber Through Bolt (4WD)	59
	Shock Absorber Upper Nut (2WD)	15
	Shock Absorber Upper Nut (4WD)	136
	Spring Hanger	70
	Steering Gear	100
	Tie Rod Adjuster Clamp	77
	Tie Rod Ball Stud	65
	Tie Rod Ball Stud, Nut	48
	Tie Rod Ball Joint, Nut	④
	Tie Rod Tube Clamp	55
	U-Bolt	92③
	Upper Control Arm	140
	Wheel Drive Shaft	155
	Wheel Hub & Bearing	133
	Wheel Speed Sensor	80①
	Wheel Speed Sensor & Brake Hose Mounting Bracket	106①
SSR		
2006	Adjuster Plug Locknut	50
	Brake Hose Bracket	89①
	Cylinder Line Nuts	23
	Flow Control Valve Fitting	55
	Lower Ball Joint To Steering Knuckle	81
	Lower Control Arm Bracket Front Mounting Bolt	192
	Lower Control Arm Bracket Rear Mounting Bolt	177
	Lower Intermediate Shaft Pinch Bolt	30
	Outer Tie Rod Retaining Nut	44
	Power Steering Gear To Frame	81
	Power Steering Pump Mounting Bolts	18
	Shock Absorber Retaining Nut	33
	Shock Module Upper Retaining Nuts	33
	Shock Module Yoke To Lower Control Arm Retaining Nut	81
	Stabilizer Shaft Insulator Clamp	41
	Stabilizer Shaft Link Retaining Nuts	74
	Upper Ball Joint Pinch Bolt	30
	Upper Control Arm Mounting Botls	111
	Wheel Hub & Bearing Mounting Bolts	77
	Wheel Lug Nut	95

TIGHTENING SPECIFICATIONS—Continued

Year	Component	Torque/Ft. Lbs.
2500HD & 3500HD		
2002–06	Anchor Plate, Bolt	12
	Anchor Plate, Nut	230
	Ball Joint	②
	Ball Joint Stud, Lower	94
	Ball Joint Stud, Upper	74
	Drive Axle Nut	165
	Hub & Bearing	133
	Intermediate Shaft Coupler Pinch Bolt	22
	Intermediate Shaft, Upper	46
	Lock Pin	29
	Pitman Arm	184
	Pitman Arm Ball Stud	46
	Pivot Bolt	101
	Power Steering Pump	37
	Power Steering Pump Hose	20
	Shock Absorber, Nut (4WD)	66
	Shock Absorber, Lower Nut	37
	Shock Absorber, Upper Nut	136
	Splash Shield	19
	Spring Hanger	70
	Stabilizer Bracket	60①
	Stabilizer Bar	29
	Stabilizer Link	50
	Steering Gear	100
	Tie Rod	35
	Tie Rod Adjuster Clamp	77
	Tie Rod Ball Stud (Except 3500HD)	40
	Tie Rod Ball Stud (3500HD)	65
	Tie Rod Ball Stud, Prevailing Torque Nut	46
	U-Bolt	92③

① — Inch lbs.

② — 2WD, 18 ft. lbs.; 4WD K1 & K2, 17 ft. lbs.; 4WD K3, 52 ft. lbs.

③ — Diagonal sequence.

④ — Axle assembly with 8100-lbs. rating, 95 ft. lbs.; all other axle assemblies 120 ft. lbs.

Front Wheel Drive

INDEX

AXLE SHAFT

REPLACE

1. Raise and support vehicle, then remove tire and wheel assembly.
2. Insert suitable drift through brake caliper and into brake rotor.
3. While holding rotor in place, remove hub nut and washer.
4. Remove drive axle flange to inboard C/V joint drive flange bolts and drift from rotor.
5. Remove stabilizer shaft bolt, spacer and nut from lower control arm.
6. Wrap shop towels around both inner and outer wheel drive shaft boots to prevent damage during removal.
7. Pull axle shaft through lower control arm opening.
8. Reverse procedure to install.

DIFFERENTIAL CARRIER

REPLACE

1. Raise and support vehicle, then remove front skid plate.
2. Drain carrier axle lubricant into suitable container.
3. Install plastic tie straps loosely over ends of front stabilizer shaft and under center of each halfshaft bar.
4. Mark relationship of propeller shaft to front axle for installation reference.
5. Remove front propeller shaft retainers.
6. Remove front propeller shaft from front axle yoke and secure it aside.
7. Remove engine oil filter.
8. Remove halfshaft flanges to differential mounting bolts.
9. Remove pitman arm from relay rod, move pitman arm towards lefthand side of vehicle for clearance.
10. Push relay rod forward and up for clearance.
11. Support front differential.
12. Remove front drive axle inner shaft housing nuts, washers and bolts from differential mounting bracket.
13. Disconnect front axle actuator electrical connector.
14. Remove front axle vent hose.
15. Place plastic tie straps around center of halfshaft, contacting only halfshaft bar. Tighten straps to support inner halfshaft ends.
16. Remove upper differential carrier mounting nut, washers and bolt.
17. Remove lower differential carrier mounting nut, washers and bolt.
18. Remove differential carrier.
19. Reverse procedure to install.

OUTPUT SHAFT

REPLACE

1. Raise and support vehicle.
2. Remove lefthand drive axle.
3. Remove lower carrier mounting bolt. Pry against lower carrier to provide clearance for output shaft removal.
4. Remove output shaft from case using slide hammer and adapter.
5. Remove deflector and seal from output shaft.
6. Reverse procedure to install. Lubricate and install new seal using suitable seal installer tool.

PINION FLANGE SEAL

REPLACE

1. Raise and support vehicle.
2. Disconnect propeller shaft from axle. Position propeller shaft aside.
3. Measure and record torque required to rotate pinion.
4. Mark pinion stem, pinion nut and companion flange, then record number of exposed thread on pinion stem.
5. Remove pinion nut using companion flange holder/remover tool No. J-8614-01, or equivalent. Four notches on tool should face flange.
6. Remove pinion flange using holder/remover tool.
7. Remove oil seal. **Do not distort or scratch aluminum case.**
8. Reverse procedure to install, noting the following:
   a. Stake new deflector at three new equally spaced positions. **Do not damage seal operating surface.**
   b. Install seal in bore, then seat seal using seal installer tool No. J-36366, or equivalent.
   c. Install pinion nut and tighten nut to original position using marks and exposed threads recorded earlier.
   d. Measure rotating torque of pinion and compare with torque recorded earlier.
   e. Tighten pinion nut until **torque** required to rotate pinion is 3 inch lbs., more than original torque.

TIGHTENING SPECIFICATIONS

Year	Component	Torque/Ft. Lbs.
2002–06	Axle Nut	165
	Axle Tube To Bracket	75
	Axle Tube To Carrier	30
	Bracket To Frame	67
	Brake Pipe Support Bracket	13
	Carrier Frame	16
	Carrier Mount	75
	Differential Carrier Shield	25
	Drain Plug	24
	Electric Motor Actuator	15
	Engagement Switch	15
	Halfshaft	58
	Lower Shock Absorber Mount	54
	Outer Tie Rod	46
	Stabilizer Bar Clamp	24
	Stabilizer Link	13
	U-Joint Clamp	15
	Upper Control Arm Stud	75

Wheel Alignment

INDEX

PRELIMINARY INSPECTION

Inspect the following components, adjust, repair or replace as required prior to performing front wheel alignment.

1. Inflate tires to cold specifications.
2. Ensure front tires are of same size, ply rating and load rating.
3. Inspect for excessive wheel bearing endplay.
4. Inspect for worn or damaged spindle ball joints.
5. Inspect steering gear mounting bolts for proper tightness.
6. Inspect radius arm or bent or damaged condition.
7. Inspect radius arm to frame bushings for looseness or wear.
8. Inspect suspension components for wear or damage.

FRONT WHEEL ALIGNMENT

Camber

2500HD & 3500HD

1. Measure camber.
2. Install adjustment kit part No. 15538596, or equivalent.
3. Reset camber to specifications.

EXCEPT SSR, 2500HD & 3500HD

1. Remove pinned adjusting cam insert.
2. Loosen upper control arm adjusting cam nuts.
3. Rotate cam bolts to required camber specification setting.
4. Maintain camber setting while tightening cam bolt nuts. **Torque** nuts to 140 ft. lbs.
5. Ensure toe, camber and caster settings after changing camber and adjust.

SSR

The caster and camber adjustments are made by loosening the lower control arm adjustment bolts and repositioning the lower control arm.

1. Loosen lower control arm adjustment bolts, **Fig. 1.**
2. Position lower control arm until alignment is within specifications. Refer to "Front Wheel Alignment Specifications" in the "Specifications" section.
3. **Torque** front lower control arm bolts to 192 ft. lbs. and rear lower control arm bolts to 177 ft. lbs.

Caster

2500HD & 3500HD

All caster specifications are given with the vehicle frame level (zero angle).

1. Position vehicle on suitable smooth level surface.
2. Correct "Z" height.
3. Measure frame angle using suitable bubble protractor or inclinometer, **Figs. 2 and 3.**
4. Record frame angle as being up in rear or down in rear.
5. Measure caster angle.
6. Determine actual (corrected) caster reading, **Fig. 3.**
7. When measuring caster, note the following:
   a. A decrease in rear frame angle must be subtracted from positive caster reading.
   b. An increase in rear frame angle must be added to positive caster reading.
   c. A decrease in rear frame angle must be added to negative caster reading.

d. An increase in rear frame angle must be subtracted from negative caster reading.

8. If caster angle is incorrect, correct caster angle by turning adjustment cam bolts.

EXCEPT SSR, 2500HD & 3500HD

1. Remove pinned adjusting cam insert.
2. Loosen upper control arm adjusting cam nuts.
3. Rotate cam bolts to required caster specification setting.
4. Maintain caster setting while tightening cam bolt nuts. **Torque** nuts to 140 ft. lbs.
5. Ensure toe, camber and caster settings after changing caster and adjust.

SSR

Refer to "Camber" under "Front Wheel Alignment" for adjustment procedure.

TOE-IN

EXCEPT RACK & PINION STEERING GEAR

1. Measure toe-in.
2. Change length of both tie rod sleeves to effect toe change.
3. Toe-in can be increased or decreased by changing length of tie rod ends. Threaded sleeve is provided for this purpose. When tie rod ends are mounted ahead of steering knuckle they must be decreased in length in order to increase toe-in. When tie rod ends are mounted behind steering knuckle they must be lengthened in order to increase toe-in. After adjusting **torque** tie rod end jam nut to 50 ft. lbs.

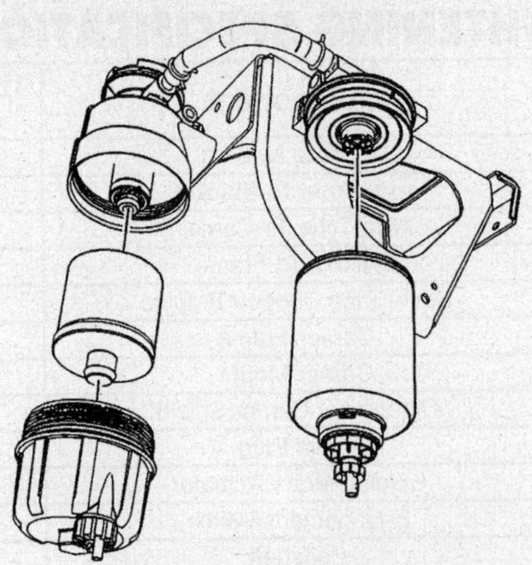

Fig. 1 Lower control arm adjustment bolts. SSR

RACK & PINION STEERING GEAR

1. Raise and support vehicle.
2. Loosen outer tie rod end jam nut.
3. Rotate inner tie rod end to correct toe setting. Refer to "Front Wheel Alignment Specifications" in the "Specifications" section.
4. **Torque** jam nut to 55 ft. lbs.

VEHICLE RIDE HEIGHT

Z HEIGHT

1. Lift front bumper of vehicle up approximately 1.5 inches.
2. Gently remove hands and allow vehicle to settle on its own.
3. Repeat this operation twice more for a total of three times.
4. Measure "Z" height, **Fig. 2.**
5. Push front bumper on vehicle down approximately 1.5 inches.
6. Gently remove hands and allow vehicle to rise on its own.
7. Repeat this operation twice more for a total of three times.
8. Measure "Z" height.
9. Find average of high and low measurements. This is "Z" height. "Z" height should be as follows:
   a. **On 2WD models,** measurement should be 3.6–3.7 inches.
   b. **On 4WD models,** measurement should be 4.3–4.8 inches.
   c. **On K3500HD models,** measurement should be 5.5–5.9 inches.

D HEIGHT

Use the procedure used in determining the "Z" height. "D" height should be the average of the high and low measurements.

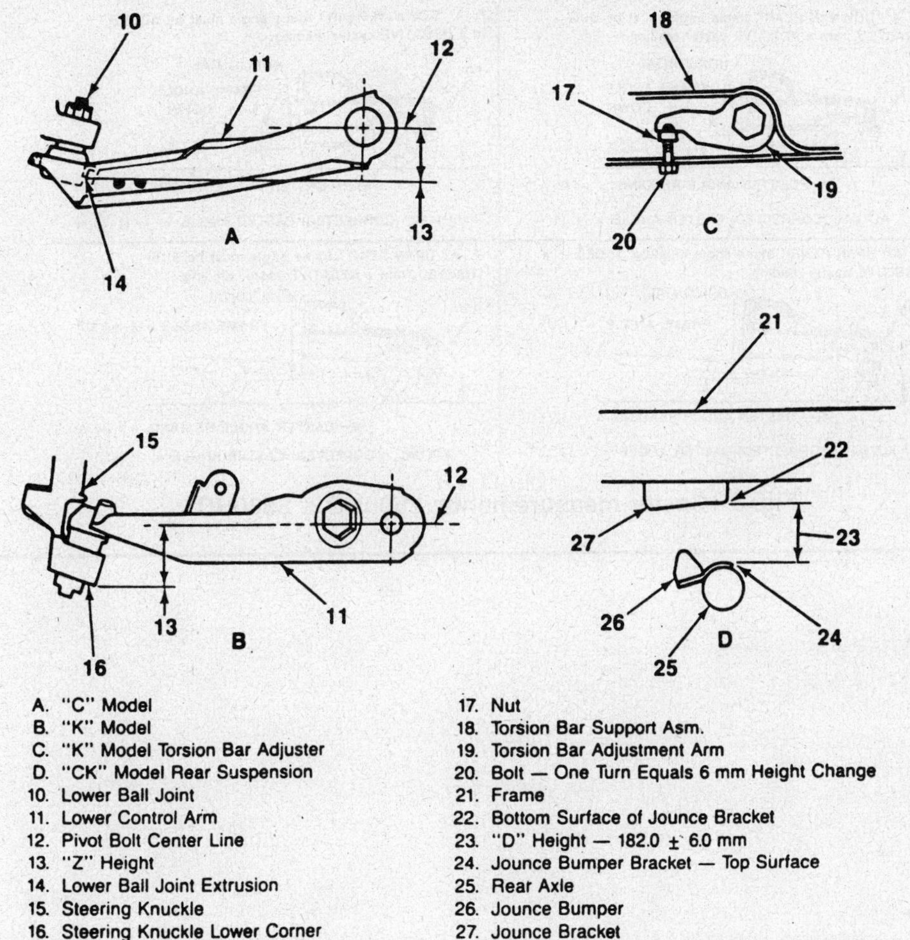

Fig. 2 Vehicle ride height location & specifications. 2500HD & 3500HD

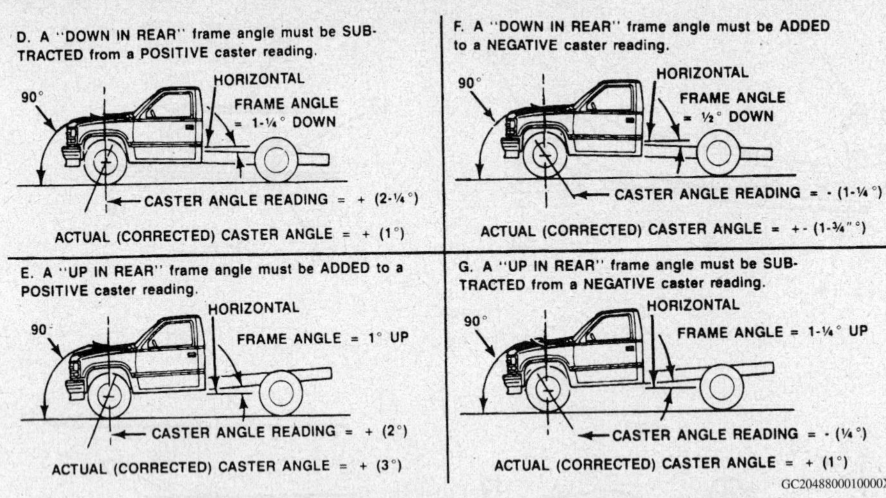

Fig. 3 Caster measurements. 2500HD & 3500HD

EXPRESS & SAVANA

NOTE: Refer To Back Of This Manual For Vehicle Manufacturer's Special Service Tool Suppliers.

INDEX OF SERVICE OPERATIONS

Specifications

GENERAL ENGINE SPECIFICATIONS

Year	Engine Liter	VIN③	Fuel System	Bore & Stroke	Comp. Ratio	Horsepower @ RPM①	Torque, Ft. Lbs. @ RPM②	Normal Oil Pressure, Lbs. @ RPM
2002	4.3L	W	SFI	4.00 x 3.48	9.2	200 @ 4400	250 @ 2800	④
	5.0L	M	SFI	3.74 x 3.48	9.4	220 @ 4600	280 @ 2800	④
	5.7L	R	SFI	4.00 x 3.48	9.4	255 @ 1600	330 @ 2800	④
	6.5L	F	③	4.06 x 3.82	19.5	195 @ 3400	430 @ 1800	40–45 @ 2000
	8.1L	G	SFI	4.25 x 4.37	9.1	340 @ 4200	455 @ 3200	—
2003–05	4.3L	X	SFI	4.00 x 3.48	9.2	200 @ 4400	250 @ 2800	④
	4.8L	V	SFI	3.78 x 3.27	9.5	270 @ 5200	285 @ 4000	④
	5.3L	T	SFI	3.78 x 3.62	9.5	285 @ 5200	325 @ 4000	④
	6.0L	U	SFI	4.00 x 3.62	9.4	300 @ 4400	360 @ 4000	④
2006	4.3L	X	SFI	4.00 x 3.48	9.2	200 @ 4400	250 @ 2800	④
	4.8L	V	SFI	3.78 x 3.27	9.5	270 @ 5200	285 @ 4000	④
	5.3L	T	SFI	3.78 x 3.62	9.5	285 @ 5200	325 @ 4000	④
	6.0L	U	SFI	4.00 x 3.62	9.4	300 @ 4400	360 @ 4000	④
	6.6L	2	③	4.06 x 3.90	17.5	300 @ 3100	520 @ 1800	⑤

SFI — Sequential Port Fuel Injection
TBI — Throttle Body Fuel Injection
① — Horsepower ratings may vary slightly depending on model application.
② — Torque ratings may vary slightly depending on model application.
③ — Electronically controlled high pressure direct injection pump.
④ — 18 psi @ 2000 RPM & 24 psi @ 4000 RPM.
⑤ — Minimum: 14psi @ idle; 42psi @ 1800 RPM.

TUNE UP SPECIFICATIONS

The following specifications are published from the latest information available. This data should only be used in the absence of a decal affixed in the engine compartment.

Year & Engine①	Spark Plug Gap	Ignition Timing BTDC				Curb Idle Speed③		Fast Idle Speed③		Fuel Pump Pressure psi.	Valve Lash, Inch
		Firing Order, Fig.	Man. Trans.	Auto. Trans.	Mark Location	Man. Trans.	Auto. Trans.	Man. Trans.	Auto. Trans.		
2002											
4.3L	.060	A	④	④	⑦	⑥	⑥	⑥	⑥	55–62⑧	②
5.0L	.060	⑤	④	④	⑦	⑥	⑥	⑥	⑥	60–66⑧	②
5.7L	.060	⑤	④	④	⑦	⑥	⑥	⑥	⑥	60–66⑧	②
8.1L	.060	⑤	④	④	⑦	⑥	⑥	⑥	⑥	55–62⑧	②
2003–06											
4.3L	.060	A	④	④	—	⑥	⑥	⑥	⑥	55–62⑧	②
4.8L	.060	⑤	④	④	—	⑥	⑥	⑥	⑥	55–62⑧	②
5.3L	.060	⑤	④	④	—	⑥	⑥	⑥	⑥	55–62⑧	②
6.0L	.060	⑤	④	④	—	⑥	⑥	⑥	⑥	55–62⑧	②

BTDC — Before Top Dead Center.

D — Drive.

N — Neutral

① — The eighth digit of VIN denotes engine code.

② — Equipped w/hydraulic valve lifters.

③ — When inspecting idle speed, set parking brake & block drive wheels.

④ — Not adjustable.

⑤ — Firing order, 1-8-7-2-6-5-4-3.

⑥ — Equipped w/Idle Speed Control (ISC) motor or Idle Air Control (IAC) valve.

⑦ — Equipped w/crankshaft position sensor.

⑧ — Wrap shop towel around engine compartment fuel pressure fitting. Connect suitable fuel pressure gauge to fuel pressure fitting. Turn ignition to On position & record fuel pressure reading.

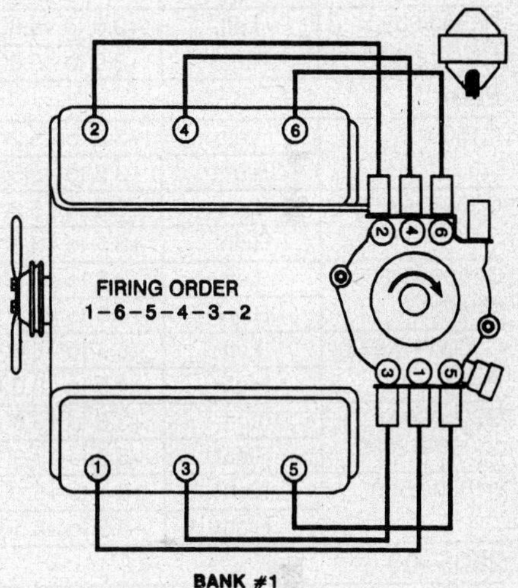

Fig. A

DIESEL ENGINE PERFORMANCE SPECIFICATIONS

Year	Engine	Injection Timing, ATDC	Curb Idle Speed	Fast Idle Speed	Fuel Pump Pressure, psi
2002	6.5L	①	②	②	5–8
2006	6.6L	—	②	②	—

ATDC — After Top Dead Center

① — Set injection timing with engine off. Injection pumps may be equipped w/dynamic injection timing marks (circle halves) or static timing marks (straight lines) on pump flange & front housing. On units w/dynamic or dynamic & static timing marks, align circle halves. On models w/static timing marks only, align scribed line marks.

② — Refer to emission control information label located in engine compartment.

FRONT WHEEL ALIGNMENT SPECIFICATIONS

Year/Model/ GVW	Side	Caster Angle, Degrees		Camber Angle, Degrees		Toe Per Wheel, Degrees①		Ball Joint Wear
		Limits	Desired	Limits	Desired	Limits	Desired	
2002								
All	Left	+2.75 to +4.75③	+3.75③	-.1 to +1.1④	+.5④	+.04 to +.44	+.24	⑤
	Right	+2.75 to +4.75③	+3.75③	-.1 to +1.1④	+.5④	+.04 to +.44	+.24	⑤
2003								
G1500	Left	+3.2 to +5.2②	+4.2②	-.35 to +.65④	+.15④	-.1 to +.3	+.1	⑤
	Right	+3.5 to +5.5②	+4.5②	-.35 to +.65④	+.15④	-.1 to +.3	+.1	⑤
G2500 W/7300	Left	+3.2 to +5.2②	+4.2②	-.35 to +.65④	+.15④	-.1 to +.3	+.1	⑤
	Right	+3.5 to +5.5②	+4.5②	-.35 to +.65④	+.15④	-.1 to +.3	+.1	⑤
G2500 W/8500/ 8600	Left	+3.6 to +5.6⑥	+4.6⑥	-.25 to +.75④	+.25④	-.1 to +.3	+.1	⑤
	Right	+4.0 to +6.0⑥	+5.0⑥	-.25 to +.75④	+.25④	-.1 to +.3	+.1	⑤
G3500 W/8600/ 9600	Left	+3.6 to +5.6⑥	+4.6⑥	-.25 to +.75④	+.25④	-.1 to +.3	+.1	⑤
	Right	+4.0 to +6.0⑥	+5.0⑥	-.25 to +.75④	+.25④	-.1 to +.3	+.1	⑤
G3500/W/ 10000–12300	Left	+3.6 to +5.6②	+4.6②	-.25 to +.75④	+.25④	-.1 to +.3	+.1	⑤
	Right	+3.9 to +5.9②	+4.9②	-.25 to +.75④	+.25④	-.1 to +.3	+.1	⑤
H1500/2500	Left	+2.6 to +4.6⑥	+3.6⑥	-.40 to +.60④	+.10④	+.1 to +.6	+.3	⑤
	Right	+3.0 to +5.0⑥	+4.0⑥	-.40 to +.60④	+.10④	+.1 to +.6	+.3	⑤
2004								
G1500	Left	+3.2 to +5.2②	+4.2②	-.35 to +.65④	+.15④	-.1 to +.3	+.1	⑤
	Right	+3.5 to +5.5②	+4.5②	-.35 to +.65④	+.15④	-.1 to +.3	+.1	⑤
G2500 W/7300	Left	+3.2 to +5.2②	+4.2②	-.35 to +.65④	+.15④	-.1 to +.3	+.1	⑤
	Right	+3.5 to +5.5②	+4.5②	-.35 to +.65④	+.15④	-.1 to +.3	+.1	⑤
G2500 W/8500/ 8600	Left	+3.6 to +5.6⑥	+4.6⑥	-.25 to +.75④	+.25④	-.1 to +.3	+.1	⑤
	Right	+4.0 to +6.0⑥	+5.0⑥	-.25 to +.75④	+.25④	-.1 to +.3	+.1	⑤
G3500 W/8600/ 9600	Left	+3.6 to +5.6⑥	+4.6⑥	-.25 to +.75④	+.25④	-.1 to +.3	+.1	⑤
	Right	+4.0 to +6.0⑥	+5.0⑥	-.25 to +.75④	+.25④	-.1 to +.3	+.1	⑤
G3500/W/ 10000–12300	Left	+3.6 to +5.6②	+4.6②	-.25 to +.75④	+.25④	-.1 to +.3	+.1	⑤
	Right	+3.9 to +5.9②	+4.9②	-.25 to +.75④	+.25④	-.1 to +.3	+.1	⑤
H1500/2500	Left	+3.1 to +5.1⑥	+4.1⑥	-.25 to +.75④	+.25④	-.1 to +.3	+.1	⑤
	Right	+3.5 to +5.5⑥	+4.5⑥	-.25 to +.75④	+.25④	-.1 to +.3	+.1	⑤
2005–06								
G10 & G20LD	Left	+3.2 to +5.2②	+4.2②	-.35 to +.65④	+.15④	-.1 to +.3	+.1	⑤
	Right	+3.5 to +5.5②	+4.5②	-.35 to +.65④	+.15④	-.1 to +.3	+.1	⑤
G20HD & G30	Left	+3.6 to +5.6⑥	+4.6⑥	-.25 to +.75④	+.25④	-.1 to +.3	+.1	⑤
	Right	+4.0 to +6.0⑥	+5.0⑥	-.25 to +.75④	+.25④	-.1 to +.3	+.1	⑤
H10 & H20	Left	+3.1 to +5.1⑥	+4.1⑥	-.25 to +.75④	+.25④	-.1 to +.3	+.1	⑤
	Right	+3.5 to +5.5⑥	+4.5⑥	-.25 to +.75④	+.25④	-.1 to +.3	+.1	⑤

GVW-Gross Vehicle Weight
G-2WD
H-All Wheel Drive
① — Toe-In (+). Toe-Out (–).
② — Cross caster: Limits, -.8° to +.2°; desired, -.3°.
③ — Cross caster: Limits, -.5° to +.5°; desired, .0°.
④ — Cross camber: Limits, -.5° to +.5°; desired, .0°.
⑤ — Refer to "Ball Joint Inspection" in "Front Suspension & Steering."
⑥ — Cross caster: Limits, -.9° to +.1°; desired, -.4°.

FLUID CAPACITIES & COOLING SYSTEM DATA

Year	Engine Liter	Cooling System Capacity, Qts. Less Rear Heater	With Rear Heater	Coolant Type	Radiator Cap Relief Pressure, Lbs.	Thermo. Opening Temp. °F	Fuel Tank Gals.	Engine Oil Refill Qts.①	Auto. Trans. Fluid, Qts.②	Rear Drive Axle Oil, Pts.
2002	4.3L	11.0	14.0	Dex-Cool	15	197	③	4.5	⑦	⑥
	5.0L	17.0	20.0	Dex-Cool	15	197	③	5.0	⑦	⑥
	5.7L	17.0	20.0	Dex-Cool	15	197	③	5.0	⑦	⑥
	6.5L⑤	23.5	27.5	Dex-Cool	15	197	③	8.0	⑦	⑥
	8.1L	23.0	26.0	Dex-Cool	15	197	③	6.5	⑦	⑥
2003	4.3L	11.0	14.0	Dex-Cool	15	197	③	4.5	⑦	⑥
	4.8L	13.4	16.4	Dex-Cool	15	197	③	6.0	⑦	⑥
	5.3L	13.4	16.4	Dex-Cool	15	197	③	6.0	⑦	⑥
	6.0L	14.8	17.8	Dex-Cool	15	197	③	6.0	⑦	⑥
2004	4.3L	11③	11③	Dex-Cool	15	197	③	4.5	⑦	④
	4.8L	13.4	16.4	Dex-Cool	15	197	③	6.0	⑦	④
	5.3L	13.4	16.4	Dex-Cool	15	197	③	6.0	⑦	④
	6.0L	14.8	17.8	Dex-Cool	15	197	③	6.0	⑦	④
2005	4.3L	11	14	Dex-Cool	15	197	⑧	4.5	⑦	④
	4.8L	13.4	16.4	Dex-Cool	15	197	⑧	6.0	⑦	④
	5.3L	13.4	16.4	Dex-Cool	15	197	⑧	6.0	⑦	④
	6.0L	14.8	17.8	Dex-Cool	15	197	⑧	6.0	⑦	④
2006	4.3L	11	14	Dex-Cool	15	197	⑧	4.5	⑦	④
	4.8L	13.4	16.4	Dex-Cool	15	197	⑧	6.0	⑦	④
	5.3L	13.4	16.4	Dex-Cool	15	197	⑧	6.0	⑦	④
	6.0L	14.8	17.8	Dex-Cool	15	197	⑧	6.0	⑦	④
	6.6L⑤	—	—	Dex-Cool	15	188	⑧	9.2	⑦	④

① — Includes filter.

② — Approximate. Make final inspection w/dipstick.

③ — Passenger & Cargo standard tank, 31 gallons; Cab & Chassis standard tank, 35 gallons; optional tank, 55 gallons.

④ — On models w/8.6 inch ring gear, 4.8 pts.; w/9.5 inch ring gear, 6.2 pts.;or 10.5 inch ring gear, 6.6 pts.

⑤ — Diesel engine.

⑥ — On models w/8.6 inch ring gear, 4.3 pts.; w/9.5 or 10.5 inch ring gear, 5.5 pts.

⑦ — 4L60-E/4L65-E pan removal, 5 qts., overhaul, 11.2 qts.; 4L80-E/4L85-E pan removal, 7.7 qts., overhaul, 13.5 qts.

⑧ — Passenger & Cargo standard tank, 31 gallons; Cab & Chassis standard tank, 33 gallons; optional tank, 57 gallons.

LUBRICANT DATA

Year	Lubricant Type: Automatic Transmission	Transfer Case	Drive Axle	Power Steering	Brake System
2002–2005	Dexron III	Dexron III	80W-90 GL-5②	①	DOT 3
2006	Dexron VI	Dexron III	75W-90 Synthetic Axle Lubricant	①	DOT 3

① — Power steering fluid GM part No. 1050017 (quart), 1052884 (pint), or equivalent.

② — On these models there may be an incompatibility situation if new Fuel Efficient SAE 75W-90 Synthetic Axle Lubricant part No. 12378261 is used in rear axles in models w/RTV differential cover sealing. Testing has proven this lubricant attacks RTV. The new lubricant is approved for use in all 8.6-inch axles as originally built. Vehicles w/9.5-inch axles can use it since they feature an upgraded gasket material. The new cover cannot be retrofitted , but a retrofit kit (part No. 12471310) will allow this conversion. All 10.5-inch axles are compatible by installing a new gasket (part No. 327739).

Electrical

NOTE: On Air Bag Equipped Models, Refer To "Air Bag System Precautions" Located In The Front Of This Manual For System Disarming & Arming Procedures.

NOTE: Refer To "Computer Relearn Procedures" Located In The Front Of This Manual When Battery Power To The Computer Has Been Interrupted.

INDEX

PRECAUTIONS

Air Bag Systems

Refer to "Air Bag System Precautions" in the front of this manual for system disarming and arming procedures.

Battery Ground Cable

Prior to service disconnect battery ground cable and isolate as required.

Radio Security System

If the Theftlock system is active when battery power is interrupted, the customers security code must be entered to restore proper function of the radio. To unlock a secured radio after power loss, proceed as follows:

1. "LOC" appears with ignition in On position.
2. Press "NM" and "000" will appear on display.
3. Press "NM" again to make last two digits agree with security code.
4. Press "HR" to make first 1 or 2 digits agree with security code.
5. Press "AM-FM" to select code entered. "SEC" will show on display indicating radio is now operable and secure.
6. If incorrect code is entered eight times, "INOP" will display. In order to reenter code, ignition must be left on for one hour before code can be entered and only three more chances to enter code are available before display reads "INOP."

FUSE PANEL & FLASHER LOCATION

2002

The instrument panel fuse panel is located behind the lefthand kick panel. The rear fuse block is located behind the lefthand side interior panel, rear of the driver's side door, above the Rear Sound Audio (RSA) module. The underhood fuse block is located on the lefthand fender.

The turn/hazard lamp flasher is located behind the center of the instrument panel, in the instrument panel relay center.

2003–06

The body fuse block is located below the driver seat. The rear fuse block is attached to the lefthand B-pillar. The underhood fuse block is located on the lefthand fender.

The turn signal/hazard flasher module is located below the center of the instrument panel, behind the left knee bolster.

RELAY CENTER LOCATION

The underhood relay center is located on the lefthand side of the engine compartment. The instrument panel relay center is located behind the center of the instrument panel.

FUEL PUMP RELAY LOCATION

The fuel pump relay is located on the lefthand side of the engine compartment, in the underhood relay center.

STARTER

REPLACE

1. Raise and support vehicle.
2. Remove starter to engine brace and heat shields.
3. Disconnect wires from solenoids.
4. Remove mounting bolts, washers and lower starter. Record position of shims, if used.
5. Reverse procedure to install, noting the following:
   a. **Torque** starter motor mounting bolts to 37 ft. lbs.
   b. **Torque** battery cable to solenoid to 89 inch lbs., and ignition wires to solenoid to 18 inch lbs.
   c. **Torque** starter motor shield bolts to 44 inch lbs., and shield nuts to 53 inch lbs.
   d. **Torque** ignition switch wires to solenoid to 18 inch lbs.

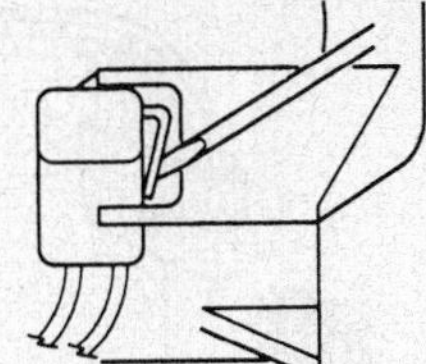

Fig. 1 Alarm switch removal

ALTERNATOR

REPLACE

Gasoline Engine

1. Remove coolant reservoir and air cleaner.
2. Remove upper fan shroud.
3. Remove drive belt as outlined in "Gasoline Engine" section.
4. Remove heater hose pipe from alternator and oil fill tubes from support bracket.
5. Remove alternator mounting bolts and alternator.
6. Disconnect electrical connectors.
7. Reverse procedure to install, noting the following:
   a. **Torque** front mounting bolt to 37 ft. lbs.
   b. **Torque** rear mounting bolt to 18 ft. lbs.

Diesel Engine

1. Remove surge tank and air cleaner.
2. Remove upper fan shroud and accessory drive belt.
3. Remove mounting bolts and alternator.
4. Disconnect electrical connectors.
5. Reverse procedure to install. **Torque** front mounting bolt to 37 ft. lbs., and rear mounting bolt to 18 ft. lbs.

Auxiliary

1. Remove drive belt.
2. Remove hoses, mounting bolts and bracket.
3. Remove mounting nut and positive battery cable.
4. Disconnect electrical connectors.
5. Remove mounting bolts, brace and alternator.
6. Reverse procedure to install. **Torque** long mounting bolt to 37 ft. lbs., and short brace mounting bolt to 18 ft. lbs.

COIL PACK

REPLACE

4.3L, 5.0L & 5.7L Engines

1. Remove air cleaner.
2. Disconnect coil electrical connectors.
3. Remove ignition coil to distributor wire.
4. Remove ignition coil bracket to intake manifold mounting studs.
5. Remove ignition coil and bracket.
6. Drill and punch out ignition coil to bracket rivets.
7. Separate ignition coil.
8. Reverse procedure to install. **Torque** ignition coil bracket to intake manifold studs to 96 inch lbs.

4.8L, 5.3L & 6.0L Engines

1. Disconnect spark plug wires at ignition coils.
2. Disconnect ignition coil harness connector.
3. Remove mounting bolts and ignition coil.
4. Reverse procedure to install. **Torque** mounting bolts to 71 inch lbs.

8.1L Engine

1. Disconnect ignition coil harness connector.
2. Remove mounting bolts and ignition coil.
3. Reverse procedure to install. **Torque** mounting bolts to 106 inch lbs.

IGNITION LOCK

REPLACE

1. Remove inner boot seal from adapter and bearing.
2. Slide boot seal down coupling and steering shaft.
3. Remove pinch bolt holding coupling and steering shaft to column.
4. Remove two lower steering column shroud mounting screws, tilt shroud downward and slide back to remove.
5. Remove two upper steering column shroud Torx screws and lift upper shroud to gain access to lock cylinder hole.
6. Hold key in START position.
7. Push on lock cylinder retaining pin using 1/16 inch Allen wrench.
8. Release key to RUN position and pull steering column lock cylinder from lock module.
9. Reverse procedure to install.

IGNITION SWITCH

REPLACE

1. Remove upper and lower steering column shrouds as outlined under "Ignition Lock, Replace."

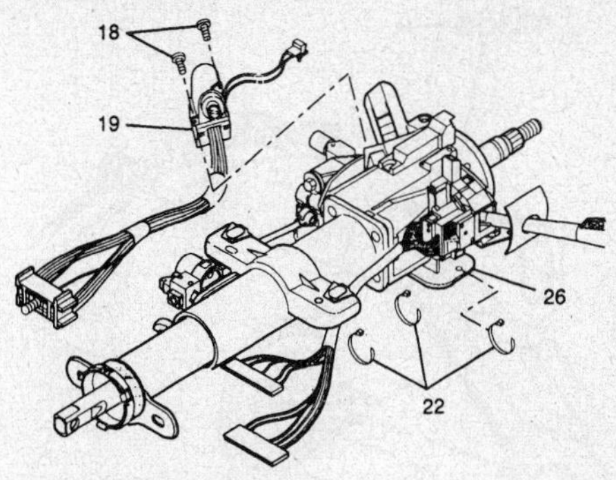

Fig. 2 Ignition & key alarm switch removal

2. Remove two plastic retaining straps from turn signal and multi-function switch wiring harness.
3. Disconnect steering column bulkhead connector from vehicle wiring harness.
4. **On models equipped with column shifter,** disconnect axial position assurance connector from BTSI actuator.
5. **On all models,** disconnect turn signal and multi-function switch connectors from steering column bulkhead connector.
6. Remove two turn signal and multi-function switch mounting screws.
7. Gently pry alarm switch retaining clip with suitable small bladed screwdriver and remove switch by rotating 1/4 turn, **Fig. 1.**
8. Remove two mounting screws, and ignition and key alarm switch from steering column, **Fig. 2.**
9. Reverse procedure to install.

NEUTRAL SAFETY SWITCH

REPLACE

1. Raise and support vehicle.
2. Disconnect shift cable end from transmission shift control lever.
3. Remove transmission shift control lever to manual shaft mounting nut.
4. Disconnect Park/Neutral position switch electrical connector.
5. Remove two mounting bolts and position switch.
6. Reverse procedure to install, noting the following:
   a. Position neutral position switch adjustment tool No. J-41364-A, or equivalent, onto Park/Neutral switch, **Fig. 3.** Ensure slots on switch are aligned with two lower tabs on tool.
   b. Rotate tool until upper locator pin on tool is aligned with slot on top of switch. **Do not remove tool during switch installation.**

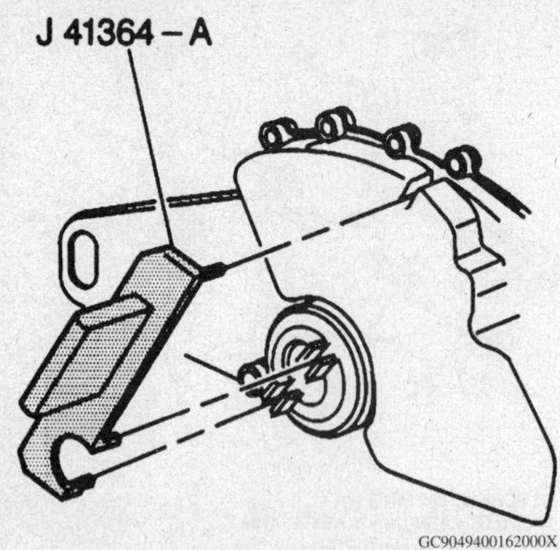

Fig. 3 Park/Neutral position switch adjustment. Automatic transmission

c. Align switch hub flats with manual shaft flats.
d. Slide switch onto manual shaft until switch mounting bracket contacts mounting bosses on transmission.
e. **Torque** switch mounting bolts to 21 ft. lbs., and remove adjustment tool.

HEADLAMP SWITCH

REPLACE

1. Pull instrument panel lower trim panel from instrument panel.
2. Pull instrument panel cluster trim panel from instrument panel by first pulling at lower lefthand, then the lower righthand corner and finally at top edge.
3. Disconnect cluster trim panel electrical connectors.
4. Move shift lever to first gear, rotate trim panel counterclockwise and lift it over steering column.
5. Release headlamp switch outboard tabs and remove switch from trim panel.
6. Reverse procedure to install.

STOP LIGHT SWITCH

REPLACE

1. Disconnect stop lamp switch electrical connector.
2. Remove retainer from brake pedal pin, **Fig. 4.**
3. Unsnap switch from pushrod.
4. Reverse procedure to install.
5. Plug connector onto switch and inspect operation. Electrical contact should be made when pedal is depressed, .45–.95 inch from its fully released position.

BACK-UP LAMP SWITCH

REPLACE

1. Disconnect switch harness.
2. Place gear selector in neutral, squeeze tangs together and remove, **Fig. 5.**
3. Reverse procedure to install, noting the following:

a. Adjust switch by moving gear selector to park.
b. Actuator will ratchet, providing proper adjustment.

MULTI-FUNCTION SWITCH

REPLACE

1. Remove steering wheel as outlined under "Steering Wheel, Replace."
2. Remove shaft lock cover. Compress lock plate and remove retaining ring using lock plate compressor tool No. J-23653-C, or equivalent, **Fig. 6.**
3. **On models equipped with standard columns,** remove shaft lock, turn signal cancelling cam assembly, upper bearing spring and thrust washer.
4. **On models equipped with tilt columns,** remove shaft lock, turn signal cancelling cam assembly, upper bearing spring, upper bearing inner race seat and inner race.
5. **On all models,** position turn signal to Right turn position and remove multi-function lever.
6. Remove mounting screw and multi-function switch.
7. Remove hazard warning button, then the turn signal and multi-function switch mounting screws.
8. Disconnect switch electrical connector from wire harness.
9. Remove turn signal and multi-function switch, pull wire harness through column.
10. Reverse procedure to install.

TURN SIGNAL SWITCH

REPLACE

Refer to "Multi-Function Switch, Replace" for replacement procedure.

DIMMER SWITCH

REPLACE

Refer to "Multi-Function Switch, Replace" for replacement procedure.

STEERING WHEEL

REPLACE

Scribe alignment marks on steering wheel and shaft to ensure correct installation.

1. Remove air bag module as outlined in "Air Bag System" chapter.
2. Remove snap ring and steering wheel mounting nut, then the horn lead.
3. Remove steering wheel using suitable puller.
4. Reverse procedure to install, ensure turn signal and multi-function is in neutral position and **torque** steering wheel nut to 30 ft. lbs.

INSTRUMENT CLUSTER

REPLACE

1. Remove instrument cluster lower trim panel as outlined under "Headlamp Switch, Replace."

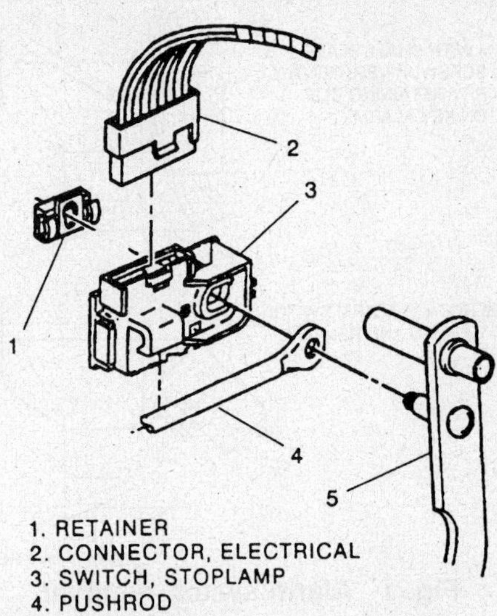

Fig. 4 Stop lamp switch removal

2. **On models equipped with tilt steering column,** tilt column fully down.
3. **On all models,** remove instrument cluster mounting screws.
4. Pull instrument cluster from instrument panel and disconnect electrical connectors.
5. Reverse procedure to install.

RADIO

REPLACE

1. Remove instrument cluster lower trim panel as outlined under "Headlamp Switch, Replace."
2. Release radio head from mounting bracket by pressing down on retaining tabs.
3. Slide radio from mounting bracket, then disconnect electrical connectors and antenna.
4. Reverse procedure to install.

WIPER MOTOR

REPLACE

1. Turn ignition switch to ACC position and set wiper switch to PULSE position.
2. Turn ignition switch off when wiper blades are in inner-wipe position.
3. Disconnect washer hose elbow from air inlet screen.
4. Remove plastic cover and wiper arm mounting nut.
5. Remove wiper arm from drive shaft.
6. Remove air inlet screen and disconnect wiper motor electrical connector.
7. Remove five mounting bolts and wiper motor.
8. Reverse procedure to install.

WIPER TRANSMISSION

REPLACE

1. Remove wiper arms from pivot shafts.
2. Remove ventilator grille to cowl mounting screws and ventilator grille.
3. Working from center of cowl, remove

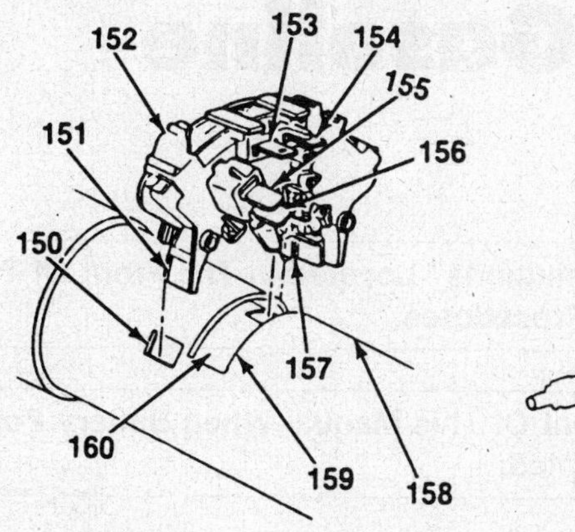

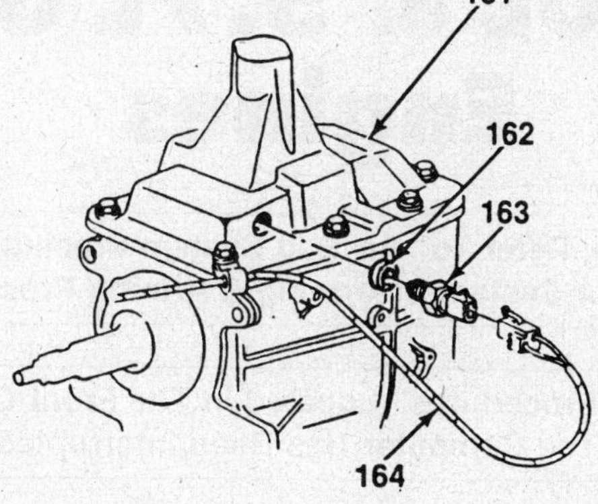

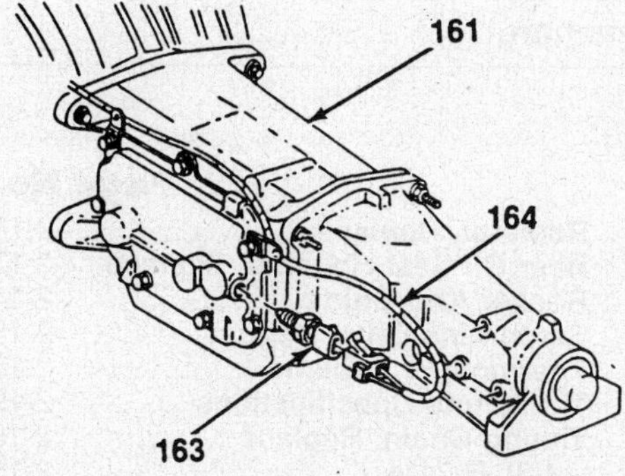

150. Rectangular Hole
151. Tang
152. Switch Assembly (Auto Trans.)
153. Back Up Switch Terminal
154. Back Up Switch Terminal
155. Park, Neutral Switch Terminal
156. Park, Neutral Switch Terminal
157. Actuator
158. Steering Column Jacket
159. Cutout
160. Shift Tube
161. Manual Transmission
162. Seal
163. Switch
164. Harness

GC9048800012000X

Fig. 5 Back-up light switch removal. Automatic transmission

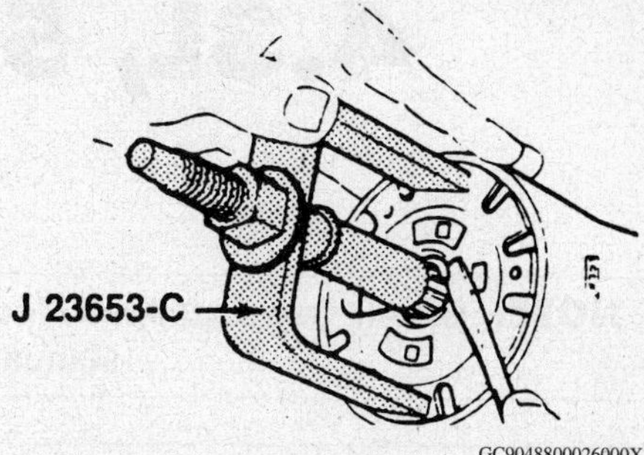

Fig. 6 Lock plate retaining ring removal

link rod to motor drive mounting nuts and disconnect link rods from pins.

4. Remove transmission pivot shaft to cowl mounting screws.
5. Remove transmission pivot shaft with link rods through opening in plenum chamber.
6. Reverse procedure to install.

BLOWER MOTOR

REPLACE

Front

1. Remove coolant recovery tank and battery.
2. **On models equipped with air conditioning,** remove air conditioning line retainers from blower insulation cover.
3. **On all models,** remove retainers and blower insulation cover from blower case.
4. Remove mounting screws and blower motor from blower case.
5. Remove mounting nut blower cage.
6. Reverse procedure to install.

Rear

1. **On models equipped with air conditioning,** recover refrigerant as outlined under "Air Conditioning."
2. **On all models,** drain cooling system into suitable container.
3. Remove lefthand rear interior trim panel.
4. Lower headliner lefthand rear corner and disconnect air duct.
5. Remove duct from rear HVAC case.
6. Remove floor air ducts and disconnect electrical connectors.
7. Remove heater and air conditioning line protective cover.
8. Remove eater and refrigerant hoses from evaporator and blower.
9. Remove rear mounting nuts and HVAC case.
10. Remove mounting screws and blower motor.
11. Reverse procedure to install.

HEATER CORE

REPLACE

Front

1. **On models equipped with air conditioning,** recover refrigerant as outlined under "Air Conditioning" then remove accumulator to gain access to heater hoses.
2. **On all models,** drain coolant into suitable container and remove coolant recovery tank.
3. Disconnect heater hoses from heater core.
4. Remove righthand kick panel and knee bolster.
5. Remove outer floor air outlet duct.
6. Remove mounting screws and heater core access cover.
7. Remove mounts, clips and heater core from case.
8. Reverse procedure to install.

Rear

1. Remove HVAC unit as outlined under "Blower Motor, Replace."
2. Remove bottom cover and heater core from HVAC case.
3. Reverse procedure to install.

EVAPORATOR CORE

REPLACE

Front

1. Recover refrigerant as outlined in "Air Conditioning" chapter.
2. Remove battery and drain engine coolant into suitable container.
3. Remove coolant recovery reservoir and disconnect electrical connectors.
4. Remove accumulator.
5. Remove blower/evaporator case insulator cover and case.
6. Separate case and remove evaporator.
7. Reverse procedure to install, using new O-rings coated with clean refrigerant oil at connections.

Rear

1. Remove HVAC unit as outlined under "Blower Motor, Replace."
2. Remove heater core as outlined under "Heater Core, Replace."
3. Remove screws and separate HVAC case.
4. Remove evaporator from case and thermal expansion valve from evaporator.
5. Reverse procedure to install.

4.3L, 5.0L & 5.7L Gasoline Engines

NOTE: On Air Bag Equipped Models, Refer To "Air Bag System Precautions" Located In The Front Of This Manual For System Disarming & Arming Procedures.

NOTE: Refer To "Computer Relearn Procedures" Located In The Front Of This Manual When Battery Power To The Computer Has Been Interrupted.

NOTE: Prior To Performing Any Service Operations Listed In This Section, Consult The "Technical Service Bulletins" In This Section For Related Information.

INDEX

PRECAUTIONS

Air Bag Systems

Refer to "Air Bag System Precautions" in the front of this manual for system disarming and arming procedures.

Battery Ground Cable

Prior to service disconnect battery ground cable and isolate as required.

Fuel System Pressure Relief

Always release residual fuel system pressure prior to disconnecting fuel lines or hoses.

1. Loosen fuel filler cap.
2. Connect suitable fuel pressure gauge to fuel pressure connection tap and install bleed hose into suitable container.
3. Open valve and bleed system pressure.

Radio Security System

If the Theftlock system is active when

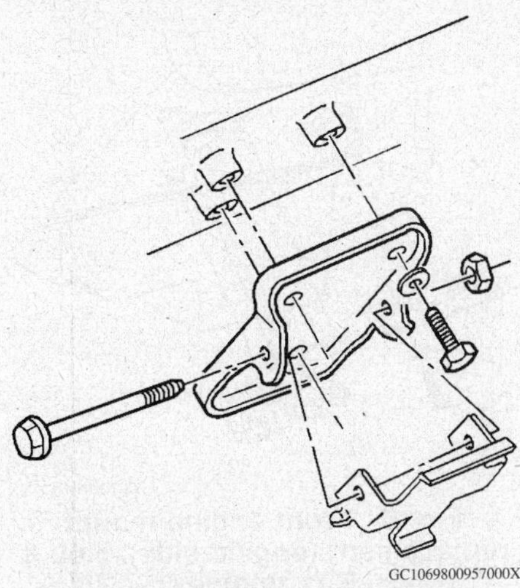

Fig. 1 Front engine mount bracket replacement. 4.3L engine

battery power is interrupted, the customers security code must be entered to restore proper function of the radio. To unlock a secured radio after power loss, proceed as follows:

1. "LOC" appears with ignition in On position.
2. Press "NM" and "000" will appear on display.
3. Press "NM" again to make last two digits agree with security code.
4. Press "HR" to make first 1 or 2 digits agree with security code.
5. Press "AM-FM" to select code entered. "SEC" will show on display indicating radio is now operable and secure.
6. If incorrect code is entered eight times, "INOP" will display. In order to reenter code, ignition must be left on for one hour before code can be entered and only three more chances to enter code are available before display reads "INOP."

COMPRESSION PRESSURE

When inspecting compression, the lowest cylinder must be within 70% of the highest and no cylinder should be less than 100 psi. Perform compression test with engine at operating temperature, all spark plugs removed and throttle wide open.

ENGINE MOUNT

REPLACE

Front

1. Support engine with suitable jack. **Do not place jack under oil pan, any sheet metal or crankshaft pulley.**
2. Remove engine mount through bolt and nut, **Figs. 1 through 6.**
3. Raise and support engine. **Raise engine only enough to gain sufficient clearance for removal. Inspect for interference between rear of engine and cowl panel.**
4. Reverse procedure to install.

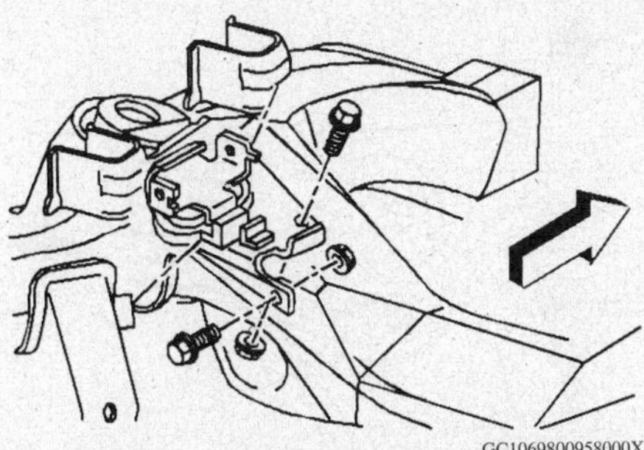

Fig. 2 Front engine mount replacement (lefthand side). 4.3L engine w/crossbrace

Rear

1. Support engine rear with suitable stand.
2. Remove rear engine mount mounting bolts and washers.
3. Raise engine enough to allow mount removal.
4. Remove mount.
5. Reverse procedure to install.

ENGINE

REPLACE

1. Remove engine cover, coolant recovery reservoir, air clearer and air cleaner intake duct.
2. Remove front bumper, grill and radiator support.
3. **On models equipped with air conditioning,** proceed as follows:
   a. Recover air conditioning refrigerant as outlined under "Air Conditioning."
   b. Remove lower hood latch cover, hood latch and lefthand headlamp housing.
   c. Remove condenser air conditioning lines.
   d. Remove mounting bolts and condenser.
4. **On all models,** remove mounting bolts, upper and lower fan shrouds, then the fan and clutch.
5. Remove clamps and upper and lower radiator hoses.
6. Disconnect radiator transmission and oil cooler lines, then remove radiator.
7. Remove ground strap and water pump fan clutch.
8. Remove engine heater hoses and wiring harness.
9. Remove accelerator control cable and cruise control cable, as required.
10. Remove alternator as outlined under "Electrical."
11. Remove mounting bolts and nut and slide alternator bracket off stud. Remove stud.
12. **On models equipped with air conditioning,** proceed as follows:
    a. Remove accumulator air conditioning lines and auxiliary hose at compressor, as required.
    b. Remove mounting bolts, nuts and air conditioning compressor brace.
    c. Remove mounting bolts and air conditioning compressor.

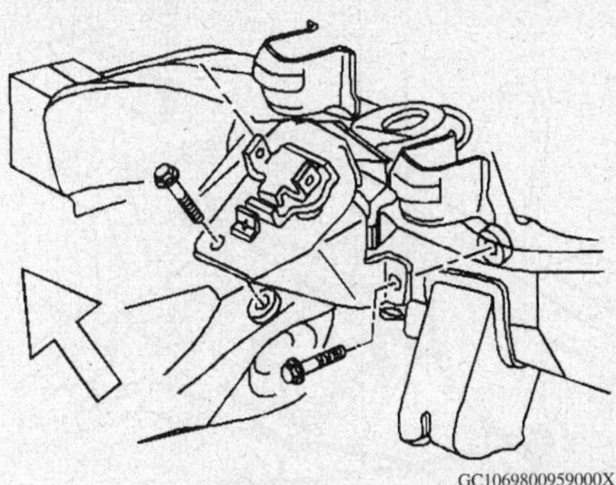

Fig. 3 Front engine mount replacement (righthand side). 4.3L engine w/crossbrace

13. **On all models,** remove power steering pump pulley.
14. Remove mounting bolts and nut and slide power steering pump brace off stud. Remove stud.
15. Remove air conditioning pressure switch, throttle position sensor, idle air control motor, SCPI injector harness connector and MAP sensor.
16. Disconnect transmission oil dipstick tube from accelerator cable bracket.
17. Disconnect fuel lines at intake manifold rear, remove mounting nuts and retainer.
18. Disconnect injector fuel inlet and outlet pipes and remove fuel line bracket.
19. Pull straight up and remove fuel pipe.
20. Remove upper intake manifold.
21. Remove fuel pipes from engine rear.
22. Remove transmission shift cable.
23. Raise and support vehicle. Drain crankcase oil into suitable container.
24. Remove exhaust pipe from exhaust manifold.
25. Remove engine oil cooler lines from mounting bracket and engine.
26. Remove flywheel cover and torque converter mounting bolts.
27. Remove starter motor and transmission cooler lines.
28. Remove transmission to engine mounting bolts.
29. Lower vehicle then install suitable chain and mounting bolt tool No. 23503910, or equivalent, to rear of lefthand cylinder head.
30. Support transmission with suitable strap between frame rails.
31. Attach suitable lifting device to chain.
32. Remove engine mount through bolts and engine mounts from frame.
33. Remove engine.
34. Reverse procedure to install.

INTAKE MANIFOLD

REPLACE

4.3L Engine

Refer to "Intake Manifold, Replace" in the "4.3L Gasoline Engine" section of the "Avalanche, Escalade EXT, Sierra, Silverado & SSR" chapter.

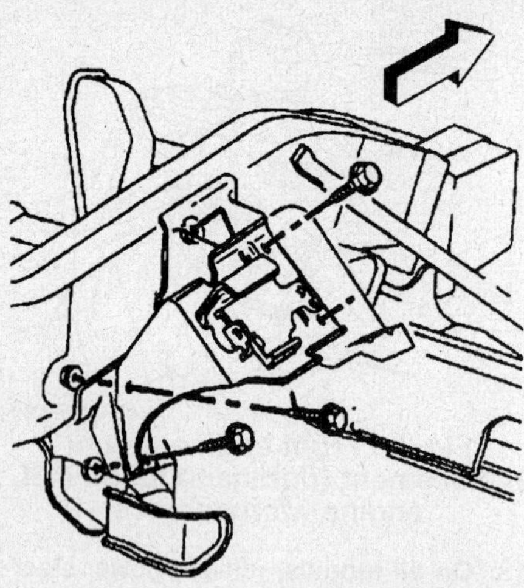

GC1069800960000X

Fig. 4 Front engine mount replacement. 4.3L engine less crossbrace

5.0L & 5.7L Engines

UPPER

1. Relieve fuel system pressure as outlined under "Precautions."
2. Remove engine cover.
3. Remove air cleaner box and intake duct.
4. Disconnect wiring harness connectors, then remove harness brackets and position harness aside.
5. Disconnect throttle linkage and bracket from throttle body.
6. **On models equipped with cruise control,** disconnect cruise control cable.
7. **On all models,** remove fuel line from throttle body to rear of intake manifold.
8. Remove fuel line bracket at rear of lower intake manifold.
9. Remove PCV hose, purge solenoid and bracket.
10. Remove upper intake manifold mounting bolts and studs. **Mark stud locations for installation reference.**
11. Remove upper intake manifold, **Fig. 7.**
12. Reverse procedure to install, noting the following:
    a. Do not pinch injector lines between upper and lower intake manifolds.
    b. Ensure studs are installed in correct positions.
    c. Align upper and lower intake manifolds by installing two corner studs first.

LOWER

1. Relieve fuel system pressure as outlined under "Precautions."
2. Remove engine cover.
3. Remove air cleaner box, intake duct and coolant reservoir.
4. Disconnect upper radiator hose from thermostat housing.
5. Disconnect heater hose from lower intake manifold.
6. Remove EGR valve and coolant bypass hose.
7. Remove fuel line bracket at rear of intake manifold.

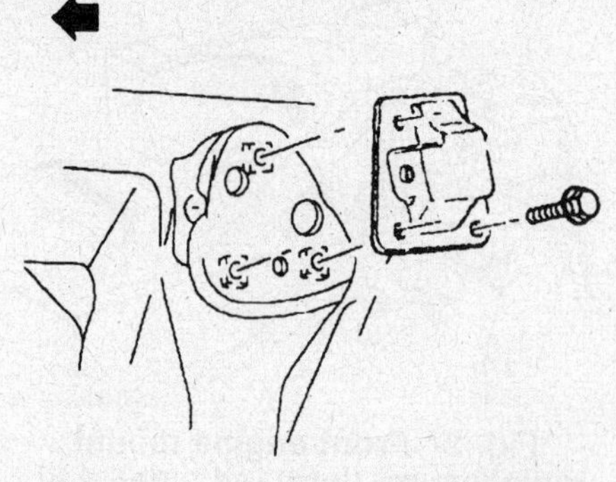

GC1069800951000X

Fig. 5 Front engine mount replacement (frame side). 5.0L & 5.7L engines

8. Disconnect wiring harness connectors, then remove harness brackets and position harness aside.
9. Disconnect throttle cable, then remove throttle cable bracket from throttle body.
10. **On models equipped with cruise control,** disconnect cruise control cable from throttle body.
11. **On all models,** remove ignition coil and bracket.
12. Remove lefthand side valve cover and oil dipstick tube.
13. Remove EGR inlet tube, clamp and bolt.
14. Disconnect PCV valve and vacuum hoses.
15. **On models equipped with air conditioning,** remove air conditioning compressor and bracket, then position aside.
16. **On all models,** remove alternator rear bracket bolt.
17. Remove mounting bolts and lower intake manifold.
18. Reverse procedure to install, noting the following:
    a. Install gaskets with port blocking plates facing rear of engine.
    b. Apply 3/16 inch bead of RTV sealant part No. 1052366, or equivalent, to front and rear sealing surfaces on block. Extend bead approximately 1/2 inch up each cylinder head to seal and retain gaskets.
    c. **Torque** mounting bolts to 27 inch lbs., in sequence, **Fig. 8.**
    d. **Torque** mounting bolts to 106 inch lbs., in sequence.
    e. Final **torque** mounting bolts to 11 inch lbs., in sequence.

EXHAUST MANIFOLD

REPLACE

4.3L Engine

Refer to "Exhaust Manifold, Replace" in the "4.3L Gasoline Engine" section of the "Avalanche, Escalade EXT, Sierra, Silverado & SSR" chapter.

5.0L & 5.7L Engines

1. Remove engine cover and raise and

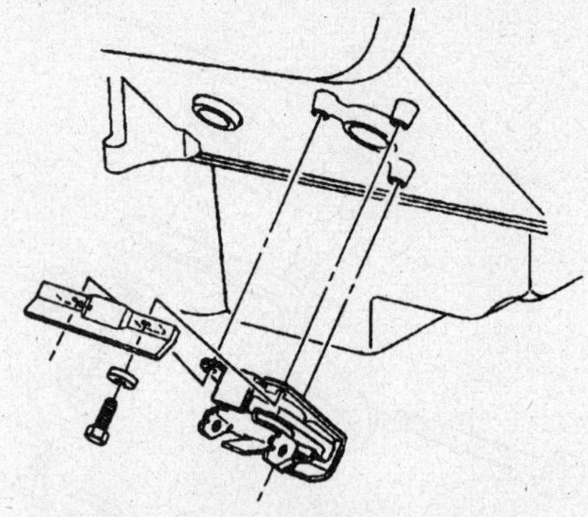

GC1069800952000X

Fig. 6 Front engine mount replacement (engine side). 5.0L & 5.7L engines

support vehicle.

2. Disconnect exhaust pipe from manifold and lower vehicle.
3. Disconnect oxygen sensor connector.
4. **On lefthand manifold,** disconnect EGR inlet pipe, then remove power steering pump bracket, alternator brace and spark plugs.
5. **On righthand manifold,** remove oil dipstick tube.
6. **On lefthand or righthand manifold,** remove exhaust manifold.
7. Reverse procedure to install.

CYLINDER HEAD

REPLACE

4.3L Engine

Refer to "Cylinder Head, Replace" in the "4.3L Gasoline Engine" section of the "Avalanche, Escalade EXT, Sierra, Silverado & SSR" chapter.

5.0L & 5.7L Engines

REMOVAL

1. Remove drive belt.
2. Recover refrigerant as outlined in "Air Conditioning" chapter and remove compressor.
3. Remove lower intake and exhaust manifolds as outlined under "Intake Manifold, Replace" and "Exhaust Manifold, Replace."
4. Remove valve cover.
5. Disconnect wires and remove spark plugs.
6. Remove rocker arms and pushrods.
7. Remove power steering pump pulley.
8. Disconnect power steering pump electrical connector and remove pump mounting nuts and bolts from bracket front.
9. Remove bracket front nut and slide power steering pump and bracket off stud. Remove stud.
10. Remove alternator as outlined under "Electrical."
11. Remove oil indicator tube.
12. Remove mounting bolts and nut, then

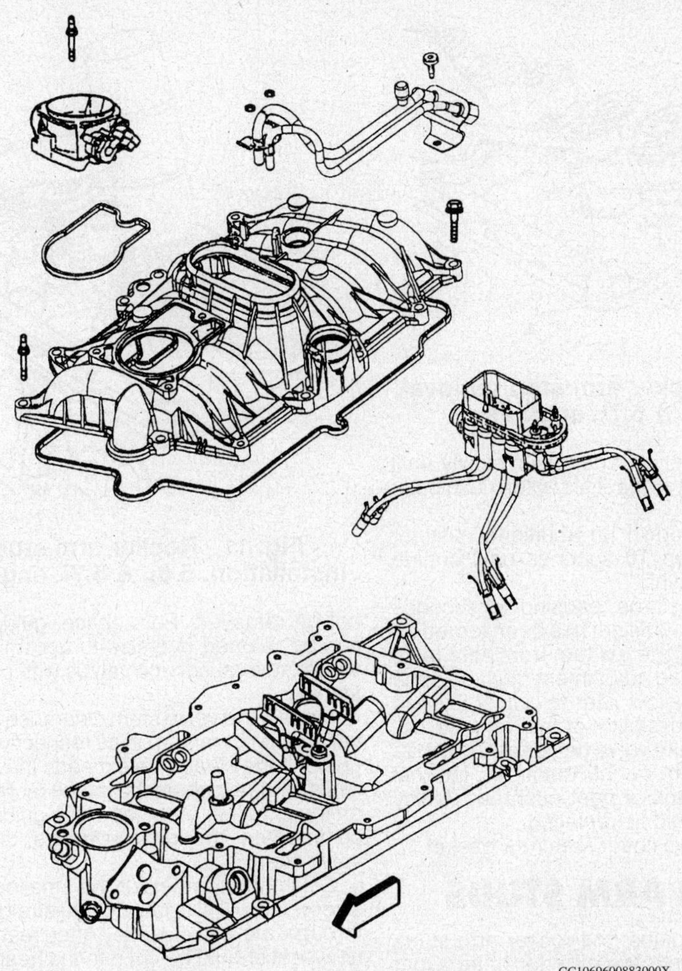

Fig. 7 Upper intake manifold. 5.0L & 5.7L engines

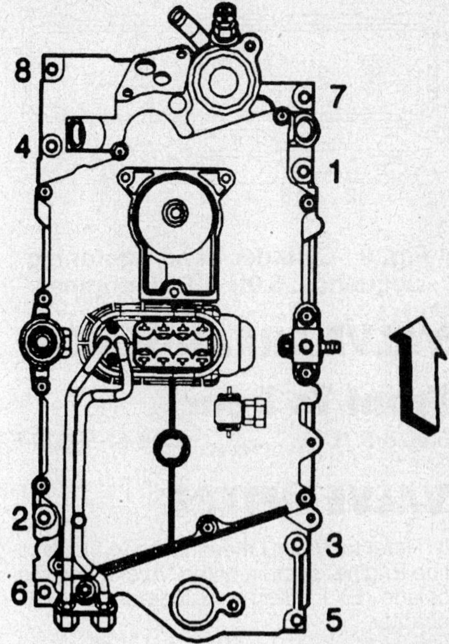

Fig. 8 Lower intake manifold bolt tightening sequence. 5.0L & 5.7L engines

the alternator bracket front and slide bracket off stud. Remove stud.

13. Remove mounting bolts and cylinder head.

INSTALLATION

1. Inspect gasket surfaces on heads and block for nicks or heavy scratches. Block bolt and cylinder head mounting bolt threads must be clean, as dirt will affect bolt holding power.
2. **On engines equipped with steel gasket,** coat both sides of gasket with suitable sealer.
3. **On engines equipped with composition steel/asbestos type gasket,** do not use sealer.
4. **On all models,** place new gasket in position over dowel pins with locating mark face up.
5. Install cylinder head over locating pins and gasket.
6. Coat cylinder head bolts threads with suitable sealer and install bolts hand tight.
7. **Torque** mounting bolts to 22 ft. lbs., in sequence, **Fig. 9.**
8. Tighten short bolts Nos. 3, 4, 7, 8, 11, 12, 15 and 16 an additional 55° using suitable torque angle meter.
9. Tighten medium bolts Nos. 14 and 17 an additional 65°.
10. Tighten long bolts Nos. 1, 2, 5, 6, 7, 10 and 13 an additional 75°.
11. Install push rods and rocket arms.
12. Install bracket and power steering pump, then the power steering pump pulley.
13. Install bracket and alternator, then the oil indicator tube.
14. Install exhaust and lower intake manifolds as outlined under "Exhaust Manifold, Replace" and "Intake Manifold, Replace."
15. Install valve covers and air conditioning compressor.
16. Install drive belt.

VALVE COVER

REPLACE

4.3L Engine

Refer to "Valve Cover, Replace" in the "4.3L Gasoline Engine" section of the "Avalanche, Escalade EXT, Sierra, Silverado & SSR" chapter.

5.0L & 5.7L Engines

LEFTHAND

1. Remove engine cover.
2. Disconnect spark plug wires from distributor cap.
3. Remove PCV valve from cover and set it aside.
4. Disconnect ECT sensor electrical connector.
5. Remove AIR bypass hose assembly.
6. **On models equipped with air conditioning,** remove air conditioning compressor as outlined under "Air Conditioning."
7. **On all models,** remove pulley from power steering pump.
8. Remove power steering pump mounting bracket, then lay power steering pump and bracket aside.
9. Remove mounting bolts, valve cover and gasket.
10. Reverse procedure to install.

RIGHTHAND

1. Remove engine cover.
2. Remove oil fill tube to alternator and drive belt tensioner bracket mounting screw.
3. Remove oil fill tube.
4. Disconnect Ignition Control Module (ICM) electrical connector.
5. Open engine electrical harness retainer.
6. Position engine electrical harness over ignition coil.
7. Disconnect spark plug wires from distributor cap.
8. Remove AIR bypass hose assembly, as required.
9. Remove crankcase vent tube from valve cover.
10. Remove mounting bolts, valve cover and gasket.
11. Reverse procedure to install.

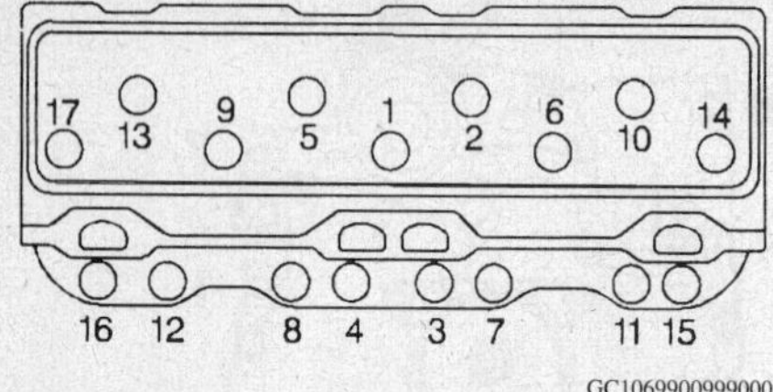

Fig. 9 Cylinder head tightening sequence. 5.0L & 5.7L engines

VALVE ARRANGEMENT

Front To Rear

5.0L & 5.7L .... E-I-I-E-E-I-I-E

VALVE LIFTERS

Refer to "Valve Lifters" in the "4.3L Gasoline Engine" section of the "Avalanche, Escalade EXT, Sierra, Silverado & SSR" chapter.

VALVE CLEARANCE SPECIFICATIONS

Net lash

5.0L & 5.7L .... .0010–.0037

VALVE ADJUSTMENT

Initial Adjustment

1. With engine in position to fire No. 1 cylinder, adjust the following valves:
   a. **On models equipped with 4.3L engine,** exhaust Nos. 1, 5 and 6; intake Nos. 1, 2 and 3.
   b. **On models equipped with 5.0L and 5.7L engines,** exhaust Nos. 1, 3, 4 and 8; intake Nos. 1, 2, 5 and 7.
   c. **On all models,** back off adjusting nut until lash is felt, (when pushrod can be rotated by hand), then tighten nut until lash is eliminated.
   d. After zero lash is obtained, tighten nut an additional one full turn.
2. Turn crankshaft one complete revolution, which will bring engine in position to fire cylinders 4 (V6) or 6 (V8).
3. With engine in this position, adjust the following valves:
   a. **On models equipped with 4.3L engine,** exhaust Nos. 2, 3 and 4; intake Nos. 4, 5 and 6.
   b. **On models equipped with 5.0L and 5.7L engines,** exhaust Nos. 2, 5, 6 and 7; intake Nos. 3, 4, 6 and 8.
   c. **On all models,** after zero lash is obtained, tighten nut an additional one full turn.

Final Adjustment

1. Warm engine operating temperature and remove valve cover.
2. With engine running at idle speed, back off valve rocker arm nut until rocker arm starts to clatter.

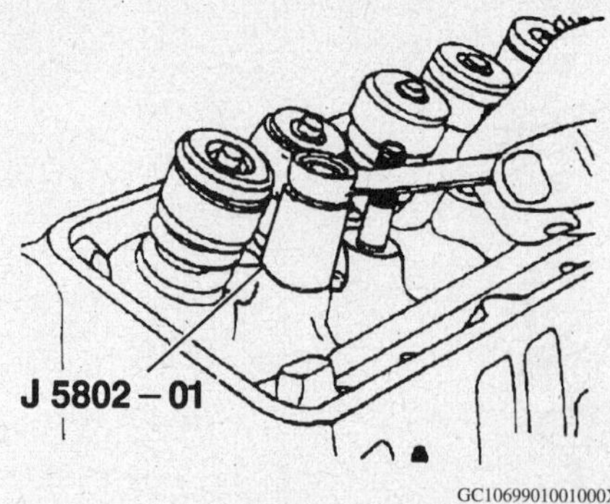

Fig. 10 Rocker arm stud removal. 5.0L & 5.7L engines

3. Turn rocker arm nut down slowly until clatter just stops. This is zero lash position.
4. Turn nut down an additional 1/4 turn, then pause 10 seconds until engine runs smoothly.
5. Repeat 1/4 turns, pausing 10 seconds each time, until nut has been turned an additional one full turn from zero lash.
6. This preload adjustment must be done slowly to allow lifter to adjust itself to prevent possibility of interference between intake valve head and top of piston, which might result in internal damage and/or bent pushrods. Noisy lifters should be replaced.
7. Install valve cover, with new gasket.

ROCKER ARM STUDS

On 4.3L engines, the rocker arm studs are threaded into the cylinder head. Coat threads on cylinder head end of stud with sealer before assembling to head. On 5.0L and 5.7L engines, replace rocker arm studs as follows:

1. Remove old stud by placing suitable spacer over stud, **Fig. 10.**
2. Install nut and flat washer on stud, then pull stud out by turning nut.
3. Ream stud hole for an oversize stud using reamer tool No. J-5715, or equivalent, for .003 inch oversize studs or tool No. J-6036, or equivalent, for .013 inch oversize stud. **Rocker arm studs that have damaged threads may be replaced with standard studs. Loose studs should be replaced with oversize studs.**
4. Coat press-fit area of new stud with rear axle lubricant.
5. Install stud using stud driver tool No. 6880, or equivalent, by driving it in until tool bottoms on head, **Fig. 11.**

PUSH RODS

When a replacement pushrod has a paint stripe at one end, this painted end must be installed in contact with the rocker arm. To provide durability a hardened insert is incorporated in the rocker arm end of these pushrods.

VALVE GUIDES

Valve guides in these engines are an integral part of the head and, therefore, can-

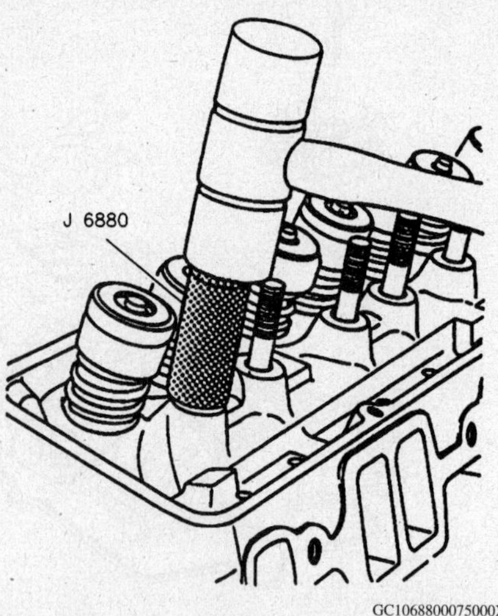

Fig. 11 Rocker arm stud installation. 5.0L & 5.7L engines

not be removed. For service, guide holes can be reamed oversize to accommodate one of several service valves with oversize stems.

Inspect the valve stem clearance of each valve (after cleaning) in its respective valve guide. If the clearance exceeds the service limits of .004 inch on the intake or .005 inch on the exhaust, ream the valve guide to accommodate the next oversize diameter valve stem.

Select the reamer for the smallest oversize which will provide a clean straight bore through the valve guide. After reaming, a new seat should be cut into the head to ensure perfect seating of the new valve.

VALVE SEATS

1. Inspect valve margin. Exhaust valve may be refaced if margin is more than .050 inch thick before grinding.
2. Reface pitted exhaust valves on suitable valve refacing machine.
3. Replace valve if margin is less than .050 inch thick after grinding.
4. If valve face has been ground, it may be required to shim valve spring to obtain proper spring installed height.
5. Inspect for loose valve seat in cylinder head. Valve seat has an interference fit to cylinder head.
6. Clean valve guide bores using suitable tool.
7. A valve guide bore that is oversized must be repaired or replaced prior to valve seat grinding.
8. Inspect valve seats. Valve seats should be concentric to .0021 inch total indicator reading.
9. If valve seat has to be ground, it may be required to shim valve spring to attain proper spring installed height.

HYDRAULIC LIFTERS

REPLACE

Removal

1. Remove cylinder head and gasket as

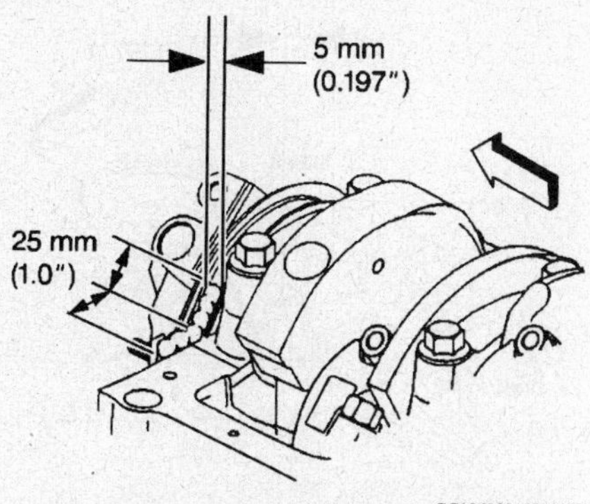

Fig. 12 Front cover adhesive installation

outlined under "Cylinder Head, Replace."

2. Remove valve lifter guide bolts and guides, as required.
3. Remove valve lifters using lifter pliers tool No. J-3049-A, or equivalent.
4. Remove valve lifters from guide.
5. Organize or mark components for installation reference.

Installation

1. Lubricate valve lifters and lifter bores with clean engine oil.
2. Insert valve lifters into lifter guides, aligning flat area on top of lifter with flat area in lifter guide bore, then push lifter completely into guide bore.
3. Install valve lifters and guide into engine block.
4. Install valve lifter guide bolt.

CRANKSHAFT DAMPER

REPLACE

1. Remove drive belt as outlined under "Serpentine Drive Belt."
2. Remove air cleaner and air intake duct.
3. Remove coolant reservoir.
4. Remove engine and transmission oil dipstick at alternator bracket mounting bolt.
5. Remove engine oil fill tube at alternator bracket mounting bolt.
6. Move oil dipstick tubes and oil fill tube away from fan shroud.
7. Remove upper fan shroud mounting bolts from top of radiator.
8. Remove upper to lower fan shroud mounting bolts.
9. **On models equipped with 4.3L engine,** push radiator intake hose aside for clearance.
10. **On all models,** remove upper fan shroud.
11. Remove fan and clutch.
12. Remove crankshaft damper using crankshaft balancer remover tool No. J-23523-F, or equivalent.
13. Reverse procedure to install.

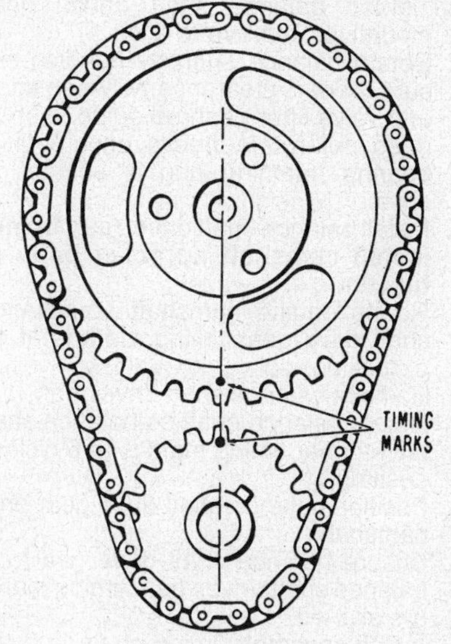

Fig. 13 Timing marks. 5.0L & 5.7L engines

FRONT COVER

REPLACE

The engine front cover gasket is reusable.

1. Remove crankshaft damper as outlined under "Crankshaft Damper, Replace."
2. Remove water pump as outlined under "Water Pump, Replace."
3. Remove oil pan as outlined under "Oil Pan, Replace."
4. Remove the Crankshaft Position (CKP) sensor from front cover.
5. Remove mounting bolts, front cover and gasket.
6. Reverse procedure to install. Apply .197 inch bead of adhesive part No. 12346141, or equivalent, in inch long to engine front cover to engine block junction at oil pan, **Fig. 12.**

FRONT COVER SEAL

REPLACE

1. Remove crankshaft damper as outlined under "Crankshaft Damper, Replace."
2. Remove seal by prying using suitable screwdriver. **Do not distort engine front cover.**
3. Install seal using cover aligner seal installer tool No. J-35468, or equivalent.

TIMING CHAIN

REPLACE

Turning either the crankshaft or the camshaft with the timing chain removed may cause the pistons to contact the valves, resulting in damage.

4.3L Engine

Refer to "Timing Chain, Replace" in the "4.3L Gasoline Engine" section of the "Avalanche, Escalade EXT, Sierra, Silverado & SSR" chapter.

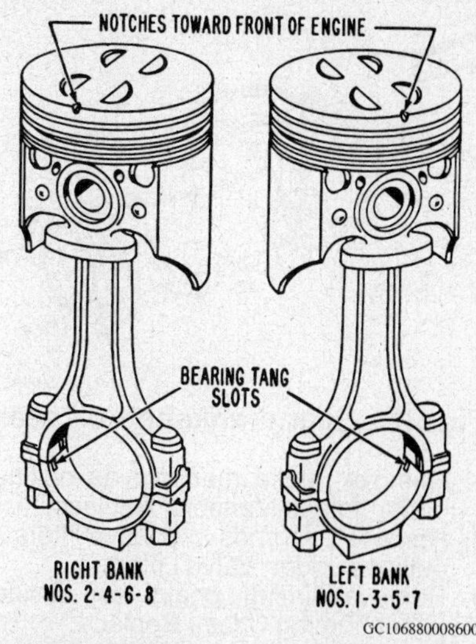

Fig. 14 Piston & rod assembly. 5.0L & 5.7L engines

5.0L & 5.7L Engines

REMOVAL

1. Remove front cover as outlined under "Front Cover, Replace."
2. Remove Crankshaft Position (CKP) sensor reluctor ring.
3. Rotate crankshaft until timing marks on both sprockets line up and cylinder No. 1 is at top dead center (TDC) of compression stroke.
4. Ensure timing marks align, **Fig. 13.**
5. Remove bolts, camshaft sprocket and camshaft timing chain.
6. Remove crankshaft sprocket using crankshaft gear remover tool No. J-5825-A, or equivalent.
7. Remove crankshaft balancer key.

INSTALLATION

1. Install crankshaft balancer key into crankshaft keyway. Key should be parallel to crankshaft or with slight incline.
2. Install crankshaft sprocket using crankshaft sprocket installer tool No. J-5590, or equivalent.
3. Ensure camshaft and crankshaft timing marks are aligned, **Fig. 13. Do not use hammer to install camshaft sprocket.**
4. Rotate crankshaft until crankshaft sprocket alignment mark is at 12 o'clock position.
5. Install camshaft sprocket and camshaft timing chain. **Install camshaft sprocket with alignment mark at 6 o'clock position.**
6. Install CKP sensor reluctor ring by aligning ring keyway with crankshaft balancer key.
7. Install front cover as outlined under "Front Cover, Replace."

CAMSHAFT

REPLACE

Depending on vehicle and engine application, the grille, engine cover, radiator and condenser may have to be removed.

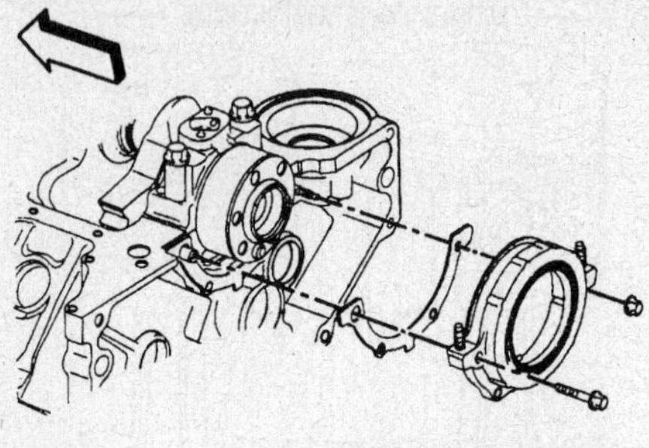

Fig. 15 Rear crankshaft oil seal

1. Remove intake manifold as outlined under "Intake Manifold, Replace."
2. Remove pushrods and valve lifters as outlined under "Valve Lifters."
3. Remove timing chain as outlined under "Timing Chain, Replace."
4. **On models equipped with 4.3L engine,** remove balance shaft gear.
5. **On all models,** install two or three 5⁄16-18 x 4–5 inch bolts into holes, then pull camshaft out of cylinder block.
6. Reverse procedure to install.

BALANCE SHAFT

REPLACE

Depending on vehicle and engine application, the grille, engine cover, radiator and condenser may have to be removed.

Removal

1. Remove valve lifter pushrod guide.
2. Hold camshaft sprocket with suitable wrench and loosen and remove balance shaft driven gear mounting bolt and washer.
3. Remove timing chain as outlined under "Timing Chain, Replace."
4. Place suitable wrench onto balance shaft near front bearing and remove driven gear mounting bolt.
5. Remove balance shaft driven gear.
6. Remove mounting bolts and balance shaft retainer.
7. Remove mounting bolts and balance shaft retainer.
8. Remove balance shaft using suitable soft-faced hammer. **Do not remove bearing.**

Installation

1. Apply clean engine oil part No. 12345610, or equivalent, to balance shaft front bearing.
2. Install balance shaft using balance shaft installer tool No. J-36996 and universal driver handle tool No. J-8092, or equivalent.
3. Install balance shaft retainer and tighten mounting bolts.
4. Install balance shaft driven gear.
5. Apply threadlock part No. 12345382, or equivalent, to balance shaft driven gear bolt threads.
6. Install balance shaft driven gear mounting bolt using suitable wrench to secure shaft. Place wrench onto shaft near front bearing.
7. Tighten balance shaft driven gear mounting. Remove wrench.
8. Rotate balance shaft by hand to ensure there is clearance between shaft and valve lifter pushrod guide. If shaft does not rotate freely, ensure front bearing retaining ring is seated on case.
9. Install balance shaft drive gear. **Do not install camshaft sprocket bolts at this time.**
10. Rotate engine camshaft so balance shaft drive gear timing mark is at 12 o'clock position.
11. Remove balance shaft drive gear.
12. Rotate balance shaft so balance shaft driven gear timing mark is at 6 o'clock position.
13. Position balance shaft drive gear onto camshaft.
14. Ensure balance shaft drive gear and balance shaft driven gear timing marks are aligned.
15. Install camshaft timing chain and the camshaft sprocket as outlined under "Camshaft, Replace."
16. Install crankshaft position reluctor ring and front cover.
17. Install valve lifter pushrod guide.

PISTON & ROD ASSEMBLY

When assembling the piston and connecting rod, the mark on the top of the piston must point to the front of the engine block. The lefthand bank connecting rods should have the flange face toward the front of the engine block. The righthand bank connecting rods should have the flange face toward the rear of the engine block. The piston pin has an interference fit into the connecting rod and is full floating in the piston. The space compression ring end gaps should be 120° apart and the oil ring end gaps should be a minimum of 90° apart. Assemble the pistons to the connecting rods, **Fig. 14.**

PISTONS, PINS & RINGS

A .001 inch oversize piston is available for service use so proper clearances can be obtained for slightly worn cylinder bores requiring only light honing. In addition, oversizes of .020 inch, .030 inch and .040 inch are available. If the cylinders have less than .005 inch taper or wear, they can be reconditioned with a hone and fitted with the .001 inch oversize piston.

MAIN & ROD BEARINGS

Main Bearings

Shell type bearings are used and if worn excessively, should be replaced. No attempt should be made to shim, file or otherwise take up worn bearings.

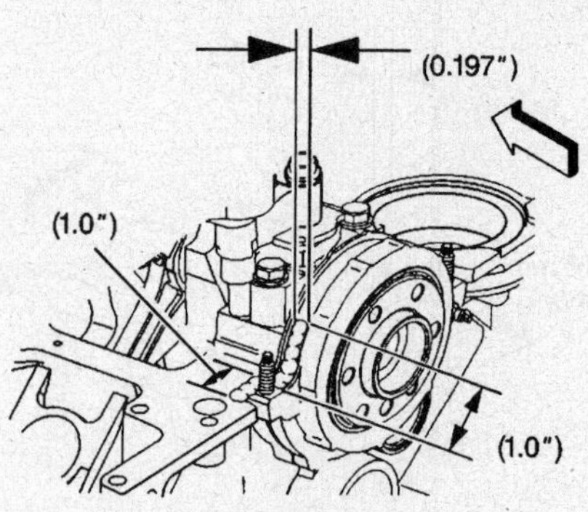

Fig. 16 Rear oil seal housing adhesive installation. 4.3L, 5.0L & 5.7L engines

Main bearings are available in standard and undersizes of .001, .002, .009, .010 and .020 inch.

INSTALLATION

1. Install crankshaft bearings.
2. Apply clean engine oil to bearings and journals.
3. Install crankshaft.
4. Install crankshaft bearings into caps.
5. Apply clean engine oil to bearings.
6. Install crankshaft bearing caps in original positions and with arrow in direction of front of engine block.
7. Install crankshaft bearing cap bolts and studs.
8. Thrust crankshaft rearward to set and align crankshaft thrust bearings and caps.
9. Thrust crankshaft forward to align rear faces of crankshaft thrust bearings.
10. Ensure crankshaft bearing caps are fully seated in engine block crankshaft bearing cap channel and are centered on engine block bulkheads.
11. **Torque** crankshaft bearing cap bolts and studs to 15 ft. lbs.
12. **On models equipped with two bolt caps,** tighten crankshaft bearing cap bolts and studs an additional 73° using electronic torque angle meter tool No. J-36660-A, or equivalent.
13. **On models equipped with four bolt caps,** proceed as follows:
    a. Tighten bearing cap outboard bolts an additional 43° using electronic torque angle meter tool No. J-36660-A, or equivalent.
    b. Tighten bearing cap inboard bolts and studs an additional 73° using electronic torque angle meter tool.

Rod Bearings

Connecting rod bearing inserts are available in standard size and undersizes of .001 inch, .002 inch, .010 inch and .020 inch. The bearings can be replaced without removing the rod assembly by removing the cap and replacing the upper and lower halves of the bearing.

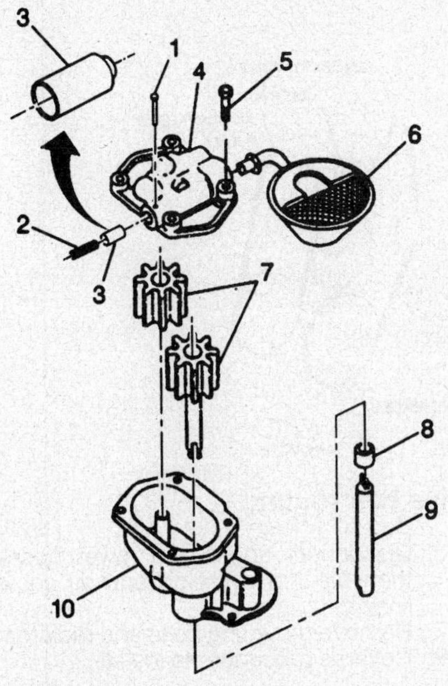

1. Retaining Pin
2. Pressure Regulator Spring
3. Pressure Regulator Valve
4. Pump Cover
5. Bolts
6. Oil Pump Screen Pickup
7. Idler Gear, Drive Gear & Shaft
8. Retainer
9. Driveshaft
10. Pump Body

GC1099900115000X

Fig. 17 Oil pump. 4.3L engine

CRANKSHAFT REAR OIL SEAL

REPLACE

Removal

1. Raise and support vehicle.
2. Remove transmission as outlined under **MOTOR's "Domestic Transmission, In-Vehicle Service" or "Transmission Service DVD."**
3. Remove flywheel or flex plate, as required.
4. Loosen oil pan.
5. Remove rear oil seal using suitable tool inserted into access notches and carefully prying seal from housing, **Fig. 15.**

Installation

1. Apply 2–3 drops of clean engine oil to rear oil seal housing bore, outside diameter of flywheel pilot flange, crankshaft seal surface and crankshaft rear oil seal O.D.
2. Apply one drop of clean engine oil to flywheel locator pin O.D.
3. **Do not allow oil or any other lubricants to contact seal lip surface of rear oil seal.**
4. Remove rear oil seal sleeve.
5. Install rear oil seal near to flush and square to crankshaft rear oil seal housing using rear main seal installer tool No. J-35621-B, or equivalent.
6. Install flywheel and transmission.

REAR OIL SEAL HOUSING

REPLACE

Do not remove the crankshaft rear oil seal housing if only replacing the crankshaft rear oil seal.

1. Remove oil pan as outlined under "Oil Pan, Replace."
2. Remove transmission as outlined under **MOTOR's "Domestic Transmission, In-Vehicle Service" or "Transmission Service DVD."**
3. Remove flywheel or flex plate, as required.
4. Remove mounting bolts, nut and rear oil seal housing.
5. Reverse procedure to install.

OIL PAN

REPLACE

4.3L Engine

1. Raise and support vehicle. Remove exhaust pipe from manifold.
2. Drain engine oil into suitable container, then remove oil filter and adapter.
3. Remove starter wire and transmission cooler pipes bracket mounting bolt .
4. Remove Crankcase Position (CKP) sensor wiring harness from retainer.
5. Remove starter motor as outlined in "Electrical" section.
6. Remove transmission cover.
7. Remove oil pan rear nuts' access plugs.
8. Remove transmission to oil pan bolts.
9. Remove and discard engine oil level sensor, as required.
10. Remove mounting bolts, nuts and oil pan. Discard oil pan gasket.
11. Reverse procedure to install, noting the following:
    a. Apply .197 inch wide and 1 inch long bead of adhesive No. 12346141, or equivalent, to engine front cover to engine block junction at oil pan sealing surfaces, **Fig. 12.**
    b. Apply .197 inch wide and 1 inch long bead of adhesive to crankshaft rear oil seal housing to engine block junction at oil pan sealing surfaces, **Fig. 16.**
    c. Install new oil pan gasket.
    d. Gasket and oil pan must be installed, and mounting bolts and nuts tightened while adhesive is still wet to touch.

5.0L & 5.7L Engines

1. Raise and support vehicle. Remove exhaust pipe from manifold.
2. Drain engine oil into suitable container, then remove oil filter and adapter.
3. Remove oil dipstick and tube.
4. Remove oil cooler pipes and retainer.
5. Remove starter motor as outlined under "Electrical."

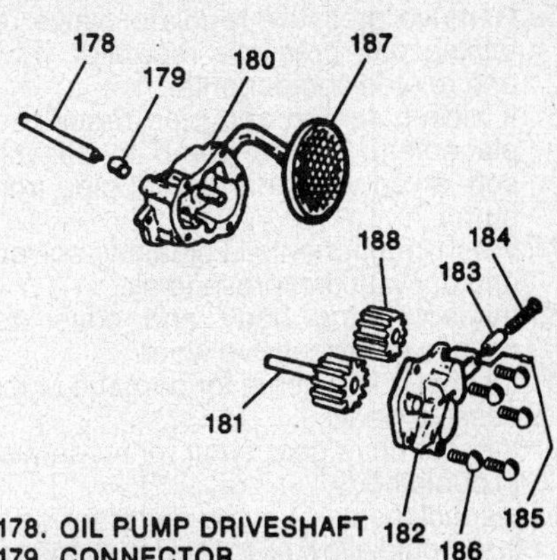

178. OIL PUMP DRIVESHAFT
179. CONNECTOR
180. BODY
181. DRIVE GEAR AND SHAFT
182. COVER
183. PRESSURE RELIEF VALVE
184. SPRING
185. SPRING RETAINING PIN
186. COVER SCREWS
187. PICK-UP SCREEN AND PIPE
188. IDLER GEAR

GC1099900116000X

Fig. 18 Oil pump. 5.0L & 5.7L engines

6. Remove engine mount through bolts.
7. Raise and support engine.
8. Remove pan mounting bolts and nuts. Record stud locations for assembly.
9. Remove pan and gasket.
10. Reverse procedure to install, noting the following:
    a. Apply .197 inch wide and 1 inch long bead of adhesive No. 12346141, or equivalent, to engine front cover to engine block junction at oil pan sealing surfaces, **Fig. 12.**
    b. Apply .197 inch wide and 1 inch long bead of adhesive to crankshaft rear oil seal housing to engine block junction at oil pan sealing surfaces, **Fig. 16.**
    c. Install new oil pan gasket.
    d. Gasket and oil pan must be installed, and mounting bolts and nuts tightened while adhesive is still wet to touch.

OIL PUMP

REPLACE

1. Remove oil pan as outlined under "Oil Pan, Replace."
2. **On models equipped with 5.0L and 5.7L engines,** remove oil deflector.
3. **On all models,** remove pump to rear main bearing cap nut, then the pump and extension shaft.
4. Reverse procedure to install.

OIL PUMP SERVICE

1. Remove oil pump as outlined under "Oil Pump, Replace."
2. Remove pump cover screws and pump cover, **Figs. 17 and 18.**
3. Mark gear teeth so they can be assembled with same teeth indexing.
4. Remove drive gear, idler gear and shaft.

5. Remove pressure regulator valve retaining pin, pressure regulator valve and related components.
6. If pickup screen and pipe require replacement, mount pump in suitable soft-jawed vise and extract pipe from pump.
7. Wash components in cleaning solvent and dry with compressed air.
8. Inspect pump body and cover for cracks and excessive wear.
9. Inspect pump gears for damage or excessive wear.
10. Inspect drive gear shaft for looseness in pump body.
11. Inspect inside of pump cover for wear that would allow oil to leak past ends of gears.
12. Inspect pickup screen and pipe for damage to screen, pipe or relief grommet.
13. Inspect pressure regulator valve for proper fit in pump housing.
14. Reverse procedure to assemble, noting the following:
    a. Turn driveshaft by hand to inspect for smooth operation.
    b. **Pump gears and body are not serviced separately. If pump gears or body are damaged or worn, pump should be replaced.**
    c. **If pickup screen was removed, it should be replaced with new one as loss of press fit condition could result in air leak and loss of oil pressure.**

SERPENTINE DRIVE BELT

These engines use a single serpentine drive belt to drive all engine-mount accessories. All belt drive accessories are rigidly mounted with belt tension maintained by a spring loaded automatic tensioner.

1. Rotate tensioner counterclockwise using suitable ½ inch breaker bar with socket placed on tensioner pulley axis bolt.
2. Remove belt from pulleys.
3. Route new belt as outlined, **Fig. 19.**
4. Rotate tensioner pulley axis bolt counterclockwise and slip belt over tensioner using suitable breaker bar and socket.
5. Release tensioner. Tensioner is spring loaded and will return to original position when released.

COOLING SYSTEM BLEED

These engines do not require a specified bleed procedure. After filling cooling system, run engine to operating temperature with radiator/pressure cap off. Air will then be automatically bled through cap opening.

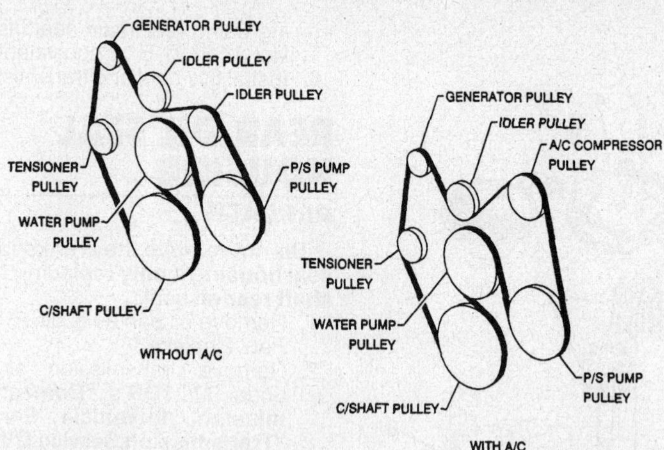

Fig. 19 Serpentine drive belt routing

THERMOSTAT

REPLACE

1. Remove engine cover, air cleaner and air inlet duct, as required.
2. Drain cooling system into suitable container until radiator coolant level is below thermostat.
3. Remove radiator hose at coolant outlet.
4. Remove thermostat housing mounting bolts and ground wire, if applicable.
5. Remove thermostat housing, thermostat and gasket.
6. Reverse procedure to install.

WATER PUMP

REPLACE

1. Drain cooling system into suitable container.
2. Remove air cleaner, duct and coolant recovery reservoir.
3. Remove upper fan shroud, fan and clutch.
4. Remove accessory drive belt(s).
5. Remove water pump pulley mounting bolts.
6. Disconnect lower radiator and upper bypass hoses from pump.
7. Remove four mounting bolts, water pump and two gaskets.
8. Reverse procedure to install.

RADIATOR

REPLACE

1. Drain coolant into a suitable container.
2. Remove air cleaner, duct and coolant recovery reservoir.
3. Remove mounting bolts, upper to lower mounting bolts and upper fan shroud.
4. Remove mounting bolts and lower fan shroud.
5. Remove fan and clutch.
6. Disconnect upper and lower hoses, then the transmission and oil cooler lines.
7. Remove mounting bolts and radiator.
8. Reverse procedure to install.

FUEL PUMP

REPLACE

1. Drain fuel tank into suitable container.
2. Remove fuel tank.
3. Remove fuel sender by turning cam lock counterclockwise using fuel tank sending unit wrench tool No. J-44402, or equivalent.
4. Remove fuel pump from sender.
5. Reverse procedure to install.

FUEL FILTER

REPLACE

Cartridge

1. Turn filter housing counterclockwise and allow remaining fuel to drain into suitable container.
2. Remove housing and gasket from base.
3. Remove cartridge.
4. Replace housing if there are signs of rust of corrosion.
5. Apply few drops of clean engine oil to new gasket and install.
6. Install new cartridge.
7. Tighten housing until gasket seats, then tighten an addition ¾ turn after gasket contacts.

Inline

1. Disconnect pipes at filter.
2. Remove mounting hardware, clamp and filter.
3. Reverse procedure to install.

TIGHTENING SPECIFICATIONS

Year	Component	Torque Ft. Lbs.
4.3L ENGINE		
2002–06	Accelerator Control Cable Bracket	106①
	Air Cleaner	18①
	Alternator	32
	Balance Shaft Driven Gear	15⑥
	Balance Shaft Retainer	106①
	Camshaft Sprocket	25
	Camshaft Thrust Plate Screws	108①
	Connecting Rod Cap Nut	45
	Crankshaft Damper	70
	Crankshaft Position Sensor	72①
	Crankshaft Pulley	43
	Cylinder Head Bolt	③
	Cylinder Head Stud	16
	Engine Mount, Front Bolt	44
	Engine Mount, Front Nut	33
	Engine Mount, Rear	35
	Engine Mount Through Bolt	70
	Engine Mount Nut	50
	Engine Oil Level Sensor	115①
	Exhaust Manifold	⑧
	Fan Shroud	71①
	Flywheel Housing	32
	Flywheel To Crankshaft	75
	Front Cover	108①
	Hydraulic Lifter Restrictor Retainer	12
	Main Bearing Cap	80
	Oil Filter Adapter	15
	Oil Level & Fill Tube	44①
	Oil Pan	18
	Oil Pan Studs	35①
	Oil Pump	66
	Oil Pump Cover	84①
	Power Brake Booster Vacuum Hose Bracket	97①
	Power Steering Pump	32
	Radiator	13
	Radiator Support	19
	Rear Oil Seal Housing (Screws & Nuts)	53①
	Rear Oil Seal Housing (Stud)	108①
	Rocker Arm Stud	35
	Rocker Cover	96①
	Rear Oil Seal Housing	106①
	Shroud To Shroud	53①
	Spark Plugs	②
	Torsional Damper	70
	Transmission Cover	106①
	Transmission Mount	35
	Transmission To Oil Pan	35
	Universal Lift Bracket	11
	Valve Cover	106①
	Water Outlet	21
	Water Pump	30

TIGHTENING SPECIFICATIONS—Continued

Year	Component	Torque Ft. Lbs.
5.0L & 5.7L ENGINES		
2002	Camshaft Sprocket	18
	Connecting Rod	45
	Crankshaft Damper	70
	Crankshaft Position Sensor	72①
	Cylinder Head	③
	Engine Mount, Rear	35
	Engine Mount, Through Bolt	70
	Engine Mount Nut	50
	Exhaust Manifold	⑧
	Fan Shroud	71①
	Flywheel Housing	32
	Flywheel To Crankshaft	75
	Front Cover	108①
	Intake Manifold (Lower)	④
	Intake Manifold (Upper)	⑦
	Main Bearing Cap	⑤
	Oil Filter Bypass Valve	18
	Oil Level & Fill Tube	44①
	Oil Pan, Bolts	106①
	Oil Pan Drain Plug	18
	Oil Pan, Nuts	18
	Oil Pan, Studs	53①
	Oil Pump	65
	Oil Pump Cover	96①
	Radiator Bracket	20
	Radiator Upper Mounting Panel	13
	Rear Oil Seal Housing	106①
	Spark Plugs	22
	Valve Cover	106①
	Vibration Damper	70
	Water Outlet	21
	Water Pump	30

① — Inch lbs.

② — New cylinder head, 22 ft. lbs.; old cylinder head, 11 ft. lbs.

③ — Refer to "Cylinder Head, Replace" for tightening procedure.

④ — Refer to "Intake Manifold, Replace" for tightening procedure.

⑤ — Refer to "Main & Rod Bearings" for tightening specifications and sequence.

⑥ — Tighten an additional 35.°

⑦ — Torque in two steps: On 4.3L engine, 1st pass to 44 inch lbs., & 2nd pass to 80 inch lbs.; on 5.0L & 5.7L engines, first pass to 44 inch lbs., & 2nd pass to 89 inch lbs.

⑧ — Torque in two steps: 1st pass to 11 ft. lbs., 2nd pass to 22 ft. lbs.

4.8L, 5.3L & 6.0L Gasoline Engines

NOTE: Refer To The "4.8L, 5.3L & 6.0L Gasoline Engines" Section Of The "Avalanche, Escalade EXT, Sierra, Silverado & SSR" Chapter For Procedures Not Included In This Section.

NOTE: On Air Bag Equipped Models, Refer To "Air Bag System Precautions" Located In The Front Of This Manual For System Disarming & Arming Procedures.

NOTE: Refer To "Computer Relearn Procedures" Located In The Front Of This Manual When Battery Power To The Computer Has Been Interrupted.

INDEX

PRECAUTIONS

Air Bag Systems

Refer to "Air Bag System Precautions" in the front of this manual for system disarming and arming procedures.

Battery Ground Cable

Prior to service disconnect battery ground cable and isolate as required.

Fuel System Pressure Relief

Always release residual fuel system pressure prior to disconnecting fuel lines or hoses.

1. Loosen fuel filler cap.
2. Connect suitable fuel pressure gauge to fuel pressure connection tap and install bleed hose into suitable container.
3. Open valve and bleed system pressure.

Radio Security System

If the Theftlock system is active when battery power is interrupted, the customers security code must be entered to restore proper function of the radio. To unlock a secured radio after power loss, proceed as follows:

1. "LOC" appears with ignition in On position.
2. Press "NM" and "000" will appear on display.
3. Press "NM" again to make last two digits agree with security code.
4. Press "HR" to make first 1 or 2 digits agree with security code.
5. Press "AM-FM" to select code entered. "SEC" will show on display indicating radio is now operable and secure.
6. If incorrect code is entered eight times, "INOP" will display. In order to reenter code, ignition must be left on for one hour before code can be entered and only three more chances to enter code are available before display reads "INOP."

COMPRESSION PRESSURE

When inspecting compression, the lowest cylinder must be within 70% of the highest and no cylinder should be less than 100 psi. Perform compression test with engine at operating temperature, all spark plugs removed and throttle wide open.

ENGINE MOUNT

REPLACE

Left

1. Raise and support vehicle, then remove front tire and wheel.
2. **On models equipped with AWD,** remove propeller shaft.
3. **On all models,** remove engine mount to frame mounting bolts through wheelwell.
4. Support engine with a suitable jack. **Do not place jack under oil pan, any sheet metal or crankshaft.**
5. Remove front engine mount to engine mounting bolts through wheelwell.
6. Remove rear engine mount to engine mounting bolts from under vehicle.
7. Remove engine mount from vehicle.
8. Reverse procedure to install.

Right

1. Raise and support vehicle.
2. Remove starter as outlined under "Electrical."
3. Remove righthand side exhaust manifold as outlined under "Exhaust Manifold, Replace."
4. Remove engine mount to frame mounting bolts.

5. Support engine with a suitable jack. **Do not place jack under oil pan, any sheet metal or crankshaft.**
6. Remove engine mount to engine mounting bolts, then the mount from vehicle.
7. Reverse procedure to install.

ENGINE

REPLACE

1. Remove engine cover, then recover air conditioning refrigerant as outlined in "Air Conditioning" chapter.
2. Raise and support vehicle, then remove splash shield.
3. Drain engine coolant into a suitable container, then remove coolant recovery reservoir.
4. Release tensioner, then remove A/C belt from pulley.
5. Remove A/C compressor retaining bolts, then the suction hose from compressor.
6. Disconnect compressor clutch and high pressure switch electrical connectors.
7. Lower vehicle, then remove fan shroud bolts, fan shroud and A/C compressor.
8. Remove battery and tray from wheelhouse, then radiator inlet and outlet hoses from water pump.
9. Remove heater hoses, then relieve fuel system pressure as outlined under "Precautions."
10. **On models equipped with cruise control,** unsnap cruise control cable from throttle body lever, bracket and sight shield retainer.
11. **On all models,**disconnect accelerator control cable from throttle body lever, bracket and sight shield.
12. Remove upper intake manifold sight shield retainer bolts and retainer.
13. Disconnect electrical connectors from EVAP canister purge solenoid and alternator.
14. Remove harness bracket nut, then the engine harness from intake manifold.
15. Remove radiator vent inlet hose from throttle body.
16. Remove alternator as outlined under "Alternator, Replace."
17. Disconnect main coil harness, then fuel injectors, electronic throttle control and EGR connectors.
18. Disconnect throttle position sensor and idle air control valve electrical connectors.
19. Disconnect manifold absolute pressure sensor and knock sensor electrical connectors.
20. Remove harness ground and negative battery cable from engine block.
21. Disconnect electrical connectors from coolant temperature sensor and Electronic variable orifice switch.
22. Disconnect electrical connectors from oil pressure sensor and camshaft position sensor.
23. Unclip all of engine harness clips from engine, then remove EVAP purge solenoid vent tube.
24. Disconnect fuel pipes, then raise and support vehicle.
25. Disconnect crankshaft position sensor, engine oil level sensor and coolant heater electrical connectors.
26. Remove battery cable channel bolt, then slide channel pin out of oil pan tab.
27. Lower vehicle, then remove rear power steering pump to engine block bolt.
28. Remove alternator bracket mounting bolts, then position bracket aside.
29. Remove vacuum brake booster hose, then the ignition coils as required.
30. Remove exhaust manifolds, then the intake manifold.
31. Install engine lift bracket bolts tool No. J 42451-1 or equivalent to cylinder head.
32. Remove left and right engine mount to engine bracket bolts.
33. Raise and support vehicle, then drain engine oil.
34. Remove starter motor as outlined under "Starter, Replace."
35. Disconnect oxygen sensors, then remove exhaust hanger bolts and hangers from vehicle.
36. Remove nuts retaining exhaust pipe flange to catalytic converter pipe, then loosen nut retaining exhaust pipe clamp to muffler.
37. Remove exhaust pipe and flange gasket from vehicle.
38. Remove positive battery cable clip bolt, clip and torque converter bolts.
39. Remove transmission oil dipstick tube.
40. **On models equipped with 4L60E transmission,** remove transmission bolt and stud on righthand side.
41. **On models equipped with 4L80E transmission,** remove transmission converter cover bolts.
42. **On all models,** remove automatic transmission bolt/stud, then separate engine from transmission.
43. Install torque converter holder tool No. J 21366 or equivalent, to transmission.
44. Lower vehicle, then install suitable engine hoist to engine and support transmission with floor jack.
45. Lift engine out of vehicle carefully.
46. Reverse procedure to install.

RADIATOR

REPLACE

1. Drain cooling system into a suitable container, then disconnect hose from coolant reservoir.
2. Remove coolant recovery reservoir retaining screws, then the coolant recovery reservoir.
3. Remove air intake duct, then disconnect mass air flow sensor electrical connector.
4. Remove MAF/IAT sensor, then pull up on air cleaner assembly to release retainers.
5. Remove mounting bolts, upper to lower mounting bolts and upper fan shroud.
6. Remove mounting bolts and lower fan shroud.
7. Remove fan and clutch.
8. Disconnect upper and lower hoses, then the transmission and oil cooler lines.
9. Remove mounting bolts and radiator.
10. Reverse procedure to install.

FUEL PUMP

REPLACE

1. Drain fuel tank into suitable container.
2. Remove fuel tank.
3. Remove fuel sender by turning cam lock counterclockwise using fuel tank sending unit wrench tool No. J-39765, or equivalent.
4. Remove fuel pump from sender.
5. Reverse procedure to install

FUEL FILTER

REPLACE

1. Relieve fuel system pressure as outlined under "Precautions" then disconnect pipes at filter.
2. Remove mounting hardware, clamp and filter.
3. Reverse procedure to install.

TIGHTENING SPECIFICATIONS

Year	Component	Torque/Ft. Lbs.
2003–06	Accelerator Control Cable Bracket	89①
	Air Conditioning Compressor	37
	Air Conditioning Compressor Bracket	37
	Air Conditioning Hose Bracket	35
	Air Conditioning Tensioner	37
	AIR Bracket	71①
	AIR Pipe To Exhaust Manifold, Nuts	18
	AIR Pipe To Exhaust Manifold, Studs	45
	Alternator & Power Steering Bracket	37
	Alternator Bracket	37
	Belt Idler Pulley	37
	Drive Belt Idler Pulley	37
	Drive Belt Tensioner	37
	Engine Shield	15
	Engine Lift Bracket, M8 Bolt	18
	Engine Lift Bracket, M10 Bolt	37
	Engine Wiring Harness Bracket	89①
	Exhaust Pipe	48
	Fan Shroud	80①
	Motor Mount	37
	Motor Mount Bracket	44
	Oil Filter	22
	Oil Filter Fitting	40
	Oil Dipstick Tube	18
	Power Steering Pump	37
	Power Steering Pump Bracket	37
	Propeller Shaft	18
	Radiator Shroud	53①
	Rear Cover	18
	Spark Plugs (New Cylinder Heads)	15
	Spark Plugs (All Subsequent Installations)	11
	Starter Bolt	37
	Radiator Support	42
	Transmission, Automatic	37
	Transmission Fluid Cooler Line	19
	Transmission To Oil Pan	97①
	Universal Lift Bracket	15

① — Inch lbs.

6.5L Diesel Engine

NOTE: On Air Bag Equipped Models, Refer To "Air Bag System Precautions" Located In The Front Of This Manual For System Disarming & Arming Procedures.

INDEX

PRECAUTIONS

Air Bag Systems

Refer to "Air Bag System Precautions" in the front of this manual for system disarming and arming procedures.

Battery Ground Cable

Prior to service disconnect battery ground cable and isolate as required.

Fuel System Pressure Bleed

1. Open air bleed valve on top of fuel manager/filter, **Fig. 1.**
2. Connect hose to air bleed valve and place other end in suitable container.
3. Disconnect engine shutoff solenoid.
4. Crank engine in 10–15 second intervals until clear fuel is observed at air bleed hose, (wait 1 minute between cranking intervals).
5. Close air bleed valve.
6. Connect engine shutoff solenoid.
7. Start engine and allow to idle for 5 minutes.
8. Inspect for fuel leaks.
9. Clear any diagnostic trouble codes.

Radio Security System

If the Theftlock system is active when battery power is interrupted, the customers security code must be entered to restore proper function of the radio. To unlock a secured radio after power loss, proceed as follows:

1. "LOC" appears with ignition in On position.
2. Press "NM" and "000" will appear on display.
3. Press "NM" again to make last two digits agree with security code.
4. Press "HR" to make first 1 or 2 digits agree with security code.
5. Press "AM-FM" to select code entered. "SEC" will show on display indicating radio is now operable and secure.
6. If incorrect code is entered eight times, "INOP" will display. In order to reenter code, ignition must be left on for one hour before code can be entered and only three more chances to enter code are available before display reads "INOP."

DESCRIPTION

The 6.5L diesel engine is both turbocharged and non-turbocharged models. In the diesel engine, air alone is compressed in the cylinder. After the air has been compressed, a charge of fuel is sprayed into the cylinder and ignition occurs because of the heat of compression. Because of the increased compression and resultant increase in combustion temperatures, major differences are evident in the cylinder heads, combustion chambers, fuel distribution system, intake manifold and engine mechanical components.

The cylinder block, crankshaft, main bearings, connecting rods, pistons and wrist pins are all heavy duty designs, because of the higher compression ratios. The main bearing caps are 4 bolt design to provide rigid crankshaft support, while minimizing stress. Roller hydraulic lifters are used to minimize wear on the forged steel camshaft and intake and exhaust valves are of special alloy material to combat the higher internal operating temperatures. Steel alloy pre-chamber inserts are installed in the combustion chambers and are serviced separately from the cylinder head. Injector nozzles and glow plugs are

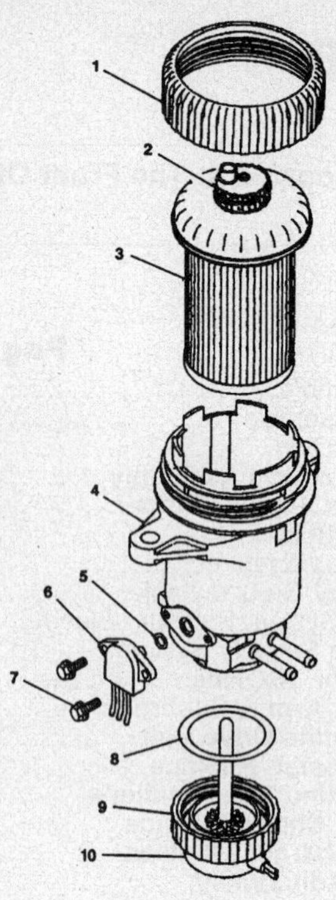

1 ELEMENT NUT
2 AIR BLEED VALVE
3 ELEMENT ASSEMBLY
4 HOUSING
5 SENSOR SEAL
6 WATER IN FUEL SENSOR
7 SENSOR MOUNTING SCREW
8 CAP SEAL
9 CAP NUT
10 FUEL HEATER

HT1029500651000X

Fig. 1 Fuel manager/filter

threaded into the cylinder head to allow direct fuel delivery and to provide chamber preheating.

The injector nozzles are spring loaded and designed to open and deliver fuel at specifically calibrated fuel pressures. Fuel is delivered into the high swirl precombustion chambers, which mix fuel and air to provide an efficient fuel burn and low emissions. The glow plugs are used to heat the pre-chambers and assist starting. In addition, a block heater is used to aid starting in cold climates. Because the intake manifold is always open to atmospheric pressures no engine vacuum supply is available and a vacuum pump is installed to supply vacuum to components such as air conditioning and cruise control.

Lubrication System

The gear-type oil pump is attached to the bottom side of the rear main bearing cap and is driven by the camshaft through an intermediate shaft. Oil flows through the pump outlet tube to the cooler located in the radiator. A bypass valve is incorporated into the system, which allows oil to bypass the cooler and continue to feed the engine should the cooler become clogged. From the cooler, the oil then flows through a cartridge type oil filter. A bypass valve is incorporated into the system to prevent oil starvation should the filter become clogged.

From the oil filter, oil then flows through the drilled galleries in the cylinder block. The rear crankshaft bearing is fed by a hole drilled from the rear main bearing bore to the main oil gallery. Oil is also pumped through the main gallery to a gallery which has been drilled the full length of the lefthand side of the block. Oil from the lefthand side gallery feeds the camshaft bearings and a gallery which runs the full length of the righthand side of the block. All other engine components are lubricated through these left and righthand main galleries.

Oil is supplied to lifters on the righthand bank from the righthand side main gallery and to lifters on the lefthand bank from the lefthand side main gallery. The lifters contain disc valves which meter oil to the hollow pushrods and provide valve train lubrication. Holes drilled from the camshaft bearing bores to the crankshaft bearing bores supply oil to main bearings 1–4. Oil flows onto the crankshaft bearings providing lubrication for the crankshaft to rotate freely in its bearings and cross drilling provides lubrication to the crankpins. As the crankshaft rotates, oil slings off the crankpins to lubricate cylinder walls, pistons and piston pins and the piston rings.

Fuel System

COMPONENTS

The fuel system consists of a tank, fuel pickup assembly, fuel filters, mechanical fuel pump, fuel line heater and an injection pump, injector lines and individual fuel injectors for each cylinder. An inline type filter is used, which combines several different functions. It acts as a two-staged fuel filter, water separator, water detector, water drain and fuel heater, **Fig. 1.** Should the fuel filter become clogged, a low pressure switch will illuminate a warning lamp.

SYSTEM OPERATION

Fuel is drawn from the fuel tank by an electric fuel pump which is located on the lefthand side of the frame rail. Fuel is then pumped through the filter/water separator. The filter/water separator is located under the rear of the air cleaner. The fuel is then transferred to the injection pump.

The injection pump is mounted on top of the engine under the intake manifold. The pump is driven by the camshaft through two gears, one attached to the front of the camshaft and the other attached to the end of the injection pump shaft. These gears are the same size and have the same number of teeth, therefore, the injection pump shaft turns at the same RPM as the camshaft. The pump rotates in the opposite direction of the camshaft and crankshaft.

The injection pump is a high pressure rotary type pump that meters, pressurizes and distributes fuel to the eight injector nozzles.

The eight high pressure lines are all the same length although shapes may be different, **Fig. 2.** This prevents timing differences between cylinders. Injection lines should not be bent to ease removal.

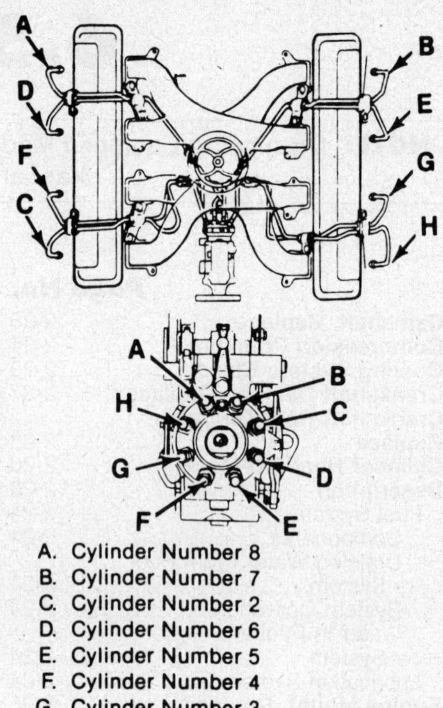

GC1028802222000X

Fig. 2 Fuel injection line routing

WATER IN FUEL WARNING SYSTEM

The water is trapped in the first stage of the fuel filter element. The water collects at the bottom of the fuel filter. When the water at the bottom of the filter reaches a certain level the "Water In Fuel Lamp" will activate. When the water in fuel lamp comes on, the filter should be drained within one to two hours of engine operation.

DRAINING WATER FROM FUEL SYSTEM

1. Block drive wheels and remove fuel filler cap to release any pressure or vacuum in fuel tank.
2. Place suitable container under filter drain hose, **Fig. 3.**
3. Start engine and open filler drain valve.
4. Once full begins to flow from drain hose, open air bleed valve on top of fuel filter and turn engine off. Opening air bleed valve will cause fuel in filter housing to siphon out drain hose.
5. Close drain valve and air bleed valve after all fuel is drained from filter housing.

COMPRESSION PRESSURE

1. Remove fuel solenoid fuse.
2. Disconnect plug wires and remove glow plugs.
3. Install compression gauge adaptor tool No. J-26999-10, or equivalent.

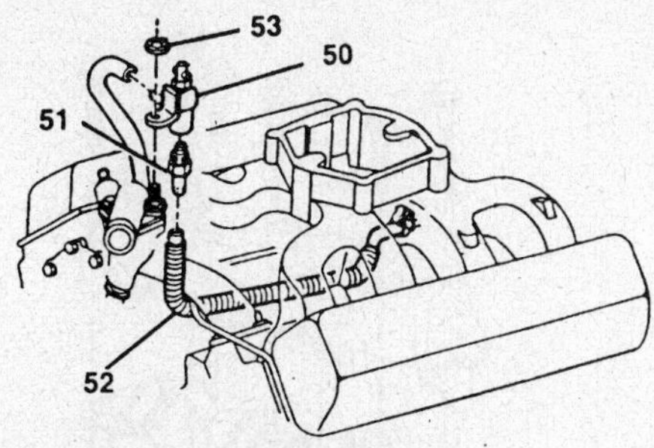

Fig. 3 Fuel filter drain valve

4. Connect compression gauge tool No. J-26999, or equivalent, **Fig. 4.**
5. Crank engine, allowing six "puffs" per cylinder.
6. Lowest cylinder compression reading should be within 80 percent of highest cylinder. No cylinder compression reading should be less than 380 psi.
   a. Normal compression builds quickly and evenly to specified compression on each cylinder. Readings should be in 380–400 psi range.
   b. Leaking compression is low on first stroke, then tends to build up on following strokes, but does not reach normal range.

ENGINE MOUNT

REPLACE

Do not use a jack under the oil pan, any sheet metal or crankshaft pulley.

Front

LEFTHAND

1. Raise and support vehicle.
2. Move front wheel to left against stop.
3. Support engine with suitable pole jack on locating tab to lefthand rear of power steering pump.
4. Remove oil cooler line and retainer from engine mount bracket.
5. Remove engine mount through bolt.
6. Raise engine only enough to remove mounting bolts.
7. Remove mounting bolts and engine block mount bracket.
8. Remove mounting bolts, nuts, washers and frame mount.
9. Reverse procedure to install.

RIGHTHAND

1. Raise and support vehicle.
2. Remove starter motor as outlined under "Electrical."
3. Support engine with suitable pole jack on locating tab to righthand rear corner above starter.
4. Remove engine mount through bolt.
5. Raise engine only enough to remove mounting bolts.
6. Remove mounting bolts and engine block mount bracket.
7. Remove mounting bolts and engine mount from frame side.
8. Reverse procedure to install.

Rear

1. Support transmission with suitable stand.
2. Remove rear mount mounting bolts and washers.
3. Raise transmission only enough to allow mount removal.
4. Remove mount.
5. Reverse procedure to install.

ENGINE

REPLACE

1. Remove hood.
2. Remove instrument panel lower extension upper trim panel.
3. Remove instrument panel lower extension mounting bolts and nuts.
4. Disconnect cigarette lighter, accessory plug and storage compartment lamp electrical connectors.
5. Remove instrument panel lower extension.
6. Disconnect retaining straps and remove engine cover.
7. Drain coolant into suitable container.
8. **On models equipped with air conditioning,** recover refrigerant as outlined in "Air Conditioning" chapter.
9. **On all models,** loose cleaner duct clamp, then remove mounting bolts and air cleaner.
10. Remove mounting bolts and front bumper.
11. Remove mounting screws, then disconnect front side marker lamps and bulb socket.
12. Remove mounting screws and park/turn signal lamp, then disconnect bulb socket.
13. Remove mounting bolts, retainers and radiator grille.
14. Remove mounting screws, retaining ring and headlamps, then disconnect electrical connector.
15. Remove push pin rivet and hood latch cover.
16. Mark hood latch and mounting bolts locations for installation.
17. Remove mounting bolts and hood latch, then disconnect release cable.
18. Raise and support vehicle.
19. Remove mounting bolts and radiator air intake baffle.
20. Disconnect lines, then remove mounting bolts and auxiliary engine oil cooler.
21. Disconnect lines, then remove mounting bolts and auxiliary transmission oil cooler.
22. Lower vehicle.
23. Remove surge tank overflow hose, then the radiator to surge tank inlet hose.
24. Remove surge tank outlet hose and disconnect coolant level sensor electrical connector.
25. Remove mounting bolt, cowl tabs and surge tank.

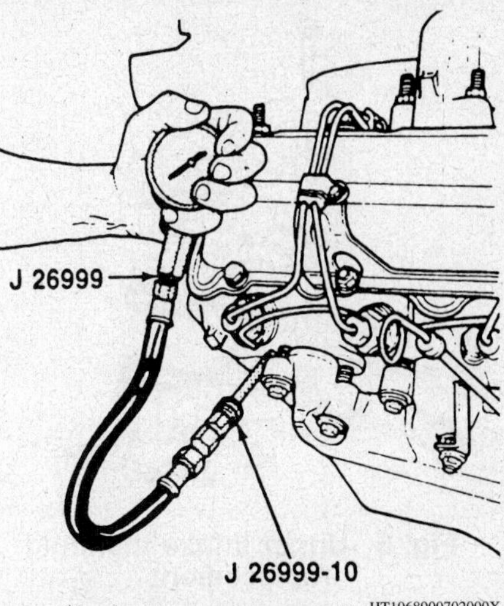

Fig. 4 Compression gauge installation

26. **On models equipped with air conditioning,** proceed as follows:
    a. Disconnect condenser A/C lines.
    b. Remove mounting bolts and condenser.
27. **On all models,** remove radiator as outlined under "Radiator, Replace."
28. Remove forward lamp harness, mounting bolts and radiator support.
29. Remove radiator hoses.
30. **On models equipped with air conditioning,** remove mounting bolts and compressor.
31. **On all models,** remove drive belt as outlined under "Serpentine Drive Belt."
32. Remove idler pulley and auxiliary alternator as outlined under "Electrical."
33. Remove thermostat housing heater hose and crossover.
34. Disconnect power steering pump hoses. Plug or cap hoses and openings.
35. Remove power steering pump pulley using power steering pump remover tool No. J-25034-C, or equivalent.
36. Remove adjusting bolts, brackets, mounting nuts and power steering pump.
37. Remove mounting bolts and lefthand accessory bracket.
38. Remove vacuum pump line, then disconnect ground strap.
39. Remove mounting bolts and vacuum pump.
40. Remove mounting bolts and righthand accessory bracket.
41. Remove left and righthand engine wiring harnesses.
42. Remove turbocharger as outlined under "Turbocharger, Replace."
43. Remove exhaust manifolds as outlined under "Exhaust Manifold, Replace."
44. Remove lower intake manifold as outlined under "Intake Manifold, Replace."
45. Raise and support vehicle.
46. Remove starter motor as outlined under "Electrical."
47. Remove transmission oil cooler lines

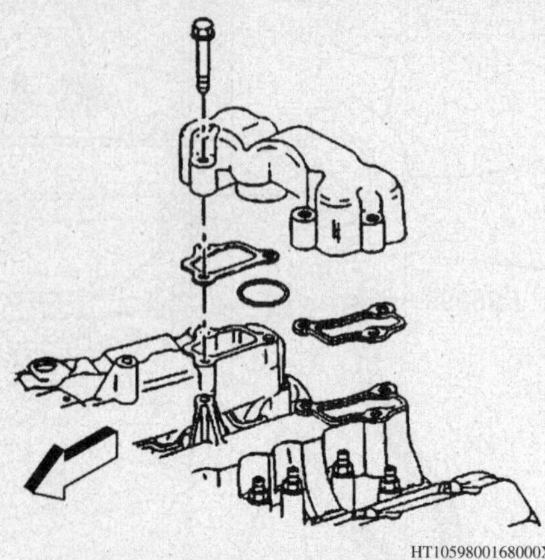

Fig. 5 Upper intake manifold replacement

from engine oil pan retainers and position aside.
48. Remove engine oil cooler lines and position aside.
49. Remove flywheel to torque converter mounting bolts.
50. Remove engine block to frame ground straps.
51. Disconnect block heater electrical connector, then remove engine oil filter.
52. Lower vehicle.
53. Install engine lift bracket tools No. J-36857, or equivalent, with suitable length of chain to rear corner of right hand cylinder head and front corner of lefthand cylinder head.
54. Support transmission and attach suitable lifting device to chain.
55. Remove engine mount through bolts and engine mounts as outlined under "Engine Mount, Replace."
56. Remove engine.
57. Flywheel may have to be removed before engine can be installed in stand.
58. Reverse procedure to install, noting the following:
    a. Install power steering pump pulley using power steering pump puller installer tool No. J-25033-C, or equivalent.

INTAKE MANIFOLD

REPLACE

Do not attempt to remove upper and lower intake manifolds as an assembly.

Upper

1. Remove engine cover and air cleaner as outlined under "Engine, Replace."
2. Remove Crankcase Depression Regulator (CDR) valve from air intake duct
3. Remove electrical harness and brackets from upper intake manifold.
4. Remove transmission oil level dipstick tube.
5. **On models equipped with air conditioning,** remove rear air conditioning line from upper intake manifold.
6. **On all models,** remove mounting bolts, upper intake manifold and gaskets, **Fig. 5.**
7. Reverse procedure to install, noting the following:
    a. Install new gasket.
    b. Coat new turbocharger O-ring with suitable clean engine oil.

Lower

1. Remove upper intake manifold outlined under "Intake Manifold, Replace Upper."
2. Disconnect gray engine harness electrical connector.
3. Remove boost sensor and glow plug relays.
4. Remove electrical harness mounting clips and ground straps.
5. Remove fuel line mounting clips.
6. Remove mounting bolt, fuel line clips, lower intake manifold and gaskets, **Fig. 6.**
7. Reverse procedure to install, noting the following:
    a. Apply suitable Teflon sealer part No. 1236004, or equivalent, on threads of studs that are second to end on both intake manifolds.
    b. Apply suitable threadlocker part No. 12345493, or equivalent, to threads of remaining studs.

EXHAUST MANIFOLD

REPLACE

1. Remove engine cover as outlined under "Engine, Replace."
2. Remove transmission oil level dipstick tube.
3. Raise and support vehicle.
4. Remove mounting bolts and clips, then the wheelhouse splash shields.
5. Remove glow plugs.
6. Remove mounting bolts and exhaust manifolds.
7. Reverse procedure to install.

CYLINDER HEAD

REPLACE

1. Remove engine cover as outlined under "Engine, Replace."
2. Remove turbocharger as outlined under "Turbocharger, Replace."
3. Remove lower intake manifold as outlined under "Intake Manifold, Replace Lower."
4. Remove front lower cylinder head bolt, insert ⅜ inch copper tube 12–18 inches long and suitable hose into bolt hole, and siphon engine block coolant.
5. Remove rocker arms, shafts and push rods as outlined under "Rocker Arm, Replace."
6. Remove exhaust manifolds as outlined under "Exhaust Manifold, Replace."
7. Remove siphon tube.
8. Remove cylinder head bolts in sequence, **Fig. 7,** then the cylinder head and gasket.
9. Reverse procedure to install, noting the following:
    a. Position cylinder head gasket over dowel pins.
    b. **Do not use any sealer on cylinder head gasket, as sealer is printed onto gaskets during manufacture. Any additional sealer will increase possibility of leakage.**
    c. Coat cylinder head bolts with suitable sealing compound part No. 1052080, or equivalent.
    d. Install lefthand rear cylinder head bolt through bolt hole and carefully guide cylinder head onto block.
    e. Using sequence **Fig. 8,** tighten cylinder head bolts in four steps: First step, **torque** bolts to 20 ft. lbs.; second step, **torque** bolts to 55 ft. lbs.; third step, **torque** bolts to 55 ft. lbs.; fourth step, tighten bolts an additional 90–100°.

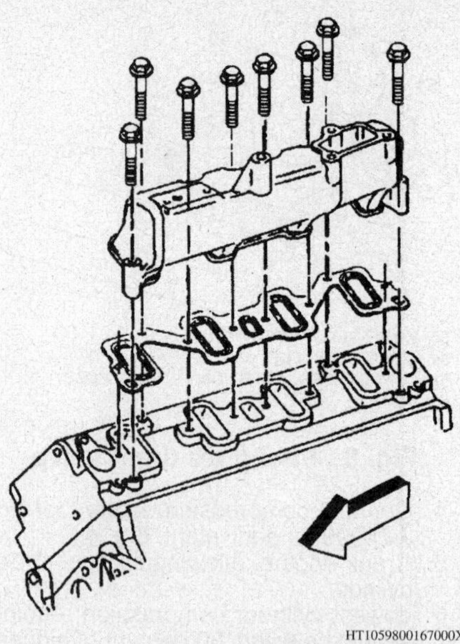

Fig. 6 Lower intake manifold replacement

ROCKER ARM & PUSHRODS

All valve train components must be assembled in exact order and position from which removed.

1. Rotate engine until crankshaft balancer mark is at 2 o'clock position.
2. Rotate engine counterclockwise 3½ inches, aligning crankshaft balancer mark with lower water pump bolt at approximately 12:30 o'clock position. At this position, no valves are close to piston crown.
3. Remove lower intake manifold as outlined under "Intake Manifold, Replace Lower."
4. Mark fuel line retaining clips and stud for assembly.
5. Remove fuel injection lines from fuel nozzles. **Do not bend fuel lines.**
6. Remove fuel return line clip at valve cover stud.
7. Remove mounting bolt rear alternator support bracket.
8. Remove mounting bolts and valve cover, noting the following:
    a. **Prying may damage valve cover sealing surface.**

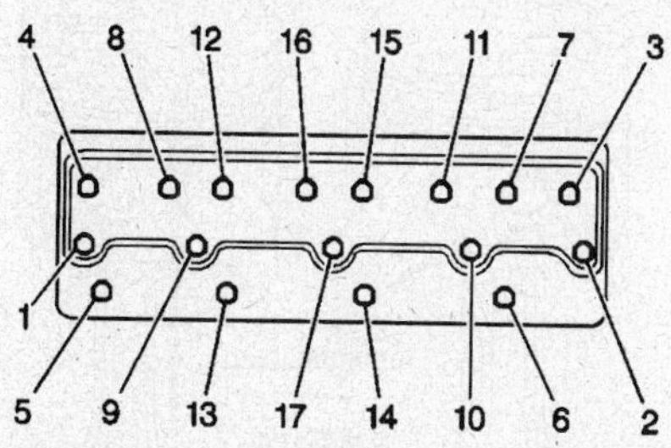

Fig. 7 Cylinder head bolt removal sequence

b. **Use suitable wood block against cover side and strike sideways with suitable hammer to shear RTV sealant.**

9. Remove mounting bolts and rocker arm shaft with rocker arms.
10. Remove push rods. Record positions for installation.
11. Break off nylon valve rocker arm retainers end from valve rocker arm shaft using suitable pliers and remove, **Fig. 9.**
12. Slide valve rocker arms from shaft.
13. Reverse procedure to install, noting the following:
    a. Install push rods in original positions and directions with painted or marked ends up.
    b. Pushrods are identified with paint stripe on upper end and hardened upper ball is darker in color than lower ball.
    c. Lubricate rocker arms with suitable clean engine oil.
    d. Install valve rocker arm with copper-colored, painted or marked end up and center rockers on corresponding shaft holes.
    e. Use at least ½ inch drift to install new retainers to valve springs.
    f. Apply 3⁄16–5⁄16 inch bead of suitable RTV sealant part No. 12345739, or equivalent, to valve covers.
    g. Sealant should follow and overlap stepped ridge.
    h. Sealer must be wet to touch when bolts are inside of bolt holes.

VALVE ARRANGEMENT

All ....I-E-I-E-I-E-I-E

VALVE ADJUSTMENT

These engines are equipped with hydraulic valve lifters. No provision for adjustment is provided.

VALVE TIMING

Intake Opens

All ....13°

VALVE GUIDES

The valve guides are an integral part of the cylinder head and are not replaceable. Inspect valve stem to guide clearance and

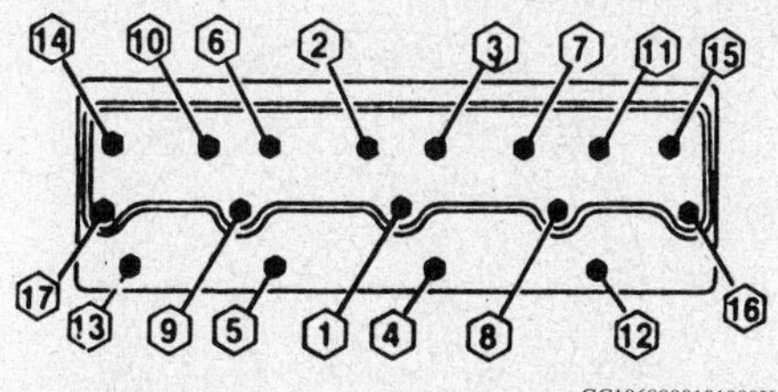

Fig. 8 Cylinder head bolt tightening sequence

compare to specifications. If clearance is excessive, ream valve guides using tool set No. J-7049, or equivalent and install oversize valves.

VALVE LIFTERS

1. Remove cylinder head as outlined under "Cylinder Head, Replace."
2. Remove mounting bolt, clamp, guide plate and lifter.
3. Reverse procedure to install, noting the following:
    a. **Lifters must be installed in original positions.**
    b. After all clamps are installed, turn crankshaft by hand two full turns, to ensure free movement of lifters in guide plate. If engine will not turn over by hand, one or more of lifters may be binding in guide plate.

CRANKSHAFT DAMPER

REPLACE

1. Remove fan shroud as outlined under "Radiator, Replace."
2. Remove drive belt as outlined under "Serpentine Drive Belt."
3. Remove fan and clutch using fan clutch wrench tool No. J-41240, or equivalent, and suitable spanner.
4. Raise and support vehicle.
5. Remove mounting bolts and crankshaft pulley.
6. Remove mounting bolt, washer and crankshaft damper using crankshaft balancer remover/installer tool No. J-23523-F, or equivalent.
7. Reverse procedure to install. **Failure to use proper installation tool may result in destroying damper tuning.**

FRONT COVER SEAL

REPLACE

1. Remove crankshaft damper as outlined under "Crankshaft Damper, Replace."
2. Remove front cover seal. **Do not damage front cover.**
3. Reverse procedure to install, noting the following:
    a. Apply small amount of suitable clean engine oil to crankshaft balancer surface and oil seal inner sealing surface.
    b. Install new seal, using seal installer tool No. J-22102, or equivalent.

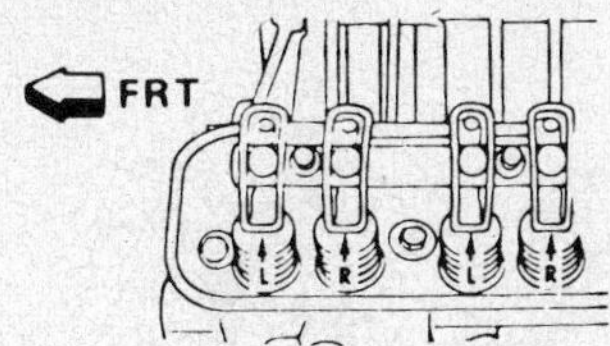

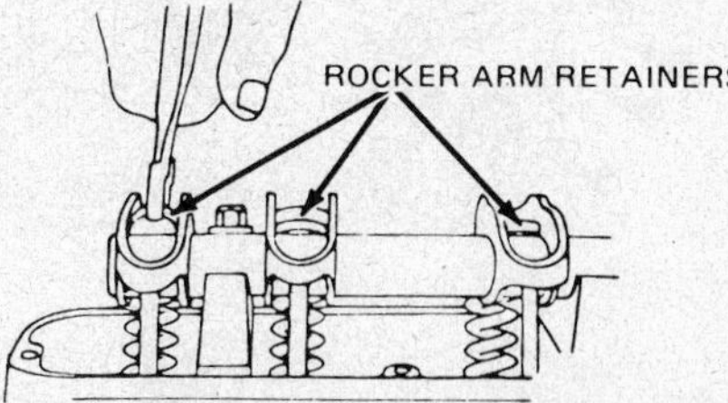

Fig. 9 Rocker arm shaft replacement

FRONT COVER

REPLACE

Perform "TDC Offset (Recovery) Adjustment" as outlined under "Fuel Injection System" if timing chain, timing gears, front cover, crankshaft position sensor, crankshaft or other timing components are replaced.

1. Drain cooling system into suitable container.
2. Remove engine oil fill tube.
3. Remove crankshaft damper as outlined under "Crankshaft Damper, Replace."
4. Remove water pump as outlined under "Water Pump, Replace."
5. Raise and support vehicle.
6. Remove crankshaft position sensor.
7. Remove fuel injection pump drive gear.
8. Mark fuel line clips and studs for installation.
9. Remove mounting bolts and front cover, **Fig. 10.**
10. Reverse procedure to install, noting the following:
    a. Install new oil seal.
    b. Apply 3⁄32 inch bead of suitable anaerobic sealant part No. 1052357, or equivalent, to front cover.
    c. Apply 3⁄16 inch bead of suitable RTV sealant around bottom front cover portion which attaches to oil pan.

TIMING CHAIN

REPLACE

Perform "TDC Offset (Recovery) Adjustment" as outlined under "Fuel Injection System" if timing chain, timing gears, front cover, crankshaft position sensor, crankshaft or other timing components are replaced.

1. Remove front cover as outlined under "Front Cover, Replace."
2. Remove camshaft sprocket mounting bolt and injection pump drive gear.
3. Remove timing chain and camshaft sprocket.

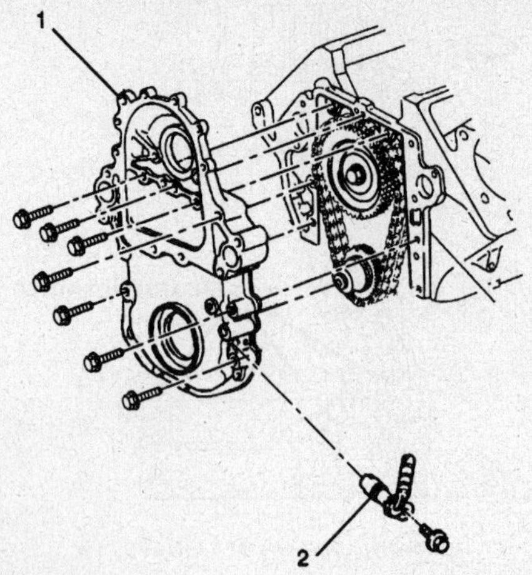

1. FRONT COVER
2. CRANKSHAFT POSITION SENSOR

GC1068800109000X

Fig. 10 Front cover replacement

4. Remove crankshaft sprocket.
5. Reverse procedure to install, noting the following:
   a. Replace crankshaft wood drift key as required.
   b. Align cam sprocket and crank sprocket timing marks, **Fig. 11**.

CAMSHAFT

REPLACE

When the camshaft is replaced, replace the valve lifters, wood drift key, oil and oil filter.

Perform "TDC Offset (Recovery) adjustment" as outlined under "Fuel Injection System" if timing chain, timing gears, front cover, crankshaft position sensor, crankshaft or other timing components are replaced.

1. Remove front cover and grille as outlined under "Engine, Replace."
2. Remove radiator as outlined under "Radiator, Replace."
3. Remove timing chain as outlined under "Timing Chain, Replace."
4. Remove mounting bolt, clamp, oil pump drive and gasket.
5. Remove valve lifters as outlined under "Valve Lifters, Replace."
6. Remove thrust bearing, retainer and camshaft spacer.
7. Remove camshaft. **Do not damage bearing.**
8. Reverse procedure to, noting the following:
   a. Coat camshaft and valve lifter lobes with suitable molybdenum based pre-lubricant part No. 1-52365, or equivalent.
   b. Lubricate camshaft bearing journals with suitable clean engine oil.
   c. Install new oil pump drive gasket.
   d. Apply small amount to suitable clean engine oil to bore and oil pump drive gear seal.
   e. Oil pump drive gear should slide into place with slight resistance. **Do not force gear into place.**

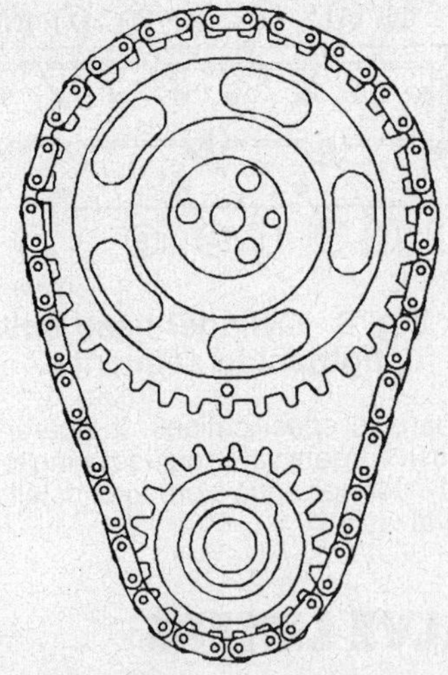

GC1060001087000X

Fig. 11 Timing chain alignment

PISTON & ROD ASSEMBLY

Assemble piston to rod and install into cylinder block. Install with depression on top of piston toward outside of engine, **Fig. 12.** Install connecting rod bearing with tang slots positioned on side opposite camshaft.

PISTONS, PINS & RINGS

Pistons are available in standard sizes and oversize of .03 inch. Rings are available in standard sizes and oversize of .03 inch.

MAIN & ROD BEARINGS

Main bearings are available in standard sizes and undersizes of .005 and .010 inch. Rod bearings are available in standard sizes and undersizes of .01 inch and .02 inch.

1. **Torque** inner bolts to 55 ft. lbs.
2. **Torque** inner bolts to 55 ft. lb., again.
3. Finally, tighten inner bolts an additional 90°.
4. **Torque** outer bolts 12 mm bolts to 48 ft. lbs.
5. **Torque** outer 12 mm bolts to 48 ft. lbs., again.
6. Finally, tighten outer 12 mm bolts an additional 90°.
7. **Torque** outer bolts 10 mm bolts to 30 ft. lbs.

CRANKSHAFT REAR OIL SEAL

REPLACE

1. Remove engine cover as outlined under "Engine, Replace."
2. Raise and support vehicle.
3. Remove starter motor as outlined under "Electrical."

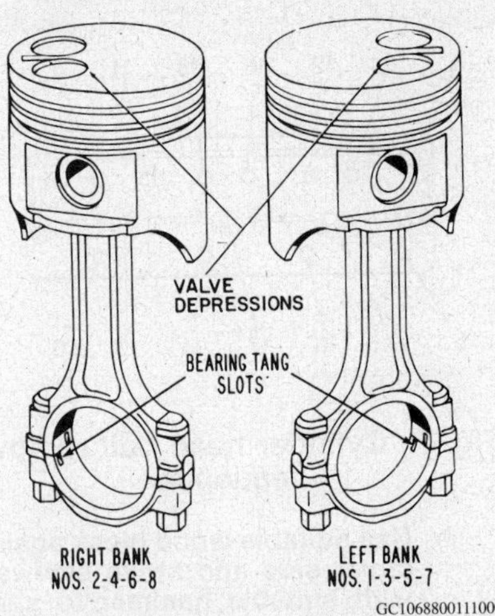

GC1068800111000X

Fig. 12 Piston & rod assembly

4. Remove transmission as outlined in **MOTOR's "Domestic Transmission, In-Vehicle Service" or "Transmission Service DVD."**
5. Remove mounting bolts and flywheel.
6. Remove rear oil seal.
7. Reverse procedure to install, noting the following:
   a. Coat crankshaft surface with suitable clean engine oil.
   b. Lightly coat new seal sealing area with suitable engine oil or grease.
   c. Do not scratch or nick sealing edge.
   d. Install seal using rear crankshaft oil seal installer tool No. J-39084, or equivalent.

OIL PAN

REPLACE

1. Remove engine oil level dipsticks and tube.
2. Remove transmission and flywheel as outlined under "Crankshaft Rear Oil Seal, Replace."
3. Drain engine oil into suitable container.
4. Remove transmission oil cooler lines from retainer.
5. Remove mounting bolts, oil pan and oil pan rear oil seal.
6. Reverse procedure to install, noting the following:
   a. Apply 3/16 inch bead of suitable RTV sealant part No. 1052915, or equivalent, to oil pan sealing surface and inboard of bolt holes.
   b. Sealer must be wet to touch when pan is installed.

OIL PUMP

REPLACE

1. Remove oil pan as outlined under "Oil Pan, Replace."
2. Remove mounting bolts and oil pump.
3. Reverse removal procedures to install, noting the following:
   a. Install new retainer between pump and hex drive shaft.
   b. Submerge pump in suitable clean engine oil, rotate hex drive by hand until oil flows from pump.

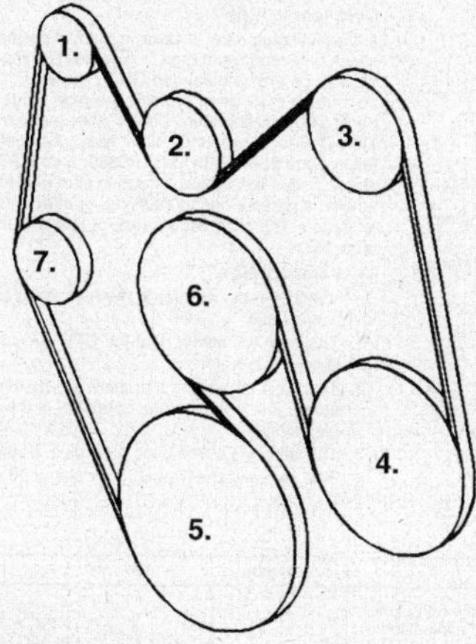

1. Alternator
2. Tensioner
3. A/C Compressor or Idler Bracket
4. Pump, Power Steering
5. Pulley, Crankshaft
6. Pump, Coolant
7. Pulley, Idler

GC1139901000000X

Fig. 13 Serpentine drive belt routing

c. Align extension shaft with drive shaft gear.
d. Pump should slide easily into place. **Do not force.**

OIL PUMP SERVICE

Disassemble

1. Remove retainer and drive shaft.
2. Remove roll pin, pressure regulator valve and spring.
3. If replacement is required, remove pickup tube and screen.
4. Remove mounting bolts, cover and spacer.
5. Mark gear teeth for installation with same teeth indexing.
6. Remove drive gear, shaft, driven gear and idler shaft.

Inspection

1. Inspect housing for scoring, damage or casting imperfections.
2. Inspect gears for chipping, galling or wear.
3. Inspect gears tops for scoring.
4. Inspect gear shaft for damage or scoring.
5. Inspect mounting bolts for damaged threads.
6. Inspect driveshaft housing bore for wear.
7. Inspect pressure relief valve for damage or sticking. Minor imperfections may be removed with fine oil stone.
8. Inspect for collapsed or broken pressure relief valve spring.

Assemble

1. Install driven gear, idler shaft and drive gear with shaft using align marks.
2. Install spacer plate and cover.

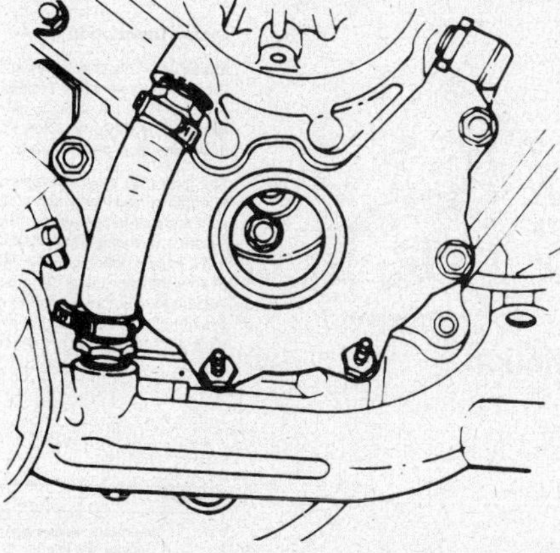

GC1028800029000X

Fig. 14 Injection pump driven gear bolt removal

3. Install pressure relief valve, new spring and roll pin.
4. If removed, install new pickup tube and screen assembly.
5. Prime pump cavity with suitable clean engine oil.
6. Turn drive shaft by hand inspecting for smooth rotation.

SERPENTINE DRIVE BELT

1. Rotate tensioner arm counterclockwise using ⅜ inch breaker bar.
2. Remove belt from pulleys.
3. Route new belt over all pulleys except tensioner arm, **Fig. 13.**
4. Rotate tensioner arm counterclockwise using ⅜ inch breaker bar.
5. Install belt over tensioner arm pulley.
6. Slowly release tensioner arm tension. Tensioner is spring loaded and will return to original position when released.

COOLING SYSTEM BLEED

This engine does not require a specified bleed procedure. After filling cooling system, run engine to operating temperature with radiator/pressure cap off. Air will automatically bleed through the cap opening.

THERMOSTAT

REPLACE

1. Remove air cleaner, duct and surge tank as outlined under "Engine, Replace."
2. Drain coolant into suitable container.
3. Disconnect thermostat housing radiator hose.
4. Remove mounting bolts and thermostat housing.
5. Remove mounting bolts, thermostat and gasket.
6. Reverse procedure to install.

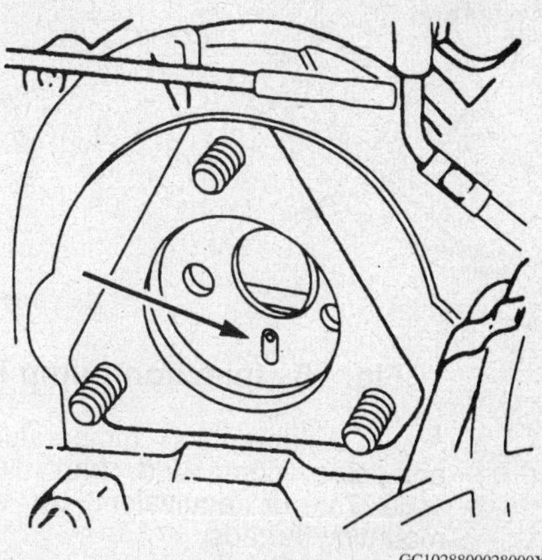

GC1028800028000X

Fig. 15 Injection pump locating pin

WATER PUMP

REPLACE

1. Drain coolant into suitable container.
2. Remove air cleaner, duct and surge tank as outlined under "Engine, Replace."
3. Remove fan shroud as outlined under "Radiator, Replace."
4. Remove fan and clutch using fan clutch wrench tool No. J-41240, or equivalent, and suitable spanner.
5. Remove serpentine drive belt as outlined under "Serpentine Drive Belt."
6. Remove mounting bolts and water pump pulley.
7. Disconnect lower radiator and bypass hoses.
8. Remove righthand and lefthand accessory brackets as outlined under "Engine, Replace."
9. Remove mounting bolts, water pump, gasket and plate.
10. Reverse procedure to install. **Do apply sealant to water pump gasket.**

RADIATOR

REPLACE

Refer to "4.3L, 5.0L & 5.7L Gasoline Engines."

TURBOCHARGER

REPLACE

1. Remove engine cover as outlined under "Engine, Replace."
2. Remove Crankcase Depression Regulator (CDR) valve.
3. Remove air cleaner intake duct from turbocharger.
4. Remove upper intake manifold as outlined under "Intake Manifold, Replace."
5. Remove mounting bolts and turbocharger heat shield.
6. Remove exhaust pipe clamps that connect turbocharger to exhaust manifold.
7. Remove mounting bolts and turbocharger.
8. Reverse procedure to install, noting the following:

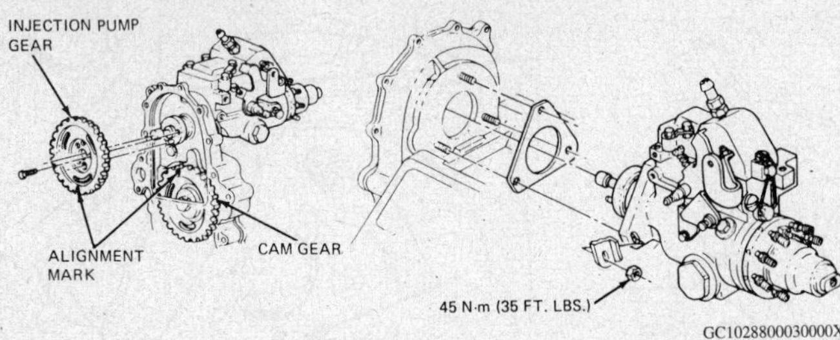

Fig. 16 Injection pump installation

Circuit Description

Important: This check only applies to the Federal Glow Plug System (the Federal Glow Plug System does not have the ability to detect for a glow plug failure). The California Glow Plug System can determine glow plug failure by setting a DTC P0380.

The glow plug system helps provide the heat required to begin combustion when starting the engine at cold ambient temperatures. The glow plugs are heated before and during cranking, as well as during the initial engine operation. The PCM controls the amount of time the glow plugs are energized by monitoring coolant temperatures and the glow plug voltage. This system check will check the glow plugs and the glow plug feed circuit coming from the relay.

Diagnostic Aids

If the glow plug relay is stuck in the ON position, check for proper operation of glow plugs. When the glow plugs are commanded ON by the scan tool, an internal PCM timer protects the glow plugs from damage by cycling them ON for 3 seconds and then OFF for 12 seconds. Most glow plug system failures are covered by DTC P0380. If no DTCs are stored,note if the vehicle is hard to start and white smoke is present during cranking, or after the vehicle is started. The most likely cause of failure is the glow plugs.

Test Description

The number(s) below refer to the number(s) on the diagnostic table.

1. This step will ensure that the OBD system check is performed.
2. This step will ensure that there are no other DTCs stored that will affect the operation of the glow plug system.
3. This step will check each glow plug for an open.
4. This step will check each glow plug feed circuit for an open.

Step	Action	Value(s)	Yes	No
1	**Important:** Before clearing the DTCs, use the Scan Tool Capture Info in order to record the Freeze Frame and the failure records for reference, as the data will be lost when the Clear Info function is used. Was the Powertrain On-Board Diagnostic (OBD) System Check performed?	—	*Go to Step 2*	Go to *A Powertrain On Board Diagnostic (OBD) System Check*
2	Is DTC: • P0117 • P0118 • P0380 stored as history or current codes?	—	Go to the Applicable DTC Table	*Go to Step 3*
3	1. Turn the ignition OFF. 2. Disconnect all of the glow plugs. 3. With a test light connected to B+, probe the spade terminal on each glow plug. Do all of the glow plugs turn the test light ON?	—	*Go to Step 4*	*Go to Step 9*
4	1. Turn the ignition ON with the engine OFF. 2. The glow plugs are still disconnected. 3. Use a test light in order to jumper each glow plug connector terminal to ground. 4. Use a Scan Tool in order to command the glow plugs ON. Does each circuit turn the test light ON?	—	*Go to Step 5*	*Go to Step 10*
5	Does the test light stay ON all the time for each glow plug terminal (even when the glow plugs aren't commanded ON)?	—	*Go to Step 6*	*Go to Step 11*

GC1060001088010X

Fig. 17 Glow plug system inspect (Part 1 of 2)

a. Apply suitable high temperature anti-seize compound part No. 1052771, or equivalent, to all mounting threads.
b. Install new O-ring.

FUEL PUMP

REPLACE

1. Disconnect electrical connector.
2. Remove fuel lines.
3. Slide pump from bracket.
4. Reverse procedure to install.

INJECTION PUMP

REPLACE

Removal

1. Remove engine cover as outlined under "Engine, Replace."
2. Remove lower intake manifold as outlined under "Intake Manifold, Replace."
3. Disconnect injection lines and fuel inlet line, then the harness connectors and hoses.
4. Disconnect electrical harness connectors and injection pump hoses.
5. Disconnect fuel return line and oil fill tube, then remove oil filler tube grommet.
6. Scribe or paint mark on front cover and injection pump flange for assembly.
7. Rotate engine to gain access to driven gear mounting bolts through oil filler neck hole, **Fig. 14. Do not use starter motor to rotate engine. Bar engine over by hand to avoid internal engine damage.**
8. Remove driven gear mounting bolts.
9. Remove injection pump flange nuts using injection pump wrench, tool No. J-41711, or equivalent.
10. Remove pump. Plug or cap lines, openings and nozzles.
11. Remove flange gasket.

Installation

1. Install new flange gasket.
2. Install pump ensuring pump hub locating pin is positioned within injection pump gear slot, **Fig. 15.**
3. Align front cover and pump flange marks, install flange nuts, **Fig. 16.**
4. Install driven gear mounting bolts. **Do not tighten until all mounting bolts are installed.**
5. Install grommet and oil filler tube.
6. Install fuel feed line and fuel return line, then the harnesses and connectors.
7. Install injector lines and intake manifold.
8. Adjust fuel injection timing as outlined under "Injection Pump Timing."

FUEL FILTER

REPLACE

1. Open fuel tank filler cap, then remove fuel filter protective shield.
2. Open fuel manager/filter air bleed valve.
3. Disconnect water-in-fuel sensor electrical connector.
4. Attach suitable flexible 1⁄4–5⁄16 inch I.D. tube or hose to water drain valve.
5. Drain filter by slowly open water drain valve. **Do not remove drain.**
6. Remove filter element, then water-in-fuel sensor.
7. Reverse procedure to install, noting the following:
   a. Install new seal.
   b. Ensure mating surface between filter element and header assembly is clean before installing filter.
   c. Align element arrow with air bleed drain valve.
   d. Tighten by hand.
   e. When clipping is heard, align locking ring arrow with element arrow.

INJECTION PUMP TIMING

A scan tool must be used to inspect or adjust injection timing. A static timing mark can be used as a reference. If a static timing mark is not present on the injection pump mounting flange, one can be scribed to assist in determining how far the pump needs to be rotated.

There will not be a change in engine performance or vehicle driveability if timing is altered during the Time Set procedure. If injection timing is not set correctly, Diagnostic Trouble Code (DTC) P0216 may be stored.

1. Start and idle engine until it reaches operating temperature.
2. Connect suitable programmed scan tool.
3. Activate Time Set. If activated correctly, Des. Inj. Time will read 0.°
4. It is normal for injection timing to fluctuate. Average timing is 3.5.°
5. If engine stalls during Time Set, slightly rotate injection pump (.039 inch equals 2°) toward driver side of vehicle.
6. If timing is more 3.5°, rotate injection pump toward passenger side of vehicle.
7. If timing is less 3.5°, rotate injection pump toward driver side of vehicle.
8. Turn engine off.

Step	Action	Value(s)	Yes	No
6	1. Disconnect the glow plug output (gray) cable from the glow plug relay. 2. Probe each glow plug terminal with a test light connected to ground. Is the test light ON for all terminals?	—	*Go to Step 7*	*Go to Step 8*
7	Repair the short to voltage on the glow plug output circuit or the short to voltage on the glow plug signal circuit. Is the action complete?	—	*Go to Step 11*	—
8	Replace the glow plug relay. Is the action complete?	—	*Go to Step 11*	—
9	Replace all of the glow plugs that do not turn the test light ON. Is the action complete?	—	*Go to Step 11*	—
10	Repair the open in each circuit that does not turn the test light ON. Is the action complete?	—	*Go to Step 11*	—
11	Operate the vehicle within the conditions under which system was noted. Does the system operate properly?	—	The System is OK	*Go to Step 1*

GC1060001088020X

Fig. 17 Glow plug system inspect (Part 2 of 2)

9. Loosen injection flange nuts using injection pump wrench tool No. J-41089, or equivalent.
10. Slightly rotate pump in desired direction.
11. Tighten flange nuts and repeat test to verify correct timing.

FUEL INJECTION SYSTEM

TDC Offset (Recovery) Adjustment

This procedure should only be used when engine, front engine cover or PCM and injection pump are replaced simultaneously.

1. Start and run engine until it reaches operating temperature (more than 170°F).
2. Turn engine off and install suitable programmed scan tool.
3. Clear all Diagnostic Trouble Codes (DTC's).
4. Turn ignition switch to On position, with engine off.
5. Hold accelerator pedal to Wide Open Throttle (WOT) for at least 45 seconds.
6. Turn ignition switch Off position for 30 seconds.
7. Start engine.
8. Ensure TDC Offset has been cleared to -.25– -.75. If not, repeat preceding steps.
9. Turn ignition switch to Off position.
10. Loosen injection flange nuts using injection pump wrench tool No. J-41089, or equivalent.
11. Slightly rotate injection pump (.039 inch equals 2°) using injection pump adjustment tool No. J-29872-A, or equivalent.
12. Rotate pump toward driver side to a positive number; rotate toward passenger side to achieve negative number.
13. Inspect TDC Offset.
14. Repeat procedure until TDC Offset is correct.

INJECTOR NOZZLE

REPLACE

1. Remove engine cover as outlined under "Engine, Replace."
2. Remove fuel return clip, then disconnect fuel return hose and fuel injection line.
3. Remove injection nozzle using nozzle socket tool No. J-29873, or equivalent.
4. Reverse procedure to install.

Circuit Description

The On Board Diagnostic (OBD) System Check is an organized approach in identifying a problem created by an electronic engine system fault. The OBD system check is the starting point for any driveability diagnosis. The OBD system check directs the service technician to the next step in diagnosing the complaint. Do not perform this check if no driveability complaint exists. Understanding the table correctly reduces the diagnostic time. Understanding the table correctly prevents the replacement of good parts.

Diagnostic Aids

Important: Do not clear the DTCs unless directed by a diagnostic procedure. Clearing the DTCs will also clear valuable freeze frame and failure records data.

Inspect all related wiring and connections including the connections at the PCM. These may cause an intermittent malfunction.

Check any circuitry that is suspected of causing an intermittent problem for the following conditions:

- Backed out terminals
- Improper mating
- Broken locks
- Improperly formed or damaged terminals
- Poor terminal to wiring connections
- Physical damage to the wiring harness
- Corrosion

Test Description

The numbers below refer to the step number in the diagnostic table.

1. This step will check for power and grounds to the Data Link Connector (DLC).
4. This step will determine if other modules on the Class 2 circuit can communicate, if no communication occurs, the class 2 circuit is grounded, open, shorted to voltage or the module is causing a communication problem.
5. This step will check for DTCs associated with the Vehicle Theft Deterrent (VTD) which will prevent the vehicle from starting. Check for Powertrain and Body DTC's.
6. Whenever multiple DTCs are stored, refer to the DTC Tables in the following order:
   1. PCM Error DTCs
   2. System voltage DTCs
   3. Component level DTCs (DTCs that indicate a malfunctioning part)
   4. System level DTCs (DTCs that indicate a system fault)
7. Checking the sensors for proper operation during warm up can be a crucial step in correctly diagnosing any driveability concern. Careful observation of these sensors during the engine warm up may reveal a slow responding sensor or a sensor that malfunctions only within a small portion of its range.

   After the engine is at the normal operating temperature, a comparison of the actual control system data with the typical values is a quick way to determine if any parameter is not within limits. Keep in mind that a base engine problem (i.e. advanced cam timing) may substantially alter sensor values.

   Check the Engine Coolant Temperature (ECT) sensor for initial coolant temperature reading at ambient. Then observe the rise in the temperature while the engine is warming up.

GC1060001089010X

Fig. 18 Powertrain On Board Diagnostic (OBD) system inspect (Part 1 of 2)

Step	Action	Value(s)	Yes	No
1	**Important:** Check for applicable service bulletins before proceeding with this diagnosis. **Important:** Do not turn the ignition OFF when performing this diagnostic. 1. Connect the scan tool to the Data Link Connector (DLC). 2. Turn the ignition ON while leaving the engine OFF. Does the scan tool power-up?	—	*Go to Step 2*	INSPECT *Data Link Connector Diagnosis*
2	Attempt to establish communications with the PCM. Does the scan tool display PCM data?	—	*Go to Step 3*	*Go to Step 4*
3	Does the engine start and continue to run?	—	*Go to Step 6*	*Go to Step 5*
4	Attempt to establish communications with other systems (Passlock/EVO, ABS controllers). Does scan tool communicate with the other systems?	—	INSPECT *Data Link Connector Diagnosis*	INSPECT *Scan Tool Does Not Communicate with Components*
5	Check for PCM DTCs using the scan tool. Were any last test failed, history, or MIL request DTCs set?	—	Go to the applicable DTC table	*Go to Step 7*
6	Is DTC P0215, P1626 or DTC P1631?	—	Go to the applicable DTC table	INSPECT *Engine Cranks but Does Not Run*
7	1. Turn ON the ignition leaving the engine OFF. 2. Check the ECT. 3. Start the engine. 4. Allow the engine temperature to reach operating temperature. 5. While the engine is reaching the operating temperature, check the ECT. 6. Compare the scan tool values of the sensors with the typical values shown in the Scan Tool Values. Are the displayed values normal or within typical ranges?	—	CHECK *Symptoms*	Go to Diagnostic Aids and Test Descriptions

GC1060001089020X

Fig. 18 Powertrain On Board Diagnostic (OBD) system inspect (Part 2 of 2)

GLOW PLUG SYSTEM

Description

The system consists of an integral electronic control/glow plug relay assembly, six-volt glow plugs, a glow plug inhibit temperature switch and a Wait lamp.

System Operation

Normal system operation is as follows:

1. Glow plugs energize (turn on) for approximately 4–6 seconds, then de-energize for approximately 4.5 seconds.
2. Glow plugs cycle on for approximately 1.5 seconds, off for approximately 4.5 seconds and continue to cycle 1.5 seconds on, then 4.5 seconds off for total duration (including initial 4–6 seconds) of approximately 20 seconds.
3. If engine is cranked during or after previous sequence, glow plugs will cycle on/off for total duration of 25 seconds after engine control switch is returned

from crank position, whether engine starts or not.
4. Engine does not have to be operating to terminate glow plug cycling.
5. Times indicated here are approximate because they vary with initial engine temperature.
6. Initial on time and cycling on/off times vary also with system voltage and/or temperature.
7. Lower temperatures will cause longer duration of cycling.

System Diagnosis

Refer to **Fig. 17** for glow plug system inspect and **Fig. 18** for Powertrain On Board Diagnostic (OBD) system inspect.

TIGHTENING SPECIFICATIONS

Year	Component	Torque Ft. Lbs.
2002	Accessory Bracket	37
	Air Cleaner	100①
	Air Cleaner Clamp	40①
	A/C Compressor	37
	A/C Hose	26
	Bell Housing	30
	Camshaft Timing Chain Sprocket	125
	Camshaft Thrust Plate & Bearing	17
	Connecting Rod Cap	48
	Coolant Crossover	31
	Coolant Drain Plug	18
	Crankcase Depression Regulator (CDR)	31
	Crankshaft Bearing Cap	②
	Crankshaft Dampener	85
	Crankshaft Pulley	30
	Crankshaft Sensor	17
	Cylinder Head	⑥
	Drive Belt Tensioner	37
	Exhaust Manifold	26
	Exhaust Manifold Heat Shield	97①
	Exhaust Pipe Clamp	90①
	Fan Shroud	53①
	Flywheel Inspection Cover	46
	Flywheel To Torque Converter	66
	Front Cover	33
	Front Engine Mount, Engine Side	40
	Front Engine Mount, Frame Side, Bolt	44
	Front Engine Mount, Frame Side, Nut	33
	Front Engine Mount Through Bolt	50
	Fuel Filter	31
	Fuel Fittings	18
	Fuel Injection Line	20
	Fuel Injection Nozzle	50
	Fuel Injection Pump Drive Gear	20
	Fuel Injection Pump, Nuts & Studs	30
	Fuel Pump Line	22
	Glow Plug	16
	Intake Manifold, Non-Turbocharged	31④
	Intake Manifold, Turbocharged Lower	31
	Intake Manifold, Turbocharged Upper	17
	Lifting Bracket	40
	Oil Cooler Line	55
	Oil Filler Tube	106①
	Oil Filler Tube Extension	27①
	Oil Pan	⑦

Continued

TIGHTENING SPECIFICATIONS—Continued

Year	Component	Torque Ft. Lbs.
2002	Oil Pump	65
	Oil Pump Cover	12
	Oil Pump Drive Clamp	31
	Power Steering Hose	20
	Power Steering Pump	37
	Radiator Mounting Bracket	13
	Rear Engine Mount	35
	Rocker Arm	40
	Surge Tank	53①
	Thermostat Housing	31
	Transmission To Engine	66
	Turbocharger	43–48
	Turbocharger Brace, Long	⑤
	Turbocharger Brace, Short	18
	Turbocharger Clamp	50①
	Turbocharger Exhaust Clamp	90①
	Turbocharger Heat Shield	③
	Turbocharger Oil Feed	21
	Turbocharger Oil Return	19
	Vacuum Pump	18
	Valve Cover	16
	Valve Lifter Guide Plate Clamp	18
	Water Pump	17
	Water Pump Backing Plate	21
	Water Pump Pulley	18

①— Inch lbs.
②— Refer to "Main & Rod Bearings" for tightening sequence.
③— Righthand & top bolts, 17 ft. lbs.; Center bolts, 17 ft. lbs.; and nuts, 22 ft. lbs.
④— Refer to "Intake Manifold, Replace" for tightening sequence.
⑤— Bolts, 37 ft. lbs.; Nuts, 25 ft. lbs.
⑥— Refer to "Cylinder Head, Replace" for tightening specifications and sequence.
⑦— Except rear bolts, 89 inch lbs.; Rear two bolts, 17 ft. lbs.

6.6L Diesel Engine

NOTE: Refer To The "6.6L Diesel Engine" Section Of The "Avalanche, Escalade EXT, Sierra, Silverado & SSR" Chapter For Procedures Not Included In This Section.

NOTE: On Air Bag Equipped Models, Refer To "Air Bag System Precautions" Located In The Front Of This Manual For System Disarming & Arming Procedures.

INDEX

PRECAUTIONS

Air Bag Systems

Refer to "Air Bag System Precautions" in the front of this manual for system disarming and arming procedures.

Battery Ground Cable

Prior to service disconnect battery ground cable and isolate as required.

Fuel System Pressure Relief

1. Loosen fuel filler cap to relieve fuel tank vapor pressure.
2. Remove instrument panel lower extension mounting bolts and nuts, then the instrument panel lower extension.
3. Remove left and right knee bolster panels from under instrument panel.
4. Disconnect retaining straps and remove engine cover.
5. Connect pressure gauge tool No. J 34730-1A, or equivalent, to fuel pressure connection.
6. Install bleed hose of gauge into an approved container.
7. Open valve on gauge in order to relieve system pressure. Fuel connections are now safe for servicing.
8. Drain any fuel remaining in gauge into an approved container.

Radio Security System

If the Theftlock system is active when battery power is interrupted, the customers security code must be entered to restore proper function of the radio. To unlock a secured radio after power loss, proceed as follows:

1. "LOC" appears with ignition in On position.
2. Press "NM" and "000" will appear on display.
3. Press "NM" again to make last two digits agree with security code.
4. Press "HR" to make first 1 or 2 digits agree with security code.
5. Press "AM-FM" to select code entered. "SEC" will show on display indicating radio is now operable and secure.
6. If incorrect code is entered eight times, "INOP" will display. In order to reenter code, ignition must be left on for one hour before code can be entered and only three more chances to enter code are available before display reads "INOP."

ENGINE MOUNT

REPLACE

Front

LEFTHAND

1. Raise and support vehicle.
2. Remove engine mount to engine mount frame bracket attaching bolts.
3. Support a suitable adjustable jack on lower engine boss, then raise engine enough to separate engine mount from frame bracket.
4. Remove engine mount to engine attaching bolts, then the engine mount.
5. Reverse procedure to install.

RIGHTHAND

1. Raise and support vehicle.
2. Disconnect transmission oil cooler lines from transmission, then position cooler lines aside. Cap lines to prevent leaking or contamination.
3. Remove starter motor as outlined in "Electrical" section.
4. Remove engine mount to engine mount bracket attaching bolts.
5. Support a suitable adjustable jack on lower engine boss, then raise engine enough to separate engine mount from frame bracket.
6. Remove engine mount to engine attaching bolts, then the engine mount.
7. Reverse procedure to install.

Rear

1. Support transmission with suitable stand.
2. Remove rear mount mounting bolts and washers.
3. Raise transmission only enough to allow mount removal.
4. Remove mount.
5. Reverse procedure to install.

ENGINE

REPLACE

1. Remove hood.
2. Remove front passenger seat.
3. Remove instrument panel lower extension upper trim panel.
4. Remove instrument panel lower extension mounting bolts and nuts, then the instrument panel lower extension.
5. Remove left and right knee bolster panels from under instrument panel.
6. Disconnect retaining straps and remove engine cover.
7. Drain coolant into suitable container.

8. Recover refrigerant as outlined in "Air Conditioning" chapter.
9. Remove mounting bolts and air cleaner.
10. Remove turbocharger as outlined under "Turbocharger, Replace."
11. Remove wiring harness connector bracket bolt and nut from top of center intake manifold.
12. Remove fuel rail clamp bolt, then the coolant inlet pipe bracket bolt.
13. Remove wiring harness connector bracket bolt and nut, then position bracket aside.
14. Disconnect engine wiring harness electrical connector from Intake Air Temperature (IAT) sensor.
15. Remove center intake manifold attaching bolts and nuts, then the center intake manifold. Remove and discard gaskets.
16. Remove charged air cooler, A/C condenser and radiator as outlined under "Radiator, Replace."
17. Remove radiator core support.
18. Remove front tire and wheel assemblies.
19. Remove wheelhouse inner panels, then disconnect cord for engine coolant heater.
20. Remove starter as outlined in "Electrical" section.
21. Remove battery cable bracket from righthand side of lower crankcase.
22. Remove auxiliary battery negative cable and engine wire harness ground wires attaching bolt from righthand side of engine. Position harness and battery cable aside.
23. Drain engine oil.
24. Remove exhaust pipe to exhaust outlet retaining clamp.
25. Place reference marks on torque converter and flywheel.
26. Remove torque converter attaching bolts through starter opening.
27. Remove transmission oil line clip nut from side of engine block.
28. Remove transmission fluid fill tube bracket retaining nuts.
29. Remove transmission to engine studs and bolts. Note location of studs and any brackets attached to studs for installation reference.
30. Working through left and right wheelhouse openings, remove engine mount to frame bracket bolts .
31. Attach engine lifting bracket tool No. J 36857, or equivalent, to left and right cylinder heads.
32. Attach a suitable engine lifting device to brackets.

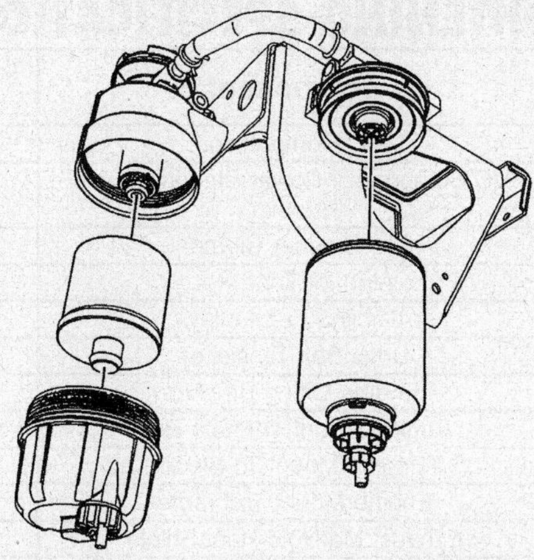

Fig. 1 Fuel filter replacement

33. Raise engine off engine mounts, then remove left and right engine mount frame brackets.
34. Remove engine from vehicle.
35. Reverse procedure to install.

RADIATOR

REPLACE

Refer to "4.3L, 5.0L & 5.7L Gasoline Engines" section.

TURBOCHARGER

REPLACE

1. Remove engine cover as outlined under "Engine, Replace."
2. Remove left and right exhaust pipes.
3. Remove EGR cooler tube.
4. Remove charge air cooler outlet pipe.
5. Disconnect engine wiring harness electrical connectors from turbocharger vane position sensor and turbocharger vane control solenoid valve.
6. Loosen charge air cooler inlet duct clamp at the turbocharger, then remove hose from turbocharger. **To prevent damage to hose, do not use a screwdriver or other tool to pry hose loose. Cover turbocharger opening with tape.**
7. Remove turbocharger upper heat shield bolts, then the upper heat shield.
8. Loosen turbocharger coolant outlet pipe clamp and remove the hose from turbocharger.
9. Remove turbocharger oil feed pipe banjo bolt and washer. Discard banjo bolt and washer.
10. Position and secure turbocharger oil feed pipe aside.
11. Remove turbocharger oil return pipe nuts at top of flywheel housing.
12. Remove turbocharger attaching bolts, then the turbocharger.
13. Remove and discard turbocharger oil return pipe gasket at flywheel housing.
14. Reverse procedure to install. Apply suitable high temperature anti-seize compound part No. 1052771, or equivalent, to all bolt threads.

FUEL PUMP

REPLACE

1. Relieve fuel system pressure as outlined under "Precautions."
2. Drain fuel tank.
3. Raise and support vehicle.
4. Loosen fuel fill hose clamp, then disconnect fuel fill hose from fuel tank.
5. Disconnect rear fuel return pipe at chassis fuel return pipe.
6. Disconnect chassis fuel feed pipe at fuel filter.
7. Disconnect electrical connector.
8. Support fuel tank with suitable jack stand.
9. Remove fuel tank strap attaching bolts, then the fuel tank straps.
10. Carefully lower fuel tank, then disconnect fuel sender and fuel pressure sensor electrical connectors.
11. Disconnect fuel lines from sending unit.
12. Remove fuel pump/sender lock ring, noting the following:
    a. Use a suitable long breaker bar and lock ring removal tool No. J-45722, or equivalent.
    b. It will take a significant amount of force to release lock ring.
    c. Before removing lock ring, secure fuel tank to prevent rotation.
13. Remove fuel pump/sender assembly.
14. Reverse procedure to install.

FUEL FILTER

REPLACE

1. Raise and support vehicle.
2. Unscrew primary and secondary fuel filters from Diesel Fuel Conditioning Module (DFCM). DFCM is located on lefthand side frame, **Fig. 1.**
3. Reverse procedure to install.

TIGHTENING SPECIFICATIONS

Year	Component	Torque Ft. Lbs.
2006	A/C Compressor	37
	A/C Compressor/Power Steering Pump Bracket	34
	Air Cleaner Clamp	71①
	Air Inlet Tube Nut	18
	Cooling Fan Pulley	30
	Drive Belt Tensioner	37
	Engine Lifting Bracket	40
	Engine Mount Through Bolt	55
	Engine Mount To Block	40
	Engine Mount To Frame	48
	Exhaust Manifold Heat Shield	89①
	Exhaust Pipe Clamp	39
	Flywheel Housing	60
	Flywheel To Torque Converter	44
	Fuel Filter Bracket	22
	Fuel Fittings	18
	Fuel Pump Line	22
	Fuel Pressure Relief Valve	74
	Oil Cooler Line	55
	Oil Drain Plug	62
	Oil Filler Tube	18
	Power Steering Hose	20
	Power Steering Pump	37
	Radiator Mounting Bracket	13
	Transmission To Engine	66
	Turbocharger	80
	Turbocharger Heat Shield	89①
	Turbocharger Oil Feed	19
	Turbocharger Oil Return	18

① — Inch lbs.

8.1L Gasoline Engine

NOTE: Refer To The "8.1L Gasoline Engine" Section Of The "Avalanche, Escalade EXT, Sierra, Silverado & SSR" Chapter For Procedures Not Included In This Section.

NOTE: On Air Bag Equipped Models, Refer To "Air Bag System Precautions" Located In The Front Of This Manual For System Disarming & Arming Procedures.

NOTE: Refer To "Computer Relearn Procedures" Located In The Front Of This Manual When Battery Power To The Computer Has Been Interrupted.

INDEX

PRECAUTIONS

Air Bag Systems

Refer to "Air Bag System Precautions" in the front of this manual for system disarming and arming procedures.

Battery Ground Cable

Prior to service disconnect battery ground cable and isolate as required.

Fuel System Pressure Relief

Always release residual fuel system pressure prior to disconnecting fuel lines or hoses.

1. Loosen fuel filler cap.
2. Remove engine cover and fuel injector sight shield.
3. Connect suitable fuel pressure gauge to fuel pressure valve and install bleed hose into suitable container.
4. Open valve and bleed system pressure.

Radio Security System

If the Theftlock system is active when battery power is interrupted, the customers security code must be entered to restore proper function of the radio. To unlock a secured radio after power loss, proceed as follows:

1. "LOC" appears with ignition in On position.
2. Press "NM" and "000" will appear on display.
3. Press "NM" again to make last two digits agree with security code.
4. Press "HR" to make first 1 or 2 digits agree with security code.
5. Press "AM-FM" to select code entered. "SEC" will show on display indicating radio is now operable and secure.
6. If incorrect code is entered eight times, "INOP" will display. In order to reenter code, ignition must be left on for one hour before code can be entered and only three more chances to enter code are available before display reads "INOP."

ENGINE MOUNT

REPLACE

1. Support engine with suitable jack stands.
2. Remove front engine mount through bolt and nut.
3. Raise engine enough to access engine mount.
4. Remove engine mount mounting bolts, nuts and washers.
5. Remove engine mount from front left-hand side of engine.
6. Reverse procedure to install.

ENGINE

REPLACE

1. Open hood and engine cover.
2. Remove battery.
3. Relieve fuel system pressure as outlined under "Precautions."
4. Remove air intake duct from throttle body and air cleaner assembly.
5. Disconnect ignition wires from coils.
6. Remove mounting bolts and ignition coil from valve rocker arm covers.
7. Drain cooling system into suitable container and remove coolant reservoir.
8. Mark location of bumper support brackets to bumper.
9. Remove bracket mounting bolts and bumper.
10. Remove side marker and front park/turn lamp assemblies from grille.
11. Remove grille to radiator support mounting bolts and grille.
12. Recover air conditioning refrigerant as outlined in "Air Conditioning" chapter.
13. Remove headlamp assemblies, hood latch cover and hood latch.
14. **On models equipped with an auxiliary oil cooler,** remove oil cooler lines and oil cooler from radiator support.
15. **On models equipped with an auxiliary transmission cooler,** remove oil cooler lines and oil cooler from radiator support.
16. **On all models,** remove air baffle from radiator support.
17. Remove air conditioning condenser and radiator from radiator support.
18. Remove mounting bolts and radiator support.
19. Rotate drive belt tensioner arm with suitable ⅜ inch drive and remove drive belt.
20. Remove fan clutch from water pump.
21. Remove radiator hoses from engine.
22. Disconnect throttle body actuator control electrical connectors.
23. Disconnect engine vacuum lines. Mark lines for installation reference.
24. Disconnect EGR valve electrical connector, then remove EGR valve and adapter.
25. Remove engine oil fill tube, then the oil dipstick and tube.
26. Remove air conditioning compressor from mounting bracket and position aside.
27. Remove hydraulic hoses from power steering pump.
28. Remove power steering pump and mounting bracket.
29. Remove air conditioning compressor mounting bracket from cylinder block.
30. Remove alternator from mounting bracket and mounting bracket from cylinder block.

31. Disconnect engine electrical harness and position aside.
32. Disconnect fuel supply lines from rear of engine.
33. Raise and support vehicle.
34. Remove ground wires from engine block.
35. Remove starter motor and flywheel inspection cover.
36. Remove torque converter to flywheel bolts.
37. Remove mounting bolts and exhaust pipe from manifold.
38. Remove transmission to engine mounting bolts.
39. Remove engine cooler lines from retaining brackets. Lower vehicle.
40. Attach engine lifting brackets tool No. J-36857, or equivalent, to rear of right-hand cylinder head and front of left-hand cylinder head.
41. Remove engine mount through bolts.
42. Remove air conditioning compressor and power steering mounting bracket from cylinder head.
43. Remove engine using suitable lifting device.
44. Reverse procedure to install.

TIGHTENING SPECIFICATIONS

Year	Component	Torque, Ft. Lbs.
2002	Air Injection Pipe, Bolt	19
	Air Injection Pipe, Nut	106①
	Air Injection Pump Pipe, Bolt	37
	Coolant Temperature Gauge Sensor	15
	Cylinder Head Coolant Hole Plug	17
	Drive Belt Tensioner	37
	EGR Vacuum Regulator Bracket	22
	EGR Valve	22
	Engine Mount, Bolt	44
	Engine Mount, Nut	33
	Flywheel	74
	Flywheel Housing, Countersunk Bolt	44
	Flywheel Housing, Hex Head Bolt	50
	Fuel Rail, Bolt	89①
	Fuel Rail, Stud	18
	Oil Dipstick Tube Bracket	13
	Oil Filler Tube	106①
	Oil Filter	28
	Oil Pan Drain Plug	21
	Transmission Convertor Cover	106①

① — Inch lbs.

Rear Axle & Suspension

NOTE: Prior To Performing Any Service Operations Listed In This Section, Consult The "Technical Service Bulletins" In This Section For Related Information.

INDEX

REAR AXLE

REPLACE

1. Raise and support vehicle.
2. Place suitable jack stands at front end of vehicle.
3. Support rear axle with suitable jack stands.
4. Remove wheel and tire assemblies.
5. Disconnect rear wheel speed sensor electrical connector.
6. Remove brake calipers from rear axle, position and support calipers aside. Do not disconnect brake hoses from calipers.
7. Disconnect propeller shaft from rear axle.
8. Disconnect park brake cables from rear axle.
9. Drain lubricant from rear axle.
10. Remove shock absorber from rear axle.
11. Remove rear leaf spring U-bolts, then the rear spring anchor plates and rear spring spacers from vehicle.
12. Remove rear axle from vehicle.
13. Reverse procedure to install.

REAR AXLE SHAFT

REPLACE

1. Raise and support vehicle, then remove tire and wheel assembly.
2. Remove brake caliper, then position and support caliper aside. Do not disconnect brake hose from caliper.
3. Drain rear axle lubricant.
4. Remove rear axle housing cover and gasket.
5. **On models not equipped with a locking differential,** remove pinion shaft locking bolt, then the pinion shaft.
6. **On models equipped with a locking differential,** proceed as follows:
   a. Remove pinion shaft locking bolt.
   b. Partially remove pinion shaft, then rotate case until pinion shaft touches housing.
   c. Rotate rear axle shaft lock until lock aligns with thrust block opening, use a screwdriver, or similar flat-bladed tool to rotate shaft lock.
   d. Push flange of axle shaft into axle housing.
7. **On all models,** remove rear axle shaft lock from button end of axle shaft.
8. Remove axle shaft from housing.
9. Reverse procedure to install, noting the following:
   a. **On models with a locking differential,** install rear axle shaft lock on axle shaft so ends are flush with thrust block.
   b. **On all models,** align hole in pinion shaft with bolt hole in differential case.

HUB & BEARING

REPLACE

1. Raise and support vehicle, then remove tire and wheel assembly.
2. Remove brake caliper, then position and support caliper aside. Do not disconnect brake hose from caliper.
3. Remove axle shaft as outlined under "Rear Axle Shaft, Replace."
4. Remove axle nut retaining ring, key and adjusting nut using wheel bearing nut wrench tool No. J 2222-C, or equivalent.
5. Remove hub from axle housing. Remove brake rotor, if necessary.
6. Remove oil seal from wheel hub.
7. Remove inner hub bearing, then the inner hub bearing cup using a suitable brass drift and hammer.
8. Remove the retaining ring from the wheel hub.
9. Remove outer hub bearing and bearing cup.
10. Reverse procedure to install.

SHOCK ABSORBER

REPLACE

1. Raise and support vehicle and rear axle.
2. **On models equipped with air lift shock absorbers,** bleed air from lines and disconnect line from shock.
3. **On all models,** remove upper and lower mounting nuts, bolts and washers.
4. Remove shock absorber.
5. Reverse procedure to install.

LEAF SPRING

REPLACE

1. Raise and support vehicle.
2. Relieve rear spring tension by supporting rear axle with suitable jack stand.
3. Remove U-bolts and anchor plate.
4. Remove spring from rear shackle, then the front hanger.
5. Remove rear shackle mounting nut and bolt, then the rear spring.
6. Reverse procedure to install, noting the following:
   a. **Torque** spring to front hanger mounting bolt to 80 ft. lbs., then tighten an additional 200°.

STABILIZER BAR

REPLACE

1. Raise and support vehicle.
2. Remove anchor plate mounting nuts, washers, bolts and brackets.
3. Remove stabilizer bar from anchor plate.
4. Remove frame mounting nuts, washers, bolts and brackets.
5. Remove stabilizer bar from frame.
6. Remove insulators from bar.
7. Reverse procedure to install.

TIGHTENING SPECIFICATIONS

Year	Component	Torque Ft. Lbs.
2002–06	Axle Flange	115
	Bearing Cap	①
	Brake Backing Plate	100
	Center Bearing	43
	Companion Flange	75
	Differential Housing Cover	④
	Drain & Fill Plugs	24
	Pinion Shaft Lock Bolt	②
	Shaft Retainer	115
	Shaft U-Bolt	
	Shock Absorber Bolts, Lower	100
	Shock Absorber Bolts, Upper	18
	Shock Absorber Mounting Nut	59
	Spring U-Bolt Retaining Nuts	③
	Spring To Hanger	107
	Spring Shackle	67
	Stabilizer Shaft Clamp	37
	Stabilizer Shaft Link	52
	U-Joint	15
	Wheel Hub Nut	52
	Wheel Lug Nut	140

① — 8½ inch ring gear, 55 ft. lbs.; 9½ & 10½ inch ring gears, 80 ft. lbs.
② — 8½ inch ring gear, 27 ft. lbs.; 9½ inch ring gear, 20 ft. lbs.
③ — 1500 series, 63 ft. lbs.; 2500 & 3500 series, 103 ft. lbs.
④ — 8½ inch ring gear, 30 ft. lbs.; 9½ & 10½ inch ring gears, 45 ft. lbs.

Front Suspension & Steering

INDEX

PRECAUTIONS

Crimped Nuts

Steering Linkage Relay Rod Assemblies Use Crimped Nuts. Whenever A Crimped Nut Is Loosened Or Removed, It Must Be Replaced With A Prevailing Torque Nut.

Air Bag Systems

Refer to "Air Bag System Precautions" in the front of this manual for system disarming and arming procedures.

DESCRIPTION

Refer to **Fig. 1** for exploded view of front suspension.

WHEEL BEARING

ADJUST

1. Raise and support vehicle.
2. Remove wheel cover and hub dust cap.
3. **Torque** hub/rotor bearing to 12 ft. lbs., while rotating wheel forward by hand.
4. Adjust nut so that it is just loose, then back nut off until spindle hole aligns with nut slot. **Do not back off nut more than ¼ flat.**
5. Install new cotter pin.
6. Ensure endplay is .001–.008 inch.

WHEEL BEARING

REPLACE

Refer to "Hub, Bearing & Seal, Replace."

HUB, BEARING & SEAL

REPLACE

Removal

1. Raise and support vehicle, then remove wheel and tire assembly.
2. Remove brake caliper as outlined under "Disc Brakes"
3. Remove dust cover, cotter pin, nut and washer.
4. Remove hub/rotor and ensure that outer wheel bearing comes free. **Do not damage steering knuckle spindle threads.**
5. Remove inner wheel bearing.

Installation

1. Fill each cone and roller assembly full of suitable high-temperature front wheel bearing grease using suitable cone-type grease machine.
2. Install inner wheel bearing into rotor and apply an additional quantity of suitable grease outboard of bearing.
3. Lubricate new seal lip with thin layer of suitable grease and install with flange using suitable flat plate or block.
4. Install hub/rotor.
5. Install outer wheel bearing, washer and nut.
6. Adjust wheel bearing as outlined under "Wheel Bearing, Adjust" then install cotter pin. **Ensure pin sends do not interfere with dust cap.**
7. Apply additional grease outboard of wheel bearing.
8. Install dust cap, caliper, and tire and wheel assembly.

BALL JOINT INSPECTION

Lower

Lower ball joints are a loose fit when not connected to the steering knuckle. Wear may be inspected without disassembling the ball stud.

1. Raise and support vehicle.
2. Support lower control arm as far outboard and near ball joint as possible with suitable floor stand or jack.
3. Adjust wheel bearing as previously outlined.
4. Position suitable dial indicator against wheel rim's lowest outboard point.
5. Rock wheel in and out while reading dial indicator.
6. If reading is more than .125 inch, position dial indicator against spindle.
7. Pry between lower control arm and out race while reading dial indicator.
8. If reading is more than .08 inch, replace ball joint.

Upper

1. Ensure ball joint is spring loaded in socket.
2. If there is any lateral movement, replace ball joint.
3. If ball joint can be twisted in socket with fingers, replace as required.

BALL JOINT

REPLACE

Lower

1. Raise and support vehicle. Remove tire and wheel assembly.
2. Support lower control arm with suitable floor jack.
3. Remove brake caliper as outlined in "Disc Brakes" chapter.
4. Remove cotter pin and nut.
5. Separate steering knuckle ball joint using ball joint separator tool No. J-23742, or equivalent.
6. Remove lower ball joint by guiding lower control arm out of splash shield with suitable screwdriver while lifting upper control arm with suitable pry bar.
7. Block knuckle assembly with suitable wood block between frame and upper control arm.
8. Remove ball joint from lower control arm using ball joint remover/installer tool No. J-9519-E, or equivalent, **Fig. 2.**

9. Reverse procedure to install, noting the following:
   a. If cotter pin does not align with stud nut, tighten nut until pin can be installed.
   b. Never loosen stud nut when installing cotter pin.

Upper

1. Raise and support vehicle. Support lower control arm with suitable floor jack.
2. Remove tire and wheel assembly.
3. Remove brake caliper as outlined under "Disc Brakes"
4. Remove wheel speed sensor harness and brake hose bracket mounting nut and bolt.
5. Center pinch ball joint mounting rivets.
6. Cut ¼ inch deep hole in rivets using ⅛ inch drill bit.
7. Drill rivet heads away using ½ inch drill bit.
8. Remove rivets by using suitable pin punch.
9. Remove cotter pin and nut.
10. Separate ball joint from steering knuckle using suitable ball joint separator tool No. J-23742, or equivalent.
11. Pull stud away from knuckle and remove ball joint.
12. Reverse procedure to install, noting the following:
    a. If cotter pin does not align with stud nut, tighten nut until pin can be installed.
    b. Never loosen stud nut when installing cotter pin.

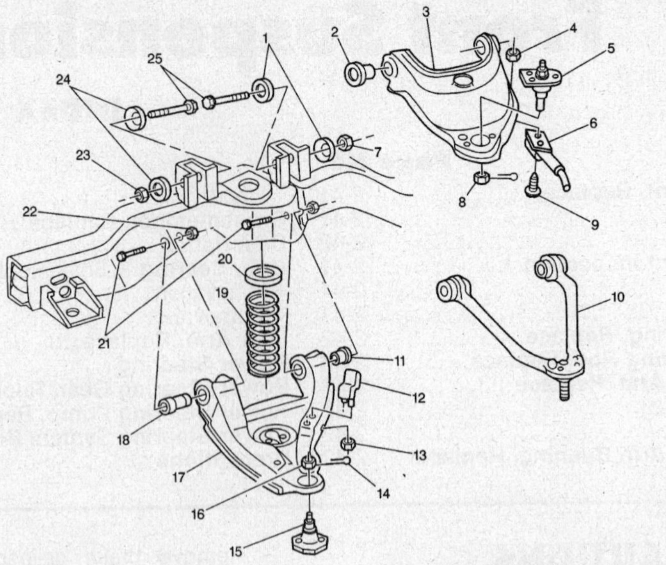

(1) Cam
(2) Upper Control Arm Bushing
(3) Upper Control Arm
(4) Nut
(5) Upper Ball Joint
(6) Brake Hose Bracket
(7) Upper Control Arm to Frame Nut
(8) Upper Ball Joint Nut
(9) Brake Hose Bracket Screw
(10) Upper Control Arm
(11) Lower Control Arm Bushing
(12) Lower Control Arm Bumper
(13) Lower Control Arm Bumper Nut
(14) Lower Ball Joint Cotter Pin
(15) Lower Ball Joint
(16) Lower Ball Joint Nut
(17) Lower Control Arm
(18) Lower Control Arm Bushing
(19) Front Coil Spring
(20) Front Coil Spring Upper Insulator
(21) Lower Control Arm to Frame Bolts
(22) Lower Control Arm to Frame Nut
(23) Upper Control Arm to Frame Nut
(24) Cams
(25) Upper Control Arm to Frame Bolts

GC2020000179000X

Fig. 1 Exploded view of front suspension

COIL SPRING

REPLACE

1. Raise and support vehicle. Allow control arm to hang free.
2. Remove tire and wheel assembly.
3. Remove stabilizer bar link pins as outlined under "Stabilizer Bar, Replace."
4. Remove shock absorbed as outlined under "Shock Absorber, Replace."
5. Cradle lower control arm using coil spring remover tool No. J-23028-01, or equivalent, and suitable jack, **Fig. 3.**
6. Secure spring using suitable safety chain through spring and lower control arm.
7. Relieve lower control arm pivot bolt tension by raising jack.
8. Remove pivot bolts and nuts.
9. Remove coil spring compression and chain.
10. Remove coil spring and insulator.
11. Reverse procedure to install.

SHOCK ABSORBER

REPLACE

1. Raise and support vehicle.
2. Relieve shock absorber tension by installing suitable jack stand under lower control arm.
3. Remove upper mounting nut. Hold shock absorber with suitable wrench.
4. Remove upper mount retainer and grommet.
5. Remove lower mounting bolts, shock absorber bushing and retainer.
6. Reverse procedure to install.

CONTROL ARM

REPLACE

Lower

1. Raise and support vehicle. Support lower control arm with suitable floor stands or jack.
2. Remove tire and wheel assembly.
3. Remove brake caliper as outlined under "Disc Brakes"
4. Remove hub and rotor as outlined under "Hub, Bearing & Seal, Replace."
5. Remove lower ball joint as outlined under "Ball Joint, Replace."
6. Remove coil spring as outlined under "Coil Spring, Replace."
7. Remove mounting nuts, bolts and lower control arm.
8. Reverse procedure to install.

Upper

1. Raise and support vehicle. Support lower control arm with floor stands between spring seats and ball joints.
2. Remove tire and wheel assembly.
3. Remove bracket mounting nuts and bolts, then tie brake hose and wheel speed sensor harness aside.
4. Remove upper ball joint as outlined under "Ball Joint, Replace."
5. Remove mounting bolts, nuts and upper control arm.
6. Reverse procedure to install.

CONTROL ARM BUSHING

REPLACE

Upper

1. Remove upper control arm as outlined under "Control Arm Replace, Upper."
2. Remove bushings using ball joint replacement tool No. J-9519-E, or equivalent.
3. Reverse procedure to install.

STEERING KNUCKLE

REPLACE

1. Raise and support vehicle.
2. Support control arms with suitable stands.
3. Remove tire and wheel assembly.
4. Remove mounting nut and disconnect tie rod ball stud using universal steering linkage puller tool No. J-24319-B, or equivalent.
5. Remove brake caliper as outlined under"Disc Brakes"
6. Remove hub and rotor as outlined under "Hub, Bearing & Seal, Replace."
7. Remove steering knuckle seal. **Do not damage seal.**
8. Remove splash shield mounting bolts.
9. Separate upper and lower ball joint studs using ball joint separator tool No. J-23742, or equivalent.
10. Remove wheel speed sensor shock tower clip mounting bolt and washer.
11. **On 7300 lbs. GVWR models,** remove

wheel speed sensor upper control arm rosebud clip.
12. **On all models,** remove wheel speed sensor wire clip upper ball joint mounting bolt.
13. Remove splash shield and wheel speed sensor.
14. Remove steering knuckle.
15. Reverse procedure to install.

STABILIZER BAR

REPLACE

1. Raise and support vehicle.
2. Remove mounting nuts, bolts and link spacer.
3. Remove mounting bolts, brackets and stabilizer bar.
4. Remove rubber insulators.
5. Reverse procedure to install.

CROSSMEMBER

REPLACE

1. Raise and support vehicle, then remove tire and wheel assemblies.
2. Remove front brake hose clip for upper control arms.
3. Disconnect brake hoses from calipers. Plug or cap lines and openings.
4. Remove mounting nuts, bolts and brackets, then disconnect stabilizer bar from lower control arms.
5. Remove mounting nuts, washer and bolts, then disconnect shock absorbers from lower control arms.
6. Remove brake line clip bolts from crossmember.
7. Remove crossmember from engine mounts.
8. Support engine and crossmember.
9. Remove mounting bolts, washers and nuts, then the suspension and crossmember.
10. Reverse procedure to install.

TIE ROD END

REPLACE

1. Raise and support vehicle.
2. Remove inner tie rod ball stud nut.
3. Remove ball stud using universal steering linkage puller tool No. J-24319-B, or equivalent.
4. Mark adjuster tube location for assembly.
5. Turn adjuster tube and remove tie rod end.
6. Remove tie rod.
7. Reverse procedure to install, noting the following:
   a. Install ball studs with appropriate sized steering linkage installer tool Nos. J-29193 or J-29194, or equivalent.
   b. Install new torque prevailing nut.

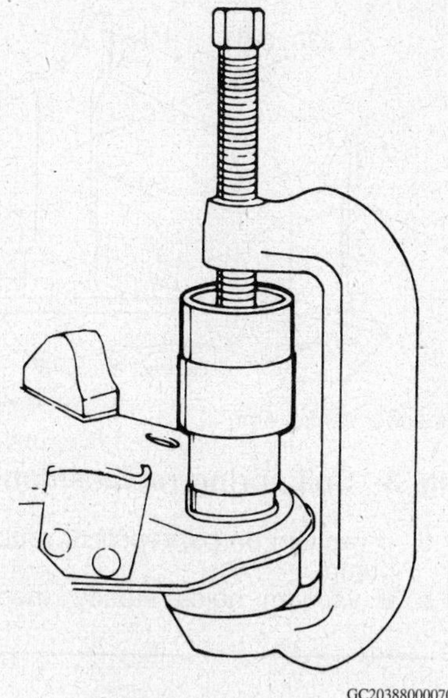

Fig. 2 Pressing lower ball joint from control arm

RELAY ROD

REPLACE

1. Raise and support vehicle.
2. Remove inner tie rod from relay rod as outlined under "Tie Rod End, Replace."
3. Remove idler arm and connecting rod ball studs' nuts.
4. Remove relay rod from idler arm using universal steering linkage puller tool No. J-24319-B, or equivalent.
5. Remove relay rod from connecting rod using universal steering linkage puller tool No. J-24319-B, or equivalent.
6. Remove relay rod.
7. Reverse procedure to install, noting the following:
   a. Install connecting rod to relay rod using appropriate sized steering linkage installer tool Nos. J-29193, J-29194, or equivalent.
   b. Install new torque prevailing nuts.

CONNECTING ROD

REPLACE

1. Raise and support vehicle.
2. Remove relay rod ball stud at pitman arm mounting nut.
3. Remove connecting rod from relay rod using universal steering linkage puller tool No. J-24319-B, or equivalent.
4. Remove connecting rod from pitman arm using universal steering linkage puller tool No. J-24319-B, or equivalent.
5. Remove connecting rod.
6. Reverse procedure to install, noting the following:
   a. Install connecting rod to pitman arm ball stud with steering linkage installer tool No. J-29193, or equivalent.
   b. Install new torque prevailing nut.
   c. Install connecting rod to pitman arm ball stud with steering linkage installer tool No. J-29193, or equivalent.
   d. Install new torque prevailing nut.

IDLER ARM

REPLACE

1. Raise and support vehicle.
2. Disconnect idler arm from frame.
3. Remove idler arm ball stud nut.
4. Separate idler arm from relay rod using universal steering linkage puller tool No. J-24319-B, or equivalent.
5. Reverse procedure to install, noting the following:
   a. Connect relay rod to idler arm ball stud with steering linkage installer tool No. J-29193, or equivalent.
   b. Install new torque prevailing nut.

STEERING DAMPER

REPLACE

1. Remove shock absorber mounting nuts.
2. Remove cotter pin and castellated nut.
3. Remove shock absorber, grommet and washer.
4. Reverse procedure to install.

POWER STEERING GEAR

REPLACE

1. Place suitable drain pan below steering gear.
2. Disconnect steering gear hoses. Cap or plug hoses and ports.
3. Mark intermediate shaft to steering gear fitting alignment for installation.
4. Remove mounting bolt and disconnect intermediate shaft.
5. Remove pitman arm as outlined under "Pitman Arm, Replace."
6. Remove mounting bolts and steering gear.
7. Reverse procedure to install.

POWER STEERING PUMP

REPLACE

1. Place suitable drain pan under pump.
2. Remove drive belt as outlined under "Serpentine Belt" in appropriate engine section.
3. Disconnect hoses at power steering pump. Cap or plug lines and ports.
4. Remove pulley using power steering pulley remover tool No. J-25034-C, or equivalent.
5. Remove adjusting bolts, nuts and brackets.
6. Reverse procedure to install, noting the following. Install pulley using power steering pump pullet installer tool No. J-25033-C, or equivalent.

POWER STEERING SYSTEM BLEED

Maintain fluid level through the bleed procedure.

1. Remove pump reservoir cap.
2. Ensure reservoir is filled to FULL COLD level.
3. Attach suitable bleeder adapter and apply not more than 20 inch Hg.
4. Typical drop is 2–3 inches Hg. in five minutes.
5. If vacuum does remain steady for five minutes, proceed as follows:
   a. Remove pressure and return hoses.
   b. Install suitable plugs in ports.
   c. Attach suitable bleeder adapter and apply not more than 20 inch Hg.

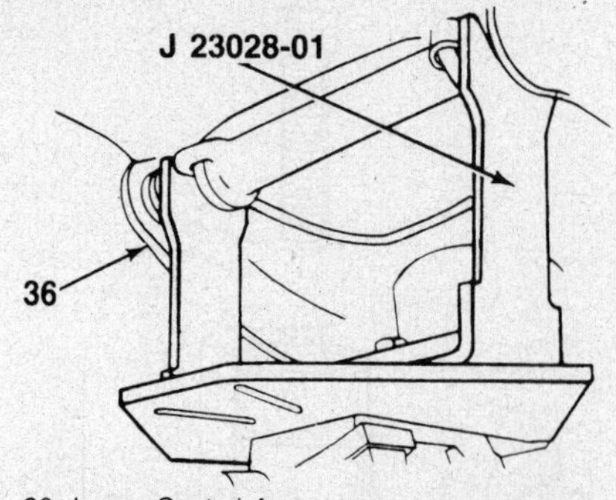

Fig. 3 Coil spring replacement

   d. If vacuum drops, repair or replace pump.
   e. If vacuum holds steady, inspect other steering system components.
6. Remove bleed adapter and install reservoir cap.
7. Start engine and idle.
8. Turn engine off.
9. Repeat previous two steps until fluid level stabilizes.
10. Start engine and idle.
11. Turn steering wheel 180–360° in both directions five times. **Do not turn steering wheel lock to lock.**
12. Turn ignition switch to Off position.
13. Verify fluid level.
14. Remove pump reservoir cap.
15. Attach suitable bleeder adapter and apply not more than 20 inch Hg.
16. If vacuum does remain steady for five minutes, inspect system. Typical drop is 2–3 inches Hg.
17. Remove bleed adapter and install reservoir cap.

TIGHTENING SPECIFICATIONS

Year	Component	Torque Ft. Lbs.
2002–06	Backing Plate	19
	Brake Hose Bracket	13
	Connecting Rod To Pitman Arm	35
	Connecting Rod To Relay Rod	35
	Coupling Shield	80
	Idler Arm To Frame	74
	Idler Arm To Relay Rod	35
	Inner Tie Rod To Relay Rod	35
	Intermediate Shaft Pinch Bolt	45
	Jounce Bumper	18
	Lower Ball Joint To Steering Knuckle	94
	Lower Control Arm	115
	Outer Tie Rod To Steering Knuckle	35
	Pitman Arm To Steering Gear	184
	Power Steering Pump Hose	20
	Power Steering Pump Bolt	37
	Power Steering Pump Brace Bolt	①
	Power Steering Pump Brace Nut	37
	Power Steering Pump Bracket	②
	Power Steering Pump Nut	30
	Power Steering Pump To Frame	43
	Shock Absorber, Lower	24
	Shock Absorber, Upper	12
	Splash Shield	19
	Stabilizer Bar	26
	Stabilizer Bar Link	13
	Steering Gear	98
	Tie Rod Adjuster Tube Clamp	18
	Tie Rod Ball Stud Prevailing Nut	35
	Tie Rod Ball Stud Tool	40
	Upper Ball Joint	18
	Upper Ball Joint To Steering Knuckle	74
	Upper Control Arm	140
	Wheel Bearing Adjuster	12
	Wheel Speed Sensor Bracket	13

① — Except 6.5L engine, 30 ft. lbs.; 6.5L engine 37 ft. lbs.
② — Except 6.5L engine, 30 ft. lbs.; 6.5L engine, 49 ft. lbs.

Front Wheel Drive

INDEX

AXLE SHAFT

REPLACE

1. Raise and support vehicle, then remove tire and wheel assembly.
2. Insert suitable drift through brake caliper and into brake rotor.
3. While holding rotor in place, remove hub nut and washer.
4. Remove drive shaft to differential flange attaching bolts, then separate drive shaft from flange.
5. Install axle remover tool No. J 45859, or equivalent, **Fig. 1.**
6. Remove front wheel drive shaft from steering knuckle.
7. Reverse procedure to install.

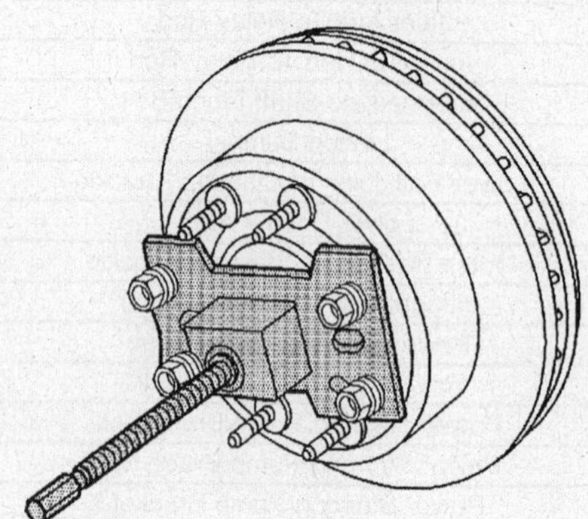

Fig. 1 Front axle removal

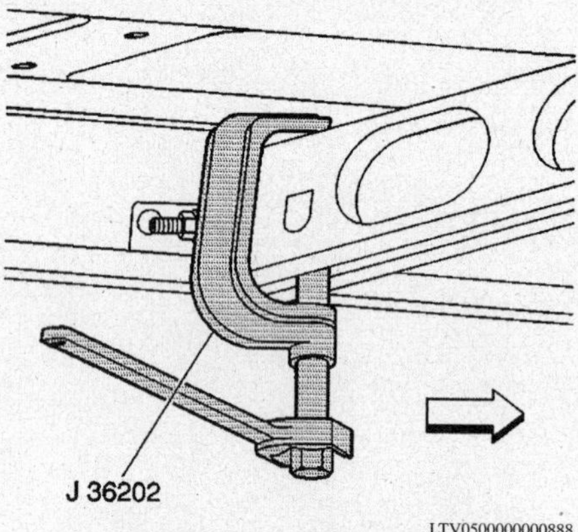

Fig. 2 Torsion bar unloading/ loading tool installation

DIFFERENTIAL CARRIER

REPLACE

1. Raise and support vehicle, then remove front skid plate.
2. Drain carrier axle lubricant into suitable container.
3. Install plastic tie straps loosely over ends of front stabilizer shaft and under center of each halfshaft bar.
4. Mark relationship of propeller shaft to front axle for installation reference.
5. Remove front propeller shaft retainers.
6. Remove front propeller shaft from front axle yoke and secure it aside.
7. Remove engine protection shield.
8. Support lower control arms with suitable jack stands.
9. Install torsion bar unloading/loading tool No. J 36202, or equivalent, to adjustment arm and support, **Fig. 2.**
10. Increase tension on adjustment arm until load is removed from adjustment bolt and nut.
11. Unload torsion bars.
12. Remove the right side differential carrier lower mounting bracket bolt and nut. Remove the right side differential carrier lower mounting bracket bolt and nut.
13. Remove left side differential carrier lower mounting bracket bolt.
14. Remove engine crossmember bolt from left lower control arm bracket.
15. Remove engine crossmember upper mounting bolts.
16. Disconnect electrical wiring harness connectors from engine crossmember.
17. Remove lower control arm nuts and washers.
18. Remove lower control arm bolts until bolts are flush with frame.
19. Remove engine crossmember.
20. Place a suitable transmission jack under differential carrier assembly.
21. Secure and support differential carrier assembly to transmission jack.
22. Place an alignment mark between drive shafts and inner shaft flanges.
23. Remove drive shaft to inner shaft bolts, then disconnect left and right side drive shafts from inner shafts.
24. Disconnect differential carrier assembly vent hose from differential carrier assembly.
25. Remove upper inner shaft housing mounting bolt.
26. Remove upper differential carrier assembly mounting bolt.
27. Remove differential carrier assembly.
28. Reverse procedure to install.

PINION FLANGE SEAL

REPLACE

1. Raise and support vehicle.
2. Disconnect propeller shaft from axle. Position propeller shaft aside.
3. Measure and record torque required to rotate pinion.
4. Mark pinion stem, pinion nut and companion flange, then record number of exposed thread on pinion stem.
5. Remove pinion nut using companion flange holder/remover tool No. J-8614-01, or equivalent. Four notches on tool should face flange.
6. Remove pinion flange using holder/ remover tool.
7. Remove oil seal. **Do not distort or scratch aluminum case.**
8. Reverse procedure to install, noting the following:
   a. Stake new deflector at three new equally spaced positions. **Do not damage seal operating surface.**
   b. Install seal in bore, then seat seal using seal installer tool No. J-36366, or equivalent.
   c. Install pinion nut and tighten nut to original position using marks and exposed threads recorded earlier.
   d. Measure rotating torque of pinion and compare with torque recorded earlier.
   e. Tighten pinion nut until **torque** required to rotate pinion is 3 inch lbs., more than original torque.

TIGHTENING SPECIFICATIONS

Year	Component	Torque/Ft. Lbs.
2002–06	Axle Nut	155
	Differential Carrier To Frame	63
	Drain Plug	24
	Drive Shaft To Inboard Flange	37
	Drive Shaft To Knuckle	58
	Lower Shock Absorber Mount	54
	Stabilizer Bar Clamp	24
	Stabilizer Link	13
	U-Joint Clamp	15

Wheel Alignment

NOTE: Prior To Performing Any Service Operations Listed In This Section, Consult The "Technical Service Bulletins" In This Section For Related Information.

INDEX

PRELIMINARY INSPECTION

Inspect the following components, adjust, repair or replace as required prior to performing front wheel alignment.

1. Inflate tires to cold specifications.
2. Ensure front tires are of same size, ply rating and load rating.
3. Inspect for excessive wheel bearing endplay.
4. Inspect for worn or damaged spindle ball joints.
5. Inspect steering gear mounting bolts for proper tightness.
6. Inspect radius arm or bent or damaged condition.
7. Inspect radius arm to frame bushings for looseness or wear.
8. Inspect suspension components for wear or damage.

FRONT WHEEL ALIGNMENT

Caster & Camber

All caster specifications are given with a frame angle of zero. Therefore, the up-in-the-rear or down-in-the-rear frame angle must be known to correct the caster reading.

1. Position vehicle on smooth and level surface.
2. Read frame angle in degree of tilt from level using suitable bubble protractor or inclinometer.
3. Determine if range is up or down-in-the-rear.
4. Determine actual, corrected caster using one of the following:
   a. Subtract down-in-rear frame angle from positive caster reading.
   b. Add up-in-rear frame angle to positive caster reading.
   c. Add down-in-rear frame angle to negative caster reading.
   d. Subtract up-in-rear frame angle from negative caster reading.
5. If caster and chamber angles are not within specifications, remove frame bracket knockouts.
6. Adjust caster and camber angles together by turning cam bolts until measurements are within specifications.

Toe-In

Toe-in can be increased or decreased by changing the length of the tie rods. A threaded sleeve is provided for this purpose. When tie rods are mounted ahead of the steering knuckle, decrease the length to increase toe-in. When tie rods are mounted behind the steering knuckle, increase the length to increase toe-in.

ESCALADE, ESCALADE ESV, SUBURBAN, TAHOE & YUKON

NOTE: Refer To The Rear Of This Manual For Vehicle Manufacturer's Special Tool Suppliers.

INDEX OF SERVICE OPERATIONS

Specifications

GENERAL ENGINE SPECIFICATIONS

Year	Engine	Engine VIN Code	Fuel System	Bore & Stroke, Inch	Compression Ratio	Horsepower @ RPM	Torque, Ft. Lbs. @ RPM	Normal Oil Pressure, psi
2002–06	4.8L	V	SFI	3.78 X 3.27	9.5	270 @ 5200	285 @ 4000	②
	5.3L	T	SFI	3.78 X 3.62	9.5	285 @ 5200	325 @ 4000	②
	6.0L	U	SFI	4.00 X 3.62	9.4	300 @ 4800	355 @ 4000	②
	8.1L	G	SFI	4.25 x 4.37	9.1	340 @ 4200	455 @ 3200	①

SFI — Sequential Fuel Injection.
① — Minimum: 5 psi @ 1000 RPM; 10 psi @ 2000 RPM.
② — Minimum: 6 psi @ 1000 RPM; 18 psi @ 2000 RPM; 24 @ 4000 RPM.

TUNE UP SPECIFICATIONS

The following specifications are published from the latest information available. This data should only be used in the absence of a decal affixed in the engine compartment.

Year & Engine①	Spark Plug Gap	Ignition Timing BTDC				Curb Idle Speed⑥		Fast Idle Speed⑥		Fuel Pump Pressure psi.	Valve Lash, Inch
		Firing Order ③	Man. Trans.	Auto. Trans.	Mark Lo-cat-ion	Man. Trans.	Auto. Trans.	Man. Trans.	Auto. Trans.		
2002–06											
4.8L	.060	⑤	④	④	⑧	⑦	⑦	⑦	⑦	55–62⑨	②
5.3L	.060	⑤	④	④	⑧	⑦	⑦	⑦	⑦	55–62⑨	②
6.0L	.060	⑤	④	④	⑧	⑦	⑦	⑦	⑦	55–62⑨	②
8.1L	.060	⑤	④	④	⑧	⑦	⑦	⑦	⑦	55–62⑨	②

BTDC — Before Top Dead Center
D — Drive
N — Neutral
① — The eighth digit of VIN denotes engine code.
② — Equipped w/hydraulic valve lifters.
③ — Before removing wires from distributor cap or coil unit, determine location of ignition wires, as position may have been altered from that outlined at end of this chart.
④ — Not adjustable.
⑤ — Firing order, 1-8-7-2-6-5-4-3.
⑥ — When inspecting idle speed, set parking brake & block drive wheels.
⑦ — Equipped w/Idle Speed Control (ISC) motor or Idle Air Control (IAC) valve.
⑧ — Equipped w/crankshaft position sensor.
⑨ — Wrap shop towel around engine compartment fuel pressure fitting. Connect suitable fuel pressure gauge to fuel pressure fitting. Turn ignition to On position & note fuel pressure reading.

FRONT WHEEL ALIGNMENT SPECIFICATIONS

Jounce vehicle three times prior to inspecting alignment to eliminate false geometry readings.

Year/ Model	Type	Side	Caster Angle, Degrees		Camber Angle, Degrees		Total Toe, Degrees①		Ball Joint Wear Limit⑦
			Limits	Desired	Limits	Desired	Limits	Desired	
2002–04									
1500	2WD Escalade	Lefthand	+3.10 to +5.10⑧	+4.10⑧	.00 to +1.00⑥	+.50⑥	-.10 to +.30	+.1	.08
		Righthand	+3.70 to +5.70⑧	+4.70⑧	.00 to +1.00⑥	+.50⑥	-.10 to +.30	+.1	.08
1500	2WD Except Escalade	Lefthand	+2.90 to +4.90④	+3.90④	-.25 to +.75⑥	+.25⑥	-.10 to +.30	+.1	.08
		Righthand	+3.70 to +5.70④	+4.70④	-.25 to +.75⑥	+.25⑥	-.10 to +.30	+.1	.08
1500	4WD w/16" tires	Lefthand	+2.50 to +4.50③	+3.50③	-.25 to +.75⑥	+.25⑥	-.10 to +.30	0	.08
		Righthand	+3.50 to +5.50③	+4.50③	-.25 to +.75⑥	+.25⑥	-.10 to +.30	0	.08

Continued

FRONT WHEEL ALIGNMENT SPECIFICATIONS—Continued

Jounce vehicle three times prior to inspecting alignment to eliminate false geometry readings.

Year/ Model	Type	Side	Caster Angle, Degrees		Camber Angle, Degrees		Total Toe, Degrees①		Ball Joint Wear Limit⑦
			Limits	Desired	Limits	Desired	Limits	Desired	
2002–04									
1500	4WD w/17" tires	Lefthand	+2.80 to +4.80②	+3.80②	-.25 to +.75⑥	+.25⑥	-.10 to +.30	0	.08
		Righthand	+3.50 to +5.50②	+4.50②	-.25 to +.75⑥	+.25⑥	-.10 to +.30	0	.08
2500	All	Lefthand	+3.50 to +5.50⑤	+4.50⑤	-.25 to +.75⑥	+.25⑥	-.10 to +.30	0	.08
		Righthand	+3.75 to +5.75⑤	+4.75⑤	-.25 to +.75⑥	+.25⑥	-.10 to +.30	0	.08
2005–06									
1500	2WD Except Police Tahoe	Lefthand	+2.90 to +4.90④	+3.90④	.00 to +1.00⑥	+.50⑥	-.20 to +.20	0	.08
		Righthand	+3.70 to +5.70④	+4.70④	.00 to +1.00⑥	+.50⑥	-.20 to +.20	0	.08
1500	2WD Police Tahoe	Lefthand	+3.35 to +5.35⑧	+4.35⑧	-1.10 to +.10⑨	+.60⑨	-.10 to +.30	+.1	.08
		Righthand	+3.85 to +5.85⑧	+4.85⑧	-.60 to +.40⑨	+.10⑨	-.10 to +.30	+.1	.08
1500	4WD w/16" tires	Lefthand	+1.60 to +3.60⑩	+2.60⑩	-.35 to +.85⑨	+.25⑨	-.10 to +.30	+.1	.08
		Righthand	+2.40 to +4.40⑩	+3.40⑩	-.35 to +.85⑨	+.25⑨	-.10 to +.30	+.1	.08
1500	4WD w/17" tires	Lefthand	+1.80 to +3.80⑪	+2.80⑪	-.35 to +.85⑨	+.25⑨	-.10 to +.30	+.1	.08
		Righthand	+3.50 to +5.50⑪	+4.50⑪	-.35 to +.85⑨	+.25⑨	-.10 to +.30	+.1	.08
1500	4WD w/20" tires	Lefthand	+2.45 to +4.45⑫	+3.45⑫	-.70 to +.50⑨	+.25⑨	-.10 to +.30	+.1	.08
		Righthand	+3.50 to +5.50⑫	+4.50⑫	-.70 to +.50⑨	+.25⑨	-.10 to +.30	+.1	.08
2500	All	Lefthand	+2.50 to +4.50⑤	+3.50⑤	-.70 to +.50⑨	+.10⑨	-.10 to +.30	+.1	.08
		Righthand	+2.75 to +4.75⑤	+3.75⑤	-.70 to +.50⑨	+.10⑨	-.10 to +.30	+.1	.08

① — Toe-In (+). Toe-Out (–).
② — Cross caster (L-R), –1.2° to –.2°, preferred, –.7°.
③ — Cross caster (L-R), –1.5° to –.5°, preferred, –.1°.
④ — Cross caster (L-R), –1.3° to –.3°, preferred, –.8°.
⑤ — Cross caster (L-R), –.75° to +.25°, preferred, –.25°.
⑥ — Cross camber (L-R), –.5° to +.5°, preferred, 0°.
⑦ — Refer to "Ball Joint Inspection" in "Front Suspension & Steering" section for inspection procedure.
⑧ — Cross caster (L-R), –1.1° to –.1°, preferred, –.6°.
⑨ — Cross camber (L-R), –.6° to +.6°, preferred, 0°.
⑩ — Cross caster (L-R), –1.55° to –.05°, preferred, –.8°.
⑪ — Cross caster (L-R), –1.45° to +.05°, preferred, –.7°.
⑫ — Cross caster (L-R), –1.05° to +.45°, preferred, –.3°.

FLUID CAPACITIES & COOLING SYSTEM DATA

Year/ Model	Engine Liter	Cooling System Capacity, Qts.		Coolant Type	Radiator Cap Relief Pressure, Lbs.	Thermo. Opening Temp. °F	Fuel Tank Gals.	Engine Oil Refill Qts.③	Transmission Oil		Transfer Case Pts.	Drive Axle Oil	
		Less A/C	With A/C						Man. Trans. Pts.	Auto. Trans. Qts. ①		Front Pts.	Rear Pts.
2002–06													
Escalade	5.3L	—	18.6	②	15	195	26	6	—	⑥	4	④	⑤
	6.0L	—	19	②	15	195	26	6	—	⑥	4	④	⑤

Continued

FLUID CAPACITIES & COOLING SYSTEM DATA—Continued

Year/ Model	Engine Liter	Cooling System Capacity, Qts.		Coolant Type	Radiator Cap Relief Pressure, Lbs.	Thermo. Opening Temp. °F	Fuel Tank Gals.	Engine Oil Refill Qts.③	Transmission Oil		Transfer Case Pts.	Drive Axle Oil	
		Less A/C	With A/C						Man. Trans. Pts.	Auto. Trans. Qts. ①		Front Pts.	Rear Pts.
2002–06													
Escalade EXV	6.0L	—	17	②	15	195	31	6	—	⑥	4	④	⑤
Suburban & Yukon XL	5.3L	—	14.4⑦	②	15	195	31	6	—	⑥	4	④	⑤
	6.0L	—	14.8	②	15	195	31	6	—	⑥	4	④	⑤
	8.1L	—	20.7	②	15	195	31	6.5	—	⑥	4	④	⑤
Tahoe & Yukon	4.8L	—	14.4	②	15	195	26	6	—	⑥	4	④	⑤
	5.3L	—	14.4⑦	②	15	195	26	6	—	⑥	4	④	⑤
	6.0L	—	14.8	②	15	195	26	6	—	⑥	4	④	⑤
Yukon Denali XL	6.0L	—	19	②	15	195	31	6	—	⑥	4	④	⑤

① — Approximate. Make final inspection w/dipstick.
② — 50/50 mixture water and GM Goodwrench DEX-COOL or Havoline DEX-COOL coolant.
③ — Includes filter.
④ — 8.25 inch ring gear, 3.5 pts.; 9.25 inch ring gear, 3.66 pts.
⑤ — 8.6 inch ring gear, 4.2 pts.; 9.5 inch ring gear, 5.5 pts.; 10.5 inch ring gear, 5.5 pts.; 11.5 inch ring gear, 7.66 pts.
⑥ — 4L60-E, pan removal, 5 qts., overhaul, 11.2 qts.; 4L80-E, pan removal, 7.7 qts., overhaul, 13.5 qts.
⑦ — With front & rear A/C, 15.8 qts.

LUBRICANT DATA

Year	Model	Lubricant Type							
		Transmission		Hydraulic Clutch Fluid	Transfer Case	Drive Axle	Power Steering	Brake System
		Manual	Automatic					
2002–05	All	—	Dexron III	DOT 3	Dexron III	②	①	DOT 3
2006	All	—	Dexron VI	DOT 3	Dexron III	②	①	DOT 3

① — Power steering fluid GM part No. 1050017 (quart), 1052884 (pint), or equivalent.
② — Front S4WD, 80W-90; Front F4WD, 75W-90; Rear 75W-90 synthetic.

Electrical

NOTE: On Air Bag Equipped Models, Refer To "Air Bag System Precautions" Located In The Front Of This Manual For System Disarming & Arming Procedures.

NOTE: Refer To "Computer Relearn Procedures" Located In The Front Of This Manual When Battery Power To The Computer Has Been Interrupted.

INDEX

PRECAUTIONS

Air Bag Systems

Refer to "Air Bag System Precautions" in the front of this manual for system disarming and arming procedures.

Battery Ground Cable

Prior to service disconnect battery ground cable and isolate as required.

Radio Security System

If the Theftlock system is active when battery power is interrupted, the customers security code must be entered to restore proper function of the radio. Use the following procedure to unlock a secured radio after a power loss. Do not wait more than 15 seconds between steps.

1. Theftlock is engaged if radio is inoperable and "LOC" appears with ignition in On position.
2. Obtain customers' code number.
3. Press "MIN" button and "000" will appear on display.
4. Press "MIN" again until last two digits displayed agree with security code.
5. Press "HR" button until first 1 or 2 digits agree with security code.
6. Press "AM-FM" to select code entered. "SEC" will display indicating radio is now operable and secure.
7. If incorrect code is entered, "SEC" will display and radio will be inoperable.
8. Radio will remain inoperable until correct code is displayed. Repeat steps until correct code is entered. If correct code cannot be obtained, contact Delco technical assistance.

FUSE PANEL & FLASHER LOCATION

The lefthand fuse block is located under the lefthand side of the instrument panel near the lefthand kick panel.

The righthand fuse block is located behind the lower righthand side of the instrument panel.

The underhood fuse block is located on the lefthand side of the engine compartment near the battery.

The turn signal/hazard flasher module is located behind the lefthand side of the instrument panel, near the lefthand fuse block.

FUEL PUMP RELAY LOCATION

The fuel pump relay is located on the lefthand side of the engine compartment, inside the underhood fuse block

RELAY CENTER LOCATION

The Underhood Bussed Electrical Center (UBEC) contains the engine compartment relays and is mounted on the lefthand wheelhouse, near the battery.

STARTER

REPLACE

4.8L, 5.3L & 6.0L Engines

1. Remove mounting bolts and engine shield,.
2. Remove mounting bolts and oil pan skid plate.
3. Remove righthand transmission cover bolt.
4. Remove front axle mounting bracket nut, then position front axle mounting bracket bolt until tip is flush with support bushing. **DO NOT remove bolt.**
5. Remove mounting bolts and slide starter forward until it clears transmission.
6. Disconnect oil level sensor electrical connector.
7. Remove starter solenoid nut and lead from stud.
8. Remove starter lead nut and the positive cable from starter stud.
9. Remove starter.

10. Reverse procedure to install, noting the following:
    a. **Torque** starter lead nut to 80 inch lbs.
    b. **Torque** starter solenoid nut 30 inch lbs.
    c. **Torque** starter mounting bolts 37 ft. lbs.
    d. **Torque** front axle mounting bracket nut 70 ft. lbs.
    e. **Torque** transmission cover bolt 80 inch lbs.
    f. **Torque** oil pan skid plate bolts to 15 ft. lbs.
    g. **Torque** engine shield bolts to 15 ft. lbs.

8.1L Engine

1. Raise and support vehicle.
2. Disconnect starter battery positive cable and wiring harness.
3. Remove starter mounting bolts, washers, shims, starter and heat shield.
4. Reverse procedure to install, noting the following:
    a. **Torque** starter shield bolts to 35 inch lbs.
    b. **Torque** starter mounting bolts to 37 ft. lbs.
    c. **Torque** battery positive cable to 89 inch lbs.
    d. **Torque** ignition switch wires to solenoid to 18 inch lbs.

ALTERNATOR

REPLACE

1. Remove air inlet duct, as required.
2. Disconnect terminal plug and battery lead connections from back of alternator.
3. Remove upper fan shroud mounting bolts and fan shroud.
4. Rotate drive belt tensioner arm counterclockwise using suitable 3/8 inch drive wrench, then remove accessory drive belt.
5. Remove mounting bolts and alternator.
6. Reverse procedure to install, noting the following:
    a. **Torque** alternator mounting bolts to 37 ft. lbs.
    b. **Torque** battery lead retaining nut to 80 inch lbs.

COIL PACK

REPLACE

4.8L, 5.3L & 6.0L Engines

1. Disconnect spark plug wires at ignition coils.
2. Disconnect ignition coil harness connector.
3. Remove mounting bolts and ignition coil.
4. Reverse procedure to install. **Torque** mounting bolts to 71 inch lbs.

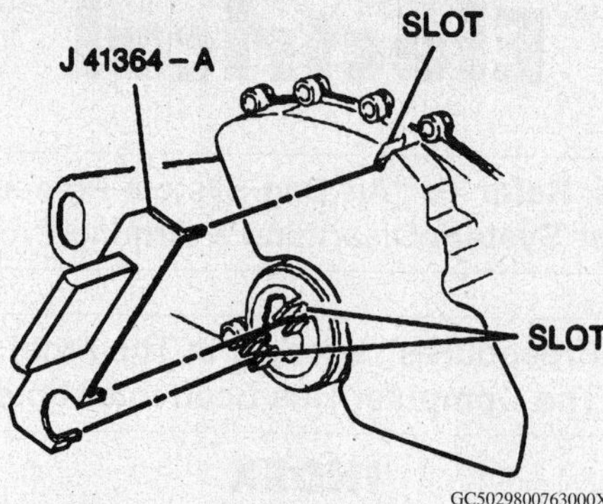

Fig. 1 Neutral safety switch installation

8.1L Engine

1. Disconnect ignition coil harness connector.
2. Remove mounting bolts and ignition coil.
3. Reverse procedure to install. **Torque** mounting bolts to 106 inch lbs.

IGNITION LOCK

REPLACE

1. Remove steering wheel as outlined under "Steering Wheel, Replace."
2. Remove tilt lever by pulling it out of steering column.
3. Remove lower steering column trim cover mounting screws.
4. Remove lower steering column trim cover by tilting it down and sliding back to disengage locking tabs.
5. Remove mounting screws and upper steering column trim cover.
6. Turn ignition lock cylinder to RUN position.
7. Insert tip of suitable awl into ignition lock cylinder access hole, then push down and hold ignition lock cylinder retaining pin.
8. Release ignition lock cylinder to RUN position and remove ignition lock cylinder by pulling it away from steering column.
9. Reverse procedure to install.

IGNITION SWITCH

REPLACE

2002

1. **On models equipped with automatic transmission,** apply parking brake and move shift lever all way down to last gear.
2. **On all models,** tilt steering wheel to full down position.
3. Remove instrument cluster trim bezel by pulling rearward on corners.
4. Remove mounting screws and knee bolster by unsnapping top.
5. Remove steering wheel as outlined under "Steering Wheel, Replace."
6. Remove tilt lever by pulling it out of steering column.
7. Remove lower steering column trim cover mounting screws.
8. Remove lower steering column trim cover by tilting it down and sliding back to disengage locking tabs.
9. Remove mounting screws and upper steering column trim cover.
10. Disconnect steering column electrical connectors.
11. Remove wire harness assembly from steering column and wire harness strap.
12. Slide two turn signal and multifunction switch connectors out of bulkhead connector.
13. Remove lock module key alarm connector by rotating connector 90° and pull key alarm connector out of lock module.
14. Remove passkey connector from lock module assembly.
15. **On models equipped floor shifters,** remove electric park lock connector.
16. **On all models,** remove ignition switch from lock module using switch connector release tool No. J-42759, or equivalent.
17. Reverse procedure to install, noting the following:
    a. **Torque** lower steering column trim cover mounting screws to 31 inch lbs.
    b. **Torque** upper steering column trim cover mounting screws to 13 inch lbs.
    c. **Torque** knee bolster screws to 18 inch lbs.

2003–06

1. Remove ignition lock as outlined under "Ignition Lock, Replace."
2. Disconnect passlock and key buzzer from lock cylinder housing.
3. Insert ignition switch connector release tool J 42759, or equivalent, into lock cylinder housing to release tabs on ignition switch.
4. Pull ignition switch out of lock cylinder housing.
5. Disconnect ignition switch electrical connector.
6. Reverse procedure to install.

NEUTRAL SAFETY SWITCH

REPLACE

Removal

1. Apply parking brake.
2. Shift transmission into neutral position, then raise and support vehicle.
3. **On models equipped with 4WD,** remove propeller shaft as outlined in "Front Wheel Drive" section.
4. **On all models,** remove transmission control to manual mounting nut and lever.
5. Disconnect park/neutral safety switch electrical connector.
6. Remove two mounting bolts and park/neutral safety switch.

Installation

1. Install adjustment tool No. J-41364-A, or equivalent, onto park/neutral safety switch. Ensure two slots on switch are lined up with lower two tabs on tool, **Fig. 1.**
2. Rotate tool until upper locator pin is lined up with slot on top of switch.
3. Install switch to transmission.
4. Install park/neutral switch to transmission mounting bolts. **Torque** bolts to 18 ft. lbs.
5. Remove adjusting tool.
6. Connect park/neutral safety switch electrical connector.
7. Install transmission control lever to manual shaft and install nut. **Torque** control lever nut to 18 ft. lbs.

HEADLAMP SWITCH

REPLACE

1. Remove instrument cluster bezel, refer to "Instrument Cluster, Replace."
2. Disconnect electrical connector from switch.
3. Remove headlamp switch by unsnapping it from instrument cluster bezel.
4. Reverse procedure to install.

STOP LIGHT SWITCH

REPLACE

1. Remove push rod retainer from brake pedal pin.
2. Unsnap stop lamp switch from pushrod.
3. Disconnect electrical connector from stop lamp switch.
4. Reverse procedure to install.

MULTI-FUNCTION SWITCH

REPLACE

1. Remove steering wheel as outlined under "Steering Wheel, Replace."
2. **On models equipped with tilt column,** remove tilt lever.
3. **On all models,** remove mounting screws and lower cover.
4. Remove two upper column cover Torx head screws.
5. Remove knee bolster mounting screws, then unsnap knee bolster from instrument panel.
6. Twist brake release cable and disengage cable from knee bolster.
7. Remove lap cooler hose and knee bolster.
8. Remove ignition lock cylinder as outlined under "Ignition Lock, Replace."
9. Remove steering column upper cover.
10. Remove two wiring harness straps from steering column wiring harness, **Fig. 2.**
11. Disconnect steering column bulkhead connector from vehicle wiring harness.
12. **On models equipped with column shift,** remove axial position assurance connector from BTSI actuator.
13. **On all models,** remove grey and black multi-function switch connectors from column bulkhead connector.
14. Remove mount screws and multi-function switch.
15. Reverse procedure to install.

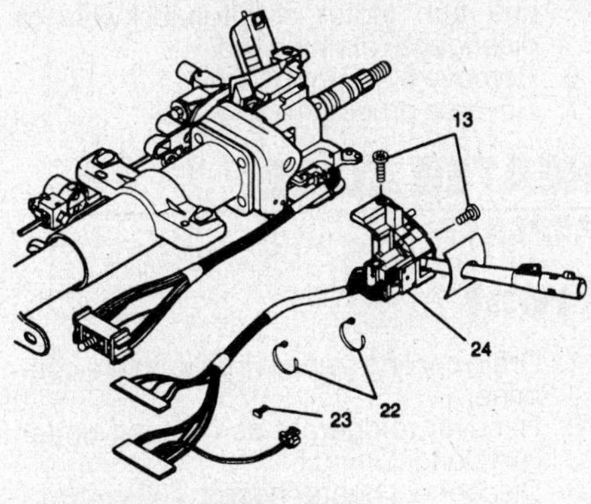

Fig. 2 Multi-function switch removal

TURN SIGNAL SWITCH

REPLACE

Refer to "Multi-Function Switch, Replace" for replacement procedures.

DIMMER SWITCH

REPLACE

Refer to "Multi-Function Switch, Replace" for replacement procedures.

STEERING WHEEL

REPLACE

1. Turn ignition switch to ON position.
2. Turn steering wheel 90° so side of SIR module is at 12 o'clock position.
3. Insert suitable screwdriver into access hole and push leaf spring to release air bag module notched pin.
4. Turn steering wheel 180° and repeat previous step.
5. Tilt air bag module top rearward and disconnect SIR lead wire from clips.
6. Disconnect Connector Position Assurance retainer from connector. Disconnect SIR connector.
7. Remove air bag module.
8. Remove horn contact plate mounting screws and plunger from steering wheel.
9. Mark steering wheel to steering shaft alignment for installation.
10. Remove steering wheel nut.
11. Remove steering wheel using steering wheel puller tool No. J-1859-A, or equivalent.
12. Reverse procedure to install, noting the following:
    a. **Torque** steering wheel nut to 30 ft. lbs.
    b. **Torque** horn contact plate mounting screws to 50 inch lbs.

INSTRUMENT CLUSTER

REPLACE

1. Engage parking brake lever.
2. Move gear shift lever and tilt steering wheel to lowest positions.
3. Remove bezel by pulling rearward on clips.
4. Remove instrument panel cluster mounting screws.
5. Disconnect instrument panel cluster electrical harness connectors.
6. Remove instrument panel cluster by tilting bottom of cluster outward.
7. Reverse procedure to install. **Torque** mounting screws to 18 inch lbs.

RADIO

REPLACE

1. Remove instrument cluster trim bezel as outlined under "Instrument Cluster, Replace."
2. Release radio assembly lock tabs using suitable screwdriver.
3. Slide radio rearward away from instrument panel and disconnect electrical connectors.
4. Remove radio.
5. Reverse procedure to install.

WIPER MOTOR

REPLACE

Front

1. Mark position of wiper blade on windshield for installation alignment.
2. Disconnect washer hose.
3. Remove cover and wiper arm nut.
4. Remove wiper arm from drive shaft using suitable battery terminal puller to remove, while rocking arm back and forth.
5. Unsnap outboard air inlet grille panel sections and remove mounting clips running along center air inlet grille panel edges.
6. Remove air inlet grille panel mounting screws on each end.
7. Disconnect windshield washer hose from nozzle underneath center air inlet grille panel.
8. Remove air inlet grille panel.
9. Remove four mounting bolts and reinforcement panel.
10. Disconnect wiper motor electrical connector.
11. Remove two mounting bolts and wiper transmission.
12. Remove drive link from wiper motor crank arm using wiper transmission separator tool No. J-39232, or equivalent.
13. Remove two mounting bolts and wiper motor.
14. Reverse procedure to install, noting the following:
    a. **Torque** wiper motor mounting bolts to 89 inch lbs.
    b. **Torque** transmission mounting bolts to 80 inch lbs.
    c. **Torque** reinforcement panel mounting bolts to 80 inch lbs.

d. **Torque** air inlet grille panel mounting screws to 18 inch lbs.
e. **Torque** wiper arm nut to 18 ft. lbs.

Rear

1. Disconnect washer hose, then remove cover, nut and wiper arm.
2. Remove wiper motor shaft nut and spacer.
3. Remove pull strap mounting screw.
4. Remove trim panel by sliding trim panel upward to disconnect mounting hooks.
5. Disconnect wiper motor electrical connector.
6. Remove two mounting screws and wiper motor.
7. Reverse procedure to install, noting the following:
   a. **Torque** wiper motor mounting screws to 14 ft. lbs.
   b. **Torque** drive shaft nut to 71 inch lbs.
   c. **Torque** wiper arm nut to 17 ft. lbs.

WIPER SWITCH

REPLACE

Front

Refer to "Multi-Function Switch, Replace" for replacement procedures.

Rear

1. Remove wiper switch from trim plate.
2. Disconnect electrical connector.
3. Reverse procedure to install.

BLOWER MOTOR

REPLACE

1. Remove hush panel from under righthand side of instrument panel.
2. Disconnect blower relay/resistor electrical connector.
3. Remove blower motor insulating cover mounting screws.
4. Disconnect blower motor electrical connector, then remove insulating cover.
5. Pull blower motor retaining tab down and turn motor counterclockwise to disengage retaining tab,
6. Remove blower motor.
7. Reverse procedure to install.

HEATER CORE

REPLACE

Front

1. Drain cooling system into suitable container.
2. Recover refrigerant as outlined under "Air Conditioning."
3. Disconnect heater hoses.
4. Remove accumulator.
5. Remove instrument panel carrier as outlined "Dash Panel Service."
6. Remove HVAC module drain hose.
7. Disconnect electrical harnesses and ground connections as needed.
8. Remove HVAC module mounting nuts and screws.
9. Remove HVAC module and set on bench.
10. Remove heater core cover screws and cover.
11. Remove heater core.
12. Reverse procedure to install. **Torque** HVAC module mounting nuts to 84 inch lbs., and bolts to 35 inch lbs.

Rear

1. Recover refrigerant from A/C system as outlined in "Air Conditioning" chapter.
2. Drain engine coolant.
3. Raise and support vehicle.
4. Disconnect heater lines and A/C lines from auxiliary HVAC module. HVAC module is located on the rear righthand side of vehicle. Heater and A/C lines are located under righthand side vehicle.
5. Remove auxiliary HVAC module retaining nuts from underside of vehicle.
6. Lower vehicle and remove right rear quarter trim panel.
7. Remove Electronic Suspension Control (ESC) module.
8. Disconnect auxiliary HVAC module electrical connectors.
9. Remove upper auxiliary air duct fastener, then carefully slide duct up and into headliner, until bottom edge of duct is above air distributor duct.
10. Remove lower auxiliary air outlet and air distributor duct fasteners, then the air distributor duct.
11. Remove auxiliary HVAC module fasteners, then the HVAC module from vehicle.
12. Remove air temperature actuator from the auxiliary HVAC module.
13. Remove heater core cover from the auxiliary HVAC module.
14. Remove heater core from auxiliary HVAC module.
15. Reverse procedure to install.

EVAPORATOR CORE

REPLACE

Front

1. Drain cooling system into suitable container.
2. Recover refrigerant as outlined in "Air Conditioning."
3. Disconnect heater hoses.
4. Remove accumulator.
5. Remove instrument panel as outlined in "Dash Panel Service."
6. Remove HVAC module drain hose.
7. Disconnect electrical harnesses and ground connections as needed.
8. Remove HVAC module mounting nuts and screws.
9. Remove HVAC module and set on bench.
10. Remove HVAC module screws and separate HVAC module.
11. Remove evaporator core.
12. Reverse procedure to install. **Torque** HVAC module mounting nuts to 84 inch lbs., and bolts to 35 inch lbs.

Rear

1. Remove auxiliary HVAC module assembly as outlined under "Heater Core, Replace."
2. Remove evaporator cowl gasket from evaporator.
3. Separate upper HVAC module assembly from the lower module assembly.
4. Remove evaporator core from upper HVAC module assembly.
5. Reverse procedure to install.

4.8L, 5.3L & 6.0L Gasoline Engines

NOTE: On Air Bag Equipped Models, Refer To "Air Bag System Precautions" Located In The Front Of This Manual For System Disarming & Arming Procedures.

NOTE: Refer To "Computer Relearn Procedures" Located In The Front Of This Manual When Battery Power To The Computer Has Been Interrupted.

NOTE: Refer To The "4.8L, 5.3L & 6.0L Gasoline Engines" Section Of The "Avalanche, Escalade EXT, Silverado, Sierra & SSR" Chapter For Any Procedures Not Found In This Section.

INDEX

PRECAUTIONS

Air Bag Systems

Refer to "Air Bag System Precautions" in the front of this manual for system disarming and arming procedures.

Battery Ground Cable

Prior to service disconnect battery ground cable and isolate, as required.

Radio Security System

If the Theftlock system is active when battery power is interrupted, the customers security code must be entered to restore proper function of the radio. To unlock a secured radio after power loss, proceed as follows:

1. "LOC" appears with ignition in On position.
2. Press "NM" and "000" will appear on display.
3. Press "NM" again to make last two digits agree with security code.
4. Press "HR" to make first 1 or 2 digits agree with security code.
5. Press "AM-FM" to select code entered. "SEC" will show on display indicating radio is now operable and secure.
6. If incorrect code is entered eight times, "INOP" will display. In order to reenter code, ignition must be left on for one hour before code can be entered and only three more chances to enter code are available before display reads "INOP."

Fuel System Pressure Relief

Prior to service, fuel pressure must be relieved by disconnecting the fuel line fittings. A small amount of fuel may still be released when the fuel line is disconnected. To reduce the chance of injury, cover the fitting(s) to be disconnected with a shop towel. Place towel in an approved container when the procedure is complete.

COMPRESSION PRESSURE

When inspecting compression, the lowest cylinder must be within 70% of the highest and no cylinder should be less than 100 psi. Perform compression test with engine at operating temperature, all spark plugs removed and throttle wide open.

ENGINE MOUNT

REPLACE

1. Raise and support vehicle.
2. Remove engine mount-to-engine mount bracket bolts.
3. Remove mounting bolts and engine shield.
4. Raise and support engine using adjustable screw type jack stands. **Do not raise and/or support engine by oil pan or crankshaft balancer.**
5. Remove mounting bolts and mount.
6. Reverse procedure to install.

ENGINE

REPLACE

1. Open hood and lace fender covers over both fenders.
2. Remove hinge bolts, raise hood until vertical and install bolts until snug.
3. Recover air conditioning refrigerant.
4. Remove drive belt as outlined under "Serpentine Drive Belt."
5. Raise and support vehicle.
6. Remove righthand front tire and wheel assembly, then the inner fender skirt.
7. Remove A/C compressor discharge and suction hoses. Discard sealing washers and cap all of openings.
8. Disconnect compressor electrical connections.
9. Remove A/C compressor mounting bolts. Lower righthand bolt will stay with compressor because of lack of clearance.
10. Remove A/C compressor from bracket through fender well. Remove A/C compressor from bottom on rear-wheel-drive 2500 series vehicles, only.
11. Remove mounting nut and bolt, support baffle and lower radiator support.
12. Disconnect clamps, then remove radiator inlet and outlet hoses from water pump.
13. Remove heater hoses.
14. Loosen mounting bolt and remove intake manifold sight shield.
15. **On models equipped with 6.0L engine,** loosen mounting bolts and remove righthand fuel rail cover.
16. **On all models,** unsnap cruise control cable from throttle body lever, then remove it from bracket. Remove clip from sight shield retainer.
17. Unsnap accelerator control cable from throttle body lever, then remove it from bracket. Remove clip from sight shield retainer.
18. Remove mounting bolts and upper intake manifold sight shield retainer.
19. Disconnect Evaporative emissions

canister purge solenoid and alternator electrical connectors.
20. Remove engine harness bracket nut.
21. Position throttle body vent inlet hose clamp aside.
22. Remove radiator vent inlet hose from throttle body.
23. Slide boot down revealing terminal stud, then remove mounting nut from terminal stud and alternator cable.
24. Disconnect main coil harness and fuel injector electrical connectors on lefthand side.
25. Disconnect main coil harness, fuel injectors and Exhaust Gas Recirculation valve electrical connectors.
26. Disconnect Throttle Position sensor and Idle Air Control valve electrical connectors.
27. Disconnect Manifold Absolute Pressure sensor and Knock Sensor electrical connectors.
28. Remove harness ground bolt.
29. Position harness ground and battery ground aside from block.
30. Disconnect coolant temperature sensor and electronic variable orifice switch electrical connectors.
31. Remove harness ground bolt at righthand rear of engine block.
32. Position harness ground and auxiliary battery ground aside.
33. Remove harness ground bolt at lefthand rear of engine block.
34. Position harness ground and engine ground strap aside.
35. Disconnect oil pressure and Camshaft Position sensors electrical connectors.
36. Unclip engine harness clips.
37. Remove battery cable junction block from bracket.
38. Remove EVAP purge solenoid vent tube end from solenoid, then remove EVAP tube end from vapor pipe.
39. Disconnect fuel pipes.
40. Raise and support vehicle.
41. Disconnect Crankshaft Position sensor, engine oil level sensor and coolant heater electrical connectors.
42. Remove battery cable channel bolt, slide channel pin out of oil pan tab, gather all branches of engine wiring harness and position aside.
43. Lower vehicle.
44. Remove rear power steering pump-to-engine block bolt, and alternator bracket mounting bolts. Position bracket aside.
45. Remove vacuum brake booster hose.
46. Remove ignition coils for proper fit of engine lifting brackets.
47. Install engine lifting brackets tools No. J-41798, or equivalent, to cylinder heads.
48. Remove left and righthand engine mount-to-engine mount bracket bolts.
49. Raise and support vehicle.
50. Remove mounting bolts and engine shield.
51. Remove mounting bolts and oil pan skid plate.
52. Drain engine oil into suitable container.
53. Remove starter motor as outlined in "Electrical" section.
54. Remove catalytic converter.
55. Remove mounting bolt and positive battery cable clip.
56. **On models equipped with automatic transmission,** proceed as follows:
    a. Remove flywheel to torque converter bolts.
    b. Remove mounting nut and transmission oil dipstick tube.
    c. **On models equipped with 4L80-E automatic transmission,** remove righthand side mounting bolt and stud.
    d. **On models equipped with 4L80-E automatic transmission,** remove converter cover bolts.
    e. **On all models,** remove mounting bolt/studs.
    f. Separate engine from automatic transmission.
    g. Hold torque converter by installing converter holding strap tool No. J-21366, or equivalent.
57. **On models equipped with manual transmission,** proceed as follows:
    a. Remove concentric slave cylinder clutch line using clutch line removal tool No. J-42371, or equivalent.
    b. Remove righthand side mounting stud.
    c. Remove mounting bolt/studs.
    d. Separate the transmission from engine.
    e. Mark flywheel and clutch pressure plate lug for installation alignment.
    f. Remove mounting bolts, clutch pressure plate and disc.
58. **On all models,** lower vehicle.
59. Install suitable engine hoist to engine lifting brackets.
60. Support transmission using suitable floor jack.
61. Remove engine. **Avoid breaking MAP sensor locating tabs.**
62. Reverse procedure to install.

TIGHTENING SPECIFICATIONS

Year	Component	Torque/Ft. Lbs.
2002–06	Alternator Bracket	37
	Accelerator Control Cable Bracket	89①
	Air Conditioning Compressor	37
	Air Conditioning Compressor Bracket	37
	Air Conditioning Hose Bracket	35
	Air Conditioning Tensioner	37
	AIR Bracket	71①
	Alternator & Power Steering Bracket	37
	Belt Idler Pulley	37
	Clutch Pressure Plate	52②
	Drive Belt Idler Pulley	37
	Drive Belt Tensioner	37
	Engine Shield	15
	Engine Lift Bracket, M8 Bolt	18
	Engine Lift Bracket, M10 Bolt	37
	Engine Wiring Harness Bracket	89①
	Exhaust Crossover Pipe	25
	Motor Mount	37
	Motor Mount Bracket	48
	Motor Mount, Lower To Upper	37
	Motor Mount, Through Bolt	68
	Motor Mount, Upper	37
	Oil Filter	22
	Oil Filter Fitting	40
	Oil Pan Drain Plug	18
	Power Steering Pump	37
	Power Steering Pump Bracket	37
	Propeller Shaft	15
	Radiator Shroud	71①
	Radiator Support	52
	Rear Engine Mount, Bolt	35
	Rear Engine Mount, Nut	40
	Rear Engine Mount, Bolt	35
	Rear Engine Mount to Crossmember	33
	Rear Engine Mount To Transmission	44
	Spark Plugs (Aluminum Cylinder Heads)	④
	Spark Plugs (Iron Cylinder Heads)	③
	Starter Cover	15
	Torque Converter	46
	Transmission	34
	Transmission Fluid Cooler Line	19
	Transmission To Oil Pan	41
	Universal Lift Bracket	15

① — Inch lbs.
② — Tighten clutch pressure plate bolts in star pattern and evenly over three increments with fourth increment to 52 ft. lbs.
③ — Spark plugs in new iron cylinder heads, 22 ft. lbs.; all subsequent installations, 11 ft. lbs.
④ — Spark plugs in new aluminum cylinder heads, 15 ft. lbs.; all subsequent installations, 11 ft. lbs.

8.1L Gasoline Engine

NOTE: Refer To The "8.1L Gasoline Engine" Section Of The "Avalanche, Escalade EXT, Silverado, Sierra & SSR" Chapter For Any Procedures Not Found In This Section.

NOTE: On Air Bag Equipped Models, Refer To "Air Bag System Precautions" Located In The Front Of This Manual For System Disarming & Arming Procedures.

NOTE: Refer To "Computer Relearn Procedures" Located In The Front Of This Manual When Battery Power To The Computer Has Been Interrupted.

NOTE: Prior To Performing Any Service Operations Listed In This Section, Consult The "Technical Service Bulletins" In This Section For Related Information.

INDEX

PRECAUTIONS

Air Bag Systems

Refer to "Air Bag System Precautions" in the front of this manual for system disarming and arming procedures.

Battery Ground Cable

Prior to service disconnect battery ground cable and isolate.

Fuel System Pressure Relief

Always release residual fuel system pressure prior to disconnecting fuel lines or hoses.

1. Loosen fuel filler cap.
2. Remove fuel injector sight shield.
3. Connect suitable fuel pressure gauge to fuel pressure valve and install bleed hose into suitable container.
4. Open valve and bleed system pressure.

COMPRESSION PRESSURE

When inspecting compression, the lowest cylinder must be within 70% of the highest and no cylinder should be less than 100 psi. Perform compression test with engine at operating temperature, all spark plugs removed and throttle wide open.

ENGINE MOUNT

REPLACE

1. Support engine assembly with suitable jack stands.
2. Remove front engine mount through bolt and nut.
3. Raise engine enough to access engine mount.
4. Remove engine mount assembly mounting bolts, nuts and washers.
5. Remove engine mount assembly from front lefthand side of engine.
6. Reverse procedure to install.

ENGINE

REPLACE

1. Raise hood, then support hood assembly at front and rear.
2. Place protective covering over cowl and fenders.
3. Remove hood ground strap, then disconnect hood lamp electrical connector.
4. Remove hood hinge to hood link assembly attaching bolt.
5. Lower and support hood.
6. Remove outboard sections from each end of cowl vent grill panel.
7. Remove pivot bolts, then the hood assembly.
8. Relieve fuel system pressure as outlined under "Precautions."
9. Remove air intake duct from throttle body, then the air cleaner assembly.
10. Disconnect ignition wires from coils.
11. Remove ignition coil attaching bolts, then the coils from valve rocker arm covers.
12. Disconnect fuel supply lines from rear of engine.
13. Drain cooling system and recover A/C refrigerant as outlined in "Air Conditioning" chapter.
14. Remove A/C compressor from mounting bracket and position aside.
15. Rotate drive belt tensioner arm with a suitable 3/8 inch drive and remove drive belt.
16. Remove fan clutch from water pump.
17. Remove radiator from vehicle.
18. Disconnect throttle body actuator control electrical connectors.
19. Disconnect engine vacuum lines. Mark lines for installation reference.
20. Disconnect EGR valve electrical connector, then remove EGR valve and adapter.
21. Remove alternator from mounting bracket and position aside.
22. Disconnect engine electrical harness and position aside.
23. Raise and support vehicle.
24. Remove hydraulic hoses from power steering pump.
25. **On models equipped with 4WD,** proceed as follows:
    a. Remove transfer case shield.
    b. Remove propeller shaft boot clamp at transfer case.
    c. Remove bolts and yoke retainers from front axle pinion yoke.
    d. Disconnect propeller shaft from front axle pinion yoke. Wrap bearing caps with suitable tape to prevent loss of bearing rollers. **Do not attempt to remove shaft by pounding on yoke ears or using a tool between yoke and universal joint. Injection joints may**

fracture and cause premature failure.

26. **On all models,** remove ground wires from engine block.
27. Remove starter motor, then the flywheel inspection cover.
28. Remove torque converter to flywheel bolts.
29. Remove exhaust pipe to manifold retaining bolts, then the exhaust pipe from manifold.
30. Remove transmission to engine attaching bolts.
31. **On models equipped with auxiliary oil cooler,** remove cooler lines from cylinder block.
32. **On all models,** lower vehicle.
33. Support transmission with a suitable jack.
34. Attach engine lifting brackets tool No. J 36857, or equivalent, to rear of right cylinder head and front of left cylinder head.
35. Remove engine mount through bolts.
36. Remove engine from vehicle using suitable lifting device.
37. Remove engine oil fill tube, then the oil dipstick and tube.
38. Remove alternator mounting bracket from cylinder block.
39. Remove A/C compressor and power steering mounting bracket from cylinder head.
40. Reverse procedure to install.

TIGHTENING SPECIFICATIONS

Year	Component	Torque, Ft. Lbs.
2002–03	Drive Belt Tensioner Bolt	37
	Engine Mount Bolt	44
	Engine Mount Nut	33
	Flywheel Cover	106①
	Flywheel Housing Bolt (Countersunk)	44
	Flywheel Housing Bolt (Hex Head)	50
	Oil Pan Drain Plug	21
	Transmission Convertor Cover Bolts	106①

① — Inch lbs.

Rear Axle & Suspension

INDEX

REAR AXLE

REPLACE

Coil Spring Suspension

1. Raise and support vehicle, then place place suitable jack stands at front end of vehicle.
2. Support rear axle with suitable jack stands, then remove tire and wheel assemblies.
3. Disconnect rear axle vent tube and wheel speed sensor electrical connector.
4. Remove propeller shaft.
5. Disconnect left and righte rear park brake cables from rear axle.
6. Remove brake calipers and suspend aside. Do not disconnect brake hydraulic lines from caliper.
7. Remove stabilizer shaft from rear axle.
8. Remove crossover brake pipe from rear axle.
9. Remove shock absorber lower mounting bolts, then the shock absorber from rear axle.
10. Remove coil springs.
11. Disconnect track bar and lower control arm from rear axle.
12. Disconnect upper control arm from rear axle.
13. Remove rear axle assembly from vehicle.
14. Reverse procedure to install.

Leaf Spring Suspension

1. Raise and support vehicle, then place place suitable jack stands at front end of vehicle.
2. Drain lubricant from rear differential.
3. Disconnect propeller shaft from rear axle.
4. Support rear axle with suitable jack stands, then remove tire and wheel assemblies.
5. Disconnect left and right parking brake cables from rear axle.
6. Remove brake line bracket bolts, then suspend brake lines from vehicle with heavy mechanics wire.
7. Remove brake calipers from brake caliper mounting brackets, then suspend calipers from vehicle with heavy mechanics wire. Do not disconnect brake lines.
8. Disconnect shock absorbers from axle brackets.
9. Remove vent hose from rear axle vent fitting.
10. Remove nuts and washers from U-bolts.
11. Remove U-bolts, spring plates and spacers form axle assembly.
12. Lower and remove axle assembly from vehicle.
13. Reverse procedure to install.

REAR AXLE SHAFT

REPLACE

1. Raise and support vehicle, then remove tire and wheel assembly.
2. Remove brake caliper, then position and support caliper aside. Do not disconnect brake hose from caliper.
3. Drain rear axle lubricant.
4. Remove rear axle housing cover and gasket.
5. **On models not equipped with a locking differential,** remove pinion shaft locking bolt, then the pinion shaft.
6. **On models equipped with a locking differential,** proceed as follows:
   a. Remove pinion shaft locking bolt.
   b. Partially remove pinion shaft, then rotate case until pinion shaft touches housing.
   c. Rotate rear axle shaft lock until lock aligns with thrust block opening, use a screwdriver, or similar flatbladed tool to rotate shaft lock.
   d. Push flange of axle shaft into axle housing.
7. **On all models,** remove rear axle shaft lock from button end of axle shaft.
8. Remove axle shaft from housing.
9. Reverse procedure to install, noting the following:
   a. **On models with a locking differential,** install rear axle shaft lock on axle shaft so ends are flush with thrust block.
   b. **On all models,** align hole in pinion shaft with bolt hole in differential case.

HUB & BEARING

REPLACE

1. Raise and support vehicle, then remove tire and wheel assembly.
2. Remove brake caliper, then position and support caliper aside. Do not disconnect brake hose from caliper.
3. Remove axle shaft as outlined under "Rear Axle Shaft, Replace."
4. Remove axle nut retaining ring, key and adjusting nut using wheel bearing nut wrench tool No. J 2222-C, or equivalent.
5. Remove hub from axle housing. Remove brake rotor, if necessary.
6. Remove oil seal from wheel hub.
7. Remove inner hub bearing, then the inner hub bearing cup using a suitable brass drift and hammer.
8. Remove the retaining ring from the wheel hub.
9. Remove outer hub bearing and bearing cup.
10. Reverse procedure to install.

SHOCK ABSORBER

REPLACE

1. Raise and support vehicle.
2. Support rear axle using suitable jack.
3. Remove mounting nuts and disconnect shock absorber from upper mounting bracket.
4. Remove lower mounting nuts and shock absorber.
5. Reverse procedure to install.

COIL SPRING

REPLACE

1. Raise and support vehicle.
2. Support rear axle using suitable jack.
3. Remove stabilizer shaft link retaining nut from frame
4. Remove lower shock absorber nut and bolt from rear axle.
5. Lower rear axle until springs are fully unloaded.
6. Remove coil spring and insulators.
7. Reverse procedure to install.

LEAF SPRING

REPLACE

1. Raise and support vehicle.
2. Support rear axle using suitable jack.
3. Remove U-bolt nuts and washers.
4. Remove anchor plate.
5. Remove U-bolts and spacer.
6. Loosen shackle to spring nut.
7. Remove shackle to rear bracket mounting nut, washer and bolt.
8. Remove spring to front bracket, nut, washers and bolt.

9. Remove spring.
10. Reverse procedure to install.

CONTROL ARM

REPLACE

Upper

1. Raise and support vehicle.
2. Support rear axle at ride height using suitable jack.
3. Remove upper control arm retaining nut and bolt from frame bracket.
4. Remove upper control arm retaining nut and bolt from axle bracket.
5. Remove upper control arm from vehicle.
6. Reverse procedure to install.

Lower

1. Raise and support vehicle.
2. Support rear axle at curb height using suitable jack.
3. Remove lower control arm retaining nuts and bolt.
4. Remove lower control arm from vehicle.
5. Reverse procedure to install.

STABILIZER SHAFT

REPLACE

1. Raise and support vehicle.
2. Remove stabilizer shaft link nut from ball stud.
3. Remove stabilizer shaft insulator bracket mounting bolts, then the stabilizer shaft.
4. Reverse procedure to install.

TIGHTENING SPECIFICATIONS

Year	Component	Torque/Ft. Lbs.
2002–06	Axle Flange	115
	Brake Backing Plate	100
	Carrier Cover	30
	Drain Plug	24
	Jounce Bumper	24
	Lower Control Arm	89
	Shackle To Frame Bracket	70
	Shackle To Spring	70
	Shock Absorber, Nut	70
	Spring To Front Hanger	92
	Stabilizer Shaft	24
	Stabilizer Shaft Link	48
	Track Bar	77
	Upper Control Arm	77
	Yoke Retainer	19

Front Suspension & Steering

NOTE: Refer To "Computer Relearn Procedures" Located In The Front Of This Manual When Battery Power To The Computer Has Been Interrupted.

INDEX

PRECAUTIONS

Battery Ground Cable

Prior to service disconnect battery ground cable and isolate, as required.

Radio Security System

If the Theftlock system is active when battery power is interrupted, the customers security code must be entered to restore proper function of the radio. Use the following procedure to unlock a secured radio after a power loss. Do not wait more than 15 seconds between steps.

1. Theftlock is engaged if radio is inoperable and "LOC" appears with ignition in On position.
2. Obtain customers' code number.
3. Press "MIN" button and "000" will appear on display.
4. Press "MIN" again until last two digits displayed agree with security code.
5. Press "HR" button until first 1 or 2 digits agree with security code.
6. Press "AM-FM" to select code entered. "SEC" will display indicating radio is now operable and secure.
7. If incorrect code is entered, "SEC" will display and radio will be inoperable.
8. Radio will remain inoperable until correct code is displayed. Repeat steps until correct code is entered. If correct code cannot be obtained, contact Delco technical assistance.

WHEEL BEARING

ADJUST

1. Raise and support vehicle.
2. Remove cap from hub/disc.
3. Remove cotter pin.
4. **Torque** adjusting nut to 12 ft. lbs., while turning wheel forward by hand, this will seat bearing.
5. Back off adjusting nut one flat. If hole in spindle lines up with slot in nut, insert cotter pin. If hole and slot do not line up, back nut off until hole and slot align. Do not back nut off more than one additional flat.
6. Install cotter pin.

HUB, BEARING & SEAL

REPLACE

1. Remove brake rotor as outlined in "Disc Brakes" chapter.
2. Remove wheel speed sensor and brake hose mounting bracket bolt from steering knuckle.
3. Disconnect wheel speed sensor electrical connection.
4. **On models equipped with 4WD,** proceed as follows:
   a. Remove cover, mounting wheel driveshaft nut and washer.
   b. Disconnect wheel driveshaft from wheel hub and bearing.
5. **On all models,** remove mounting bolts, wheel hub and bearing, then the splash shield.
6. **On 2500 series models,** remove steering knuckle bore O-ring seal.
7. **On all models,** remove wheel speed sensor mounting bolt.
8. Reverse procedure to install, noting the following:
   a. Replace O-ring seal, as required.

BALL JOINT INSPECTION

1. Wipe ball joints clean and inspect seals for damage. If seals are damaged, replace ball joint.
2. Adjust wheel bearings as outlined under "Wheel Bearing, Adjust."
3. Raise and support vehicle.
4. Place suitable dial indicator against spindle to measure vertical movement.
5. Pry between lower control arm and outer race using suitable pry bar while reading dial indicator.
6. If dial indicator reading is more than .08 inch, replace ball joint.

BALL JOINT

REPLACE

Lower

2WD MODELS

1. Raise and support vehicle, then remove tire and wheel assembly.
2. Disconnect Real Time Damping (RTD) link rod from sensor.
3. Remove lower control arm mounting nuts, washers and bolts.
4. Remove nut and disconnect the ball joint stud from steering knuckle using ball joint separator tool No. J-43631, or equivalent.
5. Remove lower control arm as outlined under "Control Arm, Replace."
6. Secure lower control arm in suitable bench vice.
7. Remove rivets and lower ball joint.
8. Reverse procedure to install.

4WD MODELS

1. Raise and support vehicle, then remove tire and wheel assembly.
2. Disconnect Real Time Damping (RTD) link rod from sensor.
3. Remove stabilizer shaft links from lower control arm.
4. Remove lower control arm as outlined under "Control Arm, Replace."
5. Remove halfshaft as outlined in "Front Wheel Drive Axles" chapter.
6. Secure lower control arm in suitable bench vice.
7. Remove lower ball joint rivets
8. Remove ball joint from lower control arm using suitable press.
9. Reverse procedure to install.

Upper

1. Raise and support vehicle, then remove tire and wheel assembly.
2. Disconnect Real Time Damping (RTD) link rod from sensor.
3. Remove brake hose and the wheel speed sensor brackets mounting bolt.

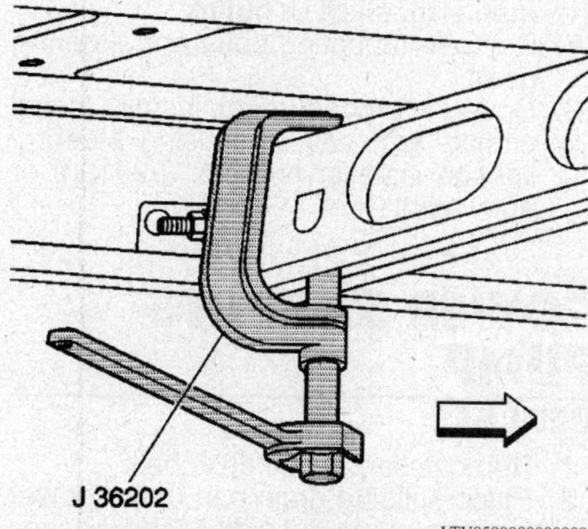

Fig. 1 Torsion bar tool installation

4. Remove halfshaft as outlined in "Front Wheel Drive Axles" chapter.
5. Remove upper control arm as outlined under "Control Arm, Replace."
6. Remove upper ball joint using suitable press.
7. Reverse procedure to install.

SHOCK ABSORBER

REPLACE

1. Raise and support vehicle, then remove tire and wheel assembly.
2. Support lower control arm with a suitable jack stand.
3. **On models equipped with Real Time Damping (RTD),** disconnect front position sensor link rod from sensor.
4. **On all models,** remove shock absorber upper retaining nut and insulator. Do not discard plastic pilot ring.
5. Remove shock absorber to lower control arm mounting bolt, then the shock absorber.
6. Reverse procedure to install.

CONTROL ARM

REPLACE

Lower

2WD MODELS

1. Raise and support vehicle, then remove tire and wheel assembly.
2. **On models equipped with Real Time Damping (RTD),** disconnect front position sensor link rod from sensor.
3. **On all models,** remove lower control arm mounting nuts, washers and bolts.
4. Remove lower ball joint stud nut.
5. Disconnect lower ball joint stud from steering knuckle using ball joint separator tool No. J-43631, or equivalent.
6. Remove lower control arm.
7. Reverse procedure to install.

4WD MODELS

1. Raise and support vehicle, then remove tire and wheel assembly
2. **On models equipped with Real Time Damping (RTD),** disconnect front position sensor link rod from sensor.

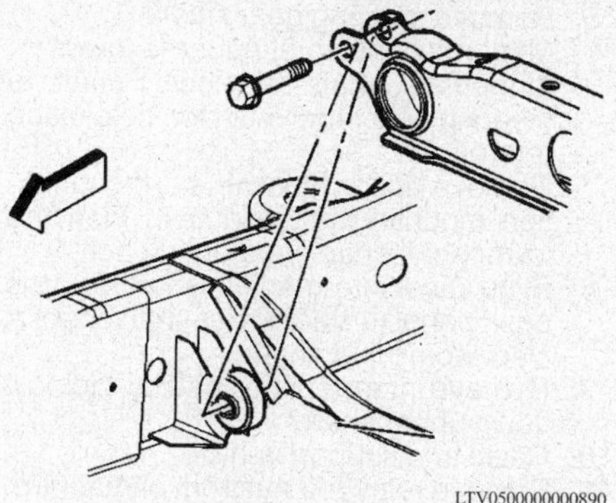

Fig. 2 Torsion bar removal

3. **On all models,** remove stabilizer shaft links from lower control arm.
4. Remove shock absorber lower mounting nut and bolt.
5. Remove torsion bars as outlined under "Torsion Bar, Replace."
6. Remove wheel drive shaft as outlined in "Front Wheel Drive Axles" chapter.
7. Remove lower ball joint stud nut.
8. Disconnect lower ball joint stud from steering knuckle using ball joint separator tool No. J-43631, or equivalent.
9. Remove mounting nuts, washers, bolts and lower control arm.
10. Reverse procedure to install.

Upper

1. Raise and support vehicle, then remove tire and wheel assembly.
2. Disconnect Real Time Damping (RTD) link rod from sensor.
3. Remove brake hose and the wheel speed sensor brackets mounting bolt.
4. Remove wheel drive shaft as outlined in "Front Wheel Drive Axles" chapter.
5. Remove upper ball joint nut . Discard nut.
6. Disconnect upper control arm from steering knuckle using ball joint separator tool No. J-43631, or equivalent.
7. Remove upper control arm mounting nuts, adjustment cams and mounting bolts.
8. Remove upper control arm.
9. Reverse procedure to install.

STEERING KNUCKLE

REPLACE

1. Raise and support vehicle, then remove tire and wheel assembly.
2. Remove wheel hub and bearing as outlined under "Hub, Bearing & Seal, Replace."
3. **On models equipped with Real Time Damping (RTD),** disconnect front position sensor link rod from sensor.
4. **On models equipped with 2WD,** support lower control arm with suitable jack.
5. **On models equipped with 4WD,** unload torsion bars.
6. **On all models,** disconnect outer tie rod from knuckle.
7. Remove brake hose bracket mounting bolt.
8. Remove mounting nut and separate upper ball joint from steering knuckle using ball joint separating tool No. J-43631, or equivalent.
9. Remove mounting nut and separate lower ball joint from steering knuckle using ball joint separating tool.
10. Remove steering knuckle.
11. Reverse procedure to install.

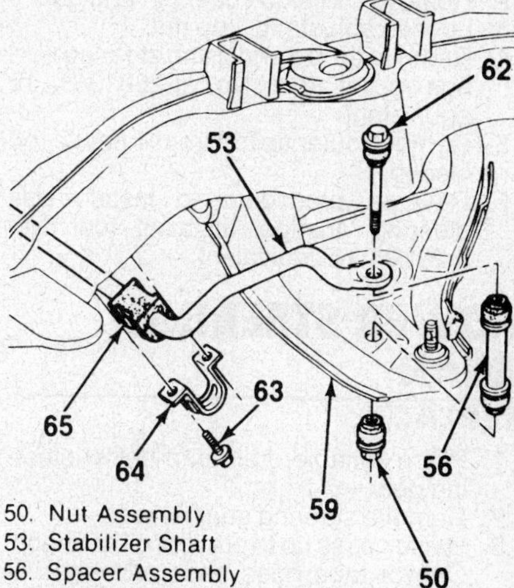

Fig. 3 Stabilizer shaft components

TORSION BAR

REPLACE

1. Raise and support vehicle.
2. Install torsion bar unloading/loading tool No. J 36202, or equivalent, to adjustment arm and crossmember, **Fig. 1.**
3. Increase tension on adjustment arm until load is removed from adjustment bolt and adjuster nut.
4. Remove adjustment bolt and adjuster nut, **Fig. 2.**
5. Remove torsion bar unloading/loading tool No. J 36202, or equivalent, to allow torsion bar to unload.
6. Remove torsion bar crossmember bolts from weld nuts.
7. Remove torsion bars from vehicle.
8. Reverse procedure to install.

STABILIZER BAR

REPLACE

1. Raise and support vehicle.
2. Remove nut from link bolt, **Fig. 3.**
3. Remove link bolt.
4. Remove spacer, mounting bolts, bracket and stabilizer shaft.
5. Remove bushing.
6. Reverse procedure to install.

TIE ROD END

REPLACE

1. Raise and support vehicle, then remove tire and wheel assembly.

2. Remove ball stud cotter pin and nut.
3. Loosen adjuster clamp nut.
4. Remove tie rod end using steering linkage puller tool No. J-26813-B, or equivalent.
5. Remove outer tie rod from inner tie rod sleeve.
6. Reverse procedure to install. Use steering linkage installer tool No. J-29194, or equivalent.

POWER STEERING GEAR

REPLACE

1. Place suitable drain pan below steering gear.
2. Remove steering gear hoses.
3. Raise hoses up to prevent oil drainage. Cap or tape hose ends and gear fittings ends.
4. Place front wheels in straight ahead position, then lock steering column by placing steering column anti-rotation pin tool No. J-42640, or equivalent, through steering column access hole.
5. Remove steering gear shield.
6. Mark relationship of upper to lower intermediate shaft and lower shaft to steering gear input shaft for installation reference.
7. Remove upper to lower shaft connection mounting nut and bolt, then the lower shaft coupler mounting bolt.
8. Slide lower intermediate shaft towards dash panel to clear lower shaft coupler clear from input shaft.
9. Remove intermediate shaft by sliding it down upper shaft.
10. Raise and support vehicle.
11. Remove relay rod nut from pitman arm ball stud. Discard nut.
12. Remove relay rod from pitman arm ball stud using universal steering linkage puller tool No. J-24319-01, or equivalent.
13. Remove pitman arm nut and washer.
14. Mark pitman arm shaft for proper installation alignment.
15. Remove pitman shaft nut or pinch bolt.
16. Remove pitman arm from shaft using pitman arm puller tool No. J-6632-01, or equivalent. **Do not hammer on pitman arm, shaft or puller.**.
17. Remove mounting bolts and steering gear.
18. Reverse procedure to install. Install pitman arm ball stud using steering linkage installer tool No. J-29193, or equivalent.

POWER STEERING PUMP

REPLACE

1. Remove serpentine drive belt.
2. Place suitable drain pan under power steering pump, then disconnect hoses from pump. Plug pump ports and hoses.
3. Remove pulley using power steering pump pulley remover tool No. J-25034-C, or equivalent.
4. Disconnect electrical connector from EVO actuator.
5. Remove front and rear mounting bolts, then the pump.
6. Reverse procedure to install.

TIGHTENING SPECIFICATIONS

Year	Component	Torque/Ft. Lbs.
2002–06	Ball Joint, Lower	52
	Ball Joint Stud, Lower	74
	Ball Joint Stud, Upper	37
	Frame Cross Bar	74
	Lower Control Arm	107
	Pivot Bolt	107
	Power Steering Pump	37
	Power Steering Pump Hose	20
	Shock Absorber Lower Control Arm, Bolt	18
	Shock Absorber Through Bolt	59
	Shock Absorber Upper Nut	15
	Spring Hanger	70
	Steering Gear	100
	Tie Rod Adjuster Clamp	77
	Tie Rod Ball Stud	65
	Tie Rod Ball Stud, Nut	48
	Tie Rod Ball Joint, Nut	②
	Tie Rod Tube Clamp	55
	Torsion Bar Crossmember Bolts	70
	Torsion Bar Support Mounting Nuts	70
	U-Bolt	92③
	Upper Control Arm To Frame	140
	Wheel Drive Shaft	155
	Wheel Hub & Bearing	133
	Wheel Speed Sensor	80①
	Wheel Speed Sensor & Brake Hose Mounting Bracket	106①

① — Inch lbs.
② — Axle assembly with 8100-lbs. rating, 95 ft. lbs.; all other axle assemblies 120 ft. lbs.
③ — Diagonal sequence.

Front Wheel Drive

INDEX

AXLE SHAFT

REPLACE

1. Raise and support vehicle, then remove tire and wheel assembly.
2. Insert suitable drift through brake caliper and into brake rotor.
3. While holding rotor in place, remove hub nut and washer.
4. Remove drive axle flange to inboard C/V joint drive flange bolts and drift from rotor.
5. Remove stabilizer shaft bolt, spacer and nut from lower control arm.
6. Wrap shop towels around both inner and outer wheel drive shaft boots to prevent damage during removal.
7. Pull axle shaft through lower control arm opening.
8. Reverse procedure to install.

DIFFERENTIAL CARRIER

REPLACE

1. Raise and support vehicle, then remove front skid plate.
2. Drain carrier axle lubricant into suitable container.
3. Install plastic tie straps loosely over ends of front stabilizer shaft and under center of each halfshaft bar.
4. Mark relationship of propeller shaft to front axle for installation reference.
5. Remove front propeller shaft retainers.
6. Remove front propeller shaft from front axle yoke and secure it aside.
7. Remove engine oil filter.
8. Remove halfshaft flanges to differential mounting bolts.
9. Remove pitman arm from relay rod, move pitman arm towards lefthand side of vehicle for clearance.
10. Push relay rod forward and up for clearance.
11. Support front differential.
12. Remove front drive axle inner shaft housing nuts, washers and bolts from differential mounting bracket.
13. Disconnect front axle actuator electrical connector.
14. Remove front axle vent hose.
15. Place plastic tie straps around center of halfshaft, contacting only halfshaft bar. Tighten straps to support inner halfshaft ends.
16. Remove upper differential carrier mounting nut, washers and bolt.
17. Remove lower differential carrier mounting nut, washers and bolt.
18. Remove differential carrier.
19. Reverse procedure to install.

OUTPUT SHAFT

REPLACE

1. Raise and support vehicle.
2. Remove lefthand drive axle.
3. Remove lower carrier mounting bolt. Pry against lower carrier to provide clearance for output shaft removal.
4. Remove output shaft from case using slide hammer and adapter.
5. Remove deflector and seal from output shaft.
6. Reverse procedure to install. Lubricate and install new seal using suitable seal installer tool.

PINION FLANGE SEAL

REPLACE

1. Raise and support vehicle.
2. Disconnect propeller shaft from axle. Position propeller shaft aside.
3. Measure and record torque required to rotate pinion.
4. Mark pinion stem, pinion nut and companion flange, then record number of exposed thread on pinion stem.
5. Remove pinion nut using companion flange holder/remover tool No. J-8614-01, or equivalent. Four notches on tool should face flange.
6. Remove pinion flange using holder/remover tool.
7. Remove oil seal. **Do not distort or scratch aluminum case.**
8. Reverse procedure to install, noting the following:
   a. Stake new deflector at three new equally spaced positions. **Do not damage seal operating surface.**
   b. Install seal in bore, then seat seal using seal installer tool No. J-36366, or equivalent.
   c. Install pinion nut and tighten nut to original position using marks and exposed threads recorded earlier.
   d. Measure rotating torque of pinion and compare with torque recorded earlier.
   e. Tighten pinion nut until **torque** required to rotate pinion is 3 inch lbs., more than original torque.

TIGHTENING SPECIFICATIONS

Year	Component	Torque/Ft. Lbs.
2002–06	Axle Nut	165
	Axle Tube To Bracket	75
	Axle Tube To Carrier	30
	Bracket To Frame	67
	Brake Pipe Support Bracket	13
	Carrier Frame	16
	Carrier Mount	75
	Differential Carrier Shield	25
	Drain Plug	24
	Electric Motor Actuator	15
	Engagement Switch	15

Continued

TIGHTENING SPECIFICATIONS—Continued

Year	Component	Torque/Ft. Lbs.
2002–06	Halfshaft	58
	Lower Shock Absorber Mount	54
	Outer Tie Rod	46
	Stabilizer Bar Clamp	24
	Stabilizer Link	13
	U-Joint Clamp	15
	Upper Control Arm Stud	75

Wheel Alignment

INDEX

PRELIMINARY INSPECTION

Inspect the following components, adjust, repair or replace as required prior to performing front wheel alignment.

1. Inflate tires to cold specifications.
2. Ensure front tires are of same size, ply rating and load rating.
3. Inspect for excessive wheel bearing endplay.
4. Inspect for worn or damaged spindle ball joints.
5. Inspect steering gear mounting bolts for proper tightness.
6. Inspect radius arm or bent or damaged condition.
7. Inspect radius arm to frame bushings for looseness or wear.
8. Inspect suspension components for wear or damage.

FRONT WHEEL ALIGNMENT

Camber

1. Remove pinned adjusting cam insert.
2. Loosen upper control arm adjusting cam nuts.
3. Rotate cam bolts to required camber specification setting.
4. Maintain camber setting while tightening cam bolt nuts. **Torque** nuts to 140 ft. lbs.

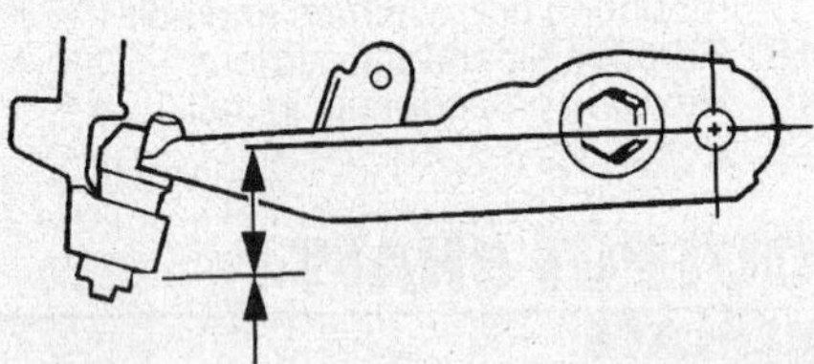

Fig. 1 Z height measurement

5. Ensure toe, camber and caster settings after changing camber and adjust.

Caster

1. Remove pinned adjusting cam insert.
2. Loosen upper control arm adjusting cam nuts.
3. Rotate cam bolts to required caster specification setting.
4. Maintain caster setting while tightening cam bolt nuts. **Torque** nuts to 140 ft. lbs.
5. Ensure toe, camber and caster settings after changing caster and adjust.

TOE-IN

1. Measure toe-in.
2. Change length of both tie rod sleeves to effect toe change.
3. Toe-in can be increased or decreased by changing length of tie rod ends. Threaded sleeve is provided for this purpose. When tie rod ends are mounted ahead of steering knuckle they must be decreased in length in order to increase toe-in. When tie rod ends are mounted behind steering knuckle they must be lengthened in order to increase toe-in. After adjusting **torque** tie rod end jam nut to 50 ft. lbs.

VEHICLE RIDE HEIGHT

Z HEIGHT

1. Lift front bumper of vehicle up approximately 1.5 inches.
2. Gently remove hands and allow vehicle to settle on its own.
3. Repeat this operation twice more for a total of three times.
4. Measure "Z" height, **Fig. 1.**
5. Push front bumper on vehicle down approximately 1.5 inches.
6. Gently remove hands and allow vehicle to rise on its own.
7. Repeat this operation twice more for a total of three times.
8. Measure "Z" height.
9. Find average of high and low measurements. This is "Z" height. "Z" height should be as follows:
   a. **On 2WD models,** measurement should be 3.6–3.7 inches.
   b. **On 4WD models,** measurement should be 4.3–4.8 inches.

D HEIGHT

Use the procedure used in determining the "Z" height. "D" height should be the average of the high and low measurements.

CANYON, COLORADO, SONOMA & S10

NOTE: Refer To The Back Of This Manual For Vehicle Manufacturer's Special Service Tool Suppliers.

INDEX OF SERVICE OPERATIONS

Specifications

GENERAL ENGINE SPECIFICATIONS

Year	Engine		Fuel System	Bore & Stroke	Compression Ratio	Net H.P. @ RPM	Maximum Torque, Ft. Lbs. @ RPM	Normal Oil Pressure, psi
	Liter	VIN Code②						
2002	2.2L	5	SFI	3.50 X 3.46	9.0	120 @ 5000	140 @ 3600	56③
	4.3L	W	SFI	4.00 X 3.48	9.2	180 @ 4400	245 @ 2800	④
2003	2.2L	5	SFI	3.50 X 3.46	9.0	120 @ 5000	140 @ 3600	56③
	4.3L	X	SFI	4.00 X 3.48	9.2	175 @ 4400	240 @ 2800	④
2004	2.8L	8	SFI	3.66 X 4.02	10.0	175 @ 5600	185 @ 2800	12①
	3.5L	6	SFI	3.66 X 4.02	10.0	220 @ 5600	225 @ 2800	12①
	4.3L	X	SFI	4.00 X 3.48	9.2	175 @ 4400	240 @ 2800	④
2005–06	2.8L	8	SFI	3.66 X 4.02	10.0	175 @ 5600	185 @ 2800	12①
	3.5L	6	SFI	3.66 X 4.02	10.0	220 @ 5600	225 @ 2800	12①

CSFI — Central Port Sequential Fuel Injection
MFI — Multi-Port Fuel Injection

① — At 1200 RPM.
② — Eighth digit denotes engine code.
③ — At 3000 RPM.
④ — Minimum hot pressures: 6.0 psi @ 1000 RPM; 18.0 psi @ 1800 RPM; 24.0 psi @ 3000 RPM.

TUNE UP SPECIFICATIONS

The following specifications are published from the latest information available. This data should only be used in the absence of a decal affixed in the engine compartment.

Engine	VIN Code①	Spark Plug Gap	Ignition Timing BTDC				Curb Idle Speed②		Fast Idle Speed②		Fuel Pump Pressure psi.	Valve Lash, Inch
			Firing Order, Fig. ③	Man. Trans.	Auto. Trans.	Mark Location	Man. Trans.	Auto. Trans.	Man. Trans.	Auto. Trans.		
2.2L	4	.040	A	⑤	⑤	⑨	⑦	⑦	⑦	⑦	41–47⑥	④
2.8L	8	.044	1-3-4-2	⑤	⑤	⑨	⑦	⑦	⑦	⑦	50–56⑧	④
3.5L	6	.044	1-3-5-4-2	⑤	⑤	⑨	⑦	⑦	⑦	⑦	50–56⑧	④
4.3L CMFI	W	.060	B	⑤	⑤	⑨	⑦	⑦	⑦	⑦	60–66⑧	④
4.3L EFI	X	.060	B	⑤	⑤	⑨	⑦	⑦	⑦	⑦	60–66⑧	④

BTDC — Before Top Dead Center
D — Drive
① — The eighth digit of VIN denotes engine code.
② — When inspecting idle speed, set parking brake & block drive wheels.
③ — Before removing wires from distributor cap or coil unit, determine location of ignition wires, as position may have been altered from that outlined at end of this chart.
④ — Equipped w/hydraulic valve lifters.
⑤ — Not adjustable.
⑥ — Loosen fuel filler cap to relieve vapor pressure in fuel tank. Wrap shop towel around engine compartment fuel pressure fitting. Connect suitable fuel pressure gauge to fuel pressure fitting. Energize fuel pump w/either suitable fuel pump test

connector or scan tool & note fuel pressure reading.

⑦ — Controlled by idle speed control (ISC) motor or Idle Air Control (IAC) valve.

⑧ — Wrap shop towel around engine compartment fuel pressure fitting. Connect suitable fuel pressure gauge to fuel pressure fitting. Turn ignition to On position & note fuel pressure reading.

⑨ — Equipped w/crankshaft position sensor.

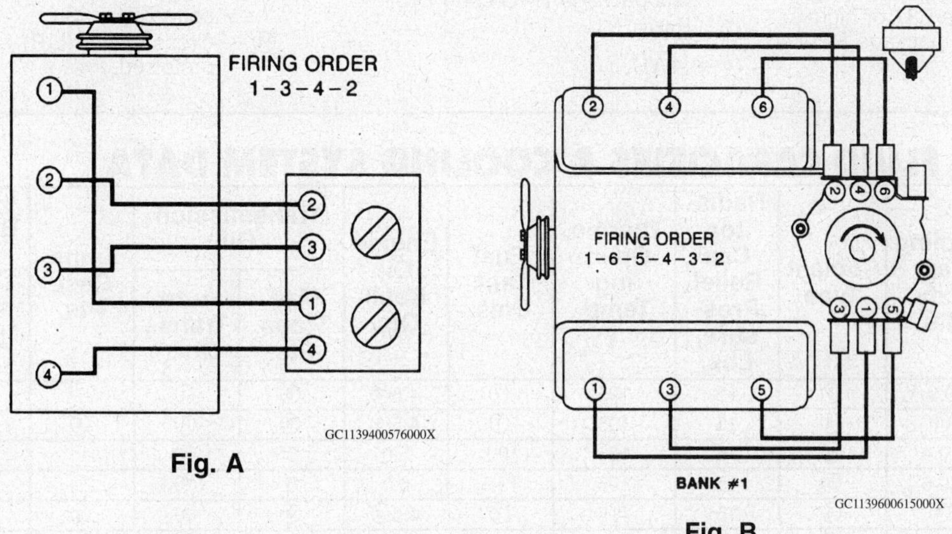

Fig. A

Fig. B

FRONT WHEEL ALIGNMENT SPECIFICATIONS

Year	Model	Side	Caster Angle, Degrees		Camber Angle, Degrees		Toe Per Wheel, Degrees①		Ball Joint Wear, Inches
			Limits	Desired	Limits	Desired	Limits	Desired	
2002–03	All④	Left	+1.8 to +3.8⑥	+2.8⑥	-1 to +1②	0②	-.1 to +.3	+.1	③
		Right	+2.3 to +4.3⑥	+3.3⑥	-1 to +1②	0②	-.1 to +.3	+.1	③
	All⑤	Left	+3.7 to +5.7⑥	+4.7⑥	-1 to +1②	0②	-.1 to +.3	+.1	③
		Right	+4.2 to +6.2⑥	+5.2⑥	-1 to +1②	0②	-.1 to +.3	+.1	③
2004–06	Canyon & Colorado⑦⑧	Left	+3.3 to +5.3⑩	+4.3⑩	-.5 to +.5②	0②	-.2 to +.2	0	③
		Right	+3.5 to +5.5⑩	+4.5⑩	-.5 to +.5②	0②	-.2 to +.2	0	③
	Canyon & Colorado⑤⑧	Left	+3.7 to +5.7⑫	+4.7⑫	.5 to +.5②	0②	-.2 to +.2	0	③
		Right	+3.7 to +5.7⑫	+4.7⑫	.5 to +.5②	0②	-.2 to +.2	0	③
	Canyon & Colorado⑧⑬	Left	+2.6 to +4.6⑭	+3.6⑭	.5 to +.5②	0②	-.2 to +.2	0	③
		Right	+3.0 to +5.0⑭	+4.0⑭	.5 to +.5②	0②	-.2 to +.2	0	③
	Canyon & Colorado⑦⑨	Left	+2.8 to +4.8⑩	+3.8⑩	.5 to +.5②	0②	-.2 to +.2	0	③
		Right	+3.0 to +5.0⑩	+4.0⑩	.5 to +.5②	0②	-.2 to +.2	0	③
	Canyon & Colorado⑨⑬	Left	+2.6 to +4.6⑩	+3.6⑩	.5 to +.5②	0②	-.2 to +.2	0	③
		Right	+3.0 to +5.0⑩	+4.0⑩	.5 to +.5②	0②	-.2 to +.2	0	③
	Sonoma & S10④	Left	+1.8 to +3.8⑥	+2.8⑥	-1 to +1②	0②	-.1 to +.3	+.1	③
		Right	+2.3 to +4.3⑥	+3.3⑥	-1 to +1②	0②	-.1 to +.3	+.1	③
	Sonoma & S10⑤	Left	+3.7 to +5.7⑥	+4.7⑥	-1 to +1②	0②	-.1 to +.3	+.1	③
		Right	+4.2 to +6.2⑥	+5.2⑥	-1 to +1②	0②	-.1 to +.3	+.1	③
	Sonoma & S10⑪	Left	+3.7 to +5.7⑥	+4.7⑥	+.5 to +1.9②	+1.2②	-.1 to +.3	+.1	③
		Right	+4.2 to +6.2⑥	+5.2⑥	+.5 to +1.9②	+1.2②	-.1 to +.3	+.1	③

CANYON, COLORADO, SONOMA & S10

① — Toe-In (+). Toe-Out (-).
② — Cross camber (L-R), -.5° to +.5°, preferred, 0°.
③ — Refer to "Ball Joint, Inspection" in "Front Suspension & Steering."
④ — Models less sport package RPO code ZQ8, low rider performance package RPO code Z87 or high wider performance package RPO code ZR2.
⑤ — Models w/sport package RPO code ZQ8 or low rider performance package RPO code Z87.
⑥ — Cross caster (L-R), -1° to 0°, preferred, -.5°.
⑦ — Models w/increased capacity chassis package RPO code Z85.
⑧ — 2WD.
⑨ — 4WD.
⑩ — Cross caster (L-R), -.7° to +.3°, preferred, -.2°.
⑪ — Models w/high wider performance package RPO code ZR2.
⑫ — Cross caster (L-R), -.5° to +.5°, preferred, 0°.
⑬ — Models w/off-road package RPO code Z71.
⑭ — Cross caster (L-R), -.9° to +.1°, preferred, -.4°.

FLUID CAPACITIES & COOLING SYSTEM DATA

Year	Engine Liter	Cooling Capacity, Qts.	Coolant Type	Radiator Cap Relief Pressure, Lbs.	Thermo. Opening Temp. °F	Fuel Tank Gals.	Engine Oil Refill Qts.	Transmission Oil		Trans. Case Pts.	Drive Axle Oil	
								Man. Trans. Pts.	Auto. Trans., Qts.①		Front Pts.	Rear Pts.
2002–03	2.2L	9.9	⑤	15	195	⑦	4.5③	⑧	④	—	—	4.0
	4.3L	⑥	⑤	15	195	⑦	4.5③	⑧	④	②	2.6	4.0
2004	2.8L	10.4	⑤	15	195	19.5	5.0	5	④	2.1	3.2	3.8
	3.5L	10.6	⑤	15	195	19.5	6.0	5	④	2.1	3.2	3.8
	4.3L	⑥	⑤	15	195	⑦	4.5③	⑧	④	②	2.6	4.0
2005–06	2.8L	10.4	⑤	15	195	19.5	5.0	5	④	2.1	3.2	3.8
	3.5L	10.6	⑤	15	195	19.5	6.0	5	④	2.1	3.2	3.8

① — Approximate make final inspection w/dipstick.
② — New Venture models 136 & 236, 4.0 pts.; New Venture model 233, 2.1 pts.
③ — Additional oil may be required w/filter change.
④ — Total capacity, 11 qts.; pan only, 5 qts.
⑤ — 50/50 mixture water and GM Goodwrench DEX-COOL or Havoline DEX-COOL coolant.
⑥ — With auto. trans., 13.8 qts.; with man. trans., 14.1 qts.
⑦ — Regular & extended cab, 18.5 gals.; crew cab, 17.8 gals.
⑧ — New Venture model 1500, 5.8 pts.; model 3500, 4.4 pts.

LUBRICANT DATA

Year	Model	Lubricant Type						
		Transmission		Hydraulic Clutch Fluid	Transfer Case	Drive Axle	Power Steering	Brake System
		Manual	Automatic					
2002–05	All	①	Dexron III	DOT 3	③	80W-90 GL-5④	②	DOT 3
2006	All	①	Dexron VI	DOT 3	③	80W-90 GL-5④	②	DOT 3

① — GM standard transmission fluid Part No. 12345349, or equivalent.
② — Power steering fluid, GM Part No. 1052884, or equivalent.
③ — Manual transfer case requires Dexron III. Automatic transfer case uses GM part No. 12378396, or equivalent.
④ — Models w/limited–slip or locking differentials, do not add limited slip additive.

Electrical

NOTE: On Air Bag Equipped Models, Refer To "Air Bag System Precautions" Located In The Front Of This Manual For System Disarming & Arming Procedures.

NOTE: Refer To "Computer Relearn Procedures" Located In The Front Of This Manual When Battery Power To The Computer Has Been Interrupted.

INDEX

PRECAUTIONS

Air Bag Systems

Refer to "Air Bag System Precautions" in the front of this manual for system disarming and arming procedures.

Battery Ground Cable

Prior to service, disconnect battery ground cable and isolate as required.

Radio Security System

THEFTLOCK

If the Theftlock system is active when battery power is interrupted, the customers security code must be entered to restore proper function of the radio. To unlock a secured radio after power loss, proceed as follows:

1. With ignition in On position, "LOC" appears on display.
2. Press "NM" button and "000" will appear on display.
3. Press "NM" until last two digits agree with security code.
4. Press "HR" button until first digit agrees with security code.
5. Press "AM-FM" to select code entered, "SEC" will appear on display indicating radio is now operable and secure.
6. If incorrect code is entered eight times, "INOP" will display. In order to reenter code, the ignition must be left on for one hour before code can be entered and only three more chances to enter code are available before display reads "INOP."

DELCO LOC II

If the Delco LOC II system is active when battery power is interrupted, the customers security code must be entered to restore proper function of the radio. To unlock a secured radio after power loss, proceed as follows:

1. Turn ignition lock to Accessory or Run position.
2. Press "SET" button and "000" will appear on display.
3. Press "SEEK" button until second and third digits of code appear.
4. Press "SCAN" button until first digit of code appears.
5. Press "AM-FM" button and "000" appears on display.
6. Press "SEEK" button until fifth and sixth digits of code appear.
7. Press "SCAN" button until fourth digit appears.
8. Press "AM-FM" button. If unlock sequence was successful, display will show "SEC," indicating unit is operational. If display shows "LOC," numbers did not match and unlock sequence was not successful.

FUSE PANEL & FLASHER LOCATION

Canyon & Colorado

The underhood fuse block is located on the lefthand side of the engine compartment.

The turn signal/hazard flasher operation is controlled by the Body Control Module (BCM). The BCM is located behind the righthand kick panel.

Sonoma & S10

The underhood fuse block is located on the lefthand side of the engine compartment.

This instrument panel fuse block is on

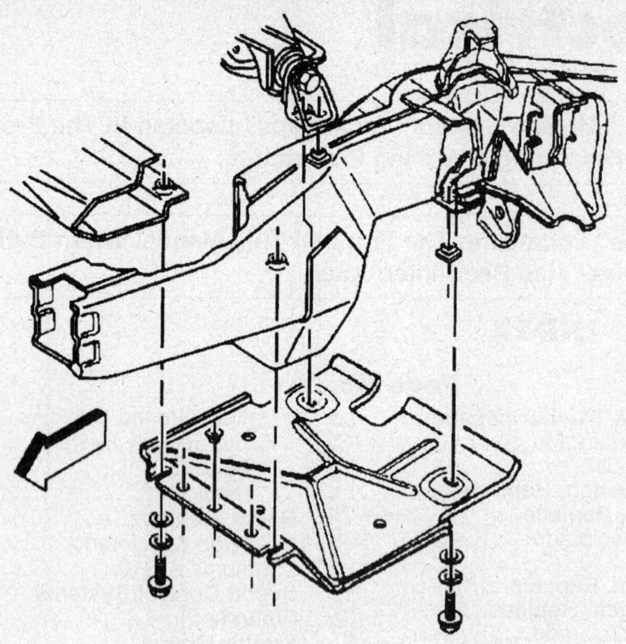

Fig. 1 Differential shield replacement. 4.3L engine

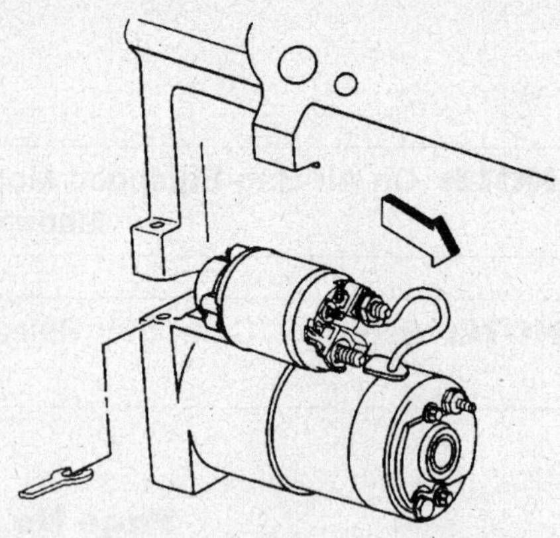

Fig. 2 Starter shim location. 4.3L engine

the lefthand side of the instrument panel, near the door jamb switch.

The hazard and turn signal flashers are located behind the righthand side of the instrument panel, mounted on the inline connector, below the recirculation door motor.

FUEL PUMP RELAY LOCATION

The fuel pump relay is located on the lefthand side of the engine compartment, in the underhood fuse block.

STARTER

REPLACE

Upon removal of starter, note if any shims are used. If shims are used, they should be installed in their original locations. After installation, if starter is noisy during cranking, remove one .015 inch double shim or add one .015 inch single shim to the outer bolt. If starter makes a high pitched whine after firing, add .015 inch double shims until noise ceases.

2.2L Engine

1. Raise and support vehicle.
2. Remove front exhaust pipe, then the engine to transmission brace rod.
3. Remove starter heat shield, then disconnect electrical connections.
4. Remove brace from brush end of starter.
5. Remove starter mounting bolts, then the starter. Note position of starter shims for installation reference.
6. Reverse procedure to install. **Torque** starter mounting bolts to 32 ft. lbs.

2.8L & 3.5L Engines

1. Remove intake manifold as oultined in "2.8L & 3.5L Gasoline Engines" section.
2. Remove starter solenoid S terminal nut and disconnect lead from starter.
3. Remove starter terminal nut and disconnect battery positive cable from starter.
4. Remove starter motor mounting nut and bolt.
5. Remove starter motor from engine.
6. Reverse procedure to install, noting the following:
   a. **Torque** starter motor mounting nut and bolt to 37 ft. lb ft.
   b. **Torque** battery positive cable to starter terminal nut to 80 inch lb.
   c. **Torque** starter solenoid S terminal nut to 31 inch lb.

4.3L Engine

1. Raise and support vehicle.
2. Remove right front tire and wheel assembly.
3. **On models equipped with 4WD,** remove differential carrier shield mounting bolts, then the shield, **Fig. 1.**
4. **On all models,** remove wires from starter solenoid.
5. Remove starter mounting bolts, then the starter. Note location of starter shims for installation reference, **Fig. 2.**
6. Reverse procedure to install, noting the following:
   a. **Torque** starter mounting bolts to 37 ft. lbs.
   b. **Torque** differential carrier shield to 18 ft. lbs.

ALTERNATOR

REPLACE

2.2L Engine

1. Remove left front wheel and tire assembly.
2. Working through wheelwell, remove alternator rear brace mounting bolts, then the brace, **Fig. 3.**
3. Remove accessory drive belt.
4. Disconnect alternator electrical connectors.
5. Remove alternator mounting bolts, then the alternator, **Fig. 4.**
6. Reverse procedure to install, noting the following:
   a. **Torque** left alternator bolt to 18 ft. lbs.
   b. **Torque** right alternator bolt to 37 ft. lbs.
   c. **Torque** alternator rear brace nuts to 18 ft. lbs.

2.8L & 3.5L Engines

1. Remove drive belt.
2. Raise and support vehicle, then remove left front wheel and tire assembly.
3. Remove left wheelhouse liner.
4. Disengage A/C compressor electrical connector from the bracket.
5. Remove lower A/C compressor mounting bolts, leave upper mounting bolt with A/C compressor.
6. Lower the vehicle.
7. Remove alternator output battery terminal nut and disconnect lead from alternator.
8. Disconnect wiring harness connector from alternator.
9. Remove alternator mounting bolts.
10. Remove engine lift bracket, then the alternator.
11. Reverse procedure to install, noting the following:
    a. **Torque** alternator mounting bolts 37 ft. lbs.
    b. **Torque** alternator output battery

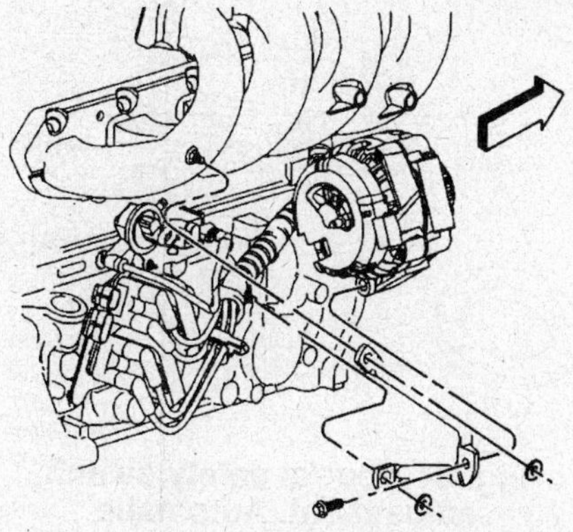

Fig. 3 Alternator brace removal. 2.2L engine

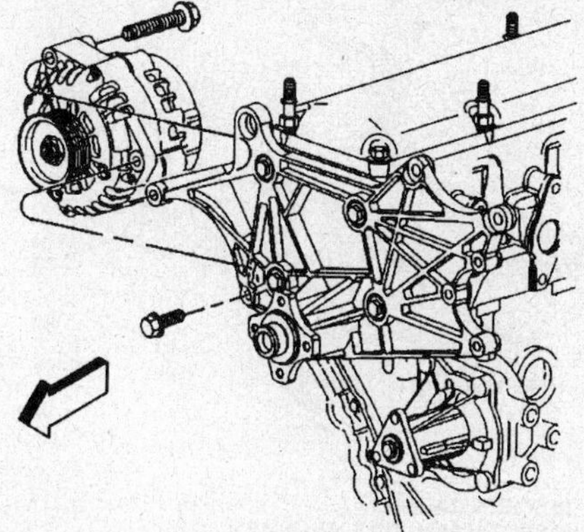

Fig. 4 Alternator removal. 2.2L engine

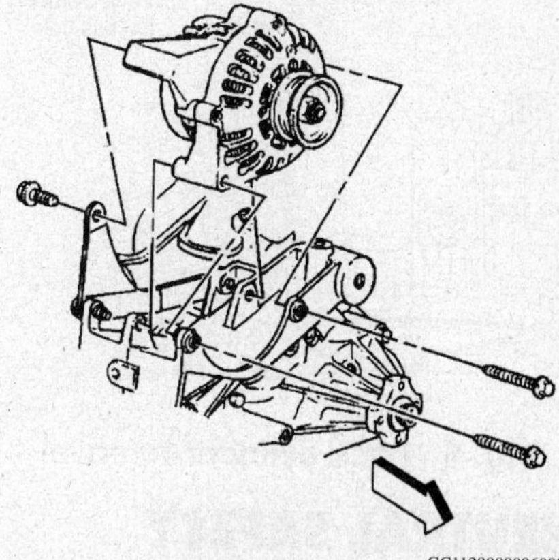

Fig. 5 Alternator removal. 4.3L engine

terminal nut to 15 ft. lbs.
   c. **Torque** A/C compressor mounting bolts to 37 ft. lbs.

4.3L Engine

1. Remove air inlet duct.
2. Remove heater hose brace bolt from rear of alternator.
3. Disconnect alternator electrical connectors.
4. Remove accessory drive belt.
5. Remove alternator mounting bolts, then the alternator, **Fig. 5.**
6. Reverse procedure to install noting the following:
   a. **Torque** front alternator bolt to 37 ft. lbs.
   b. **Torque** rear alternator bolt to 18 ft. lbs.
   c. **Torque** heater hose brace bolt to 18 ft. lbs.

5.3L ENGINE

1. Remove accessory drive belt.
2. Disconnect alternator electrical connector, then alternator cable.
3. Remove alternator bolts, then the alternator from vehicle.
4. Reverse procedure to install noting the following:
   a. **Torque** alternator bolts to 37 ft. lbs.
   b. **Torque** alternator cable nut to 80 inch lbs.

COIL PACK

REPLACE

2.2L Engine

1. Raise and support vehicle.
2. Disconnect ICM electrical connector.
3. Disconnect spark plug wires, mark wires for installation reference.
4. Remove ignition coil to engine bolts.
5. Remove coil assembly.
6. Reverse procedure to install. **Torque** ignition coil to engine bolts to 15–22 ft. lbs.

2.8L & 3.5L Engines

1. Remove air cleaner resonator and outlet duct.
2. Disconnect engine wiring harness electrical connector from oil pressure sensor.
3. Disconnect engine wiring harness retainers from power steering pump.
4. Disconnect exhaust Camshaft Position (CMP) sensor and Camshaft Position (CMP) actuator solenoid valve electrical connectors.
5. Disconnect engine wiring harness retainer from camshaft cover.
6. Disconnect Engine Coolant Temperature (ECT) sensor, fuel injector harness, ignition coils and Heated Oxygen (HO2S) sensor electrical connectors.
7. Disconnect intake Camshaft Position (CMP) sensor electrical connector, then carefully disengage engine wiring harness conduit from camshaft cover and position aside.
8. Remove ignition coil retaining bolts, then the ignition coils from camshaft cover.
9. Reverse procedure to install.

4.3L Engine

1. Disconnect electrical to coil base (ICM), then the coil high tension lead.
2. Remove studs retaining coil base to engine, then lift assembly from engine.
3. Remove heads from rivets retaining coil to base using a suitable drill motor and bit, then punch rivets out using a suitable pin punch.
4. Install new coil to base using screws supplied with new coil.
5. Reverse procedure to install. **Torque** mounting studs to 97 inch lbs.

IGNITION LOCK

REPLACE

1. Remove upper and lower steering column shrouds.
2. Turn ignition lock cylinder to start position.
3. Insert tip into ignition lock cylinder access hole using a suitable awl, **Fig. 6.**
4. Push down and hold ignition lock cylinder retaining pin.
5. Turn lock cylinder to Run position.
6. Pull lock cylinder away from steering column.
7. Reverse procedure to install.

IGNITION SWITCH

REPLACE

Sonoma & S10

1. Remove steering wheel as outlined in "Steering Wheel, Replace."
2. **On models equipped with tilt column,** remove tilt lever.
3. **On all models,** remove two tapping screws from lower column shroud, then the lower shroud.
4. Remove two Torx head screws from upper shroud.
5. Gently pry retaining clip on key alarm switch with suitable screwdriver, then rotate switch ¼ turn and remove.
6. Remove Pass Key connector from lock module assembly, **Fig. 7.**
7. Remove two tapping screws from ignition switch assembly.
8. Remove wiring harness from slot in steering column head assembly.
9. Reverse procedure to install.

Canyon & Colorado

1. Remove lock cylinder as outlined under "Ignition Lock, Replace."
2. Remove steering wheel as outlined under "Steering Wheel, Replace."
3. Remove switch mounting plate from top of steering column.
4. Remove shear bolt from ignition switch and lock housing assembly.
5. Remove ignition switch and lock housing assembly.
6. Reverse procedure to install.

CLUTCH START SWITCH

REPLACE

1. Remove lower instrument panel trim.
2. Remove clutch start switch electrical connector.
3. Remove clutch start switch from clutch pedal.
4. Reverse procedure to install.

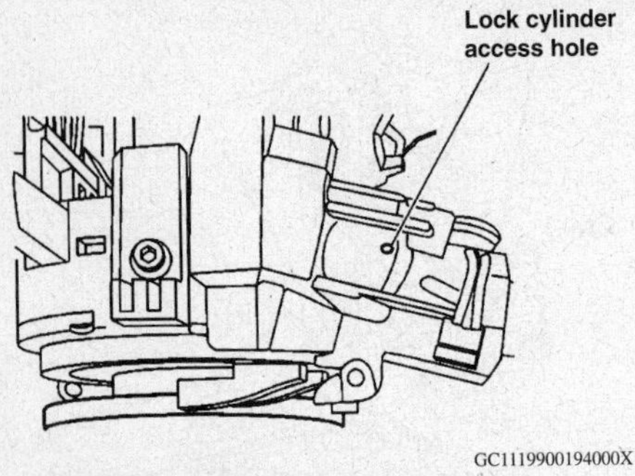

Fig. 6 Lock cylinder removal

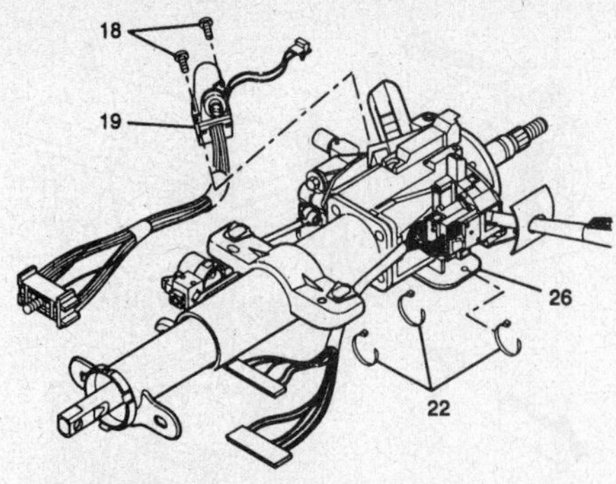

Fig. 7 Ignition switch removal. Sonoma & S10

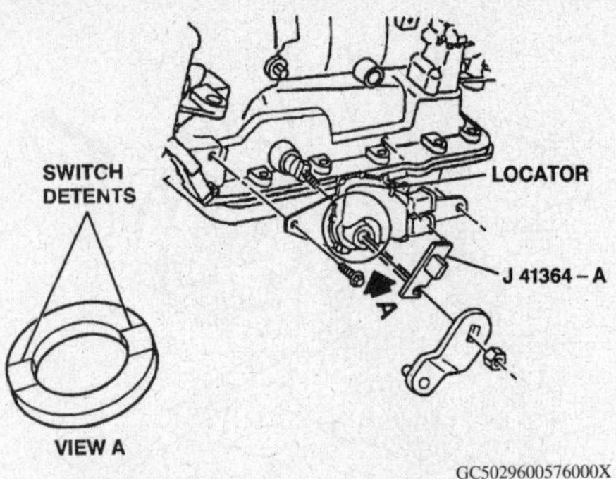

Fig. 8 Neutral safety switch adjustment. Automatic transmission

NEUTRAL SAFETY SWITCH

REPLACE

The neutral start switch also incorporates the back-up light switch in these vehicles.

Automatic Transmission

REMOVAL

1. Place transmission in neutral position, then raise and support vehicle.
2. Remove lever to transmission manual shaft retaining nut, then pull arm from shaft and let hang from shift cable.
3. Disconnect electrical connector from switch, then remove switch to transmission retaining bolts.
4. Slide switch off manual shaft. **It may be required to lightly file end of manual shaft to remove any burrs.**

INSTALLATION

1. Install alignment fixture tool, or equivalent, as outlined in **Fig. 8,** into neutral safety switch.
2. Ensure tabs of tool are fully engaged into switch detents and locator pin is engaged into locator slot on switch.
3. Ensure transmission is in neutral position.
4. Slide switch onto manual shaft, engaging switch to flats of shaft. **It may be required to lightly file end of manual shaft to remove any burrs.**
5. Seat switch against transmission, then install mounting bolts and **torque** to 21 ft. lbs.
6. Remove alignment tool.
7. Install electrical connector switch, then install control arm onto manual shaft, engaging flats of shaft to arm.
8. Install nut to shaft, then while holding arm with a suitable tool to prevent movement, **torque** nut to 21 ft. lbs.
9. Ensure vehicle will start only with shift lever in either Park or Neutral positions.

Manual Transmission

1. Disconnect back-up lamp switch electrical connector.
2. **On 4WD models,** disconnect switch wiring from transmission bracket.
3. **On all models,** remove switch from transmission.
4. Reverse procedure to install.

HEADLAMP SWITCH

REPLACE

1. Ensure headlamp switch is in Off position and ignition switch is in LOCK position.
2. Remove instrument panel accessory trim plate.
3. Disconnect headlamp switch electrical connectors.
4. Remove switch to accessory trim plate retaining screws, **Fig. 9.**
5. Remove headlamp switch.
6. Reverse procedure to install.

STOP LIGHT SWITCH

REPLACE

1. Remove left close out insulator panel from below instrument panel.
2. Disconnect stop light switch electrical connector.
3. Remove pushrod retainer from brake pedal pin.
4. Unsnap stop light switch from pushrod, then remove switch, **Fig. 10.**
5. Reverse procedure to install.

MULTI-FUNCTION SWITCH

REPLACE

1. Remove steering wheel as outlined in "Steering Wheel, Replace."
2. **On models equipped with tilt column,** remove tilt lever.
3. **On all models,** remove two tapping screws from lower column shroud, then the lower shroud.
4. Remove two Torx head screws from upper shroud.
5. Remove two wiring harness straps from steering column wiring harness, **Fig. 11.**
6. Disconnect steering column bulkhead connector from vehicle wiring harness.
7. **On models equipped with column shift,** remove axial position assurance connector from BTSI actuator.
8. **On all models,** remove grey and black multi-function switch connectors from column bulkhead connector.
9. Remove two pan head tapping screws from multi-function switch, then the switch.
10. Reverse procedure to install.

TURN SIGNAL SWITCH

REPLACE

Refer to "Multi-Function Switch, Replace" for turn signal switch replacement procedure.

DIMMER SWITCH

REPLACE

Refer to "Multi-Function Switch, Replace" for replacement procedure.

STEERING WHEEL

REPLACE

1. Remove air bag retaining bolts and air bag after disconnecting air bag wire.
2. Mark relationship of steering wheel to steering shaft.
3. Loosen steering wheel retaining nut two full turns, then carefully unseat steering wheel.
4. Remove horn lead assembly.
5. Remove steering wheel retaining nut, then the steering wheel.
6. Reverse procedure to install. **Torque** steering wheel retaining nut to 30 ft. lbs.

INSTRUMENT CLUSTER

REPLACE

Canyon & Colorado

1. Tilt steering wheel to full down position.
2. **On models equipped with a steering column mounted shift lever,** block wheels and position shift lever in FIRST gear.
3. **On all models,** carefully release clips retaining instrument cluster bezel to instrument panel, then remove bezel.
4. Remove instrument cluster to instrument panel retaining screws.

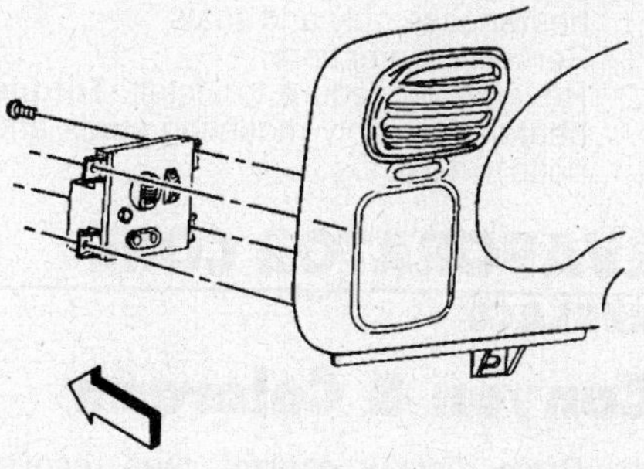

Fig. 9 Headlamp switch removal. Sonoma & S10

5. Partially remove cluster, then position Connector Position Assurance (CPA) arm away from cluster electrical harness. Note position of CPA for installation reference.
6. Disconnect cluster electrical connector, then remove cluster from vehicle.
7. Reverse procedure to install.

Sonoma & S10

1. Remove Data Link Connector (DLC) to instrument panel sound insulator retaining screws, then feed DLC lines through hole in sound insulator.
2. Remove instrument panel sound insulator to knee bolster and cowl panel retaining screws.
3. Disconnect remote control door lock receiver module electrical connectors.
4. Remove remote control door lock receiver module from instrument panel sound insulator.
5. Remove front shift handle retaining clip, then the shift handle from shift lever.
6. Open center console lid and remove console compartment inserts.
7. Remove transmission select switch.
8. Remove center console rear retaining nuts.
9. Remove cup holder insert, then the console front retaining screws.
10. Remove console from vehicle.
11. Remove screws retaining instrument panel sound insulator to knee bolster, instrument panel and heater assembly floor duct.
12. Remove instrument panel sound insulator from vehicle.
13. Disconnect electrical connector from accessory power outlet.
14. Remove park brake release cable from park brake lever.
15. Remove courtesy lamp to knee bolster retaining screw.
16. Remove knee bolster to instrument panel attaching screws, then the knee bolster from vehicle.
17. Remove instrument panel accessory trim plate retaining screws.
18. Release instrument panel accessory trim plate retaining clips.
19. Position instrument panel accessory trim plate in order to remove control switches.
20. Remove instrument cluster retaining screws, then disconnect cluster electrical connector.
21. Remove instrument cluster from instrument panel.
22. Reverse procedure to install.

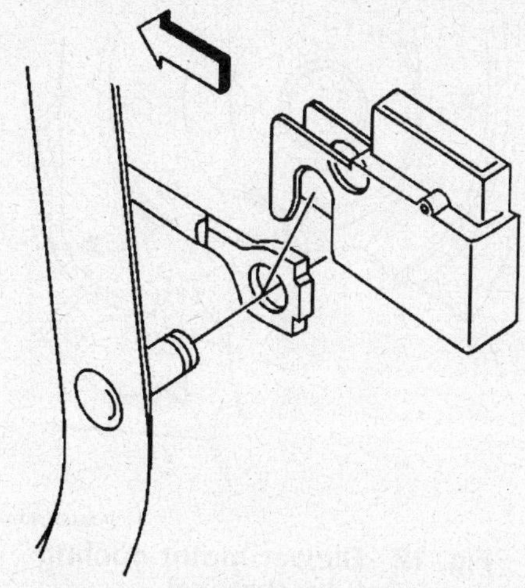

Fig. 10 Stoplight switch removal

RADIO

REPLACE

Canyon & Colorado

1. Carefully release instrument panel trim plate retaining clips using a suitable plastic flat-bladed tool.
2. Pull trim plate from center of instrument panel and disconnect electrical connectors.
3. Remove radio to instrument panel retaining screws.
4. Pull radio from instrument panel and disengage radio rear alignment locator.
5. Disconnect electrical connectors and radio antenna cable.
6. Remove radio from vehicle.
7. Reverse procedure to install.

Sonoma & S10

1. Remove Data Link Connector (DLC) to instrument panel sound insulator retaining screws, then feed DLC lines through hole in sound insulator.
2. Remove instrument panel sound insulator to knee bolster and cowl panel retaining screws.
3. Disconnect remote control door lock receiver module electrical connectors.
4. Remove remote control door lock receiver module from instrument panel sound insulator.
5. Remove screws retaining instrument panel sound insulator to knee bolster, instrument panel and heater assembly floor duct.
6. Remove instrument panel sound insulator from vehicle.
7. Disconnect electrical connector from accessory power outlet.
8. Remove park brake release cable from park brake lever.

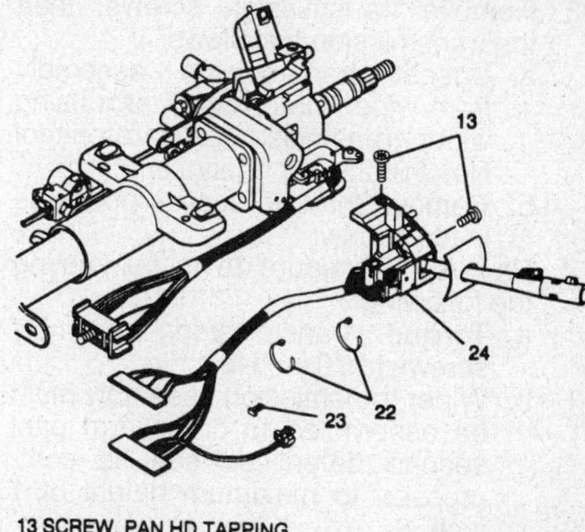

Fig. 11 Multi-function switch removal

9. Remove courtesy lamp to knee bolster retaining screw.
10. Remove knee bolster to instrument panel attaching screws, then the knee bolster from vehicle.
11. Remove instrument panel accessory trim plate retaining screws.
12. Release instrument panel accessory trim plate retaining clips.
13. Position instrument panel accessory trim plate in order to remove control switches.
14. Remove radio mounting screws.
15. Pull radio out of instrument panel, then disconnect electrical connector and antenna lead.
16. Reverse procedure to install.

WIPER MOTOR

REPLACE

1. Remove windshield wiper arms.
2. Remove cowl vent and grille.
3. Remove wiper transmission drive link to motor crank arm attaching nuts, then disconnect drive link from motor crank arm using wiper transmission separator tool No. J-39232, or equivalent.
4. Disconnect motor electrical connector and remove attaching bolts.
5. Remove motor by rotating up and outward.
6. Reverse procedure to install, noting the following:
   a. **Torque** motor attaching bolts to 57 inch lbs.
   b. Install drive link to wiper motor using wiper transmission installer tool No. J-39529, or equivalent.

WIPER SWITCH

REPLACE

Refer to "Multi-Function Switch, Replace" for front wiper switch replacement procedure.

WIPER TRANSMISSION

REPLACE

1. Remove wiper arm assembly.
2. Remove cowl vent grille.

3. Remove transmission screws, then the transmission as follows:
   a. Unseat transmission assembly from wiper motor crank arm using wiper transmission separator tool No. J-39232, or equivalent.
   b. Remove through access openings in top of cowl.
4. Reverse procedure to install, noting the following:
   a. **Torque** transmission assembly screws to 70 inch lbs.
   b. Wiper transmission assembly must be assembled to crank arm past second detent so seal is compressed to maximum height of 1 inch.

BLOWER MOTOR

REPLACE

Canyon & Colorado

1. Remove right front door sill trim plate.
2. Grasp right hinge pillar trim panel and gently pull panel away from body to release fasteners.
3. Slide hinge pillar trim panel forward so panel unhooks from around front door frame.
4. Remove right hinge pillar trim panel from vehicle.
5. Remove blower motor mounting screws.
6. Remove blower motor cooling tube, then disconnect blower motor electrical connector.
7. Remove blower motor.
8. Reverse procedure to install.

Sonoma & S10

1. Remove PCM.
2. Remove coolant reservoir.
3. Remove blower motor cooling tube, **Fig. 12.**
4. Disconnect blower motor electrical connectors.
5. Remove blower motor mounting screws, then the blower motor.
6. Reverse procedure to install.

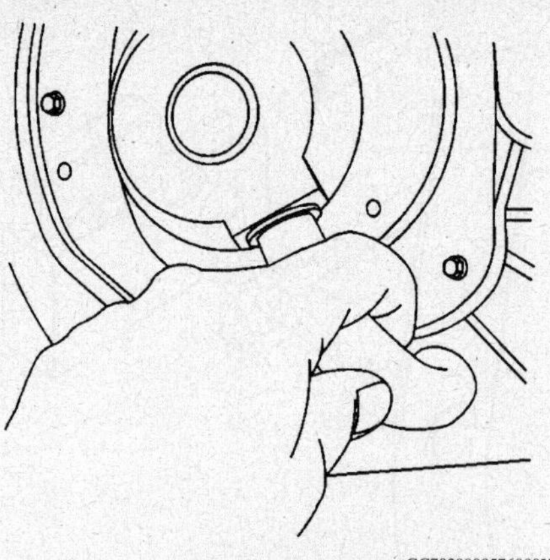

Fig. 12 Blower motor cooling tube removal

HEATER CORE

REPLACE

Canyon & Colorado

1. Drain radiator coolant, then recover A/C system refrigerant as outlined in "Air Conditioning" chapter.
2. Remove instrument panel as outlined in "Dash Panel Service."
3. Disconnect heater hose quick connects from heater core.
4. Remove retaining nut from thermo expansion valve stud.
5. Remove evaporator tube and suction hose from thermo expansion valve.
6. Remove radio antenna from HVAC module and reposition carpet.
7. Remove rear floor duct.
8. Remove HVAC module retaining nuts from cowl.
9. Remove HVAC module assembly.
10. Remove heater core pipes clamps, then the heater core from HVAC module.
11. Reverse procedure to install.

Sonoma & S10

1. Drain radiator coolant, then recover A/C system refrigerant as outlined in "Air Conditioning" chapter.
2. Disconnect heater hoses at heater core, plug core tubes.
3. Remove instrument panel as outlined in "Dash Panel Service."
4. Disconnect air inlet assembly vacuum connectors.
5. Remove air inlet assembly attaching bolts, then the assembly.
6. Disconnect heater assembly vacuum connections.
7. Remove heater assembly retaining nuts from inside engine compartment.
8. Disconnect and remove blower motor resistor.
9. Remove stud inside heater core housing that was exposed when blower motor resistor was removed.
10. Remove rear case screws, then the heater assembly and seals.
11. Remove heater core.
12. Reverse procedure to install. **Torque** heater assembly mounting studs and bolts to 17 ft. lbs.

EVAPORATOR CORE

REPLACE

Canyon & Colorado

1. Drain radiator coolant, then recover A/C system refrigerant as outlined in "Air Conditioning" chapter.
2. Remove HVAC module as outlined under "Heater Core, Replace."
3. Remove screws, then separate HVAC module assembly halves.
4. Remove evaporator temperature sensor control module screw, then position evaporator temperature sensor control module aside.
5. Separate HVAC module assembly.
6. Remove evaporator temperature sensor from evaporator.
7. Remove evaporator core from HVAC module assembly.
8. Reverse procedure to install.

Sonoma & S10

1. Remove hood from vehicle.
2. Remove righthand headlamp assembly.
3. Remove outer fender, battery tray and wheelhouse panel.
4. Disconnect evaporator tube from evaporator.
5. Remove accumulator and evaporator core heat shield.
6. Remove blower motor resistor to access heater core case to bulkhead mounting bolt.
7. Remove heater core case to bulkhead mounting bolt.
8. Remove evaporator and blower module mounting screws and nuts.
9. Remove acoustic barrier.
10. Remove lower right heater core case mounting bolts located at lower right side of instrument panel.
11. **On models equipped with 4.3L engine,** have helper lightly pull lower right corner of heater case away from bulkhead to assist in removal.
12. **On all models,** remove evaporator core assembly from vehicle, then disassemble evaporator core case sections.
13. Remove evaporator core.
14. Reverse procedure to install.

2.2L Engine

NOTE: On Air Bag Equipped Models, Refer To "Air Bag System Precautions" Located In The Front Of This Manual For System Disarming & Arming Procedures.

NOTE: Refer To "Computer Relearn Procedures" Located In The Front Of This Manual When Battery Power To The Computer Has Been Interrupted.

INDEX

PRECAUTIONS

Air Bag Systems

Refer to "Air Bag System Precautions" in the front of this manual for system disarming and arming procedures.

Battery Ground Cable

Prior to service, disconnect battery ground cable and isolate as required.

Fuel System Pressure Relief

1. Turn ignition to Off position, then disconnect battery ground cable.
2. Loosen fuel filler cap to relieve fuel tank vapor pressure.
3. Connect fuel pressure gauge to fuel pressure connection, then install bleed hose of gauge into a suitable container.
4. Open valve on gauge to bleed system pressure.

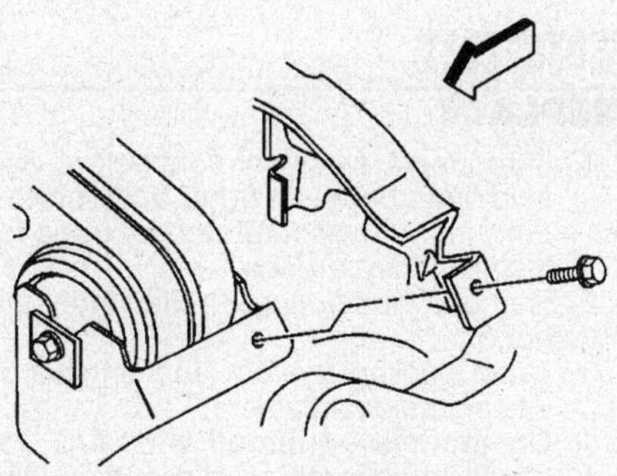

Fig. 1 Left engine mount heat shield removal

Radio Security System

THEFTLOCK

If the Theftlock system is active when battery power is interrupted, the customers security code must be entered to restore proper function of the radio. To unlock a secured radio after power loss, proceed as follows:

1. With ignition in On position, "LOC" appears on display.
2. Press "NM" button and "000" will appear on display.
3. Press "NM" until last two digits agree with security code.
4. Press "HR" button until first digit agree with security code.
5. Press "AM-FM" to select code entered, "SEC" will appear on display indicating radio is now operable and secure.
6. If incorrect code is entered eight times, "INOP" will display. In order to reenter code, the ignition must be left on for one hour before code can be entered and only three more chances to enter code are available before display reads "INOP."

DELCO LOC II

If the Delco LOC II system is active when battery power is interrupted, the customers security code must be entered to restore proper function of the radio. To unlock a secured radio after power loss, proceed as follows:

1. Turn ignition lock to Accessory or Run position.
2. Press "SET" button and "000" will appear on display.

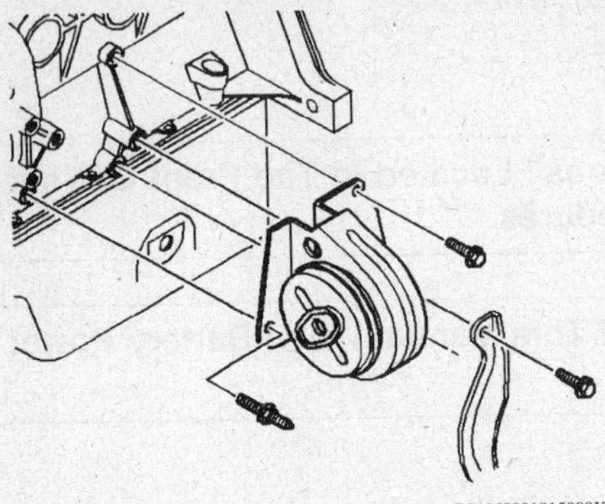

Fig. 2 Left engine mount removal

3. Press "SEEK" button until second and third digits of code appear.
4. Press "SCAN" button until first digit of code appears.
5. Press "AM-FM" button and "000" appears on display.
6. Press "SEEK" button until fifth and sixth digits of code appear.
7. Press "SCAN" button until fourth digit appears.
8. Press "AM-FM" button. If unlock sequence was successful, display will show "SEC," indicating unit is operational. If display shows "LOC," numbers did not match and unlock sequence was not successful.

COMPRESSION PRESSURE

When inspecting cylinder compression, the throttle should be open, all spark plugs removed, the battery at or near full charge and engine at operating temperature. The lowest reading cylinder should not be less than 70% of the highest and no cylinder reading should be less than 100 psi. Turn ignition key until engine cranks through four compression cycles. Normal compression builds up quickly and evenly to specified compression on each cylinder.

ENGINE MOUNT

REPLACE

Left Front

1. Raise and support vehicle.
2. Remove left side transmission brace.
3. Remove starter motor as outlined in "Starter, Replace" in "Electrical."
4. Lower vehicle.
5. Remove engine mount heat shield attaching bolt, then the shield, **Fig. 1.**
6. Install suitable lifting device through eyelet on accessory mounting bracket.
7. Raise engine enough to remove weight from engine mount.
8. Remove engine mount through bolt.
9. Remove engine mount to engine and starter support attaching bolts, **Fig. 2.**
10. Remove engine mount.
11. Reverse procedure to install.

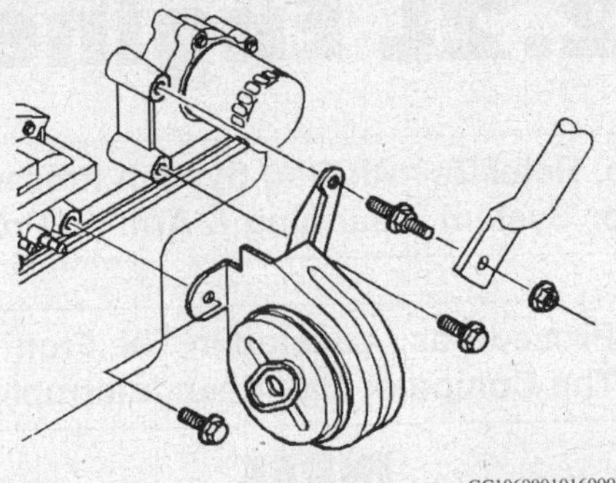

Fig. 3 Right front engine mount removal

Right Front

1. Raise and support vehicle.
2. Remove right fender wheelhouse extension.
3. Remove right side transmission support brace.
4. Remove alternator rear brace from engine.
5. Lower vehicle.
6. Install suitable lifting device through eyelet on accessory mounting bracket.
7. Raise engine enough to remove weight from engine mount.
8. Remove engine mount through bolt.
9. Remove stud and two bolts holding engine mount to engine, **Fig. 3.**
10. Reverse procedure to install.

ENGINE

REPLACE

1. Disconnect electrical connectors and fluid lines between hood and vehicle, then mark position of hood hinges for installation reference.
2. Remove hood hinge bolts, then the hood.
3. Drain cooling system and engine oil into suitable containers.
4. **On models equipped with A/C,** recover refrigerant as outlined in "Air Conditioning."
5. **On all models,** remove transmission as outlined in **MOTOR's "Domestic Transmission, In-Vehicle Service."**
6. Attach suitable lifting equipment to engine, then remove motor mount through bolts.
7. Remove radiator as outlined in "Radiator, Replace."
8. **On models equipped with A/C,** remove condenser, disconnect A/C lines from accumulator to evaporator and compressor, then the support at firewall. Cap all lines and fittings.
9. **On all models,** remove heater hoses from heater core, then disconnect throttle cable.
10. Disconnect power steering lines and drain fluid into a suitable container. Cap all lines and fittings.
11. Remove power steering filler tube.
12. Remove drive belt as outlined in "Serpentine Drive Belt," then the power steering pump and brackets.
13. Disconnect all electrical connectors

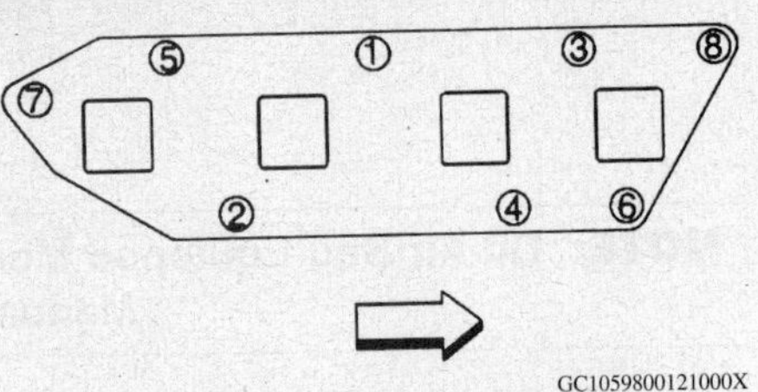

Fig. 4 Intake manifold bolt tightening sequence

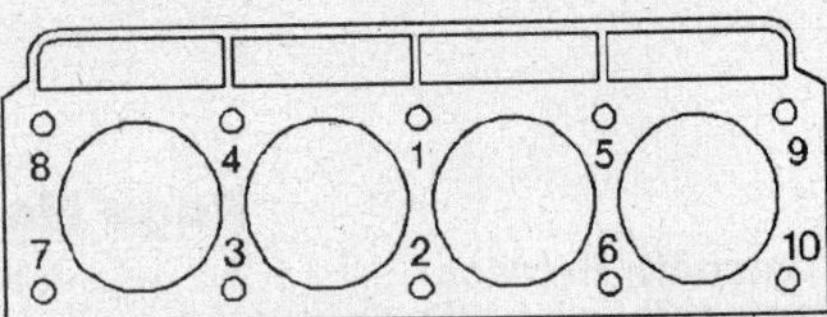

Fig. 5 Cylinder head tightening sequence

and vacuum lines between engine and vehicle. **Mark connectors and vacuum lines for installation reference.**
14. Remove engine from vehicle.
15. Remove clutch and flywheel or driveplate.
16. Reverse procedure to install.

INTAKE MANIFOLD

REPLACE

1. Remove air cleaner outlet resonator.
2. Remove EGR pipe.
3. Disconnect IAC, MAP, TP and fuel injector electrical connectors.
4. Disconnect three vacuum hoses from throttle body.
5. Remove engine harness bracket.
6. Remove transmission level indicator tube.
7. Disconnect fuel system evaporator pipe.
8. Disconnect fuel lines, accelerator cable and cruise control cable.
9. Remove throttle cable support bracket and throttle body.
10. Remove EGR pipe attaching bolts and pipe.
11. Remove intake manifold attaching bolts and nuts, then the fuel rail bracket.
12. Remove intake manifold and gasket.
13. Reverse procedure to install. Using sequence outlined in **Fig. 4,** tighten intake manifold attaching bolts.

EXHAUST MANIFOLD

REPLACE

1. Remove air cleaner and duct.
2. Disconnect oxygen sensor lead.
3. Remove oil dip stick tube.
4. Remove braces from heater hose, power steering pump and air conditioning compressor.
5. Raise and support vehicle.
6. Disconnect exhaust pipe from manifold, then lower vehicle.
7. Remove exhaust manifold bolts, then the exhaust manifold.
8. Reverse procedure to install.

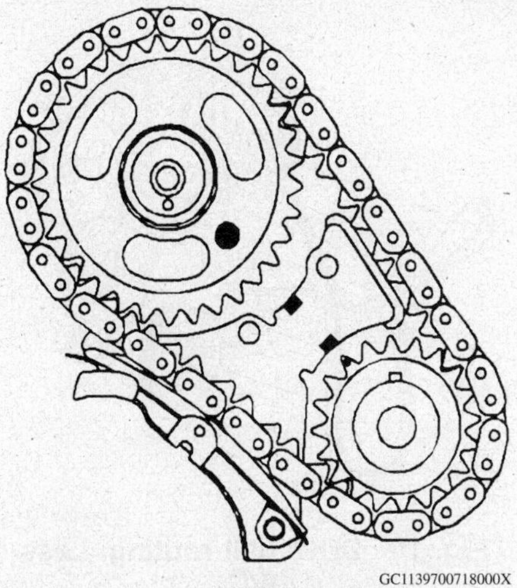

Fig. 6 Timing mark alignment

CYLINDER HEAD

REPLACE

Cylinder head bolts should only be loosened when engine is cold. **Do not reuse cylinder head bolts.**

1. Drain coolant, then remove coolant reservoir tank.
2. Remove air filter housing assembly, then remove fuel vapor pipe assembly. **Place shop towel over fuel line and fitting when disconnecting.**
3. Remove serpentine belt and front timing cover upper attaching bolts.
4. Loosen serpentine belt tensioner and place aside.
5. Remove upper radiator hose, then upper and lower fan shrouds.
6. Remove fan assembly and multiple ribbed drive belt.
7. Remove coolant pump and heater hose from intake manifold and thermostat housing.
8. Remove thermostat housing, then the alternator support brace and wires.
9. Remove power steering support brace, then A/C compressor with brackets and position aside.
10. Remove accessory support bracket with alternator and power steering pump attached. Position aside.
11. Disconnect throttle cable and support linkage.
12. Disconnect heater hose at coolant pump.
13. Remove oil fill tube, then disconnect exhaust pipe and oxygen sensor.
14. Remove exhaust manifold bolts and manifold following procedure outlined in "Exhaust Manifold, Replace."
15. Disconnect wiring and vacuum hoses from intake manifold, then remove manifold following procedures outlined in "Intake Manifold, Replace."
16. Disconnect fuel lines and spark plug wires. **Place shop towel over fuel lines and fitting when disconnecting.**
17. Remove rocker arm cover, then rocker arms and pushrods. Ensure to mark original location of rockers and pushrods for installation.
18. Disconnect engine lift bracket from rear of engine, then remove cylinder head bolts and studs. Remove cylinder head.
19. Reverse procedure to install, noting the following:
    a. Tighten cylinder head bolts in two steps using sequence outlined in, **Fig. 5.**
    b. First step, **torque** long bolts to 46 ft. lbs. and short bolts to 43 ft. lbs.
    c. Second step, tighten all bolts an additional 90.°

VALVE ARRANGEMENT

All .... I-E-I-E-E-I-E-I

CAMSHAFT LOBE LIFT SPECIFICATIONS

Valve lash is obtained through the use of hydraulic lifters. No provision for adjustment is given.

VALVE CLEARANCE SPECIFICATIONS

This engine is equipped with hydraulic lifters. No adjustment is required.

VALVE ADJUSTMENT

Valve lash is obtained through the use of hydraulic valve lifters. No adjustment is required.

VALVE GUIDES

Valve guides are not removable. If valve stem clearance becomes excessive, the valve guide should be reamed to the next oversize and the appropriate oversize valves installed. Valves are available in .00295, .0059 and .00984 inch oversizes.

HYDRAULIC LIFTERS

REPLACE

1. Remove cylinder head as outlined in "Cylinder Head, Replace."
2. Remove lifter retainer and guide
3. Remove hydraulic lifter with a suitable lifter tool and inspect as follows:
    a. Inspect for wear, scuffing and lose roller shaft.
    b. Inspect lifter bore in block for wear and scuffing.
    c. Inspect roller for freedom of movement and flat spots or pitting.
4. Reverse procedure to install.

CRANKSHAFT DAMPER

REPLACE

Removal

1. Remove serpentine belt, then raise and support vehicle.
2. Remove wheel and tire assembly, then the inner fender splash shield.
3. Remove three crankshaft pulley attaching bolts.

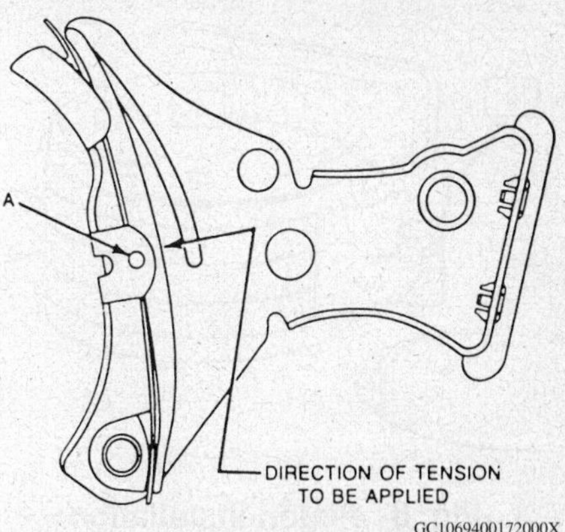

Fig. 7 Timing chain tensioner

4. Remove crankshaft pulley hub bolt, then the crankshaft pulley.
5. Install crankshaft pulley puller tool No. J 24420-B, or equivalent, on hub.
6. Turn puller screw and remove hub.

Installation

1. Coat front cover seal contact area with engine oil.
2. Apply RTV sealer No. 1052917, or equivalent, to keyway in pulley hub.
3. Place crankshaft pulley hub into position over key on crankshaft.
4. Install crankshaft pulley installer No. J 29113, or equivalent, into crankshaft so a minimum of ¼ inch of thread is engaged.
5. Pull pulley hub into position and remove tool from crankshaft.
6. Install crankshaft pulley, then the three pulley attaching bolts.
7. Install inner slash shield, then the wheel and tire assembly.
8. Lower vehicle and install serpentine belt.

FRONT COVER

REPLACE

Cover and seal must be centered to crankshaft. Alignment tool No. J 35468, or equivalent, will hold front cover and seal in correct alignment until front cover screws have been tightened.

1. Remove cooling fan and pulley.
2. Remove serpentine belt as outlined in "Serpentine Drive Belt."
3. Disconnect alternator with brackets and set aside, then remove water pump pulley as required.
4. Remove crankshaft pulley from hub, then hub from crankshaft using puller tool No. J 24420-B, or equivalent.
5. Remove engine and then oil pan as outlined in "Oil Pan, Replace."
6. Remove front cover bolts, then the cover.
7. Reverse procedure to install, noting the following:
    a. Replace front seal, if required, as outlined in "Front Cover Seal, Replace."
    b. If seal was not replaced, position driver/alignment tool No. J 35468,

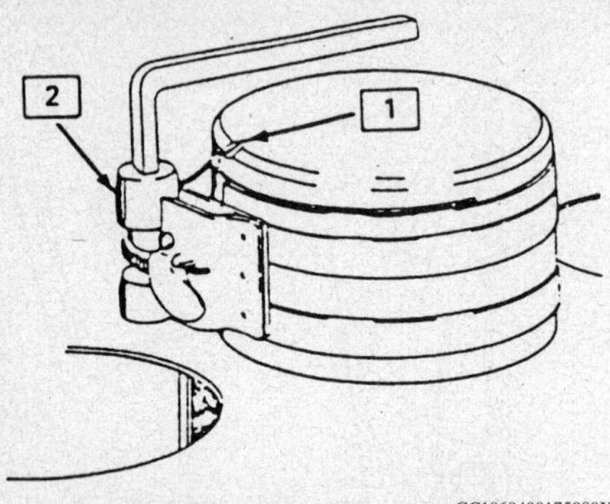

Fig. 8 Piston installation

or equivalent, into seal and leave in position until front cover is installed.
c. Apply 3/8 inch wide by 3/16 thick bead of suitable sealer to oil pan at front cover sealing surface.
d. Apply 1/4 wide by 1/8 inch thick bead of sealer to crankcase front cover at sealing surface.
e. Install crankcase front cover allowing driver/alignment tool No. J 35468, or equivalent, to center front cover.

FRONT COVER SEAL

REPLACE

1. Remove front cover as outlined in "Front Cover, Replace."
2. Pry seal from front cover, using a suitable pry bar.
3. Install new seal using driver/alignment tool No. J 35468, or equivalent. **Leave tool installed in seal until front cover has been installed.**

TIMING CHAIN

REPLACE

1. Remove front cover as outlined in "Front Cover, Replace."
2. Align marks on crank shaft sprocket and camshaft sprocket, **Fig. 6.**
3. Remove timing chain tensioner bolts, but do not remove tensioner.
4. Remove camshaft sprocket bolt, then timing chain camshaft sprocket and timing chain tensioner together.
5. If crankshaft sprocket replacement is required, pull sprocket from crankshaft using puller tool No. J-22888-20, or equivalent.
6. Reverse procedure to install, noting the following:
   a. Install tensioner to engine, compress tensioner spring, then install cotter pin or nail into hole A, **Fig. 7.**
   b. Lube timing chain and sprockets with engine oil, lube thrust surface with camshaft assembly lube part. No. 1052365, or equivalent.
   c. Align marks on camshaft and crankshaft sprockets with tabs on tensioner, **Fig. 7.**
   d. Align dowel in camshaft with dowel hole camshaft sprocket.
   e. Draw camshaft sprocket onto camshaft using mounting bolt.

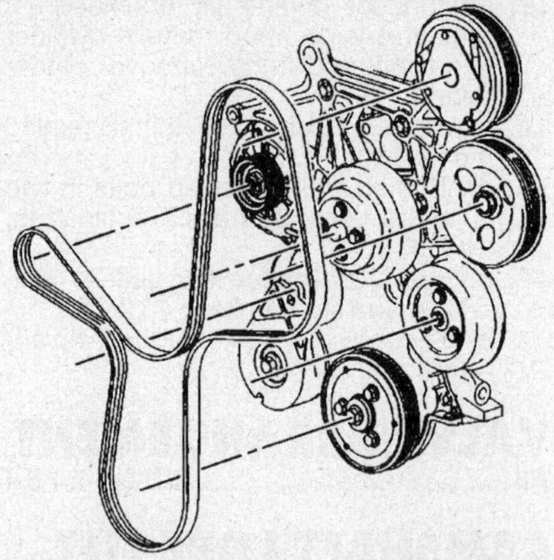

Fig. 9 Drive belt routing. With A/C

CAMSHAFT

REPLACE

1. Remove oil pan as outlined in "Oil Pan, Replace."
2. Remove crankcase front cover and valve lifters as outlined in "Front Cover, Replace" and "Hydraulic Lifters, Replace."
3. Remove oil pump and oil pump drive, then the timing chain and camshaft sprocket as outlined in "Timing Chain, Replace."
4. Remove camshaft thrust plate and camshaft. Use care not to damage camshaft bearings.
5. Inspect camshaft for wear, galling, gouges and overheating. If any of these problems exist, replace camshaft.
6. Reverse procedure to install, noting the following:
   a. Coat camshaft lobes and bearings with camshaft lube part No. 1051396 , or equivalent.
   b. **If a new camshaft was installed, replace all valve lifters.**
   c. Lifters must be installed in bores from which they were removed.

PISTON & ROD ASSEMBLY

Assemble piston to rod, with arrow on piston facing toward front of engine, **Fig. 8.** Upon installation, measure connecting rod side clearance using a feeler gauge. Side clearance should be .0039 to .0149.

Pistons are available in standard size or oversize of .020 inch (.5 mm). Piston pins are available in standard size only.

PISTONS, PINS & RINGS

Pistons are available in standard size and oversize of .020 inch (.5 mm). Piston pins are available in standard size only.

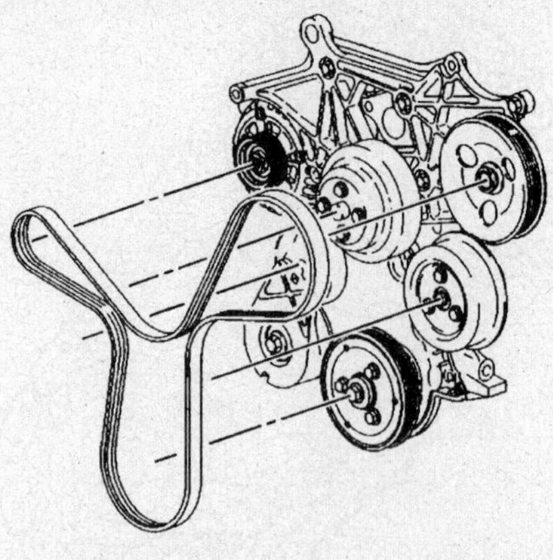

Fig. 10 Drive belt routing. Less A/C

CRANKSHAFT SEAL

REPLACE

Front

Refer to "Front Cover Seal, Replace" for procedure.

Rear

1. Raise and support vehicle.
2. **On models equipped with manual transmission,** remove transmission assembly, pressure plate, clutch and flywheel as outlined in **MOTOR's "Domestic Transmission, In-Vehicle Service."**
3. **On models equipped with automatic transmission,** remove transmission and driveplate as outlined in **MOTOR's "Domestic Transmission, In-Vehicle Service."**
4. **On all models,** pry seal from bore with tool, taking care not to mark crankshaft.
5. Thoroughly clean seal bore in block, inspect bore and crankshaft surface for nicks, burrs and wear and correct as needed.
6. Reverse procedure to install, noting the following:
   a. Apply light coat of clean engine oil to inner and outer surfaces of seal.
   b. Install seal using seal installer tool No. J-34686, or equivalent.

OIL PAN

REPLACE

1. Remove engine as outlined in "Engine, Replace."
2. Install engine into a suitable work stand.
3. Position engine in work stand to allow access to oil pan, then remove oil pan bolts and nuts.
4. Separate oil pan from block.
5. Remove rear oil pan seal and discard, then clean all old sealer from block, front cover and oil pan.
6. Apply a 1/8 inch bead of a suitable RTV sealer to side flanges and front cover

sealing surfaces. **Do not apply RTV to rear pan gasket surface.**

7. Insert a new rear pan gasket, then position pan to engine and install bolts and nuts.

OIL PUMP

REPLACE

1. Remove oil pan as outlined in "Oil Pan, Replace."
2. Remove oil pump to rear main bearing cap bolt.
3. Remove oil pump and extension shaft.
4. Remove extension shaft and retainer, being careful not to crack retainer.
5. Reverse procedure to install.

SERPENTINE DRIVE BELT

Replacement

1. Pivot tensioner and remove belt starting from alternator pulley.
2. Reverse procedure to install.

Routing

Routing belt over tensioner pulley as outlined in **Figs. 9 and 10.**

COOLING SYSTEM BLEED

After filling cooling system, start engine and allow to reach operating temperature with radiator cap removed. Air in system is bleed through radiator cap opening. Add coolant as required to bring to proper level, then install radiator cap and inspect coolant level in recovery reservoir.

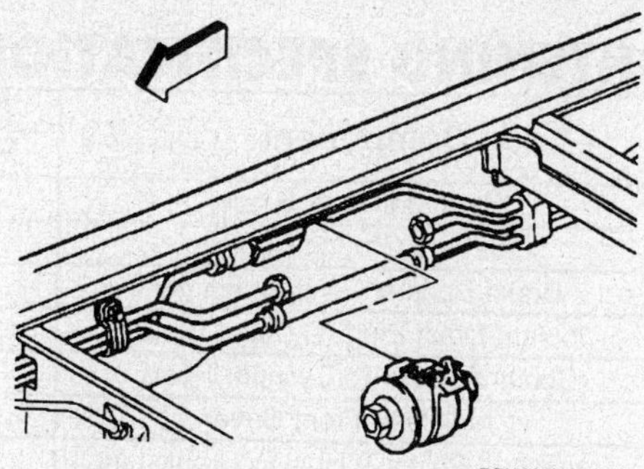

Fig. 11 Fuel filter replacement

THERMOSTAT

REPLACE

1. Drain cooling to level below thermostat.
2. Remove thermostat housing bolt.
3. Remove outlet and gasket.
4. Remove thermostat.
5. Reverse procedure to install.

WATER PUMP

REPLACE

1. Drain coolant from radiator.
2. Remove drive belt as outlined in "Serpentine Drive Belt," then the upper fan shroud.
3. Remove fan, pulley and fan clutch assembly.
4. Remove coolant pump pulley, then radiator outlet hose clamp and hose.
5. Remove bolts and studs, then coolant pump. Discard gasket.
6. Reverse procedure to install.

RADIATOR

REPLACE

1. Drain coolant from radiator, then disconnect upper coolant reservoir hose.
2. Remove upper fan shroud bolts, then the shroud.
3. **On models equipped with automatic transmission,** disconnect and plug transmission fluid cooler lines.
4. **On all models,** disconnect and plug engine oil cooler lines.
5. Raise and support vehicle, then disconnect lower radiator hose.
6. Disconnect heater hose and coolant overflow hose from radiator.
7. Remove radiator.
8. Reverse procedure to install.

FUEL PUMP

REPLACE

1. Relieve fuel system pressure as outlined in "Precautions."
2. Raise and support vehicle, remove fuel tank shields.
3. Drain fuel tank, then support tank with a suitable lifting device and remove bolts securing tank retaining straps.
4. Lower tank enough to disconnect fuel lines, ground and harness connectors, then remove tank from under vehicle.
5. Turn fuel sender unit cam lock ring counterclockwise using cam lock wrench tool No. J 36608, or equivalent, then lift sending/pump unit assembly from tank.
6. Pull fuel pump upward while pulling out from bottom and remove pump from sending unit assembly.
7. Reverse procedure to install. Use new O-ring when installing sending unit in tank.

FUEL FILTER

REPLACE

1. Relieve fuel system pressure as outlined in "Precautions."
2. Remove filler cap and fuel feed nuts from filter.
3. Loosen filter bracket clamp bolt, then remove filter from bracket, **Fig. 11.**
4. Reverse procedure to install.

TIGHTENING SPECIFICATIONS

Year	Component	Torque, Ft. Lbs.
2002–03	Alternator Rear Brace	18
	Battery Ground Cable	13
	Brake Booster Vacuum Fitting	10
	Coolant Drain Plug (Cylinder Block)	11
	Coolant Outlet To Cylinder Head	96③
	Crankcase Front Cover	96③
	Crankshaft Pulley & Hub To Crankshaft	77
	Crankshaft Pulley To Hub	37
	Cylinder Head Bolts	①
	DIS Coil Assembly	18
	Engine Mount Stud & Bolt	41
	Engine Mount Through Bolt	33
	Engine Oil Cooler Line	18
	Exhaust Heat Shield	97③
	Exhaust Manifold Nuts	10
	Exhaust Manifold Studs	10
	Exhaust Pipe To Manifold	18
	Flexplate To Crankshaft, Automatic Transmission	52
	Flywheel To Crankshaft	55
	Intake Manifold (Lower)	17②
	Intake Manifold (Upper)	23
	Main Bearing Cap Bolts	70
	Oil Filler Tube To Cylinder Block	18
	Oil Filter Adapter To Cylinder Block	18
	Oil Pan	89③
	Oil Pump Cover	84③
	Oil Pump Drive Assembly Bolt	18
	Oil Pump To Bearing Cap	32
	Pressure Plate To Flywheel	15
	Rear Engine Lift Bracket	32
	Rocker Arm Cover	89③
	Rocker Arm Nuts	22
	Rod Bearing Cap Nut	38
	Serpentine Belt Tensioner Assembly	37
	Spark Plugs	11
	Timing Chain Cover	96③
	Timing Chain Tensioner	18
	Transmission Fluid Cooler Line Nuts	18
	Water Pump	18

① — Refer to "Cylinder Head, Replace" for tightening procedure.

② — Refer to "Intake Manifold, Replace" for tightening sequence.

③ — Inch lbs.

2.8L & 3.5L Engines

NOTE: On Air Bag Equipped Models, Refer To "Air Bag System Precautions" Located In The Front Of This Manual For System Disarming & Arming Procedures.

NOTE: Refer To "Computer Relearn Procedures" Located In The Front Of This Manual When Battery Power To The Computer Has Been Interrupted.

INDEX

PRECAUTIONS

Air Bag Systems

Refer to "Air Bag System Precautions" in the front of this manual for system disarming and arming procedures.

Battery Ground Cable

Prior to service, disconnect battery ground cable and isolate as required.

Fuel System Pressure Relief

1. Turn ignition to Off position, then disconnect battery ground cable.
2. Loosen fuel filler cap to relieve fuel tank vapor pressure.
3. Connect fuel pressure gauge to fuel pressure connection, then install bleed hose of gauge into a suitable container.
4. Open valve on gauge to bleed system pressure.

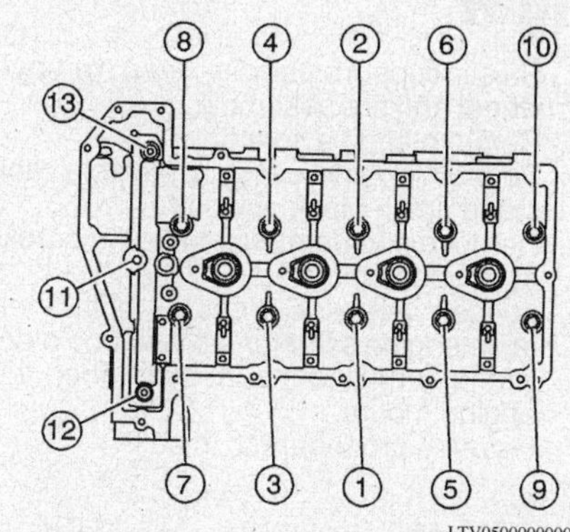

Fig. 1 Cylinder head bolt tightening sequence. 2.8L engine

Radio Security System

THEFTLOCK

If the Theftlock system is active when battery power is interrupted, the customers security code must be entered to restore proper function of the radio. To unlock a secured radio after power loss, proceed as follows:

1. With ignition in On position, "LOC" appears on display.
2. Press "NM" button and "000" will appear on display.
3. Press "NM" until last two digits agree with security code.
4. Press "HR" button until first digit agree with security code.
5. Press "AM-FM" to select code entered, "SEC" will appear on display indicating radio is now operable and secure.
6. If incorrect code is entered eight times, "INOP" will display. In order to reenter code, the ignition must be left on for one hour before code can be entered and only three more chances to enter code are available before display reads "INOP."

DELCO LOC II

If the Delco LOC II system is active when battery power is interrupted, the customers security code must be entered to restore

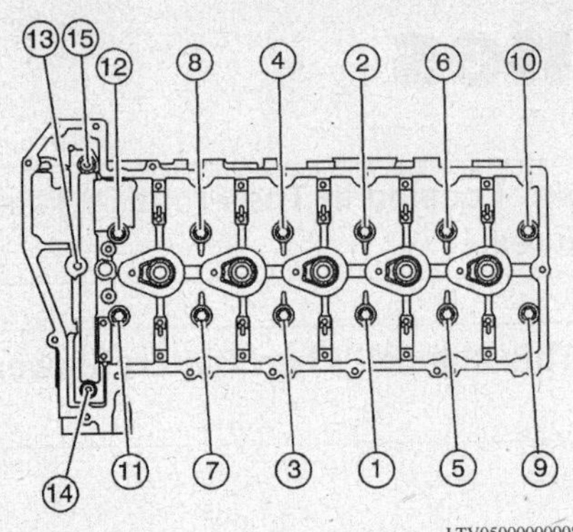

Fig. 2 Cylinder head bolt tightening sequence. 3.5L engine

proper function of the radio. To unlock a secured radio after power loss, proceed as follows:

1. Turn ignition lock to Accessory or Run position.
2. Press "SET" button and "000" will appear on display.
3. Press "SEEK" button until second and third digits of code appear.
4. Press "SCAN" button until first digit of code appears.
5. Press "AM-FM" button and "000" appears on display.
6. Press "SEEK" button until fifth and sixth digits of code appear.
7. Press "SCAN" button until fourth digit appears.
8. Press "AM-FM" button. If unlock sequence was successful, display will show "SEC," indicating unit is operational. If display shows "LOC," numbers did not match and unlock sequence was not successful.

COMPRESSION PRESSURE

1. Remove air duct from throttle control module.
2. Remove the ignition control modules and disable fuel system.
3. Remove spark plugs.
4. Firmly install compression gauge tool No. J 38722, or equivalent into spark plug hole.
5. Crank engine through at least four compression strokes.
6. Check and record readings from gauge tool at each stroke.
7. Disconnect gauge tool and repeat compression test on each cylinder.
8. Record compression readings from all cylinders.
9. Normal reading should be approximately 215 psi (1482 kPa).
10. Lowest reading should not be less than 70° of highest reading.

ENGINE MOUNT

REPLACE

Left

1. Raise and support vehicle, then remove left front wheel and tire assembly.
2. Lower vehicle and remove engine shield.
3. Turn steering wheel so front wheels are pointing straight ahead. Lock steering column by inserting locking pin tool No. J 42640, or equivalent, through access hole in lower steering column trim cover.
4. Raise and support vehicle.
5. Remove steering column upper intermediate shaft to lower intermediate shaft pinch bolt and plastic insert.
6. Disconnect upper intermediate shaft from lower intermediate shaft.
7. Remove lower intermediate shaft to power steering gear input shaft pinch bolt.
8. Disconnect lower intermediate shaft from power steering gear.
9. Remove lower intermediate steering shaft.
10. Support engine using a suitable jack stand and a block of wood.
11. Remove engine mount to frame bracket through bolt.
12. Loosen right side through bolt, then remove heater pipe bracket bolt from engine mount.
13. Raise engine using jack stand, engine will tilt to one side.
14. Remove engine mount bolts, then the engine mount.
15. Reverse procedure to install.

Right

1. Raise support vehicle, then remove wheel and tire assembly.
2. Remove engine shield.
3. Support engine using a suitable jack stand and a block of wood.
4. Remove engine mount to frame bracket through bolt.
5. Loosen left side through bolt, then raise engine so engine tilts to one side.
6. Remove engine mount bolts, then the engine mount.
7. Reverse procedure to install.

ENGINE

REPLACE

1. Disconnect electrical connectors and fluid lines between hood and vehicle, then mark position of hood hinges for installation reference.
2. Remove hood hinge bolts, then the hood.
3. Relieve fuel system pressure as outlined under "Precautions."
4. Remove battery box.
5. Drain cooling system and engine oil into suitable containers.
6. **On models equipped with A/C,** recover refrigerant as outlned in "Air Conditioning."
7. **On all models,** remove outlet radiator hose.
8. Remove cooling fan.
9. Remove air cleaner assembly, air cleaner resonator and outlet duct.
10. Remove alternator as outlined in "Electrical"

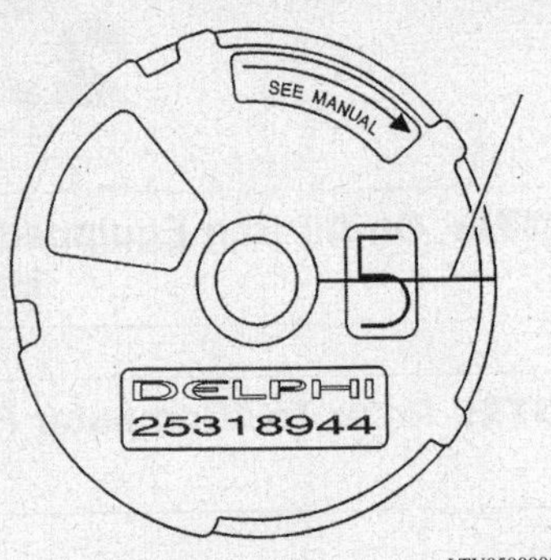

Fig. 3 Exhaust camshaft position actuator alignment

11. Remove radiator inlet hose from water outlet housing.
12. Remove washer solvent container/coolant recovery reservoir mounting bolts to gain clearance to engine wiring harness.
13. Disconnect two engine wiring harness connectors PCM.
14. Disconnect engine wiring harness retainers from the wheelhouse, then open engine wiring harness retainer.
15. Disconnect engine wiring harness retainers from power steering pump.
16. **On models equipped with 4WD,** disconnect electric motor actuator connector.
17. **On all models,** disconnect oil pressure switch, Camshaft Position (CMP) sensor and exhaust camshaft actuator.
18. Disconnect engine wiring harness connectors from Engine Coolant Temperature (ECT) sensor, fuel injector harness, ignition coils and Heated Oxygen Sensor (HO2S).
19. Disconnect engine wiring harness retainer from camshaft cover.
20. Disconnect throttle body connector.
21. Carefully disengage engine wiring harness conduit from camshaft cover.
22. Remove automatic transmission filler tube.
23. Remove studs securing secondary AIR injection (AIR) pipe cover to cylinder head.
24. Remove AIR injection pipe cover and gasket. Discard gasket.
25. Disconnect inlet heater hose quick connect from heater core and secure to engine.
26. Disconnect inlet heater hose quick connect from the heater core and secure to engine.
27. Remove power steering pump mounting bolts, then position pump aside.
28. Remove right engine mount to frame bracket bolt.
29. Disconnect engine wiring harness retainer from intake manifold. Position engine wiring harness aside.
30. Disconnect fuel feed and return pipes from fuel rail.
31. Disconnect EVAP pipe at intake manifold.
32. Remove oil level indicator and tube.
33. Disconnect brake booster hose from brake booster.
34. Remove Manifold Absolute Pressure

Fig. 4 Timing chain tensioner tee installation

(MAP) sensor.
35. Disconnect MAP sensor wiring harness retainer from intake manifold.
36. Raise and support vehicle only high enough to access the wiring harnesses through wheelhouse.
37. Disconnect wiring harness retainers from engine wiring harness bracket.
38. Remove starter solenoid "S" terminal nut and disconnect lead from starter.
39. Remove starter terminal nut and disconnect battery positive cable from starter.
40. Remove bolt securing battery negative cable to engine block.
41. Disconnect engine wiring harness connector from EVAP canister purge solenoid valve.
42. Disconnect engine wiring harness connector from Knock sensor.
43. Disconnect coolant heater cord from coolant heater.
44. Remove bolt securing heater outlet hose/pipe to left engine mount.
45. Remove heater outlet hose from heater outlet hose fitting.
46. Disconnect engine wiring harness connector from Crankshaft Position (CKP) sensor.
47. Raise and suppoprt vehicle.
48. Remove bolts securing engine wiring ground leads to engine block.
49. Disconnect engine wiring harness retainers from engine oil pan rail. Position engine wiring harness aside.
50. Remove left engine mount to frame bracket bolt.
51. Remove nuts securing fuel hose/pipe brackets to transmission.
52. Disconnect fuel hose/pipe retainer from range selector cable bracket, then position aside fuel hose/pipe bundle.
53. Remove crossmember.
54. **On models equipped with 4WD,** proceed as follows:
    a. Remove front propeller shaft as outlined in "Front Wheel Drive" section.
    b. Remove differential carrier assembly bushing to frame bolts, then position differential carrier assembly forward.
    c. Secure pinion yoke to prevent differential carrier from rotating.
55. **On all models,** remove exhaust seal.
56. Remove bolt securing transmission oil cooler pipe bracket to right side of engine oil pan rail.
57. **On models equipped with automatic transmission,** proceed as follows:
    a. Remove inspection plug from transmission, then mark torque converter to flexplate position for installation reference.
    b. Remove service slot plug.
    c. Rotate harmonic balancer center bolt clockwise to access the torque converter bolt through the service slot.
    d. Remove torque converter bolts.
58. **On all models,** remove transmission mounting bolts, then lower vehicle and place suitable jack under transmission.
59. Attach a sutiable engine lift chain to engine lift brackets.
60. Attach a suitable engine lifting device to lift chain and raise engine only enough to remove engine mounts.
61. Remove left and right engine mounts.
62. Raise engine from engine compartment, ensure transmission stays supported.
63. Reverse procedure to install.

INTAKE MANIFOLD

REPLACE

1. Remove air cleaner resonator and outlet duct.
2. Disconnect EVAP canister purge pipe from throttle control module.
3. Disconnect throttle control module electrical connector.
4. Remove throttle control module attaching bolts, then the throttle control module and seal from intake manifold.
5. Remove battery box.
6. Remove oil level indicator and tube.
7. Disconnect brake booster hose from brake booster.
8. Disconnect MAP sensor electrical connector, then the MAP sensor wiring harness retainer from intake manifold.
9. Disconnect PCV dirty air tube from camshaft cover.
10. Remove alternator as outlined in "Electrical" section.
11. Disconnect engine wiring harness retainer from intake manifold.
12. Remove engine wiring harness bracket to intake manifold upper mounting bolts.
13. Raise and support vehicle high enough to access remaining components through wheelhouse.
14. Remove left front tire and wheel assembly, then the wheelhouse liner.
15. Disconnect battery cable, engine harness and MAP sensor harness retainers from engine wiring harness bracket.
16. Remove remaining engine wiring harness bracket bolt, then the bracket from engine compartment through wheelhouse opening.
17. Remove intake manifold attaching bolts, then lower vehicle.
18. Remove intake manifold and seal from cylinder head. Discard seal.

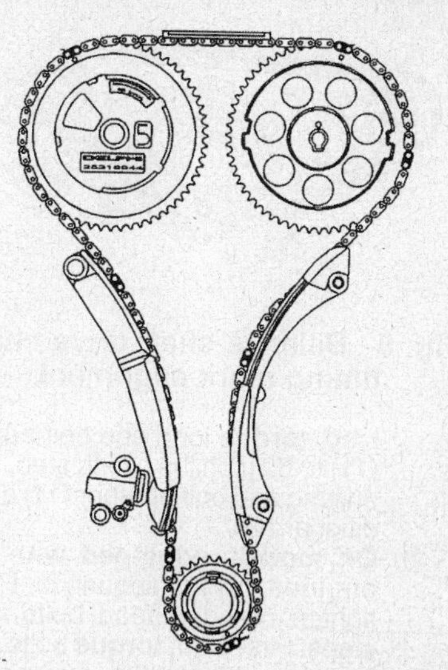

Fig. 5 Timing chain alignment

19. Cover open ports to cylinder head to prevent foreign objects from entering engine.
20. Reverse procedure to install.

EXHAUST MANIFOLD

REPLACE

1. Raise and support vehicle.
2. Remove catalytic converter to the exhaust manifold retaining nuts.
3. Position exhaust system rearward enough to remove seal, then remove seal from exhaust manifold flange. Discard seal.
4. Remove exhaust manifold heat shield retaining nuts, then the exhaust manifold heat shield.
5. Remove exhaust manifold studs and bolts.
6. Remove exhaust manifold and gasket. Discard gasket.
7. Reverse procedure to installl.

CYLINDER HEAD

REPLACE

1. Remove exhaust manifold as outlined under "Exhaust Manifold, Replace."
2. Remove timing chain and sprockets as outlined under "Timing Chain, Replace."
3. Remove and discard cylinder head attaching bolts.
4. Remove cylinder head and gasket. Discard gasket.
5. Remove all remaining gasket material from engine block.
6. Reverse procedure to install, noting the following:
    a. **On models equipped with 2.8L engines,** using sequence **Fig. 1,** tighten cylinder head bolts in six steps: First step, **torque** bolts numbered (1–10) to 22 ft. lbs.; second step, tighten bolts numbered (1–10) an additional 155°; third step, **torque** two short end bolts numbered (12–13) to 62 inch lbs.; fourth step, tighten two short end bolts (12–13) an additional 60°.; fifth

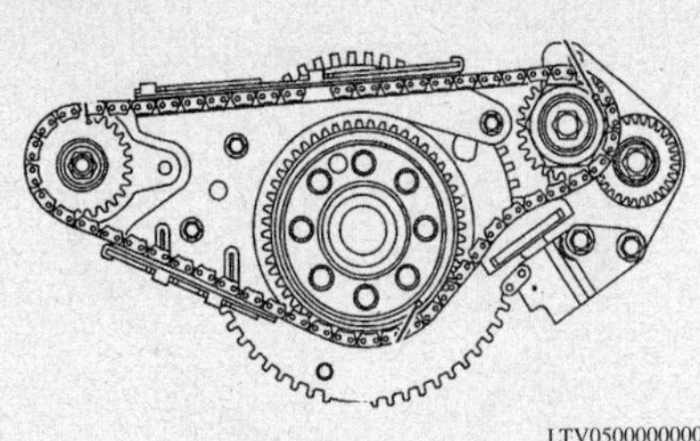

Fig. 6 Balance shaft drive chain timing mark alignment

step, **torque** long end bolt number (11) to 62 inch lbs.; sixth step, tighten long end bolt number (11) an additional 120°.

b. **On models equipped with 3.5L engines,** using sequence **Fig. 2,** tighten cylinder head bolts in six steps: First step, **torque** bolts numbered (1–12) to 22 ft. lbs.; second step, tighten bolts numbered (1–12) an additional 155°; third step, **torque** two short end bolts numbered (14–15) to 62 inch lbs.; fourth step, tighten two short end bolts (14–15) an additional 60°.; fifth step, **torque** long end bolt number (13) to 62 inch lbs.; sixth step, tighten long end bolt number (13) an additional 120°.
c. **On all models,** install timing chain and sprockets as oultined under "Timing Chain, Replace."
d. Install exhaust manifold as outlined under "Exhaust Manifold, Replace."

VALVE COVER

REPLACE

1. Remove intake manifold as oultined under "Intake Manifold, Replace."
2. Remove ignition coils as outlined in "Electrical" section.
3. Disconnect ECT sensor, fuel injector and Heated Oxygen Sensor connectors from camshaft cover.
4. Remove fuel pressure regulator screw to gain clearance to camshaft cover.
5. Remove camshaft cover bolts, then the camshaft cover and seals from cylinder head. Discard seals.
6. Reverse procedure to install.

VALVE CLEARANCE SPECIFICATIONS

This engine is equipped with hydraulic lifters. No adjustment is required.

VALVE ADJUSTMENT

Valve lash is obtained through the use of hydraulic valve lifters. No adjustment is required.

ROCKER ARMS

REPLACE

1. Remove camshafts as outlined under "Camshaft, Replace."
2. Remove valve rocker arms and lash adjusters. Place rocker arms and valve lash adjusters in order so they can be installed in their original locations.
3. Reverse procedure to install.

CRANKSHAFT BALANCER

REPLACE

1. Remove drive belt as outlined under "Serpentine Drive Belt."
2. Raise and support vehicle, then remove service slot plug from under flywheel.
3. Install flywheel holding tool No. EN 46547, or equivalent, into flywheel teeth.
4. Lower vehicle.
5. Remove crankshaft balancer retaining bolt.
6. Remove crankshaft balancer using pulling tool No. J 41816-2, or equivalent.
7. Remove crankshaft balancer friction washer.
8. Reverse procedure to install.

FRONT COVER

REPLACE

1. Remove water pump as outlined under "Water Pump, Replace."
2. Remove crankshaft balancer as outlined under "Crankshaft Balancer, Replace."
3. Remove drive belt tensioner as oultined under "Serpentine Drive Belt."
4. Remove power steering pump as outlined in "Front Suspension & Steering" section.
5. Raise and support vehicle.
6. Remove oil pump pipe and screen assembly as outlined under "Oil Pump, Replace."
7. Lower vehicle.
8. Remove engine front cover attaching bolts.
9. Install two bolts into front cover threaded holes to act as jack screws, then tighten bolts evenly to release front cover from engine block.
10. Remove engine front cover, then the two bolts from jack screw holes.
11. Reverse procedure to install. Apply a .12 inch bead of sealer to engine front cover.

TIMING CHAIN

REPLACE

Removal

1. Remove No. 1 cylinder spark plug.
2. Remove camshaft cover as outlined under "Valve Cover, Replace."
3. Disconnect exhaust CMP sensor electrical connector.
4. Remove exhaust CMP sensor retaining bolt, then the exhaust CMP sensor from cylinder head.
5. Disconnect intake CMP sensor electrical connector.
6. Remove intake CMP sensor retaining bolt, then the intake CMP sensor from cylinder head.

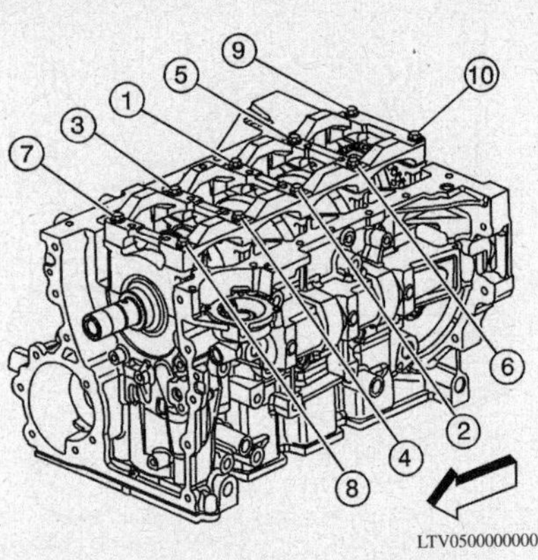

Fig. 7 Crankshaft main bearing cap bolt tightening sequence

7. Remove front cover as outlined in "Front Cover, Replace."
8. Rotate crankshaft in engine rotational direction clockwise, until No. 1 piston is at TDC on compression stroke. The word "Delphi" on exhaust camshaft position actuator should be parallel with the cylinder head to cam cover mating surface, **Fig. 3.**
9. Install camshaft holding tool No. J 44221, or equivalent, to rear of camshafts.
10. Remove timing chain tensioner bolts, but do not remove tensioner.
11. Release tension on timing chain by moving tensioner shoe inward.
12. Place tee into the tensioner to hold the shoe in place, **Fig. 4.**
13. Remove exhaust camshaft position actuator bolt, then the actuator. Discard bolt.
14. Remove intake camshaft position actuator bolt, then the actuator. Discard bolt.
15. Remove intake camshaft sprocket, timing chain and crankshaft sprocket.

Installation

1. Ensure pin on crankshaft for timing chain sprocket is straight up.
2. Install crankshaft sprocket to crankshaft snout.
3. Install intake camshaft sprocket into timing chain, align dark link of timing chain with timing mark on intake camshaft sprocket, **Fig. 5.**
4. Feed timing chain down through opening in cylinder head.
5. Install timing chain on crankshaft sprocket, align dark link of timing chain with timing mark on crankshaft sprocket, **Fig. 5.**
6. Ensure alignment pin is properly engaged with camshaft, then install intake camshaft sprocket onto intake camshaft.
7. Install the new intake camshaft sprocket bolt. Ensure camshaft actuator is fully advanced prior to installation.
8. Install exhaust camshaft actuator into timing chain, align dark link of timing chain with mark on exhaust camshaft

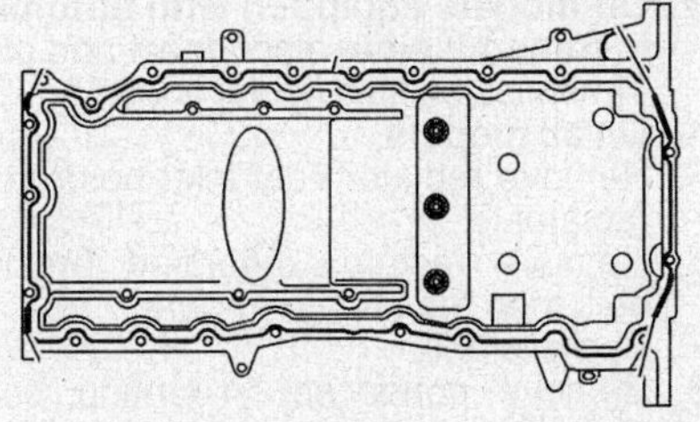

Fig. 8 Oil pan sealant application

position actuator sprocket, **Fig. 5. Engine damage may occur if camshaft actuator is not fully advanced.** Position camshaft actuator in fully advanced position as follows:

   a. Rotate camshaft using a 1 inch (25 mm) wrench on hex of camshaft until alignment pin is properly engaged with camshaft.
   b. Install exhaust camshaft actuator onto exhaust camshaft.
   c. Rotate intake camshaft back and forth (clockwise and counterclockwise) to purge oil out of camshaft position actuator.

9. Remove tee in timing chain tensioner to regain tension on timing chain.
10. Remove camshaft holding tool No. J 44221, or equivalent, from camshafts.
11. Dark links on timing chain should be aligned with marks on sprockets, , **Fig. 5.**
12. Install engine front cover as outlined under "Front Cover, Replace."
13. Install camshaft cover as outlined under "Valve Cover, Replace."

CAMSHAFT

REPLACE

1. Remove camshaft cover as oultined under "Valve Cover, Replace."
2. Remove CMP sensor, then rotate crankshaft clockwise until No. 1 piston is at TDC of compression stroke. The word Delphi on exhaust camshaft position actuator will be parallel with cylinder head to cam cover mating surface, **Fig. 3.**
3. Install camshaft holding tool No. J 44221, or equivalent, onto rear of camshafts.
4. Remove intake and exhaust camshaft sprocket bolts. Discard bolts.
5. Install camshaft sprocket holding tool No. J 44222, or equivalent, onto cylinder head and adjust horizontal bolts into camshaft sprockets to maintain chain tension and keep from disturbing timing chain components.
6. Carefully slide sprockets with timing chain from camshafts to sprocket holding tool.
7. Alternately loosen camshaft cap bolts a few turns at a time until all valve spring pressure has been released.
8. Remove the camshaft caps. Keep camshaft caps in their original positions for installation reference.
9. Remove camshaft holding tool No. J 44221, or equivalent, from camshafts.
10. Remove camshafts from cylinder head.
11. Reverse procedure to install.

BALANCE SHAFT DRIVE CHAIN

REPLACE

1. Remove crankshaft rear oil seal housing as outlined under "Crankshaft Rear Oil Seal, Replace."
2. Rotate crankshaft until 3 of 5 dark links on timing chain align with timing marks, **Fig. 6.** Lefthand balance shaft sprocket timing mark (1) is at 12:00 position, righthand balance shaft sprocket timing mark (2) is at 2:30 position and crankshaft sprocket timing mark (3) is at 4:30 position.
3. Remove balance shaft chain tensioner bolts, then the tensioner.
4. Remove balance shaft chain from balance shaft and crankshaft sprockets.
5. Reverse procedure to install.

BALANCE SHAFT

REPLACE

1. Remove balance shaft drive chain as outlined under "Balance Shaft Drive Chain, Replace."
2. Remove balance shaft retaining bolt.
3. Remove balance shaft.
4. Reverse procedure to install.

PISTON & ROD ASSEMBLY

When installing piston, the alignment mark must face the front of the engine block or the flat casting boss.

MAIN & ROD BEARINGS

Using sequence **Fig. 7, torque** crankshaft main bearing cap bolts to 18 ft. lbs., then an additional 180°.

CRANKSHAFT SEAL

REPLACE

1. Remove crankshaft balancer as outlined under "Crankshaft Balancer, Replace."
2. Pry out crankshaft front oil seal using a suitable flat-bladed tool. Discard seal.
3. Apply engine oil to outside diameter of new crankshaft front oil seal.
4. Install oil seal using seal installation tool No. J 45951, or equivalent.
5. Install crankshaft balancer as outlined under "Crankshaft Balancer, Replace."

CRANKSHAFT REAR OIL SEAL

REPLACE

1. Raise and support vehicle.
2. **On models equipped with manual transmission,** remove transmission assembly, pressure plate, clutch and

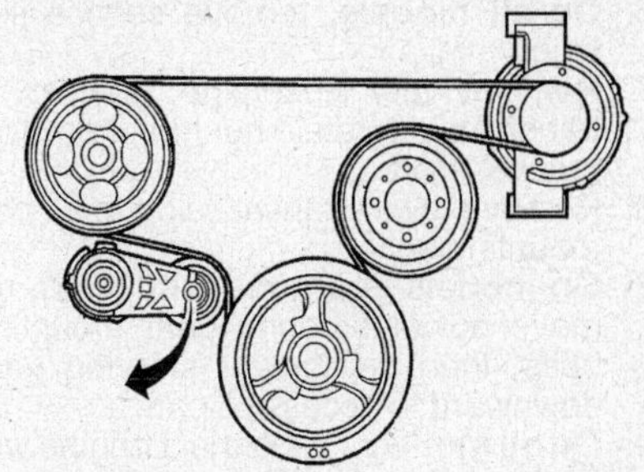

Fig. 9 Drive belt routing. Less A/C

flywheel as outlined in **MOTOR's "Domestic Transmission, In-Vehicle Service" or "Transmission Service DVD."**

3. **On models equipped with automatic transmission,** remove transmission and driveplate as outlined in **MOTOR's "Domestic Transmission, In-Vehicle Service." or "Transmission Service DVD."**
4. **On all models,** remove two bolts securing oil pan to crankshaft rear oil seal housing.
5. Remove crankshaft rear oil seal housing bolts.
6. Install two bolts into threaded holes of crankshaft rear oil seal housing to act as jack screws, then tighten bolts evenly to release housing from engine block and oil pan.
7. Remove crankshaft rear oil seal housing.
8. Remove bolts from jack screw holes.
9. Remove crankshaft rear oil seal from housing using a suitable hammer and punch. Discard seal.
10. Reverse procedure to install, noting the following:
    a. Apply a .12 inch (3 mm) bead of sealer to where crankshaft rear oil seal housing meets engine block and oil pan surface.
    b. Align housing with right alignment dowel, then tilt left side up slightly and align housing with left alignment dowel.

OIL PAN

REPLACE

1. Remove oil level indicator and tube.
2. Raise and support vehicle.
3. Remove engine protection shield, then drain engine oil.
4. **On models equipped with 2WD,** remove power steering gear as outlined in "Front Suspension & Steering" section.
5. **On models equipped with 4WD,** proceed as follows:
   a. Remove front propeller shaft and as outlined in "Front Wheel Drive" section.
   b. Remove differential carrier assembly bushing to frame bolts only.
   c. Pull differential carrier assembly downward and secure pinion yoke to prevent differential carrier from rotating.

6. **On all models,** remove service slot plug.
7. Remove fuel hose/pipe bracket to transmission retaining nuts, position bracket aside.
8. Remove lower transmission to oil pan mounting bolts.
9. **On models equipped with 4WD,** remove power steering gear mounting bolts, then pull power steering gear downward to access oil pan.
10. **On all models,** disconnect engine wiring harness retainers from oil pan.
11. Remove oil pan bolts, then install two bolts in threaded holes at rear of oil pan to act as jack screws, then tighten bolts evenly to release oil pan from engine block.
12. Remove oil pan, then the two bolts from jack screw holes.
13. Reverse procedure to install, noting the following:
    a. Apply a .22 inch bead of suitable sealer to oil pan in areas marked (1), **Fig. 8.**
    b. Apply a .12 inch bead of suitable sealer to oil pan in areas marked (2), **Fig. 8.**

OIL PUMP

REPLACE

1. Remove engine front cover as outlined under "Front Cover, Replace."
2. Remove oil pump cover bolts, then the oil pump cover.
3. Mark relationship between inner and outer gears to oil pump housing for installation reference.
4. Remove inner and outer oil pump gears.
5. Remove oil pump pressure relief valve plug, then the oil pump pressure relief valve and spring.
6. Reverse procedure to install.

SERPENTINE DRIVE BELT

Replacement

1. Rotate tensioner clockwise with a suitable 3/8 inch breaker bar.
2. Remove belt from water pump pulley.
3. Allow tensioner to return to its original position, then remove belt from remaining pulleys.
4. Reverse procedure to install.

Routing

Refer to **Figs. 9 and 10** for drive belt routing.

COOLING SYSTEM BLEED

After filling cooling system, start engine and allow to reach operating temperature with radiator cap removed. Air in system is bleed through radiator cap opening. Add

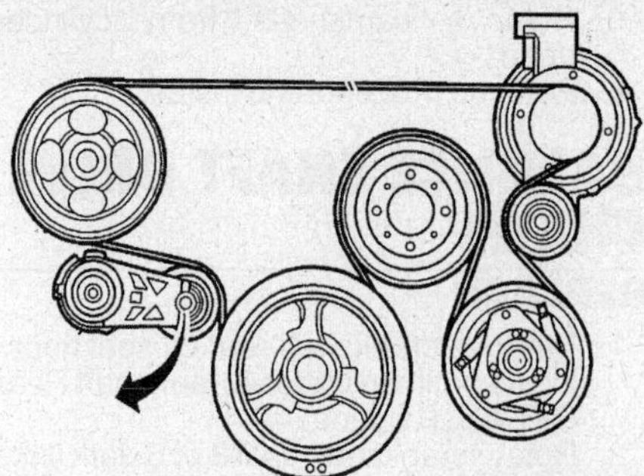

Fig. 10 Drive belt routing. With A/C

coolant as required to bring to proper level, then install radiator cap and inspect coolant level in recovery reservoir.

THERMOSTAT

REPLACE

1. Drain cooling system.
2. Raise and support vehicle high enough to access thermostat housing through wheelhouse.
3. Remove lefthand front tire and wheel assembly, then the left wheelhouse liner.
4. Remove radiator inlet hose from thermostat housing.
5. Remove thermostat housing bolts, then the thermostat housing from engine block.
6. Remove thermostat from housing.
7. Reverse procedure to install.

WATER PUMP

REPLACE

1. Drain coolant from radiator.
2. Remove radiator hose outlet from radiator.
3. Release differential vent hose, A/C suction hose and A/C discharge hose retainers from fan shroud.
4. Rotate slip ring counterclockwise from under fan shroud, then remove fan shroud.
5. Remove fan hub nut in a counterclockwise rotation, then the fan assembly.
6. Remove drive belt as outlined in "Serpentine Drive Belt."
7. Secure water pump pulley with pulley holding tool No. J 4606, or equivalent, then remove water pump pulley bolts.
8. Remove holding tool and water pump pulley.
9. Remove water pump bolts retaining bolts, then the water pump. Discard gasket.
10. Reverse procedure to install.

RADIATOR

REPLACE

1. Drain coolant from radiator, then disconnect upper coolant reservoir hose.
2. Remove upper fan shroud bolts, then the shroud.
3. **On models equipped with automatic transmission,** disconnect and plug transmission fluid cooler lines.
4. **On all models,**
5. Remove radiator vent inlet hose from radiator.
6. Remove radiator mounting bracket bolt, then the radiator mount.
7. Remove grill.
8. Remove condenser mounting bolts and separate condenser from radiator.
9. Remove radiator.
10. Reverse procedure to install.

FUEL PUMP

REPLACE

1. Relieve fuel system pressure as outlined in "Precautions."
2. Drain fuel tank.
3. Raise and support vehicle high enough to access top of fuel tank through wheelhouse liner.
4. Remove lefthand rear wheel and tire assembly, then the left rear wheelhouse liner.
5. Disconnect fuel filler hose from fuel tank.
6. Disconnect EVAP hose from filler vent tube.
7. Disconnect fuel tank pressure sensor and fuel tank module electrical connectors.
8. Disengage fuel wiring harness from retainer on fuel tank.
9. Raise vehicle fully.
10. Disconnect middle of EVAP vapor pipe located between fuel tank and EVAP canister.
11. Disconnect fuel return hose and fuel filter.
12. Remove upper fuel tank strap bolt, then the upper fuel tank strap.
13. Support fuel tank.
14. Remove lower fuel tank strap bolt, then the lower fuel tank strap.
15. Carefully lower fuel tank from vehicle.
16. Rotate cam lock ring in a counterclockwise direction using fuel sender lock nut wrench tool No. J 39765, or equivalent.
17. Remove cam lock ring from fuel tank.
18. Raise module upward from fuel tank, then tilt module to allow fuel level sensor arm and float to clear fuel tank module opening.
19. Remove and discard fuel tank module seal.
20. Reverse procedure to install.

FUEL FILTER

REPLACE

1. Relieve fuel system pressure as outlined in "Precautions."
2. Raise and support vehicle.
3. Disconnect quick-connect fittings from fuel filter. Cap fuel pipes to prevent fuel loss and fuel system contamination.
4. Pry open locking tabs enough to slide fuel filter from fuel filter bracket.
5. Drain any remaining fuel.
6. Reverse procedure to install.

TIGHTENING SPECIFICATIONS

Year	Component	Torque, Ft. Lbs.
2004–06	Air Cleaner Assembly	89③
	Alternator Mounting Bolt	37
	Balance Shaft Retaining Bolt	89③
	Balance Shaft Chain Guide Bolt	89③
	Balance Shaft Chain Tensioner Bolt	89③
	Camshaft Cap Bolt	106③
	Camshaft Cover	89③
	Camshaft Position Actuator Solenoid Valve	89③
	Camshaft Position Sensor	89③
	Connecting Rod Cap Bolt	④
	Crankshaft Balancer Bolt	⑤
	Crankshaft Main Bearing Cap Bolt	⑥
	Crankshaft Position Sensor	89③
	Crankshaft Rear Oil Seal Housing	89③
	Cylinder Head	①
	Cylinder Head Oil Gallery Plug	28
	Differential Carrier To Frame	112
	Drive Belt Idler Pulley	37
	Drive Belt Tensioner Pulley	37
	ECT Sensor	10
	Engine Block Oil Gallery Plug (Front & Rear)	60
	Engine Block Oil Gallery Plug (Side)	26
	Engine Mount Bolt	37
	Engine Mount To Frame	63
	Exhaust Camshaft Actuator	⑧
	Exhaust Manifold Bolt	15
	Flywheel	⑦
	Front Cover	89③
	Fuel Pressure Regulator Screw	71③
	Fuel Tank Strap Bolt	24
	Ignition Coil Bolt	89③
	Intake Camshaft Sprocket Bolt	②
	Intake Manifold Bolt	89③
	Oil Pan Bolt (End)	89③
	Oil Pan Bolt (Side)	18
	Oil Pan Drain Plug	19
	Power Steering Pump To Bracket	18
	Power Steering Pump Bracket	37
	Spark Plug	13
	Starter Motor	37
	Thermostat Housing	89③
	Throttle Control Module	89③
	Timing Chain Tensioner Guide	13
	Timing Chain Tensioner Shoe	18
	Timing Chain Top Guide Bolt	89③
	Torque Converter	37
	Transmission Mounting Bolts	37
	Valve Cover	89③
	Water Pump Bolt	89③
	Water Pump Pulley	18

① — Refer to "Cylinder Head, Replace" for tightening procedure.
② — First pass, 15 ft. lbs.; second pass, an additional 100°.
③ — Inch lbs.
④ — First pass, 18 ft. lbs.; second pass, an additional 110°.
⑤ — First pass, 110 ft. lbs.; second pass, an additional 180°.
⑥ — Refer to "Main & Rod Bearings" for tightening procedure.
⑦ — First pass, 30 ft. lbs.; second pass, an additional 45°.
⑧ — First pass, 18 ft. lbs.; second pass, an additional 135°.

4.3L Engine

NOTE: Refer To "4.3L Engine" In The "Avalanche, Escalade EXT, Sierra, Silverado & SSR" Chapter For Service Procedures Not Covered In This Section

NOTE: On Air Bag Equipped Models, Refer To "Air Bag System Precautions" Located In The Front Of This Manual For System Disarming & Arming Procedures.

NOTE: Refer To "Computer Relearn Procedures" Located In The Front Of This Manual For Computer Relearn Procedures.

INDEX

PRECAUTIONS

Air Bag Systems

Refer to "Air Bag System Precautions" in the front of this manual for system disarming and arming procedures.

Battery Ground Cable

Prior to service, disconnect battery ground cable and isolate as required.

Fuel System Pressure Relief

1. Turn ignition to Off position, then disconnect battery ground cable.
2. Loosen fuel filler cap to relieve fuel tank vapor pressure.
3. Connect fuel pressure gauge to fuel pressure connection, then install bleed hose of gauge into a suitable container.
4. Open valve on gauge to bleed system pressure.

Radio Security System

THEFTLOCK

If the Theftlock system is active when battery power is interrupted, the customers security code must be entered to restore proper function of the radio. To unlock a secured radio after power loss, proceed as follows:

1. With ignition in On position, "LOC" will appear on display.

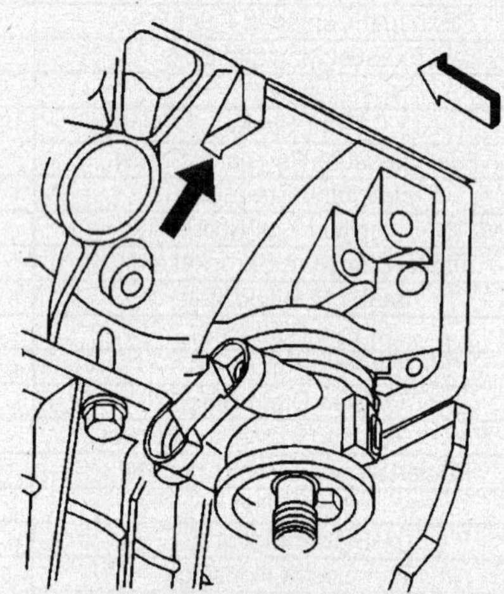

Fig. 1 Engine lifting tab

2. Press "NM" button and "000" will appear on display.
3. Press "NM" until last two digits agree with security code.
4. Press "HR" button until first digit agree with security code.
5. Press "AM-FM" to select code entered, "SEC" will appear on display indicating radio is now operable and secure.
6. If incorrect code is entered eight times, "INOP" will display. In order to reenter code, the ignition must be left on for one hour before code can be entered and only three more chances to enter code are available before display reads "INOP."

DELCO LOC II

If the Delco LOC II system is active when battery power is interrupted, the customers security code must be entered to restore proper function of the radio. To unlock a secured radio after power loss, proceed as follows:

1. Turn ignition lock to Accessory or Run position.
2. Press "SET" button and "000" will appear on display.
3. Press "SEEK" button until second and third digits of code appear.
4. Press "SCAN" button until first digit of code appears.
5. Press "AM-FM" button and "000" appears on display.
6. Press "SEEK" button until fifth and sixth digits of code appear.
7. Press "SCAN" button until fourth digit appears.
8. Press "AM-FM" button. If unlock sequence was successful, display will show "SEC," indicating unit is operational. If display shows "LOC," numbers did not match and unlock sequence was not successful.

ENGINE MOUNT

REPLACE

1. Raise and support vehicle.
2. Remove underbody shields.
3. Remove engine mount through bolt for side being replaced.
4. Raise engine enough to remove engine mount using suitable jack on square tab, **Fig. 1.**
5. Remove bolts from engine mount frame bracket.
6. Remove engine mount frame bracket.
7. Remove bolts holding engine mount to engine, **Fig. 2.**
8. Remove engine mount.
9. Reverse procedure to install.

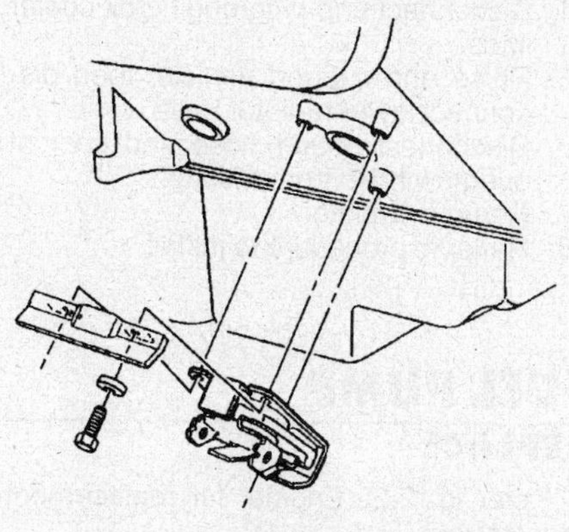

Fig. 2 Rear engine mount removal

ENGINE

REPLACE

1. Mark hood hinges for installation reference, then remove hood.
2. Raise and support vehicle, then drain engine oil and coolant into suitable containers.
3. Remove front air dam, skid plates and underbody shields.
4. Disconnect exhaust from engine, then remove exhaust system from vehicle.
5. Remove engine to transmission braces.
6. **On models equipped with manual transmission,** remove external slave cylinder or disconnect hydraulic line for internal slave cylinder, as outlined in **MOTOR's "Domestic Transmission, In-Vehicle Service" or "Transmission Service DVD."**
7. **On all models,** remove oil filter.
8. Remove fuel line clamp at bellhousing, then the starter as outlined in "Starter, Replace" in the "Electrical" section.
9. **On models equipped with automatic transmission,** remove driveplate to torque converter bolts through starter opening.
10. **On all models,** support engine with a suitable jackstand, then remove bolts for front engine mounts.
11. Remove jackstand from engine, allowing engine to rest on mount brackets.
12. Remove nut from rear transmission mount.
13. Remove all transmission to engine bolts except upper left bolt.
14. **On models equipped with 4WD,** if clearance requires, remove front propeller shaft and/or front axle mount bolts to reposition axle assembly.
15. **On all models,** remove air cleaner assembly, then coolant fan.
16. Remove drive belt as outlined in "Serpentine Drive Belt," then the pulleys for water pump and cooling fan.
17. **On models equipped with A/C,** recover refrigerant as outlined in "Air Conditioning" then remove compressor and bracket. Cap and plug all lines and connections.
18. **On models equipped with oil cooler,** disconnect and drain lines.

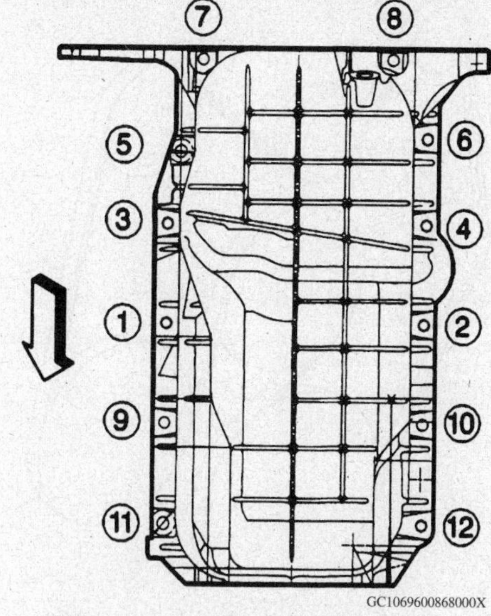

Fig. 3 Oil pan bolt tightening sequence

19. **On all models,** remove radiator as outlined in "Radiator, Replace."
20. Disconnect power steering lines from steering gear. **Cap and plug all lines and connections.**
21. Disconnect all electrical connectors and vacuum lines between engine and vehicle. **Mark connectors and vacuum lines for installation reference.**
22. Relieve fuel system pressure as outlined in "Precautions."
23. Disconnect throttle linkage and cruise control cable, then the fuel lines from engine. Position fuel lines aside.
24. Remove distributor as outlined in "Distributor, Replace" in "Electrical."
25. Pace a suitable support under transmission. **Do not support transmission under oil pan.**
26. Install engine lift bracket set, tool No. J–41427, or equivalent, to right rear and left front of intake manifold, **torque** attaching bolts to 11 ft. lbs. Bracket set is marked for installed location.
27. Attach suitable engine lifting equipment to lift brackets.
28. Remove remaining transmission to engine bolt.
29. Remove engine from vehicle.
30. Reverse procedure to install.

OIL PAN

REPLACE

Removal

2WD MODELS

1. Remove engine as outlined in "Engine, Replace."
2. Remove oil pan bolts and studs. Note stud and bolt locations for later assembly.
3. Remove oil pan and gasket. Discard gasket.

4WD MODELS

1. Remove oil dipstick tube, raise and

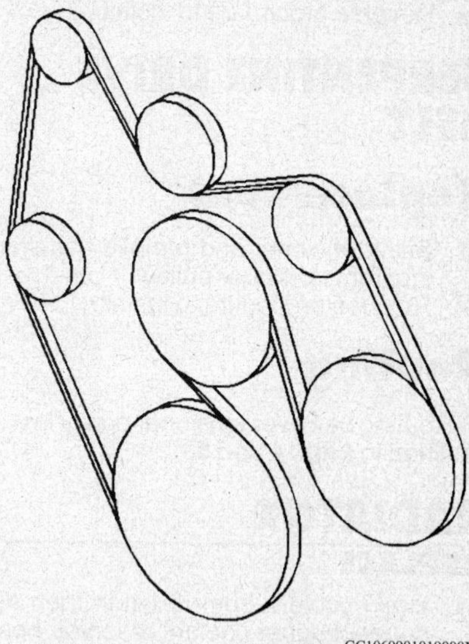

Fig. 4 Serpentine drive belt routing. Less A/C

support vehicle, then drain engine oil.
2. Remove skid plates and underbody shields as equipped.
3. Remove wiring bracket at right side of oil pan.
4. Support engine with suitable lifting equipment, then remove right and left engine mount through bolts.
5. Raise engine for clearance and block into position.
6. Remove remote oil filter adapter and lines from engine.
7. Remove pitman arm and idler arm from steering linkage and vehicle for clearance. **Mark relationship of steering components for later assembly.**
8. Remove front propeller shaft, then front axle through bolts and roll axle forward for clearance.
9. Remove oil pan bolts and studs. Note stud and bolt locations for later assembly.
10. Remove oil pan and gasket. Discard gasket.

Installation

Anytime both oil pan and transmission are removed from engine, transmission must be installed first to allow proper adjustment of oil pan as outlined below.

1. Apply a suitable RTV sealant to four places on oil pan mounting ledge where front and rear engine covers meet block.
2. Install new gasket to oil pan, then position pan to engine.
3. Install oil pan mounting bolts and studs into locations noted on removal.
4. Ensure pan is positioned as far rearward against transmission as possible.
5. Tighten oil pan bolts and studs in sequence **Fig. 3.**
6. Inspect gap between oil pan contact points at bottom of pan and transmission, gap should not exceed .010 inch.
7. If not to specification, repeat removal and installation procedures.

8. Reverse procedure to install.

SERPENTINE DRIVE BELT

Replacement

1. Pivot tensioner and remove belt starting from tensioner pulley.
2. Reverse procedure to install.

Routing

Routing belt over tensioner pulley last as outlined in **Figs. 4 and 5.**

RADIATOR

REPLACE

1. Drain coolant from radiator, then disconnect upper coolant reservoir hose.
2. Remove upper fan shroud bolts, then the shroud.
3. Disconnect and plug transmission fluid cooler lines.

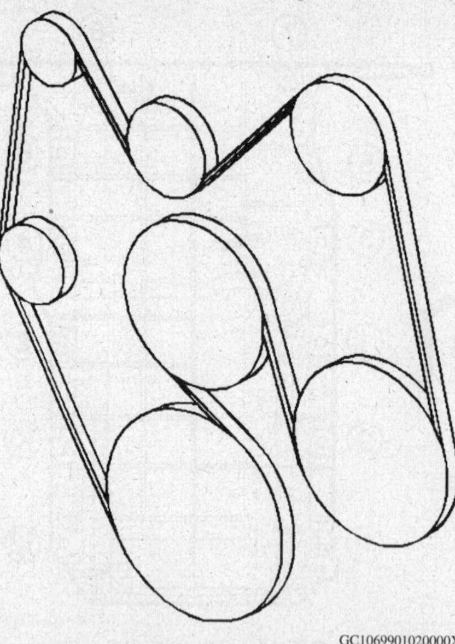

Fig. 5 Serpentine drive belt routing. With A/C

4. Disconnect and plug engine oil cooler lines.
5. Raise and support vehicle, then disconnect lower radiator hose.
6. Disconnect heater hose and coolant overflow hose from radiator.
7. Remove radiator.
8. Reverse procedure to install

FUEL PUMP

REPLACE

Refer to "2.2L Engine" for replacement procedure.

FUEL FILTER

REPLACE

Refer to "2.2L Engine" for replacement procedure.

TIGHTENING SPECIFICATIONS

Year	Component	Torque, Ft. Lbs.
2002–04	Engine Mount Through Bolts	55
	Engine Mount To Cylinder Block	41
	Engine Oil Cooler Line Nuts	18
	Flywheel	74
	Flywheel Housing	32
	Frame Bracket Bolts	33
	Oil Filter Adapter	18
	Spark Plugs	22
	Torsional Damper	70
	Transmission Fluid Cooler Line Nuts	18
	Water Outlet	21

Rear Axle & Suspension

NOTE: On Air Bag Equipped Models, Refer To "Air Bag System Precautions" Located In The Front Of This Manual For System Disarming & Arming Procedures.

INDEX

PRECAUTIONS

Air Bag Systems

Refer to "Air Bag System Precautions" in the front of this manual for system disarming and arming procedures.

Battery Ground Cable

Prior to service, disconnect battery ground cable and isolate as required.

Radio Security System

THEFTLOCK

If the Theftlock system is active when battery power is interrupted, the customers security code must be entered to restore proper function of the radio. To unlock a secured radio after power loss, proceed as follows:

1. With ignition in On position, "LOC" appears on display.
2. Press "NM" button and "000" will appear on display.
3. Press "NM" until last two digits agree with security code.
4. Press "HR" button until first digit agree with security code.
5. Press "AM-FM" to select code entered, "SEC" will appear on display indicating radio is now operable and secure.
6. If incorrect code is entered eight times, "INOP" will display. In order to reenter code, the ignition must be left on for one hour before code can be entered and only three more chances to enter code are available before display reads "INOP."

DELCO LOC II

If the Delco LOC II system is active when battery power is interrupted, the customers security code must be entered to restore proper function of the radio. To unlock a secured radio after power loss, proceed as follows:

1. Turn ignition lock to Accessory or Run position.

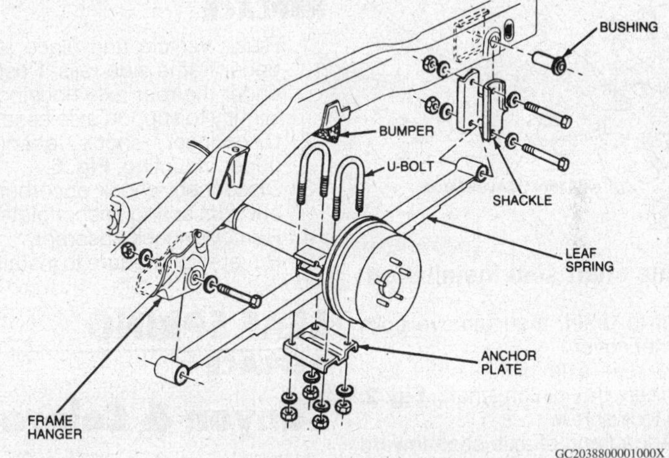

Fig. 1 Rear suspension

2. Press "SET" button and "000" will appear on display.
3. Press "SEEK" button until second and third digits of code appear.
4. Press "SCAN" button until first digit of code appears.
5. Press "AM-FM" button and "000" appears on display.
6. Press "SEEK" button until fifth and sixth digits of code appear.
7. Press "SCAN" button until fourth digit appears.
8. Press "AM-FM" button. If unlock sequence was successful, display will show "SEC," indicating unit is operational. If display shows "LOC," numbers did not match and unlock sequence was not successful.

REAR AXLE

REPLACE

Construction of the axle assembly is such that service operations may be performed with the housing installed in the vehicle or with the housing removed and installed in a holding fixture. The following procedure is required only when the housing requires replacement.

1. Raise vehicle and place jack stands under frame side rails. Position a jack under rear axle housing and raise slightly to support axle assembly.
2. Remove rear wheels, then the drums as outlined in "Drum Brakes."
3. Disconnect shock absorbers from anchor plates.
4. Scribe reference marks between propeller shaft and pinion flange for use during reassembly, then disconnect propeller shaft and position aside.
5. Disconnect brake lines from junction block and backing plates, then remove junction block attaching bolt and position aside.
6. Remove backing plates.
7. Remove U-bolts and anchor plates, **Fig. 1.**
8. Disconnect vent hose from axle housing.
9. Lower rear axle assembly, then remove lower spring shackle bolts.
10. Remove rear axle assembly.
11. Reverse procedure to install.

REAR AXLE SHAFT

REPLACE

1. Raise and support rear of vehicle, then remove wheel and brake drum on side axle is to be replaced.
2. Loosen carrier cover bolts and allow

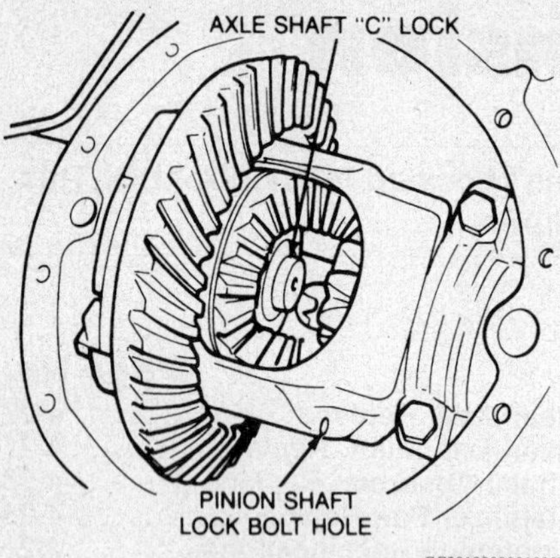

Fig. 2 Differential pinion shaft removal

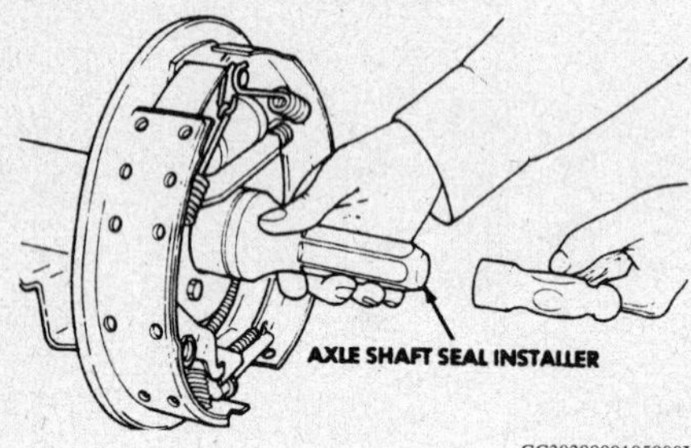

Fig. 5 Axle shaft seal installation

lubricant to drain, then remove bolts and carrier cover.
3. Remove rear axle pinion shaft lock screw, then the pinion shaft, **Fig. 2.** Discard lock screw.
4. Push flanged end of axle shaft toward center of vehicle, then remove "C" lock from button end of shaft.
5. Withdraw axle shaft from housing using caution not to damage seal.
6. Reverse procedure to install.

HUB & BEARING

REPLACE

1. Remove axle shaft as outlined in "Rear Axle Shaft, Replace."
2. Remove axle seal by prying behind seal steel case with a pry bar. Use caution to avoid damaging axle housing.
3. Remove axle bearing using a puller and slide hammer, **Fig. 3.**
4. Lubricate new bearing with gear lubricant, then install bearing in axle housing with axle shaft bearing installer tool No. J-23765, or equivalent, until bearing is seated in housing, **Fig. 4.**
5. Lubricate seal lips with gear lubricant, then position seal on axle shaft seal installer tool No. J-23771, or equivalent

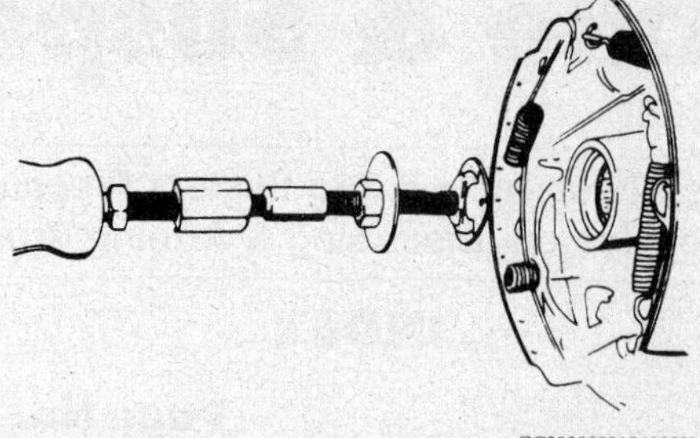

Fig. 3 Axle shaft bearing removal

and install in axle housing, tapping into place until seal is flush with axle housing, **Fig. 5.**
6. Install axle shaft.

SHOCK ABSORBER

REPLACE

1. Raise vehicle and place jack stands under frame side rails. Position a jack under the rear axle housing and raise slightly to support axle assembly.
2. Disconnect shock absorber from upper mounting, **Fig. 6.**
3. Disconnect shock absorber attaching nut from spring anchor plate.
4. Remove shock absorber.
5. Reverse procedure to install.

LEAF SPRING

REPLACE

Canyon & Colorado

1. Raise and support vehicle.
2. Support rear axle with a suitable jack to relieve tension on leaf springs.
3. Disconnect rear park brake cable.
4. Remove shock absorber lower mounting nut and bolt.
5. Remove U-bolt nuts, anchor plate and U-bolts.
6. Remove rear spring hanger bracket nut and bolt.
7. Remove front spring bracket bolt.
8. Remove leaf spring assembly from vehicle.
9. Reverse procedure to install.

Sonoma & S10

REMOVAL

1. Raise vehicle and place jack stands under frame side rails to relieve spring load. Support axle assembly.
2. Remove shock absorber.
3. Loosen, but do not remove, spring to shackle attaching nut, **Fig. 1.**

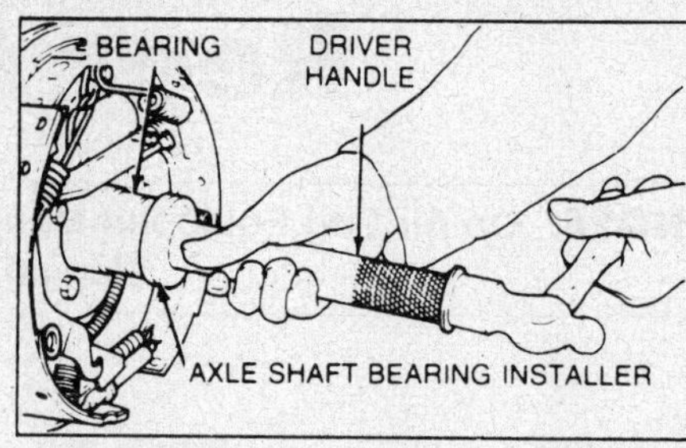

Fig. 4 Axle shaft bearing installation

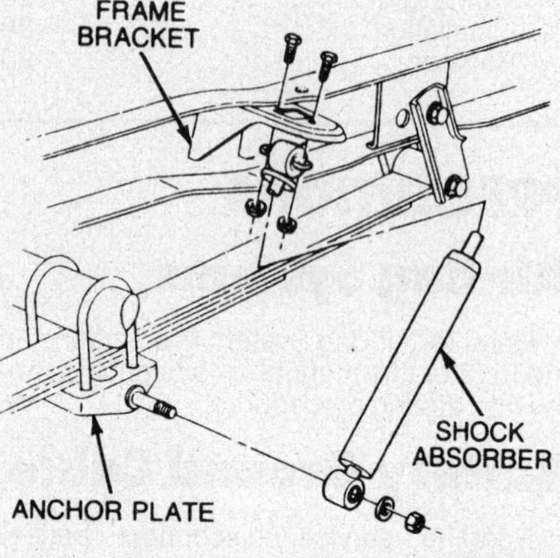

Fig. 6 Shock absorber mounting

4. Remove U-bolt attaching nuts, then the U-bolts.
5. Remove shackle to frame attaching nut and bolt. **After removing shackle to frame attaching nut and bolt, spring is free to rotate on front hanger bolt. Use restraining device to prevent rotation.**
6. Remove front spring hanger nut and bolt, then the spring.

INSTALLATION

1. Clean axle spring pad and apply a rubber lubricant to the bushing and the spring eye.
2. Install bushing to spring assembly.
3. Install spring assembly to vehicle.

STABILIZER BAR

REPLACE

1. Raise and support vehicle.
2. Remove lower nuts, washers and bolts from stabilizer links.
3. Remove nuts from U-bolts.
4. Remove U-bolts clamps and insulators.
5. Remove stabilizer.
6. Reverse procedure to install.

TIGHTENING SPECIFICATIONS

Year	Component	Torque, Ft. Lbs.
CANYON & COLORADO		
2004–06	Backing Plate Bolt	100
	Bearing Cap Bolts	55
	Differential Fill Plug	24
	Differential Housing Cover Bolts	20
	Jounce Bumper Bolts	37
	Leaf Spring To Front Bracket Nut	②
	Leaf Spring U-Bolt Nuts	56
	Pinion Shaft Lock Bolt	18
	Shock Absorber Lower Bolt	70
	Shock Absorber Upper Bolt	26
	Spring Shackle To Frame Nut	63
	Spring Shackle To Leaf Spring Nut	63
	Stabilizer Bar To Lower Link Nut	32
	Stabilizer Bar Upper Link To Frame Nut	32
	Stabilizer Clamp Bolt	37
	Wheel Lug Nut	103
SONOMA & S10		
2002–04	Axle Cover Bolts	22
	Leaf Spring U-Bolt Nuts	74
	Link To Axle	13
	Pinion Shaft Lock Screw	25
	Propeller Shaft Bolts	15
	Shackle To Frame Bolt	89
	Shackle To Front Bracket Bolt	89
	Shackle To Spring Bolt	89
	Shock Absorber Lower Mount	62
	Shock Absorber Upper Mount	18
	Stabilizer Bar Clamp	44
	Stabilizer To Link Bolt	50
	Wheel Lug Nuts	①
	Yoke Nut	25

① — Aluminum wheels, 90 ft. lbs.; steel wheels, 73 ft. lbs.
② — First pass, 59 ft. lbs.; second pass, an additional 80°.

Front Suspension & Steering

NOTE: On Air Bag Equipped Models, Refer To "Air Bag System Precautions" Located In The Front Of This Manual For System Disarming & Arming Procedures.

INDEX

WHEEL BEARING

ADJUST

Sonoma & S10

2WD MODELS

1. Raise and support front of vehicle.
2. Remove hub dust cover, then the cotter pin.
3. While rotating wheel assembly in forward direction, tighten spindle nut to specification to fully seat bearings.
4. Loosen nut to the "just loose" position, then tighten spindle nut finger tight.
5. If either spindle hole does not line up with a spindle nut slot, back off spindle nut not more than ½ nut flat.
6. Install new cotter pin, then measure hub endplay. Endplay should be .001–.005 inches when properly adjusted.
7. Install hub dust cover and lower vehicle.

4WD MODELS

These vehicles use sealed front wheel bearings which require no lubrication or adjustment.

Canyon & Colorado

These vehicles use sealed front wheel bearings which require no lubrication or adjustment.

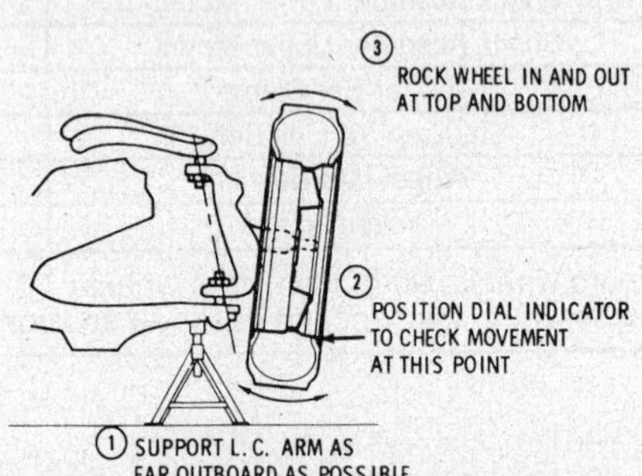

3 ROCK WHEEL IN AND OUT AT TOP AND BOTTOM
2 POSITION DIAL INDICATOR TO CHECK MOVEMENT AT THIS POINT
1 SUPPORT L. C. ARM AS FAR OUTBOARD AS POSSIBLE.
GC2028800019000X

Fig. 1 Upper ball joint inspection. 2WD models

WHEEL BEARING

REPLACE

Canyon & Colorado

1. Raise and support vehicle, then the front wheel and tire assembly.
2. Remove front brake caliper. Support and position aside.
3. Remove ABS speed sensor wiring harness from upper control arm.
4. Remove speed sensor bracket to upper control arm front retaining bolt.
5. Remove speed senor bracket from upper control arm.
6. Mark holes used to mount speed sensor electrical connector for installation reference.
7. Remove speed sensor electrical connector from body.
8. Mark location of speed sensor wiring harness to steering knuckle for installation reference.
9. **On models equipped with 4WD,** remove steering knuckle assembly as outlined under "Steering Knuckle, Replace.".
10. **On all models,** remove mounting bolts for wheel bearing/hub and brake rotor assembly.
11. Remove wheel bearing/hub and brake rotor assembly from steering knuckle.
12. Remove mounting bolt from wheel bearing/hub to brake rotor.
13. Separate wheel bearing/hub from brake rotor.
14. Reverse procedure to install.

Sonoma & S10

2WD

1. Raise and support vehicle, then the front wheel and tire assembly.
2. Remove front brake caliper. Support and position aside.
3. Remove dust cap from rotor.
4. Remove cotter pin, nut and washer.
5. Remove wheel hub and bearing from spindle.
6. Remove outer bearing and seal. Discard seal.
7. Remove inner bearing.
8. Reverse procedure to install. Adjust wheel bearing as outlined under "Wheel Bearing, Adjust."

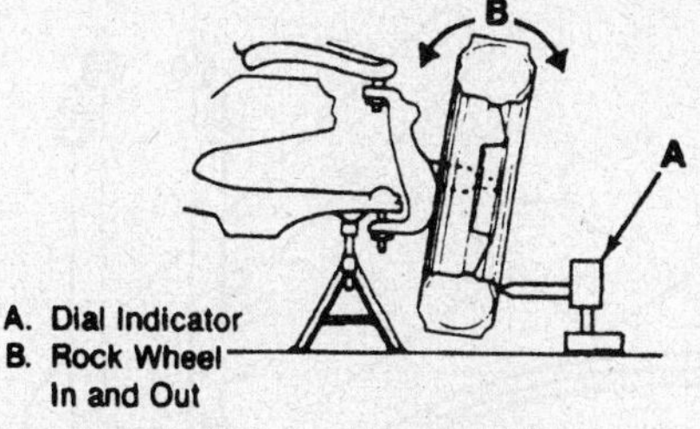

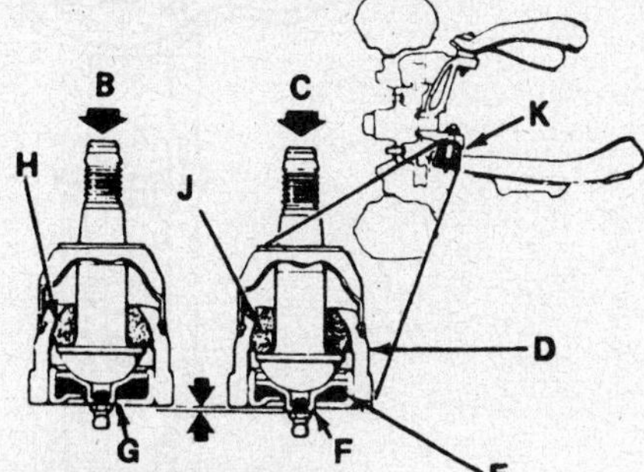

A. 1.27 mm (0.050-inch)
B. Worn Ball Joint
C. New Ball Joint
D. Housing Socket
E. Rubber Pressure Ring
F. Grease Fitting Extended When New
G. Grease Fitting Withdrawn 1.27 mm (0.050-inch) or More When Worn
H. Wear Surfaces
J. Sintered Iron Bearing
K. Joint Location

GC2028800020000X

Fig. 2 Lower ball joint wear indicator. 2WD models

4WD

1. Raise and support vehicle, then the front wheel and tire assembly.
2. Remove front brake caliper. Support and position aside.
3. Install punch in rotor vanes to prevent rotor from turning.
4. Remove drive axle nut and washer.
5. Remove brake rotor.
6. Disengage driveshaft from hub and bearing using axle remover tool No. J 45859, or equivalent.
7. Remove wheel speed sensor mounting bolt from wheel hub and bearing.
8. Remove wheel speed sensor from wheel hub and bearing.
9. Remove wheel hub and bearing to steering knuckle mounting bolts.
10. Remove wheel hub and bearing from steering knuckle.
11. Remove splash shield from steering knuckle.
12. Remove wheel hub and bearing seal from wheel hub and bearing. Discard seal.
13. Reverse procedure to install.

BALL JOINT INSPECTION

2WD Models

UPPER

Before inspecting ball joints, wheel bearings must be properly adjusted.

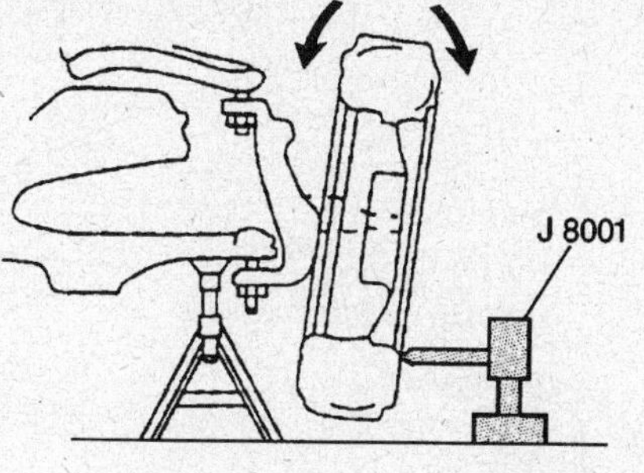

GC2029900250000X

Fig. 3 Ball joint horizontal looseness inspection. 4WD models

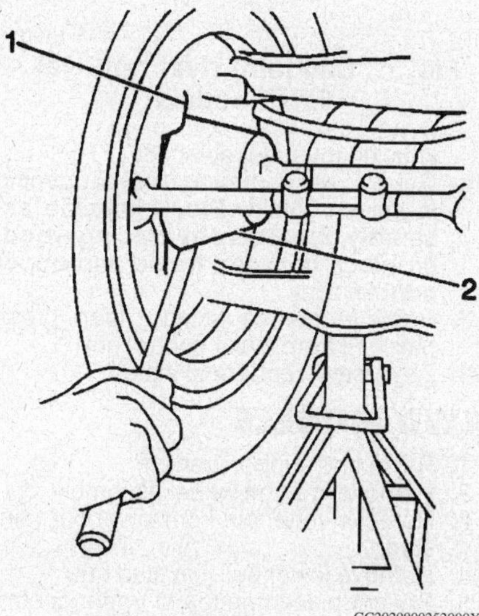

GC2029900252000X

Fig. 5 Ball joint vertical looseness inspection. 4WD models

1. Raise vehicle and position floor stands under right and left lower control arms near each lower ball joint.
2. Position dial indicator against wheel rim, **Fig. 1.**
3. Shake wheel, **Fig. 1,** and read gauge. Horizontal deflection should not exceed .125 inch.
4. If reading exceeds .125 inch or if ball stud has been disconnected from knuckle assembly and any looseness is detected or stud is loose, replace ball joint.

LOWER

The lower ball joint has a visual wear indicator, **Fig. 2.** To inspect, vehicle weight must rest on wheels to properly load ball joints.

4WD Models

1. Raise and support vehicle.
2. Support lower control arm with suitable jack stand.
3. Inspect lower ball joint for horizontal looseness as follows:
   a. Place suitable dial indicator against

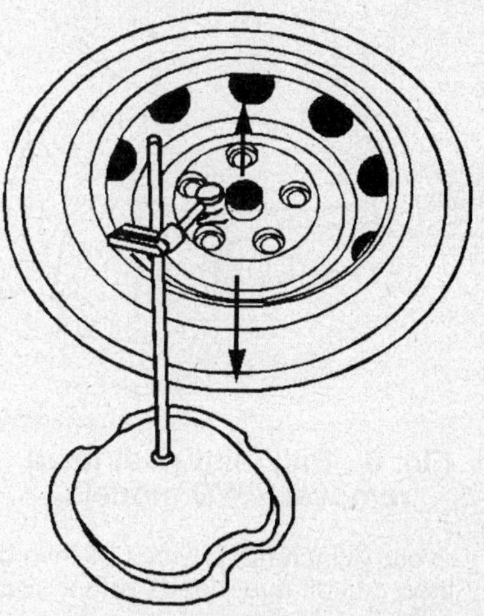

GC2029900251000X

Fig. 4 Dial indicator mounting. 4WD models

wheel rim at lowest outboard point, **Fig. 3.**
   b. Rock wheel in and out while reading dial indicator.
   c. Dial indicator reading should be no more than .125 inch.
   d. If reading is too high, inspect lower ball joint for vertical looseness.
4. Place vehicle on suitable jack stands.
5. Place suitable dial indicator against spindle, **Fig. 4.**
6. Pry between lower control arm and outer bearing race while reading dial indicator, **Fig. 5.**
7. If reading is more than .125 inch, replace lower ball joint.
8. If lower ball joint is within specification and there is too much horizontal looseness, inspect upper ball joint as follows:
   a. Disconnect ball joint from knuckle.
   b. Inspect for looseness by twisting ball joint stud with fingers, if any looseness is found replace ball joint.

BALL JOINT

REPLACE

Upper

2WD MODELS

1. Raise vehicle and support at lower control arm with jacks. **Jack must be positioned between coil spring seat and ball joint of lower control arm to obtain maximum leverage against coil spring pressure.**
2. Remove wheel and tire assembly, then the disc brake as outlined in "Disc Brakes."
3. Remove cotter pin and stud nut from ball joint.
4. Break stud loose from steering knuckle using ball joint separator tool No. J-23742, or equivalent. Support knuckle assembly to avoid damaging brake line.
5. With control arm in raised position, drill

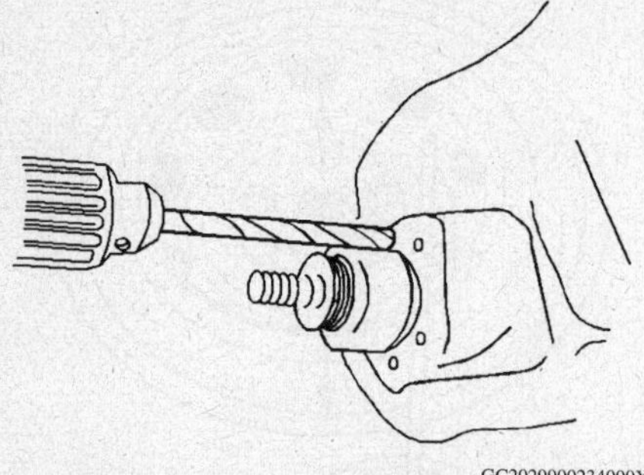

Fig. 6 Ball joint rivet head removal. 4WD models

rivets 1/4 inch deep with a 1/8 inch drill, then drill off rivet heads with a 1/2 inch drill.

6. Punch out rivets, then remove ball joint.
7. Reverse procedure to install. Replace rivets with attaching bolts and nuts.

4WD MODELS

1. Raise and support vehicle.
2. Remove tire and wheel assembly.
3. Remove wheel speed sensor electrical connector from upper control arm.
4. Disconnect wheel speed sensor electrical connector.
5. Remove cotter pin from upper ball joint stud.
6. Remove upper ball join stud nut.
7. Pry bar placed under upper control arm and on top of frame, pry upward.
8. Carefully hammer on steering knuckle in the area of upper ball joint using suitable hammer.
9. Remove upper ball joint from steering knuckle.
10. Drill approximately 1/4 inch hole in center of each ball joint attaching rivet using suitable 1/8 inch drill bit.
11. Drill rivet heads away using suitable 1/2 inch drill bit, **Fig. 6.**
12. Remove rivets using suitable punch, **Fig. 7.**
13. Remove upper ball joint from control arm.
14. Reverse procedure to install. Install upper ball joint retaining nuts and bolts as outlined in **Fig. 8.**

Lower

2WD MODELS

1. Raise vehicle and support with jack stands under frame side rails.
2. Remove front wheel, then support control arm spring seat with a jack.
3. Remove disc brake as outlined in "Disc Brakes."
4. Remove cotter pin and stud nut using ball joint separator tool No. J-23742, or equivalent, then break ball joint loose from steering knuckle.
5. Inspect and clean tapered hole in steering knuckle. If hole is out of round or damaged in any way, steering

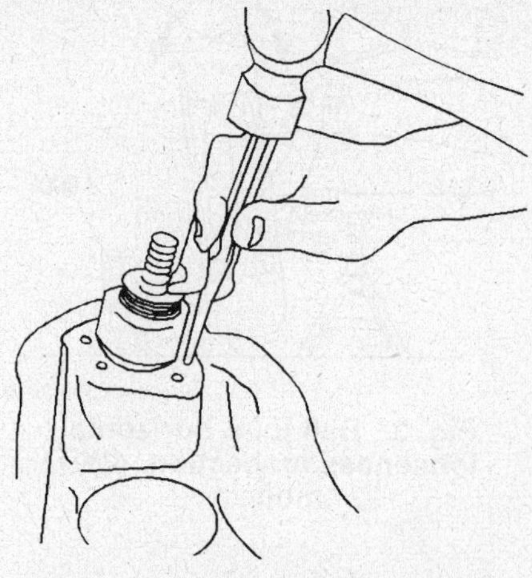

Fig. 7 Ball joint rivet removal. 4WD models

knuckle must be replaced.

6. Guide lower control arm out of opening in splash shield. **Block knuckle assembly out of way by placing wooden block between frame and upper control arm.**
7. Remove grease fittings, then press ball joint from lower control arm.
8. Reverse procedure to install.

4WD MODELS

1. Raise and support vehicle.
2. Remove tire and wheel assembly.
3. Remove cotter pin from lower ball joint stud.
4. Remove lower ball join stud nut.
5. Pry bar placed on top of upper control arm and on bottom of frame, pry downward.
6. Carefully hammer on steering knuckle in the area of lower ball joint using suitable hammer.
7. Remove lower ball joint from steering knuckle.
8. Drill approximately 1/4 inch hole in center of each ball joint attaching rivet using suitable 1/8 inch drill bit.
9. Drill rivet heads away using suitable 1/2 inch drill bit, **Fig. 6.**
10. Remove rivets using suitable punch, **Fig. 7.**
11. Remove lower ball joint from control arm.
12. Reverse procedure to install. Install lower ball joint retaining nuts and bolts as outlined in **Fig. 8.**

COIL SPRING

REPLACE

Canyon & Colorado

1. Remove shock absorber as outlined under "Shock Absorber, Replace."
2. Remove spring and mounting plate from spring compressor tool.
3. Reverse procedure to install.

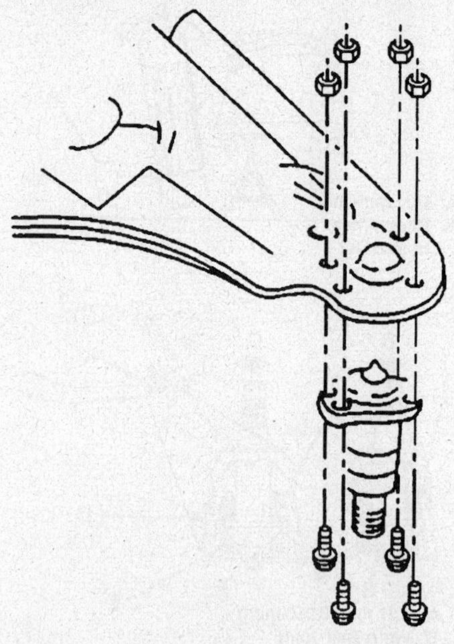

Fig. 8 Ball joint installation. 4WD models

Sonoma & S10

1. Raise and support vehicle.
2. Remove two shock absorber screws and push shock up through control arm and into spring.
3. Support vehicle so that control arms hang free.
4. Place coil spring replacement tool No. J-23028–01, or equivalent, into position cradling the inner bushings, **Fig. 9.** Tool should be secured to a jack.
5. Remove stabilizer to lower control arm attachment.
6. Raise the jack to remove tension on lower control arm pivot bolts, then install a chain around spring and through control arm and remove the nuts and bolts.
7. Lower control arm by slowly lowering jack.
8. With all pressure removed from spring, remove safety chain and spring. **Do not apply force to lower control arm and ball joint to remove spring. Proper maneuvering of spring will allow for easy removal.**
9. Reverse procedure to install, noting the following:
   a. Ensure coil spring is installed with flat coiled end with gripper notch on top and the lower coil covering all or part of one drain hole in lower control arm and with other hole exposed.
   b. Install both lower control arm bolts from front to rear to ensure adequate steering linkage clearance.
   c. Tighten stabilizer link nuts, lower vehicle and tighten lower control arm bolt nuts, after suspension has

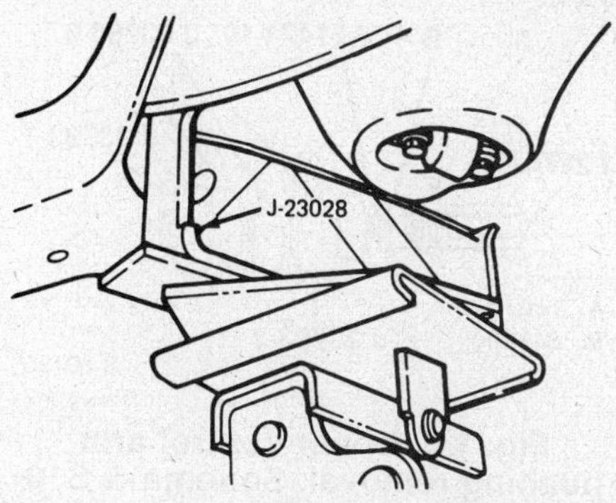

Fig. 9 Coil spring removal. Sonoma & S10

been weighted.

SHOCK ABSORBER

REPLACE

Canyon & Colorado

2WD MODELS

1. Remove absorber/spring assembly upper mounting nuts.
2. Raise and support vehicle, then remove tire and wheel assembly.
3. Remove shock absorber/spring assembly bolt and nut.
4. Remove front stabilizer link.
5. Remove shock absorber/spring assembly from vehicle.
6. Install absorber/spring assembly into spring compressor tool No. J 45400, or equivalent.
7. Turn spring compressor forcing screw until coil spring is compressed.
8. Remove shock absorber upper retaining nut, bushings and washers.
9. Remove shock absorber from assembly. Do not remove spring from compressor tool.
10. Reverse procedure to install.

4WD MODELS

1. Raise and support vehicle.
2. Support lower control arm with a suitable jack stand.
3. Hold tennon end of shock absorber with a suitable wrench while removing upper nut.
4. Remove upper insulator. Do not discard plastic pilot ring.
5. Remove shock absorber to lower control arm mounting bolts.
6. Remove shock absorber through lower control arm.
7. Reverse procedure to install.

Sonoma & S10

2WD MODELS

1. Raise and support vehicle.
2. Hold shock upper stem from turning with a wrench, then remove nut, retainer and grommet.
3. Remove lower shock pivot bolts, then the shock absorber from vehicle.
4. Reverse procedure to install.

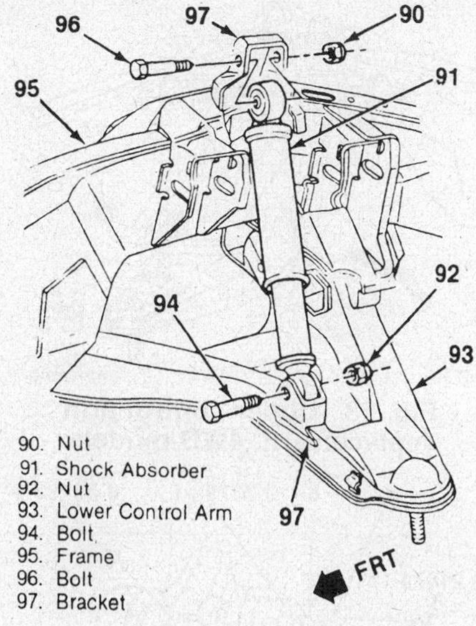

Fig. 10 Shock absorber replacement. Sonoma & S10 w/4WD

4WD MODELS

Refer to **Fig. 10** for shock absorber replacement procedure on 4WD vehicles.

CONTROL ARM

REPLACE

Canyon & Colorado

LOWER

2WD MODELS

1. Raise and support vehicle, then remove tire and wheel assembly.
2. Remove stabilizer shaft links from lower control arm.
3. Remove shock absorber nut and through bolt.
4. Remove lower ball joint stud nut, then separate lower ball joint stud from steering knuckle using joint separator tool No. J 43631, or equivalent.
5. Remove lower control arm nuts and alignment cams.
6. Remove lower control arm bolts, then the lower control arm.
7. Reverse procedure to install, noting the following:
   a. Lower control arm fasteners must be tightened in sequence: First **torque** rear nut 114 ft. lbs.; second **torque** front nut to 114 ft. lbs.
   b. Check wheel alignment as outlined in "Wheel Alignment" section.

4WD MODELS

1. Raise and support vehicle.
2. Remove steering knuckle as outlined under "Steering Knuckle, Replace."
3. Remove stabilizer shaft links from lower control arm.
4. Remove shock absorber nut and through bolt.

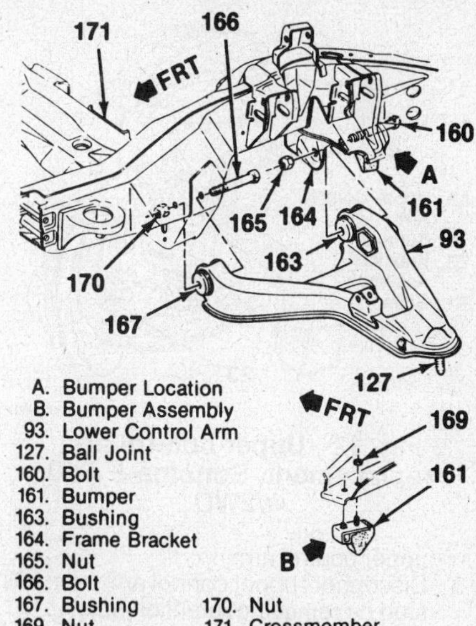

Fig. 11 Lower control arm replacement. 4WD models

5. Remove torsion bar as outlined under "Torsion Bar, Replace."
6. Remove lower control arm nuts and washers.
7. Remove lower control arm bolts, then the lower control arm.
8. Reverse procedure to install, noting the following:
   a. Lower control arm fasteners must be tightened in sequence: First **torque** rear nut 133 ft. lbs.; second **torque** front nut to 122 ft. lbs.
   b. Check wheel alignment as outlined in "Wheel Alignment" section.

UPPER

2WD MODELS

1. Raise and support vehicle, then remove tire and wheel assembly.
2. Support lower control arm at ride height with a suitable jack.
3. Remove wheel speed sensor bracket bolt.
4. Disconnect wheel speed sensor brackets, then the front brake hose from upper control arm.
5. Remove nut at upper ball joint. Discard nut.
6. Remove upper control arm bolts, then disconnect upper control arm from steering knuckle using ball joint separator tool No. J 6627-A, or equivalent.
7. Remove upper control arm.
8. Reverse procedure to install. Check wheel alignment as outlined in "Wheel Alignment" section.

4WD MODELS

1. Raise and support vehicle, then remove tire and wheel assembly.
2. Support lower control arm at ride height with a suitable jack.
3. Remove wheel speed sensor bracket bolt, then disconnect wheel speed sensor brackets.
4. Disconnect front brake hose from

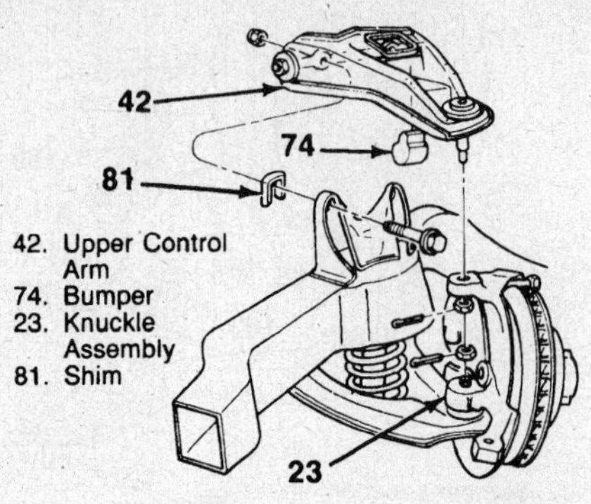

Fig. 12 Upper control arm replacement. Sonoma & S10 w/2WD

upper control arm.
5. Disconnect upper control arm from ball stud by removing retention nuts.
6. Remove upper control arm nuts and adjustment cams.
7. Remove upper control arm bolts, then the upper control arm.
8. Reverse procedure to install. Check wheel alignment as outlined in "Wheel Alignment" section.

Sonoma & S10

LOWER

2WD MODELS

1. Remove coil spring as outlined in "Coil Spring, Replace."
2. Remove lower ball joint stud, then remove lower control arm through opening in splash shield.
3. Reverse procedure to install.

4WD MODELS

Refer to **Fig. 11** for lower control arm replacement procedure on 4WD vehicles.

UPPER

2WD MODELS

1. Raise vehicle and support.
2. Support lower control arms with floor stands.
3. Remove wheel and tire assembly.
4. Disconnect upper ball joint from steering knuckle and support brake rotor to prevent damage to brake hose.
5. Remove upper control arm attaching nuts and bolts, **Fig. 12,** noting location of any shims removed.
6. Remove upper control arm.
7. Reverse procedure to install, noting the following:
   a. Install shims in their original position.
   b. Tighten control arm pivot nuts.

4WD MODELS

1. Raise vehicle and support.
2. Support at frame and raise lower control arm to relieve spring tension, placing jack stand as far out board on lower control arm as possible.
3. Remove front tire and wheel assembly.
4. Remove control arm, **Fig. 13.** Support

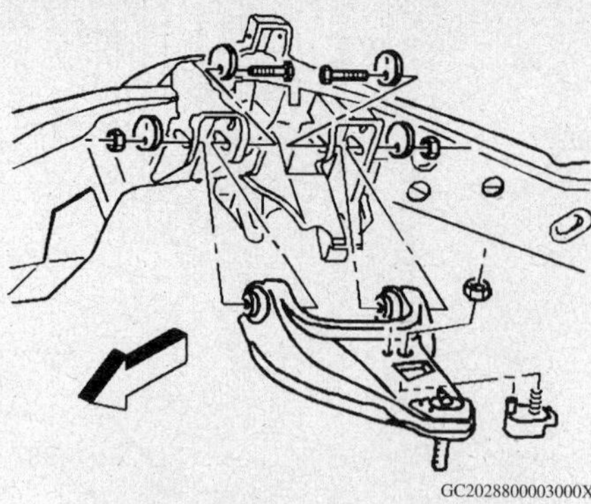

Fig. 13 Upper control arm replacement. 4WD models

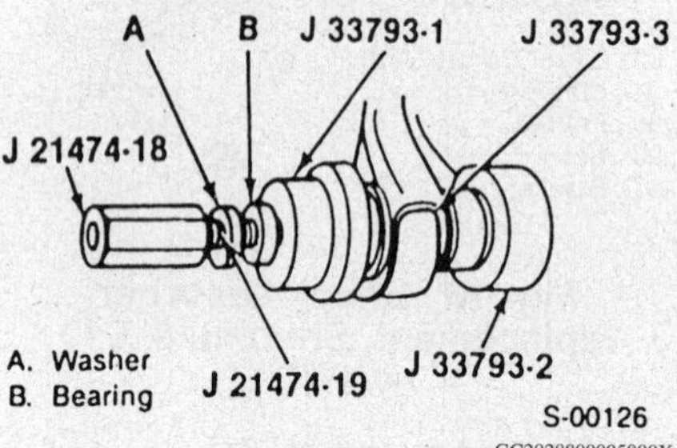

Fig. 15 Upper control arm bushing installation. Sonoma & S10

spindle to prevent damage to brake hose.
5. Reverse procedure to install.

CONTROL ARM BUSHING

REPLACE

Canyon & Colorado

LOWER

1. Remove front drive axle as outlined in "Front Wheel Drive" section.
2. Remove lower control arm as outlined under "Control Arm, Replace."
3. Prior to removing bushing, measure and record distance from bushing flange to bracket. This measured distance will be used to install new bushing.
4. Remove bushing using ball joint remover/installer tool No. J 41805, or equivalent.
5. Reverse procedure to install.

Sonoma & S10

UPPER

1. Remove upper control arm as outlined in "Control Arm, Replace."
2. **On 2WD models,** remove nuts from end of pivot shaft, then remove bushings, **Fig. 14.**
3. **On all models,** install bushings by installing pivot shaft in control arm and pressing new bushings into control arm, **Fig. 15.** Tighten pivot shaft nuts to specifications, with weight of vehicle

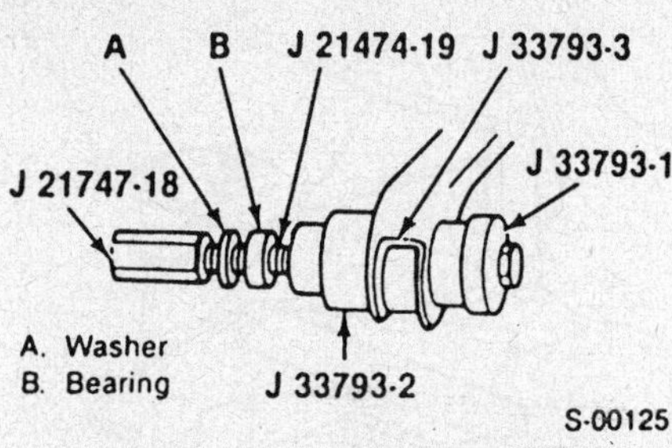

Fig. 14 Upper control arm bushing removal. Sonoma & S10 w/2WD

resting on wheels. **Both bushings must be installed .48–.52 inch from face of control arm to bushing outer sleeve.**

LOWER

2WD MODELS

1. Remove coil spring as outlined in "Coil Spring, Replace."
2. Remove lower control arm pivot bolts. Refer to "Control Arm, Replace."
3. Drive bushing flare down flush with rubber of front bushing, then remove front and rear bushings from control arm, **Figs. 16 and 17.**
4. Install front bushing, **Fig. 18,** then flare the bushing, **Fig. 19.**
5. Install rear bushings, **Fig. 20,** then the lower control arm.

4WD MODELS

1. Raise and support vehicle.
2. Remove wheel and tire assembly.
3. Unload torsion bar.
4. Remove stabilizer bar as outlined in "Stabilizer Bar, Replace."
5. Remove shock absorber as outlined in "Shock Absorber, Replace."
6. Remove control arm pivot bolts then the lower control arm.
7. Remove lower control arm front and rear bushings, **Fig. 21.**
8. Reverse procedure to install.

STEERING KNUCKLE

REPLACE

Canyon & Colorado

2WD MODELS

1. Raise and support vehicle, then remove tire and wheel assembly.
2. Support lower control arm with a suitable jack.
3. Remove wheel hub and bearing assembly as outlined under "Wheel Bearing, Replace."
4. Remove outer tie rod to steering knuckle retaining nut, then separate tie rod end from steering knuckle using ball joint separator tool No. J 6627-A, or equivalent.
5. Remove upper control arm retaining nut. Discard nut.
6. Separate upper ball joint from steering knuckle using ball joint separator tool No. J 6627-A, or equivalent.

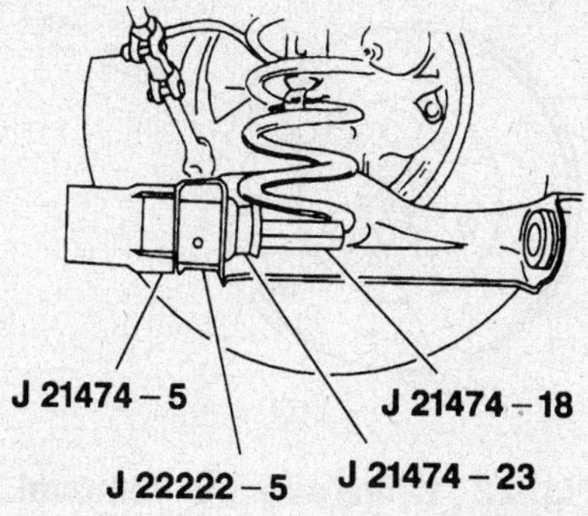

Fig. 16 Lower control arm front bushing removal. Sonoma & S10 w/2WD

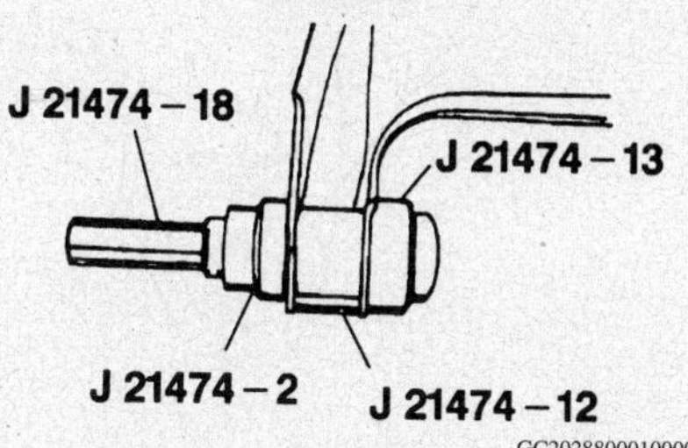

Fig. 19 Lower control arm front bushing flaring. Sonoma & S10 w/2WD

7. Remove lower control arm retaining nut. Discard nut.
8. Separate lower ball joint from steering knuckle using separator tool No. J 43631, or equivalent.
9. Remove steering knuckle.
10. Reverse procedure to install.

4WD MODELS

1. Raise and support vehicle, then remove tire and wheel assembly.
2. Support lower control arm with a suitable jack.
3. Remove drive shaft nut. Discard nut.
4. Remove brake caliper bracket.
5. Disconnect wheel speed sensor harness from chassis harness.
6. Disconnect wheel speed sensor harness from inner fender panel.
7. Remove outer tie rod to steering knuckle retaining nut, then separate tie rod end from steering knuckle using ball joint separator tool No. J 6627-A, or equivalent.
8. Remove upper control arm retaining nuts from ball joint studs.
9. Remove lower control arm retaining nut, then separate lower ball joint from steering knuckle using ball joint separator tool No. J 43631, or equivalent.
10. Remove steering knuckle assembly from vehicle.
11. Remove ball joint, then the wheel hub and bearing assembly from knuckle.
12. Reverse procedure to install.

Sonoma & S10

2WD MODELS

1. Raise and support front of vehicle, then support lower control arm with jack. **Jack must be positioned between coil spring seat and ball joint of lower control arm to obtain maximum leverage against coil spring pressure.**
2. Remove wheel and tire assembly.
3. Remove brake caliper, then the hub and rotor assembly.
4. Remove splash shield to steering knuckle attaching bolts.
5. Remove tie rod end from steering knuckle using tie rod puller tool No. J-6627, or equivalent.
6. If steering knuckle is to be replaced, remove knuckle seal.
7. Remove ball joint studs from steering knuckle using ball joint separator tool No. J-23742, or equivalent.
8. Raise upper control arm to disengage upper ball joint stud from knuckle.
9. Remove knuckle from lower ball joint stud.
10. After removal, inspect tapered holes. If holes are out of round or deformation or damage is observed, replace steering knuckle.
11. Reverse procedure to install. Install tie rod end using ball joint seating tool No. J-29193, or equivalent and **torque** to 15 ft. lbs.

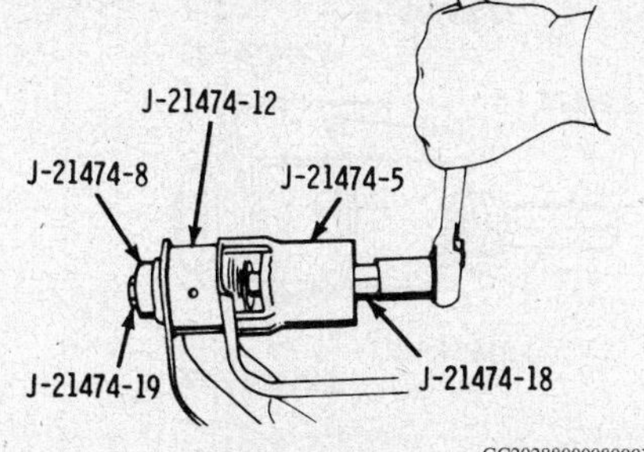

Fig. 17 Lower control arm rear bushing removal. Sonoma & S10 w/2WD

4WD MODELS

1. Raise and support vehicle.
2. Remove tire and wheel assembly.
3. Remove drive axle nut, **Fig. 22.**
4. Remove brake caliper assembly.
5. Remove hub and bearing assembly.
6. Remove cotter pin and nut from tie rod stud.
7. Remove tie rod assembly, **Fig. 23.**
8. Remove ball joints from knuckle, refer to "Ball Joint, Replace."
9. Removal knuckle from vehicle.
10. Reverse procedure to install.

TORSION BAR

REPLACE

Canyon & Colorado

1. Raise and support vehicle.
2. Allow front suspension to hang in rebound position.
3. Mark position of adjuster bolt for installation reference.
4. Remove adjuster bolt. **Record number of turns that are required to remove bolt for installation reference.**
5. Remove adjuster bolt, spacer and adjuster nut.
6. Remove adjustment arms and torsion bars as a unit, moving it rearward to disengage lower control arm.
7. Reverse procedure to install.

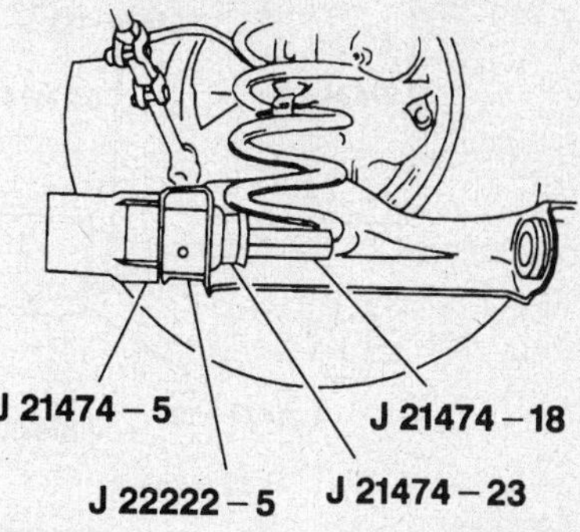

Fig. 18 Lower control arm front bushing installation. Sonoma & S10 w/2WD

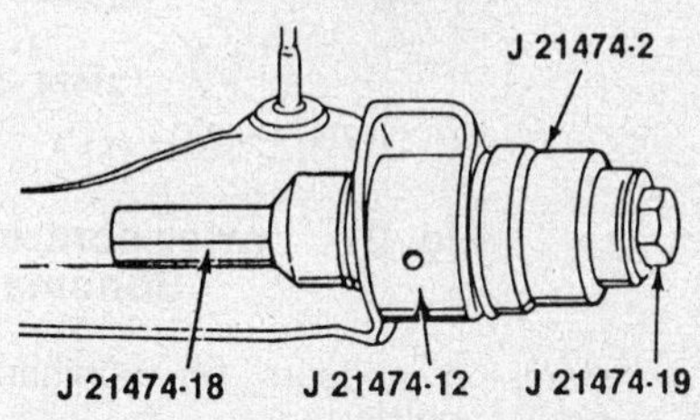

Fig. 20 Lower control arm rear bushing installation. Sonoma & S10 w/2WD

Sonoma & S10

1. Raise and support vehicle.
2. Remove transmission shield.
3. Remove both torsion bar adjusting bolts, **Fig. 24.**
4. Remove lower link mount nut from one side.
5. Remove torsion bar, **Fig. 25.**
6. Remove lower link mount nut from opposite side, then the link mount.
7. Remove upper link mount nut, then the upper link, **Fig. 26.**
8. Reverse procedure to install.

STABILIZER BAR

REPLACE

2WD Models

1. Raise and support front of vehicle.
2. Remove stabilizer link bolt nuts from both sides, then pull link bolt from linkage and remove retainers, grommets and spacers, **Fig. 27.**
3. Remove stabilizer bracket to frame or body attaching bolts, then the stabilizer bar, bushings and brackets.
4. Reverse procedure to install, noting the following:
   a. **On Sonoma and S10 models,** install stabilizer bar so identification

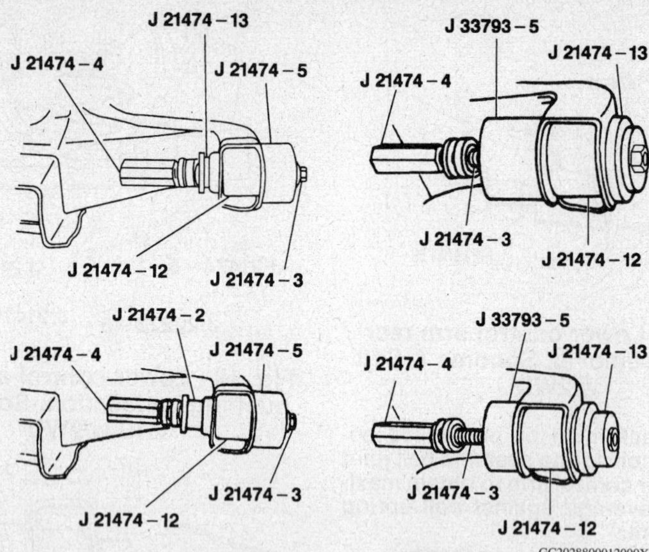

Fig. 21 Lower control arm bushing replacement. Sonoma & S10 w/4WD

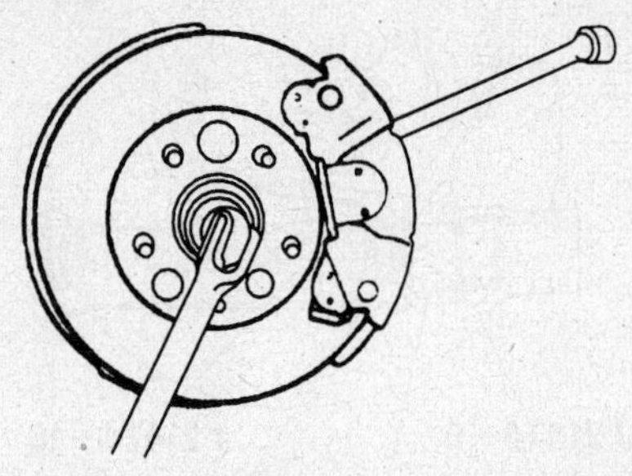

Fig. 22 Drive axle nut removal. Sonoma & S10 w/4WD

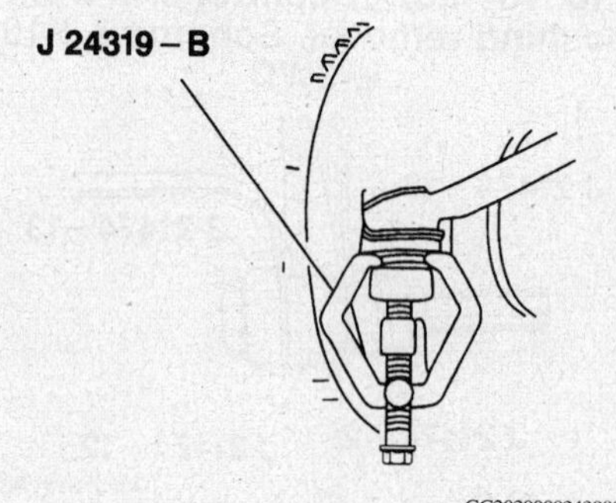

Fig. 23 Tie rod removal. Sonoma & S10 w/4WD

stamping appears on righthand side of vehicle.

b. **On all models,** position rubber bushings squarely in brackets with slit facing front of vehicle.

4WD Models

Refer to **Fig. 28** for stabilizer bar replacement procedure.

POWER STEERING GEAR

REPLACE

Canyon & Colorado

1. Raise and support vehicle, then remove both front tire and wheel assemblies.
2. Remove engine protection shield.
3. **On models equipped with 4WD,** remove front differential carrier assembly as outlined in “Front Wheel Drive” section.
4. **On all models,** disconnect outer tie rod ends from steering knuckles.
5. Place a drain pan to catch power steering fluid.
6. Disconnect power steering hose assembly from steering gear.
7. Remove coupler clamp bolt from intermediate shaft, then separate intermediate shaft from steering gear.
8. Remove steering gear vertical mounting nuts, washers and bolts.
9. Remove steering gear horizontal mounting nuts, washers and bolts.
10. **On models equipped with 2WD,** remove the crossmember mounting nuts and bolts, then the crossmember from vehicle.
11. **On all models,** remove steering gear from the vehicle.

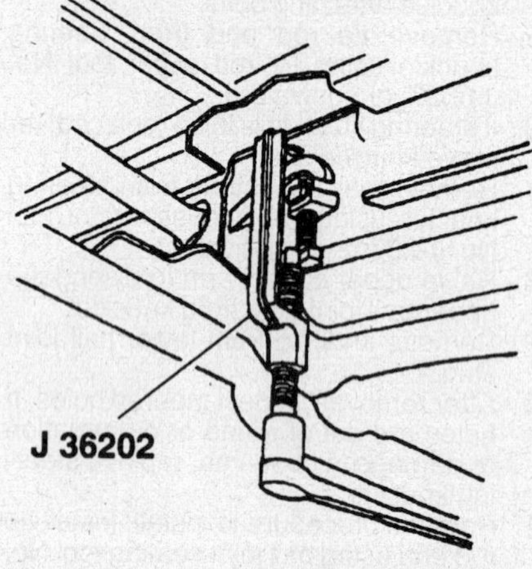

Fig. 24 Torsion bar adjusting bolt removal. Sonoma & S10

Sonoma & S10

1. Disconnect pressure and return hoses from steering gear housing, then plug hose ends and gear housing ports to prevent entry of dirt.
2. Remove coupling shield.
3. Remove retaining nuts, lock washers and bolts at steering coupling to steering shaft flange.
4. Remove pitman arm nut and washer from pitman shaft.
5. Mark relation of arm position to shaft, then remove pitman arm using suitable puller.
6. Remove screws securing steering gear to frame and remove gear from vehicle.
7. Reverse procedure to install.

POWER STEERING PUMP

REPLACE

Canyon & Colorado

1. Remove air cleaner assembly.
2. Remove drive belt.
3. Remove power steering pump pulley using power steering pump pulley remover tool No. J 25034-C, or equivalent.
4. Disconnect oil pressure sensor harness clip from pump body.
5. Place a suitable drain pan under vehicle.
6. Disconnect power steering pressure hoses from power steering pump.
7. Remove power steering pump mounting bolts, then the pump.
8. Reverse procedure to install.

Sonoma & S10

1. Disconnect pressure and return hoses from power steering pump or steering gear housing, then secure ends in raised position to prevent oil drainage. Cap all open lines and fittings.
2. Remove drive belt.
3. Remove power steering pump attaching bolts.
4. Remove power steering pump assembly, **Figs. 29 and 30.**
5. Reverse procedure to install.

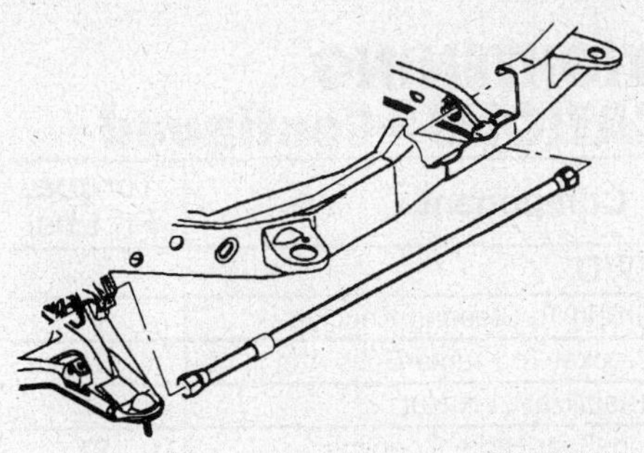

Fig. 25 Torsion bar removal. Sonoma & S10

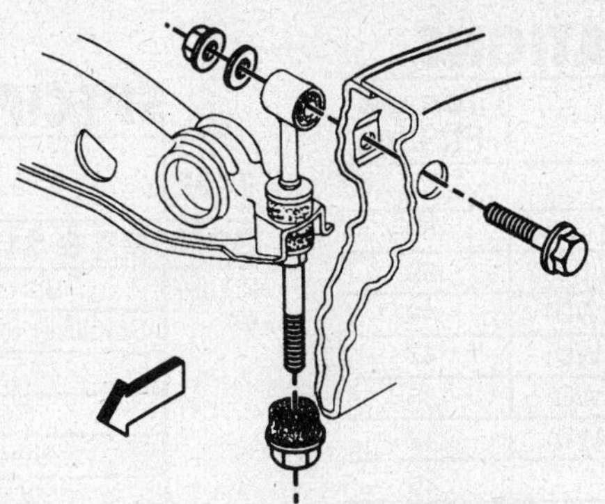

Fig. 26 Torsion bar upper link removal. Sonoma & S10

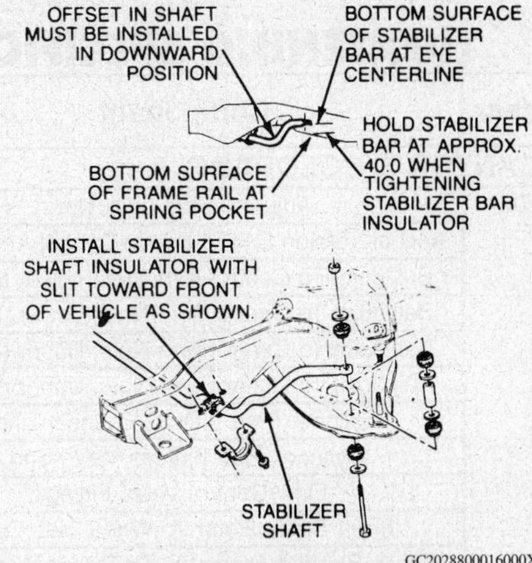

Fig. 27 Stabilizer bar replacement. 2WD models

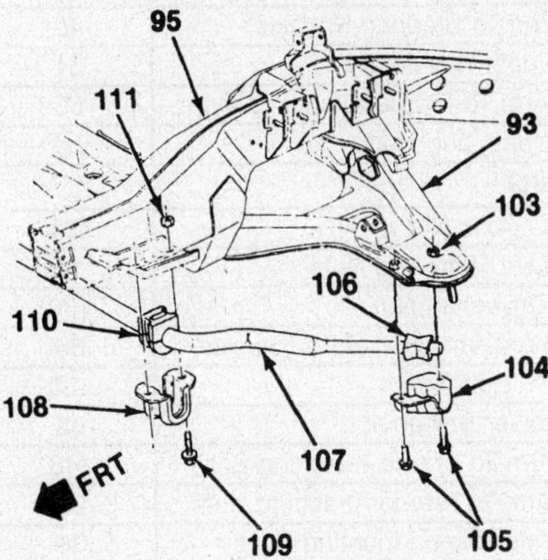

93. Lower Control Arm
95. Frame
103. Weld Nut
104. Clamp
105. Bolts
106. Insulator
107. Stabilizer Shaft
108. Clamp
109. Bolt
110. Insulator
111. Nut

GC2028800017000X

Fig. 28 Stabilizer bar replacement. 4WD models

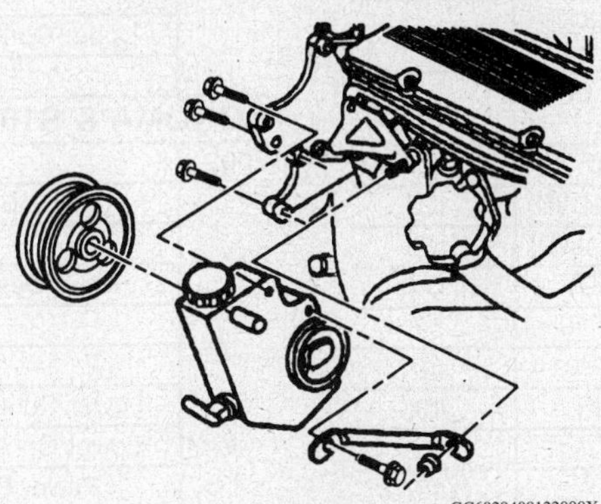

Fig. 29 Power steering pump replacement. Sonoma & S10 w/2.2L engine

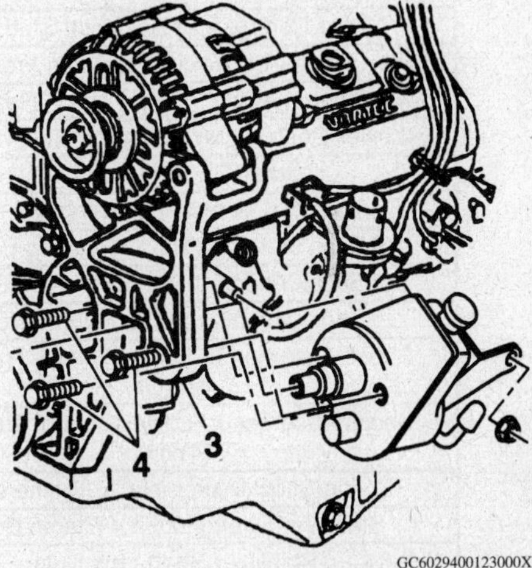

Fig. 30 Power steering pump replacement. Sonoma & S10 w/4.3L engine

TIGHTENING SPECIFICATIONS

Year	Component	Torque, Ft. Lbs.
CANYON & COLORADO		
2004–06	Adjuster Plug Lock Nut	50
	Anchor Torsion Bar To Lower Control Arm Bolts	59
	Ball Joint To Control Arm Nuts, Lower (2WD)	44
	Ball Joint To Control Arm Nuts, Lower (4WD)	47
	Ball Joint To Control Arm Nuts, Upper (4WD)	35
	Ball Joint To Control Arm Nuts, Upper (2WD)	12
	Cylinder Pipe Fittings Cylinder End	20
	Cylinder Pipe Fittings Valve End	13
	Flow Control Valve Fitting	55
	Front Brake Rotor To Wheel Hub Bolt	⑤
	Hub & Bearing Assembly To Steering Knuckle Bolts	81
	Intermediate Shaft To Steering Gear Input Shaft Pinch Bolt	33
	Lower Control Arm Ball Joint Stud Nut	107
	Lower Control Arm To Frame Bolts, Front (4WD)	122
	Lower Control Arm To Frame Bolts, Rear (4WD)	133
	Lower Control Arm To Frame Nuts (2WD)	114
	Outer Tie Rod Jam Nut	52
	Outer Tie Rod Retaining Nut	③
	Power Steering Pump Mounting Bolts	18
	Shock Absorber Tenon Nut (2WD)	15
	Shock Absorber Tenon Nut (4WD)	18
	Shock Absorber To Lower Control Arm Nut (2WD)	81
	Shock Absorber To Lower Control Arm Nut (4WD)	52
	Spring/Shock Assembly To Frame Nuts	20
	Stabilizer Shaft Insulator Clamp Bolts	37
	Stabilizer Shaft Link Nuts	32
	Steering Gear Isolator To Frame Mounting Bolts	74
	Steering Gear To Frame Mounting Bolts	96
	Steering Hose Assembly Clips To Frame Mounting Bolts	79④
	Steering Hose Assembly To Steering Gear Bolt	106④
	Steering Hose Assembly (Pressure Hose) To Pump	18
	Steering Pump Bracket Mounting Bolts	37
	Upper Control Arm Ball Joint Stud Nut	55
	Upper Control Arm To Frame Bolts (2WD)	118
	Upper Control Arm To Frame Bolts (4WD)	114
	Wheel Lug Nut	103
SONOMA & S10 2WD		
2002–04	Lower Ball Joint	83
	Lower Control Arm Bushing	20
	Lower Control Arm To Frame Attaching Nut	①
	Power Steering Pump Mounting Bolts	20
	Power Steering Pump Pressure Line Fitting	20
	Power Steering Pump Rear Brace Nut To Engine	18.5
	Rear Brace Nut To Power Steering Pump	33
	Service Ball Joint To Upper Control Arm	17
	Shock Absorber To Control Arm Bolts	20
	Shock Absorber Upper Attaching Nut	8

TIGHTENING SPECIFICATIONS—Continued

Year	Component	Torque, Ft. Lbs.
SONOMA & S10 2WD		
2002–04	Splash Shield To Steering Knuckle	10
	Stabilizer Bar Bracket To Frame Bolts And Nuts	24
	Stabilizer Link Nut	13
	Steering Gear Hose Coupling	21
	Steering Gear Lower Clamp Bolt	26
	Steering Gear Side Cover Bolts	45
	Steering Gear To Frame Bolts	55
	Tie Rod End To Steering Knuckle	40
	Upper Ball Joint	61
	Upper Control Arm To Frame Attaching Nuts	65
	Wheel Lug Nuts	②
SONOMA & S10 4WD		
2002–03	Axle Nut	180
	Ball Joint Retaining Nuts	17
	Driveshaft Nut	180
	Hub & Bearing Assembly Shield & Knuckle	86
	Hub Nut	180
	Lower Ball Joint	83
	Lower Control Arm To Frame Attaching Bolts	148
	Lower Control Arm To Frame Attaching Nuts	92
	Power Steering Pump Mounting Bolts	36
	Power Steering Pump Pressure Line Fitting	20
	Power Steering Pump Rear Brace Nut To Engine	18.5
	Rear Brace Nut To Power Steering Pump	33
	Retainer To Torsion Bar Support Bolts	26
	Service Ball Joints To Control Arm	17
	Shock Absorber Lower Attaching Nut	54
	Shock Absorber Upper Attaching Nut	54
	Stabilizer Bar Clamp To Frame Bolts	35
	Stabilizer Bar Clamp To Lower Control Arm Bolts	24
	Steering Gear Hose Coupling	21
	Steering Gear Lower Clamp Bolt	26
	Steering Gear Side Cover Bolts	45
	Steering Gear To Frame Bolts	55
	Tie Rod End To Steering Knuckle Nut	35
	Torsion Bar Support Retainer Bolts And Nuts	26
	Upper Ball Joint	61
	Upper Control Arm To Frame Attaching Nuts	70
	Wheel Lug Nuts	②

① — Front, 94 ft. lbs.; rear, 66 ft. lbs.

② — Aluminum wheels, 90 ft. lbs.; steel wheels, 73 ft. lbs.

③ — First pass, 33 ft. lbs.; second pass, an additional 95°.

④ — Inch lbs.

⑤ — First pass, 15 ft. lbs.; second pass, 81 ft. lbs.

Front Wheel Drive

NOTE: On Air Bag Equipped Models, Refer To "Air Bag System Precautions" Located In The Front Of This Manual For System Disarming & Arming Procedures.

INDEX

DESCRIPTION

Canyon & Colorado

The front axle on four wheel drive model vehicles has a central disconnect feature. The axle uses a conventional ring and pinion gear set in order to transmit the driving force of the engine to the wheels. The open differential allows the wheels to turn at different rates of speed while the axle continues to transmit the driving force. This prevents tire scuffing when going around corners and premature wear on internal axle parts. The ring and pinion set and the differential are contained within the carrier. The drive axles are completely flexible assemblies consisting of inner and outer constant velocity CV joints protected by thermoplastic boots and connected by a wheel drive shaft.

Sonoma & S10

The front differential, **Fig. 1,** is mounted to the frame, with universal joints mounted on the inner and outer ends of the axle shafts. The front axle utilizes a center disconnect system which makes shifting in or out of four-wheel drive possible at any vehicle speed. When the transfer case is shifted, a vacuum diaphragm locks or unlocks the center disconnect. This system replaces automatic-locking front hubs.

AXLE HOUSING ASSEMBLY

REPLACE

Canyon & Colorado

1. Remove wheel drive shaft as outlined under "Axle Shaft, Replace."
2. Support front drive axle assembly with a suitable jack.
3. Remove differential carrier mounting bracket to frame bolts.
4. Remove differential carrier mounting bracket to disconnect housing mounting bolts.
5. Remove left mounting bracket.
6. Remove retaining bolts from disconnect housing, then the disconnect housing.
7. Remove clutch shift fork and spring.
8. Remove thrust washer, clutch gear, clutch sleeve and gasket.
9. Remove inner drive shaft and thrust washer.
10. Remove retaining bolts from housing assembly.
11. Remove axle shaft housing assembly from differential housing, then the housing gasket.
12. Reverse procedure to install.

Sonoma & S10

REMOVAL

1. Disconnect shift cable from vacuum actuator. Disengage locking spring, then push actuator diaphragm into release cable, **Fig. 2.**
2. Unlock steering wheel so linkage is free to move.
3. Raise vehicle and place jack stands under frame side rails.
4. Remove front wheels, drive belt shield and axle skid plate as equipped.
5. Support righthand lower control arm with a jack, then disconnect right upper ball joint and remove support so that control arm hangs free.
6. Disconnect righthand drive axle shaft from tube assembly, **Fig. 3.** Insert a drift through opening in top of brake caliper and into corresponding vane of brake rotor to prevent axle from turning.
7. Disconnect four-wheel drive indicator light electrical connector from switch.
8. Remove three shift cable and switch housing to carrier bolts and pull housing out to gain access to cable locking spring. Do not remove cable coupling nut unless cable is being replaced.
9. Disconnect shift cable from fork shaft by lifting spring over slot in shift fork.
10. Remove tube bracket bolts from frame and tube assembly bolts from carrier.
11. Remove tube assembly from axle. Use care not to allow sleeve, thrust washers, connector and output shaft to fall from carrier or be damaged when removing tube.

INSTALLATION

1. Install sleeve, thrust washers, connector and output shaft in carrier. Thrust washer notch must align with tab on washer, **Fig. 4.**
2. Coat tube to carrier mating surface with Loctite 514 sealant, or equivalent.
3. Install tube and shaft assembly to carrier using only one bolt installed finger tight at one o'clock position.
4. Pull assembly down, then install cable and switch housing and four remaining bolts.
5. Install two tube to frame bolts. Tighten to specifications.
6. Inspect four wheel drive mechanism for proper operation by inserting shift cable housing installation tool No. J-33798, or equivalent, into shift fork and inspecting for rotation of axle shaft, **Fig. 5.**
7. Remove tool and install shift cable switch housing, then guide cable through housing into fork shaft hole and push cable in by sliding cable through into fork shaft hole.
8. Connect four wheel drive indicator light electrical connector to switch.
9. Support and raise righthand lower control arm using a jack and connect upper ball joint.
10. Install righthand drive axle to axle tube. Install one bolt first, then rotate axle to install five remaining bolts.
11. Install front axle skid plate, if equipped,

drive belt shield and front wheels.
12. Connect shift cable to vacuum actuator by pushing cable end into actuator shaft hole.

AXLE SHAFT

REPLACE

Canyon & Colorado

1. Raise and support vehicle, then remove tire and wheel assembly.
2. Remove drive shaft nut and washer. Discard nut.
3. Remove steering knuckle assembly as outlined in "Front Suspension & Steering" section.
4. Release wheel drive shaft by placing a suitable brass drift against tripod housing, then firmly strike brass drift with a hammer to release drive shaft.
5. Remove drive shaft from vehicle.
6. Reverse procedure to install.

PROPELLER SHAFT

REPLACE

Canyon & Colorado

1. Raise and support vehicle.
2. Mark relationship between front U-joint to pinion yoke on front differential for installation reference.
3. Mark relationship of rear U-joint to transfer case drive flange for installation reference.
4. Remove retaining nuts and bolts from drive flange.
5. Remove clamps and retaining bolts from front drive axle pinion flange.
6. Remove front propeller shaft from vehicle. Using tape and or a rubber band, wrap front U-joint bearing caps to ensure caps do not separate from U-joint.
7. Reverse procedure to install.

DIFFERENTIAL CARRIER

REPLACE

Canyon & Colorado

1. Raise and support vehicle, then remove tire and wheel assembly.
2. Drain fluid from front differential assembly.
3. Remove front propeller shaft as outlined under "Propeller Shaft, Replace."
4. Remove front wheel drive shafts as outlined under "Axle Shaft, Replace."
5. Disconnect electric motor actuator electrical connector.
6. Remove vent hose.
7. Support front differential assembly with a suitable jack.
8. Remove differential mounting bracket from vehicle.
9. Remove differential assembly from vehicle.
10. Reverse procedure to install.

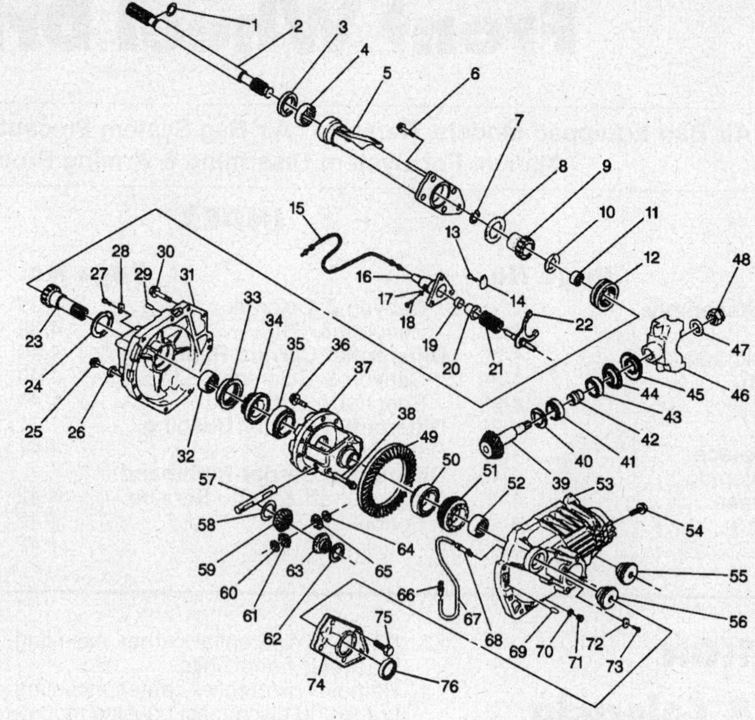

1. Retaining Ring
2. Axle Shaft
3. Seal
4. Bearing
5. Housing
6. Bolt
7. Retaining Ring
8. Washer
9. Clutch Gear
10. Washer
11. Bearing
12. Clutch Sleeve
13. Bolt
14. Lock
15. Cable
16. Housing
17. Seal
18. Switch
19. Outer Spring
20. Seal
21. Inner Spring
22. Fork
23. Clutch Shaft
24. Washer
25. Drain Plug
26. Drain Plug Gasket
27. Nut
28. Nut Lock
29. Pin
30. Bolt
31. Carrier
32. Bearing
33. Adjuster
34. Sleeve
35. Bearing
36. Bolt
37. Case
38. Bolt
39. Pinion Gear
40. Shim
41. Bearing
42. Spacer
43. Bearing
44. Seal
45. Deflector
46. Yoke
47. Washer
48. Nut
49. Ring Gear
50. Bearing
51. Insert
52. Bearing
53. Carrier
54. Bolt
55. Bushing
56. Bushing
57. Shaft
58. Washer
59. Side Gear
60. Washer
61. Pinion Gear
62. Washer
63. Side Gear
64. Washer
65. Pinion Gear
66. Vent
67. Hose
68. Hose End
69. Pin
70. Drain Plug Gasket
71. Drain Plug
72. Nut Lock
73. Nut
74. Cover
75. Bolt
76. Seal

GC3018800002000X

Fig. 1 Exploded view of front drive axle. Sonoma & S10

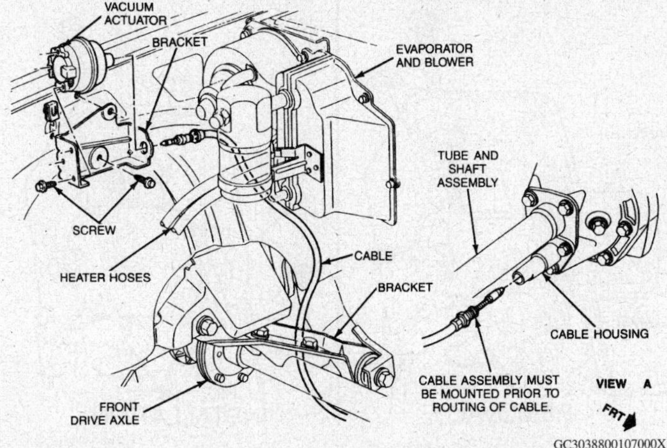

Fig. 2 Vacuum actuator. Sonoma & S10

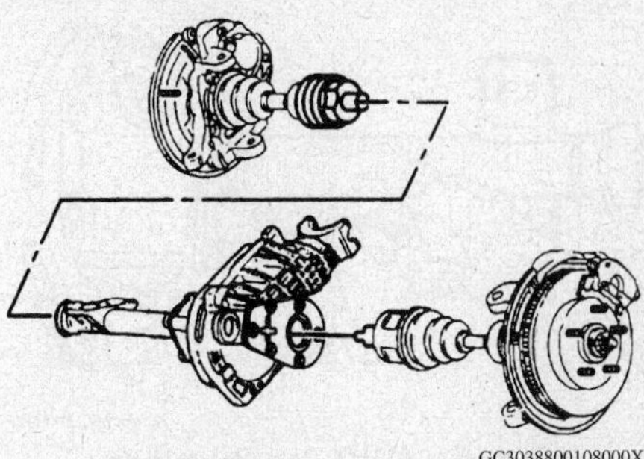

Fig. 3 Drive axle & tube assembly. Sonoma & S10

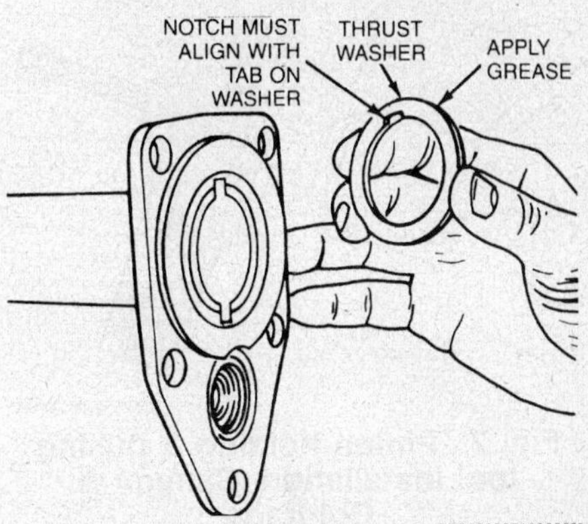

Fig. 4 Thrust washer installation. Sonoma & S10

Sonoma & S10

1. Unlock steering column so linkage is free to move, then disconnect shift cable from vacuum actuator.
2. Raise and support vehicle, then remove battery and battery tray.
3. Remove front wheels, then the front axle skid plate.
4. Remove drain plug and flat washer, then drain lubricant from carrier.
5. Remove righthand side lower shock bolt.
6. Disconnect wire from indicator switch.
7. Remove shift cable housing and shift cable from carrier housing as outlined in "Shift Cable, Replace."
8. Disconnect vent hose.
9. Disconnect steering relay rod from idler arm and pitman arm.
10. Hold left drive axle by inserting drift in top of brake caliper and into vanes in brake rotor, noting the following:
    a. It is essential positions of all driveline components relative to propeller shaft and axles be observed and accurately reference marked before disassembling. Relative components include propeller shafts, drive axles, pinion flanges, output shafts, etc.
    b. All components must be assembled in exact relationship to each other as they were before removal.
    c. Published specifications as well as any measurements made prior to disassembly must be followed.
11. Remove bolts, then the drift from brake rotor.
12. Remove bolts and nuts, then the front prop shaft, as follows:
    a. Support both lower control arms with suitable stands at edge of stabilizer shaft.
    b. Lower vehicle until front end weight is resting on stands.
13. Hold carrier upper nut with 18 mm wrench inserted through frame, then remove carrier bolts and nuts.
14. Remove carrier assembly by rolling carrier counterclockwise while lifting up to gain clearance from mounting ears.
15. Remove tube bolts from carrier.
16. Reverse procedure to install.

DIFFERENTIAL CARRIER BUSHING

REPLACE

1. Remove differential carrier as outlined in "Differential Carrier, Replace."
2. Remove bushing from carrier ear using bushing tool No. J-33791, or equivalent, **Fig. 6.**
3. Install new bushing using busing tool, **Fig. 6.** Ensure adapter tool No. J-33791-3, or equivalent, is positioned properly between bushing and carrier ear to prevent bushing from being pressed in too far.
4. Install differential carrier as outlined in "Differential Carrier, Replace."

DIFFERENTIAL OUTPUT SHAFT PILOT BEARING

REPLACE

1. Remove tube and shaft assembly as outlined in "Axle Housing Assembly, Replace."
2. Remove bearing using pilot bearing remover tool No. J-34011, or equivalent, **Fig. 1.**
3. Lubricate new bearing with suitable axle lubricant, then install bearing using pilot bearing installer tool No. J-33482, or equivalent.
4. Reverse procedure to install.

SHIFT CABLE

REPLACE

1. Remove shift cable from vacuum actuator by disengaging locking spring and pushing actuator diaphragm in to release cable.
2. Compress cable locking fingers with pliers, then remove cable from bracket.
3. Raise and support vehicle.
4. Remove switch housing mounting bolts and pull housing away from axle tube flange to gain access to cable locking spring.
5. Disconnect cable from shaft fork by lifting spring over slot in shift fork, then unscrew cable from housing and remove from vehicle.
6. Install cable following proper routing, **Fig. 2.**
7. Install cable and switch housing to carrier.
8. Slide cable through switch housing into fork shaft hole and push cable in. The cable will snap in place automatically.
9. Lower vehicle, then connect shift cable to vacuum actuator by pressing cable into bracket hole. Cable will snap in place automatically.
10. Inspect cable for proper operation.

PINION FLANGE SEAL

REPLACE

Canyon & Colorado

1. Raise and support vehicle, then remove wheel and tire assemblies.
2. Remove engine protection shield.
3. Remove front propeller shaft as outlined under "Propeller Shaft, Replace."
4. Remove brake calipers. Position and suspend calipers aside.
5. Measure torque required in order to rotate pinion using a suitable inch-pound torque wrench. Record torque value for reassembly.
6. Scribe an alignment line between pinion shaft and pinion yoke for installation reference.
7. Install flange and pulley holding tool No. J 8614-01, or equivalent, onto pinion, **Fig. 7.**

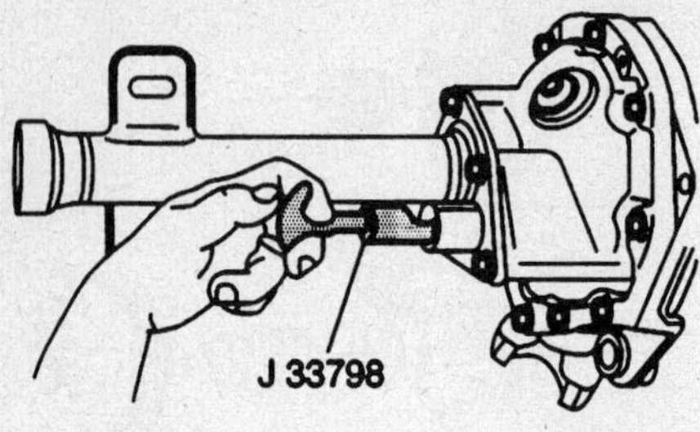

Fig. 5 4WD mechanism operational inspection. Sonoma & S10

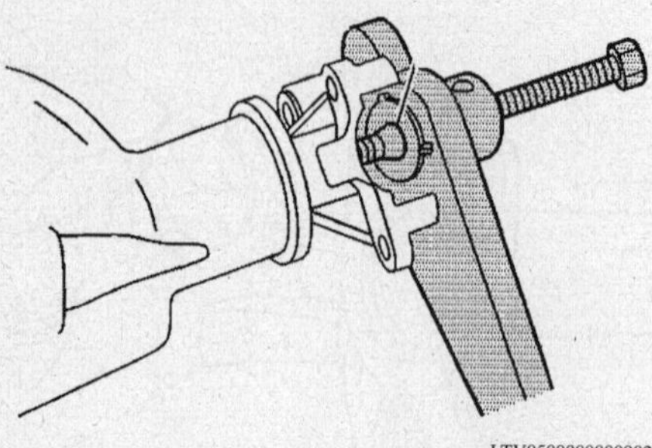

Fig. 7 Pinion holding & pulling tool installation. Canyon & Colorado

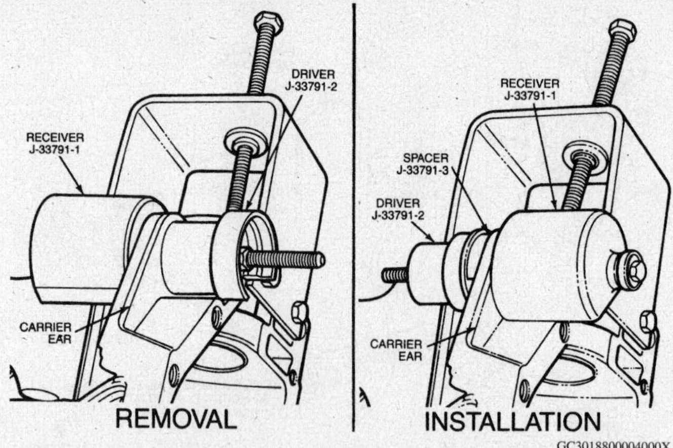

Fig. 6 Differential carrier bushing replacement

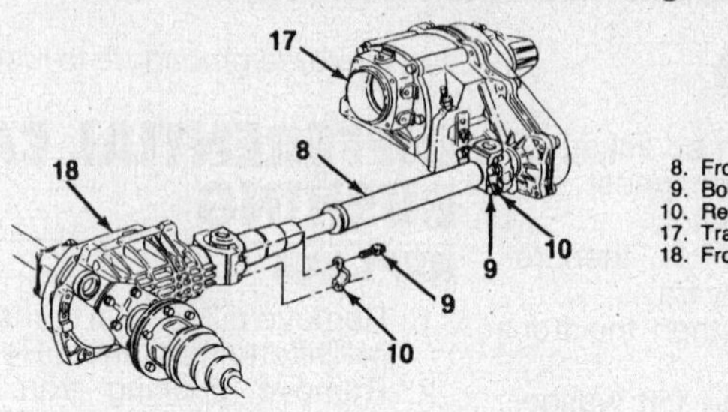

Fig. 8 Pinion flange retaining bolts

8. Remove pinion nut.
9. Install pinion pulling tool Nos. J 8614-2 and J 8614-3 into holding tool J 8614-01.
10. Remove pinon yoke by turning pulling tool clockwise.
11. Carefully remove seal from bore. **Do not distort or scratch the aluminum case.**
12. Remove oil seal using a suitable seal removal tool.
13. Remove dust deflector from pinion yoke using a soft-faced hammer.
14. Reverse procedure to install. Adjust pinion nut torque as follows:
    a. Tighten pinion nut while holding flange with pinion holding tool No. J 8614-01, or equivalent.
    b. Tighten pinion nut until pinion endplay is just taken up. Rotate pinion while tightening nut to seat bearings.
    c. Measure rotating torque of pinion using a suitable inch-pound torque wrench.
    d. Compare measurement of rotating torque to measurement recorded during removal.
    e. Rotating torque of pinion nut should be 3–5 inch lbs. greater than torque recorded during removal.
    f. If rotating torque is not as specified, continue to tighten pinion nut in small increments, as necessary, until torque required in order to rotate pinion is 3–5 inch lbs. greater than torque recorded during removal.
    g. Once specified torque is obtained, rotate pinion several times to ensure bearings have seated.
    h. Recheck rotating torque and adjust if necessary.
15. Remove crossmember and front skid plates as required.
16. Remove pinion flange bolts and retainers, **Fig. 8.**
17. Remove propeller shaft from pinion shaft and tape bearing caps to hold in place.
18. Remove pinion shaft retaining nut and washer. **Mark pinion flange, pinion shaft and pinion retaining nut to ensure proper bearing preload.**
19. Remove pinion flange using companion flange holding tool No. J-8614-01, or equivalent, **Fig. 9.**
20. Remove pinion seal using suitable seal puller.
21. Reverse procedure to install. Install pinion oil seal using seal installer tool No. J-33782, or equivalent, **Fig. 10.**

INNER TRI-POT SEAL

REPLACE

Sonoma & S10

Refer to **Figs. 11 and 12** for inner tri-pot seal replacement.

DIFFERENTIAL CARRIER RIGHTHAND OUTPUT SHAFT & TUBE SERVICE

Sonoma & S10

DISASSEMBLE

1. Remove output shaft from tube by tapping inside of flange with a rubber mallet.
2. Pry tube seal from tube, then remove bearing from tube.
3. Drive differential shift cable housing seal out of tube using a punch.

ASSEMBLE

1. Install output shaft tube bearing.
2. Install tube seal. Flange of seal must be flush with tube outer surface.
3. Install output shaft into tube by tapping flange with a rubber mallet.
4. Install differential shift cable housing seal.

CV JOINT

REPLACE

Sonoma & S10

Refer to **Figs. 13 and 14** for CV joint replacement.

Fig. 9 Pinion flange removal

Fig. 10 Pinion seal installation

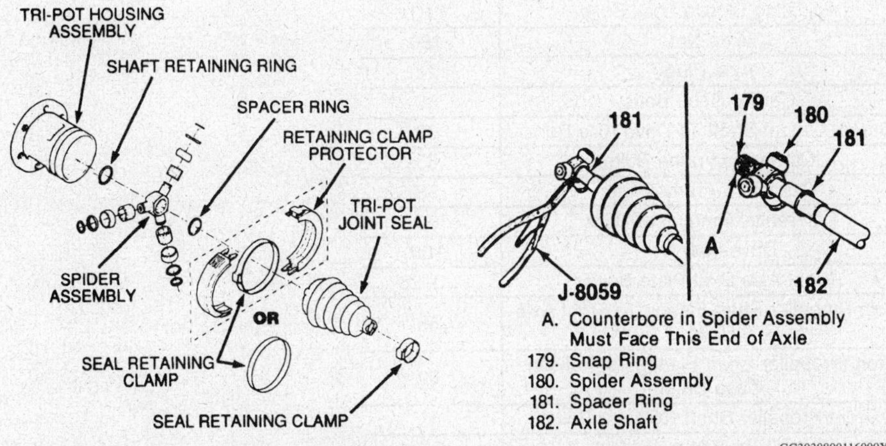

Fig. 11 Inner tri-pot seal replacement. Sonoma & S10

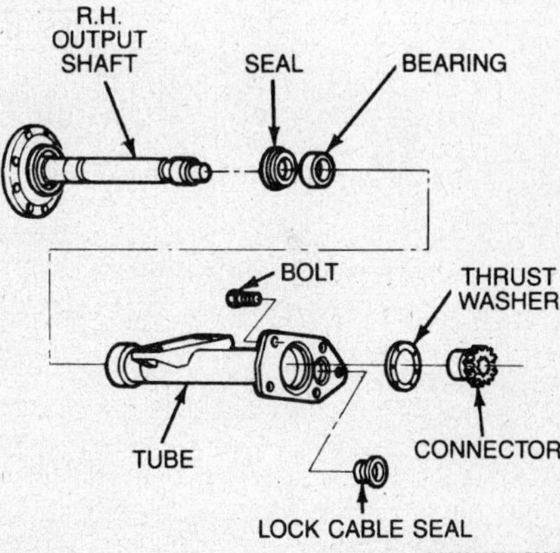

Fig. 12 Righthand output shaft & tube. Sonoma & S10

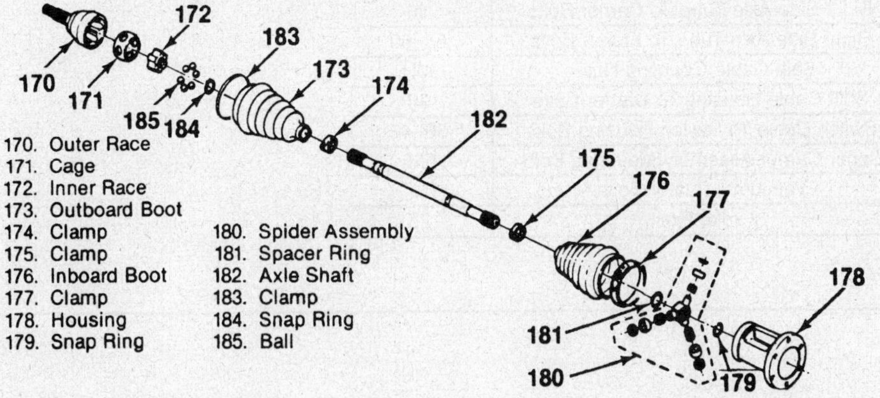

Fig. 13 Exploded view of front axle. Sonoma & S10

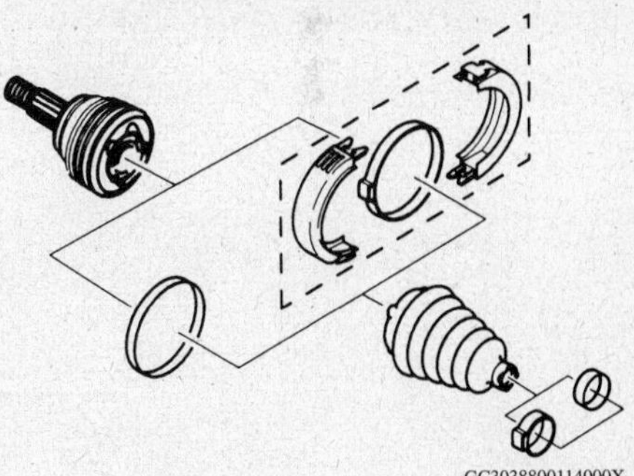
Fig. 14 Outer CV joint seal replacement. Sonoma & S10

TIGHTENING SPECIFICATIONS

Year	Component	Torque, Ft. Lbs.
CANYON & COLORADO		
2004–06	Brake Hose Retaining Bolt	18
	Differential Carrier Assembly Bearing Cap Bolts	46
	Differential Carrier Assembly Mounting Bolts	112
	Differential Housing Cover Bolts	22
	Drain & Fill Plug	24
	Electric Actuator	16
	Intermediate Shaft Housing Assembly To Axle Housing Bolts	44
	Intermediate Shaft Housing To Disconnect Housing Bolts	35
	Pinion Shaft Lock Screw/Bolt	18
SONOMA & S10		
2002–04	Adjusting Sleeve Lock Bolts	71①
	Axle Nut	180
	Axle Plug	24
	Carrier Case Bolts	35
	Carrier Output Shaft To Drive Axle Bolts	60
	Carrier To Frame Bolts	65
	Carrier To Frame Nuts	55
	Differential Ring Gear Bolts	60
	Driveshaft Nut	180
	Front Axle Skid Plate Bolts	20–28
	Front Propeller Shaft Flange To Front Axle Bolts	55
	Front Propeller Shaft Flange To Transfer Case Bolts	92
	Front Propeller Shaft Retainer Bolts	15
	Hub Nut	180
	Left Side Output Shaft Cover Bolts	18
	Lower Carrier Assembly Mounting Bolts	55
	Right Side Axle Tube To Carrier Bolts	36
	Right Side Axle Tube To Frame Bolts	54–60
	Shift Cable Coupling Nut	90①
	Shift Cable Housing To Carrier Bolts	36
	Switch Cable To Switch Housing Bolts	30–40
	Upper Carrier Assembly Mounting Bolts	636
	Vacuum Actuator Bolts	13①
	Yoke Nut	25

① — Inch lbs.

Wheel Alignment

INDEX

PRELIMINARY INSPECTION

Inspect the following components. Adjust, repair or replace as required prior to performing front wheel alignment.

1. Inflate tires to cold specifications.
2. Ensure front tires are of same size, ply rating and load rating.
3. Inspect for excessive wheel bearing endplay.
4. Inspect for worn or damaged spindle ball joints.
5. Ensure steering gear mounting bolts are tight.
6. Inspect radius arm or bent or damaged condition.
7. Inspect radius arm to frame bushings for looseness or wear.
8. Inspect suspension components for wear or damage.

FRONT WHEEL ALIGNMENT

Caster & Camber

Before inspecting or adjusting caster and camber angles, jounce vehicle at least 3 times to prevent false geometric readings.

CANYON & COLORADO

1. Caster and camber adjustments are made by rotating offset cam bolt and cam in slotted frame bracket to reposition control arm.
2. Determine caster angle.
3. Determine positive camber or negative camber angle.
4. **On models equipped with 4WD,** adjustments are made at upper control arm.
5. **On models equipped with 2WD,** adjustments are made at lower control arm.
6. **On all models,** remove pinned adjusting cam insert. **Do not reinstall the cam insert.**
7. Loosen control arm cam adjustment bolts.
8. Adjust caster and camber angle by turning cam bolts using alignment socket tool No. J 45938, or equivalent, until specifications have been met.
9. When adjustments are complete, hold the cam bolt in order to ensure cam bolt position does not change while tightening the nut. **Torque** cam nuts to 114 ft. lbs.
10. Ensure caster and camber are still within specifications.

SONOMA & S10

2WD MODELS

Caster and camber adjustments are made by shims inserted between upper control arm shaft and frame bracket, **Fig. 1.** Add, subtract or transfer shims to change readings as noted below.

To adjust caster and/or camber, loosen upper control arm shaft to frame nuts, then add or subtract shims as required and tighten upper control arm shaft to frame nuts to specification. After adjustment, the shim pack should have at least two threads of bolt exposed beyond the nut. The difference between front and rear shim packs must not exceed .40 inches.

When adjusting caster transfer shims from front to rear or rear to front. The transfer of one shim from rear to front bolt will decrease positive caster.

When adjusting camber change shims at both front and rear of shaft. Adding an equal amount of shims at both front and rear locations will decrease positive camber.

4WD MODELS

Caster and camber adjustments are made by cam mounted upper control arm attaching bolts.

To adjust caster and/or camber, loosen upper control arm to frame attaching bolt nut, then rotate cam by turning bolt head. When proper alignment settings are established, tighten upper control arm to frame attaching bolt nut to specification.

To increase positive caster, move front cam lobe inward and rear cam lobe outward.

To increase positive camber, move both front and rear cam lobes inward.

Toe-In

CANYON & COLORADO

1. Loosen jam nut on tie rod.
2. Rotate inner tie rod to specified setting.
3. Torque jam nut on tie rod to 52 ft. lbs.
4. Ensure toe setting is within specifications.

SONOMA & S10

To adjust, loosen clamp bolts at each end of steering tie rod adjustable sleeves. With steering wheel in straight ahead position, turn tie rod adjusting sleeves to obtain proper adjustment. After adjusting, inspect that number of threads showing on each end of sleeve are equal and that the tie rod end housings are at the right angles to steering arm. Position tie rod clamps and sleeves, **Fig. 2,** and tighten nuts to specification.

VEHICLE RIDE HEIGHT

Z Height

COIL SPRING SUSPENSION

MEASUREMENT

The Z dimension measurement determines proper ride height for the front end. These vehicles have no adjustment, any trim height change would require replacement of suspension components.

1. Measure Z height from center line of front lower control arm bolt down to the lower inboard corner of the ball joint, **Fig. 3.**
2. **On Canyon and Colorado models equipped with Sport suspension,** trim height should be 2.7–3.5 inches.
3. **On Canyon and Colorado models equipped with Increased Capacity suspension,** trim height should be 1.8–2.6 inches.
4. **On Sonoma and S10 models,** trim height should be 2.6–3.0 inches.

TORSION BAR SUSPENSION

MEASUREMENT

1. Lift front bumper of vehicle up about 1.5 inches, then gently remove hands and let vehicle settle by itself.
2. Repeat jounce operation two more times.
3. Measure Z dimension.
4. Push front bumper of vehicle down about 1.5 inches, then gently remove hands and let vehicle rise by itself.
5. Repeat jounce operation two more times.
6. Measure Z height from the center line of pivot bolt (1) down to lowest inboard edge of the knuckle (2), **Fig. 4.**
7. Figure average of high and low measurements to find the true dimension.
8. **On Canyon and Colorado models,** trim height should be 4.4–4.8 inches.

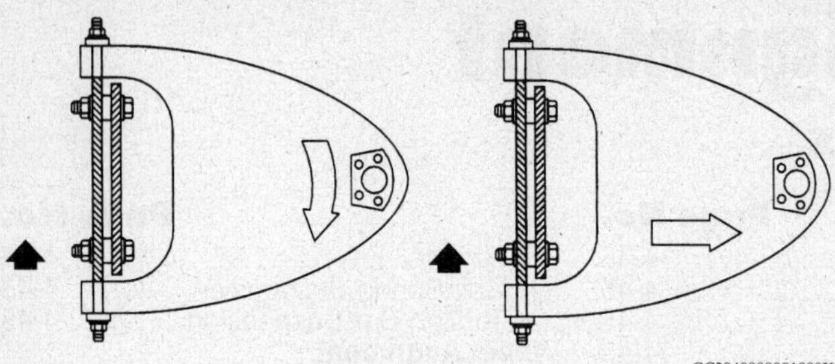

Fig. 1 Caster & camber adjustment. Sonoma & S10 w/2WD

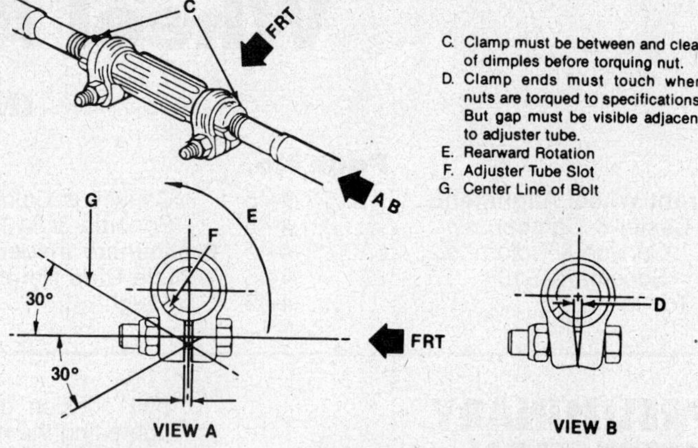

Fig. 2 Tie rod & clamp sleeve positioning. Sonoma & S10

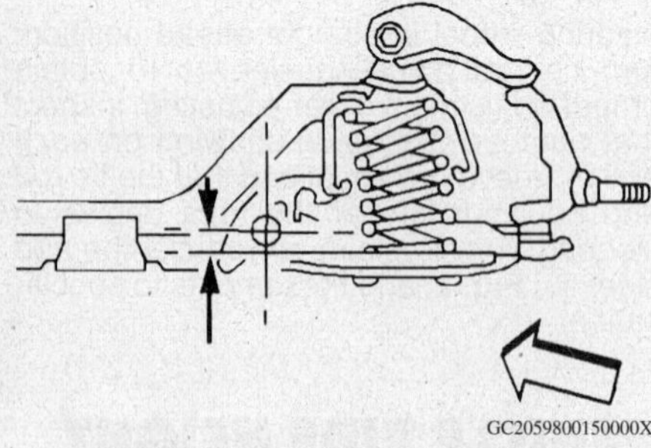

Fig. 3 Vehicle Z height measurement. Models w/coil spring suspension

9. **On Sonoma and S10 models,** trim height should be 4.6–5.0 inches.
10. **On all models,** if trim height is not within specifications, proceed to "Adjustment."

ADJUSTMENT

To adjust Z height, turn the bolt that contacts the torsion arm as required. One revolution of the bolt increases Z height by .2 inch (1) **Fig. 5.**

D Height

The D dimension measurement determines the proper rear end ride height, **Fig. 6.** There is no adjustment procedure. Repair may require replacement of suspension components.

All Vehicles require a measurement from the bumper bracket down to the top of the rear axle housing tube.

1. Lift rear bumper of vehicle up about 1.5 inches, then gently remove hands and let vehicle settle by itself.

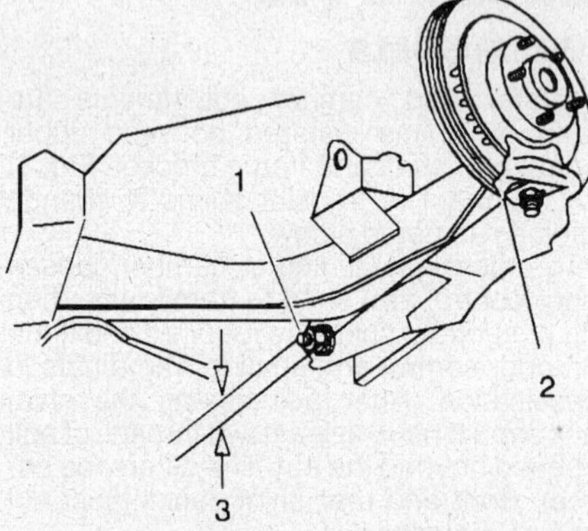

Fig. 4 Vehicle Z height measurement. Models w/torsion bar suspension

2. Repeat jounce operation two more times.
3. Measure D dimension.
4. Push rear bumper of vehicle down about 1.5 inches, then gently remove hands and let vehicle rise by itself.
5. Repeat jounce operation two more times.
6. Measure D dimension.
7. Figure average of high and low measurements to find the true dimension.
8. **On Canyon and Colorado models equipped with 2WD and Increased Capacity suspension,** D trim height should be 4.9–5.7 inches.

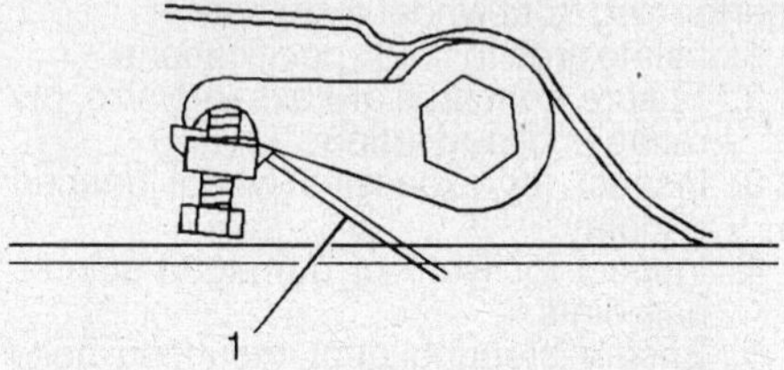

Fig. 5 Z height adjustment. Models w/torsion bar suspension

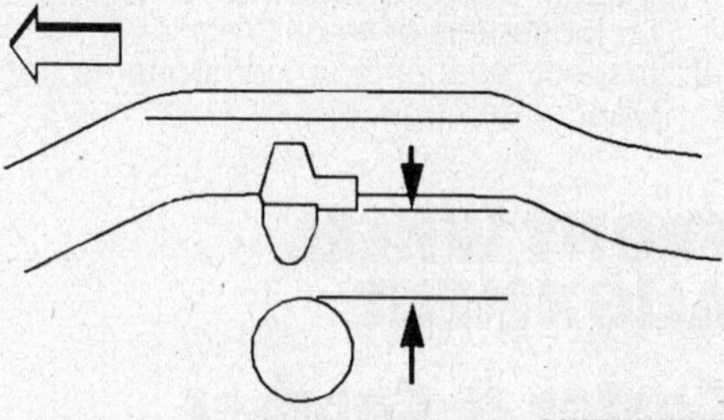

Fig. 6 D height measurement

9. **On Canyon and Colorado models equipped with 2WD and Sport suspension,** D trim height should be 5.4–6.3 inches.
10. **On Canyon and Colorado models equipped with 4WD,** D trim height should be 6.3–7.1 inches.
11. **On Sonoma and S10 models,** D trim height should be 5.1–6.4 inches.

BLAZER, BRAVADA, ENVOY, JIMMY, RAINIER & TRAILBLAZER

NOTE: Refer To The Back Of This Manual For Vehicle Manufacturer's Special Service Tool Suppliers.

INDEX OF SERVICE OPERATIONS

Specifications

GENERAL ENGINE SPECIFICATIONS

Year	Engine		Fuel System	Bore & Stroke	Compression Ratio	Net H.P. @ RPM	Maximum Torque, Ft. Lbs. @ RPM	Normal Oil Pressure, psi
	Liter	VIN Code②						
2002	4.2L	S	SFI	3.66 X 4.02	10.10	270 @ 6000	275 @ 3600	12①
	4.3L	W	SFI	4.00 X 3.48	9.20	190 @ 4400	250 @ 2800	③
2003–05	4.2L	S	SFI	3.66 X 4.02	10.10	270 @ 6000	275 @ 3600	12①
	4.3L	W	SFI	4.00 X 3.48	9.20	190 @ 4400	250 @ 2800	③
	5.3L	P	SFI	3.78 X 3.62	9.45	285 @ 5200	325 @ 4000	③
2006	4.2L	S	SFI	3.66 X 4.02	10.10	270 @ 6000	275 @ 3600	12①
	5.3L	P	SFI	3.78 X 3.62	9.45	285 @ 5200	325 @ 4000	③
	6.0L	H	SFI	4.00 X 3.62	10.9	395 @ 5400	400 @ 4400	③

CSFI — Central Port Sequential Fuel Injection
MFI — Multi-Port Fuel Injection
① — At 1200 RPM.
② — Eighth digit denotes engine code.
③ — Minimum hot pressures: 6.0 psi @ 1000 RPM; 18.0 psi @ 1800 RPM; 24.0 psi @ 3000 RPM.

TUNE UP SPECIFICATIONS

The following specifications are published from the latest information available. This data should only be used in the absence of a decal affixed in the engine compartment.

Engine	VIN Code①	Spark Plug Gap	Ignition Timing BTDC				Curb Idle Speed②		Fast Idle Speed②		Fuel Pump Pressure psi.	Valve Lash, Inch
			Firing Order, ③	Man. Trans.	Auto. Trans.	Mark Location	Man. Trans.	Auto. Trans.	Man. Trans.	Auto. Trans.		
4.2L	S	.050	⑫	—	⑦	⑨	—	⑦	—	⑦	48–54	④
4.3L	W	.060	Fig. A	⑤	⑤	⑨	⑩	⑪	⑦	⑦	60–66⑧	④
5.3L	P	.060	⑥	⑤	⑤	⑨	⑦	⑦	⑦	⑦	55–62	④
6.0L	H	.040	⑥	⑤	⑤	⑨	⑦	⑦	⑦	⑦	55–62	④

BTDC — Before Top Dead Center
D — Drive
① — The eighth digit of VIN denotes engine code.
② — When inspecting idle speed, set parking brake & block drive wheels.
③ — Before removing wires from distributor cap or coil unit, determine location of ignition wires, as position may have been altered from that outlined at end of this chart.
④ — Equipped w/hydraulic valve lifters.
⑤ — Not adjustable.
⑥ — Firing order, 1-8-7-2-6-5-4-3.
⑦ — Controlled by idle speed control (ISC) motor or Idle Air Control (IAC) valve.
⑧ — Wrap shop towel around engine compartment fuel pressure fitting. Connect suitable fuel pressure gauge to fuel pressure fitting. Turn ignition to On position & note fuel pressure reading.
⑨ — Equipped w/crankshaft position sensor.
⑩ — Under 8500 GVW, 550 RPM; Over 8500 GVW, 700 RPM. Controlled by idle speed control (ISC) motor or Idle Air Control (IAC) valve.
⑪ — Under 8500 GVW, 590D RPM; Over 8500 GVW, 650D RPM. Controlled by idle speed control (ISC) motor or Idle Air Control (IAC) valve.
⑫ — Firing order, 1-5-3-6-2-4.

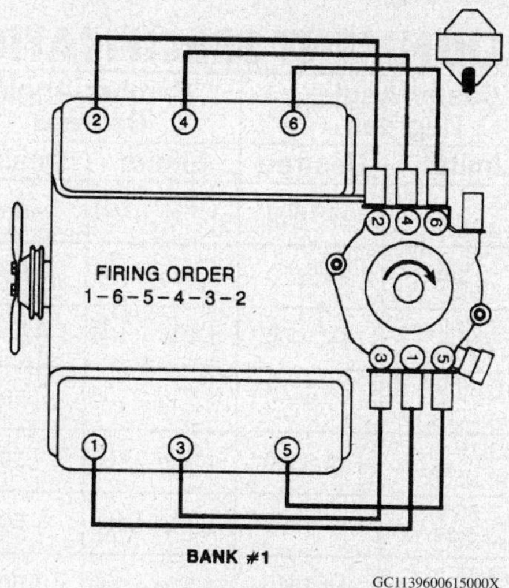

Fig. A

FRONT WHEEL ALIGNMENT SPECIFICATIONS

Year	Model	Side	Caster Angle, Degrees		Camber Angle, Degrees		Toe Per Wheel, Degrees①		Ball Joint Wear, Inches
			Limits	Desired	Limits	Desired	Limits	Desired	
2002–04	Blazer & Jimmy⑭	Lefthand	+1.80 to +3.80⑨	+2.80⑨	-1 to +1⑩	0⑩	-.1 to +.3	+.1	③
		Righthand	+2.30 to +4.30⑨	+3.30⑨	-1 to +1⑩	0⑩	-.1 to +.3	+.1	③
	Blazer & Jimmy⑮	Lefthand	+3.70 to +5.70⑨	+4.70⑨	+.5 to +2.0⑩	+1.25⑩	-.1 to +.3	+.1	③
		Righthand	+4.20 to +6.20⑨	+5.20⑨	+.5 to +2.0⑩	+1.25⑩	-.1 to +.3	+.1	③
	Bravada, Envoy, Rainier & Trailblazer	Lefthand	+3.00 to +4.00⑬	+3.50⑬	-1.0 to 0⑯	-.50⑯	-.1 to +.3	+.1	③
		Righthand	+3.50 to +4.50⑬	+4.00⑬	-1.0 to 0⑯	-.50⑯	-.1 to +.3	+.1	③
2005	Blazer & Jimmy⑭	Lefthand	+1.80 to +3.80⑨	+2.80⑨	-1 to +1⑩	0⑩	-.1 to +.3	+.1	③
		Righthand	+2.30 to +4.30⑨	+3.30⑨	-1 to +1⑩	0⑩	-.1 to +.3	+.1	③
	Blazer & Jimmy⑮	Lefthand	+3.70 to +5.70⑨	+4.70⑨	+.5 to +2.0⑩	+1.25⑩	-.1 to +.3	+.1	③
		Righthand	+4.20 to +6.20⑨	+5.20⑨	+.5 to +2.0⑩	+1.25⑩	-.1 to +.3	+.1	③
	Envoy, Rainier & Trailblazer⑰	Lefthand	+3.15 to +4.35⑪	+3.75⑪	-1.1 to +.1⑧	-.50⑧	-.1 to +.3	+.1	③
		Righthand	+3.65 to +4.85⑪	+4.25⑪	-1.1 to +.1⑧	-.50⑧	-.1 to +.3	+.1	③
	Envoy, Rainier & Trailblazer⑫	Lefthand	+3.40 to +4.60⑪	+4.00⑪	-1.1 to +.1⑧	-.50⑧	-.1 to +.3	+.1	③
		Righthand	+3.90 to +5.10⑪	+4.50⑪	-1.1 to +.1⑧	-.50⑧	-.1 to +.3	+.1	③
2006	Envoy, Rainier & Trail-blazer⑰⑦	Lefthand	+3.30 to +4.50⑤	+3.90⑤	-1.1 to +.1⑧	-.50⑧	-.1 to +.3	+.1	③
		Righthand	+3.65 to +4.85⑤	+4.25⑤	-1.1 to +.1⑧	-.50⑧	-.1 to +.3	+.1	③
	Envoy & Trailblazer ⑰⑥	Lefthand	+3.50 to +4.70④	+4.10④	-1.1 to +.1⑧	-.50⑧	-.1 to +.3	+.1	③
		Righthand	+3.30 to +4.50④	+3.90④	-1.1 to +.1⑧	-.50⑧	-.1 to +.3	+.1	③

Continued

FRONT WHEEL ALIGNMENT SPECIFICATIONS—Continued

Year	Model	Side	Caster Angle, Degrees		Camber Angle, Degrees		Toe Per Wheel, Degrees①		Ball Joint Wear, Inches
			Limits	Desired	Limits	Desired	Limits	Desired	
2006	Envoy, Rainier & Trail-blazer⑫⑦	Lefthand	+3.55 to +4.75⑤	+4.15⑤	-1.1 to +.1⑧	-.50⑧	-.1 to +.3	+.1	③
		Righthand	+3.75 to +4.95⑤	+4.35⑤	-1.1 to +.1⑧	-.50⑧	-.1 to +.3	+.1	③
	Envoy & Trailblazer ⑰⑥	Lefthand	+3.50 to +4.70④	+4.10④	-1.1 to +.1⑧	-.50⑧	-.1 to +.3	+.1	③
		Righthand	+3.30 to +4.50④	+3.90④	-1.1 to +.1⑧	-.50⑧	-.1 to +.3	+.1	③
	Envoy & Trailblazer ⑥	Lefthand	+3.75 to +4.95④	+4.35④	-1.1 to +.1⑧	-.50⑧	-.1 to +.3	+.1	③
		Righthand	+3.55 to +4.75④	+4.15④	-1.1 to +.1⑧	-.50⑧	-.1 to +.3	+.1	③
	Trailblazer SS	Lefthand	+3.65 to +4.85②	+4.25②	-1.1 to +.1⑧	-.50⑧	0 to +.4	+.2	③
		Righthand	+3.65 to +4.85②	+4.25②	-1.1 to +.1⑧	-.50⑧	0 to +.4	+.2	③

① — Toe-In (+). Toe-Out (-).
② — Cross caster (L-R), -.6° to +.6°, preferred, 0°.
③ — Refer to "Ball Joint, Inspection" in "Front Suspension & Steering."
④ — Cross caster (L-R), -.4° to +.8°, preferred, +.2°.
⑤ — Cross caster (L-R), -.8° to +.4°, preferred, -.2°.
⑥ — Long wheel base.
⑦ — Short wheel base.
⑧ — Cross camber (L-R), -.6° to +.6°, preferred, 0°.
⑨ — Cross caster (L-R), -1° to 0°, preferred, -.5°.
⑩ — Cross camber (L-R), -.5° to +.5°, preferred, 0°.
⑪ — Cross caster (L-R), -1.1° to -.1°, desired, -.5°.
⑫ — Air spring rear suspension.
⑬ — Cross caster (L-R), -.8° to -.2°, desired, -.5.
⑭ — 2WD.
⑮ — 4WD.
⑯ — Cross camber (L-R), -.3° to +.3°, preferred, 0°.
⑰ — Coil spring rear suspension.

FLUID CAPACITIES & COOLING SYSTEM DATA

Year	Engine Liter	Cooling Capacity, Qts.	Coolant Type	Radiator Cap Relief Pressure, Lbs.	Thermo. Opening Temp. °F	Fuel Tank Gals.	Engine Oil Refill Qts.⑪	Transmission Oil		Trans. Case Pts.	Drive Axle Oil	
								Man. Trans. Pts.	Auto. Trans., Qts.①		Front Pts.	Rear Pts.
2002	4.2L	13.9	⑦	15	195	18.6	7.0	—	④	4	1.7	3.6
	4.3L	⑨	⑦	15	195	⑩	4.5	⑧	④	②	2.6	4.0
2003–05	4.2L	⑥	⑦	15	195	⑤	7.0	—	④	4	1.7	3.6
	4.3L	⑨	⑦	15	195	⑩	4.5	⑧	④	②	2.6	4.0
	5.3L	③	⑦	15	195	⑤	6.0	—	④	4	1.7	4.3
2006	4.2L	⑥	⑦	15	195	⑤	7.0	—	④	4	1.7	3.6
	5.3L	③	⑦	15	195	⑤	6.0	—	④	4	1.7	4.3
	6.0L	③	⑦	15	195	⑤	6.0	—	④	4	1.7	4.3

① — Approximate make final inspection w/dipstick.
② — New Venture models 136 & 236, 4.0 pts.; New Venture model 233, 2.1 pts.
③ — Short wheel base, 15.3 qts.; long wheel base, 17.9 qts.
④ — Total capacity, 11 qts.; pan only, 5 qts.
⑤ — Short wheel base, 22 gallons; long wheel base, 25.3 gallons.
⑥ — Short wheel base, 13.9 qts.; long wheel base, 15.2 qts.
⑦ — 50/50 mixture water and GM Goodwrench DEX-COOL or Havoline DEX-COOL coolant.
⑧ — New Venture model 1500, 5.8 pts.; model 3500, 4.4 pts.
⑨ — With auto trans., 11.7 qts.; w/man. trans., 11.9 qts.
⑩ — 2 door, 19 gals.; 4 door, 18 gals.
⑪ — Includes filter.

LUBRICANT DATA

Year	Model	Lubricant Type						
		Transmission		Hydraulic Clutch Fluid	Transfer Case	Drive Axle	Power Steering	Brake System
		Manual	Automatic					
2002–05	All	①	Dexron III	DOT 3	③	80W-90 GL-5④	②	DOT 3
2006	All	①	Dexron VI	—	③	80W-90 GL-5④	②	DOT 3

①— GM standard transmission fluid Part No. 12345349, or equivalent.
②— Power steering fluid, GM Part No. 1052884, or equivalent.
③— Manual transfer case requires Dexron III. Automatic transfer case uses GM part No. 12378396, or equivalent.
④— Models w/limited–slip or locking differentials, do not add limited slip additive.

Electrical

NOTE: On Air Bag Equipped Models, Refer To "Air Bag System Precautions" Located In The Front Of This Manual For System Disarming & Arming Procedures.

NOTE: Refer To "Computer Relearn Procedures" Located In The Front Of This Manual When Battery Power To The Computer Has Been Interrupted.

INDEX

PRECAUTIONS

Air Bag Systems

Refer to "Air Bag System Precautions" in the front of this manual for system disarming and arming procedures.

Battery Ground Cable

Prior to service, disconnect battery ground cable and isolate as required.

Radio Security System

THEFTLOCK

If the Theftlock system is active when battery power is interrupted, the customers security code must be entered to restore proper function of the radio. To unlock a secured radio after power loss, proceed as follows:

1. With ignition in On position, "LOC" appears on display.
2. Press "NM" button and "000" will appear on display.
3. Press "NM" until last two digits agree with security code.
4. Press "HR" button until first digit agrees with security code.
5. Press "AM-FM" to select code entered, "SEC" will appear on display indicating radio is now operable and secure.
6. If incorrect code is entered eight times, "INOP" will display. In order to reenter code, the ignition must be left on for one hour before code can be entered and only three more chances to enter code are available before display reads "INOP."

DELCO LOC II

If the Delco LOC II system is active when battery power is interrupted, the customers security code must be entered to restore proper function of the radio. To unlock a secured radio after power loss, proceed as follows:

1. Turn ignition lock to Accessory or Run position.
2. Press "SET" button and "000" will appear on display.
3. Press "SEEK" button until second and third digits of code appear.
4. Press "SCAN" button until first digit of code appears.
5. Press "AM-FM" button and "000" appears on display.
6. Press "SEEK" button until fifth and sixth digits of code appear.
7. Press "SCAN" button until fourth digit appears.
8. Press "AM-FM" button. If unlock sequence was successful, display will show "SEC," indicating unit is operational. If display shows "LOC," numbers did not match and unlock sequence was not successful.

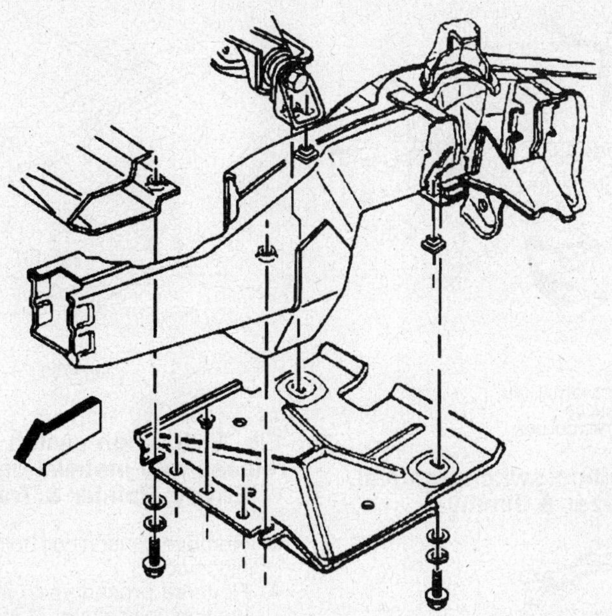

Fig. 1 Differential shield replacement. 4.2L & 4.3L engines w/4WD

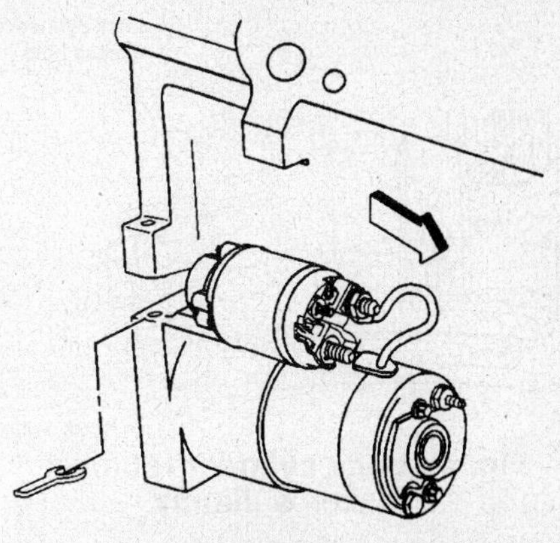

Fig. 2 Starter shim location. 4.2L & 4.3L engines

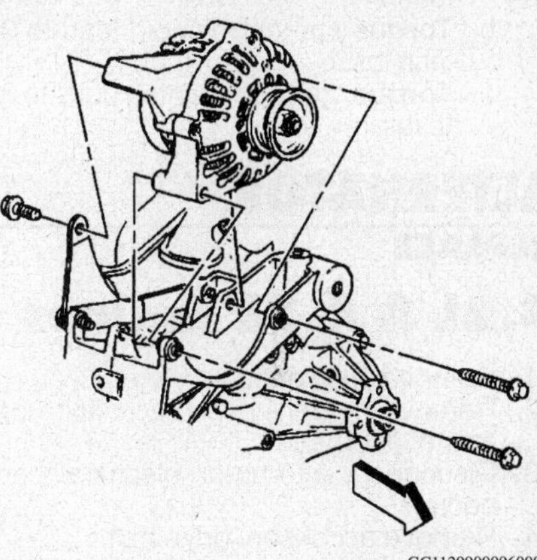

Fig. 3 Alternator removal. 4.2L & 4.3L engines

FUSE PANEL & FLASHER LOCATION

Blazer & Jimmy

The engine compartment fuse panel is located to the right of the battery.

This instrument panel fuse block is on the lefthand side of the instrument panel, near the door jamb switch.

The hazard and turn signal flashers are located behind the righthand side of the instrument panel, mounted on the inline connector, below the recirculation door motor.

Bravada, Envoy, Rainier & Trailblazer

The rear fuse block is located under the lefthand side of the rear seat. The underhood fuse block is located on the lefthand side of the engine compartment.

The turn signal/flasher module is located behind the lefthand side of the instrument panel, behind the knee bolster.

FUEL PUMP RELAY LOCATION

The fuel pump relay is located on the front lefthand side of the engine compartment, in the Underhood Bussed Electrical Center (UBEC).

RELAY CENTER LOCATION

Blazer & Jimmy

Relays are found in the Underhood Bussed Electrical Center (UBEC) or the Body Bussed Electrical Center (BBEC). The UBEC is located in the engine compartment above the left front fenderwell. The BBEC is behind the lefthand side of the instrument panel, near the fuse block.

Bravada, Envoy, Rainier & Trailblazer

Relays are located in the rear fuse block and the underhood fuse block. The rear fuse block is located under the lefthand side of the rear seat. The underhood fuse block is located on the lefthand side of the engine compartment.

STARTER

REPLACE

Upon removal of starter, note if any shims are used. If shims are used, they should be installed in their original locations. After installation, if starter is noisy during cranking, remove one .015 inch double shim or add one .015 inch single shim to the outer bolt. If starter makes a high pitched whine after firing, add .015 inch double shims until noise ceases.

4.2L & 4.3L Engines

1. Raise and support vehicle.
2. Remove right front tire and wheel assembly.
3. **On models equipped with 4WD**, remove differential carrier shield mounting bolts, then the shield, **Fig. 1**.
4. **On all models,** remove wires from starter solenoid.
5. Remove starter mounting bolts, then the starter. Note location of starter shims for installation reference, **Fig. 2.**
6. Reverse procedure to install, noting the following:
   a. **Torque** starter mounting bolts to 37 ft. lbs.
   b. **Torque** differential carrier shield to 18 ft. lbs.

5.3L & 6.0L Engines

1. Raise and support vehicle.
2. Remove front steering gear crossmember rear mounting bolts.
3. Remove rear steering gear crossmember mounting bolts, then the rear steering gear crossmember from vehicle.
4. Remove wire harness from harness retaining clips on transmission oil cooler line bracket.
5. Remove transmission oil cooler line bracket bolt.
6. Remove right transmission cover bolt.
7. Remove starter mounting bolts.
8. Move starter toward front of vehicle and remove transmission cover.
9. Remove starter solenoid heat shield.
10. Tilt and rotate starter in order to pass starter between transmission oil cooler lines and engine oil pan.
11. Remove starter solenoid nut, then the starter lead from solenoid stud.
12. Remove battery positive cable nut, then the battery positive cable from starter solenoid.
13. Remove starter from vehicle.

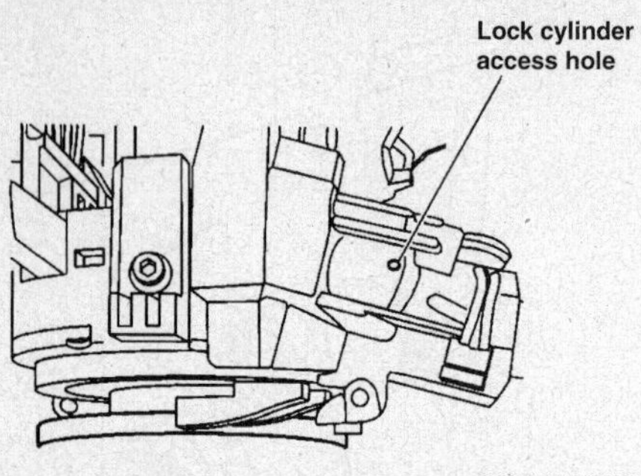

Fig. 4 Lock cylinder removal. Blazer & Jimmy

14. Reverse procedure to install, noting the following:
    a. **Torque** battery cable nut to 80 inch lbs.
    b. **Torque** starter solenoid lead to 30 inch lbs.
    c. **Torque** starter mounting bolts to 37 ft. lbs.

ALTERNATOR

REPLACE

4.2L & 4.3L Engines

1. Remove air inlet duct.
2. Remove heater hose brace bolt from rear of alternator.
3. Disconnect alternator electrical connectors.
4. Remove accessory drive belt.
5. Remove alternator mounting bolts, then the alternator, **Fig. 3.**
6. Reverse procedure to install noting the following:
    a. **Torque** front alternator bolt to 37 ft. lbs.
    b. **Torque** rear alternator bolt to 18 ft. lbs.
    c. **Torque** heater hose brace bolt to 18 ft. lbs.

5.3L & 6.0L Engines

1. Remove accessory drive belt.
2. Disconnect alternator electrical connector, then the alternator cable.
3. Remove alternator bolts, then the alternator from vehicle.
4. Reverse procedure to install noting the following:
    a. **Torque** alternator bolts to 37 ft. lbs.
    b. **Torque** alternator cable nut to 80 inch lbs.

COIL PACK

REPLACE

4.2L Engine

1. Disconnect electrical connectors from intake air temperature sensor, then the air cleaner outlet duct from resonator.
2. Disconnect fuel pressure regulator vacuum supply from air cleaner outlet resonator.
3. Disconnect crankcase ventilation hose from valve cover port.

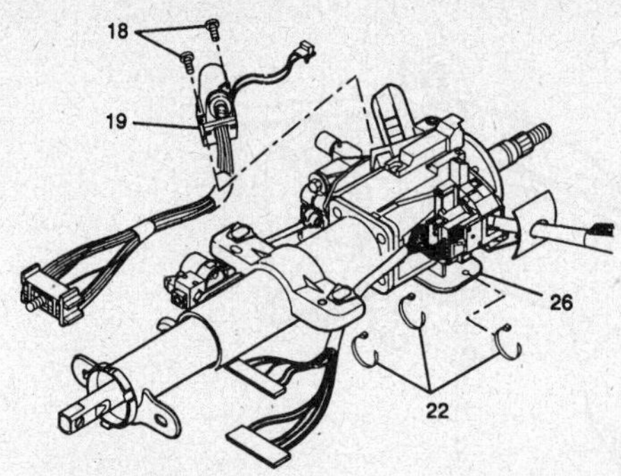

Fig. 5 Ignition switch removal. Blazer & Jimmy

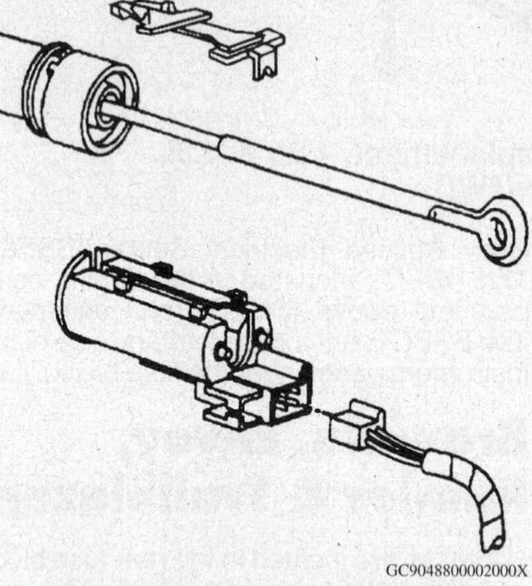

Fig. 7 Clutch start switch

4. Remove air cleaner outlet resonator assembly from engine.
5. Disconnect ignition coil connectors from ignition coils.
6. Remove ignition coils from engine.
7. Reverse procedure to install. **Torque** ignition coil retaining bolts to 89 inch lbs.

4.3L Engine

1. Disconnect electrical to coil base (ICM), then the coil high tension lead.
2. Remove studs retaining coil base to engine, then lift assembly from engine.
3. Remove heads from rivets retaining coil to base using a suitable drill motor and bit, then punch rivets out using a suitable pin punch.
4. Install new coil to base using screws supplied with new coil.
5. Reverse procedure to install. **Torque** mounting studs to 97 inch lbs.

5.3L & 6.0L Engines

1. Remove spark plug wire from ignition coil.
2. Disconnect ignition coil electrical connector.

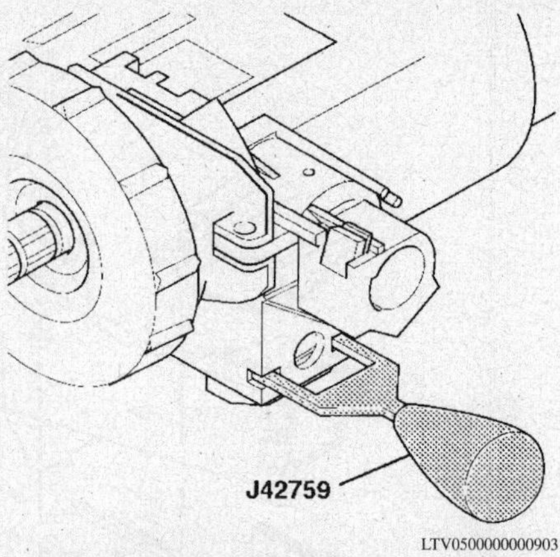

Fig. 6 Ignition switch connector release tool installation. Bravada, Envoy, Rainier & Trailblazer

3. Remove ignition coil bolts, then the ignition coil.
4. Reverse procedure to install. **Torque** ignition coil bolts to 71 inch lbs.

IGNITION LOCK

REPLACE

Blazer & Jimmy

1. Remove upper and lower steering column shrouds.
2. Turn ignition lock cylinder to start position.
3. Insert tip into ignition lock cylinder access hole using a suitable awl, **Fig. 4.**
4. Push down and hold ignition lock cylinder retaining pin.
5. Turn lock cylinder to Run position.
6. Pull lock cylinder away from steering column.
7. Reverse procedure to install.

Bravada, Envoy, Rainier & Trailblazer

1. Lower hush and knee bolster panels.
2. Remove steering column trim covers.
3. Turn ignition key to RUN position.
4. Install a suitable allen wrench into hole on top of lock cylinder housing.
5. Push down on allen wrench to release tab on lock cylinder inside lock cylinder housing.
6. Slide lock cylinder out of housing.
7. Reverse procedure to install.

IGNITION SWITCH

REPLACE

Blazer & Jimmy

1. Remove steering wheel as outlined in "Steering Wheel, Replace."
2. **On models equipped with tilt column,** remove tilt lever.
3. **On all models,** remove two tapping screws from lower column shroud, then the lower shroud.
4. Remove two Torx head screws from upper shroud.

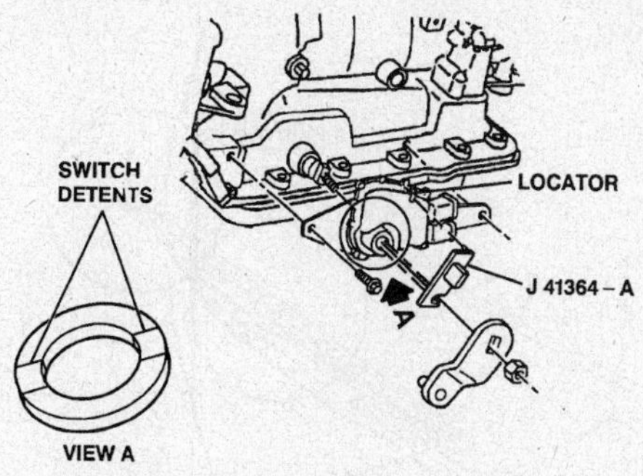

Fig. 8 Neutral safety switch adjustment. Automatic transmission

5. Gently pry retaining clip on key alarm switch with suitable screwdriver, then rotate switch ¼ turn and remove.
6. Remove Pass Key connector from lock module assembly, **Fig. 5.**
7. Remove two tapping screws from ignition switch assembly.
8. Remove wiring harness from slot in steering column head assembly.
9. Reverse procedure to install.

Bravada, Envoy, Rainier & Trailblazer

1. Remove lock cylinder as outlined under "Ignition Lock, Replace."
2. Disconnect passlock and key buzzer from lock cylinder housing.
3. Insert ignition switch connector release tool No. J 42759, or equivalent, into lock cylinder housing to release tabs on ignition switch, **Fig. 6.**
4. Pull ignition switch out of lock cylinder housing and disconnect electrical connector.
5. Reverse procedure to install.

CLUTCH START SWITCH

REPLACE

1. Remove lower instrument panel trim.
2. Remove clutch start switch electrical connector, **Fig. 7.**
3. Remove clutch start switch from clutch pedal.
4. Reverse procedure to install.

NEUTRAL SAFETY SWITCH

REPLACE

The neutral start switch also incorporates the back-up light switch in these vehicles.

Automatic Transmission

REMOVAL

1. Place transmission in neutral position, then raise and support vehicle.
2. Remove lever to transmission manual shaft retaining nut, then pull arm from shaft and let hang from shift cable.
3. Disconnect electrical connector from switch, then remove switch to transmission retaining bolts.
4. Slide switch off manual shaft. **It may be required to lightly file end of manual shaft to remove any burrs.**

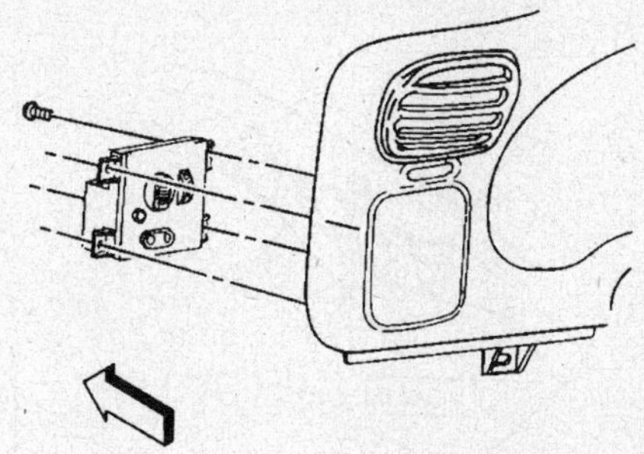

Fig. 9 Headlamp switch removal. Blazer & Jimmy

INSTALLATION

1. Install alignment fixture tool, or equivalent, as outlined in **Fig. 8,** into neutral safety switch.
2. Ensure tabs of tool are fully engaged into switch detents and locator pin is engaged into locator slot on switch.
3. Ensure transmission is in neutral position.
4. Slide switch onto manual shaft, engaging switch to flats of shaft. **It may be required to lightly file end of manual shaft to remove any burrs.**
5. Seat switch against transmission, then install mounting bolts and **torque** to 21 ft. lbs.
6. Remove alignment tool.
7. Install electrical connector switch, then install control arm onto manual shaft, engaging flats of shaft to arm.
8. Install nut to shaft, then while holding arm with a suitable tool to prevent movement, **torque** nut to 21 ft. lbs.
9. Ensure vehicle will start only with shift lever in either Park or Neutral positions.

Manual Transmission

1. Disconnect back-up lamp switch electrical connector.
2. Disconnect switch wiring from transmission bracket, four-wheel drive vehicles only.
3. Remove switch from transmission.
4. Reverse procedure to install.

HEADLAMP SWITCH

REPLACE

Blazer & Jimmy

1. Ensure headlamp switch is in Off position and ignition switch is in LOCK position.
2. Remove instrument panel accessory trim plate.

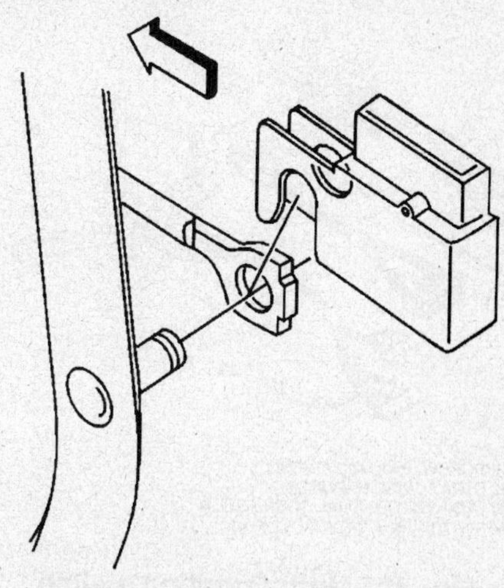

Fig. 10 Stoplight switch removal

3. Disconnect headlamp switch electrical connectors.
4. Remove switch to accessory trim plate retaining screws, **Fig. 9.**
5. Remove headlamp switch.
6. Reverse procedure to install.

Bravada, Envoy, Rainier & Trailblazer

1. Ensure headlamp switch is Off and ignition switch is in Lock position.
2. Remove left instrument panel sound insulator and knee bolster panels from under instrument panel.
3. Remove instrument panel accessory trim plate to the instrument panel retaining screws.
4. Release retaining clips, then remove instrument panel accessory trim plate.
5. Remove control switches, then disconnect electrical connectors.
6. Remove headlamp switch panel to instrument panel accessory trim plate attaching screws.
7. Remove headlamp switch panel from instrument panel accessory trim plate.
8. Reverse procedure to install.

STOP LIGHT SWITCH

REPLACE

1. Remove left close out insulator panel from below instrument panel.
2. Disconnect stop light switch electrical connector.
3. Remove pushrod retainer from brake pedal pin.
4. Unsnap stop light switch from pushrod, then remove switch, **Fig. 10.**
5. Reverse procedure to install.

MULTI-FUNCTION SWITCH

REPLACE

1. Remove steering wheel as outlined in "Steering Wheel, Replace."
2. **On models equipped with tilt column,** remove tilt lever.

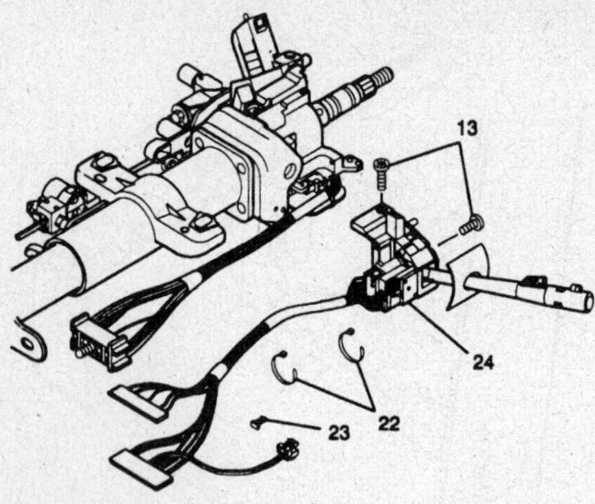

Fig. 11 Multi-Function switch removal

3. **On all models,** remove two tapping screws from lower column shroud, then the lower shroud.
4. Remove two Torx head screws from upper shroud.
5. Remove two wiring harness straps from steering column wiring harness, **Fig. 11.**
6. Disconnect steering column bulkhead connector from vehicle wiring harness.
7. **On models equipped with column shift,** remove axial position assurance connector from BTSI actuator.
8. **On all models,** remove grey and black multi-function switch connectors from column bulkhead connector.
9. Remove two pan head tapping screws from multi-function switch, then the switch.
10. Reverse procedure to install.

TURN SIGNAL SWITCH

REPLACE

Refer to "Multi-Function Switch, Replace" for turn signal switch replacement procedure.

DIMMER SWITCH

REPLACE

Refer to "Multi-Function Switch, Replace" for replacement procedure.

STEERING WHEEL

REPLACE

1. Remove air bag retaining bolts and air bag after disconnecting air bag wire.
2. Remove steering wheel retaining nut.
3. Remove horn lead assembly.
4. Mark relationship of steering wheel to steering shaft.
5. Remove steering wheel.
6. Reverse procedure to install, noting the following:
   a. **Torque** steering wheel nut to 30 ft. lbs.

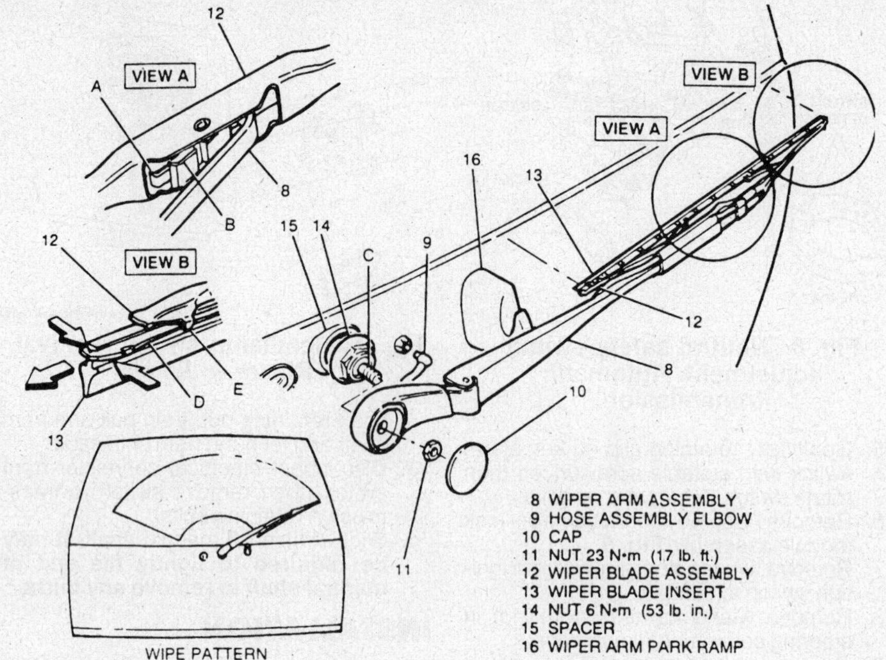

Fig. 12 Rear wiper motor replacement

INSTRUMENT CLUSTER

REPLACE

Blazer & Jimmy

1. Remove sound insulators.
2. Remove steering column nuts, then lower column for access.
3. Remove instrument cluster bezel.
4. Disconnect cluster electrical connectors.
5. Remove cluster to instrument panel screws, then the cluster from vehicle.

Bravada, Envoy, Rainier & Trailblazer

1. Remove lefthand closeout insulator and knee bolster trim panels from instrument panel.
2. Tilt steering wheel to full down position.
3. Remove instrument cluster bezel to instrument panel retaining screws, then the bezel from instrument panel.
4. Remove cluster to instrument panel retaining screws, then partially remove cluster from instrument panel in order to gain access to electrical connector.
5. Disconnect electrical connector from cluster.
6. Remove cluster from instrument panel.
7. Reverse procedure to install.

RADIO

REPLACE

Blazer & Jimmy

1. Remove accessory trim, then the HVAC control assembly.
2. Remove radio mounting screws and nuts.
3. Remove instrument panel center compartment from radio.
4. Reverse procedure to install.

Bravada, Envoy, Rainier & Trailblazer

1. **On Envoy models,** remove lower closeout/insulator panel from instrument panel.
2. **On all models,** tilt steering wheel to full down position.
3. Remove left closeout/insulator and knee bolster trim panels from lefthand side of instrument panel.
4. Remove instrument cluster bezel retaining screws, then the bezel from instrument panel.
5. Remove radio to instrument panel retaining screws.
6. Partially remove and disengage radio from rear alignment locator to access electrical connectors.
7. Disconnect electrical connectors and radio antenna cable.
8. Remove radio from vehicle.
9. Reverse procedure to install.

WIPER MOTOR

REPLACE

Front

1. Remove windshield wiper arms.
2. Remove cowl vent and grille.
3. Remove wiper transmission drive link to motor crank arm attaching nuts, then disconnect drive link from motor crank arm using wiper transmission separator tool No. J-39232, or equivalent.

4. Disconnect motor electrical connector and remove attaching bolts.
5. Remove motor by rotating up and outward.
6. Reverse procedure to install, noting the following:
   a. **Torque** motor attaching bolts to 57 inch lbs.
   b. Install drive link to wiper motor using wiper transmission installer tool No. J-39529, or equivalent.

Rear

1. Put wiper arm assembly in park position, then remove hose assembly elbow from hose connector.
2. Remove cap, then the nut from wiper arm assembly.
3. Remove wiper arm assembly from shaft.
4. Remove nut and spacer from shaft, then the interior panel from vehicle liftgate, **Fig. 12.**
5. Disconnect controller electrical connector.
6. Remove wiper motor screws, then the wiper motor from vehicle.
7. Disconnect wiper motor harness from controller, then remove controller from wiper motor.
8. Reverse procedure to install, noting the following:
   a. Position motor on vehicle with screws, while keeping shaft centered in liftgate hole. **Torque** wiper motor screws to 57 inch lbs.
   b. **Torque** shaft nut to 53 inch lbs.

WIPER SWITCH

REPLACE

Front

Refer to "Multi-Function Switch, Replace" for front wiper switch replacement procedure.

Rear

1. Remove wiper switch from trim plate, **Fig. 13.**
2. Disconnect electrical connector from wiper switch.
3. Reverse procedure to install.

WIPER TRANSMISSION

REPLACE

1. Remove wiper arm assembly.
2. Remove cowl vent grille.
3. Remove transmission screws, then unseat transmission assembly from wiper motor crank arm using wiper transmission separator tool No. J-39232, or equivalent.
4. Remove wiper transmission through access openings in top of cowl.
5. Reverse procedure to install, noting the following:
   a. **Torque** transmission assembly screws to 70 inch lbs.
   b. Wiper transmission assembly must be assembled to crank arm past second detent so seal is compressed to a maximum height of 1 inch.

GC9049500145000A

Fig. 13 Rear wiper switch replacement

BLOWER MOTOR

REPLACE

Blazer & Jimmy

1. Remove right close out insulator panel from below instrument panel.
2. Remove instrument panel storage compartment door.
3. Disconnect blower motor electrical connector, then remove blower motor mounting screws and blower motor.
4. Reverse procedure to install.

Bravada, Envoy, Rainier & Trailblazer

FRONT

1. Block wheels to prevent vehicle from moving.
2. Remove rubber ash tray inserts and rubber mat from center console.
3. Remove floor shift control knob.
4. **On Rainier models,** remove center console shift lever bezel.
5. **On all models,** remove console storage compartment.
6. Remove center console retaining screws, then adjust parking brake to full-up or fully engaged position.
7. **On Rainier models,** release two forward trim extensions ears attached to lower instrument panel.
8. **On all models,** slide console rearward and raise rear of console in order to access electrical connectors.
9. Disconnect electrical connectors, then adjust parking brake to approximately the halfway position.
10. Remove center console from vehicle.
11. Disconnect blower motor electrical connectors.
12. Remove air outlet duct from blower motor.
13. Remove blower motor retaining screws, then the blower motor.
14. Reverse procedure to install.

REAR

1. Remove cargo shade/cover from right-hand rear quarter trim panel.
2. Remove inflator access panel.
3. Remove right rear quarter upper trim panel to body retaining screws.
4. Remove cargo net retaining knobs.
5. Remove seat belt upper guide to body attaching bolt.
6. Remove rear upper quarter trim panel from vehicle.
7. Remove lift gate and right rear door sill panels.
8. Remove lower seat belt anchor bolt. Release retaining clips that retain the trim panel to the body.
9. Partially remove right rear quarter trim panel in order to remove inflator switch from inflator bezel.
10. Remove auxiliary air outlet washer and retaining nut.
11. Insert auxiliary air outlet through inflator bezel.
12. Remove inflator bezel from trim panel.
13. Disconnect 12-volt power supply electrical connector.
14. Remove right rear quarter panel retaining bolts from HVAC module.
15. Remove right rear quarter trim panel from vehicle.
16. Remove HVAC module retaining nuts from under vehicle.
17. Disconnect module electrical connectors.
18. Remove blower motor retaining screws, then the blower motor from HVAC module.
19. Reverse procedure to install.

HEATER CORE

REPLACE

Blazer & Jimmy

1. Remove instrument panel as outlined in "Dash Panel Service."
2. Remove outer cowls.
3. Disconnect washer lines and underhood lamp.
4. Remove hood and antenna.
5. Remove PCM/VCM module.
6. Drain radiator coolant and remove recovery reservoir.
7. Disconnect coolant hoses from heater core.
8. Remove righthand headlamp assembly.
9. Remove outer fender, battery tray and wheelhouse panel.
10. Evacuate and recover refrigerant.
11. Disconnect A/C lines to evaporator.
12. Remove heater box heat shield.
13. Remove heater core mounting bolts from inside and outside of vehicle.
14. With assistance inside vehicle, carefully pry back on heater box while removing evaporator housing assembly to ensure clearance of stud.
15. Remove heater case assembly and seals.
16. Remove heater core.
17. Reverse procedure to install. **Torque** heater assembly mounting studs and bolts to 40 inch lbs.

Bravada, Envoy, Rainier & Trailblazer

FRONT

1. Drain engine coolant, then recover refrigerant as outlined in "Air Conditioning."
2. Remove instrument panel as outlined in "Dash Panel Service."
3. Disconnect heater hoses from heater core, then the accumulator from evaporator.
4. Disconnect evaporator tube from evaporator, then all electrical connectors to HVAC module assembly.
5. Remove HVAC module assembly.
6. Remove heater core access cover screws, then the heater core access cover.
7. Remove heater core from HVAC module assembly.
8. Reverse procedure to install. **Torque** heater assembly mounting studs and bolts to 17 inch lbs.

REAR

1. Remove righthand rear quarter trim panel as outlined under "Blower Motor, Replace."
2. Recover A/C refrigerant as outlined in "Air Conditioning" chapter.
3. Drain cooling system, then raise and support vehicle.
4. Remove rear A/C line block fitting nuts. Cap or tape open A/C refrigerant lines.
5. Remove A/C line block fittings and discard O-ring seals.
6. Remove heater hoses from HVAC module.
7. Remove nuts from HVAC module studs, then lower vehicle.
8. Disconnect HVAC module electrical connectors.
9. Disconnect rear compartment air outlet ducts from HVAC module.
10. Remove HVAC module mounting bolts, then the module. Remove and discard module pass through seal.
11. Remove heater core cover attaching screws, then the heater core.
12. Reverse procedure to install.

EVAPORATOR CORE

REPLACE

Blazer & Jimmy

1. Remove hood from vehicle.
2. Remove righthand headlamp assembly.
3. Remove outer fender, battery tray and wheelhouse panel.
4. Disconnect evaporator tube from evaporator.
5. Remove accumulator and evaporator core heat shield.
6. Remove blower motor resistor to access heater core case to bulkhead mounting bolt.
7. Remove heater core case to bulkhead mounting bolt.
8. Remove evaporator and blower module mounting screws and nuts.
9. Remove acoustic barrier.
10. Remove lower right heater core case mounting bolts located at lower right side of instrument panel.
11. Have helper lightly pull lower right corner of heater case away from bulkhead to assist in removal.
12. Remove evaporator core assembly from vehicle, then disassemble evaporator core case sections.
13. Remove evaporator core.
14. Reverse procedure to install.

Bravada, Envoy, Rainier & Trailblazer

FRONT

1. Drain engine coolant, then recover refrigerant as outlined in "Air Conditioning."
2. Remove instrument panel as outlined in "Dash Panel Service."
3. Disconnect heater hoses from heater core, then the accumulator from evaporator.
4. Disconnect evaporator tube from evaporator, then all electrical connectors to HVAC module assembly.
5. Remove HVAC module assembly.
6. Remove screws, then separate HVAC module assembly.
7. Remove evaporator core from HVAC module assembly.
8. Remove seal between HVAC module assembly halves.
9. Reverse procedure to install.

REAR

1. Remove rear heater core as outlined under "Heater Core, Replace."
2. Remove inverted TORX studs from evaporator block.
3. Remove backing plate from evaporator core.
4. Remove evaporator core from HVAC module.
5. Carefully remove foam insulator from around evaporator core.
6. Reverse procedure to install.

4.2L Engine

NOTE: On Air Bag Equipped Models, Refer To "Air Bag System Precautions" Located In The Front Of This Manual For System Disarming & Arming Procedures.

NOTE: Refer To "Computer Relearn Procedures" Located In The Front Of This Manual When Battery Power To The Computer Has Been Interrupted.

INDEX

PRECAUTIONS

Air Bag Systems

Refer to "Air Bag System Precautions" in the front of this manual for system disarming and arming procedures.

Battery Ground Cable

Prior to service, disconnect battery ground cable and isolate as required.

Fuel System Pressure Relief

1. Remove fuel pump relay from junction box.
2. Crank engine, then allow engine to start and stall.
3. Crank engine for an additional 3 seconds to ensure relief of any remaining fuel pressure.
4. Disconnect battery ground cable.

Radio Security System

THEFTLOCK

If the Theftlock system is active when battery power is interrupted, the customers security code must be entered to restore proper function of the radio. To unlock a secured radio after power loss, proceed as follows:

1. With ignition in On position, "LOC" appears on display.

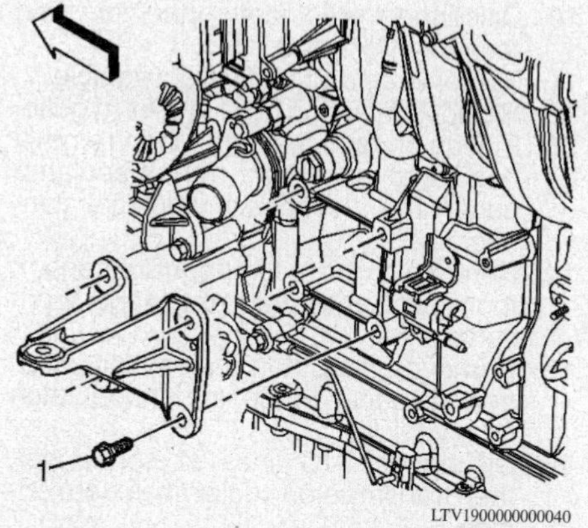

Fig. 1 Engine mount removal

2. Press "NM" button and "000" will appear on display.
3. Press "NM" until last two digits agree with security code.
4. Press "HR" button until first digit agree with security code.
5. Press "AM-FM" to select code entered, "SEC" will appear on display indicating radio is now operable and secure.
6. If incorrect code is entered eight times, "INOP" will display. In order to reenter code, the ignition must be left on for one hour before code can be entered and only three more chances to enter code are available before display reads "INOP."

DELCO LOC II

If the Delco LOC II system is active when battery power is interrupted, the customers security code must be entered to restore proper function of the radio. To unlock a secured radio after power loss, proceed as follows:

1. Turn ignition lock to Accessory or Run position.
2. Press "SET" button and "000" will appear on display.
3. Press "SEEK" button until second and third digits of code appear.
4. Press "SCAN" button until first digit of code appears.
5. Press "AM-FM" button and "000" appears on display.
6. Press "SEEK" button until fifth and sixth digits of code appear.
7. Press "SCAN" button until fourth digit appears.
8. Press "AM-FM" button. If unlock sequence was successful, display will show "SEC," indicating unit is operational. If display shows "LOC," numbers did not match and unlock sequence was not successful.

COMPRESSION PRESSURE

When inspecting cylinder compression, the throttle should be open, all spark plugs removed, the battery at or near full charge and engine at operating temperature. The lowest reading cylinder should not be less than 70% of the highest and no cylinder reading should be less than 215 psi. Turn ignition key until engine cranks through four compression cycles. Normal compression builds up quickly and evenly to specified compression on each cylinder.

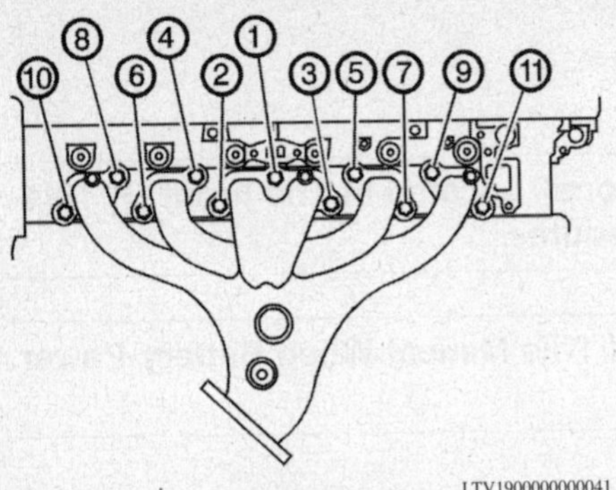

Fig. 2 Exhaust manifold tightening sequence

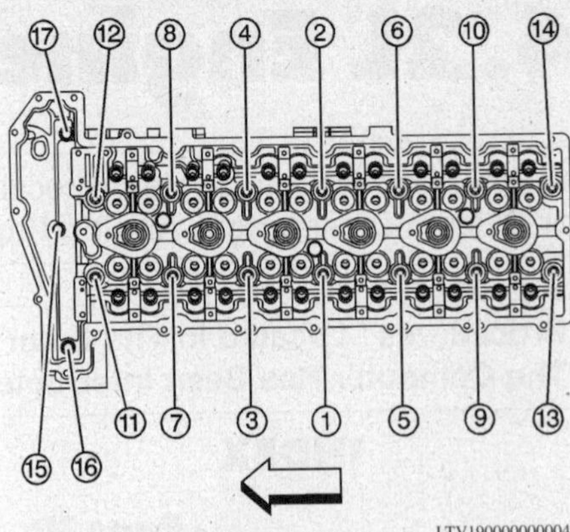

Fig. 3 Cylinder head tightening sequence

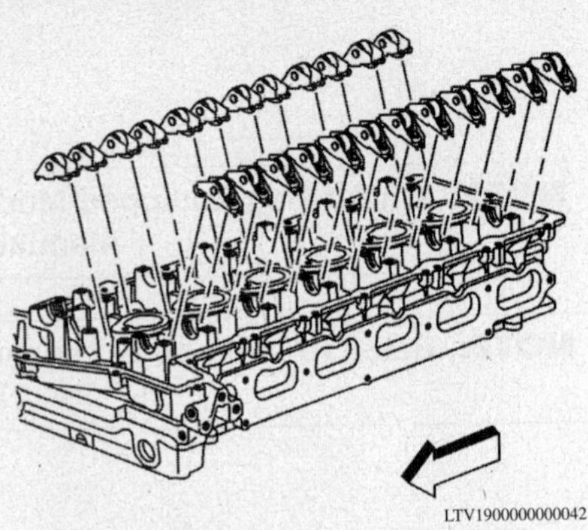

Fig. 4 Valve rocker arm removal

ENGINE MOUNT

REPLACE

1. Remove hood latch support
2. Disconnect transmission cooler lines at engine, then remove lines from fan shroud.
3. Remove upper bolts on fan shroud, then drain cooling system into a suitable container.
4. Remove upper inlet radiator hose from radiator, then the electrical connector from shroud.
5. Position water pump so bolts are aligned vertically, than remove fan hub nut from water pump shaft in a counterclockwise rotation.
6. Secure water pump pulley and loosen cooling fan hub nut from water pump shaft using tool No. J 46406 or equivalent.
7. Unclip fan shroud from radiator at side panels, then tilt radiator and condenser forward.
8. Lift fan and shroud up and out towards engine to release fan from radiator to clear radiator inlet.
9. Remove electrical connector, retainer, and MAP sensor.
10. Remove right and left upper engine mount nuts, then raise and support vehicle.
11. Remove right and left lower engine mount nuts, then engine protection shield.
12. Lower vehicle, then place a floor jack under oil pan with a block of wood and raise engine just enough to clear engine mount studs.
13. Remove engine mount from bracket, **Fig. 1.**
14. Reverse procedure to install.

ENGINE

REPLACE

1. Open hood, then release clips and remove hood molding from hood.
2. Disconnect electrical connectors and fluid lines between hood and vehicle, then mark position of hood hinges for installation reference.
3. Remove hood hinge bolts, then the hood.
4. Drain cooling system and engine oil into suitable containers.
5. **On models equipped with A/C,** recover refrigerant as outlined in "Air Conditioning."
6. **On all models,** remove two air cleaner housing/washer solvent tank assembly retaining nuts from studs.
7. Disconnect washer pump electrical connectors and hoses, then lift and remove air filter housing/washer solvent tank assembly.
8. Remove EVAP canister purge line from throttle body, then disconnect throttle body electrical connector.
9. Remove retainers, then the throttle body assembly and gasket from intake manifold.
10. Disconnect electrical connector, then remove MAP sensor.
11. Remove radiator baffle from vehicle.
12. Remove retaining clips and front grille.
13. Pull up on retaining tabs, then remove headlamp assembly from headlamp panel and disconnect electrical connectors.
14. Remove ambient temperature sensor, then bolts and headlamp panel from vehicle.
15. Remove bolts, then the radiator support diagonal brace and hood latch from vehicle.
16. Disconnect A/C lines at condenser, then transmission cooler lines from engine.
17. Remove cooling fan and shroud by tilting radiator forward, and cooling fan and shroud rearward for clearance.
18. Remove radiator with condenser and transmission cooler lines.
19. Release tensioner and remove drive belt.
20. Remove power steering pump bolts, then lay pump aside.
21. Ensure heater hoses at heater core are disconnected.
22. Remove transmission filler tube bracket nut, then the AIR adapter.
23. Install lift hook J–44220 or equivalent to AIR adapter slot.
24. Disconnect oxygen sensor electrical connector, then A/C line at accumulator.
25. Disconnect front axle actuator, then the camshaft actuator valve electrical connectors.
26. Unclip transmission cooler lines from right side of engine block, then disconnect ignition coil harness connectors.
27. Carefully disconnect harness retainer at clips and remove.
28. Remove power brake hose at booster.
29. Remove PCM harness connectors from PCM, then mounting nuts, bolts and PCM from intake manifold.
30. Disconnect fuel lines at fuel pressure regulator and cap lines.
31. Remove all harnesses from engine harness bracket, then disconnect front differential vent hose from engine harness bracket.
32. Remove engine harness bracket bolt and bracket.
33. Disconnect starter, A/C pressure sensor and clutch electrical connectors.
34. Disconnect alternator and electrical connector and battery lead.
35. Disconnect knock sensor, crankshaft sensor and camshaft sensor electrical connectors.
36. Remove grounds on left side of block, then raise and support vehicle.
37. Remove front tire and wheel assembly, then the engine protection shield.
38. Remove wheel speed sensor wiring harness from retainers and disconnect from harness.
39. Remove retaining bolt for front brake hose, then the front stabilizer bar link from lower control arm.
40. Remove upper shock module retainer from shock tower, then the outer tie rod retaining nut.
41. Disconnect outer tie rod from steering knuckle using tool No. J–24319-B or equivalent.
42. Remove left and right upper ball joint pinch bolts and nuts, then the shock module from shock tower.
43. Remove steering knuckle from upper control arm, then front wheel drive axle from steering knuckle.
44. Reference mark relationship of propeller shaft to front axle, then remove shaft from vehicle.
45. Disconnect exhaust pipe from exhaust manifold, then slide exhaust pipe backward slightly.
46. Remove fuel tank shield, then the torque converter bolt access cover.
47. Remove torque converter bolts, then place a jack on transmission oil pan for support.
48. Remove transmission support, then lower transmission enough to reach

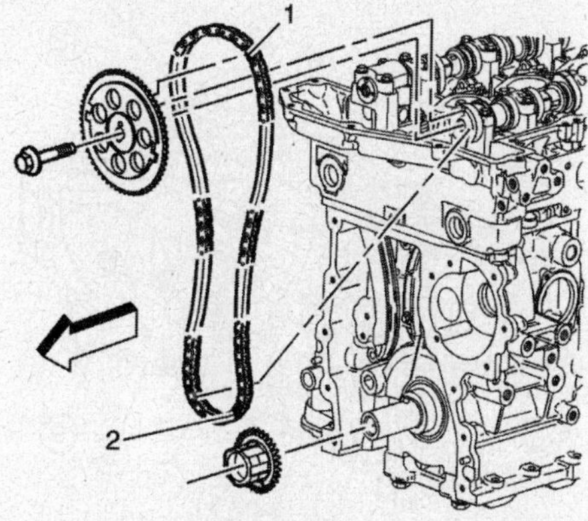

Fig. 5 Timing chain, camshaft & crankshaft sprockets removal

top bell housing bolts.
49. Remove top bell housing bolts, then raise transmission and install support using only through bolts.
50. Remove remaining bell housing bolts, then the left and right engine lower mount nuts.
51. Disconnect oil lever sensor and oil pressure switch electrical connectors.
52. Lower vehicle, and remove left and right upper engine mount nuts.
53. Install engine hoist, then raise engine out of compartment slowly keeping transmission supported.
54. Reverse procedure to install.

INTAKE MANIFOLD

REPLACE

1. Loosen air cleaner outlet duct and air cleaner outlet resonator clamps.
2. Disconnect electrical connector from IAT sensor, then the cleaner outlet duct from air cleaner outlet resonator.
3. Disconnect fuel pressure regulator vacuum supply from air cleaner outlet resonator.
4. Remove air cleaner outlet resonator to engine bolts.
5. Disconnect crankcase ventilation hose from valve cover port, then remove air cleaner outlet resonator assembly.
6. Remove EVAP canister purge line from throttle body, then disconnect throttle body electrical connector.
7. Remove throttle body assembly and gasket from intake manifold.
8. Remove PCM harness connectors from PCM, then mounting nuts, bolts and PCM from intake manifold.
9. Disconnect all harnesses from engine harness bracket.
10. Remove front differential vent hose from bracket clip.
11. Remove engine harness bracket bolt, then the bracket.
12. Disconnect MAP sensor electrical connector, then the crankcase ventilation hose and brake hose at booster.
13. Remove alternator as outlined in "Electrical."
14. Loosen, then remove intake manifold bolts and manifold.
15. Reverse procedure to install.

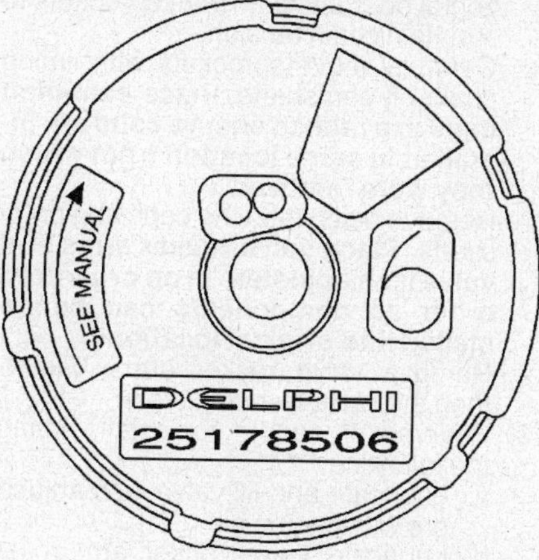

Fig. 6 Camshaft actuator installation

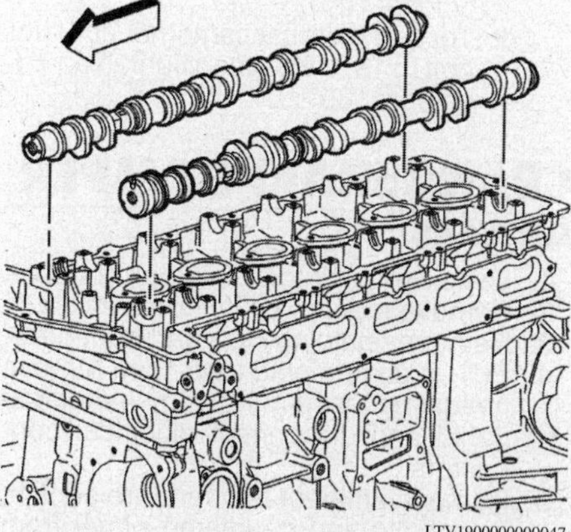

Fig. 8 Camshaft replacement

EXHAUST MANIFOLD

REPLACE

1. Loosen air cleaner outlet duct and air cleaner outlet resonator clamps.
2. Disconnect electrical connector from IAT sensor, then the cleaner outlet duct from air cleaner outlet resonator.
3. Disconnect fuel pressure regulator vacuum supply from air cleaner outlet resonator.
4. Remove air cleaner outlet resonator to engine bolts.
5. Disconnect crankcase ventilation hose from valve cover port, then remove air cleaner outlet resonator assembly.
6. Remove transmission filler tube stud nut from A.I.R. adapter, then set filler tube aside.
7. Remove A/C line bracket from oil dipstick tube stud, then disconnect O2 sensor from oil dipstick bracket.
8. Remove oil dipstick tube stud, pull indicator out of tube and tube out of block.
9. Remove oxygen sensor from exhaust manifold, then the manifold heat shield.
10. Raise and support vehicle, then remove exhaust pipe bolts from exhaust manifold.
11. Lower vehicle, then remove exhaust manifold bolts.
12. Remove exhaust manifold and gasket.

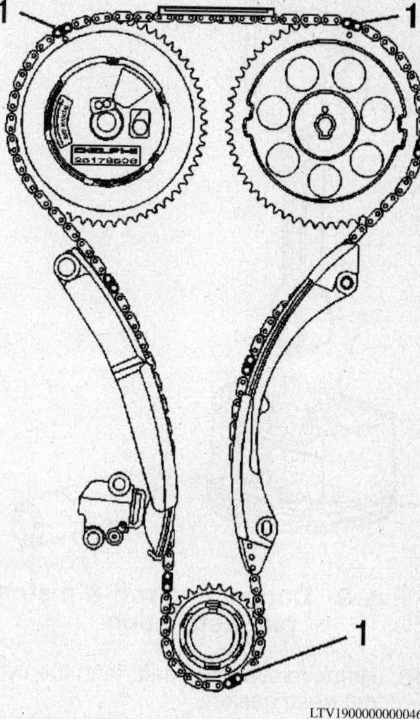

Fig. 7 Timing mark alignment

13. Reverse procedure to install, noting the following:
    a. Install a new exhaust manifold gasket.
    b. With threadlock GM P/N 12345493 on manifold bolts, install bolts onto manifold.
    c. **Torque** exhaust manifold bolts first pass in sequence, **Fig. 2,** to 15 ft. lbs.
    d. **Torque** exhaust manifold bolts second pass in sequence, to 15 ft. lbs.
    e. **Torque** exhaust manifold bolts third pass in sequence, to 15 ft. lbs.

CYLINDER HEAD

REPLACE

1. Remove intake manifold as outlined in "Intake Manifold, Replace."
2. Recover refrigerant as outlined in "Air Conditioning."
3. Remove A/C line at oil dipstick tube bracket nut, then A/C line from accumulator.
4. Remove A/C bracket bolt from engine lift hook, then the engine lift bracket.
5. Disconnect electrical connectors, then remove ignition control module.
6. Disconnect engine electrical harness housing from camshaft cover, then fuel injection harness electrical connector.
7. Remove bolts, then the camshaft cover .
8. Remove exhaust manifold as outlined in "Exhaust Manifold, Replace."
9. Remove front cover as outlined in "Front Cover, Replace."
10. Remove cylinder head access hole plugs.
11. Remove timing chain and sprockets as outlined in "Timing Chain, Replace."
12. Loosen and remove cylinder head bolts.

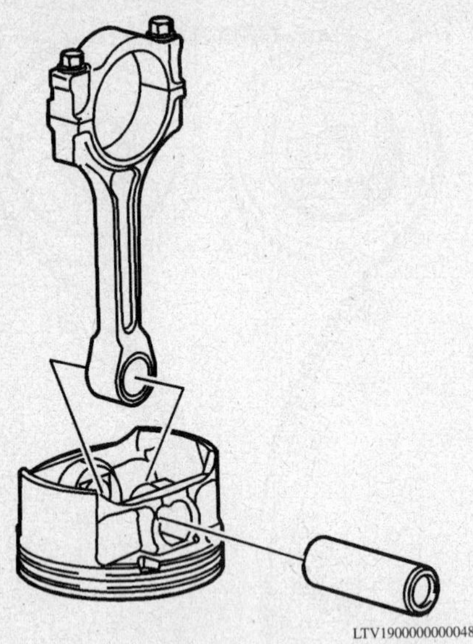

Fig. 9 Connecting rod & piston pin installation

13. Remove cylinder head, then the cylinder head gasket.
14. Reverse procedure to install noting the following:
    a. Tighten cylinder head bolts first to 22 ft. lbs., using numbered sequence, **Fig. 3.**
    b. Tighten cylinder head bolts in sequence an additional 155° using a torque angle meter.
    c. Tighten two short end bolts to 62 inch lbs., then tighten an additional 60°.
    d. Tighten one long end bolt to 62 inch lbs., then tighten an additional 120°.

VALVE CLEARANCE SPECIFICATIONS

Intake 0011–.0025
Exhaust...................................0015–.0030

VALVE ADJUSTMENT

No adjustment is required.

ROCKER ARMS

1. Remove intake manifold as outlined in "Intake Manifold, Replace."
2. Recover refrigerant as outlined in "Air Conditioning."
3. Remove A/C line at oil dipstick tube bracket nut, then A/C line from accumulator.
4. Remove A/C bracket bolt from engine lift hook, then the engine lift bracket.
5. Disconnect electrical connectors, then remove ignition control module.
6. Disconnect engine electrical harness housing from camshaft cover, then fuel injection harness electrical connector.
7. Remove bolts, then the camshaft cover .
8. Remove exhaust and intake sprocket bolts.
9. Install tool No. J–44222 or equivalent, onto cylinder head, then adjust horizontal bolts into camshaft sprockets to maintain chain tension.
10. Carefully move sprockets with timing chain off camshafts. **Place camshaft caps in a rack to ensure caps are installed in same location from which they were removed.**
11. Remove bolts, then the caps and camshafts. **Place valve rocker arms and valve lash adjusters in an organized order so components can be installed into original locations.**
12. Remove valve rocker arms, **Fig. 4.** then the valve lash adjusters.
13. Reverse procedure to install, noting the following:
    a. Lubricate and fill valve lash adjusters with engine oil.
    b. Lubricate valve rocker arm roller and coat camshaft journals with engine oil.
    c. **Torque** intake camshaft sprocket bolt to 15 ft. lbs., then tighten an additional 100°.
    d. **Torque** exhaust camshaft actuator bolt to 18 ft. lbs., then tighten an additional 135°.

CRANKSHAFT DAMPER

REPLACE

1. Drain coolant into a suitable container.
2. Remove radiator baffle from vehicle.
3. Remove retaining clips and front grille.
4. Pull up on retaining tabs, then remove headlamp assembly from headlamp panel and disconnect electrical connectors.
5. Remove ambient temperature sensor, then bolts and headlamp panel from vehicle.
6. Remove bolts, then the radiator support diagonal brace and hood latch from vehicle.
7. Remove cooling fan and shroud by tilting radiator forward, and cooling fan and shroud rearward for clearance.
8. Release tensioner and remove drive belt.
9. Remove damper bolt, then install tool No. J 41816–2 or equivalent into end of crankshaft. **Do not pull on outer edge of crankshaft balancer.**
10. Remove damper using tool No. J 44226 or equivalent.
11. Reverse procedure to install. **Torque** damper bolt to 110 ft. lbs., then tighten an additional 180°.

FRONT COVER

REPLACE

1. Remove crankshaft damper as outlined in "Crankshaft Damper, Replace."
2. Remove water pump as outlined in "Water Pump, Replace."
3. Remove power steering pump as outlined in "Power Steering Pump, Replace."
4. Remove oil pan as outlined in "Oil Pan, Replace."
5. Remove center bolt first, then the remaining bolts.
6. Place two of front cover bolts in jack

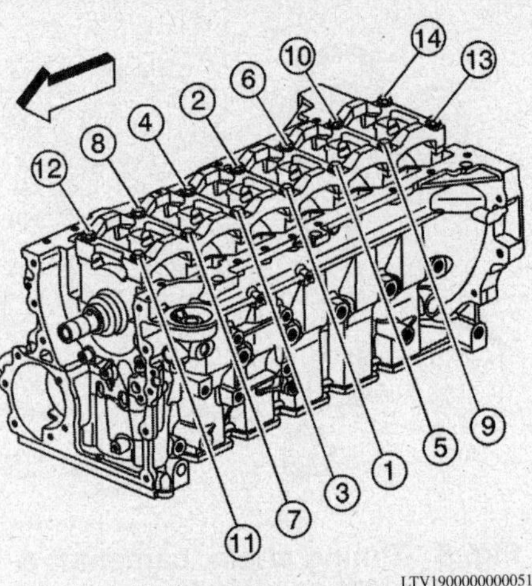

Fig. 10 Crankshaft main bearing caps tightening sequence

screw holes on front cover, then tighten bolts evenly to release front cover from engine.
7. Reverse procedure to install, noting the following:
    a. Apply a .12 inch bead of sealer GM P/N 12378521 to trace grooves on back side of engine front cover.
    b. Also apply sealant on inside three bolt hole bosses on cover.

FRONT COVER SEAL

REPLACE

1. Remove front cover as outlined in "Front Cover, Replace."
2. Pry seal from front cover, using a suitable pry bar.
3. Install new seal using a suitable driver/alignment tool **Leave tool installed in seal until front cover has been installed.**

TIMING CHAIN

REPLACE

Removal

1. Remove intake manifold as outlined in "Intake Manifold, Replace."
2. Recover refrigerant as outlined in "Air Conditioning."
3. Remove A/C line at oil dipstick tube bracket nut, then A/C line from accumulator.
4. Remove A/C bracket bolt from engine lift hook, then the engine lift bracket.
5. Disconnect electrical connectors, then remove ignition control module.
6. Disconnect engine electrical harness housing from camshaft cover, then fuel injection harness electrical connector.
7. Remove bolts, then the camshaft cover.
8. Remove front cover as outlined in "Front Cover, Replace."
9. Release tension on timing chain by moving tensioner shoe in, then place tee into tensioner to hold shoe in place.
10. Remove bolts, then the top chain guide and exhaust camshaft position actuator.

11. Remove intake camshaft sprocket, then the timing chain and crankshaft sprocket, **Fig. 5.**
12. Remove cylinder head access hole plugs, then the timing chain tensioner shoe.
13. Remove timing chain tensioner guide, then the timing chain tensioner.

Installation

Every seventh link of the timing chain is darkened to aid in aligning the timing marks.

1. Install timing chain tensioner with retaining bolts.
2. Install timing chain tensioner guide, then the timing chain tensioner shoe.
3. Install cylinder head access hole plugs, then J–44221 or equivalent with camshaft flats up and number 1 cylinder at top dead center.
4. Install crankshaft sprocket, then the intake camshaft sprocket into timing chain.
5. Align dark link of timing chain with timing mark on intake camshaft sprocket.
6. Feed timing chain down through opening in head.
7. Install timing chain on crankshaft sprocket, then align dark link of timing chain with timing mark on to crankshaft sprocket.
8. **It may be required to remove J–44221 or equivalent, to rotate and hold camshaft to align pin to camshaft sprocket.** Install intake camshaft sprocket onto intake camshaft.
9. Install intake camshaft sprocket washer and bolt.
10. Install exhaust camshaft actuator into timing chain, then align dark link of timing chain with timing mark on exhaust camshaft actuator.
11. Install exhaust camshaft actuator onto exhaust camshaft.
12. Rotate camshaft actuator clockwise until it stops, as seen from front of vehicle **Fig. 6. Camshaft actuator must be fully advanced during installation. Engine damage may occur if camshaft actuator is not fully advanced.**
13. **Torque** exhaust camshaft actuator bolt to 18 ft. lbs., then an additional 135°.
14. **Torque** intake camshaft sprocket bolt to 15 ft. lbs., then an additional 100°.
15. Remove tee in timing chain tensioner to regain tension on timing chain, then the tool.
16. Dark lines on chain should be aligned with marks on sprockets, **Fig. 7.**
17. Install top chain guide, add threadlock GM P/N 12345496 or equivalent, on top chain guide bolt threads.
18. Install engine front cover as outlined in "Front Cover, Replace."
19. Install a new camshaft cover seal, then new rubber ignition control module seals.
20. Install camshaft cover, then the ignition control modules.
21. Connect ignition control module and fuel injector electrical connectors.
22. Install engine electrical harness housing, then the A/C line bracket to oil dipstick tube stud.
23. Install engine lift bracket, then the A/C line bracket to engine lift bracket.
24. Install intake manifold as outlined in "Intake Manifold, Replace."
25. Recharge A/C system as outlined in "Air Conditioning."

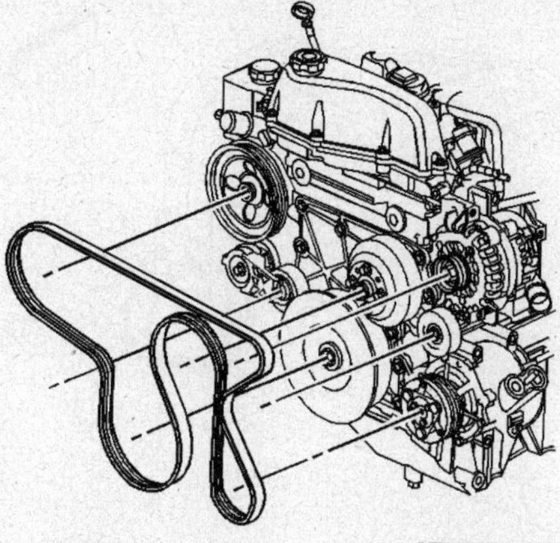

Fig. 11 Drive belt routing

CAMSHAFT

REPLACE

1. Remove intake manifold as outlined in "Intake Manifold, Replace."
2. Recover refrigerant as outlined in "Air Conditioning."
3. Remove A/C line at oil dipstick tube bracket nut, then A/C line from accumulator.
4. Remove A/C bracket bolt from engine lift hook, then the engine lift bracket.
5. Disconnect electrical connectors, then remove ignition control module.
6. Disconnect engine electrical harness housing from camshaft cover, then fuel injection harness electrical connector.
7. Remove bolts, then the camshaft cover .
8. Remove intake and exhaust camshaft sprocket bolts.
9. Install tool No. J–44222 or equivalent, onto cylinder head, then adjust horizontal bolts into camshaft sprockets to maintain chain tension.
10. Carefully move sprockets with timing chain off camshafts. **Place camshaft caps in a rack to ensure caps are installed in same location from which they were removed.**
11. Remove camshaft caps and store, then the camshaft, **Fig. 8.**
12. Reverse procedure to install noting the following:
    a. Coat camshaft journals, camshaft journal thrust face and camshaft lobes with clean engine oil.
    b. Install tool No. J–44221 or equivalent with camshaft flats up and number 1 cylinder at top dead center.
    c. **Torque** exhaust camshaft actuator bolt to 18 ft. lbs., then an additional 135°.
    d. **Torque** intake camshaft sprocket bolt to 15 ft. lbs., then an additional 100°.

PISTON & ROD ASSEMBLY

Assemble piston to rod, with arrow on piston facing toward front of engine. The piston ring end gaps must be staggered 90 degrees apart. Use a piston ring expander to install the piston rings. The rings may be damaged if expanded more than required, **Fig. 9.**

PISTONS, PINS & RINGS

Pistons are available in standard size and oversize of .020 inch (.5 mm). Piston pins are available in standard size only.

MAIN & ROD BEARINGS

1. Install upper crankshaft main bearings into block.
2. Lubricate upper crankshaft main bearing surface with clean engine oil, then install crankshaft.
3. **Refer to pin stamp on crankshaft main bearing caps for sequence and direction of installation. Pin stamp arrow points to the front of engine.** Install lower crankshaft main bearings into main bearing caps.
4. Lubricate lower crankshaft main bearing surface with clean engine oil, then install crankshaft main bearing caps.
5. Install crankshaft main bearing cap stiffener.
6. Install new crankshaft main bearing bolts, then start crankshaft main bearing cap bolts by hand.
7. Ensure bottom of crankshaft main bearing cap is parallel to block surface.
8. Tighten crankshaft main bearing cap bolts in sequence, **Fig. 10,** to 18 ft. lbs.
9. Tighten crankshaft main bearing cap bolts an additional 180°.

CRANKSHAFT SEAL

REPLACE

Front

Do not damage the engine front cover or the crankshaft.

1. Remove crankshaft damper as outlined in "Crankshaft Damper, Replace."
2. Pry out crankshaft front oil seal using a suitable tool. Use provided slots for prying out seal.
3. Reverse procedure to install. Install front oil seal using tool No. J–44218 or equivalent.

Rear

1. Remove transmission assembly, and flywheel as outlined in **MOTOR's "Domestic Transmission, In-Vehicle Service."**
2. pry seal from bore with tool, taking care not to mark crankshaft.
3. Thoroughly clean seal bore in block,

inspect bore and crankshaft surface for nicks, burrs and wear and correct as needed.
4. Reverse procedure to install. Install rear oil seal using tool No. J–44227 or equivalent.

OIL PAN

REPLACE

1. Remove A/C compressor bottom bolts and loosen top bolts.
2. Remove A/C line bracket nut, then the A/C line bracket from oil dipstick tube stud.
3. Disconnect O2 sensor electrical connector from oil dipstick bracket, then remove oil dipstick tube stud.
4. Pull indicator out of tube, then the tube out of block.
5. Raise and support vehicle, then remove tire and wheel assemblies.
6. Remove engine protection shield, then the rear lower control arm bracket to frame mounting bolts.
7. Remove mounting bolts, then the steering gear crossmember.
8. Remove wheel speed sensor wiring harness from retainers and disconnect sensor.
9. Remove retaining bolt for front brake hose, then the stabilizer shaft link to lower control arm and stabilizer shaft retaining nuts.
10. Remove stabilizer shaft link and washer.
11. Remove upper shock module retaining from shock tower, then tie rod end from steering knuckle.
12. Remove left and right upper ball joint pinch bolt and nut.
13. Remove shock module from shock tower, then the steering knuckle from upper control arm.
14. Remove the front wheel drive axle from steering knuckle
15. Support front shock module/steering knuckle to frame with mechanics wire.
16. Disconnect left and right side wheel drive shafts from differential carrier assembly using brass drift and hammer.
17. Remove wire harness clip, then the intermediate shaft bearing assembly.
18. Reference mark propeller shaft to front axle pinion yoke, then remove yoke retainer bolts and yoke retainers from front axle pinion yoke.
19. Disconnect propeller shaft from front axle pinon yoke, then remove propeller shaft from transfer case.
20. Drain engine oil into a suitable container, then unclip transmission cooler lines from engine block.
21. Remove front differential bolts and set aside front differential.
22. Remove transmission bell housing bolts that are attached to oil pan, then the remaining oil pan bolts.
23. Place two oil pan bolts in jack screws on oil pan and tighten evenly to release oil pan from engine.
24. Reverse procedure to install, noting the following:
    a. **Oil pan must be installed within 10 minutes from when sealer was applied.** Apply a .12 inch bead of sealer GM PN 12378521 or equivalent to block rather than oil pan.
    b. Tighten oil pan side bolts to 18 ft. lbs.
    c. Tighten oil pan end bolts to 89 inch lbs.

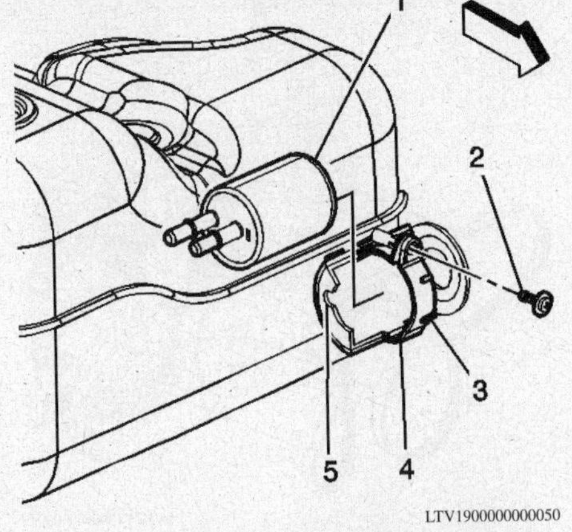

Fig. 12 Fuel filter replacement

OIL PUMP

REPLACE

1. Remove front cover as outlined in "Front Cover, Replace."
2. Remove oil pump cover, then Mark inner and outer gears in relation to oil pump housing.
3. Remove inner and outer oil pump gears, then the oil pump pressure relief valve plug.
4. Remove oil pump pressure relief valve and spring.
5. Reverse procedure to install.

SERPENTINE DRIVE BELT

Replacement

1. Pivot tensioner and remove belt starting from alternator pulley.
2. Reverse procedure to install.

Routing

Routing belt over tensioner pulley as outlined in **Fig. 11.**

COOLING SYSTEM BLEED

After filling cooling system, start engine and allow to reach operating temperature with radiator cap removed. Air in system is bleed through radiator cap opening. Add coolant as required to bring to proper level, then install radiator cap and inspect coolant level in recovery reservoir.

THERMOSTAT

REPLACE

1. Drain cooling to level below thermostat.
2. Remove alternator as outlined in "Electrical."
3. Remove thermostat housing bolt.
4. Remove outlet and gasket.
5. Remove thermostat.
6. Reverse procedure to install.

WATER PUMP

REPLACE

1. Drain coolant into a suitable container.
2. Remove radiator baffle from vehicle.
3. Remove retaining clips and front grille.
4. Pull up on retaining tabs, then remove headlamp assembly from headlamp panel and disconnect electrical connectors.
5. Remove ambient temperature sensor, then bolts and headlamp panel from vehicle.
6. Remove bolts, then the radiator support diagonal brace and hood latch from vehicle.
7. Remove cooling fan and shroud by tilting radiator forward, and cooling fan and shroud rearward for clearance.
8. Release tensioner and remove drive belt.
9. Remove water pump pulley using tool No. J–41240 or equivalent.
10. Remove bolts, then the water pump and gasket. Discard gasket.
11. Reverse procedure to install.

RADIATOR

REPLACE

1. Drain engine coolant into a suitable container.
2. Raise and support vehicle, then remove retainers and radiator support shield.
3. Remove transmission cooler lines, then the outlet hose from radiator.
4. Remove radiator baffle from vehicle.
5. Remove retaining clips and front grille.
6. Pull up on retaining tabs, then remove headlamp assembly from headlamp panel and disconnect electrical connectors.
7. Remove ambient temperature sensor, then bolts and headlamp panel from vehicle.
8. Remove bolts, then the radiator support diagonal brace and hood latch from vehicle.
9. Remove cooling fan and shroud by tilting radiator forward, and cooling fan and shroud rearward for clearance.
10. Remove upper radiator to condenser bolts, then coolant recovery line from radiator.
11. Lift upward on condenser to remove from radiator retaining tab, then radiator out of vehicle.
12. Reverse procedure to install.

FUEL PUMP

REPLACE

1. Relieve fuel system pressure as outlined in "Precautions."
2. Raise and support vehicle, remove fuel tank shields.
3. Drain fuel tank, then support tank with

a suitable lifting device and remove bolts securing tank retaining straps.
4. Lower tank enough to disconnect fuel lines, ground and harness connectors, then remove tank from under vehicle.
5. Turn fuel sender unit cam lock ring counterclockwise using cam lock wrench tool No. J–44402, or equivalent, then lift sending/pump unit assembly from tank.
6. Pull fuel pump upward while pulling out from bottom and remove pump from sending unit assembly.
7. Reverse procedure to install. Use new O-ring when installing sending unit in tank.

FUEL FILTER

REPLACE

1. Relieve fuel system pressure as outlined in "Precautions."
2. Remove filler cap and fuel feed nuts from filter.
3. Loosen filter bracket clamp bolt, then remove filter from bracket, **Fig. 12.**
4. Reverse procedure to install.

TIGHTENING SPECIFICATIONS

Year	Component	Torque, Ft. Lbs.
2002–06	A/C Line Bracket Nut	61①
	A/C Line Bracket Bolt	89①
	A/C Compressor	37
	Alternator Bolt	37
	Battery Ground Cable	11
	Brake Booster Vacuum Fitting	10
	Camshaft Cap	106①
	Camshaft Cover	89①
	Cooling Fan Hub	41
	Crankshaft Damper Bolt	④
	Crankshaft Main Bearing Caps	⑤
	Cylinder Head Bolts	③
	Engine Front Lift Bracket	37
	Engine Mount Bracket (Engine)	37
	Engine Mount Bracket (Frame)	81
	Engine Mount	52
	Exhaust Heat Shield	89①
	Exhaust Manifold	⑤
	Exhaust Camshaft Actuator	②
	Exhaust Pipe To Manifold	37
	Flywheel	⑥
	Ignition Coil	89①
	Intake Camshaft Sprocket	②
	Intake Manifold	89①
	Oil Dipstick Tube	89①
	Oil Filter Adapter	37
	Oil Pan (End)	89①
	Oil Pan (sides)	18
	Oil Pan Drain	19
	Oil Pump Cover	89①
	Power Steering Pump	18
	Power Steering Pump Bracket	37
	Spark Plugs	13
	Starter Motor	37
	Thermostat Housing	89①
	Throttle Body	89③
	Timing Chain Cover	89①
	Timing Chain Tensioner	18
	Timing Chain Guide	12
	Timing Chain Shoe	18
	Timing Chain Top Guide	89①
	Torque Converter	44

Continued

TIGHTENING SPECIFICATIONS—Continued

Year	Component	Torque, Ft. Lbs.
2002–06	Transmission Bell Housing	37
	Transmission Fluid Tube	89③
	Water Outlet	89①
	Water Pump	89①
	Water Pump Pulley	18

① — Inch lbs.
② — Refer to "Camshaft, Replace" for tightening sequence.
③ — Refer to "Cylinder Head, Replace" for tightening procedure.
④ — Refer to "Crankshaft Damper, Replace" for tightening sequence.
⑤ — Refer to "Exhaust Manifold, Replace" for tightening sequence.
⑥ — Tighten bolts in sequence, **Fig. 13,** first pass to 18 ft. lbs. Final pass an additional 50°.

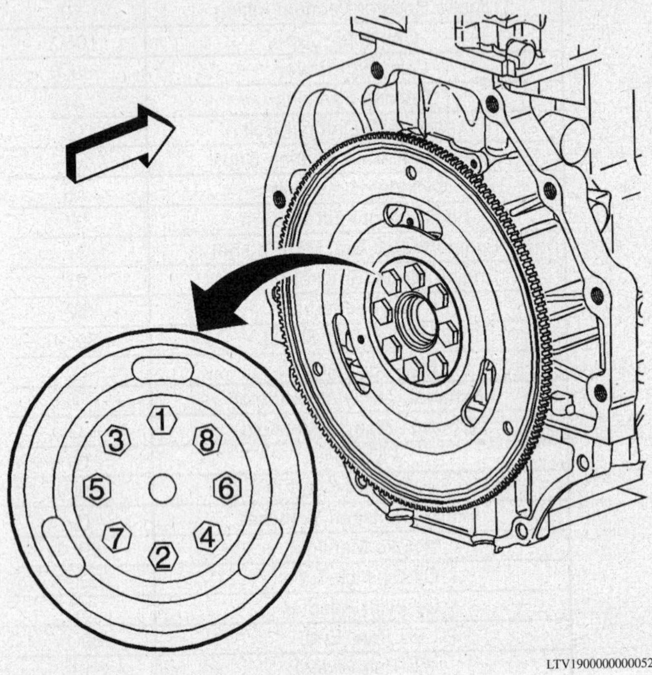

Fig. 13 Flywheel tightening sequence

4.3L Engine

NOTE: Refer To "4.3L Engine" Section In The "Avalanche, Escalade EXT, Sierra, Silverado & SSR" Chapter For Service Procedures Not Covered In This Section

NOTE: On Air Bag Equipped Models, Refer To "Air Bag System Precautions" Located In The Front Of This Manual For System Disarming & Arming Procedures.

NOTE: Refer To "Computer Relearn Procedures" Located In The Front Of This Manual For Computer Relearn Procedures.

INDEX

PRECAUTIONS

Air Bag Systems

Refer to "Air Bag System Precautions" in the front of this manual for system disarming and arming procedures.

Battery Ground Cable

Prior to service, disconnect battery ground cable and isolate as required.

Fuel System Pressure Relief

1. Turn ignition to Off position, then disconnect battery ground cable.
2. Loosen fuel filler cap to relieve fuel tank vapor pressure.
3. Connect fuel pressure gauge to fuel pressure connection, then install bleed hose of gauge into a suitable container.
4. Open valve on gauge to bleed system pressure.

Radio Security System

THEFTLOCK

If the Theftlock system is active when battery power is interrupted, the customers security code must be entered to restore proper function of the radio. To unlock a secured radio after power loss, proceed as follows:

1. With ignition in On position, "LOC" will appear on display.
2. Press "NM" button and "000" will appear on display.
3. Press "NM" until last two digits agree with security code.
4. Press "HR" button until first digit agree with security code.
5. Press "AM-FM" to select code entered, "SEC" will appear on display indicating radio is now operable and secure.
6. If incorrect code is entered eight times, "INOP" will display. In order to reenter code, the ignition must be left on for one hour before code can be entered and only three more chances to enter code are available before display reads "INOP."

DELCO LOC II

If the Delco LOC II system is active when battery power is interrupted, the customers security code must be entered to restore proper function of the radio. To unlock a secured radio after power loss, proceed as follows:

1. Turn ignition lock to Accessory or Run position.
2. Press "SET" button and "000" will appear on display.
3. Press "SEEK" button until second and third digits of code appear.
4. Press "SCAN" button until first digit of code appears.
5. Press "AM-FM" button and "000" appears on display.
6. Press "SEEK" button until fifth and sixth digits of code appear.
7. Press "SCAN" button until fourth digit appears.
8. Press "AM-FM" button. If unlock sequence was successful, display will

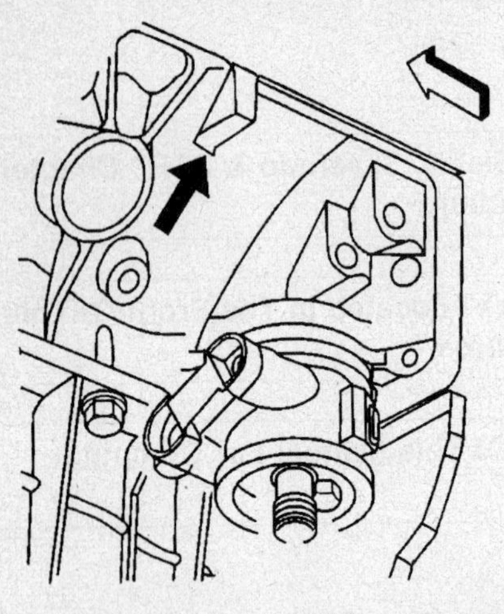

Fig. 1 Engine lifting tab

show "SEC," indicating unit is operational. If display shows "LOC," numbers did not match and unlock sequence was not successful.

ENGINE MOUNT

REPLACE

1. Raise and support vehicle.
2. Remove underbody shields.
3. Remove engine mount through bolt for side being replaced.
4. Raise engine enough to remove engine mount using suitable jack on square tab, **Fig. 1.**
5. Remove bolts from engine mount frame bracket.
6. Remove engine mount frame bracket.
7. Remove bolts holding engine mount to engine, **Fig. 2.**
8. Remove engine mount.
9. Reverse procedure to install.

ENGINE

REPLACE

1. Mark hood hinges for installation reference, then remove hood.
2. Raise and support vehicle, then drain engine oil and coolant into suitable containers.
3. Remove front air dam, skid plates and underbody shields.
4. **On models equipped with 4WD,** proceed as follows;
   a. Remove body to frame mount bolts, then place suitable jackstands under body.
   b. Raise body from frame to allow access to upper transmission to engine bolts, then remove bolts.
   c. Lower and secure body.
   d. Remove second crossmember, then fluid lines to remote oil filter.
   e. Support transmission with a suitable jack, then remove lower transmission to engine bolts.
5. **On all models,** disconnect exhaust from engine, then remove exhaust system from vehicle.
6. Remove engine to transmission braces.
7. **On models equipped with manual transmission,** remove external slave cylinder or disconnect hydraulic line for internal slave cylinder, as outlined in **MOTOR's "Domestic Transmission, In-Vehicle Service" or "Transmission Service DVD."**
8. **On all models,** remove oil filter.
9. Remove fuel line clamp at bellhousing, then remove starter as outlined in "Starter, Replace" in the "Electrical."
10. **On models equipped with automatic transmission,** remove driveplate to torque converter bolts through starter opening.
11. **On all models,** support engine with a suitable jackstand, then remove bolts for front engine mounts.
12. Remove jackstand from engine, allowing engine to rest on mount brackets.
13. **On models equipped with 2WD,** proceed as follows:
    a. Remove nut from rear transmission mount.
    b. Remove all transmission to engine bolts except upper left bolt.
14. **On models equipped with 4WD,** if clearance requires, remove front propeller shaft and/or front axle mount bolts to reposition axle assembly.
15. **On all models,** remove air cleaner assembly, then coolant fan.
16. Remove drive belt as outlined in "Serpentine Drive Belt," then the pulleys for water pump and cooling fan.
17. **On models equipped with A/C,** recover refrigerant as outlined in "Air Conditioning" then remove compressor and bracket. Cap and plug all lines and connections.
18. **On models equipped with oil cooler,** disconnect and drain lines.
19. **On all models,** remove radiator as outlined in "Radiator, Replace."
20. Disconnect power steering lines from steering gear. **Cap and plug all lines and connections.**
21. Disconnect all electrical connectors and vacuum lines between engine and vehicle. **Mark connectors and vacuum lines for installation reference.**
22. Relieve fuel system pressure as outlined in "Precautions."
23. Disconnect throttle linkage and cruise control cable, then the fuel lines from engine. Position fuel lines aside.
24. Remove distributor as outlined in "Distributor, Replace" in "Electrical."
25. **On models equipped with 2WD,** place a suitable support under transmission. **Do not support transmission under oil pan.**
26. **On all models,** install engine lift bracket set, tool No. J–41427, or equivalent, to right rear and left front of intake manifold, **torque** attaching bolts to 11 ft. lbs. Bracket set is marked for installed location.
27. Attach suitable engine lifting equipment to lift brackets.
28. **On models equipped with 2WD,** remove remaining transmission to engine bolt.
29. **On all models,** remove engine from vehicle.
30. Reverse procedure to install.

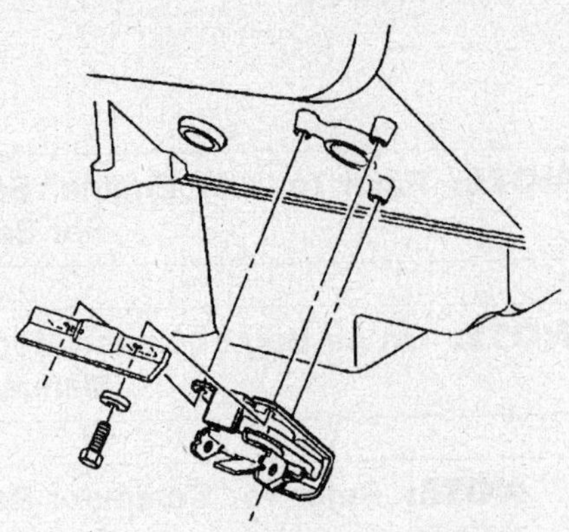

Fig. 2 Rear engine mount removal

INTAKE MANIFOLD

REPLACE

Upper

REMOVAL

1. Remove engine cover, air cleaner and intake duct, **Fig. 3.**
2. Disconnect electrical harness from manifold components and position aside.
3. Disconnect throttle linkage from upper intake manifold.
4. **On models equipped with cruise control,** disconnect cruise control linkage.
5. **On all models,** remove fuel lines and brackets at rear of lower intake manifold, then remove PCV hose.
6. Remove ignition coil, then disconnect PCV hose at upper intake manifold.
7. Remove vacuum hoses at front and rear of upper intake manifold.
8. Remove upper intake manifold attaching bolts and studs. Mark location of all studs for installation reference.
9. Remove upper intake manifold.

INSTALLATION

1. Install upper intake manifold gasket.
2. Install upper intake manifold, using care not to pinch lines and cables.
3. Install upper intake manifold bolts and studs, noting position marks made during disassembly.
4. Install purge solenoid and bracket, then the ignition coil and bracket.
5. Install PCV hose, then the fuel lines and brackets at rear of manifolds.
6. Install throttle and cruise control linkage, then connect electrical connectors to manifold components.
7. Install air cleaner and engine cover.
8. Fill cooling system, then evacuate and recharge A/C system.

Lower

REMOVAL

1. Remove upper intake manifold as outlined in "Intake Manifold Replace, Upper."

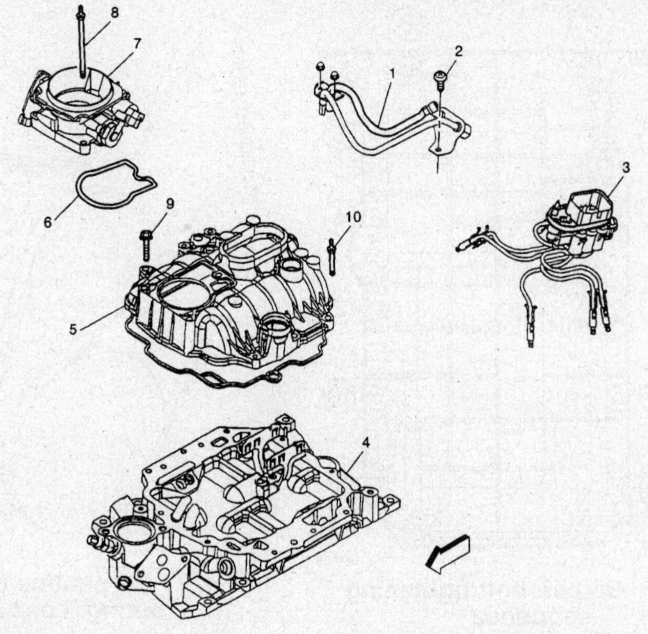

(1) Inlet and Return Fuel Pipe
(2) Fuel Pipe Assembly Screw
(3) Central Sequential Multiport Injector
(4) Lower Intake Manifold
(5) Upper Intake Manifold
(6) Throttle Body Gasket
(7) Throttle Body
(8) Throttle Body Stud
(9) Upper Intake Bolt
(10) Upper Intake Manifold Stud

GC1069600858000X

Fig. 3 Upper intake manifold replacement

2. Remove distributor assembly, mark position of distributor housing and rotor for proper installation.
3. Drain cooling system, remove upper radiator hose at thermostat housing, then disconnect heater hose at lower intake manifold.
4. Remove EGR valve, then disconnect the coolant bypass hose.
5. Disconnect electrical harness from manifold components and position aside.
6. Disconnect throttle cable.
7. **On models equipped with cruise control,** remove cable brackets from manifold.
8. **On all models,** remove transmission dipstick tube, then the EGR tube, clamp and bolt.
9. Remove PCV valve and hoses.
10. **On models equipped with air conditioning,** recover refrigerant as outlined in "Air Conditioning," then remove A/C compressor with bracket and accessory drive bracket.
11. **On all models,** remove alternator mounting bolt near thermostat housing.
12. Remove intake manifold attaching bolts, then the intake manifold.

INSTALLATION

1. Install gaskets to cylinder head, ensure port blocking plates are at rear of engine and "This Side Up" is visible.
2. Place a ¼ inch bead of Wacker T-330 RTV sealer, part No. 1234692, or equivalent, on front and rear sealing surfaces of block, **Fig. 4.** Extend bead ½ inch up onto cylinder head surfaces.
3. Position lower intake manifold into place, coat each intake manifold bolt with sealer, part No. 1052080, or equivalent, install and lightly tighten.
4. Tighten lower intake manifold in numbered sequence, **Fig. 5,** as follows:
   a. **Torque** bolts in sequence to 26 inch lbs.
   b. **Torque** bolts in sequence to 106 inch lbs.
   c. **Torque** bolts in sequence to 11 ft. lbs.
5. Install alternator bolt, then connect coolant bypass hose.
6. Connect heater hose to manifold, then the upper radiator hose to thermostat housing.
7. Connect fuel lines, then the electrical component connectors.
8. Connect throttle cable and if equipped cruise control cable and brackets.
9. Install transmission dipstick tube, then the EGR tube.
10. Install PCV valve, then the vacuum lines.
11. Install A/C compressor, bracket and accessory drive bracket.
12. Install distributor, align marks made during removal.

EXHAUST MANIFOLD

REPLACE

Refer To "4.3L Engine" Section In The "Avalanche, Escalade EXT, Sierra, Silverado & SSR" Chapter.

CYLINDER HEAD

REPLACE

Refer To "4.3L Engine" Section In The

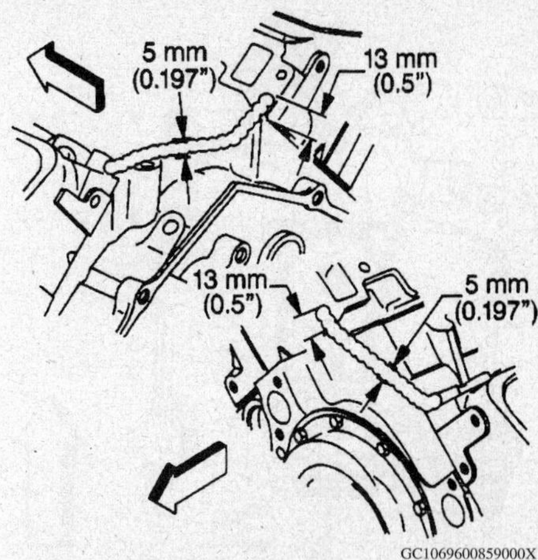

Fig. 4 Lower intake manifold sealing

"Avalanche, Escalade EXT, Sierra, Silverado & SSR" Chapter.

VALVE COVER

REPLACE

Refer To "4.3L Engine" Section In The "Avalanche, Escalade EXT, Sierra, Silverado & SSR" Chapter.

VALVE ARRANGEMENT

Refer To "4.3L Engine" Section In The "Avalanche, Escalade EXT, Sierra, Silverado & SSR" Chapter.

VALVE ADJUSTMENT

Once the rocker arms are installed and properly tightened, no additional valve adjustment is required. Refer to "Rocker Arm, Replace."

HYDRAULIC LIFTERS

REPLACE

Refer To "4.3L Engine" Section In The "Avalanche, Escalade EXT, Sierra, Silverado & SSR" Chapter.

CRANKSHAFT DAMPER

REPLACE

Refer To "4.3L Engine" Section In The "Avalanche, Escalade EXT, Sierra, Silverado & SSR" Chapter.

FRONT COVER

REPLACE

Refer To "4.3L Engine" Section In The "Avalanche, Escalade EXT, Sierra, Silverado & SSR" Chapter.

TIMING CHAIN

REPLACE

Refer To "4.3L Engine" Section In The "Avalanche, Escalade EXT, Sierra, Silverado & SSR" Chapter.

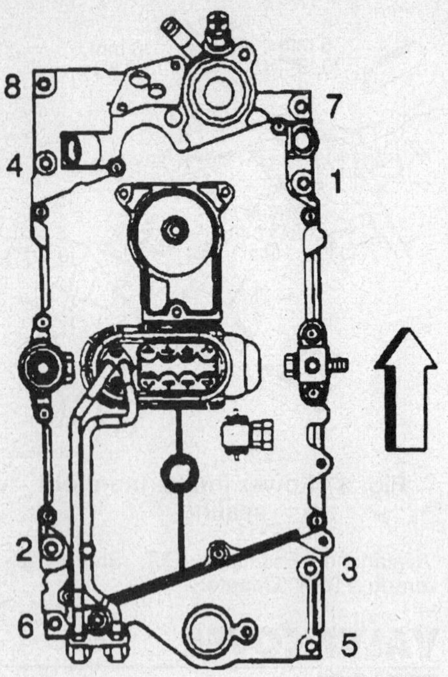

Fig. 5 Lower intake manifold bolt tightening sequence

CAMSHAFT

REPLACE

Refer To "4.3L Engine" Section In The "Avalanche, Escalade EXT, Sierra, Silverado & SSR" Chapter.

PISTON & ROD ASSEMBLY

Refer To "4.3L Engine" Section In The "Avalanche, Escalade EXT, Sierra, Silverado & SSR" Chapter.

MAIN & ROD BEARINGS

Refer To "4.3L Engine" Section In The "Avalanche, Escalade EXT, Sierra, Silverado & SSR" Chapter.

CRANKSHAFT REAR OIL SEAL

REPLACE

Refer To "4.3L Engine" Section In The "Avalanche, Escalade EXT, Sierra, Silverado & SSR" Chapter.

OIL PAN

REPLACE

Removal

2WD MODELS

1. Remove engine as outlined in "Engine, Replace."

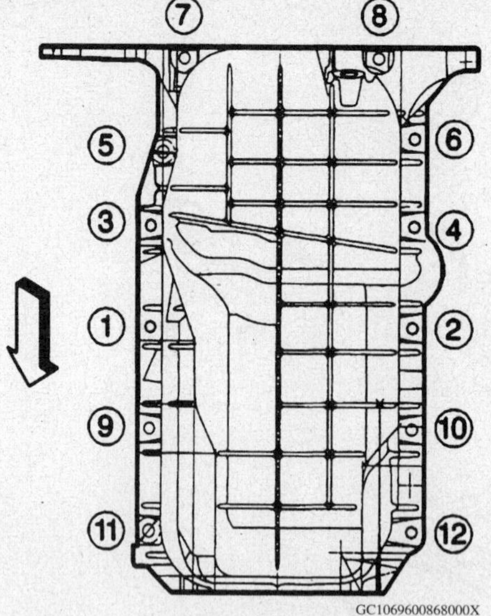

Fig. 6 Oil pan bolt tightening sequence

2. Remove oil pan bolts and studs. Note stud and bolt locations for later assembly.
3. Remove oil pan and gasket. Discard gasket.

4WD MODELS

1. Remove oil dipstick tube, raise and support vehicle, then drain engine oil.
2. Remove skid plates and underbody shields as equipped.
3. Remove wiring bracket at right side of oil pan.
4. Support engine with suitable lifting equipment, then remove right and left engine mount through bolts.
5. Raise engine for clearance and block into position.
6. Remove remote oil filter adapter and lines from engine.
7. Remove pitman arm and idler arm from steering linkage and vehicle for clearance. **Mark relationship of steering components for later assembly.**
8. Remove front propeller shaft, then front axle through bolts and roll axle forward for clearance.
9. Remove oil pan bolts and studs. Note stud and bolt locations for later assembly.
10. Remove oil pan and gasket. Discard gasket.

Installation

Anytime both oil pan and transmission are removed from engine, transmission must be installed first to allow proper adjustment of oil pan as outlined below.

1. Apply a suitable RTV sealant to four places on oil pan mounting ledge where front and rear engine covers meet block.
2. Install new gasket to oil pan, then position pan to engine.
3. Install oil pan mounting bolts and studs into locations noted on removal.

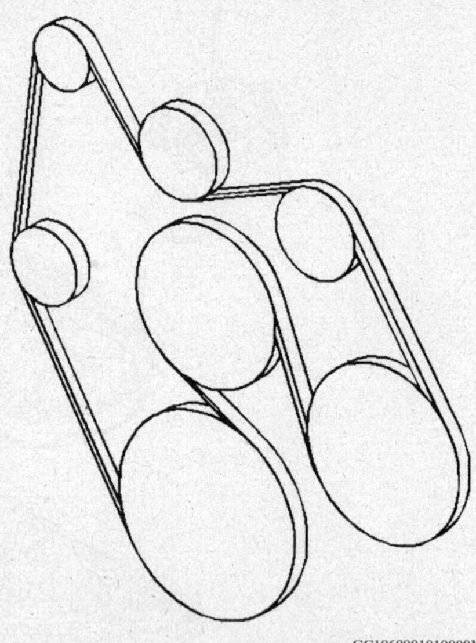

Fig. 7 Serpentine drive belt routing. Less A/C

4. Ensure pan is positioned as far rearward against transmission as possible.
5. Tighten oil pan bolts and studs in sequence, **Fig. 6.**
6. Inspect gap between oil pan contact points at bottom of pan and transmission, gap should not exceed .010 inch.
7. If not to specification, repeat removal and installation procedures.
8. Reverse procedure to install.

OIL PUMP

REPLACE

Refer To "4.3L Engine" Section In The "Avalanche, Escalade EXT, Sierra, Silverado & SSR" Chapter.

OIL PUMP SERVICE

Refer To "4.3L Engine" Section In The "Avalanche, Escalade EXT, Sierra, Silverado & SSR" Chapter.

SERPENTINE DRIVE BELT

Replacement

1. Pivot tensioner and remove belt starting from tensioner pulley.
2. Reverse procedure to install.

Routing

Routing belt over tensioner pulley last as outlined in **Figs. 7 and 8.**

COOLING SYSTEM BLEED

Refer To "4.3L Engine" Section In The "Avalanche, Escalade EXT, Sierra, Silverado & SSR" Chapter.

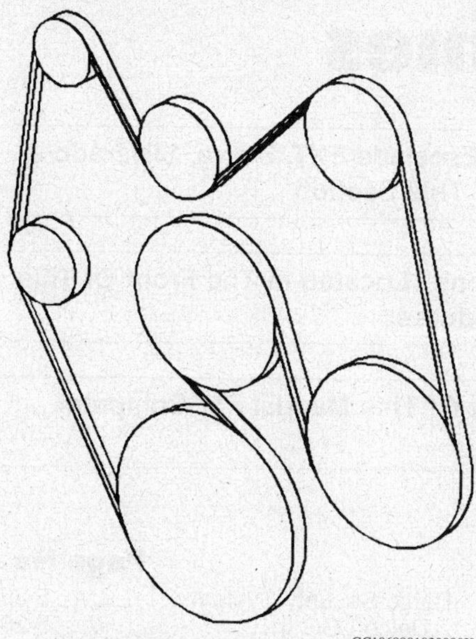

Fig. 8 Serpentine drive belt routing. With A/C

THERMOSTAT

REPLACE

Refer To "4.3L Engine" Section In The "Avalanche, Escalade EXT, Sierra, Silverado & SSR" Chapter.

WATER PUMP

REPLACE

Refer To "4.3L Engine" Section In The "Avalanche, Escalade EXT, Sierra, Silverado & SSR" Chapter.

RADIATOR

REPLACE

1. Drain coolant from radiator, then disconnect upper coolant reservoir hose.
2. Remove upper fan shroud bolts, then the shroud.
3. Disconnect and plug transmission fluid cooler lines.
4. Disconnect and plug engine oil cooler lines.
5. Raise and support vehicle, then disconnect lower radiator hose.
6. Disconnect heater hose and coolant overflow hose from radiator.
7. Remove radiator.
8. Reverse procedure to install

FUEL PUMP

REPLACE

1. Relieve fuel system pressure as outlined in "Precautions."
2. Raise and support vehicle, remove fuel tank shields.
3. Drain fuel tank, then support tank with a suitable lifting device and remove bolts securing tank retaining straps.
4. Lower tank enough to disconnect fuel lines, ground and harness connectors, then remove tank from under vehicle.

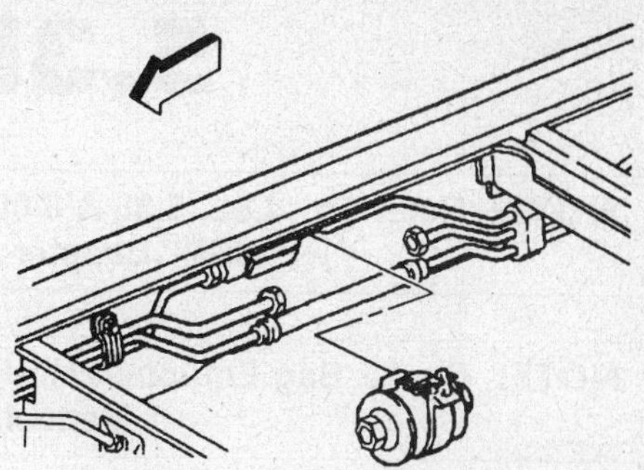

Fig. 9 Fuel filter replacement

5. Turn fuel sender unit cam lock ring counterclockwise using cam lock wrench tool No. J 36608, or equivalent, then lift sending/pump unit assembly from tank.
6. Pull fuel pump upward while pulling out from bottom and remove pump from sending unit assembly.
7. Reverse procedure to install. Use new O-ring when installing sending unit in tank.

FUEL FILTER

REPLACE

1. Relieve fuel system pressure as outlined in "Precautions."
2. Remove filler cap and fuel feed nuts from filter.
3. Loosen filter bracket clamp bolt, then remove filter from bracket, Fig. 9.
4. Reverse procedure to install.

TIGHTENING SPECIFICATIONS

Year	Component	Torque, Ft. Lbs.
2002–05	Engine Mount Through Bolts	55
	Engine Mount To Cylinder Block	41
	Engine Oil Cooler Line Nuts	18
	Exhaust Manifold	①
	Flywheel	74
	Flywheel Housing	32
	Frame Bracket Bolts	33
	Intake Manifold (Lower)	②
	Intake Manifold (Upper)	83④
	Oil Filter Adapter	18
	Oil Pan	18③
	Oil Pan Studs To Oil Seal Retainer Or Crankcase	12–24④
	Spark Plugs	22
	Torsional Damper	70
	Transmission Fluid Cooler Line Nuts	18
	Water Outlet	21

① — Center two bolts, 26 ft. lbs.; all other bolts, 20 ft. lbs.
② — Refer to "Intake Manifold, Replace."
③ — Refer to "Oil Pan, Replace" procedure for tightening sequence.
④ — Inch lbs.

5.3L & 6.0L Engines

NOTE: Refer To "4.8L, 5.3L & 6.0L Engines" Section In The "Avalanche, Escalade EXT, Sierra, Silverado & SSR" Chapter For Service Procedures Not Covered In This Section

NOTE: On Air Bag Equipped Models, Refer To "Air Bag System Precautions" Located In The Front Of This Manual For System Disarming & Arming Procedures.

NOTE: Refer To "Computer Relearn Procedures" Located In The Front Of This Manual For Computer Relearn Procedures.

INDEX

PRECAUTIONS

Air Bag Systems

Refer to "Air Bag System Precautions" in the front of this manual for system disarming and arming procedures.

Battery Ground Cable

Prior to service, disconnect battery ground cable and isolate as required.

Fuel System Pressure Relief

1. Turn ignition to Off position, then disconnect battery ground cable.
2. Loosen fuel filler cap to relieve fuel tank vapor pressure.
3. Connect fuel pressure gauge to fuel pressure connection, then install bleed hose of gauge into a suitable container.
4. Open valve on gauge to bleed system pressure.

Radio Security System

THEFTLOCK

If the Theftlock system is active when battery power is interrupted, the customers security code must be entered to restore proper function of the radio. To unlock a secured radio after power loss, proceed as follows:

1. With ignition in On position, "LOC" will appear on display.
2. Press "NM" button and "000" will appear on display.
3. Press "NM" until last two digits agree with security code.
4. Press "HR" button until first digit agree with security code.
5. Press "AM-FM" to select code entered, "SEC" will appear on display indicating radio is now operable and secure.
6. If incorrect code is entered eight times, "INOP" will display. In order to reenter code, the ignition must be left on for one hour before code can be entered and only three more chances to enter code are available before display reads "INOP."

DELCO LOC II

If the Delco LOC II system is active when battery power is interrupted, the customers security code must be entered to restore proper function of the radio. To unlock a secured radio after power loss, proceed as follows:

1. Turn ignition lock to Accessory or Run position.
2. Press "SET" button and "000" will appear on display.
3. Press "SEEK" button until second and third digits of code appear.
4. Press "SCAN" button until first digit of code appears.
5. Press "AM-FM" button and "000" appears on display.
6. Press "SEEK" button until fifth and sixth digits of code appear.
7. Press "SCAN" button until fourth digit appears.
8. Press "AM-FM" button. If unlock sequence was successful, display will show "SEC," indicating unit is operational. If display shows "LOC," numbers did not match and unlock sequence was not successful.

ENGINE MOUNT

REPLACE

2WD

1. Remove shock module upper retaining nuts.
2. Raise and support vehicle.
3. Remove tire and wheel assemblies, then the engine protection shield.
4. Remove retaining nut, then the shock module yoke from lower control arm with tool No. J–24319–B or equivalent.
5. Remove shock module from vehicle.
6. Remove lower engine mount retaining nuts from engine mount frame bracket.
7. Remove mounting bolts from upper engine mount bracket to engine block bracket.
8. Remove frame engine mount bracket retaining bolts, then install a pole jack underneath oil pan.
9. Raise engine 2 1/4 inches measuring from bottom of oil pan to front edge of transmission support crossmember.
10. Remove engine mount frame bracket from frame.
11. Remove engine mount with upper engine mount bracket as an assembly, **Fig. 1.**
12. Reverse procedure to install.

4WD

1. Remove shock module upper retaining nuts.
2. Raise and support vehicle.
3. Remove tire and wheel assemblies, then the engine protection shield.
4. Remove retaining nut, then the shock

module yoke from lower control arm with tool No. J–24319–B or equivalent.
5. Remove shock module from vehicle.
6. Remove wheel speed sensor wiring harness from retainers.
7. Disconnect wheel speed sensor from harness, then remove retaining bolt for front brake hose.
8. Remove stabilizer shaft link and washer, then the outer tie rod retaining nut.
9. Disconnect outer tie rod from steering knuckle using tool No. J–24319-B or equivalent.
10. Remove outer tie rod from inner tie rod, then the left and right upper ball joint pinch bolt and nut.
11. Remove steering knuckle from upper control arm, then the front wheel drive axle from steering knuckle.
12. Support front shock module/steering knuckle to frame.
13. Disconnect left and right side wheel drive shaft from differential carrier assembly, then remove wheel drive shafts.
14. Remove lower engine mount retaining nuts from engine mount frame bracket.
15. Remove mounting bolts from upper engine mount bracket to engine block bracket.
16. Remove frame engine mount bracket retaining bolts, then install a pole jack underneath oil pan.
17. Raise engine 2 1/4 inches measuring from bottom of oil pan to front edge of transmission support crossmember.
18. Remove engine mount frame bracket from frame.
19. Remove engine mount with upper engine mount bracket as an assembly, **Fig. 1.**
20. Reverse procedure to install.

ENGINE

REPLACE

1. Mark hood hinges for installation reference, then remove hood.
2. Recover A/C refrigerant, as outlined in "Air Conditioning."
3. Remove radiator as outlined in "Radiator, Replace."
4. Remove retaining bolts then the radiator support diagonal brace.
5. Remove engine protection shield, then drain engine oil.
6. **On models equipped with 4WD,** proceed as follows:
   a. Drain oil from front differential.
   b. Remove oil pan as outlined in "Oil Pan, Replace."
   c. Remove front differential from vehicle.
7. **On all models,** remove wheel speed sensor wiring harness from retainers.
8. Disconnect wheel speed sensor from harness, then remove retaining bolt for front brake hose.
9. Remove stabilizer shaft link and washer, then the outer tie rod retaining nut.
10. Disconnect outer tie rod from steering knuckle using tool No. J–24319-B or equivalent.
11. Remove outer tie rod from inner tie rod, then the left and right upper ball joint pinch bolt and nut.
12. Remove steering knuckle from upper control arm, then the front wheel drive axle from steering knuckle.
13. Support front shock module/steering knuckle to frame.
14. Disconnect right side wheel drive shaft from clutch fork housing assembly.
15. Remove intake manifold as outlined in "Intake Manifold, Replace."
16. Disconnect electrical connectors from oil pressure, oxygen and camshaft position sensors.
17. Remove compressor hose assembly from compressor, then the compressor suction hose from accumulator.
18. Disconnect rear auxiliary A/C compressor pipe fitting, then remove rear auxiliary A/C compressor pipe nut and bolt.
19. Tie pipe assembly out of way.
20. Disconnect engine coolant temperature sensor, then remove ground terminal bolt and retaining clips from brackets.
21. Disconnect A/C pressure switch electrical connector, then remove retaining clip from cylinder head.
22. Raise and suitably support vehicle, then remove starter as outlined in "Electrical."
23. Remove battery cable channel from oil pan, then disconnect A/C compressor electrical connector.
24. Lower vehicle, then set engine wiring harness and harness off to side.
25. Disconnect cables, then remove bracket bolts and set alternator with bracket aside.
26. Remove inlet and outlet hoses from water outlet.
27. Disconnect auxiliary heater inlet and outlet hose/pipe assembly from heater water shutoff valve pipes.
28. Remove auxiliary heater inlet and outlet hoses/pipes from water pump.
29. Remove ignition coils as outlined "Electrical."
30. Attach engine lift hook No. J–41798 or equivalent to cylinder heads.
31. Raise and support vehicle, then unscrew front and rear heated oxygen sensors from catalytic converter.
32. Remove EVAP canister from its mounting bracket. Do not disconnect canister lines.
33. Support transmission with a suitable jack, then remove bolts and transmission support from frame.
34. Reference mark propeller shaft to transmission or transfer case.
35. Remove bolts and yoke retainers from axle pinion yoke, then slide propeller shaft forward to disconnect propeller shaft from rear axle pinion yoke.
36. Slide propeller shaft rearward to disconnect propeller shaft transmission or transfer case and remove.
37. **On models equipped with 4WD,** unbolt front propeller shaft from drive axle and place propeller shaft on top of pinion yoke.
38. **On all models,** remove exhaust muffler nuts, then the left and right exhaust manifold pipe nuts.
39. Raise transmission, then angling outlet pipe toward left side of vehicle removal catalytic converter.
40. Remove lefthand and righthand frame engine mount bracket bolts.
41. Remove torque converter bolts, then the transmission oil level indicator tube.
42. Remove transmission bolt and stud on right side, then the lower transmission bolt/studs.
43. Lower vehicle, then remove upper transmission bolts/studs.
44. Install a suitable engine hoist, then a floor jack under transmission.
45. Remove engine from vehicle.
46. Reverse procedure to install.

RADIATOR

REPLACE

1. Drain coolant from radiator.
2. Raise and support vehicle.
3. Remove radiator support shield mounting nuts and bolts, then the radiator support shield.
4. Remove transmission cooler lines from radiator.
5. Remove outlet radiator hose from the radiator.
6. Lower vehicle.
7. Remove inlet radiator hose from radiator.
8. Remove air cleaner assembly and air resonator assembly.
9. Remove inlet radiator hose.
10. Remove transmission oil cooler lines from fan shroud.
11. Disconnect fan clutch electrical connector.
12. Remove fan clutch from water pump.
13. Remove upper fan shroud mounting bolts.
14. Lift and push fan shroud inward to clear filler neck on radiator.
15. Remove fan and shroud.
16. Remove windshield wiper arms.
17. Remove air inlet grille panel retaining nuts, then the air inlet grill panel push-pin retainers.
18. Disconnect washer hose and remove air inlet grille panel from vehicle.
19. Remove rear hood seal from air inlet grille panel studs.
20. Remove coolant recovery line from radiator.
21. Remove upper radiator to condenser bolts, then lift upward on condenser to remove from radiator retaining tab.
22. Remove radiator from engine compartment.
23. Reverse procedure to install.

FUEL PUMP

REPLACE

Refer to the "4.2L Engine" section.

FUEL FILTER

REPLACE

Refer to the "4.2L Engine" section.

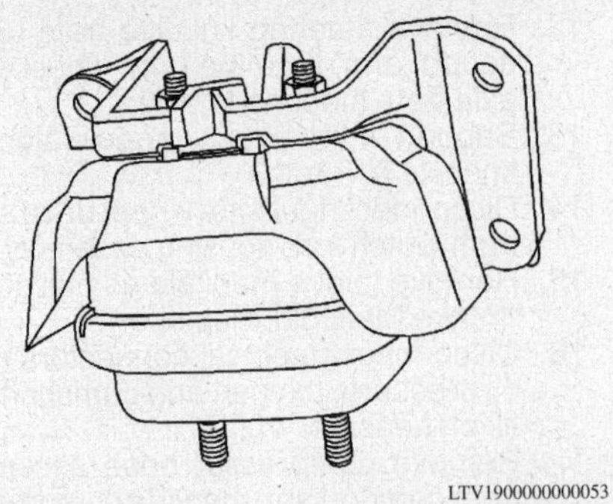

Fig. 1 Engine mount replacement

TIGHTENING SPECIFICATIONS

Year	Component	Torque/Ft. Lbs.
2003–06	Alternator Bracket	37
	Accelerator Control Cable Bracket	89①
	Air Conditioning Compressor	37
	Air Conditioning Compressor Bracket	37
	Air Conditioning Hose Bracket	35
	Air Conditioning Tensioner	37
	AIR Bracket	71①
	AIR Pipe To Exhaust Manifold, Nuts	18
	AIR Pipe To Exhaust Manifold, Studs	45
	Alternator & Power Steering Bracket	37
	Belt Idler Pulley	37
	Camshaft Retainer	18
	Camshaft Sensor	18
	Camshaft Sprocket	26
	Clutch Pressure Plate	52②
	Coolant Temperature Gauge Sensor	15
	Crankshaft Oil Deflector	18
	Crankshaft Position Sensor	18
	Crossbar	74
	Cylinder Head Coolant Plug	15
	Cylinder Head Core Hole Plug	15
	Drive Belt Idler Pulley	37
	Drive Belt Tensioner	37
	EGR Valve	③
	EGR Valve Inlet Pipe Intake Manifold	18
	EGR Valve Inlet Pipe Exhaust Manifold	22
	EGR Valve Pipe To Cylinder Head	37
	EGR Valve Pipe To Exhaust Manifold	20
	EGR Valve Pipe To Intake Manifold	89①
	Engine Block Coolant Drain Plugs	44
	Engine Lift Bracket, M8 Bolt	18
	Engine Lift Bracket, M10 Bolt	37
	Engine Oil Cooler Line Fitting	18
	Engine Oil Level Sensor	115①
	Engine Shield	15
	Engine Wiring Harness Bracket	89①
	EVAP Purge Solenoid	89①
	Exhaust Crossover Pipe	25
	Exhaust Manifold AIR Pipe	45①
	Exhaust Pipe	48

TIGHTENING SPECIFICATIONS—Continued

Year	Component	Torque/Ft. Lbs.
2003–06	Fan Clutch	17
	Fan Shroud	72①
	Front Cover	18
	Front Differential Carrier Shield	26
	Fuel Rail	89①
	Fuel Rail Cover	80①
	Fuel Rail Crossover Tube	34①
	Fuel Rail Stop Bracket	37
	Hood	18
	Ignition Coil	22①
	Intake Cover	89①
	Intake Cover Bracket	45①
	Ignition Coil To Bracket	106①
	Ignition Coil Bracket To Valve Cover	106①
	Intake Manifold Wiring Harness	89①
	Knock Sensors	15
	MAF Sensor Clamp	27–44①
	Motor Mount	37
	Motor Mount Bracket	48
	Motor Mount, Lower To Upper	37
	Motor Mount, Through Bolt	68
	Motor Mount, Upper	37
	Oil Cooler Line Clamp	80①
	Oil Cooler Line Clip	53①
	Oil Cooler Fitting	18
	Oil Filter	22
	Oil Filter Fitting	40
	Oil Dipstick Tube	18
	Oil Level Sensor	15
	Oil Pan Baffle	106①
	Oil Pan Closeout Cover	80①
	Oil Pan Drain Plug	18
	Oil Pan To Block & Front Cover	18
	Oil Pan To Rear Cover	106①
	Oil Pan Skid Plate	15
	Oil Pressure Sensor	15
	Oil Pump To Engine Block	18
	Oil Pump Cover	106①
	Oil Pump Relief Valve Plug	106①
	Oil Pump Screen	18

Continued

TIGHTENING SPECIFICATIONS—Continued

Year	Component	Torque/Ft. Lbs.
2003–06	Oil Pump Screen To Oil Pump	106①
	Oil Transfer Cover	106①
	Power Steering Pump	37
	Power Steering Pump Bracket	37
	Propeller Shaft	15
	Radiator Shroud	71①
	Rear Cover	18
	Starter Cover	15
	Radiator Support	52
	Rear Engine Mount, Bolt	35
	Rear Engine Mount, Nut	40
	Rear Engine Mount, Bolt	35
	Rear Engine Mount to Crossmember	33
	Rear Engine Mount To Transmission	44
	Throttle Body	89①

TIGHTENING SPECIFICATIONS—Continued

Year	Component	Torque/Ft. Lbs.
2003–06	Torque Converter	46
	Transmission, Automatic	34
	Transmission Fluid Cooler Line	19
	Transmission To Oil Pan	41
	Universal Lift Bracket	15
	Valley Cover	106①
	Valve Lifter Guide	106①
	Valve Rocker Arm	22
	Valve Rocker Arm Cover	106①
	Vapor Vent Pipe	106①
	Water Inlet Housing	11
	Water Pump Cover	11

①— Inch lbs.
②— Tighten clutch pressure plate bolts in star pattern & evenly over three increments with fourth increment to 52 ft. lbs.
③— First pass, 90 inch lbs.; final pass, 20 ft. lbs.

Rear Axle & Suspension

NOTE: On Air Bag Equipped Models, Refer To "Air Bag System Precautions" Located In The Front Of This Manual For System Disarming & Arming Procedures.

INDEX

PRECAUTIONS

Air Bag Systems

Refer to "Air Bag System Precautions" in the front of this manual for system disarming and arming procedures.

Battery Ground Cable

Prior to service, disconnect battery ground cable and isolate as required.

Radio Security System

THEFTLOCK

If the Theftlock system is active when battery power is interrupted, the customers security code must be entered to restore proper function of the radio. To unlock a secured radio after power loss, proceed as follows:

1. With ignition in On position, "LOC" appears on display.
2. Press "NM" button and "000" will appear on display.
3. Press "NM" until last two digits agree with security code.
4. Press "HR" button until first digit agree with security code.
5. Press "AM-FM" to select code entered, "SEC" will appear on display indicating radio is now operable and secure.
6. If incorrect code is entered eight times, "INOP" will display. In order to reenter code, the ignition must be left on for one hour before code can be entered and only three more chances to enter code are available before display reads "INOP."

DELCO LOC II

If the Delco LOC II system is active when battery power is interrupted, the customers security code must be entered to restore proper function of the radio. To unlock a secured radio after power loss, proceed as follows:

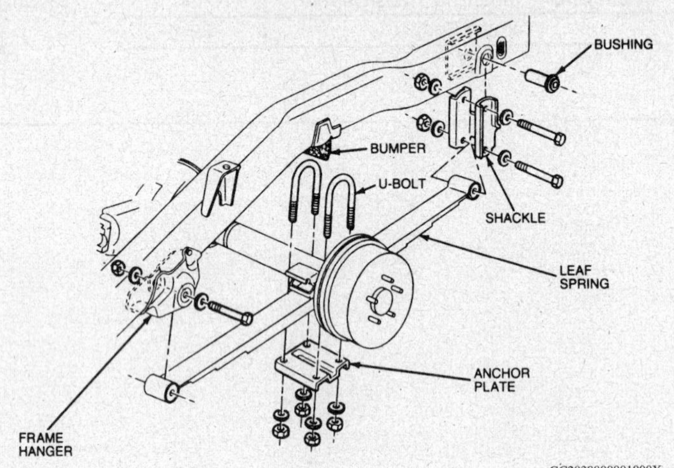

Fig. 1 Rear suspension. Blazer & Jimmy

1. Turn ignition lock to Accessory or Run position.
2. Press "SET" button and "000" will appear on display.
3. Press "SEEK" button until second and third digits of code appear.
4. Press "SCAN" button until first digit of code appears.
5. Press "AM-FM" button and "000" appears on display.
6. Press "SEEK" button until fifth and sixth digits of code appear.
7. Press "SCAN" button until fourth digit appears.
8. Press "AM-FM" button. If unlock sequence was successful, display will show "SEC," indicating unit is operational. If display shows "LOC," numbers did not match and unlock sequence was not successful.

REAR AXLE

REPLACE

Blazer & Jimmy

Construction of the axle assembly is such that service operations may be performed with the housing installed in the vehicle or with the housing removed and installed in a holding fixture. The following procedure is required only when the housing requires replacement.

1. Raise vehicle and place jack stands under frame side rails. Position a jack under the rear axle housing and raise slightly to support axle assembly.
2. Remove rear wheels, then the drums as outlined in "Drum Brakes."
3. Disconnect shock absorbers from anchor plates.
4. Scribe reference marks between driveshaft and pinion flange for use during reassembly, then disconnect driveshaft and position aside.
5. Disconnect brake lines from junction block and backing plates, then remove junction block attaching bolt and position aside.
6. Remove backing plates.
7. Remove U-bolts and anchor plates, **Fig. 1.**
8. Disconnect vent hose from axle housing.
9. Lower rear axle assembly, then remove lower spring shackle bolts.
10. Remove rear axle assembly.
11. Reverse procedure to install. Tighten shock absorber nut, U-bolt nuts and

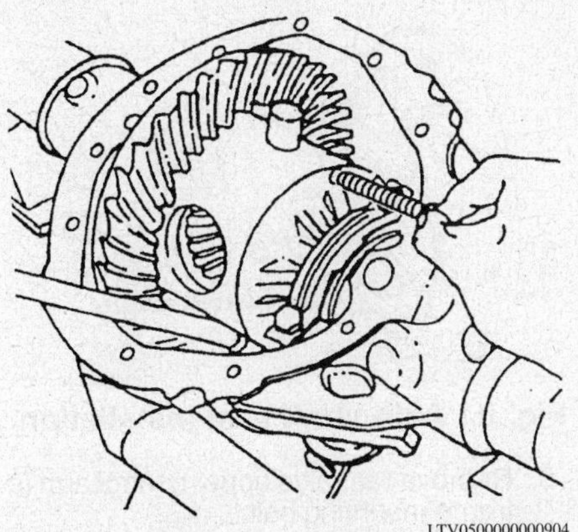

Fig. 2 Differential pinion shaft lock bolt removal

lower spring shackle bolts to specifications.

Bravada, Envoy, Rainier & Trailblazer

1. Raise and support vehicle.
2. Place suitable safety stands at front-end of vehicle.
3. Support rear axle with suitable jack stands.
4. Remove rear tire and wheel assemblies.
5. Disconnect rear axle vent tube.
6. Place reference marks on propeller shaft and rear axle pinion yoke for installation reference.
7. **On models equipped with 2WD,** place reference marks on propeller shaft and transmission yoke for installation reference.
8. **On models equipped with 4WD,** place reference marks on propeller shaft and transfer case yoke for installation reference.
9. **On all models,** slide propeller shaft forward and disconnect propeller shaft from rear axle pinion yoke.
10. Slide propeller shaft rearward in order to disconnect propeller shaft from transmission or transfer case.
11. Disconnect left rear cable of park brake from rear axle.
12. Disconnect right rear cable of park brake from rear axle.
13. Remove brake caliper assemblies. Position and suspend aside.
14. Remove stabilizer shaft from rear axle.
15. Remove coil springs as outlined under "Coil Springs, Replace."
16. Disconnect rear axle tie rod from rear axle.
17. Disconnect lower control arms from rear axle.
18. Disconnect upper control arms from rear axle.
19. Remove rear-axle assembly from vehicle.
20. Reverse procedure to install.

REAR AXLE SHAFT

REPLACE

1. Raise and support rear of vehicle.

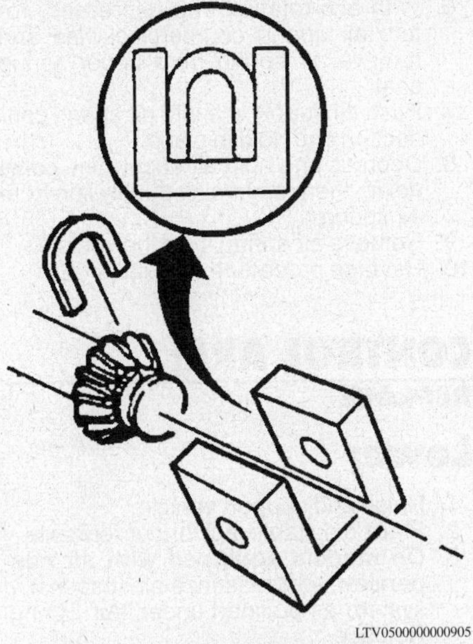

Fig. 3 Axle shaft removal. Locking differential

2. **On models equipped with disc brakes,** remove brake caliper as outlined in "Disc Brakes" chapter.
3. **On models equipped with drum brakes,** remove brake drum as outlined in "Drum Brakes" chapter.
4. **On all models,** loosen carrier cover bolts and allow lubricant to drain, then remove bolts and carrier cover.
5. Remove rear axle pinion shaft lock bolt, **Fig. 2.** Discard lock bolt.
6. **On models equipped with a standard differential,** remove pinion shaft.
7. **On models equipped with a locking differential,** proceed as follows:
   a. Remove pinion shaft part way, then rotate case until pinion shaft touches housing.
   b. Using a suitable flat-bladed tool, enter differential case and rotate rear axle shaft lock until lock aligns with thrust block, **Fig. 3.**
   c. Push flange of axle shaft inward towards differential assembly, then remove axle shaft lock from button end of axle shaft.
   d. Push flanged end of axle shaft toward center of vehicle, then remove "C" lock from button end of shaft.
8. **On all models,** pull axle shaft from housing. **Use caution not to damage seal.**
9. Reverse procedure to install.

HUB & BEARING

REPLACE

1. Remove axle shaft as outlined in "Rear Axle Shaft, Replace."
2. Remove axle seal by prying behind seal steel case with a pry bar. Use caution to avoid damaging axle housing.
3. Remove axle bearing using a puller and slide hammer, **Fig. 4.**
4. Lubricate new bearing with gear lubricant, then install bearing in axle housing with axle shaft bearing installer tool

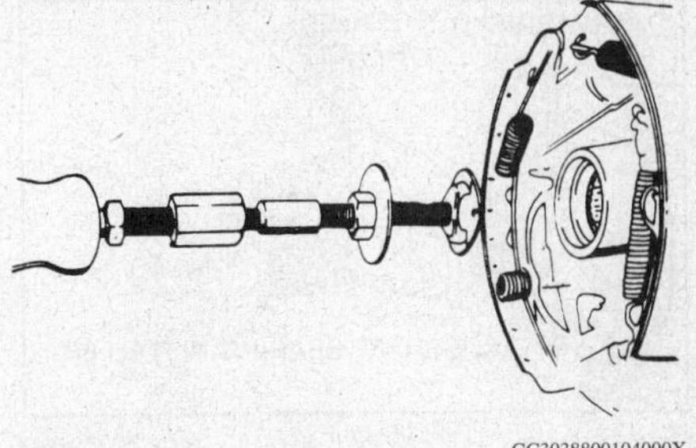

Fig. 4 Axle shaft bearing removal

No. J-23765, or equivalent, until bearing is seated in housing, **Fig. 5.**

5. Lubricate seal lips with gear lubricant, then position seal on axle shaft seal installer tool No. J-23771, or equivalent and install in axle housing, tapping into place until seal is flush with axle housing, **Fig. 6.**
6. Install axle shaft.

SHOCK ABSORBER

REPLACE

1. Raise vehicle and place jack stands under frame side rails. Position a jack under rear axle housing and raise slightly to support axle assembly.
2. Remove shock absorber upper mounting bolts.
3. **On models equipped with a leaf spring suspension,** remove shock absorber retaining nut, then the shock absorber from spring anchor plate.
4. **On models equipped with a coil spring suspension,** remove shock absorber lower mounting bolt.
5. **On all models,** remove shock absorber.
6. Reverse procedure to install.

COIL SPRING

REPLACE

1. Raise and support vehicle, then support rear axle with a suitable jack.
2. Remove shock absorber lower mounting bolts. **Do not lower rear axle so that upper control arms contact frame. Damage to upper control arms will result.**
3. Lower rear axle, the remove rear coil springs.
4. Reverse procedure to install.

LEAF SPRING

REPLACE

Removal

1. Raise vehicle and place jack stands under frame side rails to relieve spring load. Support axle assembly.
2. Remove shock absorber.
3. Loosen, but do not remove, spring to shackle attaching nut, **Fig. 1.**
4. Remove U-bolt attaching nuts, then the U-bolts.
5. Remove shackle to frame attaching nut and bolt. **After removing shackle**

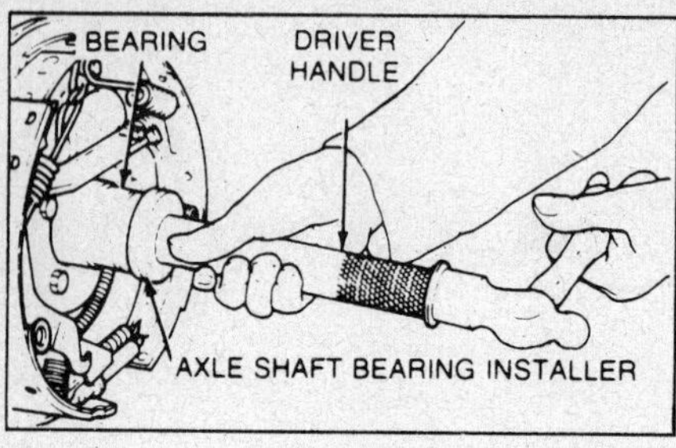

Fig. 5 Axle shaft bearing installation

to frame attaching nut and bolt, spring is free to rotate on front hanger bolt. Use restraining device to prevent rotation.

6. Remove front spring hanger nut and bolt, then the spring.

Installation

1. Clean axle spring pad and apply a rubber lubricant to the bushing and the spring eye.
2. Install bushing to spring assembly.
3. Install spring assembly to vehicle.

AIR SPRING

REPLACE

1. Remove air suspension fuse from fuse box. **Failure to remove air suspension fuse could cause damage to the air suspension system.**
2. Raise and support vehicle, then place a suitable jack under rear axle.
3. Remove air compressor mounting bolts from frame and support air compressor.
4. Loosen both air supply line connections at air compressor to depressurize air springs.
5. Depress anti-rotation peg in air spring top plate located in upper spring seat.
6. With anti-rotation peg depressed, rotate air spring counterclockwise and remove air spring from upper spring seat.
7. Push air supply line into air spring connection and hold in place.
8. Depress and hold air supply line collet down, then remove air supply line from air spring.
9. Remove air spring from the vehicle.
10. Reverse procedure to install.

CONTROL ARM

REPLACE

Lower

1. Raise and support vehicle.
2. Place a suitable jack under rear axle.
3. **On models equipped with air suspension,** depressurize air suspension system as outlined under "Air Spring, Replace."
4. **On all models,** remove rear axle lower control arm to axle mounting nut and bolt.
5. Remove rear axle lower control arm to frame mounting nut and bolt.
6. Remove lower control arm.
7. Reverse procedure to install.

Upper

1. Raise and support vehicle, then remove tire and wheel assembly.
2. Remove wheelhouse panel.
3. Place a suitable jack under rear axle.
4. **On models equipped with air suspension,** depressurize air suspension system as outlined under "Air Spring, Replace," then disconnect air suspension leveling sensor link from upper control arm.
5. **On all models,** remove rear axle upper control arm to axle mounting bolt and nut.

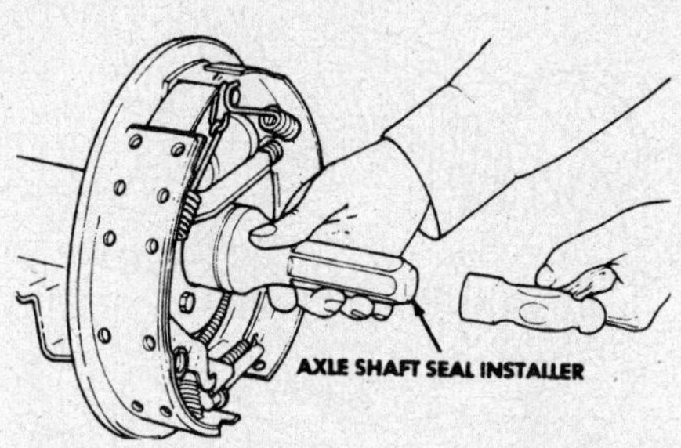

Fig. 6 Axle shaft seal installation

6. Remove rear axle upper control arm to frame mounting bolt.
7. Remove rear axle upper control arm.
8. Reverse procedure to install.

TIE ROD

REPLACE

1. Place a suitable jack under rear axle.
2. **On models equipped with air suspension,** depressurize air suspension system as outlined under "Air Spring, Replace."
3. **On all models,** remove rear axle tie rod to axle mounting bolt and nut.
4. Remove rear axle tie rod to frame mounting bolt and nut.
5. Remove rear axle tie rod from vehicle.
6. Reverse procedure to install.

STABILIZER BAR

REPLACE

1. Raise and support vehicle.
2. Remove lower nuts, washers and bolts from stabilizer links.
3. Remove nuts from U-bolts.
4. Remove U-bolts clamps and insulators.
5. Remove stabilizer.
6. Reverse procedure to install.

TIGHTENING SPECIFICATIONS

Year	Component	Torque, Ft. Lbs.
BLAZER & JIMMY		
2002–05	Axle Cover Bolts	22
	Leaf Spring U-Bolt Nuts	74
	Link To Axle	13
	Pinion Shaft Lock Screw	25
	Propeller Shaft Bolts	15
	Shackle To Frame Bolt	89
	Shackle To Front Bracket Bolt	89
	Shackle To Spring Bolt	89
	Shock Absorber Lower Mount	62
	Shock Absorber Upper Mount	18
	Stabilizer Bar Clamp	44
	Stabilizer To Link Bolt	50
	Wheel Lug Nuts	①
	Yoke Nut	25
BRAVADA, ENVOY, RAINIER & TRAILBLAZER		
2002–06	Air Spring Compressor To Frame Mounting Bolts	15
	Air Spring Leveling Sensor To Frame Mounting Bolts	71②
	Air Supply Lines To Compressor	20②
	Lower Control Arm Mounting Nut	74
	Rear Axle Brace & Tie Rod To Rear Axle Mounting Bolt	144
	Rear Axle Brace To Frame Nut	70
	Shock Absorber Lower Mounting Bolt	59
	Shock Absorber Upper Mounting Nut	59
	Stabilizer Shaft Insulator Clamp Nut	52
	Stabilizer Shaft Link Nut	74
	Tie Rod Mounting Bolt	144
	Upper Control Arm Mounting Bolt	97
	Wheel Lug Nut	103

① — Aluminum wheels, 90 ft. lbs.; steel wheels, 73 ft. lbs.
② — Inch lbs.

Front Suspension & Steering

NOTE: On Air Bag Equipped Models, Refer To "Air Bag System Precautions" Located In The Front Of This Manual For System Disarming & Arming Procedures.

INDEX

HUB & BEARING

REPLACE

2WD

1. Raise and support vehicle, then remove tire and wheel assembly.
2. Remove brake rotor as outlined in "Disc Brakes" chapter.
3. Remove ABS sensor mounting bolt, then the sensor from wheel hub and bearing.
4. Remove wheel hub and bearing to steering knuckle mounting bolts.
5. Remove wheel hub and bearing from steering knuckle.
6. Remove splash shield from steering knuckle.
7. Reverse procedure to install.

4WD

1. Remove tire and wheel center cap.
2. Remove drive axle nut.
3. Raise and support vehicle, then the tire and wheel assembly.
4. Remove brake rotor as outlined in "Disc Brakes" chapter.
5. Disengage drive shaft from steering knuckle by placing a suitable brass drift against outer end of drive shaft, then sharply strike brass drift with hammer. **Do not attempt to remove wheel drive shaft from wheel hub and bearing at this time.**
6. Remove ABS sensor mounting bolt, then the sensor from wheel hub and bearing.
7. Remove wheel hub and bearing to steering knuckle mounting bolts.
8. Remove wheel hub and bearing from steering knuckle.
9. Remove splash shield from steering knuckle.
10. Reverse procedure to install.

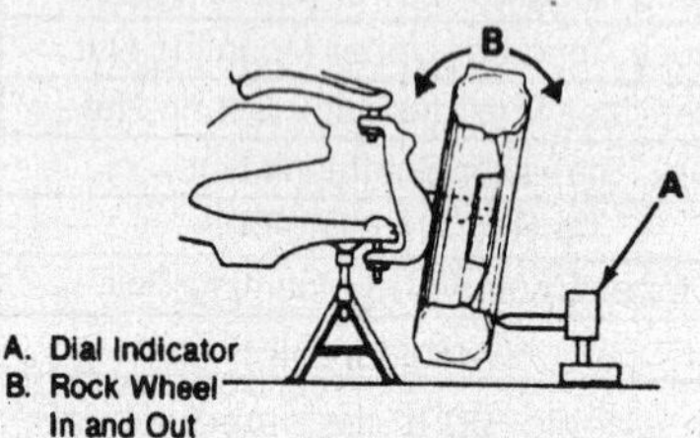

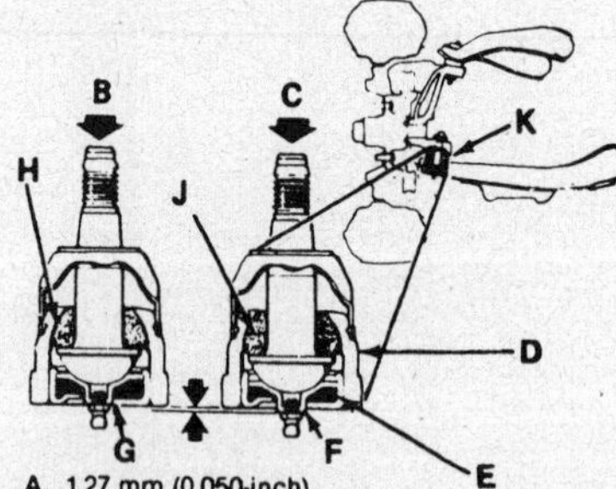

Fig. 1 Lower ball joint wear indicator. Blazer & Jimmy w/2WD

BALL JOINT INSPECTION

Blazer & Jimmy

LOWER

2WD MODELS

The lower ball joint has a visual wear indicator, **Fig. 1.** To inspect, vehicle weight must rest on wheels to properly load ball joints.

4WD MODELS

1. Raise and support vehicle.
2. Support lower control arm with suitable jack stand.
3. Inspect lower ball joint for horizontal looseness as follows:
   a. Place suitable dial indicator against wheel rim at lowest outboard point, **Fig. 2.**
   b. Rock wheel in and out while reading dial indicator.
   c. Dial indicator reading should be no more than .125 inch.
   d. If reading is too high, inspect lower ball joint for vertical looseness.
4. Place vehicle on suitable jack stands.

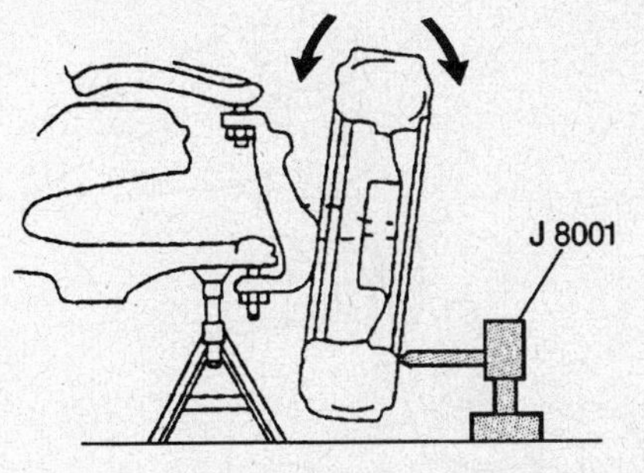

Fig. 2 Ball joint horizontal looseness inspection. Blazer & Jimmy w/4WD

5. Place suitable dial indicator against spindle, **Fig. 3.**
6. Pry between lower control arm and outer bearing race while reading dial indicator, **Fig. 4.**
7. If reading is more than .125 inch, replace lower ball joint.
8. If lower ball joint is within specification and there is too much horizontal looseness, inspect upper ball joint as follows:
   a. Disconnect ball joint from knuckle.
   b. Inspect for looseness by twisting ball joint stud with fingers, if any looseness is found replace ball joint.

UPPER

1. Raise vehicle and position floor stands under right and left lower control arms near each lower ball joint.
2. Position dial indicator against wheel rim, **Fig. 5.**
3. Shake wheel, **Fig. 5,** and read gauge. Horizontal deflection should not exceed .125 inch.
4. If reading exceeds .125 inch or if ball stud has been disconnected from knuckle assembly and any looseness is detected or stud is loose, replace ball joint.

Bravada, Envoy, Rainier & Trailblazer

1. Raise and support vehicle.
2. Support lower control arm with a floor stand or jack, as far outboard as possible.
3. Check wheel bearing for looseness.
4. Position a suitable dial indicator against lowest outboard point on wheel rim.
5. Rock wheel in and out while reading dial indicator. Dial indicator reading should be no more than .08 inch.
6. **On models equipped with 2WD,** if reading is too high, proceed to step 8. If upper ball joint is satisfactory, replace lower ball joint.
7. **On models equipped with 4WD,** if reading is too high, check lower ball joint for vertical looseness as follows:
   a. Place a suitable dial indicator against spindle to show vertical movement.

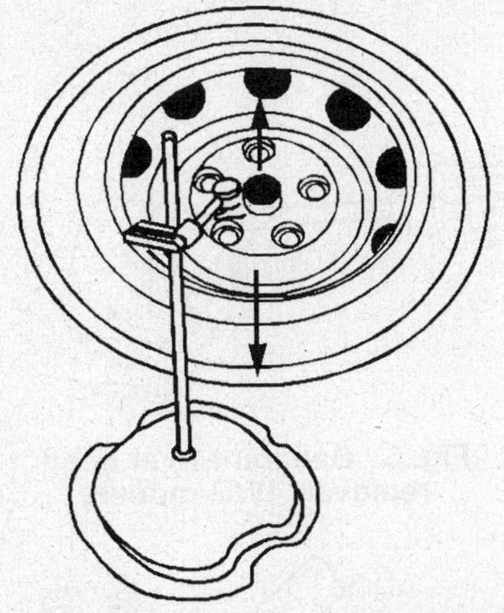

Fig. 3 Dial indicator mounting. Blazer & Jimmy w/4WD

   b. Pry between lower control arm and outer bearing race while reading dial indicator.
   c. If dial indicator reading is more than .125 inch, replace lower ball joint.
8. **On all models,** disconnect upper ball joint from steering knuckle as outlined under "Ball Joint, Replace."
9. If any looseness is found or ball joint stud can be twisted with your fingers, replace upper control arm.

BALL JOINT

REPLACE

Blazer & Jimmy

LOWER

2WD MODELS

1. Raise vehicle and support with jack stands under frame side rails.
2. Remove front wheel, then support control arm spring seat with a jack.
3. Remove disc brake as outlined in "Disc Brakes."
4. Remove cotter pin and stud nut using ball joint separator tool No. J-23742, or equivalent, then break ball joint loose from steering knuckle.
5. Inspect and clean tapered hole in steering knuckle. If hole is out of round or damaged in any way, steering knuckle must be replaced.
6. Guide lower control arm out of opening in splash shield. **Block knuckle assembly out of way by placing wooden block between frame and upper control arm.**
7. Remove grease fittings, then press ball joint from lower control arm.
8. Reverse procedure to install.

4WD MODELS

1. Raise and support vehicle.
2. Remove tire and wheel assembly.
3. Remove cotter pin from lower ball joint stud.
4. Remove lower ball join stud nut.

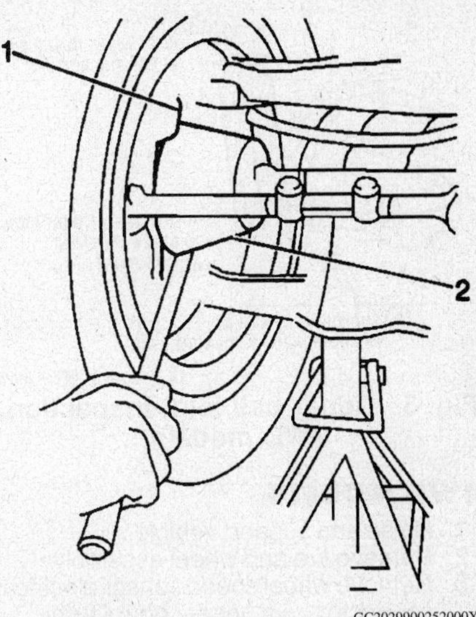

Fig. 4 Ball joint vertical looseness inspection. Blazer & Jimmy w/4WD

5. Pry bar placed on top of upper control arm and on bottom of frame, pry downward.
6. Carefully hammer on steering knuckle in the area of lower ball joint using suitable hammer.
7. Remove lower ball joint from steering knuckle.
8. Drill approximately 1/4 inch hole in center of each ball joint attaching rivet using suitable 1/8 inch drill bit.
9. Drill rivet heads away using suitable 1/2 inch drill bit, **Fig. 6.**
10. Remove rivets using suitable punch, **Fig. 7.**
11. Remove lower ball joint from control arm.
12. Reverse procedure to install. Install lower ball joint retaining nuts and bolts as outlined in **Fig. 8.**

UPPER

2WD MODELS

1. Raise vehicle and support at lower control arm with jacks. **Jack must be positioned between coil spring seat and ball joint of lower control arm to obtain maximum leverage against coil spring pressure.**
2. Remove wheel and tire assembly, then the disc brake as outlined in "Disc Brakes."
3. Remove cotter pin and stud nut from ball joint.
4. Break stud loose from steering knuckle using ball joint separator tool No. J-23742, or equivalent. Support knuckle assembly to avoid damaging brake line.
5. With control arm in raised position, drill rivets 1/4 inch deep with a 1/8 inch drill, then drill off rivet heads with a 1/2 inch drill.
6. Punch out rivets, then remove ball joint.
7. Reverse procedure to install. Replace rivets with attaching bolts and nuts.

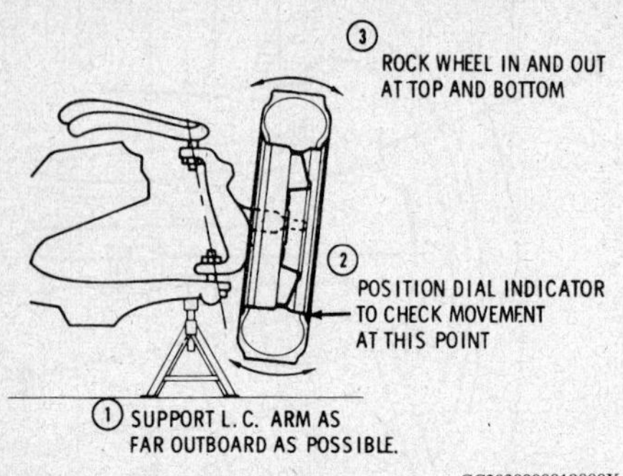
③ ROCK WHEEL IN AND OUT AT TOP AND BOTTOM
② POSITION DIAL INDICATOR TO CHECK MOVEMENT AT THIS POINT
① SUPPORT L. C. ARM AS FAR OUTBOARD AS POSSIBLE.
GC2028800019000X

Fig. 5 Upper ball joint inspection. 2WD models

4WD MODELS

1. Raise and support vehicle.
2. Remove tire and wheel assembly.
3. Remove wheel speed sensor electrical connector from upper control arm.
4. Disconnect wheel speed sensor electrical connector.
5. Remove cotter pin from upper ball joint stud.
6. Remove upper ball join stud nut.
7. Pry bar placed under upper control arm and on top of frame, pry upward.
8. Carefully hammer on steering knuckle in the area of upper ball joint using suitable hammer.
9. Remove upper ball joint from steering knuckle.
10. Drill approximately 1/4 inch hole in center of each ball joint attaching rivet using suitable 1/8 inch drill bit.
11. Drill rivet heads away using suitable 1/2 inch drill bit, **Fig. 6.**
12. Remove rivets using suitable punch, **Fig. 7.**
13. Remove upper ball joint from control arm.
14. Reverse procedure to install. Install upper ball joint retaining nuts and bolts as outlined in **Fig. 8.**

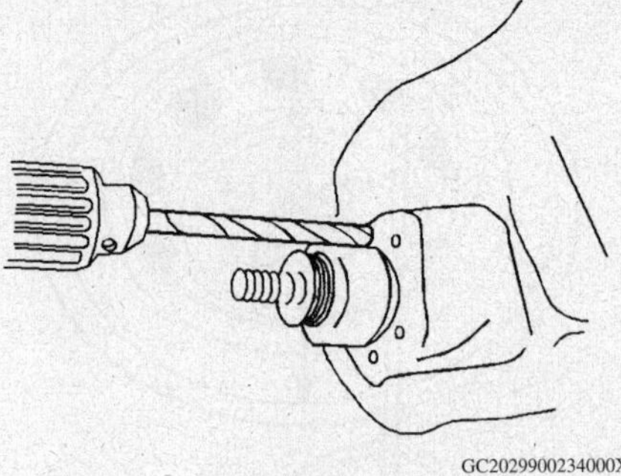
GC2029900234000X

Fig. 6 Ball joint rivet head removal. 4WD models

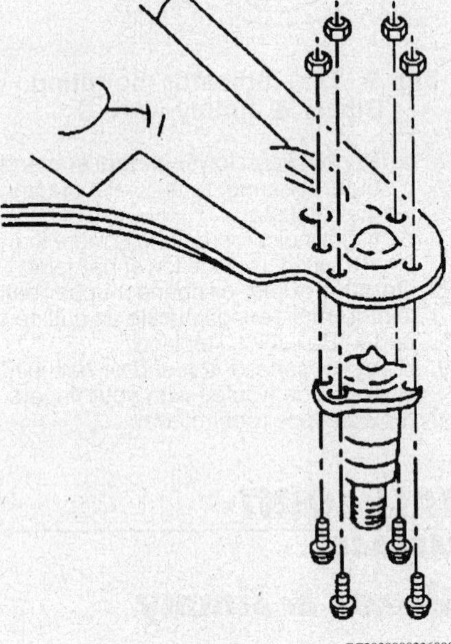
GC2029900236000X

Fig. 8 Ball joint installation. 4WD models

Bravada, Envoy, Rainier & Trailblazer

LOWER

1. Raise and support vehicle, then remove wheel and tire assembly.
2. Remove steering knuckle with wheel hub and bearing attached as outlined under "Steering Knuckle, Replace."
3. Remove lower ball joint flange with a suitable chisel.
4. Install ball joint removal tool J 9519, or equivalent, to lower ball joint.
5. Remove lower ball joint from lower control arm.
6. Reverse procedure to install.

UPPER

1. Raise and support vehicle, then remove tire and wheel assembly.
2. Remove steering knuckle with wheel hub attached as outlined under "Steering Knuckle, Replace."
3. Remove upper ball joint retaining clip, then the upper ball joint boot.
4. Remove upper ball joint from the steering knuckle using ball joint removal tool No. J 9519, or equivalent.
5. Reverse procedure to install.

COIL SPRING

REPLACE

Blazer & Jimmy

1. Raise and support vehicle.
2. Remove two shock absorber screws and push shock up through control arm and into spring.
3. Support vehicle so that control arms hang free.
4. Place coil spring replacement tool No. J-23028–01, or equivalent, into position cradling the inner bushings, **Fig. 9.** Tool should be secured to a jack.
5. Remove stabilizer to lower control arm attachment.
6. Raise the jack to remove tension on lower control arm pivot bolts, then install a chain around spring and through control arm and remove the nuts and bolts.

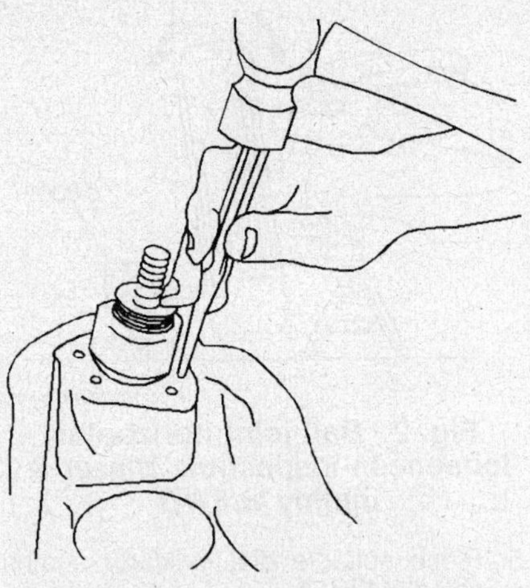
GC2029900235000X

Fig. 7 Ball joint rivet removal. 4WD models

7. Lower control arm by slowly lowering jack.
8. With all pressure removed from spring, remove safety chain and spring. **Do not apply force to lower control arm and ball joint to remove spring. Proper maneuvering of spring will allow for easy removal.**
9. Reverse procedure to install, noting the following:
   a. Ensure coil spring is installed with flat coiled end with gripper notch on top and the lower coil covering all or part of one drain hole in lower control arm and with other hole exposed.
   b. Install both lower control arm bolts from front to rear to ensure adequate steering linkage clearance.
   c. Tighten stabilizer link nuts, lower vehicle and tighten lower control arm bolt nuts, after suspension has been weighted.

Bravada, Envoy, Rainier & Trailblazer

1. Remove shock module upper retaining nuts. **Use care when handling coil springs to avoid chipping or scratching coating. Damage to coating will result in premature failure of coil springs.**
2. Raise and support vehicle, then remove tire and wheel.
3. Remove shock module yoke to lower control arm retaining nut.
4. Remove shock module yoke from lower control arm using tool No. J-24319-B, or equivalent.
5. Remove shock module from shock tower and lower control arm.
6. Remove shock module yoke to shock absorber pinch bolt and nut.
7. Spread shock module yoke at pinch bolt using a flat bladed tool.
8. Remove shock module yoke from shock absorber.
9. Install pieces of heater hose to shock module spring where tool No. J-45400,

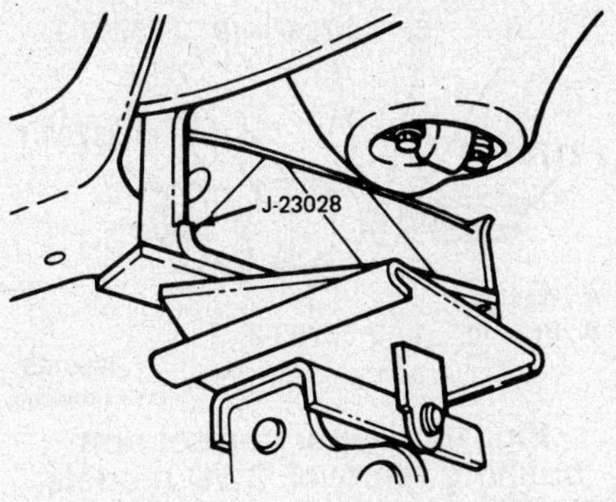

Fig. 9 Coil spring removal w/adapter tool. Blazer & Jimmy

equivalent, contacts lower part of spring.
10. Install shock module into J-45400, or equivalent, **Fig. 10.**
11. Turn spring compressor forcing screw until coil spring is compressed, then remove shock absorber from shock module.
12. Loosen compressor forcing screw until upper mounting plate and coil spring are removed.
13. Reverse procedure to install.

SHOCK ABSORBER

REPLACE

Blazer & Jimmy

2WD MODELS

1. Raise and support vehicle.
2. Hold shock upper stem from turning with a wrench and remove nut, retainer and grommet.
3. Remove lower shock pivot bolts, then remove shock absorber from vehicle.
4. Reverse procedure to install.

4WD MODELS

Refer to **Fig. 11** for shock absorber replacement procedure on 4WD vehicles.

Bravada, Envoy, Rainier & Trailblazer

Refer to "Coil Spring, Replace" for removal procedure.

CONTROL ARM

REPLACE

Blazer & Jimmy

UPPER

2WD MODELS

1. Raise vehicle and support.
2. Support lower control arms with floor stands.
3. Remove wheel and tire assembly.
4. Disconnect upper ball joint from steering knuckle and support brake rotor to prevent damage to brake hose.

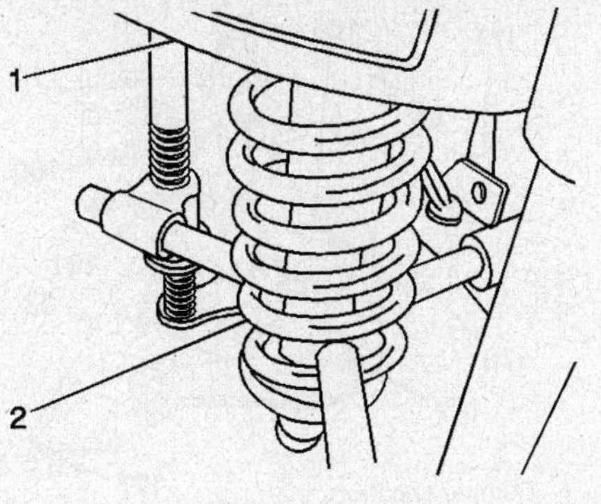

Fig. 10 Coil spring replacement. Bravada, Envoy, Rainier & Trailblazer

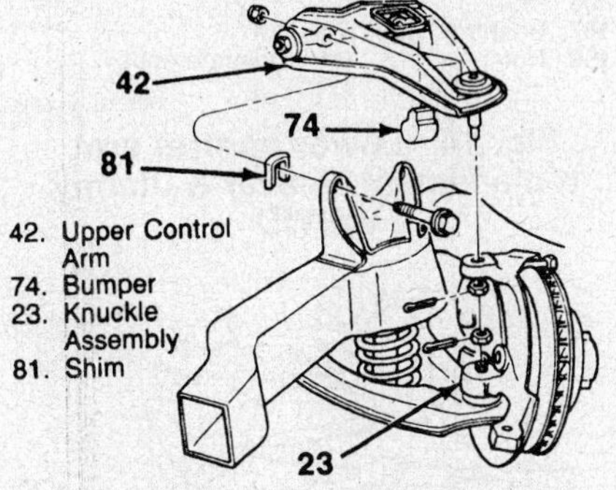

Fig. 12 Upper control arm replacement. Blazer & Jimmy w/2WD

5. Remove upper control arm attaching nuts and bolts, **Fig. 12,** noting location of any shims removed.
6. Remove upper control arm.
7. Reverse procedure to install, noting the following:
   a. Install shims in their original position.
   b. Tighten control arm pivot nuts.

4WD MODELS

1. Raise vehicle and support.
2. Support at frame and raise lower control arm to relieve spring tension, placing jack stand as far out board on lower control arm as possible.
3. Remove front tire and wheel assembly.
4. Remove and install control arm, **Fig. 13,** supporting spindle to prevent damaging brake hose.

LOWER

2WD MODELS

1. Remove coil spring as outlined in "Coil Spring, Replace."
2. Remove lower ball joint stud, then remove lower control arm through opening in splash shield.
3. Reverse procedure to install.

4WD MODELS

Refer to **Fig. 14** for lower control arm replacement procedure on 4WD vehicles.

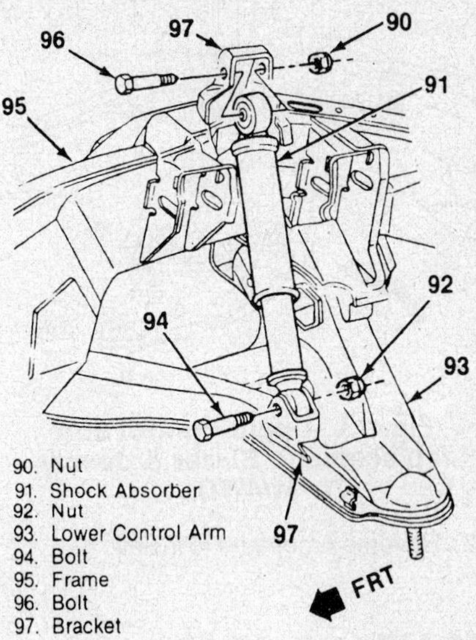

Fig. 11 Shock absorber replacement. Blazer & Jimmy w/4WD

Bravada, Envoy, Rainier & Trailblazer

LOWER

1. Raise and support vehicle, then remove tire and wheel.
2. Disconnect outer tie rod from steering knuckle using tool No. J-24319-B, or equivalent.
3. Remove stabilizer shaft link lower retaining nut, then disconnect stabilizer shaft link and washer from lower control arm.
4. Remove shock module yoke lower mounting nut, then disconnect shock module yoke from steering knuckle using tool No. J-24319-B, or equivalent.
5. Remove lower control arm to lower control arm bracket mounting nuts and bolts, **Note direction bolts are removed for installation.**
6. Remove lower ball joint retaining nut, then disconnect lower ball joint from steering knuckle using tool No. J-43631, or equivalent.
7. Pivot lower control arm outward and downward to disconnect lower control arm from lower control arm bracket.
8. Remove lower control arm from steering knuckle.
9. Reverse procedure to install.

UPPER

1. Raise and support vehicle, then remove tire and wheel.
2. Remove upper ball joint to upper control arm pinch bolt and nut.
3. Disconnect upper control arm from steering knuckle, then ABS wheel speed sensor wiring harness from upper control arm.
4. Remove mounting bolts, then the upper control arm.

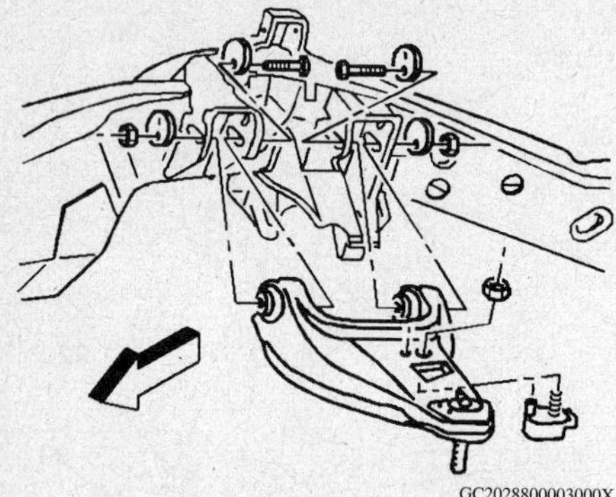

Fig. 13 Upper control arm replacement. Blazer & Jimmy w/4WD

5. Reverse procedure to install.

CONTROL ARM BUSHING

REPLACE

Upper

1. Remove upper control arm as outlined in "Control Arm, Replace."
2. **On 2WD models,** remove nuts from end of pivot shaft, then remove bushings, **Fig. 15.**
3. **On all models,** install bushings by installing pivot shaft in control arm and pressing new bushings into control arm, **Fig. 16.** Tighten pivot shaft nuts to specifications, with weight of vehicle resting on wheels. **Both bushings must be installed .48–.52 inch from face of control arm to bushing outer sleeve.**

Lower

2WD MODELS

1. Remove coil spring as outlined in "Coil Spring, Replace."
2. Remove lower control arm pivot bolts. Refer to "Control Arm, Replace."
3. Drive bushing flare down flush with rubber of front bushing, then remove front and rear bushings from control arm, **Figs. 17 and 18.**
4. Install front bushing, **Fig. 19,** then flare the bushing, **Fig. 20.**
5. Install rear bushings, **Fig. 21,** then the lower control arm.

4WD MODELS

1. Raise and support vehicle.
2. Remove wheel and tire assembly.
3. Unload torsion bar.
4. Remove stabilizer bar as outlined in "Stabilizer Bar, Replace."
5. Remove shock absorber as outlined in "Shock Absorber, Replace."
6. Remove control arm pivot bolts then the lower control arm.
7. Remove lower control arm front and rear bushings, **Fig. 22.**
8. Reverse procedure to install.

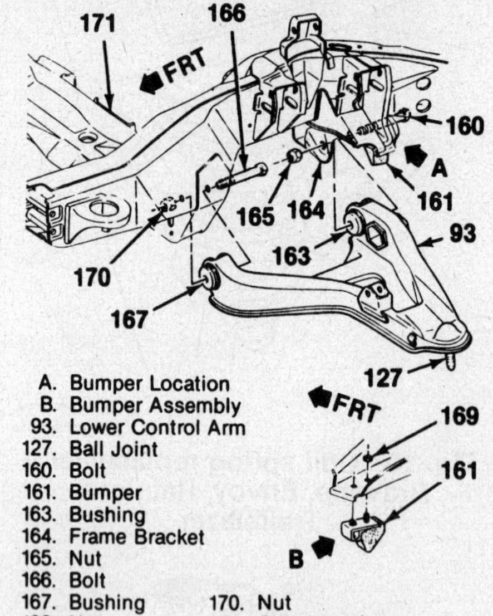

Fig. 14 Lower control arm replacement. Blazer & Jimmy w/4WD

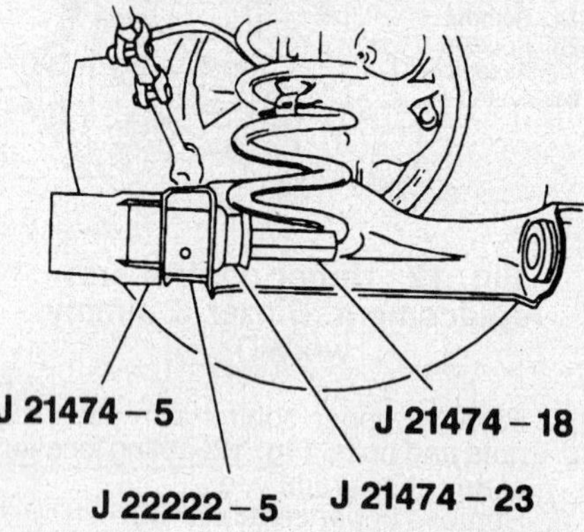

Fig. 17 Lower control arm front bushing removal. 2WD models

STEERING KNUCKLE

REPLACE

Blazer & Jimmy

2WD MODELS

1. Raise and support front of vehicle, then support lower control arm with jack. **Jack must be positioned between coil spring seat and ball joint of lower control arm to obtain maximum leverage against coil spring pressure.**
2. Remove wheel and tire assembly.
3. Remove brake caliper, then the hub and rotor assembly.
4. Remove splash shield to steering knuckle attaching bolts.
5. Remove tie rod end from steering knuckle using tie rod puller tool No. J-6627, or equivalent.
6. If steering knuckle is to be replaced, remove knuckle seal.
7. Remove ball joint studs from steering knuckle using ball joint separator tool No. J-23742, or equivalent.
8. Raise upper control arm to disengage upper ball joint stud from knuckle.
9. Remove knuckle from lower ball joint stud.
10. After removal, inspect tapered holes. If holes are out of round or deformation or damage is observed, replace steering knuckle.
11. Reverse procedure to install. Install tie rod end using ball joint seating tool No. J-29193, or equivalent and **torque** to 15 ft. lbs.

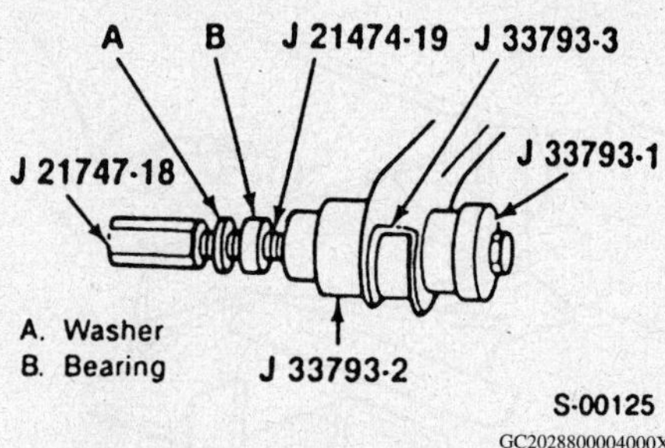

Fig. 15 Upper control arm bushing removal. 2WD models

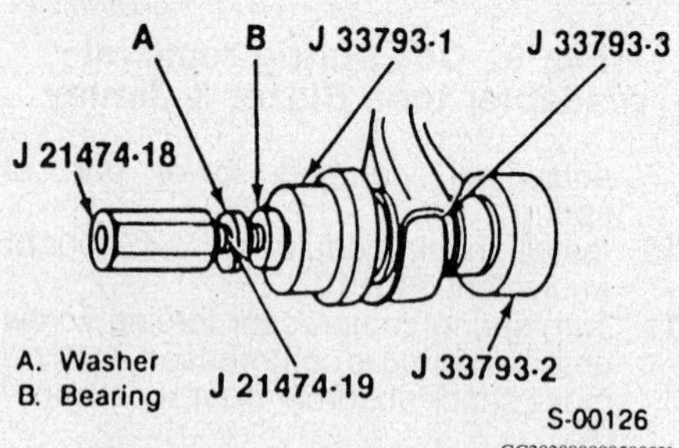

Fig. 16 Upper control arm bushing installation

4WD MODELS

1. Raise and support vehicle.
2. Remove tire and wheel assembly.
3. Remove drive axle nut, **Fig. 23.**
4. Remove brake caliper assembly.
5. Remove hub and bearing assembly.
6. Remove cotter pin and nut from tie rod stud.
7. Remove tie rod assembly, **Fig. 24.**
8. Remove ball joints from knuckle, refer to "Ball Joint, Replace."
9. Removal knuckle from vehicle.
10. Reverse procedure to install.

Bravada, Envoy, Rainier & Trailblazer

1. **On models equipped with 4WD,** remove tire and wheel center cap, then the drive axle nut.
2. **On all models,** raise and support vehicle, then remove tire and wheel assembly.
3. Remove wheel hub and bearing as outlined under "Hub & Bearing, Replace."
4. Remove outer tie rod to steering knuckle retaining nut.
5. Disconnect outer tie rod from steering

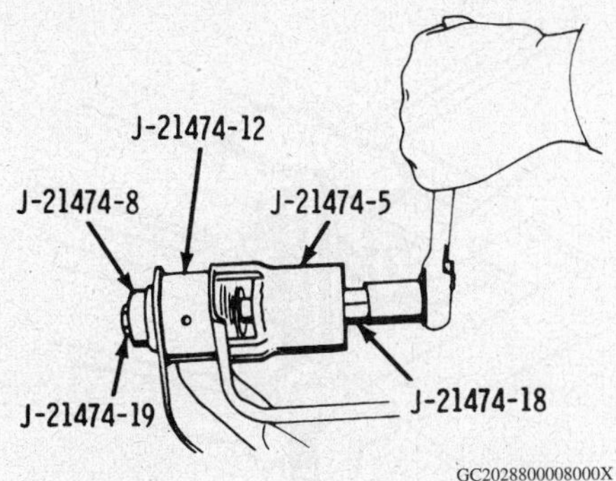

Fig. 18 Lower control arm rear bushing removal. 2WD models

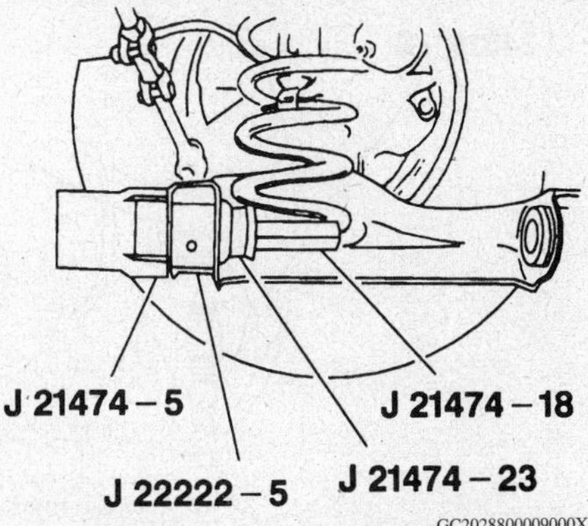

Fig. 19 Lower control arm front bushing installation. 2WD models

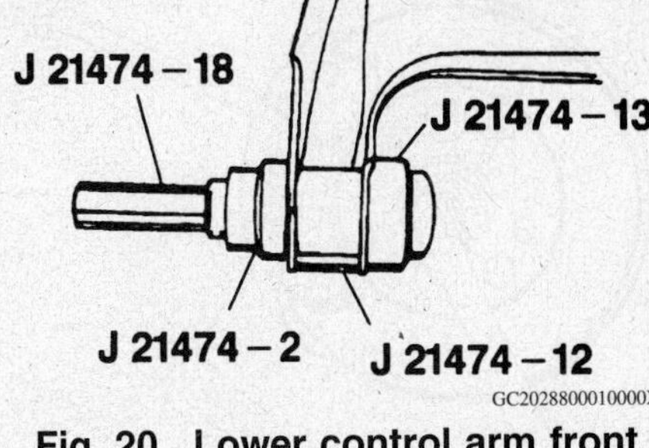

Fig. 20 Lower control arm front bushing flaring. 2WD models

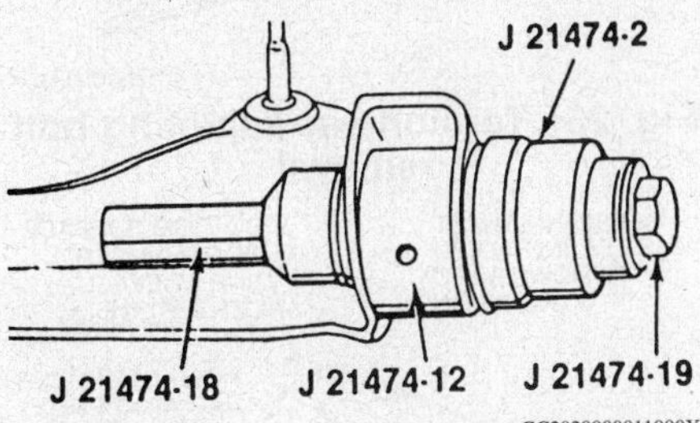

Fig. 21 Lower control arm rear bushing installation. 2WD models

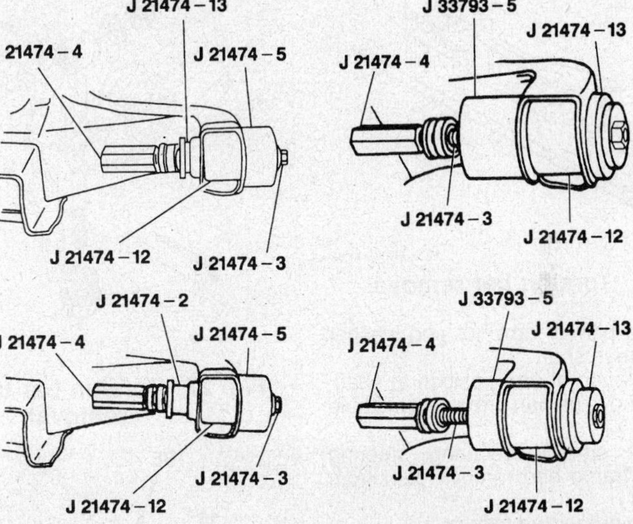

Fig. 22 Lower control arm bushing replacement. 4WD models

knuckle using joint removal tool No. J 24319, or equivalent.
6. Remove brake hose bracket retaining bolts, then the brake hose bracket from steering knuckle.
7. Disconnect ABS wheel speed sensor wiring harness bracket from steering knuckle.
8. Remove upper control arm to steering knuckle pinch bolt and nut.
9. Disconnect upper control arm from steering knuckle.
10. Remove lower ball joint to steering knuckle retaining nut, then the steering knuckle from lower control arm using ball joint separator tool No. J 43631, or equivalent.
11. Remove steering knuckle from vehicle.
12. Reverse procedure to install.

TORSION BAR

REPLACE

1. Raise and support vehicle.
2. Remove transmission shield.
3. Remove both torsion bar adjusting bolts, **Fig. 25.**
4. Remove lower link mount nut from one side.
5. Remove torsion bar, **Fig. 26.**
6. Remove lower link mount nut from opposite side, then the link mount.
7. Remove upper link mount nut, then the upper link, **Fig. 27.**
8. Reverse procedure to install.

STABILIZER BAR

REPLACE

Blazer & Jimmy

2WD MODELS

1. Raise and support front of vehicle.
2. Remove stabilizer link bolt nuts from both sides, then pull link bolt from linkage and remove retainers, grommets and spacers, **Fig. 28.**
3. Remove stabilizer bracket to frame or body attaching bolts, then the stabilizer bar, bushings and brackets.
4. Reverse procedure to install, noting the following:
   a. Install stabilizer bar so identification stamping appears on righthand side of vehicle.
   b. Position rubber bushings squarely in brackets with slit facing front of vehicle.

4WD MODELS

Refer to **Fig. 29** for stabilizer bar replacement procedure.

Bravada, Envoy, Rainier & Trailblazer

1. Raise and support vehicle, then remove tire and wheel assemblies.
2. Remove stabilizer shaft links to stabilizer shaft retaining nuts.
3. Remove stabilizer shaft insulator clamp mounting bolts.
4. Remove stabilizer shaft insulator clamp from stabilizer shaft insulator.
5. Remove stabilizer shaft insulators from stabilizer shaft.
6. Remove engine protection shield.
7. Install a suitable jack underneath oil pan and insert a block of wood between oil pan and jack.
8. Raise engine .4 inches from bottom of oil pan to rear edge of transmission support crossmember.
9. Remove stabilizer shaft from vehicle.
10. Reverse procedure to install.

POWER STEERING GEAR

REPLACE

Blazer & Jimmy

1. Disconnect pressure and return hoses from steering gear housing, then plug hose ends and gear housing ports to prevent entry of dirt.
2. Remove coupling shield.
3. Remove retaining nuts, lock washers and bolts at steering coupling to steering shaft flange.

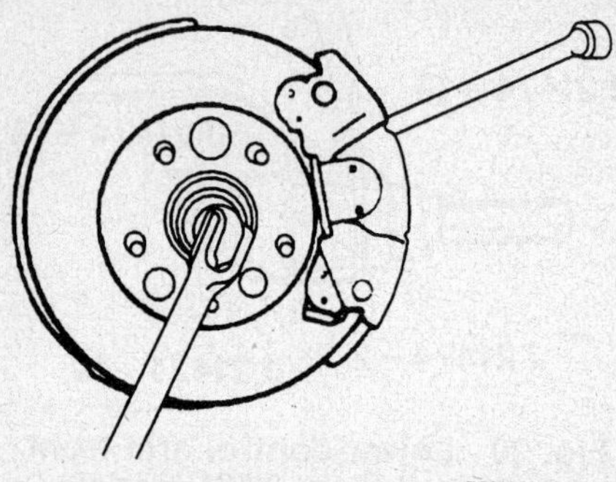

Fig. 23 Drive axle nut removal. Blazer & Jimmy w/4WD

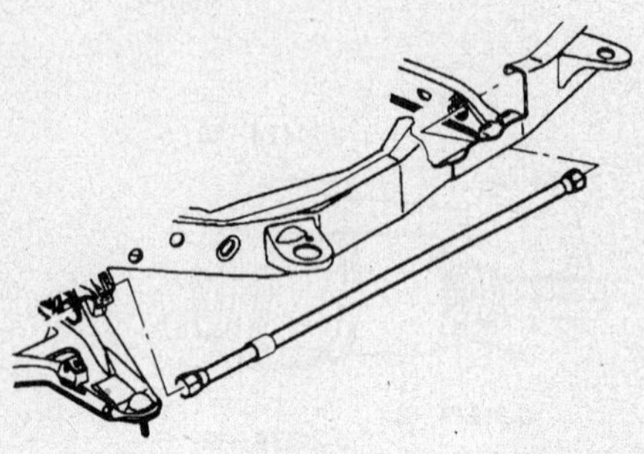

Fig. 26 Torsion bar removal

4. Remove pitman arm nut and washer from pitman shaft.
5. Mark relation of arm position to shaft, then remove pitman arm using suitable puller.
6. Remove screws securing steering gear to frame and remove gear from vehicle.
7. Reverse procedure to install.

Bravada, Envoy, Rainier & Trailblazer

1. Raise and support vehicle, then place a suitable drain pan under vehicle.
2. Remove tire and wheel assemblies.
3. Remove outer tie rod retaining to steering knuckle retaining nuts, then disconnect outer tie rods from steering knuckles using joint separator tool No. J 24319-B, or equivalent.
4. Remove engine shield mounting bolts, then the engine shield.
5. Remove rear lower control arm bracket to frame mounting bolts.
6. Remove steering gear crossmember mounting bolts, then the steering gear crossmember.
7. Disconnect lower intermediate shaft boot from power steering gear and remove intermediate shaft boot from vehicle.
8. Remove lower intermediate shaft to power steering gear input shaft pinch bolt.
9. Disconnect lower intermediate shaft from power steering gear.
10. Remove power steering hose assembly to power steering gear retaining bolt.
11. Remove power steering hose assembly from power steering gear.
12. Support power steering gear and remove power steering gear mounting bolts.
13. Remove power steering gear from vehicle.
14. Reverse procedure to install.

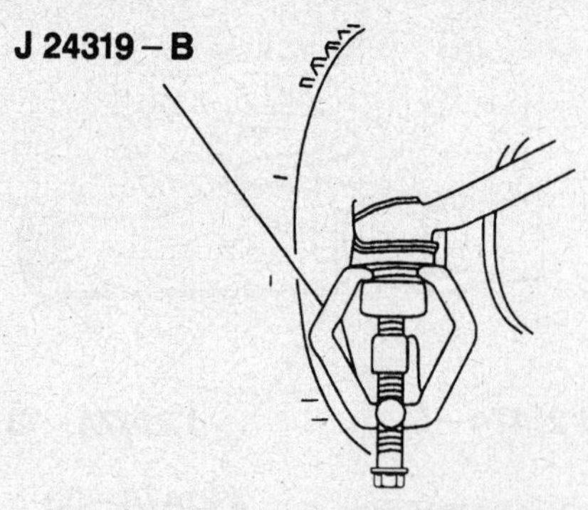

Fig. 24 Tie rod removal. Blazer & Jimmy w/4WD

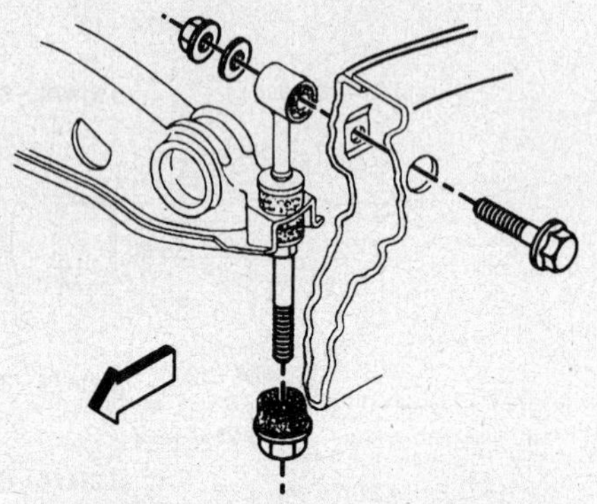

Fig. 27 Torsion bar upper link removal

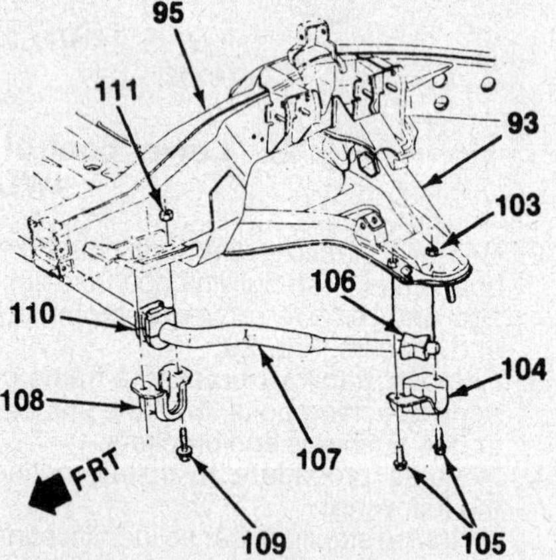

93. Lower Control Arm
95. Frame
103. Weld Nut
104. Clamp
105. Bolts
106. Insulator
107. Stabilizer Shaft
108. Clamp
109. Bolt
110. Insulator
111. Nut

GC2028800017000X

Fig. 29 Stabilizer bar replacement. 4WD models

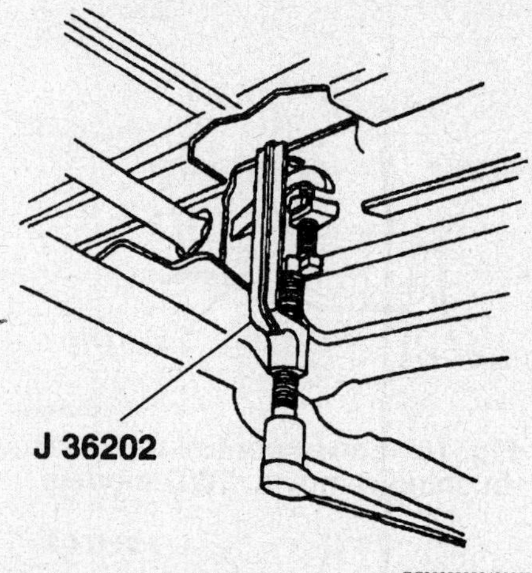

Fig. 25 Torsion bar adjusting bolt removal

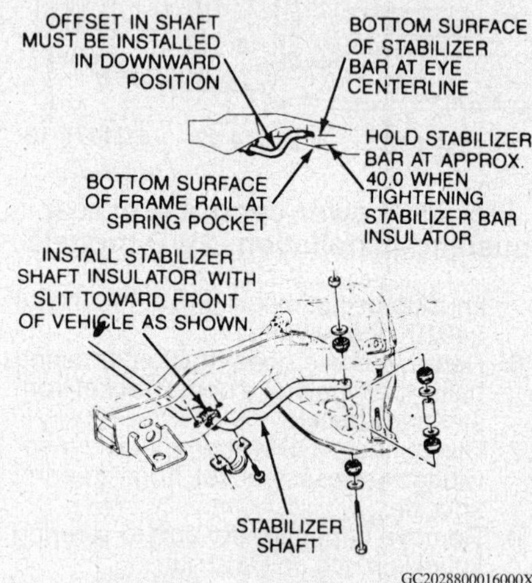

Fig. 28 Stabilizer bar replacement. 2WD models

POWER STEERING PUMP

REPLACE

1. Disconnect pressure and return hoses from power steering pump or steering gear housing, then secure ends in raised position to prevent oil drainage. Cap all open lines and fittings.
2. Remove drive belt.
3. Remove power steering pump attaching bolts.
4. Remove power steering pump assembly, **Figs. 30 through 32.**
5. **On models equipped with 4.2L, 5.3L and 6.0L engines,** remove power steering pump pulley using puller tool No. J–25034-C, or equivalent.
6. **On all models,** reverse procedure to install.

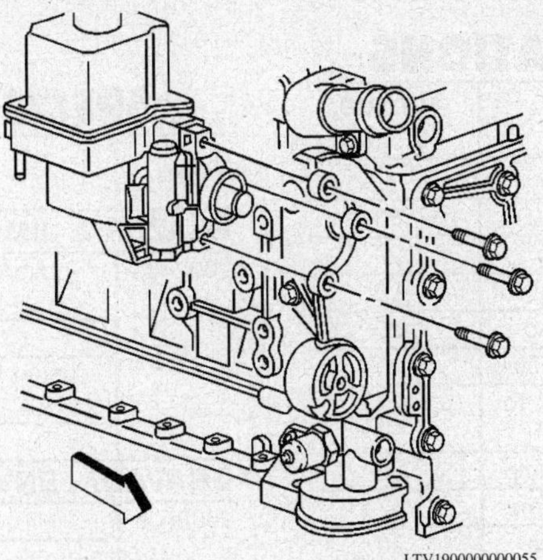

Fig. 30 Power steering pump replacement. 4.2L engine

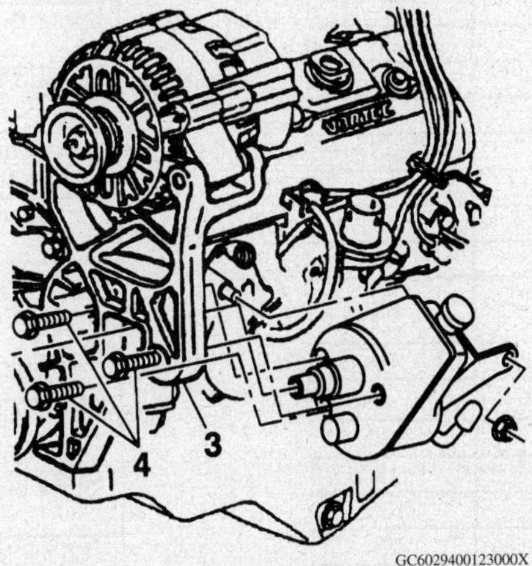

Fig. 31 Power steering pump replacement. 4.3L engine

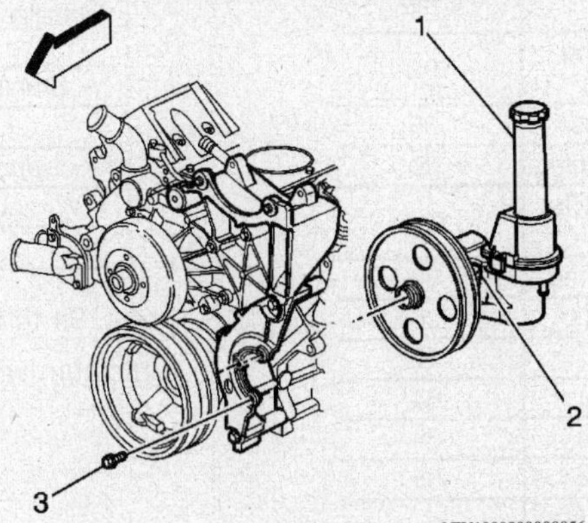

Fig. 32 Power steering pump replacement. 5.3L & 6.0L engines

TIGHTENING SPECIFICATIONS

Year	Component	Torque, Ft. Lbs.
BLAZER & JIMMY w/2WD		
2002–05	Lower Ball Joint	83
	Lower Control Arm Bushing	20
	Lower Control Arm To Frame Attaching Nut	①
	Power Steering Pump Mounting Bolts	20
	Power Steering Pump Pressure Line Fitting	20
	Power Steering Pump Rear Brace Nut To Engine	18.5
	Rear Brace Nut To Power Steering Pump	33
	Service Ball Joint To Upper Control Arm	17
	Shock Absorber To Control Arm Bolts	20
	Shock Absorber Upper Attaching Nut	8
	Splash Shield To Steering Knuckle	10
	Stabilizer Bar Bracket To Frame Bolts And Nuts	24
	Stabilizer Link Nut	13
	Steering Gear Hose Coupling	21
	Steering Gear Lower Clamp Bolt	26
	Steering Gear Side Cover Bolts	45
	Steering Gear To Frame Bolts	55
	Tie Rod End To Steering Knuckle	40
	Upper Ball Joint	61
	Upper Control Arm To Frame Attaching Nuts	65
	Wheel Lug Nuts	②
BLAZER & JIMMY w/4WD		
2002–05	Axle Nut	180
	Ball Joint Retaining Nuts	17
	Driveshaft Nut	180
	Hub & Bearing Assembly Shield & Knuckle	86
	Hub Nut	180
	Lower Ball Joint	83
	Lower Control Arm To Frame Attaching Bolts	148
	Lower Control Arm To Frame Attaching Nuts	92
	Power Steering Pump Mounting Bolts	36
	Power Steering Pump Pressure Line Fitting	20
	Power Steering Pump Rear Brace Nut To Engine	18.5
	Rear Brace Nut To Power Steering Pump	33
	Retainer To Torsion Bar Support Bolts	26
	Service Ball Joints To Control Arm	17
	Shock Absorber Lower Attaching Nut	54
	Shock Absorber Upper Attaching Nut	54
	Stabilizer Bar Clamp To Frame Bolts	35
	Stabilizer Bar Clamp To Lower Control Arm Bolts	24
	Steering Gear Hose Coupling	21
	Steering Gear Lower Clamp Bolt	26
	Steering Gear Side Cover Bolts	45
	Steering Gear To Frame Bolts	55
	Tie Rod End To Steering Knuckle Nut	35

TIGHTENING SPECIFICATIONS—Continued

Year	Component	Torque, Ft. Lbs.
BLAZER & JIMMY w/4WD		
2002–05	Torsion Bar Support Retainer Bolts And Nuts	26
	Upper Ball Joint	61
	Upper Control Arm To Frame Attaching Nuts	70
	Wheel Lug Nuts	②
BRAVADA, ENVOY, RAINIER & TRAILBLAZER		
2002–06	Adjuster Plug Locknut	50
	Drive Axle Nut	103
	Lower Ball Joint Retaining Nuts	81
	Lower Control Arm Bracket Front Mounting Bolt	195
	Lower Control Arm Bracket Rear Mounting Bolt	177
	Lower Control Arm To Bracket Mounting Nuts	96
	Lower Intermediate Shaft To Power Steering Gear Input Shaft Pinch Bolt	30
	Outer Tie Rod To Steering Knuckle Retaining Nut	44
	Outer Tie Rod To Inner Tie Rod Jam Nut	55
	Power Steering Gear To Frame Mounting Bolts	81
	Power Steering Pump Mounting Bolts	37
	Shock Absorber Retaining Nut	33
	Shock Module Upper Retaining Nuts	33
	Shock Module Yoke To Lower Control Arm Retaining Nut	81
	Shock Module Yoke To Shock Absorber Pinch Bolt	52
	Speed Sensor To Wheel Hub & Bearing Mounting Bolt	13
	Stabilizer Shaft Insulator Clamp Mounting Bolts	41
	Stabilizer Shaft Link Retaining Nuts	114
	Upper Ball Joint Pinch Bolt	30
	Upper Control Arm Mounting Bolts	111
	Wheel Hub & Bearing Mounting Bolts	77
	Wheel Lug Nut	103

① — Front, 94 ft. lbs.; rear, 66 ft. lbs.

② — Aluminum wheels, 90 ft. lbs.; steel wheels, 73 ft. lbs.

Front Wheel Drive

NOTE: On Air Bag Equipped Models, Refer To "Air Bag System Precautions" Located In The Front Of This Manual For System Disarming & Arming Procedures.

INDEX

DESCRIPTION

Blazer & Jimmy

The front differential, **Fig. 1,** is mounted to the frame, with universal joints mounted on the inner and outer ends of the axle shafts. The front axle utilizes a center disconnect system which makes shifting in or out of four-wheel drive possible at any vehicle speed. When the transfer case is shifted, a vacuum diaphragm locks or unlocks the center disconnect. This system replaces automatic-locking front hubs.

Bravada, Envoy, Rainier & Trailblazer

SELECTABLE FOUR WHEEL DRIVE (S4WD)

The front axle on Selectable Four Wheel Drive (S4WD) model vehicles uses a disconnect feature mounted on the right side of the oil pan in order to engage and disengage the front axle. When the driver engages the 4WD system, the Transfer Case Control Module sends a signal to the electric motor actuator to energize and extend the plunger inside. The extended plunger moves the clutch fork and clutch fork sleeve across from the clutch fork outer gear that is splined to the right side wheel drive shaft to the clutch fork inner gear that is splined to the inner axle shaft. The locking of the two gears allows the axle to operate in the same manner as a semi-floating rear axle. A propeller shaft connects the transfer case to the front axle. The differential carrier assembly uses a conventional ring and pinion gear set to transmit the driving force of the engine to the wheels. The ring and pinion set and the differential are contained within the carrier. The axle identification number is located on top of the differential carrier assembly or on a label on the bottom of the right half of differential carrier assembly. The wheel drive shafts are completely flexible assemblies consisting of inner and outer constant velocity CV joints protected by thermoplastic boots and connected by a wheel drive shaft

AUTOMATIC FOUR WHEEL DRIVE (A4WD)

The front axle on Automatic Four Wheel Drive (A4WD) model vehicles do not have a disconnect feature in order to engage and disengage the front axle. The Automatic Four Wheel Drive system uses the same differential carrier assembly and intermediate shaft bearing assembly, but the clutch fork, the clutch fork sleeve and the inner/outer gears have been replaced with a single splined sleeve that connects the inner axle shaft directly to the right side wheel drive shaft. This connection allows the right side wheel drive shaft and the intermediate axle shaft to be directly connected to the differential case assembly. When the transfer case is active, the clutch assembly within the transfer case controls the amount of torque applied to the front axle.

AXLE HOUSING ASSEMBLY

REPLACE

Blazer & Jimmy

4WD MODELS

REMOVAL

1. Disconnect shift cable from vacuum actuator. Disengage locking spring, then push actuator diaphragm into release cable, **Fig. 2.**
2. Unlock steering wheel so linkage is free to move.
3. Raise vehicle and place jack stands under frame side rails.
4. Remove front wheels, drive belt shield and axle skid plate as equipped.
5. Support righthand lower control arm with a jack, then disconnect right upper ball joint and remove support so that control arm hangs free.
6. Disconnect righthand drive axle shaft from tube assembly, **Fig. 3.** Insert a drift through opening in top of brake caliper and into corresponding vane of brake rotor to prevent axle from turning.
7. Disconnect four-wheel drive indicator light electrical connector from switch.
8. Remove three shift cable and switch housing to carrier bolts and pull housing out to gain access to cable locking spring. Do not remove cable coupling nut unless cable is being replaced.

9. Disconnect shift cable from fork shaft by lifting spring over slot in shift fork.
10. Remove tube bracket bolts from frame and tube assembly bolts from carrier.
11. Remove tube assembly from axle. Use care not to allow sleeve, thrust washers, connector and output shaft to fall from carrier or be damaged when removing tube.

INSTALLATION

1. Install sleeve, thrust washers, connector and output shaft in carrier. Thrust washer notch must align with tab on washer, **Fig. 4.**
2. Coat tube to carrier mating surface with Loctite 514 sealant, or equivalent.
3. Install tube and shaft assembly to carrier using only one bolt installed finger tight at one o'clock position.
4. Pull assembly down, then install cable and switch housing and four remaining bolts.
5. Install two tube to frame bolts. Tighten to specifications.
6. Inspect four wheel drive mechanism for proper operation by inserting shift cable housing installation tool No. J-33798, or equivalent, into shift fork and inspecting for rotation of axle shaft, **Fig. 5.**
7. Remove tool and install shift cable switch housing, then guide cable through housing into fork shaft hole and push cable in by sliding cable through into fork shaft hole.
8. Connect four wheel drive indicator light electrical connector to switch.
9. Support and raise righthand lower control arm using a jack and connect upper ball joint.
10. Install righthand drive axle to axle tube. Install one bolt first, then rotate axle to install five remaining bolts.
11. Install front axle skid plate, if equipped, drive belt shield and front wheels.
12. Connect shift cable to vacuum actuator by pushing cable end into actuator shaft hole.

AWD MODELS

1. Unlock steering column, then raise and support vehicle.
2. Remove right front wheel, axle nut and washer, then support lower control arm.
3. Remove lower shock bolt and nut.
4. Use posi-lock puller model No. 110, or equivalent, to push drive axle through hub.
5. Remove right drive axle, then the support bracket nuts and washers.
6. Remove tube carrier bolts, then using a slide hammer pull out output shaft.
7. Remove tube and shaft assembly.
8. Reverse procedure to install, noting the following:
   a. Apply a bead of sealer GM part No. 1052357, or equivalent, to carrier sealing surface.
   b. Add axle lubricant as required.

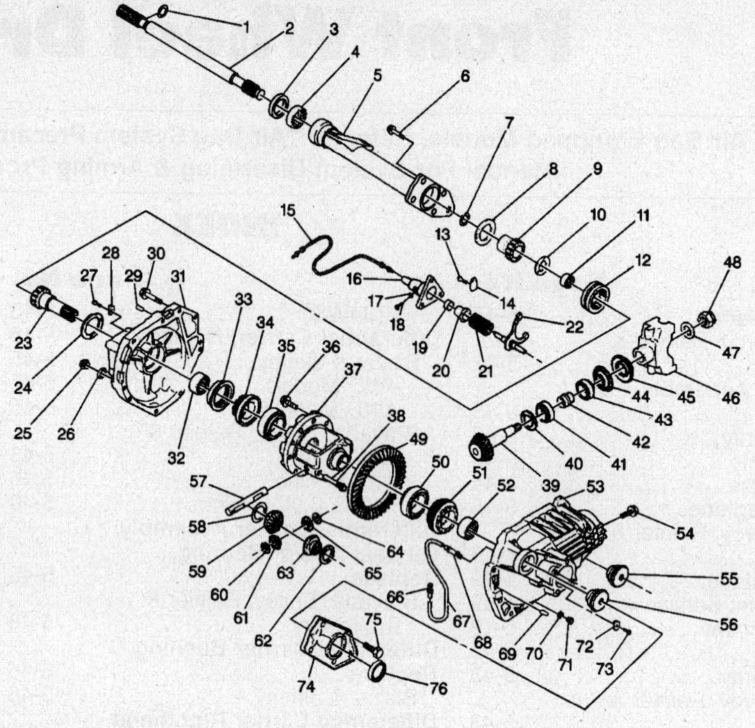

1. Retaining Ring
2. Axle Shaft
3. Seal
4. Bearing
5. Housing
6. Bolt
7. Retaining Ring
8. Washer
9. Clutch Gear
10. Washer
11. Bearing
12. Clutch Sleeve
13. Bolt
14. Lock
15. Cable
16. Housing
17. Seal
18. Switch
19. Outer Spring
20. Seal
21. Inner Spring
22. Fork
23. Clutch Shaft
24. Washer
25. Drain Plug
26. Drain Plug Gasket
27. Nut
28. Nut Lock
29. Pin
30. Bolt
31. Carrier
32. Bearing
33. Adjuster
34. Sleeve
35. Bearing
36. Bolt
37. Case
38. Bolt
39. Pinion Gear
40. Shim
41. Bearing
42. Spacer
43. Bearing
44. Seal
45. Deflector
46. Yoke
47. Washer
48. Nut
49. Ring Gear
50. Bearing
51. Insert
52. Bearing
53. Carrier
54. Bolt
55. Bushing
56. Bushing
57. Shaft
58. Washer
59. Side Gear
60. Washer
61. Pinion Gear
62. Washer
63. Side Gear
64. Washer
65. Pinion Gear
66. Vent
67. Hose
68. Hose End
69. Pin
70. Drain Plug Gasket
71. Drain Plug
72. Nut Lock
73. Nut
74. Cover
75. Bolt
76. Seal

GC3018800002000X

Fig. 1 Exploded view of front drive axle. Blazer & Jimmy

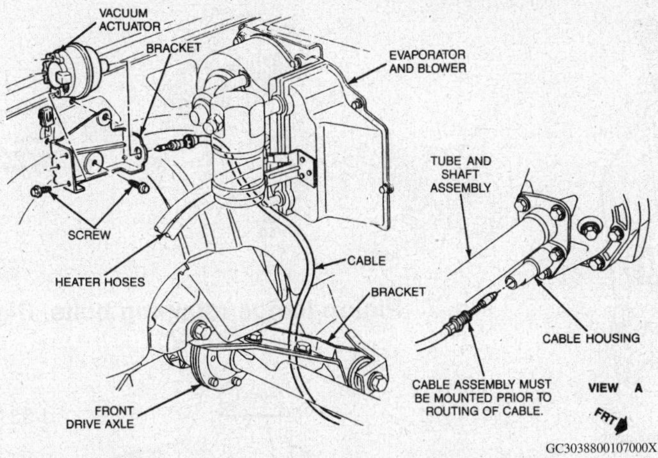

Fig. 2 Vacuum actuator. 4WD models

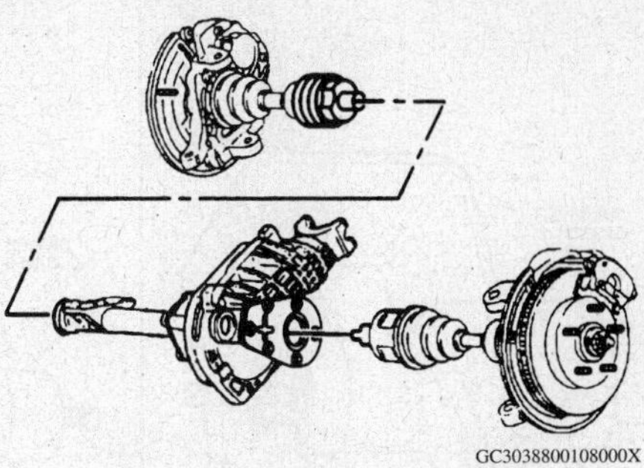

Fig. 3 Drive axle & tube assembly. 4WD models

AXLE SHAFT

REPLACE

Bravada, Envoy, Rainier & Trailblazer

1. Raise and support vehicle, then remove tire and wheel assembly.
2. Remove engine protection shield.
3. Remove wheel speed sensor wiring harness from retainers, then disconnect wheel speed sensor from harness.
4. Remove retaining bolt for front brake hose.
5. Remove front stabilizer bar link from lower control arm.
6. Remove upper shock module retaining nuts from shock tower.
7. Remove tie rod end to steering knuckle retaining nut, then separate tie rod end from steering knuckle.
8. Remove left and right upper ball joint pinch bolts and nuts.
9. Remove shock module from shock tower.
10. Remove steering knuckle from upper control arm.
11. Remove front wheel drive axle from steering knuckle.
12. Using mechanics wire or hook, support front shock module/steering knuckle to frame.
13. Disconnect left side wheel drive shaft from differential carrier assembly by placing a brass drift against tripot housing.
14. Firmly strike brass drift outward from case with a suitable hammer. Strike hard enough to overcome snap ring pressure holding in shaft.
15. **On righthand side axle shaft,** remove shaft as follows:
    a. Disconnect shaft from clutch fork housing assembly by placing a brass drift against tripot housing, then firmly strike brass drift outward from case with a suitable hammer. Strike hard enough to overcome snap ring pressure holding in shaft.
    b. Pull wheel drive shaft straight out from differential carrier assembly or clutch fork housing assembly.
16. **On lefthand or righthand axle shafts,** remove shaft from vehicle.
17. Reverse procedure to install.

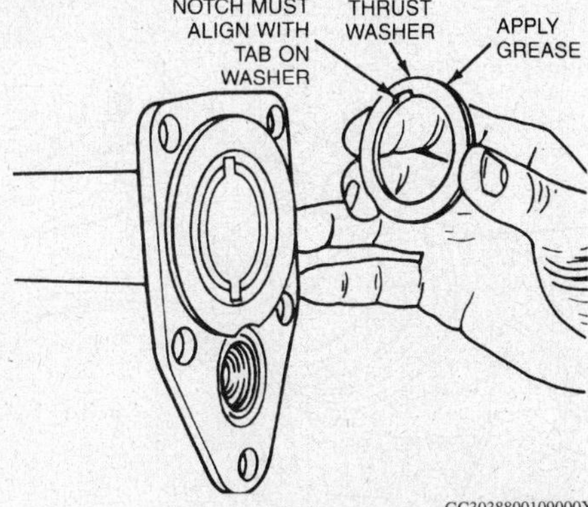

Fig. 4 Thrust washer installation. 4WD models

DIFFERENTIAL CARRIER

REPLACE

Blazer & Jimmy

4WD MODELS

1. Unlock steering column so linkage is free to move, then disconnect shift cable from vacuum actuator.
2. Raise and support vehicle, then remove battery and battery tray.
3. Remove front wheels, then the front axle skid plate.
4. Remove drain plug and flat washer, then drain lubricant from carrier.
5. Remove righthand side lower shock bolt.
6. Disconnect wire from indicator switch.
7. Remove shift cable housing and shift cable from carrier housing as outlined in "Shift Cable, Replace."
8. Disconnect vent hose.
9. Disconnect steering relay rod from idler arm and pitman arm.
10. Hold left drive axle by inserting drift in top of brake caliper and into vanes in brake rotor, noting the following:
    a. It is essential that positions of all driveline components relative to propeller shaft and axles be observed and accurately reference marked before disassembling.
    b. All components must be assembled in exact relationship to each other as they were before removal.
    c. Published specifications as well as any measurements made prior to disassembly must be followed.
11. Remove bolts, then the drift from brake rotor.
12. Remove bolts and nuts, then the front prop shaft, as follows:
    a. Support both lower control arms with suitable stands at edge of stabilizer shaft.
    b. Lower vehicle until front end weight is resting on stands.
13. Hold carrier upper nut with 18 mm wrench inserted through frame, then remove carrier bolts and nuts.
14. Remove carrier assembly by rolling carrier counterclockwise while lifting up to gain clearance from mounting ears.
15. Remove tube bolts from carrier.
16. Reverse procedure to install.

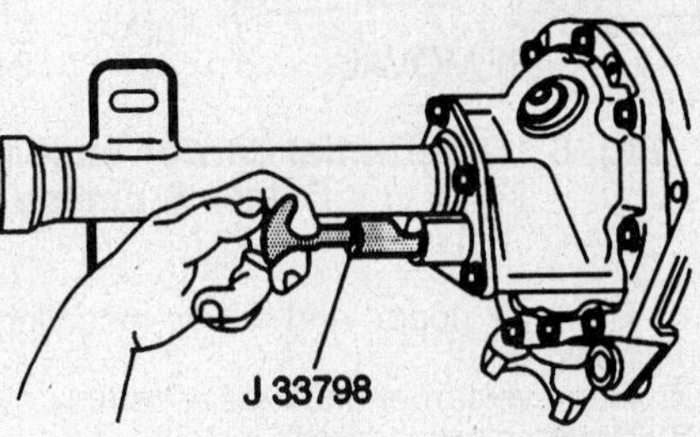

Fig. 5 4WD mechanism operational inspection. 4WD models

AWD MODELS

1. Raise and support vehicle, then remove left or right wheel.
2. Disconnect propeller shaft at front axle and support out of way.
3. Disconnect vent hose, then remove drive axle to output shaft bolts.
4. Remove tube to carrier bolts, then disconnect drive axle from output shaft and support out of way.
5. Remove axle tube support bracket to frame nuts.

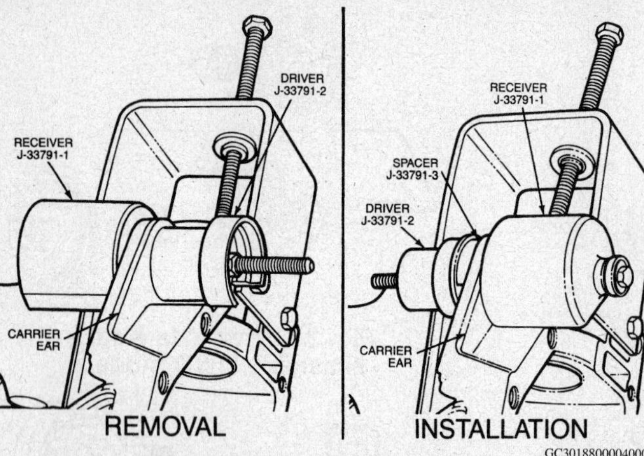

Fig. 6 Differential carrier bushing replacement. Blazer & Jimmy

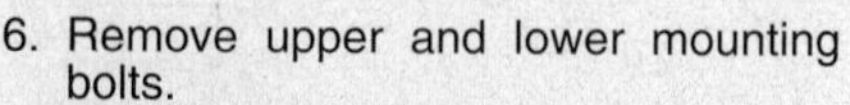

6. Remove upper and lower mounting bolts.
7. Remove carrier and tube assembly.
8. Reverse procedure to install.

Bravada, Envoy, Rainier & Trailblazer

4.2L ENGINE

1. Raise and support vehicle, then remove front tires and wheels.
2. Remove engine protection shield, then drain engine oil.
3. Drain front drive axle lubricant.
4. Remove front propeller shaft from front axle. Wrap bearing caps with tape to prevent loss of roller bearings.
5. Remove ABS wiring harness from retainers.
6. Remove brake hose retaining bolts, then the front drive axle vent hose.
7. Remove left and right upper ball joint pinch bolts and nuts.
8. Remove left and right upper shock module retaining nuts.
9. Remove front stabilizer bar links from frame.
10. Remove shock module from frame.
11. Remove steering knuckle from upper control arm.
12. Remove left and right front wheel drive shafts from front drive axle. Position and secure left and right front wheel drive shafts to frame.
13. Using mechanics wire or hook, support front shock modules and steering knuckle.
14. Remove power steering gear assembly as outlined in "Front Suspension & Steering" section.
15. Remove front drive axle from oil pan. Secure front drive axle to frame.
16. Remove engine oil pan.
17. Remove differential from vehicle.
18. Reverse procedure to install.

5.3L & 6.0L ENGINES

1. Remove tire and wheel assembly.
2. Remove engine protection shield.
3. Drain front differential.
4. Remove left and right ABS wiring harnesses from retainers.
5. Disconnect left and right wheel speed sensor electrical connectors.
6. Remove brake hose retaining bolts from frame.
7. Disconnect stabilizer bar link pins from lower control arms.
8. Remove steering gear as outlined in "Front Suspension & Steering" section.
9. Place adjustable jack stands under lower control arms.
10. Remove upper ball joint pinch bolts and nuts.
11. Remove steering knuckles from upper control arms.
12. Remove upper shock module bolts from frame.
13. Lower jack stand to allow removal of the steering knuckles from upper control arms.
14. Remove steering knuckle from the upper control arm.
15. Using a brass drift or equivalent, remove the left wheel drive shaft from the front differential.
16. Using a suitable brass drift, remove right wheel drive shaft from differential. Position axle shafts to side. Use mechanics wire or metal hooks to secure shock modules to frame. **Do not allow shock modules and steering knuckles to hang without supporting them.**
17. Remove jack stands.
18. Remove front propeller shaft from front pinion yoke. Position propeller shaft aside and secure.
19. Remove inner axle shaft.
20. Remove front differential assembly mounting bolts.
21. Remove differential assembly from oil pan.
22. Secure front differential to frame.
23. Drain engine oil, then remove engine oil pan assembly.
24. Remove differential from vehicle.
25. Reverse procedure to install.

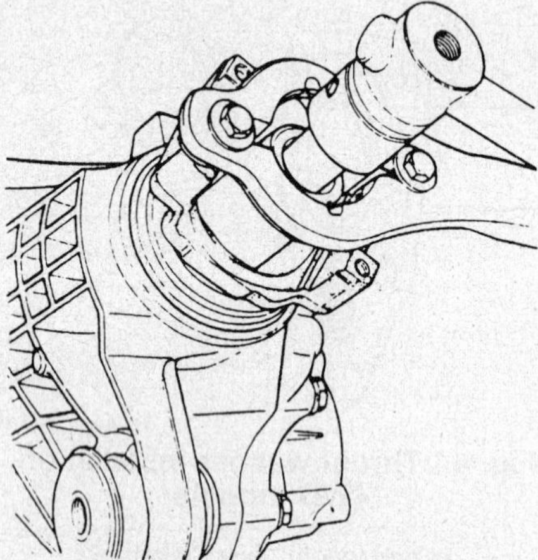

Fig. 8 Pinion flange removal. Blazer & Jimmy

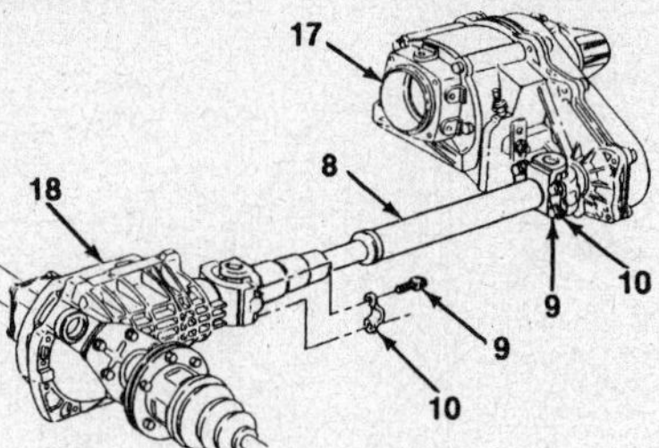

Fig. 7 Pinion flange retaining bolts. Blazer & Jimmy

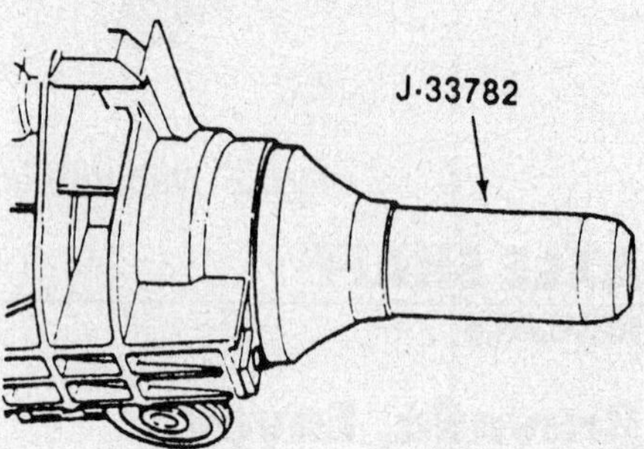

Fig. 9 Pinion seal installation. Blazer & Jimmy

DIFFERENTIAL CARRIER BUSHING

REPLACE

Blazer & Jimmy

1. Remove differential carrier as outlined in "Differential Carrier, Replace."
2. Remove bushing from carrier ear using bushing tool No. J-33791, or equivalent, **Fig. 6.**
3. Install new bushing using busing tool, **Fig. 6.** Ensure adapter tool No. J-33791-3, or equivalent, is positioned properly between bushing and carrier ear to prevent bushing from being pressed in too far.
4. Install differential carrier as outlined in "Differential Carrier, Replace."

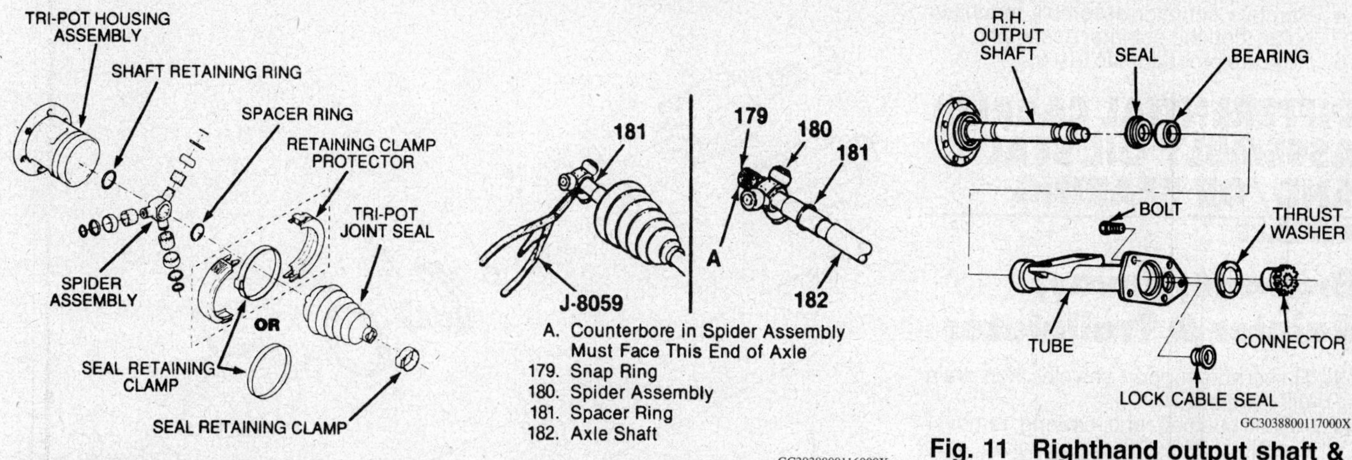

Fig. 10 Inner tri-pot seal replacement. Blazer & Jimmy

Fig. 11 Righthand output shaft & tube. Blazer & Jimmy

170. Outer Race
171. Cage
172. Inner Race
173. Outboard Boot
174. Clamp
175. Clamp
176. Inboard Boot
177. Clamp
178. Housing
179. Snap Ring
180. Spider Assembly
181. Spacer Ring
182. Axle Shaft
183. Clamp
184. Snap Ring
185. Ball

GC3038800112000X

Fig. 12 Exploded view of front axle. Blazer & Jimmy w/4WD

DIFFERENTIAL OUTPUT SHAFT PILOT BEARING

REPLACE

Blazer & Jimmy

1. Remove tube and shaft assembly as outlined in "Axle Housing Assembly, Replace."
2. Remove bearing using pilot bearing remover tool No. J-34011, or equivalent, **Fig. 1.**
3. Lubricate new bearing with suitable axle lubricant, then install bearing using pilot bearing installer tool No. J-33482, or equivalent.
4. Reverse procedure to install.

INTERMEDIATE SHAFT BEARING ASSEMBLY

REPLACE

Bravada, Envoy, Rainier & Trailblazer

AUTOMATIC 4WD (A4WD)

1. Raise and support vehicle.
2. Remove right wheel drive shaft as outlined under "Axle Shaft, Replace."
3. Remove intermediate shaft bearing assembly mounting bolts.
4. Remove wire harness clip from intermediate shaft bearing assembly. **Do not nick or cut inboard (oil pan) inner shaft seal.**
5. Remove intermediate shaft bearing assembly.
6. Reverse procedure to install.

SELECTABLE 4WD (S4WD)

1. Raise and support vehicle.
2. Remove right wheel drive shaft as outlined under "Axle Shaft, Replace."
3. Disconnect electrical connector from actuator.
4. Remove wire harness clip from intermediate shaft bearing assembly.
5. Remove intermediate shaft bearing assembly mounting bolts. **Do not nick or cut inboard (oil pan) side inner shaft seal.**
6. Remove intermediate shaft bearing assembly.
7. Remove actuator from intermediate shaft bearing assembly.
8. Reverse procedure to install.

INTERMEDIATE SHAFT BEARING ASSEMBLY OIL SEAL

REPLACE

Bravada, Envoy, Rainier & Trailblazer

1. Raise and support vehicle.
2. Remove right wheel drive shaft as outlined under "Axle Shaft, Replace."
3. Install bushing and bearing remover tool No. J 29369-2, or equivalent, into outboard wheel drive shaft side oil seal.
4. Attach a suitable slide hammer to bushing and bearing removal tool and remove outboard wheel drive shaft side inner shaft seal.
5. Remove intermediate shaft bearing assembly as outlined under "Intermediate Shaft Bearing Assembly, Replace."
6. Install intermediate shaft bearing assembly into a suitable vise, then place shop towels in vise to protect intermediate shaft bearing assembly.
7. Install bushing and bearing remover tool No. J 29369-2, or equivalent, into inboard oil seal.
8. Attach a suitable slide hammer to bushing and bearing removal tool and remove inboard inner shaft seal.
9. Reverse procedure to install.

ACTUATOR

REPLACE

Bravada, Envoy, Rainier & Trailblazer

1. Raise and support vehicle.
2. Remove engine protection shield.
3. Disconnect electrical connector from actuator assembly.

4. Remove actuator assembly mounting bolts, then the actuator assembly.
5. Reverse procedure to install.

DIFFERENTIAL CARRIER ASSEMBLY OIL SEAL AND/OR BEARING

REPLACE

Bravada, Envoy, Rainier & Trailblazer

1. Raise and support vehicle, then drain differential fluid.
2. Install bushing and bearing remover tool No. J 29369-2, or equivalent, onto backside of seal.
3. Attach a suitable slide hammer to remover tool and remove seal.
4. Place an alignment mark between differential bearing adjuster and differential carrier assembly case for installation reference.
5. Remove differential carrier assembly as outlined under "Differential Carrier, Replace."
6. Install bushing and bearing remover tool No. J 29369-2, or equivalent, onto backside of seal.
7. Attach a suitable slide hammer to remover tool and remove seal.
8. Place an alignment mark between differential bearing adjuster and differential carrier assembly case for installation reference.
9. Install bushing and bearing remover tool No. J 29369-2, or equivalent, onto backside of bearing cage.
10. Attach a suitable slide hammer to remover tool and remove bearing.
11. Reverse procedure to install.

SHIFT CABLE

REPLACE

Blazer & Jimmy

1. Remove shift cable from vacuum actuator by disengaging locking spring and pushing actuator diaphragm in to release cable.
2. Compress cable locking fingers with pliers, then remove cable from bracket.
3. Raise and support vehicle.
4. Remove switch housing mounting bolts and pull housing away from axle tube flange to gain access to cable locking spring.
5. Disconnect cable from shaft fork by lifting spring over slot in shift fork, then unscrew cable from housing and remove from vehicle.
6. Install cable following proper routing, **Fig. 2.**
7. Install cable and switch housing to carrier.

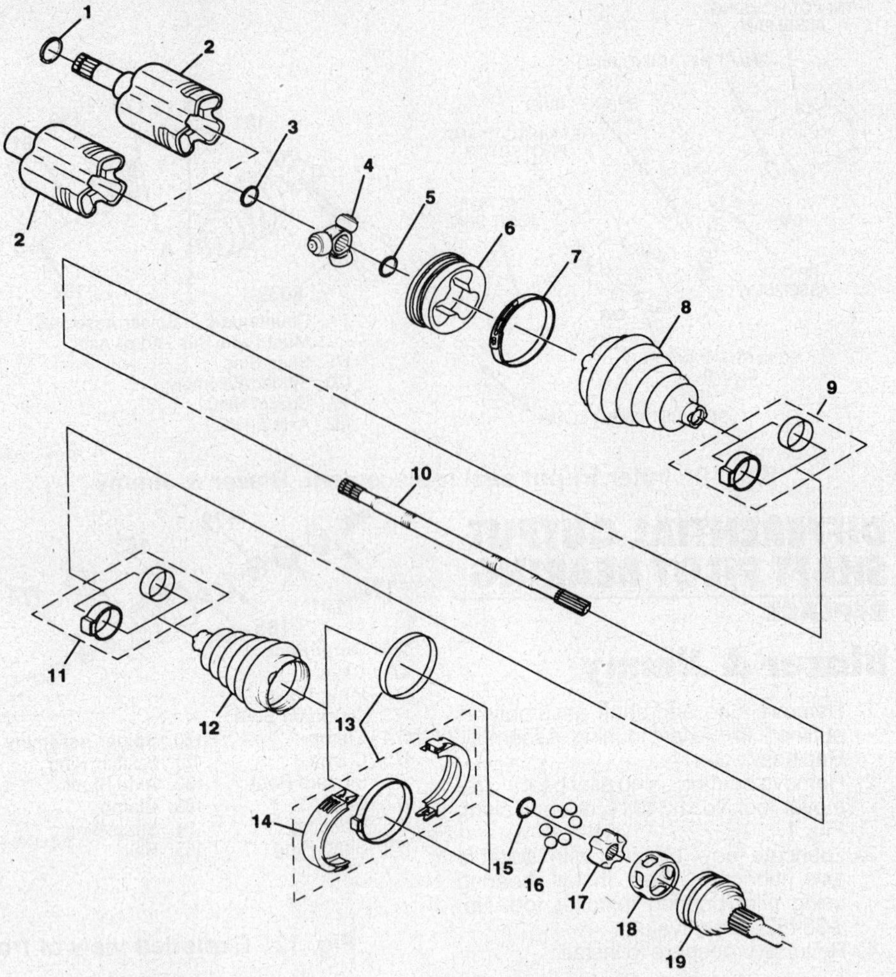

1. Ring, Diff Shaft
2. Assembly, Tripot Housing
3. Ring, Spacer
4. Spider Assembly, Tripot Joint
5. Ring, Spacer
6. Bushing, Tripot
7. Clamp, Seal Retaining
8. Seal, Tripot Joint
9. Clamp, Axle Swage
10. Shaft, Axle
11. Clamp, Small Seal Retaining
12. Seal, CV Joint
13. Ring, Swage
14. Protector, Clamp
15. Ring, Race Retaining
16. Ball
17. Race, CV Joint Inner
18. Cage, CV Joint
19. Race, CV Joint Outer

GC3038800113000X

Fig. 13 Exploded view of front axle. Blazer & Jimmy w/AWD

8. Slide cable through switch housing into fork shaft hole and push cable in. The cable will snap in place automatically.
9. Lower vehicle, then connect shift cable to vacuum actuator by pressing cable into bracket hole. Cable will snap in place automatically.
10. Inspect cable for proper operation.

PINION FLANGE SEAL

REPLACE

Blazer & Jimmy

1. Remove crossmember and front skid plates as required.
2. Remove pinion flange bolts and retainers, **Fig. 7.**
3. Remove propeller shaft from pinion shaft and tape bearing caps to hold in place.
4. Remove pinion shaft retaining nut and washer. **Mark pinion flange, pinion shaft and pinion retaining nut to ensure proper bearing preload.**
5. Remove pinion flange using companion flange holding tool No. J-8614-01, or equivalent, **Fig. 8.**
6. Remove pinion seal using suitable seal puller.
7. Reverse procedure to install. Install pinion oil seal using seal installer tool No. J-33782, or equivalent, **Fig. 9.**

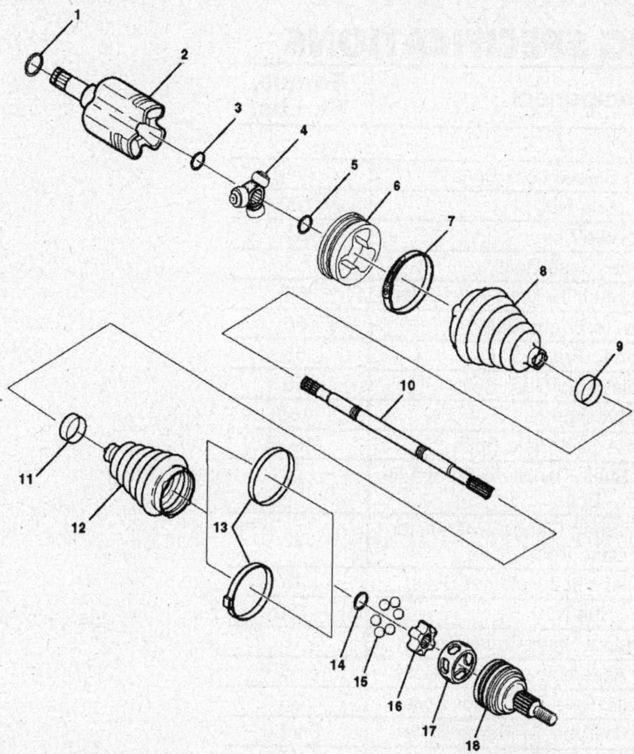

(1) Differential Shaft Ring
(2) Tripot Housing Assembly
(3) Spacer Ring
(4) Tripot Joint Spider Assembly
(5) Spacer Ring
(6) Tripot Bushing
(7) Boot Retaining Clamp
(8) Tripot Joint Boot
(9) Halfshaft Swage Ring
(10) Halfshaft Bar
(11) Halfshaft Swage Ring
(12) CV Joint Boot
(13) Swage Ring/Clamp
(14) Race Retaining Ring
(15) Ball
(16) CV Joint Inner Race
(17) CV Joint Cage
(18) CV Joint Outer Race

LTV0500000000906

Fig. 14 Exploded view of front axle. Bravada, Envoy, Rainier & Trailblazer

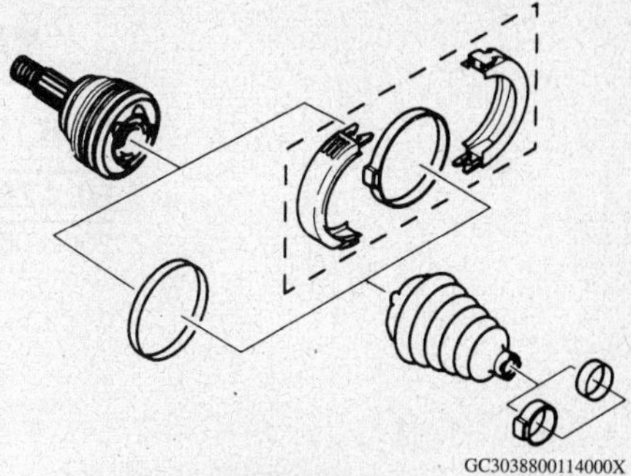

Fig. 15 Outer CV joint seal replacement

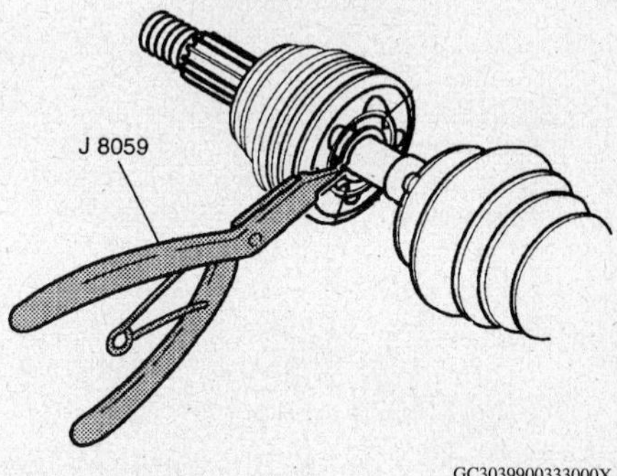

Fig. 16 Snap ring removal. Blazer & Jimmy

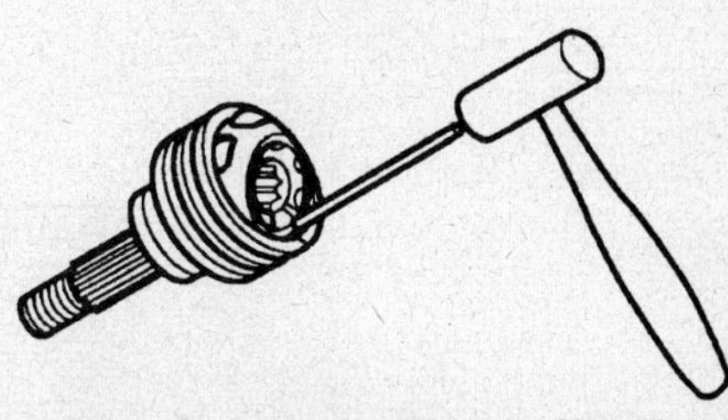

Fig. 17 CV joint ball removal. Blazer & Jimmy

INNER TRI-POT SEAL

REPLACE

Blazer & Jimmy

Refer to **Figs. 10 and 11** for inner tri-pot seal replacement.

DIFFERENTIAL CARRIER RIGHTHAND OUTPUT SHAFT & TUBE SERVICE

Blazer & Jimmy

DISASSEMBLE

1. Remove output shaft from tube by tapping inside of flange with a rubber mallet.
2. Pry tube seal from tube, then remove bearing from tube.
3. Drive differential shift cable housing seal out of tube using a punch.

ASSEMBLE

1. Install output shaft tube bearing.
2. Install tube seal. Flange of seal must be flush with tube outer surface.
3. Install output shaft into tube by tapping flange with a rubber mallet.
4. Install differential shift cable housing seal.

CV JOINT

REPLACE

Refer to **Figs. 12 through 15** for CV joint replacement.

Outer CV Joint Service

BLAZER & JIMMY

1. Place halfshaft in suitable vise.
2. Remove outer CV joint seal.
3. Locate halfshaft retaining ring and remove, **Fig. 16.**
4. Pull CV joint from halfshaft.
5. Place suitable brass drift against CV cage and tap lightly using suitable hammer in order to tilt cage, **Fig. 17.**
6. Remove CV joint ball when cage tilts.
7. Remove remaining balls using same method.
8. Pivot cage and inner race 90° to centerline of outer race.
9. Align cage windows with lands of outer race, then lift cage from inner race.
10. Reverse procedure to install.

TIGHTENING SPECIFICATIONS

Year	Component	Torque, Ft. Lbs.
BLAZER & JIMMY		
2002–05	Adjusting Sleeve Lock Bolts	71①
	Axle Nut	180
	Axle Plug	24
	Carrier Case Bolts	35
	Carrier Output Shaft To Drive Axle Bolts	60
	Carrier To Frame Bolts	65
	Carrier To Frame Nuts	55
	Differential Ring Gear Bolts	60
	Driveshaft Nut	180
	Front Axle Skid Plate Bolts	20–28
	Front Propeller Shaft Flange To Front Axle Bolts	55
	Front Propeller Shaft Flange To Transfer Case Bolts	92
	Front Propeller Shaft Retainer Bolts	15
	Hub Nut	180
	Left Side Output Shaft Cover Bolts	18
	Lower Carrier Assembly Mounting Bolts	55
	Right Side Axle Tube To Carrier Bolts	36
	Right Side Axle Tube To Frame Bolts	54–60
	Shift Cable Coupling Nut	90①
	Shift Cable Housing To Carrier Bolts	36
	Switch Cable To Switch Housing Bolts	30–40
	Upper Carrier Assembly Mounting Bolts	636
	Vacuum Actuator Bolts	13①
	Yoke Nut	25
BRAVADA, ENVOY, RAINIER & TRAILBLAZER		
2002–06	Actuator Mounting Bolts	53①
	Axle Shaft Nut	103
	Brake Caliper Mounting Bracket	52
	Brake Hose Retaining Bolt	18
	Differential Carrier Mounting Bolts	63
	Drain & Fill Plug	24
	Drive Shaft Nut	103
	Intermediate Shaft Bearing Assembly Case Bolts	35
	Intermediate Shaft Bearing Assembly Mounting Bolts	35
	Upper Shock Module Mounting Bolt	30
	Wheel Lug Nut	103

① — Inch lbs.

Wheel Alignment

INDEX

PRELIMINARY INSPECTION

Inspect the following components. Adjust, repair or replace as required prior to performing front wheel alignment.

1. Inflate tires to cold specifications.
2. Ensure front tires are of same size, ply rating and load rating.
3. Inspect for excessive wheel bearing endplay.
4. Inspect for worn or damaged spindle ball joints.
5. Ensure steering gear mounting bolts are tight.
6. Inspect radius arm or bent or damaged condition.
7. Inspect radius arm to frame bushings for looseness or wear.
8. Inspect suspension components for wear or damage.

FRONT WHEEL ALIGNMENT

Caster & Camber

Before inspecting or adjusting caster and camber angles, jounce vehicle at least 3 times to prevent false geometric readings.

BLAZER & JIMMY

2WD MODELS

Caster and camber adjustments are made by shims inserted between upper control arm shaft and frame bracket, **Fig. 1.** Add, subtract or transfer shims to change readings as noted below.

To adjust caster and/or camber, loosen upper control arm shaft to frame nuts, then add or subtract shims as required and tighten upper control arm shaft to frame nuts to specification. After adjustment, the shim pack should have at least two threads of bolt exposed beyond the nut. The difference between front and rear shim packs must not exceed .40 inches.

Caster

Transfer shims from front to rear or rear to front. The transfer of one shim from rear to front bolt will decrease positive caster.

Camber

Change shims at both front and rear of shaft. Adding an equal amount of shims at both front and rear locations will decrease positive camber.

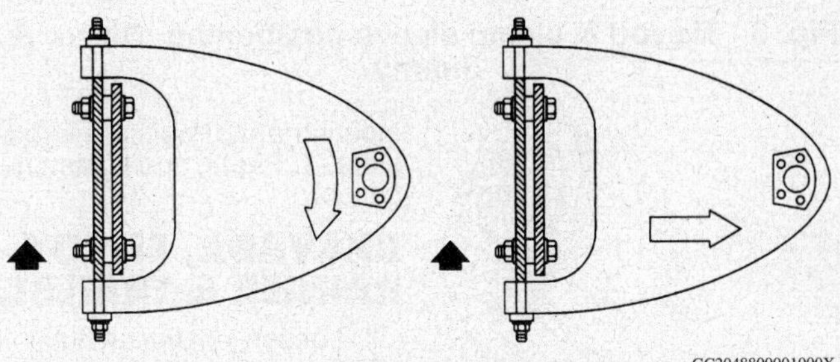

Fig. 1 Caster & camber adjustment. Blazer & Jimmy w/2WD

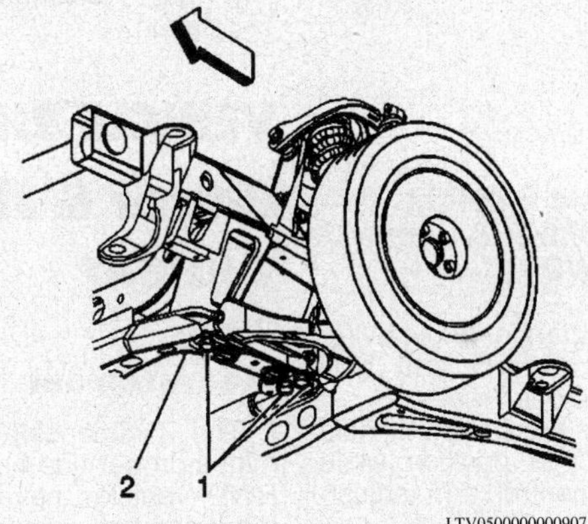

Fig. 2 Lower control arm adjustment bolts. Bravada, Envoy, Rainier & Trailblazer

4WD MODELS

Caster and camber adjustments are made by cam mounted upper control arm attaching bolts.

To adjust caster and/or camber, loosen upper control arm to frame attaching bolt nut, then rotate cam by turning bolt head. When proper alignment settings are established, tighten upper control arm to frame attaching bolt nut to specification.

Caster

To increase positive caster, move front cam lobe inward and rear cam lobe outward.

Camber

To increase positive camber, move both front and rear cam lobes inward.

BRAVADA, ENVOY, RAINIER & TRAILBLAZER

1. Loosen lower control arm adjustment bolts, **Fig. 2.**

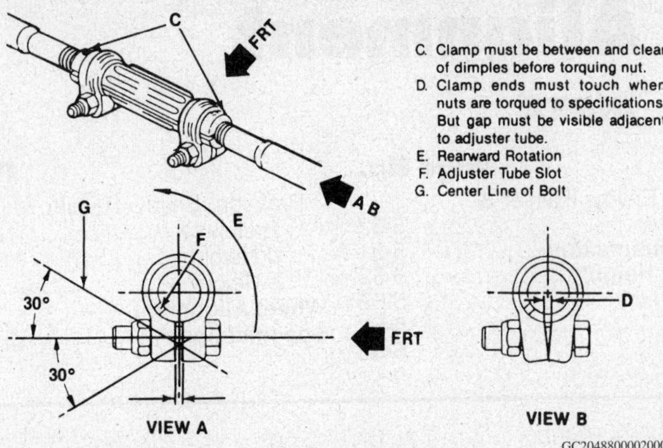
C. Clamp must be between and clear of dimples before torquing nut.
D. Clamp ends must touch when nuts are torqued to specifications. But gap must be visible adjacent to adjuster tube.
E. Rearward Rotation
F. Adjuster Tube Slot
G. Center Line of Bolt
FRT
VIEW A
VIEW B
30°
30°
GC2048800002000X

Fig. 3 Tie rod & clamp sleeve positioning. Blazer & Jimmy

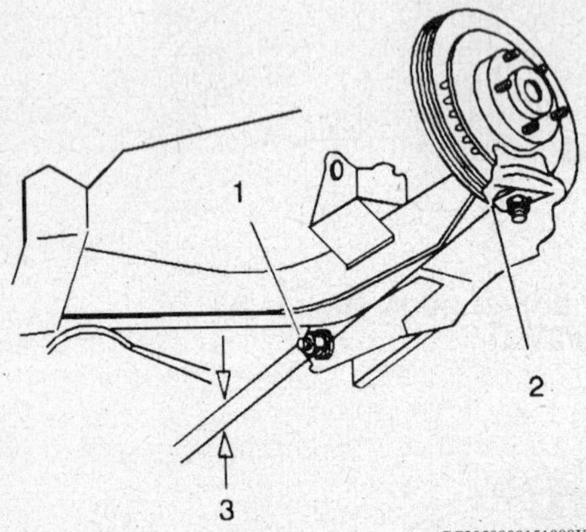
1
2
3
GC2059800151000X

Fig. 5 Vehicle Z height measurement. Blazer & Jimmy w/4WD

2. Adjust caster and camber angle by repositioning lower control arm until specifications have been met.
3. When adjustments are complete, hold lower control arm in position while tightening lower control arm adjustment bolts.
4. **Torque** front lower control arm bracket mounting bolts to 192 ft. lbs.
5. **Torque** rear lower control arm bracket mounting bolts to 177 ft. lbs.
6. Ensure caster and camber are still within specifications.

Toe-In

BLAZER & JIMMY

To adjust, loosen clamp bolts at each end of steering tie rod adjustable sleeves. With steering wheel in straight ahead position, turn tie rod adjusting sleeves to obtain proper adjustment. After adjusting, inspect that number of threads showing on each end of sleeve are equal and that the tie rod end housings are at the right angles to steering arm. Position tie rod clamps and sleeves, **Fig. 3,** and tighten nuts to specification.

BRAVADA, ENVOY, RAINIER & TRAILBLAZER

1. Loosen jam nut on outer tie rod.
2. Rotate inner tie rod until toe setting is within specification.
3. **Torque** jam nut to 55 ft. lbs.
4. Ensure toe setting is still within specification.

VEHICLE RIDE HEIGHT

Blazer & Jimmy

Z HEIGHT

2WD

Measurement

The Z dimension measurement determines proper ride height for the front end. RWD vehicles have no adjustment, any trim height change would require replacement of suspension components.

Measure Z height from center line of front lower control arm bolt down to the lower inboard corner of the ball joint, **Fig. 4.** Trim height should be 2.6–3.0 inches.

4WD

Measurement

1. Lift front bumper of vehicle up about 1.5 inches, then gently remove hands and let vehicle settle by itself.
2. Repeat jounce operation two more times.
3. Measure Z dimension.
4. Push front bumper of vehicle down about 1.5 inches, then gently remove hands and let vehicle rise by itself.
5. Repeat jounce operation two more times.

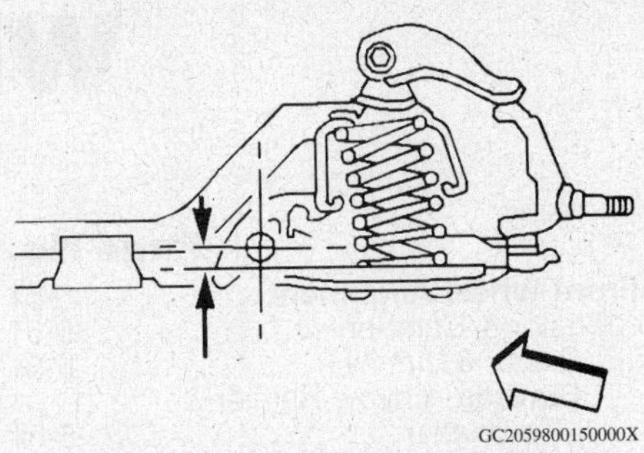
GC2059800150000X

Fig. 4 Vehicle Z height measurement. Blazer & Jimmy w/2WD

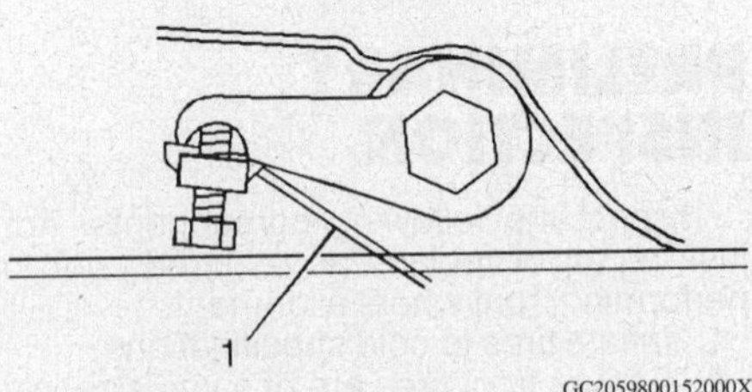
1
GC2059800152000X

Fig. 6 Z height adjustment. 4WD models

6. Measure Z height from the center line of pivot bolt (1) down to lowest inboard edge of the knuckle (2), **Fig. 5.**
7. Figure average of high and low measurements to find the true dimension.

Adjustment

Z height should be 4.6–5.0 inches. To adjust Z height, turn the bolt that contacts the torsion arm as required. One revolution of the bolt increases Z height by .2 inch (1) **Fig. 6.**

D HEIGHT

The D dimension measurement determines the proper rear end ride height, **Fig. 7.** There is no adjustment procedure. Repair may require replacement of suspension components.

All Vehicles require a measurement from the bumper bracket down to the top of the rear axle housing tube. Trim height should be 5.1–5.8 inches.

1. Lift rear bumper of vehicle up about 1.5 inches, then gently remove hands and let vehicle settle by itself.
2. Repeat jounce operation two more times.
3. Measure D dimension.
4. Push rear bumper of vehicle down about 1.5 inches, then gently remove hands and let vehicle rise by itself.
5. Repeat jounce operation two more times.
6. Measure D dimension.
7. Figure average of high and low measurements to find the true dimension.

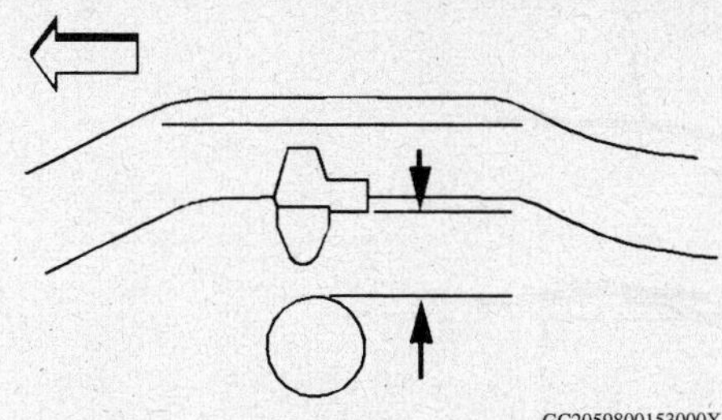

GC2059800153000X

Fig. 7 D height measurement

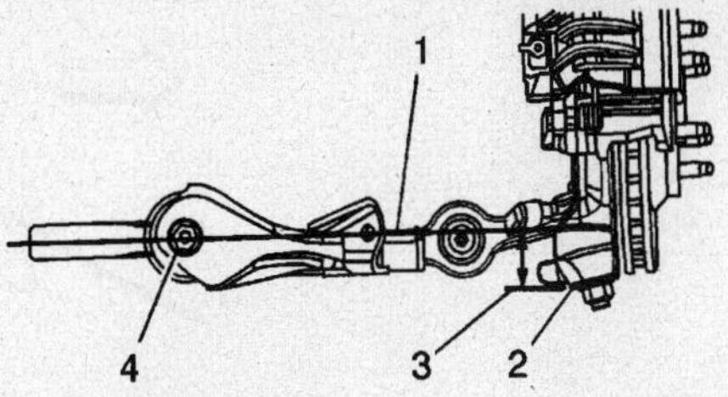

1- CENTERLINE
2- STEERING KNUCKLE
3- Z HEIGHT MEASUREMENT
4- CONTROL ARM BUSHING BOLT

LTV0500000000908

Fig. 8 Z height measurement. Bravada, Envoy, Rainier & Trailblazer

Bravada, Envoy, Rainier & Trailblazer

Z HEIGHT

The Z height measurement determines the proper ride height for the front end of the vehicle. Vehicles equipped with torsion bars use an adjusting arm to adjust the Z height. Vehicles without torsion bars have no adjustment and may require replacement of suspension components.

1. Jounce front of vehicle several times and ensure there is at least 1.5 inches of movement while jouncing.
2. Allow vehicle to settle into position.
3. Measure from centerline of lower control arm bushing bolt down to machined edge of steering knuckle, **Fig. 8.**
4. Repeat jouncing operation and measure two more times.
5. Use highest and lowest measurements to calculate average height.
6. Average height should be 2.60–3.54 inches.
7. **On 2WD models,** if average height is not within specifications, replace shock module and coil spring assembly.
8. **On 4WD models,** if average height is not within specifications, adjust torsion bars.

D HEIGHT

The D height measurement determines the proper ride height for the rear end of the vehicle. There is no adjustment procedure. Repair may require replacement of suspension components.

1. Jounce rear of vehicle several times and ensure there is at least 1.5 inches of movement while jouncing.
2. Allow vehicle to settle into position.
3. Measure vertical distance between jounce bumper reinforcement bracket on frame and top surface of axle tube, **Fig. 9.**
4. Repeat jouncing operation and measurement two more times.
5. Use highest and lowest measurements to calculate average height.
6. **On models equipped with air suspension,** average height should be 5.17–5.49 inches.
7. **On models not equipped with air suspension,** average height should be 5.88–6.35 inches.

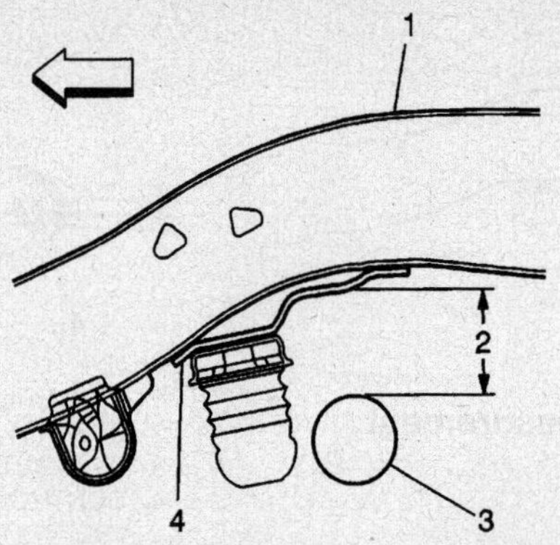

Fig. 9 D height measurement. Bravada, Envoy, Rainier & Trailblazer

EQUINOX & TORRENT

NOTE: Refer To Back Of This Manual For Vehicle Manufacturer's Special Service Tool Suppliers.

INDEX OF SERVICE OPERATIONS

Specifications

GENERAL ENGINE SPECIFICATIONS

Year	Engine Liter (VIN)	Fuel System	Bore & Stroke	Compression Ratio	Horsepower @ RPM	Torque Ft. Lbs. @ RPM	Normal Oil Pressure, psi
2005–06	3.4L (F)	SFI	3.62 X 3.31	9.6	185 @ 5200	210 @ 4000	30–35①

① — At 1850 RPM

TUNE UP SPECIFICATIONS

The following specifications are published from the latest information available. This data should only be used in the absence of a decal affixed in the engine compartment.

Year/ Engine (VIN)	Spark Plug Gap, Inch	Ignition Timing			Auto. Trans.		Fuel Pump Pressure psi.	Valve Lash, Inch
		Firing Order	Timing, BTDC	Mark Location	Curb Idle Speed	Fast Idle Speed		
3.4L (F)	.060	1-2-3-4-5-6②	①	①	①	①	50–60	③

BTDC — Before Top Dead Center

① — Controlled by the Powertrain Control Module (PCM).

② — Refer to **Fig. A** for spark plug wire & coil identification.

③ — Equipped w/hydraulic valve lifters.

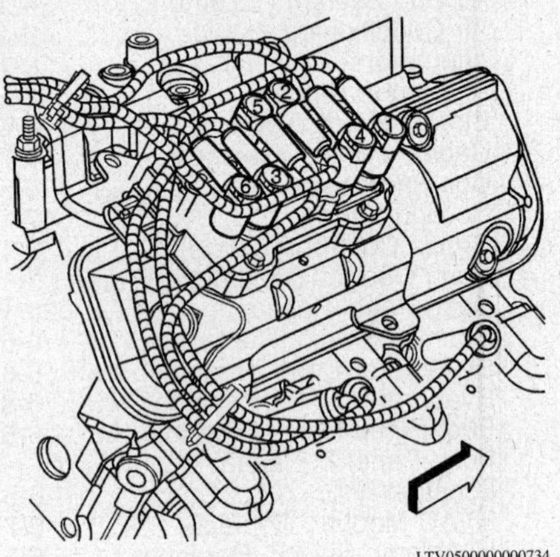

Fig. A

FRONT WHEEL ALIGNMENT SPECIFICATIONS

Year	Caster, Degree		Camber, Degree		Total Toe, Degree		Steering Wheel Angle, Degree		Ball Joint
	Limit	Desired	Limit	Desired	Limits	Desired	Limits	Desired	
2005–06	+2.25 to +2.75③	+3②	-1.35 to +.15③	-.6②	-.05 to +.35	+.15	-3.5 To +3.5	.0	①

① — Refer to "Ball Joint Inspection" in the "Front Suspension & Steering" section for ball joint specifications.

② — Desired cross tolerance, 0°.

③ — Cross tolerance limits, -.5 to + .5°.

REAR WHEEL ALIGNMENT SPECIFICATIONS

Year	Camber, Degree		Cross Camber		Toe, Degree		Thrust Angle	
	Limit	Desired	Limit	Desired	Limit	Desired	Limit	Desired
2005–06	-1.25 to + .25	-.5	-.75 to +.75	0	0 to +.40	+.2	-.2 to +.2	0

VEHICLE RIDE HEIGHT

Year	Manu-facturer's Original Tire Size	Measurement Points & Specifications①									
		Front					Rear				
		Dim.	Specifications				Dim.	Specifications			
			Inches		mm			Inches		mm	
			Limits	Desired	Limits	Desired		Limits	Desired	Limits	Desired
2005–06	②	A	15.36–17.32	16.34	390–440	415	B	16.02–17.98	17.00	407–457	432
		J	9.57–10.75	10.16	243–273	258	K	10.20–11.38	10.79	259–289	274
		Z	.36–1.14	.75	9–29	19	D	.12–.90	.51	3–23	13

Dim. — Dimension

Dim. A — Front curb height is measured 14.25 inches (362 mm) from center line of vehicle, **Fig. A.**

Dim. B — Rear curb height is measured 14.25 inches (362 mm) from center line of vehicle, , **Fig. A.**

Dim. J — Front body height is measured 17.5 inches (445 mm) rearward from center line of front wheel, **Fig. B.**

Dim. D — Rear suspension height is difference measured horizontal line thorough center of cradle mounting bolt and center of knuckle mounting bolt, **Fig. C.**

Dim. K — Rear body height is measured 17.6 inches (447 mm) rearward from center line of rear wheel, **Fig. B.**

Dim. Z — Front suspension height is vertical distance measured between centerline of lower control arm bolt and bottom of ball joint, **Fig. D.**

① — All measurements are taken with a full tank of gas.

② — Refer to door sticker or glove compartment for manufacturer's original tire size specifications.

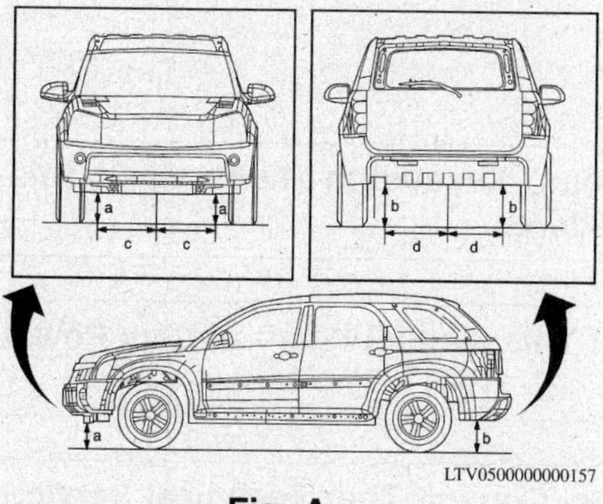

Fig. A

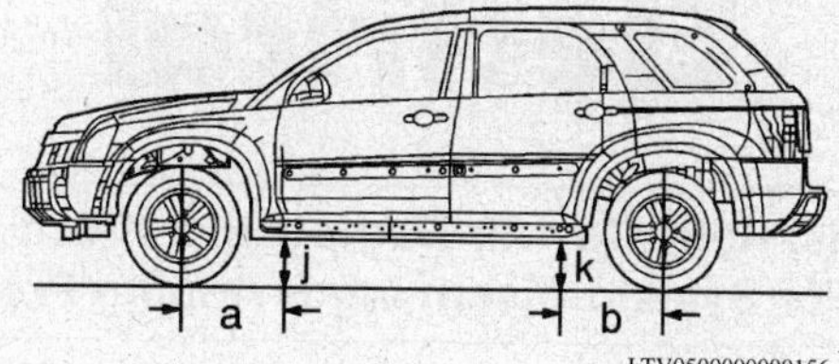

Fig. B

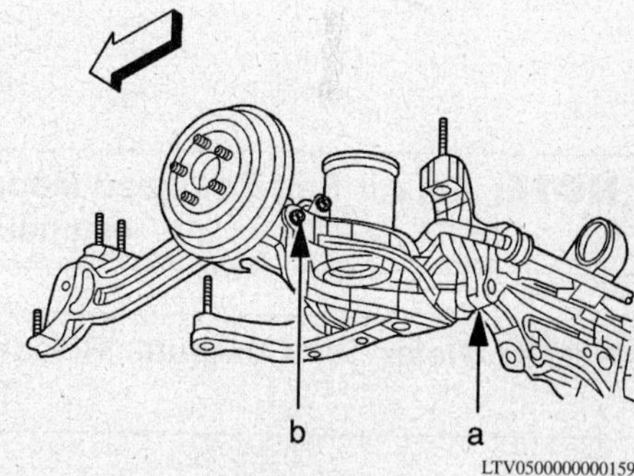

Fig. C

Fig. D

FLUID CAPACITIES & COOLING SYSTEM DATA

Year	Engine Liter	Cooling Capacity Qts.	Recommended Coolant Type	Radiator Cap Relief Pressure, psi	Thermostat Opening Temp. °F	Fuel Tank Gals.	Engine Oil Refill Qts.	Auto. Transaxle Qts.①		Transfer Case, Ounces	Differential, Ounces
								Drain & Refill	Overhaul		
2005–06	3.4L	10.6	Dex-Cool	15	188–206	16.7	4②	7.5	8.2	17	25.4

① — Approximate, make final inspect w/dipstick.

② — Includes filter.

LUBRICANT DATA

Year	Lubricant Type				
	Automatic Transaxle	Differential	Transfer Case	Power Steering	Brake System
2005–06	T-IV ATF	①	①	②	DOT 3

① — Versatrak Fluid (part No. 12378514).

② — Electric Power Steering (EPS) system uses no fluid.

Electrical

NOTE: On Air Bag Equipped Models, Refer To "Air Bag System Precautions" Located In The Front Of This Manual For System Disarming & Arming Procedures.

NOTE: Refer To "Computer Relearn Procedures" Located In The Front Of This Manual When Battery Power To The Computer Has Been Interrupted.

NOTE: Prior To Performing Any Service Operations Listed In This Section, Consult The "Technical Service Bulletins" Section For Related Information.

INDEX

PRECAUTIONS

Air Bag Systems

Refer to "Air Bag System Precautions" in the front of this manual for system disarming and arming procedures.

Battery Ground Cable

Prior to service, disconnect battery ground cable and isolate as required.

FUSE PANEL & FLASHER LOCATION

The instrument panel fuse panel is located inside in the center instrument panel, beneath the righthand side of the radio, **Fig. 1.**

The engine compartment fuse panel is located on the lefthand side of the engine compartment.

The hazard warning system uses the turn signal relay in the center of the instrument panel, behind the radio and HVAC control module, **Fig. 2.**

FUEL PUMP RELAY LOCATION

The fuel pump relay is located in the engine compartment fuse panel, **Fig. 3.**

STARTER

REPLACE

1. Raise and support vehicle.
2. Disconnect starter motor solenoid positive terminal nut and electrical wires, then the S terminal nut and electrical wire
3. Remove mounting bolt and torque converter cover.
4. Remove mounting bolts and starter motor.
5. Reverse procedure to install, noting the following:
   a. **Torque** starter motor to 32 ft. lbs.
   b. **Torque** torque converter cover mounting bolt to 71 inch lbs.
   c. **Torque** solenoid S terminal nut to 27 inch lbs.
   d. **Torque** solenoid positive terminal nut to 89 inch lbs.

ALTERNATOR

REPLACE

1. Remove terminal nut and battery positive lead electrical connector.
2. Remove serpentine drive belt as outlined under "Serpentine Drive Belt" in engine section.
3. Remove mounting bolts and alternator.
4. Reverse procedure to install.
5. Place transaxle in neutral gear position.
6. Remove engine mount strut bolts and position mount aside.
7. Install engine tilt strap tool No. J41131 or equivalent.

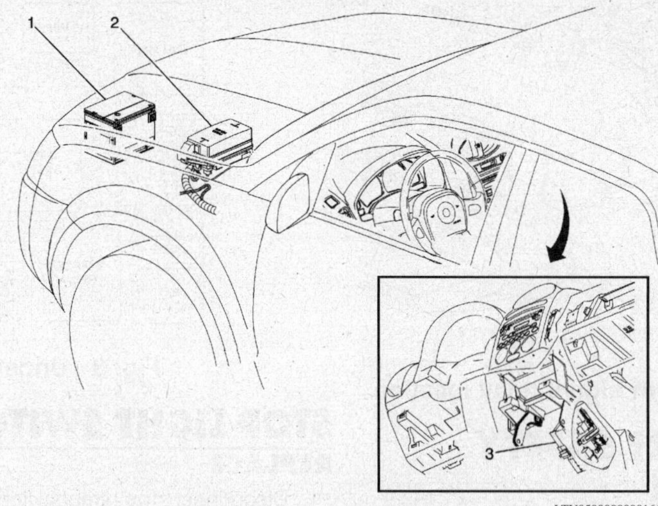

Fig. 1 Fuse panel locations

8. Rotate engine forward, then tighten engine tilt strap.
9. Disconnect alternator electrical connectors.
10. Remove accessory drive belt.
11. Remove alternator from bracket.
12. Reverse procedure to install. noting the following:
    a. **Torque** alternator mounting bolts to 37 ft. lbs.
    b. **Torque** battery positive terminal nut to 15 ft. lbs.

COIL PACK

REPLACE

1. Remove injector sight shield
2. Record positions for install alignment and disconnect spark plug wires.
3. Disconnect ignition coil control module electrical connectors.
4. Remove mounting bolts and ignition coil/control module.
5. Reverse procedure to install. **Torque** coil mounting bolts to 40 inch lbs.

IGNITION LOCK

REPLACE

1. Ensure vehicle transmission selector is in PARK position.
2. Disable air bag system as outlined in "Air Bag System Precautions" in the front of this manual.
3. Remove lower mounting screws, then the upper and lower steering column trim covers.
4. Insert ignition key, then turn lock to RUN and back to ACC position.
5. Depress locking button through hole on side of ignition module using suitable thin pick-type tool, **Fig. 4.**
6. Slide lock cylinder from ignition housing.
7. Reverse procedure to install. **Torque** steering wheel column cover mounting screws to 18 inch lbs.

IGNITION SWITCH

REPLACE

1. Disable air bag system as outlined in "Air Bag System Precautions" in the front of this manual.
2. Push driver air bag module spring fasteners inward using suitable blunt-ended too through access holes on back of steering wheel.
3. Disconnect Connector Position Assurance (CPA) retainer and electrical connector.
4. Remove driver air bag module.
5. Disconnect cruise control switch electrical connector.
6. Remove steering wheel mounting nut.
7. Remove steering wheel using steering wheel puller tool No. J1859-A and puller legs tool No. J42578, or equivalents.
8. Remove lower mounting screws, then the upper and lower steering column trim covers.
9. Remove air bag module coil harness clips from bracket below steering column, then disconnect coil and horn/cruise connectors.
10. Remove coil by prying using suitable small flat-bladed tool.
11. Disconnect multi-function turn signal switch harness connectors.
12. Depress lock tabs, then remove lefthand and righthand multi-function levers.
13. Disconnect electrical housing connectors.
14. Disconnect tabs and remove park lock cable from ignition module.
15. Remove lock housing mounting bolts.
16. Turn ignition key to ACC position and separate ignition housing from multi-function bracket.
17. Remove mounting screws and ignition switch, **Fig. 5.**
18. Reverse procedure to install, noting the following:
    a. **Torque** ignition switch mounting screws to 22 inch lbs.
    b. **Torque** housing bolts to 71 inch lbs.
    c. **Torque** steering wheel to 30 ft. lbs.

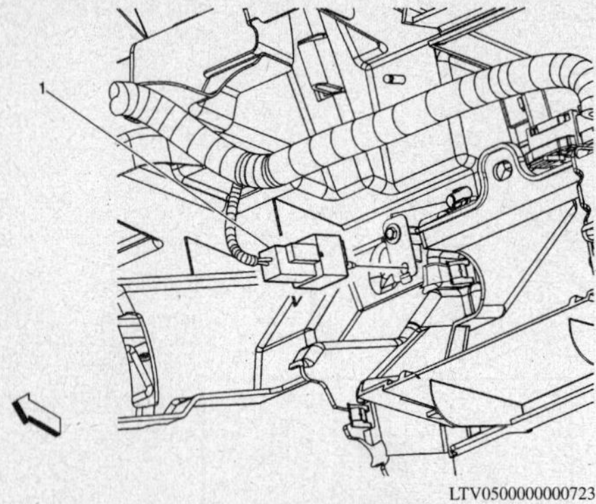

Fig. 2 Turn signal relay location

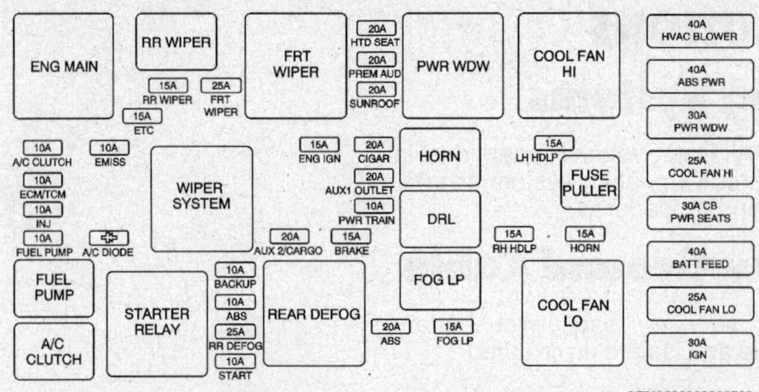

Fig. 3 Underhood fuse block relay locations

NEUTRAL SAFETY SWITCH

REPLACE

The park/neutral position switch assembly is a sliding contact switch attached to the manual shift detent lever assembly outside the transmission case.

1. Remove battery air outlet duct.
2. Remove mounting and battery tray from inner fender.
3. Disconnect shift cable from wire harness clip.
4. Apply parking brake and place control shift lever N position.
5. Disconnect transaxle range switch lever. shift control cable using fascia retainer remover tool No. J36346, or equivalent.
6. Remove mounting nut and transaxle range switch lever.
7. Disconnect transaxle range switch electrical connector.
8. Bend manual shaft nut lock washer tabs down using suitable screwdriver.
9. Remove transaxle range switch mounting bolt, stud and flat washers, then the transaxle range switch.
10. Reverse procedure to install noting the following:
    a. Ensure transaxle is in neutral position.
    b. **Torque** manual shaft mounting nut to 62 inch lbs.
    c. Ensure manual shaft is in N position.
    d. Turn transaxle range switch until neutral base line on switch lines up with indicator line on transmission indicator alignment tool No. J45404, or equivalent.
    e. **Torque** transaxle range switch mounting bolt and stud to 18 ft. lbs.
    f. **Torque** transaxle range switch lever mounting nut to 12 ft. lbs.
    g. **Torque** battery tray mounting bolts to 18 ft. lbs.

HEADLAMP SWITCH

REPLACE

Refer to "Multi-Function Switch, Replace" for headlamp switch replacement.

STOP LIGHT SWITCH

REPLACE

1. Disconnect stop lamp switch electrical connectors.
2. Rotate switch counterclockwise and remove it from retainer.
3. Reverse procedure to install, noting the following:
    a. **Do not depress brake pedal during stop lamp switch installation.**
    b. Install switch to bracket by turning and pushing it until it bottoms on brake pedal.

MULTI-FUNCTION SWITCH

REPLACE

1. Disable air bag system as outlined in "Air Bag System Precautions" in the front of this manual.
2. Remove mounting screws, then the upper and lower steering column trim covers.
3. Disconnect multi-function switch electrical connectors.
4. Depress lock tabs, then remove left-hand and righthand multi-function switches.
5. Remove switch attaching screws, then the switch.
6. Reverse procedure to install. **Torque** steering column trim cover mounting screws to 18 inch lbs.

TURN SIGNAL SWITCH

REPLACE

Refer to "Multi-Function Switch, Replace" for turn signal switch replacement.

DIMMER SWITCH

REPLACE

Refer to "Multi-Function Switch, Replace" for dimmer switch replacement.

STEERING WHEEL

REPLACE

1. Disable air bag system as outlined in "Air Bag System Precautions" in the front of this manual.
2. Push driver air bag module spring fasteners inward using suitable blunt-ended tool through access holes on back of steering wheel.
3. Disconnect Connector Position Assurance (CPA) retainer and electrical connector.
4. Remove driver air bag module.
5. Disconnect cruise control switch electrical connector.
6. Remove steering wheel mounting nut.
7. Remove steering wheel using steering wheel puller tool No. J1859-A and puller legs tool No. J42578, or equivalents.
8. Reverse procedure to install. **Torque** steering wheel to 30 ft. lbs.

INSTRUMENT CLUSTER

REPLACE

1. Disable air bag system as outlined in "Air Bag System Precautions" in the front of this manual.
2. Place steering column in lower position.
3. Remove mounting screws and remove cluster trim panel.
4. Remove lower instrument panel cluster upper and lower mounting screws, **Fig. 6.**
5. Pull cluster rearward and disconnect electrical harness.
6. Remove instrument cluster.
7. Reverse procedure to install, noting the following:
    a. **Torque** instrument cluster trim panel mounting screws to 22 inch lbs.
    b. **Torque** instrument cluster mounting screws to 18 inch lbs.

RADIO

REPLACE

1. Disconnect clips and electrical connectors, then the center trim bezel.
2. Remove radio mounting screws.
3. Pull radio rearward, then disconnect electrical connectors and antenna.
4. Disconnect ground strap and remove radio.
5. Reverse procedure to install. **Torque** radio mounting screws to 22 inch lbs.

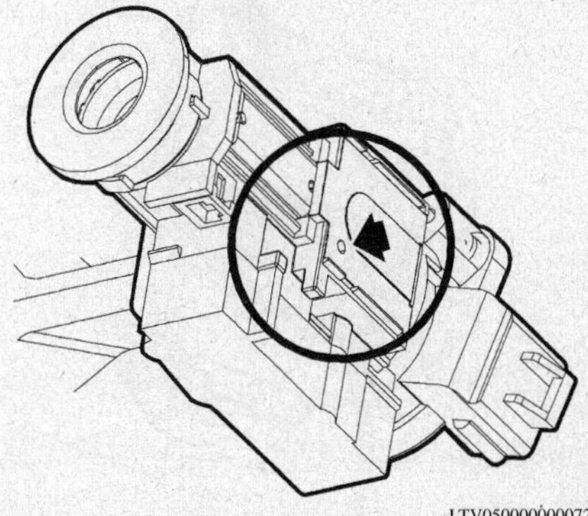
LTV0500000000726

Fig. 4 Ignition lock replacement

LTV0500000000725

Fig. 5 Ignition switch replacement

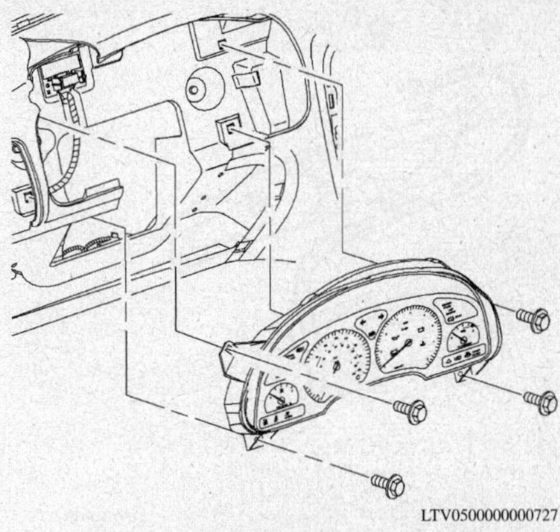
LTV0500000000727

Fig. 6 Instrument cluster replacement

WIPER MOTOR

REPLACE

1. Remove mounting nuts and wiper arms.
2. Remove push-in retainers and righthand air inlet grille.
3. Remove push-in retainers, lift lefthand air inlet griller and disconnect front washer nozzle hose.
4. Depress retaining tabs on under air inlet grille and pull front nozzles up.
5. Remove lefthand air inlet grille.
6. Remove mounting bolts and lift wiper motor module from cowl, **Fig. 7.**
7. Disconnect wiper module frame wire harness rosebud clip.
8. Disconnect wiper module motor electrical connector
9. Remove crank nut, two mounting bolts and wiper motor, **Fig. 8.**
10. Reverse procedure to install noting the following:
    a. **Torque** wiper motor mounting bolts to 71 inch lbs.
    b. **Torque** wiper motor crank arm mounting nut to 10 ft. lbs.
    c. **Torque** wiper module mounting bolts to 80 inch lbs.
    d. **Torque** wiper arm mounting nut to 21 ft. lbs.

WIPER SWITCH

REPLACE

Refer to "Multi-Function Switch, Replace" for wiper switch replacement.

WIPER MODULE

REPLACE

1. Remove mounting nuts and wiper arms.
2. Remove push-in retainers and righthand air inlet grille.
3. Remove push-in retainers, lift lefthand air inlet griller and disconnect front washer nozzle hose.
4. Depress retaining tabs on under air inlet grille and pull front nozzles up.
5. Remove lefthand air inlet grille.
6. Remove mounting bolts and lift wiper motor module from cowl, **Fig. 7.**
7. Disconnect wiper module frame wire harness rosebud clip.
8. Disconnect wiper module motor electrical connector
9. Reverse procedure to install noting the following:
    a. **Torque** wiper module mounting bolts to 80 inch lbs.
    b. **Torque** wiper arm mounting nut to 21 ft. lbs.

BLOWER MOTOR

REPLACE

1. Remove mounting screws and righthand closeout insulator panel, **Fig. 9.**
2. Disconnect electrical connector, then remove mounting screws and blower motor.
3. Reverse procedure to install, noting the following:
    a. **Torque** blower motor mounting screws to 13 inch lbs.
    b. **Torque** closeout/insulator panel to 18 inch lbs.

CABIN AIR FILTER

REPLACE

1. Remove righthand air inlet panel rear push pins.
2. Open hood, then remove righthand air inlet panel top and forward push pins.
3. Remove mounting screw and righthand air inlet panel.
4. Depress inboard edge tab and remove filter from housing.
5. Reverse procedure to install.

HVAC MODULE

REPLACE

1. Disable air bag system as outlined in "Air Bag System Precautions" in the front of this manual.
2. Recover refrigerant as outlined in "Air Conditioning" chapter.
3. Drain engine coolant into suitable container.
4. Remove mounting nut, then the outlet hose and liquid line from Thermal Expansion Valve (TXV).
5. Discard liquid line sealing washer. Cap evaporator outlet hose and liquid line.
6. Disconnect clamps, then remove heater core outlet and inlet hoses. Plug heater and evaporator cores' with suitable, clean towels.
7. Remove HVAC module front dash seal nuts.
8. Remove instrument panel as outlined in "Dash Panel Service" chapter.
9. Position front seats rearward and remove lower console mounting screws.
10. Lift center console rear and disconnect auxiliary power outlet electrical connector.
11. Slide center floor console rearward, then remove center stack mounting bolts and floor console.
12. Disconnect shift control cable from control range select lever pin using fascia retainer remover tool No. J36346, or equivalent.
13. Squeeze tabs and remove cable from shift control.
14. Disconnect park lock cable from shift control park lock lever.
15. Disconnect shift control electrical connector.
16. Remove mounting nuts and shift control.
17. Remove center floor air outlet duct by sliding it forward and up at rear.
18. Remove retainers and center instrument panel air outlet duct from tie bar.
19. Remove mounting nuts and bolts, then the instrument panel tie bar, **Fig. 10.**
20. Disconnect blower motor, resistor and HVAC module electrical connectors.
21. Remove retainer and defroster duct,
22. Disconnect instrument panel wire harness clips and remove HVAC module.
23. Remove HVAC module
24. Reverse procedure to install, noting the following:
    a. **Torque** HVAC module mounting nuts to 71 inch lbs.
    b. **Torque** instrument panel tie bar to body mounting bolts to 18 ft. lbs.
    c. **Torque** instrument panel tie bar to HVAC module mounting bolts and nuts to 36 inch lbs.
    d. **Torque** shift control mounting nuts to 18 ft. lbs.
    e. **Torque** floor console mounting screws to 22 inch lbs.
    f. **Torque** TXV mounting nut to 15 ft. lbs.

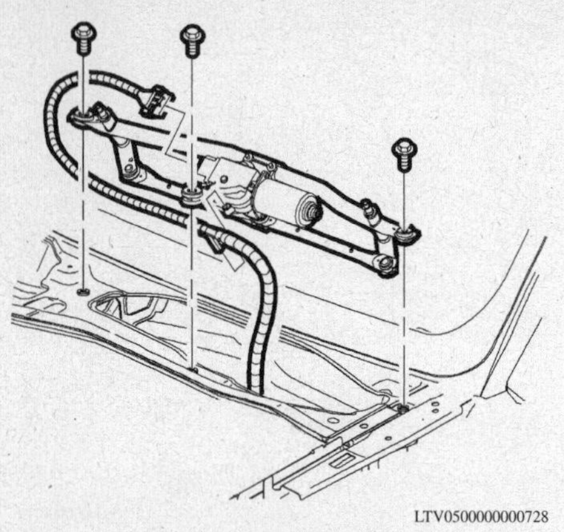

Fig. 7 Wiper module replacement

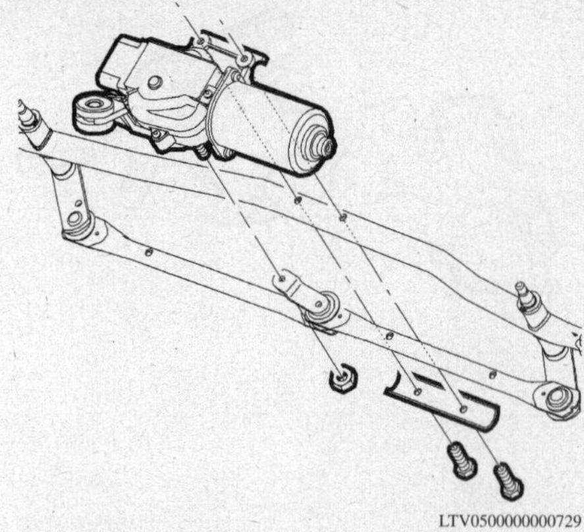

Fig. 8 Wiper motor replacement

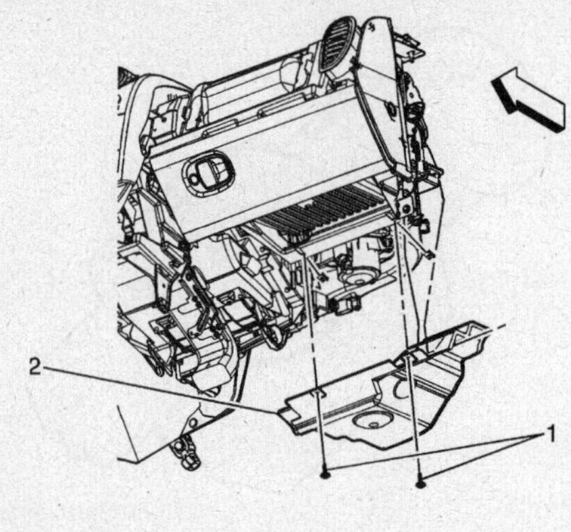

Fig. 9 Righthand closeout panel replacement

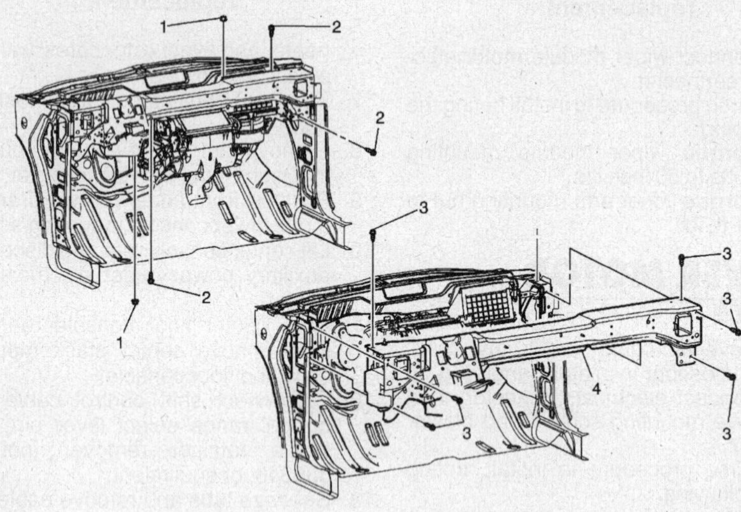

Fig. 10 Instrument panel tie bar replacement

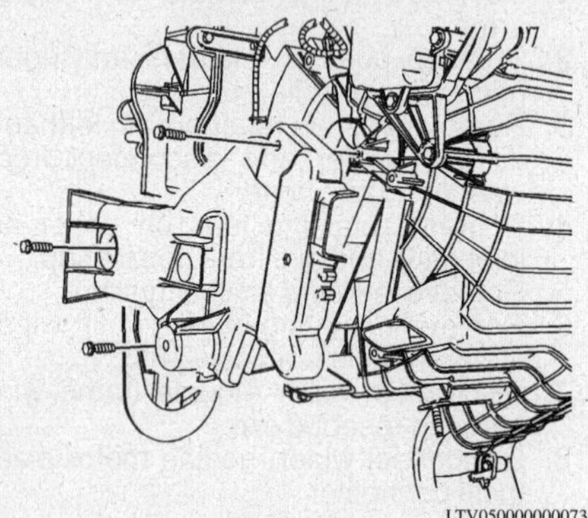

Fig. 11 Heater core cover replacement

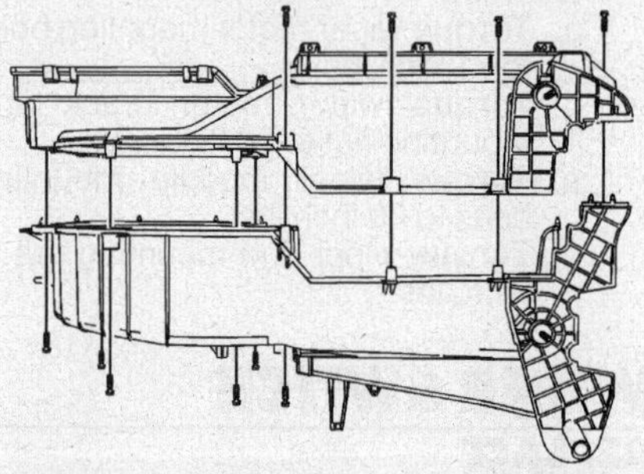

Fig. 12 Blower case separation

HEATER CORE

REPLACE

1. Remove HVAC module as outlined under "HVAC Module, Replace."
2. Remove mounting screws and cover, then the heater core, **Fig. 11.**
3. Reverse procedure to install. **Torque** heater core cover mounting screws to 13 inch lbs.

EVAPORATOR CASE

REPLACE

1. Remove HVAC module as outlined under "HVAC Module, Replace."
2. Remove mounting screws and cover, then the heater core, **Fig. 11.**
3. Remove mounting screws and evaporator case.
4. Reverse procedure to install. **Torque** heater core cover and evaporator case mounting screws to 13 inch lbs.

EVAPORATOR CORE

REPLACE

1. Remove evaporator case as outlined under "Evaporative Case, Replace."
2. Remove mounting bolts and Thermal Expansion Valve (TXV) from backing plate and evaporator pipes. Remove seal washers.
3. Remove HVAC module dash front seal.
4. Remove mounting screws and separate blower case halves, **Fig. 12.**
5. Remove evaporator core.
6. Reverse procedure to install noting the following:
   a. **Torque** blower case cover mounting screws to 13 inch lbs.
   b. **Torque** TXV mounting screws to 31 inch lbs.

TECHNICAL SERVICE BULLETINS

Intermittent No Crank, No Start

On some of these models there may be a intermittent no crank or no start condition.

This condition may be caused by the battery cable bolt.

To correct this condition, clean the battery side terminal treads and replace the cable bolt.

3.4L Engine

NOTE: On Air Bag Equipped Models, Refer To "Air Bag System Precautions" Located In The Front Of This Manual For System Disarming & Arming Procedures.

NOTE: Refer To "Computer Relearn Procedures" Located In The Front Of This Manual For Computer Relearn Procedures.

NOTE: Prior To Performing Any Service Operations Listed In This Section, Consult The "Technical Service Bulletins" Section For Related Information.

INDEX

PRECAUTIONS

Air Bag Systems

Refer to "Air Bag System Precautions" in the front of this manual for system disarming and arming procedures.

Battery Ground Cable

Prior to service, disconnect battery ground cable and isolate as required.

Fuel System Pressure Relief

1. Loosen fuel filler cap to discharge tank pressure.
2. Connect fuel pressure gauge tool No. J34730-1A, or equivalent, to fuel pressure connection. Wrap shop towel around connection while connecting gauge.
3. Install suitable bleed hose into suitable container.
4. Bleed fuel system pressure by opening valve.
5. Disconnect fuel pressure gauge.

COMPRESSION PRESSURES

No cylinder reading should be less than 100 psi.

The lowest reading should not be less than 70% of the highest reading.

ENGINE MOUNT

REPLACE

Front

1. Raise and support vehicle.
2. Remove transmission mounting bolt, **Fig. 1.**
3. Remove transmission mount-to-transmission bolts.
4. Remove transmission mount.
5. Reverse procedure to install.

Righthand

1. Loosen air cleaner intake duct clamps and remove Positive Crankcase Ventilation (PCV) fresh air pipe.
2. Remove air cleaner intake duct from Mass Air Flow (MAF) sensor and throttle body.
3. Disconnect MAF sensor electrical connector.
4. Remove mounting bolt and air cleaner assembly.
5. Remove fuel injector sight shield.
6. Pull each end of hood rear seal away from cowl panel flange near both strut towers.
7. Replace two strut bolts with studs (part No 11519137) on lefthand and righthand sides. **Torque** studs to 18 ft. lbs.
8. Install engine support fixture adapters tool No. J28467-13 and strut tower adapter tool No. J28467-5, or equivalents, to top of lefthand and righthand strut towers.
9. Install 50-inch engine support fixture cross bar transversely across vehicle

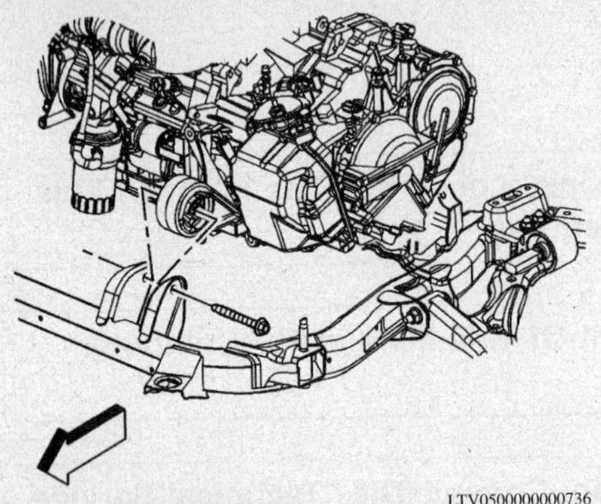

Fig. 1 Engine mount replacement. Front

between both strut tower adapters. Install safety pins.

10. Position 23-inch engine support fixture cross bar longitudinally using engine support adapter leg set tool No. J36462-A, or equivalent, next to rear engine lift bracket.
11. **If 23-inch engine support cross bar is not available it may be required to remove vehicle hood for additional clearance when using longer cross bar.**
12. Secure longitudinal mounted cross bar to transverse mounted cross bar using clamp tool No. J 28467-1A, or equivalent.
13. Connect longitudinal mounted cross bar to rear engine lift bracket using lift hook tool No. J28467-7A and bracket tool No. J28467-6, or equivalents. Remove slack.
14. Position 23-inch engine support fixture cross bar longitudinally using engine support adapter leg set tool No. J36462-A, or equivalent, next to front engine lift bracket.
15. **If 23-inch engine support cross bar is not available it may be required to remove vehicle hood for additional clearance when using longer cross bar.**
16. Secure longitudinal mounted cross bar to transverse mounted cross bar using clamp tool No. J 28467-1A, or equivalent.
17. Connect longitudinal mounted cross bar to front engine lift bracket using lift hook tool No. J28467-7A and bracket tool No. J28467-6, or equivalents. Remove slack.
18. Evenly tighten wing nuts until engine weight is supported by fixture.
19. Raise and support vehicle.
20. Remove engine mount to bracket bolts and frame rail nuts, **Fig. 2.**
21. Remove engine mount.
22. Reverse procedure to install.

ENGINE

REPLACE

1. Remove hold-down and battery.
2. Remove mounting bolt and air conditioning evaporator outlet hose.

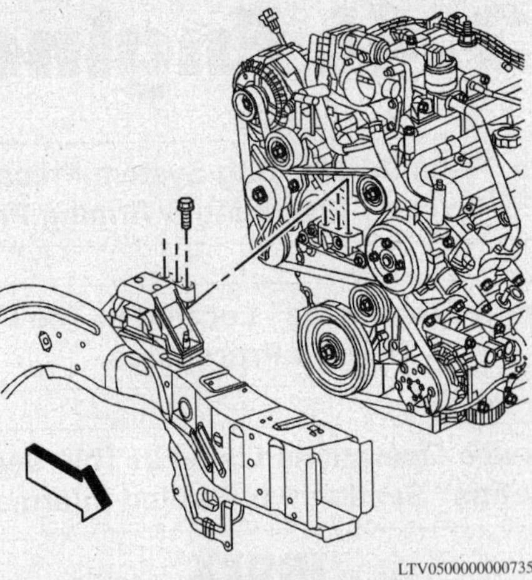

Fig. 2 Engine mount replacement. Righthand

3. Remove Underhood Fuse Block (UHFB) cover.
4. Remove mounting nut, then the positive battery cable and Electronic Power Steering (EPS) wire from UHFB B+ terminal.
5. Remove retainer and engine wire harness connector from battery box.
6. Loosen mounting bolts and clips, then remove UHFB from housing.
7. Disconnect forward lamp harness and UHFB connectors from UHFB and housing.
8. Position electrical harnesses/connectors and battery cables aside.
9. Remove mounting bolts and lift coolant surge tank aside.
10. Remove battery box mounting bolts and separate air inlet duct.
11. Remove battery box and position Engine Control Module (ECM) on top engine.
12. Remove retainers, mounting nut and battery cable from inner fender ground stud.
13. Remove fuel injector sight shield.
14. Disconnect clamp and brake booster vacuum hose from intake manifold.
15. Remove Transaxle Control Module (TCM) from bracket and set it on top of engine.
16. Loosen air cleaner intake duct clamps and remove Positive Crankcase Ventilation (PCV) fresh air pipe.
17. Remove air cleaner intake duct from Mass Air Flow (MAF) sensor and throttle body.
18. Disconnect MAF sensor electrical connector.
19. Remove mounting bolt and air cleaner assembly.
20. Relieve fuel pressure as outlined under "Precautions."
21. Disconnect Evaporative Emission (EVAP) hose/pipe from EVAP canister purge solenoid valve.
22. Disconnect engine fuel hose/pipe from chassis fuel hose/pipe.
23. Recover refrigerant as outlined in "Air Conditioning" chapter.

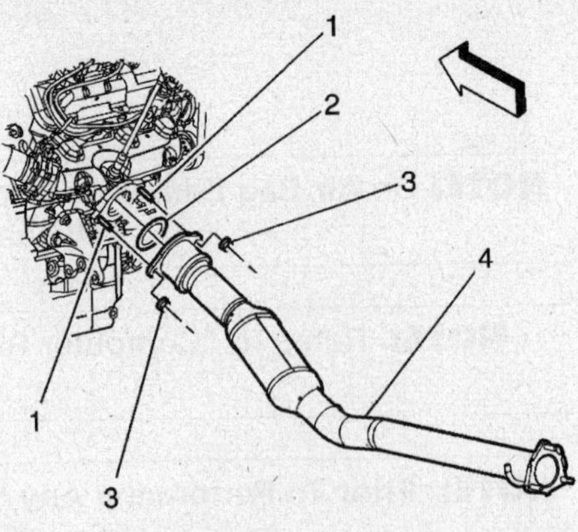

1. Exhaust Manifold Stud
2. Gasket
3. Mounting Nuts
4. Catalytic Converter

LTV0500000000743

Fig. 3 Catalytic converter replacement

24. Remove air conditioning compressor hose. Cap or plug hoses and compressor.
25. Disconnect shift control cable from transaxle range switch lever using fascia retainer remover tool No. J36346, or equivalent.
26. Disconnect engine to body inline connector.
27. Drain engine coolant into suitable container.
28. Tie radiator, condenser and fan module to upper radiator support.
29. Remove clamps, then the surge tank inlet and outlet hoses. Remove surge tank.
30. Disconnect heater hoses from engine, then the radiator inlet hose.
31. Raise and support vehicle, then remove radiator outlet hose.
32. Disconnect oil cooler lines from transaxle and remove seals. Cap oil cooler lines and plug transaxle fittings.
33. Remove push-in retainers, mounting screws and front wheelhouse liners.
34. Remove mounting screws and push-in retainers, then the front bumper fascia air deflector.
35. Disconnect Heated Oxygen Sensor (HO2S) 2 wiring harness and remove retainers.
36. Remove mounting nuts, then separate catalytic converter and exhaust system pipes, **Fig. 3.** Discard gasket.
37. **Catalytic converter flex coupler must not be deflected more than 6°.**
38. Remove mounting nuts, and separate catalytic converter from exhaust manifold. Discard gasket.
39. Separate hanger from rubber isolator and remove catalytic converter.
40. Support rear exhaust system half to vehicle underbody.
41. **On models equipped with AWD,** disconnect transfer case vent hose.
42. **On all models,** remove front tire and wheel assemblies, then the lefthand and righthand engine splash shields.

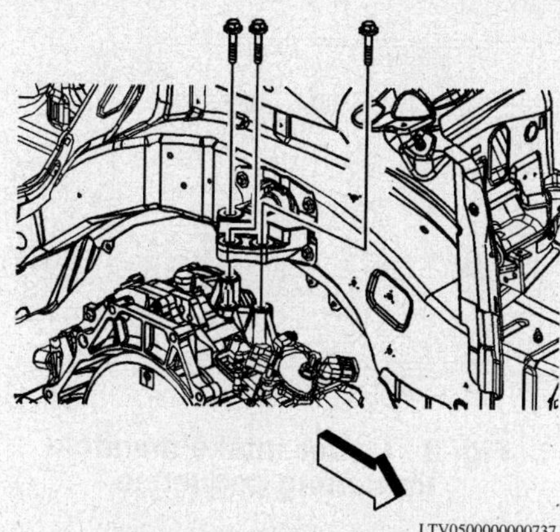

Fig. 4 Engine mount replacement. Lefthand

43. Remove steering intermediate shaft pinch bolt and discard bolt.
44. Disconnect steering intermediate shaft from steering gear.
45. Mark for installation alignment, then hold ball stud and loosen tie rod inner jam nuts.
46. Remove and discard tie rod to knuckle nuts.
47. Separate tie rods from steering knuckles using steering linkage and tie rod puller tool No. J24319-B, or equivalent. **Do not free ball stud using pickle fork or wedge-type tool.**
48. Remove outer from inner tie rods.
49. Remove mounting nuts and disconnect link from stabilizer bar.
50. Remove and discard cotter pin, then loosen steering knuckle lower ball stud nut until nut is level with top of ball stud.
51. Separate lower control arm from steering knuckle using ball joint remover tool No. J43828, or equivalent.
52. Remove lefthand and righthand front wheel drive shafts as outlined in "Front Wheel Drive" section.
53. **On models equipped with AWD,** remove rear propeller shaft as outlined in "Rear Axle & Suspension" section.
54. **On all models,** place suitable wooden support blocks between frame and engine oil pan, then between frame and transaxle.
55. Lower vehicle.
56. Remove righthand and lefthand engine mount to engine bolts, **Figs. 2 and 4**
57. Raise and support vehicle.
58. Support frame using suitable universal frame support fixture or jack stands.
59. Lower vehicle until frame contacts fixture or jack stands.
60. Remove and discard frame-to-body bolts, **Fig. 5.**
61. Ensure there is no body to powertrain contact, or entanglement of wires and hoses.
62. Carefully raise body up away from powertrain.
63. Disconnect Exhaust Gas Recirculation (EGR) valve and Throttle body.
64. Disconnect EVAP purge solenoid, then remove mounting nut and alternator battery positive lead.

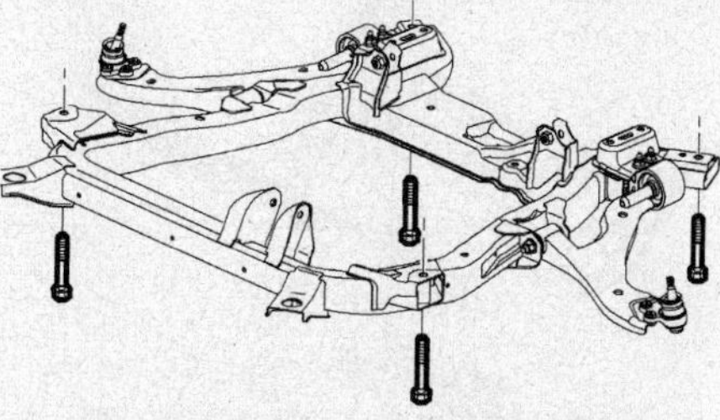

Fig. 5 Frame replacement

65. Disconnect alternator regulator and fuel injector inline connector.
66. Disconnect H2OS 1 and ignition coil/control module connectors.
67. Remove wire harness from retainers.
68. Disconnect Knock Sensor (KS) and Crankshaft Position (CKP) Sensor connector.
69. Remove mounting bolt and ground lead, then the wire harness from retainers.
70. **On model equipped with engine coolant heater,** disconnect heater cord.
71. **On all models,** disconnect air conditioning compressor clutch and refrigerant pressure sensor connectors.
72. Remove wire harness from retainer.
73. Disconnect KS and oil pressure indicator switch connectors.
74. Cover throttle body opening with suitable shop towel.
75. Disconnect TAC module electrical connector, then remove mounting bolts and throttle body. Block intake manifold opening with suitable, clean shop towel
76. Remove fuel pipe to transaxle nut and transaxle fuel pipe retainer stud.
77. **On models equipped with AWD,** remove mounting bolts and transfer case mounting bracket .
78. **On models equipped with FWD,** remove intermediate shaft as outlined in "Front Wheel Drive" section.
79. **On all models,** remove mounting nut and battery ground from transaxle stud.
80. Remove mounting bolts and engine-to-transaxle brace
81. Disconnect starter motor solenoid positive terminal nut and electrical wires, then the S terminal nut and electrical wire
82. Remove mounting bolt and torque converter cover.
83. Remove mounting bolts and starter motor.
84. Remove torque converter mounting bolts.
85. Support engine using suitable hoist and lift chain.
86. Remove automatic transaxle mounting bolts.
87. Separate automatic transaxle from engine.
88. Remove engine from frame and transaxle.
89. Reverse procedure to install.

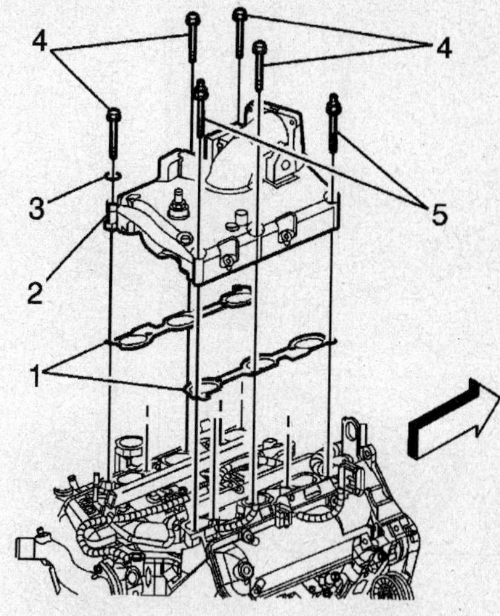

1. Upper Intake Manifold Gaskets
2. Upper Intake Manifold
3. Spark Plug Wire Retainer
4. Mounting Bolts
5. Mounting Bolts

Fig. 6 Upper intake manifold replacement

INTAKE MANIFOLD

REPLACE

Upper

1. Remove fuel injector sight shield.
2. Remove clamp and brake booster vacuum hose from intake manifold.
3. Disconnect lefthand side spark plug wires and harness clips.
4. Remove mounting bolts and position ignition control module bracket with module and spark plug wires attached aside.
5. Remove air cleaner intake duct from Mass Air Flow (MAF) sensor and throttle body.
6. Disconnect MAF sensor electrical connector.
7. Remove heater outlet pipe mounting nut from upper intake manifold, then nuts and bolt from throttle body. Position heater outlet pipe aside without disconnect hoses.
8. Remove mounting bolts and Exhaust Gas Recirculation (EGR) pipe.
9. Remove Positive Crankcase Ventilation (PCV) foul air hose.
10. Loosen alternator mounting bolt near intake manifold. **Do not completely remove bolt.**
11. Remove mounting nut and alternator brace.
12. Remove mounting bolts and spark plug retainer, then the upper intake manifold and gasket, **Fig. 6.**
13. Reverse procedure to install. Apply suitable threadlock to mounting bolts.

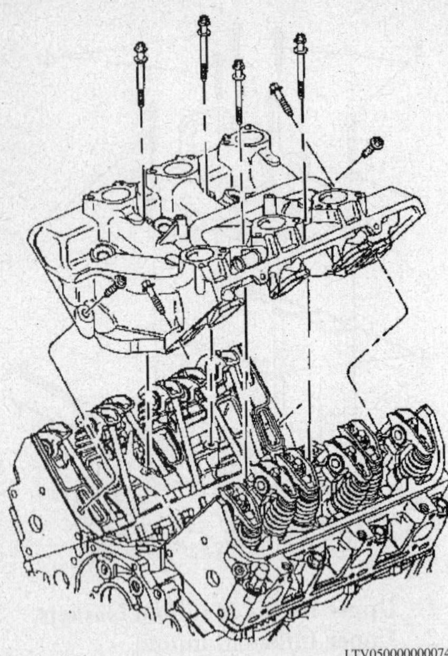

Fig. 7 Lower intake manifold replacement

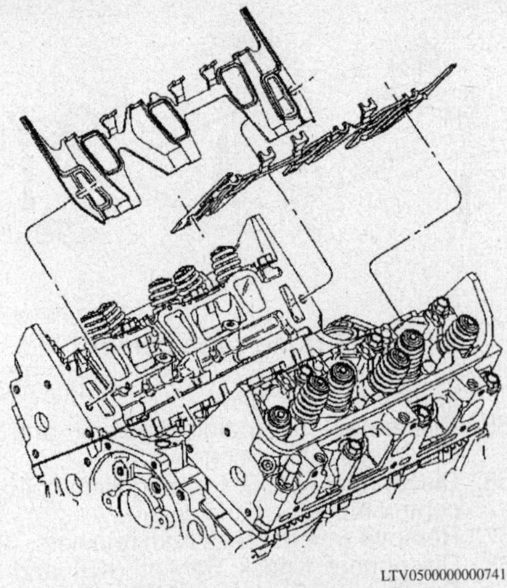

Fig. 8 Lower intake manifold gasket replacement

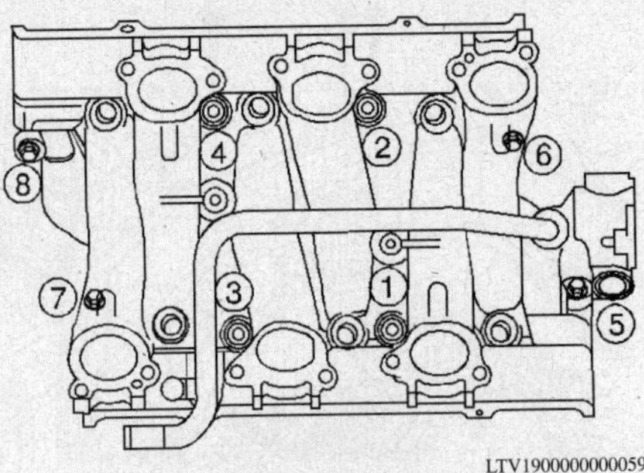

Fig. 9 Lower intake manifold tightening sequence

Lower

1. Drain cooling system into suitable container.
2. Remove upper intake manifold as outlined under "Intake Manifold, Replace."
3. Disconnect clamp and heater core inlet pipe hose, then remove mounting nut and heater inlet pipe. Remove seal.
4. Disconnect thermostat housing radiator inlet hose.
5. Relieve fuel pressure as outlined under "Precautions."
6. Disconnect engine fuel feed pipe at fuel rail
7. Disconnect main fuel injector, Engine Coolant Temperature (ECT) and Camshaft Position (CMP) sensors' connectors.
8. Disconnect fuel injectors' connectors.
9. Remove mounting bolts and fuel rail.
10. Remove mounting bolts and lower intake manifold, **Fig. 7.**
11. If replacing intake manifold, remove thermostat as outlined under "Thermostat, Replace."
12. Loosen mounting bolts and remove rocker arms.
13. Mark components for installation in original positions.
14. Remover push rods.
15. Remove lower intake manifold gasket, **Fig. 8.**
16. Reverse procedure to install, noting the following:
    a. **Do not apply Room Temperature Vulcanizing (RTV) sealer to engine block prior to installation of manifold gaskets. RTV sealer is not to be placed under lower intake manifold gaskets.**
    b. With seals in place, apply .08–.12 inch drop of RTV sealer
    c. Apply .12–.20 inch thick suitable sealer at engine block to lower intake manifold mating surfaces.
    d. **Torque** lower intake manifold mounting bolts to 115 inch lbs., in sequence, **Fig. 9.**
    e. **Torque** bolts 1–4 to 15 ft. lbs., in sequence.
    f. **Torque** bolts 5–8 to 15 ft. lbs., in sequence.

EXHAUST MANIFOLD

REPLACE

Lefthand

1. Remove three crossover pipe to lefthand exhaust manifold mounting bolts.
2. Remove mounting bolts and Exhaust Gas Recirculation (EGR) pipe.
3. Remove mounting bolts and exhaust manifold heat shield.
4. Remove mounting nuts and exhaust manifold, **Fig. 10.**
5. Reverse procedure to install.

Righthand

1. Disconnect oxygen sensor electrical connector.
2. Remove three crossover pipe to exhaust manifold mounting nuts.
3. Raise and support vehicle.
4. Remove mounting nuts, then separate catalytic converter from exhaust manifold and position it aside, **Fig. 3.**
5. Remove mounting bolts and exhaust manifold heat shield.
6. Remove mounting nuts and exhaust manifold, **Fig. 11.**
7. Reverse procedure to install.

CYLINDER HEAD

REPLACE

Lefthand

1. Drain engine coolant into suitable container.
2. Remove lefthand spark plug wires, then the mounting bolt and spark plug wire retainer support.
3. Remove lefthand hand spark plugs.
4. Remove mounting bolt, clip and foul air tube.
5. Remove mounting bolts and valve cover. Ensure gasket remains attached to cylinder head.
6. Trim valve cover gasket and sealant away from lower intake manifold gasket at cylinder head to lower intake manifold joints .
7. Remove valve rocker arm cover gasket.
8. Remove mounting bolts and valve cover.
9. Remove lower intake manifold as outlined under "Intake Manifold, Replace."
10. Remove oil dipstick, then the mounting bolts and indicator tube.
11. Remove holddown and battery.
12. Remove mounting bolt and air conditioning evaporator outlet hose.
13. Remove Underhood Fuse Block (UHFB) cover.
14. Remove mounting nut, then the positive battery cable and Electronic Power Steering (EPS) wire from UHFB B+ terminal.
15. Remove retainer and engine wire harness connector from battery box.
16. Loosen mounting bolts and clips, then remove UHFB from housing.
17. Disconnect forward lamp harness and UHFB connectors from UHFB and housing.
18. Position electrical harnesses/ connectors and battery cables aside.
19. Remove mounting bolts and lift coolant surge tank aside.
20. Remove battery box mounting bolts and separate air inlet duct.
21. Remove battery box and position Engine Control Module (ECM) on top engine.
22. Remove mounting nuts and exhaust crossover pipe.
23. Remove mounting bolts and Exhaust Gas Recirculation (EGR) pipe.
24. Remove mounting bolts and exhaust manifold heat shield.
25. Remove mounting nuts and exhaust manifold.
26. Remove mounting bolts, cylinder head and gasket. Discard cylinder head bolts.

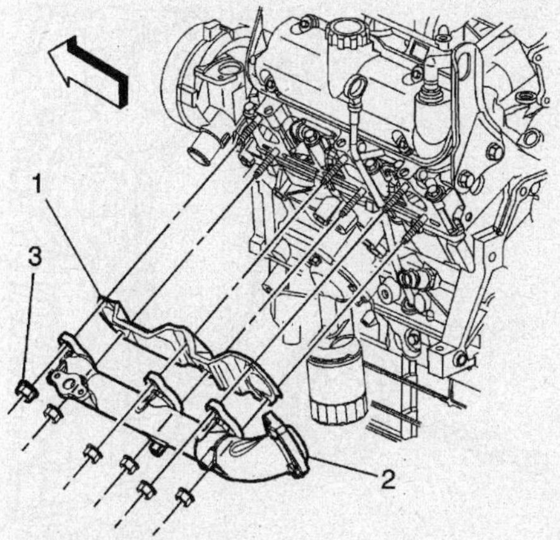

1. Gasket
2. Exhaust Manifold
3. Mounting Nut

LTV0500000000742

Fig. 10 Exhaust manifold replacement. Lefthand

27. Reverse procedure to install, noting the following:
    a. **Torque** new torque-to-yield cylinder head bolts to 44 ft. lbs., in sequence, **Fig. 12.**
    b. Final tighten head bolts an additional 95°.

Righthand

1. Drain engine coolant into suitable container.
2. Remove heater outlet pipe mounting nut from upper intake manifold, the then nuts and bolt from throttle body.
3. Remove heater outlet pipe.
4. Remove righthand cylinder head hose/pipe retainer mounting nut.
5. Disconnect electrical connector and remove ECT sensor.
6. Remove mounting bolts, ignition control module and bracket. Remove bracket studs.
7. Remove righthand wire and spark plugs.
8. Remove mounting bolt, clip and Manifold Absolute Pressure (MAP) sensor.
9. Remove clamp and hose, then the mounting nuts, bolt and heater outlet pipe.
10. Remove fresh air tube and wire harness mounting bolt.
11. Remove mounting nuts and bolts, then the ignition module with wires attached. Remove ignition module studs.
12. Remove PCV fresh air tube.
13. Remove mounting bolts and valve cover. Ensure gasket remains attached to cylinder head.
14. Trim valve cover gasket and sealant away from lower intake manifold gasket at cylinder head to lower intake manifold joints .
15. Remove valve cover gasket.
16. Remove mounting bolts and valve cover.
17. Remove mounting nuts and exhaust

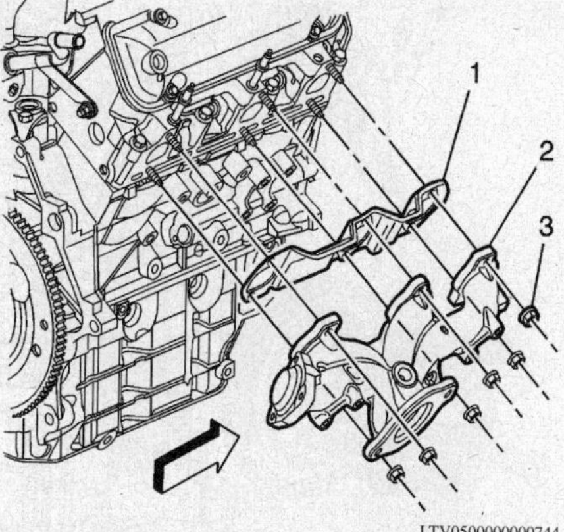

LTV0500000000744

Fig. 11 Exhaust manifold replacement. Righthand

crossover pipe.

18. Disconnect oxygen sensor electrical connector.
19. Remove mounting nuts, then separate catalytic converter from exhaust manifold and position it aside.
20. Remove mounting bolts and exhaust manifold heat shield.
21. Remove mounting nuts and exhaust manifold.
22. Remover alternator as outlined under "Alternator, Replace" in "Electrical" section.
23. Remove mounting bolt and drive belt tensioner.
24. Remove mounting bolts and alternator bracket.
25. Remove mounting bolts and
26. Drain engine oil into suitable container.
27. Lower vehicle.
28. Remove lower intake manifolds as outlined under "Intake Manifold, Replace."
29. Remove mounting bolts and exhaust crossover pipe heat shield.
30. Remove mounting nuts and exhaust crossover pipe.
31. Disconnect spark plug wires from righthand spark plugs.
32. Remove righthand exhaust manifold as outlined in "Exhaust Manifold, Replace."
33. Remove mounting bolts, cylinder head and gasket. Discard cylinder head bolts.
34. Reverse procedure to install, noting the following:
    a. **Torque** new torque-to-yield cylinder head bolts to 44 ft. lbs., in sequence, **Fig. 12.**
    b. Final tighten head bolts an additional 95°.

VALVE COVER

REPLACE

Lefthand

1. Remove mounting bolt, clip and foul air tube.
2. Remove mounting bolts and valve

LTV1900000000057

Fig. 12 Cylinder head bolt tightening sequence

cover. Ensure gasket remains attached to cylinder head.

3. Trim valve cover gasket and sealant away from lower intake manifold gasket at cylinder head to lower intake manifold joints .
4. Remove valve cover gasket.
5. Remove mounting bolts and valve cover.
6. Reverse procedure to install, noting the following:
    a. Apply suitable sealer to cylinder head to lower intake manifold joint.
    b. Install new gasket and apply suitable sealer to joint surfaces where cylinder head and intake manifold meet.

Righthand

1. Remove mounting bolt, clip and Manifold Absolute Pressure (MAP) sensor.
2. Remove clamp and hose, then the mounting nuts, bolt and heater outlet pipe.
3. Remove fresh air tube and wire harness mounting bolt.
4. Remove mounting nuts and bolts, then the ignition module with wires attached. Remove ignition module studs.
5. Remove PCV fresh air tube.
6. Remove mounting bolts and valve cover. Ensure gasket remains attached to cylinder head.
7. Trim valve cover gasket and sealant away from lower intake manifold gasket at cylinder head to lower intake manifold joints .
8. Remove valve cover gasket.
9. Remove mounting bolts and valve cover.
10. Reverse procedure to install, noting the following:
    a. Apply suitable sealer to cylinder head to lower intake manifold joint.
    b. Install new gasket and apply suitable sealer to joint surfaces where cylinder head and intake manifold meet.

CAMSHAFT LOBE LIFT SPECIFICATIONS

Intake .... **.2727 inch**
Exhaust .... **.2273 inch**

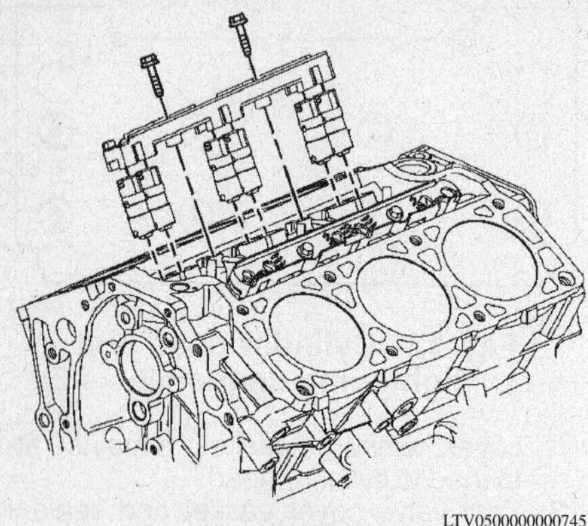

Fig. 13 Hydraulic lifter replacement

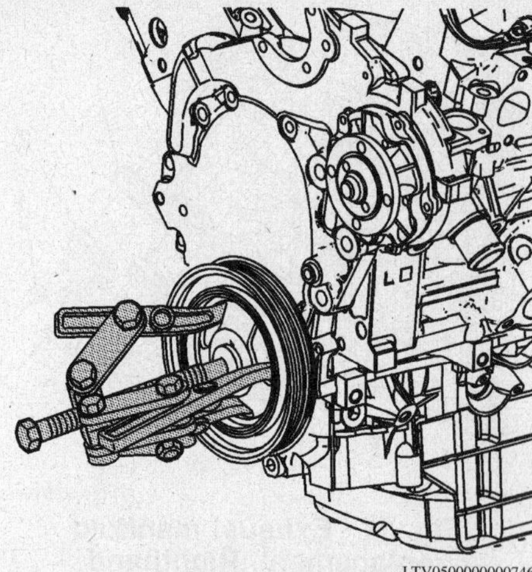

Fig. 14 Crankshaft balancer removal

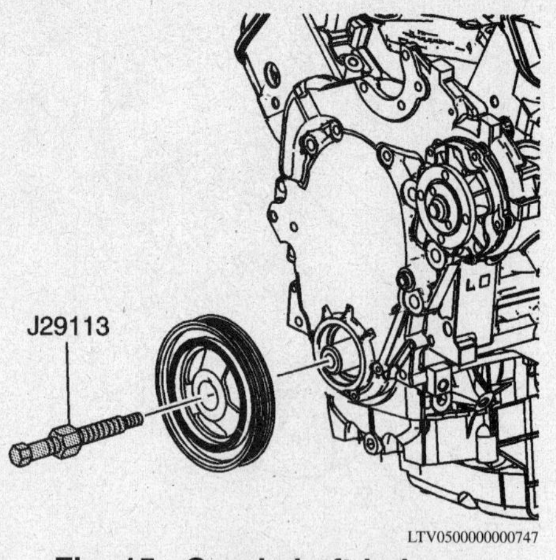

Fig. 15 Crankshaft balancer installation

VALVE CLEARANCE SPECIFICATIONS

These engines use hydraulic lifters. Valve stem to rocker arms have a clearance of zero.

VALVE ADJUSTMENT

This vehicle is equipped with hydraulic valve lifters.

ROCKER ARMS

REPLACE

1. Remove valve rocker arm cover as outlined under "Valve Cover, Replace."
2. Loosen mounting bolts and remove rocker arms.
3. Mark components for installation in original positions.
4. Reverse procedure to install.

PUSH RODS

The intake push rods measure 5.68 inches; exhaust push rods measure 6.0 inches.

1. Remove valve rocker arm cover as outlined under "Valve Cover, Replace."
2. Loosen mounting bolts and remove rocker arms.
3. Mark components for installation in original positions.
4. Remove push rods.
5. Reverse procedure to install.

HYDRAULIC LIFTERS

REPLACE

1. Remove valve cover as outlined under "Valve Cover, Replace."
2. Remove lower intake manifold as outlined under "Intake Manifold, Replace."
3. Loosen mounting bolts and remove rocker arms.
4. Mark components for installation in original positions.
5. Remove push rods.
6. Remove mounting bolts, guide and lifter, **Fig. 13.**
7. Reverse procedure to install. Coat valve lifter foot with camshaft and lifter prelube part No. 1052365, or equivalent.

CRANKSHAFT DAMPER

REPLACE

1. Relieve belt tension by rotating drive belt tensioner using serpentine belt tensioner unloader tool No. J39914, or equivalent.
2. Remove belt from righthand idler pulley.
3. Release tool and relieve spring tension.
4. Remove belt from tensioner.
5. Raise and support vehicle, then remove righthand front tire and wheel assembly.
6. Remove righthand engine splash side.
7. Remove wheelhouse liner.
8. Remove crankshaft balancer mounting bolt and washer
9. Remove crankshaft balancer using crankshaft balancer remover tool No. J41816-A and puller end protector tool No. EN46359, or equivalent, **Fig. 14. Do not use power-assisted tool with special tools.**
10. Reverse procedure to install, noting the following:
    a. Apply suitable crankshaft balancer keyway.
    b. Install crankshaft balancer using balancer and crank sprocket puller tool No. J29113, or equivalent, **Fig. 15. Do not use power-assisted tool with special tools.**
    c. **Torque** crankshaft balancer mounting bolt to 52 ft. lbs.
    d. Final tighten mounting bolt an additional 70°.

FRONT COVER

REPLACE

1. Remove drive belt tensioner as outlined under "Serpentine Drive Belt."
2. Drain cooling system into suitable container.
3. Raise and support vehicle, then remove righthand front tire and wheel assembly.
4. Remove righthand engine splash side.
5. Remove wheelhouse liner.
6. Remove crankshaft balancer mounting bolt and washer
7. Remove crankshaft balancer using crankshaft balancer remover tool No. J41816-A and puller end protector tool No. EN46359, or equivalent, **Fig. 14. Do not use power-assisted tool with special tools.**
8. Remove mounting bolt and remove lower belt idler pulley.
9. Remove oil pan as outlined under "Oil Pan, Replace."
10. Lower vehicle, then remove mounting bolt and lefthand belt idler pulley.
11. Remove mounting bolts and righthand engine mount bracket.
12. Remove mounting bolts and water pump pulley.
13. Remove mounting bolts, water pump and gasket. **Fig. 16.**
14. Disconnect clamps, then remove thermal bypass pipe and heater outlet hoses.
15. Remove mounting bolt, thermal bypass fitting and seal.
16. Remove mounting bolts, front cover and gasket, **Fig. 17.**
17. Reverse procedure to install, noting the following:
    a. Apply .2 inch wide band of suitable to both sides of front cover gasket lower tabs, **Fig. 18.**
    b. Tighten front cover immediately after installation of sealer coated gasket.
    c. Install and **torque** front cover bolts Nos. 3 and 4 to 41 ft. lbs., **Fig. 19.**
    d. Install and **torque** remaining mounting bolts to 20 ft. lbs.

TIMING CHAIN

REPLACE

Removal

1. Remove engine front cover as outlined in "Front Cover, Replace."

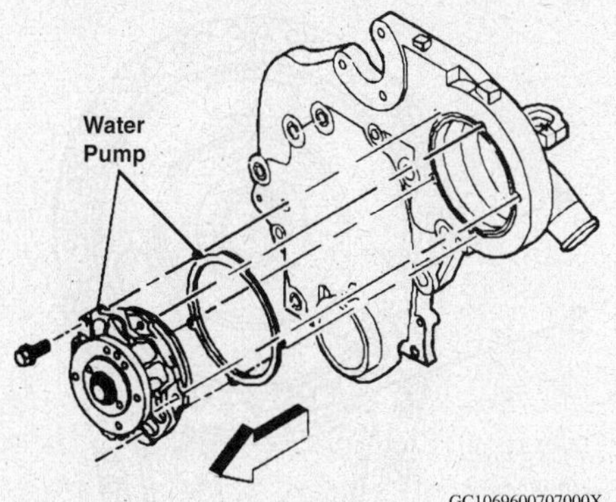

Fig. 16 Water pump replacement

2. Remove mounting bolt, camshaft sprocket and timing chain.
3. Remove crankshaft sprocket.
4. Remove mounting bolts and chain dampener.
5. Align crankshaft timing mark 2 to timing mark on bottom of timing chain dampener 1, then the timing mark on camshaft gear 4 with timing mark on top of timing chain dampener 3, **Fig. 20.**
6. Remove mounting bolt, camshaft sprocket and timing chain, **Fig. 21.**
7. Remove crankshaft sprocket using puller tool No. J5825-A, or equivalent.
8. Remove mounting bolts and timing chain dampener.

Installation

1. Install crankshaft sprocket.
2. Apply suitable lubricant to crankshaft sprocket thrust surface.
3. Install and tighten timing chain dampener.
4. Align crankshaft and timing chain dampener lower timing marks, **Fig. 22.**
5. Hold camshaft sprocket with timing chain hanging down and install timing chain to crankshaft gear.
6. Align camshaft dowel with sprocket dowel hole and draw sprocket onto camshaft using mounting bolt.
7. Coat crankshaft and camshaft sprocket with suitable engine oil.
8. Tighten camshaft sprocket mounting bolt.
9. Install front cover as outlined under "Front Cover, Replace."

CAMSHAFT

REPLACE

1. Remove timing chain as outlined in "Timing Chain, Replace."
2. Remove mounting bolt and Camshaft Position (CMP) sensor.
3. Remove mounting screws and camshaft thrust plate retaining screws and thrust plate.
4. Install sprocket bolt into camshaft hand tight.
5. Carefully rotate and remove camshaft. **Do not damage camshaft bearings.**
6. Reverse procedure to install, noting the following:
   a. Coat camshaft journals with suitable, clean engine oil.

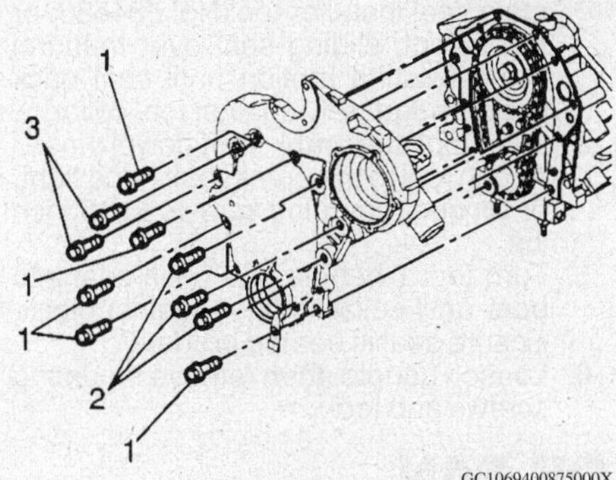

Fig. 17 Front cover bolt replacement

   b. Coat camshaft lobes with suitable prelude.

PISTON & ROD ASSEMBLY

Standard size pistons are supplied as an assembly consisting of a piston, piston pin, connecting rod and piston rings.

Assemble the piston for the specific cylinder with the connecting rod for the corresponding crankshaft journal.

Ensure that the marks on the piston and connecting rod are aligned the same as when removed.

Ensure that the arrow on top of piston faces towards the front of the engine.

If no identification marks were made during disassembly, ensure that the flat area on the bottom of the piston pin skirt is aligned with the small dimple above the connecting rod crankshaft bearing bore.

PISTONS, PINS & RINGS

1. Stagger oil control ring end gaps at least 90°.
2. Stagger compression ring end gaps at least 1 inch.

MAIN & ROD BEARINGS

Connecting Rod

1. Lightly lubricate piston, rings, cylinder bore and bearing surfaces with suitable, clean engine oil.
2. Piston alignment mark must face front of engine block.
3. Install piston and connecting rod into proper cylinder bore using connecting rod guide tool No. J41556, or equivalent.
4. Lightly tap piston top until all rings enter cylinder bore using suitable wooden hammer handle.
5. Install bearing, cap and bolts.
6. **Torque** connecting rod bearing cap bolts to 15 ft. lbs.
7. Final tighten cap bolts an additional 75°.
8. Ensure connecting rod side clearance is .007–.017 inch.

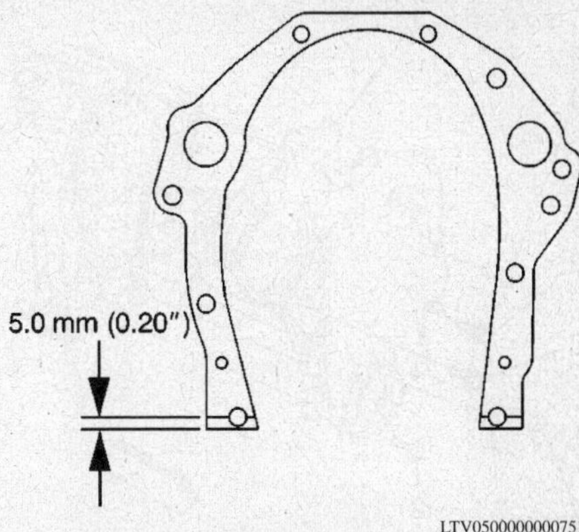

Fig. 18 Front cover gasket sealant application

Main Bearing

1. Dip crankshaft bearing cap bolts in suitable, clean engine oil.
2. Upper and lower inserts may be different. **Do not obstruct any oil passages.**
3. Place crankshaft bearing inserts into crankshaft bearing cap and block.
4. Ensure bearing inserts project an equal distance on both sides.
5. Ensure insert tangs are engaged.
6. Lubricate crankshaft main bearing surface with suitable, clean engine oil.
7. Install crankshaft.
8. Apply a .12 in bead of suitable sealant crankshaft main bearing cap No. 4 sealing surface, **Fig. 23.**
9. Tap crankshaft bearing caps into block cavity using suitable brass, lead or a leather mallet before installing bolts. **Do not use bolts to pull crankshaft bearing caps into seats.**
10. Install crankshaft main bearing caps.
11. Apply small amount of suitable sealer to rear of crankshaft main bearing cap No. 4 sealing surface, **Fig. 24.**
12. **Torque** crankshaft main bearing cap bolts to 37 ft. lbs.
13. Final tighten cap bolts an additional 77°.
14. Ensure crankshaft end play clearance is .002–.008 inch.

CRANKSHAFT SEAL

REPLACE

1. Relieve belt tension by rotating drive belt tensioner using serpentine belt tensioner unloader tool No. J39914, or equivalent.
2. Remove belt from righthand idler pulley.
3. Release tool and relieve spring tension.
4. Remove belt from tensioner.
5. Raise and support vehicle, then remove righthand front tire and wheel assembly.
6. Remove righthand engine splash side.
7. Remove wheelhouse liner.
8. Remove crankshaft balancer mounting bolt and washer
9. Remove crankshaft balancer using crankshaft balancer remover tool No.

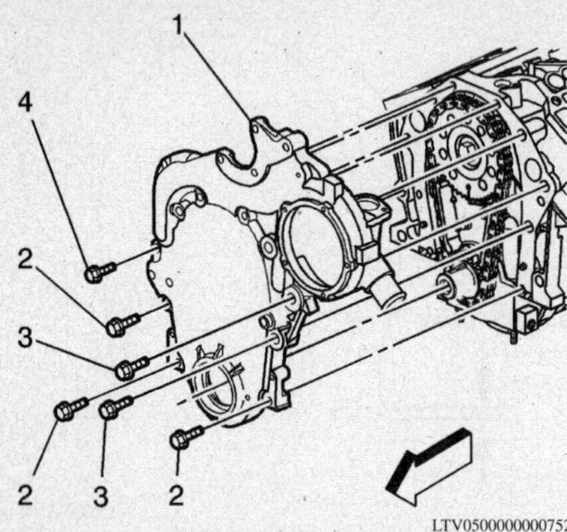

Fig. 19 Front cover tightening sequence

J41816-A and puller end protector tool No. EN46359, or equivalent, **Fig. 14. Do not use power-assisted tool with special tools.**

10. Pry crankshaft front oil seal out using suitable tool. **Do not damage engine front cover or crankshaft.**
11. Reverse procedure to install, noting the following:
    a. Install seal in front cover using cover aligner and seal installer tool No. J35468, or equivalent.
    b. Apply suitable crankshaft balancer keyway.
    c. Install crankshaft balancer using balancer and crank sprocket puller tool No. J29113, or equivalent, **Fig. 15. Do not use power-assisted tool with special tools.**
    d. **Torque** crankshaft balancer mounting bolt to 52 ft. lbs.
    e. Final tighten mounting bolt an additional 70°.

CRANKSHAFT REAR OIL SEAL

REPLACE

Removal

1. Remove transmission as outlined in **MOTOR's "Domestic Transmission, In-Vehicle Service" or "Transmission Service DVD."**
2. Remove mounting bolts and flywheel.
3. Pry crankshaft rear oil seal out using suitable tool.

Installation

Do not apply or use any oil lubrication on crankshaft rear oil seal or seal installer tool.

Do not touch the oil seal sealing lip once the protective sleeve is removed.

The new design is a reverse style as opposed to what has been used in the past. THIS SIDE OUT has been stamped into the seal, **Fig. 25.**

1. Carefully remove new crankshaft rear oil seal protection sleeve.
2. Install crankshaft rear oil seal onto rear main seal installer tool No. J34686, or equivalent, sliding seal over mandrel using twisting motion until seal back bottoms squarely against tool collar.
3. Align tool and crankshaft dowel pins.
4. Attach tool to the crankshaft hand tight, or **torque** mounting screws to 45 inch lbs.
5. Turn tool T-handle and push seal into bore until collar is tight against block. Ensure seal is seated properly.
6. Loosen handle, then remove mounting screws and tool.

OIL PAN

REPLACE

1. Recover refrigerant as outlined in "Air Conditioning" chapter.
2. Remove serpentine drive belt as outlined under "Serpentine Drive Belt."
3. Raise and support vehicle.
4. Remover mounting nut and air conditioning compressor hose.
5. Disconnect compressor electrical connector.
6. Remove and discard seal washers. Cap compressor and hose.
7. Remove mounting bolts, spacer bracket and compressor, **Fig. 26.**
8. Remove mounting bolts and engine-to-transmission brace.
9. Disconnect starter motor solenoid positive terminal nut and electrical wires, then the S terminal nut and electrical wire
10. Remove mounting bolt and torque converter cover.
11. Remove mounting bolts and starter motor.
12. **On models equipped with AWD,** remove transfer case as outlined in **MOTOR's "Domestic Transmission, In-Vehicle Service" or "Transmission Service DVD."**
13. **On models equipped with FWD,** remove intermediate shaft as outlined in "Front Wheel Drive" section.
14. **On all models,** drain engine oil into suitable container.
15. Remove side and sealing surface mounting bolts, then the oil pan, **Fig. 27.**
16. Reverse procedure to install, noting the following:
    a. If rear main bearing cap and front cover have not been removed, do not apply additional sealant.
    b. Apply suitable sealer to both sides of crankshaft rear main bearing cap, **Fig. 28,** and where engine front cover meets engine block.
    c. **Torque** air conditioning mounting bolt No. 5 to 37 ft. lbs.
    d. **Torque** air conditioning mounting bolt No. 3 to 37 ft. lbs.
    e. **Torque** air conditioning mounting bolt No. 4 to 37 ft. lbs.

OIL PUMP

REPLACE

1. Remove oil pan as outlined in "Oil Pan, Replace."

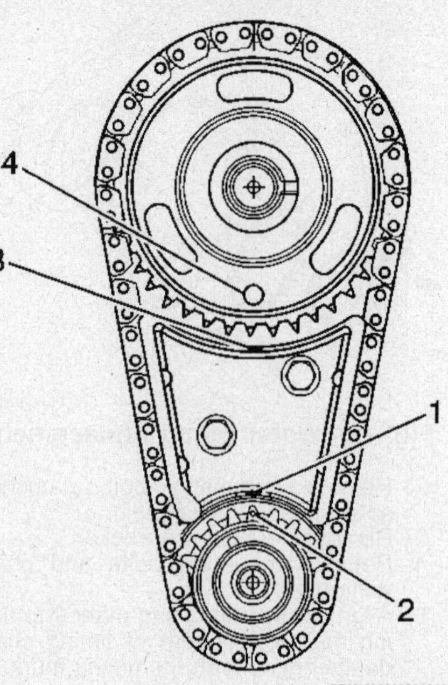

Fig. 20 Camshaft & timing chain timing marks

2. Remove mounting bolt, oil pump and oil pump driveshaft.
3. Reverse procedure to install.

OIL PUMP SERVICE

Disassemble

1. Remove driveshaft and retainer.
2. Remove mounting bolts and cover.
3. Remove drive and driven gears.
4. Remove pin and pressure regulator valve spring. **Spring is under pressure.**

Inspection

Refer to "Oil Pump" in "Engine Rebuilding Specifications" chapter for specifications.

1. Inspect pump housing and cover for: Cracks or casting imperfections; scoring and damaged threads. **Do not repair pump housing. Replace pump housing.**
2. Inspect oil pump gears for scoring and excessive wear.
3. Inspect idler shaft for looseness or scoring. If shaft is loose or damaged, replace oil pump.
4. Inspect drive gear shaft for looseness or scoring.
5. Inspect pressure regulator valve for: scoring and sticking. Burrs may be removed using suitable fine oil stone.
6. Inspect pressure regulator valve spring for: loss of tension and bending
7. Inspect suction pipe for looseness. If suction pipe is loose, bent or has been removed, replace pump body cover and suction pipe.

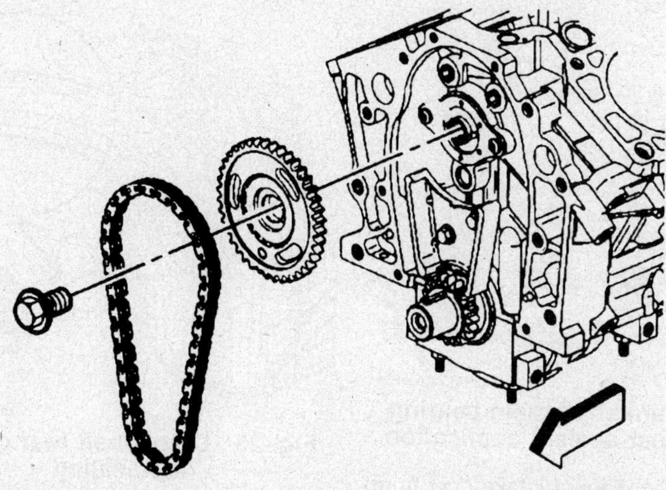

Fig. 21 Timing chain & camshaft replacement

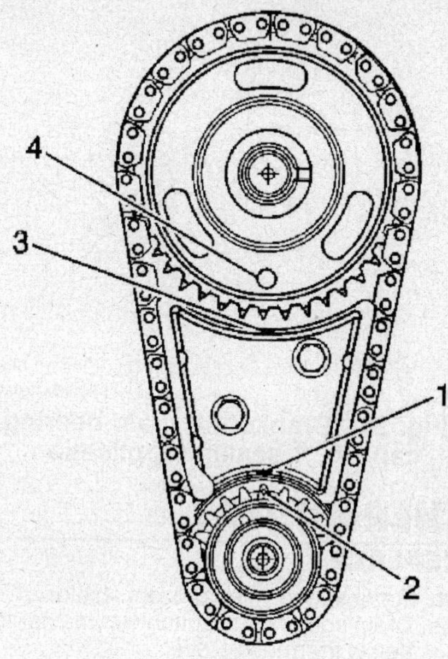

1. Dampener Timing Mark, Lower
2. Crankshaft Timing Mark
3. Dampener Timing Mark, Upper
4. Camshaft Gear Timing Mark

LTV0500000000753

Fig. 22 Timing chain alignment

8. Inspect screen for broken wire mesh or screen.
9. Measure oil pump gear lash in several places.
10. Measure oil pump housing gear pocket.
11. Measure oil pump gears.
12. Measure oil pump gear side clearance.

Assemble

Lubricate all the internal oil pump components using suitable engine oil.

1. Install gears.
2. Install cover and tighten mounting bolts.
3. Install pressure regulator valve, spring and cotter pin. **Ensure cotter pin is properly secured.**
4. Apply suitable seal to new suction pipe.
5. Tap pipe in place using oil suction pipe installer tool No. J22144, or equivalent, suitable plastic hammer and .

BELT TENSION DATA

This engine is equipped with a single serpentine drive belt. Belt tension is maintained by a spring loaded, automatic tensioner.

SERPENTINE DRIVE BELT

Belt Routing

Refer to **Fig. 29** for serpentine drive belt routing.

Belt Replacement

1. Loosen air cleaner intake duct clamps and remove Positive Crankcase Ventilation (PCV) fresh air pipe.
2. Remove air cleaner intake duct from Mass Air Flow (MAF) sensor and throttle body.
3. Disconnect MAF sensor electrical connector.
4. Remove mounting bolt and air cleaner assembly.
5. Relieve belt tension by rotating drive belt tensioner using serpentine belt tensioner unloader tool No. J39914, or equivalent.
6. Remove belt from righthand idler pulley.
7. Release tool and relieve spring tension.
8. Remove belt from tensioner.
9. **If vehicle is not to be raised and supported for additional work,** support front of engine using suitable wood block between floor jack and bottom of the engine oil pan bottom.
10. **If vehicle is to be raised and supported for additional work,** support engine using universal engine support fixture tool No, J28467, or equivalent, as outlined under "Engine Mount, Replace."
11. **On all models,** remove righthand engine mount to bracket bolts and frame rail nuts.
12. Remove righthand engine mount.
13. Remove drive belt from pulleys.
14. Reverse procedure to install, noting the following:
    a. **Torque** air cleaner assembly mounting bolt to 89 inch lbs.
    b. **Torque** air cleaner intake duct clamps to 35 inch lbs.

Tensioner Replacement

1. Remove serpentine drive belt.
2. Remove mounting bolt and tensioner.
3. Reverse procedure to install.

COOLING SYSTEM BLEED

The vehicle must be level when filling the cooling system.

1. Ensure lefthand radiator end tank drain valve is closed and engine block drain plug install.
2. Open water pump tower air bleed screw.
3. Slowly add suitable amount of antifreeze and clean water to surge tank.
4. As coolant begins to seep from air bleed, close air bleed screw.
5. Add coolant until at least 5.28 quarts is added to cooling system.
6. Start and run at idle, then add remaining coolant.
7. Install surge tank cap.
8. Run and cycle engine from idle to 3000 RPM in 30 second intervals until the engine cooling fans come ON.
9. Return engine to idle, idle for 30 seconds, then turn engine OFF.
10. Allow vehicle to cool.
11. Adjust coolant in surge tank until level is approximately one inch above top of Cold Fill Range at surge tank seam.
12. Install surge tank cap.

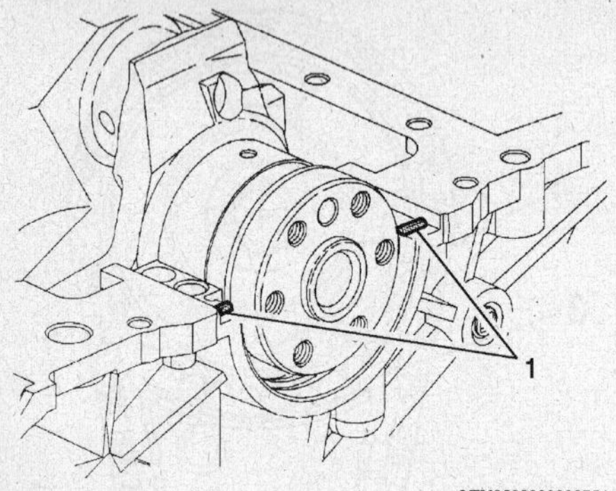

Fig. 23 Crankshaft main bearing cap No. 4 sealant application

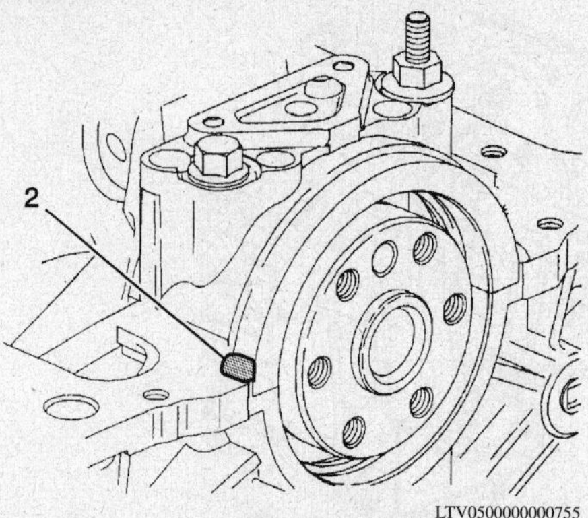

Fig. 24 Crankshaft main bearing cap No. 4 rear sealant application

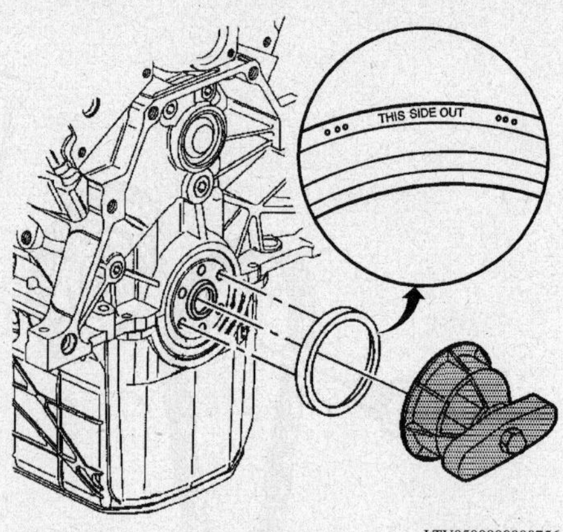

Fig. 25 Crankshaft rear oil seal installation

THERMOSTAT

REPLACE

1. Remove fuel injector sight shield.
2. Drain coolant into suitable container to below thermostat level.
3. Remove holddown and battery.
4. Remove mounting bolt and air conditioning evaporator outlet hose.
5. Remove Underhood Fuse Block (UHFB) cover.
6. Remove mounting nut, then the positive battery cable and Electronic Power Steering (EPS) wire from UHFB B+ terminal.
7. Remove retainer and engine wire harness connector from battery box.
8. Loosen mounting bolts and clips, then remove UHFB from housing.
9. Disconnect forward lamp harness and UHFB connectors from UHFB and housing.
10. Position electrical harnesses/ connectors and battery cables aside.
11. Remove mounting bolts and lift coolant surge tank aside.
12. Remove battery box mounting bolts and separate air inlet duct.
13. Remove battery box.
14. Remove mounting nuts and exhaust crossover pipe.
15. Remove radiator hose from thermostat housing.
16. Remove mounting bolts, thermostat housing and gasket.
17. Remove thermostat.
18. Reverse procedure to instal, noting the following:
    a. Apply suitable RTV sealer to thermostat housing mounting bolt threads.
    b. Maintain approximately .25 inch between thermostat housing and exhaust crossover pipe.

WATER PUMP

REPLACE

1. Drain cooling system into suitable container to below water pump level.
2. Loosen water pump pulley mounting bolts
3. Loosen air cleaner intake duct clamps and remove Positive Crankcase Ventilation (PCV) fresh air pipe.
4. Remove air cleaner intake duct from Mass Air Flow (MAF) sensor and throttle body.
5. Disconnect MAF sensor electrical connector.
6. Remove mounting bolt and air cleaner assembly.
7. Relieve belt tension by rotating drive belt tensioner using serpentine belt tensioner unloader tool No. J39914, or equivalent.
8. Remove belt from righthand idler pulley.
9. Release tool and relieve spring tension.
10. Remove belt from tensioner.
11. Remove mounting bolts and water pump pulley.
12. Remove mounting bolts, water pump and gasket. **Fig. 16.**
13. Reverse procedure to install.

RADIATOR

REPLACE

1. Drain coolant into suitable container.
2. **On Equinox models,** proceed as follows:
    a. Remove tie bar push-in retainers and fascia to fender mounting screws inside wheelhouse.
    b. Remove fascia to wheelhouse liner and vehicle push-in retainers.
    c. Pull fascia away from vehicle, near headlamps, to disconnect radiator grille strap to headlamp retainer.
    d. Slide fascia off vehicle and disconnect fog lamp from housing.
3. **On Torrent models,** proceed as follows:
    a. Remove three front fascia lower retainers.
    b. Remove two mounting bolts.
    c. Remove three upper retainers.
    d. Remove front fascia.
    e. Disconnect electrical connectors.
4. **On all models,** drain cooling system into suitable container.
5. Remove battery box air inlet duct.
6. Remove Condenser Radiator Fan Module (CRFM) closeout panel retainers from condenser.
7. Remove mounting bolts and position fan aside.
8. Remove mounting bolts and energy absorber.
9. Remove mounting bolts and impact bar.
10. Remove mounting bolts and CRFM brackets.
11. Remove clamps, then the radiator inlet and outlet hoses.
12. Disconnect radiator transmission cooler lines.
13. Remove condenser to radiator mounting bolts.
14. Position condenser and radiator assembly to righthand side for front impact bar bracket.
15. Separate condenser and remove radiator.
16. Reverse procedure to install.

FUEL PUMP

REPLACE

Ensure fuel tank is less than ¼ full.

1. Relieve fuel pressure as outlined under "Precautions."
2. Raise and support vehicle.
3. **On models equipped with AWD,** proceed as follows:
    a. Remove rear propeller shaft as outlined in "Rear Axle & Suspension" section.
    b. Remove rear drive module propeller shaft guard mounting bolts.
4. **On all models,** remove mounting nuts, then separate catalytic converter and exhaust system pipe. Discard gasket
5. Separate hangers' rubber isolators and remove exhaust system.
6. Disconnect EVAP canister fresh air hose/pipe from fuel tank air hose/pipe.
7. Disconnect EVAP canister vent and purge hose/pipes.
8. Remove mounting nuts and EVAP canister, then disconnect EVAP vent solenoid electrical connector
9. Disconnect fuel tank chassis fuel supply line.
10. Disconnect fuel tank fuel filler tube, EVAP vent hose and fresh air hose.
11. Disconnect fuel tank electrical connector and remove electrical connector retainer from rear frame.

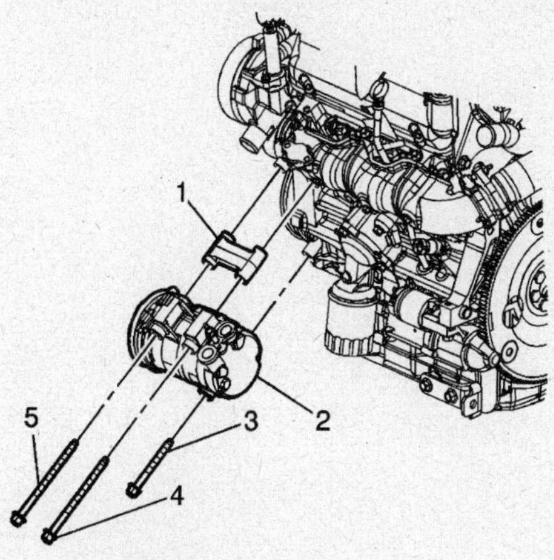

Fig. 26 Air conditioning compressor replacement

12. Support fuel tank, then remove mounting bolts and straps. **Do not bend fuel tank straps. Do not lower rear frame.**
13. Lower and remove fuel tank.
14. Disconnect EVAP vent line quick connect.
15. Remove fuel pump module retaining ring using fuel sender lock ring tool No. J39765-A, or equivalent, and suitable 12 inches, or longer, ratchet/breaker bar.
16. Disconnect secondary level sensor electrical connector and suction port tube.
17. Disconnect tank orientation tabs by lifting pump module up slightly, then rotate module 45° and remove it from tank. Discard seal
18. Remove secondary fuel pump module.
19. Disconnect primary fuel pump module and fuel tank pressure sensor electrical connectors.
20. Turn fuel sender lock ring counterclockwise using fuel sender lock ring wrench tool No. J45722, or equivalent, and suitable, long breaker-bar.
21. Disconnect fuel tank feed and vent lines.
22. Disconnect tank orientation tabs by lifting pump module up slightly, then rotate module 45° and remove it from tank. Discard seal
23. Reverse procedure to install, noting the following:

FUEL FILTER

REPLACE

The fuel filter is located on the primary fuel module, **Fig. 30.**

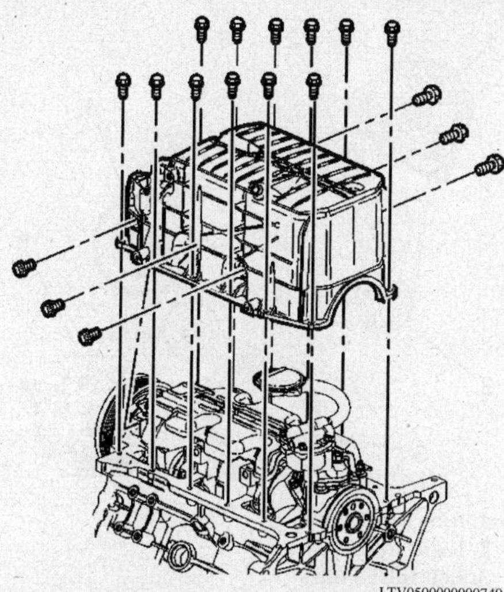

Fig. 27 Oil pan replacement

TECHNICAL SERVICE BULLETINS

External Oil Leak

2005

On some of these models there may be an external oil leak.

This condition may be caused by the crankshaft rear main oil seal.

To correct this condition, install revised crankshaft rear main oil seal (part No. 12592195) as outlined under "Crankshaft Rear Oil Seal, Replace."

Coolant Odor Under Hood

2005

Some of these models built before VIN 56172604 may have an objectionable odor coming from under the hood.

This condition may be caused by engine coolant.

To correct this condition, flush the cooling system and replace coolant hoses as follows:

1. Ensure there is at least ¼ tank of fuel before starting procedure.
2. Open radiator drain valve using suitable flat-bladed screwdriver and drain coolant into suitable container.
3. Remove surge tank cap and close radiator drain valve.
4. Raise and support vehicle.
5. Remove engine lefthand block coolant drain plug and drain coolant into suitable container. Install drain plug.
6. Remove righthand engine block heater or plug and drain coolant into suitable container. Install block heater or plug.
7. Dispose of coolant into sanitary sewer, not storm drain, etc.
8. Lower vehicle.

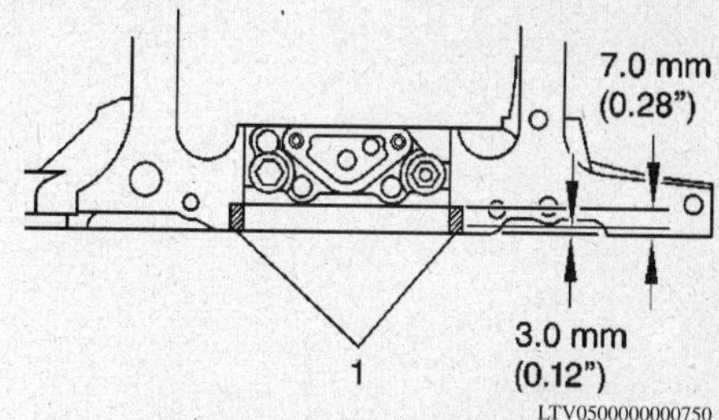

Fig. 28 Rear main bearing cap sealer application

9. Open water pump tower air bleed screw.
10. Mix cleaner (from upper part of can) in approximately three quarts of water. **Do not substitute other cleaners for Prestone Heavy Duty Cooling System Cleaner (part No. 12346500). This cleaner is in powder form and contains neutralizer.**
11. Pour mixture into surge tank. **Do not spill solution on vehicle's finish.**
12. Fill system with plain water. As water begins to seep from air bleed, close screw.
13. If surge tank fills before system, lift righthand side of vehicle and force trapped air toward air bleed.
14. Install surge tank cap and turn heater ON.
15. Run engine at fast idle for 40–60 minutes.
16. Stop and allow engine to cool.
17. Repeat previous steps using bottom part of cleaner can and run engine for 10 minutes.
18. Repeat previous steps using plain water and run engine for five minutes.
19. Completely drain system as previously outlined.
20. Remove surge tank and battery box.
21. Remove upper and lower radiator hoses, then the inlet and outlet heater core hoses.
22. Remove inlet surge tank vent hose.
23. Install new inlet surge tank vent, heater core and radiator hoses.
24. Install battery box.
25. Flush thoroughly and install coolant surge tank.
26. Fill cooling system with suitable coolant mixture. As water begins to seep from air bleed, close screw.
27. If surge tank fills before system, lift righthand side of vehicle and force trapped air toward air bleed. Vac-N-Fill tool No. GE-47716, or equivalent, may also be used to remove trapped air. **Do not use tool for cleaner or neutralizer fills.**
28. Run and cycle engine from idle to 3,000 RPM in 30 second intervals until cooling fans come on.
29. Idle engine for 30 seconds and then turn it OFF
30. Allow vehicle to cool.
31. Adjust surge tank coolant level to one inch above top of Cold Fill Range.
32. Install surge tank cap.

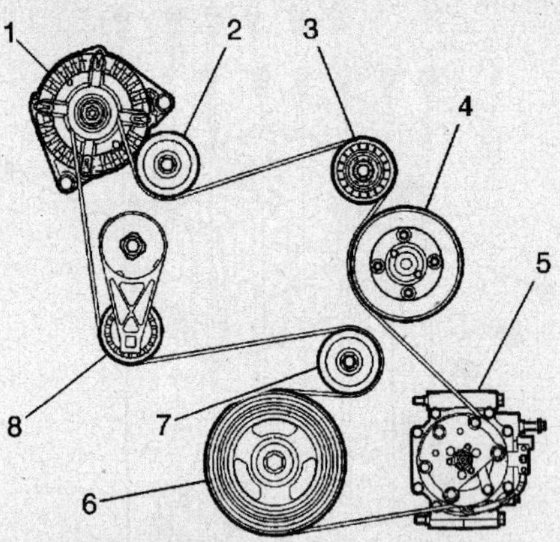

1. Alternator Pulley
2. Right Idler Pulley
3. Left Idler Pulley
4. Water Pump Pulley
5. Air Conditioning Compressor
6. Crankshaft Pulley
7. Lower Idler Pulley
8. Tensioner Pulley

LTV0500000000724

Fig. 29 Serpentine belt routing

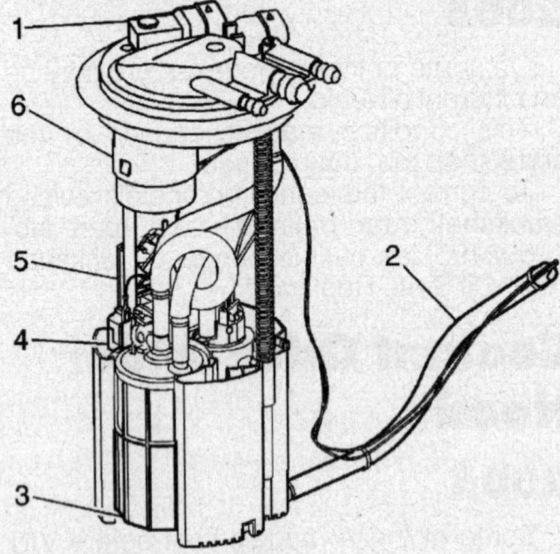

1. Fuel Pressure Sensor
2. Fuel Transfer Pipe
3. Fuel Filter
4. Fuel Level Sensor
5. Fuel Pressure Regulator
6. Fill Limiter Vent Valve

LTV0500000000757

Fig. 30 Exploded view of fuel module

TIGHTENING SPECIFICATIONS

Year	Component	Torque Ft. Lbs.
2005–06	Air Cleaner	89①
	Air Cleaner Intake Duct	35①
	Air Conditioning Compressor	⑦
	Air Conditioning Compressor Hose	16
	Air Deflector	18①
	Alternator	18
	Alternator Brace	18
	Battery Box, Inside	11
	Battery Box, Outside	89①
	Battery Cable	11
	Battery Holddown	11
	Camshaft Sprocket	103
	Camshaft Thrust Plate	89①
	Catalytic Converter	27
	CKP Sensor	98①
	CMP Sensor	89①
	Condenser	80①
	Connecting Rod	⑧
	Control Arm Ball Joint	30
	Coolant Surge Tank	53①
	Crankshaft Damper	⑤
	CRFM Bracket	89①
	Cylinder Head	②
	ECT Sensor	17
	Electronic Power Steering (EPS) Connector	11
	Engine Mount	81
	Engine Mount Bracket	41
	Engine To Transaxle Brace	37
	Evaporator Outlet Hose	11
	Exhaust Crossover Pipe	18
	Exhaust Manifold	12
	Exhaust System	27
	Exhaust Manifold Heat Shield	89①
	Fan	80①
	Frame-To-Body	114
	Front Cover	④
	Front Wheelhouse Liner	35①
	Fuel Filler Tube	44①
	Fuel Pipe	21
	Fuel Rail	89①
	Fuel Tank Strap	18
	Ground	18
	Heater Inlet Pipe	18
	Heater Outlet Pipe	89①
	Impact Bar	18
	Intake Manifold, Lower	③
	Intake Manifold, Upper	18
	Main Bearings	⑧

TIGHTENING SPECIFICATIONS—Continued

Year	Component	Torque Ft. Lbs.
2005–06	Oil Pan, Flange	18
	Oil Pan, Side	37
	Oil Pump	30
	Oil Pump Cover	89①
	PCV Fresh Air Tube	89①
	Rocker Arm	31
	Spark Plug Wire Retainer Support	18
	Stabilizer Bar Link	48
	Starter Motor	32
	Steering Intermediate Shaft	25
	Surge Tank	80①
	Thermal Bypass Fitting	106①
	Thermostat Housing	18
	Throttle Body, Bolt	89①
	Throttle Body, Stud	53①
	Tie Rod End	⑥
	Timing Chain Dampener	15
	Torque Converter	44
	Torque Converter Cover	71①
	Transfer Case	44
	Transaxle To Engine	55
	Transmission Mount	81
	Transmission Mount-To-Transmission	37
	UHFB Connector	53①
	Valve Cover	89①
	Valve Lifter Guide	89①
	Water Pump	89①
	Water Pump Pulley	19

① — Inch lbs.

② — Refer to "Cylinder Head, Replace" for tightening specifications and sequence.

③ — Refer to "Intake Manifold Replace, Lower." for tightening specifications and sequence.

④ — Refer to "Front Cover, Replace" for tightening specifications and sequence.

⑤ — Refer to "Crankshaft Damper, Replace," for tightening specifications and sequence.

⑥ — **Torque** to 18 ft. lbs, then final tighten an additional 90°.

⑦ — Refer to "Oil Pan, Replace," for tightening specifications and sequence.

⑧ — Refer to "Main & Rod Bearings" for tightening specifications and sequence.

Rear Axle & Suspension

NOTE: On Air Bag Equipped Models, Refer To "Air Bag System Precautions" Located In The Front Of This Manual For System Disarming & Arming Procedures.

NOTE: Prior To Performing Any Service Operations Listed In This Section, Consult The "Technical Service Bulletins" Section For Related Information.

INDEX

DESCRIPTION

The rear suspension system used on this vehicle is the independent link type. The rear suspension contains the following components: support assembly; coil springs; stabilizer shaft, insulators, and stabilizer links; toe link; upper and lower control arms; trailing arm; knuckles wheel bearing/hub and shock absorbers.

On models equipped with AWD, the Rear Drive Module (RDM) consists of an aluminum housing which contains a gerotor fluid pump, clutch pack and differential. It has a common fluid reservoir.

REAR AXLE SHAFT

REPLACE

1. Raise and support vehicle, then remove tire and wheel assembly.
2. Remove and discard wheel drive shaft spindle nut.
3. Remove mounting nut while holding link using suitable wrench and disconnect stabilizer link from control arm.
4. Support control arm using suitable jack stand.
5. Remove shock absorber lower mounting bolt and nut.
6. Remove toe link mounting nut, bolt and washer.
7. Loosen lower suspension jounce bumper mounting nut. **Do not remove mounting nut.**
8. Remove lower control arm-to-suspension knuckle mounting bolt and nut.
9. Slowly relieve spring tension by slowing lower support stand. Remove coil spring.
10. Loosen upper control arm-to-suspension knuckle nut. **Do not remove mounting nut.**
11. Disconnect spindle from wheel hub and bearing by tapping suitable wood block against wheel drive shaft spindle using suitable hammer.
12. Rotate suspension knuckle upward and secure using heavy mechanics wire, or equivalent.
13. Disconnect wheel drive shaft inner tripot joint from Rear Drive Module (RDM) using rear wheel drive shaft removal tool No. J453341 and slide hammer with adapter tool No. J2619-A, or equivalents, **Fig. 1.**
14. Remove wheel drive shaft. Discard retaining ring.
15. Reverse procedure to install, noting the following:
    a. Guide wheel drive shaft tripot joint squarely onto output shaft using seal protector tool No. J44394, or equivalent, **Fig. 2.**
    b. Remove tool after splined end passes oil seal.
    c. Ensure tripot joint is fully seated on output shaft.

DIFFERENTIAL CARRIER

REPLACE

1. Raise and support vehicle.
2. Remove mounting nuts, then separate catalytic converter and exhaust system pipes.
3. Separate hangers' rubber isolators and remove exhaust system.
4. Remove rear wheel drive shafts as outlined under "Rear Axle Shaft, Replace."
5. Mark propeller shaft and Rear Drive Module input flanges for installation alignment.
6. Support propeller shaft rear using suitable jack stand.
7. Remove propeller shaft flange mounting bolts.
8. Mark Power Take-Off (PTO) unit flange-to-propeller shaft constant velocity (CV) joint for installation alignment.
9. Support propeller shaft front using suitable jack stand.
10. Remove propeller shaft CV joint mounting bolts.
11. Support propeller shaft, then remove support bearing mounting bolts and propeller shaft.
12. Support and secure RDM with suitable stand.
13. Remove link to stabilizer bar nut and clamp bolts, the disconnect ball studs and remove stabilizer bar.
14. Remove RDM bracket-to-bushing mounting nut and bolt.
15. Remove mounting nut and bolt, then the RDM mounting bracket, **Fig. 3.**
16. Remove mounting nuts and bolts, then the RDM, **Fig. 4.** Discard mounting bolts and nuts.
17. Reverse procedure to install.

PROPELLER SHAFT

REPLACE

1. Place transaxle in neutral, then raise and support vehicle.
2. Mark propeller shaft to Rear Drive Module (RDM) flange for installation alignment.
3. Remove mounting bolts and underbody guard loop.
4. Support propeller shaft at RDM.
5. Remove propeller shaft yoke to RDM flange mounting bolts, **Fig. 5.**
6. Mark Power Take-Off (PTO) unit flange-to-propeller shaft constant velocity (CV) joint for installation alignment.
7. Support propeller shaft at PTO unit using suitable jack stand.
8. Remove propeller shaft to the PTO flange mounting bolts, **Fig. 6.**
9. Support propeller shaft at support bearing and remove support bearing mounting bolts.

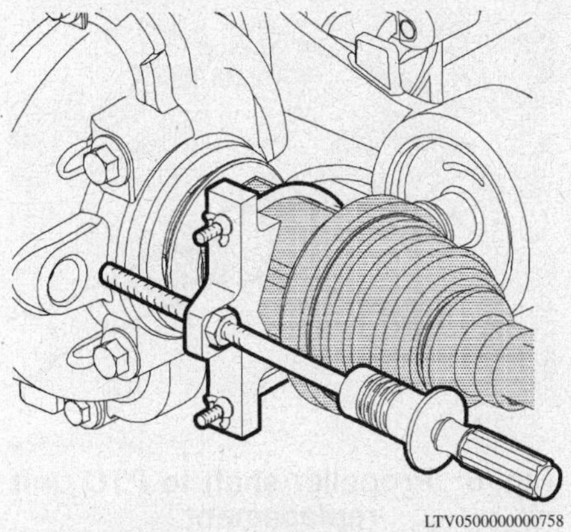

LTV0500000000758

Fig. 1 Rear axle shaft removal

10. Disconnect PTO unit constant velocity joint and remove propeller shaft rearward.
11. Reverse procedure to install.

HUB & BEARING

REPLACE

1. Release parking brake, then raise and support vehicle.
2. Remove tire and wheel assembly, then the brake drum.
3. **On models equipped with AWD,** remove wheel drive shaft spindle nut.
4. **On all models,** disconnect wheel speed sensor electrical connector.
5. **On models equipped with AWD,** support wheel drive shaft using suitable heavy mechanic's wire.
6. **On all models,** remove mounting bolts and wheel bearing/hub.
7. Reverse procedure to install.

SHOCK ABSORBER

REPLACE

1. Raise and support vehicle.
2. Remove shock absorber lower mounting bolt, **Fig. 7.**
3. If removing righthand shock absorber, remove splash shield.
4. Remove upper mounting bolt and nut, then the shock absorber, **Fig. 8.**
5. Reverse procedure to install.

COIL SPRING

REPLACE

1. Raise and support vehicle, then remove tire and wheel assembly.
2. Remove stabilizer link to lower control arm nut while holding link using suitable wrench.
3. Remove trailing arm bracket to underbody mounting bolts.
4. Support lower control arm using suitable screw-type jack stand.
5. Compress coil spring using jack stand.
6. Remove shock lower mounting bolt.
7. Loosen lower control arm to support frame mounting bolt.
8. Remove lower control arm to knuckle mounting nut and bolt.
9. Lower control arm, unload and remove coil spring.

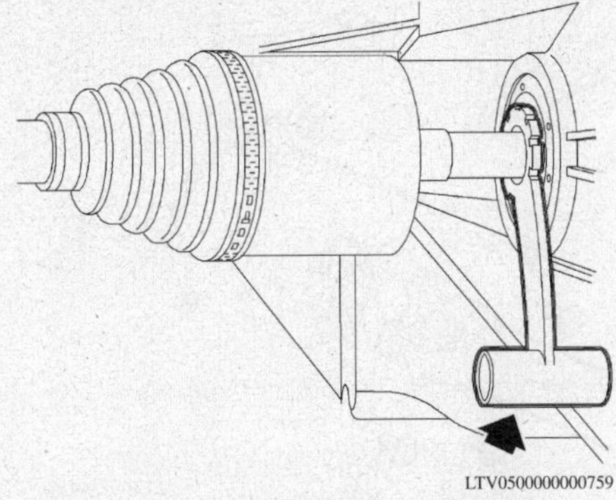

LTV0500000000759

Fig. 2 Drive shaft installation

10. Reverse procedure to install, noting the following:
    a. Fully seat top and bottom coil spring insulators to spring.
    b. Spray suitable silicon lubricant on insulators to aid in installation.

CONTROL ARM

REPLACE

Lower

1. Raise and support vehicle, then remove tire and wheel assembly.
2. Remove stabilizer link to lower control arm nut while holding link with suitable wrench.
3. Remove trailing arm bracket to underbody bolts.
4. Support lower control arm using suitable jack stand.
5. Remove shock absorber lower mounting bolt and jounce bumper nut at lower control arm.
6. Loosen lower control arm to support frame bolt.
7. Remove lower control arm to knuckle mounting nut and bolt.
8. Unload and remove coil spring by lower control arm.
9. Remove jounce bumper.
10. Remove support mounting nut and bolt, then the lower control arm, **Fig. 9.**
11. Reverse procedure to install.

Upper

1. Raise and support vehicle.
2. Remove trailing arm bracket to body mounting bolts.
3. Remove ABS brake harness from upper control arm.
4. Remove upper control arm to knuckle mounting nut and bolt.
5. Remove upper control arm to support mounting nut and bolt, **Fig. 10.**
6. Remove upper control arm.
7. Reverse procedure to install.

CONTROL ARM BUSHING

REPLACE

1. Remove lower control arm as outlined under "Control Arm, Replace."
2. Remove bushing using rear control arm bushing remover tool No. J 45097, or equivalent, **Fig. 11.**
3. Reverse procedure to install.

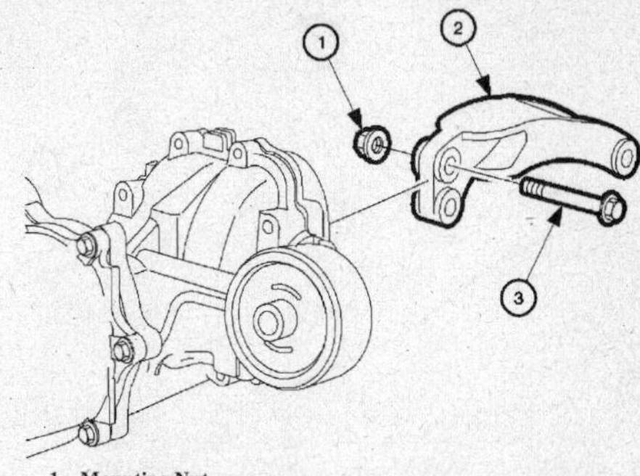

1. Mounting Nut
2. Mounting Bolt
3. RDM Mounting Bracket

LTV0500000000760

Fig. 3 RDM mounting bracket replacement

KNUCKLE

REPLACE

1. Release parking brake, then raise and support vehicle.
2. Remove tire and wheel assembly, then the brake drum.
3. **On models equipped with AWD,** remove wheel drive shaft spindle nut.
4. **On all models,** disconnect wheel speed sensor electrical connector.
5. **On models equipped with AWD,** support wheel drive shaft using suitable heavy mechanic's wire.
6. **On all models,** remove mounting bolts and wheel bearing/hub.
7. Remove upper and lower control arm to knuckle mounting bolts and nuts.
8. Remove toe link and trailing blade to knuckle mounting bolts and nuts.
9. Remove knuckle.
10. Reverse procedure to install, noting the following:
    a. Install all component to knuckle mounting bolts and nuts hand tight.
    b. Tighten knuckle to lower control arm bolt and nut.
    c. Tighten knuckle to upper control arm bolt and nut.
    d. Tighten knuckle to toe link bolt and nut.
    e. Tighten knuckle to trailing blade bolts.

TRAILING ARM

REPLACE

1. Raise and support vehicle.
2. Remove trailing arm bracket to body mounting bolts, **Fig. 12.**
3. Remove trailing arm bushing to bracket not nut and bolt
4. Remove park brake cable clip from trailing arm.
5. Remove trailing arm to knuckle mounting bolts, **Fig. 13.**
6. Remove trailing arm.
7. Reverse procedure to install.

LTV0500000000761

Fig. 4 RDM replacement

LTV0500000000762

Fig. 5 Propeller shaft to RDM replacement

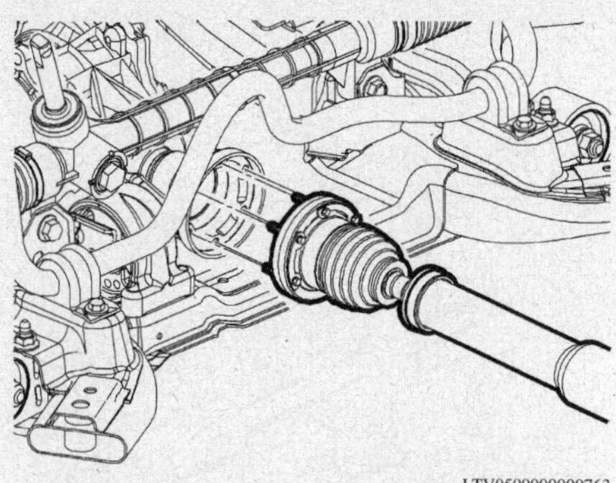
LTV0500000000763

Fig. 6 Propeller shaft to PTO unit replacement

STABILIZER SHAFT

REPLACE

1. Raise and support vehicle.
2. Remove ball shaft nut while holding shaft.
3. Remove stabilizer link to stabilizer bar nut.
4. Remove stabilizer bar clamp bolts.
5. Disconnect stabilizer bar from link ball studs, while removing stabilizer bar.
6. Reverse procedure to install.

TOE LINK

REPLACE

1. Raise and support vehicle.
2. Remove toe link to knuckle mounting nut and bolt.
3. Remove toe link to support mounting nut and bolt, **Fig. 14.**
4. Remove toe link.
5. Reverse procedure to install.

TECHNICAL SERVICE BULLETINS

Wheel Cover Rattle/ Click/Ticking

2005-06 EQUINOX w/16-INCH WHEEL COVER

On some of these models there may be a rattle/click/ticking type noise coming from the front or rear wheels. This condition is most apparent while at zero to 15 mph and is relative to wheel rotation.

This condition may be caused by hard contact between the inner edge of the wheel cover and the outer edge of the steel rim. This contact occurs when the ring comes out of its channel and separates from the wheel cover. In most cases, the delrin ring will be completely gone.

To correct, install insulators on the back side of all four wheel covers as follows:

1. Remove wheel covers.
2. Clean back side of each wheel cover using mild liquid detergent in distilled or deionized water solution.
3. Rinse each wheel cover with clean water.
4. Dry each wheel cover using compressed air or a clean, lint-free, nonabrasive cloth.
5. After wheel covers are completely dry, each wheel cover should be wiped with isopropyl alcohol on clean, lint-free, non-abrasive cloth and apply Adhesion Promoter (part No. 12378462), or equivalent, at insulator locations. Insulator location is at center of each spoke in groove.
6. Place two insulators at location where divider prevents one from going in center. Peel red non-stick backing off of insulator.
7. Carefully place insulator onto wheel cover so that area under lip is resting against corner of inside edge of wheel cover lip. This should place insulator flush with outside edge of wheel cover.
8. Press down firmly on insulator to ensure adhesive is bonding to wheel cover.
9. Place another insulator in next location by repeating.
10. There should be an insulator at each spoke location.

Growl, Groan, Moan And/Or Shudder, Binding During Parking Lot Maneuvers

2005

On some of these models with AWD built before VIN 56090271 there may be a growl, groan, moan noise and/or binding from the rear of the vehicle while making low speed parking lot maneuvers.

This condition may be caused by rear differential drum and clutch assembly. **Do not replace the complete differential/Rear Drive Module (RDM).**

To correct this condition, replace the rear differential drum and clutch assembly (part No. 15235312) as follows:

1. Raise and support vehicle.
2. Remove mounting bolts and propeller shaft underbody guard loop.
3. Mark propeller shaft flange-to-pinion flange relationship at RDM for installation alignment.
4. Remove mounting bolts and position propeller shaft aside.
5. Place suitable container under RDM, remove drain plug and drain fluid.
6. Remove mounting nut using pinion flange holder and remover tool Nos. J08614-A and J44873-2, or equivalents, then the pinion flange.
7. Remove mounting bolts and RDM housing cover.
8. Remove clutch drum from housing cover, then the filter and locating pins. **Do not gouge housing cover and RDM sealing surfaces.**
9. Remove all traces of sealer from housing cover and RDM sealing surfaces.
10. Clean housing cover and RDM sealing surfaces with denatured alcohol, or equivalent, and dry with clean, lint free cloth.
11. Inspect pinion flange sealing surface for wear or gouges; bolt threads for damage, and the pinion splines for worn or damaged splines.
12. Inspect dust deflector for cracks.
13. Inspect pinion flange seal, front and rear seals for tears, cuts and gouges on seals and sealing surfaces.
14. Install new filter (part No. 12569934) and locating pins.
15. Align new drum (part No. 15235312) clutches with pump and pump bushing.
16. Align pump and bushing using alignment tool No. J46607, or equivalent, until tool groove is flush with drum.
17. Remove tool. When properly engaged, clutch drum will be fully seated against clutch drum oil seal.
18. Install clutch drum to pinion shaft.
19. Apply continuous .098 inch bead of sealer No. 12346286, or equivalent, of equal height and width to RDM housing sealing surface.
20. Allow sealer to skin for five minutes.
21. Install seat clutch cover housing to RDM. **Do not use mounting bolts to draw cover to RDM.**
22. **Torque** clutch housing cover mounting bolts to 19 ft. lbs.

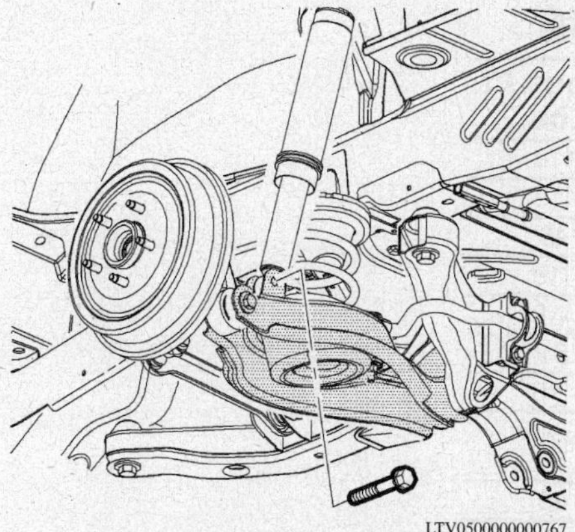

Fig. 7 Shock absorber lower mounting bolt replacement

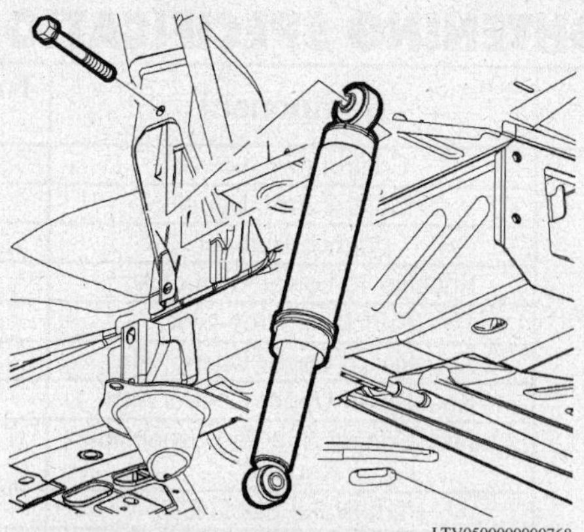

Fig. 8 Shock absorber upper mounting bolt replacement

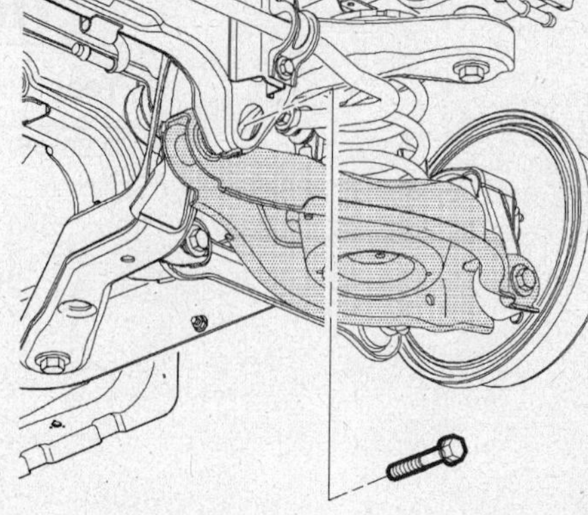

Fig. 9 Lower control arm replacement

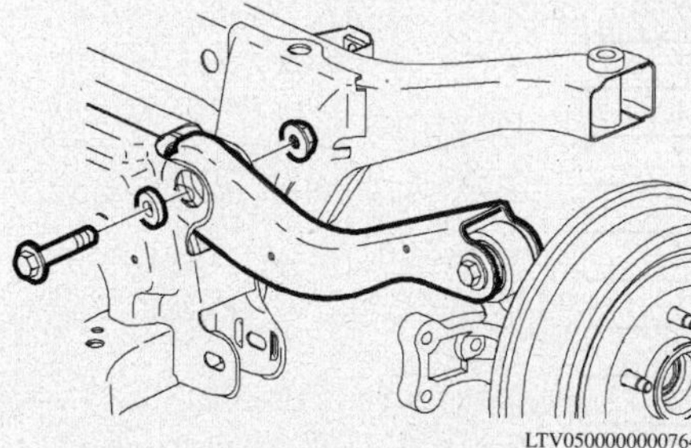

Fig. 10 Upper control arm replacement

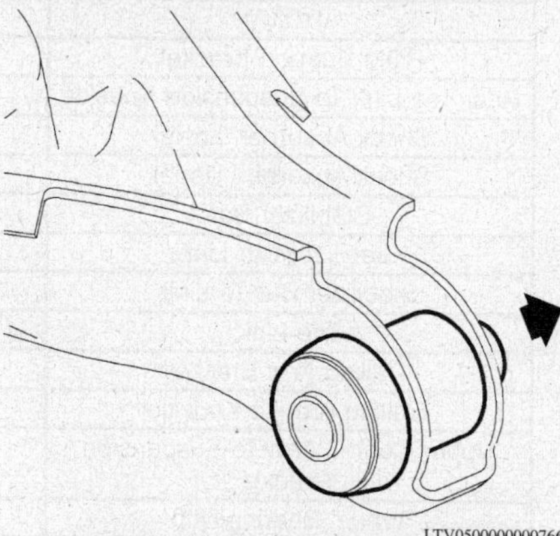

Fig. 11 Lower control arm bushing replacement

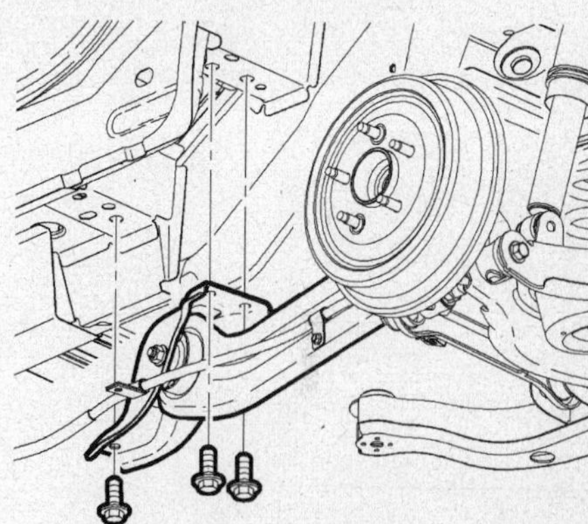

Fig. 12 Trailing arm to body replacement

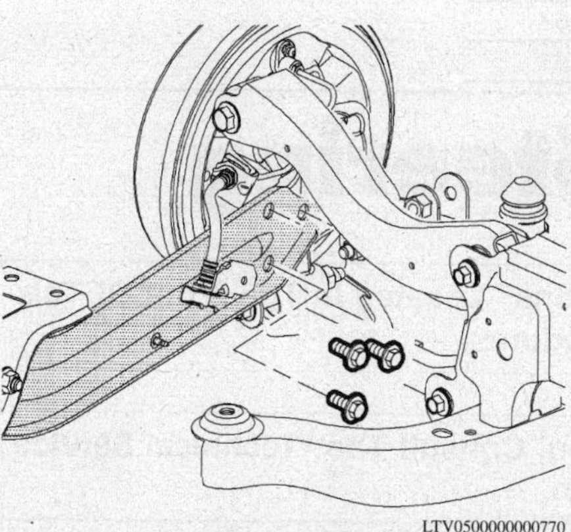

Fig. 13 Trailing arm to knuckle replacement

23. Install input flange to clutch shaft and replace pinion flange nut (part No. 12569951) to clutch shaft.
24. **Torque** pinion flange mounting nut to 150 ft. lbs., using pinion flange holder and remover tool No. J08614-A, or equivalent.
25. Clean threads and apply thread sealer No. 1234600, or equivalent, then install drain plug and **torque** it to 22 ft. lbs.
26. Remove RDM fill plug and fill RDM with suitable fluid.
27. Clean threads and apply thread sealer No. 12346004, or equivalent, then install fill plug and **torque** it to 26 ft. lbs.
28. Raise and support vehicle to point with wheels off ground, then start engine and place transmission in forward gear.
29. Slowly apply park brake until rear wheels stop rotating.
30. Carefully accelerate engine until rear wheels begin to rotate. **Do not exceed five seconds of park brake application while vehicle is in gear and engine is running.**
31. Continue allowing rear wheels to rotate for five seconds.
32. Release accelerator and apply brakes, then place transmission in park or neutral and turn engine OFF.
33. Alternatively, prime rear drive module by driving vehicle on flat, paved surface in tight, 360° circle for three consecutive revolutions at five mph.
34. Raise and support vehicle, then clean area and remove fluid fill plug.

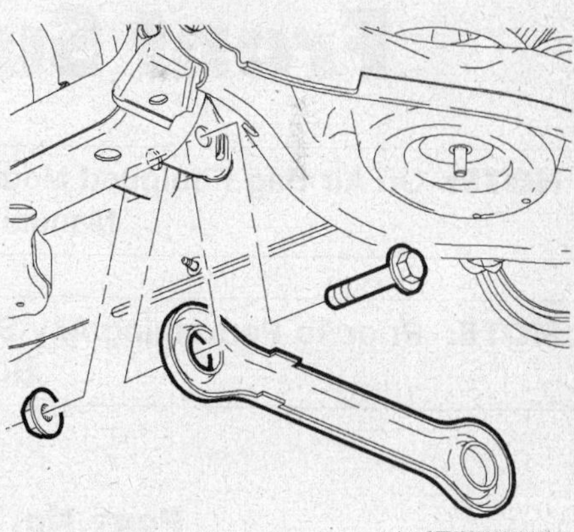

Fig. 14 Toe link replacement

35. Place 90° bend one inch for end of suitable length of heavy mechanics wire.
36. Place angled end into plug hole and rest wire squarely on threads.
37. Distance between bend and fluid level witness mark should be .32–.68 inch. Adjust fluid level.
38. **Torque** fill plug to 26 ft. lbs.

TIGHTENING SPECIFICATIONS

Year	Component	Torque Ft. Lbs.
2005–06	Control Arm, Lower	118
	Control Arm, Upper	118
	Jounce Bumper	46
	Knuckle To Lower Control Arm	118
	Knuckle To Toe Link	118
	Knuckle To Upper Control Arm	81
	Knuckle To Upper Control Arm	118
	Lower Control Arm-To-Suspension Knuckle	118
	Park Brake Cable Clip	18
	Propeller Shaft Guard Loop	19
	Propeller Shaft Support Bearing	19
	Propeller Shaft To PTO Unit	19
	Propeller Shaft To RDM	37
	RDM	77
	RDM Support Bracket	77
	Rear Toe Link To Suspension Knuckle	81
	Shock Absorber, Lower	77
	Shock Absorber, Upper	81
	Stabilizer Bar	52
	Stabilizer Bar Link	11
	Stabilizer Bar To Link	42
	Toe Link	118
	Trailing Arm Bracket	81
	Trailing Arm To Knuckle	118
	Upper Control Arm-To-Suspension Knuckle	100
	Wheel Bearing/Hub	62
	Wheel Drive Shaft Spindle	81

Front Suspension & Steering

NOTE: On Air Bag Equipped Models, Refer To "Air Bag System Precautions" Located In The Front Of This Manual For System Disarming & Arming Procedures.

NOTE: Prior To Performing Any Service Operations Listed In This Section, Consult The "Technical Service Bulletins" Section For Related Information.

INDEX

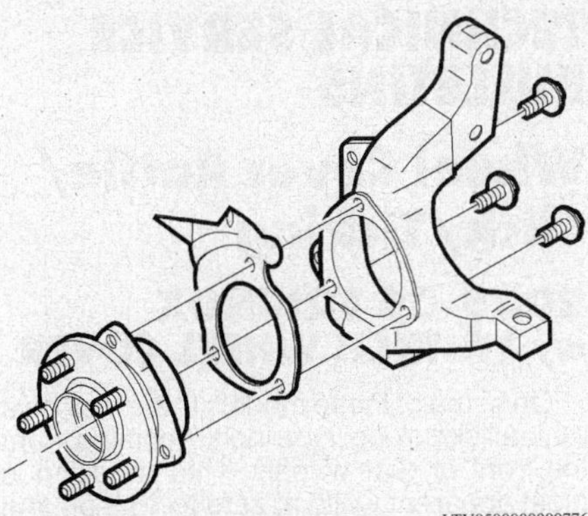

Fig. 1 Wheel bearing & hub replacement

DESCRIPTION

The Electric Power Steering (EPS) system uses the Body Control Module (BCM), Power Steering Control Module (PSCM), torque sensor, discrete battery voltage supply circuit, EPS motor, serial data bus and the Instrument Panel Cluster (IPC) message center to perform the system functions. The PSCM, torque sensor nor the EPS motor are serviced separately from each other or from the steering column. Any EPS components diagnosed to be faulting requires replacement of the steering column assembly, also known as the EPS assembly.

HUB & BEARING

REPLACE

1. Remove brake rotor as outlined in "Disc Brakes" chapter.
2. Disconnect wheel speed sensor electrical connector and remove it from connector bracket.
3. Remove front wheel drive shaft spindle nut.
4. Support wheel drive shaft using suitable, heavy mechanic's wire.
5. Remove and discard hub and bearing mounting bolts, then the wheel bearing and hub, **Fig. 1.**
6. Reverse procedure to install.

BALL JOINT INSPECTION

1. Raise and support vehicle, then inspect ball joints for seal damage.
2. Ensure wheel drive shaft nut is tightened properly.
3. Mount and secure suitable dial indicator to steering knuckle. Ensure dial indicator contacts hub vertical surface as close as possible to flange center of the flange.
4. Firmly push and pull hub flange.

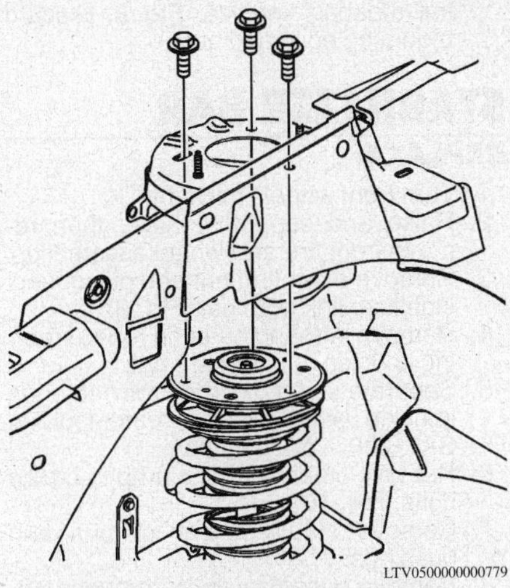

Fig. 2 Strut upper mount replacement

5. If measurement is more than .005 inch, replace bearings.
6. Position suitable dial indicator against lowest outboard point of wheel rim.
7. Rock wheel in and out .
8. If measurement is more than ,125 inch, replace lower control arm.

BALL JOINT

REPLACE

1. Remove lower control arm as outlined in "Control Arm, Replace."
2. Secure lower control arm in suitable vise.
3. Remove ball joint rivets using suitable 5⁄16 inch drill bit.
4. Mark position for installation alignment and remove ball joint from control arm.
5. Enlarge hole using suitable 31⁄64 inch drill bit. Remove burrs.
6. Reverse procedure to install.

COIL SPRING

REPLACE

Remove strut as outlined under "Strut, Replace" and replace coil spring as outlined under "Coil Spring & Strut Service."

STRUT

REPLACE

1. Raise and support vehicle.
2. Remove strut to body mounting bolts, **Fig. 2.**
3. Remove tire and wheel assemblies.
4. Remove mounting bolt and strut brake hose bracket.
5. Loosen strut to knuckle mounting bolts and nuts. **Do not remove mounting bolts and nuts.**

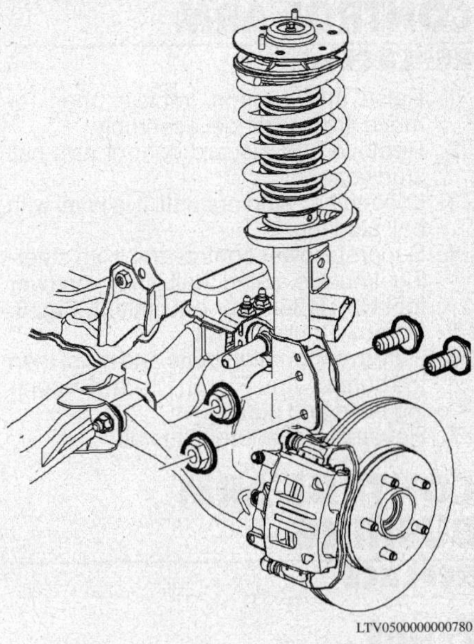

Fig. 3 Strut replacement

6. Remove mounting nut and disconnect stabilizer link.
7. Remove mounting bolts and nuts, then the strut, **Fig. 3.** Discard mounting bolts and nuts.
8. Reverse procedure to install.

COIL SPRING & STRUT SERVICE

1. Install strut assembly in strut spring compressor tool No. J45400, or equivalent.
2. Ensure strut compression leg hooks are properly installed on spring coils and strut is parallel with tool.
3. Unload upper strut mount by compressing spring.
4. **Do not allow front strut stud to rotate.**
5. Remove strut shaft nut using strut rod nut socket J42991, or equivalent.
6. Remove strut from spring, **Fig. 4.**
7. Remove upper mount, dust shield and hollow bumper.
8. Extend strut to travel limit, then install hollow bumper and dust boot.
9. Install strut into spring in compressor tool. Ensure spring identification tag is closed to bottom. Coil end sits against spring seat tab.
10. Assemble upper spring seat onto to strut shaft and align strut flat to knuckle mounting bracket.
11. Spring seat anti-rotation tab face 180° from knuckle bracket points direction.
12. Top mount metal plate flat faces same direction as spring seat anti-rotation tab.
13. Install and tighten strut shaft nut.

CONTROL ARM

REPLACE

1. Raise and support vehicle, then remove tire and wheel assembly.
2. Remove and discard control arm ball stud cotter pin
3. Loosen ball stud nut until it is level with ball stud top.
4. Separate lower control arm from steering knuckle using ball joint remover tool No. J43828, or equivalent, **Fig. 5.**
5. Remove ball stud nut.
6. Remove mounting bolts and nuts, then the control arm, **Fig. 6.** Discard mounting bolts and nuts.
7. Reverse procedure to install.

CONTROL ARM BUSHING

REPLACE

Front

1. Remove control arm as outlined in "Control Arm, Replace."
2. Remove bushing using control arm bushing remover/installer tool No. J44971, or equivalent.
3. Reverse procedure to install.

Rear

1. Remove control arm as outlined in "Control Arm, Replace."
2. Remove mounting nut and rear bushing, **Fig. 7.**
3. Reverse procedure to install.

STEERING KNUCKLE

REPLACE

1. Raise and support vehicle, then remove tire and wheel assembly.
2. Disconnect stabilizer link from strut. **Do not allow stabilizer link ball stud to rotate while removing link nut.**
3. Loosen steering knuckle to strut mounting bolts and nuts
4. Remove brake rotor as outlined in "Disc Brakes" chapter.
5. Disconnect wheel speed sensor electrical connector and remove it from connector bracket.
6. Remove front wheel drive shaft spindle nut.
7. Support wheel drive shaft using suitable, heavy mechanic's wire.
8. Remove and discard hub and bearing mounting bolts, then the wheel bearing and hub, **Fig. 1.**
9. Remove and discard control arm ball stud cotter pin
10. Loosen ball stud nut until it is level with ball stud top.
11. Separate lower control arm from steering knuckle using ball joint remover tool No. J43828, or equivalent, **Fig. 5.**
12. Remove outer tie rod end to knuckle nut.
13. Separate outer tie rod from steering knuckle using tie rod separator tool No. SA91100C, or equivalent.
14. Remove mounting bolts and nuts, then the steering knuckle, **Fig. 8.** Discard mounting bolts and nuts.

STABILIZER BAR

REPLACE

1. Turn front wheels full right.
2. Raise and support vehicle, then remove front tire and wheel assemblies.
3. Remove mounting nut and disconnect stabilizer link from bar, **Fig. 9.**
4. Remove lefthand outer tie rod to steering knuckle nut. Discard nut.
5. Separate outer tie rod from steering knuckle using tie rod separator tool No. SA91100C, or equivalent.
6. Remove stabilizer bar clamp to cradle bolts, **Fig. 10.**
7. Remove stabilizer bar clamps and bushings.
8. Remove stabilizer bar through lefthand wheel opening. **Do not catch transmission shift cable or lefthand wheel house plastic trim.**
9. Reverse procedure to install, noting the following:
   a. When tightening ball stud nut, do not allow boot to twist.
   b. Seat ball stud using steering linkage installer tool No. J44015, or equivalent.

TIE ROD END

REPLACE

1. Raise and support vehicle, then remove front tire and wheel assembly.
2. Mark jam nut for installation alignment, the loosen tie rod inner jam nut.
3. Remove tie rod to knuckle nut while holding ball stud. Discard nut.
4. Separate tie rod from steering knuckle using steering linkage and tie rod puller tool No. J24319-B, or equivalent. **Do not free ball stud by using pickle fork or wedge-type tool.**
5. Remove outer from inner tie rod.
6. Reverse procedure to install.

POWER STEERING GEAR

REPLACE

1. Raise and support vehicle, then remove front tire and wheel assemblies.
2. Remove both outer tie rod to steering knuckle nuts. Discard nuts.
3. Remove tie rod to knuckle nut while holding ball stud. Discard nut.
4. Separate tie rod from steering knuckle using steering linkage and tie rod puller tool No. J24319-B, or equivalent. **Do not free ball stud by using pickle fork or wedge-type tool.**
5. Remove pinch bolt and disconnect intermediate steering shaft from steering gear. Discard bolt.
6. Remove mounting nut and disconnect links from stabilizer bar.
7. Remove cradle mounting bolts and steering gear through righthand side, **Fig. 11.**
8. Remove heat shield.
9. Reverse procedure to install.

TECHNICAL SERVICE BULLETINS

Wheel Cover Rattle/ Click/Ticking

2005-06 EQUINOX w/16-INCH WHEEL COVER

On some of these models there may be a rattle/click/ticking type noise coming from the front or rear wheels. This condition is most apparent while at zero to 15 mph and is relative to wheel rotation.

This condition may be caused by hard contact between the inner edge of the wheel cover and the outer edge of the steel rim. This contact occurs when the delrin ring comes out of its channel and separates from the wheel cover. In most cases, the delrin ring will be completely gone.

To correct, install insulators on the back side of all four wheel covers as follows:

1. Remove wheel covers.
2. Clean back side of each wheel cover using mild liquid detergent in distilled or deionized water solution.
3. Rinse each wheel cover with clean water.
4. Dry each wheel cover using compressed air or a clean, lint-free, nonabrasive cloth.
5. After wheel covers are completely dry, each wheel cover should be wiped with isopropyl alcohol on clean, lint-free, non-abrasive cloth and apply Adhesion Promoter (part No. 12378462), or equivalent, at insulator locations. Insulator location is at center of each spoke in groove.
6. Place two insulators at location where divider prevents one from going in center. Peel red non-stick backing off of insulator.
7. Carefully place insulator onto wheel cover so that area under lip is resting against corner of inside edge of wheel cover lip. This should place insulator flush with outside edge of wheel cover.
8. Press down firmly on insulator to ensure adhesive is bonding to wheel cover.
9. Place another insulator in next location by repeating.
10. There should be an insulator at each spoke location.

Groan/Hiss/Grind Noise While Turning Steering Wheel at Low Speeds

2005

On some of these models built before VIN 56073267 there may be a groan, hiss or grind type noise while turning the steering wheel at low speeds or when the vehicle is stopped.

This condition may be caused by the front strut or stabilizer bar.

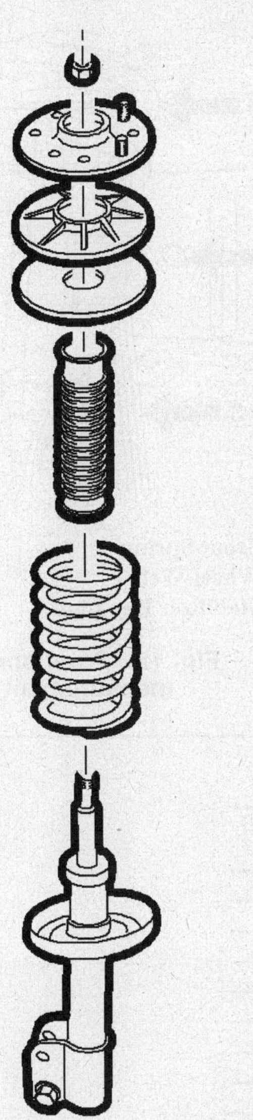

Fig. 4 Exploded view of strut

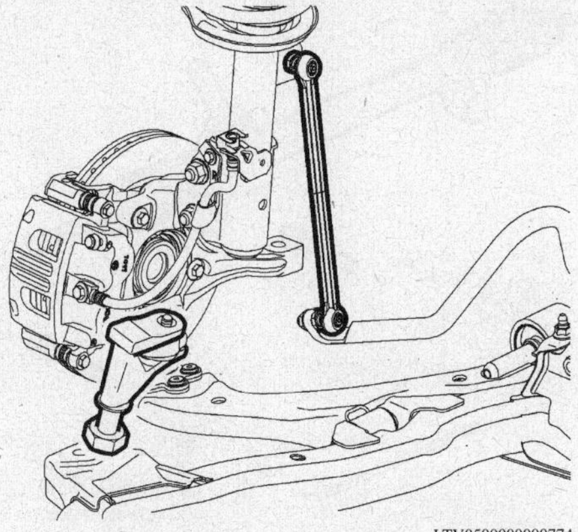

Fig. 5 Ball stud replacement

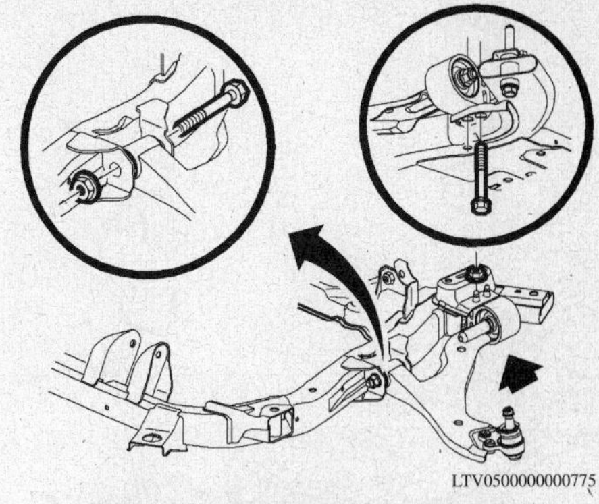

Fig. 6 Lower control arm replacement

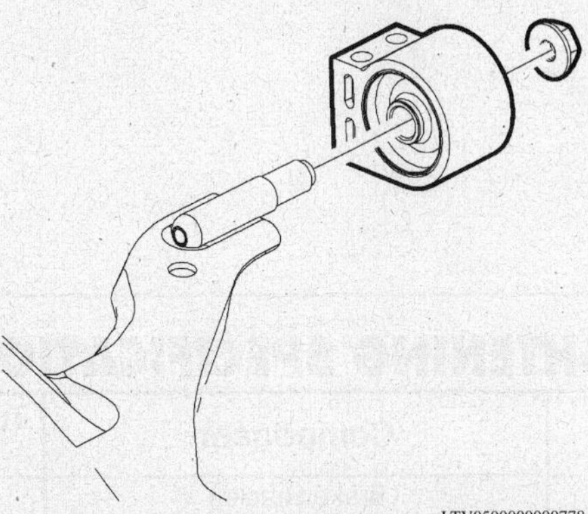

Fig. 7 Lower control arm rear bushing replacement

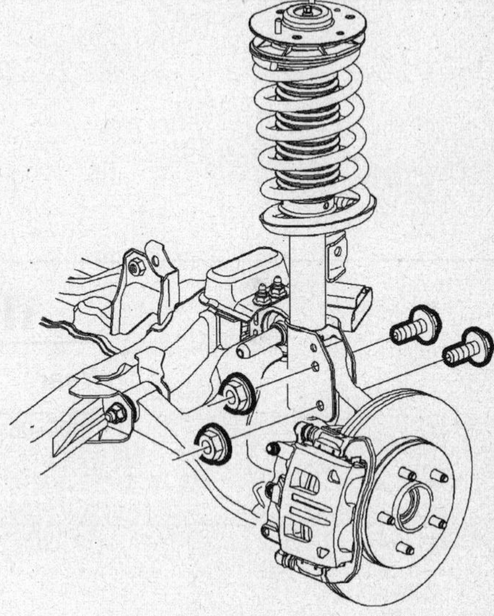

Fig. 8 Steering knuckle replacement

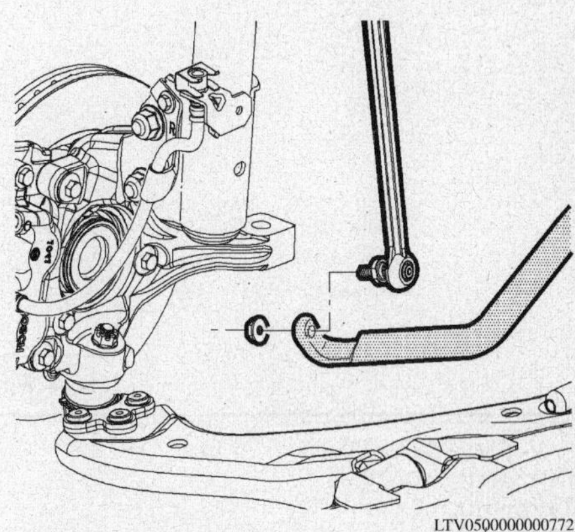

Fig. 9 Stabilizer link replacement

To correct this condition, proceed as follows:

1. Install chassis ears tool No. J 39570, or equivalent, on front springs, wheelwell and stabilizer bar link, **Fig. 12.**
2. Drive vehicle simulating parking lot maneuvers/turns.
3. If the noise is heard most predominantly through front spring, replace strut as outlined under "Strut, Replace."
4. If noise is caused by body creak, no repair is available.
5. If the noise is heard most predominantly through stabilizer shaft link, replace link as outlined under "Stabilizer Bar, Replace."

Popping Noise From Front Suspension While Driving Over Bumps

2005

On some of these models there may be a popping noise from the front suspension while driving over bumps.

This condition may be caused by the front strut or stabilizer bar.

To correct this condition, proceed as follows:

1. Raise vehicle until front wheels are off ground and slowly lower vehicle to ground.
2. Listen for popping noise as weight of vehicle settles back on suspension.
3. If no noise is heard, push down on front bumper to bounce suspension and listen for popping.
4. If pop is heard, replace strut as outlined under "Strut, Replace."

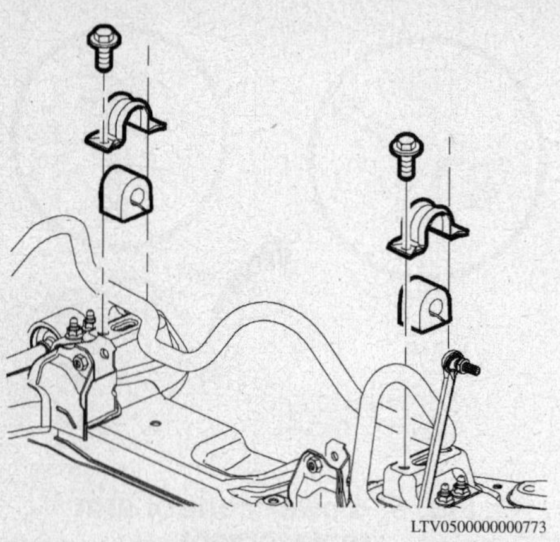

Fig. 10 Stabilizer bar replacement

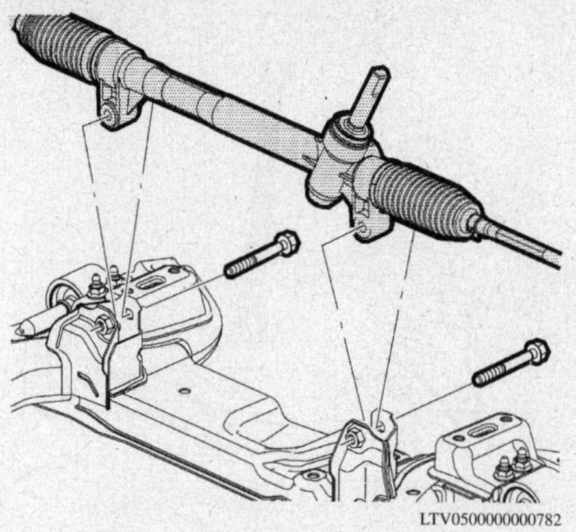

Fig. 11 Steering gear replacement

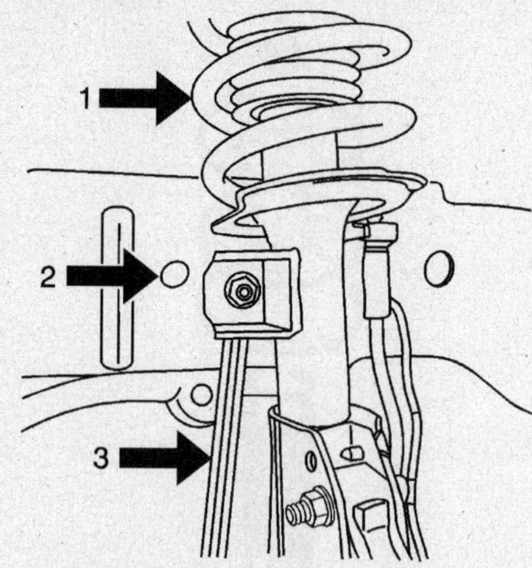

1. Front Spring
2. Wheel-Well
3. Stabilizer Bar Link

LTV0500000000160

Fig. 12 Front spring measurement

TIGHTENING SPECIFICATIONS

Year	Component	Torque Ft. Lbs.
2005–06	Brake Bracket	11
	Intermediate Shaft To Steering Gear	25
	Lower Control Arm Ball Joint	50
	Lower Control Arm Ball Stud	30
	Lower Control Arm-To-Frame, Front	89
	Lower Control Arm-To-Frame, Rear	52
	Lower Control Arm Bushing, Rear	11
	Outer Tie Rod	37
	Outer Tie Rod Ball Joint	30
	Stabilizer Bar Clamp	37
	Stabilizer Bar To Link	48
	Steering Gear	81
	Steering Knuckle	133
	Strut Shaft	55
	Strut To Body	18
	Strut To Steering Knuckle	133
	Tie Rod	18①
	Wheel Bearing & Hub	96
	Wheel Drive Shaft Spindle	151

① — Final tighten an additional 90°.

Front Wheel Drive

NOTE: On Air Bag Equipped Models, Refer To "Air Bag System Precautions" Located In The Front Of This Manual For System Disarming & Arming Procedures.

INDEX

AXLE

REPLACE

Front

1. Raise and support vehicle, then remove tire and wheel assembly.
2. Remove and discard wheel drive shaft spindle nut.
3. Remove outer tie rod end-to-steering knuckle nut while holding ball stud. **Do not loosen tie rod end jam nut.**
4. Separate tie rod from steering knuckle using steering linkage and tie rod puller tool No. J24319-B, or equivalent. **Do not free ball stud by using pickle fork or wedge-type tool.**
5. Remove and discard lower ball joint stud cotter pin.
6. Separate lower control arm ball joint stud from steering knuckle using ball joint remover tool No. J43828, or equivalent.
7. Remove nut and disconnect lower stabilizer bar link using suitable backup wrench on stud.
8. Disconnect and remove wheel drive shaft from transaxle or Power Take-Off (PTO) unit using rear wheel drive shaft removal tool No. J45341, or equivalent, **Fig. 1.**
9. **On models equipped with AWD,** cap PTO unit.
10. **On all models,** reverse procedure to install, noting the following:
    a. Install new wheel drive shaft retaining ring.
    b. Guide wheel drive shaft tripot joint squarely onto output shaft using seal protector tool No. J44394, or equivalent
    c. Remove tool after splined end passes oil seal.
    d. Pull tie rod end stud into steering knuckle using steering linkage installer tool No. J44015, or equivalent.

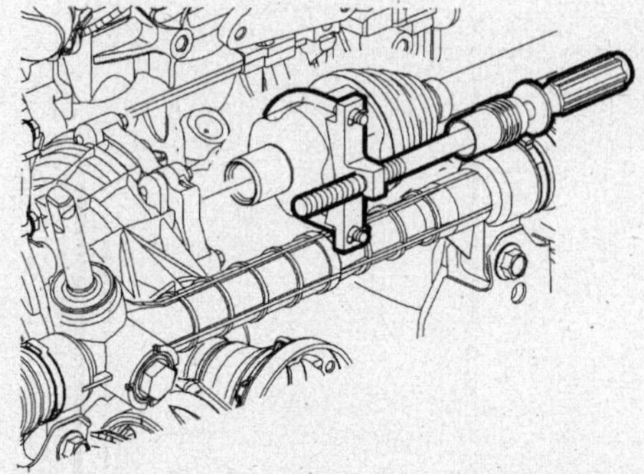

Fig. 1 Drive shaft replacement

Intermediate

1. Raise and support vehicle, then remove righthand tire and wheel assembly.
2. Remove righthand front wheel drive shaft as outlined under "Front."
3. Remove and discard wheel drive shaft retaining ring.
4. Remove intermediate drive shaft support bracket bolts at engine, **Fig. 2.**

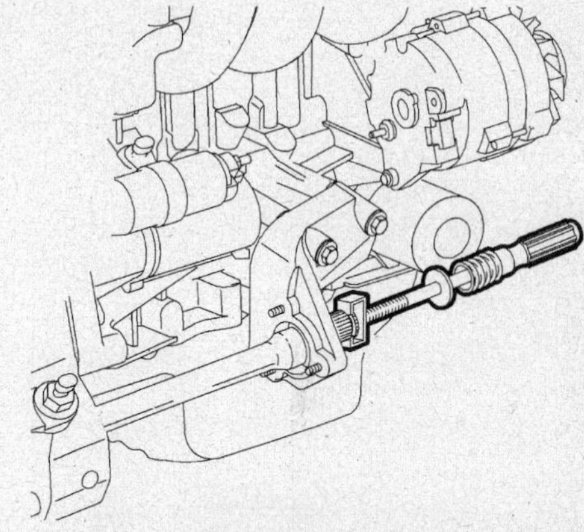

Fig. 2 Intermediate drive shaft replacement

5. Disconnect intermediate drive shaft from transaxle using output shaft assembly remover and installer tool No. J44467 and slide hammer tool No. J2619-01, or equivalents.
6. Remove intermediate drive shaft.
7. Reverse procedure to install, noting the following:
    a. Install new intermediate drive shaft O-ring seal.
    b. Guide intermediate drive shaft onto transaxle using seal protector tool No. J44394, or equivalent
    c. Remove tool after splined end passes oil seal.

TIGHTENING SPECIFICATIONS

Year	Component	Torque Ft. Lbs.
2005–06	Intermediate Drive Shaft Support Bracket	37
	Lower Control Arm Ball Joint	①
	Stabilizer Bar Link	48
	Tie Rod End	37
	Tie Rod End Stud	30
	Wheel Drive Shaft Spindle	151

① — **Torque** to 89 inch lbs., then final tighten an additional 150°.

Wheel Alignment

NOTE: On Air Bag Equipped Models, Refer To "Air Bag System Precautions" Located In The Front Of This Manual For System Disarming & Arming Procedures.

INDEX

PRECAUTIONS

Air Bag Systems

Refer to "Air Bag System Precautions" in the front of this manual for system disarming and arming procedures.

Battery Ground Cable

Prior to service, disconnect battery ground cable and isolate as required.

PRELIMINARY INSPECTION

1. Inspect tires for proper inflation and irregular tire wear.
2. Inspect runout of wheels and tires.
3. Inspect wheel bearings for backlash and excessive play.
4. Inspect ball joints and tie rod ends for looseness or wear.
5. Inspect control arms and stabilizer shaft for looseness or wear.
6. Inspect steering gear for looseness at frame.
7. Inspect struts/shock absorbers for wear, leaks and any noticeable noises.
8. Inspect vehicle trim height as outlined under "Vehicle Ride Height."
9. Inspect steering wheel for excessive drag or poor return due to stiff or rusted linkage or suspension components.
10. Ensure fuel tank should is full or vehicle has compensating load added.

FRONT WHEEL ALIGNMENT

Caster

The front caster is not adjustable. If the front caster angle is not within specifications, inspect for suspension support misalignment or front suspension damage.

Camber

1. Raise and support vehicle, then remove front tire and wheel assemblies.
2. Remove strut to knuckle mounting nuts and bolts. Discard mounting nuts and bolts.
3. Disconnect strut from knuckle.
4. If increasing negative camber, remove material from outside of lower strut hole, **Fig. 1.**
5. Maximum outboard adjustment is .0787 inch of outboard elongation or to within .433 inch from outboard edge of lower strut clevis bracket, whichever comes first.
6. If decreasing negative camber, remove material from inside of lower strut hole.
7. If increasing positive camber, .157 inch of inboard elongation.
8. Loosely install new strut to knuckle nuts and bolts.
9. Adjust camber to specifications by moving top of wheel in or out as required.
10. **Torque** strut nuts and bolts to 133 ft. lbs.

Toe

1. Position and lock steering wheel with wheels in straight forward position.
2. Loosen both inner tie rod jam nuts.
3. Loosen inner tie rod seal to boot surface. Inner tie rod must rotate freely from boot seal surface. **Do not allow boot to rotate.**
4. Increase or decrease toe angle specifications using suitable wrench on tie rod flats.
5. **Torque** cam nuts to 44 ft. lbs.

REAR WHEEL ALIGNMENT

Camber

1. Loosen upper control arm-to-frame mounting bolt and nut enough to allow movement, **Fig. 2.**
2. Rotate upper control arm-to-frame nut in direction required to correct the camber measurement. Vehicle frame is slotted, turning cam nut will move camber in to designated location.
3. Snug upper control arm mounting bolt and nut.
4. Hold nut and tighten bolt to 81 ft. lbs.

Toe

1. Loosen toe link-to-frame fastener enough to allow movement, **Fig. 3.**
2. Rotate toe link cam nut in direction required to correct toe angle. Vehicle frame is slotted, a cam nut is available for service.
3. Snug upper control arm mounting bolt and nut.
4. Hold nut and tighten bolt to 81 ft. lbs.

VEHICLE RIDE HEIGHT

Preliminary Inspection

1. Set tire pressure to certification label specifications.
2. Inspect fuel level. Add additional weight to simulate full tank.
3. Ensure passenger and rear compartments are empty, except for spare tire.
4. Ensure vehicle is on flat and level surface, such as an alignment rack.
5. Ensure all vehicle doors, hood and luggage compartment lid are securely closed.
6. Inspect for installed after market accessories or modifications that could affect trim height measurement.

Bumper Height

All dimensions are measured vertical to the ground. Trim height should be within plus or minus .87 inch to be considered correct.

1. Jounce vehicle front and rear a few times and allow suspension to settle.
2. Front bumper height measurement is taken outward 15.35 inches from center of fascia to ground level.
3. Measurements are made from inner bumper core to ground level.
4. Measure both sides and average measurements.
5. Compare measurement to front bumper curb height specification as

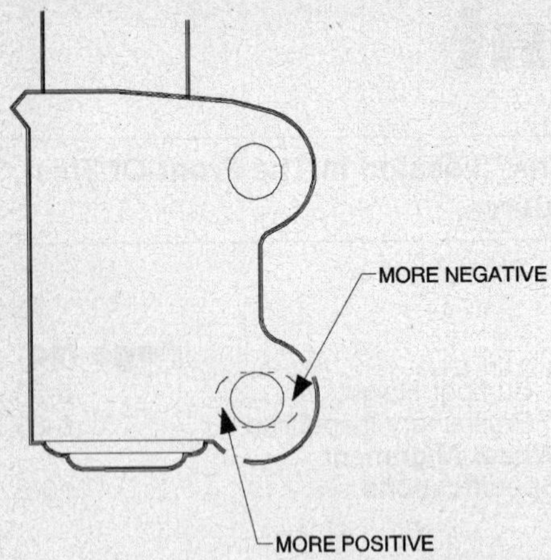

Fig. 1 Front strut camber adjustment modifications

outlined under "Vehicle Ride Height" in "Specifications" section.

6. If measurement is not within specifications, replace front springs as outlined in "Front Suspension & Steering" section.
7. Lift rear bumper approximately 1.59 inches using hands.
8. Gently remove hands and allow vehicle to lower.
9. Jounce vehicle rear downward approximately 1.59 inches using hands.
10. Gently remove your hands and allow vehicle to rise.
11. Rear bumper height measurement is taken outward 20.86 inches from center of fascia to ground level.
12. Measurements are made from inner bumper core to ground level.
13. Measure both sides and average measurements.
14. Compare measurement to rear bumper curb height specification as outlined under "Vehicle Ride Height" in "Specifications" section.
15. If measurement is not within specifications, replace rear springs as outlined in "Rear Axle & Suspension" section.

Fig. 2 Rear camber adjustment

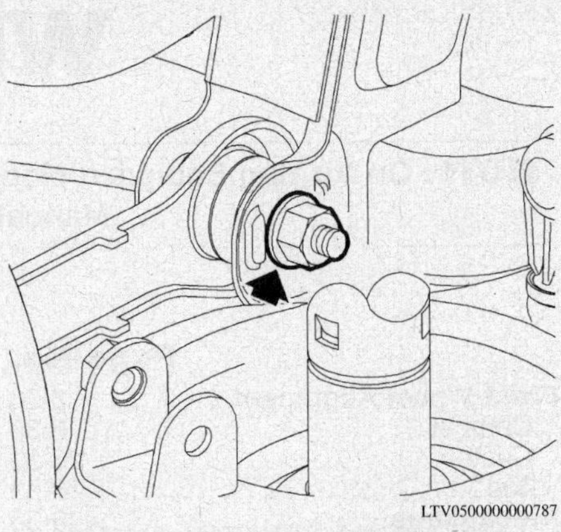

Fig. 3 Rear toe adjustment

AZTEK & RENDEZVOUS

NOTE: Refer To Back Of This Manual For Vehicle Manufacturer's Special Service Tool Suppliers.

INDEX OF SERVICE OPERATIONS

Specifications

GENERAL ENGINE SPECIFICATIONS

Year	Engine Liter	Fuel System	Bore & Stroke	Compression Ratio	Horsepower @ RPM	Torque Ft. Lbs. @ RPM	Normal Oil Pressure, psi
2002–03	3.4L	SFI	3.62 x 3.31	9.6	185 @ 5200	210 @ 4000	60①
2004–05	3.4L	SFI	3.62 x 3.31	9.6	185 @ 5200	210 @ 4000	60①
	3.6L	SFI	3.70 x 3.37	10.2	242 @ 6000	232 @ 3500	②
2006	3.5L	SFI	3.70 x 3.31	9.8	195 @ 5200	215 @ 4000	30–45①
	3.6L	SFI	3.70 x 3.37	10.2	242 @ 6000	232 @ 3500	②

① — At 1850 RPM w/5W30 motor oil.

② — At idle, 10 psi minimum; at 2,000 RPM, 20 psi minimum.

TUNE UP SPECIFICATIONS

The following specifications are published from the latest information available. This data should only be used in the absence of a decal affixed in the engine compartment.

Engine	Spark Plug Gap, Inch	Ignition Timing			Auto. Trans.		Fuel Pump ressure psi.	Valve Lash, Inch
		Firing Order	Timing BTDC	Mark Location	Curb Idle Speed	Fast Idle Speed		
3.4L	.060	1–2–3–4–5–6②	①	①	①	①	52–59	③
3.5L	.060	1–2–3–4–5–6	①	①	①	①	50–60	③
3.6L	.043	1–2–3–4–5–6	①	①	①	①	55–60	③

BTDC — Before Top Dead Center

① — PCM controlled.

② — Refer to **Figs. A and B** for spark plug wire & coil identification.

③ — Equipped w/hydraulic valve lifters.

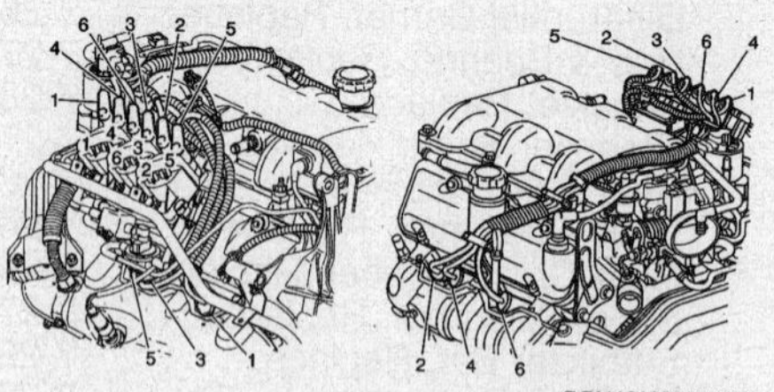

Fig. A

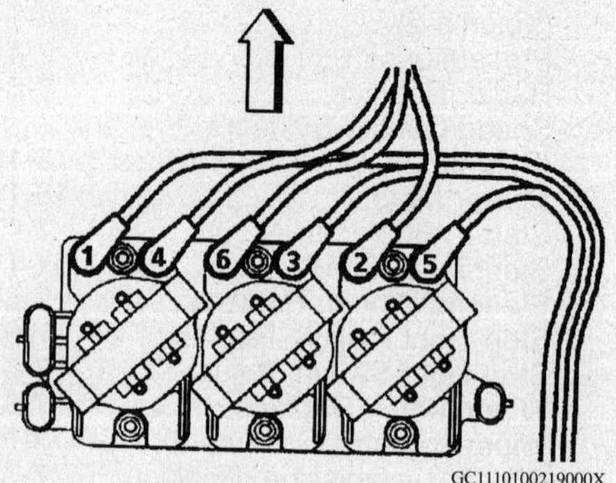

Fig. B

FRONT WHEEL ALIGNMENT SPECIFICATIONS

Year	Caster, Degree		Camber, Degree		Toe, Degree		Ball Joint
	Limit	Desired	Limit	Desired	Limits	Desired	
2002–03	+2.60 to +3.60	+3.1	-.20 to -1.20	-.70	-.2 to +.2	0	①
2004–06	+1.65 to +3.15	+2.4	-.15 to -1.15	-.65	-.2 to +.2	0	①

① — Refer to "Ball Joint Inspection" in the "Front Suspension & Steering" section for ball joint specifications.

REAR WHEEL ALIGNMENT SPECIFICATIONS

Year	Model	Camber, Degree①		Cross Camber①		Toe, Degree①	
		Limit	Desired	Limit	Desired	Limit	Desired
2002–03	AWD	+.35 to -.85	-.25	-.60 to +.60	0	-.20 to +.20	0
	FWD	-.70 to -1.30	-1.00	-.60 to +.60	0	-.30 to +.30	0
2004–05	AWD	.90 to +.30	-.30	-.75 to +.75	0	-.20 to +.20	0
	FWD	.50 to -.50	0	-.75 to +.75	0	-.30 to +.30	0
2006	All	-.90 to +.30	-.30	-.60 to +.60	0	-.20 to +.20	0

① — Not adjustable.

FLUID CAPACITIES & COOLING SYSTEM DATA

Year	Engine Liter	Cooling Capacity Qts.		Recommended Coolant Type	Radiator Cap Relief Pressure, Lbs.	Thermostat Opening Temp. °F	Fuel Tank Gals.	Engine Oil Refill Qts. ②	Auto. Transaxle Qts.①	
		Less A/C	With A/C						Drain & Refill	Overhaul
2002–03	3.4L	9.6	9.6	Dexcool	15	195	18	4.5	③	④
2004–05	3.4L	9.6	9.6	Dexcool	15	195	18	4.5	③	④
	3.6L	9.6	9.6	Dexcool	15	195	18	5.5	③	④
2006	3.5L	9.6	9.6	Dexcool	15	195	18	4.0	③	④
	3.6L	9.6	9.6	Dexcool	15	195	18	5.5	③	④

① — Approximate, make final inspect w/dipstick.
② — Includes filter.
③ — AWD, 7.8 quarts; FWD, 7.4 quarts.
④ — AWD, 10.8 quarts; FWD, 10 quarts.

LUBRICANT DATA

Year	Lubricant Type		
	Automatic Transaxle	Power Steering	Brake System
2002–05	Dexron III	①	DOT 3
2006	Dexron VI	②	DOT 3

① — GM part No. 1052884, or equivalent.
② — GM part No. 89021184, or equivalent.

Electrical

NOTE: On Air Bag Equipped Models, Refer To "Air Bag System Precautions" Located In The Front Of This Manual For System Disarming & Arming Procedures.

NOTE: Refer To "Computer Relearn Procedures" Located In The Front Of This Manual When Battery Power To The Computer Has Been Interrupted.

INDEX

PRECAUTIONS

Air Bag Systems

Refer to "Air Bag System Precautions" in the front of this manual for system disarming and arming procedures.

Battery Ground Cable

Prior to service, disconnect battery ground cable and isolate as required.

FUSE PANEL & FLASHER LOCATION

The interior fuse panel is located inside of the righthand side floor console.

The engine compartment fuse panel is located in engine compartment in front of the righthand wheelhouse, above the battery.

The flasher is located in the interior fuse panel.

FUEL PUMP RELAY LOCATION

The fuel pump relay is located in the engine compartment fuse panel.

STARTER

REPLACE

3.4L & 3.6L Engines

1. Raise and support vehicle.
2. Remove air baffle bolts, then the air baffle.
3. Remove starter motor BAT terminal nut and electrical leads.
4. **On models equipped with a 3.4L engine,** remove starter motor S terminal nut and electrical lead.
5. **On all models,** remove torque converter cover.
6. Remove starter motor mounting bolts and starter motor.
7. Reverse procedure to install, noting the following:
   a. **Torque** starter motor mounting bolts to 37 ft. lbs.
   b. **Torque** starter motor BAT terminal nut to 115 inch lbs.
   c. **Torque** air baffle bolts to 15 ft. lbs.
   d. **Torque** torque converter cover bolts to 89 inch lbs.

3.5L Engine

1. Raise and support vehicle.
2. Remove front transaxle closeout cover attaching bolt and closeout cover.
3. Remove starter solenoid BAT terminal nut.
4. Remove positive battery cable terminal from starter solenoid.
5. Remove starter solenoid S terminal nut.
6. Remove engine harness terminal from starter solenoid.
7. Remove starter bolts and starter.
   a. **Torque** starter bolts to 30 ft. lbs.
   b. **Torque** starter solenoid S terminal nut to 27 inch lbs.
   c. **Torque** starter solenoid BAT terminal nut to 115 inch lbs.
   d. **Torque** transaxle closeout cover bolt to 89 inch lbs.

ALTERNATOR

REPLACE

3.4L Engine

1. Loosen intake air duct clamps from MAF sensor and throttle body.
2. Remove IAT sensor from duct.
3. Disconnect vent tube from air intake duct.
4. Disconnect MAF sensor electrical connector.
5. Remove air intake duct and air cleaner cover.
6. Separate air intake duct from MAF sensor.
7. Set park brake and shift transaxle into Neutral.
8. Remove engine mount strut bolts and swing engine mount struts aside.
9. Install a engine tilt strap tool No. J 41131, or equivalent.
10. Pull on engine in order to rotate engine forward.
11. Tighten engine tilt strap.
12. Remove alternator B+ terminal nut and lead.
13. Disconnect alternator electrical connector.
14. Remove drive belt from alternator.
15. Remove alternator front and rear mounting bolts.
16. Remove alternator from alternator bracket and position alternator above drive axle.

17. Remove drive belt tensioner bolt and tensioner.
18. Remove alternator bracket.
19. Remove power steering pipes from power steering pipe retainer.
20. Remove fuel pressure test port (schrader valve) cap from fuel injector rail. **Do not disconnect power steering pipes from power steering pump.**
21. Remove power steering pump, then position power steering pump in front of timing chain cover to access alternator.
22. Remove electrical harness from retainer on righthand fender well and position aside.
23. Remove alternator from vehicle.
24. Reverse procedure to install, noting the following:
    a. **Torque** engine mount strut nuts to 35 ft. lbs.
    b. **Torque** alternator bolts to 37 ft. lbs.
    c. **Torque** alternator B+ terminal nut to 115 inch lbs.

3.5L Engine

1. Disconnect windshield wiper transmission link in front of wiper motor and position out of way.
2. Remove air cleaner outlet duct.
3. Set park brake and shift transaxle into Neutral.
4. Remove engine mount struts.
5. Install a engine tilt strap tool No. J 41131, or equivalent.
6. Pull on engine in order to rotate engine forward and tighten engine tilt strap.
7. Rotate engine forward, then remove drive belt.
8. Disconnect engine harness electrical connector from alternator.
9. Reposition positive battery cable boot at alternator terminal.
10. Remove positive battery cable terminal nut at alternator and cable.
11. Remove alternator lower and upper mounting bolts, then the alternator.
12. Reverse procedure to install, noting the following:
    a. **Torque** engine mount strut bolt/nut to 36 ft. lbs.
    b. **Torque** alternator mounting bolts to 37 ft. lbs.
    c. **Torque** positive battery cable terminal nut at alternator to 15 ft. lbs.

3.6L Engine

1. Remove torque struts and rotate engine to access alternator.
2. Remove alternator B+ terminal nut and battery cable from alternator.
3. Disconnect alternator electrical connector.
4. Remove drive belt from alternator.
5. Remove idler pulley.
6. Remove alternator mount bolts and alternator.
    a. **Torque** engine mount strut nuts to 35 ft. lbs.
    b. **Torque** alternator bolts to 37 ft. lbs.
    c. **Torque** alternator B+ terminal nut to 15 ft. lbs.

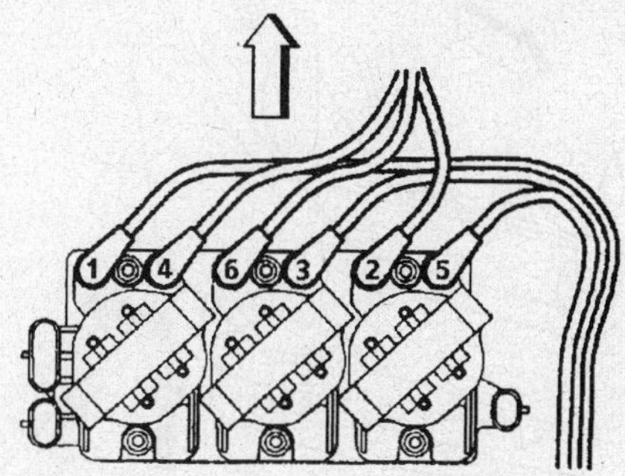

Fig. 1 Spark plug wire location. 3.4L engine

COIL PACK

REPLACE

3.4L Engine

1. Disconnect spark plug wires, **Fig. 1.**
2. Remove ignition coil from bracket.
3. Reverse procedure to install. **Torque** coil screws to 40 inch lbs.

3.5L Engine

1. Remove intake manifold cover as outlined under "Intake Manifold, Replace" in "3.5L Engine" section.
2. Disconnect engine harness electrical connector from ignition coil.
3. Disconnect spark plug wires from ignition coil.
4. Remove engine harness clip from ignition coil bracket.
5. Remove HO2S clip from ignition coil bracket.
6. Remove ignition coil bolts and nuts, then the ignition coil.
7. Remove ignition coil studs.
8. Reverse procedure to install. **Torque** ignition coil studs, bolts and nuts to 18 ft. lbs.

3.6L Engine

BANK 1

1. Raise and support vehicle.
2. Disconnect intermediate steering shaft from steering gear.
3. Remove and reposition front portion of front fender liners to gain access to frame front bolts.
4. Lower vehicle.
5. Position a floor jack at front center section of frame to support powertrain.
6. Remove frame front bolts. **Do not lower powertrain more than 4 inches.**
7. Carefully lower powertrain in order to provide access.
8. Reposition EVAP purge hoses to provide access.
9. Disconnect ignition coil electrical connectors.
10. Remove ignition coil bolts and ignition coils.
11. Reverse procedure to install, noting the following:
    a. **Torque** intermediate steering shaft lower bolt to 35 ft. lbs.
    b. **Torque** ignition coil bolts to 89 inch lbs.

BANK 2

1. Disconnect ignition coil electrical connectors.
2. Remove ignition coil bolts.
3. Remove ignition coils.
4. Reverse procedure to install. **Torque** ignition coil bolts to 89 inch lbs.

IGNITION LOCK

REPLACE

1. Remove steering wheel as outlined under "Steering Wheel, Replace."
2. Remove retaining screw from lower steering column trim covers.
3. Tilt trim cover down and slide rearward to disengage locking tabs, then remove lower steering column trim covers.
4. Remove retaining screws from upper steering column trim cover.
5. Lift trim cover to access lock cylinder access hole.
6. Insert a bent-tip awl tool No. A173A or equivalent, into access hole of ignition lock cylinder.
7. Turn ignition lock cylinder to START.
8. Use bent tip in order to push down on ignition lock cylinder retainer.
9. Release ignition lock cylinder to RUN position.
10. Remove ignition lock cylinder from lock cylinder case.
11. Reverse procedure to install, noting the following:
    a. **Torque** retaining screws to upper steering trim cover to 31 inch lbs.
    b. **Torque** lower trim cover screws to steering column to 13 inch lbs.

IGNITION SWITCH

REPLACE

1. Remove knee bolster trim panel.
2. Remove steering wheel as outlined under "Steering Wheel, Replace."
3. Remove tilt lever close out plate.
4. Remove trim cover screws from lower steering column.
5. Tilt lower trim cover down and slide lower trim cover rearward in order to disengage locking tabs.
6. Remove upper trim cover screws.
7. Remove ignition lock cylinder as outlined under "Ignition Lock Cylinder Replace".
8. Remove upper trim cover from steering column.
9. Pull theft deterrent control module away from lock cylinder housing.
10. Depress 2 white spring loaded retainers on ignition switch and slide ignition switch downward away from ignition lock cylinder case.
11. Disconnect electrical connector from ignition switch.
12. Reverse procedure to install.

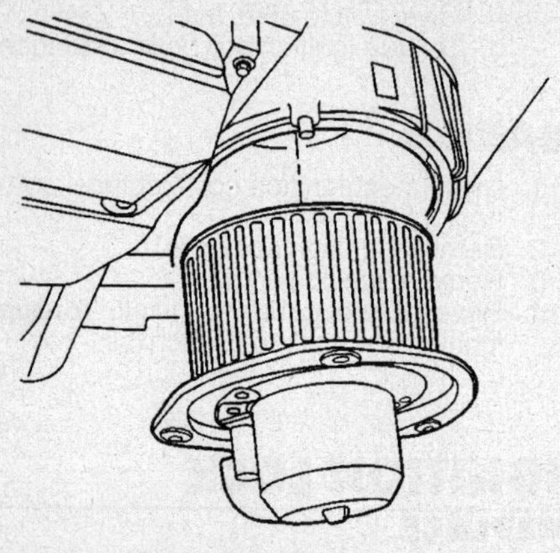

Fig. 2 Blower motor removal

NEUTRAL SAFETY SWITCH

REPLACE

1. Remove throttle body air inlet duct.
2. Disconnect shift cable from wire harness clip.
3. Remove shift cable from gear selector lever on transmission.
4. Remove neutral safety switch from transaxle.
5. Reverse procedure to install noting the following:
   a. Ensure transaxle is in neutral gear range.
   b. Align neutral safety switch using alignment tool No. J41545, or equivalent.
   c. **Torque** switch to 18 ft. lbs.

HEADLAMP SWITCH

REPLACE

1. Remove knee bolster panel.
2. Remove driver information center (DIC) switch from trim plate bezel.
3. Loosen steering column bracket and lower steering column.
4. Remove trim plate bezel from instrument panel cluster.
5. Grasp headlamp switch and pull firmly to release retaining tabs from I/P carrier.
6. Disconnect electrical connector from headlamp switch.
7. Remove headlamp switch.
8. Reverse procedure to install.

STOP LIGHT SWITCH

REPLACE

1. Remove lefthand instrument panel insulator.
2. Disconnect stop lamp switch.
3. Disconnect electrical connectors.
4. Rotate switch counterclockwise and remove from brake pedal.
5. Reverse procedure to install. Adjust switch as outlined in "Stop Light Switch, Adjust."

GC9140100261000X

Fig. 3 Floor console removal

STOP LIGHT SWITCH

ADJUST

Install switch into slotted grooves until switches are fully depressed against brake pedal, then rotate switch clockwise ¼ turn. Inspect and verify proper switch operation.

MULTI-FUNCTION SWITCH

REPLACE

1. Remove steering column trim covers.
2. Disconnect multi-function switch electrical connectors.
3. Remove wiring harness strap from steering column wiring harness.
4. Remove switch attaching screws electrical connectors, and switch.
5. Reverse procedure to install.

STEERING WHEEL

REPLACE

1. Remove driver air bag module as outlined in "Passive Restraint Systems" chapter.
2. Disconnect steering wheel electrical connector.
3. Remove steering wheel center nut.
4. Place alignment marks on steering wheel and column for installation reference.
5. Install steering wheel puller tool No. J1859–A and puller legs tool No. J42578 or equivalents to steering wheel.
6. Remove steering wheel using puller tools.
7. Reverse procedure to install. **Torque** steering wheel to 30 ft. lbs.

INSTRUMENT CLUSTER

REPLACE

1. Remove lefthand instrument panel insulator to instrument panel push-in retainers.
2. Remove instrument panel insulator to dash mat press-on retainers
3. Remove courtesy lamp from instrument panel insulator.
4. Remove insulator from instrument panel.

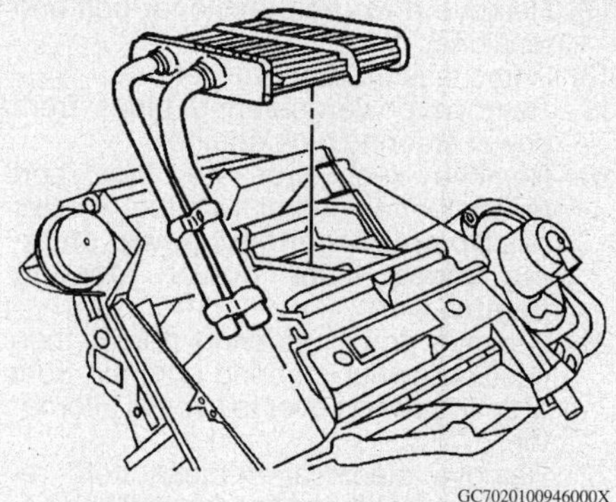

Fig. 4 Heater core removal

5. Remove bolts from bottom of knee bolster.
6. Pull on knee bolster to release upper clips, then remove bolster from instrument panel.
7. Pry cover of driver information center panel from instrument panel using a suitable flat-bladed tool.
8. Disconnect electrical connectors from driver information center panel.
9. Remove driver information center panel from instrument panel.
10. Loosen steering column bracket and lower steering column.
11. Remove trim plate bezel from instrument panel cluster.
12. Remove cluster retaining screws, then disconnect electrical connectors from cluster.
13. Remove cluster from instrument panel.
14. Reverse procedure to install.

RADIO

REPLACE

1. Apply parking brake, then place transaxle in drive.
2. Remove radio trim plate.
3. Remove radio attaching screws.
4. Pull radio from instrument panel, then disconnect electrical connectors.
5. Remove radio from instrument panel.
6. Reverse procedure to install.

WIPER MOTOR

REPLACE

1. Remove wiper arms.
2. Remove air inlet grille panel.
3. Remove underhood fuse panel cover.
4. Disconnect and isolate positive battery cable from fuse panel.
5. Loosen 4 fuse panel wire harness bolts.
6. Remove underhood fuse panel from bracket.
7. Disconnect cruise control cable from throttle body and bracket.
8. Rotate cable counterclockwise and remove from cruise control module.
9. Remove cruise control module.
10. Disconnect wiper motor cover electrical connector.
11. Remove wiper system drive module bolts.
12. Remove wiper system drive module from engine compartment.

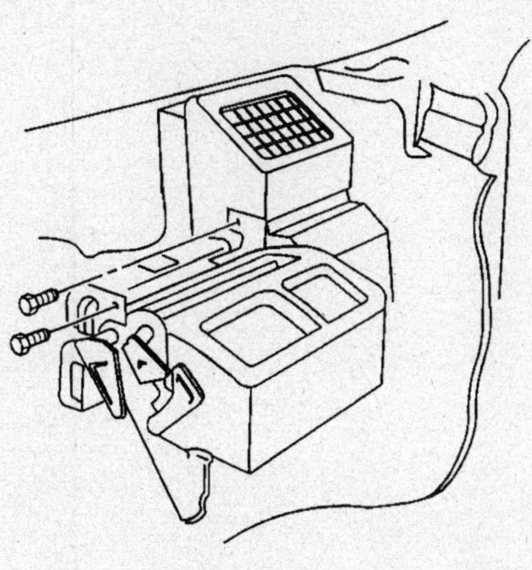

GC7020100947000X

Fig. 5 Evaporator case to cross vehicle beam attaching bolts

13. Reverse procedure to install noting the following:
    a. **Torque** wiper motor to 80 inch lbs.
    b. **Torque** fuse panel electrical connectors to 36 inch lbs.
    c. **Torque** fuse panel battery cable to 12 ft. lbs.

WIPER TRANSMISSION

REPLACE

Refer to "Wiper Motor, Replace" for procedure.

BLOWER MOTOR

REPLACE

1. Remove righthand lower instrument panel insulator.
2. Disconnect blower motor electrical connector.
3. Remove blower motor attaching screws, then motor, **Fig. 2.**
4. Reverse procedure to install.

HEATER CORE

REPLACE

1. Drain cooling system into a suitable container.
2. Remove wiper motor as outlined in "Wiper Motor, Replace."
3. Disconnect brake booster vacuum hose and position aside.
4. Remove air intake tube and air cleaner assembly.
5. Disconnect accelerator and cruise control cables from throttle body and brackets.
6. Remove transaxle dipstick, then the dipstick tube.
7. Disconnect heater hoses from heater core using suitable hose clamp pliers.
8. Place suitable plugs in heater core inlet and outlet tubes.
9. Remove righthand and lefthand lower instrument panel insulators.
10. Remove cup holder liner and screw.
11. Pull up on front floor trim plate to release from retainer clips.
12. Remove trim plate, then turn plate sideways and lift over shift lever.
13. Disconnect electrical connectors.
14. Remove nuts from floor console, then lift front of console and pull backwards to remove, **Fig. 3.**
15. Remove transaxle range selector, and floor console bracket.
16. Remove floor duct brace, and floor duct.
17. Remove heater outlet duct, and instrument panel harness to heater core cover tie strap.
18. Remove heater core cover, and heater core tube retaining clamp.
19. Remove heater core from case, **Fig. 4.**
20. Reverse procedure to install.

EVAPORATOR CORE

REPLACE

1. Recover refrigerant as outlined in "Air Conditioning" chapter.
2. Drain cooling system into a suitable container.
3. Remove wiper arm linkage nuts. Reposition lefthand wiper arm linkage to allow access.
4. Position heater controls to vent position.
5. Remove blower motor as outlined in "Blower Motor, Replace."
6. Disconnect blower motor resistor.
7. Disconnect evaporator temperature sensor.
8. Disconnect blend door electrical connectors.
9. Remove instrument panel as outlined in "Dash Panel Service" chapter.
10. Remove cup holder liner and screw.
11. Pull up on front floor trim plate to release from retainer clips.
12. Remove trim plate, then turn plate sideways and lift over shift lever.
13. Disconnect electrical connectors.
14. Remove nuts from floor console, then lift front of console and pull backwards to remove, **Fig. 3.**
15. Remove passenger air bag module as outlined in "Passive Restraint Systems" chapter.
16. Remove lefthand lower instrument panel insulator.
17. Remove brake booster pushrod from brake pedal.
18. Disconnect speed control cancel and brake lamp switches.
19. Remove righthand lower instrument panel insulator and knee bolster panel.
20. Remove brake booster and brake pedal bracket mounting nuts.
21. Remove brake pedal with bracket.
22. Disconnect transaxle shift cable and reroute through cross vehicle beam.
23. Disconnect instrument panel wiring harness clips and position harness aside.
24. Remove evaporator case to cross vehicle beam attaching bolts, **Fig. 5.**

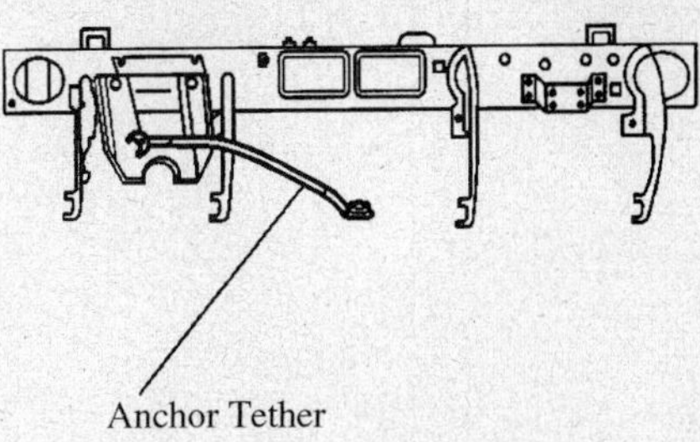

GC7020100948000X

Fig. 6 Cross vehicle beam anchor tether

25. Disconnect lefthand and righthand cross vehicle beam ground wires.
26. Disconnect cross vehicle beam anchor tether, **Fig. 6.**
27. Disconnect antenna cable from cross vehicle beam.
28. Remove evaporator case bracket from cross vehicle beam bracket.
29. **On models equipped with Heads Up Display (HUD),** remove heads up display bracket.
30. **On all models,** remove lefthand and righthand hinge pillar to cross vehicle beam bolts.
31. Remove cross vehicle beam from vehicle through main wire harness.
32. Remove defroster duct.
33. Remove evaporator outlet tube nut.
34. Disconnect evaporator inlet and outlet tubes.
35. Remove heater core inlet and outlet hoses using suitable clamp pliers.
36. Remove evaporator case to dash panel sound barrier nuts, **Fig. 7.**
37. Remove evaporator case from cowl.
38. Remove air inlet housing screws, and housing from module, **Fig. 8.**
39. Remove righthand evaporator case bracket.
40. Remove upper evaporator case retaining screw.
41. Remove evaporator case to dash panel sound barrier seal.
42. Remove lower evaporator case attaching screws, and heater core cover.
43. Remove heater core tube retaining screw.
44. Remove heater core from case, and case screw from below heater core.
45. Separate upper and lower evaporator case halves, **Fig. 9.**
46. Remove evaporator core from case.
47. Reverse procedure to install noting the following:
    a. Install new A/C O-rings lubricated with 525 viscosity refrigerant oil.
    b. **Torque** evaporator inlet and outlet tubes to 12 ft. lbs.
    c. **Torque** cross vehicle beam to hinge pillars to 18 ft. lbs.
    d. **Torque** cross vehicle beam to evaporator case to 89 inch lbs.

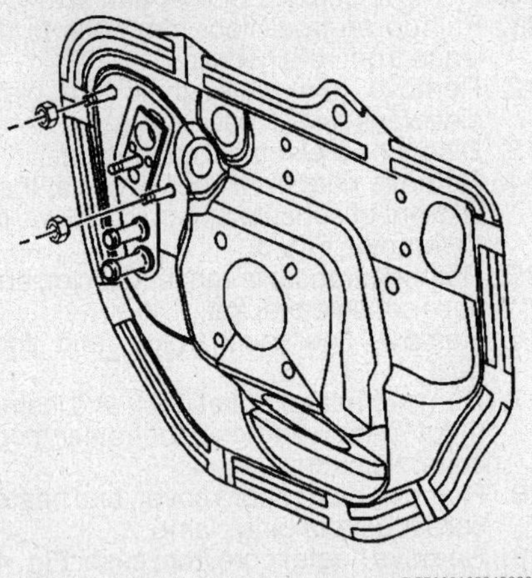
GC7020100949000X

Fig. 7 Evaporator case to dash panel sound barrier nuts

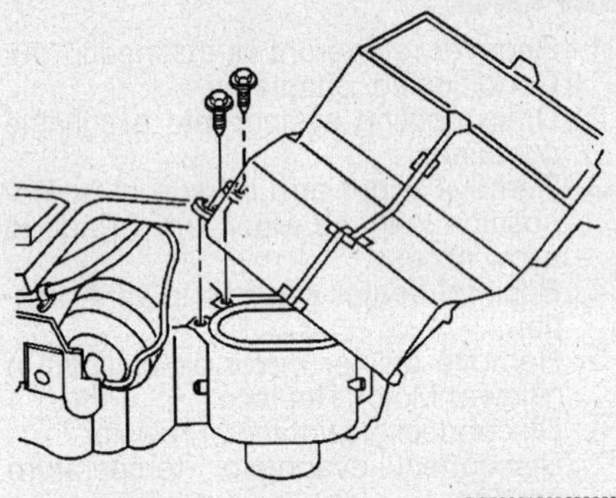
GC7020100950000X

Fig. 8 Air inlet housing

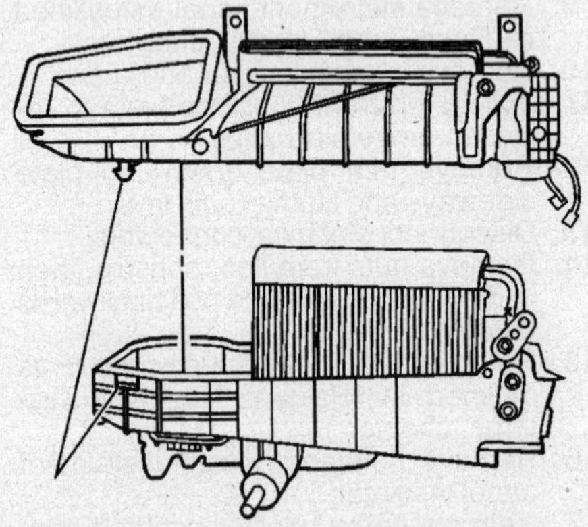
GC7020100951000X

Fig. 9 Evaporator case separation

3.4L Engine

NOTE: On Air Bag Equipped Models, Refer To "Air Bag System Precautions" Located In The Front Of This Manual For System Disarming & Arming Procedures.

NOTE: Refer To "Computer Relearn Procedures" Located In The Front Of This Manual For Computer Relearn Procedures.

INDEX

PRECAUTIONS

Air Bag Systems

Refer to "Air Bag System Precautions" in the front of this manual for system disarming and arming procedures.

Battery Ground Cable

Prior to service, disconnect battery ground cable and isolate as required.

Fuel System Pressure Relief

1. Loosen fuel filler cap to discharge tank pressure.
2. Connect fuel pressure gauge tool No. J-34730-1A, or equivalent, to fuel pressure connection. Wrap shop towel around connection while connecting fuel pressure gauge in order to avoid fuel spillage.
3. Install bleed hose into an approved container and open valve in order to bleed fuel system pressure.
4. Drain any fuel remaining in fuel pressure gauge into suitable container.

ENGINE MOUNT

REPLACE

1. Remove throttle body air inlet duct.
2. Remove lefthand and righthand engine mount strut bolts.
3. Raise and support vehicle.
4. Remove front exhaust pipe to exhaust manifold retaining nuts, then separate pipe from exhaust manifold.
5. Disconnect oxygen sensor electrical connector.
6. Remove catalytic convertor to exhaust pipe attaching bolts, and convertor from vehicle.
7. Remove righthand tire and wheel assembly.
8. Remove righthand splash shield from wheel well.
9. Remove engine mount lower retaining nuts.
10. Place a block of wood under engine oil pan, then position a suitable jack stand under block of wood and raise engine.
11. Remove engine mount bracket to oil pan bolts, and engine mount.
12. Reverse procedure to install.

ENGINE

REPLACE

1. Relieve fuel system pressure as outlined in "Precautions."
2. Remove throttle body air inlet duct.
3. Remove cruise control cable from engine and position aside.
4. Remove accelerator control cable from engine and position aside.
5. Drain engine coolant into a suitable container.
6. Disconnect radiator and heater hoses from engine.
7. Remove engine mount struts from lefthand and righthand sides of engine.
8. Disconnect fuel lines from fuel rail.
9. Disconnect engine wiring harness connectors. Mark connectors for installation reference.
10. Disconnect vacuum hoses from engine. Mark hoses for installation reference.
11. Remove vacuum hose from brake booster.
12. Remove transaxle range selector cable retaining clip, and cable from range selector.
13. Raise and support vehicle, then drain engine oil into a suitable container.
14. Remove engine wiring harness grounds.
15. Remove front exhaust pipe to exhaust manifold retaining nuts, then separate pipe from exhaust manifold.
16. Disconnect oxygen sensor electrical connector.
17. Remove exhaust pipe to catalytic convertor attaching bolts, and exhaust pipe from manifold and convertor.
18. Remove front tires and wheels.
19. Remove lefthand and righthand engine splash shields.
20. Remove stabilizer shaft links from lower control arms.
21. Remove tie rod ball stud to steering knuckle nut, then separate tie rod from steering knuckle with universal steering linkage puller tool No. J 24319-B, or equivalent.
22. Remove cotter pin from lower control

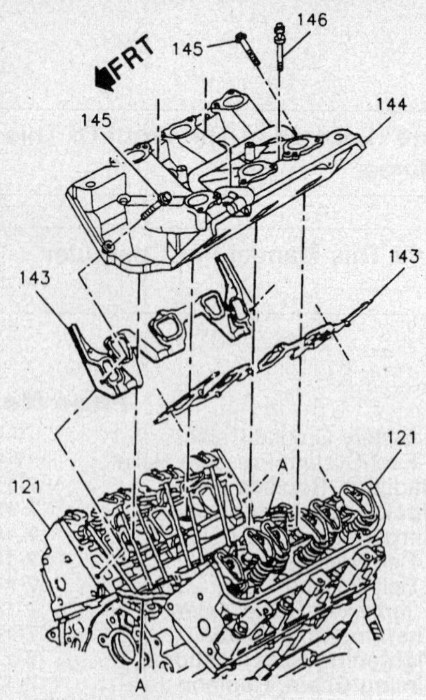

Fig. 1 Lower intake manifold & gasket replacement

arm ball joint to steering knuckle ball stud nut.

23. Loosen but do not remove control arm ball stud nut.
24. Install ball stud/joint separator tool No. J 41820, or equivalent, over ball stud nut and steering knuckle.
25. Rotate ball stud nut to separate ball joint from steering knuckle.
26. Remove lower control arm attaching bolts and nuts, and lower control arm from vehicle.
27. Remove transaxle cooler lines and bracket from transaxle.
28. Remove drive axles from transaxle as outlined in "Front Wheel Drive." Secure driveshafts to steering knuckles.
29. Apply silicone lubricant to steering column intermediate steering shaft lower seal.
30. Push intermediate shaft lower seal upward to access intermediate shaft lower bolt.
31. Remove intermediate shaft lower bolt and separate intermediate shaft from steering gear.
32. Place a transaxle support table tool No. J 39580, or equivalent, under engine and transaxle assembly, then lower vehicle until frame contacts table.
33. Remove frame bolts.
34. Raise vehicle and remove engine and transaxle.
35. Remove flywheel to torque converter bolts.
36. Remove engine to transaxle bolts and

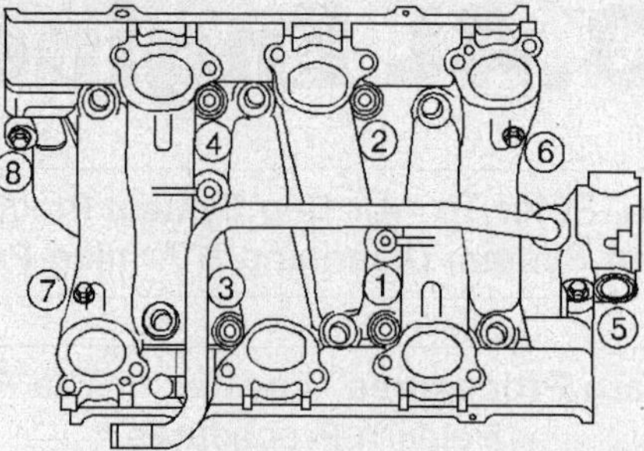

Fig. 2 Lower intake manifold tightening sequence

studs, then separate engine from transaxle.

37. Reverse procedure to install.

INTAKE MANIFOLD

REPLACE

Upper

1. Drain engine coolant into suitable container.
2. Remove throttle body air inlet duct.
3. Remove accelerator and cruise control cables with bracket from throttle body.
4. Disconnect throttle position sensor and idle air control valve wiring harness connectors from throttle body.
5. Disconnect lefthand side spark plug wires and harness attachment clip.
6. Disconnect throttle body heater hoses.
7. Disconnect EVAP canister purge solenoid valve vacuum hoses and electrical connector. Mark hose position for installation reference.
8. Release lock tab and remove EVAP canister purge solenoid valve.
9. Remove ignition coil bracket with coils.
10. Disconnect wiring harness from Manifold Air Pressure sensor.
11. Disconnect vacuum harness from MAP sensor and upper intake manifold.
12. Disconnect vacuum brake booster hose from upper intake manifold.
13. Disconnect HVAC and fuel pressure regulator vacuum hoses from intake manifold. Mark hose position for installation reference.
14. Disconnect EGR valve electrical connector.
15. Remove transaxle fluid filler tube.
16. Remove EGR pipe assembly retaining bolt, then carefully pull pipe away from valve.
17. Remove EGR valve retaining bolts, and EGR valve and gasket.
18. Disconnect MAP sensor electrical connector and vacuum hose.
19. Remove MAP sensor and bracket.
20. Remove alternator through bolt and bracket.
21. Remove mounting bolts and upper intake manifold.
22. Reverse procedure to install. Apply suitable threadlock to mounting bolts.

Lower

1. Relieve fuel pressure as outlined in

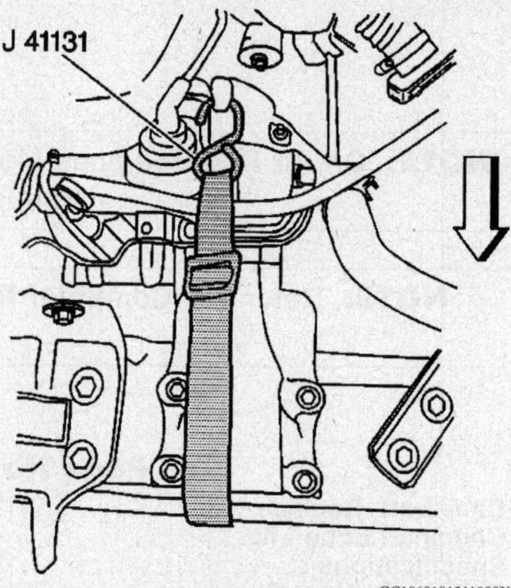

Fig. 3 Engine tilt strap installation

"Precautions."

2. Remove upper intake manifold as outlined in "Intake Manifold Replace, Upper."
3. Remove valve covers as outlined in "Valve Cover, Replace."
4. Disconnect Engine Coolant Temperature sensor wiring harness.
5. Disconnect and remove fuel injector, Manifold Air Pressure sensor and ECT wiring harnesses. Mark connectors for installation reference.
6. Remove fuel feed and return lines.
7. Remove fuel rail mounting bolts and fuel rail.
8. Remove injector O-ring seal from spray tip end of each injector.
9. Remove power steering pump from front engine cover and position aside. **Do not disconnect power steering pump hoses.**
10. Disconnect heater inlet pipe with hose from lower intake manifold and position aside.
11. Disconnect radiator inlet hose from engine, and thermostat bypass hose from lower intake manifold.
12. Remove mounting bolts and lower intake manifold, **Fig. 1.**
13. Loosen valve rocker arms and remove pushrods as outlined in "Rocker Arms, Replace."
14. Remove lower intake manifold gaskets and seals.
15. Reverse procedure to install, noting the following:
    a. Apply .08–.12 inch wide and .12–.20 inch thick suitable sealer at engine block to lower intake manifold mating surfaces.
    b. Apply suitable sealer to mounting bolt threads.
    c. Lubricate fuel injector O-rings with GM part No. 1051885, or equivalent.
    d. **Torque** bolts in sequence, **Fig. 2,** to 62 inch lbs., in first pass, then to 115 inch lbs., in final pass.

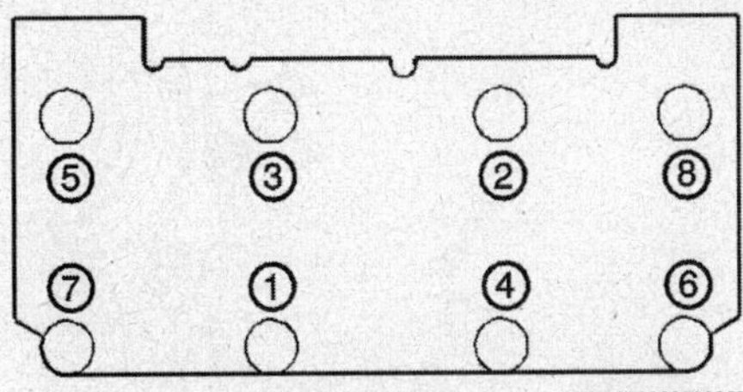

Fig. 4 Cylinder head bolt tightening sequence

EXHAUST MANIFOLD

REPLACE

Lefthand

1. Remove throttle body air inlet duct, then drain engine coolant into suitable container.
2. Remove mounting bolts and nuts from bracket on engine and upper radiator support, and righthand engine strut.
3. Remove engine oil cooler coolant line and engine wiring harness bracket bolts.
4. Remove mounting bolts, then set air conditioning compressor aside.
5. Remove engine mounting strut bracket bolt and lower engine mount strut bracket bolt from righthand engine mounting strut bracket.
6. Partially drain cooling system, then disconnect and remove inlet hose from thermostat housing and radiator.
7. Remove radiator inlet hose from engine.
8. Remove thermostat bypass hose.
9. Remove mounting bolts and exhaust crossover pipe heat shield.
10. Remove exhaust crossover pipe mounting bolts from lefthand side exhaust manifold.
11. Remove mounting nuts, and heat shield and exhaust manifold.
12. Reverse procedure to install.

Righthand

1. Remove throttle body air inlet duct, then drain engine coolant into suitable container.
2. Remove accelerator cable bracket from throttle body.
3. Disconnect MAP sensor electrical connector, then remove MAP sensor mounting screws and sensor.
4. Disconnect EGR valve electrical connector, then remove EGR valve mounting bolts and valve.
5. Set parking brake and shift transaxle to Neutral.
6. Remove engine mount strut bolts, then swing engine mounts aside.
7. Install engine tilt strap tool No. J 41131, or equivalent, to engine as outlined in **Fig. 3.**
8. Pull on strap to tilt engine forward.
9. Remove ignition module, ignition coils and bracket.
10. Remove spark plug wires from spark plugs.

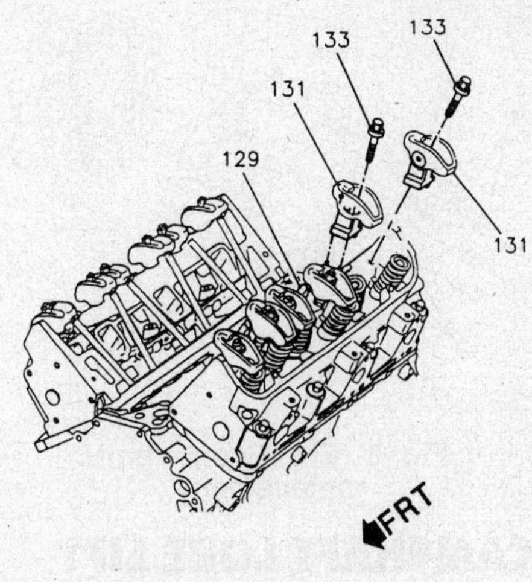

129 PUSHROD
131 ARM, ROLLER ROCKER
133 BOLT

GC1069600693000X

Fig. 5 Rocker arm replacement

11. Disconnect oxygen sensor electrical connector.
12. Remove evaporative emissions solenoid bracket.
13. Drain cooling system, then remove radiator inlet hose from engine.
14. Remove thermostat bypass hose.
15. Remove mounting bolts and exhaust crossover pipe heat shield.
16. Remove exhaust crossover pipe mounting bolts and crossover pipe.
17. Raise and support vehicle.
18. Remove three-way catalytic converter pipe from righthand exhaust manifold.
19. Remove automatic transaxle fluid filler tube.
20. Remove mounting bolts and upper heat shield.
21. Remove mounting bolts and lower heat shield.
22. Remove mounting nuts and exhaust manifold.
23. Reverse procedure to install.

CYLINDER HEAD

REPLACE

Lefthand

1. Raise and support vehicle, then drain engine coolant into suitable container.
2. Lower vehicle.
3. Remove upper and lower intake manifolds as outlined in "Intake Manifold, Replace."
4. Remove rocker arms and pushrods as outlined in "Rocker Arms, Replace."
5. Remove mounting bolts and exhaust crossover pipe heat shield.
6. Remove mounting nuts and exhaust crossover pipe.
7. Remove thermostat bypass pipe.
8. Remove mounting bolts and nuts from bracket on engine and upper radiator support, and righthand engine strut.

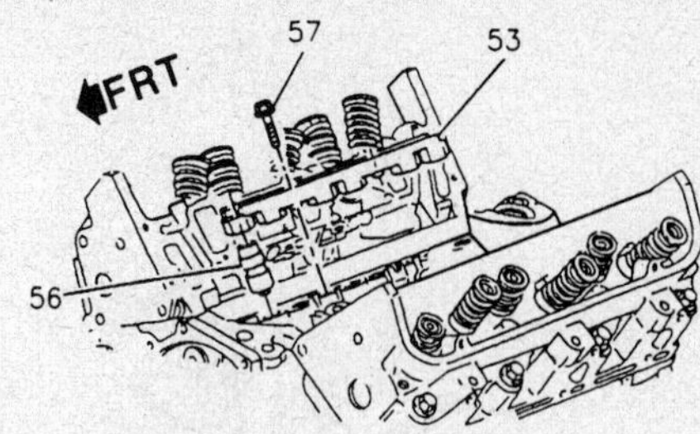

53 GUIDE, VALVE LIFTER
56 LIFTER, ROLLER VALVE
57 SCREW, VALVE LIFTER GUIDE

GC1069600694000X

Fig. 6 Valve lifter & guide replacement

9. Remove engine oil cooler coolant line and engine wiring harness brackets' bolts.
10. Remove mounting bolts, then set air conditioning compressor aside.
11. Remove vehicle engine mounting strut bracket bolt and lower engine mount strut bracket bolt from righthand engine mounting strut bracket.
12. Remove righthand engine mount strut bracket.
13. Remove oil dipstick tube.
14. Disconnect spark plug wires from lefthand spark plugs.
15. Remove lefthand exhaust manifold as outlined in "Exhaust Manifold, Replace."
16. Remove mounting bolts, cylinder head and gasket.
17. Reverse procedure to install, noting the following:
    a. Clean and remove any remaining gasket material from cylinder head and block mating surfaces.
    b. Tighten bolts in two steps using sequence outlined in **Fig. 4,** first step, **torque** bolts to 44 ft. lbs.; second step, tighten bolts an additional 95°.

Righthand

1. Raise and support vehicle.
2. Drain engine coolant into suitable container.
3. Drain engine oil into suitable container.
4. Lower vehicle.
5. Remove upper and lower intake manifolds as outlined in "Intake Manifold, Replace."
6. Remove rocker arms and pushrods as outlined in "Rocker Arms, Replace."
7. Remove mounting bolts and exhaust crossover pipe heat shield.
8. Remove mounting nuts and exhaust crossover pipe.
9. Disconnect spark plug wires from righthand spark plugs.
10. Remove righthand exhaust manifold as outlined in "Exhaust Manifold, Replace."
11. Remove mounting bolts, cylinder head and gasket.
12. Reverse procedure to install, noting the following:
    a. Clean and remove any remaining gasket material from cylinder head and block mating surfaces.

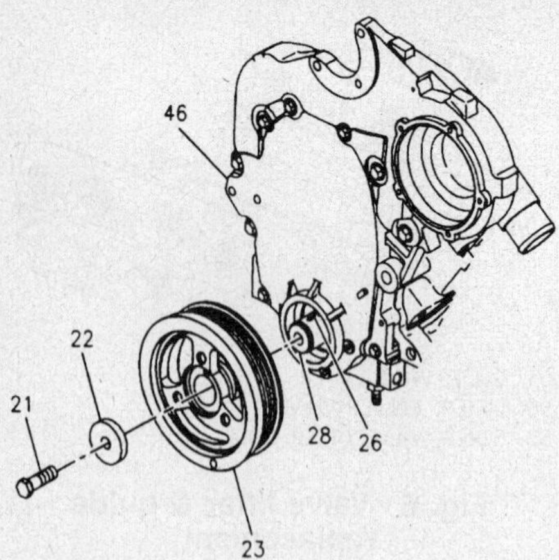

21 BOLT, CRANKSHAFT BALANCER
22 WASHER, CRANKSHAFT BALANCER
23 BALANCER, CRANKSHAFT
26 KEY, CRANKSHAFT
28 CRANKSHAFT
46 COVER, FRONT

GC1069600695000X

Fig. 7 Crankshaft dampener replacement

b. Tighten bolts in two steps using sequence outlined in **Fig. 4,** first step, **torque** bolts to 44 ft. lbs., second step, tighten bolts an additional 95°.

VALVE COVER

REPLACE

Lefthand

1. Disconnect spark plug wires from lefthand spark plugs.
2. Remove engine mount strut mounting bolts and nuts from bracket on engine and upper radiator support, and righthand engine strut.
3. Remove PCV valve from valve cover.
4. Remove mounting bolts and valve cover.
5. Reverse procedure to install. Install new gasket and apply ultra black RTV sealer, part No. 12345739, or equivalent.

Righthand

1. Remove serpentine drive belt as outlined in "Serpentine Drive Belt."
2. Remove alternator mounting bolts and bracket.
3. Disconnect wires from righthand spark plugs.
4. Disconnect vacuum hoses, then remove EVAP canister purge solenoid.
5. Remove ignition module bracket with coils.
6. Remove vacuum hose from valve cover grommet.
7. Remove mounting bolts, valve cover and gasket.
8. Reverse procedure to install. Install new gasket and apply ultra black RTV sealer, part No. 12345739, or equivalent.

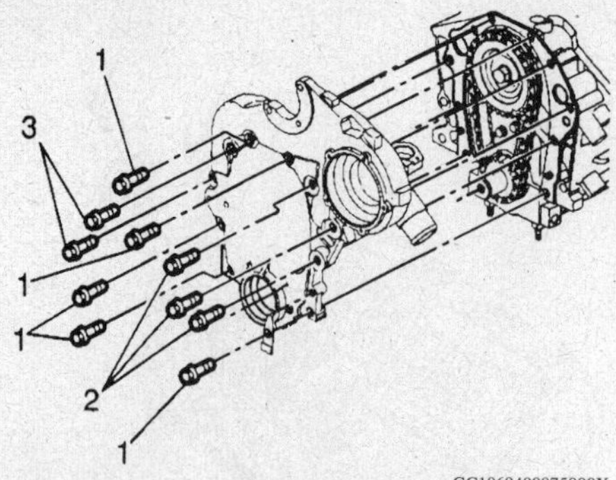

GC1069400875000X

Fig. 8 Front cover bolt replacement

CAMSHAFT LOBE LIFT SPECIFICATIONS

Intake .... .273 inch
Exhaust... .273 inch

VALVE CLEARANCE SPECIFICATIONS

These engines use hydraulic lifters. Valve stem to rocker arms have a clearance of zero.

VALVE ADJUSTMENT

This vehicle is equipped with hydraulic valve lifters.

ROCKER ARMS

REPLACE

1. Remove valve rocker arm cover as outlined in "Valve Cover, Replace."
2. Remove mounting bolts. rocker arms and pushrods, **Fig. 5.** Keep components together and mark position for assembly reference.
3. Reverse procedure to install.

VALVE GUIDES

The valve guides are an integral part of the cylinder head and cannot be replaced. If excessive valve stem clearance is observed, the valve guide must be reamed and an oversize valve installed. Valves are available in an oversize of .010 inch.

HYDRAULIC LIFTERS

REPLACE

1. Remove valve cover as outlined in "Valve Cover, Replace."
2. Remove upper and lower intake manifolds as outlined in "Intake Manifold, Replace."
3. Remove rocker arms and pushrods as outlined in "Rocker Arms, Replace."
4. Remove mounting bolts, lifter guide and lifter, **Fig. 6.**
5. Reverse procedure to install. Coat valve lifter foot with camshaft and lifter prelube part No. 1052365, or equivalent.

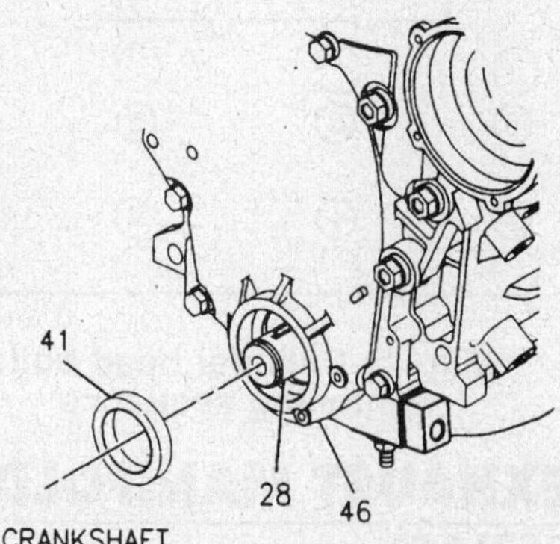

28 CRANKSHAFT
41 SEAL, FRONT COVER
46 COVER, FRONT

GC1069600697000X

Fig. 9 Front cover oil seal replacement

CRANKSHAFT DAMPER

REPLACE

1. Remove serpentine belt as outlined under "Serpentine Drive Belt."
2. Raise and support vehicle, then remove righthand front tire and wheel assembly.
3. Remove righthand engine splash side.
4. Install suitable utility stand under righthand side rail frame to support engine and frame.
5. Remove two righthand side frame mounting bolts.
6. Lower frame with utility stand to gain access to crankshaft dampener.
7. Remove and discard crankshaft dampener bolt and washer, **Fig. 7.**
8. Remove crankshaft dampener using puller tool No. J-24420-C, or equivalent.
9. Reverse procedure to install, noting the following:
   a. Apply sealer GM part No. 12345739, or equivalent, to dampener keyway.
   b. Puller dampener into place with installation tool No. J-29113, or equivalent.
   c. Tighten crankshaft damper bolts to 52 ft. lbs., then an additional 72°.
   d. Install new frame bolts.

FRONT COVER

REPLACE

1. Drain cooling system into suitable container.
2. Drain engine oil into suitable container.
3. Remove crankshaft dampener as outlined in "Crankshaft Damper, Replace."
4. Remove drive belt tensioner
5. Remove power steering pump with lines and position aside.
6. Disconnect thermostat bypass pipe and radiator outlet hose from front cover.
7. Remove water pump pulley mounting bolts and pulley.
8. Remove crankshaft position sensor wiring harness brackets.

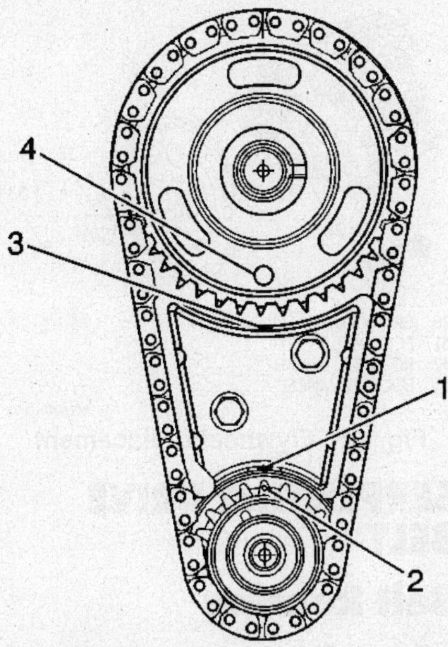

Fig. 10 Camshaft & timing chain timing marks

9. Remove oil pan as outlined in "Oil Pan, Replace."
10. Remove mounting bolts, front cover and gasket, **Fig. 8.**
11. Remove drive belt shield, crankshaft position sensor and water pump.
12. Reverse procedure to install, noting the following:
    a. Clean mating surface of front cover and cylinder block.
    b. Install new gasket.
    c. Apply .2 inch wide band of sealer part No. 1052080, or equivalent, to both sides of front cover gasket lower tabs and to engine front cover bolts.
    d. **Torque** bolts marked No. 2 in **Fig. 8** to 41 ft. lbs.
    e. **Torque** bolts marked No. 3 in **Fig. 8** to 41 ft. lbs.
    f. **Torque** bolts marked No. 1 in **Fig. 8** to 20 ft. lbs.

FRONT COVER SEAL

REPLACE

1. Remove crankshaft dampener as outlined in "Crankshaft Damper, Replace."
2. Remove front cover oil seal by prying with suitable screwdriver, **Fig. 9. Do not damage front cover.**
3. Reverse procedure to install, noting the following:
    a. Lubricate seal with clean engine oil.
    b. Install seal in front cover with lip facing engine using front cover seal installer tool No. J-34995, or equivalent.

TIMING CHAIN

REPLACE

1. Remove engine front cover as outlined in "Front Cover, Replace."

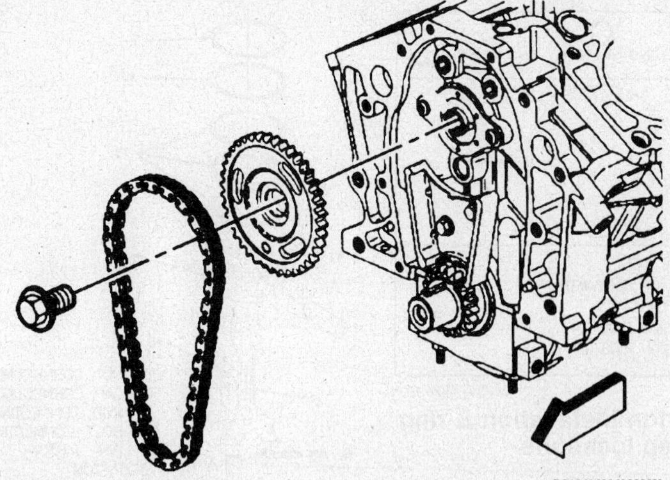

Fig. 11 Timing chain & camshaft replacement

2. Align crankshaft timing mark 2 to timing mark on bottom of timing chain dampener 1, then timing mark on camshaft gear 4 with timing mark on top of timing chain dampener 3, **Fig. 10.**
3. Remove mounting bolt, camshaft sprocket and timing chain, **Fig. 11.**
4. Remove crankshaft sprocket using puller tool No. J-5825-A, or equivalent.
5. Remove mounting bolts and timing chain dampener.
6. Reverse procedure to install, noting the following:
    a. Install crankshaft sprocket until fully seated on flange of crankshaft nose using tool No. J-38612, or equivalent.
    b. Align timing marks, **Fig. 10.**
    c. Apply prelube part No. 1052365, or equivalent, to sprocket thrust surface.

CAMSHAFT

REPLACE

1. Remove timing chain as outlined in "Timing Chain, Replace."
2. Remove mounting bolt, hold-down clamp and oil pump driven gear assembly.
3. Remove camshaft thrust plate retaining screws and thrust plate, **Fig. 11.**
4. Install suitable large screwdriver in camshaft bolt hole to help support camshaft.
5. Rotate and pull camshaft out of camshaft bearings. **Camshaft journals are all same diameter, so care must be used when removing camshaft to avoid bearing damage.**
6. Reverse procedure to install, noting the following:
    a. Coat camshaft journals with clean engine oil.
    b. Coat camshaft lobes with prelude part No. 1052365, or equivalent.

PISTON & ROD ASSEMBLY

Align pistons and rings, **Fig. 12.**

After piston and rod installation, measure connecting rod side clearance. Side clearance should be .007–.017 inch.

Torque connecting rod cap nuts to 15 ft. lbs., then tighten an additional 75.°

PISTONS, PINS & RINGS

Pistons and rings are available in standard sizes and oversizes of .010. Piston pins are supplied with the piston and are available in standard size only, **Fig. 13.**

To inspect piston fit in bore, measure bore diameter using suitable telescoping gauges and record reading. Measure piston across skirt at a point ¼ inch below piston pin center line and record reading. Subtract piston diameter from bore diameter. If measurement in between specified clearance of .0013–.0027 inch, piston is acceptable. If not within specifications, cylinder bore must be reconditioned and new oversized piston must be fitted.

MAIN & ROD BEARINGS

Main bearings are available in standard sizes and undersizes of .016 and .032 inch. Rod bearings are available in standard size and various undersizes.

CRANKSHAFT SEAL

REPLACE

Refer to "Front Cover Seal, Replace."

CRANKSHAFT REAR OIL SEAL

REPLACE

1. Remove transaxle as outlined in **MOTOR's "Domestic Transmission, In-Vehicle Service" or "Transmission Service DVD."**
2. Remove flywheel, **Fig. 14.**
3. Pry seal out with suitable tool. **Do not damage crankshaft or seal bore.**

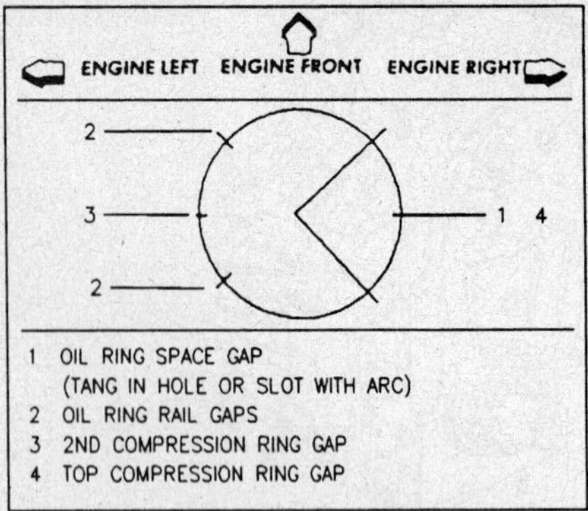

Fig. 12 Piston installation & ring gap locations

4. Reverse procedure to install, noting the following:
   a. Lubricate inside and outside seal diameters with clean engine oil.
   b. Install seal oil seal using seal installer tool No. J-34686, or equivalent, **Fig. 15.**
   c. Tighten mounting bolts to specifications.

OIL PAN

REPLACE

1. Remove engine mount struts as outlined in "Engine Mount, Replace."
2. **On models equipped with air conditioning,** remove mounting bolts and set A/C compressor aside.
3. **On all models,** install suitable engine support fixture with lift hooks and brackets.
4. Raise and support vehicle.
5. Disconnect catalytic converter pipe from righthand exhaust manifold.
6. Drain engine oil into suitable container.
7. Remove oil level sensor wiring harness connector.
8. Remove starter motor as outlined under "Starter, Replace" in "Electrical" section.
9. Remove righthand front tire and wheel assembly, and righthand engine splash shield.
10. Remove mounting bolts and transaxle brace.
11. Remove lefthand front tire and wheel assembly, and lefthand engine splash shield.
12. Support transaxle with suitable floor stands.
13. Remove transaxle mount lower nuts.
14. Remove engine mount lower nuts.
15. Raise engine to gain access to oil pan using engine support fixture.
16. Remove mounting bolts, and engine mount bracket with engine mount from oil pan.
17. Remove mounting bolts, oil pan and gasket, **Fig. 16.**
18. Reverse procedure to install, noting the following:
    a. Apply sealer part No. 1234579, or equivalent, to both side of crankshaft rear main bearing cap with suitable putty knife.

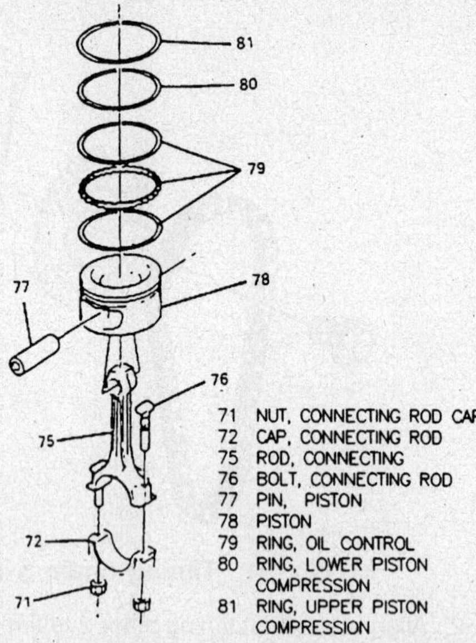

Fig. 13 Exploded view of piston & rod assembly

   b. Torque wrench adapter tool No. J-39505, or equivalent, is require to install righthand side oil pan bolts.

OIL PUMP

REPLACE

1. Remove oil pan as outlined in "Oil Pan, Replace."
2. Remove mounting bolt, oil pump and oil pump driveshaft.
3. Remove crankshaft oil deflector plate, **Fig. 17.**
4. Reverse procedure to install.

OIL PUMP SERVICE

Disassemble

1. Drain oil from pump into suitable container.
2. Remove driveshaft.
3. Remove mounting bolts and cover.
4. Remove gears.
5. Remove cotter pin and pressure regulator valve spring. **Spring is under pressure.**

Assemble

1. Lubricate internal components with clean engine oil.
2. Install gears.
3. Install cover and tighten mounting bolts to specifications.
4. Install pressure regulator valve, spring and cotter pin. **Ensure cotter pin is properly secured.**
5. Apply seal part No. 1050026, or equivalent, to new suction pipe.
6. Tap pipe in place using suitable plastic hammer and oil suction tube installer tool No. J-21882, or equivalent.

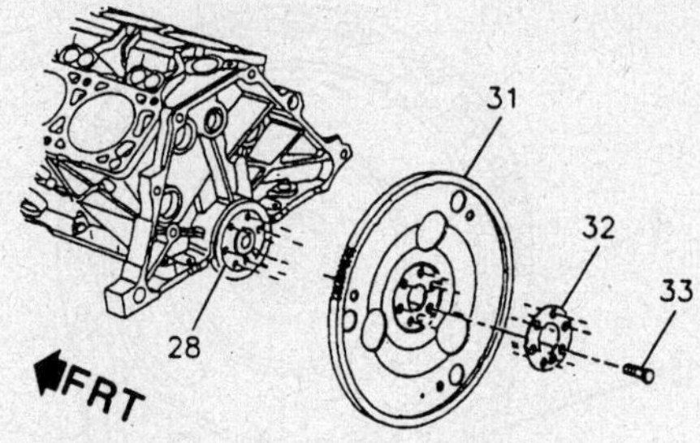

Fig. 14 Flywheel replacement

SERPENTINE DRIVE BELT

Belt Routing

Refer to **Fig. 18** for serpentine drive belt routing.

Belt Replacement

1. Release belt pressure by rotating tensioner.
2. Remove serpentine drive belt.
3. Reverse procedure to install.

Tensioner Replacement

1. Remove serpentine drive belt.
2. Remove mounting bolt and tensioner.
3. Reverse procedure to install.

COOLING SYSTEM BLEED

These engines do not require a specified bleed procedure. After filling cooling system, run engine to operating temperature with radiator/pressure cap off. Air will then be automatically bled through cap opening.

THERMOSTAT

REPLACE

1. Remove air cleaner and duct assembly.
2. Drain coolant into suitable container to below thermostat level.
3. Remove mounting nuts and exhaust crossover pipe.
4. Remove radiator hose from thermostat housing.
5. Remove mounting bolts, thermostat housing and gasket.
6. Remove thermostat.
7. Reverse procedure to install. Apply suitable RTV sealer to thermostat housing mounting bolt threads.

WATER PUMP

REPLACE

1. Drain coolant into suitable container to below water pump level.

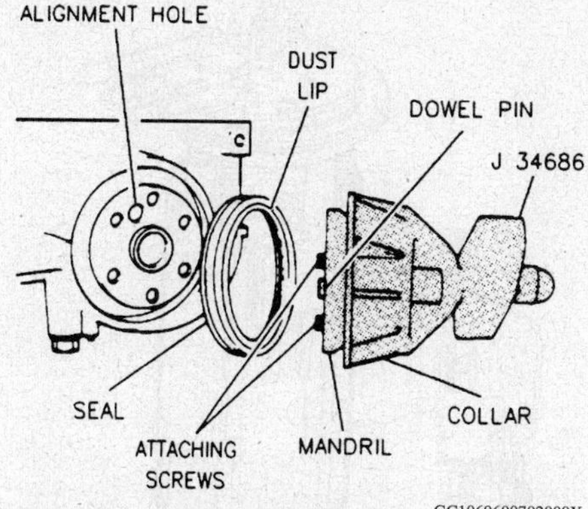

Fig. 15 Crankshaft rear oil seal installation

2. Remove drive belt guard.
3. Loosen water pump pulley bolts, **Fig. 19.**
4. Remove serpentine belt as outlined in "Serpentine Drive Belt."
5. Remove mounting bolts and water pump pulley.
6. Remove mounting bolts, water pump and gasket.
7. Reverse procedure to install.

RADIATOR

REPLACE

1. Remove air cleaner and duct assembly.
2. Drain coolant into suitable container.
3. Recover A/C refrigerant as outlined in "Air Conditioning" chapter.
4. Loosen engine mount strut to engine mount strut bracket bolts.
5. Loosen engine mount strut bracket brace bolts from upper radiator support bracket.
6. Remove mounting bolts on radiator upper support and position engine mount strut and bracket to rear.
7. Remove underhood electrical center and position aside.
8. Disconnect battery positive cable and remove battery hold-down retainer.
9. Remove battery from engine compartment.
10. Disconnect cooling fan harness electrical connector.
11. Remove cooling fans and shroud mounting bolts, and fans and shroud from engine compartment.
12. Remove lower hose from radiator.
13. Remove lines from transmission oil cooler retainers.
14. Disconnect transaxle oil cooler lines from radiator.
15. Remove A/C discharge hose from condenser block.

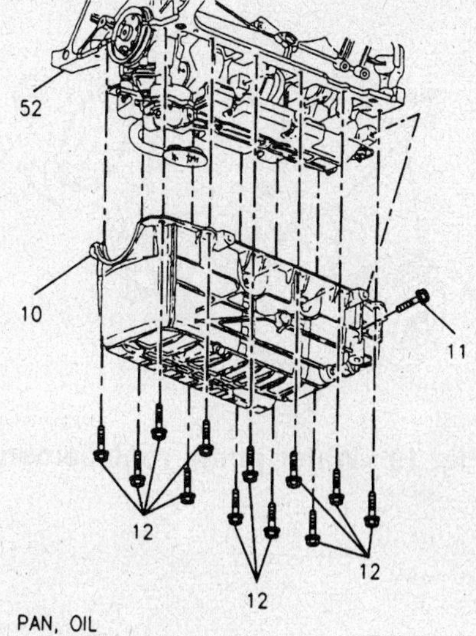

Fig. 16 Oil pan replacement

16. Remove condenser to evaporator inlet tube from condenser block.
17. Remove radiator/condenser assembly from engine compartment.
18. Remove condenser tube bracket bolt, and condenser to radiator mounting bolts.
19. Remove condenser from radiator.
20. Reverse procedure to install.

FUEL PUMP

REPLACE

1. Relieve fuel system pressure as outlined in "Precautions."
2. Loosen fuel tank fill cap.
3. Place suitable container under tank fuel filler pipe connection , then loosen clamp and remove filler pipe.
4. Draw fuel from tank into container using suitable hand pump.
5. Raise and support vehicle. **Provide addition vehicle support at front of vehicle. Chain vehicle rear frame to hoist pads.**
6. Disconnect quick-connect fittings at fuel filter inlet, return line near fuel filter and fuel tank EVAP pipe canister.
7. Remove EVAP fuel filter pipe.
8. Loosen hose clamp and remove fuel tank filler pipe.
9. Loosen hose clamp and remove fuel tank filler vent hose.
10. Support tank with suitable lifting equipment, then remove tank mounting straps.

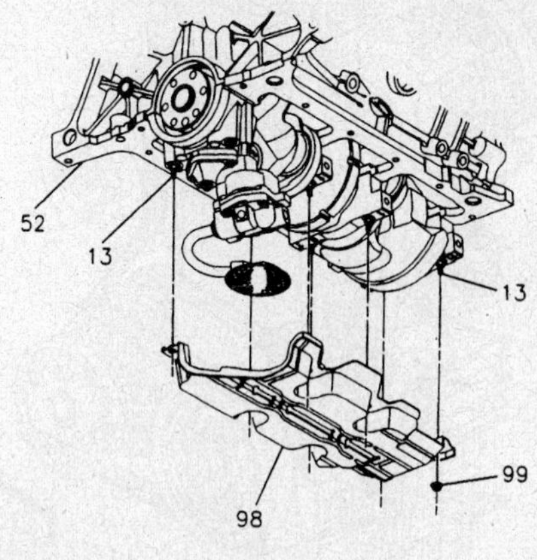

Fig. 17 Crankshaft oil deflector & oil pump replacement

11. Disconnect fuel sender and fuel tank pressure sensor electrical connectors.
12. Remove fuel tank and place on suitable work surface.
13. Clean all pipe and hose connections, as well as area surrounding connections.
14. Disconnect fuel sensor assembly quick-connect fittings.
15. Remove sender assembly mounting nut with spanner wrench tool No. J-39765, or equivalent.
16. Remove sender with O-ring.
17. Mark filter position on pump, **Fig. 20.**
18. Support reservoir with one hand and pry filter off reservoir with suitable screwdriver.
19. Reverse procedure to install, noting the following:
    a. Use new fuel pump filter screen and level meter O-ring.
    b. Ensure filter does not block full travel of float arm.

FUEL FILTER

REPLACE

1. Relieve fuel system pressure as outlined in "Precautions."
2. Raise and support vehicle.
3. Disconnect fuel line fittings using tool No. J-37088-A, or equivalent, **Fig. 21.**
4. Drain fuel into suitable container.
5. Remove mounting nut, bracket and fuel filter.
6. Remove filter from bracket, **Fig. 22.**
7. Reverse procedure to install. Apply few drops of clean engine oil to filter's tube ends to help prevent fuel leak.

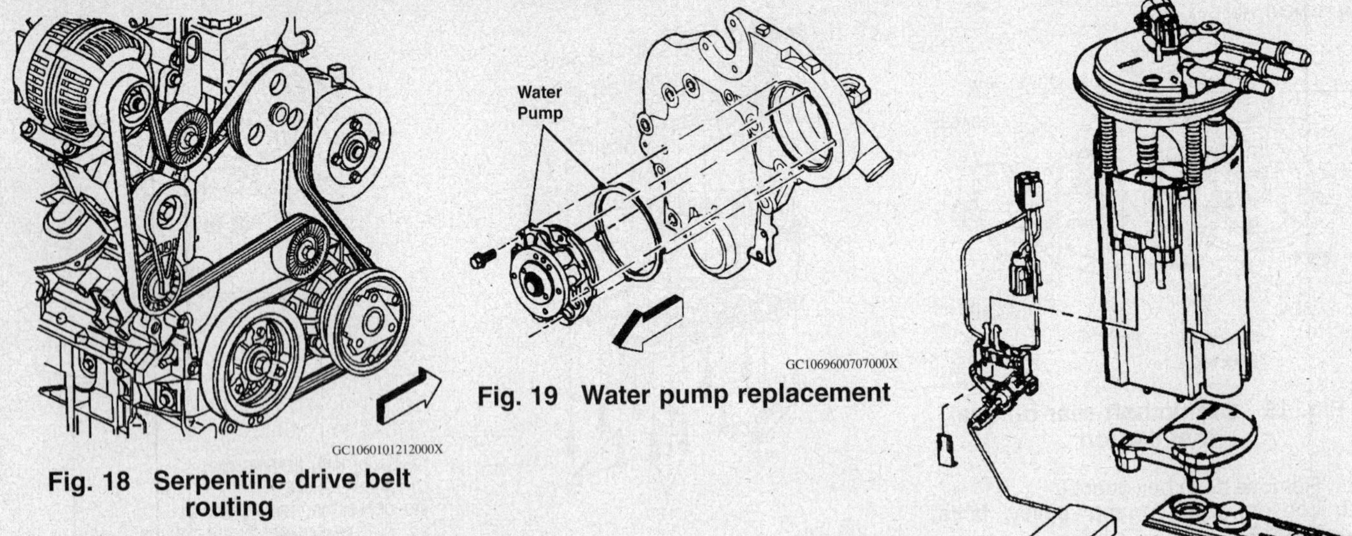

Fig. 18 Serpentine drive belt routing

Fig. 19 Water pump replacement

Fig. 20 Fuel level meter/pump assembly

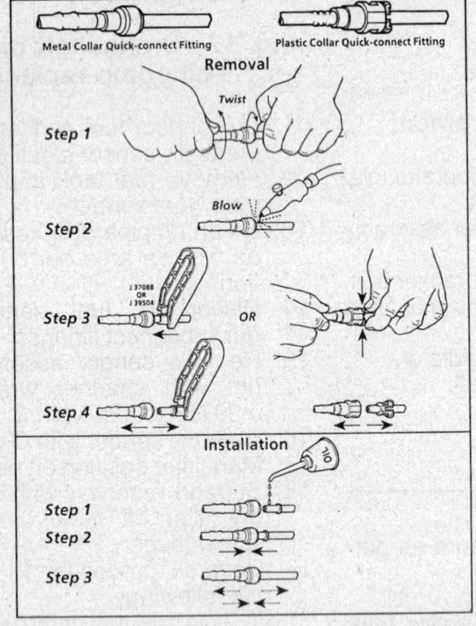

Fig. 21 Quick-connect fittings

1 FUEL FEED PIPE
2 IN-LINE FUEL FILTER
3 FUEL RETURN PIPE
4 SCREWS (2)

GC1028800046000X

Fig. 22 Fuel filter replacement

TIGHTENING SPECIFICATIONS

Year	Component	Torque Ft. Lbs.
2002–05	Accelerator Control Cable Bracket	89①
	Adapter Plate	52
	Alternator Bracket	37
	Camshaft Position Sensor	89①
	Camshaft Sprocket	103①
	Camshaft Thrust Plate	89①
	Connecting Rod Cap Nut	②
	Coolant Drain Plug	14
	Coolant Outlet	18
	Coolant Pump	89①
	Coolant Pump Pulley	18
	Coolant Temperature Sensor	17
	Crankshaft Balancer	⑨
	Crankshaft Main Bearing Cap	④
	Crankshaft Oil Deflector Nut	18
	Crankshaft Position Sensor Engine Block Side	98①
	Crankshaft Position Sensor Front Cover Bolt	89①
	Crankshaft Position Sensor Wiring Bracket	37
	Crossover Pipe	18
	Crossover Pipe Heat Shield	89①
	Cylinder Head Bolt	③
	EGR Valve	18
	Electronic Ignition Retaining Bolt & Nut	18
	Engine Mount Bracket	43
	Engine Mount Lower Nut	32
	Engine Mount Strut	35
	Engine Mount Strut, Lefthand Rear	52
	Engine Mount Strut Bracket, Righthand Side	37
	Engine Mount Strut Bracket, Upper Radiator Support	21
	Engine Mount Upper Nut	35
	Exhaust Manifold Heat Shield	89①
	Exhaust Manifold Nut	12
	Exhaust Manifold Stud	13
	Flywheel	52
	Front Cover Bolt	⑥
	Fuel Feed Pipe	13
	Fuel Injector Rail	89①
	Fuel Pipe Bracket	37
	Fuel Pipe Clip	89①
	Fuel Return Pipe	13
	Heated Oxygen Sensor	31
	Heater Inlet Pipe	18
	Heater Inlet Pipe Nipple	22
	Ignition Coil Bracket	18
	Intake Manifold Coolant Pipe	89①
	Knock Sensor	14
	Lower Intake Manifold	⑦
	Main Bearing Cap	④
	MAP Sensor	44①
	Oil Cooler Connector	37

TIGHTENING SPECIFICATIONS—Continued

Year	Component	Torque Ft. Lbs.
2002–05	Oil Cooler Hose Fitting	14
	Oil Cooler Pipe Bracket	89①
	Oil Drain Plug	18
	Oil Filter	115①
	Oil Filter Bypass Plug	14
	Oil Filter Fitting	29
	Oil Gallery Plug (¼ Inch)	14
	Oil Gallery Plug (⅜ Inch)	24
	Oil Dipstick	18
	Oil Level Sensor	89①
	Oil Pan Bottom Bolts	18
	Oil Pan Drain Plug	18
	Oil Pan Side Bolts	37
	Oil Pressure Indicator Switch	115①
	Oil Pump	30
	Oil Pump Cover	89①
	Oil Pump Drive	27
	Rear Engine Lift Bracket Bolt	37
	Rocker Arm Pivot Bolts	⑤
	Rocker Cover Retaining Bolt	89①
	Spark Plug	15
	Thermostat Body	18
	Thermostat Bypass Pipe To Cylinder Head Nut	18
	Thermostat Bypass Pipe To Front Cover	106①
	Thermostat Bypass Pipe To Throttle Body	18
	Timing Chain Dampener Bolt	15
	Upper Intake Manifold	18
	Valve Cover	89①
	Valve Lifter Guide	89①
	Valve Rocker Arm Bolt	⑧
	Valve Rocker Arm Cover	89①
	Water Outlet	18
	Water Pump	98①
	Water Pump Pulley	18
	Wiring Harness Bracket	115①

① — Inch lbs.

② — First step, 15 ft. lbs.; second step, tighten an additional 75°.

③ — Refer to "Cylinder Head, Replace" for tightening specifications.

④ — First step, 37 ft. lbs.; second step, tighten an additional 77°.

⑤ — First step, 89 inch lbs.; second step, tighten an additional 30°.

⑥ — Refer to "Front Cover, Replace" for tightening specifications.

⑦ — Refer to "Intake Manifold Replace, Lower." for tightening specifications.

⑧ — First step, 14 ft. lbs.; second step, tighten an additional 30°.

⑨ — Refer to "Crankshaft Damper, Replace," for tightening specifications.

3.5L Engine

NOTE: Refer To "3.5L Engine" Section Of "Relay, SV6, Terraza, & Uplander" Chapter In This Manual For Service Procedures & Tightening Specifications Not Found In This Section.

NOTE: On Air Bag Equipped Models, Refer To "Air Bag System Precautions" Located In The Front Of This Manual For System Disarming & Arming Procedures.

NOTE: Refer To "Computer Relearn Procedures" Located In The Front Of This Manual For Computer Relearn Procedures.

INDEX

PRECAUTIONS

Air Bag Systems

Refer to "Air Bag System Precautions" in the front of this manual for system disarming and arming procedures.

Battery Ground Cable

Prior to service, disconnect battery ground cable and isolate as required.

Fuel System Pressure Relief

1. Loosen fuel filler cap to discharge tank pressure.
2. Connect fuel pressure gauge tool No. J-34730-1A, or equivalent, to fuel pressure connection. Wrap shop towel around connection while connecting fuel pressure gauge in order to avoid fuel spillage.
3. Install bleed hose into an approved container and open valve in order to bleed fuel system pressure.
4. Drain any fuel remaining in fuel pressure gauge into suitable container.

ENGINE MOUNT

REPLACE

1. Loosen air cleaner outlet duct clamps at air cleaner and throttle body.
2. Remove PCV fresh air tube from outlet duct.
3. Remove air cleaner outlet duct from air cleaner and throttle body.
4. Remove engine mount strut bolts and struts.
5. Raise and support vehicle.
6. Remove catalytic converter.
7. Remove righthand front wheel and tire.
8. Remove righthand engine splash shield.
9. Remove engine mount lower nuts, and insert a block of wood that spans width of oil pan bottom between oil pan and jack support.
10. Remove engine mount bracket bolts.
11. Raise engine until engine mount and bracket can be removed.
12. Remove engine mount and bracket.
13. Remove engine mount bracket nuts and mount bracket.
14. Reverse procedure to install.

ENGINE

REPLACE

1. Remove intake manifold cover.
2. Remove coolant reservoir.
3. Remove lefthand front sheet metal diagonal brace.
4. Remove air cleaner side cover and air cleaner element.
5. Remove air cleaner upper cover bolts and upper cover.
6. Remove PCM and position aside with wiring harness.
7. Remove air cleaner bolts and air cleaner.
8. Drain cooling system into a suitable container.
9. Remove radiator inlet and outlet hoses.
10. Disconnect heater inlet and outlet hoses from engine.
11. Remove brake booster vacuum hose from intake manifold.
12. Disconnect fuel and EVAP line quick connect fittings at engine.
13. Disconnect automatic transaxle range selector cable from selector lever.
14. Remove selector cable from bracket.
15. Disconnect engine harness from TAC.
16. Remove engine harness clip from PCV foul air tube clip.
17. Disconnect EGR valve and EVAP canister purge solenoid.
18. Remove engine harness clips from intake manifold.
19. Disconnect engine harness electrical connector from fuel injector electrical connector.
20. Remove engine harness electrical connector clip from belt shield.
21. Remove engine harness clip from ignition coil bracket.
22. Disconnect engine harness electrical connector from ignition coil.
23. Remove engine harness clip from bracket attached to engine mount strut.
24. Disconnect engine harness electrical connector from alternator.
25. Disconnect engine harness electrical connector from transaxle.
26. Remove engine harness clip from transaxle stud.
27. Raise and suitably support vehicle.
28. Remove CPA retainer from HO2S electrical connector.
29. Disconnect engine harness electrical connector from HO2S.
30. Remove HO2S electrical connector clip from ignition coil bracket.
31. Remove engine harness clip from transaxle brace.
32. Disconnect VSS electrical connector.
33. Disconnect oil pressure switch and knock sensor electrical connectors.

34. Remove engine harness clip from oil dipstick tube.
35. Remove starter solenoid S terminal nut.
36. Remove engine harness lead from starter.
37. Remove engine harness clip from oil pan.
38. Remove engine harness nut.
39. Remove battery ground lead from stud.
40. Remove engine harness ground wires from transaxle studs.
41. Remove engine harness bolt.
42. Reposition battery ground and engine harness.
43. Disconnect engine harness electrical connector from A/C pressure sensor.
44. Disconnect engine harness electrical connector from A/C compressor.
45. Disconnect engine harness electrical connector from righthand wheel speed sensor.
46. Remove engine harness clips from lower control arm.
47. Disconnect engine harness electrical connector from lefthand wheel speed sensor.
48. Remove engine harness clips from lower control arm.
49. Remove CPA retainer from HO2S electrical connector.
50. Disconnect engine harness electrical connector from HO2S.
51. Remove engine harness clips from heat shield and underbody.
52. Disconnect knock sensor and Crankshaft Position (CKP) sensor electrical connectors.
53. Lower vehicle and remove drive belt.
54. Disconnect engine harness electrical connectors from instrument panel electrical connectors.
55. Gather all branches of engine harness and position harness to side and out of way.
56. Remove engine mount strut.
57. Raise and support vehicle.
58. Remove rear propeller shaft.
59. Remove catalytic converter.
60. Remove front tires and wheels.
61. Remove lower radiator air baffle assembly.
62. Remove engine splash shields.
63. Remove stabilizer shaft links from lower control arms.
64. Remove tie rod ends from steering knuckles.
65. Remove lower ball joints from knuckles.
66. Remove transaxle oil cooler line bracket bolt.
67. Disconnect transaxle oil cooler line quick connect fittings at transaxle.
68. Remove A/C compressor bolts and position compressor aside. **Do not discharge A/C system.**
69. Disconnect drive axles from transaxle.
70. Secure drive axles to steering knuckle/struts.
71. Remove front part of inner fender liner in order to access front cradle bolts.
72. Remove intermediate shaft pinch bolt from steering gear.
73. Install a engine support stand tool No. J 39580 or equivalent below vehicle.
74. Lower vehicle until frame contacts engine support stand.
75. Remove frame bolts.
76. Raise vehicle in order to separate powertrain/frame assembly from vehicle.
77. Remove starter motor as outlined under "Starter, Replace" in "Electrical" section.
78. Remove transaxle cover bolts.
79. Remove transaxle covers.
80. Remove torque converter bolts.
81. Remove engine mount lower nuts.
82. Remove transaxle brace bolts and brace.
83. Remove exhaust crossover pipe.
84. Install an engine hoist to engine.
85. Remove transaxle to engine bolts/stud and support transaxle.
86. Separate and remove engine from transaxle/frame.
87. Remove flywheel.
88. Reverse procedure to install.

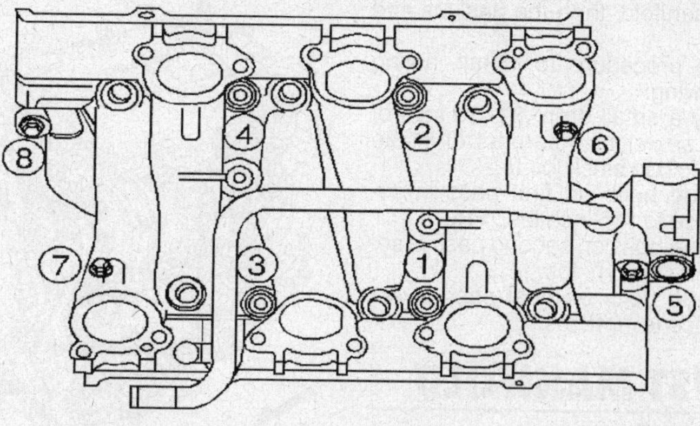

Fig. 1 Lower intake manifold bolt tightening sequence

INTAKE MANIFOLD

REPLACE

Upper

1. Drain cooling system into a suitable container.
2. Remove intake manifold cover.
3. Remove air cleaner outlet duct.
4. Disconnect EVAP canister purge solenoid valve quick connect fitting.
5. Remove PCV fresh air tube from rocker cover.
6. Reposition brake booster vacuum hose clamp at intake manifold.
7. Remove brake booster vacuum hose from intake manifold.
8. Disconnect PCM electrical connector.
9. Disconnect MAP sensor electrical connector.
10. Remove engine harness clip from PCV foul air clip.
11. Disconnect EGR valve electrical connector.
12. Disconnect EVAP canister purge solenoid valve electrical connector.
13. Remove engine harness clips from intake manifold.
14. Disconnect spark plug wires from ignition coil.
15. Remove spark plug wire harness clips from ignition coil bracket, spark plug wire support and coolant bypass pipe.
16. Disconnect spark plug wires from spark plugs.
17. Remove PCV foul air tube bolt, clip and tube.
18. Remove thermostat bypass pipe.
19. Remove ignition coil as outlined under "Ignition Coil, Replace" in "Electrical" section.
20. Remove EGR pipe bolt and carefully pull pipe assembly back.
21. Remove EGR valve studs, valve and gasket.
22. Remove alternator bracket.
23. Remove upper intake manifold bolts and stud.
24. Remove spark plug support bracket.
25. Remove upper intake manifold and gaskets.
26. Reverse procedure to install.

Lower

1. Remove upper intake manifold.
2. Remove lefthand and righthand valve rocker arm covers as outlined under "Valve Cover, Replace."
3. Relieve fuel system pressure as outlined under "Precautions."
4. Disconnect fuel feed pipe from fuel rail.
5. Disconnect EVAP pipe from EVAP canister purge solenoid valve.
6. Disconnect engine harness electrical connector from fuel injector harness electrical connector.
7. Disconnect fuel injector harness electrical connector from ECT sensor.
8. Disconnect fuel injector harness electrical connector from CMP sensor.
9. Remove fuel rail bolts and fuel rail
10. Remove fuel injector O-ring seals from spray tip end of each injector.
11. Remove fuel injectors from fuel rail.
12. Reposition radiator inlet hose clamp at thermostat housing.
13. Remove radiator inlet hose from thermostat housing.
14. Disconnect heater inlet hose quick connect.
15. Remove heater inlet pipe nut and inlet pipe from lower intake manifold.
16. Remove lower intake manifold bolts,

intake manifold, then the gaskets and seals.
17. Reverse procedure to install, noting the following:
    a. Apply a small drop .31-.39 inch of RTV sealer to 4 corners of intake manifold to block joints.
    b. **Torque** bolts on first pass in sequence to 115 inch lbs., **Fig. 1.**
    c. **Torque** bolts on second pass in sequence to 15 ft. lbs.
    d. **Torque** bolts on final pass in sequence to 18 ft. lbs.

EXHAUST MANIFOLD

REPLACE

Lefthand

1. Remove spark plug wires and spark plugs.
2. Remove exhaust manifold heat shield bolts and heat shield.
3. Remove exhaust manifold nuts and manifold.
4. Reverse procedure to install.

Righthand

1. Remove spark plug wires and spark plugs.
2. Remove EGR pipe from exhaust manifold.
3. Remove heated oxygen sensor.
4. Remove exhaust manifold heat shield bolts and heat shields.
5. Remove exhaust manifold nuts and manifold.
6. Reverse procedure to install.

SERPENTINE DRIVE BELT

Belt Routing

Refer to **Fig. 2** for serpentine drive belt routing.

Belt Replacement

1. Rotate drive belt tensioner counterclockwise in order to release tensioner spring tension.
2. Remove serpentine drive belt.
3. Reverse procedure to install.

Tensioner Replacement

1. Remove serpentine drive belt.

Fig. 2 Serpentine drive belt routing

2. Remove mounting bolt and tensioner.
3. Reverse procedure to install.

THERMOSTAT

REPLACE

1. Remove air cleaner and duct assembly.
2. Drain coolant into suitable container to below thermostat level.
3. Remove mounting nuts and exhaust crossover pipe.
4. Remove radiator hose from thermostat housing.
5. Remove mounting bolts, thermostat housing and gasket.
6. Remove thermostat.
7. Reverse procedure to install. Apply suitable RTV sealer to thermostat housing mounting bolt threads.

WATER PUMP

REPLACE

1. Drain cooling system into a suitable container.
2. Loosen water pump pulley bolts.
3. Remove drive belt as outlined under "Serpentine Drive Belt."
4. Remove water pump pulley bolts and pulley.
5. Remove water pump bolts and pump.
6. Reverse procedure to install.

RADIATOR

REPLACE

1. Recover A/C refrigerant as outlined in "Air Conditioning" chapter.
2. Drain cooling system into a suitable container.
3. Remove cooling fans with cooling fan shroud.
4. Remove air cleaner and duct assembly.
5. Remove cooling fan harness electrical connector.
6. Remove righthand side diagonal brace.
7. Loosen engine mount strut nuts.
8. Remove engine mount strut bracket brace bolts from upper radiator support and rotate struts and brackets rearward.
9. Remove upper radiator hose.
10. Remove radiator upper mount bolts and mounts.
11. Remove cooling fan shroud bolts.
12. Reposition coolant overflow hose clamp at radiator using hose clamp pliers tool No. J 38185 or equivalent.
13. Disconnect and reposition coolant overflow hose.
14. Disconnect engine wiring harness retainers at engine harness bracket and reposition engine wiring harness.
15. Remove cooling fans with cooling fan shroud.
16. Reposition hose clamp at water pump housing using hose clamp pliers.
17. Disconnect radiator outlet hose from water pump housing.
18. Remove radiator outlet hose.
19. Remove nut which secures A/C discharge hose to condenser block.
20. Disconnect A/C discharge hose from condenser block.
21. Remove and discard sealing washer.
22. Cap or tape off open A/C hose to prevent contamination.
23. Remove bolt which secures evaporator inlet tube to condenser block.
24. Disconnect evaporator inlet tube from condenser block.
25. Cap or tape off evaporator inlet tube.
26. Remove radiator and condenser assembly.
27. Remove condenser tube clip bolt.
28. Remove condenser mounting bolts.
29. Remove condenser from radiator.
30. Reverse procedure to install.

FUEL PUMP

REPLACE

Refer to "Fuel Pump, Replace" in "3.4L Engine" section for fuel pump replacement procedure.

FUEL FILTER

REPLACE

Refer to "Fuel Filter, Replace" in "3.4L Engine" chapter for fuel filter replacement procedures.

TIGHTENING SPECIFICATIONS

Year	Component	Torque Ft. Lbs.
2006	Accelerator Control Cable Bracket	89①
	Air Baffle Bolt	15
	Air Conditioning Condenser Mounting Bolt	53①
	Air Conditioning Condenser Tube Clip Bolt	22①
	Camshaft Sprocket Bolt	103
	Camshaft Thrust Plate Screw	89①
	Coolant Heater	37
	Cooling Fan Motor Screw	53①
	Cooling Fan Nut	53①
	Cooling Fan Shroud Bolt	53①
	Crankshaft Balancer Bolt	118
	Crankshaft Position Sensor Shield Nut	97①
	Crankshaft Position Sensor Stud - Side of Engine Block	97①
	Discharge Hose to Condenser Nut	12
	Drive Belt Tensioner Bolt	37
	EGR Valve Assembly Bolt	22
	EGR Valve Pipe Bolt	18
	Engine Block Drain Plug	16
	Engine Mount Strut and A/C Compressor Bracket Bolt	37
	Engine Mount Strut Bracket to Radiator Support Bolt	37
	Engine Mount Strut & Alternator Bracket Bolt	37
	Engine Mount Strut and Lift Bracket Bolt - Engine Lift Rear	52
	Engine Mount Strut Nut	35
	Engine Mount Strut and Support Bracket Bolt	18
	Engine Wiring Harness Bracket Bolt	115①
	Evaporator Inlet Tube to Condenser Bolt	12

TIGHTENING SPECIFICATIONS—Continued

Year	Component	Torque Ft. Lbs.
2006	EVAP Purge Valve Bolt	12
	Exhaust Crossover Pipe Heat Shield Bolt	89①
	Exhaust Crossover Pipe Stud/Nut	18
	Exhaust Manifold Heat Shield Bolt	89①
	Exhaust Manifold Nut	12
	Exhaust Manifold Stud	13
	Flywheel Bolt	52
	Fuel Feed Pipe to Fuel Injector Rail Bolt	89①
	Fuel Injector Rail Bolt	89①
	Heated Oxygen Sensor	31
	Heater Inlet Pipe Nut	18
	Heater Inlet Pipe Stud	26
	Ignition Coil Bracket Bolt/Nut/Stud	18
	Intake Manifold Coolant Pipe Bolt	89①
	Knock Sensor	18
	Lower Intake Manifold Bolt - Center	18
	MAP Sensor Bolt	89①
	Radiator Bracket Bolt	18
	Radiator Upper Mount Bolt	89①
	Spark Plug	11
	Thermostat Bypass Pipe Bolt/Nut	89①
	Thermostat Housing Bolt	18
	Throttle Body Bolt	89①
	Throttle Body Stud	53①
	Water Pump Bolt	89①
	Water Pump Pulley Bolt	18

① — Inch lbs.

3.6L Engine

NOTE: Refer To "3.6L Engine" Section Of "SRX" Chapter In This Manual For Service Procedures & Tightening Specifications Not Found In This Section.

NOTE: On Air Bag Equipped Models, Refer To "Air Bag System Precautions" Located In The Front Of This Manual For System Disarming & Arming Procedures.

NOTE: Refer To "Computer Relearn Procedures" Located In The Front Of This Manual For Computer Relearn Procedures.

INDEX

PRECAUTIONS

Air Bag Systems

Refer to "Air Bag System Precautions" in the front of this manual for system disarming and arming procedures.

Battery Ground Cable

Prior to service, disconnect battery ground cable and isolate as required.

Fuel System Pressure Relief

1. Loosen fuel filler cap to discharge tank pressure.
2. Connect fuel pressure gauge tool No. J-34730-1A, or equivalent, to fuel pressure connection. Wrap shop towel around connection while connecting fuel pressure gauge in order to avoid fuel spillage.
3. Install bleed hose into an approved container and open valve in order to bleed fuel system pressure.
4. Drain any fuel remaining in fuel pressure gauge into suitable container.

ENGINE MOUNT

REPLACE

1. Remove air cleaner intake duct.
2. Remove air cleaner side cover with MAF sensor.
3. Remove engine mount struts.
4. Raise and support vehicle.
5. Remove three-way catalytic converter pipe from engine righthand side exhaust manifold.
6. Remove wheel and tire.
7. Remove engine splash shield.
8. Remove engine mount lower nuts, insert a block of wood that spans width of oil pan bottom between pan and a suitable jack.
9. Raise engine to gain access.
10. Remove engine mount bracket to oil pan bolts.
11. Remove engine mount bracket to engine bolts.
12. Remove engine mount and engine mount bracket.
13. Remove engine mount upper nuts.
14. Remove engine mount from engine mount bracket.
15. Reverse procedure to install.

ENGINE

REPLACE

1. Remove throttle body air inlet duct.
2. Drain cooling system into a suitable container.
3. Disconnect radiator hoses from engine.
4. Disconnect heater hoses from engine.
5. Remove engine mount struts.
6. Relieve fuel pressure as outlined under "Precautions."
7. Disconnect fuel and EVAP pipes from engine.
8. Remove PCM chassis side electrical connector from PCM.
9. Remove wiring harness ground from transmission.
10. Remove vacuum brake booster hose from intake manifold.
11. Recover A/C system refrigerant as outlined in "Air Conditioning" chapter.
12. Disconnect discharge hose from condenser and suction hose from evaporator outlet tube.
13. Secure discharge and suction hoses aside.
14. Disconnect transaxle electrical connector.
15. Raise and support vehicle.
16. Remove torque converter bolts.
17. Drain engine oil into a suitable container.
18. **On models equipped with all wheel drive,** remove rear propeller shaft.
19. **On all models,** remove catalytic converter.
20. Remove front tires and wheels.
21. Remove lower radiator air baffle.
22. Remove engine splash shields.
23. Disconnect VSS electrical connector and secure wiring harness to vehicle.
24. Remove front wheel speed sensor wiring harnesses from lower control arms and frame.
25. Remove tie rod ends from steering knuckles.
26. Remove lower ball joints from knuckles.
27. Disconnect drive axles from transaxle.
28. Rotate struts and reposition drive axles toward rear of vehicle to provide clearance for powertrain to be removed.
29. Separate intermediate steering shaft from steering gear.
30. Remove engine mount lower nuts.
31. Remove transmission mount lower nuts.
32. Position a suitable powertrain lift table below engine assembly.
33. Lower vehicle until powertrain is supported by powertrain lift table.
34. Remove frame bolts.

35. Carefully raise vehicle or lower powertrain table in order to remove powertrain from vehicle.
36. Reverse procedure to install.

INTAKE MANIFOLD

REPLACE

1. Loosen intake air duct clamps.
2. Disconnect PCV tube from air intake duct.
3. Remove air intake duct from throttle body and MAF sensor.
4. Remove air intake duct.
5. Relieve fuel system pressure as outlined under "Precautions."
6. Disconnect fuel and EVAP hoses from engine.
7. Disconnect BARO sensor electrical connector.
8. Remove purge line from purge line retainer.
9. Remove fuel feed hose bracket bolt and reposition fuel feed hose. **Do not disconnect Powertrain Control Module (PCM) electrical connectors. Do not remove PCM from bracket.**
10. Remove PCM bracket position aside.
11. Raise and support vehicle.
12. Disconnect intermediate steering shaft from steering gear.
13. Remove and position front portion of front fender liners to gain access to frame front bolts.
14. Lower vehicle.
15. Position a suitable floor jack at front center section of frame in order to support powertrain.
16. Remove frame front bolts.
17. Carefully lower powertrain or raise vehicle enough to provide access.
18. Disconnect purge solenoid electrical connector.
19. Remove wiring harness from righthand side of intake manifold.
20. Disconnect fuel injector electrical connector.
21. Remove fuel injector electrical connector from fuel injector electrical connector bracket.
22. Disconnect intake manifold runner control solenoid electrical connector.
23. Disconnect throttle body electrical connector.
24. Remove brake booster vacuum hose and check valve from intake manifold.
25. Remove PCV hose from cylinder head and intake manifold.
26. Remove intake manifold bolts and upper intake manifold.
27. Remove and discard gasket.
28. Reverse procedure to install, noting the following:
    a. Clean and inspect intake manifold and sealing surfaces.
    b. **Torque** intake manifold bolts in sequence to 17 ft. lbs., **Fig. 1.**

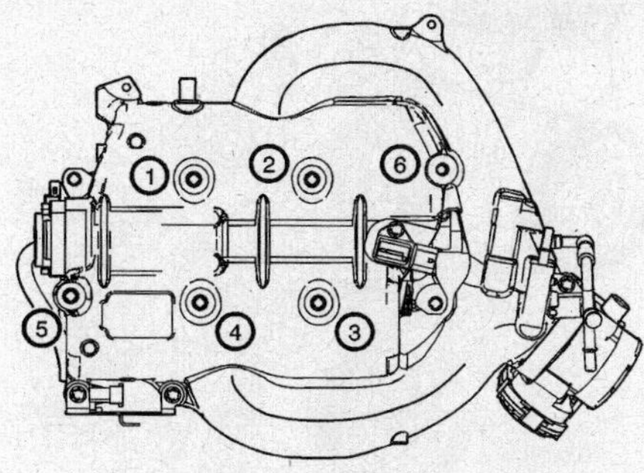

Fig. 1 Intake manifold bolt tightening sequence

EXHAUST MANIFOLD

REPLACE

Lefthand

1. Remove lefthand torque strut bracket bolts and strut bracket.
2. Remove lefthand exhaust manifold heat shield bolts and heat shield.
3. Remove ECT sensor.
4. Remove exhaust manifold and gasket.
5. Reverse procedure to install.

Righthand

1. Remove righthand exhaust manifold heat shield bolts and heat shield.
2. Remove exhaust manifold bolts from righthand cylinder head and remove righthand exhaust manifold.
3. Remove and discard exhaust manifold gasket.
4. **On models equipped with a block heater,** remove block heater cartridge.
5. **On all models,** remove righthand knock sensor bolt and knock sensor.
6. Remove CKP sensor bolt and sensor.
7. Remove and discard CKP sensor O-ring.
8. Reverse procedure to install.

SERPENTINE DRIVE BELT

Belt Routing

Refer to **Fig. 2** for serpentine drive belt routing.

Belt Replacement

1. Raise vehicle and suitably support.
2. Remove righthand engine splash shield.
3. Rotate drive belt tensioner clockwise to release drive belt tension.
4. Remove drive belt from alternator.
5. Slowly release drive belt tensioner.
6. Remove drive belt from accessory drive pulleys.
7. Reverse procedure to install.

Tensioner Replacement

1. Remove serpentine drive belt.
2. Remove idler pulley bolt and pulley.
3. Remove mounting bolt and tensioner.
4. Reverse procedure to install.

THERMOSTAT

REPLACE

1. Remove coolant reservoir.
2. Remove lefthand front sheet metal diagonal brace.
3. Remove air inlet duct.
4. Remove air cleaner upper cover bolts and upper cover.
5. Disconnect MAF sensor electrical connector.
6. Remove and reposition TCM with wiring harness to gain access. **Do not disconnect TCM electrical connector.**
7. Remove air cleaner bolts, then the air cleaner with MAF sensor.
8. Remove throttle body assembly.
9. Remove heater pipes.
10. Remove coolant outlet pipe.
11. Remove thermostat housing bolts and thermostat housing.
12. Remove and discard thermostat housing gasket.
13. Reverse procedure to install.

WATER PUMP

REPLACE

1. Drain cooling system into a suitable container.
2. Remove drive belt as outlined under "Serpentine Drive Belt."
3. Install a water pump pulley holding tool, tool No. EN 46104, or equivalent, onto water pump pulley.
4. Remove water pump pulley bolts and pump pulley.
5. Remove water pump bolts and water pump.
6. Reverse procedure to install.

RADIATOR

REPLACE

Refer to "Radiator, Replace" in "3.5L Engine" section for radiator replacement procedures.

FUEL PUMP

REPLACE

Refer to "Fuel Pump, Replace" in "3.4L Engine" section for fuel pump replacement procedures.

FUEL FILTER

REPLACE

Refer to "Fuel Filter, Replace" in "3.4L Engine" chapter for fuel filter replacement procedures.

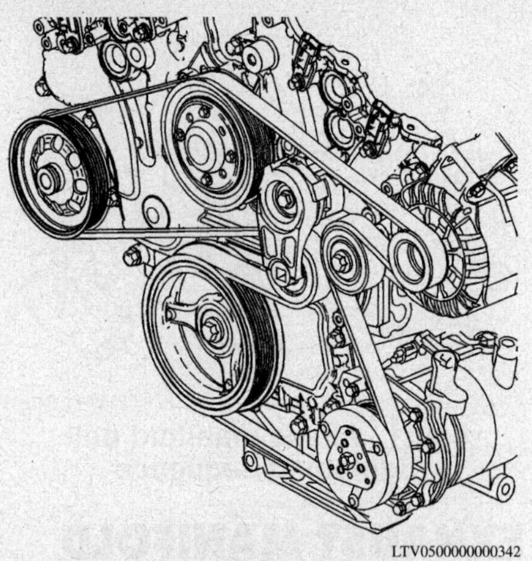

Fig. 2 Serpentine drive belt routing

TIGHTENING SPECIFICATIONS

Year	Component	Torque Ft. Lbs.
2004–06	Accelerator Control Cable Bracket	89①
	Air Baffle Bolt	15
	Air Conditioning Condenser Mounting Bolt	53①
	Air Conditioning Condenser Tube Clip Bolt	22①
	Alternator Bolt	37
	Alternator Cable Bolt	37
	Alternator Cable Nut	89①
	Camshaft Intermediate Drive Sprocket Bolt - Idler Sprocket	43
	Compressor Bolt	37
	Compressor Hose Assembly Bolt	12
	Coolant Outlet Pipe To Thermostat Housing Bolt	17
	Cooling Fan Motor Screw	53①
	Cooling Fan Nut	53①
	Cooling Fan Shroud Bolt	53①
	Crankshaft Position Sensor Bolt	89①
	Crankshaft Position Sensor/Righthand Exhaust Manifold Lower Heat Shield	②
	Discharge Hose To Condenser Nut	12
	Engine Mount Strut Bracket To Radiator Support Bolt	37
	Engine Mount Strut Nut	35
	Engine Block Drain Plug	16
	Engine Control Module Bolt	89①
	Engine Control Module Bracket Bolt - Front	17
	Engine Control Module Bracket Bolt - Side	89①
	Engine Control Module Grounding Bolt	40①
	Engine Coolant Temperature (ECT) Sensor	16
	Engine Mount Nut To Engine Mount Bracket	59
	Engine Mount Nut To Frame	59
	Engine Mount Bracket Bolt To Engine Block - M8	28
	Engine Mount Bracket Bolt To Engine Block - M10	28
	Engine Mount Bracket Bolt	43
	Engine Mount Lower Nut	35
	Engine Mount Strut Bracket Bolts - To Engine	37
	Engine Mount Strut Bracket Bolts - To Radiator Support	19
	Engine Mount Strut Nut	35
	Engine Mount Upper Nut	39
	Engine Wiring Harness Bracket Bolt - Cylinder Head Rear	89①
	Engine Wiring Harness Bracket Bolt - ECM Bracket Side	17
	Engine Wiring Harness Bracket Bolt - ECM Bracket Top	89①

TIGHTENING SPECIFICATIONS—Continued

Year	Component	Torque Ft. Lbs.
2004–06	Engine Wiring Harness Bracket Bolt - Lefthand Side Oil Pan	89①
	Engine Wiring Harness Bracket Bolt - Lefthand Side Oil Filter Adapter	89①
	Engine Wiring Harness Bracket Bolt - Near Crankshaft Position Sensor	37
	Engine Wiring Harness Bracket Bolt - Righthand Side Block Front	17
	Engine Wiring Harness Bracket Bolt - Righthand Side Head Front	89①
	Engine Wiring Harness Ground Bolt - ECM Bracket Top	89①
	Engine Wiring Harness Ground Bolt - Lefthand Cylinder Head Side	89①
	Engine Wiring Harness Ground Bolt - Righthand Cylinder Head Rear	89①
	Evaporative (EVAP) Purge Valve Bolt/Ball Stud	89①
	Exhaust Crossover Pipe Nuts	25
	Exhaust Manifold Bolt	15
	Exhaust Manifold Heat Shield Bolt	89①
	Exhaust Manifold Studs	4.4 ①
	Evaporator Inlet Tube To Condenser Bolt	12
	Fuel Rail Bolt	89①
	Heater Inlet/Outlet Pipe Assembly Bolt	89①
	Idler Pulley Bolt	37
	Ignition Coil Bolt	89①
	Knock Sensor Bolt	17
	PCV Tube Bracket Bolt/Ball Stud	89①
	Power Steering Pump Bracket To Engine Bolt	37
	Power Steering Pump Reservoir Stud	18
	Radiator Bracket Bolt	18
	Radiator Upper Mount Bolt	89①
	Tensioner Bracket Bolt	17
	Thermostat Bypass Pipe Bolt/Nut	89①
	Thermostat Housing Bolt	89①
	Water Outlet Bolt	89①
	Water Pump Bolt	89①
	Water Pump Pulley Bolt	89①

① — Inch lbs.

② — M6 bolt: 89 inch lbs.; M10 bolt: 37 ft. lbs.

Rear Axle & Suspension

NOTE: On Air Bag Equipped Models, Refer To "Air Bag System Precautions" Located In The Front Of This Manual For System Disarming & Arming Procedures.

INDEX

DESCRIPTION

All Wheel Drive

The rear suspension system used on this vehicle is an independent type suspension. The rear suspension contains the following components; crossmember, tie rod, knuckle, wheel bearing, upper and lower control arms, spindles, stabilizer shaft and shock absorbers.

Front Wheel Drive

The rear suspension system used on this vehicle is the trailing-arm axle type. Two control arms (trailing arms) mount the axle to the body. The rear suspension contains the following components; rear axle, coil springs, shock absorbers and rear axle tie rod. The rear axle contains a stabilizer shaft which is an integral part of the rear axle. A wheel bearing and hub are attached to each end of the axle. The wheel bearing and hub also contain an integral wheel speed sensor.

REAR AXLE

REPLACE

1. Raise and support vehicle.
2. Remove tires and wheels.
3. Support rear axle with suitable jack stand.
4. Remove shock absorber lower mounting bolts and nuts.
5. Remove rear axle tie rod from rear axle.
6. Lower rear axle assembly and remove coil springs, spring seats and insulators, **Fig. 1.**
7. Mark relationship between brake drum and wheel hub assembly, then remove brake drum.
8. Remove brake shoes, then park brake cable from actuator lever.
9. Remove parking brake cable from backing plate.
10. Remove brake hydraulic line from wheel cylinder.
11. Remove wheel cylinder to backing plate attaching bolts, and wheel cylinder.
12. Remove wheel bearing and hub assembly attaching bolts, and wheel bearing and hub assembly from rear axle.
13. Remove brake backing plate.
14. Disconnect intermediate brake hydraulic hoses from rear axle brake pipes.
15. Lower rear axle, then remove rear axle control arm bolts and nuts.
16. Remove control arms and rear axle assembly from vehicle.
17. Reverse procedure to install.

REAR AXLE SHAFT

REPLACE

1. Apply parking brake, then raise and support vehicle.
2. Remove tire and wheel assembly.
3. Remove driveshaft to hub assembly spindle nut.
4. Release parking brake and remove brake caliper.
5. Remove brake caliper bracket and separate tie rod end from knuckle. **Do not loosen tie rod end jam nut.**
6. Support lower control arm with suitable jack stand.
7. Disconnect wheel speed sensor electrical connector.
8. Remove parking brake cable from actuator lever.
9. Remove parking brake cable to bracket attaching bolt, then position cable aside.
10. Install hub spindle removal tool No. J 42129, or equivalent, onto wheel hub and secure with wheel nuts.
11. Begin pulling driveshaft from wheel hub and bearing assembly. Driveshaft nut can be partially installed to protect threads.
12. Remove upper control arm to knuckle attaching bolt and nut.
13. Remove and discard driveshaft spindle nut.
14. Disengage driveshaft completely from wheel and hub bearing.
15. Position steering knuckle toward rear of vehicle.
16. Attach axle shaft remover tool No. J 42129 and slide hammer tool No. J 2619-01, or equivalents, to driveshaft.
17. Remove rear axle shaft from carrier, and driveshaft from vehicle.
18. Reverse procedure to install.

DIFFERENTIAL CARRIER

REPLACE

1. Set parking brake, then raise and support vehicle.
2. Remove righthand side tire and wheel assembly.
3. Place a suitable drain pan under differential, then remove drain plug and drain differential gear oil.
4. Disconnect clutch pump check valve electrical connector.
5. Remove righthand rear wheel driveshaft as outlined in "Axle Shaft, Replace."
6. Remove front propeller shaft as outlined in "Propeller Shaft, Replace."
7. Place a suitable adjustable jack stand under torque tube.
8. Loosen, but do not remove torque tube bracket to bracket through bolts and nut, **Fig. 2.**
9. Remove bolts from torque tube bracket, **Fig. 3.**
10. Remove differential carrier to cradle mounting bolts, nuts, washers and mounts from differential.
11. While moving differential assembly towards righthand side of vehicle, disengage lefthand wheel driveshaft from differential.

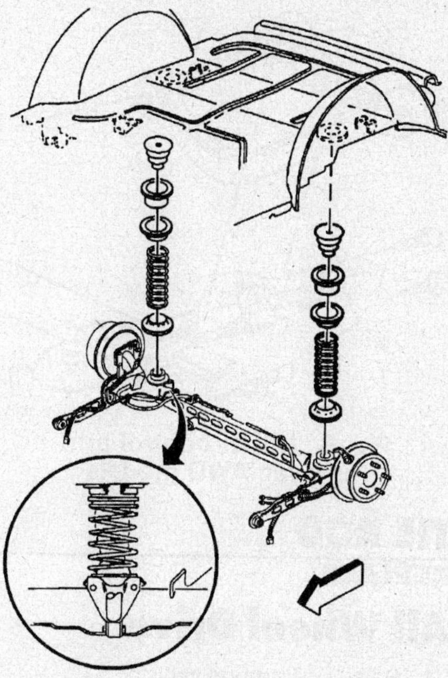

Fig. 1 Rear axle removal

12. Remove rear differential and torque tube as an assembly.
13. Remove torque tube from differential.
14. Reverse procedure to install.

PROPELLER SHAFT

REPLACE

1. Raise and support vehicle.
2. Scribe propeller shaft reference mark on transfer case flange.
3. Remove propeller shaft to transfer case flange attaching bolts.
4. Scribe propeller shaft reference mark on torque tube flange.
5. Remove propeller shaft to torque tube flange attaching bolts.
6. Push propeller shaft toward rear of vehicle, then remove propeller shaft.
7. Reverse procedure to install. Apply Loctite Dri-Loc 201, part No. 12345493, or equivalent, to bolt threads.

HUB & BEARING

REPLACE

All Wheel Drive

1. Raise and support vehicle, then remove tire and wheel assembly.
2. Release parking brake and remove brake caliper.
3. Remove brake caliper bracket and brake rotor.
4. Disconnect wheel speed sensor electrical connector, then remove speed sensor connector from connector bracket.
5. Separate driveshaft from wheel hub and bearing as outlined in "Rear Axle Shaft, Replace."
6. Remove and discard wheel bearing and hub assembly bolts.

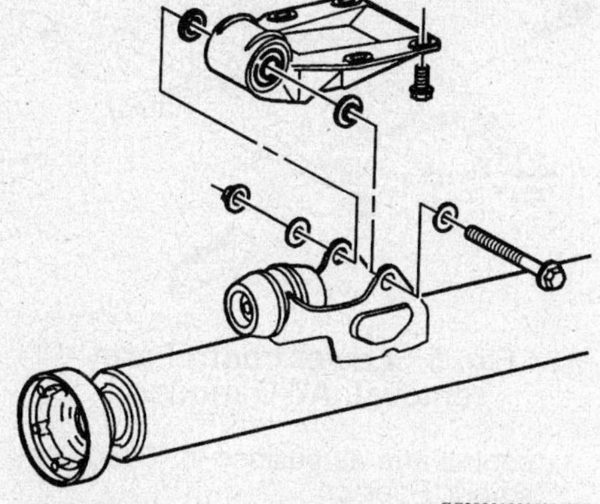

Fig. 2 Torque tube bracket. AWD models

7. Remove wheel hub and bearing assembly.
8. Reverse procedure to install. **Replace wheel hub and bearing assembly attaching bolts anytime bolts are loosened or removed. Failure to replace bolts may cause loss of vehicle control.**

Front Wheel Drive

1. Raise and support vehicle, then remove tire and wheel assembly.
2. Mark relationship of brake drum to hub assembly, then remove brake drum.
3. Remove and discard wheel bearing and hub assembly bolts.
4. Disconnect wheel speed sensor electrical connector, then remove wheel hub and bearing assembly.
5. Reverse procedure to install. **Replace wheel hub and bearing assembly attaching bolts anytime bolts are loosened or removed. Failure to replace bolts may cause loss of vehicle control.**

SHOCK ABSORBER

REPLACE

1. Raise and support vehicle.
2. **On models equipped with all wheel drive,** place a suitable jack stand under lower control arm, then raise jack stand slightly to compress coil spring and remove tension from shock absorber.
3. **On models equipped with front wheel drive,** place a suitable jack stand under rear axle, then raise jack stand slightly to compress coil spring and remove tension from shock absorber.
4. **On models equipped with Automatic Level Control (ALC),** disconnect air tube from shock absorber.
5. **On all models,** remove shock absorber upper bolt and nut.
6. Remove shock absorber lower bolts and nut, and shock absorber.
7. Reverse procedure to install.

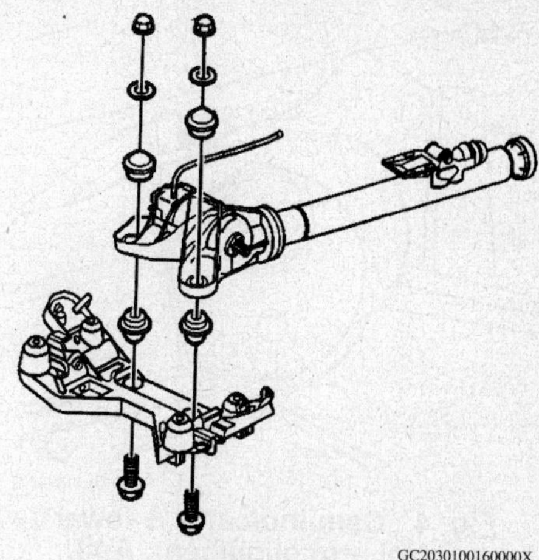

Fig. 3 Torque tube bracket & carrier to cradle mounting bolts. AWD models

COIL SPRING

REPLACE

All Wheel Drive

1. Raise and support vehicle.
2. Remove tire and wheel assembly.
3. Remove brake caliper, then position and secure caliper aside.
4. Disconnect tie rod from knuckle.
5. Support lower control arm with a suitable jack stand.
6. **On models equipped with Automatic Level Control (ALC),** disconnect height sensor link from lower control arm.
7. **On all models,** separate ball joint from knuckle using ball joint/stud separator tool No. J 41820, or equivalent.
8. Remove shock absorber to lower control arm attaching bolt and nut.
9. Lower jack stand to remove tension from coil spring, then remove coil spring and spring seats.
10. Reverse procedure to install.

Front Wheel Drive

1. Raise and support vehicle, then remove wheel and tire assemblies.
2. Remove brake caliper as outlined in "Disc Brakes" chapter.
3. Remove parking brake cable mounting bracket.
4. Remove brake caliper mounting bracket.
5. Disconnect ABS sensor electrical connector, then remove ABS electrical connector mounting bracket.
6. Support lower control arm with a suitable jack.
7. Remove stabilizer link from lower control arm.
8. Separate ball joint from knuckle using joint separator tool No. J 41820, or equivalent.
9. Lower control arm with jack to relieve coil spring tension.
10. Remove coil spring.
11. Reverse procedure to install.

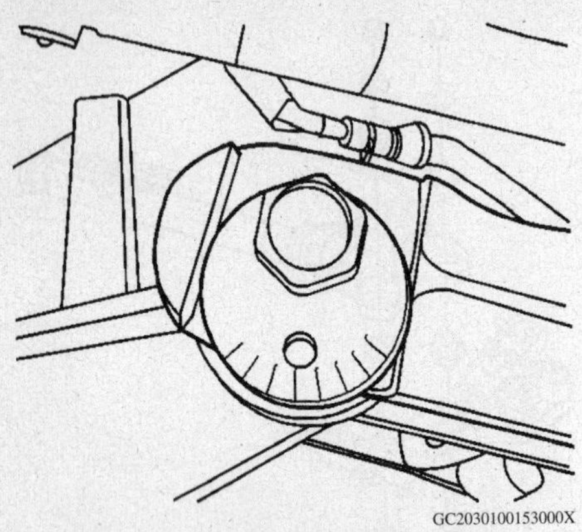

Fig. 4 Cam indicator & lower control arm alignment. AWD models

BALL JOINT

REPLACE

The ball joint is integral part of the lower control arm. Refer to "Control Arm, Replace" for ball joint replacement procedure.

CONTROL ARM

REPLACE

All Wheel Drive

LOWER

1. Raise and support vehicle, then remove rear tire and wheel assembly.
2. Remove brake caliper, then position and secure caliper aside.
3. Disconnect park brake cable from actuator and cable bracket.
4. Support lower control arm with suitable jack stand.
5. Disconnect height sensor link from lower control arm.
6. Remove shock absorber from lower control arm as outlined in "Shock Absorber, Replace."
7. Separate ball joint from lower control arm with ball joint removal tool No. J 41820, or equivalent.
8. Remove lower ball joint nut, then lower control arm to relieve coil spring tension.
9. Remove jack stand, and coil spring.
10. Place a matchmark on lower control arm at cam indicator, **Fig. 4.**
11. Remove lower control arm to crossmember attaching bolts and nuts, and control arm, **Fig. 5.**
12. Reverse procedure to install.

UPPER

1. Raise and support vehicle, then remove rear tire and wheel assembly.
2. Remove brake caliper, then position and secure caliper aside.
3. Disconnect park brake cable from actuator and cable bracket.
4. Support lower control arm with suitable jack stand.
5. Disconnect height sensor link from lower control arm.
6. Remove shock absorber from lower

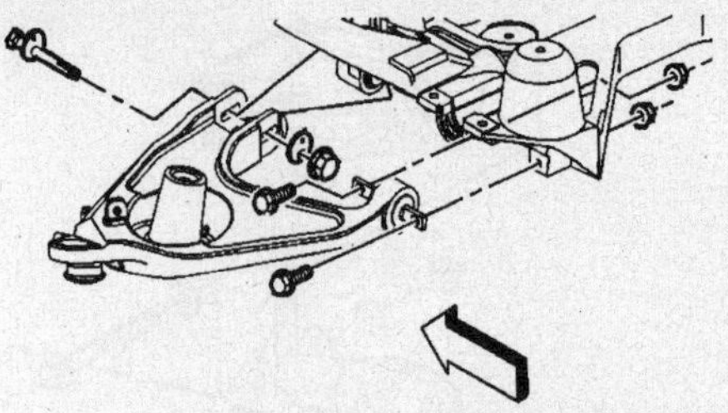

Fig. 5 Lower control arm removal. AWD models

control arm as outlined in "Shock Absorber, Replace."
7. Remove upper control arm to knuckle bolt and nut, **Fig. 6.**
8. Support rear suspension crossmember with two suitable jack stands.
9. Remove crossmember to underbody attaching bolts.
10. Slowly lower crossmember until upper control arm can be removed.
11. Remove upper control arm to crossmember attaching bolts, and crossmember from vehicle.
12. Reverse procedure to install.

CONTROL ARM BUSHING

REPLACE

All Wheel Drive

1. Remove lower control arm as outlined in "Control Arm, Replace."
2. Make a mark on lower control arm at cam indicator.
3. Remove lower control arm to crossmember mounting bolts.
4. Remove control arm bushings from crossmember using lower control arm bushing receiver tool No. J 45411, and control arm bushing set tool No. J 21474-01 or equivalent.
5. Reverse procedure to install.

Front Wheel Drive

1. Raise and support vehicle.
2. Place a suitable adjustable jack stand under lower control arm in front of coil spring.
3. Remove control arm bolts from rear axle.
4. Lower rear axle assembly enough to access control arm bushings.
5. Mark position of control arm bushing in lower control arm, **Fig. 7.**
6. Remove control arm bushing from control arm using rear suspension bushing remover/installer tool No. J 28685, or equivalent.
7. Reverse procedure to install, noting the following:
   a. Align flat edge of bushing with mark on control arm in order to install bushing on a 45° angle, **Fig. 8.**
   b. Install control arm bushing into control arm using rear suspension bushing remover/installer tool No. J 28685, or equivalent.

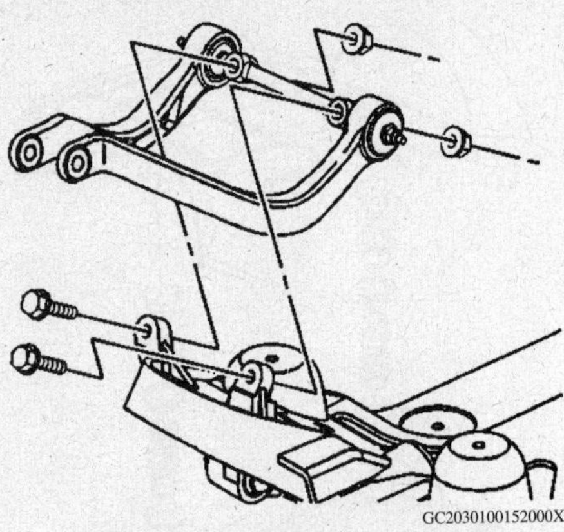

Fig. 6 Upper control arm removal. AWD models

TIE ROD

REPLACE

All Wheel Drive

1. Raise and support vehicle.
2. Remove tie rod bolt and nut, **Fig. 9.**
3. Remove tie rod from vehicle.
4. Reverse procedure to install.

Front Wheel Drive

1. Raise and support vehicle.
2. **On models equipped with Automatic Level Control (ALC),** disconnect ALC sensor electrical connector and height sensor link from tie rod.
3. **On all models,** remove rear axle tie rod bolts, and tie rod, **Fig. 10.**
4. Reverse procedure to install.

KNUCKLE

REPLACE

1. Raise and support vehicle, then remove rear tire and wheel assembly.
2. Remove brake caliper, position and secure caliper aside.
3. Remove brake caliper bracket and rotor.
4. Separate tie rod end from knuckle. **Do not loosen tie rod end jam nut.**
5. Separate driveshaft from wheel hub and bearing as outlined in "Rear Axle Shaft, Replace."
6. Remove park brake shoe and actuator.
7. Position and secure park brake cable and bracket aside.
8. Remove wheel hub and bearing assembly as outlined in "Wheel Hub & Bearing, Replace."
9. Remove brake backing plate.
10. Support lower control arm with suitable jack stand.
11. Disconnect height sensor link from lower control arm.
12. Remove shock absorber from lower control arm.
13. Separate upper control arm from knuckle as outlined in "Control Arm, Replace."
14. Separate lower ball joint from steering knuckle.

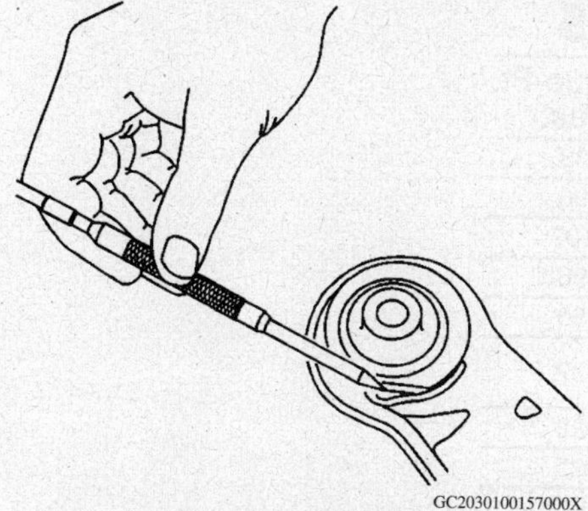

Fig. 7 Control arm bushing & control arm position mark. FWD models

15. Remove wheel speed sensor bracket from steering knuckle.
16. Remove steering knuckle.
17. Reverse procedure to install, noting the following:
    a. **Replace wheel hub and bearing assembly attaching bolts anytime bolts are loosened or removed. Failure to replace bolts may cause loss of vehicle control.**
    b. Install park brake cable end to actuator lever before you install actuator lever attaching bolts.

REAR CROSSMEMBER

REPLACE

All Wheel Drive

1. Raise and support vehicle.
2. Remove tire and wheel assemblies.
3. Place a suitable jack stand under differential carrier.
4. Remove rear differential carrier mounting bolts from crossmember.
5. Scribe crossmember mounting points to frame.
6. Remove knuckle as outlined in "Knuckle, Replace."
7. Disconnect wheel speed sensor harness from lower control arm and crossmember.
8. Remove rivets that attach park brake cable to crossmember.

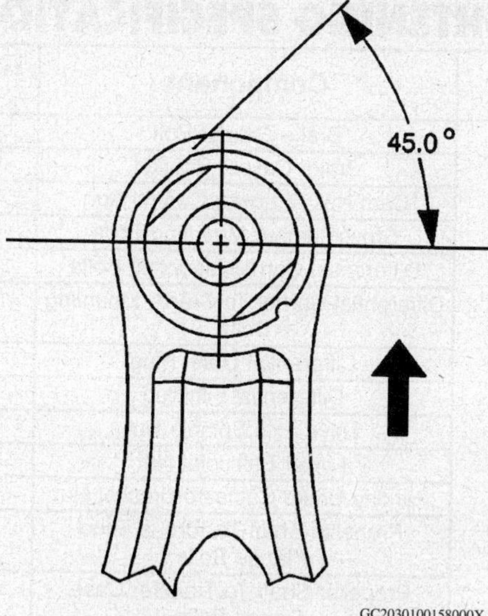

Fig. 8 Control arm bushing installation. FWD models

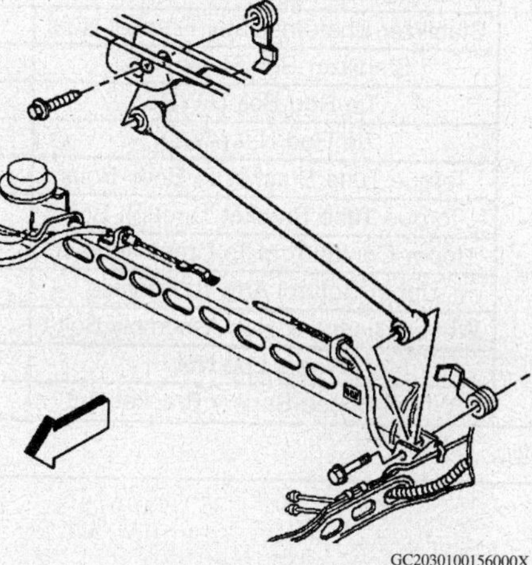

Fig. 10 Tie rod removal. FWD models

9. Support crossmember with a suitable jack stand.
10. Remove crossmember mounting bolts, then lower crossmember.
11. Remove stabilizer shaft as outlined in "Stabilizer Bar, Replace."
12. Remove upper and lower control arms from crossmember as outlined in "Control Arm, Replace."
13. Remove tie rods from crossmember as outlined in "Tie Rod, Replace."
14. Remove crossmember from vehicle.
15. Reverse procedure to install.

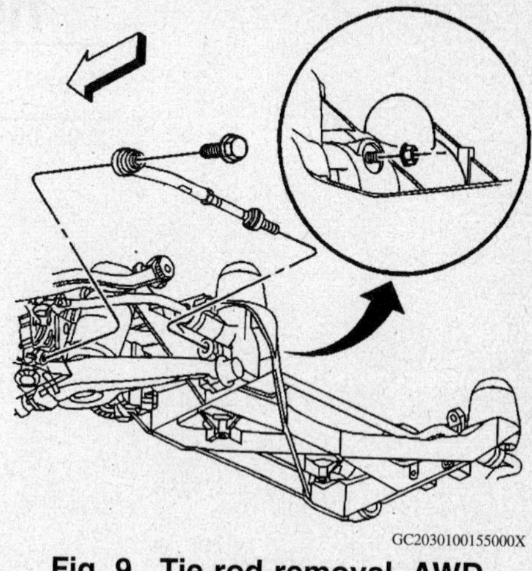

Fig. 9 Tie rod removal. AWD models

STABILIZER BAR

REPLACE

All Wheel Drive

1. Raise and suitably support vehicle.
2. Remove tires and wheels.
3. **On models equipped with Automatic Level Control (ALC),** proceed as follows:
    a. Disconnect ALC position sensor harness connector.
    b. Disconnect height sensor link from lower control arm.
    c. Remove lefthand and righthand side stabilizer shaft insulators and brackets along with ALC position sensor.
4. **On all models,** remove lefthand and righthand side stabilizer shaft insulators and brackets.
5. Remove lefthand and righthand stabilizer shaft links.
6. Remove spare tire from spare tire hoist.
7. Remove stabilizer shaft from vehicle.
8. Reverse procedure to install.

TIGHTENING SPECIFICATIONS

Year	Component	Torque Ft. Lbs.
2002–06	Brake Caliper Bolt	33
	Brake Caliper Bracket	96
	Cam Nut To Lower Control Arm	107
	Crossmember Mounting Bolts	96
	Differential Carrier Mounting Bolts	50
	Differential Carrier To Cradle Mounting Bolts	37
	Differential Drain Plug	22
	Differential Fill Plug	22
	Drive Axle Spindle Nut	192
	Lower Ball Joint Nut	63
	Parking Brake Cable To Bracket Nut	115①
	Propeller Shaft To Torque Tube Flange Bolts	24
	Propeller Shaft To Transfer Case Flange Bolts	24
	Rear Axle Tie Rod Bolts	63
	Rear Axle Tie Rod Nuts	59
	Shock Absorber Mounting Nuts	66
	Stabilizer Shaft Insulator Bracket Nuts	63①
	Stabilizer Shaft Link Nuts	29
	Tie Rod Bolt (AWD)	63
	Tie Rod Nut (AWD)	59
	Torque Tube Bracket To Body Bolts	41
	Torque Tube Bracket Through Bolt	47
	Upper Control Arm To Crossmember	55
	Upper Control Arm To Knuckle	74
	Wheel Bearing & Hub Assembly Bolts	96
	Wheel Lug Nut	100
	Wheel Speed Sensor Bracket Nut	106①

① — Inch lbs.

Front Suspension & Steering

NOTE: On Air Bag Equipped Models, Refer To "Air Bag System Precautions" Located In The Front Of This Manual For System Disarming & Arming Procedures.

INDEX

HUB & BEARING

REPLACE

1. Raise and support vehicle.
2. Remove tire and wheel assembly.
3. Disconnect wheel speed sensor electrical connector.
4. Remove wheel speed sensor connector from bracket.
5. Insert a suitable drift through brake rotor to prevent rotor from turning, then remove and discard driveshaft nut.
6. Remove brake caliper and brake rotor as outlined in "Disc Brakes" chapter.
7. Attach front hub spindle remover tool No. J 28733-B, or equivalent, then push driveshaft out of hub and bearing assembly, **Fig. 1.**
8. Remove and discard hub and bearing assembly attaching bolts.
9. Remove hub and bearing assembly from steering knuckle.

BALL JOINT INSPECTION

1. Raise and support vehicle with safety stands.
2. Support lower control arm with a jack stand. Position jack stand as far outboard as possible, near lower ball joint, **Fig. 2.**
3. Inspect ball joint for horizontal looseness as follows:
   a. Position dial indicator tool No. J 8001, or equivalent, as outlined in **Fig. 2.**
   b. Rock wheel in and out while reading indicator.
   c. **On 2002 models,** if indicator reading exceeds .125 inch, replace lower ball joint.
   d. **On 2003–06 models,** if indicator reading exceeds .0 inch, replace lower ball joint.
4. **On all models,** inspect ball joint for vertical looseness as follows:
   a. Inspect position of grease fitting to lower ball joint cover, **Fig. 3.**
   b. Grease fitting on a new ball joint projects approximately .050 inch from ball joint cover.
   c. If fitting is flush with ball joint cover, replace lower control arm.
   d. While reading dial indicator, pry between lower control arm and steering knuckle with a suitable pry bar.
   e. If indicator reading exceeds .125 inch, replace lower ball joint.

BALL JOINT

REPLACE

1. Raise and support vehicle.
2. Remove tires and wheels.
3. Remove lower control arm as outlined in "Control Arm, Replace."
4. Secure lower control arm in a suitable vise.
5. Drill out ball joint to control arm retaining rivets.
6. Use a suitable hammer and a drift punch in order to remove rivets from lower control arm.
7. Remove ball joint from lower control arm.
8. Reverse procedure to install.

COIL SPRING

REPLACE

Refer to "Coil Spring & Strut Service" for coil spring replacement.

STRUT

REPLACE

1. Remove wiper module as outlined in "Electrical" section.
2. Remove upper strut mounting nuts.
3. Raise and support vehicle, then remove tire and wheel assembly.
4. Scribe a reference mark on steering knuckle and strut assembly for installation reference, **Fig. 4.**
5. Remove strut lower mounting bolts and nuts.
6. Remove strut from vehicle.
7. Reverse procedure to install.

COIL SPRING & STRUT SERVICE

1. Mount strut assembly in a suitable spring compressor.
2. Compress spring slightly, then remove strut shaft nut using a T45-Torx and strut rod socket tool No. J 42991, or equivalents, **Fig. 5.**
3. Install strut lower adapter tool No. J 34013-971, or equivalent, to guide strut shaft out of strut upper mount, **Fig. 5.**
4. Loosen compressor forcing screw while guiding strut shaft out of upper mount, continue to loosen screw until you can remove strut and spring.
5. Reverse procedure to assemble.

CONTROL ARM

REPLACE

1. Raise and support vehicle, then remove tire and wheel assembly.
2. Disconnect wheel speed harness from lower control arm.
3. Remove stabilizer shaft link.
4. Remove cotter pin from lower ball stud, then loosen, but do not remove ball stud nut.
5. Install ball stud joint separator tool No. J 41820, or equivalent, over ball stud nut and steering knuckle, **Fig. 6.**
6. Rotate ball stud nut counterclockwise to separate ball stud from steering knuckle.
7. Remove lower control arm bolts and nuts, and lower control arm, **Fig. 7.**
8. Reverse procedure to install.

CONTROL ARM BUSHING

REPLACE

1. Remove control arm as outlined in "Control Arm, Replace."
2. Secure control arm in a suitable vice.
3. Make a reference mark on lower control arm along flat edge of bushing flange, **Fig. 8.**
4. Assemble bushing removal tool Nos. J

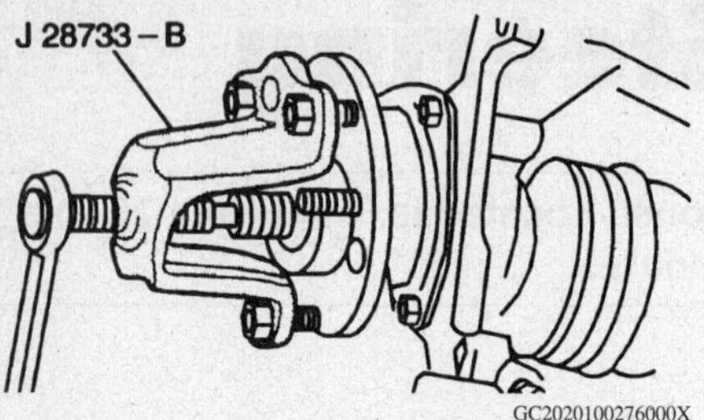

Fig. 1 Hub & bearing removal

21474-27, J 21474-13, J 34126 and J 35379, or equivalents, on bushing and control arm.
5. Remove bushing from control arm.
6. Reverse procedure to install.

STEERING KNUCKLE

REPLACE

1. Raise and support vehicle.
2. Remove tire and wheel assembly.
3. Remove hub and bearing assembly as outlined under "Hub & Bearing, Replace."
4. Separate lower ball joint from steering knuckle as outlined under "Control Arm, Replace."
5. Separate tie rod end from steering knuckle as outlined under "Tie Rod End, Replace."
6. Scribe a steering knuckle reference mark on strut assembly, **Fig. 4.**
7. Remove steering knuckle to strut attaching bolts, then the steering knuckle from strut.
8. Reverse procedure to install.

STABILIZER BAR

REPLACE

1. Raise and support vehicle.
2. Remove tire and wheel assemblies.
3. Remove stabilizer shaft links from lower control arms.
4. Remove stabilizer shaft insulator bolts and brackets, and insulators.
5. Remove stabilizer shaft from righthand side of vehicle.
6. Reverse procedure to install.

TIE ROD END

REPLACE

Inner

Refer to "Power Steering" chapter for inner tie rod end replacement.

Outer

1. Raise and support vehicle.
2. Remove tie rod end ball stud nut.
3. Separate tie rod end from steering knuckle using universal steering linkage puller tool No. J 24319-B, or equivalent.
4. Loosen tie rod end jam nut, then remove outer tie rod end from inner tie rod.

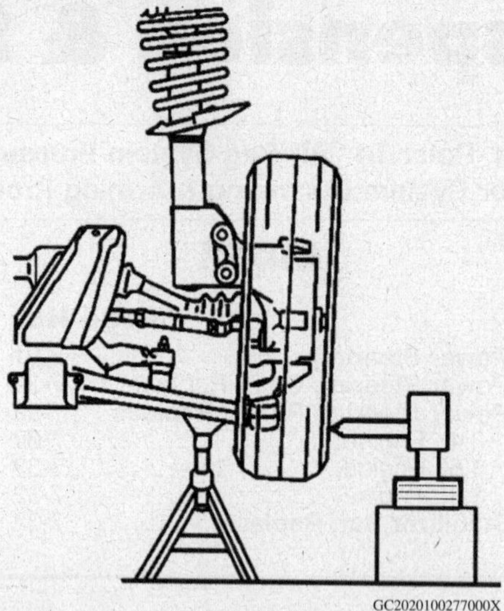

Fig. 2 Lower ball joint horizontal looseness inspection

5. Reverse procedure to install. Inspect and adjust toe setting as outlined in "Wheel Alignment."

POWER STEERING GEAR

REPLACE

1. Raise and support vehicle.
2. Remove stabilizer shaft as outlined under "Stabilizer Bar, Replace."
3. Separate tie rod end from steering knuckle as outlined under "Tie Rod End, Replace."
4. Apply silicone lubricant to steering column intermediate steering shaft lower seal.
5. Push intermediate shaft lower seal upward to access intermediate shaft lower bolt.
6. Remove intermediate shaft lower bolt and separate intermediate shaft from steering gear.
7. Support frame with a suitable adjustable jack stand as outlined in **Fig. 9.**
8. Remove and discard frame rear bolts.
9. Lower frame and powertrain with jack stand.
10. Remove power steering gear heat shield.
11. Remove cooler pipe pressure hose from steering gear.
12. Remove power steering gear retaining nuts.
13. Remove steering gear attaching bolts, and gear through lefthand wheel opening.
14. Reverse procedure to install. Use new frame bolts when installing frame.

POWER STEERING PUMP

REPLACE

3.4L Engine

1. Remove wiring harness from power steering pump wiring harness retainer.
2. Remove accessory drive belt from power steering pump pulley.
3. Remove pressure and return hoses from power steering pump.
4. Remove power steering pump mounting bolts from pump, and pump from vehicle.
5. Reverse procedure to install.

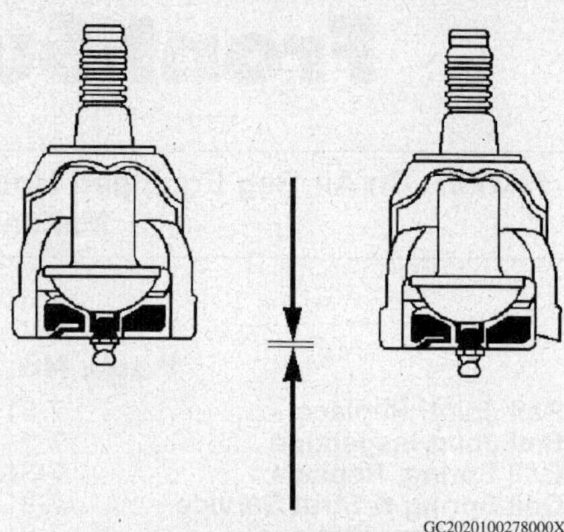

Fig. 3 Lower ball joint vertical looseness inspection

3.5L Engine

1. Remove drive belt as outlined under "Serpentine Drive Belt."
2. Remove intake manifold cover.
3. Remove power steering pump bolt.
4. Remove power steering high pressure hose fitting.
5. Remove power steering return hose clamp at pump.
6. Remove power steering pump.
7. Reverse procedure to install.

3.6L Engine

1. Turn steering wheel in order to move front of righthand wheel to outboard most position in order to allow clearance to remove power steering pump.
2. Raise vehicle and suitably support.
3. Remove front righthand wheel.
4. Remove accessory drive belt from power steering pump pulley as outlined under "Serpentine Drive Belt" in "3.6L Engine" section.
5. Remove righthand engine splash shield.
6. Remove righthand front drive shaft.
7. Disconnect power steering pump inlet hose from power steering pump.
8. Disconnect power steering pressure pipe/hose from power steering pump.
9. Remove power steering pump mounting bolts.
10. Remove power steering pump from vehicle.
11. Cap off power steering pump and hoses to prevent contamination.
12. Reverse procedure to install.

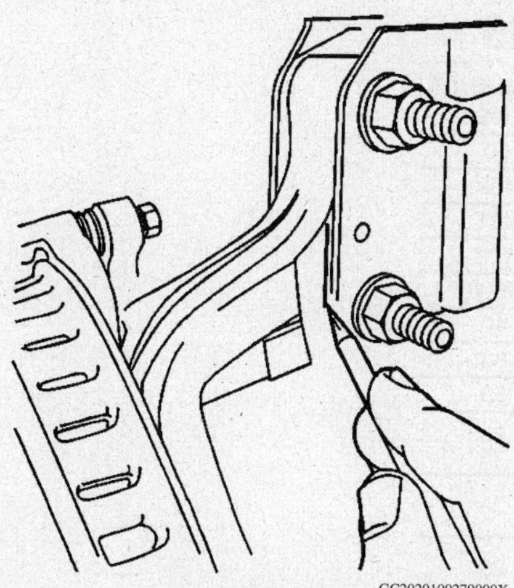

Fig. 4 Strut to steering knuckle reference mark

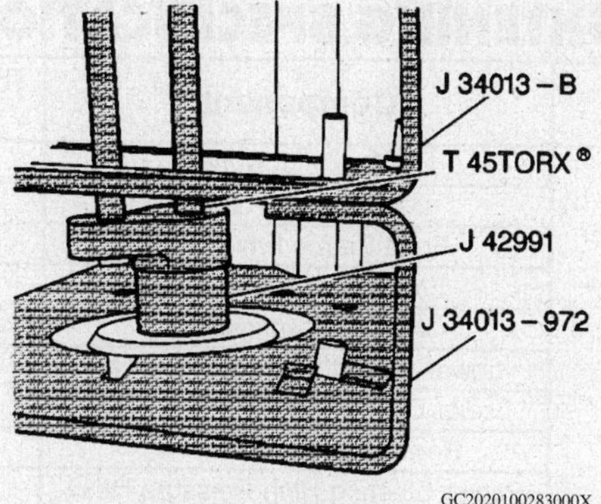

Fig. 5 Strut shaft nut removal

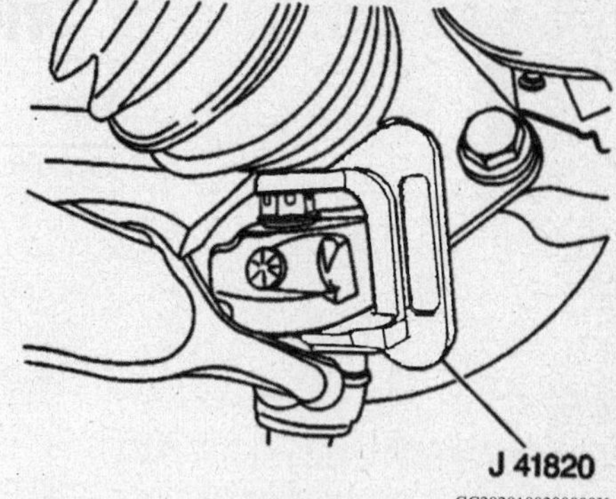

Fig. 6 Lower ball joint removal

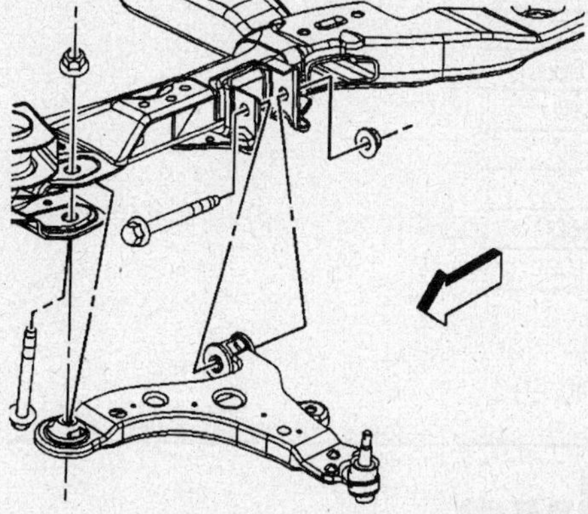

Fig. 7 Lower control arm removal

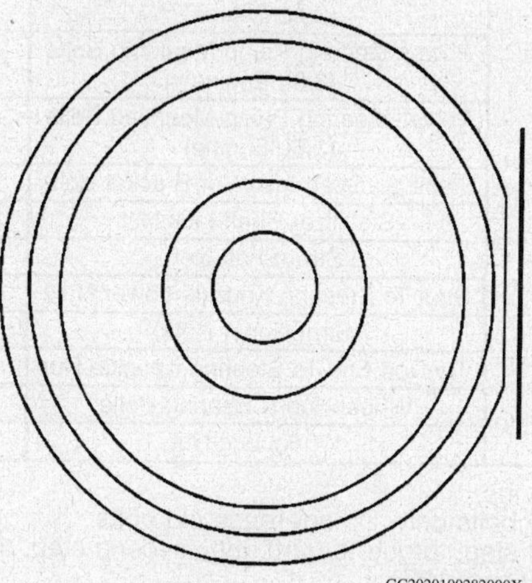

Fig. 8 Control arm bushing reference mark

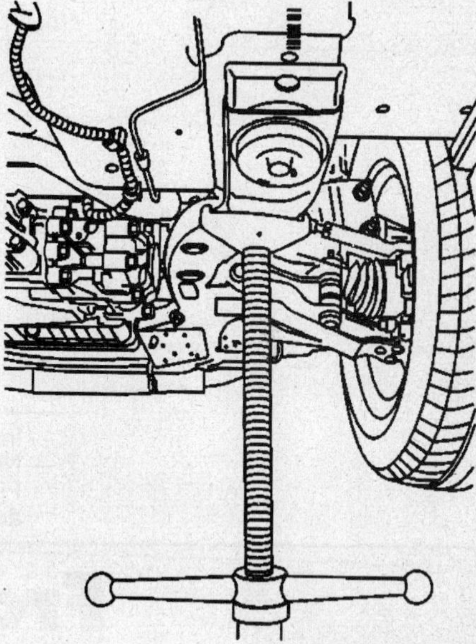

Fig. 9 Frame support location

TIGHTENING SPECIFICATIONS

Year	Component	Torque Ft. Lbs.
2002–06	Ball Joint Nuts	50
	Driveshaft Nut	192
	Front Frame Front Bolts	111
	Front Frame Rear Bolts	122
	Hub & Bearing Bolts	96②
	Lower Control Arm Ball Stud Nut	40
	Lower Control Arm To Frame Nuts	83
	Power Steering Gear Nuts	59
	Power Steering High Pressure Hose Fitting (3.5L & 3.6L Engines)	20
	Power Steering Pump Mounting Bolts (3.4L Engine)	25
	Power Steering Pump Mounting Bolts (3.5L Engine)	25
	Power Steering Pump Mounting Bolts (3.6L Engine)	37
	Stabilizer Shaft Insulator Bracket Bolts	35①
	Stabilizer Shaft Link Nut	17
	Strut Shaft Nut	63
	Strut To Steering Knuckle Lower Nuts	90
	Strut Upper Nuts	30
	Tie Rod End To Steering Knuckle Nut	③
	Wheel Hub & Bearing Bolts	96②
	Wheel Lug Nut	100

① — Inch lbs.
② — New bolts only. Do not reuse old bolts.
③ — First step, torque to 22 ft. lbs.; second step, tighten an additional 120°.

Front Wheel Drive

NOTE: On Air Bag Equipped Models, Refer To "Air Bag System Precautions" Located In The Front Of This Manual For System Disarming & Arming Procedures.

INDEX

AXLE

REPLACE

1. Raise and support vehicle, then remove tire and wheel assembly.
2. Remove engine splash shield, and stabilizer shaft link.
3. Disconnect wheel speed sensor electrical connector.
4. Insert a suitable drift through brake caliper and remove front wheel driveshaft nut.
5. Separate outer tie rod end from steering knuckle as outlined in "Tie Rod End, Replace" in "Front Suspension & Steering." **Do not loosen tie rod end jam nut.**
6. Separate lower ball joint from steering knuckle as outlined in "Lower Control Arm, Replace."
7. Attach front hub spindle remover tool No. J 42129, or equivalent, then disengage driveshaft from hub and bearing assembly.
8. Disengage driveshaft from transaxle using slide hammer tool No. J 2619-01, extension tool No. J 29794 and driveshaft remover tool No. J 33008-A, or equivalents.
9. **On righthand driveshaft,** remove and discard driveshaft retaining ring located on splined shaft of inner tripot housing.
10. **On lefthand driveshaft,** remove and discard driveshaft retaining ring located on splined transmission output shaft.
11. **On all models,** reverse procedure to install.

TIGHTENING SPECIFICATIONS

Year	Component	Torque Ft. Lbs.
2002–06	Ball Joint Nuts	50
	Driveshaft Nut	192
	Front Frame Front Bolts	111
	Hub & Bearing Bolts	96①
	Lower Control Arm Ball Stud Nut	40
	Stabilizer Shaft Link Nut	17
	Strut To Steering Knuckle Lower Nuts	90
	Tie Rod End To Steering Knuckle Nut	②
	Wheel Hub & Bearing Bolts	96①
	Wheel Lug Nut	100

① — New bolts only. Do not reuse old bolts.
② — First step, torque to 22 ft. lbs.; second step, tighten an additional 120°.

Wheel Alignment

NOTE: On Air Bag Equipped Models, Refer To "Air Bag System Precautions" Located In The Front Of This Manual For System Disarming & Arming Procedures.

INDEX

PRECAUTIONS

Air Bag Systems

Refer to "Air Bag System Precautions" in the front of this manual for system disarming and arming procedures.

Battery Ground Cable

Prior to service, disconnect battery ground cable and isolate as required.

PRELIMINARY INSPECTION

Inspect the following components, adjust, repair or replace as required prior to performing front wheel alignment.

1. Inflate tires to cold specifications.
2. Ensure tires are of same size, ply rating and load rating.
3. Inspect for excessive wheel bearing endplay.
4. Inspect for worn or damaged ball joints.
5. Inspect steering gear mounting bolts for proper tightness.
6. Inspect suspension arm or bent or damaged condition.
7. Inspect suspension arm to frame bushings for looseness or wear.
8. Inspect suspension components for wear or damage.

FRONT WHEEL ALIGNMENT

Camber

1. Raise and support vehicle.
2. Remove front tires.
3. Remove strut lower bolt and inspect oblong strut lower hole.
4. If hole is oblong, loosen strut upper bolt to adjust camber.
5. If lower hole is not oblong, proceed as follows:
   a. Remove strut assembly as outlined in "Front Suspension & Steering."
   b. Place strut in suitable soft jaw vise.
   c. File strut lower hole laterally to allow for camber adjustment, **Fig. 1.**
   d. Install strut assembly.
6. Place vehicle in suitable alignment equipment.
7. Loosen both strut-to-knuckle nuts just enough to allow movement.
8. Adjust camber to specification by moving top of wheel in or out.
9. **Torque** strut bolts to 91 ft. lbs.

Toe

1. Remove power steering gear seal small clamps.
2. Ensure steering wheel is centered and wheels are in straight ahead position.
3. Loosen lefthand and righthand tie rod jam nuts, **Fig. 2.**
4. Rotate inner tie rod end to obtain correct toe angle.
5. Ensure number of threads showing on both inner tie rod ends are approximately equal.
6. **Torque** jam nuts to 50 ft. lbs.
7. Install power steering gear seal small clamps.

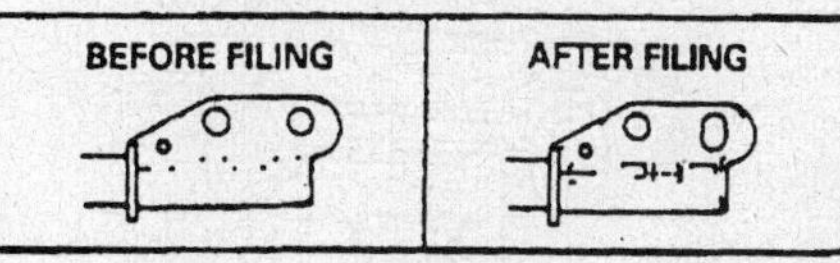

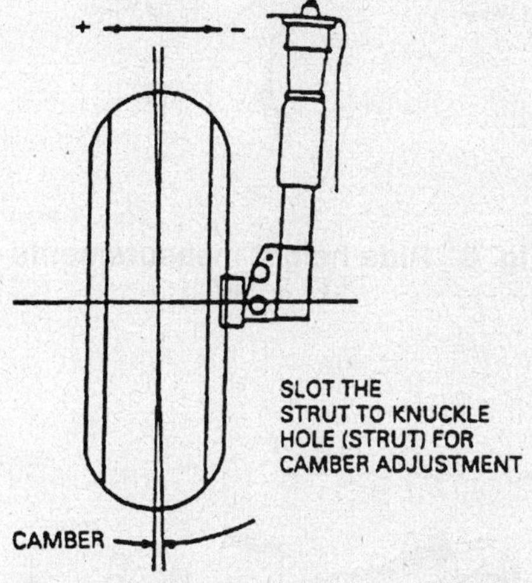

Fig. 1 Camber adjustment

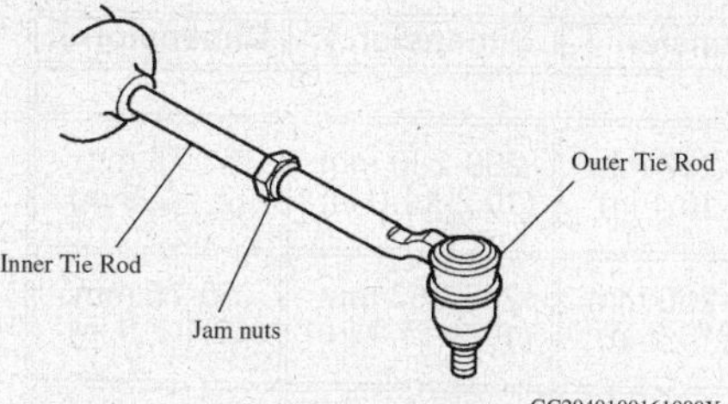

Fig. 2 Toe-in adjustment

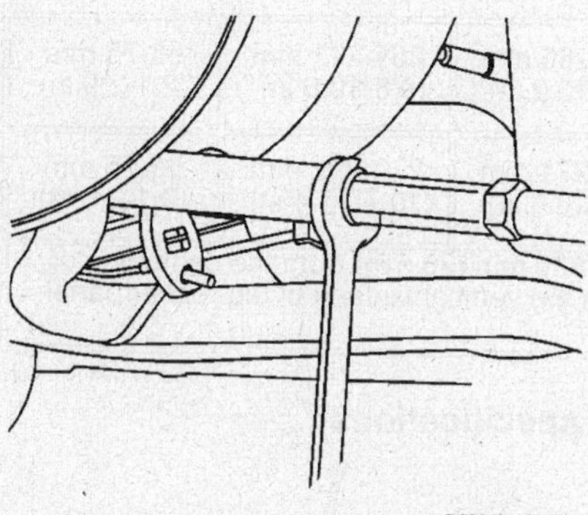

Fig. 4 Rear toe adjustment

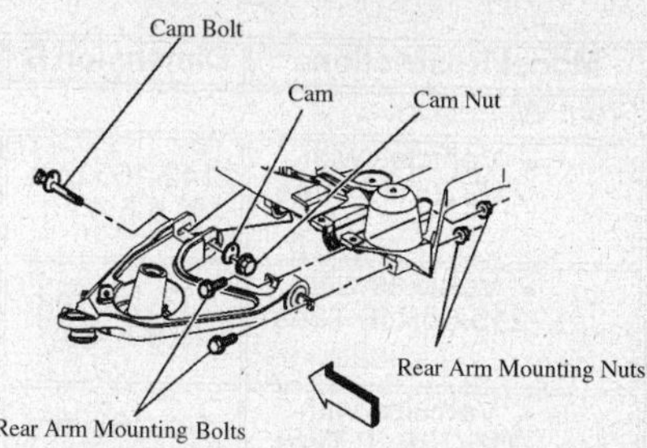

Fig. 3 Rear camber adjustment

REAR WHEEL ALIGNMENT

Camber

ALL WHEEL DRIVE

1. Raise and support vehicle, then remove tires.
2. Loosen rear lower control arm bolts, **Fig. 3.**
3. Loosen lower control arm cam bolt.
4. Install tires, then adjust camber as required.
5. **Torque** lower control arm rear bolts to 37 ft. lbs.
6. **Torque** front cam bolt to 107 ft. lbs.

Toe

1. Loosen hex nuts at rear wheel spindle rod, **Fig. 4.**
2. Adjust toe to specifications by turning adjusting nut.
3. **Torque** hex nuts to 45 ft. lbs.

VEHICLE RIDE HEIGHT

All trim height measurements are taken vertical to ground. Measurements which are within .4 inch are considered within specifications. Refer to **Fig. 5** for ride height specifications.

1. Before measuring ride height, ensure the following conditions are met:
   a. Fuel tank at least ⅛ full.
   b. Tires are of specified size as stated from manufacturer.
   c. Tire pressure at proper specifications.
   d. Ensure vehicle is on a level surface.
   e. Ensure all doors, hood and liftgate are closed.
2. Measure dimensions "J" and "K", **Fig. 6,** as follows:
   a. Lift front bumper 1.5 inches.
   b. Allow vehicle to lower to normal ride height.
   c. Push front bumper down 1.5 inches.
   d. Allow vehicle to raise to normal ride height.
   e. Measure dimension "J" on lefthand and righthand sides of vehicle 24 inches from centerline of front wheel.
   f. If ride height is not within specifications, replace front springs.
   g. Lift rear bumper 1.5 inches.
   h. Allow vehicle to lower to normal ride height.
   i. Push rear bumper down 1.5 inches.
   j. Allow vehicle to raise to normal ride height.
   k. Measure dimension "K" on lefthand and righthand sides of vehicle 22 inches from centerline of rear wheel.
   l. If ride height is not within specifications, replace rear springs.
3. Measure dimension "Z", **Fig. 7,** as follows:
   a. Lift front bumper 1.5 inches.
   b. Allow vehicle to lower to normal ride height.
   c. Push front bumper down 1.5 inches.
   d. Allow vehicle to raise to normal ride height.
   e. Measure dimension "Z" on lefthand and righthand sides of vehicle. Measurement "Z" is vertical distance measured between centerline of lower control arm bolt and bottom of ball joint.
   f. If ride height is not within specifications, replace front springs.
4. Measure dimension "D", **Figs. 8 and 9,** as follows:
   a. Lift front bumper 1.5 inches.
   b. Allow vehicle to lower to normal ride height.
   c. Push front bumper down 1.5 inches.
   d. Allow vehicle to raise to normal ride height.
   e. Measure dimension "D" on lefthand and righthand sides of vehicle. **On models equipped with FWD,** measurement "D" is vertical distance measured between frame rail and rear axle. **On models equipped with AWD,** measurement "D" is vertical distance measured between horizontal centerline of lower control arm bolt and bottom of ball joint.
   f. If ride height is not within specifications, replace rear springs.

Model/Restrictions	Dimension D	Dimension J	Dimension K	Dimension Z
Front Wheel Drive				
• Vehicles with 215/70R15 Tires	143-163 mm (5.6-6.4 in)	237-257 mm (9.3-10.1 in)[1]	260-280 mm (10.2-11.0 in)[1]	55-75 mm (2.1-2.9 in)
• Vehicles with 215/65R16 Tires	143-163 mm (5.6-6.4 in)	240-260 mm (9.4-10.2 in)[1]	263-283 mm (10.3-11.1 in)[1]	55-75 mm (2.1-2.9 in)
• Vehicles with 215/70R16 Tires	143-163 mm (5.6-6.4 in)	251-271 mm (9.8-10.6 in)[1]	274-294 mm (10.7-11.5 in)[1]	55-75 mm (2.1-2.9 in)
All Wheel Drive				
• Vehicles with 215/65R16 Tires	87-107 mm (3.4-4.2 in)	240-260 mm (9.4-10.2 in)[1]	251-271 mm (9.8-10.6 in)[1]	55-75 mm (2.1-2.9 in)
• Vehicles with 215/70R16 Tires	87-107 mm (3.4-4.2 in)	251-271 mm (9.8-10.6 in)[1]	272-292 mm (10.7-11.4 in)[1]	55-75 mm (2.1-2.9 in)

[1] Measure the J dimension and the K dimension 650 mm (25.5 in) from the centerline of the nearest wheel. These points are identified on the vertical surface of the rocker panel by a 2 mm diameter and 1 mm high circle.

GC2040100168000X

Fig. 5 Ride height specifications

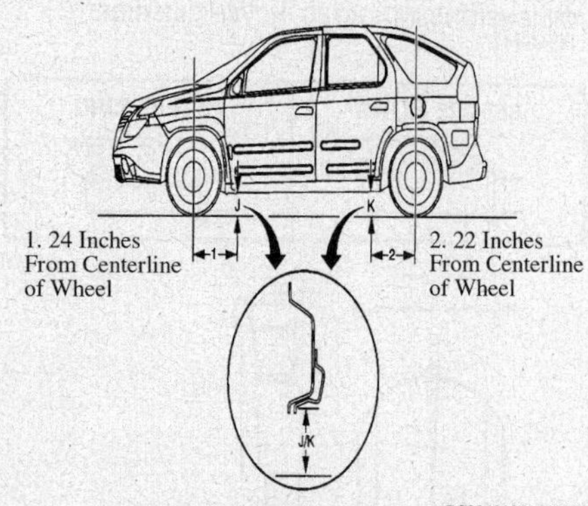

Fig. 6 Ride height measurements "J" & "K"

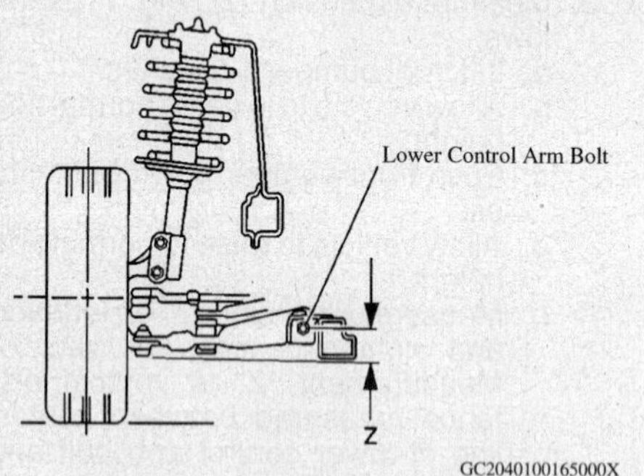

Fig. 7 Front ride height measurement "Z"

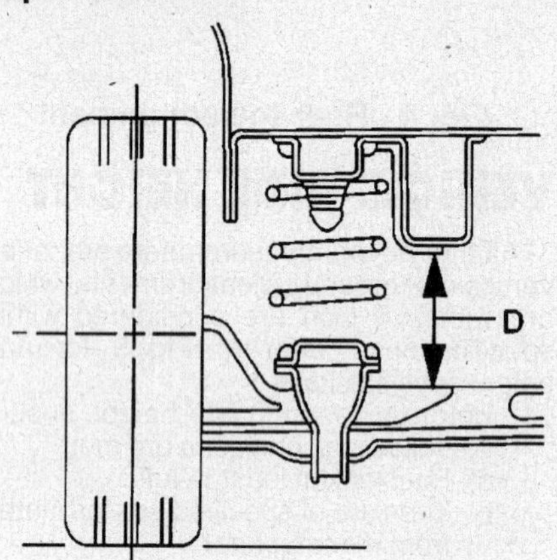

Fig. 8 Rear ride height measurement "D." Front wheel drive (FWD)

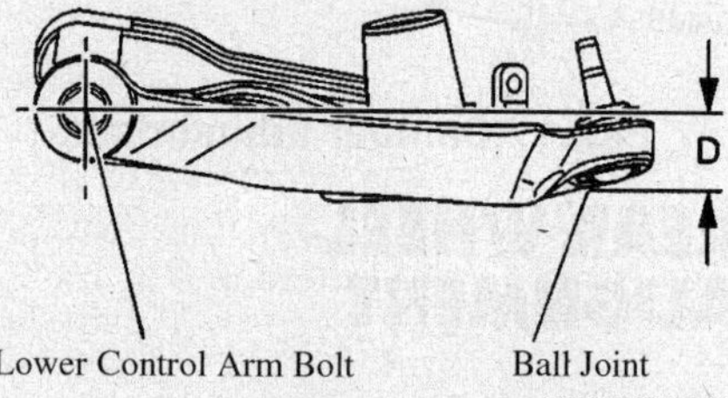

Fig. 9 Rear ride height measurement "D." All wheel drive (AWD)

HHR

NOTE: Refer To Back Of This Manual For Vehicle Manufacturer's Special Service Tool Suppliers.

INDEX OF SERVICE OPERATIONS

Specifications

GENERAL ENGINE SPECIFICATIONS

Year	Engine Liter	VIN	Fuel System	Bore & Stroke	Comp. Ratio	Horsepower @ RPM	Torque, Ft. Lbs. @ RPM	Normal Oil Pressure, Lbs. @ RPM①
2006	2.2L	F	MFI	3.39 X 3.72	10	145 @ 5600	155 @ 4000	50–80
	2.4L	B	MFI	3.47 X 3.86	10	171 @ 6200	163 @ 5000	50–80

MFI — Multi Port Fuel Injection

① — At 1000 RPM.

TUNE UP SPECIFICATIONS

The following specifications are published from the latest information available. This data should only be used in the absence of a decal affixed in the engine compartment.

Engine	Spark Plug Gap	Ignition Timing BTDC				Curb Idle Speed		Fast Idle Speed		Fuel Pump Pressure psi.	Valve Lash, Inch
		Firing Order	Man. Trans.	Auto. Trans.	Mark Location	Man. Trans.	Auto. Trans.	Man. Trans.	Auto. Trans.		
2.2L	.043	1–3–4–2	①	①	①	①	①	①	①	50–60	②
2.4L	.042	1–3–4–2	①	①	①	①	①	①	①	50–60	②

BTDC — Before Top Dead Center

① — ECM/PCM controlled.

② — Equipped w/hydraulic valve lifters.

FRONT WHEEL ALIGNMENT SPECIFICATIONS

Year	Caster Angle, Degrees		Camber Angle, Degrees		Toe Per Wheel, Degrees		Ball Joint Wear
	Limits	Desired	Limits	Desired	Limits	Desired	
2006	2.95 to 4.45	3.7	-1.8 to -.3	-1.05	+.20 to -.20	0	①

① — Refer to "Ball Joint Inspection" in the "Front Suspension & Steering" section for ball joint specifications.

REAR WHEEL ALIGNMENT SPECIFICATIONS

Year	Camber, Degree		Cross Camber		Toe, Degree	
	Limit	Desired	Limit	Desired	Limit	Desired
2006	-1.55 to -.05	-.80	—	—	+.55 to -.05	.25

FLUID CAPACITIES & COOLING SYSTEM DATA

Year	Engine Liter	Cooling Capacity Qts.	Recommended Coolant Type	Radiator Cap Relief Pressure, Lbs.	Thermostat Opening Temp. °F	Fuel Tank Gals.	Engine Oil Refill Qts.	Transmission Oil①		
								Manual Transaxle Pts.	Auto. Transaxle Qts.	
									Drain & Refill	Overhaul
2006	2.2L	7.4	DEX-COOL	15	195	16.2	5.0②	3.6	6.9	9.5
	2.4L	7.9	DEX-COOL	15	195	16.2	5.0②	3.6	6.9	9.5

① — Approximate, make final inspect w/dipstick.

② — Includes filter.

LUBRICANT DATA

Year	Lubricant Type			
	Transmission		Hydraulic Clutch Fluid	Brake System
	Manual	Automatic		
2006	Dexron-III	Dexron-VI	DOT-3	DOT-3

Electrical

NOTE: On Air Bag Equipped Models, Refer To "Air Bag System Precautions" Located In The Front Of This Manual For System Disarming & Arming Procedures.

NOTE: Refer To "Computer Relearn Procedures" Located In The Front Of This Manual When Battery Power To The Computer Has Been Interrupted.

INDEX

PRECAUTIONS

Air Bag Systems

Refer to "Air Bag System Precautions" in the front of this manual for system disarming and arming procedures.

Battery Ground Cable

Prior to service disconnect battery ground cable and isolate as required.

Radio Security System

The radio theft deterrent system is intended to disable radio functionality if incorrect vehicle information is received by the radio. The radio disables functionality if the VIN information received by the radio does not match the VIN information that has been learned by the radio. A VIN sequence is the last 6 digits of the VIN. The radio receives this information in a GMLAN frame form.

FUSE PANEL & FLASHER LOCATION

The passenger compartment fuses are located in the Body Control Module (BCM). The BCM is located under the instrument panel, below the radio on the righthand side of the center console.

The underhood fuse block is located in the engine compartment next to the lefthand strut tower.

Turn signal and hazard flasher operation is controlled by the Body Control Module (BCM). The BCM is located under the instrument panel, below the radio on the righthand side of the center console.

FUEL PUMP RELAY LOCATION

Fuel pump relay is located in the underhood fuse block.

STARTER

REPLACE

1. Raise and support vehicle.
2. Remove starter solenoid nut.
3. Remove positive/battery ground terminal from starter.
4. Remove engine harness terminal from starter.
5. Remove starter solenoid S terminal nut.
6. Remove engine harness terminal from starter solenoid.
7. Remove starter bolts and starter.
8. Reverse procedure to install, noting the following:
   a. **Torque** starter bolts to 30 ft. lbs.
   b. **Torque** starter solenoid S terminal nut to 27 inch lbs.
   c. **Torque** starter solenoid nut to 13 ft. lbs.

ALTERNATOR

REPLACE

1. Lift up rear of air cleaner assembly in order to disengage air cleaner from studs.
2. Remove PCV hose from air cleaner assembly.
3. Loosen air cleaner outlet duct clamp at throttle body.
4. Disconnect engine wiring harness

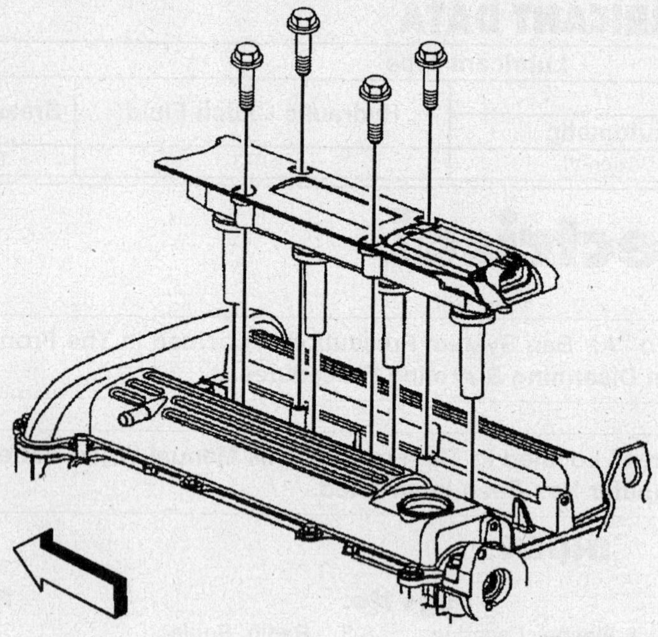

Fig. 1 Ignition coil housing

electrical connector from MAF and Intake Air Temperature (IAT) sensors.
5. Remove air cleaner assembly.
6. Remove drive belt.
7. Remove alternator terminal nut.
8. Remove engine harness terminal from alternator.
9. Remove alternator upper bolts.
10. Raise vehicle and suitably support.
11. Cut tie straps and reposition coolant heater cord.
12. Remove alternator lower bolt.
13. Disconnect alternator electrical connector and remove alternator.
14. Reverse procedure to install, noting the following:
    a. **Torque** alternator bolts to 16 ft. lbs.
    b. **Torque** alternator terminal nut to 15 ft. lbs.

COIL PACK

REPLACE

2.2L Engine

1. Lift up rear of air cleaner assembly and disengage from studs.
2. Position air cleaner assembly to access PCV hose and throttle body duct.
3. Remove PCV hose from air cleaner assembly.
4. Loosen air cleaner outlet duct clamp at throttle body.
5. Disconnect engine wiring harness electrical connector from MAF/IAT sensor.
6. Remove air cleaner assembly.
7. Disconnect ignition control module electrical connector.
8. Remove ignition coil housing bolts, **Fig. 1.**
9. Remove ignition coil housing from camshaft cover.
10. Reverse procedure to install. **Torque** ignition coil housing bolts to 89 inch lbs.

2.4L Engine

1. Lift up rear of air cleaner assembly and disengage from studs.
2. Position air cleaner assembly to access PCV hose and throttle body duct.
3. Remove PCV hose from air cleaner assembly.
4. Loosen air cleaner outlet duct clamp at throttle body.
5. Disconnect engine wiring harness electrical connector from MAF/IAT sensor.
6. Remove air cleaner assembly.
7. Disconnect ignition coil electrical connectors.
8. Remove ignition coil bolts.
9. Remove ignition coils.
10. Reverse procedure to install. **Torque** ignition coil bolts to 89 inch lbs.

IGNITION LOCK

REPLACE

1. Remove steering wheel as outlined under "Steering Wheel, Replace."
2. Remove steering column trim covers.
3. Remove theft deterrent control module.
4. Remove inflatable restraint steering wheel module coil.
5. Disconnect ignition lock cylinder solenoid harness connector.
6. Disconnect ignition switch harness connector.
7. Bite into shear bolt at a position offset from center using a suitable hammer and chisel.
8. Tap chisel to rotate and loosen bolt.
9. Ensure lock cylinder is in RUN position. If steering wheel lock bolt is engaged, it may prevent removal of lock cylinder case. If lock bolt is engaged, cut lock cylinder case housing collar at locations outlined in **Fig. 2.**
10. Remove ignition lock cylinder case housing from steering column.
11. Reverse procedure to install. Perform theft deterrent system reprogramming as follows:
    a. Connect a scan tool to vehicle.
    b. Turn ON ignition, with engine OFF.
    c. Follow scan tool instructions.

IGNITION SWITCH

REPLACE

1. Position steering column in full downward position.
2. Unsnap and remove upper steering column cover.
3. Remove lower steering column cover screws.
4. Remove lower steering column trim cover.
5. Disconnect ignition switch harness connector.
6. Turn ignition switch to run position.
7. Remove ignition switch screws. **Ignition switch must be in run position during removal in order to avoid damage to ignition switch.**
8. Remove ignition switch from steering column.
9. Reverse procedure to install.

NEUTRAL SAFETY SWITCH

REPLACE

1. Apply parking brake and place control assembly in Neutral. Transaxle manual shaft must be in Neutral position prior to installing range switch.
2. Remove shift control cable from transaxle range switch lever.
3. Disconnect electrical connectors from transaxle range switch.
4. Remove transaxle range switch lever nut and lever.
5. Remove transaxle range switch bolts and remove switch.
6. Reverse procedure to install, noting the following:
    a. **Torque** transaxle range switch bolts to 15 ft. lbs.
    b. **Torque** transaxle range switch lever retaining nut to 26 ft. lbs.

HEADLAMP SWITCH

REPLACE

Refer to "Multi-Function Switch, Replace" for replacement procedure.

STOP LIGHT SWITCH

REPLACE

1. Remove sound insulator panel from under lefthand side of instrument panel.
2. Remove knee bolster.
3. Disconnect electrical connector from stop lamp switch.
4. Remove stop lamp switch from brake pedal bracket.
5. Reverse procedure to install.

MULTI-FUNCTION SWITCH

REPLACE

1. Remove steering column trim covers.
2. Disconnect multi-function turn signal switch harness connector.
3. Depress locking tabs and remove multi-function switch from steering column.
4. Reverse procedure to install.

TURN SIGNAL SWITCH

REPLACE

Refer to "Multi-Function Switch, Replace" for replacement procedure.

STEERING WHEEL

REPLACE

1. Place wheel so that two openings on back side of steering wheel are on top.
2. Push spring fastener inward through access holes using a suitable blunt-ended tool.
3. Remove steering wheel inflatable restraint connector position assurance (CPA) retainer.
4. Disconnect electrical connectors.
5. Remove steering wheel retaining nut.
6. Remove steering wheel using countergear and steering wheel puller tool No. J 1859-A, and steering wheel puller legs tool No. J 36541-A, or equivalent.
7. Reverse procedure to install. **Torque** steering wheel nut to 30 ft. lbs.

INSTRUMENT CLUSTER

REPLACE

1. Remove instrument panel cluster trim plate retaining screws and clip.
2. Remove instrument trim plate assembly.
3. Remove instrument panel cluster retaining screws.
4. Disconnect cluster electrical connector.
5. Remove cluster assembly.
6. Reverse procedure to install.

RADIO

REPLACE

1. Remove instrument panel accessory trim plate assembly, and disconnect electrical connectors.
2. Remove heater and A/C control assembly screws.
3. Disconnect heater and A/C control assembly electrical connector, then remove assembly from instrument panel.
4. Remove radio assembly retaining screws.
5. Disconnect electrical connector and antenna cable.
6. Remove radio assembly.
7. Reverse procedure to install. **Torque** screws to 18 inch lbs.

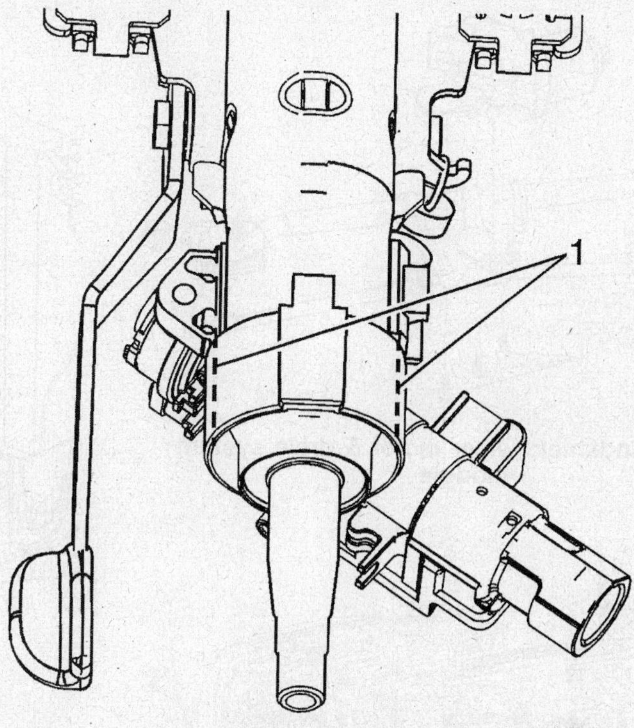

Fig. 2 Lock cylinder case housing collar cutting locations

WIPER MOTOR

REPLACE

1. Remove wiper arms.
2. Remove air inlet grille panel bolts.
3. Disconnect washer solvent hose and electrical conduit.
4. Remove air inlet grille.
5. Remove wiper drive system module bolts and module.
6. Remove windshield wiper motor attaching bolts, **Fig. 3.**
7. Separate transmission arm from wiper motor crank arm pivot.
8. Reverse procedure to install, noting the following:
   a. **Torque** windshield wiper arm nut to 11 ft. lbs.
   b. **Torque** air inlet grille bolts 89 inch lbs.
   c. **Torque** windshield wiper motor bolts to 53 inch lbs.

WIPER TRANSMISSION

REPLACE

Refer to "Wiper Motor, Replace" for replacement procedure.

BLOWER MOTOR

REPLACE

1. Remove righthand sound insulator panel from under righthand side of instrument panel.
2. Remove instrument panel compartment dampener screw.
3. Squeeze sides of instrument panel compartment assembly and pull compartment out of instrument panel opening past stops.
4. Disconnect blower motor electrical connector.
5. Remove lower blower motor cover retaining screws, then the cover.
6. Remove blower motor retaining nuts.
7. Cut through case as straight as possible because motor cup must be replaced. **In order to prevent damage to component, do not cut any deeper than required to remove motor cup, Fig. 4.**
8. Remove blower motor and cup from lower case by cutting through case between circular ribs around motor with a suitable sharp utility knife.
9. Release blower motor retaining tab and remove motor from cup.
10. Reverse procedure to install.

HEATER CORE

REPLACE

1. Drain cooling system and recover A/C system refrigerant as outlined in "Air Conditioning" chapter.
2. Remove PCV hose from air cleaner assembly.
3. Disconnect MAF/IAT sensor electrical connector.
4. Remove air cleaner assembly.
5. Remove heater inlet and outlet hoses from heater core.
6. Remove front floor console trim plate.
7. Remove front floor console side extension.
8. Loosen rear console trim plate.
9. Remove front floor console extension assembly.

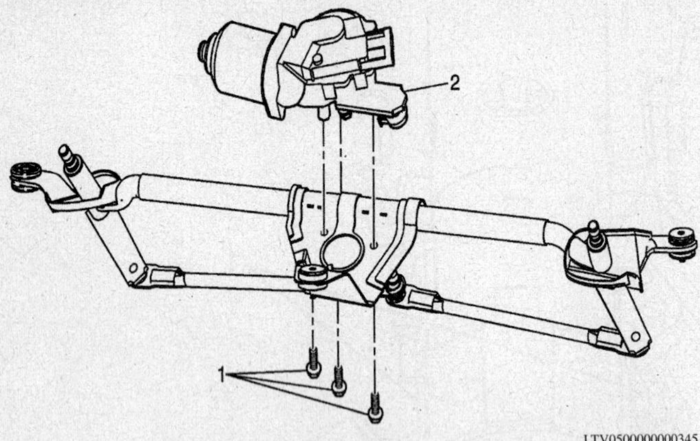

Fig. 3 Windshield wiper motor & drive system module

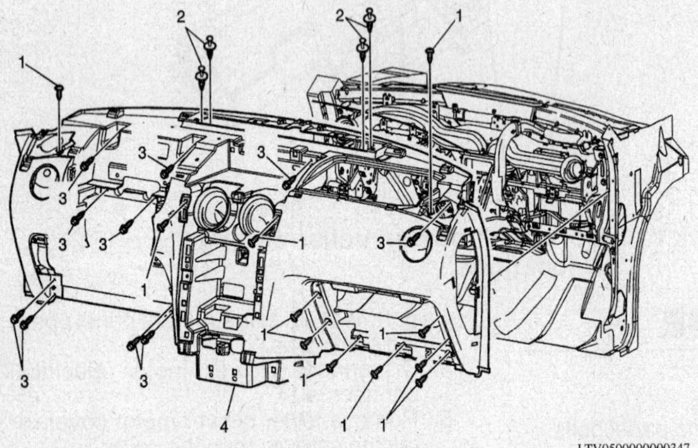

Fig. 5 Instrument panel retainer assembly

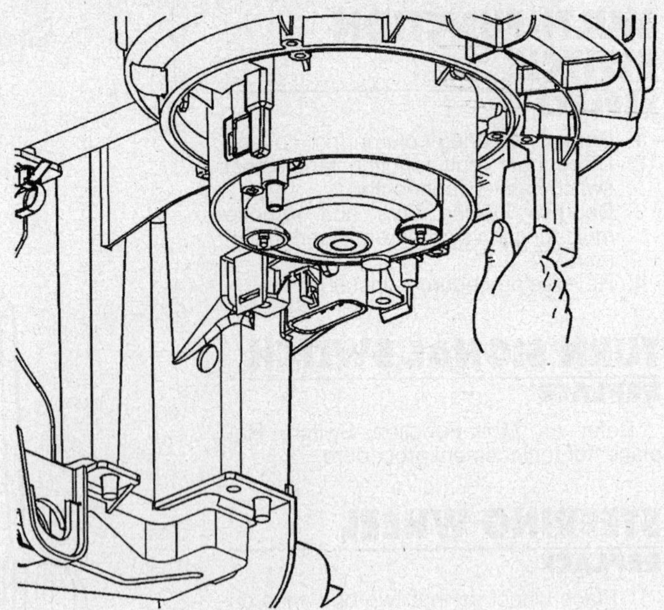

Fig. 4 Blower motor removal

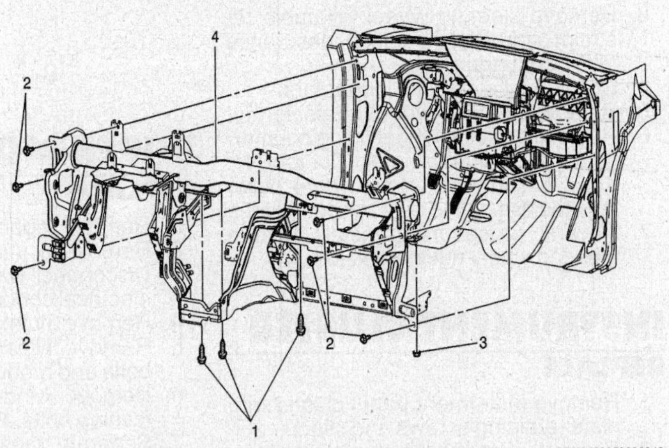

Fig. 6 Instrument panel tie bar

10. Remove rear floor console assembly nuts and assembly.
11. Disconnect shift control cables.
12. Remove Body Control Module (BCM).
13. Remove instrument panel center support bracket screws and bolts.
14. Remove instrument panel center support bracket assembly.
15. Lower steering column and position out of way.
16. Remove instrument panel cluster assembly as outlined under "Instrument Cluster, Replace."
17. Remove windshield garnish moldings.
18. Remove instrument panel cluster bezel trim plate.
19. Remove instrument panel accessory trim plate.
20. Remove instrument panel center compartment.
21. Remove instrument panel inflatable restraint as outlined in "Passive Restraint System" chapter.
22. Remove instrument panel upper trim pad screws.
23. Disconnect trim pad electrical connectors and remove trim pad.
24. Remove HVAC control module screws and control module.
25. Remove radio as outlined under "Radio, Replace."
26. Remove instrument panel compartment assembly.
27. Remove instrument panel retainer screws and bolts.
28. Disconnect electrical wiring harness connections. Note routing of wiring harness prior to removal to ensure proper reinstallation.
29. Remove instrument panel retainer assembly, **Fig. 5.**
30. Remove bolts securing brake pedal assembly to carrier.
31. Remove side window defogger ducts.
32. Remove air distribution duct assembly screws and duct assembly.
33. Remove instrument panel tie bar assembly to HVAC module bolts.
34. Remove instrument panel tie bar assembly to body bolts.
35. Remove instrument panel tie bar assembly to HVAC module nut.
36. Remove instrument panel tie bar assembly, **Fig. 6.**
37. Remove center floor air outlet duct.
38. Remove heater core cover assembly retaining screws using a suitable small chisel.
39. Remove heater core, **Fig. 7.**
40. Reverse procedure to install.

EVAPORATOR CORE

REPLACE

Refer to "Heater Core, Replace" for evaporator core replacement procedure.

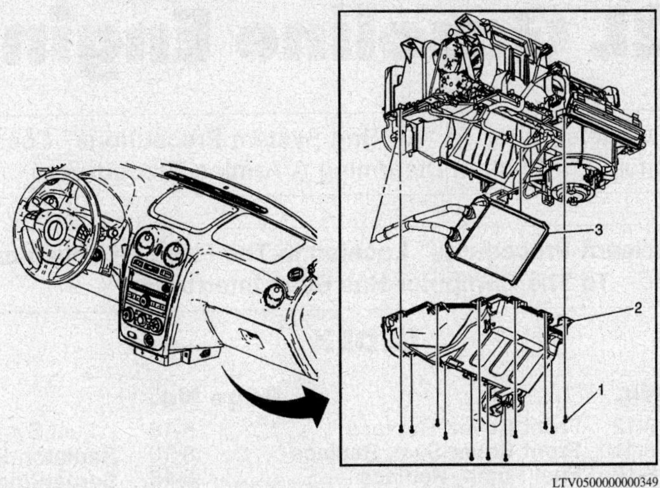

Fig. 7 Heater core assembly

2.2L Gasoline Engine

NOTE: On Air Bag Equipped Models, Refer To "Air Bag System Precautions" Located In The Front Of This Manual For System Disarming & Arming Procedures.

NOTE: Refer To "Computer Relearn Procedures" Located In The Front Of This Manual When Battery Power To The Computer Has Been Interrupted.

INDEX

PRECAUTIONS

Air Bag Systems

Refer to "Air Bag System Precautions" in the front of this manual for system disarming and arming procedures.

Battery Ground Cable

Prior to service disconnect battery ground cable and isolate as required.

Fuel System Pressure Relief

Always release residual fuel system pressure prior to disconnecting fuel lines or hoses.

1. Loosen fuel filler cap.
2. Connect suitable fuel pressure gauge to fuel pressure connection tap and install bleed hose into suitable container.
3. Open valve and bleed system pressure.

COMPRESSION PRESSURE

1. Engine should be at room temperature.
2. Disconnect wiring from ignition module.
3. Remove spark plugs.
4. Throttle body valve should be wide open.
5. Battery should be at or near full charge.
6. For each cylinder, crank engine through 4 compression strokes.
7. Lowest reading cylinder should not be less than 70 percent of highest.
8. No cylinder reading should be less than 100 psi.

ENGINE MOUNT

REPLACE

1. Gently lift up rear of air cleaner assembly to disengage air cleaner from studs.
2. Reposition air cleaner assembly in order to access positive crankcase ventilation (PCV) hose and throttle body duct.
3. Reposition PCV hose clamp at air cleaner assembly.
4. Remove PCV hose from air cleaner assembly.
5. Loosen air cleaner outlet duct clamp at throttle body.
6. Disconnect engine wiring harness electrical connector from MAF/IAT sensor.
7. Disconnect electrical connector from washer solvent reservoir pump.
8. Disconnect washer hose from container.
9. Remove windshield washer solvent container nut, and container.
10. Support engine with a suitable hydraulic floor jack. Use a piece of wood between floor jack and oil pan.
11. Remove engine mount to bracket bolts.
12. Remove engine mount to side rail nuts.
13. Remove engine mount from engine compartment.
14. Reverse procedure to install.

ENGINE

REPLACE

1. Remove air cleaner assembly as outlined under "Engine Mount, Replace."
2. Relieve fuel system pressure as outlined under "Precautions."
3. Disconnect fuel feed line from fuel rail.
4. Disconnect EVAP line from purge solenoid.
5. Disconnect washer hose from windshield washer solvent container assembly.
6. Disconnect electrical connector from windshield washer solvent container assembly.
7. Remove windshield washer solvent container assembly nut, and assembly.
8. Drain cooling system into a suitable container.
9. Remove engine drive belt as outlined under "Serpentine Drive Belt."
10. Raise and support vehicle.
11. Remove tire and wheel assembly.
12. Remove front fender liner.
13. Remove lefthand side engine splash shield retainers and splash shield.
14. Remove catalytic converter.

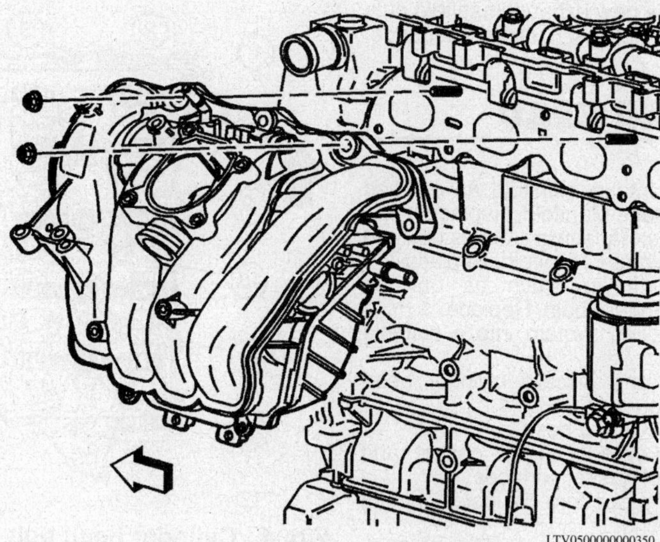

Fig. 1 Intake manifold removal

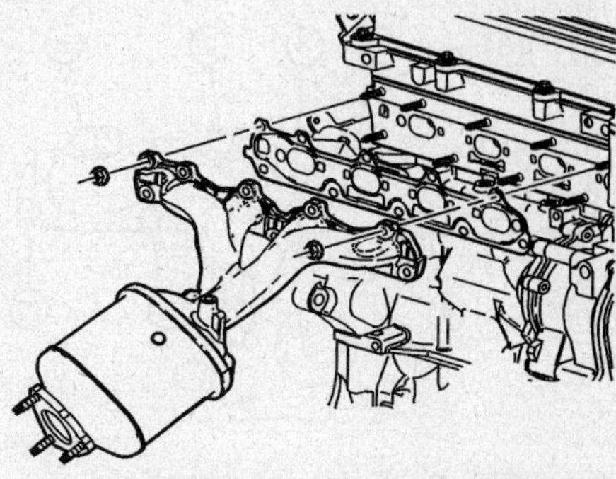

Fig. 2 Exhaust manifold removal

15. Disconnect cooling fan electrical connector.
16. Lower vehicle.
17. Remove Engine Control Module (ECM) and Transaxle Control Module (TCM) cover.
18. Disconnect body harness and engine harness electrical connectors from ECM.
19. Open junction block terminal cover.
20. Remove junction block terminal nut.
21. Remove battery cable terminal from stud.
22. Remove positive battery cable terminal from junction block stud.
23. Reposition engine harness to access ECM bracket lower bolts.
24. Remove ECM bracket nuts and bolts.
25. Lift ECM bracket off of studs and secure bracket aside.
26. Remove radiator inlet hose from engine.
27. Disconnect EVAP purge solenoid electrical connector.
28. Remove engine harness clip from EVAP purge solenoid bracket.
29. Remove radiator outlet hose from engine.
30. Remove heater inlet and outlet hose hoses from housing.
31. **On models equipped with a engine coolant heater,** disconnect engine coolant heater cord.
32. **On all models,** remove brake booster vacuum hose.
33. Disconnect Throttle Actuator Control (TAC), MAP sensor, fuel injector harness and alternator connectors.
34. Disconnect ignition control module electrical connector.
35. Remove engine harness clip from oil dipstick tube bracket and intake manifold.
36. Remove starter as outlined under "Starter, Replace" in "Electrical" section.
37. Remove battery cable ground nut and cable.
38. Remove engine harness ground terminal from stud.
39. Disconnect CKP sensor, oil pressure sensor and knock sensor electrical connectors.
40. Remove engine harness clip nut and harness clip from transaxle stud.
41. Disconnect A/C pressure switch and A/C compressor electrical connectors.
42. Remove compressor mounting bolts and reposition A/C compressor aside. Secure compressor with suitable tie straps or mechanics wire.
43. Raise and support vehicle.
44. Drain engine oil.
45. Remove engine harness ground bolt, then the harness ground from engine block.
46. Lower vehicle.
47. Remove engine harness lead terminal nut from alternator.
48. Remove engine harness clip nut from engine stud and clip from stud.
49. Disconnect Vehicle Speed Sensor (VSS) electrical connector.
50. Remove engine harness clip from speed sensor.
51. Disconnect engine harness from transaxle.
52. Disconnect Engine Coolant Temperature (ECT) sensor electrical connector.
53. Remove Connector Position Assurance (CPA) retainer.
54. Disconnect engine harness electrical connector from HO2S sensor.
55. Disconnect engine harness electrical connector from park neutral position switch.
56. Remove engine harness clip from transaxle stud and CPA retainer.
57. Remove engine harness electrical connector clip from transaxle rear mount bracket.
58. Disconnect engine harness electrical connector from HO2S.
59. **On models equipped with a manual transaxle,** proceed as follows:
    a. Disconnect engine harness electrical connector from VSS, then remove engine harness clip from transaxle and CPA retainer.
    b. Disconnect engine harness electrical connector from back up lamp switch and remove engine harness clip from transaxle.
    c. Reposition harness aside.
    d. Disconnect range selector and shift lever cables from transaxle levers.
    e. Remove range selector and shift lever cables from transaxle bracket.
60. **On models equipped with a automatic transaxle,** remove oil cooler line nut and oil cooler lines.
61. **On all models,** remove lefthand and righthand stabilizer link to strut nuts.
62. Separate stabilizer links from struts.
63. Remove lefthand and righthand steering gear outer tie rod to knuckle nuts. Discard nuts.
64. Separate outer tie rods from steering knuckles using a steering linkage and tie rod puller tool No. J 24319-B, or equivalent.
65. Remove lefthand and righthand ball joint to steering knuckle bolts and nuts, then separate lower ball joints from steering knuckles.
66. Assemble steering linkage and tie rod puller tool No. J 45341 and slide hammer tool No. J-2619-A, or equivalent.
67. Separate wheel drive shaft from transaxle using steering linkage and tie rod puller and slide hammer.
68. Secure wheel drive shafts out of way.
69. Remove lower radiator support bolts. Secure radiator assembly to radiator core support with suitable bungee cords.
70. Lower vehicle to approximately three feet off ground.
71. Position a suitable engine lift table under frame.
72. Place wood blocks on top of lift table between table and frame and lower vehicle until frame is resting on blocks of wood.
73. Remove engine mount bracket bolts.
74. Remove transaxle mount to transaxle bolts.
75. Remove front frame bolts, then the rear frame bolts.
76. Slowly raise vehicle up and away from powertrain assembly.
77. Slide lift table out from under vehicle.
78. Attach a suitable engine lift hoist to engine lift hooks.
79. **On models equipped with a automatic transaxle,** remove torque converter housing access plug, torque converter bolts and transaxle brace

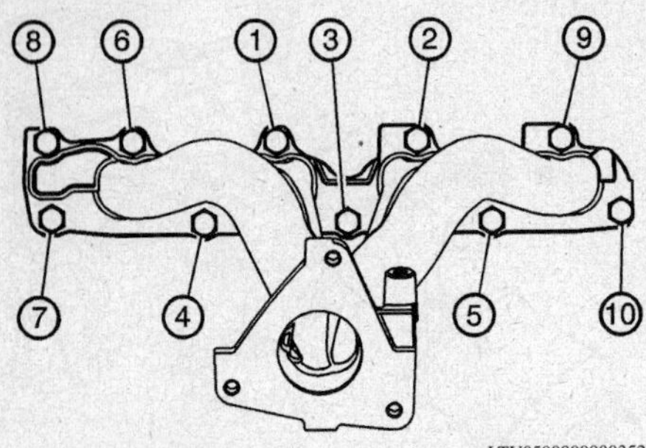

Fig. 3 Exhaust manifold tightening sequence

bolts and brace.

80. **On all models,** remove transaxle to engine bolts and studs.
81. Separate engine from transaxle.
82. **On models equipped with a manual transaxle,** remove clutch pressure plate and disc.
83. **On all models,** remove engine mount bracket and alternator.
84. Reverse procedure to install.

INTAKE MANIFOLD

REPLACE

1. Relieve fuel system pressure as outlined under "Precautions."
2. Remove air cleaner assembly.
3. Remove throttle body attaching bolts, then the throttle body.
4. Disconnect engine harness clips from the intake manifold.
5. Disconnect engine harness clip from oil dipstick tube.
6. Disconnect fuel injector electrical connector clip from intake manifold.
7. Disconnect EVAP canister purge tube from intake manifold and solenoid.
8. Remove oil dipstick tube.
9. Remove fuel pipes and clip.
10. Remove fuel rail mounting bolts and fuel rail.
11. Remove and discard fuel injector tip insulators.
12. Remove intake manifold retaining nuts and bolts, **Fig. 1.**
13. Remove intake manifold and gasket. Gasket is reusable if it is not damaged.
14. Reverse procedure to install. Lubricate new fuel injector tip insulators with clean engine oil.

EXHAUST MANIFOLD

REPLACE

1. Remove exhaust manifold heat shield.
2. **On models equipped with a block heater,** remove block heater.
3. **On all models,** remove oxygen sensor.
4. Remove and discard exhaust manifold to cylinder head retaining nuts and studs.
5. Remove exhaust manifold and catalytic converter assembly, **Fig. 2.**
6. Reverse procedure to install, noting the following:
   a. Clean all sealing surfaces.
   b. Install new exhaust manifold studs.
   c. **Torque** new exhaust manifold nuts to 10 ft. lbs., using sequence, **Fig. 3.**

CYLINDER HEAD

REPLACE

1. Remove intake manifold as outlined under "Intake Manifold, Replace."
2. Remove exhaust manifold as outlined under "Exhaust Manifold, Replace."
3. Remove timing chain as outlined under "Timing Chain, Replace."
4. Drain cooling system into a suitable container.
5. Remove and discard cylinder head bolts in sequence, **Fig. 4.**
6. Remove cylinder head.
7. Remove cylinder head gasket and clean all of gasket surfaces.
8. Reverse procedure to install, noting the following:
   a. **Torque** cylinder head bolts to 22 ft. lbs., then tighten an additional 155° using angle meter tool No. J 45059, or equivalent, using numbered sequence, **Fig. 5.**
   b. **Torque** front cylinder head bolts to 26 ft. lbs., **Fig. 6.**

VALVE COVER

REPLACE

1. Remove air cleaner assembly.
2. Remove PCV hose from valve cover.
3. Remove fuel line clip from fuel line bracket.
4. Remove fuel line bracket nut and bracket.
5. Remove ignition coil housing.
6. Remove ground strap stud from camshaft cover, then the ground strap from cover.
7. **On models equipped with a automatic transaxle,** remove engine harness clips from camshaft cover.
8. **On all models,** remove camshaft cover bolts and camshaft cover.
9. Reverse procedure to install.

HYDRAULIC LIFTERS

REPLACE

Refer to "Camshaft, Replace" for procedure.

CRANKSHAFT DAMPER

REPLACE

1. Install a crankshaft balancer holder tool No. J 38122-A, or equivalent.
2. Remove balancer retaining bolt and washer. Discard bolt.
3. Remove crankshaft balancer assembly.
4. Reverse procedure to install. Align keyway and flats on balancer with oil pump drive.

FRONT COVER

REPLACE

1. Remove drive belt tensioner as outlined under "Serpentine Drive Belt."

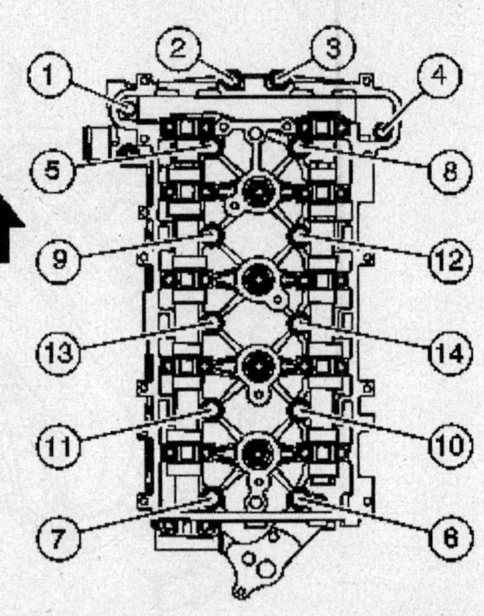

Fig. 4 Cylinder head bolt removal sequence

2. Remove crankshaft balancer as outlined under "Crankshaft Damper, Replace."
3. Remove air cleaner assembly.
4. Remove windshield washer solvent container assembly.
5. Install a suitable engine support fixture.
6. Remove engine mount to bracket bolts.
7. Remove engine mount to side rail nuts.
8. Remove engine mount from engine compartment.
9. Remove engine mount bracket to engine bolts.
10. Remove engine mount bracket.
11. Remove engine front cover to water pump bolt.
12. Raise and support vehicle.
13. Remove engine front cover bolts and cover.
14. Remove and discard engine front cover gasket.
15. Reverse procedure to install.

FRONT COVER SEAL

REPLACE

1. Remove crankshaft balancer as outlined under "Crankshaft Damper, Replace."
2. Remove seal from front cover using a suitable flat-bladed tool.
3. Reverse procedure to install. Use a camshaft/front main seal installer tool No. J 35268-A, or equivalent to install crankshaft front oil seal to engine front cover.

TIMING CHAIN

REPLACE

Removal

1. Remove camshaft cover as outlined under "Valve Cover, Replace."
2. Raise and support vehicle.
3. Remove engine front cover as outlined under "Front Cover, Replace."
4. Lower vehicle.

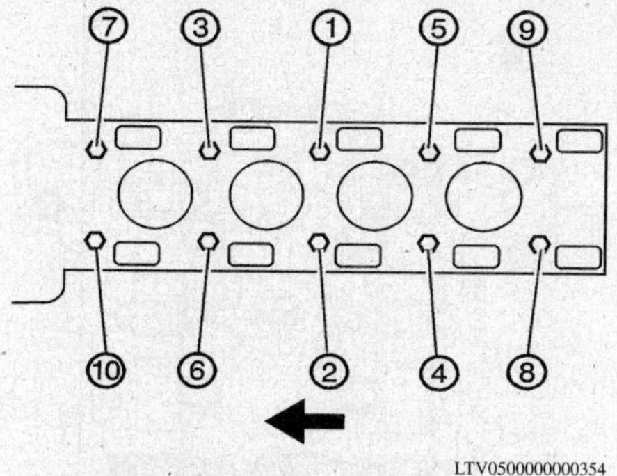

Fig. 5 Cylinder head bolt tightening sequence

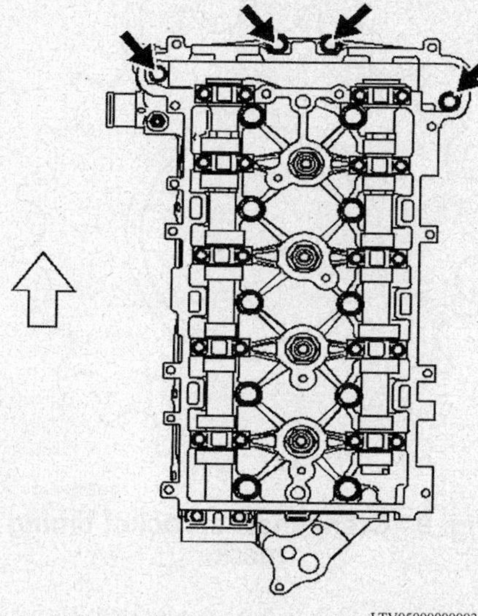

Fig. 6 Front cylinder head bolts

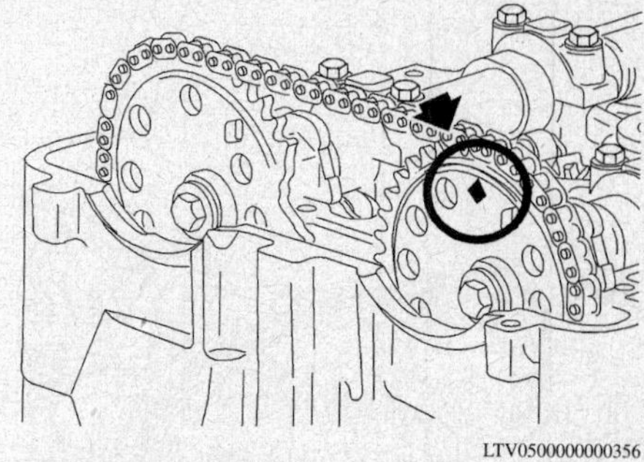

Fig. 7 Camshaft position marker

5. Remove spark plugs to ease rotation effort.
6. Rotate camshaft using a suitable 24 mm open-end wrench on camshaft flats. Camshaft should be rotated in a clockwise direction only, facing camshaft sprockets from passenger side of vehicle.
7. Locate No. 1 piston to approximately 60° before top dead center (diamond shaped hole on intake camshaft sprocket at 12 o'clock position), **Fig. 7.**
8. Remove timing chain tensioner.
9. Remove fixed timing chain guide access plug, then the timing chain guide.
10. Remove upper timing chain guide.
11. Use a suitable 24 mm wrench to prevent camshafts from turning, **Fig. 8.**
12. Remove and discard exhaust camshaft sprocket bolt, then the exhaust camshaft sprocket.
13. Remove timing chain tensioner guide.
14. Remove and discard intake camshaft sprocket bolt, then the intake camshaft sprocket.
15. Remove timing chain through top of cylinder head.
16. Remove crankshaft sprocket.
17. Remove oil nozzle and bolt.
18. Remove balance shaft drive chain tensioner.
19. Remove adjustable balance shaft chain guide.
20. Remove small balance shaft drive chain guide.
21. Remove upper balance shaft drive chain guide.
22. Remove balance shaft drive chain.

Installation

1. Install upper balance shaft chain guide bolts.
2. Install balance shaft drive chain with colored links aligned with marks on balance shaft drive sprockets and crankshaft sprocket using the following procedure:
   a. Position chain so copper colored and chrome links are visible.
   b. Place uniquely colored link so aligns with timing mark on intake side balance shaft sprocket.
   c. Working clockwise around chain, place first matching colored link in line with timing mark on crankshaft drive sprocket. (approximately 5 o'clock position on crank sprocket).
   d. Place chain on water pump drive sprocket.
   e. Align last matching colored link with timing mark on exhaust side balance shaft drive sprocket.
3. Install small balance shaft chain guide.
4. Turn tensioner plunger 90° in its bore. Compress plunger until a paper clip can be inserted through hole in plunger body and into hole in tensioner plunger.
5. Install timing chain tensioner.
6. Remove paper clip from balance shaft drive chain tensioner.
7. Install oil nozzle and bolt.
8. Install crankshaft sprocket with timing mark at 5 o'clock position, **Fig. 9.**
9. Lower timing chain through opening in top of cylinder head. Ensure chain goes around both sides of cylinder block bosses, **Fig. 10.**
10. Install intake camshaft sprocket with INT diamond at 2 o'clock position, **Fig. 11.**
11. Hand tighten a new intake camshaft sprocket bolt.
12. Route timing chain around crankshaft sprocket with matching colored link aligning with timing mark.
13. Route timing chain around intake camshaft sprocket with uniquely colored link aligning with INT diamond.
14. Install timing chain tensioner guide through opening in top of cylinder head.
15. Install exhaust camshaft sprocket and align timing chain matching colored link with sprocket EXH triangle (10 o'clock position), **Fig. 12.**
16. Use a suitable 24 mm wrench to rotate camshaft slightly, until exhaust sprocket aligns with camshaft.
17. Hand tighten exhaust camshaft sprocket bolt.
18. Install fixed timing chain guide and tighten fixed timing chain bolts.
19. Apply a suitable sealant compound to thread of timing chain guide bolt, then tighten bolt through access hole.
20. Install timing chain upper guide and bolts.
21. Measure timing chain tensioner assembly from end to end. A new tensioner should be supplied in fully compressed non-active state. A tensioner in compressed state will measure 2.83 inches from end to end. A tensioner in active state will measure 3.35 inches from end to end.
22. If timing chain tensioner is not in compressed state, perform the following:
   a. Remove piston assembly from body of timing chain tensioner by pulling it out.
   b. Install a tensioner tool, tool No. J 45027-2, or equivalent, into a vise.
   c. Install notch end of piston assembly into tensioner tool.
   d. Turn ratchet cylinder into piston.
23. Install compressed piston assembly back into timing chain tensioner body until it stops at bottom of bore. **Do not compress piston assembly against bottom of bore. This will activate tensioner, which will then need to be reset.**
24. At this point tensioner should measure approximately 2.83 inch from end to end.
25. Tighten timing chain tensioner.
26. Use a suitable 24 mm wrench to hold camshaft, then tighten camshaft sprocket bolts to specification.
27. Install camshaft cover as outlined under "Valve Cover, Replace."
28. Raise and support vehicle.
29. Install engine front cover as outlined under "Front Cover, Replace."
30. Lower vehicle.

CAMSHAFT

REPLACE

Removal

1. Remove camshaft cover as outlined under "Valve Cover, Replace."
2. Remove upper timing chain guide.
3. Install a sprocket holding tool, tool No. J 43655, or equivalent.
4. Remove both intake and exhaust camshaft sprocket bolts and discard.
5. Slide camshaft sprockets forward.
6. Mark bearing caps to ensure they are installed in original position.
7. Remove each bolt on each cap one

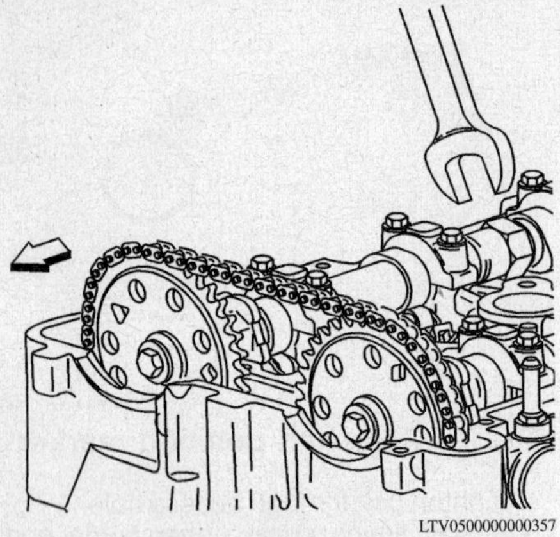

Fig. 8 Camshaft holding position

Fig. 9 Crankshaft sprocket timing mark

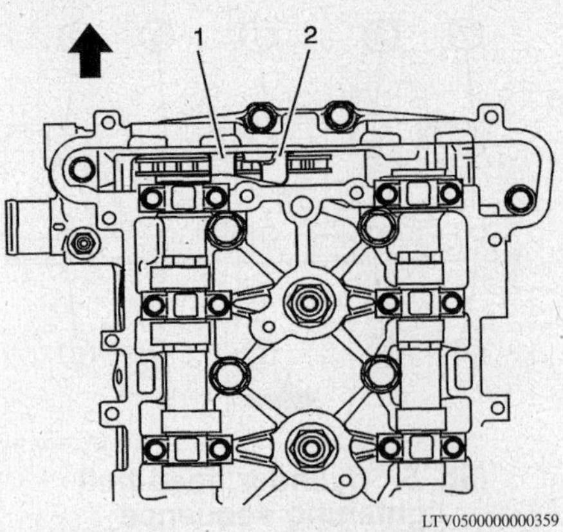

Fig. 10 Cylinder block bosses

turn at a time until there is no spring tension on camshaft.
8. Remove bearing caps.
9. Remove intake camshaft.
10. Remove camshaft roller followers.
11. Remove hydraulic lash adjusters.

Installation

1. Lubricate valve tips, **Fig. 13.**
2. Install hydraulic lash adjusters.
3. Install camshaft roller followers.
4. Ensure alignment notches are aligned with camshaft sprocket, **Fig. 14.**
5. Install camshafts.
6. Install camshaft bearing caps, then tighten camshaft bearing cap bolts in increments of three turns until they are seated.
7. Tighten camshaft bearing cap bolts.
8. Apply a .197 inch bead of permatex anaerobic gasket maker part No. 51813, or equivalent, to rear intake camshaft bearing cap.
9. Install rear intake camshaft bearing cap bolts.
10. Install camshaft sprockets onto camshafts.
11. Hand tighten new camshaft sprocket bolts.
12. Remove sprocket holding tool.
13. Tighten camshaft sprocket bolts.
14. Install upper timing chain guide and tighten.
15. Install camshaft cover as outlined under "Valve Cover, Replace."

BALANCE SHAFT

REPLACE

1. Remove timing chain as outlined under "Timing Chain, Replace."
2. Remove balance shaft bearing carrier bolts. **Do not remove bolt holding sprocket.**
3. Remove balance shaft assemblies.
4. Reverse procedure to install.

PISTON & ROD ASSEMBLY

Coat the piston pin with oil. Install one side of one piston pin retainer into the retaining groove using a piston pin retainer remover and installer tool No. EN-46745 or equivalent. Rotate the retainer until it is fully seated in the groove. Install the connecting rod and the piston pin. Push the piston pin until it bottoms in the previously installed retainer. Install the second piston pin retainer, using the piston pin retainer remover and installer tool. Ensure that the piston moves freely, **Fig. 15.**

MAIN & ROD BEARINGS

Main bearings are available in standard sizes and undersizes. Rod bearings are available in standard sizes and undersizes.

Torque crankshaft bearing bolts 15 ft. lbs., then an additional 70° using torque angle meter J 45059, or equivalent, using sequence, **Fig. 16.** Using sequence, **Fig. 17, torque** lower crankcase perimeter bolts to 18 ft. lbs.

CRANKSHAFT REAR OIL SEAL

REPLACE

1. Remove transaxle as outlined in **MOTOR's "Domestic Transmission, In-Vehicle Service" or "Transmission Service DVD."**
2. Hold crankshaft balancer, using a crankshaft balancer holder tool No. J 38122-A, or equivalent.
3. Remove flywheel bolts, then the flywheel. Discard bolts.
4. Pry out crankshaft rear oil seal using a suitable flat-bladed tool.
5. Reverse procedure to install. Install oil seal using rear main seal installer tool No. J 42067, or equivalent.

OIL PAN

REPLACE

1. Remove air cleaner assembly as outlined under "Engine Mount, Replace."
2. Remove oil dipstick.
3. Remove engine harness clip from oil dipstick tube bracket.
4. Remove A/C compressor and condenser hose clip from oil dipstick tube bracket.
5. Remove oil dipstick tube bolt, tube and O-ring seals.
6. Raise and support vehicle.
7. Drain engine oil into suitable container.
8. Remove engine drive belt as outlined under "Serpentine Drive Belt."
9. Remove lower A/C compressor bolt and lower transaxle bolts.
10. Remove oil pan bolts and oil pan.
11. Reverse procedure to install. Apply a .08 inch bead of a suitable sealant around perimeter of oil pan and oil suction port opening.

OIL PUMP

REPLACE

Refer to "Front Cover, Replace" for procedure.

OIL PUMP SERVICE

Disassemble

1. Disassemble pressure relief valve.
2. Remove oil pump gerotor cover and bolts.
3. Clean all of components in cleaning solvent. Remove varnish, sludge and dirt.

Assemble

1. Inspect oil pump for wear and scoring.
2. Replace front cover and oil pump assembly if it is out of specification or damaged.
3. Lubricate all oil pump components with engine oil.
4. Install inner gear into outer gear. If gears are improperly installed in front cover, gerotor cover will not bolt on.
5. Install gears together into front cover with hub of center gear facing front cover.
6. Install oil pump gerotor cover and bolts.
7. Install pressure relief valve piston and spring.

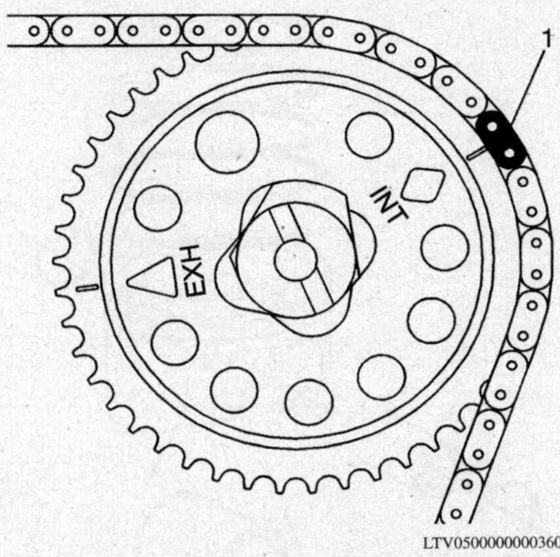

Fig. 11 Intake camshaft sprocket alignment mark

SERPENTINE DRIVE BELT

Routing

Refer to **Fig. 18** for serpentine drive belt routing.

Belt Replacement

1. Raise and support vehicle, then remove tire and wheel assembly.
2. Remove front fender liner.
3. Remove engine splash shield retainers and splash shield.
4. Install a accessory belt tensioner unloader tool No. J 44811, or equivalent, to drive belt tensioner.
5. Rotate drive belt tensioner counterclockwise to release spring tension.
6. Remove drive belt from under drive belt tensioner and accessory drive pulleys.
7. Reverse procedure to install.

Tensioner Replacement

1. Remove drive belt.
2. Insert a suitable pry bar between engine and cradle, and raise engine slightly until a socket with an extension can be installed onto drive belt tensioner bolt.
3. Remove drive belt tensioner bolt and drive belt tensioner.
4. Reverse procedure to install.

COOLING SYSTEM BLEED

These engines do not require a specified bleed procedure. After filling cooling system, run engine to operating temperature with radiator/pressure cap off. Air will then be automatically bled through cap opening.

THERMOSTAT

REPLACE

1. Drain cooling system into a suitable container.
2. Remove radiator outlet hose from thermostat housing.
3. Remove thermostat housing cover bolts and cover.
4. Remove thermostat and O-ring seal. Discard seal.
5. Reverse procedure to install.

WATER PUMP

REPLACE

1. Remove thermostat housing as outlined under "Thermostat, Replace."
2. Remove air cleaner assembly.
3. Disconnect coolant heater cord.
4. Remove coolant heater bolt and heater.
5. Remove water pump access plate from front cover.
6. Install a water pump holding tool No. J 43651, or equivalent, into position.
7. Tighten bolts on water pump holding tool into threads on water pump sprocket.
8. Install access cover bolts that were removed earlier to secure water pump holding tool to front cover assembly.
9. Remove three inner water pump sprocket to water pump bolts.
10. Remove water pump bolts.
11. Remove engine harness clip nut from water pump stud.
12. Remove engine harness clip from stud.
13. Remove water pump.
14. Reverse procedure to install.

RADIATOR

REPLACE

1. Drain cooling system into a suitable container.
2. Remove air cleaner assembly.
3. Disconnect hood latch release cable.
4. Remove hood latch bolts and hood latch.
5. Raise and support vehicle.
6. Position a suitable drain pan under transaxle cooler pipes.
7. Remove transaxle oil cooler pipes retaining nut, then the cooler pipes from transaxle.
8. Remove transaxle oil cooler pipes from fittings at radiator.
9. Remove transaxle oil cooler pipe from retaining clip at radiator.
10. Remove transaxle oil cooler pipes from vehicle.
11. Remove radiator cap and coolant recovery reservoir hose.
12. Remove radiator inlet and outlet hoses.
13. Remove radiator bracket assembly bracket assembly.
14. Remove radiator and fan assembly.
15. Separate fan assembly and condenser from radiator.
16. Reverse procedure to install.

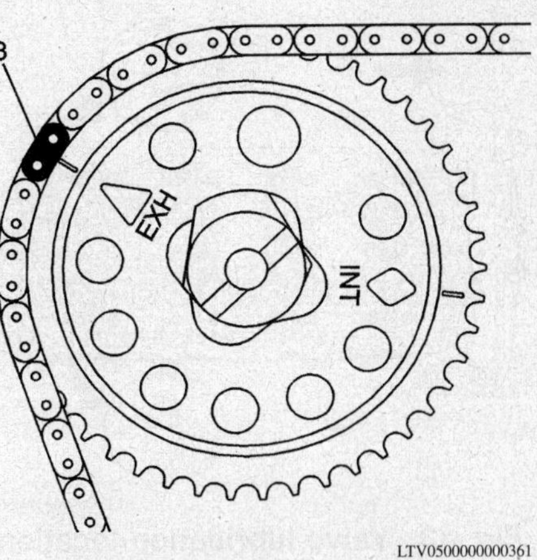

Fig. 12 Exhaust camshaft sprocket alignment mark

FUEL PUMP

REPLACE

1. Relieve fuel system pressure.
2. Drain fuel tank.
3. Raise and support vehicle.
4. Disconnect fuel tank vent pipe quick connect fittings.
5. Loosen fuel fill pipe hose clamp at fuel tank.
6. Remove fuel fill pipe hose from fuel tank.
7. Disconnect fuel tank electrical connector from pass through connector.
8. Remove exhaust pipe insulators from underbody hangers.
9. Remove muffler insulators from underbody hanger and lower exhaust. Allow exhaust to rest on rear axle beam.
10. Place a suitable adjustable jack under fuel tank.
11. Remove fuel tank strap bolts and straps.
12. Lower fuel tank away from vehicle.
13. Remove fuel feed intermediate pipe.
14. Remove fuel tank vent pipe.
15. Disconnect and remove fuel tank electrical harness.
16. Disconnect fuel pressure sensor and fuel pump module electrical connectors.
17. Disconnect fuel tank vent and feed pipe quick connect fittings.
18. Install a fuel sender lock ring wrench tool No. J 45722, or equivalent, to lock ring.
19. Turn fuel module lock ring in a counterclockwise direction.
20. Remove module lock ring.
21. Slowly raise module until fuel level sensor float arm is just visible. Ensure fuel level sensor harness connector clears tank opening, **Fig. 19.**
22. Tilt module toward rear of fuel tank to allow level sensor float arm to clear tank opening, then remove module from tank.
23. Carefully discard fuel in module reservoir bowl into an suitable container.
24. Remove and discard fuel pump module seal.
25. Reverse procedure to install.

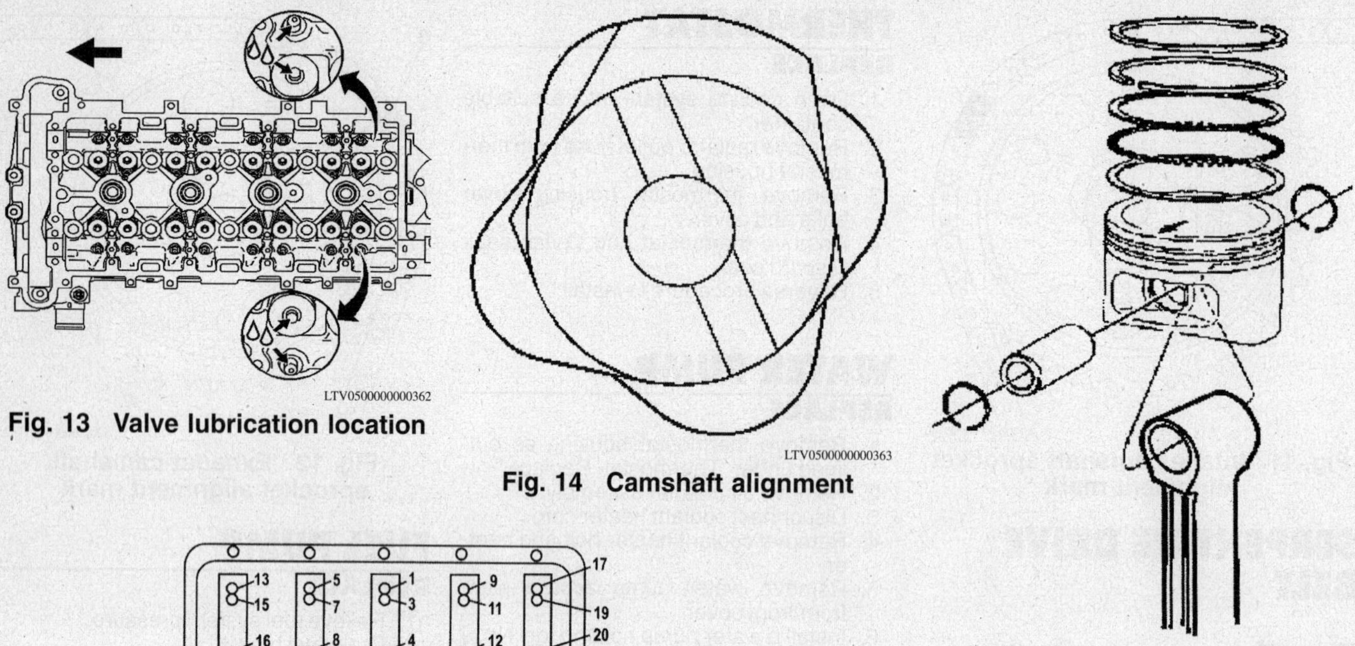

Fig. 13 Valve lubrication location

Fig. 14 Camshaft alignment

Fig. 15 Piston assembly

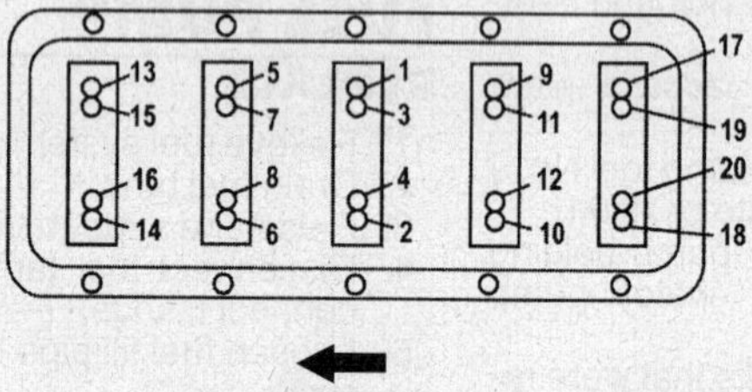

LTV0500000000910

Fig. 16 Crankshaft bearing cap bolt tightening sequence

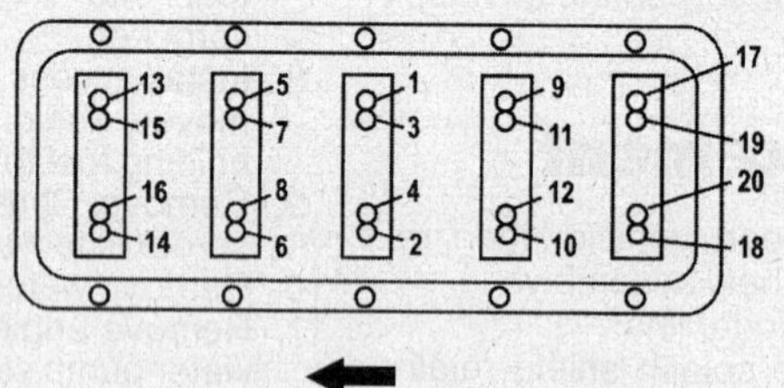

Fig. 17 Lower crankcase perimeter bolt tightening sequence

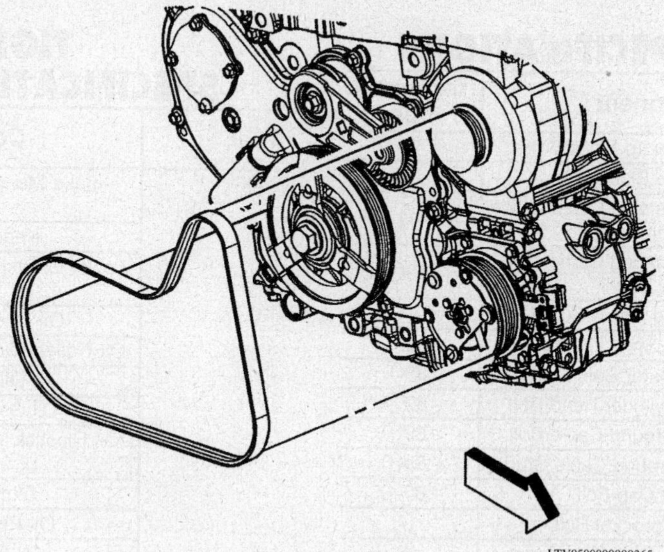

Fig. 18 Serpentine drive belt routing

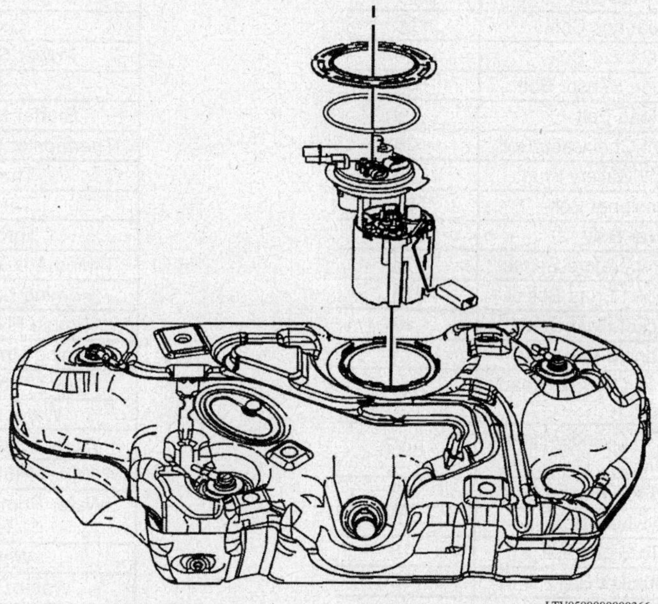

Fig. 19 Fuel pump module removal

TIGHTENING SPECIFICATIONS

Year	Component	Torque Ft. Lbs.
2006	A/C Compressor To Block Bolt	15
	Alternator To Block Bolt	17
	Balance Shaft Adjustable Chain Guide Bolt	11
	Balance Shaft Bearing Carrier To Block Bolt	89①
	Balance Shaft Fixed Chain Guide Bolt	11
	Balance Shaft Sprocket Bolt	37
	Block Heater Bolt	89①
	Cam Cover To Cylinder Head Bolt	89①
	Cam Cover To Ground Cable Bolt	89①
	Cam Cover To Ground Cable Stud	89①
	Camshaft Cap Bolt	89①
	Camshaft Sprocket Bolt	②
	Camshaft Timing Chain Tensioner	5
	Chain Guide Plug	59
	Connecting Rod Bolt	③
	Crankshaft Bearings Cap	④
	Crankshaft Balancer Bolt	⑤
	Crankshaft Position Sensor Bolt	89①
	Cylinder Head Bolt	⑥
	Cylinder Head Front Chaincase Bolt	26
	Cylinder Head Oil Gallery Plug	26
	Drive Belt Tensioner Bolt	33
	EGR Cover Bolt	18
	Engine Coolant Temperature Sensor	16
	Engine Lift Bracket Front Bolt	18
	Engine Lift Bracket Rear Bolt	18
	EVAP Purge Solenoid Valve Nut	13
	Exhaust Manifold To Cylinder Head Nut	124①
	Exhaust Manifold To Cylinder Head Stud	89①
	Exhaust Manifold Pipe Flange Stud	12
	Flexplate/Flywheel Bolt	⑦
	Front Cover To Block Bolt	18
	Front Lift Bracket Bolt	18
	Fuel Pipe Bracket Bolt	89①
	Fuel Rail Bracket Bolt	89①
	Heat Shield To Exhaust Manifold Bolt	17
	Ignition Coil Bolt	89①
	Intake Camshaft Rear Cap Bolt	89①
	Intake Manifold To Cylinder Head Bolt	89①
	Intake Manifold To Cylinder Head Nut	89①

TIGHTENING SPECIFICATIONS—Continued

Year	Component	Torque Ft. Lbs.
2006	Intake Manifold To Cylinder Head Stud	53①
	Knock Sensor Bolt	18
	Lower Crankcase To Block Perimeter Bolt	18
	Oil Filter Housing Cover	18
	Oil Gallery Gerotor Cover - Rear Bolt	53①
	Oil Gallery Plug	26
	Oil Gallery Plug - Rear	44
	Oil Dipstick Tube To Intake Manifold Bolt	89①
	Oil Pan Drain Plug	18
	Oil Pan To Block Bolts	18
	Oil Pressure Switch	16
	Oil Pump Cover Bolt	53①
	Oil Pump Pressure Relief Valve Plug	30
	Oxygen Sensor	31
	Power Steering Pump Bolt	18
	Spark Plug	15
	Starter Motor To Block Bolt	39
	Thermostat Housing To Block Bolts	89①
	Throttle Body Bolt	89①
	Throttle Body Nut	89①
	Throttle Body Stud	53①
	Timing Adjustable Chain Guide Bolt	89①
	Timing Chain Oil Nozzle Bolt	89①
	Timing Fixed Chain Guide Bolt	11
	Timing Upper Chain Guide Bolt	89①
	Vent Tube To Cylinder Head	11
	Water Jacket Drain Plug	15
	Water Pipe Support Bracket Bolt	89①
	Water Pump Access Cover Bolt	62
	Water Pump/Balance Shaft Chain Tensioner Bolt	89①
	Water Pump Bolts	18
	Water Pump Sprocket Bolt	89①

① — Inch lbs.
② — First pass, torque to 63 ft. lbs.; second pass, an additional 30°.
③ — First pass, torque to 18 ft. lbs.; second pass, an additional 100°.
④ — Refer to “Main & Rod Bearing” for tightening procedure.
⑤ — First pass, torque to 74 ft. lbs.; second pass, an additional 125°.
⑥ — Refer to “Cylinder Head, Replace” for tightening procedure.
⑦ — First pass, torque to 39 ft. lbs.; second pass, an additional 25°.

2.4L Gasoline Engine

NOTE: Refer To The "2.2L Engine" Section Of This Chapter For Service Procedures Not Found In This Section.

NOTE: On Air Bag Equipped Models, Refer To "Air Bag System Precautions" Located In The Front Of This Manual For System Disarming & Arming Procedures.

NOTE: Refer To "Computer Relearn Procedures" Located In The Front Of This Manual When Battery Power To The Computer Has Been Interrupted.

INDEX

PRECAUTIONS

Air Bag Systems

Refer to "Air Bag System Precautions" in the front of this manual for system disarming and arming procedures.

Battery Ground Cable

Prior to service disconnect battery ground cable and isolate as required.

Fuel System Pressure Relief

Always release residual fuel system pressure prior to disconnecting fuel lines or hoses.

1. Loosen fuel filler cap.
2. Connect suitable fuel pressure gauge to fuel pressure connection tap and install bleed hose into suitable container.
3. Open valve and bleed system pressure.

ENGINE MOUNT

REPLACE

Refer to the "2.2L Engine" section for engine mount replacement procedure.

ENGINE

REPLACE

Refer to the "2.2L Engine" section for engine replacement procedure.

INTAKE MANIFOLD

REPLACE

1. Relieve fuel system pressure as outlined under "Precautions."
2. Remove air cleaner outlet duct.
3. Disconnect Throttle Actuator Control (TAC) electrical connector.
4. Remove throttle body bolts and throttle body.
5. Disconnect fuel injector electrical connector.
6. Raise and support vehicle.
7. Disconnect engine harness clips from intake manifold.
8. Lower vehicle.
9. Remove air cleaner assembly.
10. Remove oil dipstick.
11. Remove engine harness clip from oil dipstick tube bracket.
12. Remove A/C compressor and condenser hose clip from oil dipstick tube bracket.
13. Remove oil dipstick tube bolt, tube and O-ring seals.
14. Disconnect fuel injector electrical connector clip from intake manifold.
15. Remove vacuum brake booster hose from intake manifold.
16. Disconnect EVAP canister purge tube from intake manifold and EVAP solenoid.
17. Disconnect fuel injector harness electrical connector.
18. Disconnect manifold absolute pressure (MAP) sensor electrical connector.
19. Remove fuel injector harness electrical connector clips from intake manifold.
20. Remove fuel rail studs.
21. Pull fuel rail back and upward in order to release fuel injectors from cylinder head ports.
22. Remove fuel rail.
23. Remove intake manifold bolt and nuts, then the intake manifold, **Fig. 1.**
24. Reverse procedure to install.

EXHAUST MANIFOLD

REPLACE

Refer to the "2.2L Engine" section for exhaust manifold replacement procedure.

CYLINDER HEAD

REPLACE

1. Drain cooling system into suitable container.
2. Remove exhaust manifold as outlined under "Exhaust Manifold, Replace."
3. Remove intake manifold as outlined under "Intake Manifold, Replace."
4. Remove radiator surge tank air bleed hose from cylinder head.
5. Remove radiator inlet hose from cylinder head.
6. Remove timing chain as outlined under "Timing Chain, Replace."
7. Remove cylinder head bolts in sequence, **Fig. 2.**
8. Remove cylinder head and gasket.
9. Reverse procedure to install, noting the following:
   a. **Torque** cylinder head bolts to 22 ft. lbs., then tighten an additional 155°

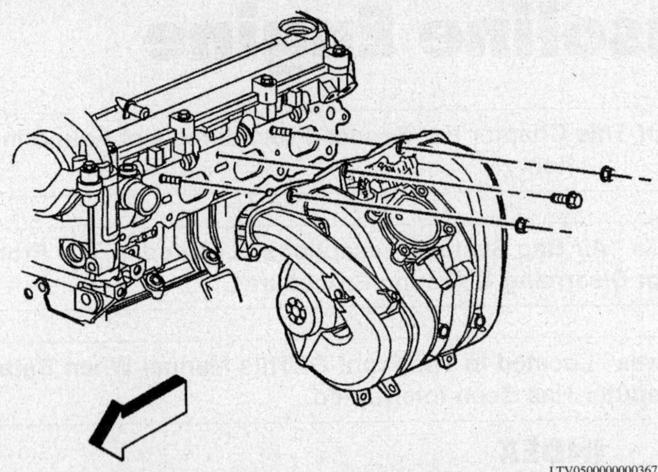

Fig. 1 Intake manifold removal

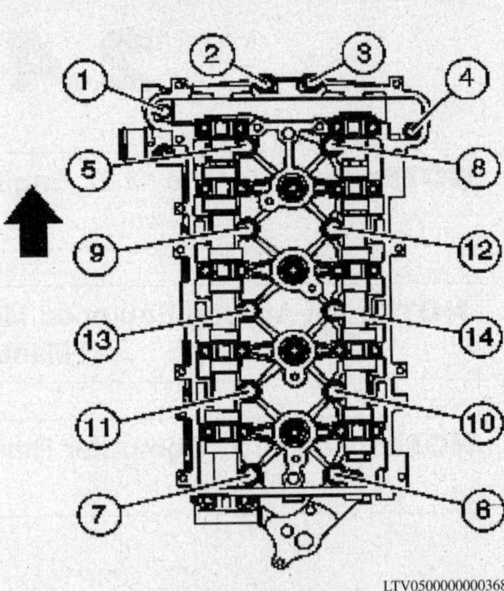

Fig. 2 Cylinder head bolt removal sequence

using a torque angle meter tool No. J 45059, or equivalent, using sequence, **Fig. 3.**

b. **Torque** front cylinder head bolts to 26 ft, lbs., **Fig. 4.**

VALVE COVER

REPLACE

1. Remove air cleaner assembly as outlined under "Intake Manifold, Replace."
2. Remove PCV hose from cover.
3. Disconnect intake and exhaust camshaft position actuator solenoid valve electrical connectors.
4. Remove ignition coils as outlined under "Ignition Coil, Replace."
5. Remove engine harness clips from cover.
6. Remove camshaft cover bolts and camshaft cover.
7. Reverse procedure to install.

HYDRAULIC LIFTERS

REPLACE

Refer to "Camshaft, Replace" for hydraulic lifter replacement procedure.

CRANKSHAFT DAMPER

REPLACE

1. Remove drive belt as outlined under "Serpentine Drive Belt."
2. Install harmonic balancer holder tool No. J 38122-A, or equivalent, to prevent crankshaft from rotating.
3. Remove and discard crankshaft balancer bolt.
4. Remove crankshaft balancer.
5. Reverse procedure to install.

FRONT COVER

REPLACE

1. Remove drive belt tensioner as outlined under "Serpentine Belt Drive."
2. Remove crankshaft balancer as outlined under "Crankshaft Damper, Replace."
3. Remove air cleaner assembly as outlined under "Intake Manifold, Replace."
4. Disconnect electrical connector from windshield washer solvent container assembly pump.
5. Disconnect washer hose from windshield washer solvent container assembly.
6. Remove windshield washer solvent container nut and container.
7. Install a suitable engine support fixture.
8. Remove engine mount to bracket bolts.
9. Remove engine mount to side rail nuts.
10. Remove engine mount from engine compartment.
11. Remove engine mount bracket to engine bolts, then the bracket.
12. Remove engine front cover to water pump bolt.
13. Raise and support vehicle.
14. Remove engine front cover bolts, front cover and gasket.
15. Reverse procedure to install.

TIMING CHAIN

REPLACE

Removal

1. Remove No. 1 cylinder spark plug.
2. Rotate crankshaft in engine rotational direction clockwise until No. 1 piston is at TDC on compression stroke.
3. Remove camshaft cover as outlined under "Valve Cover, Replace."
4. Remove engine front cover as outlined under "Front Cover, Replace."
5. Remove upper timing chain guide bolts and guide.
6. Remove timing chain tensioner.
7. Install a suitable 24 mm wrench on hex on exhaust camshaft to hold camshaft.
8. Remove and discard exhaust camshaft actuator bolt.
9. Remove exhaust camshaft actuator from camshaft and timing chain.
10. Remove timing chain tensioner guide bolt and guide.
11. Remove fixed timing chain guide access plug.
12. Remove fixed timing chain guide bolts and guide.
13. Install a suitable 24 mm wrench on hex on intake camshaft to hold camshaft.
14. Remove and discard intake camshaft actuator bolt.
15. Remove intake camshaft actuator and timing chain through top of cylinder head.
16. Remove timing chain crankshaft sprocket.
17. Remove balance shaft drive chain tensioner bolts and tensioner.
18. Remove adjustable balance shaft chain guide bolt and guide.
19. Remove small balance shaft drive chain guide bolts and guide.
20. Remove upper balance shaft drive chain guide bolts and guide.
21. Remove balance shaft drive chain.
22. Remove balance shaft drive sprocket.

Installation

1. Install balance shaft drive sprocket.
2. Install balance shaft drive chain, align colored link with marks on balance shaft sprockets and balance shaft drive sprocket. There are 3 colored links on chain. Two are chrome and one is copper, **Fig. 5.**
3. Align copper link with timing mark on intake side balance shaft sprocket.
4. Working clockwise around chain, align chrome link with timing mark on balance shaft drive sprocket (approximately 6 o'clock position on sprocket).
5. Place chain on water pump drive sprocket.
6. Align last chrome link with timing mark on exhaust side balance shaft drive sprocket.
7. Install upper balance shaft drive chain guide and bolts.
8. Install small balance shaft drive chain guide and bolts.
9. Install adjustable balance shaft chain guide and bolt.
10. Reset timing chain tensioner as follows:

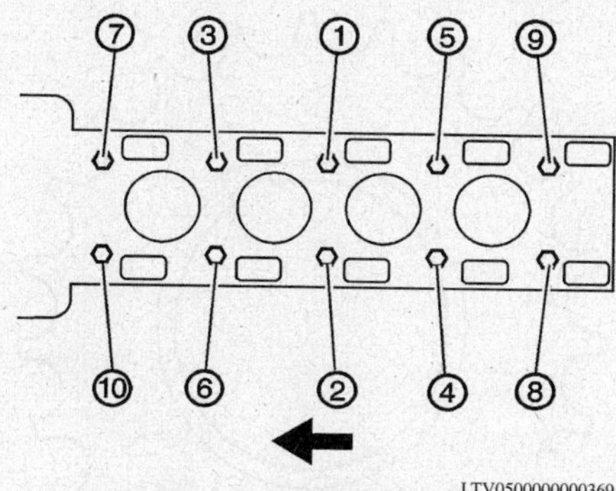

Fig. 3 Cylinder head bolt tightening sequence

a. Rotate tensioner plunger 90° in its bore and compress plunger.
b. Rotate tensioner back to original 12 o'clock position and insert a paper clip through hole in plunger body and into hose in tensioner plunger.

11. Install balance shaft drive chain tensioner and bolts.
12. Remove paper clip from balance shaft drive chain tensioner.
13. Install timing chain crankshaft sprocket onto crankshaft with timing mark in 5 o'clock position, **Fig. 6.**
14. There are 3 colored links on timing chain. Two links are pink in color and one link is blue in color. Position chain so colored links are visible.
15. Align timing chain blue colored link to intake camshaft actuator timing mark, **Fig. 7.** Install and hand tighten camshaft actuator bolt.
16. Lower timing chain through opening in cylinder head. Ensure chain goes around both sides of cylinder block bosses, **Fig. 8.**
17. Route timing chain around crankshaft sprocket and align first pink link with timing mark on crankshaft sprocket (approximately 5 o'clock position), **Fig. 9.**
18. Install adjustable timing chain guide through opening in cylinder head.
19. Install exhaust camshaft actuator.
20. Align timing mark on actuator with last pink colored link, hand tighten bolt, **Fig. 10. Do not rotate either camshaft more than half turn in either direction with crankshaft at TDC. To do so may cause valve to piston contact resulting in a damaged valve and/or a damaged piston.**
21. If camshaft is 180° out of time, realign camshaft as follows:
    a. Turn intake camshaft until alignment feature on back of camshaft actuator seats into notch in front of intake camshaft.
    b. Turn crankshaft 45° in either direction.
    c. Turn intake cam to appropriate location.
    d. Turn crankshaft back to TDC.
22. When actuator seats on cam, then hand tighten actuator bolt.
23. Ensure all colored links and appropriate timing marks are aligned.
24. Install fixed timing chain guide and bolts.
25. Install upper timing chain guide and bolts.
26. Install a suitable 24 mm wrench onto hex on intake camshaft, then tighten camshaft actuator bolt.
27. Install a suitable 24 mm wrench onto hex on exhaust camshaft, then tighten camshaft actuator bolt.
28. Remove old oil from timing chain tensioner.
29. Measure timing chain tensioner assembly from end to end. A tensioner in compressed state will measure 2.83 inch from end to end. A tensioner in active state will measure 3.35 inch from end to end.
30. If timing chain tensioner is not in compressed state, perform the following:
    a. Remove piston assembly from body of timing chain tensioner by pulling it out.
    b. Install a tensioner tool No. J 45027-2, or equivalent, into a vise.
    c. Install notch end of piston assembly into tensioner tool.
    d. Turn ratchet cylinder into piston.
31. Install compressed piston assembly back into timing chain tensioner body until assembly stops at bottom of bore. **Do not compress piston assembly against bottom of bore.**
32. At point tensioner should measure approximately 2.83 inch from end to end.
33. Ensure all dirt and debris are removed from timing chain tensioner threaded hole in cylinder head.
34. Install timing chain tensioner and tighten.
35. To release timing chain tensioner, use a suitable tool with a rubber tip on end. Feed tool down through cam drive chest to rest on cam chain. Then give a sharp jolt diagonally downwards to release tensioner.
36. Apply suitable sealant to threads and install timing chain guide bolt access hole plug and tighten.
37. Install engine front cover as outlined under "Front Cover, Replace."
38. Install camshaft cover as outlined under "Valve Cover, Replace."
39. Install No. 1 cylinder spark plug.

CAMSHAFT

REPLACE

1. Remove camshaft cover as outlined under "Valve Cover, Replace."

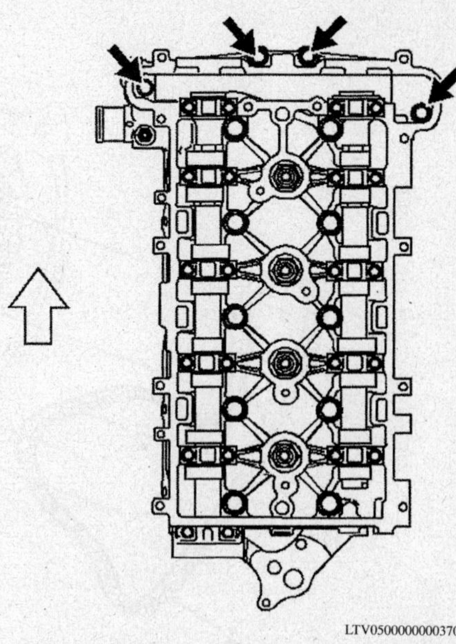

Fig. 4 Front cylinder head bolts

2. Remove upper timing chain guide bolts and guide.
3. Install a suitable 24 mm wrench onto hex onto camshaft to hold camshaft in place.
4. Loosen intake camshaft actuator bolt. **Do not remove bolt.**
5. Install a timing chain tensioner tool No. J 44217, or equivalent, onto exhaust camshaft side of timing chain assembly to retain timing chain.
6. Install timing chain tensioner tool No. J 44217, or equivalent, onto intake camshaft side of timing chain assembly to retain timing chain.
7. Mark intake and exhaust camshaft actuators and respective locations on timing chain.
8. Hold intake camshaft with a suitable 24 mm wrench, then remove intake camshaft actuator bolt.
9. Remove intake camshaft actuator from camshaft and timing chain.
10. Mark bearing caps to ensure they are installed in their original position.
11. Remove bearing cap bolts and bearing caps.
12. Remove camshaft. Keep all of roller followers and hydraulic adjusters in order so they can be installed in their original locations.
13. Remove camshaft roller followers and hydraulic lash adjusters.
14. Reverse procedure to install.

BALANCE SHAFT

REPLACE

Refer to "2.2L Engine" section for balance shaft replacement procedure.

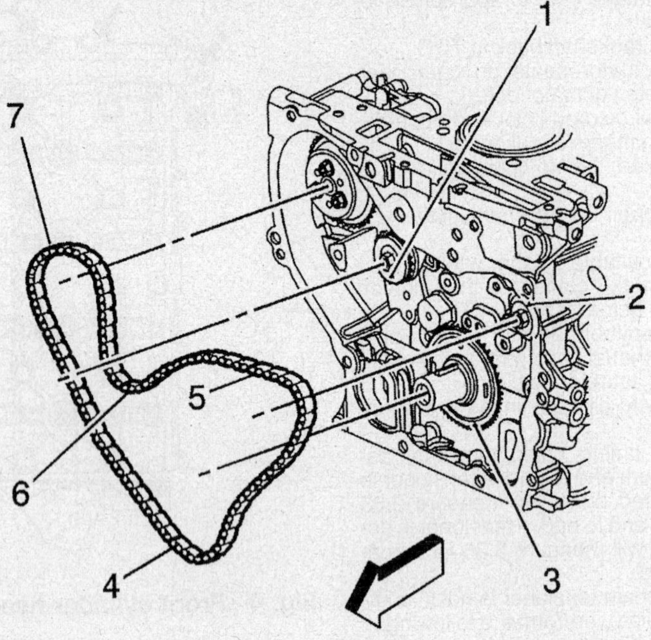

Fig. 5 Balance shaft timing chain alignment

Fig. 6 Timing chain crankshaft sprocket alignment

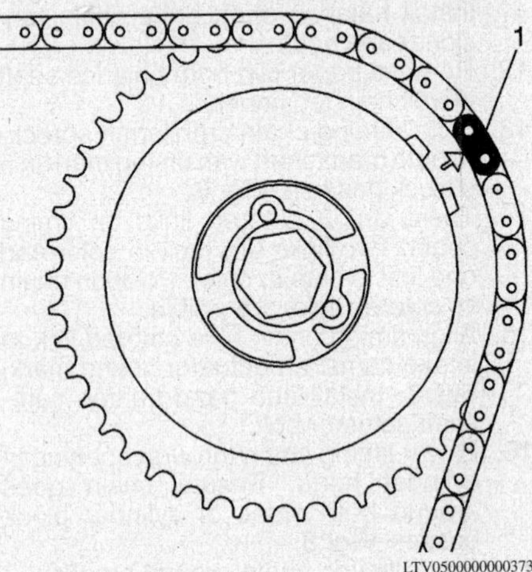

Fig. 7 Intake camshaft actuator to timing chain alignment

CRANKSHAFT REAR OIL SEAL

REPLACE

Refer to "2.2L Engine" section for crankshaft rear oil seal replacement procedure.

OIL PAN

REPLACE

1. Remove air cleaner assembly.
2. Remove oil dipstick.
3. Remove engine harness clip from oil dipstick tube bracket.
4. Remove A/C compressor and condenser hose clip from oil dipstick tube bracket.
5. Remove oil dipstick tube bolt, tube and O-ring seals.
6. Raise and support vehicle.
7. Drain engine oil into suitable container.
8. Remove engine drive belt as outlined under "Serpentine Drive Belt."
9. Remove lower A/C compressor bolt.
10. **On models equipped with a manual transaxle,** remove two lower transaxle bolts.
11. **On models equipped with a automatic transaxle,** remove four lower transaxle bolts.
12. **On all models,** remove oil pan bolts and oil pan.
13. Remove any old oil pan sealant.
14. Reverse procedure to install, noting the following:
    a. Apply a .08 inch bead of a suitable sealant around perimeter of oil pan and oil suction port opening.
    b. **Torque** oil pan bolts to 18 ft. lbs., using sequence, **Fig. 11.**

OIL PUMP

REPLACE

Refer to "Front Cover, Replace" for oil pump replacement procedure.

SERPENTINE DRIVE BELT

Refer to "2.2L Engine" section for serpentine drive belt replacement procedure.

COOLING SYSTEM BLEED

These engines do not require a specified bleed procedure. After filling cooling system, run engine to operating temperature with radiator/pressure cap off. Air will then be automatically bled through cap opening.

THERMOSTAT

REPLACE

1. Drain cooling system into a suitable container.
2. Remove radiator outlet hose from thermostat housing.
3. **On models equipped with a engine oil cooler,** remove oil cooler outlet hose from thermostat housing.
4. **On all models,** remove thermostat housing cover bolts and cover, **Fig. 12.**
5. Remove thermostat and O-ring seal.
6. Reverse procedure to install.

WATER PUMP

REPLACE

Refer to "2.2L Engine" section for water pump replacement procedure.

RADIATOR

REPLACE

Refer to "2.2L Engine" section for radiator replacement procedure.

FUEL PUMP

REPLACE

Refer to "2.2L Engine" section for fuel pump replacement procedure.

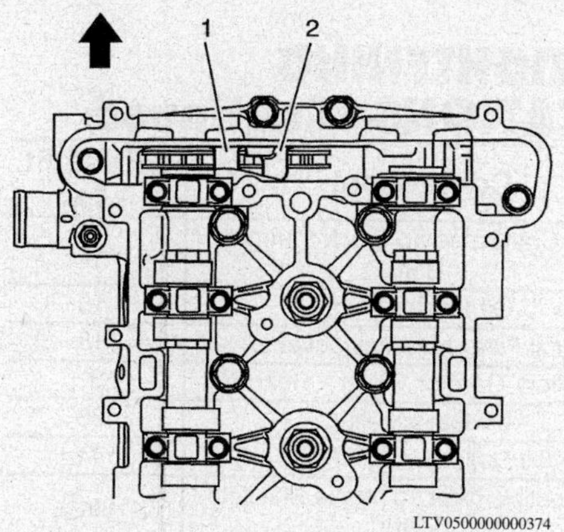

Fig. 8 Cylinder block bosses

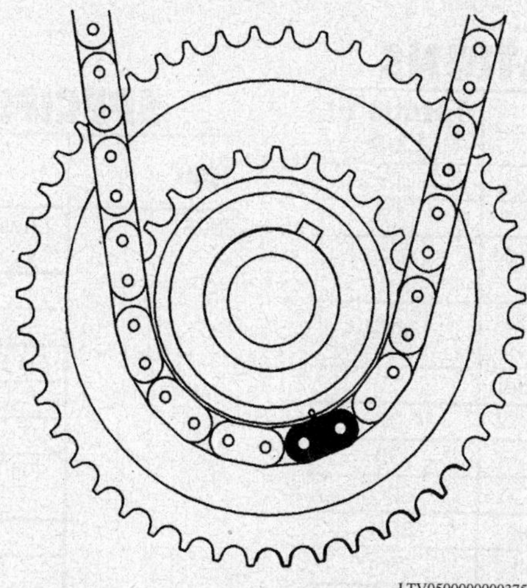

Fig. 9 Crankshaft sprocket to timing chain alignment

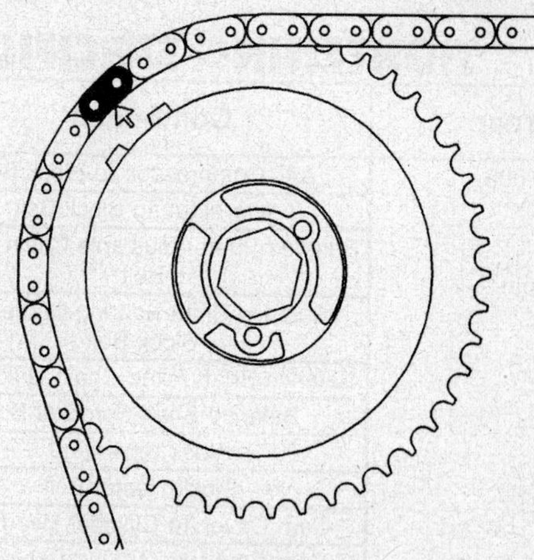

Fig. 10 Exhaust camshaft actuator to timing chain alignment

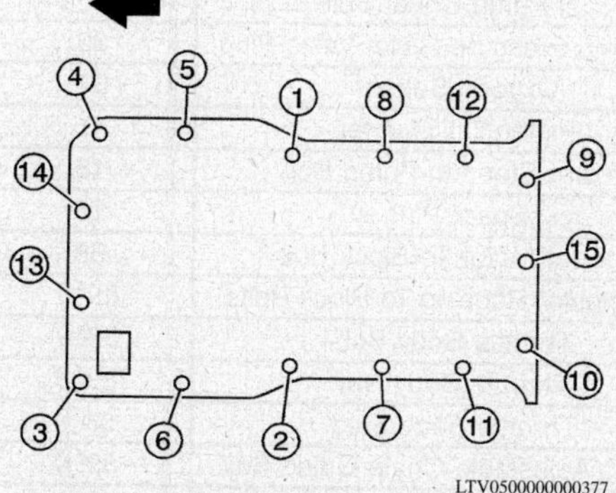

Fig. 11 Oil pan bolt tightening sequence

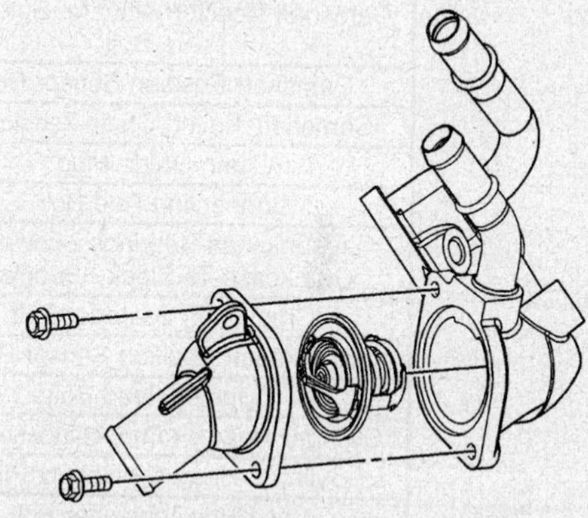

Fig. 12 Thermostat assembly

TIGHTENING SPECIFICATIONS

Year	Component	Torque Ft. Lbs.
2006	A/C Compressor To Block Bolt	15
	Alternator To Block Bolt	17
	Balance Shaft Adjustable Chain Guide Bolt	11
	Balance Shaft Bearing Carrier To Block Bolt	89①
	Balance Shaft Fixed Chain Guide Bolt	11
	Balance Shaft Sprocket Bolt	37
	Block Core Plug	30
	Block Heater Bolt	89①
	Cam Cover To Cylinder Head Bolt	89①
	Cam Cover To Ground Cable Bolt	89①
	Cam Cover To Ground Cable Stud	89①
	Camshaft Cap Bolt	89①
	Camshaft Sprocket Bolt	②
	Camshaft Position Actuator Solenoid Valve Bolt	89①
	Camshaft Position Sensor Bolt	89①
	Camshaft Timing Chain Tensioner	55
	Chain Guide Plug	59
	Connecting Rod Bolt	③
	Crankshaft Bearings - Lower Crankcase To Block - Bedplate	④
	Crankshaft Balancer Bolt	⑤
	Crankshaft Position Sensor Bolt	89①
	Cylinder Head Bolt	⑥
	Cylinder Head Front Chaincase Bolt	26
	Cylinder Head Oil Gallery Plug	26
	Drive Belt Tensioner Bolt	33
	EGR Cover Bolt	18
	Engine Coolant Temperature Sensor	15
	Engine Lift Bracket Front Bolt	18
	Engine Lift Bracket Rear Bolt	18
	EVAP Canister Valve Bolt	16
	Exhaust Camshaft Position Actuator	⑧
	Exhaust Manifold Pipe Flange Stud	12
	Exhaust Manifold To Cylinder Head Nut	124①
	Exhaust Manifold To Cylinder Head Stud	89①
	Flexplate (Automatic Transaxle) Bolt	⑦
	Flywheel (Manual Transaxle) Bolt	⑦
	Front Cover To Block Bolt	18
	Front Lift Bracket Bolt	18
	Fuel Pipe Bracket Bolt	89①
	Fuel Rail Bracket Bolt	89①
	Heat Shield To Exhaust Manifold Bolt	16
	Ignition Coil Bolt	89①
	Intake Camshaft Position Actuator	⑧
	Intake Camshaft Rear Cap Bolt	18
	Intake Manifold To Cylinder Head Bolt	89①
	Intake Manifold To Cylinder Head Nut	89①
	Intake Manifold To Cylinder Head Stud	53①
	Knock Sensor Bolt	18

TIGHTENING SPECIFICATIONS—Continued

Year	Component	Torque Ft. Lbs.
2006	Lower Crankcase To Block Perimeter Bolt	18
	Oil Cooler Bolts	16
	Oil Filter Housing Cover	18
	Oil Gallery Gerotor Cover - Rear Bolt	53①
	Oil Gallery Plug	26
	Oil Gallery Plug - Rear	44
	Oil Dipstick Tube To Intake Manifold Bolt	89①
	Oil Pan Drain Plug	18
	Oil Pan To Block Bolts	18
	Oil Pressure Switch	16
	Oil Pump Cover Bolt	53①
	Oil Pump Pressure Relief Valve Plug	30
	Oxygen Sensor	31
	Piston Oil Squirter	11
	Power Steering Pump Bolt	18
	Spark Plug	15
	Starter Motor To Block Bolt	39
	Thermostat Housing To Block Bolts	89①
	Throttle Body Bolt	89①
	Throttle Body Nut	89①
	Throttle Body Stud	53①
	Timing Adjustable Chain Guide Bolt	89①
	Timing Chain Oil Nozzle Bolt	89①
	Timing Fixed Chain Guide Bolt	11
	Timing Upper Chain Guide Bolt	89①
	Vent Tube To Cylinder Head	11
	Water Jacket Drain Plug	15
	Water Pipe Support Bracket Bolt	89①
	Water Pump Access Cover Bolt	62
	Water Pump/Balance Shaft Chain Tensioner Bolt	89①
	Water Pump Bolts	18
	Water Pump Sprocket Bolt	89①

① — Inch lbs.

② — First pass, 63 ft. lbs.; second pass, an additional 30°.

③ — First pass, 18 ft. lbs.; second pass, an additional 100°.

④ — First pass, 15 ft. lbs.; second pass, an additional 70°.

⑤ — First pass, 74 ft. lbs.; second pass, an additional 125°.

⑥ — Refer to "Cylinder Head, Replace" for tightening procedure.

⑦ — First pass, 39 ft. lbs.; second pass, an additional 25°.

⑧ — First pass, 22 ft. lbs.; second pass, an additional 100°.

Rear Axle & Suspension

INDEX

REAR AXLE

REPLACE

1. Raise and support vehicle.
2. Remove rear wheels.
3. Disconnect lefthand and righthand rear brake pipes from rear brake hoses at axle.
4. Disconnect brake hoses from axle brake hose bracket.
5. Plug brake pipes and hoses.
6. Remove brake drum as outlined in "Drum Brakes" chapter.
7. Depress retaining tab on park brake cable fitting, then tilt released side of cable end back into backing plate using a suitable flat-bladed tool.
8. Rotate park brake cable to access other retaining tab.
9. Depress retaining tab and release cable fitting from backing plate.
10. Release parking brake cable from lever, then remove cable from vehicle.
11. **On models equipped with anti-lock brakes,** disconnect anti-lock brake system ABS harness connectors.
12. **On all models,** support rear axle with a suitable hydraulic lift table.
13. Remove lower shock bolts.
14. Lower hydraulic lift table and remove rear coil springs as outlined under "Coil Spring, Replace."
15. Remove righthand and lefthand wheel bearing and hub retaining nuts.
16. Remove righthand and lefthand wheel bearing and hub assemblies, along with brake and backing plate assemblies.
17. Lower hydraulic lift table and remove rear axle.
18. Remove rear axle bushing through bolts and park brake cable brackets.
19. Reverse procedure to install.

HUB & BEARING

REPLACE

1. Raise and support vehicle, then remove tire and wheel assembly.
2. Remove rear brake drum as outlined in "Drum Brakes" chapter.
3. **On models equipped with anti-lock brakes,** disconnect electrical connector from wheel bearing and hub.
4. **On all models,** remove rear wheel bearing and hub nuts.
5. Remove rear wheel bearing and hub.
6. Reverse procedure to install.

SHOCK ABSORBER

REPLACE

1. Raise and support vehicle.
2. Remove wheel.
3. Remove upper and lower shock absorber bolts.
4. Remove rear shock absorber.
5. Reverse procedure to install.

COIL SPRING

REPLACE

1. Raise and support vehicle, then remove wheel.
2. Support rear axle with a suitable jack.
3. Remove rear shock absorber lower mounting bolt.
4. Lower jack stand to release tension on rear spring.
5. Remove rear coil spring.
6. Reverse procedure to install.

TIGHTENING SPECIFICATIONS

Year	Component	Torque Ft. Lbs.
2006	Bracket To Body Bolts	①
	Brake Hose Fittings	14
	Bushing Through Bolts	②
	Shock Bolt Lower	92
	Shock Bolt Upper	66
	Wheel Bearing/Hub Assembly Mounting Nuts	③

①— First pass, 66 ft. lbs.; second pass, an additional 45°.
②— First pass, 66 ft. lbs.; second pass, an additional 60°.
③— First pass, 33 ft. lbs.; second pass, an additional 30°.

Front Suspension & Steering

INDEX

PRECAUTIONS

Air Bag Systems

Refer to "Air Bag System Precautions" in the front of this manual for system disarming and arming procedures.

Crimped Nuts

Steering linkage relay rod assemblies use crimped nuts. Whenever a crimped nut is loosened or removed, it must be replaced with a prevailing torque nut.

DESCRIPTION

This front suspension system requires the steering knuckle be suspended between a lower control arm and a strut assembly. The lower control arm attaches from the steering knuckle at the outermost point of the control arm. The attachment is through a ball and socket type joint. The innermost end of the control arm is attached at two points to the vehicle frame through semi rigid bushings. The upper portion of the steering knuckle is attached to a strut assembly. The strut assembly then connects to the vehicle body by way of an upper bearing. The steering knuckle is allowed to travel up and down independent of the vehicle body structure and frame.

This up and down motion of the steering knuckle as the vehicle travels over bumps is absorbed predominantly by the coil spring. This spring is retained under tension over the strut assembly. A strut is used in conjunction with this system in order to dampen out the oscillations of the coil spring. Each end of the strut is designed as the connection point of the suspension system to the vehicle and acts as the coil spring seat. This allows the strut to utilize the dampening action to reduce the recoil of a spring alone. The lower control arm is allowed to pivot at the vehicle frame in a vertical fashion. The ball joint allows the steering knuckle to maintain the perpendicular relationship to the road surface.

HUB & BEARING

REPLACE

1. Raise and support vehicle.
2. Remove tire and wheels.
3. Remove brake rotor as outlined in "Disc Brakes" chapter.
4. Remove axle shaft nut.
5. Disconnect wheel speed sensor.
6. Remove wheel bearing and hub assembly bolts.
7. Remove wheel bearing and hub assembly bearing and spacer, **Fig. 1.**
8. Reverse procedure to install.

BALL JOINT INSPECTION

Refer to **Fig. 2** for ball joint inspection procedure.

BALL JOINT

REPLACE

This ball joint is an integral part of the lower control arm. Refer to "Control Arm, Replace" for ball joint replacement procedures.

COIL SPRING

REPLACE

Refer to "Coil Spring & Strut Service" for coil spring replacement.

STRUT

REPLACE

1. Remove strut upper mounting nuts.
2. Raise and support vehicle.
3. Remove tire and wheel.
4. Disconnect stabilizer shaft link from strut assembly.
5. Remove strut lower bolts, nuts and ABS wiring bracket.
6. Remove strut.
7. Reverse procedure to install.

COIL SPRING & STRUT SERVICE

1. Remove strut from vehicle as outlined under "Strut, Replace."
2. Install strut in strut spring compressor tool No. J 45400, or equivalent.
3. Turn spring compressor forcing screw until coil spring is compressed. Spring is compressed when strut moves freely.
4. Loosen compressor forcing screw until upper strut mount and coil spring may be removed.
5. Hold strut shaft with a suitable 45 Torx socket, then remove upper strut mount nut.
6. Remove upper strut mount and coil spring.
7. Reverse procedure to install.

CONTROL ARM

REPLACE

1. Raise and support vehicle.
2. Remove front tire and wheel assembly.
3. Remove ball joint to steering knuckle nut and bolt.
4. Remove lower control arm to rear frame bolt.
5. Remove lower control arm to front frame bolt.
6. Remove lower control arm.
7. Reverse procedure to install.

STEERING KNUCKLE

REPLACE

1. Raise and support vehicle.
2. Remove front tire and wheel assembly.
3. Remove brake rotor from wheel hub and bearing as outlined in "Disc Brakes" chapter.
4. Remove wheel drive shaft nut and washer.
5. Remove tie rod end to steering knuckle retaining nut.
6. Remove ball joint to steering knuckle bolt.
7. Remove strut to steering knuckle nuts and bolts.
8. Remove wheel bearing and hub bolts.
9. Disconnect wheel speed sensor.
10. Pull wheel bearing and hub from steering knuckle.
11. Remove wheel bearing and hub spacer.
12. Remove steering knuckle, **Fig. 3.**
13. Reverse procedure to install.

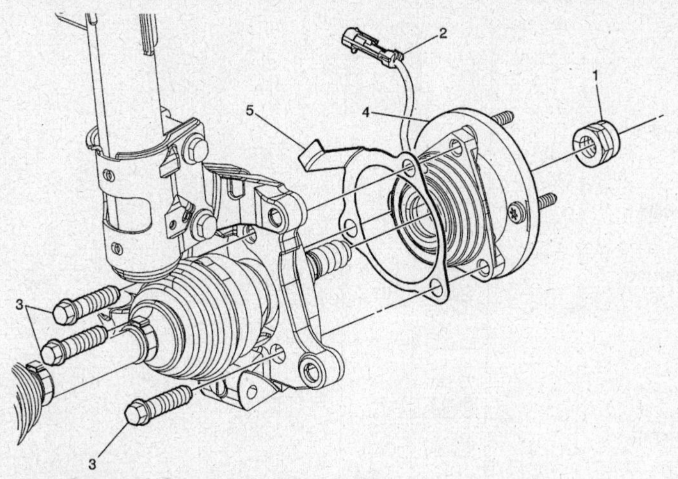

1. Axle Shaft Nut
2. Wheel Speed Sensor Connector
3. Wheel Bearing Bearing/Hub Assembly Bolt
4. Wheel Bearing/Hub Assembly Bearing
5. Wheel Bearing/Hub Assembly Spacer

LTV0500000000379

Fig. 1 Wheel bearing & hub assembly

Step	Action	Values	Yes	No
1	Did you review the General Description and perform the necessary inspections?	--	Go to Step 2	Go to Symptoms -
2	1. Raise and support the vehicle. 2. Clean the ball joint and inspect the seal for damage. Is the ball joint seal damaged?	--	Go to Step 6	Go to Step 3
3	Check the wheel bearing for looseness. Did you find and correct the condition?	--	Go to Step 7	Go to Step 4
4	**Important** Remove tension from the ball joints. Check the ball joint for horizontal looseness using the following procedure: 1. Position the J 8001 Dial Indicator against the lowest outboard point of the wheel rim. 2. Rock the wheel in and out while reading the dial indicator. Does the dial indicator measure greater than the specified value?	3.18 mm (0.125 in)	Go to Step 6	Go to Step 5

LTV0500000000380

Fig. 2 Ball joint inspection (Part 1 of 2)

STABILIZER BAR

REPLACE

1. Raise and support vehicle.
2. Remove front tire and wheel assemblies.
3. Remove front stabilizer shaft lower link nuts.
4. Remove front stabilizer shaft clamp nuts and bolts.
5. Remove front stabilizer shaft clamp.
6. Remove front stabilizer shaft insulator.
7. Remove front stabilizer shaft from righthand side of vehicle.
8. Reverse procedure to install.

TIE ROD END

REPLACE

1. Raise and support vehicle.
2. Remove front wheel.
3. Loosen outer tie rod to inner tie rod jam nut.
4. Remove tie rod to steering knuckle nut and discard.
5. Separate outer tie rod from steering knuckle using steering linkage and tie rod puller tool No. 24319-B, or equivalent.
6. Remove outer tie rod from inner tie rod. Record number of turns used to remove tie rod end for installation reference.
7. Remove outer to inner tie rod jam nut and discard.
8. Reverse procedure to install. Inspect alignment as outlined in "Wheel Alignment" section.

POWER STEERING GEAR

REPLACE

1. Turn steering wheel to straight ahead position and remove key from ignition.
2. Secure steering wheel with a suitable strap to prevent rotation.
3. Raise and support vehicle, then remove front tire and wheel assemblies.
4. Remove steering gear to intermediate shaft pinch bolt and discard.
5. Disconnect intermediate shaft from steering gear.
6. Remove both steering gear outer tie rod to knuckle nuts and discard nuts.
7. Separate outer tie rods from steering knuckles using steering linkage and tie rod puller tool No. J 24319-B, or equivalent.
8. Remove steering gear mounting bolts.
9. Remove rear transaxle mount.
10. Carefully remove steering gear through lefthand wheel opening.
11. Reverse procedure to install.

5	**Important** Remove tension from the ball joints. Check the ball joint for vertical looseness using the following procedure: 1. Install the J 8001 . 2. Move the ball joint up and down while reading the dial indicator. Does the dial indicator measure greater than the specified value?	3.18 mm (0.125 in)	Go to Step 6	Go to Step 7
6	Replace the ball joint/lower control arm. Did you complete the repair?	--	Go to Step 7	--
7	Operate the system in order to verify the repair. Did you correct the condition?	--	System OK	Go to Step 2

LTV0500000000381

Fig. 2 Ball joint inspection (Part 2 of 2)

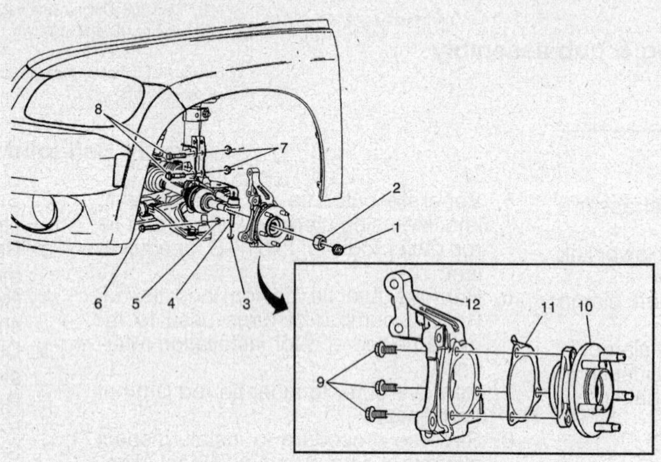

1. Wheel Drive Shaft Nut
2. Wheel Drive Shaft Washer
3. Outer Tie Rod End Nut
4. Outer Tie Rod End
5. Ball Joint to Steering Knuckle Nut
6. Ball Joint to Steering Knuckle Bolt
7. Strut to Steering Knuckle Bolt
8. Wheel Bearing/Hub Bolt
9. Wheel Bearing/Hub
10. Wheel Bearing/Hub Spacer
11. Steering Knuckle

LTV0500000000382

Fig. 3 Steering knuckle assembly

TIGHTENING SPECIFICATIONS

Year	Component	Torque Ft. Lbs.
2006	Ball Joint To Control Arm Nut & Bolts	50
	Ball Joint To Steering Knuckle Nut	②
	Control Arm To Front Frame Bolts	41
	Control Arm To Rear Frame Bolts	①
	Drive Axle Nut	155
	Frame To Chassis Bolts	①
	Intermediate Shaft Pinch Bolt	25
	Stabilizer Link To Strut Nut	59
	Stabilizer Shaft Clamp Bolt	37
	Stabilizer Shaft Clamp Nut	37
	Stabilizer Shaft Link To Stabilizer Bar Nut	89
	Strut Assembly To Steering Knuckle Nut	89
	Strut To Body Nut	15
	Strut Shaft Nut	52
	Tie Rod To Knuckle Nut	44
	Transaxle Mount Through Bolt	74
	Transaxle Mount To Frame Bolt	37
	Wheel Bearing/Hub Assembly Mounting Bolts	85

① — First pass; torque to 74 ft. lbs.; second pass, tighten an additional 180°.
② — First pass; torque to 37 ft. lbs.; second pass, reverse nut ¾ turn; third pass; tighten an additional 30°

Wheel Alignment

INDEX

PRELIMINARY INSPECTION

Before performing any adjustment affecting wheel alignment, perform the following inspections and adjustments in order to ensure correct alignment readings.

1. Inspect tires for proper inflation and irregular tire wear.
2. Inspect runout of wheels and tires.
3. Inspect wheel bearings for backlash and excessive play.
4. Inspect ball joints and tie rod ends for looseness or wear.
5. Inspect control arms and stabilizer shaft for looseness or wear.
6. Inspect steering gear for looseness at frame.
7. Inspect struts/shock absorbers for wear, leaks, and any noticeable noises.
8. Inspect vehicle trim height.
9. Inspect steering wheel for excessive drag or poor return due to stiff or rusted linkage or suspension components.
10. Inspect fuel level. Fuel tank should be full or vehicle should have a compensating load added.

FRONT WHEEL ALIGNMENT

Caster

The front caster is not adjustable. If the front caster angle is not within specifications, inspect for suspension support misalignment or front suspension damage. Replace any damaged suspension components as required.

Camber

1. Loosen both strut to knuckle nuts just enough to allow for movement.
2. If strut has not been modified previously, perform the following:
   a. Disconnect strut from knuckle as outlined under "Strut, Replace."
   b. File lower hole to groove of stamped ring around hole.
   c. Connect strut to knuckle as outlined under "Strut, Replace."
3. Adjust camber to specification by moving top of wheel in or out.

Toe-In

1. Ensure steering wheel is set in a straight ahead position.
2. Loosen tie rod jam nut.
3. Adjust toe to specification by turning inner tie rod.
4. **Torque** tie rod jam nut to 50 ft. lbs.

ASTRO & SAFARI

NOTE: Refer To Rear Of This Manual For Vehicle Manufacturer's Special Service Tool Suppliers.

INDEX OF SERVICE OPERATIONS

Specifications

GENERAL ENGINE SPECIFICATIONS

Year	Engine		Fuel System	Bore & Stroke, Inch	Compression Ratio	Net HP @ RPM	Maximum Torque, Ft. Lbs. @ RPM	Normal Oil Pressure, psi
	Liter	VIN Code②						
2002–05	4.3L	W	SFI	4.00 x 3.48	9.2:1	190 @ 4400	250 @ 2800	①

① — Minimum pressures: 6 psi @ 1000 RPM; 18 psi @ 2000 RPM; 24 psi @ 4000 RPM

② — The eighth digit denotes engine code.

TUNE UP SPECIFICATIONS

The following specifications are published from the latest information available. These data should be used only when the engine controls information decal in the engine compartment is missing or unreadable.

Year	Spark Plug Gap	Ignition Timing BTDC				Curb Idle Speed②		Fast Idle Speed②		Fuel Pump Pressure psi.	Valve Lash, Inch
		Firing Order, Fig.③	Man. Trans.	Auto. Trans.	Mark Location	Man. Trans.	Auto. Trans.	Man. Trans.	Auto. Trans.		
2002–05	.060	A	—	①	⑤	—	600D⑦	—	⑦	60–66⑥	④

BTDC — Before Top Dead Center

D — Drive

① — Not adjustable.

② — When inspecting idle speed, set parking brake & block drive wheels.

③ — Before removing wires from distributor cap or coil unit, determine location of ignition wires, as position may have been altered from that outlined at end of this chart.

④ — Equipped w/hydraulic valve lifters.

⑤ — Equipped w/crankshaft position sensor.

⑥ — Wrap shop towel around engine compartment fuel pressure fitting. Connect suitable fuel pressure gauge to fuel pressure fitting. Turn ignition to On position & note fuel pressure reading.

⑦ — Controlled by Idle Speed Control (ISC) motor or Idle Air Control (IAC) valve.

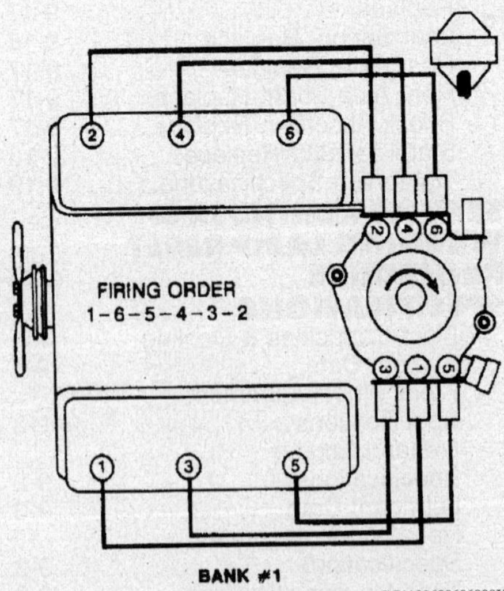

Fig. A

FRONT WHEEL ALIGNMENT SPECIFICATIONS

Year	Model	Caster Angle, Degrees		Camber Angle, Degrees		Toe Per Wheel, Degrees①	
		Limits	Desired	Limits	Desired	Limits	Desired
2002–05	AWD	④	⑤	-1.00 to +1.00	0	-.20 to +.20	0
	2WD	③	②	-.40 to +1.60	+.6	-.20 to +.20	0

① — Toe-In (+). Toe-Out (–).

② — Lefthand wheel, +3.0°; righthand wheel, +3.5°.

③ — Lefthand wheel, +2.0° to +4.0°; righthand Wheel, +2.5° to +4.5°.

④ — Lefthand wheel, +2.5° to +4.5°; righthand wheel, +3.5° to +5.5°.

⑤ — Lefthand wheel, +3.5°; righthand wheel, +4.5°.

REAR WHEEL ALIGNMENT SPECIFICATIONS

Year	Model	Camber Angle, Degrees		Total Toe, Degrees①
		Limits	Desired	
2002–05	All	-.03 to +.05	+.01	-.05 to 0

① — Toe-In (+). Toe-Out (–).

FLUID CAPACITIES & COOLING SYSTEM DATA

Year	Engine Liter	Cooling System Capacity, Qts.			Radiator Cap Relief Pressure, Lbs.	Thermo. Opening Temp. °F	Fuel Tank, Gals.	Engine Oil Refill, Qts.	Transmission Oil		Transfer Case, Pts.	Drive Axle, Pts.	
		Less A/C	With A/C	Coolant Type					Man. Trans., Pts.	Auto. Trans., Qts.①		Front	Rear
2002–05	4.3L	13.5③	13.5③	Dex-Cool	15	195	27	4.5	—	②	4.0	2.6	3.5

① — Approximate. Make final inspection w/dipstick.

② — Pan removal, 5 qts.; after overhaul, 11 qts.

③ — Add 3 qts. if equipped w/rear heater.

LUBRICANT DATA

Year	Model	Lubricant Type				
		Transmission	Transfer Case	Front & Rear Axle	Power Steering	Brake System
2002–05	All	Dexron III	Dexron III	SAE 80W-90 GL-5	GM 1052884	DOT 3

Electrical

NOTE: On Air Bag Equipped Models, Refer To "Air Bag System Precautions" Located In The Front Of This Manual For System Disarming & Arming Procedures.

NOTE: Refer To "Computer Relearn Procedures" Located In The Front Of This Manual When Battery Power To The Computer Has Been Interrupted.

INDEX

PRECAUTIONS

Air Bag Systems

Refer to "Air Bag System Precautions" in the front of this manual for system disarming and arming procedures.

Battery Ground Cable

Prior to service, disconnect battery ground cable and isolate as required.

FUSE PANEL LOCATION

The instrument panel fuse block is located under the lefthand side of the instrument panel, above the kick panel. The hazard flasher is located at the convenience center, on the lefthand side of the steering column, behind the instrument panel. The turn signal flasher is located to the righthand side of the steering column behind the instrument panel.

RELAY CENTER LOCATION

The underhood fuse/relay center is located on the righthand side of the engine compartment. The passenger compartment fuse/relay convenience center is located behind the lefthand side of the instrument panel.

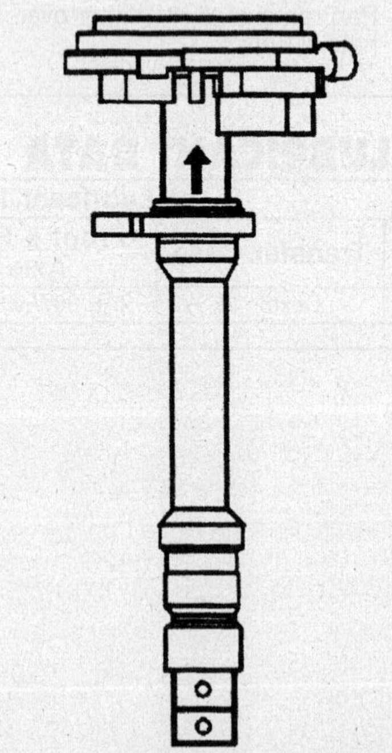

Fig. 1 Distributor alignment

FUEL PUMP RELAY LOCATION

The fuel pump relay is located on the righthand side of the engine compartment, in the underhood fuse/relay center.

STARTER

REPLACE

1. Raise and support vehicle.
2. Remove starter motor to engine mounting bolts, shims and lower starter motor.
3. Remove solenoid wires and starter.
4. Reverse procedure to install. **Torque** starter mounting bolts to 32 ft. lbs.

DISTRIBUTOR

REPLACE

1. Turn off ignition switch and remove engine cover.
2. Remove spark plug and coil wires from distributor.
3. Disconnect electrical connector from distributor base.
4. Remove two mounting screws and distributor cap.
5. Mark position of rotor to distributor housing, identify mark as No. 1.
6. Mark position of distributor housing to intake manifold.

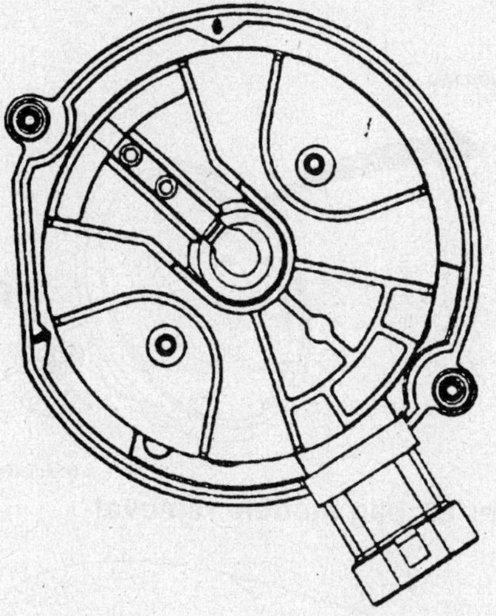

GC1119500172000X

Fig. 2 Rotor position

7. Remove mounting clamp hold-down bolt and distributor.
8. Upon removal, rotor will move 42° in counterclockwise direction, appearing to move slightly more than one clock position.
9. Record position of rotor tip; place second mark on base of distributor for proper rotor alignment upon installation. Identify second mark as No. 2.
10. Reverse procedure to install, noting the following:
    a. When installing distributor, align rotor tip No. 2 mark on base of distributor.
    b. Guide distributor in place, ensure locating slot in distributor base fits over dowel pin in intake manifold.
    c. Rotor tip will rotate 42° in clockwise direction.
    d. Ensure rotor tip aligns with No. 1 mark upon seating.
    e. **Torque** mounting clamp to 18 ft. lbs.
    f. **Torque** distributor cap screws to 42 inch lbs.

DISTRIBUTOR

ADJUST

1. Place engine in Top Dead Center (TDC) on cylinder No. 1 and remove distributor cap.
2. Align pre-drilled indent hole in distributor driven gear with arrow cast in upper shaft housing, **Fig. 1.**
3. Rotor should point to cap hold-down mount nearest flat side of housing, **Fig. 2.**
4. Align oil pump drive shaft with mating tab on distributor using suitable long screwdriver.
5. Guide distributor in place, ensure locating slot fits over dowel pin in intake manifold.
6. After distributor is fully seated, rotor tip should align with "6" pointer cast in distributor base, **Fig. 3.**
7. If rotor tip does not come within few degrees of pointer gear mesh between distributor and camshaft is off tooth or more. Repeat procedure to achieve proper alignment.

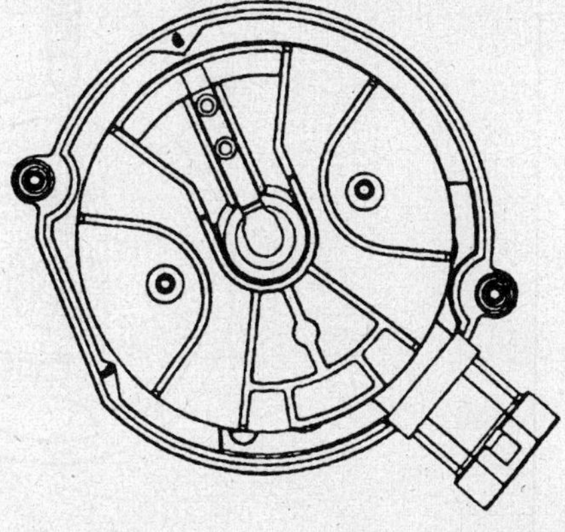

GC1119500173000X

Fig. 3 Rotor replacement position

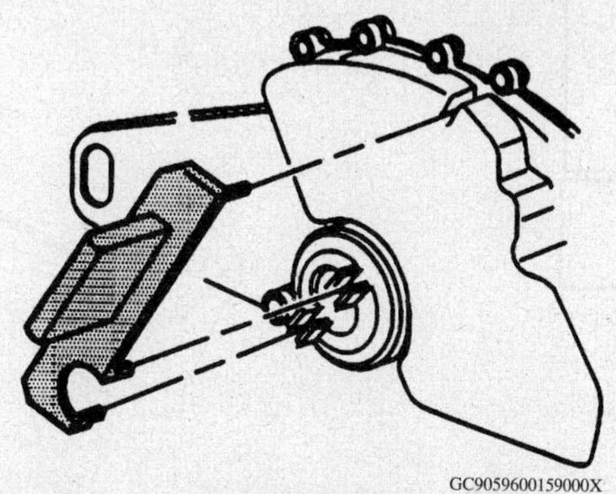

GC9059600159000X

Fig. 5 Neutral safety switch adjustment

COIL PACK

REPLACE

1. Ensure ignition is in Off position and remove engine cover.
2. Remove air cleaner.
3. Disconnect electrical connectors and high tension leads from coil.
4. Remove ignition coil and bracket mounting studs, then the coil and bracket, **Fig. 4.**
5. Remove coil to bracket rivets using suitable drill and pin punch.
6. Reverse procedure to install. **Torque** coil mounting studs to 96 inch lbs.

IGNITION LOCK

REPLACE

1. **On models equipped with tilt steering column,** position steering wheel half way between upper and lower tilt stops.
2. **On all models,** remove steering wheel as outlined in "Steering Wheel, Replace."
3. Roll shift lever seal back from upper and lower shrouds.
4. **On models equipped with tilt steering column,** remove tilt wheel lever.
5. **On all models,** set steering column on modular column holding fixture tool No. J-41352, or equivalent.

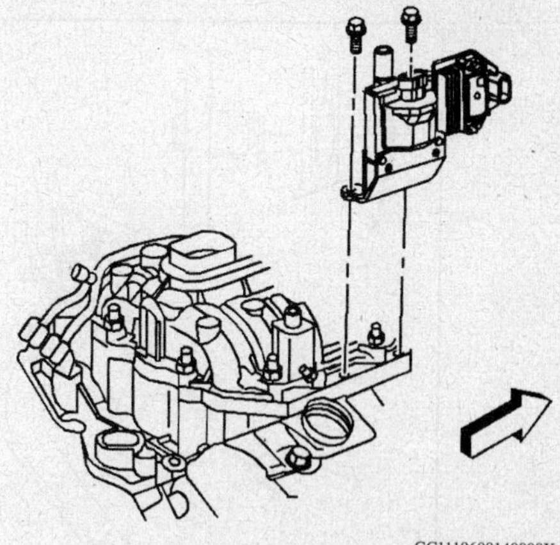

GC1119600140000X

Fig. 4 Ignition coil replacement

6. Remove mounting screws and lower steering column shroud.
7. Remove mounting screws and lift upper steering column shroud to gain access to lock cylinder access hole.
8. Inset tip of suitable bent tip awl into ignition lock cylinder access hole.
9. Turn ignition lock cylinder to Start position and push down on retaining pin using suitable awl.
10. Release ignition lock cylinder to Run position.
11. Remove ignition lock cylinder by pulling cylinder away from steering column.
12. Reverse procedure to install, noting the following:
    a. Align lock module positioning and locking tab slots with ignition lock position and locking tabs.
    b. Push cylinder in until tab locks against module.
    c. **Torque** shroud mounting screws to 31 inch lbs.

NEUTRAL SAFETY SWITCH

REPLACE

Removal

1. Apply parking brake and place transmission in neutral position.
2. Raise and support vehicle.
3. Remove transmission control lever to manual shaft mounting nut.
4. Disconnect wiring harness connector. **Disconnect harness at point near vehicle harness, not near switch lead.**
5. Remove mounting bolts and neutral safety switch. **It may be required to file burrs from selector shaft end to allow switch to slide off.**

Installation

1. Ensure transmission selector shaft is in neutral position.
2. Aligning switch hub flats with manual shaft flats.
3. Slide switch on shaft until mounting bracket contacts transmission mounting bosses.

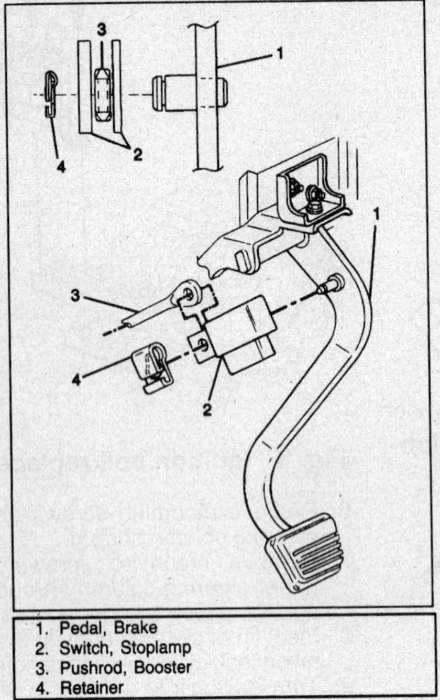

Fig. 6 Stop lamp switch replacement

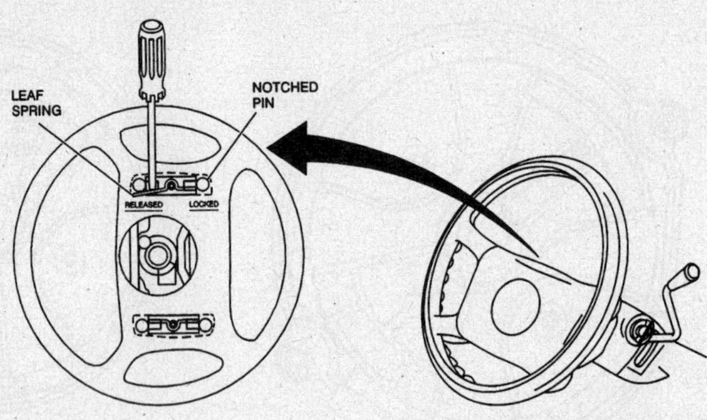

Fig. 7 Driver air bag module removal

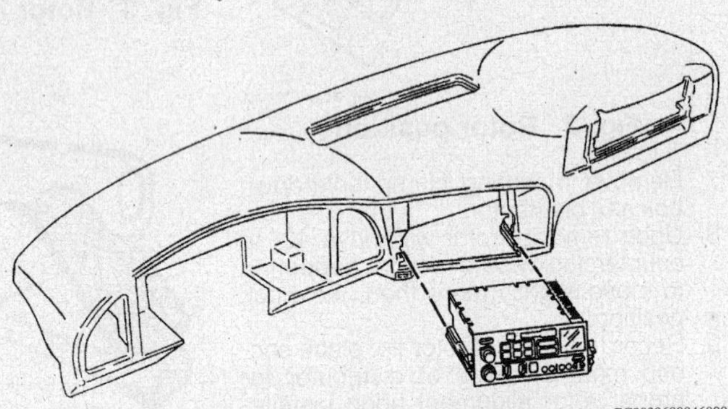

Fig. 8 Radio removal

4. Install mounting screws but do not tighten.
5. Install switch alignment tool No. J-42364-A, or equivalent, into notches of switch, **Fig. 5.**
6. Rotate tool until upper locator pin lines up with switch top slot.
7. **Torque** mounting bolts to 18 ft. lbs.
8. Remove alignment tool.
9. Connect wiring harness connector.
10. Ensure vehicle will only start in Neutral and Park positions. Adjust as required.

HEADLAMP SWITCH

REPLACE

1. Remove instrument panel cluster trim plate as outlined in "Instrument Cluster, Replace."
2. Disconnect electrical connectors at back of headlamp switch.
3. Remove switch from plate by releasing retaining tabs on sides and pulling it out.
4. Reverse procedure to install.

STOP LIGHT SWITCH

REPLACE

1. Disconnect brake pedal pin retainer, **Fig. 6.**
2. Remove stop lamp switch and brake pedal pin pushrod.
3. Disconnect electrical connector.
4. Reverse procedure to install.

MULTI-FUNCTION SWITCH

REPLACE

1. Ensure multi-function switch is in Off position.
2. **On models equipped with tilt steering column,** remove tilt wheel lever.
3. **On all models,** remove ignition lock cylinder as outlined in "Ignition Lock, Replace."
4. Remove upper steering column shroud.
5. Remove harness straps and steering column wire harness.
6. Disconnect steering column gray and black switch connectors.
7. Remove mounting screws and multi-function switch.
8. Reverse procedure to install, noting the following:
   a. Compress electrical contact using suitable small blade screwdriver.
   b. Ensure multi-function switch electrical contact rests on canceling cam.
   c. **Torque** switch mounting screws to 53 inch lbs.

TURN SIGNAL SWITCH

REPLACE

Refer to "Multi-Function Switch, Replace" for turn signal switch replacement procedure.

DIMMER SWITCH

REPLACE

Refer to "Multi-Function Switch, Replace" for dimmer switch replacement procedure.

STEERING WHEEL

REPLACE

1. Disarm air bag system system as outlined in "Precautions."
2. Unlock steering wheel by turning ignition switch to On position.
3. Turn steering wheel 90° to access driver air bag module rear shroud holes.
4. Insert suitable screw driver into access hole and push leaf spring to release pin, **Fig. 7.**
5. Turn steering wheel 180° to access remaining rear shroud holes.
6. Insert screw driver and push leaf spring to release pin.
7. Tilt driver air bag module rearward from top to access SIR wiring.
8. Disconnect SIR lead wires from driver air bag module and steering wheel clips.
9. Disconnect Connector Position Assurance (CPA) retainer and electrical connector.
10. Remove driver air bag module.
11. Remove horn plunger contact.
12. Remove mounting screws and horn contact switch.
13. Remove mounting nut and steering wheel using steering wheel puller tool No. J-1859-A, or equivalent.
14. Reverse procedure to install. **Torque** steering wheel nut to 30 ft. lbs.

INSTRUMENT CLUSTER

REPLACE

1. Set parking brake, turn ignition key to

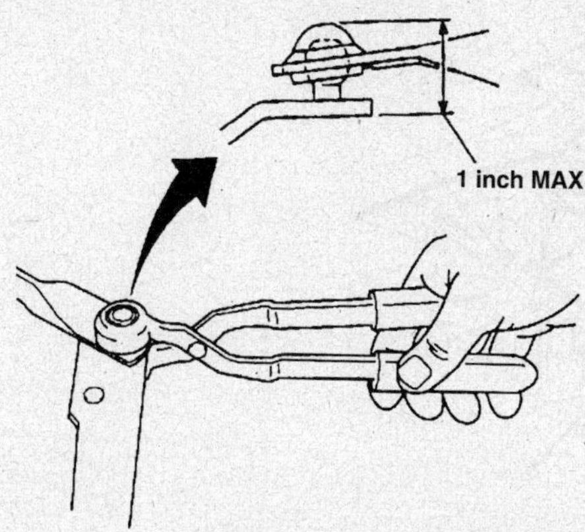

Fig. 9 Wiper transmission replacement

On position and move gear selector to first gear.

2. **On models equipped with tilt steering column,** lower column to lowest position.
3. **On all models,** remove instrument panel cluster trim plate by grasping edges until retainers release.
4. Remove accessory switches by releasing tabs on sides of each switch.
5. Disconnect headlamp and accessories electrical connectors.
6. Remove plate from instrument panel.
7. Remove mounting screws and instrument cluster.
8. Reverse procedure to install. **Torque** mounting screws to 18 inch lbs.

RADIO

REPLACE

1. Remove instrument cluster trim plate as outlined in "Instrument Cluster, Replace."
2. Squeeze clip fasteners on sides and pull radio out, **Fig. 8.**
3. Disconnect electrical and antenna connectors.
4. Remove radio.
5. Reverse procedure to install.

WIPER MOTOR

REPLACE

Front

1. Remove windshield washer hoses from wiper arms.
2. Remove wiper arms.
3. Remove antenna mast.
4. Remove mounting screws and air inlet grille panel.
5. Disconnect transmission drive link from wiper motor crank arm using wiper transmission separator tool No. J-39232, or equivalent.
6. Disconnect wiper motor electrical connector.
7. Remove transmission drive link from crank arm by prying it toward rear of vehicle.
8. Remove mounting bolts and wiper motor.
9. Reverse procedure to install, noting the following:
   a. **Torque** wiper motor mounting bolts to 62 inch lbs.
   b. Wiper transmission must be assembled to crank arm past second detent so seal is compressed to maximum height of 1 inch, **Fig. 9.**
   c. Lubricate socket inside using suitable lithium-based grease.
   d. **Torque** grille mounting screws to 18 inch lbs.
   e. **Torque** antenna mast to 44 inch lbs.

Rear

1. Remove interior handle screw cover, screws, handle and escutcheon.
2. Remove mounting screws and liftgate garnish molding.
3. Disconnect motor electrical connector.
4. Remove wiper arm.
5. Remove nut, spacer and seal.
6. Remove mounting bolts and motor.
7. Reverse procedure to install, noting the following:
   a. **Torque** motor mounting bolts to 62 inch lbs.
   b. **Torque** nut to 53 inch lbs.
   c. **Torque** garnish molding mounting screws to 18 inch lbs.
   d. **Torque** interior handle mounting screws to 53 inch lbs.

WIPER SWITCH

REPLACE

Refer to "Multi-Function Switch, Replace" for wiper switch replacement procedure.

BLOWER MOTOR

REPLACE

Front

1. Disconnect electrical connector.
2. Disconnect coolant recover reservoir hose from radiator filler neck.
3. Remove reservoir retainers and disconnect washer pump electrical connectors.
4. Remove washer pump(s) hose(s).
5. Remove recovery and windshield washer fluid reservoir.
6. Remove cover mounting screws and cut acoustic cover between ribs, **Fig. 10.**
7. Remove cut piece and retainer.
8. Remove motor cooling tube.
9. Remove mounting screws and blower motor.
10. Reverse procedure to install. **Torque** mounting screws to 18 inch lbs.

Rear

LESS AIR CONDITIONING

1. Remove intermediate seat.
2. Remove mounting screw and driver's door step well lamp.
3. Remove lefthand front body side lower trim panel using door trim pad and garnish clip remover tool No. J-38778, or equivalent.
4. Disconnect electrical connectors.
5. Record blower motor and fan orientation.
6. Remove mounting screws, blower motor and fan.
7. Reverse procedure to install. **Torque** mounting screws to 18 inch lbs.

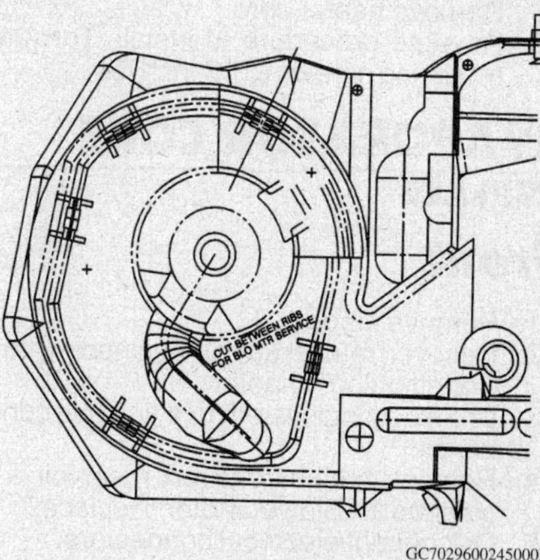

Fig. 10 Blower motor acoustic cover replacement

WITH AIR CONDITIONING

1. Remove lefthand body side trim panel.
2. Remove cooling tube from case and motor.
3. Disconnect electrical connectors.
4. Remove mounting screws, blower motor and fan.
5. Reverse procedure to install. **Torque** mounting screws to 18 inch lbs.

HEATER CORE

REPLACE

Front

1. Drain engine coolant into suitable container.
2. Disconnect heater hoses.
3. Remove cover mounting screws.
4. Remove mounting screws, straps and heater core.
5. Reverse procedure to install. **Torque** mounting screws to 18 inch lbs.

Rear

1. Drain engine coolant into suitable container.
2. Remove intermediate seat.
3. Remove mounting screw and driver's door step well lamp.
4. Remove lefthand front body side lower trim panel using door trim pad and garnish clip remover tool No. J-38778, or equivalent.
5. Remove clamps, then disconnect rear auxiliary heater pipes from heater core inlet and outlet tubes.
6. Remove mounting screws and band clamp on righthand side of core.
7. Remove mounting screw and clamp from lefthand side of core.

8. Remove heater core.
9. Reverse procedure to install. **Torque** mounting screws to 18 inch lbs.

EVAPORATOR CORE

REPLACE

Front

1. Remove air box.
2. Recover refrigerant as outlined in "Air Conditioning" chapter.
3. Drain cooling system into suitable container.
4. Remove coolant recovery reservoir, as outlined in "Blower Motor, Replace."
5. Disconnect electrical connectors.
6. Remove heater core inlet and outlet hoses.
7. Remove compressor and condenser hose from accumulator.
8. Remove relay bracket and evaporator tube.
9. Remove mounting bolts, blower and evaporator case, **Fig. 11.**
10. Separate evaporator, blower motor and acoustic case halves.
11. Remove evaporator core.
12. Reverse procedure to install, nothing the following:
    a. **Torque** evaporator and blower mounting bolts to 53 inch lbs.
    b. **Torque** evaporator and blower mounting nuts to 66 inch lbs.
    c. **Torque** evaporator to accumulator mounting bolts to 35 ft. lbs.

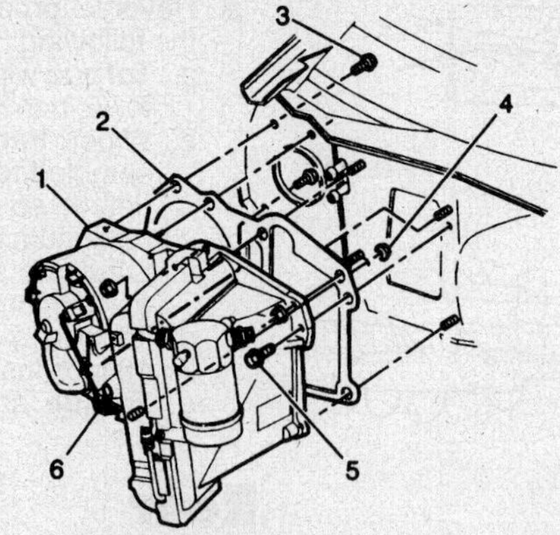

(1) Module, Blower
(2) Gasket
(3) Bolt, 6 N·m (53 lb in)
(4) Nut, 6 N·m (53 lb in)
(5) Bolt, 4.5 N·m (40 lb in)
(6) Resistor, Blower Motor

GC7028800015000X

Fig. 11 Evaporator core replacement (Front)

Rear

1. Recover refrigerant as outlined "Air Conditioning" chapter.
2. Remove lefthand body side trim panel.
3. Remove lefthand rear D pillar garnish molding.
4. Release two-piece duct set screw.
5. Slide bottom half of dust up into top half.
6. Swing duct bottom edge toward interior.
7. Pull duct top edge clear of headline duct.
8. Remove air outlet duct.
9. Remove electrical connectors.
10. Raise and support vehicle.
11. Remove auxiliary evaporator rear tube mounting nut.
12. Lower vehicle.
13. Remove evaporator case and case screws.
14. Split case, then remove seal and core.
15. Reverse procedure to install, noting the following:
    a. **Torque** case bolts to 86 inch lbs.
    b. **Torque** mounting nut to 86 inch lbs.
    c. **Torque** duct set screw to 18 inch lbs.

4.3L Engine

NOTE: Refer To "4.3L, 5.0L, 5.7L & 7.4L Gasoline Engines" Section In The "Express & Savana" Chapter For Service Procedures Not Covered In This Section

NOTE: On Air Bag Equipped Models, Refer To "Air Bag System Precautions" Located In The Front Of This Manual For System Disarming & Arming Procedures.

NOTE: Refer To "Computer Relearn Procedures" Located In The Front Of This Manual When Power To The Computer Has Been Interrupted.

INDEX

PRECAUTIONS

Air Bag Systems

Refer to "Air Bag System Precautions" in the front of this manual for system disarming and arming procedures.

Battery Ground Cable

Prior to service, disconnect battery ground cable and isolate as required.

Fuel System Pressure Relief

Prior to performing fuel system service procedures it is required to relieve fuel pressure. To relieve fuel system pressure proceed as follows:

1. Loosen fuel filler cap to relieve tank vapor pressure.
2. Connect fuel pressure gauge to fuel pressure connection tap using fuel pressure gauge tool No. J-34730-1 and adapter tool No. J-34730-25, or equivalents.
3. Wrap shop towel around connection to avoid spillage.
4. Install bleed hose in approved container and open valve to bleed fuel pressure.

COMPRESSION PRESSURE

Refer to "4.3L, 5.0L, 5.7L & 7.4L Gasoline Engines" section in "Express & Savana."

ENGINE MOUNT

REPLACE

1. Raise and support vehicle.
2. If removing righthand side engine mount proceed as follows:
   a. Remove righthand front tire and wheel assembly.
   b. Remove righthand fender wheel housing extension.
   c. Remove starter as outlined under "Starter, Replace" in "Electrical" section.
3. Remove through bolt and nut from mount, **Fig. 1.**
4. Raise engine enough to remove mount. Use suitable jack on square tab at rear of engine block, **Fig. 2. Do not use jack under oil pan, any sheet metal or crankshaft pulley.**
5. Remove mounting bolts and engine bracket.
6. Remove mounting bolts and frame bracket.
7. Reverse procedure to install.

ENGINE

REPLACE

This procedure must be performed on a side lift hoist. The engine and front frame assembly will be removed out the bottom of the vehicle. Therefore, a single post hoist or a twin point hoist cannot be used.

1. Remove engine cover.
2. Remove air cleaner and air cleaner outlet duct from throttle body.
3. Remove air filter and disconnect throttle cable.
4. Remove radiator as outlined in "Radiator, Replace."
5. **On models equipped with air conditioning,** recover refrigerant as outlined in "Air Conditioning" chapter, then disconnect air conditioning lines at accumulator and condenser.
6. **On all models,** disconnect accelerator cable from throttle shaft.

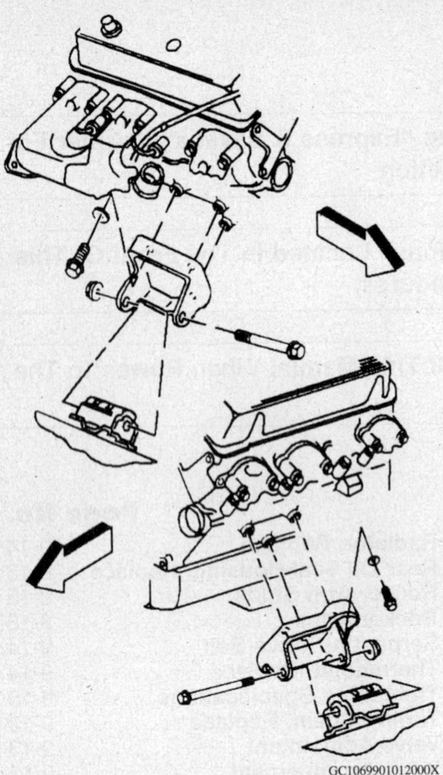

Fig. 1 Engine mount replacement

7. Drain power steering reservoir into suitable container and remove.
8. **On models equipped with cruise control,** disconnect cruise control cable and position out of way.
9. **On all models,** remove cable(s) from accelerator control cable bracket.
10. Remove power steering reservoir and drain fluid into suitable container.
11. Disconnect lines from hydro-boost unit, remove master cylinder without disconnecting lines and tie aside to oil fill tube.
12. Disconnect steering gear shaft and engine heater hoses.
13. Disconnect water control valve vacuum hose and wire connector.
14. Disconnect fuse box and wiring harness from bulkhead connector.
15. Disconnect wiring harness to body electrical connectors, including ground wires, accumulator, cruise control module and wiper motor.
16. Remove wiring harness from retainers and lay on engine.
17. If vehicle is equipped with running boards, remove front section.
18. Install body protection hoist adapter set tool No. J-41602, or equivalent, in pinch weld are on both sides of vehicle, **Fig. 3.**
19. Position front hoist arms under adapter tool and rear hoist arms.
20. Raise and support vehicle, then drain engine oil into suitable container.
21. Remove rear propeller shaft and starter motor.
22. Remove transmission cover and torque converter mounting bolts through starter motor opening.
23. Disconnect shift cable and electrical connectors from transmission.
24. Disconnect exhaust system at catalytic converter main flange.
25. Disconnect park brake bracket.
26. Disconnect rear brake line from brake pressure modulator valve.
27. Remove front bumper and disconnect power steering cooler from air deflector.
28. Disconnect front air bag sensor connector.
29. Disconnect fender wheel housing extensions from chassis.
30. **On models equipped with rear air conditioning,** disconnect lines at rear crossmember, leave lines connected to powertrain assembly.
31. **On all models,** disconnect fuel lines at fuel filter, pull fuel lines forward through crossmember and position lay on transmission.
32. Disconnect fuel tank and EVAP vent valve electrical connectors.
33. Remove EVAP vent valve bolt and ground wire.
34. Ensure all remaining connectors between powertrain and chassis are disconnected.
35. **On models equipped with AWD,** disconnect transfer case vent hose.
36. **On all models,** position universal engine support table tool No. J-39580, or equivalent, under frame.
37. Remove body mount bolts.
38. Place suitable jack stand under transmission crossmember.
39. Raise hoist to separate body from frame.
40. Install suitable support stands under rear axle.
41. Remove EGR valve inlet pipe from intake and exhaust manifolds.
42. Disconnect wires from spark plugs and remove distributor cap with wire harness.
43. Remove air condition compressor and power steering pump mounting bracket.
44. Remove righthand rear and lefthand front lower intake manifold bolts.
45. Install engine lift bracket tools No. J-41427, or equivalent, **Fig. 4. Torque** bolt to 11 ft. lbs.
46. Remove engine mount through bolts.
47. Remove fuel pipe bracket mounting bolt from rear of lefthand cylinder head.
48. Disconnect fuel lines at rear of engine.
49. Disconnect electrical harness at transmission.
50. Disconnect wire harness connections and ground wires, then move harness aside.
51. **On models equipped with AWD,** disconnect transfer case to engine brace.
52. **On all models,** raise engine slightly. Support transmission using suitable floor stand and wood block. **Do not place supports under transmission pan.**
53. Remove exhaust pipe from exhaust manifolds.
54. Remove transmission to engine bolts and separate engine from transmission.
55. Remove engine.

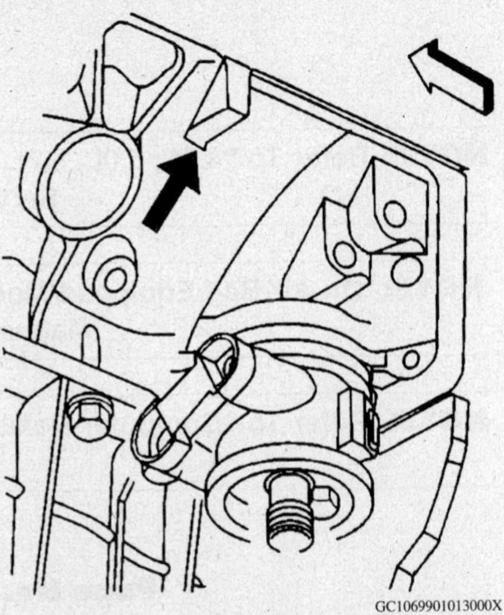

Fig. 2 Engine block square tab

56. Reverse procedure to install, noting the following:
    a. Apply suitable thread lock to lower intake manifold bolts and tighten as outlined in "Intake Manifold, Replace."
    b. **Torque** frame mounting bolts to 26 ft. lbs., in sequence, **Fig. 5.**
    c. **Torque** bolts Nos. 1 and 2 to 114 ft. lbs.
    d. **Torque** bolts Nos. 3–6 to 66 ft. lbs.
    e. Align subframe to chassis using suitable dowel pin or taper punch.
    f. Install new accelerator cable.

INTAKE MANIFOLD

REPLACE

Upper

1. Remove engine cover, air cleaner and intake duct.
2. Disconnect air condition pressure switch and throttle position sensor electrical connectors.
3. Disconnect idle air control motor and fuel meter body electrical connectors.
4. Disconnect manifold absolute pressure sensor and EVAP canister purge solenoid valve electrical connectors.
5. Remove PCV valve hose from intake manifold and rocker arm cover.
6. **On models equipped with air conditioning,** disconnect intake manifold vacuum hose.
7. **On all models,** remove engine wiring harness bracket from EVAP canister purge solenoid valve stud.
8. Remove EVAP canister purge solenoid.
9. Disconnect throttle cable from throttle shaft.
10. **On models equipped with cruise control,** disconnect cruise control cable.
11. **On all models,** remove bolt holding transmission fluid filler tube to accelerator control cable bracket.
12. Remove accelerator control cable bracket.

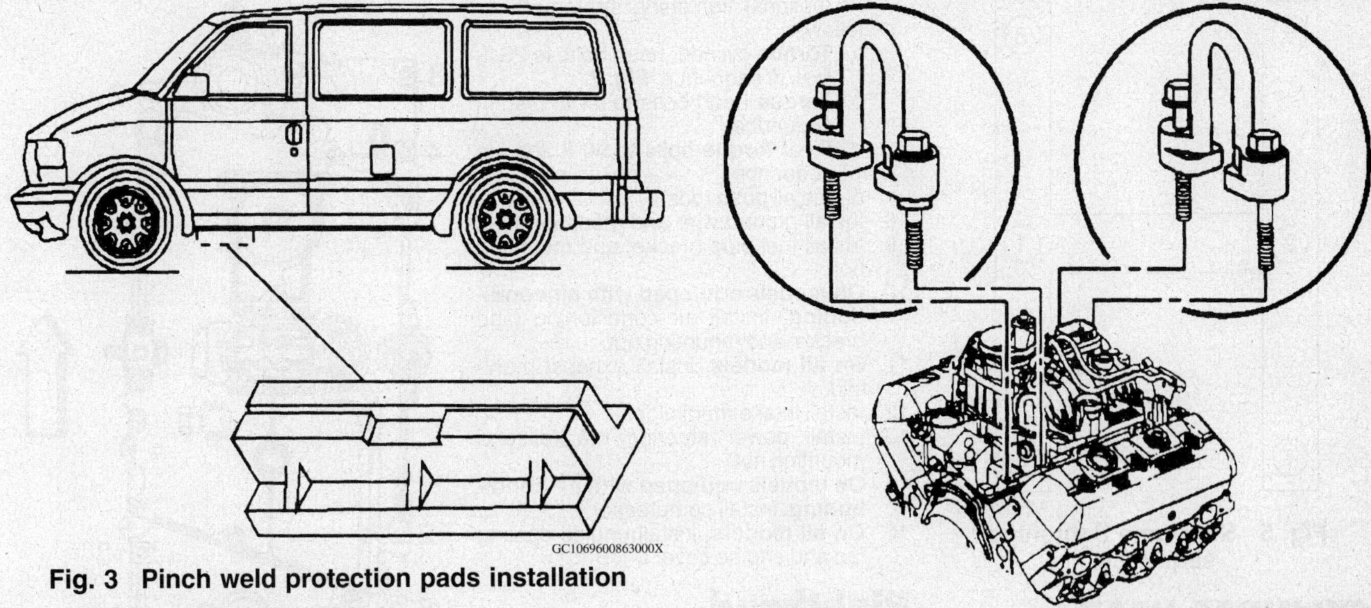

Fig. 3 Pinch weld protection pads installation

Fig. 4 Lift bracket installation

13. **On models equipped with air conditioning,** remove mounting nut and air conditioning hose bracket.
14. **On all models,** remove engine wiring harness bracket from stud.
15. Remove fuel lines from meter body.
16. Remove upper intake manifold.
17. Reverse procedure to install.

Lower

1. Remove engine cover and drain cooling system into suitable container.
2. Remove air cleaner and air cleaner outlet duct from throttle body.
3. Remove upper radiator hose at thermostat housing and disconnect heater hose at lower intake manifold.
4. Remove water pump inlet hose from intake manifold and ground wire from water outlet stud.
5. Disconnect throttle cable from throttle shaft.
6. **On models equipped with cruise control,** remove cruise control cable.
7. **On all models,** remove transmission fluid filler tube mounting bolt from throttle cable bracket.
8. Disconnect fuel meter body and EVAP canister purge solenoid valve electrical connectors.
9. Disconnect Idle Air Control motor, Throttle Position sensor and Engine Coolant Temperature gauge sensor electrical connectors.
10. **On models equipped with air conditioning,** disconnect air conditioning compressor high pressure and air conditioning clutch switches electrical connectors.
11. **On all models,** disconnect exhaust gas recirculation valve and engine coolant temperature sensor electrical connectors.
12. Remove drive belt.
13. **On models equipped with air conditioning,** remove air conditioning compressor side brace.
14. **On all models,** loosen power steering pump rear bracket nut.
15. Remove bracket mounting bolt and oil filler tube.
16. Remove power steering pump mounting bracket bolts and nut. Leave power steering pump and air conditioning compressor on bracket.
17. Slide power steering pump bracket forward to access intake manifold front bolt.
18. Remove distributor as outlined under "Distributor, Replace" in "Electrical" section.
19. Remove EGR valve inlet pipe from intake and exhaust manifolds.
20. Disconnect PCV valve hose from intake manifold and rocker arm cover.
21. **On models equipped with air conditioning,** disconnect intake manifold vacuum hose and remove air conditioning hose bracket mounting nut at intake manifold stud.
22. **On all models,** remove engine wiring harness bracket mounting nut.
23. Remove mounting bolts and set ignition control module aside.
24. Remove mounting nut and engine wiring harness bracket from EVAP canister purge solenoid valve stud.
25. Remove EVAP canister purge solenoid valve.
26. Remove mounting bolt and lower intake manifold.
27. Reverse procedure to install, nothing the following:
    a. Install gaskets to cylinder head, ensure port blocking plates are at rear of engine and "This Side Up" is visible.
    b. Place ¼ inch bead of Wacker T-330 RTV sealer, or equivalent, on front and rear sealing surfaces of block. Extend bead ½ inch up onto cylinder head surfaces.
    c. Coat intake manifold bolts with suitable sealer.
    d. **Torque** intake manifold bolts to 26 inch lbs., in sequence, **Fig. 6.**
    e. **Torque** bolts to 106 inch lbs., in sequence.
    f. Final **torque** bolts to 11 ft. lbs., in sequence.

EXHAUST MANIFOLD

REPLACE

Lefthand

1. Remove engine cover and disconnect engine coolant temperature gauge sensor.
2. Raise and support vehicle, then remove lefthand front tire and wheel assembly.
3. Remove lefthand fender wheel housing extension.
4. Remove catalytic converter.
5. Remove EGR valve inlet pipe from exhaust manifold.
6. Remove spark plugs wires and support.
7. Remove front exhaust manifold mounting bolts through wheel housing.
8. Remove rear exhaust manifold mounting bolts through engine cover.
9. Remove exhaust manifold, gaskets and spark plug wire shields.
10. Reverse procedure to install. Install new gaskets.

Righthand

1. Raise and support vehicle, then remove righthand front tire and wheel assembly.
2. Remove righthand fender wheel housing extension.
3. Disconnect wires from spark plugs.
4. Remove catalytic converter.
5. Remove mounting bolts and exhaust manifold with spark plug wire shields.
6. Reverse procedure to install. Install new gaskets.

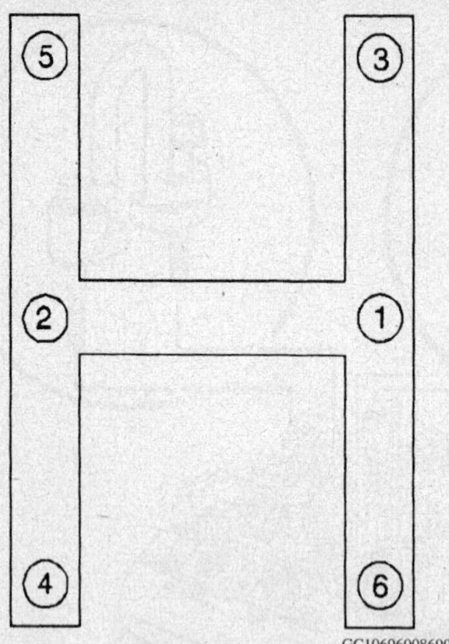

Fig. 5 Subframe tightening sequence

CYLINDER HEAD

REPLACE

Lefthand

REMOVAL

1. Remove engine cover and engine cooling fan.
2. **On models equipped with air conditioning,** remove compressor.
3. **On all models,** remove mounting nut and power steering pump rear bracket. **Pump and hoses may remain attached.**
4. Remove power steering pump mounting bracket stud from cylinder head.
5. Remove intake manifolds as outlined in "Intake Manifold, Replace."
6. Remove exhaust manifold as outlined in "Exhaust Manifold, Replace."
7. Remove ground wires from cylinder head rear.
8. **On models equipped with air conditioning,** remove air conditioning pipe bracket nut.
9. **On all models,** remove fuel line bracket at cylinder head rear.
10. Remove push rods as outlined in "Push Rods."
11. Remove mounting bolts and cylinder head.

INSTALLATION

Do not use sealer on composite type head gaskets.

1. Ensure block dowels are in place when positioning cylinder head gasket and cylinder head.
2. Coat head bolts threads with suitable sealing compound.
3. **Torque** cylinder head bolts to 22 ft. lbs., in sequence, **Fig. 7.**
4. Tighten long bolt Nos. 1, 4, 5, 8 and 9 in sequence an additional 75°.
5. Tighten medium bolt Nos. 12 and 13 in sequence an additional 65°.
6. Tighten short bolt Nos. 2, 3, 6, 7 10 and 11 in sequence an additional 55°.
7. An optional tightening strategy is as follows:
   a. **Torque** cylinder head bolts to 26 ft. lbs., in sequence, **Fig. 7.**
   b. **Torque** head bolts to 44 ft. lbs., in sequence.
   c. Final **torque** bolts to 66 ft. lbs., in sequence.
   d. Install push rods.
8. Install ground wire and mounting bolt.
9. Install fuel pipe bracket and mounting bolt.
10. **On models equipped with air conditioning,** install air conditioning pipe bracket and mounting nut.
11. **On all models,** install exhaust manifold.
12. Install intake manifolds.
13. Install power steering bracket and mounting nut.
14. **On models equipped with air conditioning,** install compressor.
15. **On all models,** install engine cooling fan and engine cover.

Righthand

REMOVAL

1. Remove engine cover and engine cooling fan.
2. Remove intake manifolds as outlined in "Intake Manifold, Replace."
3. Remove spark plug wire harness support.
4. Remove exhaust manifold as outlined in "Exhaust Manifold, Replace."
5. Remove alternator mounting bracket and bracket stud.
6. Remove push rods as outlined in "Pushrods."
7. Remove mounting bolts and cylinder head.

INSTALLATION

Do not use sealer on composite type head gaskets.

1. Ensure block dowels are in place when positioning cylinder head gasket and cylinder head.
2. Coat head bolts threads with suitable sealing compound.
3. **Torque** cylinder head bolts to 22 ft. lbs., in sequence, **Fig. 7.**
4. Tighten long bolt Nos. 1, 4, 5, 8 and 9 in sequence an additional 75°.
5. Tighten medium bolt Nos. 12 and 13 in sequence an additional 65°.
6. Tighten short bolt Nos. 2, 3, 6, 7 10 and 11 in sequence an additional 55°.
7. An optional tightening strategy is as follows:
   a. **Torque** cylinder head bolts to 26 ft. lbs., in sequence, **Fig. 7.**
   b. **Torque** head bolts to 44 ft. lbs., in sequence.
   c. Final **torque** bolts to 66 ft. lbs., in sequence.
   d. Install push rods.
8. Install exhaust manifold.
9. Install spark plug wire support.
10. Install intake manifolds.
11. Install alternator bracket.
12. Install wiring harness.
13. Install engine cooling fan and engine cover.

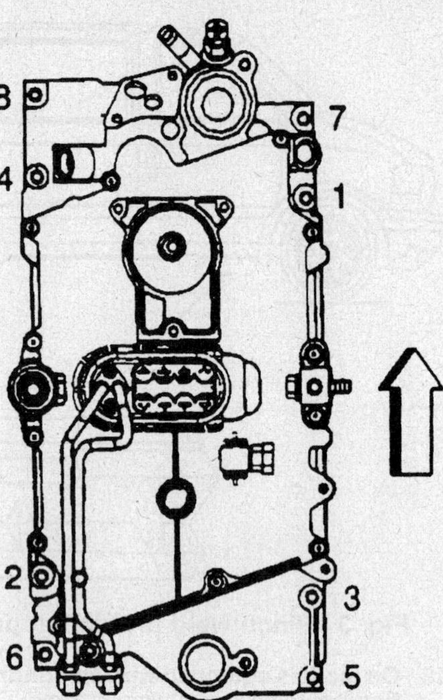

Fig. 6 Lower intake manifold bolt tightening sequence

VALVE COVER

REPLACE

Lefthand

1. Remove engine cover and disconnect engine coolant temperature gauge sensor electrical connector.
2. Remove mounting bolt and oil filler tube.
3. Remove PCV valve hose from intake manifold and rocker arm cover.
4. Remove mounting bolts, valve cover and gasket.
5. Reverse procedure to install, noting the following:
   a. Install new gasket.
   b. Install new bolt grommets.

Righthand

1. Remove engine cover.
2. Disconnect wires from spark plugs.
3. Remove PCV tube from rocker arm cover and air cleaner outlet duct.
4. Remove engine wiring harness bracket from EVAP canister purge solenoid valve stud and move aside.
5. Remove alternator wiring bracket.
6. Remove mounting bolts, valve cover and gasket.
7. Reverse procedure to install, noting the following:
   a. Install new gasket.
   b. Install new bolt grommets.

VALVE ARRANGEMENT

Refer to "4.3L, 5.0L, 5.7L & 7.4L Gasoline Engines" section in the "Express & Savana" chapter.

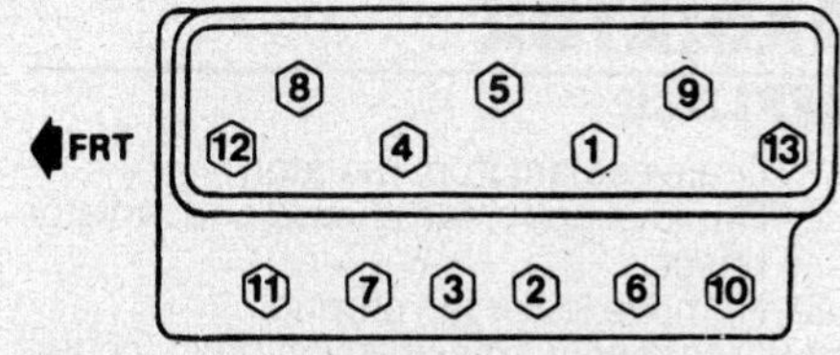

Fig. 7 Cylinder head tightening sequence

VALVE LIFTERS

Refer to "4.3L, 5.0L, 5.7L & 7.4L Gasoline Engines" section in the "Express & Savana" chapter.

VALVE CLEARANCE SPECIFICATIONS

Refer to "4.3L, 5.0L, 5.7L & 7.4L Gasoline Engines" section in the "Express & Savana" chapter.

VALVE ADJUSTMENT

Refer to "4.3L, 5.0L, 5.7L & 7.4L Gasoline Engines" section in the "Express & Savana" chapter.

ROCKER ARMS

Refer to "4.3L, 5.0L, 5.7L & 7.4L Gasoline Engines" section in the "Express & Savana" chapter.

ROCKER ARM STUDS

Refer to "4.3L, 5.0L, 5.7L & 7.4L Gasoline Engines" section in the "Express & Savana" chapter.

PUSH RODS

Refer to "4.3L, 5.0L, 5.7L & 7.4L Gasoline Engines" section in the "Express & Savana" chapter.

VALVE GUIDES

Refer to "4.3L, 5.0L, 5.7L & 7.4L Gasoline Engines" section in the "Express & Savana" chapter.

VALVE SEATS

Refer to "4.3L, 5.0L, 5.7L & 7.4L Gasoline Engines" section in the "Express & Savana" chapter.

HYDRAULIC LIFTERS

REPLACE

Refer to "4.3L, 5.0L, 5.7L & 7.4L Gasoline Engines" section in the "Express & Savana" chapter.

CRANKSHAFT DAMPER

REPLACE

1. Remove drive belt as outlined in "Serpentine Drive Belt."
2. Remove upper fan shroud and engine cooling fan.
3. Raise and support vehicle, then remove lower fan shroud.
4. Remove accessory drive pulley.
5. Remove crankshaft damper mounting bolt.
6. Remove crankshaft damper using crankshaft balancer tool No. J-39087, or equivalent.
7. Reverse procedure to install, noting the following:
   a. Install damper using stud tool No. J-23523-F, or equivalent.
   b. Seal key to keyway with small amount of suitable RTV sealant.

FRONT COVER

REPLACE

1. Remove oil pan as outlined in "Oil Pan, Replace."
2. Remove crankshaft damper as outlined in "Crankshaft Damper, Replace."
3. Remove water pump as outlined in "Water Pump, Replace."
4. Remove crankshaft position sensor.
5. Remove mounting bolts and front cover. **Do not damage oil pan seal.**
6. Reverse procedure to install, noting the following:
   a. Install new composite front cover.
   b. Install new crankshaft position sensor O-ring and lubricate with clean engine oil.
   c. Apply bead of suitable adhesive into areas where engine front cover meets oil pan surfaces.
   d. Lubricate oil pan seal with engine oil.

FRONT COVER SEAL

REPLACE

Refer to "4.3L, 5.0L, 5.7L & 7.4L Gasoline Engines" section in the "Express & Savana" chapter.

TIMING CHAIN

REPLACE

Refer to "4.3L, 5.0L, 5.7L & 7.4L Gasoline Engines" section in the "Express & Savana" chapter.

CAMSHAFT

REPLACE

Refer to "4.3L, 5.0L, 5.7L & 7.4L Gasoline Engines" section in the "Express & Savana" chapter.

BALANCE SHAFT

REPLACE

Refer to "4.3L, 5.0L, 5.7L & 7.4L Gasoline Engines" section in the "Express & Savana" chapter.

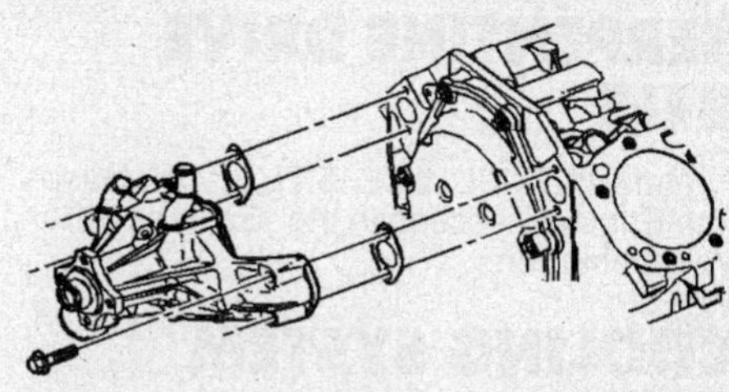

Fig. 8 Water pump replacement

PISTON & ROD ASSEMBLY

Refer to "4.3L, 5.0L, 5.7L & 7.4L Gasoline Engines" section in the "Express & Savana" chapter.

PISTONS, PINS & RINGS

Refer to "4.3L, 5.0L, 5.7L & 7.4L Gasoline Engines" section in the "Express & Savana" chapter.

MAIN & ROD BEARINGS

Refer to "4.3L, 5.0L, 5.7L & 7.4L Gasoline Engines" section in the "Express & Savana" chapter.

CRANKSHAFT REAR OIL SEAL

REPLACE

Refer to "4.3L, 5.0L, 5.7L & 7.4L Gasoline Engines" section in the "Express & Savana" chapter.

REAR OIL SEAL HOUSING

REPLACE

Refer to "4.3L, 5.0L, 5.7L & 7.4L Gasoline Engines" section in the "Express & Savana" chapter.

OIL PAN

REPLACE

Refer to "4.3L, 5.0L, 5.7L & 7.4L Gasoline Engines" section in the "Express & Savana" chapter.

OIL PUMP

REPLACE

Refer to "4.3L, 5.0L, 5.7L & 7.4L Gasoline Engines" section in the "Express & Savana" chapter.

OIL PUMP SERVICE

Refer to "4.3L, 5.0L, 5.7L & 7.4L Gasoline Engines" section in the "Express & Savana" chapter.

SERPENTINE DRIVE BELT

Refer to "4.3L, 5.0L, 5.7L & 7.4L Gasoline Engines" section in the "Express & Savana" chapter.

COOLING SYSTEM BLEED

Refer to "4.3L, 5.0L, 5.7L & 7.4L Gasoline Engines" section in the "Express & Savana" chapter.

THERMOSTAT

REPLACE

1. Drain cooling to level below thermostat.
2. Remove thermostat housing bolt.
3. Remove outlet and gasket.
4. Remove thermostat.
5. Reverse procedure to install.

WATER PUMP

REPLACE

1. Drain coolant into suitable container and remove air cleaner.

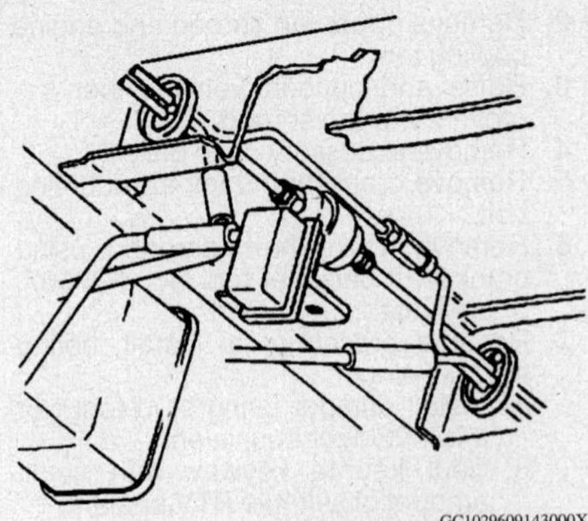

Fig. 9 Fuel filter replacement

2. Remove Mass Air Flow sensor, mounting bolts and upper fan shroud.
3. Remove drive belt as outlined in "Serpentine Drive Belt" then the fan and fan clutch.
4. Remove water pump pulley bolts and pulley, then disconnect coolant bypass hose and clamps.
5. Disconnect radiator hoses from water pump, then remove mounting bolts and water pump, **Fig. 8.**
6. Remove water pump gasket.
7. Reverse procedure to install.

RADIATOR

REPLACE

1. Drain coolant from radiator.
2. Remove upper fan shroud and radiator hoses.
3. Remove lower fan shroud.
4. Disconnect transmission fluid cooler pipes and engine oil cooler pipes.
5. Remove overflow hose and radiator grille.
6. Remove air conditioning condenser mounting bolts and radiator.
7. Reverse procedure to install.

FUEL PUMP

REPLACE

Refer to "4.3L, 5.0L, 5.7L & 7.4L Gasoline Engines" section in the "Express & Savana" chapter.

FUEL FILTER

REPLACE

1. Remove fuel tank filler cap and feed nuts.
2. Remove clamp bolt, remove filter and clamp, **Fig. 9.**
3. Reverse procedure to install.

TIGHTENING SPECIFICATIONS

Year	Component	Torque Ft. Lbs.
2002–05	Accelerator Control Cable Bracket, Nut	106①
	Accelerator Control Cable Bracket To Intake Manifold, Stud	53①
	Accelerator Control Cable Bracket To Throttle Body, Stud	106①
	Accumulator Line	35
	Air Cleaner Adapter	71①
	Air Conditioning Compressor	37
	Air Conditioning Compressor Side Brace	18
	Air Conditioning Condenser	89①
	Air Conditioning Condenser Lines	21
	Air Conditioning Hose	33
	Air Conditioning Hose Bracket To Intake Manifold	44①
	Air Conditioning Pipe Bracket	26
	Alternator	37
	Alternator Bracket	30
	Alternator Bracket Stud	15
	Alternator & Drive Belt Tensioner Bracket, Bolt & Nut	30
	Alternator & Drive Belt Tensioner Bracket, Stud	15
	Balance Shaft Drive Gear Mounting Stud	12
	Balance Shaft Driven Gear	15⑤
	Balance Shaft Retainer	106①
	Belt Idle Pulley	37
	Camshaft Retainer	106①
	Camshaft Sprocket	18
	Compressor Line	35
	Condenser Line	21
	Connecting Rod	20⑪
	Coolant Heater	18①
	Coolant Recovery Reservoir	97①
	Coolant Temperature Sensor	15
	Crankshaft Balancer	70
	Crankshaft Bearing Cap	20⑧
	Crankshaft Position (CKP) Sensor	71
	Crankshaft Pulley	43
	Crankshaft Rear Oil Seal Housing	106①
	Crankshaft Rear Oil Seal Housing Retainer	53①
	Cylinder Head	④
	Cylinder Head Core Hole Plug	15
	Distributor Cap	21①
	Distributor Clamp	18
	Drive Belt Idler Pulley	37
	Drive Belt Tensioner	37
	Drive Belt Tensioner Bracket Bolt To Engine	30
	Drive Belt Tensioner Stud To Engine	15
	EGR Valve	⑦
	EGR Valve Inlet Pipe Clamp	18
	EGR Valve Inlet Pipe At Exhaust Manifold	22
	EGR Valve Inlet Pipe At Intake Manifold	18
	Engine Block Coolant Drain Hole Plug	15

TIGHTENING SPECIFICATIONS—Continued

Year	Component	Torque Ft. Lbs.
2002–05	Engine Block Oil Gallery Plug	15
	Engine Block Oil Gallery Plug, Lefthand Rear	22
	Engine Block Oil Gallery Plug, Lefthand Side	15
	Engine Block Oil Gallery Plug, Righthand Rear	15
	Engine Coolant Temperature (ECT) Sensor	15
	Engine Lift Bracket	11
	Engine Lift Front Bracket Stud	26
	Engine Mount Bracket To Engine	47
	Engine Mount Bracket To Frame, Bolt (AWD)	35
	Engine Mount Bracket to Frame, Nut (2WD)	31
	Engine Mount Through Bolt	50
	Engine Mount To Frame (AWD)	44
	Engine Mount To Frame, Bolt (2WD)	35
	Engine Mount To Frame, Nut (2WD)	31
	Engine Oil Cooler Line Bracket	18
	Engine Oil Cooler Line Mount	26
	EVAP Line	21
	EVAP Purge Solenoid Valve	89①
	Exhaust Flange To Muffler	35
	Exhaust Manifold	③
	Exhaust Pipe Clamps	35
	Exhaust Pipe To Manifold	48
	Fan Clutch	42
	Fan Shroud	71①
	Flywheel	74
	Flywheel Housing	32
	Front Engine Cover	106①
	Fuel Line	22
	Fuel Line Bracket, Bolt	53①
	Fuel Pipe Bracket To Rear Of Cylinder Head, Stud	24
	Fuel Line Nut	27①
	Fuel Meter Body Bracket	88①
	Ground Wire To Cylinder Head Rear	26
	Ground Wire To Cylinder Water Outlet	14
	Hydraulic Lifter Restrictor Retainer	12
	Ignition Coil	106①
	Intake Manifold	⑥
	Knock Sensor	15
	Main Bearing Cap Bolt	75
	Oil Cooler Pipe Bracket	89①
	Oil Fill Tube	18
	Oil Filter Adapter	15
	Oil Filter Fitting	41
	Oil Dipstick Tube	106①
	Oil Pan	18⑩
	Oil Pan Baffle	106①
	Oil Pan Drain Plug	18
	Oil Pressure Gauge Sensor	22
	Oil Pressure Gauge Sensor Fitting	11
	Oil Pump Cover	106①

Continued

TIGHTENING SPECIFICATIONS—Continued

Year	Component	Torque Ft. Lbs.
2002–05	Oil Pump To Rear Crankshaft Bearing Cap	66
	Park Brake Bracket	18
	Power Steering Pump	37
	Power Steering Pump Bracket Stud Nut	30
	Power Steering Pump Bracket To Engine Bolt	30
	Power Steering Pump Bracket To Engine Stud	15
	Power Steering Pump Rear Bracket To Engine	30
	Power Steering Pump Rear Bracket To Power Steering Pump	37
	Pushrod Guide	12
	Radiator Hose	89①
	Radiator Support	18
	Reactor Pipe	18
	Rocker Arm Ball Stud	35
	Rocker Arm Bolt	22
	Rocker Arm Nut	18
	Seat	44
	Spark Plug	⑨
	Spark Plug Wire Support	106①
	Starter Motor	37
	Starter Motor Wiring Harness/Transmission Cooler Pipe Bracket	89
	Subframe Mounting Bolts	②
	Thermostat Housing	18
	Throttle Body	80①
	Torque Converter	55
	Transmission Control Cable Bracket	30
	Transmission Cover	106①
	Transmission Fluid Fill Tube To Accelerator Control Cable Bracket	53①
	Transmission To Engine Bolt	23
	Transmission To Oil Pan	35
	Transmission Oil Cooler	89①
	Transmission Oil Cooler Line	17

TIGHTENING SPECIFICATIONS—Continued

Year	Component	Torque Ft. Lbs.
2002–05	Transmission Oil Cooler Line Mount	80①
	Upper Radiator Hose Support Bracket to Exhaust Manifold	27
	Valve Cover	106①
	Valve Lifter Pushrod Guide	12
	Valve Rocker Arm	22
	Water Outlet	18
	Water Pump	33
	Water Pump Pulley	18
	Wiring Harness	88①
	Wiring Harness Bracket To Alternator & Drive Belt Tensioner Bracket	18
	Wiring Harness Bracket To Evaporative Emission (EVAP) Canister Purge Solenoid Valve	71⑥
	Wiring Harness Bracket to Intake Manifold	106①
	Wiring Harness Retainer To Rear Of Righthand Cylinder Head	27

①— Inch lbs.

②— Refer to "Engine, Replace" for tightening procedures & specifications.

③— Torque to 11 ft. lbs., then to 22 ft. lbs.

④— Refer to "Cylinder Head, Replace" for tightening procedures & specifications.

⑤— Then tighten an additional 35°

⑥— Refer to "Intake Manifold, Replace" for tightening procedures & specifications.

⑦— Torque to 62 inch lbs., then to 22 ft. lbs.

⑧— Then tighten an additional 73°. Optional Strategy, torque to 77 ft. lbs.

⑨— New cylinder head, 22 ft. lbs.; all subsequent installations, 11 ft. lbs.

⑩— Refer to "Oil Pan, Replace" for tightening sequence.

⑪— Then tighten an additional 70°.

Rear Axle & Suspension

INDEX

REAR AXLE

REPLACE

1. Raise vehicle and support at frame.
2. Support rear axle housing by positioning suitable jack under housing and raising slightly.
3. Remove rear wheels and brake drums, then disconnect shock absorbers from anchor plates.
4. Scribe reference marks between driveshaft and pinion flange for installation.
5. Disconnect driveshaft and secure out of way to minimize universal joint stress.
6. Disconnect brake line from axle housing and parking bracket cables.
7. Remove leaf spring U-bolts and anchor plates.
8. Remove vent hose from axle housing.
9. Remove axle housing.
10. Reverse procedure to install.

REAR AXLE SHAFT

REPLACE

1. Raise and support rear of vehicle, then remove wheel and brake drum.
2. Loosen carrier cover mounting bolts and drain lubricant into suitable container.
3. Remove mounting bolts, carrier cover and fill plug.
4. Remove rear axle pinion shaft lock bolt and pinion shaft, **Fig. 1.**
5. Remove axle shaft button end C-lock and push shaft toward vehicle center.
6. Remove axle shaft. **Do not damage seal.**
7. Reverse procedure to install, noting the following:
   a. Lubricate axle shaft wheel bearing and oil seal surfaces with suitable axle lubricant.
   b. Axle shaft splined end must engage rear axle side gear splines.
   c. Coat differential pinion shaft locking screw threads with Loctite No. 242, or equivalent.
   d. Install new housing cover gasket.
   e. Tighten carrier cover mounting bolts in crosswise pattern.

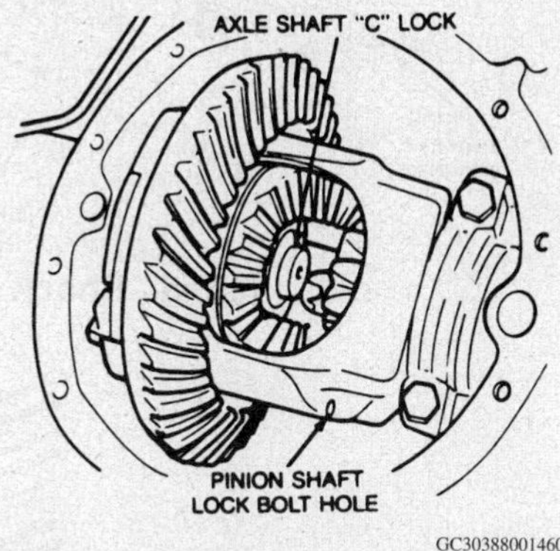

Fig. 1 Differential pinion shaft removal

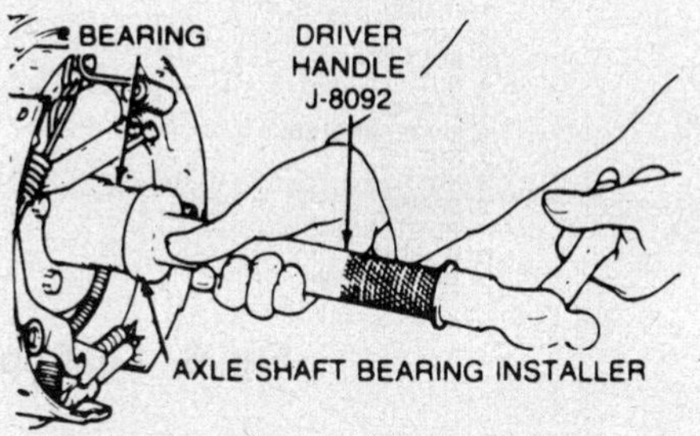

Fig. 3 Axle shaft bearing installation

AXLE SHAFT BEARINGS/SEALS

REPLACE

Removal

1. Remove axle shaft as outlined in "Rear Axle Shaft, Replace."
2. Remove seal using suitable seal removal tool behind steel case. **Do not damage housing, Fig. 2.**
3. Remove bearing using axle bearing puller tool No. J-22813-01 and slide hammer tool No. J-2619-01, or equivalents. Puller tool tangs should engage bearing outer race.

Installation

1. Install bearing in axle housing using axle shaft bearing installer tool No. J-23765, or equivalent, until tool bottoms against housing shoulder, **Fig. 3.**
2. Lubricate bearing with suitable axle lubricant.
3. Install seal using installer tool No. J-23771, or equivalent, until seal is flush with axle tube, **Fig. 4.**
4. Install axle shaft.

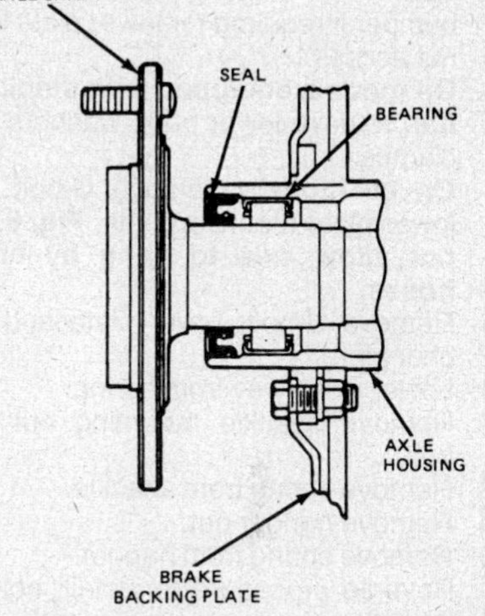

Fig. 2 Cross-sectional view of axle shaft & seal

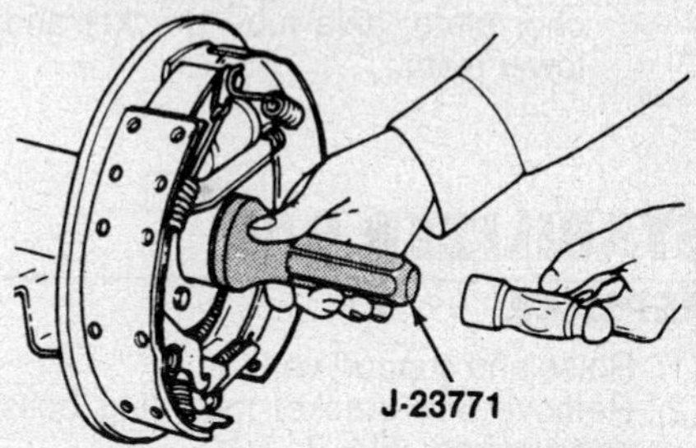

Fig. 4 Axle shaft seal installation

SHOCK ABSORBER

REPLACE

1. Raise and support vehicle.
2. Remove top shock absorber nut, washer and bolt, **Fig. 5.**

3. If removing righthand shock absorber, remove parking brake bracket.
4. Remove lower shock absorber nut, washer and bolt.
5. Remove shock absorber.
6. Reverse procedure to install.

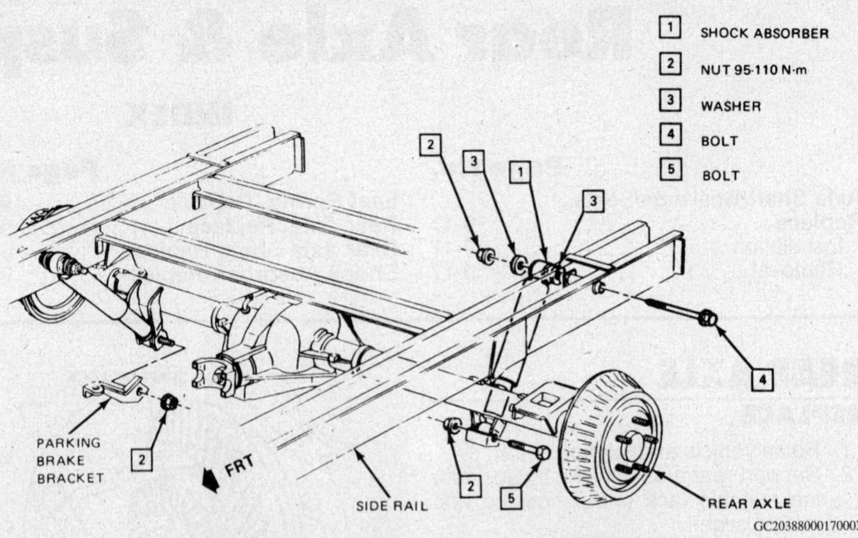

Fig. 5 Shock absorber replacement

LEAF SPRING

REPLACE

1. Raise and support vehicle. Support axle separately.
2. Remove mounting nut and axle bumper if required for lower plate front nut access.
3. **On models equipped with stabilizer bar,** remove lower nuts, washers and clamps.
4. **On all models,** remove U-bolt and lower plate mounting nuts, **Fig. 6. Do not allow axle to hang by brake hoses.**
5. Remove U-bolt, lower plate and anchor plate.
6. Lower axle away from spring.
7. Remove shackle mounting nut and bolt.
8. Remove spring from shackle.
9. Remove hanger nut.
10. Remove spring from hanger.
11. Reverse procedure to install, nothing the following:
    a. Apply suitable rubber lubricant to isolator.
    b. Ensure there is no gap between anchor plate, axle tube bracket and lower plate.

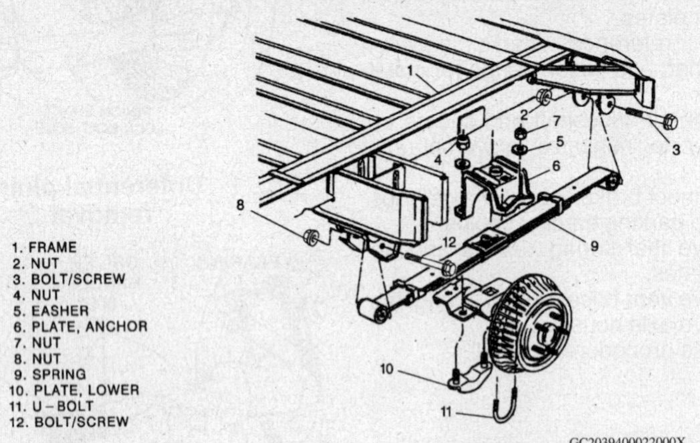

Fig. 6 Leaf spring replacement

STABILIZER BAR

REPLACE

1. Raise and support vehicle.
2. Remove link bracket mounting bolts and washers, **Fig. 7.**
3. Remove anchor block stud mounting nuts, washers and clamp. Proceed only if new stabilizer bar will be installed.
4. Remove stabilizer bar insulator.
5. Remove upper link mounting nuts, washers and bolts.
6. Remove bracket from link.
7. Remove link nuts, washers and bolts, then pry open lower link to obtain clearance from link insulator.
8. Remove stabilizer bar link insulator.
9. Reverse procedure to install.

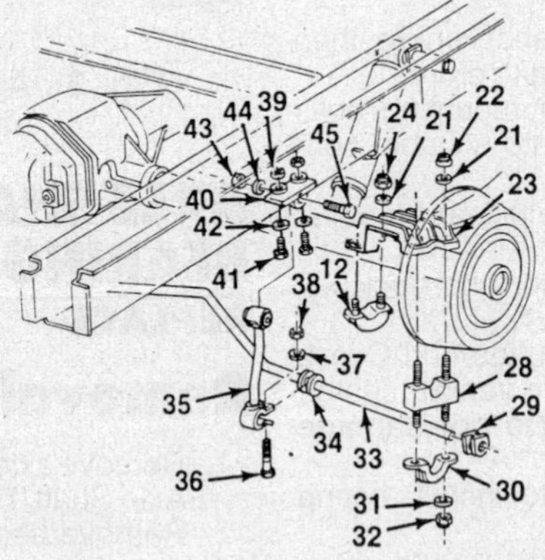

Fig. 7 Rear stabilizer replacement

TIGHTENING SPECIFICATIONS

Year	Component	Torque Ft. Lbs.
2002–05	Anchor Plate	45
	Bearing Cap	55
	Brake Pipe	13
	Bumper	33
	Cam To Hanger	24
	Differential Housing Cover	22
	Fill Plug	24
	Hanger	74
	Inner U-Bolt	41
	Line Bracket	25
	Lower Link	12
	Lower Plate	45
	Outer U-Bolt	48
	Pinion Shaft Lock	25
	Ring Gear	90
	Shackle To Frame	103
	Shackle To Spring	74
	Shock Absorber	79
	Stabilizer Link, Lower	14
	Stabilizer Link, Upper	33
	Stabilizer Shaft Clamp	44
	U-Bolt To Anchor Plate	52
	Upper Link	33
	Vent Clamp	12
	Wheel Cylinder To Backing Plate	13
	Wheel Lug Nuts	100

Front Suspension & Steering

NOTE: Refer To "Computer Relearn Procedures" Located In The Front Of This Manual When Battery Power To The Computer Has Been Interrupted.

INDEX

PRECAUTIONS

Battery Ground Cable

Prior to service, disconnect battery ground cable and isolate as required.

WHEEL BEARING

ADJUST

1. Raise and support front of vehicle.
2. Remove tire and wheel assemblies, then the hub cap.
3. Remove cotter pin and tighten spindle nut to specifications while turning wheel forward by hand.
4. Back off spindle nut until just loose. **Do not back off more than ½ flat.**
5. Hand tighten spindle nut until spindle hole aligns with nut slot.
6. Install new cotter pin, bend ends against nut and cutoff extra pin length. **Ensure cotter pin ends do not interfere with cap.**
7. Ensure endplay is .001–.005 inch.
8. Install cap.

BALL JOINT INSPECTION

Prior to inspecting ball joints, ensure wheel bearings are properly adjusted.

Upper

1. Raise vehicle and position suitable stands under lefthand and righthand lower control arms near each lower ball joint. Vehicle should not rock while on stands and upper control arm bumper must not contact frame.

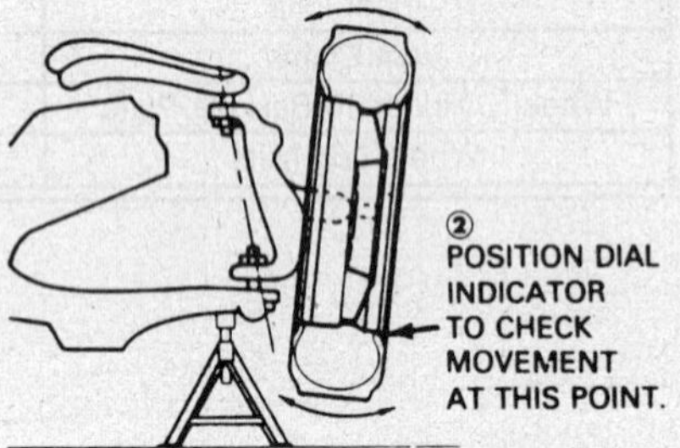

③ ROCK WHEEL IN AND OUT AT TOP AND BOTTOM.
② POSITION DIAL INDICATOR TO CHECK MOVEMENT AT THIS POINT.
① SUPPORT L. C. ARM AS FAR OUTBOARD AS POSSIBLE.
GC2028800058000X

Fig. 1 Upper ball joint inspection

2. Clean and inspect ball joint seals for cuts or tears. If seal is cut or torn, ball joint must be replaced.
3. Position dial indicator against lowest outboard point on wheel rim, **Fig. 1**.
4. Rock wheel in and out and observe gauge.
5. Replace ball joint as follows:
   a. If horizontal deflection is more than .125 inch.
   b. If ball stud had been disconnected from knuckle and any looseness is evident.
   c. If stud can be turned by hand.
   d. If round housing is flush with or inside cover surface. Normally housing project .05 inch beyond surface.

Lower

The lower ball joint is equipped with visual wear indicator, **Fig. 2.** Inspect ball joint with vehicle weight resting on wheels.

BALL JOINT

REPLACE

Upper

AWD MODELS

1. Raise and support vehicle, then remove tire and wheel assembly.
2. Unload torsion bar using torsion bar unloading/loading tool No. J-36202, or equivalent.
3. Remove brake hose and bracket from upper control arm, then the speed sensor bracket.
4. Drill rivets ¼ inch deep hole using ⅛ drill bit in rivets and heads using ½ inch drill bit.
5. Remove rivets using suitable pin punch.
6. Remove cotter pin and knurled nut.
7. Disconnect ball joint from knuckle using ball joint separator tool No, J-36607, or equivalent.
8. Support knuckle and remove ball joint.
9. Reverse procedure to install, noting the following:
   a. Tighten knurled nut with vehicle at "Z" position as outlined in "Vehicle Ride Height" in "Wheel Alignment" section.

2WD MODELS

1. Raise and support vehicle.
2. Support lower control arm using suitable jack stands between coil spring seat and ball joint of lower control arm.
3. Remove tire and wheel assembly.

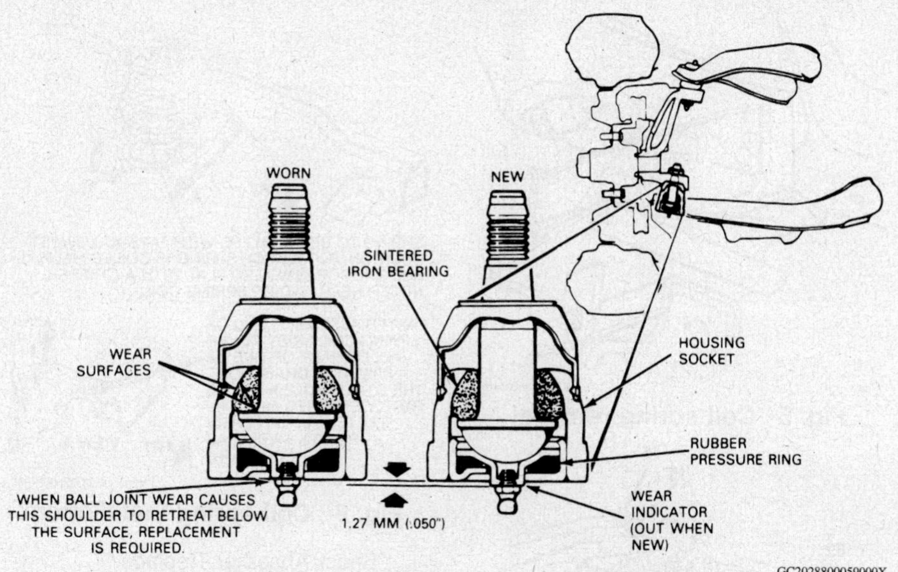

Fig. 2 Lower ball joint wear indicators

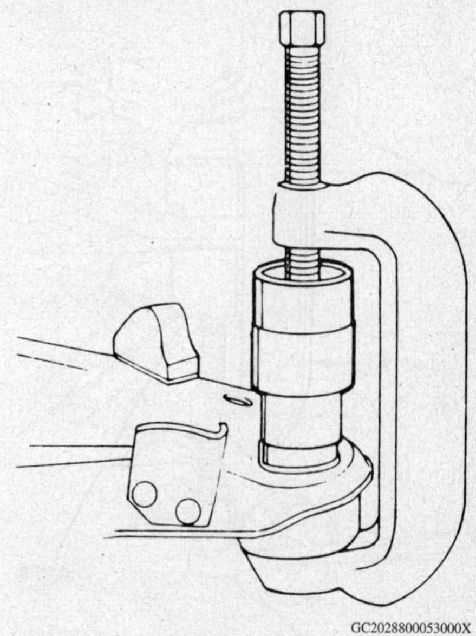

Fig. 3 Lower ball joint removal. 2WD models

4. Disconnect wheel speed sensor connector.
5. Remove ball joint cotter pin, nut and grease fitting.
6. Disconnect stud from steering knuckle using ball joint separator tool No. J-23742, or equivalent.
7. Support steering knuckle to prevent damage to brake hoses.
8. Cut ¼ inch deep holes in each rivet head center using ⅛ inch drill bit.
9. Drill off rivet heads using ½ inch drill bit.
10. Punch out rivets using suitable small pin punch and remove ball joints.
11. Reverse procedure to install. Replace rivets using suitable mounting bolts and nuts.

Lower

AWD MODELS

1. Raise vehicle and support, then remove tire and wheel assembly.
2. Remove front splash shield.
3. Remove cotter pin and castellated nut from outer tie rod.
4. Remove outer tie rod from steering knuckle using universal steering linkage puller tool No. J-24319-B, or equivalent.
5. Remove drive axle shaft nut and wash, then hub and bearing assembly mounting bolts.
6. Remove lower ball joint cotter pin and nut.
7. Mark torsion bar adjuster bolt for load and support lower control arm using suitable safety stand.
8. Unload torsion bar using torsion bar unloading/loading tool No. J-36202, or equivalent.
9. Disconnect knuckle from lower ball joint using ball joint remover tool No. J-35917, or equivalent.
10. Center punch lower ball joint rivets and drill ½ inch deep guide hole using ⅛ inch drill bit.
11. Drill rivet heads off using 5/16 inch drill bit.
12. Remove rivets using 5/16 inch pin punch.
13. Remove ball joint.
14. Reverse procedure to install, noting the following:
    a. Tighten knurled nut with vehicle at "Z" position as outlined in "Vehicle Ride Height" in "Wheel Alignment" section.

2WD MODELS

1. Raise vehicle and support, then remove tire and wheel assembly.
2. Support control arm spring seat using suitable floor jack.
3. Remove ball joint cotter pin and stud nut.
4. Break lower ball joint free from knuckle using ball joint separator tool No. J-23742, or equivalent. **Inspect and clean tapered hole in steering knuckle. If hole is out of round or damaged in any way, steering knuckle must be replaced.**
5. Pull steering knuckle free from lower ball joint.
6. Position wooden block between frame and upper control arm. Ensure brake hose is free of tension.
7. Remove lower ball joint rubber grease seal and grease fitting.
8. Press ball joint out of lower control arm using ball joint replacement tool No. J-9519-D, or equivalent, **Fig. 3.**
9. Reverse procedure to install, **Fig. 4.** Tighten lower ball joint nut, install new cotter pin.

COIL SPRING

REPLACE

1. Raise and support vehicle so control arms hang free.
2. Remove lower shock absorber bolts, then push shock up through control arm and into spring.
3. Secure spring remover tool No. J-23028-01, or equivalent, to suitable jack and position tool to cradle inner bushings, **Fig. 5.**
4. **On models equipped with 2WD,** remove stabilizer from lower control arm.
5. **On all models,** relieve lower control arm pivot bolt tension by raising jack.
6. Install suitable safety chain around spring and through control arm.
7. Remove mounting nuts and bolts. **Remove rear bolt and nut first.**
8. Slowly lower jack and control arm and remove spring. **Do not apply force to lower control arm and ball joint to remove spring. Proper maneuvering of spring will allow for easy removal.**
9. Reverse procedure to install, noting the following:
    a. Insulators must be placed on top and bottom of coil spring, **Fig. 6.**

SHOCK ABSORBER

REPLACE

AWD Models

1. Raise and support vehicle, then remove tire and wheel assembly.
2. Support lower control arm and remove inner wheel housing splash shield.
3. Remove upper and lower nuts, washers and bolts, **Fig. 7.**
4. Collapse and remove shock.
5. Reverse procedure to install.

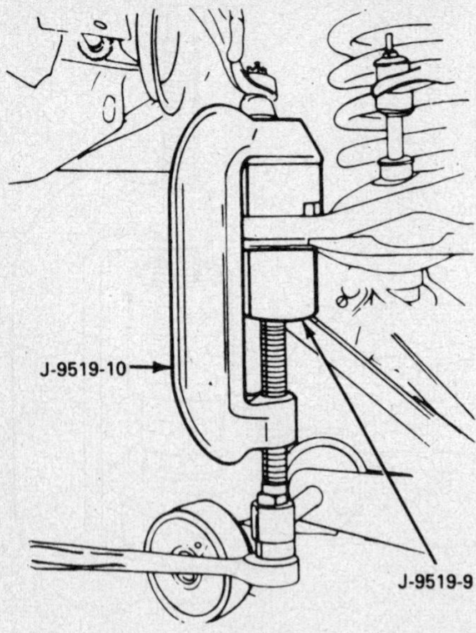
J-9519-10
J-9519-9
GC2028800054000X

Fig. 4 Lower ball joint installation. 2WD models

2WD Models

1. Raise and support vehicle, then remove tire and wheel assembly.
2. Hold shock upper stem from turning using suitable wrench, then remove nut, retainer and grommet.
3. Remove mounting bolts and shock absorber through lower control arm, **Fig. 8.**
4. Reverse procedure to install.

CONTROL ARM

REPLACE

Upper

AWD MODELS

1. Raise and support vehicle, then remove tire and wheel assembly.
2. Disconnect upper control arm brake hose and position aside.
3. Remove brake hose and speed sensor brackets.
4. Remove cotter pin and ball joint nut.
5. Disconnect upper ball joint from knuckle.
6. Remove mounting nuts, cams, bolts and upper control arm.
7. Reverse procedure to install, noting the following:
   a. Install new control arm nuts and nuts must be tightened with control arm in "Z" height as outlined in "Vehicle Ride Height" in "Wheel Alignment" section.
   b. Install new cotter pin.

2WD MODELS

1. Record shim locations for installation reference.
2. Raise and support vehicle.
3. Place suitable safety sands between lower control arm spring seat and lower ball joint.

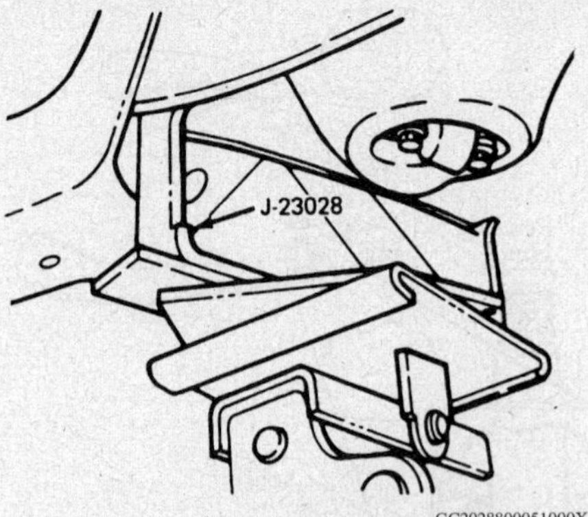
J-23028
GC2028800051000X

Fig. 5 Coil spring removal

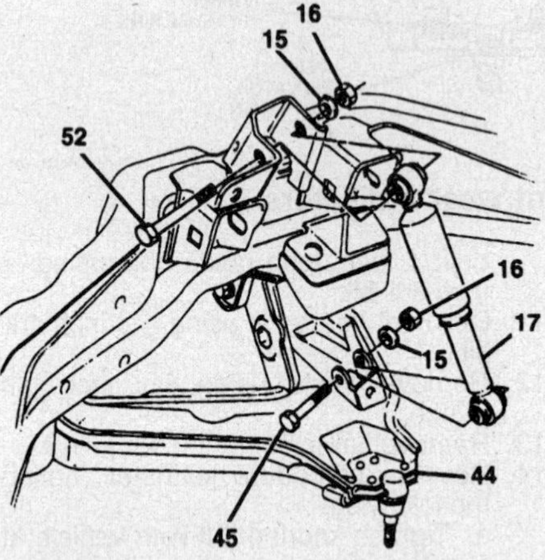
16
15
52
16
17
15
44
45
15. WASHER
16. NUT
17. ABSORBER, SHOCK
44. ARM KIT, LOWER
45. BOLT
52. BOLT
GC2029700230000X

Fig. 7 Shock absorber replacement. AWD models

4. Place suitable floor jack under lower control arm spring seat.
5. Remove tire and wheel assembly.
6. Remove wheel speed sensor harness clip rivets using 3⁄16 inch drill bit.
7. Remove cotter pin and nut to free steering knuckle.
8. Disconnect steering knuckle from upper ball joint using ball joint separator tool No. J-23742, or equivalent.
9. Lift upper control arm and support steering knuckle/hub.
10. Remove nuts and shims, **Fig. 9.**
11. Lift upper control arm to gain access and remove bolts.
12. Remove upper control arm.
13. Reverse procedure to install.

Lower

AWD MODELS

1. Raise vehicle and support, then remove tire and wheel assembly.
2. Remove mounting bolts and pivot splash shield to access tie rod and stabilizer bar.
3. Remove stabilizer bar as outlined in "Stabilizer Bar, Replace."
4. Remove shock absorber as outlined in

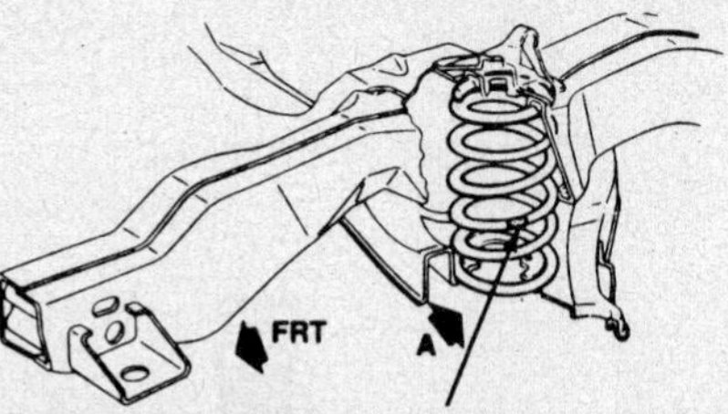
FRT
A
SPRING TO BE INSTALLED WITH TAPE AT LOWEST POSITION. BOTTOM OF SPRING IS COILED HELICAL, AND THE TOP IS COILED FLAT WITH A GRIPPER NOTCH NEAR END OF SPRING COIL.

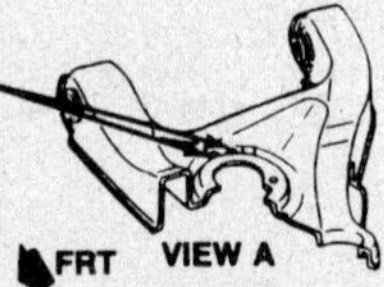
AFTER ASSEMBLY, END OF SPRING COIL MUST COVER ALL OR PART OF ONE INSPECTION DRAIN HOLE. THE OTHER HOLE MUST BE PARTLY EXPOSED OR COMPLETELY UNCOVERED. ROTATE SPRING AS NECESSARY.
FRT
VIEW A
GC2028800052000X

Fig. 6 Coil spring installation

"Shock Absorber, Replace."

5. Disconnect inner tie rod from relay rod.
6. Remove outer axle shaft nut, washer, hub and bearing assembly.
7. Unload torsion bar using torsion bar unloading/loading tool No. J-36202, or equivalent.
8. Remove adjusting arm by sliding torsion bar forward and out of rear.
9. Support lower control arm using suitable jack.
10. Remove lower ball joint cotter pin and nut.
11. Disconnect lower ball joint as outlined in "Ball Joint, Replace."
12. Remove mounting nuts, washers, bolts, lower control arm and torsion bar.
13. Separate control arm from torsion bar.
14. Reverse procedure to install, noting the following:
    a. Install new control arm nuts. Nuts must be tightened with control arm in "Z" height as outlined in "Vehicle Ride Height" in "Wheel Alignment" section.
    b. Install new cotter pin.

2WD MODELS

1. Remove coil spring as outlined in "Coil Spring, Replace."
2. Remove lower ball joint cotter pin and nut.
3. Disconnect lower ball joint from steering knuckle using ball joint separator tool No. J-23742, or equivalent.
4. Pull lower control arm free from steering knuckle.
5. Remove lower control arm, **Fig. 10.**
6. Reverse procedure to install.

CONTROL ARM BUSHING

REPLACE

Upper

AWD MODELS

1. Remove upper control arm as outlined in "Control Arm Replace, Upper."

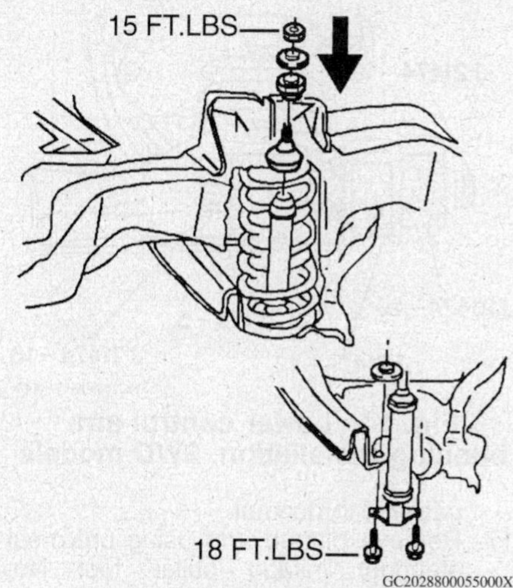
15 FT.LBS
18 FT.LBS
GC2028800055000X

Fig. 8 Shock absorber replacement. 2WD models

2. Remove bushings.
3. Reverse procedure to install.

2WD MODELS

1. Remove upper control arm as outlined in "Control Arm Replace, Upper."
2. Mount upper control arm in suitable vise.
3. Remove nuts and retainers.
4. Press bushings out of control arm using tie rod end installer tool No. J-22269, or equivalent, slotted washer and short piece of pipe slightly larger than bushing, **Fig. 11.**
5. Remove shaft from upper control arm.
6. Reverse procedure to install. Tighten tool until bushing gap is .48–.52 inch on both ends.

Lower

AWD MODELS

1. Remove lower control arm as outlined in "Control Arm Replace, Lower."
2. Unbend front bushing crimps using suitable punch.
3. Remove bushings using lower control arm bushing service set tool Nos. J-36618-2, J-36618-4, J-36618-1 and ball joint replacement tool No. J-9519-23, or equivalents.
4. Reverse procedure to install.

2WD MODELS

REMOVAL

1. Remove lower control arm as outlined in "Control Arm Replace, Lower."
2. Place lower control arm in suitable vise.
3. Drive bushing flare down flush with rubber of front bushing using suitable blunt chisel.
4. Remove bushings using control arm bushing service set tool No. J-21474-01, or equivalent, **Figs. 12 and 13.**

INSTALLATION

1. Install bushings using control arm bushing service set tool No. J-21474-01, or equivalent, **Fig. 14.**

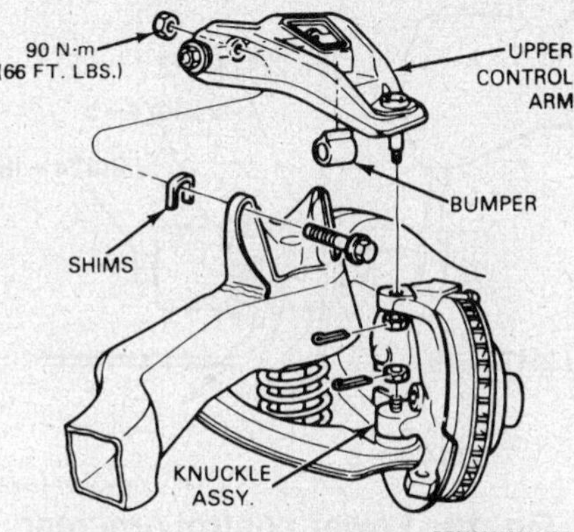
90 N·m
(66 FT. LBS.)
UPPER
CONTROL
ARM
BUMPER
SHIMS
KNUCKLE
ASSY.
GC2028800042000X

Fig. 9 Upper control arm replacement. 2WD models

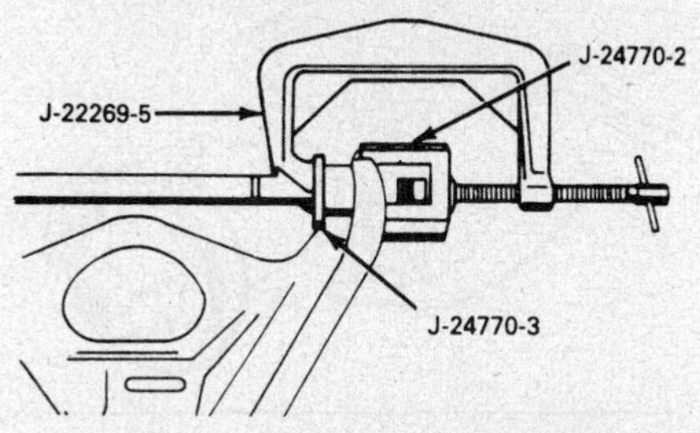
J-24770-2
J-22269-5
J-24770-3
GC2028800043000X

Fig. 11 Upper control arm bushing replacement. 2WD models

2. Tighten until bushing seats fully into lower control arm.
3. Flare front bushing approximately 45.°

STEERING KNUCKLE

REPLACE

1. Raise and support vehicle. **Do not support vehicle under lower control arms.**
2. Remove tire and wheel assembly.
3. Remove brake caliper as outlined in "Disc Brakes" chapter, then the rotor/hub.
4. Remove splash shield.
5. Disconnect tie rod end from steering knuckle using tie rod end puller tool No. J-6627, or equivalent.
6. If steering knuckle is to be repaired or replaced, remove knuckle seal.
7. Remove upper ball joint cotter pins and nuts, then the lower ball joint nut.
8. Remove ball joint studs from steering knuckle using ball joint remover tool No. J-23742, or equivalent.
9. Position suitable jack under lower control arm near spring seat.
10. Raise jack until it just supports control arm.
11. Break upper ball joint free of steering knuckle using ball joint separator toll No. J-23742, or equivalent.
12. Disconnect upper ball joint stud from knuckle by raising upper control arm.
13. Break lower ball joint free from steering knuckle using ball joint separator toll No. J-23742, or equivalent.
14. Lift steering knuckle off lower ball joint, **Fig. 15.**
15. Inspect and clean tapered hole in

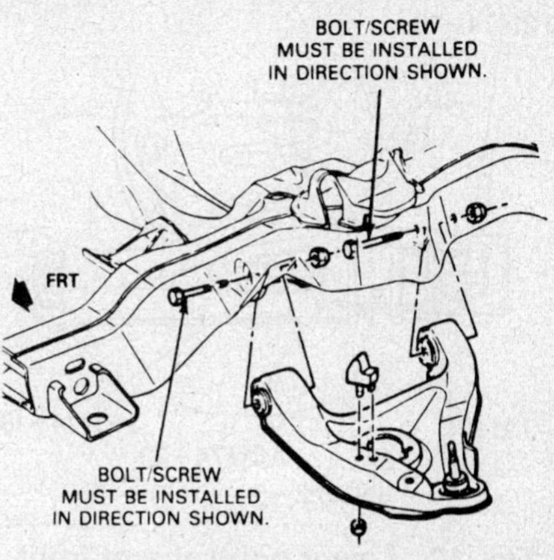
BOLT/SCREW
MUST BE INSTALLED
IN DIRECTION SHOWN.
FRT
BOLT/SCREW
MUST BE INSTALLED
IN DIRECTION SHOWN.
SUGGESTED ASSEMBLY SEQUENCE
INSTALL THE FRONT LEG OF THE LOWER CONTROL ARM INTO THE CROSSMEMBER PRIOR TO INSTALLING THE REAR LEG IN THE FRAME BRACKET.
GC2028800045000X

Fig. 10 Lower control arm replacement. 2WD models

steering knuckle. If hole is out of round or damaged in any way, knuckle must be replaced.

16. Reverse procedure to install. Install new cotter pins.

TORSION BAR

REPLACE

1. Raise and support vehicle.
2. Mark adjusting bolt position for installation.
3. Increase tension on adjustment arm using torsion bar unloading tool No. J-36202, or equivalent.
4. Remove adjustment bolt and mounting plate. Move tool aside.
5. Slide torsion bar forward and remove adjustment arms.
6. Remove torsion bar by sliding bar back partially through crossmember, dropping front end down and sliding bar forward.
7. If both torsion bars are remove, mark lefthand and righthand sides, respectively.
8. Reverse procedure to install, noting the following:
   a. Lubricate adjuster with suitable axle grease.
   b. Torsion bar rear face of should be .04–.10 inch from rear face of adjuster arm.
   c. Release tension on torsion bar until load is taken up by adjustment bolt.
   d. Lower vehicle.
   e. Inspect "Z" height as outlined in "Vehicle Ride Height" in "Wheel Alignment" section.

STABILIZER BAR

REPLACE

AWD Models

1. Raise and support vehicle, then remove tire and wheel assemblies.

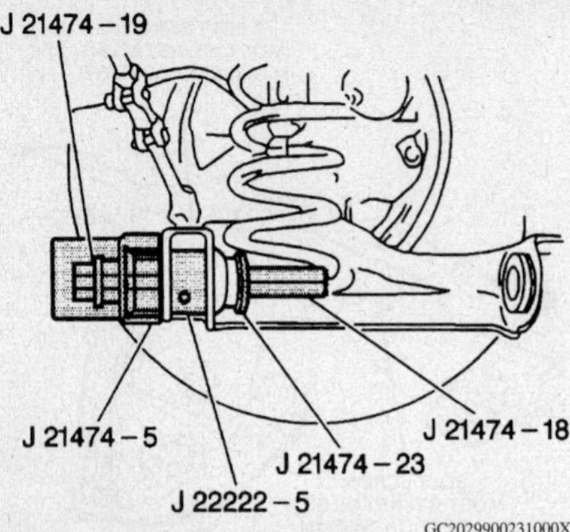

Fig. 12 Lower control arm front bushing removal. 2WD models

2. Disconnect idler arms from frame and move steering linkage to gain access to bar.
3. Remove link nuts and bolts.
4. Pull bolts up through retainers, insulators and spacers. These components will come free with ends of stabilizer.
5. Remove lefthand insulator mounting bolt and nut, then the righthand insulator mounting bolt.
6. Remove insulator clamps.
7. Remove stabilizer bar and insulators from bar.
8. Reverse procedure to install, noting the following:
   a. Install stabilizer bar insulators with slit toward front of vehicle.
   b. Stabilizer bar identification stamping appears on righthand side of vehicle.
   c. Offset bar in downward position.
   d. Position rubber bushings squarely in brackets with slit in bushings facing front of vehicle.

2WD Models

1. Raise and support vehicle, then remove tire and wheel assemblies.
2. Remove lint nuts, **Fig. 16.**
3. Pull bolts down through retainers, insulators and spacers. These components will come free with ends of stabilizer.
4. Remove bolts and insulator clamps.
5. Remove stabilizer bar and insulators.
6. Reverse procedure to install, noting the following:
   a. Install stabilizer bar insulators with slit toward vehicle front.
   b. Mount stabilizer bar identification stamping appears on righthand vehicle side.
   c. Offset bar in downward position.
   d. Position rubber bushings squarely in clamps.

POWER STEERING GEAR

REPLACE

Wheels must be straight ahead and steering column in Lock position before disconnecting steering column or intermediate shaft.

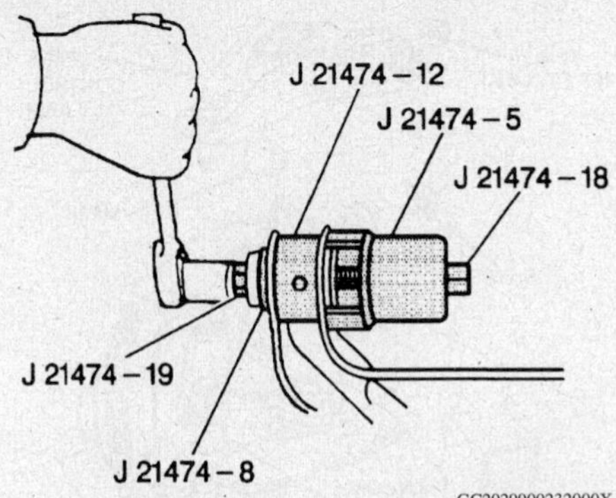

Fig. 13 Lower control arm rear bushing removal. 2WD models

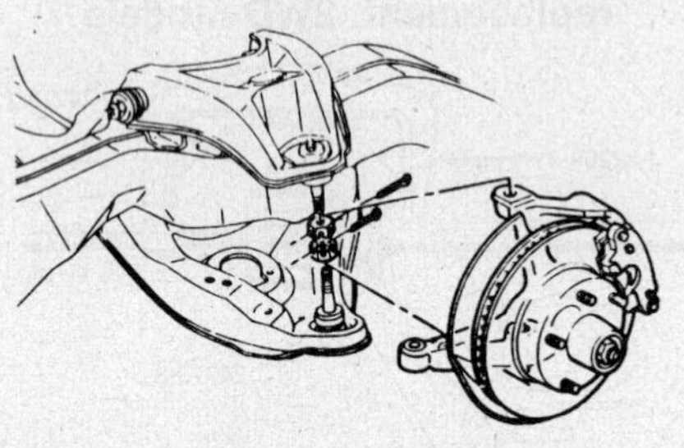

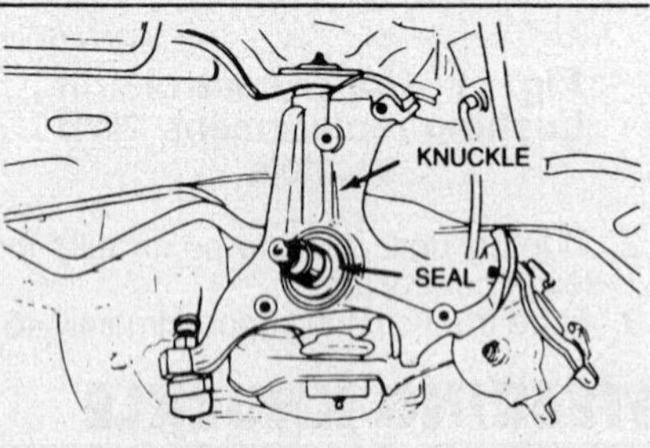

Fig. 15 Steering knuckle replacement

1. Remove air cleaner.
2. Remove mounting bolts and upper fan shroud.
3. Remove fan clutch using fan clutch wrench too No. J-41240, or equivalent.
4. Remove fan and fan blade clutch.
5. Remove lower fan shroud.
6. Mark relationship of intermediate steering shaft to steering column and steering gear shafts.
7. Install steering column anti-rotation pin tool No. C-42640, or equivalent, in steering column lower access hole.
8. Remove underhood electrical center mounting bolts and set aside.
9. Remove intermediate shaft boot from cowl.
10. Remove intermediate shaft pinch bolt at steering column.
11. Remove intermediate shaft boot from steering gear.
12. Remove pinch bolt and intermediate shaft from steering gear.
13. Place suitable container under steering gear.
14. Disconnect steering gear power steering hose and cooler line. Cap hose and gear fittings.
15. Raise and support vehicle.
16. Remove pitman arm connecting rod

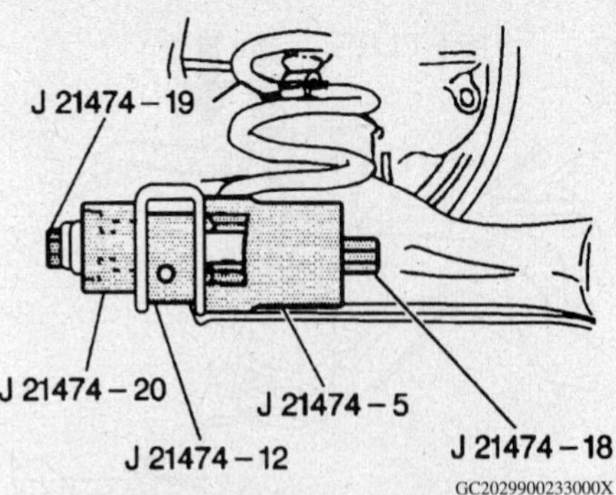

Fig. 14 Lower control arm bushing installation. 2WD models

ball stud torque nut.

17. Remove pitman arm using universal steering linkage puller tool No. J-24319-B, or equivalent.
18. Remove steering gear shaft torque nut and washer.
19. Mark pitman arm and shaft for installation alignment.
20. Remove pitman arm using pitman arm puller tool No. J-29107-A, or equivalent. **Do not hammer on arm, shaft or puller.**
21. Remove mounting bolts, washers and steering gear.
22. Reverse procedure to install. Ensure intermediate shaft angle is 38–40.°

POWER STEERING PUMP

REPLACE

1. Remove air cleaner.
2. Remove mounting bolts and upper fan shroud.
3. Remove fan clutch using fan clutch wrench tool No. J-41240, or equivalent.
4. Remove fan and fan blade clutch.
5. Remove lower fan shroud.
6. **On models equipped with air conditioning,** proceed as follows:
   a. Recover refrigerant as outlined in “Air Conditioning” chapter.
   b. Disconnect compressor electrical connectors.
   c. Remove engine cover.
   d. Remove drive belt.
   e. Remove oil filler tube.
   f. Remove compressor and condenser hose assembly.
   g. Remove mounting bolts, nuts and compressor brace.
   h. Remove mounting bolts and compressor.
7. **On all models,** remove power steering pump puller using tool No. J-25034-B, or equivalent.
8. Remove mounting bolts and nut.
9. Place suitable container under pump.
10. Disconnect hoses and remove power steering pump.
11. Reverse procedure to install. Use steering pump pulley installer tool No. J-25033-B, or equivalent.

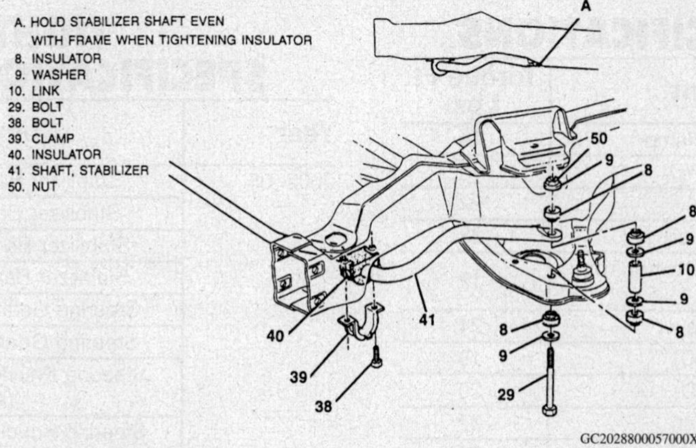

Fig. 16 Stabilizer bar replacement. 2WD models

TIGHTENING SPECIFICATIONS

Year	Component	Torque Ft. Lbs.
2002–05	Adjuster Tube Clamp	18
	Axle Shaft (AWD)	147
	Ball Joint	22
	Brake Hose To Caliper	32
	Brake Line To Upper Control Arm Bracket	12
	Brake Pedal Lever	24
	Bumper (AWD)	18
	Bumper (2WD)	20
	Caliper Mount	37
	Combination Valve Bracket	21
	Connecting Rod To Pitman Arm	48
	Connecting Rod To Relay Rod	35
	Coupling Shield Retainer & Lock	80
	Hub	12
	Hub & Bearing Mount (AWD)	66
	Hub & Bearing Mount (2WD)	133
	Idler Arm To Frame	77
	Intermediate Shaft To Steering Gear Pinch Bolt	30
	Lower Ball Joint To Steering Knuckle (AWD)	95
	Lower Ball Joint To Steering Knuckle (2WD)	90
	Lower Control Arm (2WD)	22
	Lower Control Arm Ball Joint	22
	Lower Control Arm To Frame (AWD)	98
	Lower Control Arm To Frame (2WD)	66②
	Lower Control Arm To Steering Knuckle (AWD)	95
	Master Cylinder Mounting	21
	Pitman Arm To Steering Gear	184
	Power Steering Cooler Bracket	18
	Power Steering Gear Adjuster Lock Nut	36
	Power Steering Gear Housing Cover	45
	Power Steering Hose Fitting	20
	Power Steering Hose To Steering Gear Adapter Pipe	21
	Power Steering Pressure Hose Flare Nuts	18
	Power Steering Pump, Bolt	37
	Power Steering Pump, Nut	30
	Power Steering Pump, Stud	43
	Power Steering Pump Control Valve Fitting	55
	Rack Piston Guide Clamp	43①
	Rack Piston Plug	111
	Remote Reservoir	35①
	Service Ball Joint To Upper Control Arm (2WD)	22
	Shock Absorber (AWD)	46
	Shock Absorber Lower (2WD)	18
	Shock Absorber Upper (2WD)	15
	Speed Sensor	124①
	Splash Shield	10
	Spindle	12

TIGHTENING SPECIFICATIONS—Continued

Year	Component	Torque Ft. Lbs.
2002–05	Stabilizer Bar Clamp (AWD)	41
	Stabilizer Bar Clamp (2WD)	27
	Stabilizer Bar Link Nut (AWD)	41
	Stabilizer Bar Link Nut (2WD)	13
	Steering Gear To Frame (AWD)	105
	Steering Gear To Frame (2WD)	55
	Steering Knuckle To Tie Rod End (AWD)	36
	Steering Knuckle To Tie Rod End (2WD)	35
	Tie Rod To Relay Rod	35
	Torsion Bar Retainer (AWD)	35
	Torsion Bar Retainer To Torsion Bar Support (AWD)	33
	Upper Ball Joint To Steering Knuckle (AWD)	72
	Upper Ball Joint To Steering Knuckle (2WD)	61
	Upper Control Arm Ball Joint	22
	Upper Control Arm Brake Bracket	12
	Upper Control Arm Pivot Shaft (2WD)	85
	Upper Control Arm Shaft To Frame (2WD)	81
	Upper Control Arm To Frame (AWD)	103
	Upper Control Arm To Shaft	85
	Upper Control Arm To Steering Knuckle (AWD)	66
	Wheel Lug Nuts	100
	Wheel Sensor	12
	Worm Thrust Bearing Adjuster	33

①— Inch lbs.

②— With vehicle weight on wheels.

Front Wheel Drive

NOTE: Refer To "Computer Relearn Procedures" Located In The Front Of This Manual When Battery Power To The Computer Has Been Interrupted.

INDEX

PRECAUTIONS

Battery Ground Cable

Prior to service, disconnect battery ground cable and isolate as required.

AXLE

REPLACE

Removal

1. Unlock steering column, raise and support vehicle.
2. Remove tie and wheel assembly, then the axle nut and washer, **Fig. 1.**
3. Remove upper control arm brake hose and wheel speed sensor brackets.
4. Remove brake caliper and support on wire.
5. Remove brake rotor.
6. Remove bottom shock absorber mounting nut and bolt, then compress shock absorber.
7. Strap frame to hoist and position suitable safety stand under lower control arm.
8. Support steering knuckle and lower control arm using suitable safety stand.
9. Disconnect drive axle from steering knuckle by placing suitable brass drift on shaft end and striking using suitable hammer. **Do not attempt to remove axle.**
10. Disconnect upper and lower control arm ball joints from steering knuckle as outlined under "Ball Joint, Replace" in "Front Suspension & Steering" section.
11. When lower control arm ball joint is loose from knuckle, simultaneously push axle shaft toward differential carrier.
12. Remove steering knuckle from drive axle. Support knuckle using piece of suitable wire.
13. Relieve lower control arm pressure by lowering safety stand.
14. Cover shock mounting bracket, lower control arm ball stud and other sharp edges using suitable shop towels to prevent damaging CV joint boots.

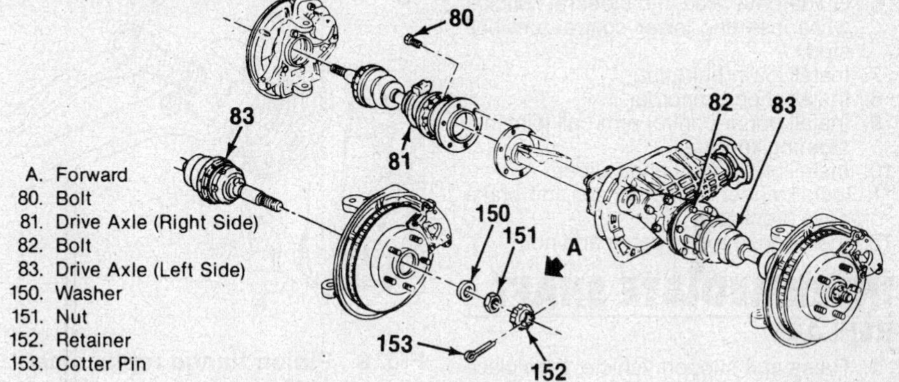

Fig. 1 Front drive axle replacement

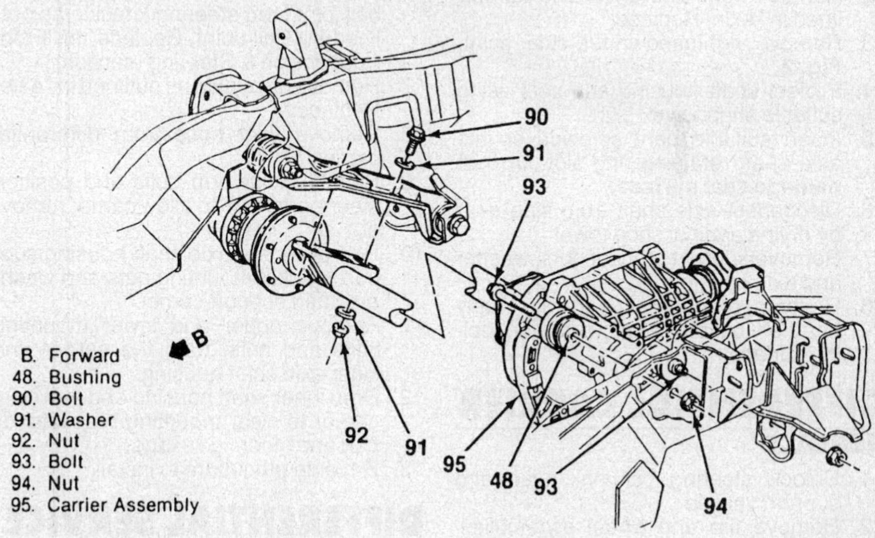

Fig. 2 Carrier & shaft assembly

15. Disconnect drive axle from front differential carrier by placing suitable brass drift or wood block on tripot housing and striking drift using suitable hammer.
16. Remove drive axle.

Installation

1. Cover shock mounting bracket, lower control arm ball stud and other sharp edges using suitable shop towels to prevent damaging CV joint boots.
2. Align shaft splines with differential housing and center drive axle into carrier.
3. Firmly push shaft straight into carrier until retaining rings sit in carrier.
4. Ensure retaining ring is properly set by pulling back on tripot housing.

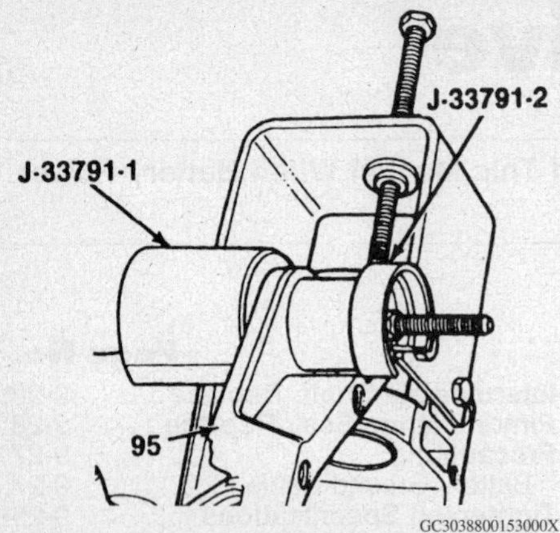

Fig. 3 Carrier bushing removal

5. Raise and support lower control arm.
6. Guide drive axle into steering knuckle while inserting lower control arm ball stud.
7. Install lower ball joint.
8. Install shock absorber.
9. Install upper control arm ball joint into steering knuckle.
10. Install brake rotor and caliper.
11. Install wheel speed sensor and brake hose brackets.
12. Install drive axle washer and nut.

INTERMEDIATE SHAFT

REPLACE

1. Raise and support vehicle, then place suitable container under shaft housing.
2. Remove righthand drive axle as outlined in "Axle, Replace."
3. Remove righthand inner axle shaft, **Fig. 2.**
4. Protect shaft housing and seal using suitable shop towel.
5. Insert suitable bent screwdriver into axle shaft retaining ring slot. **Do not damage seal surface.**
6. Disconnect axle shaft from side gear by prying against shop towel.
7. Remove support bracket nuts, washer and axle housing.
8. Reverse procedure to install. Apply bead of suitable sealer to carrier sealing surface.

DIFFERENTIAL CARRIER

REPLACE

1. Unlock steering column, raise and support vehicle.
2. Remove tire and wheel assemblies, then drain axle fluid into suitable container.
3. Mark propeller shaft and front axle flange for installation alignment.
4. Remove mounting bolts and disconnect propeller shaft from front axle. Support shaft out of way.
5. Remove upper control arm front brake hose and front wheel speed sensor brackets.

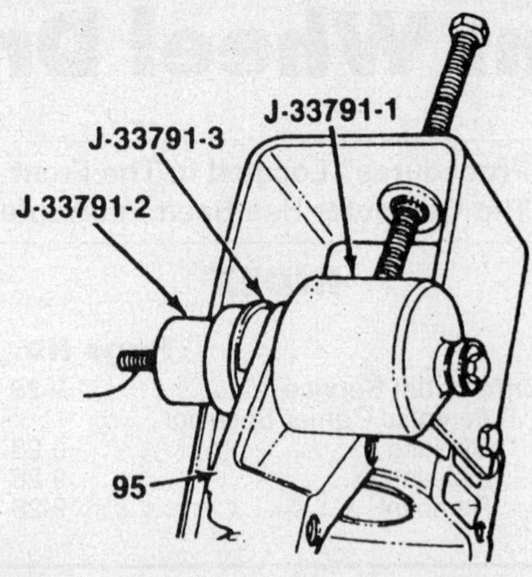

Fig. 4 Carrier bushing installation

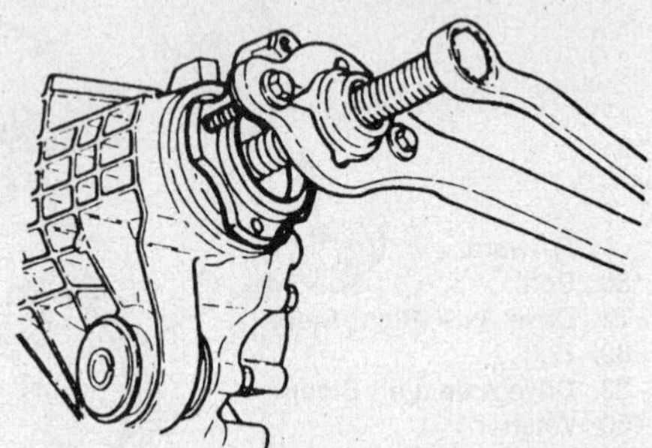

Fig. 6 Pinion flange replacement

6. Remove upper control arm ball joint cotter pin and stud nut, then the upper ball joint from steering knuckle as outlined in "Ball Joint, Replace" in "Front Suspension & Steering" section.
7. Remove drive axle as outlined in "Axle, Replace."
8. Remove vent hose from differential carrier.
9. Remove idler arm bolts and position steering linkage to allow carrier removal.
10. Remove inner axle shaft housing support bracket mounting nuts and washers, then support carrier.
11. Remove upper and lower mounting bolts and nuts, then the carrier and inner axle shaft housing.
12. Drop inner shaft housing end and twist carrier to clear mounting brackets, oil pan and steering linkage.
13. Reverse procedure to install.

DIFFERENTIAL SERVICE

Differential Carrier Bushing, Replace

REMOVAL

1. Remove differential carrier as outlined in "Differential Carrier, Replace."
2. Remove bushing using bushing replacement set tool No. J-33791, or equivalent, **Fig. 3.**

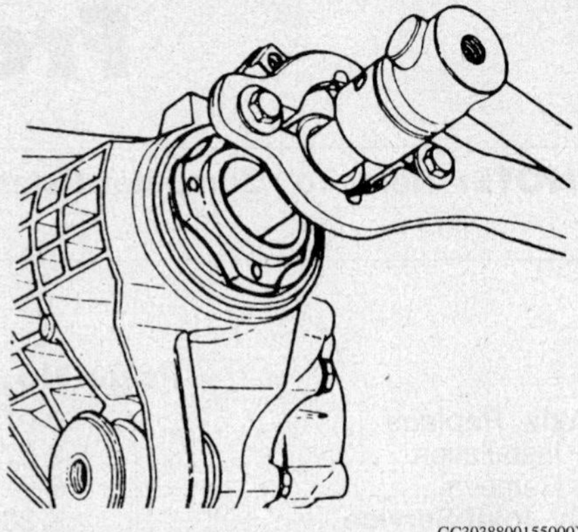

Fig. 5 Pinion nut preload measurement

INSTALLATION

1. Install bushing using tool No. J-33791, or equivalent, **Fig. 4.**
2. Ensure tool is positioned properly between bushing and carrier ear to prevent bushing from being pressed in too far.
3. Install differential carrier.

PINION FLANGE SEAL

REPLACE

1. Unlock steering column, raise and support vehicle.
2. Mark propeller shaft and front axle flange for installation alignment.
3. Remove mounting bolts and disconnect propeller shaft from front axle. Support shaft out of way.
4. Measure and record pinion shaft preload, **Fig. 5.**
5. Place suitable container under pinion.
6. Mark pinion flange, pinion shaft and pinion mounting nut for installation.
7. Hold pinion flange in place using companion flange holder tool No. J-8614-01, or equivalent, **Fig. 6.**
8. Remove mounting nuts, washers and pinion flange.
9. Drive pinion seal out of carrier using suitable blunt punch or drift.
10. Reverse procedure to install noting the following:
    a. Install pinion oil seal using pinion oil seal tool No. J-33782, or equivalent.
    b. Apply seal lubricant part No. 1050169, or equivalent, to outside of pinion flange and new seal sealing lip.

CV JOINT SERVICE

Front to "Front Wheel Drive Axle" chapter.

TIGHTENING SPECIFICATIONS

Year	Component	Torque Ft. Lbs.
2002–05	Axle Nut	160–200
	Axle Plug	22
	Brake Hose Bracket	12
	Carrier, Bolts	63
	Carrier, Nuts	54
	Carrier Output Shaft To Drive Axle	60
	Drive Axle Nut At Hub	147
	Drive Axle To Output Shaft	60
	Driveshaft Nut	160–200
	Front Propeller Shaft Flange To Front Axle	53
	Front Propeller Shaft Flange To Transfer Case	92
	Hub Nut	160–200
	Idler Arm	77
	Inner CV Joint Clamp	90
	Intermediate Shaft Housing To Frame Bracket	54
	Intermediate Shaft Housing To Carrier	36
	Propeller Shaft Flange To Front Axle	33
	Seal Clamp, Large	130
	Seal Clamp, Small	100
	Shock Absorber, Lower	46
	Righthand Side Axle Tube To Carrier	36
	Righthand Side Axle Tube To Frame Bracket	55
	Wheel Speed Sensor Bracket	12
	Wheel Lug	100
	Wheel Drive Shaft	147
	Yoke Strap	27

Wheel Alignment

INDEX

PRELIMINARY INSPECTION

Inspect the following components, adjust, repair or replace as required prior to performing front wheel alignment.

1. Inflate tires to cold specifications.
2. Ensure front tires are of same size, ply rating and load rating.
3. Inspect for excessive wheel bearing endplay.
4. Inspect for worn or damaged spindle ball joints.
5. Inspect steering gear mounting bolts for proper torque.
6. Inspect radius arm or bent or damaged condition.
7. Inspect radius arm to frame bushings for looseness or wear.
8. Inspect for loose or broken shackles.
9. Inspect for distorted or split jounce bumper.
10. Inspect suspension components for wear or damage.
11. Inspect vehicle ride height as outlined in "Vehicle Ride Height" section.
12. Ensure vehicle is on level surface when performing alignment procedure.

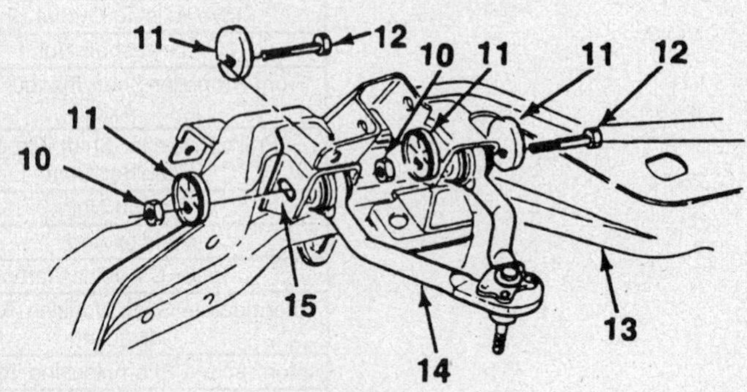

Fig. 1 Caster & camber adjustment. AWD models

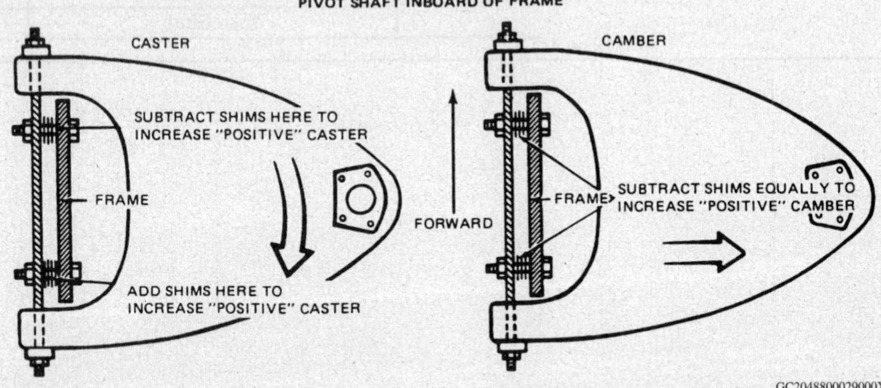

Fig. 2 Caster & camber adjustment. 2WD models

FRONT WHEEL ALIGNMENT

Caster & Camber

AWD MODELS

Before inspecting and adjusting caster and camber angles, jounce front bumper at least three times, to allow vehicle to return to normal trim height. This will prevent false readings.

Caster and camber adjustments are made by rotating the offset cam bolt and cam in slotted frame bracket to position control arm, **Fig. 1.** To adjust caster and camber, loosen upper control arm-to-frame mounting bolts. Rotate cam by rotating cam bolt head.

CAMBER

1. Hold cam bolt and loosen cam bolt nut.
2. Turn to obtain change equal to half of required correction.
3. Keep cam bolt in this position to maintain setting.
4. Obtain remaining half of correction by repeating previous steps to other cam bolt, turning cam lobe in same direction.

CASTER

1. Record camber reading.
2. Hold front cam bolt and loosen nut.
3. Turn nut to obtain change equal to ¼ of desired caster change.
4. At front cam bolt, positive camber change produces positive caster change and negative camber change produces negative caster change. Hold cam bolt in this position while tightening nut to maintain setting.
5. Hold rear cam bolt, loosen nut and turn cam bolt to return camber to setting noted by turning cam lobe in opposite direction.
6. Inspect caster setting. If not correct repeat adjustment procedure.
7. Ensure cam bolt head is secure and **torque** nut to 99 ft. lbs.

2WD MODELS

Before inspecting and adjusting caster and camber angles, jounce front bumper at least three times, to allow vehicle to return to normal trim height. This will prevent false readings.

Caster and camber adjustments are made by adding, subtracting or transfer of shims inserted between upper control arm shaft and frame bracket, **Fig. 2.**

1. To adjust caster and/or camber, loosen upper control arm shaft-to-frame nuts.
2. Add or subtract shims as required to

adjust and tighten nuts.

3. After adjustment, shim pack should have at least two threads of bolt exposed beyond nut.
4. Difference between front and rear shim packs must not be more than .4 inch.
5. When adjusting caster, proceed as follows:
   a. Transfer shims from front to rear or rear to front.
   b. Transfer of one shim from rear to front bolt will decrease positive caster.
6. When adjusting camber, proceed as follows:
   a. Change shims equally at both front and rear of shaft.
   b. Adding an equal number of shims at front and rear will decrease positive camber.
7. When performing either caster or camber adjustment, always tighten nut on thinner shim pack first to improve shaft-to-frame clamping force and torque retention.

Toe-In

1. Loosen clamp bolts at each end of steering tie rod adjusting sleeves.
2. Replace clamp bolts if breakaway is more than 80 inch lbs.
3. With steering wheel in straight ahead position, turn tie rod adjusting sleeves to obtain proper adjustment as follows:
   a. Decrease length of tie rod to increase toe-in.
   b. Increase length of tie rod to decrease toe-in.
4. After adjustment, ensure number of threads showing on inside of adjusting sleeves are equal (within three) and tie rod end stud lines up with steering knuckle.
5. Position tie rod clamps and sleeves, **Figs. 3 and 4.**
6. Centerline of clamp bolt must be within 30° of horizontal centerline.
7. **Torque** nuts to 18 ft. lbs.

VEHICLE RIDE HEIGHT

Refer to **Figs. 5 and 6** for vehicle ride height measurements and specifications.

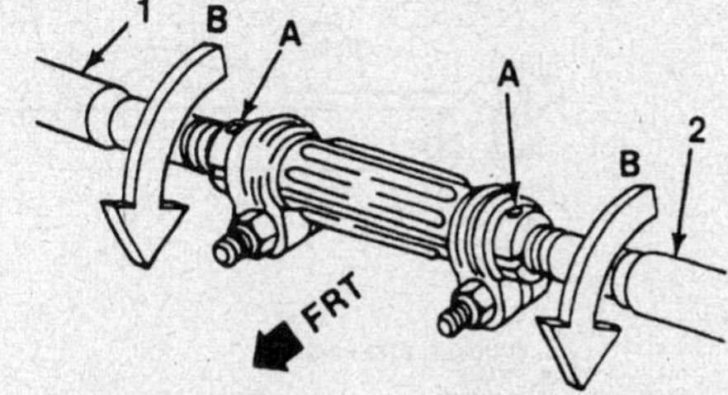

A. Clamp must be between, and clear of dimples before tightening nuts.
B. Rotate the tie rods rearward.
1. Inner Tie Rod 2. Outer Tie Rod

GC2048800031000X

Fig. 3 Tie rod adjuster tube

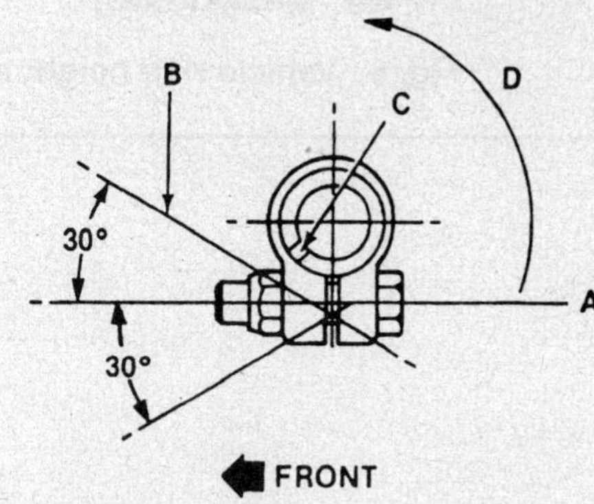

A. Horizontal
B. Centerline of bolt must be positioned within 30 degrees of the horizontal centerline.
C. Adjuster Tube Slot
D. Rearward Rotation

GC2048800032000X

Fig. 4 Clamp & sleeve orientation

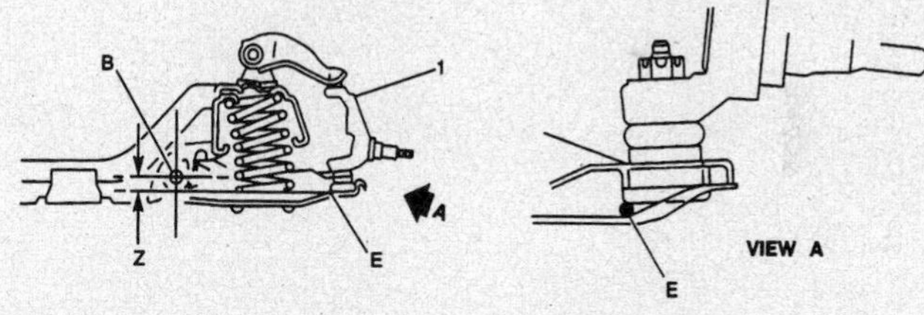

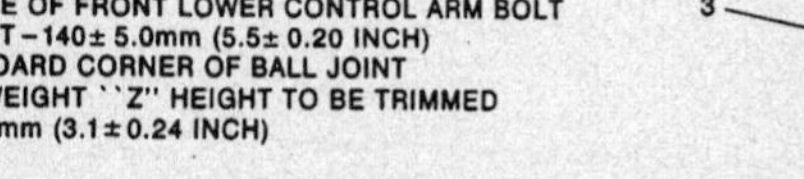

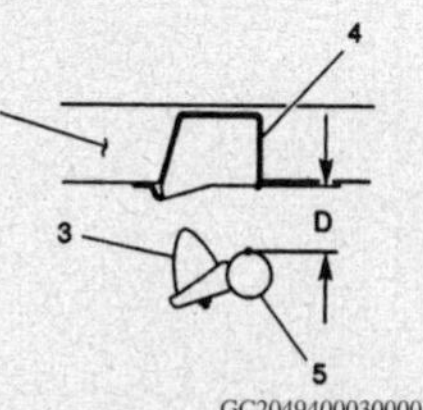

GC2049400030000X

Fig. 5 Vehicle ride height adjustment. 2WD models

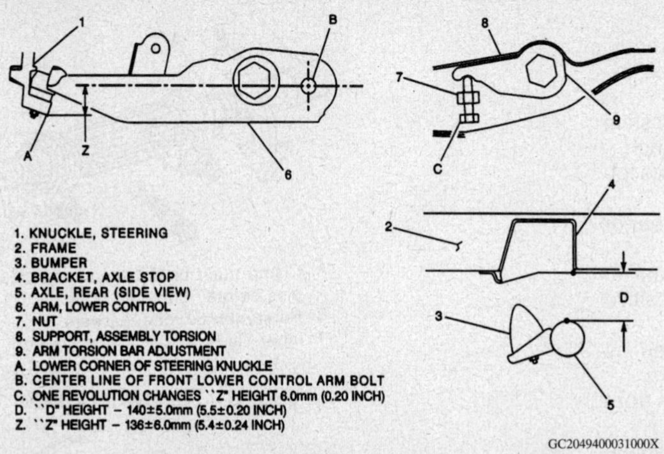

Fig. 6 Vehicle ride height adjustment. AWD models

MONTANA, SILHOUETTE & VENTURE

NOTE: Refer To The Rear Of This Manual For Vehicle Manufacturer's Special Service Tool Suppliers.

INDEX OF SERVICE OPERATIONS

Specifications

GENERAL ENGINE SPECIFICATIONS

Year	Engine Liter	Fuel System	Bore & Stroke	Compres-sion Ratio	Horsepower @ RPM	Torque Ft. Lbs. @ RPM	Normal Oil Pressure, psi
2002–04	3.4L	SFI	3.62 x 3.31	9.6	185 @ 5200	210 @ 4000	60①
2005–06	3.4L	SFI	3.62 x 3.31	9.6	185 @ 5200	210 @ 4000	60①
	3.5L w/AWD	SFI	3.70 x 3.31	9.8	201 @ 5600	240 @ 6000	30–45①
	3.5L w/FWD	SFI	3.70 x 3.31	9.8	196 @ 5600	213 @ 3200	30–45①
	3.9L	SFI	3.90 x 3.31	9.8	240 @ 6000	240 @ 4800	30–45①

① — At 1850 RPM w/10W–30 motor oil.

TUNE UP SPECIFICATIONS

The following specifications are published from the latest information available. This data should only be used in the absence of a decal affixed in the engine compartment.

Year/ Engine	Spark Plug Gap, Inch	Ignition Timing, °BTDC			Auto. Trans.		Fuel Pump Pressure psi.	Valve Lash, Inch
		Firing Order②	Auto. Trans.	Mark Location	Curb Idle Speed①	Fast Idle Speed①		
2002–05								
3.4L	.060	③	10⑧	⑦	⑥	⑥	48–55⑤	④
2005–06								
3.5L	.060	③	⑧	⑦	—	—	50–60⑤	④
3.9L	.040	③	⑧	⑦	—	—	50–60⑤	④

BTDC — Before Top Dead Center
D — Drive
N — Neutral
① — When inspecting idle speed, set parking brake & block drive wheels.
② — Before removing wires from distributor cap or coil unit, determine location of ignition wires, as position may have been altered from that outlined at end of this chart.
③ — Cylinder numbering from front of engine to rear, lefthand bank, 1-3-5; righthand bank, 2-4-6. Firing order, 1-2-3-4-5-6. Refer to **Fig. A**, for spark plug wire connections at coil unit.
④ — Equipped w/hydraulic valve lifters.
⑤ — Wrap shop towel around engine compartment fuel pressure fitting. Connect suitable fuel pressure gauge to fuel pressure fitting. Use suitable fuel pump test connector or scan tool to energize fuel pump & record fuel pressure reading.
⑥ — Controlled by Idle Air Control (IAC) valve.
⑦ — Equipped w/crankshaft position sensor.
⑧ — Non-adjustable.

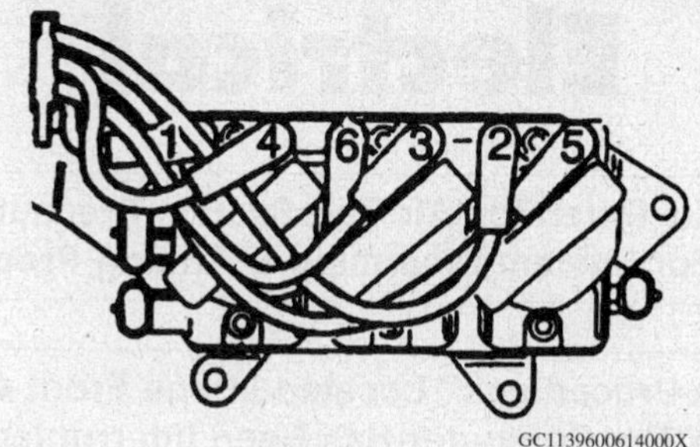

Fig. A

FRONT WHEEL ALIGNMENT SPECIFICATIONS

Year	Caster, Degree		Camber, Degree		Toe, Degree		Ball Joint
	Limit	Desired	Limit	Desired	Limits	Desired	
2002–04	+2.40 to +3.40	+2.90②	-.20 to -1.20	-.70③	+.20 to +.20	0	①
2005–06	+3.45 to +1.95	2.70②	-1.40 to +.10	-.65③	+.20 to +.20	0	①

① — Refer to "Ball Joint Inspection" in the "Front Suspension & Steering" section for ball joint specifications.

② — Cross caster, — .75° to +.75°, desired 0°.

③ — Cross camber, — .75° to +.75°, desired 0°.

REAR WHEEL ALIGNMENT SPECIFICATIONS

Year	Camber, Degree①		Toe, Degree①	Thrust Angle, Degrees
	Limits	Desired		
2002–04	-.75 to -1.25②	-1.00②	-.30 to +.30	—
2005–06	-1.50 to -.50②	-1.00②	-.30 to +.30	-.30 to +.30

① — Not adjustable.

② — Cross camber –.5° to +.5°.

FLUID CAPACITIES & COOLING SYSTEM DATA

Year	Engine Liter	Cooling Capacity Qts.		Recom-mended Coolant Type	Radiator Cap Relief Pressure, Lbs.	Thermo-stat Opening Temp. °F	Fuel Tank Gals.	Engine Oil Refill Qts.	Auto. Transaxle Qts.①	
		Less A/C	With A/C						Drain & Refill	Overhaul
2002–05	3.4L	④	④	Dexcool	15	195	③	4.5②	7.4	10⑤
2005–06	3.5L	—	⑥	Dexcool	15	195	③	4.0②	7.4	10
	3.9L	—	⑥	Dexcool	15	195	③	4.0②	7.4	10

① — Approximate, make final inspection w/dipstick.

② — Includes filter.

③ — Short wheelbase, 20 gals.; extended wheelbase, 25 gals.

④ — Less heavy duty cooling, front only, 9.6 qts.; front & rear, 11.9 qts. With heavy duty cooling, front only, 10.5 qts.; front & rear, 13.2 qts.

⑤ — AWD, pan removal 7.8 qts., and 10.4 qts., for overhaul; FWD, pan removal 7.4 qts., and 10.0 qts., for overhaul.

⑥ — With front A/C, 11.3 qts.; with front/rear A/C, 12.8 qts.

LUBRICANT DATA

Year	Model	Lubricant Type		
		Automatic Transaxle	Power Steering	Brake System
2002–06	All	Dexron III/VI	①②	DOT 3

① — Power steering fluid meeting GM specification 9985010.

② — In cold, use No. 12345867 or 12345866 (system should be drained, flushed, refilled & bled before using these fluids). Equivalent fluids may be used.

Electrical

NOTE: On Air Bag Equipped Models, Refer To "Air Bag System Precautions" Located In The Front Of This Manual For System Disarming & Arming Procedures.

NOTE: Refer To "Computer Relearn Procedures" Located In The Front Of This Manual When Battery Power To The Computer Has Been Interrupted.

INDEX

PRECAUTIONS

Air Bag Systems

Refer to "Air Bag System Precautions" in the front of this manual for system disarming and arming procedures.

Battery Ground Cable

Prior to service, disconnect battery ground cable and isolate as required.

FUSE PANEL & FLASHER LOCATION

The fuse panel is located at the righthand end of the instrument panel and is accessible through the righthand door opening. The turn signal/hazard flasher is located on the righthand side of the engine compartment, in the underhood electrical center.

RELAY CENTER LOCATION

The relay center is located on the righthand side of the engine compartment, in the underhood electrical center.

FUEL PUMP RELAY LOCATION

The fuel pump relay is located on the righthand side of the engine compartment, in the underhood electrical center.

STARTER

REPLACE

1. Raise and support vehicle.
2. Disconnect starter electrical connectors.
3. Remove converter cover.
4. Remove mounting bolts and shims, then the starter motor.
5. Reverse procedure to install. **Torque** starter motor mounting bolts to 35 ft. lbs.

COIL PACK

REPLACE

1. Disconnect spark plug wires and record positions.
2. Remove coil pack mounting screws and ignition coil assembly.
3. Reverse procedure to install. **Torque** mounting screws to 40 inch lbs.

IGNITION COIL MODULE

REPLACE

1. Remove coil pack assemblies as outlined in "Coil Pack, Replace."
2. Remove mounting bolts and ignition coil module.
3. Reverse procedure to install. **Torque** mounting bolts to 40 inch lbs.

IGNITION LOCK

REPLACE

1. Remove steering wheel as outlined in "Steering Wheel, Replace."
2. Remove tilt lever.
3. Set steering column in holding fixture, tool No. J-41352, or equivalent.
4. Remove mounting screws and lower steering column shroud.
5. Remove mounting screws, then lift upper steering column shroud to access lock cylinder access hole.
6. Insert suitable bent tip awl into access hole and turn ignition lock to Start position.
7. Push down on cylinder retainer with awl and release ignition lock to Run position.
8. Remove cylinder from lock module.
9. Reverse procedure to install, noting the following:
   a. Align lock module assembly positioning and locking tab slots with ignition lock position and locking tabs.
   b. Push cylinder into assembly until tab locks against module.
   c. **Torque** shroud mounting screws to 31 inch lbs.

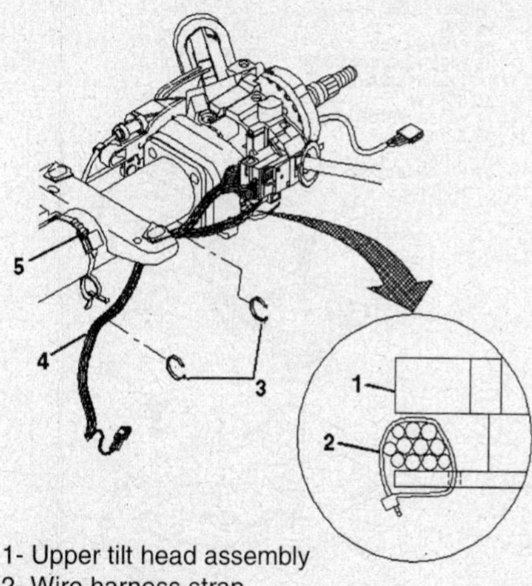

1- Upper tilt head assembly
2- Wire harness strap
3- Wire harness straps
4- Wire harness assembly
5- Wire harness strap

GC6040100316000X

Fig. 1 Steering column wiring harness

IGNITION SWITCH

REPLACE

1. Remove steering column upper and lower trim covers.
2. Remove wire harness assembly from wire harness strap, **Fig. 1.**
3. Remove wire harness retaining straps and wire harness assembly.
4. Remove wire harness strap from upper tilt head assembly.
5. Slide turn signal switch assembly connectors out of bulkhead connector.
6. Pull PASSKEY off of electronic lock module assembly, **Fig. 2.**
7. Disconnect key alarm connector from electronic lock module assembly, **Fig. 3.**
8. Remove ignition key alarm switch assembly attaching screws, then the switch assembly from steering column.
9. Reverse procedure to install.

NEUTRAL SAFETY SWITCH

REPLACE

1. Place shift lever in Neutral position.
2. Disconnect shift cable from selector shaft lever.
3. Remove lever mounting nut from selector shaft, then the lever.
4. Disconnect electrical connectors, then remove mounting screws and switch.
5. Lift switch off selector shaft.
6. Reverse procedure to install, noting the following:
   a. Ensure transaxle is in Neutral position.
   b. Install transaxle range switch with internal alignment pin. **Do not turn switch until it has been installed.**
   c. **Torque** switch mounting bolts to 18 ft. lbs.
   d. **Torque** selector shaft lever nut to 15 ft. lbs., while counter holding arm. **Do not allow shaft to turn to stop while tightening nut, internal transmission damage could occur.**

TRANSAXLE RANGE SWITCH

REPLACE

Refer to “Neutral Safety Switch, Replace” for transaxle range switch replacement procedure.

HEADLAMP SWITCH

REPLACE

1. Remove instrument cluster trim panel from instrument panel as outlined in “Instrument Cluster, Replace.”
2. Press release clips to remove headlamp switch from instrument panel.
3. Disconnect connector from headlamp switch.
4. Reverse procedure to install.

STOP LIGHT SWITCH

REPLACE

1. Remove lower lefthand side sound insulator from instrument panel.
2. Disconnect stop light switch electrical connectors, **Fig. 4.**
3. Press in on mounting clips, then remove stop light switch.
4. Reverse procedure to install, noting the following:
   a. Push and hold brake pedal depressed, then insert fully extended switch into bracket.
   b. Inspect switch operation.

MULTI-FUNCTION SWITCH

REPLACE

1. Ensure switch lever is in Off position, then remove steering wheel as outlined in “Steering Wheel, Replace.”
2. Remove mounting screws, then the lower and upper steering column shrouds.
3. Disconnect steering column electrical connectors.
4. Disconnect multi-function switch connectors from steering column electrical connector.
5. Remove mounting screws and multi-function switch.
6. Reverse procedure to install. **Torque** switch mounting screws to 62 inch lbs.

TURN SIGNAL SWITCH

REPLACE

Refer to “Multi-Function Switch, Replace” for turn signal switch replacement procedure.

DIMMER SWITCH

REPLACE

Refer to “Multi-Function Switch, Replace” for dimmer switch replacement procedure.

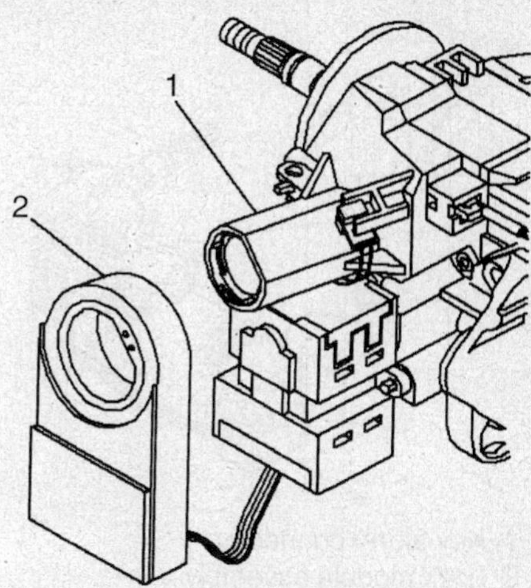

1- Lock module assembly
2- Passkey

GC6040100317000X

Fig. 2 Passkey removal

STEERING WHEEL

REPLACE

1. Remove driver air bag module as outlined in “Air Bag Systems” chapter.
2. Remove steering shaft nut, then mark shaft and wheel for assembly alignment.
3. Loosen steering wheel mounting nut and position nut flush with steering column shaft end.
4. Install puller tool No. J-1859-A, with legs tool No. J-42587, or equivalents, onto steering wheel and pull steering wheel loose from shaft.
5. Remove mounting nut and steering wheel.
6. Reverse procedure to install. **Torque** steering wheel mounting nut to 33 ft. lbs.

INSTRUMENT CLUSTER

REPLACE

1. Open ashtray and remove instrument panel trim plate mounting screws.
2. Remove instrument panel accessory trim plate upper tabs with suitable small screwdriver.
3. Disconnect electrical connectors and remove trim plate.
4. Remove mounting screws and cluster.
5. Disconnect electrical connectors.
6. Reverse procedure to install, noting the following:
   a. **Torque** cluster mounting screws to 22 inch lbs.
   b. **Torque** trim plate mounting screws to 18 inch lbs.

RADIO

REPLACE

1. Open ashtray and remove instrument panel trim plate mounting screws.
2. Remove instrument panel accessory trim plate upper tabs with suitable small screwdriver.

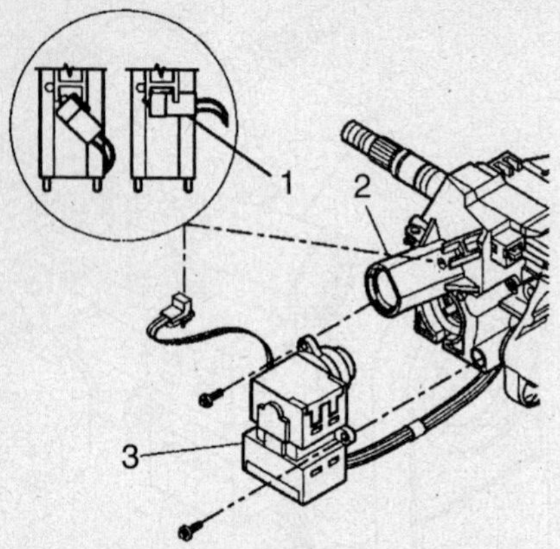

1- Key alarm connector
2- Lock module assembly
3- Ignition key & alarm switch assembly

GC6040100318000X

Fig. 3 Lock module & ignition key alarm switch

3. Disconnect electrical connectors and remove trim plate.
4. Remove radio mounting screws.
5. Remove radio by pulling straight out.
6. Disconnect electrical connectors and antenna.
7. Reverse procedure to install, noting the following:
   a. **Torque** radio mounting screws to 22 inch lbs.
   b. **Torque** trim plate mounting screws to 18 inch lbs.

WIPER MOTOR

REPLACE

Front

REMOVAL

1. Disconnect wiper motor electrical connector, **Fig. 5.**
2. Loosen mounting screws, then remove link rod from motor arm ball stud.
3. Loosen wiper motor arm mounting screw. Do not remove.
4. Pry wiper motor arm up with suitable pry bar while tapping on mounting screw with suitable soft face hammer until arm is loosened on shaft.
5. Remove mounting screw and arm.
6. Remove mounting screws and motor.

INSTALLATION

1. Install motor to wiper drive system module.
2. **Torque** mounting screws to 62 inch lbs.
3. Connect motor electrical connector, then place ignition switch in ACCY position.
4. Turn wiper switch to Pulse position and allow motor to run.
5. Turn ignition switch Off when wiper motor is in inner wipe position. **Do not allow wiper motor shaft to turn during crank arm installation.**
6. Position wiper arm on shaft so that gap of .157–.315 inch is maintained between arm and tab of wiper drive system module mounting plate, **Fig. 6.**
7. Install wiper arm mounting screw and **torque** to 10–12 ft. lbs.
8. Install wiper link rod to ball stud on wiper arm and **torque** mounting screws to 44 inch lbs.

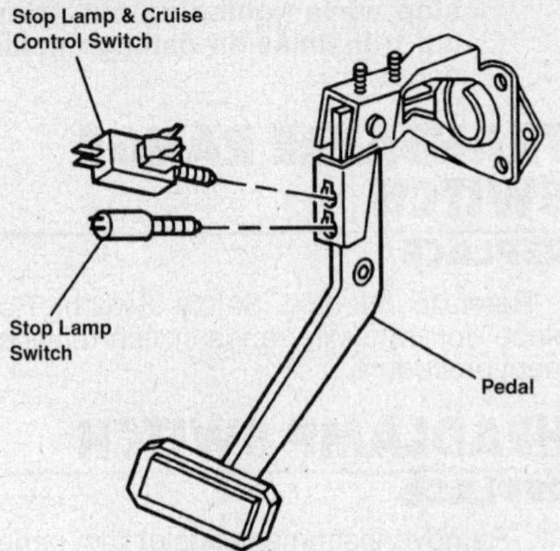

GC9048800029000X

Fig. 4 Stop light switch replacement

Rear

1. Remove shaft cap and nut, then the wiper arm.
2. Remove wiper shaft housing nut, spacer and seal.
3. Open liftgate and remove trim panel by prying loose with suitable trim panel clip removal tool.
4. Disconnect motor electrical connector.
5. Remove mounting bracket screws and motor.
6. Remove motor to bracket mounting screw, then the motor.
7. Remove shaft housing seal and spacer, then the rubber mount ring.
8. Reverse procedure to install, noting the following:
   a. **Torque** motor to bracket mounting bolt to 71 inch lbs., and bracket to liftgate mounting bolts to 49 inch lbs.
   b. Ensure wiper shaft housing seals are properly placed and that wiper motor is in park position before installing wiper arm and blade.
   c. **Torque** wiper shaft housing nut to 53 inch lbs., and wiper shaft nut to 18 inch lbs.

WIPER TRANSMISSION

REPLACE

1. Remove wiper module as outlined in "Wiper Module, Replace."
2. Remove wiper motor as outlined in "Wiper Motor, Replace."
3. Reverse procedure to install.

WIPER MODULE

REPLACE

1. Remove wiper arm shaft cap and mounting nut.
2. Remove wiper arm from shaft using puller tool No. J-6627-4, or equivalent.

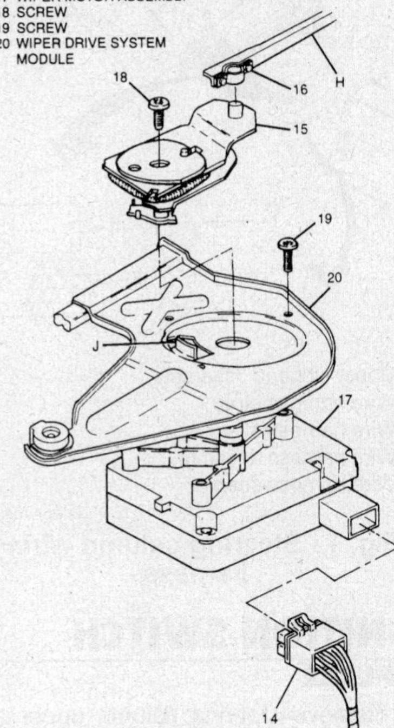

GC9029700471000X

Fig. 5 Front wiper motor replacement

3. Remove HVAC air inlet screen.
4. Disconnect motor electrical connector and remove top washer fluid reservoir mounting screws.
5. Loosen washer reservoir bottom mounting screw and rotate reservoir forward.
6. Remove module assembly mounting bolts.
7. Pull center mount from socket and rotate assembly from body.
8. Remove rubber mounts from wiper module, **Fig. 7.**
9. Reverse procedure to install, noting the following:
   a. Ensure motor is in inner wipe position before installing wiper arms and blades.
   b. Install wiper arms and blades in their normal bottom of stroke (not depressed park) position.
   c. **Torque** module mounting bolts to 90 inch lbs.
   d. **Torque** wiper shaft nut to 35 ft. lbs.

BLOWER MOTOR

REPLACE

Front

1. Remove righthand under dash insulator panel.
2. Remove blower motor cooling tube, then disconnect electrical connector.
3. Remove mounting screws and blower motor.
4. Reverse procedure to install. **Torque** mounting screws to 15 ft. lbs.

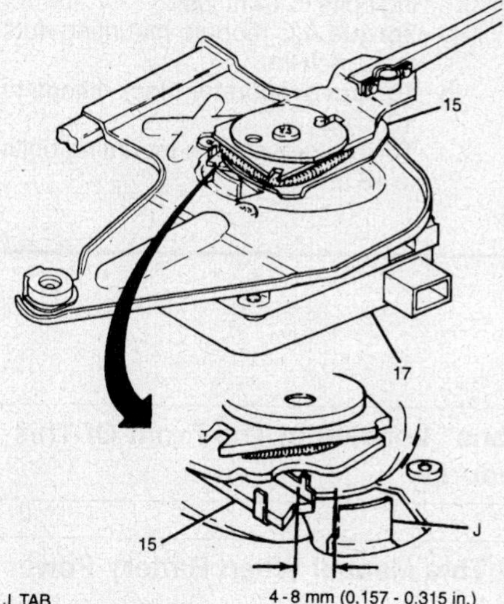

Fig. 6 Front wiper crank arm alignment

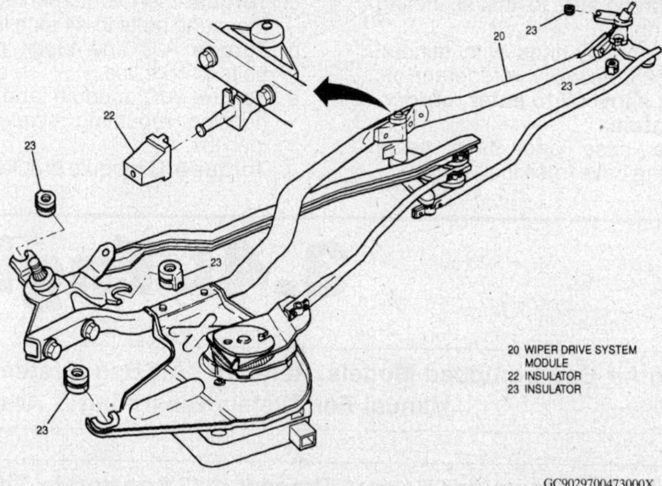

Fig. 7 Wiper module mounting replacement

Rear

1. Remove lefthand rear trim access panel.
2. Disconnect motor electrical connector.
3. Lift tabs and remove motor by turning counterclockwise.
4. Reverse procedure to install.

CABIN AIR FILTER

REPLACE

1. Open instrument panel compartment door.
2. Remove door from rear of compartment.
3. Open HVAC module assembly access door.
4. Remove righthand cabin air filter from HVAC module.
5. Slide lefthand cabin air filter to HVAC module opening.
6. Remove lefthand cabin air filter from HVAC module.
7. Reverse procedure to install.

HEATER CORE

REPLACE

Front

1. Remove air cleaner and ducts, then drain cooling system into suitable container.
2. Remove wiper linkage, then disconnect heater core hoses.
3. Pry console storage compartment loose with suitable flat tool.
4. **On models equipped with CD player,** remove CD player.
5. **On all models,** remove mounting screws and console.
6. Remove both lower dash insulator panels.
7. Remove mounting screws and heater cover.
8. Remove heater core mounting and line clamp screws.
9. Remove heater core and seals. Record seal positions for assembly.
10. Reverse procedure to install.

Rear

Refer to "Evaporator Core, Replace" for heater core replacement procedure.

EVAPORATOR CORE

REPLACE

Cap or tape A/C refrigerant lines and openings immediately.

Front

1. Drain cooling system into suitable container.
2. Recover refrigerant as outlined in "Air Conditioning" chapter.
3. Remove instrument panel as outlined in "Dash Panel Service" chapter.
4. Remove hinge pillar crossbeam tie bar.
5. Disconnect A/C lines at evaporator lock fitting.
6. Disconnect heater core hoses.
7. Remove HVAC unit mounting nuts and bolts.
8. Disconnect vacuum hoses and electrical connectors.
9. Remove HVAC module.
10. Disconnect HVAC module vacuum harness from case.
11. Remove air inlet housing and HVAC actuators.
12. Remove A/C module mounting screws.
13. Release retaining tab, then separate upper and lower modules.
14. Remove A/C module seal, then the evaporator core.
15. Remove core seals and water filter.
16. Reverse procedure to install, noting the following:
    a. Install new filter and seals.
    b. **Torque** A/C module and air inlet housing mounting screws to 13 inch lbs.
    c. **Torque** A/C module bracket mounting bolts to 14 ft. lbs.
    d. **Torque** A/C module mounting nuts to 89 inch lbs.
    e. **Torque** evaporator block fittings to 12 ft. lbs.
    f. **Torque** crossbeam mounting bolts to 18 ft. lbs.

Rear

1. Drain cooling system into suitable container.
2. Recover refrigerant as outlined in "Air Conditioning" chapter.
3. Remove instrument panel as outlined in "Dash Panel Service" chapter.
4. Remove hinge pillar crossbeam tie bar.
5. Disconnect A/C lines at evaporator lock fitting.
6. Disconnect heater core hoses.
7. Remove HVAC unit mounting nuts and bolts.
8. Disconnect vacuum hoses and electrical connectors.
9. Remove HVAC module.
10. Raise and support vehicle.
11. Remove A/C line block fitting.
12. Separate line block fitting and remove O-ring seal.
13. Lower vehicle and remove lefthand rear quarter trim panel.
14. Remove thermal expansion valve block fitting nut.
15. Pull lines up from floor.
16. Carefully remove thermal expansion valve A/C lines.
17. Remove O-ring seals.
18. Remove mounting bolts and thermal expansion valve.
19. Remove O-ring seals.
20. Disconnect mode actuator vacuum lines.
21. Remove actuator by unsnapping retainer tab.
22. Remove mounting screws and HVAC module base cover.
23. Remove mounting screws and separate case halves.
24. Remove evaporator core and insulator seal.

25. Reverse procedure to install, noting the following:
    a. Lightly coat O-rings with mineral base 525 viscosity refrigerant oil. **Do not allow oil to enter refrigerant system.**
    b. **Torque** case and base cover mounting bolts to 14 inch lbs.
    c. **Torque** thermal expansion valve mounting bolts to 44 inch lbs.
    d. **Torque** A/C line block mounting bolts to 15 ft. lbs.
    e. **Torque** A/C module and air inlet housing mounting screws to 13 inch lbs.
    f. **Torque** A/C module bracket mounting bolts to 14 ft. lbs.
    g. **Torque** A/C module mounting nuts to 89 inch lbs.
    h. **Torque** evaporator block fittings to 12 ft. lbs.
    i. **Torque** crossbeam mounting bolts to 18 ft. lbs.

3.4L Engine

NOTE: On Air Bag Equipped Models, Refer To "Air Bag System Precautions" Located In The Front Of This Manual For System Disarming & Arming Procedures.

NOTE: Refer To "Computer Relearn Procedures" Located In The Front Of This Manual When Battery Power To The Computer Has Been Interrupted.

NOTE: For Procedures Not Found In This Section, Refer To The "3.4L Engine" Section In The "Aztek & Rendezvous" Chassis Chapter.

INDEX

PRECAUTIONS

Air Bag Systems

Refer to "Air Bag System Precautions" in the front of this manual for system disarming and arming procedures.

Battery Ground Cable

Prior to service, disconnect battery ground cable and isolate as required.

Fuel System Pressure Relief

1. Loosen fuel filler cap to discharge tank pressure.
2. Connect fuel pressure gauge tool No. J-34730-1A, or equivalent, to fuel pressure connection. Wrap shop towel around connection while connecting fuel pressure gauge in order to avoid fuel spillage.
3. Install bleed hose into an approved container and open valve in order to bleed fuel system pressure.
4. Drain any fuel remaining in fuel pressure gauge into suitable container.

COMPRESSION PRESSURE

1. Operate engine until normal operating temperature is reached.
2. Turn engine off, then remove Powertrain Control Module (PCM) and ignition fuses.
3. Disconnect ignition coil positive wire plug from ignition coil.
4. Disconnect fuel injector electrical connector.
5. Remove all spark plugs.
6. Remove throttle body air duct.
7. Block throttle plate wide open.
8. Ensure battery is fully charged.
9. With compression gauge at zero, crank engine through four compression strokes.
10. Record compression at all cylinders.
11. Minimum compression recorded in any one cylinder should not be less than 70% of highest cylinder.
12. No cylinder should read less than 100 psi.

ENGINE MOUNT

REPLACE

1. Remove throttle body air inlet duct.
2. Remove engine mount strut bolts and nuts from lefthand and righthand sides, **Fig. 1.**
3. Raise and support vehicle.
4. Remove catalytic converter pipe from righthand side exhaust manifold.
5. Remove righthand front tire and wheel assembly, then the righthand engine splash shield.
6. Remove engine mount bracket to oil pan bolts.

7. Insert suitable wood block between oil pan and suitable utility stand, then raise oil pan.
8. Remove upper mounting nuts and mount bracket.
9. Reverse procedure to install.

ENGINE

REPLACE

1. Unlock tube/oil fill cap by twisting counterclockwise.
2. Remove fuel injector sight shield by lifting front and sliding tab out of engine bracket.
3. Replace tube/oil fill cap.
4. Remove throttle body air inlet duct.
5. Remove cruise control and throttle cables, then position away from engine.
6. Drain engine coolant into suitable container.
7. Disconnect radiator and heater hoses.
8. Remove engine mount struts as outlined in "Engine Mount, Replace."
9. Relieve fuel pressure as outlined in "Precautions."
10. Disconnect fuel rail lines.
11. Disconnect engine wiring harness connectors.
12. Remove brake booster vacuum hose.
13. Disconnect transaxle shift selector cable.
14. Raise and support vehicle, then drain engine oil into suitable container.
15. Disconnect wiring harness grounds.
16. Disconnect three-way catalytic converter exhaust pipe from righthand side exhaust manifold.
17. Remove front tire and wheel assemblies, then engine splash shields.
18. Remove stabilizer bar links from lower control arms as outlined in "Front Suspension & Steering."
19. Remove tie rod ends from steering knuckles as outlined in "Front Suspension & Steering."
20. Remove lower ball joints from knuckles as outlined in "Front Suspension & Steering."
21. Drain transaxle fluid into suitable container, then disconnect transaxle cooler lines and bracket.
22. Disconnect drive axles and outlined in "Front Wheel Drive Axles" then secure to steering knuckle and struts.
23. Remove intermediate shaft from steering gear.
24. Position universal engine support table tool No. J-39580, or equivalent, then lower vehicle until frame contacts table.
25. Remove frame mounting bolts.
26. Separate powertrain and frame from vehicle by raise vehicle.
27. Remove engine to transaxle mounting bolts and studs.
28. Remove torque converter mounting bolts.
29. Remove engine from transaxle/frame to suitable engine stand.
30. Reverse procedure to install, noting the following:
    a. Install new frame bolts.
    b. Ensure intermediate shaft seats to steering gear before installing pinch bolt.

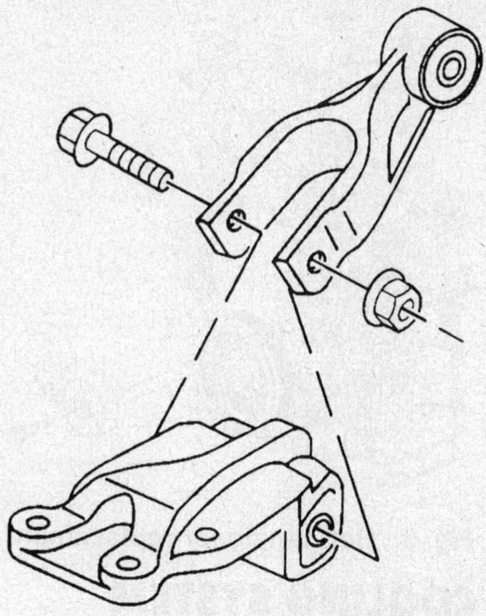

Fig. 1 Engine mount strut replacement

    c. Install new throttle cable.

INTAKE MANIFOLD

REPLACE

Refer to the "3.4L Engine" section of the "Aztek & Rendezvous" chassis chapter.

EXHAUST MANIFOLD

REPLACE

Refer to the "3.4L Engine" section of the "Aztek & Rendezvous" chassis chapter.

CYLINDER HEAD

REPLACE

Refer to the "3.4L Engine" section of the "Aztek & Rendezvous" chassis chapter.

VALVE COVER

REPLACE

Refer to the "3.4L Engine" section of the "Aztek & Rendezvous" chassis chapter.

CAMSHAFT LOBE LIFT SPECIFICATIONS

Refer to the "3.4L Engine" section of the "Aztek & Rendezvous" chassis chapter.

VALVE ADJUSTMENT

This vehicle is equipped with hydraulic valve lifters.

ROCKER ARMS

REPLACE

Refer to the "3.4L Engine" section of the "Aztek & Rendezvous" chassis chapter.

VALVE GUIDES

Refer to the "3.4L Engine" section of the "Aztek & Rendezvous" chassis chapter.

HYDRAULIC LIFTERS

REPLACE

Refer to the "3.4L Engine" section of the "Aztek & Rendezvous" chassis chapter.

CRANKSHAFT DAMPER

REPLACE

Refer to the "3.4L Engine" section of the "Aztek & Rendezvous" chassis chapter.

FRONT COVER

REPLACE

Refer to the "3.4L Engine" section of the "Aztek & Rendezvous" chassis chapter.

FRONT COVER SEAL

REPLACE

Refer to the "3.4L Engine" section of the "Aztek & Rendezvous" chassis chapter.

TIMING CHAIN

REPLACE

Refer to the "3.4L Engine" section of the "Aztek & Rendezvous" chassis chapter.

CAMSHAFT

REPLACE

Refer to the "3.4L Engine" section of the "Aztek & Rendezvous" chassis chapter.

PISTON & ROD ASSEMBLY

Refer to the "3.4L Engine" section of the "Aztek & Rendezvous" chassis chapter.

PISTONS, PINS & RINGS

Refer to the "3.4L Engine" section of the "Aztek & Rendezvous" chassis chapter.

MAIN & ROD BEARINGS

Refer to the "3.4L Engine" section of the "Aztek & Rendezvous" chassis chapter.

CRANKSHAFT SEAL

REPLACE

Refer to the "3.4L Engine" section of the "Aztek & Rendezvous" chassis chapter.

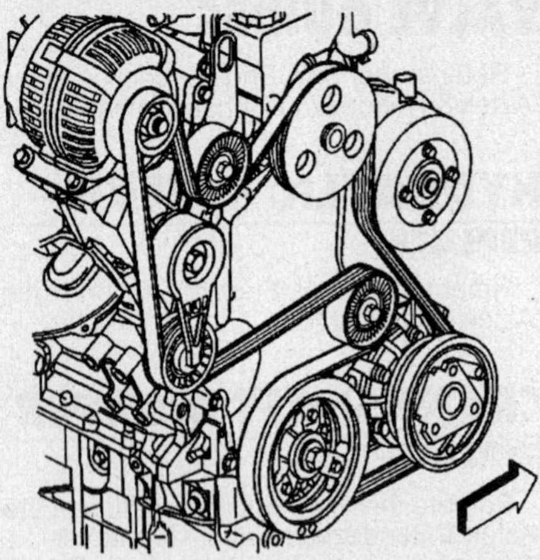
GC1069901021000X

Fig. 2 Serpentine belt routing

CRANKSHAFT REAR OIL SEAL

REPLACE

Refer to the "3.4L Engine" section of the "Aztek & Rendezvous" chassis chapter.

OIL PAN

REPLACE

Refer to the "3.4L Engine" section of the "Aztek & Rendezvous" chassis chapter.

OIL PUMP

REPLACE

Refer to the "3.4L Engine" section of the "Aztek & Rendezvous" chassis chapter.

OIL PUMP SERVICE

Refer to the "3.4L Engine" section of the "Aztek & Rendezvous" chassis chapter.

SERPENTINE DRIVE BELT

Belt Routing

Refer to **Fig. 2** for serpentine drive belt routing.

Belt Replacement

1. Release belt pressure by rotating tensioner.
2. Remove serpentine drive belt.
3. Reverse procedure to install.

Tensioner Replacement

1. Remove serpentine drive belt as outlined in "Serpentine Drive Belt."
2. Remove mounting bolt and tensioner, **Fig. 3.**
3. Reverse procedure to install.

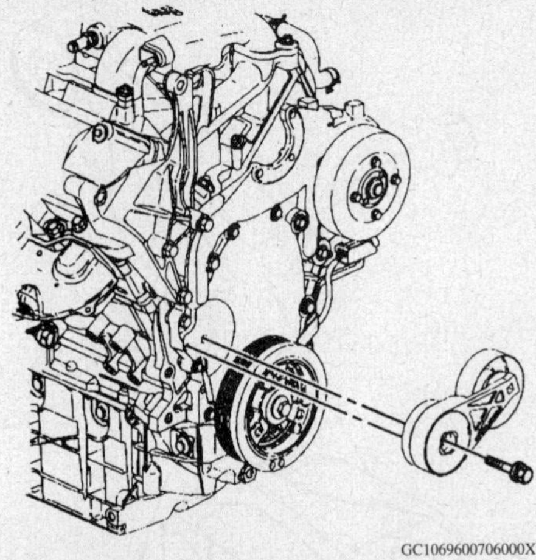
GC1069600706000X

Fig. 3 Belt tensioner replacement

COOLING SYSTEM BLEED

These engines do not require a specified bleed procedure. After filling cooling system, run engine to operating temperature with radiator/pressure cap off. Air will then be automatically bled through cap opening.

THERMOSTAT

REPLACE

1. Remove air cleaner and duct assembly.
2. Drain coolant into suitable container to below thermostat level.
3. Remove mounting nuts and exhaust crossover pipe.
4. Remove radiator hose from thermostat housing.
5. Remove mounting bolts, thermostat housing and gasket.
6. Remove thermostat.
7. Reverse procedure to install. Apply suitable RTV sealer to thermostat housing mounting bolt threads.

WATER PUMP

REPLACE

Refer to the "3.4L Engine" section of the "Aztek & Rendezvous" chassis chapter.

RADIATOR

REPLACE

1. Remove air cleaner and duct assembly.
2. Drain coolant into suitable container.
3. Loosen engine mount strut to engine mount strut bracket bolts.
4. Loosen engine mount strut bracket brace bolts from upper radiator support bracket.
5. Remove mounting bolts on radiator upper support and position engine mount strut and bracket to rear.
6. Ensure ignition switch is in Off position, then disconnect cooling fan harness electrical connector.
7. Remove cooling fan shroud mounting bolts.

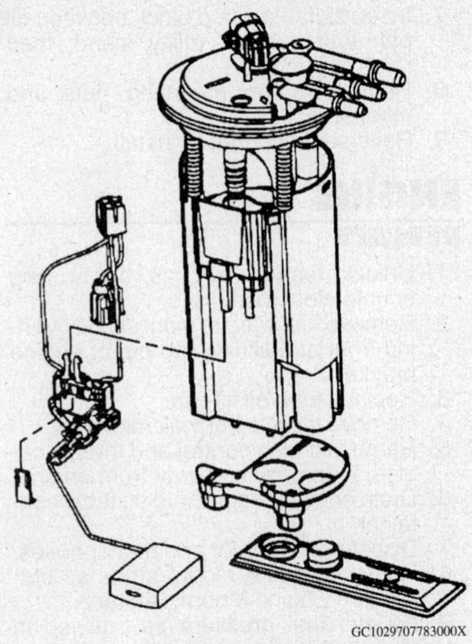
GC1029707783000X

Fig. 4 Fuel level meter/pump assembly

8. Remove lines from transmission oil cooler retainers.
9. Position upper radiator support wiring harness to gain access.
10. Remove cooling fans with shroud.
11. Remove upper and lower radiator hose.
12. Disconnect electrical connector and remove coolant level sensor.
13. Disconnect transaxle oil cooler lines from radiator.
14. Remove mounting bolts, brackets and radiator.
15. Reverse procedure to install.

FUEL PUMP

REPLACE

1. Relieve fuel system pressure as outlined in "Precautions."
2. Loosen fuel tank fill cap.
3. Place suitable container under tank fuel filler pipe connection , then loosen clamp and remove filler pipe.
4. Draw fuel from tank into container.
5. Raise and support vehicle.
6. **Provide addition vehicle support at front of vehicle. Chain vehicle rear frame to hoist pads.**
7. Disconnect quick-connect fittings at fuel filter inlet, return line near fuel filter and fuel tank EVAP pipe canister.
8. Remove EVAP fuel filter pipe.
9. Loosen hose clamp and remove fuel tank filler pipe.
10. Loosen hose clamp and remove fuel tank filler vent hose.
11. Support tank with suitable lifting equipment, then remove tank mounting straps.
12. Disconnect fuel sender and fuel tank pressure sensor electrical connectors.
13. Remove fuel tank and place on suitable work surface.
14. Clean all pipe and hose connections, as well as area surrounding connections.

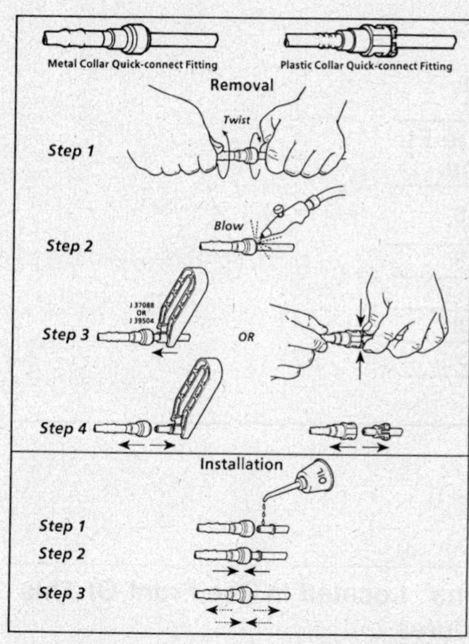

GC1028800045000X

Fig. 5 Quick-connect fittings

15. Disconnect fuel sensor assembly quick-connect fittings.
16. Remove sender assembly mounting nut with spanner wrench tool No. J-39348, or equivalent.
17. Remove sender with O-ring.
18. Mark filter position on pump, **Fig. 4.**
19. Support reservoir with one hand and pry filter off reservoir with suitable screwdriver.
20. Reverse procedure to install, noting the following:
    a. Use new fuel pump filter screen and level meter O-ring.
    b. Ensure filter does not block full travel of float arm.
    c. **Do not fold or twist filter when installing sender.**
    d. **Replace kinked nylon fuel lines. Do not straighten.**

FUEL FILTER

REPLACE

Fuel filter replacement is not a part of this vehicle's regular maintenance schedule. The filter should be replaced only when it is restricted.

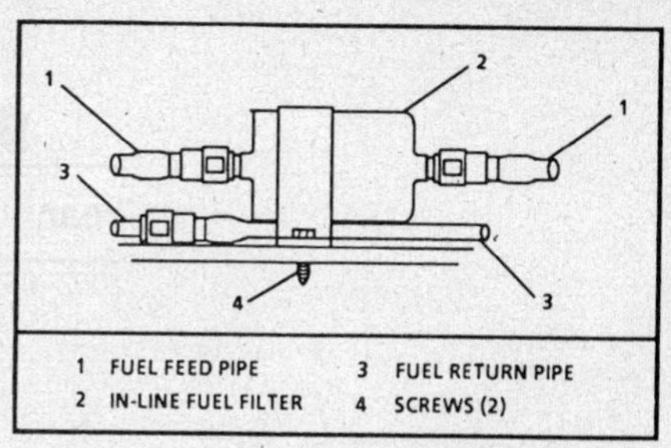

GC1028800046000X

Fig. 6 Fuel filter replacement

1. Relieve fuel system pressure as outlined in "Precautions."
2. Raise and support vehicle.
3. Disconnect fuel line fittings using tool No. J-37088-A, or equivalent, **Fig. 5.**
4. Drain fuel into suitable container.
5. Remove mounting nut, bracket and fuel filter.
6. Remove filter from bracket, **Fig. 6.**
7. Reverse procedure to install. Apply few drops of clean engine oil to filter's tube ends to help prevent fuel leak.

TIGHTENING SPECIFICATIONS

Year	Component	Torque Ft. Lbs.
2002–05	Accelerator Control Cable Bracket	89①
	Adapter Plate	52
	Alternator Bracket	37
	Coolant Drain Plug	14
	Coolant Pump Pulley	18
	EGR Valve	18
	Engine Mount Bracket	43
	Engine Mount Lower Nut	32
	Engine Mount Strut	35
	Engine Mount Strut, Lefthand Rear	52
	Engine Mount Strut Bracket, Righthand Side	37
	Engine Mount Strut Bracket, Upper Radiator Support	21
	Engine Mount Upper Nut	35
	Exhaust Manifold Stud	13
	Fuel Feed Pipe	13
	Fuel Pipe Bracket	37
	Fuel Pipe Clip	89①
	Fuel Return Pipe	13
	Ignition Coil Bracket	18
	Oil Dipstick	18
	Oil Drain Plug	18
	Oil Filter	115①
	Oil Filter Bypass Plug	14
	Oil Filter Fitting	29
	Oil Gallery Plug (¼ Inch)	14
	Oil Gallery Plug (⅜ Inch)	24
	Oil Pressure Indicator Switch	115①
	Spark Plug	15
	Thermostat Body	18
	Thermostat Bypass Pipe To Front Cover	106①

Continued

TIGHTENING SPECIFICATIONS—Continued

Year	Component	Torque Ft. Lbs.
2002–05	Thermostat Bypass Pipe To Throttle Body	18
	Water Outlet	18
	Water Pump	89①
	Water Pump Pulley	18
	Wiring Harness Bracket	115①

① — Inch lbs.

3.5L Engine

NOTE: On Air Bag Equipped Models, Refer To "Air Bag System Precautions" Located In The Front Of This Manual For System Disarming & Arming Procedures.

NOTE: Refer To "Computer Relearn Procedures" Located In The Front Of This Manual When Battery Power To The Computer Has Been Interrupted.

NOTE: For Procedures Not Found In This Section, Refer To The "3.5L Engine" In The "Relay, SV6, Terraza & Uplander" Chassis Chapter.

INDEX

PRECAUTIONS

Air Bag Systems

Refer to "Air Bag System Precautions" in the front of this manual for system disarming and arming procedures.

Battery Ground Cable

Prior to service, disconnect battery ground cable and isolate as required.

Fuel System Pressure Relief

1. Loosen fuel filler cap to discharge tank pressure.
2. Connect fuel pressure gauge tool No. J-34730-1A, or equivalent, to fuel pressure connection. Wrap shop towel around connection while connecting fuel pressure gauge in order to avoid fuel spillage.
3. Install bleed hose into an approved container and open valve in order to bleed fuel system pressure.
4. Drain any fuel remaining in fuel pressure gauge into suitable container.

COMPRESSION PRESSURE

1. Operate engine until normal operating temperature is reached.
2. Turn engine off, then remove Powertrain Control Module (PCM) and ignition fuses.
3. Disconnect ignition coil positive wire plug from ignition coil.
4. Disconnect fuel injector electrical connector.
5. Remove all spark plugs.
6. Remove throttle body air duct.
7. Block throttle plate wide open.
8. Ensure battery is fully charged.

9. With compression gauge at zero, crank engine through four compression strokes.
10. Record compression at all cylinders.
11. Minimum compression recorded in any one cylinder should not be less than 70% of highest cylinder.
12. No cylinder should read less than 100 psi.

ENGINE MOUNT

REPLACE

AWD

1. Remove air cleaner outlet duct.
2. Remove engine mount struts.
3. Raise and support vehicle.
4. Remove catalytic converter.
5. Remove righthand front wheel and tire.
6. Remove righthand engine splash shield.
7. Remove the engine mount to frame nuts. **In order to avoid oil pan damage and possible engine failure, insert a block of wood that spans width of oil pan bottom between oil pan and jack support.**
8. Place a utility stand and a block of wood under oil pan in order to raise engine.
9. Remove engine mount bracket to oil pan bolt.
10. Remove engine mount bracket to engine block bolt.
11. Remove engine mount and bracket.
12. Remove engine mount bracket to engine mount nuts.
13. Remove engine mount from the bracket.
14. Reverse procedure to install.

FWD

1. Remove throttle body air inlet duct.
2. Remove engine mount struts.
3. Raise and support vehicle.
4. Remove catalytic converter from engine exhaust manifold.
5. Remove righthand front wheel and tire.
6. Remove righthand engine splash shield.
7. Remove engine mount lower nuts.
8. Use a utility stand and a block of wood in order to raise engine.
9. Remove engine mount bracket-to-oil pan bolts.
10. Remove engine mount and engine mount bracket.
11. Remove the engine mount from the engine mount bracket.
12. Reverse procedure to install.

ENGINE

REPLACE

1. Loosen two intake air duct clamps from air cleaner housing and throttle body.
2. Remove air cleaner intake duct from air cleaner housing and throttle body.
3. Drain cooling system into suitable container.
4. Remove radiator inlet hose from engine.

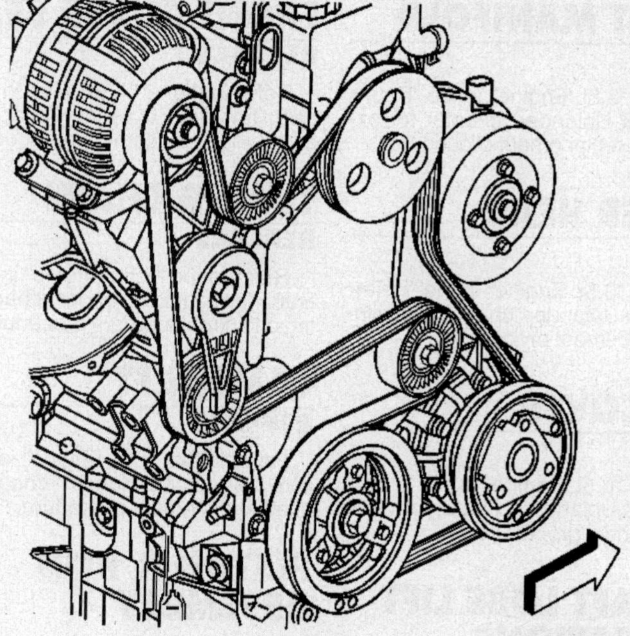

Fig. 1 Serpentine belt routing

5. Remove radiator outlet hose from engine.
6. Remove heater outlet and inlet hoses from engine.
7. Remove vacuum hoses from upper intake manifold.
8. Remove brake booster vacuum hose from upper intake manifold.
9. Remove fuel lines from fuel rail.
10. Disconnect the following electrical connectors:
    a. Knock sensor (KS).
    b. Camshaft position sensor (CMP).
    c. Crankshaft position sensor (CKP).
    d. Heated oxygen sensor (H02S).
    e. Manifold absolute pressure sensor (MAP).
    f. Exhaust gas recirculation valve (EGR).
    g. Evaporative emission canister purge solenoid (EVAP).
    h. Electrical throttle control.
    i. Ignition coil.
    j. Body wiring harness-to-engine harness.
    k. Engine wiring harness from transmission.
11. Remove engine wiring harness grounds from transaxle.
12. Remove engine mount strut.
13. Raise and support vehicle.
14. Drain engine oil.
15. Remove rear propeller shaft.
16. Remove catalytic converter.
17. Remove front tires and wheels.
18. Remove lower radiator air baffle assembly.
19. Remove engine splash shields.
20. Remove stabilizer shaft links from lower control arm.
21. Remove tie rod ends from steering knuckles.
22. Remove lower ball joints from knuckles.
23. Remove A/C compressor bolts and position compressor aside. Do not discharge A/C system. Support compressor.
24. Disconnect drive axles from transaxle.
25. Secure drive axles to steering knuckle/struts.
26. Remove intermediate shaft pinch bolt from steering gear. **Failure to disconnect intermediate shaft from rack and pinion steering gear stub shaft can result in damage to steering gear and or intermediate shaft. This damage may cause loss of steering control which could result in an accident and possible personal injury.**
27. Lower vehicle until frame contacts transaxle table.
28. Remove frame bolts.
29. Raise vehicle in order to separate powertrain frame assembly from vehicle.
30. Remove starter motor as outlined under "Starter, Replace" in "Electrical" section.
31. Remove torque converter covers.
32. Remove torque converter bolts.
33. Remove engine mount lower nuts.
34. Remove transaxle brace.
35. Remove exhaust crossover pipe.
36. Install engine hoist to engine.
37. Remove transaxle-to-engine bolts and studs.
38. Support transaxle.
39. Separate and remove engine from transaxle frame.
40. Install engine to engine stand.
41. Remove flywheel.
42. Remove drive belt.
43. Reverse procedure to install.

INTAKE MANIFOLD

REPLACE

Refer to the "3.5L Engine" in the "Relay, SV6, Terraza & Uplander" chapter for intake manifold replacement procedure.

EXHAUST MANIFOLD

REPLACE

Refer to the "3.5L Engine" in the "Relay, SV6, Terraza & Uplander" chapter for exhaust manifold replacement procedure.

CYLINDER HEAD

REPLACE

Refer to the "3.5L Engine" in the "Relay, SV6, Terraza & Uplander" chapter for cylinder head replacement procedure.

VALVE COVER

REPLACE

Refer to the "3.5L Engine" in the "Relay, SV6, Terraza & Uplander" chapter for valve cover replacement procedure.

CAMSHAFT LOBE LIFT SPECIFICATIONS

Refer to the "3.5L Engine" in the "Relay, SV6, Terraza & Uplander" chapter for camshaft lobe lift specifications.

VALVE ADJUSTMENT

This vehicle is equipped with hydraulic valve lifters.

ROCKER ARMS

REPLACE

Refer to the "3.5L Engine" in the "Relay, SV6, Terraza & Uplander" chapter for rocker arm replacement procedure.

VALVE GUIDES

Refer to the "3.5L Engine" in the "Relay, SV6, Terraza & Uplander" chapter.

HYDRAULIC LIFTERS

REPLACE

Refer to the "3.5L Engine" in the "Relay, SV6, Terraza & Uplander" chapter for hydraulic lifters replacement.

CRANKSHAFT DAMPER

REPLACE

Refer to the "3.5L Engine" in the "Relay, SV6, Terraza & Uplander" chapter for crankshaft damper replacement procedure.

FRONT COVER

REPLACE

Refer to the "3.5L Engine" in the "Relay, SV6, Terraza & Uplander" chapter for front cover replacement procedure.

FRONT COVER SEAL

REPLACE

Refer to the "3.5L Engine" in the "Relay, SV6, Terraza & Uplander" chapter for front cover seal replacement procedure.

TIMING CHAIN

REPLACE

Refer to the "3.5L Engine" in the "Relay, SV6, Terraza & Uplander" chapter for timing chain replacement procedure.

CAMSHAFT

REPLACE

Refer to the "3.5L Engine" in the "Relay, SV6, Terraza & Uplander" chapter for camshaft replacement procedure.

PISTON & ROD ASSEMBLY

Refer to the "3.5L Engine" in the "Relay, SV6, Terraza & Uplander" chapter.

PISTONS, PINS & RINGS

Refer to the "3.5L Engine" in the "Relay, SV6, Terraza & Uplander" chapter.

MAIN & ROD BEARINGS

Refer to the "3.5L Engine" in the "Relay, SV6, Terraza & Uplander" chapter.

CRANKSHAFT SEAL

REPLACE

Refer to the "3.5L Engine" in the "Relay, SV6, Terraza & Uplander" chapter for crankshaft seal replacement procedure.

CRANKSHAFT REAR OIL SEAL

REPLACE

Refer to the "3.5L Engine" in the "Relay, SV6, Terraza & Uplander" chapter for crankshaft rear oil seal replacement procedure.

OIL PAN

REPLACE

Refer to the "3.5L Engine" in the "Relay, SV6, Terraza & Uplander" chapter for oil pan replacement procedure.

OIL PUMP

REPLACE

Refer to the "3.5L Engine" in the "Relay, SV6, Terraza & Uplander" chapter for oil pump replacement procedure.

OIL PUMP SERVICE

Refer to the "3.5L Engine" in the "Relay, SV6, Terraza & Uplander" chapter for oil pump service.

SERPENTINE DRIVE BELT

Belt Routing

Refer to **Fig. 1** for serpentine drive belt routing.

Belt Replacement

1. Release belt pressure by rotating tensioner.
2. Remove serpentine drive belt.
3. Reverse procedure to install.

Tensioner Replacement

1. Remove drive belt.
2. Remove drive belt tensioner bolt.
3. Remove drive belt tensioner.
4. Reverse procedure to install.

COOLING SYSTEM BLEED

These engines do not require a specified bleed procedure. After filling cooling system, run engine to operating temperature with radiator/pressure cap off. Air will then be automatically bled through cap opening.

THERMOSTAT

REPLACE

1. Remove thermostat housing.
2. Remove thermostat.
3. Remove and discard thermostat O-ring seal.
4. Reverse procedure to install.

WATER PUMP

REPLACE

Refer to the "3.5L Engine" in the "Relay, SV6, Terraza & Uplander" chapter for water pump replacement procedure.

RADIATOR

REPLACE

1. Disconnect lower transmission oil cooler (TOC) line from radiator.
2. Remove cooling fans and shroud.
3. Remove radiator inlet hose.
4. Remove radiator outlet hose.
5. Remove bolt that secures radiator to condenser.
6. Remove the condenser tube clip screw.
7. Tilt radiator and condenser inwards toward engine and remove radiator.
8. Reverse procedure to install.

FUEL PUMP

REPLACE

1. Remove fuel tank.
2. Disconnect fuel sender electrical connections.
3. Clean all of fuel pipe connections, all of hose connections, and all of areas surrounding connections before disconnecting connections in order to avoid possible contamination of fuel system.
4. Disconnect fuel supply pipe quick-connect fitting at fuel sender assembly.
5. Disconnect evaporative emission (EVAP) pipe quick-connect fittings at fuel sender assembly.
6. Use tool No. J-45722, or equivalent, and a long breaker-bar in order to unlock fuel sender lock ring. Turn fuel sender lock ring in a counterclockwise direction. **Avoid damaging lock ring. Use only J-45722, or equivalent, to prevent damage to lock ring. Do not handle fuel sender assembly by fuel pipes. Amount of leverage generated by handling fuel pipes could damage the joints. Do NOT use impact tools. Significant force will be required to release lock ring. Use of a hammer and screwdriver is not recommended. Secure fuel tank in order to prevent fuel tank rotation.**
7. Remove fuel sender assembly and seal from fuel tank.
8. Discard fuel sender assembly seal.
9. Clean fuel sender assembly sealing surfaces.
10. Place lock ring on a flat surface. Measure clearance between to lock ring and flat surface using a feeler gage at 7 points. **Some lock rings were manufactured with DO NOT REUSE stamped into them. These lock rings may be reused if they are not damaged or warped. Inspect lock ring for damage due to improper removal or installation procedures. If damage is found, install a NEW lock ring. Inspect lock ring for flatness.**
11. If warpage is less than .016 inch, lock ring does not require replacement.
12. If warpage is greater than .016 inch, lock ring must be replaced.
13. Reverse procedure to install.

TIGHTENING SPECIFICATIONS

Year	Component	Torque Ft. Lbs.
2006	Camshaft Position Sensor Bolt	89①
	Camshaft Sprocket Bolt	103
	Camshaft Thrust Plate Screw	89①
	Connecting Rod Bearing Cap Bolt	②
	Coolant Drain Plug	14
	Coolant Temperature Sensor	17
	Crankshaft Balancer Bolt	118
	Crankshaft Main Bearing Cap Bolt/ Stud	③
	Crankshaft Oil Deflector Nut	18
	Crankshaft Position Sensor Shield Nut	97①
	Crankshaft Position Sensor Stud - Side Of Engine Block	97①
	Cylinder Head Bolt	④
	Cylinder Head Plug	15
	Drive Belt Tensioner	37
	EGR Valve Assembly Bolt	22
	EGR Valve Pipe Bolt - EGR	18
	Engine Block Plug	44
	Engine Block Heater	44
	Engine Mount Strut And A/C Compressor Bracket Bolt	37
	Engine Mount Strut And Lift Bracket Bolt - Engine Lift Rear	52
	Engine Mount Strut And Alternator Bracket Bolt	37
	Engine Mount Strut And Support Bracket Bolt	18
	Engine Oil Pressure Indicator Switch	12
	Engine Wiring Harness Bracket Bolt	115①
	EVAP Purge Valve Bolt	12
	Exhaust Crossover Pipe Heat Shield Bolt	89①
	Exhaust Crossover Pipe Stud/Nut	18
	Exhaust Manifold Heat Shield Bolt	89①
	Exhaust Manifold Nut	12
	Exhaust Manifold Stud	13
	Flywheel Bolt	52
	Front Oil Gallery Plug - Small	14
	Front Oil Gallery Plug - Large	24

Continued

TIGHTENING SPECIFICATIONS—Continued

Year	Component	Torque Ft. Lbs.
2006	Fuel Feed Pipe To Fuel Injector Rail Bolt	89①
	Fuel Injector Rail Bolt	89①
	Heated Oxygen Sensor	31
	Heater Inlet Pipe Nut	18
	Heated Inlet Pipe Stud	26
	Ignition Coil Bracket Bolt/Nut/Stud	18
	Intake Manifold Coolant Pipe Bolt	89①
	Knock Sensor	18
	Large Engine Front Cover Bolt	41
	Lower Intake Manifold Bolt - Center	15
	Lower Intake Manifold Bolt - Corner	18
	Map Sensor Bolt	89①
	Medium Engine Front Cover Bolt	41
	Oil Cooler Connector	37
	Oil Cooler Fitting	14
	Oil Cooler Pipe Bolt	89①
	Oil Filter Adapter Bolt	18
	Oil Filter	22
	Oil Filter Bypass Hole Plug	14
	Oil Filter Fitting	29
	Oil Dipstick Tube Bolt	18
	Oil Pan Bolt	18
	Oil Pan Drain Plug	18
	Oil Pan Side Bolt	37
	Oil Pump Cover Bolt	89①
	Oil Pump Drive Gear Clamp Bolt	27
	Oil Pump Mounting Bolt	30
	PCV Tube Clip Bolt - Foul Air	89①
	Piston Oil Nozzle Bolt	89①
	Rear Oil Gallery Plug - ¼ Inch	14
	Rear Oil Gallery Plug - ⅜ Inch	24
	Spark Plug	11
	Small Engine Front Cover Bolt	20
	Thermostat Bypass Pipe To Engine Front Cover Bolt	89①
	Thermostat Bypass Pipe To Throttle Body Nut/Bolt	89①
	Throttle Body Bolt	89①
	Throttle Body Stud	53①
	Timing Chain Dampener Bolt	15
	Upper Intake Manifold Bolt/Stud	18
	Valve Lifter Guide Bolt	89①
	Valve Rocker Arm Bolt	24
	Valve Rocker Arm Cover Bolt	89①
	Water Outlet Bolt	18
	Water Pump Bolt	89①
	Water Pump Pulley Bolt	18

① — Inch lbs.
② — First Pass, 18 lb. ft.; final pass 110°.
③ — First Pass, 37 lb. ft.; final pass 77°.
④ — First Pass, 44 lb. ft.; final pass 95°.

3.9L Engine

NOTE: On Air Bag Equipped Models, Refer To "Air Bag System Precautions" Located In The Front Of This Manual For System Disarming & Arming Procedures.

NOTE: Refer To "Computer Relearn Procedures" Located In The Front Of This Manual When Battery Power To The Computer Has Been Interrupted.

NOTE: For Procedures Not Found In This Section, Refer To The "3.9L Engine" In The "Relay, SV6, Terraza & Uplander" Chassis Chapter.

INDEX

PRECAUTIONS

Air Bag Systems

Refer to "Air Bag System Precautions" in the front of this manual for system disarming and arming procedures.

Battery Ground Cable

Prior to service, disconnect battery ground cable and isolate as required.

Fuel System Pressure Relief

1. Loosen fuel filler cap to discharge tank pressure.
2. Connect fuel pressure gauge tool No. J-34730-1A, or equivalent, to fuel pressure connection. Wrap shop towel around connection while connecting fuel pressure gauge in order to avoid fuel spillage.
3. Install bleed hose into an approved container and open valve in order to bleed fuel system pressure.
4. Drain any fuel remaining in fuel pressure gauge into suitable container.

COMPRESSION PRESSURE

1. Operate engine until normal operating temperature is reached.
2. Turn engine off, then remove Powertrain Control Module (PCM) and ignition fuses.
3. Disconnect ignition coil positive wire plug from ignition coil.
4. Disconnect fuel injector electrical connector.
5. Remove all spark plugs.
6. Remove throttle body air duct.
7. Block throttle plate wide open.
8. Ensure battery is fully charged.
9. With compression gauge at zero, crank engine through four compression strokes.
10. Record compression at all cylinders.
11. Minimum compression recorded in any one cylinder should not be less than 70% of highest cylinder.
12. No cylinder should read less than 100 psi.

ENGINE MOUNT

REPLACE

1. Remove air cleaner outlet duct.
2. Remove engine mount struts.
3. Raise and support vehicle.
4. Remove catalytic converter.
5. Remove righthand front wheel and tire.
6. Remove righthand engine splash shield.
7. Remove engine mount to frame nuts.
8. Place a utility stand and a block of wood under oil pan in order to raise engine. **In order to avoid oil pan damage and possible engine failure, insert a block of wood that spans width of oil pan bottom between oil pan and jack support.**
9. Remove engine mount bracket to oil pan bolts.
10. Remove engine mount and bracket.
11. Remove engine mount bracket to engine mount nuts.
12. Remove engine mount from bracket.
13. Reverse procedure to install.

ENGINE

REPLACE

1. Lock steering column by installing tool No. J-42640, or equivalent, into underside of steering column. **Front wheels of vehicle must be maintained in straight ahead position and steering column must be in LOCK position before disconnecting steering column or intermediate shaft. Failure to follow these procedures will cause improper alignment of some components during installation and result in damage to SIR coil assembly.**
2. Open hood.
3. Remove engine oil fill cap.
4. Pull up intake manifold cover in order to disengage cover from studs.
5. Disconnect battery ground.
6. Disconnect positive battery cable.
7. Disconnect battery current sensor.

8. Disconnect auxiliary ground cable on inner fender.
9. Disconnect positive battery feed at junction box.
10. Remove lower radiator air baffle.
11. Drain cooling system into suitable container.
12. Lower vehicle.
13. Reposition coolant recovery reservoir hose clamp at coolant crossover.
14. Remove coolant recovery reservoir hose from crossover.
15. Remove coolant reservoir.
16. Remove lefthand side diagonal brace.
17. Unsnap and remove junction block cover.
18. Loosen air cleaner cover bolts
19. Remove air cleaner cover.
20. Remove engine control module (ECM) from air cleaner cover.
21. Disconnect engine harness electrical connector from transaxle control module (TCM).
22. Disconnect engine harness electrical connector from instrument panel harness electrical connector.
23. Disconnect engine harness electrical connector from the I/P harness electrical connector.
24. Disconnect engine harness electrical connector from the ABS module.
25. Remove engine harness clip from air conditioning (A/C) line.
26. Remove engine harness clip from A/C line.
27. Remove underhood junction.
28. Unsnap and remove engine harness connector from junction block retainer.
29. Disconnect engine harness electrical connector from MAF/IAT sensor.
30. Disconnect positive crankcase ventilation (PCV) fresh air tube quick connect fitting from air cleaner outlet duct.
31. Loosen air cleaner outlet duct clamps at throttle body and MAF/IAT sensor.
32. Remove air cleaner outlet duct from throttle body and MAF/IAT sensor.
33. Gather outer branches of engine harness and lay them on top of engine.
34. Release tension on radiator inlet hose clamp and reposition clamp using tool No. J 38185, or equivalent.
35. Remove radiator inlet hose from coolant crossover.
36. Release tension on radiator outlet hose clamp and reposition clamp using tool No. J 38185, or equivalent.
37. Remove radiator outlet hose from thermostat housing.
38. Disconnect heater inlet and outlet hose quick connect fittings from inlet and outlet pipes.
39. Remove brake booster vacuum hose from upper intake manifold fitting.
40. Disconnect fuel feed and evaporative emission (EVAP) line quick connect fittings.
41. Remove engine mount struts.
42. Drain engine oil into suitable container.
43. Remove front wheels and tires.
44. Remove rear propeller shaft, if equipped with all wheel drive (AWD).
45. Disconnect engine harness electrical connectors from lefthand and righthand wheel speed sensors.
46. Remove drive belt.
47. Disconnect engine harness electrical connectors from A/C compressor. **It is not required to evacuate A/C system prior to repositioning A/C compressor.**
48. Remove A/C compressor front bolt and nut.
49. Remove A/C compressor rear bolt. Reposition and support A/C compressor out of way.
50. Remove catalytic converter.
51. Remove engine splash shield.
52. Remove engine harness clips from catalytic converter heat shield, if equipped with AWD.
53. Disconnect battery cable retainers at core support.
54. Remove engine harness clips from heat shield, if equipped with front wheel drive (FWD).
55. If equipped with FWD, remove stabilizer shaft link lower nuts.
56. Remove stabilizer shaft links from stabilizer shaft.
57. Remove tie rod end nuts at steering knuckles.
58. Separate outer tie rod ends from steering knuckle using tool No. J 24319-B, or equivalent. **Do not attempt to free ball stud by using a pickle fork or wedge type tool, because seal or bushing damage could result. Use proper tool to separate all ball joints.**
59. Remove lower ball joint cotter pins from ball joints.
60. Loosen lower ball joint castle nuts.
61. Install tool No. J 41820, or equivalent, over ball joint and lower control arm. **Use only recommended tools for separating ball joint from knuckle. Do NOT hammer or pry ball joint from knuckle. Failure to use recommended tools may cause damage to ball joint and seal.**
62. Rotate castle nut counterclockwise in order to separate ball joint from steering knuckle.
63. Assemble tool No. J 33008-A , J 29794 and J 2619-O1, or equivalent.
64. Disengage wheel drive shafts from transaxle using tool No. J 33008-A, J 29794 and J 2619-O1, or equivalent.
65. Secure wheel drive shafts to steering knuckle/struts.
66. Reposition intermediate steering shaft seal in order to provide access to intermediate steering shaft pinch bolt. **Failure to disconnect intermediate shaft from rack and pinion steering gear stub shaft can result in damage to steering gear and/or intermediate shaft. This damage may cause loss of steering control which could result in an accident and possible personal injury.**
67. Remove intermediate steering shaft pinch bolt.
68. Disconnect intermediate steering shaft from power steering gear.
69. Place tool No. J 39580, or equivalent, under frame.
70. Lower vehicle until frame contacts tool No. J 39580, or equivalent.
71. Remove front and rear frame bolts.
72. Remove frame rear strap bolts.
73. Remove frame rear straps.
74. Raise vehicle in order to separate powertrain/frame assembly from vehicle.
75. If required perform following steps, remove engine harness ground wire nut.
76. Remove engine harness positive battery cable from stud.
77. Disconnect engine harness electrical connector from starter.
78. Remove engine harness ground nuts from transaxle studs.
79. Remove engine harness grounds from studs.
80. Remove battery ground from transaxle stud.
81. Remove engine to transaxle brace.
82. Remove starter motor bolts and starter.
83. Remove torque converter cover bolts.
84. Remove torque converter covers.
85. Use tool No. J 37096, or equivalent, in order to hold flywheel, and also rotate flywheel to access torque converter bolts.
86. Remove torque converter bolts.
87. Remove engine mount to frame nuts.
88. Remove engine harness clips from transaxle brace.
89. Remove transaxle brace bolts and brace.
90. Remove exhaust crossover pipe shield bolts and shield.
91. Remove exhaust crossover pipe nuts and pipe.
92. Disconnect engine harness electrical connector from EVAP purge solenoid.
93. Disconnect engine harness electrical connector from the throttle actuator.
94. Disconnect engine harness electrical connector from manifold absolute pressure (MAP) sensor.
95. Disconnect engine harness electrical connector from the ignition coil.
96. Remove engine harness clip from ignition coil bracket.
97. Remove engine harness clip from engine.
98. Remove engine harness bolt.
99. Disconnect engine harness electrical connector from camshaft actuator magnet.
100. Remove engine harness bracket nut.
101. Remove engine harness bracket from stud.
102. Remove engine harness clip from bracket.
103. Disconnect engine harness electrical connector from intake manifold tuning valve.
104. Remove connector position assurance (CPA) retainer.
105. Disconnect engine harness electrical connector from fuel injector harness electrical connector.
106. Remove alternator terminal nut.
107. Remove engine harness lead from alternator.
108. Disconnect engine harness electrical connector from alternator.
109. Disconnect engine harness electrical connector from heated oxygen sensor (HO2S).
110. Remove engine harness clip from strut bracket.
111. Disconnect engine harness electrical

connector from crankshaft position (CKP) sensor.
112. Disconnect engine harness electrical connector from knock sensor.
113. Disconnect engine harness electrical connector from oil pressure sensor.
114. Disconnect engine harness electrical connector from transaxle.
115. Disconnect engine harness electrical connector from vehicle speed sensor (VSS).
116. Remove engine harness clip from stud on transaxle.
117. Remove engine harness clamp bolt from transaxle.
118. Remove engine harness clips from transaxle studs.
119. Disconnect engine harness electrical connector from oil level sensor.
120. Remove engine harness clip from oil pan.
121. Gather all branches of engine harness together and remove engine harness from engine.
122. Disconnect power steering line retainer from alternator bracket.
123. Remove power steering pressure pipe and return line from power steering pump and position out of way.
124. Install an engine hoist to engine.
125. Remove transaxle bolts and studs.
126. Support transaxle.
127. Separate and remove engine from transaxle and frame.
128. Use tool No. J 37096, or equivalent, in order to hold flywheel.
129. Loosen flywheel bolts.
130. Remove five of six flywheel bolts leaving one bolt at top of crankshaft.
131. Grip flywheel and remove remaining bolt. Do not drop flywheel when removing final bolt.
132. Remove engine flywheel.
133. Install engine to engine stand.
134. Remove engine hoist from engine.
135. Reverse procedure to install.

INTAKE MANIFOLD

REPLACE

Refer to the "3.9L Engine" in the "Relay, SV6, Terraza & Uplander" chapter for intake manifold replacement procedure.

EXHAUST MANIFOLD

REPLACE

Refer to the "3.9L Engine" in the "Relay, SV6, Terraza & Uplander" chapter for exhaust manifold replacement procedure.

CYLINDER HEAD

REPLACE

Refer to the "3.9L Engine" in the "Relay, SV6, Terraza & Uplander" chapter for cylinder head replacement procedure.

VALVE COVER

REPLACE

Refer to the "3.9L Engine" in the "Relay, SV6, Terraza & Uplander" chapter valve cover replacement procedure.

CAMSHAFT LOBE LIFT SPECIFICATIONS

Refer to the "3.9L Engine" in the "Relay, SV6, Terraza & Uplander" chapter.

VALVE ADJUSTMENT

This vehicle is equipped with hydraulic valve lifters.

ROCKER ARMS

REPLACE

Refer to the "3.9L Engine" in the "Relay, SV6, Terraza & Uplander" chapter for rocker arm replacement procedure.

VALVE GUIDES

Refer to the "3.9L Engine" in the "Relay, SV6, Terraza & Uplander" chapter.

HYDRAULIC LIFTERS

REPLACE

Refer to the "3.9L Engine" in the "Relay, SV6, Terraza & Uplander" chapter for hydraulic lifter replacement procedure.

CRANKSHAFT DAMPER

REPLACE

Refer to the "3.9L Engine" in the "Relay, SV6, Terraza & Uplander" chapter for crankshaft damper replacement procedure.

FRONT COVER

REPLACE

Refer to the "3.9L Engine" in the "Relay, SV6, Terraza & Uplander" chapter for front cover replacement procedure.

FRONT COVER SEAL

REPLACE

Refer to the "3.9L Engine" in the "Relay, SV6, Terraza & Uplander" chapter for front cover seal replacement procedure.

TIMING CHAIN

REPLACE

Refer to the "3.9L Engine" in the "Relay, SV6, Terraza & Uplander" chapter for timing chain replacement procedure.

CAMSHAFT

REPLACE

Refer to the "3.9L Engine" in the "Relay, SV6, Terraza & Uplander" chapter for camshaft replacement procedure.

PISTON & ROD ASSEMBLY

Refer to the "3.9L Engine" in the "Relay, SV6, Terraza & Uplander" chapter.

PISTONS, PINS & RINGS

Refer to the "3.9L Engine" in the "Relay, SV6, Terraza & Uplander" chapter.

MAIN & ROD BEARINGS

Refer to the "3.9L Engine" in the "Relay, SV6, Terraza & Uplander" chapter.

CRANKSHAFT SEAL

REPLACE

Refer to the "3.9L Engine" in the "Relay, SV6, Terraza & Uplander" chapter for crankshaft seal replacement procedure.

CRANKSHAFT REAR OIL SEAL

REPLACE

Refer to the "3.9L Engine" in the "Relay, SV6, Terraza & Uplander" chapter for crankshaft rear oil seal replacement procedure.

OIL PAN

REPLACE

Refer to the "3.9L Engine" in the "Relay, SV6, Terraza & Uplander" chapter for oil pan replacement procedure.

OIL PUMP

REPLACE

Refer to the "3.9L Engine" in the "Relay, SV6, Terraza & Uplander" chapter for oil pump replacement procedure.

OIL PUMP SERVICE

Refer to the "3.9L Engine" in the "Relay, SV6, Terraza & Uplander" chapter.

SERPENTINE DRIVE BELT

Belt Routing

Refer to **Fig. 1** for serpentine drive belt routing.

Belt Replacement

1. Release belt pressure by rotating tensioner.
2. Remove serpentine drive belt.
3. Reverse procedure to install.

Tensioner Replacement

1. Remove drive belt.
2. Raise and support vehicle.
3. Remove drive belt tensioner bolt by accessing it through wheelhouse opening.

4. Remove drive belt tensioner by accessing it through wheelhouse opening.
5. Reverse procedure to install.

COOLING SYSTEM BLEED

These engines do not require a specified bleed procedure. After filling cooling system, run engine to operating temperature with radiator/pressure cap off. Air will then be automatically bled through cap opening.

THERMOSTAT

REPLACE

1. Remove thermostat housing.
2. Remove thermostat.
3. Reverse procedure to install.

WATER PUMP

REPLACE

Refer to the "3.9L Engine" in the "Relay, SV6, Terraza & Uplander" chapter for water pump replacement procedure.

RADIATOR

REPLACE

1. Disconnect lower transmission oil cooler line from radiator.
2. Remove cooling fans and shroud.
3. Remove radiator inlet hose.
4. Remove radiator outlet hose.
5. Remove bolt that secures radiator to condenser.
6. Remove condenser tube clip screw.
7. Tilt radiator and condenser inwards toward engine and remove radiator.
8. Reverse procedure to install.

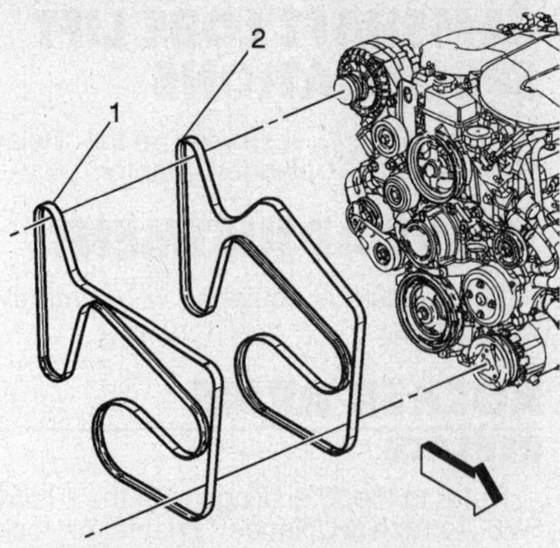

Fig. 1 Serpentine belt routing

FUEL PUMP

REPLACE

1. Remove fuel tank. **Do not handle fuel sender assembly by fuel pipes. Amount of leverage generated by handling fuel pipes could damage joints.**
2. Disconnect fuel tank harness electrical connectors from fuel tank module.
3. Clean all of fuel pipe connections, all hose connections and all areas surrounding connections before disconnecting connections in order to avoid possible contamination of fuel system.
4. Disconnect fuel feed pipe quick connect fitting from module.
5. Disconnect evaporative emission (EVAP) pipe quick connect fittings from module.
6. Use tool No. J 45722, or equivalent, and a long breaker-bar in order to unlock fuel sender lock ring. Turn fuel sender lock ring in a counterclockwise direction. **Avoid damaging lock ring. Use only tool No. J-45722, or equivalent, to prevent damage to lock ring. Do not use impact tools. Significant force will be required to release lock ring. Use of a hammer and screwdriver is not recommended. Secure fuel tank in order to prevent fuel tank rotation.**
7. Remove module and seal from fuel tank. **Drain fuel from fuel sender assembly into an approved container in order to reduce risk of fire and personal injury. Never store fuel in an open container.**
8. Discard module seal.
9. Clean module sealing surfaces.
10. Place lock ring on a flat surface. Measure clearance between lock ring and flat surface using a feeler gage at 7 points. **Some lock rings were manufactured with DO NOT REUSE stamped into them. These lock rings may be reused if they are not damaged or warped. Inspect lock ring for damage due to improper removal or installation procedures. If damage is found, install a new lock ring. Inspect lock ring for flatness.**
11. If warpage is less than .016 inch, lock ring does not require replacement.
12. If warpage is greater than .016 inch, lock ring must be replaced.
13. Reverse procedure to install.

TIGHTENING SPECIFICATIONS

Year	Component	Torque Ft. Lbs.
2006	A/C Compressor Bracket Bolt	37
	Camshaft Position Actuator Assembly Bolt	12
	Camshaft Position Actuator Magnet Bolt	89①
	Camshaft Position Sensor Bolt	89①
	Camshaft Thrust Plate Screw	89①
	Clutch Pressure Plate Bolt	18
	Connecting Rod Bearing Cap Bolt	②
	Coolant Crossover Pipe Bolt	37
	Coolant Drain Plug	14
	Coolant Temperature Sensor	15
	Coolant Vent Pipe Bolt	89①
	Crankshaft Balancer Bolt	③
	Crankshaft Main Bearing Cap Bolt/ Stud	④
	Crankshaft Oil Deflector Nut	18
	Crankshaft Position Sensor Stud	89①
	Cylinder Head Bolt	⑤
	Drive Belt Idler Pulley Bolt - 13mm	22
	Drive Belt Idler Pulley Bolt - 15mm	37

Continued

TIGHTENING SPECIFICATIONS—Continued

Year	Component	Torque Ft. Lbs.
2006	Drive Belt Tensioner Bolt	37
	Engine Block Heater/Plug	44
	Engine Front Cover Bolt	18
	Engine Lift Bracket Bolt	52
	Engine Oil Pressure Indicator Switch	12
	Engine Wiring Harness Bracket Bolt	115①
	EVAP Purge Valve Bolt	106①
	Exhaust Manifold Bolt	15
	Exhaust Manifold Heat Shield Bolt	89①
	Exhaust Manifold Lower Heat Shield Bolt	89①
	Flywheel Bolt	52
	Front Oil Gallery Plug	24
	Fuel Injector Rail Bolt	89①
	Heated Oxygen Sensor	31
	Heater Inlet And Outlet Pipe Bolt - 10mm	89①
	Heater Inlet And Outlet Pipe Bolt/Nut - 13mm	18
	Ignition Coil Bracket Bolt/Nut/Stud	18
	Knock Sensor	18
	Lower Intake Manifold Bolt - Center	⑥
	Lower Intake Manifold Bolt - Corner	⑦
	Oil Filter	22
	Oil Filter Adapter Bolt	18
	Oil Filter Fitting	29
	Oil Dipstick Tube Bolt	18
	Oil Pan Bolt	18
	Oil Pan Drain Plug	18
	Oil Pan Side Bolt	37
	Oil Pan Support Bracket Bolt	37
	Oil Pump Cover Bolt	89①
	Oil Pump Drive Bolt	27
	Oil Pump Mounting Bolt	30
	Piston Oil Nozzle Bolt	89①
	Rear Oil Gallery Plug - ⅜ Inch	24
	Spark Plug	11
	Throttle Body Bolt/Nut	89①
	Throttle Body Stud	53①
	Timing Chain Tensioner Bolt	15
	Upper Intake Manifold Bolt/Stud	18
	Valve Lifter Guide Bolt	89①
	Valve Lifter Oil Manifold Cover Plate Bolt	18
	Valve Rocker Arm Bolt	25
	Valve Rocker Arm Cover Bolt	89①
	Water Outlet Bolt/Stud	18
	Water Pump Bolt	89①
	Water Pump Pulley Bolt	18

① — Inch lbs.
② — First pass 18 lb. ft.; final pass 110°.
③ — First pass 52 lb. ft.; final pass 72°.
④ — First pass 37 lb. ft.; final pass 77°.
⑤ — First pass 44 lb. ft.; final pass 95°.
⑥ — First pass 10 lb. ft.; final pass 15 lb. ft.
⑦ — First pass 10 lb. ft.; final pass 18 lb. ft.

Rear Axle & Suspension

NOTE: On Air Bag Equipped Models, Refer To "Air Bag System Precautions" Located In The Front Of This Manual For System Disarming & Arming Procedures.

NOTE: Refer To "Computer Relearn Procedures" Located In The Front Of This Manual When Battery Power To The Computer Has Been Interrupted.

INDEX

PRECAUTIONS

Air Bag Systems

Refer to "Air Bag System Precautions" in the front of this manual for system disarming and arming procedures.

Battery Ground Cable

Prior to service, disconnect battery ground cable and isolate as required.

Electronic Level Control

On models equipped with Electronic Level Control (ELC) system, when diagnosis or repair requires raising the vehicle on a hoist, it is important that the rear axle remains in normal trim height position at all times, therefore, the hoist should support the rear wheels or axle housing. When a frame contact hoist is used, two additional jack stands should be used to support the rear axle or control arms in the normal trim height position.

Vehicle Support

When removing rear springs do not use a twin-post type hoist. The swing arc of the rear axle assembly when certain fasteners are removed may cause it to slip from hoist.

REAR AXLE

REPLACE

1. Raise and support vehicle. **When removing rear springs, do not use a twin-post type hoist. The swing arch tendency of rear axle assembly when certain fasteners are removed may cause it to slip from hoist which may cause personal injury.**
2. Remove rear tires and wheels.
3. Use a utility stand in order to support rear axle.
4. Remove rear axle coil springs, spring seats, and spring insulators.
5. Remove brake calipers.
6. Disconnect intermediate brake hoses from rear axle brake pipes.
7. Disconnect wheel speed sensor electrical connectors.
8. Use a utility stand in order to lower rear axle.
9. Remove utility stand.
10. Lower vehicle until rear axle is approximately .5 inch above ground.
11. Remove rear axle control arm bolts and nuts.
12. Remove rear axle.
13. Remove brake pipes and brake hoses from rear axle.
14. Remove wheel bearing/hub.
15. Reverse procedure to install.

HUB & BEARING

REPLACE

1. Raise and support vehicle.
2. Remove tire and wheel assembly.
3. Remove brake drum as outlined in "Drum Brakes" chapter.
4. Remove mounting bolts and bearing/hub assembly.
5. Disconnect wheel speed sensor electrical connector.
6. Reverse procedure to install. Use new bearing hub mounting bolts.

SHOCK ABSORBER

REPLACE

1. Raise and support vehicle.
2. Use a utility stand in order to slightly compress coil spring and relieve tension on shock absorber.
3. If vehicle is equipped with automatic level control, disconnect air tube connector from shock absorber.
4. Remove shock absorber upper bolt and nut.
5. Remove shock absorber lower nut.
6. Remove shock absorber.
7. Reverse procedure to install.

COIL SPRING

REPLACE

1. Raise and support vehicle.
2. Remove rear wheel.
3. Remove brake caliper and support brake caliper. Do not disconnect brake hose.
4. Disconnect tie rod from knuckle.
5. Use a utility stand in order to support lower control arm.
6. Disconnect height sensor link from lower control arm.
7. Disconnect shock absorber from lower control arm.
8. Use tool No. J 41820, or equivalent, in order to disconnect ball joint from knuckle.
9. Remove lower ball joint nut.
10. Use a utility stand in order to lower control arm and relieve coil spring tension.
11. Carefully remove coil spring and jounce bumper.
12. Remove spring insulator.
13. Remove lower control arm.
14. Reverse procedure to install.

CONTROL ARM BUSHING

REPLACE

1. Raise and support vehicle.
2. Use a utility stand in order to support control arm forward of coil spring.
3. Remove control arm bolts from rear axle.
4. Use a utility stand in order to lower rear axle enough to gain access to control arm bushing.
5. Mark orientation of control arm bushing in lower control arm.
6. Use tool Nos. J 28685 and J 9519–E, or equivalent, in order to remove control arm bushing.
7. Reverse procedure to install.

STABILIZER BAR

REPLACE

1. Raise and support vehicle.
2. Remove tire and wheel.

3. Remove load level sensor.
4. Remove clamp holding righthand park brake cable to stabilizer shaft.
5. Remove lefthand and righthand side stabilizer shaft insulators and brackets.
6. Remove lefthand and righthand stabilizer shaft links.
7. Remove spare tire from spare tire hoist.
8. Remove stabilizer shaft.
9. Reverse procedure to install.

TIGHTENING SPECIFICATIONS

Year	Component	Torque Ft. Lbs.
EXCEPT SV6		
2002–05	Axle Control	162
	Hub & Bearing Assembly	63
	Shock Absorber	63
	Stabilizer Bar	92
	Wheel Lug Nuts	100
SV6		
2005–06	Ball Joint Nut	①
	Control Arm Nut	162
	Lower Control Arm To Crossmember Bolts	37
	Lower Control Arm To Crossmember Cam Nut	107
	Rear Axle Tie Rod Bolt At Axle.	92
	Rear Axle Tie Rod Bolt At Body	100
	Rear Axle To Hub Nut	118
	Rear Crossmember To Body Mounting Bolts	96
	Shock Absorber Bolt - Axle	63
	Shock Absorber Nut And Bolt - IRS	66
	Stabilizer Shaft Insulator Bracket Nut	63
	Stabilizer Shaft Link Nuts	30
	Tie Rod Bolt	66
	Tie Rod Nut	59
	Upper Control Arm To Crossmember Nuts	55
	Upper Control Arm To Knuckle Nut	74
	Wheel Bearing/Hub Bolt - Independent Rear Suspension	96
	Wheel Bearing/Hub Bolt - Without Independent Rear Suspension (New Only)	59
	Wheel Speed Sensor Bracket Nut	106

① — First pass 26 lb. ft.; final pass 130°.

Front Suspension & Steering

NOTE: On Air Bag Equipped Models, Refer To "Air Bag System Precautions" Located In The Front Of This Manual For System Disarming & Arming Procedures.

NOTE: Refer To "Computer Relearn Procedures" Located In The Front Of This Manual When Battery Power To The Computer Has Been Interrupted.

INDEX

PRECAUTIONS

Air Bag Systems

Refer to "Air Bag System Precautions" in the front of this manual for system disarming and arming procedures.

Battery Ground Cable

Prior to service disconnect battery ground cable and isolate as required.

Drive Shaft & Boot

When performing any repair procedure near drive axles, care must be taken to prevent drive axle joints from being over extended. If either end of shaft is disconnected, over extension of joint could result in separation of internal components which could go undetected and result in failure of joint. Drive axle joint seal protectors part No. J-34754, or equivalent, should be used anytime service is performed on or near drive axles, **Fig. 1.**

DESCRIPTION

The front suspension used on these vehicles is a combination strut and spring design. The control arms pivot from frame. The frame has isolation mounts to body and rubber bushings are used for lower control arm pivots. The upper end of strut is isolated by a rubber mount and contains a bearing to allow for wheel turning.

The lower end of steering knuckle pivots on a ball joint riveted to control arm. The ball joint is fastened to steering knuckle with a pinch bolt.

HUB, BEARING & SEAL

REPLACE

1. Raise and support vehicle.

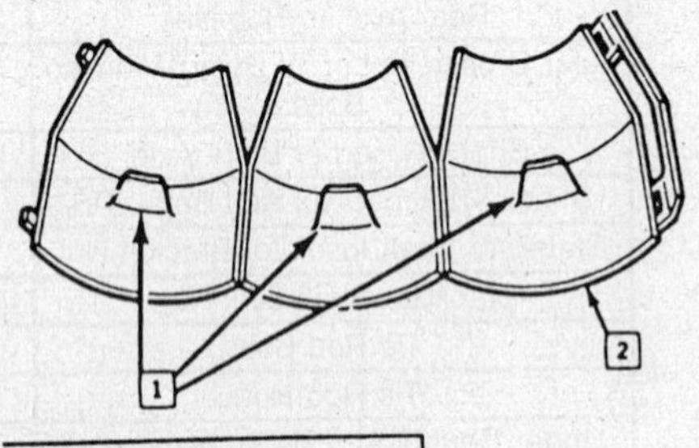

Fig. 1 Axle seal protector

2. Remove tire and wheel.
3. Disconnect wheel speed sensor electrical connector.
4. Remove wheel speed sensor electrical connector from bracket.
5. Remove brake caliper bracket with brake caliper.
6. Remove brake rotor.
7. Remove wheel drive shaft nut.
8. Use three wheel nuts in order to attach tool No. J 28733–B, or equivalent, to wheel bearing hub.
9. Use tool No. J 28733–B, or equivalent, in order to push wheel drive shaft out of wheel bearing hub.
10. Remove and discard wheel bearing hub bolts.
11. Remove wheel bearing hub. **Ensure that wheel drive shaft outer seal boot is not damaged.**
12. Reverse procedure to install.

STRUT

Care should be taken to avoid chipping or scratching spring coating when handling front suspension coil spring. Damage could cause premature failure.

1. Remove wiper module.
2. Raise and support vehicle. **Lift vehicle using only a frame-contact vehicle lift. Do not lift vehicle using a suspension-contact vehicle lift.**
3. Remove tire and wheel.
4. Lower vehicle.
5. Remove strut upper nuts.
6. Raise vehicle.
7. Scribe strut to knuckle.
8. Remove strut lower bolts and nuts.
9. Remove strut.
10. Reverse procedure to install.

STRUT ASSEMBLY SERVICE

The following procedure has been revised by a Technical Service Bulletin.

Disassemble

1. Install strut in strut compressor tool No. J-34013-B, strut lower adapter tool No. J-34013-971 and upper strut tool adapter tool No. J-34013-972, or equivalents, **Fig. 2.**
2. Rotate forcing screw until spring is slightly compressed.
3. Remove strut shaft nut with strut rod nut socket tool No. J-42991, or equivalent, and Torx T45.
4. Install alignment rod tool No. J-34013-197, or equivalent. to guide strut shaft out of upper mount.
5. Loosen compressor forcing screw while guiding strut shaft out of upper mount.
6. Continue loosening forcing screw until strut and spring can be removed.

Assemble

1. Install strut into strut compressor tool No. J-34013-B, or equivalent.

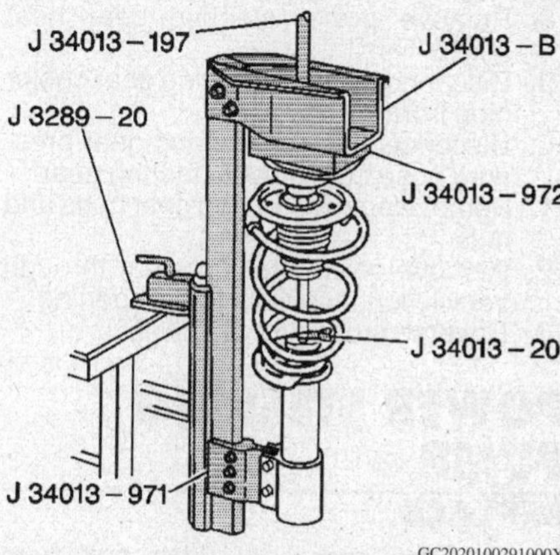

Fig. 2 Strut service

2. Install damper rod clamp tool No. J-34013-20, or equivalent.
3. Inset spring over strut in correct position.
4. Move spring upright in compressor and instal upper locking pin.
5. Install strut in strut compressor tool No. J-34013-B, strut lower adapter too No. J-34013-971 and upper strut tool adapter tool No. J-34013-972, or equivalents, **Fig. 2.**
6. Install alignment rod tool No. J-34013-197, or equivalent. through upper strut mount and into strut shaft.
7. Rotate compressor forcing screw clockwise until strut shaft threads are above strut top.
8. Install strut shaft washer and strut shaft nut.
9. Remove damper rod clamp tool.
10. Tighten strut shaft nut with strut rod nut socket tool No. J-42991, or equivalent, and Torx T45.
11. Strut shaft nuts are prevailing torque fasteners. They must develop specified torque before fastener seating. **If they do not develop proper torque before fastener seating, replace fastener.**
12. Remove strut from holding fixture.

BALL JOINT INSPECTION

1. Raise and support front of vehicle allowing front suspension to hang free.
2. Grasp tire at top and bottom and move top of tire in an in-and-out motion.
3. Observe for any horizontal movement of knuckle relative to control arm.
4. Ball joints must be replaced if any looseness is detected in joint or ball joint seal is cut.
5. Inspect ball stud tightness by shaking tire. Observe for any looseness of ball stud tightness in knuckle boss.

BALL JOINT

REPLACE

1. Remove lower control arm.
2. Secure lower control arm in a vice.
3. Drill or grind off ball stud rivet heads.
4. Use a hammer and drift punch in order to remove rivets.
5. Remove ball stud from lower control arm.
6. Reverse procedure to install.

CONTROL ARM

REPLACE

Use only recommended tools for separating ball joint from knuckle. Do not hammer or pry ball joint from knuckle. Failure to use recommended tools may cause damage to ball joint and seal.

1. Turn steering wheel in order to move front of applicable wheel to outboard most position. **Use ignition key in order to unlock steering column.**
2. Raise and support vehicle. **Use only a frame-contact type vehicle lift or a floor jack at recommended lift points. do not use a suspension-contact type vehicle lift. Do not lift vehicle by lower control arms.**
3. Remove tire and wheel.
4. Disconnect ABS wheel speed sensor connector.
5. Disconnect ABS wheel speed sensor jumper harness from harness retainer clips.
6. Remove stabilizer shaft link.
7. Remove cotter pin from ball stud.
8. Loosen ball stud nut.
9. Install tool No. J 41820, or equivalent, over ball stud and lower control arm.
10. Rotate ball stud nut counterclockwise in order to separate ball stud from steering knuckle.
11. Remove lower control arm bolts and nuts.
12. Remove lower control arm.
13. Reverse procedure to install.

CONTROL ARM BUSHING

REPLACE

Front

REMOVAL

1. Remove lower control arm.
2. Secure lower control arm in a vice.
3. Mark lower control arm along flat edge of bushing flange.
4. Assemble bushing removal tools as outlined, **Fig. 3. Apply J 23444–A, or equivalent high pressure lubricant, to threads of tool No. J 21474–27, or equivalent.**
5. Tighten tool No. J 21474–4, or equivalent, until bushing is removed from control arm.
6. Disassemble bushing removal tools.

INSTALLATION

The lower control arm vertical busing must be installed in the same position from which it was removed.

1. Align flat edge of bushing flange to mark in control arm. Ensure that flat edge of bushing flange is 30° from centerline of lower control arm. Ensure that thin slot in bushing is facing outboard.
2. Insert bushing into control arm.

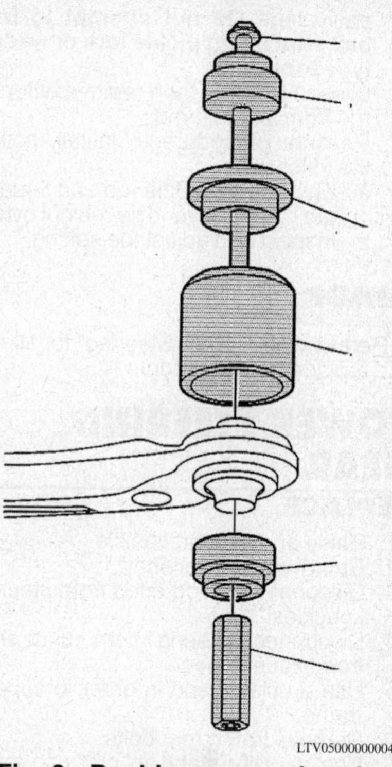

Fig. 3 Bushing removal tools description

3. Assemble bushing installation tools as outlined, **Fig. 4.**
4. Tighten tool No. J 21474–4, or equivalent, until bushing is fully seated in control arm.
5. Disassemble bushing installation tools.
6. Install lower control arm.

Rear

On these models the rear control arm rear (horizontal) bushing is not serviceable. It is replaced with the control arm as an assembly.

STABILIZER BAR

REPLACE

1. Raise and support vehicle.
2. Remove lefthand front tire and wheel.
3. Remove lefthand and righthand stabilizer shaft links.
4. Remove lefthand and righthand stabilizer shaft insulators and brackets.
5. Remove stabilizer shaft from lefthand side of vehicle.
6. Reverse procedure to install.

TIE ROD END

REPLACE

Outer

1. Remove tie rod ball stud nut.
2. separate out tire rod from steering knuckle using universal steering linkage puller tool No. J-24319-B, or

equivalent. **Do not attempt to free ball stud using pickle fork or wedge type tool.**

3. Loosen jam nut, then remove outer tie rod from inner tie rod.
4. Reverse procedure to install, noting the following:
   a. Ensure 2.5–4.5 tie rod end threads are visible beyond tie rod nut nylon.
   b. Inspect and adjust toe setting.

Inner

Refer to the "Power Steering" for tie rod end replacement procedure.

POWER STEERING GEAR

REPLACE

1. Raise and support vehicle.
2. Remove stabilizer shaft.
3. Disconnect tie rod ends from steering knuckles.
4. Disconnect steering intermediate shaft from steering gear.
5. Use a utility stand in order to support frame.
6. Remove frame rear bolts.
7. Use a utility stand in order to lower frame and powertrain. **Do not lower rear of frame too far as damage to engine components nearest to cowl may result.**

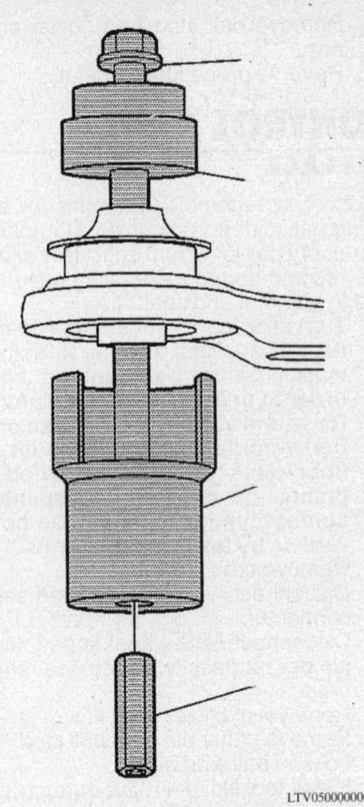

Fig. 4 Bushing installation tools

8. Remove power steering gear heat shield.
9. Disconnect power steering gear cooler pipe from steering gear.
10. Disconnect power steering gear pressure hose from power steering gear.
11. Remove power steering gear bolts and nuts.
12. Remove power steering gear through vehicle lefthand side wheel opening.
13. Reverse procedure to install.

POWER STEERING PUMP

REPLACE

1. Remove accessory drive belt from power steering pump pulley. **It is not required to completely remove drive belt from engine.**
2. Remove fuel injector sight shield.
3. Remove power steering pump pulley.
4. Disconnect power steering pressure hose form pump.
5. Disconnect power steering return hose from pump.
6. Remove engine electrical harness from reservoir retainers.
7. Remove power steering pump mounting bolts.
8. Remove power steering pump from vehicle.
9. Remove reservoir from pump.
10. Reverse procedure to install.

TIGHTENING SPECIFICATIONS

Year	Component	Torque Ft. Lbs.
EXCEPT SV6		
2002–05	Axle Nut	151
	Ball Stud Castle	③
	Brake Caliper	63
	Cooler Pipe	89①
	Control Arm Mounting	83
	Hub & Bearing	96
	Hub Nut	151
	Intermediate Shaft Lower Pinch Bolt	33
	Lower Control Arm	83
	Power Steering Cooler Hose/Pipe Fitting	20
	Power Steering Gear	59
	Power Steering Pump	25
	Rack & Pinion Mount	59
	Stabilizer Bar Insulator Bracket	35
	Stabilizer Bar Link	17
	Strut Lower Bolt	90
	Strut Upper Nut	30
	Strut Shaft	63
	Tie Rod Ball Stud	22②
	Wheel Bearing/Hub	96
	Wheel Lug Nuts	100

Continued

TIGHTENING SPECIFICATIONS—Continued

Year	Component	Torque Ft. Lbs.
SV6		
2005–06	Ball Stud Castle Nut - Lower Control Arm	④
	Ball Stud Nuts - Replacement Ball Joint	50
	Lower Control Arm Nuts - At Frame	71
	Stabilizer Shaft Insulator Bracket Bolts	35
	Stabilizer Shaft Link Nut - With Rear Twist Axle	33
	Stabilizer Shaft Link Nut - With Rear IRS	14
	Strut Lower Nuts - At Knuckle	83
	Strut Shaft Nut	63
	Strut Upper Nuts	22
	Wheel Bearing/Hub Bolts - New Only	96

①— Inch lbs.
②— Tighten an additional 120°, or two flats.
③— Used nut, 40 ft. lbs.; new nut, 50 ft. lbs.
④— First pass 22 lb. ft.; final pass add an additional 135°.

Wheel Alignment

INDEX

PRELIMINARY INSPECTION

Proper wheel alignment must be performed on a level alignment rack which is calibrated monthly. Keep turnplates clean and lubricate at least once a year.

Camber and toe are the only adjustments that can be performed on these vehicles. Before making any adjustment that affects wheel alignment, inspect the following:

1. Tires for proper inflation pressure, tread wear and that tires are same size. Inspect for tire "lead."
2. Hub and bearing assemblies for excessive wear.
3. Ball joints and tie rod ends.
4. Vehicle trim height. Refer to "Vehicle Ride Height."
5. Strut dampeners for proper operation.
6. Control arms for loose bushings.
7. Stabilizer shaft for loose or missing components.
8. Suspension and steering components for damage.
9. Inspect steering gear mounts, brackets, and bolts for looseness or damage.

FRONT WHEEL ALIGNMENT

Camber

1. Raise and support vehicle.
2. Remove tire and wheel.
3. Remove strut lower bolt in order to inspect for oblong strut lower hole. If strut lower hole is oblong, loosen strut upper bolt in order to allow for camber adjustment. If strut lower hole is not oblong, perform the following steps:
   a. Remove strut from vehicle.
   b. Secure strut in a vice.
   c. File strut lower hole laterally in order to allow for camber adjustment.
   d. Install strut to vehicle.
   e. Install strut bolts.
4. Adjust camber.
5. **Torque** strut lower nuts to 83 ft. lbs.
6. Install tire and wheel.
7. Lower vehicle.

Toe-In

1. Remove power steering gear seal small clamps.
2. Verify that steering wheel is centered and wheels are in straight ahead position.
3. Loosen lefthand and righthand tie rod jam nuts.
4. Rotate inner tie rods in order to obtain proper toe angle of 0°. **Verify that number of threads showing on both inner tie rod ends are approximately equal.**
5. **Torque** tie rod end jam nuts to 50 ft. lbs. **Use correct fastener in correct location. Replacement fasteners must be correct part number for that application. Fasteners requiring replacement or fasteners requiring use of thread locking compound or sealant are identified in service procedure. Do not use paints, lubricants, or corrosion inhibitors on fasteners or fastener joint surfaces unless specified. These coatings affect fastener torque and joint clamping force and may damage fastener. Use correct tightening sequence and specifications when installing fasteners in order to avoid damage to components and systems.**
6. Install power steering gear seal small clamps. **Verify that power steering gear seal is not twisted.**

VEHICLE RIDE HEIGHT

Refer to **Figs. 1 through 3** for vehicle ride height specifications.

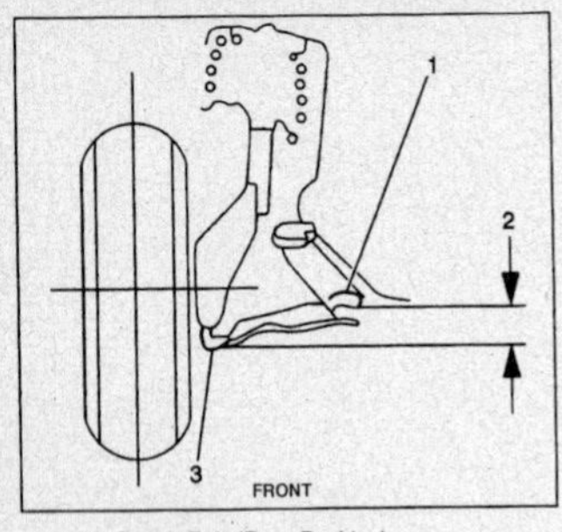

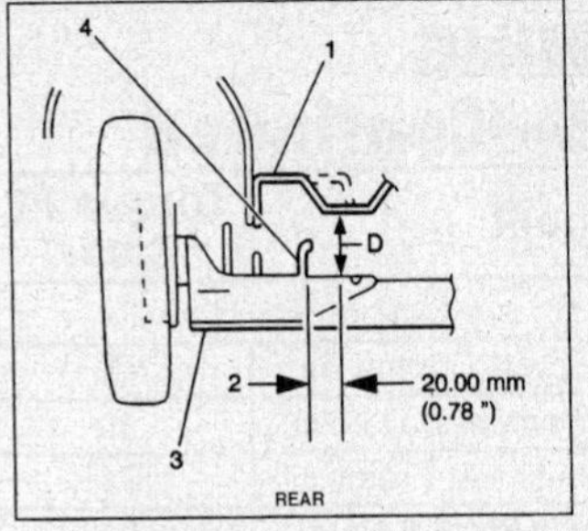

(1) Center Bolt (Rear Bushing)
(2) Z Height
(3) Lowest Point on Ball Stud

(1) Frame Rail
(2) D Height
(3) Rear Axle
(4) Coil Spring Seat Support Rail

GC2049700138020X

Fig. 1 D & Z vehicle ride height measurements

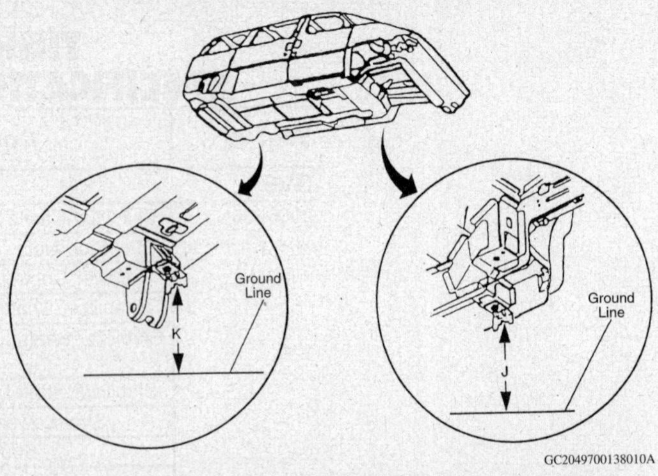

GC2049700138010A

Fig. 2 J & K vehicle ride height measurements

Year	Model	Ride Height, Inches			
		D Curb	J Curb	K Curb	Z Curb
ALL WHEEL DRIVE					
2005–06	P225/60R17 Tires	3.66	12.17	11.69	2.56
EXTENDED WHEELBASE					
2002–04	Cargo Van Less ALC	5.47–6.26	9.20–10.07	10.35–11.14	2.28–3.07
	Cargo Van w/ALC	5.78–6.57	9.44–10.23	10.98–11.77	2.28–3.07
	Non-Cargo Van	5.47–6.26	9.21–10.00	10.07–10.86	2.28–3.07
2005–06	P215/70R16 Tires	6.46	12.20	11.85	2.56
	P225/60R17 Tires	6.46	12.20	11.85	2.56
	P215/70R16 Tires	7.52	12.36	12.40	2.56
	P225/60R17 Tires	7.52	12.36	12.40	2.56
	P215/70R16 Tires	6.73	12.24	12.01	2.56
	P225/60R17 Tires	6.73	12.28	12.01	2.56
	P225/60R17 Tires	3.66	12.17	11.73	2.56
STANDARD WHEELBASE					
2002–04	P205/70R15 Tires	5.23–6.02	8.97–9.76	9.84–10.62	2.28–3.07
	P215/70R15 Tires	5.23–6.02	9.25–10.03	10.15–10.94	2.28–3.07
2005–06	P215/70R16 Tires	6.22	12.13	11.57	2.56
	P225/60R17 Tires	6.22	12.13	11.57	2.56

ALC — Automatic Level Control

Fig. 3 Vehicle ride height specifications

SRX

NOTE: Refer To Back Of This Manual For Vehicle Manufacturer's Special Service Tool Suppliers.

INDEX OF SERVICE OPERATIONS

Specifications

GENERAL ENGINE SPECIFICATIONS

Year	Engine Liter (VIN)	Fuel System	Bore & Stroke	Compression Ratio	Horsepower @ RPM	Torque Ft. Lbs. @ RPM	Normal Oil Pressure, psi
2004–06	3.6L (7)	SFI	3.7008 X 3.370	10.2	255 @ 6500	254 @ 2800	①
	4.6 (A)	SFI	3.6610 X 3.30710	10.5	320 @ 6400	315 @ 4000	②

① — 10 psi @ idle; 20 psi @ 2000 RPM.

② — 5 psi @ idle; 35 psi @ 2000 RPM.

TUNE UP SPECIFICATIONS

The following specifications are published from the latest information available. This data should only be used in the absence of a decal affixed in the engine compartment.

Year/ Engine (VIN)	Spark Plug Gap, Inch	Ignition Timing			Auto. Trans.		Fuel Pump Pressure psi.	Valve Lash, Inch
		Firing Order	Timing BTDC	Mark Location	Curb Idle Speed	Fast Idle Speed		
3.6L (7)	.0433	1-2-3-4-5-6②	①	①	①②	①	55–60	③
4.6L (A)	.0500	1-2-7-3-4-5-6-8②	①	①	①②	①	55–60	③

BTDC — Before Top Dead Center

① — Controlled by the Powertrain Control Module (PCM).

② — Air Conditioning OFF, 600 RPM; Air Conditioning ON, 700 RPM.

③ — Equipped w/hydraulic valve lifters.

FRONT WHEEL ALIGNMENT SPECIFICATIONS

Year	Caster, Degree		Camber, Degree		Total Toe, Degree		Steering Wheel Angle, Degree		Ball Joint
	Limit	Desired	Limit	Desired	Limits	Desired	Limits	Desired	
2004–06	+3.50 to +4.70②	+4.10②	-1.10 to +.10②	-.5②	0 to +.40	+.20	-3.5 To +3.5	.0	①

① — Refer to "Ball Joint Inspection" in the "Front Suspension & Steering" section for ball joint specifications.

② — Cross tolerance limits, -.6 to + .6°

REAR WHEEL ALIGNMENT SPECIFICATIONS

Year	Camber, Degree		Cross Camber		Toe, Degree		Thrust Angle	
	Limit	Desired	Limit	Desired	Limit	Desired	Limit	Desired
2004–06	-1.5 to 1.5	-1	-.75 to +.75	0	0 to +.40①	+.2①	-.2 to +.2	0

① — Individual toe to be more than or equal to -.05°.

VEHICLE RIDE HEIGHT SPECIFICATIONS

Year	Manufacturer's Original Tire Size	Measurement Points & Specifications①									
		Front					Rear				
		Dim.	Specifications				Dim.	Specifications			
			Inches		mm			Inches		mm	
			Limits	Desired	Limits	Desired		Limits	Desired	Limits	Desired
2004–06	②	Z	3.46–4.25	3.86	88–108	98	D	.2.28–3.07	2.68	58–78	68

Dim. — Dimension.

Dim. D — Rear suspension height is vertical distance between the centerline of the inboard rear lower control arm bolt and centerline of the outboard rear lower control arm bolt, **Fig. A.**

Dim. Z — Front suspension height is distance between pivot bolt center line down to the lower corner of the lower ball joint, **Fig. B.**

① — All measurements are taken with a full tank of gas.

② — Refer to door sticker or glove compartment for manufacturer's original tire size specifications.

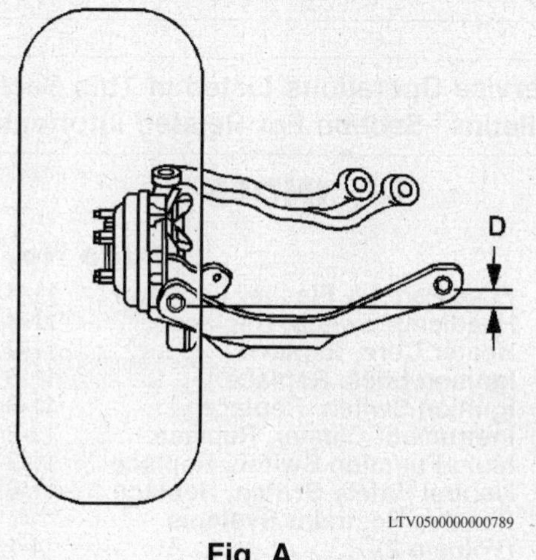

Fig. A

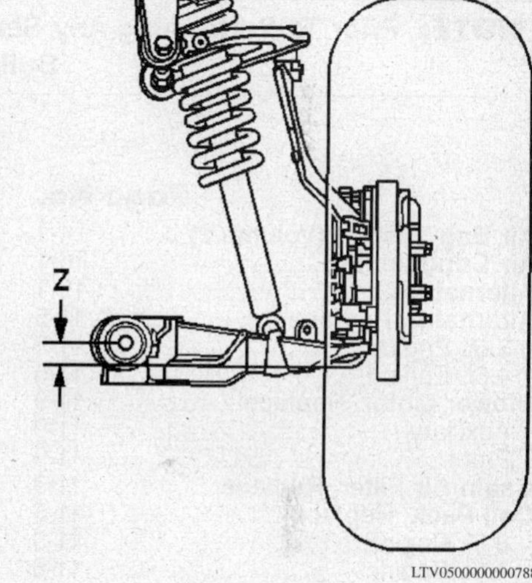

Fig. B

FLUID CAPACITIES & COOLING SYSTEM DATA

Year	Engine Liter	Cooling Capacity Qts.	Recommended Coolant Type	Radiator Cap Relief Pressure, psi	Thermostat Opening Temp. °F	Fuel Tank Gals.	Engine Oil Refill Qts.②	Auto. Transaxle Qts.①		Transfer Case, Qts	Differential, Qts.	
								Drain & Refill	Overhaul		Front	Rear
2004–06	3.6L	11.0	Dex-Cool	18	203	20.0	6.0	7.4	9.0	.53	1.37	③④
	4.6L	12.5	Dex-Cool	18	185	20.0	8.0	7.4	9.0	.53	1.37	③④

① — Approximate, make final inspect w/dipstick.
② — Includes filter.
③ — Cover removed, 1.27 Qts.; Using drain plug, 1.06 Qts.
④ — Limited Slip, add 3.38 ounces additive w/cover removed; 2.37 ounces using drain plug.

LUBRICANT DATA

Year	Lubricant Type				
	Automatic Transaxle	Differential	Transfer Case	Power Steering	Brake System
2004–06	Dextron III ATF	SAE 75W-90①	Dextron III ATF	②	DOT 3

① — Synthetic Axle Lubricant (Part No. 12378261) meeting GM specification No. 9986115.

② — GM Power Steering Fluid (Part No. 1052884), or equivalent.

Electrical

NOTE: On Air Bag Equipped Models, Refer To "Air Bag System Precautions" Located In The Front Of This Manual For System Disarming & Arming Procedures.

NOTE: Refer To "Computer Relearn Procedures" Located In The Front Of This Manual When Battery Power To The Computer Has Been Interrupted.

NOTE: Prior To Performing Any Service Operations Listed In This Section, Consult The "Technical Service Bulletins" Section For Related Information.

INDEX

PRECAUTIONS

Air Bag Systems

Refer to "Air Bag System Precautions" in the front of this manual for system disarming and arming procedures.

Battery Ground Cable

Prior to service, disconnect battery ground cable and isolate as required.

FUSE PANEL & FLASHER LOCATION

The engine compartment fuse block is located In the engine compartment, in the righthand front corner, **Fig. 1.**

The lefthand rear fuse block in located In the passenger compartment, near the lefthand side of the rear seat under the carpet.

The righthand rear fuse block in located In the passenger compartment, near the righthand side of the rear seat under the carpet.

The steering column fuse block is located behind the lefthand instrument panel knee bolster, taped to the steering column wiring harness, **Fig. 2.**

The hazard turn signal flasher is located in the lefthand front of the passenger compartment under the instrument panel, above the data link connector (DLC), **Fig. 3.**

FUEL PUMP RELAY LOCATION

The fuel pump relay is located in righthand rear fuse block, in the passenger compartment, near the righthand side of the rear seat under the carpet.

STARTER

REPLACE

3.6L Engine

1. Turn ignition switch to OFF position.
2. Remove starter solenoid electrical

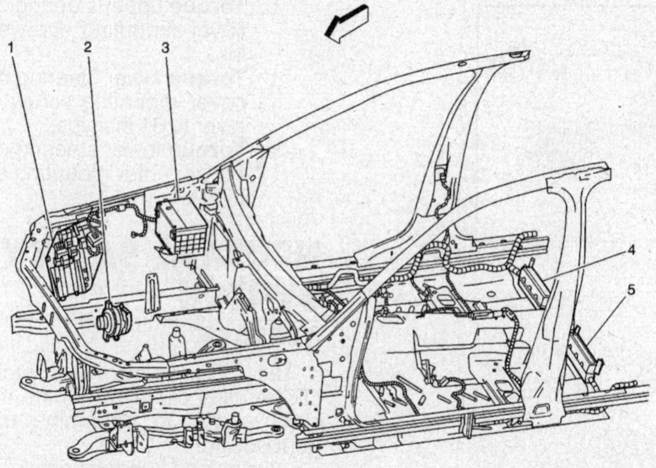

1. Underhood Fuse Block
2. Alternator
3. Battery
4. Passenger Compartment Fuse Block, Righthand Rear
5. Passenger Compartment Fuse Block, Lefthand Rear

LTV0500000000790

Fig. 1 Engine & passenger compartment fuse blocks

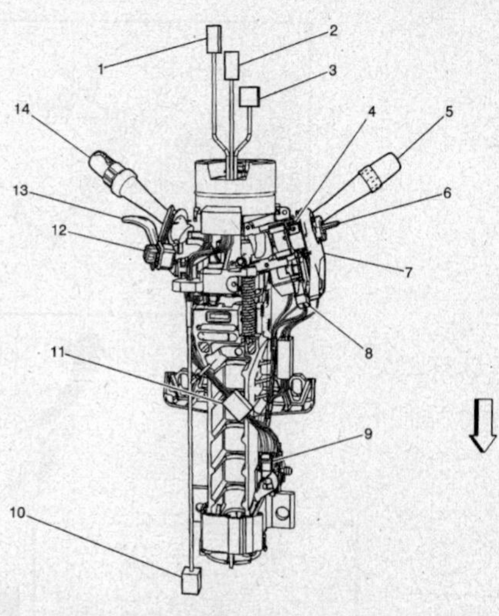

1. Inflatable Restraint Steering Wheel Module Coil Connector
2. Inflatable Restraint Steering Wheel Module Coil Connector
3. C208
4. Ignition Lock Cylinder Control Actuator
5. Windshield Wiper Washer Switch
6. Ignition Lock Cylinder Case
7. Theft Deterrent Control Module
8. Ignition Switch Connector
9. C202
10. C203
11. Fuse Block - Steering Column
12. Adjustable Pedal Switch
13. Steering Tilt Lever
14. Turn Signal/Multifunction Switch

LTV0500000000791

Fig. 2 Steering column fuse block

connector, then the terminal nut and battery positive cable.

3. Remove mounting bolts and starter motor.
4. Reverse procedure to install, noting the following:
   a. **Torque** starter motor mounting bolts to 37 ft. lbs.
   b. **Torque** starter terminal nut to 89 inch lbs.

4.6L Engine

1. Remove intake manifold as outlined under "Intake Manifold, Replace" in "4.6L Engine" section.
2. Disconnect battery positive cable and S terminal wire.
3. Remove mounting bolts and starter motor.
4. Reverse procedure to install, noting the following:
   a. **Torque** starter motor mounting bolts to 22 ft. lbs.
   b. **Torque** S terminal nut to 35 inch lbs.
   c. **Torque** battery positive cable to 89 inch lbs.

ALTERNATOR

REPLACE

3.6L Engine

1. Release drive belt tension by rotating drive belt tensioner clockwise.
2. Remove drive belt from water pump pulley.
3. Slowly release drive belt tensioner.
4. Remove drive belt from accessory drive pulleys.
5. Raise and support vehicle.
6. Disconnect alternator electrical connectors.
7. Remove boot and alternator BAT terminal nut, then the battery positive lead.
8. Remove alternator lower mounting bolts.
9. Lower vehicle.
10. Remove upper mounting bolt and alternator.
11. Reverse procedure to install, noting the following:
    a. **Torque** alternator mounting bolts to 37 ft. lbs.
    b. **Torque** battery positive lead and BAT terminal nuts to 115 inch lbs.

4.6L Engine

1. Remove alternator drive belt as outlined under "Serpentine Drive Belt" in "4.6L Engine" section.
2. Remove alternator upper mounting bolts.
3. Raise and support vehicle.
4. **On models equipped with AWD,** proceed as follows:
   a. Remove front tire and wheel assemblies.
   b. Remove push-in retainers and righthand front wheelhouse liner.
   c. Remove upper and lower mounting nuts, then the lefthand and righthand stabilizer shaft link.
   d. Remove stabilizer shaft.
5. **On all models,** cut alternator wiring harness tie strap.
6. Remove lower mounting bolt and lift alternator.
7. Disconnect alternator wire harness electrical connector.
8. Position protective boot aside, then remove output terminal nut and disconnect battery positive lead.
9. Remove alternator.
10. Reverse procedure to install, noting the following:
    a. **Torque** output terminal nut to 89 inch lbs.
    b. **Torque** alternator mounting bolts to 37 ft. lbs., in sequence, **Fig. 4.**
    c. **On models equipped with AWD, torque** stabilizer link mounting nuts to 95 ft. lbs.

COIL PACK

REPLACE

3.6L Engine

1. Remove mounting bolts and cross-vehicle brace.
2. Disengage ball studs and remove engine cover/sight shield.
3. **Do not disconnect fuel pipes and/or hoses.**
4. **If replacing ignition coil for cylinders Nos. 1, 2 or 3,** proceed as follows:
   a. Disconnect air cleaner duct from throttle body.
   b. Disconnect Positive Crankcase Ventilation (PCV) hose from righthand bank valve cover.
   c. **Do not separate upper from lower intake manifold.**
   d. Remove intake manifold mounting bolts.
   e. Remove mounting bolts and intake manifold brace.
   f. Remove and position intake manifold aside.
5. **On all models,** remove electrical connector, then the mounting bolt and ignition coil.

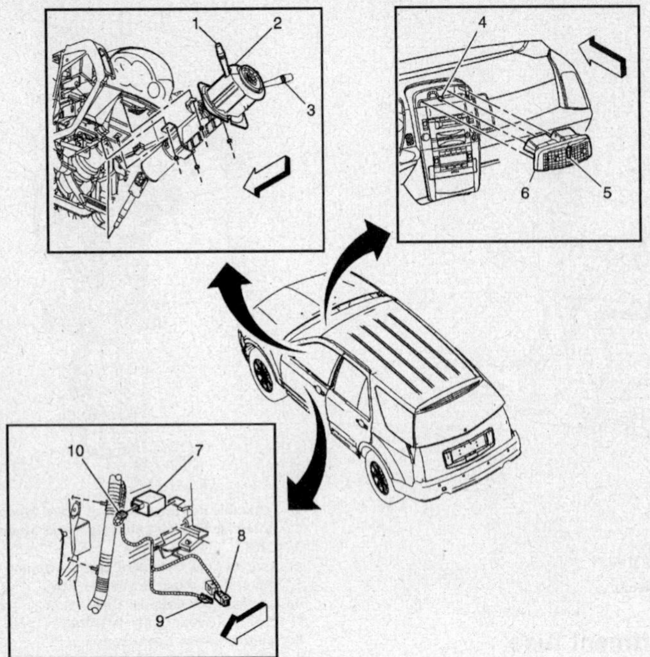

1. Turn Signal/Multifunction Switch
2. Steering Column
3. Windshield Wiper/Washer Switch
4. Hazard Switch Connector
5. Hazard Switch
6. I/P Air Deflector – Center
7. Turn Signal/Hazard Flasher Module
8. Data Link Connector (DLC)
9. Park Brake Switch Connector
10. Turn Signal/Hazard Flasher Module Connector

Fig. 3 Flasher relay location

6. Reverse procedure to install, noting the following:
   a. **Torque** ignition coil mounting bolt to 89 inch lbs.
   b. **Torque** intake manifold brace mounting bolts to 17 ft. lbs.
   c. **Torque** cross-vehicle brace mounting bolts to 83 ft. lbs.

4.6L Engine

1. Remove mounting bolts and cross-vehicle brace.
2. Remove power steering and engine oil fill caps.
3. Remove sight shield by lifting front and pull forward to disconnect rear tab.
4. Remove ignition coil cover.
5. Disconnect electrical connector, remove mounting bolt and ignition coil.
6. Reverse procedure to install. **Torque** coil mounting bolt to 89 inch lbs.

IGNITION LOCK

REPLACE

1. Turn ignition switch to START position.
2. Press release button using suitable awl through lower steering column trim cover access hole, **Fig. 5.**
3. Release ignition switch to RUN position and remove ignition lock cylinder.
4. Reverse procedure to install. Align lock module positioning locking tab slot to ignition lock cylinder positioning tab.

IGNITION SWITCH

REPLACE

1. Disarm air bag system as outlined under "Air Bag System Precautions" in the front of this manual.
2. Pull tilt lever straight out from steering column.
3. Turn ignition switch to START position.
4. Press release button using suitable awl through lower steering column trim cover access hole.
5. Release ignition switch to RUN position and remove ignition lock cylinder.
6. Disconnect adjuster pedal switch connector near ignition switch.
7. Remove two mounting screws and lower steering column trim cover.
8. Remove two mounting screws and upper steering column trim cover.
9. Remove theft deterrent control module from ignition lock cylinder case.
10. Disconnect connector near ignition switch.
11. Remove two tapping screws and ignition switch, **Fig. 6.**
12. Reverse procedure to install, noting to the following:
    a. **Torque** ignition switch tapping screws to 62 inch lbs.
    b. **Torque** upper steering column trim cover mounting screws to 9 inch lbs.
    c. **Torque** lower steering column trim cover mounting screw nearest tilt lever to 31 inch lbs.
    d. **Torque** lower steering column trim cover center mounting screw to 14 inch lbs.

NEUTRAL SAFETY SWITCH

REPLACE

The Transmission Control Module (TCM) uses signals from the manual shift shaft switch to determine transmission gear position.

1. Raise and support vehicle.
2. Remove mounting nut and disconnect shift linkage from transmission manual shift shaft.
3. Disconnect oxygen sensor electrical connector. Record wire routing and mounting points for installation alignment.
4. Remove oxygen sensors from exhaust pipe.
5. Remove two mounting bolts and tunnel brace from floor panel.
6. Support exhaust system and remove exhaust pipes to manifolds mounting nuts.
7. Pry front exhaust hangers from rear suspension hanger rods.
8. Lubricate tail pipe hanger rods and pry hangers from rods.
9. Lower exhaust system, then remove and discard seals.
10. **On models equipped with AWD,** proceed as follows:
    a. Support propeller shaft close to support bearing using suitable jack.
    b. Remove heat shield mounting bolts.
    c. Remove support bearing mounting bolts.
    d. Mark propeller shaft Consent Velocity (CV) joint to transfer case flange for installation alignment.
    e. Remove propeller shaft CV joint to transfer case flange mounting bolts.
    f. Remove propeller shaft coupler-to-differential flange mounting bolts, nuts and washers.
    g. Disconnect propeller shaft CV joint from transfer case by moving propeller shaft toward using suitable flat-bladed tool in transfer case flange.
    h. Hold and lower propeller shaft.
11. **On models equipped with RWD,** proceed as follows:
    a. Remove propeller shaft coupler-to-transmission flange mounting bolts, nuts and washers.
    b. Remove propeller shaft coupler-to-differential flange mounting bolts, nuts and washers.
    c. Support propeller shaft at support bearing.
    d. Remove support bearing mounting bolts, push front propeller shaft toward rear and disconnect it from

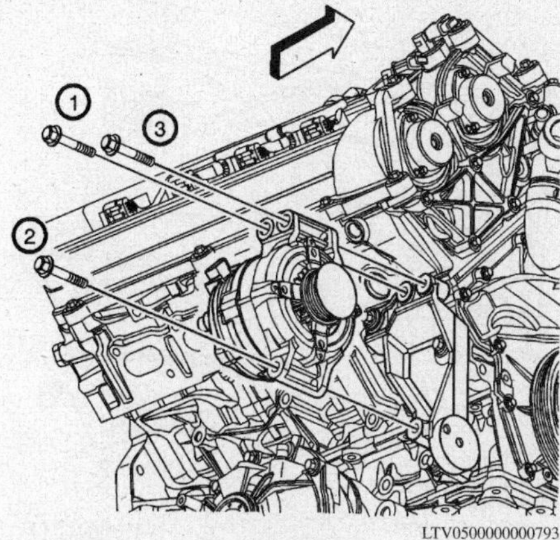

Fig. 4 Alternator tightening sequence

transmission flange.

e. Push front propeller shaft toward rear and release coupler from transmission flange.

12. **On all models,** secure front propeller shaft to shift control lever using suitable mechanics wire.
13. **Replace shaft seal and cup lug only if either is leaking.**
14. Drain transmission fluid into suitable container. Install and **torque** new drain plug to 15 ft. lbs.
15. Remove mounting bolts, then remove transmission oil pan and gasket using suitable rubber mallet.
16. Disconnect electrical connector and remove manual shift shaft position switch retaining pin using suitable pin punch.
17. Remove manual shift shaft detent spring and mounting bolts.
18. Support transmission using suitable transmission jack.
19. Remove transmission support to body mounting bolts.
20. Lower transmission rear allow manual shift shaft to clear floor pan.
21. Extract manual shift shaft from transmission case only far enough only far enough to remove manual shift shaft position switch.
22. Remove manual shift shaft position switch, detent lever, spacer and park pawl actuator, **Fig. 7.**
23. Reverse procedure to install, noting the following:
    a. **Torque** transmission support to body mounting bolts to 44 ft. lbs.
    b. Lubricate propeller shaft centering bushings.
    c. Apply suitable threadlock to propeller shaft flange bolts.
    d. **Torque** transmission oil pan to 11 ft. lbs.
    e. **Torque** heat shield mounting bolts to 71 inch lbs.
    f. **Torque** propeller shaft flange nuts and bolts to 63 ft. lbs.
    g. **Torque** propeller shaft CV joint to transfer case flange mounting bolts to 22 ft. lbs., in sequence, **Fig. 8.**
    h. **Torque** center support bearing mounting bolts to 37 ft. lbs.

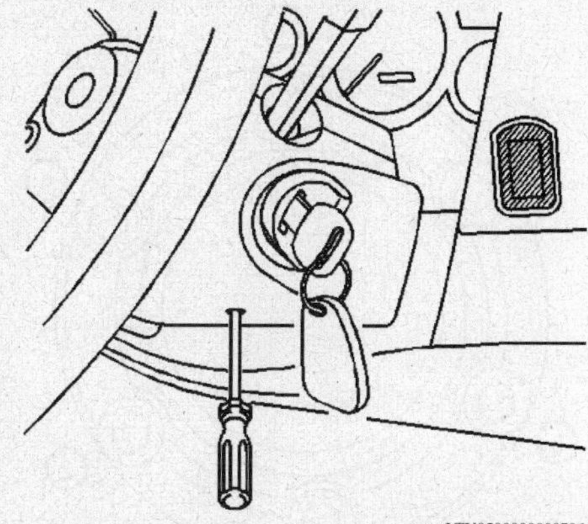

Fig. 5 Ignition lock replacement

    i. **Torque** exhaust to manifold nuts to 22 ft. lbs.
    j. **Torque** floor panel tunnel brace mounting bolts to 18 ft. lbs.
    k. **Torque** manual shaft detent spring bolts to 97 inch lbs.
    l. **Torque** manual shift shaft nut to 80 inch lbs.
    m. **Torque** oxygen sensors to 31 ft. lbs.

HEADLAMP SWITCH

REPLACE

Refer to "Multi-Function Switch, Replace" for headlamp switch replacement.

STOP LIGHT SWITCH

REPLACE

Remove

1. Remove instrument panel closeout panel mounting screws and disconnect courtesy lamp electrical connector.
2. Remove instrument panel closeout panel.
3. Remove mounting bolt, disconnect electrical connector and brake pedal position sensor.

Install

1. Connect brake pedal position sensor electrical connector.
2. Align brake panel position sensor to stud.
3. **Torque** brake pedal position sensor to 80 inch lbs.
4. Connect the courtesy lamp electrical connector.
5. Align and install closeout panel.
6. **Torque** closeout panel mounting screws to 18 inch lbs.
7. Apply parking brake and place transmission in PARK position.
8. Connect suitable programmed scan tool.
9. Turn ignition switch to ON position, with engine OFF.
10. Calibrate BPP sensor using scan tool.

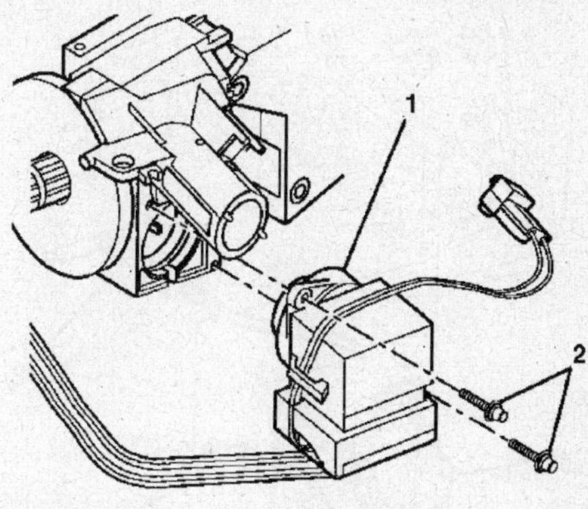

Fig. 6 Ignition switch replacement

MULTI-FUNCTION SWITCH

REPLACE

1. Disarm air bag system as outlined under "Air Bag System Precautions" in the front of this manual.
2. Pull tilt lever straight out from steering column.
3. Turn ignition switch to START position.
4. Press release button using suitable awl through lower steering column trim cover access hole.
5. Release ignition switch to RUN position and remove ignition lock cylinder.
6. Disconnect adjuster pedal switch connector.
7. Remove two mounting screws and lower steering column trim cover.
8. Remove two mounting screws and upper steering column trim cover.
9. Tilt steering column to center position.
10. Disconnect turn signal and multi-function switch connectors.
11. Remove two mounting screws, then the turn signal and multi-function switch.
12. Reverse procedure to install, noting the following:
    a. Ensure turn signal and multi-function switch electrical contact rest on turn signal cancel cam.
    b. **Torque** top mounting screw to 27 inch lbs.
    c. **Torque** front mounting screw to 62 inch lbs.
    d. **Torque** ignition switch tapping screws to 62 inch lbs.
    e. **Torque** upper steering column trim cover mounting screws to 9 inch lbs.
    f. **Torque** lower steering column trim cover mounting screw nearest tilt lever to 31 inch lbs.
    g. **Torque** lower steering column trim cover center mounting screw to 14 inch lbs.

TURN SIGNAL SWITCH

REPLACE

Refer to "Multi-Function Switch, Replace" for turn signal switch replacement.

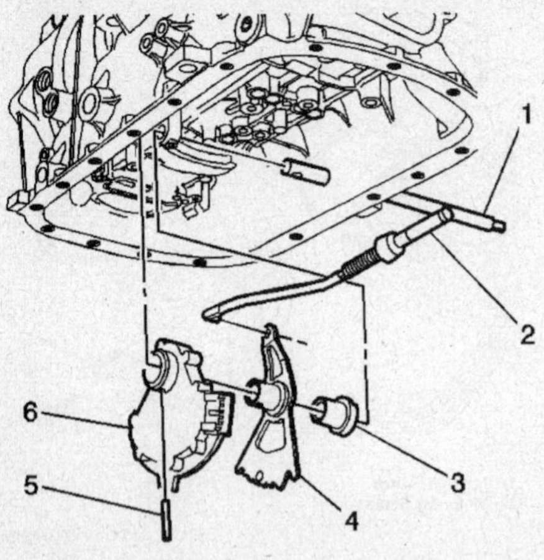

Fig. 7 Manual shift shaft position switch replacement

DIMMER SWITCH

REPLACE

Refer to "Multi-Function Switch, Replace" for dimmer switch replacement.

STEERING WHEEL

REPLACE

1. Disarm air bag system as outlined under "Air Bag System Precautions" in the front of this manual.
2. Disconnect driver air bag module spring loaded fasteners through three openings in back of steering using driver air bag removal tool No. J44298, or equivalent, one opening at a time.
3. Pull inflatable restraint module away from steering wheel and record connector positions, redundant control routing and horn wire routing for installation alignment.
4. Remove steering wheel module Connector Position Assurance (CPA) and electrical connector.
5. Remove horn contact lead and steering wheel module.
6. Disconnect steering column electrical connector.
7. Remove mounting nut and steering wheel using steering wheel puller tool No. J1859-A and legs tool No, J42578, or equivalents.
8. Reverse procedure to install. **Torque** steering wheel mounting nut to 30 ft. lbs.

INSTRUMENT CLUSTER

REPLACE

1. Tilt steering column to lowest position.
2. Remove instrument cluster trim cover using suitable, small flat bladed tool.
3. Remove mounting screws and pry instrument cluster up using suitable, small flat bladed tool, **Fig. 9.**
4. Pull cluster out and disconnect electrical connectors.

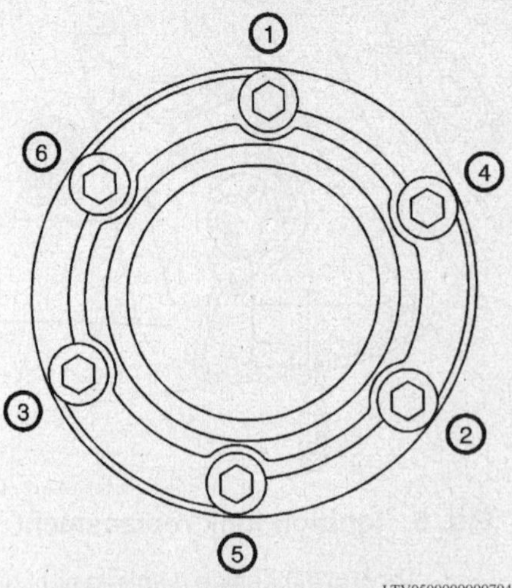

Fig. 8 Propeller shaft CV joint tightening sequence

5. Reverse procedure to install. **Torque** mounting screws to 18 inch lbs.

RADIO

REPLACE

1. Pull center instrument panel vent out and disconnect hazard switch electrical connector. Remove vent.
2. Ensure engine is off and parking brake applied with transmission in lowest gear.
3. Remove mounting screws behind ashtray, then the HVAC control module trim plate by pulling lefthand and righthand sides.
4. Disconnect HVAC control module and ash tray electrical connectors.
5. Remove mounting screws and HVAC control module, **Fig. 10.**
6. Remove four mounting screws, pull radio out and disconnect electrical connectors.
7. Remove radio.
8. Reverse procedure to install, noting the following:
   a. **Torque** radio mounting screws to 80 inch lbs.
   b. **Torque** HVAC control module mounting screws to 18 inch lbs.

WIPER MOTOR

REPLACE

Front

1. Remove wiper motor 10- and 30-amp mini fuses from underhood fuse block.
2. Set wipers in park position, then remove covers and mounting nuts from wiper arm drive spindle.
3. Remove upper hood assist rods from ball studs and support hood rearward to air inlet grille panel.
4. Remove wiper arm using wiper arm puller tool No. J39822, or equivalent.
5. Remove mounting screws and upper air inlet panel, **Fig. 11.**
6. Remove mounting screws and lower air inlet panel, **Fig. 12.**

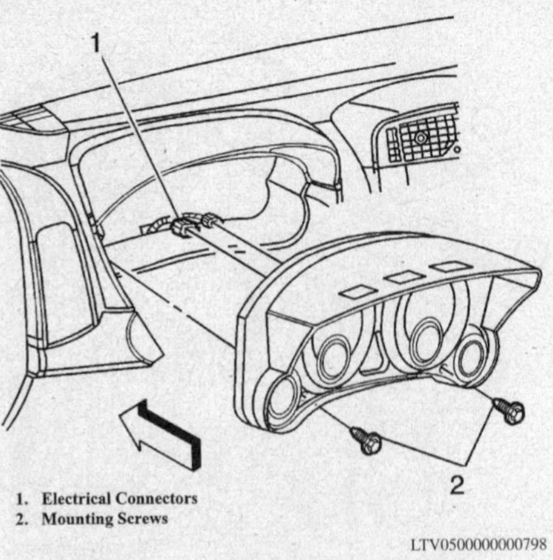

Fig. 9 Instrument cluster replacement

7. Remove wiper motor module mounting bolts and disconnect electrical connector, **Fig. 13.**
8. Remove wiper motor module.
9. Remove drive links from wiper motor crank arm using wiper linkage separator tool No. J39232, or equivalent.
10. Remove three mounting screws and wiper motor.
11. Reverse procedure to install, noting the following:
    a. **Torque** wiper motor mounting screws to 89 inch lbs.
    b. Install drive links to wiper motor crank arm using wiper linkage installer tool No. J39529, or equivalent.
    c. **Torque** wiper motor module mounting bolts to 89 inch lbs.
    d. Position righthand wiper arm so blade tip aligns with orange dot on lower outer edge of windshield.
    e. Position lefthand wiper arm so blade tip aligns with orange line on lower center of windshield.
    f. **Torque** wiper arm mounting nut to 26 ft. lbs.

Rear

1. Mark rear wiper blade to rear window position for installation alignment.
2. Pivot cap and remove rear wiper arm nut.
3. Remove rear wiper arm by rocking it until it disconnects from motor.
4. Remove liftgate mounting screw, then the cover and rod.
5. Lift panel near rear courtesy lamp and disconnect electrical connectors.
6. Remove liftgate trim panel.
7. Disconnect wiper motor fluid line and electrical connector.
8. Remove mounting bolts and wiper motor.
9. Reverse procedure to install, noting the following:
   a. Lubricate wiper motor shaft with windshield washer fluid and push it through grommet.
   b. Apply suitable threadlock to mounting bolts.
   c. **Torque** wiper motor mounting bolts to 62 inch lbs.

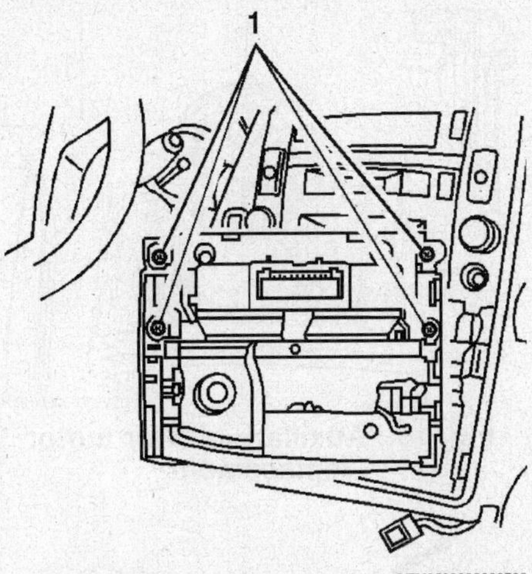

Fig. 10 HVAC control module replacement

d. **Torque** liftgate trim panel mounting screw to 18 inch lbs.
e. **Torque** wiper arm mounting nut to 13 ft. lbs.

WIPER SWITCH

REPLACE

Front

1. Disarm air bag system as outlined under "Air Bag System Precautions" in the front of this manual.
2. Pull tilt lever straight out from steering column.
3. Turn ignition switch to START position.
4. Press release button using suitable awl through lower steering column trim cover access hole.
5. Release ignition switch to RUN position and remove ignition lock cylinder.
6. Disconnect adjuster pedal switch connector .
7. Remove two mounting screws and lower steering column trim cover.
8. Remove two mounting screws and upper steering column trim cover.
9. Remove steering column wiring harness tie straps and disconnect switch connectors.
10. Depress tabs and remove switch.
11. Reverse procedure to install, noting the following:
    a. **Torque** upper steering column trim cover mounting screws to 9 inch lbs.
    b. **Torque** lower steering column trim cover mounting screw nearest tilt lever to 31 inch lbs.
    c. **Torque** lower steering column trim cover center mounting screw to 14 inch lbs.

Rear

1. Pull overhead console front edge down using fingers.
2. Disconnect electrical connectors and remove overhead console.
3. Remove rear window wiper switch.
4. Reverse procedure to install.

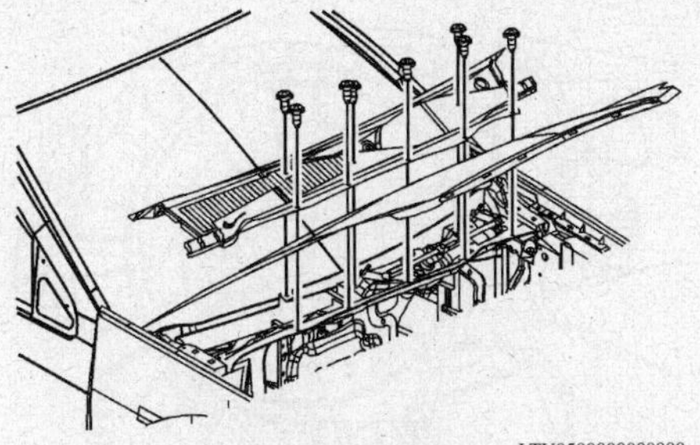

Fig. 11 Upper air inlet panel replacement

WIPER MODULE

REPLACE

1. Remove wiper motor 10- and 30-amp mini fuses from underhood fuse block.
2. Set wipers in park position, then remove covers and mounting nuts from wiper arm drive spindle.
3. Remove upper hood assist rods from ball studs and support hood rearward to air inlet grille panel.
4. Remove wiper arm using wiper arm puller tool No. J39822, or equivalent.
5. Remove mounting screws and upper air inlet panel, **Fig. 11.**
6. Remove mounting screws and lower air inlet panel, **Fig. 12.**
7. Remove wiper motor module mounting bolts and disconnect electrical connector, **Fig. 13.**
8. Remove wiper motor module.
9. Reverse procedure to install, noting the following:
    a. **Torque** wiper motor module mounting bolts to 89 inch lbs.
    b. Position righthand wiper arm so blade tip aligns with orange dot on lower outer edge of windshield.
    c. Position lefthand wiper arm so blade tip aligns with orange line on lower center of windshield.
    d. **Torque** wiper arm mounting nut to 26 ft. lbs.

BLOWER MOTOR

REPLACE

Front

1. Remove four mounting screws and pull righthand instrument panel closeout panel down.
2. Disconnect courtesy lamp electrical connector and remove righthand instrument panel closeout panel.
3. Open door, release tabs and lower glove compartment door.
4. Remove mounting screws and glove compartment.
5. Disconnect motor and processor electrical connectors, then the mounting screws and blower motor, **Fig. 14.**
6. Reverse procedure to install, noting the following:
    a. **Torque** blower motor mounting screws to 13 inch lbs.
    b. **Torque** glove compartment mounting screws to 18 inch lbs.

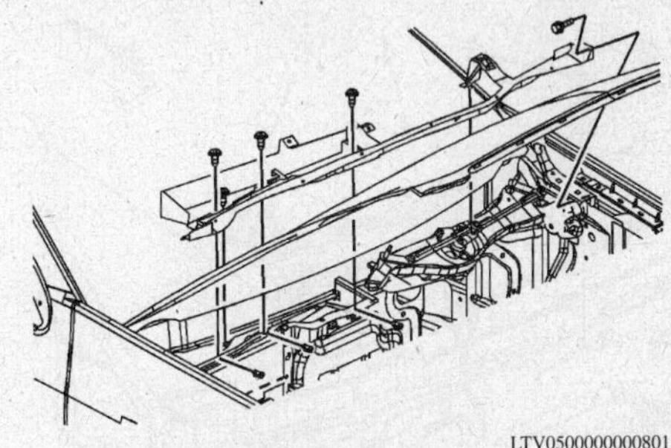

Fig. 12 Lower air inlet panel replacement

c. **Torque** closeout panel mounting screws to 18 inch lbs.

Auxiliary

1. Remove lefthand body side trim access panel.
2. Disconnect electrical connector, then remove mounting screws and blower motor, **Fig. 15.**
3. Reverse procedure to install. **Torque** blower motor mounting screws to 9 inch lbs.

CABIN AIR FILTER

REPLACE

1. Remove wiper motor 10- and 30-amp mini fuses from underhood fuse block.
2. Set wipers in park position, then remove covers and mounting nuts from wiper arm drive spindle.
3. Remove upper hood assist rods from ball studs and support hood rearward to air inlet grille panel.
4. Remove wiper arm using wiper arm puller tool No. J39822, or equivalent.
5. Remove mounting screws and upper air inlet panel, **Fig. 11.**
6. Remove mounting screws and lower air inlet panel, **Fig. 12.**
7. Disconnect tabs, then remove access cover and filter.
8. Reverse procedure to install, noting the following:
    a. Position righthand wiper arm so blade tip aligns with orange dot on lower outer edge of windshield.
    b. Position lefthand wiper arm so blade tip aligns with orange line on lower center of windshield.
    c. **Torque** wiper arm mounting nut to 26 ft. lbs.

HEATER CORE

REPLACE

1. Recover air conditioning refrigerant as outlined in "Air Conditioning" chapter.
2. Drain coolant into suitable container.
3. Disconnect heater core inlet and outlet hoses.
4. Disconnect evaporator liquid and suction lines. Discard O-rings.
5. Remove instrument panel as outlined in "Dash Panel Service" chapter.
6. Remove air inlet.
7. Disconnect HVAC module electrical connector and drain tube.

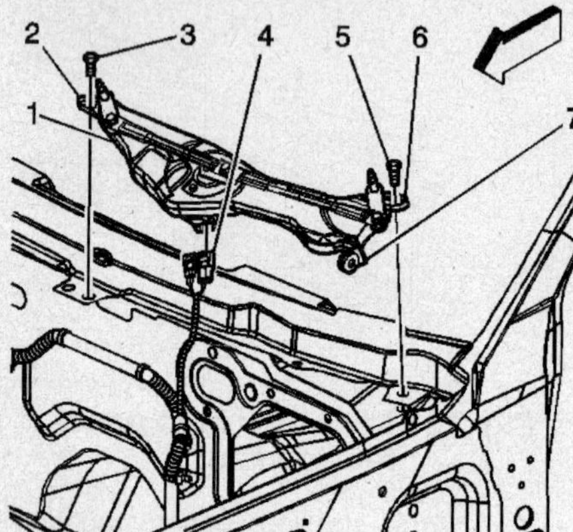

1. Wiper Motor Module
2. Wiper Motor Drive Link
3. Mounting Bolts
4. Wiper Motor Electrical Connector
5. Mounting Bolts
6. Locator Hole
7. Wiper Module Locator Hole

LTV0500000001042

Fig. 13 Wiper motor module replacement

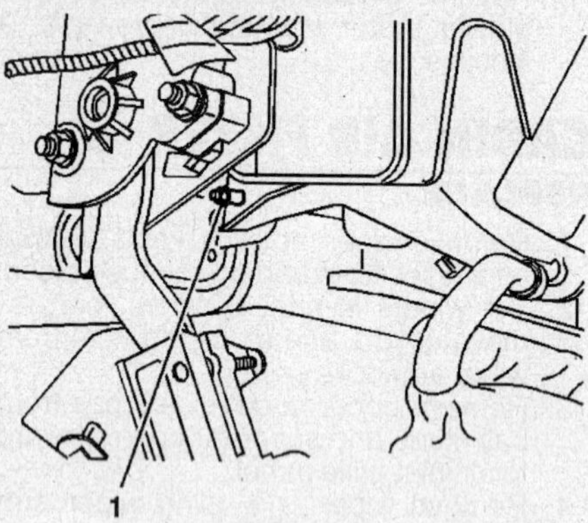

LTV0500000001045

Fig. 16 HAVC module replacement. Lower lefthand mounting nut

8. Disconnect tabs, then position lefthand and righthand rear heater ducts aside.
9. Remove lower and upper lefthand mounting nuts, **Figs. 16 and 17,** then the HVAC module.
10. Remove mounting screw and bracket, then the heater core.
11. Reverse procedure to install, noting the following:
    a. **Torque** heater core pipe bracket mounting screw to 9 inch lbs.
    b. **Torque** HVAC module mounting nuts to 80 inch lbs.

EVAPORATOR CORE

REPLACE

1. Recover air conditioning refrigerant as outlined in "Air Conditioning" chapter.
2. Remove instrument panel as outlined in "Dash Panel Service" chapter.
3. Remove Thermal Expansion Valve (TXV) insulation and HVAC line clamp.
4. Remove mounting bolts and TXV line bracket.
5. Remove TXV from evaporator core

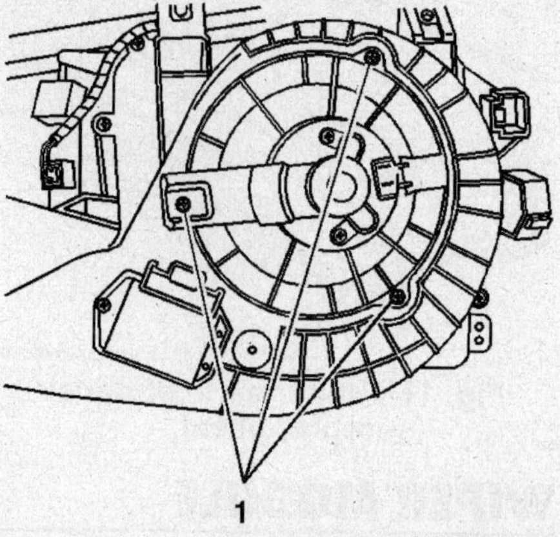

LTV0500000001043

Fig. 14 Front lower motor replacement

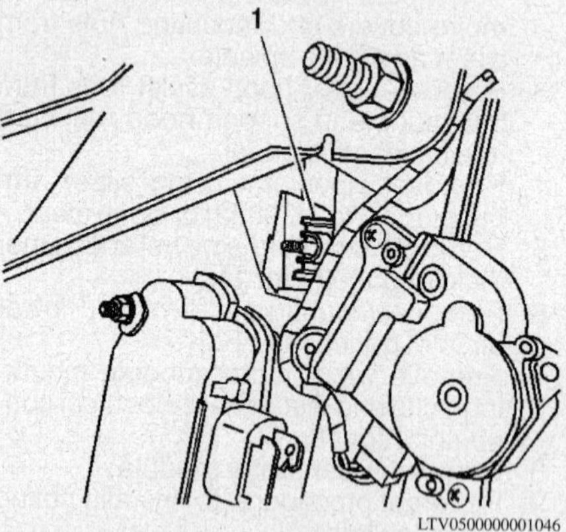

LTV0500000001046

Fig. 17 HVAC module replacement. Upper lefthand mounting nut

and disconnect from air conditioning lines. Discard O-rings.
6. Remove HVAC module case mounting screws and clips, **Fig. 18.**
7. Disconnect from righthand temperature actuator and position HVAC module wiring harness aside.
8. Disconnect and position evaporator core temperature sensor connector aside.
9. Separate HVAC module and remove evaporator core. Remove thermistor.
10. Reverse procedure to install, noting the following:
    a. **Torque** HVAC module case mounting screws to 9 inch lbs.
    b. **Torque** TXV mounting bolts to 31 inch lbs.
    c. **Torque** HVAC line clamp to 9 inch lbs.

TECHNICAL SERVICE BULLETINS

No Start, Discharged Battery

2004-05

On some of these models equipped with

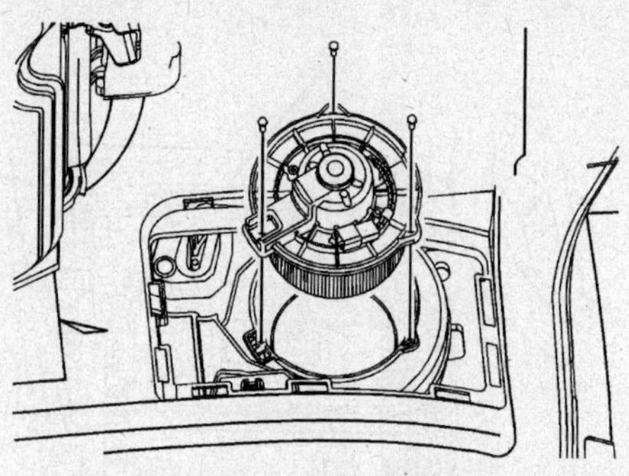

LTV0500000001044

Fig. 15 Auxiliary blower motor replacement

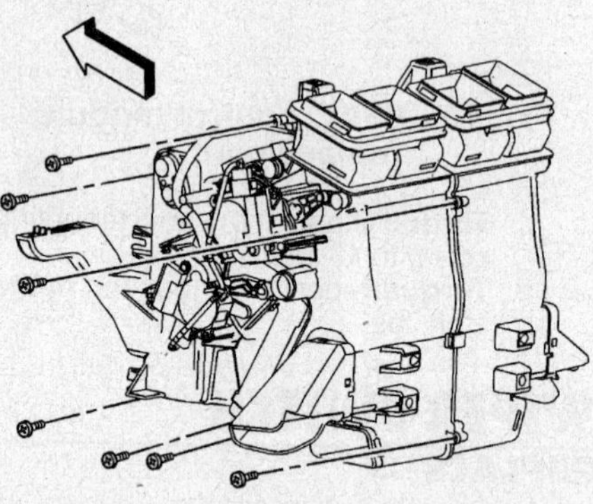

LTV0500000001047

Fig. 18 Evaporator core replacement

Tire Pressure Monitoring (TPM) system, there may be a no-start condition because of a discharged battery. This condition usually occurs after vehicle has sat of 3–4 days near other vehicle with TPM system.

This condition may be caused by RF traffic from other vehicles causing class 2 line wake up intermittently and drawing battery down.

To correct this condition, replace the remote control door lock receiver assembly (antenna module) using part No. 25771733.

Unable To Rotate Key Or Ignition Lock Jammed

2004-05

On some of these models the ignition key may not rotate in either direction, or ignition lock cylinder is jammed.

This condition may be caused by the ignition lock cylinder key guides shearing.

To correct this condition, replace the ignition lock cylinder.

3.6L Engine

NOTE: On Air Bag Equipped Models, Refer To "Air Bag System Precautions" Located In The Front Of This Manual For System Disarming & Arming Procedures.

NOTE: Refer To "Computer Relearn Procedures" Located In The Front Of This Manual When Battery Power To The Computer Has Been Interrupted.

NOTE: Prior To Performing Any Service Operations Listed In This Section, Consult The "Technical Service Bulletins" Section For Related Information.

INDEX

PRECAUTIONS

Air Bag Systems

Refer to "Air Bag System Precautions" in the front of this manual for system disarming and arming procedures.

Battery Ground Cable

Prior to service, disconnect battery ground cable and isolate as required.

Fuel Pressure Relief

1. Turn ignition in Off position.
2. Disconnect battery ground cable and isolate as required.
3. Remove mounting bolts and cross-vehicle brace.
4. Disengage ball studs and remove engine cover/sight shield.
5. Loosen fuel filler cap to relieve fuel tank vapor pressure.
6. Remove cap to fuel pressure service connection.
7. Connect suitable fuel pressure gauge to fuel pressure valve.
8. Place suitable shop towel under connections.
9. Install suitable bleed hose into suitable container.
10. Open bleed valve to relieve fuel system.

COMPRESSION PRESSURE

The minimum compression in any one cylinder should not be less than 70 percent of the highest cylinder. No cylinder should read less than 140 psi.

ENGINE MOUNT

REPLACE

Rear Wheel Drive (RWD)

1. Raise and support vehicle.
2. Support engine using suitable screw jack stand with block of wood under oil pan.
3. Remove lower engine mount mounting nut, **Fig. 1.**
4. Remove engine weight from mount by raising jack.
5. Remove upper mounting nut and engine mount.
6. Reverse procedure to install.

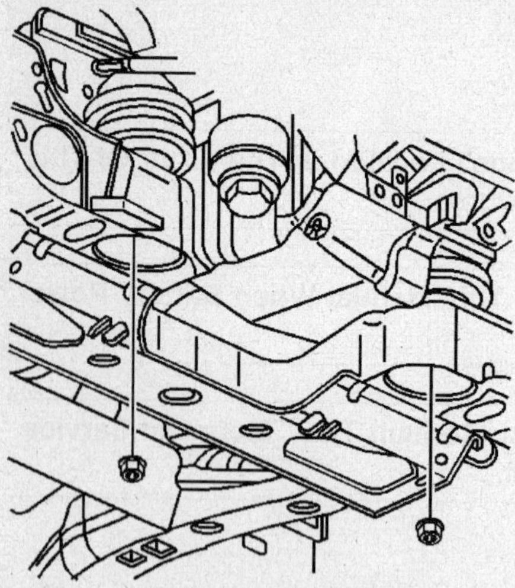

Fig. 1 Engine mounting replacement

All Wheel Drive (AWD)

LEFTHAND

1. Support engine using suitable screw jack stand with block of wood under oil pan.
2. Remove lower engine mount mounting nut, **Fig. 1.**
3. Remove engine weight from mount by raising jack.
4. Remove upper mounting nut and engine mount.
5. Reverse procedure to install.

RIGHTHAND

1. Raise and support vehicle.
2. Remove mounting bolts and exhaust manifold heat shield.
3. Remove mounting nuts and lower exhaust manifold heat shield.
4. Remove catalytic converter nuts.
5. Remove mounting bolts and exhaust manifold. Discard gasket.
6. Remove righthand cylinder head exhaust manifold studs.
7. Support engine using suitable screw jack stand with block of wood under oil pan.
8. Remove mounting nut and righthand engine mount, **Fig. 2.**
9. Remove mounting bolts and righthand engine mount bracket.
10. Reverse procedure to instal.

ENGINE

REPLACE

1. Center steering wheel and turn ignition switch to OFF position.
2. Lock steering column using steering column anti-rotation pin tool No. J42640, or equivalent.
3. Disconnect battery cables from battery, body and underhood electrical center. **Do not disconnect battery cables from engine.**
4. Secure battery cables to engine.

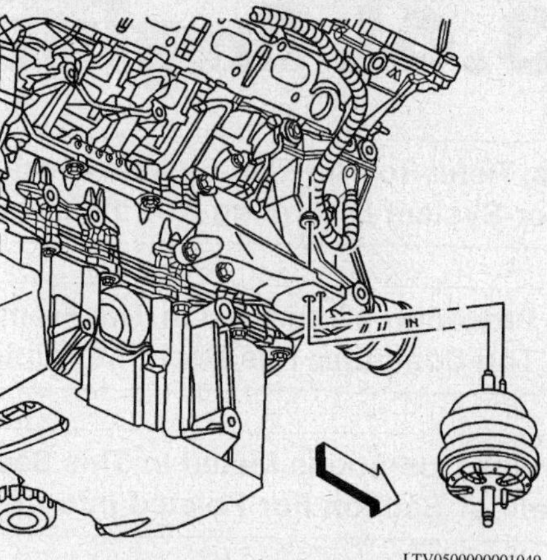

Fig. 2 Righthand engine mount replacement. AWD

5. Remove mounting bolts and cross-vehicle brace.
6. Disengage ball studs and remove engine cover/sight shield.
7. Remove wiper motor 10- and 30-amp mini fuses from underhood fuse block.
8. Set wipers in park position, then remove covers and mounting nuts from wiper arm drive spindle.
9. Remove upper hood assist rods from ball studs and support hood rearward to air inlet grille panel.
10. Remove wiper arm using wiper arm puller tool No. J39822, or equivalent.
11. Remove mounting screws and upper air inlet panel, **Fig. 3.**
12. Remove mounting screws and lower air inlet panel, **Fig. 4.**
13. Depress locking tabs and remove battery heat shield.
14. Remove mounting bolt, retainer and battery.
15. Remove air cleaner duct resonator Positive Crankcase Ventilation (PCV) hose.
16. Loosen clamps and remove air cleaner duct.
17. Disconnect electrical connectors, then remove and secure cooling fan wiring harness to vehicle.
18. Drain cooling system into suitable container.
19. Loosen clamps, then remove and secure surge tank outlet hose to engine. **Do not disconnect surge hoses from engine or radiator.**
20. Secure surge tank inlet hose to vehicle.
21. Remove mounting bolts and battery tray.
22. Remove mounting bolts and cowl panel.
23. Disconnect clamps, then the heater core inlet and outlet hoses.
24. Disconnect purge solenoid line.
25. Relieve fuel system pressure as outlined under "Precautions."
26. Disconnect fuel rail pipe. Plug or cap pipe and fuel rail.
27. Recover air conditioning refrigerant as outlined in "Air Conditioning" chapter.
28. Remove wiper motor module mounting bolts and disconnect electrical connector.

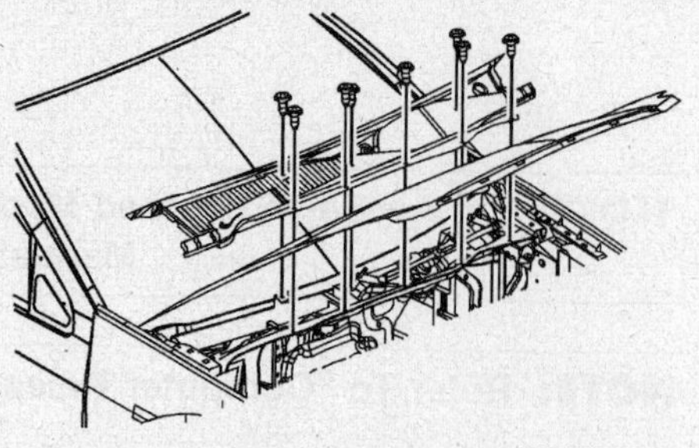

Fig. 3 Upper air inlet panel replacement

29. Remove wiper motor module.
30. Disconnect air conditioning suction hose from evaporator and remove bracket from shock tower. **Do not disconnect suction hose from compressor.** Secure hose to engine.
31. Disconnect air conditioning pressure switch electrical connector and remove liquid line. **Do not disconnect liquid line from condenser.**
32. Remove mounting bolts and radiator support brackets.
33. Disconnect brake booster check valve and vacuum hose. Secure hose to engine.
34. Disconnect master cylinder brake fluid level switch electrical connector.
35. Disconnect Mass Air Flow (MAF) sensor electrical connector.
36. Disconnect instrument panel electrical connector from engine near rear lefthand bank cylinder head and secure harness to vehicle.
37. Remove cover and disconnect underhood electrical center engine module wiring harness connectors.
38. Disconnect Transmission Control Module (TCM) wiring harness.
39. Remove ground bolt and wire, then the engine harness electrical connector from longitudinal rail.
40. Secure ground wire, then the engine and TCM harnesses to engine.
41. Remove mounting nuts and secure master cylinder to engine. **Do not disconnect master cylinder brake pipes.**
42. Raise and support vehicle.
43. Disconnect oxygen sensor electrical connector, then record wire routing and attachment points for installation alignment.
44. Remove oxygen sensors from exhaust pipe.
45. Remove two mounting bolts and tunnel brace from floor panel.
46. Support exhaust system and remove exhaust pipes to manifolds mounting nuts.
47. Pry front exhaust hangers from rear suspension hanger rods.
48. Lubricate tail pipe hanger rods and pry hangers from rods.
49. Lower exhaust system, then remove and discard seals.
50. **On models equipped with AWD,** proceed as follows:
    a. Support propeller shaft close to support bearing using suitable jack.

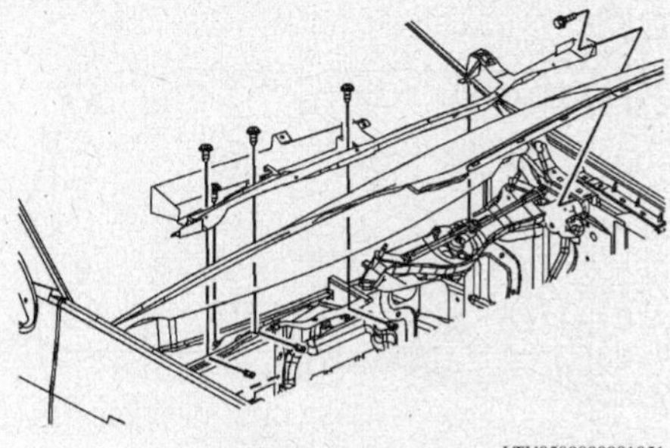

Fig. 4 Lower air inlet panel replacement

b. Remove heat shield mounting bolts.
c. Remove support bearing mounting bolts.
d. Mark propeller shaft Consent Velocity (CV) joint to transfer case flange for installation alignment.
e. Remove propeller shaft CV joint to transfer case flange mounting bolts.
f. Remove propeller shaft coupler-to-differential flange bolts, nuts and washers.
g. Disconnect propeller shaft CV joint from transfer case flange by moving shaft toward rear using suitable flat-bladed tool in transfer case flange notch.
h. Holding propeller shaft and lower support device.
i. Disconnect coupler from differential flange by moving propeller shaft forward.

51. **On models equipped with RWD,** proceed as follows:
    a. Remove propeller shaft coupler-to-transmission flange mounting bolts, nuts and washers.
    b. Remove propeller shaft coupler-to-differential flange mounting bolts, nuts and washers..
    c. Support propeller shaft at support bearing.
    d. Remove support bearing mounting bolts, push front propeller shaft toward rear and disconnect it from transmission flange.
    e. Push front propeller shaft toward rear and release coupler from transmission flange.
    f. Holding front propeller shaft, lower support and remove support bearing.
    g. Disconnect coupler from differential flange by pulling rear propeller shaft forward.
    h. Record number and location of shim packs between support bearing mounting bracket and underbody for installation alignment.
52. **On all models,** remove propeller shaft.
53. Remove push-in retainers and front air deflector.
54. Remove washer bottle bracket. **Do not remove water bottle.**
55. Disconnect radiator side air baffles.
56. Disconnect lefthand front brake pipe retainer with brake pipe from longitudinal rail and remove righthand front brake pipe from brake pipe bundle retainer.

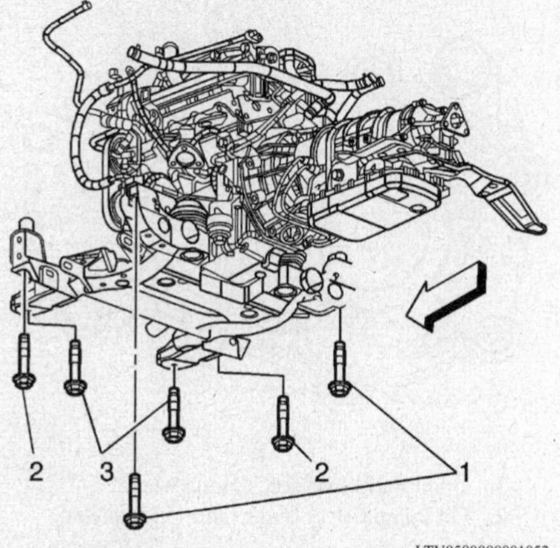

Fig. 5 Front frame tightening sequence

57. Disconnect rear brake pipes from brake modulator valve. Plug brake pipes and modulator valve.
58. Remove front tire and wheel assemblies.
59. Remove upper to center intermediate shaft and lower intermediate shaft to power steering gear mounting bolts.
60. Disconnect lower intermediate shaft from power steering gear.
61. Record center to upper intermediate shaft relationship for installation alignment.
62. Disconnect from upper intermediate shaft and remove center intermediate shaft with lower shaft attached.
63. Remove lower engine mount mounting nut, **Fig. 1.**
64. Remove nut and disconnect shift control linkage rod.
65. Disconnect low oil level sensor electrical connector. Secure connector and harness to engine mount bracket.
66. Disconnect electrical connector, then the headlamp leveling sensors ball and socket.
67. Remove mounting bolt and headlamp leveling sensors.
68. Secure shock modules to lower control arms using suitable strap.
69. Remove lefthand and righthand upper strut mounting bolts.
70. Support engine, transmission, front frame and suspension using suitable lift table.
71. Remove transmission brace to body mounting bolts.
72. Remove front frame mounting bolts, **Fig. 5.**
73. Ensure hoses, wires, pipes and struts clear vehicle during removal.
74. Remove engine, transmission, front frame and front suspension.
75. Disconnect Engine Control Module (ECM) upper electrical connector.
76. Remove lefthand exhaust manifold heat shield.
77. Remove catalytic converter mounting nuts and exhaust pipe to catalytic converter mounting bolts.

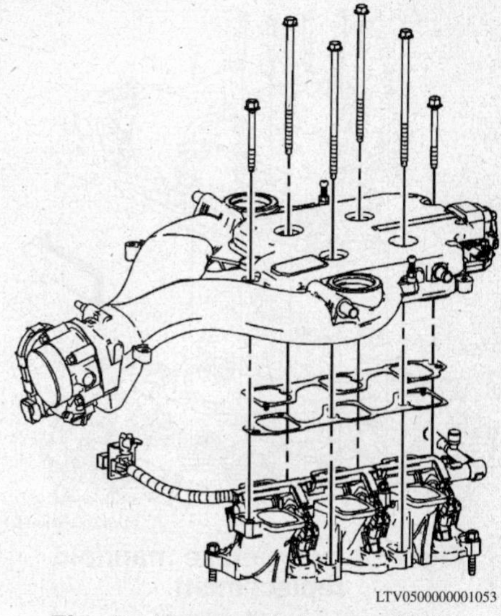

Fig. 6 Upper intake manifold replacement

78. Remove catalytic converters with seal/heat shield and oxygen sensor. **Do not remove oxygen sensors.**
79. Remove mounting bolts and heater inlet/outlet pipe. Discard O-ring and gasket.
80. Remove thermostat heater hoses and surge tank outlet hose.
81. Remove mounting bolts and starter motor.
82. Remove flywheel mounting bolts.
83. Remove HO2S connector bracket from lefthand cylinder head.
84. Disconnect transmission oil cooler pipes from engine, radiator and transmission.
85. Disconnect radiator hoses from water outlet housing and coolant inlet pipe.
86. Disconnect power steering cooler hoses from Condenser Radiator and Fan Module (CRFM). Plug hoses and pipes.
87. Remove CRFM with radiator hoses from frame.
88. Support engine using engine lift brackets tools No. EN46114, or equivalent, and suitable floor crane.
89. Support transmission using second powertrain lift table.
90. Remove mounting bolts and transmission.
91. Reverse procedure to install, noting the following:
    a. **Torque** new flywheel bolts to 22 ft. lbs.
    b. Final tighten flywheel bolts an additional 45°.
    c. **Torque** frame mounting bolts Nos. 1–2 to 141 ft. lbs.
    d. **Torque** frame mounting bolts No. 3 to 185 ft. lbs.

INTAKE MANIFOLD

REPLACE

Upper

1. Remove mounting bolts and cross-vehicle brace.

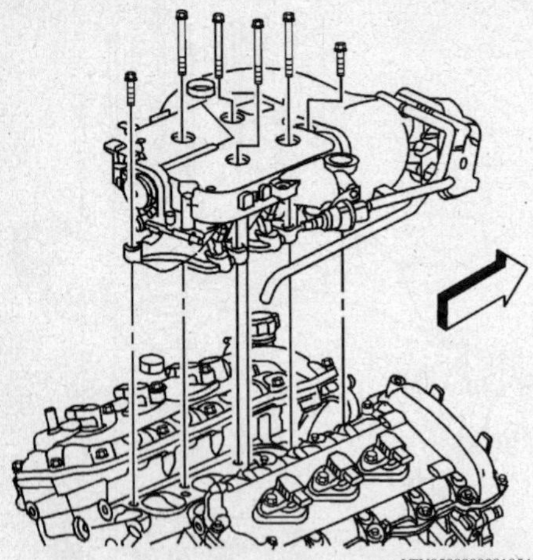

LTV0500000001054

Fig. 7 Lower intake manifold replacement

2. Disengage ball studs and remove engine cover/sight shield.
3. Remove mounting bolt, retainer and battery.
4. Remove air cleaner duct resonator Positive Crankcase Ventilation (PCV) hose.
5. Loosen clamps and remove air cleaner duct.
6. Disconnect brake booster vacuum hose from intake manifold.
7. Disconnect purge solenoid valve electrical connector and line.
8. Remove wiring harness retainer.
9. Disconnect throttle body electrical connector.
10. Remove upper intake manifold stud, mounting bolt and brace.
11. Disconnect Positive Crankcase Ventilation (PCV) hose from righthand valve cover.
12. Disconnect barometric pressure sensor and intake manifold runner control solenoid electrical connectors.
13. Remove injector harness bracket mounting bolt and lefthand ignition coil wiring harness from bracket
14. Remove mounting bolts and upper intake manifold with throttle body, **Fig. 6.** Cowl panel may have to be deflected to remove righthand rear bolt.
15. Reverse procedure to install, noting the following:
    a. Install new upper intake manifold gasket.
    b. **Torque** upper intake manifold mounting bolts to 17 ft. lbs., in circular pattern starting at center, long bolts and moving outward.

Lower

1. Remove mounting bolts and cross-vehicle brace.
2. Disengage ball studs and remove engine cover/sight shield.
3. Remove mounting bolt, retainer and battery.
4. Remove air cleaner duct resonator Positive Crankcase Ventilation (PCV) hose.

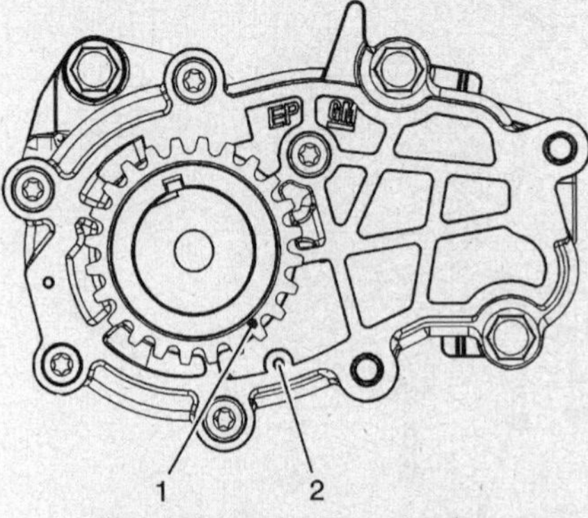

1. Crankshaft Sprocket Timing Mark
2. Oil Pump Cover Stage One Timing Mark

LTV0500000001084

Fig. 8 Stage one crankshaft alignment

5. Loosen clamps and remove air cleaner duct.
6. Disconnect brake booster vacuum hose from intake manifold.
7. Disconnect purge solenoid valve electrical connector and line.
8. Remove wiring harness retainer.
9. Disconnect throttle body electrical connector.
10. Remove upper intake manifold stud, mounting bolt and brace.
11. Remove wiring harness retainer from throttle body righthand side.
12. Disconnect Positive Crankcase Ventilation (PCV) hose from righthand valve cover.
13. Disconnect barometric pressure sensor and intake manifold runner control solenoid electrical connectors.
14. Remove lefthand ignition coil wiring harness from bracket.
15. Remove intake manifold mounting bolts, **Fig. 7. Do not remove upper to lower intake manifold bolts. Do not kink or damage fuel pipe.**
16. Position intake manifold and remove fuel feed pipe retainer, then disconnect fuel rail feed pipe.
17. Reverse procedure to install.

EXHAUST MANIFOLD

REPLACE

Lefthand

1. Center steering wheel and turn ignition switch to OFF position.
2. Lock steering column using steering column anti-rotation pin tool No. J42640, or equivalent.
3. Remove exhaust manifold heat shield mounting bolt.
4. Raise and support vehicle.
5. Remove exhaust manifold heat shield lower mounting bolt.
6. Remove mounting bolts and disconnect center from lower intermediate steering shaft.
7. Remove exhaust manifold heat shield.
8. Remove upper exhaust manifold heat shield insulator from oil dipstick tube.
9. Remove lower exhaust manifold heat shield insulator from oil dipstick and exhaust gasket.
10. Lower vehicle, then remove indicator and oil dipstick tube mounting bolt.
11. Raise and support vehicle.
12. Remove wiring harness heat shield from oil dipstick tube.
13. Disconnect electrical connector, then remove mounting bolt and Knock Sensor (KS).
14. Remove heat shield clip from oil dipstick tube.
15. Lower vehicle, then record location and orientation of secondary, small square heat shield for installation alignment.
16. Remove oil dipstick tube through exhaust manifold.
17. Remove catalytic converter mounting nuts.
18. Remove mounting bolts and exhaust manifold. Discard gasket.
19. Remove lefthand exhaust manifold mounting nuts, then the exhaust manifold.
20. Reverse procedure to install.

Righthand

1. Remove mounting bolts and exhaust manifold heat shield.
2. Remove mounting nuts and lower exhaust manifold heat shield.
3. Remove catalytic converter nuts.
4. Remove mounting bolts and exhaust manifold. Discard gasket
5. Reverse procedure to install.

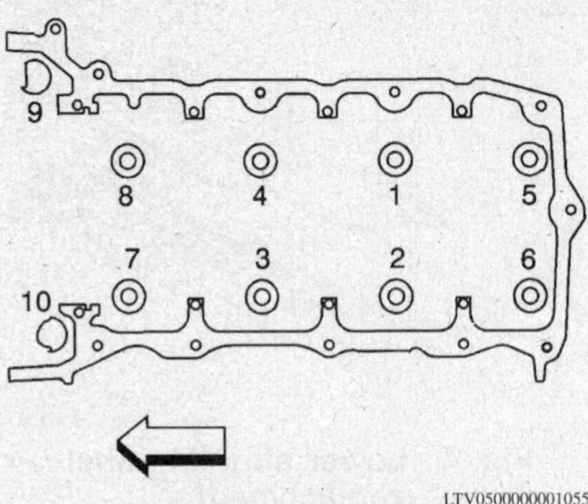

LTV0500000001055

Fig. 9 Lefthand cylinder head tightening sequence

CYLINDER HEAD

REPLACE

Lefthand

1. Remove lefthand secondary timing chain as outlined under "Timing Chain, Replace."
2. Remove upper exhaust manifold heat shield insulator from oil dipstick tube.
3. Remove lower exhaust manifold heat shield insulator from oil dipstick and exhaust gasket.
4. Lower vehicle, then remove indicator and oil dipstick tube mounting bolt.
5. Raise and support vehicle.
6. Remove coolant temperature sensor

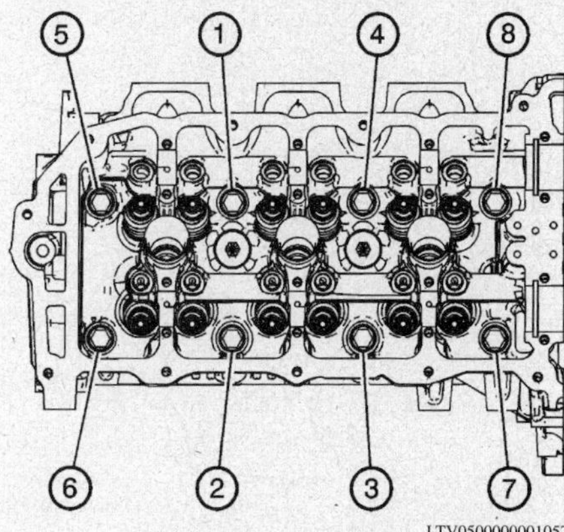

Fig. 10 Righthand cylinder head tightening sequence

heat shield and disconnect electrical connector.
7. Remove cylinder head wiring harness ground.
8. Disconnect cylinder head side wiring harness electrical connector and remove bracket.
9. Remove wiring harness connector bracket from cylinder head.
10. Remove power steering pump pulley using pulley puller tool No. J25034-C, or equivalent.
11. Remove mounting bolts and position power steering pump aside. **Do not disconnect power steering pipes or hoses.**
12. Remove surge tank hose from cylinder head rear bracket.
13. Remove wiring harness bracket from rear of cylinder head.
14. Center steering wheel and turn ignition switch to OFF position.
15. Lock steering column using steering column anti-rotation pin tool No. J42640, or equivalent.
16. Remove exhaust manifold heat shield mounting bolt.
17. Raise and support vehicle.
18. Remove exhaust manifold heat shield lower mounting bolt.
19. Remove mounting bolts and disconnect center from lower intermediate steering shaft.
20. Remove exhaust manifold heat shield.
21. Remove catalytic converter mounting nuts.
22. Disconnect oxygen sensor electrical connector.
23. Disconnect muffler pipe from lefthand and righthand catalytic converters.
24. Remove exhaust pipe to righthand catalytic converter mounting nuts.
25. Remove catalytic converter with seal/heat shield and oxygen sensor from exhaust manifold.
26. Remove wiring harness heat shield from oil dipstick tube.
27. Disconnect electrical connector, then remove mounting bolt and Knock Sensor (KS).
28. Remove heat shield clip from oil dipstick tube.
29. Remove oil filter adapter upper mounting bolt. **Do not remove oil filter adapter.**

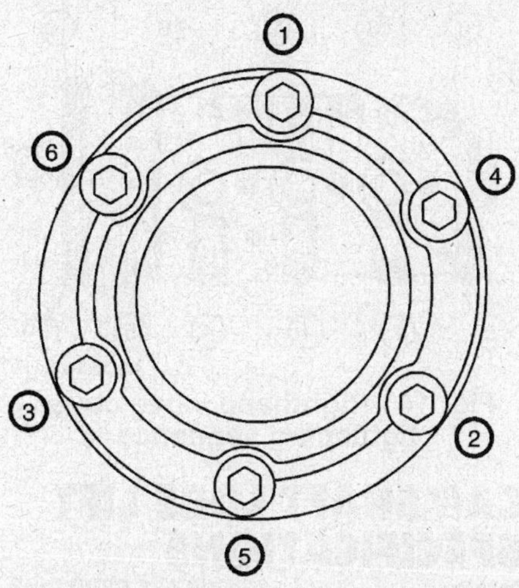

Fig. 11 Propeller shaft CV joint tightening sequence

30. Remove mounting bolts and cylinder head with exhaust manifold. Discard gasket and M11 cylinder head bolts.
31. Reverse procedure to install, noting the following:
    a. Ensure crankshaft is in stage one timing drive position using crankshaft rotation socket tool No. EN 46111, or equivalent, **Fig. 8.**
    b. **Torque** new M11 cylinder head bolts to 33 ft. lbs., in sequence, **Fig. 9.**
    c. Final tighten M11 head bolts an additional 120° in sequence.
    d. **Torque** front M8 cylinder head bolts to 11 ft. lbs., in sequence.
    e. Final tighten M8 head bolts and additional 60° in sequence.

Righthand

1. Remove righthand secondary timing chain as outlined under "Timing Chain, Replace."
2. Raise and support the vehicle.
3. Remove coolant inlet pipe to alternator bracket mounting bolt.
4. Lower vehicle and drain cooling system into suitable container.
5. Disconnect radiator outlet hose and remove wiring harnesses from coolant inlet pipe.
6. Remove coolant pipe to thermostat and cylinder head mounting bolts.
7. Position coolant inlet pipe aside.
8. Remove mounting bolts and exhaust manifold heat shield, then the mounting bolts and lower exhaust manifold heat shield.
9. Remove catalytic converter mounting nuts.
10. Raise and support vehicle.
11. **On models equipped with AWD,** proceed as follows:
    a. Remove mounting bolts and front propeller shaft Constant Velocity (CV) joint shield.
    b. Mark propeller shaft CV joint to transfer case flange for installation alignment.

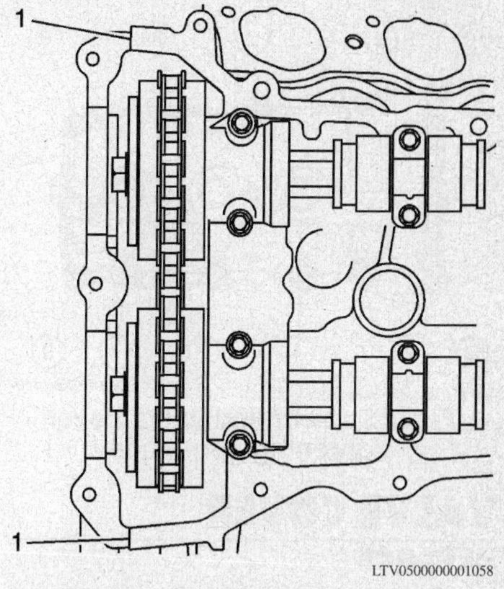

Fig. 12 Front cover sealant application

    c. Remove propeller shaft CV joint-to-differential flange mounting bolts.
    d. Disconnect propeller shaft CV joint from differential pinion flange by moving shaft toward rear using suitable flat-bladed tool in flange notch.
    e. Remove propeller shaft CV joint-to-transfer case flange mounting bolts.
    f. Disconnect propeller shaft CV joint from transfer case flange by moving shaft toward front using suitable flat-bladed tool in flange notch.
    g. Remove front propeller shaft.
12. **On all models,** disconnect oxygen sensor electrical connector.
13. Disconnect muffler pipe from lefthand and righthand catalytic converters.
14. Remove exhaust pipe to righthand catalytic converter mounting nuts.
15. Remove catalytic converter with seal/heat shield and oxygen sensor.
16. Remove cylinder head side wiring harness ground.
17. Remove upper mounting bolt and position wiring harness conduit aside.
18. Remove mounting bolt battery cable from cylinder head.
19. Remove mounting bolts and cylinder head with exhaust manifold. **Discard gasket and cylinder head M11 bolts.**
20. Reverse procedure to install, noting the following:
    a. Ensure crankshaft is in stage one timing drive position using crankshaft rotation socket tool No. EN 46111, or equivalent, **Fig. 8.**
    b. **Torque** new M11 cylinder head bolts to 33 ft. lbs., in sequence, **Fig. 10.**
    c. Final tighten M11 head bolts an additional 120° in sequence.
    d. Apply suitable threadlock to propeller shaft flange bolts.
    e. **Torque** propeller shaft to differential flange bolts to 22 ft. lbs.
    f. **Torque** propeller shaft CV joint to transfer case flange mounting bolts to 22 ft. lbs., in sequence, **Fig. 11.**

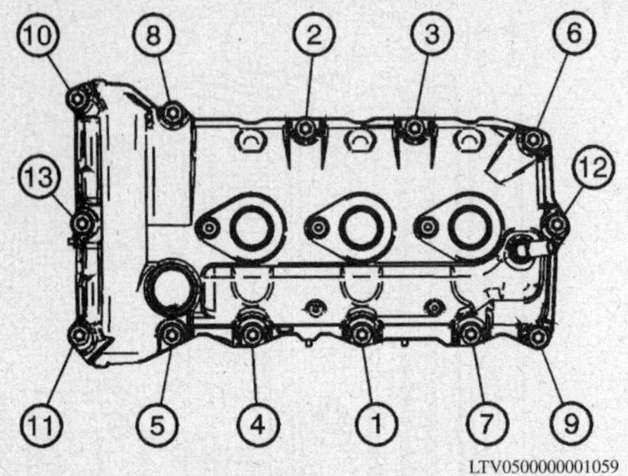

Fig. 13 Lefthand valve cover tightening sequence

VALVE COVER

REPLACE

1. Remove lower intake manifold as outlined under "Intake Manifold, Replace."
2. **Do not disconnect fuel pipes and/or hoses.**
3. **If replacing ignition coil for cylinders Nos. 1, 2 or 3,** proceed as follows:
   a. Disconnect air cleaner duct from throttle body.
   b. Disconnect Positive Crankcase Ventilation (PCV) hose from righthand bank valve cover.
   c. **Do not separate upper from lower intake manifold.**
   d. Remove intake manifold mounting bolts.
   e. Remove mounting bolts and intake manifold brace.
   f. Remove and position intake manifold aside.
4. **On all models,** remove ignition coil electrical connector.
5. Remove valve cover side wiring harness by sliding conduit down and outboard.
6. Remove valve cover wiring harness conduit retainers by rotating them counterclockwise.
7. Remove valve cover front wiring harness and position aside. **It is not required to disconnect front cover electrical connectors.**
8. Remove mounting bolts and ignition coils.
9. Remove mounting bolts and valve cover. Discard cover seal and grommets.
10. Reverse procedure to install, noting the following:
    a. Install spark plug tube seal guide tools No. EN 46101, or equivalent, onto spark plug tubes.
    b. Ensure new grommets are installed before cover mounting bolts.
    c. Apply .3150 inch diameter by .1575 inch high bead of suitable RTV sealant on engine front cover split lines, **Fig. 12.**
    d. **Torque** valve cover mounting bolts to 89 inch lbs., in sequence, **Figs. 13 and 14.**
    e. Remove tube seal guide tools and install spark plugs.

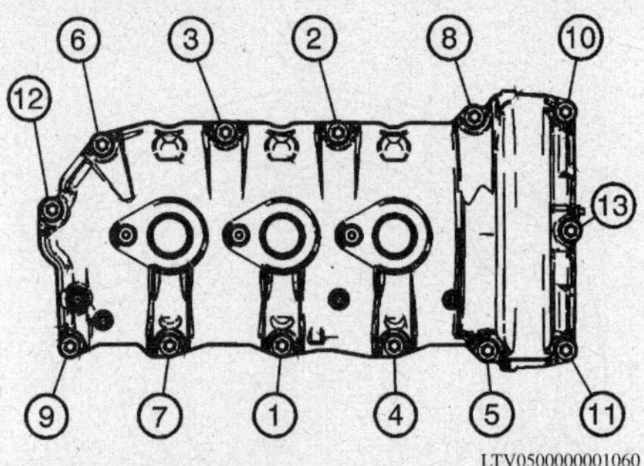

Fig. 14 Righthand valve cover tightening sequence

CAMSHAFT LOBE LIFT SPECIFICATIONS

Intake .... 1.6687–1.6805 inch
Exhaust...................... 1.6703–1.6821 inch

VALVE CLEARANCE SPECIFICATIONS

These engines are equipped with Stationary Hydraulic Lash Adjusters (SHLA). There are no provisions for adjustment.

VALVE ADJUSTMENT

This engine is equipped with Stationary Hydraulic Lash Adjusters (SHLA). There are no provisions for adjustment.

ROCKER ARMS

REPLACE

1. Remove camshaft as outlined under "Camshaft, Replace."
2. Mark rocker arms for installation in original positions.
3. Remove rocker arms.
4. Reverse procedure to install, noting the following:
   a. Apply liberal amount suitable lubricant to pivot pocket, roller and valve slot, **Fig. 15.**
   b. Follower must be positioned squarely on valve tip so full width of roller will completely contact camshaft lobe.
   c. Rounded head end goes on Stationary Hydraulic Lash Adjusters (SHLA), while flat end goes on valve tip.

HYDRAULIC LIFTERS

REPLACE

1. Remove camshaft as outlined under "Camshaft, Replace."
2. Mark rocker arms for installation in original positions.
3. Remove rocker arms.
4. Remove Stationary Hydraulic Lash Adjusters (SHLA).
5. Reverse procedure to install, noting the following:
   a. Fill SHLA with suitable, clean engine oil.
   b. Do not scratch pivot sphere area.
   c. Lubricate SHLA bores with suitable, clean engine oil.

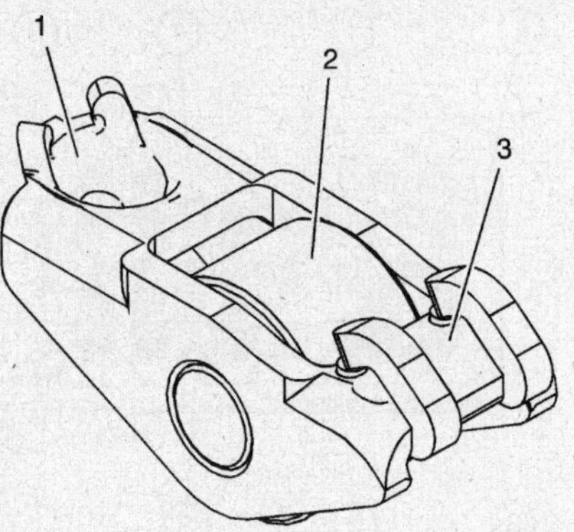

Fig. 15 Rocker arm lubrication points

   d. Apply liberal amount suitable lubricant to SHLA pivot spheres, then the rocker arm pivot pocket, roller and valve slot.
   e. Follower must be positioned squarely on valve tip so full width of roller will completely contact camshaft lobe.
   f. Rounded head end goes on SHLA, while flat end goes on valve tip.

CRANKSHAFT DAMPER

REPLACE

1. Release drive belt tension by rotating drive belt tensioner clockwise.
2. Remove drive belt from water pump pulley.
3. Slowly release drive belt tensioner.
4. Remove drive belt from accessory drive pulleys.
5. Rotate drive belt tensioner clockwise to release drive belt tension.
6. Remove drive belt from power steering pulley.
7. Slowly release drive belt tensioner and remove drive belt from accessory drive pulleys.
8. Raise and support vehicle.
9. Remove transmission bell housing inspection hole cover and install flywheel holding tool No. EN-48018, or equivalent.
10. Remove push-in retainers and front air deflector.
11. Remove crankshaft balancer mounting bolt.
12. Remove crankshaft balancer using crankshaft button tool No. J38416-2 and harmonic balancer pulling tool No. J24420-C, or equivalents.
13. Reverse procedure to install.
    a. Apply lubricant to inside of crankshaft balancer hub bore.
    b. **Do not lubricate crankshaft front oil seal or crankshaft balancer sealing surfaces. Crankshaft balancer is installed into dry seal.**
    c. Push crankshaft balancer into position using crankshaft balancer installer tool No. J41998-B, or equivalent.
    d. **Torque** mounting bolt to 74 ft. lbs.
    e. Final tighten mounting bolt an additional 150°.

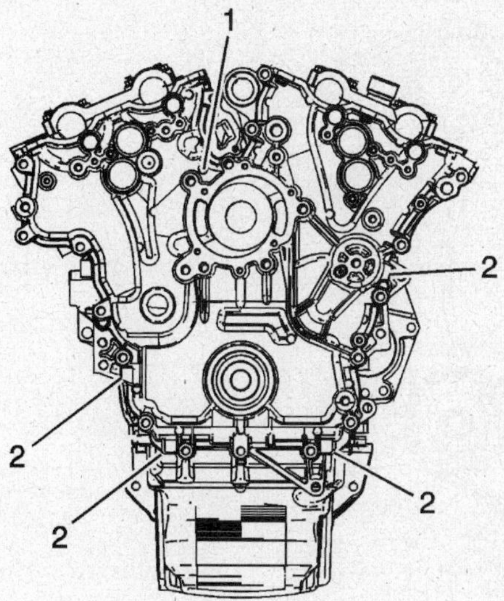

1. Jackscrew Hole
2. Pry Points

LTV0500000001063

Fig. 16 Front cover jackhole & pry points

FRONT COVER

REPLACE

1. Remove mounting bolts and cross-vehicle brace.
2. Disengage ball studs and remove engine cover/sight shield.
3. Remove valve covers as outlined under "Valve Cover, Replace."
4. Drain engine coolant into suitable container.
5. Disconnect purge vent hose from water outlet.
6. Disconnect clamps and remove water outlet radiator hose.
7. Remove mounting bolts and position water outlet housing aside. Discard seals.
8. Release drive belt tension by rotating drive belt tensioner clockwise.
9. Remove drive belt from water pump pulley.
10. Slowly release drive belt tensioner.
11. Remove drive belt from accessory drive pulleys.
12. Rotate drive belt tensioner clockwise to release drive belt tension.
13. Remove drive belt from power steering pulley.
14. Slowly release drive belt tensioner and remove drive belt from accessory drive pulleys.
15. Loosen mounting bolt, then remove air conditioning compressor and power steering belt tensioner.
16. Raise and support vehicle.
17. Disconnect alternator electrical connectors.
18. Remove boot and alternator BAT terminal nut, then the battery positive lead.
19. Remove alternator lower mounting bolts.
20. Lower vehicle.
21. Remove upper mounting bolt and alternator.

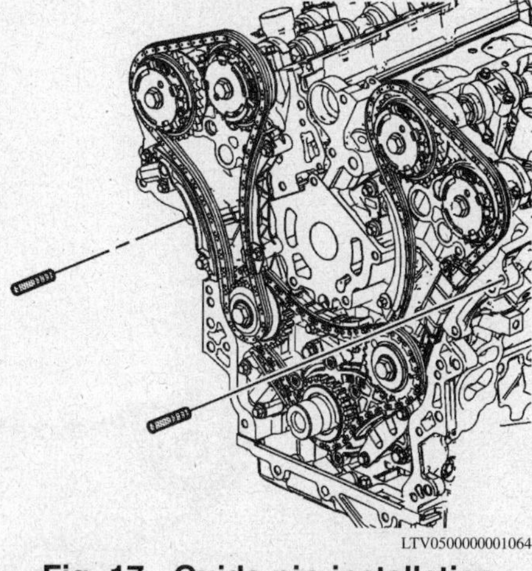

LTV0500000001064

Fig. 17 Guide pin installation

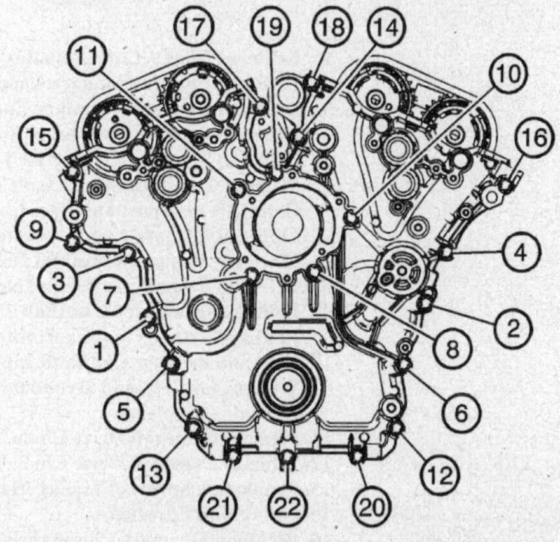

LTV0500000001588

Fig. 19 Front cover tightening sequence

22. Loosen mounting bolt and remove alternator belt tensioner.
23. Remove mounting bolts and alternator bracket.
24. Remove mounting bolts and position power steering fluid reservoir aside. **Do not disconnect power steering pipes or drain power steering fluid.**
25. Remove power steering pump pulley using pulley puller tool No. J25034-C, or equivalent.
26. Remove upper front mounting bolt and loosen remaining two mounting bolts, then and position power steering pump aside. **Do not disconnect power steering pipes or hoses.**
27. Raise and support vehicle.
28. Remove transmission bell housing inspection hole cover and install flywheel holding tool No. EN-48018, or equivalent.
29. Remove push-in retainers and front air deflector.
30. Remove crankshaft balancer mounting bolt.
31. Remove crankshaft balancer using crankshaft button tool No. J38416-2 and harmonic balancer pulling tool No. J24420-C, or equivalents.
32. Disconnect electrical connector, then remove mounting bolts and Camshaft Position (CMP) actuator valves.

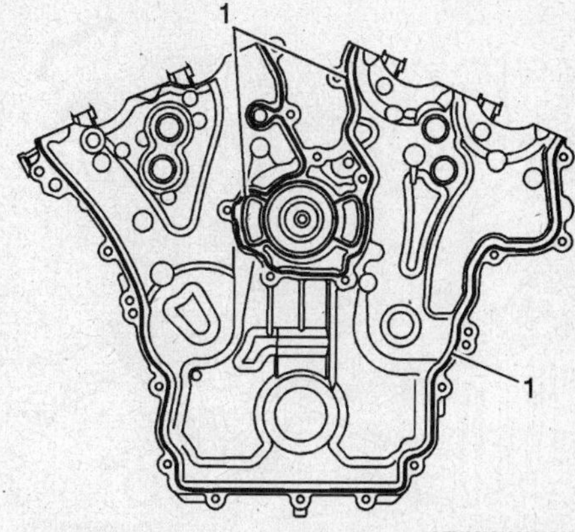

LTV0500000001065

Fig. 18 Front cover RTV sealant application

33. Remove engine front cover mounting bolts.
34. Loosely install 10 x 1.5 mm bolt in jackscrew hole and shear Room Temperature Vulcanizing (RTV) sealant using front cover edge pry points and jackscrew, **Fig. 16. Do not pry between engine front cover and CMP sensors or actuators to shear RTV.**
35. Remove front cover.
36. Rotate crankshaft using crankshaft rotation socket tool No. EN 46111, or equivalent, then align and install camshaft locking tools Nos. EN46105-02, or equivalent, into lefthand camshafts and EN46105-1, or equivalent, into righthand camshafts.
37. Reverse procedure to install, noting the following:
    a. Install .315 inch engine front cover installation guide pins tools No. EN46109, or equivalent, into cylinder block, **Fig. 17.**
    b. Install new engine front cover to cylinder block seal.
    c. Place .118 inch beat of suitable TRV sealant on front cover, **Fig. 18.**
    d. Install cover and remove guide pins, then hand start mounting bolts.
    e. **Torque** front cover mounting bolts to 17 ft. lbs., in sequence, **Fig. 19.**
    f. Install new CMP sensor O-rings.
    g. **Torque** alternator bracket mounting bolts Nos. 1 and 2 to 37 ft. lbs., **Fig. 20.**
    h. **Torque** alternator bracket mounting bolts No. 3 to 17 ft. lbs.

TIMING CHAIN

REPLACE

Primary Drive Chain

REMOVAL

1. Remove spark plugs.
2. Remove front cover as outlined under "Front Cover, Replace."
3. Remove righthand secondary camshaft drive chain as outlined under "Secondary Drive Chain."
4. Remove mounting bolts and righthand

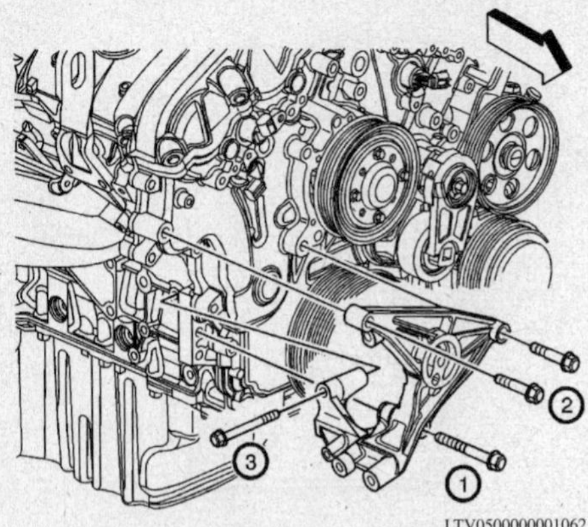

Fig. 20 Alternator bracket tightening sequence

secondary camshaft drive chain tensioner. Discard gasket.
5. Remove mounting bolt and righthand secondary timing chain shoe.
6. Remove mounting bolts and righthand secondary camshaft drive chain guide.
7. Remove righthand secondary camshaft drive chain from camshaft position actuators and righthand intermediate drive chain idler sprocket.
8. Remove mounting bolts and primary drive chain tensioner. Discard gasket.
9. Remove mounting bolts and primary camshaft drive chain upper guide.
10. Remove primary drive chain.

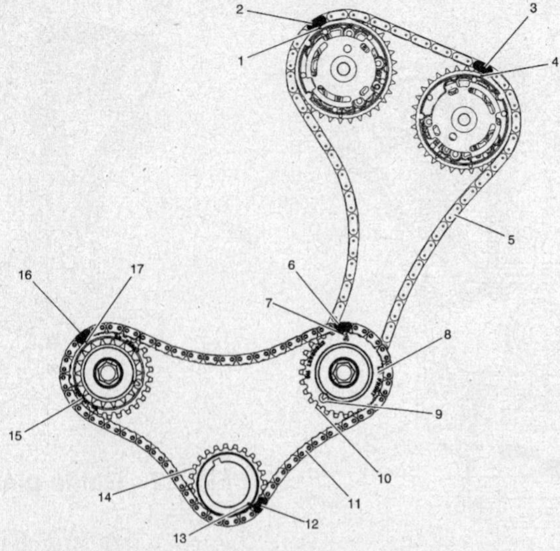

1. Lefthand Intake CMP Actuator Timing Mark
2. Lefthand Intake Secondary Camshaft Timing Drive Chain Timing Link
3. Lefthand Exhaust Secondary Camshaft Timing Drive Chain Timing Link
4. Lefthand Exhaust CMP Actuator Timing Mark
5. Lefthand Secondary Camshaft Timing Drive Chain
6. Primary Camshaft Drive Chain Timing Link for Lefthand Primary Camshaft Intermediate Drive Chain Sprocket
7. Lefthand Primary Camshaft Intermediate Drive Chain Sprocket Timing Mark for Primary Camshaft Drive Chain
8. Lefthand Primary Camshaft Intermediate Drive Chain Sprocket
9. Lefthand Secondary Camshaft Timing Drive Chain Timing Link the Lefthand Primary Camshaft Intermediate Drive Chain Sprocket
10. Lefthand Primary Camshaft Intermediate Drive Chain Sprocket Timing Window for Lefthand Secondary Camshaft Timing Drive Chain Timing Link
11. Primary Camshaft Drive Chain
12. Primary Camshaft Drive Chain Timing Link for Crankshaft Sprocket
13. Crankshaft Sprocket Timing Mark
14. Crankshaft Sprocket
15. Righthand Primary Camshaft Intermediate Drive Chain Sprocket
16. Primary Camshaft Drive Chain Timing Link for Righthand Primary Camshaft Intermediate Drive Chain Sprocket
17. Righthand Primary Camshaft Intermediate Drive Chain Sprocket Timing Mark

LTV0500000001069

Fig. 21 Timing chain stage one alignment

INSTALLATION

1. Ensure crankshaft is in stage one timing drive assembly position, **Fig. 21.**
2. Install primary camshaft drive chain.
3. Wrap chain around large sprockets of camshaft intermediate drive chain idler and crankshaft sprocket.
4. Align lefthand camshaft intermediate drive chain idler timing mark with camshaft drive chain link bright plated, **Fig. 22.**
5. Align righthand camshaft intermediate drive chain idler timing mark with bright plated camshaft drive chain link, **Fig. 23.**
6. Align crankshaft sprocket timing mark with bright plated camshaft drive chain link, **Fig. 24.**
7. Ensure timing marks properly align with chain links, **Fig. 25.**
8. Install upper primary camshaft drive chain guides and tighten mounting bolts.
9. Set primary camshaft drive chain tensioner plunger using tensioner tool No. J45027, or equivalent.
10. Install plunger into primary camshaft drive chain tensioner body.
11. Compress plunger into body and lock primary camshaft drive chain tensioner by inserting tensioner retraction pin tool No. EN46112, or equivalent, into side access hole.
12. Slowly release pressure on primary camshaft drive chain tensioner. It should remain compressed.
13. Install drive tensioner, new gasket and tighten mounting bolts loosely.
14. **Torque** primary camshaft drive chain tensioner mounting bolts to 44 inch lbs.
15. Final **torque** mounting bolts to 17 ft. lbs.
16. Release tensioner by removing pin tool.
17. Ensure primary and lefthand secondary drive chain timing marks align, **Fig. 21.**
18. Remove camshaft locking tool No. EN46105-1, or equivalent, from rear of lefthand camshafts.
19. Rotate crankshaft sprocket 115° to stage two alignment position using, crankshaft rotation socket tool No. EN 46111, or equivalent, **Fig. 26.**
20. Install camshaft locking tool EN 46105-2, or equivalent, onto the rear of the lefthand camshafts.
21. Ensure stage two alignment position and install righthand secondary camshaft drive chain.
22. Place righthand secondary camshaft drive chain around righthand side camshaft intermediate drive chain idler outer sprocket and align bright plated camshaft drive link with alignment camshaft drive chain idler inner sprocket access hole in, **Fig. 27.**
23. Wrap secondary camshaft drive chain around both righthand side actuator drive sprockets.
24. Ensure there are seven darkened links between bright plated camshaft drive chain links for camshaft position actuator sprockets, **Fig. 28.**
25. Align righthand exhaust camshaft position actuator sprocket alignment triangle mark with bright plated camshaft drive chain link, **Fig. 29.**
26. Align righthand intake camshaft position actuator sprocket alignment triangle mark with bright plated camshaft drive chain link, **Fig. 30.**
27. Ensure there are 18 links between righthand camshaft intermediate drive chain idler timing camshaft drive chain link and each righthand camshaft position actuator sprocket timing camshaft drive chain link.
28. Install righthand chain guide and tighten mounting bolts.
29. Install righthand secondary camshaft drive chain shoe and tighten mounting bolts.
30. Set righthand secondary camshaft drive chain tensioner plunger using tensioner tool No. J45027, or equivalent.

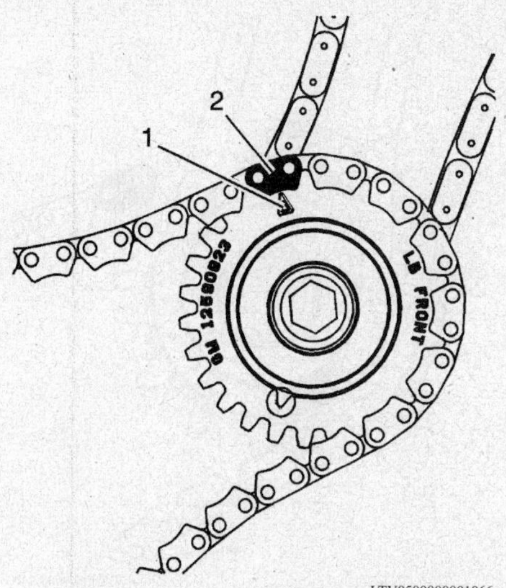

Fig. 22 Chain & lefthand intermediate idler alignment

31. Install plunger into righthand secondary camshaft drive chain tensioner body.
32. Compress plunger into body and lock righthand secondary camshaft drive chain tensioner by inserting tensioner retraction pin tool No. EN46112, or equivalent, into side access hole.
33. Slowly release pressure on righthand secondary camshaft drive chain tensioner. It should remain compressed.
34. Install drive tensioner, new gasket and tighten mounting bolts loosely.
35. **Torque** righthand secondary camshaft drive chain tensioner mounting bolts to 44 inch lbs.
36. Final **torque** mounting bolts to 17 ft. lbs.
37. Release tensioner by removing pin tool.
38. Ensure all timing marks are aligned, **Fig. 26.**
39. Install spark plugs.
40. Install front cover as outlined under "Front Cover, Replace."

Secondary Drive Chain

RIGHTHAND

Refer to "Primary Drive Chain" for secondary drive chain replacement procedures.

LEFTHAND

REMOVAL

1. Remove primary drive chain as outlined under "Primary Drive Chain."
2. Remove mounting bolts and lefthand secondary camshaft drive chain tensioner. Discard gasket.
3. Remove mounting bolts and lefthand secondary camshaft drive chain shoe.
4. Remove mounting bolts and lefthand secondary camshaft drive chain guide.
5. Remove mounting bolts and lefthand secondary camshaft drive chain idler.
6. Remove lefthand secondary camshaft drive chain from lefthand camshaft position actuators and lefthand camshaft intermediate drive chain idler sprocket.

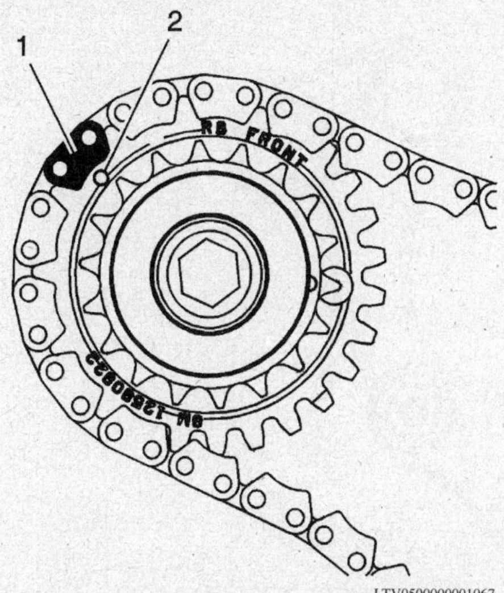

Fig. 23 Chain and righthand intermediate idler alignment

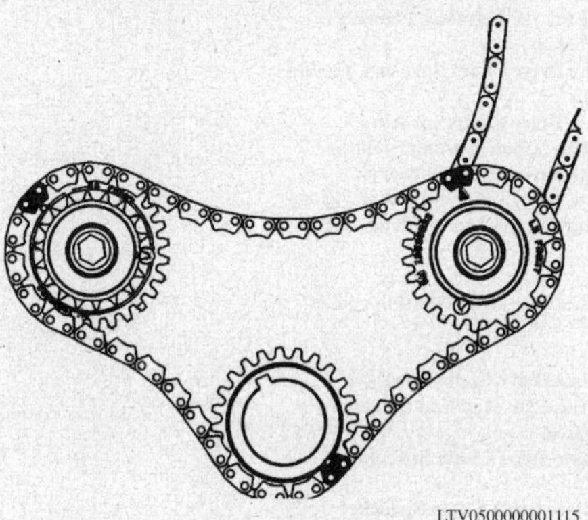

Fig. 25 Primary timing chain align

INSTALLATION

1. Hold lefthand camshafts in place by installing camshaft holding tool No. EN46105-1, or equivalent, onto rear of lefthand camshafts.
2. Ensure crankshaft is in stage one timing position crankshaft sprocket timing mark aligned to stage one timing mark on oil pump cover, **Fig. 8.**
3. Place lefthand secondary camshaft drive chain around inner sprocket of camshaft intermediate drive chain idler with bright plated drive chain link aligned to access hole in idler outer sprocket, **Fig. 31.**
4. Wrap secondary camshaft drive chain around both lefthand actuator drive sprockets.
5. Ensure there are seven darkened links between bright plated camshaft drive chain links for camshaft position actuator sprockets, **Fig. 32.**
6. Align lefthand exhaust camshaft position actuator sprocket alignment circle mark with bright plated camshaft drive chain link, **Fig. 33.**
7. Align lefthand intake camshaft position actuator sprocket alignment circle mark with bright plated camshaft drive chain link, **Fig. 34.**

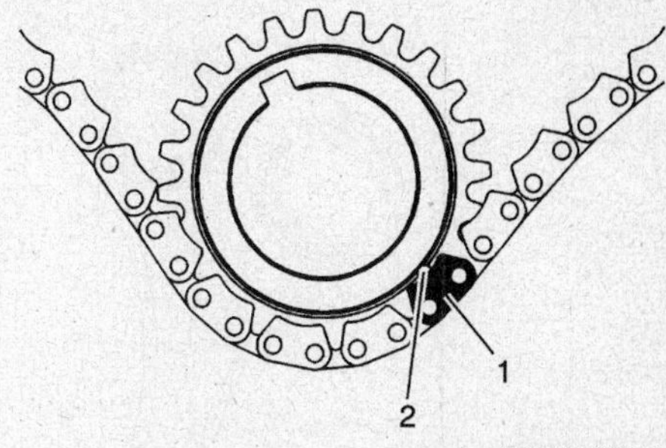

Fig. 24 Chain & crankshaft sprocket alignment

8. Ensure there are 18 links between lefthand camshaft intermediate drive chain idler timing secondary camshaft drive chain link and each lefthand camshaft position actuator sprocket timing secondary camshaft drive chain link.
9. Recessed hub and larger sprocket of lefthand camshaft intermediate drive chain idler is installed outward. Raised hub and smaller sprocket of lefthand camshaft intermediate drive chain idler is installed toward block.
10. Install lefthand camshaft intermediate drive chain idler and tighten mounting bolt.
11. Install lefthand secondary camshaft drive chain guide and tighten mounting bolts.
12. Install lefthand secondary camshaft drive chain shoe and tighten mounting bolts.
13. Set lefthand secondary camshaft drive chain tensioner plunger using tensioner tool No. J45027, or equivalent.
14. Install plunger into lefthand secondary camshaft drive chain tensioner body.
15. Compress plunger into body and lock lefthand secondary camshaft drive chain tensioner by inserting tensioner retraction pin tool No. EN46112, or equivalent, into side access hole.
16. Slowly release pressure on lefthand secondary camshaft drive chain tensioner. It should remain compressed.
17. Install drive tensioner, new gasket and tighten mounting bolts loosely.
18. **Torque** lefthand secondary camshaft drive chain tensioner mounting bolts to 44 inch lbs.
19. Final **torque** mounting bolts to 17 ft. lbs.
20. Release tensioner by removing pin tool.
21. Install righthand side camshaft secondary and primary timing chains as outlined under "Primary Drive Chain."

TIMING CHAIN TENSIONER

REPLACE

Refer to the appropriate timing chain under "Timing Chain, Replace" for tensioner replacement procedures.

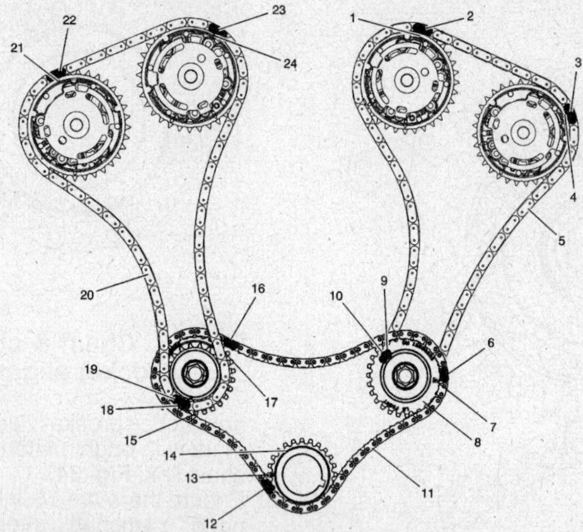

1. Lefthand Intake CMP Actuator Timing Mark
2. Lefthand Intake Secondary Camshaft Timing Drive Chain Timing Link
3. Lefthand Exhaust Secondary Camshaft Timing Drive Chain Timing Link
4. Lefthand Exhaust CMP Actuator Timing Mark
5. Lefthand Secondary Camshaft Timing Drive Chain
6. Primary Camshaft Drive Chain Timing Link for Lefthand Primary Camshaft Intermediate Drive Chain Sprocket
7. Lefthand Primary Camshaft Intermediate Drive Chain Sprocket Timing Mark for Primary Camshaft Drive Chain
8. Lefthand Primary Camshaft Intermediate Drive Chain Sprocket
9. Lefthand Secondary Camshaft Timing Drive Chain Timing Link the Lefthand Primary Camshaft Intermediate Drive Chain Sprockek
10. Lefthand Primary Camshaft Intermediate Drive Chain Sprocket Timing Window for Lefthand Secondary Camshaft Timing Drive Chain Timing Link
11. Primary Camshaft Drive Chain
12. Primary Camshaft Drive Chain Timing Link for Crankshaft Sprocket
13. Crankshaft Sprocket Timing Mark
14. Crankshaft Sprocket
15. Righthand Primary Camshaft Intermediate Drive Chain Sprocket
16. Primary Camshaft Drive Chain Timing Link for Righthand Primary Camshaft Intermediate Drive Chain Sprocket
17. Righthand Primary Camshaft Intermediate Drive Chain Sprocket Timing Mark
18. Righthand Primary Camshaft Intermediate Drive Chain Sprocket Timing Mark/Window for Righthand Secondary Camshaft Timing Drive Chain
19. Righthand Secondary Camshaft Timing Drive Chain Timing Link for Righthand Primary Camshaft Intermediate Drive Chain Sprocket
20. Righthand Secondary Camshaft Timing Drive Chain
21. Righthand Exhaust CMP Actuator Timing Mark
22. RighthandExhaust Secondary Camshaft Timing Drive Chain Timing Link
23. Righthand Intake CMP Actuator Timing Mark
24. Righthand Intake CMP Actuator Timing Mark

LTV0500000001070

Fig. 26 Timing chain stage two alignment

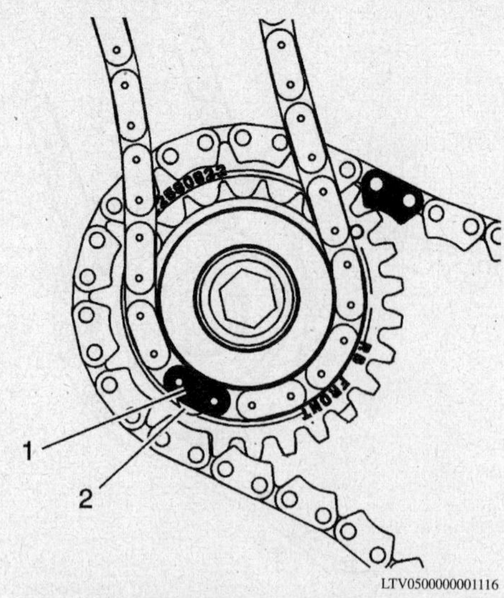

LTV0500000001116

Fig. 27 Righthand camshaft drive chain & intermediate idler sprocket alignment

CAMSHAFT

REPLACE

1. Remove camshaft cover as outlined under "Valve Cover, Replace."
2. Remove mounting bolts and position power steering fluid reservoir aside. **Do not disconnect power steering pipes or drain power steering fluid.**
3. Disconnect connectors, then remove mounting bolts and Camshaft Position (CMP) sensor.
4. Disconnect connector, then remove mounting bolts and CMP actuator solenoid.
5. Remove crankshaft balancer as outlined under "Crankshaft Damper, Replace."
6. Rotate crankshaft until camshafts are in neutral, (low tension position using crankshaft rotation socket tool No. EN 46111, or equivalent. Camshaft flats will be parallel with camshaft cover rail.
7. Hold camshafts in place with suitable open end wrench and loosen camshaft position actuator bolt.
8. Install timing chain retention tool No. 46108, or equivalent, over lefthand secondary timing chain.
9. Mark timing chain and actuators for installation alignment.
10. Remove actuator mounting bolt.
11. Remove camshaft locking tool from lefthand camshafts and position lobes in neutral position.
12. Maintain bearing caps in order for installation in original position.
13. Remove mounting bolts, bearing caps and camshafts.
14. Reverse procedure to install, noting the following:
    a. Ensure crankshaft is in stage one timing drive assembly position, **Fig. 8.**
    b. Ensure camshaft sealing rings are in place in camshaft grooves.
    c. No. 4 identification ring for lefthand intake camshaft is machined off (1); No. 5 identification ring for lefthand exhaust camshaft is machined off (2), **Fig. 35.**
    d. Apply liberal amount of suitable to camshaft journals and lefthand cylinder head camshaft carriers.
    e. Ensure bearing cap raised feature is toward center of cylinder head, **Figs. 36 and 37.**
    f. I indicates intake camshaft.
    g. E indicates exhaust camshaft.
    h. Nos. 2, 4 and 6 indicates lefthand cylinder position from front of engine.
    i. Nos. 1, 3 and 5 indicates righthand cylinder position from front of engine.
    j. Apply liberal amount of suitable lubricant to camshaft bearing caps.
    k. **Torque** camshaft bearing cap bolts to 89 inch lbs., in sequence, **Figs. 38 and 39.**
    l. Loosen center intake camshaft bearing cap bolts Nos. 1 and 2, and center exhaust camshaft bearing cap bolts No. 3 and 4.
    m. **Torque** camshaft bearing cap bolts 1, 2, 3 and 4 to 89 inch lbs.

PISTON & ROD ASSEMBLY

When installing piston and rod assemblies into cylinder block, ensure dot on top of piston faces toward front of engine, **Fig. 40.**

PISTONS, PINS & RINGS

Set the ring gaps for the oil control, second and top ring using piston location arrow for reference, **Fig. 41.**

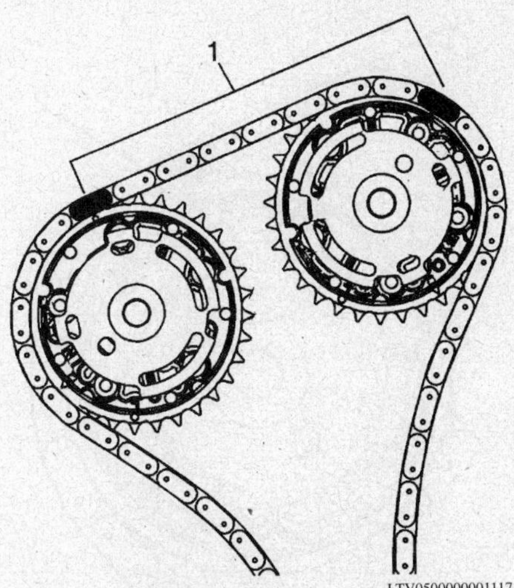

Fig. 28 Righthand camshaft drive chain installation

MAIN & ROD BEARINGS

Connecting Rod

1. **Torque** connecting rod bolts to 22 ft. lbs.
2. Loosen bolts to **torque** of zero.
3. **Torque** rod bolts to 18 ft. lbs.
4. Final tighten bolts an additional 110°.

Main Bearings

1. Install new upper crankshaft bearings into position.
2. Thrust bearing belongs in No. 3 journal.
3. Ensure upper bearing insert contains oil transfer hole and groove.
4. Roll bearing into position so lock tang engages crank slot.
5. Bearing must fit flush with upper crankcase.
6. Install new lower crankshaft bearings into position in main bearing caps.
7. Lower crankshaft bearings are identified by NO grooves or holes.
8. Bearings must fit flush with crankshaft bearing caps.
9. Apply liberal amount of suitable crankshaft prelube to upper and lower bearing surfaces.
10. Lower crankshaft into position.
11. Install main bearing caps Nos. 1–4 with arrow oriented to front of engine, **Fig. 42.** Front bearing cap is No. 1.
12. Loosely install original inner main cap bolts.
13. Loosely install new outer main cap bolts.
14. Tap crankshaft main bearing caps with suitable, soft-faced hammer.
15. Loosely install new short/inner side main cap bolts.
16. Loosely install new long/outer side main cap bolts.
17. **Torque** inboard bolts No. 1–8 to 15 ft. lbs., in sequence, **Fig. 43.**
18. Final tighten inboard bolts an additional 80° in sequence.

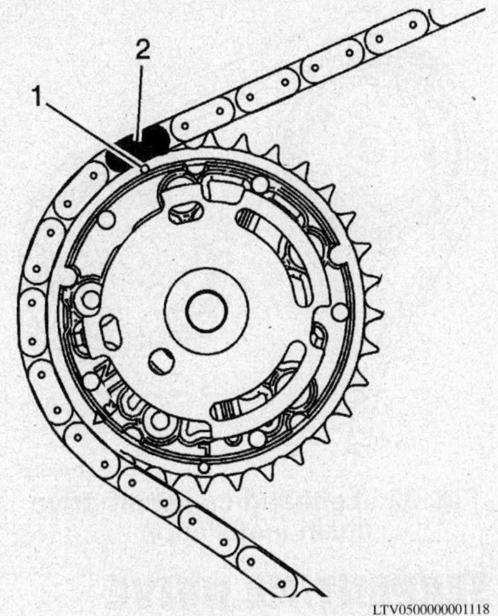

Fig. 29 Righthand camshaft drive chain & exhaust camshaft sprocket alignment

19. **Torque** outboard bolts No. 9–16 to 11 ft. lbs., **Fig. 44.**
20. Final tighten outboard bolts an additional 110° in sequence.
21. **Torque** short/inner bolts 17–20 to 22 ft. lbs., in sequence, **Fig. 45.**
22. Final tighten short/inner bolts 17–20 an additional 60° in sequence.
23. **Torque** long/inner bolts 21–24 to 22 ft. lbs., in sequence, **Fig. 45.**
24. Final tighten long/inner bolts 21–24 an additional 60° in sequence.

CRANKSHAFT SEAL

REPLACE

1. Remove crankshaft balancer as outlined under "Crankshaft Damper, Replace."
2. Remove seal using suitable flat-bladed tool.
3. Reverse procedure to install seal using oil seal installer tool No. J29184, or equivalent.

CRANKSHAFT REAR OIL SEAL

REPLACE

Removal

1. Remove transmission as outlined in **MOTOR's "Domestic Transmission, In-Vehicle Service" or "Transmission Service DVD."**
2. Remove mounting bolts and flywheel.
3. Remove oil pan as outlined under "Oil Pan, Replace."
4. Remove crankshaft rear oil seal housing mounting bolts.
5. Shear RTV sealant by prying housing at edge pry points.
6. Pry oil seal housing from cylinder block using pry points located at edge of housing.

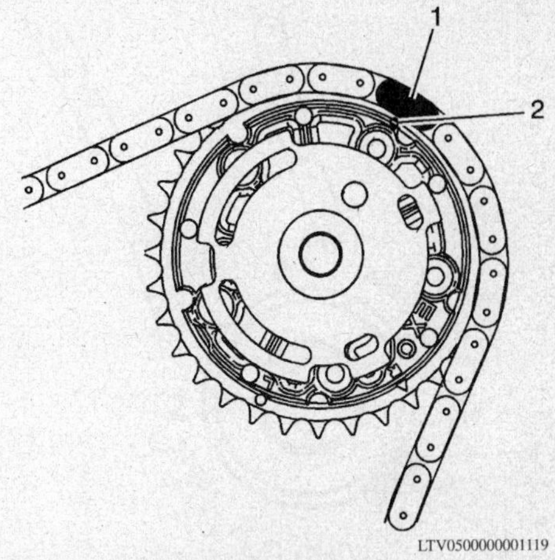

Fig. 30 Righthand camshaft drive chain & intake camshaft sprocket alignment

7. Remove and discard crankshaft rear oil seal housing.

Installation

1. Install .236 inch guides pins tools No. EN46109, or equivalent, into two crankshaft rear oil seal housing corner bolt holes of block.
2. Install crankshaft rear oil seal installation tool No. EN-47839 with handle tool No. J42183, or equivalent, onto rear of crankshaft flange.
3. Place .118 in bead of suitable RTV sealant to new crankshaft rear oil seal housing, **Fig. 46.**
4. Install crankshaft rear oil seal housing to block. **Do not allow engine oil on install area.**
5. Remove guide pins and tighten mounting bolts.
6. Install oil pan as outlined under "Oil Pan, Replace."
7. **Torque** new flywheel mounting bolts to 22 ft. lbs.
8. Final tighten bolts an additional 45°.
9. Install transmission as outlined in **MOTOR's "Domestic Transmission, In-Vehicle Service" or "Transmission Service DVD."**

OIL PAN

REPLACE

1. Remove front cover as outlined under "Front Cover, Replace."
2. Remove power steering hose retainer from air conditioning compressor bracket.
3. Remove pinch bolt and disconnect intermediate steering shaft from steering gear.
4. Remove engine mount lower nuts.
5. Remove air conditioning compressor bracket mounting bolts, then position compressor and bracket aside. **Do not disconnect air conditioning pipes and/or hoses.**
6. Drain engine oil into suitable container.
7. Remove transmission oil cooler pipe retainer from engine righthand side.

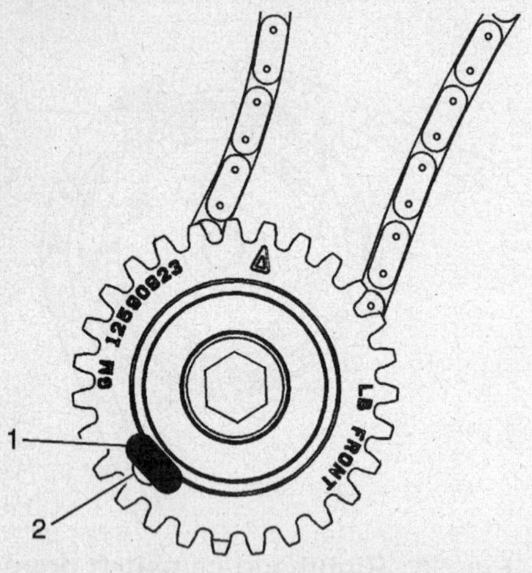

Fig. 31 Lefthand camshaft drive chain idler sprocket alignment

8. Support and raise engine using universal engine support fixture tool No. J28467-B, adapter tools No. J28467-501 and engine lift bracket tool No. J36857, or equivalent, support fixture.
9. **On models equipped with AWD,** remove front differential carrier as outlined in "Front Wheel Drive" section.
10. **On all models,** remove oil pan mounting bolts and shear RTV sealant by edge at pry points.
11. Remove oil pan.
12. Reverse procedure to install, noting the following:
    a. Install .315 inch guide pin tools No. EN46109, or equivalent, into center oil pan rail bolt hole on each side.
    b. Apply .118 inch bead suitable RTV sealant on block pan rail and crankshaft rear oil seal housing, **Fig. 47.**
    c. **Torque** oil pan 8 mm mounting bolts Nos. 1–11 to 17 ft. lbs., in sequence, **Fig. 48.**
    d. **Torque** oil pan 10 mm mounting bolts Nos. 12–13 to 89 inch lbs., in sequence.

OIL PUMP

REPLACE

1. Remove primary timing chain as outlined under "Timing Chain, Replace." **Do not remove lefthand idler sprocket.**
2. Remove crankshaft sprocket.
3. Remove oil pump bolts and the oil pump.
4. Reverse procedure to install. Ensure crankshaft is in stage one timing position with crankshaft sprocket timing mark aligned to stage one timing mark on oil pump cover, **Fig. 8.**

OIL PUMP SERVICE

There are no serviceable components within the oil pump. Disassembled oil pump must not be reused.

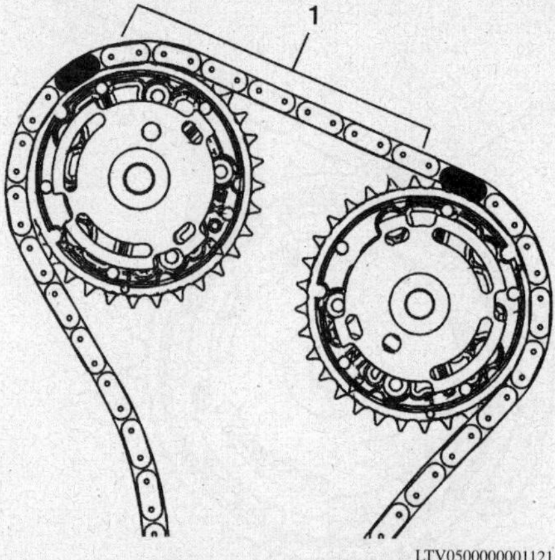

Fig. 32 Lefthand camshaft drive chain installation

SERPENTINE DRIVE BELT

Replace

ALTERNATOR & WATER PUMP

1. Release drive belt tension by rotating drive belt tensioner clockwise.
2. Remove drive belt from water pump pulley.
3. Slowly release drive belt tensioner.
4. Remove drive belt from accessory drive pulleys.
5. Reverse procedure to install.

AIR CONDITIONING & POWER STEERING

1. Remove alternator and water pump drive belt as outlined under "Alternator & Water Pump."
2. Rotate drive belt tensioner clockwise to release drive belt tension.
3. Remove drive belt from power steering pulley.
4. Slowly release drive belt tensioner and remove drive belt from accessory drive pulleys.
5. Reverse procedure to install.

Routing

Refer to **Figs. 49 and 50** for serpentine drive belts' routings.

COOLING SYSTEM BLEED

1. Slowly fill cooling system until coolant stabilizes one inch above surge tank FULL COLD mark.
2. Install surge tank cap.
3. Start and run engine at 2000–2500 RPM until it reaches normal operating temperature.
4. Idle engine for three minutes.
5. Turn engine off and allow it to cool.
6. Adjust coolant level to surge tank FULL COLD mark.

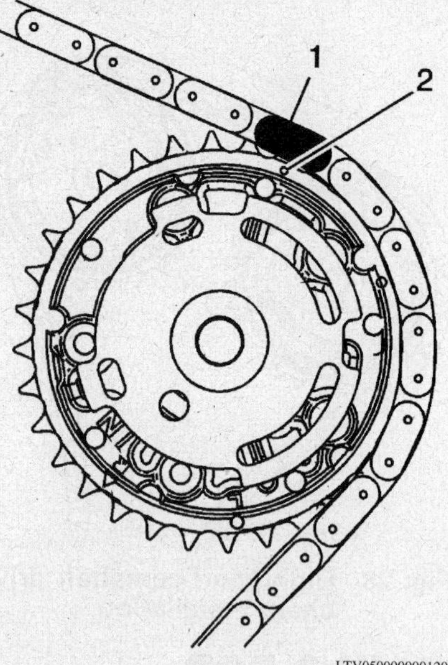

Fig. 33 Lefthand camshaft drive chain & exhaust camshaft sprocket alignment

THERMOSTAT

REPLACE

1. Remove mounting bolts and heater inlet/outlet pipe. Discard O-ring and gasket.
2. Remove mounting bolts and thermostat housing. Discard O-ring and gasket.
3. Remove mounting bolts and thermostat . Discard O-ring.
4. Reverse procedure to install.

WATER PUMP

REPLACE

1. Drain cooling system into suitable container.
2. Release drive belt tension by rotating drive belt tensioner clockwise.
3. Remove drive belt from water pump pulley.
4. Slowly release drive belt tensioner.
5. Remove drive belt from accessory drive pulleys.
6. Hold water pump pulley using pulley holding tool No. EN46104, or equivalent.
7. Remove mounting bolts and water pump pulley.
8. Remove mounting bolts and water pump. Discard seal.
9. Reverse procedure to install.

RADIATOR

REPLACE

1. Drain engine coolant into suitable container.
2. Remove Positive Crankcase Ventilation (PCV) hose from air cleaner duct resonator.
3. Loosen clamps and remove air cleaner duct.

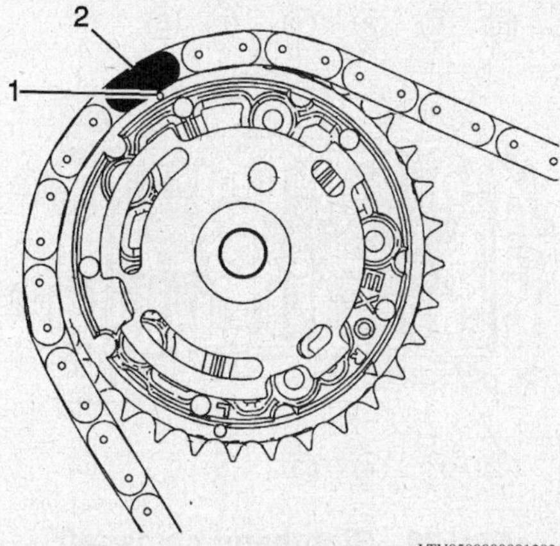

Fig. 34 Lefthand camshaft drive chain & intake camshaft sprocket alignment

4. Disconnect cooling fan electrical connectors and shroud condenser tube retainer clip.
5. Disengage surge tank inlet hose from shroud retaining and position hose aside.
6. Remove mounting bolts and cooling fan assembly.
7. Remove condenser seal, radiator mounting bolts, then the support brackets.
8. Raise and support vehicle.
9. Remove lower and upper mounting bolts, then position condenser aside.
10. Remove transmission oil cooler mounting bolts.
11. Disconnect radiator side air baffle lower retainer pins.
12. Lower vehicle.
13. Remove mounting bolts and radiator support brackets.
14. Remove radiator/condenser upper support using door trim pad clip remover tool No. J38778, or equivalent.
15. Disconnect and position radiator surge tank inlet hose aside.
16. Disconnect clamps and position radiator inlet and outlet hoses aside.
17. Disconnect side air baffle upper pins and remove radiator.
18. Reverse procedure to install.

FUEL PUMP

REPLACE

Primary

The primary fuel tank module is horizontal in the installed position, but pivots vertically for removal.

1. Drain fuel tank into suitable container.
2. Relieve fuel system pressure as outlined under "Precautions."
3. Raise and support vehicle.
4. Disconnect oxygen sensor electrical connector, then record wire routing and attachment points for installation alignment.
5. Remove oxygen sensors from exhaust pipe.
6. Remove two mounting bolts and tunnel brace from floor panel.

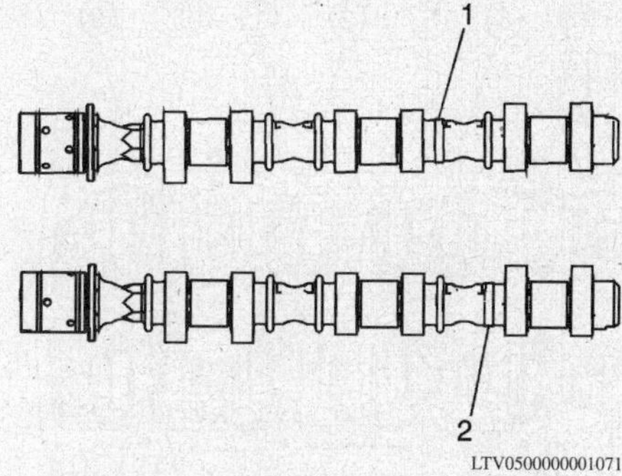

Fig. 35 Lefthand camshaft identification

7. Support exhaust system and remove exhaust pipes to manifolds mounting nuts.
8. Pry front exhaust hangers from rear suspension hanger rods.
9. Lubricate tail pipe hanger rods and pry hangers from rods.
10. Lower exhaust system, then remove and discard seals.
11. **On models equipped with AWD,** proceed as follows:
    a. Support propeller shaft close to support bearing using suitable jack.
    b. Remove heat shield mounting bolts.
    c. Remove support bearing mounting bolts.
    d. Mark propeller shaft Consent Velocity (CV) joint to transfer case flange for installation alignment.
    e. Remove propeller shaft CV joint to transfer case flange mounting bolts.
    f. Remove propeller shaft coupler-to-differential flange bolts, nuts and washers.
    g. Disconnect propeller shaft CV joint from transfer case flange by moving shaft toward rear using suitable flat-bladed tool in transfer case flange notch.
    h. Hold propeller shaft and lower support device.
    i. Disconnect coupler from differential flange by moving propeller shaft forward.
12. **On models equipped with RWD,** proceed as follows:
    a. Remove propeller shaft coupler-to-transmission flange mounting bolts, nuts and washers.
    b. Remove propeller shaft coupler-to-differential flange mounting bolts, nuts and washers.
    c. Support propeller shaft at support bearing.
    d. Remove support bearing mounting bolts, push front propeller shaft toward rear and disconnect it from transmission flange.
    e. Push front propeller shaft toward rear and release coupler from transmission flange.
    f. Holding front propeller shaft, lower support and remove support bearing.
    g. Disconnect coupler from differential flange by pulling rear propeller

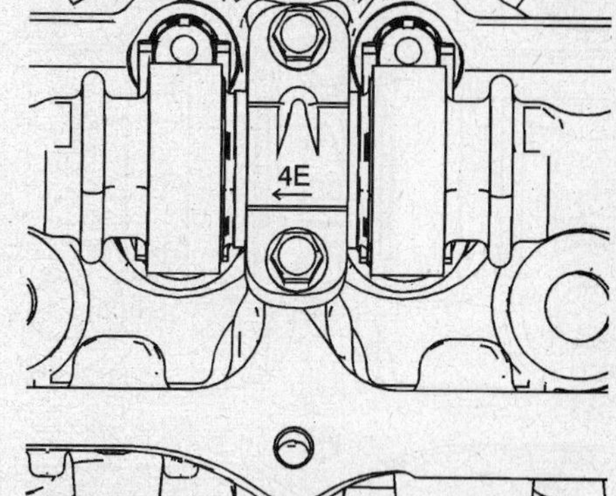

Fig. 36 Lefthand camshaft bearing cap identification

shaft forward.
    h. Record number and location of shim packs between support bearing mounting bracket and underbody for installation alignment.
13. **On all models,** remove propeller shaft.
14. Disconnect fuel tank filler hose and Evaporative Emission (EVAP) hose filler vent tube.
15. Disconnect fuel tank electrical connector and EVAP canister hoses.
16. Disconnect chassis retainer and EVAP canister electrical connector.
17. Raise lower control arms using suitable screw jack and remove shock absorber lower mounting bolts.
18. Remove screw jack.
19. Support rear fame near adjuster tie bar using suitable screw jack.
20. Remove two rear frame front mounting bolts.
21. Lower jack until there is approximately two inches between rear frame front mounting surface and chassis. **Do not over extend rear brake hoses.**
22. Remove mounting bolts and position fuel tank straps downward around rear frame. **Do not bend straps.**
23. Ensure fuel tank and EVAP wiring harness, as well as hoses at EVAP and chassis pipes are free.
24. Lower and remove fuel tank.
25. Disconnect primary fuel tank module lines and hoses from tank retainers.
26. Disconnect primary fuel tank module electrical connector.
27. Rotate and remove cam lock ring counterclockwise using fuel tank sender wrench tool No. J45747, or equivalent. **Do not allow tool to contact fuel pipes.**
28. Lift primary fuel tank module, pull licking mechanism and remove transfer tube.
29. Remove primary fuel tank module. Discard seal.
30. Reverse procedure to install, noting the following:
    a. Ensure seal bead faces fuel tank.
    b. Ensure fuel level float is free from binding.
    c. Align module to encapsulated ring.

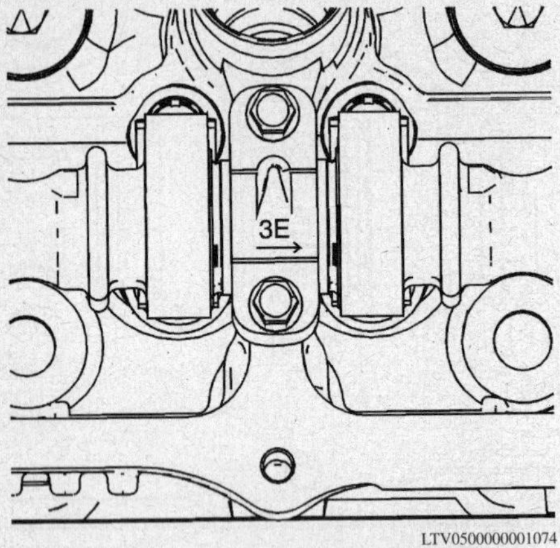

Fig. 37 Righthand camshaft bearing cap identification

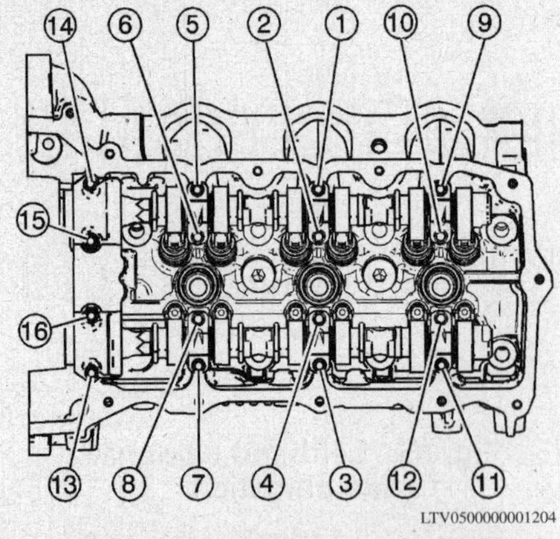

Fig. 38 Lefthand camshaft bearing cap tightening sequence

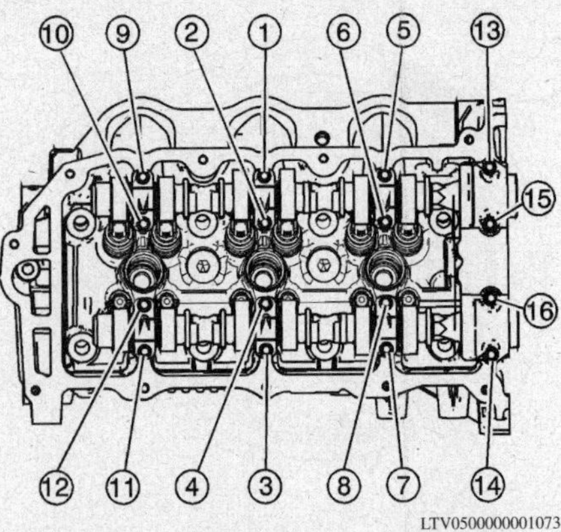

Fig. 39 Righthand camshaft bearing cap tightening sequence

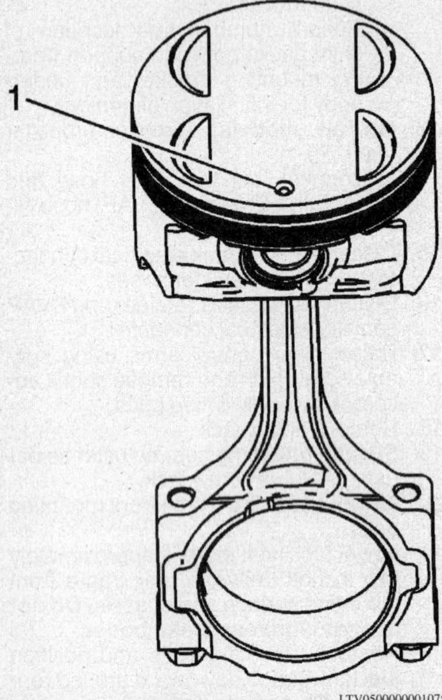

Fig. 40 Piston & rod orientation

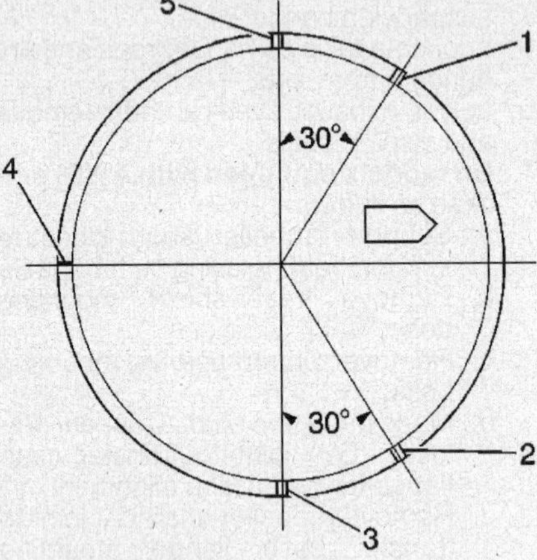

1. Lower oil control ring
2. Upper oil control ring
3. Top Ring
4. Oil control ring expander
5. Second ring

LTV0500000001076

Fig. 41 Piston ring orientation

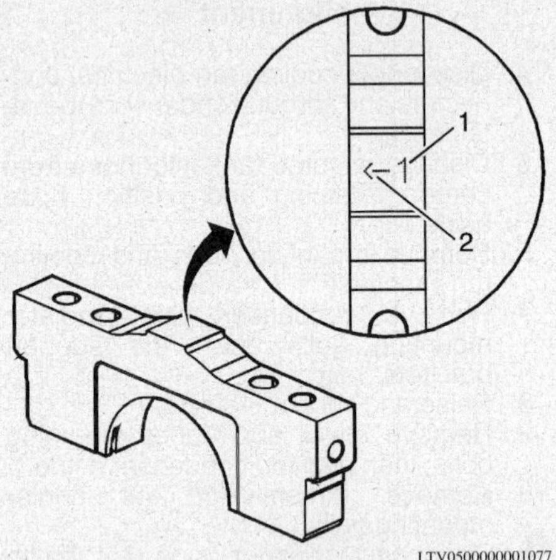

Fig. 42 Main bearing cap identification

Secondary

Replacement procedure for secondary fuel tank module is the same as for the primary fuel tank module.

FUEL FILTER

REPLACE

1. Relieve fuel system pressure as outlined under "Precautions."
2. Raise and support vehicle.
3. Disconnect fuel filter inlet quick-connect fitting.
4. Remove threaded outlet fitting using suitable primary and back-up wrenches.
5. Slide filter rearward from bracket.
6. Discard O-ring seal.
7. Reverse procedure to install. Lubricate fuel pipe new O-ring seal with suitable, clean engine oil.

TECHNICAL SERVICE BULLETINS

Whine, Whistle, Ringing From Front Of Engine

2004-05

On some of these models equipped less heavy duty cooling there may be a whine, whistle or ringing from front of engine that increases as engine RPM increases.

This condition may be caused by the harmonic balancer.

To correct this condition, replace the harmonic balancer (part No. 12597654) if the suspect balancer has three spokes. **Do not replace balancers with six spokes.**

External Oil Leak

2005

On some of these models there may be an external oil leak.

This condition may be caused by the crankshaft rear main oil seal.

To correct this condition, install revised crankshaft rear main oil seal (part No. 12592195) as outlined under "Crankshaft Rear Oil Seal, Replace."

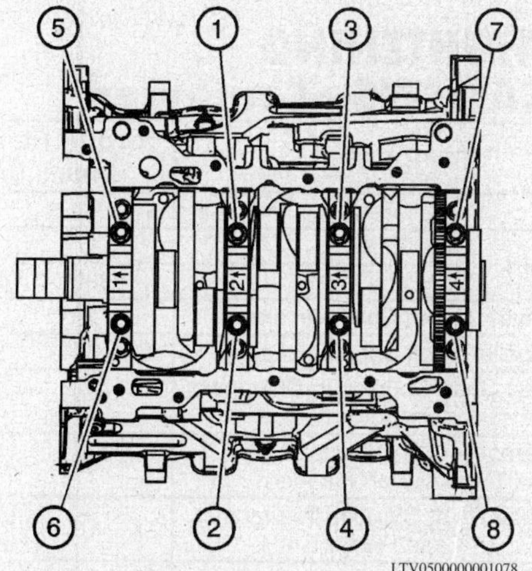

Fig. 43 Inboard main bearing cap tightening sequence

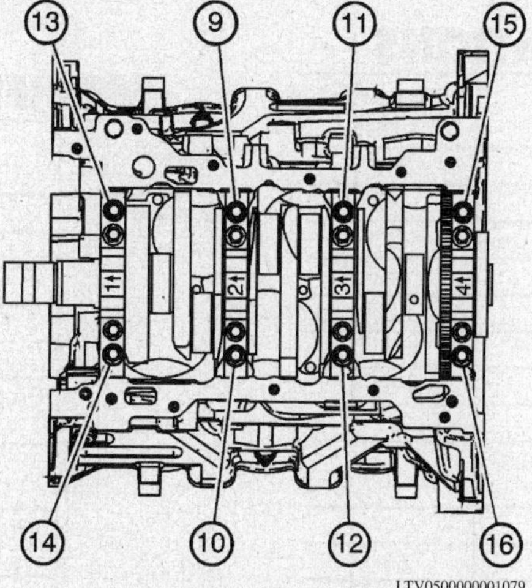

Fig. 44 Outboard main bearing cap tightening sequence

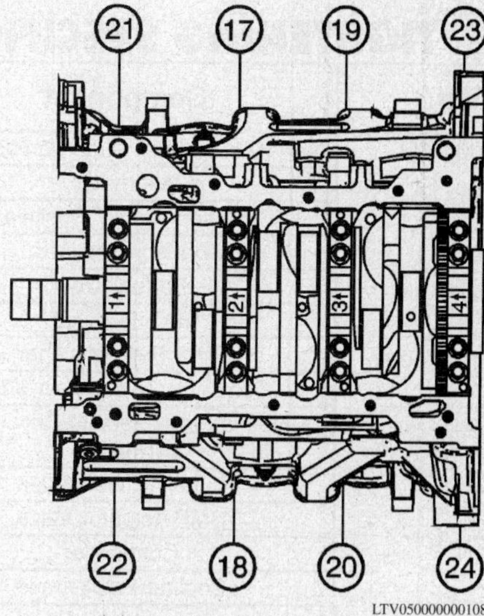

Fig. 45 Short & long/inner bolt tightening sequence

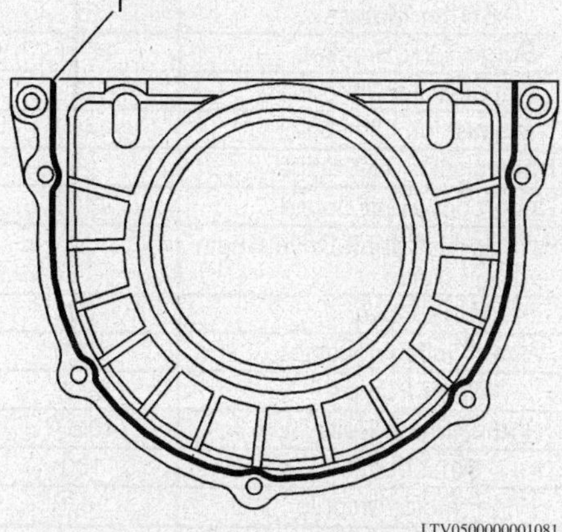

Fig. 46 Rear oil seal housing sealant application

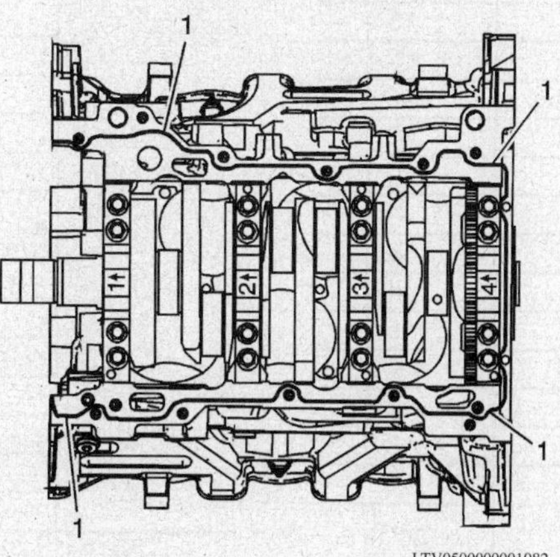

Fig. 47 Oil pan sealant application

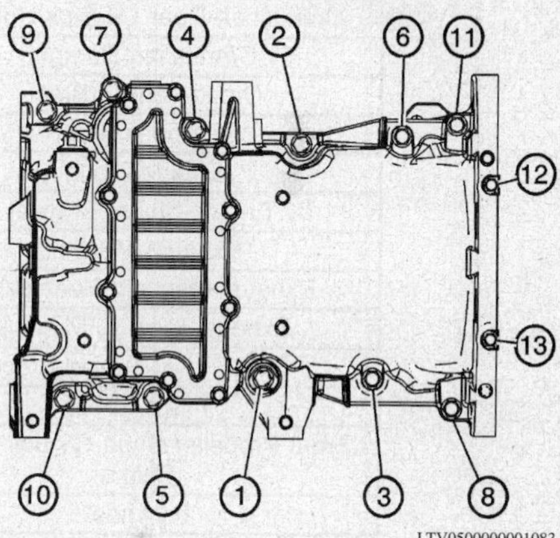

Fig. 48 Oil pan tightening sequence

Fig. 49 Alternator & water pump serpentine belt routing

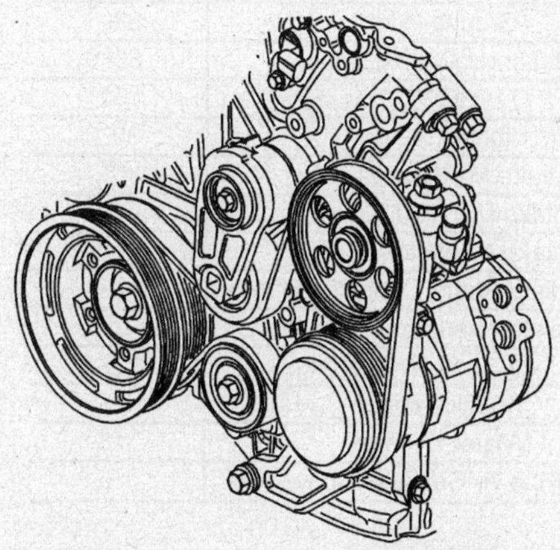

Fig. 50 Air conditioning & power steering serpentine belt routing

TIGHTENING SPECIFICATIONS

Year	Component	Torque Ft. Lbs.
2004–06	Air Cleaner Duct Clamps	35①
	Alternator	37
	Battery Cable, Positive	23
	Battery Retainer	13
	Battery Tray	53①
	BAT Terminal	115①
	Drive Belt Tensioner	37
	Camshaft Drive Chain Shoe	17
	Camshaft Intermediate Drive Chain Idler	43
	Catalytic Converter	37
	CMP Actuator Valve	89①
	Condenser	58①
	Cooling Fan Shroud	58①
	Coolant Inlet Pipe	⑥
	Cowl Panel	13
	Crankshaft Balancer	⑨
	Crankshaft Rear Oil Seal Housing	89①
	Crankshaft Damper	⑨
	Cross-Vehicle Brace	83
	Cylinder Head	⑦
	Engine Mount	59
	Engine Mount Bracket	44
	Exhaust Manifold	15
	Exhaust Manifold Heat Shield	89①
	Exhaust Pipe To Manifold	22
	Floor Panel Tunnel Brace	18
	Front Cover	⑩
	Front Propeller Shaft CV Joint Heat Shield	80①
	Flywheel	③
	Front Frame	③
	Fuel Filter Outlet	22
	Fuel Tank Strap	37
	Ground Wire	89①
	Headlamp Leveling Sensor	80①
	HO2S	31
	Ignition Coil	89①
	Intake Manifold Brace	⑤
	Intake Manifold, Lower	17
	Intake Manifold, Upper	④
	Intermediate Shaft, Center To Upper	23
	Intermediate Shaft, Lower To Center	23
	Intermediate Shaft To Steering Gear	37
	Knock Sensor	17
	Master Cylinder	18
	Muffler Pipe To Catalytic Converters	16

TIGHTENING SPECIFICATIONS—Continued

Year	Component	Torque Ft. Lbs.
2004–06	Oil Pan	⑫
	Oil Pump	17
	Oil Pump Cover	89①
	Primary Timing Chain Tensioner	⑪
	Propeller Shaft Support Bearing	37
	Propeller Shaft Coupler To Differential Flange	63
	Propeller Shaft Coupler To Transmission Flange	63
	Propeller Shaft CV Joint To Transfer Case Flange	⑦
	Radiator Support Bracket	80
	Spark Plug	15
	Strut, Upper	83
	Starter Motor	37
	Surge Tank Bracket	80①
	Transmission Mount	44
	Transmission Oil Cooler	44①
	Transmission To Engine	②
	Underbody Heat Shield	71①
	Upper Primary Camshaft Drive Chain Guide	17
	Valve Cover	⑧
	Water Outlet Housing	89①
	Water Pump	89①
	Water Pump Pulley	106①
	Wheel Lug	100
	Wiper Motor Module	89①

① — Inch lbs.
② — M10 x 1.5 bolts, 37 ft. lbs.; M12 x 1.75 bolts 55 ft. lbs.
③ — Refer to "Engine, Replace" for tightening specifications and sequence.
④ — Refer to "Intake Manifold, Replace" for tightening specifications and sequence.
⑤ — Bolt, 48 ft. lbs.; Stud, 89 inch lbs.
⑥ — To thermostat & alternator bracket, 17 ft. lbs.; to cylinder head 37 ft. lbs.
⑦ — Refer to "Cylinder Head, Replace" for tightening specifications and sequence.
⑧ — Refer to "Valve Cover, Replace" for tightening specifications and sequence.
⑨ — Refer to "Crankshaft Damper, Replace" for tightening specifications and sequence.
⑩ — Refer to "Front Cover, Replace" for tightening specifications and sequence.
⑪ — Refer to "Timing Chain, Replace" for tightening specifications and sequence.
⑫ — Refer to "Oil Pan, Replace" for tightening specifications and sequence.

4.6L Engine

NOTE: On Air Bag Equipped Models, Refer To "Air Bag System Precautions" Located In The Front Of This Manual For System Disarming & Arming Procedures.

NOTE: Refer To "Computer Relearn Procedures" Located In The Front Of This Manual When Battery Power To The Computer Has Been Interrupted.

NOTE: Prior To Performing Any Service Operations Listed In This Section, Consult The "Technical Service Bulletins" Section For Related Information.

INDEX

PRECAUTIONS

Air Bag Systems

Refer to "Air Bag System Precautions" in the front of this manual for system disarming and arming procedures.

Battery Ground Cable

Prior to service, disconnect battery ground cable and isolate as required.

Fuel System Pressure Relief

1. Turn ignition in Off position.
2. Disconnect battery ground cable and isolate as required.
3. Remove mounting bolts and cross-vehicle brace.
4. Remove power steering and engine oil fill caps.
5. Lift up and pull sight shield forward to disconnect rear tab, then remove shield.
6. Connect suitable fuel pressure gauge to fuel pressure valve.
7. Place suitable shop towel under connections.
8. Install suitable bleed hose into suitable container.
9. Open bleed valve to relieve fuel system.

COMPRESSION PRESSURE

The minimum compression in any one cylinder should not be less than 70 percent of the highest cylinder. No cylinder should read less than 140 psi.

ENGINE MOUNT

REPLACE

Lefthand

1. Raise and support vehicle.
2. Remove lefthand exhaust manifold as outlined under "Exhaust Manifold, Replace."
3. Support engine using suitable screw jack with wood block under oil pan.
4. Remove lefthand engine mount upper nut.
5. Remove mounting bolts and lefthand engine mount bracket, **Fig. 1. Do not distort or bend engine mount heat shield.**
6. Remove lower mounting nut and lefthand engine mount, **Fig. 2.**
7. Reverse procedure to install.

Righthand

1. Raise and support vehicle.
2. Remove righthand exhaust manifold as outlined under "Exhaust Manifold, Replace."
3. Support engine using suitable screw jack with wood block under oil pan.
4. Remove righthand engine mount upper nut.
5. Remove mounting bolts and righthand engine mount bracket, **Fig. 3. Do not distort or bend engine mount heat shield.**
6. Remove mounting nut and righthand engine mount, **Fig. 4.**
7. Reverse procedure to install.

ENGINE

REPLACE

1. Center steering wheel and turn ignition switch to OFF position.

2. Lock steering column using steering column anti-rotation pin tool No. J42640, or equivalent.
3. Disconnect battery cables at battery.
4. Remove mounting bolts and cross-vehicle brace.
5. Remove power steering and engine oil fill caps.
6. Lift up and pull sight shield forward to disconnect rear tab, then remove shield.
7. Disconnect Positive Crankcase Ventilation (PCV) tube from air cleaner duct.
8. Loosen clamps and remove air cleaner duct.
9. Disconnect Mass Air Flow (MAF)/ intake Air Temperature (IAT) sensor electrical connector.
10. Remove position aside coolant hose from air cleaner retainer.
11. Remove mounting screw and air cleaner.
12. Disconnect surge tank inlet hose and position aside to engine.
13. Recover air conditioning refrigerant as outlined in "Air Conditioning" chapter.
14. Disconnect air conditioning suction hose fitting at top of lefthand shock tower and remove retainer. Position hose aside to engine.
15. Disconnect condenser air conditioning liquid line and from fan shroud retainer.
16. Disconnect from brake booster and position brake booster vacuum line aside to engine.
17. Disconnect master cylinder brake fluid level switch electrical connector.
18. Remove mounting nuts and position master cylinder aside to engine. Hold master cylinder in position using suitable mechanics wire. **Do not disconnect brake lines from master cylinder.**
19. Relieve fuel system pressure as outlined under "Precautions."
20. Remove fuel line retainer from heater lines bracket on front dash.
21. Disconnect engine wiring harness connector at front of dash.
22. Disconnect underhood fuse block connector between righthand shock tower and valve cover.
23. Remove underhood electrical center cover.
24. Remove battery ground bolt and cable retainer from righthand shock tower.
25. Position battery ground aside to engine.
26. Remove mounting nut and positive battery cable from inside underhood electrical center, then position cable aside to engine.
27. Disconnect chassis electrical connector at top of righthand shock tower and position wire aside to engine.
28. Disconnect Transmission Control Module (TCM) electrical connector and position wiring harness aside to engine.
29. Disconnect engine wiring harness connector inside underhood electrical center.
30. Disconnect electrical connector at righthand frame rail.
31. Loosen fan nut from crank adapter shaft using fan clutch wrench tool No, J41240-5A, or equivalent. **Do not completely remove fan from crank adapter shaft.**

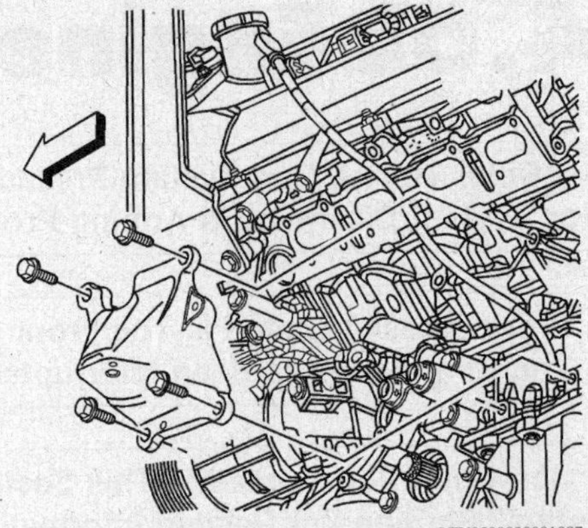

Fig. 1 Lefthand engine mount bracket replacement

32. Raise and support vehicle, then remove front tire and wheel assemblies.
33. Disconnect engine wiring harness from engine frame and position it aside.
34. Continue to loosen nut, the disconnect and remove fan.
35. **On models equipped with heavy duty electric cooling fans,** proceed as follows:
    a. Remove auxiliary cooling fan to condenser upper mounting bolts.
    b. Remove retainers and front air deflector.
    c. Disconnect auxiliary cooling fan electrical connectors.
    d. Remove lower mounting bolts and auxiliary cooling fan assembly.
36. **On all models,** remove push-in retainers, then the lefthand and righthand wheelhousing splash shields.
37. Remove push-in retainers, then the lefthand and righthand wheelhousing liners.
38. Remove windshield washer reservoir brace from front frame.
39. Disconnect transmission oil cooler lines near air conditioning compressor and drain fluid into suitable container.
40. Remove bolt and disconnect center from lower intermediate steering shaft.
41. Drain cooling system into suitable container.
42. Remove radiator power steering cooler lines mounting bolt.
43. Remove condenser upper and lower mounting bolts.
44. Disconnect radiator side air baffle lowering mounting pins.
45. Position condenser aside and remove Transmission Oil Cooler (TOC) mounting bolts.
46. Lower vehicle.
47. **On models equipped with heavy duty cooling,** proceed as follows:
    a. Disconnect condenser tube from fan shroud clip.
    b. Remove mounting bolts and cooling fan shroud.
48. **On all models,** disconnect clamps, then remove radiator outlet and inlet hoses.
49. Disconnect clamp and remove radiator surge tank inlet hose.
50. Remove mounting bolts and radiator support bracket.
51. Disconnect upper air baffle pins and remove radiator.
52. Raise and support vehicle.
53. Remove mounting bolts and position power steering cooler aside to engine. Secure cooler with suitable mechanics wire.
54. **On models equipped with AWD,** remove transfer case as outlined in **MOTOR's "Domestic Transmission, In-Vehicle Service" or "Transmission Service DVD."**
55. **On all models,** remove transmission as outlined in **MOTOR's "Domestic Transmission, In-Vehicle Service" or "Transmission Service DVD."**
56. Remove brake bundle clips from lefthand and righthand frame rails. **Do not remove clips from brake lines.**
57. Disconnect fuel filter line.
58. Disconnect Evaporative Emission (EVAP) hose connection at fuel filer rear of the fuel filter.
59. Disconnect rear brake lines from bracket above rear axle.
60. Remove fuel and brake line bundle retainers from frame rail along vehicle length. **Do not remove retainers from lines.**
61. Remove fuel filter bracket, then remove fuel and brake line bundle from righthand wheelhouse.
62. Lower vehicle.
63. Disconnect outlet hose from heater outlet pipe at righthand frame and position it aside to engine.
64. Disconnect water housing inlet hose and position it aside to vehicle.
65. **On models equipped with Magnaride,** disconnect electrical connectors from top of lefthand and righthand shock modules.
66. **On all models,** remove lefthand and righthand shock module mounting bolts.
67. Secure shock modules to front frame with suitable mechanics wire.
68. Raise vehicle and support engine, front frame and front suspension using suitable lift table.
69. Support vehicle rear with suitable jack stands.
70. Remove front frame mounting bolts.
71. Ensure all hoses, wires, pipes and shock modules clear vehicle during removal process.
72. Remove engine, front frame, fuel/ brake bundle and front suspension assembly.
73. Support engine at lefthand and righthand cylinder heads using engine lift bracket tools Nos. J28467-86 and J28467-87, or equivalent, respectively.
74. Remove engine from front frame using suitable engine lift.
75. Reverse procedure to install.

INTAKE MANIFOLD

REPLACE

1. Remove mounting bolts and cross-vehicle brace.

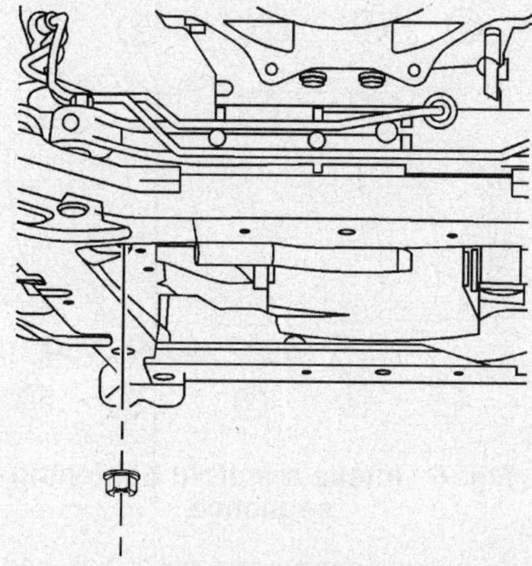

Fig. 2 Lefthand engine mount replacement

2. Remove power steering and engine oil fill caps.
3. Lift up and pull sight shield forward to disconnect rear tab, then remove shield.
4. Disconnect from lefthand valve cover and remove PCV fresh air tube from cleaner outlet duct.
5. Remove clip and disconnect from PCV orificed tube, then remove PCV dirty air tube from intake manifold.
6. Remove mounting nuts and sight shield bracket.
7. Disconnect lefthand and righthand fuel injector electrical connectors.
8. Disconnect evaporative emissions purge valve line and electrical connector.
9. Remove EVAP line from righthand cylinder head rear and position it aside.
10. Relieve fuel system pressure as outlined in "Precautions."
11. Disconnect fuel rail line and remove it from righthand cylinder head rear.
12. Remove mounting screws and fuel rail with injectors, **Fig. 5.**
13. Loosen plenum duct clamp, then remove mounting bolts and intake manifold.
14. Reverse procedure to install, noting the following:
    a. Install new gaskets.
    b. Lightly grease rubber plenum duct inside edge.
    c. **Torque** intake manifold mounting bolts to 89 inch lbs., in sequence, **Fig. 6.**

EXHAUST MANIFOLD

REPLACE

1. Disconnect heated oxygen sensor pigtail electrical connector.
2. **When removing lefthand exhaust manifold,** remove power steering gear as outlined in "Front Suspension & Steering" section.
3. **When removing righthand exhaust manifold,** disconnect alternator and bracket wire clips.
4. **On all models,** remove mounting bolts and exhaust manifold heat shield.

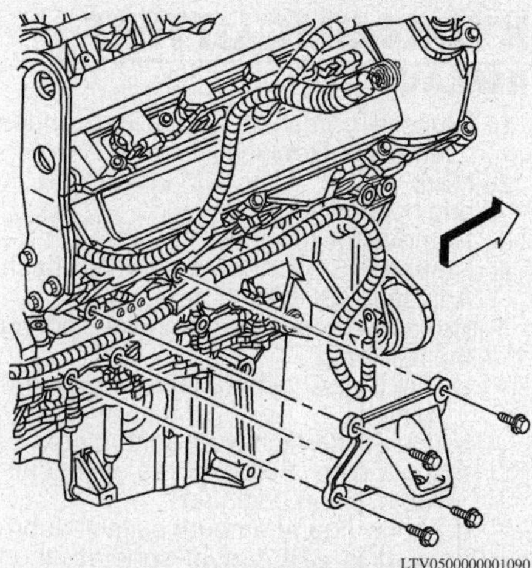

Fig. 3 Righthand engine mount bracket replacement

5. Remove heated oxygen sensor.
6. Remove mounting bolts and nuts, then the exhaust manifold. Discard mounting bolts and gasket.
7. Reverse procedure to install.

CYLINDER HEAD

REPLACE

1. Disconnect heated oxygen sensor pigtail electrical connector.
2. **When removing lefthand exhaust manifold,** remove power steering gear as outlined in "Front Suspension & Steering" section.
3. **When removing righthand exhaust manifold,** disconnect alternator and bracket wire clips.
4. **On all models,** remove mounting bolts and exhaust manifold heat shield.
5. Remove heated oxygen sensor.
6. Remove mounting bolts and nuts, then the exhaust manifold. Discard mounting bolts and gasket.
7. Drain engine coolant into suitable container.
8. Remove mounting bolts and cross-vehicle brace.
9. Remove power steering and engine oil fill caps.
10. Lift up and pull sight shield forward to disconnect rear tab, then remove shield.
11. Disconnect Positive Crankcase Ventilation (PCV) tube from air cleaner duct.
12. Loosen clamps and remove air cleaner duct.
13. Disconnect throttle body electrical connector.
14. Remove mounting bolts and throttle body. Discard gasket.
15. Disconnect electrical connector, then remove mounting bolt, bracket and Manifold Absolute Pressure (MAP) sensor.
16. Disconnect EVAP canister purge solenoid valve hose and electrical connector.
17. Disconnect clamps, then remove heater and radiator inlet hoses.
18. Disconnect clamps, then remove heater outlet, bypass and surge tank inlet hoses.

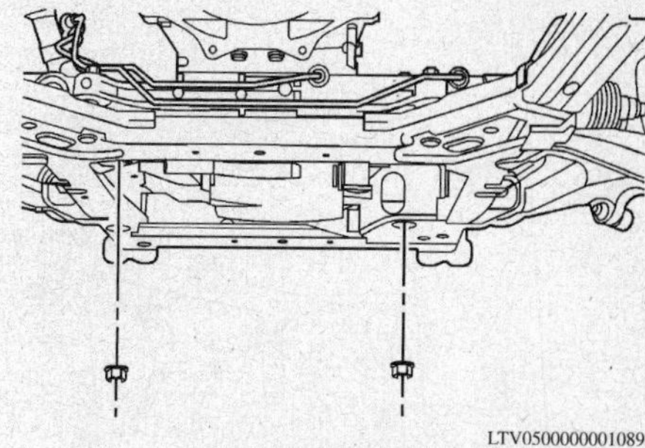

Fig. 4 Righthand engine mount replacement

19. Loosen the intake manifold duct clamp, then remove mounting bolts and water outlet housing. Discard gaskets.
20. Remove intake manifold as outlined under "Intake Manifold, Replace."
21. Remove secondary camshaft drive chain as outlined under "Timing Chain, Replace."
22. Remove camshafts as outlined under "Camshaft, Replace."
23. **If removing lefthand cylinder head,** remove power steering reservoir return hose mounting bolts.
24. **On all models,** remove three M6 external drive bolts from cylinder head front.
25. Remove ten M11 internal drive cylinder head bolts. Discard bolts.
26. Remove cylinder head and ensure no dowel guide pins are stuck in cylinder head. Discard gasket.
27. Reverse procedure to install, noting the following:
    a. Ensure locking pins are securely mounted and old thread sealant removed.
    b. **Torque** new M11 bolts to 22 ft. lbs., in sequence, **Figs. 7 and 8.**
    c. Tighten M11 head bolts an additional 60° in sequence.
    d. Tighten M11 bolts an additional 60° in sequence.
    e. Final tighten M11 bolts an additional 60° in sequence.
    f. **Torque** M6 bolts to 106 inch lbs in sequence.

VALVE COVER

REPLACE

1. Remove mounting bolts and cross-vehicle brace.
2. Remove power steering and engine oil fill caps.
3. Lift up and pull sight shield forward to disconnect rear tab, then remove shield.
4. Disconnect Positive Crankcase Ventilation (PCV) fresh air tube from lefthand valve cover.
5. Remove ignition coil cover.
6. Disconnect electrical connector, remove mounting bolt and ignition coil.
7. Remove ground strap to valve cover mounting bolt.
8. Remove mounting bolt and position oil dipstick tube aside.
9. Remove mounting bolts and valve

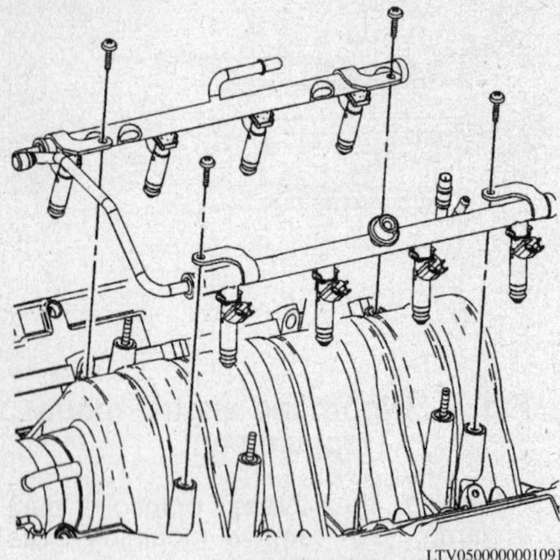

Fig. 5 Fuel rail replacement

cover, lifting camshaft drive end to clear cover. Discard gasket.

10. Reverse procedure install, noting the following:
    a. Apply small amount of suitable sealer to split line of cylinder head and camshaft position actuator housing, **Figs. 9 and 10.**

CAMSHAFT LOBE LIFT SPECIFICATIONS

Intake .... 2339 inch
Exhaust .... 2421 inch

VALVE CLEARANCE SPECIFICATIONS

These engines are equipped with Stationary Hydraulic Lash Adjusters (SHLA). There are no provision for adjustment.

VALVE ADJUSTMENT

These engines are equipped with Stationary Hydraulic Lash Adjusters (SHLA). There are no provision for adjustment.

ROCKER ARMS

REPLACE

1. Remove camshaft as outlined under "Camshaft, Replace."
2. Mark rocker arms for installation in original positions.
3. Remove rocker arms.
4. Reverse procedure to install, noting the following:
   a. Apply liberal amount suitable lubricant to pivot pocket, roller and valve slot, **Fig. 11.**
   b. Follower must be positioned squarely on valve tip so full width of roller will completely contact camshaft lobe.
   c. Rounded head end goes on Stationary Hydraulic Lash Adjusters (SHLA), while flat end goes on valve tip.

HYDRAULIC LIFTERS

REPLACE

1. Remove camshaft as outlined under "Camshaft, Replace."
2. Mark rocker arms for installation in original positions.
3. Remove rocker arms.
4. Remove Stationary Hydraulic Lash Adjusters (SHLA).
5. Reverse procedure to install, noting the following:
   a. Fill SHLA with suitable, clean engine oil.
   b. Do not scratch pivot sphere area.
   c. Lubricate SHLA bores with suitable, clean engine oil.
   d. Apply liberal amount suitable lubricant to SHLA pivot spheres, then the rocker arm pivot pocket, roller and valve slot.
   e. Follower must be positioned squarely on valve tip so full width of roller will completely contact camshaft lobe.
   f. Rounded head end goes on SHLA, while flat end goes on valve tip.

CRANKSHAFT DAMPER

REPLACE

1. Remove serpentine drive belts as outlined under "Serpentine Drive Belt."
2. Raise and support vehicle.
3. Remove transmission bell housing inspection hole cover and install flywheel holding tool No. EN48018, or equivalent.
4. Remove crankshaft balancer mounting bolt.
5. Place tool No. J38416-2 or equivalent, into end of crankshaft, then install tool No. J24420-C or equivalent on crankshaft balancer.
6. Remove crankshaft damper using crankshaft button tool No. J38416-2 and crankshaft balancer remover tool No. J24420-C, or equivalents.
7. Reverse procedure to install, noting the following:
   a. Press crankshaft balancer in place using crankshaft balancer installer No. J41998-B, or equivalent.
   b. **Torque** balancer mounting bolt to 37 ft. lbs.
   c. Final tighten mounting bolt an additional 120°.

FRONT COVER

REPLACE

1. Drain cooling system into suitable container.
2. Disconnect Positive Crankcase Ventilation (PCV) tube from air cleaner duct.
3. Loosen clamps and remove air cleaner duct.
4. Disconnect clamps, then remove thermostat housing heater and radiator hoses.
5. **On models equipped with heavy duty cooling,** proceed as follows:
   a. Disconnect clamps, then remove auxiliary water pump hoses.
   b. Disconnect electrical connector,

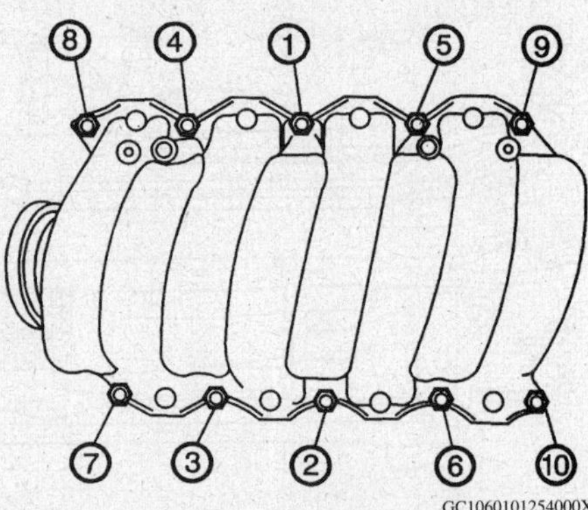

Fig. 6 Intake manifold tightening sequence

then remove mounting nuts and auxiliary water pump.

6. **On all models,** mounting bolts and drive belt tensioners.
7. Remove mounting bolts, then the drive belt idler and water pump pulleys.
8. Raise and support vehicle.
9. Remove transmission bell housing inspection hole cover and install flywheel holding tool No. EN48018, or equivalent.
10. Remove crankshaft balancer mounting bolt.
11. Place tool No. J38416-2 or equivalent, into end of crankshaft, then install tool No. J24420-C or equivalent on crankshaft balancer.
12. Remove crankshaft damper using crankshaft button tool No. J38416-2 and crankshaft balancer remover tool No. J24420-C, or equivalents.
13. Remove mounting bolts and front cover. Discard gasket.
14. Reverse procedure to install, noting the following:
    a. Apply small amount of suitable sealant to split line of upper and lower crankcases, and top of block face. **Fig. 12.**
    b. Apply suitable thread locking compound to mounting bolt threads.
    c. **Torque** front cover bolts to 11 ft. lbs., in sequence, **Fig. 13.**

TIMING CHAIN

REPLACE

Primary Drive Chain

1. Remove front cover as outlined in "Front Cover, Replace."
2. Remove three mounting bolts and pump.
3. Align primary timing marks using crankshaft socket tool No. J39946, or equivalent, **Fig. 14.**
4. Remove secondary camshaft drive chains as outlined under "Secondary Drive Chain."
5. Remove mounting bolts and primary camshaft drive chain tensioner allowing tensioner to expand as removed.
6. Remove oil outlet tube.
7. Remove mounting bolts and primary camshaft drive chain guide.

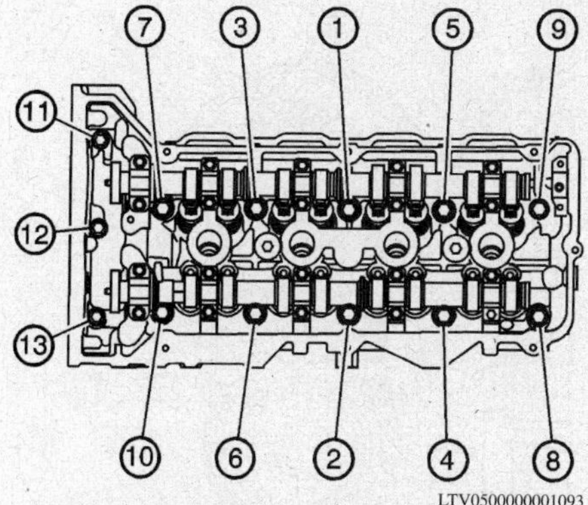

Fig. 7 Lefthand cylinder head tightening sequence

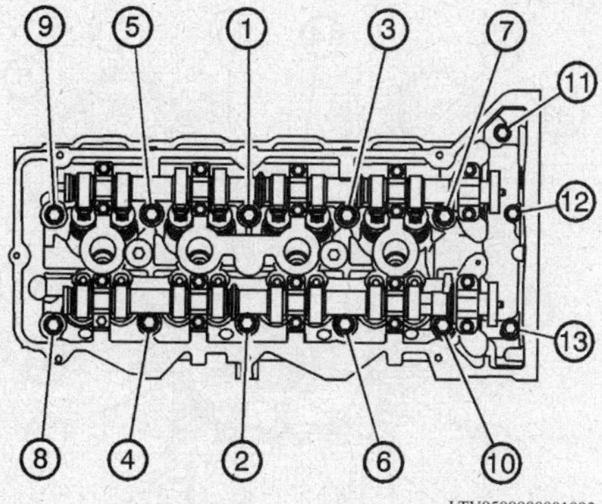

Fig. 8 Righthand cylinder head tightening sequence

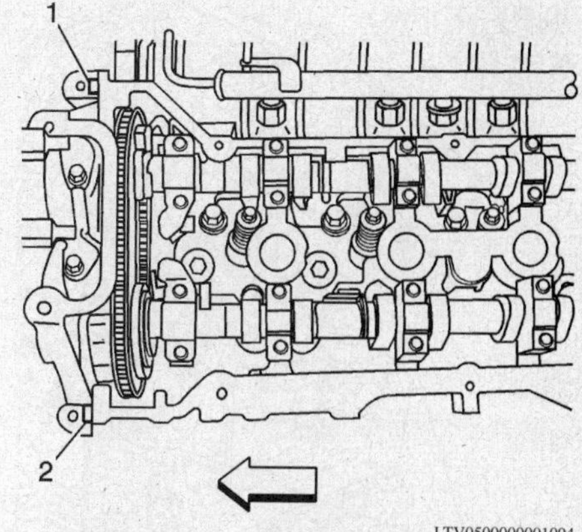

Fig. 9 Lefthand valve cover sealant application

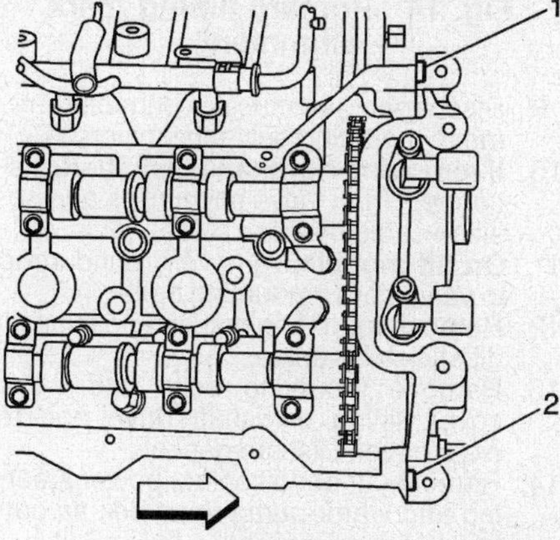

Fig. 10 Righthand valve cover sealant application

8. Remove camshaft intermediate sprocket mounting bolt.
9. Remove primary camshaft drive chain, crankshaft sprocket and camshaft intermediate sprocket.
10. Reverse procedure to install.

Secondary Drive Chain

REMOVAL

Remove the righthand secondary drive chain, then the lefthand chain using the same procedure.

1. Remove front cover as outlined in "Front Cover, Replace."
2. Remove three mounting bolts and pump.
3. Align primary timing marks using crankshaft socket tool No. J39946, or equivalent, **Fig. 14.**
4. Remove mounting bolts and cross-vehicle brace.
5. Remove power steering and engine oil fill caps.
6. Lift up and pull sight shield forward to disconnect rear tab, then remove shield.
7. Remove mounting bolts and camshaft position actuator housing. **Do not remove actuator solenoids.**
8. Lock camshaft using camshaft holding tool No. EN46328, or equivalent, then remove mounting bolts and secondary timing chain tensioner.
9. Hold exhaust camshaft hex cast using suitable open-end wrench, then remove exhaust camshaft position oil control valves.
10. Slide exhaust camshaft position actuator off of camshaft and remove secondary timing chain from camshaft actuator teeth.
11. Hold intake camshaft hex cast using suitable open-end wrench, then remove intake camshaft position oil control valves.
12. Slide intake camshaft position actuator off of camshaft and remove secondary timing chain from camshaft actuator teeth.
13. Remove secondary timing chain.

INSTALLATION

1. Install secondary timing chain to intermediate sprocket aligning sprocket LB timing mark to timing chain black link, **Fig. 15.**
2. Align lefthand intake camshaft position actuator timing mark with timing chain black link and install actuator on camshaft with actuator timing mark perpendicular (90°) to cylinder head deck surface at top of its rotation, **Fig. 16.**
3. Loosely install oil control valve.
4. Hold camshaft using suitable open-end wrench on hex cast and tighten oil control valve.
5. Align lefthand exhaust camshaft position actuator timing mark with timing chain black link and install actuator on camshaft with actuator timing mark perpendicular (90°) to cylinder head deck surface at top of its rotation.
6. Loosely install oil control valve.
7. Hold camshaft using suitable open-end wrench on hex cast and tighten oil control valve.
8. Rotate lefthand secondary camshaft chain tensioner ratchet release lever counterclockwise and hold.
9. Release ratchet lever, then collapse tensioner shoe and hold.
10. Slowly release shoe pressure until ratchet lever moves to first detent, and click is heard and felt.
11. Lock tensioner shoe in collapsed position by inserting suitable locking pin into release lever hole.

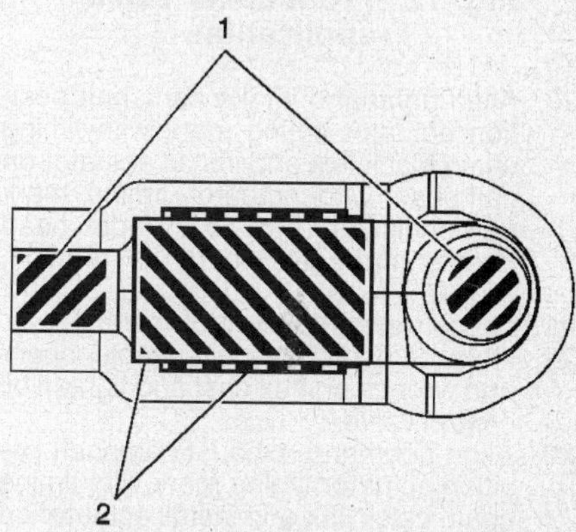

Fig. 11 Rocker arm lubrication points

12. Ensure tensioner release lever in facing outward.
13. Install tensioner and tighten mounting bolts. Remove locking pin.
14. Ensure timing marks remain aligned, **Fig. 17.**
15. Remove holding tool.
16. Install new gasket and camshaft position actuator housing, then tighten mounting bolts and studs.
17. Install camshaft position actuator housing.
18. **If camshaft position actuator solenoid were removed,** install each solenoid as follows:
    a. Apply .079 inch bead of suitable RTV around camshaft position actuator solenoid.
    b. Install camshaft position actuator solenoid.
    c. Install alignment pin (1.97 inches long piece of 15/64 inch diameter drill rod) through solenoid alignment hole and into oil control valve alignment hole.
    d. Install and tighten mounting bolts. Remove alignment pin.
    e. Install new camshaft position actuator solenoid plug.
19. **On all models,** install secondary timing chain to intermediate sprocket aligning sprocket RB timing mark to timing chain black link, **Fig. 15.**

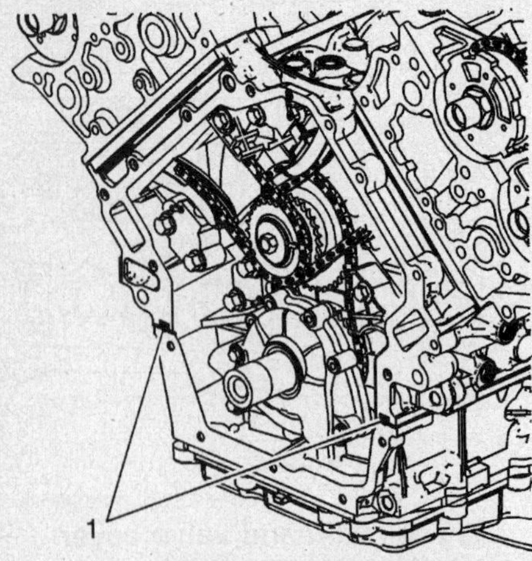

Fig. 12 Front cover sealant application

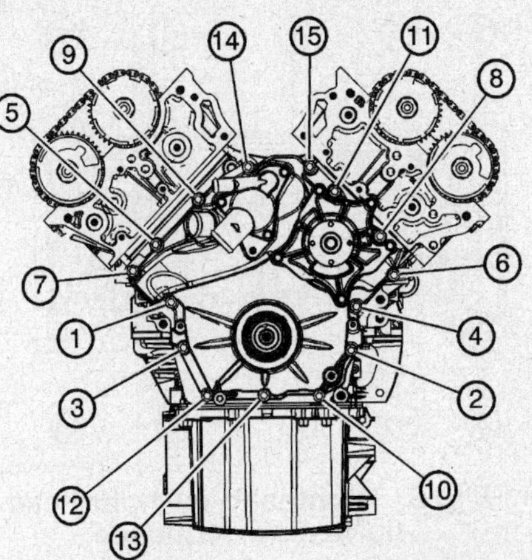

Fig. 13 Front cover tightening sequence

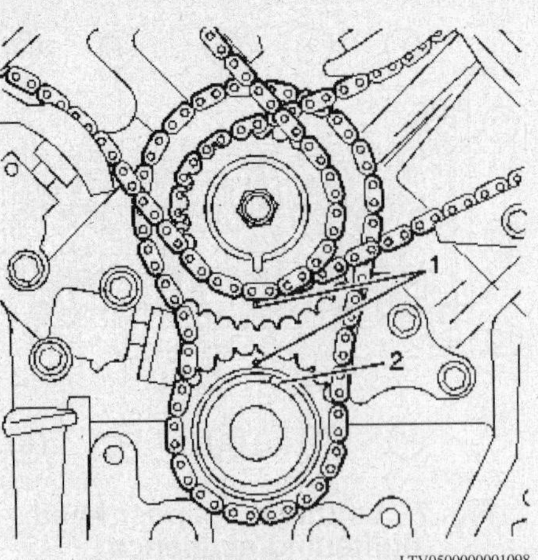

Fig. 14 Primary timing mark alignment

20. Align righthand intake camshaft position actuator timing mark with timing chain black link and install actuator on camshaft with actuator timing mark perpendicular (90°) to cylinder head deck surface at top of its rotation, **Fig. 18.**
21. Loosely install oil control valve.
22. Hold camshaft using suitable open-end wrench on hex cast and tighten oil control valve.
23. Align righthand exhaust camshaft position actuator timing mark with timing chain black link and install actuator on camshaft with actuator timing mark perpendicular (90°) to cylinder head deck surface at top of its rotation.
24. Loosely install oil control valve.
25. Hold camshaft using suitable open-end wrench on hex cast and tighten oil control valve.
26. Rotate righthand secondary camshaft chain tensioner ratchet release lever counterclockwise and hold.
27. Release ratchet lever, then collapse tensioner shoe and hold.
28. Slowly release shoe pressure until ratchet lever moves to first detent, and click is heard and felt.
29. Lock tensioner shoe in collapsed position by inserting suitable locking pin into release lever hole.
30. Ensure tensioner release lever in facing outward.
31. Install tensioner and tighten mounting bolts. Remove locking pin.
32. Ensure timing marks remain aligned, **Fig. 19.**
33. Remove holding tool.
34. Install new gasket and camshaft position actuator housing, then tighten mounting bolts and studs.
35. Install camshaft position actuator housing.
36. **If camshaft position actuator solenoid were removed,** install each solenoid as follows:
    a. Apply .079 inch bead of suitable RTV around camshaft position actuator solenoid.
    b. Install camshaft position actuator solenoid.
    c. Install alignment pin (1.97 inches long piece of 15⁄64 inch diameter drill rod) through solenoid alignment hole and into oil control valve alignment hole.
    d. Install and tighten mounting bolts. Remove alignment pin.
    e. Install new camshaft position actuator solenoid plug.

TIMING CHAIN TENSIONER

REPLACE

Refer to "Timing Chain, Replace" for tensioner replacement procedures.

CAMSHAFT

REPLACE

1. Remove mounting bolts and cross-vehicle brace.
2. Remove power steering and engine oil fill caps.
3. Lift up and pull sight shield forward to disconnect rear tab, then remove shield.
4. Disconnect Camshaft Position (CMP) sensors electrical connectors.
5. Remove mounting bolts, then lefthand exhaust and intake CMP sensors.
6. **If removing lefthand camshaft,** proceed as follows:
    a. Disconnect Positive Crankcase Ventilation (PCV) tube from air cleaner duct.
    b. Loosen clamps and remove air cleaner duct.
    c. Raise and support vehicle, then remove retainers and front air deflector.
    d. Disconnect power steering reservoir cooler and outlet hoses, then drain fluid into suitable container.
    e. Remove mounting nuts and power steering reservoir.
7. **If removing righthand camshaft,** disconnect PCV dirty air tube from valve cover
8. **On all models,** remove ignition coil cover.
9. Disconnect electrical connector, remove mounting bolt and ignition coil.
10. **If removing righthand camshaft,** disconnect front valve cover clips and position cable harness aside.
11. **On all models,** remove ground strap to valve cover mounting bolt.
12. Remove mounting bolt and position oil dipstick tube aside.
13. Remove mounting bolts and valve cover, lifting camshaft drive end to clear cover. Discard gasket.
14. Remove air conditioning, power steering and water pump drive belt as outlined under "Serpentine Drive Belt."
15. Remove mounting bolts, then the lefthand intake and exhaust CMP actuator solenoids. Discard plug.
16. Remove mounting bolts and lefthand CMP actuator housing.
17. Remove transmission bell housing inspection hole cover and install flywheel holding tool No. EN48018, or equivalent.
18. Remove crankshaft balancer mounting bolt.
19. Place tool No. J38416-2 or equivalent, into end of crankshaft, then install tool No. J24420-C or equivalent on crankshaft balancer.
20. Remove crankshaft damper using crankshaft button tool No. J38416-2 and crankshaft balancer remover tool No. J24420-C, or equivalents.
21. Turn crankshaft socket tool No. J39946, or equivalent, until both lefthand CMP actuator timing marks are perpendicular (90°) to cylinder head deck surface and near top of their rotation.
22. Lock camshaft using camshaft holding tool No. EN46328, or equivalent.
23. Mark timing chain link adjacent to each camshaft position actuator timing mark for installation alignment.
24. Hold timing chain in place using timing chain retention tools No. EN46327, or equivalent.
25. Hold camshaft using suitable open end wrench on intake and exhaust camshaft hex cast.
26. Remove lefthand oil control valves.
27. Disconnect camshaft alignment pin by pulling actuators forward.

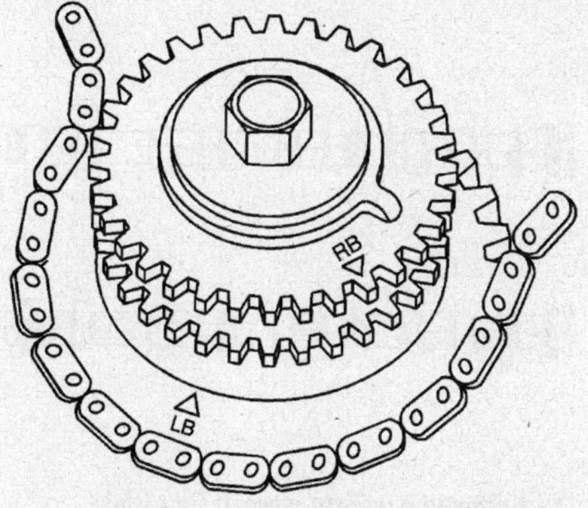

Fig. 15 Intermediate sprocket timing chain alignment

28. Disconnect secondary timing chain and remove actuators.
29. Remove bolts and camshaft bearing caps. Keep caps in order for installation in original positions.
30. Remove camshaft.
31. Reverse procedure to install, noting the following:
    a. Apply liberal amount of suitable lubricant to camshaft bearing journals, lobes, journals and bearing caps.
    b. Select proper camshaft by identifying rings cast, into the lefthand exhaust camshaft, **Figs. 20 and 21.**
    c. Camshaft can be identified by stamping near rear journal. For example: L-EXH for lefthand exhaust.
    d. Place camshaft in journals with sprocket drive pins near top of rotation and lobes in neutral position.
    e. Install camshaft bearing caps according to identifications marks, **Figs. 22 through 25.** Arrow points toward front, number indicates position from front and letter marks intake or exhaust.
    f. **Torque** camshaft cap bolts to 44 inch lbs., in sequence, **Figs. 26 through 29.**
    g. Final tightening cap bolts an additional 30° in sequence.
    h. Apply .079 inch bead of suitable RTV around camshaft position actuator solenoid.
    i. Install camshaft position actuator solenoid.
    j. Install alignment pin (1.97 inches long piece of 15⁄64 inch diameter drill rod) through solenoid alignment hole and into oil control valve alignment hole.
    k. Install and tighten mounting bolts. Remove alignment pin.
    l. Install new camshaft position actuator solenoid plug.

PISTON & ROD ASSEMBLY

1. Install piston and rod into cylinder block, ensuring dot on top of piston faces toward front of engine, **Fig. 30.**
2. Install piston and connecting rod with piston underside cast locating mark pointing toward engine front, **Fig. 31.**
3. Connecting rod cap locating notch points toward the rear on odd-numbered cylinders and front on even-numbered cylinders.

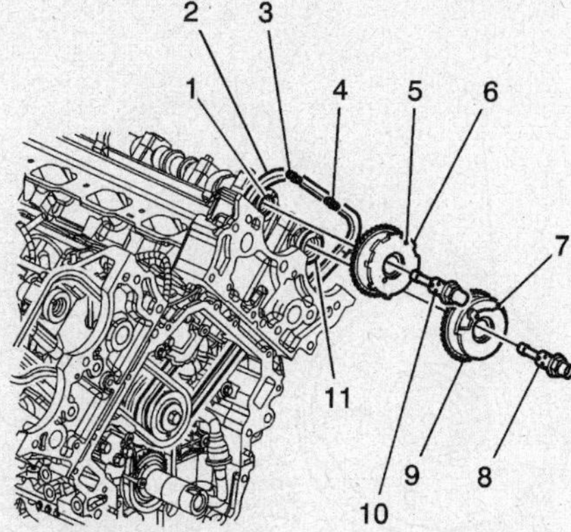

1. Intake Camshaft
2. Timing Chain
3. Timing Chain Black Link
4. Timing Chain Black Link
5. Lefthand Intake Camshaft Position Actuator Timing Mark
6. Lefthand Intake Camshaft Sprocket
7. Lefthand Exhaust Camshaft Position Actuator Timing Mark
8. Oil Control Valve
9. Lefthand Exhaust Camshaft Sprocket
10. Oil Control Valve
11. Exhaust Camshaft

LTV0500000001100

Fig. 16 Lefthand secondary timing chain alignment

PISTONS, PINS & RINGS

Refer to **Fig. 32** to set the ring gaps for the oil control, second and top ring.

MAIN & ROD BEARINGS

Connecting Rod Bearings

1. **Torque** connecting rod bolts to 22 ft. lbs.
2. Loosen connecting rod bolts until torque **torque** is zero.
3. **Torque** rod bolts to 18 ft. lbs.
4. Final tighten bolts an additional 110°.

Main Bearings

If the crankshaft bearings have been used in a running engine, they must replaced with new bearings.

1. Install new upper crankshaft bearings.
2. Thrust bearing belongs in No. 3 journal.
3. Ensure upper bearing insert contains oil transfer hole and groove.
4. Roll bearing into position so lock tang engages crank slot.
5. Bearing must fit flush with upper crankcase.
6. Install new lower crankshaft bearings into lower crankcase.

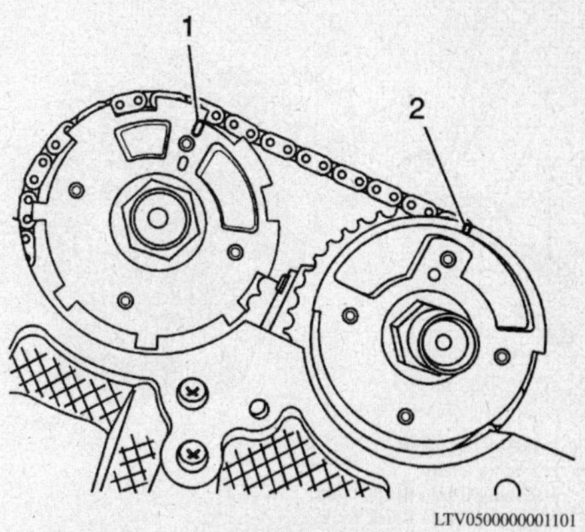

Fig. 17 Lefthand timing mark alignment

7. Lower crankcase crankshaft bearings are identified by no grooves or holes.
8. Bearings must fit flush with lower crankcase.
9. Apply liberal amount of suitable crankshaft prelube or engine oil, to upper and lower bearing surfaces.
10. Install crankshaft into cylinder block.
11. Align lower crankcase with upper dowel pins.
12. Install lower crankcase onto upper slowly until feeling positive stop. Ensure lower crankcase is fully seated on cylinder block.
13. Install oil manifold and scraper plate, then tighten mounting bolts.
14. Loosely install main bearing bolts.
15. Install single stud-end bolt to attach oil pump pipe and screen support bracket in inboard position in second set of main bearing bolts from front and lefthand side, **Fig. 33.**
16. Install lefthand and righthand upper-to-lower crankcase perimeter bolts.
17. **Torque** lower crankcase bolt Nos. 1–20 to 15 ft. lbs., in sequence, **Fig. 34.**
18. Tighten crankcase bolts Nos. 1–20 an additional 65°.
19. **Torque** upper-to-lower crankcase perimeter bolts Nos. 1–8, to 22 ft. lbs., in sequence, **Fig. 35.**

CRANKSHAFT REAR OIL SEAL

REPLACE

1. Remove transmission as outlined in **MOTOR's "Domestic Transmission, In-Vehicle Service" or "Transmission Service DVD."**
2. Remove mounting bolts and flywheel.
3. Remove rear crankshaft oil seal using rear oil seal remover tool No. J42841, or equivalent.
4. Reverse procedure to install, noting the following:
    a. Install new seal using crankshaft rear oil seal installer tool No. J45930, or equivalent.
    b. **Torque** flywheel mounting bolts to 11 ft. lbs.
    c. Final tighten mounting bolt an 50°.

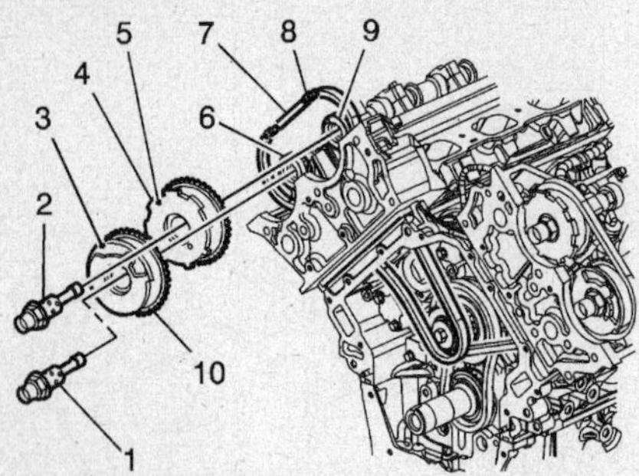

1. Intake Camshaft
2. Timing Chain
3. Timing Chain Black Link
4. Timing Chain Black Link
5. Righthand Intake Camshaft Position Actuator Timing Mark
6. Righthand Intake Camshaft Sprocket
7. Righthand Exhaust Camshaft Position Actuator Timing Mark
8. Oil Control Valve
9. Righthand Exhaust Camshaft Sprocket
10. Oil Control Valve
11. Exhaust Camshaft

LTV0500000001102

Fig. 18 Righthand secondary timing chain alignment

OIL PAN

REPLACE

1. Support engine at lefthand and righthand cylinder heads using engine lift bracket tools Nos.. J28467-86 and J28467-87, or equivalent, respectively.
2. Raise and support vehicle, then drain oil into suitable container.
3. Remove front tire and wheel assemblies, then the retainers and front air deflector.
4. Disconnect connects and wheel speed sensor harness from lower control arm.
5. Remove nut and separate outer tie rod from steering knuckle using ball joint remover tool No. J43631, or equivalent.
6. Remove power steering return and pressure hoses to frame bolts.
7. Disconnect electrical connectors and remove mounting nuts and Engine Control Module (ECM).
8. Remove mounting bolts and ECM bracket.
9. Remove power steering cooler bracket to air conditioning condenser mounting bolts.
10. Remove mounting bolts and power steering cooler from air conditioning condenser.
11. Remove power steering pressure hose to electrical harness tie strap.
12. Remove mounting bolt and disconnect pipes from power steering gear.
13. Disconnect variable effort steering electrical connector from power steering gear.
14. Remove pinch bolt and disconnect intermediate shaft from power steering gear.
15. Disconnect lines from brake hoses, then loosen mounting nuts and disconnect ABS module harness connector.
16. Remove mounting nut and separate upper ball joint ball stud from steering knuckle using ball joint remover tool. **Do not free ball stud by using pickle fork or wedge-type tool.**

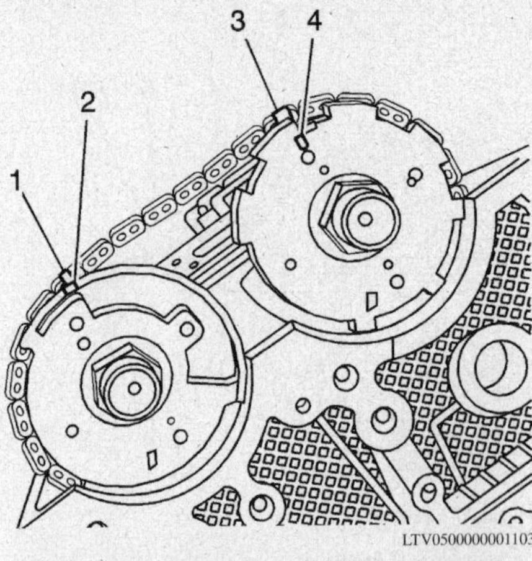

LTV0500000001103

Fig. 19 Righthand timing mark alignment

17. Remove yoke to shock mounting nut and bolt.
18. Remove washer bottle to knuckle mounting bolts.
19. Remove engine mount lower mounting nuts.
20. Support front frame using engine support stand tool No. J39580, or equivalent, and suitable frame support table.
21. Remove mounting bolts and front frame. Ensure brake pipes, steering knuckle and speed sensor harness clear frame.
22. **On models equipped with AWD,** remove front differential carrier as outlined in "Front Wheel Drive" section.
23. **On all models,** disconnect electrical connector and remove engine oil level sensor.
24. Remove mounting bolts and oil pan. **Do not remove gasket except when it is damage.**
25. Reverse procedure to install, noting the following:
    a. **Torque** oil pan mounting bolts to 11 ft. lbs., in sequence, **Fig. 36.**
    b. **Torque** oil pan mounting bolts to 18 ft. lbs., in sequence.
    c. **Torque** front frame mounting bolts Nos. 1–2 to 141 ft. lbs., in sequence, **Fig. 37.**
    d. **Torque** front frame mounting bolts Nos. 3 to 185 ft. lbs.

OIL PUMP

REPLACE

1. Remove front cover as outlined in "Front Cover, Replace."
2. Remove three mounting bolts and pump.
3. Reverse procedure to install, noting the following.
    a. **Torque** mounting bolts to 89 inch lbs., in sequence, **Fig. 38.**
    b. Final tighten mounting bolts an addition 35° in sequence.

OIL PUMP SERVICE

Disassembly

1. Remove oil pump drive spacer.

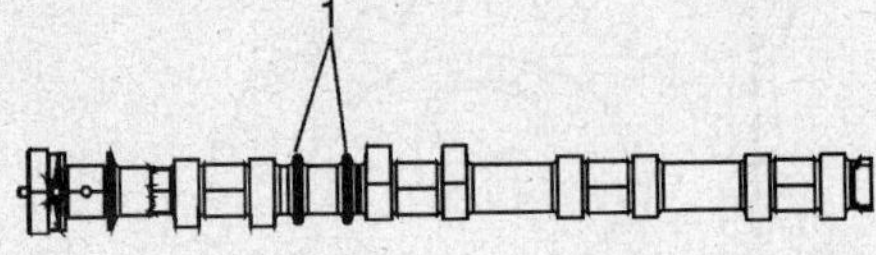

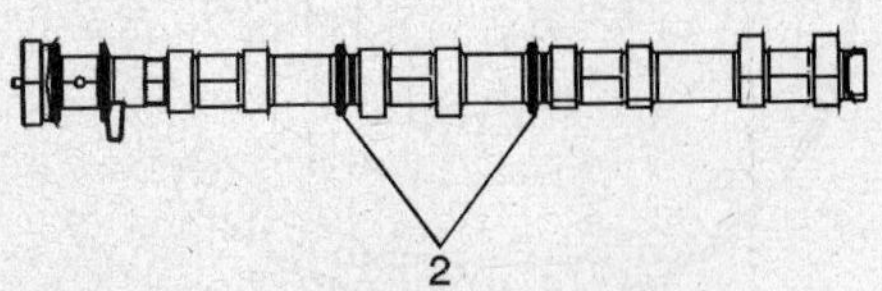

1. Lefthand Exhaust Camshaft Cast Rings
2. Lefthand Intake Camshaft Cast Rings

LTV0500000001104

Fig. 20 Lefthand camshaft ring cast identification

2. Remove mounting bolts and body cover.
3. Remove drive and driven gears.
4. Remove relief valve plug, spring and plunger.
5. Remove cover alignment dowels.

Inspection

Internal components of oil pump are not serviceable. Replace entire pump if there is wear or damage.

1. Inspect cover for cracks, scoring and casting imperfections.
2. Inspect body for cracks, scoring, casting imperfections and damaged threads.
3. Inspect gears and spacer for chipping, galling or wear.
4. Inspect relief components for embedded particles and/or damage.

Assembly

1. Install cover alignment dowels.
2. Install relief valve plunger, spring and plug, then tighten plug.
3. Install inner and outer rotors to pump cover. **Align marks made during pump disassembly.**
4. Install pressure relief valve seat, spring and pilot.
5. Install driven and drive gears. Outer driven gear has one chamfered edge that must face-down into body.
6. Pack pump body housing with suitable, clean white petroleum jelly.
7. Install cover and tighten mounting bolts.

SERPENTINE DRIVE BELT

Air Conditioning, Power Steering & Water Pump

1. Remove mounting bolts and cross-vehicle brace.
2. Remove power steering and engine oil fill caps.

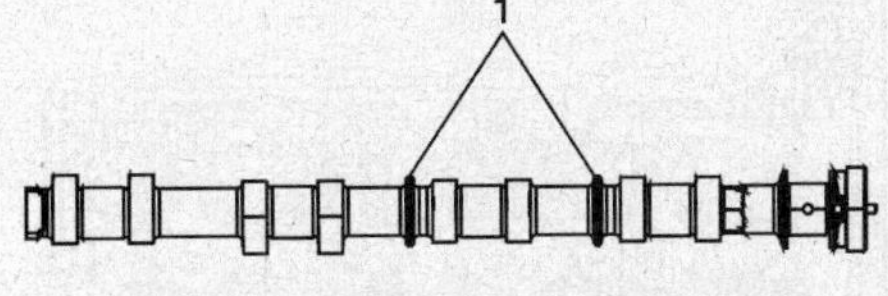

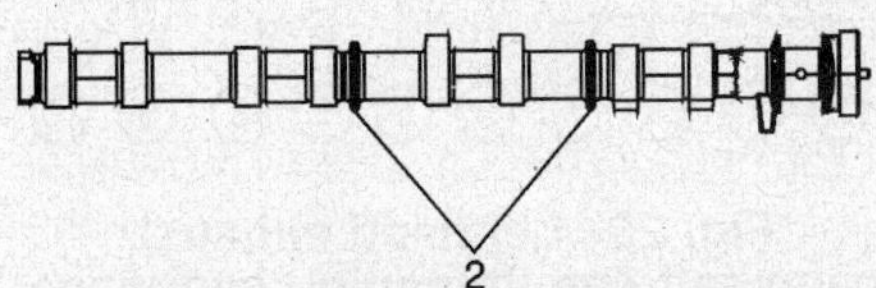

1. Righthand Intake Camshaft Cast Rings
2. Righthand Exhaust Camshaft Cast Rings

LTV0500000001109

Fig. 21 Righthand camshaft ring cast identification

3. Remove sight shield by lifting front and pull forward to disconnect rear tab.
4. Disconnect Positive Crankcase Ventilation (PCV) tube from air cleaner duct.
5. Loosen throttle body and Mass Air Flow (MAF)/Intake Air Temperature (IAT) sensor clamps, then remove air duct.
6. Raise and support vehicle, then remove push-in retainers and front air deflector.
7. Remove mounting nuts and position power steering reservoir aside with lines attached.
8. Loosen fan mounting nut from crank adapter shaft using fan clutch wrench tool No. J41240-5A, or equivalent.
9. **Do not completely remove fan from crank adapter shaft.**
10. Disconnect from frame and position engine wiring harness aside.
11. Continue loosening nut and remove fan.
12. Remove mounting bolts and fan bracket.
13. Release tension by rotating drive belt tensioner clockwise.
14. Remove drive belt from water pump pulley.
15. Slide drive belt out from behind drive belt tensioner.
16. Allow tensioner to return and remove drive belt from the remaining pulleys.
17. Reverse procedure to install.

Alternator

1. Remove air conditioning, power steering and water pump belt as outlined under "Air Conditioning, Power Steering & Water Pump."
2. Release tension by turning alternator belt tensioner clockwise.
3. Remove belt from alternator pulley.
4. Allow tensioner to return and remove belt from pulleys.
5. Reverse procedure to install.

COOLING SYSTEM BLEED

1. Slowly fill cooling system until coolant stabilizes one inch above surge tank FULL COLD mark.
2. Install surge tank cap.
3. Start and run engine at 2000–2500 RPM until it reaches normal operating temperature.
4. Idle engine for three minutes.
5. Turn engine off and allow it to cool.
6. Adjust coolant level to surge tank FULL COLD mark.

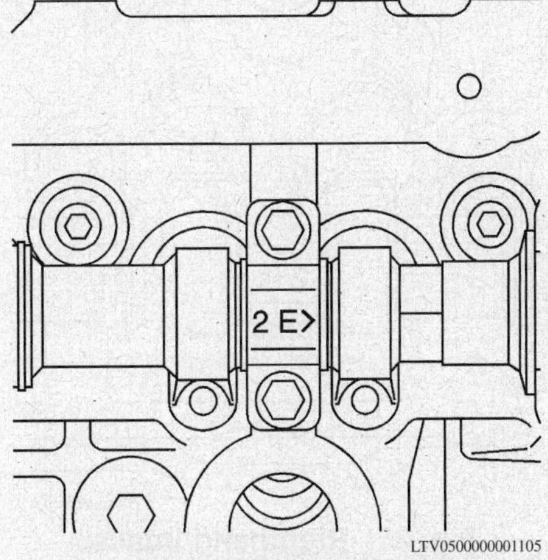

LTV0500000001105

Fig. 22 Lefthand exhaust camshaft bearing cap identification

THERMOSTAT

REPLACE

1. Drain coolant into suitable container.
2. Disconnect Positive Crankcase Ventilation (PCV) tube from air cleaner duct.
3. Loosen clamps and remove air cleaner duct.
4. Disconnect clamps, then remove thermostat housing radiator and heater hoses.
5. Remove mounting bolts and thermostat housing. Discard sealing ring.
6. Remove thermostat .
7. Reverse procedure to install.

WATER PUMP

REPLACE

1. Drain engine coolant into suitable container.
2. Remove auxiliary cooling fan to condenser upper mounting bolts.
3. Remove retainers and front air deflector.
4. Disconnect cooling fan electrical connectors.
5. Remove lower mounting bolts and cooling fan.
6. Remove water pump drive belt as outlined under "Serpentine Drive Belt."
7. Remove mounting bolt and drive belt tensioner.
8. Remove mounting bolts and water pump pulley.
9. Remove mounting bolts and water pump and seal. Discard seal.
10. Reverse procedure to install.

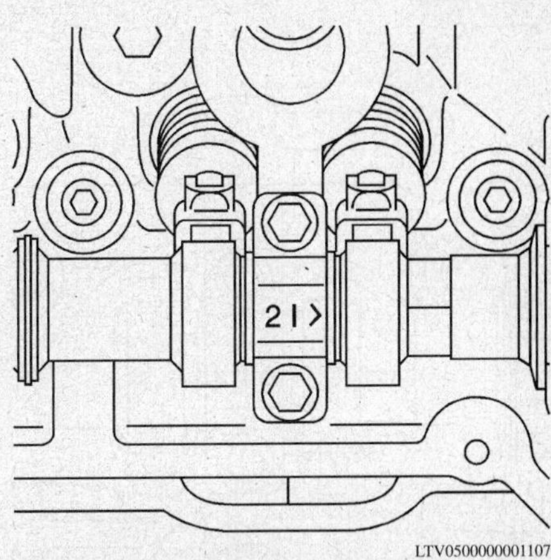

LTV0500000001107

Fig. 23 Lefthand intake camshaft bearing cap identification

RADIATOR

REPLACE

1. Drain engine coolant into suitable container.
2. Remove auxiliary cooling fan to condenser upper mounting bolts.
3. Remove retainers and front air deflector.
4. Disconnect cooling fan electrical connectors.
5. Remove lower mounting bolts and cooling fan.
6. Remove water pump drive belt as outlined under "Serpentine Drive Belt."
7. Remove upper and lower condenser mounting bolts.
8. Disconnect radiator side air baffle lower pins.
9. Remove Transmission Oil Cooler (TOC) mounting bolts.
10. Lower vehicle.
11. Disconnect clamps, then remove radiator outlet and inlet hoses.
12. Remove mounting bolts and support brackets, then the radiator.
13. Reverse procedure to install.

FUEL PUMP

REPLACE

Refer to "Fuel Pump, Replace" in "3.6L Engine" section for fuel tank module replacement procedures.

FUEL FILTER

REPLACE

1. Relieve fuel system pressure as outlined under "Precautions."
2. Raise and support vehicle.
3. Disconnect fuel filter inlet quick-connect fitting.
4. Remove threaded outlet fitting using suitable primary and back-up wrenches.
5. Slide filter rearward from bracket.
6. Discard O-ring seal.
7. Reverse procedure to install. Lubricate fuel pipe new O-ring seal with suitable, clean engine oil.

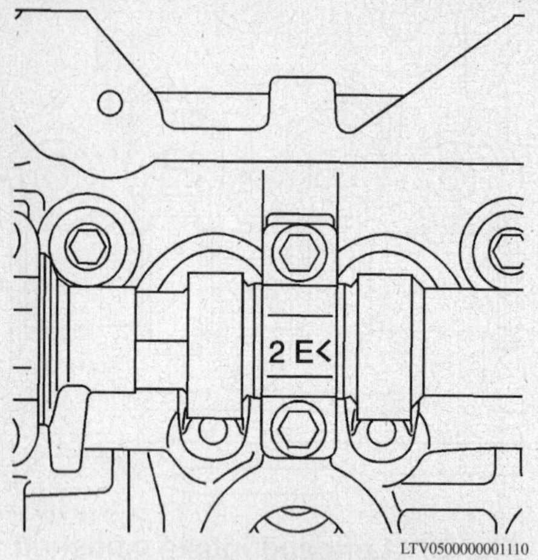

Fig. 24 Righthand exhaust camshaft bearing cap identification

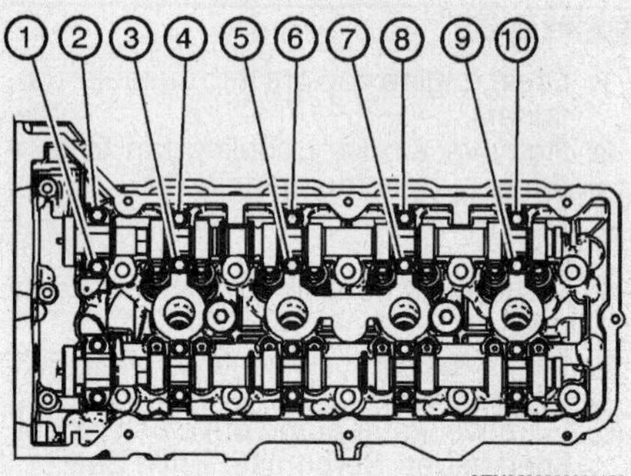

Fig. 27 Lefthand intake camshaft cap tightening sequence

TECHNICAL SERVICE BULLETINS

Engine Oil Leak

2004-05

On some of these models there may be a oil leak from the vehicle front.

This condition may be caused by the front cover or gasket.

To correct this condition, replace front cover and/or gasket, noting the following:

1. **On engine built before No. L050460029,** replace front cover and gasket.
2. **On engine built after No. L050460029,** replace front cover gasket, only.
3. **On all models,** apply .25 inch diameter bead of gray engine sealer (No. 123785321), or equivalent, to lefthand

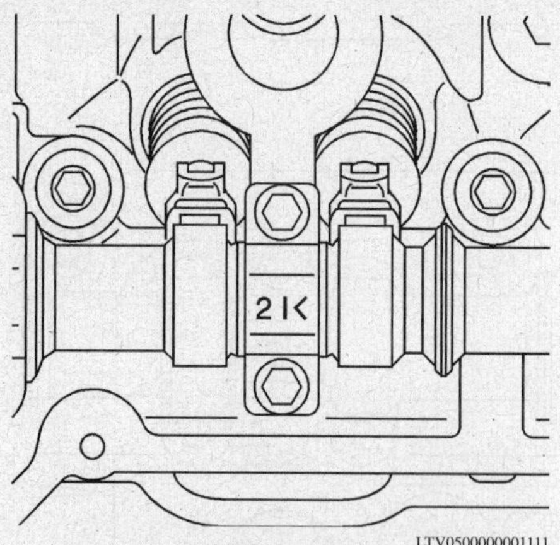

Fig. 25 Righthand intake camshaft bearing cap identification

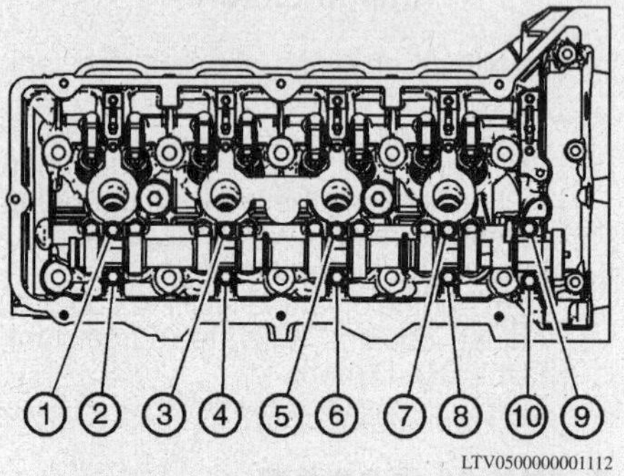

Fig. 28 Righthand exhaust camshaft cap tightening sequence

and righthand sides of front aide of gasket in area of upper and lower crankcase split.

4. Apply sealer (No. 12345382), or equivalent, to all bolts.
5. **Torque** front cover mounting bolts to 11 ft. lbs.

External Oil Leak

2005

On some of these models there may be an external oil leak.

This condition may be caused by the crankshaft rear main oil seal.

To correct this condition, install revised crankshaft rear main oil seal (part No. 12592195) as outlined under "Crankshaft Rear Oil Seal, Replace."

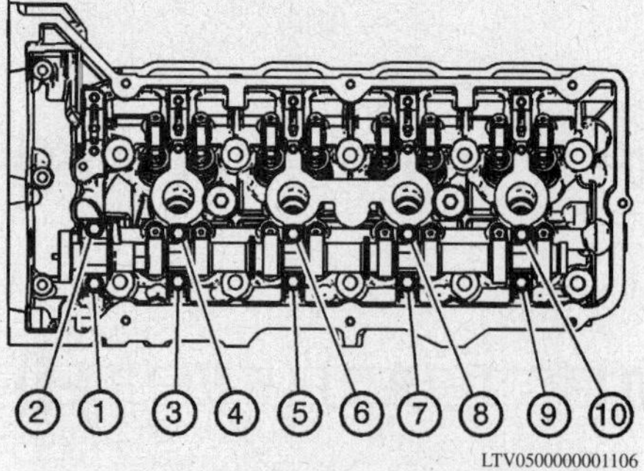

Fig. 26 Lefthand exhaust camshaft cap tightening sequence

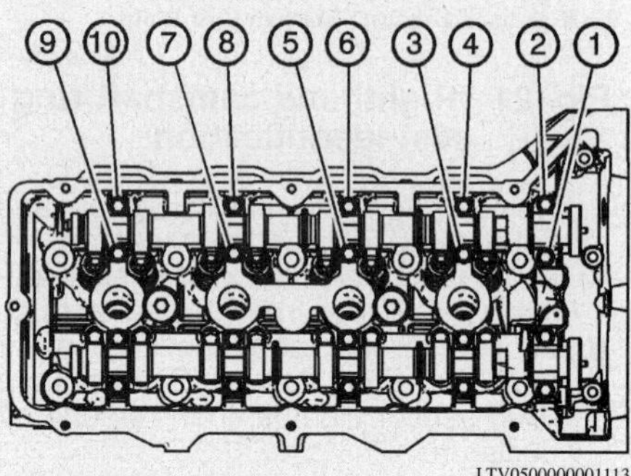

Fig. 29 Righthand intake camshaft cap tightening sequence

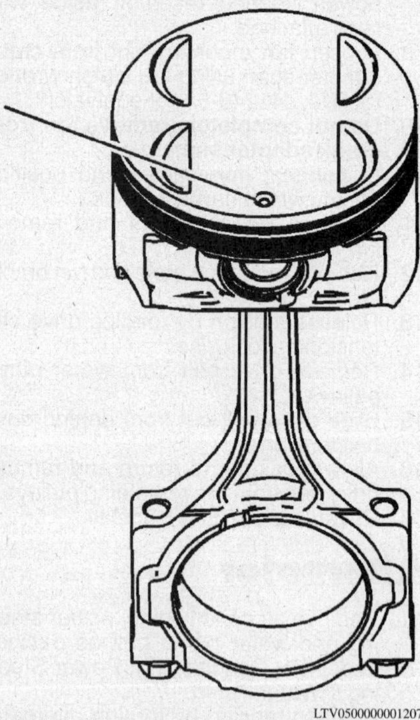

Fig. 30 Piston dot orientation

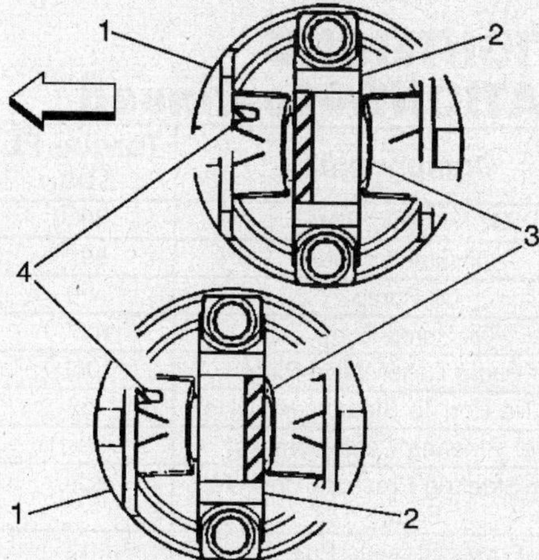

1. Piston
2. Connecting Rod
3. Locating Notch
4. Locating Mark

LTV0500000001114

Fig. 31 Piston & connecting rod orientation

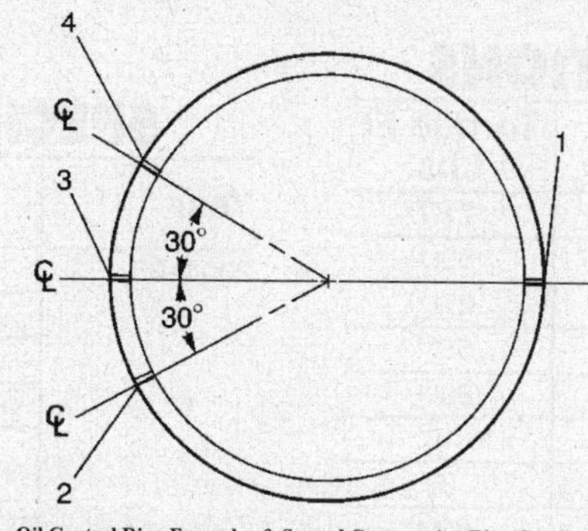

1. Oil Control Ring Expander & Second Compression Ring Gap Position
2. Upper Oil Control Ring Gap Position
3. Compression Ring Gap Position
4. Lower Control Ring Gap Position

LTV0500000001206

Fig. 32 Piston ring orientation

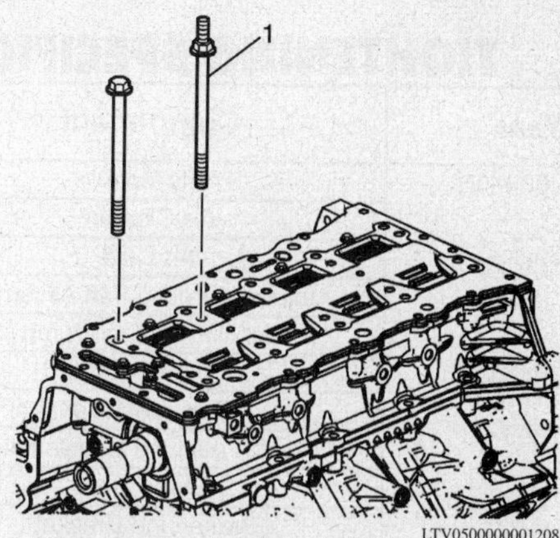

Fig. 33 Oil pump pipe & screen support bracket stud-end bolt

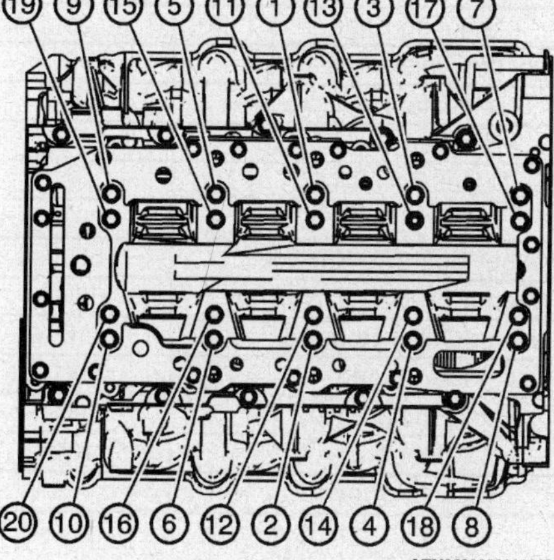

Fig. 34 Lower crankcase tightening sequence

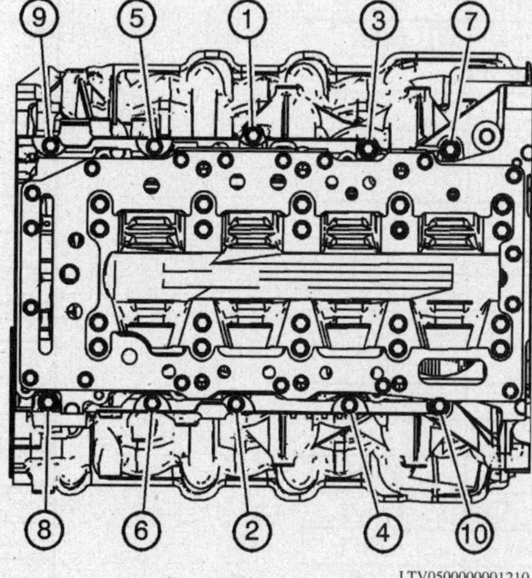

Fig. 35 Crankcase perimeter tightening sequence

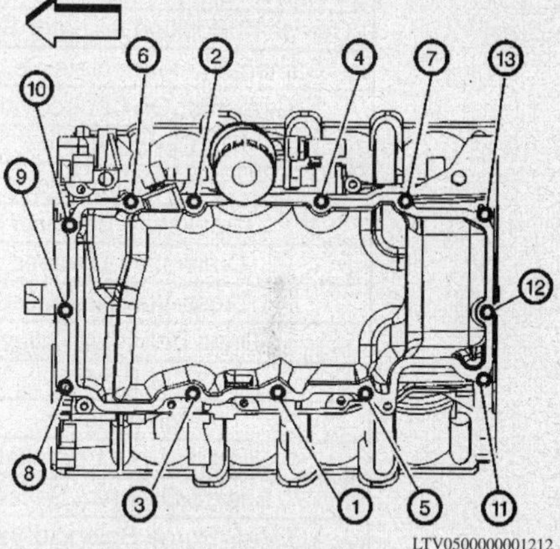

Fig. 36 Oil pan tightening sequence

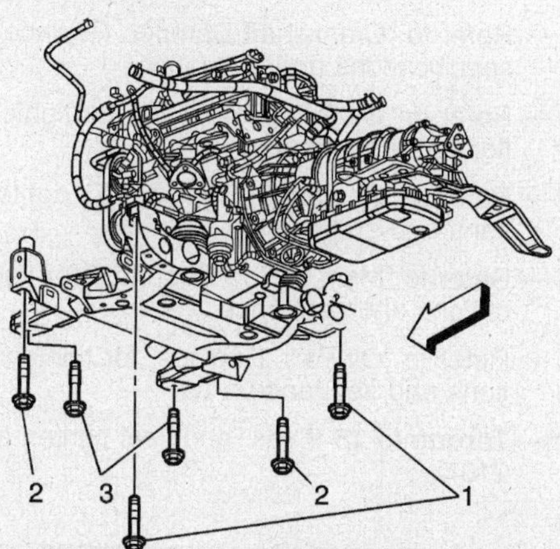

Fig. 37 Front frame tightening sequence

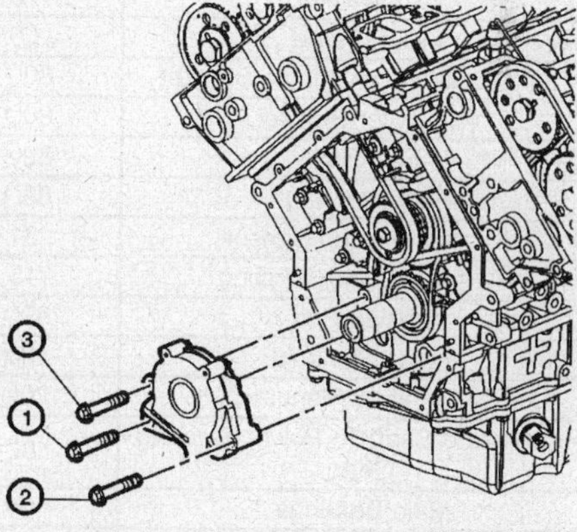

Fig. 38 Oil pump tightening sequence

TIGHTENING SPECIFICATIONS

Year	Component	Torque Ft. Lbs.
2004–06	ABS Module	71①
	Air Cleaner	89①
	Air Duct	27①
	Auxiliary Cooling Fan Assembly	58①
	Auxiliary Water Pump	80①
	Battery Cable	13
	Belt Tensioner	37
	Brake & Fuel Line Bundle Bracket	80①
	Brake Line	20
	Brake Line Bracket	80①
	Brake Master Cylinder	18
	Camshaft	⑤
	Camshaft Position Actuator Housing	89①
	Camshaft Position Actuator Solenoid	89①
	Camshaft Intermediate Sprocket	44
	Camshaft Oil Control Valve	89
	Condenser	58①
	Connecting Rod	⑥
	Crankshaft Balancer	③
	Crankshaft Damper	③
	Cross-Vehicle Brace	83
	Drive Belt Idler Pulley	37
	ECM Bracket	80①
	Engine Mount	59
	Engine Mount Bracket	44
	Engine Oil Level Sensor	89①
	EVAP Purge Solenoid Valve	106①
	Exhaust Manifold, Bolts & Nuts	18
	Exhaust Manifold, Stud	53①
	Exhaust Manifold Heat Shield	89①
	Fan	74
	Fan Bracket	18
	Front Frame	⑦
	Fuel & Brake Line Bundle Bracket	80①
	Fuel Filter Bracket	80①
	Fuel Rail	89①
	Ground Strap	89①
	Heated Oxygen Sensor	31
	Heater Inlet Hose Fitting	15
	Ignition Coil	89①
	Intake Manifold	②
	Intake Manifold Plenum Duct	20①
	Intermediate Shaft To Power Steering Gear	37
	Main Bearings	⑥
	Manifold Inlet Duct Clamp	53①
	MAP Sensor	106①
	Oil Control Valve	89①
	Oil Dipstick Tube	89①
	Oil Pan	⑦

TIGHTENING SPECIFICATIONS—Continued

Year	Component	Torque Ft. Lbs.
2004–06	Oil Manifold Plate	89①
	Oil Outlet Tube	89①
	Oil Pump	④
	Oil Pump Body	106①
	Oil Pump Relief Valve Plug	106①
	Outer Tie Rod To Steering Knuckle	52
	Power Steering Cooler Bracket	80①
	Power Steering Pressure Hose To Frame	35①
	Power Steering Pipe	17
	Power Steering Reservoir	80①
	Primary Drive Chain Guide	18
	Primary Camshaft Drive Chain Tensioner	18
	Radiator Support Bracket	80①
	Transmission Oil Cooler	44①
	Sight Shield Bracket	89①
	Shock Module, Upper	83
	Steering Reservoir	80①
	Steering Shaft	23
	Surge Tank Inlet Hose Fitting	13
	Thermostat Housing	89①
	Throttle Body	89①
	Upper Ball Joint	⑧
	Valve Cover	89①
	Washer Bottle To Knuckle	53①
	Washer Fluid Reservoir	53①
	Water Outlet Housing	18
	Water Pump	89①
	Water Pump Pulley	89①
	Wheel Lug	100
	Yoke To Shock	133

① — Inch lbs.

② — Refer to "Intake Manifold, Replace" for tightening specifications and sequence.

③ — Refer to "Crankshaft Damper, Replace" for tightening specifications and sequence.

④ — Refer to "Oil Pump, Replace" for tightening specifications and sequence.

⑤ — Refer to "Camshaft, Replace" for tightening specifications and sequence.

⑥ — Refer to "Main & Rod Bearings" for tightening specifications and sequence.

⑦ — Refer to "Oil Pan, Replace" for tightening specifications and sequence.

⑧ — **Torque** to 15 ft. lbs. and final tighten an additional 210°.

Rear Axle & Suspension

NOTE: On Air Bag Equipped Models, Refer To "Air Bag System Precautions" Located In The Front Of This Manual For System Disarming & Arming Procedures.

INDEX

DESCRIPTION

These vehicles are equipped with independent rear suspension and coil spring.

The rear suspension system on this vehicle consists of the following components:

Rear Differential
Two Coil Springs
Two Shock Absorbers
Two Toe Adjustment Links
Two Upper Control Arms
Two Lower Control Arms
Two Knuckles
Stabilizer Shaft
Two Stabilizer Shaft Links
Two Trailing Arms

All models have a 7 ⅝-inch ring gear.

REAR AXLE

REPLACE

1. Raise and support vehicle, then remove tire and wheel assembly.
2. Prevent wheel hub and bearing from turning by install suitable drift or punch into brake rotor against caliper.
3. Remove and discard wheel drive shaft spindle nut. Remove drift or punch.
4. Remove knuckle as outlined under "Knuckle, Replace."
5. Disconnect wheel drive shaft from differential enough to install seal protector tool No. J44394, or equivalent, over drive shaft and into differential output shaft seal.
6. Remove drive shaft.
7. Reverse procedure to install.

DIFFERENTIAL CARRIER

REPLACE

1. Raise and support vehicle.
2. Remove propeller shaft as outlined under "Propeller Shaft, Replace."
3. Remove righthand tire and wheel assembly.
4. Prevent wheel hub and bearing from turning by install suitable drift or punch into brake rotor against caliper.
5. Remove and discard wheel drive shaft spindle nut. Remove drift or punch.
6. Remove knuckle as outlined under "Knuckle, Replace."
7. Disconnect righthand wheel drive shaft from differential enough to install seal protector tool No. J44394, or equivalent, over drive shaft and into differential output shaft seal.
8. Remove drive shaft.
9. Support differential using suitable transmission jack.
10. Remove front support mounting bolt and nut, then the lefthand rear support bolt. **Rear differential support mounting bolts will not be able to be removed completely because of underbody interference.**
11. Remove righthand rear support mounting bolt and lower jack until front ear clears attachment point.
12. Disconnect lefthand wheel drive shaft from differential enough to install seal protector tool No. J44394, or equivalent, over drive shaft and into differential output shaft seal.
13. Remove drive shaft.
14. Lower jack while simultaneously disconnecting lefthand wheel drive shaft.
15. Remove differential. Discard wheel drive shaft retaining ring.

PROPELLER SHAFT

REPLACE

All Wheel Drive (AWD)

The propeller shaft must be supported during removal and/or installation so that the CV joint does not articulate more than 8°.

1. Raise and support vehicle.
2. Disconnect electrical connector, record oxygen sensor wire routing and attachment points for installation alignment, then remove oxygen sensor from exhaust pipe.
3. Remove the oxygen sensor.
4. Remove two mounting bolts and floor panel tunnel brace.
5. Support muffler, resonator or exhaust system pipe as a complete one-piece unit.
6. Remove exhaust pipes to manifold mounting nuts.
7. Disconnect front exhaust changes from rear suspension hanger rods.
8. Apply suitable lubricant to rods, and disconnect tail pipe hangers from rods.
9. Lower and remove exhaust system. Discard seals.
10. Support propeller shaft at support bearing.
11. Remove heat shield mounting bolts.
12. Remove support bearing mounting bolts.
13. Mark propeller shaft Consent Velocity (CV) joint to transfer case flange for installation alignment.
14. Remove propeller shaft CV joint to transfer case flange mounting bolts.
15. Remove propeller shaft coupler-to-differential flange mounting bolts. **Do not remove propeller shaft coupler.**
16. Remove propeller shaft coupler-to-differential flange mounting bolts, nuts and washers.
17. Disconnect propeller shaft CV joint from transfer case flange using suitable flat-bladed tool in transfer case flange notch to move shaft toward rear.
18. Hold front propeller shaft and lower support device.
19. Disconnect coupler from differential flange by moving shaft forward.
20. Remove propeller shaft.
21. Reverse procedure to install, noting the following:
    a. Arrows on coupler pointing toward flange.
    b. Apply small amount of suitable lubricant to rear propeller shaft centering bushings.
    c. Thoroughly clean mounting bolt and nut threads using suitable. denatured alcohol and allow to dry.
    d. Apply suitable threadlock to bolts. Ensure there are no gaps in threadlock along length of filled area.
    e. Allow threadlock to cure approximately 10 minutes before installation.
    f. **Torque** CV joint to transfer case flange mounting bolts to 22 ft. lbs., in sequence, **Fig. 1.**

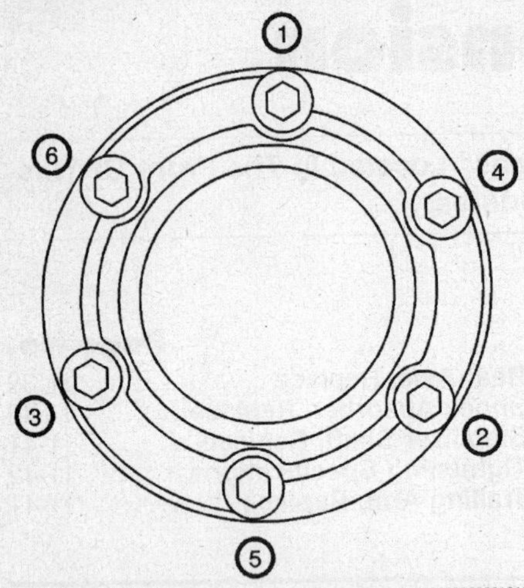

Fig. 1 CV joint to transfer case flange tightening sequence

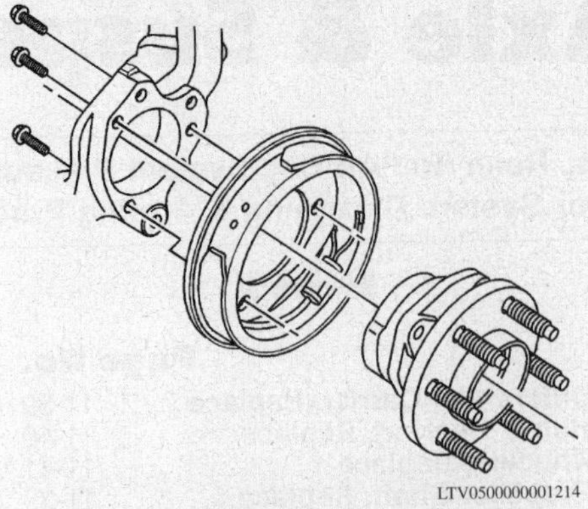

Fig. 2 Exploded view of wheel bearing/hub

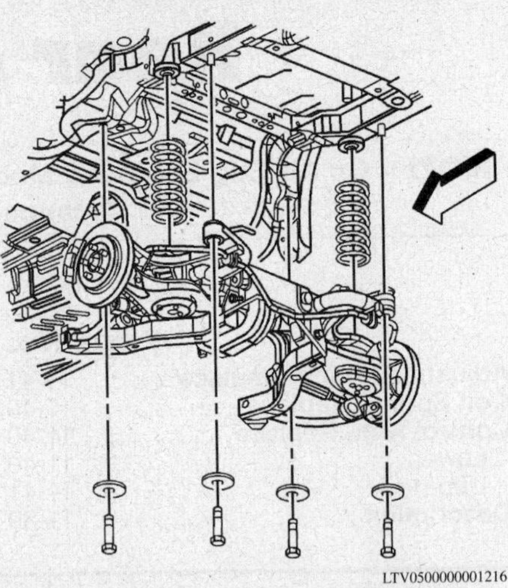

Fig. 3 Rear frame replacement

Rear Wheel Drive (RWD)

The propeller shaft must be supported during removal and/or installation so that the CV joint does not articulate more than 8°.

1. Raise and support vehicle.
2. Disconnect electrical connector, record oxygen sensor wire routing and attachment points for installation alignment, then remove oxygen sensor from exhaust pipe.
3. Remove the oxygen sensor.
4. Remove two mounting bolts and floor panel tunnel brace.
5. Support muffler, resonator or exhaust system pipe as a complete one-piece unit.
6. Remove exhaust pipes to manifold mounting nuts.
7. Disconnect front exhaust changes from rear suspension hanger rods.
8. Apply suitable lubricant to rods, and disconnect tail pipe hangers from rods.
9. Lower and remove exhaust system. Discard seals.
10. Remove propeller shaft coupler-to-transmission flange mounting bolts. **Do not remove propeller shaft coupler.**
11. Remove propeller shaft coupler-to-transmission flange mounting bolts, nuts and washers.
12. Remove propeller shaft coupler-to-differential flange mounting bolts. **Do not remove propeller shaft coupler.**
13. Remove propeller shaft coupler-to-differential flange mounting bolts, nuts and washers.
14. Support propeller shaft at support bearing.
15. Remove support bearing mounting bolts.
16. Disconnect propeller shaft coupler from transmission flange by pushing shaft toward rear.
17. Hold front propeller shaft, lower and remove support bearing from studs.
18. Disconnect coupler from differential flange by puller rear shaft forward.
19. Record number and location of support bearing mounting bracket shim packs for installation alignment.
20. Remove propeller shaft.
21. Reverse procedure to install, noting the following:
    a. Apply small amount of suitable lubricant to front and rear propeller shaft centering bushings.
    b. Thoroughly clean mounting bolt and nut threads using suitable. denatured alcohol and allow to dry.
    c. Apply suitable threadlock to bolts. Ensure there are no gaps in threadlock along length of filled area.
    d. Allow threadlock to cure approximately 10 minutes before installation.

HUB & BEARING

REPLACE

1. Raise and support vehicle, then remove rear tire and wheel assembly.
2. Compress piston into caliper bore using suitable, large C-clamp.
3. Remove pin bolts and support brake caliper aside using suitable heavy mechanic's wire. **Do not disconnect hydraulic brake flexible hose.**
4. Remove pads and retainers, then the mounting bolts and brake caliper bracket.
5. Mark brake rotor and wheel studs for installation alignment.
6. Remove mounting screws and brake rotor.
7. Disconnect wheel speed sensor electrical connector.
8. Remove and discard wheel driveshaft nut.
9. Remove mounting nut and separate upper ball joint ball stud from knuckle using ball joint remover tool No. J43631, or equivalent.
10. Remove wheel bearing/hub mounting bolts. **Do not contact to outer constant velocity boot seal.**
11. Disconnect wheel bearing/hub from drive axle using axle remover tool No. J5859, Snap-On universal hub puller tool No. CJ129, and OTC universal hub puller tool No. 7394, or equivalent, **Fig. 2.**
12. Reverse procedure to install.

SHOCK ABSORBER

REPLACE

1. Remove trim panel and shock tower sound insulator.
2. Disconnect electrical connector.
3. Remove shock absorber upper mounting nuts.
4. Raise and support vehicle.
5. Disconnect automatic level control connector.
6. Remove lower mounting bolt and shock absorber.
7. Reverser procedure to install.

COIL SPRING

REPLACE

1. Raise and support vehicle, then remove tire and wheel assembly.
2. Disconnect automatic level control sensor and headlamp adjustment links from upper control arm.
3. Support and raise lower control arm using suitable jack.
4. Remove shock absorber lower mounting bolt.
5. Lower control arm and remove support.
6. Support rear frame with suitable jack.
7. Remove frame to body side mounting bolts and washers, **Fig. 3.**
8. Lower frame and remove coil spring without going past guide pins.
9. Reverse procedure to install.

CONTROL ARM

REPLACE

Lower

1. Raise and support vehicle, then remove tire and wheel assembly.
2. Remove mounting nut and disconnect stabilizer shaft link from the lower control arm.
3. Disconnect automatic level control sensor and headlamp adjustment links from upper control arm.
4. Support and raise lower control arm using suitable jack.

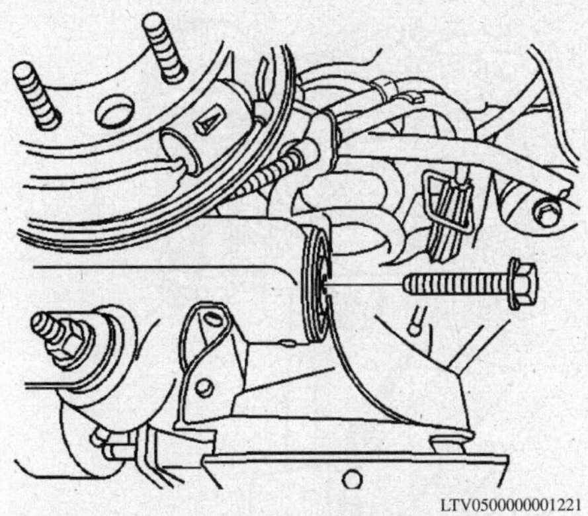

Fig. 4 Lower control arm to knuckle replacement

5. Remove shock absorber lower mounting bolt.
6. Lower control arm and remove support.
7. Support rear frame with suitable jack.
8. Remove frame to body side mounting bolts and washers, **Fig. 3.**
9. Lower frame and remove coil spring without going past guide pins.
10. Remove lower control arm to knuckle mounting bolt, **Fig. 4.**
11. Remove frame mounting bolt and nut, then the lower control arm, **Fig. 5.**
12. Reverse procedure to install. Loosely install all fasteners before tightening.

Upper

1. Raise and support vehicle, then remove tire and wheel assembly.
2. Remove upper control arm to knuckle mounting nut.
3. Disconnect upper control arm from knuckle using ball joint remover tool No. J43631, or equivalent. **Do not use pickle fork or wedge-type tool.**
4. Remove mounting nuts and bolts, then the upper control arm, **Fig. 6.** Discard nuts and bolts.
5. Reverse procedure to install, noting the following:
   a. **Torque** upper control arm to knuckle mounting nut to 15 ft. lbs.
   b. Final tighten upper control arm to knuckle mounting nut an additional 210°.

KNUCKLE

REPLACE

1. Raise and support vehicle, then remove rear tire and wheel assembly.
2. Compress piston into caliper bore using suitable, large C-clamp.
3. Remove pin bolts and support brake caliper aside using suitable heavy mechanic's wire. **Do not disconnect hydraulic brake flexible hose.**
4. Remove pads and retainers, then the mounting bolts and brake caliper bracket.
5. Mark brake rotor and wheel studs for installation alignment.

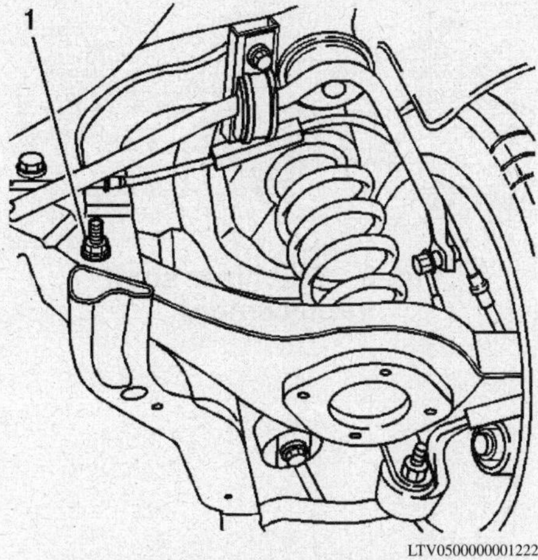

Fig. 5 Lower control arm to frame replacement

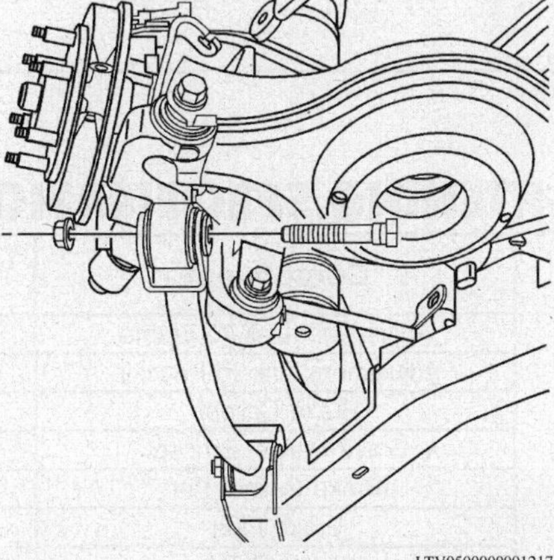

Fig. 7 Trailing link to knuckle replacement

6. Remove mounting screws and brake rotor.
7. Remove and discard wheel driveshaft nut.
8. Disconnect Anti-lock Brake System (ABS) sensor harness connector.
9. Disconnect intermediate park brake cable by pulling down near park brake cable connector.
10. Remove rear park brake cable from the bracket by depressing it using parking brake cable release tool No. J37043, or equivalent.
11. Disconnect park brake cable from actuator lever, then remove mounting bolts and park brake cable bracket.
12. Remove parking brake cable from lever.
13. Remove mounting nut and separate upper ball joint ball stud from knuckle using ball joint remover tool No. J43631, or equivalent.
14. Support lower control arm with suitable jack.
15. Remove lower shock absorber mounting bolt, then the trailing arm to knuckle mounting bolt and nut.
16. Remove lower control arm and adjustment link to knuckle mounting bolts.

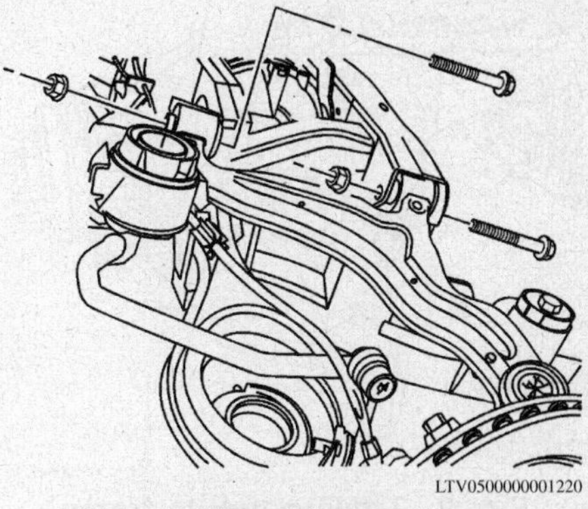

Fig. 6 Upper control arm replacement

17. Disconnect wheel bearing/hub from drive axle using axle remover tool No. J5859, Snap-On universal hub puller tool No. CJ129, and OTC universal hub puller tool No. 7394, or equivalent.
18. Remove knuckle.
19. Remove wheel bearing/hub mounting bolts, then the knuckle and backing plate from bearing/hub.
20. Reverse procedure to install.

TRAILING ARM

REPLACE

1. Raise and support vehicle, then remove tire and wheel assembly.
2. Remove automatic level control link from upper control arm.
3. Remove mounting nuts and remove brake pipe bracket.
4. Support lower control arm with suitable jack.
5. Remove trailing link to knuckle mounting nut and bolt, **Fig. 7.**
6. Remove jack.
7. Support frame with suitable jack.
8. Remove front mounting bolts and lower front of rear frame.
9. Remove trailing link to frame mounting nut and bolt, then the trailing link, **Fig. 8.**
10. Reverse procedure to instal.

STABILIZER SHAFT

REPLACE

1. Raise and support vehicle, the remove tire and wheel assemblies.
2. Remove upper mounting nuts and links from stabilizer shaft.
3. Remove mounting bolts and brackets, then the stabilizer shaft, **Fig. 9.**
4. Remove insulator from shaft.
5. Reverse procedure to install. Loosely install all components before tightening.

ADJUSTMENT LINK

REPLACE

1. Raise and support vehicle, then remove tire and wheel assembly.
2. Remove mounting bolts, nut and adjustment link, **Fig. 10.**
3. Reverse procedure to install.

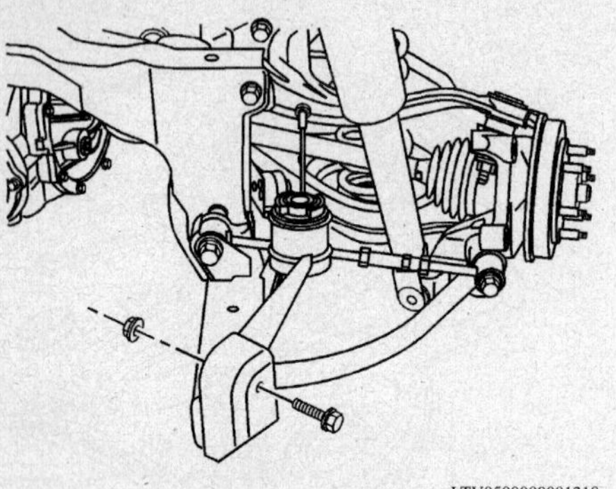

LTV0500000001218

Fig. 8 Trailing link to frame replacement

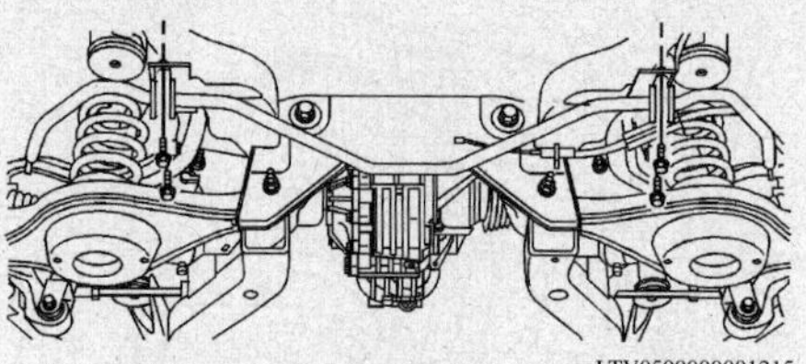

LTV0500000001215

Fig. 9 Stabilizer shaft replacement

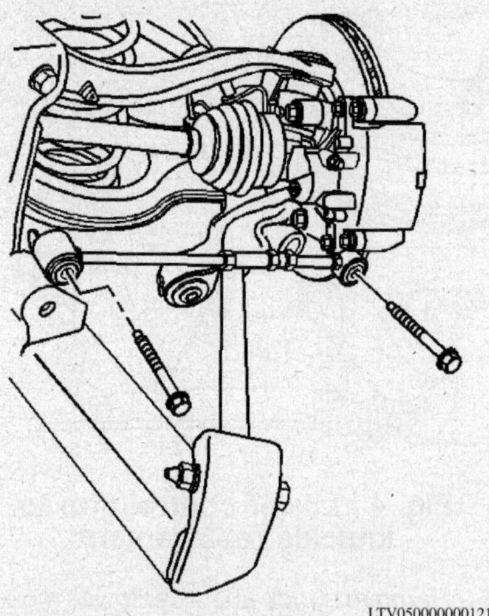

LTV0500000001219

Fig. 10 Adjustment link replacement

TIGHTENING SPECIFICATIONS

Year	Component	Torque Ft. Lbs.
2004–06	Adjustment Link To Frame	125
	Adjustment Link To Knuckle	118
	Brake Caliper	37
	Brake Caliper Bracket	88
	Brake Caliper Pin	44
	Brake Pipe	89①
	Brake Rotor	124①
	CV Joint To Transfer Case Flange	②
	Differential-To-Support	129
	Exhaust Pipes To Exhaust Manifold	22
	Floor Panel Tunnel Brace	18
	Heat Shield	71①
	HO2S	31
	Lower Control Arm To Frame	118
	Lower Control Arm To Knuckle	100
	Park Brake Cable Bracket	44
	Propeller Shaft Coupler-To-Differential Flange	63
	Propeller Shaft Coupler-To-Transmission Flange	63
	Propeller Shaft Support Bearing	37
	Rear Frame, Front	195
	Rear Frame, Rear	140
	Shock Absorber, Lower	111
	Shock Absorber, Upper	18
	Stabilizer Shaft Bracket	44
	Stabilizer Shaft Link	49
	Trailing Arm To Knuckle	125
	Trailing Arm To Frame	195
	Upper Control Arm To Frame	89
	Upper Control Arm To Knuckle	③
	Wheel Bearing/Hub	92
	Wheel Drive Shaft	118
	Wheel Lug	100

① — Inch lbs.
② — Refer to "Propeller Shaft, Replace" for tightening specifications and sequence.
③ — Refer to "Control Arm, Replace" for tightening specifications and sequence.

Front Suspension & Steering

NOTE: On Air Bag Equipped Models, Refer To "Air Bag System Precautions" Located In The Front Of This Manual For System Disarming & Arming Procedures.

NOTE: Prior To Performing Any Service Operations Listed In This Section, Consult The "Technical Service Bulletins" Section For Related Information.

INDEX

HUB & BEARING

REPLACE

1. Raise and support vehicle, then remove tire and wheel assembly.
2. **On models equipped with AWD,** remove wheel driveshaft mounting nut. Discard nut.
3. **On all models,** compress piston into caliper bore using suitable, large C-clamp.
4. Remove pin bolts and support brake caliper aside using suitable heavy mechanic's wire. **Do not disconnect hydraulic brake flexible hose.**
5. Remove brake pads and retainers from brake caliper bracket.
6. Remove guide pins and boots, then the mounting bolts and brake caliper bracket.
7. Mark brake rotor and wheel studs for installation alignment.
8. Remove mounting screws and brake rotor.
9. Disconnect and remove ABS electrical connector from splash shield.
10. **On models equipped with AWD,** remove mounting bolts and wheel bearing/hub using wheel hub remover tool No. J45859, or equivalent, **Fig. 1.**
11. **On models equipped with RWD,** remove mounting bolts and wheel bearing/hub, **Fig. 2.**
12. **On all models,** reverse procedure to install. Apply suitable threadlock to brake caliper bracket mounting bolt threads.

BALL JOINT INSPECTION

1. Raise and support vehicle, then remove tire and wheel assembly.
2. Ensure wheel drive shaft nut is properly tightened.
3. Mount suitable dial indicator to steering knuckle. Ensure instrument contacts hub vertical surface as close to center as possible.
4. Pull hub flange away from vehicle. If measurement is .005 inch, or more, replace wheel bearing/hub as outlined under "Hub & Bearing, Replace."
5. Install tire and wheel assembly.
6. Mount suitable dial indicator against lowest outboard wheel rim. If measurement is .125 inch, or more, replace lower control arm.

BALL JOINT

REPLACE

The ball joint is an integral part of the lower control arm. Refer to "Control Arm, Replace" for replacement procedure.

COIL SPRING

REPLACE

Refer to "Strut, Replace" and "Coil Spring & Strut Service" for coil spring replacement procedures.

STRUT

REPLACE

1. Raise and support vehicle, then remove tire and wheel assembly.
2. Remove push-in retainers and front air deflector.
3. Remove shock to yoke mounting nut and bolt by relieving bolt pressure by pulling up slightly lower control arm, **Fig. 3.**
4. Remove mounting nut and separate yoke from lower control arm using steering linkage and tie rod puller tool No. J24319-B, or equivalent.
5. **On models equipped with Electronic Suspension Control (ESC) Or Automatic Headlamp Aiming,** disconnect suspension position sensor link rod from upper control arm.
6. **On all models,** remove mounting nut and separate upper control arm from steering knuckle using steering linkage and tie rod puller.
7. Lower vehicle.
8. **On models equipped with ESC,** disconnect damper coil harness connector.
9. **On all models,** remove upper mounting bolts and strut.
10. Refer to "Coil Spring & Strut Service" to separate strut from assembly.
11. Reverse procedure to install.

COIL SPRING & STRUT SERVICE

1. Remove strut as outlined under "Strut, Replace."
2. Install strut in suitable spring compressor tool.
3. Mark upper control arm and insulator for installation alignment.
4. Compress coil spring and remove magnaride sensor mounting nut.
5. Remove upper mounting nut and strut from module.
6. Loosen compressor tool, then remove upper mounting plate, upper control arm bracket , insulator and coil spring.
7. Reverse procedure to install. Ensure upper control arm bracket alignment pins are orientated 90° with strut lower mounting holes.

CONTROL ARM

REPLACE

Upper

Refer to "Strut, Replace" and "Coil Spring & Strut Service" for upper control arm replacement procedures.

Lower

1. Raise and support vehicle, then remove tire and wheel assembly.
2. Remove push-in retainers and front air deflector.
3. Remove shock to yoke mounting nut and bolt by relieving bolt pressure by pulling up slightly lower control arm, **Fig. 3.**
4. Remove mounting nut and separate yoke from lower control arm using steering linkage and tie rod puller tool No. J24319-B, or equivalent.
5. Remove mounting nut and link stabilizer shaft link from lower control arm.
6. Remove ABS wire harness from lower control arm.
7. Remove mounting nut and separate lower control arm from steering knuckle using ball joint remover tool No. J43631, or equivalent.
8. Loosen mounting bolts and raise power steering gear.
9. Remove cradle mounting nuts and bolts, then the lower control arm, **Fig. 4.**
10. Reverse procedure to install.

STEERING KNUCKLE

REPLACE

1. Remove wheel bearing/hub as outlined under "Hub & Bearing, Replace."
2. Remove mounting nut and disconnect outer tie rod from steering knuckle using universal steering linkage puller tool No. J24319-B, or equivalent. **Do not use pickle fork or wedge-type tool.** Discard mounting nut.
3. Remove brake hose bracket to steering knuckle mounting bolts.
4. Remove mounting nut and separate

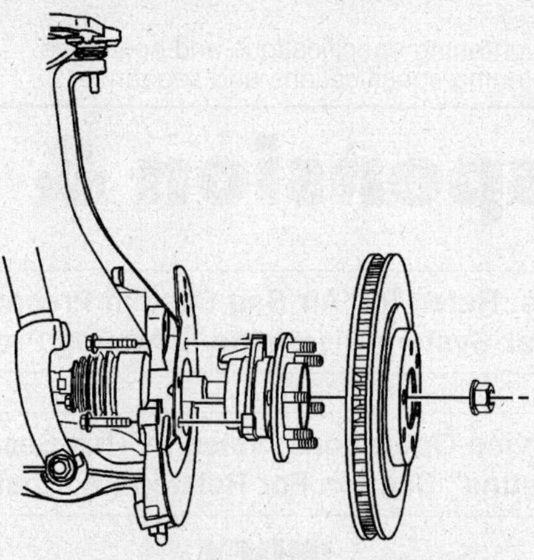

Fig. 1 Wheel bearing/hub replacement. AWD

upper control arm ball stud from steering knuckle. Discard mounting nut.
5. Remove mounting nut and separate lower control arm ball stud from steering knuckle using ball joint remover tool No. J43631, or equivalent. Discard mounting nut.
6. Remove steering knuckle, **Fig. 5.**
7. Reverse procedure to install, noting the following:
   a. **Torque** control arm ball stud mounting nuts to 15 ft. lbs.
   b. Final tighten ball stud mounting nuts an additional 210°.

STABILIZER BAR

REPLACE

1. Raise and support vehicle, then remove tire and wheel assembly.
2. Remove mounting nuts and disconnect stabilizer shaft links.
3. Remove mounting bolts and brackets, then the insulators and stabilizer shaft.
4. Reverse procedure to install. Ensure insulator slit faces rearward.

POWER STEERING GEAR

REPLACE

1. Ensure front wheels are straight-ahead and lock steering column using steering column anti-rotation pin tool No. J42640, or equivalent.
2. Raise and support vehicle, then remove tire and wheel assembly.
3. Remove push-in retainers and front air deflector.
4. Remove pinch bolt and disconnect intermediate shaft from the power steering gear.
5. Disconnect variable effort steering harness connector.
6. Remove mounting nuts and separate outer tie rod from steering knuckles using steering linkage and tie rod puller tool No. J24319-B, or equivalent.
7. Remove mounting bolt and disconnect power steering hoses from gear. Drain power steering fluid into suitable container.
8. Disconnect from line and position lefthand brake hose aside. Plug line.
9. **On models equipped with AWD,** proceed as follows:
   a. Support front differential housing using suitable jack.
   b. Loosen righthand engine mount nut.
   c. Raise differential housing.
10. **On all models,** remove power steering gear mounting bolts.
11. Remove lefthand rearward lower control arm to frame mounting nut and bolt.
12. Remove power steering gear through lefthand wheel opening.
13. Reverse procedure to install.

POWER STEERING PUMP

REPLACE

3.6L Engine

1. Raise and support vehicle, then remove push-in retainers and front air deflector.
2. Remove Positive Crankcase Ventilation (PCV) hose from resonator, then loosen clamps and remove air cleaner duct.
3. Remove drive belts as outlined under "Serpentine Drive Belt" in "3.6L Engine" section.
4. Disconnect Mass Air Flow (MAF) electrical connector, then remove mounting bolts and air cleaner.
5. Disconnect reservoir outlet and power steering pressure hoses from power steering pump. Drain fluid into suitable container.
6. Remove mounting bolts and power steering pump with bracket.
7. Reverse procedure to install. **Torque** mounting bolts to 37 ft. lbs., in sequence, **Fig. 6.**

4.6L Engine

1. Raise and support vehicle, then remove push-in retainers and front air deflector.
2. Remove mounting bolts and cross-vehicle brace.
3. Remove power steering and engine oil fill caps.
4. Lift up and pull sight shield forward to disconnect rear tab, then remove shield.
5. Disconnect Positive Crankcase Ventilation (PCV) tube from air cleaner duct.
6. Loosen throttle body and Mass Air Flow (MAF)/Intake Air Temperature (IAT) sensor clamps, then remove air cleaner duct.
7. Remove power steering pump drive belt as outlined under "Serpentine Drive Belt" in "4.6L Engine" section.
8. Remove power steering pump pulley using pulley remover tool No. J25034-C, or equivalent.
9. Disconnect Mass Air Flow (MAF)/ Intake Air Temperature (AT) electrical connector, then remove coolant hose retainer from top of air cleaner.

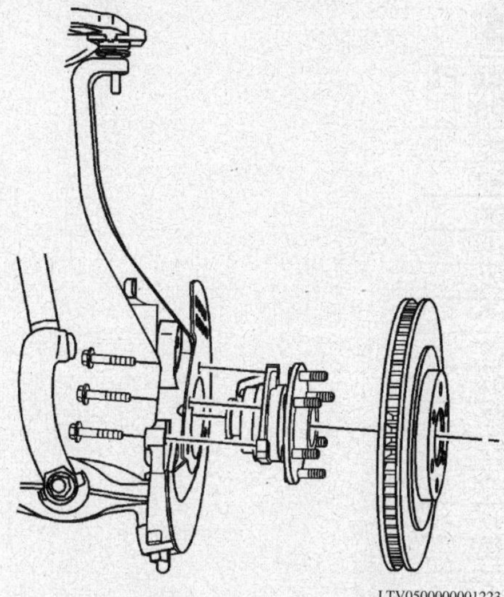

Fig. 2 Wheel bearing/hub replacement. RWD

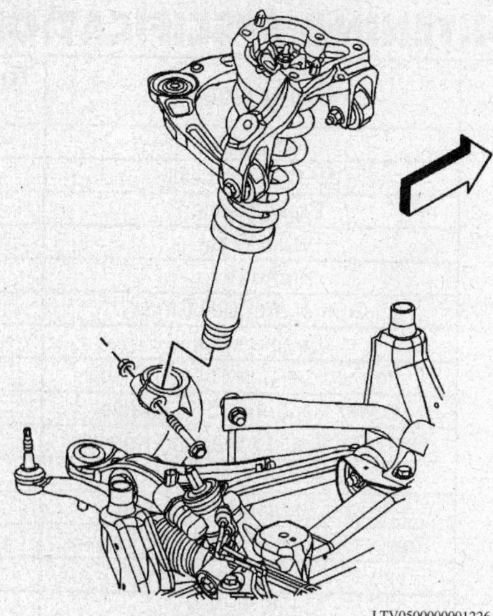

Fig. 3 Yoke replacement

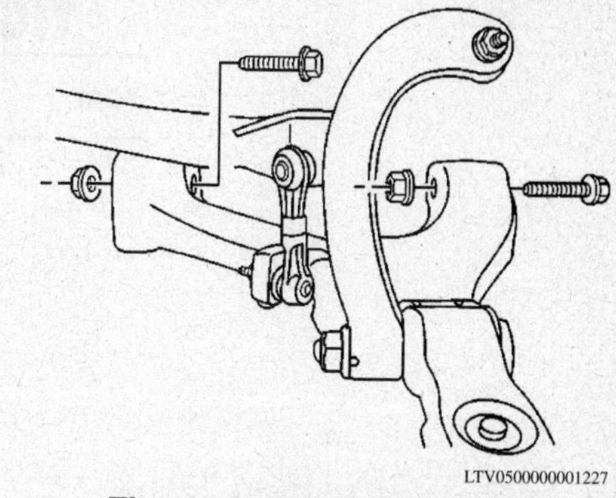

Fig. 4 Lower control arm replacement

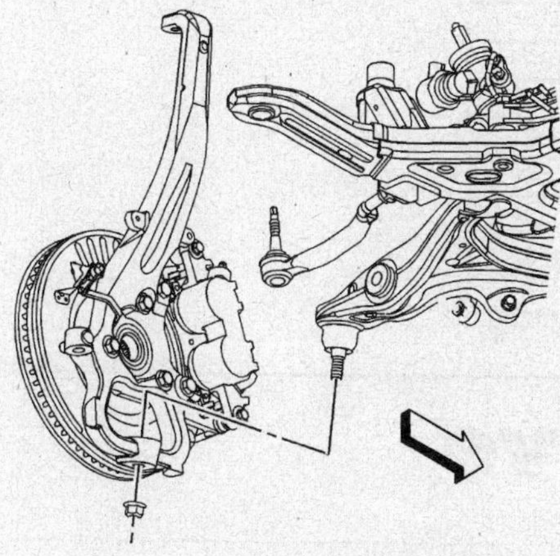

Fig. 5 Steering knuckle replacement

10. Remove mounting screws and air cleaner.
11. Disconnect reservoir outlet and power steering pressure hoses from power steering pump. Drain fluid into suitable container.
12. Remove mounting bolts and power steering pump with bracket.
13. Reverse procedure to install.

POWER STEERING SYSTEM BLEED

1. Fill pump reservoir with fluid to minimum system level, FULL COLD level or middle of hash mark on cap stick fluid level indicator.
2. **On vehicles equipped with hydro-boost,** fully charge accumulator as follows:
   a. Start engine.
   b. Firmly apply brake pedal 10–15 times.
   c. Turn engine OFF.
3. **On all models,** raise and support vehicle with front wheels off ground.
4. Turn ignition switch to OFF position.
5. Turn steering wheel stop to stop 12 times.
6. **On models equipped with hydro-boost systems or longer power steering hoses**, turn steering wheel stop to stop 15–20 time.
7. **On all models,** adjust power steering fluid level.
8. Start engine and turn steering wheel from lefthand to righthand.
9. Inspect for pump noise/whining.
10. If there are signs of cavitation or fluid aeration, adjust fluid level and repeat procedure.

TECHNICAL SERVICE BULLETINS

Rattle Or Chatter From Front At Slow Speeds

2005

On some of these models there may be a rattle or chatter from front of vehicle when driving over bumps with brakes lightly applied.

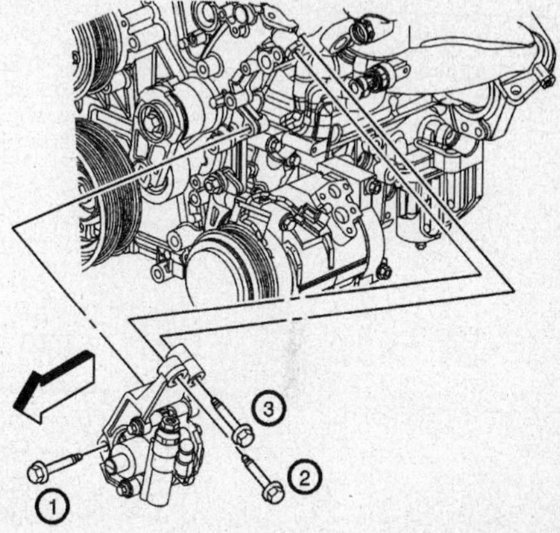

Fig. 6 Power steering pump tightening sequence. 3.6L engine

This condition may be caused by the front lower control arm hydraulic bushing.

To correct this condition, replace front lower control arm (RWD part No. 158069619 or AWD part No. 15806921).

Fluid Leak, Engine Compartment Whine, Reduced Power Steering Assist

2004

On some of these models there may be a fluid leak, excessive engine compartment whine or reduced power steering effort.

This condition may be caused by a power steering leak at the gear hose connections.

To correct this condition install replace O-rings (part No. 88964534) on power steering gear hoses.

TIGHTENING SPECIFICATIONS

Year	Component	Torque Ft. Lbs.
2004–06	Air Cleaner	78①
	Air Cleaner Duct	35①
	Brake Caliper	96
	Brake Line	20①
	Brake Rotor	124①
	Control Arm Ball Studs	②
	Engine Mount	59
	Intermediate Shaft Lower Pinch	37
	Lower Control Arm To Cradle	96
	Outer Tie Rod To Steering Knuckle	52
	Power Steering Gear	134
	Power Steering Gear Hose	17
	Power Steering Pump, 3.6L Engine	③
	Power Steering Pump	37
	Shock To Yoke	81
	Stabilizer Shaft	81
	Stabilizer Shaft Link	95
	Strut	83
	Strut Retainer	18
	Wheel Bearing/Hub	100
	Wheel Driveshaft	118
	Yoke To Lower Control Arm	133

① — Inch lbs.
② — Refer to "Steering Knuckle, Replace" for tightening specifications and sequence.
③ — Refer to "Power Steering Pump, Replace" for tightening specifications and sequence.

Front Wheel Drive

NOTE: On Air Bag Equipped Models, Refer To "Air Bag System Precautions" Located In The Front Of This Manual For System Disarming & Arming Procedures.

INDEX

AXLE SHAFT

REPLACE

Lefthand

1. Raise and support vehicle, then remove lefthand tire and wheel assembly.
2. Remove mounting nut and separate outer tie rod from steering knuckles using steering linkage and tie rod puller tool No. J24319-B, or equivalent. **Do not loosen tie rod end jam nut.**
3. Lock wheel hub and bearing from turning by installing suitable drift or punch into brake rotor against caliper mounting bracket.
4. Remove and discard wheel drive shaft spindle nut.
5. Disconnect wheel speed sensor connector and position wiring harness aside.
6. Remove mounting nut and separate upper ball joint ball stud from knuckle using ball joint remover tool No. J43631, or equivalent.
7. Disconnect lefthand front wheel drive shaft from wheel hub and bearing using wheel hub remover tool No. J45859, or equivalent. Support drive shaft.
8. Disconnect wheel drive shaft from intermediate shaft using axle shaft puller tool No. J45341, extension tool No. J29794 and slide hammer with adapter tool No. J2619-01, or equivalents.
9. Remove drive shaft.
10. Reverse procedure to install, noting the following:
    a. Install new O-rings and retaining rings.
    b. Apply small amount of suitable grease to intermediate wheel drive shaft splines.

Righthand

1. Raise and support vehicle, then remove righthand tire and wheel assembly.
2. Remove mounting nut and disconnect outer tie rod from steering knuckles

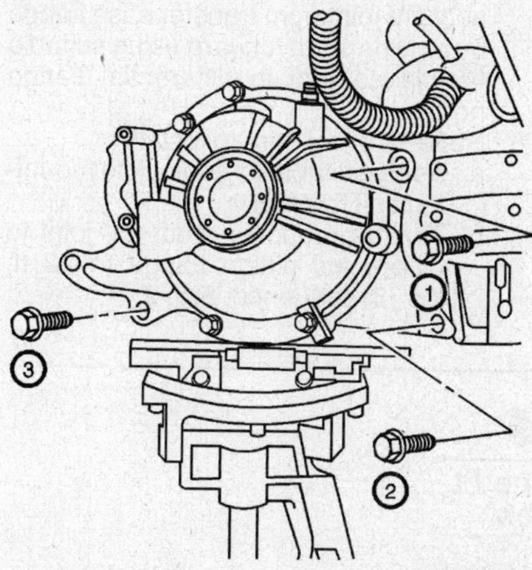

Fig. 1 Front differential tightening sequence

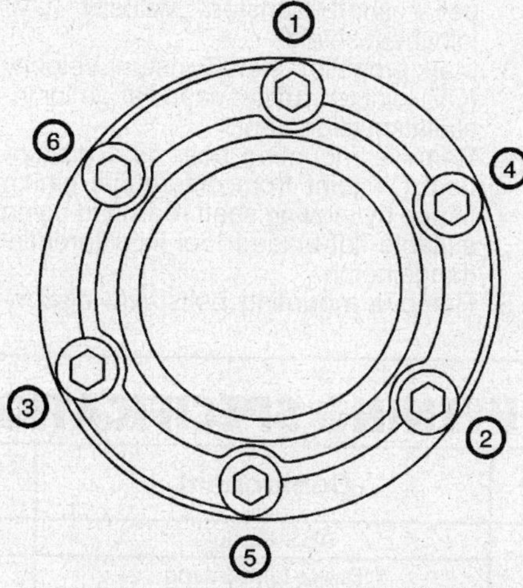

Fig. 2 CV joint tightening sequence

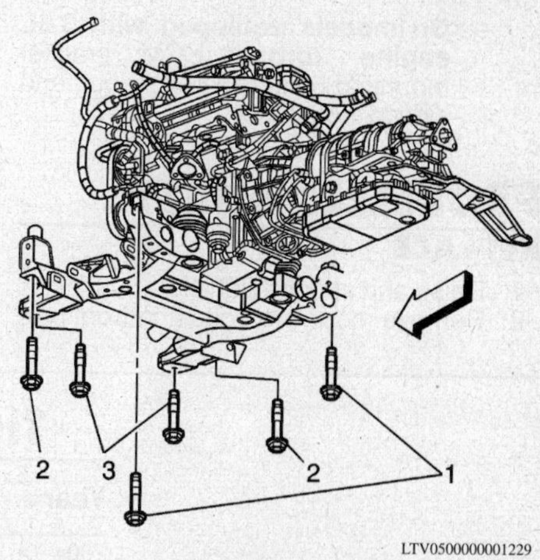

Fig. 3 Front frame tightening sequence

using steering linkage and tie rod puller tool No. J24319-B, or equivalent. **Do not loosen tie rod end jam nut.**

3. Lock wheel hub and bearing from turning by installing l suitable drift or punch into brake rotor against caliper mounting bracket.
4. Remove and discard wheel drive shaft spindle nut.
5. Disconnect wheel speed sensor connector and position wiring harness aside.
6. Remove mounting nut and separate upper ball joint ball stud from knuckle using ball joint remover tool No. J43631, or equivalent.
7. Disconnect righthand front wheel drive shaft from wheel hub and bearing using wheel hub remover tool No. J45859, or equivalent. Support drive shaft.
8. Disconnect wheel drive shaft from differential using axle shaft puller tool No. J45341, extension tool No. J29794 and slide hammer with adapter tool No. J2619-01, or equivalents.
9. Remove drive shaft.
10. Reverse procedure to install, noting the following:
    a. Install new O-rings and retaining rings.
    b. Apply small amount of suitable grease to intermediate wheel drive shaft splines.

DIFFERENTIAL CARRIER

REPLACE

1. **On models equipped with 3.6L engine,** support engine using engine lift bracket tools No. J36857, universal engine support fixture tool No. J28467-B and engine support fixture adapters tools No. J28467-501, or equivalents.
2. **On models equipped with 4.6L engine,** support engine using engine lift bracket tools No. J28467-86 and J28467-87, universal engine support fixture tool No. J28467-B and engine support fixture adapters tools No. J28467-15, or equivalents.
3. **On all models,** raise and support vehicle, then remove front tire and wheel assemblies.
4. Remove push-in retainers and front air deflector.
5. Disconnect wheel speed sensor harness connectors.
6. Remove mounting nut and separate outer tie rod from steering knuckle using ball joint remover tool No. J43631, or equivalent.
7. Remove power steering hoses to frame mounting bolts.
8. **On models equipped with 3.6L engine,** proceed as follows:
    a. Remove underhood fuse block ECM, TCM/IPC and ECM/TCM fuses.
    b. Remove chassis side upper ECM electrical connector by depressing lock lever, then simultaneously rotate clamp lever and depress lock slide.
    c. Remove body side upper and engine side lower ECM connectors.
    d. Remove ECM redundant ground wire and bolt.
    e. Remove mounting bolts and ECM.
9. **On models equipped with 4.6L engine,** disconnect electrical connector, then remove mounting nuts and ECM.
10. **On all models,** remove mounting bolts and ECM bracket.
11. Remove bracket mounting bolts and power steering cooler from air conditioning condenser.
12. Remove mounting bolt and disconnect pipes from power steering gear.
13. Disconnect power steering gear variable effort steering electrical connector.
14. Remove pinch bolt and disconnect intermediate shaft from power steering gear.
15. Disconnect lines from brake hoses.
16. Loosen ABS module mounting nuts and disconnect harness connector.
17. Remove mounting nut and separate ball stud from steering knuckle using ball joint remover tool. **Do not use pickle fork or wedge-type tool.**
18. Remove yoke to shock mounting nut and bolt.
19. Remove washer bottle to knuckle mounting bolts.
20. Remove engine mount lower mounting nuts.
21. Support frame using engine support stand tool No. J39580, or equivalent, and suitable support table.
22. Remove frame mounting bolts and raise body from frame. Ensure brake pipes, steering knuckle and wheels speed sensor electrical harness clear frame.
23. Remove mounting bolts and front propeller shaft Constant Velocity (CV) joint heat shield.
24. Remove mounting bolts and disconnect CV joint from differential pinion flange by moving shaft using suitable flat-bladed tool in differential flange notch.
25. Position propeller shaft aside.
26. Remove drive shafts as outlined under "Axle Shaft, Replace."
27. Remove and discard intermediate wheel drive shaft retaining ring, then the intermediate wheel drive shaft O-ring.
28. Remove intermediate shaft bearing mounting bolts.
29. Remove support bearing from intermediate wheel drive shaft flange and pinion cage using remover tool No. J45019, or equivalent.
30. Support differential using suitable transmission jack.
31. Remove front differential to oil pan mounting bolts.
32. Disconnect intermediate wheel drive shaft and front differential from oil pan. Remove differential.
33. Reverse procedure to install, noting the following:
    a. **Torque** differential mounting bolts to 71 ft. lbs., in sequence, **Fig. 1.**
    b. Apply suitable lubricant to intermediate wheel drive shaft splines.
    c. **Torque** propeller shaft CV joint to differential pinion flange to 22 ft. lbs., in sequence, **Fig. 2.**
    d. **Torque** frame bolts Nos. 1 and 2 to 141 ft. lbs., in sequence, then bolts No. 3 to 185 ft. lbs., **Fig. 3.**

e. **On models equipped with 3.6L engine, torque** ECM bracket mounting bolts to 88 inch lbs., and side to 17 ft. lbs.

PROPELLER SHAFT

REPLACE

1. Raise and support vehicle.
2. Remove mounting bolts and front propeller shaft Constant Velocity (CV) joint heat shield.
3. Mark propeller shaft Constant Velocity (CV) joint to transfer case flange for installation alignment.
4. Remove mounting bolts and disconnect CV joint from differential pinion flange by moving shaft rearward using suitable flat-bladed tool in differential flange notch.
5. Remove mounting bolts and disconnect CV joint from transfer case flange by moving shaft forward using suitable flat-bladed tool in differential flange notch.
6. Reverse procedure to install.
   a. Apply suitable threadlock to mounting bolt threads.
   b. **Torque** propeller shaft CV joint to differential pinion flange to 22 ft. lbs., in sequence, **Fig. 2.**

TIGHTENING SPECIFICATIONS

Year	Component	Torque Ft. Lbs.
2004–06	ABS Module	71①
	Brake Line Fitting	20
	ECM (3.6L Engine)	89①
	ECM (4.6L Engine)	71①
	ECM Bracket (3.6L Engine)	②
	ECM Bracket (4.6L Engine)	80①
	ECM Connector Bracket (3.6L Engine)	89①
	ECM Redundant Ground (3.6L Engine)	44①
	ECM Wire Harness (3.6L Engine)	17
	Engine Lift Bracket Tool	48
	Engine Mount	59
	Front Propeller Shaft CV Joint Heat Shield	80①
	Intermediate Drive Shaft Support Bearing	44
	Intermediate Shaft To Power Steering Gear	37
	Outer Tie Rod To Steering Knuckle	52
	Power Steering Cooler Bracket	80①
	Power Steering Hose To Frame	35①
	Power Steering Pipe	17
	Upper Ball Joint	③
	Washer Bottle To Knuckle	53①
	Wiring Harness Ground	89①
	Wheel Drive Shaft Spindle	118
	Yoke To Shock	133

①— Inch lbs.
②— Refer to "Differential Carrier, Replace" for tightening specifications and sequence.
③— **Torque** to 15 ft. lbs., then tighten an additional 210°.

Wheel Alignment

NOTE: On Air Bag Equipped Models, Refer To "Air Bag System Precautions" Located In The Front Of This Manual For System Disarming & Arming Procedures.

INDEX

PRECAUTIONS

Air Bag Systems

Refer to "Air Bag System Precautions" in the front of this manual for system disarming and arming procedures.

Battery Ground Cable

Prior to service, disconnect battery ground cable and isolate as required.

PRELIMINARY INSPECTION

1. Inspect tires for proper inflation and irregular tire wear.
2. Inspect runout of wheels and tires.
3. Inspect wheel bearings for backlash and excessive play.
4. Inspect ball joints and tie rod ends for looseness or wear.
5. Inspect control arms and stabilizer shaft for looseness or wear.
6. Inspect steering gear for looseness at frame.
7. Inspect struts/shock absorbers for wear, leaks and any noticeable noises.
8. Inspect vehicle trim height as outlined under "Vehicle Ride Height."
9. Inspect steering wheel for excessive drag or poor return due to stiff or rusted linkage or suspension components.
10. Ensure fuel tank is full or vehicle has compensating load added.

FRONT WHEEL ALIGNMENT

Caster

The front caster is not adjustable.

Camber

1. Install caster and camber adjusting tool No. J45845 or caster and camber adjusting tool No. J45845-10, or equivalent, **Fig. 1.**
2. Loosen lower control arm to frame mounting bolt.
3. Adjust camber angle by turn turnbuckle.
4. **Torque** mounting bolt to 96 inch lbs.
5. Ensure measurement is within specifications.

Toe

1. Loosen outer tie rod jam nut.
2. Rotate inner tie rod to required tow specification.
3. **Torque** jam nut to 41 ft. lbs.
4. Ensure toe is within specifications.

REAR WHEEL ALIGNMENT

Camber

1. Install caster and camber adjusting tool No. J45845, or equivalent, to lower control arm and frame.
2. Loosen lower control arm adjustment nuts.
3. Adjust caster and camber angle by positioning lower control arm.
4. Hold lower control arm in position and **torque** adjustment bolts to 96 ft. lbs.
5. Ensure measurements are within specifications.

Toe

Complete lefthand and righthand rear toe adjustments separately.

1. Loosen adjustment link jam nuts.
2. Rotate turnbuckle to adjust toe.
3. Hold turnbuckle and **torque** jam nuts to 30 ft. lbs.
4. Ensure measurements are within specifications.

VEHICLE RIDE HEIGHT

Preliminary Inspection

1. Set tire pressure to certification label specifications.
2. Inspect fuel level. Add additional weight to simulate full tank.
3. Ensure passenger and rear compartments are empty, except for spare tire.
4. Ensure vehicle is on flat and level surface, such as an alignment rack.
5. Ensure all vehicle doors, hood and luggage compartment lid are securely closed.
6. Inspect for installed after market accessories or modifications that could affect trim height measurement.

Bumper Height

All dimensions are measured vertical to the ground. Trim height should be within plus or minus .5 inch to be considered correct.

1. Lift front bumper up approximately 1.5 inches and allow to settle three times.
2. Measure from pivot bolt center line down to lower corner of lower ball joint.
3. Push front bumper down approximately 1.5 inches and allow to settle three times.
4. Measure from pivot bolt center line down to lower corner of lower ball joint.
5. Average measurements and compare to front bumper curb height specification as outlined under "Vehicle Ride Height" in "Specifications" section.
6. Measure from pivot bolt center line down to lower corner of lower ball joint.
7. Lift rear bumper approximately 1.5 inches and allow vehicle to settle three times.
8. Measure vertical distance between centerline of inboard rear lower control arm bolt and centerline of outboard rear lower control arm bolt.
9. Push rear bumper down approximately 1.5 inches and allow vehicle to settle three times.
10. Average measurements and compare to rear bumper curb height specification as outlined under "Vehicle Ride Height" in "Specifications" section.
11. If measurement is not within specifications, inspect for collision dame, and or worn or damaged suspension components.

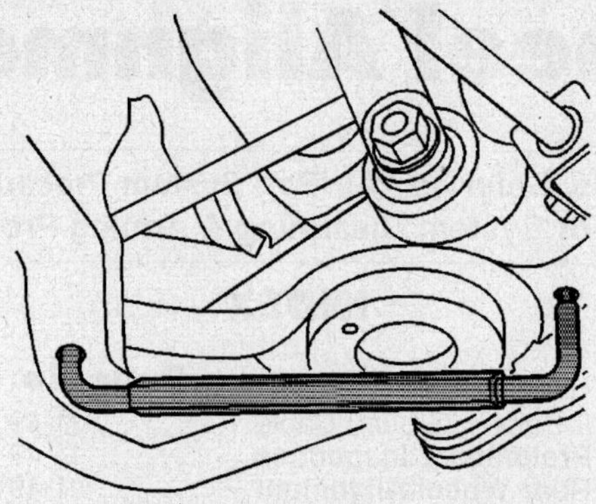

Fig. 1 Caster & camber adjustment

TRACKER

NOTE: Refer To Back Of This Manual For Vehicle Manufacturers Special Tool Suppliers.

INDEX OF SERVICE OPERATIONS

Specifications

GENERAL ENGINE SPECIFICATIONS

Year	Engine Liter	Fuel System	Bore & Stroke (Millimeters)	Comp. Ratio	Horsepower @ RPM	Torque, Ft. Lbs. @ RPM	Normal Oil Pressure, psi①
2002–04	2.0L	MFI	3.31 x 3.54	9.7	127 @ 6000	134 @ 3000	56–67
	2.5L	MFI	3.31 x 2.95	9.5	155 @ 6500	160 @ 4000	56–67

① — At 4000 RPM.

TUNE UP SPECIFICATIONS

The following specifications are published from the latest information available. This data should only be used in the absence of a decal affixed in the engine compartment.

Year & Engine	Spark Plug Gap	Ignition Timing BTDC				Curb Idle Speed④		Fast Idle Speed④		Fuel Pump Pressure psi.	Valve Lash, Inch
		Firing Order③	Man. Trans.	Auto. Trans.	Mark Location, Fig.	Man. Trans.	Auto. Trans.	Man. Trans.	Auto. Trans.		
2002–04											
2.0L	.041	①	⑦	⑦	Fig. A	⑤	⑤	⑤	⑤	36–43⑧	②
2.5L	.041	⑥	⑦	⑦	Fig. A	⑤	⑤	⑤	⑤	39–45⑧	②

BTDC — Before Top Dead Center
N — Neutral
① — Cylinder numbering from front of engine to rear, 1, 2, 3, 4. Firing order, 1-3-4-2.
② — Equipped with hydraulic lifters.
③ — Before removing wires from distributor cap, determine location of No. 1 wire in cap, as distributor position may have been altered from that outlined at end of this chart.
④ — When inspecting idle speed, set parking brake & block drive wheels.
⑤ — Controlled by idle speed control (ISC).
⑥ — Firing order, 1-6-5-4-3-2.

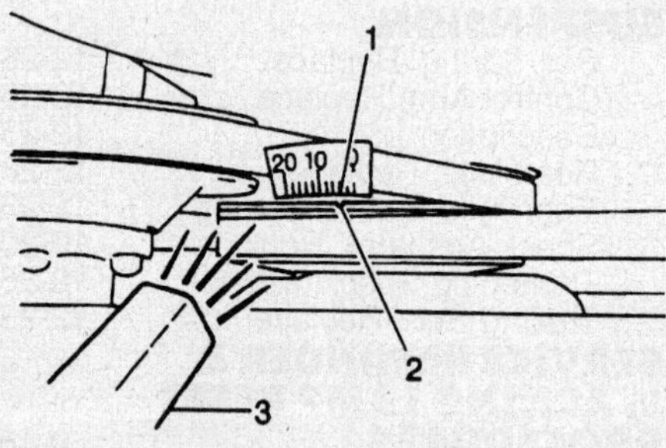

1. 5° BTDC Mark
2. "V" Mark On Crankshaft Pulley
3. Timing Light

Fig. A

⑦ — Coil on plug design, controlled by the PCM.
⑧ — Remove fuel filler cap to release pressure in tank. Remove fuel pump relay, then start engine and operate until engine stalls. Crank engine for three seconds to ensure fuel pressure is relieved. Disconnect battery ground cable. Remove fuel rail end plug bolt from fuel rail and attach suitable fuel pressure gauge. With ignition On and engine Off, read pressure at gauge.

FRONT WHEEL ALIGNMENT SPECIFICATIONS

Year	Models	Caster Angle, Degrees		Camber Angles, Degrees		Toe, Degrees①		Steering Angle, Degrees	
		Limits	Desired	Limits	Desired	Limits	Desired	Inner Wheel	Outer Wheel
2002–04	All	+1.67 to +3.67	+2.67	-1.0 to +1.0	0	-.16 to +.16	0	34.5	32.5

① — Toe-In (+). Toe-Out (–).

FLUID CAPACITIES & COOLING SYSTEM DATA

Year	Engine Liter	Cooling System Capacity Qts.		Coolant Type	Radiator Cap Relief Pressure, Lbs.	Thermo. Opening Temp. °F	Fuel Tank Gals.	Engine Oil Refill Qts.③	Transmission Oil		Transfer Case Pts.	Axle Pts.	
		Man. Trans.	Auto. Trans.						Manual Trans. Pts.	Auto. Trans. Qts.①		Front	Rear
2002–04	2.0L	6.9	6.9	Ethylene Glycol	13	179	②	5.5	⑤	④	3.6	2.2	4.6
	2.5L	8.5	8.5	Ethylene Glycol	13	179	②	5.8	⑤	④	3.6	2.2	4.6

① — Approximate. Make final inspection w/dipstick.
② — Two-door models, 14.8 gals.; Four-door models, 17.4 gals.
③ — Includes filter.
④ — Four-speed automatic, bottom pan removal, 2WD, 3.0 qts., 4WD 2.6 qts. Complete overhaul: 2.0L 2WD 7.8 qts.; 2.0L 4WD, 7.5 qts.; 2.5L 2WD, 7.8 qts.; 2.5L 4WD, 7.5 qts.
⑤ — 2WD models, 4 pts.; 4WD models, 3.2 pts.

LUBRICANT DATA

Year	Model	Lubricant Type						
		Transmission		Hydraulic Clutch Fluid	Transfer Case	Drive Axle	Power Steering	Brake System
		Manual	Automatic					
2002–04	All	75W-90 GL-4	Dexron III	①	75W-90 GL-4	80W-90 GL-5	Dexron III	DOT 3

① — GM hydraulic clutch fluid part No. 12345347, or an equivalent DOT 3 brake fluid.

Electrical

NOTE: On Air Bag Equipped Models, Refer To "Air Bag System Precautions" Located In The Front Of This Manual For System Disarming & Arming Procedures.

NOTE: Refer To "Computer Relearn Procedures" Located In The Front Of This Manual When Battery Power To The Computer Has Been Interrupted.

INDEX

PRECAUTIONS

Air Bag Systems

Refer to "Air Bag System Precautions" in the front of this manual for system disarming and arming procedures.

Battery Ground Cable

Prior to service disconnect battery ground cable and isolate as required.

FUSE PANEL LOCATION

The fuse panel and flasher are located behind the lefthand side of the instrument panel.

RELAY CENTER LOCATION

The relay center is located on the righthand side of the engine compartment, near the strut tower.

FUEL PUMP RELAY LOCATION

The fuel pump relay is located in the junction block above the lefthand side hinge pillar trim panel.

STARTER

REPLACE

2.0L Engine

1. Remove mounting nut and battery cable from starter solenoid.
2. Remove starter solenoid electrical connector.
3. Remove upper mounting nut, bolt and battery cable from starter motor.
4. Remove lower mounting nut and starter motor.
5. Reverse procedure to install, noting the following:
   a. **Torque** starter motor mounting bolts to 22 ft. lbs.
   b. **Torque** positive battery cable to starter solenoid nut to 89 inch lbs.

2.5L Engine

1. Raise and support vehicle.
2. Remove four insulator bracket mounting bolts and lower front stabilizer shaft.
3. Drain transfer case into suitable container.
4. Place index marks on pinion flange yoke and differential pinion flange.
5. Remove four yoke mounting bolts and nuts.
6. Separate pinion flange yoke from differential pinion flange and sliding yoke from transfer case.
7. Remove propeller shaft.
8. Remove front exhaust pipe.
9. Remove mounting bolt and position transmission fluid line bracket aside.
10. Disconnect starter solenoid electrical connector.
11. Remove mounting nut and positive battery cable from starter solenoid.
12. Remove two starter motor mounting bolts.
13. Move starter motor towards front of vehicle into engine mounting bracket until pinion clears transmission case.
14. Move starter motor toward back of vehicle while swinging pinion to righthand side of vehicle until starter motor clears engine mount bracket.
15. Rotate starter motor 180° so pinion faces front of vehicle.
16. Remove starter motor through area between exhaust pipe and transmission.
17. Reverse procedure to install, noting the following:
    a. **Torque** starter motor mounting bolts to 22 ft. lbs.
    b. **Torque** starter solenoid nut to 89 inch lbs.
    c. **Torque** stabilizer shaft insulator bracket mounting bolts to 11 ft. lbs.
    d. **Torque** propeller shaft bolts and nuts to 37 ft. lbs.

ALTERNATOR

REPLACE

2.0L Engine

1. Remove air cleaner hose.
2. Remove drive belt from alternator pulley.
3. Disconnect power steering pressure switch connector.
4. Disconnect alternator electrical connectors.
5. Remove vacuum line from top of EVAP canister.
6. Slide EVAP canister from mounting bracket at inner fender.
7. Remove upper and lower alternator mounting bolts.
8. Remove alternator.
9. Reverse procedure to install. **Torque** alternator mounting bolts to 17 ft. lbs.

2.5L Engine

1. Remove air cleaner hose and disconnect alternator electrical connector.
2. Remove rubber protector, nut and electrical connector from alternator B+ terminal.
3. Remove adjusting and pivot bolts, then move alternator aside.
4. Remove mounting bolts and upper alternator bracket.
5. Remove alternator.
6. Reverse procedure to install, noting the following:
   a. **Torque** alternator upper bracket mounting bolts to 32 ft. lbs.
   b. **Torque** alternator adjusting and pivot bolts to 17 ft. lbs.

DISTRIBUTOR

REPLACE

1. Disconnect electrical connection from distributor.
2. Mark distributor housing position on engine.
3. Remove distributor cap and mark rotor position on distributor housing.
4. Remove rotor, flange bolt and distributor.
5. Reverse procedure to install. Ensure removal marks are aligned.

COIL PACK

REPLACE

2.0L Engine

1. Disconnect ignition coil connector.
2. Remove bolt for each coil, **Fig. 1.**
3. Remove ignition coil.
4. Reverse procedure to install. **Torque** mounting bolt to 89 inch lbs.

2.5L Engine

1. Remove two mounting screws and ignition coil cover.

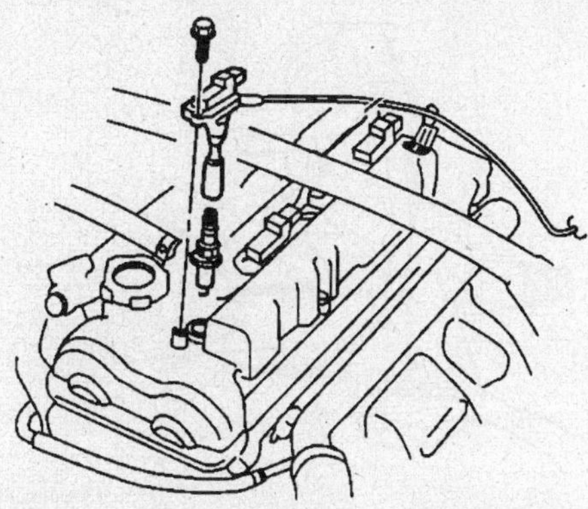

Fig. 1 Ignition coil removal. 2.0L engine

2. Disconnect ignition coil electrical connector.
3. Remove mounting bolt and ignition coil.
4. Reverse procedure to install. **Torque** mounting bolt to 26 inch lbs.

IGNITION LOCK

REPLACE

Removal

1. Remove steering wheel and signal/dimmer switch.
2. Disconnect switch lead wires from connector.
3. Remove upper steering shaft mounting bolt.
4. Remove steering column to dash and steering column to floor pan mounting bolts, then the steering column.
5. **On models equipped with automatic transmissions,** disconnect automatic lockout cable.
6. **On all models,** loosen and remove ignition lock mounting bolts using suitable center punch, **Fig. 2.**
7. Turn ignition lock cylinder to ACC or RUN position and remove lock.

Installation

1. Install steering shaft into steering column by positioning oblong hole of steering shaft into center of hole in column.
2. Turn ignition to ACC or RUN position and install steering lock onto column.
3. Turn ignition key to LOCK position and remove key.
4. Adjust hub on lock to line up with oblong hole of steering shaft. Rotate shaft to ensure steering shaft is locked, **Fig. 3.**
5. Tighten new steering lock mounting bolts until bolt head breaks off, **Fig. 4.**
6. Ensure proper operation of lock and steering shaft.
7. Install steering column.

IGNITION SWITCH

REPLACE

1. Remove ignition lock as outlined in "Ignition Lock, Replace."
2. Remove ignition switch mounting screw.
3. Reverse procedure to install. Ensure switch recess is mated with tab on bracket, **Fig. 5.**

CLUTCH START SWITCH

REPLACE

1. Disconnect Clutch Pedal Position (CPP) switch electrical connector, **Fig. 6.**
2. Loosen CPP switch locknut.
3. Remove CPP switch from clutch pedal bracket by turning counterclockwise.
4. Reverse procedure to install.

NEUTRAL SAFETY SWITCH

REPLACE

Removal

1. Remove neutral safety switch electrical connector.
2. Remove nut and washer from manual shaft.
3. Unstake lock plate behind manual shaft nut.
4. Remove lock plate.
5. Remove mounting bolt and switch from manual shaft.

Installation

1. Turn manual shaft rearward.
2. Turn manual shaft back two notches into neutral position.
3. Install switch to transmission.
4. Secure switch with one bolt.
5. Bend claws of lock plate over set nut.
6. Tightening switch mounting bolt with neutral reference line and cut out aligned, **Fig. 7.**
7. **Torque** mounting bolts to 44 inch lbs.
8. Install manual lever to manual shaft.
9. **Torque** manual shaft nut to 115 inch lbs.

HEADLAMP SWITCH

REPLACE

Replace headlamp switch as outlined in "Turn Signal Switch, Replace."

STOP LIGHT SWITCH

REPLACE

1. Disconnect stop lamp switch electrical connectors.
2. Mark depth position of switch for installation.
3. Remove mounting nut and switch.
4. Reverse procedure to install. Align depth mark.

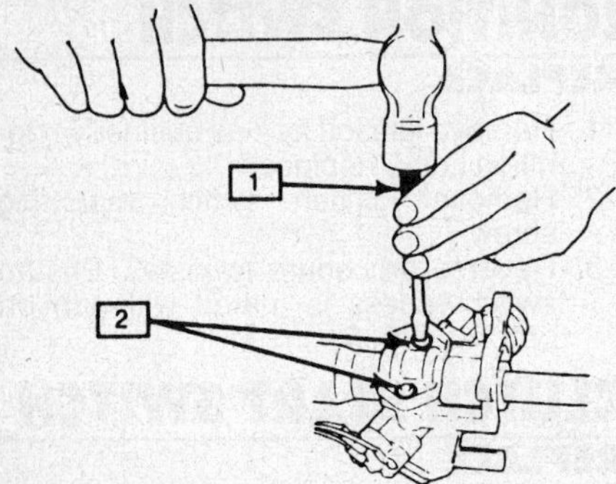

1 METAL CHISEL
2 STEERING LOCK MOUNTING BOLTS

GC9128800006000X

Fig. 2 Lock removal

TURN SIGNAL SWITCH

REPLACE

1. Remove steering wheel, upper and lower column, and steering wheel cover, **Fig. 8.**
2. Disconnect turn signal/dimmer switch connector at lead.
3. Remove mounting screws and turn signal/dimmer switch.
4. Reverse procedure to install.

DIMMER SWITCH

REPLACE

Refer to "Turn Signal Switch, Replace" for replacement procedure.

STEERING WHEEL

REPLACE

1. Remove driver air bag module as outlined in "Passive Restraint Systems" chapter.
2. Remove steering wheel mounting nut.
3. Scribe alignment mark across wheel and steering shaft, then remove steering wheel using steering wheel puller tool No. J-1859-A, or equivalent.
4. Remove horn button contact plate screws from rear of steering wheel.
5. Disconnect wire and remove contact plate.
6. Reverse procedure to install, noting the following:
   a. Align scribe marks on steering wheel and steering shaft.
   b. **Torque** steering shaft nut to 24 ft. lbs.

INSTRUMENT CLUSTER

REPLACE

1. Remove hazard lights switch knob by gently pulling out knob.
2. Remove mounting screws, steering column upper and lower covers.
3. Remove mounting screws and instrument cluster bezel.
4. Remove mounting screws and instrument cluster.

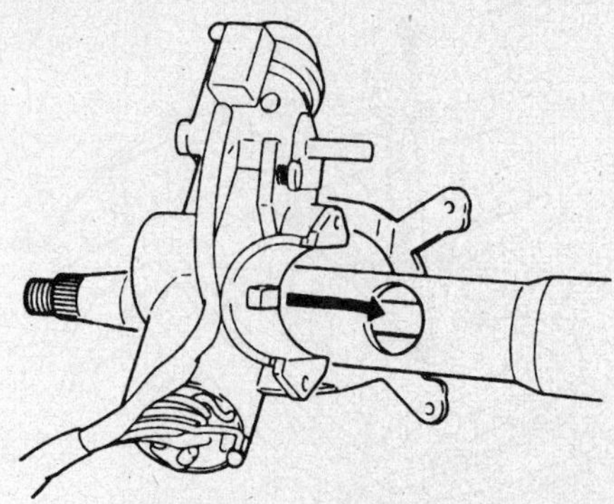

GC9128800007000X

Fig. 3 Lock alignment

5. Disconnect three electrical connectors and speedometer cable from instrument cluster.
6. Reverse procedure to install.

RADIO

REPLACE

1. Remove heater control knobs and face plate from instrument panel center trim bezel.
2. Twist off heater control unit face plate illumination bulb.
3. Remove ashtray from track.
4. Remove mounting screws and instrument panel center trim bezel.
5. Remove mounting screws from radio mounting bracket.
6. Pull radio out of instrument panel, then disconnect electrical and antenna connections.
7. Remove radio and mounting screws, then side mounting brackets from radio.
8. Reverse procedure to install.

WIPER MOTOR

REPLACE

The wiper motor crank arm is not serviced separately and should not be disconnected from the wiper motor. The crank arm is positioned on the motor to allow the wipers to return to normal park position.

Front

1. Disconnect wiper motor electrical connector.
2. Remove mounting bolts and pull wiper motor away from bulkhead.
3. Remove wiper motor linkage by gently prying off wiper motor crank arm.
4. Reverse procedure to install. **Torque** mounting bolts to 15 ft. lbs.

Rear

1. Remove plastic mounting clips and rear door inner trim panel.
2. Remove rear wiper motor mounting screws
3. Remove mounting screw and rear wiper motor ground wire from rear door.
4. Gently pry rear wiper linkage from crank arm.

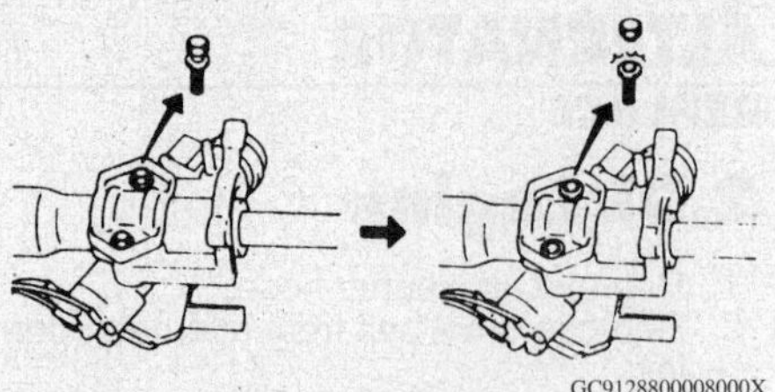

GC9128800008000X

Fig. 4 Lock assembly fastening

5. Remove rear wiper motor.
6. Reverse procedure to install.

WIPER TRANSMISSION

REPLACE

1. Push lefthand and righthand stoppers inward, then pull compartment out of instrument panel.
2. Remove instrument panel compartment hinge pins and compartment front instrument panel.
3. Disconnect blower motor and resistor electrical connectors.
4. Remove mounting screws, electrical connectors and relay bracket from blower case.
5. Disconnect fresh/recirc air control cable from blower case.
6. Remove wiring harness from blower case guide brackets.
7. Remove mounting bolts and blower case.
8. Remove blower motor cooling duct.
9. Remove mounting screws and blower motor.
10. Reverse procedure to install.

BLOWER MOTOR

REPLACE

1. Remove instrument panel as outlined in "Dash Panel Service" chapter.
2. Remove mounting nuts, screws and air box, **Fig. 9.**
3. Disconnect blower motor and resistor electrical connectors.
4. Remove fresh/recirc control cable from blower case.
5. Remove blower relay bracket mounting, relay and bracket.
6. Remove wiring harness retainers from blower case.
7. Remove PCM.
8. Remove mounting bolts and blower case, **Fig. 10.**
9. Remove mounting screws and blower motor.
10. Reverse procedure to install.

HEATER CORE

REPLACE

1. Drain cooling system into suitable container.
2. Remove instrument panel as outlined in "Dash Panel Service" chapter.
3. Remove heater hoses and clamps from heater core.
4. Disconnect air conditioning compressor control module electrical connector.

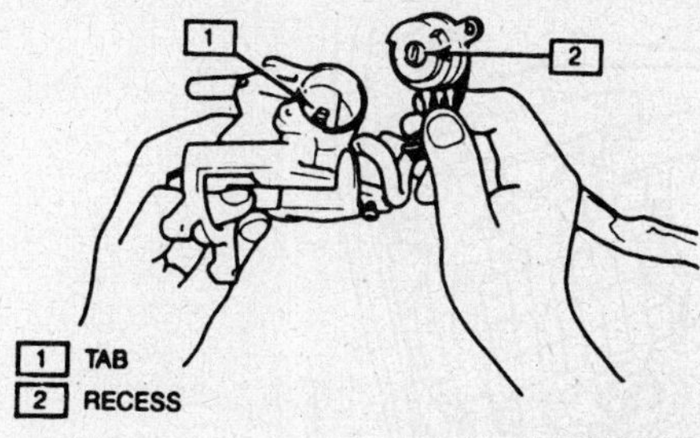

Fig. 5 Ignition switch installation

5. Remove air conditioning compressor control module.
6. Remove air box as outlined in "Blower Motor, Replace."
7. Remove mounting nut from center of bulkhead on engine side.
8. Remove heater case mounting nuts.
9. Separate floor ducts from heater case.
10. Remove heater case.
11. Remove heater case mounting clips.
12. Remove mounting screw and blend door linkages.
13. Separate case halves and remove heater core.
14. Reverse procedure to install.

EVAPORATOR CORE

REPLACE

1. Recover refrigerant as outlined in "Air Conditioning" chapter.
2. Remove instrument panel as outlined in "Dash Panel Service" chapter.
3. Remove mounting bolt and slide plate, then the evaporator inlet and outlet tubes, **Fig. 11.**
4. Disconnect evaporator temperature sensor electrical connector from compressor control module.
5. Remove mounting screws, nuts and evaporator case.
6. Remove mounting screws and insulation.
7. Separate evaporator case halves.
8. Remove mounting bolts and expansion valve.
9. Remove evaporator, **Fig. 12.**
10. Reverse procedure to install.

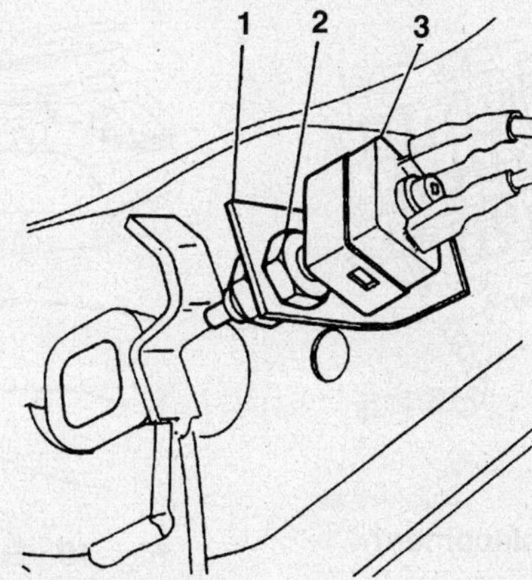

1. Clutch Pedal Bracket
2. Locknut
3. CPP Switch

GC1119900197000X

Fig. 6 CPP switch removal

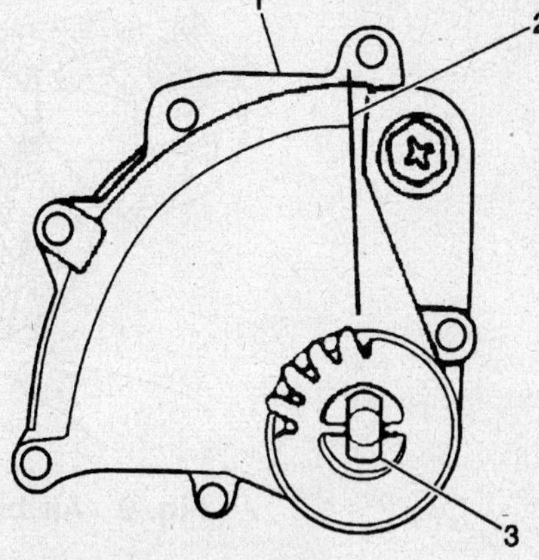

1. Switch
2. Neutral Reference Line
3. Cut Out

GC1119900196000X

Fig. 7 Neutral safety switch installation

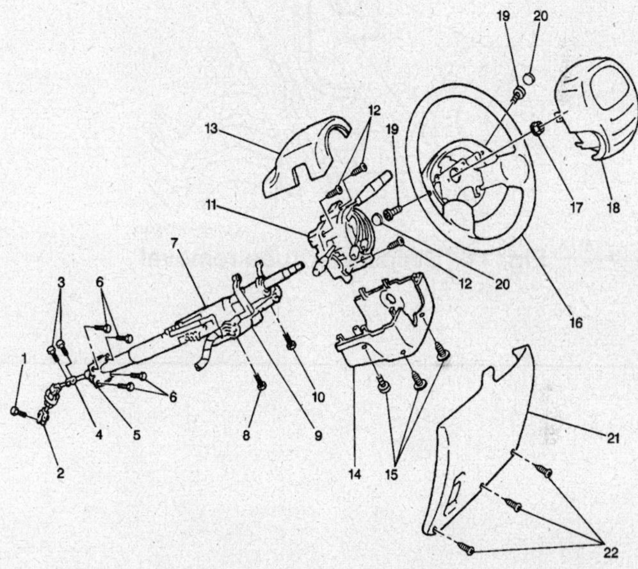

(1) Steering Shaft Coupling Bolt
(2) Lower Steering Shaft
(3) Steering Shaft Coupling Bolts
(4) Steering Shaft Coupling
(5) Steering Shaft Seal
(6) Steering Shaft Seal Bolts
(7) Steering Column
(8) Steering Column Bracket Bolt
(9) Steering Column Lock and Ignition Switch Cylinder
(10) Steering Column Bracket Bolt
(11) Turn Signal and Headlamp and Windshield Wiper and Windshield Washer Switch with Levers and Inflatable Restraint Steering Wheel Module Coil
(12) Turn Signal Base Bolts
(13) Steering Column Upper Trim Cover
(14) Steering Column Lower Trim Cover
(15) Steering Column Lower Trim Cover Bolts
(16) Steering Wheel
(17) Steering Wheel Nut
(18) Inflatable Restraint Steering Wheel Module
(19) Inflatable Restraint Steering Wheel Module Bolt
(20) Steering Wheel Opening Cover
(21) IP Steering Column Opening Trim Plate
(22) IP Steering Column Opening Trim Plate Screws

GC6040100182000X

Fig. 8 Exploded view of steering column

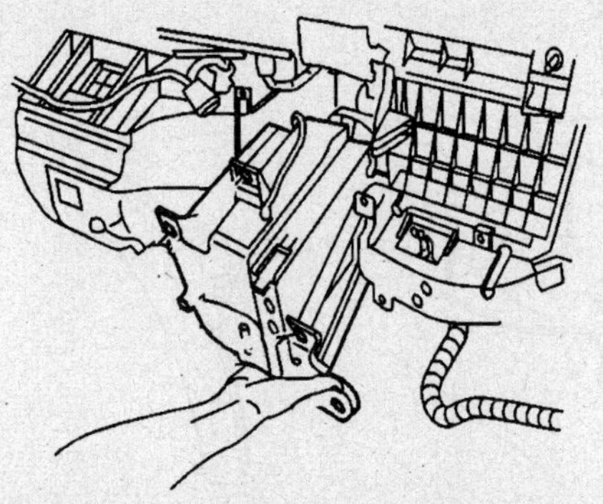
GC7029900577000X

Fig. 9 Air box replacement

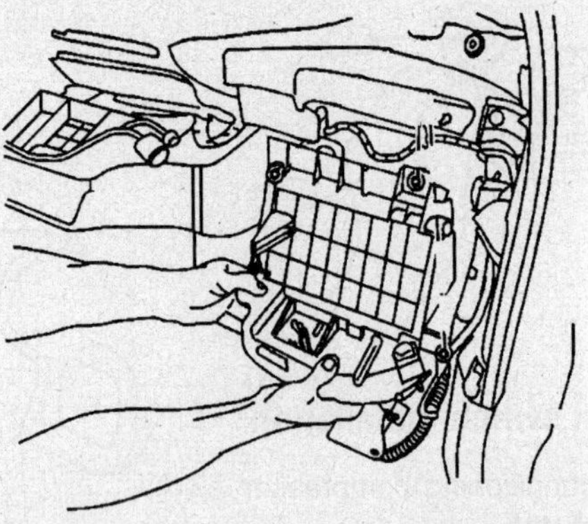
GC7029900578000X

Fig. 10 Blower case replacement

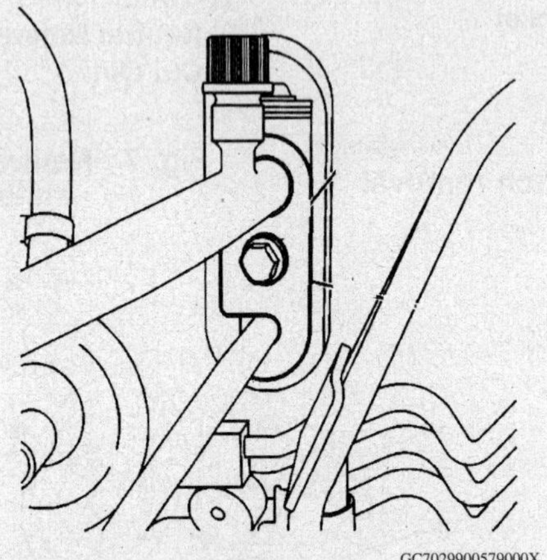
GC7029900579000X

Fig. 11 Evaporator tube removal

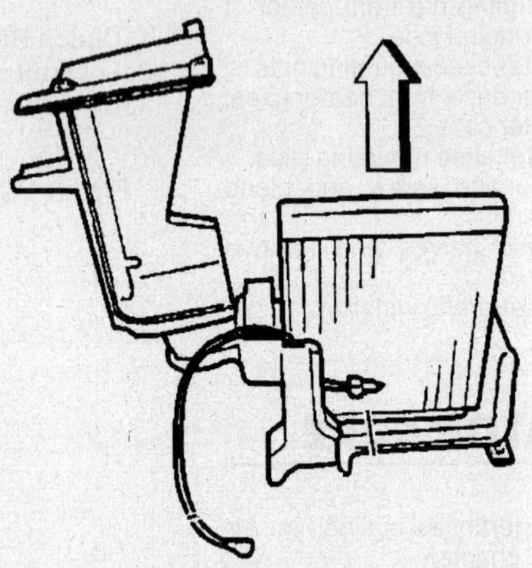
GC7029900580000X

Fig. 12 Evaporator core replacement

2.0L Engine

NOTE: On Air Bag Equipped Models, Refer To "Air Bag System Precautions" Located In The Front Of This Manual For System Disarming & Arming Procedures.

NOTE: Refer To "Computer Relearn Procedures" Located In The Front Of This Manual When Battery Power To The Computer Has Been Interrupted.

NOTE: Prior To Performing Any Service Operations Listed In This Section, Consult The "Technical Service Bulletins" Section For Related Information.

INDEX

PRECAUTIONS

Fuel System Pressure Relief

1. Place transmission in neutral or park, set parking brake and block wheels.
2. Disconnect fuel pump relay electrical connector, **Fig. 1.**
3. Remove fuel filler cap to relieve fuel tank pressure. Replace cap when pressure is released.
4. Start engine and allow to runout of fuel.
5. Crank engine an additional three seconds to discharge any remaining fuel system pressure.
6. Upon completion of servicing, connect fuel pump relay electrical connector.

Battery Ground Cable

Prior to service disconnect battery ground cable and isolate as required.

COMPRESSION PRESSURE

Standard compression pressure at 400 RPM is 199 psi. Minimum pressure at 400 RPM is 170 psi. The maximum difference at 400 RPM is 14.2 psi.

ENGINE MOUNT

REPLACE

Lefthand

1. Remove engine mount top nut.
2. Raise and support vehicle.
3. Support engine using suitable engine support.
4. Remove two bottom of engine mount nuts, **Fig. 2.**
5. Raise engine slightly to provide engine mount clearance.
6. Remove engine mount.
7. Reverse procedure to install.

Righthand

1. Remove engine mount top nut.
2. Remove engine block bracket, **Fig. 2.**
3. Raise and support vehicle.
4. Support engine using suitable engine support.
5. Remove two engine mount bottom nuts.
6. Raise engine slightly to provide clearance.
7. Remove engine mount.
8. Reverse procedure to install.

ENGINE

REPLACE

1. Relieve fuel pressure as outlined in "Precautions."
2. Raise and support vehicle, then remove front skid plate.
3. Drain engine oil and cooling system into suitable containers.
4. Remove flywheel cover.
5. **On models equipped with automatic transmission,** proceed as follows:
   a. Remove automatic transmission fluid cooler lines from radiator. Cap open lines.
   b. Remove torque converter bolts using tool No. J 35271 or equivalent.
6. **On all models,** support transmission, then remove retaining bolts and engine to transmission support bracket.
7. Remove bolts, then separate front pipe assembly from exhaust manifold.
8. Lower vehicle, then remove hood from vehicle.
9. Raise and support vehicle, then remove bolts and strut tower brace.
10. Remove engine block to catalytic converter support bracket.
11. **Do not discharge A/C system or remove refrigerant lines from compressor.**
12. Remove bolts, then the A/C compressor from its bracket and position aside.
13. Remove bolts, then the A/C compressor bracket.
14. Remove upper and lower radiator hoses from vehicle.
15. Remove radiator overflow hose from radiator, then the radiator shroud clips.

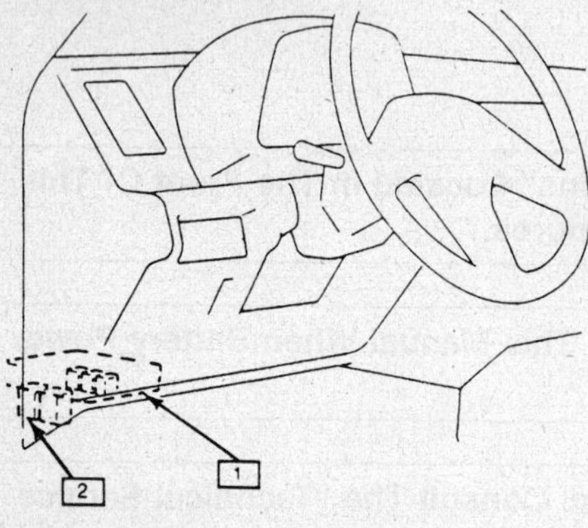

Fig. 1 Fuel pump relay connection

16. Remove bolt from radiator upper support, then lean fan shroud toward engine and lift radiator up and out of vehicle.
17. Remove fan mounting nuts, then use a second wrench to hold fan shaft.
18. Remove fan and shroud from vehicle.
19. Loosen adjusting and pivot bolts, then remove tension on fan belt by rotating tension bolt counterclockwise.
20. Remove fan belt, then the tensioner mounting bolts and tensioner.
21. Rotate belt tensioner clockwise and remove accessory drive belt.
22. Remove bolt and throttle cable bracket from intake manifold.
23. Remove cables from throttle body bellcrank and position aside.
24. Remove power steering pressure and return lines from power steering pump, then position aside.
25. Disconnect electrical connectors from intake air temperature and mass air flow sensors.
26. Remove air inlet duct from air cleaner cover, then disconnect EVAP system vent hose from air cleaner cover.
27. Remove air cleaner cover, then the air cleaner lower assembly from vehicle.
28. Remove heater hoses from heater core, then disconnect fuel feed and return hoses.
29. Disconnect electrical connectors from ignition coils, fuel injector wiring harness, throttle position and manifold absolute pressure sensors.
30. Disconnect electrical connectors from idle air control, exhaust gas recirculation valves and engine coolant temperature sensor.
31. Disconnect electrical connectors from EVAP canister purge valve, heated oxygen and camshaft position sensors.
32. Disconnect electrical connectors from power steering pressure switch, alternator and oil pressure switch.
33. Remove ground wires, then the EVAP canister purge hose from intake manifold.
34. Remove wiring harness from retaining clamps, then the brake booster vacuum line from intake manifold.
35. Remove starter motor as outlined in "Electrical" section.
36. Disconnect crankshaft position sensor electrical connector.
37. Remove cylinder block to transmission bolt and nuts, then the nuts from top side of engine mounts.
38. Install an engine hoist to engine, then remove engine assembly from vehicle.
39. Reverse procedure to install.

INTAKE MANIFOLD

REPLACE

1. Relieve fuel pressure as outlined in "Precautions."
2. Drain engine cooling system.
3. Remove air cleaner.
4. Disconnect intake manifold ground wires, MAP sensor, TP sensor, IAC valve, ECT sensor, EVAP canister purge valve and EGR valve electrical connectors.
5. Remove bolt and throttle cable bracket from manifold.
6. Remove throttle cables from bellcrank.
7. Remove EVAP canister purge hose and vacuum line from manifold.
8. Remove EVAP solenoid.
9. Remove coolant hoses from manifold and throttle body.
10. Remove brake booster hose from manifold.
11. Remove fuel line bracket to intake manifold mounting bolt and fuel return line to fuel rail mounting bolts.
12. Remove banjo fitting and washer from rear end of fuel rail.
13. Remove front support bracket from manifold, **Fig. 3.**
14. Remove intake mounting nuts, bolts and intake manifold.
15. Reverse procedure to install.

EXHAUST MANIFOLD

REPLACE

1. Remove mounting bolts, nuts and manifold heat shield.
2. Remove mounting nuts and separate front pipe from manifold.
3. Disconnect oxygen sensor.
4. Remove mounting bolt, nuts and exhaust manifold.
5. Reverse procedure to install.

CYLINDER HEAD

REPLACE

1. Relieve fuel pressure as outlined in "Precautions."
2. Drain cooling system and engine oil.
3. Remove cooling fan and shroud.
4. Remove drive belt as outlined in "Drive Belt, Replace."
5. Remove water pump as outlined in "Water Pump, Replace."
6. Remove bypass hose from coolant outlet pipe.
7. Remove crankshaft bolt and pulley.
8. Remove mounting bolts and air conditioning compressor from bracket. Set compressor aside.
9. Remove air conditioning compressor bracket.
10. Remove air cleaner hose.

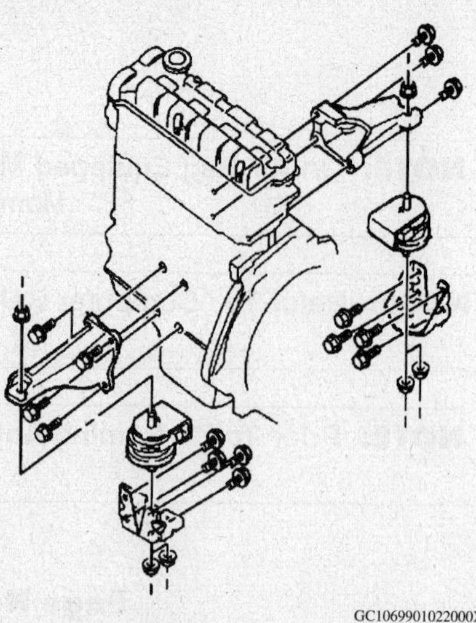

Fig. 2 Engine mounts

11. Remove intake manifold as outlined in "Intake Manifold, Replace."
12. Remove exhaust manifold as outlined in "Exhaust Manifold, Replace."
13. Remove cylinder head cover.
14. Remove spark plugs.
15. Apply match marks to camshaft sensor and cylinder head for assembly reference.
16. Remove timing chain housing.
17. Remove timing chain as outlined in "Timing Chain, Replace."
18. Remove intake camshaft and valve lifters.
19. Remove exhaust camshaft and lifters.
20. Remove cylinder head bolts in sequence, **Fig. 4.**
21. Remove cylinder head gasket.
22. Reverse procedure to install, noting the following:
    a. Clean all cylinder head and block mating surfaces.
    b. Inspect cylinder head for cracks, warpage and other damage.
    c. Replace cylinder head if warpage more than .002 inch.
    d. **Torque** cylinder head bolts to 39 ft. lbs., in sequence, **Fig. 5.**
    e. **Torque** head bolts to 61 ft. lbs., in sequence.
    f. Loosen all bolts in sequence until there is zero torque.
    g. **Torque** cylinder head bolts to 39 ft. lbs., in sequence.
    h. **Torque** head bolts to 76 ft. lbs., in sequence.
    i. **Torque** cylinder head bolt No. 11 to 84 inch lbs.

VALVE COVER

REPLACE

1. Disconnect and remove ignition coils.
2. Remove accelerator cable from clip on valve cover.
3. Remove PCV hoses.
4. Remove valve cover cap bolts and washers.
5. Remove valve cover, gasket and O-rings, **Fig. 6.**
6. Reverse procedure to install.

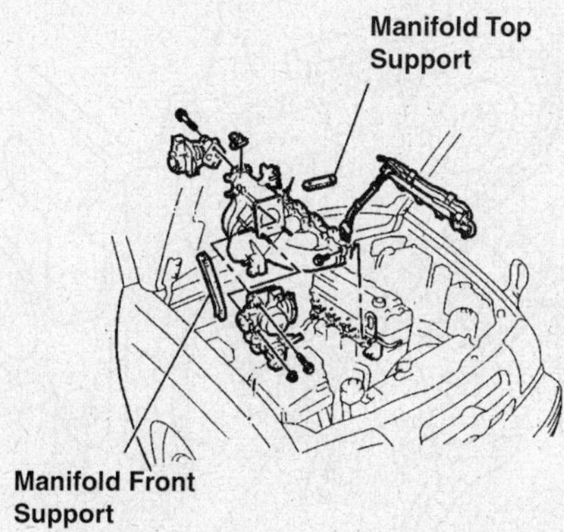

Fig. 3 Intake manifold removal

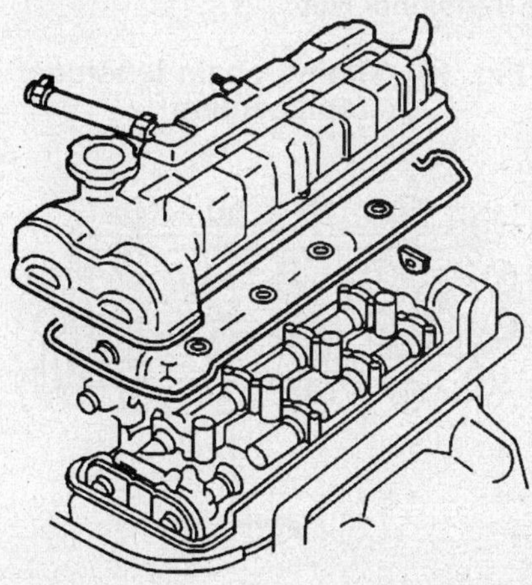

Fig. 6 Valve cover replacement

VALVE CLEARANCE SPECIFICATIONS

Engine is equipped with hydraulic lash adjusters, valve clearance is zero.

VALVE ADJUSTMENT

Engine is equipped with hydraulic lash adjusters, no adjustment is required.

FRONT COVER

REPLACE

Refer to "Timing Chain, Replace" for front cover replacement procedure.

FRONT COVER SEAL

REPLACE

1. Remove crankshaft pulley as outlined in "Timing Chain, Replace."
2. Pry seal from front cover using suitable screwdriver.
3. Lubricate new seal with suitable chassis grease.
4. Lightly tap seal into place flush with oil seal retainer using suitable hammer and seal driver, **Fig. 7.**
5. Install crankshaft pulley.

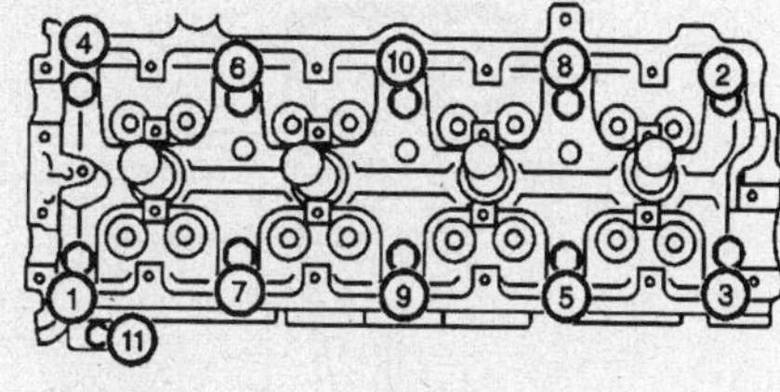

Fig. 4 Cylinder head bolt removal sequence

TIMING CHAIN

REPLACE

1. Remove steering gear as outlined in "Front Suspension & Steering" section.
2. Drain cooling system.
3. Drain engine oil.
4. Remove oil pan as outlined in "Oil Pan, Replace."
5. Remove cooling fan and shroud.
6. Remove accessory drive belt.
7. Remove drive belt idler pulley.
8. Remove mounting bolts and water pump pulley.
9. Remove bypass hose from coolant outlet pipe.
10. Remove crankshaft bolt and pulley using pinion flange holder tool No. J-8614-01, or equivalent, **Fig. 8.**
11. Remove mounting bolts and air conditioning compressor from bracket. Set compressor set aside.
12. Remove air conditioning compressor bracket.
13. Remove valve cover as outlined in "Valve Cover, Replace."
14. Remove spark plugs.
15. Remove mounting bolts and timing chain cover.
16. Align timing marks before removing timing chains.
17. Rotate crankshaft until the following conditions are met:
    a. Cylinder No. 1 is at top dead center.
    b. Crankshaft keyway aligns with engine block mark, **Fig. 9.**
    c. Arrow on idler sprocket is pointing upward.
    d. Guide pins on camshaft sprockets are aligned with notches on cylinder head.
18. Relieve tension on camshaft timing chain by turning intake camshaft slightly counterclockwise.
19. Remove nut and bolts from timing chain tensioner, **Fig. 10.**
20. Remove timing chain tensioner.
21. Holding camshaft with suitable wrench, remove camshaft sprocket bolts.
22. Remove camshaft sprockets and chain.
23. Remove mounting bolts and crankshaft timing chain tensioner, **Fig. 11.**
24. Remove mounting bolt and adjustable crankshaft timing chain guide.

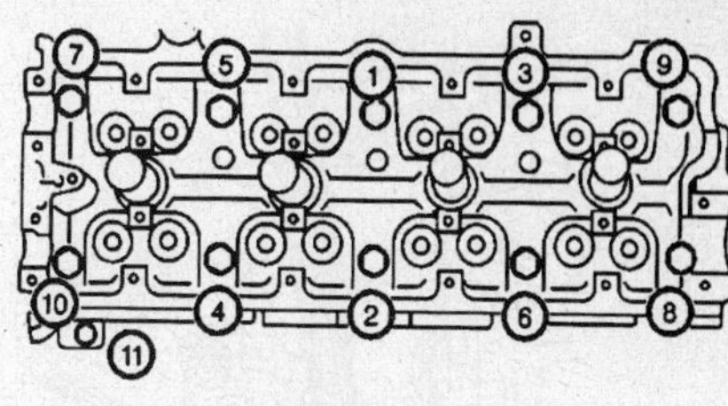

Fig. 5 Cylinder head bolt tightening sequence

Fig. 7 Front cover seal installation

25. Remove mounting bolts and fixed chain guide.
26. Remove idler sprocket and crankshaft timing chain.
27. Reverse procedure to install.

CAMSHAFT

REPLACE

1. Remove camshaft timing chain as outlined in "Timing Chain, Replace."
2. Loosen camshaft bearing caps in sequence, **Fig. 12.**
3. Remove bearing caps and camshaft.
4. Reverse procedure to install, noting the following:
    a. Ensure timing marks are properly aligned as outlined in "Timing Chain, Replace."
    b. Apply clean engine oil to all journals, lobes and lifters.
    c. **Torque** bearing caps in three progressive steps to 96 inch lbs., in sequence, **Fig. 13.**

PISTON & ROD ASSEMBLY

Pistons are available in two different oversizes, 3.3157–3.3165 inches and 3.3256–3.263 inches.

MAIN & ROD BEARINGS

Main bearings are available in three different undersizes, 2.2729–2.2731 inches, 2.2731–2.2733 inches and 2.734–2.2736 inches.

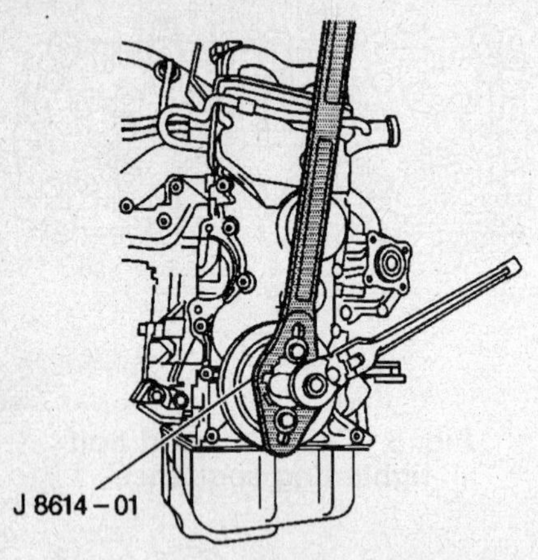

GC1069901027000X

Fig. 8 Crankshaft pulley replacement

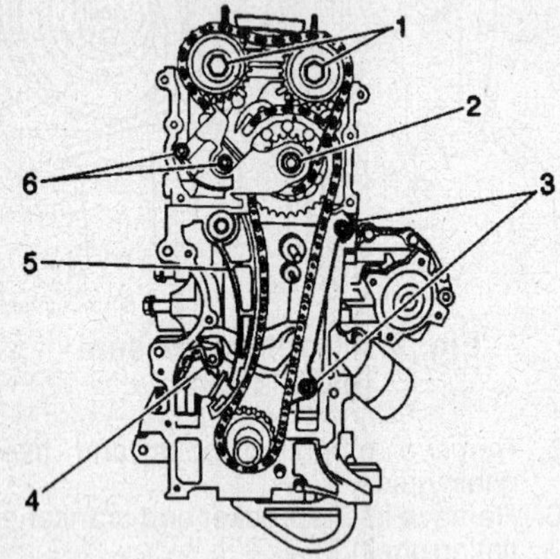

1. **Camshaft Sprocket Bolts**
2. **Camshaft Tensioner Nut**
3. **Chain Guide**
4. **Crankshaft Timing Chain Tensioner**
5. **Adjustable Chain Guide**
6. **Camshaft Tensioner Bolts**

GC1069901030000X

Fig. 11 Timing chain & related components

1. **Torque** main bearing cap bolts to 16 ft. lbs., in sequence, **Fig. 14.**
2. **Torque** bolts to 32 ft. lbs., in sequence.
3. Final **torque** bolts to 44 ft. lbs., in sequence.

CRANKSHAFT REAR OIL SEAL

REPLACE

Removal

1. Remove transmission as outlined in **MOTOR's "Domestic Transmission, In-Vehicle Service" or "Transmission Service DVD."**
2. Remove flywheel.
3. Pry out rear oil seal using suitable screwdriver.

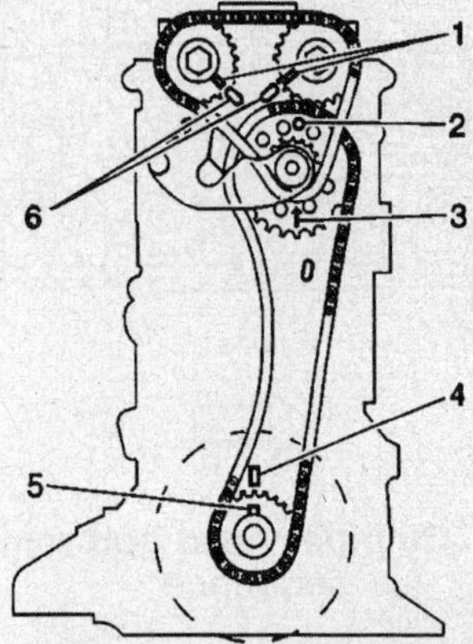

1. **Camshaft Timing Mark**
2. **Idler Sprocket Timing Mark**
3. **Idler Sprocket Arrow**
4. **Engine Block Timing Mark**
5. **Crankshaft Keyway**
6. **Cylinder Head Notches**

GC1069901028000X

Fig. 9 Timing mark alignment

Installation

1. Apply suitable multi-purpose grease to new seal.
2. Position new seal over end of crankshaft.
3. Lightly tap seal into place using seal installer tool No. J-41172, or equivalent.
4. Install flywheel and transmission.

OIL PAN

REPLACE

1. Remove oil dipstick.
2. Raise and support vehicle.
3. Remove front skid plate.
4. Remove steering gear as outlined in "Front Suspension & Steering."
5. Drain engine oil.
6. Remove flywheel inspection cover.
7. Remove oil pan mounting bolts and nuts.
8. Reverse procedure to install, noting the following:
   a. Apply continuous bead of silicon sealant to engine oil pan mating surface, **Fig. 15.**

OIL PUMP

REPLACE

1. Remove oil pan as outlined in "Oil Pan, Replace."
2. Remove three mounting bolts and oil pump strainer.
3. Remove four mounting bolts and oil pump chain cover.
4. Remove three mounting bolts and oil pump.
5. Reverse procedure to install.

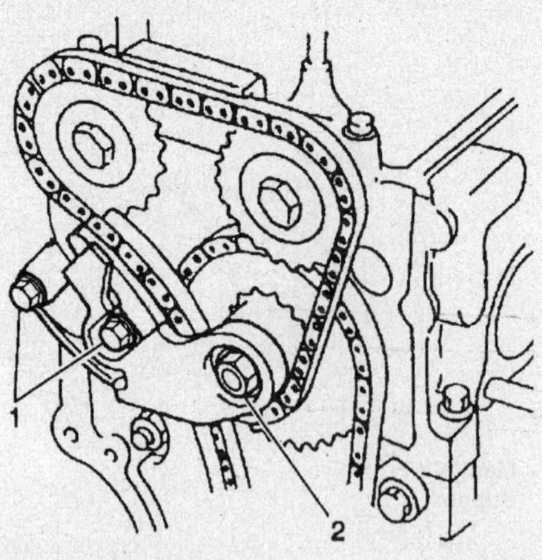

1. **Tensioner Bolts**
2. **Tensioner Nut**

GC1069901029000X

Fig. 10 Timing chain tensioner replacement

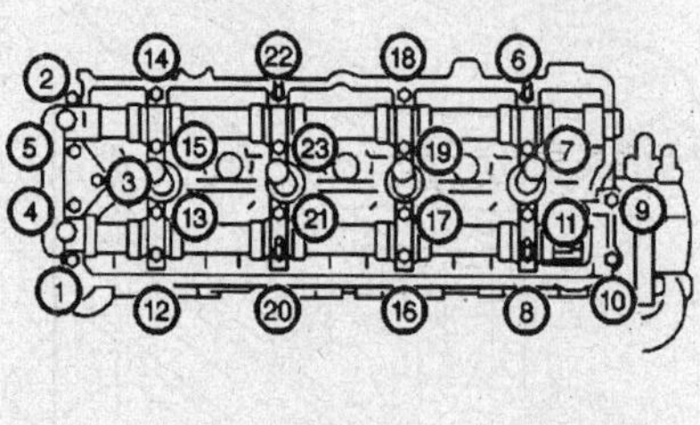

GC1069901032000X

Fig. 12 Camshaft bearing cap removal sequence

BELT TENSION DATA

Tighten new belts to a deflection of .20–.27 inch at 22 lbs., using a suitable belt tension gauge. Tighten used belts to a deflection of .24–.32 inch at 22 lbs., of tension.

COOLING SYSTEM BLEED

These engines do not require a specified bleed procedure. After filling cooling system, run engine to operating temperature with radiator/pressure cap off. Air will then be automatically bled through cap opening.

THERMOSTAT

REPLACE

1. Drain cooling system.
2. Remove clamp and radiator hose from thermostat housing.
3. Remove mounting bolts and thermostat housing.
4. Remove thermostat.
5. Reverse procedure to install.

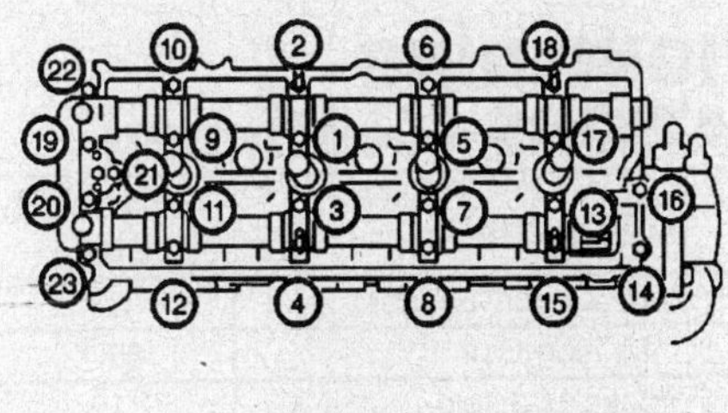

GC1069901033000X

Fig. 13 Camshaft tightening sequence

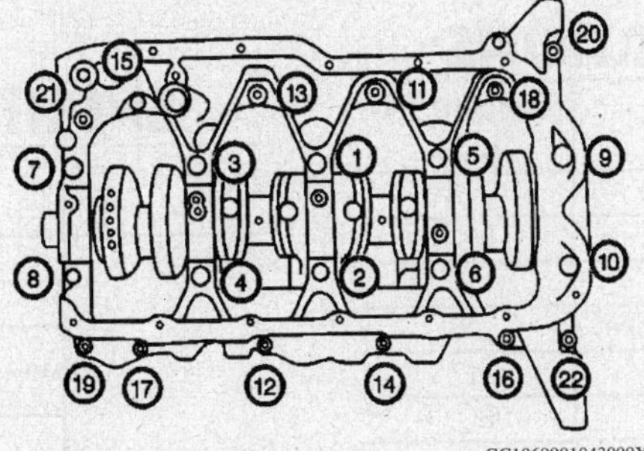
GC1069901043000X

Fig. 14 Main bearing cap bolt tightening sequence

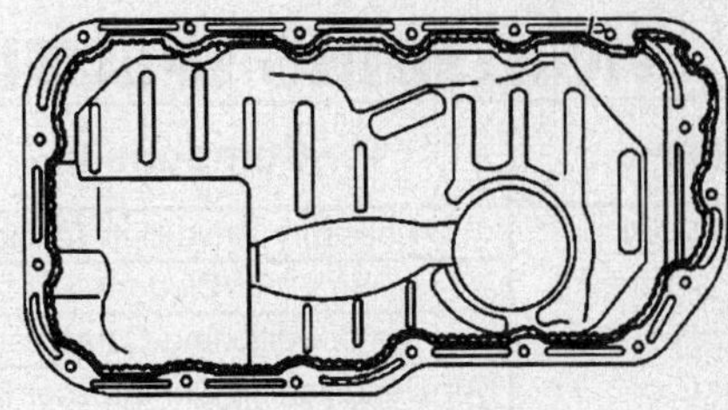
GC1069901034000X

Fig. 15 Oil pan sealant application

WATER PUMP

REPLACE

1. Drain cooling system.
2. Remove accessory drive belt.
3. Remove radiator inlet and outlet hoses.
4. Remove mounting bolt and heater outlet line from rear of water pump housing.
5. Remove mounting bolts and air conditioning compressor. Position compressor aside.
6. Remove mounting bolts and water pump.
7. Reverse procedure to install.

RADIATOR

REPLACE

Before servicing any electrical component, ignition key must be in off or lock position and all electrical loads must be off, unless instructed otherwise in these procedures. If a tool or equipment could easily come in contact with a live exposed electrical terminal, also disconnect battery ground. Failure to follow these precautions may cause personal injury and/or damage to vehicle or its components. To avoid being burned, do not remove radiator cap or surge tank cap while engine is hot. Cooling system will release scalding fluid and steam under pressure if radiator cap or surge tank cap is removed while engine and radiator are still hot.

1. Remove radiator cap.
2. Raise and support vehicle.
3. Remove lower radiator shroud clips.
4. Open drain plug.
5. Drain cooing system into a suitable container.
6. Close drain plug.
7. Remove transmission oil cooler lines from bottom of radiator (automatic transmission only). Cap open lines to prevent leakage.
8. Remove lower radiator hose.
9. Lower vehicle then remove radiator overflow hose.
10. Remove upper radiator hose.
11. Remove upper two radiator shroud clips.
12. Remove one bolt from each side of radiator.
13. Lean fan shroud toward engine and lift radiator up and out of vehicle. **Do not damage radiator on fan during removal.**
14. Reverse procedure to install.

FUEL PUMP

REPLACE

Fuel pump and fuel level sensor are integral components of fuel sender assembly. In order to service fuel pump or fuel level sensor, replace fuel sender assembly.

1. Remove fuel tank.
2. Disconnect fuel supply line from fuel sender assembly.
3. Disconnect fuel return line from fuel sender assembly.
4. Disconnect electrical connector from fuel sender assembly.
5. Remove six bolts retaining fuel sender assembly.
6. Remove fuel sender assembly.
7. Remove fuel sender assembly gasket.
8. Reverse procedure to install.

FUEL FILTER

REPLACE

1. Relieve fuel system pressure. **Before servicing any electrical component, ignition key must be in off or lock position and all electrical loads must be off, unless instructed otherwise in these procedures. If a tool or equipment could easily come in contact with a live exposed electrical terminal, also disconnect battery ground. Failure to follow these precautions may cause personal injury and/or damage to vehicle or its components.**
2. Raise and support vehicle on a hoist. **To avoid vehicle damage, serious personal injury or death when major components are removed from vehicle and vehicle is supported by a hoist, support vehicle whit jack stands at opposite end from which components are being removed.**
3. Disconnect fuel inlet hose from fuel filter.
4. Disconnect fuel outlet hose from fuel filter.
5. Remove retaining bolt from fuel filter bracket.
6. Loosen fuel filter bracket bolt and remove fuel filter from bracket.
7. Reverse procedure to install.

TIGHTENING SPECIFICATIONS

Year	Component	Torque Ft. Lbs.
2002-04	Accessory Drive Belt Tensioner	19
	Air Cleaner	89①
	Air Conditioning Compressor	17
	Air Conditioning Compressor Bracket	40
	Alternator	17
	Camshaft Bearing Cap	96①④
	Camshaft Position Sensor	11
	Camshaft Timing Sprocket	58
	Connecting Rod Cap Nuts	33
	Coolant Bypass Pipe To Cylinder Head	11
	Cooling Fan	96①
	Cooling Fan Drive Belt Tensioner	33
	Crankshaft Position Sensor	53①
	Cylinder Head	②
	Drive Belt Idler Pulley	33
	Drive Belt Tensioner	18
	Engine Ground	11
	Engine Mount Bracket, Engine Side	37
	Engine Mount Bracket, Body Side	62
	Engine Mount, Nut	37
	Engine Oil Drain Plug	26
	Exhaust Manifold Heat Shield	11
	Exhaust Manifold Flange	37
	Exhaust Manifold To Cylinder Head	37
	Exhaust Manifold To Bracket	37
	Exhaust Pipe To Catalytic Converter	37
	Flywheel	51
	Fuel Pump	60①
	Fuel Pump Inlet & Outlet Hoses	26
	Fuel Rail Banjo Fitting	22
	Fuel Rail To Cylinder Head	17
	Fuel Tank Shield	26
	Fuel Tank Strap	26

TIGHTENING SPECIFICATIONS—Continued

Year	Component	Torque Ft. Lbs.
2002–04	Heated Oxygen Sensor	33
	Ignition Coil	89①
	Intake Manifold	19
	Intake Manifold Support, Front	33
	Intake Manifold Support, Top	11
	Lower Crankcase	⑤
	Main Bearing Cap	③
	Oil Filter Adaptor	17
	Oil Pan	97①
	Oil Pressure Switch	11
	Oil Pump	20
	Oil Pump Case	106①
	Oil Pump Relief Valve Retainer	21
	Oil Pump Strainer	97①
	Oil Pump Sprocket	97①
	Power Steering Pump	19
	Spark Plugs	18
	Starter	22
	Strut Tower Brace	37
	Throttle Body	19
	Timing Chain Cover	97①
	Timing Chain Tensioner, Camshaft Bolt	97①
	Timing Chain Tensioner, Camshaft Nut	33
	Timing Chain Tensioner, Crankshaft	97①
	Timing Chain Tensioner, Guide Bolt	①
	Timing Chain Tensioner Shoe	19
	Torque Converter	47
	Transmission To Engine	62
	Transmission Bracket	37
	Water Pump	20

①— Inch lbs.
②— Refer to "Cylinder Head, Replace" for tightening procedure.
③— Refer to "Main & Rod Bearings" for tightening procedure.
④— Refer to "Camshaft, Replace" for tightening sequence.
⑤— First pass to 14 ft. lbs.; second pass to 20 ft. lbs.

2.5L Engine

NOTE: On Air Bag Equipped Models, Refer To "Air Bag System Precautions" Located In The Front Of This Manual For System Disarming & Arming Procedures.

NOTE: Refer To "Computer Relearn Procedures" Located In The Front Of This Manual When Battery Power To The Computer Has Been Interrupted.

INDEX

PRECAUTIONS

Fuel System Pressure Relief

1. Remove fuel filler cap to relieve fuel tank pressure. Replace cap when pressure is released.
2. Disconnect fuel pump relay from junction box .
3. Place transmission in neutral or park, set parking brake and block wheels.
4. Start engine and allow to runout of fuel.
5. Crank engine an additional three seconds to discharge any remaining fuel system pressure.
6. Upon completion of servicing, connect fuel pump relay electrical connector.

Battery Ground Cable

Prior to service disconnect battery ground cable and isolate as required.

COMPRESSION PRESSURE

This engine is equipped with an aluminum cylinder head. Allow the engine to cool before removing spark plugs.

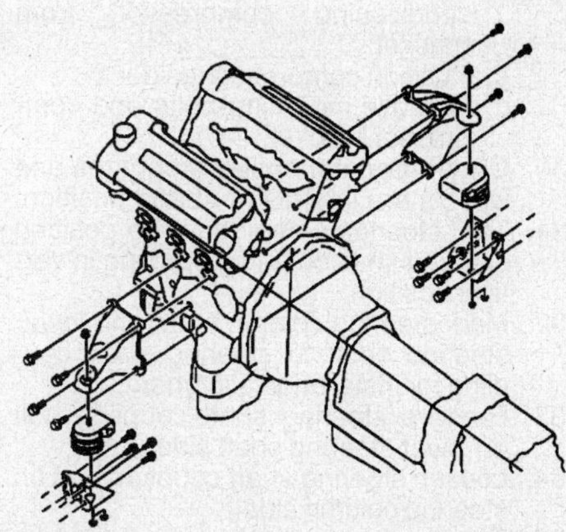

Fig. 1 Engine mount replacement

1. Remove fuel pump relay.
2. Disconnect electrical connectors and ignition coils.
3. Remove spark plugs.
4. Install suitable compression gauge into spark plug hole.
5. **On models equipped with manual transmission,** depress clutch pedal.
6. **On all models,** depress accelerator pedal to floor for Wide Open Throttle.
7. Crank engine through four compression strokes for each cylinder being tested.
8. Measure and record highest pressure reading on compression gauge, noting the following
   a. Standard compression pressure should be 199–227 psi.
   b. Minimum compression pressure should be 185 psi.
   c. Maximum allowable compression pressure difference between any two cylinders is 15 psi.

ENGINE MOUNT

REPLACE

1. Remove engine mount top nut.
2. Raise and support vehicle.
3. Support engine using suitable engine support stand.
4. Remove engine mount bottom nuts, **Fig. 1.**
5. Raise engine slightly to provide clearance.
6. Remove lefthand side engine mount.
7. Remove oil dipstick and tube mounting bolt.
8. Remove engine block bracket bolts.
9. Remove mounting bolts and body mount bracket.
10. Reverse procedure to install.

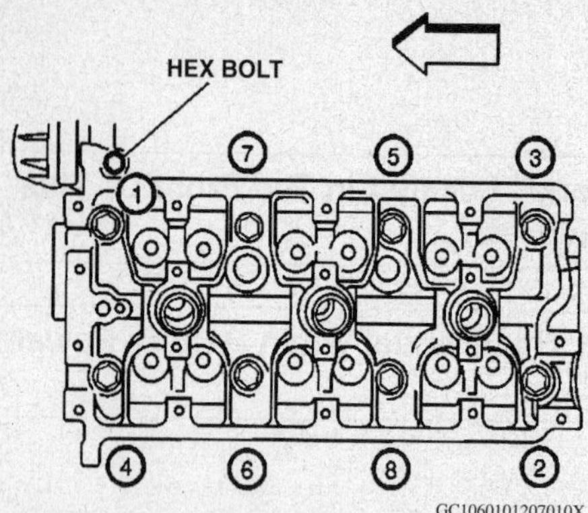

Fig. 2 Cylinder head bolt removal sequence

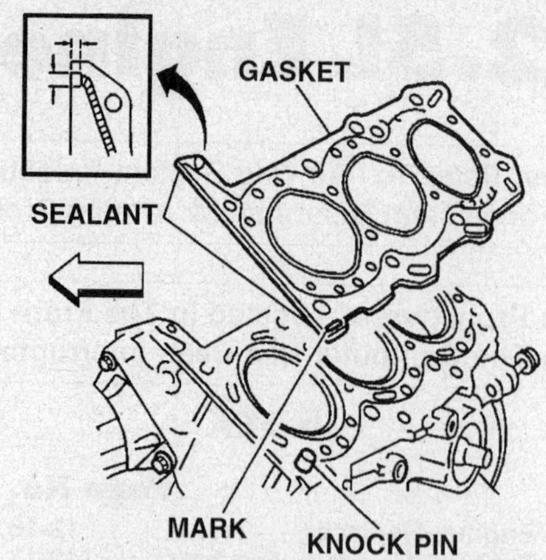

Fig. 3 Cylinder head sealant

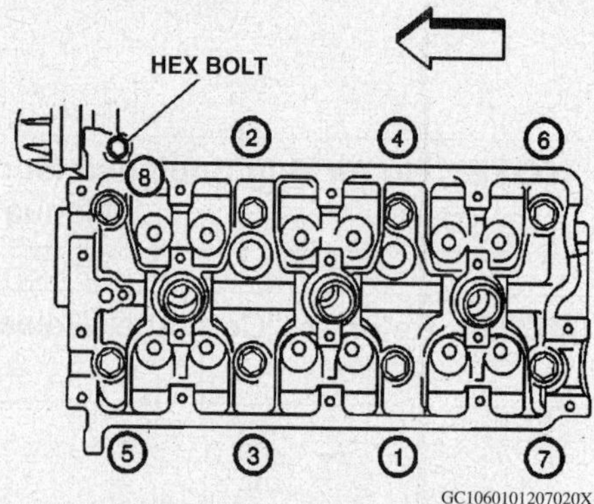

Fig. 4 Cylinder head bolt tightening sequence

ENGINE

REPLACE

1. Relieve fuel pressure as outlined in "Precautions."
2. Remove hood, then raise and support vehicle.
3. Remove front skid plate.
4. Drain engine oil and cooling system into suitable containers.
5. Remove automatic transmission fluid cooler lines from radiator. Cap open lines.
6. Lower vehicle.
7. Remove radiator as outlined in "Radiator, Replace."
8. Disconnect accelerator and automatic transmission throttle cables.
9. Raise and support vehicle.
10. Remove mounting bolts and strut tower brace.
11. Lower vehicle.
12. Remove mounting screws and surge tank cover.
13. Disconnect Intake Air Temperature sensor connector.
14. Remove surge tank pipe mounting nuts.
15. Remove air cleaner upper case, intake air hose, intake air pipe and surge tank pipe as an assembly.
16. Remove mounting bolt, engine oil dipstick and tube.
17. Remove mounting bolt, transmission fluid level indicator and tube.
18. Remove ignition coil covers.
19. Disconnect injector wire connector and brake booster vacuum hose.
20. Disconnect Camshaft Position Sensor, ignition coils, Throttle Position Sensor, Mass Air Flow sensor and Idle Air Control valve electrical connectors
21. Disconnect surge tank ground wires.
22. Remove clamp bracket, then disconnect EVAP canister purge valve, EGR valve, oxygen sensor, coolant temperature sensor, alternator wires, starter wires, oil pressure switch wire and power steering pressure switch wire electrical connectors.
23. Remove alternator bracket ground wire.
24. Remove clamp brackets, then disconnect heater hose from heater water pipe and water outlet cap, and EVAP canister hose from canister pipe.
25. Remove IAC and EVAP canister purge valves.
26. Disconnect feed hose from fuel feed pipe and return hose from fuel return pipe.
27. Remove EVAP canister.
28. Remove mounting bolts and power steering pump from bracket. Position pump aside.
29. **On models equipped with air conditioning,** proceed as follows:
    a. **Do not discharge air conditioning system or remove compressor refrigerant lines.**
    b. Remove mounting bolts and air conditioning compressor from bracket.
    c. Position compressor aside.
    d. Remove mounting bolts and compressor bracket.
30. **On all models,** ensure front tires and wheels are in straight ahead position.
31. Turn steering wheel to left to position steering shaft coupling opening in vertical position.
32. Mark steering column shaft and lower steering shaft to steering shaft coupling for installation alignment.
33. Remove steering shaft coupling bolt on lower steering shaft side.
34. Loosen steering shaft coupling bolt on steering column side.
35. Release lower steering shaft by tapping steering shaft coupling onto steering column shaft using suitable plastic hammer.
36. Secure coupling on steering column shaft with bolt.
37. Mark pinion shaft and steering gear housing to align pinion shaft during installation.
38. Remove lower bolt and lower steering shaft.
39. Raise and support vehicle.
40. **On models equipped with 4WD,** remove front axle housing as outlined in "Front Wheel Drive."
41. **On all models,** remove front exhaust pipe and exhaust manifold bracket from transmission.
42. Remove transmission fluid hose clamps from engine mounting bracket.
43. Remove flywheel cover and torque converter bolts.
44. Lock flywheel using suitable screw driver.
45. Remove mounting bolts and starting motor.
46. Lower vehicle and support transmission.
47. Remove transmission to cylinder block mounting bolts and nuts.
48. Support engine with suitable hoist.
49. Remove engine mounts top side nuts.
50. Ensure hoses, pipes, electrical wires and cables are disconnected from engine and positioned aside.
51. Remove engine assembly by sliding it toward front of engine compartment, then lift engine from vehicle, ensure clearance on all sides.
52. Reverse procedure to install, noting the following:
    a. Apply sealant No. 12345493, or equivalent, to flywheel mounting bolt threads. **Do not apply excessive sealant to flywheel mounting bolt threads.**
    b. Lock flywheel using fly wheel holder tool No. J-35271, or equivalent.

INTAKE MANIFOLD

REPLACE

1. Relieve fuel pressure as outlined in "Precautions."
2. Drain coolant into suitable container.
3. Partially raise and support vehicle. Allow suspension to hang free.
4. Remove mounting bolts and front suspension support brace.
5. Remove mounting screws and fuel injector sight shield.
6. Remove air cleaner upper case, intake air hose, intake air pipe and surge tank pipe as an assembly.
7. Disconnect accelerator and automatic transmission throttle cables from throttle body.
8. Disconnect water hoses from throttle body.
9. Disconnect injector wire coupler and brake booster hose from intake manifold.
10. Disconnect Throttle Position Sensor, Mass Air Flow sensor and Idle Air Control valve electrical connectors.
11. Disconnect intake collector ground terminal and clamp bracket.

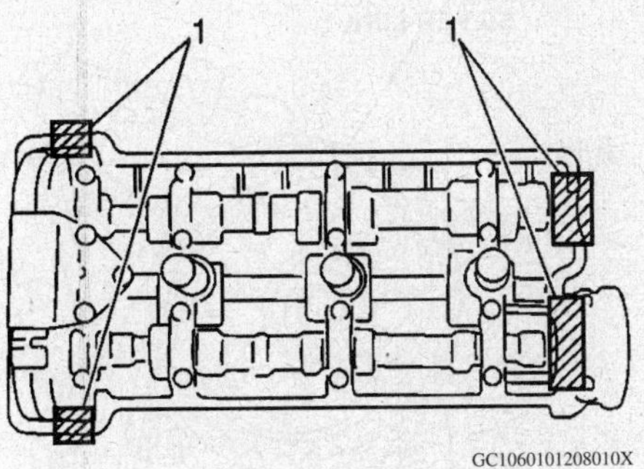

Fig. 5 Valve cover sealant application. Lefthand

12. Disconnect Manifold Differential Pressure sensor, EVAP canister purge valve and Exhaust Gas Recirculation valve electrical connectors.
13. Disconnect PCV hose from cylinder head cover, breather hose from throttle body, EVAP canister purge valve hose, water hose and heater hoses.
14. Remove EGR pipe.
15. Disconnect heater hose , EVAP canister hose, fuel feed hose, fuel return hose and tank pressure control solenoid valve hose.
16. Disconnect hose and remove Idle Air Control valve.
17. Remove mounting nuts and bolts, then the intake collector and throttle body as an assembly.
18. Remove mounting bolts, nuts and intake manifold.
19. Reverse procedure to install. Install new intake manifold and throttle body gaskets.

EXHAUST MANIFOLD

REPLACE

Left

1. Remove oil dipstick and tube.
2. Remove mounting bolts and exhaust manifold cover.
3. Detach oxygen sensor couplers from mounting bracket and disconnect oxygen sensor electrical connectors.
4. Raise and support vehicle.
5. Remove mounting bolt, nut and exhaust manifold reinforcement bracket.
6. Remove front pipe and lower vehicle.
7. Remove mounting nuts, bolts, exhaust manifold and gasket
8. Reverse procedure to install. Install new gaskets and seals.

Right

1. Remove air cleaner upper case and intake air hose, then disconnect EGR pipe.
2. Detach oxygen sensor couplers from mounting bracket and disconnect oxygen sensor electrical connectors.
3. Remove mounting bolts and exhaust manifold cover.
4. Raise and support vehicle.
5. Remove mounting bolt, nut and exhaust manifold reinforcement bracket.
6. Remove front pipe and lower vehicle.

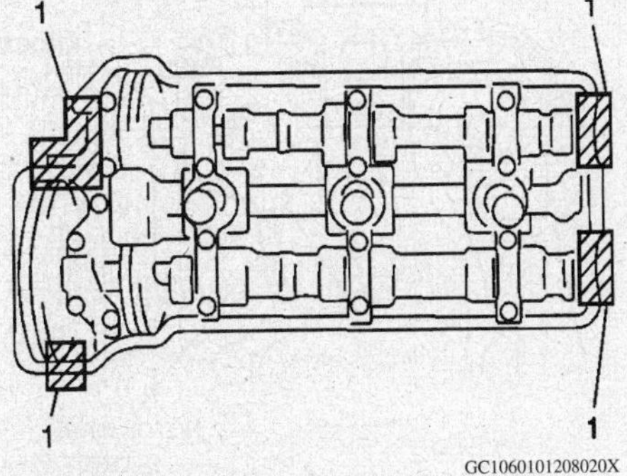

Fig. 6 Valve cover sealant application. Righthand

7. Remove mounting nuts, bolts, exhaust manifold and gasket
8. Reverse procedure to install. Install new gaskets and seals.

CYLINDER HEAD

REPLACE

1. Remove camshafts as outlined in "Camshaft, Replace."
2. Remove lifters as outlined in "Hydraulic Lifters, Replace."
3. Remove exhaust manifold as outlined in "Exhaust Manifold, Replace."
4. Drain engine coolant into suitable container.
5. Remove intake manifold as outlined in "Intake Manifold, Replace."
6. Remove throttle body water and heater outlet hoses.
7. Disconnect coolant temperature sensor electrical connector.
8. Remove bypass hoses.
9. Remove mounting nuts, bolts and water crossover.
10. Remove hex bolt, head bolts in sequence and cylinder head, **Fig. 2.**
11. Reverse procedure to install, noting the following:
    a. Install knock pin to cylinder block, **Fig. 3.**
    b. Apply sealant to cylinder head gasket.
    c. Install gasket with 86FA mark facing up.
    d. Apply clean engine oil to cylinder head bolt threads.
    e. **Torque** cylinder head bolts to 39 ft. lbs., in sequence, **Fig. 4.**
    f. **Torque** head bolts to 61 ft. lbs., in sequence.
    g. Loosen cylinder head bolts in reverse sequence to zero ft. lbs., of torque.
    h. **Torque** cylinder head bolts to 39 ft. lbs., in sequence.
    i. **Torque** head bolts to 61 ft. lbs., in sequence.
    j. **Torque** bolts to 76 ft. lbs., in sequence.
    k. **Torque** hex bolt 97 inch lbs.

VALVE COVER

REPLACE

1. Remove throttle body and intake manifold as outlined in "Intake Manifold, Replace."

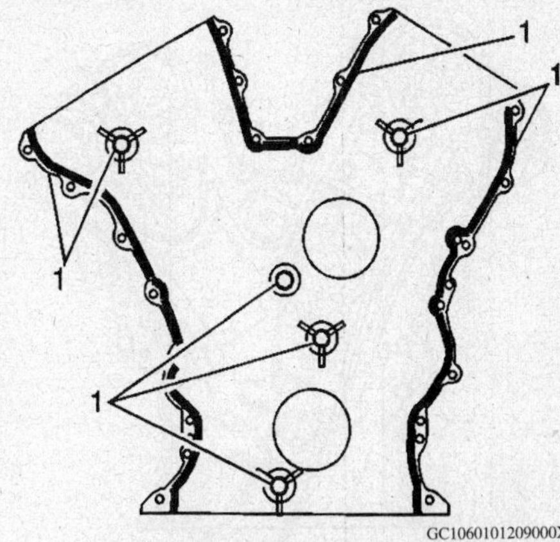

Fig. 7 Front cover sealant application

2. Remove ignition coil cover and disconnect ignition coil couplers. Remove ignition coils.
3. Remove mounting nuts and camshaft cover.
4. Reverse procedure to install, noting the following:
    a. Apply sealant part No. 12346240, or equivalent, to cylinder head, **Figs. 5 and 6.**
    b. Install new camshaft cover gasket and head side seals.

VALVE CLEARANCE SPECIFICATIONS

Engine is equipped with hydraulic lash adjusters, valve clearance is zero.

VALVE ADJUSTMENT

Engine is equipped with hydraulic lash adjusters, no adjustment is required.

HYDRAULIC LIFTERS

REPLACE

1. Remove front cover as outlined in "Front Cover, Replace."
2. Remove spark plugs.
3. Remove lefthand secondary drive chain as outlined in "Timing Chain, Replace."
4. If removing lifters from righthand side, remove primary drive chain and righthand sprocket as outlined in "Timing Chain, Replace."
5. Remove camshafts as outlined in "Camshaft, Replace."
6. Mark lifters for installation reference.
7. Remove lifters.
8. Reverse procedure to install, noting the following:
    a. Pour suitable engine oil into oil feed hole to flush debris from gallery and to prelube bore.
    b. Apply suitable engine oil to valve lifter and install in same bore from which it was removed.
    c. **Do not turn camshafts or start engine for approximately 30 minutes after replacing valve lifters and camshafts.**

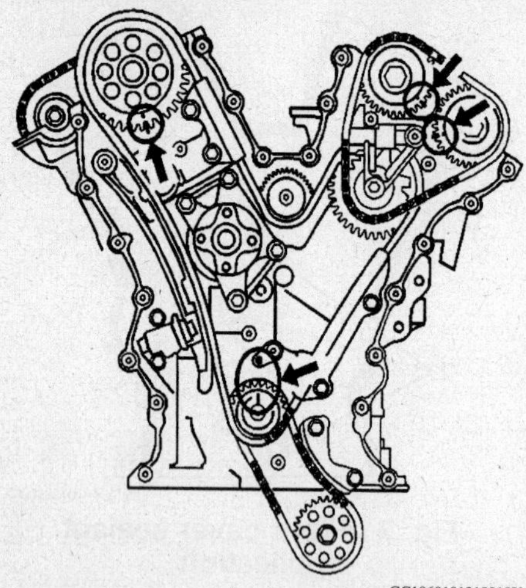

Fig. 8 Timing mark alignment

CRANKSHAFT DAMPER

REPLACE

1. Drain coolant into suitable container.
2. Remove power steering pump and cooling fan drive belts.
3. Remove fan mounting nuts and radiator shroud clips.
4. Detach power steering reservoir and position it aside.
5. Lean shroud toward engine, disconnect fan from pulley hub and remove fan/clutch assembly.
6. Remove radiator as outlined in "Radiator, Replace."
7. **Do not damage air conditioning condenser during crankshaft balancer service.**
8. Remove crankshaft damper mounting bolt using pinion flange holder tool No. J-8614-O1, or equivalent, to prevent crankshaft rotation when loosening bolt. Crankshaft may also be held by locking flywheel through access hole.
9. Remove damper.
10. Reverse procedure to install.

FRONT COVER

REPLACE

1. Drain engine oil into suitable container.
2. Remove throttle body and intake manifold as outlined in "Intake Manifold, Replace."
3. Remove lefthand and righthand valve covers as outlined in "Valve Cover, Replace."
4. Remove cooling fan and clutch as outlined in "Crankshaft Damper, Replace."
5. Remove water pump pulley.
6. Remove power steering pump and water pump drive belts.
7. Remove radiator as outlined in "Radiator, Replace."
8. Remove thermostat cap.
9. Disconnect power steering pressure switch connector.
10. Remove mounting bolts and position power steering pump aside.
11. Remove mounting bolts and power steering pump bracket.

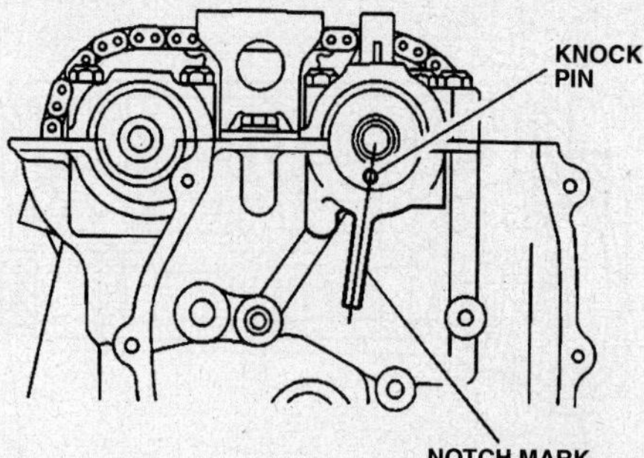

Fig. 9 Knock-pin alignment

12. Remove crankshaft damper as outlined in "Crankshaft Damper, Replace."
13. Raise and support vehicle.
14. **On models equipped with 4WD** remove front axle housing as outlined in "Front Wheel Drive."
15. **On all models,** remove oil pan as outlined in "Oil Pan, Replace."
16. Lower vehicle.
17. Disconnect connector, then remove mounting bolt and Crankshaft Position sensor.
18. Remove mounting bolts and front cover.
19. Reverse procedure to install, noting the following:
    a. Apply sealant No. 12346240, or equivalent, to front cover, **Fig. 7.**
    b. Apply engine oil to oil seal lip and water pump O-ring.
    c. Apply engine oil to CKP sensor O-ring.

FRONT COVER SEAL

REPLACE

Removal

1. Remove crankshaft damper as outlined in "Crankshaft Damper, Replace."
2. Pry crankshaft front oil seal out using suitable screwdriver with tape wrapped tip.

Installation

1. Lubricate new crankshaft front oil seal with chassis grease No. 1051344, or equivalent.
2. Lightly tap oil seal in until its surface is flush with crankshaft front oil seal retainer edge using suitable hammer and driver.
3. Install crankshaft damper.

TIMING CHAIN

REPLACE

Avoid turning the camshafts and the crankshaft once the timing chain is removed. Valve and piston damage may occur.

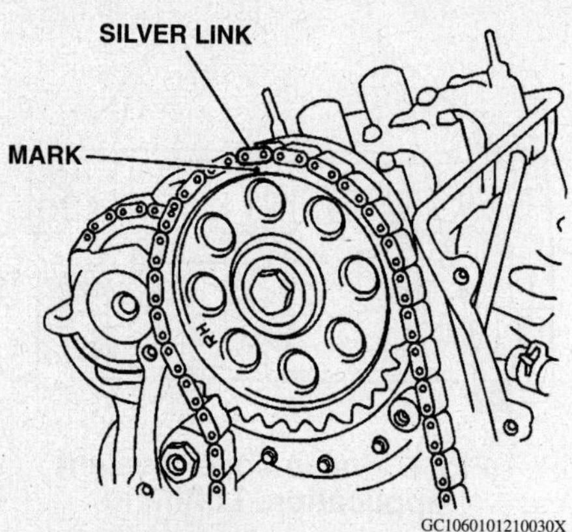

Fig. 10 Primary chain & intake sprocket alignment

Primary

REMOVAL

1. Remove front cover as outlined in "Front Cover, Replace."
2. Remove spark plugs.
3. Rotate crankshaft until timing marks are aligned, **Fig. 8.**
4. Remove lefthand secondary drive chain as outlined in "Secondary."
5. Remove drive chain guides and tensioner adjuster.
6. Remove idler sprocket and primary drive chain.
7. Remove idler sprocket and sprocket shaft.
8. Remove timing chain tensioner.
9. Remove righthand primary drive chain camshaft sprocket bolt while holding righthand intake camshaft with suitable wrench.
10. Remove righthand primary sprocket from intake camshaft.
11. Remove primary drive chain crankshaft sprocket.

INSTALLATION

1. Ensure crankshaft keyway is positioned properly.
2. Install crankshaft sprocket to crankshaft.
3. Ensure righthand intake camshaft knock-pin is aligned with match mark, **Fig. 9.**
4. Install righthand primary sprocket to intake camshaft with righthand mark facing forward.
5. Secure sprocket with bolt while holding intake camshaft with suitable wrench.
6. Install timing chain tensioner and tighten mounting nut.
7. Install primary drive chain to primary righthand intake sprocket by aligning righthand silver link on chain with sprocket mark, **Fig. 10.**
8. Apply oil to inside of idler sprocket and install it by aligning lefthand silver link with idler sprocket mark, **Fig. 11.**
9. Install primary drive chain to crankshaft sprocket by aligning chain yellow link with sprocket mark.
10. Apply oil to idler sprocket bearing, **Fig. 12.**
11. Install primary drive chain to idler

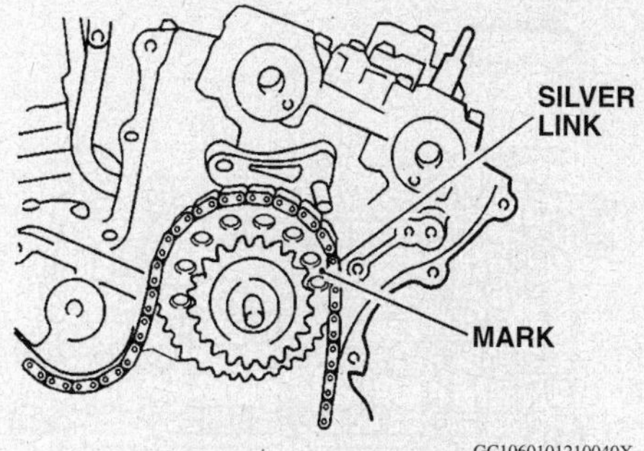

Fig. 11 Primary chain & idler sprocket alignment

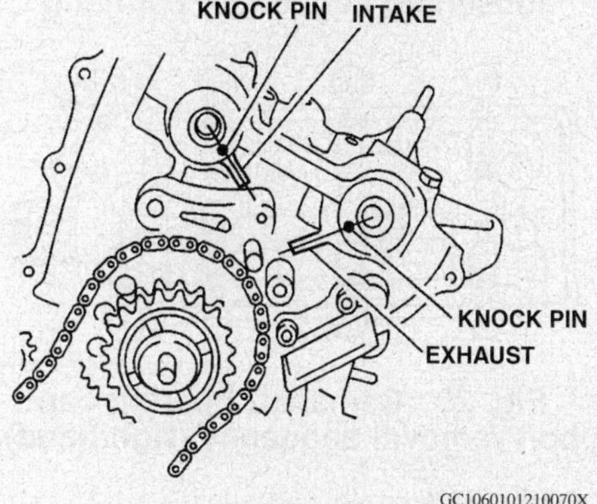

Fig. 14 Intake & exhaust camshaft knock pin alignment

sprocket and secure it with mounting bolt.

12. With tensioner adjuster latch returned and plunger pushed back into body, insert retainer (paper clip or similar tool) into set hole.
13. After inserting pin, ensure plunger will not come out.
14. Install tensioner adjuster to engine block and tensioner.
15. Secure adjuster with two bolts and tighten.
16. Remove tensioner retainer.
17. Install drive chain guides and tighten mounting bolts.
18. Ensure timing marks are properly aligned, **Fig. 8.**
19. Install lefthand secondary drive chain and tensioner.
20. Install front cover and spark plugs.

Secondary

LEFTHAND

REMOVAL

1. Remove front cover as outlined in "Front Cover, Replace."
2. Remove spark plugs.
3. Rotate crankshaft until crankshaft keyway is properly positioned, idler sprocket arrow is pointing to crankshaft and sprocket marks align with cylinder head marks, **Fig. 8.**
4. Remove mounting bolts and upper chain guide.
5. Remove mounting nut, bolts and drive chain tensioner. It may be required to slacken drive chain by turning intake camshaft counterclockwise while

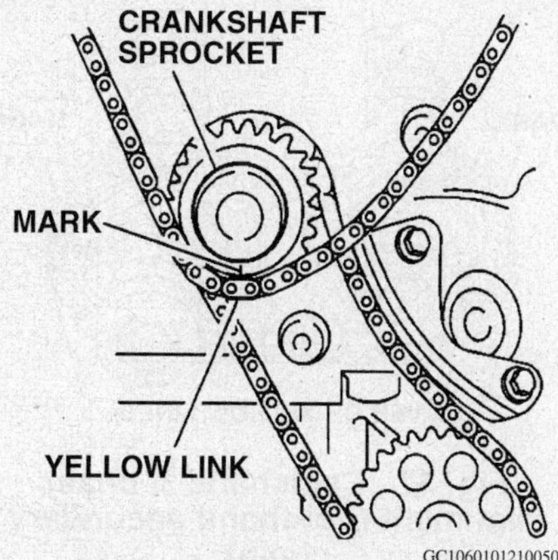

Fig. 12 Primary chain & crankshaft sprocket alignment

pushing back on tensioner pad.

6. Holding camshafts with suitable wrench, remove camshaft sprocket bolts.
7. Remove camshaft sprockets and drive chain.
8. Remove mounting bolts and side chain guide.

INSTALLATION

1. Ensure crankshaft keyway is properly aligned.
2. Ensure idler sprocket timing mark is properly aligned, **Fig. 13.**
3. Install side chain guide and tighten mounting bolts.
4. Ensure intake and exhaust camshaft knock-pins align with cylinder head match marks, **Fig. 14.**
5. Install drive chain to idler sprocket by aligning timing chain yellow link with idler sprocket mark, **Fig. 15.**
6. Install sprockets to camshafts by aligning silver links with intake and exhaust sprocket marks, **Fig. 16.**
7. Secure sprocket with bolts while holding camshafts with suitable wrench.
8. With tensioner adjuster latch returned and plunger pushed back into body, insert retainer (paper clip or similar tool) into set hole. Ensure plunger will not come out.
9. Install drive chain tensioner and tighten mounting bolt.
10. Install tensioner nuts and tighten.
11. Remove tensioner retainer.
12. Install upper chain guide and tighten mounting bolts.
13. Turn crankshaft two revolutions clockwise.
14. Align crankshaft keyway with oil jet.
15. Ensure all timing marks are properly aligned.
16. Apply engine oil to drive chains, tensioner, guides and sprockets.
17. Install spark plugs.
18. Install front cover as outlined in "Front Cover, Replace."

RIGHTHAND

REMOVAL

1. Remove front cover as outlined in "Front Cover, Replace."
2. Remove lefthand secondary drive

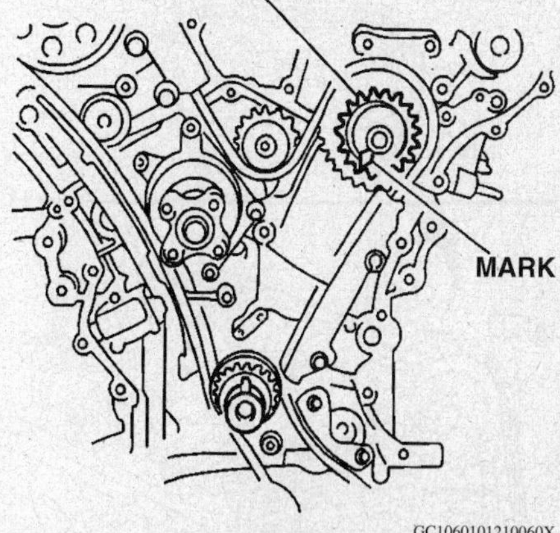

Fig. 13 Idler sprocket alignment

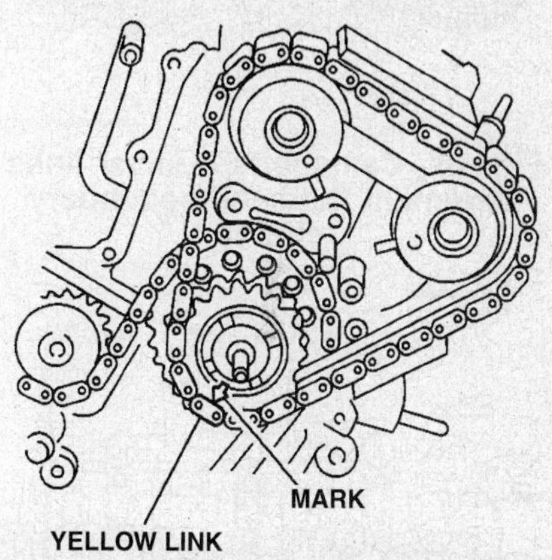

Fig. 15 Idler sprocket & yellow link alignment (lefthand secondary chain)

chain as outlined in "Timing Chain, Replace."

3. Remove primary drive chain as outlined in "Timing Chain, Replace."
4. Remove mounting bolts and drive chain guide.
5. Remove mounting bolts in sequence, then the camshaft bearing caps as outlined in "Camshaft, Replace."
6. Remove camshafts and secondary drive chain as an assembly.
7. Remove mounting bolts and drive chain tensioner.

INSTALLATION

1. Ensure crankshaft keyway is positioned properly.
2. Apply oil to secondary righthand drive chain tensioner.
3. Install drive chain tensioner and tighten mounting bolts.
4. Apply oil to camshaft lobes and journals.
5. Install righthand drive chain to camshaft sprockets by aligning silver or yellow links with camshaft sprockets marks, **Fig. 17.**
6. Install camshaft bearing cap pins.
7. Install camshafts with drive chain.
8. Apply oil to camshaft bearing cap bolts.

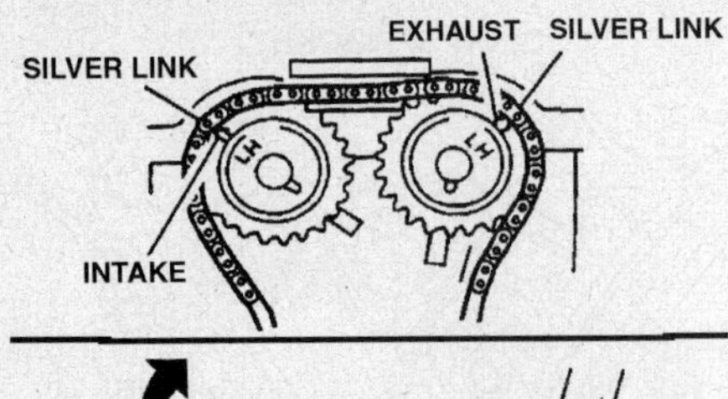

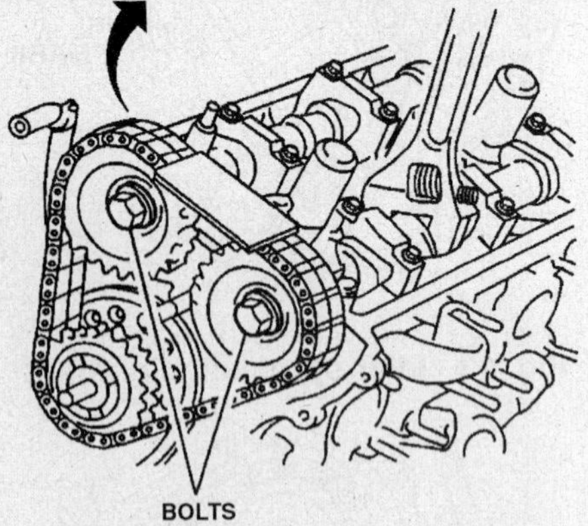

Fig. 16 Camshafts & silver links alignment (lefthand secondary chain)

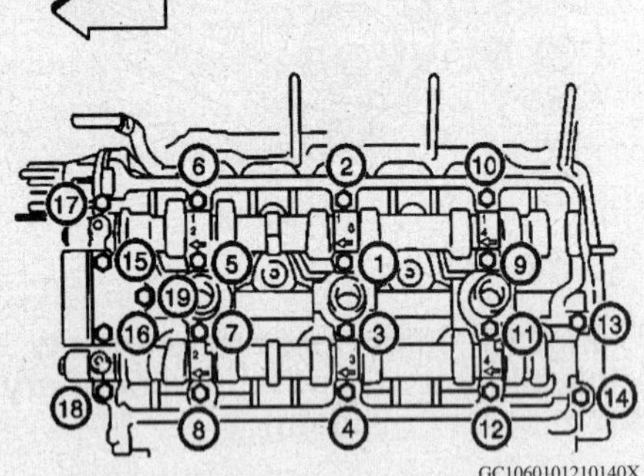

Fig. 19 Camshaft bearing cap tightening sequence. Lefthand

9. Install camshaft bearing caps. Caps are marked intake or exhaust. Ensure direction arrow on cap is pointed toward the timing chain.
10. Tighten camshaft bearing caps as outlined in "Camshaft, Replace."
11. Install righthand secondary timing chain guide and tighten mounting bolts.
12. Install primary drive and lefthand secondary drive chains as outlined in "Timing Chain, Replace."
13. Install front cover as outlined in "Front Cover, Replace."

CAMSHAFT

REPLACE

Lefthand

REMOVAL

1. Remove front cover as outlined in "Front Cover, Replace."
2. Remove spark plugs.

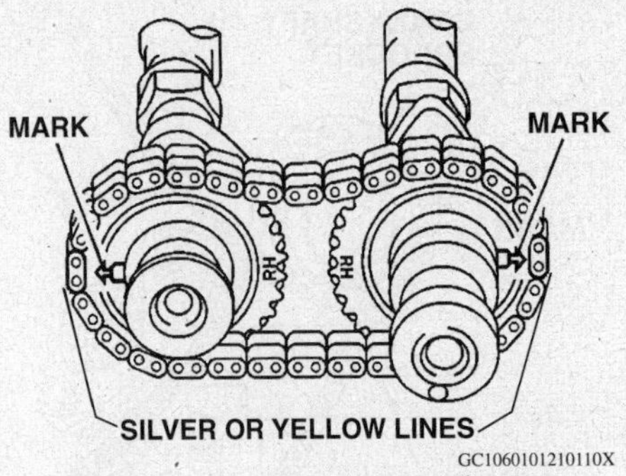

Fig. 17 Camshafts & chain alignment (righthand secondary chain)

3. Remove lefthand secondary drive chain as outlined in "Timing Chain, Replace."
4. Remove Camshaft Position sensor.
5. Loosen camshaft bearing caps in sequence, **Fig. 18.**
6. Remove bearing caps and camshafts.

INSTALLATION

1. Ensure crankshaft keyway is properly aligned.
2. Apply engine oil to camshaft journals and lobes.
3. Install camshafts aligning guide pins with marks on cylinder head, **Fig. 14.** Exhaust camshaft rear end is slotted to mate with CMP sensor.
4. Install cylinder head dowel pins.
5. Apply bead sealant part No. 12346240, or equivalent, to exhaust camshaft end housing sealing surface.
6. Install camshaft bearing caps. Caps are marked intake or exhaust, ensure direction arrow on cap is pointed toward the timing chain.
7. Apply oil to camshaft bearing cap bolts.
8. Tighten camshaft bearing caps in three progressive steps in sequence, **Fig. 19.**
9. Install CMP sensor.
10. Install lefthand secondary drive chain and tensioner as outlined in "Timing Chain, Replace."
11. Install front cover as outlined in "Front Cover, Replace."

Righthand

REMOVAL

1. Remove front cover as outlined in "Front Cover, Replace."
2. Remove spark plugs.
3. Remove lefthand secondary drive chain as outlined in "Timing Chain, Replace."
4. Remove primary drive chain and righthand sprocket as outlined in "Timing Chain, Replace."
5. Remove mounting bolts and drive chain guide.
6. Remove camshaft bearing cap bolts in sequence, **Fig. 20.**
7. Remove bearing caps, then the camshafts and secondary drive chain as an assembly.

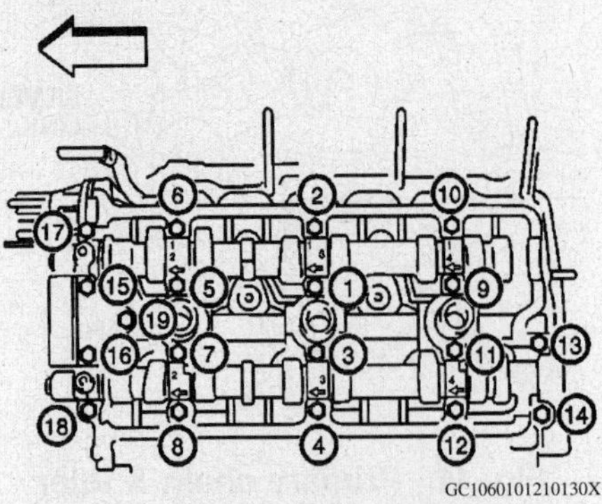

Fig. 18 Camshaft bearing cap loosening sequence. Lefthand

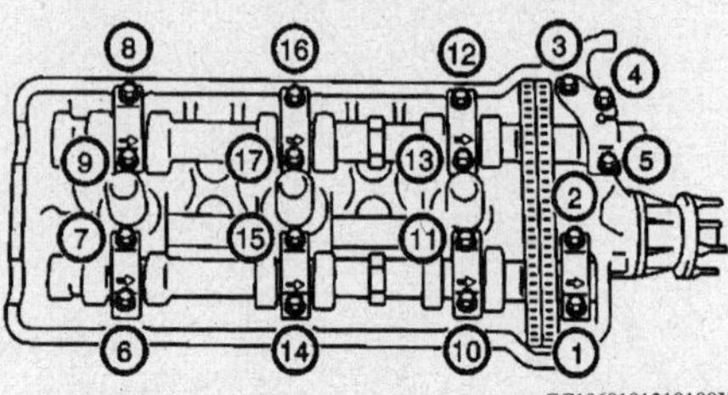

Fig. 20 Camshaft bearing cap bolt removal sequence (righthand)

INSTALL

1. Ensure crankshaft keyway is properly positioned.
2. Apply oil to camshaft lobes and journals.
3. Install righthand drive chain to camshaft sprockets by aligning silver or yellow links with camshaft sprockets marks, **Fig. 17.**
4. Install camshafts with drive chain.
5. Install cylinder head dowel pins.
6. Apply oil to camshaft bearing cap bolts.
7. Install camshaft bearing caps. Caps are marked intake or exhaust, ensure direction arrow on cap is pointed toward the timing chain.
8. Tighten camshaft bearing caps bolts in three progressive steps in sequence, **Fig. 21.**
9. Install righthand secondary timing chain guide and tighten two mounting bolts.
10. Install righthand sprocket and primary drive chain as outlined in "Timing Chain, Replace."
11. Install lefthand secondary drive chain as outlined in "Timing Chain, Replace."
12. Install engine front cover as outlined in "Front Cover, Replace."

CRANKSHAFT REAR OIL SEAL

REPLACE

1. Remove transmission assembly as outlined in **MOTOR's "Domestic Transmission, In-Vehicle Service" or "Transmission Service DVD."**
2. Remove flywheel.
3. Carefully pry out crankshaft rear oil

seal using suitable screwdriver with tape wrapped tip.

4. Reverse procedure to install, noting the following:
   a. Apply chassis grease part No. 1051344, or equivalent, to new crankshaft rear oil seal lip.
   b. Lightly tap crankshaft rear oil seal into place using suitable hammer and rear oil seal installer tool No. J-41172, or equivalent.

OIL PAN

REPLACE

1. Remove mounting bolt, then the oil dipstick and tube.
2. Remove power steering gear as outlined in "Front Suspension & Steering."
3. **On models equipped with 4WD,** remove front axle housing as outlined in "Front Wheel Drive."
4. **On all models,** drain engine oil into suitable container.
5. Remove lower oil pan from upper.
6. Remove mounting bolts and oil strainer bracket.
7. Remove radiator outlet pipe from upper oil pan.
8. Remove mounting bolts and lower upper oil pan onto crossmember.
9. Remove oil pump pipe mounting bolts.
10. Remove upper oil pan and oil strainer, together.
11. Reverse procedure to install, noting the following:
    a. Install new lower crankcase and two new oil pump pipe O-rings.
    b. Apply sealant to the upper oil pan.

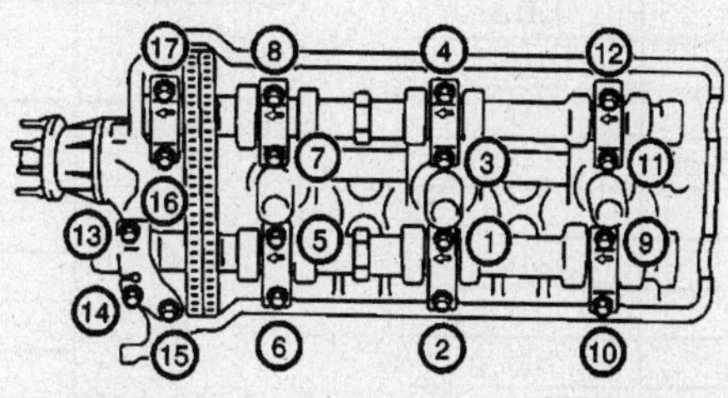

Fig. 21 Camshaft bearing cap tightening sequence (righthand)

OIL PUMP

REPLACE

1. Remove front cover as outlined in "Front Cover, Replace."
2. Remove oil pan as outlined in "Oil Pan, Replace."
3. Loosen oil pump chain guide bolts.
4. Remove mounting bolts and oil pump.
5. Reverse procedure to install.

BELT TENSION DATA

Tighten cooling fan and alternator belt to a deflection of .24–.30 inch at 22 lbs. Tighten air conditioning and power steering pump belt to a deflection of .16–.35 inch at 22 lbs., of tension.

COOLING SYSTEM BLEED

These engines do not require a specified bleed procedure. After filling cooling system, run engine to operating temperature with radiator/pressure cap off. Air will then be automatically bled through cap opening.

THERMOSTAT

REPLACE

1. Drain engine coolant into suitable container.
2. Remove lower radiator pipe bolt.
3. Remove mounting bolts, cap and the thermostat.
4. Reverse procedure to install.

WATER PUMP

REPLACE

1. Drain engine oil and coolant into suitable containers.
2. Remove front cover as outlined in "Front Cover, Replace."
3. Remove mounting bolts and water pump.
4. Reverse procedure to install. Install new O-rings.

RADIATOR

REPLACE

Refer to "Radiator, Replace" in "2.0L Engine" section.

FUEL PUMP

REPLACE

Refer to "Fuel Pump, Replace" in "2.0L Engine" section.

FUEL FILTER

REPLACE

Refer to "Fuel Pump, Replace" in "2.0L Engine" section.

TIGHTENING SPECIFICATIONS

Year	Component	Torque Ft. Lbs.
2002-04	Accessory Drive Belt Tensioner	19
	Air Conditioner Compressor	17
	Air Conditioner Compressor Bracket	40
	Alternator	17
	Alternator Terminal	71①
	Battery Ground	11
	Camshaft Bearing Cap Bolt	106①
	Camshaft Position Sensor	11
	Camshaft Timing Sprocket	58
	Connecting Rod Bearing Cap	33
	Crankshaft Damper	109
	Crankshaft Position Sensor	53①
	Crankshaft Pulley	109
	Cylinder Head	②
	Cylinder Head Cover	93①
	Cooling Fan	18
	Engine Mount	37
	Exhaust Manifold Heat Shield	89①
	Exhaust Manifold To Bracket	37
	Exhaust Manifold To Cylinder Head	22
	Front Suspension Support Brace	36
	Fuel Pump	60①
	Fuel Rail Banjo Fitting	22
	Fuel Tank Shield	26
	Fuel Tank Strap	26
	Flywheel	51⑤
	Ground Wire	11
	Heated Oxygen Sensor	33
	Ignition Coil	89①
	Intake Manifold	17
	Lower Crankcase	③

TIGHTENING SPECIFICATIONS—Continued

Year	Component	Torque Ft. Lbs.
2002–04	Main Bearing Cap Bolt	④
	Oil Drain Plug	26
	Oil Pan	97①
	Oil Pressure Switch	11
	Oil Pump	20
	Oil Pump Case	106①
	Oil Pump Strainer	97①
	Power Steering Pump	19
	Spark Plug	18
	Starter	97①
	Steering Column Shaft	18
	Strut Tower Brace	37
	Thermostat Housing	12
	Throttle Body	106①
	Timing Chain Cover	97①
	Timing Chain Tensioner, Lefthand Camshaft Bolt	106①
	Timing Chain Tensioner, Lefthand Camshaft Nut	33
	Timing Chain Tensioner, Primary	97①
	Timing Chain Tensioner, Primary Guide	97①
	Timing Chain Tensioner, Primary Shoe	20
	Timing Chain Tensioner, Righthand Camshaft Bolt	97①
	Torque Converter	47
	Transmission To Engine Mount	58
	Water Crossover	12
	Water Pump	20

① — Inch lbs.
② — Refer to "Cylinder Head, Replace" for tightening specifications and sequence.
③ — First pass, 14 ft. lbs.; Second pass, 20 ft. lbs.
④ — First pass, 31 ft. lbs.; Second pass, 42 ft. lbs.
⑤ — Cross tighten.

Rear Axle & Suspension

NOTE: Refer To "Drive Axles" Chapter For Rear Axle Service Procedures Not Covered In This Section.

INDEX

DESCRIPTION

The rigid axle unit consists of coil springs, rear axle, shock absorbers upper arms and trailing rods, **Figs. 1 and 2.** The axle has a hypoid type ring gear and drive pinion with its centerline below the centerline of the ring gear.

REAR AXLE

REPLACE

1. Drain differential gear oil into suitable container.
2. Remove brake drums and lines from rear wheel cylinders.
3. Remove rear wheel bearing retainer nuts from rear axle housing.
4. If there is no clearance between rear wheel bearing retainer and parking shoe, loosen parking cable adjusting nut and pull down brake shoe hold pin stopper plate.
5. Remove axle shaft using axle shaft pad eye tool No. J-37781 and puller tool No. J-2619-01, or equivalents.
6. Remove brake line and breather hose from rear axle.
7. Remove propeller shaft from differential and secure to one side.
8. Support rear axle beneath differential with suitable jack, then remove ball joint bracket and differential carrier.
9. Remove rear trailing rod to axle housing mounting nut. **Do not remove bolt.**
10. Remove lower shock absorber to axle housing mounting bolt.
11. Lower axle enough to relive coil spring tension and remove trailing rod from axle housing.
12. Lower and remove axle.
13. Reverse procedure to install. Apply GM sealant Vega repair No. 3997597, or equivalent, to brake backing plate bearing retainer mating surface.

REAR AXLE SHAFT

REPLACE

1. Drain differential gear oil into suitable container.
2. Raise and support vehicle.
3. Remove wheel, brake drum and rear wheel bearing retainer nuts from axle housing.
4. If there is no clearance between rear wheel bearing retainer and parking shoe, loosen parking cable adjusting nut and pull down brake shoe hold pin stopper plate.
5. Remove axle shaft using axle shaft pad eye tool No. J-37781 and puller tool No. J-2619-01, or equivalents.
6. Remove retainer ring from axle shaft using suitable grinder to flatten two components of bearing retainer ring, **Fig. 3.**
7. Remove bearing from axle shaft using suitable chisel and press.
8. Reverse procedure to install. Apply GM sealant Vega repair No. 3997597, or equivalent, to brake backing plate bearing retainer surface.

SHOCK ABSORBER

REPLACE

1. Raise vehicle and support vehicle, then remove wheel.
2. Support rear axle housing using suitable jack, then remove shock absorber upper locknut and mounting nut.
3. Remove lower mounting bolt and shock absorber.
4. Reverse procedure to install.

COIL SPRING

REPLACE

1. Raise vehicle and remove wheel.
2. Support rear axle housing with suitable jack.
3. Remove shock absorber lower mounting bolt.
4. Slowly lower rear axle housing enough to remove coil spring, then remove coil spring.
5. Reverse procedure to install.

CONTROL ARM

REPLACE

1. Raise and support vehicle.
2. Remove rear wheels.
3. Remove proportioning valve bracket.
4. Support rear axle using suitable jack.
5. Disconnect ball joint boss from differential carrier, **Fig. 4.**
6. Remove upper arm bolts and rear suspension upper arm from body.
7. Remove cotter pin and castle nut from ball joint boss.
8. Remove ball joint boss from ball joint dust seal using universal puller tool No. J-22888, or equivalent, **Fig. 5.**
9. Mount upper arm into press using control arm bushing service tool No. J-29792-1 and front control arm bushing service tool No. J-35561, or equivalents.
10. Press bushing from upper arm assembly.
11. Reverse procedure to install.

TRAILING ROD

REPLACE

1. Raise and support vehicle.
2. Remove rear wheels.
3. Disconnect parking brake cable hanger from trailing rod.
4. Support rear axle using suitable jack.
5. Remove front and rear trailing rod bolts and nuts. **Have an assistant support trailing rod when removing bolts and nuts to prevent personal injury.**
6. Mount trailing rod into suitable press using front control arm bushing service set tool No. J-29792-1 and rear suspension bushing remover tool No. J-28685-2, or equivalents.
7. Press bushing out until bushing bottoms into rear suspension bushing remover tool.
8. Release pressure, remove rear suspension bushing remover tool and install bushing remover tool No. J-28685-1, or equivalent, then press remainder of bushing out of trailing rod.
9. Reverse procedure to install.

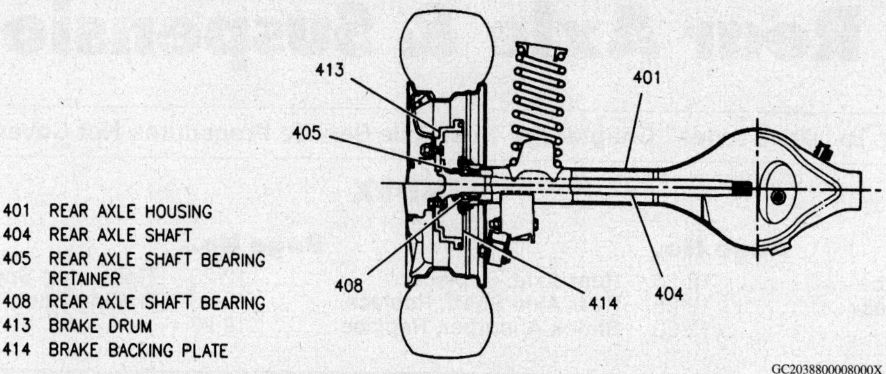

Fig. 1 Sectional view of rear axle & suspension

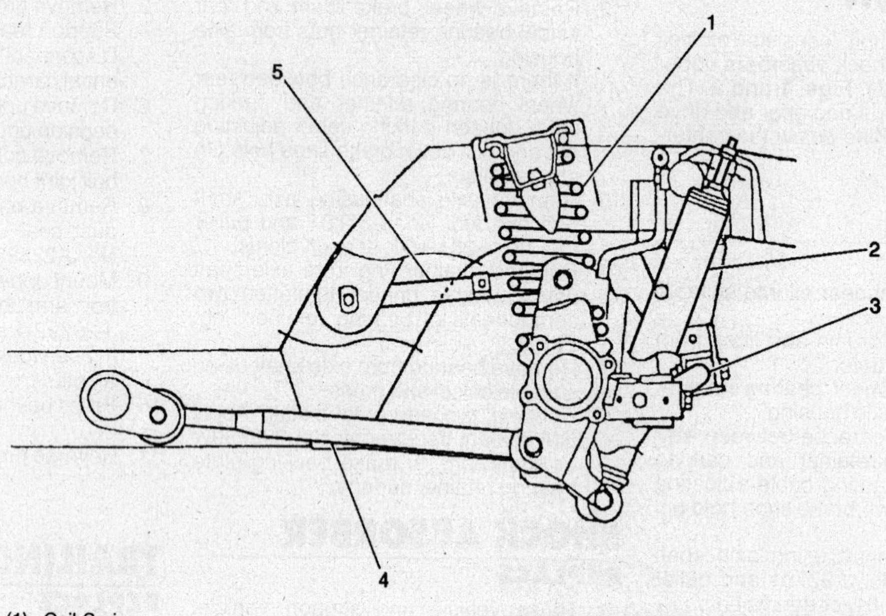

Fig. 2 Side view of rear axle & suspension

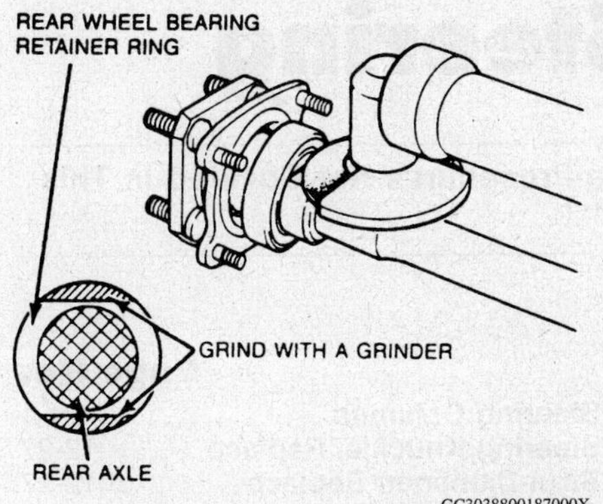

Fig. 3 Rear wheel bearing retainer ring removal

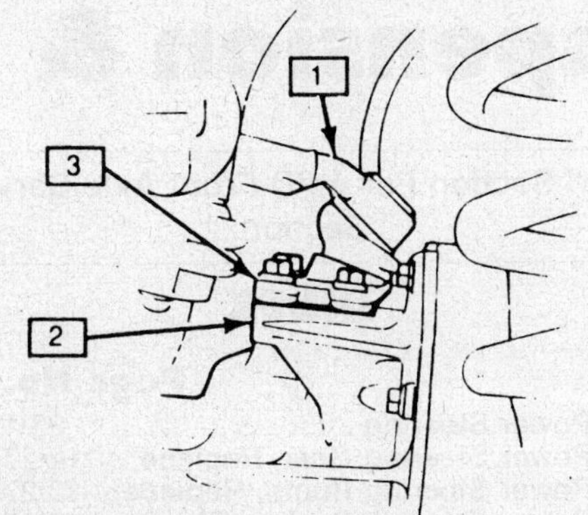

Fig. 4 Ball joint boss separation from differential carrier

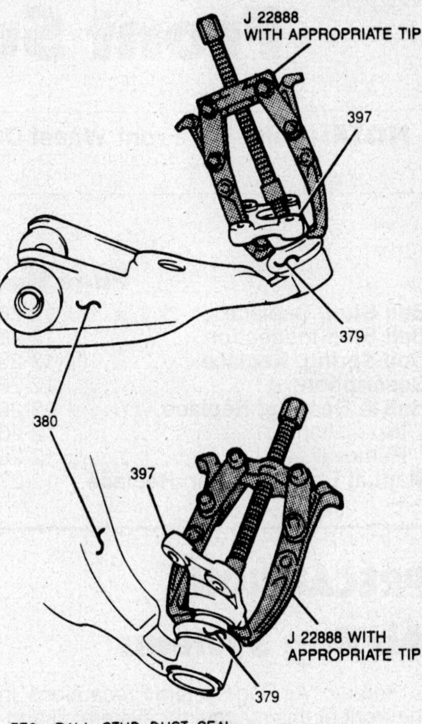

Fig. 5 Ball joint boss removal

TIGHTENING SPECIFICATIONS

Year	Component	Torque Ft. Lbs.
2002–04	ABS Speed Sensor	17
	Ball Joint	43
	Ball Joint Boss Bolt	37
	Bearing	17
	Bracket	36
	Brake Pipe Flare Nuts	11
	Carrier	16
	Control Arm	65
	Propeller Shaft	37
	Proportioning Valve Stay	17
	Rear Axle Shaft	17
	Shock Absorber Locknut	21
	Shock Absorber, Lower	62
	Shock Absorber, Upper	21
	Trailing Arm	65
	Trailing Rod Arm	66
	Wheel Lug Nut	70

Front Suspension & Steering

NOTE: Refer To "Front Wheel Drive" Section For 4WD Front Axle Service Procedures Not Covered In This Section.

INDEX

PRECAUTIONS

Air Bag Systems

Refer to "Air Bag System Precautions" in the front of this manual for system disarming and arming procedures.

Battery Ground Cable

Prior to service disconnect battery ground cable and isolate as required.

DESCRIPTION

The front suspension is a strut type independent suspension, **Fig. 1.** The upper end of the strut is secured to the body by a strut support. The lower end of the strut is connected to the upper end of the steering knuckle. A coil spring, placed between the control arm and chassis, supports the vehicle.

The rotary motion of the steering wheel is carried to the steering upper shaft, lower shaft, steering gear and pitman arm. As the pitman arm is moved, the center link moves linearly, actuating the tie rod and turning the wheels through the knuckle arms, **Fig. 2.**

HUB & BEARING

REPLACE

Removal

1. Raise and support vehicle, then remove wheel.
2. Remove brake caliper assembly as outlined in "Disc Brakes" chapter and support aside.
3. **On models equipped with 2WD,** remove hub cap.
4. **On models equipped with 4WD,** remove locking hub as outlined in "Front Wheel Drive."
5. **On all models,** install hub nut anti-rotation spring release tool and hub nut wrench tools No. J-42119-1 and J-42119-2 , **Fig. 3.**
6. Rotate hub counterclockwise two full turns to disengage lock spring from hub nut. **Do not attempt to loosen hub nut without anti-rotation lock spring release tool, spindle damage may occur.**
7. Remove lock spring release tool from hub, then the wheel bearing nut, anti-rotation lock spring and washer, **Fig. 4.**
8. Remove wheel hub assembly, **Fig. 5.** If assembly can not be removed by hand, use brake drum remover tool No. J-37781 and slide hammer tool No. J-2619-02, or equivalents, to separate hub and bearing from spindle.
9. Remove wheel bearing oil seal, then the bearing circlip.
10. Remove bearing outer race using bearing installer handle tool No. J-8092 and front wheel hub bearing remover tool No. J-37772, or equivalents.

Installation

1. Press fit bearing outer race until it is firmly seated in wheel hub using bearing installer handle tool No. J-8092 and front wheel hub bearing installer tool No. J-37777, or equivalents.
2. Pack bearing with GM wheel bearing lubricant part No. 1051344, or equivalent.
3. Install bearing circlip, then the bearing oil seal using front wheel hub and bearing oil seal installer tool No. J-37774, or equivalent.
4. Fill oil seal recess and cover oil seal lip with GM wheel bearing lubricant part No. 1051344, or equivalent.
5. Install wheel hub assembly onto front wheel spindle, then the spindle thrust washer, anti-rotation spring and hub nut. Tighten hub nut finger tight.
6. Install hub nut anti-rotation spring release tool and hub nut wrench tool Nos. J-42119-1 and J-42119-2, or equivalents, **Fig. 3. Ensure tabs of wrench properly engage slots of hub nut.**
7. Install brake disc and caliper assembly as outlined in "Disc Brakes."
8. **On models equipped with 2WD,** install hub cover, then the wheel and tighten.
9. **On models equipped with 4WD,** install locking hub, then the wheel and tighten.

BALL STUD INSPECTION

1. Raise and support vehicle so that suspension is allowed to hang free.
2. Grasp wheel and tire assembly at top and bottom, then rock top of wheel and tire assembly inward and outward.
3. While rocking wheel and tire assembly, observe movement between steering knuckle and control arm. If any horizontal movement is present, replace ball joint.
4. If ball joint is disconnected from steering knuckle, use finger to try to twist ball joint in its socket. If ball joint can be twisted in its socket, replace ball joint.

BALL STUD

REPLACE

1. Remove coil spring as outlined in "Coil Spring, Replace."
2. Remove ball stud to knuckle nut, then separate ball stud from knuckle.
3. Remove bolts mounting ball stud to control arm, then separate ball stud from control arm.
4. Reverse procedure to install.

COIL SPRING

REPLACE

1. Raise and support vehicle, then remove wheels.
2. Remove engine skid plate.
3. Support suspension arm using suitable jack.

4. Remove ball stud to suspension arm mounting bolts and separate ball stud from control arm.
5. Disconnect stabilizer bar from control arm.
6. Lower jack and remove coil spring.
7. Reverse procedure to install. Ensure larger diameter of spring is installed down against control arm.

STEERING KNUCKLE

REPLACE

1. Raise and support vehicle, then remove wheel.
2. Support suspension arm using suitable jack and remove wheel hub as outlined in "Hub & Bearing, Replace."
3. Remove wheel speed sensors and brake disc dust shield.
4. Remove wheel spindle from hub by tapping with suitable soft face hammer.
5. Remove strut to knuckle bolts, then separate strut from knuckle.
6. Remove tie rod end nut, then separate tie rod end from knuckle using tie rod end remover tool No. J-21687-02, or equivalent.
7. Remove ball stud nut, then separate steering knuckle from ball stud by tapping with suitable hammer.
8. Remove steering knuckle seal.
9. Reverse procedure to install, noting the following:
   a. Coat mating surface of wheel spindle and steering knuckle with GM Silicone Sealer part No. 1015275, or equivalent.
   b. Fill in spindle recess and knuckle seal recess with GM lubricant part No. 11052196, or equivalent.
   c. Install inner knuckle seal using driveshaft and inner oil seal installer tool No. J-37750, or equivalent.

STABILIZER BAR

REPLACE

1. Raise and support vehicle, then remove stabilizer links from front suspension arms, **Fig. 6.**
2. Remove stabilizer bar mount bushing bracket bolts.
3. Remove stabilizer bar and links.
4. Reverse procedure to install. Ensure stabilizer bar is centered, then tighten mounting bolts.

STRUT DAMPNER

REPLACE

1. Raise and support vehicle, then remove wheels.
2. Support suspension arm using suitable jack.
3. Remove brake line from strut damper bracket.
4. Remove lower strut to knuckle mounting bolts.
5. Remove upper strut mounting bolts, then the strut.
6. Reverse procedure to install.

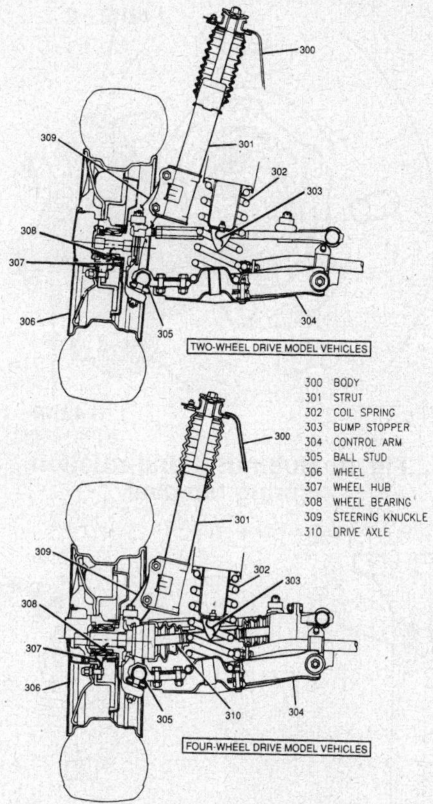

Fig. 1 Front suspension

SUSPENSION ARM

REPLACE

1. Remove coil spring as outlined in "Coil Spring, Replace."
2. Remove suspension arm to frame through bolts, then the suspension arm.
3. Reverse procedure to install.

TIE ROD

REPLACE

1. Raise and support vehicle.
2. Remove tire and wheel assembly.
3. Remove tie rod end nut.
4. Separate tie rod using suitable puller.
5. Place matchmark on tie rod thread indicating position of rod end.
6. Loosen lock nut and remove rod end from sleeve.
7. Reverse procedure to install.

POWER STEERING GEAR

REPLACE

1. Remove coolant reservoir from radiator bracket.
2. Remove and plug pressure hose from power steering gear.
3. Remove return hose from oil tank.
4. Disconnect steering column shaft from steering gear.
5. Raise and support vehicle.
6. Disconnect center link from pitman arm using pitman arm puller tool No. J-29107, or equivalent.
7. Remove steering gear mounting bolts and steering gear.
8. Mark alignment then remove pitman arm from steering gear.
9. Reverse procedure to install.

POWER STEERING PUMP

REPLACE

1. Remove coolant reservoir.
2. **On models less air conditioning,** loosen power steering adjusting and pivot bolts.
3. **On models equipped with air conditioning,** loosen compressor adjusting and pivot bolts.
4. **On all models,** remove power steering belt.
5. Disconnect power steering pressure and suction hoses.
6. Disconnect power steering pressure switch lead wire at switch terminal.
7. Drain engine oil into suitable container and remove oil filter.
8. Remove power steering pump mounting bolts and power steering pump.
9. Reverse procedure to install.

MANUAL STEERING GEAR

REPLACE

1. Disconnect steering column shaft from steering gear.
2. Raise and support vehicle.
3. Disconnect center link from pitman arm using pitman arm puller tool No. J-21687-02, or equivalent.
4. Remove steering gear mounting bolts and steering gear.
5. Note alignment then remove pitman arm from steering gear.
6. Reverse procedure to install.

POWER STEERING SYSTEM BLEED

When replacing or adding fluid, refer to "Lubricant Data" in "Specifications" section for fluid type.

1. Start engine and allow to idle, turn wheels to left to full lock.
2. Turn engine Off, fill reservoir until fluid reaches COLD mark on dipstick.
3. Start engine, run at fast idle for 15 seconds, then turn engine Off.
4. Ensure reservoir fluid level reaches COLD mark on dipstick, add fluid as required.
5. Leave filler cap off during bleeding procedures.
6. Start engine and allow to idle, slowly turn wheels full right to full left several times.
7. Inspect fluid for foaming, continue above step until fluid shows no sign of foaming.
8. Adjust fluid to correct level, then install cap.

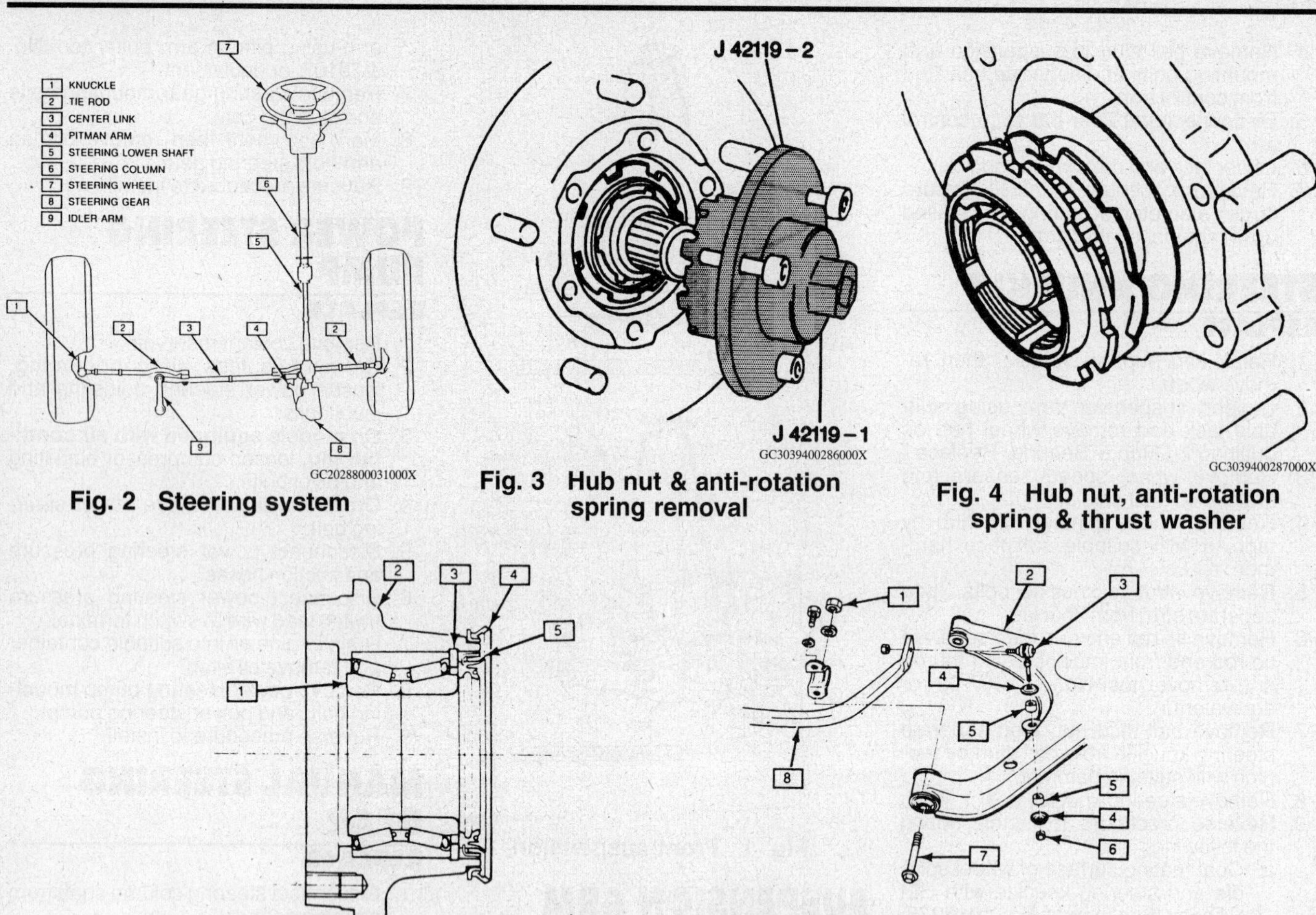

Fig. 2 Steering system

Fig. 3 Hub nut & anti-rotation spring removal

Fig. 4 Hub nut, anti-rotation spring & thrust washer

Fig. 5 Wheel hub assembly

Fig. 6 Stabilizer bar assembly

TIGHTENING SPECIFICATIONS

Year	Component	Torque Ft. Lbs.
2002–04	Axle Nut	155
	Ball Joint, Nut	63
	Ball Joint To Control Arm	63
	Ball Stud Nut	44
	Caliper	62
	Control Arm, Front	62
	Control Arm, Rear	92
	Crossmember to Frame	68
	Driveshaft Nut	155
	Freewheeling Hub	18
	Freewheeling Hub Cover	10
	Front Axle Shaft Drive Flange	35
	Front Brake Shield	37
	Hub Nut	155
	Power Steering Fluid Reservoir Bracket	96①
	Power Steering Gear Bracket	40
	Power Steering Gear Inlet Hose, Bolt	26
	Power Steering Gear Inlet Hose, Fitting	44
	Power Steering Gear Inlet Hose, Nut	29
	Power Steering Gear Outlet Hose Connector	89①
	Power Steering Pipe Clamp	97①
	Power Steering Plug	44
	Power Steering Pressure Switch	20
	Power Steering Pump	19
	Power Steering Pump Bracket w/2.0L Engine	19
	Power Steering Pump Cover	17
	Radiator Core Support To Crossmember	19
	Skid Plate	19
	Splash Shield	10
	Spring Upper Bump Stop	37
	Stabilizer Bar Insulator Bracket	17
	Stabilizer Link	21
	Stabilizer Shaft Link To Control Arm	21
	Stabilizer Shaft Link To Stabilizer Shaft	37
	Steering Gear Clamp To Crossmember	40
	Steering Shaft Coupling	18
	Strut Bracket	69
	Strut Damper Support	18
	Strut Damper To Knuckle	66
	Strut Support	40
	Suspension Brace	37
	Tie Rod End, Inner	62
	Tie Rod End, Outer	32
	Tie Rod Lock Nut	47
	Wheel Bearing	159
	Wheel Lug Nuts	69
	Yoke Nut	155

①— Inch lbs.

Front Wheel Drive

NOTE: Refer To "Drive Axles" Chapter For Front Axle Service Procedures Not Covered In This Section.

INDEX

DESCRIPTION

The righthand and lefthand front wheel drive axles consists of an inner and outer constant velocity (CV) joint connected by an axle shaft to the differential and wheel hub, **Fig. 1.**

The differential assemblies installed to the front axle use a hypoid bevel pinion and gear. The front differential is set in an aluminum housing mounted under the chassis frame, **Fig. 2.**

AXLE

REPLACE

1. Raise and support vehicle, then turn steering wheel all way to right.
2. Disconnect breather hose.
3. Remove righthand and lefthand axle driveshaft as outlined in "Axle Shaft, Replace."
4. Support differential assembly with suitable jack.
5. Remove righthand, lefthand and rear mounting bracket bolts and bracket.
6. Remove axle housing assembly.
7. Inspect condition of each bushing. If damaged or deteriorated, replace entire mount.
8. Reverse procedure to install.

AXLE SHAFT

REPLACE

1. Raise and support vehicle, then drain differential housing into suitable container.
2. Remove locking hub as outlined in "Locking Hub, Service."
3. Remove driveshaft circlip.
4. Remove tie rod end castle nut.
5. Remove disc brake caliper and support aside.
6. Support lower suspension arm with suitable jack.
7. Remove knuckle ball stud nut, then the strut to knuckle mounting bolts.
8. Remove knuckle and wheel hub assembly by lowering jack.
9. On righthand side axle shaft, proceed as follows:
   a. Separate differential side joint by prying joint away from differential assembly using axle shaft remover tool No. J-37780, or equivalent, **Fig. 3.**
   b. Remove righthand side axle shaft.
10. On lefthand side axle shaft, remove flange bolts and axle shaft.
11. Reverse procedure to install.

AXLE BEARING SEAL

REPLACE

1. Remove axle shaft as outlined in "Axle Shaft, Replace."
2. Remove oil seal from differential housing using suitable flat bladed screwdriver, **Fig. 4.**
3. Remove circlip, then the bearing from housing using bearing removal tool Nos. J-29369-1 and J-23907, or equivalents.
4. Reverse procedure to install, noting the following:
   a. Install bearing using bearing installation tool No. J-8092, or equivalent.
   b. Install oil seal with oil seal installation tool Nos. J-37770 and J-8092, or equivalents.

CV JOINT SERVICE

Disassemble

1. Remove inner and outer joint band clamp.
2. Remove drive axle end circlip.
3. Remove housing of inner joint, **Fig. 5.**
4. Remove circlip and inner ball joint, **Fig. 6. No not disassemble inner or outer ball joint. Replace these components as an assembly only.**
5. Remove outer joint assembly.
6. Remove inner and outer boots from shaft.
7. Inspect boots for breakage or corrosion. Replace as required.
8. Inspect circlip, snap ring and boot clamps for breakage or corrosion. Replace as required.
9. Clean all components, except boots, in degreaser and dry components completely with compressed air. **Clean boots with clean, damp cloth. Do not wash in degreaser.**

Assemble

1. Apply GM grease (kit No. 7805942 or equivalent,) to outer joint.
2. Assemble outer boot on shaft. Fill outer boot with grease, then fit boot on joint and install clamps.
3. Install inner boot on shaft.
4. Install inner ball joint on shaft with flat surface toward outer joint, **Fig. 6,** and apply grease to joint.
5. Install snap ring in groove on shaft.
6. Fill inner boot with grease and install housing. Assemble boot to housing and install clamps. **When clamping boot clamps, bend its end in reverse direction against drive rotating direction.**

LOCKING HUB SERVICE

Locking hubs are serviced as assemblies. Hubs may be cleaned then lubricated with hub grease part No. 1052750, or equivalent.

1. Remove hub assembly mounting bolts, then the hub cover assembly, **Figs. 7 and 8.**
2. Remove locking hub body from wheel hub assembly.
3. Reverse procedure to install, noting the following:
   a. Lubricate hub components using hub grease (part No. 1052750 or equivalent).
   b. Ensure fixed cam of hub is properly aligned with slots in spindle.

HUB & BEARING SERVICE

Refer to "Front Suspension & Steering" for procedure.

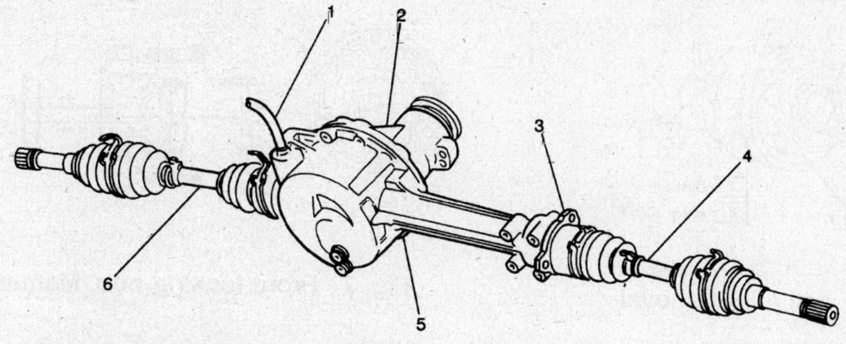

1. Front Axle Housing Breather Hose
2. Differential Carrier
3. Left Inner Axle Shaft
4. Left Drive Axle Shaft
5. Front Axle Housing
6. Right Axle Drive Shaft

GC3039900322000X

Fig. 1 Front axle assembly

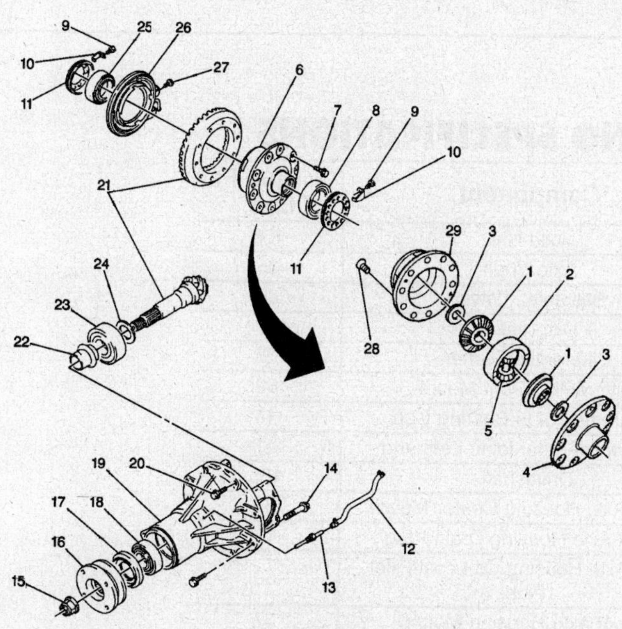

1. Differential Gear
2. Free Axle Hub
3. Thrust Washer
4. Differential Right Case
5. Differential Pinion
6. Differential Case Assembly
7. Bolt
8. Differential Side Bearing
9. Bolt
10. Lock Plate
11. Bearing Adjuster
12. Differentail Inner Air Hose
13. Air Inlet Union
14. Bearing Cap Bolt
15. Flange Nut
16. Universal Joint Flange
17. Oil Seal
18. Rear Bearing
19. Carrier Assembly
20. Bolt
21. Bevel Pinion Gear Set
22. Bevel Pinion Spacer
23. Front Bearing
24. Shim
25. Differential Side Bearing
26. Actuator
27. Bolt
28. Bolt
29. Differential Left Case

GC3039900323000X

Fig. 2 Exploded view of differential

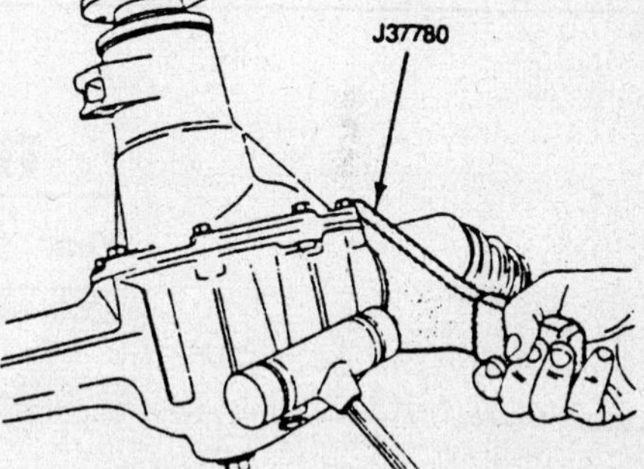

GC3038800140000X

Fig. 3 Axle shaft removal

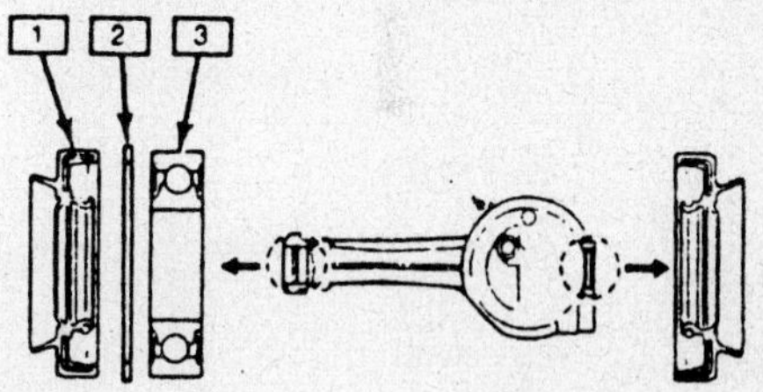

GC3038800143000X

Fig. 4 Axle shaft bearing & seal

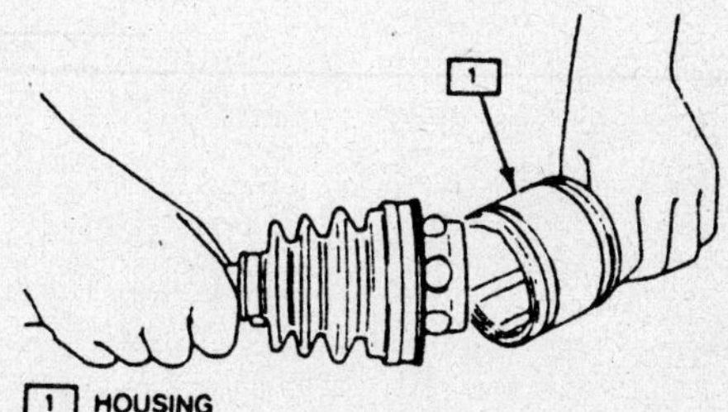

GC3038800141000X

Fig. 5 Inner CV housing removal

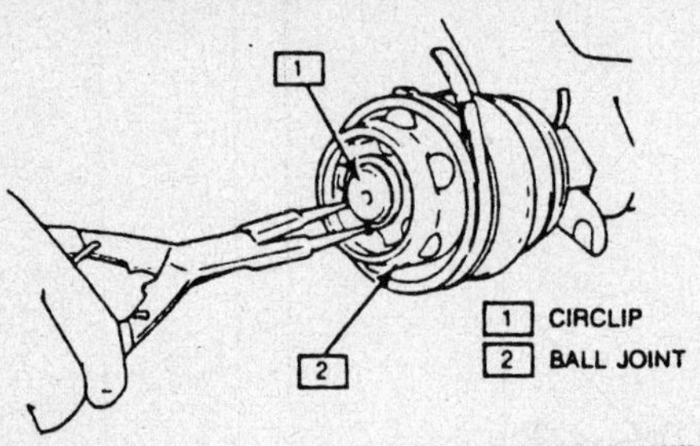

Fig. 6 Inner CV ball joint removal

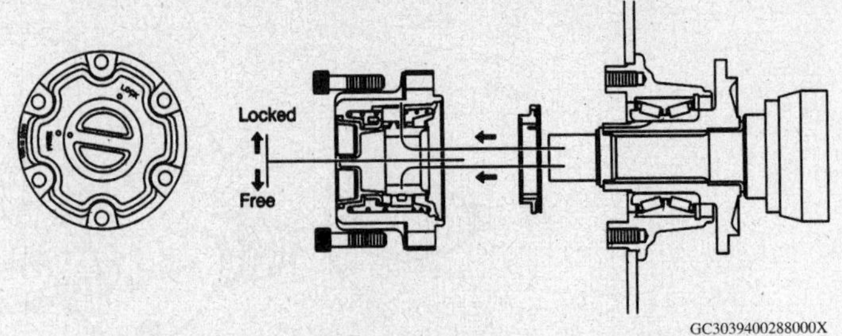

Fig. 7 Front locking hub. Manual transmission

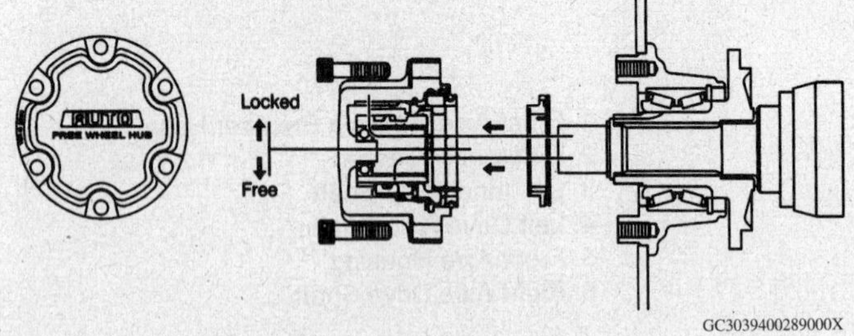

Fig. 8 Front locking hub. Automatic transmission

TIGHTENING SPECIFICATIONS

Year	Component	Torque Ft. Lbs.
2002–04	Axle Nut	155
	Axle Shaft	35
	Ball Joint, Lower	63
	Differential	37
	Differential Carrier	17
	Differential Front Mount	63
	Differential-Side Bearing Cap	44
	Differential-Side Joint, Lefthand	41
	Driveshaft	155
	Front Axle Housing Center Mount	37
	Front Axle Housing Drain Plug	17
	Front Axle Housing Oil Level/Filler Plug	30
	Front Axle Housing Mount	37
	Hub	155
	Locking Hub Cover	24
	Propeller Shaft	43
	Propeller Shaft, Front	41
	Ring Gear	70
	Side Bearing Cap	51
	Skid Plate	40
	Side Bearing Lock Plate	11
	Yoke Nut	155

Wheel Alignment

INDEX

PRELIMINARY INSPECTION

Steering and vibration complaints may be caused by conditions other than improper wheel alignment. These problems may be caused by wheel and tire imbalance. Tire lead can also cause the vehicle to deviate from a straight path. To ensure correct alignment readings and adjustments, perform the following preliminary inspection prior to beginning Front Wheel Alignment:

1. Vehicle must be on level surface while being inspected.
2. Inspect all tires for proper inflation pressures and approximate tread wear.
3. Inspect wheel bearings for looseness.
4. Inspect ball joints and tie rod ends for excessive looseness.
5. Raise vehicle front end slightly off ground.
6. Position suitable dial indicator on wheel.
7. Rotate wheel while measuring lateral runout.
8. Allowable runout is .047 inch or less.
9. Inspect vehicle for proper trim height.
10. Inspect steering gear mountings.
11. Inspect operation of struts.
12. Inspect control arms for looseness.
13. Inspect hub and bearing assemblies for excessive wear.
14. If vehicle normally carries excessive load, it should remain in vehicle during alignment inspection.

FRONT WHEEL ALIGNMENT

Caster & Camber

Refer to specification chart. Caster and camber are non-adjustable. If caster and/or camber are not within specification, locate the cause of these conditions. Damaged, loose, bent, or worn suspension components should be replaced prior to performing front wheel alignment procedure.

Toe-In

1. Loosen lefthand and righthand tie rod locknuts.
2. Rotate tie rods until within specifications. Tie rods should be of equal length after adjustment.
3. Tighten tie rod locknuts to 48 ft. lbs.

VEHICLE RIDE HEIGHT

1. Ensure tires and wheels matchsize specifications outlined on tire placard.
2. Ensure fuel tank is full or add additional weight to simulate full tank.
3. Place front seats in full rearward position.
4. Ensure rear compartment is empty except for jack and simulated fuel load.
5. Ensure spare tire is installed on spare tire carrier.
6. Ensure vehicle is on level surface, such as alignment rack.
7. Close hood, doors and rear door or tend gate.
8. All dimensions are measured vertical to ground.
9. Measure J Dimension as follows:
   a. Use hands to lift front bumper approximately 1.5 inches.
   b. Gently remove hands to allow vehicle to lower.
   c. Use hands to push front bumper down approximately 1.5 inches.
   d. Remove hands to allow vehicle to rise.
   e. Measure J dimension lefthand and righthand frame rail to ground 27.56 inches from front wheel centerline, **Fig. 1.**
   f. Compare measurement to specification, **Fig. 2.**
   g. If J dimension is not .4 inch of specification, replace front springs.
10. Measure K dimension as follows:
    a. Use hands to lift rear bumper approximately 1.5 inches.
    b. Gently remove hands to allow vehicle to lower.
    c. Use hands to push rear bumper down approximately 1.5 inches.
    d. Remove hands to allow vehicle to rise.
    e. Measure K dimension lefthand and righthand frame rail to ground 27.56 inches from rear wheel centerline, **Fig. 1.**
    f. Compare measurement to specification, **Fig. 2.**
    g. If K dimension is not .4 inch of specification, replace rear springs.
11. Measure Z dimension as follows:
    a. Use hands to lift front bumper approximately 1.5 inches.
    b. Gently remove hands to allow vehicle to lower.
    c. Use hands to push front bumper down approximately 1.5 inches.
    d. Remove hands to allow vehicle to rise.
    e. Measure Z dimension from lefthand and righthand side, **Fig. 3.**
    f. Z dimension is vertical distance measured between lower control arm rear bolt centerline and ball joint bottom.
    g. Compare measurement to specification, **Fig. 2.**
    h. If Z dimension is not .4 inch of specification, replace front springs.
12. Measure D dimension as follows:
    a. Use hands to lift rear bumper approximately 1.5 inches.
    b. Gently remove hands to allow vehicle to lower.
    c. Use hands to push rear bumper down approximately 1.5 inches.
    d. Remove hands to allow vehicle to rise.
    e. Measure D dimension from lefthand and righthand side, **Fig. 4.**
    f. D dimension is vertical distance measured between rear shock absorber reservoir top and rear axle housing top.
    g. Compare measurement to specification, **Fig. 2.**
    h. If D dimension is not .4 inch of specification, replace rear springs.

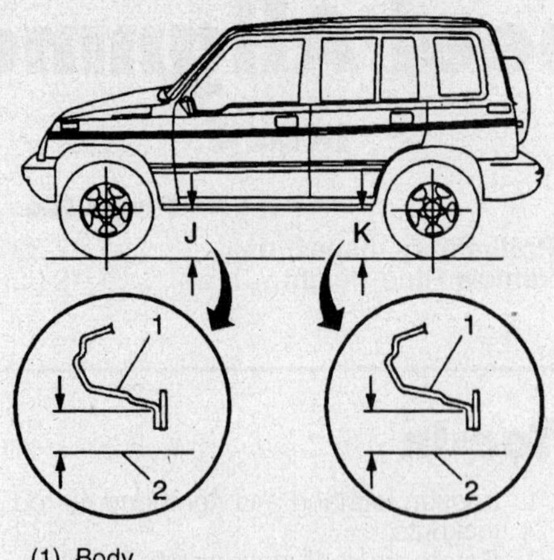

(1) Body
(2) Ground

GC2040100157000X

Fig. 1 J & K ride height measurement

Model	Drive	Dimension, Inches			
		D	J	K	Z
2002–04					
Two-Door Base	2WD	7.28	8.31	8.90	4.02
	4WD	7.28	8.58	9.17	4.02
Two-Door ZR2	4WD	7.28	9.13	9.65	4.02
Four-Door Base	2WD	7.28	8.27	8.90	4.02
	4WD	7.28	8.54	9.17	4.02
Four-Door LT	4WD	7.28	8.78	9.41	4.02
Four-Door ZR2	4WD	7.28	9.06	9.72	4.02

Fig. 2 Ride height specifications

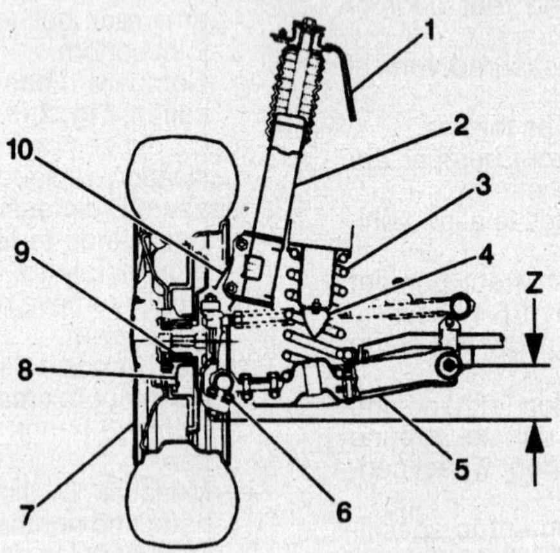

(1) Body
(2) Strut
(3) Coil Spring
(4) Bump Stopper
(5) Control Arm
(6) Ball Stud
(7) Wheel
(8) Wheel Hub
(9) Wheel Bearing
(10) Steering Knuckle

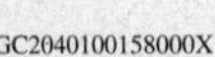
GC2040100158000X

Fig. 3 Z ride height measurement

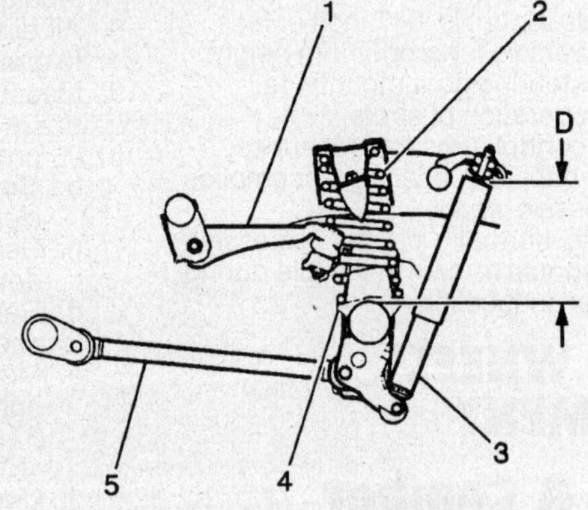

(1) Rear Suspension Upper Arm
(2) Rear Coil Spring
(3) Rear Shock Absorber
(4) Rear Axle Housing
(5) Trailing Arm

GC2040100159000X

Fig. 4 D ride height measurement

RELAY, SV6, TERRAZA & UPLANDER

NOTE: Refer To Back Of This Manual For Vehicle Manufacturer's Special Service Tool Suppliers.

INDEX OF SERVICE OPERATIONS

Specifications

GENERAL ENGINE SPECIFICATIONS

Year	Engine Liter	Fuel System	Bore & Stroke	Compression Ratio	Horsepower @ RPM	Torque Ft. Lbs. @ RPM	Normal Oil Pressure, psi
2005	3.5L	SFI	3.70 x 3.31	9.8	201 @ 5600	216 @ 4000	30–45①
2006	3.5L	SFI	3.70 x 3.31	9.8	201 @ 5600	216 @ 4000	30–45①
	3.9L	SFI	3.90 x 3.31	9.8	240 @ 6000	240 @ 4800	30–45①

① — At 1850 RPM.

TUNE UP SPECIFICATIONS

The following specifications are published from the latest information available. This data should only be used in the absence of a decal affixed in the engine compartment.

Engine	Spark Plug Gap, Inch	Ignition Timing			Auto. Trans.		Fuel Pump Pressure, psi.	Valve Lash, Inch
		Firing Order	Timing BTDC	Mark Location	Curb Idle Speed	Fast Idle Speed		
3.5L	.060	1–2–3–4–5–6	①	①	①	①	50–60	②
3.9L	.040	1–2–3–4–5–6	①	①	①	①	50–60	②

BTDC — Before Top Dead Center ① — PCM controlled. ② — Equipped w/hydraulic valve lifters.

FRONT WHEEL ALIGNMENT SPECIFICATIONS

Year	Caster, Degree		Cross Caster	Camber, Degree		Cross Camber	Toe, Degree		Ball Joint
	Limit	Desired		Limit	Desired		Limits	Desired	
2005–06	+1.95 to +3.45	+2.7	0 to +1.5	-1.4 to +.1	-.65	0 to +1.5	-.2 to +.2	0	①

① — Refer to "Ball Joint Inspection" in the "Front Suspension & Steering" section for ball joint specifications.

REAR WHEEL ALIGNMENT SPECIFICATIONS

Year	Model	Camber, Degree①		Cross Camber①		Toe, Degree①	
		Limit	Desired	Limit	Desired	Limit	Desired
2005–06	AWD	-1.0 to +.2	-.4	0 to +1.0	+.5	-.3 to +.3	0
	FWD	-1.5 to -.5	-1.0	0 to +1.2	+.6	-.3 to +.3	0

① — Not adjustable.

FLUID CAPACITIES & COOLING SYSTEM DATA

Year	Engine Liter	Cooling Capacity Qts.		Recommended Coolant Type	Radiator Cap Relief Pressure, Lbs.	Thermostat Opening Temp. °F	Fuel Tank, Gals.	Engine Oil Refill, Qts. ②	Auto. Transaxle, Qts.①	
		Less Rear A/C	With Rear A/C						Drain & Refill	Overhaul
2005–06	3.5L	11.3	12.8	Dexcool	15	195	③	4.0	7.4	10
	3.9L	10.8	12.1	Dexcool	15	195	③	4.0	7.4	10

① — Approximate, make final inspect w/dipstick.

② — Includes filter.

③ — Standard body, 20 gallons; extended body, 25 gallons.

LUBRICANT DATA

Year	Lubricant Type		
	Automatic Transaxle	Power Steering	Brake System
2005	Dexron III	①	DOT 3
2006	Dexron VI	①	DOT 3

① — GM part No. 89021184, or equivalent.

Electrical

NOTE: On Air Bag Equipped Models, Refer To "Air Bag System Precautions" Located In The Front Of This Manual For System Disarming & Arming Procedures.

NOTE: Refer To "Computer Relearn Procedures" Located In The Front Of This Manual When Battery Power To The Computer Has Been Interrupted.

INDEX

PRECAUTIONS

Air Bag Systems

Refer to "Air Bag System Precautions" in the front of this manual for system disarming and arming procedures.

Battery Ground Cable

Prior to service, disconnect battery ground cable and isolate as required.

Radio Activation

If the radio is removed, the VIN relearn procedure must be performed. The relearn procedure is located in the Module Setup section on the scan tool. Connect scan tool to the Data Link Connector (DLC) and follow scan tool instructions to perform the relearn procedure. Cycle the ignition when procedure is complete. On models equipped with an XM radio, the following procedure must be performed whenever the radio is removed:

1. Turn radio ON and tune to XM channel 0, record radio ID. Radio ID will be needed for receiver activation.
2. Call XM radio at 1-800-556-3600 to activate receiver.
3. Park vehicle outside in an area with an unobstructed view of southern sky.
4. Leave vehicle outside with ignition switch in ACC position and radio on for 30 minutes to activate XM service.
5. Once activated, radio will receive remaining XM channels.

FUSE PANEL & FLASHER LOCATION

The interior fuse block is located behind the righthand side of the instrument panel, behind the access panel.

The engine compartment fuse block is located on the righthand side of the engine compartment, on the wheelhouse.

Hazard and turn signal flasher operation is controlled by the Body Control Module (BCM). The BCM is located behind the lefthand side of the instrument panel, left of the steering column.

FUEL PUMP RELAY LOCATION

The fuel pump relay is located on the righthand side of the engine compartment, in the fuse block.

STARTER

REPLACE

1. Raise and support vehicle.
2. Remove air baffle bolts, then the air baffle.
3. Remove engine to transmission brace from rear lefthand side of engine.
4. Remove transaxle converter cover attaching bolt, then the cover.
5. Remove engine harness ground retaining nut, then the ground.
6. Disconnect engine harness electrical connector from starter.
7. Remove starter motor BAT terminal nut and electrical leads.
8. Remove starter motor S terminal nut and electrical lead.
9. Remove starter motor mounting bolts and starter motor.
10. Reverse procedure to install, noting the following:
    a. **Torque** starter motor mounting bolts to 30 ft. lbs.
    b. **Torque** starter motor BAT terminal nut to 13 ft. lbs.
    c. **Torque** air baffle bolts to 15 ft. lbs.
    d. **Torque** torque converter cover bolts to 89 inch lbs.

ALTERNATOR

REPLACE

3.5L Engine

1. Remove wiper arms.
2. Remove air inlet grill retainers, then the air inlet grill.
3. Lower washer fluid container into engine compartment.
4. Disconnect wiper motor electrical connector.
5. Remove wiper module assembly mounting bolts, then carefully guide passenger side of module out first from opening in front plenum.
6. Pull module from driver side fender flange opening, then remove module from vehicle.
7. Remove throttle body air inlet duct.
8. Set park brake and shift transaxle into Neutral.
9. Remove engine mount strut bolts, then swing engine mount struts aside.

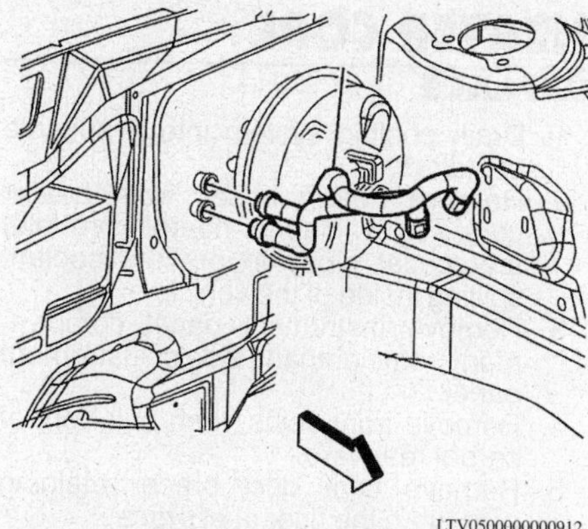

Fig. 1 Heater hose connections

10. Install a engine tilt strap tool No. J 41131, or equivalent.
11. Pull on engine in order to rotate engine forward and tighten engine tilt strap.
12. Rotate engine forward, then remove drive belt.
13. Disconnect engine harness electrical connector from alternator.
14. Reposition positive battery cable boot at alternator terminal.
15. Remove positive battery cable terminal nut at alternator and cable.
16. Remove alternator lower and upper mounting bolts, then the alternator.
17. Reverse procedure to install, noting the following:
    a. **Torque** engine mount strut bolt/nut to 36 ft. lbs.
    b. **Torque** alternator mounting bolts to 37 ft. lbs.
    c. **Torque** positive battery cable terminal nut at alternator to 15 ft. lbs.

3.9L Engine

1. Remove washer solvent container.
2. Remove wiper arms.
3. Remove air inlet grill retainers, then the air inlet grill.
4. Disconnect windshield wiper transmission link in front of wiper motor and position aside.
5. Remove throttle body air inlet duct.
6. Set park brake and shift transaxle into Neutral.
7. Remove engine mount strut bolts, then swing engine mount struts aside.
8. Install a engine tilt strap tool No. J 41131, or equivalent.
9. Pull on engine in order to rotate engine forward and tighten engine tilt strap.
10. Rotate engine forward, then remove drive belt.
11. Disconnect engine harness electrical connector from alternator.
12. Reposition positive battery cable boot at alternator terminal.
13. Remove positive battery cable terminal nut at alternator and cable.
14. Remove alternator lower and upper mounting bolts, then the alternator.
15. Reverse procedure to install, noting the following:
    a. **Torque** engine mount strut bolt/nut to 36 ft. lbs.
    b. **Torque** alternator mounting bolts to 37 ft. lbs.
    c. **Torque** positive battery cable terminal nut at alternator to 15 ft. lbs.

COIL PACK

REPLACE

3.5L Engine

1. Note position of spark plug wires for installation reference, then disconnect spark plug wires from coil.
2. Remove ignition coil to bracket retaining screws, then the coil from bracket.
3. Reverse procedure to install. **Torque** screws to 40 inch lbs.

3.9L Engine

1. Remove engine oil fill cap and oil fill pipe.
2. Pull up on intake manifold cover to disengage from studs, then remove cover from engine.
3. Disconnect brake booster vacuum hose from intake manifold.
4. Disconnect MAP sensor electrical connector.
5. Disconnect engine harness electrical connector from ignition coil.
6. Note position of spark plug wires for installation reference, then disconnect spark plug wires from coil.
7. Remove upper left coil mount bracket bolt.
8. Raise and support vehicle.
9. Disconnect wire retainers on ignition coil bracket.
10. Remove remaining bolt and two nuts on coil bracket.
11. Lower vehicle and remove ignition coil and bracket assembly.
12. Reverse procedure to install. **Torque** ignition coil studs, bolts and nuts to 15 ft. lbs.

IGNITION LOCK

REPLACE

1. Remove steering wheel as outlined under "Steering Wheel, Replace."
2. Remove retaining screw from lower steering column trim covers.
3. Tilt trim cover down and slide rearward to disengage locking tabs, then remove lower steering column trim covers.
4. Remove retaining screws from upper steering column trim cover.
5. Lift trim cover to access lock cylinder access hole.
6. Insert a bent-tip awl tool No. A173A or equivalent, into access hole of ignition lock cylinder.
7. Turn ignition lock cylinder to START.
8. Use bent tip in order to push down on ignition lock cylinder retainer.
9. Release ignition lock cylinder to RUN position.
10. Remove ignition lock cylinder from lock cylinder case.
11. Reverse procedure to install, noting the following:
    a. **Torque** retaining screws to upper steering trim cover to 31 inch lbs.

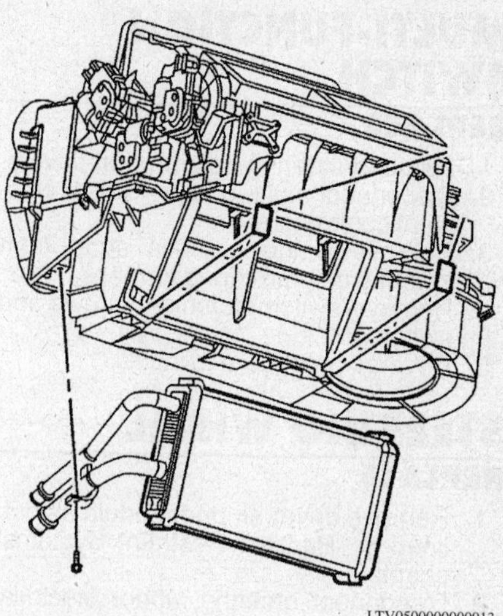

Fig. 2 Heater core removal

    b. **Torque** lower trim cover screws to steering column to 13 inch lbs.

IGNITION SWITCH

REPLACE

1. Remove ignition lock cylinder as outlined under "Ignition Lock, Replace."
2. Disconnect Theft Deterrent Module (TDM) wiring harness connector from steering column harness.
3. Pull TDM away from lock cylinder housing.
4. Remove screws from ignition switch.
5. Remove ignition switch from ignition lock cylinder case.
6. Disconnect ignition switch electrical connector.
7. Disconnect electrical connector from ignition switch.
8. Reverse procedure to install.

HEADLAMP SWITCH

REPLACE

1. Remove molding assembly from lefthand side of instrument panel on steering column opening
2. Pull outlet vent assembly from instrument panel.
3. Disconnect headlamp switch electrical connector.
4. Remove switch assembly from instrument panel.
5. Reverse procedure to install.

STOP LIGHT SWITCH

REPLACE

1. Remove lefthand instrument panel insulator.
2. Disconnect brake pedal position sensor electrical connector.
3. Remove brake pedal position sensor retaining screw, then the sensor from brake pedal.
4. Reverse procedure to install.

MULTI-FUNCTION SWITCH

REPLACE

1. Remove steering column trim covers.
2. Disconnect multi-function switch electrical connectors.
3. Remove wiring harness strap from steering column wiring harness.
4. Remove switch attaching screws and switch.
5. Reverse procedure to install.

STEERING WHEEL

REPLACE

1. Remove driver air bag module as outlined in "Passive Restraint Systems" chapter.
2. Disconnect steering wheel electrical connector.
3. Remove steering wheel center nut.
4. Place alignment marks on steering wheel and column for installation reference.
5. Install steering wheel puller tool No. J1859-A and puller legs tool No. J42578, or equivalents, to steering wheel.
6. Remove steering wheel using puller tools.
7. Reverse procedure to install. **Torque** steering wheel to 30 ft. lbs.

INSTRUMENT CLUSTER

REPLACE

1. Lower steering wheel to its lowest position.
2. Remove trim plate bezel from instrument panel cluster.
3. Remove cluster retaining screws, then disconnect electrical connectors from cluster.
4. Remove cluster from instrument panel.
5. Reverse procedure to install.

RADIO

REPLACE

1. **On models equipped with XM radio,** turn radio ON and tune to XM channel 0, record radio ID. Radio ID will be needed for receiver activation.
2. **On all models,** remove radio trim plate.
3. Remove radio attaching screws.
4. Pull radio from instrument panel, then disconnect electrical connectors.
5. Remove radio from instrument panel.
6. Reverse procedure to install. Perform the radio setup procedure as outlined under "Precautions."

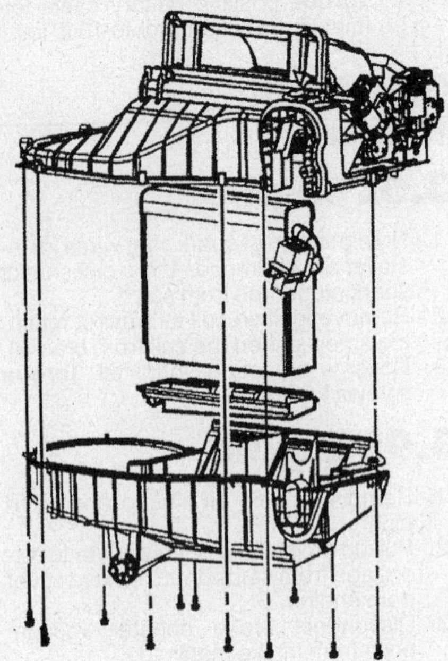

Fig. 3 Evaporator case

WIPER MOTOR

REPLACE

1. Remove wiper arms.
2. Remove air inlet grille panel.
3. Lower washer fluid container into engine compartment.
4. Disconnect wiper motor electrical connector.
5. Remove wiper module assembly mounting bolts, then carefully guide passenger side of module out first from opening in front plenum.
6. Pull module from driver side fender flange opening, then remove module from vehicle.
7. Reverse procedure to install.

WIPER TRANSMISSION

REPLACE

Refer to "Wiper Motor, Replace" for procedure.

BLOWER MOTOR

REPLACE

1. Remove righthand lower instrument panel insulator.
2. Disconnect blower motor electrical connector.
3. Remove blower motor attaching screws, then the motor.
4. Reverse procedure to install.

HEATER CORE

REPLACE

1. Drain cooling system into a suitable container.
2. Remove heater hoses from heater core, **Fig. 1.** Cap off heater core inlet and outlet pipes to prevent coolant spilling inside of the vehicle.
3. Remove instrument panel compartment from righthand side of instrument panel.
4. Remove front seats, then pull front of carpet rearward.
5. Remove floor duct brace retaining nuts, then the floor duct brace.
6. Remove floor duct from center floor duct.
7. Remove center floor duct.
8. Remove floor air outlet attaching screws, then the floor air outlet.
9. Remove heater core cover retaining screws, then the cover.
10. Remove heater core pipe clamp screw and the heater core, **Fig. 2.**
11. Reverse procedure to install.

EVAPORATOR CORE

REPLACE

1. Recover refrigerant as outlined in "Air Conditioning" chapter.
2. Drain cooling system into a suitable container.
3. Set HVAC controls in vent setting to close defroster door.
4. Remove blower motor as outlined in "Blower Motor, Replace."
5. Disconnect electrical connector from blower motor resistor.
6. Disconnect electrical connector from evaporator temperature sensor.
7. Disconnect all of HVAC actuator electrical connectors.
8. Remove instrument panel as outlined in "Dash Panel Service" chapter.
9. Remove evaporator outlet tube nut.
10. Disconnect evaporator outlet tube and evaporator inlet tube from thermal expansion valve.
11. Remove and discard sealing washers.
12. Remove heater inlet and outlet hoses.
13. Remove HVAC module nuts.
14. Remove heater outlet duct screws and the duct.
15. Remove heater core cover screws and the cover.
16. Remove heater core pipe screw, then the heater core.
17. Remove HVAC module to dash panel sound barrier seal.
18. Remove lower HVAC module screws, then separate upper and lower evaporator case halves, **Fig. 3.**
19. Remove evaporator core.
20. Reverse procedure to install.

3.5L Engine

NOTE: On Air Bag Equipped Models, Refer To "Air Bag System Precautions" Located In The Front Of This Manual For System Disarming & Arming Procedures.

NOTE: Refer To "Computer Relearn Procedures" Located In The Front Of This Manual For Computer Relearn Procedures.

INDEX

PRECAUTIONS

Air Bag Systems

Refer to "Air Bag System Precautions" in the front of this manual for system disarming and arming procedures.

Battery Ground Cable

Prior to service, disconnect battery ground cable and isolate as required.

Fuel System Pressure Relief

1. Loosen fuel filler cap to discharge tank pressure.
2. Connect fuel pressure gauge tool No. J-34730-1A, or equivalent, to fuel pressure connection. Wrap shop towel around connection while connecting fuel pressure gauge in order to avoid fuel spillage.
3. Install bleed hose into an approved container and open valve in order to bleed fuel system pressure.
4. Drain any fuel remaining in fuel pressure gauge into suitable container.

ENGINE MOUNT

REPLACE

1. Loosen air cleaner outlet duct clamps at air cleaner and throttle body.
2. Remove PCV fresh air tube from outlet duct.
3. Remove air cleaner outlet duct from air cleaner and throttle body.
4. Remove engine mount strut mounting bolts, then the struts.
5. Raise and support vehicle.
6. Remove catalytic converter.
7. Remove righthand front wheel and tire.
8. Remove righthand engine splash shield.
9. Remove engine mount lower nuts, and insert a block of wood that spans width of oil pan bottom between oil pan and suitable jack.
10. Remove engine mount bracket bolts.
11. Raise engine until engine mount and bracket can be removed.
12. Remove engine mount and bracket.
13. Remove engine mount bracket nuts and mount bracket.
14. Reverse procedure to install.

ENGINE

REPLACE

1. Drain cooling system into a suitable container.
2. Relieve fuel system pressure as outlined under "Precautions."
3. Remove intake manifold cover.
4. Remove coolant reservoir.
5. Remove lefthand front sheet metal diagonal brace.
6. Remove air cleaner side cover and air cleaner element.
7. Remove air cleaner upper cover bolts and upper cover.
8. Remove PCM and position aside with wiring harness.
9. Remove air cleaner bolts and air cleaner.
10. Remove radiator inlet and outlet hoses.
11. Disconnect heater inlet and outlet hoses from engine.
12. Remove brake booster vacuum hose from intake manifold.
13. Disconnect fuel and EVAP line quick connect fittings at engine.
14. Disconnect automatic transaxle range selector cable from selector lever.
15. Remove selector cable from bracket.
16. Remove engine wiring harness grounds from transaxle.
17. Remove engine harness clip from PCV foul air tube clip.
18. Disconnect EGR valve and EVAP canister purge solenoid.
19. Remove engine harness clips from intake manifold.
20. Disconnect engine harness electrical connector from fuel injector electrical connector.
21. Remove engine harness electrical connector clip from belt shield.
22. Remove engine harness clip from ignition coil bracket.
23. Disconnect engine harness electrical connector from ignition coil.
24. Remove engine harness clip from bracket attached to engine mount strut.
25. Disconnect engine harness electrical connector from alternator.
26. Disconnect engine harness electrical connector from transaxle.
27. Remove engine harness clip from transaxle stud.
28. Raise and suitably support vehicle.
29. Remove CPA retainer from HO2S electrical connector.
30. Disconnect engine harness electrical connector from HO2S.
31. Remove HO2S electrical connector clip from ignition coil bracket.

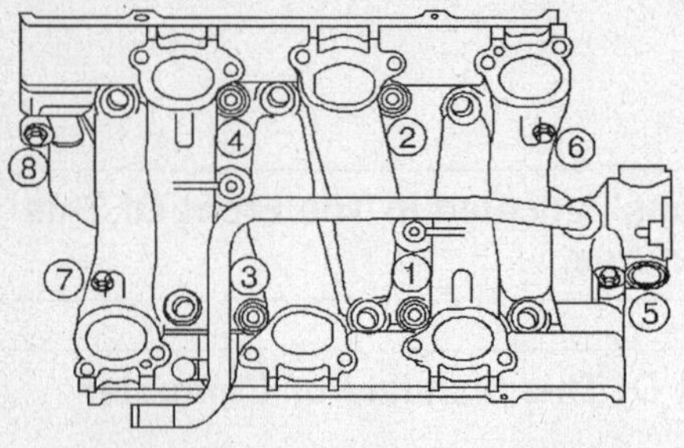

Fig. 1 Lower intake manifold bolt tightening sequence

32. Remove engine harness clip from transaxle brace.
33. Disconnect VSS electrical connector.
34. Disconnect oil pressure switch and knock sensor electrical connectors.
35. Remove engine harness clip from oil dipstick tube.
36. Remove starter solenoid S terminal nut.
37. Remove engine harness lead from starter.
38. Remove engine harness clip from oil pan.
39. Remove engine harness nut.
40. Remove battery ground lead from stud.
41. Remove engine harness ground wires from transaxle studs.
42. Remove engine harness bolt.
43. Reposition battery ground and engine harness.
44. Disconnect engine harness electrical connector from A/C pressure sensor.
45. Disconnect engine harness electrical connector from A/C compressor.
46. Disconnect engine harness electrical connector from righthand wheel speed sensor.
47. Remove engine harness clips from lower control arm.
48. Disconnect engine harness electrical connector from lefthand wheel speed sensor.
49. Remove engine harness clips from lower control arm.
50. Remove CPA retainer from HO2S electrical connector.
51. Disconnect engine harness electrical connector from HO2S.
52. Remove engine harness clips from heat shield and underbody.
53. Disconnect knock sensor and Crankshaft Position (CKP) sensor electrical connectors.
54. Lower vehicle and remove drive belt.
55. Disconnect engine harness electrical connectors from instrument panel electrical connectors.
56. Gather all branches of engine harness and position harness to side and out of way.
57. Remove engine mount strut.
58. Raise and support vehicle.
59. Remove rear propeller shaft.
60. Remove catalytic converter.
61. Remove front tires and wheels.
62. Remove lower radiator air baffle assembly.
63. Remove engine splash shields.
64. Remove stabilizer shaft links from lower control arms.
65. Remove tie rod ends from steering knuckles.
66. Remove lower ball joints from knuckles.
67. Remove transaxle oil cooler line bracket bolt.
68. Disconnect transaxle oil cooler line quick connect fittings at transaxle.
69. Remove A/C compressor bolts and position compressor aside. **Do not discharge A/C system.**
70. Disconnect drive axles from transaxle.
71. Secure drive axles to steering knuckle/struts.
72. Remove front part of inner fender liner in order to access front cradle bolts.
73. Remove intermediate shaft pinch bolt from steering gear.
74. Install a engine support stand tool No. J 39580 or equivalent below vehicle.
75. Lower vehicle until frame contacts engine support stand.
76. Remove frame bolts.
77. Raise vehicle in order to separate powertrain/frame assembly from vehicle.
78. Remove starter motor as outlined under "Starter, Replace" in "Electrical" section.
79. Remove transaxle cover bolts.
80. Remove transaxle covers.
81. Remove torque converter bolts.
82. Remove engine mount lower nuts.
83. Remove transaxle brace bolts and brace.
84. Remove exhaust crossover pipe.
85. Install an engine hoist to engine.
86. Remove transaxle to engine bolts/stud and support transaxle.
87. Separate and remove engine from transaxle/frame.
88. Remove flywheel.
89. Reverse procedure to install.

INTAKE MANIFOLD

REPLACE

Upper

1. Drain cooling system into a suitable container.
2. Remove intake manifold cover.
3. Remove air cleaner outlet duct.
4. Disconnect EVAP canister purge solenoid valve quick connect fitting.
5. Remove PCV fresh air tube from rocker cover.
6. Reposition brake booster vacuum hose clamp at intake manifold.
7. Remove brake booster vacuum hose from intake manifold.
8. Disconnect MAF sensor electrical connector.
9. Remove engine harness clip from PCV foul air clip.
10. Disconnect EGR valve electrical connector.

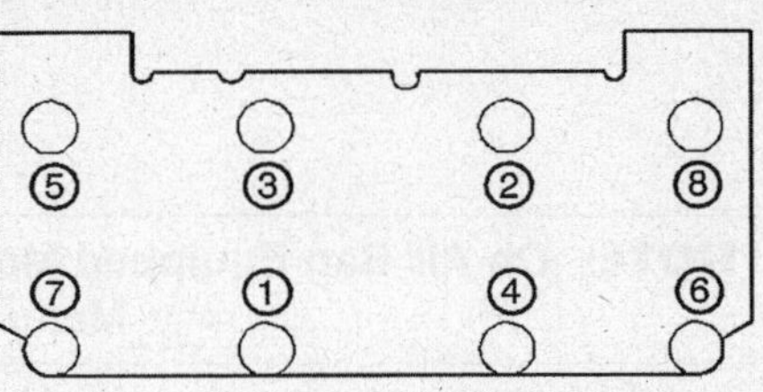

Fig. 2 Cylinder head bolt tightening sequence

11. Disconnect EVAP canister purge solenoid valve electrical connector.
12. Remove engine harness clips from intake manifold.
13. Disconnect lefthand spark plug wires from spark plugs.
14. Remove CMP sensor wiring harness and left side spark plug wire harness.
15. Remove PCV foul air tube bolt, clip and tube.
16. Remove thermostat bypass pipe.
17. Remove ignition coil as outlined under "Ignition Coil, Replace" in "Electrical" section.
18. Remove EGR pipe bolt and carefully pull pipe assembly back.
19. Remove EGR valve studs, valve and gasket.
20. Remove alternator bracket.
21. Remove upper intake manifold bolts and stud.
22. Remove spark plug support bracket.
23. Remove upper intake manifold and gaskets.
24. Reverse procedure to install.

Lower

1. Remove upper intake manifold.
2. Remove lefthand and righthand valve rocker arm covers as outlined under "Valve Cover, Replace."
3. Relieve fuel system pressure as outlined under "Precautions."
4. Disconnect fuel feed pipe from fuel rail.
5. Disconnect EVAP pipe from EVAP canister purge solenoid valve.
6. Disconnect engine harness electrical connector from fuel injector harness electrical connector.
7. Disconnect fuel injector harness electrical connector from ECT sensor.
8. Disconnect fuel injector harness electrical connector from CMP sensor.
9. Remove fuel rail bolts and fuel rail
10. Remove fuel injector O-ring seals from spray tip end of each injector.
11. Remove fuel injectors from fuel rail.
12. Reposition radiator inlet hose clamp at thermostat housing.
13. Remove radiator inlet hose from thermostat housing.
14. Disconnect heater inlet hose quick connect.
15. Remove heater inlet pipe nut and inlet pipe from lower intake manifold.
16. Remove lower intake manifold bolts, intake manifold, then the gaskets and seals.

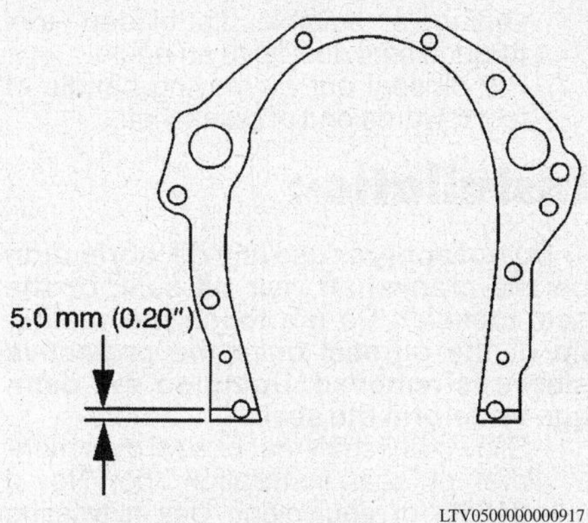

Fig. 3 Front cover sealant application

17. Reverse procedure to install, noting the following:
    a. Apply a small drop .31–.39 inch of RTV sealer to four corners of intake manifold to block joints.
    b. Using sequence, **Fig. 1,** tighten manifold bolts in three steps: First step, **torque** bolts to 115 inch lbs.; second step, **torque** bolts to 15 ft. lbs.; third step, **Torque** bolts to 18 ft. lbs.

EXHAUST MANIFOLD

REPLACE

Lefthand

1. Remove spark plug wires and spark plugs.
2. Remove exhaust manifold heat shield bolts and heat shield.
3. Remove exhaust manifold nuts and manifold.
4. Reverse procedure to install.

Righthand

1. Remove spark plug wires and spark plugs.
2. Remove EGR pipe from exhaust manifold.
3. Remove heated oxygen sensor.
4. Remove exhaust manifold heat shield bolts and heat shields.
5. Remove exhaust manifold nuts and manifold.
6. Reverse procedure to install.

CYLINDER HEAD

REPLACE

1. Raise and support vehicle.
2. Drain cooling system and engine oil.
3. Lower vehicle.
4. Remove lower intake manifold as outlined under "Intake Manifold, Replace."
5. Remove valve rocker arms and pushrods as outlined under "Rocker Arms, Replace."
6. Remove exhaust crossover pipe.
7. Remove oil level indicator tube.
8. Remove exhaust manifold as outlined under "Exhaust Manifold, Replace."
9. **On righthand side cylinder head,** remove alternator.
10. **On lefthand and righthand cylinder heads,** remove and discard cylinder head bolts.
11. **On all models,** remove cylinder head and gasket.
12. Reverse procedure to install. Using sequence shown in **Fig. 2,** tighten cylinder head bolts as follows:
    a. **Torque** bolts to 44 ft. lbs.
    b. Tighten bolts an additional 95° using torque angle wrench tool No. J 45059, or equivalent.

VALVE COVER

REPLACE

Lefthand

1. Partially drain cooling system.
2. Remove front ignition wire harness at upper intake manifold and spark plugs.
3. Remove thermostat bypass pipe, then disconnect PCV vacuum hose.
4. Remove valve rocker arm cover bolts.
5. Remove valve rocker arm cover. If cover adheres to cylinder head, bump cover with a soft rubber mallet. **When removing valve rocker arm cover, ensure gasket stays in place and attached to cylinder head.**
6. Carefully trim cover gasket and sealant away from lower intake manifold gasket and at cylinder head to lower intake manifold joints. **Failure to carefully trim gasket and sealant away from intake manifold gasket will damage gasket and cause a severe oil leak.**
7. Reverse procedure to install. Clean sealing surface on cylinder head with degreaser.

Righthand

1. Remove drive belt as outlined under "Serpentine Drive Belt."
2. Remove alternator as outlined in "Electrical" section.
3. Remove alternator bracket, then the spark plug wires.
4. Disconnect vacuum hoses from EVAP purge valve.
5. Remove EVAP purge valve, then the ignition coil bracket with coils.
6. Remove ignition coil bracket studs.
7. Remove vacuum hose from grommet in valve rocker arm cover.
8. Remove valve rocker arm cover bolts.
9. Remove valve rocker arm cover. If cover adheres to cylinder head, bump cover with a soft rubber mallet. **When removing valve rocker arm cover, ensure gasket stays in place and attached to cylinder head.**
10. Carefully trim cover gasket and sealant away from lower intake manifold gasket and at cylinder head to lower intake manifold joints. **Failure to carefully trim gasket and sealant away from intake manifold gasket will damage gasket and cause a severe oil leak.**

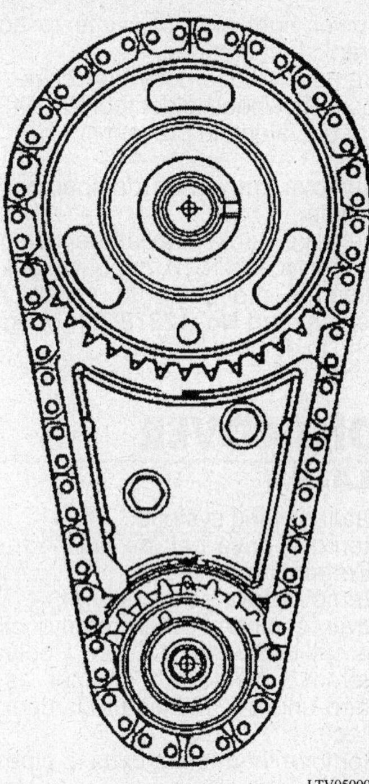

Fig. 4 Timing mark alignment

11. Reverse procedure to install. Clean sealing surface on cylinder head with degreaser.

ROCKER ARMS

REPLACE

1. Remove valve rocker arm cover as outlined under "Valve Cover, Replace."
2. Remove rocker arm bolts and the rocker arms.
3. Reverse procedure to install.

HYDRAULIC LIFTERS

REPLACE

1. Remove lower intake manifold as outlined under "Intake Manifold, Replace."
2. Remove valve rocker arms as outlined under "Rocker Arms, Replace."
3. Remove pushrods.
4. Remove the intake manifold oil splash shield.
5. Remove lifter guide bolts, then the valve lifter guides.
6. Remove valve lifters.
7. Reverse procedure to install. Coat valve lifters with suitable prelube part No. 12345501, or equivalent.

CRANKSHAFT DAMPER

REPLACE

1. Remove drive belt as outlined under "Serpentine Drive Belt."
2. Raise and support vehicle.
3. Remove right front tire and wheel.
4. Remove engine splash shield.
5. Place suitable adjustable jack stands under frame.
6. Loosen left side frame bolts, then remove right side frame bolts.

7. Lower right side of frame to access crankshaft damper.
8. Remove torque converter cover, then install flywheel holder tool No. J 43442, or equivalent, to prevent flywheel rotation.
9. Remove crankshaft damper bolt and washer.
10. Remove crankshaft damper using puller tool No. J 41816, or equivalent.
11. Reverse procedure to install. Apply sealant part No. 12378521, or equivalent, to damper keyway.

FRONT COVER

REPLACE

1. Drain cooling system.
2. Remove drive belt as outlined under "Serpentine Drive Belt."
3. Remove drive belt tensioner.
4. Drain engine oil, then remove oil pan as outlined under "Oil Pan, Replace."
5. Remove crankshaft damper as outlined under "Crankshaft Damper, Replace."
6. Remove thermostat bypass pipe from engine front cover.
7. Remove radiator outlet hose from engine front cover.
8. Remove water pump from engine front cover as outlined under "Water Pump, Replace."
9. Remove power steering pump from engine and position aside.
10. Remove front cover retaining bolts, then the front cover and gasket.
11. Reverse procedure to install, noting the following:
    a. Apply sealant part No. 12346004, or equivalent, to both sides of front cover gasket, **Fig. 3.** Apply sealer no less than .20 inch wide.
    b. Apply sealant part No. 12346004, or equivalent, to threads of front cover bolts.

TIMING CHAIN

REPLACE

1. Remove engine front cover as outlined under "Front Cover, Replace."
2. Rotate crankshaft until timing marks are aligned, **Fig. 4.**
3. Remove camshaft sprocket attaching bolt, then the camshaft sprocket with timing chain.
4. Remove crankshaft sprocket.
5. Remove timing chain damper attaching bolts, then the damper, **Fig. 5.**
6. Reverse procedure to install. Ensure timing marks are aligned, **Fig. 4.**

PISTON & ROD ASSEMBLY

Ensure the marks on the piston and connecting rod are aligned the same as when they were removed. If installing a new piston, ensure the arrow on top faces towards the front of the engine. If no identification marks were made during disassembly, ensure the flat area on the bottom of the piston pin skirt is aligned with the small dimple above the connecting rod crankshaft bearing bore.

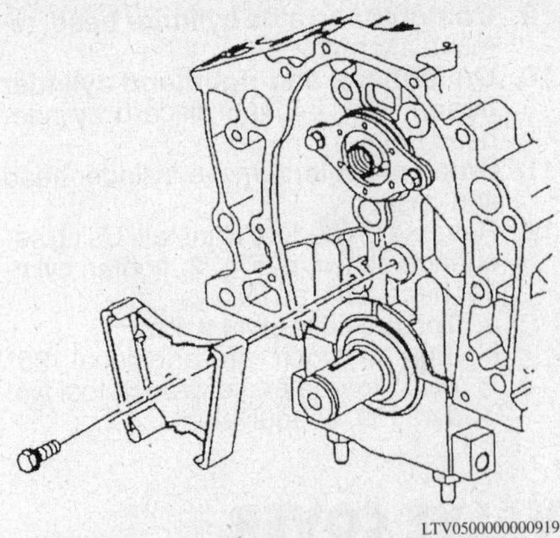

Fig. 5 Timing chain damper

MAIN & ROD BEARINGS

1. Dip bearing cap bolts in clean engine oil.
2. Apply a small amount of clean engine oil to crankshaft main bearing surface.
3. Apply a small amount of sealer part No. 1052942, or equivalent, to rear of No. 4 crankshaft main bearing cap sealing surface.
4. Tighten bearing cap bolts to specification.

CRANKSHAFT SEAL

REPLACE

1. Remove crankshaft damper as outlined under "Crankshaft Damper, Replace."
2. Remove crankshaft key from keyway.
3. Pry oil seal out of front cover using a large screwdriver.
4. Reverse procedure to install. Lubricate oil seal with clean engine oil.

CRANKSHAFT REAR OIL SEAL

REPLACE

Removal

1. Remove transaxle as outlined in **MOTOR's "Domestic Transmission, In-Vehicle Service" or "Transmission Service DVD."**
2. Install flywheel holder tool No. J 43442, or equivalent, to prevent crankshaft from rotating.
3. Loosen flywheel bolts, then remove five of six flywheel bolts leaving one bolt at top to prevent crankshaft rotation.
4. Grip flywheel and remove remaining bolt.
5. Remove engine flywheel retainer and flywheel.
6. Remove crankshaft rear oil seal by inserting a suitable flat-bladed tool through seal dust lip at an angle.
7. Pry oil seal out by moving handle of tool towards end of crankshaft.

Installation

Do not apply or use any oil lubrication on the crankshaft rear oil seal, or the seal installer. Do not touch the sealing lip of the oil seal once the protective sleeve is removed. Doing so will damage or deform the seal.

1. Slide crankshaft rear oil seal over mandrel of seal installation tool No. J 34686, or equivalent. Use a twisting motion until back of crankshaft rear oil seal bottoms squarely against collar of tool.
2. Align dowel pin of installation tool with dowel pin in crankshaft.
3. Attach seal installation tool to crankshaft by hand.
4. Turn T-handle of tool to allow collar to push seal into bore, continue to turn handle until collar is tight against engine block.
5. Ensure seal is seated properly, then remove tool.
6. Install flywheel, then the transaxle as outlined in **MOTOR's "Domestic Transmission, In-Vehicle Service" or "Transmission Service DVD."**

OIL PAN

REPLACE

1. Install engine support fixture tool No. J 28467-500, or equivalent.
2. Raise and support vehicle, then drain engine oil.
3. Remove right front tire and wheel.
4. Remove front splash shield.
5. Remove wheel speed sensor harness from right suspension support.
6. Remove right front ball joint, bolt and nut, then separate ball joint from steering knuckle.
7. Remove lower closeout panel.
8. Remove A/C compressor mounting bolts, then position compressor aside.
9. Remove braces that support engine to transmission.
10. Remove starter motor as outlined in "Electrical" section.
11. Disconnect oil level sensor.
12. Remove brake line to frame retainers.
13. Remove right side engine mount nuts and bolts, then loosen left side cradle bolts.
14. Remove frame bolts from right front and right rear.
15. Remove oil pan bolts, then the oil pan and gasket.
16. Reverse procedure to install.

OIL PUMP

REPLACE

1. Remove oil pan as outlined under "Oil Pan, Replace."
2. Remove oil pump bolt attaching bolt, then the pump and pump drive shaft.
3. Reverse procedure to install.

SERPENTINE DRIVE BELT

Belt Routing

Refer to **Fig. 6** for serpentine drive belt routing.

Belt Replacement

1. Rotate drive belt tensioner counterclockwise to release tension.
2. Remove serpentine drive belt.
3. Reverse procedure to install.

Tensioner Replacement

1. Remove serpentine drive belt.
2. Remove mounting bolt and tensioner.
3. Reverse procedure to install.

COOLING SYSTEM BLEED

1. Open cooling system bleeder screws.
2. Slowly fill cooling system with a 50/50 coolant mixture.
3. Close cooling system bleeder screws, then install pressure cap.
4. Start and run engine at 2000–2500 RPM until engine reaches normal operating temperature.
5. Allow engine to idle for three minutes, then shut engine off.
6. Allow engine to cool and top off coolant as necessary.

THERMOSTAT

REPLACE

1. Remove air cleaner intake duct.
2. Drain cooling system.
3. Remove radiator inlet hose from thermostat housing.
4. Remove thermostat housing bolts, then the thermostat housing.
5. Remove thermostat and O-ring seal. Discard O-ring seal.
6. Reverse procedure to install.

WATER PUMP

REPLACE

1. Drain cooling system.
2. Loosen water pump pulley bolts.

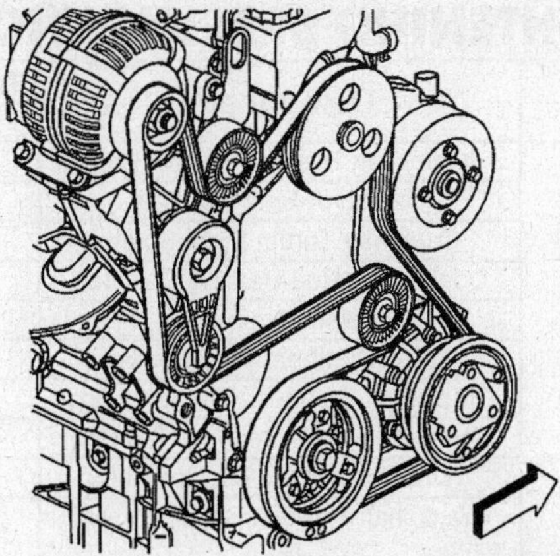

Fig. 6 Serpentine drive belt routing

3. Remove drive belt as outlined under "Serpentine Drive Belt."
4. Remove water pump pulley bolts and pulley.
5. Remove water pump bolts and pump.
6. Reverse procedure to install.

RADIATOR

REPLACE

1. Disconnect lower transmission oil cooler line from radiator.
2. Remove air cleaner and duct assembly.
3. Remove right side diagonal brace, then the radiator inlet hose.
4. Disconnect cooling fan harness electrical connector.
5. Loosen engine mount strut nuts from engine side of strut.
6. Remove engine mount strut bracket brace bolts from upper radiator support, then rotate struts and brackets rearward.
7. Reposition coolant overflow hose from reservoir.
8. Remove overflow hose from retainers, then position hose aside.
9. Remove battery.
10. Remove radiator upper mount bolts, then the mounts.
11. Remove cooling fan shroud bolts.
12. Disconnect upper transmission oil cooler line from radiator.
13. Disconnect transmission oil cooler lines from fan shroud retainer clip.
14. Remove cooling fans and shroud.
15. Remove radiator inlet and outlet hoses.
16. Remove condenser tube clip screw.
17. Tilt radiator and condenser inwards toward engine, then remove radiator.
18. Reverse procedure to install.

FUEL PUMP

REPLACE

1. Relieve fuel system fuel pressure as outlined under "Precautions."
2. Drain fuel tank, then raise and support vehicle.
3. Disconnect fuel supply pipe quick-connect fitting.
4. **On models with short wheel base,** disconnect EVAP purge pipe from canister.
5. **On all models,** loosen fuel tank filler pipe hose clamp, then disconnect fuel tank filler pipe from fuel tank.
6. Disconnect vapor recirculation pipe from filler tube.
7. Remove fuel tank shield.
8. Support fuel tank, then remove fuel tank strap attaching bolts.
9. Disconnect fuel sender and fuel tank pressure sensor electrical connectors at body pass through.
10. Remove fuel tank from vehicle.
11. Clean fuel pipe connections, hose connections and all areas surrounding connections before disconnecting connections to avoid possible fuel system contamination.
12. Disconnect fuel supply pipe quick-connect fitting at fuel sender assembly.
13. Disconnect EVAP pipe quick-connect fittings at fuel sender assembly.
14. Unlock fuel sender lock ring using fuel sender lock nut wrench tool No. J 45722, or equivalent, and a long breaker-bar.
15. Turn fuel sender lock ring in a counterclockwise direction.
16. Remove fuel sender assembly and seal from fuel tank.
17. Drain fuel from fuel sender assembly into an approved container.
18. Remove fuel sender assembly and seal from fuel tank. Discard seal.
19. Reverse procedure to install.

TIGHTENING SPECIFICATIONS

Year	Component	Torque Ft. Lbs.
2005–06	Camshaft Position Sensor Bolt	89①
	Camshaft Sprocket Bolt	103
	Camshaft Thrust Plate Screw	89①
	Connecting Rod Bearing Cap Bolt	②
	Coolant Drain Plug	14
	Coolant Temperature Sensor	17
	Crankshaft Balancer (Damper) Bolt	118
	Crankshaft Main Bearing Cap Bolt	③
	Crankshaft Oil Deflector Nut	18
	Crankshaft Position Sensor Shield Nut	97①
	Cylinder Head Bolt	④
	Cylinder Head Plug	15
	Drive Belt Tensioner Bolt	37
	EGR Valve Assembly Bolt	22
	Engine Block Plug	18
	Engine Block Heater	44
	Engine Front Cover (Large & Medium) Bolt	41
	Engine Front Cover (Small) Bolt	20
	Engine Mount Strut & A/C Compressor Bracket Bolt	37
	Engine Mount Strut & Generator Bracket Bolt	37
	EVAP Purge Valve Bolt	12
	Exhaust Crossover Pipe Stud/Nut	18
	Exhaust Manifold Nut	12
	Exhaust Manifold Stud	13
	Flywheel Bolt	52
	Intake Manifold Bolt, Lower (Center)	15
	Intake Manifold Bolt, Lower (Corner)	18
	Intake Manifold Bolt/Stud, Upper	18
	Knock Sensor	18
	MAP Sensor Bolt	89①
	Oil Pan Bolt	18
	Oil Pan Drain Plug	18
	Oil Pan Side Bolt	37
	Oil Pump Mounting Bolt	30
	Spark Plug	11
	Thermostat Bypass Pipe To Engine Front Cover Bolt	89①
	Thermostat Bypass Pipe To Throttle Body Nut/Bolt	89①
	Throttle Body Bolt	89①
	Throttle Body Stud	53①
	Timing Chain Damper Bolt	15
	Valve Lifter Guide Bolt	89①
	Valve Cover	89①
	Valve Rocker Arm Bolt	24
	Water Outlet Bolt	18
	Water Pump Bolt	89①
	Water Pump Pulley Bolt	18

① — Inch lbs.

② — First pass, 18 ft. lbs.; second pass, an additional 110°.

③ — First pass, 37 ft. lbs.; second pass, an additional 77°.

④ — Refer to “Cylinder Head, Replace” for tightening procedure.

3.9L Engine

NOTE: On Air Bag Equipped Models, Refer To "Air Bag System Precautions" Located In The Front Of This Manual For System Disarming & Arming Procedures.

NOTE: Refer To "Computer Relearn Procedures" Located In The Front Of This Manual For Computer Relearn Procedures.

INDEX

PRECAUTIONS

Air Bag Systems

Refer to "Air Bag System Precautions" in the front of this manual for system disarming and arming procedures.

Battery Ground Cable

Prior to service, disconnect battery ground cable and isolate as required.

Fuel System Pressure Relief

1. Loosen fuel filler cap to discharge tank pressure.
2. Connect fuel pressure gauge tool No. J-34730-1A, or equivalent, to fuel pressure connection. Wrap shop towel around connection while connecting fuel pressure gauge in order to avoid fuel spillage.
3. Install bleed hose into an approved container and open valve in order to bleed fuel system pressure.
4. Drain any fuel remaining in fuel pressure gauge into suitable container.

ENGINE MOUNT

REPLACE

1. Loosen air cleaner outlet duct clamps at air cleaner and throttle body.
2. Remove PCV fresh air tube from outlet duct.
3. Remove air cleaner outlet duct from air cleaner and throttle body.
4. Remove engine mount strut mounting bolts, then the struts.
5. Raise and support vehicle.
6. Remove catalytic converter.
7. Remove righthand front wheel and tire.
8. Remove righthand engine splash shield.
9. Remove engine mount lower nuts, and insert a block of wood that spans width of oil pan bottom between oil pan and suitable jack.
10. Remove engine mount bracket bolts.
11. Raise engine until engine mount and bracket can be removed.
12. Remove engine mount and bracket.
13. Remove engine mount bracket nuts and mount bracket.
14. Reverse procedure to install.

ENGINE

REPLACE

The front wheels of the vehicle must be maintained in the straight ahead position and the steering column must be in the Lock position before disconnecting the steering column or intermediate shaft. Failure to follow these procedures will cause improper alignment of some components during installation and result in damage to the SIR coil assembly.

1. Lock steering column by installing tool No. J 42640 or equivalent, into underside of steering column.
2. Open hood.
3. Remove engine oil fill cap.
4. Remove intake manifold cover.
5. Disconnect auxiliary ground cable on inner fender.
6. Disconnect positive battery feed at junction box.
7. Remove lower radiator air baffle.
8. Drain cooling system into suitable container.
9. Lower vehicle.
10. Reposition coolant recovery reservoir hose clamp at coolant crossover.
11. Remove coolant recovery reservoir hose from crossover.
12. Remove coolant reservoir.
13. Remove lefthand side diagonal brace.
14. Unsnap and remove junction block cover.
15. Loosen air cleaner cover bolts.
16. Remove air cleaner cover.
17. Remove engine control module (ECM) from air cleaner cover.
18. Disconnect engine harness electrical connector from transaxle control module (TCM), instrument panel harness electrical connector and ABS module harness electrical connector.
19. Remove engine harness clip from air conditioning line.
20. Remove engine harness clip from the A/C line.
21. Remove underhood junction.
22. Unsnap and remove engine harness connector from junction block retainer.
23. Disconnect engine harness electrical connector from mass air flow (MAF) and intake air temperature (IAT) sensor.
24. Disconnect positive crankcase ventilation (PCV) fresh air tube quick connect fitting from air cleaner outlet duct.
25. Loosen air cleaner outlet duct clamps at throttle body and MAF/IAT sensor.
26. Remove air cleaner outlet duct from throttle body and MAF/IAT sensor.
27. Gather outer branches of engine harness and lay them on top of engine.
28. Release tension on radiator inlet hose

clamp and reposition clamp using tool No. J 38185 or equivalent.
29. Remove radiator inlet hose from coolant crossover.
30. Release tension on radiator outlet hose clamp and reposition clamp using tool No. J 38185 or equivalent.
31. Remove radiator outlet hose from thermostat housing.
32. Disconnect heater inlet and outlet hose quick connect fittings from inlet and outlet pipes.
33. Remove brake booster vacuum hose from upper intake manifold fitting.
34. Disconnect fuel feed and evaporative emission line quick connect fittings.
35. Remove engine mount struts.
36. Drain engine oil into a suitable container.
37. Remove front wheels and tires.
38. **On models equipped with All Wheel Drive (AWD),** remove rear propeller shaft as outlined in "Rear Axle & Suspension" section.
39. **On all models,** disconnect engine harness electrical connectors from lefthand and righthand wheel speed sensors.
40. Remove drive belt as outlined in "Serpentine Drive Belt."
41. Disconnect engine harness electrical connectors from A/C compressor.
42. Remove A/C compressor front bolt and nut.
43. Remove A/C compressor rear bolt. Reposition and support A/C compressor out of way.
44. Remove catalytic converter.
45. Remove engine splash shield.
46. **On models equipped with All Wheel Drive (AWD),** remove engine harness clips from catalytic converter heat shield.
47. **On models equipped with Front Wheel Drive (FWD),** remove engine harness clips from heat shield.
48. **On all models,** disconnect battery cable retainers at core support.
49. **On models equipped with Front Wheel Drive (FWD),** remove stabilizer shaft link lower nuts.
50. **On all models,** remove stabilizer shaft links from stabilizer shaft.
51. Remove tie rod end nuts at steering knuckles.
52. Separate outer tie rod ends from steering knuckle using tool No. J 24319-B or equivalent. **Do not attempt to free ball stud by using a pickle fork or wedge type tool, because seal or bushing damage could result. Use proper tool to separate all ball joints.**
53. Remove lower ball joint cotter pins from ball joints.
54. Loosen lower ball joint castle nuts.
55. Install tool No. J 41820 or equivalent, over ball joint and lower control arm.
56. Rotate castle nut counterclockwise in order to separate ball joint from steering knuckle.
57. Disengage wheel drive shafts from transaxle using tool Nos., J 33008-A, J 29794 and J 2619-O1 or equivalents.
58. Secure wheel drive shafts to steering knuckle struts.
59. Reposition intermediate steering shaft seal in order to provide access to intermediate steering shaft pinch bolt. **Failure to disconnect intermediate shaft from rack and pinion steering gear stub shaft can result in damage to steering gear and/or intermediate shaft. This damage may cause loss of steering control which could result in an accident and possible personal injury.**
60. Remove intermediate steering shaft pinch bolt.
61. Disconnect intermediate steering shaft from power steering gear.
62. Place tool No. J 39580 or equivalent, under frame and lower vehicle until frame contacts tool.
63. Remove front and rear frame bolts.
64. Remove frame rear strap bolts.
65. Remove frame rear straps.
66. Raise vehicle in order to separate powertrain frame assembly from vehicle.
67. Remove engine harness ground wire nut.
68. Remove engine harness positive battery cable from stud.
69. Disconnect engine harness electrical connector from starter.
70. Remove engine harness ground nuts from transaxle studs.
71. Remove engine harness grounds from studs.
72. Remove negative battery cable from transaxle stud.
73. Remove engine to transaxle brace.
74. Remove starter motor as outlined under "Starter, Replace" in "Electrical" section.
75. Remove torque converter cover bolts.
76. Remove torque converter covers.
77. Use tool No. J 37096 or equivalent, in order to hold flywheel, and also rotate flywheel to access torque converter bolts.
78. Remove torque converter bolts.
79. Remove engine mount to frame nuts.
80. Remove engine harness clips from transaxle brace.
81. Remove transaxle brace bolts and brace.
82. Remove exhaust crossover pipe shield bolts and shield.
83. Remove exhaust crossover pipe nuts and pipe.
84. Disconnect engine harness electrical connector from EVAP purge solenoid, throttle actuator and manifold absolute pressure (MAP) sensor.
85. Disconnect engine harness electrical connector from ignition coil.
86. Remove engine harness clips from ignition coil brackets.
87. Remove engine harness clip from engine.
88. Remove engine harness bolt.
89. Disconnect engine harness electrical connector from camshaft actuator magnet.
90. Remove engine harness bracket nut.
91. Remove engine harness bracket from stud.
92. Remove engine harness clip from bracket.
93. Disconnect engine harness electrical connector from intake manifold tuning valve.
94. Remove connector position assurance (CPA) retainer from back of alternator.
95. Disconnect engine harness electrical connector from fuel injector harness electrical connector.
96. Remove alternator terminal nut.
97. Remove engine harness lead from alternator.
98. Disconnect engine harness electrical connector from generator and heated oxygen sensor (HO2S).
99. Remove engine harness clip from strut bracket.
100. Disconnect engine harness electrical connector from crankshaft position (CKP) sensor.
101. Disconnect engine harness electrical connector from knock sensor and oil pressure sensor.
102. Disconnect engine harness electrical connector from transaxle.
103. Disconnect engine harness electrical connector from vehicle speed sensor (VSS).
104. Remove engine harness clip from stud on transaxle.
105. Remove engine harness clamp bolt from transaxle.
106. Remove engine harness clips from transaxle studs.
107. Disconnect engine harness electrical connector from oil level sensor.
108. Remove engine harness clip from oil pan.
109. Remove engine harness from engine.
110. Disconnect power steering line retainer from alternator bracket.
111. Remove power steering pressure pipe and return line from power steering pump and position out of way.
112. Install an engine hoist to engine.
113. Remove transaxle bolts and studs.
114. Support transaxle, then separate and remove engine from transaxle and frame.
115. Install tool No. J 37096 or equivalent, in order to hold flywheel, then loosen flywheel bolts.
116. Remove five of six flywheel bolts leaving one bolt at top of crankshaft.
117. Hold flywheel and remove remaining bolt. **Do not drop flywheel when removing final bolt.**
118. Remove engine flywheel and install engine to engine stand.
119. Remove engine hoist from engine.
120. Reverse procedure to install, tighten to specifications.

INTAKE MANIFOLD

REPLACE

Lower

1. Remove engine oil fill cap and oil fill pipe.
2. Pull up on intake manifold cover in order to disengage cover from studs.
3. Remove alternator as outlined in "Electrical" section.
4. Remove drive belt idler pulleys.

5. Remove power steering pump as outlined in "Front Suspension & Steering" section.
6. Reposition coolant recovery reservoir inlet hose clamp at coolant crossover.
7. Remove coolant recovery reservoir inlet hose from coolant crossover.
8. Release tension on hose clamp at coolant crossover using tool No. J 38185 or equivalent.
9. Remove radiator inlet hose from crossover pipe.
10. Reposition thermal bypass hose clamp at crossover pipe.
11. Remove coolant crossover pipe bolts, then the coolant crossover pipe.
12. Remove upper intake manifold as outlined in "Intake Manifold, Replace."
13. Remove rocker arms as outlined in "Rocker Arm, Replace."
14. Disconnect engine coolant temperature (ECT) electrical connector.
15. Disconnect fuel feed line from fuel rail.
16. Remove connector position assurance (CPA) retainer, then the disconnect engine harness electrical connector from fuel injector harness electrical connector.
17. Remove fuel injector harness connector bracket bolt from intake manifold.
18. Disconnect camshaft position (CMP) sensor electrical connector.
19. Remove fuel injector rail bolts.
20. Remove fuel rail.
21. Remove lower intake manifold bolts, then the lower intake manifold.
22. Loosen valve rocker arm bolts.
23. Remove valve rocker arms, then the push rods.
24. Remove lower intake manifold gaskets and seals.
25. Clean lower intake manifold gasket and seal surfaces on cylinder heads and engine block.
26. Clean gasket and seal surfaces on lower intake manifold with degreaser.
27. Remove all loose room temperature vulcanizing sealer (RTV).
28. Reverse procedure to install. Tighten to specifications.

Upper

1. Remove engine oil fill cap and oil fill pipe.
2. Pull up on intake manifold cover in order to disengage cover from studs.
3. Drain cooling system into suitable container.
4. Remove positive crankcase ventilation (PCV) fresh air tube.
5. Remove PCV foul air tube.
6. Reposition brake booster vacuum hose clamp at intake manifold.
7. Remove vacuum hose from intake manifold.
8. Disconnect engine harness electrical connector from manifold absolute pressure (MAP) sensor.
9. Disconnect engine harness electrical connectors from electrical connector to evaporative emission (EVAP) canister purge solenoid and electronic throttle control (ETC).

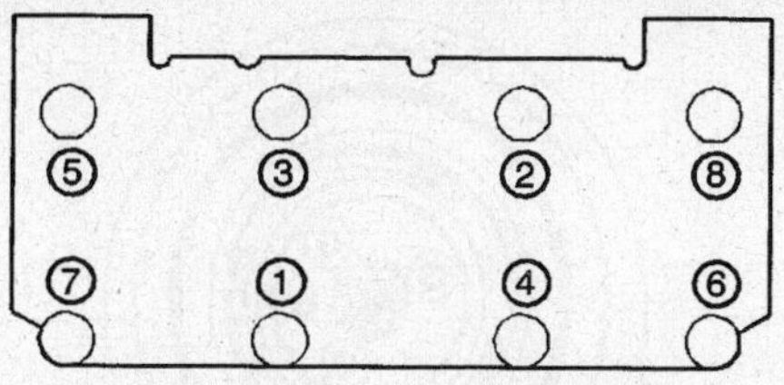

Fig. 1 Cylinder head bolt tightening sequence

10. Disconnect engine harness electrical connector from intake manifold tuning valve.
11. Remove air cleaner outlet duct.
12. Disconnect lefthand side spark plug wires from spark plugs.
13. Disconnect lefthand side spark plug wires from ignition control module.
14. Disengage spark plug wire retainer clips from intake manifold bracket and heater inlet/outlet pipe.
15. Remove lefthand side spark plug wires.
16. Remove heater inlet and outlet pipe nuts from throttle body studs.
17. Remove inlet and outlet pipe from studs.
18. Remove nut from alternator bracket to intake manifold.
19. Remove bolt connecting alternator to bracket and alternator to intake manifold.
20. Remove bracket.
21. Remove bolt holding transmission dipstick tube to upper intake manifold.
22. Remove ignition coils as outlined in "Electrical" section.
23. Remove upper intake manifold bolts and stud.
24. Separate and remove upper intake manifold from lower intake manifold.
25. Remove upper to lower intake manifold gaskets.
26. Remove inlet manifold tuning valve bolts and valve.
27. Remove EVAP canister purge solenoid valve bolt and valve.
28. Remove MAP sensor bracket bolts, bracket and sensor.
29. Remove throttle body bolts, studs and throttle body.
30. Clean upper intake to lower intake gasket mating surfaces.
31. Inspect intake manifold tuning valve seal for damage. Tuning valve blade attachment to motor should be tight, with no looseness or slack present, Replace as required.
32. Apply lubricant to nose of valve blade.
33. Reverse procedure to install, noting the following:
    a. Apply threadlock to upper intake manifold bolts and stud threads.
    b. Tighten to specifications.
    c. Fill cooling system to specifications as outlined in "Specifications" section.

EXHAUST MANIFOLD

REPLACE

Lefthand

1. Remove spark plug wires and spark plugs.
2. Remove exhaust manifold heat shield bolts and heat shield.
3. Remove exhaust manifold nuts and manifold.
4. Reverse procedure to install.

Righthand

1. Remove spark plug wires and spark plugs.
2. Remove EGR pipe from exhaust manifold.
3. Remove heated oxygen sensor.
4. Remove exhaust manifold heat shield bolts and heat shields.
5. Remove exhaust manifold nuts and manifold.
6. Reverse procedure to install.

CYLINDER HEAD

REPLACE

1. Raise and support vehicle.
2. Drain cooling system and engine oil into suitable containers.
3. Lower vehicle.
4. Remove lower intake manifold as outlined under "Intake Manifold, Replace."
5. Remove valve rocker arms and pushrods as outlined under "Rocker Arms, Replace."
6. Remove exhaust crossover pipe.
7. Remove oil level indicator tube.
8. Remove exhaust manifold as outlined under "Exhaust Manifold, Replace."
9. Remove spark plugs.
10. Remove and discard cylinder head bolts.
11. Remove cylinder head and gasket.
12. Reverse procedure to install. Using sequence shown in **Fig. 1,** tighten cylinder head bolts as follows:
    a. **Torque** bolts to 44 ft. lbs.
    b. Tighten bolts an additional 95° using torque angle wrench tool No. J 45059, or equivalent.

VALVE COVER

REPLACE

Lefthand

1. Remove intake manifold cover as outlined in "Intake Manifold, Replace."
2. Remove heater inlet and outer front pipe.
3. Disconnect positive crankcase ventilation (PCV) foul air tube from PCV valve.
4. Remove righthand side engine mount strut.
5. Remove valve rocker arm cover bolts, then the cover. **When removing valve rocker arm cover, ensure gasket stays in place attached to cylinder head.**

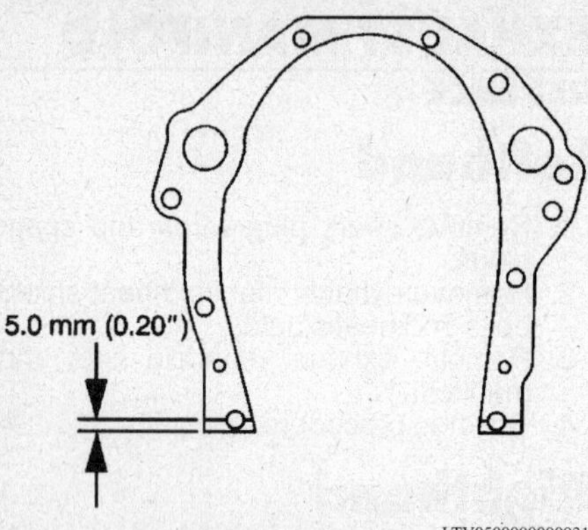

Fig. 2 Front cover gasket sealant application

6. Remove valve cover gasket.
7. Reverse procedure to install, noting the following:
   a. Clean sealing surface on cylinder head with degreaser.
   b. Install a new valve rocker arm cover gasket.
   c. Apply suitable sealant to cylinder head and surfaces where cylinder head and intake manifold contact.
   d. Tighten to specifications.

Righthand

1. Remove alternator as outlined in "Electrical" section.
2. Drain cooling system into suitable container.
3. Remove coolant crossover pipe.
4. Disconnect positive crankcase ventilation (PCV) fresh air tube from air cleaner outlet duct.
5. Remove PCV fresh air tube from righthand side valve rocker arm cover.
6. Disconnect engine harness electrical connector from manifold absolute pressure (MAP) sensor.
7. Disconnect engine harness electrical connector from ignition coil.
8. Remove heated oxygen sensor (HO2S) electrical connector clip from ignition coil bracket.
9. Remove spark plug wires from ignition coil.
10. Remove ignition coil bracket bolts and nuts.
11. Remove ignition coil with bracket from engine.
12. Remove valve rocker arm cover bolts, then the cover. **When removing valve rocker arm cover, ensure gasket stays in place attached to cylinder head.**
13. Remove valve cover gasket.
14. Reverse procedure to install, noting the following:
    a. Clean sealing surface on cylinder head with degreaser.
    b. Install a new valve rocker arm cover gasket.
    c. Apply suitable sealant to cylinder head and surfaces where cylinder head and intake manifold contact.
    d. Tighten to specifications.

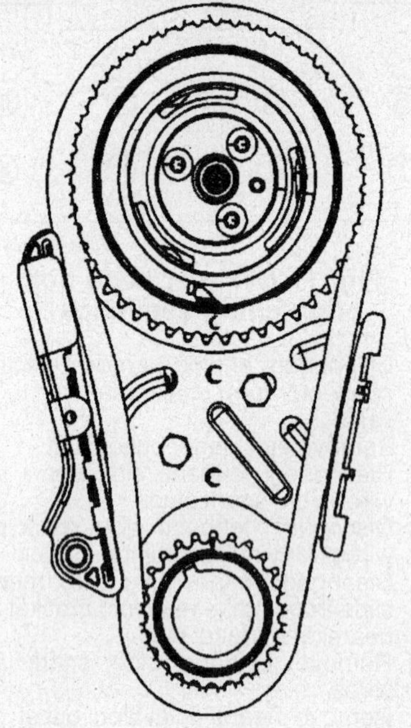

Fig. 3 Timing mark alignment

ROCKER ARMS

REPLACE

1. Remove valve rocker arm cover as outilined under "Valve Cover, Replace."
2. Remove rocker arm bolts and the rocker arms.
3. Reverse procedure to install. Tighten to specifications.

HYDRAULIC LIFTERS

REPLACE

1. Remove lower intake manifold as outlined under "Intake Manifold, Replace."
2. Remove valve rocker arms as outlined under "Rocker Arms, Replace."
3. Remove pushrods.
4. Remove the intake manifold oil splash shield.
5. Remove lifter guide bolts, then the valve lifter guides.
6. Remove valve lifters.
7. Reverse procedure to install. Coat valve lifters with suitable prelube part No. 12345501, or equivalent.

CRANKSHAFT DAMPER

REPLACE

1. Remove drive belt as outlined under "Serpentine Drive Belt."
2. Raise and support vehicle.
3. Remove right front tire and wheel.
4. Remove engine splash shield.
5. Place suitable adjustable jack stands under frame.
6. Loosen lefthand side frame bolts, then remove righthand side frame bolts.
7. Lower righthand side of frame to access crankshaft damper.
8. Remove torque converter cover, then install flywheel holder tool No. J 37096, or equivalent, to prevent flywheel rotation.

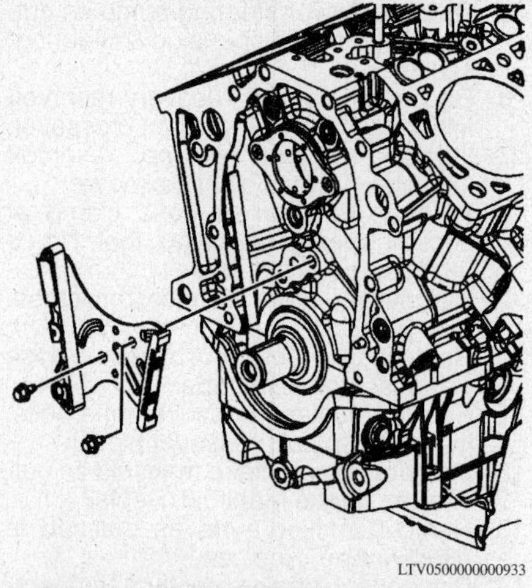

Fig. 4 Timing chain tensioner

9. Remove crankshaft damper bolt and washer.
10. Remove crankshaft damper using puller tool No. J 41816, or equivalent.
11. Reverse procedure to install, noting the following:
    a. Apply sealant part No. 12378521, or equivalent, to damper keyway.
    b. Tighten to specifications.

FRONT COVER

REPLACE

1. Drain cooling system into suitable container.
2. Remove drive belt as outlined under "Serpentine Drive Belt."
3. Remove drive belt tensioner.
4. Drain engine oil, then remove oil pan as outlined under "Oil Pan, Replace."
5. Remove crankshaft damper as outlined under "Crankshaft Damper, Replace."
6. Remove thermostat bypass pipe from engine front cover.
7. Remove radiator outlet hose from engine front cover.
8. Remove water pump from engine front cover as outlined under "Water Pump, Replace."
9. Remove power steering pump from engine and position aside.
10. Remove front cover retaining bolts, then the front cover and gasket.
11. Reverse procedure to install, noting the following:
    a. Apply sealant part No. 12346004, or equivalent, to both sides of front cover gasket, **Fig. 2.** Apply sealer no less than .20 inch wide.
    b. Apply sealant part No. 12346004, or equivalent, to threads of front cover bolts.

TIMING CHAIN

REPLACE

1. Remove engine front cover as outlined under "Front Cover, Replace."

2. Rotate crankshaft until timing marks are aligned, **Fig. 3.**
3. Remove camshaft sprocket attaching bolt, then the camshaft sprocket with timing chain.
4. Remove crankshaft sprocket.
5. Remove timing chain tensioner attaching bolts, then the tensioner, **Fig. 4.**
6. Remove and discard camshaft position actuator filter from end of camshaft.
7. Reverse procedure to install. Ensure timing marks are aligned, **Fig. 3.**

PISTON & ROD ASSEMBLY

Ensure the marks on the piston and connecting rod are aligned the same as when they were removed. If installing a new piston, ensure the arrow on top faces towards the front of the engine. If no identification marks were made during disassembly, ensure the flat area on the bottom of the piston pin skirt is aligned with the small dimple above the connecting rod crankshaft bearing bore.

MAIN & ROD BEARINGS

1. Dip bearing cap bolts in clean engine oil.
2. Apply a small amount of clean engine oil to crankshaft main bearing surface.
3. Apply a small amount of sealer part No. 1052942, or equivalent, to rear of No. 4 crankshaft main bearing cap sealing surface.
4. Tighten bearing cap bolts to specification.

CRANKSHAFT SEAL

REPLACE

1. Remove crankshaft damper as outlined under "Crankshaft Damper, Replace."
2. Remove crankshaft key from keyway.
3. Pry oil seal out of front cover using a large screwdriver.
4. Reverse procedure to install. Lubricate oil seal with clean engine oil.

CRANKSHAFT REAR OIL SEAL

REPLACE

Removal

1. Remove transaxle as outlined in **MOTOR's "Domestic Transmission, In-Vehicle Service" or "Transmission Service DVD."**
2. Install flywheel holder tool No. J 43442, or equivalent, to prevent crankshaft from rotating.
3. Loosen flywheel bolts, then remove five of six flywheel bolts leaving one bolt at top to prevent crankshaft rotation.
4. Grip flywheel and remove remaining bolt.

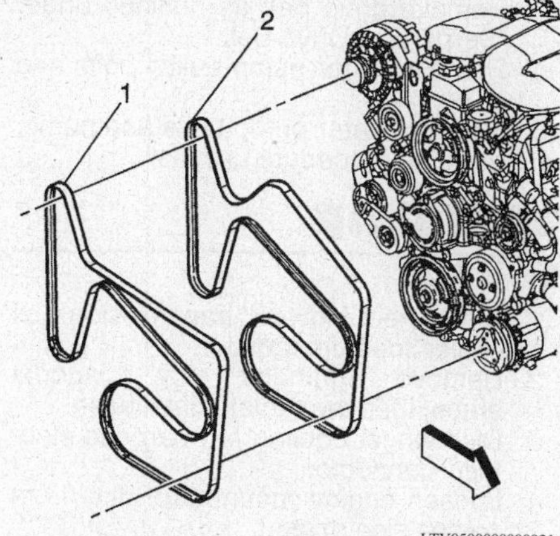

Fig. 5 Serpentine drive belt routing

5. Remove engine flywheel retainer and flywheel.
6. Remove crankshaft rear oil seal by inserting a suitable flat-bladed tool through seal dust lip at an angle.
7. Pry oil seal out by moving handle of tool towards end of crankshaft.

Installation

Do not apply or use any oil lubrication on the crankshaft rear oil seal, or the seal installer. Do not touch the sealing lip of the oil seal once the protective sleeve is removed. Doing so will damage or deform the seal.

1. Slide crankshaft rear oil seal over mandrel of seal installation tool No. J 34686, or equivalent. Use a twisting motion until back of crankshaft rear oil seal bottoms squarely against collar of tool.
2. Align dowel pin of installation tool with dowel pin in crankshaft.
3. Attach seal installation tool to crankshaft by hand.
4. Turn T-handle of tool to allow collar to push seal into bore, continue to turn handle until collar is tight against engine block.
5. Ensure seal is seated properly, then remove tool.
6. Install flywheel, then the transaxle as outlined in **MOTOR's "Domestic Transmission, In-Vehicle Service" or "Transmission Service DVD."**

OIL PAN

REPLACE

1. Install engine support fixture tool No. J 28467-500, or equivalent.
2. Raise and support vehicle, then drain engine oil.
3. Remove righthand front tire and wheel.
4. Remove righthand front splash shield.
5. Remove oil pan drain plug and drain crankcase into suitable container.
6. Install oil pan drain plug until snug.
7. Remove engine harness clips from righthand lower control arm.
8. Remove and discard lower ball joint castle nut cotter pin.
9. Remove lower ball joint castle nut.
10. Install tool No. J 41820 or equivalent over ball stud and lower control arm.
11. Rotate ball stud nut counterclockwise in order to separate ball stud from steering knuckle.
12. Remove air conditioning (A/C) compressor front bolt and nut.
13. Remove A/C compressor rear bolt and position compressor aside.
14. Remove transaxle brace to engine block oil pan bolts.
15. Remove transaxle brace to transaxle bolts.
16. Remove transaxle brace.
17. Remove transaxle brace to oil pan bolts.
18. Remove transaxle brace to transaxle bolt.
19. Remove transaxle brace.
20. Remove starter motor as outlined in "Electrical" section.
21. Disconnect engine harness electrical connector from oil level sensor.
22. Remove engine harness clip from oil pan.
23. Remove engine mount as outlined in "Engine Mount, Replace."
24. Place adjustable jack stands under frame.
25. Loosen lefthand side frame bolts and remove righthand side frame bolts.
26. Lower righthand side of frame enough to remove oil pan using jack stands.
27. Remove oil pan side bolts, then the oil pan bolts.
28. Remove oil pan, then the gasket.
29. Reverse procedure to install. Tighten to specifications.

OIL PUMP

REPLACE

1. Remove oil pan as outlined under "Oil Pan, Replace."
2. Remove oil pump bolt attaching bolt, then the pump and pump drive shaft.
3. Reverse procedure to install. Tighten to specifications.

SERPENTINE DRIVE BELT

Belt Routing

Refer to **Fig. 5** for serpentine drive belt routing.

Belt Replacement

1. Rotate drive belt tensioner clockwise in order to release tensioner spring tension.
2. **On models equipped with electric power steering,** remove serpentine drive belt No. 1 as indicated in **Fig. 5.**
3. **On models equipped with hydraulic power steering,** remove serpentine drive belt No. 2 as indicated in **Fig. 5.**
4. **On all models,** reverse procedure to install.

Tensioner Replacement

1. Remove serpentine drive belt.
2. Remove mounting bolt and tensioner.
3. Reverse procedure to install.

COOLING SYSTEM BLEED

1. Open cooling system bleeder screws.
2. Slowly fill cooling system with a 50/50 coolant mixture.
3. Close cooling system bleeder screws, then install pressure cap.
4. Start and run engine at 2,000–2,500 RPM until engine reaches normal operating temperature.
5. Allow engine to idle for three minutes, then shut engine off.
6. Allow engine to cool and top off coolant as required.

THERMOSTAT

REPLACE

1. Drain cooling system into suitable container.
2. Release tension on hose clamp at thermostat housing and reposition clamp using tool No. J 38185 or equivalent.
3. Remove radiator outlet hose from thermostat housing.
4. Remove thermostat housing bolt and stud.
5. Remove thermostat housing.
6. Reverse procedure to install.

WATER PUMP

REPLACE

1. Drain cooling system.
2. Loosen water pump pulley bolts.
3. Remove drive belt as outlined under "Serpentine Drive Belt."
4. Remove water pump pulley bolts and pulley.
5. Remove water pump bolts and pump.
6. Reverse procedure to install.

RADIATOR

REPLACE

1. Disconnect lower transmission oil cooler line from radiator.
2. Remove righthand side diagonal brace, then the radiator inlet hose.
3. Disconnect cooling fan harness electrical connector.
4. Loosen engine mount strut nuts from engine side of strut.
5. Remove engine mount strut bracket brace bolts from upper radiator support, then rotate struts and brackets rearward.
6. Reposition coolant overflow hose from reservoir.
7. Remove overflow hose from retainers, then position hose aside.
8. Remove battery.
9. Remove radiator upper mount bolts, then the mounts.
10. Remove cooling fan shroud bolts.
11. Disconnect upper transmission oil cooler line from radiator.
12. Disconnect transmission oil cooler lines from fan shroud retainer clip.
13. Remove cooling fans and shroud.
14. Remove radiator inlet and outlet hoses.
15. Remove condenser tube clip screw.
16. Tilt radiator and condenser inwards toward engine, then remove radiator.
17. Reverse procedure to install.

FUEL PUMP

REPLACE

1. Relieve fuel system fuel pressure as outlined under "Precautions."
2. Drain fuel tank, then raise and support vehicle.
3. Disconnect fuel supply pipe quick-connect fitting.
4. **On models with short wheel base,** disconnect EVAP purge pipe from canister.
5. **On all models,** loosen fuel tank filler pipe hose clamp, then disconnect fuel tank filler pipe from fuel tank.
6. Disconnect vapor recirculation pipe from filler tube.
7. Remove fuel tank shield.
8. Support fuel tank, then remove fuel tank strap attaching bolts.
9. Disconnect fuel sender and fuel tank pressure sensor electrical connectors at body pass through.
10. Remove fuel tank from vehicle.
11. Clean fuel pipe connections, hose connections and all areas surrounding connections before disconnecting connections to avoid possible fuel system contamination.
12. Disconnect fuel supply pipe quick-connect fitting at fuel sender assembly.
13. Disconnect EVAP pipe quick-connect fittings at fuel sender assembly.
14. Unlock fuel sender lock ring using fuel sender lock nut wrench tool No. J 45722, or equivalent, and a long breaker-bar.
15. Turn fuel sender lock ring in a counterclockwise direction.
16. Remove fuel sender assembly and seal from fuel tank.
17. Drain fuel from fuel sender assembly into an approved container.
18. Remove fuel sender assembly and seal from fuel tank. Discard seal.
19. Reverse procedure to install.

TIGHTENING SPECIFICATIONS

Year	Component	Torque Ft. Lbs.
2005–06	A/C Compressor Bracket Bolt	37
	Camshaft Position Actuator Assembly Bolt	12
	Camshaft Position Actuator Magnet Bolt	89①
	Camshaft Position Sensor Bolt	89①
	Camshaft Thrust Plate Screw	89①
	Clutch Pressure Plate Bolt	18
	Connecting Rod Bearing Cap Bolt	②
	Coolant Crossover Pipe Bolt	37
	Coolant Drain Plug	14
	Coolant Temperature Sensor	15
	Coolant Vent Pipe Bolt	89①
	Crankshaft Balancer Bolt	③
	Crankshaft Main Bearing Cap Bolt & Stud	④
	Crankshaft Oil Deflector Nut	18
	Crankshaft Position Sensor Stud	89①
	Cylinder Head Bolt	⑤
	Drive Belt Idler Pulley Bolt (13mm)	22
	Drive Belt Idler Pulley Bolt (15mm)	37
	Drive Belt Tensioner Bolt	37
	Engine Block Heater Plug	44
	Engine Front Cover Bolt	18
	Engine Lift Bracket Bolt	52
	Engine Oil Pressure Indicator Switch	12
	Engine Wiring Harness Bracket Bolt	115①
	EVAP Purge Valve Bolt	106①
	Exhaust Manifold Bolt	15
	Exhaust Manifold Heat Shield Bolt	89①
	Exhaust Manifold Lower Heat Shield Bolt	89①
	Flywheel Bolt	52
	Front Oil Gallery Plug	24
	Fuel Injector Rail Bolt	89①
	Heated Oxygen Sensor	31
	Heater Inlet & Outlet Pipe Bolt (10mm)	89①
	Heater Inlet & Outlet Pipe Bolt & Nut (13mm)	18
	Ignition Coil Bracket Bolt, Nut & Stud	18
	Knock Sensor	18
	Lower Intake Manifold Bolt-Center	⑥
	Lower Intake Manifold Bolt-Corner	⑦
	Oil Dipstick Tube Bolt	18
	Oil Filter	22

TIGHTENING SPECIFICATIONS—Continued

Year	Component	Torque Ft. Lbs.
2005–06	Oil Filter Adapter Bolt	18
	Oil Filter Fitting	29
	Oil Pan Bolt	18
	Oil Pan Drain Plug	18
	Oil Pan Side Bolt	37
	Oil Pan Support Bracket Bolt	37
	Oil Pump Cover Bolt	89①
	Oil Pump Drive Bolt	27
	Oil Pump Mounting Bolt	30
	Piston Oil Nozzle Bolt	89①
	Rear Oil Gallery Plug	24
	Spark Plug	11
	Throttle Body Bolt & Nut	89①
	Throttle Body Stud	53①
	Timing Chain Tensioner Bolt	15
	Upper Intake Manifold Bolt & Stud	18
	Valve Lifter Guide Bolt	89①
	Valve Lifter Oil Manifold Cover Plate Bolt	18
	Valve Rocker Arm Bolt	25
	Valve Rocker Arm Cover Bolt	89①
	Water Outlet Bolt & Stud	18
	Water Pump Bolt	89①
	Water Pump Pulley Bolt	18

① — Inch lbs.

② — First to 18 ft. lbs.; second additional 110°.

③ — First to 52 ft. lbs.; second additional 72°.

④ — First to 37 ft. lbs.; second additional 77°.

⑤ — First to 44 ft. lbs.; final additional 95°.

⑥ — First to 10 ft. lbs.; final to 15 ft. lbs.

⑦ — First to 10 ft. lbs.; final to 18 ft. lbs.

Rear Axle & Suspension

NOTE: On Air Bag Equipped Models, Refer To "Air Bag System Precautions" Located In The Front Of This Manual For System Disarming & Arming Procedures.

INDEX

DESCRIPTION

The rear suspension system on this vehicle is the trailing-arm axle type. Two control arms/trailing arms mount the axle to the vehicle body.

REAR AXLE

REPLACE

1. Raise and support vehicle using a suitable lift.
2. Remove rear tire and wheel assemblies.
3. Place a suitable jack stand under rear axle for support.
4. Remove rear axle coil springs, spring seats and spring insulators as outlined in "Coil Spring, Replace."
5. Remove rear brake calipers as outlined in "Disc Brake" chapter.
6. Disconnect intermediate brake hoses from rear axle brake pipes.
7. Disconnect wheel speed sensor electrical connectors.
8. Lower rear axle using jack stand, then remove jack stand.
9. Lower vehicle until rear axle is approximately ½ inch above ground.
10. Remove rear axle control arm bolts and nuts.
11. Remove rear axle.
12. Reverse procedure to install, noting the following:
    a. Install new control arm nuts as these are prevailing type fasteners.
    b. Bleed brake system as outlined in "Anti-Lock Brakes" chapter.
    c. Tighten to specifications.

REAR AXLE SHAFT

REPLACE

1. Set parking brake.
2. Raise and support vehicle using a suitable lift.
3. Remove rear tire and wheel assemblies.
4. Remove and discard wheel drive shaft nut. **Replace using a new nut.**
5. Release parking brake.
6. Remove and support brake caliper bracket as outlined in "Disc Brake" chapter.
7. Remove nut to parking brake cable routing bracket.
8. Remove bolt retaining rear tie rod end from rear suspension knuckle. **Do not loosen tie rod end jam nut.**
9. Loosen, but do not remove bolts to park brake cable bracket to suspension knuckle.
10. Disconnect wheel speed sensor electrical connector.
11. Install tool No. J 42129 or equivalent, to wheel hub and secure using wheel nuts.
12. Disengage wheel drive shaft from wheel hub and bearing.
13. Remove bolt and nut securing upper control arm to suspension knuckle.
14. Disengage wheel drive shaft completely from wheel hub and bearing.
15. Reposition suspension knuckle toward rear of vehicle.
16. Remove tool No. J 42129 or equivalent, from wheel hub. **Support wheel drive shaft until it is removed.**
17. Assemble tool Nos. J 33008-A, J 29794 and J 2619-01 or equivalents, and install tool No. J 33008-A or equivalent evenly onto rear beveled surface of wheel drive shaft inner joint housing.
18. Disengage wheel drive shaft from rear axle differential using tool Nos. J 33008-A, J 29794 and J 2619-01 or equivalents, then remove tool assembly.
19. Remove wheel drive shaft from vehicle.
20. Replace rear wheel drive shaft oil seal.
21. Reverse procedure to install, tighten to specifications.

DIFFERENTIAL CARRIER

REPLACE

1. Set parking brake.
2. Raise and support vehicle using a suitable lift.
3. Remove rear tire and wheel assemblies.
4. Remove differential drain plug and drain gear oil into suitable container.
5. Disconnect electrical connector from clutch pump check valve.
6. Remove righthand rear wheel drive shaft as outlined in "Rear Axle Shaft, Replace."
7. Remove front propeller shaft as outlined in "Propeller Shaft, Replace."
8. Place a suitable adjustable support under propeller shaft.
9. Loosen, do not remove propeller shaft-to-bracket through bolt and nut.
10. Remove bolts from propeller shaft bracket.
11. Remove differential carrier-to-cradle mounting bolts, nuts, washers and mounts from differential.
12. Simultaneously moving differential assembly to righthand side of vehicle, disengage lefthand side wheel drive shaft from differential.
13. Remove rear differential and propeller shaft as an assembly.
14. Remove propeller shaft from differential.
15. Reverse procedure to install, tighten to specifications.

REAR PROPELLER SHAFT

REPLACE

1. Raise and support vehicle using a suitable lift.
2. Position a suitable jack stand under front of rear differential and firmly secure differential to jack.
3. Remove front propeller shaft as outlined in "Front Propeller Shaft, Replace."
4. Remove rear propeller shaft-to-bracket through bolt and nut.
5. Remove rear propeller shaft-to-differential bolts.
6. Pull rear propeller shaft toward front of vehicle in order to disengage rear propeller shaft from differential pinion shaft.

7. Remove rear propeller shaft from differential.
8. Reverse procedure to install, tighten to specifications.

HUB & BEARING

REPLACE

Independent Rear Suspension

1. Raise and support vehicle using a suitable lift.
2. Remove tire and wheel assemblies.
3. Remove knuckle as outlined in "Knuckle, Replace."
4. Remove wheel bearing and hub assembly knuckle bolts.
5. Remove wheel bearing and hub assembly from knuckle.
6. Reverse procedure to install, tighten to specifications.

Less Independent Rear Suspension

1. Raise and support vehicle using a suitable lift.
2. Remove tire and wheel assemblies.
3. Remove brake caliper as outlined in "Disc Brakes" chapter.
4. Remove and discard wheel bearing and hub bolts.
5. Remove wheel bearing hub.
6. Disconnect wheel speed sensor electrical connector.
7. Reverse procedure to install, tighten to specifications.

SHOCK ABSORBER

REPLACE

1. Raise and support vehicle using a suitable lift.
2. Slightly compress coil spring and relieve tension on shock absorber using a suitable jack stand.
3. **On models equipped with Automatic Level Control (ALC),** disconnect air tube connector from shock absorber.
4. **On all models,** remove shock absorber upper bolt and nut.
5. Remove shock absorber lower nut
6. Remove shock absorber.
7. Reverse procedure to install, tighten to specifications.

COIL SPRING

REPLACE

All Wheel Drive

1. Raise and support vehicle using a suitable lift.
2. Remove tire and wheel assemblies.
3. Remove brake caliper and support brake caliper. **Do not disconnect brake hose.**
4. Disconnect tie rod from knuckle as outlined in "Knuckle, Replace."
5. Support lower control arm using a suitable jack stand.
6. Disconnect height sensor link from lower control arm.
7. Disconnect shock absorber from lower control arm as outlined in "Shock Absorber, Replace."
8. Disconnect ball joint from knuckle using tool No. J 41820 or equivalent.
9. Remove lower ball joint nut.
10. Lower control arm and relieve coil spring tension using suitable jack stand.
11. Remove coil spring and jounce bumper.
12. Remove spring insulator.
13. Remove lower control arm.
14. Reverse procedure to install, tighten to specifications.

Independent Rear Suspension

1. Raise and support vehicle using a suitable lift.
2. Remove tire and wheel assemblies.
3. Remove brake caliper as outlined in "Disc Brakes" chapter.
4. Remove parking brake cable mounting bracket.
5. Remove brake caliper mounting bracket.
6. Disconnect ABS electrical connector.
7. Remove ABS electrical connector mounting bracket.
8. Support lower control arm using a suitable jack stand.
9. Remove stabilizer link from lower control arm.
10. Disconnect ball joint from knuckle using tool No. J 41820 or equivalent.
11. Lower the lower control arm and relieve coil spring tension using a suitable jack stand.
12. Remove coil spring.
13. Reverse procedure to install, tighten to specifications.

CONTROL ARM

REPLACE

Lower

1. Raise and support vehicle using a suitable lift.
2. Remove tire and wheel assemblies.
3. Remove brake caliper as outlined in "Disc Brakes" chapter.
4. Support lower control arm using a suitable jack stand.
5. Disconnect height sensor link from lower control arm.
6. Disconnect speed sensor harness from control arm.
7. Disconnect speed sensor harness connector.
8. Remove speed sensor connector mounting bracket.
9. Remove stabilizer shaft link from lower control arm as outlined in "Stabilizer Bar, Replace."
10. Disconnect shock absorber from lower control arm as outlined in "Shock Absorber, Replace."
11. Disconnect ball joint from knuckle using tool No. J 41820 or equivalent.
12. Remove lower ball joint nut.
13. Lower control arm and relieve coil spring tension using suitable jack stand.
14. Remove jack stand.
15. Carefully remove coil spring.
16. Place a suitable matchmark on lower control arm at cam indicator.
17. Remove lower control arm to crossmember mounting bolts.
18. Remove lower control arm.
19. Reverse procedure to install, tighten to specifications.

Upper

1. Raise and support vehicle using a suitable lift.
2. Remove tire and wheel assemblies.
3. Remove brake caliper as outlined in "Disc Brakes" chapter.
4. Disconnect park brake cable from park brake actuator and park brake cable bracket.
5. Support lower control arm using a suitable jack stand.
6. Disconnect height sensor link from lower control arm.
7. Disconnect shock absorber from lower control arm as outlined in "Shock Absorber, Replace."
8. Remove upper control arm to knuckle nut and bolt.
9. Support crossmember using two suitable jack stands.
10. Remove crossmember to underbody bolts.
11. Slowly lower crossmember until there is enough clearance to remove upper control arm.
12. Remove upper control arm to crossmember bolts and nuts.
13. Remove upper control arm.
14. Reverse procedure to install, tighten to specifications.

CONTROL ARM BUSHING

REPLACE

1. Raise and support vehicle using a suitable lift.
2. Support control arm forward of coil spring using a suitable jack stand.
3. Remove control arm bolts from rear axle as outlined in "Rear Axle, Replace."
4. Lower rear axle enough to gain access to control arm bushing using a suitable jack stand.
5. Place a suitable matchmark on control arm bushing in lower control arm.
6. Remove control arm bushing using tool Nos., J 28685 and J 9519-E, or equivalents.
7. Reverse procedure to install, noting the following:
   a. Align flat edge of bushing to be 90° to fluid axis. Fluid axis is 9° from center line of control arm, **Fig. 1.**
   b. Bushing must extend 1.18 inch from control arm.
   c. Tighten to specifications.

TIE ROD

REPLACE

Independent Rear Suspension

1. Raise and support vehicle using a suitable lift.
2. Remove tire and wheel assemblies.
3. Remove tie rod bolt and nut, then the tie rod.
4. Reverse procedure to install, tighten to specifications.

Less Independent Rear Suspension

1. Raise and support vehicle using a suitable lift.
2. **On models equipped with Automatic Level Control (ALC),** disconnect ALC sensor link from sensor and height sensor link from rear axle tie rod.
3. **On all models,** remove rear axle tie rod bolts, then the tie rod from vehicle.
4. Reverse procedure to install, tighten to specifications.

KNUCKLE

REPLACE

1. Raise and support vehicle using a suitable lift.
2. Remove tire and wheel assemblies.
3. Remove brake caliper as outlined in "Disc Brakes" chapter.
4. Remove brake caliper bracket.
5. Remove brake rotor as outlined in "Disc Brakes" chapter.
6. Remove tie rod from knuckle as outlined in "Tie Rod, Replace."
7. Disconnect stabilizer shaft link at lower control arm as outlined in "Stabilizer Bar, Replace."
8. Disconnect drive axle from wheel bearing and hub.

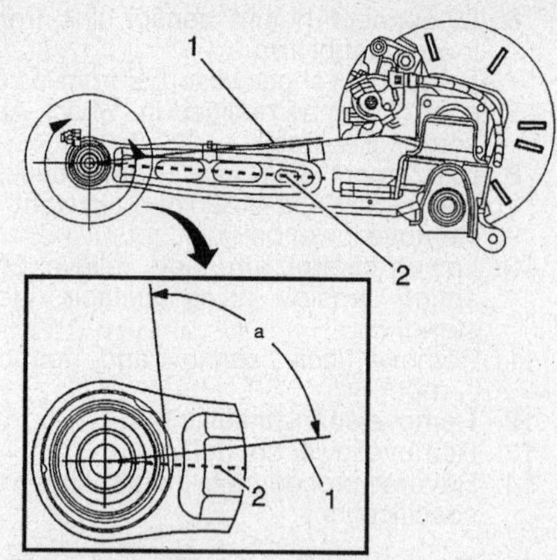

Fig. 1 Center line of control arm installation

9. Position park brake cable and park brake cable bracket aside.
10. Remove wheel bearing and backing plate as outlined in "Hub & Bearing, Replace."
11. Support lower control arm using a suitable jack stand.
12. Disconnect height sensor link from lower control arm.
13. Disconnect shock absorber from lower control arm as outlined in "Shock Absorber, Replace."
14. Disconnect upper control arm from knuckle as outlined in "Control Arm Replace."
15. Disconnect lower ball joint from knuckle using tool No. J 41820 or equivalent.
16. Remove knuckle from vehicle.
17. Remove wheel speed sensor connector bracket from knuckle.
18. Reverse procedure to install, tighten to specifications.

STABILIZER BAR

REPLACE

1. Raise and support vehicle using a suitable lift.
2. Remove tire and wheel assemblies.
3. Remove load level sensor.
4. Remove clamp holding righthand park brake cable to stabilizer shaft.
5. Remove lefthand and righthand side stabilizer shaft insulators and brackets.
6. Remove lefthand and righthand stabilizer shaft links as outlined in "Stabilizer Shaft Link, Replace."
7. Remove spare tire from hoist.
8. Remove stabilizer shaft.
9. Reverse procedure to install, tighten to specifications.

STABILIZER SHAFT INSULATOR

REPLACE

1. Raise and support vehicle using a suitable lift.
2. Remove load level sensor from lefthand side.
3. Remove stabilizer shaft insulator bracket bolts, nuts then the bracket.
4. Remove stabilizer shaft insulators from stabilizer shaft.
5. Reverse procedure to install, tighten to specifications.

STABILIZER SHAFT LINK

REPLACE

1. Raise and support vehicle using a suitable lift.
2. Remove stabilizer shaft link nuts using a suitable wrench.
3. Remove stabilizer shaft link.
4. Reverse procedure to install, tighten to specifications.

TIGHTENING SPECIFICATIONS

Year	Component	Torque Ft. Lbs.
2005–06	Ball Joint Nut	②
	Control Arm Nut	162
	Crossmember To Underbody Bolts	96
	Differential Carrier To Cradle Mounting Bolts	37
	Drain Plug	23
	Driveshaft Bolt To Differential Carrier Bolts	18
	Driveshaft To Transfer Case Bolts	24
	Driveshaft Bracket To Body Bolts	41
	Driveshaft Bracket Through Bolt & Nut	47
	Fill Plug	23
	Lower Control Arm To Crossmember Bolts	37
	Lower Control Arm To Crossmember Cam Nut	107
	Park Brake Cable Bracket Nut	89①
	Rear Axle Tie Rod Bolt At Axle	92
	Rear Axle Tie Rod Bolt At Body	100
	Rear Axle To Hub Nut	118
	Rear Crossmember To Body Mounting Bolts	96
	Shock Absorber Bolts To Axle	63
	Shock Absorber Nut & Bolt (IRS)	66
	Stabilizer Shaft Insulator Bracket Nut	63
	Stabilizer Shaft Ling Nuts	30
	Tie Rod Bolt	66
	Tie Rod Nut	59
	Tie Rod To Knuckle Bolt	63
	Upper Control Arm To Crossmember Nuts	55
	Upper Control Arm To Knuckle Bolt & Nut	63
	Upper Control Arm To Knuckle Nut	74
	Wheel Bearing Hub Bolts (IRS)	96
	Wheel Bearing Hub Bolts (Less IRS)	59
	Wheel Drive Shaft Spindle Nut	192
	Wheel Speed Sensor Bracket Nut	106①

① — Inch lbs.

② — First pass, torque to 26 ft. lbs.; second pass, an additional 130°.

Front Suspension & Steering

NOTE: On Air Bag Equipped Models, Refer To "Air Bag System Precautions" Located In The Front Of This Manual For System Disarming & Arming Procedures.

INDEX

HUB & BEARING

REPLACE

1. Raise and support vehicle.
2. Remove tire and wheel assembly.
3. Disconnect wheel speed sensor electrical connector.
4. Remove wheel speed sensor connector from bracket.
5. Insert a suitable drift through brake rotor to prevent rotor from turning, then remove and discard driveshaft nut.
6. Remove brake caliper and brake rotor as outlined in "Disc Brakes" chapter.
7. Attach front hub spindle remover tool No. J 28733-B, or equivalent, then push driveshaft out of hub and bearing assembly, **Fig. 1.**
8. Remove and discard hub and bearing assembly attaching bolts.
9. Remove hub and bearing assembly from steering knuckle.

BALL JOINT INSPECTION

1. Raise and support vehicle with safety stands.
2. Support lower control arm with a jack stand. Position jack stand as far outboard as possible, near lower ball joint, **Fig. 2.**
3. Inspect ball joint for horizontal looseness as follows:
   a. Position dial indicator tool No. J 8001, or equivalent, as outlined in **Fig. 2.**
   b. Rock wheel in and out while reading indicator.
   c. **On 2002 models,** if indicator reading exceeds .125 inch, replace lower ball joint.
   d. **On 2003–06 models,** if indicator reading exceeds .0 inch, replace lower ball joint.
4. **On all models,** inspect ball joint for vertical looseness as follows:
   a. Inspect position of grease fitting to lower ball joint cover, **Fig. 3.**
   b. Grease fitting on a new ball joint projects approximately .050 inch from ball joint cover.
   c. If fitting is flush with ball joint cover, replace lower control arm.
   d. While reading dial indicator, pry between lower control arm and steering knuckle with a suitable pry bar.
   e. If indicator reading exceeds .125 inch, replace lower ball joint.

BALL JOINT

REPLACE

1. Raise and support vehicle.
2. Remove tires and wheels.
3. Remove lower control arm as outlined in "Control Arm, Replace."
4. Secure lower control arm in a suitable vise.
5. Drill out ball joint to control arm retaining rivets.
6. Use a suitable hammer and a drift punch in order to remove rivets from lower control arm.
7. Remove ball joint from lower control arm.
8. Reverse procedure to install.

COIL SPRING

REPLACE

Refer to "Coil Spring & Strut Service" for coil spring replacement.

STRUT

REPLACE

1. Remove wiper module as outlined in "Electrical" section.
2. Remove upper strut mounting nuts.
3. Raise and support vehicle, then remove tire and wheel assembly.
4. Scribe a reference mark on steering knuckle and strut assembly for installation reference, **Fig. 4.**
5. Remove strut lower mounting bolts and nuts.
6. Remove strut from vehicle.
7. Reverse procedure to install.

COIL SPRING & STRUT SERVICE

1. Mount strut assembly in a suitable spring compressor.
2. Compress spring slightly, then remove strut shaft nut using a T45-Torx and strut rod socket tool No. J 42991, or equivalents, **Fig. 5.**
3. Install strut lower adapter tool No. J 34013-971, or equivalent, to guide strut shaft out of strut upper mount, **Fig. 5.**
4. Loosen compressor forcing screw while guiding strut shaft out of upper mount, continue to loosen screw until you can remove strut and spring.
5. Reverse procedure to assemble.

CONTROL ARM

REPLACE

1. Raise and support vehicle, then remove tire and wheel assembly.
2. Disconnect wheel speed harness from lower control arm.
3. Remove stabilizer shaft link.
4. Remove cotter pin from lower ball stud, then loosen, but do not remove ball stud nut.
5. Install ball stud joint separator tool No. J 41820, or equivalent, over ball stud nut and steering knuckle, **Fig. 6.**
6. Rotate ball stud nut counterclockwise to separate ball stud from steering knuckle.
7. Remove lower control arm bolts and nuts, and lower control arm, **Fig. 7.**
8. Reverse procedure to install.

CONTROL ARM BUSHING

REPLACE

1. Remove control arm as outlined in "Control Arm, Replace."
2. Secure control arm in a suitable vice.
3. Make a reference mark on lower control arm along flat edge of bushing flange, **Fig. 8.**
4. Assemble bushing removal tool Nos. J

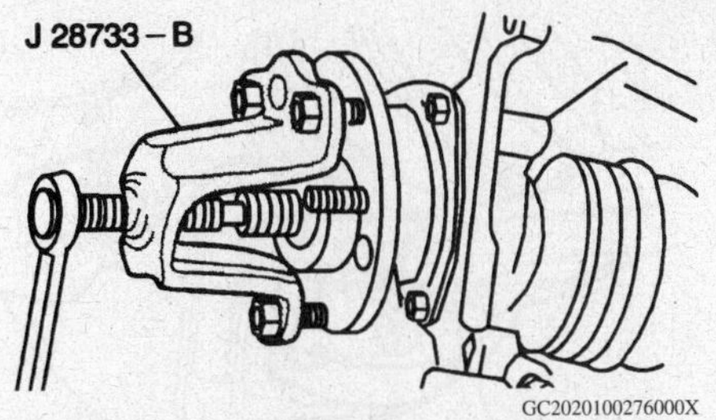

Fig. 1 Hub & bearing removal

21474-27, J 21474-13, J 34126 and J 35379, or equivalents, on bushing and control arm.
5. Remove bushing from control arm.
6. Reverse procedure to install.

STEERING KNUCKLE

REPLACE

1. Raise and support vehicle.
2. Remove tire and wheel assembly.
3. Remove hub and bearing assembly as outlined under "Hub & Bearing, Replace."
4. Separate lower ball joint from steering knuckle as outlined under "Control Arm, Replace."
5. Separate tie rod end from steering knuckle as outlined under "Tie Rod End, Replace."
6. Scribe a steering knuckle reference mark on strut assembly, **Fig. 4.**
7. Remove steering knuckle to strut attaching bolts, then the steering knuckle from strut.
8. Reverse procedure to install.

STABILIZER BAR

REPLACE

1. Raise and support vehicle.
2. Remove tire and wheel assemblies.
3. Remove stabilizer shaft links from lower control arms.
4. Remove stabilizer shaft insulator bolts and brackets, and insulators.
5. Remove stabilizer shaft from righthand side of vehicle.
6. Reverse procedure to install.

TIE ROD END

REPLACE

Inner

Refer to "Power Steering" chapter for inner tie rod end replacement.

Outer

1. Raise and support vehicle.

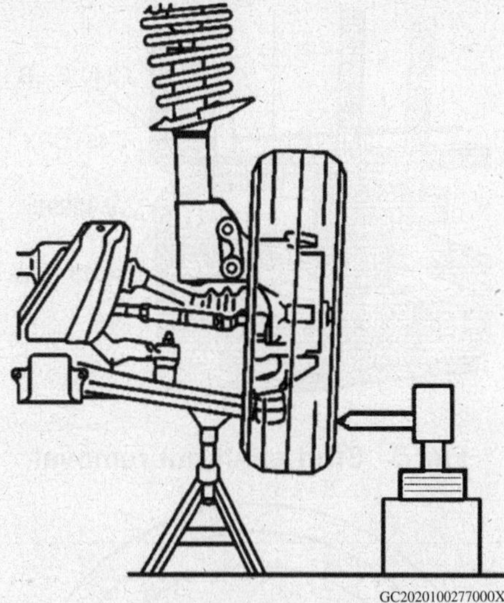

Fig. 2 Lower ball joint horizontal looseness inspection

2. Remove tie rod end ball stud nut.
3. Separate tie rod end from steering knuckle using universal steering linkage puller tool No. J 24319-B, or equivalent.
4. Loosen tie rod end jam nut, then remove outer tie rod end from inner tie rod.
5. Reverse procedure to install. Inspect and adjust toe setting as outlined in "Wheel Alignment."

POWER STEERING GEAR

REPLACE

1. Raise and support vehicle.
2. Remove stabilizer shaft as outlined under "Stabilizer Bar, Replace."
3. Separate tie rod end from steering knuckle as outlined under "Tie Rod End, Replace."
4. Apply silicone lubricant to steering column intermediate steering shaft lower seal.
5. Push intermediate shaft lower seal upward to access intermediate shaft lower bolt.
6. Remove intermediate shaft lower bolt and separate intermediate shaft from steering gear.
7. Support frame with a suitable adjustable jack stand, **Fig. 9.**
8. Remove and discard frame rear bolts.
9. Lower frame and powertrain with jack stand.
10. Remove power steering gear heat shield.
11. Remove cooler pipe pressure hose from steering gear.

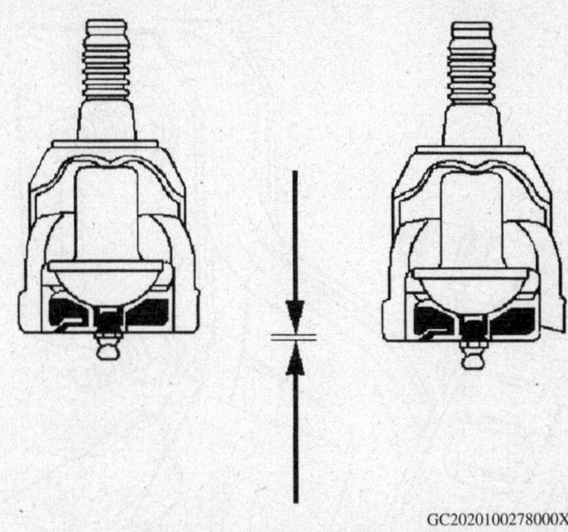

Fig. 3 Lower ball joint vertical looseness inspection

12. Remove power steering gear retaining nuts.
13. Remove steering gear attaching bolts, and gear through lefthand wheel opening.
14. Reverse procedure to install. Use new frame bolts when installing frame.

POWER STEERING PUMP

REPLACE

3.5L Engine

1. Remove drive belt as outlined under "Serpentine Drive Belt."
2. Remove intake manifold cover.
3. Remove power steering pump bolt.
4. Remove power steering high pressure hose fitting.
5. Remove power steering return hose clamp at pump.
6. Remove power steering pump.
7. Reverse procedure to install.

3.9L Engine

1. Remove accessory drive belt from power steering pump pulley as outlined in "Serpentine Drive Belt."
2. Remove fuel injector sight shield.
3. Remove power steering pump pulley.
4. Disconnect power steering pressure hose from pump.
5. Disconnect power steering return hose from pump.
6. Remove engine electrical harness from reservoir retainers.
7. Remove power steering pump mounting bolts.
8. Remove power steering pump from vehicle.
9. Reverse procedure to install.

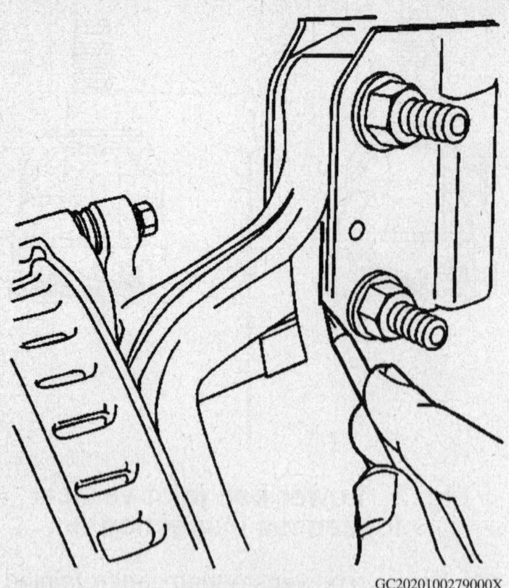
GC2020100279000X

Fig. 4 Strut to steering knuckle reference mark

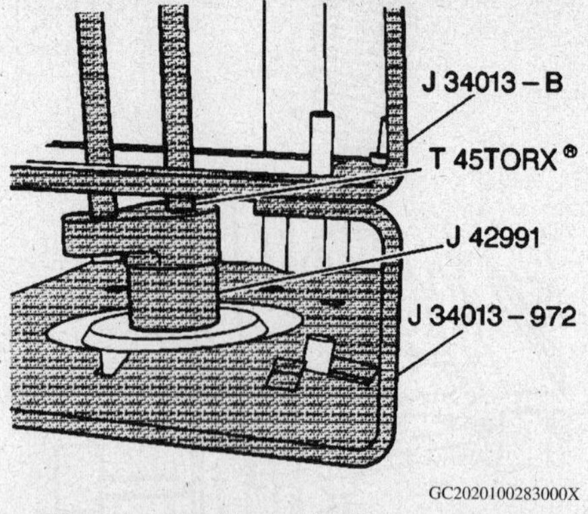

GC2020100283000X

Fig. 5 Strut shaft nut removal

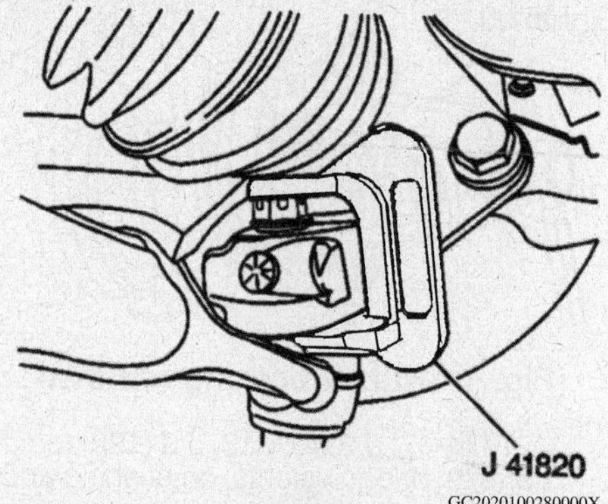

GC2020100280000X

Fig. 6 Lower ball joint removal

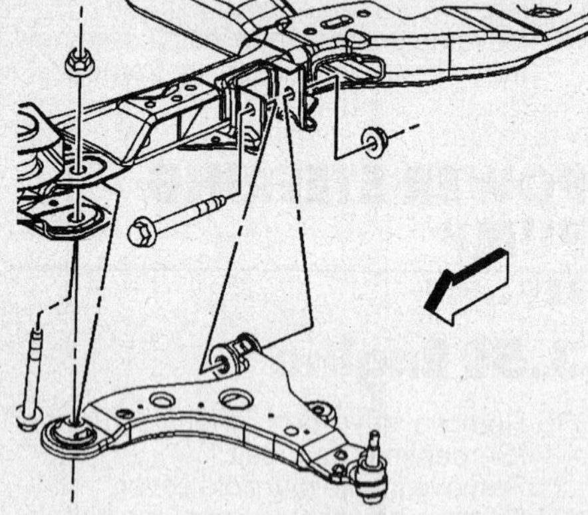
GC2020100281000X

Fig. 7 Lower control arm removal

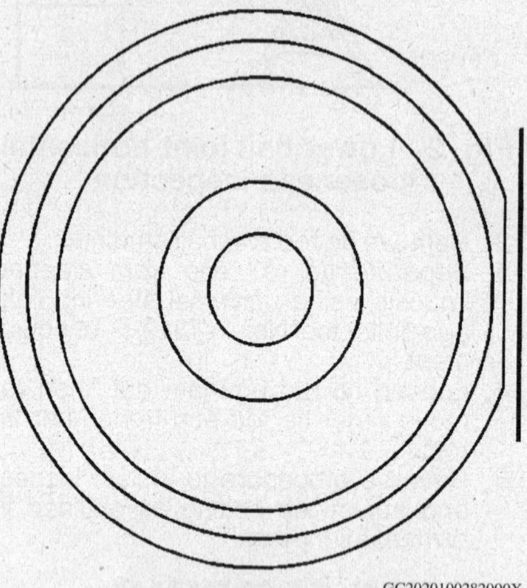
GC2020100282000X

Fig. 8 Control arm bushing reference mark

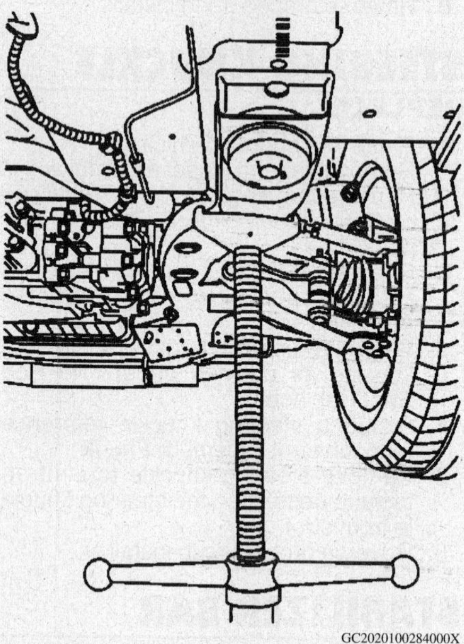
GC2020100284000X

Fig. 9 Frame support location

TIGHTENING SPECIFICATIONS

Year	Component	Torque Ft. Lbs.
2005–06	Ball Stud Castle Nut To Lower Control Arm	①
	Ball Stud Nuts To Ball Joint	50
	Lower Control Arm Nuts To At Frame	71
	Power Steering Pressure Hose To The Pump	20
	Power Steering Pump Bolts	25
	Stabilizer Shaft Insulator Bracket Bolts	35
	Stabilizer Shaft Link Nut (With Rear Twist Axle)	33
	Stabilizer Shaft Link Nut (With Rear IRS)	14
	Strut Lower Nuts At Knuckle	83
	Strut Shaft Nut	63
	Strut Upper Nuts	22
	Wheel Bearing & Hub Bolts	96

① — First step to 22 ft. lbs.; second step, an additional 135°.

Front Wheel Drive

NOTE: On Air Bag Equipped Models, Refer To "Air Bag System Precautions" Located In The Front Of This Manual For System Disarming & Arming Procedures.

INDEX

Page No.

AXLE SHAFT

REPLACE

1. Raise and support vehicle, then remove tire and wheel assembly.
2. Remove engine splash shield.
3. Insert a suitable drift or punch through brake caliper and into brake rotor to prevent wheel hub and bearing from turning.
4. Remove wheel drive shaft spindle nut.
5. Remove stabilizer shaft link.
6. Disconnect outer tie rod end from steering knuckle. **Do not loosen tie rod end jam nut.**
7. Disconnect wheel speed sensor electrical connector, then reposition wiring harness away from ball joint.
8. Disconnect lower ball joint from steering knuckle.
9. Install wheel hub remover tool No. J 42129, or equivalent, onto wheel hub and secure with wheel nuts. Ensure to support drive axle until it is fully removed from vehicle.
10. Separate drive axle from wheel hub and bearing.
11. Separate drive axle from transaxle using suitable puller and slide hammer.
12. Reverse procedure to install. **Torque drive axle nut to 118 ft. lbs.**

Wheel Alignment

NOTE: On Air Bag Equipped Models, Refer To "Air Bag System Precautions" Located In The Front Of This Manual For System Disarming & Arming Procedures.

INDEX

PRECAUTIONS

Air Bag Systems

Refer to "Air Bag System Precautions" in the front of this manual for system disarming and arming procedures.

Battery Ground Cable

Prior to service, disconnect battery ground cable and isolate as required.

PRELIMINARY INSPECTION

Inspect the following components, adjust, repair or replace as required prior to performing front wheel alignment.

1. Inflate tires to cold specifications.
2. Ensure tires are of same size, ply rating and load rating.
3. Inspect for excessive wheel bearing endplay.
4. Inspect for worn or damaged ball joints.
5. Inspect steering gear mounting bolts for proper tightness.
6. Inspect suspension arm or bent or damaged condition.
7. Inspect suspension arm to frame bushings for looseness or wear.
8. Inspect suspension components for wear or damage.

FRONT WHEEL ALIGNMENT

Camber

1. Raise and support vehicle.
2. Remove front tires.
3. Remove strut lower bolt and inspect oblong strut lower hole.
4. If hole is oblong, loosen strut upper bolt to adjust camber.
5. If lower hole is not oblong, proceed as follows:
   a. Remove strut assembly as outlined in "Front Suspension & Steering."
   b. Place strut in suitable soft jaw vise.
   c. File strut lower hole laterally to allow for camber adjustment, **Fig. 1.**
   d. Install strut assembly.
6. Place vehicle in suitable alignment equipment.
7. Loosen both strut-to-knuckle nuts just enough to allow movement.
8. Adjust camber to specification by moving top of wheel in or out.
9. **Torque** strut bolts to 83 ft. lbs.

Toe

1. Remove power steering gear seal small clamps.
2. Ensure steering wheel is centered and wheels are in straight ahead position.
3. Loosen lefthand and righthand tie rod jam nuts, **Fig. 2.**
4. Rotate inner tie rod end to obtain correct toe angle.
5. Ensure number of threads showing on both inner tie rod ends are approximately equal.
6. **Torque** jam nuts to 50 ft. lbs.
7. Install power steering gear seal small clamps.

REAR WHEEL ALIGNMENT

Camber

1. Raise and support vehicle, then remove tires.
2. Loosen rear lower control arm bolts, **Fig. 3.**
3. Loosen lower control arm cam bolt.
4. Install tires, then adjust camber as required.
5. **Torque** lower control arm rear bolts to 37 ft. lbs.
6. **Torque** front cam bolt to 107 ft. lbs.

Toe

1. Loosen hex nuts at rear wheel spindle rod, **Fig. 4.**
2. Adjust toe to specifications by turning adjusting nut.
3. **Torque** hex nuts to 45 ft. lbs.

VEHICLE RIDE HEIGHT

Inspection

Perform the following steps before measuring the trim height:

1. Inspect fuel level, ensure a fuel tank weight is obtained.
2. Ensure that correct size tires are on vehicle.
3. Set tire pressures to pressure shown on tire placard.
4. The tire placard is located on driver's door.
5. The spare tire and tools are properly located and secured.
6. **On models equipped with Automatic Level Control (ALC),** ensure system is active.
7. **On all models,** ensure a flat and level surface.
8. Close doors, hood and liftgate.

FRONT AND REAR SUSPENSION ARE HELD TO DIMENSIONS INDICATED IN "VEHICLE RIDE HEIGHT".

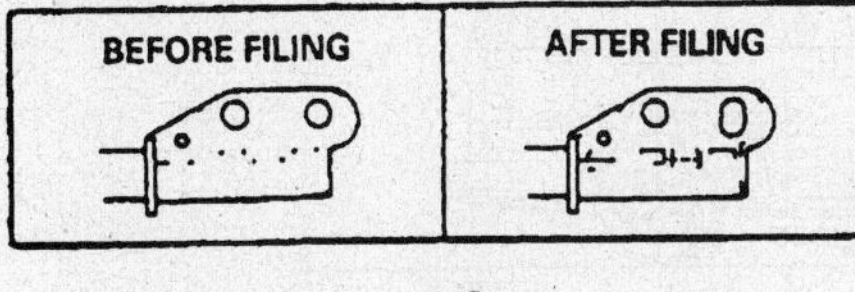

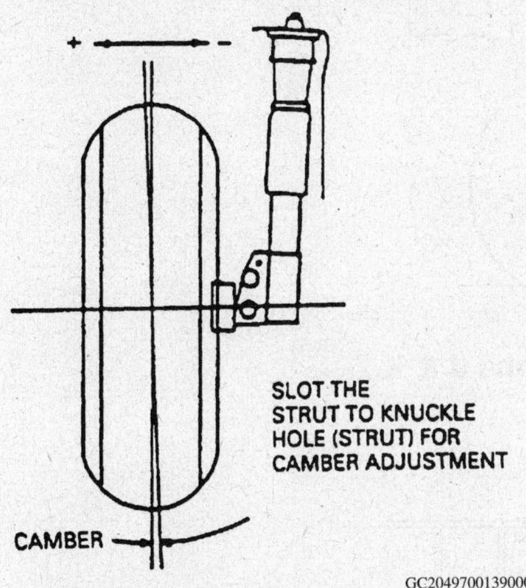

Fig. 1 Camber adjustment

Measuring Dimensions

DIMENSIONS J & K

1. Use hands in order to lift front bumper of vehicle up approximately 1.5 inch. Gently remove hands in order to allow vehicle to settle.
2. Use hands in order to push front bumper of vehicle down approximately 1.5 inch. Remove hands in order to allow vehicle to rise.
3. Measure J dimension for lefthand and righthand side of vehicle 24 inches from centerline of FRONT wheel, **Fig. 5.**
4. Replace front springs to correct front trim height as required.
5. Use hands in order to lift rear bumper of vehicle up approximately 1.5 inch. Gently remove hands in order to allow vehicle to settle.
6. Use hands in order to push front bumper of vehicle down approximately 1.5 inch. Remove hands in order to allow vehicle to rise.
7. Measure K dimension for lefthand and righthand side of vehicle 22 inches from centerline of REAR wheel, **Fig. 5.**
8. Replace rear springs to correct rear trim height as required.

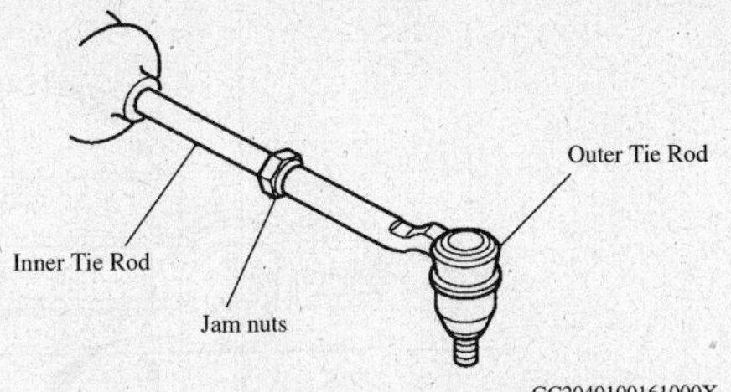

Fig. 2 Toe-in adjustment

DIMENSION Z

1. Use hands in order to lift front bumper of vehicle up approximately 1.5 inch. Gently remove hands in order to allow vehicle to lower.
2. Use hands in order to push front bumper of vehicle down approximately 1.5 inch. Remove hands in order to allow vehicle to rise.
3. Measure Z dimension for lefthand and righthand side of vehicle. Z dimension is vertical distance measured between centerline of lower control arm bolt and bottom of ball joint, **Fig. 6.**
4. Replace front springs to correct low front trim height as required.

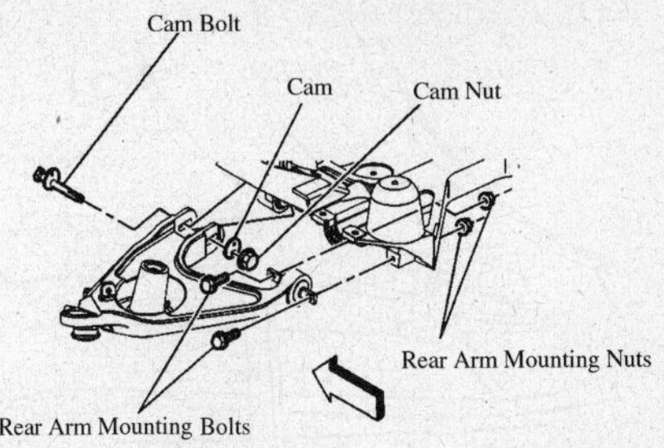

Fig. 3 Rear camber adjustment

DIMENSION D

1. Use hands in order to lift rear bumper of vehicle up approximately 1.5 inch. Gently remove hands in order to allow vehicle to lower.
2. Use hands in order to push rear bumper of vehicle down approximately 1.5 inch. Remove hands in order to allow vehicle to rise.
3. Measure D dimension for lefthand and righthand side of vehicle as follows:
   a. D dimension for twist axle vehicles is vertical distance measured between frame rail and rear axle, **Fig. 7.**
   b. D dimension for independent rear suspension (IRS) vehicles is vertical distance measured between horizontal centerline of lower control arm bolt and bottom of ball joint, **Fig. 7.**
4. Replace rear springs to correct low rear trim height as required.

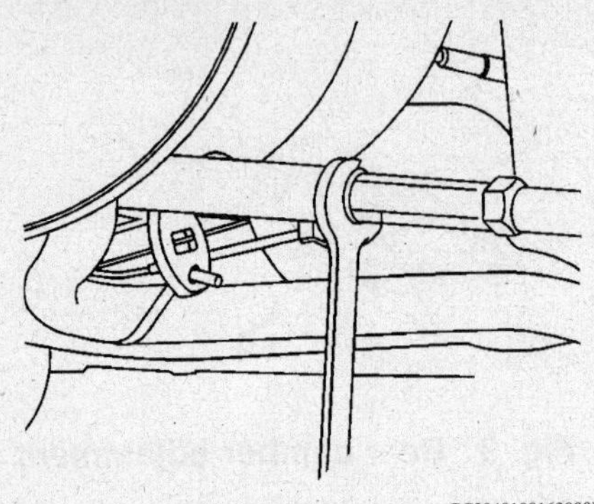

Fig. 4 Rear toe adjustment

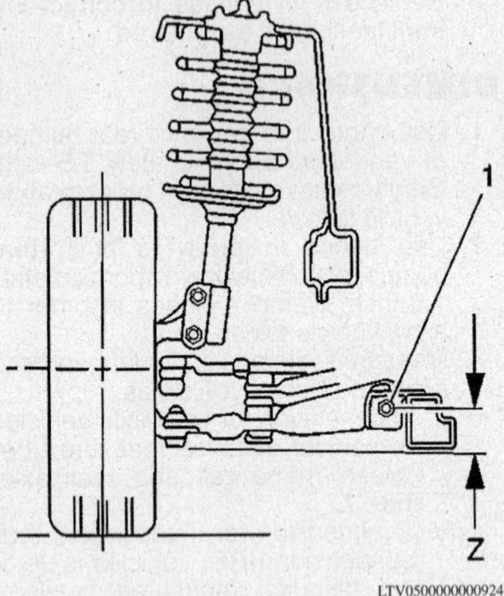

Fig. 6 Dimension Z

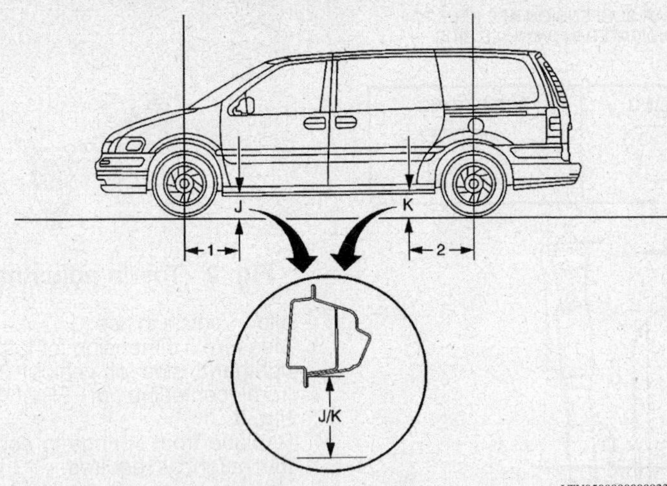

Fig. 5 Dimensions J & K

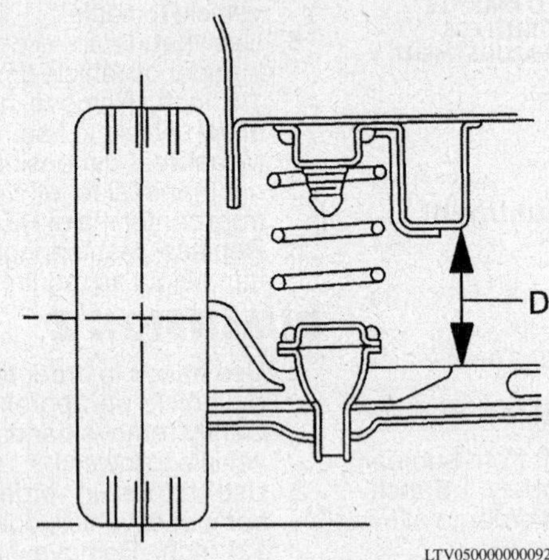

Fig. 7 Dimension D

HUMMER H2 & H3

NOTE: Refer To The Rear Of This Manual For Vehicle Manufacturer's Special Tool Suppliers.

INDEX OF SERVICE OPERATIONS

Specifications

GENERAL ENGINE SPECIFICATIONS

Year	Engine	Engine VIN Code	Fuel System	Bore & Stroke, Inch	Compres-sion Ratio	Horse-power @ RPM	Torque, Ft. Lbs. @ RPM	Normal Oil Pressure, psi
2003–04	6.0L	U	SFI	4.00 X 3.62	9.4	316 @ 5200	360 @ 4000	①
2005–06	6.0L	U	SFI	4.00 X 3.62	9.4	325 @ 5200	365 @ 4000	①
2006	3.5L	6	MFI	3.66 X 4.02	10	220 @ 5600	225 @ 2800	②

SFI — Sequential Fuel Injection

MFI — Multi-Port Fuel Injection

① — Minimum: 6 psi @ 1000 RPM; 18 psi @ 2000 RPM; 24 @ 4000 RPM.

② — Minimum: 12 psi @ 1200 RPM.

TUNE UP SPECIFICATIONS

The following specifications are published from the latest information available. This data should only be used in the absence of a decal affixed in the engine compartment.

Year & Engine①	Spark Plug Gap	Ignition Timing BTDC				Curb Idle Speed⑩		Fast Idle Speed⑩		Fuel Pump Pressure psi.⑥	Valve Lash, Inch
		Firing Order ③	Man. Trans.	Auto. Trans.	Mark Location	Man. Trans.	Auto. Trans.	Man. Trans.	Auto. Trans.		
2003–06											
6.0L	.060	⑤	④	④	⑧	⑦	⑦	⑦	⑦	55–62⑨	②
2006											
3.5L	.048	1-3-5-4-2	④	④	⑧	⑦	⑦	⑦	⑦	50–57	②

BTDC — Before Top Dead Center
D — Drive
N — Neutral
① — The eighth digit of VIN denotes engine code.
② — Equipped w/hydraulic valve lifters.
③ — Before removing wires from coil unit, determine location of ignition wires.
④ — Not adjustable.
⑤ — Firing order, 1-8-7-2-6-5-4-3.
⑥ — Wrap shop towel around fuel hose to steel line connection in engine compartment to prevent fuel spillage. Disconnect hose from steel line & install suitable fuel pressure gauge between hose & line. Ensure pressure gauge connections are tight, then start engine & inspect fuel pressure readings.
⑦ — Equipped w/Idle Speed Control (ISC) motor or Idle Air Control (IAC) valve.
⑧ — Equipped w/crankshaft position sensor.
⑨ — Wrap shop towel around engine compartment fuel pressure fitting. Connect suitable fuel pressure gauge to fuel pressure fitting. Turn ignition to On position & note fuel pressure reading.
⑩ — When inspecting idle speed, set parking brake & block drive wheels.

FRONT WHEEL ALIGNMENT SPECIFICATIONS

Jounce vehicle three times prior to inspecting alignment to eliminate false geometry readings.

Year	Model	Side	Caster Angle, Degrees		Camber Angle, Degrees		Total Toe, Degrees①		Ball Joint Wear Limit
			Limits	Desired	Limits	Desired	Limits	Desired	
2003	H2	Lefthand	+3.25 to +5.25	+4.25	-.25 to +.75	+.25	-.1 to +.3	+.10	②
		Righthand	+3.75 to +5.75	+4.75	-.25 to +.75	+.25	-.1 to +.3	+.10	②

Continued

FRONT WHEEL ALIGNMENT SPECIFICATIONS—Continued

Jounce vehicle three times prior to inspecting alignment to eliminate false geometry readings.

Year	Model	Side	Caster Angle, Degrees		Camber Angle, Degrees		Total Toe, Degrees①		Ball Joint Wear Limit
			Limits	Desired	Limits	Desired	Limits	Desired	
2004–05	H2	Lefthand	+3.25 to +5.25	+4.25	-.35 to +.85	+.25	-.1 to +.3	+.10	②
		Righthand	+3.75 to +5.75	+4.75	-.35 to +.85	+.25	-.1 to +.3	+.10	②
2006	H2	Lefthand	+2.25 to +4.25	+3.25	-.35 to +.85	+.25	-.1 to +.3	+.10	②
		Righthand	+2.75 to +4.75	+3.75	-.35 to +.85	+.25	-.1 to +.3	+.10	②
	H3	Lefthand	+1.80 to +3.80	+2.80	0	0	0	0	②
		Righthand	+2.10 to +4.10	+3.10	0	0	0	0	②

①— Toe-In (+). Toe-Out (–).

②— Refer to "Ball Joint Inspection" in "Front Suspension & Steering" section for inspection procedure.

FLUID CAPACITIES & COOLING SYSTEM DATA

Year	Model	Engine Liter	Cooling System Capacity, Qts.		Coolant Type	Radiator Cap Relief Pressure, Lbs.	Thermo. Opening Temp. °F	Fuel Tank Gals.	Engine Oil Refill Qts.②	Transmission Oil		Transfer Case Pts.	Drive Axle Oil	
			Less A/C	With A/C						Man. Trans. Pts.	Auto. Trans. Qts. ①		Front Pts.	Rear Pts.
2003	H2	6.0L	—	14.8	③	15	195	32	6	—	5	3	5.5	3.66
2004–06	H2	6.0L	—	13.0	③	15	195	32	6	—	5	3	5.5	3.66
2006	H3	3.5L	—	10.6	③	—	194	23	6	④	5	3.2	⑤	⑤

①— Approximate. Make final inspection w/dipstick.

②— Includes filter.

③— 50/50 mixture water and GM Goodwrench DEX-COOL or Havoline DEX-COOL coolant.

④— On models equipped with RWD, 4.6 pts.; With 4WD, 4.8 pts.

⑤— Fill fluid to 0–.4 inch below the fill plug opening.

LUBRICANT DATA

Year	Model	Lubricant Type						
		Transmission		Hydraulic Clutch Fluid	Transfer Case	Drive Axle	Power Steering	Brake System
		Manual	Automatic					
2003–05	H2	—	Dexron III ATF	—	Dexron III ATF	75W-90 Synthetic	GM PSF	DOT 3
2006	H2	—	Dexron VI	—	Dexron III ATF	75W-90 Synthetic	GM PSF	DOT 3
	H3	MTF	Dexron VI	DOT 3	Dexron III ATF	75W-90 Synthetic	GM PSF	DOT 3

ATF — Automatic Transmission Fluid

MTF — Manual Transmission Fluid GM P/N 89021806 or equivalent.

PSF — Power Steering Fluid

Electrical

NOTE: On Air Bag Equipped Models, Refer To "Air Bag System Precautions" Located In The Front Of This Manual For System Disarming & Arming Procedures.

NOTE: Refer To "Computer Relearn Procedures" Located In The Front Of This Manual When Battery Power To The Computer Has Been Interrupted.

INDEX

PRECAUTIONS

Air Bag Systems

Refer to "Air Bag System Precautions" in the front of this manual for system disarming and arming procedures.

Battery Ground Cable

Prior to service disconnect battery ground cable and isolate as required.

FUSE PANEL LOCATION

The body junction block is located under the lefthand side of the instrument panel near the lefthand kick panel.

The instrument panel junction block is located in the lower righthand side of the instrument panel.

The instrument panel fuse block is located on the lower lefthand side of the instrument panel.

The underhood fuse block is located on the lefthand side of the engine compartment near the battery.

The rear lamps junction block is located in the front of the rear bumper on the crossmember.

FUEL PUMP RELAY LOCATION

The fuel pump relay is located on the lefthand side of the engine compartment, inside the underhood fuse block

RELAY CENTER LOCATION

The Underhood Bussed Electrical Center (UBEC) contains the engine compartment relays and is mounted on the lefthand wheelhouse, near the battery. The convenience center is located just below the lefthand side of the instrument panel.

STARTER

REPLACE

H2

1. Remove mounting bolts and engine shield, as required.
2. Remove mounting bolts and oil pan skid plate, as required.
3. Remove righthand transmission cover bolt.
4. Remove front axle mounting bracket nut, then position front axle mounting bracket bolt until tip is flush with support bushing. **Do not remove bolt.**
5. Remove mounting bolts and slide starter forward until it clears transmission.
6. Disconnect oil level sensor electrical connector.
7. Remove starter solenoid nut and lead from stud.
8. Remove starter lead nut and the positive cable from starter stud.
9. Remove starter.

10. Reverse procedure to install, noting the following:
    a. **Torque** starter lead nut to 80 inch lbs.
    b. **Torque** starter solenoid nut 30 inch lbs.
    c. **Torque** starter mounting bolts 37 ft. lbs.
    d. **Torque** front axle mounting bracket nut 70 ft. lbs.
    e. **Torque** transmission cover bolt 80 inch lbs.
    f. **Torque** oil pan skid plate bolts to 15 ft. lbs.
    g. **Torque** engine shield bolts to 15 ft. lbs.

H3

1. Remove intake manifold as outlined in "Intake Manifold, Replace."
2. Remove starter solenoid S terminal nut and disconnect lead from starter.
3. Remove starter terminal nut and disconnect battery positive cable from starter.
4. Remove starter motor nut and bolt, then the starter motor.
5. Reverse procedure to install, noting the following:
    a. **Torque** starter motor bolt and nut to 37 ft. lbs.
    b. **Torque** battery positive cable to 80 inch lbs.
    c. **Torque** starter solenoid S nut to 31 inch lbs.

ALTERNATOR

REPLACE

H2

1. Remove air inlet duct, as required.
2. Disconnect terminal plug and battery lead connections from back of alternator.
3. Remove upper fan shroud mounting bolts and fan shroud.
4. Remove accessory drive belt using suitable 3/8 inch drive wrench to rotate tensioner arm counterclockwise.
5. Remove mounting bolts and alternator.
6. Reverse procedure to install, noting the following:
    a. **Torque** alternator mounting bolts to 37 ft. lbs.
    b. **Torque** battery lead mounting nut to 80 inch lbs.

H3

1. Remove drive belt as outlined in "Serpentine Drive Belt."
2. Raise and support vehicle high enough to access air conditioning compressor through wheelhouse.
3. Remove lefthand front wheel.
4. Remove lefthand wheelhouse liner.
5. Disengage A/C compressor electrical connector from bracket.
6. Recover A/C system as outlined in "Air Conditioning" chapter.
7. Disconnect A/C condenser and evaporator lines from compressor.

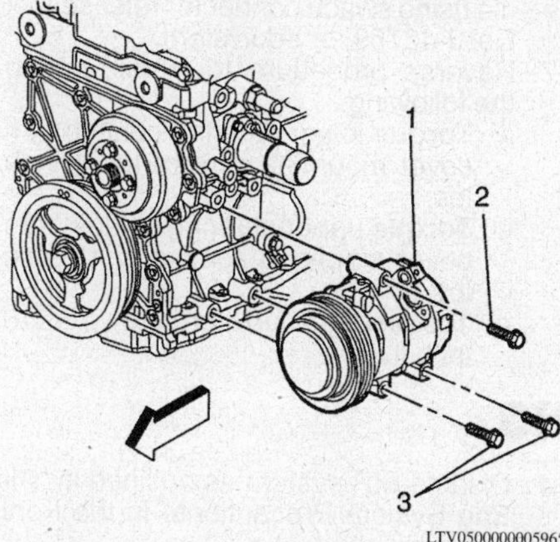

Fig. 1 A/C compressor removal. H3

8. Remove A/C compressor mounting bolts (2 and 3), **Fig. 1.** Upper mounting bolt (2) will remain with A/C compressor.
9. Lower vehicle.
10. Reposition protective boot from alternator output BAT terminal.
11. Remove alternator output BAT terminal nut and remove alternator lead from alternator.
12. Disconnect alternator electrical connector.
13. Remove three alternator bolts.
14. Position A/C compressor forward, in order to gain clearance to remove alternator.
15. Remove alternator assembly.
16. Reverse procedure to install, noting the following:
    a. **Torque** three alternator bolts to 37 ft. lbs.
    b. **Torque** alternator output BAT nut to 15 ft. lbs.
    c. **Torque** A/C compressor bolts to 37 ft. lbs.
    d. Charge A/C system as outlined in "Air Conditioning" chapter.

COIL PACK

REPLACE

H2

1. Disconnect spark plug wires at ignition coils.
2. Disconnect ignition coil harness connector.
3. Remove mounting bolts and ignition coil.
4. Reverse procedure to install. **Torque** mounting bolts to 71 inch lbs.

H3

1. Loosen air cleaner outlet duct clamps.
2. Remove air cleaner outlet duct from air cleaner assembly and air cleaner resonator.
3. Loosen air cleaner resonator outlet duct clamp.
4. Remove two air cleaner resonator bolts.
5. Lift upward on air cleaner resonator and outlet duct assembly.
6. Disconnect crankcase ventilation hose from camshaft cover and outlet duct from throttle body.
7. Remove assembly from engine.
8. Disconnect engine wiring harness electrical connector from oil pressure sensor.
9. Disconnect engine wiring harness retainers from power steering pump.
10. Disconnect engine wiring harness electrical connectors from following:
    a. Exhaust camshaft position (CMP) sensor.
    b. Camshaft position (CMP) actuator solenoid valve.
11. Disconnect engine wiring harness retainer from camshaft cover.
12. Disconnect engine wiring harness electrical connectors from following:
    a. Engine coolant temperature (ECT) sensor.
    b. Fuel injector harness.
    c. Ignition coils.
    d. Heated oxygen sensor (HO2S).
13. Disconnect engine wiring harness electrical connector from intake camshaft position (CMP) sensor.
14. Disengage engine wiring harness conduit from camshaft cover and place aside.
15. Remove ignition coil bolts.
16. Remove ignition coils from camshaft cover.
17. Reverse procedure to install, noting the following:
    a. **Torque** ignition coil bolts to 89 inch lbs.
    b. **Torque** air cleaner resonator clamp and bolts to 53 inch lbs.

IGNITION LOCK

REPLACE

H2

1. Remove steering wheel as outlined under "Steering Wheel, Replace."
2. Remove tilt lever by pulling it out of steering column.
3. Remove lower steering column trim cover mounting screws.
4. Remove lower steering column trim cover by tilting it down and sliding back to disengage locking tabs.
5. Remove mounting screws and upper steering column trim cover.
6. Turn ignition lock cylinder to START position.
7. Insert tip of suitable awl into ignition lock cylinder access hole, then push down and hold ignition lock cylinder retaining pin.
8. Release ignition lock cylinder to RUN position and remove ignition lock cylinder by pulling it away from steering column.
9. Reverse procedure to install, noting the following:
    a. **Torque** lower steering column trim cover mounting screws to 31 inch lbs.
    b. **Torque** upper steering column trim cover mounting screws to 13 inch lbs.

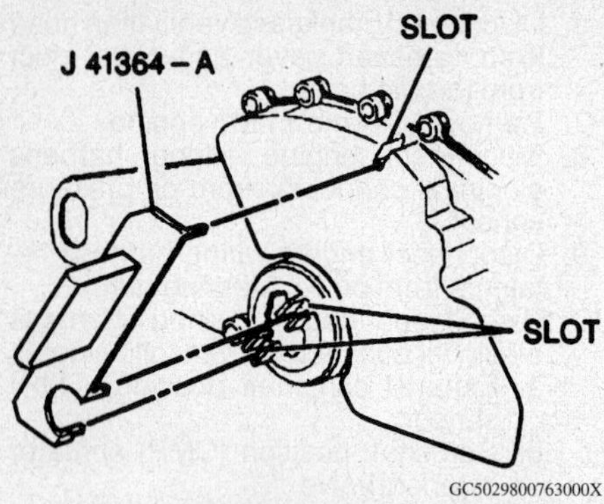

Fig. 2 Neutral safety switch installation. H2

H3

1. Remove steering column trim covers.
2. Turn ignition lock cylinder to accessory (ACC) position.
3. Lock cylinder access hole is just under driver air bag coil on righthand side center of column housing.
4. Insert 90° tip of a pick type tool into access hole of ignition lock cylinder.
5. Push down and hold retaining pin of ignition lock cylinder.
6. Remove ignition lock cylinder by pulling cylinder away from steering column.
7. Reverse procedure to install.

IGNITION SWITCH

REPLACE

H2

1. Apply parking brake and move shift lever all way down to last gear.
2. Tilt steering wheel to full down position.
3. Remove instrument cluster trim bezel by pulling rearward on corners.
4. Remove mounting screws and knee bolster by unsnapping top.
5. Remove steering wheel as outlined under "Steering Wheel, Replace."
6. Remove tilt lever by pulling it out of steering column.
7. Remove lower steering column trim cover mounting screws.
8. Remove lower steering column trim cover by tilting it down and sliding back to disengage locking tabs.
9. Remove mounting screws and upper steering column trim cover.
10. Disconnect steering column electrical connectors.
11. Remove wire harness assembly from steering column and wire harness strap.
12. Slide two turn signal and multi-function switch connectors out of bulkhead connector.
13. Remove lock module key alarm connector by rotating connector 90° and pull key alarm connector out of lock module.
14. Remove passkey connector from lock module assembly.
15. Remove electric park lock connector.
16. Remove ignition switch from lock module using switch connector release tool No. J-42759, or equivalent.
17. Reverse procedure to install, noting the following:
    a. **Torque** lower steering column trim cover mounting screws to 31 inch lbs.
    b. **Torque** upper steering column trim cover mounting screws to 13 inch lbs.
    c. **Torque** knee bolster screws to 18 inch lbs.

H3

1. Disable SIR system as outlined in "Air Bag System Precautions" in the front of this manual.
2. Remove lock cylinder as outlined in "Ignition Lock, Replace."
3. Remove two washer head screws from switch mounting plate.
4. Slide switch mounting plate from steering column shaft.
5. Remove shear bolt from ignition switch and lock housing assembly using a suitable hammer and chisel.
6. Remove ignition switch and lock housing assembly.
7. Reverse procedure to install, noting the following:
    a. Relearn theft deterrent system using a suitably programmed scan tool.
    b. Enable SIR system as outlined in "Air Bag System Precautions" in the front of this manual.

NEUTRAL SAFETY SWITCH

REPLACE

H2

REMOVAL

1. Apply parking brake.
2. Shift transmission into neutral position, then raise and support vehicle.
3. Remove transmission control to manual mounting nut and lever.
4. Disconnect park/neutral safety switch electrical connector.
5. Remove two mounting bolts and park/neutral safety switch.

INSTALLATION

1. Install adjustment tool No. J-41364-A, or equivalent, onto park/neutral safety switch. Ensure two slots on switch are lined up with lower two tabs on tool, **Fig. 2.**
2. Rotate tool until upper locator pin is lined up with slot on top of switch.
3. Install switch to transmission.
4. Install park/neutral switch to transmission mounting bolts. **Torque** bolts to 18 ft. lbs.
5. Remove adjusting tool.
6. Connect park/neutral safety switch electrical connector.
7. Install transmission control lever to manual shaft and install nut. **Torque** control lever nut to 18 ft. lbs.

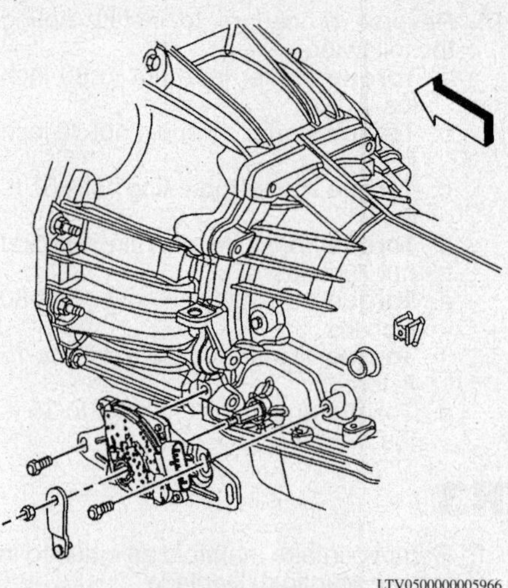

Fig. 3 Neutral safety switch installation. H3

H3

REMOVAL

1. Apply parking brake.
2. Shift transmission into neutral position.
3. Raise and support vehicle using a suitable lift.
4. Remove nut securing transmission control lever to manual shaft.
5. Remove transmission control lever from manual shaft.
6. Disconnect electrical connector from switch.
7. Remove bolts securing neutral back up switch to transmission.
8. Remove neutral back up switch from manual shaft.

INSTALLATION

1. Install neutral back up switch to transmission manual shaft by aligning switch hub flats with manual shaft flats, **Fig. 3.**
2. Slide switch onto transmission manual shaft until switch mounting bracket contacts mounting bosses on transmission.
3. Loosely install two neutral back up switch bolts.
4. Position tool No. J 41364-A or equivalent, onto neutral back up switch, **Fig. 4.** Ensure that 2 slots on switch where manual shaft is inserted are lined up with lower 2 tabs on tool.
5. Rotate switch until upper locator pin on tool is lined up with slot on top of switch. **Torque** neutral back up switch bolts to 20 ft. lbs.
6. Remove tool No. J 41364-A or equivalent, from switch. If installing a new switch, remove positive assurance bracket at this time.
7. Connect electrical connector to switch.
8. Install transmission control lever to manual shaft with nut. **Torque** control lever nut to 15 ft. lbs.
9. Lower vehicle.
10. Adjust automatic transmission range selector cable.
11. Inspect switch for proper operation.

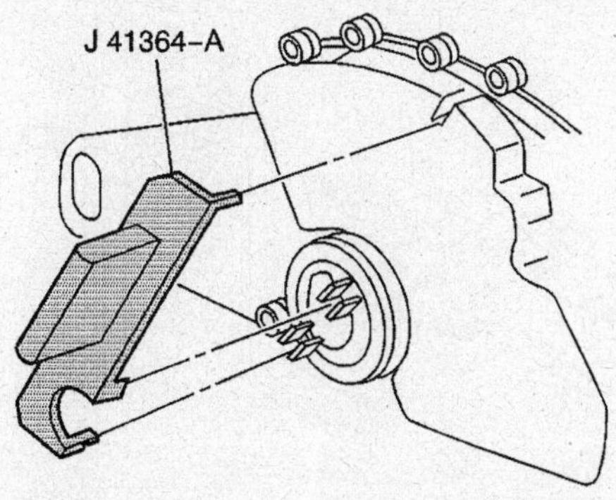

Fig. 4 Neutral safety switch tool installation. H3

Engine must start in P or N positions only. If proper operation of switch can not be obtained, replace switch.

HEADLAMP SWITCH

REPLACE

H2

1. Remove instrument cluster bezel as outlined in "Instrument Cluster, Replace."
2. Disconnect electrical connector from switch.
3. Remove headlamp switch by unsnapping it from instrument cluster bezel.
4. Reverse procedure to install.

H3

1. Remove instrument panel outer cover.
2. Remove trim clip retainers.
3. Remove hood release handle.
4. Remove park brake release handle assembly.
5. Remove driver instrument panel knee bolster cover.
6. Remove trim clip retainers.
7. Remove headlamp switch screw, then the headlamp switch assembly.
8. Reverse procedure to install.

STOP LIGHT SWITCH

REPLACE

H2

1. Remove push rod retainer from brake pedal pin, **Fig. 5.**
2. Unsnap stop lamp switch from pushrod.
3. Disconnect electrical connector from stop lamp switch.
4. Reverse procedure to install.

H3

1. Disconnect stop lamp switch electrical connectors from under driver side instrument panel at top of brake pedal bracket.
2. Rotate switch counterclockwise.
3. Remove switch from bracket.
4. Remove switch from vehicle.
5. Remove switch retainer.
6. Reverse procedure to install.

MULTI-FUNCTION SWITCH

REPLACE

H2

1. Remove steering wheel as outlined under "Steering Wheel, Replace."
2. Remove tilt lever.
3. Remove mounting screws and lower cover.
4. Remove two upper column cover Torx head screws.
5. Remove knee bolster mounting screws, then unsnap knee bolster from instrument panel.
6. Twist brake release cable and disengage cable from knee bolster.
7. Remove lap cooler hose and knee bolster.
8. Remove ignition lock cylinder as outlined under "Ignition Lock, Replace."
9. Remove steering column upper cover.
10. Remove two wiring harness straps from steering column wiring harness, **Fig. 6.**
11. Disconnect steering column bulkhead connector from vehicle wiring harness.
12. Remove grey and black multi-function switch connectors from column bulkhead connector.
13. Remove mount screws and multi-function switch.
14. Reverse procedure to install.

H3

1. Disable SIR system as outlined in "Air Bag System Precautions" in the front of this manual.
2. Remove steering wheel as outlined in "Steering Wheel, Replace."
3. Remove steering column trim covers.
4. Remove wire harness straps from wire harness assembly.
5. Disconnect multi-function switch SIR coil assembly connector from base of column.
6. Remove multi-function switch SIR coil assembly lead from wire harness assembly.
7. Remove three pan head tapping screws from multi-function switch SIR coil assembly, **Fig. 7.**
8. Slide multi-function switch SIR coil assembly off of steering column. Discard multi-function switch SIR coil assembly if replacing.
9. Reverse procedure to install, noting the following:
   a. A new multi-function switch SIR coil assembly will come precentered with a centering tab attached. Do not remove centering tab until installation is complete.

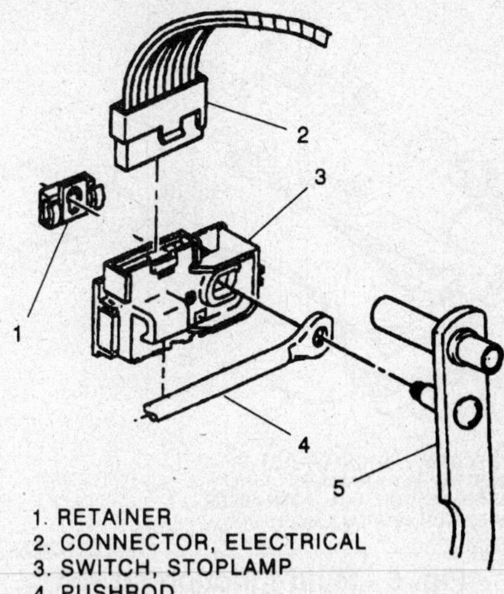

Fig. 5 Stop lamp switch removal. H2

   b. Failure to follow procedure will cause a misalignment to SIR coil and centering will be required.
   c. If reusing existing multi-function switch SIR coil assembly, you must center SIR coil as outlined in "Passive Restraint Systems" chapter.
   d. **Torque** pan head tapping screws to 30 inch lbs.
   e. Enable SIR system as outlined in "Air Bag System Precautions" in the front of this manual.

TURN SIGNAL SWITCH

REPLACE

Refer to "Multi-Function Switch, Replace" for turn signal switch replacement procedures.

DIMMER SWITCH

REPLACE

Refer to "Multi-Function Switch, Replace" for dimmer switch replacement procedures.

STEERING WHEEL

REPLACE

H2

1. Turn ignition switch to ON position.
2. Turn steering wheel 90° so side of SIR module is at 12 o'clock position.
3. Insert suitable screwdriver into access hole and push leaf spring to release air bag module notched pin.
4. Turn steering wheel 180° and repeat previous step.
5. Tilt air bag module top rearward and disconnect SIR lead wire from clips.
6. Disconnect Connector Position Assurance retainer from connector. Disconnect SIR connector.

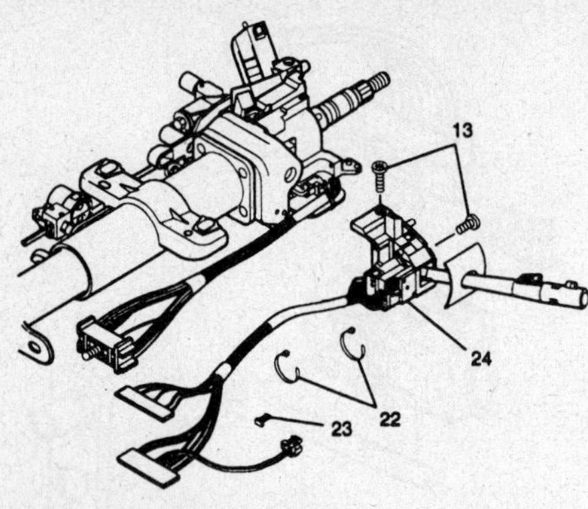

Fig. 6 Multi-function switch removal. H2

7. Remove air bag module.
8. Remove horn contact plate mounting screws and plunger from steering wheel.
9. Mark steering wheel to steering shaft alignment for installation.
10. Remove steering wheel nut.
11. Remove steering wheel using steering wheel puller tool No. J-1859-A, or equivalent.
12. Reverse procedure to install, noting the following:
    a. **Torque** steering wheel nut to 30 ft. lbs.
    b. **Torque** horn contact plate mounting screws to 50 inch lbs.

H3

1. Set front wheels in straight-ahead position.
2. Disable SIR system as outlined in "Air Bag System Precautions" in the front of this manual.
3. Lock steering column through access hole in lower steering column trim cover using tool No. J 42640 or equivalent.
4. Remove driver air bag module as outlined in "Passive Restraint Systems" chapter.
5. Place an alignment mark in order to note relationship of steering wheel to steering shaft.
6. Loosen steering wheel nut two complete revolutions, **Fig. 8.**
7. Carefully unseat steering wheel from steering column.
8. Remove steering wheel nut, then the steering wheel from steering column, **Fig. 8.**
9. Reverse procedure to install, noting the following:
    a. Improper alignment of steering wheel to steering column shaft will cause vehicle damage. In order to prevent vehicle damage, ensure that steering wheel is properly indexed to steering column before tightening steering wheel nut.
    b. **Torque** steering wheel nut to steering shaft to 26 ft. lbs.
    c. Enable SIR system as outlined in "Air Bag System Precautions" in the front of this manual.

INSTRUMENT CLUSTER

REPLACE

H2

1. Engage parking brake lever.
2. Move gear shift lever and tilt steering wheel to lowest positions.
3. Remove bezel by pulling rearward on clips , **Fig. 9.**
4. Remove instrument panel cluster mounting screws, **Fig. 10.**
5. Disconnect instrument panel cluster electrical harness connectors.
6. Remove instrument panel cluster by tilting bottom of cluster outward.
7. Reverse procedure to install. **Torque** mounting screws to 18 inch lbs.

H3

1. Remove instrument panel cluster trim plate assembly.
2. Remove trim clip retainer.
3. Remove instrument panel cluster screw.
4. Remove instrument panel cluster assembly and disconnect electrical connector.
5. Reverse procedure to install, noting the following:
    a. The odometer will read zero miles after instrument panel cluster is replaced. Body control module (BCM) stores mileage information for odometer. Vehicle will have to be driven for BCM to send out a mileage update to IPC. IPC should then display current mileage.
    b. **Torque** instrument panel cluster screws to 18 inch lbs.

RADIO

REPLACE

H2

1. Remove instrument cluster trim bezel as outlined under "Instrument Cluster, Replace."
2. Release radio assembly lock tabs using suitable screwdriver.
3. Slide radio rearward away from instrument panel and disconnect electrical connectors.
4. Remove radio.
5. Reverse procedure to install.

H3

REMOVAL

1. Remove instrument panel center accessory trim plate assembly.
2. Disconnect electrical connectors to rear wiper washer switch, HVAC control module, instrument panel accessory switch, 12-volt accessory power

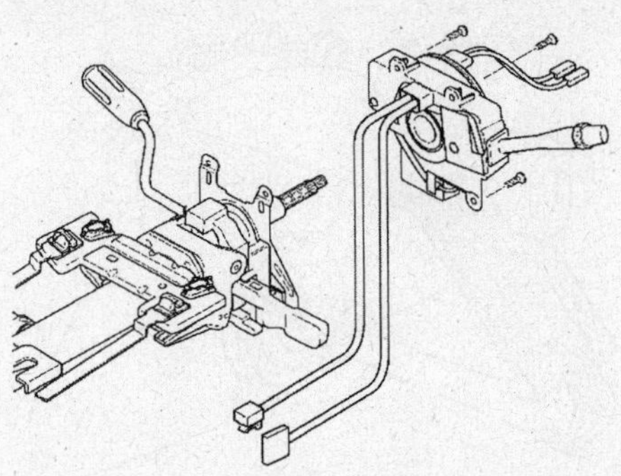

Fig. 7 Multi-function switch removal. H3

outlets, HVAC center air outlets, and if equipped off road lamp switches.
3. Remove four screws that retain radio to instrument panel.
4. Partially remove radio disengaging radio rear alignment locator to gain access to electrical connectors.
5. Disconnect radio antenna cable.
6. Disconnect electrical connectors to radio.
7. Remove radio from vehicle.

INSTALLATION

1. Connect electrical connectors to radio.
2. Connect radio antenna cable.
3. Install radio and **torque** radio screws to 18 inch lbs.
4. Connect electrical connectors to rear wiper washer switch, HVAC control module, instrument panel accessory switch, 12-volt accessory power outlets, HVAC center air outlets, and if equipped off road lamp switches.
5. Install instrument panel center accessory trim plate assembly.
6. Complete following procedure using a scan tool in order to properly set up communication:
    a. At Main Menu screen, select: Diagnostics.
    b. At Vehicle Identification screens, build vehicle.
    c. At System Selection Menu screen, select: Body and Accessories.
    d. At Body Screen, select: Entertainment.
    e. At Entertainment screen, select appropriate radio.
    f. At Radio screen, select: Module Setup.
    g. At Module Replacement screen, select appropriate module to setup.
    h. Press EXIT on scan tool and cycle ignition.

WIPER MOTOR

REPLACE

H2

FRONT

1. Mark position of wiper blade on windshield for installation alignment.
2. Disconnect washer hose.

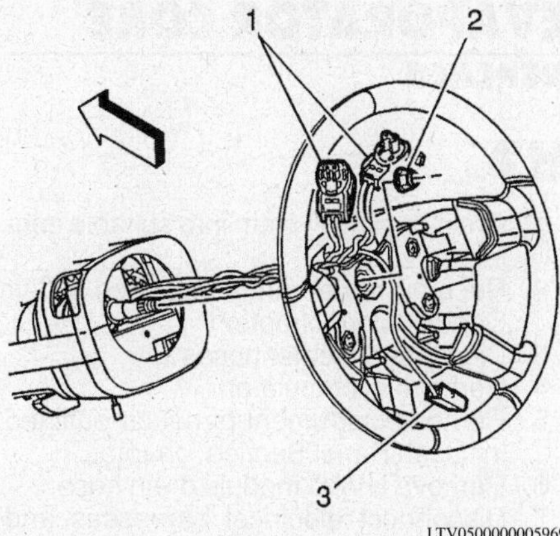

Fig. 8 Steering wheel & component removal. H3

3. Remove cover and wiper arm nut.
4. Remove wiper arm from driveshaft using suitable battery terminal puller to remove, while rocking arm back and forth.
5. Unsnap outboard air inlet grille panel sections and remove mounting clips running along center air inlet grille panel edges.
6. Remove air inlet grille panel mounting screws on each end.
7. Disconnect windshield washer hose from nozzle underneath center air inlet grille panel.
8. Remove air inlet grille panel.
9. Remove four mounting bolts and reinforcement panel.
10. Disconnect wiper motor electrical connector.
11. Remove two mounting bolts and wiper transmission.
12. Remove drive link from wiper motor crank arm using wiper transmission separator tool No. J-39232, or equivalent.
13. Remove two mounting bolts and wiper motor.
14. Reverse procedure to install, noting the following:
    a. **Torque** wiper motor mounting bolts to 89 inch lbs.
    b. **Torque** transmission mounting bolts to 80 inch lbs.
    c. **Torque** reinforcement panel mounting bolts to 80 inch lbs.
    d. **Torque** air inlet grille panel mounting screws to 18 inch lbs.
    e. **Torque** wiper arm nut to 18 ft. lbs.

REAR

1. Disconnect washer hose, then remove cover, nut and wiper arm.
2. Remove wiper motor shaft nut and spacer.
3. Remove pull strap mounting screw.
4. Remove trim panel by sliding trim panel upward to disconnect mounting hooks.
5. Disconnect wiper motor electrical connector.
6. Remove two mounting screws and wiper motor.
7. Reverse procedure to install, noting the following:
    a. **Torque** wiper motor mounting screws to 14 ft. lbs.
    b. **Torque** driveshaft nut to 71 inch lbs.
    c. **Torque** wiper arm nut to 17 ft. lbs.

H3

FRONT

1. Remove wiper arm cap and nut, then the wiper arm.
2. Remove upper cowl panel using care when pulling away from clips.
3. Disconnect wiper motor electrical connector.
4. Remove wiper motor module.
5. Remove transmission to wiper motor bolts, then the wiper motor.
6. Reverse procedure to install, noting the following:
    a. **Torque** transmission to wiper motor bolts to 89 inch lbs.
    b. **Torque** windshield wiper transmission grommet bolts to 89 inch lbs.
    c. **Torque** wiper arm nuts to 38 ft. lbs.

REAR

1. Remove spare wheel from spare tire carrier.
2. Remove rear window wiper arm.
3. Remove sheep hook tab.
4. Remove rear window wiper blade.
5. Remove rear wiper arm finish cover.
6. Remove rear window wiper motor nut.
7. Remove rear wiper washer hose.
8. Remove rear window wiper assembly arm.
9. Remove jack stowage cover.
10. Remove jack stowage tool kit.
11. Remove rear wiper motor bolts, then the wiper motor.
12. Reverse procedure to install, noting the following:
    a. **Torque** rear window wiper motor nuts to 80 inch lbs.
    b. **Torque** rear window wiper motor bolts to 89 inch lbs.

WIPER SWITCH

REPLACE

H2

FRONT

Refer to "Multi-Function Switch, Replace" for wiper switch replacement procedures.

REAR

1. Remove wiper switch from trim plate.
2. Disconnect electrical connector.
3. Reverse procedure to install.

H3

FRONT

Refer to "Multi-Function Switch, Replace" for wiper switch replacement procedures.

REAR

1. Remove instrument panel center accessory trim plate assembly as outlined in "Radio, Replace."
2. Remove rear wiper washer switch screw.
3. Remove rear wiper washer switch assembly.
4. Reverse procedure to install. **Torque** switch screws to 18 inch lbs.

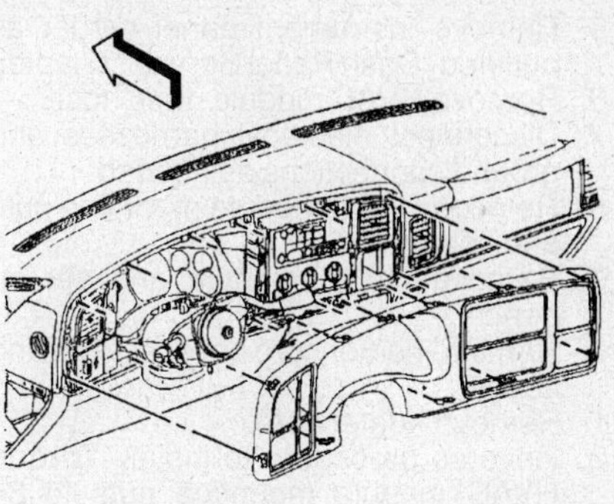

Fig. 9 Instrument cluster bezel removal. H2

BLOWER MOTOR

REPLACE

H2

1. Remove hush panel from under right-hand side of instrument panel.
2. Disconnect blower relay/resistor electrical connector.
3. Remove blower motor insulating cover mounting screws.
4. Disconnect blower motor electrical connector, then remove insulating cover.
5. Pull blower motor retaining tab down and turn motor counterclockwise to disengage retaining tab,
6. Remove blower motor.
7. Reverse procedure to install.

H3

1. Remove front side door sill trim plate assembly.
2. Remove door trim clips.
3. Remove cowl side trim panel, then the panel cowl side trim clip.
4. Disconnect blower motor resistor electrical connector.
5. Remove blower motor resistor screw.
6. Remove blower motor resistor.
7. Remove three blower motor screws.
8. Remove blower motor assembly.
9. Reverse procedure to install.

HEATER CORE

REPLACE

H2

1. Drain cooling system into suitable container.
2. Recover refrigerant as outlined under "Air Conditioning" chapter.
3. Disconnect heater hoses.
4. Remove accumulator.

5. Remove instrument panel carrier as outlined "Dash Panel Service" chapter.
6. Remove HVAC module drain hose.
7. Disconnect electrical harnesses and ground connections as needed.
8. Remove HVAC module mounting nuts and screws.
9. Remove HVAC module and set on bench.
10. Remove heater core cover screws and cover.
11. Remove heater core.
12. Reverse procedure to install. **Torque** HVAC module mounting nuts to 84 inch lbs., and bolts to 35 inch lbs.

H3

1. Drain cooling system into suitable container.
2. Recover refrigerant system as outlined in "Air Conditioning" chapter.
3. Remove air cleaner assembly.
4. Remove front grille assembly.
5. Remove evaporator tube and condenser nut, then the sealing washer.
6. Remove thermal expansion valve nut and sealing washer.
7. Remove evaporator tube assembly.
8. Remove alternator as outlined in "Alternator, Replace."
9. Remove transmission as outlined in **MOTOR's "Domestic Transmission, In-Vehicle Service" or "Transmission Service DVD."**
10. Reposition hose clamp at heater outlet fitting using tool No. J 38185 or equivalent.
11. Remove heater inlet hose from heater outlet fitting.
12. Remove heater inlet hose from heater core.
13. Remove transmission housing bolt.
14. Remove heater inlet hose.
15. Remove heater outlet hose assembly.

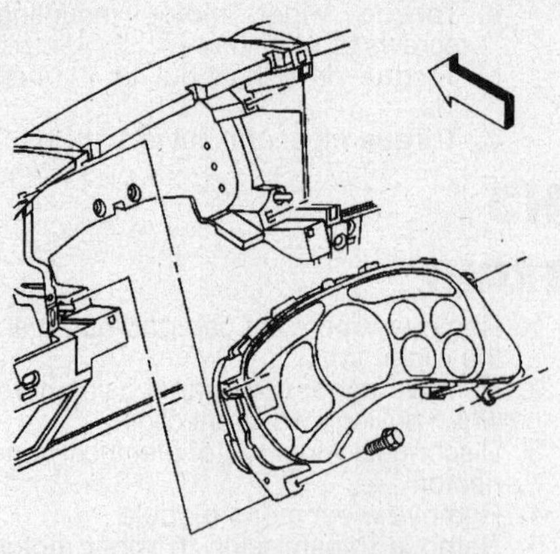

Fig. 10 Instrument cluster removal. H2

16. Remove instrument panel carrier as outlined in "Dash Panel Service" chapter.
17. Disconnect HVAC module assembly electrical connectors.
18. Remove HVAC module assembly nut, then the HVAC module.
19. Disconnect actuator electrical connectors from recirculation case.
20. Remove heater core cover screw, heater core cover and heater core pass through seal.
21. Remove rear floor air outlet duct screw and air outlet duct.
22. Remove air distribution case screw and air distribution case.
23. Remove heater core bracket screw, heater core bracket and heater core.
24. Reverse procedure to install, noting the following:
    a. **Torque** evaporator tube and condenser nut to 21 ft. lbs.
    b. Charge refrigerant system as outlined in "Air Conditioning" chapter.

EVAPORATOR CORE

REPLACE

H2

1. Drain cooling system into suitable container.
2. Recover refrigerant as outlined in "Air Conditioning" chapter.
3. Disconnect heater hoses.
4. Remove accumulator.
5. Remove instrument panel as outlined in "Dash Panel Service" chapter.
6. Remove HVAC module drain hose.
7. Disconnect electrical harnesses and ground connections as needed.
8. Remove HVAC module mounting nuts and screws.
9. Remove HVAC module and set on bench.
10. Remove HVAC module screws and separate HVAC module.
11. Remove evaporator core.
12. Reverse procedure to install. **Torque** HVAC module mounting nuts to 84 inch lbs., and bolts to 35 inch lbs.

H3

1. Remove HVAC module as outlined in "Heater Core, Replace."
2. Remove evaporator case seal.
3. Remove thermal expansion valve bolts, then the valve.
4. Remove sealing washer.
5. Remove rear air outlet duct screw and rear air outlet duct.
6. Remove evaporator case screw, then the evaporator lower case.
7. Remove air conditioning evaporator.
8. Reverse procedure to install.

3.5L Engine

NOTE: On Air Bag Equipped Models, Refer To "Air Bag System Precautions" Located In The Front Of This Manual For System Disarming & Arming Procedures.

NOTE: Refer To "Computer Relearn Procedures" Located In The Front Of This Manual When Battery Power To The Computer Has Been Interrupted.

INDEX

PRECAUTIONS

Air Bag Systems

Refer to "Air Bag System Precautions" in the front of this manual for system disarming and arming procedures.

Battery Ground Cable

Prior to service disconnect battery ground cable and isolate, as required.

Fuel System Pressure Relief

1. Turn ignition to Off position, then disconnect battery ground cable.
2. Loosen fuel filler cap to relieve fuel tank vapor pressure.
3. Connect fuel pressure gauge to fuel pressure connection, then install bleed hose of gauge into a suitable container.
4. Open valve on gauge to bleed system pressure.

COMPRESSION PRESSURE

1. Remove air duct from throttle control module.
2. Remove the ignition control modules and disable fuel system.
3. Remove spark plugs.
4. Firmly install compression gauge tool No. J 38722, or equivalent into spark plug hole.
5. Crank engine through at least four compression strokes.
6. Inspect and record readings from gauge tool at each stroke.
7. Disconnect gauge tool and repeat compression test on each cylinder.
8. Record compression readings from all cylinders.
9. Normal reading should be approximately 215 psi.
10. Lowest reading should not be less than 70° of highest reading.

ENGINE MOUNT

REPLACE

1. Raise and support vehicle using a suitable lift.
2. Remove front tire and wheel assemblies.
3. Remove engine shield.
4. If removing lefthand side mount, remove intermediate steering shaft as outlined in "Steering Columns" chapter.
5. Support engine using a suitable jack stand and block of wood.
6. Remove engine mount to frame bracket through bolt.
7. Loosen side through bolt.
8. Raise engine using suitable jack stand so engine tilts to one side.
9. Remove engine mount bolts, then the engine mounts.
10. Reverse procedure to install, tighten to specifications.

ENGINE

REPLACE

1. Remove hood. Place matchmarks on hinge and hood for installation alignment.
2. Recover air conditioning system as outlined in "Air Conditioning" chapter.
3. Remove drive belt as outlined in "Serpentine Drive Belt."
4. Remove battery tray.
5. Remove battery cable harness clips from battery tray.
6. Lift lower battery box upward from battery tray.
7. Drain engine coolant into suitable container.
8. Remove lefthand front wheelhouse panel.
9. Remove engine shield.
10. Remove radiator outlet hose.
11. Remove radiator as outlined in "Radiator, Replace."
12. Remove fan shroud.
13. Loosen fan clutch using tool Nos., J 41240 and J 46406 or equivalents.
14. Remove fan hub nut in a counterclockwise rotation.
15. Remove cooling fan from fan clutch.
16. Remove air cleaner assembly.
17. Remove air cleaner resonator and outlet duct.
18. Position tool No. J 38185 or equivalent, to clamp in order to remove radiator inlet hose from water outlet housing.
19. Remove washer solvent container and coolant recovery reservoir mounting bolts only in order to gain clearance to remove engine wiring harness.
20. Remove two engine wiring harness connectors from powertrain control module (PCM).
21. Remove engine wiring harness clips from wheelhouse.

22. Remove engine wiring harness retainers from power steering pump, **Fig. 1.**
23. Remove engine wiring harness connectors from electric motor actuator connector and oil pressure switch.
24. Remove engine wiring harness retainer from camshaft cover.
25. Remove engine wiring harness connectors from exhaust camshaft position (CMP) sensor and exhaust camshaft actuator.
26. Remove engine wiring harness connectors from engine coolant temperature (ECT) sensor, fuel injector harness, ignition coils and heated oxygen sensor (HO2S).
27. Remove engine wiring harness retainer from camshaft cover.
28. Remove engine wiring harness connector from throttle body.
29. Remove engine wiring harness connector from intake CMP sensor.
30. Remove engine wiring harness conduit from camshaft cover.
31. Remove transmission filler tube.
32. Remove air conditioning compressor evaporator hose bracket bolt from cylinder head.
33. Drain engine oil into suitable container.
34. Remove studs securing secondary air injection (AIR) pipe cover to cylinder head.
35. Remove AIR pipe cover and gasket. Discard gasket.
36. Install tool No. J 44220 or equivalent, in place of AIR adapter.
37. Remove inlet heater hose quick connect from heater core, and secure to engine.
38. Remove power steering pump mounting bolts only, and position aside.
39. Remove righthand side engine mount-to-frame bracket bolt.
40. Remove engine wiring harness retainer from engine wiring harness bracket.
41. Position engine wiring harness aside.
42. Remove fuel feed pipe from fuel rail.
43. Remove evaporative emission (EVAP) pipe at purge solenoid.
44. Remove fuel lines from the retainers at the oil dipstick bracket and intake manifold.
45. Remove oil dipstick from tube.
46. Remove oil dipstick tube bolt.
47. Remove oil dipstick tube from engine oil pan.
48. Remove manifold absolute pressure (MAP) sensor.
49. Remove MAP sensor wiring harness retainer from intake manifold.
50. Raise and support vehicle only high enough to access wiring harnesses through wheelhouse.
51. Remove A/C condenser line bolt at A/C compressor, then the line from compressor.
52. Remove A/C evaporator line bolt at A/C compressor, then the line from compressor.
53. Remove A/C compressor bolts and compressor.
54. Disconnect battery cable and MAP sensor wiring harness retainers from engine wiring harness bracket.
55. Remove starter solenoid S terminal nut and disconnect lead from starter.

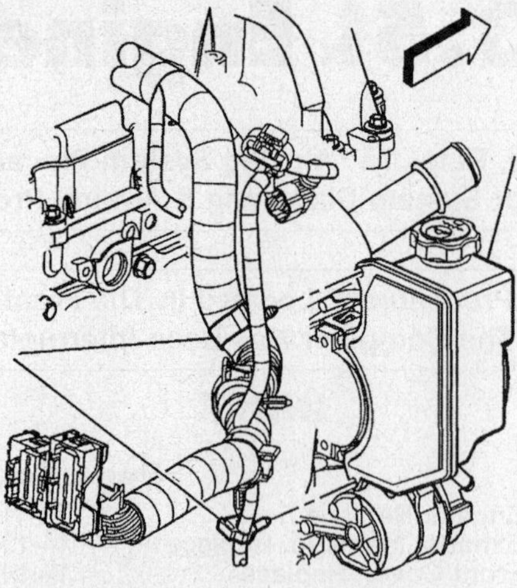

Fig. 1 Power steering pump harness connections

56. Remove starter terminal nut and disconnect battery positive cable from starter.
57. Remove bolt securing battery ground cable ground terminal to engine block.
58. Remove engine wiring harness connector from EVAP canister purge solenoid valve.
59. Remove engine wiring harness connector from No. 2 knock sensor (KS).
60. Remove coolant heater cord from coolant heater.
61. Remove engine wiring harness retainers from A/C compressor and engine oil pan rail.
62. Position tool No. J 38185 or equivalent, to clamp in order to remove heater outlet hose from heater outlet hose fitting.
63. Remove engine wiring harness connector from crankshaft position (CKP) sensor.
64. Raise vehicle completely.
65. Remove three bolts securing engine wiring ground leads to engine block.
66. Remove engine wiring harness retainer from engine oil pan rail.
67. Position engine wiring harness aside.
68. Remove fuel line clips from brackets on transmission.
69. Remove engine shield.
70. Remove oil pan skid plate.
71. Support front differential assembly using suitable jack.
72. Remove front differential assembly bolt.
73. Remove crossmember nut, bolt then the crossmember.
74. Remove front propeller shaft as outlined in "Front Suspension & Steering" section.
75. Remove differential carrier assembly bushing to frame bolts only.
76. Position differential carrier assembly forward.
77. Secure pinion yoke in order to prevent differential carrier from rotating.
78. Remove exhaust seal.
79. **On models equipped with automatic transmission,** remove bolt securing transmission oil cooler pipe bracket to righthand side of engine oil pan rail.
80. **On models equipped with manual transmission,** remove inspection plug from transmission.
81. **On models equipped with manual transmission,** mark torque converter to flexplate/flywheel orientation to ensure proper realignment.
82. **On all models,** remove service slot plug.
83. **On models equipped with automatic transmission,** rotate harmonic balancer center bolt clockwise only in order to access torque converter bolts through service slot. Remove torque converter bolts.
84. **On all models,** lower transmission slightly.
85. Remove transmission bolts.
86. Lower vehicle.
87. Remove lefthand engine mount-to-frame bracket bolt.
88. Place a suitable jack under transmission for support.
89. Remove remaining transmission mounting bolts.
90. Install an engine lift chain to engine lift brackets and attach to an engine lift device.
91. Raise engine to remove engine mounts using engine lift device.
92. Remove engine mounts as outlined in "Engine Mount, Replace."
93. Carefully raise engine from engine compartment, ensuring transmission stays supported.
94. Install engine to an engine stand.
95. Remove engine lift chain from engine lift brackets.
96. Reverse procedure to install, noting the following:
    a. With ignition Off or disconnected, crank engine several times. Listen for any unusual noises or evidence that any components are binding.
    b. Start engine and listen for abnormal conditions.
    c. Inspect vehicle oil pressure gage or light and confirm that engine has acceptable oil pressure.
    d. Run engine at approximately 1000 RPM until engine reaches normal operating temperature.
    e. While engine continues to idle raise and support vehicle.
    f. Inspect for oil, coolant, transmission fluid and exhaust leaks while engine is at idle.
    g. Lower vehicle.
    h. Perform CKP variation learn procedure using a suitable programmed scan tool.
    i. Perform a final inspection for proper engine oil, transmission fluid and coolant levels.
    j. Road test vehicle.

INTAKE MANIFOLD

REPLACE

1. Remove air cleaner resonator and outlet duct assembly.
2. Disconnect EVAP canister purge pipe from throttle control module.
3. Disconnect throttle body electrical connector.

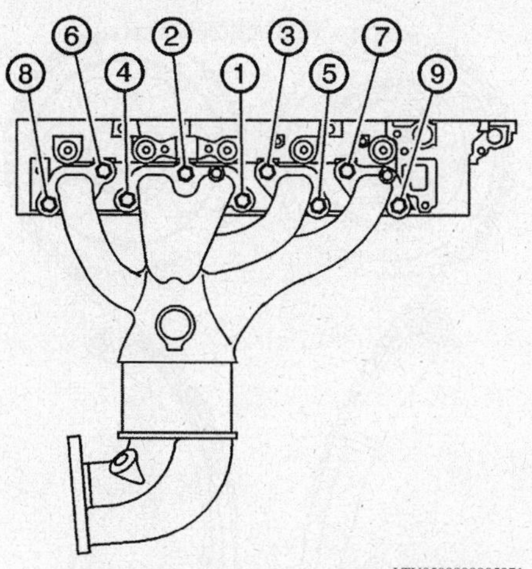

Fig. 2 Exhaust manifold tightening sequence

4. Remove throttle body bolts, then the throttle body and seal from intake manifold. **Ensure a clean gasket surface for installation.**
5. Remove battery box.
6. Remove oil dipstick indicator and tube.
7. Disconnect MAP sensor electrical connector.
8. Disconnect MAP sensor wiring harness retainer from intake manifold.
9. Disconnect PVC dirty air tube from camshaft cover.
10. Remove alternator as outlined under "Alternator, Replace" in "Electrical" section.
11. Remove engine wiring harness retainer from engine wiring harness bracket.
12. Remove two upper bolts securing engine wiring harness bracket to intake manifold.
13. Raise and support vehicle using a suitable lift to access remaining components through wheelhouse.
14. Remove lefthand side front wheel.
15. Remove lefthand side front wheelhouse.
16. Disconnect battery cable, engine and MAP sensor wiring harness retainers from engine wiring harness bracket.
17. Remove remaining lower engine wiring harness bracket bolt.
18. Remove bracket from engine compartment through wheelhouse opening.
19. Remove intake manifold bolts.
20. Lower vehicle.
21. Remove intake manifold from cylinder head.
22. Remove and discard gasket from intake manifold.
23. Cover open ports to cylinder head using suitable tape.
24. Clean and inspect intake manifold.
25. Reverse procedure to install, noting the following:
    a. Install a new gasket onto intake manifold.
    b. Tighten to specifications.

EXHAUST MANIFOLD

REPLACE

1. Raise and support vehicle using a suitable lift.
2. Remove catalytic converter to exhaust manifold nuts.
3. Place exhaust system rearward to allow clearance to remove seal.
4. Remove and discard exhaust manifold seal.
5. Remove air cleaner outlet duct and air cleaner assembly.
6. **On models equipped with automatic transmission,** remove transmission filler tube bracket nut from secondary air injection adapter and position aside.
7. **On all models,** remove heated oxygen sensor (HO2S) from exhaust manifold.
8. Remove nuts securing heat shield to exhaust manifold, then the exhaust manifold heat shield.
9. Remove exhaust manifold bolts, then the exhaust manifold.
10. Remove and discard exhaust manifold gasket.
11. Clean and inspect exhaust manifold.
12. Reverse procedure to install, noting the following:
    a. Install a new exhaust manifold gasket onto cylinder head.
    b. Tighten exhaust manifold bolts in numbered sequence as indicated, **Fig. 2. Torque** first sequence to 15 ft. lbs.; second sequence to 15 ft. lbs., and final sequence to 15 ft. lbs.
    c. Tighten remaining nuts and bolts to specifications.

CYLINDER HEAD

REPLACE

1. Remove intake manifold as outlined in "Intake Manifold, Replace."
2. Remove exhaust manifold as outlined in "Exhaust Manifold, Replace."
3. Remove timing chain and sprockets as outlined in "Timing Chain, Replace."
4. Remove and discard cylinder head bolts.
5. Remove cylinder head.
6. Reverse procedure to install, noting the following:
    a. Place cylinder head on a flat, clean surface with combustion chambers facing upward.
    b. Remove and discard cylinder head gasket.
    c. Remove all gasket material from engine block.
    d. Inspect cylinder head gasket mating surface on engine block.
    e. Clean and inspect cylinder head.
    f. Ensure number one cylinder is at top-dead-center.
    g. Install new cylinder head gasket onto engine block.
    h. Install new torque-to-yield bolts.
    i. Tighten cylinder head bolts in numbered sequences as follows, **Fig. 3. Torque** bolts 1–12 first pass in sequence to 22 ft. lbs., using tool No. J 45059 or equivalent, tighten bolts 1–12 final pass in sequence an additional 155°. **Torque** 2 short bolts 14 and 15 first pass to 62 inch lbs., using tool No. J 45059 or equivalent, tighten bolts 14 and 15 final pass an additional 60°. **Torque**

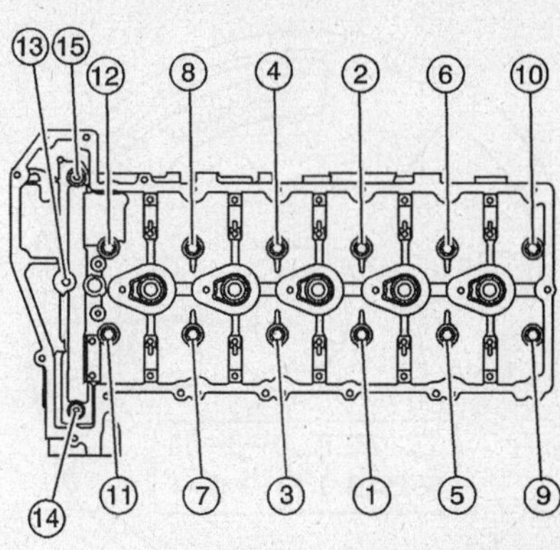

Fig. 3 Cylinder head bolt tighten sequence

1 long bolt 13 first pass to 62 inch lbs., using tool No. J 45059 or equivalent, tighten bolt 13 final pass an additional 120°.
    j. Tighten remaining nuts and bolts to specifications.

VALVE COVER

REPLACE

1. Remove intake manifold as outlined in "Intake Manifold, Replace."
2. Remove ignition coils as outlined under "Ignition Coil, Replace" in "Electrical" section.
3. Disconnect ECT sensor, fuel injector and HO2S from camshaft cover.
4. Remove fuel pressure regulator screw.
5. Remove camshaft cover bolts.
6. Remove camshaft cover from cylinder head.
7. Reverse procedure to install, noting the following:
    a. Remove and discard gasket from camshaft cover.
    b. Clean and inspect cylinder head sealing surface.
    c. Clean and inspect camshaft cover.
    d. Install new camshaft cover gasket into camshaft cover groove.
    e. Install new ignition control module gaskets into camshaft cover grooves.
    f. Tighten to specifications.

VALVE CLEARANCE SPECIFICATIONS

This engine is equipped with hydraulic lifters. No adjustment is required.

VALVE ADJUSTMENT

Valve lash is net build and no valve adjustment is required on these models.

ROCKER ARMS

1. Remove camshafts as outlined under "Camshaft, Replace."
2. Remove valve rocker arms and lash adjusters. Place rocker arms and valve lash adjusters in order so they can be installed in their original locations.
3. Reverse procedure to install.

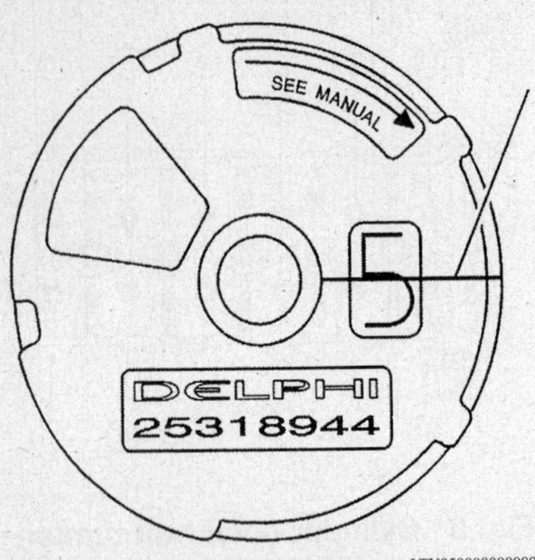

Fig. 4 Exhaust camshaft position actuator alignment

CRANKSHAFT BALANCER

REPLACE

1. Remove drive belt as outlined under "Serpentine Drive Belt."
2. Raise and support vehicle, then remove service slot plug from under flywheel.
3. Install flywheel holding tool No. EN 46547, or equivalent, into flywheel teeth.
4. Lower vehicle.
5. Remove fan and fan shroud.
6. Drain engine cooling system into suitable container.
7. Remove radiator as outlined in "Radiator, Replace."
8. Remove crankshaft balancer retaining bolt.
9. Remove crankshaft balancer using pulling tool No. J 41816-2, or equivalent.
10. Remove crankshaft balancer friction washer.
11. Reverse procedure to install, tighten to specifications.

FRONT COVER

REPLACE

1. Remove water pump as outlined under "Water Pump, Replace."
2. Remove crankshaft balancer as outlined under "Crankshaft Balancer, Replace."
3. Remove drive belt tensioner as outlined under "Serpentine Drive Belt."
4. Remove power steering pump as outlined in "Front Suspension & Steering" section.
5. Raise and support vehicle.
6. Remove oil pump pipe and screen assembly as outlined under "Oil Pump, Replace."
7. Lower vehicle.
8. Remove engine front cover attaching bolts.
9. Install two bolts into front cover threaded holes to act as jack screws, then tighten bolts evenly to release front cover from engine block.

Fig. 5 Timing chain tensioner tee installation

10. Remove engine front cover, then the two bolts from jack screw holes.
11. Reverse procedure to install, noting the following:
    a. Apply a .12 inch bead of sealer to engine front cover.
    b. Tighten to specifications.

TIMING CHAIN

REPLACE

Removal

1. Remove No. 1 cylinder spark plug.
2. Remove camshaft cover as outlined under "Valve Cover, Replace."
3. Disconnect exhaust CMP sensor electrical connector.
4. Remove exhaust CMP sensor retaining bolt, then the exhaust CMP sensor from cylinder head.
5. Disconnect intake CMP sensor electrical connector.
6. Remove intake CMP sensor retaining bolt, then the intake CMP sensor from cylinder head.
7. Remove front cover as outlined in "Front Cover, Replace."
8. Rotate crankshaft in engine rotational direction clockwise, until No. 1 piston is at TDC on compression stroke. The word "Delphi" on exhaust camshaft position actuator should be parallel with the cylinder head to cam cover mating surface, **Fig. 4.**
9. Install camshaft holding tool No. J 44221, or equivalent, to rear of camshafts.
10. Remove timing chain tensioner bolts, but do not remove tensioner.
11. Release tension on timing chain by moving tensioner shoe inward.
12. Place tee into the tensioner to hold the shoe in place, **Fig. 5.**
13. Remove exhaust camshaft position actuator bolt, then the actuator. Discard bolt.
14. Remove intake camshaft position actuator bolt, then the actuator. Discard bolt.
15. Remove intake camshaft sprocket, timing chain and crankshaft sprocket.

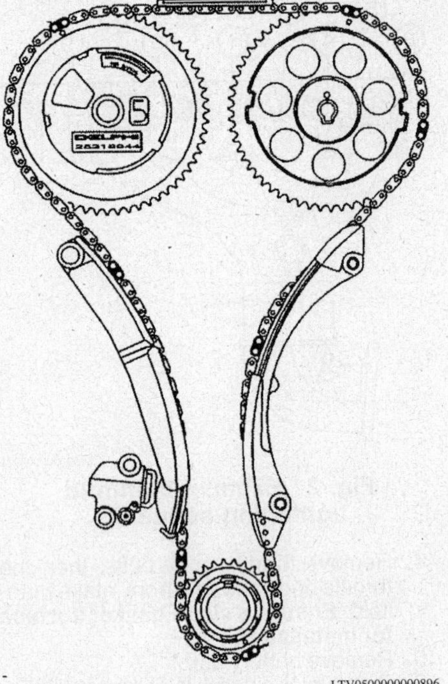

Fig. 6 Timing chain alignment

Installation

1. Ensure pin on crankshaft for timing chain sprocket is straight up.
2. Install crankshaft sprocket to crankshaft snout.
3. Install intake camshaft sprocket into timing chain, align dark link of timing chain with timing mark on intake camshaft sprocket, **Fig. 6.**
4. Feed timing chain down through opening in cylinder head.
5. Install timing chain on crankshaft sprocket, align dark link of timing chain with timing mark on crankshaft sprocket, **Fig. 6.**
6. Ensure alignment pin is properly engaged with camshaft, then install intake camshaft sprocket onto intake camshaft.
7. Install the new intake camshaft sprocket bolt. Ensure camshaft actuator is fully advanced prior to installation.
8. Install exhaust camshaft actuator into timing chain, align dark link of timing chain with mark on exhaust camshaft position actuator sprocket, **Fig. 6. Engine damage may occur if camshaft actuator is not fully advanced.** Position camshaft actuator in fully advanced position as follows:
    a. Rotate camshaft using a 1 inch (25 mm) wrench on hex of camshaft until alignment pin is properly engaged with camshaft.
    b. Install exhaust camshaft actuator onto exhaust camshaft.
    c. Rotate intake camshaft back and forth (clockwise and counterclockwise) to purge oil out of camshaft position actuator.
9. Remove tee in timing chain tensioner to regain tension on timing chain.
10. Remove camshaft holding tool No. J

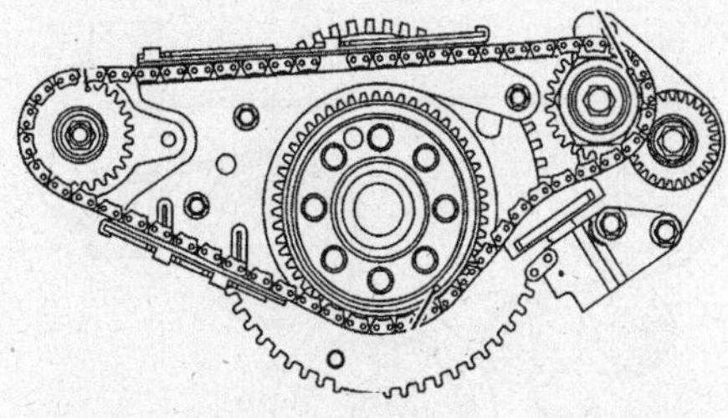

Fig. 7 Balance shaft drive chain timing mark alignment

44221, or equivalent, from camshafts.
11. Dark links on timing chain should be aligned with marks on sprockets, **Fig. 6.**
12. Install engine front cover as outlined under "Front Cover, Replace."
13. Install camshaft cover as outlined under "Valve Cover, Replace."

CAMSHAFT

REPLACE

1. Remove camshaft cover as outlined under "Valve Cover, Replace."
2. Remove CMP sensor, then rotate crankshaft clockwise until No. 1 piston is at TDC of compression stroke. The word Delphi on exhaust camshaft position actuator will be parallel with cylinder head to cam cover mating surface, **Fig. 4.**
3. Install camshaft holding tool No. J 44221, or equivalent, onto rear of camshafts.
4. Remove intake and exhaust camshaft sprocket bolts. Discard bolts.
5. Install camshaft sprocket holding tool No. J 44222, or equivalent, onto cylinder head and adjust horizontal bolts into camshaft sprockets to maintain chain tension and keep from disturbing timing chain components.
6. Carefully slide sprockets with timing chain from camshafts to sprocket holding tool.
7. Alternately loosen camshaft cap bolts a few turns at a time until all valve spring pressure has been released.
8. Remove the camshaft caps. Keep camshaft caps in their original positions for installation reference.
9. Remove camshaft holding tool No. J 44221, or equivalent, from camshafts.
10. Remove camshafts from cylinder head.
11. Reverse procedure to install, tighten to specifications.

BALANCE SHAFT DRIVE CHAIN

REPLACE

1. Remove crankshaft rear oil seal housing as outlined under "Crankshaft Rear Oil Seal, Replace."
2. Rotate crankshaft until 3 of 5 dark links on timing chain align with timing marks, **Fig. 7.** Lefthand balance shaft sprocket timing mark (1) is at 12:00 position, righthand balance shaft sprocket timing mark (2) is at 2:30 position and crankshaft sprocket timing mark (3) is at 4:30 position.
3. Remove balance shaft chain tensioner bolts, then the tensioner.
4. Remove balance shaft chain from balance shaft and crankshaft sprockets.
5. Reverse procedure to install.

BALANCE SHAFT

REPLACE

1. Remove balance shaft drive chain as outlined under "Balance Shaft Drive Chain, Replace."
2. Remove balance shaft retaining bolt.
3. Remove balance shaft.
4. Reverse procedure to install.

PISTON & ROD ASSEMBLY

When installing piston, the alignment mark must face the front of the engine block or the flat casting boss.

MAIN & ROD BEARINGS

Torque crankshaft main bearing cap bolts to 18 ft. lbs., then an additional 180° using sequence, **Fig. 8.**

CRANKSHAFT SEAL

REPLACE

1. Remove crankshaft balancer as outlined under "Crankshaft Balancer, Replace."
2. Pry out crankshaft front oil seal using a suitable flat-bladed tool. Discard seal.
3. Apply engine oil to outside diameter of new crankshaft front oil seal.
4. Install oil seal using seal installation tool No. J 45951, or equivalent.
5. Install crankshaft balancer as outlined under "Crankshaft Balancer, Replace."

CRANKSHAFT REAR OIL SEAL

REPLACE

1. Raise and support vehicle.
2. **On models equipped with manual transmission,** remove transmission assembly, pressure plate, clutch and flywheel as outlined in **MOTOR's "Domestic Transmission, In-Vehicle Service" or "Transmission Service DVD."**
3. **On models equipped with automatic transmission,** remove transmission and driveplate as outlined in **MOTOR's "Domestic Transmission, In-Vehicle Service." or "Transmission Service DVD."**
4. **On all models,** remove two bolts securing oil pan to crankshaft rear oil seal housing.
5. Remove crankshaft rear oil seal housing bolts.
6. Install two bolts into threaded holes of crankshaft rear oil seal housing to act as jack screws, then tighten bolts evenly to release housing from engine block and oil pan.
7. Remove crankshaft rear oil seal housing.
8. Remove bolts from jack screw holes.
9. Remove crankshaft rear oil seal from housing using a suitable hammer and punch. Discard seal.
10. Reverse procedure to install, noting the following:
    a. Apply a .12 inch (3 mm) bead of sealer to where crankshaft rear oil seal housing meets engine block and oil pan surface.
    b. Align housing with righthand alignment dowel, then tilt lefthand side up slightly and align housing with lefthand alignment dowel.
    c. Tighten to specifications.

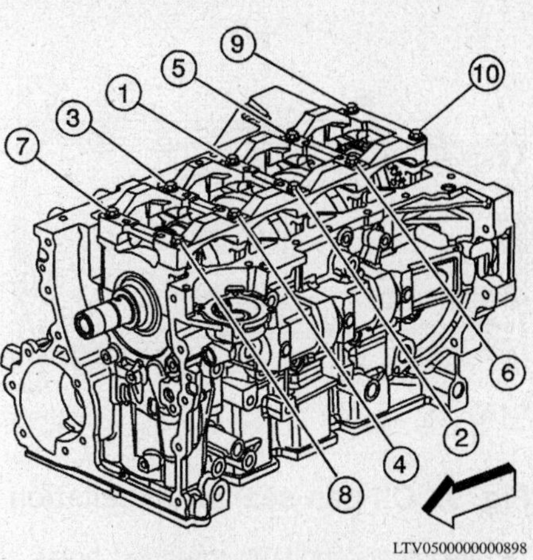

Fig. 8 Crankshaft main bearing cap bolt tightening sequence

OIL PAN

REPLACE

1. Remove oil dipstick and tube.
2. Remove oil pane skid plate bolts, then the skid plate.
3. Drain engine oil into suitable container.
4. Support front differential assembly using a suitable jack stand or lift.
5. Remove front differential assembly nut, crossmember bolt then the crossmember.
6. Remove differential carrier assembly bushing to frame bolts only.
7. Pull differential carrier assembly downward.
8. Secure pinion yoke, in order to prevent differential carrier from rotating.
9. Remove service slot plug.
10. Remove nuts securing fuel hose pipe bracket to transmission and place aside.
11. Remove four lower transmission mounting bolts that are attached to oil pan.
12. Remove power steering gear as outlined in "Front Suspension & Steering-"section.
13. Pull power steering gear downward in order to gain access to oil pan.
14. Disconnect engine wiring harness retainers from oil pan.
15. Remove oil pan bolts.

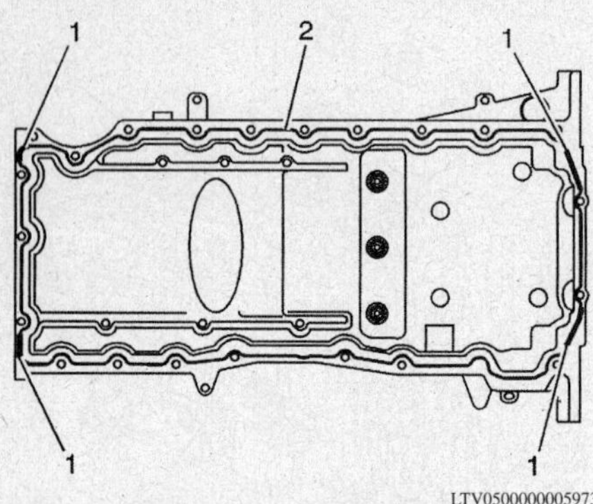

Fig. 9 Oil pan sealant installation

16. Install two bolts in threaded holes at rear of oil pan to act as jack screws and tighten evenly to release oil pan from engine block.
17. Remove oil pan.
18. Remove two bolts from jack screw holes.
19. Clean and inspect oil pan.
20. Clean and inspect engine block sealing surface.
21. Reverse procedure to install, noting the following:
    a. Apply a .22 inch bead of sealer to oil pan in areas marked (1), **Fig. 9.**
    b. Apply a .12 inch bead of sealer to oil pan in area marked (2), **Fig. 9.**
    c. Tighten to specifications.

OIL PUMP

REPLACE

1. Remove engine front cover as outlined under "Front Cover, Replace."
2. Remove oil pump cover bolts, then the oil pump cover.
3. Mark relationship between inner and outer gears to oil pump housing for installation reference.
4. Remove inner and outer oil pump gears.
5. Remove oil pump pressure relief valve plug, then the oil pump pressure relief valve and spring.
6. Reverse procedure to install.

SERPENTINE DRIVE BELT

Replacement

1. Rotate tensioner clockwise with a suitable ⅜ inch breaker bar.
2. Remove belt from water pump pulley.
3. Allow tensioner to return to its original position, then remove belt from remaining pulleys.
4. Reverse procedure to install.

Routing

Refer to **Figs. 10 and 11** for drive belt routing.

COOLING SYSTEM BLEED

After filling cooling system, start engine and allow to reach operating temperature with radiator cap removed. Air in system is bled through radiator cap opening. Add coolant as required to bring to proper level, then install radiator cap and inspect coolant level in recovery reservoir.

THERMOSTAT

REPLACE

1. Drain cooling system.
2. Raise and support vehicle high enough to access thermostat housing through wheelhouse.
3. Remove lefthand front tire and wheel assembly, then the lefthand wheelhouse liner.
4. Remove radiator inlet hose from thermostat housing.
5. Remove thermostat housing bolts, then the thermostat housing from engine block.
6. Remove thermostat from housing.
7. Reverse procedure to install.

WATER PUMP

REPLACE

1. Drain coolant from radiator.
2. Remove radiator hose outlet from radiator.
3. Release differential vent hose, A/C suction hose and A/C discharge hose retainers from fan shroud.
4. Rotate slip ring counterclockwise from under fan shroud, then remove fan shroud.
5. Remove fan hub nut in a counterclockwise rotation, then the fan assembly.
6. Remove drive belt as outlined in "Serpentine Drive Belt."
7. Secure water pump pulley with pulley holding tool No. J 4606, or equivalent, then remove water pump pulley bolts.
8. Remove holding tool and water pump pulley.
9. Remove water pump bolts retaining bolts, then the water pump. Discard gasket.
10. Reverse procedure to install, tighten to specifications.

RADIATOR

REPLACE

1. Drain coolant from radiator into suitable container.
2. Raise and support vehicle using a suitable lift.
3. **On models equipped with automatic transmission,** remove transmission cooler lines from radiator.
4. **On all models,** reposition radiator outlet hose clamp from radiator using tool No. J 38185 or equivalent.
5. Remove radiator outlet hose from radiator, then lower vehicle.
6. Remove cooling fan as outlined in "Cooling Fans" chapter.
7. Reposition radiator inlet hose clamp using tool No. J 38185 or equivalent.
8. Remove radiator inlet hose from radiator.
9. Remove radiator vent inlet hose from radiator.

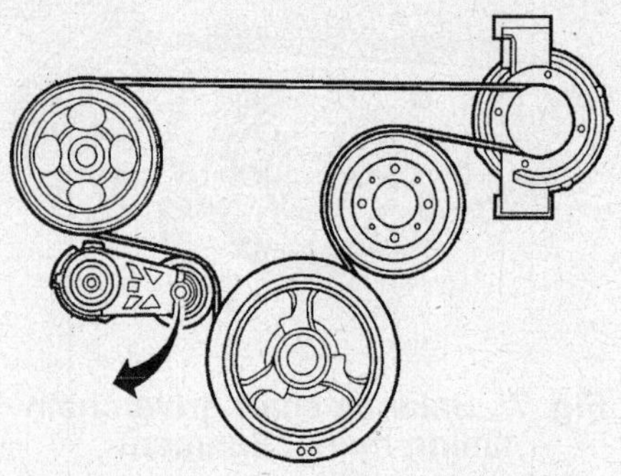

Fig. 10 Drive belt routing. Less A/C

10. Remove fan shroud from radiator.
11. Remove condenser to radiator retaining bolts.
12. Remove radiator support bracket retaining bolt, then the radiator support bracket.
13. Reposition condenser from radiator.
14. Remove radiator from vehicle.
15. Reverse procedure to install, noting the following:
    a. Fill coolant system to specifications.
    b. Tighten to specifications.

FUEL PUMP

REPLACE

1. Relieve fuel system pressure as outlined in "Precautions."
2. Drain fuel tank into suitable container.
3. Raise and support vehicle to access top of fuel tank through wheelhouse liner.
4. Remove lefthand side rear wheelhouse liner.
5. Loosen fuel fill hose clamp at fuel tank.
6. Remove fuel fill hose from fuel tank.
7. Disconnect EVAP vapor line from fuel fill neck vapor line.
8. Completely raise vehicle.
9. Remove fuel tank shield rear upper bolt.
10. Remove fuel tank shield lower bolts.
11. Remove fuel tank shield.
12. Place adjustable jack under fuel tank for support.
13. Remove upper fuel tank strap bolt, then the upper fuel tank strap.
14. Remove fuel tank front strap bolt, then the fuel tank front strap.
15. Remove fuel tank rear strap bolt.
16. Remove fuel tank rear strap.
17. With aid of an assistant, carefully lower fuel tank until electrical connections can be accessed.
18. Disconnect fuel tank pressure sensor and fuel tank module electrical connectors from fuel tank.
19. Disconnect fuel feed line at fuel tank.
20. Completely lower fuel tank and place fuel tank in a suitable work area.
21. Disconnect fuel feed line fitting from fuel tank module using a suitable flare nut wrench and a back up wrench.
22. Disconnect EVAP vapor line from fuel tank vent valve.

23. Disconnect EVAP vapor line quick connect from fuel tank module.
24. Reposition fuel feed and EVAP lines in order to access lock ring.
25. Use tool No. J 45722 or equivalent, and a long breaker-bar in order to unlock fuel sender lock ring. Turn tool No. J 45722 or equivalent, fuel sender lock ring in a counterclockwise direction.
26. Remove cam lock ring from fuel tank.
27. Raise fuel tank module upward far enough to access vapor line quick connect under module cover.
28. Disconnect vapor line quick connect from fuel tank module.
29. Tilt module to allow fuel level sensor arm and float to clear fuel tank module opening.
30. Remove fuel tank module from fuel tank.

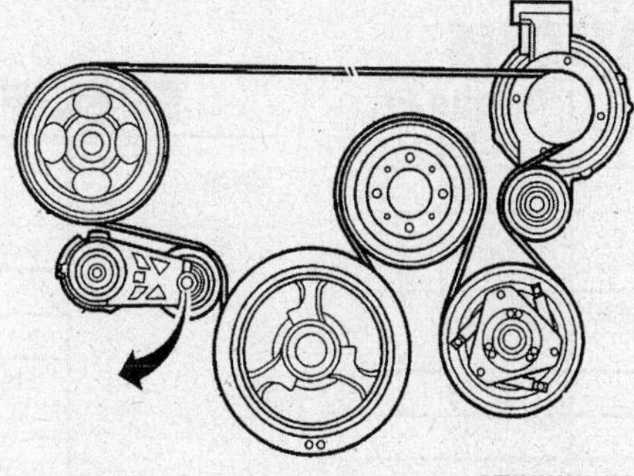

Fig. 11 Drive belt routing. With A/C

31. Remove fuel tank module seal. **Do not reuse seal.**
32. Clean fuel module sealing surfaces.
33. Place lock ring on a flat surface. Measure clearance between lock ring and flat surface using a suitable feeler gage at seven points.
34. If warpage is greater than .016 inch, lock ring must be replaced.
35. Reverse procedure to install, noting the following:
    a. In order to reduce risk of fire and personal injury that may result from a fuel leak, always replace fuel sender gasket when installing fuel sender assembly.
    b. Ensure lock ring is installed with correct side facing upward. A correctly installed lock ring will only turn in a clockwise direction.
    c. Inspect for leaks.
    d. Tighten to specifications.

TIGHTENING SPECIFICATIONS

Year	Component	Torque Ft. Lbs.
2006	A/C Compressor Bolts	37
	A/C Compressor Evaporator Hose Bracket To Cylinder Head Bolt	80①
	A/C Evaporator Line To Compressor Bolt	12
	AIR Cover Studs	18
	Alternator Mounting Bolt	37
	Automatic Transmission Filler Tube Bracket Nut	111①
	Balance Shaft Chain Guide Bolt	89①
	Balance Shaft Chain Tensioner Bolt	89①
	Balance Shaft Retaining Bolt	89①
	Battery Ground Cable To Engine Block	26
	Battery Positive Cable To Starter Nut	80①
	Camshaft Cap Bolts	106①
	Camshaft Cover Bolts	89①
	Camshaft Position Actuator Valve Bolt	89①
	Catalytic Converter To Exhaust manifold Nuts	37
	Condenser To Radiator Bolts	21
	Connecting Rod Cap Bolt	18⑥
	Coolant Temperature Sensor	12
	Crankshaft Balancer Bolt	110⑦
	Crankshaft Position Sensor Bolt	89①
	Crankshaft Rear Oil Seal Housing Bolts	89①
	Cylinder Head Access Hole Plug	44①
	Cylinder Head Bolts	③
	Cylinder Head Oil Gallery Plug	28
	Differential Carrier To Frame Bolts	112
	Drive Belt Idler Pulley Bolt	37
	Drive Belt Tensioner Bolt	37
	Engine Block Coolant Plug	37
	Engine Block Oil Gallery Plug-Side	26
	Engine Front Cover Bolts	89①
	Engine Front Cover Small Center Bolt	71①
	Engine Front Cover Spacer Bolt	89①
	Engine Mount Bolts	37
	Engine Mount To Frame Bracket Bolts	63
	Engine Wiring Ground Lead Bolts	15
	Engine Wiring Harness Bracket Bolts	89①
	EVAP Purge Solenoid Valve Bolt	89①
	Exhaust Camshaft Actuator Bolt	18⑤
	Exhaust Camshaft Position Sensor Bolt	89①
	Exhaust Manifold Bolt	⑧
	Exhaust Manifold Heat Shield Nut & Stud	89①
	Fuel Feed Line Fitting To Fuel Tank Module	22
	Fuel Fill Hose Clamp	22①
	Fuel Hose Pipe Bracket Nuts	15
	Fuel Injector Rail Bolt	89①
	Fuel Pressure Regulator Screw	71①
	Fuel Tank Shield Bolts	89①

TIGHTENING SPECIFICATIONS—Continued

Year	Component	Torque Ft. Lbs.
2006	Fuel Tank Strap Bolts	24
	Heater Inlet Pipe Bolt	89①
	Heater Outlet Fitting	33
	Heater Outlet Hose Pipe Bracket To Lefthand Engine Mount Bolt	80①
	Ignition Control Module Bolt	89①
	Intake Camshaft Position Sensor Bolt	89①
	Intake Camshaft Sprocket Bolt	15④
	Intake Manifold Bolts	②
	Knock Sensor	18
	Lower Transmission Mounting Bolts	37
	Oil Dipstick Tube Bolt	89①
	Oil Filter	22
	Oil Filter Adapter	37
	Oil Filter Bypass Hole Plug	10
	Oil Pan Drain Plug	19
	Oil Pan End Bolts	89①
	Oil Pan Side Bolts	18
	Oil Pressure Switch	15
	Oil Pump Cover Bolts	89①
	Oil Pump Pipe & Screen Bolt	89①
	Oil Pump Pressure Relief Valve Plug	10
	Power Steering Pump Mounting Bolts	18
	Power Steering Pump Bracket Bolt	37
	Radiator Support Bracket Retaining Bolt	18
	Spark Plug	13
	Starter Solenoid S Nut	31①
	Thermostat Housing Bolt	89①
	Throttle Body Bolts	89①
	Timing Chain Tensioner Bolt	18
	Timing Chain Tensioner Guide Bolt	13
	Timing Chain Tensioner Shoe Bolt	18
	Timing Chain Top Guide Bolt	89①
	Torque Converter Bolts	44
	Transmission Mounting Bolts	37
	Transmission Oil Cooler Pipe Bracket Bolt	15
	Water Outlet Bolt	89①
	Water Pump Bolt	89①
	Water Pump Pulley Bolt	18

① — Inch lbs.

② — Torque from inside to outside to 89 inch lbs.

③ — Refer to “Cylinder Head, Replace” for tightening torque and sequence.

④ — Final pass additional 100°.

⑤ — Final pass additional 135°.

⑥ — Final pass additional 110°.

⑦ — Final pass additional 180°.

⑧ — Refer to “Exhaust Manifold, Replace” for tightening torque and sequence.

6.0L Engine

NOTE: On Air Bag Equipped Models, Refer To "Air Bag System Precautions" Located In The Front Of This Manual For System Disarming & Arming Procedures.

NOTE: Refer To "Computer Relearn Procedures" Located In The Front Of This Manual When Battery Power To The Computer Has Been Interrupted.

NOTE: Refer To The "Gasoline Engines" Section Of "Express & Savana" For Any Procedures Not Found In This Section.

INDEX

PRECAUTIONS

Air Bag Systems

Refer to "Air Bag System Precautions" in the front of this manual for system disarming and arming procedures.

Battery Ground Cable

Prior to service disconnect battery ground cable and isolate, as required.

Fuel System Pressure Relief

Prior to service, fuel pressure must be relieved by disconnecting the fuel line fittings. A small amount of fuel may still be released when the fuel line is disconnected. To reduce the chance of injury, cover the fitting(s) to be disconnected with a shop towel. Place towel in an approved container when the procedure is complete.

COMPRESSION PRESSURE

When inspecting compression, the lowest cylinder must be within 70% of the highest and no cylinder should be less than 100 psi. Perform compression test with engine at operating temperature, all spark plugs removed and throttle wide open.

ENGINE MOUNT

REPLACE

1. Raise and support vehicle.
2. Remove engine mount-to-engine mount bracket bolts.
3. Remove mounting bolts and engine shield.
4. Raise and support engine using adjustable screw type jack stands. **Do not raise and/or support engine by oil pan or crankshaft balancer.**
5. Remove mounting bolts and mount.
6. Reverse procedure to install.

ENGINE

REPLACE

1. Open hood, then disconnect underhood electrical connectors and remove wiring harness from hood.
2. With hood supported, then remove hood support cable pins and cables.
3. Remove hood hinges, then the hood from vehicle with aid of assistants.
4. Remove hood from cowl, then A/C condenser mounting bolts and secure to frame rail.
5. Remove all accessories from radiator support, then the retainers and radiator support.
6. Drain engine coolant into a suitable container, then remove radiator hoses from water pump.
7. Disconnect heater hoses from heater core using tool No. J 43181 or equivalent.
8. Remove intake manifold sight shield, then disconnect throttle body, EVAP canister and alternator electrical connectors.
9. Remove harness bracket nut then the engine harness from intake manifold.
10. Remove radiator vent inlet hose from throttle body, then alternator cable from alternator.
11. Disconnect main coil harness and fuel injector electrical connectors on lefthand side.
12. Disconnect main coil harness, fuel injectors and exhaust gas recirculation valve electrical connectors.
13. Disconnect manifold absolute pressure sensor and knock sensor electrical connectors.
14. Remove harness ground bolt then reposition harness ground and battery

ground from block.
15. Disconnect coolant temperature sensor and electronic variable orifice switch electrical connectors.
16. Remove harness ground bolt at righthand rear of engine block and set aside.
17. Disconnect electrical connectors from oil pressure and camshaft position sensors.
18. Unclip all of engine harness clips from engine, then remove battery cable junction block from junction block bracket.
19. Remove EVAP tube end from solenoid, then the EVAP tube end from vapor pipe.
20. Disconnect fuel pipes, then raise and support vehicle.
21. Disconnect electrical connectors from crankshaft position, engine oil level and coolant heater sensors.
22. Remove battery cable channel bolt, then slide channel pin out of oil pan tab and move all wiring harness aside.
23. Lower vehicle, then remove rear power steering pump to engine block bolt.
24. Remove alternator bracket mounting bolts, set bracket aside.
25. Remove ignition coil, then install tool No. J 41798 or equivalent engine lift bracket to cylinder heads.
26. Remove lefthand and righthand engine mount to engine mount bracket bolts, then raise and support vehicle.
27. Remove engine shield bolts and shield, then the ladder shields bolts and plate.
28. Drain engine oil, then remove flywheel to torque converter bolts.
29. Remove transmission oil dipstick tube nut and oil dipstick tube.
30. **On models equipped with 4L60-E automatic transmission,** remove transmission bolt and stud on righthand side.
31. **On all models,** remove automatic transmission bolt and studs.
32. Separate engine from transmission, then install converter holding strap No. J 21366 or equivalent.
33. Lower vehicle, then install a suitable engine hoist and a floor jack under transmission for support.
34. Remove engine from vehicle. **Avoid breaking MAP sensor locating tabs.**
35. Reverse procedure to install.

INTAKE MANIFOLD

REPLACE

1. **On models equipped with Electronic Throttle Control (ELC),** proceed as follows:
   a. Partially drain cooling system into suitable container.
   b. Disconnect Intake Air Temperature sensor harness connector.
   c. Remove air intake duct.
   d. Disconnect throttle actuator motor and Throttle Position sensor harness connectors.
   e. Disconnect crankcase ventilation hose from throttle body.

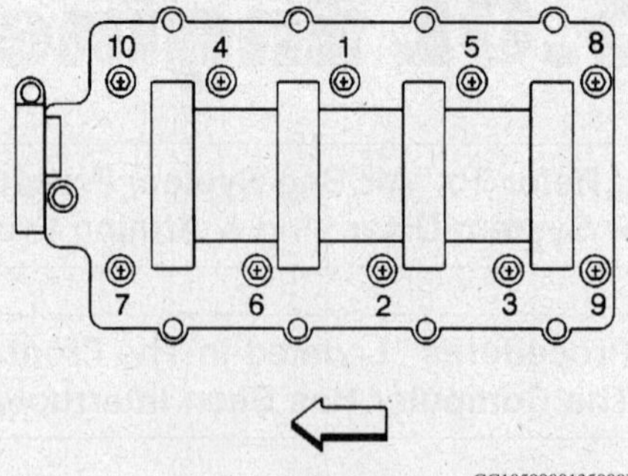

Fig. 1 Intake manifold tightening sequence

2. **On models equipped less Electronic Throttle Control (ELC),** proceed as follows:
   a. Remove air intake duct.
   b. Disconnect accelerator and cruise control cables from throttle body.
   c. Disconnect vacuum hose from throttle body.
   d. Disconnect Throttle Position sensor and Idle Air Control valve harness connectors.
   e. Disconnect coolant hose from throttle body and vapor vent pipe.
3. **On all models,** remove engine sight shield.
4. Disconnect accelerator and cruise control cables from cable bracket and throttle body.
5. Remove upper engine wire harness mounting nut.
6. Disconnect Evaporative Emission purge solenoid electrical connector.
7. Position upper engine wire harness aside.
8. Identify connectors to their corresponding injectors to ensure correct sequential injector firing order after installation.
9. Pull top portion of injector connectors up. **Do not pull past top of white portion.**
10. Release connectors from injector by pushing tab on lower side.
11. Disconnect fuel feed and return pipes from fuel rail.
12. Disconnect fuel pressure regulator vacuum line.
13. Loosen crossover tube to righthand fuel rail mounting screw.
14. Disconnect Manifold Absolute Pressure sensor, Knock Sensor and Exhaust Gas Recirculation valve electrical connectors.
15. Remove knock sensor harness electrical connector from intake manifold. Set electrical harness aside.
16. Remove EGR pipe to intake manifold, cylinder head and exhaust manifold mounting bolts, then the EGR pipe with valve. Remove EGR pipe gasket.
17. Remove vacuum brake booster hose from rear of intake manifold.
18. Remove Positive Crankcase Ventilation hose with valve.
19. Remove MAP sensor from intake manifold.
20. Remove mounting bolts and accelerator control cable bracket .
21. Remove Evaporative Emission purge solenoid vent tube end.
22. Squeeze connect fitting retainer and remove VEEP tube end from the vapor pipe.
23. Remove mounting bolt. EVAP purge solenoid and isolator.
24. Remove mounting bolts, intake manifold and gaskets. Discard gaskets.
25. Reverse procedure to install, noting the following:
   a. Install new intake manifold-to-cylinder head gaskets.
   b. Apply .20 inch band of threadlock part No. 12345382, or equivalent, to intake manifold bolts' threads.
   c. **Torque** intake manifold mounting bolts to 44 inch lbs., in sequence, **Fig. 1.**
   d. Final **torque** mounting bolts to 89 inch lbs.
   e. Install new intake manifold gaskets.
   f. Apply .20 inch band of threadlock No. 12345382, or equivalent, to intake manifold bolts' threads.
   g. Lightly coat MAP sensor seal with clean engine oil.

EXHAUST MANIFOLD

REPLACE

Lefthand

1. Raise and support vehicle.
2. Remove mounting nuts and separate exhaust pipe from manifold.
3. Lower vehicle and remove spark plugs.
4. Remove air injection reaction center pipe bolt.
5. Loosen hose clamps and remove hose.
6. Remove AIR pipe, nuts, studs and gasket.
7. Remove spark plugs' ignition wires.
8. Remove exhaust manifold bolts, manifold and gasket. Discard gasket.
9. Reverse procedure to install.

Righthand

1. Raise and support vehicle.
2. Remove mounting nuts and separate exhaust pipe from manifold.
3. Lower vehicle and remove spark plugs.
4. Remove EGR valve, gasket and bolts.
5. Remove EGR pipe bolt from intake manifold.
6. Remove EGR pipe bolts and gasket from exhaust manifold.
7. Remove EGR pipe bolts from cylinder head.
8. Remove EGR pipe from intake manifold.
9. Remove O-ring seal from EGR pipe. Discard gasket and O-ring seal.
10. Remove AIR pipe, nuts and gasket from righthand exhaust manifold.
11. Remove exhaust manifold, bolts and gasket. Discard gasket.
12. Reverse procedure to install.

CYLINDER HEAD

REPLACE

Lefthand

1. Remove alternator and mounting bracket as outlined under "Electrical" section.
2. Remove intake manifold as outlined under "Intake Manifold, Replace."
3. Remove coolant air bleed pipe bolts and pipe. Remove and discard gaskets.
4. Remove exhaust manifold as outlined under "Exhaust Manifold, Replace."
5. Remove pushrods as outlined under "Rocker Arms & Pushrods, Replace."
6. Remove cylinder head bolts and discard M11 bolts.
7. Remove cylinder head and gasket. Discard gasket.
8. Reverse procedure to install, noting the following:
   a. Apply .20 inch band of threadlock part No. 12345382, or equivalent, to threads of M8 cylinder head bolts.
   b. **Torque** M11 bolts to 22 ft. lbs., in sequence, **Fig. 2.**
   c. Tighten bolts an additional 90°.
   d. Tighten bolts Nos. 1–8 an additional 90°, bolts Nos. 9 and 10 an additional 50°.
   e. **Torque** M8 bolts to 22 ft. lbs., beginning with center bolts and working outward.

Righthand

1. Remove mounting and oil dipstick tube.
2. Remove intake manifold as outlined under "Intake Manifold, Replace."
3. Remove exhaust manifold as outlined under "Exhaust Manifold, Replace."
4. Remove pushrods as outlined under "Rocker Arms & Pushrods, Replace."
5. Remove cylinder head bolts. Discard M11 bolts.
6. Remove cylinder head and gasket. Discard gasket.
7. Reverse procedure to install, noting the following:
   a. Apply .20 inch band of threadlock part No. 12345382, or equivalent, to threads of M8 cylinder head bolts.
   b. **Torque** new M11 bolts to 22 ft. lbs., in sequence, **Fig. 2.**
   c. Tighten bolts an additional 90°.
   d. Tighten bolts Nos. 1–8 an additional 90°, bolts Nos. 9 and 10 an additional 50°.
   e. **Torque** M8 bolts to 22 ft. lbs., beginning with center bolts and working outward, alternating side-to-side.

VALVE COVER

REPLACE

1. Remove ignition coil as outlined under "Electrical" section.

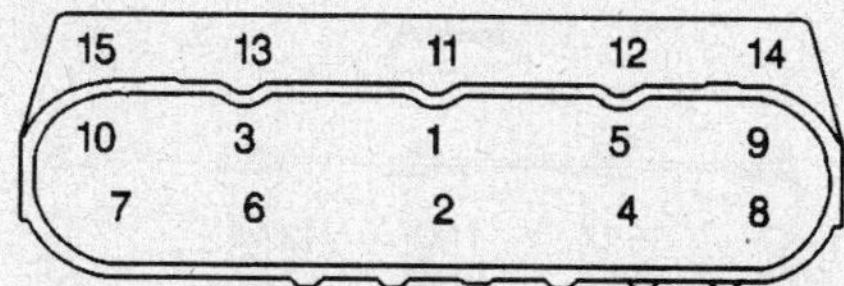

Fig. 2 Cylinder head tightening sequence

2. Remove PVC valve and hose from lefthand side valve cover.
3. Remove oil fill cap and tube from righthand side valve cover.
4. Remove mounting bolts, covers and gaskets. Discard gaskets.
5. Reverse procedure to install.

VALVE ARRANGEMENT

Front To Rear

Lefthand Side......................I-E-I-E-I-E-I-E
Righthand Side....................E-I-E-I-E-I-E-I

VALVE ADJUSTMENT

Valve lash is net build and no valve adjustment is required on these models.

PUSH RODS

Removal

1. Remove valve cover as outlined under "Valve Cover, Replace."
2. Remove bolts and rocker arms.
3. Remove rocker arm pivot support.
4. Remove pushrods.

Installation

1. Lubricate rocker arms and pushrods with clean engine oil.
2. Lubricate flange of rocker arm bolts with clean engine oil.
3. Install valve rocker arm pivot support.
4. Install pushrods. Ensure pushrods are seated properly in valve lifter sockets.
5. Install rocker arms and bolts, but do not tighten bolts at this time. Ensure pushrods seat properly to ends of rocker arms.
6. Rotate crankshaft until piston No. 1 is at top dead center of compression stroke with crankshaft and camshaft sprocket marks aligned.
7. With engine in No. 1 firing position, tighten exhaust rocker arm bolts 1, 2, 7 and 8, then intake rocker arm bolts 1, 3, 4 and 5 to specifications.
8. Rotate crankshaft 360,° then tighten exhaust rocker arm bolts 3, 4, 5 and 6, then intake rocker arm bolts 2, 6, 7 and 8 to specifications.
9. Install valve cover as outlined under "Valve Cover, Replace."

HYDRAULIC LIFTERS

REPLACE

1. Remove cylinder head and gasket as outlined under "Cylinder Head, Replace."
2. Remove mounting bolts and valve lifter guide.
3. Remove valve lifters using lifter pliers tool No. J-3049-A, or equivalent.
4. Remove valve lifters from guide. Keep lifters in order, to ensure they are installed in their original position.
5. Reverse procedure to install. Lubricate valve lifter with clean engine oil.

CRANKSHAFT DAMPER

REPLACE

Removal

1. Remove drive belt as outlined under "Serpentine Drive Belt."
2. Remove upper fan shroud.
3. Remove engine cooling fan.
4. Remove starter motor as outlined under "Electrical" section.
5. Install flywheel holder tool No. J-42386-A, or equivalent.
6. Remove crankshaft damper bolt.
7. Remove crankshaft damper using puller tool Nos. J-41816 and J-41816-2, or equivalents.

Installation

1. Install damper onto end of crankshaft.
2. Install damper using crankshaft damper installation tool No. J-41665, or equivalent.
3. Remove damper installation tool and install crankshaft damper bolt.
4. Remove crankshaft damper bolt and measure for correctly installed damper. Nose of crankshaft should be recessed .094–.176 inch into damper bore.
5. If damper is not installed properly, repeat installation procedure.
6. Tighten new crankshaft damper.
7. Remove flywheel holder tool.

FRONT COVER

REPLACE

Removal

1. Remove water pump as outlined under "Water Pump, Replace."
2. Remove the crankshaft balancer as outlined under "Crankshaft Damper, Replace."
3. Remove oil pan-to-front cover mounting bolts.
4. Remove mounting bolts, front cover and gasket. Discard gasket.

INSTALLATION

1. Apply .20 inch bead of sealant No. 12378190, or equivalent, .80 inch long to oil pan to engine block junction.
2. Install new gasket and front cover.
3. Install mounting bolts until snug. **Do not overtighten.**
4. Install oil pan-to-front cover bolts until snug. **Do not over tighten.**
5. Install front and rear cover alignment tool No. J 41476, or equivalent, to front

cover. Align tapered legs with machined alignment surfaces on front cover.
6. Install crankshaft balancer bolt until snug. **Do not overtighten.**
7. Tighten oil pan to front cover and front cover mounting bolts.
8. Remove alignment tool.
9. Install new crankshaft front oil seal.
10. Install water pump.

FRONT COVER SEAL

REPLACE

1. Remove crankshaft damper as outlined under "Crankshaft Damper, Replace."
2. Remove crankshaft front oil seal.
3. Reverse procedure to install, noting the following:
   a. Lubricate outer edge of new oil seal and front cover seal bore with clean engine oil.
   b. Install seal into front cover using front oil seal installer tool No. J-41478, or equivalent.

TIMING CHAIN

REPLACE

Removal

1. Remove oil pump as outlined under "Oil Pump, Replace."
2. Rotate crankshaft until timing marks on crankshaft and camshaft sprockets are aligned.
3. Remove mounting bolts, camshaft sprocket and timing chain.
4. Remove crankshaft sprocket using crankshaft sprocket puller tool Nos. J-41558, J-41816-2 and J-8433-1, or equivalents.
5. Remove crankshaft key.

Installation

1. Install key into keyway, if removed.
2. Install crankshaft sprocket onto front of crankshaft. Align crankshaft key with crankshaft sprocket keyway.
3. Install sprocket onto crankshaft until fully seated against crankshaft flange using sprocket installer tool No. J-41665, or equivalent.
4. Rotate crankshaft sprocket until alignment mark is in 12 o'clock position.
5. Install camshaft sprocket and timing chain, noting the following:
   a. Locate camshaft sprocket locating pin with camshaft sprocket alignment hole.
   b. Locate camshaft sprocket alignment mark in 6 o'clock position.
6. Rotate camshaft or crankshaft sprockets to align timing marks.
7. Install camshaft sprocket mounting bolts.

CAMSHAFT

REPLACE

1. Raise hood to servicing position as outlined under "Engine, Replace."

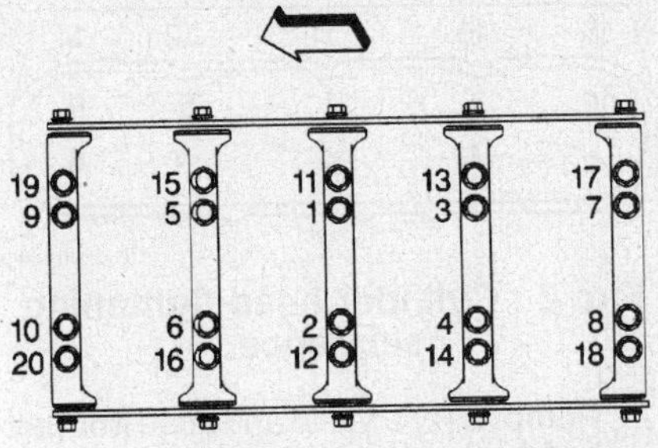

Fig. 3 Main bearing cap tightening sequence

2. Remove radiator support as outlined under "Engine, Replace."
3. Remove timing chain as outlined under "Timing Chain, Replace."
4. Remove valve lifters as outlined under "Valve Lifters, Replace."
5. Remove mounting bolt and camshaft sensor .
6. Remove mounting bolts and camshaft retainer.
7. Install three M8-1.25 x 4.0 inch bolts in camshaft front bolt holes.
8. Rotate and pull camshaft out of engine block using bolts as handle.
9. Remove bolts from front of camshaft.
10. Reverse procedure to install, noting the following:
    a. If camshaft replacement is required, valve lifters must also be replaced.
    b. Lubricate camshaft journals and bearings with clean engine oil.
    c. Install retainer plate with sealing gasket facing engine block.
    d. Lubricate camshaft sensor seal with clean engine oil.

PISTON & ROD ASSEMBLY

When assembling the piston and connecting rod, the mark on the top of the piston must point to the front of the engine block. Lefthand bank connecting rods should have the flange face toward front of engine block. Righthand bank connecting rods should have flange face toward rear of the engine block. The piston pin has an interference fit into the connecting rod and is full floating in the piston. Space compression ring end gaps a minimum of one inch apart and oil ring end gaps a minimum of 90° apart.

PISTONS, PINS & RINGS

A .001 inch oversize piston is available so proper clearance can be obtained for slightly worn cylinder bores requiring light honing, only. If the cylinder have less than .005 inch taper or wear, they can be reconditioned with a hone and fitted with the .001 inch oversize piston.

In addition, oversizes of .020, .030 and .040 inch are available.

MAIN & ROD BEARINGS

Main Bearings

Shell type bearings are used and if worn excessively, should be replaced. No attempt should be made to shim, file or otherwise take up worn bearings.

Main bearings are available in standard and undersides of .001, .002, .009, .010 and .020 inch.

Bearing caps must be installed in proper location and direction.

1. Install crankshaft bearing caps with bearings into engine block.
2. Start M10 bolts and bolt/studs.
3. Tap bearing caps into place suitable plastic-faced hammer.
4. Install new M8 bearing cap side bolts.
5. **Torque** inner M10 bearing cap bolts to 15 ft. lbs., in sequence. **Fig. 3.**
6. Tap crankshaft rearward then forward to align thrust bearings using suitable plastic faced hammer.
7. Tighten inner M10 bolts an additional 80° in sequence using torque angle meter tool No. J-36660-A, or equivalent.
8. **Torque** outer M10 bolts/studs to 60 inch lbs., in sequence.
9. Tighten outer M10 bolts/studs an additional 53° in sequence 53° using torque angle meter tool.
10. **Torque** bearing cap side M8 bolts to 18 ft. lbs. Tighten bolt on one side of bearing cap and then tighten bolt on opposite side of same bearing cap.

CRANKSHAFT REAR OIL SEAL

REPLACE

Removal

1. Remove transmission as outlined under **MOTOR's "Domestic Transmission, In-Vehicle Service" or "Transmission Service DVD."**
2. Remove mounting bolts and flywheel.
3. Remove crankshaft rear oil sea from rear cover.

Installation

Do not lubricate the oil seal inside diameter or the crankshaft surface.

1. Remove flywheel spacer.
2. Lubricate outside diameter of oil seal with clean engine oil. **Do not allow oil or other lubricants to contact seal surface.**
3. Lubricate rear cover oil seal bore with clean engine oil. **Do not allow oil or other lubricants to contact crankshaft surface.**
4. Install tapered cone tool No. J 41479, or equivalent, and mounting bolts onto crankshaft rear.
5. Tighten bolts until snug. **Do not overtighten.**
6. Install rear oil seal onto tapered cone and push seal to rear cover bore.

7. Thread tool rod into tapered cone until tool contacts oil seal.
8. Align oil seal into tool.
9. Rotate tool handle tool clockwise until seal enters rear cover and bottoms into cover bore.
10. Remove tool.
11. Instal flywheel.
12. **Torque** flywheel mounting bolts to 15 ft. lbs., then to 37 ft. lbs., and finally to 74 ft. lbs.
13. Install transmission as outlined under **MOTOR's "Domestic Transmission, In-Vehicle Service" or "Transmission Service DVD."**

OIL PAN

REPLACE

1. Remove front differential as outlined in "Front Wheel Drive Axles" chapter.
2. Remove starter motor as outlined in "Electrical" section.
3. Remove mounting bolts and engine shield.
4. Remove mounting bolts and oil pan skid plate.
5. Remove mounting bolts and crossbar.
6. Remove mounting bolt and transmission cover.
7. Drain engine oil into suitable container and remove engine oil filter.
8. Install drain plug and oil filter until snug.
9. **On models equipped with 4L60-E automatic transmission,** remove righthand side transmission mounting bolt and stud, then the bottom lefthand side mounting bolt.
10. **On models equipped with the 4L80-E automatic transmission,** remove transmission converter cover bolts.
11. **On models equipped with manual transmission,** remove two bottom bellhousing bolts.
12. **On all models,** disconnect oil level sensor electrical connector.
13. Remove battery cable channel bolt and slide channel pin out of oil pan tab.
14. Remove wiring harness and positive battery cable clips.
15. Remove engine oil cooler lines from positive battery cable clip.
16. Remove positive battery cable clip bolt and clip.
17. Remove mounting bolts and oil pan.
18. Drill out oil pan gasket retaining rivets and remove gasket. Discard gasket and rivets.
19. Reverse procedure to install, noting the following
    a. It is not required to rivet new gasket to oil pan.
    b. Apply .20 inch bead of sealant No. 12378190, or equivalent, .8 inch long to engine block.
    c. Apply sealant directly onto tabs of front and rear cover gaskets that protrudes into the oil pan surface.

OIL PUMP

REPLACE

1. Remove oil pan as outlined under "Oil Pan, Replace."
2. Remove front cover as outlined under "Front Cover, Replace."
3. Remove mounting bolt, nuts and oil pump screen with O-ring seal. Discard seal
4. Remove mounting nuts and crankshaft oil deflector.
5. Remove mounting bolts and oil pump.
6. Reverse procedure to install.

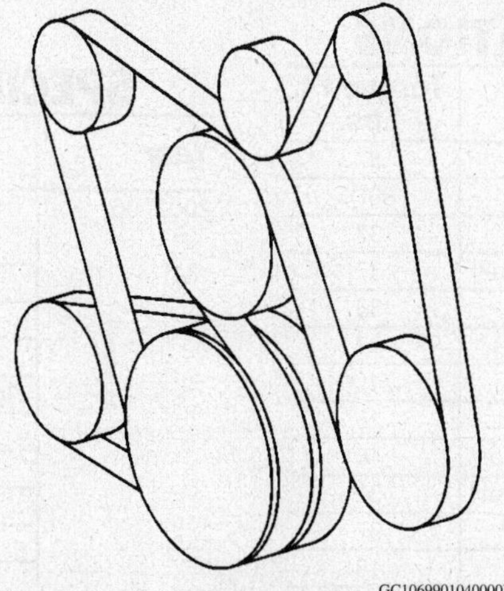

Fig. 4 Serpentine drive belt routing

SERPENTINE DRIVE BELT

Routing

Refer to **Fig. 4** for serpentine drive belt routing.

Replacement

1. Rotate tensioner clockwise to release belt tension using suitable wrench, then remove belt.
2. Route belt over pulleys except belt tensioner.
3. Rotate tensioner to released position and slide belt over tensioner pulley.
4. Ensure belt has correct groove tracking around each pulley.

COOLING SYSTEM BLEED

These engines do not require a specified bleed procedure. After filling cooling system, run engine to operating temperature with radiator/pressure cap off. Air will then be automatically bled through cap opening.

THERMOSTAT

REPLACE

1. Remove radiator outlet hose.
2. Remove mounting bolts, then the water pump inlet and thermostat from water pump.
3. Reverse procedure to install.

WATER PUMP

REPLACE

1. Drain engine coolant into suitable container.
2. Loosen throttle body Mass Air Flow/ Intake Air Temperature (MAF/IAT) sensor air cleaner outlet duct clamps, then remove air cleaner outlet duct.
3. Remove engine sight shield.
4. Remove radiator vent inlet hose from clips.
5. Remove water pump inlet hose.
6. Remove upper fan shroud.
7. Remove fan using fan clutch remover and installer tool No. J-41240, or equivalent.
8. Remove accessory drive belt as outlined under "Serpentine Drive Belt."
9. Remove water pump outlet, surge tank outlet hose and heater inlet hoses.
10. Remove mounting bolts and water pump pulley.
11. Remove mounting bolts, water pump and gaskets. Discard gaskets.
12. Reverse procedure to install. Use new gaskets and tighten mounting bolts.

RADIATOR

REPLACE

1. Drain radiator coolant into suitable container.
2. Remove upper and lower radiator hoses.
3. Remove mounting bolts and lower fan shroud.
4. Remove engine vent hose and surge take hose.
5. Disconnect engine oil cooler lines. Cap lines.
6. Disconnect transmission fluid cooler lines.
7. Remove radiator mounting bolts.
8. Tilt radiator towards engine, then pull up to remove it from support.
9. Reverse procedure to install.

FUEL PUMP

REPLACE

1. Release fuel system pressure as outlined under "Precautions."
2. Drain fuel tank into suitable container.
3. Remove fuel tank.
4. Remove fuel sender by turning cam lock counterclockwise using tool No. J-39765, or equivalent.
5. Remove fuel pump from sender.
6. Reverse procedure to install.

FUEL FILTER

REPLACE

1. Release fuel system pressure as outlined under "Precautions."
2. Remove fuel filler cap, then disconnect fuel feed nuts.
3. Remove clamp bolt, filter and clamp.
4. Remove clamp from filter.
5. Reverse procedure to install.

TIGHTENING SPECIFICATIONS

Year	Component	Torque Ft. Lbs.
2003–06	Alternator Bracket	37
	Accelerator Control Cable Bracket	89①
	Air Conditioning Compressor	37
	Air Conditioning Compressor Bracket	37
	Air Conditioning Hose Bracket	35
	Air Conditioning Tensioner	37
	AIR Bracket	71①
	AIR Pipe To Exhaust Manifold, Nuts	18
	AIR Pipe To Exhaust Manifold, Studs	45
	Alternator & Power Steering Bracket	37
	Belt Idler Pulley	37
	Camshaft Retainer	18
	Camshaft Sensor	18
	Camshaft Sprocket	26
	Clutch Pressure Plate	52⑭
	Connecting Rod	15⑨
	Coolant Temperature Gauge Sensor	15
	Crankshaft Bearing Cap	②
	Crankshaft Damper	37③
	Crankshaft Oil Deflector	18
	Crankshaft Position Sensor	18
	Crossbar	74
	Cylinder Head	④
	Cylinder Head Coolant Plug	15
	Cylinder Head Core Hole Plug	15
	Drive Belt Idler Pulley	37
	Drive Belt Tensioner	37
	Engine Block Coolant Drain Plugs	44
	Engine Oil Cooler Line Fitting	18
	Engine Oil Level Sensor	115①
	Engine Shield	15
	Engine Lift Bracket, M8 Bolt	18
	Engine Lift Bracket, M10 Bolt	37
	Engine Wiring Harness Bracket	89①
	EGR Valve	⑥
	EGR Valve Inlet Pipe Intake Manifold	18
	EGR Valve Inlet Pipe Exhaust Manifold	22
	EGR Valve Pipe To Cylinder Head	37
	EGR Valve Pipe To Exhaust Manifold	20
	EGR Valve Pipe To Intake Manifold	89①
	Exhaust Crossover Pipe	25
	Exhaust Manifold AIR Pipe	45①
	Exhaust Manifold	⑦
	Exhaust Manifold Heat Shield	80①
	Exhaust Pipe	48
	EVAP Purge Solenoid	89①
	Fan Clutch	17
	Fan Shroud	72①
	Flywheel	⑤
	Front Cover	18
	Front Differential Carrier Shield	26
	Fuel Rail	89①
	Fuel Rail Cover	80①
	Fuel Rail Crossover Tube	34①
	Fuel Rail Stop Bracket	37

TIGHTENING SPECIFICATIONS—Continued

Year	Component	Torque Ft. Lbs.
2003–06	Hood	18
	Ignition Coil	22①
	Intake Cover	89①
	Intake Cover Bracket	45①
	Ignition Coil To Bracket	106①
	Ignition Coil Bracket To Valve Cover	106①
	Intake Manifold	⑧
	Intake Manifold Wiring Harness	89①
	Knock Sensors	15
	Main Bearing Cap	②
	MAF Sensor Clamp	27–44①
	Motor Mount	37
	Motor Mount Bracket	48
	Motor Mount, Lower To Upper	37
	Motor Mount, Through Bolt	68
	Motor Mount, Upper	37
	Oil Cooler Line Clamp	80①
	Oil Cooler Line Clip	53①
	Oil Cooler Fitting	18
	Oil Filter	22
	Oil Filter Fitting	40
	Oil Dipstick Tube	18
	Oil Level Sensor	15
	Oil Pan Baffle	106①
	Oil Pan Closeout Cover	80①
	Oil Pan Drain Plug	18
	Oil Pan To Block & Front Cover	18
	Oil Pan To Rear Cover	106①
	Oil Pan Skid Plate	15
	Oil Pressure Sensor	15
	Oil Pump To Engine Block	18
	Oil Pump Cover	106①
	Oil Pump Relief Valve Plug	106①
	Oil Pump Screen	18
	Oil Pump Screen To Oil Pump	106①
	Oil Transfer Cover	106①
	Power Steering Pump	37
	Power Steering Pump Bracket	37
	Propeller Shaft	15
	Radiator Shroud	71①
	Rear Cover	18
	Spark Plugs (Aluminum Cylinder Heads)	⑩
	Spark Plugs (Iron Cylinder Heads)	⑪
	Starter Cover	15
	Radiator Support	52
	Rear Engine Mount, Bolt	35
	Rear Engine Mount, Nut	40
	Rear Engine Mount, Bolt	35
	Rear Engine Mount to Crossmember	33
	Rear Engine Mount To Transmission	44
	Throttle Body	89①
	Torque Converter	46
	Transmission, Automatic	34

Continued

TIGHTENING SPECIFICATIONS—Continued

Year	Component	Torque Ft. Lbs.
2003–06	Transmission, Manual	35
	Transmission Fluid Cooler Line	19
	Transmission To Oil Pan	41
	Universal Lift Bracket	15
	Valley Cover	106①
	Valve Lifter Guide	106①
	Valve Rocker Arm	22
	Valve Rocker Arm Cover	106①
	Vapor Vent Pipe	106①
	Water Inlet Housing	11
	Water Pump	⑫
	Water Pump Cover	11
	Water Pump Pulley	⑬

①— Inch lbs.
②— Refer to "Main & Rod Bearings."
③— Tighten an additional 140°.
④— Refer to "Cylinder Head, Replace."
⑤— Refer to "Crankshaft Rear Oil Seal, Replace"
⑥— First pass, 90 inch lbs.; final pass, 20 ft. lbs.
⑦— First pass, 11 ft. lbs.; final pass, 18 ft. lbs.
⑧— Refer to "Intake Manifold, Replace."
⑨— Tighten additional 60°.
⑩— Spark plugs in new aluminum cylinder heads, 15 ft. lbs.; all subsequent installations, 11 ft. lbs.
⑪— Spark plugs in new iron cylinder heads, 22 ft. lbs.; all subsequent installations, 11 ft. lbs.
⑫— First pass, 11 ft. lbs.; final pass, 22 ft. lbs.
⑬— First pass, 90 inch lbs.; final pass, 18 ft. lbs.
⑭— Tighten clutch pressure plate bolts in star pattern and evenly over three increments with fourth increment to 52 ft. lbs.

Rear Axle & Suspension

INDEX

REAR AXLE

REPLACE

H2

1. Raise and support vehicle. Support rear axle using suitable jack.
2. Drain axle fluid into suitable container.
3. Mark driveshaft to flange, disconnect driveshaft and tie driveshaft to side rail or crossmember.
4. Tape bearing cups to prevent loss of rollers.
5. Remove wheel and brake drum or hub and drum.
6. Disconnect parking brake cable from lever and brake flange plate.
7. Disconnect and cap hydraulic brake lines from connectors.
8. Remove shock absorbers from axle brackets, **Fig. 1.**
9. Disconnect vent line from vent fitting.
10. Remove height sensing and brake proportional valve brackets.
11. Remove nuts, washers, U-bolts, spring plates, spacers and axle.
12. Reverse procedure to install.

H3

1. Raise and support vehicle using a suitable lift.
2. Drain rear axle lubricant into suitable container.
3. Remove rear propeller shaft as outlined in "Propeller Shaft, Replace."
4. Remove vent tube.
5. Remove retaining bolts from park brake cables at rear leaf springs.
6. Remove clips retaining rear brake lines to rear axle housing.
7. Remove bolts retaining rear brake lines to rear axle jounce bumper mounting brackets.
8. Remove bolt retaining rear brake line to differential cover.
9. Remove bolt retaining brake junction block to rear axle.
10. Remove rear axle shafts as outlined in "Rear Axle Shaft, Replace."
11. Remove mounting bolts to backing plates.
12. Relocate rear shoe assemblies to side and support using suitable wire.
13. Remove lower shock absorber mounting bolt and nut.
14. Remove U-bolt nuts, then the anchor plate.
15. Remove U-bolts from rear axle housing.
16. With aid of an assistant, remove rear axle assembly from vehicle.
17. Reverse procedure to install, noting the following:
    a. Fill rear axle with suitable fluid to specifications.
    b. Tighten to specifications.

REAR AXLE SHAFT

REPLACE

H2

1. Raise and support vehicle, then remove tire and wheel assembly.
2. Remove axle shaft mounting bolts.
3. Tap axle shaft flange lightly using suitable soft-faced hammer to loosen shaft, **Figs. 2 and 3.**
4. Remove axle shaft by twisting flange using suitable locking pliers.
5. Remove gasket and RTV.
6. Reverse procedure to install. Install new gasket and RTV.

H3

1. Raise and support vehicle using a suitable lift.
2. Remove tire and wheel assembly.
3. Remove brake caliper as outlined in "Disc Brakes" chapter.
4. Remove bolt for rear brake pipe retainer.
5. Remove bolt for mounting bracket.
6. Remove mounting brackets from rear axle cover.
7. Position a suitable drain pan under axle.
8. Remove rear cover mounting bolts.
9. Remove rear cover and gasket from differential housing.
10. Drain rear axle.
11. Remove pinion shaft locking bolt.
12. **On models less locking differential,** remove pinion shaft.
13. **On all models,** push flange of axle shaft toward differential.
14. Remove C-lock from button end of axle shaft.
15. Remove axle shaft from housing.
16. Reverse procedure to install.
    a. Fill rear axle with suitable fluid to specifications.
    b. Tighten to specifications.

PROPELLER SHAFT

REPLACE

1. Place transmission in neutral position.
2. Release park brake, if applied.
3. Raise and support vehicle using a suitable lift.
4. Mark front universal joint to driveshaft flange.
5. Remove retaining bolts and straps.
6. Remove propeller shaft from front pinion drive flange.
7. Remove propeller shaft retaining bolts.
8. Remove propeller shaft CV joint from transmission transfer case flange.
9. Wrap U-Joint bearing caps to ensure bearing caps do not separate from U-Joint.
10. Reverse procedure to install, tighten to specifications.

HUB & BEARING

REPLACE

H2

1. Raise and support vehicle.
2. Remove axle shaft as outlined under "Rear Axle Shaft, Replace."
3. Remove retaining ring and key.
4. Remove adjusting nut and washer.
5. Remove hub and drum.
6. Remove oil seal.
7. **On models equipped with 10 ½-inch ring gear,** proceed as follows:
    a. Remove inner bearing and cup using suitable drill.
    b. Remove retaining ring using suitable snap ring pliers.
8. **On models equipped with 11-inch ring gear,** proceed as follows:
    a. Lay drum on suitable flat surface, then place suitable shop towel under drum to catch inner bearing and seal.
    b. Remove bearing cup and seal using suitable drift.
    c. Remove retaining ring using suitable snap ring pliers.

9. **On all models,** drive outer bearing and cup from hub using bearing remover tool Nos. J-8092 and J-24426, or equivalents.
10. Reverse procedure to install.

H3

1. Raise and support vehicle using a suitable lift.
2. Remove tire and wheel assembly.
3. Remove rear axle housing cover as outlined in "Rear Axle Shaft, Replace."
4. Remove axle shaft as outlined in "Rear Axle Shaft, Replace."
5. Remove axle shaft seal and bearing from axle housing using tool Nos. J 44685 and J 2619-01 or equivalents.
6. Reverse procedure to install, noting the following:
   a. Fill rear axle with suitable fluid to specifications.
   b. Tighten to specifications.

WHEEL BEARING

ADJUST

H2

Ensure brakes are completely released and do not drag. Inspect wheel bearing play by grasping the tire at the top and pulling and pushing back and forth, or by using a pry bar under the tire. If the wheel bearings are properly adjusted, movement of the brake drum in relation to the brake flange plate will be barely noticeable and the wheel will turn freely. If the movement is excessive, adjust the bearings.

10½-INCH RING GEAR

1. Raise and vehicle until wheel is free to spin.
2. Remove axle shaft as outlined under "Axle Shaft, Replace."
3. Clean adjusting nut and threads.
4. Remove retaining ring and key.
5. **Torque** adjusting nut to 50 ft. lbs., while turning drum in opposite direction.
6. Ensure inner bearing roller assembly is seated against spindle shoulder.
7. Loosen adjusting nut ¼ turn, then **torque** adjusting nut to 13 ft. lbs.
8. Align closest adjusting nut slot with keyway in axle spindle.
9. Install key into keyway and adjusting nut slot.
10. Install retaining ring and axle shaft.

11-INCH RING GEAR

1. Raise and vehicle until wheel is free to spin.
2. Remove axle shaft as outlined under "Axle Shaft, Replace."
3. **Torque** adjusting nut to 50 ft. lbs., while rotating hub in opposite direction.
4. Ensure bearing cones are seated and in contact with spindle shoulder.
5. Loosen adjusting nut, then tighten nut while rotating hub.
6. Loosen adjusting nut, then **torque** nut to 35 ft. lbs., while rotating hub.

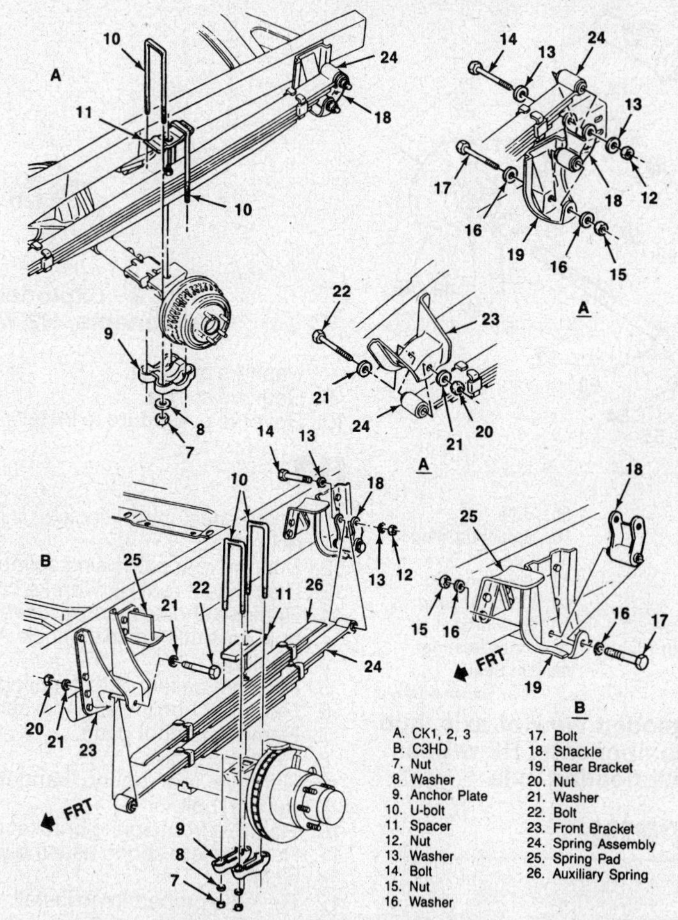

Fig. 1 Exploded view of axle components. H2

7. Loosen adjusting nut 135–150°.
8. Install lock washer, then bend one tang of retaining washer over flat on adjusting nut to minimum of 30°.
9. Install outer mounting nut and **torque** to 65 ft. lbs.
10. Bend one tang of retaining washer over flat of outer nut to minimum of 60°.
11. Add wheel bearing grease to bearings, then install axle shaft as outlined under "Rear Axle Shaft, Replace."

H3

Ensure brakes are completely released and do not drag. Inspect wheel bearing play by grasping the tire at the top and pulling and pushing back and forth, or by using a pry bar under the tire. If the wheel bearings are properly adjusted, movement of the brake drum in relation to the brake flange plate will be barely noticeable and the wheel will turn freely. If the movement is excessive, adjust the bearings.

SHOCK ABSORBER

REPLACE

H2

1. Raise and support vehicle.
2. Support rear axle using suitable jack.
3. Remove mounting nuts and disconnect shock absorber from upper mounting bracket.
4. Remove lower mounting nuts and shock absorber.
5. Reverse procedure to install.

H3

1. Raise and support vehicle.
2. Support rear axle at ride height using suitable jack.
3. Remove upper absorber bolts.
4. Remove lower absorber nut and bolt.
5. Remove shock absorber.
6. Reverse procedure to install, tighten to specifications.

COIL SPRING

REPLACE

1. Raise and support vehicle.
2. Support rear axle using suitable jack.
3. Remove stabilizer shaft link retaining nut from frame
4. Remove lower shock absorber nut and bolt from rear axle.
5. Lower rear axle until springs are fully unloaded.
6. Remove coil spring and insulators.
7. Reverse procedure to install.

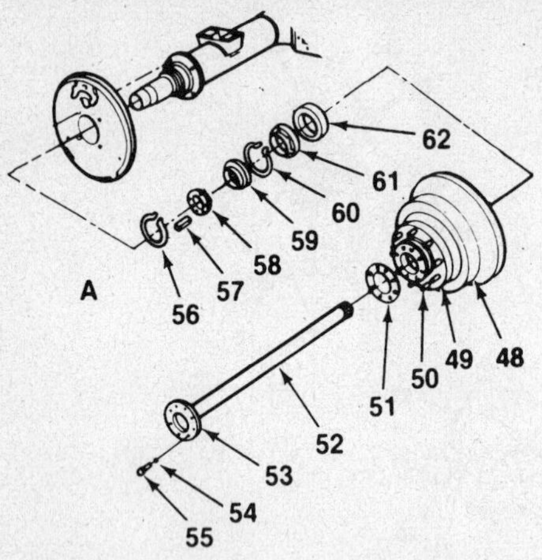

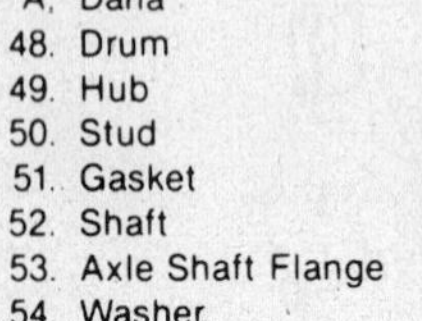

A. Dana	55. Bolt
48. Drum	56. Retaining Ring
49. Hub	57. Key
50. Stud	58. Adjusting Nut
51. Gasket	59. Outer Bearing
52. Shaft	60. Retaining Ring
53. Axle Shaft Flange	61. Inner Bearing
54. Washer	62. Oil Seal

GC3038800123000X

Fig. 2 Exploded view of axle, hub & drum components. H2 w/Dana full floating axle

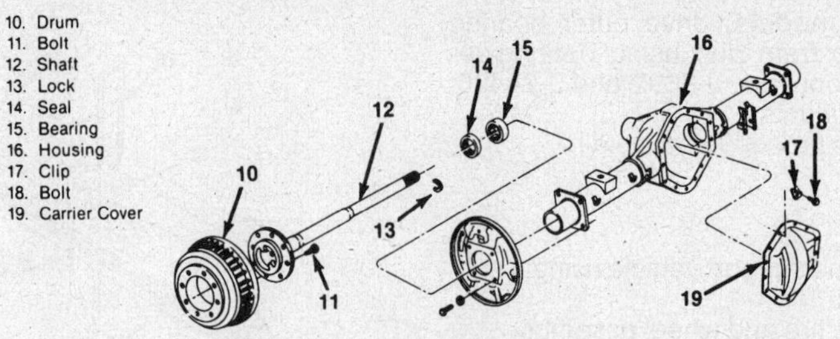

Fig. 3 Exploded view of axle shaft & housing components. H2 w/Saginaw semi-floating type axle

LEAF SPRING

REPLACE

H2

1. Raise and support vehicle.
2. Support rear axle using suitable jack.
3. Remove U-bolt nuts and washers.
4. Remove anchor plate.
5. Remove U-bolts and spacer.
6. Loosen shackle to spring nut.
7. Remove shackle to rear bracket mounting nut, washer and bolt.
8. Remove spring to front bracket, nut, washers and bolt.
9. Remove spring.
10. Reverse procedure to install.

H3

1. Raise and support vehicle using a suitable lift.
2. Support rear axle using suitable jack.
3. Disconnect rear park brake cable.
4. Remove shock absorber lower nut and bolt as outlined in “Shock Absorber, Replace.”
5. Remove trailer hitch, if equipped.
6. Remove U-bolt nuts and washers.
7. Remove anchor plate.
8. Remove U-bolts.
9. Remove rear spring hanger bracket nut and bolt.
10. Remove front spring bracket bolt.
11. Remove leaf spring assembly from vehicle.
12. Reverse procedure to install, tighten to specifications.

CONTROL ARM

REPLACE

Upper

1. Raise and support vehicle.
2. Support rear axle at ride height using suitable jack.
3. Remove upper control arm retaining nut and bolt from frame bracket.
4. Remove upper control arm retaining nut and bolt from axle bracket.
5. Remove upper control arm from vehicle.
6. Reverse procedure to install.

Lower

1. Raise and support vehicle.
2. Support rear axle at curb height using suitable jack.
3. Remove lower control arm retaining nuts and bolt.
4. Remove lower control arm from vehicle.
5. Reverse procedure to install.

STABILIZER SHAFT

REPLACE

1. Raise and support vehicle using a suitable lift.
2. Support rear axle at curb height using a suitable jack.
3. Remove stabilizer shaft to link nut.
4. Remove stabilizer shaft insulator bracket mounting bolts.
5. Remove stabilizer shaft, insulator brackets and insulators.
6. Reverse procedure to install, tighten to specifications.

TIGHTENING SPECIFICATIONS

Year	Component	Torque Ft. Lbs.
H2		
2003–06	Axle Flange	148
	Brake Backing Plate	103
	Carrier Cover	30
	Drain Plug	24
	Jounce Bumper	24
	Lower Control Arm	89
	Shackle To Frame Bracket	70
	Shackle To Spring	70
	Shock Absorber, Nut	70
	Spring To Front Hanger	92
	Stabilizer Shaft	24
	Stabilizer Shaft Link	48
	Track Bar	77
	U-Bolt	①
	Wheel Axle Hub	52
	Upper Control Arm	77
	Yoke Retainer	19
H3		
2006	Backing Plate Bolt	100
	Bearing Cap Bolts	55
	Differential Housing Cover Bolts	18
	Fill Plug/Drain Plug	24
	Front Propeller Shaft CV Joint To Transfer Case Drive Flange Bolt	51
	Front Propeller Shaft To Front Pinion Yoke Bolt	18
	Leaf Spring To Front Bracket Nut	66
	Leaf Spring U-Bolt Nuts	53
	Pinion Shaft Lock Bolt	18
	Rear Propeller Shaft Retainer Bolt	18
	Ring Gear Bolts	89
	Spring Shackle To Frame Nut	70
	Spring Shackle To Leaf Spring Nut	66
	Shock Absorber Lower Bolts	70
	Shock Absorber Upper Bolts	26
	Stabilizer Bar Lower Link Nut	59
	Stabilizer Bar Upper Link To Frame Nut	59
	Stabilizer Clamp Bolts	37
	Wheel Speed Sensor Bolt	13

① — Less washers, 101 ft. lbs; w/washers, 53 ft. lbs.

Front Suspension & Steering

NOTE: Refer To "Computer Relearn Procedures" Located In The Front Of This Manual When Battery Power To The Computer Has Been Interrupted.

INDEX

PRECAUTIONS

Battery Ground Cable

Prior to service disconnect battery ground cable and isolate as required.

Radio Security System

If the Theftlock system is active when battery power is interrupted, the customers security code must be entered to restore proper function of the radio. Use the following procedure to unlock a secured radio after a power loss. Do not wait more than 15 seconds between steps.

1. Theftlock is engaged if radio is inoperable and "LOC" appears with ignition in On position.
2. Obtain customers' code number.
3. Press "MIN" button and "000" will appear on display.
4. Press "MIN" again until last two digits displayed agree with security code.
5. Press "HR" button until first 1 or 2 digits agree with security code.
6. Press "AM-FM" to select code entered. "SEC" will display indicating radio is now operable and secure.
7. If incorrect code is entered, "SEC" will display and radio will be inoperable.
8. Radio will remain inoperable until correct code is displayed. Repeat steps until correct code is entered. If correct code cannot be obtained, contact Delco technical assistance.

WHEEL BEARING

ADJUST

1. Raise and support vehicle.
2. Remove cap from hub/disc.
3. Remove cotter pin.
4. **Torque** adjusting nut to 12 ft. lbs., while turning wheel forward by hand, this will seat bearing.
5. Back off adjusting nut one flat. If hole in spindle lines up with slot in nut, insert cotter pin. If hole and slot do not line up, back nut off until hole and slot align. Do not back nut off more than one additional flat.
6. Install cotter pin.

HUB, BEARING & SEAL

REPLACE

H2

1. Remove brake rotor as outlined in "Disc Brakes" chapter.
2. Remove wheel speed sensor and brake hose mounting bracket bolt from steering knuckle.
3. Disconnect wheel speed sensor electrical connection.
4. Remove cover, mounting wheel driveshaft nut and washer.
5. Disconnect wheel driveshaft from wheel hub and bearing.
6. Remove mounting bolts, wheel hub and bearing, then the splash shield.
7. Remove wheel speed sensor mounting bolt.
8. Reverse procedure to install, noting the following:
   a. Replace O-ring seal, as required.
   b. Tighten to specifications.

H3

1. Raise and support vehicle using a suitable lift.
2. Remove tire and wheel assembly.
3. Remove brake rotor as outlined in "Disc Brakes" chapter.
4. Remove wheel speed sensor.
5. Remove retaining nut and washer for wheel driveshaft.
6. Remove wheel driveshaft from wheel hub and bearing. **The wheel driveshaft does not have to be removed from vehicle, just reposition to gain access to mounting bolts for wheel hub.**
7. Remove wheel driveshaft from wheel hub and bearing.
8. Remove wheel hub and bearing mounting bolts.
9. Remove wheel hub and bearing and splash shield from vehicle.
10. Reverse procedure to install, tighten to specifications.

BALL JOINT INSPECTION

1. Wipe ball joints clean and inspect seals for damage. If seals are damaged, replace ball joint.
2. Adjust wheel bearings as outlined under "Wheel Bearing, Adjust."
3. Raise and support vehicle.
4. Place suitable dial indicator against spindle to measure vertical movement.
5. Pry between lower control arm and outer race using suitable pry bar while reading dial indicator.
6. If dial indicator reading is more than .08 inch, replace ball joint.

BALL JOINT

REPLACE

H2

LOWER

1. Raise and support vehicle, then remove tire and wheel assembly.
2. Disconnect Real Time Damping (RTD) link rod from sensor.

3. Remove stabilizer shaft links from lower control arm.
4. Remove shock absorber lower mounting nut and bolt.
5. Remove torsion bars.
6. Remove halfshaft as outlined in "Front Wheel Drive Axles" chapter.
7. Remove nut and disconnect the ball joint stud from steering knuckle using ball joint separator tool No. J-43631, or equivalent.
8. Remove lower control arm mounting nuts, washers and bolts.
9. Remove lower control arm.
10. Secure lower control arm in suitable bench vice.
11. Remove lower ball joint rivets
12. Remove ball joint from lower control arm using suitable press.
13. Reverse procedure to install.

UPPER

1. Raise and support vehicle, then remove tire and wheel assembly.
2. Disconnect Real Time Damping (RTD) link rod from sensor.
3. Remove brake hose and the wheel speed sensor brackets mounting bolt.
4. Remove halfshaft as outlined in "Front Wheel Drive Axles" chapter.
5. Remove upper ball joint mounting nut. Discard nut.
6. Disconnect upper control arm from steering knuckle using ball joint separator tool No. J-43631, or equivalent.
7. Remove upper control arm mounting nuts, bolts and adjustment cams.
8. Remove upper control arm.
9. Remove upper ball joint using suitable press.
10. Reverse procedure to install.

H3

1. Raise and support vehicle using a suitable lift.
2. Remove tire and wheel assembly.
3. Remove lower control arm as outlined in "Control Arm, Replace."
4. Place lower control arm in a suitable vice.
5. Remove securing crimps from ball joint body using a suitable chisel.
6. Remove ball joint from lower control arm using a suitable press.
7. Reverse procedure to install, tighten to specifications.

COIL SPRING

REPLACE

1. Raise and support vehicle, then remove engine protection shield.
2. Remove tire and wheel assembly.
3. Remove shock absorber as outlined under "Shock Absorber, Replace."
4. Remove front stabilizer shaft link.
5. Install coil spring replacement tool No. J-23028-15, or equivalent using outboard locating tab on 1500 series models and inboard locating tab on 2500 series.
6. Attach retaining hook to control arm and tighten wing nut to eliminate freeplay.
7. Securely attach coil spring replacement tool No. J-23028-01, or equivalent, to suitable transmission jack.
8. Relieve spring tension from lower control arm pivot bolts by raising jack.
9. Remove lower control arm pivot bolt nuts, then rear and front pivot bolts.
10. Slowly lower transmission jack to unload front coil spring.
11. Remove coil spring and insulator.
12. Reverse procedure to install.

SHOCK ABSORBER

REPLACE

H2

1. Raise and support vehicle, then remove tire and wheel assembly.
2. Remove mounting nut and washer, then shock absorber from leaf spring spacer.
3. Remove mounting nut, washer and bolt, then the shock absorber from frame.
4. Reverse procedure to install.

H3

1. Raise and support vehicle using a suitable lift.
2. Support lower control arm using a suitable jack stand.
3. Hold tennon end using a suitable wrench while removing nut.
4. Remove upper shock absorber nut.
5. Remove upper insulator.
6. Remove shock absorber mounting bolts at lower control arm.
7. Remove shock absorber through lower control arm from below.
8. Reverse procedure to install, tighten to specifications.

LEAF SPRING

REPLACE

1. Raise and support vehicle.
2. Support axle separately to eliminate any load on springs.
3. Remove tire and wheel assembly.
4. Remove mounting nut, washer and shock absorber from axle.
5. Remove mounting nut, washer and stabilizer link from shaft using wheel stud and tie rod remover tool No. J-6627-A, or equivalent, to separate stabilizer shaft from link.
6. Remove mounting nut, retainer and insulator, then the stabilizer link from axle. Pull link free from axle. **Do not lose other insulator and retainer.**
7. Remove mounting nuts, washers and U-bolts.
8. Remove spacer and spring spacer.
9. Remove leaf spring from axle.
10. Remove mounting nut, washers and bolt, then separate spring from rear shackle.
11. Remove mounting nut, washers and bolt, then separate spring from front hanger.
12. Remove leaf spring from frame by pulling back and out.
13. Reverse procedure to install.

CONTROL ARM

REPLACE

H2

LOWER

1. Raise and support vehicle, then remove tire and wheel assembly
2. Disconnect Real Time Damping (RTD) link rod from sensor.
3. Remove stabilizer shaft links from lower control arm.
4. Remove shock absorber lower mounting nut and bolt.
5. Remove torsion bars.
6. Remove wheel driveshaft as outlined in "Front Wheel Drive Axles" chapter.
7. Remove lower ball joint stud nut.
8. Disconnect lower ball joint stud from steering knuckle using ball joint separator tool No. J-43631, or equivalent.
9. Remove mounting nuts, washers, bolts and lower control arm.
10. Reverse procedure to install.

UPPER

1. Raise and support vehicle, then remove tire and wheel assembly.
2. Disconnect Real Time Damping (RTD) link rod from sensor.
3. Remove brake hose and the wheel speed sensor brackets mounting bolt.
4. Remove wheel driveshaft as outlined in "Front Wheel Drive Axles" chapter.
5. Remove upper ball joint nut . Discard nut.
6. Disconnect upper control arm from steering knuckle using ball joint separator tool No. J-43631, or equivalent.
7. Remove upper control arm mounting nuts, adjustment cams and mounting bolts.
8. Remove upper control arm.
9. Reverse procedure to install.

H3

LOWER

1. Raise and support vehicle using a suitable lift.
2. Remove steering knuckle as outlined in "Steering Knuckle, Replace."
3. Remove stabilizer shaft links from lower control arm.
4. Remove shock absorber as outlined in "Shock Absorber, Replace."
5. Allow front suspension to hang in rebound position. Place a matchmark on adjuster bolt.
6. Remove adjuster bolt, spacer and adjuster nut.
7. Remove adjustment arms and torsion bars as a unit, moving it rearward to disengage lower control arm.
8. Remove lower control arm nuts and washers.
9. Remove lower control arm bolts.
10. Remove lower control arm.
11. Reverse procedure to install, tighten to specifications.

UPPER

1. Raise and support vehicle using a suitable lift.
2. Remove tire and wheel assembly.
3. Support lower control arm at ride height.
4. Remove wheel speed sensor bracket bolt.
5. Disconnect wheel speed sensor brackets.
6. Disconnect front brake hose from upper control arm.
7. Disconnect upper control arm from ball stud, removing pinch bolt.
8. Remove upper control arm nuts and adjustment cams.
9. Remove upper control arm bolts, then the arms.
10. Reverse procedure to install, noting the following:
    a. Inspect wheel alignment as outlined in "Wheel Alignment" section.
    b. Tighten to specifications.

STEERING KNUCKLE

REPLACE

H2

1. Raise and support vehicle, then remove tire and wheel assembly.
2. Remove wheel hub and bearing as outlined under "Hub, Bearing & Seal, Replace."
3. Disconnect Real Time Damping (RTD) link rod from sensor.
4. Unload torsion bars.
5. Disconnect outer tie rod from knuckle.
6. Remove brake hose bracket mounting bolt.
7. Remove mounting nut and separate upper ball joint from steering knuckle using ball joint separating tool No. J-43631, or equivalent.
8. Remove mounting nut and separate lower ball joint from steering knuckle using ball joint separating tool.
9. Remove steering knuckle.
10. Reverse procedure to install.

H3

1. Raise and support vehicle using a suitable lift.
2. Remove tire and wheel assembly.
3. Support lower control arm using a suitable jack stand.
4. Remove wheel driveshaft nut. Discard nut.
5. Disconnect wheel speed sensor harness from chassis harness.
6. Disconnect wheel speed sensor harness from inner fender panel.
7. Remove outer tie rod retaining nut.
8. Disconnect outer tie rod from steering knuckle using tool No. J 24319-B or equivalent.
9. Loosen jam nut and remove outer tie rod from inner tie rod. Discard jam nut.
10. Disconnect outer tie rod from steering knuckle.
11. Remove upper control arm pinch bolt from ball joint.

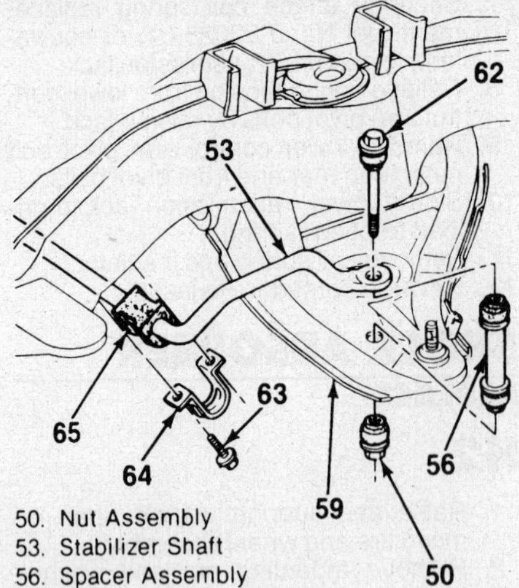

Fig. 1 Stabilizer shaft components. H2

12. Remove lower control arm retaining nut.
13. Separate lower ball joint from steering knuckle using tool No. J 43631 or equivalent.
14. Remove steering knuckle assembly from vehicle and set on a bench.
15. Remove ball joint using tool No. J 6627-A or equivalent.
16. Remove wheel hub and bearing assembly as outlined in "Hub, Bearing & Seal, Replace."
17. Reverse procedure to install, noting the following:
    a. Inspect wheel alignment as outlined in "Wheel Alignment" section.
    b. Tighten to specifications.

STABILIZER BAR

REPLACE

H2

1. Raise and support vehicle.
2. Remove nut from link bolt, **Fig. 1.**
3. Remove link bolt.
4. Remove spacer, mounting bolts, bracket and stabilizer shaft.
5. Remove bushing.
6. Reverse procedure to install.

H3

1. Raise and support vehicle using a suitable lift.
2. Remove nuts from stabilizer link assemblies, then the link.
3. Remove insulator clamp bolts, then the clamps.
4. Remove stabilizer shaft and insulators.
5. Reverse procedure to install, noting the following:
    a. Inspect all components for wear and damage.
    b. Tighten to specifications.

TIE ROD END

REPLACE

1. Raise and support vehicle, then remove tire and wheel assembly.
2. Remove ball stud cotter pin and nut.
3. Loosen adjuster clamp nut.
4. Remove tie rod end using steering linkage puller tool No. J-26813-B, or equivalent.
5. Remove outer tie rod from inner tie rod sleeve.
6. Reverse procedure to install. Use steering linkage installer tool No. J-29194, or equivalent.

POWER STEERING GEAR

REPLACE

H2

1. Place suitable drain pan below steering gear.
2. Remove steering gear hoses.
3. Raise hoses up to prevent oil drainage. Cap or tape hose ends and gear fittings ends.
4. Place front wheels in straight ahead position, then lock steering column by placing steering column anti-rotation pin tool No. J-42640, or equivalent, through steering column access hole.
5. Remove steering gear shield.
6. Mark relationship of upper to lower intermediate shaft and lower shaft to steering gear input shaft for installation reference.
7. Remove upper to lower shaft connection mounting nut and bolt, then the lower shaft coupler mounting bolt.
8. Slide lower intermediate shaft towards dash panel to clear lower shaft coupler clear from input shaft.
9. Remove intermediate shaft by sliding it down upper shaft.
10. Raise and support vehicle.
11. Remove relay rod nut from pitman arm ball stud. Discard nut.
12. Remove relay rod from pitman arm ball stud using universal steering linkage puller tool No. J-24319-01, or equivalent.
13. Remove pitman arm nut and washer.
14. Mark pitman arm shaft for proper installation alignment.
15. Remove pitman shaft nut or pinch bolt.
16. Remove pitman arm from shaft using pitman arm puller tool No. J-6632-01, or equivalent. **Do not hammer on pitman arm, shaft or puller.** .
17. Remove mounting bolts and steering gear.
18. Reverse procedure to install. Install pitman arm ball stud using steering linkage installer tool No. J-29193, or equivalent.

H3

1. Raise and support vehicle using a suitable lift.
2. Remove both front tire and wheel assemblies.
3. Remove engine shield bolts, then the engine shield.
4. Remove front differential carrier assembly as outlined in "Front Wheel Drive" section.
5. Disconnect outer tie rod end from steering knuckle as outlined in "Steering Knuckle, Replace."
6. Place a suitable drain pan to catch fluid during removal of power steering gear.
7. Disconnect power steering hose assembly from power steering pump.
8. Raise vehicle and support with suitable safety stands.
9. Remove power steering hose assembly bracket retaining bolts.
10. Remove power steering hose assembly to power steering gear retaining bolt.
11. Disconnect power steering hose assembly from the power steering gear.
12. Remove power steering hose assembly from vehicle.
13. Remove coupler clamp bolt from intermediate shaft.
14. Separate intermediate shaft from steering gear.
15. Remove steering gear vertical mounting nuts, then the washers and bolts.
16. Remove steering gear horizontal mounting nuts, then the washers and bolts.
17. Remove steering gear from vehicle.
18. Reverse procedure to install, noting the following:
    a. Bleed power steering system as outlined in "Power Steering" chapter.
    b. Tighten to specifications.

POWER STEERING PUMP

REPLACE

H2

1. Remove serpentine drive belt as outlined under "Serpentine Drive Belt."
2. Place suitable drain pan under power steering pump, then disconnect hoses from pump. Plug pump ports and hoses.
3. Remove pulley using power steering pump pulley remover tool No. J-25034-C, or equivalent.
4. Disconnect electrical connector from EVO actuator.
5. Remove front and rear mounting bolts, then the pump.
6. Reverse procedure to install.

H3

1. Disconnect electrical connector from MAF/IAT sensor.
2. Loosen clamp and disconnect air cleaner outlet duct from air cleaner assembly.
3. Remove bolts and nut securing air cleaner assembly to wheel house.
4. Remove air cleaner assembly from vehicle.
5. Remove drive belt as outlined in "Serpentine Drive Belt" of "3.5L Engine" section.
6. Remove power steering pump pulley using tool No. J 25034-C or equivalent.
7. Remove pulley from pump shaft.
8. Disconnect oil pressure sensor harness clip from pump body.
9. Install a suitable drain pan under vehicle.
10. Disconnect power steering pressure hoses from power steering pump.
11. Remove power steering pump mounting bolts, then the power steering pump.
12. Reverse procedure to install, noting the following:
    a. Bleed power steering system as outlined in "Power Steering" chapter.
    b. Tighten to specifications.

TIGHTENING SPECIFICATIONS

Year	Component	Torque Ft. Lbs.
H2		
2003–06	Ball Joint, Lower	52
	Ball Joint Stud, Lower	74
	Frame Cross Bar	74
	Lower Control Arm	107
	Pivot Bolt	107
	Power Steering Pump	37
	Power Steering Pump Hose	20
	Shock Absorber Lower Control Arm, Bolt	18
	Shock Absorber Lower Nut	37
	Shock Absorber Through Bolt	59
	Shock Absorber Upper Nut	136
	Spring Hanger	70
	Steering Gear	100
	Tie Rod Adjuster Clamp	77
	Tie Rod Ball Stud	65
	Tie Rod Ball Stud, Nut	48
	Tie Rod Ball Joint, Nut	120
	Tie Rod Tube Clamp	55
	U-Bolt	92②
	Upper Control Arm	140
	Wheel Driveshaft	155
	Wheel Hub & Bearing	133
	Wheel Speed Sensor	80①
	Wheel Speed Sensor & Brake Hose Mounting Bracket	106①
H3		
2006	Hub & Bearing Mounting Bolts	133
	Insulator Clamp Bolts	37
	Link Assembly Nuts	32
	Lower Ball Joint To Steering Knuckle Nut	107
	Lower Control Arm Front Nut	122
	Lower Control Arm Rear Nut	133
	Power Steering Pump Mounting Bolts	18
	Power Steering Pressure Hose	18
	Shock Absorber To Lower Control Arm Bolts	52
	Steering Gear Vertical Long Mounting Nuts & Bolts	96
	Steering Gear Vertical Isolator Clamp Mounting Bolts	74
	Tennon End Nut	18
	Upper Ball Joint To Steering Knuckle Bolt	55
	Upper Control Arm Nuts To Adjustment Cams	114
	Upper Control Arm To Ball Stud Bolt	47
	Wheel Driveshaft To Steering Knuckle	173
	Wheel Lug Nuts	103
	Wheel Speed Sensor Bracket Bolt	15

① — Inch lbs.
② — Diagonal sequence.

Front Wheel Drive

INDEX

AXLE SHAFT

REPLACE

H2

1. Raise and support vehicle, then remove tire and wheel assembly.
2. Insert suitable drift through brake caliper and into brake rotor.
3. While holding rotor in place, remove hub nut and washer.
4. Remove drive axle flange to inboard C/V joint drive flange bolts and drift from rotor.
5. Remove stabilizer shaft bolt, spacer and nut from lower control arm.
6. Wrap shop towels around both inner and outer wheel driveshaft boots to prevent damage during removal.
7. Pull axle shaft through lower control arm opening.
8. Reverse procedure to install.

H3

1. Raise and support vehicle, then remove tire and wheel assembly.
2. Remove wheel driveshaft nut and washer.
3. Remove steering knuckle as outlined under "Steering Knuckle, Replace" in "Front Suspension & Steering" section.
4. Release wheel driveshaft by placing a brass drift against tripod housing. Firmly strike brass drift with a hammer to release driveshaft.
5. Remove front wheel driveshaft from vehicle.
6. Reverse procedure to install, noting the following:
   a. Inspect fluid level of front differential.
   b. Tighten to specifications.

DIFFERENTIAL CARRIER

REPLACE

H2

1. Raise and support vehicle, then remove front skid plate.
2. Drain carrier axle lubricant into suitable container.
3. Install plastic tie straps loosely over ends of front stabilizer shaft and under center of each halfshaft bar.
4. Mark relationship of propeller shaft to front axle for installation reference.
5. Remove front propeller shaft retainers.
6. Remove front propeller shaft from front axle yoke and secure it aside.
7. Remove engine oil filter.
8. Remove halfshaft flanges to differential mounting bolts.
9. Remove pitman arm from relay rod, move pitman arm towards lefthand side of vehicle for clearance.
10. Push relay rod forward and up for clearance.
11. Support front differential.
12. Remove front drive axle inner shaft housing nuts, washers and bolts from differential mounting bracket.
13. Disconnect front axle actuator electrical connector.
14. Remove front axle vent hose.
15. Place plastic tie straps around center of halfshaft, contacting only halfshaft bar. Tighten straps to support inner halfshaft ends.
16. Remove upper differential carrier mounting nut, washers and bolt.
17. Remove lower differential carrier mounting nut, washers and bolt.
18. Remove differential carrier.
19. Reverse procedure to install.

H3

1. Remove front and rear engine protection shields.
2. Drain front drive axle fluid into suitable container.
3. Remove front wheel driveshafts as outlined in "Front Wheel Drive Axles" chapter.
4. Remove crossmember to front drive axle mounting bolt.
5. Remove crossmember to frame mounting bolts.
6. Remove crossmember to frame nut.
7. Remove transfer case crossmember.
8. Remove mounting bracket bolts. Support front drive axle using a suitable transmission jack stand.
9. Remove front drive axle.
10. Reverse procedure to install, tighten to specifications.

FRONT PROPELLER SHAFT

REPLACE

1. Place transmission in neutral.
2. Release park brake, if applied.
3. Raise and support vehicle using a suitable lift.
4. Place a matchmark on front universal joint to driveshaft flange.
5. Remove retaining bolts and straps.
6. Remove propeller shaft from front pinion drive flange.
7. Remove propeller shaft retaining bolts.
8. Remove propeller shaft/CV joint from transmission/transfer case flange.
9. Wrap U-Joint bearing caps to ensure bearing caps do not separate from U-Joint using suitable tape or a rubber band.
10. Reverse procedure to install, tighten to specifications.

OUTPUT SHAFT

REPLACE

1. Raise and support vehicle.
2. Remove lefthand drive axle.
3. Remove lower carrier mounting bolt. Pry against lower carrier to provide clearance for output shaft removal.
4. Remove output shaft from case using slide hammer and adapter.
5. Remove deflector and seal from output shaft.
6. Reverse procedure to install. Lubricate and install new seal using suitable seal installer tool.

PINION FLANGE SEAL

REPLACE

H2

1. Raise and support vehicle.
2. Disconnect propeller shaft from axle. Position propeller shaft aside.
3. Measure and record torque required to rotate pinion.
4. Mark pinion stem, pinion nut and companion flange, then record number of exposed thread on pinion stem.
5. Remove pinion nut using companion flange holder/remover tool No. J-8614-01, or equivalent. Four notches on tool should face flange.
6. Remove pinion flange using holder/remover tool.
7. Remove oil seal. **Do not distort or scratch aluminum case.**
8. Reverse procedure to install, noting the following:
   a. Stake new deflector at three new equally spaced positions. **Do not damage seal operating surface.**
   b. Install seal in bore, then seat seal using seal installer tool No. J-36366, or equivalent.

c. Install pinion nut and tighten nut to original position using marks and exposed threads recorded earlier.
d. Measure rotating torque of pinion and compare with torque recorded earlier.
e. Tighten pinion nut until **torque** required to rotate pinion is 3 inch lbs., more than original torque.

H3

1. Raise and support vehicle using a suitable lift.
2. Remove engine protection shields.
3. Remove front propeller shaft as outlined in "Front Propeller Shaft, Replace."
4. Remove brake calipers as outlined in "Disc Brakes" chapter.
5. Measure torque required in order to rotate pinion. Using an inch-pound torque wrench, record torque value for reassembly. This will give combined preload for following components:
   a. Pinion bearings.
   b. Pinion seal.
   c. Carrier bearings.
   d. Axle bearings.
   e. Axle seals.
6. Scribe an alignment line between pinion shaft and pinion yoke.
7. Install tool No. J 8614-01 or equivalent, onto pinion.
8. Remove pinion nut while holding tool No. J 8614-01 or equivalent.
9. Install tool Nos., J 8614-2 and J 8614-3 or equivalent, into tool No. J 8614-01 or equivalent.
10. Remove pinon yoke by turning tool No. J 8614-3 or equivalent, clockwise while holding tool No. J 8614-01 or equivalent.
11. Remove oil seal using a suitable seal removal tool.
12. Remove dust deflector from pinion yoke using a soft-faced hammer.
13. Reverse procedure to install, tighten to specifications.

TIGHTENING SPECIFICATIONS

Year	Component	Torque Ft. Lbs.
H2		
2003–06	Axle Nut	165
	Axle Tube To Bracket	75
	Axle Tube To Carrier	30
	Bracket To Frame	67
	Brake Pipe Support Bracket	13
	Carrier Frame	16
	Carrier Mount	75
	Differential Carrier Shield	25
	Drain Plug	24
	Electric Motor Actuator	15
	Engagement Switch	15
	Halfshaft	58
	Lower Shock Absorber Mount	54
	Outer Tie Rod	46
	Stabilizer Bar Clamp	24
	Stabilizer Link	13
	U-Joint Clamp	15
	Upper Control Arm Stud	75
H3		
2006	Crossmember To Front Drive Axle Bolt	74
	Crossmember To Frame Bolts	118
	Mounting Bracket Bolts	112
	Propeller Shaft/CV Joint Bolts	51
	Strap & Retaining Bolts	18

Wheel Alignment

INDEX

PRELIMINARY INSPECTION

Inspect the following components, adjust, repair or replace as required prior to performing front wheel alignment.

1. Inflate tires to cold specifications.
2. Ensure front tires are of same size, ply rating and load rating.
3. Inspect for excessive wheel bearing endplay.
4. Inspect for worn or damaged spindle ball joints.
5. Inspect steering gear mounting bolts for proper tightness.
6. Inspect radius arm or bent or damaged condition.
7. Inspect radius arm to frame bushings for looseness or wear.
8. Inspect suspension components for wear or damage.

FRONT WHEEL ALIGNMENT

Camber

1. Remove pinned adjusting cam insert.
2. Loosen upper control arm adjusting cam nuts.
3. Rotate cam bolts to required camber specification setting.
4. **On H2 models,** maintain camber setting while tightening cam bolt nuts. **Torque** nuts to 140 ft. lbs.
5. **On H3 models,** maintain camber setting while tightening cam bolt nuts. **Torque** nuts to 114 ft. lbs.
6. **On all models,** ensure toe, camber and caster settings after changing camber and adjust.

Caster

1. Remove pinned adjusting cam insert.
2. Loosen upper control arm adjusting cam nuts.
3. Rotate cam bolts to required caster specification setting.
4. Maintain caster setting while tightening cam bolt nuts. **Torque** nuts to 140 ft. lbs.
5. Ensure toe, camber and caster settings after changing caster and adjust.

Toe-In

1. Measure toe-in.
2. Change length of both tie rod sleeves to effect toe change.
3. Toe-in can be increased or decreased by changing length of tie rod ends. Threaded sleeve is provided for this purpose. When tie rod ends are mounted ahead of steering knuckle they must be decreased in length in order to increase toe-in. When tie rod ends are mounted behind steering knuckle they must be lengthened in order to increase toe-in. After adjusting **torque** tie rod end jam nut to 50–52 ft. lbs.

VEHICLE RIDE HEIGHT

Z Height

H2

1. Lift front bumper of vehicle up approximately 1.5 inches.
2. Gently remove hands and allow vehicle to settle on its own.
3. Repeat this operation twice more for a total of three times.
4. Measure "Z" height, **Fig. 1.**
5. Push front bumper on vehicle down approximately 1.5 inches.
6. Gently remove hands and allow vehicle to rise on its own.
7. Repeat this operation twice more for a total of three times.
8. Measure "Z" height.
9. Find average of high and low measurements. This is "Z" height. "Z" height should be 4.3–4.8 inches.

H3

When adjusting either the righthand or lefthand rear trim height the opposite side trim height will be effected. Trim height should be measured with a full tank of gas and zero passengers or cargo. An alignment hoist should be inspected periodically to assure that both runners are the same height off the ground, side-to-side and front-to-rear.

1. Place vehicle on an alignment rack.
2. Set tire air pressure to proper pressure.
3. Manually lift rear of vehicle up approximately 1½ inch, gently remove hands and let vehicle settle.
4. Repeat above step two more times for a total of three times.
5. Measure distance between lowest point of ball joint and center of front side of lower control arm mounting bolt using tool No. J 42854 or equivalent.
6. Manually push rear of vehicle down approximately 1½ inch, gently remove hands and let vehicle settle.
7. Repeat above step two more times for a total of three times.
8. Measure both righthand and lefthand sides of vehicle to specifications of 6 inches.

D Height

H2

Use the procedure used in determining the "Z" height. "D" height should be the average of the high and low measurements.

H3

Use the procedure used in determining the "Z" height. "D" height should be 6.7 inches.

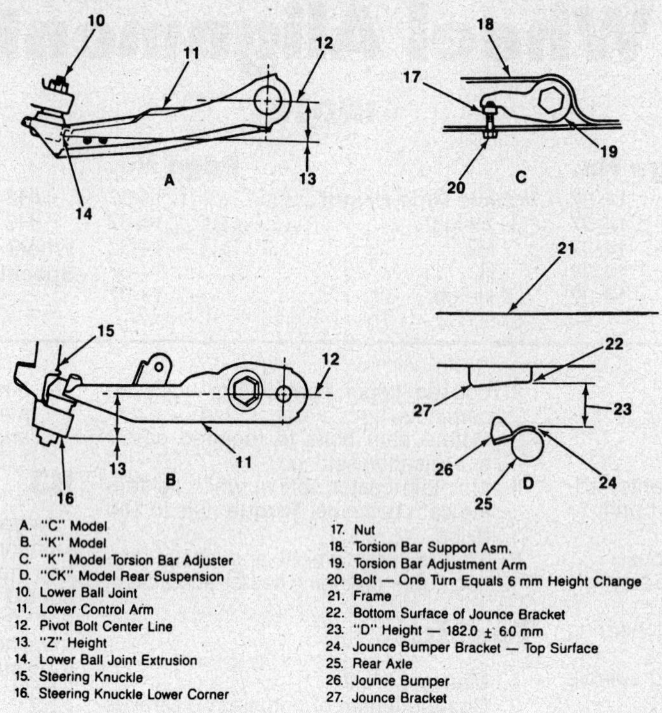
10
11
12
13
14
A
18
17
19
20
C
21
15
12
22
27
23
13
11
B
16
26
D
24
25
A. "C" Model
B. "K" Model
C. "K" Model Torsion Bar Adjuster
D. "CK" Model Rear Suspension
10. Lower Ball Joint
11. Lower Control Arm
12. Pivot Bolt Center Line
13. "Z" Height
14. Lower Ball Joint Extrusion
15. Steering Knuckle
16. Steering Knuckle Lower Corner
17. Nut
18. Torsion Bar Support Asm.
19. Torsion Bar Adjustment Arm
20. Bolt — One Turn Equals 6 mm Height Change
21. Frame
22. Bottom Surface of Jounce Bracket
23. "D" Height — 182.0 ± 6.0 mm
24. Jounce Bumper Bracket — Top Surface
25. Rear Axle
26. Jounce Bumper
27. Jounce Bracket
GC2048800009000X

Fig. 1 Z height. H2

VUE

NOTE: Refer To Back Of This Manual For Vehicle Manufacturers Special Tool Suppliers.

INDEX OF SERVICE OPERATIONS

Specifications

GENERAL ENGINE SPECIFICATIONS

Year	Engine Liter	Fuel System	Bore & Stroke (Millimeters)	Comp. Ratio	Horsepower @ RPM	Torque, Ft. Lbs. @ RPM	Normal Oil Pressure, psi
2002–03	2.2L	SPFI	3.39 x 3.72	10.0	140 @ 5600	150 @ 4000	50–80③
	3.0L	SPFI	3.39 x 2.34	10.1	182 @ 6000	184 @ 3600	50–80①
2004–06	2.2L	SPFI	3.39 x 3.72	10.0	140 @ 5600	150 @ 4000	50–80③
	3.5L	SPFI	3.50 x 3.66	10.0	250 @ 5800	242 @ 4500	71②

① — At 4000 RPM.

② — At 3000 RPM.

③ — At 1000 RPM.

TUNE UP SPECIFICATIONS

The following specifications are published from the latest information available. This data should only be used in the absence of a decal affixed in the engine compartment.

Year & Engine	Spark Plug Gap	Ignition Timing BTDC				Curb Idle Speed		Fast Idle Speed		Fuel Pump Pressure psi.	Valve Lash, Inch
		Firing Order	Man. Trans.	Auto. Trans.	Mark Location	Man. Trans.	Auto. Trans.	Man. Trans.	Auto. Trans.		
2002–03											
2.2L	.045	②	①	①	—	①	①	①	①	50–60	④
3.0L	.039	③	—	①	—	①	①	①	①	50–60	④
2004–06											
2.2L	.045	②	①	①	—	①	①	①	①	50–60	④
3.5L	.051	1-4-2-5-3-6	⑤	⑤	—	⑥	⑥	①	①	50–60	④

① — Computer controlled and not adjustable.

② — Firing order, 1-3-4-2.

③ — Firing order, 1-2-3-4-5-6.

④ — Equipped with hydraulic lash adjusters.

⑤ — 8–12 BTDC at 680–780 RPM.

⑥ — 680–780 RPM.

FRONT WHEEL ALIGNMENT SPECIFICATIONS

Year	Models	Side	Caster Angle, Degrees②		Camber Angles, Degrees③		Toe, Degrees①		Steering Angle, Degrees	
			Limits	Desired	Limits	Desired	Limits	Desired	Inner Wheel	Outer Wheel
2002–03	All	All	+2.6 to +3.4	+3	-1 to -.2	-.6	+1 to +.3	+.2	—	—
2004–06	Except Redline	Righthand	2.15 to 3.65	2.90	-1.35 to +.15	-.6	+.30 to .0	+.15	-2.50 to +2.50	-2.50 to +2.50
		Lefthand	2.40 to 3.90	3.15	-1.35 to +.15	-.6	+.30 to .0	+.15	-2.50 to +2.50	-2.50 to +2.50
	Redline	Righthand	3.85 to 2.35	3.10	-1.65 to -.15	-.90	+.30 to .0	+.15	-2.50 to +2.50	-2.50 to +2.50
		Lefthand	2.60 to 4.10	3.35	-1.65 to -.15	-.90	+.30 to .0	+.15	-2.50 to +2.50	-2.50 to +2.50

① — Toe-In (+). Toe-Out (–).

② — Cross caster, -.5° to +1.0°; Desired, .25°.

③ — Cross camber, -.75° to +.75°; Desired, 0°.

REAR WHEEL ALIGNMENT SPECIFICATIONS

Year	Model	Camber Angle, Degrees		Total Toe, Degrees①
		Limits	Desired	
2002–03	All	-.55 to -.45	-.05	-.20 to +.20
2004–06	All	-1.10 to .40	-.35	.0 to .50

① — Toe-In (+). Toe-Out (-).

FLUID CAPACITIES & COOLING SYSTEM DATA

Year	Engine Liter	Cooling System Capacity Qts.			Radiator Cap Relief Pressure, Lbs.	Thermo. Opening Temp. °F	Fuel Tank, Gals.	Engine Oil Refill, Qts.	Transaxle Oil		Transfer Case, Pts.	Axle Pts.
		Man. Trans.	Auto. Trans.	Coolant Type					Manual Trans., Pts.	Auto. Trans., Qts.①		Rear
2002–03	2.2L	7.40	7.40	Dexcool	13–17	186	15.5	5②	3.6	④	1.06	1.59
	3.0L	8.45	8.45	Dexcool	13–17	186	15.5	5②	—	③	1.06	1.59
2004–06	2.2L	7.40	7.40	Dexcool	13–17	194	16.5	5②	—	④	1.06	1.59
	3.5L	9.7	9.7	Dexcool	13–17	194	16.5	4.5②	—	⑤	1.14	1.59

① — Approximate. Make final inspection w/dipstick.

② — Includes filter.

③ — Fluid change, 4.2 qts.; after overhaul, 7.5 qts.

④ — Fluid change, 6.9 qts.; after overhaul, 8.1 qts.

⑤ — Fluid change, 6.9 qts.; after overhaul, 9.5 qts.

LUBRICANT DATA

Year	Model	Lubricant Type						
		Transmission		Hydraulic Clutch Fluid	Transfer Case	Drive Axle	Power Steering	Brake System
		Manual	Automatic					
2002–06	All	Dexron III	Dexron III	—	①	①	—	DOT 3

① — Use Versa-Tank fluid, Part No. 12378514.

Electrical

NOTE: On Air Bag Equipped Models, Refer To "Air Bag System Precautions" Located In The Front Of This Manual For System Disarming & Arming Procedures.

NOTE: Refer To "Computer Relearn Procedures" Located In The Front Of This Manual When Battery Power To The Computer Has Been Interrupted.

INDEX

PRECAUTIONS

Air Bag Systems

Refer to "Air Bag System Precautions" in the front of this manual for system disarming and arming procedures.

Battery Ground Cable

Prior to service disconnect battery ground cable and isolate as required.

FUSE PANEL LOCATION

The engine compartment fuse block is located at the lefthand rear corner engine compartment. The instrument panel fuse block is located in the center of instrument panel, on the righthand front side of the center console.

RELAY CENTER LOCATION

The relay center is located at the lefthand rear corner engine compartment.

FUEL PUMP RELAY LOCATION

The fuel pump relay is located in the relay center. Refer to "Relay Center Location."

STARTER

REPLACE

2.2L Engine

1. Raise and support vehicle.
2. Disconnect electrical connectors and position aside.
3. Remove mounting bolts and starter.
4. Reverse procedure to install. **Torque** starter mounting bolts to 30 ft. lbs.

3.0L Engine

1. Raise and support vehicle.
2. Disconnect electrical connectors and position aside.
3. Remove upper starter assembly to engine block bolt.
4. Move starter right, clearing engine block, then lefthand and out of engine block.
5. Reverse procedure to install. **Torque** starter mounting bolts to 26 ft. lbs.

3.5L Engine

1. Remove B+ battery cable nut at starter.
2. Remove S-terminal connector.
3. Remove lower starer assembly to transmission bolt and oxygen sensor connector bracket.
4. Remove upper starter assembly to transmission bolt.
5. Remove starter.
6. Reverse procedure to install. **Torque** starter mounting bolts to 33 ft. lbs.

ALTERNATOR

REPLACE

2.2L Engine

1. Remove throttle body air duct and accessory drive belt.
2. Disconnect alternator electrical connectors.
3. Remove mounting bolts and alternator.
4. Reverse procedure to install. **Torque** alternator mounting bolts to 16 ft. lbs.

3.0L Engine

1. Remove accessory drive belt and belt tensioner.
2. Remove belt tensioner to engine block bolts, then the tensioner.
3. Disconnect alternator electrical connections, then remove upper alternator to engine block bolts.
4. Raise and support vehicle.
5. Turn steering wheel towards righthand side to access lower alternator bolt.
6. Remove lower alternator bolt. Lower vehicle.
7. Separate alternator from engine block.
8. Disconnect electrical connectors and remove alternator.
9. Reverse procedure to install. **Torque** alternator mounting bolts to 26 ft. lbs.

3.5L Engine

1. Remove air cleaner assembly.
2. Remove accessory drive belt tensioner.
3. Install engine support fixture.
4. Remove front of engine mount throughbolt and raise engine for proper clearance.
5. Disconnect alternator electrical connections.
6. Remove alternator to engine block bolts and alternator.
7. Reverse procedure to install. **Torque** alternator mounting bolts to 33 ft. lbs.

COIL PACK

REPLACE

2.2L Engine

1. Remove accelerator cable from bracket, then the cable bracket.
2. Disconnect ignition module electrical connector.
3. Remove mounting screws and electronic ignition module.
4. Remove mounting bolts and coil pack.
5. Reverse procedure to install, noting the following:
    a. **Torque** coil pack bolts to 89 inch lbs.
    b. **Torque** electronic ignition module mounting screws to 13 inch lbs.

3.0L Engine

1. Turn ignition switch to Off position.
2. Remove upper intake manifold runner as outlined under "Intake Manifold, Replace" in "3.0L Engine" section.
3. Disconnect electrical connector, then remove ignition coil and gasket.
4. Reverse procedure to install. **Torque** ignition module to 71 inch lbs.

3.5L Engine

RIGHTHAND

1. Disconnect electrical connectors.
2. Remove engine coil bolts.
3. Remove engine coils.
4. Reverse procedure to install. **Torque** ignition module to 106 inch lbs.
5.

LEFTHAND

1. Remove air cleaner outlet duct assembly.
2. Disconnect electrical connectors.
3. Remove engine coil bolts.
4. Remove engine coils.
5. Reverse procedure to install. **Torque**-ignition module to 106 inch lbs.

IGNITION LOCK

REPLACE

1. Disable air bag system as outlined under "Air Bag System" chapter.

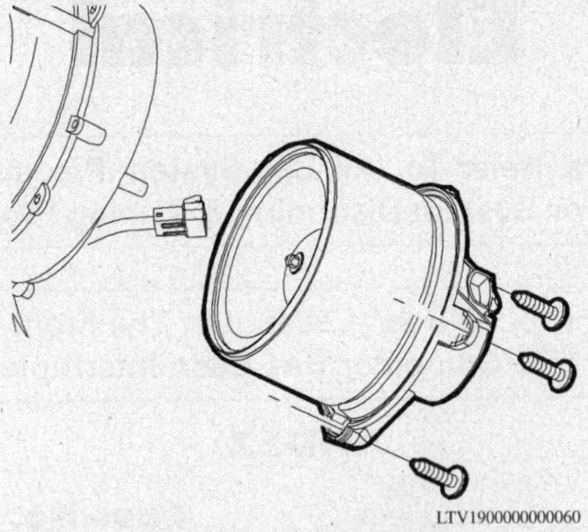

Fig. 1 Blower motor replacement

2. Remove upper steering column covers, then the lower steering column cover screws.
3. Lower steering column adjusting handle, then remove lefthand right lower steering column covers.
4. Turn ignition lock cylinder to RUN position.
5. Depress locking retainers through housing access hole, then remove lock cylinder.
6. Reverse procedure to install.

IGNITION SWITCH

REPLACE

1. Remove steering column upper shroud.
2. Remove ignition switch retainers, then the switch.
3. Disconnect electrical connector from ignition switch.
4. Reverse procedure to install.

CLUTCH START SWITCH

REPLACE

1. Remove lower instrument panel closeout panel.
2. Remove clutch start switch from clutch pedal assembly by sliding it upward.
3. Disconnect clutch start switch connector from switch.
4. Reverse procedure to install.

TRANSAXLE RANGE SWITCH

REPLACE

1. Remove battery cover, then disconnect cables.
2. Loosen battery hold down screws, then remove battery.
3. Remove underhood fuse block cover, then the positive battery cable and electronic power steering wire from terminal at fuse block.
4. Open all retainer clips, then remove all cables, lines and harnesses from battery cooling box.
5. Remove fuse block connector retaining bolts, then the block from housing. Disconnect electrical connector.
6. Pull inlet duct away , then remove battery cooling box.
7. Remove battery tray bracket, then the control cable from transaxle range switch lever.
8. Remove transaxle range switch lever nut and lever.
9. Reverse procedure to install.

HEADLAMP SWITCH

REPLACE

Refer to "Multi-Function Switch, Replace" for replacement procedure.

STOP LIGHT SWITCH

REPLACE

1. Disconnect electrical connectors from stop lamp switch.
2. Rotate stop lamp switch counterclockwise, then remove switch from switch retainer.
3. Compress locking tabs on switch retainer and remove switch retainer from brake pedal assembly.
4. Reverse procedure to install.

MULTI-FUNCTION SWITCH

REPLACE

1. Remove steering column covers.
2. Disconnect multi-function and headlamp/turn signal connectors.
3. Remove multi-function and headlamp/turn from steering column.
4. Reverse procedure to install.

TURN SIGNAL SWITCH

REPLACE

Refer to "Multi-Function Switch, Replace" for replacement procedure.

STEERING WHEEL

REPLACE

1. Remove driver air bag module as outlined in "Air Bag System" chapter.
2. **On models equipped with cruise control,** disconnect switch connector from steering column.
3. **On all models,** remove steering wheel nut.
4. Remove steering wheel using tool No. J-42578 and J 1859–A or equivalents.
5. Reverse procedure to install. **Torque** steering wheel nut to 30 ft. lbs.

INSTRUMENT CLUSTER

REPLACE

1. Disable air bag system as outlined under "Air Bag System" chapter.
2. Place steering column in lowest position, then remove cluster trim panel screws and pull out panel.
3. Remove retainers from cluster, then pull rearward to remove cluster. Disconnect electrical connector.
4. Reverse procedure to install.

RADIO

REPLACE

1. Set park brake, then move shifter to neutral position.
2. Starting at most forward end, pull up and remove bezel. Disconnect electrical connectors.
3. Remove instrument panel storage compartment screws and storage compartment.
4. Starting at bottom, pull to disengage trim bezel clips and disconnect HVAC control head connections.
5. Disconnect electrical connectors from bezel mounted switches and remove center trim bezel.
6. Remove radio screws, then disconnect radio electrical connectors and antenna.
7. Disconnect ground strap and remove radio from vehicle.
8. Reverse procedure to install.

WIPER MOTOR

REPLACE

1. Open hood to access wiper arm nut and remove.
2. Lift wiper arm assembly away from windshield, then remove wiper arm from pivot shaft.
3. Remove retainers, then the air inlet grilles from vehicle.
4. Remove wiper module bolts, then lift wiper motor module away from cowl.
5. Disconnect wire harness rosebud clip from wiper module frame then the electrical connector at motor.
6. Reverse procedure to install. **Torque** wiper motor module mounting bolts to 108 inch lbs., and wiper arm mounting nuts to 20 ft. lbs.

WIPER TRANSMISSION

REPLACE

Refer to "Wiper Motor, Replace" for wiper motor transmission replacement procedure.

BLOWER MOTOR

REPLACE

1. Disconnect electrical connector from blower motor.
2. Remove blower motor from HVAC module, **Fig. 1.**
3. Reverse procedure to install. **Torque** blower motor retaining screws to 108 inch lbs.

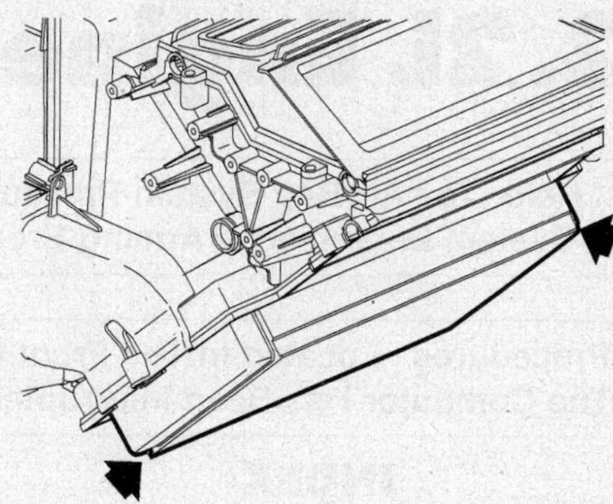

Fig. 2 Heater core replacement

CABIN AIR FILTER

REPLACE

1. Remove push pins from air filter access panel.
2. Remove air filter panel, then the air filter from housing.
3. Reverse procedure to install.

HEATER CORE

REPLACE

1. Disable air bag system as outlined under "Air Bag System" chapter.
2. Recover refrigerant as outlined under "Air Conditioning" chapter.
3. Drain engine coolant into a suitable container, then remove suction and liquid lines at TXV. Cap suction lines.
4. Disconnect TXV temperature sensor connector, then remove inlet and outlet heater hoses from heater core.
5. Remove instrument panel as outlined under "Dash Panel Service" chapter.
6. Remove screws, then the console and disconnect shifter cable from control assembly pin.
7. Remove shifter cable retainer clip, then the cable from control assembly. Discard clip.
8. Disconnect park lock cable assembly from pin on control assembly.
9. Depress tab on park lock cable, then remove cable from control assembly. Discard park lock cable clip.
10. Remove indicator bulb by rotating bulb a quarter turn and pulling out then disconnect electrical connectors.
11. Remove nuts, then the control assembly, transaxle control bracket and bolts.
12. Remove front rear duct by sliding forward on heater duct then up at rear and then rearward.
13. Remove auxiliary duct assembly then disconnect harnesses at blower motor and blower motor resistor connectors.
14. Disconnect instrument panel harness at HVAC module connectors.
15. Remove defroster duct to HVAC module nuts and defroster duct.
16. Remove lefthand HVAC module to cross vehicle beam bracket from HVAC module and cross vehicle beam.
17. Remove remaining HVAC module to cross vehicle beam and front of dash retainers, then the HVAC module.
18. Remove TXV to backing plate attaching bolts, then the TXV and backing plate.
19. Remove O-rings from evaporator pipes and caps to prevent system contamination.
20. Remove HVAC module front of dash seal, then the heater duct.
21. Disconnect HVAC module harness from mode actuators, then remove panel, defrost and floor mode actuators.
22. Remove heater core cover, then the heater core pipe cover, pipe seal and heater core, **Fig. 2.**
23. Remove evaporator cover assembly, pipe retainer and evaporator core.
24. Reverse procedure to install.

EVAPORATOR CORE

REPLACE

Refer to "Heater Core, Replace," for replacement procedure.

2.2L Engine

NOTE: On Air Bag Equipped Models, Refer To "Air Bag System Precautions" Located In The Front Of This Manual For System Disarming & Arming Procedures.

NOTE: Refer To "Computer Relearn Procedures" Located In The Front Of This Manual When Battery Power To The Computer Has Been Interrupted.

INDEX

PRECAUTIONS

Air Bag Systems

Refer to "Air Bag System Precautions" in the front of this manual for system disarming and arming procedures.

Battery Ground Cable

Prior to service, disconnect battery ground cable and isolate as required.

Fuel System Pressure Relief

1. Connect tool No. 34730–1A, or equivalent, to fuel pressure connection.
2. Place end of bleed hose into suitable container and open valve to bleed system pressure.
3. Remove gauge and replace cap.

COMPRESSION PRESSURE

1. Start and run engine until it reaches normal operating temperature.
2. Turn engine off, disconnect ignition module wiring and remove spark plugs.
3. Install suitable compression gauge tool in spark plug hole.
4. Ensure battery is charged and throttle is fully open.
5. Crank engine through four compression strokes for each cylinder.
6. Lowest reading cylinder should be within 70% of highest.
7. No cylinder should read less than 100 psi.
8. Place shop towel over spark plug holes and crank engine a few seconds without compression gauge or spark plugs installed.
9. Repeat compression measuring steps on all cylinders.

ENGINE MOUNT

REPLACE

1. Disconnect intake air temperature sensor connector, then loosen clamp at the cleaner assembly.
2. Remove outlet resonator duct from air cleaner, then loosen clamp at throttle body assembly and disconnect PCV hose.
3. Remove retaining bolts, then the air cleaner.
4. Place a jack with a wood block under engine oil pan to support powertrain.
5. Remove engine mount to bracket fasteners.
6. Remove engine mount to body mounting bolts, **Fig. 1.**
7. Remove engine mount.
8. Reverse procedure to install.

ENGINE

REPLACE

1. Disconnect intake air temperature sensor connector, then loosen clamp at the cleaner assembly.
2. Remove outlet resonator duct from air cleaner, then loosen clamp at throttle body assembly and disconnect PCV hose.
3. Remove retaining bolts, then the air cleaner.
4. Remove any dirt around throttle body, intake manifold and cylinder head.
5. Remove underhood fuse block cover, then the inner fuse cover and loosen connectors through bolts at top of fuse block.
6. Remove battery and electronic power steering feed wire connection nut, then the wire from fuse block stud.
7. Disconnect electrical connectors fuse block and remove from vehicle.
8. Remove battery cable and harness attachment clips on battery tray and fuse block bracket assembly.
9. Remove main connectors from fuse block housing, then lay battery positive cable wire over engine.
10. Remove electrical harness clips on battery tray, then the fuse block and battery tray.
11. Disconnect electrical connectors at transaxle connector, then remove engine to body ground bolt.
12. Disconnect connector for rear O2 sensor, then remove vacuum hose with check valve from booster and lay on engine.
13. Disconnect eight-way electrical connector, then remove main engine harness Gray connector and lay over engine.
14. **Do not remove shifter cable from bracket before removing cable from transaxle range switch. Damage to manual shift linkage may occur.**
15. **On models equipped with automatic transaxle,** pry out shifter cable from transaxle range switch.
16. **On models equipped with manual transaxle,** proceed as follows:
    a. Pry out shift lever cables from shift control housing and shift lever cable bracket using Tool No.

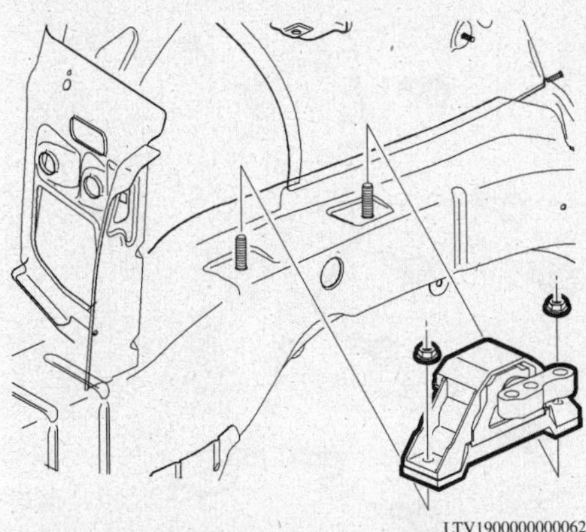

Fig. 1 Engine mount replacement

J–36346 or equivalent.
 b. Disconnect pressure line from clutch actuator cylinder.
 c. Disconnect back-up lamp switch and front wheel speed sensor.
17. **On all models,** drain engine coolant into a suitable container and disconnect upper and lower radiator hoses.
18. Disconnect hoses from surge tank, then heater hoses from heater core.
19. Relieve fuel system pressure as outlined under "Precautions."
20. Disconnect fuel line transfer line at quick connect from fuel line using tool No. SA9805E or equivalent.
21. Disconnect purge hoses at rear of purge solenoid, then remove headlamp assemblies.
22. Secure radiator and condenser fan assembly to radiator support assembly.
23. Raise and support vehicle, then remove front wheels and wheel inner splash shields.
24. Install a piece of hardwood 1 x 2 x 4 between transaxle case and engine cradle assembly.
25. Install a piece of hardwood 1 x 2 x 4 between engine oil pan and engine cradle assembly near crankshaft.
26. Remove accessory drive belt, using tool No. J-44811 or equivalent.
27. Disconnect electrical connectors A/C compressor, remove bolts and support with straps.
28. Remove pushpin retainers from air deflector assembly to cradle.
29. Drain transaxle fluid.
30. **On models equipped with automatic transaxle,** disconnect transaxle lines from transaxle.
31. **On all models,** remove exhaust pipe to manifold flange bolts, then the exhaust pipe to intermediate pipe nuts.
32. Remove converter pipe assembly and support intermediate pipe assembly.
33. **On models equipped with AWD,** proceed as follows:
 a. Remove propshaft bolts to power takeoff unit, then the propshaft bolts at rear axle assembly.
 b. Remove propshaft support bracket to body bolts, then the propshaft assembly.
34. **On models equipped with automatic transaxle,** remove shifter cable from bracket assembly.
35. **On all models,** remove steering gear to intermediate shaft bolt, then the tie rod to knuckle nuts.
36. Separate tie rod assemblies from knuckle assemblies using tool No. SA91100C or equivalent.
37. Remove lower control arm cotter pins and nuts to knuckle assembly, then separate using tool No. J–43828 or equivalent.
38. Remove lower stabilizer link nuts to stabilizer bar, then the lefthand axle shaft assembly from transaxle.
39. Disconnect righthand shaft assembly from intermediate drive shaft using tool No. J–45341 or equivalent.
40. Lower vehicle, remove righthand engine mount to engine bracket bolts. Engine should rest on wood blocks.
41. Remove lefthand transaxle mount to transaxle bolts, transaxle should rest on wood blocks.
42. Raise and support engine. **During powertrain removal support vehicle body by placing a jack at rear of vehicle.**
43. Position engine support table, then fully raise table to contact with powertrain assembly.
44. Remove cradle to body retaining bolts.
45. Lower engine table, then raise body on hoist until powertrain and cradle assembly is free from vehicle.
46. Reverse procedure to install.

INTAKE MANIFOLD

REPLACE

1. Disconnect intake air temperature sensor connector, then loosen clamp at the cleaner assembly.
2. Remove outlet resonator duct from air cleaner, then loosen clamp at throttle body assembly and disconnect PCV hose.
3. Remove retaining bolts, then the air cleaner.
4. Remove any dirt around throttle body, intake manifold and cylinder head.
5. Disconnect harness connector at throttle body, then remove bolts, throttle body and gasket.
6. Cover intake manifold opening with a clean shop towel.
7. Remove engine control module bolts and set ECM aside.
8. Disconnect electrical connectors from side of manifold and set aside.
9. Disconnect manifold absolute pressure sensor, then the purge hose.
10. Disconnect electrical attachment bolt at bottom of manifold, then raise and support vehicle.
11. Disconnect electrical harness clips at bottom of manifold and lower vehicle.
12. Remove oil level tube bolt and rotate tube away from manifold.
13. Remove intake manifold bolts and nuts, then pull away from cylinder head.
14. Disconnect brake booster hose at manifold, then remove intake manifold from vehicle. Discard gasket.
15. Reverse procedure to install.

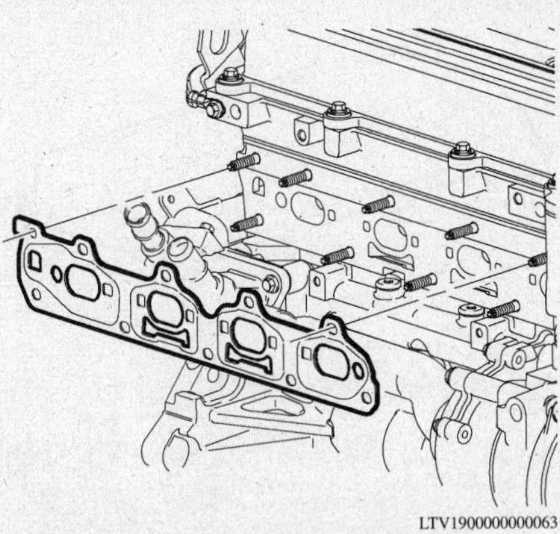

Fig. 2 Exhaust manifold replacement

EXHAUST MANIFOLD

REPLACE

1. Disconnect intake air temperature sensor connector, then loosen clamp at the cleaner assembly.
2. Remove outlet resonator duct from air cleaner, then loosen clamp at throttle body assembly and disconnect PCV hose.
3. Remove retaining bolts, then the air cleaner.
4. Remove exhaust manifold heat shield, then disconnect O2 sensor and remove using tool No. J-39194-C or equivalent.
5. Raise and support vehicle, then remove exhaust pipe to manifold and pipe to resonator nuts.
6. Remove exhaust manifold pipe to resonator pipe nuts behind the converter, then disconnect rear O2 sensor wire from heat shield.
7. Separate exhaust manifold pipe and resonator pipe. Discard gaskets.
8. Remove exhaust manifold assembly and discard gasket, **Fig. 2.**
9. Reverse procedure to install.

CYLINDER HEAD

REPLACE

1. Disconnect intake air temperature sensor connector, then loosen clamp at the cleaner assembly.
2. Remove outlet resonator duct from air cleaner, then loosen clamp at throttle body assembly and disconnect PCV hose.
3. Remove retaining bolts, then the air cleaner.
4. Remove ignition module assembly, then disconnect ECM electrical connector and ground.
5. Remove oil dipstick bolt to manifold, then disconnect electrical connector from throttle body.
6. Disconnect electrical connector from fuel injector harness, then the attachment at bottom of intake manifold.
7. Disconnect electrical connectors from purge solenoid and MAP sensor, then brake booster vacuum hose.
8. Disconnect coolant pipe bracket bolts

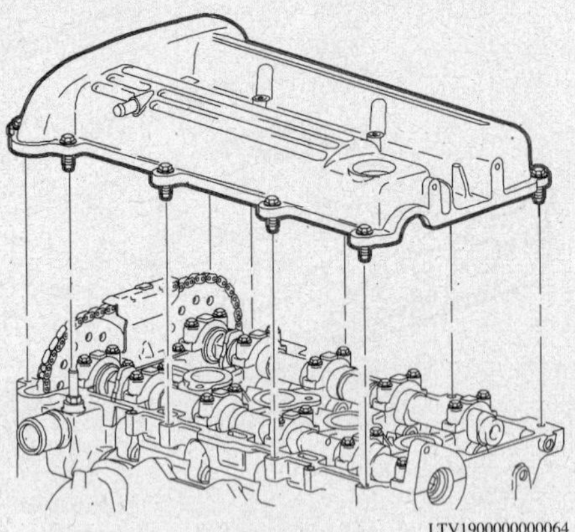

Fig. 3 Cam cover assembly removal

to front of cylinder head, then the hose at clamp from cylinder head and unclip from fuel rail.

9. Disconnect ground strap from rear of cam cover assembly.
10. Relieve fuel system as outlined under "Precautions."
11. Disconnect fuel rail bracket and bolt at the rear cam cover.
12. While supporting fuel rail assembly, loosen transfer line fitting at fuel rail.
13. Position fuel line away from cam cover assembly, then remove cam cover assembly. **Fig. 3.**
14. Locate No. 1 piston to approximately 60° before top dead center, diamond shaped hole on intake camshaft sprocket at 12 o'clock position and remove spark plugs.
15. Remove upper timing chain guide, **Fig. 4.**
16. Remove timing chain tensioner, then the fixed timing chain guide access plug.
17. Remove upper fixed guide bolt.
18. Install engine support fixture, then remove righthand engine mount assembly and bracket.
19. Raise and support vehicle, then remove righthand side wheel and splash shield.
20. Install block of wood between oil pan and cradle, then remove accessory drive belt.
21. Remove tensioner bolt through access hole at engine rail, then the tensioner assembly.
22. Remove crankshaft balancer pulley bolt and pulley using tool No. J–38122–A or equivalent. Discard the pulley bolt.
23. Remove front cover assembly bolts, then lower water pump assembly bolt.
24. Remove front cover assembly and gasket, **Fig. 5.**
25. Remove adjustable guide bolt, then the lower fixed guide.
26. Use a 24 mm wrench to hold camshaft assembly, then remove bolt and exhaust sprocket. Discard bolt.
27. Remove adjustable guide through top of cylinder head.
28. Use a 24 mm wrench to hold camshaft assembly, then remove bolt and intake sprocket. Discard bolt.

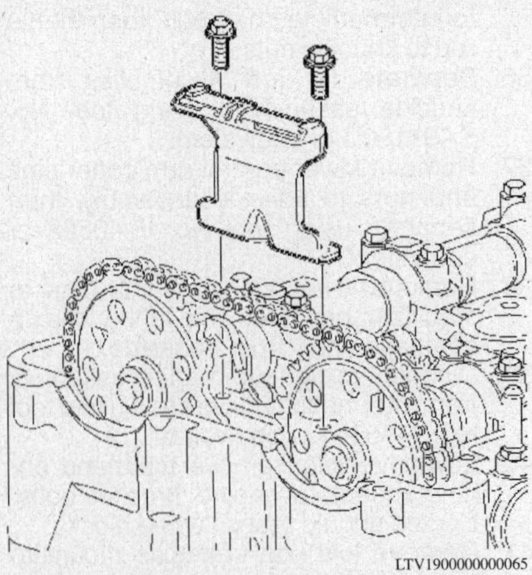

Fig. 4 Upper timing chain guide removal

29. Remove timing chain assembly through top of cylinder head, **Fig. 6.**
30. Remove timing chain drive sprocket from crankshaft, then the timing chain oiler nozzle and bolt.
31. **Replace timing chain guides if wear exceeds .045 inch.**
32. Support engine at center of pan using floor jack and block of wood.
33. Remove engine three bar engine support fixture for access.
34. Remove cylinder head bolts in sequence, **Fig. 7.**
35. Remove cylinder head from block with exhaust and intake manifold attached.
36. Reverse procedure to install noting the following:
    a. Use new cylinder head bolts.
    b. **Torque** cylinder head bolts in sequence, **Fig. 8,** to 22 ft. lbs., and an additional 155°.
    c. Coat front cylinder head crankcase bolts with Permatex Threadlocker Blue P/N 21485278, or equivalent.
    d. **Torque** cylinder head front chain case bolts to 24 ft. lbs., **Fig. 9.**

VALVE ADJUSTMENT

This engine is equipped with hydraulic lifters and no adjustment is required.

VALVE GUIDES

Valve guides are an integral part of the cylinder head and are pressed in. If valve stem clearance becomes excessive, the valve guides must be hand reamed to the oversize using valve guide reamer tool J-42096, or equivalent. Service valves are available in standard and .003 inch oversize.

FRONT COVER

REPLACE

Refer to "Cylinder Head, Replace" for replacement procedure.

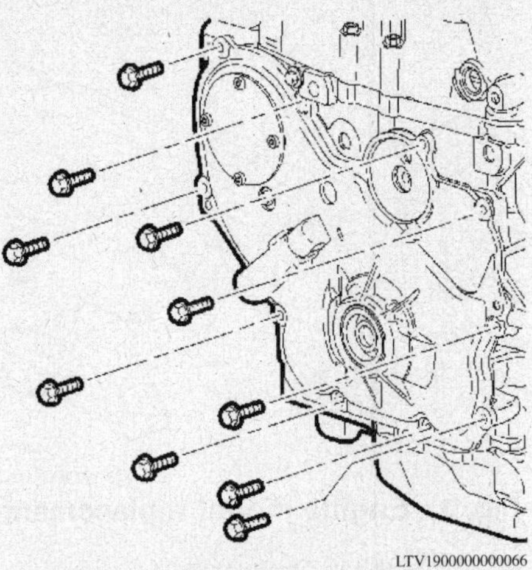

Fig. 5 Engine front cover bolts removal

TIMING CHAIN

REPLACE

Refer to "Cylinder Head, Replace" for replacement procedure.

CAMSHAFT

REPLACE

1. Disconnect intake air temperature sensor connector, then loosen clamp at the cleaner assembly.
2. Remove outlet resonator duct from air cleaner, then loosen clamp at throttle body assembly and disconnect PCV hose.
3. Remove retaining bolts, then the air cleaner.
4. Remove ignition module assembly, then disconnect ECM electrical connector and ground.
5. Remove oil dipstick bolt to manifold, then disconnect electrical connector from throttle body.
6. Disconnect electrical connector from fuel injector harness, then the attachment at bottom of intake manifold.
7. Disconnect electrical connectors from purge solenoid and MAP sensor, then brake booster vacuum hose.
8. Disconnect coolant pipe bracket bolts to front of cylinder head, then the hose at clamp from cylinder head and unclip from fuel rail.
9. Disconnect ground strap from rear of cam cover assembly.
10. Relieve fuel system as outlined under "Precautions."
11. Disconnect fuel rail bracket and bolt at the rear cam cover.
12. While supporting fuel rail assembly, loosen transfer line fitting at fuel rail.
13. Position fuel line away from cam cover assembly, then remove cam cover assembly. **Fig. 3.**
14. Locate No. 1 piston to approximately 60° before top dead center, diamond shaped hole on intake camshaft sprocket at 12 o'clock position and remove spark plugs.
15. Remove upper timing chain guide, **Fig. 4.**

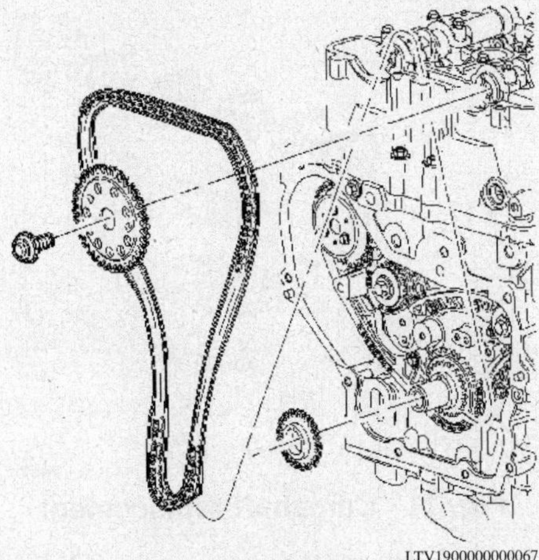

Fig. 6 Timing chain assembly removal

16. Remove front camshaft caps. **Lubricate sprocket pins with clean motor oil. This will allow sprockets to easily slide on sprocket pins.**
17. Install J–43655 or equivalent, through sprocket holes from timing side of sprocket towards rear of engine **Fig. 10.**
18. With guide pin installed in sprocket, align guide pins into slots on support plate. Tighten support plate to 89 inch lbs.
19. Hold each camshaft in place using a 24 mm open end wrench, then remove camshaft sprocket timing retaining bolts and washers. Discard torque to yield bolts.
20. Slide camshaft sprockets away from camshafts.
21. After camshaft is disengaged from sprocket, rotate camshaft using a 24 mm wrench to a neutral position to release spring tension.
22. Uniformly loosen, then remove remaining camshaft bearing cap bolts.
23. Carefully pull camshafts straight up to avoid damaging cylinder head thrust surfaces, **Fig. 11.**
24. Reverse procedure to install.

PISTON & ROD ASSEMBLY

Install the piston onto the connecting rod with the arrow pointed toward the front of the engine.

PISTONS, PINS & RINGS

Replace any pistons that show signs of damage or excessive wear. Piston pin bores and pins must be free of varnish or scuffing. Use an outside micrometer to measure the piston contact areas and piston pin bore. Subtract the measurement of the piston pin bore from the piston pin.

MAIN & ROD BEARINGS

1. Install crankshaft bearing caps using

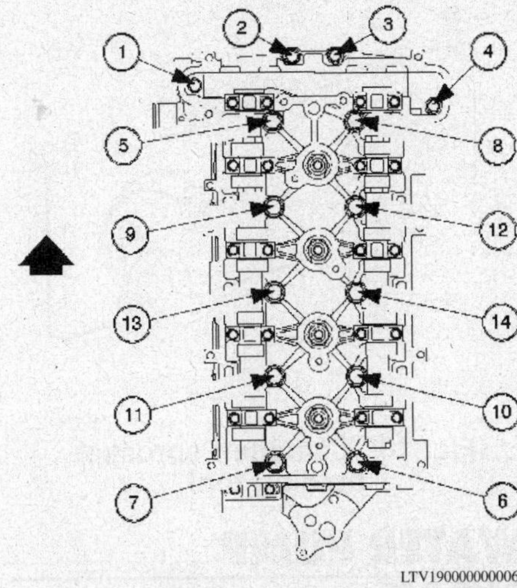

Fig. 7 Cylinder head loosening sequence

suitable brass, lead, leather, or equivalent soft-faced mallet. **Do not use lower crankcase bolts to pull bearing caps into seats.**

2. **Torque** lower crankcase inner bolts to 15 ft. lbs., in sequence, **Fig. 12.**
3. **Torque** lower crankcase outer bolt to 18 ft. lbs., in sequence, **Fig. 13.**

CRANKSHAFT REAR OIL SEAL

REPLACE

1. Remove transaxle as outlined in **MOTOR's "Domestic Transmission, In-Vehicle Service" or "Transmission Service DVD."**
2. Remove flywheel and cover.
3. Insert suitable screwdriver into pry tangs of seal carrier and remove seal.
4. Apply suitable clean engine oil to seal lip and inside diameter of seal carrier.
5. Install seal using seal installer tool No. J-42067, or equivalent.
6. Install transaxle and flywheel.

OIL PAN

REPLACE

1. Remove oil dipstick assembly, then the oil level tube.
2. Install a suitable engine support fixture, then remove righthand side engine mount.
3. Raise engine approximately three inches using support tool, then raise vehicle.
4. Remove lower A/C compressor bolt to oil pan, then drain engine oil.
5. Remove oil pan retaining bolts, then use pry points to separate from engine block, **Fig. 14.**
6. Reverse procedure to install.

OIL PUMP

REPLACE

Refer to "Cylinder Head, Replace" for replacement procedure.

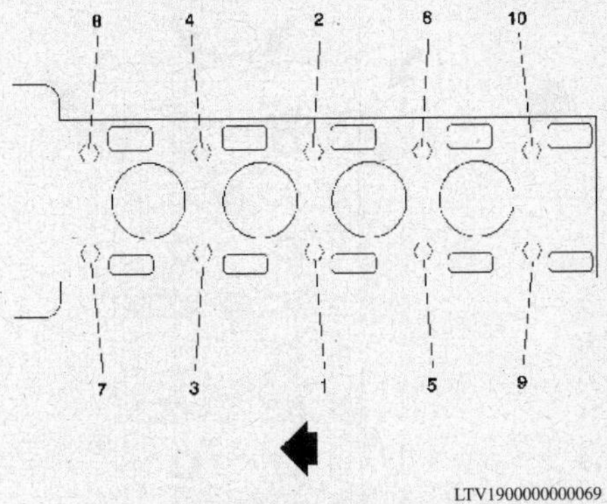

Fig. 8 Cylinder head tightening sequence

OIL PUMP SERVICE

Disassemble

1. Remove cover plate mounting bolts.
2. Mark drive and driven rotors for assembly.
3. Remove drive and driven rotors, then the pressure relief valve.

Inspection

1. Measure clearance between driven rotor and pump body, **Fig. 15.** Replace oil pump if clearance is more than .011 inch.
2. Inspect clearance between both tips, **Fig. 16.** Replace oil pump if clearance is more than .006 inch.
3. Measure clearance between side of drive and driven rotors, and oil pump cover plate, **Fig. 17.** Replace oil pump is clearance is more than .003 inch.

Assemble

1. Remove front cover oil seal using suitable screwdriver or punch.
2. Install new oil seal using oil seal installer tool No. J-35268-A, or equivalent, and suitable press.
3. Install pressure relief valve, valve spring and oil pump pressure relief valve plug.
4. Lubricate drive and driven rotors with clean engine oil, then align marks on drive and driven rotors.
5. Install drive and driven rotors into pump body.
6. Fill oil pump with petroleum jelly to prime oil pump.
7. Install oil pump gear cover plate screws.

SERPENTINE DRIVE BELT

Belt Routing

Refer to **Fig. 18** for accessory drive belt routing.

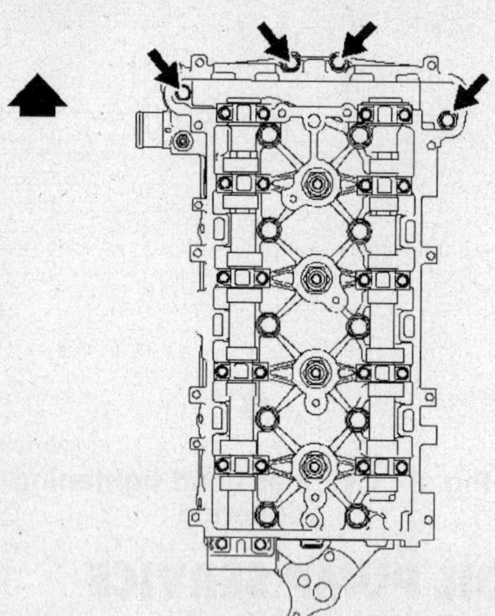

Fig. 9 Front cylinder head bolt locations

Tensioner Replacement

1. Raise and support vehicle, then remove righthand side wheel and splash shield.
2. Install tool No. J–44811 or equivalent onto tensioner, unload tension and remove drive belt.
3. Remove mounting bolt, then the tensioner assembly, **Fig. 19.**

Drive Belt Replacement

Refer to "Tensioner Replacement" for procedure.

COOLING SYSTEM BLEED

These engines do not require a special bleed procedure. After filling cooling system, start and run engine until it reaches normal operating temperature with pressure cap off. Air will then automatically bleed through cap opening.

THERMOSTAT

REPLACE

1. Drain engine coolant into a suitable container.
2. Remove exhaust heat shield, then raise and support vehicle.
3. Drain coolant from water pump drain plug.
4. Remove thermostat cover from thermostat housing and discard housing O-seal.
5. Remove water pipe from water pump assembly, then discard seals from water pipe.
6. Remove inner thermostat sleeve, then the thermostat assembly.
7. Reverse procedure to install.

Fig. 10 Camshaft sprocket holding tool

WATER PUMP

REPLACE

1. Drain engine coolant into a suitable container.
2. Remove thermostat housing pipe to cylinder bolt near front of engine.
3. Remove exhaust manifold heat shield, then the water pump access plate from front cover.
4. Remove righthand wheel, then inner splash shield.
5. Drain coolant from plug at the bottom of water pump, then disconnect ECT sensor electrical connector.
6. Remove thermostat housing bolts, then move housing toward lefthand vehicle while twisting water feed pipe from rear of water pump assembly.
7. Leave coolant hoses and thermostat housing cover connected, then remove water feed pipe. Discard water pipe seals.
8. Install water pump holding tool No. J-43651 or equivalent, then remove sprocket access plate.
9. Remove water pump assembly bolts, then the water pump assembly and water pump O-seal.
10. Reverse procedure to install.

RADIATOR

REPLACE

1. Remove front fascia, then drain coolant into suitable container.
2. Disconnect cooling fans electrical connectors and slide electrical connectors out of retainers.
3. Remove pusher fan electrical harness from fan shroud retaining tabs.
4. Remove wiring harness from clamp on fan shroud.
5. **On models equipped with automatic transaxle,** remove upper transaxle cooler lines from radiator end tank. Cap line.
6. **On all models,** remove upper radiator hose from radiator.
7. Remove mounting bolts and fan shroud.
8. Remove forward wiring harness from retaining clips and lower radiator hose from radiator.
9. **On models equipped with automatic transaxle,** remove lower transaxle cooler line. Cap line.

Fig. 11 Camshaft replacement

10. **On all models,** remove mounting bolts, upper bracket and rubber mounts.
11. Secure condenser away from upper rail using suitable tie strap.
12. Raise and support vehicle.
13. Remove condenser mounting bolts.
14. Pull condenser and pusher fan down slightly to disconnect radiator tabs.
15. Lower vehicle.
16. Remove radiator.
17. Remove upper radiator to condenser gaskets.
18. Reverse procedure to install.

FUEL PUMP

REPLACE

1. Ensure that fuel level in tank is less than 1/4 full.
2. Relieve fuel system pressure as outlined under "Precautions," then raise and support vehicle.
3. Remove rubber exhaust hangers, allowing exhaust system to drop slightly.
4. Remove propeller shaft guard, then index mark relationship of propeller shaft to rear drive module flange.
5. Remove underbody guard loop, then place a support under propeller shaft at rear drive module.
6. Remove bolts securing propeller shaft yoke flange to rear drive module flange.
7. Index mark relationship of propeller shaft to power take-off unit flange.
8. Place a support under propeller shaft at PTU, then remove bolts securing propeller shaft to PTU flange.
9. Remove bolts securing propeller shaft support bearing to vehicle underbody.
10. While supporting propeller shaft, move propeller shaft rearward to disengage and remove.
11. Disconnect EVAP canister vent and fresh air hoses.
12. Remove fuel filler pipe, EVAP vent hose, and fresh air hose from fuel tank.
13. Disconnect chassis fuel supply line from fuel filter outlet, then the fuel tank ground strap fastener and connector.
14. Support fuel tank, then remove fuel tank strap bolts and fuel tank straps.
15. Lower fuel tank from underbody of vehicle.

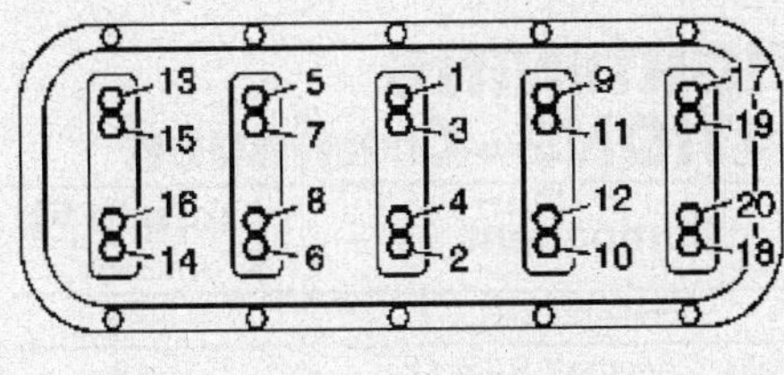

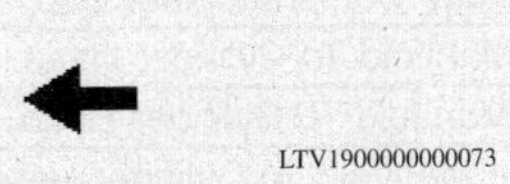

Fig. 12 Lower crankcase inner bolt tightening sequence

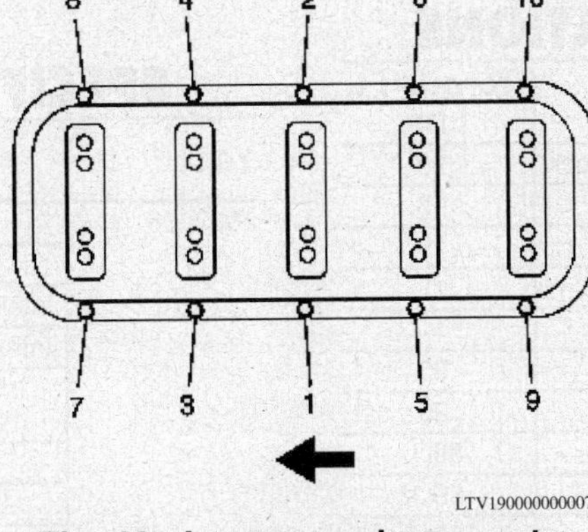

Fig. 13 Lower crankcase outer bolt tightening sequence

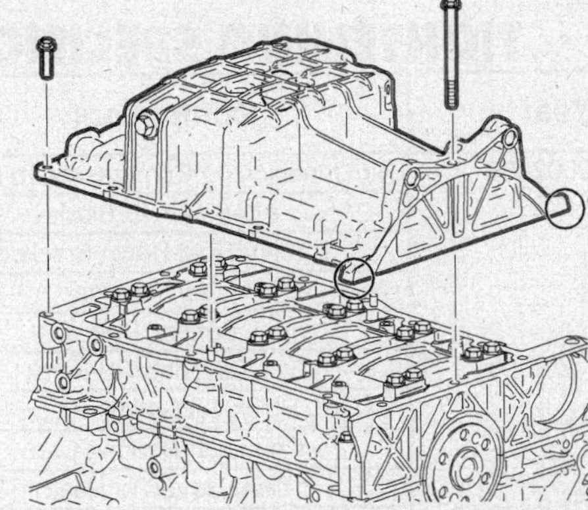

Fig. 14 Oil pan pry points

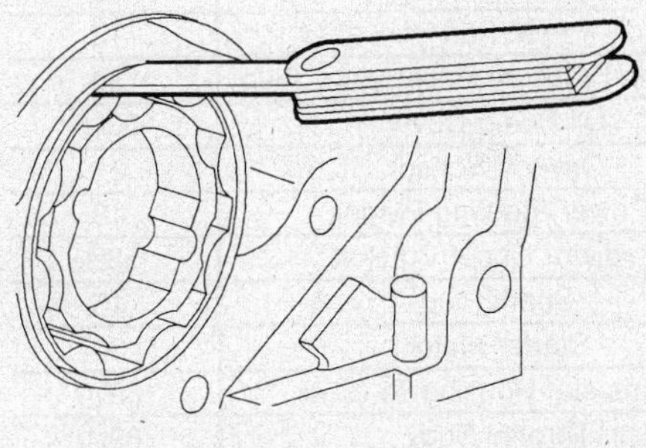

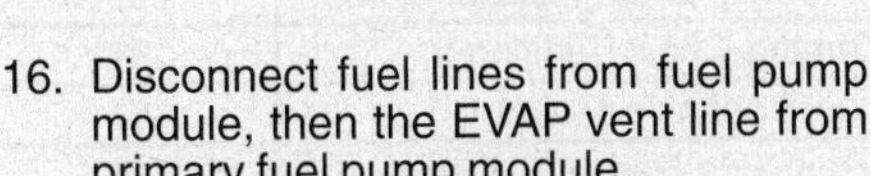

Fig. 15 Oil pump body clearance measurement

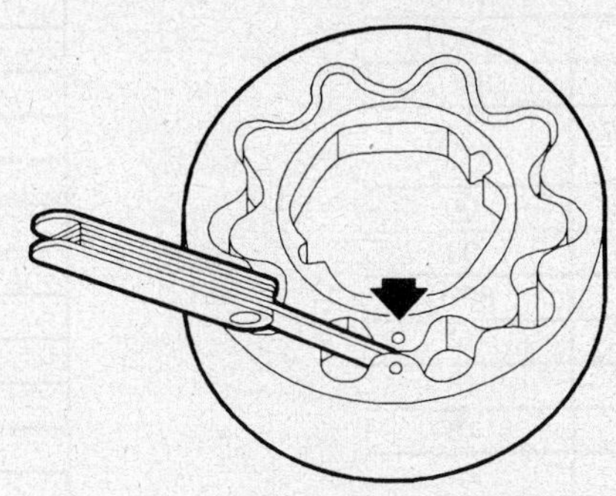

Fig. 16 Oil pump tip clearance measurement

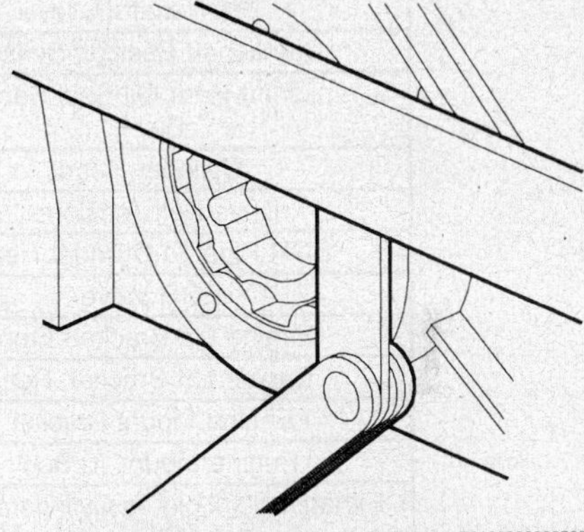

Fig. 17 Oil pump end to end clearance measurement

16. Disconnect fuel lines from fuel pump module, then the EVAP vent line from primary fuel pump module.
17. Disconnect electrical connector from primary fuel pump module.
18. Remove fuel pump module retaining ring using tool No. SA9156E or equivalent.
19. Remove primary fuel pump module, then disconnect fuel level sender and fuel tank pressure sensor electrical connectors.
20. Remove fuel pump module retaining ring using tool No. SA9156E or equivalent.
21. Remove secondary fuel pump module, then discard fuel pump module to tank seal.
22. Reverse procedure to install.

FUEL FILTER

REPLACE

1. Raise and support vehicle.
2. Remove fuel filter bracket screw, then disconnect fuel lines from inlet and outlet sides of fuel filter.
3. Slide fuel filter out of bracket.
4. Reverse procedure to install.

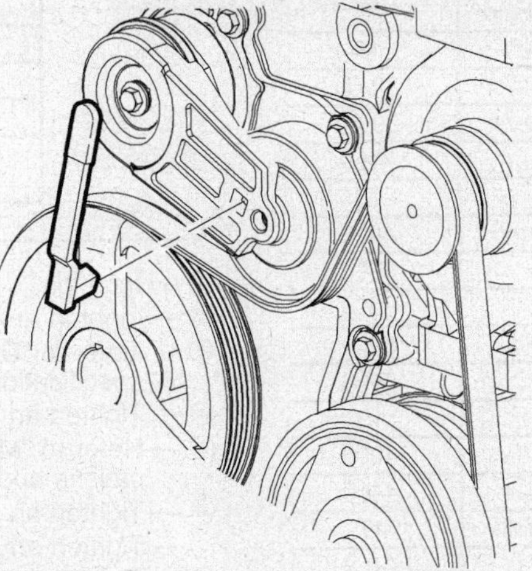

Fig. 18 Accessory drive belt routing

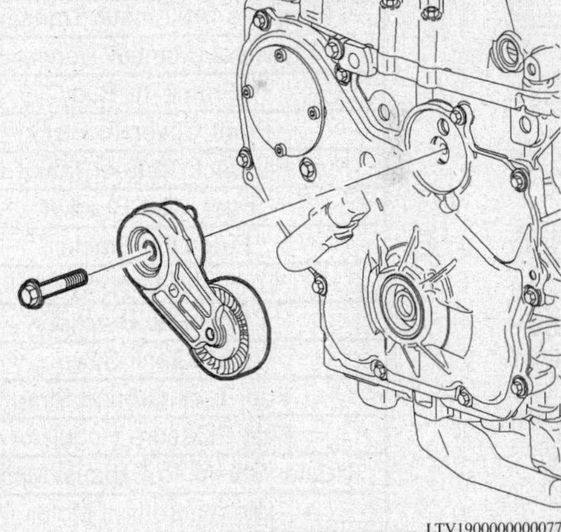

Fig. 19 Drive belt tensioner replacement

TIGHTENING SPECIFICATIONS

Year	Component	Torque Ft. Lbs.
2002–06	Air Conditioning Compressor To Block	15
	Alternator To Block	18
	Battery Hold-Down Bracket	15
	Battery Terminal	13
	Battery Tray	11
	Belt Tensioner To Block	33
	Block Oil Gallery Plug	26
	Camshaft Bearing Cap	89①
	Cam Cover To Head	89①
	Camshaft Sprocket	63②
	Chain Guide Plug	59
	Connecting Rod	18⑧
	Crankshaft Pulley	74⑦
	Crankshaft Position Sensor	89①
	Crankshaft Rear Oil Seal Carrier To Block	89①
	Cylinder Head	③
	Drive Belt Tensioner	33
	EGR Pipe To Cylinder Head	89①
	EGR Valve	18
	Engine Lift Bracket, Front	18
	Engine Lift Bracket, Rear	18
	Engine Mount Bracket	74
	Engine Mount To Body	74
	Exhaust Manifold To Cylinder Head, Stud	18
	Exhaust Manifold To Cylinder Head, Nut	108①
	Exhaust Manifold Pipe Flange	12
	Flexplate (Automatic Transaxle)	39 ⑥
	Flywheel (Manual Transaxle)	39 ⑥
	Frame To Body	74④
	Front Cover To Block	18
	Fuel Fill Neck To Fuel Tank Clamp	44①
	Fuel Filter Bracket	35①
	Fuel Line Bracket	89①
	Fuel Line Support Clip	89①
	Fuel Rail Bracket	89①
	Fuel Tank Strap	19
	Fuel Tank Ground Strap	40①
	Fuel Pressure Regulator	44①
	Heater Shield To Exhaust Manifold	17
	Idle Air Control Motor	27①

TIGHTENING SPECIFICATIONS—Continued

Year	Component	Torque Ft. Lbs.
2002–06	Ignition Coil	89①
	Intake Camshaft Rear Cap	18
	Intake Manifold To Cylinder Head, Bolt	89①
	Intake Manifold To Cylinder Head, Nut	89①
	Intake Manifold To Cylinder Head, Stud	53
	Knock Sensor	18
	Main Bearings	⑤
	Oil Drain Plug	18
	Oil Pan	18
	Oil Pump Pressure Relief Valve Plug	30
	Oil Pump Cover	53①
	Oxygen Sensor	31
	Power Steering Pump	18
	Radiator Upper Bracket	53①
	Spark Plug	15
	Starter Motor	30
	Thermostat Housing To Block	89①
	Throttle Body	89①
	Throttle Position Sensor	18①
	Timing Chain Guides	89①
	Timing Chain Nozzle	89①
	Timing Chain Tensioner	55
	Transaxle Mount	41
	Transaxle Range Switch	18
	Transaxle Range Switch Lever	26
	Vent Tube To Cylinder Head	11
	Water Pump Access Cover	89①
	Water Pump	18
	Water Pump/Balance Shaft Chain Tensioner	89①
	Water Pump Sprocket	89①

①— Inch lbs.
②— Tighten an additional 30°.
③— Refer to "Cylinder Head, Replace" for tightening specifications and sequence.
④— Tighten an additional 180°.
⑤— Refer to "Main & Rod Bearings" for tightening specifications and sequence.
⑥— Tighten an additional 25°
⑦— Tighten an additional 75°.
⑧— Tighten an additional 100°.

3.0L Engine

NOTE: For Procedures Not Found In This Section, Refer To The "2.2L Engine" Section.

NOTE: On Air Bag Equipped Models, Refer To "Air Bag System Precautions" Located In The Front Of This Manual For System Disarming & Arming Procedures.

NOTE: Refer To "Computer Relearn Procedures" Located In The Front Of This Manual When Battery Power To The Computer Has Been Interrupted.

INDEX

PRECAUTIONS

Air Bag Systems

Refer to "Air Bag System Precautions" in the front of this manual for system disarming and arming procedures.

Battery Ground Cable

Prior to service, disconnect battery ground cable and isolate as required.

Fuel System Pressure Relief

1. Connect J–34730-1A or equivalent to fuel pressure connection.
2. Install bleed hose into an approved container and open valve to bleed system pressure.
3. Disconnect fuel pressure gage from fuel pressure connection.

COMPRESSION PRESSURE

1. Start and run engine until it reaches normal operating temperature. Turn engine off.
2. Remove ignition modules and spark plugs.
3. Connect compression gauge tool No. SA-9127-E, or equivalent, into spark plug hole.
4. Open throttle fully.
5. Crank engine at not less than 250 RPM.
6. Measure compression while cranking engine. Prior to reading compression gauge needle should bounce at least 10 times.
7. Repeat previous steps for each cylinder.
8. Minimum compression on any one cylinder should not be less than 70% of highest cylinder. No cylinder should read less than 100 psi.
9. Place shop towel over spark plug holes and crank engine over a few seconds without compression gauge or spark plugs installed.
10. Repeat compression measuring steps on each cylinder.

ENGINE MOUNT

REPLACE

1. Loosen clamp at air cleaner assembly, then remove outlet resonator duct assembly from air cleaner.
2. Disconnect electrical connector at mass air flow sensor, then release clamps on side of air cleaner assembly.
3. Remove upper air cleaner lid, then the air filter assembly.
4. Place a floor jack with wood block under engine oil pan to support powertrain.
5. Remove mount to mount bracket bolts, then the mount to frame rail nuts and mount.
6. Reverse procedure to install.

ENGINE

REPLACE

1. Remove battery cover and battery.
2. Loosen clamp at air cleaner assembly, then remove outlet resonator duct assembly from air cleaner.
3. Disconnect electrical connector at mass air flow sensor, then release clamps on side of air cleaner assembly.
4. Remove upper air cleaner lid, then the air filter assembly.
5. Remove underhood fuse block fuse cover, then the inner cover.
6. Loosen three connector through bolts at top of fuse block.
7. Remove battery and electronic power steering feed wire connection nut, then the wire from fuse block stud.
8. Release tabs, then raise fuse block from connectors, disconnect electrical connector and remove from vehicle.
9. Remove battery cable and harness attachment clips on side of battery tray bracket assembly.
10. Remove main connectors from fuse block housing, lay battery positive cable over engine.

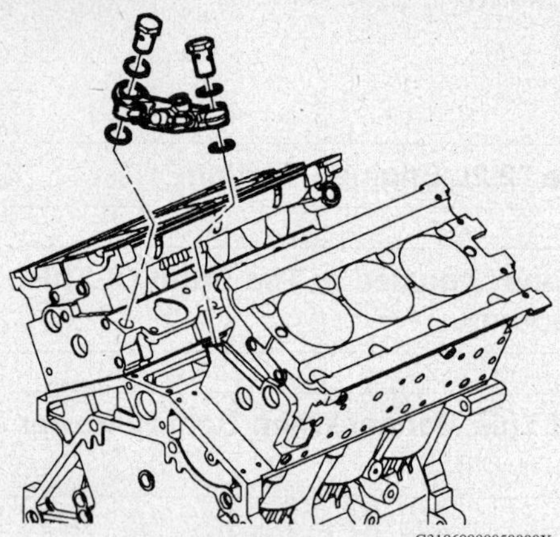
G31069900059000X

Fig. 1 Coolant bridge replacement

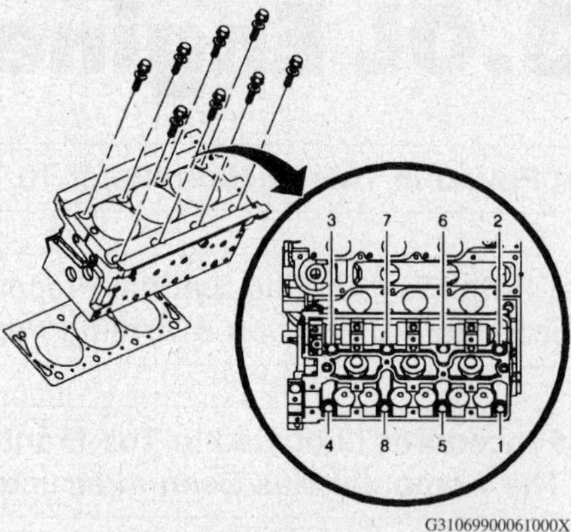

Fig. 2 Cylinder head bolt loosening sequence

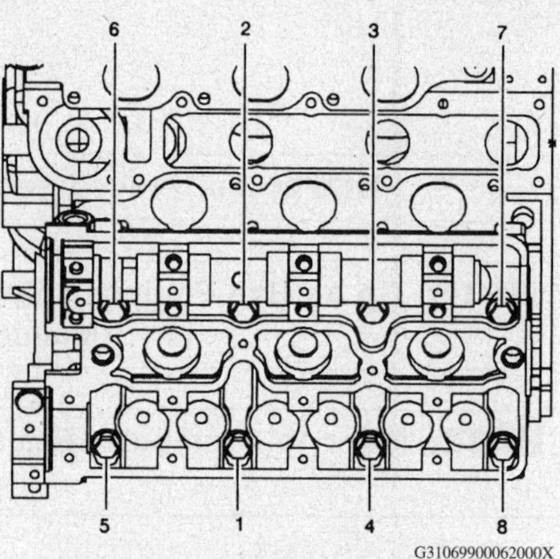

Fig. 3 Cylinder head bolt tightening sequence

11. Disconnect electrical connectors at transaxle controller near brake booster, then the electrical connector for rear O2 sensor and cut tie strap to heater hoses.
12. Remove vacuum hose from check valve and brake booster, lay across engine.
13. Disconnect main engine harness gray connector and lay over engine assembly.
14. Remove fuse block and battery tray bolts, then the battery tray and ground wire.
15. Slightly pry between shifter cable plastic retainer and PRNDL switch to disconnect.
16. Drain engine coolant into a suitable container, then disconnect upper radiator hose from cylinder head lower radiator hose from radiator.
17. Disconnect hoses from surge tank, then heater hoses from heater core.
18. Relieve fuel system pressure as outlined under "Precautions."
19. Disconnect fuel transfer line using tool No. SA9805E or equivalent, then purge hoses from purge solenoid.
20. Secure radiator and condenser fan assembly to body.
21. Recover refrigerant as outlined in "Air Conditioning" chapter. Disconnect A/C transducer and compressor.
22. Raise and support vehicle.
23. Remove front wheels and inner splash shields.
24. Install a piece of hardwood 1 X 2 X 4 between transaxle case and engine cradle assembly.
25. Remove compressor and support A/C line.
26. Remove push pins that retain air deflector assembly to cradle.
27. Disconnect transaxle lines from transaxle, then remove exhaust manifold to pipe flange bolts.
28. Remove exhaust pipe to muffler pipe nuts, then the converter pipe assembly. Support muffler and pipe assembly.
29. Remove propshaft bolts at power take unit, then the propshaft bolt at rear axle assembly.
30. Remove propshaft assembly, then the shifter cable bracket assembly nut and free bracket with cable from transaxle.
31. Remove steering gear to intermediate shaft bolt, then tie rod to knuckle nuts.
32. Separate tie rod assemblies form knuckle assemblies using tool No. SA91100C or equivalent.
33. Remove lower control arm cotter pins and nuts to knuckle assembly.
34. Separate lower controls arms from knuckle assemblies using tool No. J–43828 equivalent.
35. Remove lower stabilizer link nuts to stabilizer bar, then disconnect lefthand axle shaft assembly from transaxle.
36. Disconnect righthand shaft assembly from intermediate drive shaft using tool No. J–45341 or equivalent.
37. Support axle shaft by using tie straps, then lower vehicle.
38. Remove righthand engine mount to engine bracket bolts, then the lefthand transaxle mount to transaxle bolts. **Engine should rest on wood blocks.**
39. Raise vehicle, then position engine support table under powertrain assembly.
40. With table positioned, fully raise table to contact with powertrain assembly and remove cradle to body bolts.
41. Lower engine table, then raise body on a hoist until powertrain and cradle assembly is free from vehicle.
42. Reverse procedure to install.

INTAKE MANIFOLD

REPLACE

1. Loosen clamp at air cleaner assembly, then remove outlet resonator duct assembly from air cleaner.
2. Disconnect electrical connector at mass air flow sensor, then release clamps on side of air cleaner assembly.
3. Remove upper air cleaner lid, then the air filter assembly.
4. Remove resonator outlet duct assembly bracket from manifold.
5. Relieve fuel system pressure as outlined under "Precautions."
6. Disconnect fuel transfer line at the quick connect from the fuel line using J 37088-A , or equivalent blue tool.
7. Disconnect fuel transfer line using tool No. J-37088 or equivalent.
8. Disconnect electrical harness attachment from manifold and lay aside.
9. Disconnect attachment of purge solenoid line from rear of manifold.
10. Disconnect brake booster line from intake manifold, then the fuel injector and intake manifold control solenoid connectors.
11. Remove PCV fresh air hose, then the throttle body retaining bolts and cooling hose bracket bolts from throttle body.
12. With coolant lines connected to throttle body, lay throttle body assembly over mast cylinder.
13. Remove upper manifold to spacer plate bolts, then the lower intake manifold bolt near throttle body.
14. Remove intake manifold assembly, then the lower intake manifold spacer plate.
15. Reverse procedure to install.

EXHAUST MANIFOLD

REPLACE

1. Loosen clamp at air cleaner assembly, then remove outlet resonator duct assembly from air cleaner.
2. Disconnect electrical connector at mass air flow sensor, then release clamps on side of air cleaner assembly.
3. Remove upper air cleaner lid, then the air filter assembly.
4. Disconnect purge solenoid from manifold.
5. Disconnect front 02 sensor from connector at side of engine, then remove front 02 sensor using tool No. J–39119 or equivalent.
6. Remove coolant extension pipe and engine lift bracket bolt, then the oil dipstick and tube.
7. Remove upper exhaust manifold nuts to cylinder head, then raise vehicle.
8. Remove exhaust pipe flange to front exhaust manifold nuts, then the exhaust pipe crossover flange nuts.
9. Remove lefthand and righthand side lower stabilizer link to stabilizer nuts, then the righthand side stabilizer bar to cradle bolts.

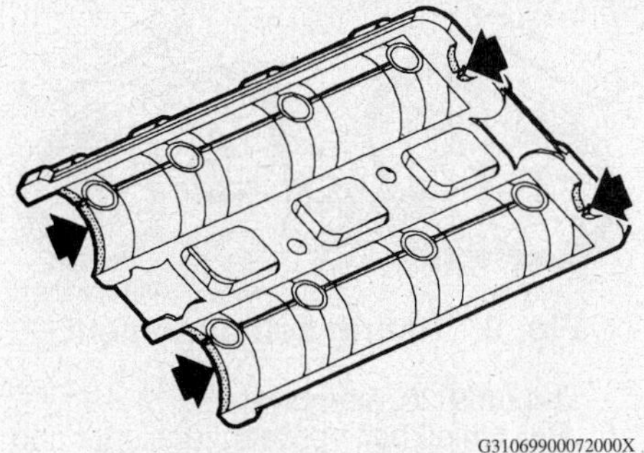

Fig. 4 Valve cover sealant application points

10. Rotate stabilizer bar upward to provide clearance for exhaust pipe removal.
11. Separate downpipe from exhaust pipe, twist and rotate to clear rear flange and remove.
12. Remove bolts, then the shield and righthand side manifold.
13. Remove righthand splash shield, then loosen accessory drive belt from pulleys.
14. Disconnect electrical connector at A/C compressor and pressure transducer.
15. Remove A/C compressor to bracket bolts, then the A/C compressor and support it with straps.
16. Remove lefthand exhaust manifold assembly and gasket.
17. Reverse procedure to install.

CYLINDER HEAD

REPLACE

1. Loosen clamp at air cleaner assembly, then remove outlet resonator duct assembly from air cleaner.
2. Disconnect electrical connector at mass air flow sensor, then release clamps on side of air cleaner assembly.
3. Remove upper air cleaner lid, then the air filter assembly.
4. Remove intake manifold as outlined under "Intake Manifold, Replace."
5. Remove coolant intake and heater hoses.
6. Remove coolant bridge and seals, **Fig. 1.**
7. Drain coolant into suitable container.
8. Remove upper radiator hose.
9. Remove exhaust manifold heat shield.
10. Remove exhaust pipe to exhaust manifold mounting nuts.
11. Remove front exhaust pipes from exhaust manifolds.
12. Support powertrain using suitable floor jack under oil pan.
13. Remove front transaxle mount bolt.
14. Raise powertrain using floor jack to gain access to coolant extension housing.
15. Remove oil dipstick tube.
16. Twist and remove coolant extension housing.
17. Remove grounds from front lift bracket.
18. Disconnect oxygen sensor connector.
19. Remove EGR to exhaust manifold pipe.
20. Remove camshaft cover.

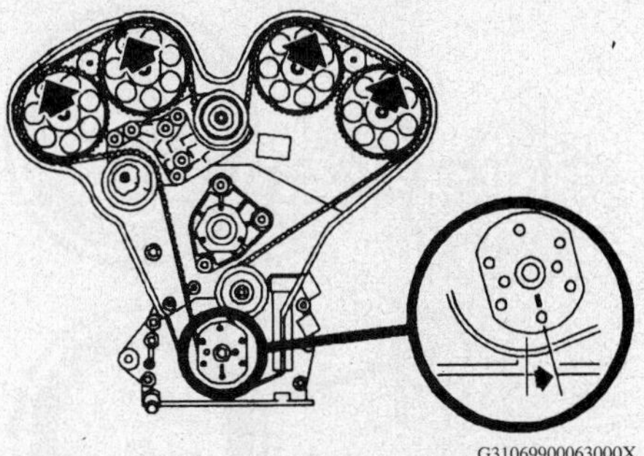

Fig. 5 Crankshaft alignment to 60° BTDC

21. Remove front timing belt cover as outlined under "Front Cover, Replace."
22. Remove timing belt as outlined under "Timing Belt, Replace."
23. Remove timing belt tensioner bracket.
24. Remove rear timing belt cover as outlined under "Front Cover, Replace."
25. Disconnect camshaft sensor connector.
26. Remove exhaust camshaft as outlined under "Camshaft, Replace."
27. Loosen and remove cylinder head bolts in several steps in sequence, **Fig. 2.**
28. Remove cylinder head and gasket.
29. Remove exhaust manifold.
30. Clean and inspect cylinder head and sealing surfaces.
31. Reverse procedure to install, noting the following:
    a. Ensure new cylinder head gasket part number imprint is facing towards top of engine.
    b. **Torque** cylinder head bolts to 18 ft. lbs., in sequence, **Fig. 3.**
    c. Tighten cylinder head bolts an additional 90° in sequence.
    d. Tighten head bolts an additional 90° in sequence.
    e. Tighten bolts an additional 90° in sequence.
    f. Finally, tighten cylinder head bolts an additional 15° in sequence.
    g. Replace sealing rings on coolant pipe and lubricate with coolant.
    h. Replace sealing rings on coolant pipe and lubricate with coolant.

VALVE COVER

REPLACE

1. Remove intake manifolds as outlined under "Intake Manifold, Replace."
2. Remove ignition coils module.
3. Remove rear cover knock sensor wire harness and disconnect camshaft position sensor.
4. Remove cover and O-ring seals. Ensure O-rings are accounted for.
5. Clean cover and sealing surfaces.
6. Reverse procedure to install. Apply thin coat of Loctite 5900, or equivalent, to front and rear of cover, **Fig. 4.**

CAMSHAFT LOBE LIFT SPECIFICATIONS

Exhaust cam lobe lift rise .3409–.3441 inch, minimum service limit is .3390 inch.

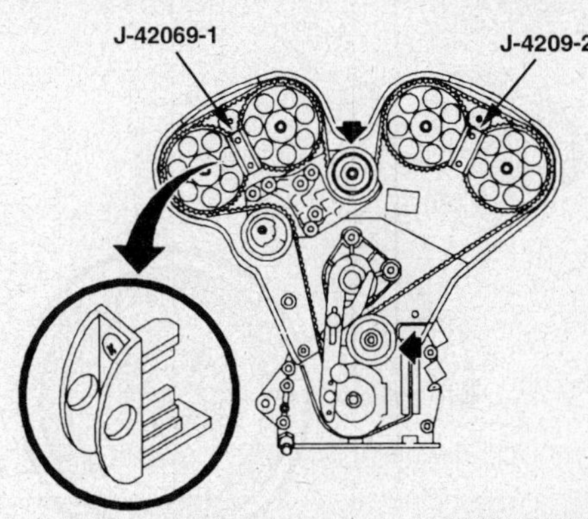

Fig. 6 Camshaft gear locking tool installation

VALVE ADJUSTMENT

Engine is equipped with hydraulic lifters, no adjustment is required.

FRONT COVER

REPLACE

1. Loosen clamp at air cleaner assembly, then remove outlet resonator duct assembly from air cleaner.
2. Disconnect electrical connector at mass air flow sensor, then release clamps on side of air cleaner assembly.
3. Remove upper air cleaner lid, then the air filter assembly.
4. Raise and support vehicle, then remove righthand front wheel and splash shield.
5. Lower vehicle, then loosen but do not remove water pump pulley bolts.
6. Install engine support fixture and adapters.
7. Remove serpentine belt as outlined under "Serpentine Drive Belt."
8. Remove water pump and idler pulleys.
9. Remove serpentine belt tensioner and crankshaft balancer.
10. Disconnect air conditioning pressure connector to allow additional slack in harness, remove wiring harness channel from front cover and position away from front of engine.
11. Remove timing belt front cover.
12. Inspect outer edge sealing strip on front timing cover for cracks or tears and replace as required.
13. Remove timing belt as outlined under "Timing Belt, Replace."
14. To prevent valve to piston contact, rotate crankshaft counterclockwise to 60° BTDC, **Fig. 5.**
15. Remove camshaft gears using camshaft lock tools Nos. J-42069-1 and J-42069-2, or equivalents, when initially loosening camshaft bolts, **Fig. 6.**
16. Remove timing belt tensioner bracket.
17. Remove timing belt idler pulley for camshaft Nos. 3 and 4, **Fig. 7.**
18. Remove mounting bolts, threaded pin and rear timing belt cover.
19. Reverse procedure to install, noting the following:
    a. Install threaded pin with Loctite 242, or equivalent.

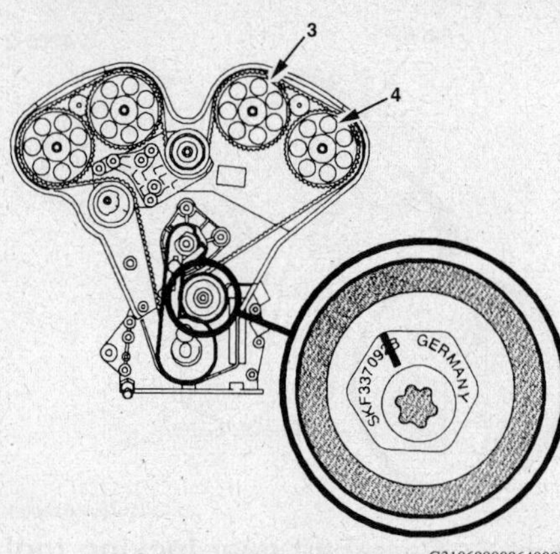

Fig. 7 Camshaft Nos. 3 & 4 idler pulley replacement

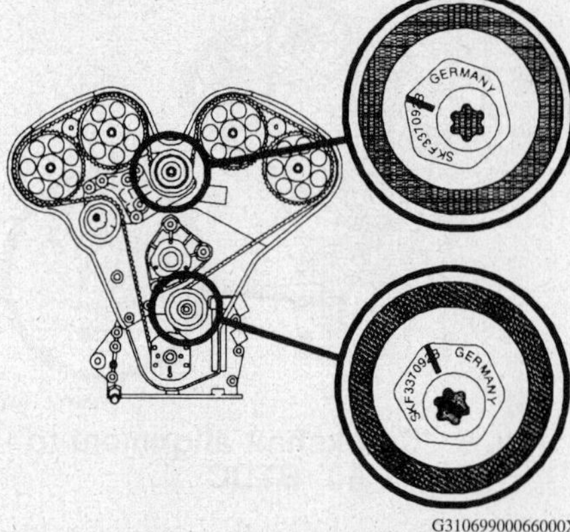

Fig. 8 Upper & lower idler pulleys alignment

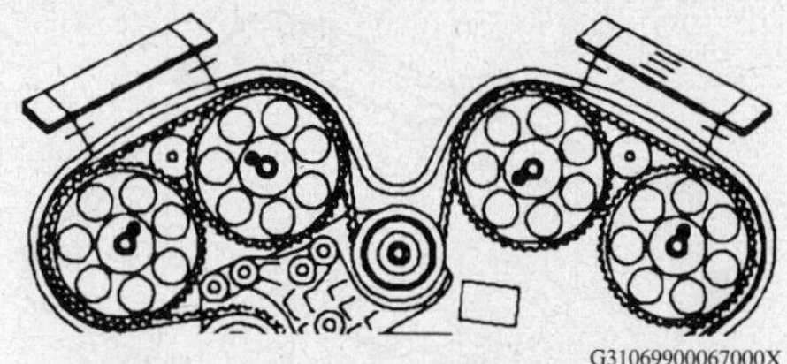

Fig. 9 Timing belt alignment

b. Tighten timing belt idler pulley until snug. After final timing belt adjustments are made, tighten to specifications.
c. Adjust timing belt as outlined under "Timing Belt, Replace."
d. Install new camshaft gear bolts.

TIMING BELT

REPLACE

Removal

1. Remove timing belt front cover as outlined "Front Cover, Replace."
2. Rotate crankshaft using crank hub Torx socket tool No. J-42098, or equivalent, until cylinder No. 1 is at 60° BTDC, **Fig. 5.**
3. Install crankshaft locking tool No. J-42069-10, or equivalent.
4. Rotate crankshaft clockwise using crank hub Torx socket tool No. J-42098, or equivalent, until cylinder No. 1 is at TDC and tighten lever arm to water pump pulley flange.
5. Ensure alignment of crankshaft is not 180° off. Alignment marks must align with corresponding notches on rear timing belt cover.
6. Install camshaft gear locking tools Nos. J-42069-1 and J-42069-2, or equivalents, **Fig. 6.**
7. Remove upper and lower idler pulleys.
8. Remove timing belt tensioner.
9. Remove timing belt.
10. Do not rotate crankshaft if camshaft locking tools are not in place.
11. Do not rotate camshafts unless crankshaft is at 60° BTDC.

Installation

1. Remove crankshaft locking tool.
2. Mark furthest point from Torx head bolt on upper and lower idler pulleys, **Fig. 8.**
3. Idler pulleys provide adjustment by rotating eccentric circle around mounting bolt.
4. Install lower idler pulley allowing pulley to rotate with slight resistance using idler pulley wrench tool No. J-42069-40, or equivalent.

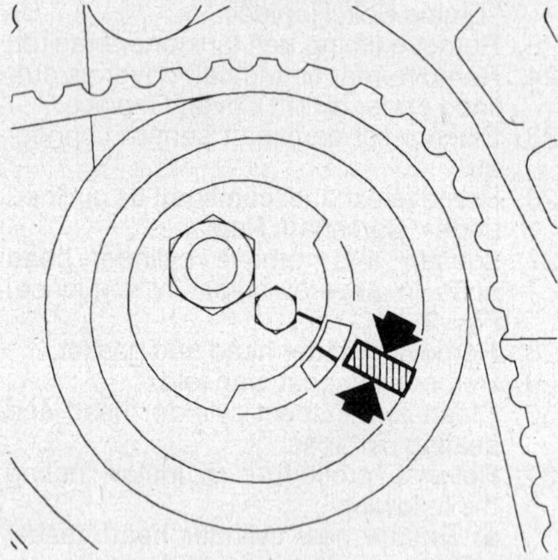

Fig. 10 Timing belt tensioner alignment

5. Align marks on timing belt with marks on camshaft sprockets Nos. 3 and 4, **Fig. 9.**
6. Route timing belt around lower idler pulley and crankshaft sprocket. Ensure timing belt and crankshaft sprocket marks align.
7. Lock timing belt to crankshaft sprocket using plastic wedge tool No. J-42069-30, or equivalent.
8. Route belt around timing belt tensioner, then around Nos. 1 and 2 camshaft sprockets. Ensure timing belt and sprockets' marks align.
9. Install upper idler pulley using idler pulley wrench tool No. J-42069-40, or equivalent. Allow pulley to rotate.
10. Install crankshaft locking tool No. J-42069-10, or equivalent, and tighten lever arm to water pump pulley flange.
11. Adjust timing belt tensioner alignment mark 1/8 inch above mark on spring loaded idler, **Fig. 10.**
12. Adjust mark on upper idler pulley to 10 o'clock position to align Nos. 1 and 2 timing marks close to settings. Snug but do not fully tighten pulley.
13. Adjust mark on lower idler pulley to 11 o'clock position to align Nos. 3 and 4 timing marks close to settings. Snug but do not fully tighten pulley.
14. Remove camshaft locking tools and install inspecting gauge tool No. J-42069-20, or equivalent.
15. Pull timing belt between tensioner and crankshaft sprocket to remove slack between camshaft Nos. 3 and 4 and lower idler pulley. Ensure timing marks on camshaft Nos. 3 and 4 are .0394 inch on retard side, **Fig. 11.** If timing marks are not .0394 inch on retard side, turn lower idler clockwise and repeat procedure.
16. Remove crankshaft locking tool.
17. Rotate crankshaft 1¾ turns clockwise and install crankshaft locking tool at TDC.
18. Tighten lever arm to water pump pulley flange.
19. If TDC is passed, do not rotate counterclockwise, rotate crankshaft an additional two turns.
20. Rotate lower idler pulley counterclockwise until timing marks on camshaft sprocket Nos. 3 and 4 align with marks on inspecting gauge tool.
21. Hold idler pulley using idler pulley wrench tool and tighten.
22. Remove crankshaft locking tool.
23. Rotate crankshaft 1¾ turns clockwise and install crankshaft locking tool. Stop at TDC and tighten lever arm to water pump pulley flange. If TDC is passed, do not rotate counterclockwise, rotate crankshaft an additional two turns.
24. Inspect alignment marks on camshaft Nos. 3 and 4, realign if required.
25. Install inspecting gauge tool on camshaft Nos. 1 and 2, then install camshaft locking tool on camshaft Nos. 2 and 4.
26. Rotate upper idler pulley counterclockwise until timing marks on camshaft sprocket Nos. 1 and 2 align with marks on inspecting gauge tool.
27. Hold idler pulley and tighten using idler pulley wrench tool.
28. Remove camshaft and crankshaft locking tools.
29. Rotate crankshaft 1¾ turns clockwise and install crankshaft locking tool. Stop at TDC and tighten lever arm to water pump pulley flange. If TDC is passed, do not rotate counterclockwise, rotate crankshaft an additional two turns.
30. Inspect both pairs of camshaft timing marks using inspecting gauge tool. Adjust as required.
31. Adjust timing belt tensioner mark 1/8 inch above alignment mark on spring loaded idler, **Fig. 10.**
32. Remove crankshaft locking tool and inspecting gauge tool.
33. Install timing belt front cover.

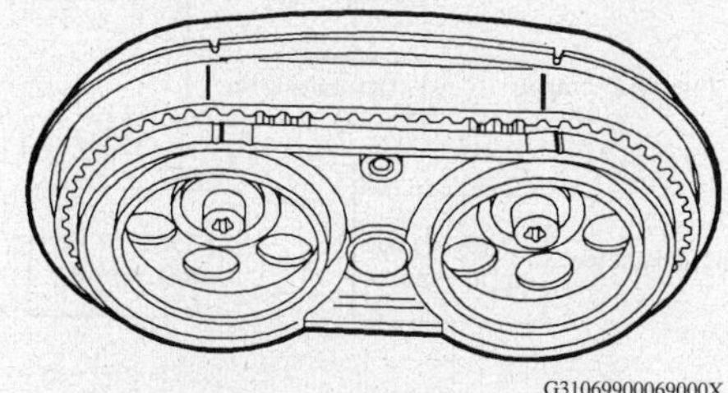

Fig. 11 Timing belt alignment retarded .0394 inch

CAMSHAFT

REPLACE

Removal

1. Remove intake manifold as outlined under "Intake Manifold, Replace."
2. Remove timing belt cover as outlined under "Front Cover, Replace."
3. Remove timing belt as outlined "Timing Belt, Replace."
4. Rotate crankshaft counterclockwise to 60° BTDC to prevent valve to piston contact, **Fig. 5.**
5. Remove gear bolt and gear using camshaft locking tools Nos. J-42069-1 and J-42069-2, or equivalents.
6. Ensure camshaft is not under load from lifters.
7. Remove bearing cap bolts, starting in center and moving outward in spiral direction, in stages of ½–1 turn.
8. Code marks on bearing caps are as follows:
   a. Rear cylinder head cylinders Nos. 1, 3 and 5 bearing caps are marked with L followed by a number.
   b. Front cylinder head cylinders Nos. 2, 4 and 6 bearing caps are marked with R followed by a number.
9. Remove camshaft with seal, then clean bearing and sealing surfaces.

Installation

1. Lubricate camshaft bearing surfaces with oil.
2. Install camshafts as follows:
   a. **When installing rear exhaust camshaft,** ensure pin points towards 1 o'clock position.
   b. **When installing rear intake camshaft,** ensure pin points towards 11 o'clock position.
   c. **When installing front exhaust camshaft,** ensure pin points toward 12 o'clock position.
   d. **When installing front intake camshaft,** ensure pin points toward 7 o'clock position.
3. Apply sealant Loctite 573, or equivalent, to forward edge of front bearing cap, ensure sealant does not enter oil journal.
4. Install bearing caps in appropriate positions, **Figs. 12 and 13.**
5. Tighten bearing caps, starting in center and moving outward in spiral direction.
6. Coat lip of camshaft seal with engine oil and tap into place using camshaft front seal installer tool No. J-35268-A, or equivalent, ensure seal is fully seated.
7. Install camshaft gear with new bolts and camshaft locking tool.
8. Install new camshaft gear mounting bolts.
9. Install and adjust timing belt.
10. Install valve cover.
11. Install intake manifold.

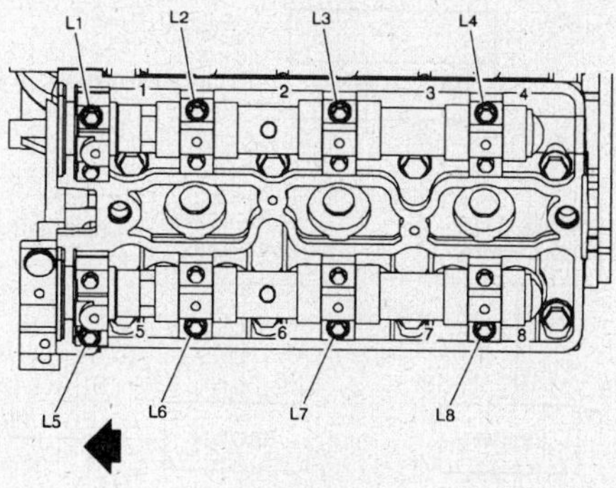

Fig. 12 Rear cylinder head bearing cap locations

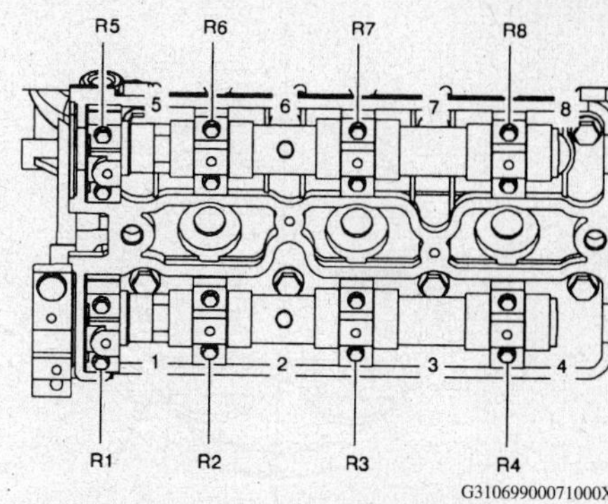

Fig. 13 Front cylinder head bearing cap locations

CYLINDER BORE	PISTON SIZE
(8) 85.976 - 85.985 mm (3.3848 - 3.3852 inch)	(8) 85.940 - 85.950 mm (3.3834 - 3.3838 inch)
(99) 85.985 - 85.995 mm (3.3852 - 3.3856 inch)	(99) 85.950 - 85.960 mm (3.3838 - 3.3842 inch)
(00) 85.995 - 86.005 mm (3.3856 - 3.3860 inch)	(00) 85.960 - 85.970 mm (3.3842 - 3.3846 inch)
(01) 86.005 - 86.015 mm (3.3860 - 3.3864 inch)	(01) 85.970 - 85.980 mm (3.3846 - 3.3850 inch)
(02) 86.015 - 86.025 mm (3.3864 - 3.3868 inch)	(02) 85.980 - 85.990 mm (3.3850 - 3.3854 inch)
† (7 + 0.5) 86.465 - 86.475 mm (3.4041 - 3.4045 inch)	† (7 + 0.5) 86.430 - 86.440 mm (3.4027 - 3.4031 inch)

GC1069700845000X

Fig. 14 Piston selection chart

PISTON & ROD ASSEMBLY

Ensure arrow on piston head faces towards front of engine and bump on connecting rod face towards rear of engine.

PISTONS, PINS & RINGS

1. If cylinders have been honed, proper size piston must be selected for each bore from chart, **Fig. 14.**
2. If piston must be separated from connecting rod.
3. Remove and install piston pin clips using piston pin clip replacement tool No. J-43654, or equivalent.
4. Remove or install piston from connecting rod using piston pin remover/installer tool No. SA-9101-E, or equivalent.
5. Ensure arrow on top of piston and bump on connecting rod face in opposite directions when assembling piston and rod. Arrow on piston will face front of engine block, bump on connecting rod will face rear of engine block.
6. Measure piston pin bore to piston pin clearance. Replace piston and piston pin if clearance is not .0001–.0003 inch.
7. Hone cylinders.
8. Install 1st and 2nd compression rings in cylinder bore. Gap should be .0118–.0196 inch.
9. Install oil control ring in cylinder bore. Gap should be .0157–.0551 inch.
10. Replace rings if end gap clearance is more than specified.
11. First and 2nd compression ring groove clearance should be .0008–.0015 inch.
12. Oil control ring groove clearance should be .0004–.0012 inch.
13. Replace piston if ring groove clearance is more than specified.
14. Refer to **Fig. 15** for piston ring orientation.

MAIN & ROD BEARINGS

The crankshaft main bearing caps are numbered 1, 2 and 3 from the front of the engine. The rear bearing cap is not numbered and contains the thrust bearings. The Nos. 2 and 3 bearing shells do not have oil grooves on the cap sides.

There is a 0 or 1 stamped on the cylinder block oil pan mating flange near the end of each main bearing cap. This is the Determining No. The Determining No. corresponds to each crankshaft main bearing size and color to be installed. The main journal diameter for a determining No. 0 is 2.8368–2.8371 inches. The main journal diameter for a determining No. 1 is 2.8371–2.8373 inches.

To select the correct main bearing, measure crankshaft main bearing journal diameter and refer to main bearing selective fits chart, **Fig. 16.**

Tighten connecting rod caps as follows:

1. **Torque** to 26 ft. lbs.
2. Tighten an additional 45°.
3. Finally, tighten an additional 15°.

Tighten main bearings as follows:

1. **Torque** main bearing cap bolts to 37 ft. lbs.
2. Tighten mounting bolts an additional 60°.
3. Finally, tighten an additional 15°.

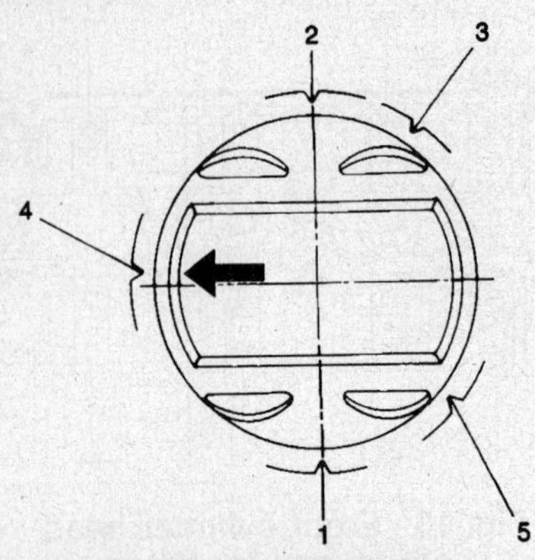

Fig. 15 Piston ring orientation

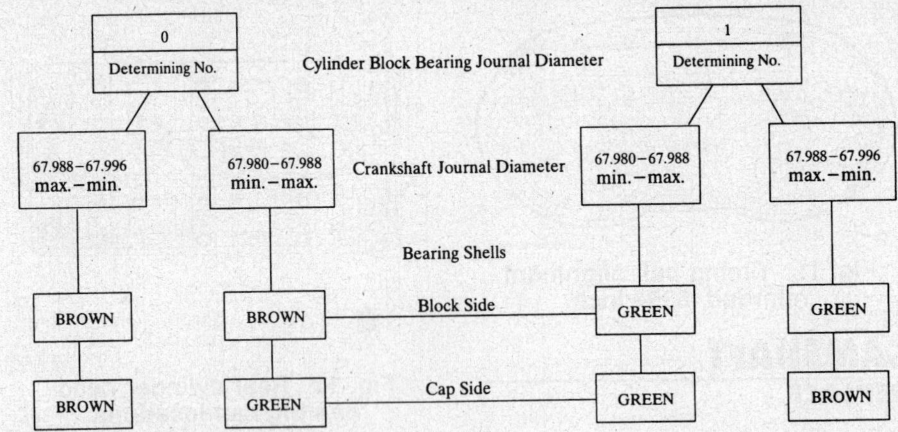

Fig. 16 Main bearing selective fits chart

CRANKSHAFT REAR OIL SEAL

REPLACE

1. Remove transaxle as outlined in **MOTOR's "Domestic Transmission, In-Vehicle Service" or "Transmission Service DVD."**
2. Counterhold crankshaft using crank hub Torx socket tool No. J–42098 or equivalent, remove flexplate.
3. Center punch steel ring in rear oil seal, then drill small, shallow pilot hole in steel ring.
4. Screw self tapping screw into steel ring and remove rear oil seal using suitable pliers.
5. Reverse procedure to install, noting the following:
   a. Coat lip of rear oil seal with suitable clean engine oil.
   b. Install rear oil seal using rear main oil seal installer tool No. J-42067, or equivalent.

OIL PAN

REPLACE

1. Raise and support vehicle.
2. Drain engine oil into a suitable container.
3. Remove lower transaxle flange to oil pan bolts.
4. Remove oil pan using RTV cutter tool No. SA-9123-E, or equivalent, to break pan loose from engine block.
5. Reverse procedure to install using Loctite 5900, or equivalent, .118 inch from inside edge of oil pan.

OIL PUMP

REPLACE

1. Drain coolant into suitable container.
2. Loosen clamp at air cleaner assembly, then remove outlet resonator duct assembly from air cleaner.
3. Disconnect electrical connector at mass air flow sensor, then release clamps on side of air cleaner assembly.
4. Remove upper air cleaner lid, then the air filter assembly.
5. Remove timing belt front and rear covers as outlined under "Front Cover, Replace."
6. Remove timing belt as outlined under "Timing Belt, Replace."
7. Remove and position air conditioning compressor and power steering pump aside.
8. Pivot alternator aside.
9. Remove oil pan as outlined under "Oil Pan, Replace," then the oil pump pick-up tube.
10. Hold crankshaft drive gear using crank hub holding tool No. J-42065, or equivalent.
11. Remove drive gear using crank hub Torx socket tool No. J-42098, or equivalent.
12. Remove oil pan housing bolts and oil pump.
13. Remove front main oil seal and collar from oil pump.
14. Reverse procedure to install, noting the following:
    a. Coat pump side of new oil pump gasket with anaerobic sealant Loctite 518, or equivalent.
    b. Install oil pump and align using guide pins. Apply thread sealant Loctite 242, or equivalent, to bolts.
    c. Coat lip of front main oil seal with suitable clean engine oil, then install using front main seal installer tool No. J-35268-A, or equivalent. Ensure seal is seated fully and evenly.
    d. Install new crankshaft drive gear bolt.
    e. Tighten oil pump after alternator and drive belt idler pulley for camshafts Nos. 3 and 4 have been tightened.
    f. Fill and bleed cooling system, as required.

BELT TENSION DATA

1. Allow engine to run for approximately 10 minutes with accessories turned on to ensure engine is warmed up.
2. Rotate tensioner arm clockwise until belt becomes loose and slowly apply tension back on belt.
3. Marking on tensioner arm must fall within two marks on tensioner body. Replace drive belt if tensioner marks fall outside operating range.
4. Record belt tension at midspan using calibrated belt tension gauge tool No. SA-9181-NE, or equivalent. This inspection can be performed with engine removed. If engine is in vehicle, upper engine mount must be removed.
5. Repeat previous steps three times. Determine average belt tension.
6. New belt tension should be 50–65 lbs. Used belt should be at least 45 lbs.

SERPENTINE DRIVE BELT

Belt Routing

Refer to **Fig. 17** for serpentine belt routing.

Belt Replacement

1. Remove righthand front engine mount as outlined under "Engine Mount, Replace."
2. Remove belt by rotate tensioner pulley clockwise and sliding drive belt off tensioner or water pump.
3. Reverse procedure to install.

COOLING SYSTEM BLEED

Run engine until thermostat opens, then cycle engine speed from idle to 3000 RPM in 30 second intervals. Add coolant as required to bring level to cold line on reservoir after engine has cooled.

THERMOSTAT

REPLACE

1. Remove thermostat housing extension bolt.
2. Remove extension by pulling it out from thermostat housing.
3. Remove thermostat housing and thermostat.
4. Reverse procedure to install.

WATER PUMP

REPLACE

1. Drain engine coolant into a suitable container.
2. Remove front timing belt cover as outlined under "Front Cover, Replace."
3. Remove water pump retaining bolts, then the water pump.
4. Remove water pump and O-ring.

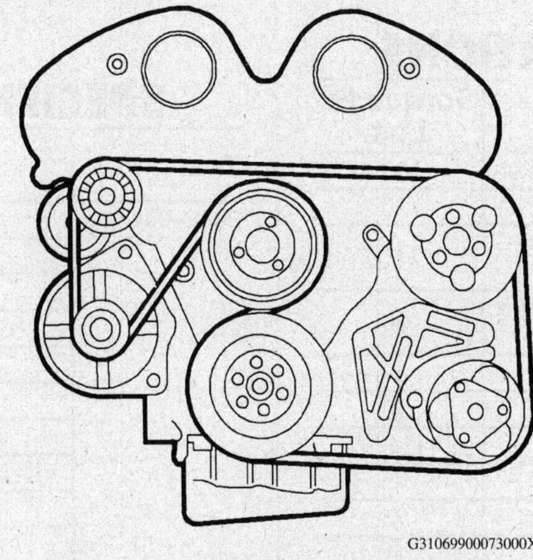

Fig. 17 Serpentine drive belt routing

5. Reverse procedure to install.

RADIATOR

REPLACE

Refer to the "2.2L Engine" section for replacement procedure.

FUEL PUMP

REPLACE

Refer to the "2.2L Engine" section for replacement procedure.

FUEL FILTER

REPLACE

Refer to the "2.2L Engine" section for replacement procedure.

TIGHTENING SPECIFICATIONS

Year	Component	Torque Ft. Lbs.
2002–03	Air Conditioning Compressor Bracket	30
	Air Conditioning Compressor	15
	Air Conditioning Compressor Hose Support Strap	71①
	Accessory Bracket, Air Conditioning & Power Steering	30
	Accessory Drive Belt Tensioner	30
	Alternator	30
	Battery Ground To Chassis	114①
	Battery Hold Down Bracket	15
	Battery Terminal	13
	Battery Tray	11
	Belt Tensioner	30
	Camshaft Bearing	71①
	Camshaft Cover	71①
	Camshaft Gear	37⑤
	Camshaft Position Sensor	71①
	Catalytic Converter	15
	Catalytic Converter Hanger	15
	Connecting Rod Cap	②
	Coolant Bridge	22
	Crankshaft Balancer	15
	Crankshaft Main Bearing	②
	Crankshaft Bearing Bridge	15
	Crankshaft Drive Gear	184⑥
	Crankshaft Position Sensor	71①
	Crankshaft Reluctor Ring	11
	Cylinder Head	④
	Drive Belt Tensioner	30
	Engine Control Module	71①
	Engine Coolant Temperature Sensor	13
	Engine Mount	41
	Engine Mount Bracket	41
	Engine Oil Cooler Cover	15
	Engine Oil Cooler Inlet & Outlet	22
	Engine Rear Cover	71①
	Engine Rear Cover Threaded Pin	89①
	Exhaust Manifold	15
	Flexplate	65③
	Front Timing Belt Cover	71①
	Fuel Filter Bracket	35①
	Fuel Line Stone Chip Guard	106①

TIGHTENING SPECIFICATIONS—Continued

Year	Component	Torque Ft. Lbs.
2002–03	Fuel Rail	71①
	Fuel Tank Mounting Strap	19
	Fuel Tank Pressure Sensor	18①
	Heated Oxygen Sensor	37
	Ignition Coil	71①
	Ignition Module	71①
	Intake Manifold	15
	Intake Manifold Spacer	25
	Intake Runner Bracket	15
	Knock Sensors	15
	Main Bearing	②
	Manifold Absolute Pressure Sensor	44①
	Oil Cooler Inlet & Outlet	15
	Oil Filter Cap	19
	Oil Filter Cartridge Housing to Engine Block	33
	Oil Pan	11
	Oil Pan Drain Plug	18
	Oil Pressure Switch	30
	Oil Pump	21
	Oxygen Sensors, Exhaust Manifold	37
	Power Steering Pump Pulley	15
	Spark Plug	18
	Starter	30
	Thermostat Housing	15
	Throttle Boot	71①
	Timing Belt Idler Pulley	30
	Timing Belt Tensioner Bracket	30
	Timing Belt Tensioner	15
	Torque Convertor Bolt	48
	Transaxle Cooler Line, Lower	36①
	Transaxle Cooler Line, Upper	18
	Transaxle Range Switch	18
	Transaxle Range Switch Lever	26
	Water Pump	18
	Water Pump Pulley	71①
	Wheel Bolt	92
	Wiring Channel	71①

①— Inch lbs.
②— Refer to "Main & Rod Bearings" for tighten specifications & sequence.
③— Tighten an additional 30° and final tighten an additional 15°.
④— Refer to "Cylinder Head, Replace" for tighten specifications & sequence.
⑤— Tighten an additional 60° and final tighten an additional 15°.
⑥— Tighten an additional 45° and final tighten an additional 15°.

3.5L Engine

NOTE: For Procedures Not Found In This Section, Refer To The "3.5L Engine" In The "Relay, SV6, Terraza & Uplander" Chapter.

NOTE: On Air Bag Equipped Models, Refer To "Air Bag System Precautions" Located In The Front Of This Manual For System Disarming & Arming Procedures.

NOTE: Refer To "Computer Relearn Procedures" Located In The Front Of This Manual When Battery Power To The Computer Has Been Interrupted.

INDEX

PRECAUTIONS

Air Bag Systems

Refer to "Air Bag System Precautions" in the front of this manual for system disarming and arming procedures.

Battery Ground Cable

Prior to service, disconnect battery ground cable and isolate as required.

Fuel System Pressure Relief

1. Connect J–34730-1A or equivalent to fuel pressure connection.
2. Install bleed hose into an approved container and open valve to bleed system pressure.
3. Disconnect fuel pressure gage from fuel pressure connection.

COMPRESSION PRESSURE

1. Start and run engine until it reaches normal operating temperature. Turn engine off.
2. Remove ignition modules and spark plugs.
3. Connect compression gauge tool No. SA-9127-E, or equivalent, into spark plug hole.
4. Open throttle fully.
5. Crank engine at not less than 250 RPM.
6. Measure compression while cranking engine. Prior to reading compression gauge needle should bounce at least 10 times.
7. Repeat previous steps for each cylinder.
8. Minimum compression on any one cylinder should not be less than 70% of highest cylinder. No cylinder should read less than 100 psi.
9. Place shop towel over spark plug holes and crank engine over a few seconds without compression gauge or spark plugs installed.
10. Repeat compression measuring steps on each cylinder.

ENGINE MOUNT

REPLACE

1. Remove air cleaner assembly.
2. Support engine.
3. Raise and support vehicle.
4. Remove engine mount to bracket bolts.
5. Remove engine mount to frame rail nuts.
6. Remove engine mount from vehicle.
7. Reverse procedure to install.

ENGINE

REPLACE

1. With tires in straight forward position, remove key from ignition.
2. Disconnect battery ground.
3. Remove air cleaner assembly.
4. Secure cooling module to upper body structure.
5. Remove battery and battery tray.
6. Disconnect transmission shifter cable.
7. Disconnect wiring harness from underhood junction block.
8. Evacuate A/C system.
9. Drain cooling system into suitable container.
10. Remove powertrain control module.
11. Remove A/C low pressure tube at front lift bracket.
12. Disconnect alternator positive battery cable.
13. Disconnect A/C high pressure switch harness.
14. Remove A/C tube from A/C compressor.
15. Disconnect A/C line from condenser to compressor.
16. Disconnect coolant reservoir hose from engine to reservoir.
17. Disconnect radiator inlet and outlet hoses from engine.
18. Remove inlet and outlet heater hoses.
19. Remove starter positive cable.
20. Relieve fuel pressure.
21. Disconnect fuel feed line.
22. Disconnect fuel EVAP line.
23. Raise and support vehicle.
24. Remove lower transaxle-to-engine bolts.
25. Remove PTU.
26. Remove torque convertor inspection cover.
27. Remove torque convertor to flywheel bolts.
28. Remove front wheels.

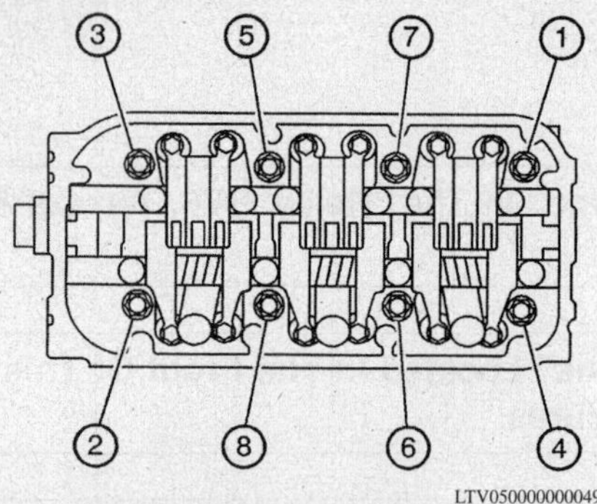

Fig. 1 Lefthand cylinder head bolt removal sequence

29. Remove lefthand wheelhouse liner.
30. Disconnect transmission cooler lines from transmission and bracket.
31. Remove lefthand and righthand tie rod ends from steering knuckle.
32. Remove lefthand and righthand stabilizer bar links.
33. Disconnect lefthand and righthand lower ball joints.
34. Remove lefthand and righthand axle shaft nuts.
35. **On AWD models,** remove propeller shaft completely from vehicle.
36. **On all models,** disconnect intermediate shaft from steering gear. **In order to prevent possible SIR system deployment, do not attempt to rotate steering shaft.**
37. Remove front exhaust pipe.
38. Remove three front fender pushpins to allow front fender to flex.
39. Use a paint pen or magic marker to mark frame to body position.
40. Support engine in cradle with wood blocks.
41. Disconnect front engine mount from body.
42. Position engine support table under powertrain assembly. **During powertrain removal, support vehicle body by placing a jack at rear of vehicle.**
43. With table positioned, fully raise table to contact with powertrain assembly.
44. Remove cradle bolts.
45. Slowly lower table to floor.
46. Remove starter.
47. Recover refrigerant.
48. Remove accessory drive belt.
49. Disconnect electrical connector from compressor.
50. Remove compressor hose bolt from compressor.
51. Remove compressor hose from compressor.
52. Remove and discard O-rings from compressor.
53. Install a cap to compressor hose to prevent moisture or contamination from entering A/C system.
54. Place an adjustable jack or lifting device under front edge of engine frame.
55. Loosen, but do not remove, front engine frame mounting bolts.
56. Lower forward edge of engine frame approximately .5 in.
57. Remove compressor bolts from engine.
58. Remove compressor from vehicle.
59. Remove alternator.
60. Remove front covers.
61. Remove rocker covers.
62. Remove catalytic converters.
63. Remove timing belt.
64. Loosen lefthand cylinder head bolts one-third of a turn at a time, in sequence, until all bolts are loosened, **Fig. 1.**
65. Remove bolts.
66. Remove lefthand cylinder head, gasket and pins.
67. Loosen righthand cylinder head bolts one-third of a turn at a time in sequence, until all bolts are loosened, **Fig. 2.**
68. Remove bolts.
69. Remove cylinder head, gasket and pins.
70. Remove front engine mount from engine.
71. Remove righthand engine mount.
72. Separate engine from transmission.
73. Reverse procedure to install.

INTAKE MANIFOLD

REPLACE

Refer to the "3.5L Engine" in the "Relay, SV6, Terraza & Uplander" chapter for intake manifold replacement procedure.

EXHAUST MANIFOLD

REPLACE

Refer to the "3.5L Engine" in the "Relay, SV6, Terraza & Uplander" chapter for exhaust manifold replacement procedure.

CYLINDER HEAD

REPLACE

Refer to the "3.5L Engine" in the "Relay, SV6, Terraza & Uplander" chapter for cylinder head replacement procedure.

VALVE COVER

REPLACE

Refer to the "3.5L Engine" in the "Relay, SV6, Terraza & Uplander" chapter for valve cover replacement procedure.

CAMSHAFT LOBE LIFT SPECIFICATIONS

Refer to the "3.5L Engine" in the "Relay, SV6, Terraza & Uplander" chapter for camshaft lobe lift specifications.

VALVE ADJUSTMENT

Refer to the "3.5L Engine" in the "Relay, SV6, Terraza & Uplander" chapter for valve adjustment procedure.

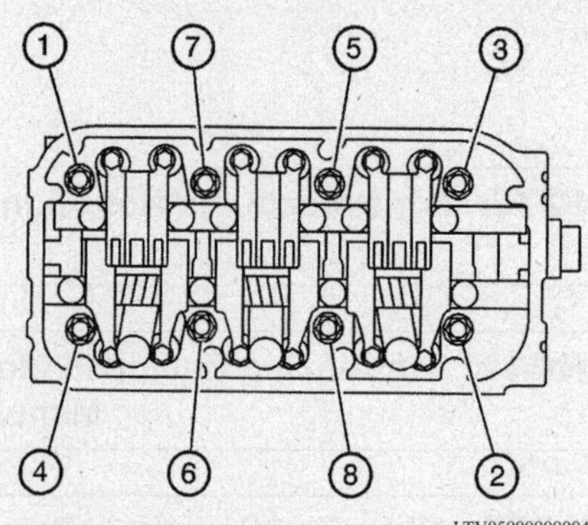

Fig. 2 Righthand cylinder head bolt removal sequence

FRONT COVER

REPLACE

Refer to the "3.5L Engine" in the "Relay, SV6, Terraza & Uplander" chapter for front cover replacement procedure.

TIMING BELT

REPLACE

Refer to the "3.5L Engine" in the "Relay, Terraza, Uplander & SV6" chapter for timing belt replacement procedure.

CAMSHAFT

REPLACE

Refer to the "3.5L Engine" in the "Relay, SV6, Terraza & Uplander" chapter for camshaft replacement procedure.

PISTON & ROD ASSEMBLY

Refer to the "3.5L Engine" in the "Relay, SV6, Terraza & Uplander" chapter for piston & rod assembly.

PISTONS, PINS & RINGS

Refer to the "3.5L Engine" in the "Relay, SV6, Terraza & Uplander" chapter.

MAIN & ROD BEARINGS

Refer to the "3.5L Engine" in the "Relay, SV6, Terraza & Uplander" chapter.

CRANKSHAFT REAR OIL SEAL

REPLACE

Refer to the "3.5L Engine" in the "Relay, SV6, Terraza & Uplander" chapter for crankshaft rear oil seal replacement procedure.

OIL PAN

REPLACE

Refer to the "3.5L Engine" in the "Relay, SV6, Terraza & Uplander" chapter for oil pan replacement procedure.

OIL PUMP

REPLACE

Refer to the "3.5L Engine" in the "Relay, SV6, Terraza & Uplander" chapter for oil pump replacement procedure.

BELT TENSION DATA

Refer to the "3.5L Engine" in the "Relay, SV6, Terraza & Uplander" chapter for belt tension data.

SERPENTINE DRIVE BELT

Belt Routing

Refer to **Fig. 3** for serpentine drive belt routing.

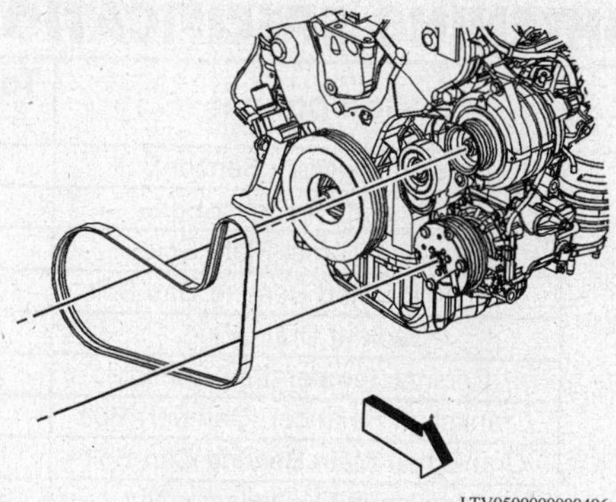

Fig. 3 Serpentine drive belt routing

Belt Replacement

1. Remove air cleaner assembly.
2. Loosen drive belt tensioner by rotating tensioner pulley clockwise while sliding drive belt off tensioner.
3. Remove drive belt.
4. Clean and inspect serpentine drive belt surfaces.
5. Reverse procedure to install.

COOLING SYSTEM BLEED

Run engine until thermostat opens, then cycle engine speed from idle to 3000 RPM in 30 second intervals. Add coolant as required to bring level to cold line on reservoir after engine has cooled.

THERMOSTAT

REPLACE

Refer to the "3.5L Engine" in the "Relay, SV6, Terraza & Uplander" chapter for thermostat replacement procedure.

WATER PUMP

REPLACE

Refer to the "3.5L Engine" in the "Relay, SV6, Terraza & Uplander" chapter for water pump replacement procedure.

RADIATOR

REPLACE

1. Drain cooling system into suitable container.
2. Remove front fascia.
3. Remove condenser radiator fan module closeout retainers from condenser.
4. Remove CRFM closeout panel from condenser.
5. Remove fan assembly bolts from radiator.
6. Lift fan assembly to disengage lower retention tabs.
7. Position fan assembly away from radiator.
8. Lift condenser while holding upper retention tabs forward.
9. Position condenser away from radiator.
10. Disconnect transmission cooler liners from radiator.
11. Remove CRFM bracket bolts from radiator support.
12. Remove CRFM brackets from radiator.
13. Remove radiator inlet hose clamp from radiator.
14. Remove radiator inlet hose from radiator.
15. Remove radiator outlet hose clamp from radiator.
16. Remove radiator outlet hose from radiator.
17. Remove radiator from vehicle.
18. Remove radiator seals from radiator.
19. Reverse procedure to install.

FUEL PUMP

REPLACE

Whenever fuel line fittings are loosened or removed, wrap a shop cloth around fitting and have an approved container available to collect any fuel. Clean all fuel pipe and hose connections and surrounding areas before disassembling to avoid possible contamination of fuel system. Spray fuel pump module cam-lock ring tang with penetrating oil prior to attempting removal.

1. Remove fuel tank.
2. Disconnect EVAP vent line quick connect.
3. Use tool no. SA9156E, or equivalent, and remove fuel pump module retaining ring. **To prevent retainer damage, do not attempt to remove retainer with a 12 in. or shorter ratchet/breaker bar.**
4. Disconnect secondary level sensor electrical connector.
5. Disconnect suction port attaching tube by pressing down on tab.
6. Remove secondary fuel pump module. **To prevent bending of sending unit float arm during removal, lift pump module up slightly to disengage orientation tabs in tank and rotate module 45°.**
7. Disconnect electrical connector from primary fuel pump module and fuel tank pressure sensor.
8. Use tool no. J 45722, or equivalent, and a long breaker-bar in order to unlock fuel sender lock ring. **Avoid damaging lock ring. Use only tool no. J-45722, or equivalent, to prevent damage to lock ring. Do not handle fuel sender assembly by fuel pipes. Amount of leverage generated by handling fuel pipes could damage joints. Do not use impact tools. Significant force will be required to release lock ring. Use of a hammer or screwdriver is not recommended. Secure fuel tank in order to prevent fuel tank rotation.**
9. Disconnect fuel feed and vent lines from fuel tank.
10. Remove primary fuel pump module assembly. **To prevent bending of sending unit float arm during removal, lift pump module up slightly to disengage orientation tabs in tank and rotate module 45°.**
11. Discard fuel pump module-to-tank seal. **Always replace fuel pump module-to-tank seal, O-ring, when fuel pump module is removed.**
12. If fuel level sending unit is being replaced, remove fuel level sender.
13. Place lock ring on a flat surface. Measure clearance between lock ring and flat surface using a feeler gage at 7 points. **Some lock rings were manufactured with DO NOT REUSE stamped into them. These lock rings may be reused if they are not damaged or warped. Inspect lock ring for damage due to improper removal installation procedures. If damage is found, instal a new lock ring. Inspect lock ring for flatness.**
14. If warpage is less than .016 in., lock ring does not require replacement.
15. If warpage is greater than .016 in., lock ring must be replaced.
16. Reverse procedure to install.

TIGHTENING SPECIFICATIONS

Year	Component	Torque Ft. Lbs.
2005–06	Camshaft Position Sensor Bolt	89①
	Camshaft Sprocket Bolt	103
	Camshaft Thrust Plate Screw	89①
	Connecting Rod Bearing Cap Bolt	②
	Coolant Drain Plug	14
	Coolant Temperature Sensor	17
	Crankshaft Balancer (Damper) Bolt	118
	Crankshaft Main Bearing Cap Bolt	③
	Crankshaft Oil Deflector Nut	18
	Crankshaft Position Sensor Shield Nut	97①
	Cylinder Head Bolt	④
	Cylinder Head Plug	15
	Drive Belt Tensioner Bolt	37
	EGR Valve Assembly Bolt	22
	Engine Block Plug	18
	Engine Block Heater	44
	Engine Front Cover (Large & Medium) Bolt	41
	Engine Front Cover (Small) Bolt	20
	Engine Mount Strut & A/C Compressor Bracket Bolt	37
	Engine Mount Strut & Generator Bracket Bolt	37
	EVAP Purge Valve Bolt	12
	Exhaust Crossover Pipe Stud/Nut	18
	Exhaust Manifold Nut	12
	Exhaust Manifold Stud	13
	Flywheel Bolt	52
	Intake Manifold Bolt, Lower (Center)	15
	Intake Manifold Bolt, Lower (Corner)	18
	Intake Manifold Bolt/Stud, Upper	18
	Knock Sensor	18
	MAP Sensor Bolt	89①
	Oil Pan Bolt	18
	Oil Pan Drain Plug	18
	Oil Pan Side Bolt	37
	Oil Pump Mounting Bolt	30
	Spark Plug	11
	Thermostat Bypass Pipe To Engine Front Cover Bolt	89①
	Thermostat Bypass Pipe To Throttle Body Nut/Bolt	89①
	Throttle Body Bolt	89①
	Throttle Body Stud	53①
	Timing Chain Damper Bolt	15
	Valve Lifter Guide Bolt	89①
	Valve Cover	89①
	Valve Rocker Arm Bolt	24
	Water Outlet Bolt	18
	Water Pump Bolt	89①
	Water Pump Pulley Bolt	18

① — Inch lbs.
② — First pass, 18 ft. lbs.; second pass, an additional 110°.
③ — First pass, 37 ft. lbs.; second pass, an additional 77°.
④ — Refer to "Cylinder Head, Replace" for tightening procedure.

Rear Axle & Suspension

NOTE: On Air Bag Equipped Models, Refer To "Air Bag System Precautions" Located In The Front Of This Manual For System Disarming & Arming Procedures.

INDEX

DESCRIPTION

The rear suspension system used on this vehicle is an independent link type suspension. The rear suspension contains the following components; Support assembly, coil springs, stabilizer shaft, insulators, stabilizer links, upper and lower control arms, trailing arm, knuckles, wheel bearing/hub and shock absorbers.

REAR AXLE SHAFT

REPLACE

1. Raise and support vehicle, then remove tire and wheel.
2. Remove and discard wheel drive shaft spindle nut.
3. Disconnect stabilizer link from lower control arm.
4. Place a stand under lower control arm for support, then remove lower shock absorber mounting bolt and nut.
5. Remove toe link nut, bolt, and washer.
6. Loosen, but do not remove lower suspension jounce bumper nut.
7. Remove lower control arm to suspension knuckle bolt and nut.
8. Slowly lower support stand until coil spring tension is relieved, then remove coil spring.
9. Loosen, but do not remove upper control arm to suspension knuckle nut.
10. Place a block of wood against wheel drive shaft spindle, then tap with a hammer to release spindle from wheel hub and bearing assembly.
11. Rotate suspension knuckle upward, then secure with mechanics wire.
12. Assemble tool Nos. J-45341 and SA9173 or equivalents, to wheel drive shaft inner tripot joint.
13. Disengage tripot joint from rear drive module.
14. Remove wheel drive shaft from vehicle.
15. Reverse procedure to install.

DIFFERENTIAL CARRIER

REPLACE

1. Raise and support vehicle.
2. Remove rear exhaust pipe flange to intermediate pipe nuts.
3. Separate hangers from rubber isolators, then remove muffler and pipe assembly.
4. Remove rear wheel drive shafts as outlined under "Rear Axle Shaft, Replace."
5. Remove propeller shaft as outlined under "Propeller Shaft, Replace."
6. Support rear drive module, then remove rear exhaust pipe flange to intermediate pipe nuts.
7. Separate hangers from rubber isolators, then remove muffler and pipe assembly.
8. Remove stabilizer bar as outlined under "Stabilizer Bar, Replace."
9. Remove RAM bracket to bushing mounting nut and bolt, then the bracket.
10. Remove rear drive module mounting nuts and bolts, then the module from vehicle.
11. Reverse procedure to install.

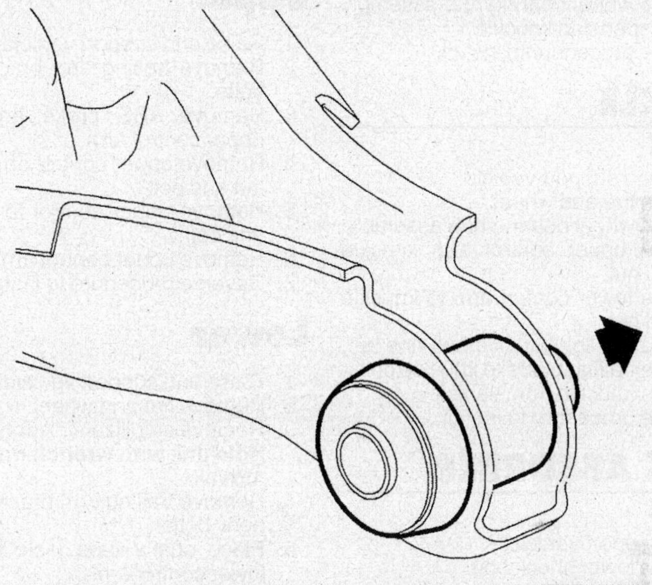

Fig. 1 Lower control arm bushing removal

PROPELLER SHAFT

REPLACE

1. Place transmission in neutral, then raise and support vehicle.
2. Index mark relationship of propeller shaft to rear drive module flange.
3. Remove bolts, then the underbody guard loop.
4. Support propeller shaft at rear drive module.
5. Remove bolts securing propeller shaft yoke flange to rear drive module flange.
6. Index mark relationship of propeller shaft to power take off unit flange.
7. Support propeller shaft at PTU, then remove bolts securing propeller shaft to PTU flange.
8. Support propeller shaft at support bearing, then remove bolts securing

propeller shaft support bearing to vehicle underbody.
9. Move propeller shaft rearward to disengage constant velocity joint from PTU flange.
10. Remove propeller shaft from vehicle.
11. Reverse procedure to install.

HUB & BEARING

REPLACE

1. Remove rear brake drum.
2. On vehicles with all-wheel drive, remove wheel drive shaft spindle nut.
3. Disconnect wheel speed sensor electrical sonneteer, if equipped.
4. Support wheel drive shaft with heavy mechanic's wire, or equivalent. **Do not damage wheel drive shaft joint seal.**
5. Remove wheel bearing/hub mounting bolts.
6. Remove wheel bearing/hub assembly from suspension knuckle.
7. Reverse procedure to install.

KNUCKLE

REPLACE

1. Raise and support vehicle.
2. Remove tire and wheel.
3. Remove wheel bearing/hub assembly.
4. Remove upper control arm knuckle bolt and nut.
5. Remove lower control arm to knuckle bolt and nut.
6. Remove toe link knuckle bolt and nut.
7. Remove trailing blade to knuckle bolts.
8. Remove knuckle from vehicle.
9. Reverse procedure to install.

SHOCK ABSORBER

REPLACE

1. Raise support vehicle.
2. Remove lower shock bolt.
3. Remove wheelhouse liner.
4. Remove upper shock bolt.
5. Remove shock from vehicle.
6. Reverse procedure to install.

COIL SPRING

REPLACE

1. Raise support vehicle.
2. Remove tire and wheel.
3. Remove stabilizer link lower control arm nut. **Hold link with a wrench during nut removal.**
4. Remove trailing arm bracket to underbody bolts.
5. Place screw-type jackstand under lower control arm.
6. Compress coil spring.
7. Remove lower shock bolt.
8. Loosen lower control arm to support frame bolt.
9. Remove lower control arm knuckle nut and bolt.
10. Lower control arm in order to unload coil spring.
11. Remove coil spring.
12. Reverse procedure to install.

CONTROL ARM

REPLACE

Upper

1. Raise and support vehicle.
2. Remove trailing arm bracket to body bolts.
3. Remove ABS brake harness from upper control arm.
4. Remove upper control arm to knuckle nut and bolt.
5. Remove upper control to support nut and bolt.
6. Remove upper control arm.
7. Reverse procedure to install.

Lower

1. Raise and support vehicle.
2. Remove tire and wheel.
3. Remove stabilizer link control arm nut. **Hold link with wrench during nut removal.**
4. Remove trailing arm bracket to underbody bolts.
5. Place screw type jack stand under lower control arm.
6. Compress coil spring.
7. Remove lower shock bolt.
8. Remove jounce bumper nut at lower control arm.
9. Loosen lower control arm to support frame bolt.
10. Remove lower control arm to knuckle nut and bolt.
11. Lower control arm in order to unload coil spring.
12. Remove coil spring.
13. Remove jounce bumper.
14. Remove control arm support nut and bolt.
15. Remove lower control arm.
16. Reverse procedure to install.

CONTROL ARM BUSHING

REPLACE

1. Remove lower control arm as outlined under "Control Arm Replace, Lower."
2. Remove bushing in direction of arrow, **Fig. 1,** using tool no. J 45097, or equivalent.
3. Install push out socket against bushing from flanged side of control arm.
4. Install through bolt with washer and bearing against push out socket.
5. Install backing socket against control arm, opposite of flange.
6. Install stabilizer between control arm ears.
7. Install flat washer and nut.
8. Tighten nut until bushing is removed. **Apply high pressure lube to threads of tool.**
9. Reverse procedure to install.

TRAILING ARM

REPLACE

1. Raise and support vehicle.
2. Remove trailing arm bracket to body bolts.
3. Remove trailing arm bushing to bracket nut and bolts.
4. Remove park brake cable clip from trailing arm.
5. Remove trailing arm knuckle bolts.
6. Remove trailing arm.
7. Reverse procedure to install.

STABILIZER BAR

REPLACE

1. Raise and support vehicle.
2. Remove stabilizer link to stabilizer bar nut. **Hold ball shaft secure with a torx bit, when removing nut.**
3. Remove stabilizer bar clamp bolts.
4. Disengage stabilizer bar from stabilizer link ball studs, while removing stabilizer bar from vehicle.
5. Reverse procedure to install.

TIGHTENING SPECIFICATIONS

Year	Component	Torque Ft. Lbs.
2002–06	Drive Module Bracket To Drive Module Bolts	92
	Drive Module Bracket To Support Assembly Nut	92
	Jounce Bumper To Lower Control Arm Nut	46
	Knuckle To Lower Control Arm Nut	81
	Knuckle To Toe Link Bolt	118
	Knuckle To Trailing Arm Bolt	100
	Knuckle To Upper Control Arm Bolt	118
	Lower Control Arm To Support Assembly Bolt	81
	Lower Shock Bolt	77
	Park Brake Cable Clip	18
	Stabilizer Link To Lower Control Arm Nut	11
	Stabilizer Link To Stabilizer Shaft Nut	35
	Stabilizer Shaft Clamp Bolt	52
	Support To Body Bolts	125
	Toe Link To Support Bolts	118
	Trailing Arm Bracket To Body Bolts	81
	Trailing Arm Bushing To Bracket Bolts	118
	Upper Control Arm Support Bolts	118
	Upper Shock Bolts	77
	Wheel Bearing/Hub Mounting Bolts Rear	62
	Wheel Bearing/Hub To Steering Knuckle Bolts	96
	Wheel Drive Shaft Spindle Nut	92

Front Suspension & Steering

INDEX

HUB & BEARING

REPLACE

1. Remove front brake rotor.
2. Disconnect wheel speed sensor electrical connector.
3. Remove wheel speed sensor electrical connector from connector bracket.
4. Remove front wheel drive shaft spindle nut.
5. Support wheel drive shaft with heavy mechanic's wire or equivalent.
6. Remove and discard wheel bearing/hub mounting bolts.
7. Remove wheel bearing/hub assembly from steering knuckle.
8. Reverse procedure to install.

BALL JOINT

REPLACE

1. Remove lower control arm as outlined under "Control Arm, Replace."
2. Place control arm in a vise or suitable holding device.
3. Remove ball joint rivets using the following procedure:
   a. Drill through rivets using a 5⁄16 inch drill bit.
   b. Enlarge hole using a 31⁄64 inch drill bit.
   c. Remove any remaining burs from control arm.
4. Remove ball joint from control arm. Note position of ball joint for reassembly.
5. Reverse procedure to install.

COIL SPRING

REPLACE

Refer to "Coil Spring & Strut Service" for coil spring replacement.

STRUT

REPLACE

1. Install strut assembly in tool no J 45400, or equivalent, using the following procedure:
   a. Adjust lower legs of tool no. J 45400, or equivalent, to lowest possible coil of spring.
   b. Adjust upper legs of tool no. J 45400, or equivalent, to highest possible coil of spring.
   c. Inspect strut assembly to insure hooks on strut compress legs are properly installed on spring coils.
   d. Verify strut assembly is parallel with tool no. J 4540, or equivalent.
2. Compress spring enough to unload upper strut mount.
3. Remove strut shaft nut.
4. Lower strut from spring assembly. **Leave spring in spring compressor.**
5. Remove upper mount assembly, inspect for damage and deterioration. Replace as required.
6. Remove strut dust shield and inspect for damage and deterioration. Replace as required.
7. Remove hollow bumper from strut shaft and inspect for damage and deterioration. Replace as required.
8. Inspect spring for damage. Replace as required.
9. Reverse procedure to install.

COIL SPRING & STRUT SERVICE

1. Remove strut assembly as outlined under "Strut, Replace."
2. Install strut assembly in spring compressing tool No. J-45400 or equivalent.
3. Compress spring enough to unload upper strut mount, then remove strut shaft nut.
4. Lower strut from spring assembly, inspect for damage and deterioration.
5. Reverse procedure to install.

CONTROL ARM

REPLACE

1. Raise and support vehicle.
2. Remove wheel and tire assembly.
3. Remove control arm ball stud cotter pin. Discard cotter pin.
4. Loosen ball stud nut until nut is level with top of ball stud.
5. Separate lower control arm from steering knuckle using tool no. J 43828, or equivalent.
6. Remove ball stud nut.
7. Remove control arm-to-frame bolt and nut. Discard bolt and nut.
8. Remove control arm-to-frame rear bolts and nuts. Discard bolts and nuts.
9. Remove control arm.
10. Reverse procedure to install.

CONTROL ARM BUSHING

REPLACE

Front

1. Raise and support vehicle.
2. Remove front tire wheel assembly.
3. Remove lower control arm as outlined in "Control Arm Replace, Lower".
4. Place control arm in a vise or suitable holding device.
5. Use tool no. J 44971, or equivalent, to press out front control arm bushing.
6. Reverse procedure to install.

Rear

1. Raise and support vehicle.
2. Remove front tire and wheel assembly.
3. Remove lower control arm as outlined in "Control Arm Replace, Lower".
4. Remove rear bushing nut.
5. Remove rear bushing.
6. Reverse procedure to install.

STEERING KNUCKLE

REPLACE

1. Raise and support vehicle.
2. Remove tire and wheel.
3. Disconnect stabilizer link from strut assembly. **Do not allow stabilizer ball stud to rotate while removing link nut.**
4. Loosen steering knuckle to strut bolts and nuts.
5. Remove wheel bearing/hub assembly.
6. Remove and discard lower ball joint cotter pin.
7. Loosen ball joint stud nut, until level with top of ball stud.
8. Separate lower control arm from steering knuckle using tool no. J 43828, or equivalent.
9. Remove lower control arm and nut from steering knuckle.
10. Remove outer tie rod end to knuckle nut.
11. Separate outer tie rod from steering knuckle using tool no. SA91100C, or equivalent.
12. Remove steering knuckle to strut bolts and nuts. Discard bolts and nuts.
13. Remove steering knuckle from vehicle.
14. Reverse procedure to install.

STABILIZER BAR

REPLACE

1. Turn front wheel to full righthand position.
2. Raise and support vehicle.
3. Remove front tire and wheels.
4. If equipped with a 2.2L engine, remove front exhaust pipe.
5. Disconnect stabilizer link from stabilizer bar.
6. Remove lefthand outer tie rod to steering knuckle nut. Discard nut.
7. Separate outer tie rod from steering knuckle using tool no. SA91100C, or equivalent.
8. Remove stabilizer bar clamp to cradle bolts.
9. Remove stabilizer bar clamps and bushings from stabilizer bar.
10. Remove stabilizer bar from vehicle through lefthand wheel opening. **Take care not to catch transmission shift cable or lefthand wheel house plastic trim when removing stabilizer bar.**
11. Reverse procedure to install.

TIE ROD

REPLACE

1. Raise and support vehicle.
2. Remove front tire assembly.
3. Loosen tie rod inner jam nut. **Mark location of jam nut for installation.**
4. Remove tie rod to knuckle nut. Discard nut. **Hold ball stud to prevent turning during removal of nut.**
5. Use SA91100C to separate tie rod from steering knuckle. **Do not free ball stud by using a pickle fork or wedge-type tool. Damage to seal or bushing may result.**
6. Remove outer tie rod end from inner tie rod.
7. Reverse procedure to install.

POWER STEERING GEAR

REPLACE

1. Raise and support vehicle.
2. Remove front tires.
3. Remove both outer tie rod to steering knuckle nuts. Discard nuts.
4. Separate tie rods from steering knuckles using tool no. SA91100C, or equivalent. **Do not free ball stud by using a pickle fork or a wedge-type tool. Damage to seal or bushing may result. Hold ball stud to prevent turning during removal of nut.**
5. Rotate intermediate steering shaft in order to gain access to intermediate shaft pinch bolt.
6. Remove intermediate to steering gear pinch bolt. Discard bolt.
7. Disconnect intermediate shaft from steering gear.
8. Disconnect stabilizer links from stabilizer bar.
9. On CVT equipped vehicle, remove shift cable clip from steering gear.
10. Remove steering gear cradle mounting bolts.
11. Remove steering gear through righthand side of vehicle.
12. With heat shield equipped steering gears, remove heat shield. Save for installation.
13. Reverse procedure to install.

TIGHTENING SPECIFICATIONS

Year	Component	Torque Ft. Lbs.
2002–06	Ball Joint To Control Arm Bolt And Nut	50
	Brake Bracket Bolt	11
	Control Arm To Frame Front Bolt	148
	Control Arm To Frame Rear Nuts	52
	Intermediate Steering Shaft Pinch Bolt	25
	Lower Control Arm Ball Stud Nut	30
	Outer Tie Rod Retention Nut	18①
	Rear Bushing To Lower Control Arm Nut	110
	Stabilizer Bar Clamp Bolt	37
	Stabilizer Link Nuts	48
	Steering Gear To Cradle Mounting Bolt	81
	Strut Shaft Nut	55
	Strut To Body Nuts And Bolts	18
	Strut To Steering Knuckle Bolt And Nut	133
	Tie Rod Retention Nut	44
	Wheel Bearing/Hub Mounting Bolt	96
	Wheel Drive Shaft Spindle Nut	157

① — Plus an additional 90°.

Wheel Alignment

INDEX

PRECAUTIONS

Air Bag Systems

Refer to "Air Bag System Precautions" in the front of this manual for system disarming and arming procedures.

Battery Ground Cable

Prior to service, disconnect battery ground cable and isolate as required.

PRELIMINARY INSPECTION

Inspect the following components, adjust, repair or replace as required prior to performing front wheel alignment.

1. Inflate tires to cold specifications.
2. Ensure tires are of same size, ply rating and load rating.
3. Inspect runout of wheels and tires.
4. Inspect for excessive wheel bearing endplay.
5. Inspect ball joints and tie rod ends for looseness or wear.
6. Inspect control arms and stabilizer shaft for looseness or wear.
7. Inspect steering gear for looseness at the frame.
8. Inspect struts/shock absorbers for wear, leaks, and any noticeable noises.
9. Inspect the vehicle trim height.
10. Inspect fuel level. Fuel tank should be full or vehicle should have a compensating load added.

FRONT WHEEL ALIGNMENT

Caster

The front caster is not adjustable. If the front caster angle is not within specifications, inspect for suspension support misalignment or front suspension damage. Replace any damaged suspension components as required.

Camber

1. Raise and support vehicle.
2. Remove front tires.
3. Remove strut to knuckle nuts and bolts, discard nuts and bolts.
4. If strut has not been modified, proceed as follows:
   a. Remove strut assembly as outlined under "Front Suspension & Steering."
   b. If increasing negative camber, remove material from outside of lower strut hole.
   c. If decreasing negative camber, remove material from inside of lower strut hole, **Fig. 1.**
   d. Install strut assembly.
5. Place vehicle in suitable alignment equipment.
6. Loosen both strut-to-knuckle nuts just enough to allow movement.
7. Adjust camber to specification by moving top of wheel in or out.
8. **Torque** strut bolts to 133 ft. lbs.

Toe

1. Position and lock steering wheel with vehicle wheels in straight forward position.
2. Loosen both inner tie rod jam nuts, **Fig. 2.**
3. Use a wrench on tie rod flats to increase or decrease toe angle specifications.
4. **Torque** jam nuts to 44 ft. lbs.
5. Inspect toe angle to ensure proper adjustment and adjust as required.

REAR WHEEL ALIGNMENT

Camber

1. Loosen upper control arm to frame bolt enough to allow movement, **Fig. 3.**
2. **Frame in this vehicle is slotted, turning cam nut will move camber in to designated location.**
3. Rotate upper control arm to frame bolt in direction required to correct camber measurement.
4. Snug upper control arm to frame bolt, do not tighten at this time.
5. Inspect rear camber specifications and adjust as required.
6. **Torque** upper control arm to frame bolts to 81 ft. lbs.

Toe

1. Loosen toe link to frame bolt enough to allow for movement, **Fig. 4.**
2. Adjust toe to specifications by turning adjusting nut.
3. **Torque** cam nuts to 81 ft. lbs.

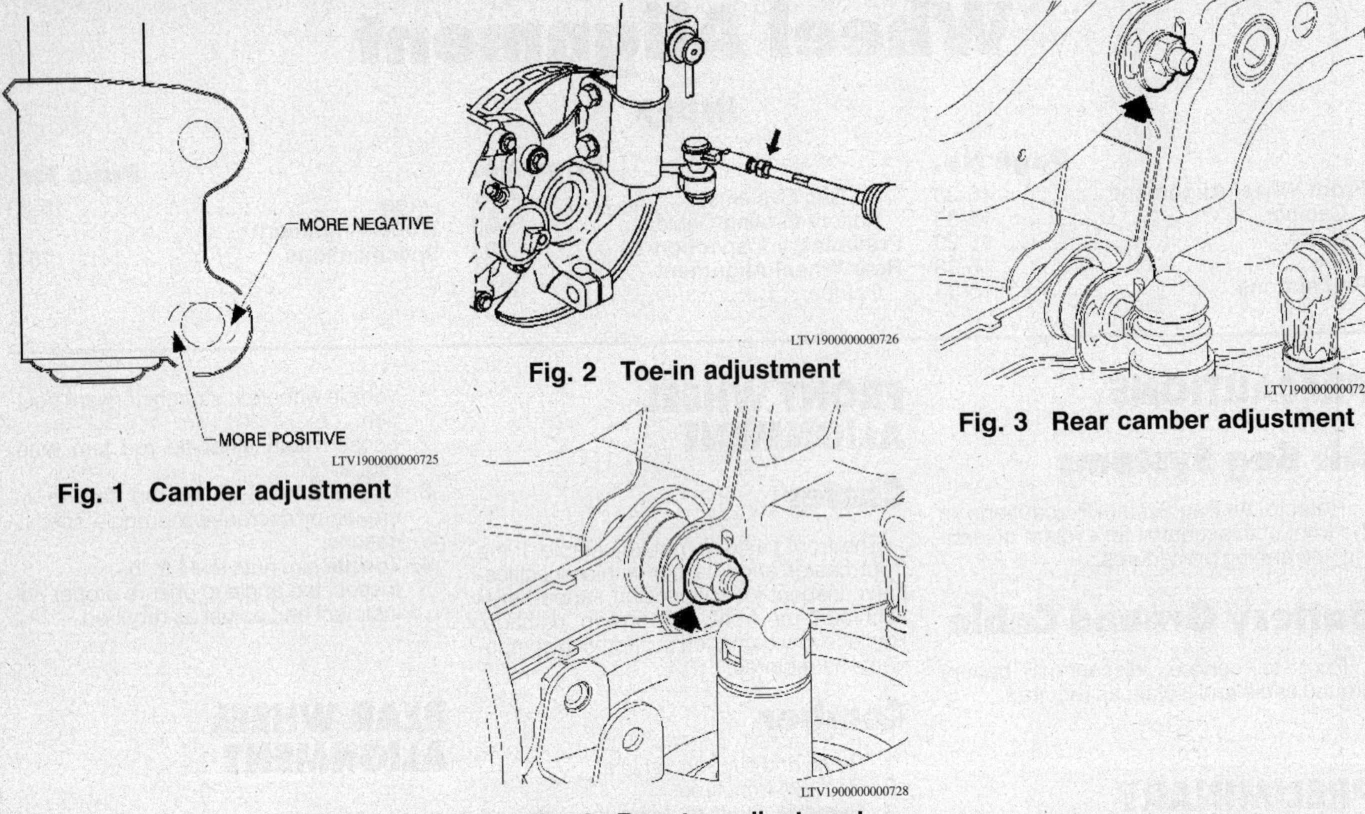

Fig. 1 Camber adjustment

Fig. 2 Toe-in adjustment

Fig. 3 Rear camber adjustment

Fig. 4 Rear toe adjustment

AIR CONDITIONING

TABLE OF CONTENTS

System Testing

INDEX

PRECAUTIONS

Battery Ground Cable

Prior to service disconnect battery ground cable and isolate as required.

Product Compatibility

Before replenishing refrigerant oil, ensure product compatibility with the system being serviced.

R-134a

R-134a refrigerant is a non-toxic, nonflammable, clear, colorless and odorless liquefied gas.

R-134a refrigerant is not compatible with R-12 refrigerant. Even a small amount of R-12 in an R-134a system will cause lubricant contamination, compressor failure and or improper A/C performance. Never add R-12 to an R-134a system.

New service ports have been added to the compressor to prevent charging the system with R-12 refrigerant. **R-134a systems require a special compressor lubricant. Use recommended compressor oil when servicing system.**

Avoid breathing R-134a A/C refrigerant and lubricant vapor or mist. Exposure may irritate eyes, nose and throat. Use only approved service equipment to discharge R-134a systems.

Always wear eye protection when servicing the air conditioning system. Serious injury may result from eye contact with refrigerant. If this occurs, seek prompt medical attention.

Safety

Protective goggles should be worn when opening any refrigerant lines. A bottle of sterile mineral oil and a quantity of weak boric acid solution must always be kept nearby when servicing air conditioning system. **If liquid coolant does touch eyes, immediately use a few drops of sterile mineral oil to wash them out, then wash eyes clean with weak boric acid solution. Seek a doctor's aid immediately even though irritation may have ceased.**

Freon used in vehicle A/C systems will usually be in a vapor state when being handled in a repair shop. Should a portion of liquid coolant come in contact with hands or face, **note that its temperature momentarily will be at least 22°F below zero.**

When inspecting a system for leaks with a torch type leak detector, **do not breathe vapors coming from flame.** Do not recover refrigerant in area of a live flame. A poisonous phosgene gas is produced when refrigerant is burned. While small amount of gas is produced by a leak detector this is not harmful unless inhaled directly at flame.

Never allow temperature of refrigerant drums to exceed 125°F. Resultant increase in temperature will cause a corresponding increase in pressure which may cause safety plug to release or drum to burst.

If it is required to heat a drum of refrigerant when charging a system, drum should be placed in water that is no hotter than 125°F. Never use a blowtorch, or other open flame. If possible, a pressure release mechanism should be attached before drum is heated.

Cleanliness

Air conditioning systems are extremely sensitive to moisture and dirt. The importance of clean working conditions is extremely important, as the smallest particle of foreign matter in an air conditioning system will contaminate the refrigerant, causing rust, ice or damage to the compressor. For this reason, all replacement components are sold in vacuum sealed containers and should not be opened until they are to be installed in the system. If, for any reason, a part has been removed from its container for any length of time, the part must be completely flushed to remove any dust or moisture that may have accumulated during storage. In cases of collision repairs where the system has been open for any length of time, the entire system must be purged completely and a new receiver/drier must be installed because the element of the existing unit will have become saturated and unable to remove any moisture from the system once the system is recharged.

When making gauge connections, purge the gauge lines first by cracking the charging valve and allowing a small amount of refrigerant to flow through the lines, then connect the lines immediately.

Cleanliness is especially important when servicing compressors because of the very close tolerances used in these units. Consequently, repairs to the compressor itself should not be attempted unless all proper

Step	Action	Value(s)	Yes	No
1	Inspect the following components of the A/C system: • The fuses • The wire connectors • The blower fan operation Did you find and repair a condition?	—	System OK	Go to *Step 2*
2	Is the drive belt loose, missing, or damaged?	—	Go to *Step 4*	Go to *Step 3*
3	**Important:** The ambient temperature must be above 10°C (50°F) for completion of this diagnostic procedure. Inspect the compressor clutch engagement by following these steps: 1. Start the engine. 2. Idle the engine at approximately 1000 RPM. 3. Set the A/C control assembly to the NORM position. 4. Set the blower to the HIGH position. 5. Place an auxiliary fan in front of the vehicle. 6. Observe the clutch operation for a period of 5 minutes. Does the clutch engage or cycle?	—	Go to *Step 7*	Go to *Step 11*
4	Has the compressor seized?	—	Go to *Step 5*	Go to *Step 6*

GC7029900586010A

Fig. 1 CCOT troubleshooting (Part 1 of 4)

Step	Action	Value(s)	Yes	No
5	1. Replace the compressor assembly. 2. Replace the orifice. 3. Recover the refrigerant. 4. Evacuate the system. 5. Charge the system. Does the air conditioning system operate properly?	—	System OK	Go to *Step 6*
6	Tighten or replace the belt, as needed. Does the air conditioning system operate properly?	—	System OK	Go to *Step 3*
7	Feel the liquid line before the orifice tube. Is the liquid line cold?	—	Go to *Step 8*	Go to *Step 9*
8	1. Inspect the high side of the system for a frost spot in order to locate a restriction. 2. Repair the restriction. 3. Recover the refrigerant. 4. Evacuate the system. 5. Charge the system. Is the air condition system operating properly?	—	System OK	Go to *Step 9*
9	1. Feel the evaporator inlet pipe. 2. Feel the evaporator outlet pipe. Is the inlet pipe colder than the outlet pipe?	—	Go to *Step 10*	Go to *Step 24*
10	1. Conduct a leak test of the system. Refer to *Vacuum System*. 2. Repair any leaks, as necessary. 3. If you repaired a leak, complete the following steps: 3.1. Recover the refrigerant. 3.2. Evacuate the system. 3.3. Charge the system. Is the air condition system operating properly?	—	System OK	Go to *Step 20*
11	1. Connect a fused jumper wire from the compressor hot lead to the positive battery post. 2. Observe the compressor operation. Does the compressor clutch engage?	—	Go to *Step 12*	Go to *Step 18*
12	1. Remove the jumper. 2. Measure the pressure at the accumulator fitting. Is the pressure below the specified value?	345 kPa (50 psi)	Go to *Step 13*	Go to *Step 15*
13	Measure the refrigerant pressure on the high side of the system. Is the pressure above the specified value?	345 kPa (50 psi)	Go to *Step 14*	Go to *Step 10*
14	1. Recover the refrigerant. 2. Inspect for the following conditions: 2.1. A plugged orifice 2.2. A restriction in the high side of the system 3. Complete the necessary repairs, or replace the orifice. 4. Evacuate the system. 5. Charge the system. Is the air condition system operating properly?	—	System OK	Go to *Step 10*
15	Connect a fused jumper wire between the pressure switch and the positive battery post. Does the compressor operate?	—	Go to *Step 16*	Go to *Step 17*

GC7029900586020A

Fig. 1 CCOT troubleshooting (Part 2 of 4)

tools are at hand and a virtually spotless work area is provided.

General Service

Use care when disconnecting or connecting refrigerant lines; **always use a back-up wrench and be careful not to overtighten any connection.** Overtightening may result in a line or flare seat distortion and a system leak.

When making pressure inspects on systems having service valves, be sure valve is in the intermediate position. If turned in too far, the hose connection will be closed, a position used for isolating the compressor. **When closing the gauge port, do not overtighten the valve or damage to the seat will result.**

After disconnecting gauge lines, inspect the valve areas to be sure service valves are correctly seated and Schraeder valves, if used, are not leaking.

DESCRIPTION

Cycling Clutch Orifice Tube (CCOT)

The Cycling Clutch Orifice Tube (CCOT) refrigeration system is designed to cycle a compressor on and off to maintain desired cooling and to prevent evaporator freeze-up. Passenger compartment comfort is maintained by the temperature select bar on the controller.

Control of the refrigeration cycle (on and off operation of the compressor) is done with a switch that senses low side pressure as an indicator of evaporator pressure. During air temperatures of 60–80°F, the equalized pressures within the charged air conditioning system will close contacts of the pressure switch.

When an air conditioning mode is selected, voltage is supplied to the compressor clutch coil. As the compressor reduces the evaporator pressure to approximately 25 psi, the pressure switch will open, de-energizing the compressor clutch. As system equalizes and the pressure reaches approximately 46 psi, the pressure switch contacts close, energizing the clutch coil.

When the engine is turned off with the air conditioning system operating, the refrigerant in the system will flow from the high pressure side of the expansion tube (orifice) to the low pressure side until the pressure is equalized. This may be detected as a hissing sound for 30–60 seconds and is considered a normal condition.

Variable Displacement Orifice Tube (VDOT)

The Variable Displacement Orifice Tube (VDOT) refrigeration system employs the constant run V-5 compressor. The V-5 is a variable displacement compressor which can match A/C demand under all conditions without cycling. The basic compressor mechanism is a variable angle wobble-plate with five axial oriented cylinders. The compressor displacement center of control is a bellows actuated control valve located in the rear head of the compressor which senses compressor suction pressure. The wobble plate angle and compressor displacement are controlled by the crankcase suction pressure differential. When the air conditioning capacity demand is high, the suction pressure will be above the control point and the valve will maintain a bleed from crankcase to suction. When no crankcase suction pressure differential exists, the compressor will have maximum displacement.

When the air conditioning capacity demand is lower and the suction pressure reaches the control point, the valve will bleed discharge gas into the crankcase and close off a passage from the crankcase to the suction plenum. The angle of the wobble-plate is controlled by a force balance on the five pistons. A slight elevation of the crankcase suction pressure differential creates a total force on the pistons, resulting in a movement about the wobble-plate pivot pin, reducing the plate angle.

When the engine is turned off with the A/C system operating, the refrigerant in the system will flow from the high pressure side of the orifice tube to the low pressure side until the pressure is equalized. This may be detected as a faint sound of liquid flowing (hissing) for 30–60 seconds and is a normal condition.

TROUBLESHOOTING

Refer to **Figs. 1 through 8** for system troubleshooting procedures.

EXERCISE SYSTEM

An important fact most owners ignore is that A/C units must be used periodically. Manufacturers caution when the air conditioner is not used regularly, particularly during cold months, it should be turned on for a few minutes once every two or three weeks while the engine is running. This keeps the system in good operating condition.

Step	Action	Value(s)	Yes	No
16	**Important:** Do not recover the refrigerant. The fitting has a Schrader Valve®. Replace the pressure switch. Is the air condition system operating properly?	—	System OK	Go to *Step 7*
17	1. Inspect the pressure switch for an open circuit or a broken wire. 2. Complete any necessary repairs. Is the air condition system operating properly?	—	System OK	Go to *Step 7*
18	Apply an external ground to the compressor. Does the compressor clutch engage?	—	System OK	Go to *Step 19*
19	Rebuild the compressor. Is the air condition system operating properly?	—	System OK	Go to *Step 12*
20	1. Add 0.45 kg (1 lb) of refrigerant to the system. 2. Inspect the clutch cycle rate. Is the clutch cycle rate greater than the specified value?	8 cycles/minute	Go to *Step 21*	Go to *Step 22*
21	1. Recover the refrigerant. 2. Inspect the system for a plugged orifice. 3. Repair the orifice as necessary. 4. Evacuate the system. 5. Charge the system. Does the air conditioning system operate properly?	—	System OK	Go to *Step 11*
22	1. Feel the evaporator inlet pipe. 2. Feel the evaporator outlet pipe. Is the inlet pipe colder than the outlet pipe?	—	Go to *Step 23*	System OK
23	1. Add 0.45 kg (1 lb) of refrigerant to the system. 2. Feel the evaporator inlet pipe. 3. Feel the evaporator outlet pipe. Is the inlet pipe colder than the outlet pipe?	—	Go to *Step 21*	System OK
24	1. Install a gauge set. 2. Inspect the compressor cycling pressure. Does the compressor cycle on within the specified value range?	280–350 kPa (41–51 psi)	Go to *Step 25*	Go to *Step 27*
25	Does the compressor cycle off within the specified value range?	140–190 kPa (20–28 psi)	Go to *Step 26*	Go to *Step 27*
26	1. Set the A/C control assembly to the MAX position. 2. Set the temperature setting to full cold position. 3. Set the blower to the HIGH position. 4. Stabilize the engine speed for 5 minutes. 5. Install a thermometer in the A/C outlet. 6. Perform the Performance Test. Refer to *System Performance Test.* Is the temperature performance within the limits of the test specifications?	—	System OK	Go to *Step 10*
27	Does the compressor cycle high on above the specified value?	350 kPa (51 psi)	Go to *Step 28*	Go to *Step 29*
28	Does the compressor cycle OFF below the specified value?	140 kPa (20 psi)	Go to *Step 16*	Go to *Step 29*
29	1. Disconnect the blower wire. 2. Determine when the compressor cycles OFF. Does the compressor cycle off below the specified value range?	140 kPa (20 psi)	Go to *Step 16*	Go to *Step 30*
30	Reconnect the blower motor wire. Is the wire reconnected?	—	Go to *Step 26*	—

GC7029900586030A

Fig. 1 CCOT troubleshooting (Part 3 of 4)

Step	Action	Value(s)	Yes	No
31	Observe the compressor cycling. Does the compressor cycle ON continuously?	—	Go to *Step 32*	Go to *Step 21*
32	1. Recover the refrigerant. 2. Inspect the orifice. Is the orifice missing?	—	Go to *Step 33*	Go to *Step 34*
33	1. Install the orifice. 2. Evacuate the system. 3. Charge the system. Does the air conditioning system operate properly?	—	System OK	Go to *Step 34*
34	Inspect the suction line. Is the suction line restricted?	—	Go to *Step 35*	Go to *Step 36*
35	1. Repair the suction line, as required. 2. Evacuate the system. 3. Charge the system. Does the air conditioning system operate properly?	—	System OK	Go to *Step 36*
36	1. Evacuate the system 2. Charge the system Does the air conditioning system operate properly?	—	System OK	—

GC7029900586040A

Fig. 1 CCOT troubleshooting (Part 4 of 4)

Inspecting out the system for the effects of insufficient use before the onset of summer is one of the most important aspects of A/C servicing.

First clean out the condenser core, mounted in all cases at the front of the radiator. All obstructions, such as leaves, bugs, and dirt, must be removed, as they will reduce heat transfer and impair the efficiency of the system. Ensure the space between the condenser and the radiator also is free of foreign matter.

Make certain the evaporator water drain is open. Certain systems have two evaporators, one in the engine compartment and one toward the rear of the vehicle. The evaporator cools and dehumidifies the air before it enters the passenger compartment, where the refrigerant changes from a liquid to a vapor. As the core cools the air, moisture condenses on it but is prevented from collecting in the evaporator by the water drain.

PERFORMANCE TEST

Prior to the performance test, a functional test should be performed.

1. Test must be performed with vehicle in a shaded area.
2. Open windows to ventilate interior, then connect suitable A/C service gauge set.
3. Determine relative humidity and ambient temperature and record.
4. **On Vue models,** disconnect vehicle thermal expansion valve (TXV) electrical connector, then connect a thermistor exposed to ambient air.
5. **On all models,** close hood, windows and doors, ensure gauge hoses are not pinched.
6. Set mode switch to A/C, blower switch to High and temperature to full cold.
7. Ensure all A/C outlets are open, then place a suitable thermometer in the righthand center air outlet.
8. **On all models except S & T,** start engine and run at about 2000 RPM for three minutes, then record outlet temperature.
9. **On S & T models,** start engine and run at about 1500 RPM for three minutes, then record outlet temperature.
10. **On all models,** refer to system performance charts to determine if system is operating satisfactorily, **Figs. 9 through 19.**

LEAK TEST

Testing the refrigerant system for leaks is one of the most important phases of troubleshooting. One or more of the methods outlined will prove useful in detecting leaks or inspecting connections if service work is performed. Before beginning any leak test, attach a manifold gauge set and note pressure. If little or no pressure is indicated, a partial charge must be installed. Inspect all connections, compressor head gasket, oil filler plug and compressor shaft seal for leaks.

For R-134a system an electronic type leak detector is recommended.

Flame Type (Halide) Leak Detectors

Avoid inhaling fumes produced by burning refrigerant when using flame type detectors. Use caution when using detector near flammable materials such as interior trim components. Do not use flame type detector where concentrations of combustible or explosive gases, dusts or vapors may exist.

1. Light leak detector and adjust flame as low as possible to obtain maximum sensitivity.
2. Allow detector to warm until copper element is cherry-red. Flame should be almost colorless.
3. Test reaction plate sensitivity by passing end of sensor hose near an opened can of refrigerant. Flame should react violently, turning bright blue.
4. If flame does not change color, replace reaction plate following manufacturer's instructions.
5. Allow flame to clear, then slowly move sensor hose along areas suspected of leakage while observing flame. **Position sensor hose under areas of suspected leakage, as refrigerant is heavier than air.**
6. Move sensor hose under all lines, fittings and components. Insert hose into evaporator case, if possible, and inspect compressor shaft seal.
7. The presence of refrigerant will cause flame to change color as follows: pale blue, no refrigerant; yellow-yellow/green, slight leak; bright blue-purple/blue, major leak or concentration of refrigerant.
8. If detector indicates a large leak or heavy concentration of refrigerant, ventilate area using a small fan in order to pinpoint leak.
9. Repair leaks as needed, recover and recharge system, then reinspect system for leaks.

Step	Action	Value(s)	Yes	No
Checking the compressor clutch for engagement.				
1	Were you sent here from the VDOT Refrigerant Charge Diagnostic Table?	—	Go to Step 2	Go to the System Performance Test
2	1. Let the engine run at idle speed. 2. Set the A/C control head in the A/C mode. 3. Set the blower motor speed to high. 4. Set the temperature control to full cold. Does the clutch engage?	—	Go to Step 3	Go to Step 4
3	Check for noise coming from the compressor or the A/C drive belt area. Is there noise coming from the compressor or the belt?	—	Go to Step 4	Go to System Performance Table
4	Is the noise due to belt slippage?	—	Go to Step 5	Go to Step 6
5	Replace the belt. Is the repair complete?	—	System OK	Go to Step 9
6	Is the noise coming from the compressor?	—	Go to Step 7	Go to Step 9
7	Check the A/C lines for contact with other components. Is there contact with other components?	—	Go to Step 8	Go to Step 9
8	Reposition or replace the A/C lines as necessary. Is the repair complete?	—	System OK	Go to System Performance Table
9	Is the noise coming from the compressor?	—	Go to Step 10	Go to System Performance Table
10	Replace the compressor. Is the noise still present?	—	Go to System Performance Table	System OK
11	1. Turn the ignition OFF. 2. Disconnect the clutch wires at the compressor. 3. Connect a jumper wire from ground to one of the compressor clutch terminals. 4. Connect a fused-jumper wire from the positive battery post to the other compressor clutch terminal. Does the clutch engage?	—	Go to Step 12	Go to Step 13

GC7029900588010X

Fig. 2 VDOT troubleshooting chart (Part 1 of 2). Compressor clutch engagement

Step	Action	Value(s)	Yes	No
12	1. Repair the electrical circuit to the compressor clutch. 2. Let the engine run at idle speed. 3. Set the A/C control head in the A/C mode. 4. Set the blower motor speed to high. 5. Set the temperature control to full cold. Does the clutch engage?	—	System OK	Go to System Performance Table
13	Replace the clutch coil. Is the repair complete?	—	System OK	Go to System Performance Table

GC7029900588020X

Fig. 2 VDOT troubleshooting chart (Part 2 of 2). Compressor clutch engagement

Step	Action	Value(s)	Yes	No
VDOT control valve diagnosis.				
1	Were you sent here from the Low Side Pressure Table?	—	Go to Step 2	Go to System Performance Test
2	1. Connect high and low side pressure gages. 2. Close all the vehicle doors and windows. 3. Run the engine at 2000 rpm to 5 minutes. 4. Set the A/C control head to the A/C mode. 5. Set the temperature control to full cold. 6. Set the blower motor speed on low. Is the low side pressure within the value(s)?	172 to 241 kPa (25 to 35 psi)	Go to System Performance Test	Go to Step 3

GC7029900592010X

Fig. 3 VDOT troubleshooting (Part 1 of 2). Control valve

Step	Action	Value(s)	Yes	No
3	1. Recover the refrigerant. 2. Replace the control valve. Is the repair complete?	—	Go to Step 4	—
4	Evacuate and charge the A/C system. Is the repair complete?	—	System OK	Go to System Performance Test

GC7029900592020X

Fig. 3 VDOT troubleshooting (Part 2 of 2). Control valve

Electronic Leak Detectors

There are a number of electronic leak detectors available to perform leak tests. Refer to operating instructions for the unit being used and observe these general procedures:

1. Move the detector probe one inch per second in areas of suspected leaks.
2. Position the probe below the test point, as refrigerant gas is heavier than air.
3. Ensure to inspect service access gauge port valve fittings, particularly when valve caps are missing, as dirt accumulations can destroy the sealing area of valve core when manifold gauge set is attached. Replace missing valve caps after cleaning valve core area. **Valve caps should only be finger tightened. Using pliers to tighten valve caps may distort sealing surface of valve.**
4. Inspect for leaks in manifold gauge set and hoses, as well as the rest of the system.

Fluid Type Leak Detectors

Apply leak detector solution around joints to be tested. A cluster of bubbles will form immediately if there is a leak. A white foam that forms after a short while will indicate an extremely small leak. In some confined areas such as sections of the evaporator and condenser, electronic leak detectors will be more useful.

REFRIGERANT RECOVERY

R-134a systems require the use of special service equipment designed specifically for R-134a systems. R-12 servicing equipment cannot be used on R-134a systems.

R-12 recovery stations cannot be used on R-134a systems. A separate recovery station must be used on R-134a systems. The refrigerants are not compatible and will contaminate the R-12 recovery station.

The use of refrigerant recovery and recycling stations allows the recovery and reuse of refrigerant after contaminants and moisture have been removed.

When using a recovery or recycling station, follow the manufacturer's operating instructions, noting the following:

1. **Use extreme caution and observe all safety and service precautions related to use of refrigerants.**
2. Connect refrigerant recycling station hose(s) to vehicle A/C service port(s) and recovery station inlet fitting. Hoses used should have shutoff devices or check valve within 12 inches of hose ends to minimize introduction of air into recycling station and to minimize amount of refrigerant release when hose(s) is disconnected.
3. Turn recycling station On to start recovery process. Allow recycling station to pump refrigerant from A/C system until station pressure gauge indicates vacuum.
4. After vehicle A/C system has been recovered, close station inlet valve, if equipped.
5. Turn station Off. On some stations the pump will automatically be turned Off by a low pressure switch.
6. Allow vehicle A/C system to remain closed for approximately two minutes. Observe vacuum level indicated on gauge. If pressure does not rise, disconnect recycling station hose(s).
7. If system pressure rises, repeat previous until vacuum level remains stable for two minutes.
8. Service A/C system as required, then recover and recharge A/C system.

CHARGING SYSTEM

Refer to A/C System Specifications Chart in the "Specifications" section for refrigerant capacities.

Use instructions provided with charging station. Follow these procedures to prevent

Step	Action	Value(s)	Yes	No
Right area diagnosis and service.				
1	Were you sent here from the VDOT System Performance Table?	—	Go to Step 2	Go to the System Performance Test
2	1. Start the engine. 2. Close all the vehicle doors and windows. 3. Set the A/C control head in the A/C mode. 4. Set the blower motor speed to high. 5. Set the temperature control to full cold. 6. Open the hood. 7. Feel the liquid line between the condenser and the expansion tube. Is the liquid line cold?	—	Go to Step 3	Go to Step 7
3	Check the cooling fans. Are the cooling fans operating?	—	Go to Step 4	Go to Step 5
4	Check the airflow at the condenser for restrictions. Is the airflow at the condenser restricted?	—	Go to Step 6	Go to the System Performance Test
5	Repair or replace the cooling fans as necessary. Is the repair complete?	—	System OK	—
6	Remove the restriction. Is the repair complete?	—	System OK	—
7	Check the A/C system for an overcharge of refrigerant. Is the A/C system overcharged?	—	Go to Step 8	Go to Step 9
8	1. Recover the refrigerant. 2. Evacuate and charge the A/C system. Is the repair complete?	—	System OK	Go to the System Performance Test

GC7029900590010X

Fig. 4 VDOT troubleshooting chart (Part 1 of 2). High side pressure

Step	Action	Value(s)	Yes	No
Left area diagnosis and service.				
1	Were you sent here from the VDOT System Performance Table?	—	Go to Step 2	Go to the System Performance Test
2	With the engine running, connect high and low side pressure gages. Are the high and low side pressures within the values?	207 kPa (30 psi)	Go to Step 3	Go to Step 8
3	1. Close all the vehicle doors and windows. 2. Run the engine at 2000 rpm. 3. Set the temperature control to full cold. 4. Set the blower motor speed to high. 5. Cycle the mode button from vent to A/C every 20 seconds for 3 minutes. Are the high and low side pressures within the value?	207 kPa (30 psi)	Go to Step 4	—
4	Does the pressure rise slow on both the high and low side gages? Is the compressor suction line warm and the discharge line very hot?	—	Go to Step 5	Go to Step 6
5	Replace the compressor. Is the repair complete?	—	System OK	—
6	Turn the engine OFF. With the compressor clutch disengaged, does the compressor clutch driver (not the pulley) turn freely by hand?	—	Go to Step 5	Go to Step 7
7	Check the low side pressure. Is there a rapid rise in the low side pressure with the engine rpm between the value(s)?	2000 and 2800 rpm	Go to the VDOT Control Valve Table	Go to Step 5

GC7029900591010X

Fig. 5 VDOT troubleshooting chart (Part 1 of 2). Low side pressure

Step	Action	Value(s)	Yes	No
9	Check for air in the A/C system. Is there air in the A/C system?	—	Go to Step 10	Go to the System Performance Test
10	Leak test the A/C system. Is there a leak in the A/C system?	—	Go to Step 11	Go to the System Performance Test
11	1. Recover the refrigerant. 2. Repair the leak in the A/C system. 3. Evacuate and charge the A/C system. 4. Is the repair complete?	—	System OK	—

GC7029900590020X

Fig. 4 VDOT troubleshooting chart (Part 2 of 2). High side pressure

Step	Action	Value(s)	Yes	No
8	Is the low side pressure within the values?	172 to 241 kPa (27 to 38 psi)	Go to Step 9	Go to the VDOT Control Valve Table
9	Feel the liquid line before the expansion (orifice) tube. Is the liquid cold?	—	Go to Step 10	Go to Step 12
10	Check the liquid line for a restriction before the expansion (orifice) tube. Is there a restriction in the liquid line before the expansion (orifice) tube?	—	Go to Step 11	Go to the System Performance Test
11	Repair the restriction or replace the liquid line before the expansion (orifice) tube. Is the repair complete?	—	System OK	Go to System Performance Test
12	Add.40 kg (14 oz) of refrigerant to the system. Does the cooling improve?	—	Go to Step 13	Go to Step 15
13	Perform a leak test. Is there a leak?	—	Go to Step 14	System OK
14	1. Repair the leak. 2. Evacuate and charge the A/C system. Is the repair complete?	—	System OK	—
15	1. Recover the refrigerant. 2. Check the expansion (orifice) tube. Is the expansion (orifice) tube plugged?	—	Go to Step 16	—
16	Remove and clean or replace the expansion (orifice) tube as necessary. Is the repair complete?	—	Go to Step 17	—
17	Evacuate and charge the A/C system. Is the repair complete?	—	System OK	Go to System Performance Test

GC7029900591020X

Fig. 5 VDOT troubleshooting chart (Part 2 of 2). Low side pressure

charging station from being accidentally exposed to high-side vehicle system pressure:

1. Do not connect high pressure line to A/C system.
2. Always keep high pressure valve closed on charging station.
3. Perform all evacuation and charging through receiver/drier low-side pressure service fitting.

SYSTEM INSPECTION

While a detailed diagnostic procedure for all air conditioning systems would be impractical due to the many variations in construction and operation, there are three fundamental components of a total diagnosis:

1. Refrigerant systems must have an adequate, but not excessive charge.
2. Determination must be made whether the refrigerant system is governed by a cycling clutch compressor or by valves which control evaporator pressure.
3. The air distribution system (blower motor, switches, vacuum lines and air ducts) must be operational before inspecting the refrigerant system.

Inspect the blower; if inoperative, examine switches, fuses, connections, wiring and the blower motor. If blower is operating but the air output is low, inspect for loose wire connections or shorts, undercharged battery, dirty or loose switch contacts, or a faulty blower motor. Inspect the air distribution system for obstructions and ensure proper door operation.

If the blower is circulating the air but there is no cooling, inspect the compressor drive belt; ensure it is not broken or slipping. If the pulley is turning but the compressor shaft is not, inspect the magnetic clutch. On models equipped with a cycling clutch, the following hand inspect method will determine whether the problem lies in the refrigerant system or further testing of the distribution system is required.

1. With engine warmed up and at normal idle, set selector lever to Norm, temperature lever to Cold and blower on Hi.
2. Place one hand on the evaporator inlet pipe and the other on the receiver/drier surface with the compressor engaged.
3. If both surfaces are the same temperature and colder than ambient temperature, refrigerant system is normal.
4. If the inlet pipe is cooler than the receiver/drier surface, refrigerant system is low on charge. Add small amounts of refrigerant until both feel the same temperature. Then add 14 oz. (one can) of additional refrigerant.
5. If inlet pipe is frosted over and receiver/drier surface is warmer, proceed as in step 4.

The individual components of the refrigerant system will often give clear signs of their faults. Use the following general descriptions to pinpoint faulty components.

Compressor

A faulty compressor will display one or more of the following symptoms: noise, seizure, leakage or low inlet and discharge pressure. A steady, resonant noise from the compressor is not necessarily an indication of a problem, but irregular metallic rattling

Step	Action	Value(s)	Yes	No
Checking the refrigerant charge.				
1	Were you sent here from the System Performance Test?	—	Go to Step 2	Go to the System Performance Test
2	With the ignition OFF, connect the A/C gages. Are the high and low side pressures approximately equal to the value specified?	345 kPa (50 psi)	Go to the Compressor Clutch	Go to Step 3
3	Are the high and low side pressures above the value specified?	345 kPa (50 psi)	System OK	Go to Step 4
4	1. Add.45 kg (1 lb.) of R-134a. 2. Check the system for leaks. Is there a leak?	—	Go to Step 6	Go to Step 5
5	Are the high and low side pressures between the value specified?	69 and 345 kPa (10 and 50 psi)	Go to Step 6	System OK
6	Repair the leak. Is the repair done?	—	Go to Step 7	—
7	Evacuate and charge the A/C system. Are the high and low side pressures above the value specified?	345 kPa (50 psi)	System OK	Go to the Compressor Clutch

GC7029900587000X

Fig. 6 VDOT troubleshooting chart. Refrigerant charge

Step	Action	Value(s)	Yes	No
Checking the VDOT system performance.				
1	Were you sent here from the Compressor Clutch Engagement Table?	—	Go to Step 2	Go to the System Performance Test
2	1. Close all the vehicle windows and doors. 2. Set A/C control head in the A/C mode. 3. Set the blower motor speed to high. 4. Set the temperature control to full cold. 5. Let the engine run at idle speed for five minutes. 6. Feel the liquid line on both sides of the expansion (orifice) tube. Is the temperature the same on both sides of the expansion (orifice) tube?	—	Go to Step 3	Go to Step 8
3	1. Recover the refrigerant. 2. Check for a missing expansion (orifice) tube or O-ring. Is the expansion (orifice) tube or O-ring missing?	—	Go to Step 4	Go to Step 5
4	Replace the missing expansion (orifice) tube or O-ring. Is the repair complete?	—	Go to Step 6	—
5	Check for a restriction in the highside line. Is there a restriction?	—	Go to Step 7	—
6	1. Evacuate and charge the A/C system. 2. Leak test the system. 3. Check the discharge temperature. Is the discharge temperature within specs?	—	System OK	Go to Step 8

GC7029900589010X

Fig. 7 VDOT troubleshooting chart (Part 1 of 2). System performance

Step	Action	Value(s)	Yes	No
7	Repair the restriction in the high-side line. Is the repair done?	—	System OK	—
8	1. Operate the A/C system for five minutes or longer. 2. Record the low and high side pressures. 3. On engines equipped with electric cooling fans, record the pressures with the fans ON. 4. Locate the intersection of the low and high side pressures. Do the low and high side pressures intersect on the left side or right side of the chart.	—	If on the right side: Go to High Side Pressure Table	If on the left side: Go to High Side Pressure Table

GC7029900589020X

Fig. 7 VDOT troubleshooting chart (Part 2 of 2). System performance

may indicate broken components and should be investigated. A thumping noise from the compressor and a cool, sweating suction line into it may indicate an overcharged system. Inspect seizure by disengaging the magnetic clutch and rotating the driven plate. If the compressor is seized, the driven plate will not rotate.

False compressor seizure may occur after an extended period of disuse or storage. Lubricating oil drains away from the polished surfaces of ball seats and axial plate and the compressor appears to be seized. Use a clutch hub holding tool to turn the compressor in the opposite direction of rotation at least three revolutions. Inspect for false compressor seizure if compressor has not been used in a month or longer.

If compressor is not seized but will not rotate, inspect for current at magnetic coil. Low discharge pressure may be caused by faulty seals within the compressor, a restriction in the compressor or elsewhere, or by a low refrigerant charge. The compressor must have the correct amount of the proper viscosity oil. Excess oil will restrict refrigerant circulation and reduce compressor outlet pressure.

Condenser

The condenser may faulty either due to leakage or restriction. If restricted, compressor discharge pressure will be excessive. Icy or frosty spots on the condenser will indicate a partial restriction within the condenser. Ensure all foreign matter is removed from the front of the condenser. Similarly, bent cooling fins will block air flow through the condenser and result in high discharge pressures.

Evaporator

A faulty evaporator will provide insufficient cooling to the vehicle. The core may be restricted with dirt, the case may be cracked, or a seal may be leaking sufficiently to prevent cooling. If evaporator restriction is due to icing, the expansion valve, capillary tube or suction throttling valve, if equipped, may be at fault and should be investigated.

Since there is a constant condensation of atmospheric moisture on the outside of the evaporator coils, ensure the draining system is unobstructed and clean. Some vehicles have an auxiliary evaporator in the trunk or between the headliner and the roof.

Receiver/Drier

A restriction inside the receiver-dehydrator will result in high head pressures if the restriction is on the inlet side of the unit. A restriction at the outlet side will cause low head pressures and little or no cooling. An exceedingly cold receiver-dehydrator may be restricted.

If the system has been in service for a considerable amount of time, the desiccant element may have lost its moisture absorbing ability. This condition is indicated by the constant presence of small bubbles in the sight glass if equipped and a wide difference in temperature between the inlet and outlet receiver-dehydrator lines.

Thermostatic Expansion Valve

Faulty expansion valves will be indicated by low suction and discharge pressures on the manifold gauge set. In most cases the power element fails and the valve closes. Occasionally the inlet screen becomes clogged with contamination or desiccant beads loose in the system.

Refrigerant Line Restrictions

1. A restricted suction line is indicated by low suction pressure at the compressor, low discharge pressure and little or no cooling.
2. A restricted discharge line will usually cause the pressure relief valve to open.
3. A restricted liquid line will cause low suction and discharge pressures and little or no cooling.

PRESSURE GAUGE INDICATION

Due to the different types of models and systems, the following typical pressure gauge indications should be used as a guide only, **Fig. 20.** Refer to the "Performance Tests" or "System Pressure Check" for the particular model being tested. When indications other than normal are encountered, these typical indication charts will assist in diagnosing the refrigerant system. It should be noted that pressures may vary slightly above or below due to changes in ambient temperature and relative humidity.

Step	Action	Value	Yes	No
1	Check air outlet temperature at rear compartment air outlet (roof) duct with thermometer. Is air outlet temperature within specifications?		Go to Step 2	Go to Step 3
2	Familiarize vehicle owner with rear heating and A/C system operation and performance capability.	—	—	—
3	Is the rear heating and A/C fan (blower motor) operating properly?	—	Go to Step 4	Go to Step 5
4	Toggle system mode back and forth between LOWER and UPPER while checking airflow from the body side window defogger outlet duct. Does the airflow pattern match the rear A/C function test?	—	Go to Step 6	Go to Step 7
5	Refer to blower motor diagnosis.	—	—	—
6	Check for restriction in A/C condenser (condenser to evaporator) tube, A/C evaporator (inlet front-to-rear) tube, rear evaporator inlet tube, or thermal expansion valve inlet tube. Do any frost spots appear on A/C tubes during system operation?	—	Go to Step 13	Go to Step 12
7	Check for leaking or improperly installed air distribution ducts. Are all ducts intact and properly installed?	—	Go to Step 8	Go to Step 9
8	Check heater and A/C control vacuum hose to rear temperature valve actuator for leaks, restrictions or improper installation. Is the vacuum hose intact and properly installed?	—	Go to Step 10	Go to Step 11
9	Repair, replace and/or correct installation of ducts as necessary.	—	—	—
10	Replace the rear temperature valve vacuum operator.	—	—	—
11	Repair, replace and/or correct installation of vacuum hose as necessary.	—	—	—
12	Check for restriction in the rear evaporator outlet tube, A/C evaporator (outlet rear-to-front) tube, and A/C compressor and condenser hose. Do any frost spots appear on the A/C tubes/hoses during system operation?	—	Go to Step 14	Go to Step 15
13	Replace restricted A/C tube.	—	—	—
14	Replace restricted A/C tube.	—	—	—

GC7029900593010X

Fig. 8 VDOT troubleshooting (Part 1 of 2). Rear A/C

Ambient Air Temperature	Relative Humidity	Service Port Pressure		Maximum Left Center Discharge Air Temperature
		Low Side	High Side	
13-18°C (55-65°F)	0-100%	197-225 kPa (29-33 psi)	1100-1230 kPa (160-178 psi)	9°C (48°F)
19-23°C (66-75°F)	Below 40%	191-228 kPa (28-33 psi)	1060-1230 kPa (154-178 psi)	10°C (50°F)
	Above 40%	202-246 kPa (29-36 psi)	1100-1370 kPa (160-199 psi)	12°C (54°F)
24-29°C (76-85°F)	Below 35%	194-230 kPa (28-33 psi)	1130-1220 kPa (164-177 psi)	11°C (52°F)
	35-60%	198-246 kPa (29-36 psi)	1090-1320 kPa (158-191 psi)	12°C (54°F)
	Above 60%	236-311 kPa (34-45 psi)	1140-1580 kPa (165-229 psi)	15°C (59°F)
30-35°C (86-95°F)	Below 30%	208-256 kPa (30-37 psi)	1230-1370 kPa (178-199 psi)	14°C (57°F)
	30-50%	215-284 kPa (31-41 psi)	1180-1540 kPa (171-223 psi)	16°C (61°F)
	Above 50%	236-311 kPa (34-45 psi)	1290-1750 kPa (187-254 psi)	18°C (64°F)
36-40°C (96-105°F)	Below 20%	235-298 kPa (34-43 psi)	1340-1600 kPa (194-232 psi)	17°C (63°F)
	20-40%	246-315 kPa (36-46 psi)	1340-1700 kPa (194-247 psi)	18°C (64°F)
	Above 40%	260-348 kPa (38-51 psi)	1410-1940 kPa (204-281 psi)	21°C (70°F)
41-46°C (106-115°F)	Below 20%	266-339 kPa (39-49 psi)	1550-1820 kPa (225-264 psi)	21°C (70°F)
	Above 20%	280-369 kPa (41-54 psi)	1530-2000 kPa (222-290 psi)	23°C (73°F)
47-49°C (116-120°F)	Below 30%	304-378 kPa (44-55 psi)	1870-2020 kPa (271-293 psi)	24°C (75°F)

GC7010100274000X

Fig. 9 A/C system performance test specifications. Aztek

Step	Action	Value	Yes	No
15	Disassemble the evaporator and blower module. Check thermal expansion valve installation. Is the thermal expansion valve capillary tube properly clipped to the evaporator outlet tube?	—	Go to Step 16	Go to Step 17
16	Remove the evaporator core and check for restrictions. Were any restrictions found?	—	Go to Step 18	Go to Step 19
17	Fasten the thermal expansion valve capillary tube securely to the evaporator core outlet tube with retaining clip. Reassemble system and test performance.	—	—	—
18	Replace evaporator core.	—	—	—
19	Replace thermal expansion valve.	—	—	—

GC7029900593020X

Fig. 8 VDOT troubleshooting (Part 2 of 2). Rear A/C

Ambient Air Temperature	Relative Humidity	Service Port Pressure		Maximum Left Center Discharge Air Temperature
		Low Side	High Side	
13-18°C (55-65°F)	0-100%	131-172 kPa (19-25 psi)	1000-1276 kPa (135-175 psi)	4°C (40°F)
19-24°C (66-75°F)	Below 40%	165-207 kPa (24-30 psi)	1103-1379 kPa (160-200 psi)	7°C (44°F)
	Above 40%	165-207 kPa (24-30 psi)	1172-1448 kPa (170-210 psi)	7°C (44°F)
25-29°C (76-85°F)	Below 35%	179-221 kPa (26-32 psi)	1310-1586 kPa (190-230 psi)	8°C (47°F)
	35-60%	200-241 kPa (29-35 psi)	1344-1620 kPa (195-235 psi)	10°C (50°F)
	Above 60%	207-248 kPa (30-36 psi)	1344-1620 kPa (195-235 psi)	11°C (51°F)

LTV1900000000410

Fig. 10 A/C system performance test specifications (Part 1 of 2). Astro & Safari w/front A/C

30-35°C (86-95°F)	Below 30%	234-276 kPa (34-40 psi)	1620-1896 kPa (235-275 psi)	12°C (54°F)
	30-50%	262-303 kPa (38-44 psi)	1793-2068 kPa (260-300 psi)	16°C (60°F)
	Above 50%	276-324 kPa (40-47 psi)	1793-2068 kPa (260-300 psi)	16°C (60°F)
36-41°C (96-105°F)	Below 20%	262-317 kPa (38-46 psi)	1793-2068 kPa (260-300 psi)	15°C (59°F)
	20-40%	255-310 kPa (37-45 psi)	1586-1862 kPa (230-270 psi)	14°C (57°F)
	Above 40 %	296-352 kPa (43-51 psi)	1999-2275 kPa (290-330 psi)	17°C (63°F)
42-46°C (106-115°F)	Below 20%	262-317 kPa (38-46 psi)	1758-2034 kPa (255-295 psi)	15°C (59°F)
	Above 20%	269-324 kPa (39-47 psi)	1758-2034 kPa (255-295 psi)	16°C (60°F)
47-49°C (116-120°F)	Below 30%	296-352 kPa (43-51 psi)	1931-2206 kPa (280-320 psi)	18°C (64°F)

LTV1900000000411

Fig. 10 A/C system performance test specifications (Part 2 of 2). Astro & Safari w/front A/C

Ambient Air Temperature	Relative Humidity	Service Port Pressure		Maximum Rear Discharge Air Temperature
		Low Side	High Side	
13-18°C (55-65°F)	0-100%	131-172 kPa (19-25 psi)	1000-1276 kPa (135-175 psi)	4°C (40°F)
19-24°C (66-75°F)	Below 40%	165-207 kPa (24-30 psi)	1103-1379 kPa (160-200 psi)	7°C (44°F)
	Above 40%	165-207 kPa (24-30 psi)	1172-1448 kPa (170-210 psi)	7°C (44°F)
25-29°C (76-85°F)	Below 35%	179-221 kPa (26-32 psi)	1310-1586 kPa (190-230 psi)	8°C (47°F)
	35-60%	200-241 kPa (29-35 psi)	1344-1620 kPa (195-235 psi)	10°C (50°F)
	Above 60%	207-248 kPa (30-36 psi)	1344-1620 kPa (195-235 psi)	11°C (51°F)

LTV1900000000412

Fig. 11 A/C system performance test specifications (Part 1 of 2). Astro & Safari w/front & rear A/C

Ambient Air Temperature	Relative Humidity	Service Port Pressure		Maximum Left Center Discharge Air Temperature
		Low Side	High Side	
13-16°C (55-65°F)	0-100%	175-206 kPa (25-30 psi)	340-850 kPa (49-123 psi)	7°C (45°F)
19-24°C (66-75°F)	Below 40%	175-215 kPa (25-31 psi)	430-930 kPa (62-135 psi)	6°C (43°F)
	Greater than 40%	175-254 kPa (25-37 psi)	570-1070 kPa (83-155 psi)	9°C (48°F)
25-29°C (76-85°F)	Below 35%	175-249 kPa (25-36 psi)	760-1410 kPa (147-205 psi)	9°C (48°F)
	35-60%	175-261 kPa (26-38 psi)	830-1180 kPa (120-171 psi)	10°C (50°F)
	Greater than 60%	185-286 kPa (27-42 psi)	880-1250 kPa (128-181 psi)	11°C (52°F)

LTV1900000000402

Fig. 12 A/C system performance test specifications (Part 1 of 2). C, G, K, Sierra & Silverado Series w/front A/C

30-35°C (86-95°F)	Below 30%	234-276 kPa (34-40 psi)	1620-1896 kPa (235-275 psi)	12°C (54°F)
	30-50%	262-303 kPa (38-44 psi)	1793-2068 kPa (260-300 psi)	16°C (60°F)
	Above 50%	276-324 kPa (40-47 psi)	1793-2068 kPa (260-300 psi)	16°C (60°F)
36-41°C (96-105°F)	Below 20%	262-317 kPa (38-46 psi)	1793-2068 kPa (260-300 psi)	15°C (59°F)
	20-40%	255-310 kPa (37-45 psi)	1586-1862 kPa (230-270 psi)	14°C (57°F)
	Above 40%	296-352 kPa (43-51 psi)	1999-2275 kPa (290-330 psi)	17°C (63°F)
42-46°C (106-115°F)	Below 20%	262-317 kPa (38-46 psi)	1758-2034 kPa (255-295 psi)	15°C (59°F)
	Above 20%	269-324 kPa (39-47 psi)	1758-2034 kPa (255-295 psi)	16°C (60°F)
47-49°C (116-120°F)	Below 30%	296-352 kPa (43-51 psi)	1931-2206 kPa (280-320 psi)	18°C (64°F)

LTV1900000000413

Fig. 11 A/C system performance test specifications (Part 2 of 2). Astro & Safari w/front & rear A/C

30-35°C (86-95°F)	Below 30%	193-293 kPa (28-43 psi)	1010-1410 kPa (146-205 psi)	12°C (54°F)
	30-50%	228-269 kPa (30-44 psi)	1050-1440 kPa (153-209 psi)	13°C (55°F)
	Greater than 50%	221-324 kPa (32-47 psi)	1100-1470 kPa (160-213 psi)	14°C (58°F)
36-41°C (96-105°F)	Below 20%	241-337 kPa (35-47 psi)	1310-1700 kPa (190-246 psi)	16°C (61°F)
	20-40%	247-345 kPa (36-50 psi)	1320-1700 kPa (190-230 psi)	16°C (61°F)
	Greater than 40%	259-353 kPa (37-52 psi)	1350-1690 kPa (196-246 psi)	16°C (61°F)
42-46°C (106-115°F)	Below 20%	292-378 kPa (42-55 psi)	1630-1950 kPa (238-283 psi)	17°C (62°F)
	Greater than 20%	297-383 kPa (43-55 psi)	1620-1930 kPa (235-280 psi)	19°C (66°F)
47-49°C (116-120°F)	Below 30%	338-405 kPa (50-59 psi)	187-2080 kPa (271-302 psi)	20°C (68°F)

LTV1900000000403

Fig. 12 A/C system performance test specifications (Part 2 of 2). C, G , K, Sierra & Silverado Series w/front A/C

Ambient Air Temperature	Relative Humidity	Service Port Pressure		Maximum Discharge Air Temperature	
		Low Side	High Side	Left Center	Rear Center
13-18°C (55-65°F)	0-100%	175-205 kPa (25-30 psi)	420-860 kPa (61-125 psi)	6°C (43°F)	9°C (48°F)
19-24°C (66-75°F)	Below 40%	175-240 kPa (25-35 psi)	610-1080 kPa (89-157 psi)	8°C (46°F)	11°C (52°F)
	Above 40%	175-267 kPa (25-39 psi)	680-1170 kPa (99-170 psi)	10°C (50°F)	13°C (55°F)
25-29°C (76-85°F)	Below 35%	184-284 kPa (27-41 psi)	940-1330 kPa (136-193 psi)	11°C (52°F)	14°C (57°F)
	35-50%	197-293 kPa (29-43 psi)	990-1360 kPa (144-197 psi)	12°C (54°F)	15°C (59°F)
	Above 50%	207-310 kPa (30-45 psi)	1020-1430 kPa (148-208 psi)	13°C (55°F)	16°C (61°F)

LTV1900000000404

Fig. 13 A/C system performance test specifications (Part 1 of 2). C, G , K, Sierra & Silverado Series w/front & rear A/C

30-35°C (86-95°F)	Below 30%	233-339 kPa (34-49 psi)	1210-1640 kPa (176-238 psi)	15°C (59°F)	18°C (64°F)
	30-50%	241-348 kPa (35-51 psi)	1240-1680 kPa (180-244 psi)	16°C (61°F)	19°C (66°F)
	Above 50%	253-362 kPa (37-53 psi)	1280-1730 kPa (186-251 psi)	18°C (64°F)	21°C (70°F)
36-41°C (96-105°F)	Below 20%	289-392 kPa (42-57 psi)	1520-1940 kPa (221-282 psi)	19°C (66°F)	21°C (70°F)
	20-40%	294-399 kPa (43-58 psi)	1540-1980 kPa (224-287 psi)	20°C (68°F)	22°C (72°F)
	Above 40%	303-407 kPa (44-59 psi)	1580-2010 kPa (229-294 psi)	21°C (70°F)	24°C (75°F)
42-46°C (106-115°F)	Below 20%	348-440 kPa (51-64 psi)	1840-2210 kPa (267-321 psi)	23°C (73°F)	24°C (75°F)
	Above 20%	352-446 kPa (51-65 psi)	1860-2240 kPa (270-325 psi)	24°C (75°F)	26°C (79°F)
47-49°C (116-120°F)	Below 30%	400-472 kPa (58-69 psi)	2130-2380 kPa (309-345 psi)	25°C (77°F)	27°C (81°F)

LTV1900000000405

Fig. 13 A/C system performance test specifications (Part 2 of 2). C, G, K, Sierra & Silverado Series w/front & rear A/C

Ambient Temperature	Relative Humidity	Low Side Service Port Pressure	High Side Service Port Pressure	Maximum Left Center Discharge Air Temperature
13-18°C (55-65°F)	0-100%	175-207 kPa (25-30 psi)	1030-1220 kPa (135-175 psi)	7°C (45°F)
19-24°C (66-75°F)	Below 40%	175-254 kPa (25-37 psi)	1200-1430 kPa (160-200 psi)	11°C (52°F)
	Above 40%	175-262 kPa (25-38 psi)	1170-1400 kPa (170-210 psi)	11°C (52°F)
25-29°C (76-85°F)	Below 35%	208-288 kPa (30-42 psi)	1370-1570 kPa (150-190 psi)	14°C (57°F)
	35-50%	213-292 kPa (31-42 psi)	1350-1570 kPa (160-200 psi)	14°C (57°F)
	Above 50%	216-300 kPa (31-44 psi)	1340-1550 kPa (160-200 psi)	15°C (59°F)

LTV1900000000416

Fig. 15 A/C system performance test specifications (Part 1 of 2). Bravada, Envoy & Trailblazer Series w/front A/C

Ambient Air Temperature	Relative Humidity	Service Port Pressure		Maximum Left Center Discharge Air Temperature
		Low Side	High Side	
13-18°C (55-65°F)	0-100%	145-186 kPa (21-27 psi)	931-1207 kPa (135-175 psi)	6°C (43°F)
19-24°C (66-75°F)	Below 40%	172-214 kPa (25-31 psi)	1103-1379 kPa (160-200 psi)	7°C (45°F)
	Above 40%	172-214 kPa (25-31 psi)	1172-1448 kPa (170-210 psi)	8°C (46°F)
25-29°C (76-85°F)	Below 35%	179-221 kPa (26-32 psi)	1034-1310 kPa (150-190 psi)	9°C (48°F)
	35-60%	186-228 kPa (27-33 psi)	1103-1379 kPa (160-200 psi)	10°C (50°F)
	Above 60%	193-234 kPa (28-34 psi)	1103-1379 kPa (160-200 psi)	9°C (49°F)

LTV1900000000414

Fig. 14 A/C system performance test specifications (Part 1 of 2). S Series

30-35°C (86-95°F)	Below 30%	241-283 kPa (35-41 psi)	1379-1655 kPa (200-240 psi)	13°C (55°F)
	30-50%	241-283 kPa (35-41 psi)	1379-1655 kPa (200-240 psi)	13°C (56°F)
	Above 50%	255-296 kPa (37-43 psi)	1379-1655 kPa (200-240 psi)	14°C (57°F)
36-41°C (96-105°F)	Below 20%	255-310 kPa (37-45 psi)	1655-1931 kPa (240-280 psi)	16°C (60°F)
	20-40%	283-338 kPa (41-49 psi)	1689-1965 kPa (245-285 psi)	18°C (64°F)
	Above 40%	310-365 kPa (45-53 psi)	1724-1827 kPa (250-265 psi)	16°C (61°F)
42-46°C (106-115°F)	Below 20%	303-359 kPa (40-48 psi)	1724-1999 kPa (250-290 psi)	17°C (62°F)
	Above 20%	303-359 kPa (44-52 psi)	1793-2068 kPa (260-300 psi)	19°C (67°F)
47-49°C (116-120°F)	Below 30%	324-379 kPa (47-55 psi)	1999-2275 kPa (290-330 psi)	21°C (70°F)

LTV1900000000415

Fig. 14 A/C system performance test specifications (Part 2 of 2). S Series

30-35°C (86-95°F)	Below 30%	242-328 kPa (35-48 psi)	1510-1750 kPa (200-240 psi)	17°C (63°F)
	30-50%	246-335 kPa (36-49 psi)	1500-1740 kPa (200-240 psi)	17°C (63°F)
	Above 50%	252-346 kPa (37-50 psi)	1490-1730 kPa (200-240 psi)	19°C (66°F)
36-41°C (96-105°F)	Below 20%	281-366 kPa (41-53 psi)	1680-1920 kPa (240-280 psi)	19°C (66°F)
	20-40%	285-374 kPa (41-54 psi)	1670-1920 kPa (245-285 psi)	21°C (70°F)
	Above 40%	292-383 kPa (42-56 psi)	1670-1910 kPa (250-265 psi)	22°C (72°F)
42-46°C (106-115°F)	Below 20%	322-400 kPa (47-58 psi)	1850-2070 kPa (250-290 psi)	22°C (72°F)
	Above 20%	326-410 kPa (47-60 psi)	1840-2060 kPa (260-300 psi)	23°C (73°F)
47-49°C (116-120°F)	Below 30%	360-426 kPa (52-62 psi)	1990-2150 kPa (290-330 psi)	24°C (75°F)

LTV1900000000417

Fig. 15 A/C system performance test specifications (Part 2 of 2). Bravada, Envoy & Trailblazer Series w/front A/C

Ambient Air Temperature	Relative Humidity	Service Port Pressure		Maximum Discharge Air Temperature	
		Low Side	High Side	Left Center	Rear Center
13-18°C (55-65°F)	0-100%	184-273 kPa (27-40 psi)	600-1080 kPa (87-157 psi)	19°C (66°F)	17°C (62°F)
19-24°C (66-75°F)	Below 40%	227-335 kPa (33-49 psi)	720-1210 kPa (105-176 psi)	19°C (66°F)	20°C (68°F)
	Above 40%	234-349 kPa (34-51 psi)	840-1330 kPa (122-193 psi)	22°C (72°F)	21°C (70°F)
25-29°C (76-85°F)	Below 35%	286-383 kPa (42-56 psi)	1050-1440 kPa (152-209 psi)	21°C (70°F)	23°C (73°F)
	35-50%	293-390 kPa (43-57 psi)	1110-1470 kPa (161-213 psi)	22°C (72°F)	23°C (73°F)
	Above 50%	298-403 kPa (43-59 psi)	1160-1550 kPa (168-225 psi)	24°C (75°F)	24°C (75°F)

LTV1900000000418

Fig. 16 A/C system performance test specifications (Part 1 of 2). Bravada, Envoy & Trailblazer Series w/front & rear A/C

Ambient Air Temperature	Relative Humidity	Service Port Pressure		Maximum Left Center Discharge Air Temperature
		Low Side	High Side	
13-18°C (55-65°F)	0-100%	197-225 kPa (29-33 psi)	1100-1230 kPa (160-178 psi)	9°C (48°F)
19-23°C (66-75°F)	Below 40%	191-228 kPa (28-33 psi)	1060-1230 kPa (154-178 psi)	10°C (50°F)
	Above 40%	202-246 kPa (29-36 psi)	1100-1370 kPa (160-199 psi)	12°C (54°F)
24-29°C (76-85°F)	Below 35%	194-230 kPa (28-33 psi)	1130-1220 kPa (164-177 psi)	11°C (52°F)
	35-60%	198-246 kPa (29-36 psi)	1090-1320 kPa (158-191 psi)	12°C (54°F)
	Above 60%	236-311 kPa (34-45 psi)	1140-1580 kPa (165-229 psi)	15°C (59°F)

LTV1900000000406

Fig. 17 A/C system performance test specifications (Part 1 of 2). Montana, Silhouette, Trans Sport & Venture w/front A/C

30-35°C (86-95°F)	Below 30%	334-440 kPa (49-64 psi)	1310-1720 kPa (190-250 psi)	24°C (75°F)	27°C (81°F)
	30-50%	341-452 kPa (51-68 psi)	1340-1750 kPa (195-254 psi)	25°C (77°F)	27°C (81°F)
	Above 50%	350-469 kPa (51-68 psi)	1390-1800 kPa (202-261 psi)	27°C 81°F)	28°C (82°F)
36-41°C (96-105°F)	Below 20%	388-492 kPa (56-71 psi)	1600-2000 kPa (232-290 psi)	27°C (81°F)	30°C (86°F)
	20-40%	394-506 kPa (57-73 psi)	1620-2020 kPa (235-293 psi)	28°C (82°F)	31°C (88°F)
	Above 40%	406-520 kPa (59-76 psi)	1660-2040 kPa (241-296 psi)	29°C (84°F)	32°C (90°F)
42-46°C (106-115°F)	Below 20%	445-541 kPa (65-79 psi)	1910-2260 kPa (277-328 psi)	30°C (86°F)	34°C (93°F)
	Above 20%	452-557 kPa (66-81 psi)	1920-2260 kPa (279-328 psi)	31°C (88°F)	34°C (93°F)
47-49°C (116-120°F)	Below 30%	501-579 kPa (73-84 psi)	2180-2410 kPa (316-350 psi)	32°C (90°F)	36°C (97°F)

LTV1900000000419

Fig. 16 A/C system performance test specifications (Part 2 of 2). Bravada, Envoy & Trailblazer Series w/front & rear A/C

30-35°C (86-95°F)	Below 30%	208-256 kPa (30-37 psi)	1230-1370 kPa (178-199 psi)	14°C (57°F)
	30-50%	215-284 kPa (31-41 psi)	1180-1540 kPa (171-223 psi)	16°C (61°F)
	Above 50%	236-311 kPa (34-45 psi)	1290-1750 kPa (187-254 psi)	18°C (64°F)
36-40°C (96-105°F)	Below 20%	235-298 kPa (34-43 psi)	1340-1600 kPa (194-232 psi)	17°C (63°F)
	20-40%	246-315 kPa (36-46 psi)	1340-1700 kPa (194-247 psi)	18°C (64°F)
	Above 40%	260-348 kPa (38-51 psi)	1410-1940 kPa (204-281 psi)	21°C (70°F)
41-46°C (106-115°F)	Below 20%	266-339 kPa (39-49 psi)	1550-1820 kPa (225-264 psi)	21°C (70°F)
	Above 20%	280-369 kPa (41-54 psi)	1530-2000 kPa (222-290 psi)	23°C (73°F)
47-49°C (116-120°F)	Below 30%	304-378 kPa (44-55 psi)	1870-2020 kPa (271-293 psi)	24°C (75°F)

LTV1900000000407

Fig. 17 A/C system performance test specifications (Part 2 of 2). Montana, Silhouette, Trans Sport & Venture w/front A/C

Ambient Air Temperature	Relative Humidity	Service Port Pressure: Low Side	Service Port Pressure: High Side	Maximum Left Center A/C Discharge Air Temperature	Maximum Left/Top Rear A/C Discharge Air Temperature
13-18°C (55-65°F)	0-100%	251-270 kPa (36-39 psi)	650-990 kPa (94-144 psi)	12°C (54°F)	18°C (64°F)
19-23°C (66-75°F)	Below 40%	257-282 kPa (37-41 psi)	680-1190 kPa (99-173 psi)	13°C (55°F)	19°C (66°F)
	Above 40%	262-368 kPa (38-53 psi)	740-1230 kPa (107-178 psi)	22°C (72°F)	25°C (77°F)
24-29°C (76-85°F)	Below 35%	255-310 kPa (37-45 psi)	970-1370 kPa (141-199 psi)	16°C (61°F)	21°C (70°F)
	35-60%	256-337 kPa (37-49 psi)	1010-1430 kPa (147-207 psi)	18°C (64°F)	23°C (73°F)
	Above 60%	262-422 kPa (38-61 psi)	1100-1380 kPa (160-200 psi)	26°C (79°F)	29°C (84°F)

LTV1900000000408

Fig. 18 A/C system performance test specifications (Part 1 of 2). Montana, Silhouette, Trans Sport & Venture w/front & rear A/C

30-35°C (86-95°F)	Below 30%	280-348 kPa (41-51 psi)	1180-1570 kPa (171-228 psi)	19°C (66°F)	24°C (75°F)
	30-50%	280-406 kPa (41-59 psi)	1200-1610 kPa (174-234 psi)	24°C (75°F)	29°C (84°F)
	Above 50%	309-456 kPa (41-59 psi)	1290-1590 kPa (187-231 psi)	28°C (82°F)	32°C (90°F)
36-40°C (96-105°F)	Below 20%	312-387 kPa (45-56 psi)	1370-1770 kPa (1992-257 psi)	23°C (73°F)	28°C (82°F)
	20-40%	312-446 kPa (45-65 psi)	1370-1830 kPa (199-265 psi)	27°C (81°F)	33°C (91°F)
	Above 40%	342-496 kPa (50-72 psi)	1470-1810 kPa (213-263 psi)	31°C (88°F)	36°C (97°F)
41-46°C (106-115°F)	Below 20%	350-456 kPa (51-66 psi)	1550-2030 kPa (225-295 psi)	28°C (82°F)	34°C (93°F)
	Above 20%	359-493 kPa (52-72 psi)	1630-2050 kPa (236-297 psi)	31°C (88°F)	37°C (99°F)
47-49°C (116-120°F)	Below 30%	405-543 kPa (59-79 psi)	1840-2180 kPa (267-316 psi)	34°C (93°F)	42°C (108°F)

LTV1900000000409

Fig. 18 A/C system performance test specifications (Part 2 of 2). Montana, Silhouette, Trans Sport & Venture w/front & rear A/C

NORMAL SYSTEM PERFORMANCE SERVICE STALL

If the ambient air temperature is …		The low side gauge should read…		The high side gauge should read…		The right center air temperature should be…	
DEGREES		**SUCTION**		**DISCHARGE**		**OUTLET**	
°C	**(°F)**	**kPa**	**(psi)**	**kPa**	**(psi)**	**°C**	**(°F)**
21	(70)	131–186	(19–27)	765–1130	(111–164)	1–8	(33–46)
27	(80)	131–186	(19–27)	896–1193	(130–173)	1–9	(33–49)
32	(90)	131–186	(19–27)	1151–1462	(167–212)	2–9	(34–49)
38	(100)	144–193	(21–28)	1456–1751	(211–254)	3–10	(37–51)
43	(110)	144–193	(21–28)	1599–1938	(232–281)	3–10	(37–51)

IMPORTANT: To ensure accurate pressure and temperature readings make sure the vehicle is properly set up to run the performance test. **All test parameters must be followed to obtain accurate readings.**

IMPORTANT: Use a refrigerant identifier to verify refrigerant purity. Non-condensable gases or refrigerant substitutes will affect system pressure/temperature readings.

NORMAL SYSTEM PERFORMANCE SERVICE STALL HIGH HUMIDITY

If the ambient air temperature is …		The low side gauge should read…		The high side gauge should read…		The right center air temperature should be…	
DEGREES		**SUCTION**		**DISCHARGE**		**OUTLET**	
°C	**(°F)**	**kPa**	**(psi)**	**kPa**	**(psi)**	**°C**	**(°F)**
21	(70)	138–193	(20–28)	807–1124	(117–163)	2–9	(36–48)
27	(80)	138–193	(20–28)	1075–1358	(156–197)	2–10	(36–50)
32	(90)	144–193	(21–28)	1489–1793	(216–260)	5–12	(40–53)
38	(100)	144–193	(21–28)	1627–1994	(236–289)	6–13	(43–55)
43	(110)	144–200	(21–29)	1917–2303	(278–334)	6–14	(43–56)

- High humidity conditions affect system performance by increased heat load on system. This extra heat load will increase discharge pressure and outlet temperature. High humidity is defined as a relative humidity higher than 70 percent at 21° C (70°F), 60 percent at 27° C (80°F), 50 percent at 32° C (90°F), 40 percent at 38° C (100°F), and 20 percent at 43° C (110°F).
- This chart illustrates the effect high humidity has on the Saturn VUE air conditioning system. Use this chart to determine normal system performance under high humidity conditions.

G37010200050000X

Fig. 19 A/C system performance test. Vue

GAUGE READINGS	OTHER SYMPTOMS	DIAGNOSIS	CORRECTION
1 Low side NORMAL High side NORMAL 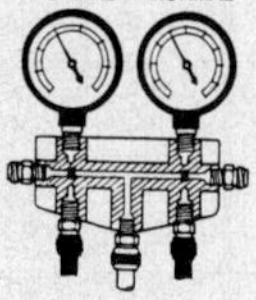	• Discharge air: slightly cool. • Thermostatic switch (with thermistor): Low side gauge doesn't fluctuate with switch "ON" and "OFF" cycle.	Some air and moisture in system.	1. Leak test system. 2. Discharge refrigerant from system. 3. Repair leaks as located. 4. Replace receiver-drier.(The drier is probably saturated with moisture.) 5. Evacuate the system for at least 30 minutes. 6. Charge system with refrigerant. 7. Operate system and check performance.
2 Low side NORMAL High side NORMAL 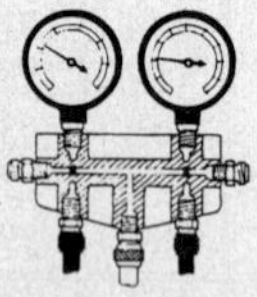	• Discharge air: Becomes warm as low side cycles into vacuum. • Discharge air: Becomes warm all the time during hot part of day.	Excessive moisture in system	1. Discharge refrigerant 2. Replace receiver-drier 3. Evacuate system with a vacuum pump. 4. Recharge system to proper capacity. 5. Operate system and check performance.
3 Low side NORMAL High side NORMAL 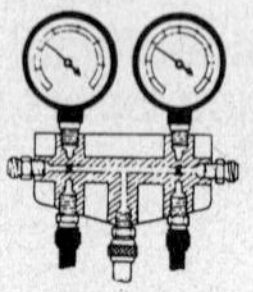	• Compressor: Cycles on and off too fast. • Low side gauge: Not enough range shown on low side gauge.	Defective thermostatic switch	1. Stop engine and turn air conditioning "OFF" 2. Replace thermostatic switch when installing new thermostatic switch. Make sure that thermister tube is installed in the same position and to the same depth in evaporator core as old switch tube. 3. Operate system and check performance.

HY7029600095010X

Fig. 20 Pressure gauge indication chart (Part 1 of 4)

GAUGE READINGS	OTHER SYMPTOMS	DIAGNOSIS	CORRECTION
4 Low side NORMAL to HIGH High side NORMAL 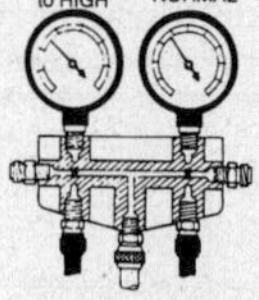	• Compressor: low side pressure builds too high before compressor turns on (cycle "ON" point too high)	Faulty thermostatic switch	1. Stop engine and turn air conditioning "OFF" 2. Repair or replace thermostatic switch with thermistor (make sure that all wiring is positioned so that no short circuiting can occurred.) 3. Operate system and check performance.
5 Low side LOW High side LOW 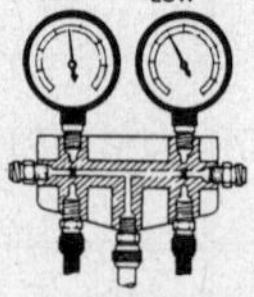	• Discharge air: Slightly cool.	System slightly low on refrigerant	1. Check leaks. 2. Discharge refrigerant. 3. Repair leaks. 4. Check compressor oil level. 5. Evacuate system using a vacuum pump. 6. Charge system with refrigerant. 7. Operate system and check performance.
6 Low side LOW High side LOW 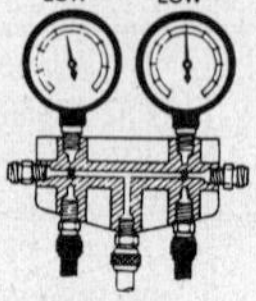	• Discharge air: Warm	• System very low on refrigerant • Possible leak in system.	1. Check leaks. 2. Leak test compressor seal area very carefully. 3. Discharge refrigerant. 4. Check compressor oil level. 5. Evaporate system using a vacuum pump. 6. Charge system with refrigerant. 7. Operate system and check performance.
7 Low side LOW High side LOW 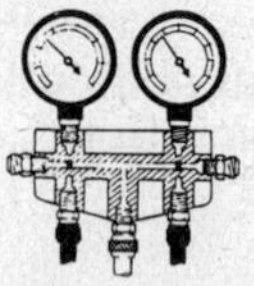	• Discharge air: Slightly cool. • Expansion valve: Sweating or frost build up.	• Expansion valve stuck closed. • Screen plugged. • Sensing bulb malfunction.	1. Discharge system. 2. Disconnect inlet line at expansion valve and remove and inspect screen. 3. Clean and replace screen and reconnect inlet line. 4. Evacuate system using a vacuum pump. 5. Charge system with refrigerant.

HY7029600095020X

Fig. 20 Pressure gauge indication chart (Part 2 of 4)

GAUGE READINGS	OTHER SYMPTOMS	DIAGNOSIS	CORRECTION
8 Low side LOW High side LOW 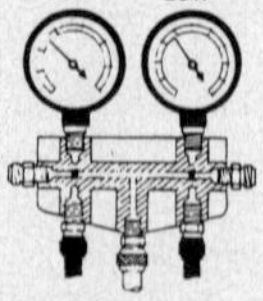	• Discharge air: slightly cool. • High side pipe: Cool and also shows sweating or frost.	Restriction in high side of system	1. Discharge system. 2. Remove and replace receiver-drier, liquid pipes or other defective components. 3. Evacuate system using a vacuum pump. 4. Charge system with refrigerant. 5. Operate system and check performance.
9 Low side HIGH High side LOW 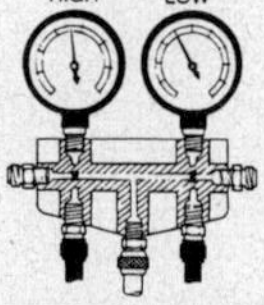	• Compressor :Noisy	Compressor malfunction	1. Isolate compressor. 2. Remove compressor cylinder head and inspect compressor. 3. Check compressor oil level. 4. Replace receiver-drier 5. Operate system and check performance.
10 Low side HIGH High side HIGH 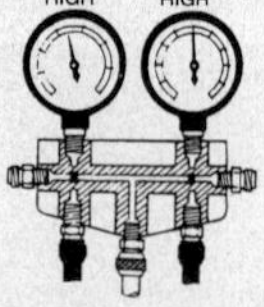	• Discharge air: Warm. High side pipe : Very hot	Malfunctioning condenser overcharge.	1. Check for loose or worn fan belt. 2. Inspect condenser for clogged air passage. 3. Inspect condenser mounting for proper radiator clearance. 4. Check for refrigerant overcharge. 5. Operate system and check performance.
11 Low side HIGH High side HIGH 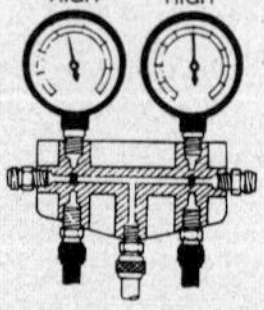	• Discharge air: Slightly cool.	Large amount of air and moisture	1. Discharge refrigerant from system. 2. Replace receiver-drier which may be saturated with moisture. 3. Evacuate system using vacuum pump. 4. Charge system with refrigerant. 5. Operate system and check performance.

HY7029600095030X

Fig. 20 Pressure gauge indication chart (Part 3 of 4)

GAUGE READINGS	OTHER SYMPTOMS	DIAGNOSIS	CORRECTION
12 Low side HIGH High side HIGH 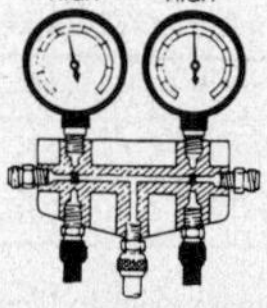	• Discharge air: Warm • Evaporator: Sweating or frost.	Expansion valve stuck open	1. Discharge system. 2. Replace expansion valve, making sure all contacts are clean and secure. 3. Evacuate system using vacuum pump, then recharge system with refrigerant. 4. Operate system and check performance.

HY7029600095040X

Fig. 20 Pressure gauge indication chart (Part 4 of 4)

System Service

NOTE: Prior To Performing Any Service Operations Listed In This Section, Consult The "Technical Service Bulletins" Section For Related Information.

INDEX

OIL CHARGE

Recover refrigerant, then measure amount of oil collected. **If more than .5 oz. is collected when recovering system, an equal amount of new refrigeration oil must be added to system.**

On Tracker models, if refrigerant charge is abruptly lost because of a large refrigerant leak, add 1.3 oz. of oil to system plus amount required for any component replaced.

On all models except Tracker, if refrigerant charge was abruptly lost because of a large refrigerant leak, add 3.0 oz. of oil to system plus amount required for any component replaced.

Remove faulty components. Add the proper amount of oil to each replacement component using the following procedures.

Except Tracker

Drain oil from old compressor and measure, then drain new compressor. If more than 1.0 oz. is drained from old compressor, add same amount to new compressor. If less than 1.0 oz. is drained from old compressor, add 2.0 oz.

When other air conditioning system components are replaced add the following quantities of refrigerant oil: Front evaporator, 3.0 oz.; condenser, 1.0 oz.; receiver/drier, 3.5 oz.

On all models except Montana, Venture, Silhouette and Trans Sport , add 3.0 oz. when replacing rear evaporator.

On Montana, Venture, Silhouette and Trans Sport models, add 2.0 oz. of oil when replacing rear evaporator and 1.0 oz. when replacing rear evaporator pipes.

Tracker

Drain oil from old compressor and measure, then drain new compressor. Add same amount drained from old compressor to new compressor, ensuring 4.0 oz., of oil has been added.

When other air conditioning system components are replaced add the following quantities of refrigerant oil: evaporator, .7–1.0 oz.; condenser, .7–1.0 oz.; receiver/drier, .3 oz.

Component Replacement

If there are no external signs of oil leakage from the A/C system, maintain the proper system oil charge by adding new refrigeration oil during component replacement as follows:

1. Discharge system as outlined, then measure amount of oil collected in discharge container. **If more than ½ ounce of oil is collected when discharging system, an equal amount of new refrigeration oil must be added to the system.**
2. Remove faulty components. Drain and measure oil remaining in compressor or accumulator, if removed.
3. Add the proper amount of oil to each replacement component as follows:
   a. If accumulator is being replaced, add the same amount of oil that was drained from the faulty accumulator plus 2 additional ounces.
   b. If compressor is replaced, add the same amount of oil that was drained from faulty compressor plus 3.5 ounces in the HR-6 model and one ounce is all other models.
   c. If condenser is replaced, add one ounce of oil to replacement condenser.
   d. If evaporator is replaced, add one ounce of oil to the V-5 model evaporator and 3 ounces of oil to all other model replacement evaporators.
   e. If receiver/drier is replaced, add one ounce of oil to replacement receiver/drier.

Oil Level Check-Leak Condition

If external oil leakage is evident, inspect compressor oil level using the following procedures.

1. Discharge system as outlined, then measure amount of oil collected in discharge container. **If more than ½ ounce of oil is collected when discharging system, an equal amount of new refrigeration oil must be added to the system.**
2. **On models with A-6 axial compressor,** proceed as follows:
   a. Remove compressor and accumulator, drain oil from components into a suitable container and measure amount of oil recovered.
   b. If more than 4 ounces are recovered, add the same amount of new refrigeration oil to system.
   c. If less than 6 ounces are recovered, add 6 ounces.
3. **On models with R-4 or HR-6 compressors,** proceed as follows:
   a. Remove accumulator, drain oil remaining in accumulator into a suitable container and measure amount of oil recovered. **These compressors do not have an oil sump, therefore it is unnecessary to drain this compressor to inspect system oil level.**
   b. If the amount of oil recovered is 3 ounces or more, add the same amount of new refrigeration oil to system.

   c. If less than 3 ounces of oil are recovered, add 3 ounces of new refrigeration oil to system.
4. **On all models,** add refrigeration oil, as needed, to compressor sump or accumulator. Reinstall components, then recover and recharge system.

OIL LEVEL CHECK

Refer to "A/C System Specifications" for oil level specifications.

The Frigidaire/Delco Air axial six cylinder and radial four cylinder compressors must be removed from vehicle and drained to inspect the oil level. Refer to "Oil Charge" for service procedures.

TECHNICAL SERVICE BULLETINS

Loss Of HVAC Modes Or Temperature Control

AVALANCHE, DENALI, ESCALADE, SILVERADO, SIERRA, SUBURBAN, TAHOE, YUKON

On some of these models there may be loss of HVAC modes. This loss of function will cause loss of control of the HVAC systems modes or temperature control.

This condition may be caused by poor terminal contact or bent connectors on HVAC controller or excessive tension on the wire harness due to misrouted in the instrument panel carrier may have cause these conditions.

To correct this condition as follows:

1. Disarm air bag system as outlined in "Precautions."
2. Disconnect steering wheel and instrument panel (IP) air bag connectors then remove IP upper trim pad.
3. Locate connector w/6 pin or 8 pin connectors. The connector is attached to a metal brace on far righthand side of the IP carrier above the IP air distributor duct.
4. Inspect routing of the wiring harness to the connector. The correct routing of the wiring harness is above the air distributor duct with no tension on wires in the connector. The routing is improper if wire harness is below the air distributor duct resulting in excessive tension on the terminals in the connector. This could cause poor terminal contact, causing in open circuit, in the connector.
5. If harness is routed correctly, contact Technical Assistance for further information.
6. If harness is routed incorrectly, remove connector from the brace.
7. Disconnect the connector.
8. Perform a pin drag test on the female terminals.
9. Inspect the male terminals for straightness.
10. Inspect wire terminal connections at connector.
11. Reroute wiring harness above air distributor duct.
12. Reconnect connector.
13. Reattach connector to metal brace.
14. Install the IP upper trim pad.
15. Turn Off ignition and reconnect steering wheel and IP air bags.
16. Install Air Bag fuse, then inspect that air bag light flashes seven times then goes out.
17. Clear any diagnostic trouble codes that could have set.
18. Inspect for proper operation of HVAC system mode and temperature controls.

Air Conditioning Odor

EXCEPT TRACKER

On some of these models odors may be emitted from the air conditioning system, primarily at start-up in hot humid climates.

This condition may be caused by microbial growth on the evaporator core. When the blower motor fan is turned on, the microbial growth may release an unpleasant, musty odor into the passenger compartment.

To correct this condition, proceed as follows:

1. Visually inspect air conditioning evaporator drain hose for obstructions and/or working condition. Repair as required.
2. Apply evaporator core cooling coil coating (part No. 12377951 or AC Delco No. 15-102) as outlined in instructions supplied with kit.
3. Install the electronic evaporator dryer (part No. 12346377 or AC Delco No. 12346378). Complete detailed installation instructions and wire connectors are supplied with electronic evaporator dryer.
4. Ground wire should be attached to body ground source.
5. If required, evaporator dryer can be installed underhood away from extreme heat conditions (i.e. exhaust manifolds) and/or water splash areas.

Insufficient A/C Cooling

ASTRO & SAFARI w/REAR A/C SYSTEM

On some of these models there may comment on no A/C.

This condition may be caused by loss of A/C refrigerant because of the A/C compressor and condenser hose assembly rubbing at the lefthand rear area of the engine block, causing a hole.

To correct this condition, proceed as follows:

1. Recover A/C system, then raise and support vehicle.
2. Inspect hose at lefthand rear engine block for signs of rub through.
3. Disconnect A/C compressor and condenser hose assembly from auxiliary evaporator line.
4. Remove A/C compressor and condenser hose assembly to chassis clip mounting bolts.
5. Remove A/C compressor and condenser hose assembly to bell housing stud mounting nut.
6. Lower vehicle, then remove engine cover and air cleaner.
7. Remove grille.
8. Remove A/C compressor and condenser hose assembly to intake manifold stud mounting nut.
9. Remove A/C compressor and condenser hose assembly to compressor mounting bolt.
10. Disconnect hose assembly from condenser and accumulator, then remove it.
11. Install revised A/C compressor and condenser hose assembly (part No. 15049493) with tighter routing.

Lack Of Performance

SILHOUETTE & VENTURE

On some of these models equipped with front air conditioner and manual controls built before VIN breakpoint YD150489 there may be a lack of performance in hot, humid weather.

This condition may be caused by an undercharged air conditioning system.

To correct this condition recover and recharge the A/C system with 2.375 lbs. of R-134a.

A/C Not Cold Enough/Inoperative

TRACKER

On some of these models the air conditioning does not seem cold enough or is inoperative.

This condition may be caused by a low refrigerant charge because of a leak in the system.

To correct this condition, proceed as follows:

1. Recover system.
2. Lightly coat new O-rings with suitable 525 mineral oil.
3. **Discard all old bolts and replace with new ones.**
4. Replace both evaporator O-rings.
5. Replace both compressor O-rings.
6. Replace condenser discharge hose O-rings.
7. Install washer behind A/C hose mounting bolts at compressor and evaporator blocks.
8. Install evaporator inlet and outlet tubes to expansion valve. **Torque** new mounting bolts to 26 ft. lbs.
9. Install discharge hose to condenser. **Torque** new mounting to 19 ft. lbs.**Torque** evaporator blocks to 26 ft. lbs.
10. Install discharge and suction hoses to compressor. **Torque** two new mounting bolts to 19 ft. lbs.
11. Refill system with proper amount of R-134a refrigerant.

A/C Compressor Inoperative

AZTEK, MONTANA w/MITSUBISHI A/C COMPRESSOR & RENDEZVOUS, VENTURE & SILHOUETTE

On some of these models there may be an intermittent air conditioning system operation DTC P0530 may be set.

To correct this condition, proceed as follows:

1. Perform a leak test on A/C system.
2. Inspect the A/C high pressure valve for leaks located on the A/C compressor.
3. If the A/C high pressure valve is the source of the leak, continue with next step if high pressure valve is not the source of the leak refer to A/C diagnosis.
4. Recover the refrigerant from the system.
5. Remove and replace the A/C high pressure valve from compressor.
6. Vacuum and recharge A/C system.
7. Connect scan tool and inspect for trouble code P0530 clear trouble code, then operate the vehicle to conditions for running the DTC trouble code.

A/C Not Cold Enough

SIERRA & SILVERADO w/6.6L DIESEL

On some of these models A/C performance will be poor when ambient temperature is above 194°F.

To correct this condition, proceed as follows:

1. If normal diagnostics do not correct then perform the following A/C system inspections.
2. Calibrate the actuators.
3. Inspect the lower A/C condenser deflector for proper installation.
4. Inspect the engine cooling fan clutch for proper operation.
5. Inspect vehicle license plate bracket is installed upside down if so it will block the two fresh air intake holes in the bumper.
6. Some improvements have been seen by lowering the A/C charge from 1.8 lbs to 1.6 lbs. When recovering the A/C recovery must be pulled for at least 45 minutes.
7. Inspect low pressure cycling switch for correct operation. The low pressure switch opens at 21.5 psi, which stops compressor then closes when the low pressure side reaches 40 psi. This results for the A/C compressor to turn back on.
8. When performing the A/C performance test. Refer to A/C system performance test for specifications.

AZTEK, MONTANA, RENDEZVOUS, SILHOUETTE & VENTURE

On some of these models A/C performance will be poor do to cracked and leaking condenser leaking at the lower righthand attachment bracket.

To correct this condition, proceed as follows:

1. Recover system.
2. Replace condenser with new (part No. 10339103 or 10339104).
3. Refill system with proper amount of R-134a refrigerant.

Insufficient A/C Performance

ENVOY XL & TRAILBLAZER EXT

On some of these models A/C Performance will be poor due to an overcharged system. If system is overcharged this may cause A/C to stop blowing cold air after extend idle at high ambient temperatures. It has been found that the under hood A/C specifications label containing the A/C charge is incorrect. The correct specification should read Front and Rear 2.65 lbs.

A/C System Inoperative

BRAVADA, ENVOY, TRAILBLAZER

On some of these models A/C system becomes inoperative at any time during the drive cycle and at any temperature setting, the returns to normal after the vehicle has been turned off then restarted. To correct this condition update the HVAC control module with new software update. Then perform the HVAC Diagnostic system test inspection.

Inoperative Rear A/C Controls

ENVOY XL & TRAILBLAZER EXT w/AUTOMATIC TEMPERATURE CONTROL

On some of these models built in May 2002 or prior rear A/C may become inoperative. The controls may appear not to be respond or have very slow response for about one minute from starting the vehicle with limited temperature mode range of the controller. Diagnostic trouble code (DTC) B0150 may be stored in history. This could be caused do to servicing of battery or battery being disconnected resulting in at the first key on the rear HVAC controller will reset and perform a test, ranging the temperature and mode doors to full range of there travel or beyond there range of travel, (DTC) B0150 will be set and this code will disable the rear HVAC control. Do to productions variances, the mode doors and temp doors may be traveling beyond their programed range. To correct this condition a revised rear HVAC controller has been released that eliminates (DTC) B0150 and has updated programming to allow for increased range of temp doors travel. GM part No of HVAC Control module part No. 15184851 w/o rear audio, part No. 15184098 w/rear audio. If the part number matches the revised part No. listed this Technical Service Bulletin does not apply to these vehicles.

Specifications

INDEX

A/C SPECIFICATIONS

Model	Year	Refrigerant		Compressor Oil Viscosity	Total System Oil Capacity, Oz.	Compressor Clutch Air Gap, Inch
		Capacity, Lbs.	Type			
BUICK						
Rainier w/Front A/C Only	2004	1.90	R-134a	③	7.40	—
	2005–06	1.90	R-134a	③	8.00	—
Rainier w/Front & Rear A/C	2004	3.00	R-134a	③	8.45	—
	2005–06	2.65	R-134a	③	8.00	—
Rendezvous	2002–06	1.68	R-134a	⑦	7.10	.015–.020
Terraza w/Front A/C Only 3.5L	2005–06	1.68	R-134a	⑦	7.10	—
Terraza w/Front & Rear A/C 3.5L	2005–06	2.20	R-134a	⑦	7.70	—
Terraza w/Front A/C Only 3.9L	2005–06	1.68	R-134a	⑦	7.10	—
Terraza w/Front & Rear A/C 3.9L	2005–06	1.98	R-134a	⑦	7.70	—
CADILLAC						
Escalade w/Front A/C Only	2002	1.80	R-134a	③	8.00	.020–.030
	2003–04	1.60	R-134a	⑦	8.00	—
	2005–06	1.60	R-134a	⑦	7.10	—
Escalade w/Front & Rear A/C	2002	2.70	R-134a	③	11.00	.020–.030
	2003–06	2.70	R-134a	⑦	11.00	—
Escalade ESV	2004–06	2.70	R-134a	⑦	11.00	—
Escalade EXT w/Front A/C Only	2002	1.80	R-134a	③	8.00	.020–.030
	2003–04	1.60	R-134a	⑦	8.00	—
	2005–06	1.60	R-134a	⑦	7.10	—
Escalade EXT w/Front & Rear A/C	2002	2.70	R-134a	③	11.00	.020–.030
	2003–06	3.00	R-134a	⑦	11.00	—
SRX w/Front A/C Only	2004–06	1.26	R-134a	⑦	6.09	—
SRX w/Front & Rear A/C	2004–06	1.76	R-134a	⑦	6.09	—
CHEVROLET						
Astro w/Front A/C Only	2002	2.00	R-134a	③	8.00	.015–.020
	2003	2.00	R-134a	⑦	8.00	.015–.020
	2004–05	2.00	R-134a	③	8.00	.015–.020
Astro w/Front & Rear A/C	2002	3.00	R-134a	③	11.00	.015–.020
	2003	3.00	R-134a	⑦	11.00	.015–.020
	2004–05	3.00	R-134a	③	11.00	.015–.020
Avalanche w/Front A/C Only	2002	1.80	R-134a	③	8.00	.020–.030
	2003–04	1.60	R-134a	⑦	8.00	—
	2005–06	1.60	R-134a	⑦	7.10	—
Avalanche w/Front & Rear A/C	2002	2.70	R-134a	③	11.00	.020–.030
	2003–06	2.70	R-134a	⑦	11.00	—
Blazer S/T	2002	1.75	R-134a	③	①	.020–.030
	2003	1.75	R-134a	⑦	①	⑤
	2004–05	1.75	R-134a	②	8.00	.020–.030
Colorado	2004–06	1.60	R-134a	⑦	4.00	—
C4/5	2003–06	2.125	R-134a	⑦	8.00	.020–.030

Continued

A/C SPECIFICATIONS—Continued

Model	Year	Refrigerant		Compressor Oil Viscosity	Total System Oil Capacity, Oz.	Compressor Clutch Air Gap, Inch
		Capacity, Lbs.	Type			
CHEVROLET						
Equinox	2005	1.75	R-134a	⑦	7.00	.014–.030
	2006	1.30	R-134a	⑦	4.40	.012–.024
Express w/Front A/C Only	2002	2.00	R-134a	③	8.00	.020–.030
	2003–06	2.00	R-134a	⑦	8.00	—
Express w/Front & Rear A/C	2002	3.50	R-134a	③	11.00	.020–.030
	2003–06	3.00	R-134a	⑦	11.00	—
G Series w/Front A/C Only	2002	2.00	R-134a	③	8.00	.020–.030
	2003–06	2.00	R-134a	⑦	8.00	—
G Series w/Front & Rear A/C	2002	3.50	R-134a	③	11.00	.020–.030
	2003–06	3.00	R-134a	⑦	11.00	—
HHR	2006	.90	R-134a	⑦	5.00	.012–.024
Silverado	2002	1.80	R-134a	⑦	8.00	.020–.030
	2003–04	1.60	R-134a	⑦	8.00	—
	2005–06	1.60	R-134a	⑦	7.10	—
SSR	2003–04	1.80	R-134a	⑦	7.40	—
	2005–06	1.20	R-134a	⑦	7.40	—
S/T Pickup w/2.2L	2002	1.75	R-134a	③	9.00	.015
	2003	1.75	R-134a	⑦	9.00	.015
S/T Pickup w/4.3L	2002	1.75	R-134a	③	8.00	.020.–030
	2003	1.75	R-134a	⑦	8.00	.020.–030
	2004–05	1.75	R-134a	②	8.00	.020.–030
Suburban w/Front A/C Only	2002	1.80	R-134a	③	8.00	.020–.030
	2003–04	1.60	R-134a	⑦	8.00	—
	2005–06	1.60	R-134a	⑦	7.10	—
Suburban w/Front & Rear A/C	2002	3.00	R-134a	③	11.00	.020–.030
	2003–06	3.00	R-134a	⑦	11.00	—
Tahoe w/Front A/C Only	2002	1.80	R-134a	③	8.00	.020–.030
	2003–04	1.60	R-134a	⑦	8.00	—
	2005–06	1.60	R-134a	⑦	7.10	—
Tahoe w/Front & Rear A/C	2002	2.70	R-134a	③	11.00	.020–.030
	2003–06	2.70	R-134a	⑦	11.00	—
Tracker	2002–04	.77–.99	R-134a	③	3.50	.012–.020
Trailblazer w/Front A/C Only	2002–03	1.80	R-134a	⑦	7.40	—
	2004	1.90	R-134a	③	7.40	—
	2005–06	1.90	R-134a	③	8.00	—
Trailblazer w/Front & Rear A/C	2002–03	2.65	R-134a	⑦	8.45	—
	2004	3.00	R-134a	③	8.45	—
	2005–06	2.65	R-134a	③	8.00	—
Uplander w/Front A/C Only 3.5L	2005–06	1.68	R-134a	⑦	7.10	—
Uplander w/Front & Rear A/C 3.5L	2005–06	2.20	R-134a	⑦	7.70	—
Uplander w/Front A/C Only 3.9L	2005–06	1.68	R-134a	⑦	7.10	—
Uplander w/Front & Rear A/C 3.9L	2005–06	1.98	R-134a	⑦	7.70	—
Venture w/Front A/C Only	2002	1.68	R-134a	③	7.10	—
	2003–05	1.68	R-134a	⑦	7.10	—
Venture w/Front & Rear A/C	2002	2.20	R-134a	③	7.77	—
	2003–05	2.20	R-134a	⑦	7.77	—
3500HD	2002	2.00	R-134a	③	8.00	—
GMC						
Canyon	2004–06	1.60	R-134a	⑦	4.00	—
C4/5	2003–06	2.125	R-134a	⑦	8.00	.020–.030

Continued

A/C SPECIFICATIONS—Continued

Model	Year	Refrigerant Capacity, Lbs.	Refrigerant Type	Compressor Oil Viscosity	Total System Oil Capacity, Oz.	Compressor Clutch Air Gap, Inch
GMC						
Denali w/Front A/C Only	2002	2.00	R-134a	③	8.00	.020–.030
	2003–04	1.60	R-134a	⑦	8.00	—
	2005–06	1.60	R-134a	⑦	7.10	—
Denali w/Front & Rear A/C	2002	2.70	R-134a	③	11.00	.020–.030
	2003–06	2.70	R-134a	⑦	11.00	—
Denali XL w/Front & Rear A/C	2002	3.00	R-134a	③	11.00	.020–.030
	2003–06	3.00	R-134a	⑦	11.00	—
Envoy w/Front A/C Only	2002–03	1.80	R-134a	⑦	7.40	—
	2004	1.90	R-134a	③	7.40	—
	2005–06	1.90	R-134a	③	8.00	—
Envoy w/Front & Rear A/C	2002–03	2.65	R-134a	⑦	8.45	—
	2004	3.00	R-134a	③	8.45	—
	2005–06	2.65	R-134a	③	8.00	—
G Series w/Front A/C Only	2002	2.00	R-134a	③	8.00	.020–.030
	2003–05	2.00	R-134a	⑦	8.00	—
G Series w/Front & Rear A/C	2002	3.50	R-134a	③	11.00	.020–.030
	2003–05	3.00	R-134a	⑦	11.00	—
Jimmy S/T	2002	1.75	R-134a	③	①	.020–.030
	2003	1.75	R-134a	⑦	①	⑤
	2004–05	1.75	R-134a	②	8.00	.020–.030
Safari w/Front A/C Only	2002	2.00	R-134a	③	8.00	.015–.020
	2003	2.00	R-134a	⑦	8.00	.020–.030
	2004–05	2.00	R-134a	③	8.00	.020–.030
Safari w/Front & Rear A/C	2002	3.00	R-134a	③	11.00	.015–.020
	2003	3.00	R-134a	⑦	11.00	.020–.030
	2004–05	3.00	R-134a	③	11.00	.020–.030
Savana w/Front A/C Only	2002	2.00	R-134a	③	8.00	.020–.030
	2003–06	2.00	R-134a	⑦	8.00	—
Savana w/Front & Rear A/C	2002	3.50	R-134a	③	11.00	.020–.030
	2003–06	3.00	R-134a	⑦	11.00	—
Sierra	2002	2.00	R-134a	③	8.00	.020–.030
	2003–04	1.60	R-134a	⑦	8.00	—
	2005–06	1.60	R-134a	⑦	7.10	—
Sonoma w/2.2L	2002	1.75	R-134a	③	9.00	.015
	2003	1.75	R-134a	⑦	9.00	.015
Sonoma w/4.3L	2002	1.75	R-134a	③	8.00	.020.–030
	2003	1.75	R-134a	⑦	8.00	.020.–030
	2004–05	1.75	R-134a	②	8.00	.020.–030
Yukon w/Front A/C Only	2002	1.80	R-134a	③	8.00	.020–.030
	2003–04	1.60	R-134a	⑦	8.00	—
	2005–06	1.60	R-134a	⑦	7.10	—
Yukon w/Front & Rear A/C	2002	2.70	R-134a	③	11.00	.020–.030
	2003–06	2.70	R-134a	⑦	11.00	—
Yukon XL w/Front A/C Only	2002	1.80	R-134a	③	8.00	.020–.030
	2003–04	1.60	R-134a	⑦	8.00	—
	2005–06	1.60	R-134a	⑦	7.10	—
Yukon XL w/Front & Rear A/C	2002	3.00	R-134a	③	11.00	.020–.030
	2003–06	3.00	R-134a	⑦	11.00	—
3500HD	2002	2.00	R-134a	③	8.00	—

Continued

A/C SPECIFICATIONS—Continued

Model	Year	Refrigerant Capacity, Lbs.	Refrigerant Type	Compressor Oil Viscosity	Total System Oil Capacity, Oz.	Compressor Clutch Air Gap, Inch
HUMMER						
H2	2003–04	1.60	R-134a	⑦	8.00	—
	2005–06	1.60	R-134a	⑦	7.10	—
H3	2006	1.50	R-134a	⑦	4.00	—
OLDSMOBILE						
Bravada w/Front A/C Only	2002–03	1.80	R-134a	⑦	7.40	—
	2004	1.90	R-134a	③	7.40	—
Bravada w/Front & Rear A/C	2002–03	2.65	R-134a	⑦	8.45	—
	2004	3.00	R-134a	③	8.45	—
Silhouette w/Front A/C Only	2002	1.68	R-134a	③	7.10	—
	2003–04	1.68	R-134a	⑦	7.10	—
Silhouette w/Front & Rear A/C	2002	2.20	R-134a	③	7.77	—
	2003–04	2.20	R-134a	⑦	7.77	—
PONTIAC						
Aztek	2002–05	1.68	R-134a	③	7.40	.015–.020
Montana & Trans Sport w/Front A/C Only	2002	1.68	R-134a	③	7.10	—
	2003–06	1.68	R-134a	⑦	7.10	—
Montana & Trans Sport w/Front & Rear A/C	2002	2.20	R-134a	③	7.77	—
	2003–05	2.20	R-134a	⑦	7.77	—
Montana SV6 w/Front A/C Only 3.5L	2005–06	1.68	R-134a	⑦	7.10	—
Montana SV6 w/Front & Rear A/C 3.5L	2005–06	2.20	R-134a	⑦	7.70	—
Montana SV6 w/Front A/C Only 3.9L	2005–06	1.68	R-134a	⑦	7.10	—
Montana SV6 w/Front & Rear A/C 3.9L	2005–06	1.98	R-134a	⑦	7.70	—
Torrent	2006	1.30	R-134a	⑦	4.40	.012–.024
SATURN						
Relay w/Front A/C Only 3.5L	2005–06	1.68	R-134a	⑦	7.10	—
Relay w/Front & Rear A/C 3.5L	2005–06	2.20	R-134a	⑦	7.70	—
Relay w/Front A/C Only 3.9L	2005–06	1.68	R-134a	⑦	7.10	—
Relay w/Front & Rear A/C 3.9L	2005–06	1.98	R-134a	⑦	7.70	—
Vue	2002–03	1.50	R-134a	③	7.00	.014–.030
	2004–06	⑥	R-134a	④	7.00	.014–.030

① — V-7 compressor, 9 oz.; HT-6 compressor, 8.00 oz.

② — PAG (Polyalkaline Glycol) synthetic refrigerant oil (GM part number 1237852), or equivalent.

③ — PAG (Polyalkaline Glycol) synthetic refrigerant oil (GM part number 12345923), or equivalent.

④ — PAG (Polyalkaline Glycol) synthetic refrigerant oil (GM part number 22695048), or equivalent.

⑤ — V-7 compressor, .015 inch; HT-6 compressor, .020–.030 inch.

⑥ — 2.2L engine, 1.50 lbs.; 3.5L engine, 1.75 lbs.

⑦ — PAG (Polyalkaline Glycol) synthetic refrigerant oil (GM part number 12378526), or equivalent.

CHARGING VALVE LOCATION

The high pressure fitting is located either in the high pressure vapor line or muffler, while the low pressure fitting is located on the accumulator.

BELT TENSION

Belt tension is maintained by a spring tensioned idler pulley. No adjustment of the serpentine belt is required.

COOLING FANS

TABLE OF CONTENTS

Variable Speed Fans

INDEX

PRECAUTIONS

Do not operate engine until fan has first been inspected for cracks and/or separations. If a fan blade is found to be bent or damaged in any way, do not attempt to repair or reuse damaged part. Proper balance is essential in fan assembly operation. Balance cannot be ensured once a fan assembly has been found to be bent or damaged and failure may occur during operation, creating an extremely dangerous condition. Always replace damaged fan assembly.

DESCRIPTION

The fan drive clutch is a fluid coupling containing silicone oil. Fan speed is regulated by the torque-carrying capacity of the silicone oil. The more silicone oil in the coupling, the greater the fan speed, and the less silicone oil, the slower the fan speed.

The fan drive clutch uses a heat-sensitive, coiled bimetallic spring connected to an opening plate which regulates the flow of silicone oil into the coupling from a reserve chamber. The silicone oil is returned to the reserve chamber through a bleed hole when the valve is closed. This unit causes the fan speed to increase with a rise in temperature and to decrease as temperature decreases.

TROUBLESHOOTING

Fan Clutch Noise

Fan clutch noise can sometimes be noticed when clutch is engaged for maximum cooling. Clutch noise is also noticeable within the first few minutes after starting engine while clutch is redistributing the silicone fluid back to its normal, disengaged operating condition after settling for long periods of time (overnight). However, continuous fan noise or an excessive roar indicates the clutch assembly is locked-up due to internal failure. This condition can be inspected by attempting to manually rotate fan. If fan cannot be rotated manually or there is a rough, abrasive feel as fan is rotated, the clutch should be replaced.

Fan Looseness

Lateral movement can be observed at the fan blade tip under various temperature conditions because of the type bearing used. This movement should not exceed 1/4 inch (6.5 mm) as measured at the fan tip. If this lateral movement does not exceed specifications, there is no cause for replacement.

Clutch Fluid Leak

Small fluid leaks do not generally affect the operation of the unit. These leaks generally occur around the area of the bearing assembly, but if the leaks appear to be excessive, engine overheating may occur. Clutch and fan free-wheeling can cause overheating. To inspect for clutch and fan free-wheeling, turn the motor off. Spin the fan and clutch assembly by hand. If the fan spins five or more times before it stops, replace the clutch.

Engine Overheating

1. Start with cool engine to ensure complete fan clutch disengagement.
2. If fan and clutch assembly free wheels with no drag (revolves more than five times when spun by hand), replace clutch. If clutch performs properly with slight drag, proceed to following step.
3. Position thermometer so it is located between fan blades and radiator, noting the following:
   a. Insert thermometer sensor through one of existing holes in fan shroud or place between radiator and shroud. It may be required to drill a 3/16 inch hole in fan shroud to insert thermometer.
   b. Inspect for adequate clearance between fan blades and thermometer sensor before starting engine, as damage could occur.
4. With thermometer in position, cover radiator grill sufficiently to induce high engine temperature.
5. Start engine, then turn on air conditioning and operate at 2000 RPM.
6. Observe thermometer reading when clutch disengages, noting the following:
   a. It will take approximately 5–10 minutes for temperature to become high enough to allow engagement of fan clutch. This will be indicated by a 5–15°F drop in thermometer reading.
   b. If clutch did not engage between 150–195°F, unit should be replaced. Ensure fan clutch was disengaged at beginning of test.
   c. If no sharp increase in fan noise or temperature drop was observed and fan noise level was constantly high from start of test to 190°F, unit should be replaced. Do not continue this test past thermometer reading of 190°F to prevent engine overheating.
7. As soon as clutch engages, remove radiator grille cover and turn A/C off to assist in engine cooling. Run engine at approximately 1500 RPM.
8. After several minutes, fan clutch should disengage as indicated by reduction in fan speed and roar. If fan clutch fails to function as described, replace.

COMPONENT REPLACEMENT

Cooling Fan

ASTRO, AVALANCHE, CANYON, COLORADO, ESCALADE, HUMMER H2, HUMMER H3, SAFARI, SIERRA, SILVERADO, SUBURBAN, TAHOE & YUKON

GASOLINE ENGINE

1. Remove upper fan shroud.
2. Install a fan clutch remover and installer tool No. J 46406 to fan clutch.
3. Remove fan hub nut from water pump in a counterclockwise rotation.
4. Remove fan clutch bolts from rear of fan blade.
5. Separate fan clutch from fan blade.
6. Reverse procedure to install, noting the following:
   a. **Torque** fan clutch bolts to 17 ft lbs.
   b. **Torque** fan clutch nut to 41 ft lbs.
   c. **On H2 model, torque** fan clutch nut to 44 ft lbs.
   d. **On Colorado and Canyon models, torque** fan blade bolts to 20 ft lbs.
   e. **On Astro and Safari models, torque** fan blade bolts to 24 ft lbs. and fan clutch assembly bolts to 41 ft lbs.

DIESEL ENGINE

1. Remove upper fan shroud.
2. Remove engine cooling fan shroud bolts.
3. Position engine cooling fan shroud forward to radiator.
4. Install a suitable long pin bar into fan hub.
5. Remove fan hub nut from hub in a counterclockwise rotation using fan clutch wrench tool No. J 41240-5A, or equivalent.
6. Remove fan and engine cooling fan shroud as an assembly.
7. Remove fan clutch bolts from rear of fan blade.
8. Separate fan clutch from fan blade.
9. Reverse procedure to install, noting the following:
   a. **Torque** fan clutch bolts to 17 ft lbs.
   b. **Torque** fan clutch hub nut clockwise to 41 ft lbs.
   c. **Torque** engine cooling fan shroud bolts 71 inch lbs.

BLAZER, JIMMY, S10 & SONOMA

1. **On models equipped with 2.2L engine,** remove air intake duct assembly.
2. **On all models,** remove upper fan shroud bolts.
3. Remove coolant recovery reservoir hose from lower fan shroud.
4. Remove upper fan shroud.
5. Lift lower fan shroud enough to disengage locating tabs from radiator.
6. Remove lower fan shroud from vehicle.
7. Remove fan clutch from water pump in a counterclockwise direction using a fan clutch wrench tool No. J 46406, or equivalent.
8. Remove fan clutch assembly.
9. Remove fan blade mounting bolts.
10. Remove fan blade from fan clutch.
11. Reverse procedure to install, noting the following:
    a. **Torque** fan blade mounting bolts to 24 ft lbs.
    b. **Torque** fan clutch nut to 40 ft lbs.

BRAVADA, ENVOY, RAINIER, & TRAILBLAZER

1. Drain cooling system into a suitable container.
2. Remove air cleaner assembly.
3. Remove air resonator assembly.
4. Remove inlet radiator hose.
5. Remove transmission oil cooler lines from fan shroud.
6. Disconnect fan clutch electrical connector.
7. Remove fan clutch from water pump using a fan clutch remover and installer tool No. J 46406, or equivalent.
8. Remove mounting bolts from upper fan shroud.
9. Lift and push fan shroud inward to clear filler neck on radiator.
10. Remove fan and shroud.
11. Remove cooling fan and shroud.
12. Remove push-pin and release fan clutch electrical connector from fan shroud.
13. Remove fan clutch from fan shroud.
14. Remove bolts retaining fan blade to fan clutch.
15. Separate fan blade from fan clutch.
16. Reverse procedure to install, noting the following:
    a. **Torque** fan blade bolts to 20 ft lbs.
    b. **Torque** upper fan shroud bolts to 21 ft lbs.

EXPRESS, SAVANNA

2002

1. Remove air cleaner and duct.
2. Partially drain engine coolant into a suitable container.
3. Remove overflow hose from top of surge tank.
4. Remove inlet hose from top of radiator and from surge tank.
5. Remove outlet hose from bottom of surge tank.
6. Disconnect coolant level sensor electrical connector.
7. Remove surge tank retaining bolt.
8. Remove surge tank from cowl tabs.
9. Remove surge tank from vehicle.
10. Remove upper radiator shroud from radiator.
11. **On models equipped with 4.3L, 5.0L and 5.7L engines,** remove engine oil fill tube and transmission oil level indicator to alternator bracket retaining bolts.
12. **On models equipped with 6.5L engines,** remove wiring harness clip retainers from fan shroud.
13. **On all models,** remove upper fan shroud retaining bolts from top of radiator.
14. Remove upper to lower fan shroud retaining bolts.
15. Remove upper fan shroud from vehicle.
16. Remove fan and clutch from engine.
17. Remove lower fan shroud retaining bolts.
18. Remove lower fan shroud from vehicle.
19. Remove fan clutch assembly on using a fan clutch wrench tool No. J 41240-5A, or equivalent.
20. Remove retaining bolts from fan and clutch.
21. Remove fan from clutch.
22. Reverse procedure to install.

2003–05

1. Remove fan shroud bolts from top and sides of radiator support.
2. Remove upper fan shroud.
3. Secure pulley using a fan clutch remover and installer tool No. J 41240, or equivalent.
4. Remove fan clutch assembly.
5. Remove bolts from fan clutch.
6. Separate fan clutch from fan blade.
7. Reverse procedure to install, noting the following:
   a. **Torque** fan clutch bolts 18 ft lbs.
   b. **Torque** fan clutch nut 70 ft lbs.
   c. **Torque** fan shroud bolts 53 inch lbs.

2006

Gasoline Engine

1. Remove coolant recovery reservoir.
2. Remove air cleaner assembly.
3. Remove fan shroud bolts, fan shroud, and upper fan shroud.
4. Secure pulley using a fan clutch remover and installer tool No. J 41240, or equivalent.
5. Remove fan clutch assembly.
6. Remove cooling fan from fan clutch.
7. Reverse procedure to install. **Torque** fan clutch nut to 70 ft lbs.

Diesel Engine

1. Remove surge tank.
2. Remove charge air cooler inlet and outlet hoses.
3. Remove air cleaner assembly.
4. Disconnect fan clutch electrical connector.
5. Remove upper fan shroud to core support bolts.
6. Remove fan clutch electrical wiring harness routing clip.
7. Remove upper fan shroud to lower fan shroud bolts.
8. Secure pulley using a fan clutch remover and installer tool No. J 41240, or equivalent.
9. Remove fan clutch assembly.
10. Remove cooling fan from fan clutch.
11. Reverse procedure to install. **Torque** fan clutch nut to 70 ft lbs.

TRACKER

1. Remove fan nuts and clips.
2. Remove power steering reservoir and reposition aside.

3. Lean shroud toward engine.
4. Detach fan from pulley hub and remove fan/clutch assembly.
5. Remove fan clutch mounting bolts and separate fan from clutch.
6. Inspect fan for cracks and broken blades.
7. Inspect fan clutch for cracks, binding and a worn bearing.
8. Reverse procedure to install.

Electric Fans

NOTE: "Electrical Symbol & Wire Color Code Identification" Located In The Front Of This Manual Can Be Used As An Aid When Using Wiring Circuits Found In This Section.

NOTE: Refer To "Computer Relearn Procedures" Located In The Front Of This Manual When Battery Power To The Computer Has Been Interrupted.

NOTE: On Air Bag Equipped Models, Refer To "Air Bag System Precautions" Located In The Front Of This Manual For System Disarming & Arming Procedures.

INDEX

PRECAUTIONS

Air Bag Systems

Refer to "Air Bag System Precautions" in the front of this manual for system disarming and arming procedures.

Battery Ground Cable

Prior to service, disconnect battery ground cable and isolate as required.

DESCRIPTION

The engine cooling fan system consists of electrical cooling fans and fan relays. The relays are arranged in a series/parallel configuration that allows the Powertrain Control Module (PCM) to operate both fans together at low or high speeds.

SYSTEM DIAGNOSIS & TESTING

Diagnostic Trouble Codes

Code	Description
P0480	Low Speed Cooling Fan Relay Control Circuit
P0481	High Speed Cooling Fan Relay Control Circuit

COMPONENT REPLACEMENT

Cooling Fan

AZTEK & RENDEZVOUS

1. Remove air cleaner and duct assembly.
2. Remove cooling fan harness electrical connector.
3. Remove right side diagonal brace.
4. Loosen engine mount strut nuts.
5. Remove engine mount strut bracket brace bolts from upper radiator support and rotate struts and brackets rearward.
6. Remove upper radiator hose.
7. Remove radiator upper mount bolts.
8. Remove radiator upper mounts.
9. Remove cooling fan shroud bolts.
10. Reposition coolant overflow hose clamp at radiator using hose clamp pliers tool No. J 38185, or equivalent.
11. Disconnect and reposition coolant overflow hose.
12. Disconnect upper TOC line from radiator.
13. Raise vehicle and suitably support.
14. Disconnect TOC lines from fan module retainer clip.
15. Lower vehicle.
16. Disconnect engine wiring harness retainers at engine harness bracket.
17. Reposition engine wiring harness.
18. Remove cooling fans with cooling fan shroud.
19. Reverse procedure to install, noting the following:
    a. **Torque** cooling fan shroud bolts to 53 inch lbs.
    b. **Torque** radiator upper mount bolts to 88 inch lbs.
    c. **Torque** engine mount strut bracket brace bolts to 21 ft lbs.
    d. **Torque** engine mount strut nuts to 35 ft lbs.

EQUINOX & TORRENT

1. Remove front fascia.
2. Drain coolant into a suitable container.
3. Disconnect electrical connectors from fan motors.
4. Unclip wire harness from fan assembly.
5. Remove Condenser Radiator Fan Module (CRFM) closeout panel retainers from condenser.
6. Remove CRFM closeout panel from condenser.
7. Remove front impact bar.
8. Remove CRFM mounting bracket bolts from radiator support.
9. Remove CRFM mounting brackets from radiator support.
10. Remove radiator inlet hose clamp from radiator.
11. Remove radiator inlet hose from radiator.
12. Disconnect transmission cooler lines from radiator.
13. Unclip transmission cooler lines from

fan assembly.

14. Remove fan assembly bolts from radiator.
15. Remove fan assembly from radiator.
16. Position condenser and radiator assembly forward of right hand front impact bar bracket.
17. Remove fan assembly from vehicle.
18. Reverse procedure to install, noting the following:
    a. **Torque** fan assembly bolts to 80 inch lbs.
    b. **Torque** CRFM mounting bracket bolts to 89 inch lbs.

HHR

1. Remove air cleaner assembly.
2. Remove coolant recovery reservoir.
3. Remove hood latch from tie bar and set aside.
4. Remove radiator inlet hose from radiator.
5. Remove upper radiator air baffle.
6. Remove radiator support brackets.
7. Disconnect cooling fan motor electrical connector.
8. Remove transmission line connector from fan shroud.
9. Lift radiator out of support bracket and pull toward front of vehicle.
10. Lift up on fan shroud assembly to release from radiator.
11. Remove fan assembly with shroud.
12. Reverse procedure to install. **Torque** hood latch bolts to 19 ft lbs.

MONTANA, SILHOUETTE & VENTURE

1. Remove fastener from coolant tank.
2. Remove coolant tank and set aside.
3. Remove 3 bolts from support brace and remove brace.
4. Disconnect MAF sensor electrical connector.
5. Remove air inlet duct and MAF sensor assembly.
6. Unsnap latches and remove air cleaner housing cover.
7. Remove air filter element.
8. Unsnap latch on upper cover and remove cover.
9. Carefully remove Powertrain Control Module (PCM) leaving harnesses connected and position aside.
10. Remove bolts from air cleaner assembly and remove housing.
11. Remove hood latch support bolts, then the support.
12. Remove cooling fan harness electrical connector.
13. Remove right side diagonal brace.
14. Loosen engine mount strut nuts from engine.
15. Remove engine mount strut bracket brace bolts from upper radiator support, then rotate struts and brackets rearward.
16. Remove upper radiator hose.
17. Remove radiator upper mount bolts and upper mounts.
18. Remove cooling fan shroud bolts.
19. Disconnect and reposition coolant overflow hose.
20. Disconnect upper transmission oil cooler line from radiator.
21. Disconnect transmission oil cooler lines from fan module retainer clip.
22. Remove cooling fans with cooling fan shroud.
23. Reverse procedure to install, noting the following:
    a. **Torque** cooling fan shroud bolts to 53 inch lbs.
    b. **Torque** radiator upper mount bolts to 88 inch lbs.
    c. **Torque** engine mount strut bracket brace bolts to 21 ft lbs.
    d. **Torque** engine strut mount nuts to 35 ft lbs.
    e. **Torque** hood latch support bolts to 18 ft lbs.

RELAY, SV6, TERRAZA & UPLANDER

1. Remove air cleaner and duct assembly.
2. Remove right side diagonal brace.
3. Remove radiator inlet hose.
4. Disconnect cooling fan harness electrical connector.
5. Loosen engine mount strut to engine retaining nuts.
6. Remove engine mount strut bracket brace bolts from upper radiator support, then rotate struts and brackets rearward.
7. Remove overflow hose from retainers.
8. Disconnect radiator outlet hose retainer from fan shroud.
9. Remove battery.
10. Remove radiator upper mount bolts and mount.
11. Remove cooling fan shroud bolts.
12. Disconnect upper transmission oil cooler line from radiator.
13. Raise and support vehicle.
14. Remove radiator air baffle.
15. Disconnect transaxle oil cooler lines from fan shroud retainer clip.
16. Lower vehicle.
17. Remove cooling fan shroud and fans.
18. Reverse procedure to install, noting the following:
    a. **Torque** cooling fan shroud bolts to 53 inch lbs.
    b. **Torque** radiator upper mount bolts to 88 inch lbs.
    c. **Torque** engine mount strut bracket brace bolts to 21 ft lbs.
    d. **Torque** engine strut mount nuts to 35 ft lbs.

SSR

1. Remove air filter housing.
2. Disconnect cooling fan electrical connector.
3. Reposition tie straps that secure cooling fan assembly to radiator.
4. Pull up on cooling fan assembly.
5. Remove cooling fan assembly.
6. Reverse procedure to install.

VUE

1. Remove front fascia.
2. Drain engine coolant.
3. Disconnect fan motor wiring harness.
4. Unclip transmission cooler line from fan assembly.
5. Remove battery box air intake duct.
6. Remove condenser splash shield.
7. Remove radiator hoses.
8. Remove upper CRFM brackets.
9. Lift out CRFM assembly from vehicle.
10. Remove cooling fan assembly mounting bolts, and fan.
11. Reverse procedure to install. **Torque** fan motor screws to fan shroud screws to 71 inch lbs.

Cooling Fan Motor

AZTEK, HHR & RENDEZVOUS

1. Turn ignition off.
2. Remove cooling fan and shroud assembly.
3. Remove cooling fan nut.
4. Remove cooling fan from shroud.
5. Disconnect electrical connector from cooling fan motor.
6. Remove screws from cooling fan motor.
7. Remove cooling fan motor.
8. Reverse procedure to install.
    a. **Torque** cooling fan motor screws to 53 inch lbs.
    b. **Torque** cooling fan nut to 53 inch lbs.

EQUINOX, & TORRENT

This vehicle is equipped with counter-rotating engine cooling fans. The right hand fan will require the use of cooling fan socket tool No. GE-47827 or equivalent for fan blade removal. The left hand fan blade can be removed using a suitable normal six point socket.

1. Remove fan shroud assembly from vehicle.
2. Hold fan blade to prevent rotation. Turn fan motor drive plate in opposite direction of arrow stamped on fan blade. Using a suitable six point socket.
3. Remove and discard fan blade.
4. Tape off all entry points to cooling fan motor.
5. Center punch each of rivets from rear of motor using a suitable punch.
6. Drill head of rivets from fan motor using a suitable 0.25 inch drill bit.
7. Tap rivets out of fan shroud.
8. Remove fan motor from fan shroud.
9. Remove tape covering entry points from fan motor.
10. Reverse procedure to install, noting the following:
    a. **Torque** cooling fan motor nuts to 53 inch lbs.
    b. Using hot tap water at a minimum of 120°F, hold new fan blade hub under running water for a minimum of 60 seconds to hear fan blade to temperature of water. Immediately after heating, position fan blade on fan motor drive plate.

STARTER MOTORS

TABLE OF CONTENTS

Delco-Remy Starters

INDEX

APPLICATION CHART

Year	Engine	Model
ASTRO & SAFARI		
2002–05	4.3L	PG-260
AZTEK		
2002–05	3.4L	PG-260D
BRAVADA & ENVOY		
2002–06	2.2L	PG-260F
2002–06	4.3L	PG-260G
C & K SERIES, AVALANCHE, DENALI, ESCALADE, SIERRA, SILVERADO, SSR & YUKON		
2002–06	4.3L	PG-260G
	4.8L	PG-260F2
	5.3L	PG-260F2
	6.0L	PG-260M
	6.5L	MT-28
	8.1L	PG-260M
COLORADO, CANYON & S10		
2002–06	4.3L	PG-260
	2.8L	PG
	3.5L	PG
G SERIES		
2002	4.3L	PG-260G
	5.0L	PG-260M
	5.7L	PG-260M
	6.5L	MT-28
	8.1L	PG-260M
2003–06	4.3L	PG-260G
	4.8L	PG-260G
	5.3L	PG-260G
	6.0L	PG-260L
HHR		
2006	2.2L	PG
	2.4L	PG
MONTANA, SILHOUETTE & VENTURE		
2002–04	3.4L	PG-260D
2005–06	3.9L	PG-260D

Continued

APPLICATION CHART—Continued

Year	Engine	Model
SRX		
2004–06	3.6L	PG-260M
	4.6L	PG-260L
TRAILBLAZER, BLAZER & RAINER		
2002–03	4.2L	PG-260L
2003	5.3L	PG-260G
2004–06	6.0L	PG
VUE		
2002–06	All	PG-260D

DESCRIPTION

The Delco-Remy starter motor has the solenoid shift lever mechanism and the solenoid plunger enclosed in the drive housing to protect them from exposure to road dirt, icing conditions and splash, **Figs. 1 through 6.** They have an extruded field frame and an overrunning clutch type drive. The overrunning clutch is operated by a solenoid switch mounted to a flange on the drive housing. The permanent magnet gear reduction starter has a gear reduction assembly to achieve free speed of up to 7000 RPM. The MT-28 diesel starter has a center bearing.

The solenoid is attached to the drive end housing by two screws, **Fig. 7.** The cover can be removed to inspect the contacts and contact disc, but the switch is serviced as an assembly only.

Most motors of this type have graphite and oil impregnated bronze bearings which ordinarily require no added lubrication except at time of overhaul when a few drops of light engine oil should be placed on each bearing before reassembly.

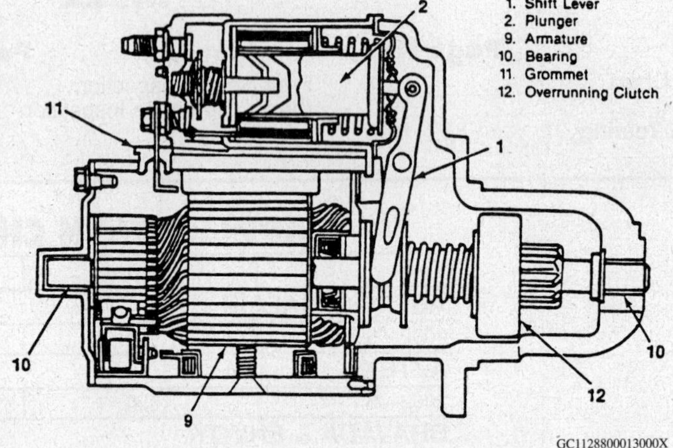

Fig. 1 SD-205 standard duty starter

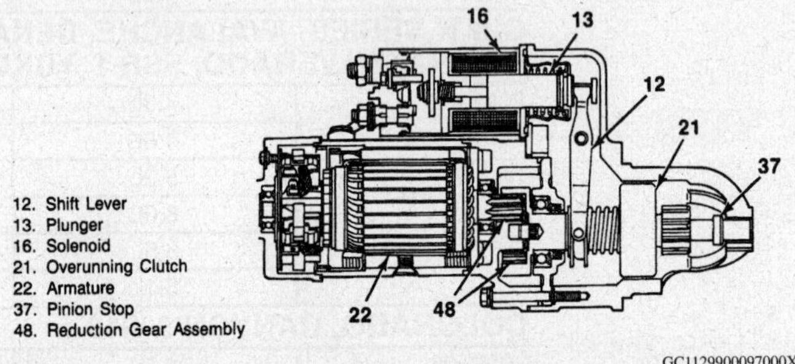

Fig. 2 MT-28 gear reduction starter

DIAGNOSIS & TESTING

When diagnosing starter motors, refer to **Figs. 8 through 11** for diagnostic procedures.

FREE SPEED INSPECTION

This test is performed during bench testing. With the circuit connected, **Fig. 12,** use a tachometer to measure armature revolutions per minute. Failure of the motor to perform to specifications may be because of light or dry bearings or high resistance connections. Starter motors do not require lubrication except during overhaul. At this time a couple drops of light oil may be applied to bearings.

STARTER DRAW TEST

1. Disable fuel system by removing fuel solenoid fuse.
2. Calculate current draw and select 200 A or 2000 A scale on current clamp and meter, tool Nos. J-35590 and J-39200, or equivalent.
3. Zero current clamp. Clamp tool to battery ground cable.
4. Crank engine and observe meter readings, noting the following:
   a. Reading should be 330–360 amperes.
   b. If amperage is more than 360 amperes, an internal starter failure may be at fault.
   c. If amperage is less than 330 amperes, battery cable or connection may be at fault.

PINION CLEARANCE INSPECTION

There is no provision for adjusting pinion clearance on this motor, but clearance should be inspected after motor reassembly on all models except the MT-28 (which is not serviceable). When the shift lever is assembled properly, pinion clearance should be .01–.06 inch. When clearance is not within specifications, it may indicate excessive wear of the solenoid linkage or the shift lever yoke buttons. Inspect pinion clearance as follows:

1. Disconnect motor field coil connector from solenoid motor terminal, then insulate end carefully.
2. Connect one battery lead to solenoid switch terminal, then the other lead to the solenoid frame, **Fig. 13.**
3. Connect jumper lead to solenoid motor terminal. Momentarily flash lead to solenoid frame. This will shift pinion into cranking position until battery is disconnected.
4. Push pinion back toward commutator end as far as possible to take up any slack movement, then inspect clearance with feeler gauge, **Fig. 14.**

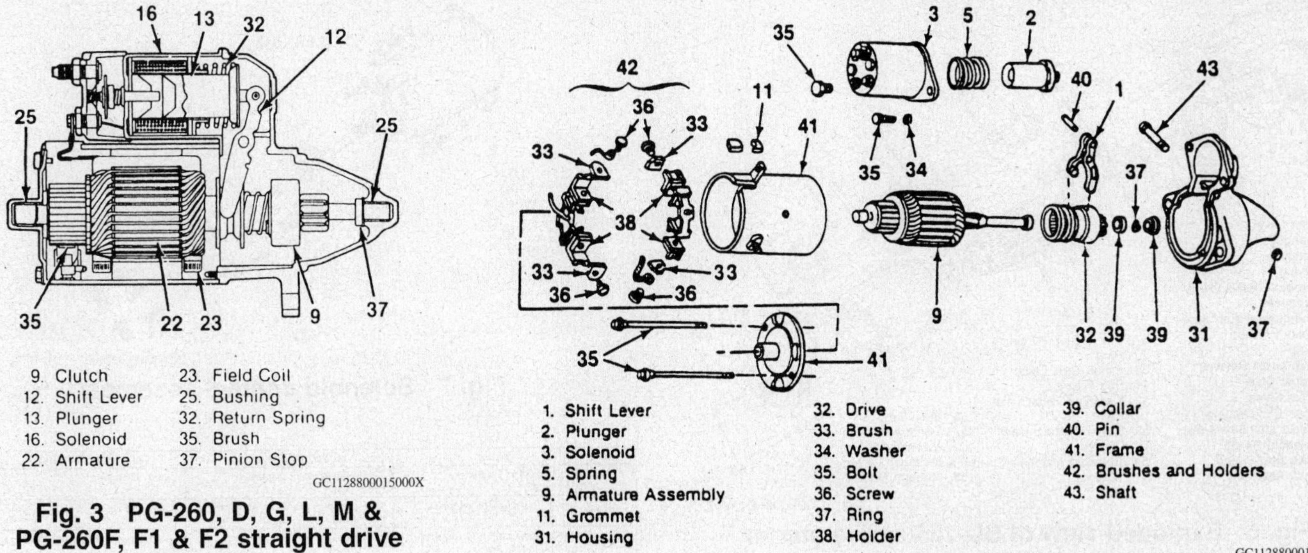

9. Clutch
12. Shift Lever
13. Plunger
16. Solenoid
22. Armature
23. Field Coil
25. Bushing
32. Return Spring
35. Brush
37. Pinion Stop

GC1128800015000X

Fig. 3 PG-260, D, G, L, M & PG-260F, F1 & F2 straight drive starters

1. Shift Lever
2. Plunger
3. Solenoid
5. Spring
9. Armature Assembly
11. Grommet
31. Housing
32. Drive
33. Brush
34. Washer
35. Bolt
36. Screw
37. Ring
38. Holder
39. Collar
40. Pin
41. Frame
42. Brushes and Holders
43. Shaft

GC1128800017000X

Fig. 4 Exploded view of SD-205 series starter motor

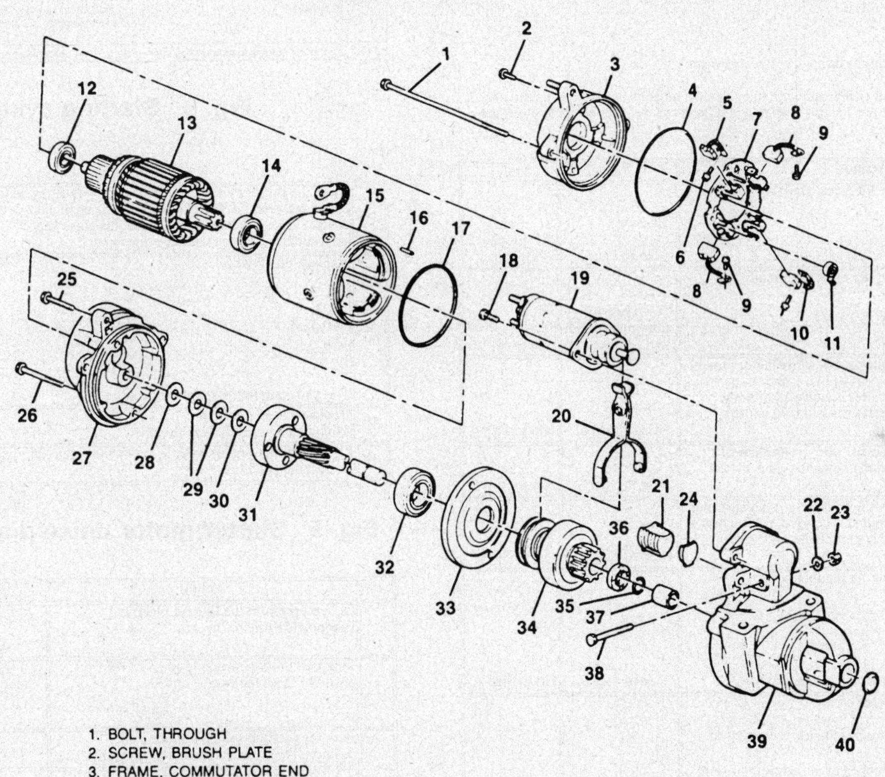

1. BOLT, THROUGH
2. SCREW, BRUSH PLATE
3. FRAME, COMMUTATOR END
4. SEAL, O-RING (C.E. END)
5. BRUSH (GROUNDED)
6. SCREW, GROUNDED BRUSH
7. ASSEMBLY, BRUSH HOLDER
8. BRUSH (INSULATED)
9. SCREW, INSULATED BRUSH
10. BRUSH (GROUNDED)
11. SPRING, BRUSH
12. BEARING, C.E. ARMATURE
13. ARMATURE
14. BEARING, D.E. ARMATURE
15. ASSEMBLY, FRAME AND FIELD
16. PIN, DOWEL
17. SEAL, O-RING (FIELD FRAME)
18. SCREW, SOLENOID
19. ASSEMBLY, SOLENOID
20. LEVER, SHIFT
21. PLUG, DRIVE HOUSING
22. WASHER, SHIFT LEVER
23. NUT, SHIFT LEVER
24. PLATE (IF USED)
25. BOLT, DRIVE HOUSING (SHORT ON SOME MODELS)
26. BOLT, DRIVE HOUSING (LONG)
27. BRACKET, ARMATURE SUPPORT
28. WASHER, (FIBER)
29. WASHER, THIN (ONE OR TWO MAY BE USED)
30. WASHER, THICK
31. SHAFT, DRIVE
32. BEARING, CENTER SUPPORT
33. SUPPORT, DRIVE SHAFT
34. ASSEMBLY, CLUTCH DRIVE
35. RING, STOP
36. STOP, PINION
37. BUSHING, D.E. HOUSING
38. SCREW, SHIFT LEVER
40. PLUG, BUSHING (IF USED)

GC1129100062000X

Fig. 5 Exploded view of MT-28 series starter motor

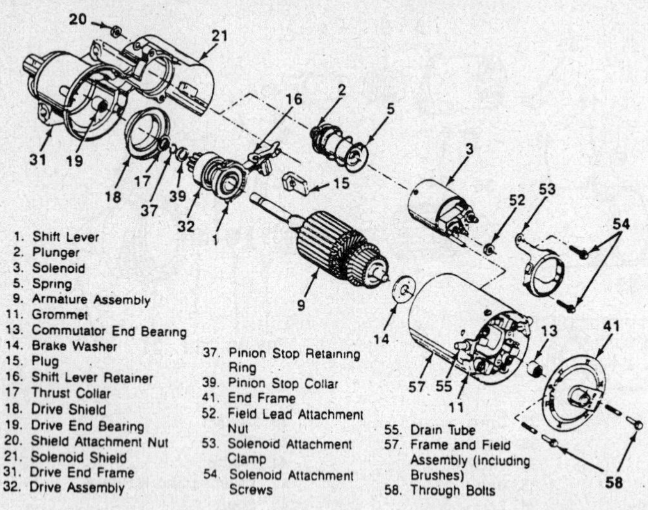

Fig. 6 Exploded view of SD-255 series starter motor

Diagnostic Aids

- Inspect the flywheel ring gear for damage or unusual wear.
- Shim the starter as required.
- In order to add pinion to ring gear clearance a full size shim must be used. Do not shim only 1 starter mounting bolt. There are 3 shims available in different shapes (for clearance). All are 1 mm thick.

Step	Action	Yes	No
1	Did you perform the Engine Electrical Diagnostic System Check?	Go to Step 2	Check Engine Electrical
2	Start the engine. Does the starter operate normally?	Test for Intermittent and Poor Connections	Go to Step 3
3	Start the engine while listening to the starter motor turn. Is there a loud "whoop" (it may sound like a siren if the engine is revved while the starter is engaged) after the engine starts, but while the starter is still held in the engaged position?	Go to Step 6	Go to Step 4
4	Do you hear a "rumble", a "growl", or, in some cases, a "knock" as the starter is coasting down to a stop after starting the engine?	Go to Step 7	Go to Step 5
5	(This is often diagnosed as a starter drive gear hang-in or a weak solenoid.) When the engine is cranked, do you hear a high-pitched whine after the engine cranks and starts normally?	Go to Step 8	Go to Step 7
6	Inspect the flywheel ring gear for the following: • Chipped gear teeth • Missing gear teeth • Milled teeth Is the flywheel bent, or does it have damaged teeth?	Go to Step 9	Go to Step 10
7	1. Remove the starter motor. 2. Inspect the starter motor bushings and clutch gear. Does the clutch gear have chipped or milled teeth or worn bushings?	Go to Step 10	Go to Step 9

GC1120100121010X

Fig. 9 Starter motor noise diagnosis (Part 1 of 2)

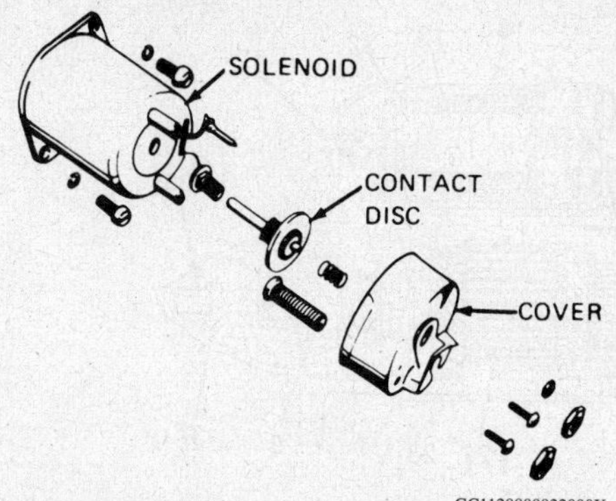

Fig. 7 Solenoid contact assembly

Step	Action	Normal Result(s)	Abnormal Result(s)*
1	Visually inspect the battery hydrometer.	battery hydrometer displays a green eye.	*Battery Charging*
2	Visually inspect battery cables.	Battery cables are clean and tightly connected.	*Battery Cable*
3	Inspect fuse, crank fuse, gauges fuse and fusible link.	Fuses are not open.	Repair source of overload and Replace fuse
4	Inspect all grounds.	All grounds are clean and tightly connected.	Clean and tighten grounds.
5	Inspect starter motor and starter solenoid.	Both starter motor and starter solenoid are properly mounted and starter solenoid terminals are clean and tight.	Ensure proper mounting and clean and tighten terminals.

* Refer to the appropriate symptom diagnostic table for the applicable abnormal result.

GC1120000102000X

Fig. 8 Starting system check

Step	Action	Yes	No
8	Shim the starter motor away from the flywheel by adding shims between the starter motor and the engine block one at a time. Flywheel runout may make this noise appear to be intermittent. Did you complete the repair?	Go to Step 11	--
9	Replace the flywheel. Did you complete the replacement?	Go to Step 11	--
10	Replace the starter motor. Did you complete the replacement?	Go to Step 11	--
11	Operate the system in order to verify the repair. Did you correct the condition?	System OK	Go to Step 3

GC1120100121020X

Fig. 9 Starter motor noise diagnosis (Part 2 of 2)

Step	Action	Yes	No
1	Did you preform the Engine Electrical Diagnostic System Check?	Go to Step 2	Check Engine Electrical
2	Turn the ignition switch to the START position. Does the engine crank?	Test Intermittent and Poor Connections	Go to Step 3
3	Turn the ignition switch to the START position. Does the starter motor relay click?	Go to Step 7	Go to Step 4
4	1. Remove the starter motor relay. 2. Connect a test light from the supply voltage circuit of the starter motor relay coil circuit to ground. 3. With the transmission in park, or clutch pedal depressed, turn the ignition switch to the START position. Does the test light illuminate?	Go to Step 5	Go to Step 6
5	1. Connect a test light from the supply voltage circuit of the starter motor relay coil circuit to the control circuit of the starter motor relay coil circuit. 2. With the transmission in park, or clutch pedal depressed, turn the ignition switch to the START position. Does the test light illuminate?	Go to Step 13	Go to Step 10

GC1120100122010X

Fig. 10 Starter solenoid does not click (Part 1 of 3)

6	1. Turn OFF the ignition. 2. Disconnect the Park Neutral Position (PNP) or the Clutch Pedal Position switch 3. Turn ON the ignition, with the engine OFF. 4. Connect a 10 amp fused jumper between the starter motor relay coil control circuits of the PNP switch or clutch pedal position switch. 5. With the transmission in park, or clutch pedal depressed, turn the ignition switch to the START position. Does the test lamp illuminate?	Go to Step 14	Go to Step 11
7	1. Turn OFF the ignition. 2. Disconnect the starter motor relay. 3. Connect a test lamp between the battery positive voltage circuit of the starter motor relay switch circuit and a good ground. Does the test lamp illuminate?	Go to Step 8	Go to Step 17
8	Connect a 30 amp fused jumper between the battery positive voltage circuit of the starter motor relay switch circuit and the supply voltage circuit of the starter solenoid. Does the engine crank?	Go to Step 13	Go to Step 9
9	Does the fuse in the jumper open?	Go to Step 18	Go to Step 12
10	Test the control circuit of the starter motor relay for an open or high resistance. Did you find and correct the condition?	Go to Step 23	Go to Step 19
11	Test the supply voltage circuit of the starter motor relay coil circuit for an open or high resistance. Did you find and correct the condition?	Go to Step 23	Go to Step 15
12	Test the supply voltage circuit of the starter solenoid for an open or high resistance. Did you find and correct the condition?	Go to Step 23	Go to Step 16
13	Inspect for poor connections at the starter motor relay. Did you find and correct the condition?	Go to Step 23	Go to Step 19
14	• If equipped with an Automatic Transmission, inspect for poor connection at the PNP switch harness connector. • If equipped with a Manual Transmission, inspect for poor connection at the clutch pedal position switch harness connector. Did you find and correct the condition?	Go to Step 23	Go to Step 20

GC1120100122020X

Fig. 10 Starter solenoid does not click (Part 2 of 3)

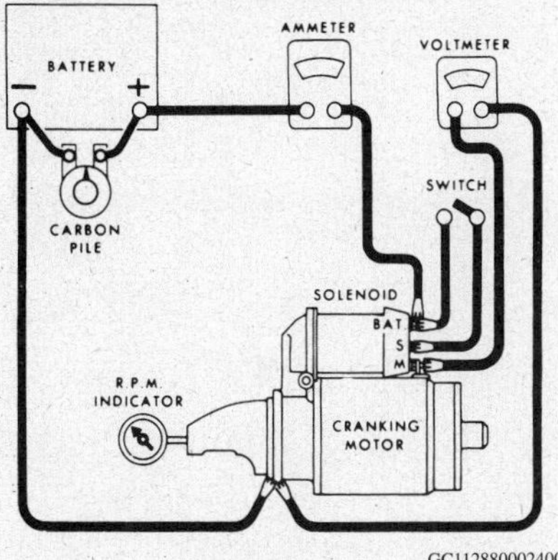

GC1128800024000X

Fig. 12 Motor free speed inspection

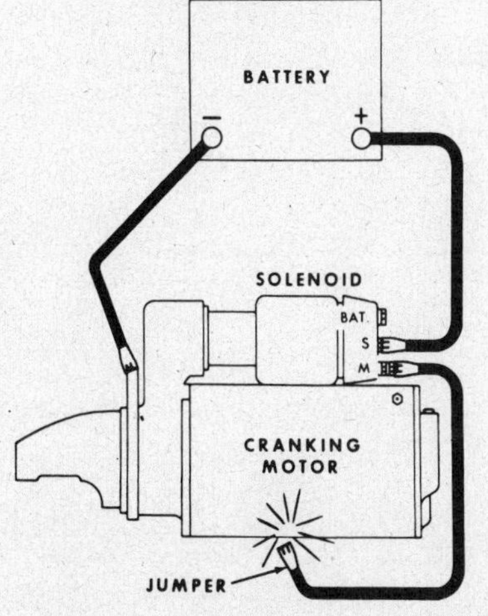

GC1128800025000X

Fig. 13 Pinion clearance inspection connections

15	Inspect for poor connections at the ignition switch harness connector. Did you find and correct the condition?	Go to Step 23	Go to Step 21
16	Inspect for poor connections at the starter solenoid. Did you find and correct the condition?	Go to Step 23	Go to Step 22
17	Repair the open or high resistance in the battery positive voltage circuit of the Starter Motor relay switch circuit. Did you complete the repair?	Go to Step 23	--
18	Repair the short to ground in the supply voltage circuit of the starter solenoid. Did you complete the repair?	Go to Step 23	--
19	Replace the starter motor relay. Did you complete the replacement?	Go to Step 23	--
20	1. Replace the PNP switch. 2. Replace the clutch pedal position switch. Did you complete the replacement?	Go to Step 23	--
21	Replace the Ignition Switch. Did you complete the replacement?	Go to Step 23	--
22	Replace the starter. Did you complete the replacement?	Go to Step 23	--
23	Operate the system for which the symptom occurred. Did you correct the condition?	System OK	Go to Step 2

GC1120100122030X

Fig. 10 Starter solenoid does not click (Part 3 of 3)

Step	Action	Yes	No
1	Did you perform the Engine Electrical Diagnostic System Check?	Go to Step 2	Check Engine Electrical
2	Turn the ignition to the START position. Did the starter solenoid click?	Go to Step 3	Go to Starter Solenoid Does Not Click
3	Inspect the engine and belt drive system for mechanical binding (seized engine, seized generator). Does the engine move freely?	Go to Step 4	Check Engine Mechanical Condition
4	Test the battery positive cable between the battery and the starter solenoid for high resistance. Did you find and correct the condition?	Go to Step 8	Go to Step 5
5	Test the ground circuit between the battery and the starter motor for a high resistance. Did you find and correct the condition?	Go to Step 8	Go to Step 6
6	Inspect for poor connections at the starter. Did you find and correct the condition?	Go to Step 8	Go to Step 7
7	Replace the Starter. Did you complete the replacement?	Go to Step 8	--
8	Operate the system for which the symptom occurred. Did you correct the condition?	System OK	Go to Step 2

GC1120100123000X

Fig. 11 Starter solenoid clicks, engine does not crank

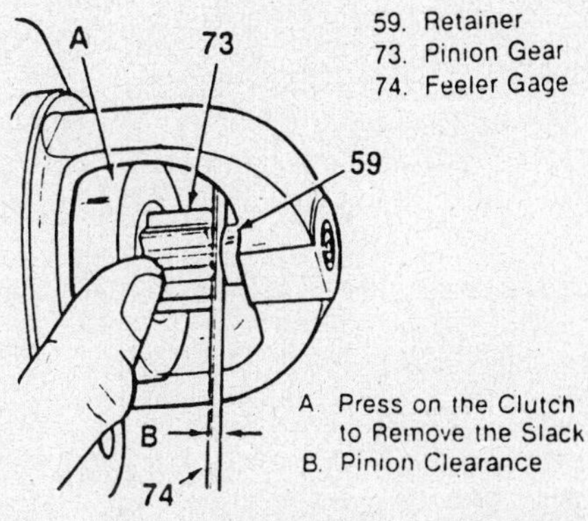

GC1128800026000X

Fig. 14 Pinion clearance inspection

STARTER SPECIFICATIONS

Model	Free Speed Test			Solenoid	
	Amps	Volts	RPM	Hold-In Windings, Amps	Pull-In Windings, Amps
MT-28	130–190	10	2300–5600	12–14	52–59
PG-260	65–95	10	2825–3275	12–14	52–59
PG-260F1	40–90	10	3200–4800	6–12	30–45
SD-205	60–85	10	6100–12,900	—	—
SD-255	47–70	10	6500–11,000	10–12	60–85

Mitsubishi Starters

INDEX

APPLICATION CHART

Year	Engine	Model
TRACKER		
2002	1.6L	Mitsubishi Reduction Gear
	2.0L	Mitsubishi Reduction Gear
	2.5L	Mitsubishi Reduction Gear
2003–04	2.0L	Mitsubishi Reduction Gear
	2.5L	Mitsubishi Reduction Gear

DESCRIPTION

The Mitsubishi starter motor is a high torque, permanent magnet, 12 volt electric motor, **Fig. 1.** When the ignition switch is turned to the start position, a circuit is closed from the battery positive post through the starter solenoid coil to ground. With battery voltage applied, the coil in the starter solenoid becomes an electromagnet and pulls the plunger into the solenoid assembly. As the plunger is pulled in, the pinion drive lever moves the pinion out to mesh with the flywheel, the main starter solenoid contacts close, battery voltage is applied directly to the starter motor and the engine cranks until the circuit is broken by releasing the ignition switch to the Run position.

DIAGNOSIS & TESTING

When diagnosing starter motors, refer to **Figs. 2 through 4** for diagnostic procedures.

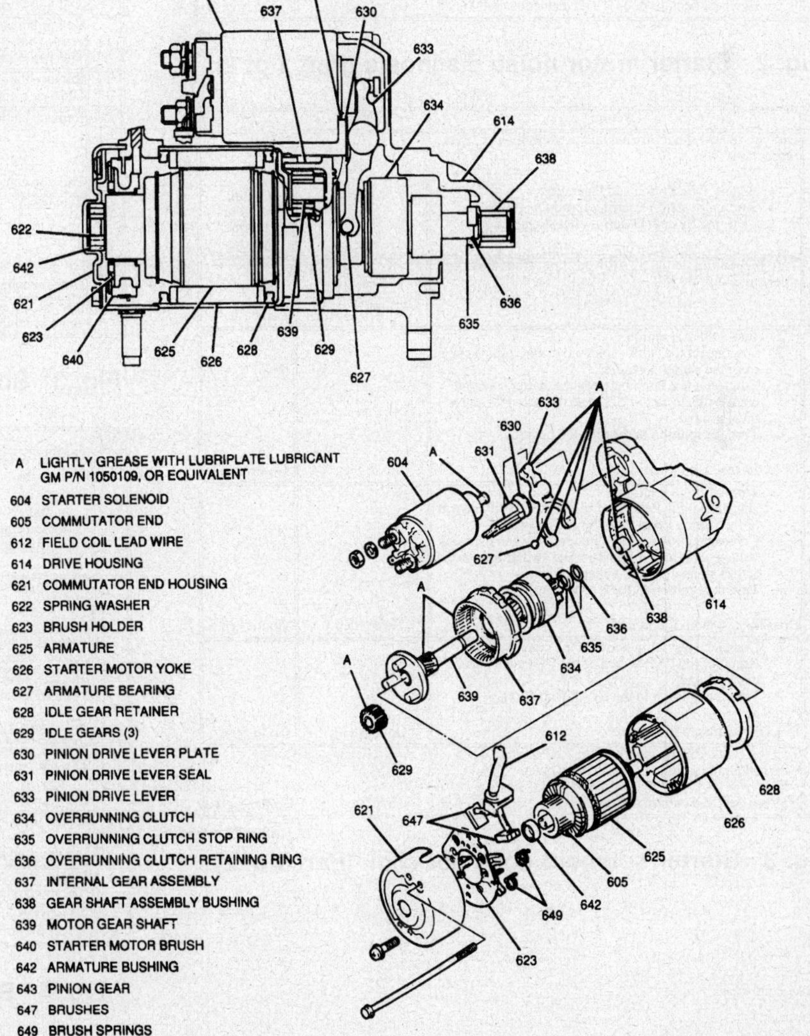

Fig. 1 Exploded view of Mitsubishi starter motor

Diagnostic Aids

Inspect the flywheel ring gear for damage or unusual wear.

Shim the starter as required.

In order to add pinion to ring gear clearance a full size shim must be used. Do not shim only one starter mounting bolt. There are three shims available in different shapes (for clearance); all are 1 mm thick.

Step	Action	Yes	No
1	Did you review the Battery Operation, the Starting System Operation and the Charging System Operation and perform the necessary inspections?	Go to Step 2	Check Engine Electrical
2	Start the engine. Does the starter operate normally?	Test Intermittent and Poor Connections	Go to Step 3
3	Start the engine while listening to the starter motor turn. Is there a loud "whoop" (it may sound like a siren if the engine is revved while the starter is engaged) after the engine starts, but while the starter is still held in the engaged position?	Go to Step 6	Go to Step 4
4	Do you hear a "rumble", a "growl", or, in some cases, a "knock" as the starter is coasting down to a stop after starting the engine?	Go to Step 7	Go to Step 5
5	When the engine is cranked, do you hear a high-pitched whine after the engine cranks and starts normally? (This is often diagnosed as a starter drive gear hang-in or a weak solenoid.)	Go to Step 8	Go to Step 7
6	Inspect the flywheel ring gear for the following: • Chipped gear teeth • Missing gear teeth • Milled teeth Is the flywheel bent, or does it have damaged teeth?	Go to Step 9	Go to Step 10
7	1. Remove the starter motor. 2. Inspect the starter motor bushings and clutch gear. Does the clutch gear have chipped or milled teeth or worn bushings?	Go to Step 10	Go to Step 9
8	Shim the starter motor away from the flywheel by adding shims between the starter motor and the engine block one at a time. Flywheel runout may make this noise appear to be intermittent. Did you complete the repair?	Go to Step 11	--
9	Replace the flywheel. Did you complete the replacement?	Go to Step 11	--
10	Replace the starter motor. Did you complete the replacement?	Go to Step 11	--
11	Operate the system in order to verify the repair. Did you correct the condition?	System OK	Go to Step 3

GC1120100124010X

GC1120100124020X

Fig. 2 Starter motor noise diagnosis (Part 1 of 2)

Fig. 2 Starter motor noise diagnosis (Part 2 of 2)

Step	Action	Yes	No
1	Did you review the following and perform the necessary inspections? • Battery Description and Operation • Starting System Description and Operation • Charging System Description and Operation	Go to Step 2	Check Symptoms Engine Electrical
2	Turn the ignition to the START position. Does the starter solenoid click?	Test for Intermittent and Poor Connections	Go to Step 3
3	1. Turn OFF the ignition. 2. Disconnect the starter solenoid crank voltage circuit from the starter solenoid. 3. Connect a test lamp between the starter solenoid crank voltage circuit of the starter solenoid and a good ground. 4. Turn the ignition to the START position. Does the test lamp illuminate?	Go to Step 7	Go to Step 4
4	1. Turn OFF the ignition. 2. Disconnect the Park/Neutral Position (PNP) switch or the Clutch Pedal Position (CPP) switch. 3. Connect a 10 Amp fused jumper between the crank voltage circuit of the appropriate switch and the starter solenoid crank voltage circuit. 4. Turn the ignition to the START position. Does the test lamp illuminate?	Go to Step 8	Go to Step 5
5	1. Connect a test lamp between the crank voltage circuit of the PNP switch or the CPP switch and a good ground. 2. Turn the ignition to the START position. Does the test lamp illuminate?	Go to Step 11	Go to Step 6
6	Test the crank voltage circuit of the PNP switch or the CPP switch for a high resistance or an open. Did you find and correct the condition?	Go to Step 15	Go to Step 10
7	Inspect for poor connection at starter solenoid. Did you find and correct the condition?	Go to Step 15	Go to Step 12
8	Inspect the PNP switch or the CPP switch for proper operation. Did you find and correct the condition?	Go to Step 15	Go to Step 9
9	Inspect for poor connection at the PNP switch or the CPP switch. Did you find and correct the condition?	Go to Step 15	Go to Step 13
10	Inspect for poor connection at the ignition switch. Did you find and correct the condition?	Go to Step 15	Go to Step 14
11	Repair the high resistance or open in the starter solenoid crank voltage circuit. Did you complete the repair?	Go to Step 15	--
12	Replace the starter. Did you complete the replacement?	Go to Step 15	--
13	Replace the PNP switch or the CPP switch. Did you complete the replacement?	Go to Step 15	--
14	Replace the ignition switch. Did you complete the replacement?	Go to Step 15	--
15	Operate the system for which the symptom occurred. Did you correct the condition?	System OK	Go to Step 3

GC1120100125010X

GC1120100125020X

Fig. 3 Starter solenoid does not click (Part 1 of 2)

Fig. 3 Starter solenoid does not click (Part 2 of 2)

Step	Action	Yes	No
1	Did you review the following description and operations and perform the necessary inspections? • Battery Description and Operation • Starting System Description and Operation • Charging System Description and Operation	Go to Step 2	Inspect - Engine Electrical
2	Turn the ignition to the START position. Did the starter solenoid click?	Go to Step 3	Go to Starter Solenoid Does Not Click
3	Inspect the engine and belt drive system for mechanical binding (seized engine, seized generator). Does the engine move freely?	Go to Step 4	Go to Engine Mechanical
4	Test the battery positive cable between the battery and the starter solenoid for high resistance. Did you find and correct the condition?	Go to Step 8	Go to Step 5
5	Test the ground circuit between the battery and the starter motor for a high resistance. Did you find and correct the condition?	Go to Step 8	Go to Step 6
6	Inspect for poor connections at the starter. Did you find and correct the condition?	Go to Step 8	Go to Step 7
7	Replace the Starter. Did you complete the replacement	Go to Step 8	--
8	Operate the system for which the symptom occurred. Did you correct the condition?	System OK	Go to Step 3

GC1120100126000X

Fig. 4 Starter solenoid clicks, engine does not crank

STARTER SPECIFICATIONS

Engine	Model	Cranking Amps Draw Test	Free Speed Test			
			Amps①	Volts	RPM②	
					Auto. Trans.	Manual Trans.
All	Mitsubishi Reduction Drive	90③	300	11	2500	3000

① — Maximum current draw. ② — Minimum speed. ③ — No load.

Hitachi Starter

INDEX

APPLICATION CHART

Year	Engine	Model
C & K SERIES		
2002–06	6.6L	Hitachi-S14-100B

DESCRIPTION

The Hitachi-S14-100B is a non-repairable starter motor. It has pole pieces that are arranged around the armature within the starter housing. When the solenoid windings are energized, the pull-in winding circuit is completed to ground through the starter motor. The hold-in winding circuit is completed to ground through the solenoid. The windings work together magnetically to pull in and hold in the plunger. The plunger moves the shift lever. This action causes the starter drive assembly to rotate on the armature shaft spline as it engages with the flywheel ring gear on the engine. At the same time, the plunger closes the solenoid switch contacts in the starter solenoid. Full battery voltage is then applied directly to the starter motor and it cranks the engine.

DIAGNOSIS & TESTING

Refer to "Delco-Remy Starters."

ALTERNATORS

TABLE OF CONTENTS

Bosch & Delcotron/Delphi & Valeo Integral Charging Systems

NOTE: Refer To "Computer Relearn Procedures" Located In The Front Of This Manual When Battery Power To The Computer Has Been Interrupted.

INDEX

APPLICATION CHART

Year	Engine	Alternator Model
ASTRO & SAFARI		
2002–05	All	Delphi AD-230
AVALANCHE, ESCALADE, SILVERADO, SIERRA, SUBURBAN, TAHOE & YUKON		
2002–06	All	AD-230
		AD-244
		Bosch No. 15755900
AZTEK & RENDEZVOUS		
2002–06	All	Valeo SG10
		Valeo SG12
BRAVADA		
2002–04	All	Delphi AD-244
CANYON & COLORADO		
2004–06	All	Delphi AD-244
ENVOY, RAINIER & TRAILBLAZER		
2002–05	All	Delphi AD-244
2006	All	DR44G
EQUINOX & TORRENT		
2005–06	3.4L Early	Valeo SG10
	3.4L Late	Denso SC2
EXPRESS & SAVANNA		
2002–06	All	Delphi AD-230
		Delphi AD-244
HHR		
2006	All	Denso SC0
H2 & H3		
2003–05	All	Delphi AD244

Continued

APPLICATION CHART—Continued

Year	Engine	Alternator Model
H2 & H3		
2006	H2	DR44M
2006	H3	Valeo TG13
MONTANA, SILHOUETTE & VENTURE		
2002	All	Bosch KCB2
		Bosch NCB1
2003–05	All	Valeo SG-10
		Valeo SG-12
RELAY, SV6, TERRAZA, & UPLANDER		
2005–06	All	Valeo TG10
		Valeo TG13
S & T SERIES		
2002–05	All	Delphi CS-130D
SSR		
2003–05	All	Delphi AD-230
2006	All	Remy DR44G
VUE		
2002–06	2.2L	Valeo SG10
	3.0L & 3.5L	Valeo SG12

PRECAUTIONS

Battery Ground Cable

Prior to service, disconnect battery ground cable and isolate as required.

DESCRIPTION

These units, feature a high ampere output-to-weight ratio. The Delcotron/Delphi alternators are electrically similar to standard units, however they do not contain a diode trio. The voltage setting of the integral regulator varies with temperature and limits system voltage by controlling rotor field current.

The regulator has four terminals; "P," "L," "I," and "S." The "P" terminal is not used. The "L" terminal may be connected to the instrument cluster for charging indicator and voltmeter. The "I" terminal provides a voltage feed for the heated oxygen sensor, variable throttle control relay, and electronic automatic transmission. The "S" terminal is not used.

The CS-130D, AD-230 and AD-244 alternators are serviceable only by complete replacement. No periodic maintenance is required. They should not be disassembled for any reason.

The CS-130 and 144 alternators feature a high amphere output per pound of weight. The alternator uses a conventional fan and pulley. An internal fan cools the slip rings, the end frame, the rectifier bridge and the regulator. The CS-130 is not be disassembled for any reason. Unlike the CS-130, the CS-144 is serviceable. The CS-144 alternator, with an internal regulator, does not have a diode trio. The delta stator, the rectifier bridge and the rotor with slip rings and brushes, are electrically similar to other CS Series alternators. The CS-144 alternator requires no periodic maintenance or adjustment.

The Valeo A13VI alternator incorporates a load response control function that "ramps up" loads. This feature provides a gradual loading of the charging system when large, transient electrical loads are encountered. A four-way Packard regulator connector provides interface for the lamp "L" and sense "S" terminals. The two terminals are not used.

The Valeo SG10 and SG12 alternators are electrically similar to earlier models. The alternators feature the following major components: delta stator, rectifier bridge, rotor with slip rings and brushes, a conventional pulley, dual internal fans and regulator. The pulley and the fan cool the slip ring and the frame. The alternators feature permanently lubricated bearings. Service should only include tightening of mount components. Otherwise, replace the alternator as a complete unit, only.

The Bosch KCB2 and NCB1 alternators create a magnetic field when current flows through the rotor. The magnetic field rotates while the rotor is driven by the engine. This rotation creates an alternating current voltage in the stator windings. The rectifier bridge converts the current voltage to direct current.

The alternators digital regulator uses digital techniques in order to supply the rotor current and control output voltage. The only serviceable parts on the alternators are the voltage regulator and the rear cover.

The Leece-Neville model 4884JB is a 200 amp, air-cooled, belt-driven unit that is designed for heavy-duty diesel engine applications. This unit features an integral voltage regulator, fully-enclosed brushes, built-in rectifier assemblies with extra large heat sinks, a dynamically balanced rotor and a heavy-duty stator and bearings. It has extended one-quarter inch AC terminals that are provided for accessories, such as converters, power packs, etc. The alternator has an extra terminal (marked TO #1 TERM. OF DUVAC) for used with DUVAC and battery isolator systems. The DUVAC terminal is internally connected to the regulator positive terminal. This connection allows the regulator to monitor output voltage and provides a source of current for field excitation. The integral voltage regulator is accessible without removing or disconnecting the unit and is fully adjustable. No other maintenance or adjustments are required on this alternator. Except for adjusting the voltage regulator, it is serviceable by replacement only.

DIAGNOSIS & TESTING

Alternator Noise Diagnosis

Refer to **Fig. 1** for alternator noise diagnosis.

Charging System Test

Refer to **Fig. 2** for charging system test.

Intermittents

Most intermittent malfunction conditions are caused by poor electrical connections, defective or improperly routed wiring. The cause for most intermittent malfunctions can be located by performing a thorough visual inspection of system wiring harnesses and/or by road testing vehicle while monitoring the suspected circuit with suitable testing equipment.

Diagnostic Aids

Noise from a generator may be due to electrical or mechanical noise. Electrical noise (magnetic whine) usually varies with the electrical load placed on the generator and is a normal operating characteristic of all generators. When diagnosing a noisy generator, it is important to remember that loose or misaligned components around the generator may transmit the noise into the passenger compartment and that replacing the generator may not solve the problem.

Step	Action	Yes	No
1	Test the generator for proper operation using the Generator Tester. Is the generator operating properly?	Go to Step 2	Go to Step 11
2	1. Start the engine. Verify that the noise can be heard. 2. Turn OFF the engine. 3. Disconnect the 4-way connector from the generator. 4. Start the engine. 5. Listen for the noise. Has the noise stopped?	Go to Step 11	Go to Step 3
3	1. Turn OFF the engine. 2. Remove the drive belt. 3. Spin the generator pulley by hand. Does the generator shaft spin smoothly and without any roughness or grinding noise?	Go to Step 4	Go to Step 11
4	Inspect the generator for a loose pulley and/or pulley nut. Is the generator pulley or pulley nut loose?	Go to Step 11	Go to Step 5
5	1. Loosen all of the generator mounting bolts. 2. Tighten the generator mounting bolts to specifications and in the proper sequence (if necessary). 3. Install the drive belt. 4. Start the engine. Has the noise decreased or stopped?	System OK	Go to Step 6

GC1120100134010X

Fig. 1 Alternator Noise Diagnosis (Part 1 of 2)

Step	Action	Yes	No
6	Inspect the generator for the following conditions: • Strained or stretched electrical connections. • Hoses or other vehicle equipment resting on the generator (which may cause the noise to be transmitted into the passenger compartment) Are any electrical connections pulling on the generator or are any hoses, etc. resting on the generator?	Go to Step 7	Go to Step 8
7	1. Reroute the electrical connections to relieve the tension. 2. Reroute the hoses, etc. away from the generator. 3. Start the engine. Has the noise decreased or stopped?	System OK	Go to Step 8
8	Inspect the drive belt for proper tension. Is the drive belt loose?	Go to Step 9	Go to Step 10
9	1. Replace the drive belt tensioner. 2. Start the engine. Has the noise decreased or stopped?	System OK	Go to Step 11
10	Compare the vehicle with a known good vehicle. Do both vehicles make the same noise?	System OK	Go to Step 11
11	**Important** If no definite generator problems were found, be sure that all other possible sources of objectionable noise are eliminated before replacing the generator. Replacing the generator may not change the noise level if the noise is a normal characteristic of the generator or the generator mounting. Replace the generator. Has the noise decreased or stopped?	Go to Step 12	--
12	Operate the system in order to verify the repair. Did you correct the condition?	System OK	Go to Step 2

GC1120100134020X

Fig. 1 Alternator Noise Diagnosis (Part 2 of 2)

Step	Action	Normal Result (s)	Abnormal Result(s)*
1	Perform the battery check. Refer to Battery Check .	Battery OK.	Battery Not Operating Properly .
2	Turn the ignition ON.	The charge indicator is on.	The charge indicator is off. Charge Indicator Inoperative .
3	Start the engine.	The charge indicator is off.	The charge indicator is on. Charge Indicator Always On .
4	1. Turn on all of the following electrical accessories. o Headlights o Wipers o HVAC Blower on High o Rear Defogger 2. Apply the parking brake and the regular brake. 3. Shift the transmission into Drive. 4. Allow the engine to idle.	The charge indicator is off.	The charge warning is on. Charge Indicator Always On .

GC1120100139000X

Fig. 2 Charging System Test

ALTERNATOR SPECIFICATIONS

Year	Model or Part No.	Option Code	Rated Hot Output, Amps	Load Test Output Amps
ASTRO & SAFARI				
2002–05	Delphi AD-230	—	105	73
AVALANCHE, ESCALADE, SILVERADO, SIERRA, SUBURBAN, TAHOE & YUKON				
2002–06	Bosch No. 15755900	—	130	91
	Delphi AD-230	K68	102	71
	Delphi AD-244	8A7	130	91
AZTEK & RENDEZVOUS				
2002–06	Valeo SG-10	K68	105	73
	Valeo SG-12	KG7	125	87
BRAVADA				
2002–04	Delphi AD-244	—	150	105
CANYON & COLORADO				
2004–06	Delphi AD-244	—	100	70

Continued

ALTERNATOR SPECIFICATIONS—Continued

Year	Model or Part No.	Option Code	Rated Hot Output, Amps	Load Test Output Amps
ENVOY & TRAILBLAZER				
2002–05	Delphi AD-244	—	150	105
2006	DR44G	—	150	105
EQUINOX & TORRENT				
2005–06	Valeo SG10	—	145	69
	Denso SC2	—	155	75
EXPRESS & SAVANNA				
2003–06	Delphi AD-230	—	105	73
	Delphi AD-244	—	145	102
2002	Delphi AD-244		130	91
HHR				
2006	Denso SC0	—	130	91
H2 & H3				
2003–05	Delphi AD244	—	145	102
2006	DR44M	—	160	112
2006	Valeo TG13	—	125	70
MONTANA, SILHOUETTE & VENTURE				
2002	Bosch KCB2	K68	105	70
	Bosch NCB1	KG9	125	87.5
2003–05	Valeo SG-10	K68	105	70
	Valeo SG-12	KG9	125	87.5
S & T SERIES				
2002–04	Delphi CS-130D	K60	100	70
SSR				
2003–05	Delphi AD230	—	102	71
2006	Remy DR44G	—	145	105
VUE				
2002–03	Valeo SG10	—	105	73
	Valeo SG12	—	125	87

Mitsubishi Alternator

INDEX

APPLICATION CHART

Year	Engine	Alternator Model
TRACKER		
2002–04	All	—

Diagnostic Aids

Noise from a generator may be due to electrical or mechanical noise. Electrical noise (magnetic whine) usually varies with the electrical load placed on the generator and is a normal operating characteristic of all generators. When diagnosing a noisy generator, it is important to remember that loose or misaligned components around the generator may transmit the noise into the passenger compartment and that replacing the generator may not solve the problem.

Step	Action	Yes	No
1	Test the generator for proper operation using the Generator Tester. Is the generator operating properly?	Go to Step 2	Go to Step 11
2	1. Start the engine. Verify that the noise can be heard. 2. Turn OFF the engine. 3. Disconnect the connector from the generator. 4. Start the engine. 5. Listen for the noise. Has the noise stopped?	Go to Step 11	Go to Step 3
3	1. Turn OFF the engine. 2. Remove the drive belt. 3. Spin the generator pulley by hand. Does the generator shaft spin smoothly and without any roughness or grinding noise?	Go to Step 4	Go to Step 11
4	Inspect the generator for a loose pulley and/or pulley nut. Is the generator pulley or pulley nut loose?	Go to Step 11	Go to Step 5
5	1. Loosen all of the generator mounting bolts. 2. Tighten the generator mounting bolts to specifications and in the proper sequence (if necessary). 3. Install the drive belt. 4. Start the engine. Has the noise decreased or stopped?	System OK	Go to Step 6
6	Inspect the generator for the following conditions: • Strained or stretched electrical connections. • Hoses or other vehicle equipment resting on the generator (which may cause the noise to be transmitted into the passenger compartment) Are any electrical connections pulling on the generator or are any hoses, etc. resting on the generator?	Go to Step 7	Go to Step 8

GC1120100127010X

Fig. 1 Alternator noise diagnosis (Part 1 of 2)

PRECAUTIONS

Battery Ground Cable

Prior to service, disconnect battery ground cable and isolate as required.

DESCRIPTION

The Mitsubishi integral charging system consists of an alternator and an IC integral regulator. All regulator components are enclosed in a solid mold and are mounted inside the alternator.

The stator windings are assembled on the inside of a laminated core that forms part of the alternator frame. A rectifier bridge containing eight diodes is connected to the stator windings, which changes AC voltage to DC voltage which is available at the output terminal. The diode trio serves to convert the voltage fluctuation at the neutral point to direct current for increasing the general output.

The alternator is also equipped with a condenser mounted in the rear housing that suppresses radio noise. Maintenance or adjustments of any kind are not required on this unit.

DIAGNOSIS & TESTING

Refer to **Figs. 1 through 5** for diagnosis and testing procedures.

Step	Action	Yes	No
7	1. Reroute the electrical connections to relieve the tension. 2. Reroute the hoses, etc. away from the generator. 3. Start the engine. Has the noise decreased or stopped?	System OK	Go to Step 8
8	Inspect the drive belt for proper tension. Is the drive belt loose?	Go to Step 9	Go to Step 10
9	1. Replace the drive belt tensioner. 2. Start the engine. Has the noise decreased or stopped?	System OK	Go to Step 11
10	Compare the vehicle with a known good vehicle. Do both vehicles make the same noise?	System OK	Go to Step 11
11	**Important** If no definite generator problems were found, be sure that all other possible sources of objectionable noise are eliminated before replacing the generator. Replacing the generator may not change the noise level if the noise is a normal characteristic of the generator or the generator mounting. Replace the generator. Has the noise decreased or stopped?	Go to Step 12	--
12	Operate the system in order to verify the repair. Did you correct the condition?	System OK	Go to Step 2

GC1120100127020X

Fig. 1 Alternator noise diagnosis (Part 2 of 2)

Step	Action	Normal Result(s)	Abnormal Result(s)*
1	Inspect the for the following conditions: 1. Proper battery installation. 2. Proper battery terminal installation. 3. Proper battery cable installation. 4. Clean and tight ground connections. 5. Excessive battery terminal corrosion. 6. Cracking or other damage. 7. Correct battery voltage. 8. The battery hydrometer for a green dot. 9. The generator wiring for damage or poor connections. 10. The generator mounting bolts for proper torque. 11. The generator drive belt for proper installation.	• The battery is properly installed. • The battery terminals are properly installed. • The battery cables are properly installed. • The ground connections are clean and tight. • The battery terminals are clean and tight. • The battery is not physically damaged. • Battery voltage is approximate 11.5-13.0 volts. • The battery hydrometer displays a green dot. • the wiring is in serviceable condition.	• Battery Hydrometer Displays Dark or Yellow Dot . • Battery Common Causes of Failure . • Battery Load Test . • Battery Charging . • Clean, tighten or repair the wiring and connections as necessary. • Battery Not Operating Properly . • Battery Check . • Battery Terminal Check . • Battery Hydrometer Displays Yellow Dot . • Generator Replacement . • Drive Belt Replacement
2	Turn the ignition switch to the key ON engine OFF position	The charge indicator lamp lights.	Charge Indicator Inoperative
3	Start the engine	The charge indicator lamp goes out after the engine starts.	Charge Indicator Always On

GC1120100128000X

Fig. 2 Charging system test.

Step	Action	Value (s)	Yes	No
1	Did you review the following and perform the necessary inspections? • Battery Description and Operation • Starting System Description and Operation • Charging System Description and Operation	--	Go to Step 2	Go to Symptoms
2	Start the engine. Does the battery charge indicator remain illuminated after the five second bulb check?	--	Go to Step 3	Go to Testing for Intermittent and Poor Connections
3	1. Install a scan tool 2. With a scan tool, observe the Battery Voltage parameter in the Powertrain data list. Does the voltage measure within the normal operating range?	10 V-15 V	Go to Step 4	Go to Charging System Test
4	Test the charge indicator ground circuit for a short to ground. Did you find and correct the condition?	--	Go to Step 5	--
5	Operate the system in order to verify the repair. Did you correct the condition?	--	System OK	Go to Step 3

LTV1900000000429

Fig. 3 Charge indicator always on

Step	Action	Value (s)	Yes	No
1	Did you review the Description and perform the necessary inspections?	--	Go to Step 2	Check Engine Electrical
2	1. Turn OFF all electrical loads. 2. Start the engine. 3. Install a scan tool. 4. With a scan tool view the Battery Voltage parameter in the Powertrain data list. Does the scan tool indicate the voltage is within the specified value?	11.0-15.5 V	Go to Step 3	Test for Intermittent and Poor Connections
3	1. Turn OFF the ignition. 2. Connect a charging system tester to the battery (follow the manufacturer's instructions). 3. Operate the engine at 2500 RPM. 4. Adjust the carbon pile as necessary in order to obtain the maximum current output. Is the generator output within 10 A of the specified value?	89 A	Go to Step 9	Go to Step 4
4	1. Maintain the engine speed at 2500 RPM and continue to operate the generator at the load test value. 2. Measure the voltage drop between the generator output terminal and the battery positive terminal. Is the voltage above the specified value?	0.5 V	Go to Step 6	Go to Step 5
5	1. Maintain the engine speed at 2500 RPM and continue to operate the generator at the load test value. 2. Measure the voltage drop between the battery negative terminal and the generator metal housing. Is the voltage above the specified value?	0.5 V	Go to Step 7	Go to Step 8
6	Test the battery positive circuit between the generator output terminal and the battery positive terminal for a high resistance. Did you find and correct the condition?	--	Go to Step 9	Go to Step 7
7	Repair the high resistance in the ground circuit between the generator housing and the battery negative terminal. Did you complete the repair?	--	Go to Step 9	--
8	Replace the generator. Did you complete the repair?	--	Go to Step 9	--
9	Operate the system in order to verify the repair. Did you correct the condition?	--	System OK	Go to Step 3

GC1120100129010X

Fig. 4 Charging system test (Part 1 of 2)

GC1120100129020X

Fig. 4 Charging system test (Part 2 of 2)

Step	Action	Yes	No
1	Did you review the following description and operations and perform the necessary inspections? • Battery Description and Operation • Starting System Description and Operation • Charging System Description and Operation		Check Engine Electrical
2	Turn ON the ignition, with the engine OFF. Does the battery charge indicator illuminate for five seconds during bulb check?	Test for Intermittent and Poor Connections	Go to Step 3
3	1. Disconnect the generator connector. 2. Connect a 20 amp fused jumper to the charge indicator ground circuit. 3. Turn the ignition switch to the ON position. Does the battery charge indicator illuminate?	Go to Step 4	Go to Step 6
4	Test the generator supply voltage circuit for an open. Did you find and correct the condition?	Go to Step 9	Go to Step 5
5	Replace the IC voltage regulator. Did you complete the replacement?	Go to Step 9	--
6	1. Inspect the charge indicator bulb and replace as necessary. 2. Test the charge indicator supply voltage circuit for an open. Did you find and correct the condition?	Go to Step 9	Go to Step 7
7	Test the charge indicator ground circuit for an open. Did you find and correct the condition?	Go to Step 9	Go to Step 8
8	Repair or replace the instrument cluster printed circuit. Did you complete the replacement?	Go to Step 9	--
9	Operate the system in order to verify the repair. Did you correct the condition?	System OK	Go to Step 2

GC1120100132000X

Fig. 5 Charge indicator inoperative

ALTERNATOR SPECIFICATIONS

Year	Alternator				Regulated Voltage
	Engine	Normal Operating Voltage	Maximum Alternator Output, Amps	No Load Alternator Speed, RPM	
2002–04	1.6L	12	60	1300	14.4–15.0
	2.0L	12	70	1300	14.4–15.0
	2.5L	12	85	1300	14.4–15.0

DASH PANEL SERVICE

NOTE: On Air Bag Equipped Models, Refer To "Air Bag System Precautions" Located In The Front Of This Manual For System Disarming & Arming Procedures.

NOTE: Refer To "Computer Relearn Procedures" Located In The Front Of This Manual When Battery Power To The Computer Has Been Interrupted.

INDEX

PRECAUTIONS

Air Bag Systems

Refer to "Air Bag System Precautions" in the front of this manual for system disarming and arming procedures.

Battery Ground Cable

Prior to service disconnect battery ground cable and isolate as required.

Electrostatic Discharge (ESD)

Many solid state electrical components, such as those found in the instrument panel and the radio, can be damaged by Electrostatic Discharge (ESD). Some will display a label, but many will not. In order to avoid possible damage to any components, observe the following:

1. Body movement produces electrostatic charge. To discharge personal static electricity, touch ground point (metal) on vehicle. This should be done any time you slide across seat, sit down, get up or do any walking.
2. Do not touch exposed electric terminals on components with your finger or any tools. The connector being inspected might be tied into a circuit which, in turn, could be damaged by electrostatic discharge.
3. When using a screwdriver or similar tool to disconnect a connector, never let tool come in contact with or come between exposed terminals.
4. Never jump, ground or use test equipment probes on any components or connectors unless specified in diagnosis. **When using test equipment, always connect ground lead first.**
5. Do not remove solid state component from protective packaging until ready to install.
6. Always touch solid state component's package to ground before opening. Solid state components can also be damaged if bumped or dropped.
7. Do not allow solid state components to come into contact with metal work benches or electronic components such as a television, radio or oscilloscope.

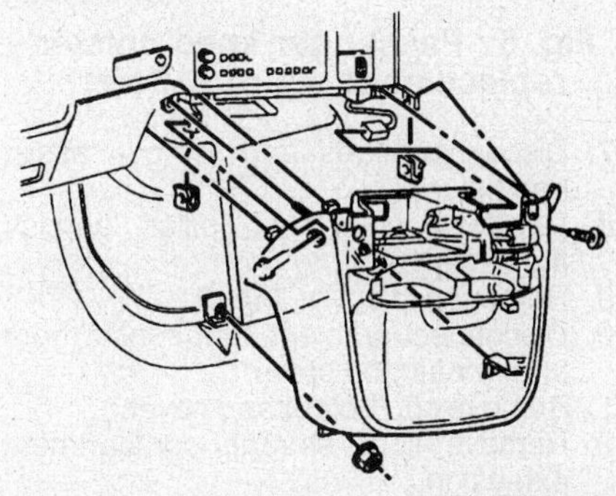

Fig. 1 Instrument panel extension replacement. Astro & Safari

DASH PANEL

REPLACE

Astro & Safari

1. Remove two instrument panel extension side mounting screws and bottom mounting nuts, **Fig. 1.**
2. Remove extension from instrument panel by pulling rearward to disconnect fasteners.

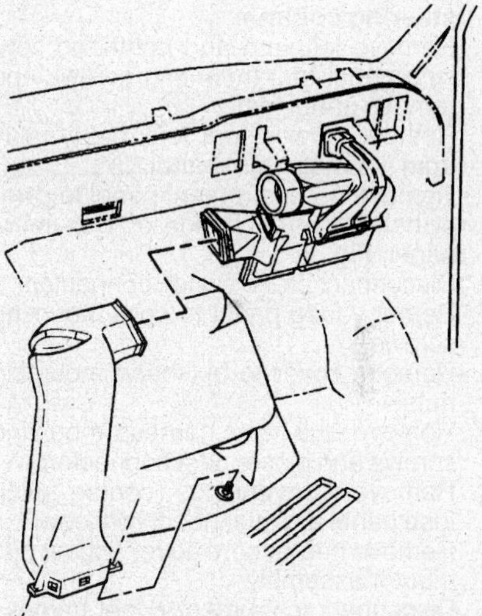

Fig. 2 Center floor air outlet replacement. Astro & Safari

3. Disconnect electrical harness.
4. Remove windshield defroster grille.
5. Remove instrument panel to defroster nozzle fasteners.
6. Remove instrument panel carrier mounting screw.
7. Rotate defrost nozzle down and away from instrument panel carrier.
8. Remove two floor outlet duct to instrument panel carrier mounting screws, **Figs. 2 through 4.**
9. Remove side glass defrost ducts and air outlet.
10. Loosen engine cover mounting bolts and rotate brackets aside.

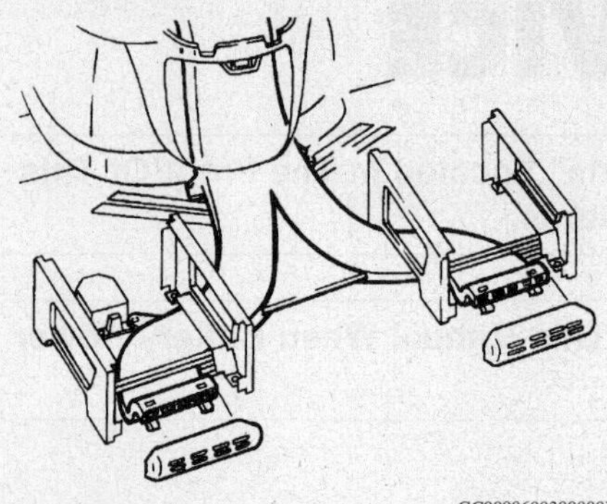

Fig. 3 Rear seat floor air outlet replacement. Astro & Safari

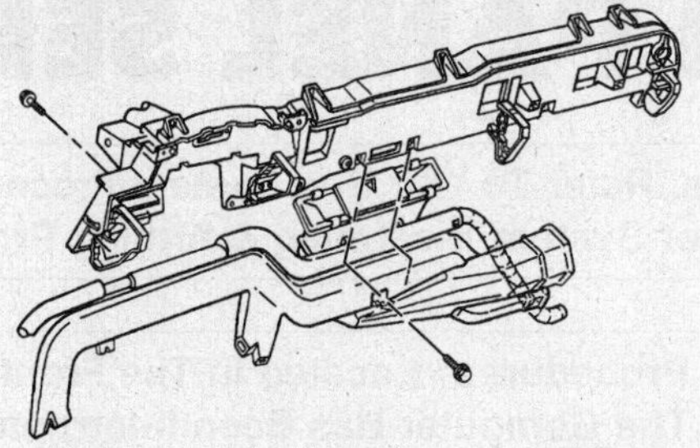

Fig. 4 Lefthand floor air outlet replacement. Astro & Safari

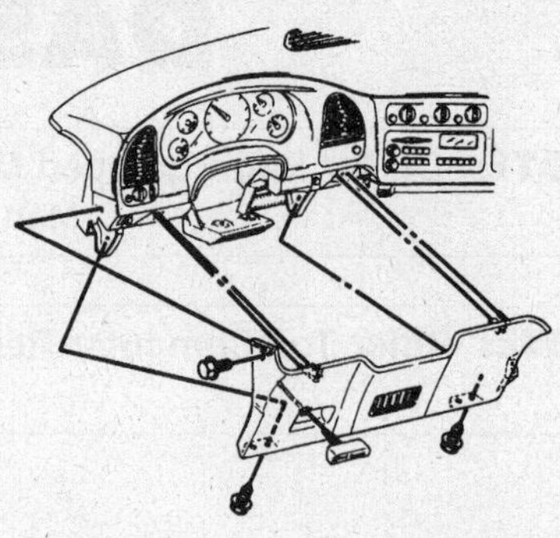

Fig. 5 Driver knee bolster replacement. Astro & Safari

11. Disconnect latches and remove mounting screws.
12. Remove mounting screws, then pull driver and passenger knee bolster rearward to disconnect fasteners, **Figs. 5 and 6.**
13. Disconnect parking brake lever.
14. Disconnect steering column harness by removing one bolt in center of connector, then disconnecting upper and lower fasteners.
15. Support steering column and remove two upper and lower mounting bolts, **Fig. 7. Do not remove or rotate steering column.**
16. Remove lefthand and righthand cowl side panel trim mounting screws and remove panel trim.
17. Remove power door lock delay relay from righthand trim panel.
18. Remove two instrument panel to carrier bolts from each side of instrument panel, **Fig. 8.**
19. Disconnect brake switch connector.
20. Remove fuse panel to cowl mounting screws.
21. Remove cover to bulkhead mounting nuts.
22. Remove bulkhead harness mounting screws and disconnect connector.
23. Remove convenience center, mini-fuse panel and bulkhead from cowl.
24. Remove heater core cover and air distributor assembly.
25. Disconnect instrument panel harness from instrument panel.
26. Slide instrument panel harness away from cowl, then lift it up and off pivot points.
27. Reverse procedure to install.

Avalanche, Escalade EXT, Sierra & Silverado

1. **On models equipped with air conditioning,** set air flow control to vent position.
2. **On all models,** apply parking brake.
3. Move shift lever all way down.
4. Remove instrument panel cluster trim plate bezel.
5. Remove end panels.
6. Remove righthand side air outlets.

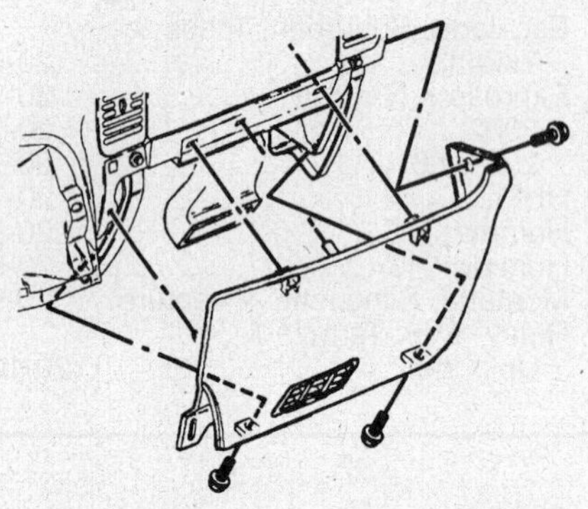

Fig. 6 Passenger knee bolster replacement. Astro & Safari

7. Disconnect tabs and remove assist handle.
8. Remove windshield pillar garnish moldings.
9. Remove top cover, **Fig. 9.**
10. Disconnect ambient light sensor from underneath top cover.
11. Remove cup holder and cover.
12. Remove floor storage compartment extension.
13. Remove Data Link Connector (DLC).
14. Remove lefthand knee bolster.
15. Remove lower instrument panel trim panel.
16. Remove passenger air bag module as outlined in "Passive Restraint Systems" chapter.
17. Remove knee bolster deflector.
18. Remove steering column.
19. Disconnect body control module with bracket.
20. Remove lefthand accessory switch bracket.
21. Remove instrument cluster.
22. Remove radio and HVAC control head.
23. Remove righthand accessory switch housing and disconnect electrical connection.
24. Remove instrument panel upper bracket and disconnect wiring harness.
25. Disconnect remote function actuator.
26. Disconnect righthand bussed electrical center.
27. Disconnect righthand courtesy lamp and instrument cluster electrical connectors.
28. Remove parking brake release handle.
29. Remove instrument panel from carrier support.
30. Reverse procedure to install.

Aztek & Rendezvous

1. Remove covers from lefthand and righthand instrument panel access hole.
2. Remove instrument panel insulator retainers, **Fig. 10.**
3. Remove instrument panel insulators.
4. Remove Data Link Connector (DLC).
5. Remove windshield side upper garnish moldings.
6. Lift panel up two inches and pull rearward to disconnect retainers.
7. Remove daytime running lamp sensor.
8. Remove sun load sensor.
9. Remove instrument panel upper trim panel.
10. Remove cup holder liner and screw.
11. Pull up on front floor trim plate to disconnect retainer clips.
12. Remove trim plate, turn it sideways and lift it over shift lever.
13. Disconnect electrical connectors.
14. Remove mounting nuts, then lift console front and pull it backwards to remove, **Fig. 11.**
15. Remove knee bolster panel.
16. Remove lower steering column mounting bolts and upper column mounting nuts.
17. Lower steering column.
18. Remove base mounting bolts, cable and hood release handle.
19. Remove accessory trim plate.
20. Remove instrument panel cluster trim plate mounting screws at assist handle.
21. Pull out instrument cluster trim plate to disconnect retainers.
22. Disconnect electrical connectors and remove instrument cluster trim plate.
23. Remove instrument panel cluster.
24. Remove radio assembly disconnecting electrical connectors.
25. Remove heater air conditioning control unit disconnecting electrical connectors.
26. Remove end gate switch bank.
27. Remove glove compartment, **Fig. 12.**
28. Remove glove compartment lamp switch using suitable screwdriver.

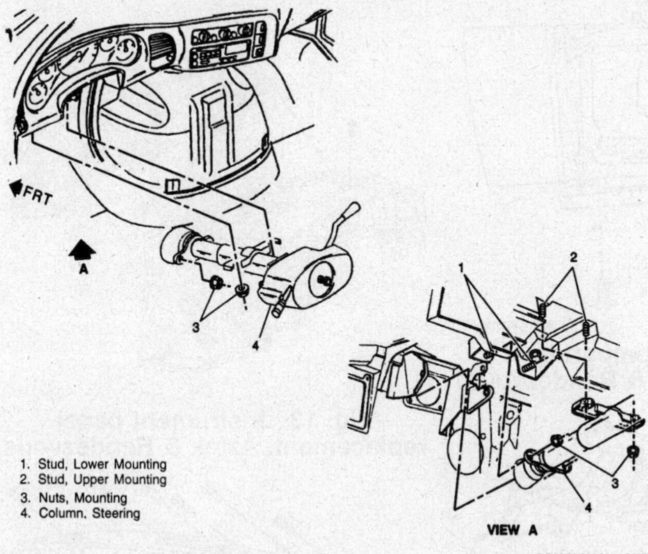

Fig. 7 Steering column replacement. Astro & Safari

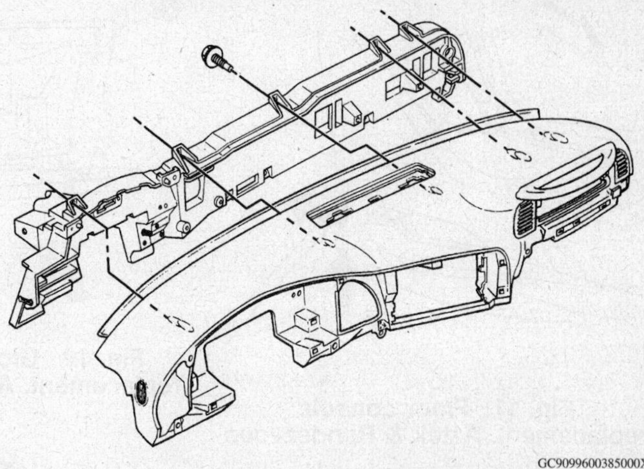

Fig. 8 Exploded view of instrument panel. Astro & Safari

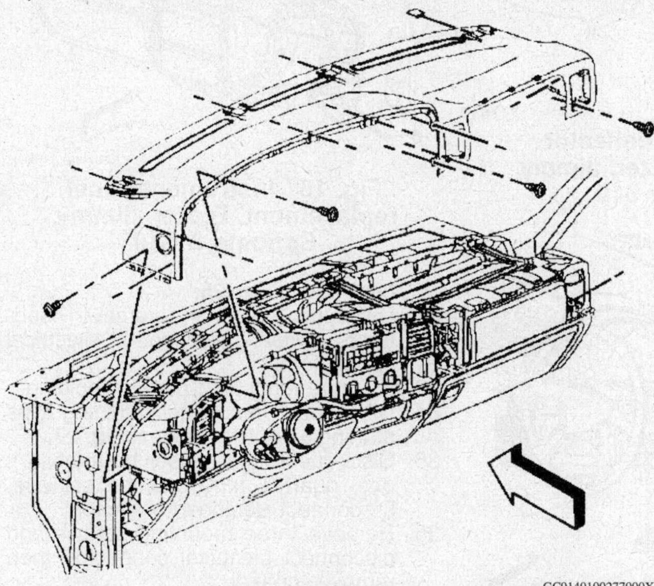

Fig. 9 Top cover replacement. Avalanche, Escalade, Escalade EXT, Sierra, Silverado, Suburban, Tahoe, Yukon & Yukon XL

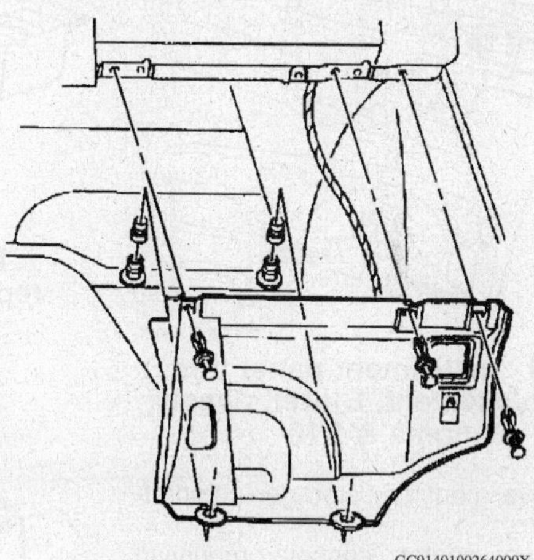

Fig. 10 Instrument panel insulator retainer replacement. Aztek & Rendezvous

29. Remove instrument panel mounting screws.
30. Disconnect electrical connectors and remove instrument panel, **Fig. 13.**
31. Reverse procedure to install.

Blazer, Jimmy, Sonoma & S10

1. **On models equipped with manual transmission,** remove shift lever.
2. **On models equipped with automatic transmission,** place transmission in Low position.
3. **On all models,** remove righthand instrument panel sound insulator and storage compartment.
4. Remove lower righthand instrument panel mounting bolt, then the lefthand and righthand speaker and speaker grilles.
5. Remove windshield defroster grille using suitable flat-bladed tool and center sound insulator.
6. Remove lefthand sound insulator and park brake release handle.
7. Remove knee bolster and lower lefthand instrument panel mounting bolt.
8. Remove truck body control module and instrument panel accessory trim plate, **Fig. 14.**
9. Remove instrument cluster and audio system.
10. Remove knee deflector and driver knee bolster brackets, **Fig. 15.**
11. Disconnect electrical connectors, then remove mounting nuts and lower steering column.
12. Remove HVAC control assembly.
13. Remove instrument panel mounting screws, **Fig. 16.**
14. Remove instrument panel.
15. Reverse procedure to install.

Bravada, Envoy, Rainier & Trailblazer

1. Remove mounting screw and disconnect clips, then remove insulator panel, **Fig. 17.**
2. Remove mounting screws and disconnect clips, then remove trim panel, **Fig. 18.**
3. Remove lefthand HVAC push pin and floor duct, **Fig. 19.**
4. Disconnect steering column electrical connector.
5. Disconnect body wiring harness connector from steering column lower bracket, **Fig. 20.**
6. Remove steering column intermediate shaft bolt, **Fig. 21.**
7. Remove mounting nuts and steering column, **Fig. 22.**
8. Remove rubber ashtray inserts and mat from console.
9. Remove floor shift control knob and center console shift lever bezel.

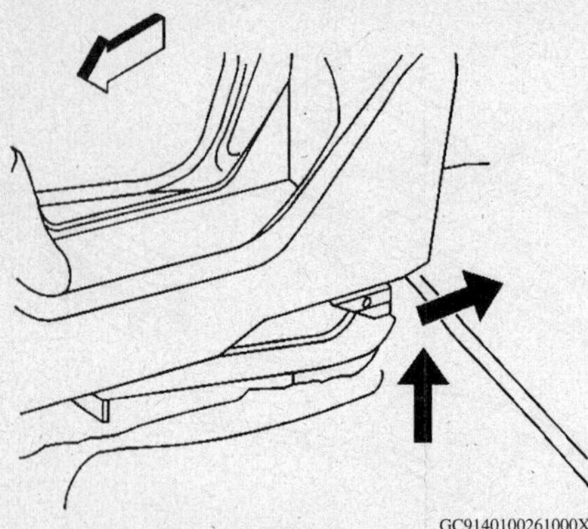

Fig. 11 Floor console replacement. Aztek & Rendezvous

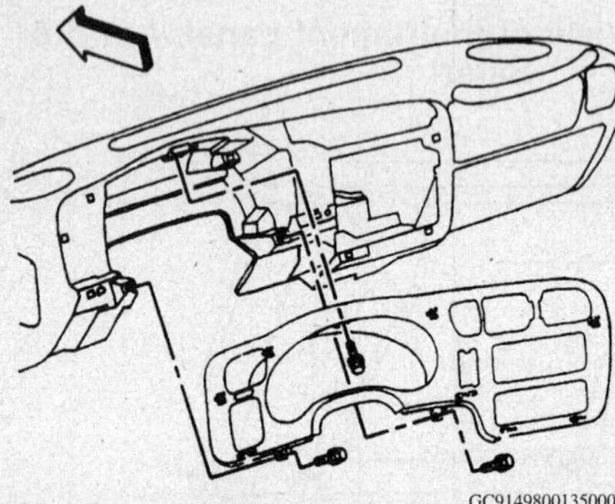

Fig. 14 Instrument panel trim plate replacement. Blazer, Jimmy, Sonoma & S10

10. Remove console storage compartment.
11. Remove center console mounting screws, **Fig. 23.**
12. Adjust parking brake to fully engaged position.
13. Slide console rearward, raise rear of console and disconnect electrical connectors.
14. Adjust parking brake to halfway position.
15. Remove center console.
16. Remove four mounting screws and closeout panel, **Fig. 24.**
17. **On Envoy models,** proceed as follows:
    a. Remove lower trim plate mounting screws.
    b. Release two lower retaining clips, two intermediate retaining clips and three upper retaining clips from trim plate.
    c. Disconnect electrical connectors.
18. **On all models,** remove mounting screws and instrument panel cluster bezel.
19. Remove mounting screws and instrument panel cluster.
20. Remove two mounting screws and disconnect electrical connector, then remove insulator panel.
21. Remove righthand insulator panel.
22. Remove mounting screws and glove compartment.
23. Remove five glove compartment jamb trim panel mounting screws.

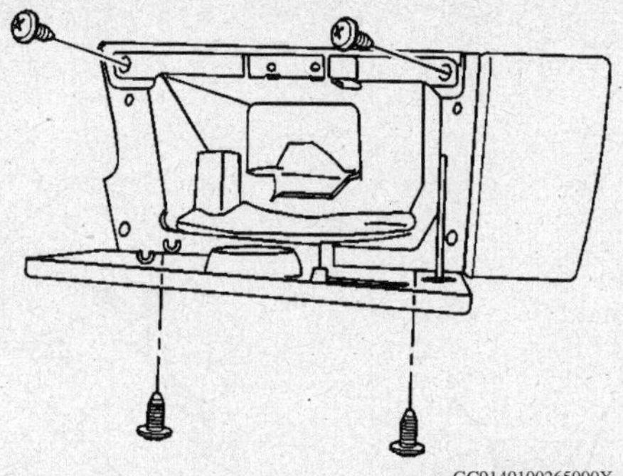

Fig. 12 Glove compartment replacement. Aztek & Rendezvous

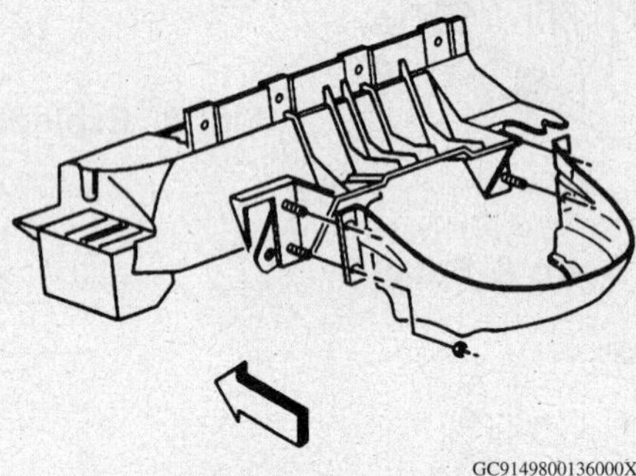

Fig. 15 Knee deflector replacement. Blazer, Jimmy, Sonoma & S10

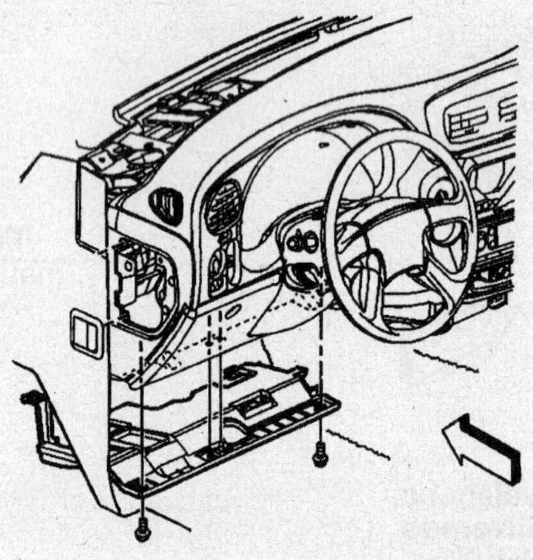

Fig. 17 Lefthand insulator panel replacement. Bravada, Envoy, Rainier & Trailblazer

24. Disconnect socket electrical connector.
25. Remove trim panel from instrument panel.
26. Disconnect tabs and remove socket assembly.
27. Remove three mounting screws and disconnect electrical connectors, then remove radio.
28. Remove mounting screws and disconnect tabs, then remove HVAC control module.
29. Disconnect electrical connectors.
30. Remove HVAC control module wiring harness attachment from instrument panel substrate, **Fig. 25.**
31. Remove lefthand instrument panel access cover, **Fig. 26.**

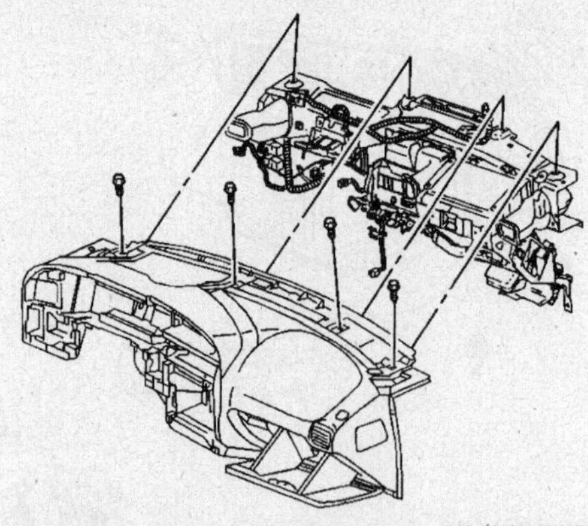

Fig. 13 Instrument panel replacement. Aztek & Rendezvous

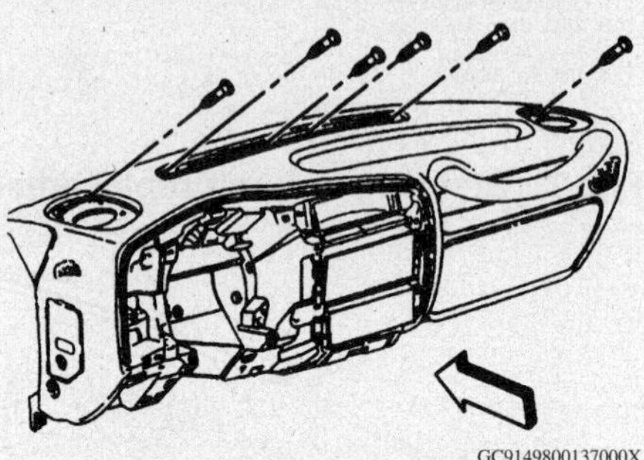

Fig. 16 Instrument panel replacement. Blazer, Jimmy, Sonoma & S10

32. Disconnect tabs and remove headlamp switch. Disconnect electrical connectors.
33. Remove windshield garnish molding.
34. Disconnect trim panel retaining clips starting on outside edges, **Fig. 27.**
35. Disconnect light sensor by rotating it one quarter turn counterclockwise. Disconnect electrical connector.
36. Remove three mounting screws and disconnect electrical connector, then remove speaker.
37. Remove righthand instrument panel access cover.
38. Remove side window defroster outlet, **Fig. 28.**
39. Remove lower instrument panel mounting bolts, **Fig. 29.**
40. Remove instrument panel middle and upper mounting bolts, **Fig. 30.**
41. Remove instrument panel.
42. Reverse procedure to install.

Canyon & Colorado

1. Remove mounting screws, open door and remove glove compartment.
2. Remove cover, mounting bolt and windshield garnish molding.
3. Remove lefthand and righthand front door sill plates.
4. Remove lefthand and righthand hinge pillar trim panels.
5. Remove push-pins using suitable trim tool and lower center instrument panel trim.
6. Disconnect clips using suitable plastic

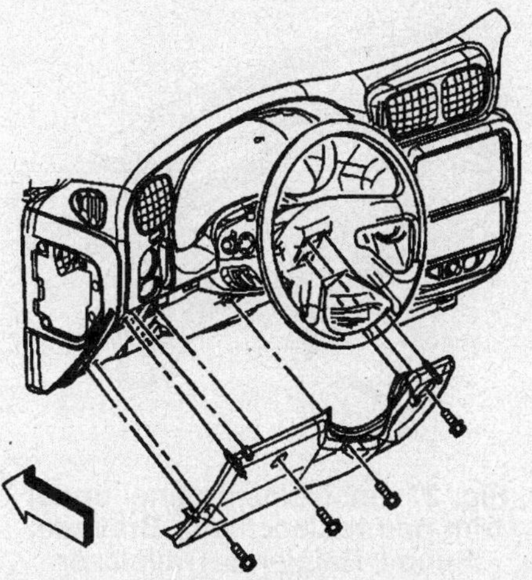
GC9140200327000X

Fig. 18 Knee bolster panel replacement. Bravada, Envoy, Rainier & Trailblazer

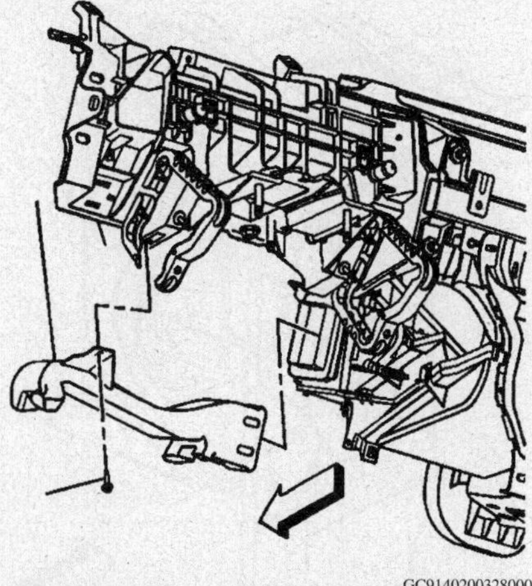
GC9140200328000X

Fig. 19 HVAC component replacement. Bravada, Envoy, Rainier & Trailblazer

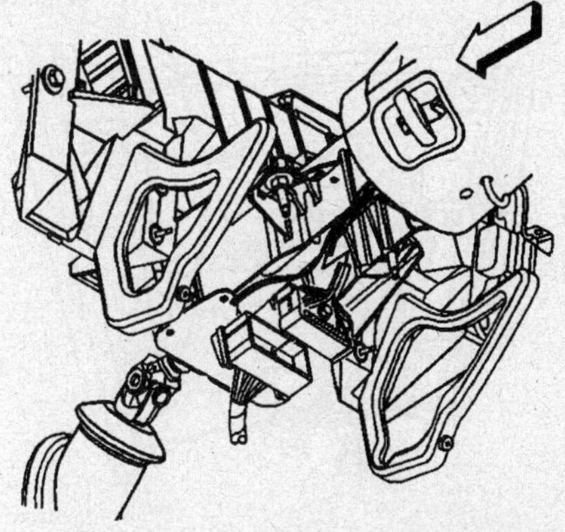
GC9140200329000X

Fig. 20 Steering column component replacement. Bravada, Envoy, Rainier & Trailblazer

GC9140200330000X

Fig. 21 Steering column intermediate shaft bolt replacement. Bravada, Envoy, Rainier & Trailblazer

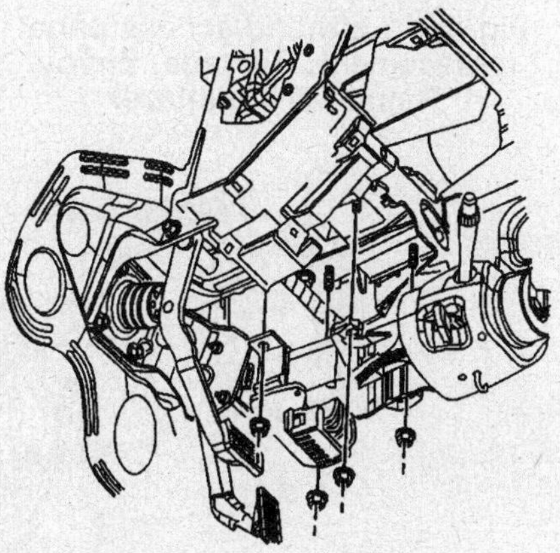
GC9140200331000X

Fig. 22 Steering column replacement. Bravada, Envoy, Rainier & Trailblazer

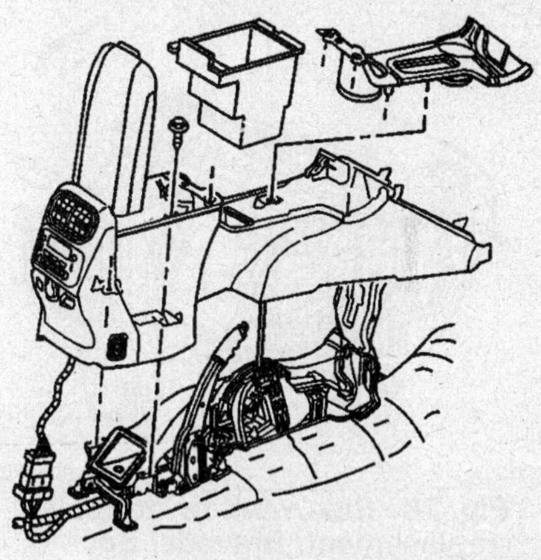
GC9140200324000X

Fig. 23 Floor console replacement. Bravada, Envoy, Rainier & Trailblazer

flat-bladed tool and remove accessory trim panel. Disconnect electrical connectors.

7. Remove three mounting screws and disconnect radio from alignment locator.
8. Disconnect antenna cable and electrical connectors, then remove radio.
9. Remove mounting screws and HVAC control assembly.
10. Disconnect mode and temperature cables, then the HVAC electrical connectors.
11. Disconnect tabs using suitable flat-bladed plastic tool, then remove lefthand and righthand air outlet.
12. Remove mounting screws and hood release lever.
13. Remove mounting screws, disconnect clips and remove knee bolster trim panel.
14. Remove park brake release handle from cable using suitable flat-bladed tool.
15. Remove cable by rotating it clockwise past moulded bumps, then remove knee bolster trim panel.
16. Disconnect tab and remove Data Link Communication (DLC) connector.
17. Remove mounting screws and disconnect hangers, then the knee bolster.
18. Tilt steering wheel to full down position.
19. **On models equipped with steering column mounted shift lever,** block wheels and position shift lever in FIRST gear.

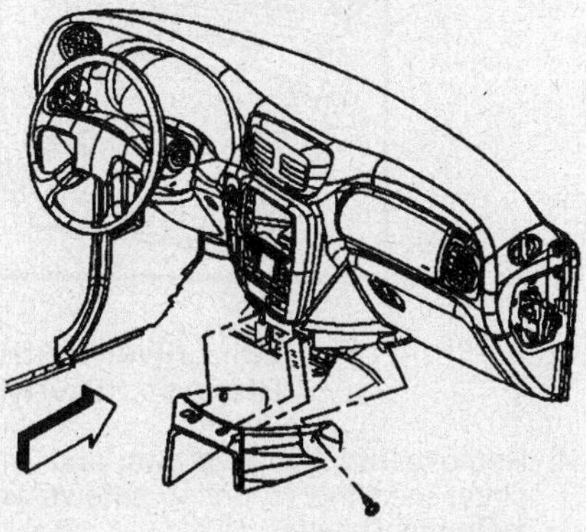
GC9140200332000X

Fig. 24 Instrument panel lower insulator replacement. Bravada, Envoy, Rainier & Trailblazer

20. **On all models,** disconnect clips and remove instrument cluster bezel.
21. Remove mounting screws and partially remove instrument cluster.
22. Disconnect electrical connector.
23. Record location for installation alignment and position Connector Position Assurance (CPA) arm aside. Disconnect electrical connector.
24. Remove instrument cluster.
25. Remove mounting screw and partially remove headlamp switch.
26. Disconnect electrical connectors and remove headlamp switch.
27. Remove Daytime Running Lamp (DRL) sensor using suitable flat-bladed tool. Disconnect electrical connector.
28. Remove covers and three upper instrument panel to bulkhead mounting nuts, **Fig. 31.**
29. Remove three upper HVAC duct mounting screws.
30. Remove mounting screws behind instrument cluster.
31. Remove two glove compartment door latch mounting screws and three lower panel mounting screws, **Fig. 32.**
32. Remove hazard switch harness from routing hole.
33. Remove mounting screws and digital radio receiver.
34. Remove mounting bolts and nuts, then partially remove passenger air bag module.

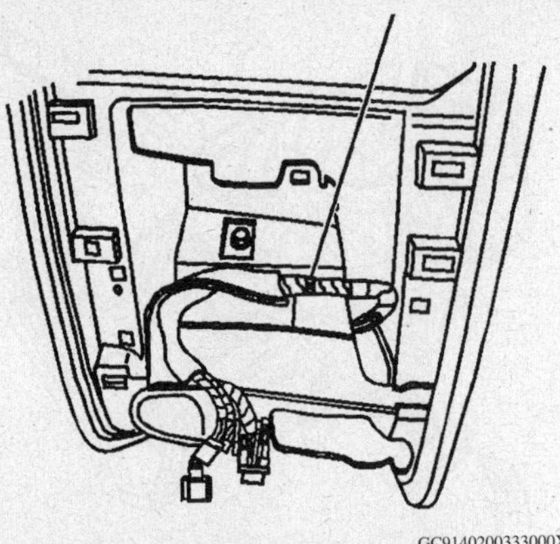

Fig. 25 HVAC control module wire harness. Bravada, Envoy, Rainier & Trailblazer

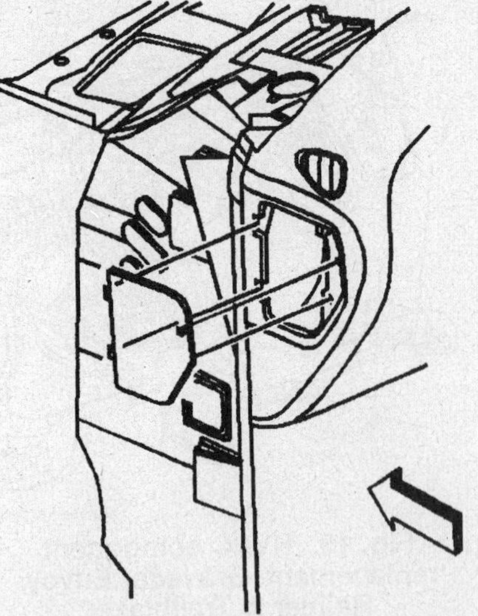

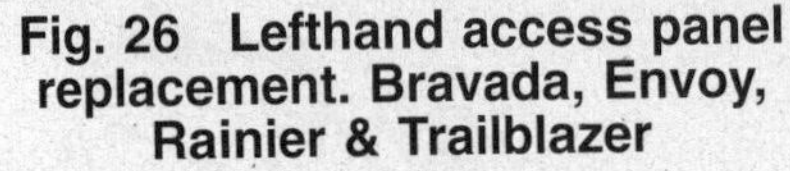

Fig. 26 Lefthand access panel replacement. Bravada, Envoy, Rainier & Trailblazer

Fig. 27 Instrument panel upper trim pad replacement. Bravada, Envoy, Rainier & Trailblazer

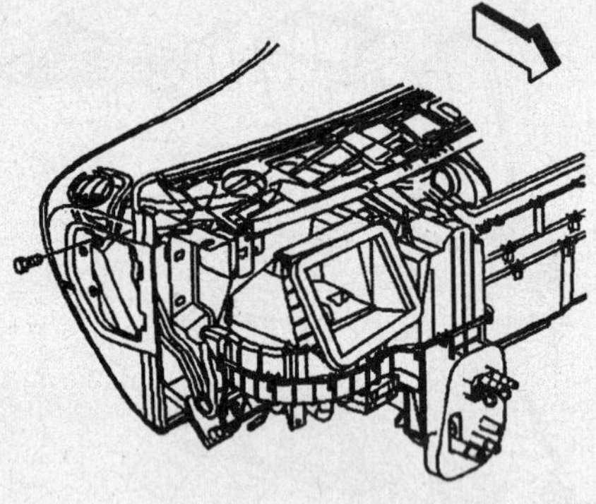

Fig. 28 Side window defroster replacement. Bravada, Envoy, Rainier & Trailblazer

35. Disconnect CPA connector and remove passenger air bag module.
36. Remove two mounting screws in passenger air bag module opening and end cap mounting screw.
37. Pull compartment folding panel down and remove instrument panel mounting screw.
38. Disconnect accessory power outlet electrical connectors.
39. Disconnect clips by pulling lower center edge, then the lower righthand edge rearward.
40. Remove wiring harness clips and instrument panel.
41. Reverse procedure to install.

Escalade, Suburban, Tahoe & Yukon

Refer to "Avalanche, Escalade EXT, Sierra & Silverado" for instrument panel replacement procedures.

Equinox & Torrent

1. Remove cover, mounting screw and windshield upper garnish molding.
2. Remove covers, mounting bolts and upper trim panel.
3. Place steering column in lowest position.

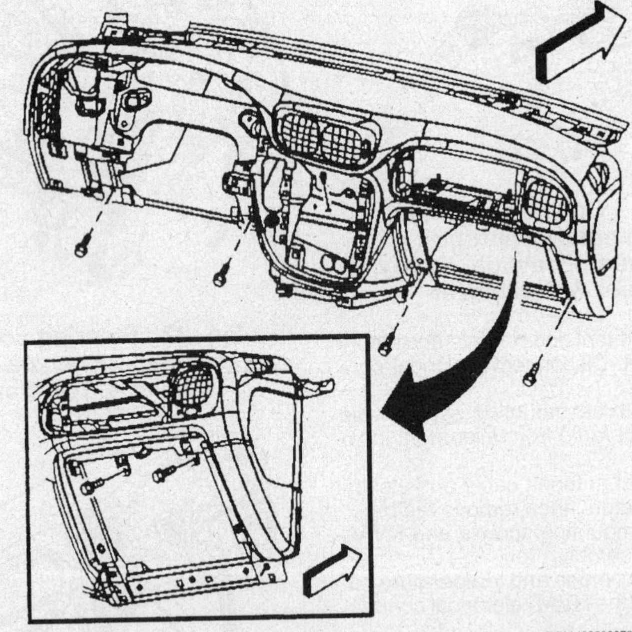

Fig. 29 Lower instrument panel replacement. Bravada, Envoy, Rainier & Trailblazer

4. Remove mounting screws and trim plate, then the mounting screws and instrument cluster.
5. Disconnect clips and electrical connectors, then remove center trim bezel.
6. Remove mounting, then disconnect radio electrical connectors and antenna.
7. Disconnect ground strap and remove radio.
8. Disconnect electrical harness and remove Body Control Module (BCM).
9. Move front seats rearward and remove center trim panel.
10. Remove mounting screws, then the lefthand and righthand console trim panels.
11. Open door and remove glove compartment pivot pins.
12. Turn and remove stops, then the glove compartment.
13. Remove mounting screws and disconnect clips, then remove steering column filler panel.
14. Remove power mirror and dimmer switches panel.
15. Remove passenger air bag module as outlined in "Passive Restraint Systems" chapter.
16. Remove lefthand and righthand carpet clips.

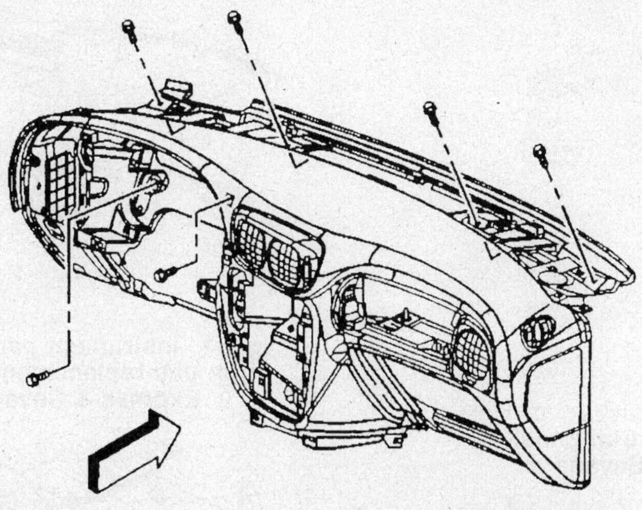

Fig. 30 Middle & upper instrument panel replacement. Bravada, Envoy, Rainier & Trailblazer

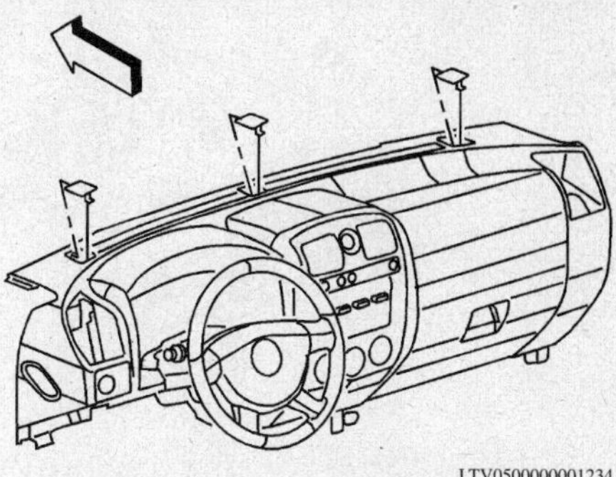

Fig. 31 Upper instrument panel mounting nut replacement. Canyon & Colorado

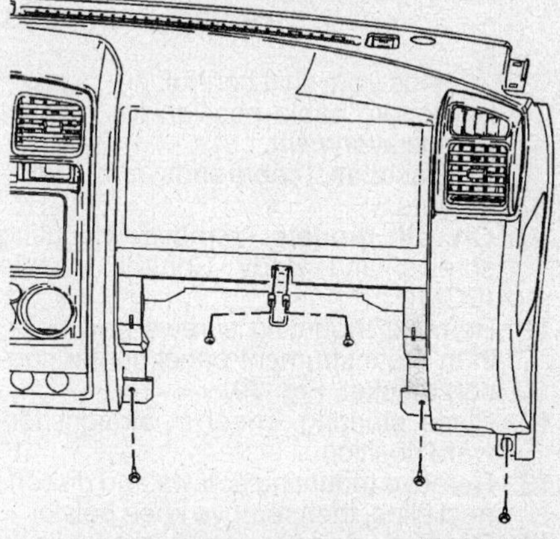

Fig. 32 Glove compartment area mounting screw replacement. Canyon & Colorado

17. Remove retainer to cross-beam mounting bolts and instrument panel.
18. Reverse procedure to install.

Express & Savana

2002

1. With engine off, set parking brake and move gear selector to first gear position.
2. Remove instrument cluster lower trim filler panel.
3. Remove instrument cluster lower trim panel, **Fig. 33.**
4. Remove lower instrument panel center trim.
5. Remove lefthand knee bolster.
6. Remove righthand knee bolster and brackets.
7. Remove instrument panel assist handle.
8. Remove instrument panel upper front trim panel.
9. Remove instrument panel upper trim pad, **Fig. 34.**
10. Remove instrument panel lower extension.
11. Remove engine cover.
12. Remove radio, CD player and mounting brackets.
13. Remove instrument panel storage compartments.
14. Remove HVAC control head.
15. Remove push-in fasteners mounting radio and HVAC wiring harnesses to instrument panel carrier.
16. Remove steering column to instrument panel carrier mounting bolts.
17. Remove instrument panel gauge cluster and disconnect electrical connectors.
18. Remove instrument panel carrier mounting bolts.
19. Rotate instrument panel carrier downward and disconnect wiring harness retainers from carrier.
20. Disconnect HVAC vacuum harness connector at lower righthand cowl area.
21. Remove air duct to instrument panel carrier mounting screws.
22. Remove instrument panel carrier.
23. Reverse procedure to install.

2003-06

1. Remove righthand knee bolster.
2. Remove body control module.
3. Remove lefthand knee bolster and brackets.
4. Lock steering column through access hole in lower steering column trim cover using steering column anti-rotation pin tool No. J42640, or equivalent.
5. Remove body control bracket.
6. Disconnect transmission shift cable.
7. Disconnect electrical connectors and wire harness retaining pin from instrument panel.
8. Remove pinch bolt and disconnect upper intermediate shaft from steering column.
9. Remove lower and lower steering column mounting bolts and nuts.
10. Remove support bracket and steering column.
11. Remove instrument panel cluster trim plate bezel.
12. Remove instrument cluster.
13. Remove lefthand and righthand hinge pillar trim panels.
14. Remove righthand knee bolster bracket.
15. Remove SIR module.
16. Remove upper instrument panel trim pad to body mounting bolts and screws, **Fig. 35.**
17. Remove engine cover.
18. Remove radio and mounting bracket.
19. Remove glove compartment.
20. Remove heater and air conditioning controls.
21. Remove instrument panel to mounting bolts, **Fig. 36.**
22. Rotate instrument panel out and downward.
23. Remove mounting bolts and remove air duct.
24. Remove wiring harness and instrument panel.
25. Reverse procedure to install.

HHR

1. Remove mounting screws and console accessory switch mount plate.
2. Apply parking brake and place shifter in NEUTRAL position.
3. Disconnect clips and remove front floor console side extension.
4. Remove mounting bolts and front seat armrests.
5. Disconnect clips and remove rear console trim plate.
6. Remove mounting screws and center console extension, **Fig. 37.**
7. Remove mounting screws and front floor console, **Fig. 38.**
8. **On models equipped with automatic transaxle,** proceed as follows:
   a. Raise and support vehicle.
   b. Remove shift cable mounting nut near exhaust heat shield.
   c. Remove shift cable from transmission cable bracket.
   d. Disconnect shift cable from park/neutral position switch.
   e. Disconnect shift cable from shift control.
9. **On models equipped with manual transaxle,** proceed as follows:
   a. Lift retainers and disconnect cable

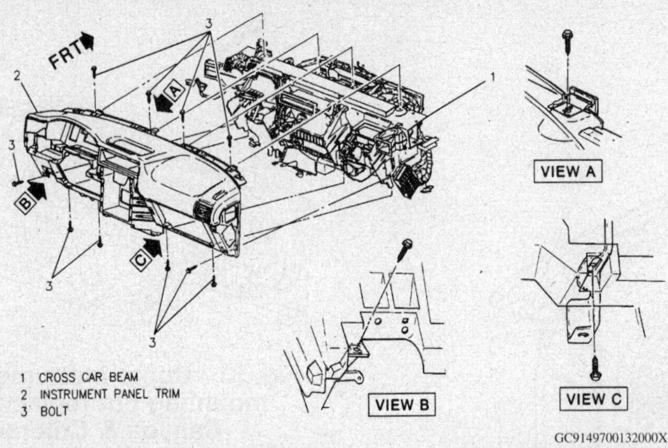

Fig. 33 Instrument cluster lower trim panel replacement. 2002 Express & Savana

ends from shift control.

b. Record cable position for installation alignment.
c. Disconnect cable ends from shift levers.

10. **On all models,** remove mounting screws and Body Control Module (BCM).
11. Remove mounting screws and bolts, then the instrument panel center support bracket, **Fig. 39.**
12. Place steering wheel in straight forward position.
13. Remove mounting screws and disconnect clips, then remove knee bolster.
14. Remove mounting screws and knee bolster reinforcement.
15. Remove driver air bag module as outlined in "Passive Restraint Systems" chapter.
16. Remove mounting nut and steering wheel using countergear and steering wheel puller tool No. J1859-A and steering wheel puller legs tools No. J36541-A, or equivalents.
17. Position steering column in full down position, then disconnect and remove upper steering column cover.
18. Remove mounting screws and lower steering column trim cover.
19. Disconnect headlamp/turn signal, wiper/washer harness and SIR coil module connectors.
20. Disconnect tabs using suitable, small flat-bladed tool and remove SIR coil module.
21. Disconnect ignition lock cylinder and switch connectors.
22. Mark intermediate shaft to steering column for installation alignment.
23. Remove and discard pinch bolt, then disconnect intermediate shaft from steering column.
24. Disconnect EPS control module harness connectors.
25. Remove pivot and mounting bolts, then lower steering column.
26. Remove mounting screws and instrument cluster trim plate.
27. Remove mounting screws and disconnect clips, then remove instrument cluster.

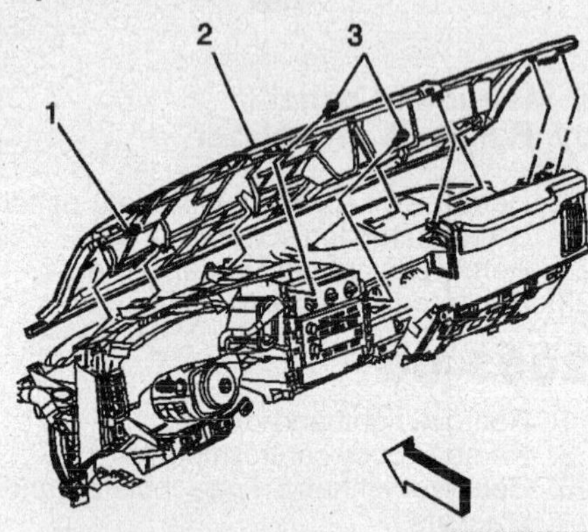

Fig. 35 Instrument panel upper trim pad replacement. 2003–06 Express & Savana

28. Remove covers and mounting screws. then disconnect clips and remove windshield garnish moldings.
29. Disconnect clips and remove instrument panel accessory trim plate.
30. Remove mounting screws and instrument panel center compartment.
31. Remove passenger air bag module as outlined in "Passive Restraint Systems" chapter.
32. Remove mounting screws and disconnect clips, then remove instrument panel upper trim pad, **Fig. 40.**
33. Remove mounting screws and HVAC control assembly.
34. Remove mounting screws and radio. Disconnect electrical connectors and antenna cable.
35. Disconnect clips, then remove lefthand and righthand instrument panel end covers.
36. Record wiring harness routing for installation alignment.
37. Remove glove compartment dampener mounting screw.
38. Squeeze sides and remove glove compartment past stops.
39. Remove mounting screws and bolts, then the instrument panel, **Fig. 41.**
40. Reverse procedure to install

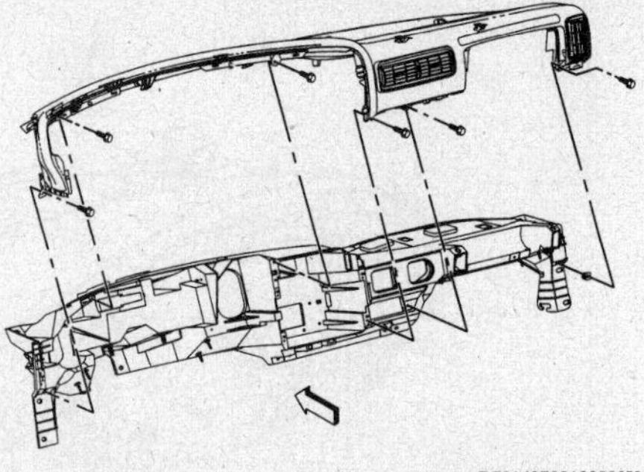

Fig. 34 Instrument panel upper trim pad replacement. 2002 Express & Savana

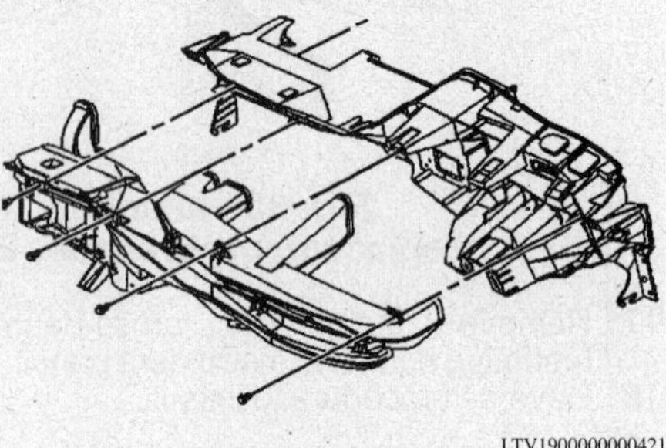

Fig. 36 Instrument panel lower trim panel replacement. 2003–06 Express & Savana

Hummer H2

1. Remove mounting bolts and insulator.
2. Disconnect brake release lever.
3. Remove diagnostic connection from bottom of lefthand side instrument panel.
4. Loosen set screw and remove shift control knob.
5. Remove screw, storage bin and shifter.
6. Disconnect clips and electrical connector, then remove cup holder.
7. Remove upper console trim panel and disconnect electrical connector.
8. Remove mounting bolts and center console, **Fig. 42.**
9. Remove screws and center trim.
10. Remove lefthand and righthand instrument panel side trims, then the assist handle.
11. Remove hinge mounting screws, door and glove compartment.
12. Remove instrument panel cluster trim.
13. Remove mounting bolts and screws, then the lefthand knee bolster trim.
14. Remove lefthand and righthand accessory trim plates and panel.
15. Remove connector and passenger air bag module.
16. Lock steering column through access hole in lower steering column trim cover using steering column anti-rotation pin tool No. J42640, or equivalent.
17. Remove knee bolster deflector and

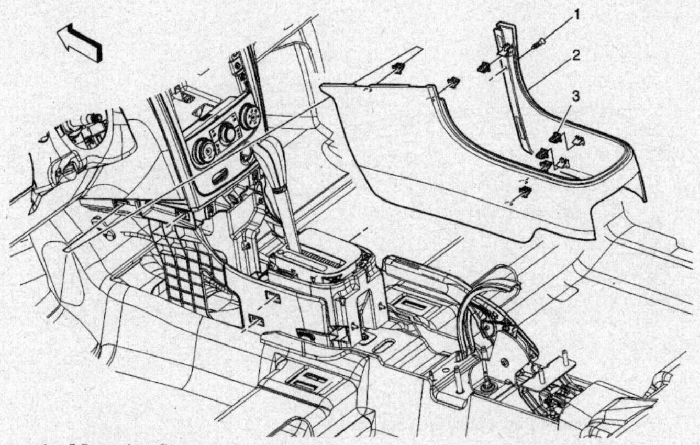

1 Mounting Screws
2 Front Floor Console Extension Assembly
3 Retainer Clip

LTV0500000001239

Fig. 37 Center console extension replacement. HHR

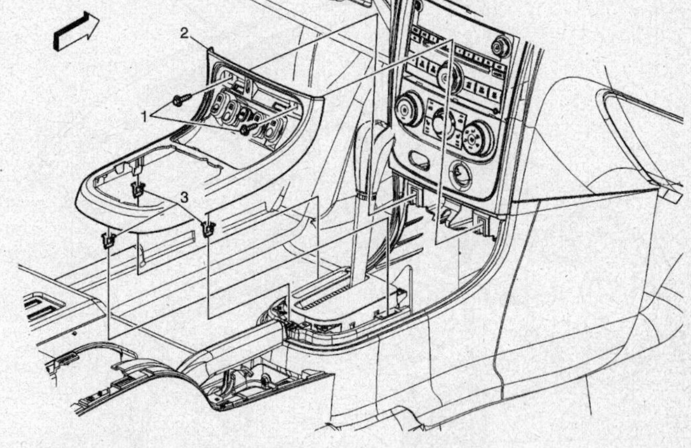

1. Front Floor Console Screws
2. Front Floor Console
3. Retainer Clips

LTV0500000001240

Fig. 38 Front console replacement. HHR

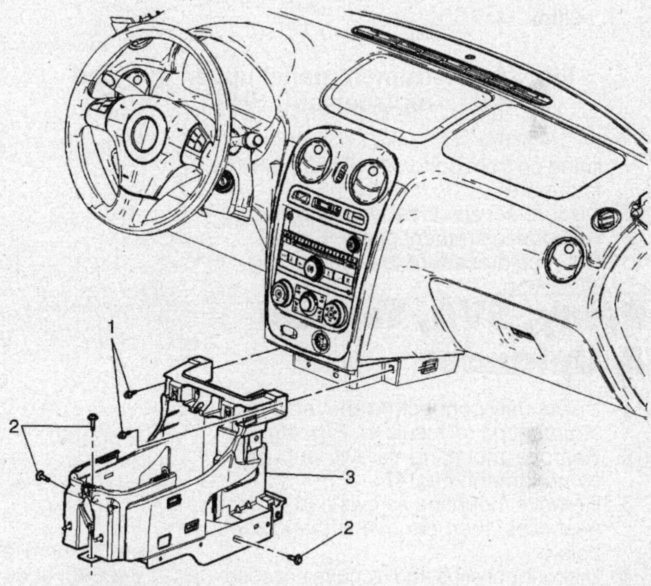

1. Mounting Screws
2. Mounting Bolts
3. Center Support Bracket

LTV0500000001238

Fig. 39 Center support bracket replacement. HHR

transfer case electronic control module.

18. Disconnect steering column lower bracket electrical and body wiring harness connectors.
19. Remove intermediate shaft bolt, then the mounting bolts and steering column.
20. Remove mounting screws and instrument cluster. Disconnect connectors.
21. Remove upper trim pad, **Fig. 43.**
22. Remove windshield garnish molding and disconnect speaker connector.
23. Remove mounting bolts, disconnect electrical and antenna connectors, then pull radio out.
24. Remove mounting screws and disconnect tabs, then remove HVAC control module. Disconnect electrical connectors.
25. Remove mounting crews and OnStar button assembly. Disconnect electrical connectors.
26. Remove traction control air ride and transfer case control switch modules.
27. Remove wiper/washer switch and disconnect electrical connectors.
28. Disconnect clips and remove headlamp switch. Disconnect connector.
29. Disconnect electrical connector, then remove upper and lower air temperature sensors.
30. Remove center support mounting nut and upper instrument panel carrier mounting bolts.
31. Remove lefthand and righthand carrier mounting bolts, then disconnect body control module electrical connectors.
32. Remove wiring harnesses and instrument panel.
33. Reverse procedure to install.

Hummer H3

Refer to "Bravada, Envoy, Rainier & Trailblazer" for instrument panel replacement procedure.

Montana, Silhouette & Venture

1. Remove instrument panel insulator and knee bolster.
2. Remove instrument panel accessory trim plate.
3. Tilt steering wheel to lowest position.
4. Starting near headlamp switch and working toward center of instrument panel, remove cluster trim cluster trim plate by pulling on release clips.
5. Remove mounting screws and instrument cluster. Disconnect electrical connectors
6. Open ashtray and remove instrument panel trim plate mounting screws.
7. Disconnect upper tabs and electrical connectors, then remove instrument panel accessory trim plate.
8. Remove lefthand and righthand instrument panel insulators.
9. Remove instrument panel upper trim panel.
10. Remove switch bank, audio system and HVAC controls.
11. Remove headlamp switch and hood release lever.
12. Remove instrument panel trim pad mounting bolts and screws, **Fig. 44.**
13. Remove instrument panel trim pad by

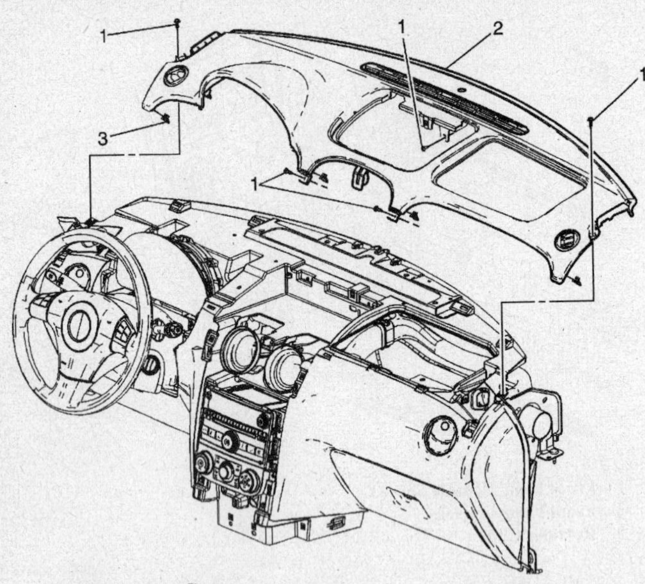

1. Mounting Screws
2. Instrument Panel Upper Trim Pad
3. Clips

LTV0500000001241

Fig. 40 Instrument panel upper trim pad replacement. HHR

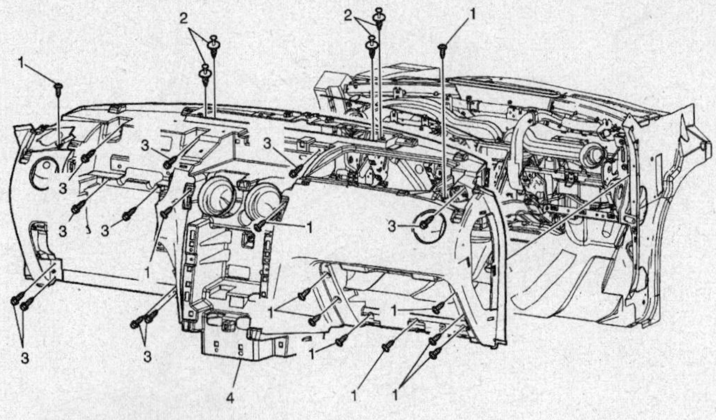

1. Instrument Panel Retainer Screws
2. Push Pin Fasteners
3. Instrument Panel Retainer Bolts
4. Instrument Panel Retainer

LTV0500000001237

Fig. 41 Instrument panel replacement. HHR

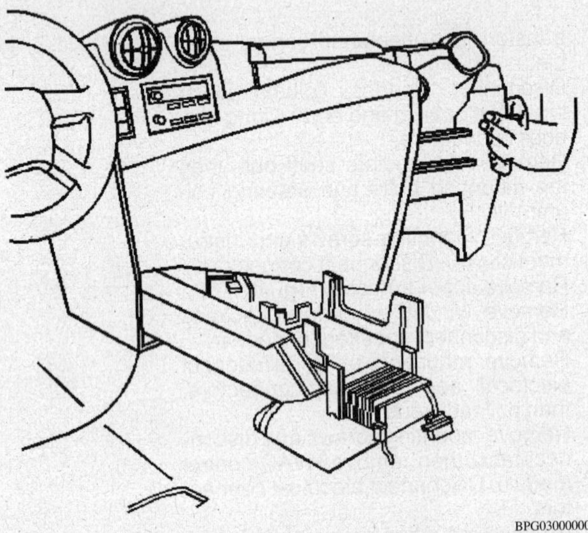

BPG0300000000181

Fig. 42 Floor console replacement. Hummer H2

lifting up from bottom to disconnect top fasteners.

14. Disconnect electrical wiring harness.
15. Remove instrument panel, **Fig. 45.**
16. Reverse procedure to install.

Relay, SV6, Terraza & Uplander

1. Disconnect connectors and remove instrument panel insulator, **Fig. 46.**
2. Remove mounting screws and glove compartment, **Fig. 47.**
3. Remove mounting screws and disconnect clips, then remove lefthand knee bolster.
4. Disconnect clips and remove accessory trim plate.
5. Remove mounting bolts and screws, then the HVAC control module. Disconnect electrical connectors.
6. Remove mounting screws and radio. Disconnect antenna cable and electrical connector.
7. Pull air conditioning center outlet rearward and disconnect electrical connectors from switches.
8. Remove mounting screws and driver information center.
9. Remove mounting screws and trim plate, then the mounting screws and instrument cluster.
10. Disconnect clips and remove lower trim molding.
11. Disconnect clips and remove sterling column opening moldings.
12. Disconnect clips and remove windshield pillar garnish moldings.
13. Disconnect clips and remove upper trim pad, **Fig. 48.**
14. Ensure front wheels are straight ahead and lock steering column using steering column anti-rotation pin tool No. J42640, or equivalent.
15. Remove driver air bag module as outlined in "Passive Restraint Systems" chapter.
16. Disconnect steering wheel control electrical connector.
17. Remove mounting nut, then the steering wheel using steering wheel puller tool No. J1859-A and leg tools No. J42578, or equivalent.
18. Raise and support vehicle.
19. Remove lower pinch bolt and disconnect intermediate steering shaft from power steering gear stub shaft.
20. Lower vehicle.
21. Remove upper pinch bolt and disconnect intermediate steering shaft from steering column.
22. Disconnect transaxle shift cable from linear shift ball stud, then remove clip and transaxle shift cable from bracket.
23. Remove mounting bolts and nuts, then the steering column.
24. Disconnect clips and remove front floor console, **Fig. 49.**
25. Remove lefthand and righthand trim panels, then the mounting screws and front floor console reinforcement.
26. Remove mounting nuts and front floor console bracket.
27. Remove passenger air bag module as outlined in "Passive Restraint Systems" chapter.
28. Remove mounting screws and hood release handle.
29. Remove Data Link Connector (DLC) mounting screws.
30. Remove mounting screws and instrument panel carrier cover, **Fig. 50.**
31. Remove mounting screws and lower extension panel.
32. Lift instrument panel and disconnect wiring harness retainers.
33. Remove instrument panel.
34. Reverse procedure to install.

SRX

1. Remove center console.
2. Pull center instrument panel vent out disconnect hazard switch electrical connector.

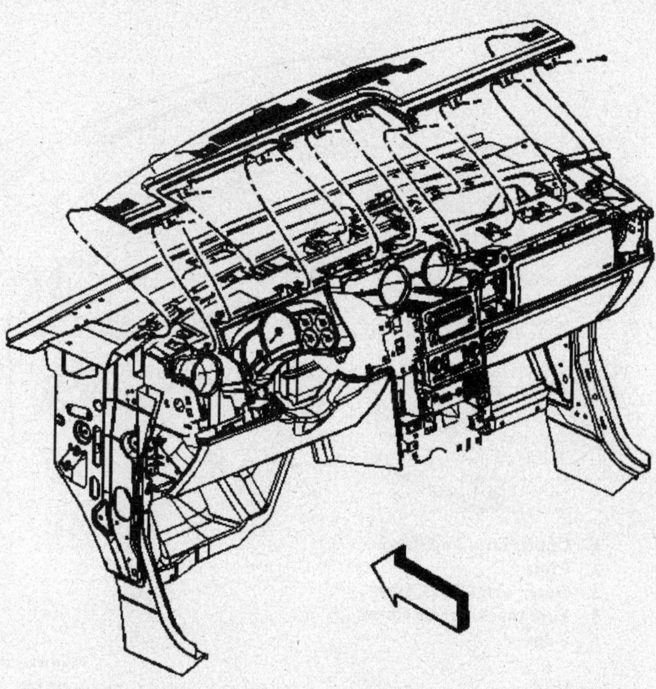

Fig. 43 Instrument panel upper trim removal. Hummer H2

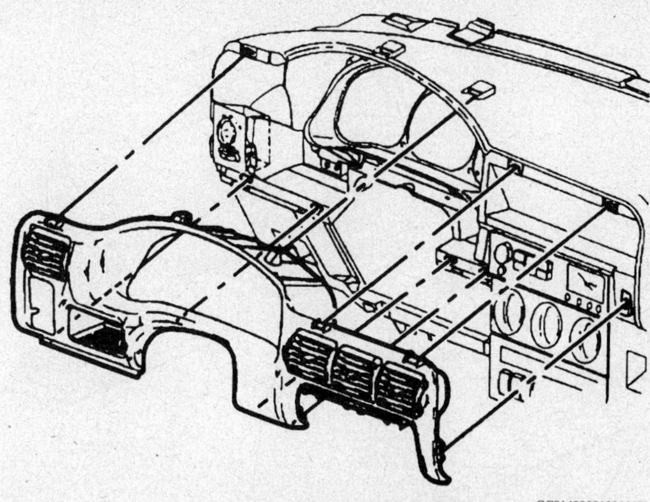

Fig. 44 Instrument panel trim plate replacement. Montana, Silhouette & Venture

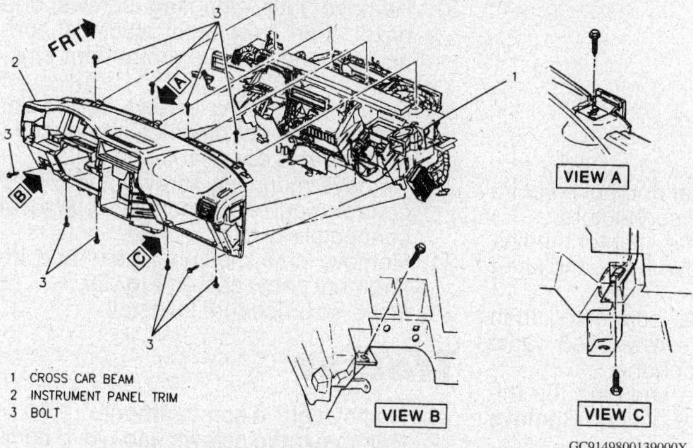

Fig. 45 Instrument panel replacement. Montana, Silhouette & Venture

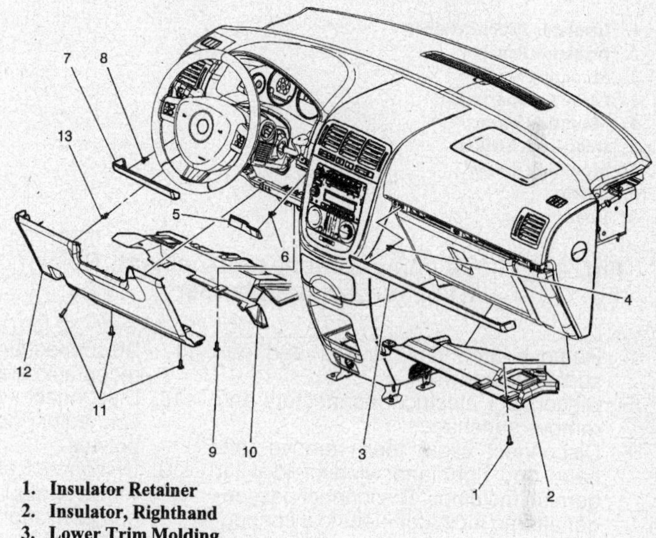

Fig. 46 Knee bolster, insulator & molding replacement. Relay, SV6, Terraza & Uplander

3. Remove screw behind ashtray.
4. Remove HVAC control module by pulling outward on lefthand and righthand side.
5. Disconnect HVAC control module electrical connector.
6. Disconnect ashtray electrical connector.
7. Remove mounting screws and HVAC control module, **Fig. 51.**
8. Remove four mounting screws and remove radio. Disconnect connector and antenna.
9. Open door and press tabs, then remove mounting screws and glove compartment, **Fig. 52.**
10. Tilt steering column to lowest position.
11. Remove trim cover, remove mounting screws and instrument cluster. Disconnect electrical connectors.
12. Pry grille up to disconnect clips, **Fig. 53.**
13. Disconnect sunload sensor wiring connector and remove defroster grille.
14. Remove four mounting screws and disconnect tabs, then disconnect electrical connector and remove righthand closeout panel, **Fig. 54.**
15. Remove four mounting screws and disconnect tabs, then disconnect electrical connector and remove lefthand closeout panel, **Fig. 55.**
16. Lower steering column.
17. Remove lower retainer support bracket mounting bolts, **Fig. 56.**
18. Remove lower center stack mounting screws, **Fig. 57.**
19. Remove mounting screws behind glove compartment.
20. Remove mounting screws and instrument panel, **Fig. 58.**
21. Reverse procedure to install.

SSR

1. Block wheels and move shift lever to FIRST position, then lower convertible top.
2. Tilt steering wheel to full down position.
3. Remove mounting screws and sunshade anchors.

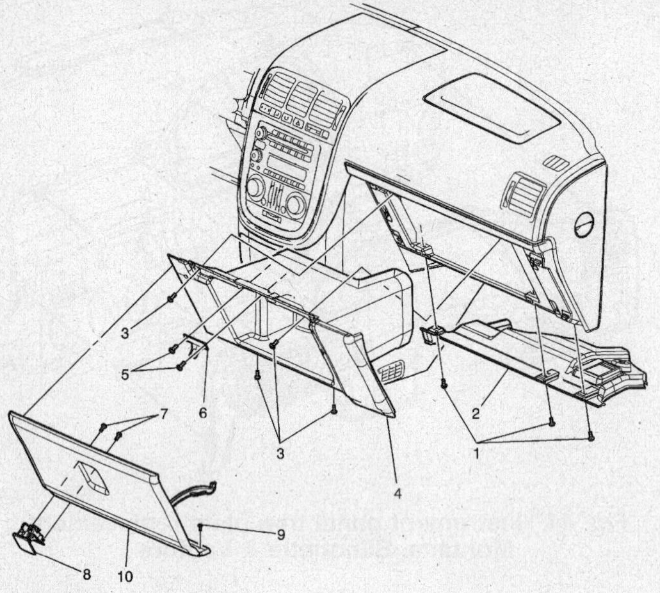

1. Insulator Panel Retainer
2. Insulator Panel
3. Mounting Screw
4. Glove Compartment
5. Mounting Screw
6. Door Lock Striker
7. Mounting Screw
8. Latch
9. Door

LTV0500000001243

Fig. 47 Glove compartment replacement. Relay, SV6, Terraza & Uplander

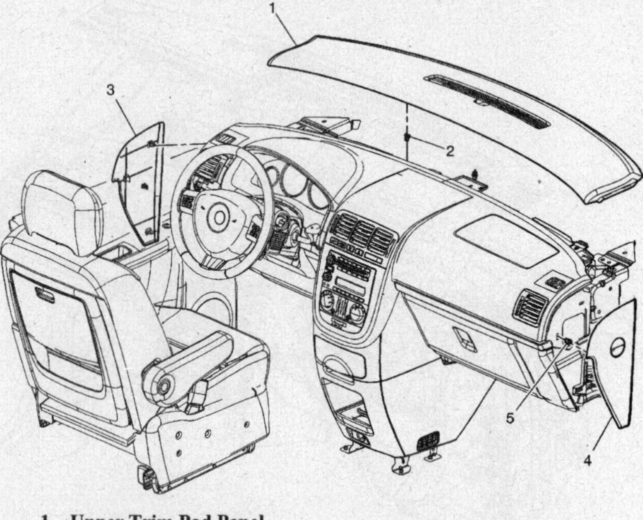

1. Upper Trim Pad Panel
2. Clips
3. Outer Trim Pad Cover
4. Fuse Block Access Cover
5. Clips

LTV0500000001244

Fig. 48 Upper trim pad replacement. Relay, SV6, Terraza & Uplander

4. Remove mounting screws and pull sunshades down.
5. Disconnect electrical connectors and remove sunshades.
6. Disconnect clips, then remove lefthand and righthand windshield pillar garnish moldings. Disconnect passenger air bag indicator electrical connector.
7. Disconnect clips and remove upper trim panel.
8. Disconnect clips and remove lefthand trim panel.
9. Remove HVAC knobs, then disconnect clips and remove righthand trim panel.
10. Remove passenger air bag module as outlined in "Passive Restraint Systems" chapter.
11. Remove three mounting bolts and lefthand knee bolster. Disconnect headlamp switch electrical connector.
12. Remove three mounting screws, then open and remove storage compartment.
13. Remove two mounting screws and ash tray door. Disconnect electrical connector
14. Remove righthand knee bolster mounting screws.
15. Disconnect tabs and remove inflatable restraint instrument panel module disable switch.
16. Disconnect inflatable restraint instrument panel module disable switch and glove compartment lamp electrical connectors.
17. Disconnect bed cover and power point receptacle electrical connectors.
18. Disconnect cigarette lighter in-line connector and remove righthand knee bolster.
19. Disconnect electrical connector, then remove mounting screws and radio compensation microphone.
20. Remove the screws securing the microphone to the knee bolster. Remove the microphone
21. Remove two Data Link Connector (DLC) mounting screws.
22. Remove seven mounting screws and lefthand knee bolster bracket.
23. Remove set screw and gear shift knob.
24. Disconnect clips and power switch module electrical connector, then remove floor console bezel to the floor console.
25. Fold lefthand and righthand seats forward.
26. Remove two upper console mounting screws and console trim to base by shift bezel lever mounting screw.
27. Remove parking brake handle bezel, open storage bin cover and remove two mounting screws.
28. Disconnect tabs and remove console trim.
29. Remove two mounting screws and disconnect clips, then remove ambient light sensor and instrument panel upper trim plate.
30. Remove five mounting screws and disconnect clips, then remove instrument cluster trim panel and seal.
31. Remove four mounting screws and bezel, then disconnect electrical connectors and remove instrument cluster.
32. Remove mounting screws and radio, then disconnect electrical connectors and antenna coax cable.
33. Remove mounting screws and HVAC control module. Disconnect electrical connector.
34. Remove nine mounting bolts and instrument panel carrier, **Fig. 59.**
35. Reverse procedure to install.

Tracker

1. Remove glove compartment.
2. Remove three screws and glove compartment trim plate, **Fig. 60.**
3. Remove passenger air bag module as outlined in "Passive Restraint Systems" chapter.
4. Position front seats forward and remove park brake lever.
5. Remove two rear console mounting screws and disconnect accessory socket electrical connector.
6. Remove rear floor console.
7. Remove front floor console mounting bolts, then lift and disconnect power/normal electrical switch.
8. Remove front floor console.
9. Remove ashtray and guide, then the lamp and housing.
10. Remove radio, then disconnecting electrical connectors and antenna.
11. Remove cigarette lighter bulb socket. Disconnect electrical connector
12. Remove mounting screws and disconnect electrical connectors, then remove instrument cluster.
13. Remove two instrument panel accessory trim plate switch hole covers.
14. Remove hazard warning switch and

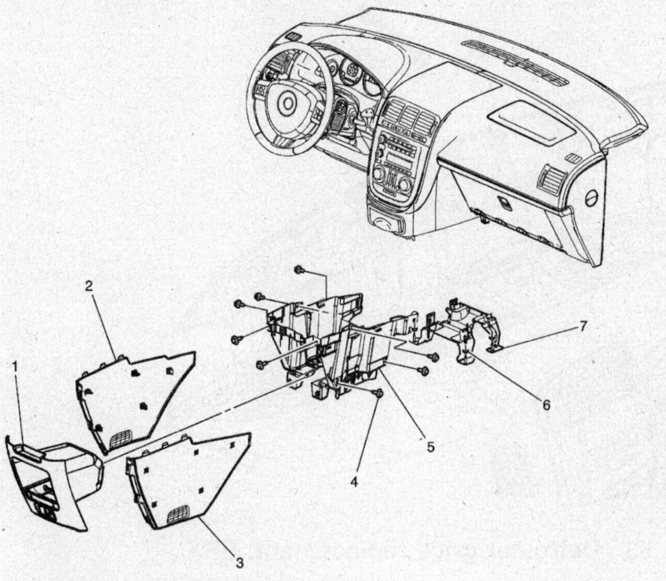

1. Front Floor Console Compartment
2. Front Floor Console Left Side Trim Panel
3. Front Floor Console Right Side Trim Panel
4. Front Floor Console Reinforcement Screw
5. Front Floor Console Reinforcement
6. Front Floor Console Bracket Nut
7. Front Floor Console Bracket

LTV0500000001245

Fig. 49 Front floor console replacement. Relay, SV6, Terraza & Uplander

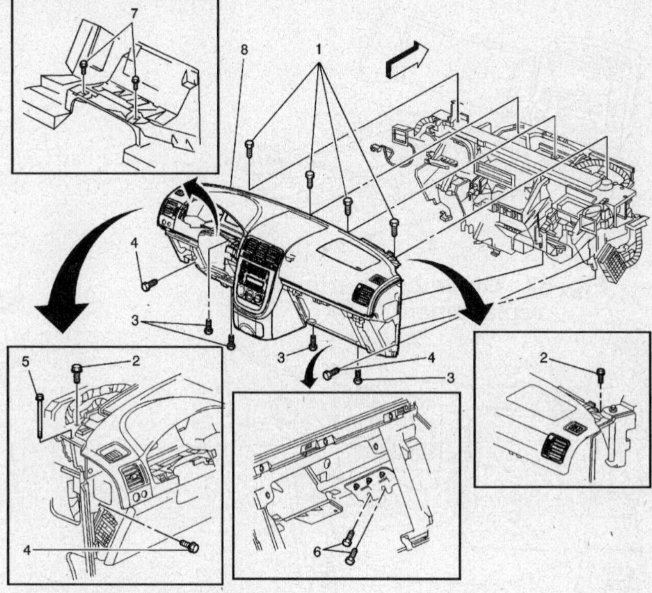

1. Carrier Trim Cover Mounting Screw
2. Carrier Mounting Bolt
3. Carrier Mounting Screw
4. Carrier Mounting Screw
5. Carrier Pivot Mounting Bolt
6. Passenger Air Bag Module
7. Carrier Mounting Screw
8. Instrument Panel

LTV0500000001236

Fig. 50 Instrument panel replacement. Relay, SV6, Terraza & Uplander

disconnect electrical connector.

15. Remove rear window defogger switch and disconnect electrical connector.
16. Remove instrument panel lamp dimmer control.
17. Remove mode control cable at heater case.
18. Disconnect, then remove screws and defroster switch.
19. Remove temperature and fresh/recirc control cables at heater case.
20. Disconnect air conditioning switch electrical connector.
21. Remove instrument cluster trim bezel.
22. Remove control knobs and heater control fascia.
23. Tilt heater control unit and disconnect electrical connectors.
24. **On models equipped with cruise control,** release upper and lower retaining tabs and remove cruise control switch. Disconnect electrical connector.
25. **On all models,** release upper and lower retaining tabs, then remove outside remote control rearview mirror switch.
26. Disconnect tabs and remove rear window wiper/washer switch.
27. Remove instrument panel accessory trim plate switch hole located lefthand of instrument panel.
28. Remove driver knee bolster panels.
29. Rotate steering wheel until steering shaft coupling is in vertical position.
30. Marks steering column shaft and lower steering shaft for installation alignment.
31. Turn ignition to Lock position and rotate steering wheel to lock column.

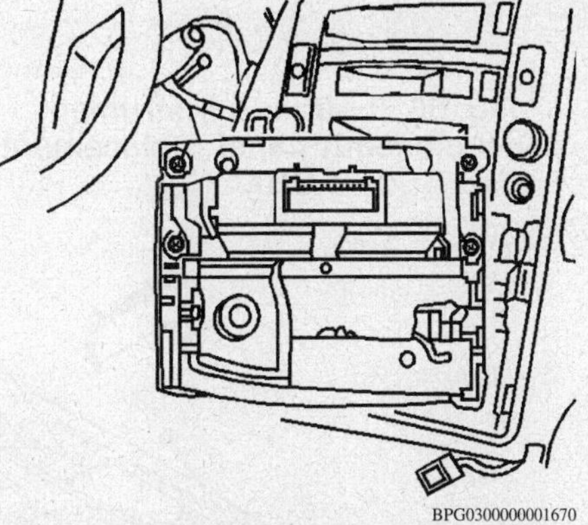

BPG0300000001670

Fig. 51 HVAC control module replacement. SRX

32. Remove driver air bag module as outlined in "Passive Restraint Systems" chapter.
33. Remove mounting nuts and steering wheel using suitable puller tool.
34. Remove steering wheel trim covers.
35. Remove turn signal, headlamp and windshield washer switch with air bag module coil.
36. Remove and disconnect automatic transmission park lock cable.
37. Remove coupling bolt and disconnect steering column shaft.
38. Remove mounting bolts and steering column.
39. Remove hood latch release handle.
40. Remove windshield side garnish moldings.

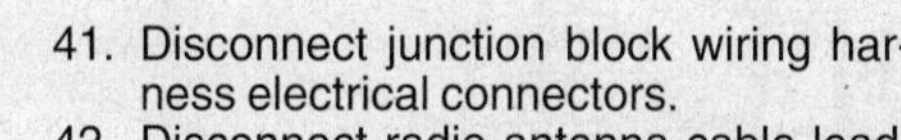

41. Disconnect junction block wiring harness electrical connectors.
42. Disconnect radio antenna cable lead.
43. Remove Connector Position Assurance (CPA) from inflatable restraint Sensing And Diagnostic Module (SDM).
44. Remove instrument panel wiring harness ground wire.
45. Remove ambient light sensor.
46. Remove mounting bolts and instrument panel, **Fig. 61.**
47. Reverse procedure to install.

Vue

1. Remove covers mounting screws and A-pillar trim panel, **Fig. 62.**
2. Remove lower panel/knee bolster mounting screws, **Fig. 63.**
3. Remove lefthand instrument panel end trim panel by pulling outward on rear edge to disconnect clips.
4. Disconnect door open indicator switch electrical connector and remove end panel.
5. Remove righthand instrument panel end trim panel by pulling outward on rear edge to disconnect clips.
6. Open glove compartment and remove two forward facing push pins from end panel.
7. Disconnect door open indicator switch electrical connector and remove panel, **Fig. 64.**
8. Remove glove compartment stops by turning them ¼ turn, **Fig. 65.**

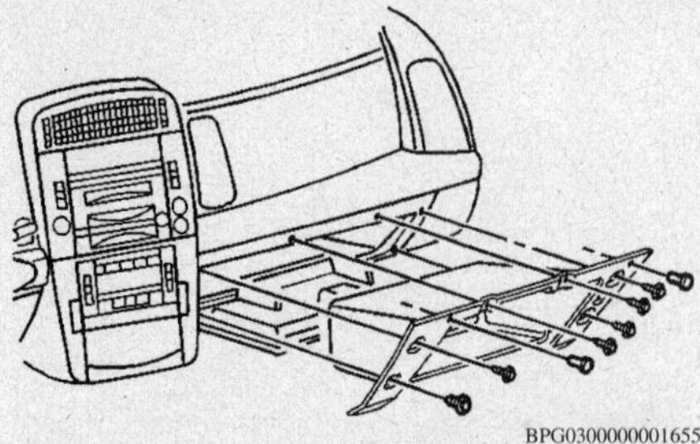

Fig. 52 Glove compartment replacement. SRX

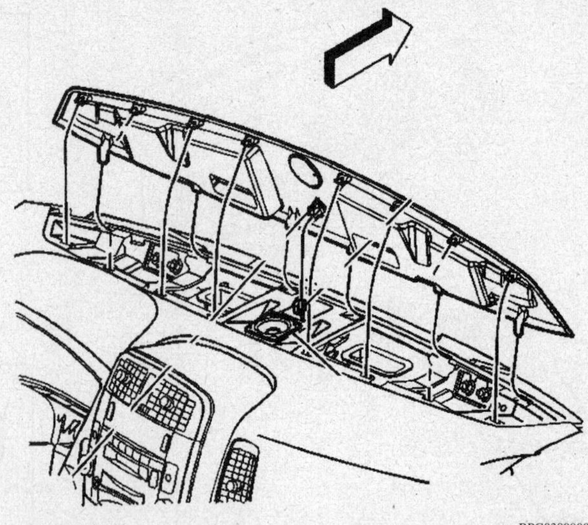

Fig. 53 Defroster grille replacement. SRX

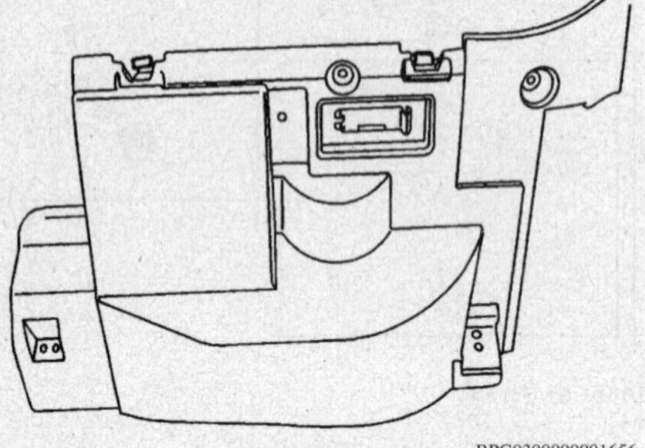

Fig. 54 Righthand instrument panel closeout panel replacement. SRX

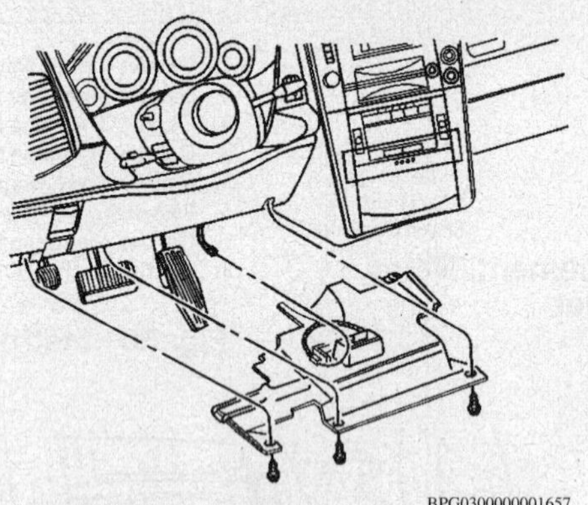

Fig. 55 Lefthand instrument panel closeout panel replacement. SRX

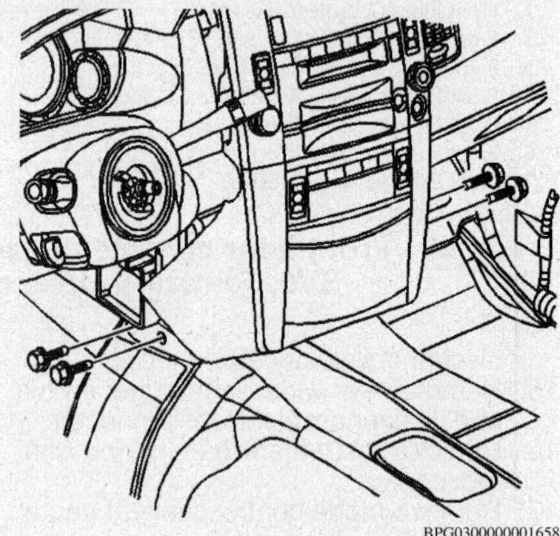

Fig. 56 Lower retainer support bracket. SRX

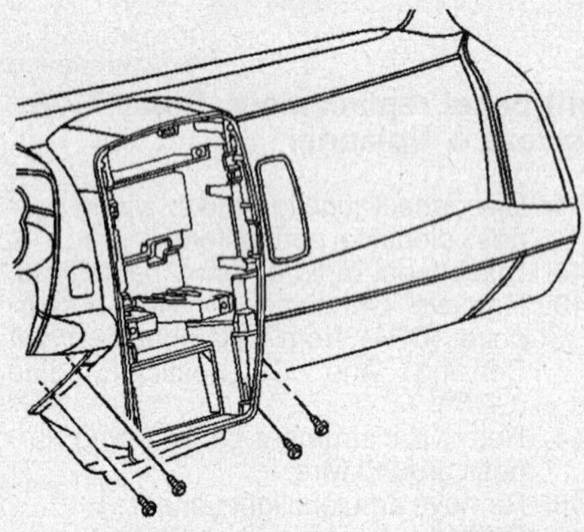

Fig. 57 Lower center stack mounting screws. SRX

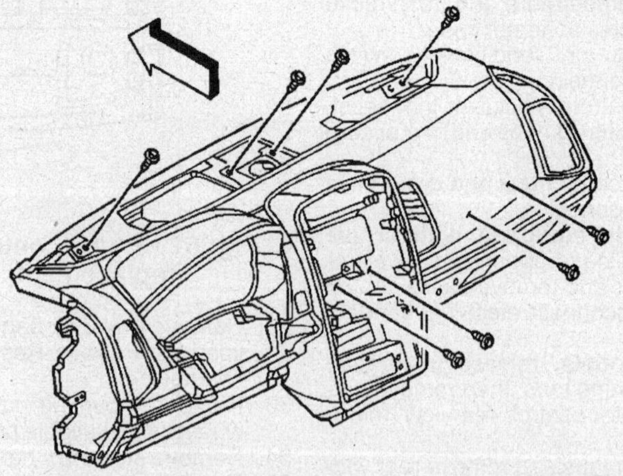

Fig. 58 Instrument panel mounting bolts (Part 1 of 2). SRX

9. Push center portion of pivot pins toward inside and remove glove compartment.
10. Remove shifter bezel and console trim.
11. Remove mounting bolt and lower instrument panel storage compartment.
12. Remove radio/accessory panel mounting screws, pull outward at lower edge and upper edge of panel to disconnect clips.
13. Disconnect temperature cable.
14. Disconnect blower switch electrical connector and 20-way connector, **Fig. 66,** as follows:
15. Disconnect air bag telltale lamp and fog lamp/traction switch, then the dimmer and hazard lamp switches electrical connectors.
16. Remove radio/accessory panel.
17. Remove upper and lower steering column shroud, **Fig. 67.**
18. Remove instrument cluster trim mounting screws.
19. remove instrument cluster trim by disconnecting clips.
20. Remove mounting bolts and righthand air conditioning air deflector.
21. Remove instrument panel mounting bolts, **Fig. 68.**
22. Lifting upward on passenger side and position instrument cluster opening around steering wheel, then remove it through door opening.
23. Reverse procedure to install.

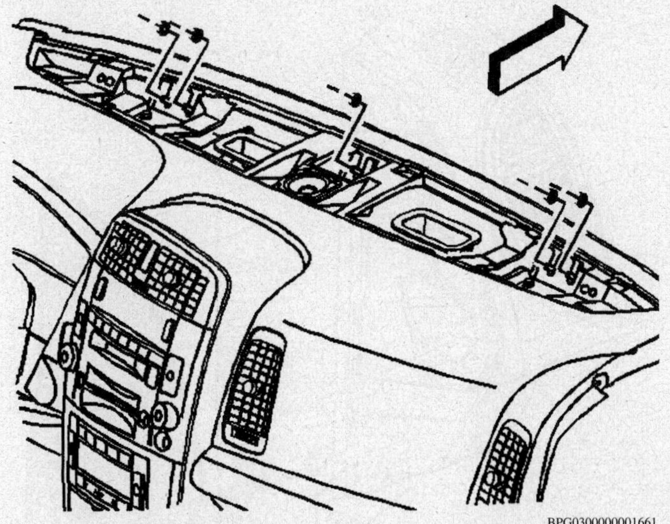

Fig. 58 Instrument panel mounting bolts (Part 2 of 2). SRX

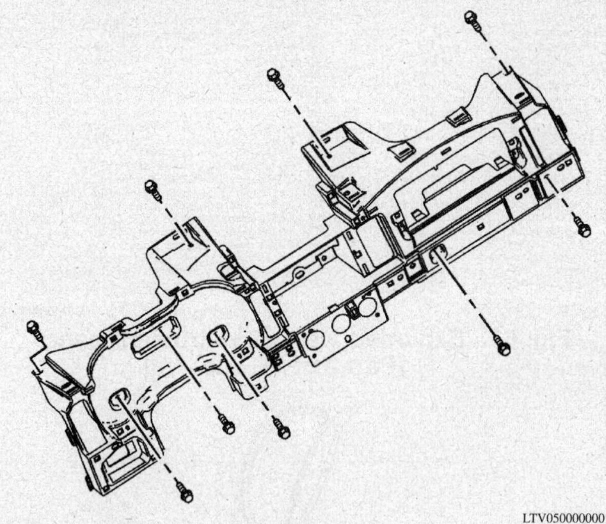

Fig. 59 Instrument panel carrier replacement. SSR

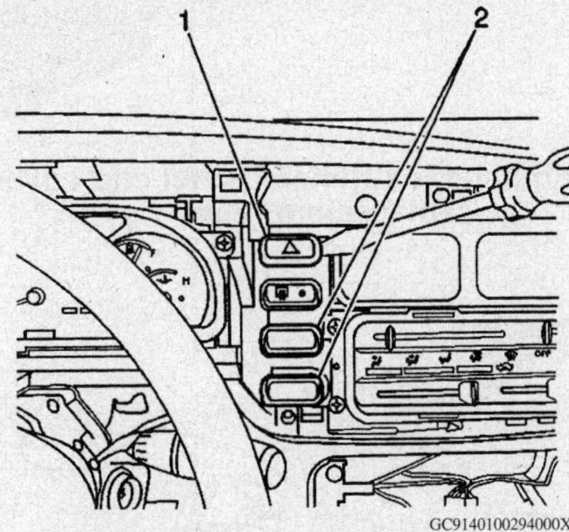

Fig. 60 Glove compartment trim plate replacement. Tracker

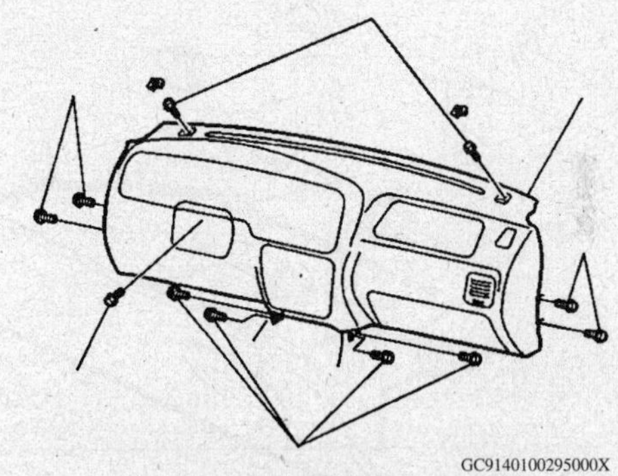

Fig. 61 Instrument panel replacement. Tracker

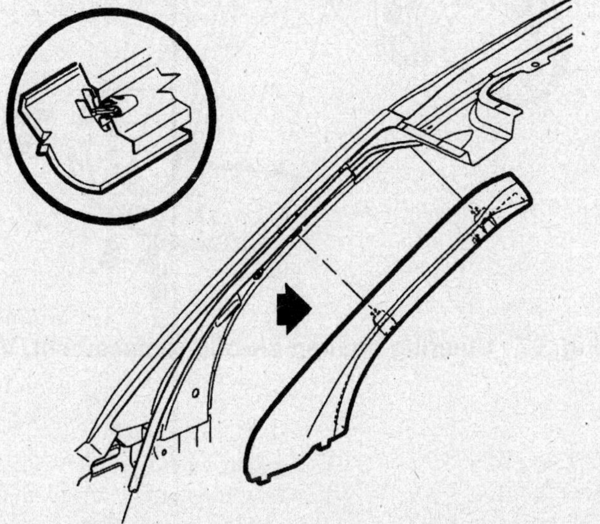

Fig. 62 A-pillar trim replacement. Vue

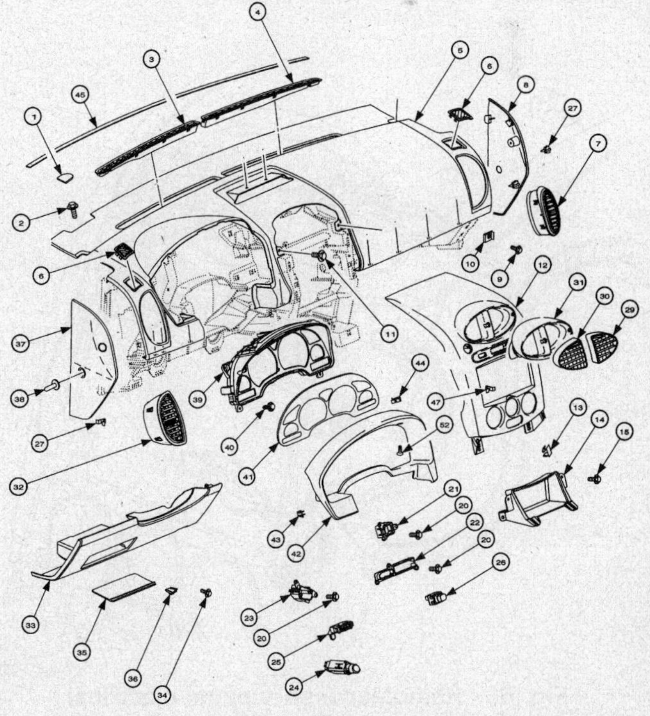

Fig. 63 Exploded view of instrument panel (Part 1 of 2). Vue

1. Bolt cap
2. Upper carrier bolt
3. Lefthand defroster grill
4. Righthand defroster grill
5. Instrument panel assembly
6. Side window defogger outlet grill
7. Righthand A/C outlet deflector
8. Righthand end trim panel
9. A/C outlet deflector retaining bolt
10. A/C outlet deflector blind nut/clip
11. Instrument panel retaining bolt
12. Radio/Accessory panel
13. Radio/Accessory panel bezel clip
14. Instrument panel storage compartment
15. Floor compartment retaining screw
20. Fog lamp bezel retaining screw
21. Fog lamp inner bezel
22. Outer switch bezel
23. Accessory switch inner bezel
24. Hazard lamp switch
25. Instrument panel dimmer switch
26. Fog lamp, traction control switch
27. Side trim retaining clip
29. A/C righthand center deflector
30. A/C lefthand center deflector
31. A/C distribution duct
32. Lefthand A/C outlet deflector
33. Lower instrument panel cover (knee bolster)
34. Knee bolster retaining bolt
35. Instrument panel lower compartment
36. Knee bolster retaining clip
37. Lefthand end trim panel
38. Door open indicator switch
39. Instrument cluster assembly
40. Instrument cluster retaining screw
41. Instrument cluster lens cover
42. Instrument cluster trim bezel
43. Instrument cluster retaining clip
44. Instrument cluster bezel clip
45. Instrument panel upper trim seal
47. Radio/Accessory panel bezel clip
52. Instrument cluster trim bolt

G39140100062020X

Fig. 63 Exploded view of instrument panel (Part 2 of 2). Vue

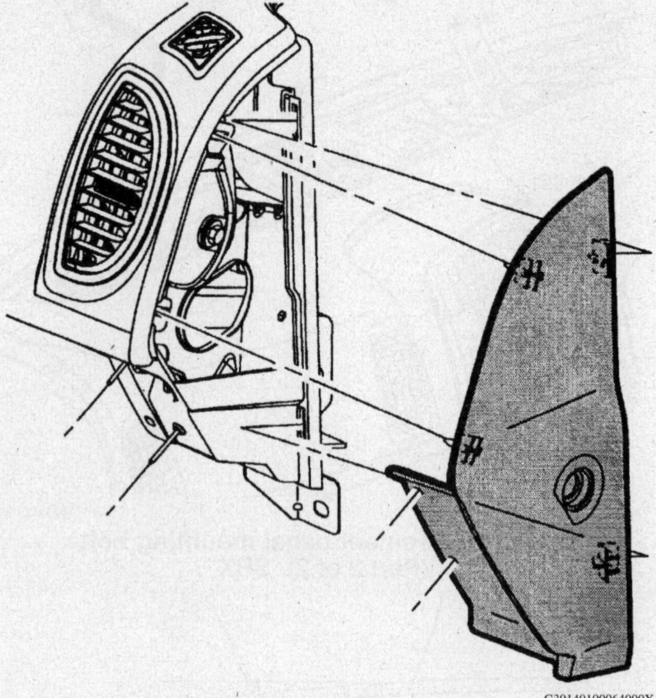

Fig. 64 Righthand instrument panel end cover trim replacement. Vue

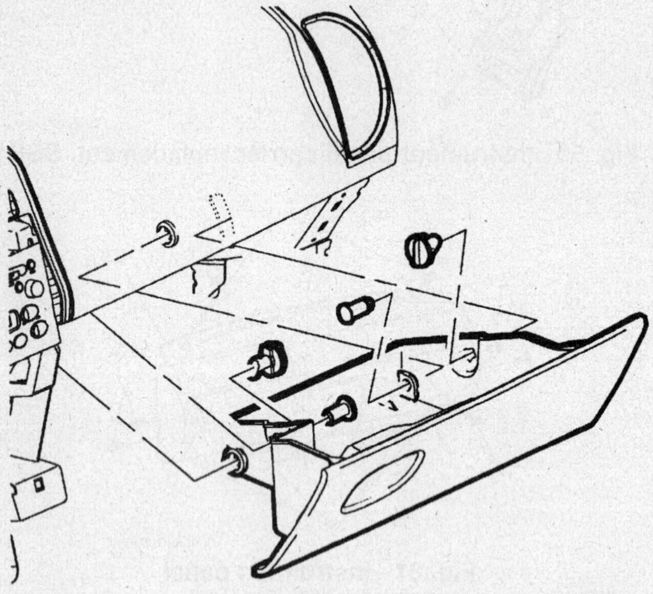

Fig. 65 Glove compartment replacement. Vue

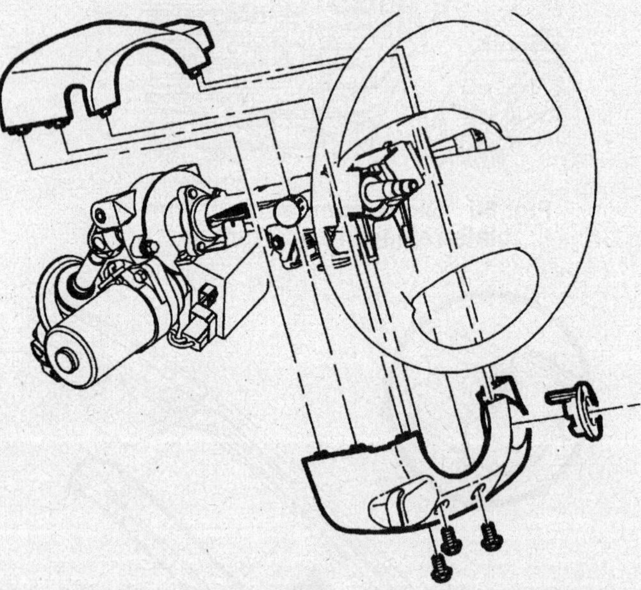

Fig. 67 Steering column shroud replacement. Vue

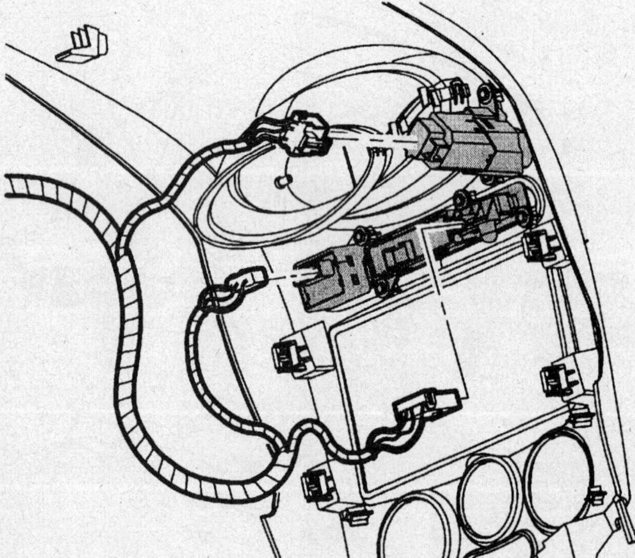

Fig. 66 Radio/accessory panel electrical connections. Vue

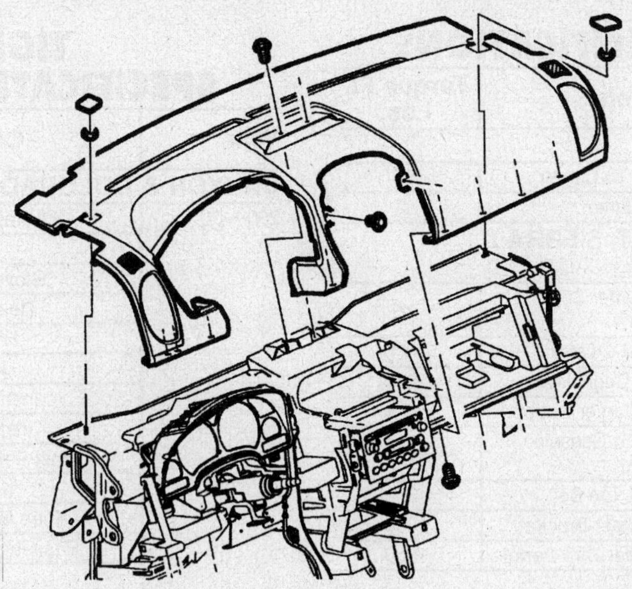

Fig. 68 Instrument panel mounting bolt locations. Vue

TIGHTENING SPECIFICATIONS

Year	Component	Torque Ft. Lbs.
ASTRO & SAFARI		
2002–05	Instrument Panel To Carrier	33
	Steering Column	22
AVALANCHE, ESCALADE EXT, SIERRA & SILVERADO		
2002–06	Instrument Panel Center Support Bracket	18
	Instrument Panel Cluster	18①
	Instrument Panel Cupholder	18①
	Instrument Panel To Carrier Support	80①
	Instrument Panel To Console Extension	18①
	Instrument Panel Top Bolt	37
	Instrument Panel Upper Bracket	18①
	Lower Instrument Panel Trim Panel	18①
AZTEK & RENDEZVOUS		
2002–06	Hood Release Base	18①
	Instrument Panel Cluster Trim Plate	18①
	Glove Compartment Hinge	35①
	Glove Compartment Trim Pad	18①
	Instrument Cluster Pocket Trim Pad	44①
	Trim Pad At Windshield	44①
	Steering Column	18
BLAZER, JIMMY, SONOMA & S10		
2002–05	Accelerator Pedal	35①
	HVAC Control	17①
	Instrument Panel, Lower	11①
	Instrument Panel, Top	17①
	Instrument Panel, Upper	66①
	Instrument Panel Support	66①
	Knee Bolster	84①
	Knee Bolster Bracket	56①
	Speaker Grille	17①
	Steering Column	18①
BRAVADA, ENVOY, RAINIER & TRAILBLAZER		
2002–06	Cowl Side Carrier Bracket	36
	Defogger Duct	22①
	Floor Console Bracket To Floor Panel	18
	Floor Console Bracket Instrument Panel Bracket	88①
	Floor Console & Storage Bin	22①
	Instrument Cluster	22①
	Instrument Panel	22①
	Instrument Panel Support	62①
	Knee Bolster	88①
	Knee Bolster Trim Panel	22①
	Steering Column Support	36
	Trim Plate	22①

TIGHTENING SPECIFICATIONS—Continued

Year	Component	Torque Ft. Lbs.
CANYON & COLORADO		
2004–06	Digital Radio Receiver	27①
	End Cap	27①
	Glove Compartment	27①
	Headlamp Switch	22①
	HVAC Control	18①
	HVAC Duct	27①
	Instrument Cluster	22①
	Instrument Panel	27①
	Instrument Panel, Upper	80①
	Knee Bolster	80①
	Knee Bolster Trim Panel	22①
	Passenger Air Bag Module	80①
	Radio	18①
	Windshield Garnish Molding	79①
ESCALADE, SUBURBAN, TAHOE & YUKON		
2002–06	Instrument Panel Center Support Bracket	18
	Instrument Panel Cluster	18①
	Instrument Panel Cupholder	18①
	Instrument Panel To Carrier Support	80①
	Instrument Panel To Console Extension	18①
	Instrument Panel Top Bolt	37
	Instrument Panel Upper Bracket	18①
	Lower Instrument Panel Trim Panel	18①
EQUINOX & TORRENT		
2005–06	Instrument Cluster	18①
	Instrument Cluster Trim Plate	22①
	Console Trim Panel	22①
	Instrument Panel	89①
	Radio	22①
	Steering Column Filler Panel	22①
	Upper Trim Panel	89①
	Windshield Upper Garnish Molding	18①
EXPRESS & SAVANA		
2002	Instrument Cluster	97①
	Instrument Panel Carrier	37
	Glove Compartment	18
	Instrument Panel Knee Bolster	35①
	Knee Bolster Bracket	89①
	Knee Bolster Trim Panel	11
	Steering Column	35
	Upper Trim Pad	18①
2003–06	Instrument Cluster	18①
	Instrument Panel Carrier	37
	Glove Compartment	18
	Instrument Panel Knee Bolster	31①
	Knee Bolster Brackets	88①
	Knee Bolster Trim Panel	80①
	Steering Column	22
	Steering Column Intermediate Shaft	47①
	Upper Trim Pad	18①

Continued

TIGHTENING SPECIFICATIONS—Continued

Year	Component	Torque Ft. Lbs.
HHR		
2006	Body Control Module	18①
	Glove Compartment Dampener	18①
	HVAC Control Assembly	22①
	Instrument Cluster	18①
	Instrument Panel Center Compartment.	18①
	Instrument Cluster Trim Plate	18①
	Instrument Panel Upper Trim Pad	18①
	Intermediate Shaft Pinch	25
	Knee Bolster	18①
	Knee Bolster Reinforcement	18①
	Radio	18①
	Seat Armrest	80①
	Shift Cable	89①
	Steering Column	18
	Steering Column Trim Cover.	17①
	Steering Wheel	30
	Windshield Garnish Moldings	80①
HUMMER H2		
2003–06	Instrument Panel Carrier, Bolt	37
	Instrument Panel Carrier, Nut	80①
	Intermediate Shaft	37
	Knee Bolster	18①
	Passenger Air Bag Module	89①
	Steering Column	20
	Trim Panel	53①
HUMMER H3		
2006	Cowl Side Carrier Bracket	36
	Defogger Duct	22①
	Floor Console Bracket To Floor Panel	18
	Floor Console Bracket Instrument Panel Bracket	88①
	Floor Console & Storage Bin	22①
	Instrument Cluster	22①
	Instrument Panel	22①
	Instrument Panel Support	62①
	Knee Bolster	88①
	Knee Bolster Trim Panel	22①
	Steering Column Support	36
	Trim Plate	22①

TIGHTENING SPECIFICATIONS—Continued

Year	Component	Torque Ft. Lbs.
RELAY, SV6, TERRAZA & UPLANDER		
2005–06	Carrier, Bolt	89①
	Carrier, Screw	25①
	Carrier Pivot	18
	Carrier Trim	18①
	Driver Information Center Display Switch	18①
	Front Floor Console Bracket	25①
	Front Floor Console Reinforcement.	18①
	Hood Release Handle	18①
	HVAC Control Module	22①
	Instrument Cluster	18①
	Instrument Cluster Trim Plate	18①
	Intermediate Steering Shaft	35
	Passenger Air Bag Module	25①
	Radio	18①
	Steering Column	18
	Steering Wheel	30
SILHOUETTE, VENTURE & MONTANA		
2002–05	Glove Compartment	22①
	Instrument Panel	89①
	Instrument Panel Accessory Trim Plate	18①
	Instrument Panel Cluster	22①
	Instrument Panel Lower Brace	18①
	Knee Bolster	22①
SRX		
2004–06	Center Support Bracket	80①
	Console	18
	Instrument Panel	80①
	Instrument Panel Carrier	18
	Knee Bolster Bracket	80①
	Knee Bolster Trim	18①
	Radio	80①
SSR		
2003–06	Ashtray Door	22①
	Console Trim	22①
	HVAC Control Module	14①
	Instrument Cluster	22①
	Instrument Cluster Trim Panel	22①
	Instrument Panel	22①
	Knee Bolster	22①
	Radio	80①
	Storage Compartment	22①
	Sunshade	18①
	Trim Plate	22①

Continued

TIGHTENING SPECIFICATIONS—Continued

Year	Component	Torque Ft. Lbs.
TRACKER		
2002–04	Automatic Transmission Park Lock Cable To Ignition Switch	20①
	Instrument Panel Handle	15
	Instrument Panel	17
	Passenger Air Bag Module	17
	Steering Column	17
	Steering Shaft Coupling	18

TIGHTENING SPECIFICATIONS—Continued

Year	Component	Torque Ft. Lbs.
VUE		
2002–06	Console To Floor	19①
	Instrument Cluster	18
	Radio/Accessory Panel	22①
	Speaker, Front	20①
	Speaker, Rear	22①
	Steering Column Shroud	13①
	Storage Tray	22①

① — Inch lbs.

STEERING COLUMNS

NOTE: On Air Bag Equipped Models, Refer To "Air Bag System Precautions" Located In The Front Of This Manual For System Disarming & Arming Procedures.

NOTE: Refer To "Computer Relearn Procedures" Located In The Front Of This Manual When Battery Power To The Computer Has Been Interrupted.

INDEX

PRECAUTIONS

Air Bag Systems

Refer to "Air Bag System Precautions" in the front of this manual for system disarming and arming procedures.

Battery Ground Cable

Prior to service, disconnect battery ground cable and isolate as required.

Steering Column Damage

Use care when handling a removed steering column. Such actions as a sharp blow on the end of the steering shaft or shift levers, leaning on the column assembly or dropping of the assembly could loosen or shear the plastic shear joints or rivets used to maintain column rigidity. **Hammering, jolting or bumping the steering shaft and gearshift tube must be avoided during all service operations. If the shear pins are broken, the controlled length of the telescoping design will be altered making these components unfit for further service. When removing the steering wheel, only a steering wheel puller designed for this purpose may be used.**

It is important that only the specified screws, bolts and nuts be used during the assembly procedure and tightened to specifications to ensure proper breaking action of the column under impact. Avoid using excessively long bolts or fasteners as they may prevent a portion of the steering column from collapsing. When replacing fasteners, replace with the same part number or equivalent.

DESCRIPTION

The energy absorbing function of the steering column allows the column to collapse at a controlled rate during a severe collision. The collapsing action reduces the possibility of the steering wheel being driven rearward towards the driver. If the driver is thrown forward into the steering wheel, the column can collapse even further at the same controlled rate, thereby reducing the force of impact.

Several designs of steering column jackets are used: the slip-tube design held together with plastic inserts or rivets that shear upon impact and allow column to collapse, slotted or corrugated mesh design and bellows type shortens in length during impact.

The shift tube is a two piece design held together by injections of plastic that form interconnecting inserts and shear pins. Under impact, there is a gradual paring away of the inserts by the knife-like edge in the adjoining tube section.

The steering shaft is a two-piece assembly. The upper piece is solid and has a double flattened lower end. The lower piece is hollow and formed to fit over the double flattened section of the upper piece. The purpose of the double flattened section is to provide continued steering action even though the shaft is completely collapsed. Upon impact, the shear pins break off and the shaft gradually telescopes against resistance provided by the plastic injections.

The steering column mounting bracket prevents the column from being shifted toward the driver during impact. It uses two breakaway capsules that allow the mounting bracket to slip off its attaching points, allowing the steering column to compress or yield in a forward direction under a severe impact from the driver's end.

When removing or installing the steering wheel, ignition switch, lock cylinder, turn signal switch, neutral start switch, back-up lamp switch or adjusting column shift manual transmission linkage refer to the appropriate vehicle chapter.

TROUBLESHOOTING

Refer to **Figs. 1 through 7** when troubleshooting steering column faults.

STEERING COLUMN

REPLACE

Astro, Express, Safari & Savana

1. Remove driver air bag module as outlined in "Air Bag System" chapter.
2. Remove steering wheel as outlined in "Electrical" section of appropriate vehicle chapter.
3. **On Express & Savana,** proceed as follows:
   a. Remove steering column trim panel.
   b. Remove lower steering column brace to steering column mounting bolts as outlined in **Fig. 8.**
   c. Remove lower steering column brace attaching bolts, then the lower steering column brace.
   d. Remove lower Cardan joint pinch bolt from intermediate shaft. Mark alignment of Cardan joint yoke to steering shaft.
   e. Remove upper steering column bracket.
4. **On Astro and Safari,** proceed as follows:
   a. Remove transmission control linkage from column shaft tube levers, **Fig. 9.**

Step	Action	Yes	No
1	Did you review the Ignition Lock System Description and perform the necessary inspections?	Go to Step 2	
2	Verify that the lock system does not unlock. Does the lock system operate normally?	System OK	Go to Step 3
3	Inspect for an incorrect, worn, or damaged key. Is the key incorrect, worn, or damaged?	Go to Step 8	Go to Step 4
4	Inspect for a faulty lock cylinder. Is the lock cylinder damaged?	Go to Step 9	Go to Step 5
5	Inspect the automatic transmission shift lock control adjustment. Is the automatic transmission shift lock control adjusted incorrectly?	Go to Step 10	Go to Step 6
6	Inspect the lock module assembly for damage. Is the lock module assembly damaged?	Go to Step 11	Go to Step 7
7	Inspect the ignition switch assembly for damage. Is the ignition switch assembly damaged?	Go to Step 12	Go to Step 3
8	Replace the key. Did you complete the repair?	Go to Step 13	--
9	Replace the lock cylinder. Did you complete the repair?	Go to Step 13	--

GC6040100306010X

Fig. 1 Lock system does not unlock (Part 1 of 2)

Step	Action	Yes	No
10	Adjust the automatic transmission shift lock control. Did you complete the repair?	Go to Step 13	--
11	Tighten the lock module assembly. Did you complete the repair?	Go to Step 13	--
12	Replace the ignition switch. Did you complete the repair?	Go to Step 13	--
13	Operate the system in order to verify the repair. Did you correct the condition?	System OK	Go to Step 3

GC6040100306020X

Fig. 1 Lock system does not unlock (Part 2 of 2)

Step	Action	Yes	No
1	Did you review the ignition lock system description and perform the necessary inspections?	Go to Step 2	
2	Verify that the lock system does not lock. Does the lock system operate normally?	System OK	Go to Step 3
3	Inspect for an incorrect, worn, or damaged key. Is the key incorrect, worn, or damaged?	Go to Step 9	Go to Step 4
4	Inspect for a faulty lock cylinder or release button. Is the lock cylinder or release button damaged?	Go to Step 10	Go to Step 5
5	Inspect the shift linkage adjustment. Is the shift linkage adjusted incorrectly?	Go to Step 11	Go to Step 6
6	Inspect the automatic transmission shift lock control for damage. Is the automatic shift lock control damaged?	Go to Step 12	Go to Step 7
7	Inspect the ignition switch for damage. Is the ignition switch damaged?	Go to Step 13	Go to Step 8
8	Inspect the park lock for damage. Is the park lock damaged?	Go to Step 14	Go to Step 3
9	Replace the key. Did you complete the repair?	Go to Step 15	--

GC6040100307010X

Fig. 2 Lock system does not lock (Part 1 of 2)

b. Remove upper Cardan joint pinch bolt from intermediate shaft. Mark alignment of universal yoke to steering shaft.

5. **On all models,** remove capsule nuts and lower steering column.
6. Disconnect steering column electrical connector.
7. Remove shift cable retaining clip and shift cable.
8. Remove steering column assembly, rotating column so shift lever clears cowl opening.
9. Reverse procedure to install.

Avalanche, Escalade, Sierra, Silverado, SSR, Suburban, Tahoe, Yukon & Yukon XL

1. Set front wheels straight ahead and steering wheel to the locked position.
2. Disable air bag as outlined in "Air Bag System" chapter.
3. Remove knee bolster assembly.
4. Disconnect transmission control cable from steering column.
5. Disconnect steering column harness connectors.
6. Remove body control module bracket.
7. Remove bolt from upper to lower shaft connection.
8. Remove nuts from upper and lower support brackets as outlined in **Fig. 10.**
9. Insert anti rotation pin tool No. J 42640, or equivalent into steering column.
10. Lower steering column assembly.
11. Remove column from vehicle.
12. Reverse procedure to install.

Aztek, Montana, Rendezvous, Silhouette & Venture

Steering must be centered straight ahead and ignition switch in Lock position before performing the following procedure. Failure to do so may allow damage to the air bag coil.

Never allow column assembly to hang from one set of mounting brackets or damage to column will occur.

1. Remove steering wheel as outlined in "Electrical" section of appropriate vehicle chapter.
2. Remove lefthand under instrument panel, then the trim panel below steering column.
3. Push down intermediate shaft boot, then remove upper coupling pinch bolt.
4. Disconnect shift cable from ball stud on shifter arm, then unclip and remove cable from column.
5. While supporting column, remove bolts from upper and lower column mounting brackets, **Fig. 11,** then lower column.
6. Loosen retaining screw, then disconnect electrical connectors.
7. Disconnect steering shaft from upper coupling. If required, spread coupling with a suitable pry bar.
8. Remove column from vehicle.
9. Reverse procedure to install.

Equinox & Torrent

1. Set tires in straight ahead position.
2. Remove steering wheel.
3. Remove trim covers.
4. Remove SIR coil.
5. Remove knee bolster screws. Unsnap knee bolster.
6. Remove multi-function levers.

10	Replace the lock cylinder. Did you complete the repair?	Go to Step 15	--
11	Adjust the shift linkage. Did you complete the repair?	Go to Step 15	--
12	Replace the automatic transmission shift lock control. Did you complete the repair?	Go to Step 15	--
13	Replace the ignition switch. Did you complete the repair?	Go to Step 15	--
14	Replace the park lock. Did you complete the repair?	Go to Step 15	--
15	Operate the system in order to verify the repair. Did you correct the condition?	System OK	Go to Step 3

GC6040100307020X

Fig. 2 Lock system does not lock (Part 2 of 2)

Step	Action	Yes	No
1	Did you review the Ignition Lock System Description and perform the necessary inspections?	Go to Step 2	
2	Verify that the lock system sticks in the START position. Does the lock system operate normally?	System OK	Go to Step 3
3	Inspect the lock module assembly for damage. Is the lock module assembly damaged?	Go to Step 6	Go to Step 4
4	Inspect the lock cylinder for damage. Is the lock cylinder damaged?	Go to Step 7	Go to Step 5
5	Inspect the ignition switch for damage. Is the ignition switch damaged?	Go to Step 8	Go to Step 3
6	Tighten the lock module assembly mounting bolts. Did you complete the repair?	Go to Step 9	--
7	Replace the lock cylinder. Did you complete the repair?	Go to Step 9	--
8	Replace the ignition switch. Did you complete the repair?	Go to Step 9	--
9	Operate the system in order to verify the repair. Did you correct the condition?	System OK	Go to Step 3

GC6040100308000X

Fig. 3 Lock system sticks in start

7. Disconnect ignition housing electrical connectors.
8. Disengage retaining tabs on park lock cable assembly. Remove assembly from ignition module.
9. Remove lock housing bolts.
10. Remove lock housing. Slide bracket from column.
11. Disconnect EPS electrical connectors from EPS controller.
12. Remove and discard column to I-shaft bolt. **Rotating steering wheel while it is disconnected from steering gear may cause damage to SIR coil. Place a scribe mark on column to I-shaft connection for reassembly alignment.**
13. Remove lower column pivot bolt.
14. Remove upper column attachment bolts.
15. Remove steering column.
16. Reverse procedure to install.

HHR

1. Place steering wheel in straight forward position.
2. Remove knee bolster.
3. Remove knee bolster reinforcement.
4. Remove steering wheel.
5. Remove column trim covers.
6. Disconnect head lamp turn signal harness connector from SIR coil module assembly.
7. Disconnect wiper washer harness connector from SIR coil module assembly.
8. Disconnect SIR coil harness connector from SIR coil module assembly.
9. Remove SIR coil module assembly.
10. Disconnect ignition lock cylinder harness connector.
11. Disconnect ignition switch harness connector.
12. Place scribe marks on intermediate shaft to steering column, for use during assembly.
13. Remove intermediate shaft pinch bolt at steering column and discard.
14. Slide intermediate shaft off steering column.
15. Disconnect EPS control module power feed harness connector.
16. Disconnect EPS control module small harness connector.
17. Remove steering column pivot bolt.
18. Remove steering column mounting bolts.
19. Remove column from vehicle and place on a bench.
20. Remove ignition lock cylinder case from steering column.
21. Reverse procedure to install.

Hummer H2

Once steering column is removed from vehicle, column is extremely susceptible to damage. Dropping column assembly on end could collapse steering shaft or loosen plastic injections, which maintain column rigidity. Leaning on column assembly could cause jacket to bend or deform. Any of above damage could impair columns collapsible design. Do not hammer end of shaft, because hammering could loosen plastic injections, which maintain column rigidity.

Front wheels of vehicle must be maintained in straight ahead position and steering column must be in lock position before disconnecting steering column or intermediate shaft. Failure to follow these procedures will cause improper alignment of some components during installation and result in damage to SIR coil assembly.

1. Disable SIR system as outlined in "Precautions."
2. Lock steering column through access hole in lower steering column trim cover using J 42640, or equivalent.
3. Remove knee bolster deflector.
4. Remove transfer case electronic control module.
5. Disconnect HVAC duct and move out of way.
6. Remove transfer case electronic control module bracket bolts and lower bracket out of way.
7. Disconnect steering column electrical connector.
8. Disconnect wiring harness connector from back of fuse block.
9. Remove intermediate shaft bolt from steering column.
10. Remove steering column mounting nuts.
11. Remove steering column from vehicle.
12. Reverse procedure to install.

Hummer H3

Once steering column is removed from vehicle, column is extremely susceptible to damage. Dropping column assembly on end could collapse steering shaft or loosen plastic injections, which maintain column rigidity. Leaning on column assembly could cause jacket to bend or deform. Any of above damage could impair columns collapsible design. Do not hammer end of shaft, because hammering could loosen plastic injections, which maintain column rigidity.

Front wheels of vehicle must be maintained in straight ahead position and steering column must be in lock position before disconnecting steering column or intermediate shaft. Failure to follow these procedures will cause improper alignment of some components during installation and result in damage to SIR coil assembly.

1. Disable SIR system as outlined in "Precautions."
2. Lock steering column through access

Step	Action	Yes	No
1	Did you review the Ignition Lock System Description and perform the necessary inspections?	Go to Step 2	
2	Verify that the key cannot be removed from the lock cylinder in the OFF position. Does the lock system operate normally?	System OK	Go to Step 3
3	Inspect for incorrect, worn, or damaged key. Is the key incorrect, worn, or damaged?	Go to Step 5	Go to Step 4
4	Inspect for a faulty lock cylinder or release button. Is the lock cylinder or release button damaged?	Go to Step 6	Go to Step 3
5	Replace the key. Did you complete the repair?	Go to Step 7	--
6	Replace the lock cylinder. Did you complete the repair?	Go to Step 7	--
7	Operate the system in order to verify the repair. Did you correct the condition?	System OK	Go to Step 3

GC6040100309000X

Fig. 4 Key cannot be removed in the off lock position

Step	Action	Yes	No
1	Did you review the Ignition Lock System Description and perform the necessary inspections?	Go to Step 2	
2	Verify that the lock system has a high lock effort. Does the lock system operate normally?	System OK	Go to Step 3
3	Inspect for an incorrect, worn, or damaged key. Is the key incorrect, worn, or damaged?	Go to Step 7	Go to Step 4
4	Inspect for a faulty lock cylinder. Is the lock cylinder damaged?	Go to Step 8	Go to Step 5
5	Inspect the lock module assembly for damage. Is the lock module assembly damaged?	Go to Step 9	Go to Step 6
6	Inspect the ignition switch assembly for damage. Is the ignition switch assembly damaged?	Go to Step 10	Go to Step 7
7	Replace the key. Did you complete the repair?	Go to Step 11	--
8	Replace the lock cylinder. Did you complete the repair?	Go to Step 11	--
9	Tighten the lock module assembly. Did you complete the repair?	Go to Step 11	--
10	Replace the ignition switch. Did you complete the repair?	Go to Step 11	--
11	Operate the system in order to verify the repair. Did you correct the condition?	System OK	Go to Step 3

GC6040100310000X

Fig. 5 High lock effort

hole in lower steering column trim cover using J 42640, or equivalent.
3. Remove steering wheel.
4. Remove knee bolster.
5. Disconnect steering column electrical connector.
6. Remove upper intermediate shaft to steering column retaining bolt.
7. Remove steering column mounting bolts.
8. Remove steering column from vehicle.
9. Reverse procedure to install.

Relay, SV6, Terraza & Uplander

1. Disable SIR system.
2. Install tool No. J 42640, or equivalent, to steering column. **Wheels of vehicle must be straight ahead and steering column in lock position before disconnecting steering column or intermediate shaft from steering gear. Failure to do so will cause SIR coil assembly to become uncentered, which may cause damage to coil assembly.**
3. Remove steering wheel.
4. Remove lefthand knee bolster.
5. Remove intermediate steering shaft from steering column.
6. Disconnect transaxle shift cable from linear shift assembly ball stud.
7. Remove transaxle shift cable retaining clip.
8. Remove transaxle shift cable from shift cable bracket.
9. Disconnect steering column electrical connectors.
10. Remove steering column bolts.
11. Remove steering column nuts.
12. Remove steering column. **Once steering column is removed from car, column is extremely susceptible to damage. Dropping column on its end could collapse steering shaft or loosen plastic injections which maintain column rigidity. Leaning on column could cause jacket to bend or deform. Any of above damage could impair column's collapsible design. If it is required to remove steering wheel, use only specified steering wheel puller. Under no conditions should end of shaft be hammered upon as hammering could loosen plastic injections which maintain column rigidity.**
13. Reverse procedure to install.

SRX

Once steering column is removed from vehicle, column is extremely susceptible to damage. Dropping column assembly on end could collapse steering shaft or loosen plastic injections, which maintain column rigidity. Leaning on column assembly could cause jacket to bend or deform. Any of above damage could impair columns collapsible design. Do not hammer on end of shaft, because hammering could loosen plastic injections, which maintain column rigidity.

Front wheels of vehicle must be maintained in straight ahead position and steering column must be in lock position before disconnecting steering column or intermediate shaft. Failure to follow these procedures will cause improper alignment of some components during installation and result in damage to SIR coil assembly.

1. Disable SIR system.
2. Turn steering wheel so that front wheels are pointing straight ahead.
3. Turn ignition lock cylinder to lock position and remove key.
4. Insert tool No. J 42640, or equivalent, into steering column access hole in order to lock steering column. This will maintain correct orientation.
5. Raise and support vehicle.
6. Remove retaining bolt that secures intermediate upper to intermediate shaft center.
7. Lower vehicle.
8. Remove knee bolster.
9. Remove steering column trim covers.
10. Disconnect steering column electrical connectors.
11. Support steering column. **Stabilize studs in order to remove nuts securing steering column to instrument panel.**
12. Remove steering column mounting nuts.
13. Remove steering column.
14. Remove retaining bolt that secures upper intermediate shaft to steering column.
15. Remove upper intermediate shaft from steering column.
16. Reverse procedure to install.

Step	Action	Yes	No
1	Did you review the Steering Wheel and Column Description and perform the necessary inspections?	Go to Step 2	
2	Verify that noise is present in the steering column during operation. Is noise present in the steering column during operation?	Go to Step 3	System OK
3	Inspect the steering column components for looseness. Is the steering column components loose?	Go to Step 10	Go to Step 4
4	Inspect the SIR/SRS coil for noise. Is the SIR/SRS coil noisy?	Go to Step 11	Go to Step 5
5	Inspect the horn contact ring for lubrication. Is the horn contact ring lubricated?	Go to Step 12	Go to Step 6
6	Inspect the lock plate retaining ring for the correct installation. Is the lock plate retaining ring installed properly?	Go to Step 13	Go to Step 7
7	Inspect the shaft bearing for the following conditions: • Damage • Lubrication • Wear • Proper seating Are the bearings in need of repair or replacement?	Go to Step 14	Go to Step 8
8	Inspect the spherical joint for lubrication. Is the spherical joint lubricated?	Go to Step 15	Go to Step 9

GC6040100311010X

Fig. 6 Noise in steering column (Part 1 of 2)

Step	Action	Yes	No
9	Inspect the steering column coupling for looseness. Is the steering column coupling loose?	Go to Step 16	Go to Step 3
10	Tighten the steering column components to specifications. Did you complete the repair?	Go to Step 17	--
11	Replace the SIR coil. Did you complete the repair?	Go to Step 17	--
12	Lubricate the horn contact ring. Did you complete the repair?	Go to Step 17	--
13	Install the lock plate retaining ring properly. Did you complete the repair?	Go to Step 17	--
14	Repair the shaft bearings as necessary. Did you complete the repair?	Go to Step 17	--
15	Lubricate the spherical joints. Did you complete the repair?	Go to Step 17	--
16	Tighten the steering column coupling to specifications. Did you complete the repair?	Go to Step 17	--
17	Operate the system in order to verify the repair. Did you correct the condition?	System OK	Go to Step 3

GC6040100311020X

Fig. 6 Noise in steering column (Part 2 of 2)

S & T Series

REMOVAL

1. Set front wheels in straight ahead position.
2. Disconnect transmission control cable from column shift lever.
3. Remove steering column trim panels.
4. Remove steering wheel as outlined in "Steering Wheel, Replace" in "Electrical" section of chassis chapter.
5. Remove steering column floor/toe plate.
6. Remove support bracket nuts, then lower steering column as outlined in **Fig. 12.**
7. Disconnect steering column electrical connectors.
8. Remove steering column assembly by rotating column so shift lever clears instrument panel opening.

INSTALLATION

1. Lower end of steering column through instrument panel opening, then connect steering column electrical connectors.
2. Raise steering column into place.
3. Connect shift indicator cable to shift bowl.
4. Install two upper column and two lower column nuts.
5. Install steering column floor/toe plate bolts/screws.
6. Install transmission control cable.
7. Install steering wheel as outlined in "Steering Wheel, Replace."

Tracker

1. Remove steering wheel as outlined in "Electrical" section of appropriate vehicle chapter.
   a. Remove upper and lower column covers, then the access cover.
   b. Disconnect lead wire from turn signal/dimmer switch.
   c. Remove assembly screws, then the signal/dimmer assembly.
2. Disconnect lead wires from ignition switch at connector.
3. Remove column assembly lower bolts.
4. **On models equipped with automatic transmission,** remove transmission lockout cable.
5. **On all models,** remove column upper bolts, then remove column assembly.
6. Reverse procedure to install.

Vue

1. Set tires in a straight ahead position, then center steering wheel.
2. Remove steering wheel as outlined in "Electrical" section of chassis chapter.
3. Remove steering column covers, then disconnect electrical connectors from coil module.
4. Remove coil assembly screw, then using a small flat-bladed tool pry retaining tabs away and slide coil assembly off steering column.
5. Remove lock cylinder bezel, then the upper and lower shrouds.
6. Depress tabs on multi-function levers, then remove multi-function levers.
7. Disconnect electrical housing electrical connectors.
8. Disengage retaining tabs on park lock cable assembly, then remove assembly from ignition module.
9. Disconnect ignition switch electrical connector, then remove lock housing bolts.
10. Remove lock housing, then slide bracket from column.
11. Remove knee bolster, then disconnect EPS electrical connectors. **Rotating steering wheel while it is disconnected from steering gear may cause damage to coil.**
12. Remove lower column mounting bolt, index mark column to I-shaft connection for reassembly alignment.
13. Remove and discard column to I-shaft bolt.
14. Remove upper column attachment bolts, then the steering column.
15. Reverse procedure to install.

STEERING COLUMN SERVICE

Standard & Tilt Steering Column

When servicing steering columns, refer to **Figs. 13 through 35.**

Step	Action	Yes	No
1	Did you review the Steering Wheel and Column - Tilt Description and Operation and perform the necessary inspections?	Go to Step 2	
2	Verify that the steering column tilt function is inoperative. Does the steering column tilt function operate normally?	System OK	Go to Step 3
3	Verify that the shoe is not seized on the pivot pin. Is the shoe seized on the pivot pin?	Go to Step 9	Go to Step 4
4	Inspect the shoe grooves for dirt, burrs, or rust. Are the shoe grooves free of dirt, burrs, and rust?	Go to Step 9	Go to Step 5
5	Inspect weak or broken shoe lock spring. Is the shoe lock spring weak or broken?	Go to Step 9	Go to Step 6
6	Inspect the pivot pins for binding. Are the pivot pins binding?	Go to Step 10	Go to Step 7
7	Inspect for a weak or broken wheel tilt spring. Is the wheel tilt spring weak or broken?	Go to Step 11	Go to Step 8
8	Inspect the steering column wiring harness for tightness. Is the steering column wiring harness too tight?	Go to Step 12	Go to Step 3
9	Replace the tilt head. Is the repair complete?	Go to Step 13	--
10	Replace the pivot pins. . Is the repair complete?	Go to Step 13	--
11	Replace the tilt spring. Is the repair complete?	Go to Step 13	--

GC6040100312010X

Fig. 7 Steering column tilt function inoperative (Part 1 of 2)

Step	Action	Yes	No
12	Reroute the steering column wiring harness to the correct location. Is the steering column wiring harness routed properly?	Go to Step 13	--
13	Operate the steering column tilt function in order to verify the repair. Did you correct the condition?	System OK	Go to Step 3

GC6040100312020X

Fig. 7 Steering column tilt function inoperative (Part 2 of 2)

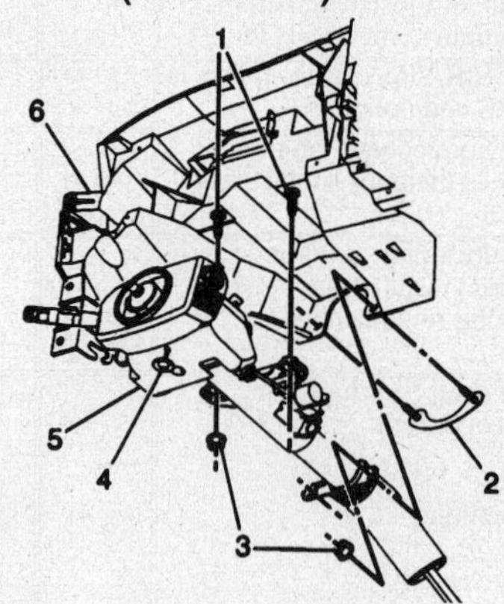

(1) Stud, Instrument Panel Carrier
(2) Plate, Steering Column Mounting
(3) Nut, Steering Column Retaining 47 N.m (35 lb. ft.)
(4) Pin, Anti Rotation
(5) Column, Steering
(6) Carrier, Instrument Panel

GC6049600218000X

Fig. 8 Steering column removal. Express & Savana

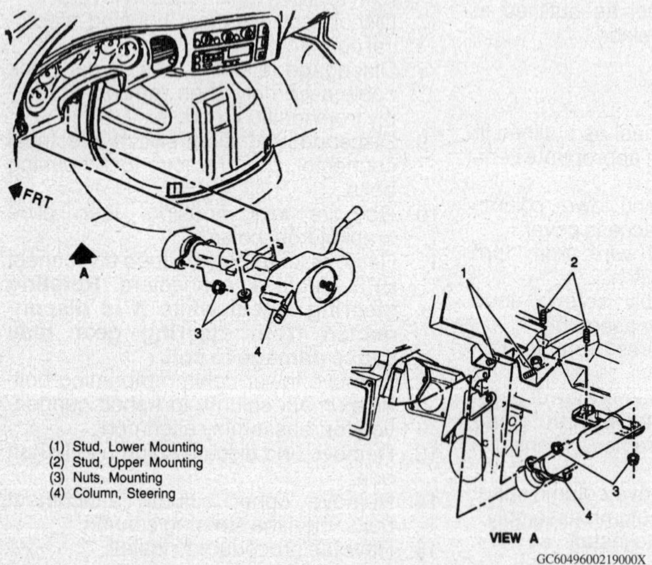

GC6049600219000X

Fig. 9 Steering column removal. Astro & Safari

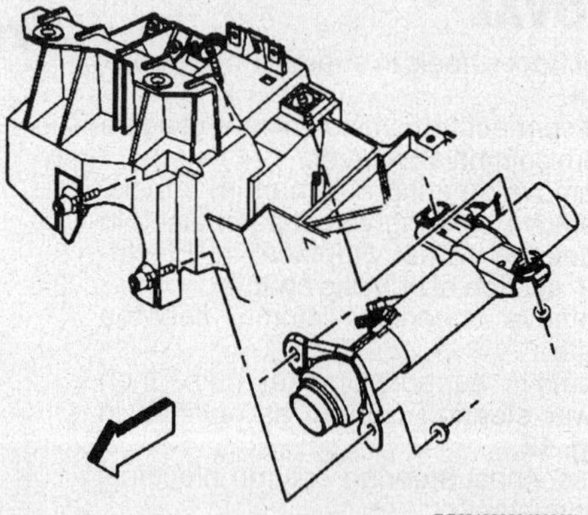

GC6049900260000X

Fig. 10 Steering column removal. Avalanche, Escalade, Sierra, Silverado, Suburban, Tahoe, Yukon & Yukon XL

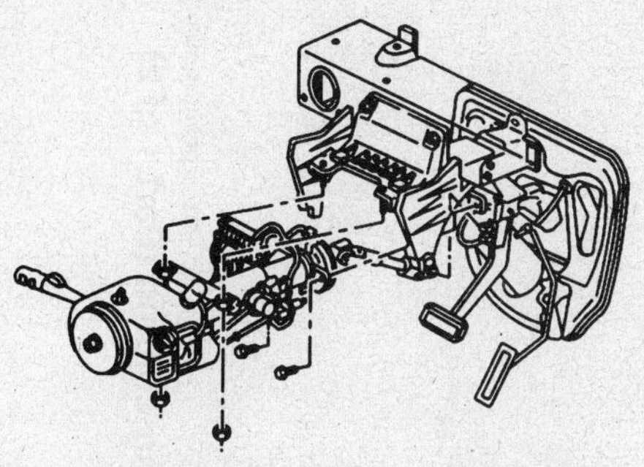

Fig. 11 Steering column replacement. Aztek, Montana, Rendezvous, Silhouette & Venture

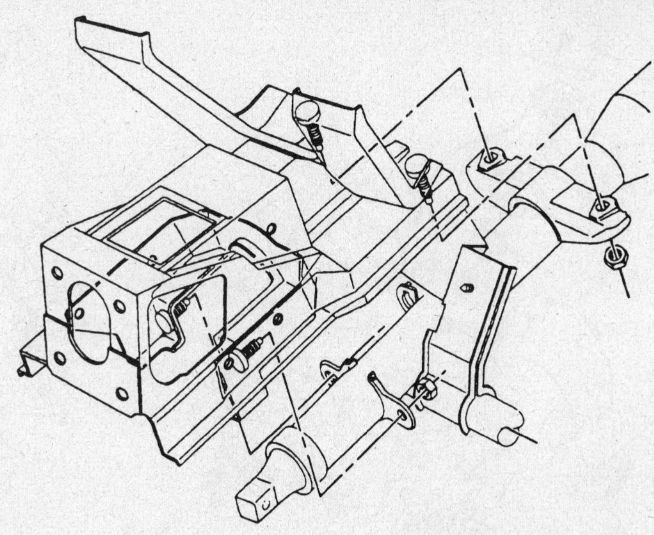

Fig. 12 Steering column to bracket assembly. S & T Series

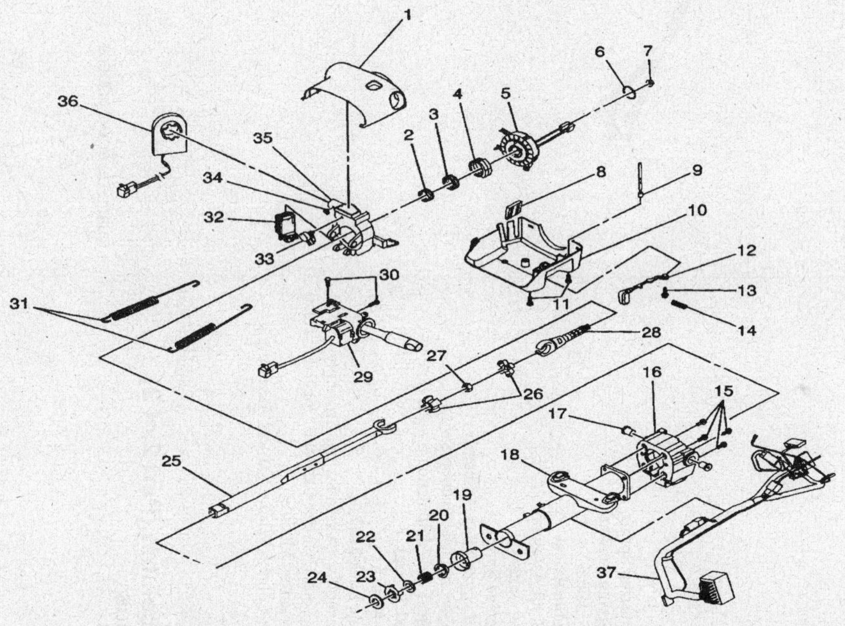

Fig. 13 Exploded view of steering column (Part 1 of 2). Aztek & Rendezvous

(1) Upper Trim Cover
(2) Upper Bearing
(3) Upper Bearing Spring
(4) Turn Signal Cancel Cam
(5) Inflatable Restraint Steering Wheel Module Coil
(6) Bearing Retainer
(7) Steering Wheel Nut
(8) Trim Cover Protector
(9) Anti-Rotation Pin
(10) Lower Trim Cover
(11) Lower Trim Cover Screws
(12) Tilt Lever
(13) Tilt Lever Bolt
(14) Tilt Lever Spring
(15) Lower Tilt Head Mounting Bolts
(16) Lower Tilt Head
(17) Tilt Head Pivots
(18) Steering Column Jacket Assembly
(19) Adapter and Bearing Assembly
(20) Lower Bearing Seat
(21) Lower Bearing Spring
(22) Lower Spring Retainer
(23) Sensor Retainer
(24) Steering Shaft Seal
(25) Lower Shaft Assembly
(26) Centering Sphere
(27) Joint Preload Spring
(28) Race and Upper Shaft Assembly
(29) Turn Signal and Malfunction Switch
(30) Turn Signal and Malfunction Switch Screws
(31) Tilt Head Springs
(32) Ignition Switch
(33) Electronic Lock Module
(34) Ignition and Key Alarm Switch Assembly
(35) Ignition Lock Cylinder Case and Upper Tilt Head
(36) Theft Deterrent Module
(37) Steering Column Wiring Harness Assembly

GC6040100305020X

Fig. 13 Exploded view of steering column (Part 2 of 2). Aztek & Rendezvous

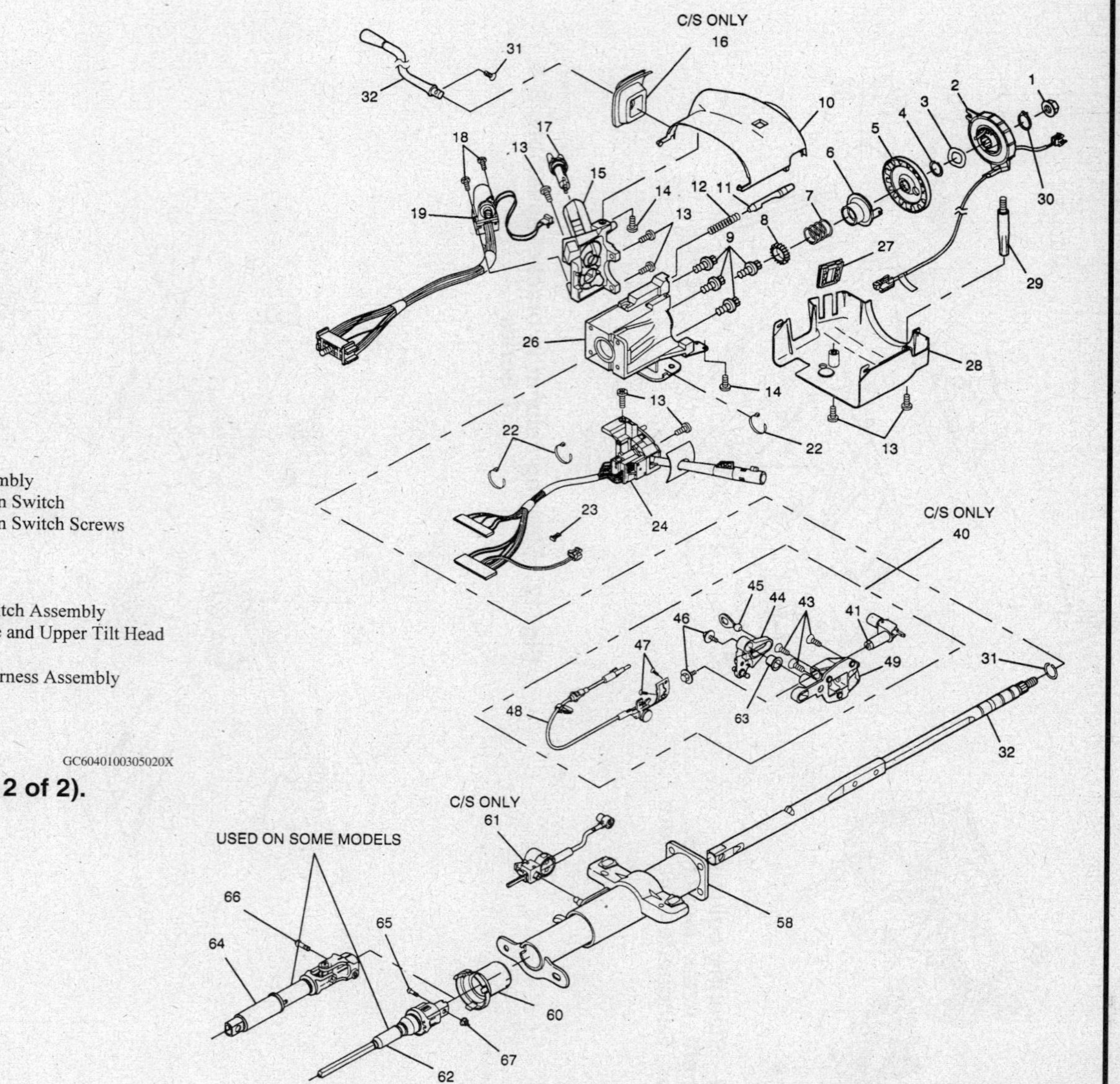

Fig. 14 Exploded view of standard steering column (Part 1 of 2). S & T Series

1- NUT, HEXAGON LOCKING (M14x1.5)
2- COIL ASM, SIR
3- WASHER, WAVE
4- RING, RETAINING
5- SHIELD ASM, SHAFT LOCK
6- CAM ASM, T/SIG CANCEL
7- SPRING, UPPER BEARING
8- WASHER, THRUST
9- SCREW, TORX HEAD
10- SHROUD, UPPER
11- BOLT ASM, LOCK
12- SPRING, LOCK BOLT
13- SCREW, PAN HD TAPPING
14- SCREW, TORX HEAD
15- MODULE ASM, LOCK
16- SEAL, SHIFT LEVER
17- LOCK CYL SET, STRG COLUMN
18- SCREW, TAPPING
19- SWITCH ASM, IGN & KEY ALARM
22- STRAP, WIRE HARNESS
23- CONNECTOR, AXIAL POSN ASSUR
24- SWITCH ASM, T/S & MULTIFUNC
26- HOUSING ASM, STRG COLUMN
27- PROTECTOR, SHROUD
28- SHROUD, LOWER
29- STUD, SHROUD MOUNTING
30- RING, RETAINING
31- RING, RETAINING
32- SHAFT ASM, STEERING
33- SCREW, SHIFT LEVER
34- LEVER ASM, AUTO TRANS CONTROL
40- SHIFT ASM, LINEAR
41- CLEVIS, SHIFT LEVER
43- SCREW, FLAT HD 6-LOBED SOC TAP
44- CAM ASM, CABLE SHIFT
45- ACTUATOR ASM, BALL &
46- BOLT, HEX FLANGE HEAD
47- SCREW, OVAL HD 6-LOBED SOC TAP
48- CABLE ASM, PARK LOCK
49- BRACKET, G/S LEVER ASM SUPPORT
58- JACKET ASM, STRG COL
60- BEARING ASM, ADAPTER &
61- ACTUATOR, ELECTRICAL (BTSI)
62- SHAFT ASM, CPLG & STRG
63- BUSHING, CAM
64- SHAFT ASM, YOKE & INTER STRG
65- BOLT, ROUND HD LOCKING
66- BOLT, PINCH
67- NUT, HEX HD

GC6049600180020X

Fig. 14 Exploded view of standard steering column (Part 2 of 2). S & T Series

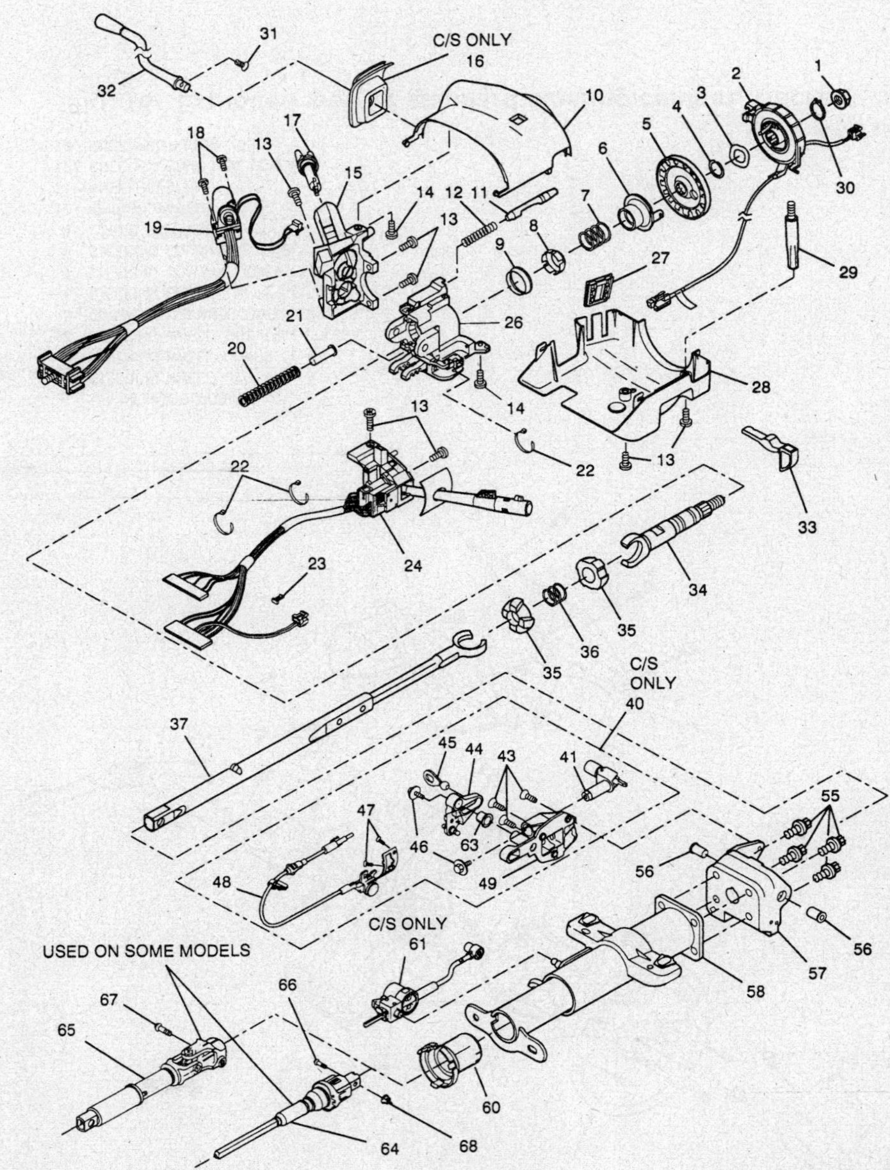

Fig. 15 Exploded view of tilt steering column (Part 1 of 2). S & T Series

1-NUT, HEXAGON LOCKING (M14x1.5)
2-COIL ASM, SIR
3-WASHER, WAVE
4-RING, RETAINING
5-SHIELD ASM, SHAFT LOCK
6-CAM ASM, T/SIG CANCEL
7-SPRING, UPPER BEARING
8-SEAT, UPPER BEARING INNER RACE
9-RACE, INNER
10-SHROUD, UPPER
11-BOLT ASM, LOCK
12-SPRING, LOCK BOLT
13-SCREW, PAN HD TAPPING
14-SCREW, TORX HEAD
15-ASM, LOCK MODULE
16-SEAL, SHIFT LEVER
17-LOCK CYL SET, STRG COLUMN
18-SCREW, TAPPING
19-SWITCH ASM, IGN & KEY ALARM
20-SPRING, TILT
21-GUIDE, SPRING
22-STRAP, WIRE HARNESS
23-CONNECTOR, AXIAL POSN ASSUR
24-SWITCH ASM, T/S & MULTIFUNCTION
26-TILT HEAD ASM, STRG COL
27-PROTECTOR, SHROUD
28-SHROUD, LOWER
29-STUD, SHROUD MOUNTING
30-RING, RETAINING
31- SCREW, SHIFT LEVER
32-LEVER ASM, A/TRNS CONTROL
33- LEVER ASM, TILT
34-SHAFT ASM, RACE & UPPER
35-SPHERE, CENTERING
36-SPRING, JOINT PRELOAD
37-SHAFT ASM, LOWER STRG
40-SHIFT ASM, LINEAR
41-CLEVIS, SHIFT LEVER
43-SCREW, FLAT HD 6-LOBED SOC TAP
44-CAM ASM, CABLE SHIFT
45-ACTUATOR ASM, BALL &
46-BOLT, HEX FLANGE HEAD
47-SCREW, OVAL HD 6-LOBED SOC TAP
48-CABLE ASM, PARK LOCK
49-BRACKET, G/S LEVER ASM SUPPORT
55-SCREW, TORX HEAD
56-PIN, PIVOT
57-SUPPORT ASM, STRG COL
58-JACKET ASM, STRG COL
60-BEARING ASM, ADAPTER &
61-ACTUATOR, ELECTRICAL (BTSI)
63-BUSHING, CAM
64-SHAFT ASM, CPLG & STRG
65-SHAFT ASM, YOKE & INTER STRG
66-BOLT, ROUND HD LOCKING
67-BOLT, PINCH
68-NUT, HEX HD

GC6049600179020X

Fig. 15 Exploded view of tilt steering column (Part 2 of 2). S & T Series

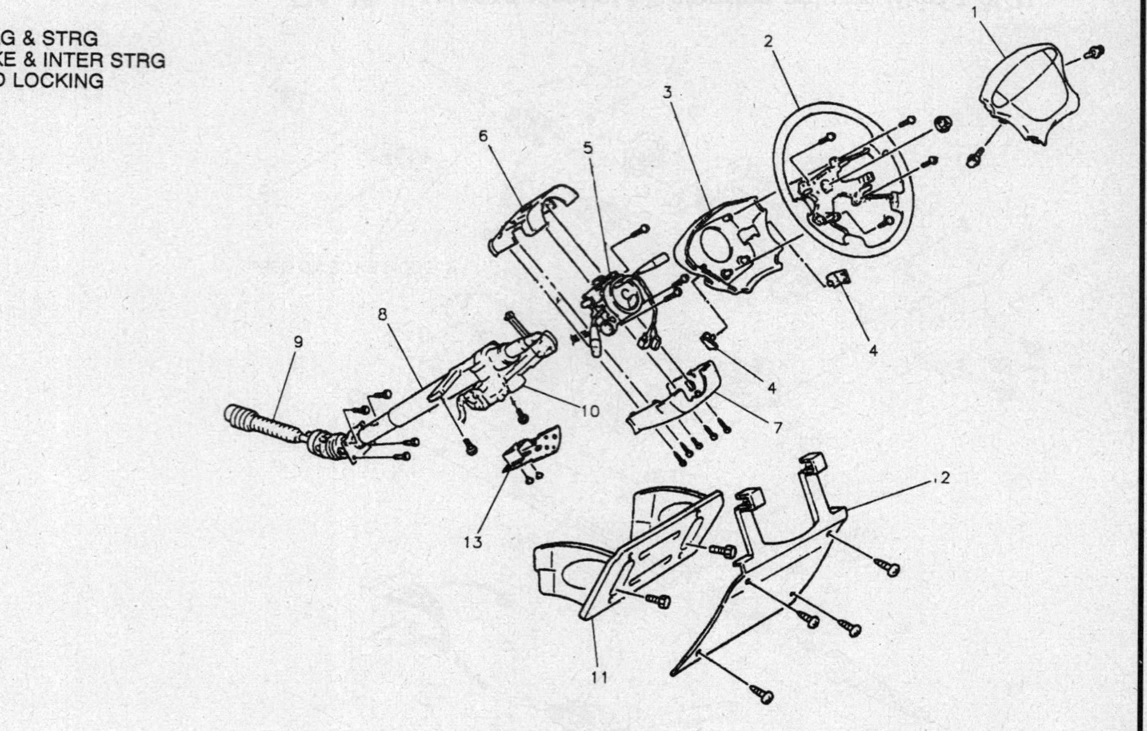

1 SIR INFLATOR MODULE
2 STEERING WHEEL
3 STEERING WHEEL LOWER COVER
4 STEERING WHEEL SIDE TRIM COVERS
5 CONTACT COIL AND COMBINATION SWITCH ASSEMBLY
6 STEERING COLUMN UPPER COVER
7 STEERING COLUMN LOWER COVER
8 STEERING COLUMN ASSEMBLY
9 LOWER STEERING SHAFT
10 IGNITION SWITCH
11 KNEE BOLSTER
12 KNEE BOLSTER TRIM COVER
13 KNEE PROTECTOR

GC6049600177000X

Fig. 16 Exploded view of standard steering column. Tracker

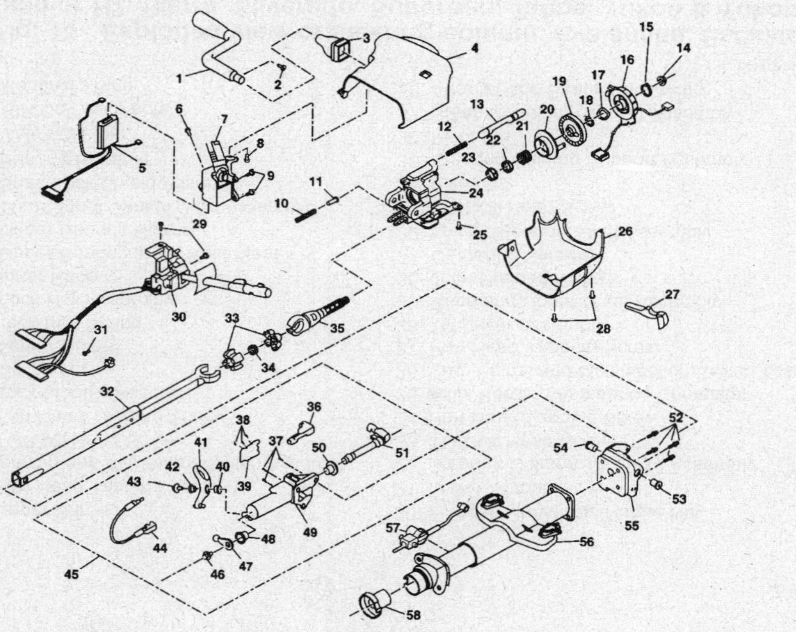

1. Automatic Transmission Control Lever Assembly (Shift Lever Assembly)
2. Shift Lever Screw
3. Shift Lever Seal
4. Upper Shroud
5. Ignition and Key Alarm Switch Assembly
6. Pan Head Tapping Screw
7. Lock Module Assembly
8. TORX® Head Screw
9. Pan Head Tapping Screw
10. Tilt Spring
11. Spring Guide
12. Lock Bolt Spring
13. Lock Bolt Assembly
14. Flanged Prevailing Torque Nut
15. Retaining Ring
16. SIR Coil Assembly
17. Wave Washer
18. Bearing Retainer
19. Shaft Lock Shield Assembly
20. Turn Signal Cancel Cam Assembly
21. Upper Bearing Spring
22. Upper Bearing Inner Race Seat
23. Inner Race
24. Steering Column Tilt Head Assembly
25. TORX® Head Screw
26. Lower Shroud
27. Tilt Lever Assembly
28. Pan Head Tapping Screw
29. Pan Head Tapping Screw
30. Turn Signal and Multifunction Switch Assembly
31. Axial Position Assurance Connector
32. Lower Steering Shaft Assembly

GC6049900261010X

Fig. 17 Exploded view of steering column (Part 1 of 2). Avalanche, Escalade, Hummer H2, Sierra, Silverado, Suburban, Tahoe, Yukon & Yukon XL w/column shift

33. Centering Sphere
34. Joint Preload Spring
35. Race and Upper Shaft Assembly
36. Park Position Switch Assembly
37. Flat Head 6-Lobed Socket Tapping Screw
38. Oval Head Socket Tapping Screw
39. Shift Lever Gate
40. Cam Bushing
41. Linear Shift Cam Assembly
42. Cam Bushing
43. Hexagon Flange Head Bolt
44. Park Lock Cable System
45. Linear Shift Assembly
46. Hexagon Flange Head Bolt
47. Ball and Actuator Assembly
48. Actuator Bushing
49. Linear Shift Bracket Assembly
50. Actuator Bushing
51. Linear Shift Shaft Assembly
52. TORX® Head Screw
53. Pivot Pin
54. Pivot Pin
55. Steering Column Support Assembly
56. Steering Column Jacket Assembly
57. Electrical (BTSI) Actuator
58. Adapter and Bearing Assembly

GC6049900261020X

Fig. 17 Exploded view of steering column (Part 2 of 2). Avalanche, Escalade, Hummer H2, Sierra, Silverado, Suburban, Tahoe, Yukon & Yukon XL w/column shift

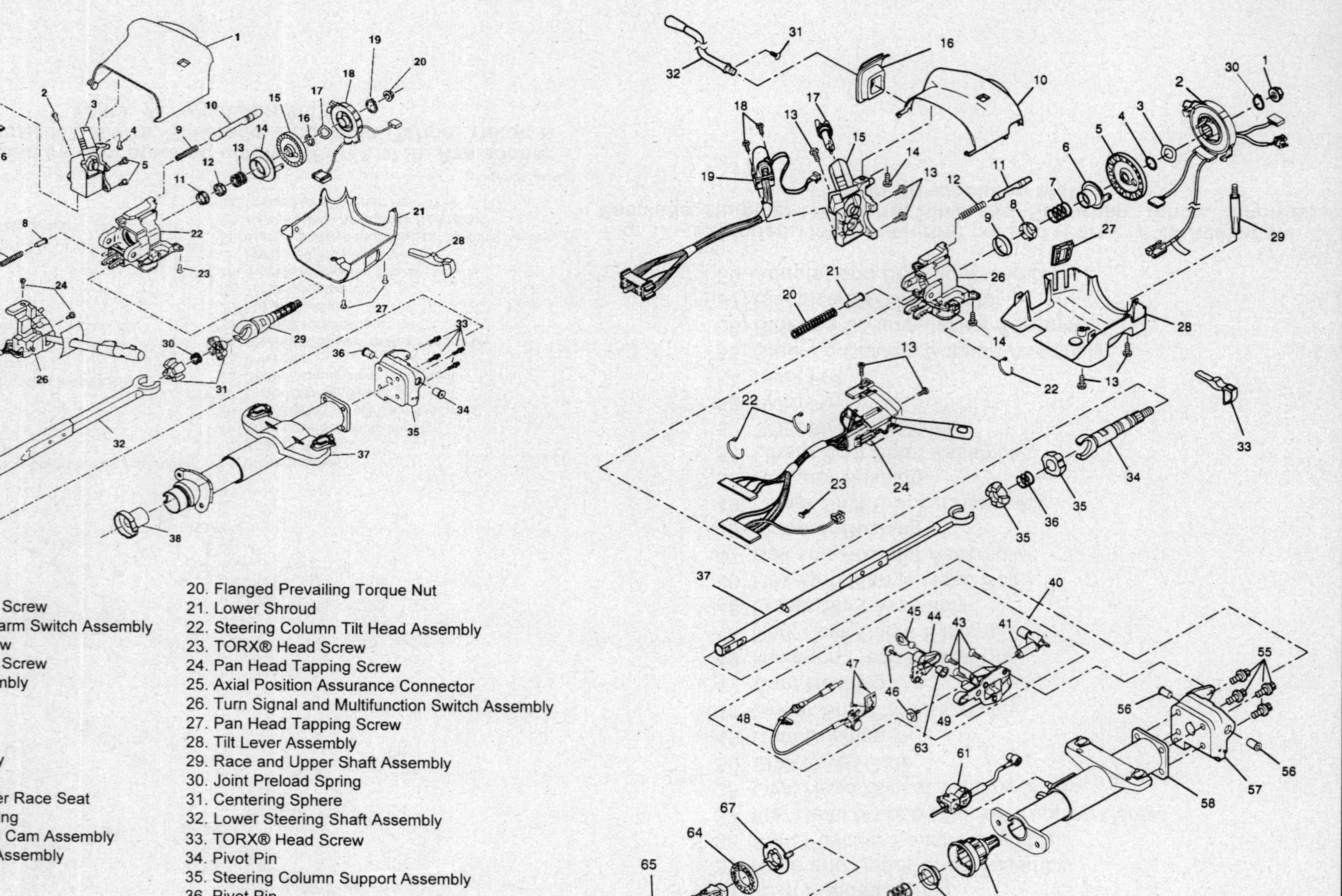

1. Upper Shroud
2. Pan Head Tapping Screw
3. Ignition and Key Alarm Switch Assembly
4. TORX® Head Screw
5. Pan Head Tapping Screw
6. Lock Module Assembly
7. Tilt Spring
8. Spring Guide
9. Lock Bolt Spring
10. Lock Bolt Assembly
11. Inner Race
12. Upper Bearing Inner Race Seat
13. Upper Bearing Spring
14. Turn Signal Cancel Cam Assembly
15. Shaft Lock Shield Assembly
16. Bearing Retainer
17. Wave Washer
18. SIR Coil Assembly
19. Retaining Ring
20. Flanged Prevailing Torque Nut
21. Lower Shroud
22. Steering Column Tilt Head Assembly
23. TORX® Head Screw
24. Pan Head Tapping Screw
25. Axial Position Assurance Connector
26. Turn Signal and Multifunction Switch Assembly
27. Pan Head Tapping Screw
28. Tilt Lever Assembly
29. Race and Upper Shaft Assembly
30. Joint Preload Spring
31. Centering Sphere
32. Lower Steering Shaft Assembly
33. TORX® Head Screw
34. Pivot Pin
35. Steering Column Support Assembly
36. Pivot Pin
37. Steering Column Jacket Assembly
38. Adapter and Bearing Assembly

GC6049900274010X

Fig. 18 Exploded view of steering column. Avalanche, Escalade, Hummer H2, Sierra, Silverado, Suburban, Tahoe, Yukon & Yukon XL w/floor shift

GC6049700217010X

Fig. 19 Exploded view of tilt steering column (Part 1 of 2). Montana, Silhouette & Venture

1-NUT, HEXAGON LOCKING (M14x1.5)
2-COIL ASM, SIR
3-WASHER, WAVE
4-RING, RETAINING
5-SHIELD ASM, SHAFT LOCK
6-CAM ASM, T/SIG CANCEL
7-SPRING, UPPER BEARING
8-SEAT, UPPER BEARING INNER RACE
9-RACE, INNER
10-SHROUD, UPPER
11-BOLT ASM, LOCK
12-SPRING, LOCK BOLT
13-SCREW, PAN HD TAPPING
14-SCREW, TORX HEAD
15-ASM, LOCK MODULE
16-SEAL, SHIFT LEVER
17-LOCK CYL SET, STRG COLUMN
18-SCREW, TAPPING
19-SWITCH ASM, IGN & KEY ALARM
20-SPRING, TILT
21-GUIDE, SPRING
22-STRAP, WIRE HARNESS
23-CONNECTOR, AXIAL POSN ASSUR
24-SWITCH ASM, T/S & MULTIFUNCTION
26-TILT HEAD ASM, STRG COL
27-PROTECTOR, SHROUD
28-SHROUD, LOWER
29-STUD, SHROUD MOUNTING
30-RING, RETAINING
31-SCREW, SHIFT LEVER
32-LEVER ASM, A/TRNS CONTROL
33-LEVER ASM, TILT
34-SHAFT ASM, RACE & UPPER
35-SPHERE, CENTERING
36-SPRING, JOINT PRELOAD
37-SHAFT ASM, LOWER STRG
40-SHIFT ASM, LINEAR
41-CLEVIS, SHIFT LEVER
43-SCREW, FLAT HD 6-LOBED SOC TAP
44-CAM ASM, CABLE SHIFT
45-ACTUATOR ASM, BALL &
46-BOLT, HEX FLANGE HEAD
47-SCREW, OVAL HD 6-LOBED SOC TAP
48-CABLE ASM, PARK LOCK
49-BRACKET, G/S LEVER ASM SUPPORT
55-SCREW, TORX HEAD
56-PIN, PIVOT
57-SUPPORT ASM, STRG COL
58-JACKET ASM, STRG COL
60-BEARING ASM, ADAPTER &
61-ACTUATOR, ELECTRICAL (BTSI)
63-BUSHING, CAM
64-SEAL, STRG SHAFT
65-SHAFT ASM, INTER STRG
66-BOLT, PINCH
67-RETAINER, SENSOR
68-SEAT, LOWER BEARING
69-SPRING, LOWER BEARING
70-RETAINER, LOWER SPRING

GC6049700217020X

Fig. 19 Exploded view of tilt steering column (Part 2 of 2). Montana, Silhouette & Venture

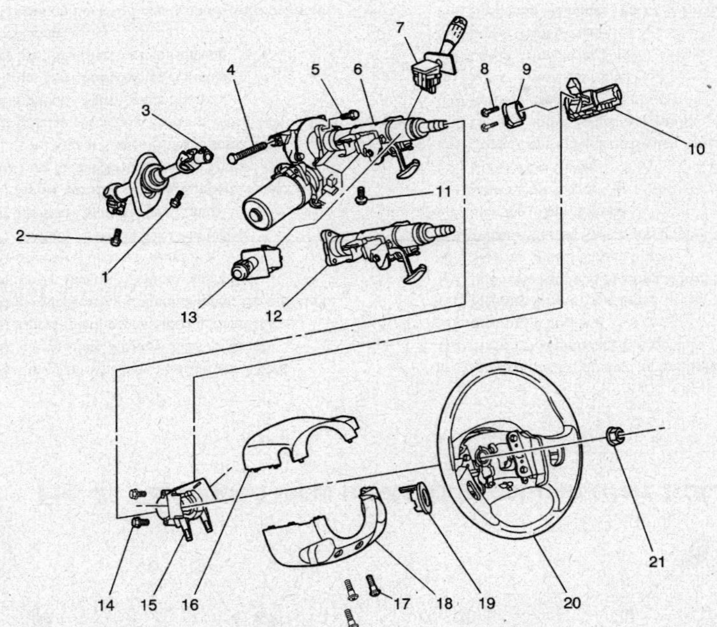

Fig. 20 Exploded view of steering column (Part 1 of 2). Vue

(1) Upper Intermediate Shaft Bolt
(2) Lower Intermediate Shaft Bolt
(3) Intermediate Shaft Assembly
(4) Lower Steering Column Support Bracket Bolt
(5) Lower Steering Column Jacket Bolt
(6) Steering Column Assembly
(7) Wiper/Washer Switch Assembly
(8) Ignition Start Switch Screw
(9) Ignition Start Switch Assembly
(10) Ignition Start Switch Housing Assembly
(11) Upper Steering Column Support Bracket Bolt
(12) Steering Column Jacket Assembly
(13) Headlamp/Dimmer/Park/Turn Signal Switch Assembly
(14) Ignition Start Switch Bracket Bolt
(15) Wiper/Washer Switch and Headlamp/Dimmer/Park/Turn Signal Switch Bracket
(16) Steering Column Shroud Assembly
(17) Lower Steering Column Shroud Screw
(18) Steering Column Shroud
(19) Ignition Start Switch Bezel
(20) Steering Wheel Assembly
(21) Steering Wheel Nut

LTV1900000000730

Fig. 20 Exploded view of steering column (Part 2 of 2). Vue

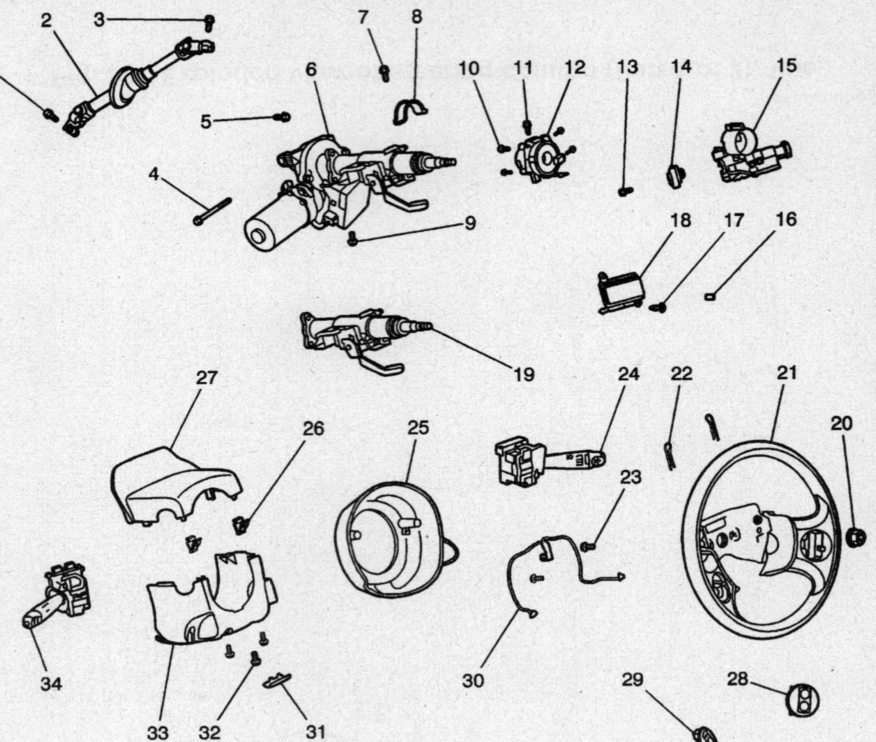

Fig. 21 Exploded view of steering column (Part 1 of 2). HHR

(1) Lower Intermediate Steering Shaft Bold
(2) Intermediate Steering Shaft Assembly
(3) Upper Intermediate Steering Shaft Bolt
(4) Lower Steering Column Support Bracket Bolt
(5) Lower Steering Column Jacket Bolt
(6) Steering Column Assembly
(7) Ignition / Start Switch Clamp Bolt
(8) Ignition / Start Switch Clamp
(9) Upper Steering Column Support Bracket Bolt
(10) Turn Signal Switch Bracket Screw
(11) Turn Signal Switch Bracket Screw
(12) Inflatable Restraint Steering Wheel Module Coil Assembly
(13) Ignition / Start Switch Screw
(14) Ignition / Start Switch Assembly
(15) Ignition / Start Switch Housing
(16) Spring
(17) Ignition Lock Cylinder Control Solenoid Screw
(18) Ignition Lock Cylinder Control Solenoid Assembly
(19) Steering Column Jacket Assembly
(20) Steering Wheel Nut
(21) Steering Wheel Assembly
(22) Inflatable Restraint Steering Wheel Module Retainer
(23) Steering Wheel Shroud Screw
(24) Wiper / Washer Switch Assembly
(25) Steering Wheel Shroud
(26) Lower Trim Cover Clip
(27) Upper Trim Cover
(28) Cruise Control Resume Switch Assembly
(29) Cruise Control Switch Assembly
(30) Harness Assembly
(31) Lower Trim Cover Plug
(32) Lower Trim Cover Screw
(33) Lower Trim Cover
(34) Headlamp / Dimmer / Park / Turn Signal Switch Assembly

LTV0500000000499

Fig. 21 Exploded view of steering column (Part 2 of 2). HHR

LTV0500000000500

Fig. 22 Exploded view of steering column (Part 1 of 2). SSR

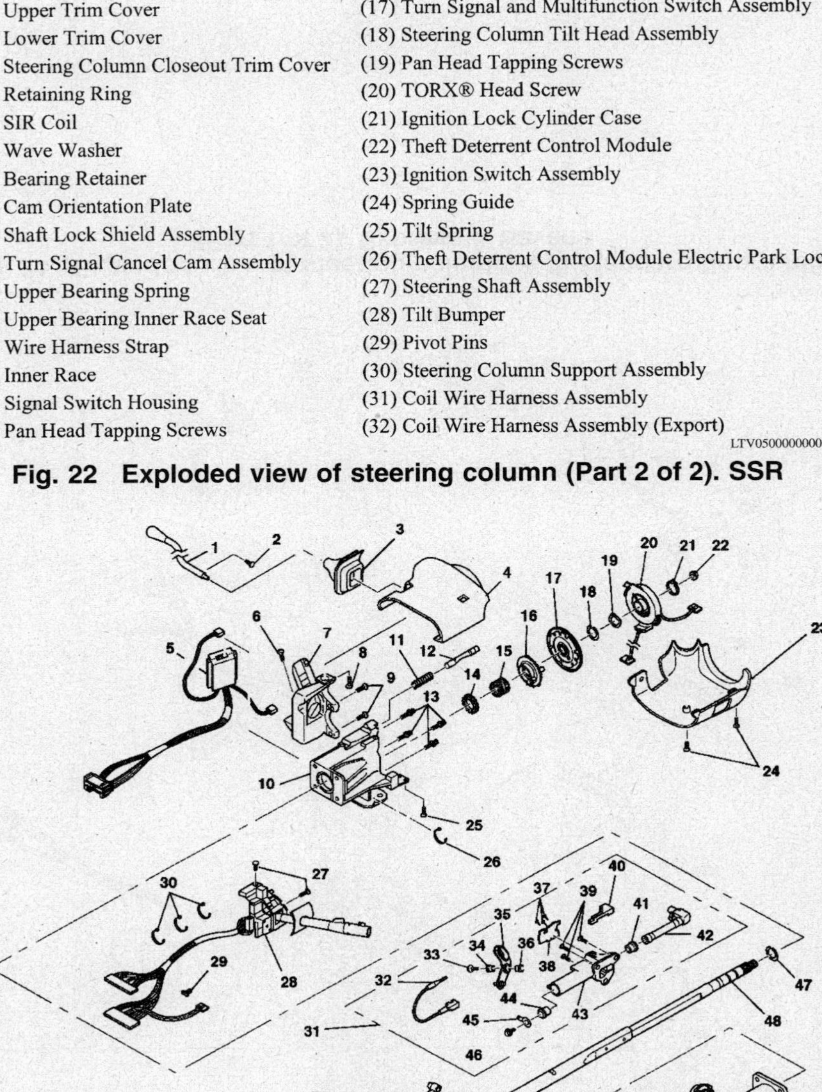

(1) Upper Trim Cover
(2) Lower Trim Cover
(3) Steering Column Closeout Trim Cover
(4) Retaining Ring
(5) SIR Coil
(6) Wave Washer
(7) Bearing Retainer
(8) Cam Orientation Plate
(9) Shaft Lock Shield Assembly
(10) Turn Signal Cancel Cam Assembly
(11) Upper Bearing Spring
(12) Upper Bearing Inner Race Seat
(13) Wire Harness Strap
(14) Inner Race
(15) Signal Switch Housing
(16) Pan Head Tapping Screws
(17) Turn Signal and Multifunction Switch Assembly
(18) Steering Column Tilt Head Assembly
(19) Pan Head Tapping Screws
(20) TORX® Head Screw
(21) Ignition Lock Cylinder Case
(22) Theft Deterrent Control Module
(23) Ignition Switch Assembly
(24) Spring Guide
(25) Tilt Spring
(26) Theft Deterrent Control Module Electric Park Lock
(27) Steering Shaft Assembly
(28) Tilt Bumper
(29) Pivot Pins
(30) Steering Column Support Assembly
(31) Coil Wire Harness Assembly
(32) Coil Wire Harness Assembly (Export)

LTV0500000000501

Fig. 22 Exploded view of steering column (Part 2 of 2). SSR

LTV0500000000502

Fig. 23 Exploded view of steering column with standard column shift (Part 1 of 2). Express & Savana

(1) Shift Lever Assembly
(2) Shift Lever Screw
(3) Shift Lever Seal
(4) Upper Trim Cover
(5) Ignition Switch Assembly
(6) Pan Head Tapping Screw
(7) Ignition Lock Cylinder Case
(8) TORX® Head Screw
(9) Pan Head Tapping Screws
(10) Steering Column Housing Assembly
(11) Lock Bolt Spring
(12) Lock Bolt Assembly
(13) TORX® Head Screws
(14) Thrust Washer
(15) Upper Bearing Spring
(16) Turn Signal Cancel Cam Assembly
(17) Shaft Lock Shield Assembly
(18) Bearing Retainer
(19) Wave Washer
(20) SIR Coil
(21) Retaining Ring
(22) Flanged Prevailing Torque Nut
(23) Lower Trim Cover
(24) Pan Head Tapping Screws
(25) TORX® Head Screw
(26) Wire Harness Strap
(27) Pan Head Tapping Screws
(28) Turn Signal and Multifunction Switch Assembly
(29) Axial Position Assurance Connector
(30) Wire Harness Straps
(31) Linear Shift Assembly
(32) Park Lock Cable Assembly
(33) Hexagon Flange Head Bolt
(34) Cam Bushing
(35) Cable Shift Cam Assembly
(36) Cam Bushing
(37) Oval Head 6-Lobed Socket Tapping Screws
(38) Shift Lever Gate
(39) Flat Head Tapping Screws
(40) Park Position Switch Assembly
(41) Actuator Bushing
(42) Shift Lever Clevis
(43) Gear Shift Lever Assembly Support Bracket Assembly
(44) Actuator Bushing
(45) Ball and Actuator Assembly
(46) Hex Flange Head Bolt
(47) Retaining Ring
(48) Steering Shaft Assembly
(49) Steering Column Jacket Assembly
(50) Adapter and Bearing Assembly
(51) Shaft Seal Retainer
(52) Steering Shaft Seal
(53) Inner Boot Seal
(54) Large Flange Hexagon Nut
(55) Coupling and Steering Shaft Assembly
(56) Round Head Locking Bolt
(57) Electrical (BTSI) Actuator

LTV0500000000503

Fig. 23 Exploded view of steering column with standard column shift (Part 2 of 2). Express & Savana

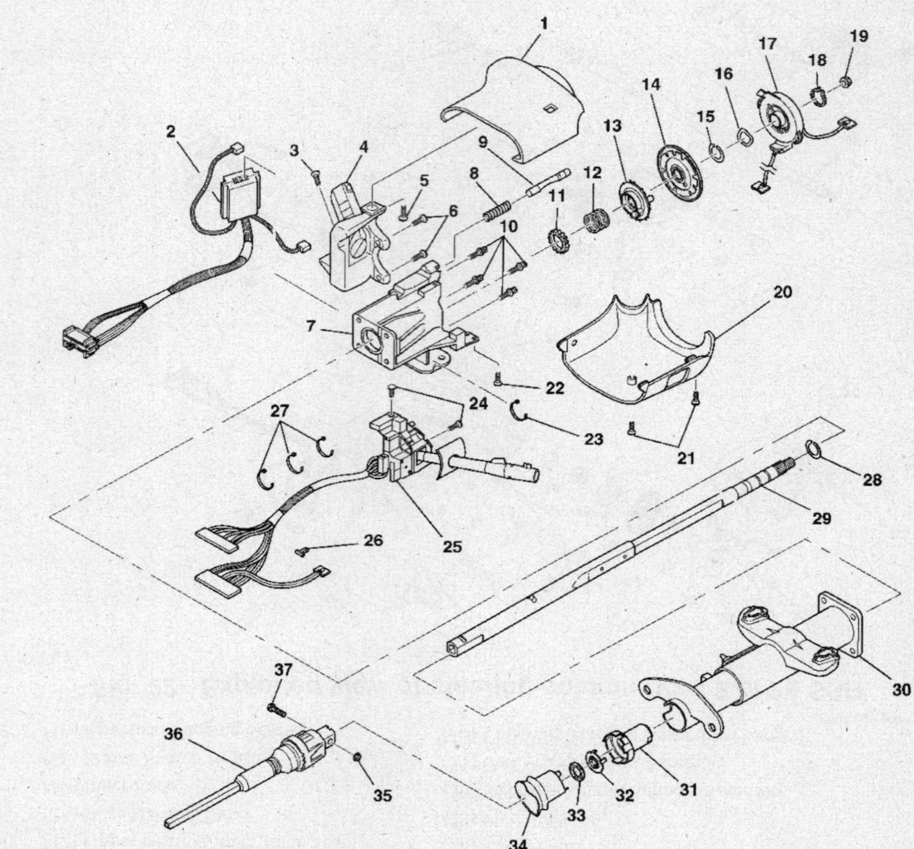

Fig. 24 Exploded view of steering column with standard floor shift (Part 1 of 2). Express & Savana

(1) Upper Trim Cover
(2) Ignition Switch Assembly
(3) Pan Head Tapping Screw
(4) Ignition Lock Cylinder Case
(5) TORX® Head Screw
(6) Pan Head Tapping Screws
(7) Steering Column Housing Assembly
(8) Lock Bolt Spring
(9) Lock Bolt Assembly
(10) TORX® Head Screws
(11) Thrust Washer
(12) Upper Bearing Spring
(13) Turn Signal Cancel Cam Assembly
(14) Shaft Lock Shield Assembly
(15) Bearing Retainer
(16) Wave Washer
(17) SIR Coil
(18) Retaining Ring
(19) Flanged Prevailing Torque Nut
(20) Lower Trim Cover
(21) Pan Head Tapping Screws
(22) TORX® Head Screw
(23) Wire Harness Strap
(24) Pan Head Tapping Screws
(25) Turn Signal and Multifunction Switch Assembly
(26) Axial Position Assurance Connector
(27) Wire Harness Straps
(28) Bearing Retainer
(29) Steering Shaft Assembly
(30) Steering Column Jacket Assembly
(31) Adapter and Bearing Assembly
(32) Shaft Seal Retainer
(33) Steering Shaft Seal
(34) Inner Boot Seal
(35) Large Flange Hexagon Nut
(36) Coupling and Steering Shaft Assembly
(37) Round Head Locking Bolt

LTV0500000000505

Fig. 24 Exploded view of steering column with standard floor shift (Part 2 of 2). Express & Savana

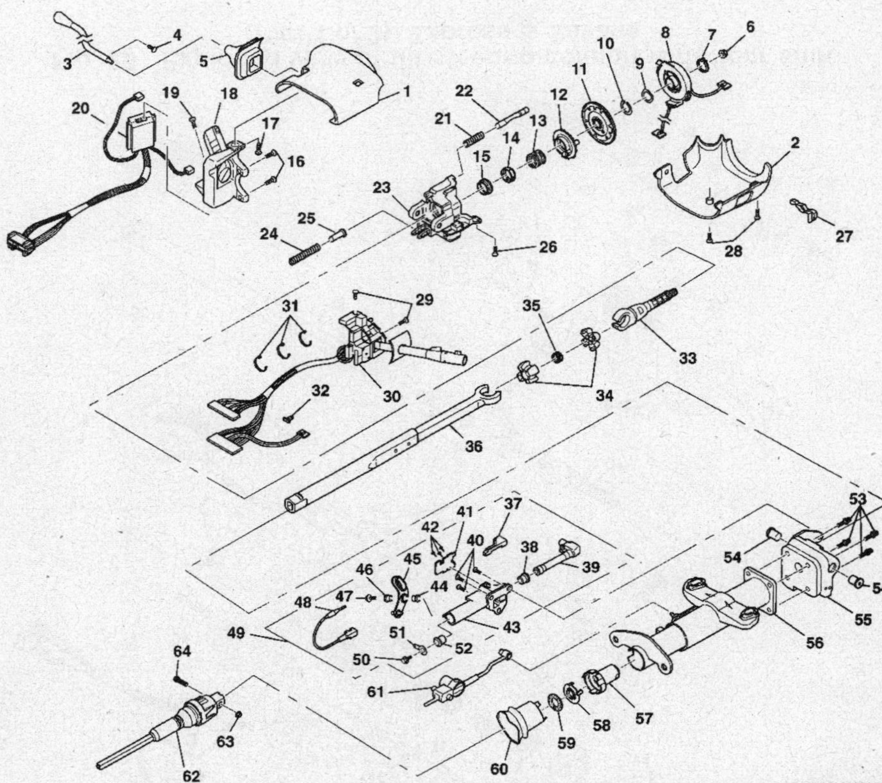

Fig. 25 Exploded view of steering column with tilt steering (Part 1 of 2). Express & Savana

(1) Upper Trim Cover
(2) Lower Trim Cover
(3) Shift Lever Assembly
(4) Shift Lever Screw
(5) Shift Lever Seal
(6) Flanged Prevailing Torque Nut
(7) Retaining Ring
(8) SIR Coil
(9) Wave Washer
(10) Bearing Retainer
(11) Shaft Lock Shield Assembly
(12) Turn Signal Cancel Cam Assembly
(13) Upper Bearing Spring
(14) Upper Bearing Inner Race Seat
(15) Inner Race
(16) Pan Head Tapping Screws
(17) TORX® Head Screw
(18) Ignition Lock Cylinder Case
(19) Pan Head Tapping Screw
(20) Ignition Switch Assembly
(21) Lock Bolt Spring
(22) Lock Bolt Assembly
(23) Steering Column Tilt Head Assembly
(24) Tilt Spring
(25) Spring Guide
(26) TORX® Head Screw
(27) Tilt Lever Assembly
(28) Pan Head Tapping Screws
(29) Pan Head Tapping Screws
(30) Turn Signal and Multifunction Switch Assembly
(31) Wire Harness Straps
(32) Axial Position Assurance Connector
(33) Race and Upper Shaft Assembly
(34) Centering Sphere
(35) Joint Preload Spring
(36) Lower Steering Shaft Assembly
(37) Shift Lever Clevis
(38) Cam Bushing
(39) Linear Shift Shaft Assembly
(40) Flat Head Tapping Screws
(41) Shift Lever Gate
(42) Oval Head 6-Lobed Socket Tapping Screws
(43) Gear Shift Lever Support Bracket
(44) Actuator Bushing
(45) Cable Shift Cam Assembly
(46) Actuator Bushing
(47) Hexagon Flange Head Bolt
(48) Park Lock Cable Assembly
(49) Linear Shift Assembly
(50) Hexagon Flange Head Bolt
(51) Ball and Actuator Assembly
(52) Actuator Bushing
(53) TORX® Head Screws
(54) Pivot Pins
(55) Steering Column Support Assembly
(56) Steering Column Jacket Assembly
(57) Adapter and Bearing Assembly
(58) Shaft Seal Retainer
(59) Steering Shaft Seal
(60) Inner Boot Seal
(61) Automatic Transmission Shift Lock Control
(62) Coupling and Steering Shaft Assembly
(63) Large Flange Hexagon Nut
(64) Round Head Locking Bolt

LTV0500000000507

Fig. 25 Exploded view of steering column with tilt steering (Part 2 of 2). Express & Savana

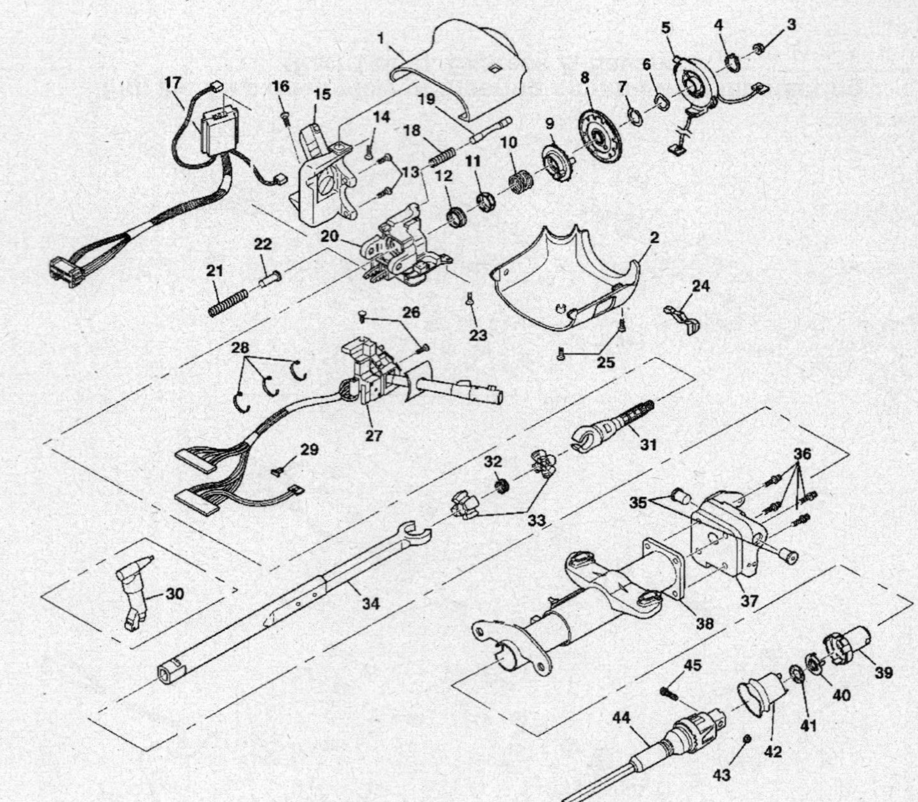

Fig. 26 Exploded view of tilt steering column with floor shift (Part 1 of 2). Express & Savana

(1) Upper Trim Cover
(2) Lower Trim Cover
(3) Flanged Prevailing Torque Nut
(4) Retaining Ring
(5) SIR Coil
(6) Wave Washer
(7) Bearing Retainer
(8) Shaft Lock Shield Assembly
(9) Turn Signal Cancel Cam Assembly
(10) Upper Bearing Spring
(11) Upper Bearing Inner Race Seat
(12) Inner Race
(13) Pan Head Tapping Screws
(14) TORX® Head Screw
(15) Ignition Lock Cylinder Case
(16) Pan Head Tapping Screw
(17) Ignition Switch Assembly
(18) Lock Bolt Spring
(19) Lock Bolt Assembly
(20) Steering Column Tilt Head Assembly
(21) Tilt Spring
(22) Spring Guide
(23) TORX® Head Screw
(24) Tilt Lever Assembly
(25) Pan Head Tapping Screws
(26) Pan Head Tapping Screws
(27) Turn Signal and Multifunction Switch Assembly
(28) Wire Harness Straps
(29) Axial Position Assurance Connector
(30) Steering Column Electric Park Lock
(31) Race and Upper Shaft Assembly
(32) Joint Preload Spring
(33) Centering Spheres
(34) Lower Steering Shaft Assembly
(35) Pivot Pins
(36) TORX® Head Screws
(37) Steering Column Support Assembly
(38) Steering Column Jacket Assembly
(39) Adapter and Bearing Assembly
(40) Sensor Retainer
(41) Shaft Seal Retainer
(42) Steering Shaft Boot
(43) Large Flange Hexagon Nut
(44) Coupling and Steering Shaft Assembly
(45) Round Head Locking Bolt

LTV0500000000509

Fig. 26 Exploded view of tilt steering column with floor shift (Part 2 of 2). Express & Savana

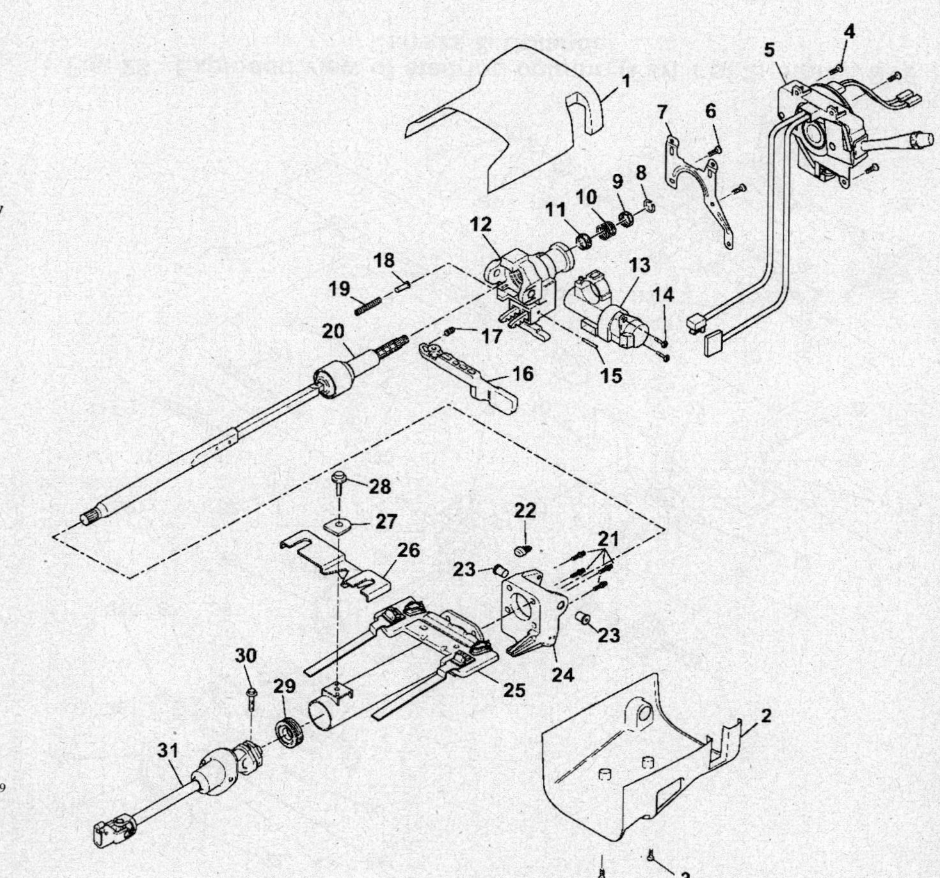

Fig. 27 Exploded view of steering column (Part 1 of 2). H3

(1) Upper Trim Cover
(2) Lower Trim Cover
(3) Shoulder Tapping Screws
(4) Pan Head Tapping Screws
(5) Multifunction Switch Assembly
(6) Washer Head Screws
(7) Switch Mounting Plate
(8) Bearing Retainer
(9) Spring Retainer
(10) Upper Bearing Spring
(11) Inner Race Seat
(12) Steering Column Housing Assembly
(13) Ignition Switch and Lock Housing Assembly
(14) Set Screws
(15) Release Lever Pin
(16) Lever Spring Assembly
(17) Release Lever Spring
(18) Spring Guide
(19) Tilt Spring
(20) Steering Shaft Assembly
(21) Torque Head Screws
(22) Tilt Bumper
(23) Pivot Pin
(23) Pivot Pins
(24) Steering Column Support Assembly
(25) Bracket and Upper Jacket Assembly
(26) Lower Column Support Bracket
(27) Lower Bracket Retainer Spacer
(28) Washer and Bolt Assembly
(29) Lower Shaft Bearing Assembly
(30) Bolt and Retainer Assembly
(31) Intermediate Steering Shaft Assembly

LTV0500000000511

Fig. 27 Exploded view of steering column (Part 2 of 2). H3

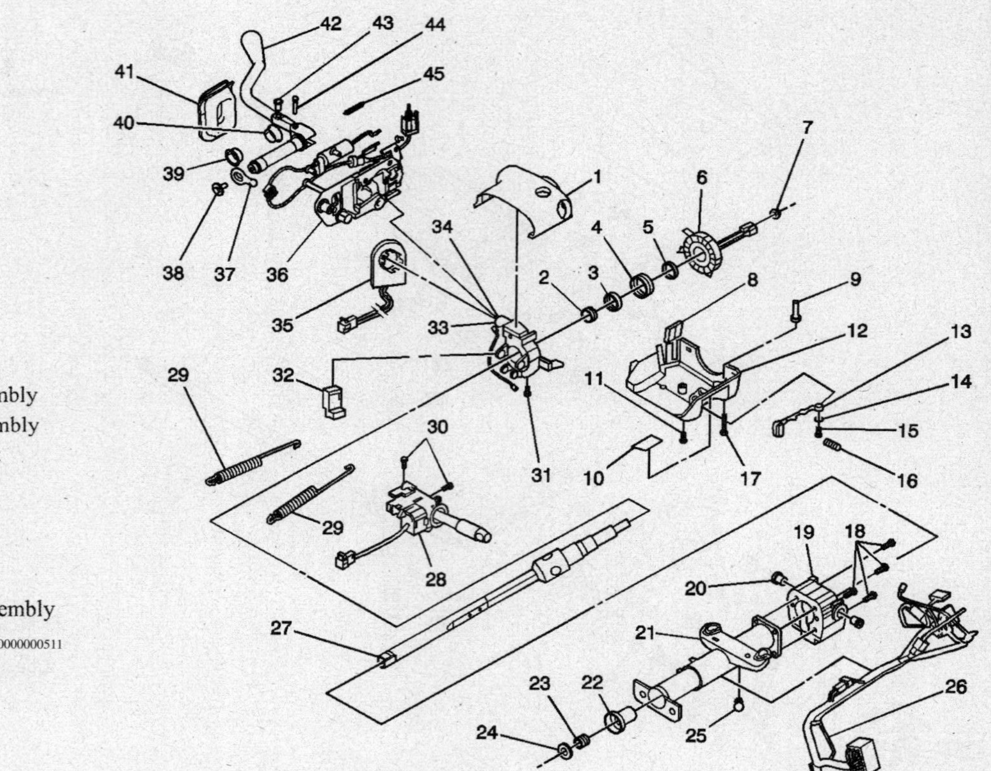

Fig. 28 Exploded view of steering column (Part 1 of 2). Relay, SV6, Terraza & Uplander

(1) Upper Trim Cover
(2) Upper Bearing
(3) Upper Bearing Seat
(4) Steering Shaft Upper Bearing Spring
(5) Bearing Retainer
(6) Inflatable Restraint Steering Wheel Module Coil
(7) Steering Wheel Nut
(8) Trim Cover Protector
(9) Sleeve
(10) Cover, Housing Trim Extension
(11) Lower Trim Cover Screws
(12) Lower Trim Cover
(13) Tilt Lever
(14) Tilt Lever Spring
(15) Tilt Lever Bolt
(16) Tilt Lever Spring
(17) Lower Trim Cover Screw
(18) Lower Tilt Head Mounting Bolts
(19) Lower Tilt Head
(20) Tilt Head Pivot Pins
(21) Steering Column Jacket Assembly
(22) Adapter and Bearing Assembly
(23) Lower Bearing Seat
(24) Lower Bearing Retainer
(25) Wire Harness Retainer
(26) Wire Harness Assembly
(27) Shaft Assembly
(28) Multifunction Switch
(29) Tilt Head Springs
(30) Multifunction Switch Screws
(31) Trim Cover Screw
(32) Ignition Switch
(33) Ignition Key Alarm
(34) Upper Tilt Head
(35) Theft Deterrent Module
(36) Control Assembly
(37) Shift Lever Pivot Pin
(38) Pivot Pin Bolt
(39) Lower Shift Lever Bushing
(40) Upper Shift Lever Bushing
(41) Steering Column Boot
(42) Shift Lever
(43) Shift Lever Screw
(44) Shift Lever Pin
(45) Shift Lever Spring

LTV0500000000513

Fig. 28 Exploded view of steering column (Part 2 of 2). Relay, SV6, Terraza & Uplander

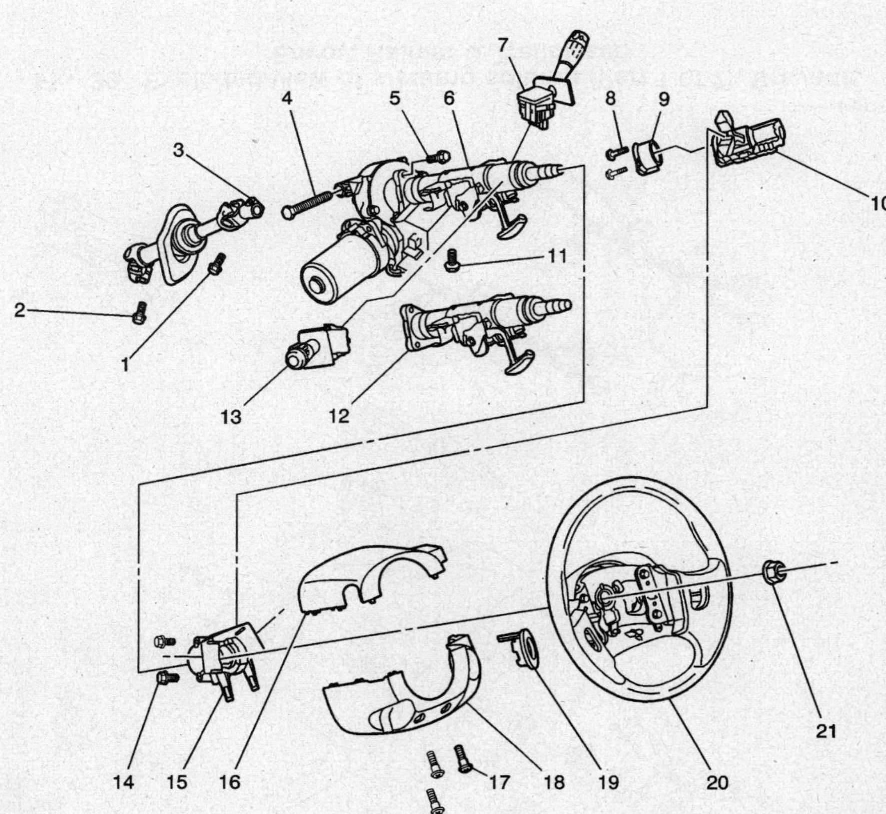

Fig. 29 Exploded view of steering column (Part 1 of 2). Equinox & Torrent

(1) Upper Intermediate Shaft Bolt
(2) Lower Intermediate Shaft Bolt
(3) Intermediate Shaft Assembly
(4) Lower Steering Column Support Bracket Bolt
(5) Lower Steering Column Jacket Bolt
(6) Steering Column Assembly
(7) Wiper/Washer Switch Assembly
(8) Ignition Start Switch Screw
(9) Ignition Start Switch Assembly
(10) Ignition Start Switch Housing Assembly
(11) Upper Steering Column Support Bracket Bolt
(12) Steering Column Jacket Assembly
(13) Headlamp/Dimmer/Park/Turn Signal Switch Assembly
(14) Ignition Start Switch Bracket Bolt
(15) Wiper/Washer Switch and Headlamp/Dimmer/Park/Turn Signal Switch Bracket
(16) Steering Column Shroud Assembly
(17) Lower Steering Column Shroud Screw
(18) Steering Column Shroud
(19) Ignition Start Switch Bezel
(20) Steering Wheel Assembly
(21) Steering Wheel Nut

LTV0500000000517

Fig. 29 Exploded view of steering column (Part 2 of 2). Equinox & Torrent

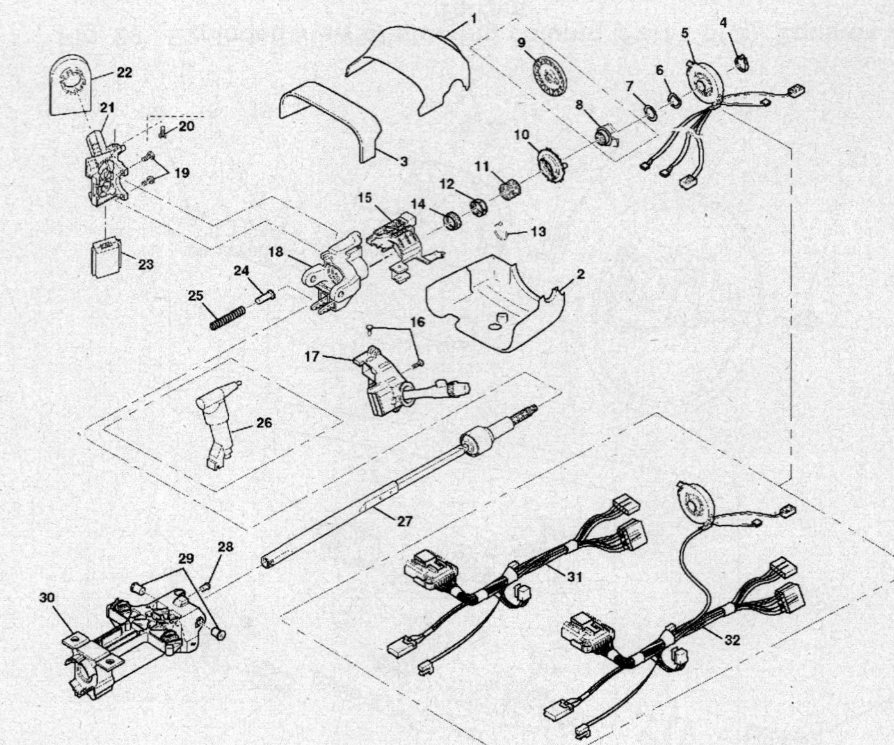

Fig. 30 Exploded view of steering column (Part 1 of 2). Bravada, Envoy, Rainier & Trailblazer

(1) Upper Trim Cover
(2) Lower Trim Cover
(3) Steering Column Closeout Trim Cover
(4) Retaining Ring
(5) SIR Coil
(6) Wave Washer
(7) Bearing Retainer
(8) Cam Orientation Plate
(9) Shaft Lock Shield Assembly
(10) Turn Signal Cancel Cam Assembly
(11) Upper Bearing Spring
(12) Upper Bearing Inner Race Seat
(13) Wire Harness Strap
(14) Inner Race
(15) Signal Switch Housing
(16) Pan Head Tapping Screws
(17) Turn Signal and Multifunction Switch Assembly
(18) Steering Column Tilt Head Assembly
(19) Pan Head Tapping Screws
(20) TORX® Head Screw
(21) Ignition Lock Cylinder Case
(22) Theft Deterrent Control Module
(23) Ignition Switch Assembly
(24) Spring Guide
(25) Tilt Spring
(26) Theft Deterrent Control Module Electric Park Lock
(27) Steering Shaft Assembly
(28) Tilt Bumper
(29) Pivot Pins
(30) Steering Column Support Assembly
(31) Coil Wire Harness Assembly
(32) Coil Wire Harness Assembly (Export)

LTV0500000000519

Fig. 30 Exploded view of steering column (Part 2 of 2). Bravada, Envoy, Rainier & Trailblazer

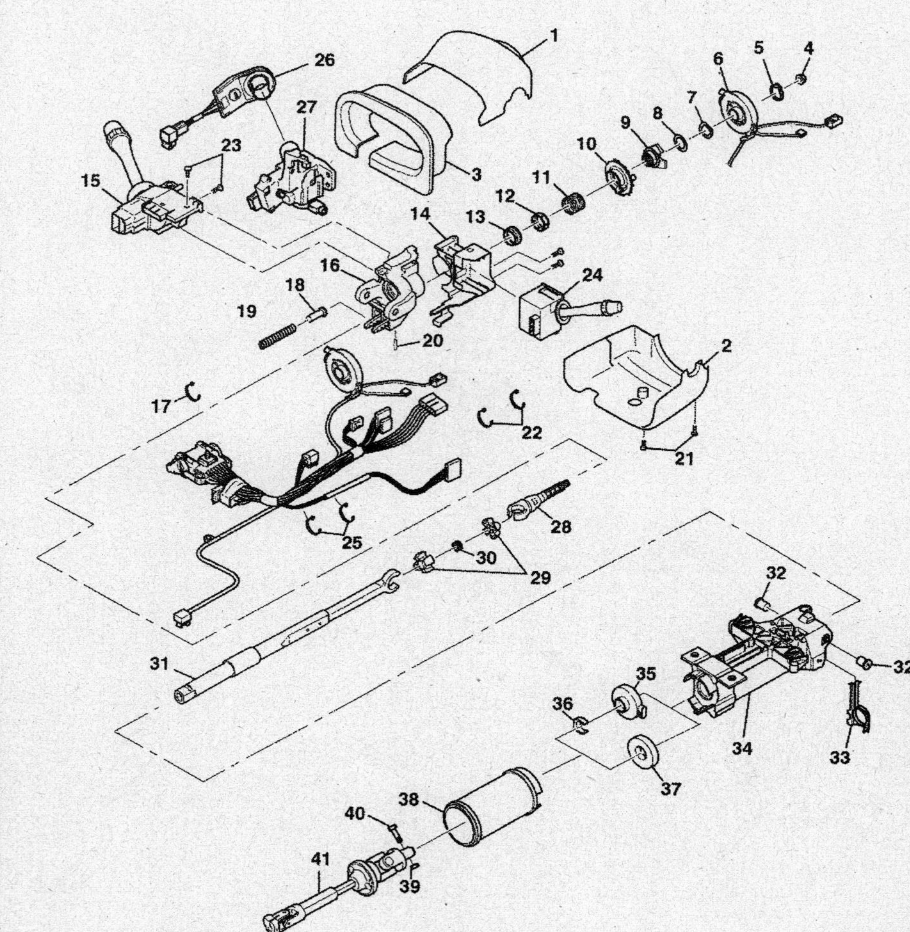

Fig. 31 Exploded view of steering column (Part 1 of 2). SRX

(1) Upper Trim Cover
(2) Lower Trim Cover
(3) Steering Column Closeout Trim
(4) Flange Prevailing Torque Nut
(5) Retaining Ring
(6) SIR Coil
(7) Wave Washer
(8) Bearing Retainer
(9) Cam Orientation Plate
(10) Turn Signal Cancel Cam
(11) Upper Bearing Spring
(12) Upper Bearing Inner Race
(13) Inner Race
(14) Switch Mounting Bracket
(15) Turn Signal and Multifunction Switch Assembly
(16) Steering Column Tilt Head Assembly
(17) Wire Strap
(18) Spring Guide
(19) Tilt Spring
(20) Release Lever Pin
(21) Pan Head Tapping Screws
(22) Wire Straps
(23) Pan Head Tapping Screws
(24) Window Washer and Wiper Switch Assembly
(25) Wire Straps
(26) Theft Deterrent
(27) Ignition Lock Cylinder Case
(28) Race and Upper Shaft
(29) Centering Sphere
(30) Joint Preload Spring
(31) Lower Steering Shaft
(32) Pivot Pins
(33) Wire Strap
(34) Steering Column Jacket Assembly
(35) Steering Column Position Sensor
(36) Sensor Clip
(37) Sensor Seal
(38) Boot
(39) Bolt Retainer
(40) Pinch Bolt
(41) Intermediate Shaft Assembly

LTV0500000000521

Fig. 31 Exploded view of steering column (Part 2 of 2). SRX

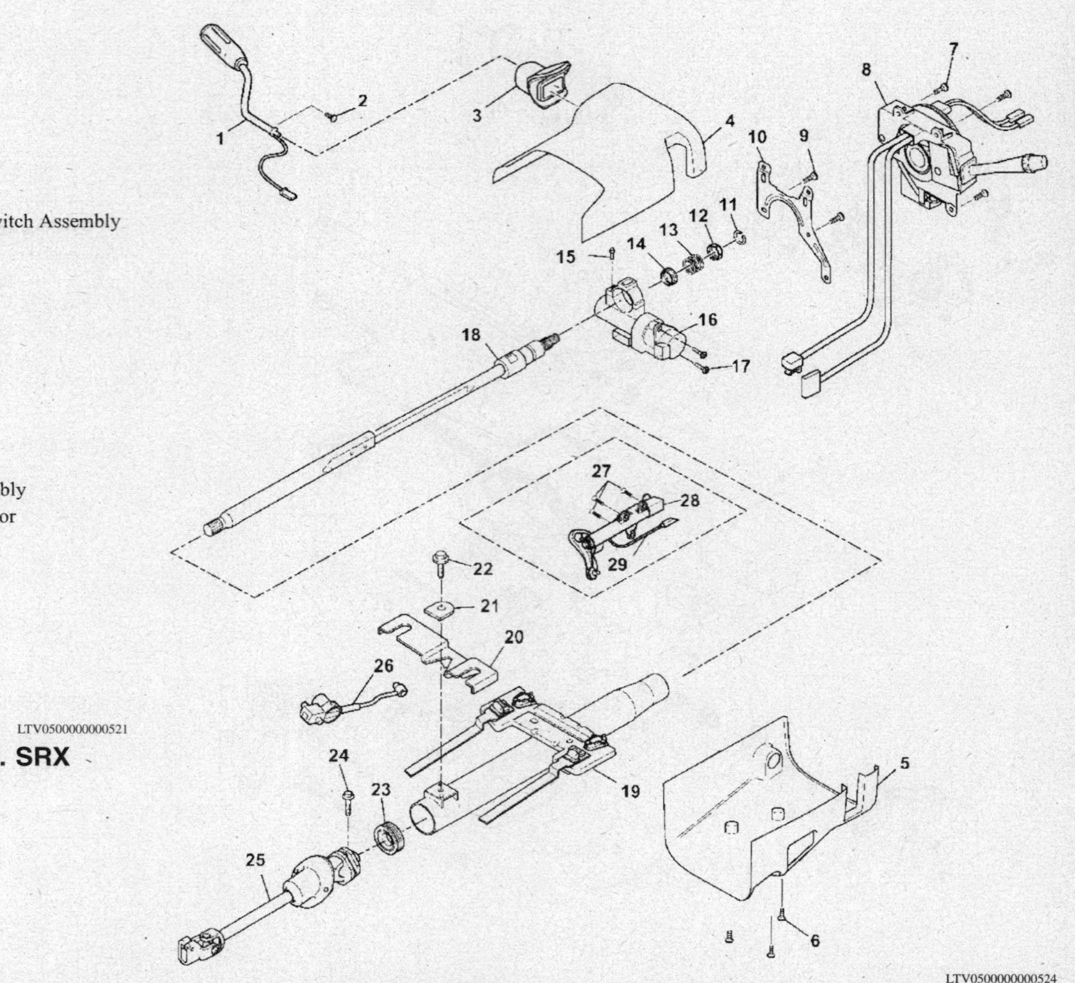

LTV0500000000524

Fig. 32 Exploded view of steering column with standard shift (Part 1 of 2). Colorado & Canyon

(1) Shift Lever
(2) Shift Lever Screw
(3) Shift Lever Seal
(4) Upper Trim Cover
(5) Lower Trim Cover
(6) Shoulder Tapping Screws
(7) Pan Head Tapping Screws
(8) Multifunction Switch Assembly
(9) Washer Head Screws
(10) Switch Mounting Plate
(11) Bearing Retainer
(12) Spring Retainer
(13) Upper Bearing Spring
(14) Inner Race Seat
(15) Shear Bolt Washer
(16) Ignition Switch and Lock Housing
(17) Set Screws
(18) Steering Shaft Assembly
(19) Bracket and Upper Jacket Assembly
(20) Lower Column Support Bracket
(21) Lower Bracket Retainer Spacer
(22) Washer and Bolt Assembly
(23) Lower Shaft Bearing Assembly
(24) Bolt and Retainer Assembly
(25) Intermediate Steering Shaft Assembly
(26) Electrical (BTSI) Actuator
(27) Oval Head Tapping Screws
(28) Linear Shift Assembly
(29) Park Lock Cable

LTV0500000000525

Fig. 32 Exploded view of steering column with standard shift (Part 2 of 2). Colorado & Canyon

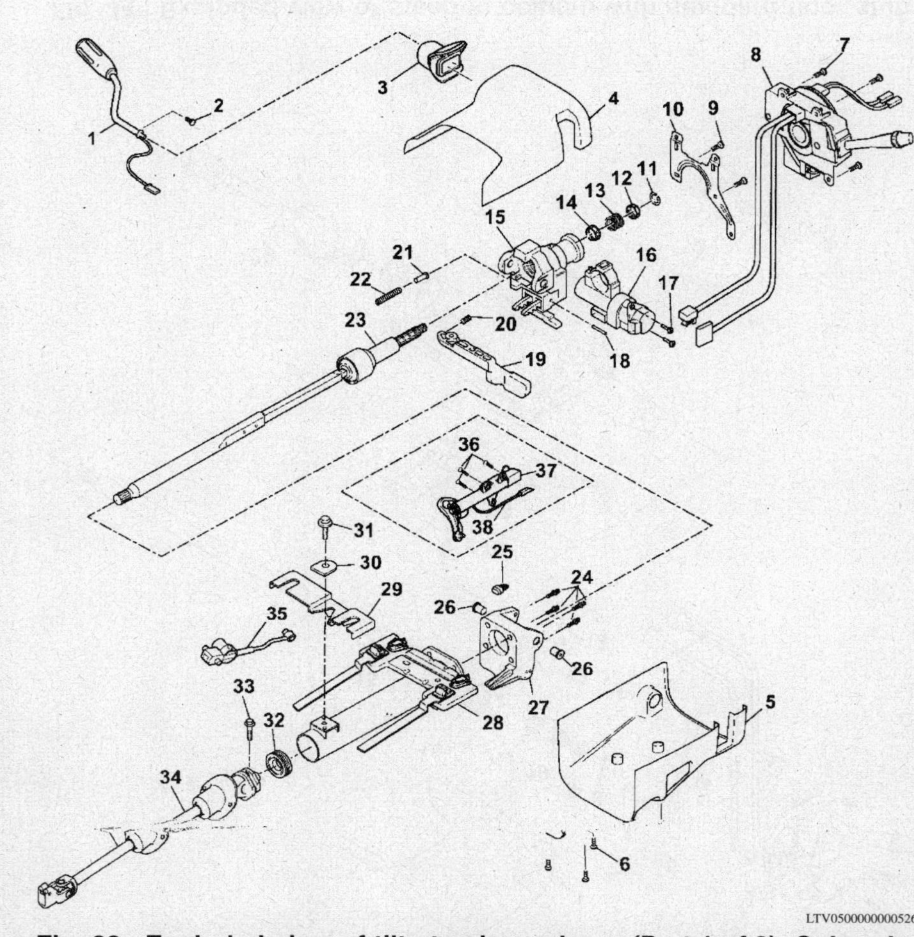

Fig. 33 Exploded view of tilt steering column (Part 1 of 2). Colorado & Canyon

(1) Shift Lever
(2) Shift Lever Screw
(3) Shift Lever Seal
(4) Upper Trim Cover
(5) Lower Trim Cover
(6) Shoulder Tapping Screws
(7) Pan Head Tapping Screws
(8) Multifunction Switch Assembly
(9) Washer Head Screws
(10) Switch Mounting Plate
(11) Bearing Retainer
(12) Spring Retainer
(13) Upper Bearing Spring
(14) Inner Race Seat
(15) Steering Column Housing Assembly
(16) Ignition Switch and Lock Housing Assembly
(17) Set Screws
(18) Release Lever Pin
(19) Lever and Spring Assembly
(20) Release Lever Spring
(21) Spring Guide
(22) Tilt Spring
(23) Steering Shaft Assemby
(24) Torque Head Screws
(25) Tilt Bumper
(26) Pivot Pins
(26) Pivot Pins
(27) Steering Column Support Assembly
(28) Bracket and Upper Jacket Assembly
(29) Lower Column Support Bracket
(30) Lower Bracket Retainer Spacer
(31) Washer and Bolt Assembly
(32) Lower Shaft Bearing Assembly
(33) Bolt and Retainer Assembly
(34) Intermediate Steering Shaft Assembly
(35) Electrical (BTSI) Actuator
(36) Oval Head Tapping Screws
(37) Linear Shift Assembly
(38) Park Lock Cable

LTV0500000000527

Fig. 33 Exploded view of tilt steering column (Part 2 of 2). Colorado & Canyon

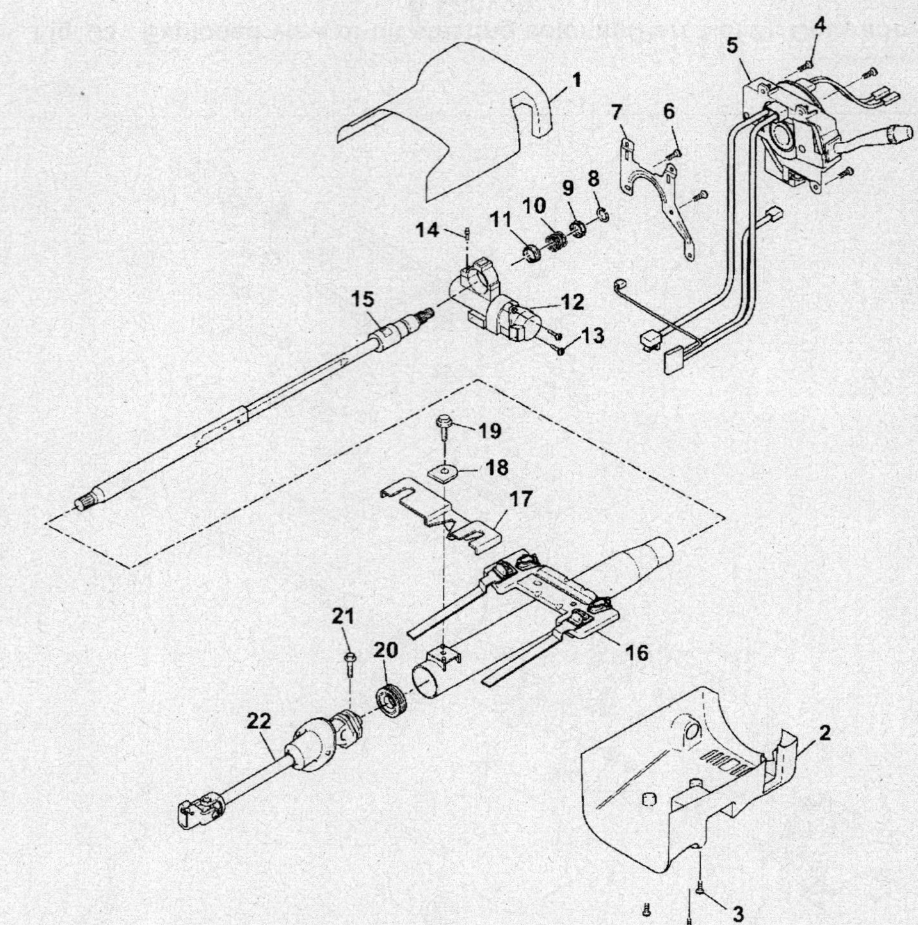

Fig. 34 Exploded view of steering column with standard floor shift (Part 1 of 2). Colorado & Canyon

(1) Upper Trim Cover	(12) Ignition Switch and Lock Housing Assembly
(2) Lower Trim Cover	(13) Set Screws
(3) Shoulder Tapping Screws	(14) Shear Bolt and Washer Assembly
(4) Pan Head Tapping Screws	(15) Steering Shaft Assembly
(5) Multifunction Switch Assembly	(16) Steering Column Jacket Assembly
(6) Washer Head Screws	(17) Lower Column Support Bracket
(7) Switch Mounting Plate	(18) Lower Bracket Retainer Spacer
(8) Bearing Retainer	(19) Washer and Bolt Assembly
(9) Spring Retainer	(20) Lower Shaft Bearing Assembly
(10) Upper Bearing Spring	(21) Bolt and Retainer Assembly
(11) Inner Race Seat	(22) Upper Steering Shaft Assembly

LTV0500000000529

Fig. 34 Exploded view of steering column with standard floor shift (Part 2 of 2). Colorado & Canyon

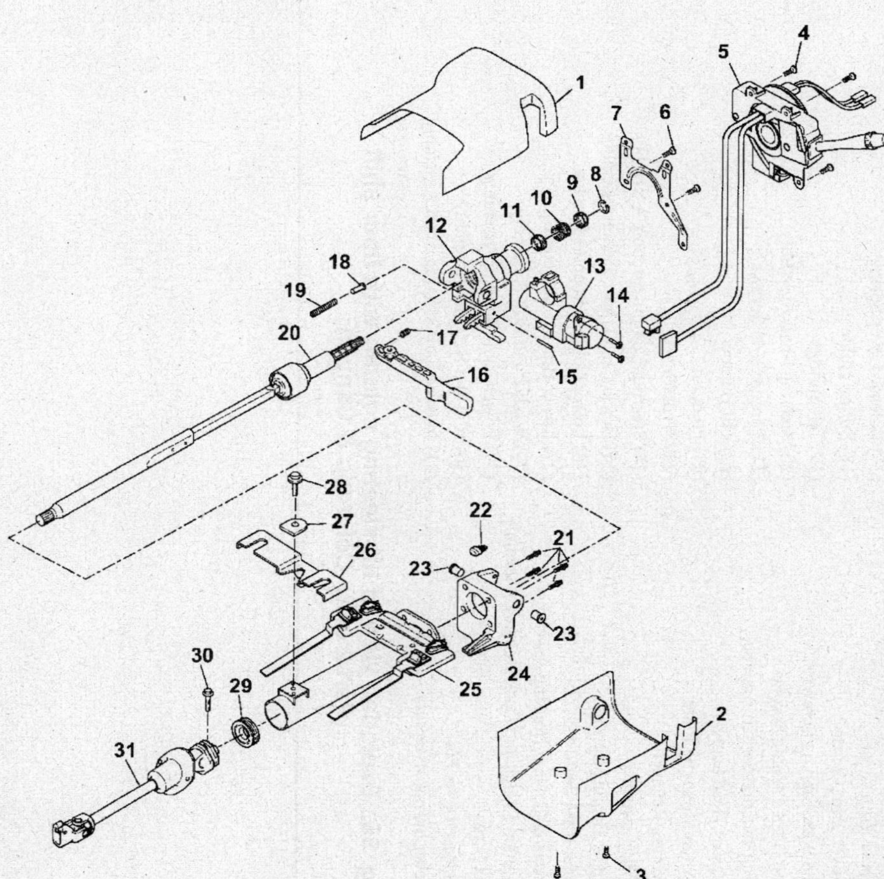

Fig. 35 Exploded view of tilt steering column with floor shift (Part 1 of 2). Colorado & Canyon

(1) Upper Trim Cover
(2) Lower Trim Cover
(3) Shoulder Tapping Screws
(4) Pan Head Tapping Screws
(5) Multifunction Switch Assembly
(6) Washer Head Screws
(7) Switch Mounting Plate
(8) Bearing Retainer
(9) Spring Retainer
(10) Upper Bearing Spring
(11) Inner Race Seat
(12) Steering Column Housing Assembly
(13) Ignition Switch and Lock Housing Assembly
(14) Set Screws
(15) Release Lever Pin
(16) Lever Spring Assembly
(17) Release Lever Spring
(18) Spring Guide
(19) Tilt Spring
(20) Steering Shaft Assembly
(21) Torque Head Screws
(22) Tilt Bumper
(23) Pivot Pin
(23) Pivot Pins
(24) Steering Column Support Assembly
(25) Bracket and Upper Jacket Assembly
(26) Lower Column Support Bracket
(27) Lower Bracket Retainer Spacer
(28) Washer and Bolt Assembly
(29) Lower Shaft Bearing Assembly
(30) Bolt and Retainer Assembly
(31) Intermediate Steering Shaft Assembly

LTV0500000000531

Fig. 35 Exploded view of tilt steering column with floor shift (Part 2 of 2). Colorado & Canyon

TIGHTENING SPECIFICATIONS

Year/ Model	Component	Torque Ft. Lbs.
ASTRO & SAFARI		
2002–06	Cable Shift Cam Screws	13
	G/S Lever Support Bracket Screws	89①
	Housing Assembly To Jacket Screws	80①
	Ignition Switch Screws	12①
	Key Alarm Switch Screws	12①
	Lock Cylinder Module Screws	30①
	Lower Column Mounting Nuts	22
	Lower Shroud Screws	30①
	Multi-Function Switch Screws	30①
	Shift Lever Clevis Screws	13
	Shift Lever Gate Screws	58①
	Steering Shaft Nut	30
	Steering Shaft Pinch Bolt	30
	Steering Wheel Nut	30
	Turn Signal Switch Screws	30①
	Upper Column Mounting Nuts	22
	Upper Shroud Screws	12①
AVALANCHE, ESCALADE, HUMMER H2, SIERRA, SILVERADO, SUBURBAN, TAHOE, YUKON & YUKON XL		
2002–06	Horn Contact Plate Screws	53①
	Intermediate Shaft Coupler Bolt	35①
	Lower Column Cover Screws	25①
	Multi-Function Switch Screws	53①
	Shift Lever Screws	16
	Steering Column Bracket Nuts	22
	Steering Column Seal Nuts	25
	Steering Wheel Nut	29
	Upper Column Covers	15①
	Upper To Lower Intermediate Shaft Pinch Bolt	37
AZTEK & RENDEZVOUS		
2002–06	Anchor Cable Nut At Console Support Bracket	89①
	Intermediate Steering Shaft Bolts	35
	Intermediate Steering Shaft Seal Bolts	27①
	Steering Column Bolts At IP Lower Bracket	18
	Steering Column Support Bolts, Internal	13
	Steering Column Nuts At IP Upper Bracket	18
	Steering Column Tilt Lever Bolt	89①
	Steering Wheel Nut	30
	Trim Cover Screws, Lower	31①
	Trim Cover Screws, Upper	13①
	Turn Signal Switch Screws	62①
BRAVADA		
2002–04	Horn Plate Switch Crews	49①
	HVAC Floor Duct Mounting Screw	17①
	Ignition Lock Cylinder Case Screws	62①
	Intermediate Shaft To Steering Column Pinch Bolt	37
	Intermediate Shaft To Steering Gear Pinch Bolt	29

TIGHTENING SPECIFICATIONS—Continued

Year/ Model	Component	Torque Ft. Lbs.
BRAVADA		
2002–04	Steering Column Electrical Connector Screw	53①
	Steering Column Mounting Nuts	20
	Steering Column Trim Cover Screws Lower	31①
	Steering Column Trim Cover Screws Upper	9①
	Steering Wheel Nut	30
	Steering Wheel Shroud Screws	18①
	Turn Signal Multi-Function Switch Screws Side	62①
	Turn Signal Multi-Function Switch Screws Top	27①
	Upper Intermediate Shaft To Lower Intermediate Shaft Pinch Bolt	37
C & K SERIES		
2002–06	Cable Shift Cam Screws	13
	Gear Shift Lever Support Bracket Screws	89①
	Hazard Switch Screws	53①
	Hex Head Nut	46
	Housing Assembly To Jacket Screws	80①
	Ignition & Key Alarm Switch Screws	12①
	Intermediate Shaft Coupler Pinch Bolt	22
	Intermediate Shaft Upper Pinch Bolt	46
	Lock Cylinder Module Screws	53①
	Lower Column Cover Screws	53①
	Multi-Function Switch Screws	53①
	Pinch Bolt	35
	Round Head Locking Bolt	35
	Shift Lever Gate Screws	58①
	Shift Lever Screws	16
	Steering Column Bracket Nuts	22
	Steering Shaft Nut	29
	Steering Wheel Nut	29
	Support Bracket Bolts	22
	Turn Signal Switch Screws	53①
	Upper Column Cover Screws	12①
COLORADO & CANYON		
2004–06	Column Support Bracket Nuts	22
	Horn Contact Plate Screws	50①
	Ignition Lock Cylinder Case Shear Bolt	②
	Intermediate Shaft To Steering Column Pinch Bolt	17
	Intermediate Shaft To Steering Gear Pinch Bolt	33
	Linear Shift Assembly To Steering Column Mounting Screws	89①
	Lower Intermediate Shaft To Upper Intermediate Shaft Pinch Bolt	17
	Lower Mounting Bracket	75①
	Shift Lever Screw	15
	Steering Column Bulkhead Connector Screw	53①

Continued

TIGHTENING SPECIFICATIONS—Continued

Year/ Model	Component	Torque Ft. Lbs.
COLORADO & CANYON		
2004–06	Steering Column Mounting Bolts	20
	Steering Column Support Screws	14
	Steering Column Toe Plate Nuts	22
	Steering Column Trim Cover Screws Lower	31①
	Steering Wheel Nut	26
	Switch Mounting Bracket	22①
	Turn Signal Multi-Function Switch Screws	40①
	Upper Intermediate Shaft To Dash Stud Nuts	17
	Upper Intermediate Shaft To Lower Intermediate Shaft Pinch Bolt	17
ENVOY, RAINIER & TRAILBLAZER		
2002–06	Adapter Support Plate	62①
	Horn Plate Switch Screws	49①
	HVAC Floor Duct Mounting Screw	17①
	Ignition Shaft To Steering Column Pinch Bolt	62①
	Intermediate Shaft To Steering Column Pinch Bolt	37
	Intermediate Shaft To Steering Gear Pinch Bolt	29
	Steering Column Electrical Connector Screw	53①
	Steering Column Mounting Nuts	20
	Steering Column Trim Cover Screws Lower	31①
	Steering Column Trim Cover Screws Upper	9①
	Steering Wheel Nut	30
	Steering Wheel Shroud Screws	18①
	Turn Signal Multi-Function Switch Screws Side	62①
	Turn Signal Multi-Function Switch Screws Top	27①
	Upper Intermediate Shaft To Lower Intermediate Shaft Pinch Bolt	37
EQUINOX & TORRENT		
2005–06	Ignition Lock Cylinder Solenoid Screw	17①
	Ignition Switch Lock Housing Bolts	71
	Ignition Switch Screws	22①
	Intermediate Shaft Pinch Bolt	25
	Multi-Function Turn Signal Headlamp Switch Screw	17①
	Steering Column Mid Pivot Bolt	18
	Steering Column Mounting Bolt	18
	Steering Column Trim Cover Screws	17①
	Steering Column Upper Jacket Bolt	97①
	Steering Wheel Nut	31

TIGHTENING SPECIFICATIONS—Continued

Year/ Model	Component	Torque Ft. Lbs.
EXPRESS & SAVANA		
2003–06	Column Support Bracket Nuts	22
	Cruise Control Module Mounting Nuts	44①
	Horn Contact Plate Screws	49①
	Ignition Lock Cylinder Case Screws	115①
	Intermediate Shaft Bearing Bracket Retaining Nuts	22
	Intermediate Shaft Bearing Lower Brace Retaining Nut	22
	Intermediate Shaft Seal Bolts	18①
	Intermediate Shaft To Steering Column Pinch Bolt	46
	Intermediate Shaft To Steering Gear Pinch Bolt	45
	Linear Shaft Assembly To Steering Column Mounting Screws	115①
	Lower Intermediate Shaft To Intermediate Shaft Bearing Retaining Bolt	22
	Shift Lever Screw	15
	Steering Column Bulkhead Connector Screw	53①
	Steering Wheel Nut	30
	Turn Signal Multi-Function Switch Screws	9①
	Upper Intermediate Shaft To Intermediate Shaft Bearing Retaining Bolt	22
HHR		
2006	Ignition Lock Cylinder Solenoid Screw	18①
	Ignition Switch Screws	18①
	Intermediate Shaft Pinch Bolt	25
	Steering Column Mid Pivot Bolt	18
	Steering Column Mounting Bolt	18
	Steering Column Trim Cover Screws	18①
	Steering Column Upper Jacket Bolt	97①
	Steering Wheel Control Switch	16①
	Steering Wheel Horn Switch Bolts	62①
	Steering Wheel Nut	31
HUMMER H3		
2006	Column Support Bracket Nuts	20
	Horn Contact Plate Screws	50①
	Ignition Lock Cylinder Case Shear Bolt	②
	Intermediate Shaft To Steering Column Pinch Bolt	45
	Intermediate Shaft To Steering Gear Pinch Bolt	33
	Lower Intermediate Shaft To Upper Intermediate Shaft Pinch Bolt	17
	Steering Column Bulkhead Connector Screw	53①
	Steering Column Support Screws	13
	Steering Column Toe Plate Nuts	22
	Steering Column Trim Cover Screws	30①

Continued

TIGHTENING SPECIFICATIONS—Continued

Year/ Model	Component	Torque Ft. Lbs.
HUMMER H3		
2006	Steering Column Trim Cover Screws Upper	13①
	Steering Wheel Nut	26
	Turn Signal Multi-Function Switch Mounting Bracket	22
	Turn Signal Multi-Function Switch Screws	62①
MONTANA, SILHOUETTE, TRANS SPORT & VENTURE		
2002–06	Air Bag Module To Steering Wheel	22
	Bolt At Rack & Pinion	35
	Cable Shift Cam Screw	13
	Gear Shift Lever Support Bracket Screw	89①
	Ignition & Key Alarm Switch Screws	12①
	Lock Module Screws	53①
	Lower Column Cover Bolts Or Screws	36①
	Lower Steering Column Bolts	18
	Multi-Function Switch Screws	53①
	Pinch Bolt	35
	Shift Lever Clevis Screw	13
	Shift Lever Gate	58①
	Shift Lever Screw	15
	Steering Column Intermediate Shaft Coupling Bolt	35
	Steering Column Support Screw	80①
	Steering Shaft Nut	35
	Steering Wheel Nut	35
	Transmission Range Selector Lever Screw	14
	Turn Signal Switch Screws	53①
	Upper Steering Column Bolt	18
	Upper Steering Column Cover Screws	36①
RELAY, SV6, TERRAZA & UPLANDER		
2005–06	Anchor Cable Nut At Console Support Bracket	89①
	Ignition Switch Screws	11①
	Intermediate Steering Shaft Bolt	35
	Intermediate Steering Shaft Bolt At Gear	35
	Intermediate Steering Shaft Seal Bolts	27①
	Linear Shift Assembly Screw	89①
	Multi-Function Switch Screws	26①
	Shift Lever Set Screw	62①
	Steering Column Bolts At Instrument Panel Lower Bracket	18
	Steering Column Nuts At Instrument Panel Upper Bracket	18
2005–06	Steering Column Support Bolts Internal	13
	Steering Column Tilt Lever Bolt	89①
	Steering Wheel Nut	30③
	Steering Wheel Rear Bezel Screws	27①
	Trim Cover Screws Lower	13①
	Trim Cover Screws Upper	31①

TIGHTENING SPECIFICATIONS—Continued

Year/ Model	Component	Torque Ft. Lbs.
SSR		
2003–06	Horn Contact Plate Screws	49①
	HVAC Floor Duct Mounting Screw	17①
	Ignition Lock Cylinder Case Screws	62①
	Intermediate Shaft To Steering Column Pinch Bolt	37
	Intermediate Shaft To Steering Gear Pinch Bolt	37
	Steering Column Electrical Connector Screw	53①
	Steering Column Mounting Nuts	20
	Steering Column Trim Cover Screws Lower	31①
	Steering Column Trim Cover Screws Upper	9①
	Steering Wheel Nut	30
	Steering Wheel Shroud Screws	18①
	Turn Signal Multi-Function Switch Screws Side	62①
	Turn Signal Multi-Function Switch Screws Top	27①
	Upper Intermediate Shaft To Lower Intermediate Shaft Pinch Bolt	37
SRX		
2004–06	Ignition Lock Cylinder Case Screws	62①
	Intermediate Shaft Bolts	22
	Intermediate Shaft To Steering Column Pinch Bolt	35
	Intermediate Shaft To Steering Gear Pinch Bolt	37
	Steering Column Mounting Nuts	18
	Steering Column Trim Cover Screws Lower In Center Of Cover	31①
	Steering Column Trim Cover Screws Lower Nearest Tilt Lever	14①
	Steering Column Trim Cover Screws Upper	9①
	Steering Wheel Control Harness Retainer Screws	20①
	Steering Wheel Control Switch Screws	20①
	Steering Wheel Nut	30
	Turn Signal Multi-Function Switch Screw Side	62①
	Turn Signal Multi-Function Switch Screw Top	27①
	Upper Intermediate Shaft To Lower Intermediate Shaft Pinch Bolt	22

Continued

TIGHTENING SPECIFICATIONS—Continued

Year/ Model	Component	Torque Ft. Lbs.
S & T SERIES		
2002–06	Gear Shift Lever Support Bracket Screws	89①
	Ignition & Key Alarm Switch Screws	12①
	Intermediate Shaft Seal Bolt	27①
	Lock Module Assembly Screws	53①
	Lower Brace Screws	10
	Lower Intermediate Shaft Rag Joint Bolt	25
	Lower Steering Column Mounting Nuts	22
	Multi-Function Switch Screws	53①
	Pinch Bolt	35
	Shift Lever Clevis & Cable Shift Cam Screws	13
	Shift Lever Gate	58①
	Steering Column Support Screws	80①
	Steering Shaft Nut	30
	Steering Wheel Nut	30
	Turn Signal Switch Screws	53①
	Upper Steering Column Mounting Nut	22
TRACKER		
2002–05	Air Bag Module Retaining Bolts	17
	Steering Column Bolts	17
	Steering Shaft Joint Bolts	18
	Steering Shaft Nut	24
	Steering Wheel Nut	24

TIGHTENING SPECIFICATIONS—Continued

Year/ Model	Component	Torque Ft. Lbs.
VUE		
2002–06	Ignition Lock Cylinder Solenoid	17①
	Ignition Switch	17①
	Ignition Lock Cylinder Case Shear Bolt	15
	Intermediate Shaft Pinch Bolt	25
	Multi-Function Turn Signal/Headlamp Switch	17①
	Steering Column Mid Pivot Bolt	18
	Steering Column Mounting Bolt	18
	Steering Column Trim Cover	17①
	Steering Column Upper Jacket Bolt	97①
	Steering Wheel Nut	31

① — Inch lbs.

② — Tighten until bolt head breaks off

③ — This fastener may be reused only if fastener and its counterpart are clean and free from rust. Fastener develops a specified amount of torque against its counterpart prior to fastener seating.

POWER STEERING

TABLE OF CONTENTS

Application Chart

Model	Steering Gear	Steering Pump
Astro & Safari	Saginaw 700 Series Integral	Constant Displacement Vane-Type Pump
Avalanche, Escalade, Suburban, Tahoe & Yukon①	Saginaw 670 & 700 Series Integral	Constant Displacement Vane-Type Pump
Aztek & Rendezvous	Saginaw Rack & Pinion	Constant Displacement Vane-Type Pump
Blazer, Jimmy, Sonoma & S10	Saginaw 700 Series Integral	Constant Displacement Vane-Type Pump
Bravada, Envoy, Rainier & Trailblazer	Saginaw Rack & Pinion	Constant Displacement Vane-Type Pump
Canyon & Colorado	Saginaw Rack & Pinion	Constant Displacement Vane-Type Pump
Equinox & Torrent	Electric Power Steering (EPS) System	Electric Power Steering (EPS) System
Express & Savana	Saginaw 700 Series Integral	Constant Displacement Vane-Type Pump
HHR	Electric Power Steering (EPS) System	Electric Power Steering (EPS) System
Hummer H2	Saginaw 700 Series Integral	Constant Displacement Vane-Type Pump
Hummer H3	Saginaw Rack & Pinion	Constant Displacement Vane-Type Pump
Montana, Silhouette & Venture	Saginaw Rack & Pinion	Constant Displacement Vane-Type Pump
Relay, SV6, Terraza & Uplander	Saginaw Rack & Pinion	Constant Displacement Vane-Type Pump
Sierra & Silverado 2WD C1500	Saginaw Rack & Pinion	Constant Displacement Vane-Type Pump
Sierra & Silverado Except 2WD C1500	Saginaw 670 & 700 Series Integral	Constant Displacement Vane-Type Pump
SRX②	Saginaw Rack & Pinion	Constant Displacement Vane-Type Pump
SSR	Saginaw Rack & Pinion	Constant Displacement Vane-Type Pump
Tracker	Tracker Rack & Pinion	Koyo Seiko
Vue	Electric Power Steering (EPS) System	Electric Power Steering (EPS) System

① — These 2002 models are available w/Variable Effort Steering (VES) system.

② — These models are available w/Variable Effort Steering (VES) system.

Power Steering Pressure Specifications

Year	Models	Engine Size	High Flow, GPM	Pressure Relief, psi
ASTRO & SAFARI				
2002–05	All	4.3L	3.10/3.50	1350
AVALANCHE				
2002–06	All	5.3L & 8.1L	3.50/3.90	1425/1525
AZTEK & RENDEZVOUS				
2002–05	All	3.4L	1.70/2.10	1350/1500
		3.6L	3.36	1350/1500
2006	All	3.5L	1.70/2.10	1350/1500
		3.6L	3.36	1350/1500
BLAZER, JIMMY, SONOMA & S10				
2002–03	RWD	2.2L	2.40/2.80	1100/1250
	RWD	4.3L	2.50/2.90	1100/1250
	4WD	4.3L	2.90/3.30	1350/1500
2004–05	ALL	4.3L	2.90/3.30	1350/1500
BRAVADA, ENVOY, RAINIER & TRAILBLAZER				
2002	Five-Passenger	4.2L	2.70/3.10	1500/1600
	Seven-Passenger	4.2L	3.10/3.50	1500/1600
2003–04	Five-Passenger	4.2L	2.70/3.10	1500/1600
	Seven-Passenger	4.2L & 5.3L	3.10/3.50	1500/1600
2005	Five-Passenger	4.2L & 5.3L	2.70/3.10	1500/1600
	Seven-Passenger	4.2L & 5.3L	3.10/3.50	1500/1600
2006	Five-Passenger	4.2L & 5.3L	2.70/3.10	1500/1600
	Seven-Passenger	4.2L & 5.3L	3.10/3.50	1500/1600
	SS	6.0L	2.70/3.10	1400/1500
CANYON & COLORADO				
2004–06	All	2.8L & 3.5L	2.40/2.80	1350/1450
ESCALADE & ESCALADE EXT				
2002–06	All	5.3L	2.70/3.10	1475/1525
		6.0L	3.50/3.90	1425/1525
EXPRESS & SAVANA				
2002	G 10/20 Series 7200/8600 GVW w/vacuum brakes	4.3L, 5.0L & 5.7L	2.70/3.10	1425/1525
	G 20/30 Series Above 8600 GVW w/hydroboost	6.5L Diesel & 8.1L	3.10/3.50	1425/1525
2003–05	All	4.3L, 4.8L, 5.7L & 6.0L	2.70/3.10	1425/1525
2006	All	4.3L, 4.8L, 5.7L, 6.0L & 6.6L	2.70/3.10	1425/1525
HUMMER H2				
2003–06	All	6.0L	3.50/3.90	1425/1525
HUMMER H3				
2006 (1560641)	All	3.5L	2.50/2.90	1350/1450
MONTANA, SILHOUETTE & VENTURE				
2002–05	All	3.4L	1.70/2.10	1200/1300
RELAY, SV6, TERRAZA & UPLANDER				
2005	All	3.5L	1.70/2.10	1350/1500
2006	All	3.5L & 3.9L	1.70/2.10	1350/1500

Continued

Year	Models	Engine Size	High Flow, GPM	Pressure Relief, psi
SIERRA & SILVERADO				
2002	C15 With Vacuum Brakes & New Style Flow Control Valve Has "AA" Stamped Into The Fitting	4.3L, 4.8L & 5.3L	2.90/3.30	1425/1525
	C15 With Vacuum Brakes & Old Style Flow Control Valve Has "O" Stamped Into The Fitting	4.3L, 4.8L & 5.3L	3.50/3.90	1425/1525
	C/K 25/35	8.1L	3.50/3.90	1425/1525
	C/K 35 w/Hydroboost	6.6L Diesel	3.50/3.90	1425/1525
	K15 w/Vacuum Brakes	4.3L, 4.8L, 5.3L & 6.0L	2.70/3.10	1425/1525
2003–06	C15 w/Vacuum Brakes, 7200 GVW	4.3L, 4.8L & 5.3L	2.90/3.30	1425/1525
	K15 w/Vacuum Brakes, 7200 GVW	4.3L, 4.8L & 5.3L	2.70/3.10	1425/1525
	K15 & Sierra Denali w/Vacuum Brakes	6.0L	3.50/3.90	1425/1525
	C/K 15HD/25/25HD/35 w/Hydroboost	6.0L	3.50/3.90	1425/1525
	C/K 25/25HD/35	6.6L Diesel & 8.1L	3.50/3.90	1425/1525
SRX				
2004–06	All	3.6L & 4.6L	2.84/3.24	1668/1770
SSR				
2003–06	All	5.3L	3.10/3.50	1500/1600
SUBURBAN, TAHOE & YUKON				
2002	C15 w/Vacuum Brakes	5.3L	2.70/3.10	1425/1525
	C25 & K15 w/Hydroboost	5.3L & 6.0L	3.50/3.90	1425/1525
	K15 w/Vacuum Brakes	4.8L, 5.3L & 6.0L	1.65/3.80	1425/1525
2003–06	Vacuum Brakes	4.8L & 5.3L	2.70/3.10	1475/1525
	Hydroboost	6.0L & 8.1L	3.50/3.90	1425/1525
TRACKER				
2002–04	Tracker, Tracker ZR2	2.0L	1.70/2.10	972/1088
	Tracker LT, Tracker ZR2 V6	2.5L	1.20/2.10	1044/1160

GPM — Gallons Per Minute

Constant Displacement Vane-Type Pump

INDEX

DESCRIPTION

The hydraulic pump is a submerged, vane-type design. Submerged pumps have a housing and internal components inside the reservoir and operate submerged in fluid.

There are two openings at the rear of the pump housing. The larger opening contains the cam ring, pressure plate, thrust plate, rotor and vane assembly and the end plate. The smaller opening contains the pressure line union, flow control valve, and spring. The flow control orifice is part of the pressure line union. The pressure relief valve, located inside the flow control valve, limits pump pressure.

DIAGNOSIS & TESTING

Symptom Based Diagnosis

Refer to **Figs. 1 through 10** for symptom based diagnosis. Perform the "Power Steering System Test" first.

Power Steering System Test

Refer to **Fig. 11** for power steering system test.

DIAGNOSTIC CHART INDEX

Description	Page No.	Fig. No.
ASTRO & SAFARI		
Power Steering System Test Procedure	22-11	11
Power Steering Fluid Leaks	22-7	1
Rattle, Clunk Or Shudder Noise From Power Steering System	22-8	4
Steering Effort Hard In One Or Both Directions	22-10	9
Steering Effort Too Easy In One Or Both Directions	22-10	10
Whine Or Growl Noise From Power Steering System	22-10	7
AVALANCHE, ESCALADE EXT, ESCALADE, SUBURBAN, TAHOE & YUKON		
Power Steering System Test Procedure	22-11	11
Power Steering Fluid Leaks	22-7	3
Rattle, Clunk Or Shudder Noise From Power Steering System	22-9	6
Steering Effort Hard In One Or Both Directions	22-10	9
Steering Effort Too Easy In One Or Both Directions	22-10	10
Whine Or Growl Noise From Power Steering System Less Hydraulic Brake Booster	22-10	8
Whine Or Growl Noise From Power Steering System w/Hydraulic Brake Booster	22-10	7
AZTEK & RENDEZVOUS		
Power Steering System Test Procedure	22-11	11
Power Steering Fluid Leaks	22-7	1
Rattle, Clunk Or Shudder Noise From Power Steering System	22-9	5
Steering Effort Hard In One Or Both Directions	22-10	9
Steering Effort Too Easy In One Or Both Directions	22-10	10
Whine Or Growl Noise From Power Steering System	22-10	8
BLAZER, JIMMY, SONOMA & S10		
Power Steering System Test Procedure	22-11	11
Power Steering Fluid Leaks	22-7	1

Continued

DIAGNOSTIC CHART INDEX—Continued

Continued

DIAGNOSTIC CHART INDEX—Continued

Step	Action	Yes	No
1	Did you review the Power Steering System General Description	Go to Step 2	Check Symptoms
2	Verify that power steering fluid leaks are present. Is the power steering system leaking?	Go to Step 3	System OK
3	Inspect the power steering system fittings. Are the fittings leaking?	Go to Step 8	Go to Step 4
4	Inspect the power steering hoses. Are the hoses leaking?	Go to Step 9	Go to Step 5
5	Inspect the power steering sensors. Are the sensors leaking?	Go to Step 10	Go to Step 6
6	Inspect the power steering pump, shaft seal, and the reservoir for leaks. Is the power steering pump, shaft seal, or reservoir leaking?	Go to Step 11	Go to Step 7
7	Inspect the power steering gear for leaks. Is the power steering gear leaking?	Go to Step 12	Go to Step 8
8	Tighten the fittings. Did you complete the repair?	Go to Step 13	--
9	Replace the power steering hoses. Did you complete the repair?	Go to Step 13	--
10	Replace the power steering sensors. Did you complete the repair?	Go to Step 13	--

LTV0500000001537

Fig. 1 Power Steering Fluid Leaks (Part 1 of 2). Astro, Aztek, Blazer, Bravada, Envoy, Jimmy, Rainier, Rendezvous, Safari, Sonoma, SRX, SSR, S10 & Trailblazer

Step	Action	Yes	No
1	Did you review the Power Steering System General Description	Go to Step 2	Symptoms
2	Verify that power steering fluid leaks are present. Is the power steering system leaking?	Go to Step 3	System OK
3	Inspect the power steering system fittings. Are the fittings leaking?	Go to Step 7	Go to Step 4
4	Inspect the power steering hoses. Are the hoses leaking?	Go to Step 8	Go to Step 5
5	Inspect the power steering pump and the reservoir for leaks. Is the power steering pump or reservoir leaking?	Go to Step 9	Go to Step 6
6	Inspect the power steering gear for leaks. Is the power steering gear leaking?	Go to Step 10	--
7	Tighten the fittings. Did you complete the repair?	Go to Step 11	--
8	Replace the power steering hoses. Did you complete the repair?	Go to Step 11	--
9	Replace the power steering pump. Did you complete the repair?	Go to Step 11	--
10	Replace the power steering gear. Did you complete the repair?	Go to Step 11	--
11	Operate the system in order to verify the repair. Did you correct the condition?	System OK	Go to Step 3

LTV0500000001548

Fig. 2 Power Steering Fluid Leaks. Canyon, Hummer H3 & Colorado

Step	Action	Yes	No
11	Replace the power steering pump, shaft seal, or reservoir. Did you complete the repair?	Go to Step 13	--
12	Replace the power steering gear. Did you complete the repair?	Go to Step 13	--
13	Operate the system in order to verify the repair. Did you correct the condition?	System OK	Go to Step 3

LTV0500000001538

Fig. 1 Power Steering Fluid Leaks (Part 2 of 2). Astro, Aztek, Blazer, Bravada, Envoy, Jimmy, Rainier, Rendezvous, Safari, Sonoma, SRX, SSR, S10 & Trailblazer

Test Description

The numbers below refer to the step numbers on the diagnostic table.

5. This step tests the system for restrictions.
7. This step tests the following components for the following conditions:
   - The pump for internal leaks
   - The power steering pipes for kinks
8. This step tests the ability of the pump to regulate flow at maximum pressure.
10. This step tests the ability of the pump to regulate flow under normal operating conditions.
12. This step tests the internal components of the pump and the gear.

Step	Action	Value(s)	Yes	No
DEFINITION: The Power Steering System Test Procedure will perform the following functions: • Test the operation of the hydraulic power steering system. • Test the operation of the power steering pump and power steering gear. • Identify restrictions in the system.				
1	Inspect the power steering fluid for the following indications of contamination • Milky fluid-water • Brown fluid-burnt • Debris in fluid-plastic or dirt Is the fluid free of contamination?	--	Go to Step 3	Go to Step 2
2	Flush the power steering system. Did you complete the procedure?	--	Go to Step 3	--
3	**Important:** In order to accurately diagnose the system, the malfunction must be present during the test procedure. Attempt to duplicate the condition. Is the condition present?	--	Go to Step 4	System OK

LTV0500000001549

Fig. 3 Power Steering Fluid Leaks (Part 1 of 3). Avalanche, Escalade, Express, Hummer H2, Montana, Relay, Savana, Sierra, Silhouette, Silverado, Suburban, SV6, Tahoe, Terraza, Uplander, Venture & Yukon

Step	Action	Yes	No
4	Inspect the power steering hoses. Are the hoses leaking?	Go to Step 10	Go to Step 5
5	Inspect the power steering pump and the reservoir for leaks. Is the power steering pump or reservoir leaking?	Go to Step 11	Go to Step 6
6	Inspect the power steering gear for leaks. Is the power steering gear leaking?	Go to Step 12	Go to Step 7
7	Inspect the hydraulic brake booster assembly for leaks. Is the hydraulic brake booster assembly leaking?	Go to Step 13	Go to Step 8
8	Inspect the power steering cooler for leaks. Is the power steering cooler leaking?	Go to Step 14	Go to Step 3
9	Tighten the fittings. Did you complete the repair?	Go to Step 15	--
10	Replace the power steering hoses. Refer to the appropriate procedure(s): Did you complete the repair?	Go to Step 15	--
11	Replace the power steering pump or reservoir. Refer to Power Steering Pump Replacement or Power Steering Reservoir Replacement - Off Vehicle . Did you complete the repair?	Go to Step 15	--

LTV0500000001587

Fig. 3 Power Steering Fluid Leaks (Part 2 of 3). Avalanche, Escalade, Express, Hummer H2, Montana, Relay, Savana, Sierra, Silhouette, Silverado, Suburban, SV6, Tahoe, Terraza, Uplander, Venture & Yukon

Step	Action	Yes	No
1	Did you review the Power Steering System General Description	Go to Step 2	Check Symptoms -
2	Verify that a rattle, clunk or shudder noise is present. Is a rattle, clunk or shudder noise present?	Go to Step 3	System OK
3	Inspect the power steering hoses for proper routing and clearance. Is the routing or clearance of the power steering hoses incorrect?	Go to Step 12	Go to Step 4
4	Inspect the engine drive belt for cracking or excessive wear. Is the drive belt cracked or excessively worn?	Go to Step 13	Go to Step 5
5	Inspect the power steering pump pulley for damage. Is the power steering pump pulley damaged?	Go to Step 14	Go to Step 6
6	Inspect the power steering pump and the power steering mounting bracket/brace for the proper installation. Is the power steering pump installation incorrect?	Go to Step 15	Go to Step 7
7	Inspect the power steering gear for the proper installation. Is the power steering gear installation incorrect?	Go to Step 16	Go to Step 8
8	Inspect the steering gear bearing preload for the proper adjustment. Is the steering gear bearing preload adjustment incorrect?	Go to Step 17	Go to Step 9
9	Inspect the steering linkage. Is the steering linkage worn?	Go to Step 18	Go to Step 10
10	Inspect the suspension. Is the suspension worn?	Go to Step 19	Go to Step 11
11	Inspect the intermediate shaft. Is the intermediate shaft worn?	Go to Step 20	Go to Step 3

LTV0500000001531

Fig. 4 Rattle, Clunk Or Shudder Noise From Power Steering System (Part 1 of 2). Astro, Blazer, Jimmy, Safari, Sierra, Silverado, Sonoma & S10

Step	Action	Yes	No
12	Replace the power steering gear. Did you complete the repair?	Go to Step 15	--
13	Replace the hydraulic brake booster assembly. Did you complete the repair?	Go to Step 15	--
14	Replace the power steering cooler Did you complete the repair?	Go to Step 15	--
15	Operate the system in order to verify the repair. Did you correct the condition?	System OK	Go to Step 3

LTV0500000001550

Fig. 3 Power Steering Fluid Leaks (Part 3 of 3). Avalanche, Escalade, Express, Hummer H2, Montana, Relay, Savana, Sierra, Silhouette, Silverado, Suburban, SV6, Tahoe, Terraza, Uplander, Venture & Yukon

Step	Action	Yes	No
12	Adjust or replace the hoses. Did you complete the repair?	Go to Step 21	
13	Replace the engine drive belt. Did you complete the repair?	Go to Step 21	--
14	Replace the power steering pump pulley. Did you complete the repair?	Go to Step 21	--
15	Install the power steering pump correctly. Did you complete the repair?	Go to Step 21	--
16	Install the power steering gear correctly. Did you complete the repair?	Go to Step 21	--
17	Adjust the steering gear bearing preload. Did you complete the repair?	Go to Step 21	--
18	Replace the worn steering linkage. Refer to Steering Linkage Inspection in Steering Linkage. Did you complete the repair?	Go to Step 21	--
19	Replace the worn suspension components. Did you complete the repair?	Go to Step 21	--
20	Replace the intermediate shaft. Did you complete the repair?	Go to Step 21	--
21	Operate the system in order to verify the repair. Did you correct the condition?	System OK	Go to Step 3

LTV0500000001532

Fig. 4 Rattle, Clunk Or Shudder Noise From Power Steering System (Part 2 of 2). Astro, Blazer, Jimmy, Safari, Sierra, Silverado, Sonoma & S10

Step	Action	Yes	No
1	Did you review the Power Steering System General Description	Go to Step 2	Check Symptoms
2	Verify that a rattle, clunk or shudder noise is present. Is a rattle, clunk or shudder noise present?	Go to Step 3	System OK
3	Inspect the power steering hoses for proper routing and clearance. Is the routing or clearance of the power steering hoses incorrect?	Go to Step 10	Go to Step 4
4	Inspect the engine drive belt for cracking or excessive wear. Is the drive belt cracked or excessively worn?	Go to Step 11	Go to Step 5
5	Inspect the power steering pump pulley for damage. Is the power steering pump pulley damaged?	Go to Step 12	Go to Step 6
6	Inspect the power steering pump and the power steering mounting bracket/brace for the proper installation. Is the power steering pump installation incorrect?	Go to Step 13	Go to Step 7
7	Inspect the power steering gear for the proper installation Is the power steering gear installation incorrect?	Go to Step 14	Go to Step 8
8	Inspect the suspension. Is the suspension worn?	Go to Step 15	Go to Step 9
9	Inspect the intermediate shaft. Is the intermediate shaft worn?	Go to Step 16	Go to Step 3
10	Adjust or replace the hoses. Did you complete the repair?	Go to Step 17	--
11	Replace the engine drive belt. Did you complete the repair?	Go to Step 17	--

LTV0500000001539

Fig. 5 Rattle, Clunk Or Shudder Noise From Power Steering System (Part 1 of 2). Aztek, Rendezvous & SRX

Step	Action	Yes	No
1	Did you review the Power Steering System Description	Go to Step 2	Check Symptoms -
2	Verify that a rattle, clunk or shudder noise is present. Is a rattle, clunk or shudder noise present?	Go to Step 3	System OK
3	Inspect the power steering hoses for proper routing and clearance. Is the routing or clearance of the power steering hoses incorrect?	Go to Step 11	Go to Step 4
4	Inspect the engine drive belt for cracking or excessive wear. Is the drive belt cracked or excessively worn?	Go to Step 12	Go to Step 5
5	Inspect the power steering pump pulley for damage. Is the power steering pump pulley damaged?	Go to Step 13	Go to Step 6
6	Inspect the power steering pump and the power steering mounting bracket/brace for the proper installation. Is the power steering pump installation incorrect?	Go to Step 14	Go to Step 7
7	Inspect the power steering gear for the proper installation. Is the power steering gear installation incorrect?	Go to Step 15	Go to Step 8
8	Inspect the power steering gear rack bearing preload for the proper adjustment. Is the power steering gear rack bearing preload adjustment incorrect?	Go to Step 16	Go to Step 9
9	Inspect the suspension. Is the suspension worn?	Go to Step 17	Go to Step 10
10	Inspect the intermediate shaft. Is the intermediate shaft worn?	Go to Step 18	Go to Step 3
11	Adjust or replace the power steering hoses. Did you complete the repair?	Go to Step 19	--

LTV0500000001543

Fig. 6 Rattle, Clunk Or Shudder Noise From Power Steering System (Part 1 of 2). Avalanche, Bravada, Canyon, Colorado, Envoy, Escalade, Express, Hummer H2, Hummer H3, Montana, Rainier, Relay, Savana, Silhouette, SSR, Suburban, SV6, Terraza, Tahoe, Trailblazer, Uplander, Venture & Yukon

Step	Action	Yes	No
12	Replace the power steering pump pulley. Did you complete the repair?	Go to Step 17	--
13	Install the power steering pump correctly. Did you complete the repair?	Go to Step 17	--
14	Install the power steering gear correctly. Did you complete the repair?	Go to Step 17	--
15	Replace the worn suspension components. Did you complete the repair?	Go to Step 17	--
16	Replace the intermediate shaft. Did you complete the repair?	Go to Step 17	--
17	Operate the system in order to verify the repair. Did you correct the condition?	System OK	Go to Step 3

LTV0500000001540

Fig. 5 Rattle, Clunk Or Shudder Noise From Power Steering System (Part 2 of 2). Aztek, Rendezvous & SRX

Step	Action	Yes	No
12	Replace the engine drive belt. Did you complete the repair?	Go to Step 19	--
13	Replace the power steering pump pulley. Did you complete the repair?	Go to Step 19	--
14	Install the power steering pump correctly. Did you complete the repair?	Go to Step 19	--
15	Install the power steering gear correctly. Did you complete the repair?	Go to Step 19	--
16	Adjust the power steering gear rack bearing preload. Did you complete the repair?	Go to Step 19	--
17	Replace the worn suspension components. Did you complete the repair?	Go to Step 19	--
18	Replace the intermediate shaft. Did you complete the repair?	Go to Step 19	--
19	Operate the system in order to verify the repair. Did you correct the condition?	System OK	Go to Step 3

LTV0500000001544

Fig. 6 Rattle, Clunk Or Shudder Noise From Power Steering System (Part 2 of 2). Avalanche, Bravada, Canyon, Colorado, Envoy, Escalade, Express, Hummer H2, Hummer H3, Montana, Rainier, Relay, Savana, Silhouette, SSR, Suburban, SV6, Terraza, Tahoe, Trailblazer, Uplander, Venture & Yukon

Step	Action	Yes	No
1	Did you review the Power Steering System General Description	Go to Step 2	Check Symptoms -
2	Verify that a whine or growl noise is present. Is a whine or growl noise present?	Go to Step 3	System OK
3	Perform the power steering test procedure in order to diagnose a hydraulic condition and repair or replace a component. Did you repair or replace a power steering system component?	Go to Step 12	Go to Step 4
4	Using J 39570 , inspect the power steering gear for a whine or growl noise. Is the noise present at the power steering gear?	Go to Step 8	Go to Step 5
5	Using J 39570 , inspect the power steering pump for a whine or growl noise. Is the noise present at the power steering pump?	Go to Step 9	Go to Step 6
6	Inspect the power steering hoses for a whine or growl noise using J 39570 . Is the noise present at the power steering hoses?	Go to Step 10	Go to Step 7
7	Inspect the hydraulic brake booster for a whine or growl noise using J 39570 . Is the noise present at the hydro boost?	Go to Step 11	Go to Step 3
8	Replace the power steering gear. Did you complete the repair?	Go to Step 12	--
9	Replace the power steering pump. Did you complete the repair?	Go to Step 12	--
10	Adjust the routing of the power steering hoses. Did you complete the repair?	Go to Step 12	--
11	Diagnose the hydraulic brake booster. Did you correct the condition?	Go to Step 12	--
12	Operate the system in order to verify the repair. Did you correct the condition?	System OK	Go to Step 3

LTV0500000001533

Fig. 7 Whine Or Growl Noise From Power Steering System. Astro, Avalanche, Escalade, Hummer H2, Safari, Suburban, Tahoe & Yukon w/Hydraulic Brake Booster

Step	Action	Yes	No
1	Did you review the Power Steering System Description	Go to Step 2	Check Symptoms -
2	Verify that a whine or growl noise is present. Is a whine or growl noise present?	Go to Step 3	System OK
3	Perform the power steering test procedure in order to diagnose a hydraulic condition and repair or replace a component. Did you repair or replace a power steering system component?	Go to Step 10	Go to Step 4
4	Using the J 39570 Chassis Ear, inspect the power steering gear for a whine or growl noise. Is the noise present at the power steering gear?	Go to Step 7	Go to Step 5
5	Using the J 39570 , inspect the power steering pump for a whine or growl noise. Is the noise present at the power steering pump?	Go to Step 8	Go to Step 6
6	Using the J 39570 , inspect the power steering hoses for a whine or growl noise. Is the noise present at the power steering hoses?	Go to Step 9	Go to Step 2
7	Replace the power steering gear. Did you complete the repair?	Go to Step 10	--
8	Replace the power steering pump. Did you complete the repair?	Go to Step 10	--
9	Adjust the routing of the power steering hoses. Did you complete the repair?	Go to Step 10	--
10	Operate the system in order to verify the repair. Did you correct the condition?	System OK	Go to Step 3

LTV0500000001541

Fig. 8 Whine Or Growl Noise From Power Steering System. Avalanche, Aztek, Bravada, Blazer, Canyon, Colorado, Envoy, Escalade, Express, Hummer H3, Jimmy, Montana, Rainier, Relay, Rendezvous, Savana, Sierra, Silhouette, Silverado, Sonoma, SRX, SSR, Suburban, SV6, S10, Terraza, Tahoe, Trailblazer, Uplander, Venture & Yukon Less Hydraulic Brake Booster

Step	Action	Yes	No
1	Did you review the Power Steering System General Description	Go to Step 2	Go to Symptoms
2	Verify that the steering effort is hard in one or both directions. Does the system operate normally?	System OK	Go to Step 3
3	Perform the power steering test procedure. Did you complete the procedure?	Go to Step 4	--
4	Operate the system in order to verify the repair. Did you correct the condition?	System OK	Go to Step 3

LTV0500000001534

Fig. 9 Steering Effort Hard In One Or Both Directions

Step	Action	Yes	No
1	Did you review the Power Steering System Description	Go to Step 2	Symptoms
2	Verify that the steering effort is too easy in one or both directions. Does the system operate normally?	System OK	Go to Step 3
3	Perform the power steering test procedure. Did you complete the procedure?	Go to Step 4	--
4	Operate the system in order to verify the repair. Did you correct the condition?	System OK	Go to Step 3

LTV0500000001535

Fig. 10 Steering Effort Too Easy In One Or Both Directions

Test Description

The numbers below refer to the step numbers on the diagnostic table.

5. This step tests the system for restrictions.
7. This step tests the following components for the following conditions:
   - The pump for internal leaks
   - The power steering pipes for kinks
8. This step tests the ability of the pump to regulate flow at maximum pressure.
10. This step tests the ability of the pump to regulate flow under normal operating conditions.
12. This step tests the internal components of the pump and the gear.

Step	Action	Value(s)	Yes	No
DEFINITION: The Power Steering System Test Procedure will perform the following functions: • Test the operation of the hydraulic power steering system. • Test the operation of the power steering pump and power steering gear. • Identify restrictions in the system.				
1	Inspect the power steering fluid for the following indications of contamination: • Milky fluid - water • Brown fluid - burnt • Debris in fluid - plastic or dirt Is the fluid free of contamination?	--	Go to Step 3	Go to Step 2
2	Flush the power steering system. Did you complete the procedure?	--	Go to Step 3	--
3	**Important:** In order to accurately diagnose the system, the malfunction must be present during the test procedure. Attempt to duplicate the condition. Is the condition present?	--	Go to Step 4	System OK

LTV0500000001527

Fig. 11 Power Steering System Test Procedure (Part 1 of 4)

Step	Action	Value(s)	Yes	No
4	1. Turn the ignition switch to the OFF position. 2. Place a drain pan under the vehicle in order to catch any power steering fluid. 3. Disconnect the power steering pressure pipe/hose from the power steering pump or the power steering gear as necessary. 4. Install the J 44721 Power Steering System Analyzer . 5. Fill the power steering system. Did you complete the installation?	--	Go to Step 5	--
5	1. Fully open the J 44721 valve. 2. Start the engine. **Notice:** Do not hold the steering wheel in the full turn position longer than 5 seconds, as damage to the steering pump may result. 3. Turn the steering wheel and BRIEFLY hold the steering wheel against the steering stop in order to release any trapped air from the system. 4. Inspect and ensure that all of the power steering pipe/hose connections are not leaking. 5. Observe the pressure reading. Is the pressure reading greater than the specified value?	1379 kPa (200 psi)	Go to Step 6	Go to Step 7
6	**Important:** A restriction may be present in the power steering system. Turn off the engine IMMEDIATELY. Locate and repair the restriction. Did you complete the repair?	--	Go to Step 18	--
7	1. Allow the engine to run until the engine reaches full operating temperature. 2. Record the pressure reading and flow reading. 3. Partially close the J 44721 valve until the system pressure reaches the specified value, then record the FLOW reading. 4. Subtract second flow reading from the first flow reading. Is the flow DECREASE greater than 3.8 L (1 gal) per minute?	4827 kPa (700 psi)	Go to Step 13	Go to Step 8
8	**Notice:** Do not leave the valve fully closed for more than 5 seconds, or the pump could be damaged internally. Fully close then open the J 44721 valve 3 times. Record all of the high pressure readings. Are the three high pressure readings within specifications?	--	Go to Step 9	Go to Step 15

LTV0500000001528

Fig. 11 Power Steering System Test Procedure (Part 2 of 4)

POWER STEERING SYSTEM BLEED

1. Fill pump reservoir with fluid to minimum system level, FULL COLD level, or middle of hash mark on cap stick fluid level indicator.
2. **On models equipped with hydro-boost,** the oil level will appear falsely high i hydro-boost accumulator is not fully charged. **Do not apply brake pedal with engine OFF.** Proceed as follows:
   a. Start engine.
   b. Firmly apply brake pedal 10–15 times.
   c. Turn engine OFF.
3. **On all models,** raise and support front end of vehicle.
4. Turn steering wheel from stop to stop 12 times. On models equipped with hydro-boost systems or longer length power steering hoses may require turns up to 15–20 stop to stops.
5. Ensure power steering fluid lever in correct.
6. Fill pump fluid reservoir to proper level.
7. Start engine.
8. Turn steering wheel from lefthand to righthand side.
9. Inspect for sign of cavitation or fluid aeration (pump noise/whining).
10. Ensure fluid level is correct.

Component Service

Do not disassemble the power steering pump.

Refer to **Figs. 12 through 15** for exploded view of power steering pumps.

9	Are the three high pressure readings within 245 kPa (50 psi) of each other?	-	Go to Step 10	Go to Step 14
10	1. Increase the engine speed to approximately 1500 RPM. 2. Record the flow reading. Is the actual flow reading within specifications?	-	Go to Step 11	Go to Step 13
11	Is the difference between the actual flow reading and the maximum flow specification more than 3.8 L (1 gal) per minute?	-	Go to Step 16	Go to Step 12
12	**Notice:** Do not hold the steering wheel in the full turn position longer than 5 seconds, as damage to the steering pump may result. Turn the steering wheel from steering stop to steering stop and record the FLOW readings at each stop. Is the flow LOWER than 3.8 L (1 gal) per minute?	-	Go to Step 18	Go to Step 17
13	Replace the power steering pump. Did you complete the replacement?	-	Go to Step 18	--
14	1. Remove the power steering pump flow control valve. 2. Inspect the flow control valve. If any burrs or scratches are noticed on the flow control valve, replace the flow control valve. Do NOT attempt to clean the flow control valve. 3. Inspect the flow control valve bore. If any burrs or scratches are present in the control valve bore, replace the power steering pump. Did you complete the repair?	-	Go to Step 18	--
15	Replace the power steering pump flow control valve. Did you complete the replacement?	-	Go to Step 18	--
16	1. Remove the power steering pump flow control valve and inspect for any wear or damage. Do NOT disassemble the flow control valve. 2. If the flow control valve is worn damaged, replace the flow control valve. Did you complete the repair?	-	Go to Step 18	--
17	The power steering gear is leaking across the piston or bypassing the valve circuit. Replace the power steering gear. Did you complete the replacement?	-	Go to Step 18	--

LTV0500000001529

Fig. 11 Power Steering System Test Procedure (Part 3 of 4)

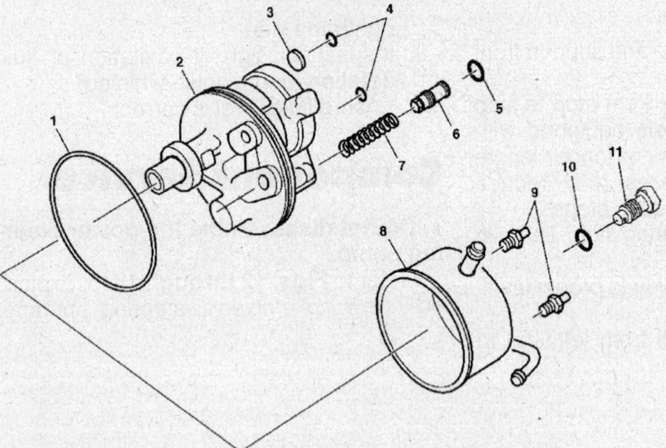

1. O-ring Seal
2. Hydraulic Pump Housing Assembly
3. Magnet
4. Rectangular Section Seal
5. Rectangular Section Seal
6. Control Valve Assembly
7. Flow Control Spring
8. Hydraulic Pump Reservoir Assembly
9. Pump Mounting Studs
10. O-ring Seal
11. Connector & Fitting Assembly

LTV0500000001526

Fig. 12 Exploded view of vane-type power steering pump w/integral reservoir. Astro, Express, Safari & Savana

18	Test the power steering system for the original condition. Does the original condition still exist?	--	Go to Step 5	Go to Step 19
19	1. Disconnect and remove the J 44721 from the vehicle. 2. Connect the vehicle power steering pipes/hoses. 3. Bleed the power steering system and add fluid as necessary. Did you complete the repair?	--	System OK	--

LTV0500000001530

Fig. 11 Power Steering System Test Procedure (Part 4 of 4)

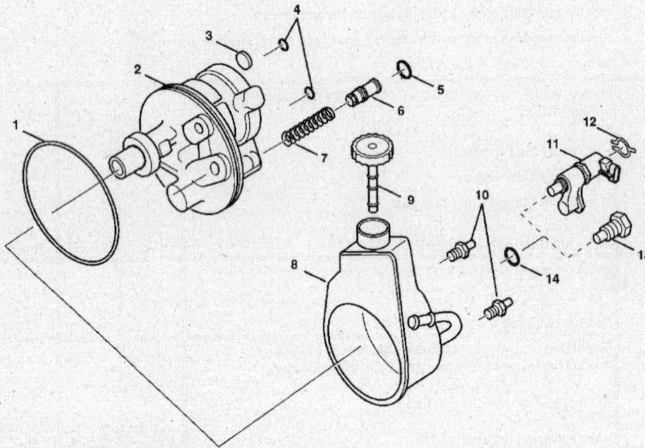

1. O-ring Seal
2. Hydraulic Pump Housing Assembly
3. Magnet
4. O-ring Seals
5. Rectangular Section Seal
6. Control Valve
7. Flow Control Spring
8. Reservoir Assembly
9. Reservoir Capstick
10. Pump Mounting Studs
11. Variable Assist Steering Actuator
12. Retaining Ring
13. Connector & Fitting Assembly
14. O-ring Seal

LTV0500000001547

Fig. 13 Exploded view of power steering pump less integral reservoir. Avalanche, Escalade EXT, Escalade, Hummer H2, Sierra, Silverado, Suburban, Tahoe & Yukon

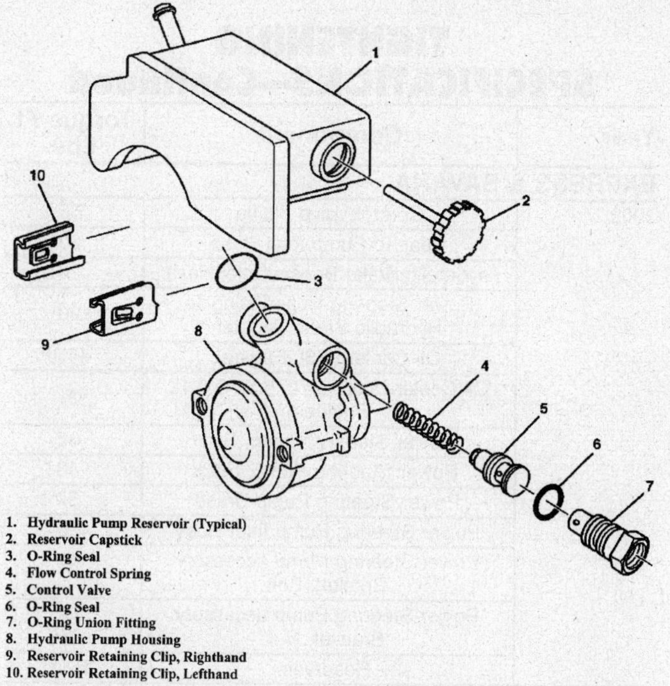

1. Hydraulic Pump Reservoir (Typical)
2. Reservoir Capstick
3. O-Ring Seal
4. Flow Control Spring
5. Control Valve
6. O-Ring Seal
7. O-Ring Union Fitting
8. Hydraulic Pump Housing
9. Reservoir Retaining Clip, Righthand
10. Reservoir Retaining Clip, Lefthand

LTV0500000001536

Fig. 14 Exploded view of CB series power steering pump less integral reservoir. Aztek, Bravada, Blazer, Canyon, Colorado, Envoy, Hummer H3, Jimmy, Montana, Rainier, Relay, Rendezvous, Silhouette, Sonoma, SSR, SV6, Terraza, Trailblazer, Uplander, Venture & S10

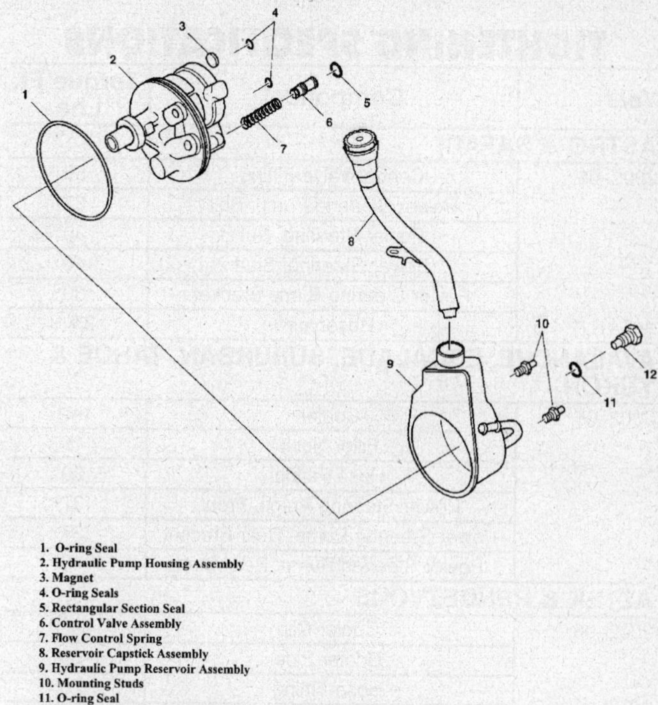

1. O-ring Seal
2. Hydraulic Pump Housing Assembly
3. Magnet
4. O-ring Seals
5. Rectangular Section Seal
6. Control Valve Assembly
7. Flow Control Spring
8. Reservoir Capstick Assembly
9. Hydraulic Pump Reservoir Assembly
10. Mounting Studs
11. O-ring Seal
11. 12. Connector & Fitting Assembly

LTV0500000001542

Fig. 15 Exploded view of P series power steering pump less integral reservoir. Sonoma & S10 w/2.2L Engine

TIGHTENING SPECIFICATIONS

Year	Component	Torque Ft. Lbs.
ASTRO & SAFARI		
2002–05	Control Valve Fitting	55
	Power Steering Pump, Bolt	37
	Power Steering, Nut	30
	Power Steering, Stud	43
	Power Steering Pump Bracket	30
	Reservoir	35①
AVALANCHE, ESCALADE, SUBURBAN, TAHOE & YUKON		
2002–06	Cooler	44①
	Filler Neck	18
	Hose Fitting	20
	Power Steering Pump, Front	37
	Power Steering Pump, Rear Bracket	37
	Power Steering Pump, Rear Stud	43
AZTEK & RENDEZVOUS		
2002–06	Cooler Clip	89①
	Cooler Pipe	20
	Hose Fitting	20
	O-Ring Union Fitting	55
	Power Steering Pump (3.4L Engine)	25
	Power Steering Pump (3.6L Engine)	37
	Power Steering Pump To Bracket (3.6L Engine)	15
	Pressure Hose/Pipe	19
	Reservoir	19
	Reservoir Bracket	53①
BLAZER, JIMMY, SONOMA & S10		
2002–05	Cooler	89①
	Flow Control Valve	55
	Hose Clamp	18①
	Power Steering Pump, Front (2.2L Engine)	18
	Power Steering Pump, Front Bolt (4.3L Engine)	37
	Power Steering Pump, Front Nut (4.3L Engine)	31
	Power Steering Pump, Rear Mount Bracket (2.2L Engine)	37
	Power Steering Pump, Rear Mount Bracket (4.3L Engine)	31
	Power Steering Pump, Stud	43
	Pressure Hose	18
BRAVADA, ENVOY, RAINIER & TRAILBLAZER		
2002–06	Flow Control Valve	55
	Hose Bracket	89①
	Power Steering Pump	18
	Power Steering Pump Bracket	37
	Pressure Hose	22
CANYON & COLORADO		
2004–06	Flow Control Valve	55
	Hose Clip	79①
	Power Steering Pump	18
	Power Steering Pump Bracket	37
	Pressure Hose To Pump	18

TIGHTENING SPECIFICATIONS—Continued

Year	Component	Torque Ft. Lbs.
EXPRESS & SAVANA		
2002	Control Valve Fitting	55
	Gear To Pump Inlet Hose	20
	Hydraulic Brake Booster Inlet Hose	20
	Power Steering Hose Fitting To Hydraulic Brake Booster	20
	Oil Cooler (4.3L Engine)	44①
	Oil Cooler (5.0L, 5.7L, 6.5L & 8.1L Engines)	21
	Power Steering Pump, Bolt	37
	Power Steering Pump, Stud	43
	Power Steering Pump Brace	37
	Power Steering Pump Inlet Hose	20
	Power Steering Pump accessory Bracket, Bolt	37
	Power Steering Pump accessory Bracket, Nut	30
	Reservoir	62①
2003–06	Accessory Mounting Bracket	37
	Cooler (Axle Rear 3.73 Ratio)	44①
	Cooler (4.10 Rear Axle Ratio)	21
	Flow Control Valve	55
	Hydraulic Brake Booster Inlet/Outlet Fitting	24
	Power Steering Pump, Bracket	37
	Power Steering Pump, Front	37
	Power Steering Pump, Lower & Rear (4.3L Engine)	30
	Power Steering Pump, Stud	43
	Power Steering Pump, Rear (4.8L, 5.3L & 6.0L Engines)	30
	Reservoir	58①
HUMMER H2		
2003–06	Cooler	44①
	Power Steering Pump, Bolt	37
	Power Steering Pump, Stud	44
	Power Steering Pump Bracket	37
	Power Steering Pump Connector & Fitting	55
	Pressure Hose	21
HUMMER H3		
2006	Power Steering Pump	18
	Power Steering Pump Bracket	37
	Pressure Hose	18
MONTANA, SILHOUETTE & VENTURE		
2002–05	Cooler Pipe	89①
	Flow Control Valve	55
	Hose/Pipe	20
	Power Steering Pump	25
RELAY, SV6, TERRAZA & UPLANDER		
2005–06	Cooler Pipe	89①
	Flow Control Valve	55
	Hose/Pipe Fitting	20
	Power Steering Pump	25

Continued

TIGHTENING SPECIFICATIONS—Continued

Year	Component	Torque Ft. Lbs.
SIERRA & SILVERADO		
2002–06	Accessory Mounting Bracket, Bolt	37
	Accessory Mounting Bracket, Nut	30
	Battery Junction Block	80①
	Cooler	44①
	Connector Fitting	55
	Hose Connection	20
	Hose Fitting (Parallel Hybrid)	18
	Power Steering Pump, Front (Gasoline Engines)	37
	Power Steering Pump (Diesel Engine)	34
	Power Steering Pump (Parallel Hybrid)	18
	Power Steering Pump Bracket (Diesel engine)	34
	Power Steering Pump Bracket (Parallel Hybrid)	18
	Power Steering Pump, Stud	43
	Power Steering Pump, Rear Bracket	37

TIGHTENING SPECIFICATIONS—Continued

Year	Component	Torque Ft. Lbs.
SRX		
2004–06	Cooler Hose/Line To Frame	35①
	Cooler To Bracket	80①
	Hose To Frame	40①
	Power Steering Pump Bracket	37
	Power Steering Pump To Bracket	18
	Power Steering Pump To Engine	37
	Pressure Hose To Frame	40①
	Pressure Hose To Pump	28
	Reservoir	80①
	Return Line	35①
SSR		
2003–06	Cooler	15
	Flow Control Valve	55
	Hose Bracket	89①
	Power Steering Pump	18
	Pressure Hose	18

① — Inch lbs.

Saginaw Integral Power Steering Gears

INDEX

DESCRIPTION

These power steering gears have a recirculating ball system which acts as a rolling thread between the worm shaft and the rack piston. The worm shaft is supported by a thrust bearing preload and two conical thrust races at the lower end, and a bearing assembly in the adjuster plug at the upper end, **Figs. 1 and 2.**

The control valve in the steering gear directs the power steering fluid to either side of the rack piston. The rack piston converts the hydraulic pressure into a mechanical force. If the steering system loses hydraulic pressure, the vehicle can be controlled manually.

When the worm shaft is turned right, the rack piston moves up in the gear while turning left moves the rack piston down in the gear. The rack piston teeth mesh with the pitman shaft sector. Turning the worm shaft turns the pitman shaft, which turns the wheels through the steering linkage.

DIAGNOSIS & TESTING

Refer to "Constant Displacement Vane-Type Pump" section for power steering system diagnosis and testing.

POWER STEERING SYSTEM SERVICE

Power Steering System Flush

Refer to "Constant Displacement Vane-Type Pump" section for power steering system for flushing procedures.

POWER STEERING SYSTEM BLEED

Refer to "Constant Displacement Vane-Type Pump" section for power steering system for bleeding procedures.

Component Service

If broken components or foreign materials are found during disassembly of the gear, the hydraulic system should be inspected, cleaned and flushed before service is complete.

The ball nut and control rings are not generally replaced unless cut or damaged. If replacing, inspect all mating components for burrs, cracks, scratches or damage. Replace or repair as needed.

670 SERIES GEAR

STUB SHAFT HOUSING, REPLACE

1. Remove mounting bolts, then the housing from gear.
2. Remove O-rings and retaining ring.
3. Reverse procedure to install. Use new rings.

PITMAN SHAFT & SIDE COVER, REPLACE

1. Remove stub shaft housing as outlined in "Stub Shaft Housing, Replace."
2. Remove pitman arm from steering gear.
3. Rotate stub shaft with suitable wrench from stop to stop.
4. Count number of turns, then rotate shaft back half total number of turns.
5. Remove pitman shaft cover mounting bolts.
6. Remove lash adjuster nut.
7. Remove shaft and cover assembly.
8. Reverse procedure to install. Use new O-ring.

PITMAN SHAFT SEALS & BEARING, REPLACE

1. Remove pitman shaft and side cover as outlined in "Pitman Shaft & Side Cover, Replace."
2. Clean exposed end of pitman shaft.
3. Clean splines with suitable wire brush.
4. Clean steering gear housing.
5. Remove pitman shaft boot and dust seal. **Do not score housing bore.**
6. Remove pitman shaft retaining ring with internal snap ring pliers No. J4245, or equivalent.
7. Remove backup washer from housing.
8. Pry pitman shaft seal from housing with suitable screwdriver.
9. Inspect housing and remove burrs.
10. Reverse procedure to install, noting the following:
    a. Drive needle bearing into housing until shoulder seats against housing using pitman shaft bearing remover and installer tool No. J6278, or equivalent.
    b. Coat pitman shaft seal and backup washer with suitable grease.

RACK PISTON & WORM SHAFT, REPLACE

1. Remove pitman shaft and side cover as outlined in "Pitman Shaft & Side Cover, Replace."
2. Remove pitman seals and bearing as outlined in "Pitman Shaft Seals & Bearing, Replace."
3. Remove stub shaft housing as outlined in "Stub Shaft Housing, Replace."
4. Turn stub shaft counterclockwise until rack piston begins to come out of steering gear housing.
5. Install rack piston arbor tool No. J21552, or equivalent, into rack piston bore.
6. Force rack piston into tool, by holding tool firmly against worn shaft while turning shaft counterclockwise.
7. Remove rack piston, balls and tool.
8. Remove tool from rack piston.
9. Remove Telfon ring and O-ring from housing.
10. Reverse procedure to install, noting the following:
    a. Lubricate O-ring and Teflon ring.
    b. Ensure balls remain in place.
    c. Install rack piston to worm shaft with rack piston Teflon ring compressor tool No. J8947, or equivalent.

700 SERIES GEAR

STUB SHAFT HOUSING, REPLACE

1. Remove stub shaft housing bolts from housing, **Fig. 3.**
2. Remove stub shaft housing.
3. Remove stub shaft housing O-rings.
4. Remove retaining ring.
5. Reverse procedure to install.

PITMAN SHAFT & SIDE COVER, REPLACE

1. Remove adjuster lock nut, **Fig. 4.**
2. Remove four bolts from side cover.
3. Rotate and center steering gear stub shaft using 12-point socket.
4. Remove following as an assembly:
    a. Side cover.
    b. Gasket.
    c. Pitman shaft.
5. Remove pitman shaft at side cover.
6. Reverse procedure to install.

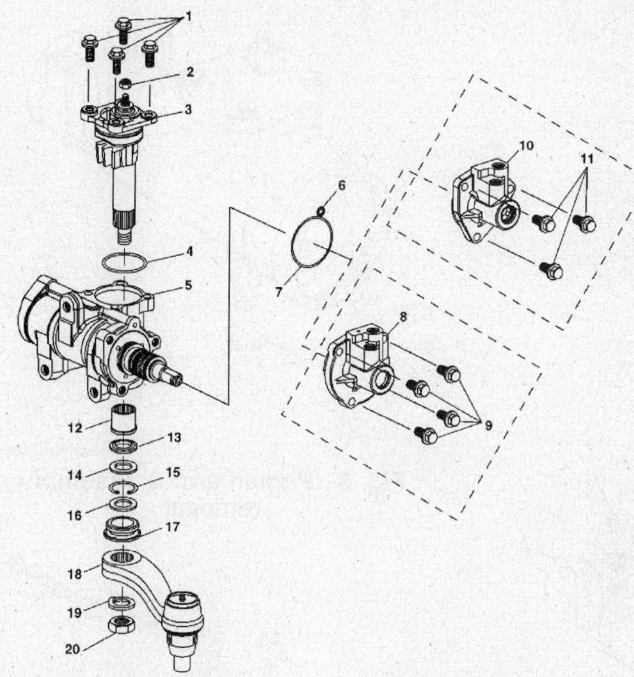

1. Hexagon Bolt
2. Lash Adjuster Nut
3. Pitman Shaft and Cover Assembly
4. O-Ring Seal
5. Steering Gear Housing Assembly
6. O-Ring Seal
7. O-ring Seal
8. Stub Shaft Housing (680 Gear)
9. Hexagon Bolt
10. Stub Shaft Housing (670 Gear)
11. Hexagon Bolt
12. Needle Bearing Assembly
13. Pitman Shaft Seal
14. Backup Washer
15. Retaining Ring
16. Dust Seal
17. Putman Shaft Boot
18. Pitman Arm Assembly
19. Lock Washer
20. Pitman Arm Nut

LTV0500000001525

Fig. 1 Exploded view of 670 series power steering gear

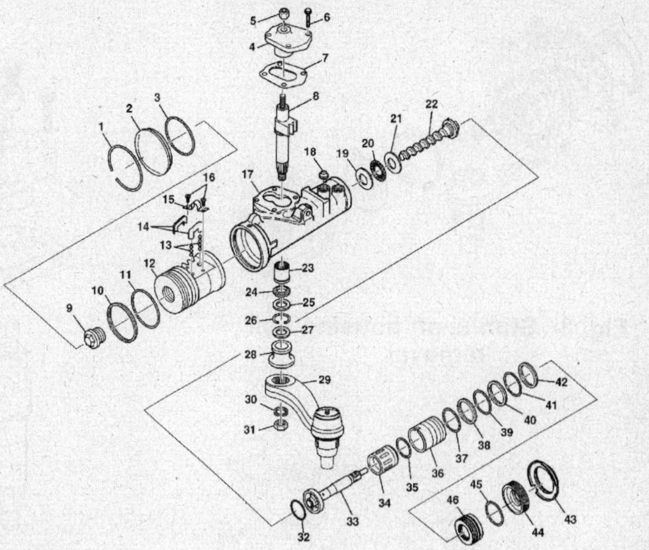

1 Retaining Ring
2 Plug
3 O-ring Seal
4 Side Cove
5 Adjuster Lock Nut
6 Bolt
7 Gasket
8 Pitman Shaft
9 Steering Gear Housing End Plug
10 Teflon Ring
11 O-ring Seal
12 Rack Piston
13 Balls
14 Ball Guide
15 Clamp
16 Screw
17 Housing
18 Check Valve
19 Flat Race
20 Thrust Bearing
21 Flat Race
22 Worm Shaft
23 Needle Bearing
24 Pitman Shaft Seal
25 Backup Washer
26 Retaining Ring
27 Dust Seal
28 Pitman Shaft Boot
29 Pitman Shaft Arm
30 Lock Washer
31 Nut
32 Seal
33 Stub Shaft
34 Valve Spool
35 Seal
36 Valve Body
37 O-ring Seal
38 Valve Body Ring
39 O-ring Seal
40 Valve Body Ring
41 O-ring Seal
42 Valve Body Ring
43 Coupling Shield Retainer and Lock Nut
44 Adjuster Nut Assembly
45 O-ring Seal
46 Thrust Support Assembly

LTV0500000001524

Fig. 2 Exploded view of 700 series power steering gear

PITMAN SHAFT SEALS & BEARING, REPLACE

1. Remove locknut and washer, then the pitman arm from steering gear, **Fig. 5.**
2. Remove pitman shaft and side cover as outlined in "Pitman Shaft & Side Cover, Replace."
3. Clean exposed end of pitman shaft and housing.
4. Remove dust seal.
5. Remove retaining nut using internal snap ring pliers tool No. J4245, or equivalent.
6. Remove backup washer and double lip seal using suitable screwdriver.
7. Remove steering gear housing.
8. Drive out needle bearing using pitman shaft bearing replacement tool No. J6278, or equivalent.
9. Reverse procedure to install.

RACK PISTON & WORM SHAFT, REPLACE

1. Remove pitman shaft and side cover as outlined in "Pitman Shaft & Side Cover, Replace."
2. Remove housing end plug, **Fig. 6.**
3. Turn stub shaft counterclockwise until rack piston begins to come out of steering gear housing.
4. Remove rack piston plug.
5. Install rack piston arbor tool No. J21552, or equivalent into bore of rack piston.
6. Hold rack piston arbor tool No. J21552, or equivalent tightly against worm shaft while turning stub shaft counterclockwise. Turning stub shaft forces race piston onto rack piston arbor tool No. J21552, or equivalent, leaving rack balls in place.
7. Remove following as assembly:
   a. Rack piston.
   b. Rack piston balls.
   c. Rack piston arbor tool No. J21552, or equivalent.
8. Remove steering gear valve.
9. Remove worm shaft, **Fig. 7.**
10. Remove thrust bearing and flat washer, **Fig. 7.**
11. Remove rack piston arbor tool No. J21552, or equivalent for rack piston.
12. Remove rack piston balls, **Fig. 7.**
13. Remove following components from rack piston:
    a. Screws.
    b. Clamps.
    c. Ball guide.
14. Remove teflon ring, O-ring seal, then clean all components.
15. Reverse procedure to install.

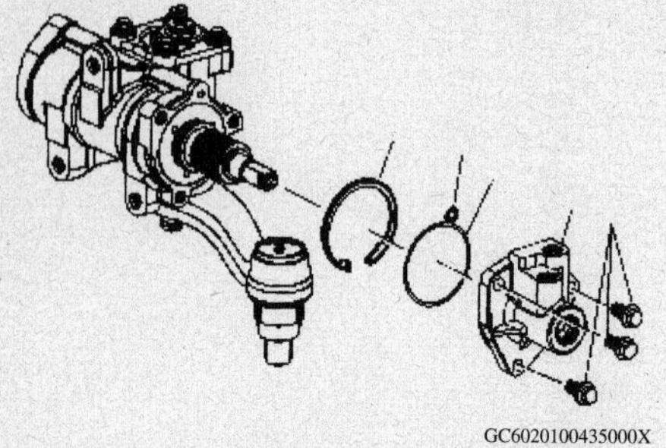
GC6020100435000X

Fig. 3 Stub shaft housing bolt removal

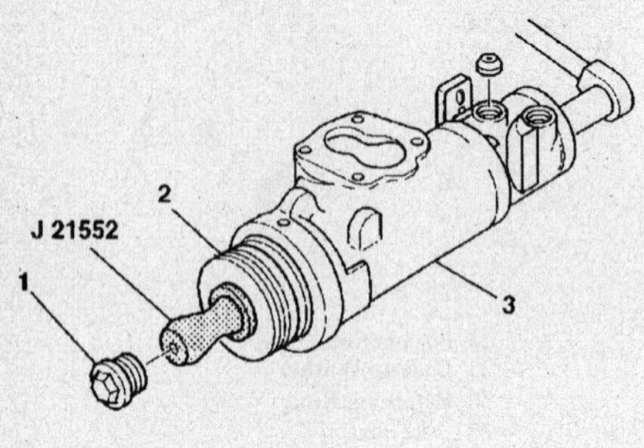

1. Housing end plug.
2. Bore of the rack piston.
3. Steering gear housing.

GC6020100438000X

Fig. 6 Housing end plug removal

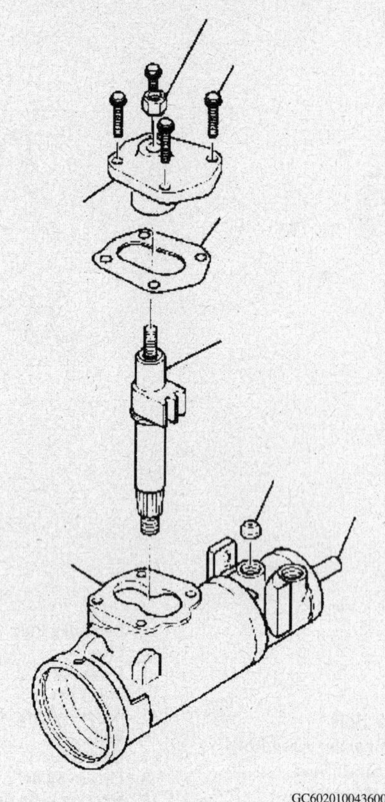
GC6020100436000X

Fig. 4 Adjuster lock nut removal

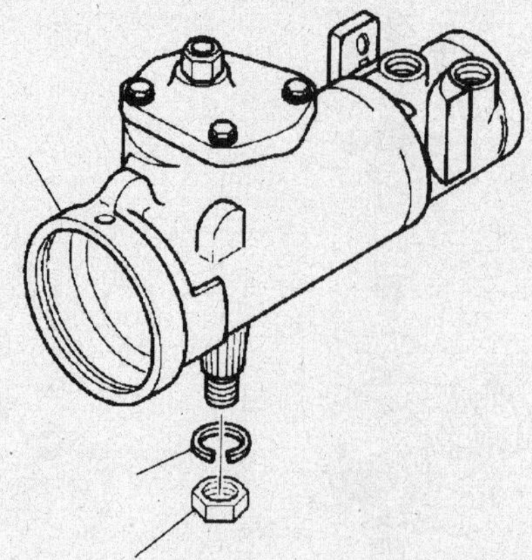
GC6020100437000X

Fig. 5 Pitman arm & assembly removal

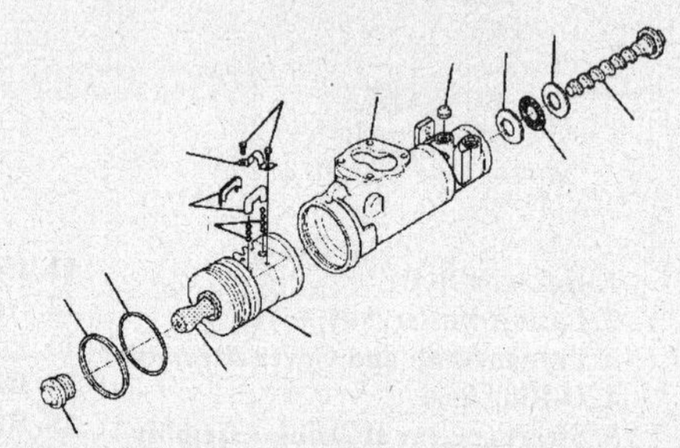
GC6020100439000X

Fig. 7 Worm shaft & component removal

TIGHTENING SPECIFICATIONS

Year	Component	Torque Ft. Lbs.
ASTRO & SAFARI		
2002–05	Housing Cover	45
	Hose Fitting	20
	Intermediate Shaft To Gear	30
	Pitman Arm To Connecting Rod	48
	Pitman Arm To Gear	184
	Power Steering Gear (AWD)	106
	Power Steering Gear (RWD)	55
	Power Steering Gear (4WD)	106
	Rack Piston Guide Clamp	53①
	Rack Piston Plug	111
	Worm Thrust Bearing Adjuster	22
AVALANCHE, ESCALADE, SUBURBAN, TAHOE & YUKON		
2002–06	Adjuster	20
	Adjuster Lock	36
	Ball Guide	53①
	Cooler	44①
	Coupler Shield	80
	Hose Fitting	20
	Pitman Arm To Relay Rod	46
	Pitman Arm To Steering Gear	184

TIGHTENING SPECIFICATIONS—Continued

Year	Component	Torque Ft. Lbs.
AVALANCHE, ESCALADE, SUBURBAN, TAHOE & YUKON		
2002–06	Power Steering Gear	110
	Rack Piston	111
	Rear Fitting	55
	Shaft Cover (670 Gear)	46
	Shaft Cover (700 Gear)	45
	Stub Shaft Housing	46
	Steering Gear Side Cover	46
BLAZER, JIMMY, SONOMA & S10		
2002–05	Adjuster Lock (2002–03)	36
	Adjuster Lock (2004–05)	32
	Ball Guide Clamp	53
	Cooler	89①
	Coupling Shield	80
	Front Differential Carrier Shield	18
	Gear Side Cover	45
	Hose Clamp	18①
	Lower Intermediate Shaft To Gear	26
	Pitman Arm To Gear	184
	Pitman Arm Ball Stud	61

Continued

TIGHTENING SPECIFICATIONS—Continued

Year	Component	Torque Ft. Lbs.
BLAZER, JIMMY, SONOMA & S10		
2002–05	Power Steering Gear	55
	Power Steering Gear Return Hose	18
	Pressure Hose (2.2L Engine)	18
	Pressure Hose (4.3L Engine)	22
	Rack Piston Plug	111
	Rack Piston Guide Clamp	53①
EXPRESS & SAVANA		
2002	Ball Guide Clamp	43
	Cooler (Axle Rear 3.73 Ratio)	44①
	Cooler (4.10 Rear Axle Ratio)	21
	Coupling Shield	80
	Gear Inlet/Outlet Hose	20
	Gear To Pump Inlet Hose	20
	Outlet Hose To Gear	24
	Pitman Shaft & Housing Cover	45
	Pitman Shaft Preload Adjustment Lock	23
	Power Steering Gear	111
	Rack Piston Plug	111
	Steering Gear To Frame	98
	Thrust Bearing Preload Adjustment	22
2003–06	Adjuster Lock	32
	Adjuster Plug Lock	50
	Ball Guide Clamp	80①
	Cooler Hose To Gear	24
	Coupling Shield	80
	Cylinder Liner To Gear, Cylinder End	20
	Cylinder Liner To Gear, Valve End	13
	Inner Tie Rod To Gear	74
	Lower Intermediate Steering Shaft To Gear	45
	Outer tie Rod To Steering Knuckle	47
	Pitman Arm To Gear	184
	Pitman Arm To Relay Rod	47
	Pitman Shaft Side Cover	45

TIGHTENING SPECIFICATIONS—Continued

Year	Component	Torque Ft. Lbs.
HUMMER H2		
2003–06	Adjuster Lock	32
	Ball Guide Clamp	53①
	Coupling Shield	80
	Cooler	44①
	Pitman Arm To Gear	184
	Power Steering Gear	111
	Pressure Hose	21
	Rack Piston Plug	111
	Side Cover	45
	Worm Thrust Preload Adjustment	22
SIERRA & SILVERADO		
2002–06	Ball Guide Clamp	53
	Cooler	44①
	Coupling Shield	80
	Hose Connection	20
	Inner Tie Rod	74
	Intermediate Shaft To Gear	33
	Outer Tie Rod To Steering Knuckle	37
	Pitman Arm To Gear	184
	Pitman Arm To Relay Rod	46
	Pitman Shaft Cover (670 Gear)	46
	Pitman Shaft Cover (700 Gear)	45
	Power Steering Gear	110
	Thrust Bearing Adjuster	23
SSR		
2003–05	Adjust Plug	50
	Cylinder Line	23
	Cylinder Line Plate	12
	Hose Bracket	89①
	Inner Tie Rod Housing	74
	Lower Intermediate Shaft To Gear	30
	Power Steering Gear	81
	Power Steering Gear Hose	106①

① — Inch lbs.

Saginaw Rack & Pinion Steering Gear

INDEX

DESCRIPTION

The power rack and pinion steering system has a rotary control valve which directs hydraulic fluid coming from the pump to one or the other side of the rack piston. The piston is attached to the rack. The piston converts hydraulic pressure to a linear force which moves the rack left or right. The force is then transmitted through the inner and outer tie rods to the steering knuckles, which turn the wheels, **Figs. 1 and 2.**

If hydraulic assist is not available, manual control is maintained, however more steering effort is required. The movement of the steering wheel is transferred to the pinion. The movement of the pinion is transferred through the pinion teeth, which mesh with teeth on the rack, causing the rack to move.

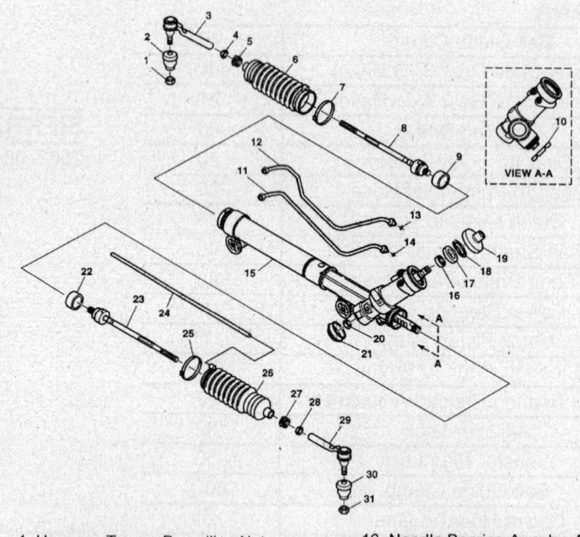

1. Hexagon Torque Prevailing Nut
2. Tie Rod Seal
3. Outer Tie Road Assembly
4. Hexagon Jam Nut
5. Tie Rod End Clamp
6. Rack and Pinion Boot
7. Boot Clamp
8. Inner Tie Rod Assembly
9. Shock Dampener Ring
10. Adjuster Plug Lock Nut
11. Cylinder Line Assembly (RH)
12. Cylinder Line Assembly (LH)
13. O-Ring Seal
14. O-Ring Seal
15. Rack and Pinion Gear Assembly (Partial)
16. Needle Bearing Annulus Assembly
17. Seal Adapter
18. Retaining Ring
19. Spool Shaft Seal
20. Hexagon Lock Nut
21. Dust Cover
22. Shock Dampener Ring
23. Inner Tie Rod Assembly
24. Breather Tube
25. Boot Clamp
26. Rack and Pinion Boot
27. Tie Rod End Clamp
28. Hexagon Jam Nut
29. Outer Tie Rod Assembly
30. Tie Rod Seal
31. Hexagon Torque Prevailing Nut

GC6029900391000X

Fig. 1 Exploded view of rack & pinion steering gear. Aztek, Canyon, Colorado, Montana, Relay, Rendezvous, Silverado, Sierra, Silhouette, SV6, Terraza, Uplander & Venture

DIAGNOSIS & TESTING

Refer to "Constant Displacement Vane-Type Pump" section for power steering system diagnosis and testing.

POWER STEERING SYSTEM SERVICE

Power Steering System Flush

Refer to "Constant Displacement Vane-Type Pump" section for power steering system for flushing procedures.

POWER STEERING SYSTEM BLEED

Refer to "Constant Displacement Vane-Type Pump" section for power steering system for bleeding procedures.

Component Service

Do not disassemble the power rack and pinion steering gear.

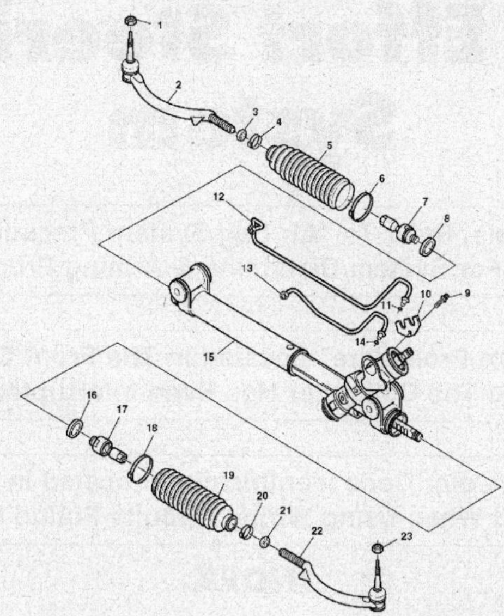

1. Torque Prevailing Nut
2. Outer Tie Rod Assembly
3. Hexagon Jam Nut
4. Tie Rod End Clamp
5. Rack and Pinion Boot
6. Boot Clamp
7. Inner Tie Rod Assembly
8. Shock Dampener Ring
9. External TORX Screw
10. Cylinder Line Retaining Plate
11. O-ring Seal
12. Righthand Cylinder Line
13. Lefthand Cylinder (LH) Line
14. O-ring Seal
15. Rack and Pinion Gear (Partial)
16. Shock Dampener Ring
17. Inner Tie Rod Assembly
18. Boot Clamp
19. Rack and Pinion Boot
20. Tie Rod End Clamp
21. Hexagon Jam Nut
22. Outer Tie Rod Assembly
23. Torque Prevailing Nut

LTV0500000001523

Fig. 2 Exploded view of rack & pinion steering gear. Bravada, Envoy, Hummer H3, Rainier, SSR & Trailblazer

Variable Effort Steering (VES) System

NOTE: On Air Bag Equipped Models, Refer To "Air Bag System Precautions" Located In The Front Of This Manual For System Disarming & Arming Procedures.

NOTE: Refer To "Computer Relearn Procedure" Located In The Front Of This Manual When Battery Power To The Computer Has Been Interrupted.

NOTE: Electrical Symbol & Wire Color Code Identification Located In The Front Of This Manual May Be Used As An Aid When Using Wiring Circuits Found In This Section.

INDEX

DESCRIPTION

The Variable Effort Steering (VES) system controls the amount of steering effort needed to steer the vehicle as vehicle speed and steering wheel position and turning speed changes.

The Body Control Module (BCM) or Electronic Suspension Control (ESC) module, vehicles equipped with Real Time Damping (RTD), controls an electronic Variable Orifice (EVO) solenoid located in the power steering pump's output fluid orifice. The solenoid consists of a pintle valve which moves in and out of the orifice, regulating power steering fluid flow. The BCM/ESC module varies the amount of steering effort by commanding more or less current to the solenoid.

At low speeds, no current is commanded and the pintle is fully retracted which provides maximum fluid flow and maximum steering assist for easy turning and parking maneuvers. At high speeds, more current is commanded to the solenoid and the pintle moves closer to the orifice, decreasing fluid flow, providing firmer steering (road feel) and directional stability.

The VES system uses the Steering Wheel Position sensor input to calculate lateral acceleration during abrupt driving maneuvers. The system also uses the Vehicle Speed Sensor (VSS) signal from the Powertrain Control Module (PCM) via a class 2 serial data circuit. The control module is constantly monitoring these inputs to achieve the desired current to the EVO solenoid. The BCM/ESC module has the ability to detect faults within the VES system. Any faults detected will cause the EVO outputs to be disabled.

DIAGNOSIS & TESTING

Accessing Diagnostic Trouble Codes

Connect a suitably programmed scan tool to Diagnostic Link Connector (DLC) and follow scan tool manufacturer's instructions.

Diagnostic Trouble Code Interpretation

Refer to **Fig. 1** for Diagnostic Trouble Code (DTC) interpretation.

Wiring Diagrams

Refer to **Figs. 2 through 4** for wiring diagrams.

Diagnostic Tests

Refer to **Figs. 5 through 12** for diagnostic tests.

Intermittents & Poor Connections

Faulty electrical connections and wiring cause most intermittent faults, although a damaged EVO/Passlock module can occasionally be at fault.

1. Poor mating of connector halves, or terminals not fully seated in connector body. Inspect wiring and connectors for the following:
2. Dirt or corrosion on terminals.
3. Damaged connector body.
4. Improperly formed or damaged terminals.
5. Poor terminal to wire connection.
6. Rubbed through wiring insulation.
7. Wiring broken inside insulation.

Clearing Diagnostic Trouble Codes

Follow scan tool manufacturer's instructions.

Code	Interpretation
C0450	Open, Short VES Actuator Or Circuits
C0470	Steering Wheel Position Sensor Voltage Fault
C0472	Steering Wheel Speed Sensor Signal Voltage Fault
C0473	Steering Wheel Speed Sensor Signal Voltage Fault
C0495	EVO Tracking Error
C0496	Steering Assist Control Actuator Feed Circuit
C0498	Steering Assist Control Actuator Feed Circuit
C0499	Steering Assist Control Actuator Feed Circuit
C0501	Steering Assist Control Solenoid Return Circuit
C0503	Steering Assist Control Solenoid Return Circuit
C0504	Steering Assist Control Solenoid Return Circuit
C0506	Steering Wheel Position Sensor Voltage Fault
C0521	Steering Wheel Position Sensor Circuit

Fig. 1 DTC interpretation

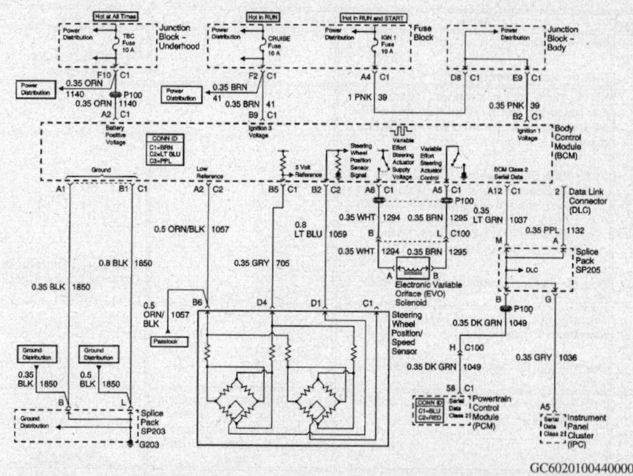

Fig. 2 VES wiring diagram. 2002 Avalanche, Escalade, Suburban, Tahoe & Yukon less RTD

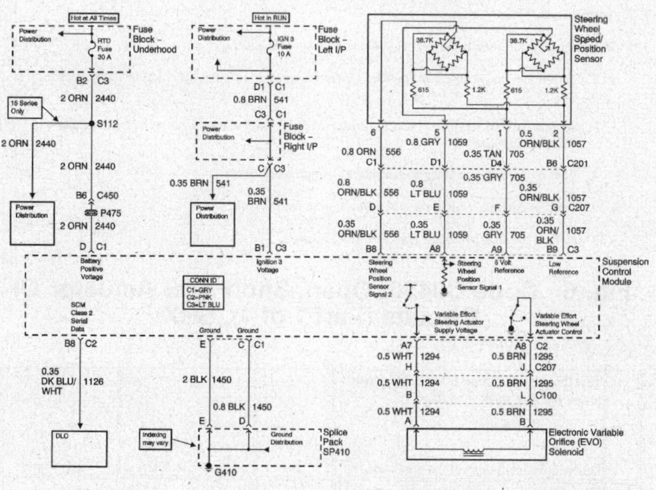

Fig. 3 VES wiring diagram. 2002 Avalanche, Escalade, Suburban, Tahoe & Yukon w/RTD

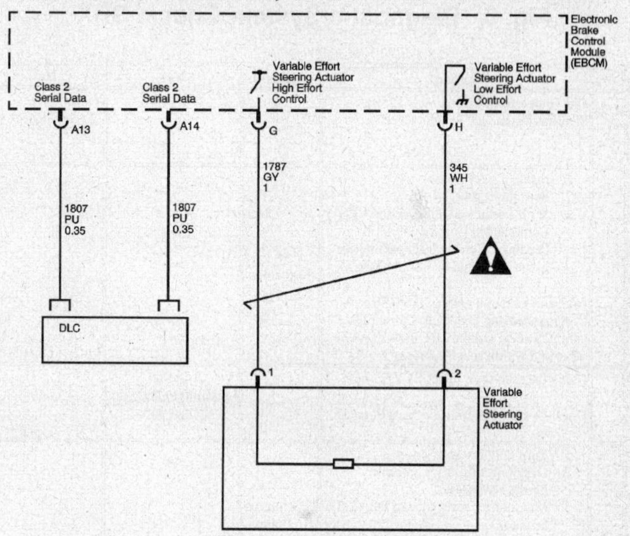

Fig. 4 VES wiring diagram. SRX

DIAGNOSTIC CHART INDEX

Code	Description	Page No.	Fig. No.
AVALANCHE, ESCALADE, SUBURBAN, TAHOE & YUKON			
—	Diagnostic System Check	22-24	5
C0470	Steering Wheel Position Sensor Voltage Fault	22-25	7
C0472	Steering Wheel Speed Sensor Signal Voltage Fault	22-25	8
C0473	Steering Wheel Speed Sensor Signal Voltage Fault	22-25	8
C0495	EVO Tracking Error	22-26	9
C0496	Steering Assist Control Actuator Feed Circuit	22-26	10
C0498	Steering Assist Control Actuator Feed Circuit	22-26	10
C0499	Steering Assist Control Actuator Feed Circuit	22-26	10
C0501	Steering Assist Control Solenoid Return Circuit	22-27	11
C0503	Steering Assist Control Solenoid Return Circuit	22-27	11
C0504	Steering Assist Control Solenoid Return Circuit	22-27	11
C0506	Steering Wheel Position Sensor Voltage Fault	22-25	7
C0521	Steering Wheel Position Sensor Circuit	22-27	12
SRX			
—	Diagnostic System Check	22-24	5
C0450	Open, Short VES Actuator Or Circuits	22-24	6

Step	Action	Yes	No
1	Install a scan tool. Does the scan tool power up?	Go to Step 2	Go to Scan Tool Does Not Power Up
2	NOTE: The BCM/ESC stores the DTCs scan tool data and special functions. However, the scan tool menu to access variable effort steering is located in chassis. 1. Turn ON the ignition, with the engine OFF. 2. Attempt to establish communication with the Electronic Suspension Control (ESC) Module, vehicles equipped with Real Time Damping (RTD), or the Body Control Module (BCM), vehicles W/O RTD. Does the scan tool communicate with the ESC module, or BCM?	Go to Step 3	Go to Scan Tool Does Not Communicate with Class 2 Device
3	Select the ESC module, or BCM Display DTCs function on the scan tool. Does the scan tool display any DTCs that begin with a "U"?	Go to Diagnostic Trouble Code (DTC) List	Go to Step 4
4	Does the scan tool display any BCM, or RTD, if equipped DTCs?	Go to Diagnostic Trouble Code (DTC) List in Body Control System, or Diagnostic Trouble Code (DTC) List in Real Time Damping	Go to Step 5
5	Does the scan tool display any VES DTCs?	Go to Diagnostic Trouble Code (DTC) List	System OK

LTV1900000000732

Fig. 5 Diagnostic System Check. SRX

Step	Action	Values	Yes	No
1	Did you perform the Variable Effort Steering Diagnostic System Check?	--	Go to Step 2	Go to System Check -
2	1. Install a scan tool. 2. Start the engine. 3. With a scan tool, observe the VES Commanded Current and VES Feedback Current Data parameters in the VES data list for the EBCM. Does the scan tool display the VES Commanded and Feedback Current Data parameters are within 0.03 amps of each other and within specified range?	0.90 to 1.00 amps	Go to Step 3	Go to Step 4
3	Using the scan tool, select F1 VES Test. Does the scan tool indicate, Test Passed?	--	Test for Intermittent and Poor Connections	Go to Step 4
4	1. Turn OFF the ignition. 2. Disconnect the VES actuator harness connector. 3. Measure the resistance of the VES actuator. Does the resistance measure within specified range?	5.0ohms to 10.0ohms	Go to Step 5	Go to Step 12
5	Test the VES actuator and actuator harness for a short to ground. Was a short to ground located?	--	Go to Step 6	Go to Step 78
6	Visually inspect the actuator harness for any cut, chaffed or damaged wires. Did you find and correct the condition?	--	Go to Step 15	Go to Step 14
7	Test the control circuit of the VES actuator for a short to ground. Did you find and correct the condition?	--	Go to Step 15	Go to Step 8

LTV0500000001262

Fig. 6 Code C0450: Open, Short VES Actuator Or Circuits (Part 2 of 4). SRX

Circuit Description

The electronic brake control module (EBCM) commands current from 0-1 amp to the VES actuator, depending on vehicle speed. At low speeds, 1 amp of current is commanded to the actuator and the actuator valve is fully closed. A speed increases, less current is commanded to the actuator and the valve opens, allowing pressure to bleed off through a power steering fluid orifice. The EBCM monitors and compares the Commanded and Feedback Current parameters to detect malfunctions in the VES system.

Conditions for Running the DTC

- Ignition voltage between 10.5-17.0 volts
- Off state test - Initial ignition ON, no engine RPM or vehicle speed present.
- On state test - If off state test passes, engine RPM and vehicle speed present.

Conditions for Setting the DTC

An open, short to ground or short to voltage in the VES actuator or the circuits to the actuator.

Action Taken When the DTC Sets

- A DTC C0450 is stored in memory.
- The DIC displays the SERVICE STEERING SYSTEM warning message.
- The VES system is disabled for the remainder of the ignition cycle.

Conditions for Clearing the DTC

- A current DTC will clear when the malfunction is no longer present.
- A history DTC will clear after 100 consecutive ignition cycles with the malfunction no longer present.
- Using a scan tool.

Diagnostic Aids

The vehicle may need to be driven to view full VES Commanded and Feedback Data parameters

Test Description

The numbers below refer to the step numbers on the diagnostic table.

2. Tests if the Commanded and Feedback Current parameters are within specification in there active state.
3. Perform the VES test located under Special Functions. This test may indicate if the VES actuator is mechanically bound.
4. Tests if the resistance of the VES actuator is within specification.
7. Tests the control circuit of the VES actuator for a short to ground.
13. Perform the setup procedure after EBCM replacement.

LTV0500000001261

Fig. 6 Code C0450: Open, Short VES Actuator Or Circuits (Part 1 of 4). SRX

8	Test the control circuit of the VES actuator for an open or short to voltage. Did you find and correct the condition?	--	Go to Step 15	Go to Step 9
9	Test the return circuit of the VES actuator for a short to ground. Did you find and correct the condition?	--	Go to Step 15	Go to Step 10
10	Test the return circuit of the VES actuator for an open or a short to voltage. Did you find and correct the condition?	--	Go to Step 15	Go to Step 11
11	Inspect for poor connections at the harness connector of the EBCM. Did you find and correct the condition?	--	Go to Step 15	Go to Step 13
12	Inspect for poor connections at the harness connector of the VES actuator. Did you find and correct the condition?	--	Go to Step 15	Go to Step 14
13	**Important** Always perform the setup procedure for the EBCM. 1. Replace the EBCM. 2. Perform the setup procedure for the EBCM. Did you complete the replacement?	--	Go to Step 15	--

LTV0500000001263

Fig. 6 Code C0450: Open, Short VES Actuator Or Circuits (Part 3 of 4). SRX

Step	Action	Value(s)	Yes	No
14	Replace the VES actuator. Did you complete the replacement?	-	Go to Step 15	--
15	1. Use the scan tool in order to clear the DTCs. 2. Operate the vehicle within the Conditions for Running the DTC. Does the DTC reset?	-	Go to Step 2	System OK

LTV0500000001264

Fig. 6 Code C0450: Open, Short VES Actuator Or Circuits (Part 4 of 4). SRX

Step	Action	Value(s)	Yes	No
6	Test the 5 volt reference circuit of the steering wheel position sensor for a short to ground or an open. Did you find and correct the condition?	-	Go to Step 15	Go to Step 12
7	Test the 5 volt reference circuit of the steering wheel position sensor for a short to voltage, a high resistance, or an open. Did you find and correct the condition?	-	Go to Step 15	Go to Step 11
8	Test the signal 1/signal 2 circuit of the steering wheel position sensor for a short to ground. Did you find and correct the condition?	-	Go to Step 15	Go to Step 12
9	Test the signal 1/signal 2 circuit of the steering wheel position sensor for a short to voltage, a high resistance, or an open. Did you find and correct the condition?	-	Go to Step 15	Go to Step 10
10	Test the low reference circuit of the steering wheel position sensor for a high resistance, a short to voltage or an open. Did you find and correct the condition?	-	Go to Step 15	Go to Step 12
11	Inspect for poor connections at the harness connector of the steering wheel position sensor. Did you find and correct the condition?	-	Go to Step 15	Go to Step 13
12	Inspect for poor connections at the harness connector of the Suspension Control Module. Did you find and correct the condition?	-	Go to Step 15	Go to Step 14
13	Replace the steering wheel position sensor. Did you complete the replacement?	-	Go to Step 15	--
14	**Important** After replacement, use the scan tool to perform the setup procedure located under Special Functions (F8: Recalibration) for the suspension control module. Replace the suspension control module. Did you complete the replacement?	-	Go to Step 15	--
15	1. Use the scan tool in order to clear the DTCs. 2. Operate the vehicle within the Conditions for Running the DTCs as specified in the supporting text. Does the DTC reset?	-	Go to Step 2	System OK

LTV1900000000734

Fig. 7 Codes C0470 & C0506: Steering Wheel Position Sensor Voltage Fault (Part 2 of 2). Avalanche, Escalade, Suburban, Tahoe & Yukon

Step	Action	Value (s)	Yes	No
1	If DTC C0870 is present perform the diagnosis for that DTC before proceeding. Did you perform the Variable effort Steering Diagnostic System Check?	--	Go to Step 2	Go to Diagnostic System Check
2	1. Install a scan tool. 2. Turn ON the ignition, with the engine OFF. 3. With a scan tool, observe the steering wheel position signal 1/signal 2 data parameter in the suspension Control Module data list. Does the scan tool indicate that the steering wheel position signal 1/signal 2 data parameter is within the specified range?	0.35-4.7 V	Test for Intermittent and Poor Connections	Go to Step 3
3	1. Turn OFF the ignition. 2. Disconnect the steering wheel position sensor harness connector. 3. Turn ON the ignition, with the engine OFF. 4. With a scan tool, observe the steering wheel position signal 1/signal 2 data parameter. Does the scan tool indicate that the steering wheel position signal 1/signal 2 data parameter is greater than the specified value?	4.7 V	Go to Step 4	Go to Step 8
4	1. Turn OFF the ignition 2. Connect a 3 amp fused jumper wire between the signal 1/signal 2 circuit and the low reference circuit of the steering wheel position sensor harness connector. 3. Turn ON the ignition, with the engine OFF. 4. With a scan tool, observe the steering wheel position signal 1/signal 2 data parameter. Does the scan tool indicate that the steering wheel position signal 1/signal 2 data parameter is less than the specified value?	0.35 V	Go to Step 5	Go to Step 9
5	1. Turn OFF the ignition. 2. Disconnect the fused jumper wire. 3. Connect a 3 amp fused jumper wire between the 5 volt reference circuit and the signal 1/signal 2 circuit of the steering wheel position sensor harness connector. 4. Turn ON the ignition, with the engine OFF. 5. With a scan tool, observe the steering wheel position signal 1/signal 2 data parameter. Does the scan tool indicate that the steering wheel position signal 1/signal 2 data parameter is greater than the specified value?	4.7 V	Go to Step 7	Go to Step 6

LTV1900000000733

Fig. 7 Codes C0470 & C0506: Steering Wheel Position Sensor Voltage Fault (Part 1 of 2). Avalanche, Escalade, Suburban, Tahoe & Yukon

Step	Action	Value (s)	Yes	No
1	Did you perform the Variable Effort Steering Diagnostic System Check?	--	Go to Step 2	Go to Diagnostic System Check
2	1. Install a scan tool. 2. Turn ON the ignition, with the engine OFF. 3. With a scan tool, observe the steering wheel position sensor data parameter in the Electronic Variable Orifice data list. Does the scan tool display the steering wheel position sensor data parameter is within the specified range?	0.35-4.7 V	Test for Intermittent and Poor Connections	Go to Step 3
3	1. Turn OFF the ignition. 2. Disconnect the steering wheel position sensor harness connector. 3. Turn ON the ignition, with the engine OFF. 4. With a scan tool, observe the steering wheel position sensor data parameter. Does the scan tool indicate that the steering wheel position sensor data parameter is greater than specified value?	0.0 V	Go to Step 4	Go to Step 8
4	1. Turn OFF the ignition. 2. Connect a 3 amp fused jumper wire between the signal circuit and the low reference circuit of the steering wheel position sensor harness connector. 3. Turn ON the ignition, with the engine OFF. 4. With a scan tool, observe the steering wheel position sensor data parameter. Does the scan tool indicate that the steering wheel position sensor data parameter is less than specified value?	0.35 V	Go to Step 5	Go to Step 9
5	1. Turn OFF the ignition. 2. Disconnect the fused jumper wire. 3. Connect a 3 amp fused jumper wire between the 5 volt reference circuit and the signal circuit of the steering wheel position sensor harness connector. 4. Turn ON the ignition, with the Engine OFF. 5. With a scan tool, observe the steering wheel position sensor data parameter. Does the scan tool indicate that the steering wheel position sensor data parameter is greater than the specified value?	4.7 V	Go to Step 7	Go to Step 6
6	Test the 5 volt reference circuit of the steering wheel position sensor for a short to ground. Did you find and correct the condition?	--	Go to Step 15	Go to Step 12

LTV1900000000735

Fig. 8 Codes C0472 & C0473: Steering Wheel Speed Sensor Signal Voltage Fault (Part 1 of 2). Avalanche, Escalade, Suburban, Tahoe & Yukon

7	Test the 5 volt reference circuit of the steering wheel position sensor for a short to voltage or an open. Did you find and correct the condition?	-	Go to Step 15	Go to Step 11
8	Test the signal circuit of the steering wheel position sensor for a short to ground. Did you find and correct the condition?	-	Go to Step 15	Go to Step 12
9	Test the signal circuit of the steering wheel position sensor for a short to voltage or an open. Did you find and correct the condition?	-	Go to Step 15	Go to Step 10
10	Test the low reference circuit of the steering wheel position sensor for a short to voltage or an open. Did you find and correct the condition?	-	Go to Step 15	Go to Step 12
11	Inspect for poor connections at the steering wheel position sensor harness connector. Did you find and correct the condition?	-	Go to Step 15	Go to Step 13
12	Inspect for poor connections at the BCM harness connector. Did you find and correct the condition?	-	Go to Step 15	Go to Step 14
13	Replace the steering wheel position sensor. Did you complete the replacement?	-	Go to Step 15	--
14	Replace the BCM. Did you complete the replacement?	-	Go to Step 15	--
15	1. Use the scan tool in order to clear the DTCs. 2. Operate the vehicle within the conditions for running the DTC as specified in the supporting text. Does the DTC reset?	-	Go to Step 2	System OK

LTV1900000000736

Fig. 8 Codes C0472 & C0473: Steering Wheel Speed Sensor Signal Voltage Fault (Part 2 of 2). Avalanche, Escalade, Suburban, Tahoe & Yukon

6	Does the test lamp remain on continuously with the ignition ON or OFF?	-	Go to Step 7	Go to Step 10
7	Test the EVO solenoid supply circuit for a short to voltage. Did you find and correct the condition?	-	Go to Step 10	Go to Step 9
8	Replace the EVO solenoid. Did you complete the replacement?	-	Go to Step 10	--
9	Replace the BCM/ESC module. Did you complete the replacement?	-	Go to Step 10	--
10	1. Use the scan tool in order to clear the DTCs . 2. Operate the vehicle within the Conditions for Running the DTC as specified in the supporting text. Does the DTC reset?	-	Go to Step 2	System OK

LTV1900000000738

Fig. 9 Code C0495: EVO Tracking Error (Part 2 of 2). Avalanche, Escalade, Suburban, Tahoe & Yukon

Step	Action	Value (s)	Yes	No
1	**Important:** If DTC C0501 is also set, perform the diagnostic procedure for C0501 before proceeding. Did you perform the Variable Effort Steering Diagnostic System Check?	--	Go to Step 2	Go to Diagnostic System Check
2	1. Install a scan tool. 2. Turn ON the ignition, with the engine OFF. 3. With a scan tool, command the EVO solenoid ON and OFF. Does the EVO solenoid turn ON and OFF with each command?	--	Test for Intermittent and Poor Connections	Go to Step 3
3	1. Turn OFF the ignition. 2. Disconnect the EVO solenoid harness connector. 3. Measure the resistance of the EVO solenoid. Does the resistance measure within the specified value?	11-13 ohms	Go to Step 4	Go to Step 8
4	Inspect for poor connections at the EVO solenoid harness connector. Did you find and correct the condition?	--	Go to Step 10	Go to Step 5
5	1. Probe the EVO solenoid supply circuit at the solenoid harness connector with a test lamp connected to ground. 2. Turn ON the ignition, with the engine OFF. Does the test lamp turn on when the ignition is turned ON?	--	Go to Step 9	Go to Step 6

LTV1900000000737

Fig. 9 Code C0495: EVO Tracking Error (Part 1 of 2). Avalanche, Escalade, Suburban, Tahoe & Yukon

Step	Action	Value (s)	Yes	No
1	Did you perform the Variable Effort Steering Diagnostic System Check?	--	Go to Step 2	Go to Diagnostic System Check
2	1. Install a scan tool. 2. Turn ON the ignition, with the engine OFF. 3. With a scan tool, command the EVO solenoid ON and OFF. Does the EVO solenoid turn ON and OFF with each command?	--	Test for Intermittent and Poor Connections	Go to Step 3
3	1. Turn OFF the ignition. 2. Disconnect the EVO solenoid. 3. Turn ON the ignition, with the engine OFF. 4. With a test lamp connected to a ground probe the EVO solenoid supply circuit at the solenoid harness connector. 5. With a scan tool, command the EVO solenoid ON. Does the test lamp turn ON with initial command?	--	Go to Step 4	Go to Step 5
4	1. Connect a test lamp between the EVO solenoid supply circuit and the EVO solenoid control circuit of the solenoid harness connector. 2. With a scan tool, command the EVO solenoid ON. Does the test lamp turn ON with initial command?	--	Go to Step 8	Go to Step 10
5	Does the test lamp remain illuminated continuously with each command?	--	Go to Step 7	Go to Step 6
6	Test the EVO solenoid supply circuit for a short to ground. Did you find and correct the condition?	--	Go to Step 14	Go to Step 9

LTV1900000000739

Fig. 10 Codes C0496, C0498 & C0499: Steering Assist Control Actuator Feed Circuit (Part 1 of 2). Avalanche, Escalade, Suburban, Tahoe & Yukon

Step	Action	Value(s)	Yes	No
7	Test the EVO solenoid supply circuit for a short to voltage or an open. Did you find and correct the condition?	--	Go to Step 14	Go to Step 9
8	Inspect for poor connections at the harness connector of the EVO solenoid . Did you find and correct the condition?	--	Go to Step 14	Go to Step 11
9	Inspect for poor connections at the harness connector of the BCM/suspension control module. Did you find and correct the condition?	--	Go to Step 14	Go to Step 13
10	Repair the control circuit of the EVO solenoid. Did you complete the repair?	--	Go to Step 14	--
11	Measure the resistance of the EVO solenoid. Does the resistance measure within the specified value?	11-13 ohms	Go to Step 13	Go to Step 12
12	Replace the EVO solenoid. Did you complete the replacement?	--	Go to Step 14	--
13	Replace the BCM/ESC module. Did you complete the replacement?	--	Go to Step 14	--
14	1. Use the scan tool in order to clear the DTCs. 2. Operate the vehicle within the Conditions for Running the DTC as specified in the supporting text. Does the DTC reset?	--	Go to Step 2	System OK

LTV1900000000740

Fig. 10 Codes C0496, C0498 & C0499: Steering Assist Control Actuator Feed Circuit (Part 2 of 2). Avalanche, Escalade, Suburban, Tahoe & Yukon

Step	Action	Value(s)	Yes	No
7	1. Turn ON the ignition, with the engine OFF. 2. With the scan tool, command the EVO solenoid OFF. Does the test light turn OFF with initial command?	-	Go to Step 13	Go to Step 8
8	Test the EVO solenoid control circuit for a short to ground. Did you find and correct the condition?	-	Go to Step 13	Go to Step 12
9	Test the EVO solenoid control circuit for a short to voltage or an open. Did you find and correct the condition?	-	Go to Step 13	Go to Step 10
10	Inspect the Suspension Control Module/BCM harness connector control circuit for poor connections. Did you find and correct the condition?	-	Go to Step 13	Go to Step 12
11	Replace the EVO solenoid. Did you complete the replacement?	-	Go to Step 13	--
12	Replace the ESC module/BCM. Did you complete the replacement?	-	Go to Step 13	--
13	1. Use the scan tool in order to clear the DTCs. 2. Operate the vehicle within the Conditions for Running the DTC as specified in the supporting text. Does the DTC reset?	-	Go to Step 2	System OK

LTV1900000000742

Fig. 11 Codes C0501, C0503 & C0504: Steering Assist Control Solenoid Return Circuit (Part 2 of 2). Avalanche, Escalade, Suburban, Tahoe & Yukon

Step	Action	Value (s)	Yes	No
1	Did you perform the Variable Effort Steering Diagnostic System Check?	--	Go to Step 2	Go to Diagnostic System Check
2	1. Install a scan tool. 2. Turn ON the ignition, with the engine OFF. 3. With a scan tool, command the EVO solenoid from OFF to ON. Does the EVO solenoid turn OFF and ON with each command?	--	Test for Intermittent and Poor Connections	Go to Step 3
3	1. Turn OFF the ignition. 2. Disconnect the EVO solenoid. 3. Measure the resistance of the EVO solenoid. Does the resistance measure within the specified value?	11-13ohms	Go to Step 4	Go to Step 11
4	Inspect the EVO solenoid harness connector control and supply circuits for poor connections. Did you find and correct the condition?	--	Go to Step 13	Go to Step 5
5	1. Probe the EVO solenoid control circuit at the solenoid harness connector with a test lamp connected to battery voltage. 2. Turn ON the ignition, with the engine OFF. Does the test lamp turn ON when the ignition is turned ON?	--	Go to Step 7	Go to Step 6
6	Does the test lamp remain on continuously with the ignition ON or OFF?	--	Go to Step 8	Go to Step 9

LTV1900000000741

Fig. 11 Codes C0501, C0503 & C0504: Steering Assist Control Solenoid Return Circuit (Part 1 of 2). Avalanche, Escalade, Suburban, Tahoe & Yukon

Step	Action	Value(s)	Yes	No
1	Did you perform the Variable Effort Steering Diagnostic System Check?	--	Go to Step 2	Go to Diagnostic System Check
2	1. Install a scan tool. 2. Turn ON the ignition, with the engine on. 3. Center the steering wheel. 4. With a scan tool, observe the Steering Wheel Position Sensor signal 1 and Steering Wheel Position Sensor signal 2 data parameters in the RTD/EVO data list. Does the scan tool display the signal 1 and signal 2 data parameters at the specified value?	signal 1: 4.0 V signal 2: 2.0 V	Go to Step 3	Go to Step 5
3	Slowly turn the steering wheel to full left lock while observing the signal 1 and signal 2 data parameters. Do the signal 1 and signal 2 data parameters change state in synchronization with each other and reach the specified value?	signal 1: 2.5 V signal 2: 4.5 V	Go to Step 4	Go to Step 5
4	Slowly turn the steering wheel to full right lock while observing the signal 1 and signal 2 data parameters. Do the signal 1 and signal 2 data parameters change state in synchronization with each other and reach the specified value?	signal 1: 1.6 V signal 2: 1.6 V	Test for Intermittent and Poor Connections	Go to Step 5
5	Inspect for poor connections at the harness connector of the Steering Wheel Position Sensor. Did you find and correct the condition?	--	Go to Step 7	Go to Step 6
6	Replace the Steering Wheel Position Sensor. Did you complete the replacement?	--	Go to Step 7	--
7	1. Use the scan tool in order to clear the DTCs. 2. Operate the vehicle within the Conditions for Running the DTC as specified in the supporting text. Does the DTC reset?	--	Go to Step 2	System OK

LTV1900000000743

Fig. 12 Code C0521: Steering Wheel Position Sensor Circuit. Avalanche, Escalade, Suburban, Tahoe & Yukon

POWER STEERING SYSTEM SERVICE

Component Service

REPLACEMENT

SOLENOID ACTUATOR

1. Disconnect power steering solenoid actuator electrical connector.
2. Remove power steering pump as outlined under "Front Suspension & Steering" in appropriate chassis chapter.
3. Remove retaining ring and solenoid.
4. Record actuator discharge fitting orientation for installation alignment.
5. Remove power steering solenoid actuator and O-ring.
6. Reverse procedure to install, noting the following:
   a. Lubricate and install new O-ring seal using suitable power steering fluid.
   b. **Torque** power steering solenoid actuator to 46 ft. lbs.

STEERING WHEEL POSITION SENSOR

1. Set front wheels in straight ahead position and lock steering wheel.
2. Remove upper to lower steering shaft connection nut and bolt.
3. Disconnect position sensor connector.
4. Position sensor connector by using suitable tool to pull connector down around righthand side of steering column.
5. Remove sensor and bearing assembly from steering column jacket by pulling them straight out.
6. Remove position sensor for bearing assembly clips.
7. Reverse procedure to install.

TIGHTENING SPECIFICATIONS

Year	Component	Torque Ft. Lbs.
AZTEK & RENDEZVOUS		
2002–06	Bearing Preload Adjust Lock	50
	Cooler Pipe Clip	89①
	Cooler Pipe Fitting	20
	Cylinder End Fitting	20
	Front Frame	114
	Hose Fitting	20
	Inner Tie Rod	74
	Intermediate Shaft To Gear	33
	O-Ring Union	55
	Pinion Lock	22
	Power Steering Gear	59
	Power Steering Gear Heat Shield	124①
	Pressure Hose/Pipe	19
	Rear Frame	177
	Tie Rod Ball Stud	③
	Valve End Fitting	13
BRAVADA, ENVOY, RAINIER & TRAILBLAZER		
2002–06	Adjust Plug Lock	50
	Cooler	15
	Cylinder End Fitting	20
	Cylinder Valve End Fitting	13
	Hose Bracket	89①
	Inner Tie Rod Housing	74
	Lower Intermediate Shaft To Gear	30
	Outer Tie Rod	33
	Outer To Inner Tie Rod, Jam	55
	Power Steering Gear	81
	Power Steering Gear Hose	106①
CANYON & COLORADO		
2004–06	Adjuster Plug Lock	50
	Cylinder Pipe Fitting, Cylinder End	20
	Cylinder Pipe Fitting, Valve End	13
	Hose Clip	79①
	Inner Tie Rod End	74
	Lower Intermediate Shaft To Gear	33
	Outer Tie Rod, Jam Nut	52
	Outer Tie Rod, Retaining Nut	④
	Power Steering Gear	96
	Power Steering Gear Hose	106①
	Power Steering Gear Isolator	74
HUMMER H3		
2006	Adjuster Plug	50
	Cylinder Pipe Fitting, Cylinder End	20
	Cylinder Pipe Fitting, Valve End	13
	Hose Clip	79①
	Hose To Steering Gear	106①
	Lower Intermediate Shaft To Steering Gear	33
	Inner Tie Rod End	65
	Outer Tie Rod, Jam Nut	52
	Outer Tie Rod, Retaining Nut	④
	Power Steering Gear	96
	Power Steering Gear Insulator	74

TIGHTENING SPECIFICATIONS—Continued

Year	Component	Torque Ft. Lbs.
MONTANA, SILHOUETTE & VENTURE		
2002–05	Adjuster Plug	50
	Cooler Pipe	89①
	Cylinder Line Fitting (2002)	12
	Cylinder Line Fitting (2003–05)	20
	Heat Shield	124①
	Hose/Pipe Fitting	20
	Inner Tie Rod	74
	Intermediate Shaft	33
	Power Steering Gear To Frame (2002)	59
	Power Steering Gear To Frame (2003–05)	②
	Power Steering Gear Stub Shaft	22
	Power Steering Gear Valve End	13
	Rear Frame To Body	122
	Tie Rod Ball Stud	③
RELAY, SV6, TERRAZA & UPLANDER		
2005–06	Adjust Plug	50
	Cooler Pipe	89①
	Cylinder Line Fitting	20
	Frame To Body	134
	Heat Shield	124①
	Hose/Pipe Fitting	20
	Inner Tie Rod	74
	Power Steering Gear	②
	Tie Rod Ball Stud	③
	Valve End Fitting	13
SIERRA & SILVERADO		
2002–06	Adjuster Lock	36
	Cooler	44①
	Cylinder End Fitting	20
	Hose Connection	20
	Inner Tie Rod	74
	Intermediate Shaft To Gear	33
	Outer Tie Rod To Steering Knuckle	37
	Pinion Adjuster	50
	Piston Plug	111
	Pitman Arm To Gear	184
	Pitman Arm To Relay Rod	46
	Power Steering Gear	136
	Power Steering Gear Stub Shaft	46
	Valve End Fitting	13
SRX		
2004–06	Cooler To Bracket	80①
	Cooler Hose/Pipe To Frame	35①
	Intermediate Shaft	37
	Lower Engine Mount	59
	Outer Tie Rod To Knuckle	25
	Power Steering Gear	134
	Power Steering Gear Hose	17
	Pressure Hose To Frame	40①
	Return Line To Frame	35①

① — Inch lbs.
② — **Torque** new mounting nut to 44 ft. lbs., then tighten an additional 60°.
③ — **Torque** to 22 ft. lbs., then tighten an additional 120°. Ensure 2.5–4.5 tie rod end threads are visible beyond tie rod ball stud nut nylon.
④ — **Torque** to 33 ft. lbs., then tighten an additional 95°.

Tracker Power Steering Pump

INDEX

DESCRIPTION

The power steering pump is a vane-type pump driven by belt from the crankshaft pulley.

As the discharge rate of the power steering pump increases in proportion to the pump revolution speed, a flow control valve is utilized to control the maximum amount of fluid needed for steering operation. Within the flow control valve is a pressure relief valve which controls the maximum amount of pressure supplied to the power steering gear.

DIAGNOSIS & TESTING

Symptom Based Diagnosis

Refer to **Figs. 1 through 5** for symptom based diagnosis. Perform the "Power Steering System Test" first.

Power Steering System Test

Refer to **Fig. 6** for power steering system test.

DIAGNOSTIC CHART INDEX

Description	Page No.	Fig. No.
Power Steering System Test	22-31	6
Power Steering Fluid Leaks	22-30	1
Rattle, Clunk or Shudder Noise From Power Steering System	22-30	2
Steering Effort Hard In One or Both Directions	22-31	4
Steering Effort Too Easy In One Or Both Directions	22-31	5
Whine or Growl Noise From Power Steering System	22-30	3

Step	Action	Yes	No
1	Did you review the Power Steering System Description	Go to Step 2	Go to Symptoms -
2	Verify that power steering fluid leaks are present. Is the power steering system leaking?	Go to Step 3	System OK
3	Inspect the power steering system hose clamps and fittings. Is the power steering system leaking at the hose clamps or the fittings?	Go to Step 8	Go to Step 4
4	Inspect the power steering pipes and hoses. Is the power steering system leaking from the pipes or the hoses?	Go to Step 9	Go to Step 5
5	Inspect the power steering fluid reservoir for leaks. Is the reservoir leaking?	Go to Step 10	Go to Step 6
6	Inspect the power steering pump for leaks. Is the power steering pump leaking?	Go to Step 11	Go to Step 7
7	Inspect the power steering gear for leaks. Is the power steering gear leaking?	Go to Step 12	Go to Step 8
8	Did you complete the repair?	Go to Step 13	--
9	Replace the power steering hoses. Did you complete the repair?	Go to Step 13	--
10	Replace the power steering fluid reservoir. Did you complete the repair?	Go to Step 13	--

LTV0500000001252

Fig. 1 Power Steering Fluid Leaks (Part 1 of 2)

Step	Action	Yes	No
11	Overhaul or replace the power steering pump as necessary. Did you complete the repair?	Go to Step 13	--
12	Replace the power steering gear. Did you complete the repair?	Go to Step 13	--
13	Operate the system in order to verify the repair. Did you correct the condition?	System OK	Go to Step 3

LTV0500000001253

Fig. 1 Power Steering Fluid Leaks (Part 2 of 2)

Step	Action	Yes	No
1	Did you review the Power Steering System Description	Go to Step 2	Check Symptoms -
2	Verify that a rattle, clunk or shudder noise is present. Is a rattle, clunk or shudder noise present?	Go to Step 3	System OK
3	Inspect the power steering hoses for proper routing and clearance. Is the routing or clearance of the power steering hoses incorrect?	Go to Step 10	Go to Step 4
4	Inspect the engine drive belt for cracking or excessive wear. Is the drive belt cracked or excessively worn?	Go to Step 11	Go to Step 5
5	Inspect the power steering pump pulley for damage. Is the power steering pump pulley damaged?	Go to Step 12	Go to Step 6
6	Inspect the power steering pump and the power steering pump bracket for the proper installation. Is the power steering pump installation incorrect?	Go to Step 13	Go to Step 7
7	Inspect the power steering gear for the proper installation. Is the power steering gear installation incorrect?	Go to Step 14	Go to Step 8
8	Inspect the suspension. Is the suspension worn?	Go to Step 15	Go to Step 9
9	Inspect the lower steering shaft. Is the lower steering shaft worn?	Go to Step 16	Go to Step 2

LTV0500000001254

Fig. 2 Rattle, Clunk or Shudder Noise From Power Steering System (Part 1 of 2)

Step	Action	Yes	No
10	Adjust or replace the hoses as necessary. Did you complete the repair?	Go to Step 17	--
11	Replace the engine drive belt. Did you complete the repair?	Go to Step 17	--
12	Replace the power steering pump pulley. Did you complete the repair?	Go to Step 17	--
13	Install the power steering pump correctly. Did you complete the repair?	Go to Step 17	--
14	Install the power steering gear correctly. Did you complete the repair?	Go to Step 17	--
15	Replace the worn suspension components. Did you complete the repair?	Go to Step 17	--
16	Replace the lower steering shaft. Did you complete the repair?	Go to Step 17	--
17	Operate the system in order to verify the repair. Did you correct the condition?	System OK	Go to Step 3

LTV0500000001255

Fig. 2 Rattle, Clunk or Shudder Noise From Power Steering System (Part 2 of 2)

Step	Action	Yes	No
1	Did you review the Power Steering System Description	Go to Step 2	Go to Symptoms -
2	Verify that a whine or growl noise is present. Is a whine or growl noise present?	Go to Step 3	System OK
3	Perform the power steering test procedure in order to diagnose a hydraulic condition and repair or replace a component. Did you repair or replace a power steering system component?	Go to Step 10	Go to Step 4
4	Use the J 39570 Chassis Ear in order to inspect the power steering gear for a whine or a growl noise. Is the noise present at the power steering gear?	Go to Step 7	Go to Step 5
5	Use the J 39570 in order to inspect the power steering pump for a whine or a growl noise. Is the noise present at the power steering pump?	Go to Step 8	Go to Step 6
6	Use the J 39570 in order to inspect the power steering pipes and hoses for a whine or a growl noise. Is the noise present at the power steering pipes and hoses?	Go to Step 9	Go to Step 2
7	Replace the power steering gear. Did you complete the repair?	Go to Step 10	--
8	Replace the power steering pump. Did you complete the repair?	Go to Step 10	--
9	Adjust the routing of the power steering pipes and hoses. Did you complete the repair?	Go to Step 10	--
10	Operate the system in order to verify the repair. Did you correct the condition?	System OK	Go to Step 3

LTV0500000001256

Fig. 3 Whine or Growl Noise From Power Steering System

Step	Action	Yes	No
1	Did you review the Power Steering System Description	Go to Step 2	Go to Symptoms -
2	Verify that the steering effort is hard in one or both directions. Is the steering effort hard in one or both directions?	Go to Step 3	System OK
3	Perform the power steering system test procedure in order to diagnose and correct a hydraulic condition. Did you diagnose and correct a hydraulic condition?	Go to Step 5	Go to Step 4
4	Review the Diagnostic Starting Point in Suspension General Diagnosis in order to diagnose and correct a mechanical condition. Did you diagnose, repair, or replace a component?	Go to Step 5	Go to Step 2
5	Operate the system in order to verify the repair. Did you correct the condition?	System OK	Go to Step 2

LTV0500000001257

Fig. 4 Steering Effort Hard In One or Both Directions

Test Description

The numbers below refer to the step numbers on the diagnostic table.

5. This step tests the system for restrictions.
7. This step tests the following components for the following conditions:
   - The pump for internal leaks
   - The power steering pipes for kinks
8. This step tests the ability of the pump to regulate flow at maximum pressure.
10. This step tests the ability of the pump to regulate flow under normal operating conditions.
12. This step tests the internal components of the pump and the gear.

Step	Action	Value(s)	Yes	No
	DEFINITION: The Power Steering System Test Procedure will perform the following functions: • Test the operation of the hydraulic power steering system. • Test the operation of the power steering pump and power steering gear. • Identify restrictions in the system.			
1	Inspect the power steering fluid for the following indications of contamination • Milky fluid-water • Brown fluid-burnt • Debris in fluid-plastic or dirt Is the fluid free of contamination?	--	Go to Step 3	Go to Step 2
2	Flush the power steering system. Did you complete the procedure?	--	Go to Step 3	--
3	**Important:** In order to accurately diagnose the system, the malfunction must be present during the test procedure. Attempt to duplicate the condition. Is the condition present?	--	Go to Step 4	System OK

LTV0500000001249

Fig. 6 Power Steering System Test (Part 1 of 3)

Step	Action	Yes	No
1	Did you review the Power Steering System Description	Go to Step 2	Go to Symptoms
2	Verify that the steering effort is too easy in one or both directions. Is the steering effort too easy in one or both directions?	Go to Step 3	System OK
3	Perform the power steering test procedure. Did you complete the procedure?	Go to Step 4	--
4	Operate the system in order to verify the repair. Did you correct the condition?	System OK	Go to Step 3

LTV0500000001258

Fig. 5 Steering Effort Too Easy In One Or Both Directions

Step	Action	Value(s)	Yes	No
4	1. Turn the ignition switch to the OFF position. 2. Place a drain pan under the vehicle in order to catch any power steering fluid. 3. Disconnect the power steering pressure pipe from the power steering pump. 4. Install the J 44721 Power Steering System Analyzer. 5. Fill the power steering system. 6. Bleed the power steering system. Did you complete the installation?	--	Go to Step 5	--
5	1. Fully open the J 44721 valve. 2. Start the engine. **Notice:** Do not hold the steering wheel in the full turn position longer than 5 seconds, as damage to the steering pump may result. 3. Turn the steering wheel and BRIEFLY hold the steering wheel against the steering stop in order to release any trapped air from the system. 4. Inspect and ensure that all of the power steering pipe/hose connections are not leaking. 5. With the steering wheel OFF the steering stop, observe the pressure reading. Is the pressure reading greater than the specified value?	1379 kPa (200 psi)	Go to Step 6	Go to Step 7
6	**Important:** A restriction may be present in the power steering system. Turn off the engine IMMEDIATELY. Locate and repair the restriction. Did you complete the repair?	--	Go to Step 15	--
7	1. Allow the engine to run until the engine reaches full operating temperature. 2. Record the pressure reading and the flow reading. 3. Partially close the J 44721 valve until the system pressure reaches the specified value, then record the FLOW reading. 4. Subtract the second flow reading from the first flow reading. Is the flow DECREASE greater than 3.8 L (1 gal) per minute?	4827 kPa (700 psi)	Go to Step 11	Go to Step 8

LTV0500000001250

Fig. 6 Power Steering System Test (Part 2 of 3)

Step	Action	Value(s)	Yes	No
8	**Notice:** Do not leave the valve fully closed for more than 5 seconds, or the pump could be damaged internally. Fully close then open the J 44721 valve 3 times. Record all of the high pressure readings. Refer to Power Steering Pump Specifications for power steering system pressure relief specifications. Are the three high pressure readings within specifications?	- -	Go to Step 9	Go to Step 13
9	Are the three high pressure readings within 245 kPa (50 psi) of each other?	- -	Go to Step 10	Go to Step 13
10	1. Increase the engine speed to approximately 1500 RPM. 2. Record the flow reading. Is the actual flow reading within specifications?	- -	Go to Step 11	Go to Step 13
11	Is the difference between the actual flow reading and the maximum flow specification more than 3.8 L (1 gal) per minute?	- -	Go to Step 13	Go to Step 12
12	**Notice:** Do not hold the steering wheel in the full turn position longer than 5 seconds, as damage to the steering pump may result. Turn the steering wheel from steering stop to steering stop and record the FLOW readings at each stop. Is the flow LOWER than 3.8 L (1 gal) per minute?	- -	Go to Step 15	Go to Step 14
13	Replace the power steering pump. Did you complete the replacement?	- -	Go to Step 15	--
14	The power steering gear is leaking across the piston or bypassing the valve circuit. Replace the power steering gear. Did you complete the replacement?	- -	Go to Step 15	--
15	Test the power steering system for the original condition. Does the original condition still exist?	- -	Go to Step 5	Go to Step 16
16	1. Disconnect and remove the J 44721 from the vehicle. 2. Connect the vehicle power steering pipes/hoses. 3. Fill the power steering system. 4. Bleed the power steering system . Did you complete the repair?	- -	System OK	--

LTV0500000001251

Fig. 6 Power Steering System Test (Part 3 of 3)

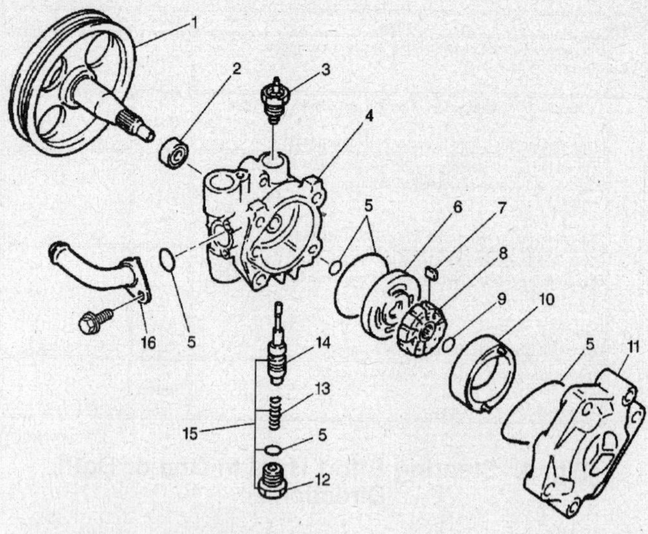

1. Power Steering Pump Pulley
2. Power Steering Pump Seal
3. Idle Speed Control Power Steering Pressure Switch
4. Power Steering Pump Body
5. Power Steering Pump Seal
6. Power Steering Pump Side Plate
7. Power Steering Pump Vane
8. Power Steering Pump Rotor
9. Snap Ring
10. Power Steering Pump Cam Ring
11. Power Steering Pump Cover
12. Flow Control Valve Plug
13. Flow Control Valve Spring
14. Flow Control Valve (Relief Valve)
15. Flow Control Valve Assembly
16. Power Steering Pump Inlet Hose Connector

LTV0500000001248

Fig. 7 Exploded view of power steering gear

POWER STEERING SYSTEM BLEED

1. Remove reservoir cap and adjust fluid level. Install cap.
2. Start and idle engine.
3. Turn engine off.
4. Remove reservoir cap and adjust fluid level. Install cap.
5. Start and idle engine.
6. Partially raise and support vehicle.
7. Turn steering wheel 180–360° in both directions five times. **Do not turn steering wheel to lock.**
8. Turn the ignition switch OFF
9. Remove reservoir cap and adjust fluid level. Install cap.

Component Service

DISASSEMBLE

1. Mount pump in suitable table vise, then remove suction hose connector bolt, connector and O-ring.
2. Remove pressure switch and flow control valve, **Fig. 7.**
3. Remove mounting bolts in sequence, then the rear pump cover and O-ring seal, **Fig. 8.**
4. Remove cam ring and vanes. Ensure vanes are kept together so they can be installed in original positions.
5. Snap ring and rotor, then the side plate and O-rings.
6. Remove shaft with pulley attached.
7. Remove oil seal.
8. Reverse procedure to install.

INSPECTION

1. Inspect power steering pump body and cover for cracks or leaks. If there is excessive wear, cracks or leaks, replace power steering pump.
2. Inspect side plate and shaft for excessive wear and damage. If any defect is found, replace pump.
3. Inspect cam ring for excessive wear and damage. If any defect is found, replace pump.
4. Inspect sliding surfaces of rotor and vane for wear and damage. If wear or damage is present, replace rotor and vanes with power steering pump seal kit.
5. Measure vane-to-rotor clearance. If clearance is more than 0006–.0011 inch, replace rotor and vanes with power steering pump seal kit.
6. Inspect relief valve fluid passage and connector orifice for obstructions.
7. Inspecting relief valve sliding surface for wear and damage.
8. Measure flow control valve spring free length. If measurement is not .748–.866 inch, replace power steering pump.

ASSEMBLE

1. Apply suitable wheel bearing lubricant to oil seal lip.
2. Apply Dexron-III ATF, or equivalent, to shaft sliding surface.
3. Install pulley shaft from oil seal side of pump body.
4. Apply Dexron-III ATF, or equivalent, to O-rings. Install O-rings to pump body.
5. Install side plate to pump body. Align dowel pins on side plate with bolt hole.
6. Apply Dexron-III ATF, or equivalent, to rotor sliding surface.
7. Install rotor to shaft with dot side facing upward to shaft.
8. Install new snap ring.
9. Apply Dexron-III ATF, or equivalent, to cam ring sliding surface.
10. Install cam ring to pump body with tapered end facing side plate.
11. Apply Dexron-III ATF, or equivalent, to vanes.

12. Install vanes to rotor and snap ring to shaft.
13. Apply Dexron-III ATF, or equivalent, to O-ring. Install O-ring to pump body.
14. Apply Dexron-III ATF, or equivalent, to pump cover and rotor sliding surfaces.
15. Match dowel pins to holes of the and install cover to body.
16. Gradually **torque** mounting bolts to 17 ft. lbs., in sequence, **Fig. 8.**
17. Apply Dexron-III ATF, or equivalent, to pressure switch O-ring. Install and tighten pressure switch.
18. Apply Dexron-III ATF, or equivalent, to relief valve.
19. Install relief valve and flow control spring.
20. Apply Dexron-III ATF, or equivalent, to plug O-rings. Install O-rings and tighten plug.

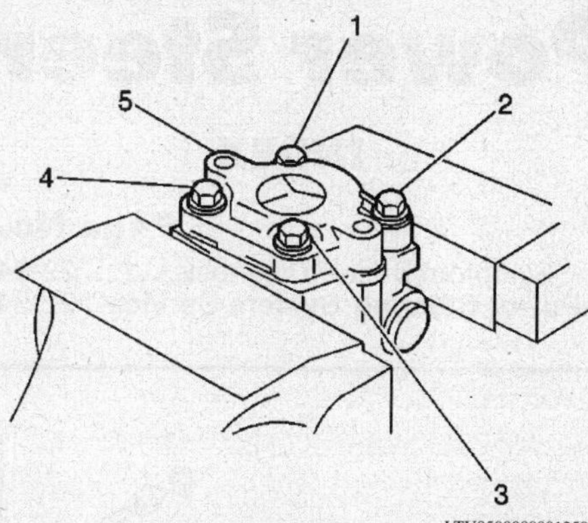

Fig. 8 Rear pump cover loosening & tightening sequence

21. Apply Dexron-III ATF, or equivalent, to suction connector O-ring. Install O-rings and tighten plug.
22. Install and tighten outlet hose connector.

TIGHTENING SPECIFICATIONS

Year	Component	Torque Ft. Lbs
2002–04	Alternator	17
	Power Steering Pump	18
	Power Steering Fluid Reservoir Bracket	96①
	Power Steering Pressure Switch	20
	Power Steering Pump Bracket (2.0L Engine)	18
	Power Steering Pump Bracket (2.5L Engine)	33
	Power Steering Pump Cover	②
	Power Steering Pump Fitting	44
	Power Steering Pump Lug	44
	Steering Shaft Coupling	18

① — Inch lbs.
② — Refer to "Component Service" for tightening specifications and sequence.

Tracker Power Steering Gear

INDEX

DESCRIPTION

The steering gear is a rack and pinion type steering system. The steering gear has a control valve which directs the fluid to either side of the rack piston. The piston uses hydraulic pressure to move the rack to the left and to the right, **Fig. 1**.

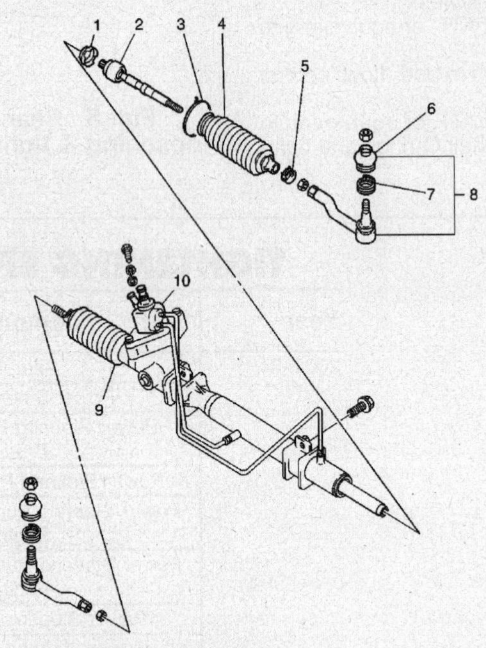

1. Inner Tie Rod Washer
2. Inner Tie Rod
3. Steering Gear Boot Retaining Ring
4. Steering Gear Boot
5. Steering Gear Boot Clamp
6. Outer Tie Rod Seal
7. Tie Rod Seal Retainer
8. Outer Tie Rod Kit
9. Steering Gear Boot
10. Steering Gear

LTV0500000001247

Fig. 1 Exploded view of power steering gear

DIAGNOSIS & TESTING

Symptom Based Diagnosis

Refer to "Tracker Power Steering Pump" for Tractor power steering diagnosis.

POWER STEERING SYSTEM SERVICE

Do not disassemble the power steering gear.

Power Steering System Bleed

Refer to "Tracker Power Steering Pump" for power steering system bleeding procedure.

TIGHTENING SPECIFICATIONS

Year	Component	Torque Ft. Lbs
2002–04	Power Steering Gear Bracket	40
	Power Steering Gear Inlet Hose, Bolt	26
	Power Steering Gear Inlet Hose, Fitting	44
	Power Steering Gear Inlet Hose, Nut	29
	Power Steering Pipe Clamp	96①
	Power Steering Pressure Switch	20
	Tie Rod, Inner	62
	Tie Rod, Lock	47
	Tie Rod, Outer	32

① — Inch lbs.

Electronic Power Steering (EPS)

NOTE: On Air Bag Equipped Models, Refer To "Air Bag System Precautions" Located In The Front Of This Manual For System Disarming & Arming Procedures.

NOTE: Refer To "Computer Relearn Procedures" Located In The Front Of This Manual When Battery Power To The Computer Has Been Interrupted.

NOTE: "Electrical Symbol & Wire Color Code Identification" Located In The Front Of This Manual May Be Used As An Aid When Using Wiring Circuits Found In This Section.

INDEX

DESCRIPTION

This Electric Power Steering (EPS) system uses the Under Hood Fuse Block (UHFB), Instrument Panel Fuse Block (IPFB), Power Steering Control Module (PSCM), torque sensor, discrete battery voltage supply circuit, EPS motor, class 2 serial data circuit and the Instrument Panel Cluster (IPC) message center to perform system functions.

The PSCM, torque sensor, nor the EPS motor are serviced separately from each other or from steering column. All EPS components diagnosed as faulting requires the steering column assembly to be replaced.

The PSCM uses a torque sensor as it's main input for determining the amount of steering assists. When steering wheel is turned, the PSCM uses signal voltage from the torque sensor to detect the amount of torque being applied to steering column shaft and amount of current to command to the EPS motor.

Code	Interpretation
C0000	No Vehicle Speed Message From ECM
C0176	System Thermal Error
C0475	EPS Motor Circuit Short Or Open
C0476	PSCM Detects High System Temperature
C0545	Torque Sensor Input Out Of Range
C0551	PSCM Not Configured With Proper Tuning Profile.
C0845	Device Ignition 1 Circuit
C0847	Ignition Voltage Circuit Shorted To Ground
C0848	Ignition Voltage Circuit Shorted To Voltage
C0895	EPS System Battery Voltage
C0896	EPS System Voltage Is 9–11 Volts
C0899	EPS System Voltage Is Less Than 8 Volts
C0900	EPS System Voltage Is Greater Than 17 Volts

Fig. 1 DTC interpretation

DIAGNOSIS & TESTING

Accessing Diagnostic Trouble Codes

Connect a suitably programmed scan tool to Diagnostic Link Connector (DLC) and follow scan tool manufacturer's instructions.

Diagnostic Trouble Code Interpretation

Refer to **Fig. 1** for Diagnostic Trouble Code (DTC) interpretation

Wiring Diagrams

Refer to **Figs. 2 and 3** for wiring diagrams.

Symptom Based Diagnosis

Refer to **Figs. 4 through 7** for symptom based diagnosis.

Diagnostic Tests

Refer to **Figs. 8 through 21** for diagnostic tests.

Clearing Diagnostic Trouble Codes

Follow the scan tool manufacturer's instructions to clear DTCs.

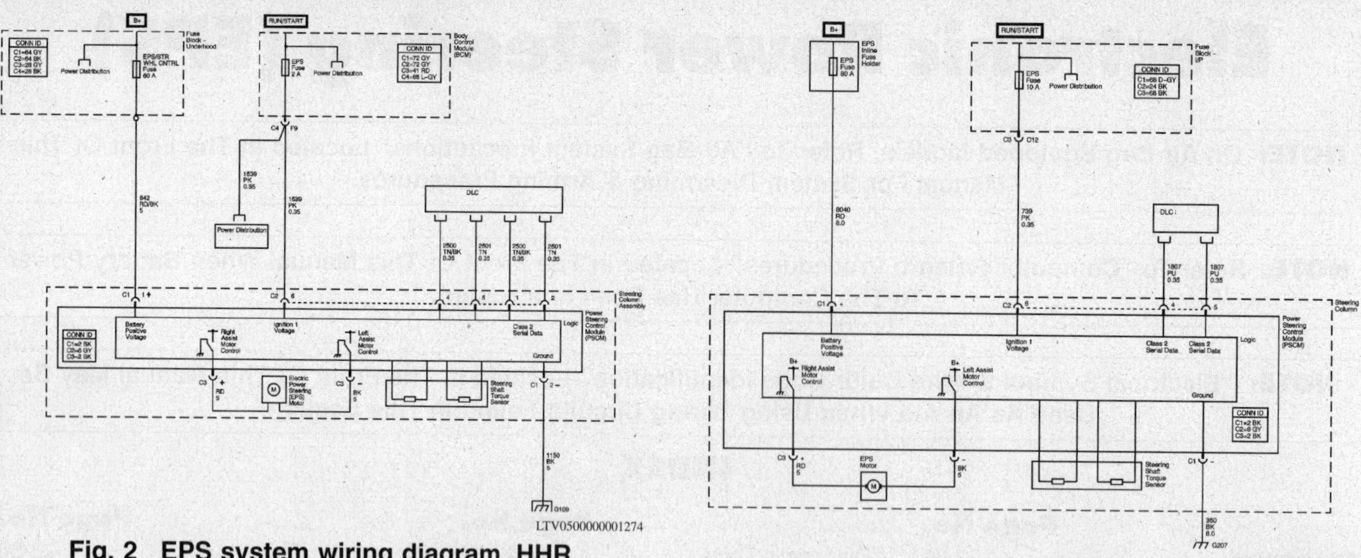

Fig. 2 EPS system wiring diagram. HHR

Fig. 3 EPS system wiring diagram. Equinox, Torrent & VUE

DIAGNOSTIC CHART INDEX

Code	Description	Page No.	Fig. No.
—	Diagnostic System Check	22-38	8
—	Increase In Effort While Turning Steering Wheel	22-37	5
—	Poor Return Of Steering Wheel	22-37	6
—	Rattle, Clunk Or Shudder Noise From Power Steering System	22-37	4
—	Steering Wheel Surges/Jerks While Turning	22-37	7
C0000	No Vehicle Speed Message From ECM	22-38	9
C0176	System Thermal Error	22-39	10
C0475	EPS Motor Circuit Short Or Open	22-39	11
C0476	PSCM Detects High System Temperature	22-40	12
C0545	Torque Sensor Input Out Of Range	22-40	13
C0551	PSCM Not Configured w/ Proper Tuning Profile	22-41	14
C0845	Device Ignition 1 Circuit	22-41	15
C0847	Ignition Voltage Circuit Shorted To Ground	22-42	16
C0848	Ignition Voltage Circuit Shorted To Voltage	22-42	17
C0895	EPS System Battery Voltage	22-43	18
C0896	EPS System Voltage Is 9–11 Volts	22-43	19
C0899	EPS System Voltage Is Less Than 8 Volts	22-44	20
C0900	EPS System Voltage Is Greater Than 17 Volts	22-45	21

Step	Action	Yes	No
1	Did you review the Power Steering System General Description	Go to Step 2	Go to Symptoms
2	Verify that a rattle, clunk or shudder noise is present. Is a rattle, clunk or shudder noise present?	Go to Step 3	System OK
3	Inspect the power steering gear for the proper installation. Is the power steering gear installation incorrect?	Go to Step 6	Go to Step 4
4	Inspect the intermediate shaft. Is the intermediate shaft worn?	Go to Step 8	Go to Step 5
5	Inspect the suspension. Is the suspension worn?	Go to Step 7	Diagnose noise
6	Install the power steering gear correctly. Did you complete the repair?	Go to Step 9	--
7	Replace the worn suspension components. Did you complete the repair?	Go to Step 9	--
8	Replace the intermediate shaft. Did you complete the repair?	Go to Step 9	--
9	Operate the system in order to verify the repair. Did you correct the condition?	System OK	Go to Step 3

LTV0500000001266

Fig. 4 Rattle, Clunk Or Shudder Noise From Power Steering System

Step	Action	Yes	No
1	Did you review the Power Steering System Description	Go to Step 2	Go to Description
2	Verify that there is an increase in effort while turning is present. Does the system operate normally?	System OK	Go to Step 3
3	Check for the following tire related conditions: • Incorrect tire inflation • Improper tire size Did you find and correct the condition?	Go to Step 10	Go to Step 4
4	1. Raise and support the vehicle. 2. Check for a binding or worn tie rod end. Is the tie rod binding or worn?	Go to Step 7	Go to Step 5
5	Check for a worn or binding intermediate shaft. Is the intermediate shaft worn or binding?	Go to Step 8	Go to Step 6
6	Check for a worn or binding steering gear. Is the steering worn or binding?	Go to Step 9	System OK
7	Replace the outer tie rod end. Did you complete the repair?	Go to Step 10	--
8	Replace the intermediate shaft. Did you complete the repair?	Go to Step 10	--
9	Replace the steering gear. Did you complete the repair?	Go to Step 10	--
10	Operate the system in order to verify the repair. Did you correct the condition?	System OK	Go to Step 3

LTV0500000001267

Fig. 5 Increase In Effort While Turning Steering Wheel

Step	Action	Yes	No
1	Did you review the Power Steering System Description	Go to Step 2	Go to Description
2	Verify a poor return of the steering wheel is present. Does the system operate normally?	System OK	Go to Step 3
3	Check for incorrect tire inflation. Did you find and correct the condition?	Go to Step 11	Go to Step 4
4	1. Raise and support the vehicle. 2. Check for a binding or worn tie rod end. Is the tie rod binding or worn?	Go to Step 8	Go to Step 5
5	Check for a worn or binding intermediate shaft. Is the intermediate shaft worn or binding?	Go to Step 9	Go to Step 6
6	Check for worn a or binding ball joint. Are the ball joints worn or binding?	Go to Step 10	Go to Step 7
7	Check for proper alignment of the front suspension. Did you complete the wheel alignment?	Go to Step 11	--
8	Replace the outer tie rod end. Did you complete the repair?	Go to Step 11	--
9	Replace the intermediate shaft. Did you complete the repair?	Go to Step 11	--
10	Replace the ball joint. Did you complete the repair?	Go to Step 11	--
11	Operate the system in order to verify the repair. Did you correct the condition?	System OK	Go to Step 3

LTV0500000001268

Fig. 6 Poor Return Of Steering Wheel

Step	Action	Yes	No
1	Did you review the Power Steering System Description	Go to Step 2	Go to Description
2	Verify that the steering wheel surges/jerks while turning. Does the system operate normally?	System OK	Go to Step 3
3	Check for worn or binding front suspension components. Did you find and correct the condition?	Go to Step 15	Go to Step 4
4	1. Raise and support the vehicle. 2. Check for a binding or worn tie rod end. Is the tie rod binding or worn?	Go to Step 11	Go to Step 5
5	Check for a worn or binding intermediate shaft. Is the intermediate shaft worn or binding?	Go to Step 12	Go to Step 6
6	Check for worn a binding steering gear. Is the steering gear worn or binding?	Go to Step 13	Go to Step 7
7	Check for a worn or binding steering column. Is the steering column worn or binding?	Go to Step 14	Go to Step 8
8	Check for excessive heat in the EPS motor. Does the EPS appear to be overheated?	Go to Step 09	Go to Step 10
9	**Important** • Do not perform excessive parking lot maneuvers during testing. • Excessive parking lot maneuvers can cause the EPS motor to heat up. Allow the EPS motor to cool and retest the system. Did you find and correct the condition?	Go to Step 15	Go to Step 10
10	Check for low battery voltage. Did you find and correct the condition?	Go to Step 15	System OK

LTV0500000001269

Fig. 7 Steering Wheel Surges/Jerks While Turning (Part 1 of 2)

11	Replace the outer tie rod end. Did you complete the repair?	Go to Step 15	--
12	Replace the intermediate Shaft. Did you complete the repair?	Go to Step 15	--
13	Replace the steering gear. Did you complete the repair?	Go to Step 15	--
14	Replace the steering column. Did you complete the repair?	Go to Step 15	--
15	Operate the system in order to verify the repair. Did you correct the condition?	System OK	Go to Step 3

LTV0500000001270

Fig. 7 Steering Wheel Surges/Jerks While Turning (Part 2 of 2)

Step	Action	Value(s)	Yes	No
1	Install a scan tool. Does the scan tool turn on?	--	Go to Step 2	Scan Tool Does Not Power Up
2	1. Turn ON the ignition, with the engine OFF. 2. Attempt to establish communication with the Power Steering Control Module (PSCM). Does the scan tool communicate with the PSCM?	--	Go to Step 3	Scan Tool Does Not Communicate with Class 2 Device
3	Select the Diagnostic Trouble Codes (DTC) function on the scan tool. Does the scan tool display any DTCs that begin with a U?	--	Diagnostic Trouble Code (DTC)	Go to Step 4

ARM66GC000000451

Fig. 8 Diagnostic System Check (Part 1 of 2)

4	Does the scan tool display DTC C0550, or any DTCs that begin with a B?	--	Diagnostic Trouble Code (DTC)	Go to Step 5
5	Does the scan tool display any EPS DTCs?	--	Diagnostic Trouble Code (DTC)	Go to Step 6
6	1. Start the engine. 2. Turn the steering wheel 90° to the left, then 90° to the right, then return the steering wheel to center. 3. remove hands from steering wheel and ensure no force is being applied to the steering wheel. 4. Using the scan tool observe the Steering Shaft Torque data parameter in the EPS data list 2. Does the scan tool indicate that the Steering Shaft Torque data parameter is within the specified range?	< + or - 1 N·m (0.7 lb ft)	Power Steering System	Replace Steering Column

ARM66GC000000452

Fig. 8 Diagnostic System Check (Part 2 of 2)

Circuit Description

The Power Steering Control Module (PSCM) receives a class 2 vehicle speed message from the Engine Control Module (ECM) via a class 2 serial data circuit. The PSCM uses this vehicle speed message, and other inputs, to determine the desired amount of steering assist.

Conditions for Running the DTC

- The ignition is ON.
- DTC U1300, U1301, or U2100 are not set.
- Vehicle speed is greater than 8.1 km/h (5 mph).

Conditions for Setting the DTC

The PSCM receives an invalid, or no vehicle speed message from the ECM.

Action Taken When the DTC Sets

- DTC C0000 is stored in memory.
- The IPC message center displays the PWR STR warning message.
- Steering assist level defaults to 120 km/h (74.5 mph) vehicle speed level of assist.

Conditions for Clearing the DTC

- A current DTC will clear on the next consecutive malfunction free ignition cycle.
- A history DTC will clear after 100 consecutive malfunction free ignition cycles.
- Using a scan tool

Test Description

2. tests for the presence of vehicle speed related DTCs in the control modules where the vehicle speed message originates.

ARM66GC000000453

Fig. 9 Code C0000: No Vehicle Speed Message From ECM (Part 1 of 2)

Step	Action	Yes	No
1	Did you perform the Power Steering System Diagnostic System Check?	Go to Step 2	Go to Diagnostic System Check -
2	1. Install a scan tool. 2. Turn ON the ignition, with the engine OFF. 3. With the scan tool, select the Engine, or Transmission Diagnostic Trouble Codes (DTC) function in Powertrain. Does the scan tool indicate the presents of any ECM, or TCM DTCs?	Diagnostic Trouble Code (DTC)	Go to Step 3
3	1. Use the scan tool in order to clear the EPS DTCs 2. Operate the vehicle within the conditions for running the DTC. Does the DTC reset?	Go to Step 2	System OK

ARM66GC000000454

Fig. 9 Code C0000: No Vehicle Speed Message From ECM (Part 2 of 2)

Circuit Description

The power steering control module (PSCM) monitors the temperature of the Power Steering System. The PSCM uses voltage, current levels and input from an internal temperature sensor to calculate an estimated system temperature. If the PSCM detects a high system temperature event is occurring, the amount of assist is reduced to lower system temperature to prevent thermal damage to the power steering components.

DTC Descriptor

This diagnostic procedure supports the following DTC:

DTC C0176 System Thermal Error

This vehicle has DTCs which include DTC symptoms. For more information on DTC symptoms, refer to DTC Symptom Description in Vehicle DTC Information.

DTC Symptom	DTC Symptom Descriptor
54	Temperature High

Condition for Running the DTC

- The ignition is ON, with the engine ON.
- Power Steering System voltage is 9-16 volts.
- Repetitive steering input is present.

Conditions for Setting the DTC

The PSCM detects a high system temperature.

Action Taken When the DTC Sets

- DTC C0176 54 is stored in memory.
- Steering assist is reduced.

Conditions for Clearing the DTC

- A current DTC will clear when the Power Steering System temperature returns to normal.
- A history DTC will clear after 100 consecutive malfunction-free ignition cycles.
- Using a scan tool

Diagnostic Aids

- DTC C0176 54 does not indicate that a malfunction has occurred. Rather that the PSCM had to limit current to the power steering motor to avoid thermal damage to the Power Steering System components.
- Inspect the under dash area around the steering column assembly. Ensure that no other components have come in contact with the power steering motor and module assembly, such as under dash insulation, or other electrical components.
- Ensure that no steering components down stream of the power steering column assembly, such as

LTV0500000001275

Fig. 10 Code C0176: System Thermal Error (Part 1 of 2)

Circuit Description

The Power Steering Control Module (PSCM) continuously monitors the voltage and current levels being commanded to the Electric Power Steering (EPS) motor. The PSCM compares the desired and actual current levels to detect malfunctions in the EPS motor, or the circuits to the motor.

Conditions for Running the DTC

- The ignition is ON.
- No voltage DTCs are present.

Conditions for Setting the DTC

A short to ground, short to voltage, or an open in the EPS motor, or the circuits to the motor.

Action Taken When the DTC Sets

- A DTC C0475 is stored in memory.
- The IPC message center displays the PWR STR warring message.
- No steering assist is provided.

Conditions for Clearing the DTC

- A current DTC will clear on the next malfunction free ignition cycle.
- A history DTC will clear after 100 consecutive malfunction free ignition cycles.
- Using a scan tool

ARM66GC000000455

Fig. 11 Code C0475: EPS Motor Circuit Short Or Open (Part 1 of 2)

ball joints, tie rod ends, universal joints, or the steering gear assembly, are mechanically binding.

Test Description

The number below refers to the step number on the diagnostic table.

2. This step tests if the high system temperature is driving condition related.

Step	Action	Yes	No
1	Did you perform the Diagnostic System Check	Go to Step 2	Go to Diagnostic System Check -
2	Since most occurrences of the DTC are caused by excessive static steering, such as parking maneuvers and high ambient temperatures, review the Power Steering System with the customer to determine the conditions under which the DTC set. Did steering conditions and/or high ambient temperatures cause the DTC to set?	Go to Step 3	Go to Diagnostic Aids
3	1. Use the scan tool in order to clear the DTCs. 2. Operate the vehicle within normal conditions. Does the DTC reset?	Go to Step 2	System OK

LTV0500000001276

Fig. 10 Code C0176: System Thermal Error (Part 2 of 2)

Step	Action	Yes	No
1	Did you perform the Power Steering Diagnostic System Check?	Go to Step 2	Go to Diagnostic System Check
2	Inspect for poor connections at the EPS motor harness connector. Did you find and correct the condition?	Go to Step 6	Go to Step 3
3	Test the EPS motor control circuits for a short to ground or an open. Did you find and correct the condition?	Go to Step 6	Go to Step 4
4	Test the EPS motor control circuits for a short to voltage. Did you find and correct the condition?	Go to Step 6	Go to Step 5
5	Replace the EPS assembly. Did you complete the repair?	Go to Step 6	--
6	1. Use the scan tool in order to clear the DTCs. 2. Operate the vehicle within the Conditions for Running the DTC. Does the DTC reset?	Go to Step 2	System OK

ARM66GC000000456

Fig. 11 Code C0475: EPS Motor Circuit Short Or Open (Part 2 of 2)

Circuit Description

The Power Steering Control Module (PSCM) monitors the temperature of the Electric Power Steering (EPS) system. The PSCM uses voltage and current levels to calculate an estimated system temperature. If the PSCM detects a high system temperature event is occurring the amount of assist is reduced to lower the EPS system temperature to prevent system thermal damage.

Condition for Running the DTC

The ignition is ON.

Conditions for Setting the DTC

The PSCM detects a high system temperature.

Action Taken When the DTC Sets

- A DTC C0476 is stored in memory.
- Steering assist is reduced.

Conditions for Clearing the DTC

- A current DTC will clear when the EPS system temperature returns to normal.
- A history DTC will clear after 100 consecutive malfunction free ignition cycles.
- Using a scan tool

Diagnostic Aids

- DTC C0476 does not indicate that a malfunction has occurred. Rather that the PSCM had to limit current to the EPS motor to avoid system thermal damage.
- Inspect the under dash area around the EPS assembly. ensure that no other components have come in contact with the EPS assembly such as under dash insulation or other electrical components.
- Ensure that no steering components down stream of the EPS assembly, such as ball joints, tie rod ends, universal joints, or the steering rack and pinion are mechanically binding.

Test Description

The number below refer to the step number on the diagnostic table.

2. Tests if the high system temperature is system, or driving condition related.

ARM66GC000000457

Fig. 12 Code C0476: PSCM Detects High System Temperature (Part 1 of 2)

Circuit Description

The electric power steering (EPS) system uses a torque sensor to detect the amount of torque being applied to the steering column shaft when the steering wheel is turned. The power steering control module (PSCM) uses this sensor as it's main input in determining the amount of steering assist needed.

Condition for Running the DTC

The ignition, and the engine are ON.

Condition for Setting the DTC

- The PSCM's torque sensor input is greater than 20.70 N·m (15.2 lb ft) during a right turn.
- The PSCM's torque sensor input is less than -20.70 N·m (15.2 lb ft) during a left turn.
- The difference between the 2 torque sensor coils is greater than 2.4 N·m (1.7 lb ft).

Action Taken When the DTC Sets

- A DTC C0545 is stored in memory.
- The IPC message center displays the PWR STR warning message.
- No steering assist is provided.

Conditions for Clearing the DTC

- A current DTC will clear on the next malfunction free ignition cycle.
- A history DTC will clear after 100 consecutive malfunction free ignition cycles.
- Using a scan tool

Diagnostic Aids

The torque sensor is hard wired to the PSCM, thus no connector, or circuit testing can be performed. if an intermittent malfunction is suspected with the torque sensor, or the circuits to the torque sensor, replace the EPS assembly. The scan tool can be used to view the torque sensor value.

Test Description

The number below refers to the step number on the diagnostic table.

2. Tests the torque sensor in its active state.

ARM66GC000000459

Fig. 13 Code C0545: Torque Sensor Input Out Of Range (Part 1 of 2)

Step	Action	Yes	No
1	Did you perform the Power Steering Diagnostic System Check?	Go to Step 2	Go to Diagnostic System Check -
2	Since most occurrences of the DTC are caused by frequent static steering, such as parking maneuvers and high ambient temperatures, review the EPS system with the customer to determine the conditions under which the DTC set. Did steering conditions, or high ambient temperatures cause the DTC to set?	Go to Step 3	Go to Diagnostic Aids
3	1. Use the scan tool in order to clear the DTCs. 2. Operate the vehicle within the Conditions for Running the DTC. Does the DTC reset?	Go to Step 2	System OK

ARM66GC000000458

Fig. 12 Code C0476: PSCM Detects High System Temperature (Part 2 of 2)

Step	Action	Values	Yes	No
1	Did you perform the Power Steering Diagnostic System Check?		Go to Step 2	Go to Diagnostic System Check -
2	1. Install a scan tool 2. Start the engine. 3. With the scan tool, observe the Steering Shaft Torque data parameter in the EPS Data List 2. 4. Turn the steering wheel 90 degrees to the right and hold the steering wheel position. Does the scan tool indicate that the Steering Shaft Torque data parameter changes state wile turning the steering wheel and is less than the specified value?	20.70 N·m (15.2 lb ft)	Go to Diagnostic Aids	Go to Step 3
3	Replace the EPS assembly. Did you complete the repair?		Go to Step 4	--
4	1. Use the scan tool in order to clear the DTCs. 2. Operate the vehicle within the Conditions for Running the DTC. Does the DTC reset?		Go to Step 2	System OK

ARM66GC000000460

Fig. 13 Code C0545: Torque Sensor Input Out Of Range (Part 2 of 2)

Circuit Description

After replacement of the electric power steering (EPS) assembly and the power steering control module (PSCM) must be configured with the proper tuning profile using the Saturn Service Stall.

DTC Descriptor

This diagnostic procedure supports the following DTC:

DTC C0551 Option Configuration Error

Conditions for Running the DTC

The ignition is ON.

Conditions for Setting the DTC

The PSCM has not been configured with the proper tuning profile.

Action Taken When the DTC Sets

- DTC C0551 is stored in memory.
- The instrument panel cluster (IPC) displays the SERVICE VEHICLE SOON warning indicator.
- Steering assist is set to a default level.

Conditions for Clearing the DTC

- A current DTC will clear after the PSCM has been configured with the proper tuning profile.
- A history DTC will clear after 100 consecutive malfunction free ignition cycles from when the PSCM has been configured.
- Using a scan tool

Diagnostic Aids

A newly replaced EPS assembly will set DTC C0551 on it's initial ignition ON cycle.

LTV0500000001271

Fig. 14 Code C0551: PSCM Not Configured w/Proper Tuning Profile (Part 1 of 2).

Test Description

The numbers below refer to the step numbers on the diagnostic table.

2. Tests if the condition is current.

Step	Action	Yes	No
1	Did you perform the Diagnostic System Check	Go to Step 2	Go to Diagnostic System Check
2	1. Install a scan tool. 2. Turn ON the ignition, with the engine OFF. 3. With a scan tool, observe the Tuning Profile parameter in the electric power steering (EPS) data list. Does the scan tool display number 0?	Go to Step 3	Go to Step 4
3	Configure the power steering control module (PSCM). Did you complete the repair?	Go to Step 4	--
4	1. Use the scan tool in order to clear the DTCs. 2. Operate the vehicle within the Conditions for Running the DTC. Does the DTC reset?	Go to Step 2	System OK

LTV0500000001272

Fig. 14 Code C0551: PSCM Not Configured w/ Proper Tuning Profile (Part 2 of 2).

Circuit Description

The body control module (BCM) contains the 2-amp EPS fuse. This fuse and the ignition 1 voltage circuit supply ignition voltage to the power steering control module (PSCM). This ignition voltage is used to wake up the PSCM. The PSCM receives a class 2 power moding message from the BCM to determine the position of the ignition switch. When a power mode message is received, the PSCM monitors the ignition 1 voltage circuit to detect if a short to voltage, short to ground, or an open exists.

DTC Descriptor

This diagnostic procedure supports the following DTC:

DTC C0845 Device Ignition 1 Circuit

This vehicle has DTCs which include DTC symptoms.

DTC Symptom	DTC Symptom Descriptor
01	Short to Battery +
06	Short to Ground or Open

Conditions for Running the DTC

The PSCM has 9-16 volts.

Conditions for Setting the DTC

- The class 2 power mode message indicates OFF, and the ignition 1 voltage circuit is shorted to voltage.
- The class 2 power mode message indicates ON, and the ignition 1 voltage circuit is shorted to ground or open.
- DTCs U1300 and U1301 are not set.

Action Taken When the DTC Sets

- DTC C0847 is stored in memory.
- The instrument panel cluster (IPC) message center displays the PWR STR warning message.
- The EPS system is disabled.

Conditions for Clearing the DTC

- A current DTC will clear when the malfunction is no longer present.
- A history DTC will clear after 100 consecutive malfunction free ignition cycles.
- Using a scan tool

Diagnostic Aids

LTV0500000001277

Fig. 15 Code C0845: Device Ignition 1 Circuit (Part 1 of 3)

The ignition 1 voltage circuit supplies several other control modules with ignition voltage. Before preceding with the diagnostic table below, ensure no other control modules that use the ignition 1 circuit for their ignition voltage supply have any ignition voltage malfunctions present, such as the sensing and diagnostic module (SDM) or the cruise control module (CCM). Refer to Power Distribution Schematics . If an intermittent malfunction exists, refer to Testing for Intermittent Conditions and Poor Connections for further diagnosis.

Test Description

The numbers below refer to the step numbers on the diagnostic table.

2. This step tests if the malfunction is intermittent.

5. This step tests if a short to ground exists in the ignition 1 voltage circuit, or in the PSCM.

Step	Action	Yes	No
1	Did you perform the Diagnostic System Check	Go to Step 2	Go to Diagnostic System Check
2	1. Install a scan tool. 2. Turn ON the ignition, with the engine OFF. 3. With a scan tool, attempt to establish communication with the power steering control module (PSCM). Does the scan tool communicate with the PSCM?	Go to Step 6	Go to Step 3
3	1. Turn OFF the ignition. 2. Inspect the 2 A EPS fuse for an open. Is the fuse open?	Go to Step 4	Go to Step 7
4	1. Replace the 2 A EPS fuse. 2. Turn ON the ignition, with the engine OFF. Does the fuse open?	Go to Step 5	Go to Diagnostic Aids
5	Test the ignition 1 voltage circuit of the PSCM for a short to ground. Did you find and correct the condition?	Go to Step 11	Go to Step 10
6	Test the ignition 1 voltage circuit for a short to voltage. Did you find and correct the condition?	Go to Step 11	Go to Diagnostic Aids
7	Test the ignition 1 voltage circuit of the PSCM for an open. Did you find and correct the condition?	Go to Step 11	Go to Step 8

LTV0500000001278

Fig. 15 Code C0845: Device Ignition 1 Circuit (Part 2 of 3)

Step	Action	Yes	No
8	Inspect for poor connections at the harness connector of the body control module (BCM). Did you find and correct the condition?	Go to Step 11	Go to Step 9
9	Inspect for poor connections at the harness connector of the PSCM. Did you find and correct the condition?	Go to Step 11	Go to Step 10
10	Replace the electronic power steering (EPS) assembly. Did you complete the replacement?	Go to Step 11	--
11	1. Use the scan tool in order to clear the DTCs. 2. Operate the vehicle within the Conditions for Running the DTC. Does DTC C0845 reset?	Go to Step 2	System OK

LTV0500000001279

Fig. 15 Code C0845: Device Ignition 1 Circuit (Part 3 of 3)

Step	Action	Yes	No
1	Did you perform the Power Steering Diagnostic System Check?	Go to Step 2	Go to Diagnostic System Check -
2	1. Install a scan tool. 2. Turn ON the ignition, with the engine OFF. 3. With a scan tool, attempt to establish communication with the PSCM. Does the scan tool communicate with the PSCM?	Go to Diagnostic Aids	Go to Step 3
3	1. Turn OFF the ignition. 2. Inspect the 2 A EPS fuse for an open. Is the fuse open?	Go to Step 4	Go to Step 6
4	1. Replace the 2 A EPS fuse. 2. Turn ON the ignition, with the engine OFF. Does the fuse open?	Go to Step 5	Go to Diagnostic Aids
5	Test the ignition 1 voltage circuit of the PSCM for a short to ground. Did you find and correct the condition?	Go to Step 10	Go to Step 9

ARM66GC000000462

Fig. 16 Code C0847: Ignition Voltage Circuit Shorted To Ground (Part 2 of 3)

Step	Action	Yes	No
6	Test the ignition 1 voltage circuit of the PSCM for an open. Did you find and correct the condition?	Go to Step 10	Go to Step 7
7	Inspect for poor connections at the harness connector of the BCM. Did you find and correct the condition?	Go to Step 10	Go to Step 8
8	Inspect for poor connections at the harness connector of the PSCM. Did you find and correct the condition?	Go to Step 10	Go to Step 9
9	Replace the EPS assembly. Did you complete the replacement?	Go to Step 10	--
10	1. Use the scan tool in order to clear the DTCs. 2. Operate the vehicle within the Conditions for Running the DTC. Does the DTC reset?	Go to Step 2	System OK

ARM66GC000000463

Fig. 16 Code C0847: Ignition Voltage Circuit Shorted To Ground (Part 3 of 3)

Circuit Description

The Body Control Module (BCM) contains the 2 amp EPS fuse. This fuse and the ignition 1 voltage circuit supply ignition voltage to the Power Steering Control Module (PSCM). This ignition voltage is used to wake up the PSCM.

Conditions for Running the DTC

The ignition is ON.

Conditions for Setting the DTC

- The ignition 1 voltage circuit is shorted to ground or open.
- DTCs U1300 and U1301 are not set.

Action Taken When the DTC Sets

- DTC C0847 is stored in memory.
- The IPC message center displays the PWR STR warning message.
- The EPS system is disabled.

Conditions for Clearing the DTC

- A current DTC will clear when the malfunction is no longer present.
- A history DTC will clear after 100 consecutive malfunction free ignition cycles.
- Using a scan tool

Diagnostic Aids

The Ignition 1 voltage circuit supplies several other control modules with ignition voltage. Before preceding with the diagnostic table below, ensure no other control modules that use the ignition 1 circuit for their ignition voltage supply have any ignition voltage malfunctions present, such as the Sensing and Diagnostic Module (SDM), or the Cruise Control Module (CCM).

Test Description

The numbers below refer to the step numbers on the diagnostic table.

2. Tests if the malfunction is intermittent.

5. Tests if a short to ground exists in the ignition 1 voltage circuit, or in the PSCM.

ARM66GC000000461

Fig. 16 Code C0847: Ignition Voltage Circuit Shorted To Ground (Part 1 of 3)

Circuit Description

The Power Steering Control Module (PSCM) receives a class 2 power moding message from the Body Control Module (BCM) to determine the position of the ignition switch. After a power mode OFF message is received, the PSCM monitors the ignition 1 voltage circuit to detect if a short to voltage fault exists.

Conditions for Running the DTC

- The ignition is OFF.
- The class 2 power mode message indicates OFF.

Conditions for Setting the DTC

- The PSCM ignition 1 voltage circuit is shorted to voltage.
- DTCs U1300 and U1301 are not set.

Action Taken When the DTC Sets

- DTC C0848 is stored in memory.
- The IPC message center displays the PWR STR warning message.

Conditions for Clearing the MIL/DTC

- A current DTC will clear on the next consecutive malfunction free ignition cycle.
- A history DTC will clear after 100 consecutive malfunction free ignition cycles.
- Using a scan tool

Step	Action	Yes	No
1	Did you perform the Power Steering Diagnostic System Check?	Go to Step 2	Go to Diagnostic System Check
2	Test the ignition 1 voltage circuit for a short to voltage. Did you find and correct the condition?	Go to Step 3	Test for Intermittent and Poor Connections
3	1. Use the scan tool in order to clear the DTCs. 2. Operate the vehicle within the Conditions for Running the DTC. Does the DTC reset?	Go to Step 2	System OK

ARM66GC000000464

Fig. 17 Code C0848: Ignition Voltage Circuit Shorted To Voltage

Circuit Description

The power steering control module (PSCM) has a discrete battery positive voltage supply circuit. The PSCM monitors the voltage level on this circuit to ensure the electric power steering (EPS) system has adequate voltage levels to perform the system functions.

DTC Descriptor

This diagnostic procedure supports the following DTC:

DTC C0895 Device Voltage

This vehicle has DTCs which include DTC symptoms. For more information on DTC symptoms, refer to DTC Symptom Description .

DTC Symptom	DTC Symptom Descriptor
03	Voltage Below Threshold
11	Above Maximum Threshold
12	Below Minimum Threshold

Conditions for Running the DTC

The ignition is ON.

Conditions for Setting the DTC

EPS system battery voltage is less than 9.55 volts or greater than 17.5 volts.

Action Taken When the DTC Sets

- DTC C0896 is stored in memory.
- The instrument panel cluster (IPC) message center displays the PWR STR warning message.
- Steering assist is reduced.

Conditions for Clearing the DTC

- A current DTC will clear when EPS system voltage is 9.55-17.5 volts.
- A history DTC will clear after 100 consecutive ignition cycles with EPS system voltage between 9.55-17.5 volts.

Diagnostic Aids

The scan tool can be used to view the number of times a low battery voltage incident has occurred.

Test Description

LTV0500000001280

Fig. 18 Code C0895: EPS System Battery Voltage (Part 1 of 3)

The numbers below refer to the step number on the diagnostic table.

2. This step tests if the malfunction exists in the vehicles charging system.

3. This step tests if the malfunction is intermittent.

Step	Action	Yes	No
1	Did you perform the Diagnostic System Check	Go to Step 2	Go to Diagnostic System Check
2	1. Install a scan tool. 2. Turn ON the ignition, with the engine OFF. 3. With a scan tool, observe the Battery Voltage parameter in the engine control module (ECM) Data List. Does the scan tool display 9.55-17.5 volts?	Go to Step 3	Go to Diagnostic System Check -
3	With a scan tool, observe the Battery Voltage parameter in the electric power steering (EPS) Data List 1. Does the scan tool display 9.55-17.5 volts?	Go to Diagnostic Aids	Go to Step 4
4	Test the battery positive voltage circuit of the power steering control module (PSCM) for a high resistance. Did you find and correct the condition?	Go to Step 10	Go to Step 5
5	Test the ground circuit of the PSCM for a high resistance. Did you find and correct the condition?	Go to Step 10	Go to Step 6
6	Inspect for poor connections at the harness connector of the underhood fuse block stud terminal. Did you find and correct the condition?	Go to Step 10	Go to Step 7
7	Inspect for poor connections at the harness connector of the PSCM. Did you find and correct the condition?	Go to Step 10	Go to Step 8
8	Inspect for poor connections at the ground terminal G109 . Did you find and correct the condition?	Go to Step 10	Go to Step 9

LTV0500000001281

Fig. 18 Code C0895: EPS System Battery Voltage (Part 2 of 3)

Step	Action	Yes	No
9	Replace the EPS assembly. Did you complete the replacement?	Go to Step 10	--
10	1. Use the scan tool in order to clear the DTCs. 2. Operate the vehicle within the Conditions for Running the DTC. Does DTC C0895 reset?	Go to Step 2	System OK

LTV0500000001522

Fig. 18 Code C0895: EPS System Battery Voltage (Part 3 of 3)

Circuit Description

The Power Steering Control Module (PSCM) has a discrete battery positive voltage supply circuit. The PSCM monitors the voltage level on this circuit to ensure the Electric Power Steering (EPS) system has adequate voltage levels to perform the system functions.

Conditions for Running the DTC

The ignition is ON.

Conditions for Setting the DTC

EPS system battery voltage is 9-11 volts.

Action Taken When the DTC Sets

- DTC C0896 is stored in memory.
- The IPC message center displays the PWR STR warning message.
- Steering assist is reduced.

Conditions for Clearing the DTC

- A current DTC will clear when EPS system voltage is greater than 11 volts.
- A history DTC will clear after 100 consecutive ignition cycles with EPS system voltage greater than 11 volts.
- Using a scan tool

Diagnostic Aids

The scan tool can be used to view the number of times a low battery voltage incident has occurred.

Test Description

The number below refers to the step number on the diagnostic table.

2. Tests if the malfunction exists in the vehicles charging system.

3. Tests if the malfunction is intermittent.

ARM66GC000000465

Fig. 19 Code C0896: EPS System Voltage Is 9–11 Volts (Part 1 of 3)

Step	Action	Yes	No
1	Did you perform the Power Steering Diagnostic System Check?	Go to Step 2	Go to Diagnostic System Check
2	1. Install a scan tool. 2. Turn ON the ignition, with the engine OFF. 3. With a scan tool, observe the Battery Voltage parameter in the ECM Data List. Does the scan tool display greater than 11 volts?	Go to Step 3	Go to Diagnostic System Check
3	With a scan tool, observe the Battery Voltage parameter in the EPS Data List 1. Does the scan tool display greater than 11 volts?	Go to Diagnostic Aids	Go to Step 4
4	Test the battery positive voltage circuit of the PSCM for a high resistance. Did you find and correct the condition?	Go to Step 10	Go to Step 5
5	Test the ground circuit of the PSCM for a high resistance. Did you find and correct the condition?	Go to Step 10	Go to Step 6

ARM66GC000000466

Fig. 19 Code C0896: EPS System Voltage Is 9–11 Volts (Part 2 of 3)

Step	Action	Yes	No
6	Inspect for poor connections at the harness connector of the underhood fuse block stud terminal. Did you find and correct the condition?	Go to Step 10	Go to Step 7
7	Inspect for poor connections at the harness connector of the PSCM. Did you find and correct the condition?	Go to Step 10	Go to Step 8
8	Inspect for poor connections at the ground terminal G109 . Did you find and correct the condition?	Go to Step 10	Go to Step 9
9	Replace the EPS assembly. Did you complete the replacement?	Go to Step 10	--
10	1. Use the scan tool in order to clear the DTCs. 2. Operate the vehicle within the Conditions for Running the DTC. Does the DTC reset?	Go to Step 2	System OK

ARM66GC000000467

Fig. 19 Code C0896: EPS System Voltage Is 9–11 Volts (Part 3 of 3)

Circuit Description

The Power Steering Control Module (PSCM) has a discrete battery positive voltage supply circuit. The PSCM monitors the voltage level on this circuit to ensure the Electric Power Steering (EPS) system has adequate voltage levels to perform the system functions.

Conditions for Running the DTC

The ignition is ON.

Conditions for Setting the DTC

EPS system voltage is less than 8 volts

Action Taken When the DTC Sets

- DTC C0899 is stored in memory.
- The IPC message center displays the PWR STR warning message.
- No steering assist is provided.

Conditions for Clearing the DTC

- A current DTC will clear when EPS system voltage is greater than 8.65 volts.
- A history DTC will clear after 100 consecutive ignition cycles with the EPS system voltage greater than 8.65 volts.
- Using a scan tool

Diagnostic Aids

The scan tool can be used to view the number of times a low battery incident has occurred.

Test Description

The numbers below refer to the step numbers on the diagnostic table.

2. Tests if the malfunction exsists in the vehicles charging system.

3. Tests if the malfunction is in the EPS system.

ARM66GC000000468

Fig. 20 Code C0899: EPS System Voltage Is Less Than 8 Volts (Part 1 of 3)

Step	Action	Yes	No
1	Did you perform the Power Steering Diagnostic System Check?	Go to Step 2	Go to Diagnostic System Check
2	1. Install a scan tool. 2. Turn ON the ignition, with the engine OFF. 3. Turn ON the scan tool Does the scan tool power up and communicate with the Engine Control Module (ECM)?	Go to Step 3	Go to Diagnostic System Check
3	With the scan tool observe the Battery Voltage parameter in the EPS Data List 1. Does the scan tool display less than 8 Volts?	Go to Step 3	Go to Diagnostic Aids
4	Test the battery positive voltage circuit of the PSCM for a high resistance. Did you find and correct the condition?	Go to Step 10	Go to Step 5
5	Test the ground circuit of the PSCM for a high resistance . Did you find and correct the condition?	Go to Step 10	Go to Step 6

ARM66GC000000469

Fig. 20 Code C0899: EPS System Voltage Is Less Than 8 Volts (Part 2 of 3)

Step	Action	Yes	No
6	Inspect for poor connections at the harness connector of the PSCM. Did you find and correct the condition?	Go to Step 10	Go to Step 7
7	Inspect for poor connections at the harness connector of the underhood fuse block stud terminal . Did you find and correct the condition?	Go to Step 10	Go to Step 8
8	Inspect for poor connections at the ground connector, G109. Did you find and correct the condition?	Go to Step 10	Go to Step 9
9	Replace the EPS assembly. Did you complete the replacement?	Go to Step 10	--
10	1. Use the scan tool in order to clear the DTCs. 2. Operate the vehicle within the Conditions for Running the DTC. Does the DTC reset?	Go to Step 2	System OK

ARM66GC000000470

Fig. 20 Code C0899: EPS System Voltage Is Less Than 8 Volts (Part 3 of 3)

Circuit Description

The Power Steering Control Module (PSCM) has a discrete battery voltage supply circuit. The PSCM monitors the voltage level on this circuit to protect itself against high voltage damage.

Conditions for Running the DTC

The ignition is ON.

Conditions for Setting the DTC

EPS system voltage is greater than 17 volts.

Action Taken When the DTC Sets

- DTC C0900 is stored in memory.
- The IPC message center displays the PWR STR warning message.
- The PSCM is disabled to protect itself.

Conditions for Clearing the MIL/DTC

- A current DTC will clear when the EPS system voltage returns to less than 15.5 volts.
- A history DTC will clear after 100 consecutive ignition cycles with the EPS system voltage less than 15.5 volts.
- Using a scan tool

Diagnostic Aids

Jump starting the vehicle can cause DTC C0900 to set.

ARM66GC000000471

Fig. 21 Code C0900: EPS System Voltage Is Greater Than 17 Volts (Part 1 of 2)

Step	Action	Values	Yes	No
1	Did you perform the Power Steering Diagnostic System Check?	--	Go to Step 2	Go to Diagnostic System Check
2	1. Install a scan tool. 2. Turn ON the ignition, with the engine OFF. 3. With a scan tool, observe the Battery Voltage parameter in the Engine Control Module (ECM) data list. Does the scan tool display greater than the specified value?	17 V	Check Engine Electrical	Go to Step 3
3	Test the ground circuit of the PSCM for a high resistance. Did you find and correct the condition?		Go to Step 4	Go to Diagnostic Aids
4	1. Use the scan tool in order to clear the DTC. 2. Operate the vehicle within the conditions for running the DTC. Does the DTC reset?		Go to Step 2	System OK

ARM66GC000000472

Fig. 21 Code C0900: EPS System Voltage Is Greater Than 17 Volts (Part 2 of 2)

POWER STEERING SYSTEM SERVICE

Component Service

The power steering gear on these models cannot be disassembled. Refer to the "Front Suspension & Steering" section of the appropriate chassis chapter for power steering gear replacement procedure.

TIGHTENING SPECIFICATIONS

Year	Component	Torque Ft. Lbs.
2002–06	Intermediate Steering Shaft To Gear	25
	Outer Tie Rod	①
	Steering Gear To Cradle	81

① — **Torque** to 18 ft. lbs, then tighten an additional 90°.

DISC BRAKES

TABLE OF CONTENTS

Application Chart

Year	Model	Brake Type	
		Front	Rear
2002	Astro & Safari	Delco Single Piston Sliding Caliper	—
	Avalanche, Escalade, Escalade EXT, Sierra, Silverado, Suburban, Tahoe & Yukon	Delco Dual Piston Sliding Caliper	Delco Dual Piston Sliding Caliper
	Aztek & Rendezvous	Delco Single Piston Sliding Caliper	Delco Single Piston Sliding Caliper
	Blazer, Bravada, Envoy, Jimmy, Trailblazer, Sonoma & S10	Delco Single Piston Sliding Caliper	Delco Single Piston Sliding Caliper
	Blazer, Bravada, Envoy, Jimmy, Trailblazer, Sonoma & S10	Delco Dual Piston Sliding Caliper	Delco Single Piston Sliding Caliper
	Express & Savana	Delco Single Piston Sliding Caliper	—
	Montana, Silhouette & Venture	Delco Single Piston Sliding Caliper	Delco Single Piston Sliding Caliper
	Tracker	Tokico	—
	Vue	Delco Single Piston Sliding Caliper	—
2003	Astro & Safari	Delco Dual Piston Sliding Caliper	Delco Single Piston Sliding Caliper
	Avalanche, Escalade, Escalade EXT, Sierra, Silverado, Suburban, Tahoe & Yukon	Delco Dual Piston Sliding Caliper	Delco Dual Piston Sliding Caliper
	Aztek & Rendezvous	Delco Single Piston Sliding Caliper	Delco Single Piston Sliding Caliper
	Blazer, Bravada, Envoy, Jimmy, Trailblazer, Sonoma & S10	Delco Single Piston Sliding Caliper	Delco Single Piston Sliding Caliper
	Blazer, Bravada, Envoy, Jimmy, Trailblazer, Sonoma, S10, & SSR	Delco Dual Piston Sliding Caliper	Delco Single Piston Sliding Caliper
	Express & Savana	Delco Single Piston Sliding Caliper	Delco Single Piston Sliding Caliper
	Hummer H2	Delco Dual Piston Sliding Caliper	Delco Dual Piston Sliding Caliper
	Montana, Silhouette & Venture	Delco Single Piston Sliding Caliper	Delco Single Piston Sliding Caliper
	Tracker	Tokico	—
	Vue	Delco Single Piston Sliding Caliper	—

Continued

Year	Model	Brake Type	
		Front	Rear
2004	Astro & Safari	Delco Dual Piston Sliding Caliper	Delco Single Piston Sliding Caliper
	Avalanche, Escalade, Escalade EXT, Sierra, Silverado, Suburban, Tahoe & Yukon	Delco Dual Piston Sliding Caliper	Delco Dual Piston Sliding Caliper
	Aztek & Rendezvous	Delco Single Piston Sliding Caliper	Delco Single Piston Sliding Caliper
	Blazer, Bravada, Envoy, Jimmy, Trailblazer, Sonoma & S10	Delco Single Piston Sliding Caliper	Delco Single Piston Sliding Caliper
	Blazer, Bravada, Envoy, Jimmy, Rainier, Trailblazer, Sonoma, S10, & SSR	Delco Dual Piston Sliding Caliper	Delco Single Piston Sliding Caliper
	Canyon & Colorado	Delco Dual Piston Sliding Caliper	—
	Express & Savana (1500)	Delco Dual Piston Sliding Caliper	Delco Single Piston Sliding Caliper
	Express & Savana (2500 & 3500)	Delco Dual Piston Sliding Caliper	Delco Dual Piston Sliding Caliper
	Hummer H2	Delco Dual Piston Sliding Caliper	Delco Dual Piston Sliding Caliper
	Montana, Silhouette & Venture	Delco Single Piston Sliding Caliper	Delco Single Piston Sliding Caliper
	SRX	Delco Dual Piston Sliding Caliper	Delco Single Piston Sliding Caliper
	Tracker	Tokico	—
	Vue	Delco Single Piston Sliding Caliper	—
2005	Astro & Safari	Delco Dual Piston Sliding Caliper	Delco Single Piston Sliding Caliper
	Avalanche, Escalade, Escalade EXT, Sierra, Silverado, Suburban, Tahoe & Yukon	Delco Dual Piston Sliding Caliper	Delco Dual Piston Sliding Caliper
	Aztek & Rendezvous	Delco Single Piston Sliding Caliper	Delco Single Piston Sliding Caliper
	Blazer, Envoy, Jimmy & Trailblazer	Delco Single Piston Sliding Caliper	Delco Single Piston Sliding Caliper
	Blazer, Envoy, Jimmy, Rainier, Trailblazer & SSR	Delco Dual Piston Sliding Caliper	Delco Single Piston Sliding Caliper
	Canyon & Colorado	Delco Dual Piston Sliding Caliper	—
	Equinox & Torrent	Delco Single Piston Sliding Caliper	—
	Express & Savana (1500)	Delco Dual Piston Sliding Caliper	Delco Single Piston Sliding Caliper
	Express & Savana (2500 & 3500)	Delco Dual Piston Sliding Caliper	Delco Dual Piston Sliding Caliper
	Hummer H2	Delco Dual Piston Sliding Caliper	Delco Dual Piston Sliding Caliper
	Montana & Venture	Delco Single Piston Sliding Caliper	Delco Single Piston Sliding Caliper
	Relay, Terraza, SV6 & Uplander	Delco Single Piston Sliding Caliper	Delco Single Piston Sliding Caliper
	SRX	Delco Dual Piston Sliding Caliper	Delco Single Piston Sliding Caliper
	Vue	Delco Single Piston Sliding Caliper	—
2006	Avalanche, Escalade, Escalade EXT, Sierra, Silverado, Suburban, Tahoe & Yukon	Delco Dual Piston Sliding Caliper	Delco Dual Piston Sliding Caliper
	Canyon & Colorado	Delco Dual Piston Sliding Caliper	—
	Envoy, Rainier, SSR & Trailblazer	Delco Dual Piston Sliding Caliper	Delco Single Piston Sliding Caliper
	Express & Savana (1500)	Delco Dual Piston Sliding Caliper	Delco Single Piston Sliding Caliper
	Express & Savana (2500 & 3500)	Delco Dual Piston Sliding Caliper	Delco Dual Piston Sliding Caliper
	HHR	Delco Single Piston Sliding Caliper	—
	HHR	Delco Single Piston Sliding Caliper	Delco Single Piston Sliding Caliper
	Hummer H2	Delco Dual Piston Sliding Caliper	Delco Dual Piston Sliding Caliper
	Hummer H3	Delco Dual Piston Sliding Caliper	Delco Single Piston Sliding Caliper
	Relay, Terraza, SV6 & Uplander	Delco Single Piston Sliding Caliper	Delco Single Piston Sliding Caliper
	Rendezvous	Delco Single Piston Sliding Caliper	Delco Single Piston Sliding Caliper
	SRX	Delco Dual Piston Sliding Caliper	Delco Single Piston Sliding Caliper
	Vue	Delco Single Piston Sliding Caliper	—

Delco Single Piston Sliding Caliper

INDEX

PRECAUTIONS

Brake Lines & Linings

Remove one of the front wheels and inspect the brake disc, caliper and linings.

Do not allow any oil or grease on the linings. It is recommended that linings be replaced in sets when worn or damaged.

If the caliper is cracked or fluid leakage through the casting is evident, it must be replaced as a unit.

Brake Roughness

The most common cause of brake chatter on disc brakes is a variation in thickness of the disc. If roughness or vibration is encountered during highway operation or if pedal pumping is experienced at low speeds, the disc may have excessive thickness variation. To inspect for this condition, measure the disc at 12 points with a micrometer at a radius approximately one inch from edge of disc. If thickness measurements vary more than specifications allow, the disc should be replaced with a new one.

Excessive lateral runout of braking disc may cause a knocking back of the pistons, possibly creating increased pedal travel and vibration when brakes are applied.

Before inspecting the runout, wheel bearings should be adjusted. Ensure adjustments are made according to the recommendations given in the individual truck chapters.

Brake Disc Service

Disc brake service is extremely critical because of the close tolerances required in matching the brake disc to ensure proper brake operation.

The maintenance of these close controls on the friction surfaces is required to prevent brake roughness. In addition, the surface finish must be non-directional and maintained at a micro-inch finish. This close control of the rubbing surface finish is required to avoid pulls and erratic performance and promote long lining life and equal lining wear of both lefthand and righthand brakes.

Because of these close tolerances, refinishing of the rubbing surfaces should not be attempted unless precision equipment capable of measuring in micro-inches is available.

To inspect runout of a disc, mount a dial indicator on a convenient part (steering knuckle, tie rod, disc brake caliper housing) so that the plunger of the dial indicator contacts the disc at a point one inch from the outer edge. If the total indicated runout exceeds specifications, install a new disc.

General

1. Grease or any other foreign material must be kept off caliper, surfaces of disc and external surfaces of hub during service procedures. Avoid deformation of disc and nicking or scratching of brake linings when handling brake discs and calipers.
2. If inspection reveals rubber piston seals are worn or damaged, they should be replaced immediately.
3. Do not interfere with or damage caliper splash shield or bleeder screw during wheel assembly removal and installation.
4. Front wheel bearings should be adjusted to specifications.
5. Ensure vehicle is centered on hoist before servicing any of front end components to avoid bending or damaging disc splash shield on full lefthand or righthand wheel turns.
6. Before vehicle is moved after any brake service work, ensure to obtain firm brake pedal.
7. Two caliper housings mounting bolts should not be disturbed unless caliper requires service.

DESCRIPTION

The caliper assembly slides on its mounting surfaces, **Fig. 1.** Upon brake application, hydraulic pressure against the piston forces the inboard pad against the inboard side of the disc. This action causes the caliper assembly to slide until the outboard pad comes into contact with the disc, which in turn creates a slowing or stopping action.

TROUBLESHOOTING

Excessive Pedal Travel

1. Worn brake linings.
2. Disc pads knock back after cornering or rough road travel.
3. Piston and linings not properly seated or positioned.
4. Insufficient fluid in system.
5. Loose wheel bearing adjustment.
6. Damaged or worn caliper piston seal.
7. Improper booster pushrod adjustment.
8. Pads out of flat more than .005 inch.
9. Rear brake automatic adjusters inoperative.
10. Improperly ground rear brake shoes.

Brake Roughness Or Chatter; Pedal Pumping

1. Excessive lateral runout of rotor.
2. Rotor excessively out of parallel.

Excessive Pedal Effort

1. Frozen or seized pistons.
2. Brake fluid, oil or grease on linings.
3. Linings worn below specifications.
4. Proportioning valve fault.
5. Booster inoperative.
6. Leaking booster vacuum check valve.

Pull, Uneven Or Grabbing Brakes

1. Frozen or seized pistons.
2. Brake fluid, oil or grease on linings.
3. Caliper out of alignment with rotor.
4. Loose caliper attachment.
5. Front tire pressure not equalized.
6. Incorrect front end alignment.
7. Linings improperly bonded.

Brake Rattle

1. Excessive clearance between pad and caliper.
2. Hardware missing or improperly positioned.

Heavy Brake Drag

1. Frozen or seized pistons.
2. Operator riding brake pedal.
3. Incomplete brake pedal return because of linkage interference.
4. Faulty booster check valve holding pressure in hydraulic system.
5. Residual pressure in front brake hydraulic system.

Caliper Brake Fluid Leak

1. Damaged or worn caliper piston seal.
2. Scores in cylinder bore.
3. Corrosion build-up in cylinder bore or on piston surface.

No Braking Effect When Brake Pedal Is Depressed

1. Piston and linings not properly seated or positioned.
2. Insufficient fluid in system.
3. Damaged or worn caliper piston seal.
4. Bleeder screw open.
5. Air in hydraulic system.

Rear Brakes Locking On Application

On brake system equipped with a proportioning or rear pressure regulator valve, should the valve fault, rear brakes may receive excessive pressure, resulting in wheel lock-up.

BRAKE SYSTEM BLEED

Refer to "Hydraulic Brake Systems" chapter for brake system bleed procedures.

BRAKE PAD SERVICE

Removal

1. Remove caliper as outlined in "Caliper Service."
2. Remove inboard pad with retainer spring.
3. Remove outboard pad and position caliper on front suspension so brake hose will not support weight of caliper.
4. Remove two sleeves from inboard ears of caliper.
5. Remove four rubber bushings from grooves in each of caliper ears.

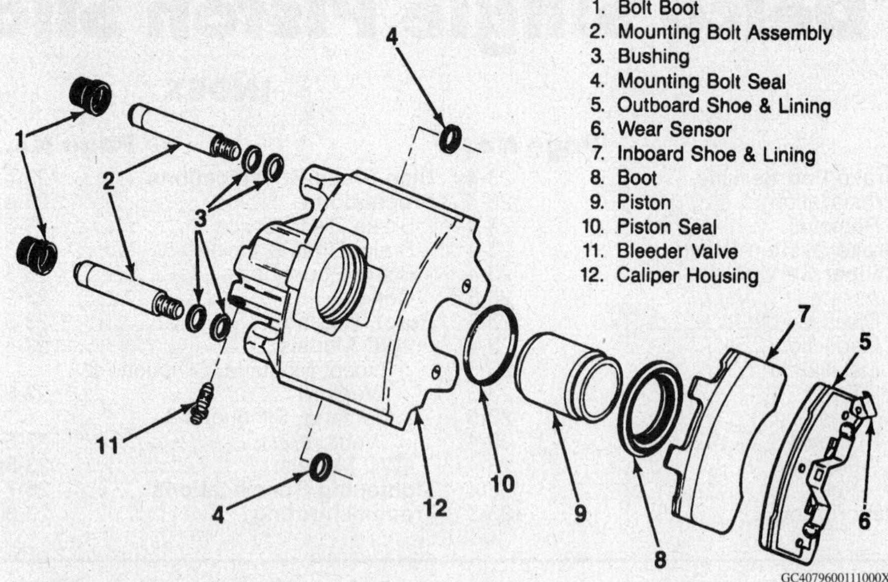

Fig. 1 Exploded view of disc brake caliper

Installation

1. Lubricate new sleeves, rubber bushings, bushing grooves and mounting bolt ends with lubricant part No. 19010909, or equivalent.
2. Install new bushings and sleeves in caliper ears. Position sleeve so end toward pad is flush with machined surface of ear.
3. Install retainer spring on back of inboard pad.
4. Position inboard pad with ears up and retainer spring facing piston.
5. Press pad into piston bore until seated.
6. Position outboard pad to caliper interior with pad ears over caliper ears and tab at bottom of pad is seated in caliper cutout.
7. Install caliper as outlined in "Caliper Service."
8. Seat outboard pad to caliper by grasping ears with channel lock type pliers and pressing together firmly, **Fig. 2.**

CALIPER SERVICE

Removal

FRONT

1. Siphon brake fluid out of master cylinder until fluid level is approximately ⅓ full, this will prevent fluid overflow when caliper piston is pushed back into its bore.
2. Raise and support vehicle, then remove wheels.
3. Push piston back into its bore using suitable C-clamp, **Fig. 3.**
4. Remove brake caliper hose bolt, then two metal gaskets from brake caliper bolt.
5. Remove two caliper mounting bolts and lift caliper off of rotor.

REAR

1. Siphon brake fluid out of master cylinder until fluid level is approximately ⅓ full, this will prevent fluid overflow when caliper piston is pushed back into its bore.
2. Raise and support vehicle, then remove wheels.
3. Push piston back into its bore using suitable C-clamp.
4. Remove mounting bolt and disconnect brake hose fitting from caliper. Discard gaskets and plug brake hose fitting.
5. Remove two caliper mounting bolts and lift caliper off rotor.

Inspection

Should it become required to remove the caliper for installation of new components, clean components in denatured alcohol, wipe dry using lint-free cloths. Blow out drilled passages and holes using compressed air. Inspect dust boots for punctures or tears. If punctures or tears are evident, new boots should be installed upon assembly.

Inspect piston bores in both housings for scoring or pitting. Bores that show light scratches or corrosion can usually be cleaned with crocus cloth. However, bores that have deep scratches or scoring may be honed, provided the diameter of the bore is not increased more than .002 inch. If the bore does not clean up within this specification, a new caliper housing should be installed (black stains on the bore walls are caused by piston seals and will do no harm).

When using a hone, ensure to install the

hone baffle before honing bore. The baffle is used to protect the hone stones from damage. Use extreme care in cleaning the caliper after honing. Remove dust and grit by flushing the caliper with denatured alcohol. Wipe dry with clean lint-free cloth and then clean a second time in the same manner.

Disassemble

1. Remove caliper as outlined in "Caliper, Replace."
2. Drain caliper brake fluid into suitable container.
3. Pad caliper interior with clean shop towels and apply regulated compressed air to remove piston, **Fig. 4.** Use just enough air pressure to ease piston out of bore. **When applying compressed air do not place fingers in front of piston in an attempt to catch or protect it as this could result in serious injury.**
4. Carefully pry dust boot out of bore.
5. Remove piston seal from bore using suitable small piece of wood or plastic. **Do not use metal tool of any kind to remove seal.**
6. Remove bleeder valve.

Assemble

1. Lubricate caliper piston bore and new piston seal with clean brake fluid. Position seal in bore groove.
2. Lubricate piston with clean brake fluid and assemble new boot into groove in piston so fold faces open end of piston.
3. Insert piston into bore and force piston to bottom. **Do not unseat seal.**
4. Position dust boot in caliper counterbore and install, **Fig. 5.**
5. Inspect boot installation and ensure retaining ring molded into boot is not bent and boot is installed below caliper face and evenly all around. If boot is not fully installed, dirt and moisture may enter bore and cause corrosion.
6. Use new copper washers and install brake hose to caliper.
7. Install pads and caliper.

Installation

FRONT

1. Lubricate new bushings, bolt seals and housing cavities between bushings with silicone lubricant part No. 19010909, or equivalent.
2. Position caliper over disc and line up mounting holes in caliper with holes in mounting bracket. If brake hose was not disconnected during removal, ensure hose did not kink during installation.
3. Start mounting bolts through sleeves in inboard caliper ears and mounting bracket. Ensure bolt ends pass under

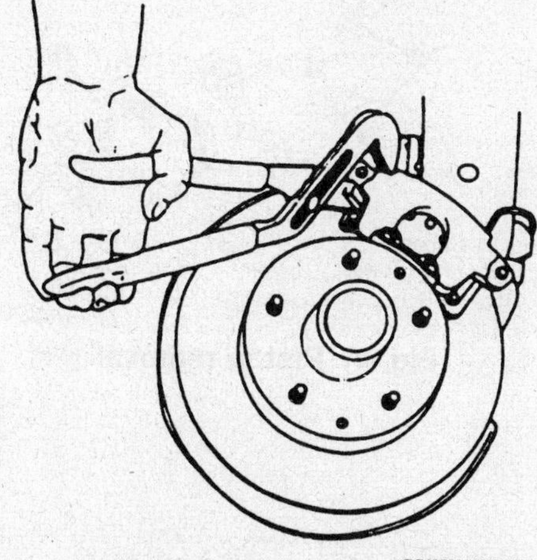

Fig. 2 Disc brake pad installation

ears on inboard shoe. **Lefthand and righthand calipers must not be interchanged.**

4. Push mounting bolts through to engage holes in outboard ears and thread mounting bolts into bracket.
5. Tighten mounting bolts to specifications.
6. Connect brake hose and bleed calipers.
7. Replace front wheels, lower vehicle and add brake fluid to master cylinder to bring level to 1/4 inch from top. **Before moving vehicle, pump brake pedal several times to ensure it is firm. Do not move vehicle until firm pedal is obtained.**

REAR

1. Install caliper housing over rotor and onto anchor bracket.
2. Install new upper and lower caliper mounting bolts.
3. Install brake hose fitting, two new gaskets and brake hose fitting mounting bolt.
4. Bleed brake hydraulic system as outlined in "Hydraulic Brake Systems" chapter.
5. Install tire and wheel assembly, then lower vehicle.
6. Start engine and pump brake pedal several times.
7. Inspect for brake fluid leaks.

ROTOR

REPLACE

2WD Models

EXCEPT MONTANA, SILHOUETTE & VENTURE

FRONT

1. Raise and support vehicle.
2. Remove tire and wheel assembly.
3. Remove caliper as outlined in "Caliper Service."
4. Remove grease cap from hub/rotor, **Fig. 6.**
5. Remove cotter pin, nut and washer.
6. Remove hub/rotor from spindle, being careful not to damage spindle threads or outer bearing.
7. Reverse procedure to install, noting the following:
   a. Apply high-temperature wheel bearing grease to inner and outer wheel bearings.
   b. **Torque** nut to 12 ft. lbs., while turning wheel assembly forward by hand, back nut off one flat or until hole in spindle aligns with hole in nut. Insert cotter pin.

REAR

1. Raise and support vehicle.
2. Remove tire and wheel assembly.
3. Remove caliper as outlined in "Caliper Service."
4. Remove caliper mounting bracket bolts from backing plate.
5. Remove brake pads from mounting bracket.
6. Remove clips from inside ends of caliper mounting bracket, discard clips.
7. While slowly turning rotor, remove rotor from axle.

MONTANA, SILHOUETTE & VENTURE

1. Raise and support vehicle.
2. Remove tire and wheel assembly.
3. Remove caliper as outlined in "Caliper Service."
4. Remove two mounting bolts and caliper bracket.
5. Remove rotor.
6. Reverse procedure to install.

4WD Models

1. Raise and support vehicle.
2. Remove tire and wheel assembly.
3. Remove caliper as outlined in "Caliper Service."
4. Remove rotor from hub, **Fig. 7.**
5. Reverse procedure to install.

DISC BRAKE SPECIFICATIONS

Refer to "Disc Brake Specifications" section in this chapter.

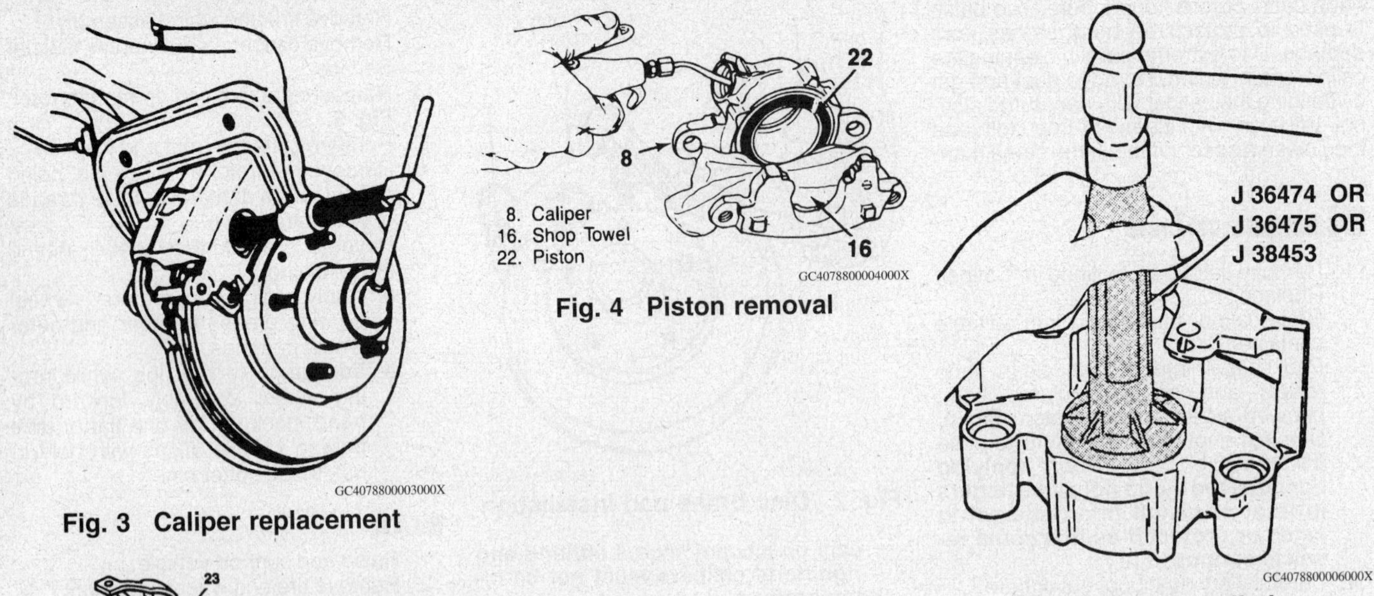

Fig. 3 Caliper replacement

Fig. 4 Piston removal

Fig. 5 Boot installation

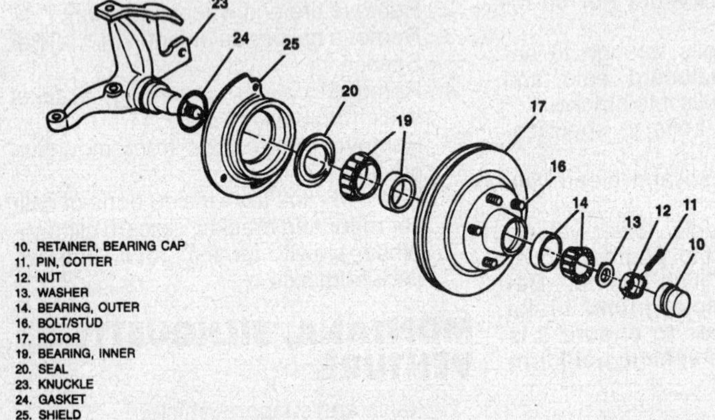

Fig. 6 Exploded view of front hub assembly. 2WD models except Montana, Silhouette & Venture

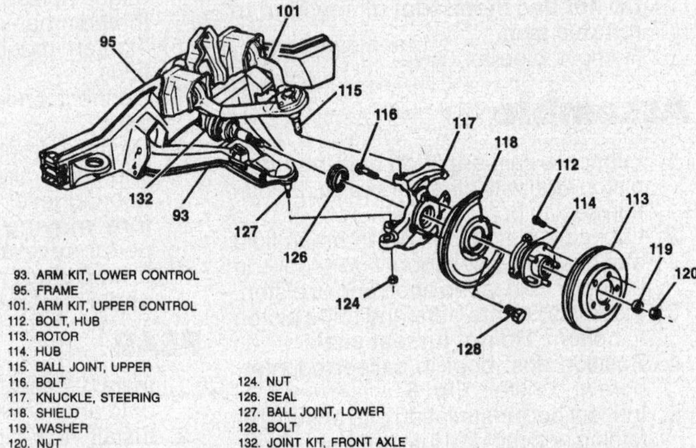

Fig. 7 Exploded view of hub assembly

TIGHTENING SPECIFICATIONS

Year	Component	Torque Ft. Lbs.
ASTRO & SAFARI		
2002–05	Bleeder Valve	115①
	Brake Booster	20
	Brake Booster To Gear Line	25
	Brake Hose To Caliper	32
	Caliper	38
	Master Cylinder	21
	Wheel Lug Nuts	100
BLAZER, BRAVADA, ENVOY, JIMMY, SONOMA , S10 & TRAILBLAZER		
2002–06	ABS Sensor Wire	13
	Bleeder Valve (Front Wheel)	110①
	Bleeder Valve (Rear Wheel)	110①
	Brake (Rear Wheel)	47
	Brake Hose Fitting (Rear Wheel)	40
	Caliper Bracket To Knuckle (Dual Piston Front Caliper)	133
	Caliper Bracket to Mounting Plate	52
	Caliper Guide Pin (Dual Piston Front Caliper)	85
	Caliper Mounting (Two-Wheel Disc Brake)	38
	Front Flex Hose Bolt	40
	Guide Pin (Rear Caliper)	23
	Wheel Lug Nuts	95
EXPRESS & SAVANA		
2002–06	Bleeder Valve	114①
	Brake Booster	21
	Brake Booster To Gear Line	25
	Brake Hose To Caliper	32
	Brake Line	12
	Caliper	38
	Power Steering Pump To Booster Line	25
	Return Line At Booster & Gear	25
	Wheel Lug Nuts	②
MONTANA, SILHOUETTE & VENTURE		
2002–06	Bleeder Valve	10
	Brake Hose	40
	Caliper (Front)	63
	Caliper (Rear)	33
	Caliper Bracket (Front)	137
	Caliper Bracket (Rear)	92
	Master Cylinder Mounting Nut	20
	Wheel Lug Nuts	100

① — Inch lbs.
② — Five stud wheels, 100 ft. lbs.; eight stud wheels, 120 ft. lbs.

Delco Dual Piston Sliding Caliper

INDEX

PRECAUTIONS

Brake Lines & Linings

Remove one of the front wheels and inspect the brake disc, caliper and linings.

Do not allow any oil or grease on the linings. It is recommended that linings be replaced in sets when worn or damaged.

If the caliper is cracked or fluid leakage through the casting is evident, it must be replaced as a unit.

Brake Roughness

The most common cause of brake chatter on disc brakes is a variation in thickness of the disc. If roughness or vibration is encountered during highway operation or if pedal pumping is experienced at low speeds, the disc may have excessive thickness variation. To inspect for this condition, measure the disc at 12 points with a micrometer at a radius approximately one inch from edge of disc. If thickness measurements vary more than specifications allow, the disc must be replaced.

Excessive lateral runout of braking disc may cause a knocking back of the pistons, possibly creating increased pedal travel and vibration when brakes are applied.

Before inspecting the runout, wheel bearings should be adjusted. Ensure adjustments are made according to the recommendations given in the individual truck chapters.

Brake Disc Service

Disc brake service is extremely critical because of the close tolerances required in matching the brake disc to ensure proper brake operation.

The maintenance of these close controls on the friction surfaces is required to prevent brake roughness. In addition, the surface finish must be non-directional and maintained at a micro-inch finish. This close control of the rubbing surface finish is required to avoid pulls and erratic performance and promote long lining life and equal lining wear of both lefthand and righthand brakes.

Because of these close tolerances, refinishing of the rubbing surfaces should not be attempted unless precision equipment capable of measuring in micro-inches is available.

To inspect runout of a disc, mount a dial indicator on a convenient part (steering knuckle, tie rod, disc brake caliper housing) so that the plunger of the dial indicator contacts the disc at a point one inch from the outer edge. If the total indicated runout exceeds specifications, replace.

General

1. Grease or any other foreign material must be kept off caliper, surfaces of disc and external surfaces of hub during service procedures. Avoid deformation of disc and nicking or scratching of brake linings when handling brake discs and calipers.
2. If inspection reveals rubber piston seals are worn or damaged, they should be replaced immediately.
3. Do not interfere with or damage caliper splash shield or bleeder screw during wheel assembly removal and installation.
4. Front wheel bearings should be adjusted to specifications.
5. Ensure vehicle is centered on hoist before servicing any of front end components to avoid bending or damaging disc splash shield on full lefthand or righthand wheel turns.
6. Before vehicle is moved after any brake service work, ensure to obtain firm brake pedal.
7. Two caliper housings mounting bolts should not be disturbed unless caliper requires service.

DESCRIPTION

The caliper mounts in a way that allows the caliper to move laterally inboard as the brake pads wear. The caliper housing is a one piece casting with the inboard side containing the piston bore. The piston seal also acts as a return mechanism for the piston.

Applying the brake pedal causes the hydraulic pressure that moves the caliper piston. The piston then forces the inboard brake pad against the inboard braking surface of the rotor. Increasing the force against the rotor causes the caliper to move inboard. The outer brake pad then contacts the outboard braking surface of the rotor.

The force of the two brake pads being squeezed against the rotor provides the desired braking forces to be generated. Releasing the brake pedal relieves the pressure applied on the piston.

The square cut seal on the piston relaxes and pulls the caliper piston back into the bore slightly. This allows running clearance between the brake pads and the rotor.

TROUBLESHOOTING

Refer to "Troubleshooting" as outlined in "Delco Single Piston Sliding Caliper" section.

BRAKE SYSTEM BLEED

Refer to "Hydraulic Brake Systems" chapter for brake system bleed procedures.

BRAKE PAD SERVICE

The procedures to remove and install the brake pads are outlined in "Caliper Service." It is not required to disconnect the brake hose. **Do not twist or kink the hose.**

CALIPER SERVICE

Removal

1. Siphon ⅔ of the brake fluid from master cylinder.
2. Raise and support vehicle.
3. Remove tire and wheel assembly.
4. Compress caliper pistons until they bottom in bores using suitable clamp, **Fig. 1.**
5. Disconnect brake hose at caliper by removing inlet fitting bolt.
6. Remove mounting bolts and caliper.

Inspection

Should it become required to remove the caliper for installation of new components, clean components in denatured alcohol, wipe dry using lint-free cloths. Blow out drilled passages and holes using compressed air. Inspect dust boots for punctures or tears. If punctures or tears are evident, new boots should be installed upon assembly.

Inspect piston bores in both housings for scoring or pitting. Bores that show light scratches or corrosion can usually be cleaned with crocus cloth. However, bores that have deep scratches or scoring may be honed, provided the diameter of the bore is

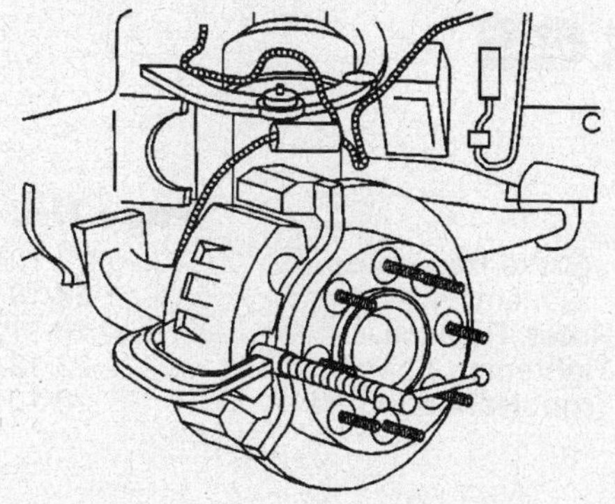

GC4079900138000X

Fig. 1 C-clamp installation

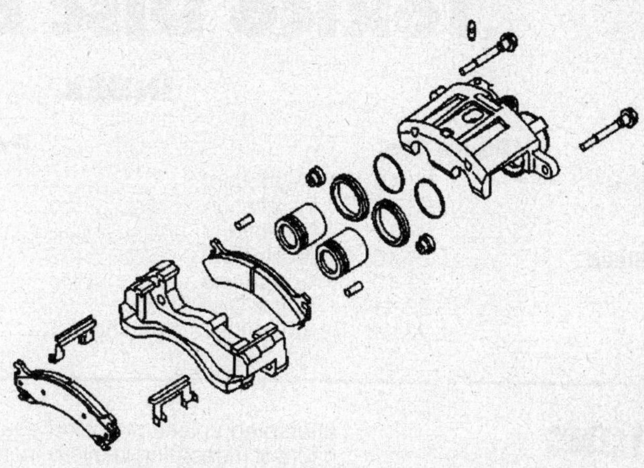

GC4079900140000X

Fig. 2 Exploded view of caliper

not increased more than .002 inch. If the bore does not clean up within this specification, a new caliper housing should be installed (black stains on the bore walls are caused by piston seals and will do no harm).

When using a hone, ensure to install the hone baffle before honing bore. The baffle is used to protect the hone stones from damage. Use extreme care in cleaning the caliper after honing. Remove dust and grit by flushing the caliper with denatured alcohol. Wipe dry with clean lint-free cloth and then clean a second time in the same manner.

Disassemble

1. Remove brake fluid from caliper.
2. Place suitable thin piece of wood in front of pistons to prevent damage during removal.
3. Remove pistons by directing compressed air into brake hose inlet fitting.
4. Remove piston seals from groove in brake caliper bore using suitable pointed piece of wood or plastic, **Fig. 2.**
5. Remove bleeder valve.
6. Clean components using brake components cleaner part No. 12345754, or equivalent.

Assemble

1. Install brake caliper bleed screw.
2. Install new piston seals in seal grooves of piston bores.
3. Lubricate pistons and bores with new brake fluid and gently push pistons into bores.
4. Rotate pistons slightly to prevent dislodging of seals and press dust boots into counterbore in brake caliper housing.
5. Ensure boot seats properly into piston groove and into groove in caliper bore.

Installation

1. Install inner and outer brake pads onto caliper.
2. Install brake caliper.
3. Connect brake hose and install caliper.
4. Install caliper mounter bolts and fill master cylinder with brake fluid.
5. Bleed brake system as outlined in "Brake System Bleed."
6. Install tire and wheel assemblies, then lower vehicle.

ROTOR

REPLACE

1. Raise and support vehicle, then remove wheel and tire assemblies.
2. Compress caliper pistons until they bottom in bores using suitable clamp.
3. Remove caliper and mounting bracket as an assembly and position aside. **Do not disconnect brake hose from caliper.**
4. While slowly turning remove rotor.
5. Reverse procedure to install.

DISC BRAKE SPECIFICATIONS

Refer to "Disc Brake Specifications" section in this chapter.

TIGHTENING SPECIFICATIONS

Year	Component	Torque Ft. Lbs.
2002–06	Brake Hose To Caliper (Front)	33
	Brake Hose To Caliper (Rear)	18
	Caliper Guide Pin	80
	Caliper Mounting Bracket	122
	Caliper Mounting Bracket To Knuckle	221
	Wheel Lug Nuts	140

Tokico Disc Brakes

INDEX

PRECAUTIONS

Brake Lines & Linings

Remove one of the front wheels and inspect the brake disc, caliper and linings.

Do not allow any oil or grease on the linings. It is recommended that linings be replaced in sets when worn or damaged.

If the caliper is cracked or fluid leakage through the casting is evident, it must be replaced as a unit.

Brake Roughness

The most common cause of brake chatter on disc brakes is a variation in thickness of the disc. If roughness or vibration is encountered during highway operation or if pedal pumping is experienced at low speeds, the disc may have excessive thickness variation. To inspect for this condition, measure the disc at 12 points with a micrometer at a radius approximately one inch from edge of disc. If thickness measurements vary more than specifications allow, the disc should be replaced with a new one.

Excessive lateral runout of braking disc may cause a knocking back of the pistons, possibly creating increased pedal travel and vibration when brakes are applied.

Before inspecting the runout, wheel bearings should be adjusted. Ensure adjustments are made according to the recommendations given in the individual truck chapters.

Brake Disc Service

Disc brake service is extremely critical because of the close tolerances required in matching the brake disc to ensure proper brake operation.

The maintenance of these close controls on the friction surfaces is required to prevent brake roughness. In addition, the surface finish must be non-directional and maintained at a micro-inch finish. This close control of the rubbing surface finish is required to avoid pulls and erratic performance and promote long lining life and equal lining wear of both lefthand and righthand brakes.

Because of these close tolerances, refinishing of the rubbing surfaces should not be attempted unless precision equipment capable of measuring in micro-inches is available.

To inspect runout of a disc, mount a dial indicator on a convenient part (steering knuckle, tie rod, disc brake caliper housing) so that the plunger of the dial indicator contacts the disc at a point one inch from the outer edge. If the total indicated runout exceeds specifications, install a new disc.

General

1. Grease or any other foreign material must be kept off caliper, surfaces of disc and external surfaces of hub during service procedures. Avoid deformation of disc and nicking or scratching of brake linings when handling brake discs and calipers.
2. If inspection reveals rubber piston seals are worn or damaged, they should be replaced immediately.
3. Do not interfere with or damage caliper splash shield or bleeder screw during wheel assembly removal and installation.
4. Front wheel bearings should be adjusted to specifications.
5. Ensure vehicle is centered on hoist before servicing any of front end components to avoid bending or damaging disc splash shield on full lefthand or righthand wheel turns.
6. Before vehicle is moved after any brake service work, ensure to obtain firm brake pedal.
7. Two caliper housings mounting bolts should not be disturbed unless caliper requires service.

DESCRIPTION

The caliper assembly slides on its mounting surfaces, **Fig. 1.** When the brakes are applied, hydraulic pressure against the caliper piston forces the inboard pad against the inboard side of the disc. This action causes the caliper assembly to slide until the outboard pad comes into contact with the disc.

TROUBLESHOOTING

Refer to "Troubleshooting" as outlined in "Delco Single Piston Sliding Caliper."

BRAKE SYSTEM BLEED

Refer to "Hydraulic Brake Systems" chapter for brake system bleed procedures.

BRAKE PAD SERVICE

Removal

1. Raise and support vehicle.
2. Remove wheel assembly.
3. Remove brake line, mounting bolts and caliper. Hang caliper with suitable wire hook, or equivalent, to prevent brake hose from bending or twisting excessively. **Do not depress brake pedal with pads removed.**
4. Remove disc pads and pad retaining clips.
5. Remove rotor retaining screws and rotors.
6. Clean and inspect components.
7. Resurface rotors.

Installation

1. Install rotors and rotor retaining screws.
2. Install pad retaining clips.
3. Install pads and caliper.
4. Install brake line, **Fig. 2.**
5. Bleed brake hydraulic system.
6. Install wheel assembly. Inspect brakes for proper operation.

CALIPER SERVICE

Removal

1. Raise and support vehicle.
2. Remove tire and wheel assembly.
3. Remove brake hose mounting bolt from caliper.
4. Remove mounting bolts and caliper.

Inspection

Should it become required to remove the caliper for installation of new components, clean components in denatured alcohol, wipe dry using lint-free cloths. Blow out

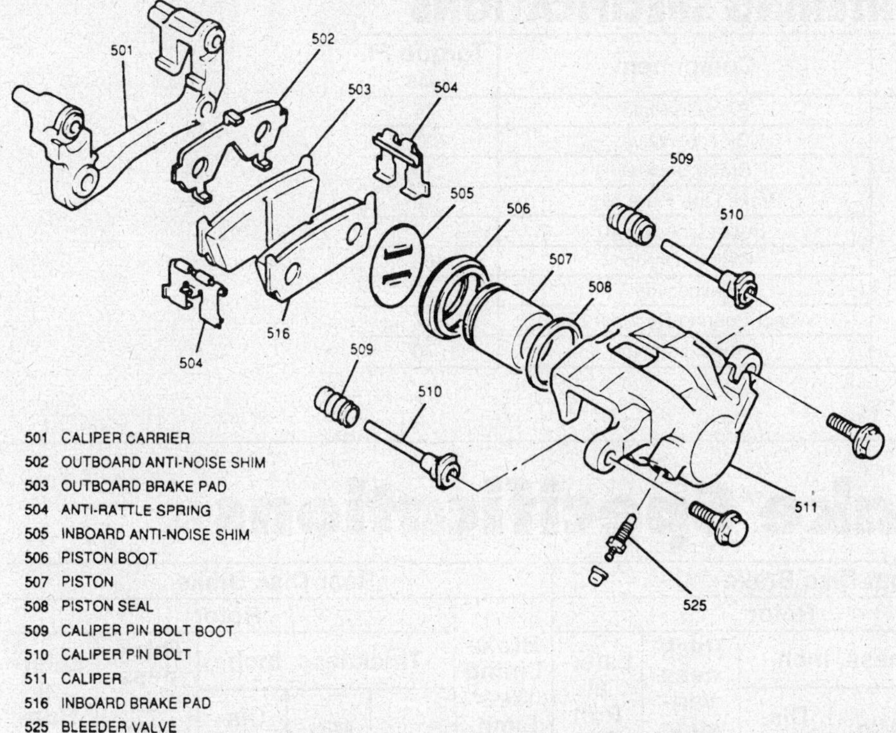

Fig. 1 Exploded view of front disc brake

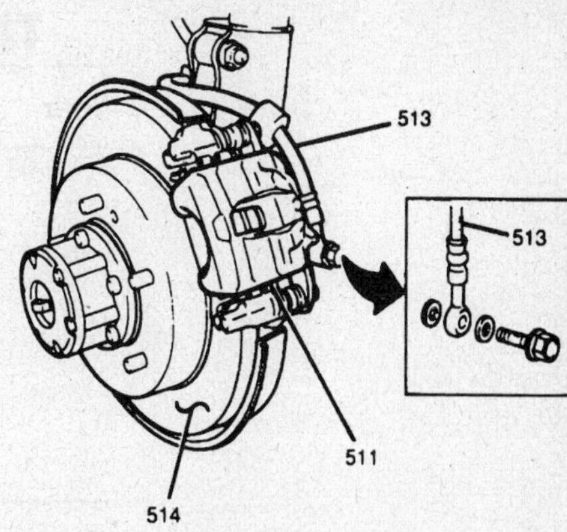

Fig. 2 Brake hose installation

drilled passages and holes using compressed air. Inspect dust boots for punctures or tears. If punctures or tears are evident, new boots should be installed upon assembly.

Inspect piston bores in both housings for scoring or pitting. Bores that show light scratches or corrosion can usually be cleaned with crocus cloth. However, bores that have deep scratches or scoring may be honed, provided the diameter of the bore is not increased more than .002 inch. If the bore does not clean up within this specification, a new caliper housing should be installed (black stains on the bore walls are caused by piston seals and will do no harm).

When using a hone, ensure to install the hone baffle before honing bore. The baffle is used to protect the hone stones from damage. Use extreme care in cleaning the caliper after honing. Remove dust and grit by flushing the caliper with denatured alcohol. Wipe dry with clean lint-free cloth and then clean a second time in the same manner.

Disassemble

1. Drain caliper brake fluid into suitable container.
2. Pad caliper interior with clean shop towels and apply compressed air to remove piston, **Fig. 3.** Use just enough air pressure to ease piston out of bore. **When applying compressed air, do not place fingers in front of piston in an attempt to catch or protect it, as this could cause serious injury.**
3. Carefully pry dust boot out of bore.
4. Remove piston seal from bore using suitable small piece of wood or plastic. **Do not use metal tool of any kind to remove seal.**
5. Remove bleeder valve.

Assemble

1. Lubricate caliper piston bore and new piston seal with clean brake fluid and position seal in bore groove.
2. Lubricate piston with clean brake fluid and install new boot into groove in piston with fold facing open end of piston.
3. Insert piston into bore and force piston to bottom. **Do not unseat seal.**
4. Position dust boot in caliper counterbore and install. Ensure retaining ring molded into boot is not bent , and boot is installed below caliper face and set evenly all around.

Installation

1. Install caliper to caliper carrier, **Fig. 2.**
2. Install pin and tighten bolts.
3. Connect brake hose to caliper,
4. Fill reservoir with brake fluid and bleed brake system. Inspect brakes for leaks and proper operation.

ROTOR

REPLACE

1. Remove ⅔ of brake fluid from master cylinder reservoir with siphon.

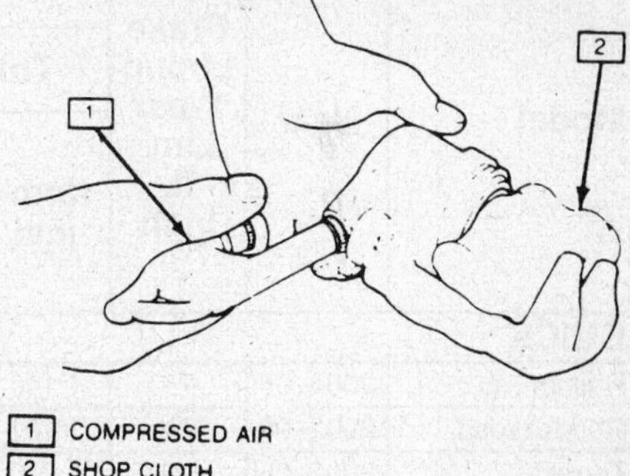

Fig. 3 Piston removal w/compressed air

2. Raise and support vehicle.
3. Remove tire and wheel.
4. Position C-clamp around outer brake pad and caliper and tighten until caliper piston is recessed completely into its bore.
5. Remove brake hose E-clip.
6. Remove two caliper carrier mounting bolts.
7. Lift caliper and caliper carrier along with brake pads, off of brake rotor and suspend with wire to prevent damage to brake hose.
8. Remove brake rotor from wheel hub. If rotor cannot be removed by hand, install two 8 mm bolts into threaded holes in rotor. Tightening bolts will force rotor off of wheel hub.
9. Reverse procedure to install.

DISC BRAKE SPECIFICATIONS

Refer to "Disc Brake Specifications" section in this chapter.

TIGHTENING SPECIFICATIONS

Year	Component	Torque Ft. Lbs.
2002–04	Backing Plate	16
	Bleeder Valve	89①
	Brake Booster	10
	Brake Line Flare Nut	12
	Brake Line Union	17
	Caliper Carrier	63
	Caliper Pin	20
	Wheel Bearing Retainer Nut	17
	Wheel Lug Nut	70

① — Inch lbs.

Disc Brake Specifications

Model	Year	Front Disc Brake						Rear Disc Brake					
			Rotor						Rotor				
		Brake Lining Wear Limit, Inch ②	Thickness, Inch			Thickness Variation Parallelism Inch	Lateral Run Out (T.I.R.) Inch	Brake Lining Wear Limit, Inch ②	Thickness, Inch			Thickness Variation Parallelism Inch	Lateral Run-Out (T.I.R.) Inch
			Nominal	Min. Refinish	Discard Limit ①				Nominal	Min. Refinish	Discard Limit ①		
BUICK													
Rainier	2004–06	.030	1.140	1.080	—	.001	.002	.030	.787	.728	—	.0010	.0020
Rendezvous	2002–06	.030	1.181	1.118	1.063	.001	.002	.030	.430	.420	.350	.0010	.0020
Terreza	2005–06	.030	1.270	1.220	1.210	.001	.002	.030	.472	.425	.413	.0010	.0020
CADILLAC													
Escalade	2002–06⑤	.030	1.142	1.102	1.083	.0010	.005	.030	1.181	1.142	1.122	.0010	.0050
	2002–06⑥	.030	1.496	1.457	1.437	.0010	.005	.030	1.142	1.102	1.083	.0010	.0050
SRX	2004–06	.030	1.267	1.209	1.209	.001	.002	.030	1.020	.9440	.940	.0010	.0020
CHEVROLET													
Astro Van 2WD	2002	.030	1.040	.980	.965	.0010	.002	—	—	—	—	—	—
	2003–06	.030	1.142	1.102	1.083	.0010	.005	.030	.7870	.7480	.7280	.0010	.0050
Astro Van AWD	2002	.030	1.250	1.230	1.215	.0010	.002	—	—	—	—	—	—
	2003–06	.030	1.142	1.102	1.083	.0010	.002	.030	.7870	.7480	.7280	.0010	.0050
Avalanche	2002–06⑤	.030	1.142	1.102	1.083	.0010	.005	.030	1.181	1.142	1.122	.0010	.0050
	2002–06⑥	.030	1.496	1.457	1.437	.0010	.005	.030	1.142	1.102	1.083	.0010	.0050
Blazer	2002–05④	.030	1.030	.980	.965	.0010	.002	—	—	—	—	—	—
	2002–05③	.030	1.140	1.100	1.080	.0010	.002	.030	.787	.748	.728	.0010	.0020
Colorado	2005–06	.030	1.060	—	1.00	.0020	.0020	—	—	—	—	—	—
Eqinox	2005–06	.080	1.024	.960	.960	.0010	.0020	—	—	—	—	—	—
Express/Van 1500	2002	.030	1.250	1.230	1.215	.0005	.003	—	—	—	—	—	—
Express/Van 2500 (8600 Lbs. GVW) Gasoline	2002	.030	1.260	1.230	1.215	.0005	.003	—	—	—	—	—	—
Express/Van 2500 (8600 Lbs. GVW) Diesel	2002	.030	1.500	1.480	1.465	.0005	.003	—	—	—	—	—	—

Continued

Model	Year	Front Disc Brake						Rear Disc Brake					
		Brake Lining Wear Limit, Inch ②	Rotor					Brake Lining Wear Limit, Inch ②	Rotor				
			Thickness, Inch			Thickness Variation Parallelism Inch	Lateral Run Out (T.I.R.) Inch		Thickness, Inch			Thickness Variation Parallelism Inch	Lateral Run-Out (T.I.R.) Inch
			Nominal	Min. Refinish	Discard Limit ①				Nominal	Min. Refinish	Discard Limit ①		
CHEVROLET													
Express/Van 3500	2002	.030	1.500	1.480	1.465	.0005	.003	—	—	—	—	—	—
Express (1500, 2500 & 3500 SRW)	2003–06	.030	1.142	1.102	1.083	.0010	.005	.030	1.181	1.142	1.122	.0010	.0050
Express (2500 & 3500 DRW)	2003–06	.030	1.496	1.457	1.437	.0010	.005	.030	1.181	1.142	1.122	.0010	.0050
HHR	2006⑦	.039	.933	.896	.870	.0010	.0020	—	—	—	—	—	—
	2006⑧	.039	1.023	.906	.898	.0010	.0020	.039	.551	.472	.465	.0010	.0020
SSR	2004–06	.030	1.140	1.130	1.080	.0010	.0020	.030	.787	.748	.728	.0010	.0020
Silverado⑨	2002–06	.030	1.140	1.100	1.082	.0010	.005	.030	1.181	1.142	1.122	.0010	.0050
Silverado⑩	2002–06	.030	1.181	1.100	1.100	.0010	.005	—	—	—	—	—	—
Silverado⑪	2002–06	.030	1.140	1.100	1.082	.0010	.005	.030	.787	.748	.728	.0010	.0020
Silverado⑫	2002–06	.030	1.150	1.460	1.437	.0010	.005	.030	1.141	1.102	1.082	.0010	.0050
Silverado⑬	2002–06	.030	1.150	1.460	1.437	.0010	.005	.030	1.181	1.142	1.122	.0010	.0020
Suburban	2002–06⑤	.030	1.142	1.102	1.083	.0010	.005	.030	1.181	1.142	1.122	.0010	.0050
	2002–06⑥	.030	1.496	1.457	1.437	.0010	.005	.030	1.142	1.102	1.083	.0010	.0050
S10 2WD	2002–04	.030	1.030	.980	.965	.0010	.002	—	—	—	—	—	—
S10 2WD 4WD	2002–04	.030	1.140	1.130	1.080	.0010	.002	.030	.787	.748	.728	.0010	.0020
Tahoe	2002–06⑤	.030	1.142	1.102	1.083	.0010	.005	.030	1.181	1.142	1.122	.0010	.0050
	2002–06⑥	.030	1.496	1.457	1.437	.0010	.005	.030	1.142	1.102	1.083	.0010	.0050
Tracker Four-Door	2002–04	.080	.670	—	.590	.0005	.006	—	—	—	—	—	—
Tracker Two-Door	2002–04	.080	.670	—	.590	.0005	.006	—	—	—	—	—	—
Trailblazer	2002–06	.030	1.140	1.130	1.080	.0010	.002	.030	.787	.748	.728	.0010	.0020
Uplander	2005–06	.030	1.270	1.220	1.210	.0010	.002	.030	.472	.425	.413	.0010	.0020
Venture AWD	2002–05	.030	1.181	1.118	1.063	.0010	.002	.030	.433	.390	.354	.0010	.0020
Venture FWD	2002–05	.030	1.270	1.220	1.210	.0010	.002	.030	.433	.390	.354	.0010	.0020
GMC													
Canyon	2005–06	.030	1.060	—	1.00	.0020	.0020	—	—	—	—	—	—
Denali	2002–06⑤	.030	1.142	1.102	1.083	.0010	.005	.030	1.181	1.142	1.122	.0010	.0050
	2002–06⑥	.030	1.496	1.457	1.437	.0010	.005	.030	1.142	1.102	1.083	.0010	.0050
Envoy	2002–06	.030	1.140	1.130	1.080	.0010	.002	.030	.787	.748	.728	.0010	.0020
Jimmy	2002–05④	.030	1.030	.980	.965	.0010	.002	—	—	—	—	—	—
	2002–05③	.030	1.140	1.100	1.080	.0010	.002	.030	.787	.748	.728	.0010	.0020
Safari Van AWD	2002	.030	1.250	1.230	1.215	.0010	.002	—	—	—	—	—	—
	2003–06	.030	1.142	1.102	1.083	.0010	.002	.030	.7870	.7480	.7280	.0010	.0050
Safari Van 2WD	2002	.030	1.040	.980	.965	.0010	.002	—	—	—	—	—	—
	2003–06	.030	1.142	1.102	1.083	.0010	.005	.030	.7870	.7480	.7280	.0010	.0050
Savana 1500	2002	.030	1.250	1.230	1.215	.0005	.003	—	—	—	—	—	—
Savana 2500 (8600 Lbs. GVW) Gasoline	2002	.030	1.260	1.230	1.215	.0005	.003	—	—	—	—	—	—

Continued

Model	Year	Front Disc Brake						Rear Disc Brake					
		Brake Lining Wear Limit, Inch ②	Rotor					Brake Lining Wear Limit, Inch ②	Rotor				
			Thickness, Inch			Thickness Variation Parallelism Inch	Lateral Run Out (T.I.R.) Inch		Thickness, Inch			Thickness Variation Parallelism Inch	Lateral Run-Out (T.I.R.) Inch
			Nominal	Min. Refinish	Discard Limit ①				Nominal	Min. Refinish	Discard Limit ①		
GMC													
Savana 2500 (8600 Lbs. GVW) Diesel	2002	.030	1.500	1.480	1.465	.0005	.003	—	—	—	—	—	—
Savana 3500	2002	.030	1.500	1.480	1.465	.0005	.003	—	—	—	—	—	—
Savana (1500, 2500 & 3500 SRW)	2003–06	.030	1.142	1.102	1.083	.0010	.005	.030	1.181	1.142	1.122	.0010	.0050
Savana (2500 & 3500 DRW)	2003–06	.030	1.496	1.457	1.437	.0010	.005	.030	1.181	1.142	1.122	.0010	.0050
Sierra⑨	2002–06	.030	1.140	1.100	1.082	.0010	.005	.030	1.181	1.142	1.122	.0010	.0050
Sierra⑩	2002–06	.030	1.181	1.100	1.100	.0010	.005	—	—	—	—	—	—
Sierra⑪	2002–06	.030	1.140	1.100	1.082	.0010	.005	.030	.787	.748	.728	.0010	.0020
Sierra⑫	2002–06	.030	1.150	1.460	1.437	.0010	.005	.030	1.141	1.102	1.082	.0010	.0050
Sierra⑬	2002–06	.030	1.150	1.460	1.437	.0010	.005	.030	1.181	1.142	1.122	.0010	.0020
Sonoma 2WD	2002–04	.030	1.030	.980	.965	.0010	.002	—	—	—	—	—	—
Sonoma 4WD	2002–04	.030	1.140	1.130	1.080	.0010	.002	.030	.787	.748	.728	.0010	.0020
Suburban	2002–06⑤	.030	1.142	1.102	1.083	.0010	.005	.030	1.181	1.142	1.122	.0010	.0050
	2002–06⑥	.030	1.496	1.457	1.437	.0010	.005	.030	1.142	1.102	1.083	.0010	.0050
Yukon	2002–06⑤	.030	1.142	1.102	1.083	.0010	.005	.030	1.181	1.142	1.122	.0010	.0050
	2002–06⑥	.030	1.496	1.457	1.437	.0010	.005	.030	1.142	1.102	1.083	.0010	.0050
HUMMER													
H2	2003–06	.030	1.496	1.457	1.437	.0010	.005	.030	1.142	1.102	1.083	.0010	.0050
H3	2005–06	.030	1.100	1.060	1.040	.0010	.002	.030	.472	.433	.413	.0010	.0020
OLDSMOBILE													
Bravada	2002–04	.030	1.140	1.130	1.080	.0010	.002	.030	.787	.748	.728	.0010	.0020
Silhouette AWD	2002–04	.030	1.181	1.118	1.063	.0010	.002	.030	.433	.390	.354	.0010	.0020
Silhouette FWD	2002–04	.030	1.270	1.220	1.210	.0010	.002	.030	.433	.390	.354	.0010	.0020
PONTIAC													
Aztek	2002–03	.030	1.181	1.125	1.063	.0010	.002	.030	.430	.420	.350	.0010	.0020
Montana AWD	2002–04	.030	1.181	1.118	1.063	.0010	.002	.030	.433	.390	.354	.0010	.0020
Montana FWD	2002–04	.030	1.270	1.220	1.210	.0010	.002	.030	.433	.390	.354	.0010	.0020
SV6	2005–06	.030	1.270	1.220	1.210	.0010	.002	.030	.472	.425	.413	.0010	.0020
SATURN													
Vue	2002–06	.080	1.024	.960	.960	.0010	.002	—	—	—	—	—	—
Relay	2005–06	.030	1.270	1.220	1.210	.0010	.002	.030	.472	.425	.413	.0010	.0020

AWD — All Wheel Drive
DRW — Dual Rear Wheels
GVW — Gross Vehicle Weight
SRW — Single Rear Wheels
2WD — Two Wheel Drive
4WD — Four Wheel Drive
① — Discard thickness is stamped on rotor.
② — Above rivet head or backing plate. Original equipment type brake lining.
③ — Models w/4 wheel disc brakes.
④ — Models w/front disc brakes & rear drum brakes.
⑤ — Except JH6 brake system.
⑥ — JH6 brake system.
⑦ — J41/JM4 brake system.
⑧ — JL9 brake system.
⑨ — JC4 brake system.
⑩ — JF4/JF7 brake system.
⑪ — JH1 brake system.
⑫ — JH6 brake system.
⑬ — JH7 brake system.

DRUM BRAKES

INDEX

PRECAUTIONS

When working on or around brake assemblies, care must be taken to prevent breathing asbestos dust, as many manufacturers incorporate asbestos fibers in the production of brake linings. During routine service operations, the amount of asbestos dust from brake lining wear is at a low level because of a chemical breakdown during use and a few precautions will minimize exposure. **Do not sand or grind brake linings unless suitable local exhaust ventilation equipment is used to prevent excessive asbestos exposure.**

1. Wear suitable respirator approved for asbestos dust use during all repair procedures.
2. When cleaning brake dust from brake components, use vacuum cleaner with highly efficient filter system or denatured alcohol. **Do not use compressed air or dry brush to clean brake components.**
3. Keep work area clean, using same equipment as for cleaning brake components.
4. Properly dispose of rags and vacuum cleaner bags by placing them in plastic bags.
5. Do not smoke or eat while working on brake systems.

INSPECTION

General System

1. Inspect components for damage or unusual wear. Replace as required.
2. Inspect backing plate mounting bolts and ensure they are tight.
3. Inspect wheel cylinders. Excessive fluid indicates cup leakage and need for wheel cylinder replacement. Slight amount of fluid is always present and is considered normal, acting as lubricant for cylinder pistons.
4. Inspect adjuster screw operation. If satisfactory, lightly lubricate adjusting screw and washer with suitable brake lube. If operation is unsatisfactory, replace.
5. Clean rust and dirt from shoe contact surfaces on backing plate using fine emery cloth or other suitable abrasive.

Brake Drums

Any time the brake drums are removed for brake service, the braking surface diameter should be inspected with a suitable brake drum micrometer at several points to determine if they are within the safe, oversize limit stamped on the brake drum outer surface. If the braking surface diameter exceeds specifications, the drum must be replaced. If the braking surface diameter is within specifications, drums should be cleaned and inspected for cracks, scores, deep grooves, taper, out-of-roundness and heat spotting. If drums are cracked or heat spotted, they must be replaced. Grooves and large scores can only be removed by machining with special equipment, as long as the braking surface is within specifications stamped on brake drum outer surface. Any brake drum sufficiently out of round to cause vehicle vibration or noise while braking, or showing taper should also be machined, removing only enough stock to true up the brake drum.

After a brake drum is machined, wipe the braking surface diameter with a cloth soaked in denatured alcohol. Brake drums should always be machined in pairs and within allowable side to side specifications to maintain equal braking forces.

Brake Linings & Springs

Inspect brake linings for excessive wear, damage, oil, grease or brake fluid contamination. If any of the proceeding conditions exist, brake linings should be replaced. Brake shoes should always be replaced as an axle set to maintain equal braking pressures. Examine brake shoe webbing and hold-down/return springs for signs of overheating, indicated by a slight blue color. If any component shows signs of overheating, replace it. Overheated springs lose their strength and could cause brake linings to wear out prematurely. Inspect all springs for sags, bends or external damage and replace them as required.

Inspect hold-down retainers and pins for bends, rust and corrosion. If any of the proceeding conditions exist, replace retainers and pins.

Backing Plate

Inspect backing plate shoe contact surface for grooves that may restrict shoe movement and cannot be removed by lightly sanding with emery cloth or other suitable abrasive. If backing plate exhibits proceeding condition, it should be replaced. Also inspect for signs of cracks, warpage and excessive rust, indicating need for replacement.

Adjuster Mechanism

Inspect all components for rust, corrosion, bends and fatigue. Replace as required. On adjuster mechanism equipped with adjuster cable, inspect cable for kinks, fraying or elongation of eyelet and replace as required.

Parking Brake Cable

Inspect parking brake cable end for kinks, fraying or elongation and replace as required. Compress clamp where it enters backing plate to remove using suitable small hose clamp.

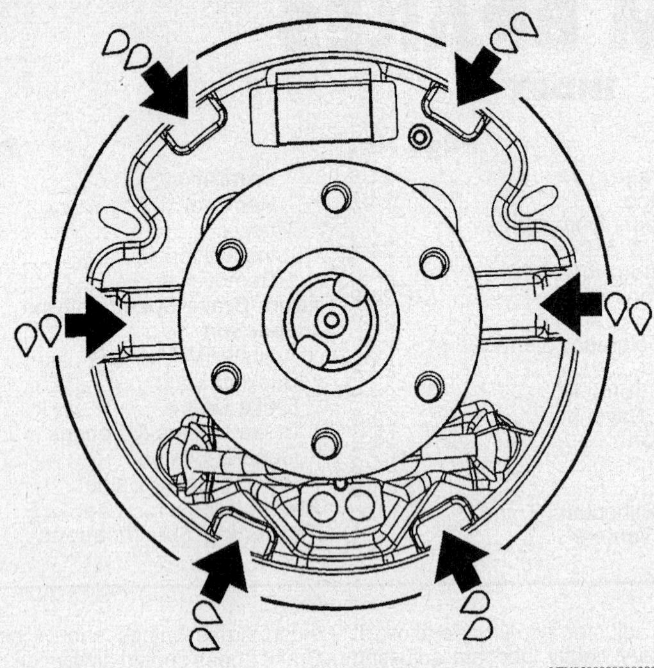

Fig. 1 Backing plate lubrication location

BRAKE SERVICE

Astro, Blazer, Jimmy, Safari, Sonoma & S10

1. Raise vehicle and suitably support.
2. Remove tire and wheel assembly.
3. Mark relationship of brake drum to axle.
4. Remove brake drum.
5. Remove brake shoe return springs.
6. Remove brake shoe guide.
7. Remove hold down springs.
8. Remove hold down pins.
9. Remove actuator lever and actuator lever pivot.
10. Remove actuator lever and lever pivot.
11. Remove lever return spring.
12. Remove parking brake strut and strut spring.
13. Remove parking brake lever.
14. Remove brake shoes.
15. Remove adjusting screw assembly and adjusting screw spring from brake shoes.
16. Inspect all parts for discoloration due to heat, worn, or stress.
17. Inspect wheel cylinder for signs of leakage and brake drum for scoring and machining tolerance.
18. Reverse procedure to install. Lubricate brake shoe backing plate, adjusting screw threads, socket and socket face with a thin coat of Suitable high temperature silicone lubricant.

Aztek, Rendezvous & Vue

REMOVAL

1. Raise and support vehicle.
2. Mark relationship of drum to hub.
3. Remove and discard retaining clip.
4. Remove brake drum. If brake drum does not come off easily, proceed as follows:
   a. Loosen parking brake cable.
   b. Remove backing plate access hole plug.
   c. Disengage self adjuster by inserting suitable flat-bladed tool through backing plate access hole.
   d. Loosen adjuster screw by inserting another flat-bladed tool through access hole .
   e. Install access hole plug.
   f. Apply small amount of penetrating oil around brake drum center hole.
   g. Remove brake drum.
5. Disengage adjuster spring hook end from tab on adjuster actuator. **Do not over stretch adjuster spring.**
6. Remove straight end of adjuster spring from brake shoe.
7. Remove adjuster actuator from brake shoe.
8. Remove return spring from brake shoes.
9. Remove park brake cable from park brake actuator lever.
10. Remove brake shoe hold-down springs and retainers from brake shoes.
11. Remove adjuster from brake shoes and park brake actuator lever.
12. Remove horseshoe clip retaining park brake actuator lever to brake shoe.
13. Remove park brake actuator lever and wave washer from brake shoe.

INSTALLATION

1. Apply brake lubricant No. 1052196, or equivalent, to brake shoe contact points on backing plate, adjuster screw threads and adjuster socket inside diameter.
2. Install park brake actuator lever and wave washer to brake shoe.
3. Install horseshoe clip to park brake actuator lever pivot pin.
4. Install brake shoes to brake backing plate.
5. Install brake shoe hold-down pins, springs and retainers to brake shoes.
6. Install park brake cable to park brake actuator lever.
7. Install adjuster screw to brake shoe and park brake actuator. **Ensure adjuster engages brake shoe and park brake actuator properly.**
8. Apply brake lubricant No. 1052196, or equivalent, to adjuster actuator/brake shoe interface.
9. Install adjuster actuator to brake shoe.
10. Install straight end of adjuster spring to brake shoe. **Do not over stretch adjuster spring.**
11. Install adjuster spring hook end to tab on adjuster actuator.
12. Install return spring to brake shoes.
13. Move park brake actuator lever to spread brake shoes apart. Adjuster actuator lever should move downward, then upward as park brake actuator lever is released, forcing adjuster wheel to rotate. If adjuster does not operate properly, remove and install adjuster. **Ensure adjuster operates properly.**
14. Adjust brake shoes as and park brake cable as outlined under "Adjustments."
15. Align marks on brake drum and hub made during removal.
16. Install brake drum.
17. Install tire and wheel assembly.

Canyon, Colorado, Sierra & Silverado

1. Raise and support vehicle.
2. Remove rear tire and wheel.
3. Remove brake drum retainer and brake drum.
4. If brake drum cannot be removed, proceed as follows:
   a. Remove rubber plug from backing plate.
   b. Insert a suitable screwdriver until contact has been made with adjuster lever. Slightly push adjuster lever away from adjuster.
   c. Rotate adjuster in a upward motion

until adjuster is seated using a second screwdriver.
d. Remove rear brake drum.
5. Adjust brake shoe to lowest setting.
6. Remove adjuster spring, brake adjuster lever and adjuster assembly.
7. Remove retractor spring from secondary brake shoe, then the secondary brake shoe from backing plate.
8. Remove retractor spring from primary brake shoe, then the primary brake shoe from backing plate.
9. Remove return spring.
10. Press and hold lock tab for park brake cable using a suitable small flat-blade screwdriver.
11. Push park brake cable forward and remove from lever.
12. Reverse procedure to install, noting the following:
    a. Apply a small amount of suitable high temperature silicone grease or equivalent to contact areas between rear brake shoes and backing plate, **Fig. 1.**
    b. Adjust rear brake shoes using a suitable measuring tool, **Fig. 2.**

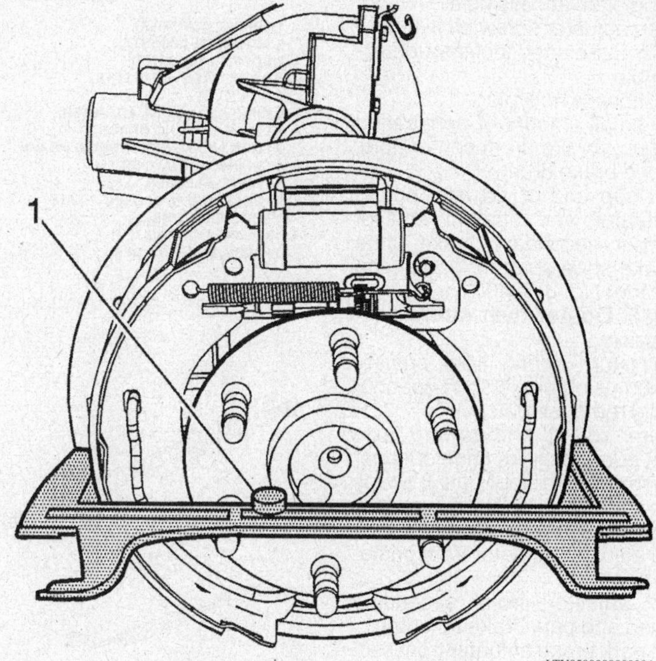

Fig. 2 Brake measurement

Equinox & Torrent

1. Raise and support vehicle.
2. Remove brake drum.
3. Remove spring hook end of adjuster from tab on adjuster actuator.
4. Remove straight end of adjuster spring from brake shoe.
5. Remove adjuster actuator from brake shoe.
6. Remove return spring from brake shoes.
7. Remove park brake cable from park brake actuator lever.
8. Remove brake shoe hold-down springs and retainers from brake shoes.
9. Remove adjuster from brake shoes and park brake actuator lever.
10. Remove horseshoe clip retaining park brake actuator lever to brake shoe.
11. Remove park brake actuator lever and wave washer from brake shoe.
12. Reverse procedure to install. Apply a thin coat of suitable high temperature silicone brake lubricant to brake shoe contact points, adjuster screw threads and adjuster socket.

Express & Savana

REMOVAL

1. Raise and support vehicle, then remove tire and wheel assembly.
2. Install park brake lever pin.
3. Mark relationship of rear brake drum to axle.
4. Remove rear brake drum retainer, then the brake drum.
5. Remove rear brake shoe return springs.
6. Remove hold-down springs and pins.
7. Remove shoe guide, rear brake shoe actuator and spring.
8. Remove rear brake shoe actuator link.
9. Remove rear parking brake lever strut and spring.
10. Remove rear brake shoe adjuster spring and adjuster.
11. Remove rear brake shoes.

INSTALLATION

1. Lubricate rear brake backing plate and adjusting screw threads with thin coat of suitable white lithium grease.
2. Install rear brake shoes.
3. Install rear brake shoe adjuster.
4. Install rear brake shoe adjuster spring. **Do not interchange left and right-hand brake shoe adjusting screws.** Coils of adjusting screw spring must not touch adjusting screw.
5. Install rear park brake lever strut and spring.
6. Install rear brake shoe actuator link.
7. Install rear brake shoe actuator and spring.
8. Install shoe guide, hold-down pins and springs.
9. Install rear brake shoe return springs.
10. Locate relationship mark and install brake drum to axle.
11. Install rear brake drum retainers, as required.
12. Remove park brake lever pin.
13. Install tire and wheel assembly.
14. Adjust rear brakes as outlined under "Adjustments."
15. Adjust parking brake as outlined under "Adjustments."
16. Lower vehicle.

HHR

1. Raise and support vehicle.
2. Remove tire and wheel assembly.
3. Remove brake drum and adjuster spring.
4. Disengage spring hook end of adjuster from tab on adjuster actuator lever, then release spring from brake shoe web hole.
5. Remove adjuster actuator lever from pivot.
6. Spread top of brake shoes apart using brake shoe spanner and spring remover tool No. J 38400, or equivalent.
7. Remove adjuster assembly from brake shoes.
8. Position hook end of brake shoe spanner and spring remover under universal spring and lightly pull universal spring end out of shoe web hole. Hold universal spring while removing trailing brake shoe.
9. Release park brake cable from park brake lever on trailing shoe.
10. Position hook end of brake shoe spanner and spring remover under universal spring and lightly pull universal spring end out of shoe web hole. Hold universal spring while removing leading brake shoe.
11. Reverse procedure to install. Apply a thin coat of suitable high temperature silicone brake lubricant to brake shoe to backing plate contact surfaces.

Montana, Silhouette, Trans Sport & Venture

REMOVAL

1. Release parking brake.
2. Raise and support vehicle, then remove wheel and tire assembly.
3. Mark relationship of drum to hub.
4. Remove and discard retaining clip.
5. Remove brake drum. If brake drum is hard to remove, proceed as follows:
    a. Loosen parking brake cable.
    b. Remove backing plate access hole plug.
    c. Disengage self adjuster by inserting suitable flat-bladed tool through

backing plate access hole.
   d. Loosen adjuster screw by inserting another flat-bladed tool through access hole .
   e. Install access hole plug.
   f. Apply small amount of penetrating oil around brake drum center hole.
   g. Remove brake drum.
6. Remove loop end of adjuster spring from actuator and straight end of spring from secondary brake shoe using brake shoe spanner and spring remover tool No. J-38400, or equivalent, **Fig. 3. Do not over stretch adjuster spring.**
7. Remove return spring from primary brake shoe using brake shoe spanner and spring remover tool.
8. Pry return spring end toward axle using flat edge of brake shoe spanner and spring remover tool until it snaps off brake shoe.
9. Remove primary brake shoe.
10. Remove adjuster actuator from primary brake shoe.
11. Remove adjuster from secondary brake shoe and park brake actuator.
12. Remove park brake actuator from secondary brake shoe.
13. Remove return spring from secondary brake shoe using brake shoe spanner and spring remover tool.
14. Pry return spring end toward axle using flat edge of brake shoe spanner and spring remover tool.
15. Remove secondary brake shoe.
16. Remove return spring from backing plate.

INSTALLATION

1. Apply brake lubricant No. 1052196, or equivalent, to six brake shoe contact points on backing plate, adjuster screw threads and adjuster socket inside diameter.
2. Install return spring to backing plate.
3. Install secondary brake shoe to backing plate.
4. Install return spring into secondary brake shoe using brake shoe spanner and spring remover tool No. J-38400, or equivalent.
5. Install park brake actuator to secondary brake shoe.
6. Install adjuster screw to secondary brake shoe and park brake actuator. **Ensure adjuster engages brake shoe and park brake actuator properly.**
7. Apply suitable brake lubricant to adjuster actuator/primary brake shoe interface.
8. Install adjuster actuator to primary brake shoe.
9. Install primary brake shoe with adjuster actuator to backing plate.
10. Install return spring into primary brake shoe using brake shoe spanner and spring remover tool. **Ensure adjuster engages brake shoe and adjuster actuator properly.**
11. Install straight end of adjuster spring into secondary brake shoe and loop end to actuator using brake shoe spanner and spring remover tool. **Do not over stretch adjuster spring.**

1 SPRING, ACTUATOR
2 ACTUATOR, ADJUSTER
3 SOCKET, ADJUSTER
4 BOLT/SCREW, ADJUSTER
5 NUT, PIVOT
6 SHOE AND LINING, ADJUSTER
7 LEVER, PARKING BRAKE
8 SHOE AND LINING, PARKING BRAKE
9 SPRING, RETRACTOR
10 VALVE, BLEEDER
11 BOLT/SCREW, BACKING PLATE
12 CYLINDER, WHEEL
13 PLATE, BACKING
14 PLUG, ACCESS HOLE

GC4089200005000X

Fig. 3 Drum brake assembly. Montana, Silhouette, Trans Sport & Venture

12. Move park brake actuator to spread brake shoes apart. Adjuster actuator tab should move up, forcing adjuster wheel to rotate. If adjuster does not operate properly, remove adjuster, then install, again. **Ensure adjuster operates properly.**
13. Adjust brake shoes as outlined under "Adjustments."
14. Adjust park brake cable as outlined under "Adjustments."
15. Align brake drum and hub marks, then install brake drum.
16. Install tire and wheel assembly, then lower vehicle.

Tracker

REMOVAL

1. Remove four mounting screws and two clips, then lift up console.
2. Loosen parking brake cable lock nut.
3. Raise and support vehicle, then remove tire and wheel assembly.
4. Remove locking washers from wheel studs.
5. Remove drum from axle hub. If drum cannot be removed by hand, force drum off hub by installing two 8 mm bolts into drum and tightening.
6. To increase brake shoe to drum clearance, pull shoe hold-down pin approximately .197 inch.
7. Release shoe hold down springs by turning pins.
8. Remove shoe hold-down springs, **Fig. 4.**
9. Remove upper return spring, strut, adjuster, adjuster lever, adjuster spring, strut spring and pawl lever.
10. Remove lower return spring.
11. Disconnect parking brake cable from shoe lever.
12. Remove brake shoes with park brake shoe lever attached.
13. Disconnect park brake cable from shoe lever.
14. Remove brake shoes.
15. Remove park brake shoe lever and retainer from brake shoe.

INSTALLATION

Apply suitable white lithium grease to all of the brake component metal contact points where the brake shoe metal contacts the backing plate, the wheel cylinder, the adjustment strut, etc. prior to installation.

1. Install parking brake lever to shoe with C-clip.
2. Install strut and springs.
3. Install brake shoes with park brake shoe lever.
4. Connect parking brake cable to shoe lever and install brake shoes.
5. Install upper return spring, strut, adjuster, adjuster lever, adjuster spring, strut spring and pawl lever.
6. Install shoe hold-down springs. Secure shoe hold down springs by turning pins.
7. Measure brake shoes outer diameter. If outer diameter is not 8.638–8.650 inches, turn adjuster.
8. Install brake drum and locking washers to wheel studs.
9. Install tire and wheel assembly.
10. Lower vehicle.
11. Press brake pedal 3–10 times with approximately 66 lbs. pressure to obtain proper drum-to-shoe clearance.
12. Adjust parking brake as outlined under "Adjustments."
13. Install console.

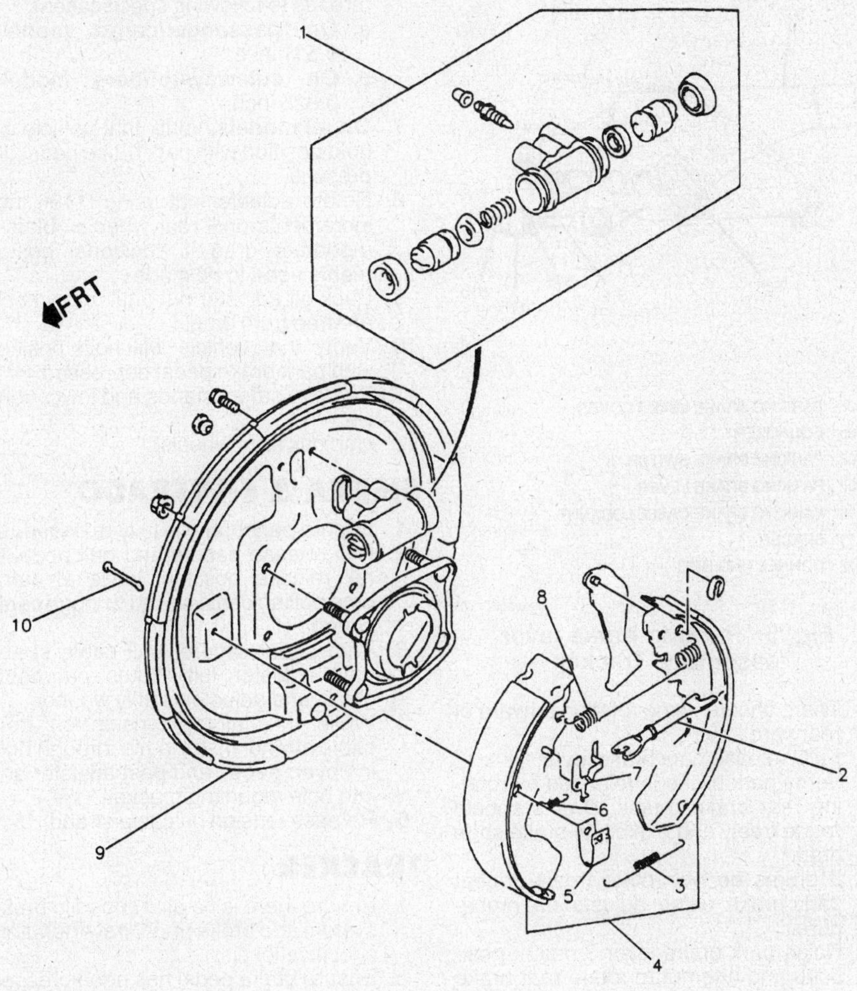

Fig. 4 Exploded view of drum brake assembly. Tracker

ADJUSTMENTS

Service Brake

The following procedure has been revised by a technical service bulletin.

These brakes have self-adjusting shoe mechanisms that ensure correct lining-to-drum clearances at all times. The automatic adjusters operate only when the brakes are applied as the vehicle is moving rearward or when the vehicle comes to an uphill stop.

Although the brakes are self-adjusting, an initial adjustment is required after the brake shoes have been relined or replaced, or when the length of the adjusting screw has been changed during some other service operation.

Frequent usage of an automatic transmission forward range to halt reverse vehicle motion may prevent the automatic adjusters from functioning, thereby inducing low pedal heights. Should low pedal heights be encountered, it is recommended that numerous forward and reverse stops be made until satisfactory pedal height is obtained.

If a low pedal condition cannot be corrected by making numerous reverse stops (provided the hydraulic system is free of air) it indicates that the self-adjusting mechanism is not functioning. Therefore it will be required to remove the brake drum, clean, free up and lubricate the adjusting mechanism. Then adjust the brakes, ensuring the parking brake is fully released.

1. Knock out lanced area in backing plate or drum using suitable punch. If drum is installed on vehicle when this is done, remove drum and clean brake compartment of all metal. **When adjustment is completed, new hole cover must be installed in backing plate.**
2. Turn brake adjusting screw to expand brake shoes at each wheel until wheel can just be turned by hand using suitable tool. Drag should be equal on all wheels.
3. Back off adjusting screw at each wheel three notches.
4. If shoe still drags slightly on drum, back off adjusting screw an additional 1–2 notches.
5. When adjusting screw has been backed off correctly, brakes should be free of drag. Heavy drag at this point indicates tight parking brake cable.
6. Install adjusting hole cover in brake backing plate.
7. Inspect parking brake for proper adjustment.

Manual Parking Brake

ASTRO, BLAZER, BRAVADA, JIMMY, SAFARI, SONOMA & S10 SERIES

The park brake must be adjusted any time the park brake cables have been replaced or disconnected, or if under heavy foot pressure the pedal travel is less than half the pedal total travel. The rear brakes must be adjusted properly before adjusting the park brake.

1. Block front wheels.
2. Raise rear axle and support rear axle with suitable safety stands.
3. Loosen equalizer nut.
4. Fully release park brake pedal.
5. Tighten equalizer nut until rear wheels will not rotate without excessive force in a forward direction.
6. Loosen equalizer nut until there is little or no drag when rear wheels are rotated in a forward direction.
7. Lower vehicle and remove blocks from front wheels.

AZTEK, MONTANA, RENDEZVOUS, SILHOUETTE, TRANS SPORT, VENTURE & VUE

1. Raise and support vehicle.
2. Release all tension in parking brake cable.
3. Ensure both levers are against stops.
4. Adjust rear service brakes as outlined under "Service Brake."
5. Adjust parking brake by turning nut on equalizer while spinning both rear wheels. When rear wheel develops drag, stop adjusting and back off one full turn.
6. Apply parking brake to four clicks and inspect rear wheel rotation.
7. Ensure wheel does not move when attempting to rotate it by hand in forward direction.

8. Ensure wheel drags or does not move when attempting to rotate in rearward direction.
9. Release parking brake and inspect for free wheel rotation.
10. Apply parking brake to 10 clicks and release. Repeat five times.
11. Inspect parking brake for full release.
12. Turn ignition On and ensure Brake indicator lamp is Off.
13. If light is On and brake appears to be released, ensure pedal is in release mode and fully returned to stop and pull down on parking brake cable to take up slack.
14. Lower vehicle.

CANYON & COLORADO

1. Release park brake pedal.
2. Raise and support vehicle.
3. Clean threads on front park brake cable.
4. Adjust park brake until right rear brake is locked.
5. Apply and release park brake five times.
6. With park brake in release position, adjust park brake until right rear brake develops a slight drag.
7. Back off adjusting nut two complete turns.

EQUINOX, HHR & TORRENT

1. Apply and fully release park brake several times. Verify that park brake lever releases completely.
2. Turn ON ignition. Verify red BRAKE warning lamp is not illuminated.
3. If red BRAKE warning lamp is illuminated, verify the following:
   a. Park brake lever is in fully released position and against stop.
   b. There is no slack in park brake cable.
4. Turn OFF ignition.
5. Disable supplemental inflatable restraint (SIR) system as outlined under "Passive Restraint Systems"
6. Remove front floor console.
7. With park brake lever in released position, loosen adjusting nut completely to end of front cable threaded rod using suitable hand tools.
8. Raise vehicle and suitably support.
9. Remove rear tire and wheel assemblies.
10. Adjust rear drum brakes.
11. Ensure there is no brake shoe drag after adjustment by rotating brake drums. If drag exists, re-center brake shoes and perform brake shoe adjustment again.
12. Install 2 wheel nuts to wheel studs and firmly hand tighten in order to retain brake drums.
13. Lower vehicle to permit access to park brake lever.
14. Raise park brake lever 1 detent position.
15. Tighten park brake cable adjusting nut until light to moderate drag is exhibited while rotating rear brake drums using suitable hand tools.
16. Attempt to rotate rear brake drums. There should be no rotation forward or rearward.
17. Fully release park brake lever.
18. Verify park brake is released by rotating rear brake drums. Drums should rotate freely and exhibit no brake shoe drag.
19. If drums do not rotate freely, repeat park brake cable adjustment procedure.
20. Raise park brake lever 3 detent positions and attempt to rotate rear brake drums:
    a. One of brake drums should not rotate forward or rearward.
    b. Other brake drum should not rotate forward or rearward, or should require substantial effort to rotate.
21. Raise vehicle and suitably support.
22. Remove wheel nuts retaining brake drums.
23. Install rear tire and wheel assemblies and lower vehicle.
24. Install front floor console.
25. Release park brake lever.
26. Enable SIR system as outlined under "Passive Restraint System."

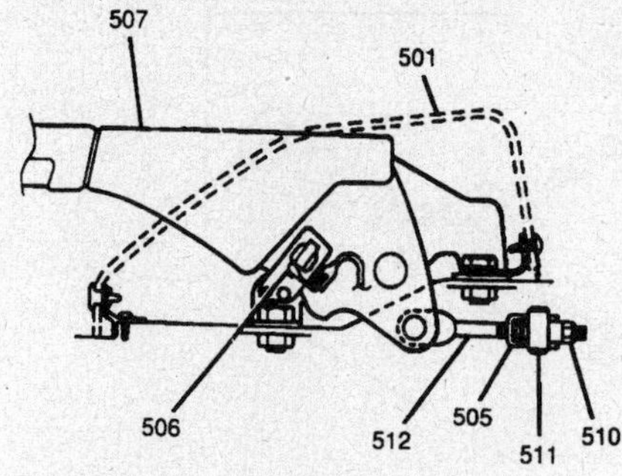

501 PARKING BRAKE LEVER COVER
505 EQUALIZER
506 PARKING BRAKE SWITCH
507 PARKING BRAKE LEVER
510 PARKING BRAKE CABLE LOCKNUT
511 SPACER
512 CONNECTING ROD

GC4089600043000X

Fig. 5 Parking brake lever assembly. Tracker

EXPRESS & SAVANA

The cable tension is self adjusting. However, during normal brake lining wear, it is possible that the cable tension may need adjustment due to the increased pedal travel.

1. Inspect rear brake shoe for wear. Rear brake shoe thickness should not be more than 80 percent worn.
2. Make sure system is free from corrosion and free from sticking or binding.
3. Block front wheels.
4. Raise and suitably support vehicle.
5. Place park brake pedal to FULL up position.
6. Measure threads on equalizer. Adjust threads to following specifications:
   a. **On passenger/cargo models,** 0.511 inch.
   b. **On cutaway/upfitters models,** 0.826 inch.
7. **On all models,** verify that vehicle will hold position with park brake pedal depressed.
8. Rotate adjuster nut using 0.196 inch increments until rear wheels obtain a moderate drag if additional adjustments need to be made.
9. Back off adjuster nut until rear wheels are free from drag.
10. Verify that vehicle will hold position with park brake pedal depressed.
11. Remove safety stands and lower vehicle.
12. Unblock front wheels.

SIERRA & SILVERADO

1. Ensure park brake is fully released.
2. Pull release handle and pull pedal to full release position, while at same time pulling cable strand through cable conduit.
3. With pedal secure, pull cable strand until adjuster fully takes out cable slack, and adjuster is fully wound.
4. While maintaining tension on front cable strand, install a pin through hole in cover, pedal, and past adjuster and into hole mounting bracket.
5. Release tension on cable strand.

TRACKER

1. Ensure there is no air trapped in brake system and brake pedal travel is within specifications.
2. Ensure brake pedal has been pressed a few times with approximately 66 lbs. load and parking brake lever has been pulled up a few times with approximately 44 lbs. of force and completely released.
3. Ensure rear brake shoes are not worn beyond limit and self-adjusting mechanism operates properly.
4. Adjust parking brake by adjusting self locking nut located on parking brake adjusting rod on parking brake lever until parking brake engages within 7–9 notches when being pulled with approximately 40 lbs. of force, **Fig. 5.**

Automatic Apply Parking Brakes

CONTROL ROD

1. Place parking brake control valve lever in its park detent position.
2. Place selector in park position.
3. Install rod end into control valve lever and mounting nut. **Torque** nut to 124 ft. lbs.
4. Turn rod clockwise until it is in line with transmission control equalizer lever hole.
5. Install mounting nut. **Torque** nut to 124 ft. lbs., and jam nuts to 13 ft. lbs.

DRUM BRAKE SPECIFICATIONS

Model	Year	Brake Lining Wear Limit, Inch②	Brake Drum Inside Diameter, Inches			Drum Runout Limit, Inch	Drum Maximum Out Of Roundness, Inch②
			Nominal	Maximum Refinish	Maximum Inside Diameter (Discard Limit)①		
Astro Van & Safari	2002	.030	9.50	9.56	9.59	.0060	—
Aztek & Rendezvous	2002–05	.059	—	9.88	9.90	.0060	—
Blazer & Jimmy	2002–04	.030	—	9.50	9.50	.0060	—
Canyon & Colorado	2004–06	.030	—	—	11.67	.0060	—
Express & Savanna (1500)	2002–04	.030	11.15	11.21	11.24	.0060	—
Express & Savanna (2500 & 3500)	2002–04	.030	13.00	13.06	13.09	.0060	—
HHR	2006	.020	9.06	9.07	9.09	.004	—
Sierra & Silverado	2004–06	.030	—	—	11.67	.0024	—
Sonoma & S10	2002–04	.030	—	9.50	9.50	.0060	—
Tracker	2002–04	.040	8.66	—	8.74	.002	—
Venture, Silhouette & Montana	2002–05	.059	8.86	8.91	8.92	.0060	—

① — Maximum brake drum inside diameter (discard limit) is stamped on drum.

② — Above rivet head or shoe. Original equipment type brake linings.

TIGHTENING SPECIFICATIONS

Year	Component	Torque, Ft. Lbs.
ASTRO & SAFARI		
2002	Backing Plate	35
	Bleeder Valve	62①
	Brake Pipe Fittings	13
	Wheel Cylinder	13
AZTEK, MONTANA, RENDEZVOUS, SILHOUETTE & VENTURE		
2002–05	Bleeder Valve	62①
	Brake Pipe To Wheel Cylinder	12
	Wheel Cylinder Bolts	110①
BLAZER, JIMMY, SONOMA & S10		
2002–03	Backing Plate	35
	Bleeder Valve	62①
	Brake Line Fitting	16
	Wheel Cylinder	13
CANYON & COLORADO		
2004–06	Backing Plate Mounting Bolts	100
	Bleeder Valve	80①
	Rear Brake Pipe Fitting	14
	Wheel Cylinder Mounting Bolts	13
EQUINOX & TORRENT		
2005–06	Brake Pipe Fitting At Wheel Cylinder	14
	Wheel Cylinder Bleeder Valve	71①
	Wheel Cylinder Mounting Bolts	11
EXPRESS & SAVANA		
2002–04	Rear Brake Anchor Pin (1500)	146
	Rear Brake Anchor Pin (2500 & 3500)	220
	Rear Brake Backing Plate Retaining Bolts	104
	Rear Brake Pipe To Rear Brake Cylinder	13
	Rear Brake Bleeder Valve	100①
	Rear Brake Cylinder Retaining Bolts	15
HHR		
2006	Brake Pipe Fitting At Wheel Cylinder, First Or Second Design	14
	Wheel Cylinder Bleeder Valve	71①
	Wheel Cylinder Mounting Bolts	12
SIERRA & SILVERADO		
2005–06	Backing Plate Bolts	100
	Bleeder Valve	80 ①
	Brake Pipe Fittings	14
	Wheel Cylinder	13
TRACKER		
2002–04	Backing Plate	17
	Brake Line Flare Nut	12
	Wheel Cylinder Bleeder Plug	66①
	Wheel Cylinder	75①

① — Inch lbs.

HYDRAULIC BRAKE SYSTEMS

INDEX

DESCRIPTION

Master Cylinder

Some vehicles use a conventional tandem master cylinder with two hydraulic pistons operating in-line. The primary piston controls the front brake system and the secondary piston controls the rear brake system.

Other models use a master cylinder that operates the same as the conventional master cylinder, but also incorporates a quick take-up feature in the rear chamber to reduce excessive pedal travel which may result from increased fluid displacement required to move the low drag caliper piston out against the rotor.

The quick take-up uses a spring-loaded ball check valve to hold pressure in the large diameter rear chamber when the brakes are first applied. At initial application, movement of the rear piston causes fluid to be displaced forward past the primary piston seal into the primary high pressure chamber. At a specified pressure, the ball unseats and fluid from the large rear bore is displaced past the primary piston seal into the primary high pressure chamber. At a specified pressure, the ball unseats and fluid from the large rear bore is displaced past the bore into the reservoir. When the brake pedal is released, suction generated in the large bore chamber replenishes its fluid supply by drawing fluid from the reservoir around the quick take-up lip seal and through a small bleed orifice in the ball seat.

Hydraulic Control Valves

These vehicles use either a two function or three function combination valve. Some vehicles use a height sensitive proportioning valve in addition to the combination valve.

The two function combination valve consists of a metering valve and a brake failure warning switch. The hydraulic brake lines are routed through this valve to the wheel cylinders or calipers. The metering portion of this valve assists in providing balanced front to rear braking by delaying full hydraulic fluid pressure to the front disc brakes until the rear drum brakes overcome return spring tension and the linings contact the drums. The brake failure warning switch

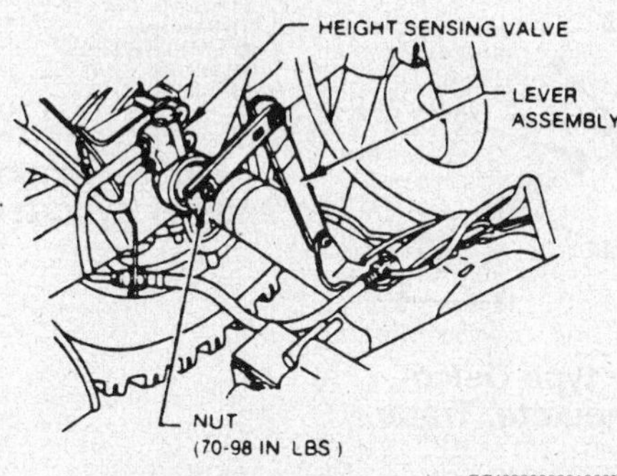

Fig. 1 Height sensing proportioning valve

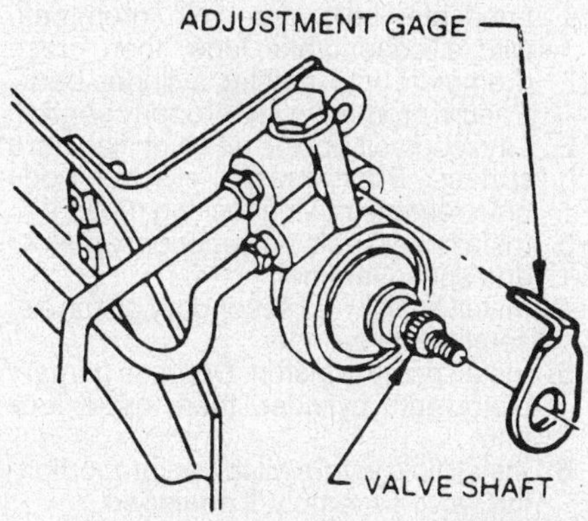

Fig. 2 Adjustment gauge installation

portion of the valve activates the brake warning lamp when there is a loss of pressure in either the front of the rear braking system.

The three function combination valve consists of a metering valve, a brake failure warning switch and a proportioning valve. The metering valve and brake failure warning switch operate the same as those in the two function combination valve previously outlined.

The proportioning section of the valve proportions outlet pressure to the rear brakes after a certain rear input pressure has been reached, preventing rear wheel lock-up.

The height sensitive proportioning valve provides ideal brake balance according to weight at the rear axle. This valve is mounted on the frame and responds to changes in vehicle trim height in relation to rear axle load. Mechanical linkage connects the valve to a bracket attached to the rear axle.

ADJUSTMENTS

Height Sensing Proportioning Valve

The height sensing proportioning valve must be adjusted whenever the valve and/or linkage is disassembled or removed for service. In addition, adjustment should be inspected if excessive front wheel lock-up is experienced with a lower than desired brake application rate when vehicle is at or near maximum GVWR.

1. Raise and support vehicle, leave wheels on and allow axle to hang freely.
2. Remove lever retaining nut and disconnect lever from valve shaft, **Fig. 1.**
3. Rotate valve shaft to permit installation of correct adjustment gauge, **Fig. 2,** ensure D shaped hole of gauge is properly seated on valve shaft and that gauge tang engages mounting hole in valve. **Adjustment gauges vary depending upon vehicle application. Correct gauge must be used to ensure proper operation of braking system.**
4. Install lever on valve shaft by pressing plastic bushing and clip assembly over shaft serrations using C-clamp or suitable pliers. **Do not press lever onto shaft using retaining nut. Adjustment of valve will be disturbed.**
5. Install lever retaining nut and **torque** to 72–96 inch lbs.
6. Cut tang off adjustment gauge and allow valve to rotate freely.
7. Lower vehicle and test brakes.

COMPONENT REPLACEMENT

Master Cylinder

1. **On models equipped with manual brake system,** disconnect master cylinder pushrod from brake pedal.
2. **On all models,** disconnect all wire connectors from master cylinder components.

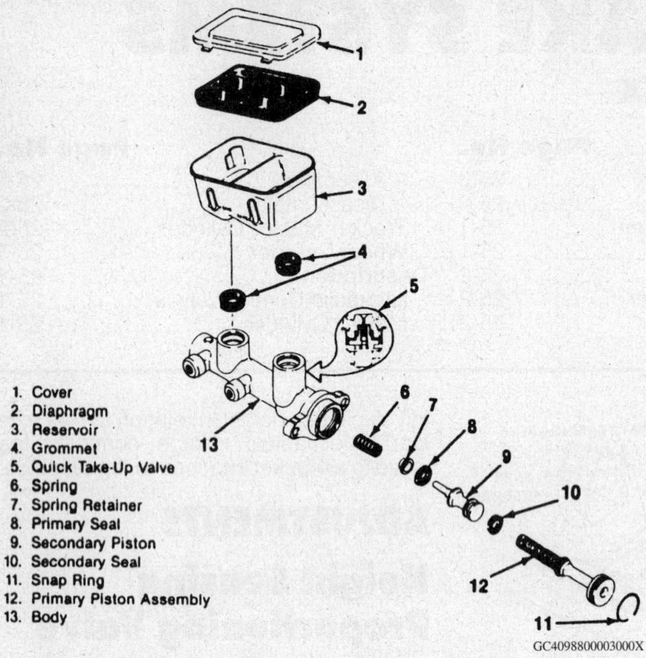

Fig. 3 Exploded view of composite type Delco master cylinder. Except Montana, Silhouette, Trans Sport & Venture

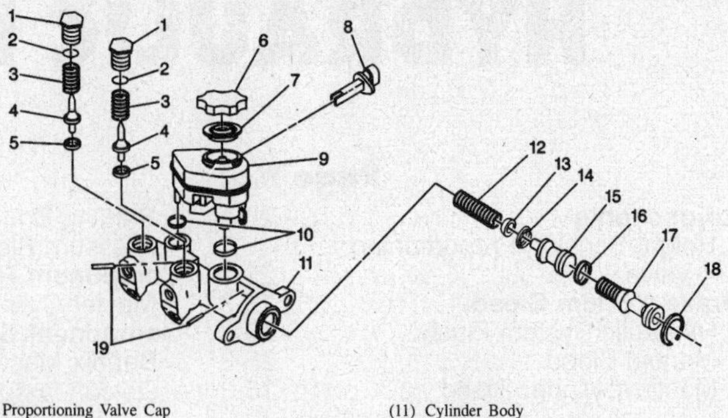

(1) Proportioning Valve Cap
(2) O-Ring
(3) Spring
(4) Proportioning Valve Piston
(5) Proportioning Valve Seal
(6) Reservoir Cap
(7) Diaphragm
(8) Fluid Level Sensor
(9) Reservoir
(10) O-Ring
(11) Cylinder Body
(12) Spring
(13) Spring Retainer
(14) Primary Seal
(15) Secondary Piston
(16) Secondary Seal
(17) Primary Piston
(18) Retainer
(19) Spring Pin

GC4098800004000A

Fig. 4 Exploded view of composite type Delco master cylinder. Montana, Silhouette, Trans Sport & Venture

3. Disconnect brake lines from master cylinder.
4. Remove master cylinder mounting nuts, and master cylinder.
5. Reverse procedure to install.

COMPONENT SERVICE

Delco Master Cylinder

When performing the following procedures, refer to **Figs. 3 and 4,** noting that the composite reservoir may vary in design.

DISASSEMBLE

1. Remove master cylinder from vehicle.
2. Remove reservoir cover and diaphragm. Discard old brake fluid in reservoir.
3. Inspect cover and diaphragm. Replace if cut, cracked or deformed.
4. Remove fluid level switch and proportioning valve assembly, if equipped.
5. Depress primary piston and remove lock ring.
6. Plug primary fluid outlet (outlet nearest to cowl when master cylinder is installed), then apply compressed air into secondary fluid outlet to remove primary and secondary pistons.
7. Remove spring retainer and seals from secondary piston.
8. Clamp master cylinder in a vise, then remove reservoir using a pry bar. Remove reservoir grommets.
9. Inspect master cylinder bore for corrosion. **Do not use abrasive material on master cylinder bore.** Replace if bore is corroded.

ASSEMBLE

Clean all components not included in repair kit with brake fluid. **Do not dry with compressed air.** Lubricate all rubber components with clean brake fluid prior to installation.

1. Lubricate new reservoir grommets with silicone brake lube, then press grommets into master cylinder body. Ensure grommets are properly seated.
2. Lay reservoir upside down on flat, hard surface. Press master cylinder body onto reservoir using rocking motion.
3. Install new seals on secondary piston, and spring retainer.
4. Install spring and secondary piston assembly into cylinder.
5. Install primary piston. Depress primary piston into cylinder, then install lock ring.
6. Install fluid level switch and proportioning valve assembly, if equipped.
7. Fit diaphragm into reservoir cover, then install cover onto reservoir.
8. Install master cylinder in vehicle.

Bendix Master Cylinder

Refer to **Fig. 5** when performing the following procedure.

1. Remove master cylinder from vehicle.
2. Clean outside of master cylinder, then remove reservoir cover and diaphragm.
3. Drain brake fluid from reservoir, then remove reservoir attaching bolts and reservoir.
4. Remove O-ring, compensating valve seals, valve poppets and springs.
5. Depress primary piston, then remove snap ring.
6. Remove primary piston assembly and piston return spring.
7. Remove secondary piston assembly by applying small amount of air pressure to front compensating valve port. Ensure front port is plugged.
8. Remove secondary spring.
9. Reverse procedure to assemble, noting the following:
   a. Inspect cylinder bore for scoring and corrosion. Replace master cylinder if required.
   b. Clean all metal components in denatured alcohol.
   c. Clean all rubber components in clean brake fluid.
   d. Polish discolored or stained cylinder with crocus cloth, then rinse in clean brake fluid. Ensure compensating port is clean.

Tracker Master Cylinder

Refer to **Fig. 6** while performing the following procedures.

1. Remove master cylinder from vehicle.
2. Remove pressure limit valve and proportioning/differential valve, if equipped.
3. Depress primary piston, then remove snap ring.
4. Remove primary piston stopper, cylinder cup and plate, and primary piston.
5. Remove secondary stopper bolt.
6. Remove secondary piston assembly by applying small amount of air pressure to stopper bolt hole.
7. Remove secondary return spring.
8. Reverse procedure to assemble, noting the following:
   a. Inspect cylinder bore for scoring and corrosion. Replace master cylinder if required.
   b. Clean all metal components in denatured alcohol.
   c. Clean all rubber components in clean brake fluid.
   d. Polish discolored or stained cylinder with crocus cloth, then rinse in clean brake fluid. Ensure compensating port is clean.

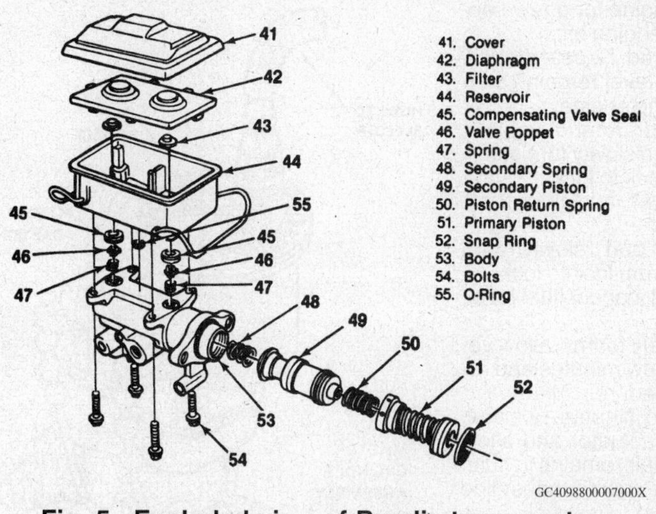

Fig. 5 Exploded view of Bendix type master cylinder

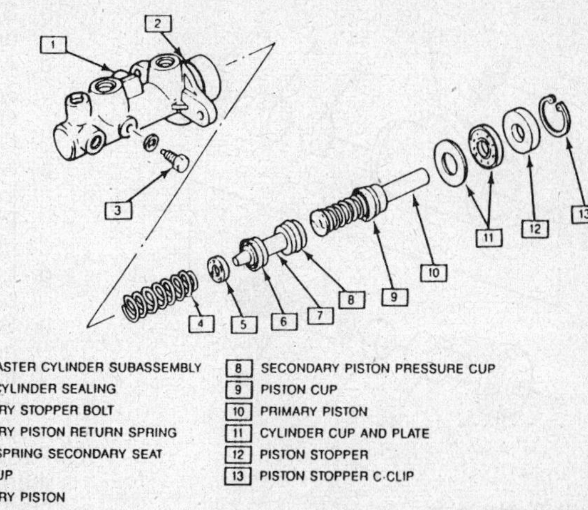

Fig. 6 Exploded view of Tracker master cylinder

Wheel Cylinder

1. Raise and support vehicle.
2. Remove wheel, drum and brake shoes.
3. Disconnect hydraulic line at wheel cylinder.
4. Remove wheel cylinder attaching screws, then remove wheel cylinder.
5. Strip cylinder of boots, pistons, springs and seals, **Fig. 7.**
6. Inspect cylinder bore for scoring and corrosion. Discoloration is a sign that springs have been damaged by heat, replace them if required.
7. Clean cylinder bore with crocus cloth. If cleaning does not remove scoring, replace cylinder.
8. Lubricate cylinder bore and seals with brake fluid, then reassemble cylinder.
9. Reverse procedure to install. Bleed system as outlined under "Brake System Bleed."

BRAKE SYSTEM BLEED

Manual Bleed

1. If vehicle is equipped with power brakes, remove vacuum reserve by applying brakes several times with engine off.
2. Fill master cylinder reservoirs with suitable brake fluid. **Ensure to always keep master cylinder reservoirs at least half full during entire bleeding procedure.**
3. If master cylinder is suspected to have air in bore, it must be bled first. To bleed master cylinder, proceed as follows:
   a. Disconnect forward brake pipe connection at master cylinder.
   b. Allow brake fluid to fill master cylinder bore until it begins to flow from forward pipe connector port.
   c. Connect and tighten forward brake pipe at master cylinder.
   d. Depress brake pedal slowly one time and hold, then loosen forward brake pipe connection at master cylinder to purge air from bore. Tighten connection, then release brake pedal slowly and wait 15 seconds.
   e. Repeat steps "a" though "e," until all air is purged from bore.
   f. Bleed rear bore by repeating steps "a" though "e."
4. Bleed right rear brake as follows:
   a. Depress brake pedal slowly one time and hold.
   b. Loosen bleeder valve to purge air from brake.
   c. Tighten bleeder valve and slowly release pedal, then wait 15 seconds.
   d. Repeat steps "a" through "c," until all air is purged.
5. Bleed left rear, right front, and left front brakes, in that order, using same method as for right rear brake.
6. Inspect brake operation and ensure pedal is firm. Also inspect master cylinder fluid level and add fluid as required.
7. Turn off brake warning light by applying moderate pressure to brake pedal several times.
8. Road test vehicle.

Pressure Bleed

1. Loosen, then slightly retighten bleeder valves at all four wheels. Repair any broken, stripped or frozen valves at this time.
2. Install suitable bleeder adapter to master cylinder using a diaphragm type pressure bleeder, **Fig. 8.**
3. Charge bleeder ball to 20–25 psi, then depress and hold valve stem on combination valve.
4. Connect pressure bleeder line to adapter.
5. Open line valve on pressure bleeder, then depress bleed-off valve on adapter until a small amount of brake fluid is released.
6. Raise and support vehicle.
7. Bleed right rear, left rear, right front and left front brakes, in that order.
8. Place transparent tube over bleeder valve, then allow tube to hang down into transparent container. Ensure end of tube is submerged in clean brake fluid.
9. Open bleeder valve ½–¾ turn and allow fluid to flow into container until all air is purged from line.

Hydraulic System Flush

If brake fluid is old, rusty or contaminated, or whenever new components are installed in the hydraulic system, the system must be flushed. Bleed brakes, allowing at least one quart of clean brake fluid to pass through system. Any rubber components in hydraulic system which were exposed to contaminated fluid must be replaced.

Master Cylinder Bleed

This procedure can be performed with master cylinder on or off vehicle.

1. Disconnect brake lines at master cylinder, if required.
2. Connect suitable lengths of brake lines to master cylinder and immerse other ends of lines in master cylinder reservoirs.
3. Apply master cylinder pushrod or brake pedal with full strokes until air bubbles have disappeared in reservoirs. It may require 20–30 applications to fully eliminate air bubbles.
4. Remove bleeding lines from master cylinder, then install master cylinder on vehicle, if required, and connect brake lines. **It is not required to bleed entire hydraulic system after replacing master cylinder, providing master cylinder has been bled and filled during installation.**

Parking Brake Bleed

1. Ensure shift and control levers are in park.

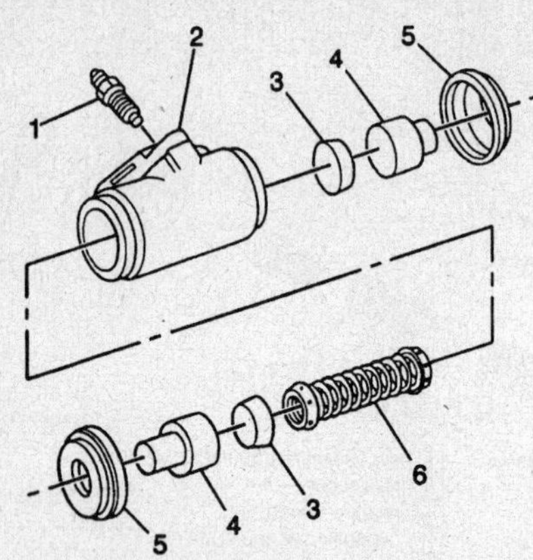

(1) Bleeder Valve
(2) Wheel Cylinder
(3) Seal
(4) Piston
(5) Boot
(6) Spring

GC4098800009000X

Fig. 7 Disassembled view of typical wheel cylinder

2. Bleed power steering system as follows:
   a. Fill pump reservoir to proper level. Let fluid settle for at least two minutes.
   b. Start and run engine for a few seconds, then turn engine off.
   c. Add fluid if required. Repeat steps A and B until fluid level remains constant after running engine.
   d. Raise and support front of vehicle.
   e. Start engine, then slowly turn steering wheel from lock to lock.
   f. Inspect fluid level, add fluid if required.
   g. Lower vehicle and slowly turn steering wheel from lock to lock.
   h. Stop engine and inspect fluid level, add as required.
   i. If fluid is extremely foamy, allow vehicle to stand a few minutes and repeat above procedure.
3. Reset shift lever to Neutral position, then open port on actuator and allow fluid to flow until no air remains in fluid.
4. Tighten port. Crack open exhaust line fitting to control valve.
5. Put control valve in park position. Allow small amount of fluid to bleed out of fitting.
6. Tighten fitting. Cycle system and observe any noise which indicates trapped air.
7. Repeat procedure as required. **System is filled properly when inspected in neutral gear and manual parking brake is applied. Fluid level should be 7.12 inches from top of reservoir.**

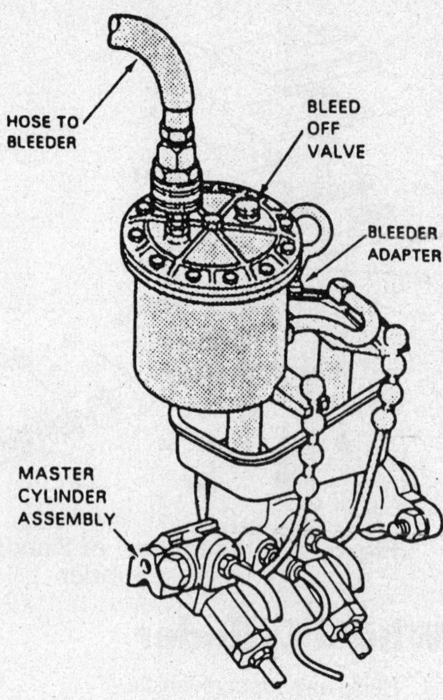

GC4098800010000X

Fig. 8 Pressure bleeder adapter installation

POWER BRAKE UNITS

TABLE OF CONTENTS

Delco Brake Booster

INDEX

DESCRIPTION

In order to properly service power brake systems, a thorough understanding of the various power assist systems is required. These systems provide a mechanical assist, acting to increase the force applied to the master cylinder piston by the driver while decreasing the effort required to obtain acceptable stopping performance. Two basic types of power assist mechanisms are used: vacuum assist diaphragm assemblies which use engine vacuum and in some cases vacuum from an external vacuum pump, and hydraulic assist assemblies which use hydraulic pressure developed by an external pump (usually the power steering pump).

Vacuum assist units are similar in operation, using vacuum applied to a diaphragm or piston in opposition to atmospheric pressure in order to increase the force applied to the master cylinder piston. However, two types of vacuum assist assemblies are used, the air suspended type and the vacuum suspended type. Air suspended units are under atmospheric pressure until the brakes are applied, then engine vacuum is admitted causing the piston or diaphragm to move and apply force to the master cylinder pushrod. Vacuum suspended types are balanced with engine vacuum until the brake pedal is depressed, allowing atmospheric pressure to unbalance the unit and apply force to the brake system.

Single Diaphragm Type

These power brake units are a combination vacuum-hydraulic brake booster of the vacuum suspended type which use engine intake manifold vacuum and atmospheric pressure for its power.

These units consist of a vacuum power section and an hydraulic master cylinder section. The vacuum power section contains a power piston with rolling diaphragm mechanism and power piston return spring.

The control valve is made up of an air valve and floating vacuum control valve assembly. The reaction mechanism consists of an hydraulic piston, reaction plate and a series of levers. The valve operating rod, which operates the air valve, projects from the power section and is connected to the brake pedal linkage.

The hydraulic pushrod operates against the master cylinder piston. A split system (tandem piston) or (duel piston) type master cylinder is incorporated into some units. The front half of the master cylinder in the split system operates the rear brakes while the rear half of the master cylinder operates the front brakes.

A vacuum check valve, attached to the front vacuum chamber and connected to the intake manifold, traps vacuum in.

OPERATION

As the brakes are applied by the driver, the valve operating rod and control piston move forward in the power piston assembly to compress the valve return spring and bring the poppet valve into contact with the vacuum valve seat in the valve housing to close the vacuum post. Any additional movement of the valve operating rod in the applied direction moves the control valve away from the poppet valve to open the atmospheric port and admit air through the air filter and passages to the chamber at the right of the vacuum power piston assembly. With vacuum on the left side of the diaphragm and atmospheric pressure on the right side of the diaphragm, a force is developed to move the vacuum power piston assembly, hydraulic pushrod, and hydraulic piston to the left to close the compensating port and force hydraulic fluid under pressure through the residual check valve and brake tubes into the brake wheel cylinders.

Tandem (Dual) Diaphragm Type

These units have a vacuum power chamber that consists of a front and rear shell, a housing divider, front and rear diaphragm and plate assemblies, a hydraulic pushrod and a diaphragm return spring.

The unit operates in much the same manner as the single diaphragm unit outlined above. The diaphragm and plate assemblies use the pressure differential created by the engine intake manifold vacuum and atmospheric pressure to assist the hydraulic pushrod.

TROUBLESHOOTING

Hard Pedal

1. Internal vacuum leak.
2. Faulty control valve.
3. Broken or damaged hydraulic brake lines.
4. Collapsed or damaged vacuum hose.
5. Plugged or loose vacuum fitting.
6. Bad stud welds on front or rear housing on power head.
7. Faulty booster diaphragm.
8. Restricted air filter element.
9. Worn or distorted reaction plate or levers.
10. Cracked or broken power pistons or retainers.

Brakes Grab

1. Faulty control valve.
2. Broken or damaged hydraulic brake lines.
3. Faulty master cylinder seals.
4. Cracked master cylinder casting.
5. Air in hydraulic system.

Slow Or No Release

1. Faulty pushrod adjustment.
2. Binding linkage.
3. Blocked passage in power piston.
4. Air valve sticking shut.
5. Broken piston return spring or air valve spring.

GENERAL SERVICE

Certain general service procedures apply, regardless of whether the brakes are vacuum or hydraulically assisted. Only top quality, clean brake fluid should be used. More seals and valves are used with power brake systems than with ordinary brakes, so an inferior brake fluid will do much more damage. For the same reason, ensure all dirt is kept out of the system. Additionally, on models with hydraulic assist brakes, care must be taken not to mix the fluids of the booster hydraulic system and brake hydraulic system as the fluids are not compatible.

If the power unit fails, the brakes will still operate, as the conventional brake system is left intact and a power unit is simply added to the existing system. Troubleshooting is then exactly the same up to the power unit. As with conventional hydraulic brakes, a spongy pedal with power brakes is caused by air in the system and grease on the linings will cause the brakes to grab. However, power brakes develop higher line pressure, thus making leaks more critical.

Do not immediately replace the power unit if the brakes grab. First look for all the usual causes, such as greasy linings or scored drums. If the hydraulic system is satisfactory, diagnosis of the power unit is required.

POWER BRAKE UNIT SERVICE

The power brake unit is not serviceable and must be replace as an assembly.

POWER BRAKE UNIT

REPLACE

Astro & Safari

Refer to "Avalanche, Escalade EXT, Sierra, Silverado & SSR" for procedure.

Aztek & Rendezvous

1. Remove coolant reservoir, then relieve fuel system pressure as outlined under "Precautions."
2. Remove cruise control cable from module, then disconnect electrical connector from cruise control module.
3. Remove cruise control module from bracket, then the front end sheet metal diagonal brace.
4. Remove PCM cover from air cleaner housing, then the PCM and set aside.
5. Remove air cleaner intake duct, then bolts from air cleaner assembly and housing.
6. Remove fuel lines from pipes and vapor line, then disconnect fluid level sensor switch from brake master cylinder.
7. Disconnect brake lines from master cylinder, then remove master cylinder.
8. Remove vacuum hose from vacuum check valve, reposition vacuum hose.
9. Remove brake lines from ABS module, then the ABS module and bracket.
10. Remove retaining clip and washer, then the brake booster push rod from brake pedal.
11. Remove mounting nuts, then the brake booster.
12. Reverse procedure to install, noting the following:
    a. **Torque** booster retaining nuts to 18 ft. lbs.
    b. **Torque** master cylinder retaining nuts to 18 ft. lbs.

Avalanche, Escalade EXT, Sierra, Silverado & SSR

1. Apply parking brake.
2. Remove master cylinder retaining nuts and bracket.
3. Pull master cylinder forward so it clears mounting studs and move to one side. Support cylinder to avoid stress on hydraulic lines.
4. Remove vacuum hose from check valve.
5. Remove stop lamp switch from brake pedal support.
6. Remove brake pedal pushrod retainer and disconnect pushrod from pin.
7. Remove booster to dash retaining nuts.
8. Remove booster from vehicle.
9. Reverse procedure to install, noting the following:
    a. **Torque** booster retaining nuts to 26 ft. lbs.
    b. **Torque** master cylinder retaining nuts to 20 ft. lbs.
    c. Bleed brake system as outlined in "Hydraulic Brake Systems" chapter.

Blazer, Bravada, Envoy, Jimmy, Rainier & Trailblazer

1. Apply parking brake.
2. Remove master cylinder mounting nuts.
3. Position and support master cylinder away from booster.
4. Disconnect vacuum hose from booster.
5. Remove lefthand closeout insulator panel as outlined in "Dash Panel Service" chapter.
6. Remove pushrod retainer and stop lamp switch from brake pedal.
7. **On models equipped with manual transmission,** remove pushrod from clutch pedal.
8. **On models except Envoy & TrailBlazer,** proceed as follows:
    a. Remove steering column support retaining nuts and bolts.
    b. Remove brake pedal from steering column support, then the support bracket from vehicle.
9. **On all models,** remove booster attaching nuts from inside of vehicle, then the booster.
10. Reverse procedure to install, noting the following:
    a. **Torque** steering column support retaining nuts and bolts to 18 ft. lbs.
    b. **Torque** booster attaching nuts to 30 ft. lbs.
    c. **Torque** master cylinder retaining nuts to 27 ft. lbs.
    d. **Torque** brake pipe fittings to 13 ft. lbs.
    e. Bleed brake system as outlined in "Hydraulic Brake Systems" chapter.

Canyon, Colorado, Sonoma & S10

Refer to "Blazer, Bravada, Envoy, Jimmy, Rainier & Trailblazer" for procedure.

Equinox & Torrent

Refer to "Blazer, Bravada, Envoy, Jimmy, Rainier & Trailblazer" for procedure.

Express & Savana

1. Remove brake pipes from master cylinder. Plug pipes to prevent fluid contamination.
2. Remove master cylinder attaching nuts and position master cylinder aside.

3. Disconnect stop lamp switch electrical connector.
4. Remove stop lamp switch retainer from brake pedal pin, then the stop lamp switch from brake pedal support.
5. Disconnect power brake unit pushrod from brake pedal.
6. Remove attaching nuts, then the power brake unit.
7. Reverse procedure to install.
   a. **Torque** booster retaining nuts to 27 ft. lbs.
   b. **Torque** master cylinder retaining nuts to 27 ft. lbs.
   c. **Torque** brake pipe fittings to 22 ft. lbs.
   d. Bleed brake system as outlined in "Hydraulic Brake Systems" chapter.

Escalade, Suburban, Tahoe & Yukon

Refer to "Avalanche, Escalade EXT, Sierra, Silverado & SSR" for procedure.

HHR

Refer to "Avalanche, Escalade EXT, Sierra, Silverado & SSR" for procedure.

Hummer H2

1. Disconnect rear and left front brake pipes from brake master cylinder.
2. Disconnect right front brake pipe from brake master cylinder.
3. Disconnect electrical connectors at brake pressure modulator valve and for fluid level sensor.
4. Remove knee bolster panel, then the bracket.
5. Remove clevis pin retainer from clevis pin, then the clevis pin from master cylinder push rod.
6. Remove mounting nuts, then the master cylinder assembly.
7. Remove power brake booster pump fluid accumulator fitting.
8. Hold brake master cylinder with power brake booster and chassis control module in a vise using tool No CH-47830 or equivalent.
9. Remove brake booster inlet and outlet hoses.
10. Remove plugs and retaining screws, then black negative wire and red positive wire.
11. Remove mounting bolts, then the brake booster pump.
12. Remove retainer ring for mounting bracket by breaking retaining ring for damper.
13. Remove mounting bracket.
14. Reverse procedure to install, noting the following:
    a. Install mounting bracket on hydraulic booster pump.
    b. Install NEW retainer ring.
    c. **Torque** brake booster pump bracket mounting bolts to 27 ft. lbs.

Hummer H3

Refer to "Avalanche, Escalade EXT, Sierra, Silverado & SSR" for procedure.

Montana, Silhouette & Venture

1. Remove air cleaner and duct assembly.
2. Remove vacuum hose from vacuum check valve and position aside.
3. Remove accelerator cable cross slug from throttle body slot.
4. Depress tangs and remove accelerator cable from accelerator cable bracket.
5. Remove accelerator cable bracket to throttle body attaching nuts and bolts.
6. Remove accelerator cable bracket from throttle body.
7. Drain cooling system.
8. Remove heater inlet hose from inlet pipe.
9. Remove heater inlet pipe mounting nut.
10. Remove inlet pipe from disconnect nipple, then the inlet pipe from vehicle.
11. Relieve fuel system pressure as follows:
    a. Loosen fuel filler cap to relieve tank vapor pressure.
    b. Connect fuel pressure gauge tool No. J 34730–1A, or equivalent, to fuel pressure connection on fuel rail. Wrap a shop towel around connection to prevent spillage.
    c. Insert bleed hose of fuel pressure gauge into a suitable container.
    d. Open valve and bleed system pressure.
12. Remove fuel line quick-connect fittings, then plug chassis fuel feed and return pipes to prevent fuel system contamination.
13. Disconnect vacuum lines from upper intake manifold.
14. Disconnect MAP sensor electrical connector, then remove MAP sensor from intake manifold.
15. Remove EGR valve pipe from exhaust manifold.
16. Remove EGR valve attaching bolts, then the EGR valve, gasket and valve pipe.
17. Remove spark plug wires.
18. Remove ignition control module attaching bolts and nuts, then the module from the intake manifold.
19. Remove upper intake manifold bolts and nuts.
20. Remove upper intake manifold and gasket.
21. Remove engine fuel return pipe from fuel pressure regulator.
22. Remove engine fuel feed pipe from fuel rail.
23. Perform "Gear Tension Relief Sequence" using a suitable scan tool.
24. Disconnect two brake solenoid valve electrical connectors.
25. Disconnect brake fluid level indicator sensor connector.
26. Disconnect ABS brake motor pack 6-way electrical connector.
27. Remove brake pipes from brake modulator/master cylinder assembly.
28. Remove brake modulator/master cylinder assembly to power booster retaining nuts.
29. Remove inlet radiator hose from engine.
30. Remove transaxle vacuum modulator pipe from transaxle.
31. Remove thermostat bypass hose.
32. Remove exhaust crossover heat shield bolts, then the crossover head shield.
33. Remove exhaust crossover pipe bolts, then the crossover pipe.
34. Remove transaxle fluid filler tube from transaxle.
35. Remove instrument panel insulator from under lefthand side of instrument panel.
36. Remove steering column opening filler panel from under steering column.
37. Remove instrument panel bracket.
38. Remove steering column mounting bolts.
39. Remove brake booster pushrod from brake pedal.
40. Remove brake booster mounting nuts, then the brake booster.
41. Reverse procedure to install, noting the following:
    a. **Torque** booster mounting nuts to 18 ft. lbs.
    b. **Torque** exhaust crossover pipe bolts to 18 ft. lbs.
    c. **Torque** exhaust crossover pipe heat shield bolts to 84 inch lbs.
    d. **Torque** brake modulator/master cylinder assembly attaching nuts to 20 ft. lbs.
    e. **Torque** brake pipe to brake modulator/master cylinder assembly nuts to 18 ft. lbs.
    f. Install new O-rings for fuel feed and return pipes.
    g. **Torque** upper intake manifold bolts and studs to 18 ft. lbs.
    h. **Torque** accelerator cable bracket nuts and bolts to 96 inch lbs.
    i. Bleed brake system as outlined in "Hydraulic Brake Systems" chapter.

Relay, Terraza, SV6 & Uplander

1. Relieve fuel system as outlined under "Relay, Terraza, SV6 & Uplander" chassis chapter.
2. Drain cooling system into a suitable container.
3. Remove hose from reservoir, the coolant recovery reservoir retainer and reservoir.
4. Remove left front cross brace, then the PCM cover from air cleaner housing.
5. Remove PCM and set aside, it is not required to disconnect electrical connector.
6. Loosen intake air duct clamps from air cleaner housing and throttle body.
7. Remove air cleaner intake duct from air cleaner housing and throttle bottle.
8. Remove fuel feed pipe retaining clip,

then disconnect engine fuel feed pipe from fuel rail.

9. Disconnect EVAP pipe from EVAP canister purge solenoid valve. Cap fuel pipes as needed to stop any fuel leakage.
10. Remove heater hose from coolant cross over pipe and reposition out of way.
11. Unclip fuel lines from shock tower for easier access to brake pipes.
12. Disconnect fluid level sensor switch and brake lines from brake master cylinder, then remove master cylinder.
13. Remove brake modulator assembly as outlined under "Anti-Lock Brake Systems" chapter, then the bracket.
14. Remove brake booster vacuum hose from vacuum brake booster check valve. Reposition vacuum hose.
15. Remove driver side knee bolster, then the booster push pin retaining clip and washer from brake pedal assembly.
16. Remove brake booster push rod from brake pedal.
17. Remove brake booster mounting nuts, then the nuts from engine mount struts at right and left engine mount strut brackets on engine.
18. Remove bolts and nuts from engine mount struts at engine mount strut brackets on upper radiator support, then the engine mount struts.
19. Rotate engine forward to gain access to brake booster removal.
20. Remove brake booster from vehicle.
21. Reverse procedure to install noting the following:
    a. When replacing power booster brake, ensure that cruise control cable is not routed between booster and cowl.
    b. **Torque** booster mounting nuts to 18 ft. lbs.
    c. **Torque** brake master cylinder assembly attaching nuts to 21 ft. lbs.
    d. **Torque** brake pipe to brake master cylinder assembly to 24 ft. lbs.

SRX

1. Remove left closeout/insulator panel, then the vacuum brake booster push rod retaining clip.
2. Remove vacuum brake booster pushrod from brake pedal.
3. Remove cross vehicle brace, **it is not required to disconnect brake pipes from master cylinder.**
4. Remove master cylinder from vacuum brake booster and position master cylinder aside.
5. Remove air inlet grille panel, to access vacuum brake booster locking tab.
6. **It is not required to drain coolant or disconnect surge tank outlet hose from surge tank.**
7. Disconnect surge tank inlet hose and position out of way.
8. Remove coolant surge tank bolts and position coolant surge tank out of way.
9. Connect surge tank inlet hose to prevent coolant loss.
10. Disconnect vacuum brake booster check valve from vacuum brake booster and position out of way.
11. Attach tool No. J–22805-B or equivalent, to vacuum brake booster using master cylinder mounting nuts.
12. Unlock vacuum brake booster from front of cowl. Use a flat bladed tool to depress vacuum brake booster locking tab out of cowl mounting flange, while turning vacuum brake booster counter clockwise with a ratchet on tool.
13. Carefully remove vacuum brake booster from cowl mounting flange.
14. Support vacuum brake booster, then push vacuum brake booster foam filter in enough to access vacuum brake booster retaining clip.
15. Carefully lift longer leg of retaining clip upward, then remove pushrod from vacuum brake booster.
16. Reverse procedure to install.

Vue

1. Disconnect , then remove battery and underhood fuse block cover.
2. Remove positive battery cable electronic power steering wire from underhood fuse block.
3. Open all retainer clips, then remove all cables, lines and harnesses from battery cooling box.
4. Remove retainers, then disconnect electrical connectors, pull out ducts and box.
5. Disconnect coolant surge hose from surge tank and position aside.
6. Remove master cylinder mounting nuts, do not disconnect brake pipes from master cylinder.
7. Pull master cylinder away from vacuum booster and position aside.
8. Release retaining clamp, then remove vacuum hose from vacuum port on engine.
9. Remove check valve and hose from brake booster, then the transaxle control module and position over engine.
10. Remove brake modulator assembly as outlined under "Anti-Lock Brake Systems" chapter, then the bracket.
11. Remove brake booster push rod to brake pedal retaining clip, then the foam washer from brake pedal assembly.
12. Remove brake booster mounting nuts. **Ensure that foam insulator on mounting surface of brake booster withdraws with booster.**
13. Disengage brake booster from front of dash and brake pedal bracket, then remove from vehicle.
14. Reverse procedure to install. **Torque** brake booster and master cylinder mounting bolts to 18 ft. lbs.

Tracker Brake Booster

INDEX

DESCRIPTION

Vacuum assist units are similar in operation, using vacuum applied to a diaphragm or piston in opposition to atmospheric pressure in order to increase the force applied to the master cylinder piston. However, two types of vacuum assist assemblies are used, the air suspended type and the vacuum suspended type. Air suspended units are under atmospheric pressure until the brakes are applied, then engine vacuum is admitted causing the piston or diaphragm to move and apply force to the master cylinder pushrod. Vacuum suspended types are balanced with engine vacuum until the brake pedal is depressed, allowing atmospheric pressure to unbalance the unit and apply force to the brake system.

This unit uses a single vacuum diaphragm with an effective diameter of 7 inches to mechanically increase brake application force with engine vacuum.

The diaphragm and plate assemblies use the pressure differential created by engine vacuum and atmospheric pressure to assist in applying the master cylinder pushrod.

POWER BRAKE UNIT

REPLACE

Removal

1. Remove fluid from reservoir using a syringe.
2. **On models equipped with anti-lock brakes,** proceed as follows:
   a. Remove three-way joint attaching bolt and position joint aside.
   b. Remove two brake pipe flare nuts, then disconnect brake pipes from master cylinder. Plug lines.
3. **On models not equipped with anti-lock brakes,** remove three flare nuts and disconnect three brake fluid lines from master cylinder assembly. Plug lines.
4. **On all models,** disconnect fluid level switch electrical connector.
5. Remove two master cylinder attaching nuts and washers, then the master cylinder from booster.
6. Disconnect vacuum hose from brake booster, **Fig. 1.**
7. Remove cotter pin and clevis pin from brake pedal pushrod clevis.
8. **On models equipped with anti-lock brakes,** remove brake modulator assembly as follows:
   a. Perform "Gear Tension Relief" procedure with a suitable programmed scan tool.
   b. Disconnect motor pack, ABS solenoid and shuttle switch electrical connectors.
   c. Place a shop towel below modulator brake pipes to prevent fluid from contaminating motor pack or electrical connectors.
   d. Disconnect brake pipes from modulator and shutter valves. Plug pipes.
   e. Remove modulator assembly mounting bolts, then the modulator and motor pack from vehicle.
9. **On all models,** remove power unit retaining nuts from bulkhead, then the power unit.

Installation

1. Measure pushrod clevis length, **Fig. 2,** then install pushrod clevis so correct length of 4.96–5.00 inches is obtained. **Torque** clevis locknut to 19 ft. lbs.
2. Adjust booster piston rod to master cylinder piston clearance as follows:
   a. Push booster piston rod several times to ensure reaction disc is in place.
   b. Set booster piston rod height gauge tool No. J 39567, or equivalent, on master cylinder, **Fig. 3.**
   c. Push gauge tool downward until pin touches master cylinder piston, then remove tool from master cylinder.
   d. Turn gauge tool upside down and set it on booster, then measure clearance between pin and booster piston rod, **Fig. 4.**
   e. **On 2-door models less anti-lock brakes** clearance should be .01–.02 inch.
   f. **On 2-door models with anti-lock brakes and all 4-door models,** clearance should be .060–.014 inch.
   g. **On all models,** if clearance is not within specifications, hold booster piston rod in place with pushrod adjustment tool No. J 37767, or equivalent, then turn adjustment nut until correct clearance is reached, **Fig. 5.**
3. Apply suitable silicone grease to master cylinder piston.
4. Install brake booster to bulkhead, but do not tighten nuts at this time.
5. **On models equipped with anti-lock brakes,** install brake modulator as follows:
   a. Install brake modulator/motor pack to vehicle and **torque** retaining bolts to 48 inch lbs.
   b. Install brake pipes and **torque** nuts to 11 ft. lbs.
   c. Connect motor pack, ABS solenoids and shuttle valve switch electrical connectors.
6. **On all models,** attach pushrod clevis to brake pedal with clevis pin, then install cotter pin.
7. **Torque** booster assembly retaining nuts to 115 inch lbs.
8. Install master cylinder with new gasket, **torque** master cylinder mounting nuts to 115 inch lbs.
9. Connect brake pipes and **torque** flare nuts to 12 ft. lbs.
10. **On models equipped with anti-lock brakes,** install three-way joint to master cylinder.
11. **On all models,** connect battery ground cable and bleed brake hydraulic system as outlined in "Hydraulic Brake Systems" chapter.

POWER BRAKE UNIT SERVICE

The power brake unit is not serviceable and must be replace as an assembly.

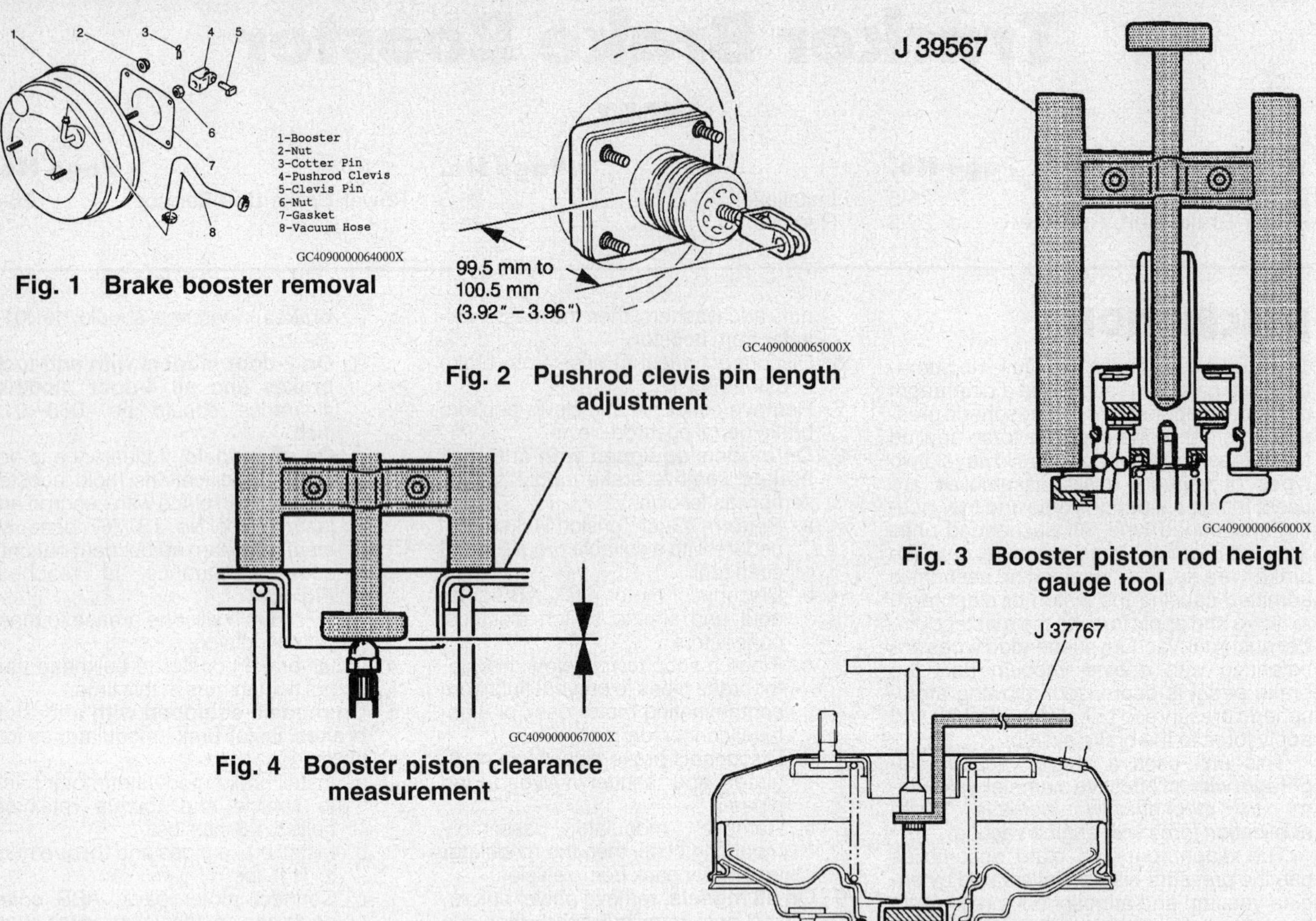

Fig. 1 Brake booster removal

Fig. 2 Pushrod clevis pin length adjustment

Fig. 3 Booster piston rod height gauge tool

Fig. 4 Booster piston clearance measurement

Fig. 5 Booster piston clearance adjustment

VACUUM PUMPS

INDEX

PRECAUTIONS

Battery Ground Cable

Prior to service, disconnect battery ground cable and isolate as required.

DESCRIPTION

These vehicles use a belt driven vacuum pump to either aid the engine or operate independently to maintain a proper vacuum level for the power brake system, emission controls or other vacuum powered accessories.

DIAGNOSIS & TESTING

1. Block wheels, apply parking brake, and place gear shift lever in Park or Neutral.
2. Connect vacuum gauge to vacuum pump inlet (lower port).
3. Disconnect outlet hose from outlet tube (upper port) and plug end of hose. **Do not plug vacuum pump outlet tube.**
4. Start engine and run at idle. Vacuum should read as indicated within 30 seconds, **Fig. 1.**
5. If vacuum is below specification, or gauge reading fluctuates, proceed as follows:
   a. Inspect gauge and connections for leaks, correcting as required.
   b. Inspect belt tension and pulley fit to pump, repairing or replacing as required.
   c. Inspect idle speed and correct as required.
   d. If vacuum is still below specifications or gauge still fluctuates, replace vacuum pump and repeat procedure.
6. If vacuum is within specifications, proceed as follows:
   a. Remove plug from outlet hose and connect hose to pump outlet tube.
   b. Connect vacuum inlet hose to pump with a T-fitting and vacuum gauge located near pump inlet.
   c. Start engine and run at idle for one minute.
   d. If vacuum is three inches Hg lower than original reading, vacuum pump is not faulty.
   e. If vacuum is more than three inches Hg lower than original reading, inspect all attaching hoses for leaks, correcting as required.
   f. If vacuum is still too low, inspect all vacuum accessories for leaks, repairing or replacing as required.

VACUUM PUMP

REPLACE

Removal

1. Disconnect vacuum hose.
2. Loosen and remove vacuum pump belt.
3. Remove vacuum pump pulley to hub attaching bolt.
4. Remove pump from mounting bracket on engine.
5. Remove hub from pump, using pump pulley removal tool No. J25034-B, or equivalent. **Hub must be used on replacement unit.**

Installation

1. Press vacuum pump pulley onto pump as follows:
   a. Place vacuum pump in vise.
   b. Attach pulley installer tool No. J25033-B, or equivalent, to pulley.
   c. Install pulley onto vacuum pump.
   d. Remove installation tool from pulley and install pulley to hub attaching bolt.
   e. Remove pump from vise.
2. Install pump to mounting bracket on engine.
3. Connect vacuum hose to pump.
4. Install vacuum pump belt and adjust belt tension.

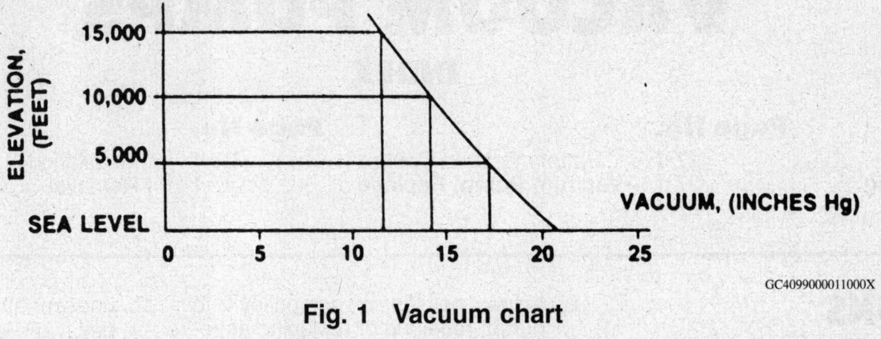

Fig. 1 Vacuum chart

TRANSFER CASES

TABLE OF CONTENTS

Application Chart

Year	Transfer Case	RPO	
		Code	Description
ASTRO & SAFARI			
2002–05	New Venture Gear (NVG) 136	NP4	Transfer Case—Active, All Wheel Drive (AWD)
AVALANCHE, ESCALADE, SUBURBAN, TAHOE & YUKON			
2002	New Venture Gear (NVG) 236/246	NP8	Transfer Case—(Active) — Push Button Control, Two-Speed
2003–05	New Venture Gear (NVG) 246 (Two-Speed Automatic)	NP8	Transfer Case—(Active) — Push Button Control, Two-Speed
	Borg-Warner (BW) 4482	NR4	Transfer Case—4 Wheel Drive (4WD), Open Differential, Two-Speed
2006	New Venture Gear (NVG) 246	NP8	Transfer Case—(Active) — Push Button Control, Two-Speed
	Borg-Warner (BW) 4481	NR3	Transfer Case—All Wheel Drive (AWD), Open Differential, Single Speed
	Borg-Warner (BW) 4482	NR4	Transfer Case—4 Wheel Drive (4WD), Open Differential, Two-Speed
AZTEK & RENDEZVOUS			
2002–06	Steyr	M76	Transmission—Auto Four-Speed, HMD, 4T65-E PTU, O/D
BLAZER, JIMMY, SONOMA & S10			
2002–05	New Venture Gear (NVG) 233	MP1	Transfer Case—Electric Shift Control, Two-Speed
	New Venture Gear (NVG) 236	NP8	Transfer Case—Active, Two-Speed, Push Button Control
BRAVADA, ENVOY, RAINIER & TRAILBLAZER			
2002	New Venture Gear (NVG) 226	NP8	Transfer Case—Active, Two Speed, Push Button Control
2003–04	New Venture Gear (NVG) 126	NP4	Transfer Case—Active, All Wheel Drive (AWD)
	New Venture Gear (NVG) 226	NP8	Transfer Case—Active, Two Speed, Push Button Control
2004–05	New Venture Gear (NVG) 226	NP8	Transfer Case—Active, Two Speed, Push Button Control
2006	New Venture Gear (NVG) 120	NR9	Transfer Case—All Wheel Drive (AWD), Open Diff, Torque Biased Single Speed
	New Venture Gear (NVG) 126	NP4	Transfer Case—Active, All Wheel Drive (AWD)
	New Venture Gear (NVG) 226	NP8	Transfer Case—Active, Two Speed, Push Button Control
CANYON & COLORADO			
2004–06	Isuzu T150	NP1	Transfer Case—Electric Shift Control, Two-Speed
EQUINOX & TORRENT			
2005–06	New Venture Gear (NVG) 900	—	—
EXPRESS & SAVANA			
2003–06	Borg-Warner (BW) 4473	NP3	Transfer Case—One Speed Automatic All Wheel Drive (AWD)

Continued

Year	Transfer Case	RPO Code	RPO Description
HUMMER H2			
2003–06	Borg-Warner (BW) 4484	NR4	Transfer Case—BW 4484 Two-Speed full time 4WD
HUMMER H3			
2006	Borg-Warner (BW) 4493/4494	NR4	Transfer Case—Four Wheel Drive (4WD) Open Diff, Two Speed
		NR6	Transfer Case—Four Wheel Drive (4WD) Open Diff, Two Speed, High Ratio
MONTANA, SILHOUETTE & VENTURE			
2002–05	Steyr	M76	Transmission—Auto Four-Speed, HMD, 4T65-E PTU, O/D
RELAY, SV6, TERRAZA & UPLANDER			
2005–06	Steyr	M76	Transmission—Auto Four-Speed, HMD, 4T65-E PTU, O/D
SIERRA & SILVERADO			
2002–06	New Venture Gear (NVG) 149	NP3	Transfer Case—All-Wheel Drive (AWD)
	New Venture Gear (NVG) 236/246	NP8	Transfer Case—(Active) — Push Button Control, Two-Speed
	New Venture Gear (NVG) 261	NP2	Transfer Case—(Manual) — Full Range
	New Venture Gear (NVG) 263	NP1	Transfer Case—(Electric) — Full Range
SRX			
2004–06	Borg-Warner (BW) 4476/79	MV3	Transmission—AUTO Five-Speed, HMD< 5L50-E PTU, Electronic, O/D
		MX5	Transmission—AUTO Five-Speed, HMD, 5L40-E PTU, O/D
		MX7	Merchandised TRANS—AUTO Provisions, O/D, All Wheel Drive
TRACKER			
2002–04	Tracker Transfer Case	—	—
VUE			
2002–03	New Venture Gear (NVG) 900	M16	Transmission—Continuously Variable Ratio, GM, X15F-PTU Electronic
2004–06	New Venture Gear (NVG) 900	M16	Transmission—Continuously Variable Ratio, GM, X15F-PTU, VT25-E AWD, Electronic
	Honda AWD Transfer Case	MJ8	Transmission—Auto Five-Speed, Honda, 5AT, PTU

Borg-Warner 4473

INDEX

DISASSEMBLE

1. Mount holding fixture tool No. J3289-20, or equivalent, to suitable, sturdy workbench.
2. Attach assembly fixture tool No. J45759, or equivalent, to transfer case, then the assembly to holding fixture.
3. Remove drain plug and drain fluid into suitable container, **Fig. 1.**
4. Remove front input shaft seal using suitable flat-tipped screwdriver and pry inner seal race forward.
5. Remove inner seal race from front input shaft using suitable, small pry bar.
6. Remove front output shaft seal using suitable flat-tipped screwdriver or small pry bar between lip of outer lip of front output shaft seal and transfer case. **Front output shaft seal is two-piece internal seal, force fit.**
7. Remove remaining part of front output shaft seal from transfer case.
8. Remove Vehicle Speed Sensor (VSS) with O-ring seal.
9. Remove rear output shaft seal by prying out with suitable, flat-blade screwdriver.
10. Remove transfer case mounting bolts and washers,
11. Mark bracket locations for assembly alignment.
12. Shear case halves sealer using case spreader tool No. J45358, or equivalent, between case halves tabs.
13. Remove case from locating pins using suitable pry bars at each side.
14. Remove rear case half from front case half. Rear output shaft will come out with rear case half.
15. Remove thrust washer and planetary carrier.
16. Remove sun gear thrust washer and front input shaft.
17. If front output shaft cup plug is leaking, remove it using suitable brass drift.
18. Mark chain to sprockets relationship for assembly alignment, **Fig. 2.**
19. Remove chain with driven sprocket.
20. Remove sun gear with drive gear and viscous coupling by lifting sun gear up while tapping down on input shaft with suitable soft-face hammer.
21. Remove sun gear bearing using rear pinion and axle bearing remover tool No. J22912-01, or equivalent, and suitable hydraulic press.
22. Remove drive gear and viscous coupling from sun gear.
23. Remove input shaft from front case.
24. Remove seal using output shaft oil seal remover tool No. J36825 and slide hammer with bearing adapter tool No. J23907, or equivalents.
25. Remove front output shaft bearing from front case half using a brass drift.
26. Remove front case half vent.
27. Spread outer retaining ring and remove rear output shaft rear bearing using suitable soft-face hammer tapped on shaft end.
28. Remove retaining ring and rear output shaft from annulus gear.

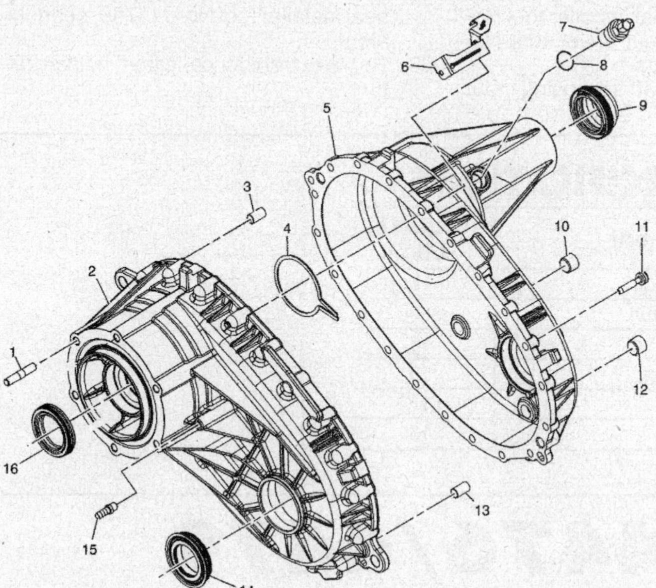

1. Adapter Stud
2. Front Case Half
3. Locating Pin
4. Rear Output Shaft Bearing Out Retaining Ring
5. Rear Case Half
6. Wiring Harness Bracket
7. Vehicle Speed Sensor (VSS)
8. VSS O-Ring
9. Rear Output Shaft Seal
10. Oil Fill Plug
11. Case Half Bolt
12. Oil Drain Plug
13. Locating Pin'
14. Front Output Shaft Seal
15. Vent
16. Input Shaft Seal

LTV0500000001565

Fig. 1 Exploded view of case components

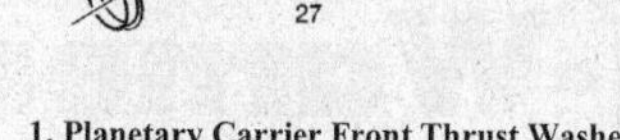

1. Planetary Carrier Front Thrust Washer
2. Planetary Pinion Gear Thrust Washer
3. Planetary Pinion Gear
4. Planetary Pinion Gear Thrust Washer
5. Planetary Pinion Gear Shaft
6. Planetary Carrier Rear Thrust Washer
7. Input Shaft Rear Support Bearing
8. Rear Output Shaft
9. Annulus Gear
10. Annulus Gear Retaining Ring
11. Rear Output Shaft Bearing
12. Rear Output Shaft Bearing Retaining Ring
13. Speed Reluctor Wheel
14. Rear Output Shaft Shipping Seal
15. Sun Gear Bushing
16. Sun Gear
17. Viscous Coupling
18. Drive Sprocket
19. Driven Sprocket
20. Front Output Shaft
21. Front Output Shaft Cup Plug
22. Front Output Shaft Rear Bearing
23. Drive Chain
24. Front Output Shaft Front Bearing
25. Sun Gear Bearing
26. Oil Restrictor
27. Input Shaft
28. Input Shaft Bushing
29. Oil Scoop

LTV0500000001566

Fig. 2 Exploded view of internal components

29. If rear output shaft bearing is faulty, remove it using bearing remover tool No. J45849, or equivalent.
30. Remove retaining ring for rear output shaft bearing and speed reluctor wheel.
31. Remove speed reluctor wheel and rear output shaft bearing using axle bearing remover tool No. J22912-01, or equivalent, and suitable hydraulic press. Discard speed reluctor wheel.
32. Remove front output shaft rear bearing from rear case, using 3–4 inch bushing and bearing remove tool No. J26941, or equivalent, and slide hammer with bearing adapter.

ASSEMBLE

Lubricate all bearings and bearing journals with suitable transfer case fluid during installation.

1. Install and tighten transfer case mounting studs.
2. Mount holding fixture tool No. J3289-20, or equivalent, to suitable, sturdy workbench.
3. Attach assembly fixture tool No. J45759, or equivalent, to transfer case, then the assembly to holding fixture.
4. Apply suitable pipe sealant to threads and install vent.
5. Install front output shaft rear bearing in rear case half using suitable hammer and brass drift on outer bearing race. Ensure bearing is kept square to bore.
6. Install input shaft bushing in front case half using input sun gear ball bearing installer tool No. J36373, or equivalent, and suitable hammer.
7. Install front output shaft front bearing in front case half using suitable hammer and brass drift on outer bearing race. Ensure bearing is kept square to bore.
8. Install input shaft rear support bearing in rear output shaft using bearing installer tool No. J45848 and non-threaded universal driver handle tool No. J42176, or equivalents.
9. Install rear output shaft bearing with retaining ring groove towards gear using input and countershaft race installer tool No. J22828, or equivalent, and suitable hydraulic press.
10. Install new speed reluctor wheel using input and countershaft race installer tool No. J22828, or equivalent, and suitable hydraulic press.
11. Install new rear output shaft bearing retaining ring and rear output shaft in annulus gear.
12. Install new annulus gear retaining ring.
13. Spread rear output shaft rear bearing outer retaining ring and install rear output shaft in rear case using suitable soft-face hammer to tap shaft. Ensure retaining ring is in groove.
14. Install input shaft in front case and viscous coupling on sun gear.
15. Install drive gear on sun gear.
16. Install bearing on sun gear using tone ring and bearing installer tool No. J45540 and rear pinion bearing race installer tool No. J5590, or equivalents. and suitable hammer. Ensure bearing is fully seated against drive gear.
17. Install sun gear with drive gear and viscous coupling, on input gear.
18. If shaft is new or if cup plug was removed, install cup plug in front output shaft using suitable driver. Cup plug should be .039 inch from flush with end of shaft.
19. **Ensure to align marks of drive chain and sprockets.**
20. Install drive chain with blue link facing up and alignment disassembly marks.
21. Install driven sprocket and chain.
22. Install front output shaft in driven sprocket and bearing.
23. Lubricate sun gear thrust washer with suitable transjel transmission assembly lubricant. Install sun gear thrust washer.
24. Install planetary carrier and thrust washer lubricated with suitable transjel transmission assembly lubricant.
25. Install front case locating pins.
26. Apply ⅛ inch bead of suitable Room Temperature Vulcanizing (RTV) sealant to front case half mating surfaces.
27. Lower rear case half into place, then install bolts, washers and brackets. Tighten mounting bolts.
28. Install rear output shaft seal using rear output shaft seal installer tool No. J45756, or equivalent.
29. Install VSS with new O-ring seal. Tighten VSS.

30. Apply suitable pipe sealant to threads, then install and tighten drain and fill plugs.
31. Install front output shaft seal using front output shaft seal installer tool No. J43484 and universal driver tool No. J8092, or equivalents.
32. Install front input shaft seal using input seal installer tool No. J45758, or equivalent.
33. Remove transfer case from holding fixture.

TIGHTENING SPECIFICATIONS

Year	Component	Torque/Ft. Lbs.
2003–06	Case, Bolt	15
	Case, Stud	89①
	Drain Plug	18
	Fill Plug	18
	Vent	53①
	VSS	13

① — Inch Lbs.

Borg-Warner 4476/4479

INDEX

DISASSEMBLE

1. Remove mounting bolts and dampener, **Fig. 1.**
2. Remove drain and fill plugs, then drain fluid into suitable container.
3. Remove case mounting bolts, then separate case and cover apart using suitable screwdriver at pry points. Remove alignment dowel.
4. Remove chain snubber.
5. Install split plate set tool No. DT-47752, or equivalent, perpendicular to chain and rotate tool 180°.
6. Install second split plate perpendicular to chain and secure with short plate bolts.
7. Install split plate and two jaw puller tool No. J8433, or equivalent, onto front output shaft.
8. Install split plate set tool No. DT-47752-3, or equivalent, into input shaft.
9. Remove sprockets, chain and carrier using split plate set tool No. DT-47752-2, or equivalent, and impact wrench, **Fig. 2.**
10. Remove special tools.
11. Record blue chain link position for assembly alignment.
12. Remove lower sprocket, chain and carrier as an assembly.
13. Remove snap ring and push front output shaft from case.
14. Remove mounting bolt and vent baffle.
15. Remove front output and input seals from case using suitable hammer and driver.
16. **Only remove bearing that must be replaced.**
17. Remove front output and input bearings using suitable hammer and punch.
18. Remove and discard vent.
19. Remove carrier thrust washer.
20. Remove input shaft from carrier using suitable press.
21. Remove carrier direction for assembly alignment. Groove around 50/50 and 40/60 ratios splines face towards output shaft.
22. Remove sun gear from ear output shaft using universal two-jaw puller tool No. J22888-20A and side bearing puller pilot tool No. J8107-2, or equivalent.
23. Remove output shaft snap ring using suitable snap ring pliers.
24. Push output shaft from cover.
25. Drive out rear output seal and outside output bearing from inside cover using suitable hammer and punch.
26. Drive out inner output shaft bearing from outside cover and output shaft bore using suitable hammer and punch.
27. Remove front output cover bearing from cover using bushing and bearing remover tool No. J29369-1 and slide hammer with adapter tool No. J-2619-A, or equivalents.

ASSEMBLE

Lubricate all bearings and bearing journals with suitable transfer case fluid.

1. Install input shaft bearing into case using suitable hammer and brass driver on outer bearing race. Ensure bearing is kept square to bore.
2. Install front output shaft bearing into case.
3. Install input shaft oil seal using input seal installer tool No. J46269 and driver handle tool No. J8092, or equivalents.
4. Install front output shaft oil seal using output seal installer tool No. J46268 and driver handle tool No. J8092, or equivalents.
5. Install chain snubber, then apply suitable sealant to threads and tighten bolts.
6. Install vent baffle, then apply suitable sealant to threads and tighten bolt.
7. With planetary differential thrust washer side facing down, align pinion gears marks, **Fig. 3.** Position alignment marks with planetary differential area that can be reference for all gears.
8. Input shaft must be installed to carrier with raised bosses facing up and thrust washer groove facing down.
9. Press input shaft to carrier.
10. Lubricate and install thrust washer over input shaft rear into carrier groove.
11. Install sun gear into carrier. Ensure carrier rotates freely.
12. Remove sun gear from carrier.
13. Install front output shaft to case and snap ring.
14. Install chain, upper planetary gear and lower sprocket to case.
15. Press to fully seat lower sprocket to front output shaft using rear pinion bearing race installer tool No. J5590, or equivalent, while guiding planetary input shaft until it is seated to case.
16. Install rear output shaft bearing using suitable hammer and brass drift only on outer bearing race. Ensure bearing is kept square to bore.
17. Install the rear output oil seal using output seal installer tool J46268 and driver handle tool No. J8092, or equivalents.

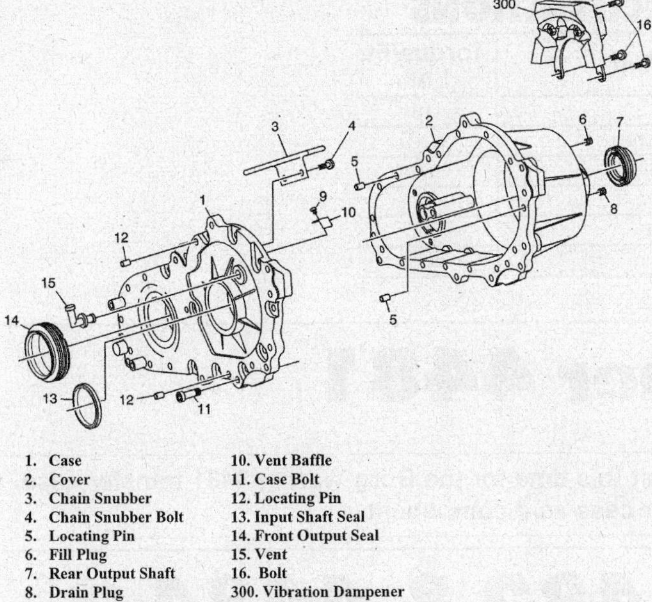

1. Case
2. Cover
3. Chain Snubber
4. Chain Snubber Bolt
5. Locating Pin
6. Fill Plug
7. Rear Output Shaft
8. Drain Plug
9. Vent Baffle Bolt
10. Vent Baffle
11. Case Bolt
12. Locating Pin
13. Input Shaft Seal
14. Front Output Seal
15. Vent
16. Bolt
300. Vibration Dampener

LTV0500000001567

Fig. 1 Exploded view of case components

18. Install inner output shaft bearing using suitable hammer and brass drift only on outer bearing race. Ensure bearing is kept square to bore.
19. Install front output shaft bearing using suitable hammer and brass drift only on outer bearing race. Ensure bearing is kept square to bore.
20. Install rear output shaft by pushing it in through bearings.
21. Install rear output shaft snap ring in output shaft lower groove.
22. Install sun gear to output shaft. Use pinion cone and side bearing installer tool No. J24433, or equivalent, and suitable press.
23. Install cover dowel pins.
24. Apply ⅛ inch bead of suitable RTV sealant to cover mating surfaces.
25. Lower cover over case. Turn rear output shaft to align splines and shaft into cover bearing.
26. Hand start mounting bolts. **Do NOT use power-assisted tools to install bolts.**
27. Tighten case bolts in criss-cross pattern.
28. Install vent breather by pushing it into hole. Align vent and case flats.
29. Apply suitable pipe sealant to threads, then install and tighten drain plug.
30. Fill transfer case with suitable fluid. Apply suitable pipe sealant to threads, then install and tighten fill plug.
31. Install dampener and tighten mounting bolts.

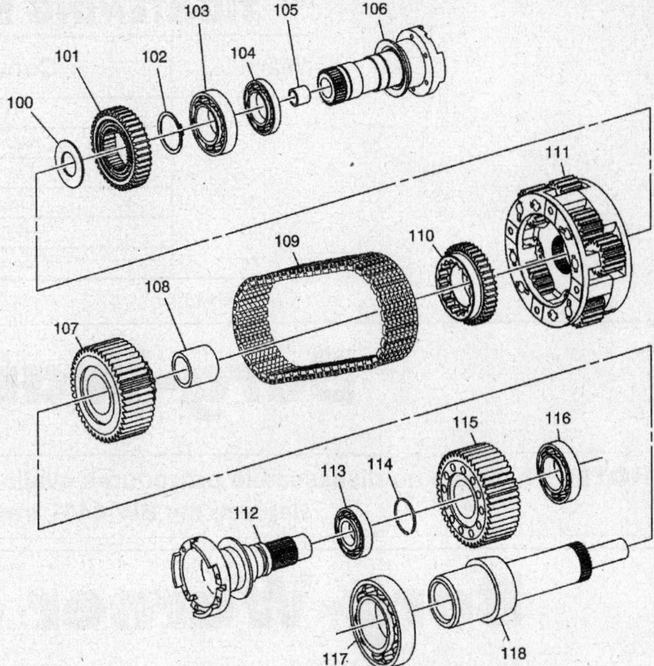

100. Thrust Washer
101. Sun Gear
102. Rear Output Shaft Snap Ring
103. Rear Output Shaft Bearing
104. Rear Output Shaft Bearing
105. Rear Output Shaft Bushing
106. Rear Output Shaft
107. Upper Sprocket
108. Upper Sprocket Bushing
109. Chain
110. Sun Gear
111. Carrier
112. Front Output Shaft
113. Front Output Shaft Bearing
114. Front Output Shaft Snap Ring
115. Lower Sprocket
116. Front Output Shaft Bearing
117. Input Shaft Bearing
118. Input Shaft

LTV0500000001568

Fig. 2 Exploded view of internal components

LTV0500000001569

Fig. 3 Pinion gear marks

TIGHTENING SPECIFICATIONS

Year	Component	Torque/Ft. Lbs.
2004–06	Case	18
	Chain Snubber	62①
	Dampener	20
	Drain Plug	18
	Fill Plug	18
	Vent Baffle	62①

① — Inch Lbs.

Borg-Warner 4481

NOTE: There are no disassemble procedures available at this time for the Borg-Warner 4481 transfer case. Replace the BW 4481 transfer case as a component.

Borg-Warner 4482 & 4484

INDEX

DISASSEMBLE

1. Mount holding fixture tool No. J3289-20, or equivalent, to suitable, sturdy workbench.
2. Attach assembly fixture tool No. J45759, or equivalent, to transfer case, then the assembly to holding fixture.
3. Remove drain and fill plugs, then drain fluid into suitable container, **Figs. 1 and 2.**
4. Remove front output shaft seal by inserting suitable screwdriver behind inner race of seal and pry it forward.
5. Move inner seal race forward on front output shaft using suitable small pry bar.
6. Remove inner seal race from front output shaft. **Front output shaft seal is two-piece internal seal that is force fit on front output shaft.**
7. Insert suitable screwdriver or small pry bar between outer lip of front output shaft seal and transfer case.
8. Remove remaining part of front output shaft seal from transfer case.
9. Remove bracket bolt and mounting bolts, then the encoder motor.
10. Remove Vehicle Speed Sensor (VSS) and O-ring seal.
11. Remove rear output shaft seal by prying it out using suitable flat-balded screwdriver.
12. Remove shipping seal from rear output shaft.
13. Remove transfer case mounting bolts and washers. Mark bracket location of assembly alignment.
14. Shear case halves sealer using case spreader tool No. J45358, or equivalent.
15. Remove case from locating pins using suitable pry bars at each side.
16. Remove rear from front case half. Rear output shaft will come with rear case half.
17. Remove shift fork shaft spring.
18. Remove rear sun gear, **Figs. 3 and 4.**
19. Remove rear output shaft thrust washer.
20. Remove planetary differential.
21. Remove front sun gear.
22. Remove chain with drive and driven sprockets. **Mark chain to sprockets relationship for assembly alignment.**
23. Remove drive sprocket thrust washer.
24. Remove lockup shift and mode shift fork. Remove fork from lockup shift.
25. If lockup shift disassembly is required, proceed as follows:
    a. Remove sleeve retainer.
    b. Remove hub.
    c. Remove spring.
26. Remove inner lockup hub and magnet.
27. Remove oil pump with hose and screen.
28. Disconnect oil pump hose from oil pump screen and oil pump.
29. Remove shift fork shaft.
30. Rotate high/low shift fork roller from shift detent lever.
31. Lift straight up and remove shift detent lever. **Do not allow shift detent lever to tilt.**
32. If shift detent lever disassembly is required, proceed as follows:
    a. Hold shift detent lever by one spring tab in suitable vise.
    b. Rotate other spring tab and slide detent lever cam off shaft.
    c. Remove sleeve.
    d. Push shaft out of spring,
33. Remove mainshaft.
34. Remove high/low range sleeve with high/low range shift fork.
35. Remove range shift fork from range shift sleeve, then the input shaft thrust washer.
36. Remove high/low planetary carrier.
37. Remove mainshaft front support bearing from planetary carrier using suitable brass drift and hammer.
38. Remove front output shaft.
39. If cup plug in front output shaft is leaking, remove plug using suitable brass drift.
40. Remove input seal using suitable hammer and punch.
41. Remove input shaft bearing from front case half using suitable hammer and brass drift.
42. Remove front output shaft bearing from front case half using suitable brass drift.
43. Remove retaining ring and annulus gear from front case half.
44. Remove front case half vent and rear output shaft from rear case half.
45. Spread retaining ring and remove rear output shaft rear bearing by taping end using suitable soft-face hammer.
46. Tap on end of rear output shaft, then remove.
47. Remove speed reluctor wheel using rear pinion and axle bearing remover tool No. J22912-01, or equivalent, and suitable hydraulic press. Discard reluctor wheel.

48. Remove retaining ring then the rear output shaft bearing using suitable hydraulic press.
49. Remove mainshaft rear support bushing from rear output shaft using slide hammer tool No. J2619-01 and mainshaft support bushing/bearing remover tool No. J45548, or equivalents.
50. Remove front output shaft rear bearing from rear case using 3–4 inch bushing and bearing remover tool No. J26941 and slide hammer with bearing adapter tool No. J23907, or equivalents.
51. Remove seal for shift detent lever shaft seal by prying it out from case.

ASSEMBLE

1. Install and tighten transfer case mounting studs.
2. Mount holding fixture tool No. J3289-20, or equivalent, to suitable, sturdy workbench.
3. Attach assembly fixture tool No. J45759, or equivalent, to transfer case, then the assembly to holding fixture.
4. Install shift detent lever shaft seal using hand pressure. Spring side or opened side of seal faces outward.
5. Apply suitable pipe sealant to threads, then install and tighten vent.
6. Install annulus gear in front case half and new retaining ring.
7. Lubricate all bearings and journals with suitable transfer case fluid.
8. Install input shaft bearing in front case half using suitable hammer and brass drift only on outer bearing race. Ensure bearing is kept square to bore.
9. Install front bearing for front output shaft front bearing in front case halfsoling suitable hammer and brass drift only on outer bearing race. Ensure bearing is kept square to bore.
10. If using new shaft or if cup plug was removed, apply suitable threadlocker then install cup plug in front output shaft cup plug should be .039 inch from flush with end of shaft.
11. Install front output shaft.
12. Install mainshaft front support bearing in high/low planetary carrier using mainshaft support bushing and bearing installer tool No. J45757 and nonthreaded universal driver handle tool No. J42176, or equivalents.
13. Install high/low planetary carrier, then lubricate using suitable transjel lubricant and install input shaft thrust washer.
14. Install new shift fork pads.
15. Install shift sleeve in range fork.
16. Align range shift sleeve gear teeth to planetary carrier.
17. Install fork and range shift sleeve.
18. Install mainshaft.
19. If required, assemble shift detent lever . as follows:
    a. Mount spring by one tab in suitable vise.
    b. Install sleeve in spring.
    c. Install shaft partially in spring.
    d. Install shift detent lever cam on shaft.

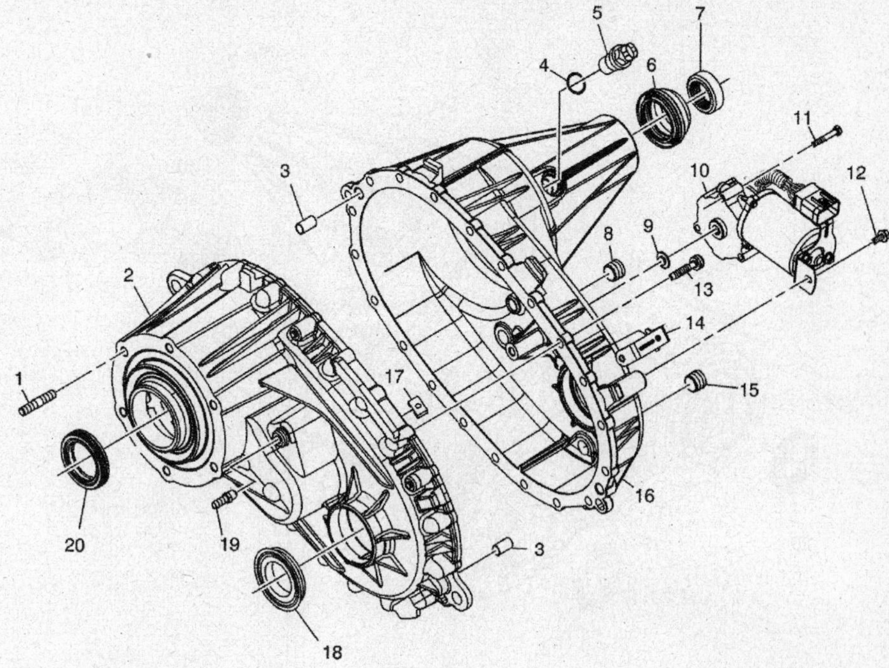

1. Adapter Stud
2. Front Case Half
3. Location Pin
4. Vehicle Speed Sensor O-Ring Seal
5. Vehicle Speed Sensor
6. Rear Output Shaft Seal
7. Shipping Seal
8. Fill Plug
9. Shift Detent Lever Seal
10. Encoder Motor
11. Encoder Motor Bolt
12. Encoder Motor Bracket Bolt
13. Case Half Bolt
14. Wiring Harness Bracket
15. Drain Plug
16. Rear Case Half
17. Magnet
18. Front Output Shaft Seal
19. Vent
20. Input Shaft Seal

LTV0500000001570

Fig. 1 Exploded view of case components. BW 4482 transfer case

    e. Rotate spring and install tab on shift detent lever between spring tabs.
    f. Install shaft and align lever between spring tabs.
20. Install shift detent lever. **Do not tilt lever.**
21. Rotate high/low shift fork to position fork in detent lever slot.
22. Install shift fork shaft.
23. Connect oil pump hose to screen and oil pump.
24. Install oil pump with hose and screen.
25. Align oil pump gear square boss with mainshaft flat area.
26. Install oil pump screen in front case half slot. Ensure wear clip is on oil pump.
27. Install oil pump screen in front case half.
28. Install magnet.
29. Install inner lockup hub.
30. Install spring in sleeve, then the hub with external tabs towards spring and retainer ring in sleeve.
31. Slide shift fork over shaft, then turn mainshaft to align slot on inner lockup hub with lockup shift large tooth area.
32. Lubricate drive sprocket thrust washer with suitable transjel transmission assembly lubricant and install washer
33. Install drive chain and sprockets with chain blue link facing up.
34. Align drive sprocket engagement and lockup shift assembly hub teeth.
35. Install front sun gear.
36. With rear side of planetary differential facing up, align pinion gears. Position alignment marks with planetary differential that can be reference for all gears.
37. Do not rotate planetary differential pinion gears when installing. Alignment marks are still in position.
38. Single row pinion gears face rearward, or up and double row pinion gears face forward or down.
39. Lubricate rear output shaft thrust washer with suitable transjel transmission assembly lubricant and install washer.
40. Install rear sun gear with shoulder side facing up. **Do not rotate differential pinion gears.**
41. Temporarily install rear output shaft to planetary differential and rear sun gear.
42. Rotate rear output shaft 3–4 revolutions to rotate planetary differential pinion gears. Pinion gears should rotate freely.
43. Remove rear output shaft without disturbing rear sun gear.
44. Install shift fork shaft spring.
45. Install front output shaft rear bearing in rear case half using suitable hammer and brass drift only on outer bearing

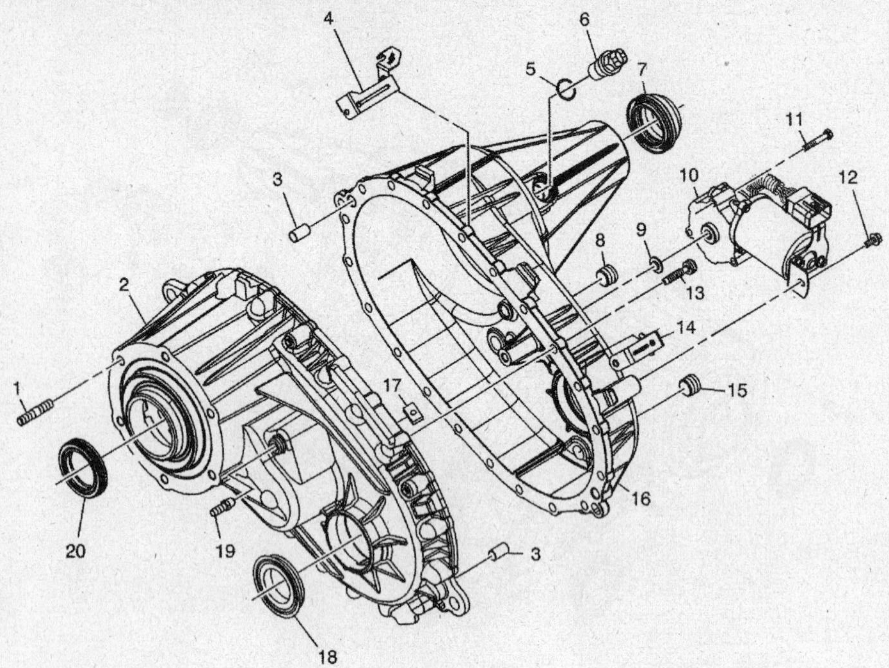

1. Adapter Stud
2. Front Case Half
3. Location Pin
4. Fuel Line Bracket
5. Vehicle Speed Sensor O-Ring Seal
6. Vehicle Speed Sensor
7. Rear Output Shaft Seal
8. Fill Plug
9. Shift Detent Lever Seal
10. Encoder Motor
11. Encoder Motor Bolt
12. Encoder Motor Bracket Bolt
13. Case Half Bolt
14. Wiring Harness Bracket
15. Drain Plug
16. Rear Case Half
17. Magnet
18. Front Output Shaft Seal
19. Vent
20. Input Shaft Seal

LTV0500000001572

Fig. 2 Exploded view of case components. BW 4484 transfer case

race. Ensure bearing is kept square in bore.

46. Install rear output shaft bearing using rear pinion and axle bearing remover tool No. J22912-01, or equivalent, and suitable hydraulic press.
47. Bearing retaining ring groove goes toward input end or forward.
48. Use suitable press plate on rear output shaft end and ensure bearing is supported on inner race.
49. Install new rear output shaft bearing retaining ring.
50. Install new speed reluctor wheel using suitable hydraulic press.
51. Install mainshaft rear support bushing in rear output shaft mainshaft support bushing and bearing installer tool No. J45757 and non-threaded universal driver handle tool No. J42176, or equivalents.
52. Install rear output shaft rear in rear case half.
53. Spread rear output shaft rear bearing outer retaining ring and install rear output shaft bearing outer retaining ring until it is seated in bearing groove.
54. Install locating pins in front and rear case halves.
55. Apply ⅛ inch bead of suitable RTV Sealant GM to front case half mating surfaces.
56. Lower rear case half into place. Rotate rear output shaft to align teeth with planetary differential.
57. Replace case bolts if there is any damage to nylon coating.
58. Install and tighten case bolts with washers and brackets. **Do not use power assisted tools to install bolts.**
59. Install and tighten vehicle speed sensor with new O-ring seal.
60. Apply ⅛ inch bead of suitable RTV sealant to encoder motor sealing surface.
61. Install encoder motor and rotate shift detent lever to align to encoder motor.
62. Loosely install encoder motor mounting bolts and bracket bolt. Tighten mounting bolts.
63. Install rear output shaft seal using rear output shaft seal installer tool No. J45756, or equivalent.
64. Apply pipe suitable sealant to threads, then install and tighten drain and fill plugs.
65. Install front output shaft seal using front output shaft seal installer tool No. J43484 and universal driver handle tool No. J8092, or equivalents.
66. Install front input shaft seal using seal installer tool No. J42738, or equivalent.

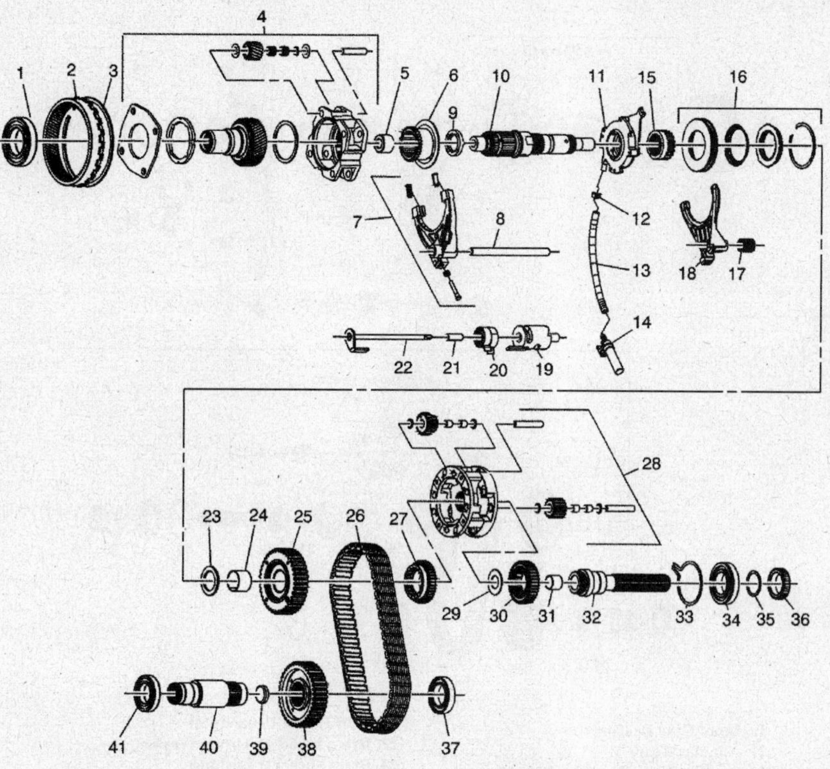

1. Input Gear Bearing
2. Annulus Gear
3. Annulus Gear Retaining Ring
4. High/Low Planetary Carrier Assembly
5. Mainshaft Front Support Bearing
6. High/Low Range Sleeve
7. High/Low Range Shift Fork Assembly
8. Shift Fork Shaft
9. Input Gear Thrust Washer
10. Mainshaft
11. Oil Pump
12. Oil Pump Hose Clamp
13. Oil Pump Hose
14. Oil Pump Screen
15. Inner Lockup Hub
16. Lockup Shift Assembly
17. Shift Fork Shaft Spring
18. Lockup Shift Fork
19. Shift Detent Lever Cam
20. Shift Detent Lever Shaft Spring
21. Shift Detent Lever Shaft Sleeve
22. Shift Detent Lever Shaft
23. Drive Sprocket Thrust Washer
24. Drive Sprocket Bushing
25. Drive Sprocket
26. Drive Chain
27. Front Sun Gear
28. Planetary Differential Assembly
29. Rear Output Shaft Thrust Washer
30. Rear Sun Gear
31. Mainshaft Rear Support Bushing
32. Rear Output Shaft
33. Rear Output Shaft Bearing Outer Retaining Ring
34. Rear Output Shaft Bearing
35. Rear Output Shaft Bearing Retaining Ring
36. Speed Reluctor Wheel
37. Front Output Shaft Rear Bearing
38. Driven Gear
39. Front Output Shaft Cup Plug
40. Front Output Shaft
41. Front Output Shaft Front Bearing

LTV0500000001571

Fig. 3 Exploded view of internal components. BW 4482 transfer case

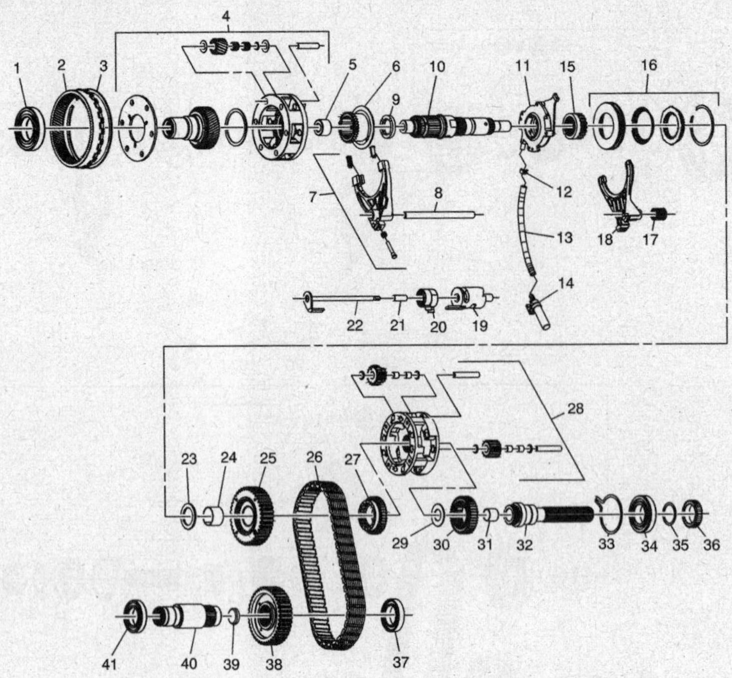

1. Input Gear Bearing
2. Annulus Gear
3. Annulus Gear Retaining Ring
4. High/Low Planetary Carrier Assembly
5. Mainshaft Front Support Bearing
6. High/Low Range Sleeve
7. High/Low Range Shift Fork Assembly
8. Shift Fork Shaft
9. Input Gear Thrust Washer
10. Mainshaft
11. Oil Pump
12. Oil Pump Hose Clamp
13. Oil Pump Hose
14. Oil Pump Screen
15. Inner Lockup Hub
16. Lockup Shift Assembly
17. Shift Fork Shaft Spring
18. Lockup Shift Fork
19. Shift Detent Lever Cam
20. Shift Detent Lever Shaft Spring
21. Shift Detent Lever Shaft Sleeve
22. Shift Detent Lever Shaft
23. Drive Sprocket Thrust Washer
24. Drive Sprocket Bushing
25. Drive Sprocket
26. Drive Chain
27. Front Sun Gear
28. Planetary Differential Assembly
29. Rear Output Shaft Thrust Washer
30. Rear Sun Gear
31. Mainshaft Rear Support Bushing
32. Rear Output Shaft
33. Rear Output Shaft Bearing Outer Retaining Ring
34. Rear Output Shaft Bearing
35. Rear Output Shaft Bearing Retaining Ring
36. Speed Reluctor Wheel
37. Front Output Shaft Rear Bearing
38. Driven Gear
39. Front Output Shaft Cup Plug
40. Front Output Shaft
41. Front Output Shaft Front Bearing

LTV0500000001573

Fig. 4 Exploded view of internal components. BW 4484 transfer case

TIGHTENING SPECIFICATIONS

Year	Component	Torque/Ft. Lbs.
2003–06	Case, Bolt	15
	Case, Stud	89①
	Drain Plug	18
	Encoder Motor	89①
	Encoder Motor Bracket	89①
	Fill Plug	18
	Vent	53①
	VSS	13

① — Inch Lbs.

Borg-Warner 4493/4494

INDEX

DISASSEMBLE

1. Mount holding fixture tool No. J3289-20, or equivalent, to suitable, sturdy workbench.
2. Attach assembly fixture tool No. J45759, or equivalent, to transfer case, then the assembly to holding fixture.
3. Remove drain and fill plugs, then drain fluid into suitable container, **Fig. 1.**
4. Remove bracket bolt, mounting bolts and encoder motor.
5. Remove rear Vehicle Speed Sensor (VSS) and O-ring seal.
6. Remove rear output shaft seal using seal remover tool No. J45278 and slide hammer tool No. J2619-01, or equivalents.
7. Loosen front output shaft flange nut while holding flange using flange and pulley holding tool No. J8614-01, or equivalent.
8. Remove nut, washer, seal and front output shaft flange.
9. Remove front output shaft seal using universal seal remover tool No. J2312 and slide hammer with adapter tool No. J6125-1B, or equivalents.
10. Remove transfer case mounting bolts and washers. Mark brackets locations for assembly alignment.
11. Shear case halves sealer using case spreader tool No. J45358, or equivalent, between tabs.
12. Remove case from locating pins using suitable pry bars at each side of case.
13. Remove rear from front case half. Rear output shaft is removed with rear case half.
14. Remove shift fork shaft spring, **Fig. 2.**
15. Remove rear output sun gear and shaft thrust washer, then the planetary differential and front output sun gear.
16. Mark chain to sprockets relationship for assembly alignment.
17. Remove chain with drive and driven sprockets.
18. Remove lockup shift collar and fork, then the fork from collar.
19. If lockup shift collar disassembly is required, proceed as follows:
    a. Remove retainer ring from sleeve.
    b. Remove hub.
    c. Remove spring.
20. Remove inner lockup hub and upper thrust washer, then the magnet.
21. Remove center bearing support and lower thrust washer.
22. Spread snap ring using suitable needle-nose pliers, and remove bearing from support.
23. Remove oil pump with hose and screen.
24. Disconnect hose from screen and oil pump.
25. Remove shift fork shaft.
26. Rotate high/low shift fork roller from shift cam, then remove shift cam and shaft. **Keep shaft straight. Do not tilt.**
27. Remove mainshaft.
28. Remove high/low range sleeve with high/low range shift fork, then the fork from range shift sleeve.
29. Remove input shaft needle thrust bearing and high/low planetary carrier, **Fig. 3.**
30. Remove mainshaft front support bearing from planetary carrier using suitable brass drift and hammer.
31. Remove front output shaft.
32. Remove input shaft seal using suitable hammer and punch.
33. Remove input gear bearing from front case half using suitable hammer and brass drift.
34. Remove front output shaft bearing from front case half using suitable brass drift.
35. Remove retaining ring and ring gear from front case half.
36. Remove front case half vent.
37. Remove rear output shaft bushing using transfer case rear bushing remover and installer tool No. J45380, or equivalent.
38. Remove rear output shaft from rear case half.
39. Spread rear bearing outer retaining ring, then the rear output shaft using suitable soft-face hammer.
40. Remove speed sensor tone wheel using split plate bearing puller tool No. J22912-01, or equivalent, and suitable hydraulic press. Discard speed sensor tone wheel.
41. Remove retaining ring, then the rear output shaft bearing using suitable hydraulic press.
42. Remove mainshaft rear support bushing from rear output shaft using mainshaft support bushing/bearing remover tool No. J45548 and slide hammer tool No. J2619-01, or equivalent.
43. Remove front output shaft rear bearing from rear case using bushing and bearing remover tool No. J29369-1 and slide hammer with bearing adapter tool No. J23907, or equivalents.
44. Remove shift shaft seal by prying it out of case.

ASSEMBLE

Lubricate all of bearings and journals with transfer case fluid during installation.

1. Install and tighten transfer case mounting studs.
2. Mount holding fixture tool No. J3289-20, or equivalent, to suitable, sturdy workbench.
3. Attach assembly fixture tool No. J45759, or equivalent, to transfer case, then the assembly to holding fixture.
4. Apply suitable threadlock to threads and install vent.
5. Install right gear and new retaining ring in front case half.
6. Install input shaft bearing in front case half using suitable hammer and brass drift only on outer bearing race. Ensure bearing is kept square to bore.
7. Install front output shaft front bearing in front case half using suitable hammer and brass drift only on outer bearing race. Ensure bearing is kept square to bore.
8. Install front output shaft.
9. Install mainshaft front support bearing in high/low planetary carrier using bearing installer tool No. DT-47946 and non-threaded universal driver handle tool No. J42176, or equivalents, noting the following:
    a. **On BW 4493 models,** using short reach end of bearing installer tool No. DT-47946.
    b. **On BW 4494 models,** using long reach end of bearing installer tool No. DT-47946.
10. **On all models,** install high/low planetary carrier.
11. Lubricate and install input shaft needle thrust bearing using suitable transjel lubricant, or equivalent.
12. Install new shift fork pads, then the high/low range sleeve in high/low range fork.
13. Align high/low range shift sleeve gear teeth to high/low planetary carrier, then install high/low range shift fork and range sleeve.
14. Install mainshaft.
15. Install shift cam and shaft straight, with tip into case hole. **Keep shaft straight and do not tilt.**
16. Rotate high/low range shift fork to position shift fork roller in shift cam slot.
17. Install shift fork shaft.
18. Connect hose to screen and oil pump.
19. Align square boss of oil pump gear with mainshaft flat area and install oil pump in front case half slot. Ensure wear clip is on oil pump.
20. Install oil pump screen in front case half.
21. Install magnet.
22. Install lower center support bearing

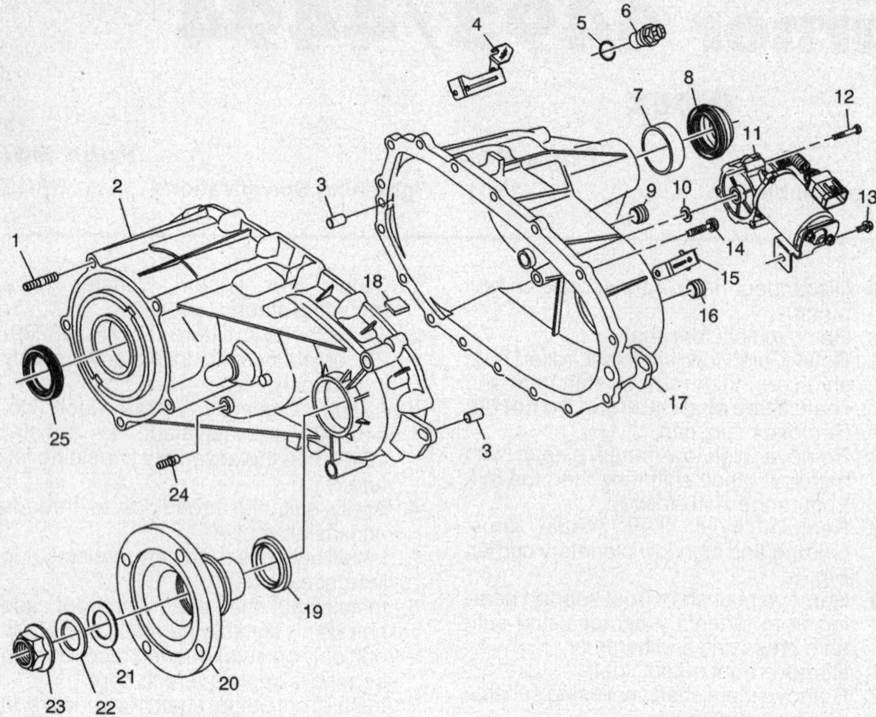

1. Adapter Stud
2. Front Case Half
3. Location Pin
4. Fuel Line Bracket
5. Vehicle Speed Sensor O-Ring Seal
6. Vehicle Speed Sensor
7. Output Shaft Bushing
8. Rear Output Shaft Seal
9. Fill Plug
10. Shift Shaft Seal
11. Encoder Motor
12. Encoder Motor Bolt
13. Encoder Motor Bracket Bolt
14. Case Half Bolt
15. Wiring Harness Bracket
16. Drain Plug
17. Rear Case Half
18. Magnet
19. Front Output Shaft Seal
20. Front Output Shaft Flange
21. Front Output Shaft Flange Seal
22. Front Output Shaft Flange Washer
23. Front Output Shaft Flange Nut
24. Vent
25. Input Shaft Seal

LTV0500000001575

Fig. 1 Exploded view of case components

thrust washer and center bearing support, then the upper center bearing support thrust washer and inner lockup hub.

23. Install spring in lockup mode shift collar and hub with external tabs toward spring. Install collar retainer ring.
24. Install fork to lockup mode shift collar.
25. Slide shift fork and collar over shift fork shaft, then turn mainshaft to align inner lockup hub slot with lockup shift collar hub large tooth area.
26. Install drive chain and sprockets, aligning drive sprocket engagement teeth with lockup shift hub teeth. Chain blue link faces up.
27. Install front output sun gear.
28. With planetary differential rear side facing up, align pinion gears marks, **Fig. 4.** Position the alignment marks with planetary differential area that can be reference for all gears.
29. Install planetary differential. **Do not rotate planetary differential pinion gears when installing.** Ensure alignment marks are in position, single row pinion gears face rearward or up, while double row pinion gears face forward or down.
30. Lubricate and install rear output shaft thrust washer using suitable transjel lubricant, or equivalent.
31. Install rear output sun gear. Shoulder side of gear faces up. **Do not rotate differential pinion gears.**
32. Temporarily install rear output shaft to planetary differential and rear output sun gear.
33. Rotate rear output shaft 3–4 revolutions to rotate planetary differential pinion gears. Pinion gears should rotate freely and there should be no binding.
34. Remove rear output shaft without disturbing rear sun gear.
35. Install shift fork shaft spring.
36. Install front output shaft rear bearing in rear case half using suitable hammer and brass drift only on outer bearing race. Ensure bearing is kept square to bore.
37. Install shift shaft seal using hand pressure. Spring or opened side faces outward.
38. Install rear output shaft bearing using split plate bearing puller tool No. J22912-01, or equivalent, and suitable hydraulic press with suitable press plate on shaft end. Retaining ring groove goes toward input end or forward. Ensure bearing is supported on inner race.
39. Install new rear output shaft bearing retaining ring.
40. Install new speed sensor tone wheel using suitable hydraulic press.
41. Install mainshaft rear support bushing in rear output shaft using mainshaft support bushing and bearing installer tool No. J45757 and non-threaded universal driver handle tool No. J42176, or equivalents.
42. Spread and install outer retaining ring until it is seated in bearing groove.
43. Install locating pins in front and rear cases halves.
44. Apply ⅛ inch bead of suitable Room Temperature Vulcanizing (RTV) sealant to front case half mating surfaces.
45. Lower rear case half into place. Rotate rear output shaft to align with planetary differential teeth.
46. Replace case mounting bolts if there is any damage to nylon coating.
47. Install and tighten mounting bolts with washers and brackets. **Do not use power assisted tools to install mounting bolts.**
48. Install output shaft bushing using transfer case rear bushing remover and installer tool No. J45380, or equivalent.
49. Install rear output shaft seal using rear output shaft seal installer tool No. J45756, or equivalent.
50. Install and tighten vehicle speed sensor with new O-ring seal.
51. Apply ⅛ inch bead of suitable RTV sealant to encoder motor sealing surface.
52. Rotate shift detent lever to align and install encoder motor, then loosely install motor and bracket mounting bolts. Tighten mounting bolts.
53. Apply suitable pipe sealant to threads, then install and tighten drain and fill plugs.
54. Install front output shaft seal using front output shaft seal installer tool No. DT-47847, or equivalent.
55. Install front output shaft flange.
56. Install front output shaft flange seal. Ensure seal is fully seated.
57. Install front output shaft flange washer and new nut.
58. Tighten front output shaft flange nut while holding flange using flange and pulley holding tool No. J8614-01, or equivalent.
59. Remove holding tool and install input shaft seal.

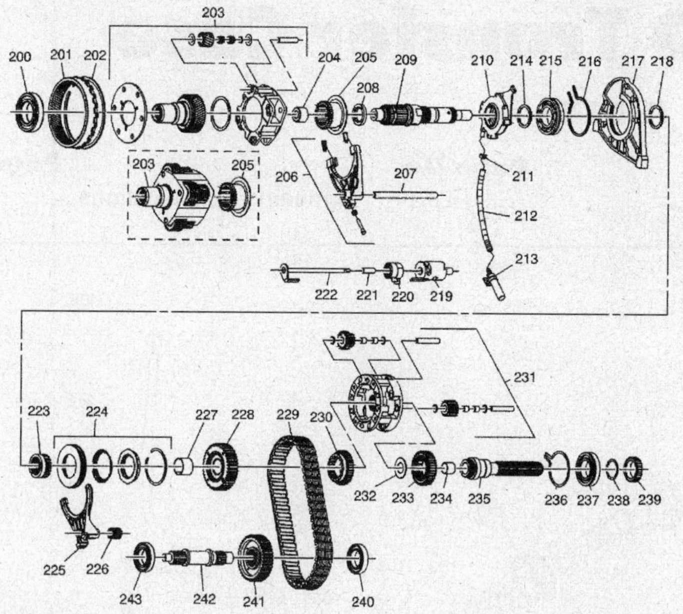

200. Input Gear Bearing
201. Ring Gear
202. Ring Gear Retaining Ring
203. High/Low Planetary Carrier Assembly
204. Mainshaft Front Support Bearing
205. High/Low Range Sleeve
206. High/Low Range Shift Fork Assembly
207. Shift Fork Shaft
208. Input Gear Thrust Bearing
209. Mainshaft
210. Oil Pump
211. Oil Pump Hose Clamp
212. Oil Pump Hose
213. Oil Pump Screen
214. Upper Center Bearing Support Thrust Washer
215. Bearing
216. Snap Ring
217. Center Bearing Support
218. Lower Center Support Bearing Thrust Washer
219. Shift Cam
220. Shift Shaft Torsional Spring
221. Shift Shaft Spacer
222. Shift Shaft
223. Inner Lockup Hub
224. Lockup Mode Shift Collar Assembly
225. Lockup Mode Shift Fork
226. Shift Fork Shaft Spring
227. Drive Sprocket Bushing
228. Drive Sprocket
229. Drive Chain
230. Front Output Sun Gear
231. Planetary Differential Assembly
232. Rear Output Shaft Thrust Washer
233. Rear Output Sun Gear
234. Mainshaft Rear Support Bushing
235. Rear Output Shaft
236. Rear Output Shaft Bearing Outer Retaining Ring
237. Rear Output Shaft Bearing
238. Rear Output Shaft Bearing Retaining Ring
239. Speed Sensor Tone Wheel
240. Front Output Shaft Rear Bearing
241. Driven Gear
242. Front Output Shaft
243. Front Output Shaft Front Bearing

LTV0500000001576

Fig. 2 Exploded view of internal components

1. BW 4494
2. BW 4493

LTV0500000001577

Fig. 3 High/low planetary carrier replacement

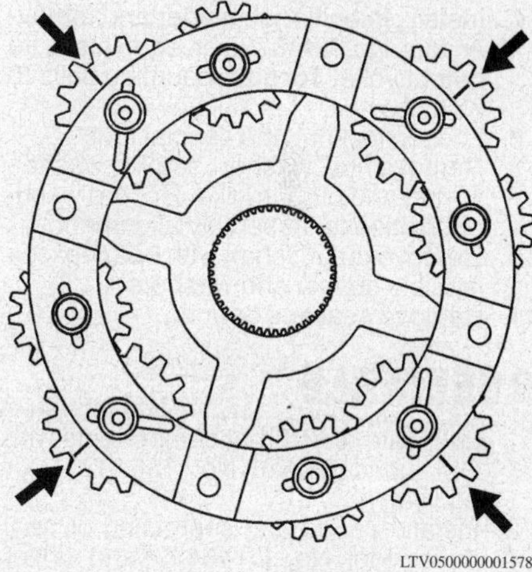

LTV0500000001578

Fig. 4 Pinion gear alignment

TIGHTENING SPECIFICATIONS

Year	Component	Torque/Ft. Lbs.
2006	Adapter Stud	10
	Case	18
	Drain Plug	12
	Encoder Motor	89①
	Encoder Motor Bracket	89①
	Fill Plug	12
	Front Output Shaft Flange	235
	Speed Sensor	13
	Vent	53①

① — Inch Lbs.

Honda AWD Transfer Case

INDEX

DISASSEMBLE

1. Remove ventilation valve , hose and clamps.
2. Remove drain and fill plugs and washers, **Fig. 1.**
3. Remove mounting bolts and cover, then the seal, O-ring and locating pin.
4. Remove input gear, bearing and shim. Mark shim for assembly alignment.
5. Secure case using suitable side with soft jaws.
6. Cut locknut tab using suitable chisel.
7. Install pinion flange holder and remover tool No. J44873, or equivalent, to output yoke. **Torque** mounting bolts to 35 ft. lbs.
8. Loosen locknut and special tool.
9. Remove nut , washer , sealing washer, O-ring and output yoke. Record washer position for assembly alignment.
10. Remove output shaft with bearing, collapsible spacer and washers.
11. Remove seal and bearing.

ASSEMBLE

1. Lubricate all internal components with GM lubricant part No. 12578261, or equivalent.
2. Install bearing and seal using oil seal driver tool No. DT46429 and driver handle tool No. EN46342, or equivalent.
3. Install output shaft with bearing, new collapsible spacer and washers, **Fig. 2.**
4. Lubricate output shaft threads using GM part No. 1237826, or equivalent.
5. Install output yoke, then new O-ring, sealing washer, washer and locknut, **Fig. 3.**
6. Secure case in suitable vise with soft jaws.
7. Install pinion flange holder and remover tool No. J44873, or equivalent, to output yoke. **Torque** mounting bolts to 35 ft. lbs.
8. Rotate output yoke several times in both directions to seat tapered roller bearings.
9. Tighten locknut while measuring rotating torque. Rotating **torque** should be 10.2–15.1 inch lbs. If rotating torque is more than 15.1 inch lbs., replace collapsible spacer.
10. Remove special tool and stake locknut using suitable .138 inch punch.
11. Install input gear with shim and bearing into case, **Fig. 4.**
12. Install oil seal using oil seal driver tool No. DT46429 and driver handle tool No. EN46342, or equivalent until seal flat surface is zero to .04 inch flush or above cover surface.
13. Install new O-ring and cover, **Fig. 5.** Tighten bolts.
14. Install locating pin.
15. Install and tighten fill and drain plugs with new washers.
16. Install ventilation valve, hose and clamps.

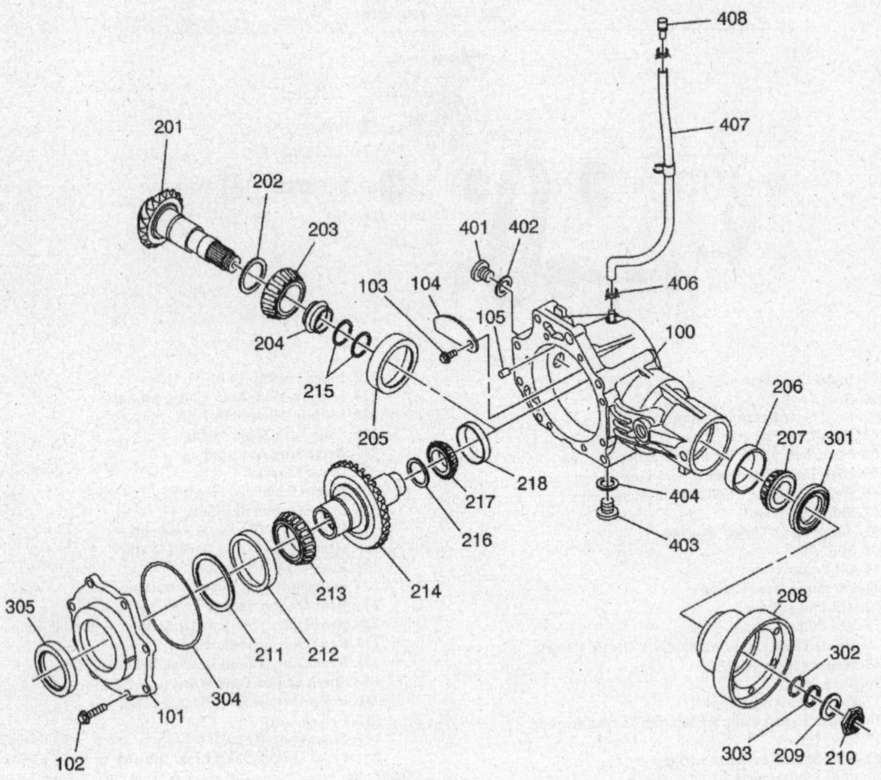

100. Case
101. Cover
102. Bolt
103. Bolt
104. Ventilation Baffle
105. Locating Pin - Transfer Case-to-Transaxle
201. Output Shaft
202. Shim - 40 mm
203. Bearing
204. Space
205. Race
206. Race
207. Bearing
208. Output Yoke
209. Washer
210. Nut
211. Shim – 80mm
212. Race
213. Bering
214. Input Gear
215. Washer
216. Shim – 25mm
217. Bearing
218. Race
301. Seal – Output Shaft
302. O-Ring
303. Sealing Washer
304. O-Ring
305. Seal – Input Shaft
401. Fill Plug
402. Washer
403. Drain Plug
404. Washer
406. Clamp
407. Ventilation Hose
408. Ventilation Valve

LTV0500000001574

Fig. 1 Exploded view of transfer case

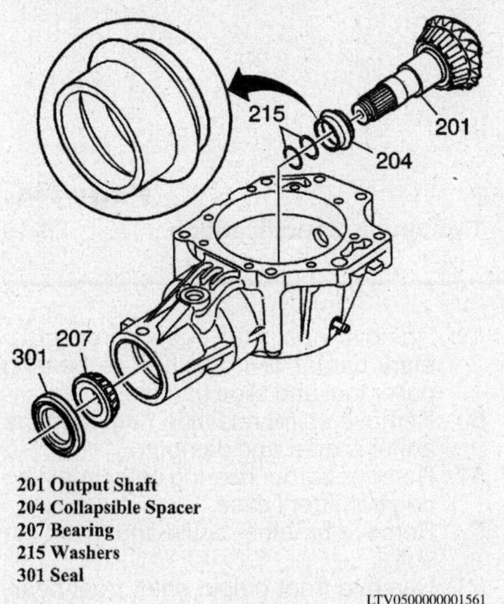

201 Output Shaft
204 Collapsible Spacer
207 Bearing
215 Washers
301 Seal

LTV0500000001561

Fig. 2 Output shaft replacement

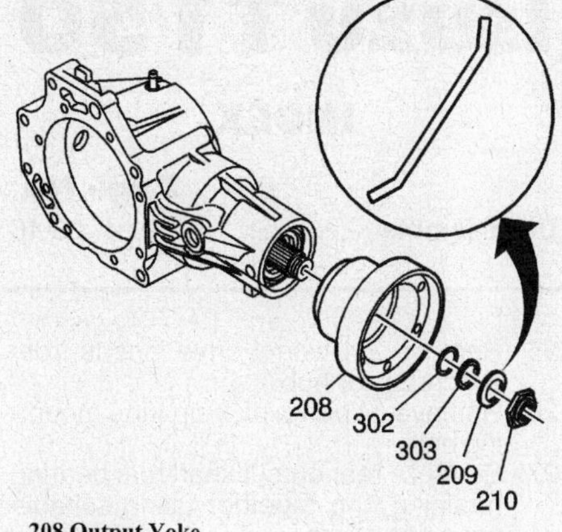

208 Output Yoke
209 Washer
210 Locknut
302 O-ring
303 Seal Washer

LTV0500000001562

Fig. 3 Output yoke replacement

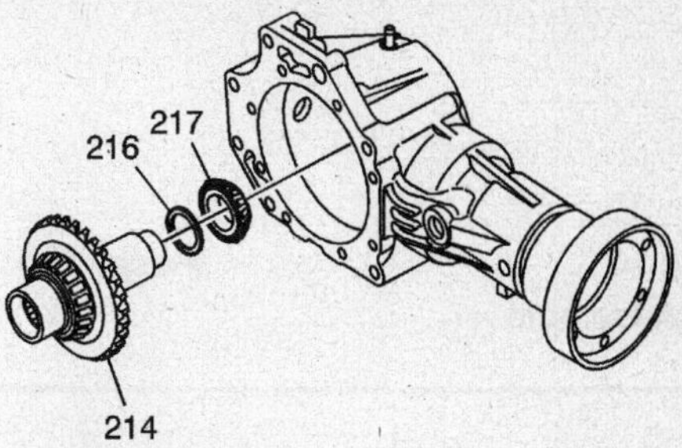

214 Input Gear
216 Shim
217 Bearing

LTV0500000001563

Fig. 4 Input gear replacement

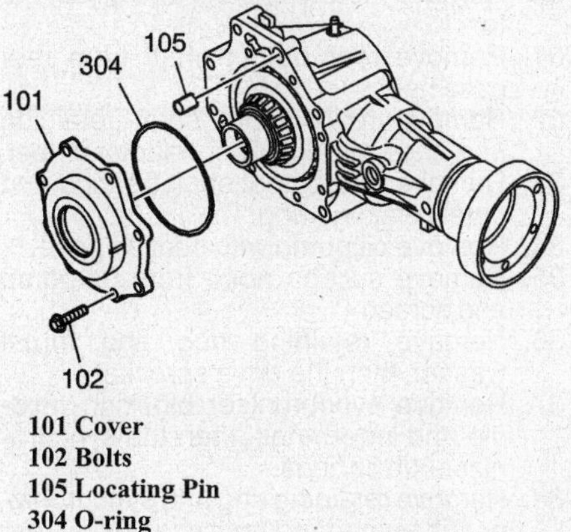

101 Cover
102 Bolts
105 Locating Pin
304 O-ring

LTV0500000001564

Fig. 5 Cover replacement

TIGHTENING SPECIFICATIONS

Year	Component	Torque/Ft. Lbs.
2004–06	Cover	20
	Drain Plug	33
	Output Yoke Locknut	76–217

Isuzu T150

INDEX

DISASSEMBLE

1. Install assembly fixture tool No. J45759, or equivalent, to transfer case and mount fixture and transfer case to holding fixture tool No, J3289-20, or equivalent on sturdy workbench.
2. Remove drain and fill plugs, then drain oil into suitable container, **Fig. 1.**
3. Remove vehicle speed sensor and O-ring seal.
4. Remove rear output shaft seal.
5. Remove actuator assembly vent hose and breather hose.
6. Remove mounting bolts and wire harness bracket, then the actuator and O-ring seal.
7. Remove switches wiring harness connectors and bracket.
8. Remove mounting bolts, then the connector bracket and spacer.
9. Remove 2/4 switch with copper gasket.
10. Remove neutral start switch with copper gasket.
11. Remove detent plugs, springs and balls. **Transfer case may or may not have additional spring nesting inside high/low shift shaft detent.**
12. Bend yoke flange nut stakes out using suitable punch.
13. Loosen yoke flange nut using flange and pulley holding tool J8614-01, or equivalent.
14. Remove nut, O-ring seal and front output yoke flange. Discard O-ring seal and mounting nut.
15. Remove case half mounting bolts.
16. Shear case half sealer using suitable soft face hammer on rear case half.
17. Separate case halve using suitable soft face hammer on front output shaft end.
18. Carefully remove rear from front case half. **Hold rear case half straight.**
19. Only input shaft, with planetary carrier assembly, will remain in front case half. **Reach in and hold shift forks in position. Watch for pieces to fall out of cases, if not removed straight and if shift forks bind.**
20. Remove high/low shift fork, with high/low range sleeve and fork, from output shaft, **Fig. 2. 2/4 synchronizer sleeve may have to be moved forward and roller on shift fork may fall off.**
21. Remove high/low shift fork from range sleeve.
22. Remove 2/4 wheel drive shift fork and synchronizer sleeve. **Shift fork roller may fall off.**
23. Remove shift fork from sleeve.
24. Remove control actuator shaft and cam.
25. Remove 2/4 wheel drive inserts from synchronizer hub.
26. Remove oil pump pick-up tube mounting bolt.
27. Squeeze rear output shaft rear bearing retaining ring together using suitable snap ring pliers.
28. Remove rear output shaft until rear output shaft bearing is just out of case using suitable soft face hammer on rear output shaft.
29. Remove front output shaft and drive chain.
30. Remove mounting bolts and oil deflector.
31. Remove rear output shaft from rear case half.
32. Remove rear output shaft retaining ring and speed sensor reluctor wheel.
33. Remove rear output shaft bearing and outer retaining ring.
34. Remove oil pump with suction hose.
35. Remove suction hose from oil pump and screen.
36. Remove retaining ring and thrust washer, then the drive sprocket.
37. Remove synchronizer blocking, middle and inner rings, then the synchronizer hub springs.
38. Remove retaining ring and synchronizer hub from rear output shaft using rear pinion and axle bearing remover tool No. J22912-01, or equivalent, and suitable hydraulic press.
39. Remove rear output shaft front support bearing from inside of input shaft.
40. Remove input shaft seal using slide hammer with bearing adapter tool No. J23907 and seal remover tool No. J45278, or equivalents. **There is no shoulder to prevent seal from going into case.**
41. Spread planetary carrier bearing retaining ring using suitable large pair of snap ring pliers. **Ensure snap ring pliers do not catch on case ribs.**
42. With ring spread, remove planetary carrier using a suitable soft face hammer on input shaft.
43. Mark planetary carrier low gear to planetary carrier relationship for assembly alignment.
44. Remove retaining ring and planetary carrier low gear.
45. Remove input shaft from planetary carrier.
46. Remove input shaft thrust bearing.
47. Remove planetary carrier bearing retaining ring.
48. Remove planetary carrier bearing using transfer case assembly/disassembly kit tool Nos. J45933-1 and J22912-01, or equivalents, and suitable hydraulic press.
49. Remove input shaft bearing from planetary carrier using split plate bearing puller tool and slide hammer.
50. Remove spiral retaining ring, then the annulus gear and damper.
51. Remove carrier bearing outer retaining ring from front case.
52. Remove breather baffle and mounting bolt.
53. Remove front output shaft front bearing retaining ring.
54. Remove front output shaft seal and front case half from assembly fixture tool.
55. Remove front output shaft bearing using universal driver tool No. J8092 and front output shaft bearing remover and installer tool No. J46199, or equivalents. Discard bearing.
56. Remove oil pump retaining ring from rear case half.
57. Remove front output shaft rear bearing from rear case half using bushing and bearing remover tool J29369-2, or equivalent, and slide hammer. Discard bearing.
58. Remove control actuator shaft seal from rear case.
59. If rear bushing is faulty, remove it using tool No. J45933 Isuzu transfer case assembly/disassembly kit tools No. J45933, J45933-3 and J45933-4, or equivalents. **Use thrust bearing between tool No. J45933-4 and washer. Ensure threaded shaft threads are lubricated with kit supplied lubricant.**
60. If required, remove shift shaft plugs, then the vent or breather hose pipes.
61. If component replacement is required, disassemble shift forks as follows:
    a. Disassemble high/low shift fork by compressing spring in suitable vise.
    b. Remove shift shaft retaining ring.
    c. Remove shift fork from vise, then the shift block.
    d. Compress spring in high/low shift block using suitable, small socket and vise.
    e. Remove shift block inner retaining ring.
    f. Remove shift block from vise.
    g. Remove shift block spring seat, spring and block collar.
    h. Remove high/low shift fork roll pin.
    i. Remove shift shaft fork.
    j. Disassemble 2/4 shift fork by compressing spring in suitable vise.
    k. Remove shift shaft retaining ring.
    l. Remove shift shaft 2/4 shift fork and spring.

ASSEMBLE

1. If disassembled, assemble shift forks as follows:
   a. Install 2/4 shift fork and spring on shift shaft.
   b. Compress spring on 2/4 shift fork in suitable vise.
   c. Install retaining ring.
   d. Install high/low shift fork on shift shaft.
   e. Install roll pin in shift fork until flush.
   f. Install spring seat, spring and block collar in shift block.
   g. Install inner retaining ring over suitable socket.
   h. Install socket and block in suitable vise and compress spring.
   i. Install inner retaining ring in block.
   j. Compress high/low shift block spring using suitable vise.
   k. Install shift rail retaining ring.
2. If removed, install the vent or breather hose pipes using suitable retaining compound. Ensure pipes are properly aligned.
3. Mount front case half to assembly fixture tool No. J45759, or equivalent.
4. Install assembly fixture tool into holding fixture tool No. J3289-20, or equivalent.
5. Install control actuator shaft bushing using control actuator shaft bushing installer tool No. J45936, or equivalent.
6. Install breather baffler and tighten mounting bolt.
7. Install new front output shaft front bearing in front case half using output shaft bearing installer tool No. J36371, or equivalent. Install new retaining ring.
8. Install carrier bearing outer retaining ring in front case half.
9. Lubricate annulus gear damper with suitable transfer case fluid. Install damper in case.
10. Install annulus gear in front case. Ensure damper is in correct position.
11. Compress damper until retaining ring groove is exposed using Isuzu transfer case assembly/disassembly kit tool No. J45933-2, or equivalent, in annulus gear step and tool No. J45933-3, or equivalent, in input seal bore.
12. Install annulus gear spiral retaining ring.
13. Remove Isuzu transfer case assembly/disassembly kit tools and ensure spiral retaining ring is sully seated.
14. Holding nut and threaded shaft in suitable vise, and stack Isuzu transfer case assembly/disassembly kit tool No. J45933-2 and planetary carrier over threaded shaft.
15. Side of Isuzu transfer case assembly/disassembly kit tool No. J45933-1 with step against bearing
16. Install planetary carrier input shaft bearing.
17. Install planetary carrier bearing using Isuzu transfer case assembly/disassembly kit tools Nos. J45933-2, or equivalent.
18. Install planetary carrier bearing retaining ring.

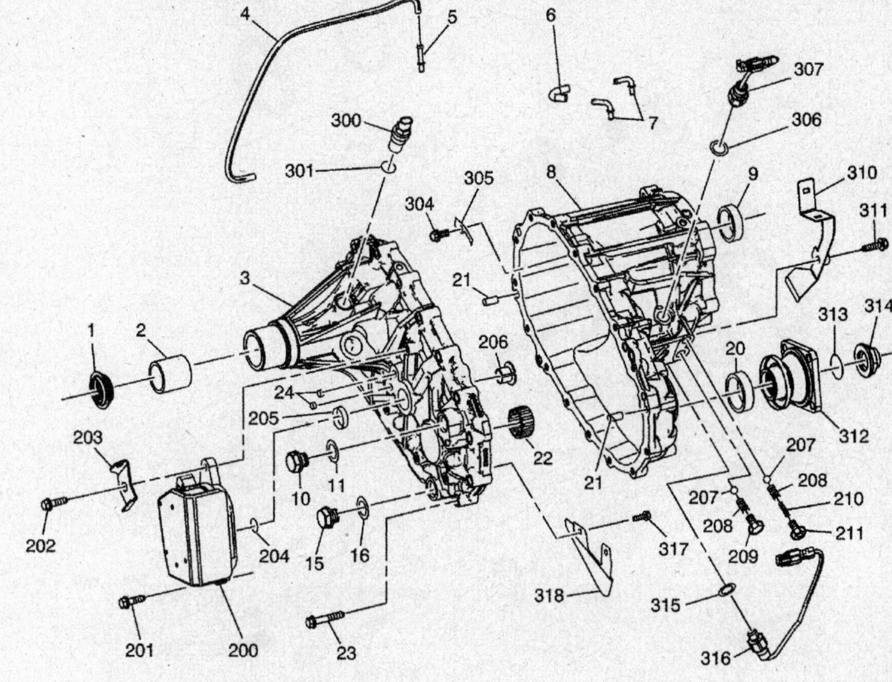

1. Rear Output Shaft Seal
2. Rear Bushing
3. Rear Case Half
4. Vent Hose
5. Vent Hose Pipe
6. Breather Hose
7. Breather Hose Pipe
8. Front Case Half
9. Input Shaft Seal
10. Oil Fill Plug
11. Oil Fill Plug Gasket
15. Oil Drain Plug
16. Oil Drain Plug Gasket
20. Front Output Shaft Seal
21. Location Pin
22. Front Output Shaft Rear Bearing
23. Case Half Bolt
24. Shift Shaft Plug
200. Actuator Assembly
201. Actuator Assembly Bolt
202. O2 Sensor Wiring Harness Bracket Bolt
203. O2 Sensor Wiring Harness Bracket
204. Actuator Assembly O-Ring Seal
205. Control Actuator Shaft Seal
206 Control Actuator Shaft Bushing
207 Shift Shaft Detent Ball
208. Shift Shaft Detent Spring
209. Shift Shaft Detent Plug
210. Shift Shaft Detent Spring
211. Shift Shaft Detent Plug
300. Vehicle Speed Sensor
301. Vehicle Speed Sensor O-Ring Seal
304. Breather Baffle Bolt
305 Breather Baffle
306. Transfer Case NEUTRAL Switch Gasket
307. Transfer Case NEUTRAL Switch
310. Switch Connector Bracket
311. Switch Connector Bracket Bolt
312. Front Output Yoke Flange
313 Yoke Flange O-Ring Seal
314. Yoke Flange Nut
315. 2/4 Indicator Switch Gasket
316. 2/4 Indicator Switch
317. Oil Deflector Bolt

LTV0500000001558

Fig. 1 Exploded view of case components

19. Install input shaft thrust bearing.
20. Install input shaft in planetary carrier.
21. Install planetary carrier low gear with thrust surface facing toward input shaft. Install retaining ring.
22. Spread carrier bearing retaining ring using suitable large snap ring pliers and install planetary carrier. Ensure snap ring pliers do not catch on case ribs. Ensure retaining ring is secured on planetary carrier bearing.
23. Install rear output shaft front support bearing.
24. Pack bearing using transjel lubricant tool No. J36850, or equivalent.
25. Install 2/4 synchronizer hub using suitable hydraulic press. Hub non-shoulder side aligns to rear of rear output shaft. Ensure hub is supported on shoulder flange, not on external hub teeth.
26. Install synchronizer hub retaining ring.
27. Install rear spring on synchronizer hub.
28. Align spring ends by insert slots.
29. Install front spring on synchronizer hub with ends opposite from rear spring.
30. Align spring ends by insert slots.
31. Install three inserts in synchronizer hub.
32. Install synchronizer sleeve with shoulder groove aligned forward and flat teeth with insert. Push in on inserts.
33. Install high/low range sleeve.
34. Install high/low shift fork to high/low range sleeve and 2/4 shift fork to 2/4 synchronizer sleeve.

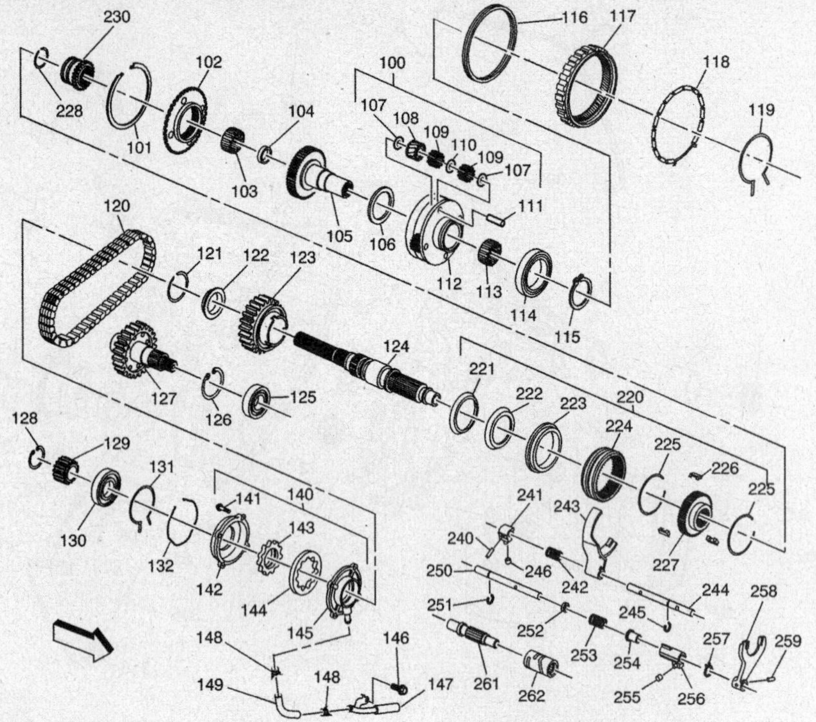

100. High/Low Planetary Carrier Assembly
101. Planetary Carrier Low Gear Retaining Ring
102. Planetary Carrier Low Gear
103. Rear Output Shaft Front Support Bearing
104. Input Shaft Plug
105. Input Shaft
106. Input Shaft Thrust Bearing
107. Pinion Gear Thrust Washer
108. Pinion Gear
109. Pinion Gear Bearing
110. Pinion Gear Shaft Spacer
111. Pinion Gear Shaft
112. Planetary Carrier
113. Input Shaft Bearing
114. Planetary Carrier Bearing
115. Planetary Carrier Bearing Retaining Ring
116. Annulus Gear Retaining Ring
117. Annulus Gear
118. Annulus Gear Damper
119. Carrier Bearing Outer Retaining Ring
120. Drive Chain
121. Drive Sprocket Retaining Ring
122. Drive Sprocket Thrust Washer
123. Drive Sprocket
124. Rear Output Shaft
125. Front Output Shaft Front Bearing
126. Front Output Shaft Front Bearing Retaining Ring
127. Front Output Shaft
128. Rear Output Shaft Retaining Ring
129. Speed Sensor Reluctor Wheel
130. Rear Output Shaft Bearing
131 Rear Output Shaft Bearing Retaining Ring
132. Oil Pump Retaining Ring
140. Oil Pump Assembly
141. Oil Pump Case Screw
142. Oil Pump Rear Case
143. Oil Pump Gear
144. Oil Pump Rotor
145. Oil Pump Front Case
146. Oil Pump Screen Bolt
147. Oil Pump Screen
148. Oil Pump Suction Hose Clamp
149. Oil Pump Suction Hose
220.2 /4 Wheel Drive Synchronizer Assembly
221. Synchronizer Inner Ring
222. Synchronizer Outer Ring
223. Synchronizer Blocking Ring
224. Synchronizer Sleeve
225. Synchronizer Insert Spring
226. Synchronizer Insert
227. Synchronizer Hub
228. Synchronizer Assembly Retaining Ring
230. High/Low Range Sleeve
240. 2/4 Wheel Drive Shift Block Pin
242. 2/4 Wheel Drive Shift Shaft Spring
243. 2/4 Wheel Drive Shift Fork
244. 2/4 Wheel Drive Shift Shaft
245. 2/4 Wheel Drive Shift Fork Retaining Ring
246. 2/4 Wheel Drive Shift Fork Roller
250. High/Low Shift Shaft
251. High/Low Shift Fork Retaining Ring
252. High/Low Shift Shaft Spring Seat
253. High/Low Shift Shaft Spring
254. High/Low Shift Block Collar
255. High/Low Shift Fork Roller
256. High/Low Shift Block
257. High/Low Shift Block Retaining Ring
258. High/Low Shift Fork
259. High/Low Shift Fork Pin
261. Control Actuator Shaft
262. Control Actuator Cam

LTV0500000001559

Fig. 2 Exploded view of internal components

35. Align shift blocks.
36. Lubricate front shift shaft holes with suitable transfer case fluid.
37. Hold shift forks in position to sleeves and install shift shafts in front case half holes.
38. Align high/low range sleeve teeth with planetary low gear teeth and install rear output shaft in front case half.
39. Install shift forks rollers.
40. Install control actuator cam with smaller recess up and facing toward shift rails.
41. Rotate control actuator cam to align to shift forks.
42. Install control actuator shaft aligning large spline with cam large groove.
43. Install 2/4 synchronizer blocking ring aligning tabs ring with synchronizer hub insert grooves.
44. Install 2/4 synchronizer middle and inner rings.
45. Lubricate rear output shaft drive sprocket journal with suitable transfer case fluid.
46. Install chain drive and driven sprockets with blue link pointing to rear case.
47. Rotate drive gear to align with 2/4 synchronizer rings' tabs.
48. Ensure chain links are parallel to case sealing flange when viewed from chain side.
49. Install drive gear thrust washer aligning teeth with rear output shaft flat area.
50. Install new, thickest drive sprocket retaining ring that fits groove.
51. Measure retaining ring outside diameter. If measurement is more than 1.769–2.169 inches, select thinner retaining ring.
52. Install rear bushing in rear case, using Isuzu transfer case assembly/disassembly kit tools Nos. J45933-3 and J45933-4, or equivalent. Use thrust bearing between J45933-4 and washer. Ensure threaded shaft threads are lubricated with kit supplied lubricant.
53. Align bushing holes with case oil grooves and install bushing to just past case shoulder.
54. Install shift shaft plugs using suitable threadlocker.
55. Install front output shaft rear bearing using universal driver tool No. J8092 and front output shaft bearing remover and installer tool No. J46199, or equivalents. Bearing part numbers align away from case to toward tool.
56. Position speed sensor reluctor wheel in rear case half with oil grooved side toward inside of rear case half.
57. Install rear output shaft bearing in rear case half with single shoulder side of Isuzu transfer case assembly/disassembly kit tool No. J45933-3, or equivalent, in rear seal bore.
58. Ensure bearing is installed square to bore and install until it bottoms in bore using Isuzu transfer case assembly/disassembly kit tool No. J45933-1, or equivalent.
59. Install rear output shaft bearing retaining ring.
60. Install oil pump wire retaining ring with ends aligning in larger open area of bore.
61. Prelube oil pump by pouring small quantity of suitable transfer case fluid in oil suction pipe fitting and rotating oil pump gear a few turns.
62. Install oil pump suction hose to oil pump and screen.
63. Install oil pump with screen in rear case half. Push on oil pump and it will snap into position. Tighten oil pump suction tube mounting bolt.

64. Install oil deflector and tighten mounting bolts.
65. Apply ⅛ inch bead of suitable flange sealant to rear case half sealing flange, **Fig. 3.** Apply sealer evenly to inside surface of bolt holes with no gaps.
66. Install location pins in front case half.
67. Rotate input shaft to allow rear output shaft to align with speed sensor reluctor wheel splines and lightly tap down on rear case half to fully install on locating pins. Tighten mounting bolts.
68. Position new rear output shaft retaining ring over rear output shaft.
69. Tap lightly, or use hand pressure on rear output shaft retaining ring installer tool No. J45937, or equivalent, until retaining ring installs in groove.
70. Install rear output shaft seal using oil pump seal installer tool No. J35582, or equivalent, and suitable hammer.
71. Install control actuator shaft seal flush to case surface. Spring side installs to inside.
72. Install input shaft seal using input seal installer tool No. J45934, or equivalent, and suitable hammer.

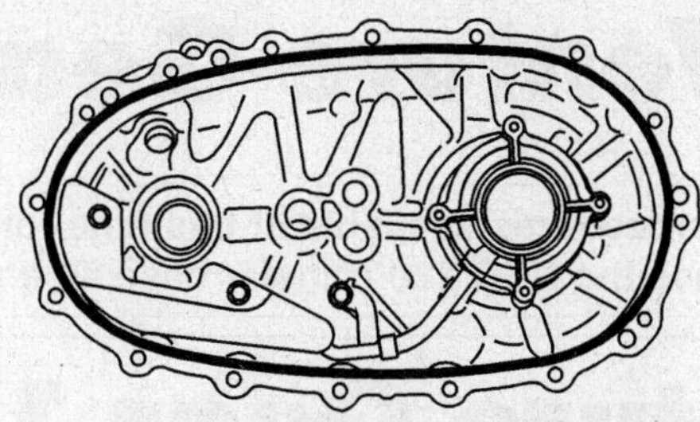

Fig. 3 Rear case half sealant application

73. Install front output shaft seal using front output shaft seal installer tool No. J37212, or equivalent, and suitable hammer.
74. Install detent springs and balls. Transfer case may or may not have additional spring nesting inside high/low shift shaft detent.
75. Apply suitable lubricant to threads, then install and tighten detent plugs.
76. Install yoke flange on front output shaft.
77. Lightly lubricate new yoke flange O-ring with transfer case fluid. Install O-ring.
78. Install and tighten new yoke flange nut using flange and pulley holding tool No. J8614-01, or equivalent.
79. Remove special tool and stake yoke flange nut in two places.
80. Install 2/4 switch with copper gasket. Tighten 2/4 switch.
81. Install neutral start switch with copper gasket. Tighten switch.
82. Install witch connector bracket and spacer. Tighten mounting bolt.
83. Install wiring harness connectors into switch connector bracket.
84. Install actuator and new O-ring seal. **Do not rotate actuator shaft to align with control actuator shaft.**
85. Install mounting bolts and wire harness bracket. Tighten mounting bolts.
86. Install vent and breather hoses, then the Vehicle Speed Sensor (VSS) and O-ring seal. Tighten VSS.
87. Install new O-ring gaskets, then tighten drain and fill plugs.

TIGHTENING SPECIFICATIONS

Year	Component	Torque/Ft. Lbs.
2004–06	Actuator	18
	Breather Baffle	56①
	Case Half	16
	Connector Bracket	11
	Deflector	11
	Detent Plugs	14
	Drain & Fill Plugs	29
	Neutral Switch	29
	Suction Tube	11
	VSS	13
	Yoke Flange	101
	2/4 Switch	29

① — Inch Lbs.

New Venture Gear 120

NOTE: There are no disassemble procedures available at this time for the New Venture Gear 120 transfer case. Replace the NVG 120 transfer case as a component.

New Venture Gear 126/226

INDEX

DISASSEMBLE

1. Mount front case half to assembly fixture tool No. J45759, or equivalent.
2. Install assembly fixture tool into holding fixture tool No. J3289-20, or equivalent.
3. Remove drain plug and drain fluid into suitable container, **Fig. 1.**
4. Loosen front input shaft seal using suitable fine flat-bladed screwdriver and mallet.
5. Remove front input shaft seal using suitable small wooden block and large flat-bladed screwdriver.
6. Remove front output shaft dust seal. Do not remove front output shaft oil seal now.
7. Mark location for assembly alignment and remove wiring harness bracket mounting bolt.
8. Remove mounting bolts and encoder/motor.
9. Remove both Vehicle Speed Sensors (VSS) and O-ring seals from rear extension.
10. Remove rear output shaft seal.
11. Remove rear output shaft bushing using transfer case rear bushing remover and installer tool No. J45380, or equivalent.
12. Remove rear extension and case half mounting bolts.
13. Shear front and rear case half sealer using case spreader tool No. J45358, or equivalent. **Do not use screwdrivers or pry bars to separate transfer case halves.**
14. Separate front input shaft from front output shaft bearing and input shaft from output shaft using suitable prying tools.
15. Remove front from rear case half. Only input gear will remain with front case half.
16. Mark drive chain to sprockets position for assembly alignment.
17. Remove front output shaft from rear bearing, **Fig. 2.**
18. Remove chain from drive gear on output shaft and driven gear on front output shaft.
19. Remove rear extension from rear case half using suitable screwdriver in rear extension slot.
20. Remove speed sensor reluctor wheel from rear output shaft using T-bar push puller tool No. J44707, Adapter 3/8 NC to 5/8 NF tool No. J44759 and gear and bearing separator plate tool No. J36513, or equivalents. Discard speed sensor reluctor wheel.
21. Remove rear output shaft and clutch lever.
22. Remove mounting bolts and oil pump cover, the then oil pump drive gear inner rotor and oil pump driven gear outer rotor.
23. Remove clutch pressure plate bearing retaining ring while pushing down on clutch apply plate, **Fig. 3.**
24. Remove inner plate, pressure plate bearing and clutch apply plate.
25. Remove spring, hub retaining ring and clutch housing.
26. Hold clutch plates and turn housing over on workbench.
27. Remove clutch housing from plates and clutch hub, then the clutch hub from plates.
28. Remove retaining ring and drive sprocket from clutch housing.
29. Remove clutch housing retaining ring and rear output shaft rear thrust washer.
30. Support front case half on press plates, then remove input gear using suitable adapter and press.
31. If input gear bearing came out with input gear, remove input gear bearing using suitable press.
32. Remove thrust bearing from input gear.
33. Remove retaining ring and driver gear from front output shaft.
34. Remove front speed sensor reluctor wheel using suitable adapter and hydraulic press.
35. Remove vent only if damaged.
36. Remove front output shaft VSS and O-ring seal from rear case.
37. Remove chip collector magnet from rear case.
38. Remove oil pump suction pipe with screen.
39. Remove retaining ring and control actuator lever shaft. Discard retaining ring.
40. Only remove bearings if they are faulty, noting the following:
    a. Remove rear bearing for front output shaft using 3–4 inch bushing/bearing remover tool No. J26941 and slide hammer with bearing adapter tool No. J23907, or equivalents.
    b. Remove rear output shaft bearing from rear case using 3–4 inch bushing/bearing remover tool No. J26941 and slide hammer tool No. J23907, or equivalents.
    c. Ensure tool No. J26941 jaws are between bearing and oil pump bushing. **Tool jaws must not contact oil pump bushing surface.**
    d. Remove control actuator lever shaft bearing using shift rail bearing remover tool No. J44737 and T-bar push puller tool No. J44707, or equivalents.
    e. Remove front output shaft seal using suitable prying tool.
    f. Remove front output shaft front bearing from front case using suitable hammer and punch.

ASSEMBLE

1. Install input gear seal after transfer case is assembled.
2. **Do not cock bearings when installing.**
3. Install rear output shaft bearing using suitable bearing installer against outer race.
4. Install front output shaft rear bearing into rear case half using output shaft bearing installer tool No. J36371, or equivalent.
5. Install control actuator lever shaft bearing until it bottoms in bore using needle bearing installer tool No. J45239 and universal driver handle tool No. J8092, or equivalents. Bearing seal side faces encoder motor.
6. Install control actuator lever shaft and new retaining ring in rear case half.
7. Install screen and hose to oil pump suction pipe. Install new O-ring lightly lubricated with suitable transfer case oil.
8. Install oil pump suction pipe in rear case half. Ensure suction pipe is fully seated.

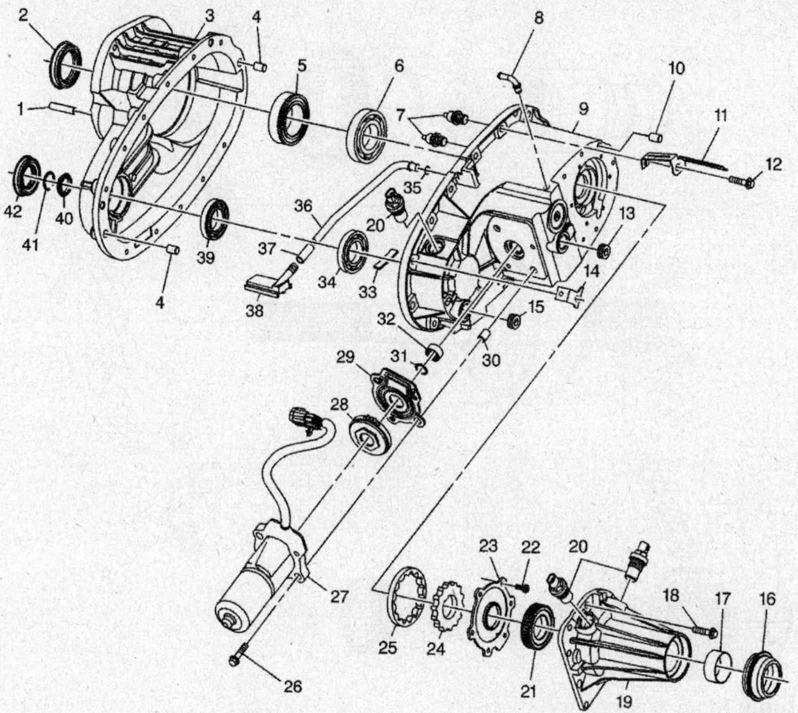

1. Adapter Stud
2. Input Shaft Seal
3. Front Case Half
4. Location Pin
5. Front Input Bearing
6. Rear Output Rear Bearing
7. Control Lever Studs
8. Vent Pipe
9. Rear Case Half
10. Location Pin
11. Wiring Harness Bracket
12. Case Half Bolt
13. Oil Fill Plug
14. Bracket
15. Oil Drain Plug
16. Rear Output Shaft Seal
17. Rear Extension Bushing
18. Rear Extension Bolt
19. Rear Extension
20. Vehicle Speed Sensor
21. Output Shaft Speed Reluctor Wheel
22. Oil Pump Cover Bolt
23. Oil Pump Cover
24. Oil Pump Drive Gear
25. Oil Pump Driven Gear
26. Encoder Motor Bolt
27. Encoder Motor
28. Encoder Sensor
29. Insulator
30. Location Pin
31. Actuator Lever Shaft Retaining Ring
32. Actuator Lever Shaft Bearing
33. Chip Collector Magnet
34. Front Output Shaft Rear Bearing
35. Oil Pump Suction Pipe Seal O-Ring
36. Oil Pump Suction Pipe
37. Oil Pump Suction Hose
38. Oil Pump Screen
39. Front Output Shaft Front Bearing
40. Front Output Shaft Dust Seal
41. Front Output Shaft Ring
42. Front Output Shaft Seal

LTV0500000001579

Fig. 1 Exploded view of case components

9. Install chip collector magnet in rear case half.
10. Apply thin layer of suitable retaining compound and tap vent into case.
11. Install front output shaft seal after transfer case is assembled.
12. Install front output shaft front bearing into front case using output shaft bearing installer tool No. J36371, or equivalent.
13. Install input gear bearing into front case using suitable press and plates to fit bearing outer race.
14. Install input gear thrust bearing into input gear using input gear thrust bearing installer tool No. J45237 and universal driver handle tool No. J8092, or equivalents.
15. Install input gear into bearing while supporting front case half on press plates that allow gear to protrude. Support input gear bearing inner race and use suitable press plate on gear end. Press gear until fully seated against input gear bearing.
16. Install rear output shaft thrust washer aligning tabs with shaft splines.
17. Install new clutch housing retaining ring on rear output shaft. Ensure retaining ring is properly installed in groove.
18. Install drive sprocket and new retaining ring onto clutch housing.
19. Lightly lubricate clutch housing inner bearing with suitable transfer case fluid.
20. Install clutch housing onto rear output shaft.
21. Install hub into clutch housing.
22. Install an outer disc into clutch housing with friction material facing down.
23. Install an inner disc into clutch housing with friction material facing down.
24. Continue to install outer and inner clutch discs, alternating until nine of each are installed.
25. Install new clutch hub retaining ring onto rear output shaft.
26. Install clutch spring.
27. Install clutch apply plate aligning apply plate tabs with hub. Ensure clutch spring is seated properly in clutch apply plate underside groove.
28. Install clutch pressure plate bearing, fitting flush to inner plate.
29. Install clutch inner plate.
30. Align clutch pressure plate bearing markings, then install the clutch apply plate retaining ring while pushing down on clutch apply plate, **Fig. 4.**
31. Position clutch lever onto two pivot pins and shift control actuator lever shaft to neutral position, then install clutch lever to rear case half.
32. Install rear output shaft. Ensure rear output shaft flat area aligns with shift fork.
33. Install new front speed sensor reluctor wheel onto front output shaft using input sun gear ball bearing installer tool No. J36373 , or equivalent and suitable hydraulic press .
34. Install driven sprocket and new retaining ring onto front output shaft.
35. Position drive chain on front output shaft driven sprocket , then on rear output shaft drive sprocket.
36. Install front output shaft into front output shaft rear bearing.
37. Mount front case half to assembly fixture tool No. J45759, or equivalent.
38. Install assembly fixture tool into holding fixture tool No. J3289-20, or equivalent.
39. Apply ⅛ inch bead of suitable sealant onto the rear case half, **Fig. 5.**
40. Install front case half location pins.
41. Install front to rear case half, rotating output shaft to align with input gear splines.
42. Install and tighten case half mounting bolts.
43. Install oil pump driven gear outer rotor and drive gear, inner rotor. Inner rotor flat aligns to rear output shaft flat area.
44. Install cover and tighten mounting bolts. **Do not use sealer on oil pump cover.**
45. Install new rear output shaft speed sensor reluctor wheel.
46. Install rear speed sensor reluctor wheel to proper specifications using rear speed sensor reluctor wheel installer tool No. J45235, or equivalent.
47. Install rear case half location pins.
48. Apply ⅛ inch bead of suitable sealant onto rear extension.
49. Install rear extension and tighten mounting bolts.
50. Shift control detent into neutral position, then install location pins and motor/encoder. Tighten mounting bolts.
51. Install motor/encoder wiring harness bracket and tighten case bolt.

52. Install and tighten front and rear Vehicle Speed Sensors (VSS).
53. Install front output shaft seal using front output shaft seal installer tool No. J45236-2, or equivalent.
54. Install front input shaft seal using seal installer tool No. J42738, or equivalent.
55. Install new rear output shaft bushing using transfer case rear bushing remover and installer tool No. J45380, or equivalent, and suitable hammer.
56. Install rear output shaft seal with tab at top and weep hole at bottom using seal installer tool No. J37668-A, or equivalent, aligning tool notch with seal tab.
57. Apply suitable pipe sealant to threads, then install and tighten fill and drain plugs.

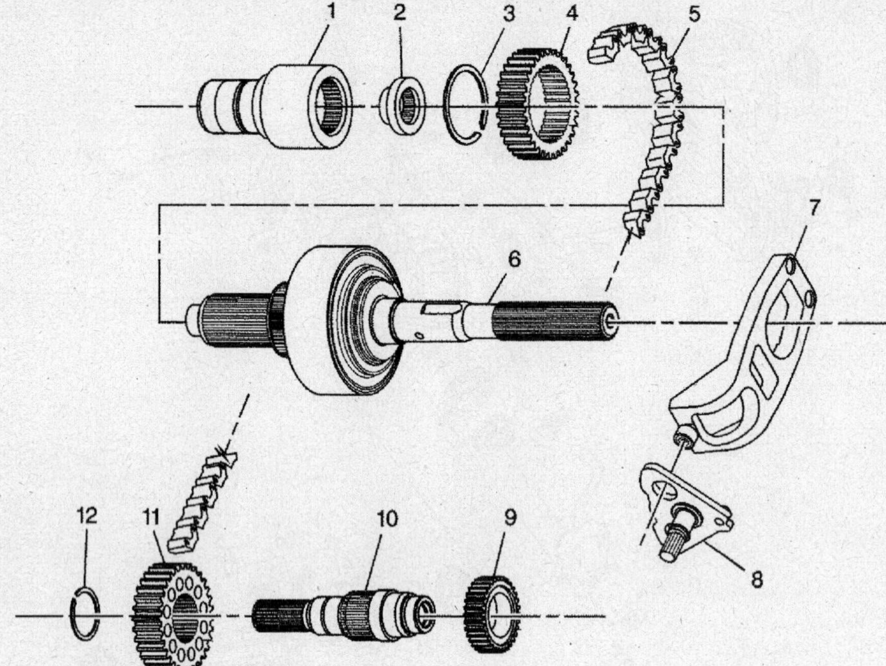

1. Input Shaft Gear
2. Input Gear Thrust Bearing
3. Drive Sprocket Retaining Ring
4. Drive Sprocket
5. Drive Chain
6. Rear Output Shaft
7. Clutch Lever
8. Control Actuator Lever Shaft
9. Front Output Shaft Speed Reluctor Wheel
10. Front Output Shaft
11. Driven Sprocket
12. Driven Sprocket Retaining Ring

LTV0500000001580

Fig. 2 Exploded view of internal components

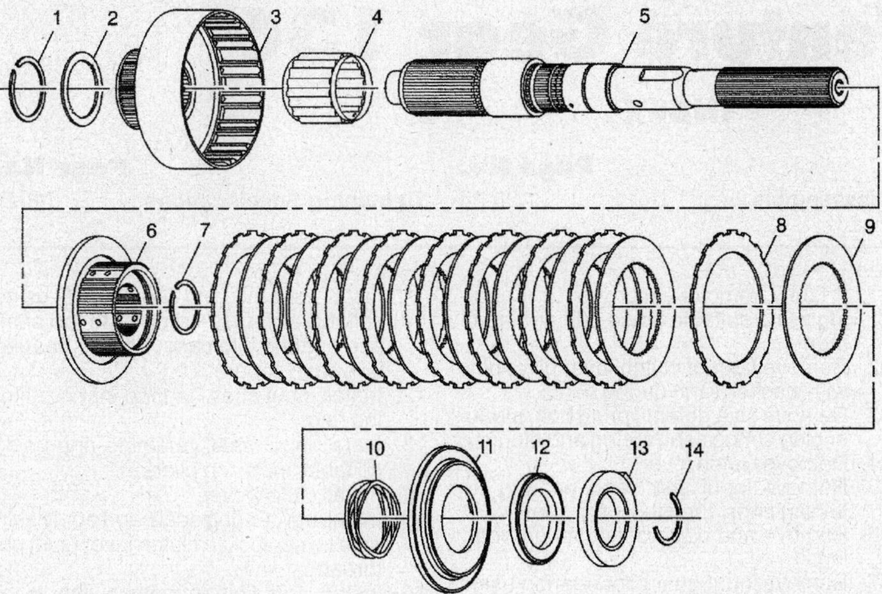

1. Clutch Retaining Ring
2. Rear Output Shaft Thrust Washer
3. Clutch Housing
4. Clutch Housing Bearing
5. Rear Output Shaft
6. Clutch Hub
7. Clutch Retaining Ring
8. Clutch Pressure Plate – Outer
9. Clutch Pressure Plate – Inner
10. Clutch Spring
11. Clutch Pressure Plate – Apply
12. Clutch Pressure Plate Bearing
13. Clutch Inner Plate
14. Clutch Pressure Plate Bearing Hub Retaining Ring

LTV0500000001581

Fig. 3 Exploded view of rear output shaft

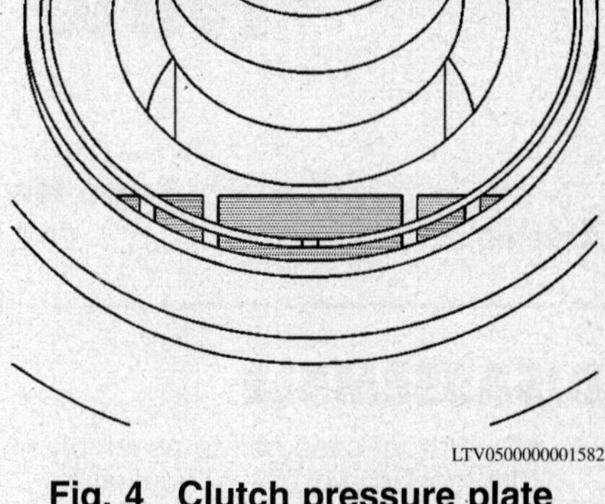

LTV0500000001582

Fig. 4 Clutch pressure plate bearing alignment

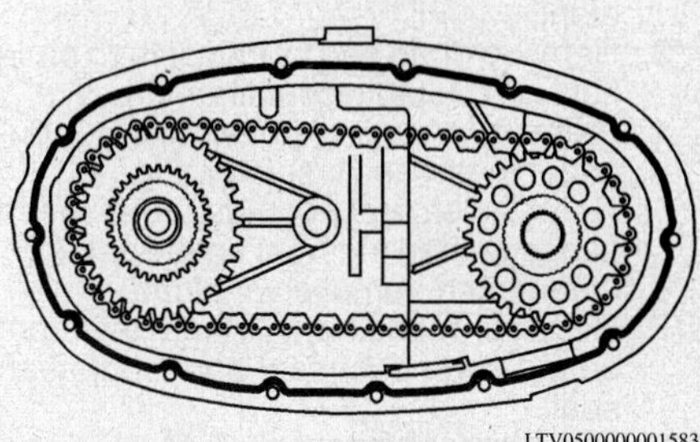

LTV0500000001583

Fig. 5 Rear case sealant application

TIGHTENING SPECIFICATIONS

Year	Component	Torque/Ft. Lbs.
2003–06	Case Half	16
	Drain Plug	20
	Fill Plug	20
	Motor/Encoder	12
	Oil Pump Cover	97①
	Rear Extension	16
	VSS	13

① — Inch lbs.

New Venture Gear 136

INDEX

DISASSEMBLE

1. Mount front case half to assembly fixture tool No. J45759, or equivalent.
2. Install assembly fixture tool into holding fixture tool No. J3289-20, or equivalent.
3. Remove drain and fill plugs, then drain fluid into suitable container, **Fig. 1.**
4. Remove mounting bolts, actuator encoder motor and insulator, **Fig. 2.**
5. Remove left and righthand rear speed sensors, then the front speed sensor.
6. If damaged, remove vent tube.
7. Remove rubber plug, then the front output shaft dust seal and input shaft seal.
8. Remove rear output shaft seal.
9. Remove rear output bushing transfer case rear bushing remover and installer tool No. J45380, or equivalent.
10. Remove transfer case mounting bolts and studs. Mark studs and brackets for assembly alignment.
11. Separate front and rear case halves using suitable flat-blade screwdrivers on left and righthand sides.
12. Open rear output shaft bearing retaining ring using suitable snap ring pliers and remove rear from front case.
13. If worn or damaged, remove oil pump wear sleeve.
14. Remove retaining ring and rear output shaft bearing.
15. Remove rear output shaft speed sensor reluctor wheel and magnet.
16. Remove oil pump suction pipe. **Do not remove screen.**
17. Remove oil pump, **Fig. 3.**
18. Remove oil pump suction pipe seal.
19. Remove drive and driven sprocket retaining rings.
20. Mark drive chain to sprocket relationship for assembly alignment.
21. Remove drive chain and sprockets, then the rear output shaft.
22. Mount rear output shaft in suitable soft-jaw vise with input end up.
23. Remove retaining ring, then the clutch pressure plate and spring.
24. Remove bearing, with inner support from clutch pressure plate.
25. If faulty, remove clutch pressure plate bearing from inner support using suitable hydraulic press and adapter.
26. Remove retaining ring, then the clutch housing and hub from ear output shaft.
27. Turn clutch over and remove housing.
28. Remove clutch hub. **Do not remove oil restrictor plate.**
29. Separate clutch plates, then remove and discard shims.
30. If replace rear output shaft, remove oil restrictor.
31. If faulty, remove clutch housing bearing using suitable brass drift and hammer.
32. Remove both of clutch lever pivot pins with washers and O-ring seals.
33. Remove shift detent spring bolt, plunger plug O-ring seal, spring and plunger.
34. Remove clutch lever.
35. Remove input shaft and bearing retaining rings, then the input shaft.
36. Remove and discard input shaft bearing.
37. Remove input gear pilot bearing using suitable brass drift. Discard bearing.
38. Remove retaining ring and front output shaft.
39. If damaged, remove speed sensor reluctor wheel from front output shaft using suitable a hydraulic press.
40. Remove retaining ring and front output shaft bearing.
41. If faulty, remove front output shaft rear bearing using 3–4 inch bushing and bearing remover tool No. J26941 and slide hammer with bearing adapter tool No. J23907, or equivalents.
42. Remove retaining ring and control actuator lever shaft.
43. If leaking or fault, remove control actuator lever bearing.

ASSEMBLE

1. Install mounting studs at 1.16–1.20 inches high.
2. Mount front case half to assembly fixture tool No. J45759, or equivalent.
3. Install assembly fixture tool into holding fixture tool No. J3289-20, or equivalent.
4. Install front output shaft bearing and retaining ring.
5. Install front output shaft rear bearing using drive sprocket needle bearing installer tool No. J36370 and universal driver tool No. J8092, or equivalents.
6. Install control actuator lever shaft bearing using sector bearing installer tool No. J42737, or equivalent.
7. Lubricate bearing, then install control actuator lever shaft and new retaining ring.
8. Install front output shaft tone wheel using mainshaft bushing installer tool No. J22873, or equivalent, and suitable hydraulic press.
9. Install front output shaft using suitable soft-face hammer to tap shaft into bearing. Install retaining ring.
10. Install input shaft pilot bearing to 1.30 inches from gear face or just below bore taper using input gear thrust bearing installer tool No. J45237 and universal driver tool No. J8092, or equivalents.
11. Install bearing and input shaft using suitable soft-face hammer to tap shaft and bearing into case. Ensure bearing is in case square.
12. Install input shaft bearing inner retaining ring.
13. Install input shaft retaining ring using suitable snap ring pliers.
14. Install clutch lever.
15. Install new O-ring seals and apply suitable threadlock to clutch lever pivot pin threads.
16. Install and tighten both clutch lever pivot pins with aluminum washers and O-ring seals.
17. Install shift detent plunger and spring.
18. Lightly lubricate new shift detent plunger O-ring seal with suitable transfer case fluid.
19. Install O-ring seal, then install and tighten shift detent spring bolt in front transfer case.
20. **If installing new rear output shaft,** install rear output shaft oil restrictor flush with end of shaft.
21. **On all models,** install clutch housing bearing using drive sprocket needle bearing installer tool No. J36370 and universal driver tool No. J8092, or equivalents. Ensure double shoulder of tool No. J36370 is against bearing.
22. Clamp rear output shaft in suitable soft-jaw vise with front end facing up.
23. Install clutch housing and hub.
24. Install friction, then steel clutch pressure plate. Continue install friction and steel clutch plates, alternating until eight friction plates and seven steel plates are installed.
25. Install clutch hub retaining ring.
26. Securely install clutch pack shimming kit tool No. J44295, or equivalent, base plate of in suitable vise, with machined surface of locating tabs facing up.
27. Install assembled mainshaft with drum, inner clutch plates and outer separator plates, on base plate.
28. Install clutch pack shimming kit tool No. J44295, or equivalent, weight on top of assembled clutch plates.
29. Place clutch pack shimming kit tool No. J44295, or equivalent, gage block on base plate locating tabs.
30. Place clutch pack shimming kit tool No. J44295, or equivalent, space under gage block.
31. Measure distance between gage block and spacer on all three base plate locating tabs.
32. Required shim thickness is average of measurements. Measure shims in center. **Shims may not be combined.**
33. Remove tool weight and install shim.

Do not remove clutch plates from drum.

34. Press clutch bearing inner support in clutch pressure plate bearing using suitable press plate and hydraulic press. Ensure bearing inner bearing race is supported.
35. Install bearing with inner support, in pressure plate.
36. Install clutch pressure plate and spring.
37. Install clutch pressure plate align lugs with hub slots in the hub. Spring installs in plate groove.
38. Push down on clutch pressure plate and install retaining ring.
39. Align clutch bearing inner support tab between clutch lever.
40. Install rear output shaft turning rear output shaft to align with input shaft splines.
41. Install drive chain and sprockets. Chain blue links must face up toward case rear.
42. Install drive and driven sprocket retaining rings.
43. Install new O-ring on suction pipe, then install oil pump.
44. Install screen in case and suction pipe to oil pump.
45. Install magnet.
46. Install rear output shaft speed sensor reluctor wheel.
47. Install ear output shaft bearing with retaining ring groove facing up. Install retaining ring.
48. Install oil pump wear sleeve.
49. Install front case locating pins.
50. Apply ⅛ inch bead of suitable RTV sealant to front case sealing surface.
51. Ensure rear output shaft bearing outer retaining ring aligns with access opening and install rear case half.
52. Open rear output shaft bearing outer retaining ring using suitable snap ring pliers, then insert suitable rubber coasted screwdriver into speed sensor holes, lift up speed reluctor wheel and seat retaining ring.
53. Install and tighten case half bolts/studs with cup washers.
54. Install input shaft seal using seal installer tool No. J42738, or equivalent.
55. Install new rear output shaft bushing using transfer case rear bushing remover and installer tool No. J45380 , or equivalent, and suitable hammer.
56. Install rear output shaft seal with drain hole facing down using output shaft seal installer tool No. J37668-A, or equivalent.
57. Install dust seal.

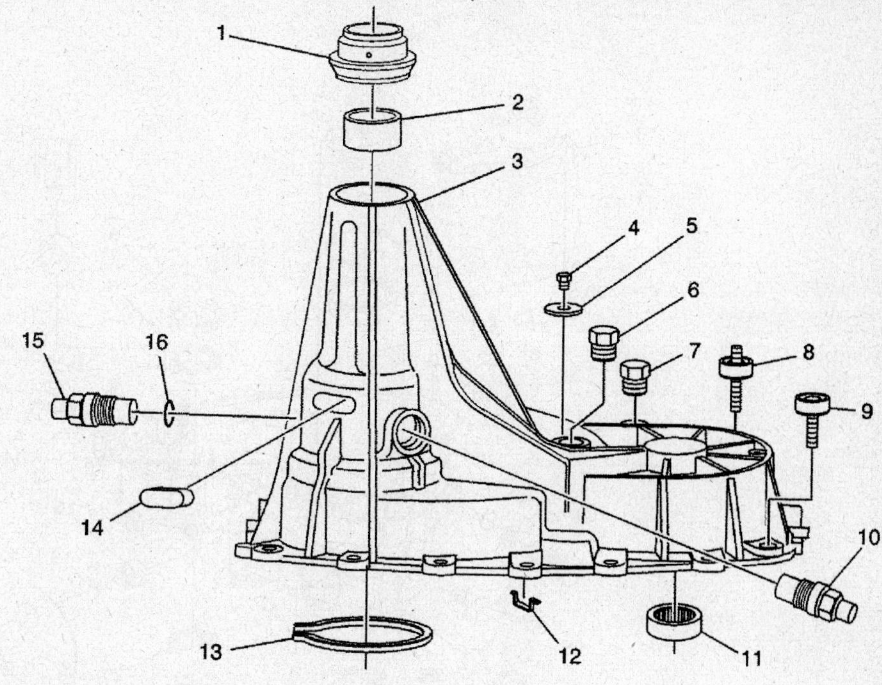

1. **Rear Output Shaft Seal**
2. **Rear Bushing**
3. **Rear Case Half**
4. **Screw**
5. **Identification Tag**
6. **Oil Fill Plug**
7. **Oil Drain Plug**
8. **Case Half Stud**
9. **Case Half Bolt**
10. **Speed Sensor**
11. **Front Output Shaft Rear Bearing**
12. **Oil Pump Wear Sleeve**
13. **Rear Output Bearing Outer Retaining Ring**
14. **Rubber Plug**
15. **Speed Sensor**
16. **Speed Sensor O-Ring Seal**

LTV0500000001586

Fig. 1 Exploded view of rear case half

58. Install front output shaft seal installer tool No. J44636-2, or equivalent, on front output shaft and seal on installer tool.
59. Install front output shaft seal using front output shaft seal protector tool No. J44636-1, or equivalent.
60. Install new O-ring seals on Vehicle Speed Sensors (VSS) and lubricate seals with suitable transfer case fluid.
61. Install and tighten VSSs.
62. Install vent tube elbow.
63. Install insulator and rotate control actuator shaft to align actuator encoder motor output shaft.
64. Install actuator encoder motor and tighten mounting bolts.
65. Install rubber plug.

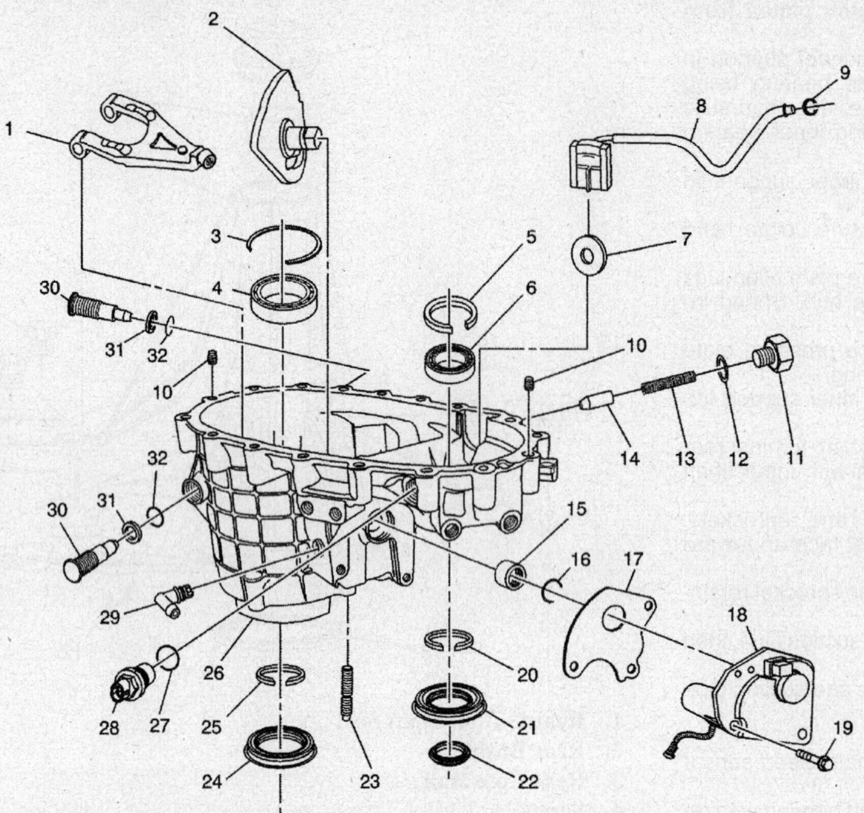

1. Clutch Lever
2. Control Actuator Lever
3. Input Gear Bearing Retaining Ring
4. Input Gear Bearing
5. Front Output Bearing Retaining Ring
6. Front Output Shaft Front Bearing
7. Magnet
8. Oil Pump Suction Pipe Assembly
9. Oil Pump Suction Pipe Seal
10. Location Pin
11. Shift Detent Spring Bolt
12. Shift Detent Plunger Plug O-Ring
13. Shift Detent Spring
14. Shift Detent Plunger
15. Control Actuator Lever Bearing
16. Control Actuator Lever Retaining Ring
17. Actuator Insulator
18. Actuator Encoder Motor
19. Actuator Encoder Motor Bolt
20. Front Output Shaft Bearing Retaining Ring
21. Front Output Shaft Seal
22. Front Output Shaft Dust Seal
23. Adapter Stud
24. Input Shaft Seal
25. Input Gear Bearing Outer Retaining Ring
26. Front Case Half
27. Vehicle Speed Sensor (VSS) O-Ring Seal
28. VSS – Front
29. Vent
30. Clutch Lever Pivot Pin
31. Clutch Lever Pivot Pin Washer
32. Clutch Lever Pivot Pin O-Ring Seal

LTV0500000001584

Fig. 2 Exploded view of front case half

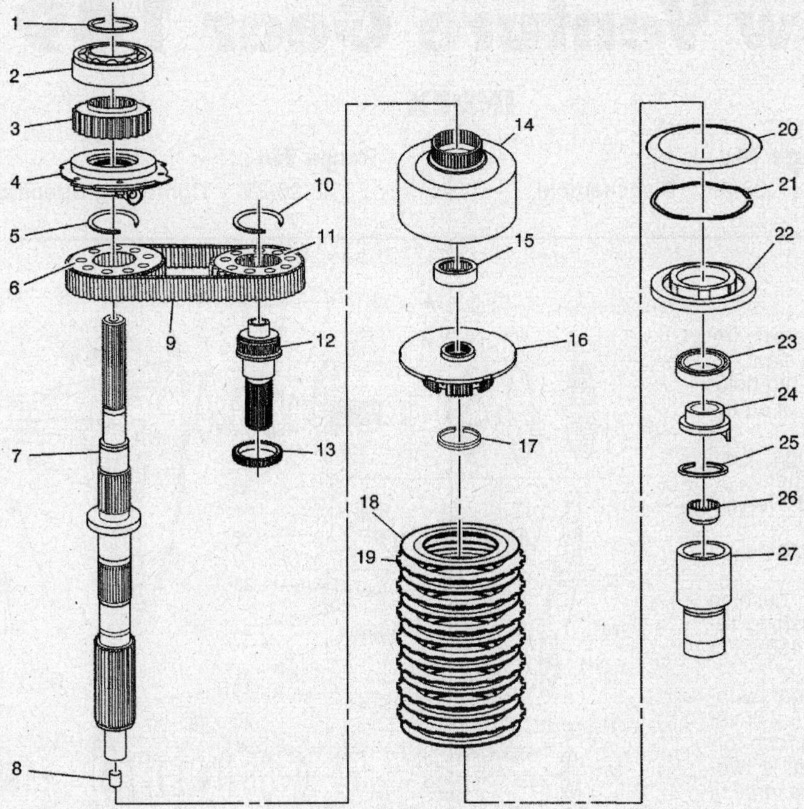

1. Rear Output Shaft Rear Bearing Retaining Ring
2. Rear Output Shaft Rear Bearing
3. Rear Output Shaft Speed Reluctor Wheel
4. Oil Pump
5. Drive Sprocket Retaining Ring
6. Drive Sprocket
7. Rear Output Shaft
8. Oil Restrictor
9. Chain
10. Driven Sprocket Retaining Ring
11. Driven Sprocket
12. Front Output Shaft
13. Front Output Shaft Speed Reluctor Wheel
14. Clutch Housing
15. Clutch Housing Bearing
16. Clutch Hub
17. Clutch Hub Retaining Ring
18. Clutch Press Plate – Friction
19. Clutch Press Plate – Steel
20. Clutch Shim
21. Clutch Spring
22. Clutch Pressure Plate
23. Clutch Pressure Plate Bearing
24. Clutch Bearing Inner Support
25. Clutch Assembly Retaining Ring
26. Input Shaft Pilot Bearing
27. Input Gear

LTV0500000001585

Fig. 3 Exploded view of internal components

TIGHTENING SPECIFICATIONS

Year	Component	Torque/Ft. Lbs.
2002–05	Actuator Encoder Motor	15
	Case Half	27
	Clutch Lever Pivot Pin	45
	Shift Detent Spring	13
	VSS	11

New Venture Gear 149

INDEX

DISASSEMBLE

1. Mount front case half to assembly fixture tool No. J45759, or equivalent.
2. Install assembly fixture tool into holding fixture tool No. J3289-20, or equivalent.
3. Remove drain and full plugs, then drain fluid into suitable container.
4. Remove access plug and vehicle speed sensor, **Fig. 1.**
5. Remove input and rear output shaft seals.
6. Remove rear output shaft bushing using transfer case rear bushing remover and installer tool No. J45380, or equivalent.
7. Remove front output shaft seal by inserting suitable flat-tipped screwdriver in inner seal race and prying race forward. Front output shaft seal is two-piece internal style seal and is force fit on front output shaft.
8. Remove inner seal race forward using suitable small pry bar.
9. Remove remaining part of front output seal by inserting suitable flat-tipped screwdriver or small pry bar between lip of front output shaft seal outer lip and transfer case.
10. Mark brackets' locations for assembly alignment.
11. Remove transfer case mounting bolts, washers and brackets.
12. Insert suitable flat-blade screwdrivers in left and righthand slots, then press screwdrivers down equally.
13. Open outer rear output shaft bearing retaining ring using suitable snap ring pliers in slot.
14. Remove rear from front case half.
15. Remove oil pump screen.
16. Hold planetary carrier in place and remove rear output shaft.
17. Remove retaining ring, then the output shaft bearing using flat side of split-plate bearing puller tool No. J22912-01, or equivalent, and suitable press.
18. Move oil pump retaining ring down and away from tone wheel.
19. Remove speed reluctor wheel using split-plate bearing puller tool No. J22912-01, or equivalent, and suitable press. Discard speed reluctor wheel.
20. Remove retaining ring and oil pump.
21. Unseat and remove annulus retaining ring using suitable screwdriver.
22. Remove rear output shaft.
23. Remove mainshaft rear bearing using mainshaft support bushing/bearing remover tool No. J45548 and slide hammer tool No. J2619-01, or equivalents.
24. Remove planetary carrier by tapping on end of mainshaft with suitable soft-face hammer while lifting off planetary carrier.
25. Remove planetary carrier thrust washer and sun gear.
26. Remove carrier retaining ring and mainshaft.
27. Remove planetary carrier sun gear bearing.
28. Remove driven sprocket retaining ring and drive chain.
29. Remove viscous coupling.
30. Remove retaining ring from groove

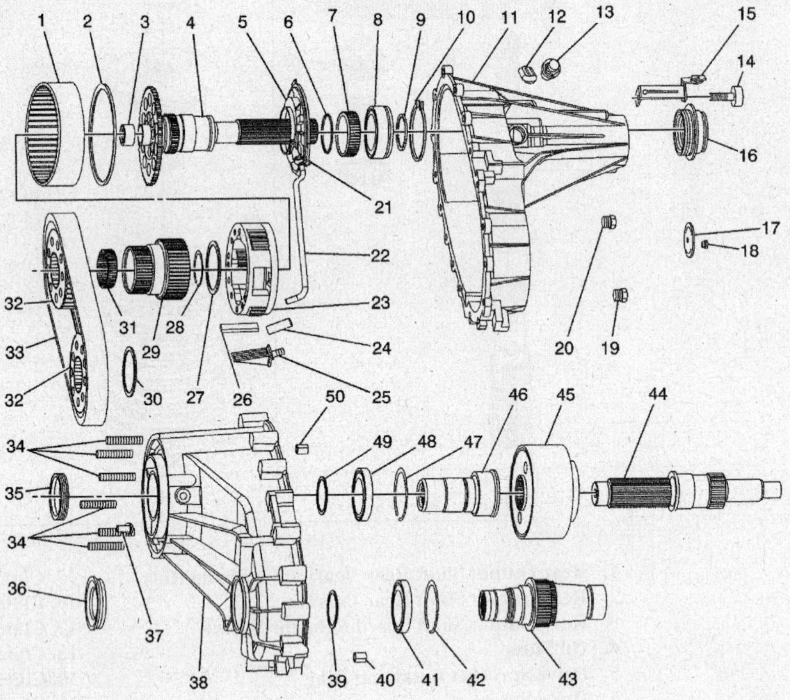

1. Annulus Gear
2. Retaining Ring
3. Mainshaft Rear Bushing
4. Rear Output Shaft
5. Oil Pump Assembly
6. Retaining Ring
7. Tone Wheel
8. Rear Output Shaft Bearing
9. Retaining Ring
10. Retaining Ring
11. Rear Case
12. Plug
13. Speed Sensor
14. Bolt
15. Bracket
16. Rear Output Shaft Seal
17. Identification Tag
18. Screw
19. Drain Plug
20. Fill Plug
21. Oil Seal
22. Oil Tube
23. Carrier Assembly
24. Connector Tube
25. Oil Screen
26. Magnet
27. Sun Gear Thrust Washer
28. Retaining Ring
29. Sun Gear
30. Retaining Ring
31. Needle Roller Bearing
32. Sprocket
33. Chain
34. Stud
35. Input Gear Seal
36. Front Output Seal
37. Vent Assembly
38. Front Case
39. Retaining Ring
40. Split Dowel
41. Front Output Bearing
42. Retaining Ring
43. Front Output Shaft
44. Mainshaft
45. Viscous Coupling
46. Input Gear
47. Retaining Ring
48. Input Gear Bearing
49. Retaining Ring
50. Split Dowel

LTV0500000001589

Fig. 1 Exploded view of transfer case

using suitable flat-bladed screwdriver and input gear.

31. Remove retaining ring and input gear bearing using suitable press.
32. Remove retaining ring and front output shaft.
33. Remove retainer ring and front output shaft bearing.
34. Remove front output shaft bearing from rear case using 3–4 inch bushing and bearing remover too No. J26941 and slide hammer with bearing adapter tool No. J23907, or equivalents.

ASSEMBLE

1. Install mounting studs at 1.16–1.20 inches high.
2. Mount front case half to assembly fixture tool No. J45759, or equivalent.
3. Install assembly fixture tool into holding fixture tool No. J3289-20, or equivalent.
4. Install input bearing facing toward front of input gear using suitable press and ensure bearing is supported by internal race. Install new retaining ring.
5. Install input gear and new retaining ring.
6. Install front output shaft bearing with cafe side facing inside front case and new retaining ring.
7. Install front output shaft and new retaining ring.
8. Install viscous coupling and mainshaft.
9. Install drive chain and sprockets. Blue colored link faces up or toward rear of case.
10. Install driven sprocket and carrier retaining rings.
11. Lubricate and install planetary carrier sun gear bearing with suitable transfer case fluid.
12. Install sun gear ensuring spline engages with both sprocket and viscous coupling cover. Sub gear shoulder must bottom on sprocket.
13. Install sun gear thrust washer
14. Install carrier. Snap should be felt and heard when carrier is properly seated.
15. Install mainshaft rear bearing in rear output shaft using mainshaft support bearing installer tool No. J45549 and universal driver handle tool No. J8092, or equivalents.
16. Install rear output shaft in annulus gear and new retaining ring.
17. Install oil pump and new speed reluctor wheel retaining ring.
18. Install speed reluctor wheel until it is just contacting retaining ring using tone ring and bearing installer tool No. J45540 and rear pinion bearing race installer tool No. J5590, or equivalents.
19. Install rear output shaft bearing using tone ring and bearing installer tool No. J45540 and rear pinion bearing race installer tool No. J5590, or equivalents. Ensure rear output shaft bearing retaining ring groove is facing toward rear of rear output shaft.
20. Install new rear output shaft bearing new retaining ring.
21. Install rear output shaft.
22. Install front output shaft rear bearing using drive sprocket needle bearing installer tool No. J36370 and universal driver handle tool No. J8092, or equivalents.
23. Install wear clip in rear case half.
24. Install O-ring , then oil pump screen and tube.
25. Install chip collector magnet.
26. Apply ⅛ inch bead of suitable RTV sealant to front case half.
27. Install front case half locating pins in and align rear case on rear output shaft bearing, then install rear case half.
28. Open outer rear output shaft bearing retaining ring and lower rear case on to rear output shaft bearing. Remove snap ring pliers.
29. Lower rear case on to alignment dowels. Ensure rear case is squarely seated on dowels.
30. Position brackets to proper bolt hole, then install and tighten new case half mounting bolts and washers.
31. Install new rear output shaft bushing, using transfer case rear bushing remover and installer tool No. J45380, or equivalent, and suitable hammer.
32. Install input seal, using seal installer tool No. J42738, or equivalent.
33. Install rear output shaft seal with bottom drain hole forcing down toward ground using output shaft seal installer tool No. 37668-A or equivalent.
34. Install front output shaft seal using front output shaft seal installer tool No. J43484 and universal driver handle tool No. J8092, or equivalents.
35. Install and tighten transfer case speed sensor.
36. Install and tighten drain and fill plugs. **Only use aluminum drain and fill plugs.**
37. Install access plug.

TIGHTENING SPECIFICATIONS

Year	Component	Torque/Ft. Lbs.
2002–06	Case Half	27
	Drain Plug	15
	Fill Plug	15
	Speed Sensor	11

New Venture Gear 233

INDEX

DISASSEMBLE

1. Remove vehicle speed sensor assembly, **Fig. 1.**
2. Remove mounting bolts and motor/encoder.
3. Remove detent plug, O-ring, spring and plunger.
4. Remove retainer rings, plastic washer and front output shaft seal.
5. Remove mounting bolts and rear extension housing.
6. Remove retaining ring, mounting bolts and output bearing cover.
7. Remove snap ring and tone wheels from rear and output shafts.
8. Record bracket mounting bolt positions for assembly.
9. Remove case halves mounting bolts.
10. Separate case halves, by inserting suitable screwdrivers into cast slots and prying apart, noting the following:
    a. **Do not damage oil pump.**
    b. **Do not wedge halves apart at any point on mating surface.**
11. Remove rear case and oil pump as assembly, **Fig. 2.**
12. Disconnect from tube and remove oil pump.
13. Remove oil pump, O-ring, rubber tube, pickup screen and tube.
14. Remove front output shaft and drive chain from case and mainshaft.
15. Remove mainshaft and mode shift fork.
16. Remove mode shift fork spring and retaining spring cover from fork shaft.
17. Remove mode fork from mainshaft.
18. Remove low range fork, sleeve and hub from planetary assembly.
19. Remove range shift hub from low range fork.
20. Remove shift lever nut, washer, shift lever, plastic washer and O-ring, then the sector.
21. Remove mounting bolts and input bearing retainer.
22. Remove input gear snap ring.
23. Remove planetary assembly.
24. Remove retaining and stop rings, then the synchronizer/sleeve assembly and drive sprocket.
25. Remove synchronizer hub clutch sleeve, retaining ring and studs.
26. Turn synchronizer over and remove stud retaining ring.
27. Remove snap ring for planetary carrier, then the steel spacer and fiber washer from input gear.
28. Remove input gear and fiber washer from planetary carrier.
29. Remove input bearing retainer seal.
30. Remove output shaft extension housing oil seal.
31. Remove input gear bearing using output shaft bearing remover tool No. J29369-1, adapter tool No. J9276-21 and slide hammer tool No. J2619, or equivalents.
32. Remove front output shaft retaining ring.
33. Remove front output shaft bearing using bearing remover tool No. J33790 and universal driver handle tool No. J8092, or equivalents.
34. Remove front output shaft rear roller bearing using bearing remover tool No. J29369-2 and universal driver handle tool No. J8092, or equivalents.
35. Remove rear output bearing using bearing remover tool No. J33790 and universal driver handle tool No. J8092, or equivalents.
36. Remove bearing retaining ring.
37. Remove front input bearing using bearing remover tool No. J33790 and universal driver handle tool No. J8092, or equivalents.

ASSEMBLE

1. Install bearing retaining ring, then the front input shaft bearing using tool No. J36370 and universal driver handle tool No. J8092, or equivalents.
2. Install output shaft rear bearing using front and rear output shaft bearing installer tool No. J36371, or equivalent.
3. Install front output shaft rear roller bearing using bearing installer tool No. J33832 and universal driver handle tool No. J8092, or equivalents.
4. Install output shaft front bearing using front and rear output shaft bearing installer tool No. J36371, or equivalent.
5. Install front output shaft front bearing retaining ring.
6. Install input gear bearing using input gear ball bearing installer tool No. J36373 and universal driver handle tool No. J8092, or equivalents.
7. Lubricate rear extension oil seal with suitable ATF and install using extension housing seal installer tool No. J33843, or equivalent.
8. Install fiber washer and input gear into planetary gear.
9. Install fiber washer and steel spacer onto input gear.
10. Install planetary carrier snap ring. Set planetary gear and input gear aside.
11. Install input bearing retainer seal using seal installer tool No. J33831, or equivalent.
12. Install retaining ring hook end into strut and hold in place, then install remaining synchronizer struts into hub and ring.
13. Turn synchronizer over and install second retaining ring. Ensure second retaining ring hook end is not installed in same strut as first ring.
14. Install clutch sleeve over synchronizer hub, noting the following:
    a. Ensure clutch sleeve spline is aligned with strut.
    b. Ensure struts are in sleeve strut pocket recesses.
15. Install drive sprocket, synchronizer and sleeve assembly, and snap and retaining rings, noting the following:
    a. Ensure drive sprocket with cone end clutch teeth is toward mainshaft input end.
    b. Ensure synchronizer stop ring is onto drive sprocket cone.
    c. Ensure clutch teeth mate with drive sprocket teeth.
16. Slip and lock mainshaft retaining ring.
17. Install planetary gear assembly into front case, then instal input shaft snap ring.
18. Apply suitable RTV sealant to bearing retainer mating surfaces and Loctite 242, or equivalent threadlock, to mounting bolt threads.
19. Install input bearing retainer.
20. Install sector into front case through sector hole, then the O-ring and plastic washer.
21. Install shift lever onto shaft and flush against plastic washer.
22. Install shift lever washer and nut.
23. Install new low range and mode fork pads.
24. Install range shift hub into low range fork.
25. Install low range fork, sleeve and hub onto planetary assembly and case. Ensure sleeve roller is on sector slot.
26. Install mode shift fork onto mainshaft.
27. Install mainshaft and mode shift fork, noting the following:
    a. Ensure mainshaft is in hub and planetary assembly.
    b. Ensure mode fork shaft is in sleeve assembly.
28. Install mode fork retaining spring and cover onto mode shift shaft.
29. Install front output shaft and drive chain into front case and mainshaft.
30. Install rubber tube, oil pickup screen, O-ring and oil pump. Secure oil pickup tube to pump.
31. Apply suitable RTV sealant to case mating surfaces.
32. Install rear case onto front case.
33. Install case halves mounting bolts, noting the following:
    a. Apply Loctite 242, or equivalent threadlock, to mounting bolts.

b. Longer case bolts and their washers are placed in doweled case holes or in original attaching brackets holes.

34. Install retaining ring and rear output shaft tone wheel. Ensure tine wheel is flash against retaining ring.
35. Install second retaining ring. Ensure ring is in groove.
36. Apply thin coat of suitable RTV sealant to rear output shaft bearing cover mating surface. Ensure not RTV is applied or pushed into oil return port.
37. Install rear output shaft bearing cover.
38. Install rear output shaft bearing retaining ring.
39. Install rear extension housing onto bearing cover with weep hole down.
40. Install front output shaft seal using extension housing seal installer tool No. J33843, or equivalent.
41. Install output shaft retaining ring and plastic washer, then the second retainer ring.
42. Install motor/encoder and tighten mounting bolts.
43. Install detent plunger, spring, O-ring seal and plug.
44. Install vehicle speed sensor.

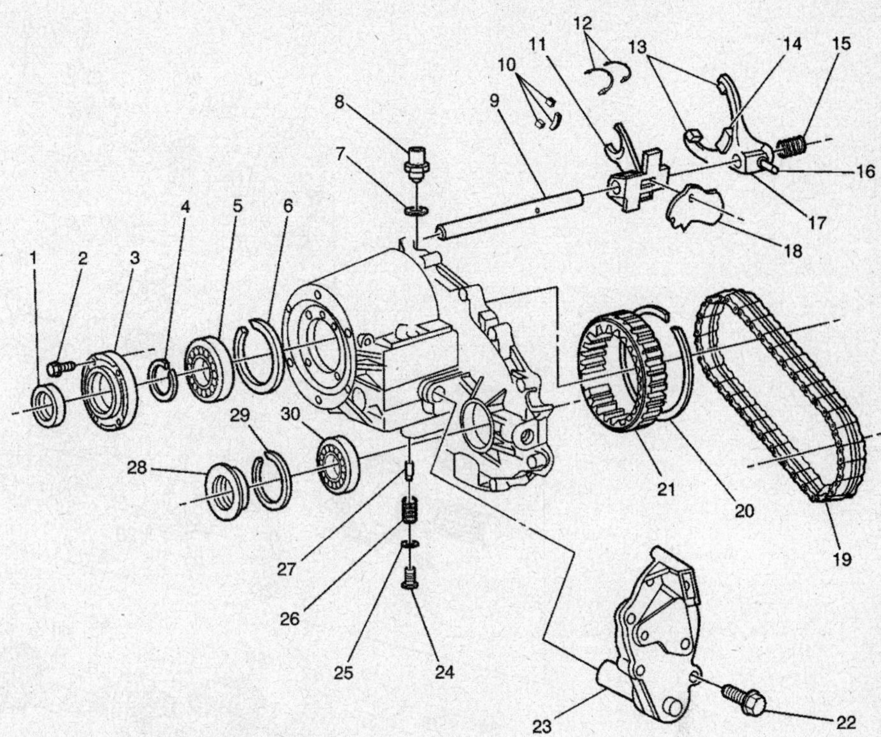

1. Input Bearing Retainer Seal
2. Input Gear Bearing Retainer Bolt
3. Input Bearing Retainer
4. Input Bearing Retaining Ring
5. Front Input Bearing
6. Bearing Retainer Ring
7. Switch Seal
8. Vacuum Switch
9. Shift Rail
10. Range Shift Fork Pads, 1st Design
11. Range Shift Fork
12. Range Shift Fork Pads, 2nd Design
13. Mode Shift Fork Side Pad
14. Mode Shift Fork Center Pad
15. Shift Fork Spring
16. Shift Fork Pin
17. Mode Shift Fork
18. Sector Shaft
19. Drive Chain
20. Annulus Gear Retainer Ring
21. Annulus Gear
22. Encoder Motor Bolt
23. Encoder Motor
24. Detent Bolt
25. Detent Plunger Bolt O-Ring
26. Detent Plunger Spring
27. Detent Plunger
28. Front Output Shaft Seal
29. Front Output Bearing Retaining Ring
30. Front Output Bearing

LTV0500000001597

Fig. 1 Exploded view of case components

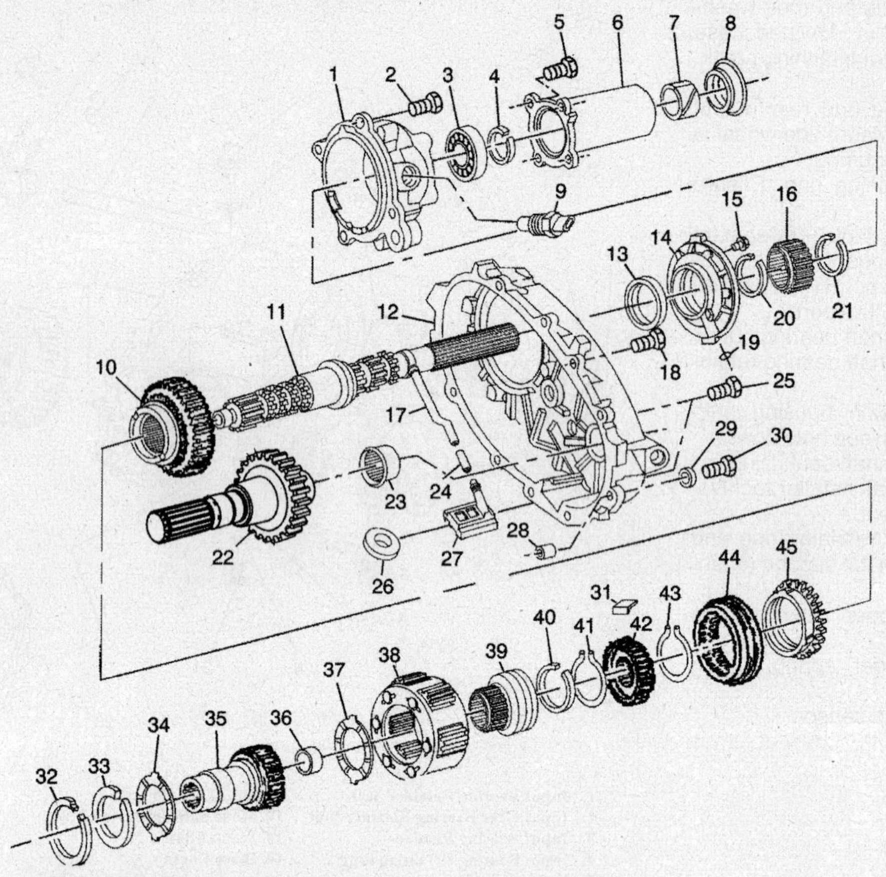

1. Rear Output Shaft Bearing Retainer
2. Retainer Housing Bolt
3. Rear Output Shaft Bearing
4. Rear Output Shaft Rear Bearing Retaining Ring
5. Extension Housing Bolt
6. Rear Extension
7. Rear Extension Bushing
8. Rear Output Shaft Seal
9. Speed Sensor
10. Drive Sprocket
11. Rear Output Shaft
12. Rear Half Case
13. Oil Pump Seal
14. Oil Pump
15. Bolt
16. Speed Sensor Reluctor Wheel
17. Oil Pump Suction Tube Bolt
18. Bolt
19. Oil Pump Suction Tube Seal
20. Speed Sensor Reluctor Wheel Retaining Ring
21. Speed Sensor Reluctor Wheel Retaining Ring
22. Front Output Shaft
23. Front Output Shaft Rear Bearing
24. Oil Pump Suction Hose
25. Oil Fill Plug
26. Magnet
27. Oil Pump Screen
28. Case Half Dowel
29. Case Half Washer
30. Bolt
31. Synchronizer Inserts
32. Planetary Carrier Retaining Ring
33. Planetary Carrier Shaft Retaining Ring
34. Input Gear Thrust Washer
35. Input Gear
36. Input Gear Bearing
37. Input Gear Thrust Washer
38. Planetary Carrier
39. Range Sleeve
40. Synchronizer Retaining Ring
41. Synchronizer Spring
42. Synchronizer Hub
43. Synchronizer Spring
44. Synchronizer Sleeve
45. Synchronizer Blocker Ring

LTV0500000001598

Fig. 2 Exploded view of rear case & drivetrain components

TIGHTENING SPECIFICATIONS

Year	Component	Torque/Ft. Lbs.
2002–05	Actuator Switch	17
	Case Half	23
	Detent Plug	11
	Drain Plug	35
	Encoder Motor	13
	Fill Plug	35
	Front Yoke Nut	148
	Input Shaft Bearing	14
	Mainshaft Extension Housing	23
	Rear Extension Housing	23
	Rear Retainer Housing	30
	Shift Select Lever	20
	Speed Sensor	23
	Vacuum Switch	17
	4WD Indicator Switch	17

New Venture Gear 236/246

INDEX

DISASSEMBLE

1. Remove mounting bolts, motor/encoder and gasket, **Fig. 1.**
2. Remove drain and fill plugs.
3. If vent tube is damaged, remove it and O-ring.
4. Remove rear speed sensors.
5. Remove rear case rubber plug.
6. Remove front speed sensor.
7. Remove front case input shaft studs.
8. Remove shield mounting bracket studs.
9. Remove front and rear case mounting bolts, studs and washers.
10. Spread rear output bearing retaining ring and separate case halves using suitable rubber mallet.
11. Remove front case alignment dowels.
12. Remove oil pump retainer tab from rear case, **Fig. 2.**
13. Remove magnet from front case.
14. Remove tone wheel, rear output bearing and retaining ring.
15. Remove oil pump pickup tube from pump inlet hole and O-ring.
16. Remove oil screen from front case and then from nylon tube.
17. Remove oil pump, then the inlet hole O-ring.
18. Remove gerotor pump retaining ring.
19. Remove drive and driven sprocket retaining rings.
20. Remove drive chain with drive and driven sprockets.
21. Remove sprockets from chain.
22. Remove mainshaft.
23. Remove retaining ring, thrust bearing, inner and outer bearing support plates and inner clutch drum, **Fig. 3.**
24. Remove inner bearing support from thrust bearing using suitable press.
25. Remove inner clutch and outer separator plates.
26. Remove clutch drum flange and inner clutch drum retaining ring.
27. Remove return spring and clutch inner drum.
28. Remove clutch drum.
29. Remove clutch inner drum.
30. Remove second clutch out drum bearing using suitable press.
31. Remove clutch outer drum bearing using suitable press.
32. If replacing mainshaft, remove oil restrictor.
33. Remove clutch lever and insets.
34. Remove shift rail.
35. Remove plunger, spring, O-ring and poppet bolt.
36. Remove range fork and shift sleeve from planetary gear, then the shift sleeve from range fork.
37. Remove front output shaft oil seal.
38. Remove front input case bearing retaining ring using suitable snap-ring pliers. **Do not scratch/damage seal surface.**
39. Remove front output shaft oil seal and retaining ring.
40. Remove front output shaft and bearing.
41. Remove driven sprocket and retaining ring.
42. Remove tone wheel and cap from front output shaft.
43. Remove input shaft and bearing.
44. Remove input shaft pilot bearing using suitable press.
45. Remove planetary and input gear retaining ring and thrust plate.
46. Remove planetary and input gear second thrust plate.
47. Remove input gear and thrust washer from planetary gear.
48. Remove rear output bearing.
49. Remove front output shaft rear bearing.
50. Remove rear output shaft seal.
51. Remove rear retainer bushing using suitable press.
52. Remove sector shaft retaining ring and sector.
53. Remove sector bearing using sector bearing installer tool No. J42737, or equivalent.
54. Remove front output shaft bearing retaining ring.
55. Remove front output shaft bearing using suitable press.
56. Remove input bearing gear retaining ring.
57. Remove input gear bearing using suitable press.

ASSEMBLE

1. Install input gear bearing using suitable press. Install retaining ring.
2. Install front output shaft bearing using suitable press. Install retaining ring.
3. Install sector bearing using sector bearing installer tool No. J42737, or equivalent. Ensure bearing seal is outward and bearing lettering inward.
4. Install sector and shaft retaining ring.
5. Install rear retainer bushing flush with case half bushing opening using suitable press.
6. Install rear output shaft seal using rear

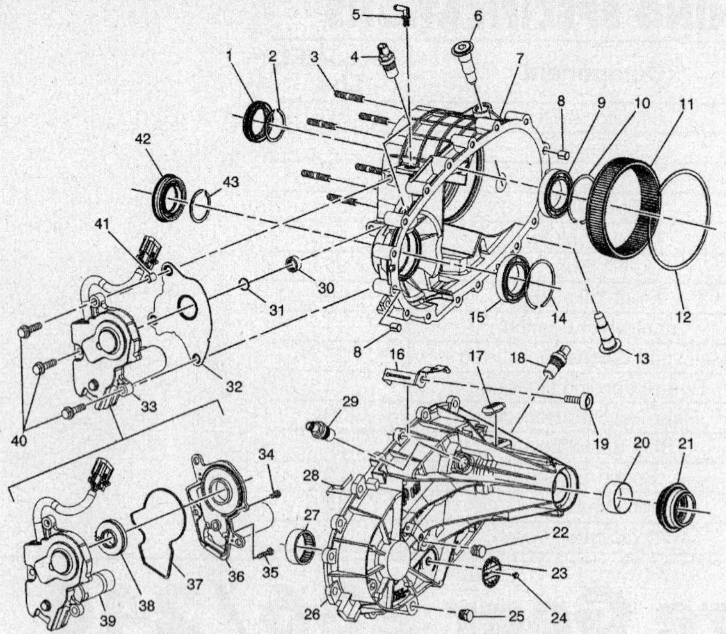

1. Input Shaft Seal
2. Input Gear Bearing Outer Retaining Ring
3. Adapter Stud
4. Front Vehicle Speed Sensor
5. Vent
6. Clutch Lever Pivot Pin
7. Front Case Half
8. Location Pin
9. Input Gear Bearing
10. Input Gear Bearing Retaining Ring
11. Annulus Gear
12. Annulus Gear Retaining Ring
13. Clutch Lever Pivot Pin
14. Front Output Shaft Bearing Retaining Ring
15. Front Output Shaft Front Bearing
16. Bracket
17. Access Hole Plug
18. Right Vehicle Speed Sensor
19. Case Half Bolt
20. Rear Bushing
21. Rear Output Shaft Seal
22. Fill Plug
23. ID Tag
24. ID Tag Screw
25. Drain Plug
26. Rear Case Half
27. Front Output Shaft Rear Bearing
28. Wear Clip
29. Left Vehicle Speed Sensor
30. Control Actuator Lever Bearing
31. Control Actuator Lever Retaining Ring
32. Actuator Encoder Motor Insulating Spacer
33. Actuator Encoder Motor
34. Housing Screw
35. Motor Cover Screw
36. Actuator Cover Plate
37. Actuator Seal
38. Range Select Position Sensor
39. Actuator Housing
40. Actuator Encoder Motor Bolt
41. Actuator Encoder Motor Location Pin
42. Front Output Shaft Seal
43. Front Output Shaft Bearing Retaining Ring

LTV0500000001592

Fig. 1 Exploded view of case components

output shaft seal installer tool No. J29162, or equivalent, noting the following:
   a. Align seal driver with rear output shaft seal notches.
   b. Align rear output seal drain tube with rear case half drain channel.
7. Install front output shaft rear bearing using bearing installer tool No. J33832 and universal driver handle tool No. J8092, or equivalents, noting the following:
   a. Ensure bearing rounded side is inward toward rear case half.
   b. Ensure bearing lettering side is outward away from rear case half.
8. Install drain and fill plugs and tighten to specifications, noting the following:
   a. Ensure plugs are aluminum. Steel plugs will destroy magnesium case integrity with accelerated corrosion.
   b. Do not use impact tool to install plugs.
9. Install rear output bearing retaining ring.
10. Install planetary gear thrust washer.
11. Install input gear pilot bearing to ground mark point using suitable press. Bearing top should align with input gear bottom edge.
12. Install input gear into planetary gear.
13. Install thrust washer, plate and retaining ring over input gear. Ensure thrust plate surface lettering is upward.
14. Install input shaft through bearing. Tap shaft lightly until flush against bearing.
15. Install front output shaft cap using suitable press.
16. Install front output shaft tone wheel using suitable press.
17. Install front output shaft driven sprocket.
18. Install front output shaft through case and bearing. **Do not overpress shaft into bearing.**
19. Install front output shaft retaining ring.
20. Install front output shaft oil seal using front output shaft seal installer tool No. J35870, or equivalent.
21. Install front output gear case bearing retaining ring using suitable snap-ring pliers. **Do not scratch/damage seal surface.**
22. Install front input gear oil seal with part numbers outward using front input shaft seal installer tool No. J33831, or equivalent.
23. Install shift rail into range fork. Ensure rail fits into machined hole at case bottom.
24. Install clutch lever and insets inserts.
25. Tighten clutch insets to specifications, noting the following:
   a. Ensure clutch lever roller is resting on sector.
   b. Ensure clutch lever is free to move.
26. If installing new mainshaft, install oil restrictor with top flush to funneled chamber bottom.
27. Install clutch outer drum bearing using suitable press, noting the following:
   a. Ensure gear side faces down.
   b. Bearing numbered side must face drum outside.
   c. Ensure bearing is flush with clutch drum bottom.
28. Install clutch drum.
29. Install inner drum and clutch drum. Inner drum should rest on outer drum top.
30. Install clutch washer into inner drum, noting the following:
   a. Ensure return spring prongs are upward and away from inner drum.
   b. Ensure return spring flat side is down against inner drum.
31. Install inner clutch drum retaining ring.
32. Install clutch drum flange, noting the following:
   a. Ensure flange is installed with counter bore side facing down.
   b. Align flange teeth with inner clutch drum slots.
33. Install inner clutch plates over clutch drum flange.
34. Install outer separator plate over inner clutch plate.
35. Continue installing inner clutch and outer separator plates until 10 inner clutch plates and nine outer separator plates are installed. All separator plate tabs should be aligned.
36. Install shim clutch pack.
37. Install inner bearing support into thrust bearing.
38. Install thrust bearing, and inner bearing support plate into outer bearing support plate. Ensure preload spring is in groove.
39. Install thrust bearing, and inner and outer bearing support plate into outer bearing support plate. Ensure all tabs align.
40. Install clutch retaining ring.
41. Install mainshaft, noting the following:
   a. Align inner bearing support tabs with clutch lever insets.
   b. Clutch drum should align with front case.
   c. Align mainshaft teeth with input gear inside teeth.
   d. Ensure inner bearing support lug aligns and fits between fork.
42. Install sprockets on chain.

43. Install drive chain with drive and driven sprockets. If there are three off colored chain links, ensure chain is installed with off colored links toward case rear.
44. Install drive and driven sprocket retaining rings.
45. Install gerotor pump retaining ring. Ensure retaining ring is not over mainshaft oil hole.
46. Install oil pump inlet hole O-ring.
47. Install oil pump, noting the following:
    a. Ensure pump seats on mainshaft flange.
    b. Ensure inlet hole is pointing toward front output shaft.
48. Install oil pump pickup tube into pump inlet hole and O-ring.
49. Position pickup tube under chain.
50. Install oil screen in front case and secure with nylon tube.
51. Install magnet in front case.
52. Install wave washer, tone wheel, rear output bear and retaining ring on mainshaft.
53. Install oil pump retainer tab using a thin coat of suitable RTV.
54. Install front case alignment dowels.
55. Apply suitable RTV sealant to front and rear case mating surfaces.
56. Spread rear output bearing retaining ring and assemble case halves using suitable rubber mallet.
57. Install case mounting bolts, studs and washers, noting the following:
    a. **Do not use steel bolts, studs or washers.**
    b. **Steel fasteners will destroy magnesium case integrity with accelerated corrosion, cause severe oil leakage and transfer case fault.**
    c. Ensure bolt and stud threads are clean and free of pre-applied thread fastener compounds, corrosion and debris.
    d. Apply Loctite PST 565, PST 242, or equivalent.
    e. Install and tighten bolts and studs within 10 minutes of applying thread fastener.
    f. Install bolts and studs in original positions.
    g. Transfer case may not have had aluminum washers. Aluminum washers were added during early to mid-year production.
58. Install shield mounting bracket studs, noting the following:
    a. Ensure stud threads are clean and free of pre-applied thread fastener compounds, corrosion and debris.
    b. Apply Loctite PST 565, PST 242, or equivalent.
    c. Install and tighten studs within 10 minutes of applying thread fastener.
59. Install front output shaft oil seal using front output shaft oil seal installer tool No. J33834, or equivalent.
60. Install rear speed sensors and tighten to specifications.
61. Install front speed sensor and tighten to specifications.
62. Ensure rear output bearing retaining ring is properly seated in groove and install rear case rubber plug.
63. If vent tube was damaged, install new one and O-ring.
64. Install plunger, spring, O-ring and poppet bolt, noting the following:
    a. Ensure bolt has O-ring position under head.
    b. Apply light coat of suitable transfer case oil to mating surface.
    c. Align sector notch with poppet plunger.
    d. **Do not use impact tool to install bolt.**
    e. Ensure poppet plunger remains in sector not during spring and bolt installation.
    f. Tighten poppet bolt to specifications.
65. Install motor/encoder and gasket, noting the following:
    a. Align mounting holes.
    b. Ensure gasket remains aligned.

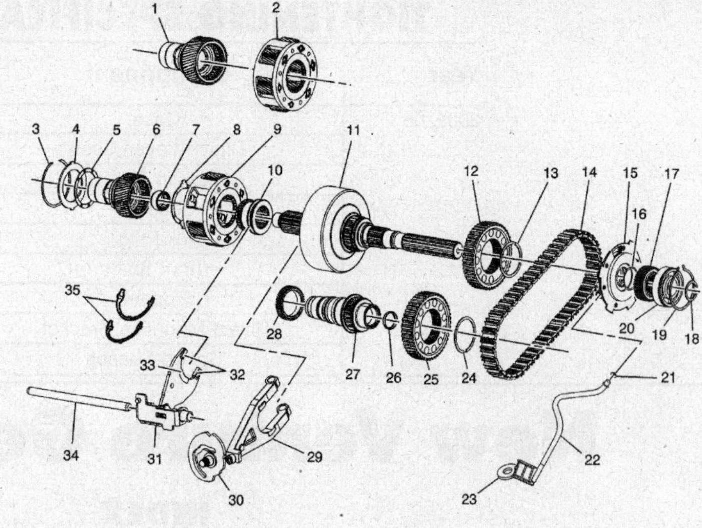

1. Input Gear 32 Teeth
2. High/Low Planetary Carrier 6 Pinion Gears
3. Planetary Gear Shaft Retaining Ring
4. Planetary Carrier Lock Ring
5. Input Gear Front Thrust Washer
6. Input Gear 27 Teeth
7. Input Gear Pilot Bearing
8. Input Gear Rear Thrust Washer
9. High/Low Planetary Carrier 3 Pinion Gears
10. High/Low Range Sleeve
11. Rear Output Shaft Assembly
12. Drive Sprocket
13. Drive Sprocket Retaining Ring
14. Drive Chain
15. Oil Pump
16. Oil Pump Wave Spring
17. Rear Output Shaft Speed Reluctor Wheel
18. Rear Output Shaft Rear Bearing Retaining Ring
19. Rear Output Shaft Rear Bearing Outer Retaining Ring
20. Rear Output Shaft Rear Bearing
21. Oil Pump Suction Pipe O-Ring Seal
22. Oil Pump Screen and Suction Pipe
23. Magnet
24. Driven Sprocket Retaining Ring
25. Driven Sprocket
26. Front Output Shaft Cup Plug
27. Front Output Shaft
28. Front Output Shaft Speed Reluctor Wheel
29. Clutch Lever
30. Control Actuator Lever
31. Range Fork
32. Shift Fork Pad, 1st Design
33. Center Shift Fork Pad, 1st Design
34. Shift Fork Shaft
35. Shift Fork Pads, 2nd Design

LTV0500000001593

Fig. 2 Exploded view of internal components

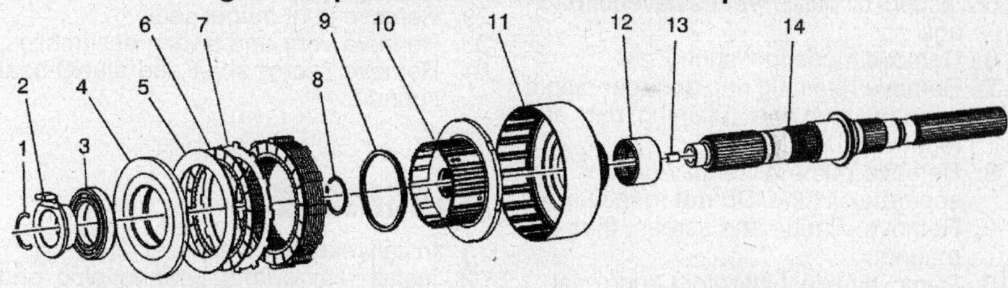

1. **Clutch Retaining Ring**
2. **Clutch Bearing Inner Support**
3. **Clutch Apply Plate Bearing**
4. **Clutch Apply Plate**
5. **Shims**
6. **Clutch Inner Plate Friction**
7. **Clutch Outer Plate Steel**
8. **Clutch Hub Retaining Ring**
9. **Clutch Return Spring**
10. **Clutch Hub**
11. **Clutch Housing**
12. **Clutch Housing Bearing**
13. **Oil Restrictor**
14. **Rear Output Shaft**

LTV0500000001594

Fig. 3 Exploded view of clutch components

TIGHTENING SPECIFICATIONS

Year	Component	Torque/Ft. Lbs.
2002–06	Case	27
	Clutch Lever Insert	35
	Drain Plug	15
	Encoder	27
	Fill Plug	15
	Input Shaft	27
	Poppet	15
	Shield Mounting Bracket	27
	Speed Sensor	23

New Venture Gear 261

INDEX

DISASSEMBLE

1. Remove rear speed sensors.
2. Remove rear output bearing plug and separate rear output retaining ring, **Fig. 1.**
3. Remove front and rear case mounting bolts.
4. Separate case halves by prying at slots provided.
5. Inspect oil pump wear sleeve for damage.
6. Remove mode fork spring.
7. Remove retaining ring and rear output bearing, then the retaining ring and tone wheel,
8. Remove pump assembly-gerotor and separate oil tube. **Do not lose O-ring.**
9. Remove oil tube and screen, then the magnet.
10. Remove mainshaft rotor O-ring seal.
11. Remove driven and drive sprocket retaining rings.
12. Remove sprockets and drive chain as assembly.
13. Remove mode fork assembly and mainshaft as assembly.
14. Remove mode fork and shift rail, then separate rail from fork.
15. Remove synchronizer clutch gear.
16. Remove retaining ring and synchronizer assembly.
17. Remove outer ring, middle ring and inner core.
18. Remove synchronizer hub, **Fig. 2.**
19. Remove screw-O-ring, spring and poppet plunger.
20. Remove range fork and range shift sleeve.
21. Remove retaining ring and sector shaft.
22. Remove retaining ring, sector shaft front bearing and internal case retaining ring.
23. Remove lever assembly, mounting bolt and sector.
24. Remove front input oil seal and retaining ring.
25. Remove input gear and planetary assembly.
26. Remove retaining ring, separate input gear and planetary assembly.
27. Remove lock plate carrier and input gear/planetary housing thrust washers.
28. Remove retaining ring and front input bearing.
29. Remove front output seal.
30. Remove vent and switch assemblies.
31. Remove sector shaft and stat-O-seal support.

ASSEMBLE

1. Install rear speed sensors.
2. Install rear output bearing plug and separate rear output retaining ring.
3. Install front and rear case mounting bolts.
4. Separate case halves by prying at slots provided.
5. Inspect oil pump wear sleeve for damage.
6. Install mode fork spring.
7. Install retaining ring and rear output bearing, then the retaining ring and tone wheel.
8. Install pump asm-gerotor and separate oil tube. **Do not lose O-ring.**
9. Install lock plate carrier and input gear/ planetary housing thrust washers.
10. Install sector shaft and stat-O-seal support assemblies.
11. Install switch assembly.
12. Install front output seal.
13. Install front input bearing and retaining ring.
14. Install rear case extension area seal using rear output shaft seal installer tool No. J29162, or equivalent.
15. Install thrust washer and input gear into planetary gear, then the thrust washer onto input gear and inside planetary gear.
16. Install carrier ring onto input gear and inside planetary gear, then the carrier lock ring.
17. Install planetary assembly.
18. Install retaining ring and front input oil seal.
19. Install sector.
20. Install front bearing and retaining ring.
21. Install retaining ring and front output shaft.
22. Install range fork and range shift sleeve.
23. Install screw-O-ring, spring and poppet plunger.
24. Install inner core, middle ring and outer ring onto mainshaft.
25. Hold other struts from front with retaining ring.
26. Install retaining ring and synchronizer assembly.
27. Install synchronizer retaining ring hook end into first strut to hold in place.
28. Turn synchronizer over and install second retaining ring. Ensure hook end is not installed on same strut as first retaining ring.
29. Install clutch sleeve of synchronizer hub, noting the following:
    a. Ensure clutch sleeve spline aligned with strut.
    b. Ensure struts position in clutch sleeve strut pocket recesses.
30. Install synchronizer assembly and retaining ring.
31. Install synchronizer clutch gear with collar side out and flat side in.
32. Install shift rail into to mode fork, then the mode fork and shift rail onto synchronize clutch sleeve.
33. Install mainshaft, mode fork and shift rail as assembly.
34. Inspect drive chain for off colored links. Position off colored links toward rear case.
35. Install drive and driven sprockets into

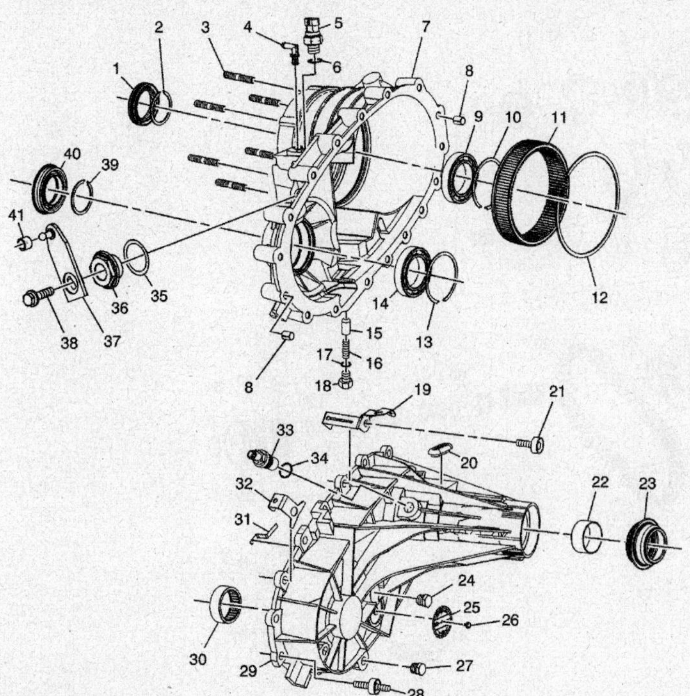

1. Input Shaft Seal
2. Input Gear Bearing Outer Retaining Ring
3. Adapter Stud
4. Vent
5. Gear Indicator Switch
6. Gear Indicator Switch Seal
7. Front Case Half
8. Locating Pin
9. Input Gear Bearing
10. Input Gear Bearing Retaining Ring
11. Annulus Gear
12. Annulus Gear Retaining Ring
13. Front Output Shaft Bearing Retaining Ring
14. Front Output Shaft Bearing
15. Shift Detent Plunger
16. Shift Detent Spring
17. Shift Detent Plunger Plug O-Ring Seal
18. Shift Detent Spring Bolt
19. Wiring Harness Bracket
20. Access Hole Plug
21. Case Half Bolt
22. Rear Bushing
23. Rear Output Shaft Seal
24. Fill Plug
25. ID Plate
26. ID Plate Screw
27. Drain Plug
28. Case Half Stud
29. Rear Case Half
30. Front Output Shaft Rear Bearing
31. Oil Pump Wear Sleeve
32. Bracket
33. Vehicle Speed Sensor
34. Vehicle Speed Sensor O-Ring Seal
35. Shift Detent Lever Seal
36. Shift Control Lever Shaft Support
37. Shift Control Lever
38. Shift Control Lever Bolt
39. Front Output Shaft Bearing Outer Retaining Ring
40. Front Output Shaft Seal
41. Foam Seal

LTV0500000001595

Fig. 1 Exploded view of case components

chain, then onto mainshaft and front output shaft.

36. Install driven and drive sprocket retaining rings.
37. Install mainshaft rotor O-ring seal.
38. Install oil pump onto main shaft, then the tube, rubber hose and screen.
39. Install metal debris magnet.
40. Install tone wheel and retaining ring.
41. Install rear output bearing. Ensure bearing retaining ring groove is toward case rear.
42. Install rear output bearing retaining ring.
43. Install mode fork spring.
44. Apply suitable RTV sealant to front and rear case mating surfaces.
45. Spread rear output bearing retainer ring and position case halves together.
46. Install rear output bearing plug.
47. Install speed sensor.
48. Install sector bolt.

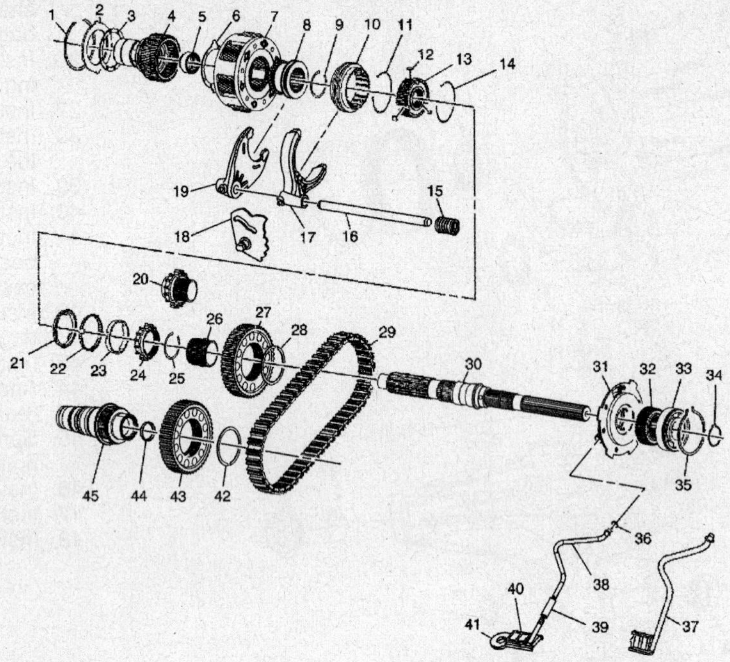

1. Planetary Carrier Internal Gear Retaining Ring
2. Planetary Carrier Lock Plate
3. Input Gear Front Thrust Washer
4. Input Gear
5. Input Gear Needle Bearing
6. Input Gear Rear Thrust Washer
7. High/Low Planetary Carrier
8. High/Low Range Sleeve
9. Synchronizer Retaining Ring
10. Synchronizer Sleeve
11. Synchronizer Insert Spring
12. Synchronizer Insert
13. Synchronizer Hub
14. Synchronizer Insert Spring
15. Shift Fork Shaft Spring
16. Shift Shaft
17. 2/4 Wheel Drive Mode Shift Fork
18. Shift Detent Lever
19. High/Low Range Shift Fork
20. 2/4 Wheel Drive Synchronizer Gear, 2nd Design
21. Synchronizer Outer Ring
22. Synchronizer Middle Ring
23. Synchronizer Inner Ring
24. 2/4 Wheel Drive Synchronizer Gear, 1st Design
25. Drive Sprocket Front Retaining Ring, 1st Design
26. Drive Sprocket Sleeve, 1st Design
27. Drive Sprocket
28. Drive Sprocket Rear Retaining Ring
29. Chain
30. Rear Output Shaft
31. Oil Pump
32. Speed Reluctor Wheel
33. Rear Output Shaft Bearing
34. Rear Output Shaft Bearing Retaining Ring
35. Rear Output Shaft Bearing Outer Retaining Ring
36. Oil Pump Suction Pipe O-Ring Seal
37. Oil Pump Suction Pipe Assembly, 2nd Design
38. Oil Pump Suction Pipe, 1st Design
39. Connector Hose, 1st Design
40. Oil Pump Screen, 1st Design
41. Magnet
42. Driven Sprocket Retaining Ring
43. Driven Sprocket
44. Front Output Shaft Cup Plug
45. Front Output Shaft

LTV0500000001596

Fig. 2 Exploded view of internal components

TIGHTENING SPECIFICATIONS

Year	Component	Torque/Ft. Lbs.
2002–06	Case Half	23
	Detent Plug	11
	Drain Plug	35
	Fill Plug	35
	Front Propeller Shaft Yoke	148
	Input Shaft Bearing	14
	Mainshaft Extension Housing	23
	Rear Retainer Housing	30
	Shift Select Lever	20
	Speed Sensor	23
	4WD Indicator Switch	17

New Venture Gear 263

INDEX

DISASSEMBLE

1. Remove mounting bolts, motor/ encoder and gasket, **Fig. 1.**
2. Remove drain and fill plugs.
3. If vent tube is damaged, remove it and O-ring.
4. Remove rear speed sensors.
5. Remove rear case rubber plug.
6. Remove front speed sensor.
7. Remove front case input shaft studs.
8. Remove shield mounting bracket studs.
9. Remove front and rear case mounting bolts, studs and washers.
10. Spread rear output bearing retaining ring and separate case halves using suitable rubber mallet.
11. Remove front case alignment dowels.
12. Remove oil pump retainer tab from rear case, **Fig. 2.**
13. Remove magnet from front case.
14. Remove tone wheel, rear output bearing and retaining ring.
15. Remove oil pump pickup tube from pump inlet hole and O-ring.
16. Remove oil screen from front case and then from nylon tube.
17. Remove oil pump, then the inlet hole O-ring.
18. Remove gerotor pump retaining ring.
19. Remove drive and driven sprocket retaining rings.
20. Remove drive chain with drive and driven sprockets.
21. Remove sprockets from chain.
22. Remove mainshaft.
23. Remove retaining ring, thrust bearing, inner and outer bearing support plates and inner clutch drum.
24. Remove inner bearing support from thrust bearing using suitable press.
25. Remove inner clutch and outer separator plates.
26. Remove clutch drum flange and inner clutch drum retaining ring.
27. Remove return spring and clutch inner drum.
28. Remove clutch drum.
29. Remove clutch inner drum.
30. Remove second clutch out drum bearing using suitable press.
31. Remove clutch outer drum bearing using suitable press.
32. If replacing mainshaft, remove oil restrictor.
33. Remove clutch lever and insets.
34. Remove shift rail.
35. Remove plunger, spring, O-ring and poppet bolt.
36. Remove range fork and shift sleeve from planetary gear, then the shift sleeve from range fork.
37. Remove front output shaft oil seal.
38. Remove front input case bearing retaining ring using suitable snap-ring pliers. **Do not scratch/damage seal surface.**
39. Remove front output shaft oil seal and retaining ring.
40. Remove front output shaft and bearing.
41. Remove driven sprocket and retaining ring.
42. Remove tone wheel and cap from front output shaft.
43. Remove input shaft and bearing.
44. Remove input shaft pilot bearing using suitable press.
45. Remove planetary and input gear retaining ring and thrust plate.
46. Remove planetary and input gear second thrust plate.
47. Remove input gear and thrust washer from planetary gear.
48. Remove rear output bearing.
49. Remove front output shaft rear bearing.
50. Remove rear output shaft seal.
51. Remove rear retainer bushing using suitable press.
52. Remove sector shaft retaining ring and sector.
53. Remove sector bearing using sector bearing installer tool No. J42737, or equivalent.
54. Remove front output shaft bearing retaining ring.
55. Remove front output shaft bearing using suitable press.
56. Remove input bearing gear retaining ring.
57. Remove input gear bearing using suitable press.

ASSEMBLE

1. Install input gear bearing using suitable press. Install retaining ring.
2. Install front output shaft bearing using suitable press. Install retaining ring.
3. Install sector bearing using sector bearing installer tool No. J42737, or equivalent. Ensure bearing seal is outward and bearing lettering inward.
4. Install sector and shaft retaining ring.
5. Install rear retainer bushing flush with case half bushing opening using suitable press.
6. Install rear output shaft seal using rear output shaft seal installer tool No. J29162, or equivalent, noting the following:
   a. Align seal driver with rear output shaft seal notches.
   b. Align rear output seal drain tube with rear case half drain channel.
7. Install front output shaft rear bearing using bearing installer tool No. J33832 and universal driver handle tool No. J8092, or equivalents, noting the following:
   a. Ensure bearing rounded side is inward toward rear case half.
   b. Ensure bearing lettering side is outward away from rear case half.
8. Install drain and fill plugs and tighten to specifications, noting the following:
   a. Ensure plugs are aluminum. Steel plugs will destroy magnesium case integrity with accelerated corrosion.
   b. Do not use impact tool to install plugs.
9. Install rear output bearing retaining ring.
10. Install planetary gear thrust washer.
11. Install input gear pilot bearing to ground mark point using suitable press. Bearing top should align with input gear bottom edge.
12. Install input gear into planetary gear.
13. Install thrust washer, plate and retaining ring over input gear. Ensure thrust plate surface lettering is upward.
14. Install input shaft through bearing. Tap shaft lightly until flush against bearing.
15. Install front output shaft cap using suitable press.
16. Install front output shaft tone wheel using suitable press.
17. Install front output shaft driven sprocket.
18. Install front output shaft through case and bearing. **Do not overpress shaft into bearing.**
19. Install front output shaft retaining ring.
20. Install front output shaft oil seal using front output shaft seal installer tool No. J35870, or equivalent.
21. Install front output gear case bearing retaining ring using suitable snap-ring pliers. **Do not scratch/damage seal surface.**
22. Install front input gear oil seal with part numbers outward using front input shaft seal installer tool No. J33831, or equivalent.
23. Install shift rail into range fork. Ensure rail fits into machined hole at case bottom.
24. Install clutch lever and insets inserts.
25. Tighten clutch insets to specifications, noting the following:
   a. Ensure clutch lever roller is resting on sector.
   b. Ensure clutch lever is free to move.
26. If installing new mainshaft, install oil restrictor with top flush to funneled chamber bottom.
27. Install clutch outer drum bearing using suitable press, noting the following:

a. Ensure gear side faces down.
b. Bearing numbered side must face drum outside.
c. Ensure bearing is flush with clutch drum bottom.
28. Install clutch drum.
29. Install inner drum and clutch drum. Inner drum should rest on outer drum top.
30. Install clutch washer into inner drum, noting the following:
a. Ensure return spring prongs are upward and away from inner drum.
b. Ensure return spring flat side is down against inner drum.
31. Install inner clutch drum retaining ring.
32. Install clutch drum flange, noting the following:
a. Ensure flange is installed with counter bore side facing down.
b. Align flange teeth with inner clutch drum slots.
33. Install inner clutch plates over clutch drum flange.
34. Install outer separator plate over inner clutch plate.
35. Continue installing inner clutch and outer separator plates until 10 inner clutch plates and nine outer separator plates are installed. All separator plate tabs should be aligned.
36. Install shim clutch pack.
37. Install inner bearing support into thrust bearing.
38. Install thrust bearing, and inner bearing support plate into outer bearing support plate. Ensure preload spring is in groove.
39. Install thrust bearing, and inner and outer bearing support plate into outer bearing support plate. Ensure all tabs align.
40. Install clutch retaining ring.
41. Install mainshaft, noting the following:
a. Align inner bearing support tabs with clutch lever insets.
b. Clutch drum should align with front case.
c. Align mainshaft teeth with input gear inside teeth.
d. Ensure inner bearing support lug aligns and fits between fork.
42. Install sprockets on chain.
43. Install drive chain with drive and driven sprockets. If there are three off colored chain links, ensure chain is installed with off colored links toward case rear.
44. Install drive and driven sprocket retaining rings.
45. Install gerotor pump retaining ring. Ensure retaining ring is not over mainshaft oil hole.
46. Install oil pump inlet hole O-ring.
47. Install oil pump, noting the following:
a. Ensure pump seats on mainshaft flange.
b. Ensure inlet hole is pointing toward front output shaft.
48. Install oil pump pickup tube into pump inlet hole and O-ring.
49. Position pickup tube under chain.
50. Install oil screen in front case and secure with nylon tube.
51. Install magnet in front case.
52. Install wave washer, tone wheel, rear output bear and retaining ring on mainshaft.
53. Install oil pump retainer tab using a thin coat of suitable RTV.
54. Install front case alignment dowels.
55. Apply suitable RTV sealant to front and rear case mating surfaces.
56. Spread rear output bearing retaining ring and assemble case halves using suitable rubber mallet.
57. Install case mounting bolts, studs and washers, noting the following:
a. **Do not use steel bolts, studs or washers.**
b. **Steel fasteners will destroy magnesium case integrity with accelerated corrosion, cause severe oil leakage and transfer case fault.**
c. Ensure bolt and stud threads are clean and free of pre-applied thread fastener compounds, corrosion and debris.
d. Apply Loctite PST 565, PST 242, or equivalent.
e. Install and tighten bolts and studs within 10 minutes of applying thread fastener.
f. Install bolts and studs in original positions.
g. Transfer case may not have had aluminum washers. Aluminum washers were added during early to mid-year production.
58. Install shield mounting bracket studs, noting the following:
a. Ensure stud threads are clean and free of pre-applied thread fastener

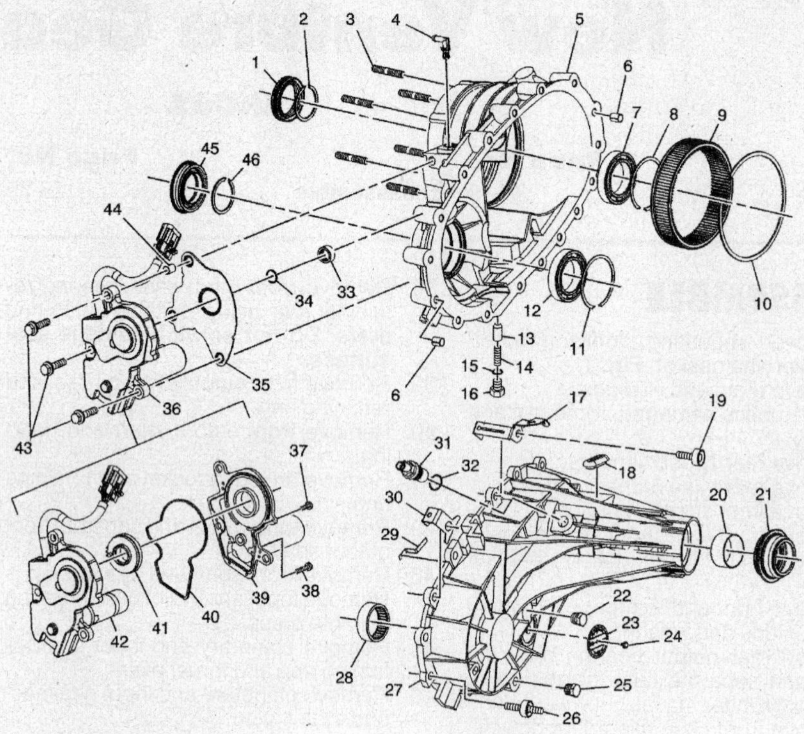

1. Input Shaft Seal
2. Input Gear Bearing Outer Retaining Ring
3. Adapter Studs
4. Vent
5. Front Case Half
6. Locating Pin
7. Input Gear Bearing
8. Input Gear Bearing Retaining Ring
9. Annulus Gear
10. Annulus Gear Retaining Ring
11. Front Output Shaft Bearing Retaining Ring
12. Front Output Shaft Bearing
13. Shift Detent Plunger
14. Shift Detent Spring
15. Shift Detent Plunger Plug O-Ring Seal
16. Shift Detent Spring Bolt
17. Wiring Harness Bracket
18. Access Hole Plug
19. Case Half Bolt
20. Rear Bushing
21. Rear Output Shaft Seal
22. Fill Plug
23. ID Plate
24. ID Plate Screw
25. Drain Plug
26. Case Half Stud
27. Rear Case Half
28. Front Output Shaft Rear Bearing
29. Oil Pump Wear Sleeve
30. Bracket
31. Vehicle Speed Sensor
32. Vehicle Speed Sensor O-Ring Seal
33. Shift Detent Lever Bearing
34. Shift Detent Lever Retaining Ring
35. Actuator Insulator
36. Actuator Encoder Motor
37. Housing Screw
38. Motor Cover Screw
39. Actuator Cover Plate
40. Actuator Seal
41. Range Select Position Sensor
42. Actuator Housing
43. Actuator Encoder Motor Bolts
44. Actuator Encoder Motor Locating Pin
45. Front Output Shaft Seal
46. Front Output Shaft Bearing Outer Retaining Ring

LTV0500000001590

Fig. 1 Exploded view of case components

compounds, corrosion and debris.

b. Apply Loctite PST 565, PST 242, or equivalent.

c. Install and tighten studs within 10 minutes of applying thread fastener.

59. Install front output shaft oil seal using front output shaft oil seal installer tool No. J33834, or equivalent.
60. Install rear speed sensors and tighten to specifications.
61. Install front speed sensor and tighten to specifications.
62. Ensure rear output bearing retaining ring is properly seated in groove and install rear case rubber plug.
63. If vent tube was damaged, install new one and O-ring.
64. Install plunger, spring, O-ring and poppet bolt, noting the following:
    a. Ensure bolt has O-ring position under head.
    b. Apply light coat of suitable transfer case oil to mating surface.
    c. Align sector notch with poppet plunger.
    d. **Do not use impact tool to install bolt.**
    e. Ensure poppet plunger remains in sector not during spring and bolt installation.
    f. Tighten poppet bolt to specifications.
65. Install motor/encoder and gasket, noting the following:
    a. Align mounting holes.
    b. Ensure gasket remains aligned.

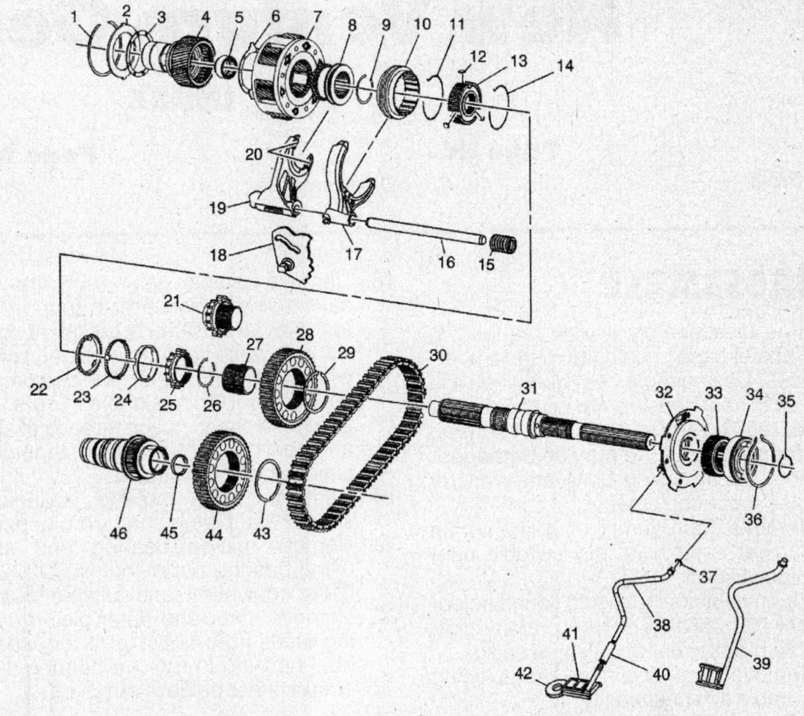

1. Planetary Carrier Internal Gear Retaining Ring
2. Planetary Carrier Lock Plate
3. Input Gear Front Thrust Washer
4. Input Gear
5. Input Gear Needle Bearing
6. Input Gear Rear Thrust Washer
7. High/Low Planetary Carrier
8. High/Low Range Sleeve
9. Synchronizer Retaining Ring
10. Synchronizer Sleeve
11. Synchronizer Insert Spring
12. Synchronizer Insert
13. Synchronizer Hub
14. Synchronizer Insert Spring
15. Shift Fork Shaft Spring
16. Shift Shaft
17. 2/4 Wheel Drive Mode Shift Fork
18. Shift Detent Lever
19. High/Low Range Shift Fork
20. High/Low Range Shift Fork Pads
21. 2/4 Wheel Drive Synchronizer Gear, 2nd Design
22. Synchronizer Outer Ring
23. Synchronizer Middle Ring
24. Synchronizer Inner Ring
25. 2/4 Wheel Drive Synchronizer Gear, 1st Design
26. Drive Sprocket Front Retaining Ring, 1st Design
27. Drive Sprocket Sleeve, 1st Design
28. Drive Sprocket
29. Drive Sprocket Rear Retaining Ring
30. Chain
31. Rear Output Shaft
32. Oil Pump
33. Speed Reluctor Wheel
34. Rear Output Shaft Bearing
35. Rear Output Shaft Bearing Retaining Ring
36. Rear Output Shaft Bearing Outer Retaining Ring
37. Oil Pump Suction Pipe O-Ring Seal
38. Oil Pump Suction Pipe, 1st Design
39. Oil Pump Suction Pipe Assembly, 2nd Design
40. Connector Hose, 1st Design
41. Oil Pump Screen, 1st Design
42. Magnet
43. Driven Sprocket Retaining Ring
44. Driven Sprocket
45. Front Output Shaft Cup Plug
46. Front Output Shaft

LTV0500000001591

Fig. 2 Exploded view of internal components

TIGHTENING SPECIFICATIONS

Year	Component	Torque/Ft. Lbs.
2002–06	Case	27
	Clutch Lever Insert	35
	Drain Plug	15
	Encoder	27
	Fill Plug	15
	Input Shaft	27
	Poppet	15
	Shield Mounting Bracket	27
	Speed Sensor	23

New Venture Gear 900

INDEX

DISASSEMBLE

During disassembly it may required to heat transfer case housing to remove bearing races. Use suitable heat gun when it is required to heat housing. **Do not heat case above (250° F). Do not use torches, transfer case housing may be damaged.**

1. Remove mounting bolts and transfer case mounting bracket.
2. Remove drain and fill plug, then drain transfer case fluid into suitable container, **Fig. 1.**
3. Remove pinion nut using flange holder tool No. J8614-2, or equivalent, suitable breaker bar and 27 mm socket.
4. Removal tool to pinion flange using suitable flywheel/pulley.
5. Remove mounting bolts and separate cover from housing using suitable screwdriver at pry point relief slot.
6. Remover carrier from transfer case housing.
7. Remove and discard ring gear mounting bolts. **Ring gear bolts have lefthanded threads.**
8. Remove right and lefthand side bearing using differential installer tool No. J44879 and bearing puller tool No. J22912-01 or equivalents, and suitable press
9. Remove ring gear from carrier.
10. Remove stub shaft inner bearing from carrier using universal bearing/ bushing removal tool No. J29369-1, or equivalent.
11. Remove pinion seal from housing.
12. Remove bearing race, shim and seal from side cover. It may be required to heat housing to remove bearing race.
13. Remove axle seal from side cover.
14. Remove carrier bearing race and shim from transfer case housing, It may be required to heat housing to remove bearing race.
15. Remove pinion shaft oil seal and oil slinger from housing.
16. Remove pinion gear from transfer case using pinion press support bar tool No. J44882, or equivalent, gear will spin while tightening forcing screw, when gear stops teeth will be contacting housing. **Do not use air tools.**
17. Install old pinion nut on threads of shaft and hold gear head face up, then drive pinion shaft out of case.
18. Remove pinion bearing, collapsible spacer and pinion shaft from housing.
19. Remove pinion bearing and shim using bearing puller tool No. J22912-01, or equivalent, and suitable press.
20. Remove inner and outer pinion bearing races from housing. If required to heat housing to remove bearing race, ensure inner baffle is removed.

ASSEMBLE

Before installation of bearing races, heat transfer case housing to (250° F), using suitable heat gun, **Do not heat case above (250° F). Do not use torches.**

1. Install inner and outer bearing races, using bearing race installer tool No. J44884, or equivalent.
2. Install shim and bearing onto pinion shaft.
3. Position pinion shaft into transfer case housing and install outer bearing with new collapsible spacer on pinion shaft.
4. Install oil slinger and new pinion seal using pinion seal installer tool No. J44872, or equivalent.
5. Install pinion flange and new nut onto pinion shaft.
6. Position transfer case with pinion flange facing up support pinion gear.
7. Install flange holder tool No. J8614-2 and shoulder bolts, part No. J44873, or equivalents, then tighten pinion nut slowly to **rotating torque**of 14 inch lbs., using suitable breaker bar and 27 mm socket.
8. Install axle shaft needle bearing into carrier until bearing is fully seated using needle bearing installer tool No. J4972-4, or equivalent, and suitable driver handle.
9. Install and tighten ring gear onto carrier using new bolts. **Ring gear bolts have lefthanded threads.**
10. Install lefthand side carrier bearing onto carrier assembly using lefthand side bearing installer tool No. J44874, or equivalent, and suitable press.
11. Install righthand side carrier bearing onto carrier assembly using righthand side bearing installer tool No. J44875, or equivalent, and suitable press.
12. Install lefthand side shim, bearing cup and vent baffle into housing, using lefthand bearing race installer tool No. J44874, or equivalent.
13. Install righthand side output shaft seal from outside of transfer case housing using output shaft seal installer tool No. J44871, or equivalent. **Do not install seal from inside of housing.**
14. Install side cover inner oil seal using output shaft seal installer tool No. J44871, or equivalent. Bearing cup must be removed before seal can be installed.
15. Install side cover shim and bearing cup using righthand side bearing race installer tool No. J44875 or equivalent, and suitable handle.
16. Install axle shaft oil seal into side cover using output shaft seal installer tool No. J29162, or equivalent.
17. Lubricate seal lips, with suitable grease and install carrier assembly into transfer case housing.
18. Apply .08–.12 inch. bead of suitable sealer to transfer case side cover mating surface.
19. Install side cover and tighten mounting bolts, with dowel pins first, then alternating remaining bolts from side to side.
20. Install mounting bracket and tighten mounting bolts.

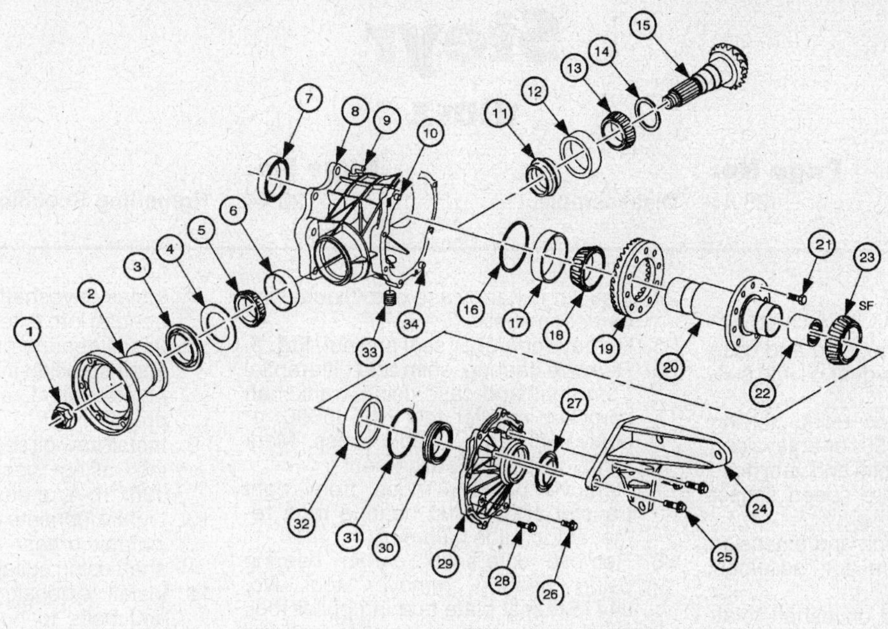

(1)	Nut	(19)	Ring Gear
(2)	Flange	(20)	Carrier
(3)	Oil Seal	(21)	Bolt
(4)	Slinger Washer	(22)	Bearing
(5)	Bearing	(23)	Bearing
(6)	Bearing Race	(24)	Bracket
(7)	Axle Shaft Oil Seal (Left Side)	(25)	Bolts
(8)	Housing	(26)	Fill Plug
(9)	Vent	(27)	Axle Shaft Oil Seal (Right Side)
(10)	Hollow Dowel	(28)	Bolt
(11)	Collapsible Spacer	(29)	Side Cover
(12)	Bearing Race	(30)	Side Cover Seal
(13)	Bearing	(31)	Shim
(14)	Shim	(32)	Bearing Race
(15)	Pinion Shaft	(33)	Drain Plug
(16)	Shim	(34)	Hollow Dowel
(17)	Bearing Race		
(18)	Needle Bearing		

G33040200001000X

Fig. 1 Exploded view of transfer case

TIGHTENING SPECIFICATIONS

Year	Component	Torque/Ft. Lbs.
2002–06	Drain Plug	18
	Fill Plug	11
	Pinion Flange	14
	Ring Gear	48
	Side Cover	25

Steyr

INDEX

DISASSEMBLE

1. Remove extension housing and case drain plugs and drain gear oil into suitable container.
2. Support transfer case using holding fixture tool No. J44755, or equivalent.
3. Remove mounting bolts and vent hose with bracket, then the speed sensor and O-ring seal.
4. Remove mounting bolt and extension housing. Mark shim for assembly alignment.
5. Measure and record driveshaft rotating torque in both directions for assembly alignment.
6. Install extension housing onto holding fixture
7. Remove mounting nut and bolts, then the extension housing from holding fixture tool.
8. Position extension housing into suitable press, then remove flange, spacer and shaft, **Fig. 1.** Discard spacer.
9. Remove oil seal and bearing.
10. Remove bearing races from housing using bearing race remover tool No. J44380 and slide hammer tool No. J2619-01, or equivalents.
11. Remove shaft bearing using split plate bearing puller tool No. J22912-01, or equivalent, and suitable press.
12. Remove mounting bolts, housing, shim and O-ring seal from lefthand case, **Fig. 2.** Mark shim for assembly alignment,
13. Remove righthand case mounting bolts rotate holding fixture 90°.
14. Separate transfer case halves, **Fig. 3. Do not insert screwdriver or prying tool between case sealing surfaces.**
15. Remove idler gear from righthand case. Mark idler gear for assembly alignment.
16. Remove idler gear bearings using split plate bearing puller tool and suitable press.
17. Install lefthand case half onto holding fixture aligning tool notches with driveshaft flat areas, **Fig. 4.**
18. Remove driveshaft nut and position lefthand case into press.
19. Remove gear, bearing, shim and shaft from lefthand case. Mark shim for assembly alignment.
20. Remove outer and inner bearing races from lefthand case using bearing race tool and slide hammer.
21. Remove lefthand case oil seals.
22. Remove shaft bearing using split plate bearing puller tool and suitable press.
23. Remove idler gear bearing race from lefthand case using bearing race tool and slide hammer.
24. Install righthand case onto fixture with carrier on post.
25. Remove carrier oil seal and nut, **Fig. 5.**
26. Remove bearing, shim and differential from righthand case using crankshaft sprocket installer tool No. J5590, or equivalent, and suitable press. Mark shim for assembly alignment.
27. Remove bearing races from right transfer case using bearing race remover tool slide hammer.
28. Remove differential carrier bearing using bearing remover tool No. J44754, split plate bearing puller tool, crankshaft sprocket installer tool and suitable press.
29. Remove righthand case idler gear bearing race using bearing race remover tool, slide hammer and bearing race remover tool. Mark shim for assembly alignment.
30. Remove driveshaft bearing using bearing remover tool No. J44737, or equivalent, and side hammer.
31. Remove roll pin and shaft from differential carrier.
32. Remove side and pinion gears, then the carrier washers.
33. Remove ring, then the pin, gear and washers from carrier.
34. Remove needle bearings and washers from gear, **Fig. 6.**

ASSEMBLE

Lightly lubricate bearing races, bearings, gears and oil seals with suitable lubricant. Components in the transaxle portion of transfer case should be lubricated with Dexron III, or equivalent. Components in the hypoid gear portion of the transfer case should be lubricated with GM part No. 12378514, or equivalent. **Do not assemble internal components dry.**

1. Install needle bearings and washer, then the pin, gear, washers and ring to carrier, **Fig. 6.**
2. Install side and pinion gears, then the carrier washers.
3. Install shaft and roll pin to carrier, **Fig. 7.**
4. Install outer and inner bearing races to extension housing using bearing race installer tool No. J44908, or equivalent, and suitable hydraulic press.
5. **If driveshaft has plus, minus or zero value etched onto gear end, Fig. 8** measure and record distance between flange on driven shaft and end of pinion.
6. **On all models,** install driveshaft inner bearing using bearing installer tool No. J44907, or equivalent, and suitable hydraulic press.
7. Install driveshaft and new spacer and bearing into extension housing, **Fig. 1.**
8. Install bearing onto shaft using crankshaft sprocket installer tool No. J5590, or equivalent, and suitable hydraulic press.
9. Install new oil seal into extension housing using seal installer tool No. J36797-A, or equivalent.
10. Lightly lubricate driveshaft splines with suitable grease and install flange onto shaft using suitable hydraulic press.
11. Install extension housing assembly and bolts to holding fixture tool No. J44753, or equivalent.
12. Install and tighten new shaft nut.
13. Remove extension housing and bolts from holding fixture.
14. Measure rotating torque of driveshaft in both directions. New bearing should have rotating torque of 13 inch lbs. Used bearing should have rotating torque equal to value recorded during disassembly.
15. Tighten flange nut to achieve proper rotating torque. **Loosening pinion nut to achieve proper rotating torque requires installation of new spacer.**
16. Measure and record distance between pinion end and extension housing seal surface.
17. Install shim selection kit tool No. J4757-3 into bore and mounting No. J44757-9, or equivalents, with bolts to housing, **Fig. 9.**
18. Measure distance between shim kit parts.
19. Add measured value to 2.65 inches.
20. **If driveshaft has plus, minus or zero value etched onto gear end, Fig. 8,** calculate extension housing shim thickness as follows:
    a. Subtract pinion thickness from 2.24 inches.
    b. Add pinion installed height.
    c. Subtract driveshaft housing calculated value.
    d. Add or subtract the plug, minus or zero value etched on end of driveshaft to determine extension housing shim thickness.
21. **If driveshaft has four-digit number etched onto gear end, Fig. 8,** calculate extension housing shim thickness as follows:
    a. Add driveshaft end value measurement to pinion installed height.
    b. Subtract pinion calculated height determined in previous step from driveshaft housing calculated value to determine extension housing shim thickness.

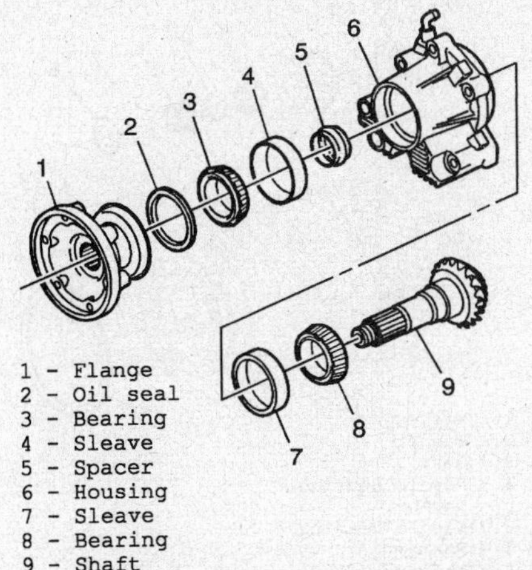

Fig. 1 Exploded view of extension housing

22. **On all models,** install idler gear bearings using crankshaft sprocket installer tool and suitable hydraulic press.
23. Install bearing race into lefthand case cover using bearing, race, and seal installer tool No. J44752 , or equivalent, and suitable hydraulic press
24. Install idler gear and bearing race to lefthand case.
25. Ensure side gear with long flange area is installed onto righthand case.
26. Install shim selection kit tool No. J44757-1, or equivalent, to idler gear and race.
27. Install righthand cover and mounting bolts, then the shim selection kit tool No. J44757-8, or equivalent, to lefthand case.
28. Measure gap in shim selection kit to determine idler gear bearing shim, thickness, **Fig. 10.**
29. Separate righthand from lefthand case, and remove tools.
30. Install selected shim and bearing race to righthand case using bearing and race installer too, and suitable hydraulic press.
31. Install driveshaft bearing to righthand case.
32. Install bearing to righthand case using bearing and seal installer tool No. J44753, or equivalent, and suitable hydraulic press
33. Install transaxle and gear oil side oil seals using bearing and seal installer tool , until seal bottoms in lefthand case bore.
34. Install outer and inner bearing races to lefthand case using bearing race installer tool and suitable hydraulic press.
35. Press shaft, shim selection kit tool No. J44757-7, or equivalent, and bearing to lefthand case using crankshaft sprocket installer tool and suitable hydraulic press.
36. Install and tighten snug shim selection kit tool No. J44757-2, or equivalent.
37. Install shim selection kit tool Nos. J44757-6 and J44757-8, bolts, nuts and washers.
38. Rotate driveshaft multiple times in both

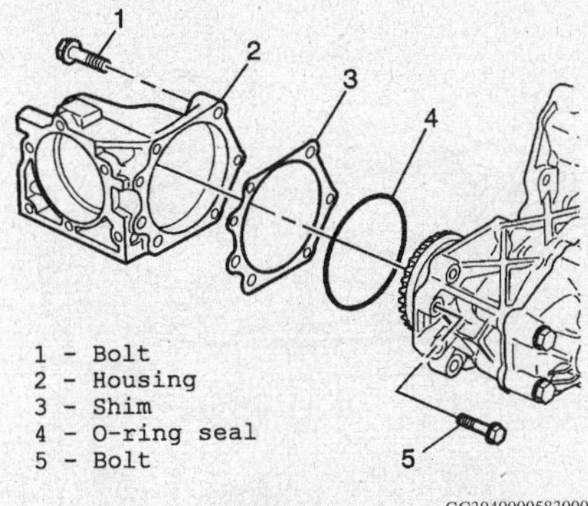

Fig. 2 Extension housing replacement

directions to ensure bearing rollers are seated to bearing races.
39. Install suitable dial indicator set onto shim selector tool No. J44757-6, or equivalent, position dial indicator tip onto end of shim selector tool No. J44757-2, or equivalent.
40. Tighten lower nut to preload bearings and position shaft at bottom of travel.
41. Hold shim selector tool No. J44757-2, or equivalent, using second wrench and when dial indicator needle movement stops shaft is at bottom travel, **Fig. 11.** Zero dial indicator
42. Loosen lower nut, then tighten upper nut to preload bearings and position shaft at top of travel. Hold J44757-2 shaft using second wrench.
43. Subtract measured value from .236 inch to determine driveshaft shim required for proper bearing installation and preload.
44. Disassemble shaft, bearing and shim from lefthand case, then install proper size shim, shaft, bearing and gear to lefthand case, **Fig. 12.**
45. Lightly lubricate driveshaft splines with suitable grease.
46. Install bearing, shim and gear on shaft using crankshaft sprocket tool and suitable hydraulic press.
47. Install lefthand case onto holding fixture and align tool notched area with driveshaft flat areas.
48. Install and tighten new driveshaft nut.
49. Measure rotating torque of driveshaft. Measurement should be 13 in. lbs.
50. Install carrier inner and outer bearing race to righthand case using bearing, race and seal installer tool and suitable hydraulic press.
51. Install inner bearing to differential carrier using bearing, race and seal installer tool and suitable hydraulic press.
52. Install carrier, shim selection kit tool No. J44757-4, or equivalent, shim and bearing to righthand case using bearing, race, and seal installer tool and suitable hydraulic press
53. Install righthand case onto holding fixture and position carrier onto fixture post,
54. Install and tighten snug selected shim tool No. J44757-5, or equivalent, onto carrier .

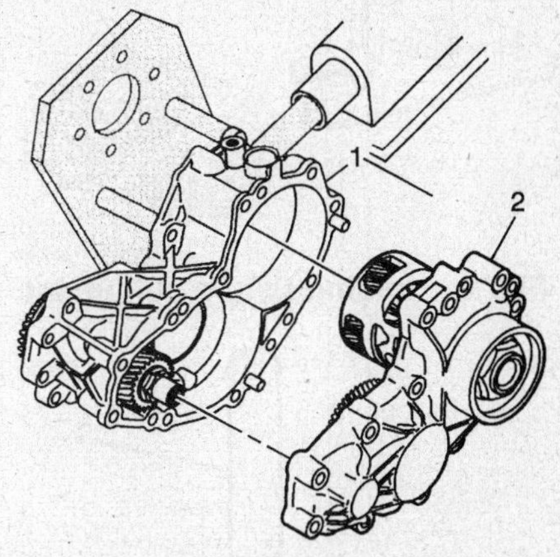

Fig. 3 Transfer case halves separation

55. Install shim selection tool No. J44757-6 and J44757-8, or equivalents, then the bolts, washers and nuts to righthand case.
56. Rotate differential carrier multiple times in both directions to ensure bearing rollers are seated to bearing races.
57. Install suitable dial indicator set onto shim selector tool No. J44757-6, or equivalent, position dial indicator tip onto end of shim selector tool No. J44757-5, or equivalent.
58. Tighten lower nut to preload bearings and position differential carrier at bottom of travel.
59. Hold shim selector tool No. J44757-5, or equivalent, using second wrench and when dial indicator needle movement stops carrier is at bottom travel, **Fig. 11.** Zero dial indicator
60. Loosen lower nut, then tighten upper nut to preload bearings and position carrier at top of travel. Hold J44757-5 shaft using second wrench.
61. Subtract measured value from .394 inch to determine driveshaft shim required for proper bearing installation and preload.
62. Disassemble carrier, bearing and shim from righthand case, then install shaft, proper size shim and bearing to righthand case using bearing, race, and seal installer and suitable hydraulic press.
63. Install and tighten differential carrier nut .
64. Measure and ensure carrier rotating torque is 13 inch lbs.
65. Stake nut flange to carrier shaft groove.
66. Install seal to righthand case using bearing and race installer tool.
67. Remove righthand case and carrier from holding fixture.
68. Install random size shim and extension housing, then **torque** M8 bolts to 23 ft. lbs. and M10 bolts to 44 ft. lbs.
69. Apply suitable sealant to both sides of shim, then install housing and shim. **Torque** mounting bolts to 23 ft. lbs.
70. Install bolt into threaded hole in flange and position dial indicator top against bolt flat area.

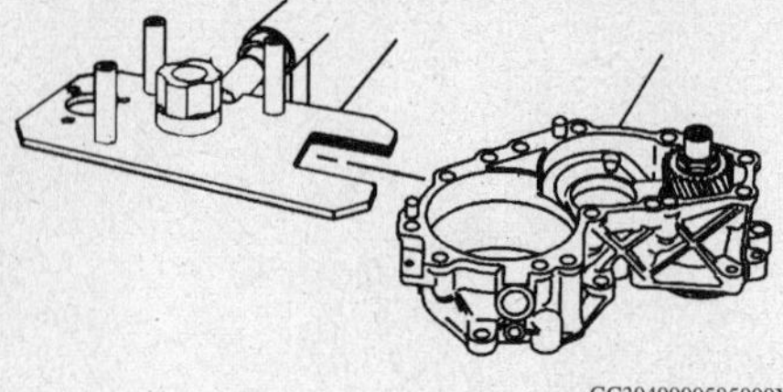

Fig. 4 Holding fixture alignment

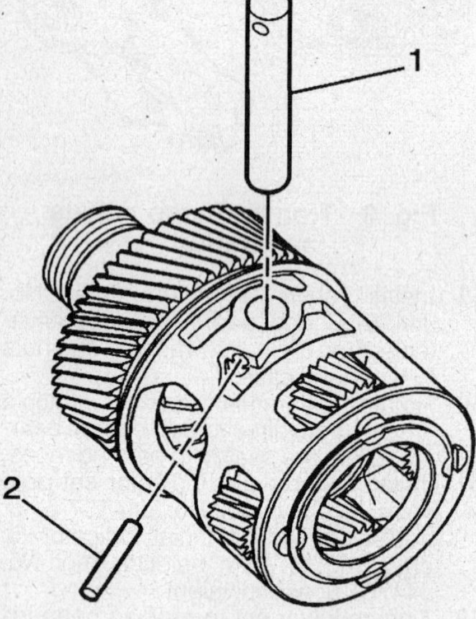

Fig. 7 Shaft & roll pin replacement

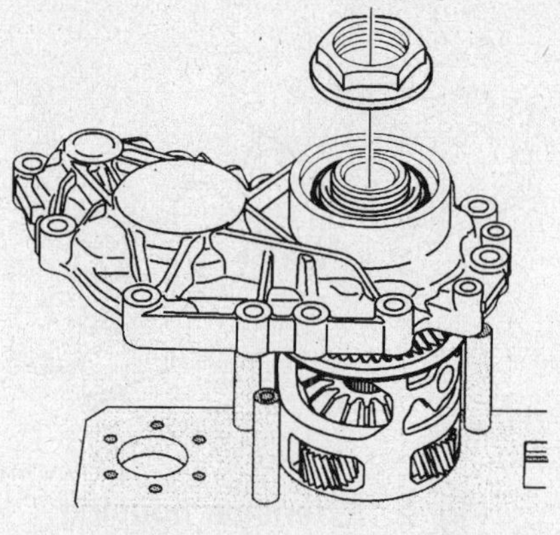

Fig. 5 Carrier nut replacement

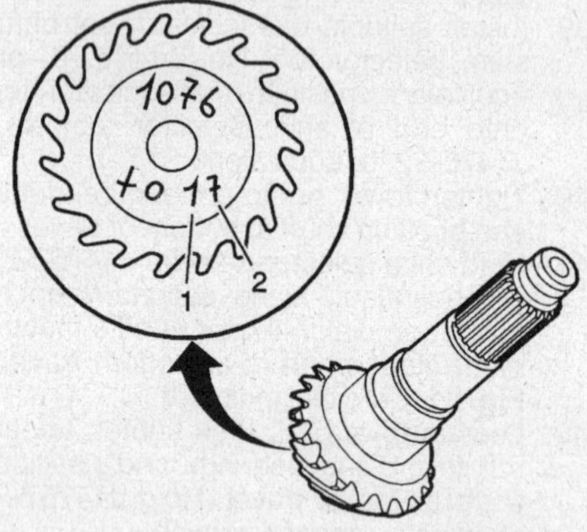

Fig. 8 Driveshaft gear marking

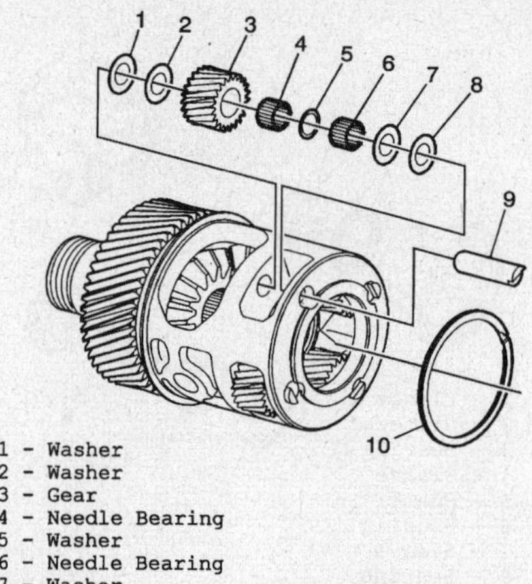

Fig. 6 Exploded view of carrier

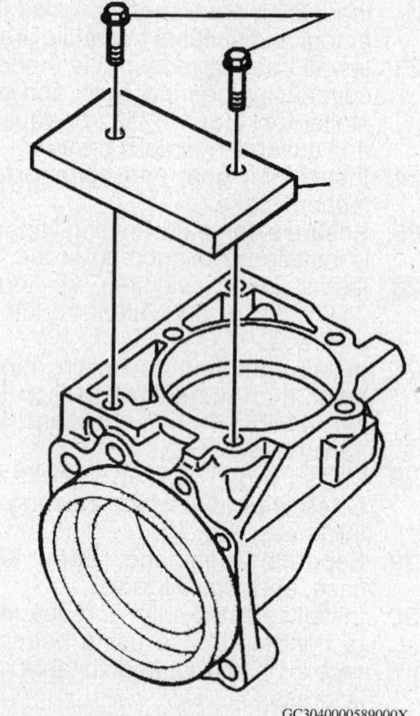

Fig. 9 Shim selection kit

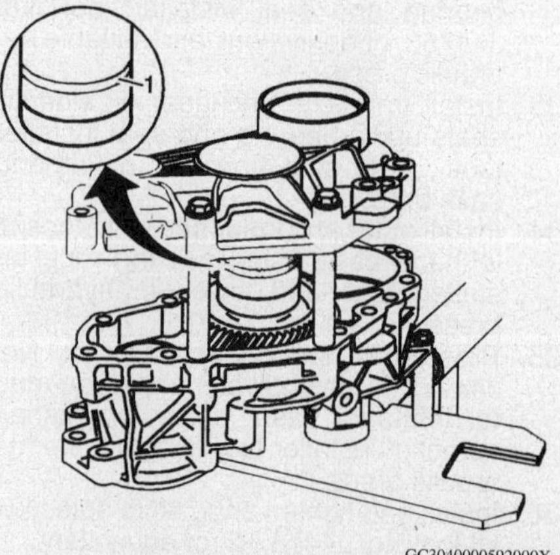

Fig. 10 Idler gear bearing shim thickness measurement

71. Hold driveshaft nut using suitable wrench or socket. **Do not allow shaft to rotate or move when measuring backlash.**
72. Rotate flange left and right, then measure drive and driveshafts gear backlash.
73. Select, and install shim to obtain backlash of .0078–.0118 inch. Thicker shim increases backlash and thinner will decrease backlash.
74. Apply suitable sealant to righthand case sealing surfaces and install idler gear. Gear flange area is installed into righthand case.
75. Rotate holding fixture 90°, then install right to lefthand transfer case.
76. **Torque** M8x40 case bolt to 24 ft. lbs., **Fig. 13.**
77. **Torque** M10x60 case bolts to 44 ft. lbs.
78. **Torque** M10x50 case bolt to 44 ft. lbs.
79. **Torque** M10x75 case stud bolts to 44 ft. lbs.
80. Install speed sensor and O-ring.
81. Install vent hose and clamp, then tighten bolt.
82. Install transmission and gear oil drain plugs and gaskets. Tighten plugs

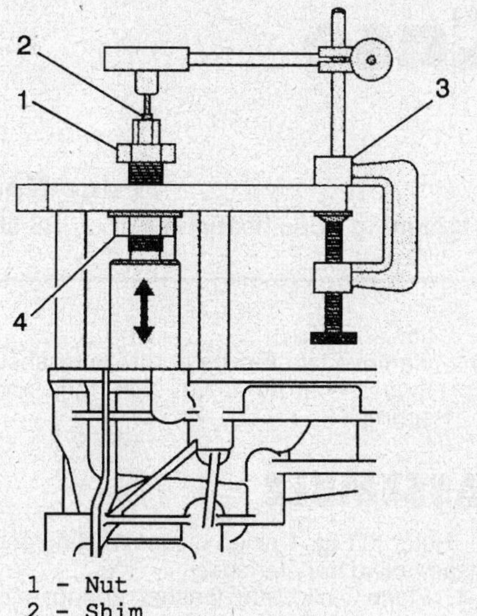

Fig. 11 Driveshaft shim measurement

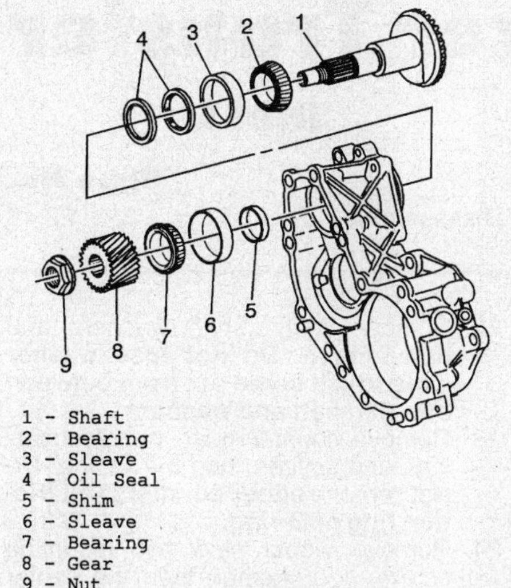

Fig. 12 Driveshaft replacement

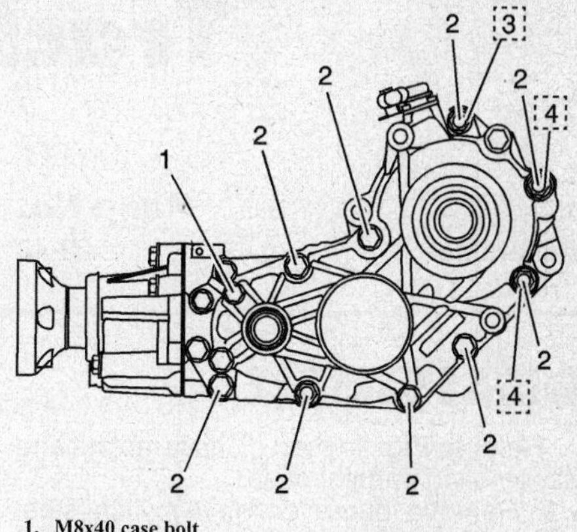

Fig. 13 Case tightening sequence

TIGHTENING SPECIFICATIONS

Year	Component	Torque/Ft. Lbs.
2002–06	Case	①
	Differential Carrier Nut	369
	Drain Plug	24
	Driveshaft Nut	372
	Extension Housing	21
	Flange, New Bearings	185
	Flange, Used Bearings	148
	Holding Fixture, M8	18
	Holding Fixture, M10	37
	Output Driveshaft M10	40
	Output Driveshaft M8	21
	Vent Hose/Speed Sensor	22

① — Refer to "Assemble" for tightening specifications and sequence.

Tracker Transfer Case

INDEX

DISASSEMBLE

Refer to **Fig. 1** when disassembling and assembling transfer case.

1. Remove four-wheel drive switch, steel ball and O-ring, then the four-wheel drive lover switch, steel ball and O-ring.
2. Remove mounting bolt, speedometer driven gear case and O-ring.
3. Remove five mounting bolts, then the gearshift bracket and lever case.
4. Remove mounting bolt and washer, then the select return spring, ball and pin, **Fig. 2.**
5. Drive reduction shift yoke roll pin into transfer case using suitable drift punch and hammer.
6. Slide yoke rearward off reduction shift shaft and out of rear case.
7. Remove 15 mounting bolts and separate rear from center case using case separator tool No. J37637, or equivalent. **Remove shift yoke roll pin from inside rear transfer case using suitable a magnet.**
8. Remove rear output shaft rear bearing selective shim.
9. Remove C-clip and speedometer drive gear using output shaft ring remover tool No. J34757, or equivalent.
10. Remove rear output shaft drive gear ball.
11. Remove rear output shaft rear bearing C-clip using output shaft ring remover tool.
12. Remove rear output shaft rear bearing using bearing puller tool No. J8433 and output shaft bearing puller adapter tool No. J37756, or equivalent.
13. Remove drive sprocket bushing output shaft and drive sprocket needle bearing output shaft. **Do not lose rear output shaft washer ball underneath drive sprocket bushing.**
14. Remove two mounting screws and rear output shaft synchronizing plate.
15. Remove rear and front output shafts' drive sprocket and chain, then the rear output shaft washer ball.
16. Remove rear output shaft oil seal using needle bearing puller tool No. J26941 and slide hammer tool No. J23907, or equivalents.
17. Remove mounting bolt and rear case oil guide.
18. Remove rear output shaft needle bearing using needle bearing puller tool and slide hammer.
19. Remove mounting washer and countershaft case plate from front case.
20. Remove nine mounting bolts and separate front from center case.
21. Remove countershaft.
22. Remove countershaft washers and balls, **Fig. 3. Do not lose washer balls which come out from between countershaft and washers.**
23. Remove counter gear, needle bearings and spacer, then the O-ring. **Do not remove either countershaft friction ring or O-ring.**
24. Remove rubber plug, two mounting screws and washer, then the center case locating springs and balls.
25. Record caged needle bearing, reduction clutch sleeve and hub, and front drive clutch sleeve and hub for assembly alignment.
26. Remove rear output shaft reduction shift shaft, fork and clutch sleeve from center case.
27. Remove interlock ball from center case passage.
28. Remove rear output shaft reduction hub C-clip using output shaft ring remover tool.
29. Remove rear output shaft reduction clutch hub, low output gear and needle bearing.
30. Remove rear output shaft from center case using suitable plastic mallet.
31. Remove rear output shaft front bearing using split plate tool No. J22912-O1, or equivalent, and suitable press arbor.
32. Remove front output shaft and bearings from center case using suitable plastic mallet.
33. Remove mounting bolt and center case gutter.
34. Remove front output shaft oil seal from center case using needle bearing puller tool and slide hammer.
35. Remove front output shaft needle bearing from center case using needle bearing puller tool and slide hammer.
36. Remove front output shaft bearings using split plate tool and front shaft bearing remover tool No. J34844, or equivalent.
37. Loosen center bearing snap ring within input gear. **Snap ring cannot be removed now.**
38. Remove input gear from front case using suitable plastic mallet.
39. Remove input gear oil seal from front case using needle bearing puller tool and slide hammer.
40. Remove input gear snap ring using suitable snap ring pliers.
41. Remove input gear bearing using split plate tool No. J22912-O1, or equivalent, input gear bearing remover tool No. J28496, or equivalents and suitable press arbor.
42. Remove center bearing snap ring from input gear.
43. Remove roll pin and fork from reduction shift shaft.
44. Remove two E-clips and stop washer, then the front drive shift fork and spring.

ASSEMBLE

Refer to **Fig. 1** when disassembling and assembling transfer case.

1. Place C-clip, stop washer, spring, shift fork and stop washer on front drive shaft.
2. Install fork and roll pin onto reducation shift shaft.
3. Install input gear bearing using bearing race installer tool No. J6133-A, or equivalent, and suitable press arbor. Install snap ring.
4. Install input gear oil seal into front case using oil seal installer tool No. J37752, or equivalent.
5. Apply Loctite 414, or equivalent, to threads, then install oil guide in rear case and tighten mounting bolt.
6. Install input gear into front case using countershaft front bearing installer tool No. J35871, or equivalent, and suitable press arbor. Install C-clip.
7. Install front output shaft bearings onto front output shaft using press tube/ bearing installer tool No. J35664, split plate tool No. J22912-O1, or equivalents, and suitable press arbor.
8. Install front output shaft needle bearing into center case using needle bearing installer tool No. J37757, or equivalent.
9. Install front output shaft oil seal into center case using oil seal installer tool No. J37751, or equivalent.
10. Install center case gutters, mounting bolt and screw.
11. Install front output shaft into center case using suitable plastic mallet.
12. Install rear output shaft front bearing using bearing installer tool No. J37753, split plate and suitable press arbor.
13. Install front bearing, gear needle bearing and low output gear, then the reduction clutch hub and snap ring onto rear output shaft, **Fig. 4.**
14. Install rear output shaft into center case using input shaft press tube tool No. J36183, or equivalent.
15. Apply suitable transjel transmission assembly lubricant to low output gear needle bearing.
16. Press-fit needle bearing into center case using bearing installer tool and suitable press. **Do not press-fit bearing further than limit line.**
17. Install rear output shaft reduction hub C-clip.

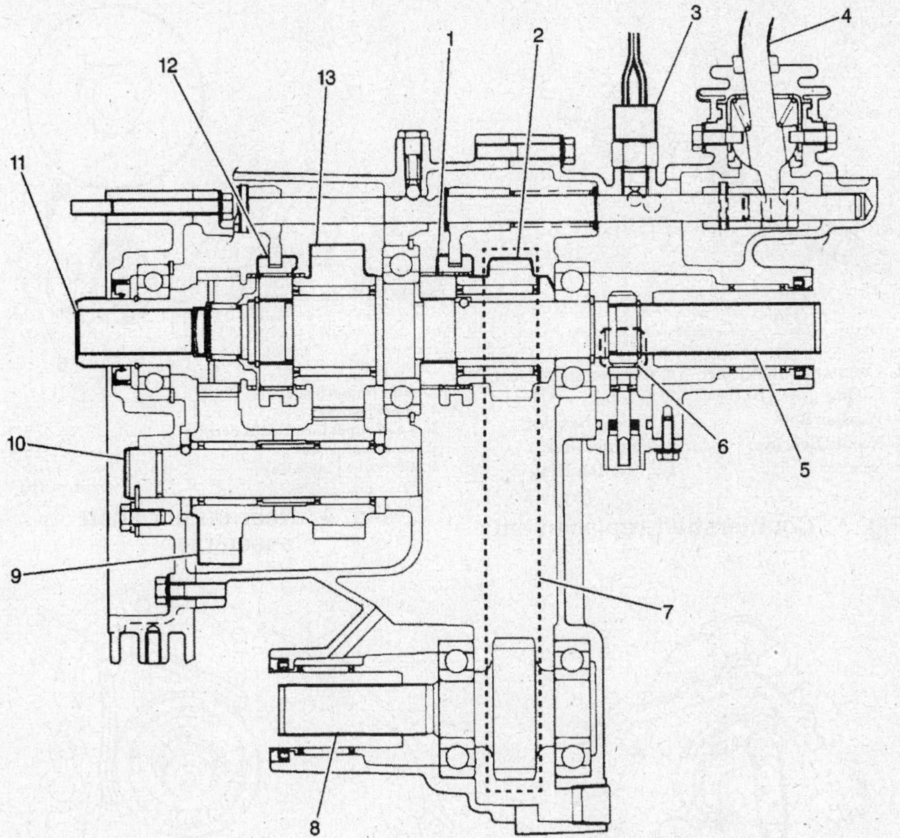

1. **Front Drive Clutch**
2. **Drive Sprocket**
3. **Four-Wheel Drive Switch**
4. **Gearshift Control Lever**
5. **Rear Output Shaft**
6. **Speedometer Driven Gear**
7. **Drive Chain**
8. **Front Output Shaft**
9. **Counter Gear**
10. **Countershaft**
11. **Input Gear**
12. **Reduction Clutch Sleeve**
13. **Low Output Gear**

LTV0500000001555

Fig. 1 Cross-sectional view of Tracker transfer case

18. Install caged needle bearing.
19. Install interlock ball into enter case passage, then push against interlock notch of front drive shift shaft.
20. Position front drive shift shaft at 4WD position.
21. Install front drive shift shaft and fork, then the clutch sleeve and hub on rear output shaft, **Fig. 5.** Align clutch hub and sleeve marks.
22. Place reduction shift shaft at 4WD position.
23. Install reduction shift shaft, fork and sleeve onto rear output shaft in front center case, **Fig. 6.**
24. Align reduction clutch hub and the sleeve marks.
25. Apply Loctite 599, or equivalent, RTV silicone sealer, to rubber plug.
26. Apply Loctite pipe sealant, or equivalent, to mounting screw threads.
27. Install two locating balls and springs, then the rubber plug and washer. Tighten two locating screws.
28. Install spacer, needle bearings and counter gear, then the balls and washers on countershaft, **Fig. 3.**
29. Install countershaft into center case.
30. Apply Loctite 599, or equivalent RTV silicone sealer, to front and center cases' mating surfaces.
31. Install front to center case and tighten nine mounting bolts.
32. Apply Loctite 414, or equivalent, to threads, then install countershaft case plate and tighten mounting bolt.
33. Install rear output shaft needle bearing in rear case using needle bearing installer tool.
34. Install rear output shaft oil seal into rear case using oil seal installer tool.
35. Hold shaft ball in place on rear output shaft using suitable transjel transmission assembly lubricant.
36. Install washer ball, drive sprocket and chain onto rear and front output shafts.
37. Install synchronizer plate to front output shaft case.
38. Apply Loctite 414, or equivalent, to threads and secure plate with two mounting screws.
39. Apply suitable transjel transmission assembly lubricant to drive sprocket needle bearing.
40. Install drive sprocket needle bearing and bushing.
41. Install rear output shaft rear bearing onto rear output shaft using tube/ bearing installer tool.
42. Install rear output shaft rear bearing C-clip onto rear output shaft.
43. Install speedometer drive gear and C-clip on output rear shaft.
44. Measure and record rear case bearing bore depth using suitable straight edge and vernier caliper.
45. Press-fit needle bearing into rear case using bearing installer tool and suitable press. **Do not press-fit bearing further than tool limit line.**
46. Measure and record rear case rear output shaft rear bearing on rear output shaft depth and width using suitable straight edge and vernier caliper.
47. Subtract height of bearing on rear output shaft from rear of case bearing bore depth to determine shim clearance. **No shim is needed if clearance is less than .0005 inch.**
48. Install selected shim to rear output shaft rear bearing top and hold in place using suitable transjel transmission assembly lubricant.
49. Apply Loctite 599, or equivalent RTV silicone sealer, to rear case mating surface.
50. Install rear to center case and tighten 15 mounting bolts.
51. Install yoke and roll pin onto reduction shift shaft in rear case.
52. Apply light coat of Loctite pipe sealant, or equivalent, to select return spring bolt threads.
53. Install pin, select return ball and washer, then washer and spring. Tighten select return spring bolt.
54. Apply Loctite 599, or equivalent RTV silicone sealer, to rear and gearshift lever case's mating surfaces.
55. Install gearshift lever case to rear case and tighten five mounting bolts.
56. Apply suitable transjel transmission assembly lubricant to speedometer driven gear case O-ring.
57. Install speedometer driven gear case and tighten mounting bolt.
58. Apply suitable transjel transmission assembly lubricant to four-wheel drive switch O-ring.
59. Install steel ball and four-wheel drive switch, then tighten switch.
60. Apply suitable transjel transmission assembly lubricant to four-wheel drive low switch O-ring.
61. Install steel ball and four-wheel drive switch, then tighten switch.

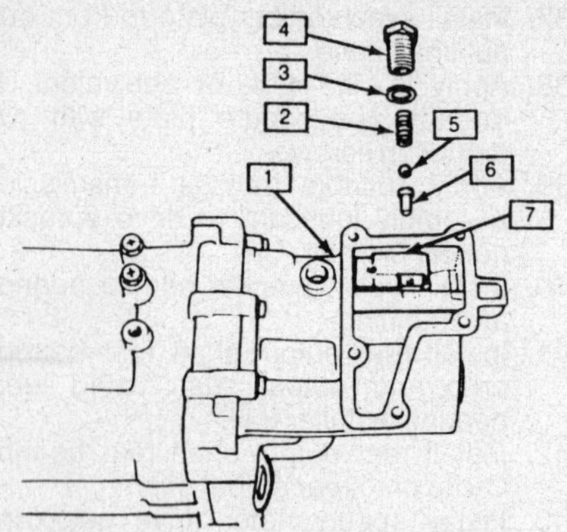

1 REAR CASE
2 SELECT RETURN SPRING
3 WASHER (ALUMINUM)
4 RETURN SPRING BOLT
5 BALL
6 SELECT RETURN PIN
7 REDUCTION SHIFT YOKE

GC3048800108000X

Fig. 2 Gear select return replacement

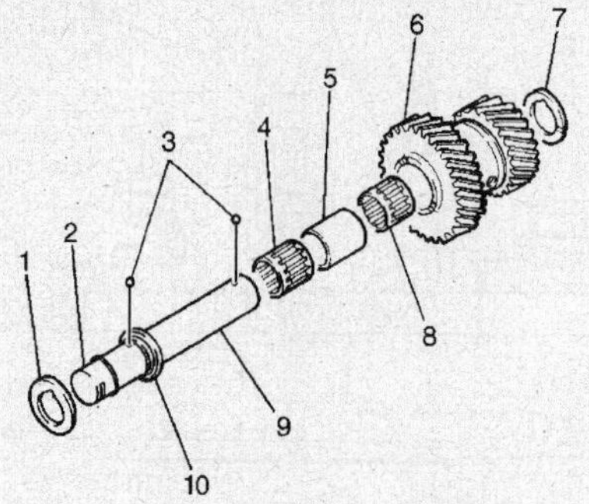

1. Countershaft Washer
2. O-ring
3. Washer Ball
4. Needle Bearing
5. Spacer
6. Countershaft Gear
7. Washer
8. Needle Bearing
9. Countershaft
10. Friction Ring

LTV0500000001551

Fig. 3 Countershaft replacement

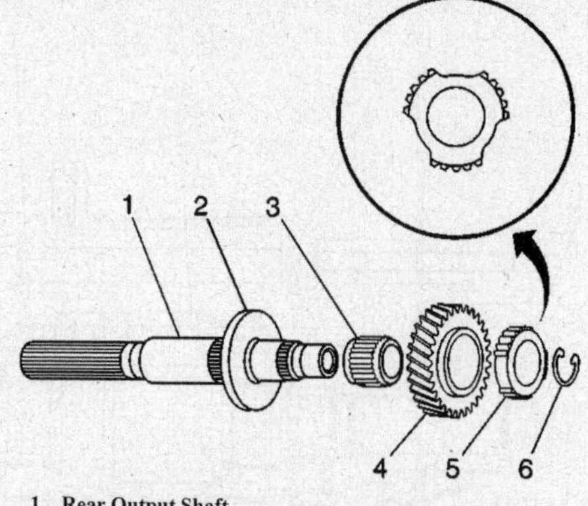

1. Rear Output Shaft
2. Front Bearing
3. Low Output Gear Needle Bearing
4. Low Output Gear
5. Reduction Clutch Hub

LTV0500000001552

Fig. 4 Rear output shaft assembly

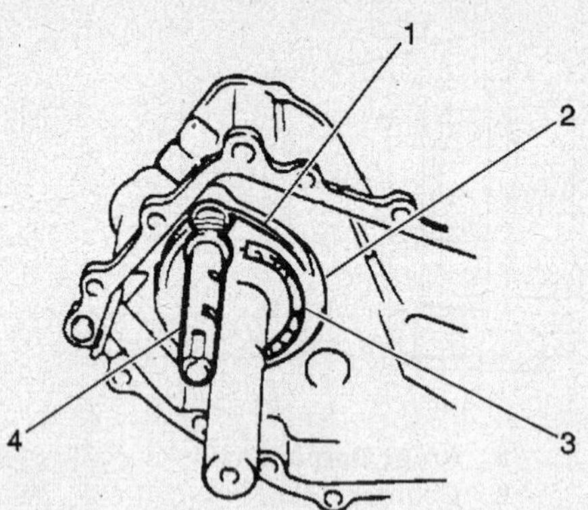

1. Front Drive Shift Fork
2. Front Drive Clutch Sleeve
3. Front Drive Clutch Hub
4. Front Drive Shift Shaft

LTV0500000001553

Fig. 5 Rear output shaft in rear center case assembly

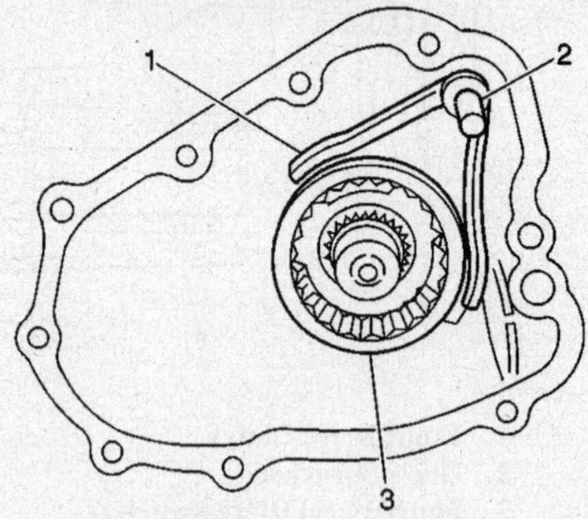

1. Reduction Shift Fork
2. Reduction Clutch Sleeve
3. Reduction Shift Shaft

LTV0500000001554

Fig. 6 Rear output shaft in front center case assembly

TIGHTENING SPECIFICATIONS

Year	Component	Torque/Ft. Lbs.
2002–04	Case	17
	Case Gutter	106①
	Countershaft Case Plate	17
	Gearshift Lever Case	12
	Locating Screws	18
	Oil Guide	89①
	Select Return Spring	25
	Speedometer Driven Gear Case	89①
	4WD Drive Low Switch	14
	4WD Drive Switch	14

① — Inch lbs.

FRONT WHEEL DRIVE AXLES

NOTE: For Service Procedures On Rear Wheel And Four Wheel Drive Vehicles, Refer To "Drive Axles" Chapter.

INDEX

PRECAUTIONS

Battery Ground Cable

Prior to service, disconnect battery ground cable and isolate as required.

DESCRIPTION

Front drive axles are completely flexible assemblies consisting of an inner and outer constant velocity joint connected by an axle shaft, **Fig. 1.** The inner joint is completely flexible and has the capability of in-and-out movement. The outer joint is also flexible but cannot move in-and-out. All drive axles, except the left hand inboard end on automatic transaxles models, incorporate a male spline and interlock with the transaxle gears through the use of barrel-type snap rings. The left hand inboard shaft attachment on automatic transaxle models, utilizes a female spline which installs over a stub shaft extending out of the transaxle.

The drive axle spline that mates with the knuckle and hub assembly is a helical type spline which provides a tight press fit and ensures that no endplay will exist between the hub bearing and driveshaft assembly.

TROUBLESHOOTING

Clicking Noise In Turns

1. Worn or damaged outboard joints.
2. Cut or damaged seals.

Shudder Or Vibration During Acceleration

1. Excessive joint angle.
2. Excessive toe.
3. Incorrect trim height.
4. Worn or damaged joints.
5. Sticking spider assembly.

Vibration At Highway Speeds

1. Out of balance tires or wheels.
2. Out of round front tires.
3. Worn joint.
4. Binding or tight joint.

Clunk When Accelerating From Coast

1. Loose driveshaft to hub assembly nut.
2. Damaged inner CV joint.

DRIVESHAFT REPLACE

Care must be exercised to prevent over extending the tri-pot joints. When either end of the drive axle is disconnected, over extension of the joint may result in separation of the internal components and possible joint failure. Drive axle joint seal protectors should be used any time service is performed.

Removal

1. Raise and support vehicle, then remove front tire and wheel assembly.
2. Insert drift or screwdriver into caliper and rotor to prevent rotor from turning, then remove shaft nut and washer. Discard nut.
3. Remove caliper from steering knuckle and suspend caliper with wire, then remove brake rotor from hub and bearing assembly.
4. Remove lower ball joint then the steering knuckle nut.
5. Install seal protector tool No. J-34754, or equivalent. Seal protector should be modified as outlined, **Fig. 2,** and installed on any dive axle prior to service procedures on or near drive axle. Failure to do so may result an seal damage and possible joint failure.
6. Remove ball joint from steering knuckle.
7. Remove drive axle from hub and bearing using front hub spindle remover tool No. J-28733-A, or equivalent, then the drive axle from transaxle using axle shaft remover tool No. J-33008, or equivalent, with suitable slide hammer and extension.

Installation

1. Carefully guide axle shaft splines past lip seal. Do not allow shaft splines to contact any part of seal surface, as seal damage will occur.
2. Install axle to transaxle, then axle shaft to hub.
3. Install lower control arm ball joint to steering knuckle, then **torque** steering knuckle nut to 56 ft. lbs.
4. Install brake rotor, then the caliper.
5. Insert drift or screwdriver to caliper, then install drive axle washer and nut. **Torque** nut to 104 ft. lbs.
6. Remove drift or screwdriver from caliper and rotor, then seat drive axle into transaxle by placing a screwdriver into groove on joint housing and tapping until seated.
7. Pull outward on tri-pot housing to ensure drive axle is fully seated into transaxle. **Do not pull on axle shaft.**
8. Install wheel and tire assembly, then lower vehicle.

DRIVESHAFT SERVICE

Refer to **Fig. 1** for drive axle overhaul procedures. When assembling the inboard thermoplastic seal, the joint must be collapsed to 5 1/16 inch prior to crimping the clamps. This procedure will prevent ballooning of the seal.

Outer Joint Seal

1. Remove and discard retaining clamps from CV joint and axle shaft with side cutter.
2. Separate joint seal from CV joint race at large diameter and slide seal away from joint along axle shaft, then wipe grease from face of CV joint inner race.
3. Spread ears on race retaining ring with snap ring pliers, then remove CV joint assembly from axle shaft.
4. Remove seal from axle shaft, then disassemble joint and flush grease prior to installing new seal as outlined under "Outer Joint Assembly."
5. Reverse procedure to install.

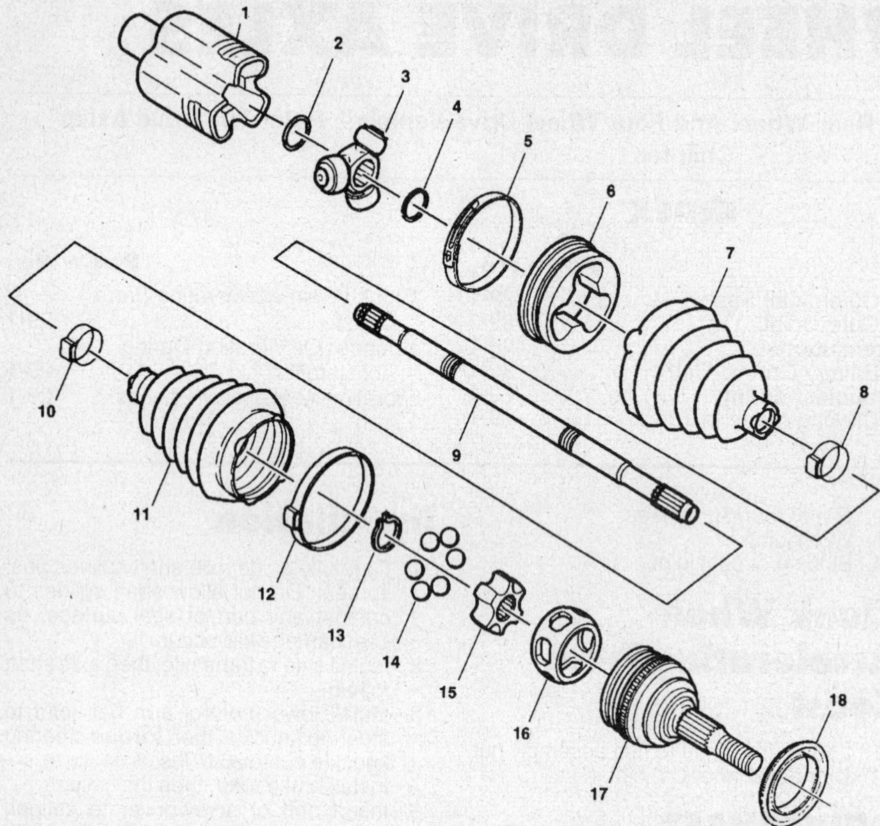

(1) Tripot Housing Assembly
(2) Spacer Ring
(3) Tripot Joint Spider Assembly
(4) Spacer Ring
(5) Tripot Bushing
(6) Boot Retaining Clamp
(7) Tripot Joint Boot
(8) Small Boot Retaining Clamp
(9) Halfshaft Bar
(10) Small Boot Retaining Clamp
(11) CV Joint Boot
(12) Swage Ring
(13) Race Retaining Ring
(14) Ball
(15) CV Joint Inner Race
(16) CV Joint Cage
(17) CV Joint Outer Race
(18) Deflector Ring

GC3030000374000X

Fig. 1 Exploded view of tri-pot drive axle

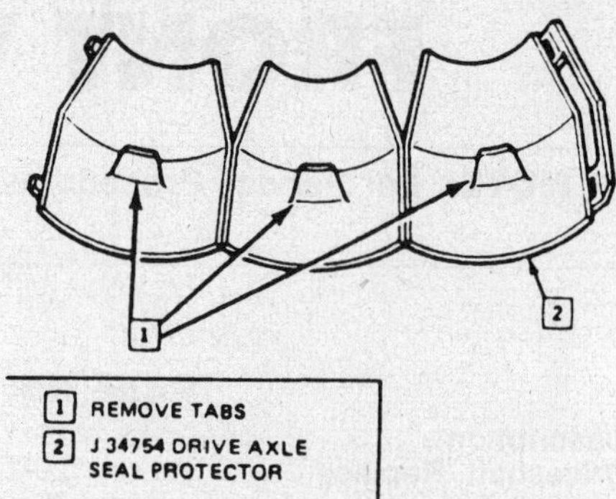

GC3038800096000X

Fig. 2 Seal protector modification

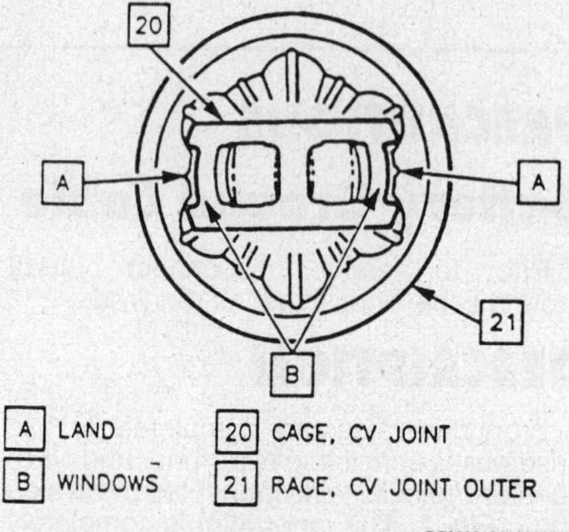

GC3039100190000X

Fig. 3 Outer race & cage separation

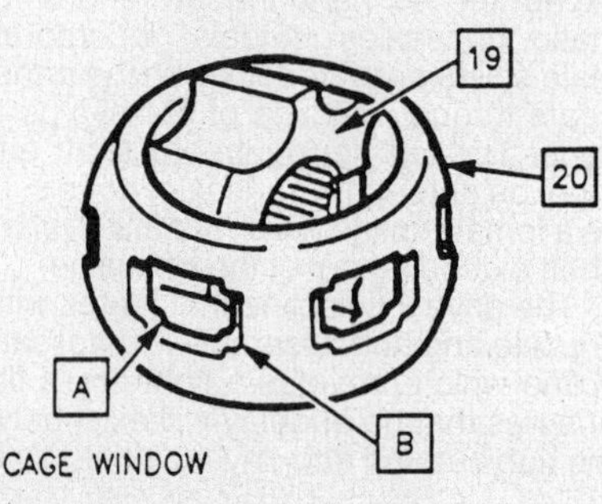

GC3039100191000X

Fig. 4 Inner race & cage separation

Outer Joint

1. Remove outer joint seal as outlined in, "Outer Joint Seal."
2. Use a brass drift and hammer to gently tap on CV joint cage until cage is tilted enough to remove first ball, then tilt cage in opposite direction to remove opposing ball. Remove remaining balls in same manner.
3. Position cage and inner race 90° to centerline of outer race and align cage windows with lands of outer race. Remove cage and inner race from outer race, **Figs. 3 and 4.**
4. Rotate inner race 90° to centerline of cage with lands of inner race aligned with windows of cage, then pivot inner race into cage window and remove inner race.
5. Reverse procedure to install ensure retaining ring side of inner race faces axle shaft.

Inner Tri-Pot Seal & Joint

1. Remove large boot clamp from tri-pot seal.
2. Remove tri-pot housing and bushing from axle shaft, then the small clamp from tri-pot seal.
3. Slide tri-pot seal up axle shaft, away from tri-pot spider assembly toward end of axle shaft.
4. Remove tri-pot spider assembly spacer ring using snap ring pliers tool No. J 8059, or equivalent, then the retaining ring, spider assembly, spacer ring and tri-pot seal.
5. Inspect joint seal, spider, and housing for damage or wear.
6. Reverse procedure to install. Ensure counterbored face of tri-pot spider faces end of shaft.

ALL-WHEEL DRIVE SYSTEMS

NOTE: On Air Bag Equipped Models, Refer To "Air Bag System Precautions" Located In The Front Of This Manual For System Disarming & Arming Procedures.

NOTE: Refer To "Computer Relearn Procedures" Located In The Front Of This Manual When Battery Power To The Computer Has Been Interrupted.

INDEX

PRECAUTIONS

Air Bag Systems

Refer to "Air Bag System Precautions" in the front of this manual for system disarming and arming procedures.

Battery Ground Cable

Prior to service, disconnect battery ground cable and isolate as required.

Balance

Mark all driveline components relationships including propeller shafts, drive axles, pinion flanges, output shafts, etc., for assembly and to maintain factory set system balance. Specifications, torque values and measurements must be followed to maintain balance.

DESCRIPTION

The front axle on all-wheel drive models uses a conventional ring and pinion gear to transmit the engine driving force to the wheels. The axle remains in constant drive operation with no disconnect feature.

TROUBLESHOOTING

When an axle is suspected of being noisy, make a thorough test to determine whether noise originates in the tires, road surface, wheel bearings, engine, transmission, propeller shaft, or front or rear axle assembly. Road testing vehicle with rear propeller shaft removed is helpful in separating front from rear axle noise.

Tire Noise

1. Inspect tires for irregular wear and improper tire pressure.
2. Temporarily inflate all tires to 50 psi. This will alter tire noise but will not effect axle noise.
3. Drive over different road surfaces. Smooth asphalt minimizes tire noise.
4. Cross switch tires.
5. Mud and snow tires cause added noises.

Road Noise

1. Inspect axle lubricant level.
2. Drive to warm front axle to operating temperature.
3. Test at various speeds.

Engine Or Transmission Noise

1. Note engine and vehicle speed and conditions when noise is most pronounced.
2. Shift transmission to neutral at speed.
3. Let engine speed drop to idle.
4. Stop vehicle and run engine at speed.

Wheel Bearing Noise

1. Drive vehicle at low speed on smooth road.
2. Turn vehicle to change noise with cornering loads.
3. Jack wheels up an verify rough or brindled, or loose wheel bearings.

Gear Teeth Noise

Broken, bent or forcibly damaged gear teeth produce a very audible noise over entire speed range.

1. Rough running or whine noise should increase with speed.
2. Noise pitch should be higher than differential noise.
3. Perform test on smooth road to minimize tire noise.
4. Perform test at various speeds in drive, float and coast, with and without rear propeller shaft.
5. Rear pinion bearing noise may be louder on deceleration.
6. Front gear noise will still be present with rear propeller shaft removed.

AXLE SHAFT

REPLACE

Removal

EXPRESS & SAVANA

1. Raise and support vehicle.
2. Drain differential carrier assembly.
3. Remove engine protection shield.
4. Disconnect wheel drive shaft from inner axle shaft as follows:
   a. Remove tire and wheel assembly.
   b. Remove wheel drive shaft nut.
   c. Remove wheel drive shaft retaining bolts.
   d. Remove lefthand wheel drive shaft from differential flange.
   e. Remove righthand wheel drive shaft from differential flange.
   f. Install tool No. J 45859, or equivalent.
   g. Remove front wheel drive shaft from steering knuckle using tool No. J 45859, or equivalent.
   h. Remove lefthand wheel drive shaft from vehicle.

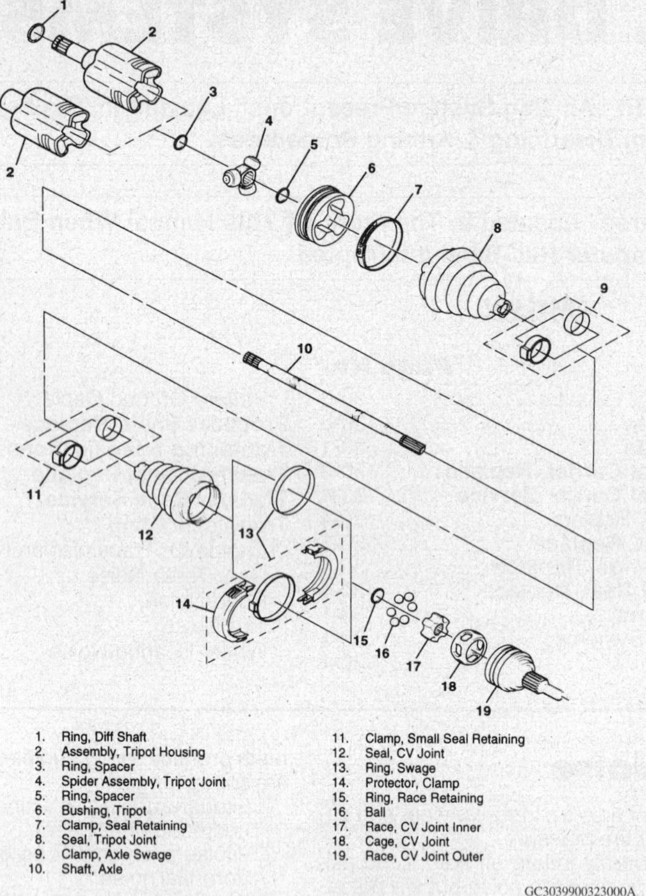

Fig. 1 Axle shaft service

i. Remove righthand wheel drive shaft from vehicle.
5. Place a pry bar between inner axle shaft flange and inner axle shaft housing.
6. Disconnect inner axle shaft from differential case side gear using pry bar. Do not remove inner axle shaft at this time.
7. Install a support jack underneath differential carrier assembly.
8. Remove upper inner shaft housing bushing bolt and nut.
9. Remove lower inner shaft housing bushing bolt and nut.
10. Remove inner axle shaft housing bolts from differential carrier assembly.
11. Remove inner axle shaft and inner axle shaft housing from vehicle.
12. Remove inner axle shaft from inner axle shaft housing.
13. Remove inner axle shaft seal and bearing from inner axle shaft housing.

H2 & H3

1. Remove lefthand differential carrier mounting bracket. **When servicing inner drive shaft housing, inner drive shaft bearing must be replaced. Bearing is not serviced with inner drive shaft housing.**
2. Remove retaining bolts from disconnect housing.
3. Remove coupling housing.
4. Remove coupler.
5. Remove gasket.
6. Remove intermediate housing retaining bolts.
7. Remove intermediate housing.
8. Remove intermediate housing gasket.
9. Install intermediate shaft housing in suitable clamping device.
10. Remove inner drive shaft bearing using tool No. J 29369–1 and J 2619–01, or equivalents.

RAINIER

1. Raise and support vehicle.
2. Drain lubricant from differential carrier assembly.
3. Remove intermediate shaft bearing assembly.
4. Install tool No. J 45104 to tool No. J 6125–B, or equivalent.
5. Install J 45104 and J 6125–B into threaded hole on inner axle shaft.
6. Remove inner axle shaft using tool No. J 6125–B and tool No. J 45104, or equivalent. Support inner axle shaft as required in order to pull inner axle shaft from differential carrier assembly and evenly through oil pan. **Do not nick or cut inboard side differential carrier assembly oil seal.**

Installation

EXPRESS & SAVANA

1. Install new inner axle shaft bearing and new seal to inner axle shaft housing.
2. Install inner axle shaft into inner axle housing. Do not install inner axle shaft completely into inner axle shaft housing at this time. **Do not nick or cut inner axle shaft oil seal.**
3. Apply sealant GM P/N 1052942, or equivalent to inner axle housing to differential carrier sealing surface.
4. Install inner axle shaft housing with inner axle shaft to differential carrier assembly.
5. Install inner axle shaft housing bolts. Tighten to specification.
6. Install lower inner axle shaft housing bushing bolt and nut.
7. Install upper inner axle shaft housing bushing bolt and nut. Tighten to specification.
8. Remove support jack.
9. Install inner axle shaft into differential case side gear by doing the following:
   a. Carefully guide inner axle shaft through inner axle housing until retaining ring on inner axle shaft contacts differential case side gear.
   b. Install inner axle shaft into differential case side gear by tapping retaining ring into retaining groove using soft-faced mallet and until retaining ring on inner axle shaft is fully seated within groove in differential case side gear.
   c. Pull back on inner axle shaft to ensure that inner axle shaft is properly retained in differential case side gear.
10. Install wheel drive shaft to inner axle shaft.
11. Fill differential carrier assembly with axle lubricant.
12. Lower vehicle.

H2 & H3

1. Install inner drive shaft bearing using tool No. J 45232 and J 8092, or equivalents.
2. Apply a small amount of clean grease on housing gasket to hold it in place.
3. Install intermediate housing. **Clean thread locking material from bolts. Apply new thread locking material to bolts.**
4. Install retaining bolts. Tighten to specification.
5. Install intermediate shaft.
6. Apply a small amount of grease to housing gasket to hold it in place.
7. Install coupler.
8. Position coupler housing on intermediate housing.
9. Install retaining bolts. Tighten to specification.
10. Install lefthand differential carrier mounting bracket.
11. Lower vehicle.

RAINIER

1. Install tool Nos. J 45104 and J 6125–B, or equivalent to inner axle shaft.
2. While supporting tool Nos. J 6125–B and J 45104, or equivalent, with inner axle shaft, place inner axle shaft into inner axle shaft opening in oil pan.
3. Carefully guide inner axle shaft through oil pan and differential carrier assembly oil seal into differential side gear turning as required in order to

align inner axle shaft splines with differential side gear splines using tool No. J 6125–B and J 45104, or equivalent.
4. Push axle shaft into differential side gear until retaining ring snaps inner axle shaft in place using tool No. J 6125–B, or equivalent. Pull on inner axle shaft to ensure that it is locked into position.
5. Remove tool Nos. J 45104 and J 6125–B, or equivalent.
6. Install intermediate shaft bearing assembly.
7. Add lubricant to differential carrier assembly. Use proper fluid.
8. Lower vehicle.

AXLE SHAFT SERVICE

Refer to **Fig. 1** when servicing axle shaft.

Inspection

1. Wipe knuckle wheel bearing seal area clean.
2. Inspect seal for cuts or tears. If cut or torn, inspect wheel bearing for damage and replace seal.
3. Lubricate seal lip.

CV Joint Replacement

INNER

1. Cut and remove clamps.
2. Remove axle shaft with spider assembly.
3. Slide spacer ring and spider assembly back, and snap ring using suitable snap ring pliers.
4. Remove spider assembly.
5. Reverse procedure to install, noting the following:
   a. Clean housing and inboard boot.
   b. Ensure snap ring counterbore faces axle housing end.
   c. Pack housing with half of boot kit supplied grease. Use remaining grease in boot and to coat inside of boot sealing lips.
   d. Use clamp tool No. J-35910, or equivalent.

OUTER

1. Cut and remove clamps.
2. Remove snap ring using suitable snap ring pliers.
3. Remove axle shaft joint assembly.
4. Tap cage with suitable brass drift and hammer until it tilts enough to remove first ball, then remove other balls similarly.
5. Pivot cage with inner race 90° to outer race centerline, align cage windows with outer race lands, and lift cage with inner race.
6. Rotate inner race up and out of cage.
7. Reverse procedure to install, noting the following:
   a. Clean all components except outboard boot with suitable solvent.
   b. Apply suitable grease to inner and outer race ball grooves.
   c. Ensure inner race retaining ring faces out.
   d. Pack joint with suitable grease.
   e. Use clamp tool No. J-35910, or equivalent.

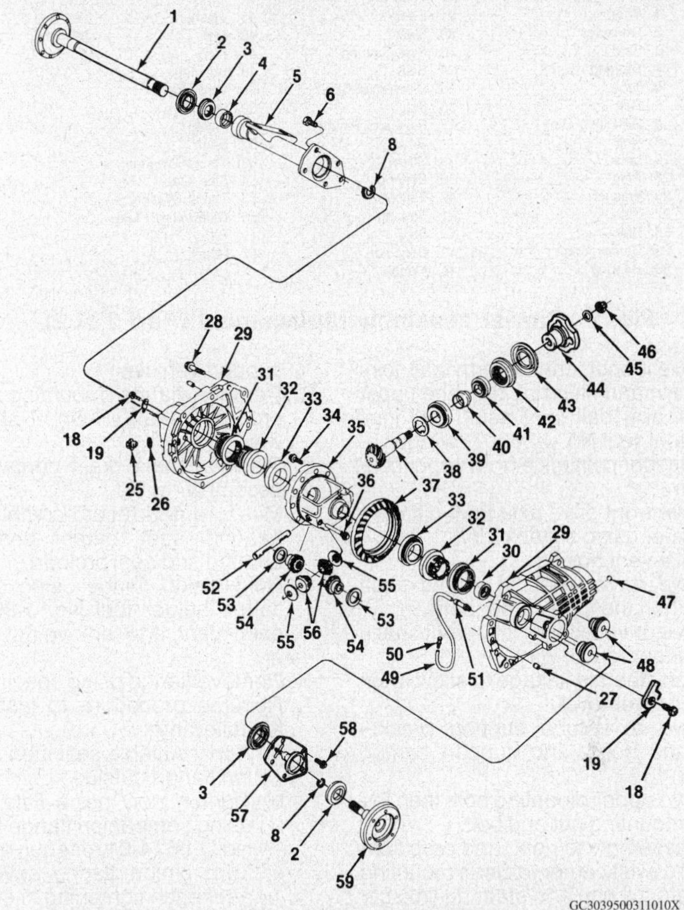

Fig. 2 Carrier assembly replacement (Part 1 of 2)

DRIVESHAFT

REPLACE

1. Remove righthand drive axle as outlined under "Axle Shaft, Replace."
2. Position suitable drain container under housing, and protect inner axle shaft housing and seal with suitable shop towel.
3. Insert suitable bent screwdriver into shaft retaining ring slot and pry against shop towel to disengage inner axle shaft from side gear.
4. Remove support bracket nuts and washers, **Fig. 2.**
5. Remove tube to carrier mounting bolts.
6. Remove tube and shaft.
7. Strike shaft flange inside with suitable brass hammer to dislodge shaft.
8. Carefully pull splined shaft through seal diameter to avoid cutting seal.
9. Remove seal and bearing using countershaft roller bearing tool No. J-29369-2 and slide hammer tool No. J-29307, or equivalents.
10. Remove differential pilot bearing using pilot bearing tool No. J-34011, or equivalent.
11. Reverse procedure to install, noting the following:
    a. Lubricate seal lips, bearings and bearing surfaces with suitable axle lubricant.
    b. Use pilot bearing tool No. J-33842, or equivalent.
    c. Use bearing tool No. J-42211, or equivalent.
    d. Use shaft seal tool Nos. J-33893 or J-42212, or equivalents.
    e. Clean sealing surfaces with suitable chlorinated solvent.
    f. Apply bead of suitable sealer to carrier sealing surface.

DIFFERENTIAL CARRIER

REPLACE

1. Unlock steering column, raise and support vehicle.
2. Drain fluid from axle into suitable container.
3. Remove lefthand or righthand front wheel.
4. Insert suitable drift through brake caliper top opening into brake rotor vane to keep axle from turning.
5. Remove propeller shaft at front axle and support out of way.
6. Remove brake hose and wheel speed sensor wire upper control arm brackets.

1. Shaft
2. Deflector
3. Seal
4. Bearing
5. Tube
6. Bolt
8. Retaining Ring
18. Bolt
19. Lock
25. Plug
26. Washer
27. Pin
28. Bolt
29. Carrier Case
30. Bearing
31. Insert
32. Sleeve
33. Side Bearing
34. Bolt
35. Differential Case
36. Bolt
37. Ring and Pinion Gears
38. Shim
39. Bearing
40. Spacer
41. Bearing
42. Seal
43. Deflector
44. Flange
45. Washer
46. Nut
47. Plug
48. Bushing
49. Vent Hose
50. Vent
51. Fitting
52. Shaft
53. Thrust Washer
54. Side Gear
55. Thrust Washer
56. Differential Pinion Gear
57. Cover
58. Bolt
59. Shaft

GC3039500311020X

Fig. 2 Carrier assembly replacement (Part 2 of 2)

7. Remove upper control arm ball joint cotter pin and stud nut, then the upper control arm ball joint using ball joint separator tool No. J-36607, or equivalent. Suspend knuckle from upper control arm.
8. Remove front drive axle from differential carrier using suitable drift.
9. Remove vent hose.
10. Remove drive axles to output shaft bolts, then the tube carrier bolts.
11. Remove drive axles from output shafts and support out of way.
12. Position steering linkage to allow room for carrier removal.
13. Remove axle tube support bracket nuts and bolts, and support carrier, **Fig. 3.**
14. Remove upper mounting bolt, then the lower mounting nut and bolt.
15. Slide assembly to right, and drop tube end and twist carrier to clean mounting brackets, oil pan and steering linkage.
16. Reverse procedure to install.

DIFFERENTIAL CARRIER SERVICE

Bushing, Replace

1. Remove differential carrier assembly as outlined under "Differential Carrier, Replace."
2. Remove bushing using bushing replacement set tool No. J-33791, or equivalent, **Fig. 4.**
3. Install bushing using bushing replacement set tool No. J-33791, or equivalent.
4. Install differential carrier assembly as outlined under "Differential Carrier, Replace."

PINION FLANGE

REPLACE

1. Unlock steering column, raise and support vehicle.
2. Remove flange mounting bolts and propeller shaft. Support shaft out of way.
3. Place suitable drain container under assembly.
4. Measure and record combined pinion bearing, seal, carrier bearing, axle bearing and seal preload.
5. Hold pinion flange using companion flange holder tool No. J-8614-01, or equivalent, and remove nut and washer.
6. Remove flange using special tool.
7. Reverse procedure to install, noting the following:
   a. Apply suitable seal lubricant to pinion flange outside.
   b. Tighten new nut a little at a time using companion flange holder tool No. J-8614-01, or equivalent.
   c. Turn pinion flange several times after each tightening to set rollers.
   d. Measure bearing preload after each tightening until preload is 3–5 inch lbs., more than recorded during removal.

PINION OIL SEAL

REPLACE

1. Remove pinion flange mounting bolts.
2. Remove propeller shaft and support out of way.
3. Mark pinion flange, shaft and nut.
4. Measure and record bearing preload.
5. Place suitable drain container under assembly.
6. Hold pinion flange using companion flange holder tool No. J-8614-01, or equivalent, and remove nut and washer. Count and record number of turns required to remove nut.
7. Remove flange using special tool.
8. Drive seal out of carrier with suitable blunt punch or drift. Be careful to not damage carrier.
9. Reverse procedure to install, noting the following:
   a. Apply suitable seal lubricant to pinion flange outside.
   b. Install flange in exact spline relationship to removal using same number of turns to install as to remove.
   c. Turn pinion flange several times after each tightening to set rollers.
   d. Measure bearing preload after each tightening until preload is 3–5 inch lbs., more than recorded during removal.

PROPELLER SHAFT

REPLACE

1. Raise and support vehicle.
2. Remove front axle bolts.
3. Remove transfer case bolts.
4. Remove propeller shaft.
5. Reverse procedure to install.

TRANSFER CASE

REPLACE

1. Raise and support vehicle.
2. Remove engine brace mounting bolts, then the engine brace.
3. Remove transfer case shield.
4. Remove front and rear propeller shaft assemblies.
5. Remove motor encoder electrical connector.
6. Remove transfer case electrical harness.
7. Remove transfer case vent hose.
8. Support transmission using a suitable transmission jack, then remove transmission mount retaining nuts and mount.
9. Remove transfer case bottom retaining nut.
10. Install transmission mount, then remove transmission jack stand.
11. Remove transfer case upper retaining nuts.
12. Install suitable transmission jack to transfer case.
13. Remove transfer case assembly.
14. Reverse procedure to install.

TRANSFER CASE SERVICE

Refer to "Transfer Cases" chapter.

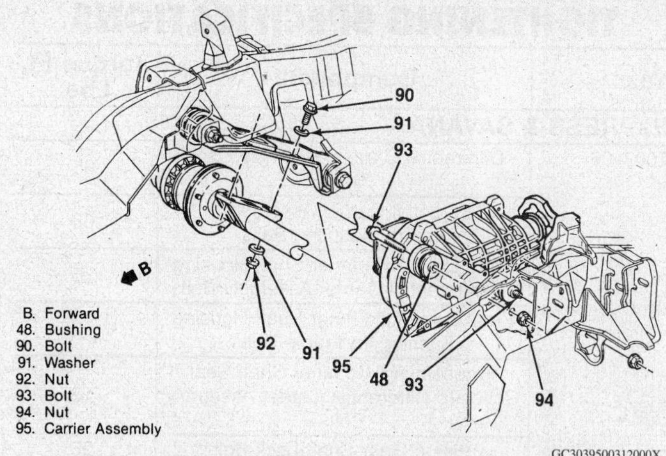

Fig. 3 Differential carrier replacement

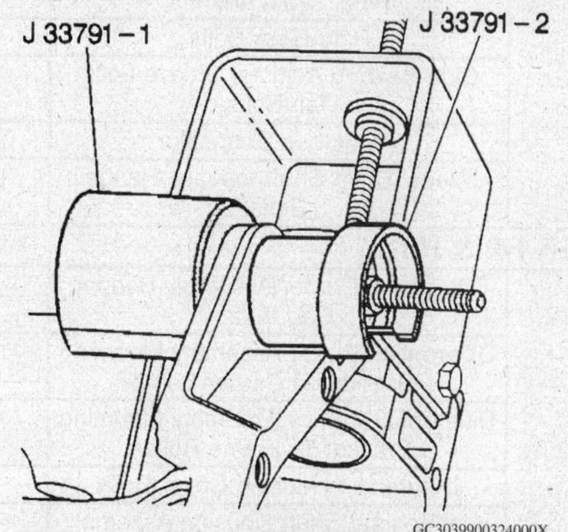

Fig. 4 Differential carrier bushing removal

TIGHTENING SPECIFICATIONS

Year	Component	Torque Ft. Lbs.
EXPRESS & SAVANA		
2002–06	Differential Carrier Assembly Case Bolts	35
	Differential Carrier Assembly To Frame Mounting Bolts	63
	Front Drive Axle Inner Shaft Housing To Differential Carrier Assembly Bolts	35
	Front Drive Axle Inner Shaft Housing Bushing To Frame Bolts	63
	Front Drive Axle Inner Shaft Seal Cover To Differential Carrier Assembly Bolts	13
	Pinion Gear Shaft Lock Bolt	26
	Pinion Yoke Retainer Bolts	18
	Plug, Drain And Fill	24
	Ring Gear Bolts	62
	Side Bearing Adjuster Sleeve Lock Tab Bolts	71①
	Vent Hose Connector	30
	Wheel Drive Shaft Inboard Flange Bolts	37
HUMMER H2 & H3		
2003–06	Differential Carrier Assembly Bearing Cap Bolts	46
	Differential Carrier Assembly Mounting Bracket To Carrier Bolts	114
	Differential Carrier Assembly Mounting Bracket To Frame Bolts	114
	Differential Housing Cover Bolts	22
	Intermediate Shaft Housing Assembly To Axle Housing Bolts	49
	Intermediate Shaft Housing To Outer Housing Bolts	35
	Pinion Shaft Lock Screw/Bolt	18
	Plug, Drain And Fill	24
	Ring Gear Bolts	89
	Third Point Mount Bolt	81
RAINIER		
2004–06	Actuator Mounting Bolts	53①
	Brake Hose Retaining Bolt	18
	Differential Carrier Assembly Case Bolts	35
	Differential Carrier Assembly Mounting Bolts	63
	Intermediate Shaft Bearing Assembly Case Bolts	35
	Intermediate Shaft Bearing Assembly Mounting Bolts	35
	Pinion Shaft Lock Screw	26
	Plug, Drain And Fill	24
	Ring Gear Bolts	61
	Upper Shock Module Mounting Bolt	30

① — Inch lbs.

DRIVE AXLES

NOTE: For Service Procedures On Front Wheel Drive Vehicles, Refer To "Front Wheel Drive" Section.

TABLE OF CONTENTS

IDENTIFICATION

Axle codes are identified by either a stamp on the axle tube or the size of the ring gear.

Application Chart

Model	Axle
Astro	7 ½ & 10 ½
Avalanche	8⅝, 9½ & 10½
Aztec	Versatrak
Blazer	7 ½ & 8 ⅝
Bravada	8 & 8⅝
Canyon	8
Colorado	8
Envoy	8 & 8⅝
Equinox	Versatrak
Escalade	8⅝, 9½ & 10½
Express	8⅝, 9¾ & 10½
Jimmy	7 ½ & 8 ⅝
Montana	Versatrak
Rainier	8 & 8⅝
Relay	Versatrak
Rendezvous	Versatrak
Safari	7 ½ & 10 ½
Savana	8⅝, 9¾ & 10½

Model	Axle
Sierra	8⅝, 9¾, 10½ & 11½
Silhouette	Versatrak
Silverado	8⅝, 9¾, 10½ & 11½
Sonoma	7 ½ & 8 ⅝
SRX	7 ½
SSR	8⅝
Suburban	8⅝, 9½ & 10½
SV6	Versatrak
S10	7 ½ & 8 ⅝
Tahoe	8⅝, 9½ & 10½
Terraza	Versatrak
Torrent	Versatrak
Trailblazer	8 & 8⅝
Uplander	Versatrak
Venture	Versatrak
Vue	Vue
Yukon	8⅝, 9½ & 10½

American/GM Front & Rear Drive Axles w/8 Inch Ring Gears

INDEX

STANDARD DIFFERENTIAL

Disassemble

1. Install differential assembly in a suitable vise.
2. Install a side bearing puller kit tool No. J 22888-20A, or equivalent.
3. Remove differential side bearings using a side bearing puller kit.
4. Remove differential assembly from vise.
5. Remove differential side bearings.
6. Remove and discard ring gear bolts. **Do not pry ring gear from differential case. Prying ring gear from differential case may cause damage to ring gear and/or differential case. Ring gear bolts have left-hand threads.**
7. Remove ring gear from differential case, then drive ring gear off with a suitable brass drift.
8. Mark pinion gears top and bottom and differential side gears left and right for assembly reference.
9. Remove pinion shaft lock bolt, then the pinion shaft.
10. Roll differential pinion gears out of case with pinion gear thrust washers.
11. Remove differential side gears and side gear thrust washers.

Assemble

1. Lubricate pinion and side gears using axle lubricant. Using a suitable fluid.
2. Install differential side gear thrust washers to differential side gears.
3. Install differential side gears and thrust washers into differential case. If same differential side gears and thrust washers are being used, install gears and thrust washers to their original locations.
4. Position one pinion gear between differential side gears.
5. Position second pinion gear between differential side gears directly opposite of first gear.
6. Rotate differential side gears until pinion gears is directly opposite opening in differential case.
7. Install thrust washers. Rotate pinion gears toward differential opening in order to permit sliding in of thrust washers.
8. Install pinion shaft.
9. Install a new pinion shaft lock bolt and **torque** to 18 ft. lbs.
10. Install ring gear to differential case. **Ring gear bolts have left-hand threads.**
11. Install new ring gear bolts. Hand start each bolt to ensure ring gear is properly installed to differential case.
12. **Torque** ring gear bolts alternately and in stages, gradually pulling ring gear onto differential case to 89 ft. lbs.
13. Install differential side bearings.

LOCKING DIFFERENTIAL

Disassemble

1. Remove governor bushing using a locking differential governor remover tool No. J 26252 or equivalent.
2. Remove governor assembly. To aid in removal of governor assembly, turn side gear as necessary to position governor assembly between two of side gear teeth.
3. Remove latching bracket assembly bushing using locking differential governor remover. To aid in removal of latching bracket assembly, turn side gear as necessary to position latching bracket assembly between two of side gear teeth.
4. Remove pinion shaft lock bolt and pinion shaft.
5. Remove differential pinion gears and thrust washers. Rotate pinion gears and roll pinion gears and thrust washers out of case through differential window. Mark pinion gears and thrust washers accordingly for re-assembly.
6. Remove thrust block.
7. Remove right side gear and clutch discs assembly.
8. Remove right side shim.
9. Remove left side gear (cam unit) and clutch discs assembly.
10. Remove left side gear thrust washer.

Cleaning & Inspection

1. Clean components in suitable solvent and blow dry with compressed air, noting the following:
   a. Do not use brush when cleaning bearings.
   b. Do not spin dry bearings, as bearings will be damaged.
   c. Lightly lubricate components after cleaning to retard corrosion.
   d. Keep all components in order to ensure proper assembly.
2. Inspect gears for cracks, chipped teeth, wear and scoring, and damaged bearing or mounting surfaces. Replace gears that are damaged or excessively worn. **Ring gear and pinion must be replaced as an assembly.**
3. Inspect differential case for cracks, damage, worn side gear bores and scored bearing surfaces and replace as needed.
4. Inspect housing for scored bearing mount surfaces, cracks and distortion and replace as needed.
5. Inspect bearing rollers and races for pitting, scoring, overheating and damage.
6. Mate bearing with race and inspect operation.
7. Replace any bearing that is damaged, excessively worn or that fails to operate smoothly.
8. Mount differential case along with side bearings and ring gear in housing and inspect runout with side bearings adjusted for zero preload and suitable dial indicator positioned against machined edge of ring gear.
9. If runout exceeds .003 inch and gear cannot be repositioned to eliminate runout, ring gear and/or case should be replaced.

Adjustments

DIFFERENTIAL SIDE BEARING PRELOAD

The differential side bearing preload adjustment must be completed before the backlash adjustment can be started. In order to maintain the original backlash, adjust the differential case side bearing preload by changing the thickness of the left and the right side shim packs equally. Measure the service shims and the spacers one at a time. Add the measurements together in order to obtain the total thickness of the left or the right side shim pack. Do not use or reuse the original cast iron production shims. Use service shims and spacers instead.

1. Install drive pinion.
2. Measure rotating torque of drive pinion using a suitable inch-pound torque wrench. Rotating torque of drive pinion should be 15–30 inch lbs for new bearings or 10–30 inch lbs. for used bearings.
3. Record measurement.
4. Install differential assembly with side bearings and bearing cups into axle housing.
5. Insert one .17 inch thick service spacer into left side of axle housing.
6. Slide differential assembly towards service spacer in order to hold spacer in place.
7. Install side bearing backlash gauge tool No. J 22779, or equivalent, between right side differential side bearing cup and axle housing.
8. Tighten knob on side bearing backlash gauge tool until there is a moderate drag when side bearing backlash gauge is moved.
9. Remove side bearing backlash gauge.
10. Remove service spacer.
11. Measure thickness of side bearing backlash gauge in three locations using a suitable micrometer. Calculate average of three measurements and record measurement.
12. Measure thickness of service spacer using a suitable micrometer. Record measurement.
13. Add thickness of service spacer to average thickness of side bearing backlash gauge. Resulting value is total service shim thickness without preload for axle.
14. Insert one .04 inch service shim between right side differential side bearing cup and axle housing.
15. Insert one bent .04 inch service shim between right side differential side bearing cup and service shim.
16. Install side bearing backlash gauge on left side of differential assembly.
17. While rotating ring gear back and forth, tighten knob on side bearing backlash gauge until there is approximately .001–.002 inch of backlash between ring gear and drive pinion.
18. Remove side bearing backlash gauge.
19. Remove differential case with differential side bearings and bearing cups.
20. Remove service shims.
21. Measure thickness of side bearing backlash gage in three locations using a suitable micrometer.
22. Calculate average of three measurements. This average value is left side service shim thickness without preload.
23. Subtract service shim thickness for left side of axle from total service shim thickness. This value is service shim thickness for right side of axle without preload.
24. In order to initially set preload of differential side bearings and backlash to approximately .005–.009 inch, take previous value determined and add .008 inch service shim thickness to this amount.
25. Assemble left side shim pack using one .170 inch service spacer and appropriate amount of selective service shims equaling thickness determined. Measure service spacer and service shims separate, then add measurements together in order to determine total shim pack thickness.
26. Assemble right side shim pack using one .170 inch service spacer and appropriate amount of selective service shims. Measure service spacer and service shims separately, then add measurements together in order to determine total shim pack thickness.
27. Install differential assembly with differential side bearings and differential side bearing cups.
28. Install left side service spacer between axle housing and differential assembly.
29. Install left side selective service shim or shims. service shim or shims must be installed between service spacer and differential side bearing cup.
30. Install right side service spacer between axle housing and differential assembly.
31. Install right side selective service shim or shims using a side bearing shim installer tool No. J 25588 , or equivalent. Service shim or shims must be installed between service spacer and differential side bearing cup.
32. Install differential bearing caps and **torque** differential bearing cap bolts to 55 ft lbs.
33. Measure drive pinion and differential side bearing preload using a suitable inch-pound torque wrench.
34. Rotate pinion several times to ensure differential side bearings have seated.
35. Rotating torque of drive pinion and differential side bearings should be 30–55 inch lbs. for new bearings or 25–45 inch lbs. for used bearings.
36. Record measurement.
37. Calculate differential side bearing preload by subtracting drive pinion preload from drive pinion and differential case bearing preload. Multiply value obtained by axle ratio. Differential case side bearing preload should be 15-35 inch lbs.
38. If differential side bearing preload is not within specifications, add or subtract shim thickness equally from each shim pack as necessary in order to increase or decrease side bearing preload.
39. Once differential side bearing preload is correct, measure backlash and adjust, if necessary.
40. Once differential side bearing preload and backlash is correct, perform a gear tooth contact pattern check in order to ensure proper alignment between ring and pinion gears.

DRIVE PINION DEPTH

1. Lubricate pinion bearings with suitable axle lubricant.
2. Install pinion bearings into axle housing.
3. Assemble pinion setting gauge block tool No. J 45230, or equivalent, into axle housing.
4. Install a suitable inch-pound torque wrench on nut of pinion setting gauge block. Torque nut on pinion setting gauge block until a rotating torque of 15–25 inch lbs. is obtained.
5. Rotate assembly several times in both directions in order to seat pinion bearings.
6. Check rotating torque of assembly. If torque is less than 15 inch lbs. continue to tighten nut on pinion setting gauge block until a rotating torque of 15–25 inch lbs. is obtained.
7. Assemble pinion setting gauge block.
8. Rotate pinion setting gauge block. Pinion setting gauge block must rotate back and forth freely within discs. If pinion setting gauge block does not rotate freely, disassemble components and inspect for proper seating and/or mis-aligned components and reassemble.
9. Align plunger of pinion setting gauge block.
10. Install dial indicator set tool No. J 800, or equivalent, to pinion setting gauge block as follows:
    a. Loosely clamp dial indicator set onto stem on pinion setting gage block.
    b. Place contact pad of dial indicator set onto mounting post of pinion setting gage block.
    c. With contact pad of dial indicator set touching mounting post of pinion setting gage block, loosen lock nut on dial indicator set and push down on dial indicator set until needle of dial indicator set has turned ¾ of a turn clockwise.
    d. Tighten clamp on dial indicator set finger tight.
11. Move plunger of pinion setting gage block back and forth until needle of dial indicator set indicates greatest deflection. Deflection is point where needle changes direction.
12. At greatest point of deflection, move housing of dial indicator set until needle indicates zero.
13. Move plunger of pinion setting gage block back and forth again to verify zero setting. Adjust housing of dial indicator set as necessary to set needle to zero.
14. Rotate plunger of pinion setting gage block away from pinion setting gage block until it no longer touches pinion setting gage block.
15. Value indicated on dial indicator set is thickness of shim needed in order to set depth of pinion.
16. Select shim that indicates proper thickness. Measure shim with a micrometer in order to verify that thickness is correct.
17. Remove pinion depth setting tools and pinion bearings.
18. Install pinion shim between pinion gear and inner pinion bearing.

BACKLASH

1. Install guide pins tool No. J 25025-1 and dial indicator set tool No. J 800, or

equivalent, to axle housing.

2. Place indicator stem of dial indicator at heel end of a gear tooth.
3. Set dial indicator so stem is aligned with gear rotation and perpendicular to tooth angle.
4. Preload dial of dial indicator. Align needle and dial face of dial indicator to zero.
5. While holding drive pinion stationary, move ring gear back and forth. Measure and record backlash.
6. Repeat measuring procedure at eight points around ring gear. Difference between backlash at all of measuring points should not vary by more than .002 inch.
7. If difference between backlash at all of measuring points varies by more than .002 inch, inspect for burrs, distorted case flange, uneven bolting. If difference between all measuring points is within specifications, backlash at minimum lash should be between .003–.010 inch with a preferred backlash of .005–.007 inch. **Do not use original cast iron production shims to adjust backlash. Use service shims and spacers instead.**
8. Adjust thickness of shim pack on each side of differential in equal amounts. This will maintain correct axle side bearing preload. Moving .002 inch of shim thickness from one side of differential to other will change backlash adjustment approximately .001 inch.
9. If backlash is too small, increase backlash using the following procedure:
   a. Remove bearing cap bolts and bearing caps. Mark bearing caps left or right.
   b. Remove differential case assembly with bearing cups and shims. Mark bearing cups and shims left or right.
   c. Measure thickness of left side shim pack. Measure production shim or shim and service spacer in three locations. Measure each shim separately.
   d. Calculate average of three measurements for each shim, then add average of each of shim measurements together and record measurement. This is thickness for left side shim pack.
   e. Assemble a new left side shim pack by decreasing appropriate amount of thickness from original left side shim pack. If original shim is cast iron production shim, assemble shim pack using a service spacer and service shims. For example, to increase backlash by 0.002 inch, remove 0.004 inch of thickness from left side shim pack.
   f. Measure thickness of right side shim pack. Measure shim or shim and service spacer in three locations and measure each shim separately.
   g. Calculate average of three measurements for each shim, then add average of each of shim measurements together and record measurement. This is thickness for right side shim pack.
   h. Assemble a new right side shim pack by increasing appropriate amount of thickness to original right side shim pack. If original shim is cast iron production shim, assemble shim pack using a service spacer and service shims. For example, to increase backlash by 0.002 inch, add 0.004 inch of thickness to right side shim pack.
10. If backlash is too large, decrease backlash using following procedure:
    a. Remove bearing cap bolts and bearing caps. Mark bearing caps left or right.
    b. Remove differential case assembly with bearing cups and shims. Mark bearing cups and shims left or right.
    c. Measure thickness of left side shim pack. Measure production shim or shim and service spacer in three locations. Measure each shim separately.
    d. Calculate average of three measurements for each shim, then add average of each of shim measurements together and record measurement. This is thickness for left side shim pack.
    e. Assemble a new left side shim pack by increasing appropriate amount of thickness to original left side shim pack. If original shim is cast iron production shim, assemble shim pack using a service spacer and service shims. For example, to increase backlash by 0.002 inch, add 0.004 inch of thickness to left side shim pack.
    f. Measure thickness of right side shim pack. Measure shim or shim and service spacer in three locations. Measure each shim separately.
    g. Calculate average of three measurements for each shim, then add average of each of shim measurements together and record measurement. This is thickness for right side shim pack.
    h. Assemble a new right side shim pack by decreasing appropriate amount of thickness to original right side shim pack. If original shim is cast iron production shim, assemble shim pack using a service spacer and service shims. For example, to decrease backlash by 0.002 inch, remove 0.004 inch of thickness to right side shim pack.
11. Install differential case assembly with bearing cups. Install left side service spacer between axle housing and differential case. Install right side service spacer between axle housing and differential case.
12. Install left side service shim using side bearing shim installer tool No. J 25588, or equivalent. Service shim must be installed between service spacer and differential bearing cup.
13. Install right side service shim between service spacer and differential bearing cup.
14. Install bearing caps and bolts, **torque** bolts to 55 ft. lbs.
15. Once backlash is correct, perform a gear tooth contact pattern check in order to ensure proper alignment between ring and pinion gears.

Assemble

PINION INSTALLATION

1. Install outer pinion bearing cup using a outer bearing race installer tool No. J 7817, and universal driver handle 3/4 inch tool No. J 8092, or equivalents.
2. Install inner pinion bearing cup using rear pinion bearing race installer tool No. J 8608, or equivalent, and universal driver handle tool.
3. Determine selective shim thickness for pinion.
4. Install selective shim between inner pinion bearing and shoulder on gear.
5. Install inner pinion bearing using pinion cone and side bearing installer tool No. J 24433, or equivalent. Press bearing on until cone seats on pinion shim.
6. Install a new collapsible spacer.
7. Lubricate pinion bearings with suitable axle lubricant. Use proper fluid.
8. Install pinion into axle housing.
9. Install outer pinion bearing onto pinion.
10. Install a new pinion oil seal using a pinion oil seal installer tool No. J 33782, or equivalent.
11. Apply a suitable sealant to splines of pinion yoke.
12. Install pinion yoke and align marks made during removal.
13. Seat pinion yoke onto pinion shaft by tapping it with a suitable soft-faced hammer until a few pinion shaft threads show through yoke.
14. Install washer and a new pinion nut.
15. Install a flange and pulley holding tool No. J 8614-01, or equivalent, onto pinion yoke.
16. While holding flange and pulley holding tool, tighten pinion nut until pinion end play is just taken up. Rotate pinion while tightening nut to seat bearings.
17. Measure rotating torque of pinion using a suitable inch-pound torque wrench. Rotating torque of pinion should be 10–25 inch lbs. for used bearings, or 15–30 inch lbs. for new bearings.
18. If rotating torque measurement is below 10 inch lbs. for used bearings, or 15 inch lbs. for new bearings, continue to tighten pinion nut in small increments, as needed, until torque required to rotate pinion is 10-25 inch lbs. for used bearings, or 15-30 inch lbs. for new bearings.
19. Once specified torque is obtained, rotate pinion several times to ensure bearings have seated.

DIFFERENTIAL CASE ASSEMBLE

1. Install left side gear thrust washer.
2. Install left side gear (cam unit) and clutch disc assembly.
3. Install right side gear thrust washer.
4. Install right side clutch pack assembly.
5. Install right side gear. If original pinion

gears and thrust washers are being reused, install pinion gears and thrust washers on same side as removed.
6. Install pinion gear and pinion thrust washers. Place pinion gears and pinion thrust washers 180° apart.
7. Rotate pinion gears and pinion thrust washers 90° and align pinion gears with pinion shaft opening in differential case. Install thrust block. Open side of thrust block must face window opening.
8. Install pinion shaft.
9. Install new pinion shaft lock bolt. Tighten lock bolt finger tight.
10. Install governor assembly.
11. Install governor bushing using a hammer and a suitable brass drift. Press bushing into place until there is .01—.03 inch of shaft endplay.
12. Install latching bracket assembly. Straight end of latching bracket spring must be over and outside governor assembly shaft.
13. Install latching bracket bushing using a hammer and a brass drift. Press bushing into place until there is .0–.002 inch of shaft endplay.
14. **Torque** pinion shaft lock bolt to 27 ft lbs.

American/GM Front & Rear Drive Axles w/9½ Inch Ring Gears

INDEX

OVERHAUL

Standard Differential

DISASSEMBLE

1. Install differential assembly into a suitable vise.
2. Install a side bearing puller pilot tool No. J 36597 and side bearing puller kit tool No. J 22888-20A, or equivalent.
3. Remove differential side bearings using a side bearing puller kit tool No. J 22888-20A, or equivalent.
4. Remove gear bolts and discard. **Ring gear bolts have lefthand threads.**
5. Remove ring gear from differential case using a suitable brass drift.
6. Remove pinion shaft lock bolt and pinion shaft.
7. Drive pinion gear thrust washer out from differential case using a suitable hammer and brass drift.
8. Roll differential pinion gears out of differential case.
9. Remove differential side gears and side gear thrust washers. Mark pinion gears top and bottom and differential side gears left and right.

ASSEMBLE

1. Lubricate pinion and side gears using a suitable axle lubricant.
2. Install differential side gear thrust washers to differential side gears.
3. Install differential side gears and thrust washers into differential case. If same differential side gears and thrust washers are being used, install gears and thrust washers to their original locations.
4. Position one of pinion gears between differential side gears.
5. Install second pinion gear directly opposite of first gear between differential side gears.
6. Rotate differential side gears until pinion gears are directly opposite opening in differential case.
7. Install pinion gear thrust washers using a suitable hammer and a suitable brass drift.
8. Install pinion shaft and lock bolt, **torque** bolt to 37 ft lbs.
9. Install ring gear to differential case. Ring gear bolts have left-hand threads.
10. Install new ring gear bolts. Hand start each bolt to ensure ring gear is properly installed.
11. **Torque** ring gear bolts alternately and in stages to 103 ft. lbs.
12. Install a 9.25 inch side bearing puller pilot tool No. J 29710 and a ¾ universal driver handle tool No. J 8092, or equivalents, onto differential case bearing, **Fig. 1.**
13. Drive bearing into case.

Limited Slip Differential

DISASSEMBLE

1. Remove ring gear.
2. Remove differential side bearings.
3. Remove pinion shaft roll pin using a suitable brass drift.
4. Remove pinion shaft.
5. Install a limited slip differential overhaul tool No. J 45709-4, or equivalent, into a suitable vise.
6. Install differential assembly onto limited slip differential overhaul tool No. J 45709-4, or equivalent.
7. Compress side gear clutch disc packs.
8. Remove pinion gear thrust washers.
9. Turn forcing screw of limited slip differential overhaul tool No. J 45709-4, or equivalent, counterclockwise to relieve tension of clutch disc packs against differential case.
10. Once tension between clutch disc packs and differential case has been relieved, rotate differential case.
11. Remove differential pinion gears.
12. Remove limited slip differential overhaul tool.
13. Remove differential side gears and clutch disc pack assemblies.
14. Remove upper differential side gear and clutch disc pack.
15. Remove lower differential side gear and clutch disc pack.

ASSEMBLE

The clutch discs are replaceable as complete sets only. If one clutch disc pack requires replacement, both packs must be replaced. New clutch discs and clutch plates need to be soaked in the lubricant that is provided in the kit for 20 minutes before the clutch packs can be assembled.

1. Soak clutch discs and clutch plates in a suitable lubricant provided with kit for 20 minutes.
2. Assemble components, **Fig. 2,** of each clutch pack onto left and right side differential side gear in the following order:
   a. Limited slip clutch disc spacer.
   b. 1st non-eared clutch disc.
   c. 1st eared clutch plate.
   d. 2nd non-eared clutch disc.
   e. 2nd eared clutch plate.
   f. 3rd non-eared clutch disc.
   g. 3rd eared clutch plate.
   h. 4th non-eared clutch disc.
   i. 4th non-eared clutch disc.
   j. 4th eared clutch plate.

3. Install two differential clutch retainers to each of clutch packs. Ensure differential clutch retainers are fully seated onto ears of clutch plates.
4. Install left side differential side gear and clutch pack into flange end of differential case.
5. Install right side differential side gear and clutch pack into bell end of differential case.
6. While holding bell end differential side gear in position, install limited slip differential overhaul tool into differential case.
7. Tighten limited slip differential overhaul tool until there is enough clearance to install pinion gears.
8. While holding pinion gears against side gears, rotate differential until pinion gears align with pinion shaft bore.
9. Lubricate differential pinion gear thrust washers with suitable lubricant.
10. Install differential pinion gear thrust washers. If thrust washers cannot be installed, continue to tighten limited slip differential tool until thrust washers can be installed.
11. Remove limited slip differential overhaul tool.
12. Install pinion shaft.
13. Using a suitable brass drift, drive roll pin into differential case until it is approximately 1.75 inch below surface of differential case.
14. Install differential side bearings and ring gear.

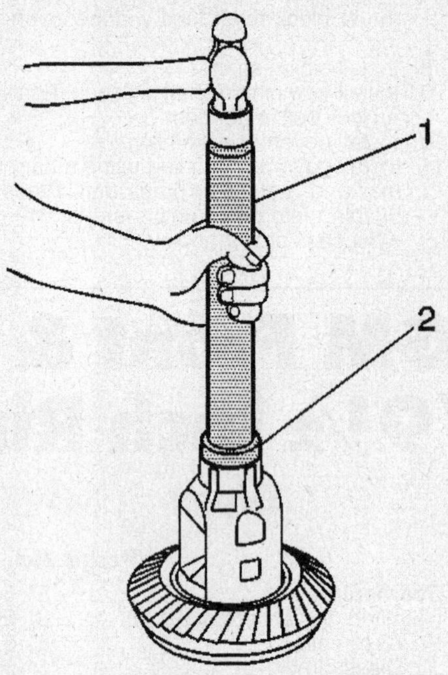

Fig. 1 Differential side bearing installation

Locking Differential

DISASSEMBLE

1. Remove ring gear.
2. Remove governor bushing using a locking differential governor remover tool No. J 26252, or equivalent.
3. Turn side gear to position governor assembly between two of side gear teeth, then remove governor assembly.
4. Remove latching bracket assembly bushing using locking differential governor remover tool No. J 26252, or equivalent. To aid in removal of latching bracket assembly, turn side gear as necessary to position latching bracket assembly between two of side gear teeth.
5. Remove pinion shaft lock bolt and pinion shaft.
6. Rotate pinion gears and roll pinion gears and thrust washers out of case through differential window. Mark pinion gears and thrust washers for assembly reference.
7. Remove thrust block.
8. Remove right side gear, clutch disc assembly and shim.
9. Remove left side gear (cam unit), clutch disc assembly and thrust washer.

ASSEMBLE

1. Install left side gear thrust washer, clutch disc assembly and left side gear (cam unit).
2. Install right side gear thrust washer, clutch disc assembly and right side gear.
3. Install pinion gear and pinion thrust washers. Place pinion gears and pinion thrust washers 180° apart.
4. Rotate pinion gears and pinion thrust washers 90° and align pinion gears with pinion shaft opening in differential case.
5. Install thrust block. Open side of thrust block must face window opening.
6. Install pinion shaft, then the new pinion shaft lock bolt, tighten finger tight.
7. Install governor assembly, then the governor bushing using a suitable hammer and brass drift. Press bushing into place until there is .01–.03 inch of shaft endplay.
8. Install latching bracket assembly. Straight end of latching bracket spring must be over and outside governor assembly shaft.
9. Install latching bracket bushing using a suitable hammer and brass drift. Press bushing into place until there is 0–.002 inch of shaft endplay.
10. **Torque** pinion shaft lock bolt to 37 ft lbs.
11. Install ring gear.

CLEANING & INSPECTION

1. Clean components in suitable solvent and blow dry with compressed air, noting the following:
   a. Do not use brush when cleaning bearings.
   b. Do not spin dry bearings, as bearings will be damaged.
   c. Lightly lubricate components after cleaning to retard corrosion.
   d. Keep all components in order to ensure proper assembling.
2. Inspect gears for cracks, chipped teeth, wear and scoring, and damaged bearing or mounting surfaces. Replace gears that are damaged or excessively worn. **Ring gear and pinion must be replaced as an assembly.**
3. Inspect differential case for cracks, damage, worn side gear bores and scored bearing surfaces and replace as needed.
4. Inspect housing for scored bearing mount surfaces, cracks and distortion and replace as needed.
5. Inspect bearing rollers and races for pitting, scoring, overheating and damage.
6. Mate bearing with race and inspect operation.
7. Replace any bearing that is damaged, excessively worn or that fails to operate smoothly.
8. Mount differential case along with side bearings and ring gear in housing and inspect runout with side bearings adjusted for zero preload and suitable dial indicator positioned against machined edge of ring gear.
9. If runout exceeds .003 inch and gear cannot be repositioned to eliminate runout, ring gear and/or case should be replaced.

ADJUSTMENTS

Differential Side Bearing Preload

The drive pinion bearing preload must be within specifications before the differential side bearing preload adjustment can be performed. The differential side bearings must be initially preloaded in order to determine the backlash of the gear set. After the backlash is set, the final bearing preload is set.

1. Measure rotating torque of drive pinion bearing using a suitable inch-pound torque wrench. Rotating torque of drive pinion should be 15–30 inch lbs. for new bearings or 10–20 inch lbs. for used bearings.
2. If rotating torque of drive pinion is less than 15 inch lbs. for new bearings or 10 inch lbs. for used bearings, tighten pinion in small increments until specified rotating torque is obtained.
3. If rotating torque of drive pinion is greater than 30 inch lbs. for new bearings or 20 inch lbs. for used bearings, remove drive pinion and replace collapsible spacer and re-install drive pinion.
4. Support differential assembly in order

to prevent differential assembly from falling out of axle housing.

5. Slide differential case assembly towards right side axle housing until ring gear contacts drive pinion. This is zero backlash point. If zero backlash cannot be obtained, turn differential bearing adjuster nut into axle housing using a side bearing backlash spanner tool No. J 24429, or equivalent, until ring gear fully contacts drive pinion to obtain zero backlash.
6. While holding ring gear against pinion, turn differential bearing adjuster nut out from axle housing using side bearing backlash spanner tool No. J 24429, or equivalent, until it contacts differential side bearing.
7. Turn adjuster nut out from axle housing an additional two slots using side bearing backlash spanner tool No. J 24429, or equivalent, in order to obtain initial backlash adjustment.
8. Install adjuster nut lock and adjuster nut lock bolt.
9. Remove left side differential bearing cap bolts.
10. Remove left side differential bearing cap.
11. Install a side bearing backlash gauge tool No. J 22779, or equivalent, into left side axle housing between differential bearing bore and differential bearing cup.
12. Tighten knob of side bearing backlash gauge until there is moderate drag when side bearing backlash gauge is moved.
13. Remove side bearing backlash gauge, then measure side bearing backlash gauge in three locations.
14. Calculate average of three measurements. Resulting value is shim thickness required in order to set initial backlash of differential assembly.
15. Select a service shim of approximately same thickness to install into axle housing. Verify thickness of service shim using a suitable micrometer.
16. Install service shim into axle housing between differential bearing bore and differential bearing cup.
17. Install left side differential bearing cap.
18. Install left side differential bearing cap bolts finger tight.
19. Remove differential bearing adjuster nut lock bolt and nut lock.
20. Firmly tighten differential bearing adjuster nut using side bearing backlash spanner tool No. No. J 24429, or equivalent, to force differential case assembly into solid contact with service shim.
21. Rotate pinion several times in order to seat bearings.
22. Loosen differential bearing adjuster nut using J side bearing backlash spanner until nut is free from differential side bearing.
23. Tighten differential bearing adjuster nut using J side bearing backlash spanner tool No. J 24429, or equivalent, until differential bearing adjuster nut contacts bearing.
24. On new bearings, once right differential bearing adjuster contacts differential bearing, tighten differential bearing adjuster nut using side bearing backlash spanner tool No. J 24429, or equivalent, an additional three slots.
25. On old bearings, once right differential bearing adjuster contacts differential bearing, tighten differential bearing adjuster nut using side bearing backlash spanner tool No. J 24429, or equivalent, an additional two slots.
26. Install right differential bearing adjuster nut lock and bolt.
27. **Torque** bearing cap bolts to 63 ft lbs.
28. **Torque** differential bearing adjuster nut lock bolt to 19 ft lbs.
29. Measure drive pinion and differential case side bearing preload using a suitable inch-pound torque wrench. Rotate pinion several times to ensure bearings have seated. Rotating torque of drive pinion and differential case bearings should be 30–55 inch lbs. for new bearings or 25–45 inch lbs. for used bearings.
30. Calculate differential side bearing preload by subtracting drive pinion preload, from drive pinion and differential case bearing preload. Multiply value obtained by axle ratio. Differential case side bearing preload should be 15–35 inch lbs.
31. If differential case side bearing preload is not within specification, increase or decrease shim thickness as necessary in order to increase or decrease side bearing preload.
32. Once differential side bearing preload is correct, measure drive pinion to differential assembly backlash and adjust, **Fig. 3.**

Fig. 2 Differential clutch pack assembly

Drive Pinion Depth

1. Lubricate pinion bearings with a suitable axle lubricant.
2. Install pinion bearings into axle housing.
3. Assemble side bearing disc tool No J 21777-8, or equivalent.
4. While holding side bearing disc stationary, install a suitable inch-pound torque wrench on nut of side bearing disc and tighten nut until a rotating torque 15 inch lbs. is obtained. Rotate assembly several times in both directions in order to seat pinion bearings.
5. If rotating torque is less than 15 inch lbs., tighten nut on side bearing disc until a rotating torque of 15–20 inch lbs. is obtained.
6. Assemble side bearing disc.
7. **Torque** bearing cap bolts to 55 ft lbs.
8. Rotate side bearing disc back and forth within discs. If side bearing disc does not rotate freely, disassemble components, inspect for proper seating and/or mis-aligned components and reassemble.
9. Install a dial indicator set tool No. J 8001, or equivalent, to side bearing disc as follows:
   a. Loosely clamp dial indicator set onto stem on side bearing disc tool.
   b. Place contact pad of dial indicator set onto mounting post of side bearing disc.
   c. With contact pad of dial indicator set touching mounting post of dial indicator set, loosen locknut on dial indicator set and push down on dial indicator set until needle dial indicator set has turned ¾ of a turn clockwise.
   d. Tighten clamp on dial indicator set finger tight.
10. Move plunger of side bearing disc back and forth until needle of dial indicator set indicates greatest deflection. Deflection is point where needle changes direction.
11. At greatest point of deflection, move housing of dial indicator set until needle indicates zero.
12. Move plunger of side bearing disc back and forth again to verify zero setting. Adjust housing of dial indicator set as necessary to set needle to zero.
13. Rotate plunger of side bearing disc away from pinion setting gage block tool No. J 45108, or equivalent, until it no longer touches pinion setting gauge block.
14. Value indicated on dial indicator set is thickness of shim needed in order to set depth of pinion.
15. Select shim that indicates proper thickness. Measure shim with a micrometer in order to verify thickness is correct.
16. Remove pinion depth setting tools and pinion bearings.
17. Install pinion shim between pinion gear and inner pinion bearing.

Backlash

Ensure the side bearing surfaces in the axle housing are clean and free of burrs. If the original bearings are to be reused, the original bearing cups must also be used. The differential side bearings must be initially preloaded in order to determine the backlash of the gear set. After the backlash is set, the final bearing preload is set.

1. Measure rotating torque of drive pinion

and differential assembly using a suitable inch-pound torque wrench. Rotating torque of drive pinion and differential assembly should be 30–55 inch lbs. for new bearings or 25–45 inch lbs. for used bearings.

2. If rotating torque is too low, tighten differential bearing adjuster nut in one slot increments until specified rotating torque is obtained.
3. If rotating torque is too high, loosen differential bearing adjuster nut in one slot increments until specified rotating torque is obtained.
4. If specification for rotating torque of drive pinion and differential assembly cannot be obtained by adjusting differential bearing adjuster nut, remove differential assembly.
5. Install guide pins tool No. J 25025-1 and dial indicator set tool No. J 8001-3, or equivalents, to axle housing.
6. Place indicator stem of dial indicator set at heel end of a gear tooth.
7. Set dial indicator set so stem is aligned with gear rotation and perpendicular to tooth angle.
8. Preload dial of dial indicator set approximately ¾ of a turn. Align needle and dial face of dial indicator set to zero.
9. While holding drive pinion stationary, move ring gear back and forth. Measure and record backlash.
10. Repeat measuring procedure at eight points around ring gear. Difference between backlash at all of measuring points should not be more than .002 inch.
11. If difference between backlash at all of measuring points is more than .002 inch, inspect for burrs, distorted case flange and uneven bolting.
12. If difference between all measuring points is within specification, backlash between ring gear and drive pinion should be between .003–.010 inch with a preferred backlash of .005–.007 inch.
13. If backlash is not within specification, adjust backlash as follows:
    a. Remove differential bearing adjuster nut retainer bolt.
    b. Remove differential bearing adjuster nut retainer.
    c. Loosen bearing cap bolts. **Do not remove bearing cap bolts.**
    d. Loosen differential bearing adjuster nut using side bearing backlash spanner tool No. J 24429, or equivalent.
    e. Remove differential side bearing shim.
    f. Measure thickness of shim three locations.
    g. Calculate average of three measurements and record measurement.
    h. If backlash is too small, select a smaller shim than one that was removed. To increase backlash by .002 inch, select a shim that is .004 inch thinner than shim that was removed.
    i. Install shim.
14. Tighten differential bearing adjuster nut using a side bearing backlash spanner tool No. J 24429, or equivalent, until differential bearing adjuster nut is seated against bearing cup.
15. Once differential bearing adjuster is seated against differential bearing, tighten differential bearing adjuster nut the following additional amounts:
    a. For used bearings, tighten differential bearing adjuster nut an additional two slots.
    b. For new bearings, tighten differential bearing adjuster nut an additional three slots.
16. **Torque** differential bearing cap bolts to 63 ft lbs.
17. Install differential bearing adjuster nut retainer and bolt, **torque** bolt to 19 ft. lbs.
18. Perform a gear tooth contact pattern check in order to ensure proper alignment between ring and pinion gears.

Shim Sizes

- 0.220 in
- 0.222 in
- 0.224 in
- 0.226 in
- 0.228 in
- 0.230 in
- 0.232 in
- 0.234 in
- 0.236 in
- 0.238 in
- 0.240 in
- 0.242 in
- 0.244 in
- 0.246 in
- 0.248 in
- 0.250 in
- 0.252 in
- 0.254 in
- 0.256 in
- 0.258 in

LTV0500000000388

Fig. 3 Differential selective shim size

American/GM Front & Rear Drive Axles w/8⅝ Inch Ring Gears

INDEX

STANDARD DIFFERENTIAL

1. Remove differential side bearings using suitable puller.
2. Remove differential pinion shaft lock bolt and pinion shaft, **Fig. 1.**
3. Remove differential pinions and thrust washers, side gears and side gear thrust washers, noting installation position for assembling. Keep thrust washers with respective gears.
4. Remove ring gear bolts, ring gear and driving ring gear from case using suitable drift and hammer. **Ring gear bolts have lefthand threads. Do not pry between ring gear and case, as mating surfaces will be damaged.**
5. Inspect components and replace as needed.
6. Install thrust washers on side gears and mount side gears in case. **Lubricate all components with specified gear lubricant prior to assembling.**
7. Position one differential pinion (less thrust washer) between side gears and rotate gears until pinion is directly opposite case loading opening.
8. Install other pinion with pinion shaft holes aligned, then rotate side gears and ensure pinions align with shaft openings in case.
9. When pinions are properly aligned, rotate pinions toward loading opening just enough to allow thrust washer installation, install washers.
10. Align pinions with shaft opening in case, insert pinion shaft through case, install new lock bolt.
11. Ensure ring gear and case mating surfaces are clean and free from burrs, mount gear on case, install two new retaining bolts at opposite sides of gear and alternately tighten bolts to draw gear on case.
12. Install remaining ring gear bolts hand tight and ensure gear is squarely seated on case. **Always use new bolts of proper type when installing ring gear. Do not reuse old bolts.**
13. Alternately **torque** ring gear bolts to 90 ft. lbs.
14. Press side bearings onto case. If old bearings are reused, ensure bearings are installed in original position.

LIMITED SLIP DIFFERENTIAL

1. Remove ring gear and side bearings, then the pinion shaft, **Fig. 2.**
2. Remove preload spring from case using a brass drift drive.
3. Support an axle shaft in a vise and slide case into shaft, then turn case to remove both pinions and thrust washers.
4. Remove case from axle shaft, then both side gears, clutch packs and shims. Mark gears, clutch packs and shims for installation in same position.
5. Inspect gears, bearings and case, replace as needed.
6. Inspect clutch plates and spacers and replace if worn or overheated.
7. Replace preload spring if force required to compress spring to height of 1$\frac{5}{16}$ inches is not 270–330 lbs.
8. Lubricate clutch discs and plates with limited slip lubricant.
9. Alternately position clutch plates and discs on a side gear, beginning and ending with a clutch plate, **Fig. 2.**
10. Position side gear, clutch pack and original shim into case.
11. Install both pinion gears, thrust washers and pinion shaft into case.
12. Install case onto an axle shaft supported in a vise.
13. Insert a screwdriver between pinion shaft and face of side gear. Force screwdriver in until clutch pack is compressed.
14. Inspect backlash between side gear and pinion gears. If backlash is not .005–.008 inch, adjust shim dimension as required. Increasing shim thickness will decrease backlash; decreasing shim thickness will increase backlash. Service shims are available in sizes from .070–.122 inch, in increments of .004 inch.
15. Remove pinion shaft, pinion gears, side gear, clutch pack and shim from case.
16. Install opposite gear, clutch pack and original shim into opposite side of case. Place both pinion gears and thrust washers into place and install pinion shaft.
17. Follow procedure in steps 12 through 14 to determine proper shim dimension.
18. When proper shim dimensions have been determined, remove pinion gears and pinion shaft and install both side gears, shims and clutch packs into case.
19. Mount case onto axle shaft locked in a vise. Place both pinions and thrust washers into position 180° apart and carefully roll in by turning case on shaft. A large C-clamp may be used to apply slight compression against pinion gears to aid rolling in procedure.
20. Tap preload spring into place with a hammer.
21. Install pinion shaft and lock screw.
22. Install side bearings and ring gear using procedure outlined for conventional units.
23. Place differential unit in carrier and adjust ring gear and pinion backlash and gear tooth pattern.

LOCKING DIFFERENTIAL

Differential Case Disassemble

1. Note position of governor and latching bracket for assembly reference, then remove side bearings and ring gear.
2. Remove governor assembly and latching bracket by pulling retaining bushings from case, **Fig. 3.** Pull latching bracket spring aside when removing bushings to prevent damage.
3. Remove lock screw and pinion shaft, **Fig. 4.**
4. Roll differential pinions to access window by turning side gears, then remove pinions.
5. Remove pinion thrust washers and thrust block. Keep all components in order for assembly.
6. Remove right side gear, disc pack/shim assembly and guide clips.
7. Remove left cam gear/disc pack assembly along with shim and guide clips.
8. Replace components that are damaged, deformed or excessively worn.

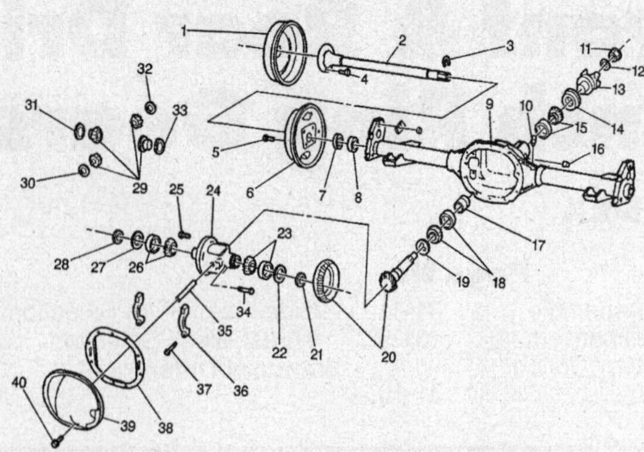

(1) Brake Drum
(2) Axle Shaft
(3) C Lock
(4) Wheel Stud
(5) Backing Plate Bolt
(6) Brake Assembly
(7) Axle Shaft Oil Seal
(8) Axle Shaft Bearing
(9) Axle Housing
(10) Axle Air Vent
(11) Pinion Nut
(12) Washer
(13) Pinion Flange
(14) Pinion Oil Seal
(15) Pinion Outer Bearing
(16) Plug
(17) Collapsable Spacer
(18) Pinion Inner Bearing
(19) Shim
(20) Pinion and Ring Gear Set
(21) Spacer
(22) Shim
(23) Differential Side Bearing and Cup
(24) Differential Case
(25) Ring Gear Bolt
(26) Differential Side Bearing and Cup
(27) Shim
(28) Spacer
(29) Differential Gears
(30) Pinion Thrust Washer
(31) Side Gear Thrust Washer
(32) Pinion Thrust Washer
(33) Side Gear Thrust Washer
(34) Pinion Shaft Lock Bolt
(35) Pinion Shaft
(36) Bearing Cap
(37) Bolt
(38) Gasket
(39) Cover
(40) Bolt

GC3038800002000A

Fig. 1 Exploded view of standard differential/axle assembly

Cam Gear Clutch Service

1. Remove retaining ring from end of cam gear, **Fig. 4.**
2. Remove discs and cam plate from gear, keeping all components in order.
3. Clean and inspect components, replace any that are damaged, distorted or excessively worn. If cam gear must be replaced, refer to "Cam Gear Shim Selection" for shim selection procedures prior to case assemby.
4. Position gear on flat surface with hub end up, then assemble cam plate onto gear with cam form down to mate with cam form on gear.
5. Assemble two eared discs, one splined disc and one wave washer on cam gear, starting with eared disc, **Fig. 4.**
6. Alternately assemble three eared discs and two splined discs on cam gear hub, starting with eared discs.
7. Install retaining ring, ensure retainer is fully seated.

Righthand Side Gear Clutch Service

1. Remove disc pack and shim from side gear, keeping components in order.
2. Clean and inspect components. Replace any components that are damaged, deformed or excessively worn. If side gear must be replaced, refer to "Side Gear Shim Selection" for shim selection prior to case assembly. If side gear hub is scored or worn, inspect bore in case and replace assembly if bore is damaged or worn.
3. Alternately assemble eared discs and splined discs on side gear hub, starting with eared disc, **Fig. 4.**

Cam Gear Shim Selection

1. Install cam gear assembly in case using original thrust washer or washer of equal thickness.
2. Mount differential pinions and thrust washers in proper installed position in case, manually depress cam gear into bore and insert pinion shaft through case and pinion assemblies and secure shaft with lockscrew. **If pinion shaft cannot be inserted, replace cam gear shim with one of less thickness.**
3. Index one tooth of pinion gear nearest shaft lock screw so tooth points downward, perpendicular to case flange.
4. Wedge large tapered screwdriver between cam gear and pinion shaft to hold gear compressed in bore.
5. Mount suitable dial indicator on case with pointer bearing against indexed differential pinion tooth, **Fig. 5.**
6. Ensure pinion is firmly pulled back in seat, then rock pinion back and forth, read backlash clearance from dial indicator and note reading.
7. Index tooth of opposite differential pinion as outlined in step 3, then repeat steps 5 and 6.
8. Replace cam gear assembly shim as needed to obtain differential pinion backlash of .010–.018 inch. **If cam gear is replaced, perform "Thrust Block Selection" procedure during case assembly to ensure proper case assembly clearances.**

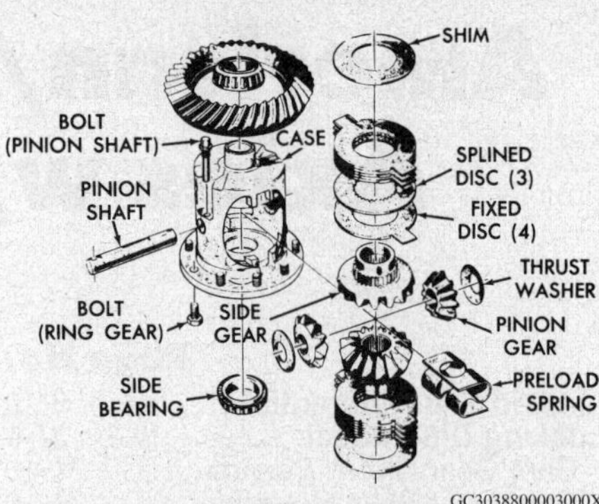

GC3038800003000X

Fig. 2 Exploded view of GM disc type limited slip differential

Side Gear Shim Selection

When side gear is replaced, or if side gear shim is damaged and proper thickness must be determined, select proper side gear shim thickness by measuring backlash between side gear and differential pinions. Follow procedure outlined for "Cam Gear Shim Selection," using fully assembled side gear properly installed in case and select a shim that will provide .002–.010 inch backlash between side gear and differential pinions.

Thrust Block Selection

If cam gear and/or side gear have been replaced, or if it is required to replace thrust

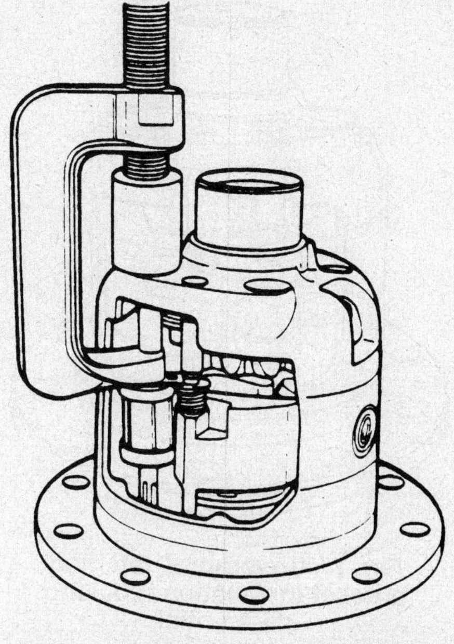

GC3038800007000X

Fig. 3 Governor & latch bracket bushing removal. Locking differential

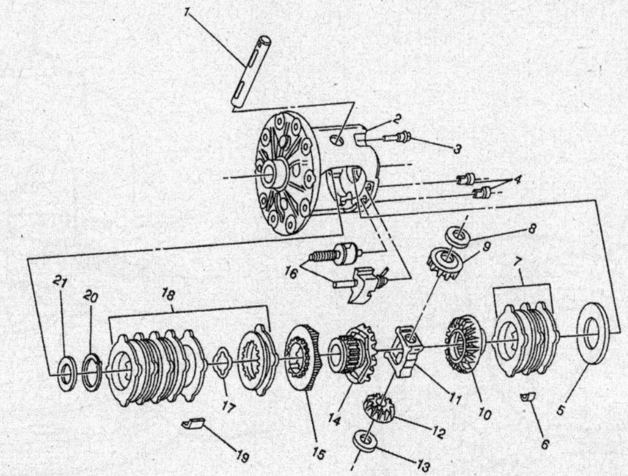

(1) Differential Pinion Gear Shaft
(2) Differential Housing
(3) Differential Pinion Gear Shaft Lock Bolt
(4) Locking Differential Lockout Bushing
(5) Locking Differential Clutch Disc Thrust Washer
(6) Locking Differential Clutch Disc Guide
(7) Locking Differential Clutch
(8) Differential Pinion Gear Thrust Washer
(9) Differential Pinion Gear
(10) Locking Differential Side Gear
(11) Locking Differential Thrust Block
(12) Differential Pinion Gear
(13) Differential Pinion Gear Thrust Washer
(14) Locking Differential Side (Can Faced) Gear
(15) Locking Differential Cam
(16) Locking Differential Governor
(17) Wave Washer
(18) Locking Differential Clutch Disc Set
(19) Locking Differential Clutch Disc Guide
(20) External Snap Ring M46 Diameter Shaft Retainer
(21) Locking Differential Clutch Disc Thrust Washer

GC3038800008000X

Fig. 4 Exploded view of locking differential

block and original dimension cannot be determined, use the following procedure during differential case assembly to determine proper thrust block dimension.

1. Install cam gear and side gear assemblies into case, insert differential pinion shaft through case bores and secure with lock screw.
2. Wedge large tapered screwdrivers, or equivalent, tools between cam gear, side gear and pinion shaft to seat gears in case.
3. Measure distance between face of cam gear and face of side gear using suitable gauge as shown, **Fig. 6.** Record measurement. **Ensure gauge ends rest on gear faces, not gear teeth when measuring side gear spread.**
4. Measure thickness of original thrust block at outer corner and record dimension.
5. Select a thrust block with a thickness 0–.006 inch less than side gear spread measured in step 3. **If original thrust block is serviceable, but does not provide specified zero to .006 inch clearance, righthand side gear can be shimmed to provide proper thrust block clearance as long as side gear backlash is maintained within specified .002–.010 inch.**

Differential Case Assemble

1. Install four clutch pack guide clips on cam gear clutch pack, using heavy grease to retain clips.
2. Install cam gear assembly along with shim in flange end of case, **Fig. 4.**
3. Install four guide clips on assembled side gear clutch pack using grease to retain clips.
4. Install side gear assembly in case along with shim. If side gear has been replaced, perform shim selection procedure prior to installation.
5. Lock axle shaft in vise with sufficient portion of spline protruding from vise to engage side gear, then mount case assembly on axle and engage axle with side gear.
6. Install thrust washers on back of differential pinions using grease to adhere washers.
7. Install one pinion assembly through small case opening while simultaneously installing remaining pinion and thrust block through large opening.
8. Rotate assembly approximately 90° to position open side of thrust block toward small opening in case and pinions in proper installed position. If side gears and/or thrust block have been replaced, refer to "Thrust Block Selection Procedure" to ensure proper assembly clearances.
9. Insert pinion shaft ensuring pinion thrust washers are properly positioned, then install new lock screw and **torque** screw to 20 ft. lbs.
10. Insert governor assembly and latching bracket into case as outlined in **Fig. 7,** positioning straight end of latching bracket spring over and to outside of engagement shaft to preload bracket against governor.
11. Press governor assembly bushing into case to a depth that will allow .004–.020 inch shaft endplay.
12. Press latching bracket bushing into case to a depth that will provide 0–.003 inch shaft endplay.
13. Install ring gear and bearings as outlined for standard differentials. **Always use new bolts of proper type when installing ring gear. Do not reuse old bolts.**

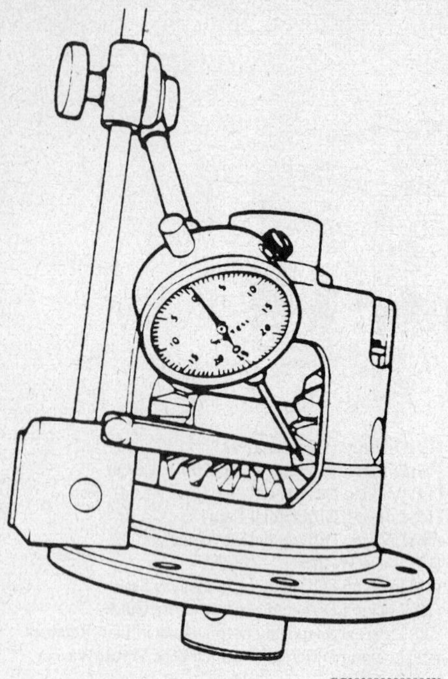

Fig. 5 Differential pinion backlash inspection

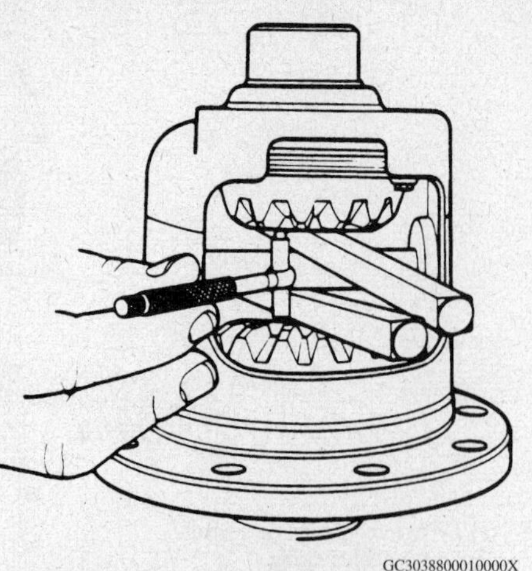

Fig. 6 Side gear spread inspection. Locking differential

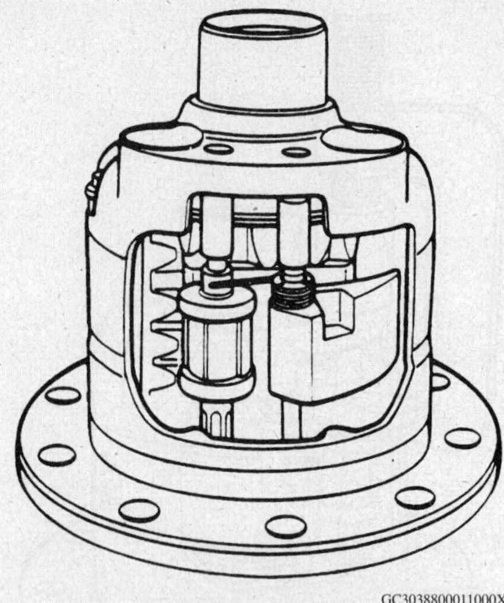

Fig. 7 Governor & latching bracket installation. Locking differential

GM Drive Axle w/10½ Inch Ring Gear

INDEX

DIFFERENTIAL OVERHAUL

Standard Differential

1. Mount axle assembly in suitable holding fixture, remove rear cover and gasket as outlined in **Fig. 1,** and drain lubricant.
2. Measure ring gear and pinion backlash using suitable dial indicator and record reading to aid assembling.
3. Remove adjusting nut lock retainers, then mark installation position of side bearing caps. **Keep all components in order during disassembling so that any component to be reused can be installed in original position.**
4. Remove side bearing caps, then loosen bearing adjusters using side bearing adjustment spanner tool No. J-24429, or equivalent, then lift differential assembly from housing.
5. Remove side bearing outer races and place with respective bearing caps.
6. Measure pinion rotating torque using suitable torque wrench. If no bearing preload is present, or if endplay is evident, pinion bearings may require replacement.
7. Remove pinion bearing retainer bolts, then the pinion assembly, tapping on pilot end of pinion to free assembly from housing.
8. Measure and record thickness of shim installed between pinion bearing retainer and housing and retain shims for assembling.
9. Inspect components as outlined in "Cleaning & Inspection," and replace as needed.
10. If side bearings are to be replaced, remove bearings using suitable puller, ensuring puller jaws are seated in case notches and pulling against side bearing inner race.
11. Remove ring gear retaining bolts and lockwashers, then the ring gear, using soft faced hammer to tap gear from case. **Do not pry gear from case as machined surfaces will be damaged.**

12. Scribe matching mark between differential case halves, then separate cover from case.
13. Remove differential pinion, pinion yoke, side gears and thrust washers from case, noting installation position for assembling.
14. Inspect components as outlined in "Cleaning & Inspection," and replace as needed. **If components are to be reused, they must be installed in original position. Coat all components with specified lubricant prior to installation.**
15. Install differential pinions and thrust washers on yoke.
16. Install side gears and thrust washers in case halves, then position yoke and pinion assembly on flanged case half.
17. Hold side gear into case cover and join case halves, ensuring matching marks are aligned and that gears are properly meshed.
18. Install ring gear, retaining bolts and lock washers, then evenly **torque** ring gear bolts to 110 ft. lbs.
19. Install case side bearings, using suitable driver to seat bearings. **Support case on suitable pilot when installing second side bearing to prevent damaging bearing already installed.**

Locking Differential

CASE DISASSEMBLE

1. Mount axle assembly in suitable holding fixture, remove rear cover and gasket as outlined in **Fig. 1,** and drain lubricant.
2. Measure ring gear and pinion backlash using suitable dial indicator and record reading to aid assembling.
3. Remove adjusting nut lock retainers, then mark installation position of side bearing caps. **Keep all components in order during disassembling so that any component to be reused can be installed in original position.**
4. Remove side bearing caps, then loosen bearing adjusters using side bearing adjustment spanner tool No. J-24429, or equivalent, then lift differential assembly from housing.
5. Remove side bearing outer races and place with respective bearing caps.
6. Measure pinion rotating torque using suitable torque wrench. If no bearing preload is present, or if endplay is evident, pinion bearings may require replacement.
7. Remove pinion bearing retainer bolts, then the pinion assembly, tapping on pilot end of pinion to free assembly from housing.
8. Measure and record thickness of shim installed between pinion bearing retainer and housing and retain shims for assembling.
9. Inspect components as outlined in "Cleaning & Inspection," and replace as needed.
10. Remove side bearings and ring gear as outlined for standard differential.
11. Remove three case retaining screws from ring gear mounting flange, then set unit on right case half, **Fig. 2.**
12. Carefully pry case apart at yoke opening, hold side gear assembly in case, then remove left case half.
13. Note installation position, then remove governor and latching bracket.
14. Remove thrust blocks, yoke and differential pinions, noting installation position for assembling.
15. Remove cam gear and disc assembly, shim and guide clips from right case half.
16. Remove side gear, disc pack and shim and guide clips from left case half.
17. Clean and inspect all components, keeping components in order for proper assembling. Replace any components that are damaged, distorted or excessively worn.

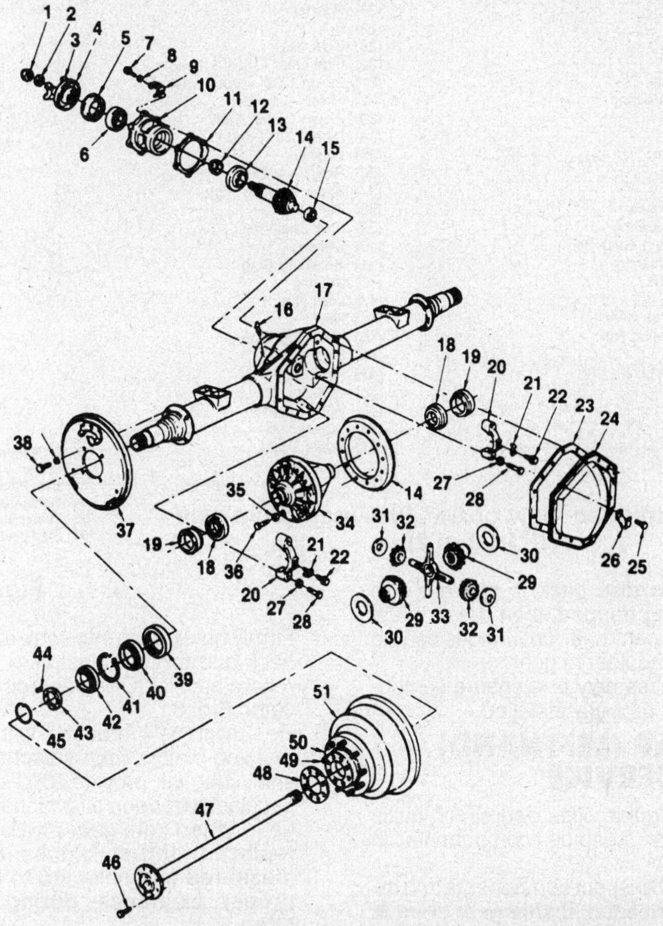

Fig. 1 Exploded view of GM 10½ inch drive axle (Part 1 of 2)

CAM GEAR CLUTCH SERVICE

1. Measure and record overall length of cam gear assembly from front face of gear to back face of thrust ring, including shim.
2. Compress disc pack and insert jaws of bearing separator tool No. J-22912, or equivalent between thrust ring and top clutch disc with chamfer of separator facing thrust ring.
3. Support separator in press and press cam gear from thrust ring using suitable spacer as outlined in **Fig. 3,** keeping components in order as cam gear is removed.
4. Remove discs, spring and cam plate from gear as outlined in **Fig. 4,** clean and inspect components and replace any that are damaged or excessively worn. **Do not replace cam gear and/or thrust ring unless required. If ring or gear is excessively worn or scored, inspect bore in case. If case bore is scored, differential assembly must be replaced. If cam gear or thrust ring is replaced, shim thickness must be selected to provide original assembly dimension and proper differential pinion backlash.**
5. Position cam gear with hub facing up and install cam plate with cam form down to mesh with form on gear.
6. Assemble two eared discs and one disc with large splines on cam plate, starting with eared disc as outlined in **Fig. 4,** then install wave spring. **If components are reused, they must be installed in original position.**
7. Assemble four eared discs and three splined discs on cam gear, starting with eared disc, **Fig. 4.**
8. Position cam gear assembly in press and install thrust ring on hub of gear, ensuring ring is square with hub.

(1) Pinion Nut
(2) Washer
(3) Pinion Flange
(4) Slinger
(5) Pinion Oil Seal
(6) Pinion Front Bearing
(7) Bolt
(8) Washer
(9) Brake Line Clip
(10) Pinion Cage
(11) Shim
(12) Collapsible Spacer
(13) Pinion Rear Bearing
(14) Pinion and Ring Gear Set
(15) Pinion Pilot Bearing
(16) Axle Vent Tube
(17) Axle Housing
(18) Differential Side Bearing
(19) Bearing Adjusting Nut
(20) Bearing Cap
(21) Adjusting Nut Lock
(22) Bolt
(23) Gasket
(24) Cover
(25) Bolt
(26) Brake Line Clip
(27) Washer
(28) Bolt
(29) Side Gear
(30) Side Gear Thrust Washer
(31) Pinion Gear Thrust Washer
(32) Pinion Gear Set
(33) Pinion Cross Shaft
(34) Differential Case
(35) Washer
(36) Ring Gear Bolt
(37) Brake Backing Plate
(38) Bolt
(39) Axle Shaft Seal
(40) Bearing
(41) Retaining Ring
(42) Bearing
(43) Lock Nut
(44) Key
(45) Retaining Ring
(46) Bolt
(47) Axle Shaft
(48) Gasket
(49) Wheel Stud
(50) Wheel Hub
(51) Brake Drum

GC3039900326020X

Fig. 1 Exploded view of GM 10½ inch drive axle (Part 2 of 2)

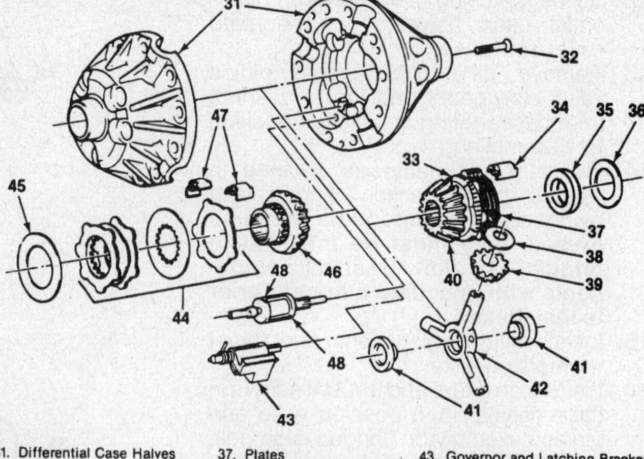

31. Differential Case Halves
32. Screw
33. Cam Plate
34. Guide Clip
35. Thrust Sleeve
36. Side Gear Thrust Washer
37. Plates
38. Pinion Thrust Washer
39. Pinion Gear
40. Side Cam Gear
41. Reaction Block
42. Pinion Yoke
43. Governor and Latching Bracket
44. Plates
45. Side Gear Thrust Washer
46. Side Gear
47. Guide Clip
48. Governor

GC3038800032000X

Fig. 2 Exploded view of Locking differential

9. Compress disc pack to prevent disc from being trapped, then press thrust ring onto cam gear until ring is seated against shoulder of gear.
10. Inspect assembly and ensure components are properly installed.

SIDE GEAR (LEFTHAND) CLUTCH SERVICE

1. Remove guide clips and clutch discs from gear keeping components in order.
2. Clean and inspect components and replace as needed. **If side gear shim is faulty, it must be replaced with one of equal thickness. If side gear is replaced and/or if side gear shim thickness cannot be determined, perform "Side Gear Shim Selection" procedure.**
3. Install eared and splined clutch discs on side gear, starting with eared disc, **Fig. 2.** If components are reused, they must be installed in original position.
4. Install selected shim on side gear.

CAM GEAR SHIM SELECTION

If cam gear is replaced or if original cam gear shim thickness cannot be determined, shim must be selected to maintain proper backlash with differential pinions using following procedure.

1. Install six guide clips on cam gear clutch ears, then insert cam gear assembly into right case half.
2. Clamp cam gear assembly securely in case pocket using suitable bolt, nut and washers, **Fig. 5.**
3. Install all three differential pinions and thrust washers on yoke and firmly seat pinion and yoke assembly in case, tapping assembly with suitable hammer.
4. Slightly loosen bolt clamping cam gear into case and index one pinion gear tooth so that it points downward, perpendicular to parting line of case, then retighten cam gear clamping bolt.
5. Mount suitable dial indicator on case with plunger contact bearing against tooth indexed in step 4.
6. Firmly hold pinion into seat, rock pinion back and forth against cam gear and record backlash reading from dial indicator, **Fig. 6.**
7. Repeat steps 4 through 6 with each remaining pinion, then select cam gear shim that will provide .010–.018 inch backlash between all pinions and cam gear. **When cam gear and/or shim is replaced, thrust blocks must be measured and selected to maintain proper clearance during assembling.**

SIDE GEAR SHIM SELECTION

If side gear is replaced, or if original shim thickness cannot be measured, select proper side gear shim thickness by measuring backlash between side gear and differential pinions. Follow procedure for "Cam Gear Shim Selection," using fully assembled side gear installed in left case half. Select a shim that will provide .002–.010 inch backlash between side gear and differential pinions. If side gear and/or shim is replaced, refer to "Thrust Block Selection" during case assembly in order to install thrust block that will maintain proper assembly clearances.

THRUST BLOCK SELECTION

If cam gear, side gear and/or shims are replaced, or if thrust blocks must be replaced and original dimension cannot be determined, use following procedure during case assembly to determine proper thrust block size.

1. Secure fully assembled cam gear and side gear assemblies into respective case halves as outlined in shim selection procedure.
2. Measure distance from each gear face to case mounting surface as outlined in **Fig. 7,** and record dimension.
3. Add together cam gear and side gear depth measurements to obtain side gear spread. **When adding dimensions measured in step 2, be sure to subtract thickness of gauge block from each measurement.**
4. Select two thrust blocks with combined thickness of zero to .006 inch less than side gear spread measurement, measuring thrust blocks as outlined, **Fig. 8. Original thrust blocks can be used if they are undamaged and will provide specified 0–.006 inch clearance. In addition, left side gear can be shimmed to provide proper thrust block clearance as long as specified .002–.006 inch backlash is maintained between side gear and differential pinions.**

CASE ASSEMBLE

Coat components with specified axle lubricant during assembling. If components are reused, they should be installed in original position.

1. Install six guide clips on ears of cam gear disc pack, using grease to retain clips.
2. Install cam gear assembly along with selected shim into right case half. **If cam gear thrust ring was replaced, measure length of assembly from front face of cam gear to rear face of thrust ring, including shim. Select a shim that will provide a measurement as close to measurement made during disassembling as possible.**
3. Install selected right side thrust block on cam gear face with button side of block facing up. **If cam or side gears or thrust block was replaced, select thrust block thickness as outlined in "Thrust Block Selection." Improper thrust block clearance will result in differential fault.**
4. Assemble differential pinions and thrust washers on yoke, index yoke to proper position, then install yoke in right side of case.
5. Ensure yoke is centered over thrust block button and seat yoke in housing by tapping lightly with hammer.

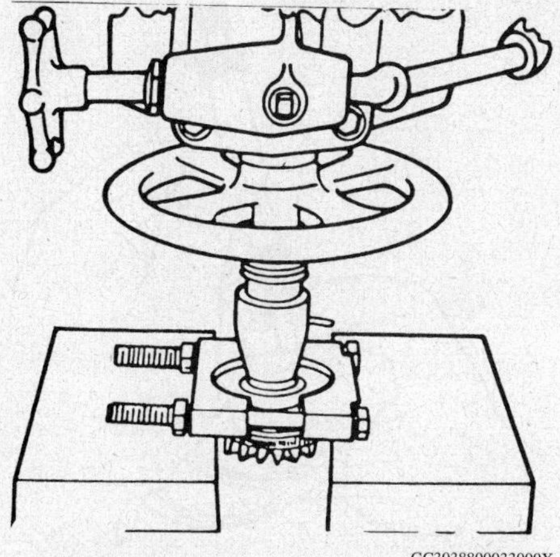

Fig. 3 Cam gear thrust ring removal. Locking differential

6. Install left side thrust block, ensuring thrust block button is seated in yoke. Ensure thrust block is of proper thickness as outlined in selection procedure.
7. Install governor and latching bracket in respective positions as outlined in **Fig. 2,** and position straight end of latching bracket spring over and to outside of governor shaft to preload bracket against governor.
8. Install six guide clips on ears of side gear disc pack using grease to retain clips.
9. Install selected shim in left case half.
10. Carefully remove disc pack from side gear and lower assembly into right case half, ensuring guide clips are properly positioned.
11. Insert side gear through disc pack into left case half, rotating gear as needed to align splines.
12. Hold side gear into case, then lower left case assembly onto right case half, ensuring bores for governor and latching bracket shafts are properly aligned.
13. Invert assembly taking care not to dislodge internal components, then install three retaining screws.
14. Mount axle shaft in vise with spline protruding enough to engage side gear.
15. Install case assembly over axle shaft and rotate case to inspect operation. Assembly should rotate smoothly, without binding or locking-up.
16. Install differential pinions and thrust washers on yoke.
17. Install side gears and thrust washers in case halves, then position yoke and pinion assembly on flanged case half.
18. Hold side gear into case cover and join case halves, ensuring matching marks are aligned and that gears are properly meshed.
19. Install ring gear, retaining bolts and lock washers, then evenly **torque** ring gear bolts to 110 ft. lbs.
20. Install case side bearings, using suitable driver to seat bearings. **Support case on suitable pilot when installing second side bearing to prevent damaging bearing already installed.**

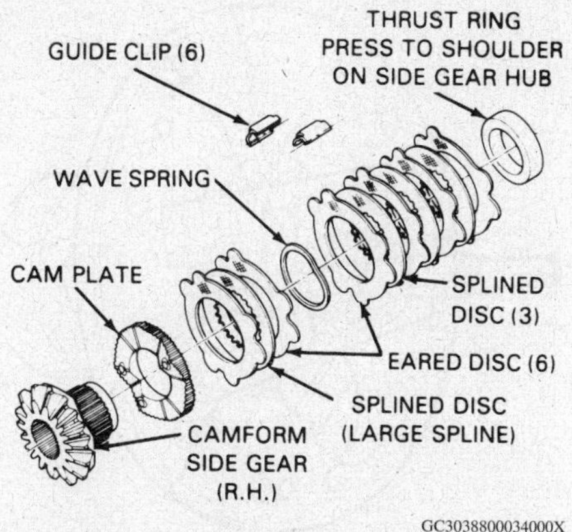

Fig. 4 Exploded view of cam gear assembly. Locking differential

DRIVE PINION & BEARING SERVICE

Disassemble

1. Clamp pinion assembly in vise taking care not to damage housing or gear.
2. Hold driveshaft flange with suitable tool, then remove pinion nut and washer.
3. Remove driveshaft flange from pinion shaft using suitable puller.
4. Support housing in press as outlined in **Fig. 9,** and press pinion from housing. Do not allow pinion to drop on floor.
5. Separate pinion flange, oil seal, front bearing and bearing retainer, driving seal from housing with suitable drift.
6. Remove bearing races from housing using suitable drift and place front bearing race with bearing.
7. Press rear bearing from pinion and place bearing with race.
8. Remove straddle bearing from axle housing using suitable drift, **Fig. 10.**
9. Inspect components as outlined in "Cleaning & Inspection," keeping all components in order and replace as needed.

Assemble & Preload Adjustment

Coat components with specified lubricant during assembling. If components are reused, they should be installed in original position.

1. Press rear bearing onto pinion using suitable spacers.
2. Install front and rear bearing races in housing, using suitable drivers to ensure races are properly seated.
3. Install straddle bearing in axle housing using straddle bearing installer tool No. J-23322, or equivalent, to ensure bearing is properly seated.
4. Insert pinion through housing, install new collapsible spacer and front bearing over pinion shaft, support pinion and press front bearing onto shaft.
5. Lubricate lips of new seal with grease and install seal using suitable driver to seat seal against shoulder of housing.

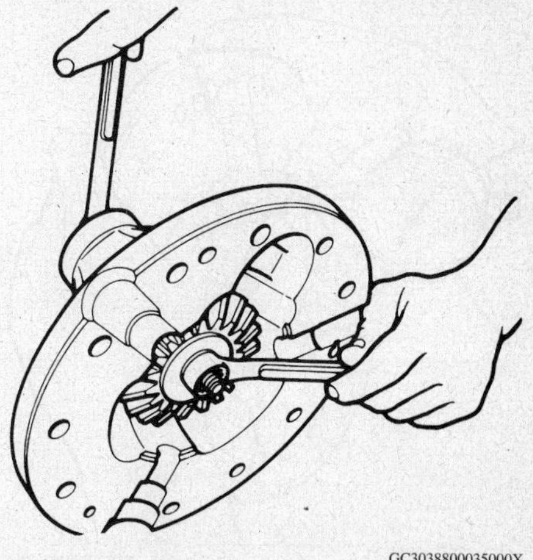

Fig. 5 Cam/side gear installation for assembly clearance measurement. Locking differential

6. Install driveshaft companion flange, washer and new pinion nut.
7. Clamp housing in vise, hold flange with suitable tool and tighten pinion nut just until all endplay is removed.
8. Inspect pinion bearing preload (rotating torque) using suitable torque wrench.
9. Continue tightening pinion nut in small increments until specified preload is obtained, inspecting preload after each adjustment. **Exceeding specified preload will collapse spacer too far to be reused. If preload specification is exceeded, spacer must be replaced and adjustment procedure must be repeated. Do not loosen pinion nut to reduce bearing preload.**

CLEANING & INSPECTION

1. Clean components in suitable solvent and blow dry with compressed air, noting the following:
   a. Do not use brush when cleaning bearings.
   b. Do not spin dry bearings as they will be damaged.
   c. Lightly lubricate components after cleaning to retard corrosion.
   d. Keep all components in order to ensure proper assembling.
2. Inspect gears for cracks, chipped or broken teeth, wear and scoring. Replace gears that are damaged or excessively worn. **Ring gear and pinion must be replaced as an assembly.**
3. Inspect differential case for cracks, damage, distortion, and worn or scored side gear bores and bearing surfaces. Replace case if damaged or scored.
4. Inspect axle and pinion housings for scored bearing mount surfaces, cracks and distortion and replace as needed. Ensure housing is clean and free from foreign material.
5. Inspect bearing rollers and races for pitting, scoring, overheating and damage.

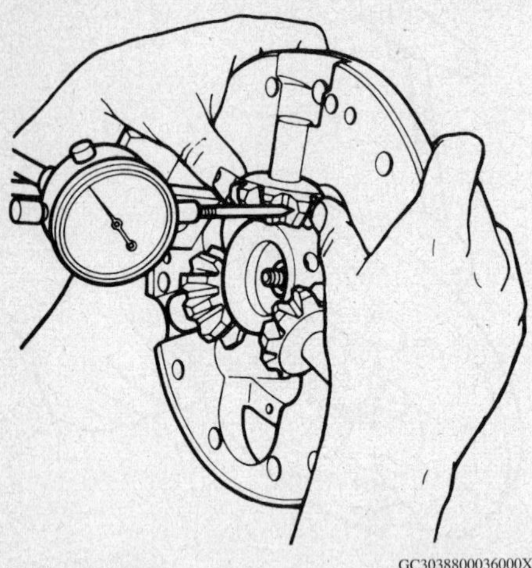
GC3038800036000X

Fig. 6 Differential pinion backlash measurement. Locking differential

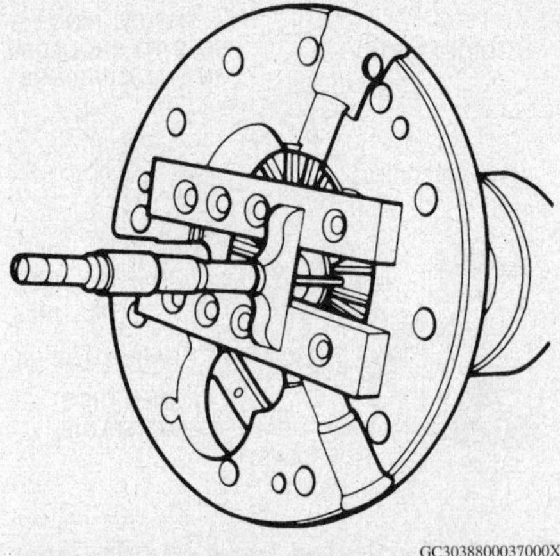
GC3038800037000X

Fig. 7 Cam/side gear depth measurement. Locking differential

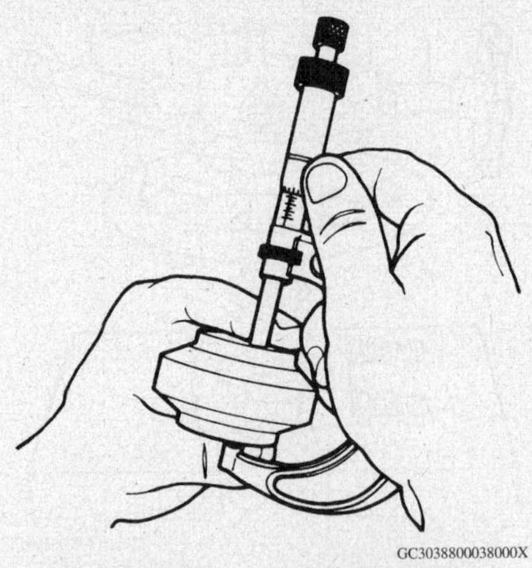
GC3038800038000X

Fig. 8 Thrust block thickness measurement. Locking differential

6. Mate each bearing with race and inspect operation.
7. Replace any bearing assembly that is damaged, excessively worn, or that fails to operate smoothly.
8. Mount differential case along with ring gear and side bearings in housing, adjust side bearings to zero preload and inspect ring gear runout with dial indicator bearing against machined edge of gear.
9. If ring gear runout exceeds .003 inch and gear cannot be repositioned to reduce runout, replace ring gear and/or case assembly.

FINAL ADJUSTMENTS & MEASUREMENTS

1. Inspect head of drive pinion for pinion depth code number. **Pinion may be stamped with either plus (+) or minus (–) number, indicating required modification of shim thickness to ensure proper engagement.**
2. Compare depth code number with number on original pinion and use chart as outlined in **Fig. 11,** to select proper shim thickness for preliminary pinion depth adjustment as follows:
   a. Refer to thickness of shims removed during disassembling and add or subtract value outlined in chart.
   b. If original pinion, housing and rear bearing is to be reused, install shims of original thickness.
3. Position selected shim on axle housing, ensure bolt holes are aligned, then install pinion assembly and **torque** retaining bolts to 65 ft. lbs., in crossing pattern.
4. Place outer races over differential case bearings, mount differential assembly in housing and install bearing caps and tighten cap bolts snug.
5. Loosen right bearing adjusting nut and tighten left nut using suitable tool as outlined in **Fig. 12,** until ring gear contacts pinion. **Do not force gears into contact. Tighten left nut just enough to obtain zero backlash without binding gears.**
6. Loosen left adjusting nut approximately two notches, then install adjusting nut lock.
7. Firmly tighten right adjusting nut to force case against left nut, then loosen nut until clearance exists between right nut and bearing race.
8. Tighten right adjusting nut until it just contacts bearing race (zero preload), then tighten nut an additional two slots for used bearings or three slots for new bearings and secure position with locking retainer. **At this point differential bearing preload is properly set. If any additional adjustments are required, ensure preload remains as established. If one adjusting nut is loosened, other nut must be tightened an equal amount in order to maintain preload.**
9. Mount suitable dial indicator on housing with plunger contact bearing against ring gear tooth, **Fig. 13.**
10. Hold pinion and rock ring gear back and forth, reading backlash from dial indicator.
11. Backlash should be .003–.012 inch, with .005–.008 inch preferred setting. **If original ring gear and pinion are used, set backlash to amount measured during disassembling to avoid changing gear contact pattern.**
12. If backlash is not within specifications, proceed as follows:
    a. If backlash is greater than .012 inch, loosen right adjusting nut one notch and tighten left nut one notch.
    b. If backlash is less than .003 inch, loosen left adjusting nut one notch, then tighten right nut one notch. **Always rotate adjusting nuts equal amounts in opposite directions to maintain differential bearing preload.**
    c. Inspect backlash after each adjustment and correct as needed.
    d. When proper backlash has been obtained, install adjusting nut locks to secure adjustment.
13. **Torque** side bearing cap bolts to 135 ft. lbs., then inspect gear tooth contact pattern as follows. **Gear tooth contact pattern must be inspected to verify correct relationship between ring gear and pinion in order to ensure pinion depth is set properly.**
    a. Ensure ring gear is clean and free from oil.
    b. Apply suitable marking compound to coat drive and coast face of each ring gear tooth.
    c. Apply braking force to differential case in order to load gears, then turn pinion to rotate ring gear one full revolution in each direction. **If inspect is made without loading gears, a satisfactory pattern cannot be obtained. Excessive rotation of ring gear is not recommended.**
    d. Inspect contact pattern on ring gear and correct differential adjustments, if required, **Fig. 14.**
    e. Clean marking compound from gears.

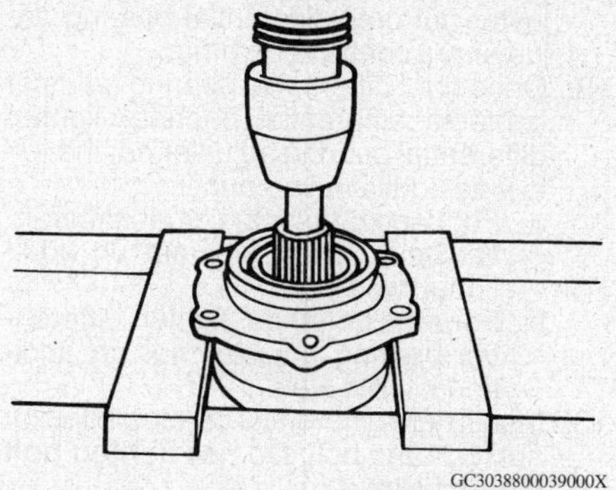

Fig. 9 Drive pinion removal

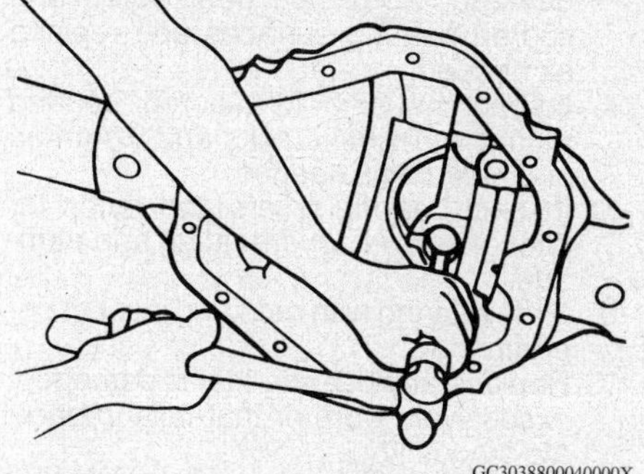

Fig. 10 Pinion straddle bearing removal

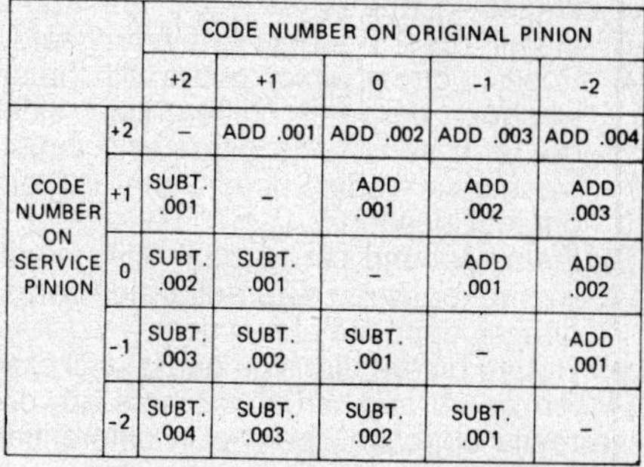

Code number on service pinion		Code number on original pinion				
		+2	+1	0	-1	-2
	+2	–	ADD .001	ADD .002	ADD .003	ADD .004
	+1	SUBT. .001	–	ADD .001	ADD .002	ADD .003
	0	SUBT. .002	SUBT. .001	–	ADD .001	ADD .002
	-1	SUBT. .003	SUBT. .002	SUBT. .001	–	ADD .001
	-2	SUBT. .004	SUBT. .003	SUBT. .002	SUBT. .001	–

Fig. 11 Pinion depth shim selection chart

Fig. 12 Side bearing preload adjustment

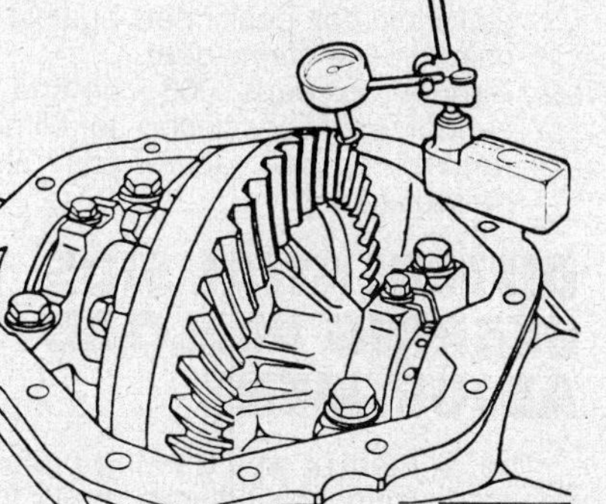

Fig. 13 Ring gear & pinion backlash measurement

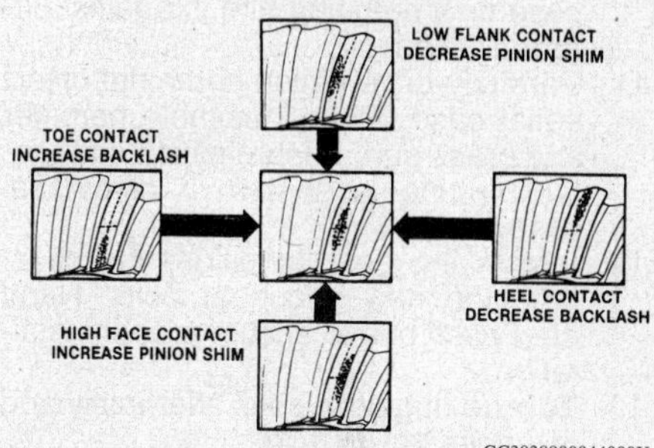

Fig. 14 Ring gear & pinion tooth contact inspection

American/GM Front & Rear Drive Axles w/11½ Inch Ring Gears

INDEX

STANDARD DIFFERENTIAL OVERHAUL

Disassemble

1. Install differential assembly into a suitable vise.
2. Remove rear axle housing cover and gasket.
3. Remove differential bearing adjuster nut retainers.
4. Remove bearing caps and bolts. Mark bearing caps left and right.
5. Loosen adjusters using a side bearing backlash spanner tool No. J 24429, or equivalent.
6. Remove bearing cups. Mark cups left and right. Place cups with bearing caps.
7. Install a side bearing remover tool No. 22888-20A, or equivalent, then remove differential side bearings.
8. Remove ring gear bolts and discard.
9. Remove ring gear from differential case using a suitable brass drift.
10. Locate end of pinion shaft pilot hole.
11. Place a brass drift onto end of pinion shaft with pilot hole, then drive pinion shaft through differential case using a suitable hammer.
12. Remove and discard retaining ring from pinion shaft.
13. Remove differential pinion gears and pinion gear thrust washers by rolling gears out through differential case opening.
14. Remove differential side gears and thrust washers. Mark pinion gears top and bottom and differential side gears left and right.

Assemble

1. Install new retaining onto pinion shaft.
2. Lubricate pinion and side gears using a suitable axle lubricant.
3. Install differential side gear thrust washers to differential side gears.
4. Install differential side gears and thrust washers into differential case in their

original locations.
5. Install thrust washers to pinion gears.
6. Position one of pinion gears with thrust washer between differential side gears. If same side gears and thrust washers are being used, install in their original locations.
7. Install second pinion gear with thrust washer between differential side gears directly opposite of first gear.
8. Rotate differential side gears until pinion gears and thrust washers are directly opposite opening in differential case.
9. Insert side of pinion shaft with pilot hole into differential case.
10. Slide pinion shaft through differential case until retaining ring is against differential case.
11. Carefully drive pinion shaft into differential case using a suitable hammer and brass drift. Ensure pinion shaft retaining ring is seated in differential case channel.
12. Install ring gear to differential case, then the new ring gear bolts. Hand start each bolt to ensure proper installation.
13. **Torque** ring gear bolts alternately and in stages to 175 ft. lbs.
14. Install a differential bearing and hub seal installer tool No. J 44420 and 3/4 inch universal driver handle tool No. J 8092, or equivalents, onto differential case bearing, then drive bearing onto case.

LIMITED SLIP DIFFERENTIAL

Refer to "American/GM Drive Axle w/9½ Inch Ring Gear" for disassembly and assembly procedures.

LOCKING DIFFERENTIAL

Refer to "American/GM Drive Axle w/9½ Inch Ring Gear" for disassembly and assembly procedures.

CLEANING & INSPECTION

1. Clean components in suitable solvent and blow dry with compressed air, noting the following:
   a. Do not use brush when cleaning bearings.
   b. Do not spin dry bearings, as bearings will be damaged.
   c. Lightly lubricate components after cleaning to retard corrosion.
   d. Keep all components in order to ensure proper assembling.
2. Inspect gears for cracks, chipped teeth, wear and scoring, and damaged bearing or mounting surfaces. Replace gears that are damaged or excessively worn. **Ring gear and pinion must be replaced as an assembly.**
3. Inspect differential case for cracks, damage, worn side gear bores and scored bearing surfaces and replace as needed.
4. Inspect housing for scored bearing mount surfaces, cracks and distortion and replace as needed.
5. Inspect bearing rollers and races for pitting, scoring, overheating and damage.
6. Mate bearing with race and inspect operation.
7. Replace any bearing that is damaged, excessively worn or that fails to operate smoothly.
8. Mount differential case along with side bearings and ring gear in housing and inspect runout with side bearings adjusted for zero preload and suitable dial indicator positioned against machined edge of ring gear.
9. If runout exceeds .003 inch and gear cannot be repositioned to eliminate runout, ring gear and/or case should be replaced.

DIFFERENTIAL SIDE BEARING PRELOAD ADJUSTMENT

The differential side bearing preload is adjusted using two adjusting nuts in the bearing bore. The bore and the bearing cap provide the mating threads for the bearing nut. The differential must be initially preloaded in order to determine the backlash of the gear set. After the backlash is set, the final bearing preload is set. The rotating torque of the drive pinion must be within specifications before the pinion gear bearing retainer can be installed.

1. Install drive pinion, differential side bearings and adjuster nuts.
2. Install differential bearing caps and bolts, finger tighten bolts.
3. Slide differential case assembly towards right side axle housing until ring gear contacts pinion. This is zero backlash point. If zero backlash cannot be obtained, turn right side differential bearing adjuster nut inward towards axle housing until ring gear fully contacts pinion.
4. While holding ring gear against pinion, turn left differential bearing adjuster nut out from axle housing using side bearing backlash spanner tool No. J 24429, or equivalent, until it contacts differential side bearing.
5. Turn right differential bearing adjuster nut out from axle housing until it contacts differential side bearing.
6. Back off left adjusting nut approximately two slots in order to obtain initial backlash adjustment.
7. Install left adjuster nut lock and bolt.
8. Firmly tighten right differential bearing adjuster nut to force differential case assembly into solid contact with left differential adjuster nut.
9. Rotate pinion several times in order to seat bearings.
10. Loosen right differential bearing adjuster nut until nut is free from differential side bearing.
11. Tighten right differential bearing adjuster nut until differential bearing adjuster nut contacts bearing.
12. Once right differential bearing adjuster contacts differential bearing, tighten differential bearing adjuster nut the following additional amounts:
    a. For used bearings, tighten differential bearing adjuster nut an additional two slots.
    b. For new bearings, tighten differential bearing adjuster nut an additional three slots.
13. Install right differential bearing adjuster nut lock and bolt. **Do not tighten bolt at this time.**
14. **Torque** bearing cap bolts to 153 ft. lbs.
15. **Torque** differential bearing adjuster nut lock bolts to 20 ft. lbs.
16. Measure ring gear to pinion backlash.

FINAL ADJUSTMENTS & MEASUREMENTS

Ensure the side bearing surfaces in the axle housing are clean and free of burrs. If the original bearings are to be reused, the original bearing cups must also be used. The differential side bearings must be initially preloaded in order to determine the backlash of the gear set. After the backlash is set, the final bearing preload is set.

1. Measure rotating torque of drive pinion and differential assembly using an suitable inch-pound torque wrench. Rotating should be 30–55 inch lbs. for new bearings or 25—45 inch lbs. for used bearings.
2. If rotating torque is too low, tighten differential bearing adjuster nuts in one slot increments until specified rotating torque is obtained.
3. If rotating torque is too high, loosen differential bearing adjuster nuts in one slot increments until specified rotating torque is obtained.
4. If specification for rotating torque of drive pinion and differential assembly cannot be obtained by adjusting differential bearing adjuster nut, measure rotating torque of drive pinion and adjust as necessary.
5. Install guide pins tool No. J 25025-1 and dial indicator set tool No. J 8001, or equivalents, to axle housing.
6. Place indicator stem of dial indicator set at heel end of a gear tooth.
7. Set dial indicator set so stem is aligned with gear rotation and perpendicular to tooth angle.
8. Preload dial of dial indicator set. Align needle and dial face of dial indicator set to zero.
9. While holding drive pinion stationary, move ring gear back and forth. Measure and record backlash.
10. Repeat measuring procedure at eight points around ring gear. Difference between measuring points should not vary by more than .002 inch.
11. If difference between backlash is more than .002 inch, inspect for burrs, distorted case flange and uneven bolting.
12. If difference between all measuring points is within specifications, backlash at minimum lash point measured

should be between .003–.010 inch with a preferred backlash of .005–.007 inch.

13. If backlash is not within specifications, adjust as follows:
    a. Remove differential bearing adjuster nut retainer bolts and retainers.
    b. Remove bearing cap bolts and bearing caps. Mark bearing caps left and right.
    c. If backlash is too small, increase backlash by turning left differential bearing adjuster in one slot and right differential bearing adjuster out one slot until correct backlash is obtained.
    d. If backlash is too large, decrease backlash by turning right differential bearing adjuster in one slot and left differential bearing adjuster out one slot until correct backlash is obtained.
14. Install bearing cap bolts and **torque** to 153 ft lbs.
15. Install differential bearing adjuster nut retainers.
16. Install differential bearing adjuster nut retainer bolts and **torque** to 20 ft lbs.
17. Measure drive pinion and differential case side bearing preload.
18. Once backlash and bearing preload is correct, perform a gear tooth contact pattern check in order to ensure proper alignment between ring and pinion gears.

American/GM Aluminum Case w/7½ & 8¼ Inch Front Drive Axle

NOTE: For Front Axle Shaft Service Procedures On 4 Wheel Drive Vehicles, Refer To Appropriate Truck Chapter.

INDEX

DIFFERENTIAL CARRIER, OVERHAUL

Disassemble

1. Remove left output shaft tube and shaft as outlined in **Figs. 1 through 3.** Pry between shaft flange, carrier bolt and tapping flange with soft-faced hammer.
2. Remove lefthand side cover from carrier, then the seal from cover.
3. Remove bolts holding carrier cover halves together, then insert screwdriver in slots and pry cover halves apart, **Fig. 4.**
4. Remove differential case from carrier. **For service procedures on differential case, refer to "Differential Case, Disassemble."**
5. Remove two side bearing adjusting locks.
6. Remove both differential side bearing races using side bearing adjuster wrench tool, No. J-33792, or equivalent, for 7¼ inch axles or No. J-36599, or equivalent for 8 ¼ inch axles.
7. Remove pinion flange nut using pinion flange remover tool No. J-8614-01, or equivalent, then install pinion bearing cup remover and installer tool No. J-33837, or equivalent, for 7¼ inch axles or No. J-36598, or equivalent, for 8¼ inch axles, **Fig. 5. On ½ axles, adapter tool No. J-36598-6, or equivalent, will be needed.**
8. Remove pinion from carrier by turning bolt on pinion bearing cup remover and installer tool, then the pinion flange.
9. Install pinion bearing cup remover and installer tool, then remove outer pinion bearing, pinion bearing race and pinion seal.
10. Install pinion bearing cup remover and installer tool, then remove inner pinion bearing race from carrier.
11. Remove inner drive pinion using differential side bearing remover tool No. J-22912-01, or equivalent.

Assemble

Lubricate all bearings, races and seals with axle lubricant before installing in differential.

1. Install outer pinion bearing race, then inner race using pinion bearing cup remover and installer tool No. J-33837-4, or equivalent.
2. Set pinion depth and install correct shim on drive pinion as outlined under "Pinion Depth, Adjust."
3. Install inner pinion bearing on pinion using pinion bearing installer tool No. J-33785, or equivalent.
4. Install a new collapsible spacer on pinion, then position pinion assembly in carrier.
5. Install outer pinion bearing in carrier, then install bearing seal using pinion oil seal installer tool No. J-33782, or equivalent.
6. Install pinion flange, washer and nut, then the holder pinion flange remover tool No. J-8614-01, or equivalent, on flange. Tighten nut until no endplay is detectable.
7. Inspect preload and set to 15–25 inch lbs. **When setting preload, tighten pinion nut in small increments and inspect setting frequently. If preload specifications are exceeded, collapsible spacer will be compressed beyond limits and will have to be replaced.**
8. Rotate pinion several times to ensure bearings have been seated, then inspect preload and correct as required.
9. Install output shaft bearings and adjusting sleeves in inserts in carrier and tighten finger tight.
10. Install differential side bearing race into carrier using bearing cup installer tool No. J-23423-A, or equivalent. If differential output shaft bearings or adjusting sleeve inserts must be replaced, proceed as follows:
    a. Remove differential output shaft bearing from adjusting sleeve using output shaft bearing remover tool No. J-21551, or equivalent.
    b. Install new bearings into adjusting sleeves using output shaft bearing installer tool No. J-33788, or equivalent.
    c. Install sleeve and bearing into insert and tighten finger tight, then install complete assembly into carrier using bearing cup installer tool No. J-23423-A, or equivalent.
11. Install differential case in carrier, then adjust differential backlash as outlined under "Differential Backlash, Adjust."
12. Install lefthand carrier cover seal using suitable tool. Support cover when installing seal to avoid bending cover.

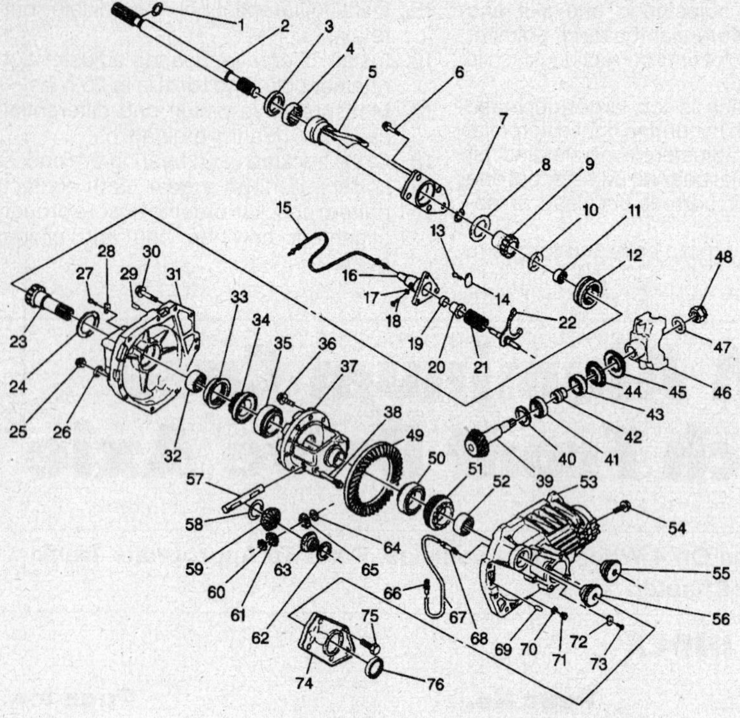

1. Retaining Ring
2. Axle Shaft
3. Seal
4. Bearing
5. Housing
6. Bolt
7. Retaining Ring
8. Washer
9. Clutch Gear
10. Washer
11. Bearing
12. Clutch Sleeve
13. Bolt
14. Lock
15. Cable
16. Housing
17. Seal
18. Switch
19. Outer Spring
20. Seal
21. Inner Spring
22. Fork
23. Clutch Shaft
24. Washer
25. Drain Plug
26. Drain Plug Gasket
27. Nut
28. Nut Lock
29. Pin
30. Bolt
31. Carrier
32. Bearing
33. Adjuster
34. Sleeve
35. Bearing
36. Bolt
37. Case
38. Bolt
39. Pinion Gear
40. Shim
41. Bearing
42. Spacer
43. Bearing
44. Seal
45. Deflector
46. Yoke
47. Washer
48. Nut
49. Ring Gear
50. Bearing
51. Insert
52. Bearing
53. Carrier
54. Bolt
55. Bushing
56. Bushing
57. Shaft
58. Washer
59. Side Gear
60. Washer
61. Pinion Gear
62. Washer
63. Side Gear
64. Washer
65. Pinion Gear
66. Vent
67. Hose
68. Hose End
69. Pin
70. Drain Plug Gasket
71. Drain Plug
72. Nut Lock
73. Nut
74. Cover
75. Bolt
76. Seal

GC3039900327000X

Fig. 1 Exploded view of 7¼ inch front drive axle. Except AWD models

13. Apply sealer No. 1052366, or equivalent, to carrier mating surface, then install cover. **Torque** bolts to 15–20 ft. lbs.

PINION DEPTH

ADJUST

The drive pinions used are "nominal" or "zero" pinions and are not marked. The thickness of the shim used will be equal to the dial indicator gauge reading.

1. Lubricate inner and outer pinion bearings with axle lubricant, then while holding bearings in place install pinion shim setting gauge tool No. J-33838, or equivalent, **Fig. 6.**
2. **Torque** preload of pinion bearings to 15–25 inch lbs. by tightening mounting bolt on tool while holding end of tool shaft with a wrench.
3. Zero dial indicator, then install it on pinion shim setting gauge tool No. J-33838, or equivalent. Push dial indicator down until needle rotates approximately three turns clockwise and tighten dial indicator in this position.
4. Position button of pinion shim setting gauge tool No. J-33838, or equivalent, in differential bearing bore, then rotate tool back and forth until lowest point of bore is indicated on dial indicator.
5. Zero dial indicator, then repeat rocking action of tool to verify zero setting.
6. When zero setting has been obtained and verified, move tool button out of bearing bore and record dial indicator reading. Select shim equal to this reading.
7. Install shim on drive pinion, then install pinion in carrier as outlined under "Differential Carrier Assemble."

DIFFERENTIAL BACKLASH

ADJUST

1. Turn lefthand adjusting sleeve in toward differential case using side bearing adjuster wrench tool No. J-33792, or equivalent, until backlash is felt between ring and pinion gears.
2. Clean carrier half mating surfaces, then install halves together without using any sealer and install four case bolts as outlined in **Fig. 7,** and **torque** to 37 ft. lbs. **If carrier halves will not make complete contact, back righthand adjusting sleeve outward.**
3. Tighten righthand adjusting sleeve using side bearing adjuster wrench tool No. J-33792, or equivalent, until no backlash is present (approximately 100 ft. lbs.), then **torque** lefthand adjusting sleeve to approximately 100 ft. lbs.
4. Mark relation of adjusting sleeves to carrier halves so that notches in adjusting sleeves can be counted when turned.
5. Turn righthand adjusting sleeve out two notches and lefthand sleeve in one

notch using side bearing adjuster wrench tool No. J-33792, or equivalent.

6. Rotate axle case several times to seat bearings, then mount dial indicator.
7. Install a small button on indicator stem and position so that contact can be made near heel end of tooth angle. This will provide an accurate backlash reading. Backlash should be .003–.010 inch, with a preferred reading of .005–.007 inch.
8. If backlash is not within specifications, readjust adjusting sleeves as required. Do not install adjusting sleeve locks at this time.
9. Mark position of righthand adjusting sleeve, then loosen sleeve to relieve contact between righthand side bearing and differential case.
10. Remove four carrier bolts and separate carrier halves.
11. Apply sealer No. 1052357, Loctite 514, or equivalent, to mating surface of one carrier half, then assemble two halves together with all ten attaching bolts. **Torque** bolts to 30–40 ft. lbs.
12. Set righthand adjusting sleeve in position according to mark made previously, then install both adjusting sleeve locks and **torque** to 62–88 inch lbs.

DIFFERENTIAL CASE, OVERHAUL

Disassemble

1. Remove side bearings using differential side bearing remover tool No. J-22912-01, or equivalent.
2. Remove pinions, side gears and thrust washers from case. Mark relation between side gears and case for reference during assembly.
3. If ring gear is to be replaced, remove ring gear bolts (righthand thread). If ring gear is tight on case, drive it off using a suitable brass drift and hammer. **Do not pry between ring gear and case.**

Assemble

Prior to assembling the differential case, lubricate all components with axle lubricant.

1. Install thrust washers on side gear hubs, then the side gears into case.
2. Install one pinion, without thrust washer, between side gears and turn gears until pinion is directly opposite loading opening in case.
3. Install other pinion between side gears so pinion shaft holes are aligned. Rotate gears to ensure holes in pinions will align with holes in case. If holes align, turn pinions back toward loading opening just enough to permit installation of pinion thrust washers.

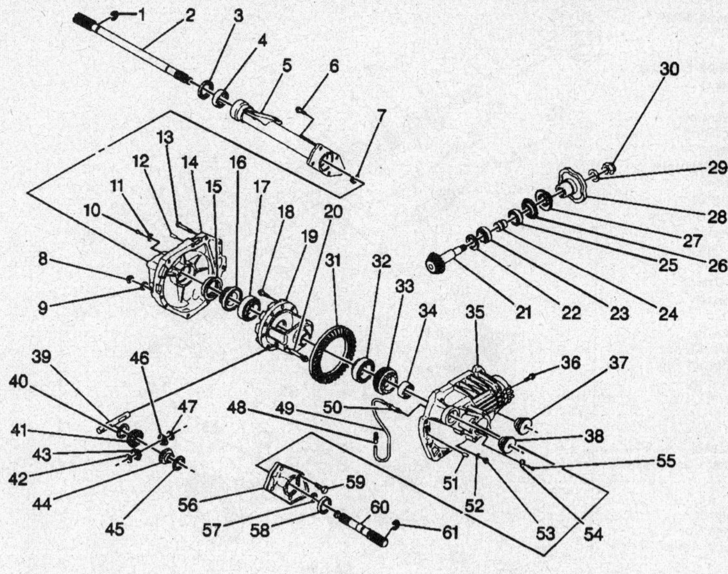

1. Retaining Ring
2. Axle Shaft
3. Seal
4. Bearing
5. Inner Axle Shaft Housing
6. Bolt
7. Retaining Ring
8. Plug
9. Washer
10. Bolt
11. Lock
12. Pin
13. Bolt
14. Carrier Case
15. Insert
16. Sleeve
17. Side Bearing
18. Bolt
19. Differential Case
20. Bolt
21. Pinion Gear
22. Shim
23. Bearing
24. Spacer
25. Bearing
26. Seal
27. Deflector
28. Pinion Flange
29. Washer
30. Nut
31. Ring Gear
32. Side Bearing
33. Insert
34. Bearing
35. Carrier Case
36. Plug
37. Bushing
38. Bushing
39. Shaft
40. Thrust Washer
41. Side Gear
42. Thrust Washer
43. Pinion Gear
44. Side Gear
45. Thrust Washer
46. Pinion Gear
47. Thrust Washer
48. Vent
49. Vent Hose
50. Fitting
51. Pin
52. Washer
53. Plug
54. Lock
55. Bolt
56. Cover
57. Retaining Ring
58. Seal
59. Bolt
60. Axle Shaft
61. Retaining Ring

GC3039900328000X

Fig. 2 Exploded view of 7¼ inch front drive axle. AWD models

4. Ensure ring gear and case mating surfaces are clean and free of burrs, then thread two bolts into opposite ends of ring gear and install gear on case.
5. Install new ring gear retaining bolts and **torque** alternately to 52–66 ft. lbs., on 7¼ inch axles and 88 ft. lbs., on 8 ¼ inch axles.
6. Install case side bearings using differential side bearing installer tool No. J-33790, or equivalent.

1. Right Output Shaft
2. Deflector
3. Seal
4. Output Shaft Bearing
5. Axle Tube
6. Bolt
7. Thrust Washer
8. Retaining Ring
9. Connector
10. Differential Actuator
11. *Washer
12. *Retaining Ring
13. Engagement Switch
14. Shifter Fork Spring
15. Shifter Shaft Ring
16. Shift Fork
17. Damper Spring
18. Shifter Shaft
20. Shim
21. Pilot Bearing
22. Differential Sleeve
23. *Inner Output Shaft
25. Fill/Drain Plug
26. Washer
27. Pin
28. Bolt
29. Carrier Case
30. Differential Case Bearing
31. Insert
32. Sleeve
33. Side Bearing
34. Ring Gear Bolt
35. Differential Case
36. Pin
37. Ring and Pinion Gears
38. Pinion Shim
39. Pinion bearing
40. Spacer
41. Pinion Bearing
42. Seal
43. Deflector
44. Pinion Flange
45. Washer
46. Nut
48. Mounting Bushing
51. Lock
52. Pinion Shaft
53. Thrust Washer
54. Side Gear
55. Thrust Washer
56. Differential Pinion Gear
57. *Spacer
59. Left Output Shaft
60. Vent Plug
61. *Adjuster
62. *O-Ring
63. *Retainer Tab
64. *Bolt

*Components Unique to K3

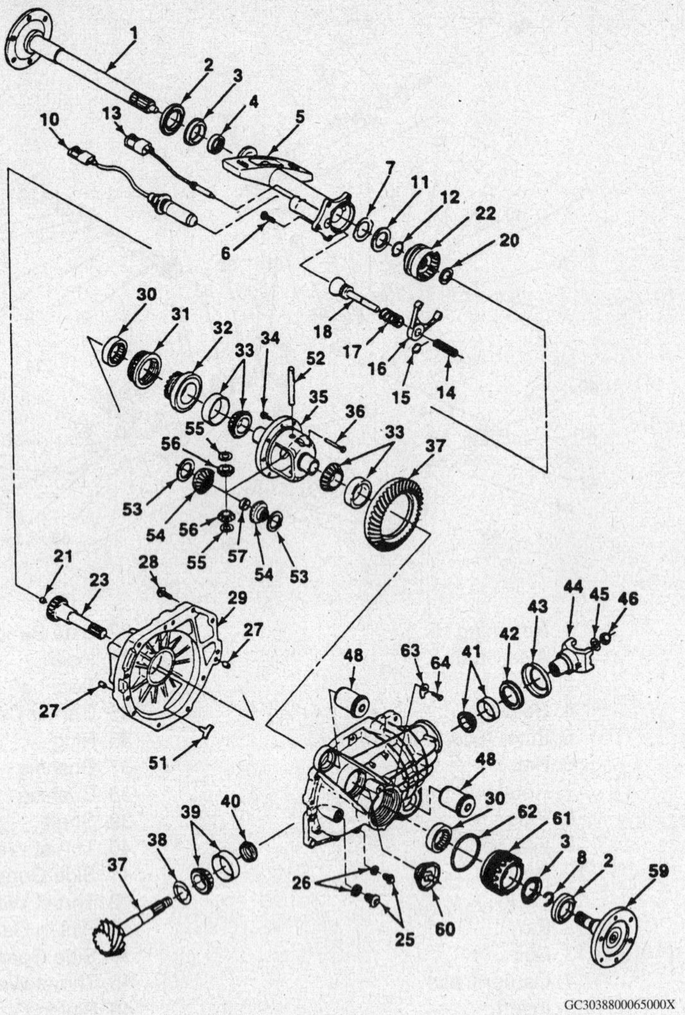

GC3038800065000X

Fig. 3 Exploded view of 8¼ inch front drive axle

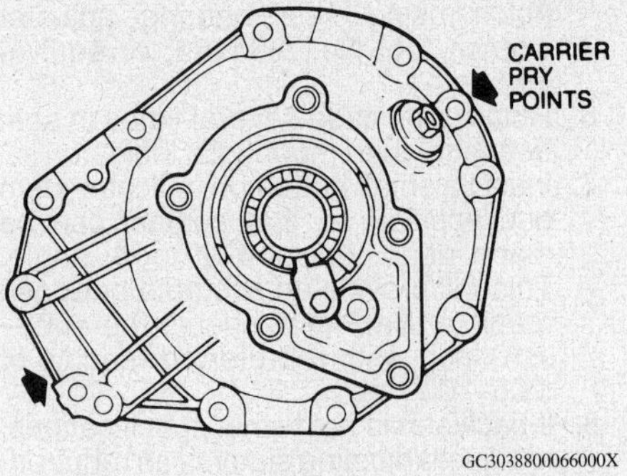

GC3038800066000X

Fig. 4 Differential carrier pry points

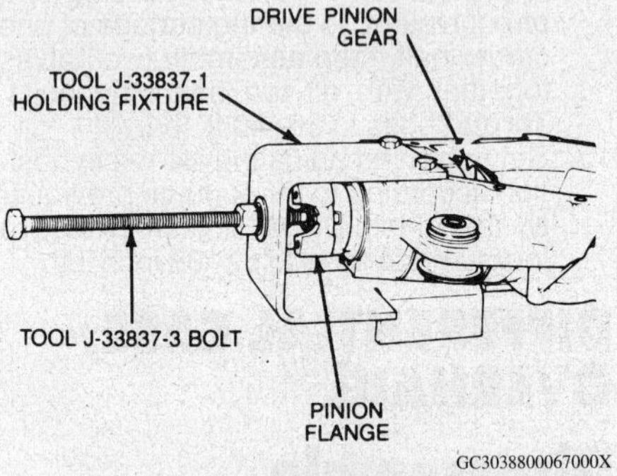

GC3038800067000X

Fig. 5 Drive pinion removal

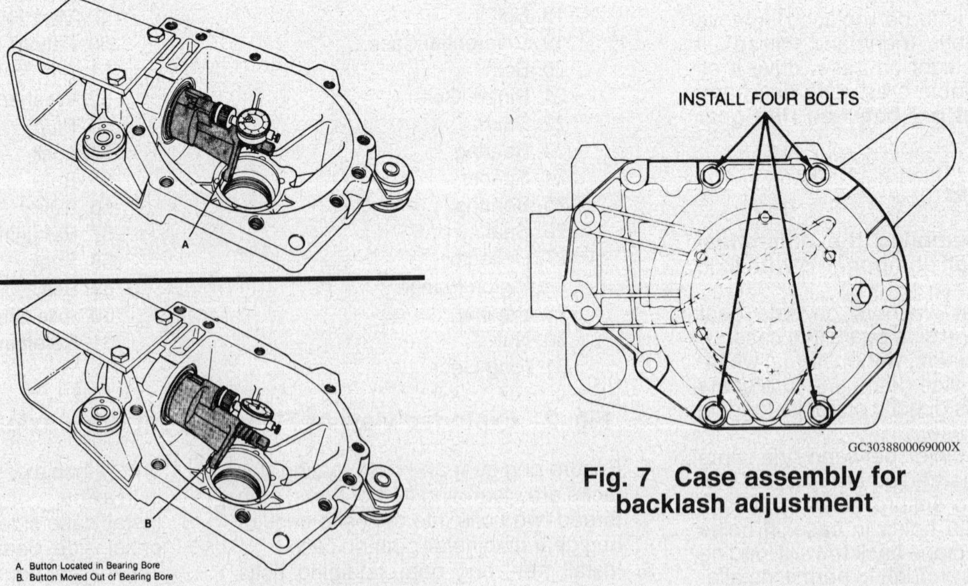

Fig. 6 Pinion depth setting

Fig. 7 Case assembly for backlash adjustment

Dana Model 80 Drive Axle

INDEX

AXLE, DISASSEMBLE

1. Remove axle shafts as outlined in specific vehicle repair section.
2. Remove plug and drain lubricant from carrier.
3. Remove carrier cover attaching screws, then the cover and gasket, **Fig. 1.**
4. Mark one side of carrier and matching bearing cap for assembly reference, then remove bearing caps.
5. Spread carrier a maximum of .015 inch using differential carrier spreader tool No. J-24385, or equivalent, and a suitable dial indicator, **Fig. 2.**
6. Remove dial indicator, then lift differential case from carrier using a suitable prybar. Measure and record dimensions and note location of side bearing shims for assembly reference, then remove spreader tool.
7. Measure pinion rotating torque with suitable torque wrench. If no preload is present, shake companion flange to inspect for looseness of pinion assembly. If pinion assembly is loose, bearing must be replaced.
8. Install holder tool No. J-8614-11, or equivalent, on flange using two bolts and flat washers. Position tool with four notches toward flange, then remove and discard pinion nut and washer.
9. Remove companion flange using tools outlined in **Fig. 3.**
10. Remove drive pinion from carrier, tapping with a soft-faced hammer, if required.
11. Tap on inner race of outer pinion bearing, using a long drift and remove pinion oil seal, slinger, gasket, outer pinion cone and roller and shim pack. Mark and retain shim pack for assembly.
12. If required, drive pinion bearing cups out of carrier, then remove shims and oil slinger from behind inner bearing cup. Mark shims and retain for assembling.
13. Inspect components as outlined under "Cleaning & Inspection" and replace as required.

DIFFERENTIAL OVERHAUL

1. Remove differential side bearings using a suitable puller or press.
2. Remove ring gear attaching bolts and ring gear.
3. Scribe an alignment mark on both case halves, then remove bolts holding case halves together.
4. Tap top half of case loose from bottom, then remove top half and all internal components.
5. Position new washers on side gears, using a small amount of lubricant on side gear hubs.
6. Install pinion gears and new washers onto cross shaft.
7. Assemble top half of case to bottom half, using alignment marks made during disassembling. Tighten bolts alternately and evenly.
8. Install ring gear and alternately **torque** bolts in stages to 110 ft. lbs. On 10½ inch axles, 220 ft. lbs., on 11 inch.
9. Position side bearings onto case and seat bearings using a suitable driver. When installing second bearing, support case with suitable pilot to prevent damaging case of opposite bearing.
10. Determine side bearing shim requirements as follows:
    a. Place bearing cups over side bearings and install differential case into carrier, with pinion removed from carrier.
    b. Position original shim in ring gear side, then install bearing caps and tighten just enough to retain in place.
    c. Install a dial indicator on carrier with indicator button contacting back surface of ring gear.
    d. Position two screwdrivers between bearing shim and carrier on ring gear side of case. Apply force to screwdrivers to move differential case as far as possible away from dial indicator. With force still applied, set dial indicator to zero.
    e. Reposition screwdrivers on opposite side of differential case and force differential case back toward dial indicator. Repeat sequence several times until same reading is obtained.
    f. Add thickness of shim to dial indicator reading and record result.

CLEANING & INSPECTION

1. Clean components in suitable solvent and blow dry with compressed air, noting the following:
    a. Do not use brush when cleaning bearings.
    b. Do not spin dry bearings as bearings will be damaged.
    c. Lightly lubricate components after cleaning to retard corrosion.
    d. Keep all components in order to ensure proper assembling.
2. Inspect gears for cracks, chipped or broken teeth, wear and scoring. Replace gears that are damaged or excessively worn.
3. Inspect differential case for cracks, damage, distortion, worn side gear bores and scored bearing surfaces and replace as needed.
4. Inspect housing for scored bearing mount surfaces, cracks and distortion and replace as needed. Ensure housing is clean and free from foreign material.
5. Inspect bearing rollers and races for pitting, scoring, overheating and damage.
6. Mate each bearing with race and inspect operation.
7. Replace any bearing assembly that is damaged, excessively worn, or that fails to operate smoothly.
8. Mount differential case along with side bearings and ring gear in housing, adjust side bearings to zero preload and inspect ring gear runout with dial indicator bearing against machined edge of gear.

PINION DEPTH

ADJUST

If original ring gear and pinion are to be reused, then the original shim pack must also be reused. **No adjustment is required.**

Ring gears and pinions are supplied in matched sets only. If a new gear is being used, verify numbers on pinion and ring gear before proceeding with assembling.

On the button end of the pinion there is a (+), (–), or "0" number which indicates the best running position for each particular gear set. This position is controlled by shims installed behind the inner bearing cup. **If baffles or oil slingers are used, they are considered part of the adjusting shim pack.**

1. Install inner bearing cup using handle tool No. J 39708 and cup installer tool No. 39707, or equivalents.
2. Install outer bearing cup using rear bearing cup installer tool No. J 7818 and driver handle tool No. 8092, or equivalents.
3. Install inner bearing cone into inner bearing cup, then outer bearing cone into outer bearing cup using adapter cone tool No. J 41691, or equivalent.
4. Install master pinion block tool No. J 41690, and pinion height block tool No. J 41689, or equivalents, into carrier

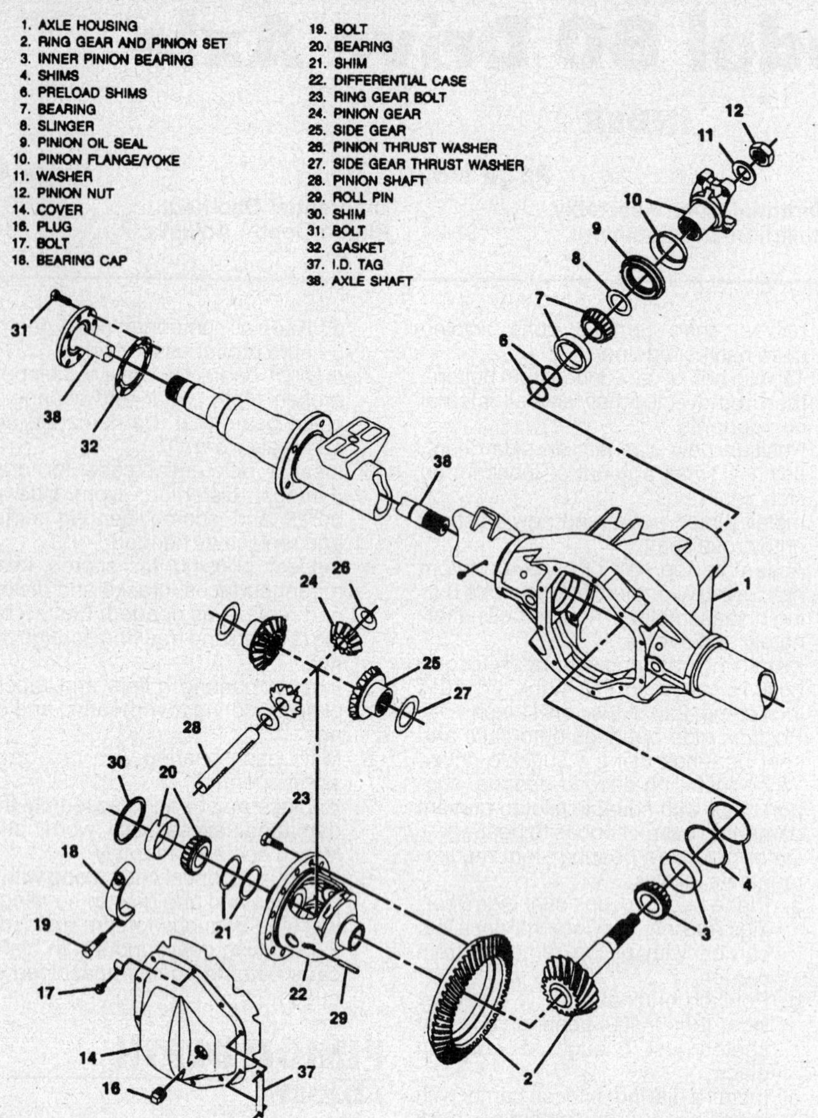

Fig. 1 Exploded view of Dana model 80 drive axle w/11 inch ring gear

housing using adapter cone and threaded rod tool No. J 41692, or equivalent.

5. Tighten adapter cone by hand until all endplay is removed, then install arbor tool No. J 39702, and master discs tool No. J 39701, or equivalents, into carrier housing.
6. Place dial indicator tool No. J 39704, or equivalent, on upper step of pinion height block as outlined in **Fig. 4,** then set dial indicator by pressing down on pinion height block to apply pressure to block of dial indicator and set dial indicator at zero.
7. Slide dial indicator over arbor as outlined in **Fig. 5,** then record reading at point of greatest deflection when needle of dial indicator is centered between movement to left and right. **This reading determines amount of shims needed for a nominal pinion setting. Pinion marking may change pinion depth by adding or deleting shims.**

DIFFERENTIAL CASE ASSEMBLY, INSTALLATION & ADJUSTMENT

1. Install differential case with side bearings and cups in position, into carrier.
2. Place smallest of original shims between bearing cup and carrier on ring gear side of case. This shim will act as a gauging shim.
3. Install bearing caps in proper position and tighten just enough to retain in place.
4. Install a dial indicator on ring gear side of carrier with indicator button contacting back of ring gear.
5. Position two screwdrivers between bearing cup and housing on side opposite ring gear.
6. Apply force to screwdrivers to move differential case as far as possible toward indicator.
7. Set dial indicator to zero with force still applied to screwdrivers.
8. Reposition screwdrivers on ring gear side of case, then force ring gear into mesh with drive pinion and note dial indicator reading. Repeat sequence several times until same reading is obtained. Add this reading to "gauging" shim thickness to determine shim required on ring gear side of case.
9. Remove "gauging" shim and install correct thickness shim between bearing cup and carrier on ring gear side of case.
10. To determine correct dimension for remaining shim, subtract size of shim already installed from reading obtained in step 10 of "Differential Overhaul" procedure. On 10½ inch axles, add an .006 inch to this figure to compensate for preload and backlash, on 11 inch, add .010 inch.
11. Spread differential carrier as outlined in **Fig. 2,** then install shim between bearing cup and carrier.
12. Remove spreader tool and dial indicator, then install bearing caps and **torque** cap bolts to 85 ft. lbs.
13. Install dial indicator and inspect ring gear backlash at four equidistant points on ring gear. Backlash must measure .004–.009 inch and must not vary more than .002 inch between inspecting points. If backlash is not within specifications, adjust differential bearing shim pack as required. **If backlash is less than specifications, decrease shim on ring gear side and increase shim on opposite side an equal amount. If backlash exceeds specifications, increase shim on ring gear side and decrease shim on opposite side an equal amount.**
14. Ensure ring gear teeth are clean and free from oil, then coat drive and coast face of each tooth with suitable marking compound.
15. Apply braking force to ring gear, then turn pinion to rotate ring gear one complete revolution in each direction. **Accurate contact pattern cannot be obtained unless gears are "loaded" when rotated.**
16. Examine gear tooth contact pattern as outlined in **Fig. 6,** and correct assembly adjustments as needed.
17. Install housing cover, using a new gasket and **torque** attaching bolts to 35 ft. lbs.
18. Install rear universal joint, then axle shafts as outlined in specific vehicle repair section.
19. Fill axle with specified lubricant.

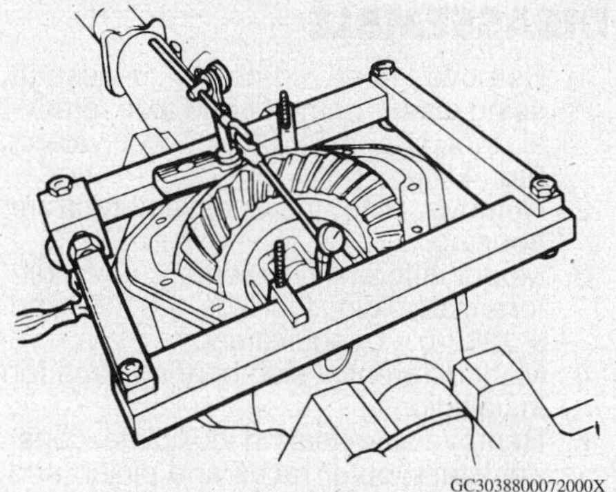

Fig. 2 Differential carrier spreading

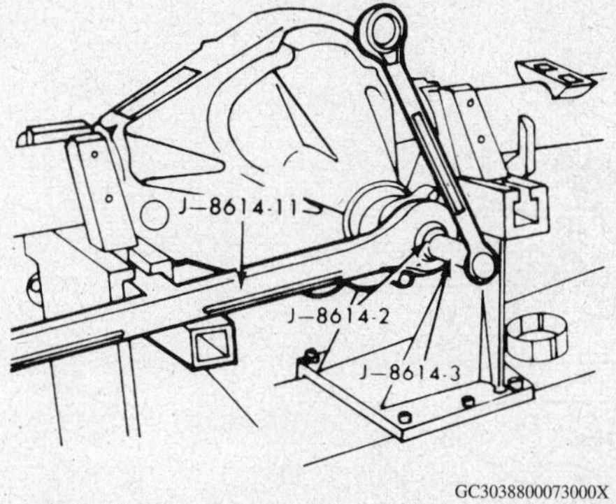

Fig. 3 Companion flange removal

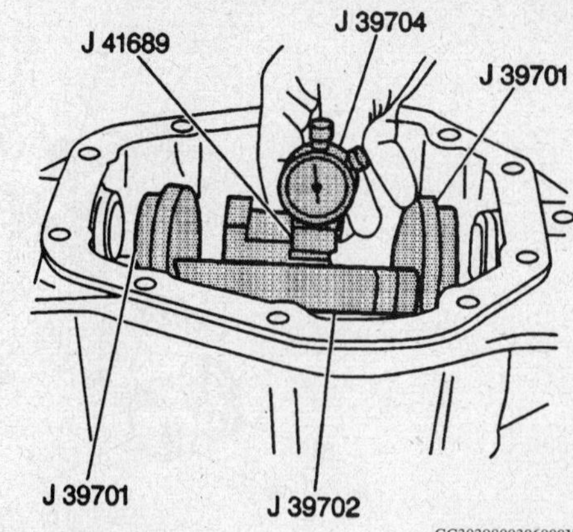

Fig. 4 Dial indicator installation

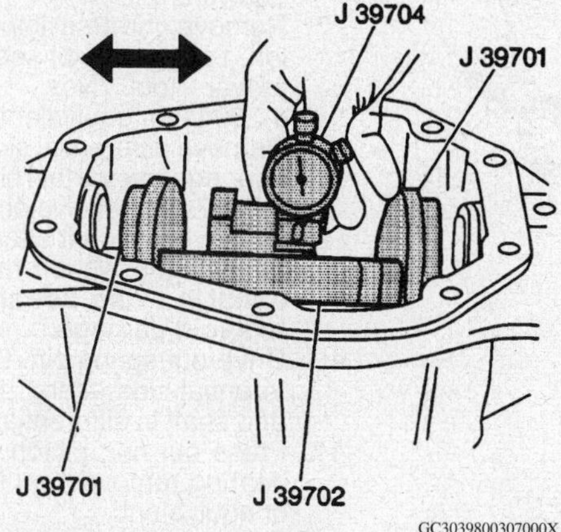

Fig. 5 Pinion depth measurement

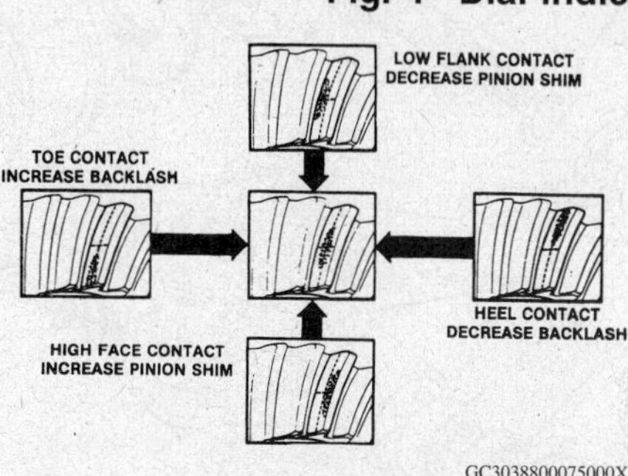

Fig. 6 Gear tooth contact pattern inspection

Tracker Front & Rear Axles

INDEX

DESCRIPTION

The differential assemblies installed to the front and rear axles use a hypoid bevel pinion and gear. The rear differential as outlined in **Fig. 1,** is set in an axle housing. The front differential as outlined in **Fig. 2,** is set in an aluminum housing mounted under the chassis frame. The reduction ratio for manual transmission equipped vehicles is different from automatic transmission equipped vehicles.

All adjustments outlined for front and rear differentials are the same.

DIFFERENTIAL FRONT

REPLACE

Front

1. Raise and support vehicle.
2. Disconnect breather hose.
3. Disconnect and support propeller shaft.
4. Remove four left mounting bracket bolts and three driveshaft flange bolts, **Fig. 3.**
5. Support differential and remove bolts from crossmember and right end of housing.
6. Disconnect right side driveshaft joint and remove housing assembly using suitable pry bars.
7. Reverse procedure to install, noting the following:
   a. **Torque** all mounting bracket bolts to 37 ft. lbs.
   b. **Torque** front driveshaft flange bolts to 37 ft. lbs.
   c. **Torque** propeller shaft flange bolts to 41 ft. lbs.

Rear

1. Raise and support vehicle.
2. Remove right and left axle shafts.
3. Remove propeller shaft bolts and shaft.
4. Support axle assembly and remove four upper arm mounting bolts and lower axle. **Rear shock absorbers must remain installed during this process. Without them, axle may**

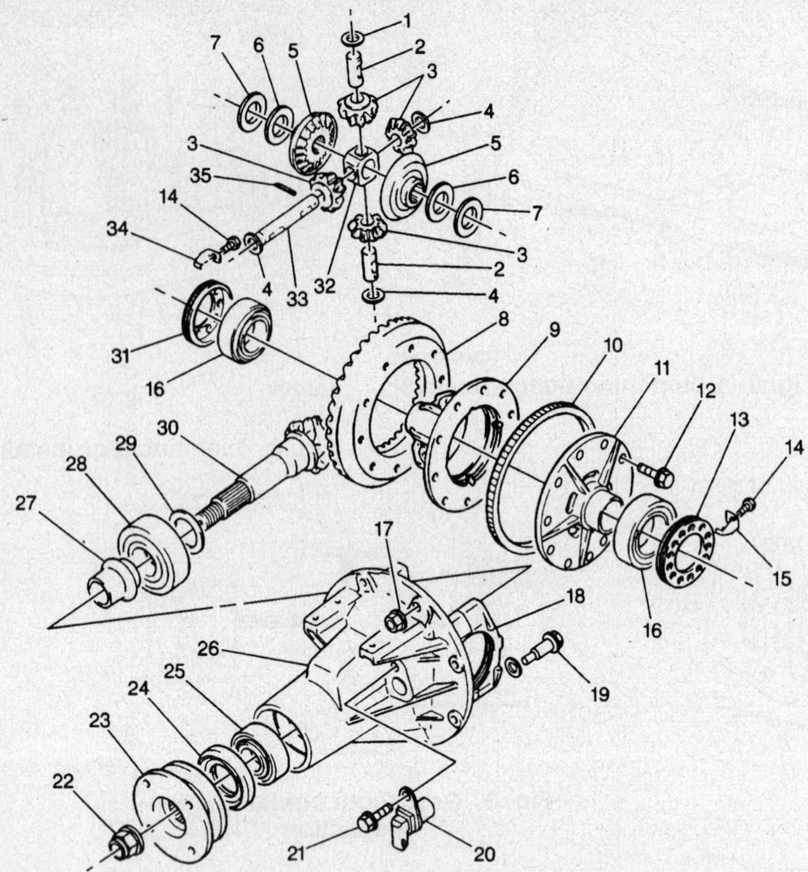

(1) Pinion Washer
(2) Pinion Cross Shaft (Short)
(3) Differential Pinion Gear
(4) Pinion Washer
(5) Side Gear
(6) Side Gear Spring Washer
(7) Side Gear Washer
(8) Ring Gear
(9) Right Differential Case
(10) Rear Wheel Speed Sensor Exciting Ring
(11) Left Differential Case
(12) Ring Gear Bolts
(13) Left Side Bearing Adjuster
(14) Side Bearing Lock Plate Bolt
(15) Side Bearing Lock Plate
(16) Side Bearing
(17) Differential Carrier Nuts
(18) Side Bearing Cap
(19) Side Bearing Cap Bolt
(20) Rear Wheel Speed Sensor
(21) Rear Wheel Speed Sensor Bolt
(22) Pinion Flange Nut
(23) Pinion Flange
(24) Pinion Seal
(25) Outer Pinion Bearing
(26) Differential Carrier
(27) Collapsible Spacer
(28) Inner Pinion Bearing

GC3038800248000A

Fig. 1 Exploded view of rear differential

fall and cause personal injury.

5. Remove differential fastening nuts and differential.
6. Reverse procedure to install noting the following:
   a. Clean all mating surfaces and apply GM sealant (Part No. 3997597).
   b. **Torque** rear differential carrier nuts to 41 ft. lbs.
   c. **Torque** upper arm bolts to 37 ft. lbs.
   d. **Torque** propeller shaft flange bolts to 41 ft. lbs.
   e. Fill axle with SAE 75W-90 hypoid gear oil and **torque** fill plug to 32 ft. lbs.

ADJUSTMENTS

Front and rear differential backlash, bearing preload and pinion depth can be found under "Assemble" procedure of "Differential Service"

DIFFERENTIAL SERVICE

Front

Refer to **Fig. 2** when performing the following procedures.

DISASSEMBLE

1. Remove front righthand driveshaft using plastic hammer and axle removal tool No. J-37780, or equivalent, **Fig. 4.**
2. Remove differential assembly from housing.
3. Mount differential assembly, using differential holding tool Nos. J-37769 and J-3289-01, or equivalent.
4. Mark differential side bearing caps for installation.
5. Remove side bearing lock plate, caps, adjusters, outer races and pinion and ring gear assembly.
6. Rotate differential assembly using flange holding tool No. J-8614-01, or equivalent.
7. Remove universal joint flange nut, pinion, flange and oil seal using seal removal tool Nos. J-8614-01 and J-26941, or equivalent.
8. Remove differential side bearing using bearing removal tool Nos. J-22888 and J-8107-4, or equivalent.
9. Remove ring gear attaching bolts, then gear, **Fig. 5. When mounting differential in a vise, use aluminum plates to avoid damage.**
10. Drive out spring pin. Disassemble differential side gears, pinions, washers and shaft in differential case.
11. Press out ring pinion gear using side bearing remover tool No. J-22912-01, or equivalent.
12. Drive out pinion bearing outer race using suitable tools. **Ring gear and pinion must be replaced as a set.**

ASSEMBLE

1. Assemble pinion bearing outer races using bearing installer tool Nos. J-8092, J-37759 and J-37758, or equivalents.
2. Assemble differential side gear and side pinion with pinion shaft.
3. Mount dial indicator to top surface of side gear. Move lower end of side gear up and down, noting movement of indicator, **Fig. 6.**
4. Install a .043 inch thrust washer and ensure a .005–.014 inch side gear thrust play is obtained.
5. Drive spring pin in until it is flush with differential case surface.
6. Install ring gear to differential case and **torque** bolts to 70 ft. lbs. **Use GM Loctite thread locking kit (Part No. 1052624) for ring gear bolts.**
7. Mount dial indicator tool to back of side gear, **Fig. 7.**
8. Install a .043 inch thrust washer and side thrust gear installation tool No. J-35138, or equivalent, onto differential side gear.
9. Move tool up and down in a straight forward manner and ensure a side gear thrust play of .005–.014 inch is obtained.
10. Install side bearings using bearing installation tool Nos. J-8092 and J-24433, or equivalents. **Be sure to use side bearing removal tool No. J-8107-4, or equivalent, to protect**

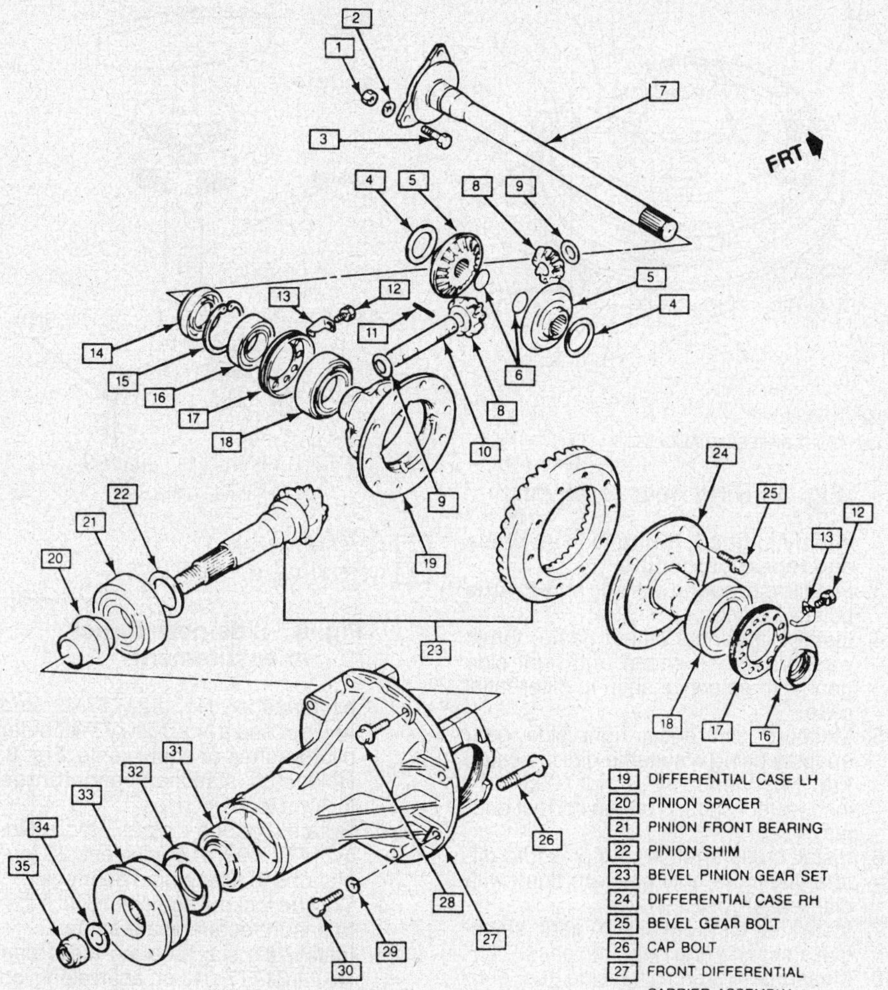

1. SHAFT NUT
2. LOCK WASHER
3. SHAFT BOLT
4. WASHER
5. DIFFERENTIAL GEAR
6. SHAFT SNAP RING
7. FRONT DRIVE SHAFT
8. DIFFERENTIAL PINION
9. PINION WASHER
10. DIFFERENTIAL PINION SHAFT
11. SHAFT PIN
12. BEARING BOLT
13. BEARING BACK PLATE
14. DIFFERENTIAL OUTPUT OIL SEAL
15. BEARING CIRCLIP
16. DRIVE SHAFT BEARING
17. BEARING ADJUSTER
18. DIFFERENTIAL SIDE BEARING
19. DIFFERENTIAL CASE LH
20. PINION SPACER
21. PINION FRONT BEARING
22. PINION SHIM
23. BEVEL PINION GEAR SET
24. DIFFERENTIAL CASE RH
25. BEVEL GEAR BOLT
26. CAP BOLT
27. FRONT DIFFERENTIAL CARRIER ASSEMBLY
28. CARRIER BOLT
29. LOCK WASHER
30. CARRIER KNOCK BOLT
31. PINION REAR BEARING
32. PINION OIL SEAL
33. UNIVERSAL JOINT FLANGE
34. FLANGE WASHER
35. FLANGE NUT

GC3038800086000X

Fig. 2 Exploded view of front differential

lower bearing.

11. Install depth gauge setting tool No. J-21777, or equivalent, while holding bearing in position, **Fig. 8.** Use low step on gauge plate.
12. **Torque** tool nut to 19 inch lbs. and rotate gauge plate several times to seat bearings.
13. **Torque** tool nut to 19 inch lbs. or until gauge plate rotates smoothly with torque wrench.
14. Install pinion setting gauge tool No. J-23597, or equivalent and assemble gauge shaft in carrier so that dial indicator rod is centered on gauging area of gauge block.
15. Install side bearing caps and **torque** bolts to 63 ft. lbs.
16. Adjust dial indicator until a zero reading is obtained.
17. Adjust position of gauge shaft mounting post so contact button touches indicator pad.
18. Push dial indicator downward into gauge plate until needle rotates ¾ of a turn then tighten in this position.
19. Slowly rotate gauge shaft back and forth. At point of greatest deflection, reset dial indicator to zero. Repeat and ensure zero reading.
20. Rotate gauge shaft until dial indicator rod no longer touches gauge plate.
21. Read movement on dial indicator. Total movement on dial indicator indicates thickness of shim required.
22. Assemble pinion rear bearing, pinion shim and pinion assembly.
23. Install front bearing to differential carrier with new spacer inserted.
24. Install oil seal into differential carrier until seal is flush with carrier end. Apply grease to lip of seal.
25. Install pinion washer and nut. Hold pinion flange and rotate pinion to seat bearing. Tighten pinion flange nut until endplay is taken up. **Preload specification is reached when endplay is no longer detectable. No further tightening should be attempted until preload has been inspected.**

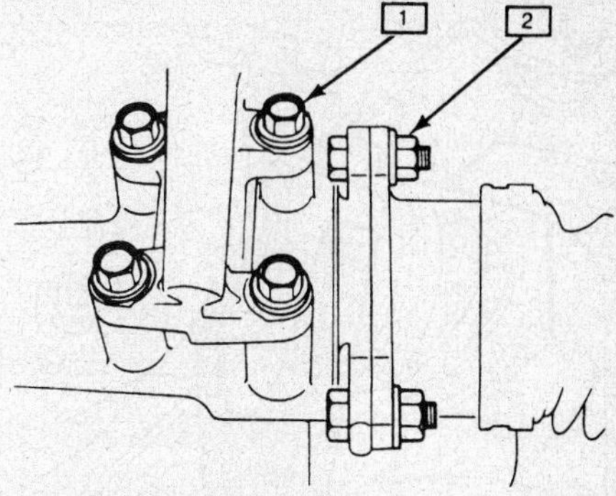

1. MOUNTING BRACKET BOLT
2. DRIVE SHAFT FLANGE BOLT AND NUT

GC3038800087000X

Fig. 3 Front differential left mounting bracket

26. Adjust bearing preload **torque** to 11 inch lbs.
27. Install ring gear and differential case assembly, side bearing outer races, bearing adjusters and bearing caps, noting alignment mark.
28. **Torque** bearing caps bolts to 63 ft. lbs.
29. Turn bearing adjuster to push side bearing lightly so that outer races are in contact with inner races, **Fig. 9.**
30. Measure preload of pinion with an inch pound torque wrench.
31. Adjust side bearing until gear backlash and bearing preload are within specifications, **Fig. 10.**
32. Install bearing lock plates.
33. Clean mating surfaces of housing and carrier and apply GM silicone sealer (Part No. 1052917).
34. Position differential assembly in housing with two reamer bolts, then install six bolts, **torquing** to 17 ft. lbs.

Rear

Refer to **Fig. 1** when performing the following procedures.

DISASSEMBLE

1. Mount differential carrier in holding fixture tool No. J-34162-A, or equivalent, using differential housing adapter tool No. J-37769, or equivalent.
2. Mount differential carrier and holding tool in a suitable vise.
3. Scribe alignment marks in differential side bearing caps for assembling reference.
4. Remove side bearing lock plate and caps.
5. Remove side bearing adjusters and outer bearing races.
6. Remove rear wheel speed sensor.
7. Remove 10 ring gear assembly attaching bolts.
8. Separate differential left case with rear

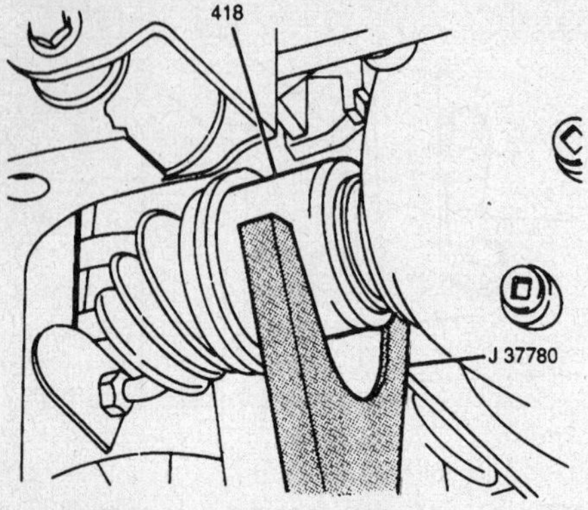

418 DIFFERENTIAL-SIDE JOINT HOUSING

GC3038800088000A

Fig. 4 Axle shaft removal

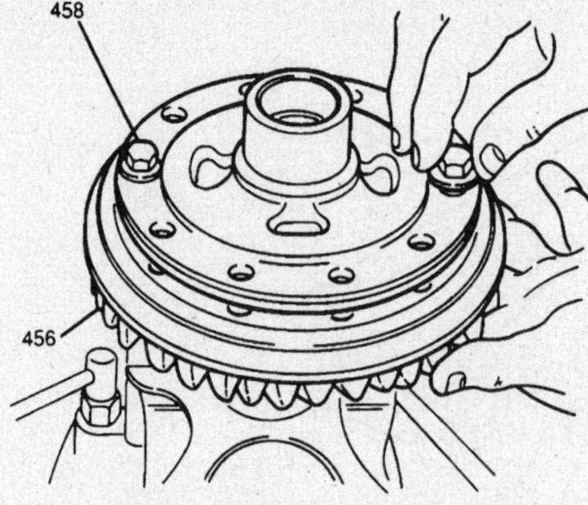

456 RING GEAR
458 RIGHT DIFFERENTIAL CASE

GC3038800089010A

Fig. 5 Ring gear removal

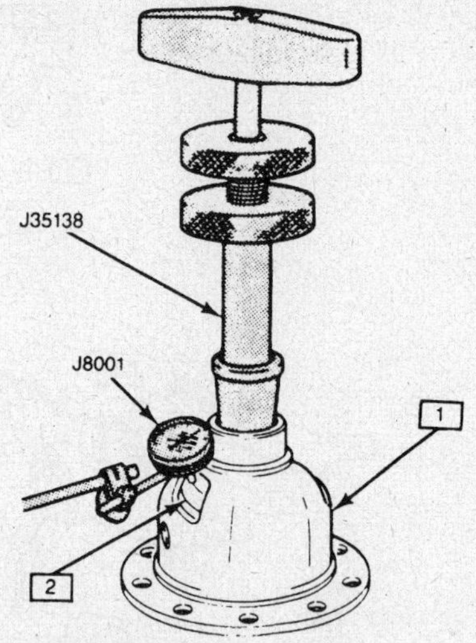

1 DIFFERENTIAL CASE
2 DIFFERENTIAL SIDE GEAR

GC3038800090000X

Fig. 6 Side gear thrust measurement

wheel anti-lock brake exciter ring from right case.

9. Remove exciter ring from left case using a suitable copper hammer. **Tap evenly along outer edge of exciter ring.**
10. Turn differential carrier in fixture 90.°
11. Remove universal joint flange nut using pinion flange holder J-8614-01, or equivalent.
12. Remove universal joint flange and pinion shaft.
13. Remove pinion shaft oil seal using oil seal remover tool No. J-26941 and slide hammer tool No. J-23907, or equivalents.
14. Remove outer pinion bearing from differential case.
15. Remove outer and inner pinion bearing races.
16. Remove differential side bearings using side bearing puller tool No. J-22888-D and side bearing remover pilot tool No. J-8107-4, or equivalents, **Fig. 11.**
17. Remove shaft spring pins using an arbor punch and a hammer.
18. Remove differential side gears, selective shims, pinion gears, thrust washers and cross shafts.
19. Remove collapsible spacer and inner pinion bearing using a suitable press and inner pinion bearing cone remover tool No. J-22912-01, or equivalent, **Fig. 12.** Discard collapsible spacer.

ASSEMBLE

Ring gear and pinion must be replaced as a set. Taper roller bearings and races must be replaced as a set.

1. Install anti-lock brake exciter ring to differential left case using exciter ring installer tool No. J-38891, differential side bearing remover tool No. J-8107-4 and a suitable press, or equivalents.
2. Install rear wheel anti-lock brake exciter ring using exciter ring installer tool No. J-38891, or equivalent, a differential side bearing installer tool No. J-8107-04, or equivalent, and a press, **Fig. 13. Pressure exerted on exciter ring should not exceed 1102 lbs. If more than 1102 lbs. of pressure is needed for press fitting, left case and exciter ring are probably not evenly aligned. Remove from press and repeat procedure.**
3. Install rear speed sensor and **torque** bolt to 17 ft. lbs.
4. Install differential pinion gears, thrust washers, cross shafts and right side gear with selective shim in differential case.
5. Measure differential right side gear endplay using a suitable dial indicator, **Fig. 14.** If endplay is not .005–.014 inch, select shim to obtain correct endplay.
6. Install cross shaft spring pins into differential case until pins are flush with differential case surface.
7. Install left differential side gear, selective shim and ring gear into case.
8. Measure differential left side gear endplay using a suitable dial indicator and universal endplay measuring tool No. J-35138, or equivalent, **Fig. 7.** If endplay is not .005–.014 inch, select shim to obtain correct endplay.
9. Coat ring gear bolts with sealant part No. 1052624, or equivalent, then install bolts and **torque** to 63 ft. lbs.
10. Install differential right side bearing, using bearing cone installer tool No. J-24433, driver handle tool No. J-8092, or equivalents, and a suitable press.
11. Install differential left side bearing, using bearing cone installer tool No. J-37758, driver handle tool No. J-8092, or equivalents, and a suitable press.
12. Install bearing plug tool No. J-8107-4, or equivalent, on lower bearing to protect side bearing from damage.
13. Install pinion gear inner race using inner bearing race installer tool No. J-37759 and driver handle tool No. J-8092 or, equivalents.
14. Install pinion gear outer bearing race using outer bearing race installer tool No. J-37758 and driver handle tool No. J-8092 or, equivalents.
15. **Set pinion depth as follows:**
    a. Lubricate inner and outer pinion bearings with GM part No. 1050010, or equivalent lubricant.
    b. While holding pinion bearings in position, install a No. J-21777-102 gauge plate, No. J23597-12 inner pilot washer, No. J-21777-43 stud and nut and a No. J-21777-42 outer pilot washer, or equivalents, **Fig. 8.**
    c. Hold stud stationary and **torque** locknut to 18 inch lbs.
    d. Rotate gauge plate tool No. J-21777-102, or equivalent, 25 revolutions to seat pinion bearings.
    e. **Torque** locknut again to 18 inch lbs. to ensure bearings are seated.
    f. Install two side bearing discs part No. J-21777-01, or equivalent, on side bearing bores using arbor tool No. J-23597-1, or equivalent.
    g. Rotate gauge plate tool No. J-21777-102, or equivalent, until gauging areas are parallel with two side bearing discs.
    h. Position dial indicator rod over 97 mm portion of the gauging plate.
    i. Connect dial indicator tool No. J-8001, or equivalent, to arbor tool No. J-23597-1, or equivalent, and position gauge shaft over dial indicator rod.
    j. Install side bearing caps and **torque** bolts to 63 ft. lbs.
    k. Set dial indicator to zero.
    l. Slowly rotate arbor on 97 mm step of gauge plate to determine point of greatest deflection. Reset dial indicator to zero.
    m. Slowly rotate arbor until dial indicator is no longer in contact with gauge plate.
    n. Record dial indicator reading. This reading indicates the selective shim required for correct pinion depth. Refer to selective shim chart as outlined in **Fig. 15** for correct shim.
16. Install pinion selective shim on pinion gear shaft.
17. Press pinion bearing on pinion gear shaft using bearing installer tool No. J-6133-01, or equivalent.

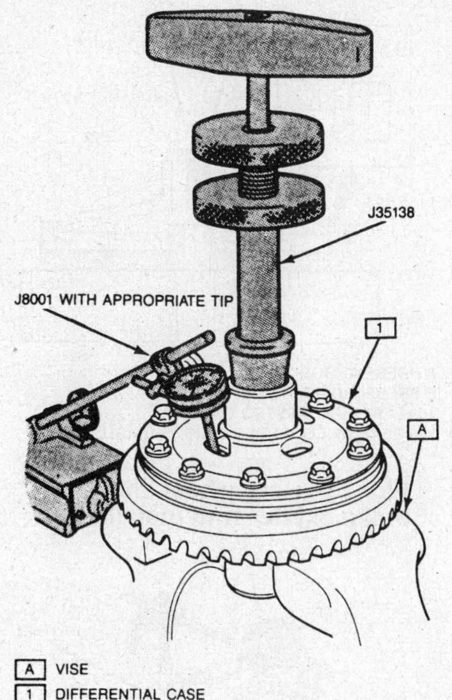

Fig. 7 Bearing preload adjustment

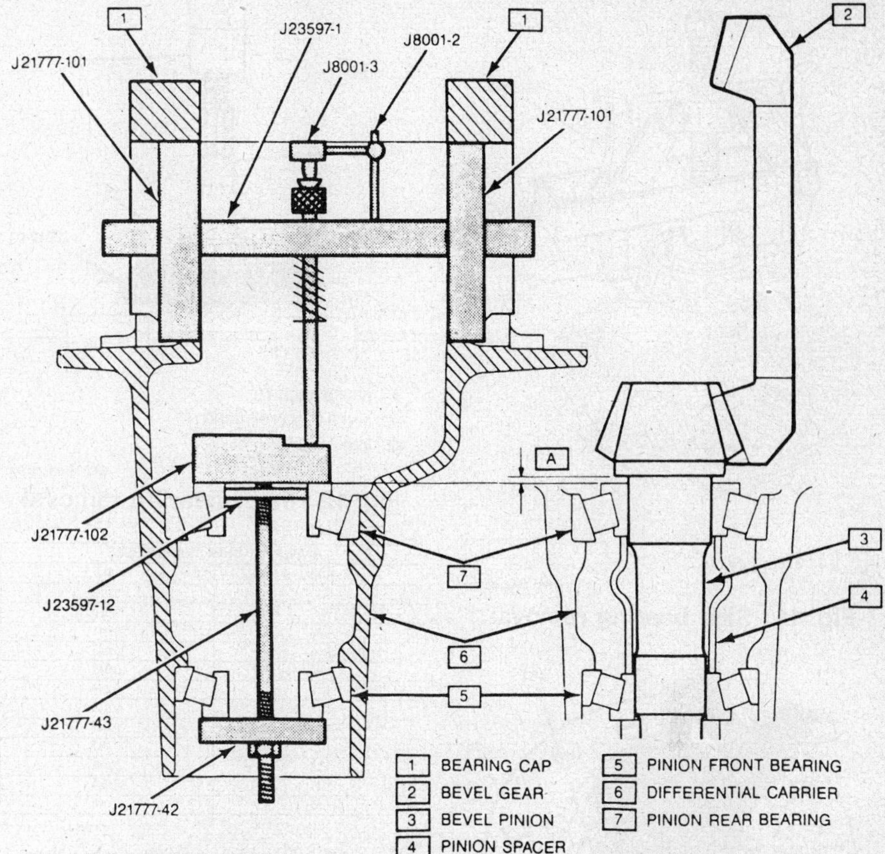

Fig. 8 Pinion depth measurement

18. Install new collapsible spacer on pinion gear shaft.
19. Install pinion outer bearing into differential carrier.
20. Lubricate pinion oil seal with part No. 1050010, or equivalent, then install pinion oil seal using seal installer tool No. J-25273, or equivalent, and a plastic hammer.
21. Install pinion flange, washer and flange nut using pinion flange holder tool No. J-8614-01, or equivalent. **Tightening flange nut will preload pinion bearings. Exceeding preload specification will compress collapsible spacer too far and require installation of a new spacer. Adjust pinion bearing preload to 11 ft. lbs., starting torque not rotating torque. Measure pinion bearing preload again after rotating pinion several times to ensure bearings have been seated. If preload has been reduced, reset preload to specification.**
22. Install side bearing races on differential side bearings.
23. Install differential case on differential carrier.
24. Install side bearing adjusters, then align bearing caps with marks made during disassembling and **torque** cap bolts to 65 ft. lbs.
25. **Adjust backlash and differential bearing preload as follows:**
    a. Left bearing adjuster nut is located on ring gear side of carrier, right bearing adjuster nut is located on pinion gear side of carrier.
    b. Loosen right adjuster nut until it does not contact side bearing race

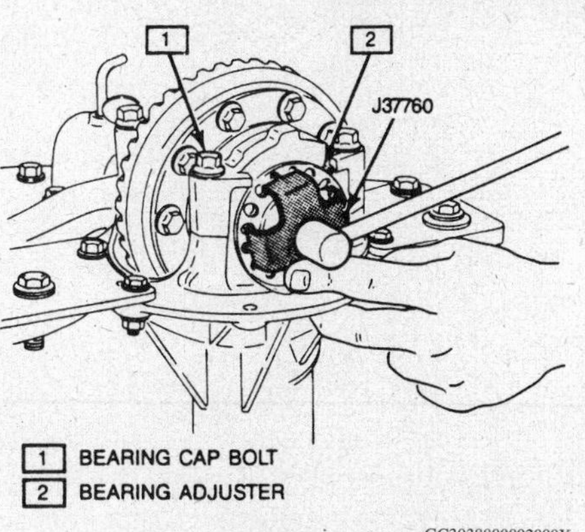

Fig. 9 Side bearing pre-adjustment

using spanner wrench tool No. J-37760, or equivalent.

c. Using spanner wrench, tighten left adjuster nut until ring gear is fully engaged into pinion gear with zero backlash.
d. Ensure right adjuster nut is still not in contact with side bearing race.
e. Rotate pinion gear to ensure there is no binding.
f. Install dial indicator to differential carrier, **Fig. 16.**
g. Tighten right adjuster nut until it contacts side bearing race using spanner wrench tool No. J-37760, or equivalent.

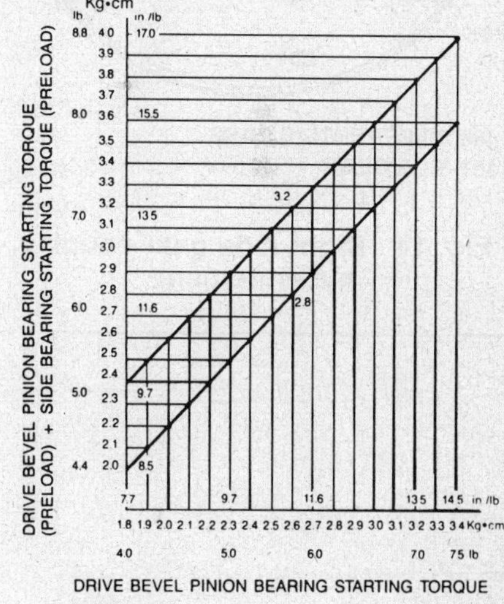

Fig. 10 Combination of preloads

h. Set dial indicator to zero against side bearing cap.
i. Adjust side bearing preload by tightening right adjuster nut until dial indicator reads .002–.006, case spread.
j. Rotate pinion gear to ensure side bearings seat.

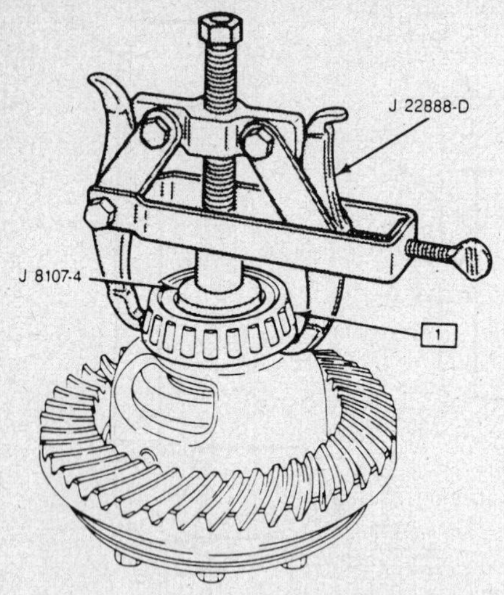

1 SIDE BEARING

GC3038800250000X

Fig. 11 Side bearing removal

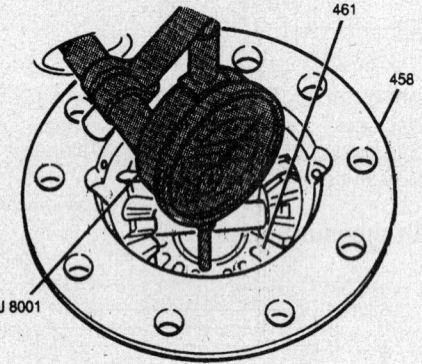

458 DIFFERENTIAL CASE
461 SIDE GEAR

GC3038800253000A

Fig. 14 Right side gear endplay measurement

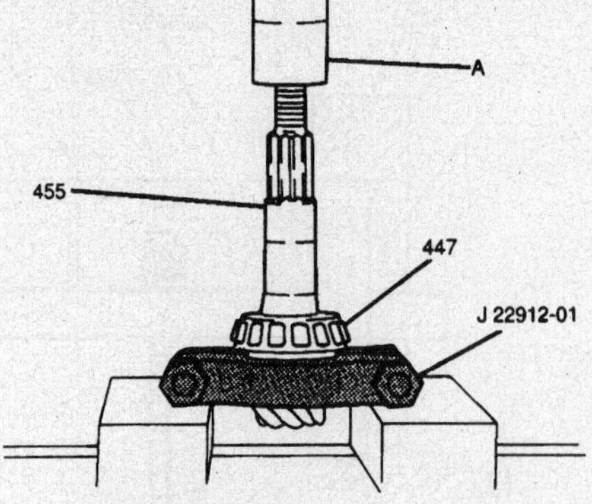

A PRESS ARBOR
447 INNER PINION BEARING
455 PINION GEAR

GC3038800251000X

Fig. 12 Inner bearing removal

AVAILABLE SHIM THICKNESSES	
mm	in.
0.30	0.012
1.00	0.039
1.03	0.041
1.06	0.042
1.09	0.043
1.12	0.044
1.15	0.045
1.18	0.046
1.21	0.047
1.24	0.048
1.27	0.049
1.30	0.050

GC3038800254000X

Fig. 15 Pinion depth selective shims

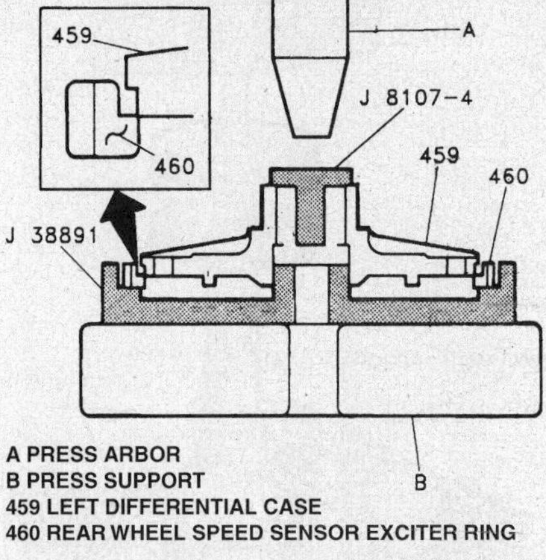

A PRESS ARBOR
B PRESS SUPPORT
459 LEFT DIFFERENTIAL CASE
460 REAR WHEEL SPEED SENSOR EXCITER RING

GC3038800252000X

Fig. 13 Rear wheel anti-lock brake exciter ring installation

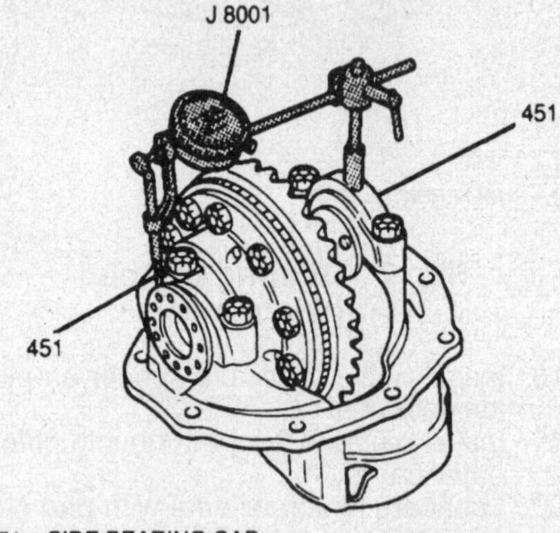

451 SIDE BEARING CAP

GC3038800255000X

Fig. 16 Side bearing preload dial indicator setting

Versatrak

INDEX

DESCRIPTION

The rear differential assembly consists of a torque tube assembly, three-piece differential housing, ring and pinion with differential carrier assembly, **Fig. 1.** The propeller shaft on the Versatrak system is constantly rotating and spins at a rate equal to an average of the two front wheels. Under normal conditions, the external and internal gears of the differential gerotor pumps are rotating at an equal rate of speed.

DISASSEMBLE

Do not disassemble side cover or differential assembly. Oil seal damage or entry of foreign material into hydraulic system may effect system operation.

1. Remove drain plug and gasket, **Fig. 2.**
2. Remove clamp and vent hose assembly, **Fig. 3.**
3. Remove clutch pump check valve bolts, **Fig. 4.**
4. Remove O-ring seal from check valve.
5. Remove bracket assembly from tube, **Fig. 5.**
6. Remove differential bolts, then separate torque tube from differential.
7. Remove bolts from differential.
8. Remove pinion, housing and shim assembly, **Fig. 6.**
9. Remove oil seal and O-ring from pinion housing.
10. Remove left axle shaft oil seal from differential, **Fig. 7.**
11. Remove right axle shaft oil seal from differential, **Fig. 8.**
12. Inspect components as outlined under "Cleaning & Inspecting" and replace as required.

CLEANING & INSPECTION

1. Clean components in suitable solvent and blow dry with compressed air, noting the following:
   a. Do not use brush when cleaning bearings.
   b. Do not spin dry bearings as bearings will be damaged.
   c. Lightly lubricate components after cleaning to retard corrosion.
   d. Keep all components in order to ensure proper assembling.
2. Inspect gears for cracks, chipped or broken teeth, wear and scoring. Replace gears that are damaged or excessively worn.
3. Inspect differential case for cracks, damage, distortion, worn side gear bores and scored bearing surfaces and replace as needed.
4. Inspect housing for scored bearing mount surfaces, cracks and distortion and replace as needed. Ensure housing is clean and free from foreign material.
5. Inspect bearing rollers and races for pitting, scoring, overheating and damage.
6. Mate each bearing with race and inspect operation.
7. Replace any bearing assembly that is damaged, excessively worn, or that fails to operate smoothly.
8. Mount differential case along with side bearings and ring gear in housing, adjust side bearings to zero preload and inspect ring gear runout with dial indicator bearing against machined edge of gear.

ASSEMBLE

1. Install righthand axle shaft oil seal using tool No. J-44809, or equivalent, **Fig. 8.**
2. Install lefthand axle shaft oil seal using tool No. J-44809, or equivalent, **Fig. 7.**
3. Lubricate O-ring seal and oil seal sealing surface using GM P/N 12378514, or equivalent.
4. Install seal into groove of pinion housing using tool No. J-44915, or equivalent, **Fig. 6.**
5. Install pinion, housing and shim assembly to differential.
6. Install bolts to differential, and tighten to specification.
7. Attach torque tube to differential, and tighten to specification.
8. Install spacers, then attach bracket, bolt, washers and nut to torque tube, **Fig. 5.**
9. Install O-ring seals onto clutch pump check valve.
10. Install valve and bolts to differential, and tighten to specification.
11. Install vent hose assembly and clamp to differential.
12. Install drain plug and gasket to differential, and tighten to specification.

DIFFERENTIAL ASSEMBLY

REPLACE

Refer to "Rear Axle & Suspension" section under "Aztek & Rendezvous" chassis chapter.

AXLE SHAFT SEAL

REPLACE

1. Raise and support vehicle.
2. Remove rear wheel assembly.
3. Remove and discard wheel drive shaft nut.
4. Release parking brake.
5. Support brake caliper using suitable wire, then remove brake pads from caliper bracket.
6. Remove brake pad retainers from caliper bracket.
7. Remove brake caliper bolts, then bracket.
8. Remove park cable brake routing nut.
9. Remove bolt retaining rear tie rod end from rear suspension knuckle, **Fig. 9.**
10. Loosen, but do not remove, bolts securing park brake cable bracket to suspension knuckle.
11. Disconnect wheel speed sensor electrical connector.
12. Install tool No. J-42129, or equivalent onto wheel hub and secure with wheel nuts, then begin to disengage wheel drive shaft from wheel hub and bearing, **Fig. 10.**
13. Remove upper control arm to suspension knuckle bolt.
14. Disengage wheel drive shaft from wheel hub and bearing.
15. Position and support suspension knuckle, then remove tool No. J-42129, or equivalent from wheel hub.
16. Assemble tool Nos. J-33008-A, J-29794 and J-2619-01, or equivalents, then install tool No. J-33008-A, or equivalent evenly onto rear wheel drive shaft inner joint housing.
17. Disengage wheel drive shaft from rear axle differential using tool Nos. J-33008-A, J-29794 and J-2619-01, or equivalents, then remove tool assembly.
18. Remove wheel drive shaft assembly from vehicle.
19. Reverse procedure to install, tighten to specifications.

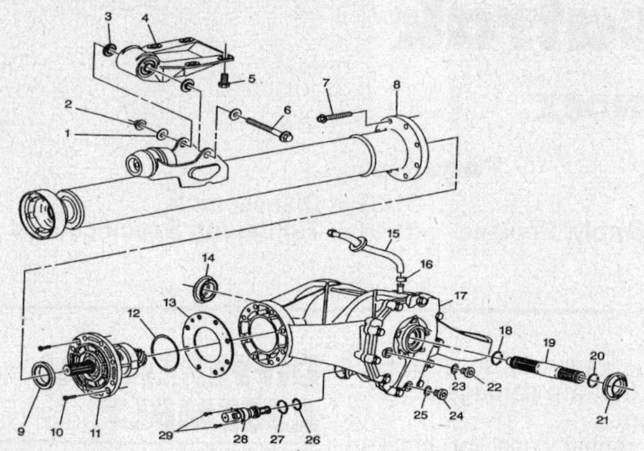

(1) Washer
(2) Nut
(3) Spacer
(4) Bracket
(5) Bolt
(6) Bolt
(7) Bolt
(8) Torque Tube Assembly
(9) Oil Seal
(10) Bolt
(11) Pinion and Housing Assembly
(12) O-Ring
(13) Shim
(14) Oil Seal (Right)
(15) Vent Hose Assembly
(16) Clamp
(17) Differential Assembly
(18) Snap Ring
(19) Axle Shaft
(20) Snap Ring
(21) Oil Seal (Left)
(22) Fill Plug
(23) Gasket
(24) Drain Plug
(25) Gasket
(26) O-Ring
(27) O-Ring
(28) Clutch Pump Check Valve
(29) Bolts

GC3030100388000X

Fig. 1 Exploded view of Versatrak rear differential

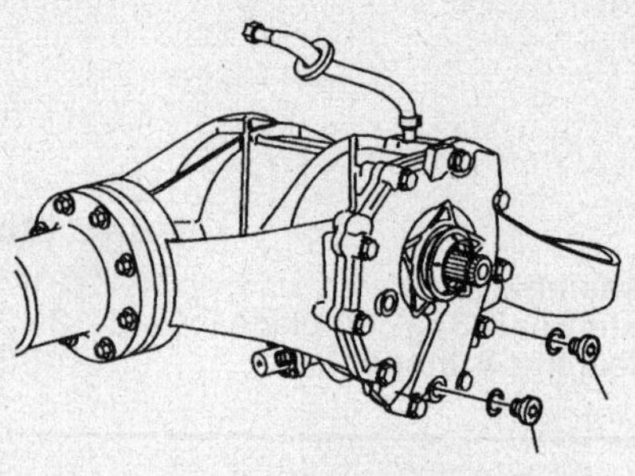

GC3030100389000X

Fig. 2 Drain plug & gasket removal

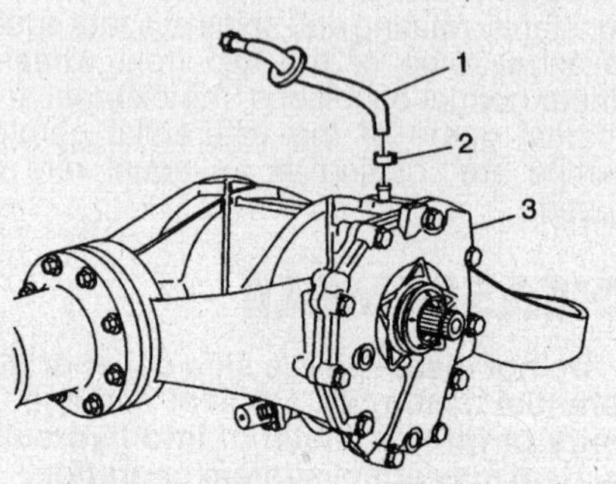

GC3030100390000X

Fig. 3 Clamp & vent hose removal

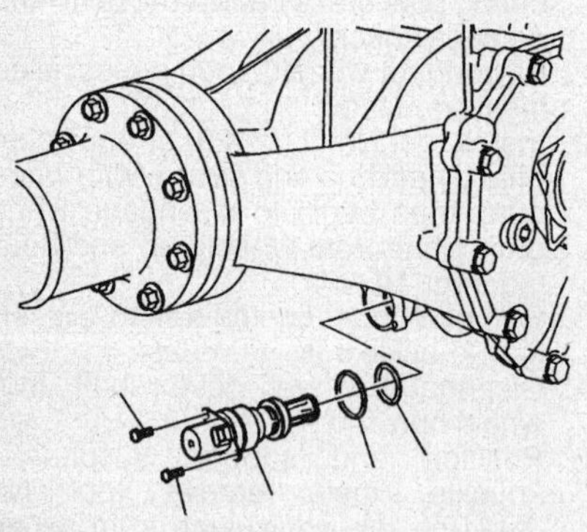

GC3030100391000X

Fig. 4 Check valve bolt removal

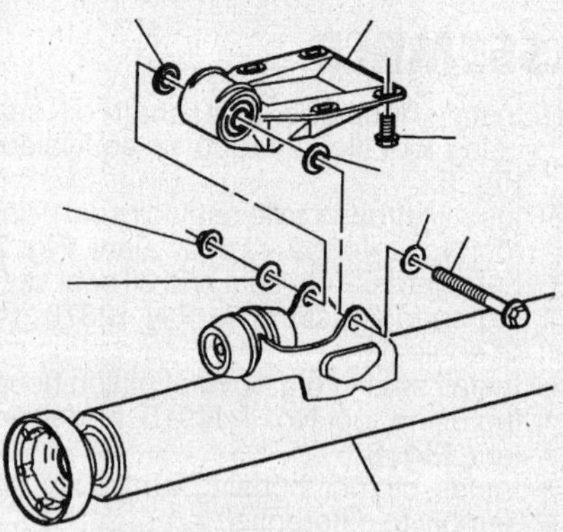

GC3030100392000X

Fig. 5 Bracket assembly removal

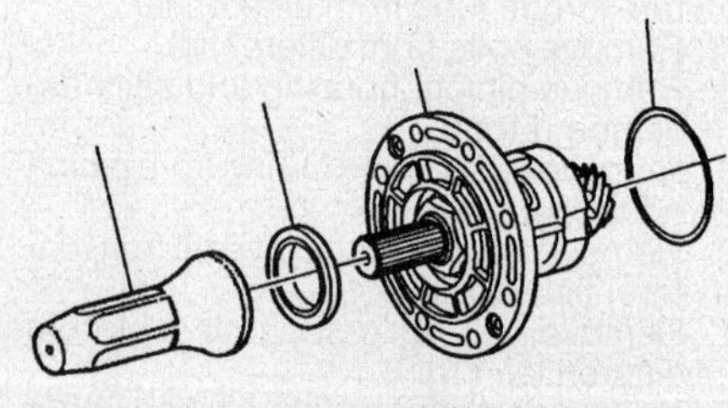

GC3030100393000X

Fig. 6 Pinion, housing & shim assembly removal

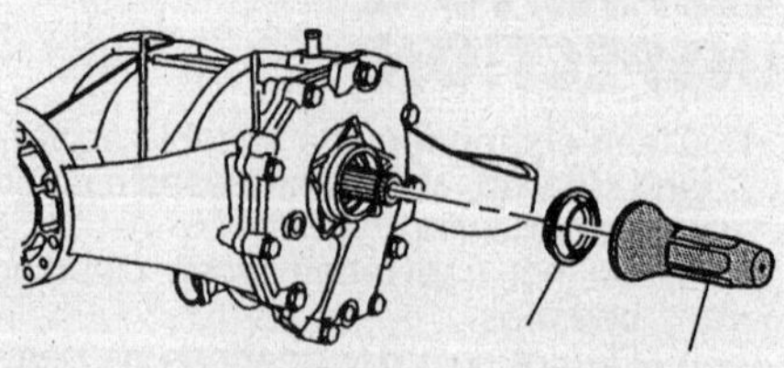

GC3030100394000X

Fig. 7 Lefthand axle shaft oil seal removal

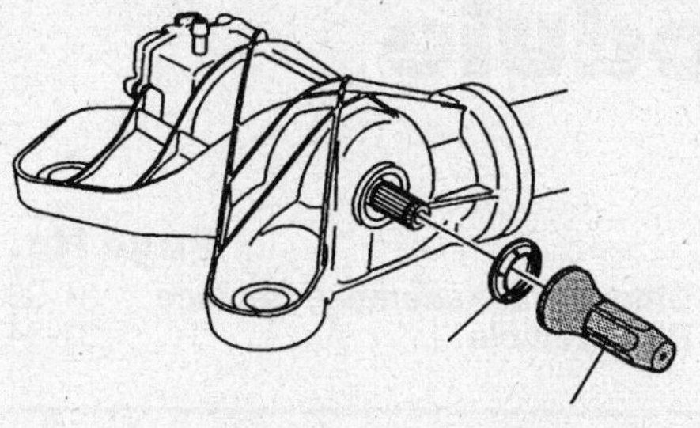

Fig. 8 Righthand axle shaft oil seal removal

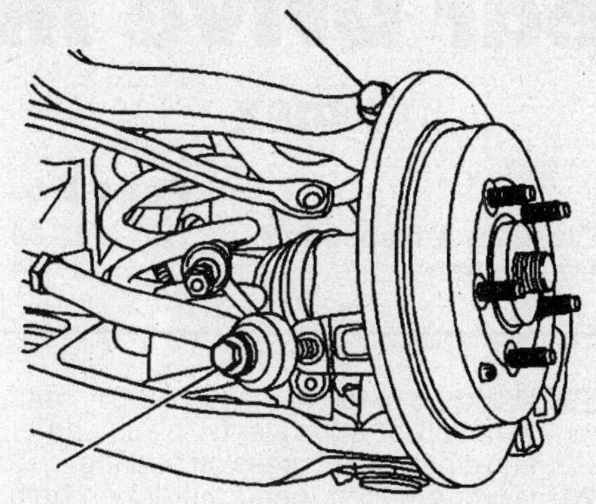

Fig. 9 Rear tie rod end bolt removal

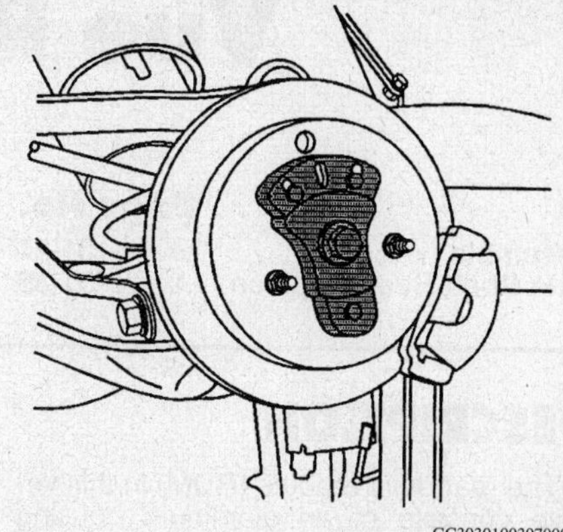

Fig. 10 Wheel drive shaft & wheel hub bearing removal

TIGHTENING SPECIFICATIONS

Year	Component	Torque Ft. Lbs.
AZTEC, MONTANA, RELAY, RENDEZVOUS, SILHOUETTE, SV6, TERRAZA, UPLANDER & VENTURE		
2002–06	Brake Caliper Bracket Bolts	92①
	Differential Carrier-To-Cradle Mounting Bolts	37
	Drain Plug	23
	Park Brake Cable Routing Bracket Nut	89①
	Tie Rod To Knuckle Bolt	63
	Torque Tube Bracket-To-Body Bolts	41
	Torque Tube-To-Bracket Through Bolt And Nut	47
	Upper Control Arm To Suspension Knuckle Bolt	63
	Wheel Drive Shaft Spindle Nut	192
EQUINOX & TORRENT		
2005–06	Lower Control Arm-To-Suspension Knuckle Bolt And Nut	118
	Lower Jounce Bumper Nut	46
	Lower Shock Absorber Mounting Bolt And Nut	77
	RDM Mounting Nuts	77
	Stabilizer Bar Link Nut	11
	Suspension Knuckle And Toe Link Bolt And Nut.	81
	Upper Control Arm-To-Suspension Knuckle Bolt And Nut	100
	Wheel Drive Shaft Spindle Nut	81

① — Inch lbs.

Vue Rear Drive Module

INDEX

DESCRIPTION

The rear drive module (RDM) in this vehicle consists of an aluminum housing which contains a gerotor fluid pump, clutch pack and a differential, **Fig. 1.** It has a common fluid reservoir. The on-demand rear differential distributes variable torque/ power to the rear wheels via individual axle shafts. The system has an integral protection device that reduces rear wheel torque when excessive heat is generated, thus protecting the rear wheel drive module (RDM).

DISASSEMBLE

1. Remove drain plug and drain fluid.
2. Remove fill plug, then rear mounting bracket and bolts **Fig. 2.**
3. Install J–44873 or equivalent to pinion flange using two prop shaft bolts, then attach half drive breaker bar to hold pinion flange and remove nut.
4. Remove nut and flange, then discard used nut.
5. Remove dust deflector from flange, then input flange oil seal from clutch cover **Fig. 3.**
6. Remove bolts and clutch cover from differential housing, then filter assembly and dowel pins.
7. **Do not submerge clutch drum in solvent. This will damage friction material and geroter pump. Clutch drum is not serviceable. If inoperative conditions are found, replace unit.**
8. Remove clutch drum, then snap ring from clutch cover.
9. Remove bearing only if being replaced, it must be pressed out by inner race.
10. Remove clutch drum rear oil seal from housing.
11. Attach assembly to holding fixture, then remove rear cover bolts.
12. Remove rear cover by prying it off at pry point locations, **Fig. 4.**
13. Remove right and left axle shaft oil seals, then differential carrier.
14. Place a screw driver in axle differential bore and pry up, **Fig. 5.**
15. Mark or tag bearing races and shims for assembly, then remove.
16. **Ring gear bolts are not to be reused. Use new bolts during assembly.** Remove bolts and ring gear from carrier.
17. Identify lock pin location within differential case, **Fig. 6.**
18. Drive pinion shaft roll pin from access hole until pinion shaft can be removed from differential case.
19. Using J–44854, J–22912-01 and J–44855 or equivalents, place carrier into a press and press off bearing.
20. Using a punch, bend out flat on both sides of pinion nut.
21. Place J–44864 or equivalent over pinion shaft, then turn shaft to align hex nut with flat on assembly holding fixture.
22. Place J–44865 or equivalent and breaker bar over pinion splines, then remove nut.
23. **Pinion nut is not reuseable.** Remove J–44864 or equivalent and nut.
24. Remove bolts from holding fixture, then remove from housing.
25. Position differential housing into a press and remove pinion shaft.
26. **Collapsible spacer is not reusable.** Remove front bearing, then collapsible spacer and pinion shaft.
27. If dowel pins are still in housing, remove them before pressing. Pressing on dowels will damage housing.
28. Place J–3940 or equivalent behind front bearing race in grooves, then spread arms and tighten lock bolt.
29. Place housing in a press and remove race.
30. Using J–44858 and J–22912-01 or equivalents, place V of split plate in groove of tool and tighten nuts.
31. Pinion shim is located under bearing, measure and mark or tag when removed.
32. Place pinion shaft and tools in a press, then remove bearing and shim.

CLEANING & INSPECTION

Do not use any type of motored cleaning device, air tools or drills.

1. Inspect all drive unit components before assembly. Thorough inspection of drive components for wear and stress with subsequent replacement of worn components eliminates costly drive component repair after assembly.
2. Clean housings in solvent and remove all sealant material from sealing surfaces.
3. Inspect clutch and differential housings for damaged sealing surfaces, worn or scored bearing race bores, damaged bolt, drain plug, or fill plug hole threads.
4. Inspect clutch and differential housings for porosity, damage to exterior of housings, damaged, restricted or missing vent tube and worn mounting bracket bushings.
5. Clean and inspect vent passage and oil return passage, then vent passage in rear cover.
6. Clean and inspect drain plug threads and inspect welch plug for leakage, rust holes and looseness.
7. Clean gears and shafts in solvent.
8. Ring gear and pinion must be inspected for proper wear pattern.
9. End of gear tooth farthest away from center of ring gear is heel end of tooth.
10. End of gear tooth nearest to center of ring gear is toe end of tooth.
11. Side of tooth that curves inward or is concave is considered coast side of tooth.
12. Side of tooth that curves outward or is convex is considered drive side of tooth.
13. Inspect pinion shaft for worn or damaged splines, bearings, wear, pitting, or discoloration by heat.
14. Inspect pinion shaft for damaged threads, worn or scored shaft.
15. Inspect bearings for a bent bearing cage.
16. Inspect bearing rollers and races for pitting, scoring, grooves and excessive wear or other damage.
17. Inspect bearing rollers and races for heat discoloration, which ranges from a faint yellow to a dark blue color.
18. Inspect pinion flange sealing surface for wear, damaged bolt threads and worn or damaged splines.
19. Wipe with a clean lint free towel and inspect pinion nut threads, bearing surface, front sealing surface, and rear sealing surface.
20. Clean differential case in solvent.
21. Inspect side bearing mounting surfaces, differential pin bores, ring gear mounting surfaces, side and spider gear thrust washer surfaces for cracking or scoring.
22. Replace differential carrier assembly as required.
23. Inspect side gear thrust washers, side gears, spider gear thrust washers, pinion gears, Pinion shaft pin and lock pin for scoring, pitted teeth and cracks.

ASSEMBLE

Do not use excessive amounts of sealer. Excess sealer could plug the vent passage, the oil pump, and/or the oil pump screen causing internal damage. **Sealer cure time is 8 hours prior to a fluid fill. Ensure sealing surface is still clean and oil free.**

1. Apply sealer Saturn P/N 12346240 or equivalent to rear housing sealing surface, do not apply sealer to vent walls.

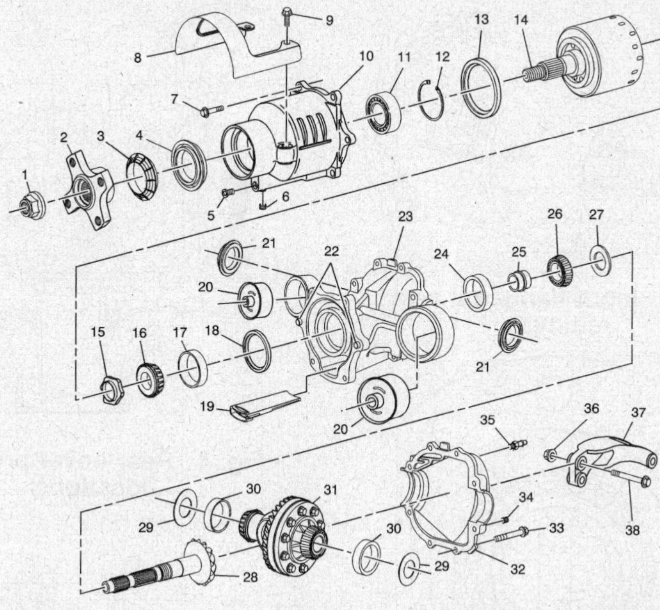

Fig. 1 Exploded view of Vue rear differential (Part 1 of 2)

Apply a constant bead of sealer .098 inch wide and thick.

2. Install dial indicator on cover at top of bearing bore, preload indicator and zero it out.
3. Install J–44868 or equivalent on cover.
4. Spread cover while measuring movement, do not spread cover more than .012–0.016 inch.
5. After spread is reached, remove dial indicator and install cover.
6. Install M8 cover bolts and tighten in a criss-cross pattern to 18 ft. lbs.
7. Remove housing spreader, then install M10 cover bolts and tighten in a criss-cross pattern to 38 ft. lbs.
8. Using J–44853 or equivalent, install clutch drum rear oil seal to differential housing **Fig. 7.**
9. Install bearing and snap ring to clutch cover using SA9114T from SA1991T2 automatic transmission tool kit or equivalent.
10. Using J–44852 or equivalent, install front clutch drum oil seal.
11. Install filter assembly, then dowel pins.
12. Install clutch drum on pinion shaft, **Fig. 8.**
13. It will be required to shake and twist clutch drum back and forth to engage splines into pump rotor and bushing.
14. A properly installed clutch drum will be fully engaged seal.
15. Apply sealant Saturn P/N 12346240 or equivalent, to sealing surface of differential housing and apply a constant bead of sealer .098 inch wide and thick.
16. Install clutch cover and bolts (2) to differential housing and tighten bolts to 18 ft. lbs.
17. Install dust deflector to flange, then using J–44851 or equivalent seal into housing.
18. Install flange and a new nut to pinion shaft.
19. Install J–44873 or equivalent to pinion flange using two prop shaft bolts.
20. Attach half drive breaker bar to hold pinion flange to tighten nut to 150 ft. lbs.
21. Using J–44809 or equivalent, install right axle shaft oil seal into differential housing.
22. Install rear mounting bracket, bolts and new nuts to differential housing and tighten bolt to 77 ft. lbs. **Fig. 9.**
23. Apply Saturn P/N 21485278 or equivalent on threads, then install vent and drain plug to differential housing and tighten to 22 ft. lbs.
24. Apply sealant Saturn P/N 21485278 or equivalent to threads of fill plug.
25. Install or 25.4 oz GM VERSATRAK fluid Saturn P/N 12378514 equivalent after axle is in vehicle.
26. Install fill plug and tighten to 26 ft. lbs.

DIFFERENTIAL ASSEMBLY

REPLACE

1. Raise and support vehicle, then remove wheel and tire assembly.
2. Disconnect, then remove intermediate exhaust pipe and muffler assembly from front pipe.
3. Remove, then discard wheel drive shaft spindle nut.
4. While holding stabilizer link with a wrench, remove stabilizer link-to-lower control arm nut.
5. Place a stand under lower control arm to support.
6. Remove lower shock absorber mounting bolt and nut, then toe link nut, bolt, and washer.
7. Loosen, but do not remove lower suspension jounce bumper nut.
8. Remove lower control arm to suspension knuckle bolt and nut.

(1) Nut
(2) Input Flange
(3) Dust Shield
(4) Oil Seal
(5) Drain Plug
(6) Plug
(7) Bolt
(8) Shield
(9) Bolt
(10) Clutch Cover
(11) Bearing
(12) Snap Ring
(13) Seal
(14) Clutch Drum
(15) Pinion Nut
(16) Bearing
(17) Cup
(18) Seal
(19) Filter
(20) Mount
(21) Axle Seals
(22) Hollow Dowel
(23) Differential Carrier
(24) Cup
(25) Collapsible Spacer
(26) Bearing
(27) Shim
(28) Pinion Gear
(29) Shim
(30) Cup
(31) Differential Carrier Assembly
(32) Cover
(33) Bolt
(34) Fill Plug
(35) Vent
(36) Nut
(37) Bracket
(38) Bolt

LTV1900000000784

Fig. 1 Exploded view of Vue rear differential (Part 2 of 2)

9. Slowly lower support stand until coil spring tension is relieved and remove coil spring.
10. Loosen, but do not remove upper control arm to suspension knuckle nut.
11. **Support wheel drive shaft while it is disengaged from wheel hub and bearing assembly to avoid damaging seals.**
12. Place a block of wood against wheel drive shaft spindle and tap with a hammer to release spindle from wheel hub and bearing assembly.
13. Rotate suspension knuckle upward and secure with heavy mechanics wire, or equivalent.
14. Assemble J–45341 and SA9173G or equivalents to wheel drive shaft inner tripod joint.
15. Disengage tripot joint from rear drive module, then remove wheel drive shaft from vehicle.
16. Reference mark propeller shaft flange to rear drive module input flange, then

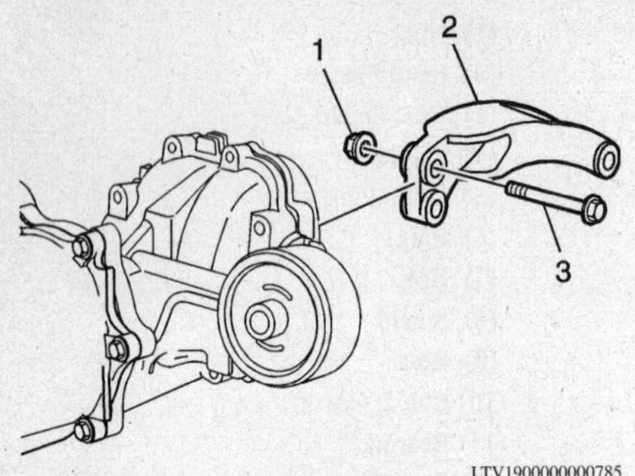

Fig. 2 Rear mounting bracket removal

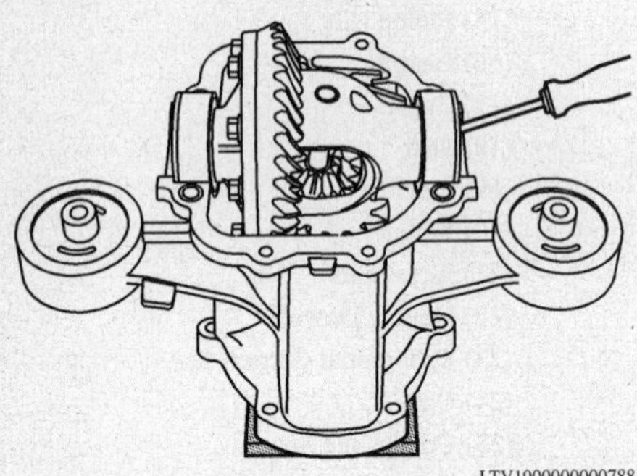

Fig. 5 Differential carrier removal

place a support stand under rear of propeller shaft.
17. Remove propeller shaft flange mounting bolts.
18. Reference mark power take off unit flange to propeller shaft constant velocity joint.
19. Place a support stand under front of propeller shaft, then remove propeller shaft CV joint mounting bolts.
20. While supporting propeller shaft, remove support bearing mounting bolts from vehicle underbody.
21. Remove propeller shaft from vehicle, then place a support stand under RDM to secure.
22. Remove RDM bracket to bushing mounting nut and bolt.
23. Remove nut and bolt from RDM mounting bracket then bracket.
24. Remove RDM support mounting nuts and discard nut.
25. Remove RDM mounting bolts, then RDM from vehicle.

AXLE SHAFT SEAL

REPLACE

1. Raise and support vehicle, then remove wheel and tire assembly.
2. Remove rear wheel drive shaft as outlined under "Differential Assembly, Replace."
3. Carefully pry out output shaft seal and discard.
4. Reverse procedure to install. Use tool No. J-44809 or equivalent to install seal.

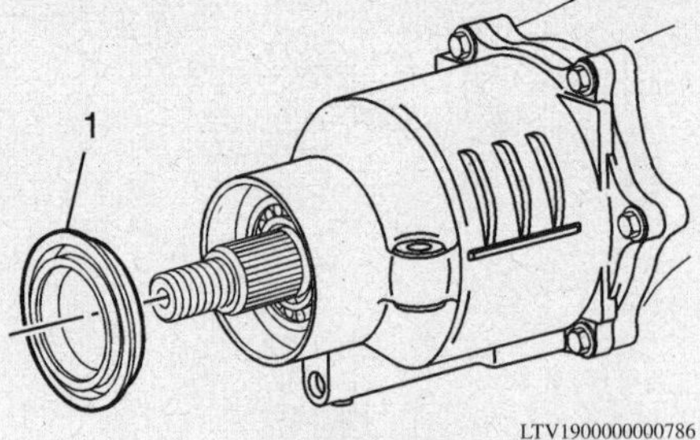

Fig. 3 Input flange oil seal removal

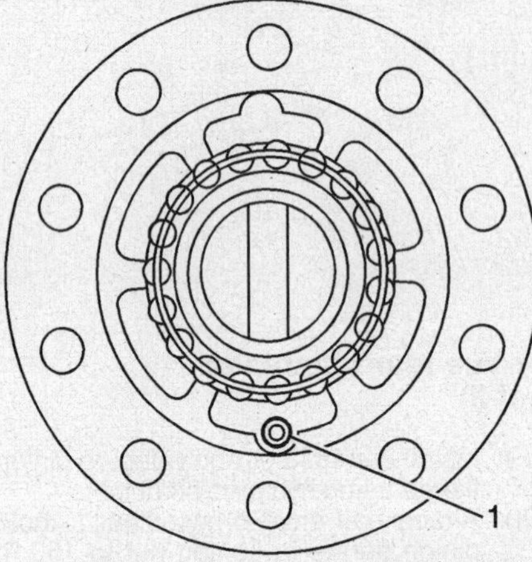

Fig. 6 Lock pin location

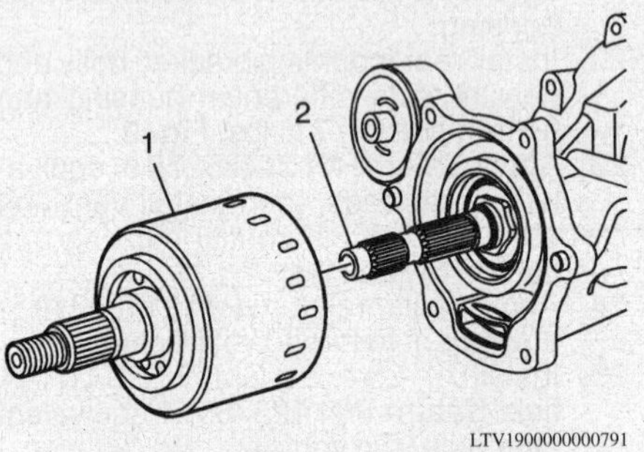

Fig. 8 Clutch drum installation

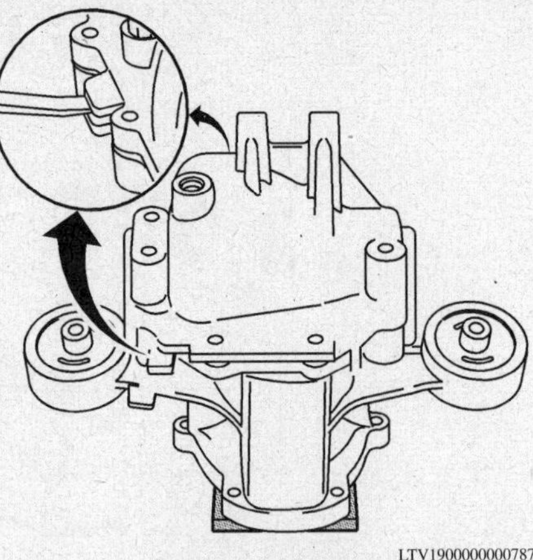

Fig. 4 Rear cover pry point locations

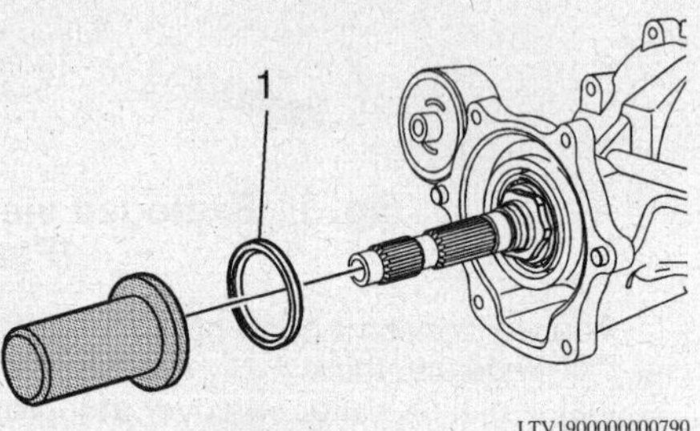

Fig. 7 Clutch drum rear oil seal installation

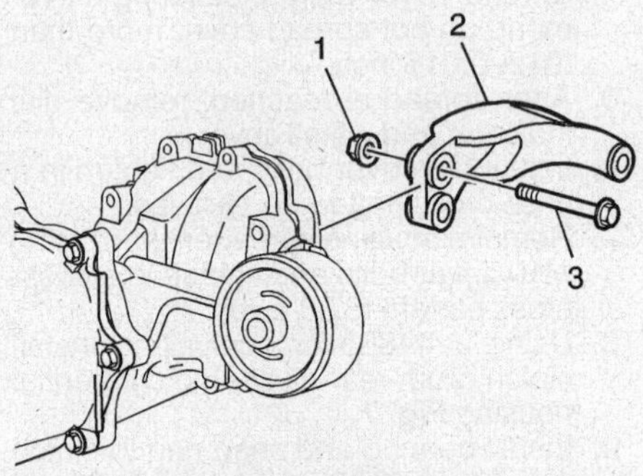

Fig. 9 Rear mounting bracket installation

UNIVERSAL JOINTS

INDEX

CONSTANT VELOCITY (CV)

Refer to "Front Wheel Drive Axles" chapter under "Inner Tri-Pot Seal & Joint,""Outer Joint" and "Outer Joint Seal" for Constant Velocity (CV) joint service.

CROSS & ROLLER

Precautions

Avoid jamming, bends or over-angulation of any propeller shaft components during removal and installation.

Avoid damaging the propeller weld yokes and slip yoke ears during removal and installation.

Never clamp propeller shaft tubing in a vice. Always clamp one of the yokes and support shaft horizontally.

Avoid damaging slip yoke sealing surface. Nicks may damage the bushing or cut the lip seal.

Description

The cross and roller type universal joint is a cross-shaped spider joint connecting two Y-shaped yokes, **Fig. 1.** Four caps with needle bearings and grease seals are mounted on the cross or spider trunnions. The bearings and caps are pressed into the yokes and held in place with either snap rings or injected plastic.

When design angles of more than 3–4° are exceeded, joints wear faster than normal.

Original equipment joints are lubricated for life and cannot be lubricated on the vehicle. A service kit consisting of a spider bearing and snap rings may be installed if a universal joint becomes worn or noisy. The propeller shaft must be removed to replace the universal joint. Refer to the appropriate chassis section for propeller shaft removal and installation.

Production universal joints cannot be reassembled because the bearing caps do no have bearing retainer grooves.

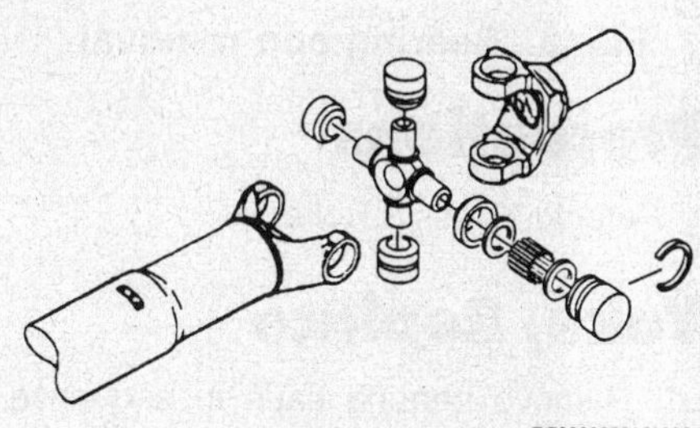

Fig. 1 Cross & roller type universal joint

Component Replacement

REMOVAL

EXTERNAL SNAP RING

1. Mark shaft for assembly reference.
2. Support shaft in horizontal line with suitable press table.
3. Remove snap rings, **Fig. 2.** If ring does not snap out of groove, relieve pressure on ring by tapping lightly on bearing cup.
4. Place joint so lower ear is supported with suitable 1⅛ inch socket and press lower bearing cup out of yoke ease using in universal joint bearing separator tool No. J-9522-3, or equivalent, **Fig. 3.**
5. If cup is not completely removed, insert spacer tool No. J-9522-5, or equivalent, between seal and bearing cup then continue to press cup of yoke, **Fig. 4.**
6. Rotate propeller shaft and press opposite cup out, then remove cross from yoke.
7. Remove reaming universal joint components from yoke.
8. If removing front universal joint, remove slip yoke bearings cups in same manner.

NYLON INJECTED RING

1. Mark shaft for assembly reference.
2. Support shaft in horizontal line with suitable press table.
3. Place joint so lower ear is supported with suitable 1⅛ inch socket and press lower bearing cup out of yoke ease shearing plastic retaining ring using in universal joint bearing separator tool No. J-9522-3, or equivalent, **Fig. 3.**
4. If cap is not completely removed, insert spacer tool No. J-9522-5, or equivalent, between seal and bearing cup then continue to press cup of yoke, **Fig. 4.**
5. Rotate propeller shaft and press opposite cup out, then remove cross from yoke.
6. Remove reaming universal joint components from yoke.
7. If removing front universal joint, remove slip yoke bearing cups in same manner.
8. Clean sheared plastics from bearing retainer groves. **Sheared plastic may prevent proper seating of new bearing cups.**

INSPECTION

1. Inspect retaining ring groves for dirt, corrosion or old ring pieces.
2. Inspect bearing cup bores for burrs or imperfections.

INSTALLATION

1. Coat needle bearings with thin layer of suitable grease using finger.
2. Put one bearing cup part way into one side of yoke and insert cross into cup so trunnion seats freely into cup, **Fig. 5.**
3. Turn yoke sear towards bottom.
4. Press cross and cap into yoke until cup is flush with yoke ear.
5. Press opposite cup into yoke, ensure trunnion alignment, **Fig. 6.**
6. Continue to press cup into yoke ear while working cross to ensure free, unbinding movement until retainer groove clears inside of yoke. **If binding occurs, stop pressing and inspect for misaligned bearings.**
7. Snap retainers into place, **Fig. 7.** Yoke can be sprung slightly with firm hammer blow if retainer is difficult to seat, **Fig. 8.**

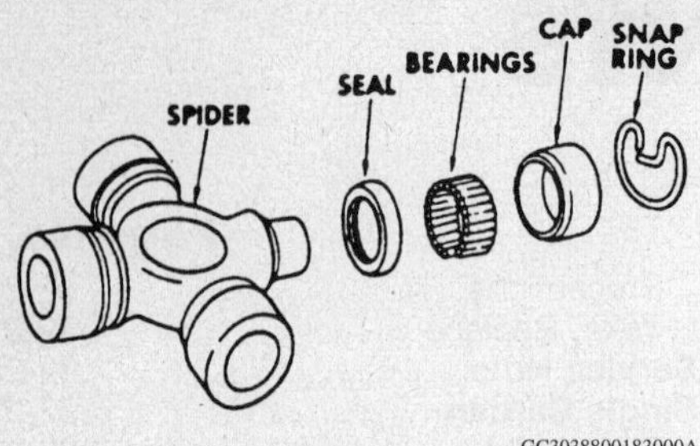

Fig. 2 External snap ring universal joint

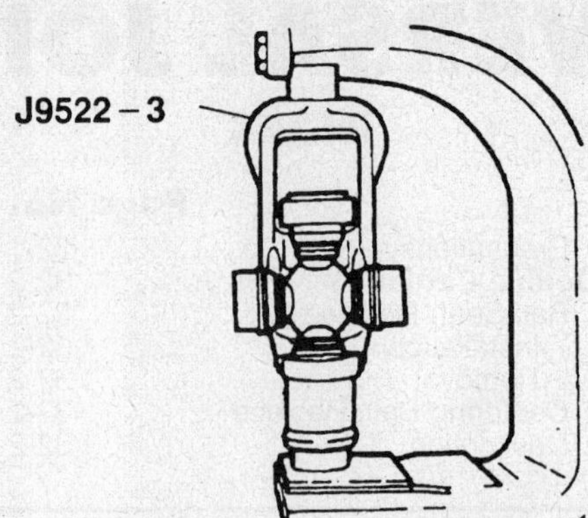

Fig. 3 Bearing cup removal

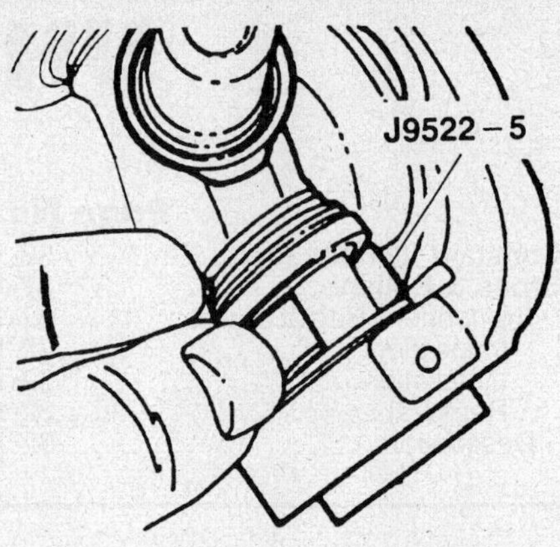

Fig. 4 Bearing cup removal w/spacer

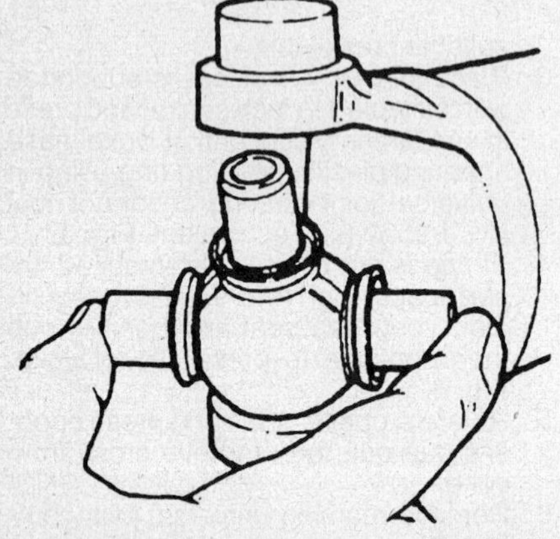

Fig. 5 Cross into cup installation

SINGLE CARDAN

Precautions

Refer to "Cross & Roller."

Description

A single Cardan universal joint and splined slip yoke are located at the transmission or transfer case output shaft where they are held in alignment by a bushing. The slip yoke permits fore and aft movement of the propeller shaft as the differential assembly moves up and down.

Lubricate the spline internally with transmission lubricant. An oil seal prevents leakage and protects the slip yoke from dust, dirt and other harmful material.

DOUBLE CARDAN

Description

A double Cardan joint consists of two single joints connected by a special link yoke. A ball and socket centering device is located between the cross to maintain their relative positions. The double Cardan joint attaches a propeller shaft rear to the differential assembly. A second universal joint may be used where the propeller shaft flange mates with the pinion flange.

Precautions

Refer to "Cross & Roller."

Yoke, Replace

1. Remove bearing caps in sequence, **Fig. 9.**
2. Mark yoke for installation reference.
3. Remove cross & roller.
4. Reverse procedure to install.

Centering Ball, Replace

1. Disassemble flange yoke.
2. Inspect ball seat bushing for wear. Replace yoke and cross as required.
3. Inspect seal and ball seats with spring and washers. Replace entire set as required.
4. Inspect centering ball surface. Replace as required.
5. Clean all plastic from yokes grooves by driving suitable small pin or punch through injection holes.
6. Disassemble shaft in suitable bench vise.
7. Remove ball from stud using ball puller tool No. J-23996-2, or equivalent, **Fig. 10.**
8. Reverse procedure to install. Position new ball on stud and drive until bottomed using CV replacement ball installer tool No. J-23996-1, or equivalent, and suitable hammer, **Fig. 11.**

Ball Seat, Replace

REMOVAL

1. Remove centering ball.
2. Pry grease seal from ball housing. **Do not damage seal bore.**
3. Remove large washer, seats, small washer and spring.
4. Wash housing thoroughly using suitable mineral spirits.
5. Dry bore with compressed air.

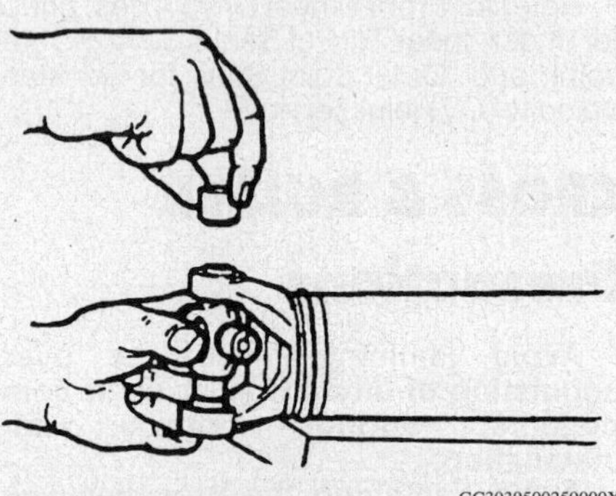

Fig. 6 Cross trunnions between cups alignment

INSTALLATION

1. Liberally grease ball seat housing with suitable grease.
2. Grease and install new spring, small washer, seats and large washer.
3. Install grease seal with lip facing down and using seal installer tool No. J-23694, or equivalent, and suitable hammer to tap until flush with housing, **Fig. 12.**
4. Liberally lubricate seat assembly and seal with suitable grease.
5. Align ball support yoke and cross assembly reference marks in flange yoke, then install bearing cups.

SERVICE NOTE

Before disassembling any universal joint, examine the assembly carefully and note the position of the grease fitting (if used). Also, be sure to mark the yokes in relation to the propeller shaft for assembly reference. Failure to observe these precautions may produce rough vehicle operation resulting in rapid wear and components failure, as well as placing an unbalanced load on transmission, engine and rear axle.

When universal joints are disassembled for lubrication or inspection, and the old components are to be installed, special care must be exercised to avoid damage to universal joint spider or cross and bearing cups.

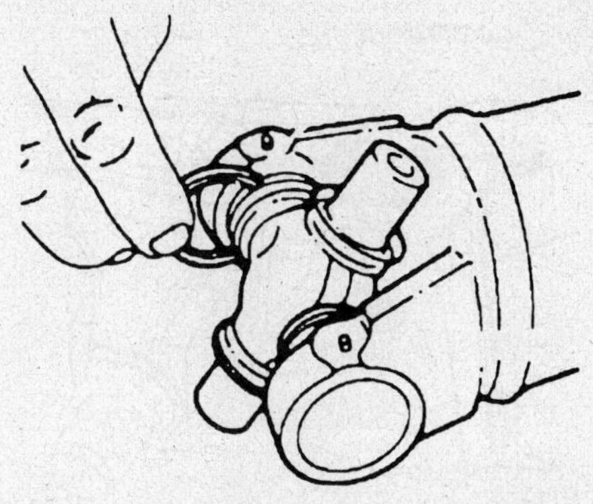

Fig. 7 Retaining ring installation

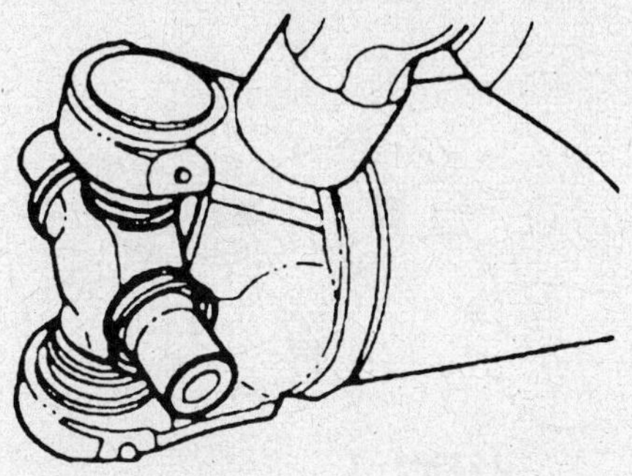

Fig. 8 Snap ring seating

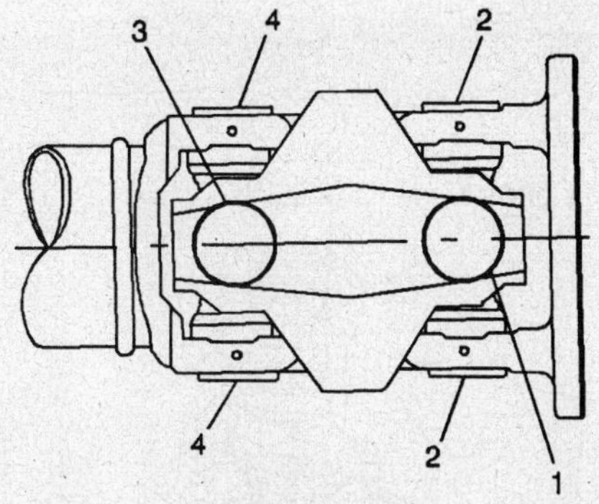

Fig. 9 Bearing cap removal sequence

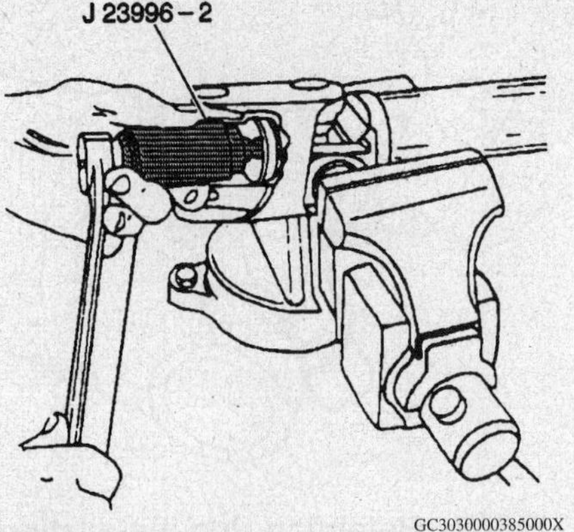

Fig. 10 Centering ball removal

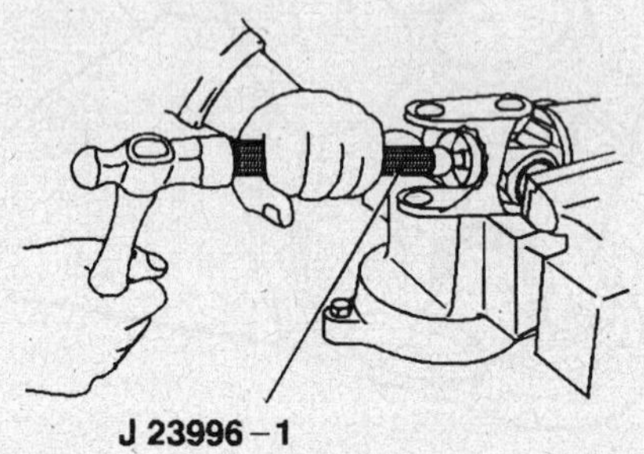

Fig. 11 Centering ball installation

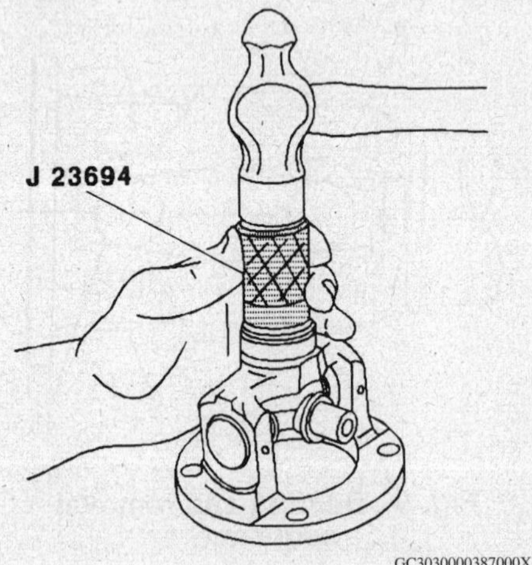

Fig. 12 Seal installation

ENGINE REBUILDING SPECIFICATIONS

INDEX

CYLINDER HEAD, VALVE GUIDE & VALVE SEATS

All specifications given in inches, unless otherwise noted.

Engine Liter	Year	Cylinder Head Warpage Limit	Valve Guides			Valve Seats			
			Inside Diameter	Stem To Guide Clearance		Seat Angle, Degrees	Seat Contact Width		Runout
				Intake	Exhaust		Intake	Exhaust	
2.0L	2002–04	.0020	.23620–.23660	.0008–.0027	.0018–.0035	45	.0430–.0512	.0430–.0512	.0030
2.2L (L4)	2002–03	.0100	.27500–.27600	.0007–.0020	.0014–.0029	45	.1100	.1380	.0020
2.2L (L61)	2002–06	.0040	.23620–.23670	.0012–.0022	.0020–.0026	—	—	—	.0020
2.4L	2006	.0040	.23620–.23670	.0012–.0022	.0020–.0026	—	—	—	.0020
2.5L	2002–04	.0020	.23620–.23670	.0008–.0027	.0018–.0035	45	.0433–.0512	.0433–.0512	—
2.8L	2004–06	.0030	—	.0011–.0025	.0015–.0030	—	—	—	.0020
3.0L	2002–03	.0020	.23620–.23670	.0012–.0022	.0016–.0026	45	—	—	—
3.4L	2002–06	.0050	.31500	.0010–.0027	.0010–.0027	45	.0610–.0710	.0670–.0790	.0015
3.5L (LX9)	2004–06	.0040	—	.0010–.0027	.0010–.0027	46	.0610–.0710	0670–.0790	—
3.5L (L52)	2004–06	.0030	—	.0011–.0025	.0015–.0030	—	—	—	.0020
3.6L	2004–06	.0030	.23620–.23670	.0010–.0026	.0014–.0030	45	.0394–.0551	.0551–.0709	.0020
3.9L	2004–06	.0040	—	.0010–.0027	.0010–.0027	46	.0610–.0710	.0670–.0790	—
4.2L	2002–06	.0030	—	.0011–.0025	.0015–.0030	—	—	—	.0020
4.3L	2002–05	.0040	—	.0010–.0037	.0010–.0037	46	.0400–.0650	.0650–.0980	.0020
4.6L	2004–06	.0020	—	.0011–.0043	.0020–.0047	46	.0165–.0323	.0512–.0669	.0020
4.8L	2002–06	②	—	.0010–.0037	.0010–.0037	46	.0400	.0700	.0020
5.0L	2002	.0040	—	.0010–.0037	.0010–.0037	46	.0450–.0700	.0650–.0980	.0020
5.3L	2002–06	②	—	.0010–.0037	.0010–.0037	46	.0400	.0700	.0020
5.7L	2002	.0040	—	.0010–.0037	.0010–.0037	46	.0400–.0650	③	.0020
6.0L	2002–06	②	—	.0010–.0037	.0010–.0037	46	.0400	.0700	.0020
6.5L①	2002	④	—	.0010–.0027	.0010–.0027	46	.0351–.0603	.0618–0930	.0020
6.6L①	2002–06	.0030	—	.0079	.0079	45	.0984	.0984	—
8.1L	2002–06	⑤	—	.0010–.0039	.0012–.0041	46	.0030–.0060	.0060–.0950	.0020

① — Diesel engine.
② — Within 6-inch area, .004 inch; overall length .008 inch.
③ — Light duty, .065–.098 inch; heavy duty, .059–.101 inch.
④ — Replace head if warpage exceeds .003 inch laterally or .006 inch longitudinally. Resurfacing is not recommended.
⑤ — .002 inch over 6 inches, .004 inch over entire face.

VALVE SPRINGS

All specifications given in inches, unless otherwise noted.

Engine Liter	Year	Free Length	Out Of Square Limit	Installed Height	Pressure, Lbs. @ Inches			
					Closed		Open	
					Intake	Exhaust	Intake	Exhaust
2.0L	2002–04	②	.0790	—	③	③	—	—
2.2L (L4)	2002–03	1.9100	—	1.7010	73.1–81.2 @ 1.6000	72.8–81.2 @ 1.6000	201–215 @ 1.175	201–215 @ 1.175
2.2L (L61)	2002–06	—	—	—	—	—	—	—
2.4L	2006	—	—	—	—	—	—	—
2.5L	2002–04	⑤	④	—	—	—	—	—
2.8L	2004–06	—	—	—	47.4–52.4 @ 1.379	47.4–52.4 @ 1.379	130–142 @ .965	130–142 @ .965
3.0L	2002–03	—	—	—	—	—	—	—
3.4L	2002–06	1.8900	—	1.7010	75 @ 1.7010	75 @ 1.7010	230 @ 1.260	230 @ 1.260
3.5L (LX9)	2004–06	1.9100	—	1.7400	77 @ 1.7400	77 @ 1.7400	234 @ 1.299	234 @ 1.299
3.5L (L52)	2004–06	—	—	—	47.4–52.4 @ 1.379	47.4–52.4 @ 1.379	130–142 @ .965	130–142 @ .965
3.6L	2004–06	1.6555-1.7657	—	—	56-61 @ 1.378	56-61 @ 1.378	134–149 @ .945	134–149 @ .945
3.9L	2004–06	1.8900	—	1.7010	75 @ 1.7010	75 @ 1.7010	230 @ 1.260	230 @ 1.260
4.2L	2002–06	—	—	—	47.5–52.5 @ 1.7010	47.5–52.5 @ 1.7010	130–142 @ 1.260	130–142 @ 1.260
4.3L	2002–05	2.0200	—	1.6700–1.7000	76–84 @ 1.7000	76–84 @ 1.7000	187–203 @ 1.270	187–203 @ 1.270
4.6L	2004–06	1.6059-1.7201	—	—	47.4–52.4 @ 1.379	47.4–52.4 @ 1.379	130–142 @ .965	130–142 @ .965
4.8L	2002–06	2.0800	—	1.8000	76 @ 1.8000	76 @ 1.8000	220 @ 1.320	220 @ 1.320
5.0L	2002	2.0200	—	1.6700–1.7000	76–84 @ 1.7000	76–84 @ 1.7000	187–203 @ 1.270	187–203 @ 1.270
5.3L	2002–06	2.0800	—	1.8000	76 @ 1.8000	76 @ 1.8000	220 @ 1.320	220 @ 1.320
5.7L	2002	2.0200	—	1.6700–1.7000	76–84 @ 1.7000	76–84 @ 1.7000	187–203 @ 1.270	187–203 @ 1.270
6.0L	2002–06	2.0800	—	1.8000	76 @ 1.8000	76 @ 1.8000	220 @ 1.320	220 @ 1.320
6.5L①	2002	—	—	1.8110	80 @ 1.8000	80 @ 1.8000	230 @ 1.400	230 @ 1.400
6.6L①	2002–06	2.2283	.0787	1.6142	71 @ 1.6142	71 @ 1.6142	—	—
8.1L	2002–06	2.2180	—	1.8080–1.8380	86–94 @ 1.8080	86–94 @ 1.8080	216–236 @ 1.338	216–236 @ 1.338

① — Diesel engine.
② — Inner 1.3780–1.4204 inches; outer 1.5441–1.5921 inches.
③ — Inner, 15.1–17.5 lbs. @ 1.08 inches; Outer, 33.9–39.2 lbs. @ 1.25 inches.
④ — Inner: .063 inch. Outer: .070 inch.
⑤ — Inner: 1.3780 inches. Outer: 1.5441 inches.

VALVES

All specifications given in inches, unless otherwise noted.

Engine Liter	Year	Stem Diameter Std.		Installed Height	Guide Protrusion	Maximum Tip Refinish	Face Angle, Degrees	Margin⑤		Valve Lash④
		Intake	Exhaust					Intake	Exhaust	
2.0L	2002–04	.2339–.2344	.2348–.2354	—	.5300	—	45	.0240–.0390	.0280–.0470	—
2.2L (LN2)	2002–03	—	—	—	—	—	45	.0400–.0610	.0870–.0800	—
2.2L (L61)	2002–06	.2344–.2355	.2337–.2343	—	—	—	—	—	—	—
2.4L	2006	.2344–.2355	.2337–.2343	—	—	—	—	—	—	—
2.5L	2002–04	.2348–.2354	.2339–.2344	—	—	—	45	—	—	—
2.8L	2004–06	—	—	—	—	—	—	—	—	—
3.0L	2002–03	.2344–.2350	.2341–.2346	1.54300	1.5430	—	45	—	—	—

Continued

VALVES—Continued

All specifications given in inches, unless otherwise noted.

Engine Liter	Year	Stem Diameter Std.		Installed Height	Guide Protrusion	Maximum Tip Refinish	Face Angle, Degrees	Margin⑤		Valve Lash④
		Intake	Exhaust					Intake	Exhaust	
3.4L	2002–06	—	—	1.70100	—	—	45	.0830	.1060	②
3.5L (LX9)	2004–06	—	—	—	—	—	—	—	—	—
3.5L (L52)	2004–06	—	—	—	—	—	—	—	—	—
3.6L	2004–06	.2344–.2352	.2341–.2348	—	—	—	45	—	—	—
3.9L	2004–06	—	—	1.70100	—	—	45	—	—	—
4.2L	2002–06	—	—	—	—	—	—	—	—	—
4.3L	2002–05	—	—	1.69000–1.78000	—	—	45	.3100	.3100	②
4.6L	2004–06	.2331–.2339	.2331–.2339	—	—	—	45	—	—	—
4.8L	2002–06	.3130–.3140	.3130–.3140	—	—	—	45	.0500	.0500	②
5.0L	2002	.3410–.3416	.3410–.3416	—	—	③	45	.3100	.3100	②⑥
5.3L	2002–06	.3130	.3130	.71200–.75200	—	—	45	.0500	.0500	②
5.7L	2002	.3410–.3416	.3410–.3416	.03937–.07874	—	③	45	.3100	.3100	②⑥
6.0L	2002–06	.3130–.3140	.3130–.3140	.71200–.75200	—	—	45	.0500	.0500	②
6.5L①	2002	—	—	1.80000	.4800–.3800	③	45	—	—	—
6.6L①	2002–06	.2800	.2800	—	—	—	45	.0287	.0394	—
8.1L	2002–06	.3715–.3722	.3713–.3720	—	—	—	45	—	—	—

① — Diesel engine.
② — Net lash, no adjustment.
③ — Grind only enough to provide true surface. After grinding valve stems, ensure sufficient clearance remains between rocker arm & valve spring cap or rotator.
④ — Cold.
⑤ — Minimum.
⑥ — One turn after lash is removed.

CAMSHAFT

All specifications given in inches, unless otherwise noted.

Engine Liter	Year	Camshaft Journal Diameter	Camshaft Bearing Clearance	Camshaft Endplay	Camshaft Runout (Max.)	Lifter Bore Diameter	Lifter Diameter	Lifter To Bore Clearance
2.0L	2002–04	1.0220–1.0228	.0008–.0047	—	.0039	1.2205–1.2214	1.2189–1.2194	.0059
2.2L (LN2)	2002–03	1.8680–1.8690	.0015–.0035	—	.0010	—	—	—
2.2L (L61)	2002–06	1.0604–1.0614	—	.0016–.0057	—	—	—	—
2.4L	2006	1.0604–1.0614	—	.0016–.0057	—	—	—	—
2.5L	2002–05	1.0220–1.0228	.0008–.0047	—	.0039	1.2205–1.2214	1.2188–1.2194	—
2.8L	2004–06	⑤	.0015–.0033	⑥	—	—	—	—
3.0L	2002-03	1.0990–1.1000	.0015–.0020	.0016–.0057	—	—	1.2820–1.2980	.0010–.0026
3.4L	2002–06	1.8680–1.8690	.0010–.0039	—	.0010	—	—	—
3.5 (LX9)	2004–06	1.8680–1.8690	—	—	.0001	.8430–.8440	—	—

Continued

CAMSHAFT—Continued

All specifications given in inches, unless otherwise noted.

Engine Liter	Year	Camshaft Journal Diameter	Camshaft Bearing Clearance	Camshaft Endplay	Camshaft Runout (Max.)	Lifter Bore Diameter	Lifter Diameter	Lifter To Bore Clearance
3.5 (L52)	2004–06	⑤	.0015–.0033	⑥	—	—	—	—
3.6L	2004–06	④	.0016–.0033	.0018–.0085	.0002	—	.4523–.4724	.0015–.0016
3.9L	2004–06	2.0240–2.0250	—	—	.0010	.8430–.8440	—	—
4.2L	2002–06	⑤	.0015–.0033	⑥	—	—	—	—
4.3L	2002–05	1.8677–1.8696	—	.0010–.0090	.0026	—	—	—
4.6L	2004–06	1.0610-1.0619	.0016–.0035	0050–.0087	.0002	.4730–.4739	.4719–.4724	.0015–.0016
4.8L	2002–06	2.1640–2.1660	—	.0010–.0120	.0020	.8430–.8440	—	—
5.0L	2002	1.8677–1.8697	—	.0020–.0120	.0026	—	—	—
5.3L	2002–06	2.1640–2.1660	—	.0010–.0120	.0010	.8430–.8440	—	—
5.7L	2002	1.8677–1.8697	—	.0040–.0120	.0026	—	—	—
6.0L	2002–06	2.1640–2.1660	—	.0010–.0120	.0020	.8430–.8440	—	—
6.5L①	2002	③	②	.0020–.0120	—	—	—	—
6.6L①	2002–06	2.3984–2.4001	—	.0079	.0020	—	—	—
8.1L	2002–06	1.9477–1.9497	—	—	.0030	.8430–.8440	—	—

① — Diesel engine.
② — Except No. 5, .0010–.0046 inches; No. 5, .0008–.0044 inches.
③ — Except No. 5, 2.1642–2.1659 inches; No. 5, 2.0069–2.0086 inches.
④ — Front number 1, 1.3779-1.3787 inches; middle and rear numbers 2-4, 1.0605-1.0614 inches.
⑤ — All intake and exhaust cylinders 2–7, 1.0612–1.0622 inches; exhaust cylinder #1, 1.1794–1.1804 inches.
⑥ — Exhaust, .0017–.0084 inch; intake, .0020–.0079 inch.

CRANKSHAFT, BEARINGS & RODS

All specifications given in inches, unless otherwise noted.

Engine Liter	Year	Crankshaft Journals				Bearing Clearance			Connecting Rods	
		Main Bearing Journal Diameter	Connecting Rod Journal Diameter	Maximum Out Of Round All	Runout Service Limit	Main Bearings	Connecting Rod Bearings	Thrust Bearing	Pin Clearance	Side Clearance
2.0L	2002–04	④	⑫	.00040	.0023	.0010–.0023	.00180–.00310	.0039–.0165	—	.00990–.01770
2.2L (L4)	2002–03	2.4945–2.4954	1.9983–1.9994	.00019	—	.0006–.0019	.00098–.00310	—	.00040–.00090	.00390–.01490
2.2L (L61)	2002–06	2.2045–2.2050	1.9291–1.9297	—	—	.0012–.0026	.00110–.00270	—	—	—
2.4L	2006	2.2045-2.2050	1.9291-1.9297	—	—	.0012–.0026	.0011–.0027	—	—	.0028–.0146
2.5L	2002–04	—	—	.00040	—	.0016–.0022	.00990–.01570	—	—	—
2.8L	2004–06	2.7567-2.7574	—	.0002	—	.0004–.0025	.00080–.00250	—	—	—
3.0L	2002–03	⑨	1.9270–1.9280	.00120	—	.0006–.0017	—	—	—	—
3.4L	2002–06	2.6473–2.6483	1.9987–1.9994	.00020	.0016	0008–.0025	.00070–.01700	.0012–.0030	.00060–.00180	.00700–.01700
3.5L (LX9)	2004–06	2.6473-2.6483	2.2480-2.2490	.00020	.0016	.0008–.0025	.00070–.01700	—	—	.0080–.0090

Continued

CRANKSHAFT, BEARINGS & RODS—Continued

All specifications given in inches, unless otherwise noted.

Engine Liter	Year	Crankshaft Journals				Bearing Clearance			Connecting Rods	
		Main Bearing Journal Diameter	Connecting Rod Journal Diameter	Maximum Out Of Round All	Runout Service Limit	Main Bearings	Connecting Rod Bearings	Thrust Bearing	Pin Clearance	Side Clearance
3.5L (L52)	2006	2.7567-2.7574	—	.0002	—	.0004–.0025	.00080–.00250	—	—	—
3.6L	2004–06	2.6768-2.6775	2.2044–2.2050	.0002	.0012	.0004–.0024	.0004–.0028	.0030–.0120	—	.0374–.0140
3.9L	2004–06	2.6473-2.6483	2.2480-2.2490	.0002	.0016	⑭	.00070–.01700	—	—	.0080–.0090
4.2L	2002–06	2.7567–2.7574	—	.00020	—	.0004–.0025	.00080–.00250	—	—	—
4.3L	2002–05	⑪	2.2487–2.2497	.00100	.0010	⑦	.00100–.00250	—	00080–.00160⑩	.00600–.01700
4.6L	2004–06	2.5335-2.5341	2.1239-2.1245	.00020	.0016	.0006–.0025	.0010–.0030	—	—	.0079–.0197
4.8L	2002–06	2.5580–2.5593	2.0987–2.1000	.00040	.0020	.0008–.0025	.00090–.00300	—	.00078–.00169⑩	.00430–.02000
5.0L	2002	⑥	2.0986–2.0998	.00100	.0015	⑧	.00100–.00250	—	.00080–.00160⑩	.00600–.02700
5.3L	2002–06	2.5580–2.5593	2.0987–2.1000	.00015–.00030	.0002	.0008–.0025	.00090–.00300	—	.00078–.00169⑩	.00433–.02000
5.7L	2002	⑥	2.0986–2.0998	.00100	.0015	⑧	.00100–.00250	—	.00080–.00160⑩	.00600–.02700
6.0L	2002–06	2.5580–2.5593	2.0987–2.1000	.00300	.0002	.0008–.0025	.00090–.00300	—	.00078–.00169⑩	.00433–.02000
6.5L①	2002	③	②	.00033	—	⑤	.00700–.02500	—	.00020–.00120	.00670–.02500
6.6L①	2002–06	3.1453–3.1466	2.4756–2.4772	—	.0173	.0015–.0055	.00140–.00390	—	—	.01220–.02130
8.1L	2002–06	2.7482–2.7489	2.1990–2.1996	.00040	.0020	⑬	.00080–.00320	—	—	.01510–.02700

① — Diesel engine.
② — Yellow, 2.3987–2.3991 inches; green, 2.3990–2.4000 inches.
③ — Blue: except No. 5, 2.9517–2.9520 inches; No. 5, 2.9515–2.9518 inches. Orange or red: except No. 5, 2.9520–2.9524 inches; No. 5, 2.9518–2.9522 inches. White: except No. 5, 2.9524–2.9527 inches; No. 5, 2.9522–2.9525 inches.
④ — Journal No. 1, 2.2832–2.2834 inches; Journal No. 2, 2.2830–2.3832 inches, & Journal No. 3, 2.2828–2.2829 inches.
⑤ — Journal Nos. 1–4, .0018–.0033 inch; No 5, .0022–.0037 inch.
⑥ — Journal No. 1, 2.4484–2.4493 inches; Journals Nos. 2–4 , 2.4481–2.4491 inches; Journal No. 5, 2.4482–2.4491 inches.
⑦ — Journal No. 1, .0010–.0020 inch; Journals Nos. 2–4 , .0010–.0025 inch.
⑧ — Journal No. 1, .001–.002 inch; Journals Nos. 2–4 , .0010–.0025 inch; Journal No. 5, .0015–.0025 inch.
⑨ — Green, 2.6763–2.6766 inch; brown, 2.6766–2.6770 inch.
⑩ — Interference fit.
⑪ — Journal No. 1, 2.4488–2.4495 inches; Journals Nos. 2 & 3, 2.4485–2.4494 inches; Journal No. 4, 2.4480–2.4489 inches.
⑫ — Letter A, 2.4409–2.4411 inches; Letter B, 2.4412–2.4414 inches, & Letter C, 2.4414–2.4416 inches.
⑬ — Number 1, 2, 3, & 4 journals, .0008–.0035 inch; number 5 journal, .0014–.0040 inch.
⑭ — Crankshaft main bearing clearance except #3, .0008–.0025 inches; crankshaft main bearing clearance - #3, 0012–.0030 inches

BALANCE SHAFT

All specifications given in inches, unless otherwise noted.

Engine Liter	Year	Journal Bearing Diameter		Rear Bearing Journal Clearance
		Front	Rear	
2.2L (L61)	2002–06	①	①	—
2.4L	2006	①	①	.0012–.0025
4.3L	2002–06	2.1648–2.1654	1.4994–1.5000	.0010–.0035

① — Bearing journal diameter, .7874–.7882 inch; bushing journal diameter, 1.4458–1.4466 inch.

PISTONS, PINS & RINGS

All specifications given in inches, unless otherwise noted.

Engine Liter	Year	Piston Diameter (Std.)③	Piston Clearance	Piston Pin Diameter (Std.)	Pin To Piston Bore Clearance	Piston Rings End Gap②		Piston Rings Side Clearance	
						Comp.	Oil	Comp.	Oil
2.0L	2002–04	3.3063–3.3066	.00080–.00150	.8267–.8268	.00010–.00050	.0079–.0276	.0079–.0709	.0012–.0027	.00080–.00230
2.2L (L4)	2002–03	3.5036–3.5043	.00059–.00185	.8001–.8002	.00031–.00071	.0100–.0200	.0100–.0300	.0020–.0035	.00050–.00870
2.2L (L61)	2002–06	3.3845–3.3851	.00040–.00160	.7872–.7874	.00010–.00050	.0080–.0160	.0100–.0300	.0015–.0031	.00350–.00420
2.4L	2006	3.3845–3.3851	.00040–.00160	.7872–.7874	.00010–.00050	.0080–.0160	.0100–.0300	.0015–.0031	.00350–.00420
2.5L	2002–04	3.3063–3.3067	.00080–.00150	.8266–.8268	.00010–.00050	.0079–.0137	.0079–.0275	.0008–.0023	—
2.8L	2004–06	3.6603-3.6616	0.0006-0.0014	.9054–.9055	.00012–.0005	⑱	.0098–.0299	⑲	.0023–.0085
3.0L	2002–03	⑩	.00100–.00180	.8267	.00010–.00030	.0118–.0196	.0157–.0551	.0008–.0015	.00040–.00120
3.4L	2002–06	⑪	.00130–.00270	.9052–.9054	.00040–.00080	.0060–.0140	.0098–.0303	.0020–.0330	.02800–.003700
3.5L (LX9)	2004–06	3.6990	.0030	.9447–.9448	.0003–.0006	㉑	.0100–.0290	㉒	.0040
3.5L (L52)	2004–06	3.6627-3.6633	0004–.0017	.9054–.9055	.00012–.0005	⑳	.0098–.0299	⑲	.0023–.0085
3.6L	2004–06	3.6990-3.6998	.0010–.0021	.9448–.9449	.0002–.0005	㉕	.0059–.0236	㉖	.0012–.0067
3.9L	2004–06	3.8950	.0030	.9420–.9430	.00008–.0004	㉓	.060–.0250	㉔	.0040
4.2L	2002	3.6603–3.6616	.00060–..00140	.9054–.9055	.00012–.00050	.0059–.0018	.0098–.0299	.0017–.0037	.00230–.00850
4.3L	2002–05	—	.00070–.00290	.9270–.9271	.00050–.00100	⑫	.0100–.0290	.0012–.0033	.00300–.00790
4.6L	2004–06	3.6597-3.6603	—	.9053–.9055	.0001–.0005	⑧	.0098–.0299	.0016–.0037	—
4.8L	2002–06	3.7790–3.7800	.00140–.0060	.9447–.9448	.00027–.00082	⑬	.0070–.0320	⑭	.00050–.00780
5.0L	2002	—	.00070–.00260	.9270–.9271	.00050–.00100	.0100–.0250	.0100–.0350	.0015–.0030	.00200–.00900
5.3L	2002–06	3.7800	.00140–.00280	.9447–.9448	.00027–.00082	⑬	.0070–.0320	⑭	.00050–.00780
5.7L	2002	—	.00070–.00260	.9270–.9271	.00050–.00100	.0090–.0190	.0100–.0350	.0012–.0035	00180–.00390
6.0L	2002–06	⑮	.00090–.00280	.9447–.9448	.00040–.00080	.0125–.0189	.0125–.0320	.00157–.00346	.00040–.00866
6.5L①	2002	⑥	④	⑨	00040–.00060	⑤	.0098–.02001	.0015–.0031	.00160–.00350
6.6L①	2002–06	4.0531–4.0535	—	1.3563	.00070	⑯	.0059–.0472	⑰	.00040–.00470
8.1L	2002–03	—	—	1.0400–1.0401	—	⑦	.0150–.0450	.0012–.0029	.00200–.00800

① — Diesel engine.
② — Minimum.
③ — Measured at 90° angle to piston pin.
④ — Cylinders Nos. 1–6, .0035–.0049 inch; Cylinders Nos. 7 & 8, .0040–.0054 inch.
⑤ — Piston Nos. 1–6, .0100–.0224 inch; piston Nos. 7 & 8, .0115–.0240 inch.
⑥ — Production standard, 4.0498–4.0505 inches; Service Hi Limit, 4.00513–4.0520 inches.
⑦ — First compression ring, .018–.027 inch; second compression ring, .026–.039 inch.
⑧ — First compression ring, .0098–.0157 inch; second compression ring, .0138–.0020 inch.
⑨ — Green, 1.2203–1.2204 inches; orange, 1.2204–1.2205 inches.
⑩ — Select fit designation stamped on top of piston. (8), 3.3834–3.3828 inch, (99), 3.3838–3.3842 inch, (00), 3.3842–3.3846 inch, (01), 3.3846–3.3850 inch, (02), 3.3850–3.3854 inch.
⑪ — Cylinders 1–4, 3.621–3.622 inch, cylinders 5–6, 3.621–3.623 inches.
⑫ — First compression ring, .010–.020 inch; second compression ring, .015–.031 inch.
⑬ — First compression ring, .009–.0196 inch; second compression ring, .0173 inch–.030 inch.
⑭ — First compression, .00157–.00335 inch; second compression, .00157–.0031 inch.
⑮ — 4.0002–4.0016 inch measured over skirt coating.
⑯ — First compression ring, .0118–.0539 inch; second compression ring, .0197–.0531 inch.
⑰ — First compression ring, .0030–.0102 inch; second compression ring, .0004–.0039 inch.

⑱ — First compression ring, .00787-.0157 inch; second compression ring, .0142–.0201 inch.
⑲ — First compression ring, .0017–.0037 inch; second compression ring, .0021–.0037 inch.
⑳ — First compression ring, .00790-.0157 inch; second compression ring, .0142–.0201 inch.
㉑ — First compression ring, .0070–.0150 inch; second compression ring, .0190–.0290 inch.
㉒ — First compression ring, .0010–.0030 inch; second compression ring, .0020–.0030 inch.
㉓ — First compression ring, .0060–.0110 inch; second compression ring, .0020–.0030 inch.
㉔ — First compression ring, .0010–.0020 inch; second compression ring, .0007–.0020 inch.
㉕ — First compression ring, .0059–.0118 inch; second compression ring, .0110–.0189 inch.
㉖ — First compression ring, .0012–.0026 inch; second compression ring, .0006–.0024 inch.

CYLINDER BLOCK

All specifications given in inches, unless otherwise noted.

Engine Liter	Year	Bore Diameter (Std.)	Out Of Round (Max.)	Taper (Max.)	Deck Warpage Limit
2.0L	2002–04	3.3071–3.3090	.0039	.0039	.0024
2.2L (L4)	2002–03	3.5036–3.5043	.0005	.0005	②
2.2L (L61)	2002–06	3.3861	.0004	.0004	.0031
2.4L	2006	3.4668-3.4675	.0004	.0004	.0031
2.5L	2002–04	3.3075–3.3078	.0039	.0039	.0024
2.8L	2004–06	3.6638-3.6644	.0005	.0005	.0030
3.0L	2002–03	③	.0026	.0003	—
3.4L	2002–06	3.6220–3.6230	.0010	.0010	.0050
3.5L (LX9)	2004–06	3.8970-3.8980	.0011	.0011	⑦
3.5L (L52)	2004–06	3.6638-3.6644	.0005	.0005	.0030
3.6L	2004–06	3.7005-3.7011	.0005	.0005	—
3.9L	2004–06	3.8970-3.8980	.0011	.0011	⑦
4.2L	2002–03	3.6638-3.6644	.0005	—	.0030
4.3L	2002–05	4.0007–4.0017	.0020	.0010	.0020–.0060
4.6L	2004–06	3.6611-3.6617	.0039	.0039	.0039
4.8L	2002–06	3.7799–3.7806	—	.0007	④
5.0L	2002	3.7360–3.7381	.0020	.0010	.0040
5.3L	2002–06	3.7799–3.7806	—	.0007	④
5.7L	2002	4.0007–4.0017	.0020	.0010	—
6.0L	2002–03	4.0007–4.0017	—	④	.0030
6.5L①	2002	⑤	.0008⑥	.0008⑥	.0030
6.6L①	2002–06	4.0551–4.0594	.0006	.0006	—
8.1L	2002–06	4.2496–4.2516	.0020	.0020	.0040

① — Diesel engine.
② — Maximum resurface, .010 inch.
③ — Select fit stamped on block. (8), 3.3848–3.3852 inch, (99), 3.3852–3.3856 inch, (00), 3.3856–3.3860 inch, (01), 3.3860–3.3864 inch, (02), 3.3864–3.3868 inch.
④ — .004 inch in 6-inch area; .008 overall.
⑤ — Production standard (mark J): Cylinders Nos. 1–6, 4.0540–4.0547 inches; Cylinders Nos. 7 & 8, 4.0545–4.0552 inches. Production O.S. (mark S): Cylinders Nos. 1–6, 4.0597–4.0602 inches; Cylinders Nos. 7 & 8, 4.0602–40607 inches.
⑥ — Add .0005 inch for cylinders Nos. 7 & 8.
⑦ — .0019 inch per 5.905 inches.

ENGINE REBUILDING SPECIFICATIONS

OIL PUMP

All specifications given in inches, unless otherwise noted.

Engine Liter	Year	Rotor Backlash	Rotor To Body Clearance	Rotor End Clearance②	Gear Pocket		Rotor Thickness	Rotor Diameter	Relief Valve To Body Clearance
					Depth	Diameter			
2.0L	2002–04	—	.0043	.0059	—	—	—	—	—
2.2L (L4)	2002–03	.0091–.0201	.0010–.0040	.0020–.0070	1.195–1.198	1.50300–1.50600	1.199–1.200	1.498–1.500	.0015–.0035
2.2L (L61)	2002–06	—	—	—	—	—	—	—	—
2.4L	2006	—	—	—	—	—	—	—	—
2.5L	2002–04	—	.0059	.0043	—	—	—	—	—
2.8L	2004–06	—	—	—	.614–.615	3.429–3.430	④	⑤	.1010–.0640
3.0L	2002–03	—	.0110	.0060	—	—	—	—	—
3.4L	2002–06	.0037–.0077	.0010–.0030	.0020–.0050	1.202–1.204	1.50300–1.50500	1.199–1.200	1.498–1.500	.0015–.0035
3.5L (LX9)	2004–06	.0037–.0077	.0010–.0030	.0020–.0050	1.202–1.204	1.50300–1.50500	1.199–1.200	1.498–1.500	.0015–.0035
3.5L (L52)	2004–06	—	—	—	.614–.615	3.42900–3.43000	④	⑤	.1010–.0640
3.6L	2004–06	—	—	—	.6128–.6142	3.4360–3.4380	.6107–.6117	2.0988–2.0998	.0018–.0043
3.9L	2004–06	.0037–.0077	.0010–.0030	.0020–.0050	1.202–1.204	1.50300–1.50500	1.199–1.200	1.498–1.500	.0015–.0035
4.2L	2002–06	—	—	—	.614–.615	3.42900–3.43000	④	⑤	.5750–.5740
4.3L	2002–06	③	③	③	③	③	③	③	③
4.6L	2004–06	③	③	③	③	③	③	③	③
4.8L	2002–06	③	③	③	③	③	③	③	③
5.0L	2002	③	③	③	③	③	③	③	③
5.3L	2002–06	③	③	③	③	③	③	③	③
5.7L	2002	③	③	③	③	③	③	③	③
6.0L	2002–06	③	③	③	③	③	③	③	③
6.5L①	2002	③	③	③	③	③	③	③	③
6.6L①	2002–06	—	.0049–.0087	—	—	.78784	—	—	—
8.1L	2002–03	—	—	—	—	—	—	—	—

① — Diesel engine.

② — Measured between pump cover mating surface & end of rotors using straight edge & suitable feeler gauges.

③ — Pump rotor & body are not serviced separately. If inspection reveals damaged or worn components, the pump must be replaced as a complete assembly.

④ — Drive gear, .611–.613 inch; driven, .605–.611 inch.

⑤ — Drive, 2.893–2.891 inch; driven, 3.428–3.426 inch.

ABBREVIATIONS & ACRONYMS

AAC: Auxilliary Air Control
AAV: Anti Afterburn Valve
ABS: Anti-Lock Brake System
A/C: Air Conditioning
A/C ATS: A/C Ambient Temperature Switch
ACC: Accessory Position
ACL: Air Cleaner
ACM: Air Bag Control Module
ACR-4: Air Conditioning Refrigerant, Recovery, Recycling, Recharging
ACT: Air Charge Temperature
A/D: Analog to Digital
AECM: Air Bag Electronic Control Module
A/F: Air/Fuel
AIR: Secondary Air Injection
AIRB: Secondary Air Injection Bypass
AIRD: Secondary Air Injection Diverter
AIS: Air Injection System
AIS: Automatic Idle Speed
ALDL: Assembly Line Diagnostic Link
AM1: Thermactor Air Management 1
AM2: Thermactor Air Management 2
AP: Accelerator Pedal
API: American Petroleum Institute
APP: Accelerator Pedal Position
APPS: Accelerator Pedal Position Sensor
ARS: Automatic Restraint System
ASD: Auto Shutdown Device
ASDM: Air Bag System Diagnostic Module
ASR: Automatic Slip Regulation
AT: Automatic Transmission
ATC: Active Transfer Case
ATDC: After Top Dead Center
AWD: All Wheel Drive
B+: Battery Positive Voltage
B-: Battery Negative Voltage
BAP: Barometric Atmosphere Pressure
BAR: Bureau Of Auto Repair
BARO: Barometric Pressure
BB: Barrel
BCDD: Boost Control Deceleration Device
BCI: Battery Council International
BCM: Body Control Module
BID: Breakerless Inductive Discharge
BOB: Breakout Box
BOO: Brake On/Off
BP: Barometric Pressure
BPA: Bypass Air
BPT: Backpressure Transducer
BTDC: Before Top Dead Center
BTS: Battery Temperature Sensor
BVSV: Bi-Metal Vacuum Switching Valve
BVT: Backpressure Variable Transducer
B+: Battery Positive Voltage
C: Continuous Memory
CA: California
CAA: Clean Air Act
CAB: Controller Anti-Lock Brakes
CAC: Charge Air Cooler
CALPAK: Device On FI To Allow Fuel Delivery In Event Of PROM Or ECM Malfunction
CANP: Canister Purge
CARB: California Air Resources Board
CAT: Catalytic Converter
CAT: Charge Air Temperature
CBD: Closed Bowl Distributor
CC: Catalytic Converter
CCA: Center Control Assembly
CCC: Computer Command Control
CCC: Converter Clutch Control Solenoid
CCCI: Computer Controlled Coil Ignition
CCD: Chrysler Collision Detection
CCD: Computer Controlled Dwell
CCD+: Chrysler Collision Detection Bus (+)
CCD–: Chrysler Collision Detection Bus (–)
CCECS: Computer Controlled Emission Control System
CCO: Converter Clutch Overdrive Solenoid
CCOT: Cycling Clutch Orifice Tube
CCP: Carbon Canister Purge
CCRM: Constant Control Relay Module
CEC: Computerized Emission Control System
CES: Clutch Engage Switch
CFI: Continuous Fuel Injection
CFRM: Condenser Fan Relay Module
CID: Cubic Inch Displacement
CID: Cylinder Identification
CIS: Constant Injection System
CIS-E: Constant Injection System Electronic
CKP: Crankshaft Position Sensor
CKT: Circuit
CL: Closed Loop
CLECS: Closed Loop Emission Control System
CLFCS: Closed Loop Fuel Control System
CMFI: Central Multi-Port Fuel Injection
CMP: Camshaft Position Sensor
CMTC: Compass/Mini-Trip Computer
CNG: Compressed Natural Gas
CO: Carbon Monoxide
COP: Coil On Plug
CO2: Carbon Dioxide
CP: Canister Purge
CPP: Clutch Pedal Position
CPS: Crankshaft Position Sensor
CPU: Central Processing Unit
CSF: Crankshaft Speed Fluctuation
CSFI: Central Sequential Fuel Injection
CTM: Central Timer Module
CTO: Coolant Temperature Override
CTOX: Continuous Trap Oxidizer
CTP: Closed Throttle Position
CTS: Coolant Temperature Sensor
CV: Constant Velocity
CVCC: Compound Vortex Controlled Combustion
CVVT: Continuous Variable Valve Timing
CYL: Cylinders
CYP: Cylinder Position
C3: Computer Command Control
C3I: Computer Controlled Computer Ignition
C-4: Computer Controlled Catalytic Convertor
DAB: Driver Air Bag
DCL: Data Communications Link
DCP: Duty Cycle Purge
DDS: Driveline Disengagement Switch
DEC: Diesel Engine Control
DERM: Diagnostic Energy Reserve Module
DFI: Direct Fuel Injection
DI: Distributor Ignition
DIC: Driver Information Center
DIS: Direct Or Distributorless Ignition System
DLC: Data Link Connector
DME: Digital Motor Electronics
DMIVA: Distributor Mounted Ignition Vacuum Advance
DOHC: Dual Overhead Camshaft
DPFE: Differential Pressure Feedback EGR
DPI: Dual Plug Ignition
DRB: Diagnostic Readout Box
DRB II: Diagnostic Readout Box II
DRB II: Diagnostic Readout Box II
DRB III: Diagnostic Readout Box III
DRL: Daytime Running Lamps
DS-I: Dura Spark I Ignition System
DS-II: Dura Spark II Ignition System
DSAS: Deceleration Spark Advance System
DTC: Diagnostic Trouble Code
DTM: Diagnostic Test Mode
DVOM: Digital Volt Ohm-Meter
EAT: Electronically Controlled Automatic Transaxle Or Transmission
EATXII: Electronic Automatic Transmission Controller 2nd Generation
EBCM: Engine Brake Control Module
EBL: Electric Back Lite
EBP: Exhaust Back Pressure
ECA: Electronic Control Assembly
ECCS: Electronic Concentrated Engine Control System
ECI: Electronic Control Injection
ECITS: Electronic Ignition Timing System
ECL: Engine Coolant Level
ECM: Engine Control Module
ECS: Evaporative Control System
ECT: Engine Coolant Temperature Sensor
ECTF: Cooling Fan Engine Coolant Temperature
ECU: Engine Control Unit
EDF: Electro Drive Fan
EDFI: Electronic Diesel Fuel Injection
EDI: Electronic Controlled Direct Ignition System
EDIS: Electronic Distributorless Ignition System
EDL: Engine Data Line
EEC: Electronic Engine Control
EEC-I: Electronic Engine Control I
EEC-II: Electronic Engine Control II
EEC-III: Electronic Engine Control III
EEC-IV: Electronic Engine Control IV
EEC-V: Electronic Engine Control V
EEGR: Electronic EGR Valve
EEPROM: Electronic Erasable Programmable Read Only Memory
EET: Electronic EGR Transducer
EETS: Electric EGR Transducer Solenoid
EFC: Electronic Fuel Control
EFE: Early Fuel Evaporation
EFI: Electronic Fuel Injection
EGO: Exhaust Gas Oxygen Sensor
EGR: Exhaust Gas Recirculation
EGRC: EGR Control
EGRT: EGR Temperature
EGRV: EGR Vent
EI: Electronic Ignition
EIC: Electronic Instrument Cluster
EICU: Electronic Ignition Control Unit
EITC: Electronic Ignition Timing Control
ELB: Electronic Lean Burn System
ELC: Electronic Level Control
ELCD: Evaporative Loss Control Device

ABBREVIATIONS & ACRONYMS

ELD: Electric Load Detector
EM: Engine Modification
EMCC: Electronic Modulated Converter Clutch
EMI: Electromagnetic Interference
EMR: Electronic Module Retard
EOP: Engine Oil Pressure
EOT: Engine Oil Temperature
EPA: Environmental Protection Agency
EPC: Electronic Pressure Control
EPP: Engine Position Pulse
EPR: Exhaust Back Pressure Regulator
EPT: EGR Pressure Transducer
ESA: Electronic Spark Advance
ESC: Electronic Spark Control
ESS: Engine Speed Sensor
EST: Electronic Spark Timing
ETC: Electronic Temperature Control
ETCS-i: Electronic Throttle Control System-Itelligent
ETW: Equivalent Test Weight
EVAP: Evaporative Emission
EVIC: Electronic Vehicle Information Center
EVO: Electronic Variable Orifice
EVP: EGR Valve Position
EVR: Electronic Voltage Regulator
EVSV: Electronic Vacuum Switching Valve
EWL: Engine Warning Lamp
EWMA: Exponentially Weighted Moving Average
EZL: Electronic Ignition System With Variable Characteristics
FC: Fan Control
FDCS: Fuel Demand Command Signal
FED: Federal (49 State)
FEEPROM: Flash Electrically Erasable Programmable Read Only Memory
FEPROM: Flash Electrically Programmable Read Only Memory
FF: Flexible Fuel
FI: Fuel Injected Or Fuel Injection
FMEM: Failure Mode Effects Management
FMI: Failure Mode Identifiers
FPCM: Fuel Injection Pump Control Module
FPM: Fuel Pump Monitor
FPRC: Fuel Pressure Regulator Control
FR: Fillpipe Restrictor
FSS: Flexible Service System
FTP: Federal Test Procedure
FWD: Front Wheel Drive
GEN: Generator
GFD: Generic Field Data
GFP: Gaseous Fuel Prep
GPC: Glow Plug Control
GPL: Glow Plug Wait Lamp
GPM: Gallons Per Minute
gpm: Grams Per Million
GPR: Glow Plug Relay
GVW: Gross Vehicle Weight
GVWR: Gross Vehicle Weight Rating
HAI: Heated Air Intake
HC: Hydrocarbon
HCU: Hydraulic Control Unit
HD: Heavy Duty
HDC: Heavy Duty Emission Cycle
HE: Hall Effect
HEDF: High Electro Drive Fan
HEGO: Heated Exhaust Gas Oxygen Sensor
HEI: High Energy Ignition
HEUI: Hydraulically Actuated Electronically Controlled Unit Injectors
HF: High Fuel Economy
HFAN: High Speed Cooling Fan
HFC: High Fan Control
HFM: Hot Film Air Mass Sensor
Hg: Mercury
HIC: Hot Idle Compensation
HO2S: Heated Oxygen Sensor
HO: High Output
HPTBI: High Pressure TBI
HSC: High Swirl Combustion
HSIA: High Speed Inlet Air Conditioning
HVS: High Voltage Switch Ignition System
H2O: Water Column
IAC: Idle Air Control
IACV-AAC: Idle Air Control Valve-Auxilliary Air Control Valve
IAT: Intake Air Temperature
IC: Ignition Control
ICM: Ignition Control Module
ICP: Injector Control Pressure
ICS: Ignition Control System
ICTO: Ignition Coolant Temperature Overide
ID: Inner Diameter
IDI: Integrate Direct Ignition
IDM: Injector Driver Module
IDM: Ignition Diagnostic Monitor
IFI: Indirect Fuel Injection
IFS: Inertial Fuel Shutoff
ILC: Idle Load Compensator
ILEV: Inherently Low Emission Vehicle
I/M: Inspection & Maintenance Testing
IMRC: Intake Manifold Runner Control
IMT: Intake Manifold Temperature
IOD: Ignition Current Off Draw
IPR: Ignition Control Pressure Regulator
ISA: Idle Speed Actuator
ISC: Idle Speed Control
ISS: Integrated Idle Stabilization System
ITS: Idle Tracking Switch
IVS: Idle Validation Switch
JTEC: Combined Engine And Transmission Control Module
JTEC: Jeep Truck Powertrain Control Module System
KAM: Keep Alive Memory
KOEO: Key On Engine Off
KOER: Key On Engine Running
KS: Knock Sensor
L: Liter
LCD: Liquid Crystal Display
LD: Light Duty
LDP: Leak Detection Pump
LED: Light Emitting Diode
LEV: Low Emissions Vehicle
LFAN: Low Speed Cooling Fan
LH: Lefthand
LPG: Liquid Propane Gas
LPT: Light Pressure Turbo
LPTBI: Low Pressure TBI
LSIACV: Linear Solenoid Idle Air Control Valve
LTW: Low Tire Warning
LUS: Lock-Up Solenoid
LVW: Loaded Vehicle Weight
MAF: Mass Air Flow
MAP: Manifold Absolute Pressure
MAT: Manifold Absolute Temperature
MBEC: Multiple Board Engine Controller
MC: Mixture Control
MCC: Manifold Catalytic Converter
MCCA: Message Center Control Assembly
M/CCC: Modulated Converter Clutch Control
MCS: Mixture Control System
MCU: Microprocessor Control Unit
MC-VAF: Measuring Core Volume Air Flow
MDP: Manifold Differential Pressure
MDS2: Mopar Diagnostic System 2nd Generation
MEMCAL: Memory Calibration Unit
MFI: Multi-Point Fuel Injection
MIC: Mechanical Instrument Cluster
MID: Message Identifier
MIL: Malfunction Indicator Lamp
MLP: Manual Level Position
MLUS: Modulator Lock-Up Solenoid
MPFI: Multi-Point Fuel Injection
MPI: Multi-Port Injection
MST: Intake Manifold Surface Temperature
MT: Manual Transmission
MTA: Managed Thermactor Air
MTV: Manifold Tuning Valve
MVLPS: Manual Valve Lever Position Switch (See Also PNP Switch)
MUI: Mechanical Unit Injection
MUT II: Multi-Use Tool, Second Edition
MVZ: Manifold Vacuum Zone
NGC: Next Generation Controller
NGS: New Generation Star Tester
NGV: Natural Gas Vehicle
NOx: Oxides Of Nitrogen
NTC: Negative Temperature Coefficient
NVLD: Natural Vacuum Leak Detection
NVRAM: Non-Volatile Random Access Memory
O: Key On Engine Off
OBD: On-Board Diagnostic
OBD II: On-Board Diagnostic Class II
OC: Oxidation Catalytic Converter
OCC: Output Circuit Check
OD: Outer Diameter
ODM: Output Driver Module
ODO: Odometer
OHC: Overhead Cam
OL: Open Loop
ORVR: On Board Refueling Vapor Recovery
OSAC: Orifice Spark Advance Control
OSC: Output State Control
OSS: Output Shaft
OSS: Output Speed Sensor
OTIS: Overhead Travel Information System
OWL: Oil/Water Warning Lamp
O2: Oxygen Sensor
O2S: Oxygen Sensor (Left Sensor When Two Sensors Are Used)
O2SR: Right Oxygen Sensor
PAB: Passenger Air Bag
PAD: Passenger Air Bag Disable
PAG: Polyalkaline Glycol
PAIR: Pulse Secondary Air Injection
PCI: Programmable Communications Interface
PCM: Powertrain Control Module
PCV: Positive Crankcase Ventilation
PDC: Power Distribution Center
PEP: Peripheral Expansion Port
PFE: Pressure Feedback EGR
PG: Pulse Generator
PGM-FI: Programmed Fuel Injection
PGM-IG: Programmed Ignition
PID: Parameter Identifier
PIP: Profile Ignition Pickup
PNP: Park/Neutral Position
PPM: Parts Per Million
PPS: Proportional Purge Solenoid
PRC: Pressure Regulator Control

PROM: Programmable Read Only Memory
PSI: Pounds Per Square Inch
PSP: Power Steering Pressure
PTC: Positive Temperature Coefficient
PTEC: Powertrain Electronic Controller Management System
PTO: Power Take Off
PTOX: Periodic Trap Oxidizer
PVS: Ported Vacuum Switch
PWM: Pulse-Width Modulation
R: Key On Engine Running
RABS: Rear Anti-Locking Braking System
RAM: Random Access Memory
RAP: Retained Accessory Power
RDS: Radio Data System
REDOX: Reduction Oxydation Catalytic Converter
REGT: Recirculated Exhaust Gas Temperature
RFI: Radio Frequency Interference
RH: Righthand
RKE: Remote Keyless Entry
RM: Relay Module
ROM: Read Only Memory
RON: Research Octane Number
RPM: Revolutions Per Minute
RPS: Revolutions Per Second
RWAL: Rear Wheel Anti-Lock Brakes
RWD: Rear Wheel Drive
SAE: Society Of Automotive Engineers
SAS: Speed Adjusting Screw
SAW: Spark Angle Word
SBEC: Single Board Engine Controller (PCM)
SBEC II: Single Board Engine Controller II
SC: Supercharger
SCB: Supercharger Bypass
SCC: Spark Control Computer
SCCS: Speed Control Command Switches
SCI: Serial Communications Interface
SCS: Speed Controlled Spark
SCW: Similar Conditions Window
SFI: Sequential Multi-Port Fuel Injection
SFTP: Supplementary Federal Test Procedure
SHO: Super High Output
SID: Subsystem Identifier
SIL: Shift Indicator Lamp
SIR: Supplemental Inflatable Restraint
SKIM: Sentry Key Immobilizer Module
SKIS: Sentry Key Immobilizer System
SMEC: Single Module Engine Controller
SOHC: Single Overhead Camshaft
SO2: Sulfur Dioxide
SPCS: Spark Plug Switching Control System
SPI: Serial Peripheral Interface
SPK: Spark Control
SPL: Smoke Puff Limiter
SPOUT: Spark Output
SRI: Service Reminder Indicator
SRS: Supplemental Restraint System
SRT: System Readiness Test
SRV: Short Runner Valve
SS: Shift Solenoid
SSI: Solid State Ignition
SST: Special Service Tool
ST: Scan Tool
STAR: Self-Test Automatic Readout
STC: Spark Timing Control
STI: Self-Test Input
STO: Self-Test Output
SULEV: Super Ultra Low Emissions Vehicle
SVO: Special Vehicle Operations
SVT: Special Vehicle Team
TAB: Thermactor Air Bypass Vacuum Solenoid Valve
TAC: Thermal Air Control
TAD: Thermactor Air Diverter Valve
TBI: Throttle Body Injection
TC: Turbocharged
TCC: Torque Converter Clutch
TCM: Transmission Control Module
TCS: Transmission Controlled Spark
TDC: Top Dead Center
TFI-I: Thick Film I Ignition System
TFI-IV: Thick Film IV Ignition System
TFT: Transmission Fluid Temperature
TI: Transistor Ignition System
TLEV: Transitional Low Emission Vehicle
TOT: Transmission Oil Temperature
TP: Throttle Position
TPI: Tuned Port Injection
TPMS: Tire Pressure Monitoring System
TPOUT: Throttle Position Output
TPS: Throttle Position Sensor
TPT: Throttle Position Transducer
TR: Transmission Range
TRS: Transmission Range Sensor
TSB: Technical Service Bulletin
TSP: Throttle Solenoid Positioner
TSS: Transmission Speed Sensor
TSS: Turbine Speed Sensor
TTS: Transaxle Temperature Switch
TV: Throttle Valve
TVP: Throttle Valve Potentiometer
TVS: Thermal Vacuum Switch
TVSV: Thermal Vacuum Shutoff Valve
TVV: Thermal Vacuum Valve
TWC: Three-Way Catalyst
TWC+OC: Three-Way+Oxidation Catalytic Converter
TWC: Three-Way Catalytic Converter
UIC: Universal Integrated Circuit Ignition
ULEV: Ultra Low Emissions Vehicle
UVC: Under Valve Cover
V: Volt
VAF: Volume Air Flow
VANOS: Double Variable Camshaft Control
VAT: Vane Air Temperature
VCM: Vehicle Controll Module
VCRM: Variable Control Relay Module
VCV: Vacuum Control Valve
VDV: Vacuum Delay Valve
VECI: Vehicle Emission Control Information
VEPS: Vehicle Electronic Programming System
VFD: Vacuum Fluorescent Display
VIC: Vehicle Information Center
VICS: Variable Inertia Charging System
VIN: Vehicle Identification Number
VIT: Vehicle Interface Tool
VOM: Volt-Ohm Meter
VOTM: Vacuum Operated Throttle Modulator
VPM: Vehicle Personality Module
VP-20: Bosch VP-20 Diesel Engine Control System
VR: Voltage Regulator
VRE: Vehicle Retarder Enable
V-REF: Voltage Reference
VRV: Vacuum Regulator Valve
VSC: Vehicle Speed Control
VSS: Vehicle Speed Sensor
VTEC: Variable Valve Timing & Valve Lift Electronic Control
VTSS: Vehicle Theft Security System
VVTI: Variable Valve Timing With Intelligence
WAC: Wide Open Throttle A/C Cutoff
WOT: Wide Open Throttle
WOTPS: Wide Open Throttle Position Switch
WSS: Wheel Speed Sensor
WU-OC: Warm Up Oxidation Catalytic Converter
WU-TWC: Warm Up Three-Way Catalytic Converter
X: Equipped
ZEV: Zero Emissions Vehicle
2VH: 2 Valve Head
2WD: Two-Wheel Drive
4VH: 4 Valve Head
4WD: Four-Wheel Drive

NOTES

DECIMAL & MILLIMETER EQUIVALENTS

Inch	Inch	mm
1/64	.015625	.397
1/32	.03125	.794
3/64	.046875	1.191
1/16	.0625	1.587
5/64	.078125	1.984
3/32	.09375	2.381
7/64	.109375	2.778
1/8	.125	3.175
9/64	.140625	3.572
5/32	.15625	3.969
11/64	.17185	4.366
3/16	.1875	4.762
13/64	.203125	5.159
7/32	.21875	5.556
15/64	.234375	5.953
1/4	.25	6.350
17/64	.265626	6.747
9/32	.28125	7.144
19/64	.296875	7.541
5/16	.3125	7.937
21/64	.328125	8.334
11/32	.34375	8.731

Inch	Inch	mm
23/64	.359375	9.128
3/8	.375	9.525
25/64	.390625	9.922
13/32	.40625	10.319
27/64	.421875	10.716
7/16	.4375	11.113
29/64	.453125	11.509
15/32	.46875	11.906
31/64	.484375	12.303
1/2	.5	12.700
33/64	.515625	13.097
17/32	.53125	13.494
35/64	.546875	13.890
9/16	.5625	14.287
37/64	.578125	14.684
19/32	.59375	15.081
39/64	.609375	15.478
5/8	.625	15.875
41/64	.640625	16.272
21/32	.65625	16.669
43/64	.671875	17.065

Inch	Inch	mm
11/16	.6875	17.462
45/64	.703125	17.859
23/32	.71875	18.265
47/64	.734375	18.653
3/4	.75	19.505
49/64	.765625	19.447
25/32	.78125	19.884
51/64	.796875	20.240
13/16	.8125	20.637
53/64	.828125	21.034
27/32	.84375	21.431
55/64	.859375	21.828
7/8	.875	22.225
57/64	.890625	22.622
29/32	.90625	23.019
59/64	.921875	23.415
15/16	.9375	23.812
61/64	.953125	24.209
31/32	.96875	24.606
63/64	.984375	25.003
1	1	25.400

Special Service Tools

Throughout this manual references are made to and illustrations may depict the use of special tools required to perform certain jobs. These special tools can generally be ordered through the dealers of the make vehicle being serviced. It is also suggested that you check with local automotive supply firms as they also supply tools manufactured by other firms that will assist in the performance of these jobs. The vehicle manufacturers special tools are supplied by:

Chrysler Corporation .... Miller Special Tools
OTC Division
28635 Mound Rd.
Warren, Michigan 48092-3499

Ford Motor Company .... SPX Corporation, OTC
ATTN: Ford Rotunda
28635 Mound Rd.
Warren, Michigan 48092-3499

General Motors Corporation .... Kent-Moore
SPX Corporation
28635 Mound Rd.
Warren, Michigan 48092-3499

Manual Information Loca

Front Wheel Drive Models

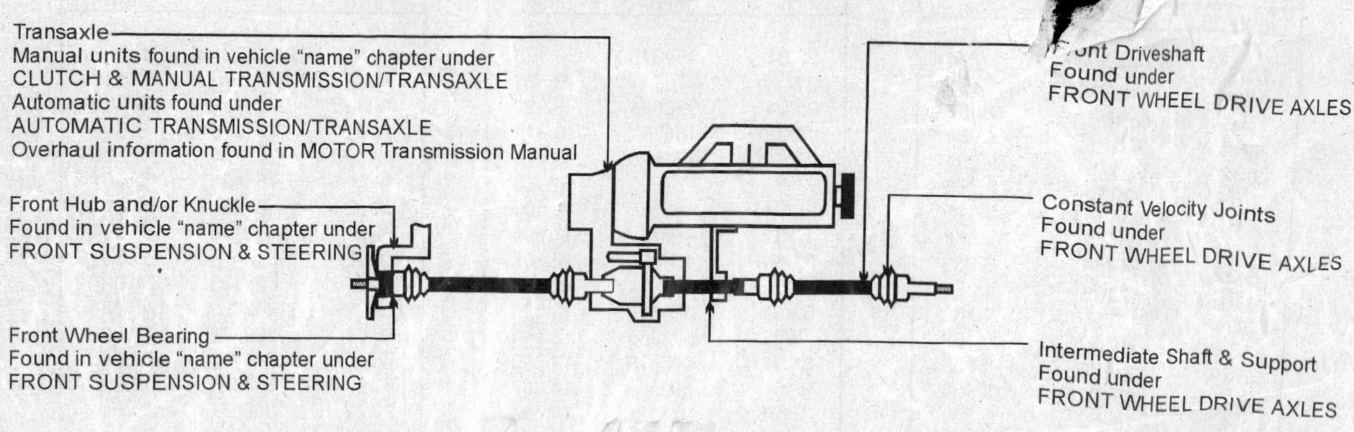

Four Wheel Drive Models

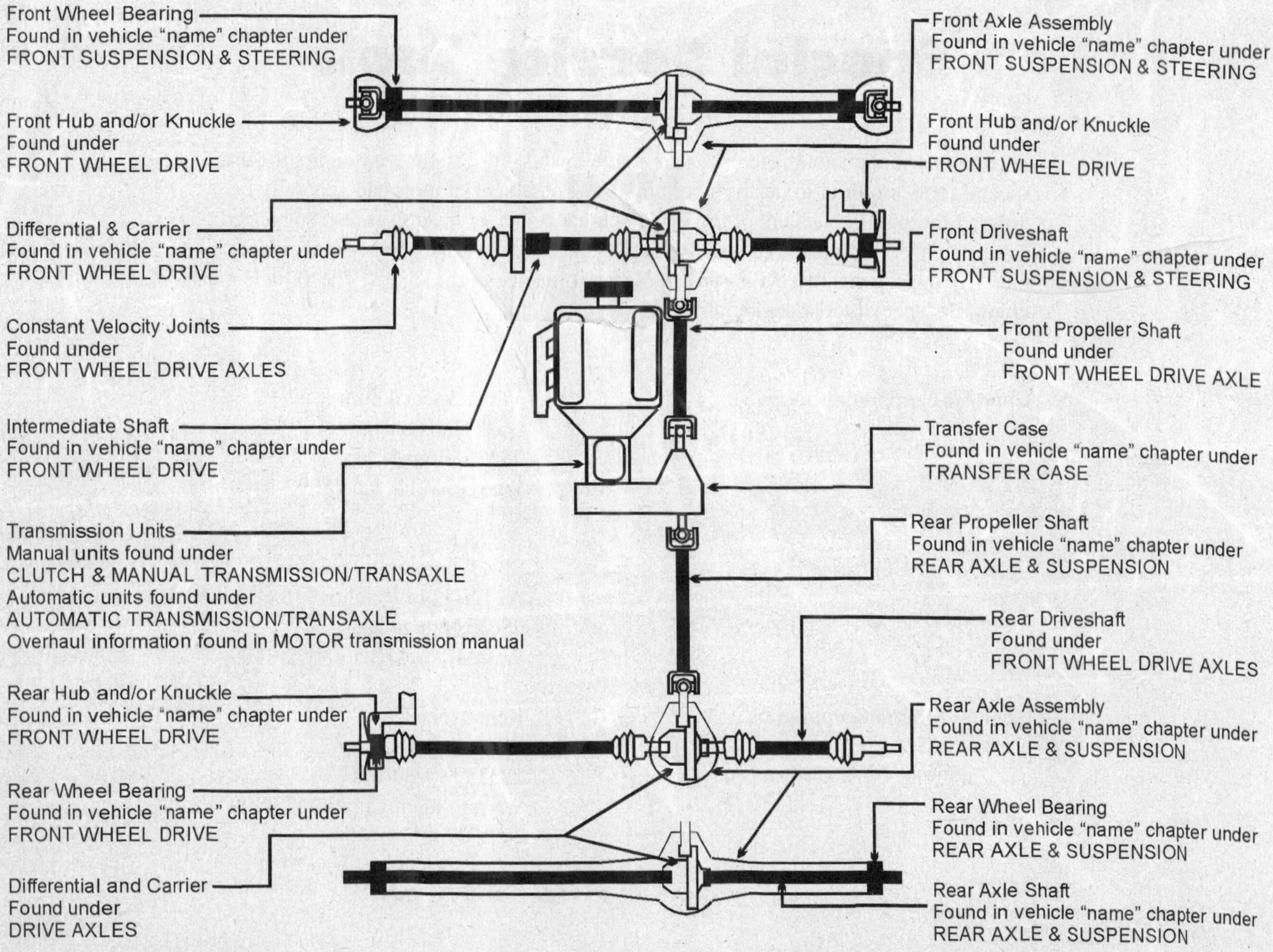

Front Wheel Bearing
Found in vehicle "name" chapter under
FRONT SUSPENSION & STEERING

Front Hub and/or Knuckle
Found under
FRONT WHEEL DRIVE

Differential & Carrier
Found in vehicle "name" chapter under
FRONT WHEEL DRIVE

Constant Velocity Joints
Found under
FRONT WHEEL DRIVE AXLES

Intermediate Shaft
Found in vehicle "name" chapter under
FRONT WHEEL DRIVE

Transmission Units
Manual units found under
CLUTCH & MANUAL TRANSMISSION/TRANSAXLE
Automatic units found under
AUTOMATIC TRANSMISSION/TRANSAXLE
Overhaul information found in MOTOR transmission manual

Rear Hub and/or Knuckle
Found in vehicle "name" chapter under
FRONT WHEEL DRIVE

Rear Wheel Bearing
Found in vehicle "name" chapter under
FRONT WHEEL DRIVE

Differential and Carrier
Found under
DRIVE AXLES

Front Axle Assembly
Found in vehicle "name" chapter under
FRONT SUSPENSION & STEERING

Front Hub and/or Knuckle
Found under
FRONT WHEEL DRIVE

Front Driveshaft
Found in vehicle "name" chapter under
FRONT SUSPENSION & STEERING

Front Propeller Shaft
Found under
FRONT WHEEL DRIVE AXLE

Transfer Case
Found in vehicle "name" chapter under
TRANSFER CASE

Rear Propeller Shaft
Found in vehicle "name" chapter under
REAR AXLE & SUSPENSION

Rear Driveshaft
Found under
FRONT WHEEL DRIVE AXLES

Rear Axle Assembly
Found in vehicle "name" chapter under
REAR AXLE & SUSPENSION

Rear Wheel Bearing
Found in vehicle "name" chapter under
REAR AXLE & SUSPENSION

Rear Axle Shaft
Found in vehicle "name" chapter under
REAR AXLE & SUSPENSION

Manual Information Locator

All Wheel Drive Models

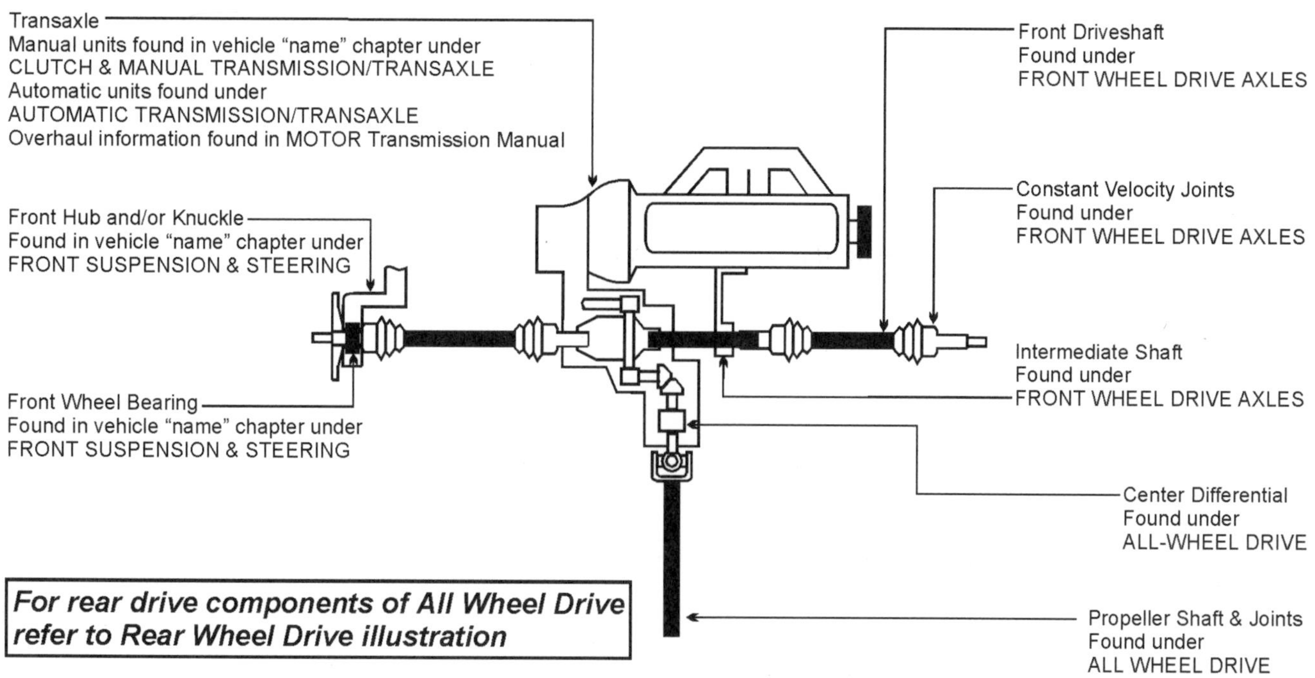

For rear drive components of All Wheel Drive refer to Rear Wheel Drive illustration

Rear Wheel Drive Models

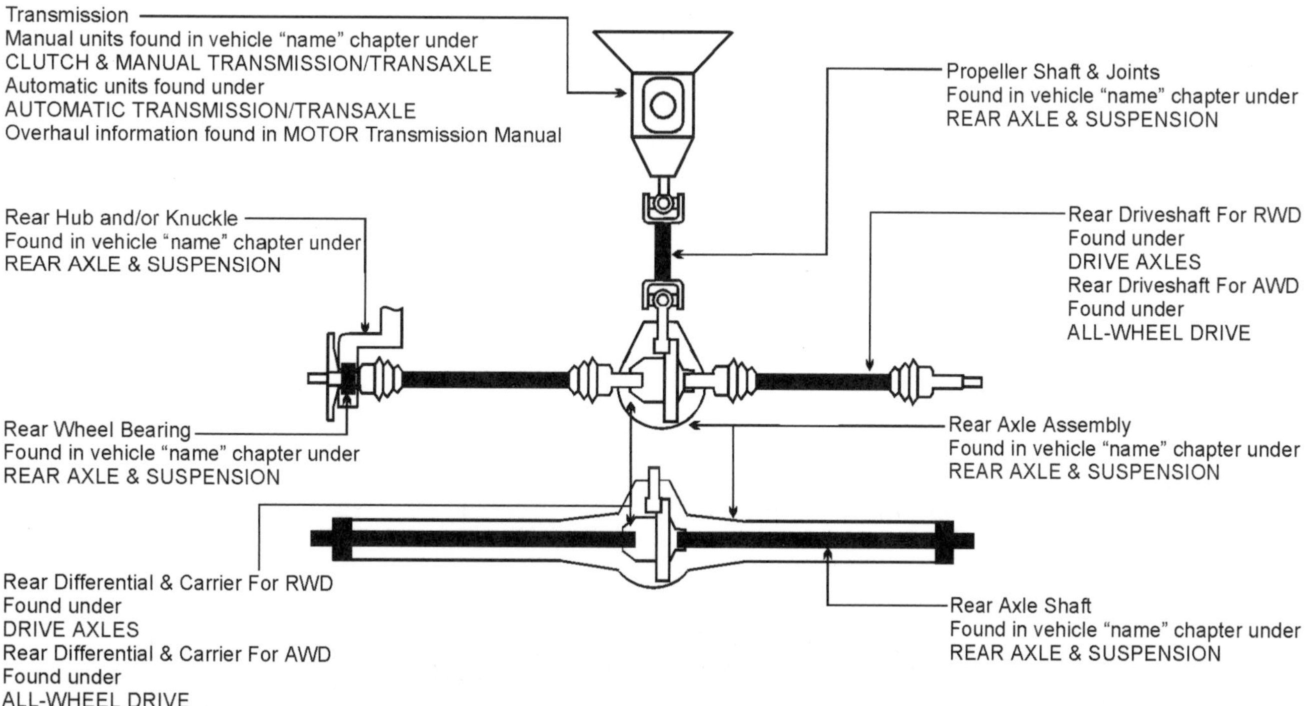

MANUAL INFORMATION LOCATOR—Continued

Operation/Subject/Topic	Light Truck & Van Repair Manual Mechanical Repair	Light Truck & Van Repair Manual ABS/ Electrical	Engine Performance & Driveability Product
Air Bags	—	X	—
Air Bag System Precautions	X	X	X
Air Conditioning	X	—	—
AIR Systems	—	—	X
All-Wheel Drive Systems	X	—	—
Alternator Specifications	X	—	—
Alternator Systems	X	—	—
Anti-Lock Brake Systems	—	X	—
Automatic Seat Belts	—	X	—
Automatic Transaxle In-Vehicle Service	X	—	—
Automatic Transmission In-Vehicle Service	X	—	—
Axle Shaft Service	X	—	—
Back-Up Light Switch, Replace	X	—	—
Balance Shaft Service	X	—	—
Ball Joint Service	X	—	—
Belt Tension Data	X	—	—
Blower Motor, Replace	X	—	—
Brake Booster Service	X	—	—
Brake Service	X	—	—
Camber Adjustment	X	—	—
Camshaft Service	X	—	—
Capacity Data	X	—	—
Caster Adjustment	X	—	—
Catalytic Converters	—	—	X
Clutch Service	X	—	—
Clutch Start Switch, Replace	X	—	—
Coil Pack, Replace	X	—	X
Coil Spring, Replace	X	—	—
Compression Check	X	—	X
Compression Pressures	X	—	X
Computer Relearn Procedures	X	X	X
Computerized Engine Control Systems	—	—	X
Control Arm Service	X	—	—
Cooling System Bleed	X	—	—
Cooling System Data	X	—	—
Crankshaft Pulley, Replace	X	—	—
Crankshaft Rear Oil Seal Service	X	—	—
Cruise Control Systems	—	X	—
Cylinder Block Specifications	X	—	—
Cylinder Head Service	X	—	—
Cylinder Head Specifications	X	—	—
Cylinder Head, Replace	X	—	—
Cylinder Liner, Replace	X	—	—
Dash Panel Service	X	—	—
Differential Service	X	—	—
Dimmer Switch, Replace	X	—	—
Disc Brake Service	X	—	—
Distributor Service	—	—	X
Distributor, Replace	X	—	X
Distributorless Ignition Systems	—	—	X
Drive Axle Service	X	—	—
Drive Belt Tension Data	X	—	—
Drum Brake Service	X	—	—
EGR System	—	—	X
Electric Engine Cooling Fans	X	—	—
Electric Fuel Pumps	X	—	X
Electrical Symbol Identification	X	X	X
Electronic Fuel Injection	—	—	X
Electronic Ignition	—	—	X
Electronic Instrumentation	—	—	X
Electronic Level Controls	—	X	—
Emission Control Application Charts	—	—	X
Emission Controls	—	—	X
Emission Vacuum Hose Routings	—	—	X
Engine Compartment Reference Diagrams	—	—	X
Engine Cooling Fans	X	—	—
Engine Control Module, Replace	—	—	X
Engine Control Unit, Replace	—	—	X
Engine Front Cover Service	X	—	—
Engine Mounts, Replace	X	—	—
Engine Oil Seal Service	X	—	—
Engine Rebuilding Specifications	X	—	—
Engine Repairs	X	—	—
Engine Sensor Location	—	—	X
Engine Sensor Replacement	—	—	X
Engine Sensor Specifications	—	—	X
Engine System Identification Charts	—	—	X
Engine Tightening Specifications	X	—	—
Engine, Replace	X	—	—
Evaporator Core, Replace	X	—	—
Exhaust Gas Recirculation (EGR) Systems	—	—	X
Exhaust Manifold, Replace	X	—	—
Fast Idle Speed Adjustment	—	—	X
Federal Air Quality Standards	—	—	X
Flasher Location	X	—	—
Front Drive Axle Service	X	—	—
Front Wheel Alignment	X	—	—
Fuel Control System Identification	—	—	X
Fuel Filter, Replace	X	—	—
Fuel Injection Systems	—	—	X
Fuel Injector Cleaning Procedures	—	—	X
Fuel Injector, Replace	—	—	X
Fuel Pump Pressure Specifications	X	—	X
Fuel Pump Pressure Test	—	—	X
Fuel Pump Relay Location	X	—	X
Fuel Pump Replacement	X	—	X
Fuse Panel Location	X	—	—
General Engine Specifications	X	—	—
Headlight Switch, Replace	X	—	—
Heated Air Cleaners	—	—	X
Heater Core, Replace	X	—	—
Hub & Bearing Assembly Service	X	—	—
Hydraulic Brake System Service	X	—	—
Hydraulic Engine Cooling Fans	X	—	—
Hydraulic Valve Lifter Service	X	—	—
Idle Mixture Adjustments	—	—	X
Idle Speed Adjustments	—	—	X
Ignition Lock, Replace	X	—	—
Ignition Switch, Replace	X	—	—
Ignition System Application	—	—	X
Ignition Timing Procedures	—	—	X
Instrument Cluster, Replace	X	—	—
Intake Manifold, Replace	X	—	—
Intermittent Malfunction Computer Diagnosis	—	—	X
Knock Sensor, Replace	—	—	X
Leaf Spring, Replace	X	—	—
Lift Point Illustrations	X	X	—
Locking Differential Service	X	—	—
Locking Hub Service	X	—	—
Lower Ball Joint, Replace	X	—	—